THE CHARLTON STANDARD CATALOGUE OF
HOCKEY CARDS

SIXTH EDITION
1995

W. K. CROSS
Publisher

TORONTO, ONTARIO
BIRMINGHAM, MICHIGAN

COPYRIGHT NOTICE

Copyright 1995 Charlton International Inc. All Rights Reserved

TRADEMARK NOTICE

The terms Charlton, Charlton's, The Charlton Press, and the Charlton Cataloguing System and abbreviations thereof, are trademarks of Charlton International Inc. and shall not be used without written consent from Charlton International Inc.

While every care has been taken to ensure accuracy in the compilation of the data in this catalogue, the publisher cannot accept responsibility for typographical errors.

No part of this publication may be reproduced, stored in a retrieval system, or transmitted in any form or by any means, electronic, mechanical, photocopying, recording, or otherwise without the prior written permission of the copyright owner.

Permission is hereby given for brief excerpts to be used for the purpose of reviewing this publication in newspapers, magazines, periodicals and bulletins, other than in the advertising of items for sale, provided the source of the material so used is acknowledged in each instance.

All hockey cards illustrated on the covers or in the text of this catalogue are done so with the express permission of the card manufacturers. Trademarks, copyrights and logos remain the property of the card manufacturer and must not be reproduced without their written permission.

Canadian Cataloguing in Publication Data

Main entry under title:
The 1991/1992 Charlton hockey card price guide

1st ed.
ISSN 1183-3033
ISBN 0-88968-114-7 (4th ed.)
Continues: Charlton Standard Catalogue of Hockey Cards
ISBN 0-88968-136-8 (6th ed.)

1. Hockey cards - Catalogs. 2. Hockey cards - Prices - Canada. I. Charlton hockey card price Guide. II. Hockey card price guide.

GV847.C48 1991 769.　4'9796962'029471
　　　　　　　　　　　　　　　C91-093835-0

Printed in Canada
in the Province of Quebec

The Charlton Press

Editorial Office
2010 Yonge Street,
Toronto, Ontario M4S 1Z9
Telephone (416) 488-4653 Fax: (416) 488-4656

EDITORIAL

Editor	W. K. Cross	Editorial Assistant	Davina Rowan
Associate Editor	Jean Dale	Layout	Frank van Lieshout
Director of Research and Pricing	Joel Spillman		

CONTRIBUTORS

The Charlton Press would like to thank the following for their generous contributions to this Sixth Edition:

DEALERS

Ed Agopian, Imperial Cards, Burlington, Ontario; **Ross Arnott**, Bluenose Coin & Stamp, Pointe Claire, Quebec; **Brian Bell**, Twin B Hockey Cards, Moncton, N.B.; **Bob Boin**, Prime TimeSportscard, Oakville, Ontario; **Edwin Borau**, Hockey Immortals, Penticton, b.C.; **Hersh Borenstein**, Frozen Pond Collectibles, Toronto, Ontario; **John Brenner**, Lookin' For Heroes, Kitchener, Ontario; **Sandy Campbell**, Proof Positive, Baddeck, Nova Scotia; **Dave's Sports Collectibles Inc.**, Kentville, Nova Scotia; **Diamond Connection**, Centerline, MI; **Ben Doyon**, Cartes Timbres Monnaies, Ste.-Foy, Quebec; **Andrew Driega**, Sears Coins and Stamp Shop, Ottawa, Ontario; **Ron Emery**, Toronto, Ontario; **Joseph E. Filion**, Cartomania, Cheneville, Quebec; **Bill Foot & Gerry Soble**, Foot's Sports Collectables & Comics, Delta, B.C.; **Bill Fougere**, Mr. Wax, Armdale, Nova Scotia; **Barry Gibson**, Heroes of Overtime; **Harvey Goldfarb**; A. J. Cards; **Andrew Kossman**, Action Coin and Card, Toronto, Ontario; **George Kumagei**, Major Leagues, Burlington, Ontario; **Gary Lane**, Georgetown, Ontario; **Frank Leardi**, Frank Leardi Sportscards, Toronto, Ontario; **Barry McGlynn**, Sterling Cards, Cornwall, Ontario; **Dennis Mitri**, Pit Bull Collectibles, London, Ontario; **Daniel Naiman**, Sports Collector's Heaven, North York, Ontario; **Leandre Normand**, Promodium, Montreal, Quebec; **Jean-Guy Pichette**, Mon Hobby My Passion, Laval, Quebec; **Richard Plett**, Trueman's Sports Cards, Mississauga, Ontario; **Len Pottie**, Windsor Junction, Nova Scotia; **Chris Rogers**, Hab-It Sportscards, Orillia, Ontario; **Angelo Savelli**, Canada's Number One King of Cards, Hamilton, Ontario; **Ronald Villeneuve**, Collection de Sport AZ, Inc., St.-Eustache, Quebec; **Mike Wrobleski**, Merri-Seven Coins, Liviona, Michigan

COLLECTORS

Terry W. Allen, Edmonton,Alberta; **Seth Aberbach**, Huntington, New York; **Dave Allison**, Sherwood Park, Alberta; **Alain Arsenault**, Bonaventure, Quebec; **T. A. Bailey, Ottawa**, Ontario; **Brad Bakken**, Shaunavon, Saskatchewan; **John Beaulieu**, Lewiston, Maine; **Francois Beaumier Jr.**, Victoria, British Columbia; **William Binka**, Kitchener, Ontario; **Brian Bishop**, Hamilton, Ontario; **Vern Blais**, Coquitlam, British Columbia; **Joseph Bonett**, Forest Hills, N.Y.; **Bill Boucher**, Moncton, N.B.; **Tony Bowman**, Delta, British Columbia; **Michel Boyer**, Montreal, Quebec; **Chris Brunette**, Ottawa, Ontario; **Robert Byce**, Sault Ste. Marie, Ontario; **Martin Cann**, Beamsville, Ontario; **Donald Coleman**, Toronto, Ontario; **Ken Collins**, Sudbury, Ontario; **Normand Comtois**, Aylmer, Quebec; **Tim Crane**, Fredericton, New Brunswick; **Lyne Cyr**, Gloucester, Ontario; **Pierre Dansereau**, Montreal, Quebec; **Michael Darling**, London, Ontario; **Danny Dill**, Windsor, Ontario; **Tony Duszik**; **Kate Dwyer**, Thunder Bay, Ontario; **Graham Esler**, Curator, Bank of Canada; **Travis Favretto**, Sault Ste. Marie, Ontario; **Aubrey Ferguson**, Peterborough, Ontario; **Alan Fewster**, Woodstock, Ontario; **Eric Fiander**, Fredericton, New Brunswick; **Bob Fitzgerald**, Mississauga, Ontario; **Mike Fudali**, Abbotsford, British Columbia; **Randy Gardner**, Ottawa, Ontario; **Emile O. Gionet**, Caraquet, N.B.; **Sylvie Guenett-Craig**, Nepean, Ontario; **Jens Gustavsen**, Toronto; **Tony Hager**, Port Alberni, British Columbia; **Alex Horkay**, London, Ontario; **D. Tod Hughes**, Bremerton, Washington; **Bill Irvine**, Niagara Falls, Ontario; **Bertrand Jetté**, Hawksbury, Ontario; **Bob Johnson**, Peterborough, Ontario; **Tony Kelly**, Ottawa, Ontario; **David Kyle**, Lively, Ontario; **Eric Laberge**, Ontario; **Alice Lake**, Toronto, Ontario; **Andre Lamirande**, Jonquier, Quebec; **John Landry**, Gloucester, Ontario; **Cheryl A. Lemmens**, Toronto, Ontario; **William LeRoy**, Halifax, Nova Scotia; **Glenn Lockhart**, Fort Frances, Ontario; **Jay Lombardi**, Milford, Connecticut; **Mike Loncar**, Hamilton, Ontario; **Paul Major**, Belleville, Ontario; **Jennifer Matis**, Coaldale, Alberta; **Daniel McLeod**, Vancouver, British Columbia; **Dave McPherson**, Ontario; **Scott McRae**, Kitchener, Ontario; **Clark Muldavin**, Sacramento. CA; **Robert Murray**, Abbotsford, British Columbia; **Troy Nass**, Newburne, Newfoundland; **Kevin Nelson**, Lethbridge, Alberta; **Chip Orlando**, Williamsville, New York; **R. V. Perrier**, Castlegar, B.C.; **Randy Peters**, Richmond, British Columbia; **Donald Plesh**, Swan River, Manitoba; **Larry Purdy**, Paradise, Newfoundland; **Ron Robert**, Winnipeg, Manitoba; **Elliot Schwartzkopf**, Beaverton, Oregon; **M.S. Sekersky**, Windsor, Ontario; **Greg Sladics**, London, Ontario; **J. Donald Smith**, Davidson, Alberta; **Philip Sommers**, Highland, N.Y.; **Jasse Tuukki**, Finland; **Roderick Van Rhyn**, Prince George, British Columbia; **Jason Verner**, Gloucester, Ontario; **Jacques Vincent**, Fredericton, New Brunswick; **Wyamn and Barb Walek**, Dart, N.S.; **Jim Wallace**, Tillsonburg, Ontario; **Mrs. A. White**, Elgin, Ontario; **Dr. Roger Wray**, Nepean, Ontario; **Bruce Yourex**, Calgary, Alberta

CORPORATIONS

Noella Barkoulas, Panini Canada, St. Laurent, Quebec; **Bowman**, Brooklyn, New York; **Steve Charendoff**, Classic Inc., Cherry Hill, New Jersey; **Elizabeth Coogan**, Philadelphia Flyers, Philadelphia, PA; **France La Monde**, Kraft General Foods, Don Mills, Ontario; **Fleer Ltd.**, Weston, Ontario; **Diane Gordon**, Zellers, Montreal, Quebec; **Howard Granner**, Leaf Canada; **Highliner Foods**; **Phil Loeper**, Kellogg's Canada, Toronto, Ontario; **Susan Martenson**, Baybank, Waltham, Massachusettes; **O-Pee-Chee Company**, London, Ontario; **Dr. Brian Price**, President of Parkhurst.; **Pro Set Inc.**, Dallas, Texas; **Pinnacle Brands**, Dallas, Texas; **Phil Carter**, Topps Gum Company, Brooklyn, New York; **Upper Deck Company**, Yorba Linda, California; **Casey White**, **Albalene Sales & Promotion**, Delta, British Columbia.

The publisher would also like to thank both **Brian "Chappie" Chapman**, the authority on Bee Hives; **Don Graham**, Slapshot Ventures Inc., Kitchener; **Frank Leardi**, Leardi Coins and Cards, Toronto; **Neil Getz**, Sportsworld, Toronto; **Gerald Higgs**, Ben Wheeler, Texas; **Carlton McDiarmid**, The Post Card King.

AMERI-CAN SPORTSCARDS

✪ *One of Canada's Finest Selections of Rare Sportscards*

✪ *We Stock all Years of Hockey Cards in Singles & Sets in All Grades*

✪ *We Solicit & Fulfill All Want Lists at Very Competitive Prices*

✪ *We are Serious Buyers of all Larger Collections & Estates*

Monday to Friday, 10:00am to 6:00pm
Saturday, 9:00am to 5:00pm
300 John Street, Suite #409
Thornhill, Ontario L3T 5W4
(905) 764-2620
Plenty of free parking

(1 mile north of Steeles, N/E corner of Bayview Avenue & John Street, 4th Floor of Thornhill Square Mall)

TABLE OF CONTENTS

INTRODUCTION
- Pricing in this Catalogue xvi
- History of the Hockey Card xvi
- The Market xviii
  - Buying and Selling Cards xviii
- Card Care xviii
- Card Grading
  - Border Conformity xx
  - Corner Wear xx
  - Creases xx
  - Alterations xx
  - Surface Wear xx
  - Mishandling Defects xx
- Condition Guide xvi
- Counterfeit Cards xviii

CHAPTER ONE
ADVERTISING TRADE CARDS
BUFFORD LITHO
- 1879 - 1882 Issue 3

THE GREAT ATLANTIC AND PACIFIC TEA CO.
- 1888 Issue 4

F. MAYER BOOT & SHOE CO.
- 1890 Issue 4

GOTTMANN & KRETCHMER
- Circa 1900 Issue 5

CHAPTER TWO
POSTCARDS
WARWICK BRO'S. & RUTTER LTD
- Circa 1896 Issue 9

NORTHERN HARDWARE COMPANY
- 1907 - 08 Issue 9

CALUMEL HOCKEY CLUB OF LAURIUM
- 1912 - 13 Issue 10

A. R. CLARKE & CO. LIMITED
- 1912 - 13 Issue 10

CHAPTER THREE
TOBACCO CARDS, FLANNELS AND SILKS
HAMILTON KINGS CIGARETTES
- 1902 Issue 13

MURAD CIGARETTES COLLEGE SERIES
- 1908 Flannel Issue 13
- 1909 - 10 College Series - Cards ... 14
- 1910 - 11 College Series Premiums - Cards 15
- 1912 - 15 College Seal Series - Large Silks 15
- 1912 - 15 College Seal Series - Small Silks 16

IMPERIAL TOBACCO
- 1910 - 11 Regular Issue 17
- 1910 - 11 Postcard Issue 17
- 1911 - 12 Regular Issue 18
- 1912 - 13 Regular Issue 18

CHAMP'S CIGARETTE CARDS
- 1924 - 25 Regular Issue 20

SWEET CAPORAL
- 1934 - 35 Photo Issue 20

CHAPTER FOUR
NATIONAL HOCKEY LEAGUE
WILLIAM PATERSON LTD
- 1923 - 24 Regular Issue 25

MAPLE CRISPETTE
- 1924 - 25 Regular Issue 26

ANONYMOUS
- 1925 - 26 "Borderless" Issue 26
- 1926 - 27 "Borders" Issue 27

DOMINION CHOCOLATE
- 1925 Dominion Athletic Stars 27
- 1926 Dominion Athletic Stars - New Series 27

WILLARD CHOCOLATE
- 1925 Sporting Champions 28

LA PRESSE
- 1927 - 32 Issue 28

O'KEEFE BEVERAGES
- 1932 - 33 Issue 28

CANADIAN CHEWING GUM SALES LTD
- 1933 - 34 Regular Issue 29

CANADIAN CYCLE AND MOTOR COMPANY (CCM)
- 1933 - 36 Issue 29

THE DIAMOND MATCH COMPANY
- 1933 - 35 "Silver Hockey Issue" 30
- 1936 - 39 "Tan" Hockey Issue 31

GOUDEY GUM CO.
- 1933 Sports Kings 33

HAMILTON GUM
- 1933 - 34 Regular Issue 33

O-PEE-CHEE
- 1933 - 34 Regular Issue Series A ... 33
- 1934 - 35 Regular Issue Series B ... 34
- 1935 - 36 Regular Issue Series C ... 34
- 1936 - 37 Regular Issue Series D ... 35
- 1937 - 38 Regular Issue Series E ... 35
- 1939 - 40 Regular Issue 36
- 1940 - 41 Regular Issue 37
- 1968 - 69 Regular Issue 37
- 1968 - 69 Puck Stickers 40
- 1969 - 70 Regular Issue 40
- 1969 - 70 Stamps 43
- 1969 - 70 Quad Ministicker Cards .. 43
- 1969 - 70 Mini-Card Albums 43
- 1970 - 71 Regular Issue 44
- 1970 - 71 Deckle Edge 46
- 1970 - 71 Sticker Stamps 47
- 1971 - 72 Regular Issue 47
- 1971 - 72 Booklets 49
- 1971 - 72 Posters 49
- 1972 - 73 Regular Issue 50
- 1972 - 73 Player Crest Stickers 52
- 1972 - 73 Team Logo Stickers 52
- 1973 - 74 Regular Issue 53
- 1973 - 74 Team Logo Stickers 55
- 1973 - 74 Rings 55
- 1974 - 75 Regular Issue 55
- 1975 - 76 Regular Issue 58
- 1976 - 77 Regular Issue 62
- 1977 - 78 Regular Issue 65
- 1977 - 78 Glossy Photos 68
- 1978 - 79 Regular Issue 68
- 1979 - 80 Regular Issue 72
- 1980 - 81 Regular Issue 75
- 1981 - 82 Regular Issue 78
- 1982 - 83 Regular Issue 82
- 1983 - 84 Regular Issue 86
- 1984 - 85 Regular Issue 90
- 1985 - 86 Regular Issue 93
- 1986 - 87 Regular Issue 95
- 1987 - 88 Regular Issue 97
- 1988 - 89 Regular Issue 99
- 1989 - 90 Regular Issue 102

- 1990 - 91 Regular Issue 104
- 1990 - 91 Insert Set - Central Red Army 106
- 1990 - 91 Premier Issue 106
- 1991 - 92 Regular Issue 107
- 1991 - 92 Insert Set - San Jose / Russia 110
- 1991 - 92 Premier Issue 110
- 1992 Promotional Sheet 111
- 1992 - 93 Regular Issue 111
- 1992 - 93 Insert Set - 25th Anniversary ... 113
- 1992 - 93 Premier Issue 113
- 1992 - 93 Premier Insert Set - Star Performers .. 114
- 1992 - 93 Insert Set - Top Rookies . 114
- 1993 Hockey Fanfest Promotional Sheet 114
- 1993 - 94 Premier Issue 114
- 1993 - 94 INSERT SETS
- 1993- 94 Black Gold 117
- 1993 - 94 Finest Hockey Roster 117
- 1993 - 94 Finest Redemption Card . 117
- 1993 - 94 Team Canada 118
- 1993 - 94 Stadium Club and First Day Production 118
- 1993 - 94 Stadium Club Insert Set .. 119
- 1994 - 95 Regular Issue 119
- 1994 - 95 Insert Set 121

O-PEE-CHEE MISCELLANEOUS ISSUES
- 1980 - 81 Photos 122
- 1981 - 82 Stickers 122
- 1982 - 83 Stickers 124
- 1983 - 84 Stickers 125
- 1984 - 85 Stickers 127
- 1985 - 86 Box Bottoms 129
- 1985 - 86 Stickers 129
- 1986 - 87 Box Bottoms 131
- 1986 - 87 Stickers 131
- 1987 - 88 Hockey Leaders 132
- 1987 - 88 Box Bottoms 133
- 1987 - 88 Stickers 133
- 1988 - 89 NHL All Stars 134
- 1988 - 89 Box Bottoms 135
- 1988 - 89 Stickers 135
- 1988 - 89 Future Stars 137
- 1989 - 90 Box Bottoms 137
- 1989 - 90 Stickers 137
- 1989 - 90 Future Stars 139
- 1990 - 91 Box Bottoms 139
- 1992 - 93 Box Bottoms 139

WORLD WIDE GUM
- 1933 - 34 Ice Kings 140
- 1933 - 34 Ice Kings Premium 140
- 1936 - 37 Regular Issue 140

V129 ANONYMOUS
- 1933 - 34 Issue 141

ST. LAWRENCE STARCH COMPANY
- Bee Hive Photos 143
- Bee Hive Variations 144
- Group One Photos 1934 to 1944 ... 145
- Group Two 1944 to 1963 147
- Group Three 1964 to 1967 151

CANADA STARCH
- 1935 - 1940 Crown Brand 152

AMALGAMATED PRESS
- 1935 - 36 Champion Magazine 153
- 1935 - 36 Triumph Magazine 153

QUAKER OATS
- 1938 - 39 Photo Issue 153
- 1945 - 54 Photos 154
- 1955 - 56 Regular Issue 155

CHLP / CKAC / CKVL RADIO
- 1943 - 47 Parade Sportive 156

BERK ROSS
- 1951 Hit Parade of Champions 157

PARKHURST
- 1951 - 52 Regular Issue 157
- 1952 - 53 Regular Issue 158
- 1953 - 54 Regular Issue 159
- 1954 - 55 Regular Issue 160

1955 - 56 Regular Issue	161
1957 - 58 Regular Issue	162
1958 - 59 Regular Issue	162
1959 - 60 Regular Issue	163
1960 - 61 Regular Issue	163
1961 - 62 Regular Issue	164
1962 - 63 Regular Issue	165
1963 - 64 Regular Issue	165
1991 - 92 Promotional Cards	167
1991 - 92 Regular Issue - Series One	167
1991 - 92 Regular Issue - Series Two	168
1991 - 92 Insert Set	170
1991 - 92 Final Update	170
1992 - 93 Regular and Emerald Ice	171
1992 - 93 Parkhurst Reprint Cards	174
1992 - 93 Don Cherry Reprint Card	174
1992 - 93 Cherry Picks	174
1992 - 93 Don Cherry Redemption Card	174
1992 - 93 Final Update and Emerald Ice	174
1992 - 93 Final Update Insert Card	175
1992 - 93 Commemorative Sheets	175
1992 - 93 Maple Leafs Alumni Game Sheet	175
1992 - 93 Limited Edition Canadian Tour Sheets	175
1992 - 93 Cherry Picks Sheets	175
1993 - 94 Regular Issue and Emerald Ice	177
1993 - 94 Insert Set - East/West Stars	180
1993 - 94 Calder Candidates	180
1993 - 94 Cherry's Playoff Heroes	180
1993 - 94 Firsts Overall	181
1993 - 94 Parkies Reprints	181
1993 - 94 Parkie Case Inserts	181
1993 - 94 U.S.A. and Canada Gold Foil	181
1993 - 94 The Missing Link Promotional Cards	182
1993 - 94 Missing Link Promotional Sheet	182
1993 - 94 1956 - 57 Missing Link	182
1993 - 94 INSERT SETS	
1993 - 94 Autographed Cards	183
1993 - 94 Future Cards	183
1993 - 94 US and Canadian Pop Up Greats	183
1993 - 94 NHL All-Star Redemption Sheet	183
1994 - 95 Gold and Silver Parkies	184
1994 - 95 Insert Set "Crash the Game"	186
1994 - 95 Vintage Parkhurst	186

LA PATRIE

1951 - 54 Issues	187

ROYAL DESSERTS

1952 Royal Stars of Hockey	187

TOPPS

1954 - 55 Regular Issue	188
1957 - 58 Regular Issue	188
1958 - 59 Regular Issue	188
1959 - 60 Regular Issue	190
1960 - 61 Regular Issue	190
1961 - 62 Regular Issue	191
1961 - 62 Stamps	192
1962 - 63 Regular Issue	192
1962 - 63 Hockey Bucks	193
1963 - 64 Regular Issue	193
1964 - 65 Regular Issue	194
1965 - 66 Regular Issue	195
1966 - 67 Regular Issue	196
1966 - 67 USA Test	198
1967 - 68 Regular Issue	198
1968 - 69 Regular Issue	200
1969 - 70 Regular Issue	201
1970 - 71 Regular Issue	202
1970 - 71 Deckle Edge	204
1970 - 71 Sticker Stamps	204
1971 - 72 Regular Issue	204
1971 - 72 Booklets	205
1972 - 73 Regular Issue	206
1973 - 74 Regular Issue	207
1974 - 75 Regular Issue	209
1975 - 76 Regular Issue	211
1976 - 77 Regular Issue	214
1976 - 77 Glossy Insert Set	216
1977 - 78 Regular Issue	216
1977 - 78 Glossy Photos	219
1978 - 79 Regular Issue	219
1978 - 79 Team Inserts	221
1979 - 80 Regular Issue	221
1979 - 80 Helmet and Stick Decals Insert Set	223
1980 - 81 Regular Issue	224

1980 - 81 Team Posters	226
1981 - 82 Regular Issue	226
1984 - 85 Regular Issue	228
1985 - 86 Regular Issue	230
1985 - 86 Sticker Inserts	231
1986 - 87 Regular Issue	232
1986 - 87 Sticker Inserts	233
1987 - 88 Regular Issue	234
1987 - 88 Sticker Inserts	235
1988 - 89 Regular Issue	235
1988 - 89 Sticker Inserts	237
1989 - 90 Regular Issue	238
1989 - 90 Sticker Inserts	238
1990 - 91 Regular Issue	239
1990 - 91 Insert Set - 1989-90 Team Leaders	241
1991 Promotional Cards	241
1991 - 92 Regular Issue	241
1991 - 92 Insert Set - 1990-91 Team Leaders	244
1991 - 92 Stadium Club	244
1991 - 92 Stadium Club Charter Member	246
1992 - 93 Regular and Gold Issue	246
1992 - 93 Stadium Club	249
1992 - 93 Stadium Club Members Only	251
1993 - 94 Promotional Sheet	251
1993 - 94 Premier Regular and Gold	251
1993 - 94 INSERT SETS	
1993 - 94 Black Gold	254
1993 - 94 Black Gold Redemption Cards	254
1993 - 94 Premier Finest	254
1993 - 94 Finest Redemption Card	254
1993 - 94 Team U.S.A.	154
1993 - 94 Stadium Club and First Day Production	254
1993 - 94 INSERT SETS	
1993 - 94 Master Photos	257
1993 - 94 NHL All Star 1992 - 1993	257
1993 - 94 Master Photo Winner Cards	258
1993 - 4 Stadium Club Team U.S.A.	258
1994 - 95 Regular Issue	258
1994 - 95 Insert Set	260

TOPPS MISCELLANEOUS ISSUES

1982 - 83 Stickers	260
1983 - 84 Stickers	261
1985 - 86 Box Bottoms	263
1986 - 87 Box Bottoms	264
1989 - 90 Box Bottoms	264
1990 - 91 Box Bottoms	264

THE TORONTO STAR

1954 - 67 Weekend Magazine Issue	265
1957 - 67 Daily Star Hockey Photos	266
1963 - 64 Hockey Stars in Action	267
1964 - 65 Regular Issue	268

NABISCO

1955 - 56 Issue	268

ADVENTURE GUM

1956 Issue	269

SHIRRIFF

1960 - 61 Hockey Coins	269
1961 - 62 Shirriff / Salada Hockey Coins	270
1962 - 63 Hockey Coins	271
1968 - 69 Hockey Coins	271

WONDER BREAD

1960 Wrapper Issue	273
1960 Premium Photos	273

YORK PEANUT BUTTER

1960 - 61 Premiums	273
1961 - 62 Yellow Backs	273
1962 - 63 Iron-on Transfers	274
1963 - 64 White Backs	274
1967 - 68 Hockey Action	274

EL PRODUCTO

1962 - 63 Issue	275
1962 - 63 Disks	275

CHEX

1963 - 65 Photos	275

COCA-COLA

1964 - 65 Caps	276
1965 - 66 Regular Issue	277
1966 Booklets	277
1977 - 78 Mini Issue	278

EATON'S

1964 - 67 Gordie Howe "Sports Adviser"	278

POST CEREAL

1966 - 67 Hockey Tips Large Size	278
1966 - 67 Hockey Tips Small Size	278
1967 - 68 Issue	279
1968 - 69 Marbles	279
1972 - 73 Hockey Action Transfers	279
1981 - 82 NHL Stars In Action	279
1982 - 83 Issue	280

BAUER SKATES

1968 - 69 Issue	282

EDDIE SARGENT PROMOTIONS LTD

1969 Stickers	283
1970 - 71 Stickers	283
1971 - 72 Stickers	285
1972 - 73 Stickers	286

COLGATE

1970 - 71 Stamps	289
1971 - 72 Heads	289

DAD'S COOKIES

1970 - 71 Issue	290

ESSO

1970 - 71 Power Players	291
1983 - 84 Issue	293
1988 - 89 All Star Stickers	293

BAZOOKA

1971 - 72 Issue	293

KELLOGG'S

1971 Iron On Transfers	294
1984 Puck Issue	294
1992 Issue	296
1992 Rice Krispies	296
1992 - 93 Posters	296

TORONTO SUN

1971 - 72 Issue	296

DIMANCHE / DERNIERE HEURE

1972 - 84 Issues	298

TOWERS / BONIMART

1972 Hockey Instruction Booklets	301

LETRASET

1973 Action Replay Transfers	301

MAC'S MILK

1973 - 74 Issue	302

LIPTON SOUP

1974 - 75 Issue	302

LOBLAWS

1974 - 75 NHL Action Players	302

POPSICLE

1975 - 76 Issue	305
1976 - 77 Issue	305

SPORTSCASTER CARDS

1977 - 79 Issue	305

PEPSICO

1980 - 81 Caps	306

TCMA LTD

1981 Issue	307

McDONALD'S RESTAURANTS

1982 - 83 Stickers	308
1991 - 92 All-Stars	308
1992 - 93 Issue	308
1993 - 94 Issue	309
1993 - 94 Redemption Cards	309

HOCKEY HALL OF FAME

1983 Regular Issue	309
1983 Postcards	311
1987 Regular Issue	312

FUNMATE CANADA LTD

1983 - 84 Puffy Stickers	314

VACHON FOODS

1983 - 84 Issue	316

7-ELEVEN
- 1984 - 85 Sticker Disks 317
- 1985 - 86 Credit Cards 318

KRAFT
- 1986 - 87 Drawings 318
- 1986 - 87 Posters 319
- 1990 Regular Issue 319
- 1990 Stickers 320
- 1990 - 91 Regular Issue 320
- 1991 - 92 Special Edition 321
- 1993 Regular Issue 322
- 1994 Regular Issue 323

PANINI
- 1987 - 88 Stickers 324
- 1988 - 89 Stickers 326
- 1989 - 90 Stickers 328
- 1990 - 91 Stickers 330
- 1991 - 92 Stickers 332
- 1992 - 93 Stickers English and French Issue . . 334
- 1992 - 93 Insert Sets English and French 336
- 1992 - 93 Action Freaks 336
- 1993 - 94 Stickers 337
- 1993 - 94 Insert Set 338

CELEBRITY WATCH INC.
- 1988 Pro-Sport Autograph Collection 339

FRITO-LAY
- 1988 - 89 Stickers 339

ACTION PACKED
- 1989 - 90 Promotional Set 339
- 1993 Promotionl Set 339

BOWMAN
- 1990 - 91 Issue 340
- 1990 - 91 Insert Set Hat Tricks 341
- 1991 Promotional Cards 341
- 1991 - 92 Regular Issue 342
- 1992 - 93 Regular Issue 344

PRO SET
- 1990 Promotional Card 346
- 1990 - 91 Series One 346
- 1990 - 91 Series Two 350
- 1990 - 91 Player of the Month 352
- 1991 - NHL Awards Special 352
- 1991 - NHL Sponsor Awards 352
- 1991 - 12th Annual National 352
- The 1991 Hockey Hall of Fame Dinner 352
- 1991 - Hockey Hall of Fame 75th Anniversary . 353
- 1991 - Promotional Cards 353
- 1991 St. Louis Blues Mid West Collector Show . 353
- 1991 - 1992 National Hockey Tour Promo Card . 353
- 1991 - 92 Regular Issue 353
- 1991 - 92 Insert Set Collector Cards . . . 357
- 1991 - 92 75th Anniversary Hologram . . 357
- 1991 - 92 Autographed Card Patrick Roy . 357
- 1991 - 92 Pro Set Platinum 355
- 1991 - 92 Insert Set Platinum Collectibles . 360
- 1991 - 92 Player Of The Month 360
- 1992 Pro Set Gazette Collectibles 360
- 1992 The Puck Promotional Cards 360
- 1992 The Puck Series One 360
- 1992 - 93 Regular Issue 361
- 1992 - 93 Insert Set - Award Winners 362
- 1992 - 93 Rookie Goal Leaders 1991 - 92 . . . 362
- 1992 - 93 Team Leaders 1991 - 92 363
- 1992 - 93 Parkhurst Previews 363

SCORE
- 1990 American Promotional Cards 364
- 1990 Canadian Promotional Cards 364
- 1990 - 91 Regular Issue 364
- 1990 - 91 Eric Lindros 366
- 1990 Rookie And Traded 366
- 1990 Young Superstars 367
- 1990 - 91 Hockey's 100 Hottest and Rising Stars 367
- 1991 Promotional Cards 368
- 1991 - 92 American Promotional Cards . 368
- 1991 - 92 American Issue 368
- 1991 - 92 Promotional Cards Canadian and Bilingial 370
- 1991 - 92 Regular Issue Series One Canadian and Bilingual 371

1991 - 92 INSERT SETS
- 1991 - 92 Bobby Orr Collector Cards 374
- 1991 - 92 Insert Set Hot Cards 374
- 1991 - 92 Rookie and Traded 374
- 1991 - 92 Young Superstars 375

PINNACLE ISSUE
- 1991 - 92 English and French 375

PINNACLE INSERT SETS
- 1991 - 92 Team Pinnacle English and French 377
- 1991 - 92 Eric Lindros Fire on Ice 378
- 1992 Lindros Joining the Flyers 378
- 1992 - 93 Promotional Cards Canadian Issue . 378
- 1992 - 93 Regular Issue 378

CANADIAN INSERT SETS
- 1992 - 93 Olympic Heroes 381
- 1992 - 93 Maurice Richard Collectors Set . . . 381
- 1992 - 93 Sharp Shooters 381

AMERICAN INSERT SETS
- 1992 - 93 U.S.A. Greats 381
- 1992 - 93 Four Card Promotional Sheets . . . 382
- 1992 - 93 Six Card Promotional Sheet 382

PINNACLE ISSUE
- 1992 - 93 American and Canadian 382

PINNACLE INSERT SETS
- 1992 - 93 American and Canadian Team Pinnacle 384
- 1992 - 93 American and Canadian Team 2000 384
- 1993 - 94 Promotional Cards - American . . . 385

PINNACLE REGULAR ISSUE
- 1993 - 94 American and Canadian Series One . 385
- 1993 - 94 American abd Canadian Series Two . 387

1993 - 94 PINNACLE INSERT SETS
- 1993 - 94 Eric Lindros All Star Game 1994 . . . 388
- 1993 - 94 Gold Rush Set - American and Canadian 388
- 1993 - 94 Dream Team - Canadian . . . 389
- 1993 - 94 Dynamic Duos - Canadian . . 389
- 1993 - 94 Dynamic Duos - American . . 389
- 1993 - 94 The Franchise - American . . . 389
- 1993 - 94 44th All Star Game - American and Canadian 390
- 1993 - 94 International Stars American and Canadian 390
- 1993 Commemorative Sheets 390
- 1993 - 94 American Promotional Cards 390

1993 - 94 PINNACLE ISSUE
- 1993 - 94 Series One 390
- 1993 - 94 Series Two 391

PINNACLE INSERT SETS
- 1993 - 94 Autographs 393
- 1993 - 94 Team Captains 393
- 1993 - 94 Expansion - American 393
- 1993 - 94 Masks 393
- 1993 - 94 Nifty Fifty 393
- 1993 - 94 Super Rookies - American . . 394
- 1993 - 94 Team Pinnacle 394
- 1993 - 94 Team 2001 394
- 1993 - 94 Lindros Brothers 394
- 1993 - 94 Draft Day Card Alexandre Daigle . . 395
- 1994 - 95 Promotional Cards 395
- 1994 - 95 Pinnacle Regular And Gold Issue . . 395
- 1994 - 95 American and Canadian 395

PINNACLE INSERT SETS
- 1994 Canadian Team 396
- 1994 Dream Team 397
- 1994 Check It 397
- 1994 Franchise 397
- 1994 90 + Club 397
- 1994 Pro Debut 397

UPPER DECK
- 1990 Promotional Cards 398
- 1990 Hockey Superstars Stereograms 398
- 1990 - 91 Issue English and French . . . 398
- 1991 - 92 Regular Issue English and French . . 401
- 1991 Collector Card Hockey Superstars 404
- 1991 - 92 Insert Set Hockey Heroes . . . 404
- 1991 - 92 Autographed Card Brett Hull 405
- 1991 - 92 Award Winners Holograms . . 405
- 1991 - 92 Euro Stars 405
- 1992 - 93 Regular Issue 406
- 1992 -93 Insert Set Hockey Heroes W. Gretzky . 408
- 1992 - 93 Hockey Heroes Gordie Howe 409
- 1992 - 93 Collectors Card 409

- 1992 - 93 Euro Rookies 409
- 1992 - 93 Calder Candidates 409
- 1992 - 93 Euro Stars 409
- 1992 - 93 Amer / Can Rookie Team Holograms . 410
- 1992 - 93 All Rookie Team 410
- 1992 - 93 Euro - Rookie Team 410
- 1992 - 93 All World Team 410
- 1992 - 93 World Junior Grads Class of '92 . . . 410
- 1992 - 93 Gordie Howe Selects 411
- 1992 - 93 44th AllStar Game 411
- 1992 - 93 Autographed Gordie Howe . . 411
- 1992 - 93 Commemorative Sheets . . . 411
- 1992 - 93 Upper Deck Flyers Team Set . 412
- 1993 - 94 Regular Issue 412
- 1993 - 94 Insert Set Award Winners . . . 414
- 1993 - 94 Collectors Card 415
- 1993 - 94 Future Heroes 415
- 1993 - 94 Gretzky's Great Ones 415
- 1993 - 94 Hat Tricks 415
- 1993 - 94 Next In Line 415
- 1993 - 94 NHL's Best 416
- 1993-94 Program of Excellence 416
- 1993 - 94 Silver Skates 416
- 1993 - 94 Gold and Silver Skates 416
- 1993 - 94 Special Print 416
- 1994 Upper Deck World Cup Soccer 417
- 1993 - 94 Roots "Be A Player" NHLPA 418

GILLETTE
- 1991 - 92 Issue 419

ABALENE SALES AND PROMOTIONS LTD
- 1992 - 93 Artcard Issue 419
- 1992 - 93 Greeting Card Issue 419

DURIVAGE
- 1992 - 93 Les Grand Hockeyeurs Quebecois . 420
- 1992 - 93 Patrick Roy Autograph 420
- 1993 - 94 Des Grands Hockeyeurs Quebecois . 420
- 1993 - 94 Autograph Cards 420

FLEER ULTRA
- 1992 - 93 Series One 421
- 1992 - 93 Series Two 422

1992 - 93 INSERT SETS
- 1992 - 93 Jeremy Roenick Highlights . . 423
- 1992 - 93 Jeremy Roenick Autograph . 423
- 1992 - 93 Rookies 423
- 1992 - 93 NHL All Star 424
- 1992 - 93 Award Winners 424
- 1992 - 93 Imports 424
- 1993 - 94 Promotional Sheet 424
- 1993 - 94 Series One 424
- 1993 - 94 Series Two 425

1993 - 94 INSERT SETS
- 1993 - 94 Adam Oates Career Highlights . . . 427
- 1993 - 94 Adam Oates Autographed Card . . . 427
- 1993 - 94 All Rookie 427
- 1993 - 94 All Stars 427
- 1993 - 94 Award winners 428
- 1993 - 94 Premier Pivots 428
- 1993 - 94 Prospects 93-94 428
- 1993 - 94 Red Light Specials 428
- 1993 - 94 Scoring Kings 428
- 1993 - 94 Speed Kings 428
- 1993 - 94 Wave of The Future 429
- 1993 - 94 Power Play Series One 429
- 1993 - 94 Power Play Series Two 431

1993 - 94 POWER PLAY INSERT SETS
- 1993 - 94 Gamebreakers 432
- 1993 - 94 Global Greats 432
- 1993 - 94 Netminders 432
- 1993 - 94 Point Leaders 433
- 1993 - 94 Rising Stars 433
- 1993 - 94 Rookie Standouts 433
- 1993 - 94 Second Year Stars 433
- 1993 - 94 Slapshot Artists 433
- 1994 - 95 Issue 434

1994 - 95 INSERT SETS
- 1994 - 95 NHL All Stars 435
- 1994 - 95 Performance Highlights Sergei Fedorov 436
- 1994 - 95 Premier Pad Men 436
- 1994 - 95 Ultra Power 438
- 1994 - 95 Scoring Kings 436

HIGHLINER
- 1992 - 93 Centennial Collector Series 436
- 1993 - 94 Greatest Goalies 437

HOCKEY HALL OF FAME and MUSEUM
- 1992 Legends of Hockey 437

HUMPTY DUMPTY
- 1992 - 93 Issue Series One 437
- 1992 - 93 Issue Series Two 437

SEASON'S
- 1992 - 93 Action Players Patches 438
- 1993 - 94 Action Players Patches 438

ULTIMATE TRADING CARD COMPANY
- 1992 Promotional Cards 438
- 1992 Original Six 438

ZELLERS
- 1992 - 93 Masters of Hockey 439
- 1993 - 94 Masters of Hockey 439
- 1994 - 95 Masters of Hockey 440

DONRUSS
- 1993 - 94 Regular Issue 440
- 1993 - 94 Update Set 442

1993 - 94 INSERT SETS
- 1993 - 94 Conference Inserts 443
- 1993 - 94 Elite Series 443
- 1993 - 94 Ice Kings 443
- 1993 - 94 Rated Rookies 443
- 1993 - 94 Special Print - Premier Edition 444
- 1993 - 94 1994 World Junior Championships . . 444

KENNER
- 1993 - 94 Starting Line Up 444

HOCKEYWIT
- 1993 - 94 Issue 444

SEGA - E M SPORTS
- 1993 - 94 Issue 445

LEAF
- 1993 Promotional Sheet Mario Lemieux 447
- 1993 - 94 Regular Issue Series One 447
- 1993 - 94 Regular Issue Series Two 448

1993 - 94 INSERT SETS
- 1993 - 94 Freshman Phenoms 449
- 1993 - 94 Gold All-Stars 449
- 1993 - 94 Gold Leaf Rookies 1992/93 449
- 1993 - 94 Hat Trick Artists 449
- 1993 - 94 Mario Lemieux Collection 449
- 1993 - 94 Mario Lemieux Autograph Card 450
- 1993 - 94 Painted Warriors 450
- 1993 - 94 Studio Signature 450
- 1994 - 95 Regular Issue Series One 450

1994 - 95 INSERT SETS
- 1994 - 95 Gold Leaf Stars 452
- 1994 - 95 Fire on Ice 452
- 1994 - 95 Leaf Limited 452
- 1994 - 95 Gold Leaf Rookies 452

NHA and NHL ALPHABETICAL INDEX
- A to Z 455

CHAPTER FIVE
NHL TEAM SETS

ATLANTA FLAMES

COCA-COLA
- 1978 - 79 Postcard Issue 579
- 1979 - 80 Issue 759

BOSTON BRUINS

TEAM SETS
- 1970 - 71 Stanley Cup Champions - 1970 580
- 1984 - 85 Issue 580
- 1988 - 89 Issue 580

SPORTS ACTION
- 1988 - 89 Regular Issue 580
- 1989 - 90 Regular Issue 580
- 1990 - 91 Regular Issue 581
- 1991 - 92 Regular Issue 581

PRO SHOP
- 1991 - 92 Boston Bruins Legends 581

BAYBANK
- 1992 - 93 Boby Orr 581

BUFFALO SABRES

TEAM ISSUES
- 1972 - 73 Postcard Issue 582
- 1973 - 74 Postcard Issue 582
- 1974 - 75 Postcard Issue 582
- 1986 - 87 Postcard Issue 582

BELLS MARKETS
- 1973 - 74 Postcard Issue 582
- 1979 - 80 Issue 582

LINNETT
- 1975 - 76 Issue 582

WENDZ
- 1980 - 81 Issue 583
- 1981 - 82 Issue 583
- 1982 - 83 Issue 583
- 1984 - 85 Photo Issue 583

BLUE SHIELD
- 1984 - 85 Issue 583
- 1985 - 86 Regular Issue 583
- 1985 - 86 Postcard Issue 583
- 1986 - 87 Postcard Issue 584
- 1987 - 88 Postcard Issue 584
- 1988 - 89 Postcard Issue 584
- 1989 - 90 Postcard Issue 584
- 1990 - 91 Postcard Issue 584
- 1991 - 92 Postcard Issue 585
- 1992 - 93 Postcard Issue 585

WONDER BREAD / HOSTESS CAKES
- 1987 - 88 Regular Issue 585
- 1988 - 89 Regular Issue 585

CAMPBELL'S
- 1989 - 90 Regular Issue 586
- 1990 - 91 Regular Issue 586
- 1991 - 92 Regular Issue 586

JUBILEE FOODS
- 1992 - 93 Regular Issue 586

NOCO EXPRESS SHOP
- 1993 - 94 Regular Issue 587

CALGARY FLAMES

TEAM ISSUES
- 1980 - 81 Postcard Issue 588
- 1981 - 82 Postcard Issue 588
- 1982 - 83 Postcard Issue 588

STATER MINT LTD
- 1982 - 83 Hockey Dollars 588
- 1983 - 84 Hockey Dollars 588

RED ROOSTER
- 1985 - 86 Issue 588
- 1986 - 87 Issue 589
- 1987 - 88 Issue 589

I.G.A.
- 1990 - 91 Issue 589
- 1991 - 92 Issue 589

CHICAGO BLACK HAWKS

TEAM ISSUES
- 1979 - 80 Postcard Issues 590
- 1980 - 81 Postcard Issues 590
- 1981 - 82 Postcard Issue 590
- 1982 - 83 Postcard Issue 590
- 1983 - 84 Postcard Issue 590

COCA-COLA
- 1986 - 87 Postcard Issue 590
- 1987 - 88 Postcard Issue 591
- 1988 - 89 Postcard Issue 591

COLORADO ROCKIES

TEAM ISSUES
- 1979 - 80 Postcard Issue 592
- 1981 - 82 Postcard Issue 592

DETROIT RED WINGS

TEAM ISSUES
- 1956 - 57 Postcard Issue 593
- 1958 - 59 Postcard Issue 593
- 1959 - 60 Postcard Issue 593
- 1964 - 65 Postcard Issue 593
- 1968 Photo Issue 593
- 1972 - 73 Photo Issue 593
- 1974 - 75 Postcard Issue 593
- 1976 Regular Issue 595
- 1979 - 80 Postcard Issue 595
- 1980 - 81 Photo Issue 595
- 1988 - 89 Postcard Issue 595

MARATHON
- 1970 - 71 Photo Issue 595

LITTLE CAESARS PIZZA
- 1987 - 88 Postcard Issue 595

MCDONALDS
- Hockey Heroes - Gordie Howe 595

EDMONTON OILERS

TEAM ISSUES
- 1979 - 80 Postcard Issue 596
- 1984 - 85 Postcard Issue 596
- 1986 - 87 Postcard Issue 596
- 1987 - 88 Postcard Issue 596
- 1988 - 89 Postcard Issue 597
- 1988 - 89 Tenth Anniversary Action Magazine . 597

RED ROOSTER
- 1981 - 82 Regular Issue 597
- 1982 - 83 Regular Issue 598
- 1984 - 85 Regular Issue 598
- 1985 - 86 Regular Issue 598
- 1986 - 87 Regular Issue 598
- 1993 - 94 Photo Issue 599

NEILSON'S
- 1982 - 1983 Wayne Gretzky 599

McDONALD'S RESTAURANTS
- 1983 - 84 Buttons 599
- 1984 Regular Issue 600

STATER MINT LTD
- 1983 - 84 Hockey Dollars 600

I.G.A.
- 1990 - 91 Regular Issue 600
- 1991 - 92 Regular Issue 600

HARTFORD WHALERS

TEAM ISSUES

THE JUNIOR WHALERS
- 1983 - 84 Junior Issue 601
- 1988 - 89 Ground Round Postcard Issue 601
- 1989 - 90 Real Milk Postcard Issue 601
- 1990 - 91 7-Eleven Postcard Issue 601
- 1991 - 92 7-Eleven Postcard Issue 601

COURANT
- 1982 - 83 Postcard Issue 602

THOMAS
- 1982 - 83 Junior Issue 602

WENDY'S
- 1984 - 85 Junior Issue 602
- 1985 - 86 Junior Issue 602

COCA-COLA
- 1993 - 94 Regular Issue 602

DAIRYMART
- 1992 - 93 Regular Issue 602

LOS ANGELES KINGS

CARD NIGHT
- 1980 - 81 Regular Issue 603

SMOKEY
- 1984 - 85 Issue 603
- 1988 - 89 Regular Issue 603
- 1989 - 90 Regular Issue 603
- 1989 - 90 Gretzky 604

1990 - 91 Regular Issue 604	**PROVIGO**	**CLARK BUNS**
1991 - 92 Issue 604	1985 - 86 Issue 614	1993 Mario Lemieux 626
NORTHWEST AIRLINES	**VACHON**	**QUEBEC NORDIQUES**
1990 - 91 Issue 604	1988 Super Collection 614	**TEAM ISSUES**
TARGET	**O-PEE-CHEE**	1980 - 81 Postcard Issue 627
1991 - 92 Issue 604	1993 Hockeyfest Promotional Sheet 615	1981 - 82 Postcard Issue 627
UPPER DECK	1993 Hockeyfest 615	1982 - 83 Postcard Issue 627
1991 - 92 Season Ticket Holders 604	**NEW JERSEY DEVILS**	1983 - 84 Postcard Issue 627
1992 - 93 Season Ticket Holders 604	**TEAM ISSUES**	1985 - 86 Postcard Issue 627
COCA-COLA	1983 - 84 Postcard Issue 616	1986 - 87 Postcard Issue 628
1993 - 94 Wayne Gretzky Pog Set 604	1984 - 85 Postcard Issue 616	1987 - 88 Postcard Issue 628
MINNESOTA NORTH STARS	1985 - 86 Postcard Issue 616	1988 - 89 Postcard Issue 628
TEAM ISSUES	1989 - 90 Regular Issue	1989 - 90 Postcard Issue 629
1973 - 74 Postcard Issue 605	1990 - 91 Regular Issue 616	**YUM-YUM**
1978 Postcard Issue 605	**POLICE**	1984 - 85 Issue 629
1979 - 80 Postcard Issue 605	1986 - 87 Regular Issue 617	1987 - 88 Issue 629
1980 - 81 Postcard Issue 605	**CARRETTA TRUCKING**	**GENERAL FOODS**
1981 - 82 Postcard Issue 605	1988 - 89 Regular Issue 617	1985 - 86 Issue 629
1982 - 83 Postcard Issue 605	**NEW YORK ISLANDERS**	1986 - 87 Issue 629
1983 - 84 Postcard Issue 606	**TEAM ISSUES**	1987 - 88 Issue 629
1986 - 87 Issue 606	1979 - 80 Postcard Issue 618	1987 - 88 Postcard Issue 629
1987 - 88 Postcard Issue 606	**ISLANDER NEWS**	1988 - 89 Issue 629
CLOVERLEAF DAIRY	1984 Regular Issue 618	**PROVIGO FOODS**
1978 - 79 Issue 606	1984 - 85 Regular Issue 618	1985 - 86 Sticker Issue 629
1979 - 80 Issue 606	1985 Bryan Trottier 618	**ST. LOUIS BLUES**
7 - ELEVEN	**NEW YORK RANGERS**	**TEAM ISSUES**
1984 - 85 Regular Issue 606	**MARINE MIDLAND**	1978 - 79 Postcard Issue 630
1985 - 86 Regular Issue 606	1989 - 90 Regular Issue 620	1979 - 80 Issue 630
1986 - 87 Regular Issue 607	**OTTAWA SENATORS**	1981 - 82 Issue 630
MONTREAL CANADIENS	**TEAM ISSUES**	1982 - 83 Issue 630
TEAM ISSUES	1992 - 93 Postcard Issue 621	1988 - 89 Issue 630
1967 - 68 Postcard Issue 608	**PHILADELPHIA FLYERS**	**KODAK**
1970 - 71 Postcard Issue 608	**TEAM ISSUES**	1987 - 88 Regular Issue 630
1971 Pins Issue 608	1981 - 82 Ticket Issue 622	1988 - 89 Regular Issue 630
1971 - 72 Issue 608	1986 - 87 Postcard Issue 622	1989 - 90 Regular Issue 630
1973 - 74 Postcard Issue 608	1992 - 93 Photo Issue 622	1990 - 91 Regular Issue 630
1974 - 75 Postcard Issue 608	1993 - 94 Photo Issue 622	**McDONALD'S / UPPER DECK**
1974 - 75 Photo Issue 608	**MIGHTY MILK**	1967 - 92 The Best of the Blues 631
1975 - 76 Postcard Issue 609	1972 - 73 Issue 623	**SAN JOSE SHARKS**
1976 - 77 Postcard Issue 609	**SCORE PINNACLE**	**TEAM ISSUES**
1977 - 78 Postcard Issue 609	1993 Eric Lindros 623	1991 - 92 Regular Issue 632
1978 - 79 Postcard Issue 609	**J.C. PENNY STORES**	1991 - 92 Photo Issue 632
1979 - 80 Postcard Issue 609	1993 - 94 Postcard Issue 623	1993 - 94 Commemorative Sheets 632
1980 - 81 Postcard Issue 609	**PITTSBURGH PENGUINS**	1993 - 94 Coming Home to a New Beginning . 632
1981 - 82 Poscard Issue Set No. 1 610	**TEAM ISSUES**	1993 - 94 Single Ticket New Beginning 632
1981 - 82 Postcard Issue Set No. 2 610	1971 - 72 Postcard Issue 624	1993 - 94 Season Ticket Limited Edition 632
1982 - 83 Postcard Issue 610	1974 - 75 Postcard Issue 624	Commemorative Sheet
1983 - 84 Postcard Issue 610	1983 - 84 Postcard Issue 624	1993 - 94 Gameline Photo Inserts 632
1984 - 85 Postcard Issue 610	**McDONALD'S RESTAURANTS**	**TORONTO MAPLE LEAFS**
1985 - 86 Postcard Issue 610	1977 - 78 Puck Bucks 624	**TEAM ISSUES**
1985 - 86 Placemats 611	**COCA-COLA**	1940 - 1950 Exhibit Cards 635
1986 - 87 Postcard Issue Set No. 1 611	1983 - 84 Issue 624	1964 - 65 Postcard Issue Set A Circa 635
1986 - 87 Postcard Issue Set No. 2 611	**HEINZ**	1865 - 66 Postcard Issue Set B Circa 635
1987 - 88 Postcard Issue 611	1983 - 84 Issue 624	1965 - 66 Postcard Issue Set C 635
1988 - 89 Postcard Issue 611	**KODAK**	1965 - 66 Postcard Issue Set D 635
1989 - 90 Postcard Issue Set No. 1 612	1986 - 87 Regular Issue 624	1962-63 to 1967-68 Postcard Issue 635
1989 - 90 Postcard Issue Set No. 2 612	1987 - 88 Regular Issue 624	1964 - 65 Postcard Issue 635
LA PATRIE	**ELBY'S / BIG BOY**	1968-69 to 1970-71 Postcard Issue 635
1927 - 28 Photo Issue 612	1989 - 90 Postcard Issue 625	1971-72 to 1972-73 Postcard Issue 636
PLAYING CARDS	**ELBY'S / COCA COLA**	1972 - 73 Postcard Issue 636
1927 Circa 612	1991 - 92 Postcard Issue 625	1973-74 to 1974-75 Postcard Issue 636
MOLSON'S	**FOODLAND**	1975 - 76 Postcard Issue 636
1953 - 67 Photo Issue 612	1989 - 90 Regular Issue 625	1976 - 77 Postcard Issue 50th Anniversary Year 636
IGA	1990 - 91 Regular Issue 625	1977 - 78 Posrcard Issue 636
1967 - 68 Regular Issue 612	1991 - 92 Regular Issue 25th Anniversary . 625	1978 - 79 Postcard Issue 636
1968 - 69 Regular Issue 613	1991 - 92 Sticker Issue 625	1979 - 80 Postcard Issue 637
PRO STAR PROMOTIONS	1993 - 94 Regular Issue 626	1980 - 81 Postcard Issue 637
1969 - 70 Postcard Issue 613		1981 - 82 Postcard Issue 637
1970 - 71 Postcard Issue 613		1982 - 83 Postcard Issue 637
1971 - 72 Postcard Issue 613		1983 - 84 Postcard Issue 637
1971 - 72 Postcard Updated Issue 613		1984 - 85 Postcard Issue 638
1972 - 73 Postcard Issue 613		1985 - 86 Postcard Issue 638
STEINBERG		1986 - 87 Postcard Issue 638
1982 - 83 Issue 614		1987 - 88 Photo Issue 638
1983 - 84 Issue 614		1988 - 89 Postcard Set 638

O'KEEFE BEVERAGES
- 1932 - 33 Coaster Issue 638

ESSO HOCKEY TALKS
- 1966 - 67 Coaster Issue 639

POLICE LAW AND YOUTH
- 1987 - 88 Regular Issue 639
- 1988 - 89 Regular Issue 639
- 1990 - 91 Regular Issue 639

TIM HORTON
- 1991 Regular Issue 639

KODAK
- 1992 - 93 Photo Issue 640

BLACK'S PHOTOGRAPHY
- 1993 - 94 Pop-Up Issue 640

VANCOUVER CANUCKS

TEAM ISSUES
- 1979 - 80 Postcard Issue 641
- 1980 Postcard Issue 641
- 1981 - 82 Postcard Issue 641
- 1982 - 83 Postcard Issue 641
- 1983 - 84 Postcard Issue 641
- 1984 - 85 Postcard Issue 642
- 1985 - 86 Regular Issue 642
- 1986 - 87 Regular Issue 642
- 1987 - 88 Issue 642
- 1991 - 92 Issue 642
- 1991 - 92 Autographed Cards 642
- 1992 - 93 Postcard Issue 642

ROYAL BANK
- 1970 - 71 Postcard Issue 642
- 1971 - 72 Postcard Issue 643
- 1972 - 73 Postcard Issue 643
- 1973 - 74 Postcard Issue 643
- 1974 - 75 Postcard Issue 643
- 1975 - 76 Postcard Issue 643
- 1976 - 77 Postcard Issue 643
- 1977 - 78 Postcard Issue 644
- 1978 - 79 Postcard Issue 644

NALLEY'S BOX
- 1972 - 73 Issue 644

POLICE SET
- 1979 - 80 Issue 644

SILVERWOOD DAIRIES
- 1980 - 81 Regular Issue 644
- 1981 - 82 Regular Issue 644

SHELL OIL
- 1986 - 87 Issue 645
- 1987 - 88 Regular Issue 645

MOHAWK
- 1988 - 89 Regular Issue 645
- 1989 - 90 Regular Issue 645
- 1990 - 91 Issue 645

MOLSON
- 1990 - 91 Issue 645
- 1991 - 92 Issue 645

VANCOUVER MILLIONAIRS

TEAM ISSUES
- 1919 Postcard Issue 646

WASHINGTON CAPITALS

TEAM ISSUES
- Postcard Issue 647
- 1978 - 79 Postcard Issue 647
- 1979 - 80 Postcard Issue 647
- 1979 - 80 Issue 647
- 1980 - 81 Postcard Issue 647
- 1981 - 82 Postcard Issue 647
- 1982 - 83 Postcard Issue 647
- 1990 - 91 Postcard Issue 647

PIZZA HUT
- 1984 - 85 Issue 648
- 1985 - 86 Issue 648

KODAK
- 1986 - 87 Regular Issue 648
- 1987 - 88 Regular Issue 648
- 1989 - 90 Regular Issue 648
- 1990 - 91 Regular Issue 648
- 1991 - 92 Issue 648
- 1992 - 93 Regular Issue 649

POLICE
- 1986 - 87 Regular Issue 649

SMOKEY
- 1988 - 89 Regular Issue 649
- 1990 - 91 Regular Issue 649

WINNIPEG JETS

TEAM SETS
- 1979 - 80 Postcard Issue 650
- 1980 - 81 Postcard Issue 650
- 1981 - 82 Postcard Issue 650
- 1982 - 83 Postcard Issue 650
- 1983 - 84 Postcard Issue 650
- 1985 - 86 Postcard Issue 651
- 1986 - 87 Postcard Issue 651
- 1987 - 88 Postcard Issue 651
- 1988 - 89 Postcard Issue 651

ANONYMOUS
- 1982 - 83 Postcard Issue 651

STATER MINT LTD
- 1983 - 84 Hockey Dollars 651

POLICE
- 1984 - 85 Regular Issue 652
- 1985 - 86 Regular Issue 652
- 1988 - 89 Regular Issue 652

SILVERWOOD DAIRY
- 1985 - 86 Issue 653

SAFEWAY
- 1989 - 90 Issue 653

I.G.A.
- 1990 - 91 Issue 653

RUFFLES
- 1993 - 94 Postcard Issue 653

CHAPTER SIX
WORLD HOCKEY ASSOCIATION

O-PEE-CHEE
- 1972 - 73 Team Logo Stickers 657
- 1972 - 73 World Hockey Association .. 657
- 1973 - 74 Posters 657
- 1974 - 75 Regular Issue 657
- 1975 - 76 Regular Issue 658
- 1976 - 77 Regular Issue 659
- 1977 - 78 Regular Issue 660

QUAKER OATS
- 1973 - 74 Issue 661

WHA TEAM SETS

CLEVELAND CRUSADERS
- 1972 - 73 Postcard Issue 662

HOUSTON AREOS
- 1975 - 76 Postcard Issue 662

LOS ANGELES SHARKS
- 1972 - 73 Issue 662

NEW ENGLAND WHALERS
- 1972 - 73 Issue 662

OTTAWA NATIONALS
- 1972 - 73 Issue 663

PHEONIX ROADRUNNERS
- 1975 - 76 Issue 663
- 1976 - 77 Issue 663

QUEBEC NORDIQUES
- 1972 - 73 Issue 663
- 1973 - 74 Postcard Issue 663

- 1976 - 77 Marie Antoinette 664
- 1976 - 77 Postcard Issue 664

VANCOUVER BLAZERS
- 1973 - 74 Postcard Issue 664

WINNIPEG JETS
- 1978 - 79 Postcard Issue 664

WHA ALPHABETICAL INDEX
- Christer Abrahamsson to Bill Young .. 666

CHAPTER SEVEN
TEAM CANADA

O-PEE-CHEE
- 1972 - 73 Team Canada 671

SCOTIA BANK
- 1972 Postcard Issue 671
- 1974 Postcard Issue 671

FUTURE TRENDS

'72 HOCKEY CANADA
- 1991 Promotional Cards 671
- 1991 Issue 671
- 1991 Autographed Cards 672

CANADA CUP 76
- Commemorative Sheets 672
- Canada Cup 76 672
- Canada Cup 76 Autographed Cards 673

ALBERTA LOTTERIES
- Alberta International Hockey Tour '91 . 673
- Canada'a National Team Collectors Edition ... 673

CHAPTER EIGHT
WORLD HOCKEY

RUSSIAN TEAM SETS
- 1978 Soviet National Team - Prague .. 677
- 1979 Soviet National Team - Moscow .. 677
- 1988 History of Soviet Team In Olympics . 677
- 1989 - 90 Stars of Soviet Hockey 677

IVAN FIODOROV PRESS
- 1991 Sport Unites Hearts 677

RED ACE INTERNATIONAL
- 1991 Russian NHL Stars 677
- 1992 Russian NHL Stars 678
- 1992 Russian Stars 678

TRI-GLOBE INTERNATIONAL
- 1992 Sergei Fedorov 678
- 1992 Magnificent Five 678
- 1992 From Russia with Puck 678

PANINI
- 1979 Stickers 679

U.S.A. OLYMPIC TEAM
- 1979- 80 Issue 681

CHAPTER NINE
WORLD JUNIOR HOCKEY

CANADA JUNIOR TEAM
- 1982 Celebration 685
- 1982 World Champions 685
- 1983 Postcard Issue 685
- 1983 Team Photo 685

UPPER DECK
- 1991 - 92 World Junior Championships . 685

LEAF
- 1993 - 94 Finland 686
- 1994 - 95 Finland 688

CHAPTER TEN
MINOR LEAGUES

AMERICAN AND INTERNATIONAL HOCKEY LEAGUES

PROCARDS
- 1988 - 89 AHL 693
- 1988 - 1989 IHL 694
- 1989 - 90 AHL 695
- 1989 - 1990 IHL 697
- 1990 - 1991 AHL / IHL 698
- 1991 - 1992 AHL / IHL 701

SAFEWAY
- 1992 - 93 Phoenix Roadrunners .. 705

NHL DRAFT PICKS

ARENA HOLOGRAMS
- 1991 Regular Issue 706
- 1991 Insert Set Autographed Cards ... 706

CLASSIC GAMES
- 1991 Promotional Cards 706
- 1991 Regular Issue 706
- 1991 FOUR SPORT DRAFT PICKS
  - 1991 Promotional Cards 707
  - 1991 Promotional Sheet 707
  - 1991 Regular Issue 707
- 1992 HOCKEY DRAFT PICKS
  - 1992 Promotional Cards 707
  - 1992 Hockey Draft Picks Collection ... 707
- 1992 - 93 HOCKEY DRAFT PICKS INSERT SETS
  - 1992 Mario Lemieux 708
  - 1992 Exclusive Limited Print Insert Cards ... 708
- 1992 - 93 FOUR SPORT DRAFT PICKS
  - 1992 Promotional Cards 708
- 1992 - 93 CLASSIC FOUR SPORT
  - 1992 - 93 Draft Pick Collection ... 708
- 1992 - 93 DRAFT PICK COLLECTION INSERT SETS
  - Autographed Cards 709
  - 1992 - 93 Bonus Cards 709
  - 1992 Exclusive Limited Print Cards ... 709
- 1993 HOCKEY PRO PROSPECTS
  - Promotional Cards 709
  - 1993 Hockey Pro Prospects 709
- 1992 - 93 INSERT SETS
  - Autograph Card 710
  - 1992 Exclusive Limited Print Cards ... 710
  - 1992 - 93 Bonus Cards 711
  - 1993 Hockey Draft 711
- 1993 INSERT SETS
  - Classic Autographed Cards 712
  - Class of 1994 712
  - Classic Crash 712
  - Team Canada 712
  - Classic Top Ten 712
  - 1994 Classic Pro Hockey Prospects ... 713
  - 1994 Pro Prospects International Heroes ... 714
  - 1994 Autographed Cards 714

STAR PICS
- 1991 Promotional Cards 714
- 1991 Regular Issue 714

ULTIMATE TRADING CARD COMPANY
- 1991 Promotional Cards 715
- 1991 Regular Issue 715

MEMORIAL CUP

7TH INNING SKETCH
- 1990 Regular Issue 716
- 1991 Regular Issue 716

ONTARIO AND QUEBEC HOCKEY LEAGUES

ANONYMOUS
- 1952 - 53 Issue 718

ONTARIO HOCKEY LEAGUE

7TH INNING SKETCH
- 1989 - 90 Regular Issue 719
- 1990 - 91 Promotional Card 721
- 1990 - 91 Regular Issue 721
- 1991 - 92 Regular Issue 726
- 1991 - 92 Insert Set The Teams .. 729
- 1991 CHL Award Winners 729

QUEBEC HOCKEY LEAGUE

LAVAL DAIRY
- 1951 - 52 Issue 730
- 1951 - 52 Update 731
- 1951 - 52 Lac St. Jean 731

ST. LAWRENCE SALES AGENCY
- 1952 - 53 Issue 732

7TH INNING SKETCH
- 1990 - 91 Regular Issue 733
- 1991 - 92 Regular Issue 736
- 1991 - 92 Insert Set The Teams .. 739

WESTERN CANADIAN HOCKEY LEAGUE AND WESTERN HOCKEY LEAGUES

CRESCENT ICE CREAM
- 1923 - 24 Selkirks Hockey Club .. 740
- 1924 - 25 Selkirks Hockey Club .. 740
- 1924 - 25 Falcon Tigers Hockey Club ... 740

HOLLAND CREAMERIES
- 1924 - 25 Western 740

PAULINS CANDY
- 1923 - 24 Issue 740
- 1928 - 29 Issue 741

7TH INNING SKETCH
- 1990 - 91 Regular Issue 742
- 1991 - 92 Regular Issue 743
- 1991 - 92 Insert Set The Teams .. 746

SASKATCHEWAN JUNIOR HOCKEY LEAGUE

AIR CANADA
- 1991 - 92 Regular Issue 747

MPS PHOTOGRAPHICS
- 1993 Issue 748

SLAPSHOT IMAGES LTD
- 1993 - 94 Regular Issue 749

CHAPTER ELEVEN
MINOR LEAGUE TEAM SETS

BALTIMORE SKIPJACKS
- 1991 - 92 Regular Issue 755

BELLEVILLE BULLS
- 1983 - 84 Regular Issue 755
- 1984 - 85 Regular Issue 755

BRANDON WHEAT KINGS
- 1982 - 83 Regular Issue 755
- 1983 - 84 Regular Issue 755
- 1984 - 85 Regular Issue 756
- 1985 - 86 Regular Issue 756
- 1988 - 89 Regular Issue 756
- 1989 - 90 Regular Issue 756

BRANTFORD ALEXANDERS
- 1983 - 84 Regular Issue 757

BROCKVILLE BRAVES
- 1987 - 88 Regular Issue 757
- 1988 - 89 Regular Issue 757
- 1990 - 91 Regular Issue 757

CHICOUTIMI SAGUENEURS
- 1984 - 85 Regular Issue 757

CORNWALL ROYALS
- 1991 - 92 R.A.I.D. 757

FLINT SPRINTS
- 1987 - 88 Regular Issue 758

- 1988 - 89 Regular Issue 758

FREDERICTON EXPRESS
- 1981 - 82 Regular Issue 758
- 1982 - 83 Regular Issue 758
- 1983 - 84 Regular Issue 758
- 1984 - 85 Regular Issue 758
- 1985 - 86 Regular Issue 758
- 1986 - 87 Regular Issue 758

FREDERICTON CANADIENS
- 1992 - 93 Regular Issue 759

HALIFAX CITADELS
- 1989 - 90 Regular Issue 760
- 1990 - 91 Issue 760

HAMILTON CANUCKS
- 1992 - 93 Regular Issue 760

HAMILTON FINCUPS
- 1975 - 76 Regular Issue 760

HAMILTON STEEL CITY
- Date Unknown 760

L'OUTAOUAIS OLYMPIQUES DE HULL
- 1987 - 88 Regular Issue 761

HULL OLYMPICS
- 1980 Regular Issue 761

INDIANAPOLIS CHECKERS
- 1982 - 83 Regular Issue 761
- 1982 - 83 Regular Issue 761

KAMLOOPS BLAZERS
- 1985 - 86 Issue 761
- 1986 - 87 Regular Issue 761
- 1987 - 88 Regular Issue 761
- 1988 - 89 Regular Issue 762
- 1989 - 90 Regular Issue 762

KELOWNA WINGS
- 1984 - 85 Photo Issue - Esso 762
- 1984 - 85 Regular Issue 762

KINGSTON CANADIENS
- 1979 - 80 Issue 762
- 1980 - 81 Issue 762
- 1981 - 82 Issue 762
- 1982 - 83 Regular Issue 763
- 1983 - 84 Regular Issue 763
- 1984 - 85 Regular Issue 763
- 1985 - 86 Regular Issue 763
- 1986 - 87 Regular Issue 764
- 1987 - 88 P.L.A.Y. 764

KITCHENER RANGERS
- 1982 - 83 Regular Issue 764
- 1983 - 84 Regular Issue 764
- 1984 - 85 Regular Issue 765
- 1985 - 86 Regular Issue 765
- 1986 - 87 Regular Issue 765
- 1987 - 88 P.L.A.Y. 765
- 1988 - 89 Regular Issue 766
- 1990 - 91 Regular Issue 766

LETHBRIDGE HURRICANES
- 1988 - 89 Regular Issue 766
- 1989 - 90 Regular Issue 767
- 1990 - 91 Issue 767
- 1991 - 92 Issue 767
- 1992 - 93 Regular Issue 767

LONDON KNIGHTS
- 1985 - 86 Regular Issue 767
- 1986 - 87 Regular Issue 767

MAINE BLACK BEARS
- 1992 - 93 Regular Issue Series Two ... 768

MEDICINE HAT TIGERS
- 1982 - 83 Regular Issue 768
- 1983 - 84 Regular Issue 768
- 1985 - 86 Regular Issue 768

MILWAUKEE ADMIRALS
- 1981 - 82 Regular Issue 768

MONCTON ALPINES
- 1982 - 83 Regular Issue 768

1983 - 84 Regular Issue 768
MONCTON GOLDEN FLAMES
1984 - 85 Regular Issue 769
1985 - 86 Regular Issue 769
1986 - 87 Regular Issue 769
MONCTON HAWKS
1987 - 88 Regular Issue 769
1990 - 91 Regular Issue 770
1991 - 92 Regular Issue 770
MONTREAL JUNIORS
1979 - 80 Postcard Issue Black and White 770
1979 - 80 Postcard Issue Four Colour 770
NASHVILLE KNIGHTS
1989 - 90 Regular Issue 770
NIAGARA FALLS THUNDER
1988 - 89 Regular Issue 771
1989 - 90 Regular Issue 771
NORTH BAY CENTENNIALS
1982 - 83 Regular Issue 771
1983 - 84 Regular Issue 771
NOVA SCOTIA OILERS
1984 - 85 Regular Issue 771
1985 - 86 Regular Issue 772
NOVA SCOTIA VOYAGEURS
1983 - 84 Regular Issue 772
OSHAWA GENERALS
1980 - 81 Regular Issue 772
1981 - 82 Regular Issue 772
1982 - 83 Regular Issue 773
1983 - 84 Regular Issue 773
1989 - 90 Regular Issue 773
1990 - 91 Regular Issue 773
1991 - 92 Regular Issue 774
OTTAWA 67'S
1981 - 82 Photo Issue 774
1982 - 83 Regular Issue 774
1983 - 84 Regular Issue 774
1984 - 85 Regular Issue 775
1985 - 86 Regular Issue 775
1992 - 93 25th Anniversary 775
PETERBOROUGH PETES
1991 - 92 Regular Issue 775
1992 Regular Issue 776

PORTLAND WINTERHAWKS
1986 - 87 Regular Issue 776
1988 - 89 Regular Issue 776
1989 - 90 Regular Issue 776
1993 - 94 Regular Issue 776
PRINCE ALBERT RAIDERS
1984 - 85 Sticker Issue 776
QUEBEC RAMPARTS
1980 - 81 Regular Issue 776
RAYSIDE BALFOUR JUNIOR A CANADIANS
1990 - 91 Regular Issue 777
1991 - 92 Regular Issue 777
REGINA PATS
1981 - 82 Regular Issue 777
1982 - 83 Regular Issue 777
1983 - 84 Regular Issue 777
1985 - 86 Regular Issue 778
1986 - 87 Regular Issue 778
1987 - 88 Regular Issue 778
1988 - 89 Regular Issue 778
1989 - 90 Regular Issue 778
RICHMOND RENEGADES
1990 - 91 Issue 778
LES RIVERAIRES DE RICHELIEU
1988 - 89 Regular Issue 778
SAGINAW GEARS
1978 - 79 Regular Issue 779
SAGINAW HAWKS
1988 - 89 Regular Issue 779
SALT LAKE GOLDEN EAGLES
1988 - 89 Regular Issue 779
SASKATOON BLADES
1981 - 82 Regular Issue 779
1983 - 84 Regular Issue 779
1984 - 85 Regular Issue 780
1986 - 87 Photo Issue 780
SAULT STE. MARIE GREYHOUNDS
1980 - 81 Regular Issue 780
1981 - 82 Regular Issue 780
1982 - 83 Regular Issue 780
1983 - 84 Regular Issue 780
1987 - 88 Regular Issue 781

SHAWINNIGAN FALLS CATARACTS
1980 Regular Issue 781
SHERBROOKE CANADIENS
1986 - 87 Regular Issue 781
SPOKANE CHIEFS
1989 - 90 Regular Issue 781
SPRINGFIELD INDIANS
1983 - 84 Regular Issue 781
1984 - 85 Regular Issue 782
SUDBURY WOLVES
1984 - 85 Postcard Issue 782
1985 - 86 Regular Issue 782
1986 - 87 Regular Issue 782
1987 - 88 Regular Issue 782
1988 - 89 Regular Issue 783
1989 - 90 Regular Issue 783
1990 - 91 Regular Issue 783
1991 - 92 Regular Issue 783
1992 - 93 Regular Issue 783
TORONTO MARLBOROUGHS
Date Unknown 784
VICTORIA COUGARS
1981 - 82 Regular Issue 784
1982 - 83 Regular Issue 784
1983 - 84 Police 784
1984 - 85 Regular Issue 784
1989 - 90 Regular Issue 785
WHEELING THUNDERBIRDS
1992 - 93 Regular Issue 785
WINDSOR SPITFIRES
1989 - 90 Regular Issue 785
EAST COAST HOCKEY LEAGUE TOLEDO STORM
1992 - 93 Regular Issue 785
UNIVERSITY OF MINNESOTA - DULUTH - MINNESOTA BULLDOGS
1985 - 86 Issue 786
UNIVERSITY OF ARIZONA - ARIZONA ICECATS
1985 - 86 Regular Issue 786
APPENDIX . . . .
GLOSSARY OF TERMS . . . .
ABBREVIATIONS . . . .
ALPHABETICAL INDEX OF ISSUERS . . . . . .

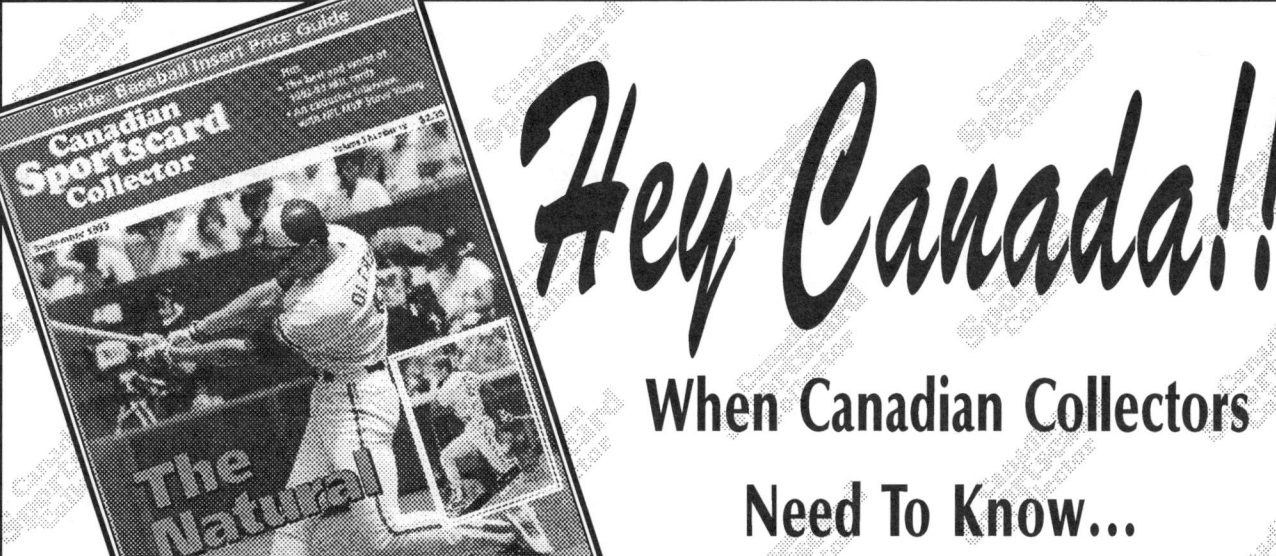

HOCKEY CARD ISSUES

INTRODUCTION

This price guide offers the hockey card collector the most comprehensive guide to modern hockey cards produced and distributed by a host of companies covering a span of over eighty years, from the 1879 season up to 1995. Whether a novice collector or a seasoned pro, this book will be an invaluable aid and source of reference.

Everyone is a collector of something. People collect things for a variety of reasons; for investment purposes, the joy of the hunt, for sentimental reasons, or just for the thrill of owning something rare or limited.

Those just starting out will soon discover that collecting sports memorabilia can become an addictive pastime that has many variations whatever its theme.

Deciding what to collect is a totally personal choice. It's impossible to collect everything. Collectors should focus on a particular era, player, team, company, or issue year. They may focus on a certain type of card; such as, all star, all-time great, highlight, MVP, record breaker, rookie, team leader, or superstar card.

Whatever you decide to collect, enjoy the wonderful world of hockey card collecting.

PRICING IN THIS CATALOGUE

The purpose of this catalogue is to give the most accurate, up-to-date retail prices for hockey cards. These individual market results are drawn from both dealer and collector activity and are averaged to reflect the current marketplace. Regional price differences will occur due to team and player popularity across the country. The early cards in mint condition will command premiums of two or three times NRMT prices.

A necessary word of caution. No catalogue can or should propose to be a fixed price list. Except in the case of newly issued cards (where the published price is actually a manufacturer's suggested retail price) collector interest, rarity factors and other vagaries of the hobby itself invariably dictate true retail values.

This catalogue then, should be considered as a guide, indicating current retail prices possible for the collector and dealer alike to use as a starting point for a buy/sell transaction.

HISTORY OF THE HOCKEY CARD

Manufactured in Canada long before the arrival of baseball and football cards, the first card sets were distributed in cigarette packages during the 1910-13 era. Only three C sets were produced before WW I, with cards measuring 1 1/2" X 2 1/2". The backs of these cards list the player's team membership history.

The first set issued for the 1910-11 season, titled "Hockey Series", featured coloured portraits of the leading players. The "Hockey Players" series of the 1911-12 season is the easiest of the earlier sets to complete and featured players from the Quebec, Ottawa, Renfrew, Wanderers, and Montreal teams. The scarce 1912-13 "Hockey Series" issue featured black and white portraits of players from eastern and western Canadian teams.

After WW I, only one more cigarette set was issued - during the 1924-25 season by Champ's Cigarettes of Hamilton, Ontario. The sepia-toned set featured players from the six NHL teams.

Several food and candy manufacturers produced sets during the '20s. Paulin's Candy, Maple Crispette, Crescent, Holland Creameries and La Patrie are among those known to have issued sets. The backs of the cards contain information on promotional gift offers available by returning a complete card set to the company. On receiving the completed sets, the companies would stamp or punch the cards and return them along with the gift. For this reason, mint condition cards of these sets are very difficult to find. The sets of the '20s are the scarcest because their distribution was regional.

Four gum manufacturers—Canadian Chewing Gum, Hamilton Chewing Gum, O-Pee-Chee Co., and World Wide Chewing Gum Co.—appeared on the scene during the 1933-34 season. O-Pee-Chee outskated its rivals by producing cards with a variety of background colours and more attractive designs, and was the only chewing gum company to issue cards up to the 1940-41 season, when production stopped because of WW II.

Hockey cards didn't appear again until the 1951-52 season. A number of food companies joined the popular game with brief promotional appearances. Of these, three of the common household names were York Peanut Butter, Shirriff Desserts and Post Cereal.

Parkhurst Products of Toronto, Ontario, was the major unchallenged issuer for the first three seasons starting in 1951. O-Pee-Chee of London, Ontario and Topps of Brooklyn, New York, entered the picture during the 1954-55 season.

Topps and O-Pee-Chee missed the next two years, then started up again during the 1957-58 season. The Parkhurst issues lacked originality and had more regional distribution. In contrast, Topps and O-Pee-Chee distributed issues featuring more colourful cards and more player information across the nation. By the end of the 1963-64 season, Parkhurst was forced to take a permanent leave of absence from the arena.

Since affiliating in 1968, the Topps/O-Pee-Chee alliance has become the dominant North American supplier of hockey cards, with O-Pee-Chee supplying Canada, and Topps supplying the United States.

NO ORDER IS TOO SMALL WITH

CARTOMANIA

MONEY BACK GUARANTEE IF NOT SATISFIED

"ONLY HOCKEY" 1951 to Date ❖ BUY – SELL – TRADE

SINGLES - SETS - WAX BOXES

JOSEPH E. "JOE" FILION, Proprietor
819-428-7053 Fax 819-428-1241

Fan's items such as: JERSEYS, HATS, T-SHIRTS, GLASSES, PENNANTS, MINI STICKS, KEY RINGS, PINS, PUCKS, Etc.
82 PRINCIPALE, CHENEVILLE QUEBEC J0V 1E0
Other Location: HAWKESBURY MALL, 400 SPENCE ST., HAWKESBURY, ONT. (613) 632-7141
— FREE CATALOGUE ON REQUEST —

HOCKEY IMMORTALS

- SETS AND SINGLES FROM PRE WAR, PARKHURST, TOPPS AND OPC •
- BEE HIVE PHOTOS • DIAMOND MATCHBOOKS • QUAKER OATS •
- ESSO • TORONTO STAR • WONDER BREAD • LA PATRIE • SHIRRIFF •
- YORK • COCA COLA • EATONS • POST CEREAL • LIPTON •
- LOBLAWS • KRAFT • 7 ELEVEN • McDONALDS • FUN MATE •
- PANINI AND OPC STICKERS • WRAPPERS • VACHON • RED ROOSTER •
- POSTCARDS • IGA • STEINBERG • SHELL • JERSEYS • MAGAZINES •
- PROGRAMS • UNOPENED WAX • MEMORABILIA •

WANT LISTS WELCOMED
ORDERS SHIPPED FROM CANADA OR U.S.
100% MONEY BACK IF NOT SATISFIED
ALWAYS INTERESTED IN BUYING QUALITY
HOCKEY MATERIAL

P.O. BOX 23023
PENTICTON B.C.
V2A 8L7

or

P.O. BOX 1594
OROVILLE, WA
U.S.A. 98844

 TELEPHONE 604-492-2072 FAX 604-493-9327
ERWIN BORAU — OWNER

SEND $2 FOR MY EXTENSIVE CATALOGUE PUBLISHED QUARTERLY,
CONTAINING ALL THE ABOVE ITEMS AS WELL AS OPC BASEBALL,
CFL FOOTBALL, SPECIALS & CLEAROUT ITEMS.
CATALOGUE COST REFUNDABLE WITH ANY PURCHASE.

THE MARKET

Like all businesses, the value of hockey cards is determined by the law of supply and demand. The supply of available cards is less than the quantity produced because a certain percentage of cards are thrown away or destroyed. Not all purchasers of hockey cards are serious collectors intent on preserving the quality of their cards. However, more and more people are becoming aware of the appreciative value of mint condition sports cards every year.

The supply is almost impossible to determine since private companies are not required by law to divulge information on the quantity of cards they produce. Variations in supply have gradually been noted over the years.

Experienced dealers have noted supply differences in the O-Pee-Chee issues between 1979 and 1987. It was noted that the three issues between 1979 and 1982 were short-supplied. The three issues between 1982 and 1985 were over-supplied compared to the 1985-86 and 1986-87 issues.

A similar discrepancy is noted in some Topps issues prior to 1973. In this case, certain issues had a scarcity of higher numbered cards. This occurred because the issue was printed and distributed in two series, with the second series being printed at a later date in a smaller quantity, presumably because the first series sales did not meet forecast expectations.

Hockey card production has increased in recent years. The fact that more and more dealers are opening stores offering sports cards and supplies confirms that the demand is strong. Interest in hockey card collecting is increasing in the United States, where the O-Pee-Chee Canadian issues are beginning to gain popularity because the sets are larger than those issued by Topps.

Several factors determine the demand of any given card; the number of cards produced, the popularity of the player depicted on the card, the age of the card, the condition of the card and the card's over-all attractiveness. Rookie cards consistently demand a higher value, even for common players.

The primary focus of demand continues to be centred around the two main issuers, O-Pee-Chee and Topps. Parkhurst does, however, retain its share of dedicated collectors. The standard size waxpack card issues enjoy greater popularity among collectors than do the various insert sets which are comprised of stickers, box bottoms and the two or four player on one standard size card format. Promotional and community issues are primarily of regional interest only. Non-standard size cards and those produced by small manufacturers tend to be sold at a higher price as complete sets. But still, a diehard collector will buy almost anything.

The demand for cards will vary regionally across the nation. Human nature dictates that cards depicting local or hometown players and teams will demand a higher price locally than in other regions.

Although one would think that a complete set would cost more than the total price of the individual cards, this is usually not the case. This trend began with the growing interest among collectors in individual player cards, specifically rookie, star, and superstar cards. Because the same quantity of each card in a series was produced, it became more difficult to complete a set because of the shortage of certain individual player cards. With the decreased demand for sets, dealers were more inclined to let a set go at a lower price in order to get rid of a large stock of less desirable cards. The older cards, however, still sell better individually because the sets are very difficult to complete.

BUYING AND SELLING CARDS

Several avenues are available as sources for buying, selling, or trading individual cards and sets.

Naturally, like any business person, you want to sell your cards for the highest possible price and purchase them at the lowest possible price. Using this price guide as a reference, you will have to shop around to become familiar with pricing differences among the various sources. The sports card market is not as liquid as the stock market and a certain degree of patience is necessary to sell your cards at what you think is a fair price.

It's a good idea to keep abreast of the changing market by regularly reading the several monthly sports periodicals available. These publications are very useful in keeping up-to-date on pricing fluctuations, collectors' personal advertisements and the dates and locations of shows, auctions, and conventions.

Shows and conventions offer you the best opportunity to shop around and meet a wide range of dealers and collectors assembled under one roof. Not only do you have a huge selection of older cards to choose from, but you may also buy unopened product by the single pack or by the box.

You may wish to maximize your profit by selling your cards on your own. You may advertise in a local newspaper or sports periodical or rent a booth space at a card show if you have a large collection to sell. But before you set out, take into consideration the time you must invest - advertising costs, miscellaneous expenses, your sales ability, and your knowledge of card collecting will all dictate your success.

For the collector who enjoys assembling a collection slowly, piece by piece, gum waxpacks are usually available at your local convenience store.

If you are in a hurry to make a transaction, or you don't want the hassle of selling your cards yourself, you may choose a dealer as a source. Dealers are in touch with an extensive network of collectors and suppliers and are more knowledgeable at identifying potential buyers for your cards, or locating the owners of elusive cards. You must be fully aware, however, that a dealer has to cover expenses, and his primary reason for setting up shop is to make a profit. Dealers will pay anywhere from 20% to 75% of the book value depending on demand (measured as the time it takes the dealer to sell the item). You may also arrange for a dealer to accept your cards on consignment. This assures you that he will attempt to obtain the highest possible price, since he will charge a percentage of the sale price as his fee.

Direct mail is another source for obtaining cards. If you choose this route, it would be wise to start off buying small quantities of cards until you become accustomed with the quality of cards purchased unseen.

CARD CARE

In order to ensure the continued appreciation in value of your cards, you must keep card handling to a minimum. It is highly recommended that you obtain suitable storage containers to preserve the condition of your delicate cards. Items such as sleeves, boxes and binder sheets are commercially available in specific sizes in which to safely store your prized collectibles.

Card sleeves are handy for displaying single cards. Sleeves are made of various materials, ranging from pliable polypropylene and polyethylene, to a stiffer mylar, to hard acrylic and Plexiglass.

Specially designed cardboard boxes enable you to store hundreds of cards and also facilitate transportation or storage. Try to use boxes with flat bottoms as boxes with bottom flaps can damage your cards. Since some cardboard boxes may contain an element of acid, you may wish to insert your cards into individual sleeves before placing them in boxes. As an added precaution, take care not to place your valuable cards at either end of the box.

Plastic three-ring binder sheets with pockets are a popular means of holding and displaying cards. Make certain that the pockets will hold your cards snugly but not tightly, as some sheets are designed to hold a specific size of card. Sheets made of polyvinyl chloride (PVC) are less flexible and more transparent, but contain certain oils which may after long periods of time damage your cards. PVC may be detected by its customary vinyl odour, whereas polypropylene and polyethylene are odourless.

Needless to say, mint condition cards do not have foreign substances applied to them. Adding glue, tape, protective coating, or writing; removing tabs; applying elastic bands to stacks of cards; or using photograph corners to store cards in a scrap album are all taboo.

Extreme environmental conditions will, in time, adversely affect the condition of your cards. Prolonged direct sunlight will remove the gloss from and fade the colours on cards. High humidity or extreme changes in humidity will result in gradual deterioration and warping, while excessive heat will increase the rate of decomposition.

It's not necessary to handle cards with gloves or tongs, just be aware of the adverse affects of mishandling and take a realistic approach to preserving the condition of your cards.

A.J. Cards – NOW BUYING –

BUYING HOCKEY SETS

	EX-MT	NM-MT
1910-11	$4,950	$6,930
1911-12	$4,950	$6,930
1933-34 OPC	$5,225	$6,380
1934-35 OPC	$2,035	$2,915
1935-36 OPC	$1,623	$2,310
1936-37 OPC	$6,050	$8,635
1937-38 OPC	$3,245	$4,620
1939-40 OPC	$2,778	$4,043
1940-41 OPC	$2,833	$4,043
1951-52 PARKHURST	$6,500	$9,000
1952-53 PARKHURST	$3,500	$5,850
1953-54 PARKHURST	$2,825	$3,870
1955-56 PARKHURST	$1,625	$2,700
1957-58 PARKHURST	$1,100	$1,800
1958-59 PARKHURST	$800	$1,350
1959-60 PARKHURST	$650	$1,100
1960-61 PARKHURST	$875	$1,450
1961-62 PARKHURST	$675	$1,125
1962-63 PARKHURST	$800	$1,350
1963-64 PARKHURST	$975	$1,625
1954-55 TOPPS	$2,400	$4,000
1957-58 TOPPS	$1,080	$1,800
1958-59 TOPPS	$1,950	$3,250
1959-60 TOPPS	$1,080	$1,800
1960-61 TOPPS	$1,080	$1,800
1961-62 TOPPS	$870	$1,450
1962-63 TOPPS	$700	$1,170
1963-64 TOPPS	$540	$900
1964-65 TOPPS	$3,500	$5,850
1965-66 TOPPS	$1,450	$2,425
1966-67 TOPPS	$2,160	$3,600
1967-68 TOPPS	$1,460	$2,430
1968-69 OPC	$800	$1,350
1969-70 OPC	$650	$1,170
1970-71 OPC	$600	$1,000
1971-72 OPC	$700	$1,100
1972-73 OPC	$600	$975
1973-74 OPC	$200	$320
1974-75 OPC	$225	$360
1975-76 OPC	$135	$220
1979-80 OPC	$450	$920
1986-87 OPC	$125	$200

BUYING WAX BOXES

	NR-MT
1977-78	$300 BOX
1978-79	$180 BOX
1979-80	$2,700 BOX
1980-81	$1,200 BOX
1981-82	$840 BOX
1982-83	$180 BOX
1983-84	$180 BOX
1984-85	$600 BOX
1985-86	$900 BOX
1986-87	$720 BOX
1987-88	$335 BOX
1988-89	$180 BOX

BUYING

SHIRRIFF COINS	NR-MT
1960-61	$320
1961-62	$250
1962-63	$395
1968-69	$4,700

YORK PEANUT BUTTER	NR-MT
1960-61	$320
1961-62	$450
1962-63 IRON ON	$1,600
1963-64	$500
1967-68	$325

ALSO BUYING

	NR-MT
1961-62 STAMPS TOPPS	$750
1970-71 DECLE EDGE OPC	$200
1970-71 STICKER STAMPS OPC	$200
1968-69 PUCK STICKERS OPC	$200
1969-70 STAMPS OPC	$40
1969-70 4 IN 1 SET OPC	$600
1969-70 MINI CARD ALBUM OPC	$40
1962-63 HOCKEY BUCKS TOPPS	$600

BUYING: BEEHIVE, CANADA, STARCH, QUAKER OATS PHOTOS

A.J. Cards

530 Rowntree Dairy Rd., Unit #3
Woodbridge, Ontario L4L 8II2
Tel: (416) 740-3642   Fax: (905) 851-9259
1-800-263-2307

CARD GRADING

Grading the value of any collectible item is always a subjective decision, but the most important criteria in grading is the condition of the item.

Physical defects decreasing the value of a card may be the result of printing errors, collector mishandling, or natural environmental deterioration.

The main criteria for judging the condition of a card are border conformity (centering), corner wear, creases, alterations, and surface wear.

BORDER CONFORMITY

Border conformity is one defect beyond the control of the card purchaser. Whereas a mint card is generally thought to be one which is in the same condition as when issued, printing errors and poor quality control may devalue a card before it is even packaged. A mint card has opposing borders of equal width. Width differences in adjacent borders are acceptable. The degree of border conformity defects vary from slightly off-centred to blatently miscut.

- **Slightly Off-centred:** One border width is barely smaller than its opposite border.
- **Off-centred:** One border width is noticeably larger than the opposite border.
- **Badly Off-centred:** A border is barely perceptible on one side of the card.
- **Miscut:** The card is cut so badly that one border is missing, and the opposite border shows part of the adjacent card of a print sheet.

CORNER WEAR

The degree of rounding and fraying (paper layer separation) of the corners on square edge cards decreases the value proportionately. Corner wear may be expressed in the following degrees of seriousness: sharp corners with slight fraying, slightly rounded corners, rounded corners, and badly rounded corners.

CREASES

Creases range in severity from light to heavy, and may even occur during the printing process.

- **Light Crease:** This crease is barely perceptible, and is not as serious if on the back of the card.
- **Medium Crease:** This crease is noticeable, but is not the length of the card or deep enough to break the surface of the face of the card.
- **Heavy Crease:** The crease breaks through the face surface.

ALTERATIONS

Buyers must take special care to ensure that purchased cards have not been trimmed or touched-up in an attempt to improve the appearance.

- **Trimming:** This is an attempt by the owner to remove rounding, fraying, and uneven border defects by cutting away parts of the card. The safest way to check this suspicion is to measure the card with a ruler.
- **Touch-up:** This is an attempt to enhance faded areas on a card by covering up obvious defects with the use of some sort of colouring device.

SURFACE WEAR

Cards that are mishandled or handled too often will show signs of surface wear. Prolonged direct exposure to sunlight will remove the gloss and cause discolouration to the face of the card. Warping and water staining resulting from improper storage are considered to be major defects.

MISHANDLING DEFECTS

Poor handling habits and improper storage of cards will cause several other defects. Common flaws include tape or paste marks, pin holes, tears, fuzzy or worn edges, rubber band marks, smoke stains, writing, and removal of perforated tabs or coupons. Improper manufacturer packaging may also cause gum staining.

CONDITION GUIDE

The following eight categories are commonly used to describe the condition of a card.

- **MINT (MT):** A card containing no defects. The picture is in focus, the borders are even, the corners are sharp, the edges are smooth, the surface contains no creases and has its orignal gloss, and there are no printing defects.
- **NEAR MINT (NRMT):** A card with one of the very slight defects previously mentioned. This would include printer's lines or spots.
- **EXCELLENT-MINT (EX-MT):** A card with two or three very slight defects.
- **EXCELLENT (EX):** A card with only a few minor defects; such as, stains, writing, or marks on the back of the card, loss of gloss, and only slight rounding, off-centring, or creasing.
- **VERY GOOD (VG):** A card displaying one major or several minor defects which are noticeable but not serious; such as, some corner rounding, loss of surface gloss, off-centred or discoloured borders, minor creases, or picture slightly out of focus.
- **GOOD (G):** A card showing the results of much handling, with two or three major defects. Common major flaws include deceptive trimming, badly off-centred borders showing signs of browning, and a higher degree of corner rounding and layering, creasing, scuffing of the card face, and edge notching.
- **FAIR (F):** A card with one serious defect or several major defects. Serious defects include writing on the front, miscutting, large holes, noticeable trimming, heavy creases, and tears.
- **POOR (P):** A card with two or more serious defects. If it has any value at all, it would only be as a filler until a replacement card is found.

CONDITION MUST BE DETERMINED BEFORE A CARD CAN BE PRICED.

AVAILABLE IN APRIL!

THE CHARLTON STANDARD CATALOGUE OF CANADIAN BASEBALL & FOOTBALL CARDS

CFL Cards From 1952!
Baseball Cards From 1912!
Over 100,000 Prices!

4 EDITION 1995

For Canadian Baseball and Football Card Collectors this catalogue has it all!

IMPERIAL TOBACCO * MAPLE CRISPETTE
PARKHURST * O-PEE-CHEE * CANADA STARCH
STUART * POST TOPPS * WORLD WIDE GUM
NALLEYS * DONRUSS - LEAF * EDDIE SARGENT
PROVIGO WILLARD * NABISCO * TORONTO BLUE
JAYS STANDARD OIL * BLUE RIBBON TEA * PANINI
GENERAL MILLS * SCORE * EXHIBITS * HOSTESS
PURITAN MEATS * GULF CANADA * JOGO
VACHON * ROYAL STUDIOS * NEILSON'S * BEN'S
AULT FOODS * COCA-COLA * BAZOOKA * KFC
And All Other Major Manufacturers...

BASEBALL CARDS FROM 1912   FOOTBALL CARDS FROM 1949

✓ Complete price listings for all Major League Baseball and Canadian Football League cards!
✓ Comprehensive baseball and football minor league card listings!
✓ Regular issues, stickers, inserts, subsets, transfers and much, much more!
✓ All major manufacturers!
✓ Current Pricing for all cards in up to three grades of condition - VG, EX, and NRMT!
✓ All rookie, last, pitcher, quarterback, error and variation cards identified and priced!
✓ Plus Charlton's Fabulous Alphabetical Index!

★ OVER 300 PAGES ★ 60,000 PRICES ★
★ NEW, LARGER 8 1/2 x 11" FORMAT ★

RESERVE YOUR COPY TODAY DIRECTLY FROM THE PUBLISHER!!
THE CHARLTON PRESS, 2010 YONGE STREET, TORONTO, ONTARIO M4S 1Z9.

---------- *Photocopy and Fax or Mail* ----------

✓ **YES!** I'd like to order ___ copy (ies) of *The Charlton Standard Catalogue of Canadian Baseball and Football Cards - 4th Edition* @ only $ 29.95 per copy, plus postage.

I have enclosed $ _____ for _____ copy (ies) plus $5 per copy for postage.

NAME _____   ADDRESS_____

_____   CITY _____ PROV./STATE _____

POSTAL/ZIP CODE _____   Enclosed is my cheque for $ _____

Please charge my   ☐ VISA   ☐ AMEX Acc. # _____

EXP. DATE _____   SIGNATURE _____

FOR TOLL FREE ORDERING PHONE 1-800-442-6042   FAX 1-800-442-1542 From anywhere in Canada or the U.S.

COUNTERFEIT CARDS

The following pages contain photographs and information that outline the differences you must look for to distinguish counterfeit from authentic cards. Study these points carefully. They will be extremely helpful when you enter the market to either buy or sell cards.

Parkhurst 1951-52
CARD #18

MAURIE "ROCKET" RICHARD and TERRY SAWCHUK

Card No. 4
Maruice "Rocket" Richard

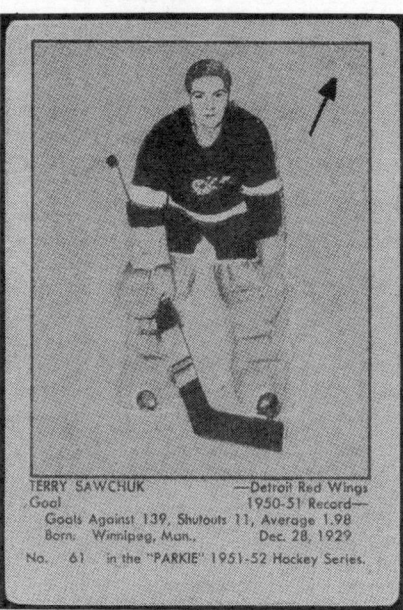

Card No. 61,
Terry Sawchuk

FACE

This is a very good job of counterfeiting. The photographic detail is very good but colours are not as strong as the genuine cards and the paper on which they are printed is thicker. The edges look like they have just been cut but the corners have been artifically rounded to make the cards look old.

There are even small printers marks very much like those on the originals. Look for small creases which have been photographically produced.

BACK
Blank

Note: Due to the high price of this set collectors are warned to be very careful. It is believed that every card in this set has been counterfeited.

O-Pee-Chee 1979-80
CARD #18

WAYNE GRETZKY

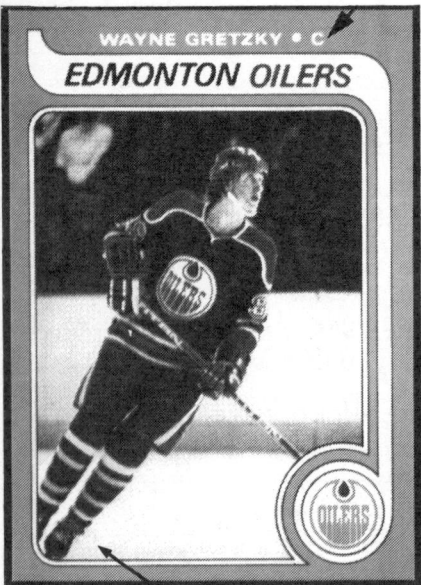

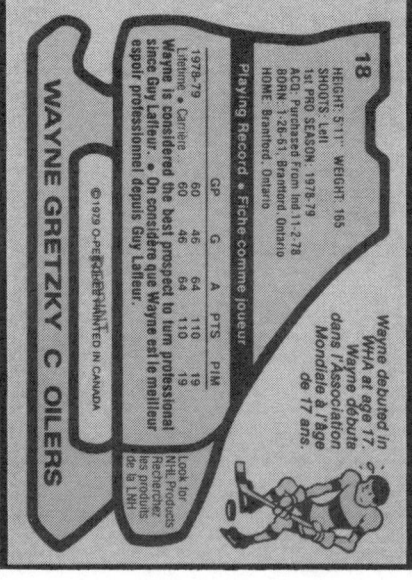

FACE

"Wayne Gretzky . C" on the original card face has clear, sharp, wide lettering. The counterfeit has small fuzzy lettering. Each letter under magnification on the reproduction will have jagged outlines.

On the original, Gretzky's skate laces will show individual lace strands while the reproduction will show a blurr with no definition of the individual strands.

The colours on the original are more subdued and the border a powder blue versus a sky blue border on the original.

BACK

The skate on the original must be sky blue in colour. The counterfeit has a turquoise coloured skate. Also the skate outline on the original has a brown/black border while the reproduction has only a brown border

The "WH" of "WHA" is joined on the counterfeit and separate on the original. Some of the reproductions have been stamped reprint over the O-Pee-Chee copyright

Note: Due to printing variations that occur over a long run of card sheets it's a good rule of thumb to have confirmation of two or more of the above points before a card is classified as counterfeit.

KITCHENER COIN SHOP

SPECIALIZING IN HOCKEY & BASEBALL

We Also Carry Football & Basketball

WAX PACKS SETS & SINGLES

19 Scott Street, Kitchener, Ontario N2H 2P6
(519) 742-9181   Est. 1965

TOPPS UPPER DECK BOWMAN TOPPS PARKHURST O-PEE-CHEE PRO SET

TORONTO SPORTSCARDS COMPANY INC.

— *David Chu* —

Specializing in Buying and Selling Hockey Cards

*Buy-Sell-Trade
We Do Mail Order
Send Us Your Want Lists!*

- *BEST SELECTION OF WAX PACKS IN THE CITY*
  - *WE CATER TO REGIONAL COLLECTORS*
  - *INSERTS, SETS, HARD TO FIND COMMONS*
    Huge Inventory of European Players - All Years

363 Yonge Street, Second Floor, Downtown Toronto, Ontario M5B 1S1
Between Hockey Hall of Fame & Maple Leaf Gardens
Phone (416) 979-0860 Fax (416) 340-7132

LEAF DONRUSS PRO SET CLASSIC SCORE PARKHURST UPPER DECK

UPPER DECK AUTHENTICATED — *O-PEE-CHEE UPPER DECK SCORE*

O-Pee-Chee 1980-81
CARD #140

RAY BOURQUE

FACE

The face of the card has poor flesh tones and the face of the player is paler than the original. There is also less detail in both the photograph and the type. This gives the card an overall fuzzy appearance. The counterfeit appears to have been printed on card stock that is lighter in colour than that of the original.

BACK

The edge of the puck containing the number of the player is fuzzy and is lighter than the original. Since the counterfeit has been printed on card stock of a lighter colour, unprinted surfaces appear white rather than the darker shade found in the authentic card. The green ink on the back of the card is much lighter than the darker green found on the original. The yellow areas of the counterfeit are much more of an intense yellow than authentic cards.

O-Pee-Chee 1980-81
CARD #289

MARK MESSIER

 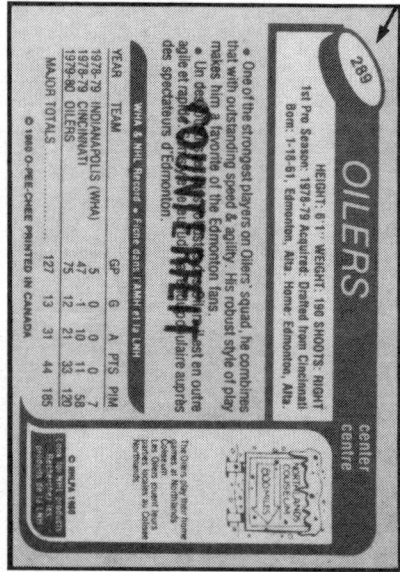

FACE

The face of the card has poor flesh tones and the face of the player is paler than the original. There is also less detail in both the photograph and the type. This gives the card an overall fuzzy appearance. The counterfeit appears to have been printed on card stock that is lighter in colour than that of the original.

BACK

The edge of the puck containing the number of the player is fuzzy and is lighter than the original. Since the counterfeit has been printed on card stock of a lighter colour, unprinted surfaces appear white rather than the darker shade found in the authentic card. The green ink on the back of the card is much lighter than the darker green found on the original. The yellow areas of the counterfeit are much more of an intense yellow than authentic cards.

Note: Due to printing variations that occur over a long run of card sheets it's a good rule of thumb to have confirmation of two or more of the above points before a card is classified as counterfeit.

RONALD VILLENEUVE

COLLECTION DE SPORT AZ INC.

809 Fresniere, St-Eustache
Quebec, Canada J7R 4K3

Telephone 514-473-2822   Fax 514-623-7454
In Business Since 1980
Sales and Auction Lists Four Times A Year

Subscription of $3.00 for One Sales & Auction List

ALWAYS INTERESTED IN BUYING QUALITY HOCKEY MATERIAL
✧ **UNOPENED PACKS** ✧ **WRAPPERS** ✧ **SETS** ✧ **STARS PRE 1971** ✧

IMPERIAL COIN & CARD

Hamilton & Area's Largest Selection of Sportscards!

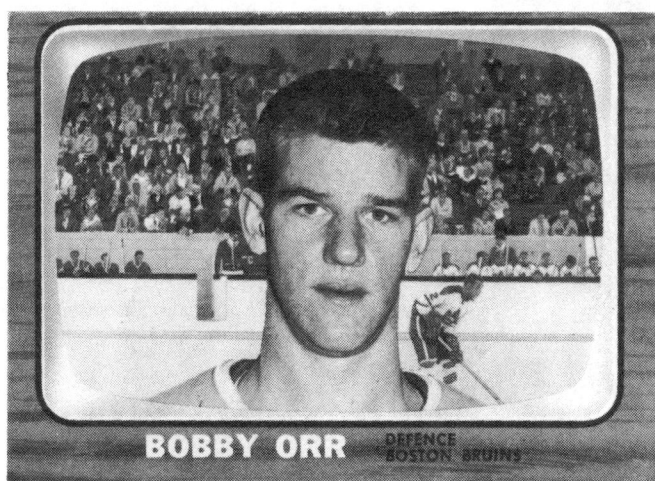

"OVER
10 MILLION
SINGLE CARDS
IN STOCK"

**IMPERIAL
COIN & CARD CO.**

White Oaks Plaza,
195 Plains Road East
Burlington, Ontario L7T 2C4
(905) 639-4614

*Others Claim It!
Come and See It!*

O-Pee-Chee 1981-82
CARD #111

PAUL COFFEY

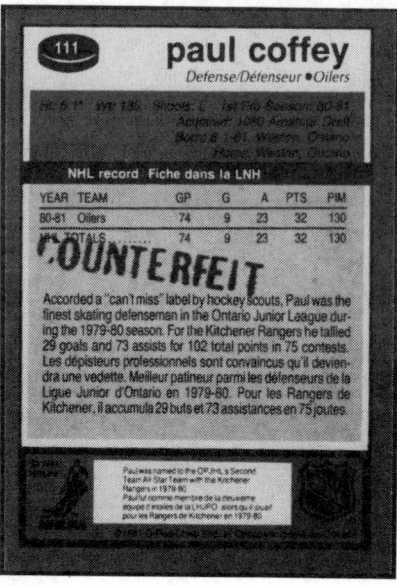

FACE

The counterfeit card actually features sharper photographic detail than the original. Borders are cut more sharply and are whiter than those of the authentic cards. This counterfeit, like that of the OPC counterfeit 1980-81 cards, seems to have been printed with slightly more yellow. The yellow word "OILERS" on the face is slightly more intense than on the original authentic card.

BACK

The counterfeit, again, seems to have been printed on card stock that is whiter than that of the authentic issue. Unprinted surfaces appear much whiter than those of original cards. The blue on the back is more of a royal blue and is darker than the original. There is a white or knock-out box at the bottom of the card which, on the authentic card is sharply bordered. The border on the counterfeit is fuzzy.

O-Pee-Chee 1985-86
CARD #9

MARIO LEMIEUX

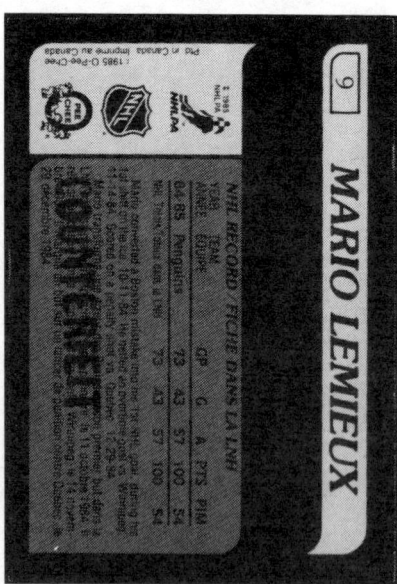

FACE

This counterfeit is again trimmed more sharply than the authentic issue and has a more yellowish tint. The photograph is fuzzy and there is a bluish tint to the background behind Lemieux that does not exist on the original. The photo on the counterfeit has less detail and the type and artwork are blurred.

BACK

The red border on the original card is a less intense colour. On the counterfeit the red is more of a deep red wine colour and the area containing the player's statistics is more of an orange than the original's pink colour. The screen used on the back of the counterfeit is much more apparent than on the authentic issue. All unprinted areas appear white on the counterfeit instead of the original's light grey-brown shade.

Note: Due to printing variations that occur over a long run of card sheets it's a good rule of thumb to have confirmation of two or more of the above points before a card is classified as counterfeit.

TRUEMAN'S SPORTS CARDS

Mailing Address: 1755 Rathburn Rd. E., Unit 26, Mississauga, Ontario L4W 2M8

Specializing in Canadian Only Issues

Hard to Find Current Insert Cards You Have Been Looking For

CALL US!
WE HAVE THEM!

* Call/Write/Fax Us for a list of cards of your favourite players. (Gretzky, Roy, Lemieux, Potvin, Bure, Selanne, Hull, Jagr, Lindros, Leetch, Belfour, Yzerman, Modano, Roenick, Joseph, Bourque, Gilmour & many more).

Satisfaction Guaranteed!

Phone: (905) 629-8309 Fax: (905) 206-0244

FROZEN POND

We carry the largest quality assortment of Hockey Autographs on the Continent. From Abel to Zezel, we have them all. Please call or write for our latest catalogue.

Come visit our new showroom at
112 Merton St., Suite One, in mid-town Toronto.

Frozen Pond,
7B Pleasant Blvd., Suite 989,
Toronto, Ontario, M4T 1K2

Tel. 416-488-9903
Fax 416-488-9430

PRIME TIME
SPORTS CARDS
BUY ❖ SELL ❖ TRADE

BOB BOIN
(905) 844-2161
PAGER (416) 329-6103

OAKVILLE PLACE MALL
240 LEIGHLAND AVE.
(QEW at Trafalgar Rd.)
OAKVILLE, ONT. L6H 3H6

FRANK LEARDI SPORTSCARDS

One of Canada's Largest
Mail Order Companies
- FULL SERVICE DEALER
- CUSTOMER SATISFACTION GUARANTEED
- FREE PRICE LIST ON REQUEST

Specializing in all Hockey!

Try us out! You'll be glad you did!

FRANK LEARDI SPORTSCARDS
416-781-0127   416-781-3170
P.O. Box 361, Station T, Toronto Ontario M6B 4A3

O-Pee-Chee 1986-87
CARD #3

WAYNE GRETZKY

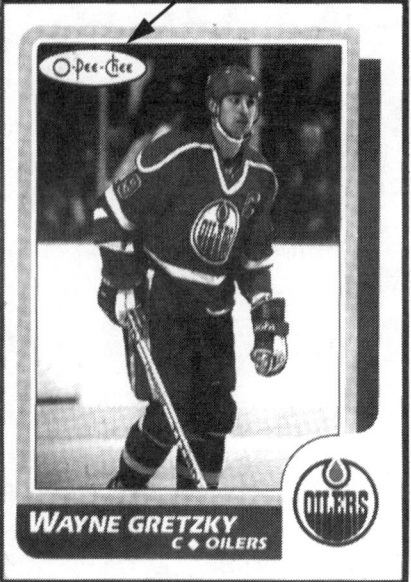 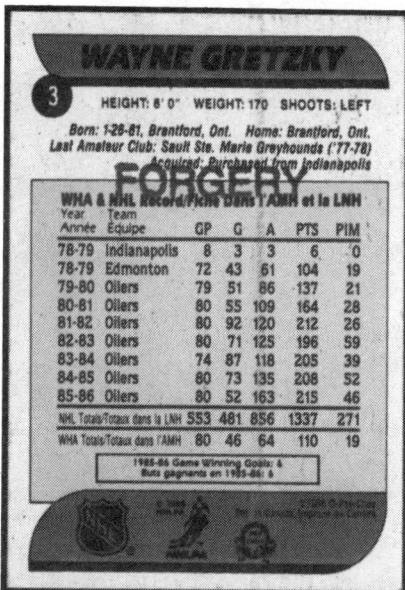

FACE

The counterfeit cards have a blueish tinge. This effect colours anything appearing white or grey on the orginal card, blue on the counterfeit card. The white border, the grey ice, the white stripes in the Oilers uniform all have a blueish tinge on the counterfeit card.
Both cards have a gloss finish.
O-Pee-Chee on the forgery has a reddish hue to the letters and naturally each letter is fuzzy and irregular. This is better seen under magnification.
The facial tones of Gretzky have again a reddish tinge, except now there can be seen a red dot on the left side of Wayne's nose.
The Oilers uniform colours are darker on the counterfeit than on the original.

BACK

The blue tint that carried over to all the white and grey sections on the face does the same on the back. The grey card stock of the orginal has a overall blueish tint on the forgery.

O-Pee-Chee 1987-88
CARD #42

LUC ROBITAILLE

 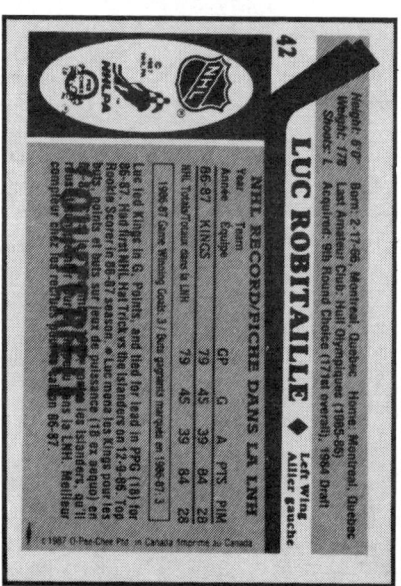

FACE

The photograph, type and artwork on the counterfeit are just slightly inferior to that of the oringial but the colours are a near match. Examination of the OPC logo on the counterfeit will, however, reveal less detail. Again, the counterfeits appear to be more sharply trimmed than the original.

BACK

The overall pink colour on the back more closely matches that of the original. However, the back of the counterfeit card is slightly lighter than the authentic issue. Also, there is less detail in the type and artwork and the black ink underneath the hockey stick is not as solid as that on the original card. Again, unprinted areas of the cards appear much whiter than those on the authentic card.

Note: Due to printing variations that occur over a long run of card sheets it's a good rule of thumb to have confirmation of two or more of the above points before a card is classified as counterfeit.

SPORTSCARD SHOWS

WHOLESALE TO THE PUBLIC!

EVERY MONDAY
6pm to 10pm
Leaside
Community
Gardens
1073 Millwood Road
at Laird Drive

EVERY TUESDAY
6pm to 10pm
Thornhill
Community Centre
7755 Bayview
(at John)
2 lights North of Steeles

Tables & Information:
905-844-2161
or 416-329-6103

BOB BOIN PROMOTIONS

CARDS PLUS

Mail Order

Wax Boxes, Singles, Autographs, & Collectables

Vintage to Present

Rare Cards & Memorabilia

| Bowman | Fleer | O-Pee-Chee | Pinnacle | Topps |
| Donruss | Leaf | Parkhurst | Score | Upper Deck |

U.S. Orders Welcome
"Quality Guaranteed"

Call (905) 886-1117

6021 Yonge Street, Suite 119,
Toronto, Ontario M2M 3W2
Canada

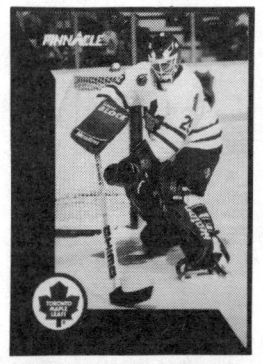

O-Pee-Chee 1987-88
CARD #53

WAYNE GRETZKY

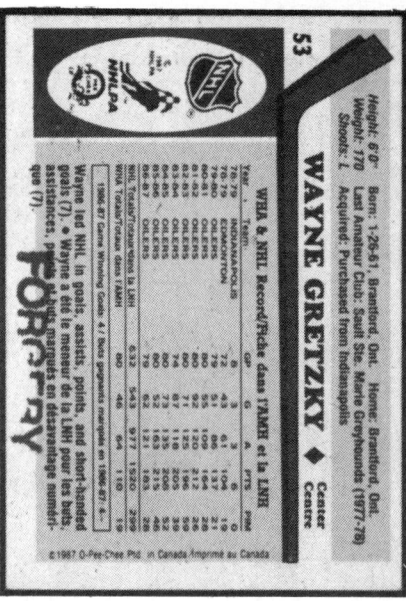

FACE

The original card is printed on a matte white card stock. It has no gloss or shine to the surface. The counterfeit card is printed on a glossy white card stock with the final step in the printing process being the application of a varnish. This gives the surface of the counterfeit card an even higher gloss than original.
The O-Pee-Chee logo, while white on the original, is filled with blue and red dots on the counterfeit.
The white border under magnification of the countefeit card is again cluttered with blue dots.
The colours of the orginal card are soft with all the folds and creases in Gretzky's uniform clear. On the counterfeit cards the colours are darker with a loss of folds and creases in the uniform. Gretzky's facial tones have a reddish tinge on the forgeries.

BACK

Again the difference in the card stock can be seen on the back of the counterfeit card which has a grey overall tint while the original has the standard beige tint.
The logos; NHL, NHLPA and O-Pee-Chee are all missing different pieces, depending on how fine the orginal lines

O-Pee-Chee 1987-88
CARD #123

ADAM OATES

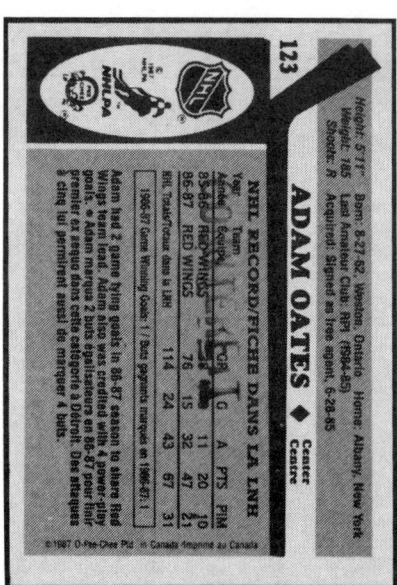

FACE

The photograph, type and artwork on the counterfeit are inferior to that of the original but the colours are a near match. Examination of the O-Pee-Chee logo on the counterfeit will, however, reveal less detail and it is darker due to bad printing registration. Again, the counterfeits appear to be more sharply trimmed than the original.

BACK

The overall pink colour on the back more closely matches that of the original. However, the back of the counterfeit card featuring the player's statistics is slightly lighter than the authentic issue. Also, there is less detail in the type and artwork and the black ink underneath the hockey stick is not as solid as that on the authentic cards. Again, unprinted areas of the cards appear much whiter than those on the authentic card.

Note: Due to printing variations that occur over a long run of card sheets it's a good rule of thumb to have confirmation of two or more of the above points before a card is classified as counterfeit.

O-Pee-Chee 1988-89
CARD #1

MARIO LEMIEUX

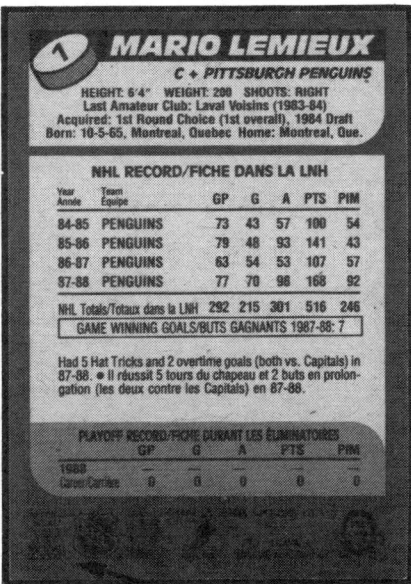

FACE

There is a series of black dots under the player's name on the face of the card intended to look like a shadow. These dots run into the top left corner of the player's picture. On the original the dots remain solid in colour and round, whereas on the forgery the dots have ragged edges and appear to be made from a cluster of smaller dots. Magnification is required to see this difference.

On the front of the original card the O-Pee-Chee logo is a solid cyan (blue), however on the forgery it is made up of process dots. Magnification is required to detect this difference.

BACK

The edges of the original are slightly ragged due to the slitting operation they are put through. The fake card has cleaner edges and also shows traces of the orange ink from the backs. The fakes were probably guillotine cut and may have been slightly wet resulting in the orange edges and traces of offsetting. The orange edges are visible to the naked eye but magnification is required to see the other differences.

On the back of the card next to the NHL logo are the words "NATIONAL HOCKEY LEAGUE LIGUE NATIONALE DE HOCKEY". On the original the "A"

O-Pee-Chee 1988-89
CARD #16

JOE NIEUWENDYK

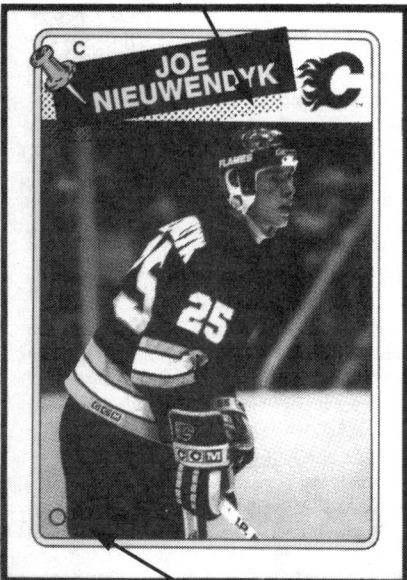

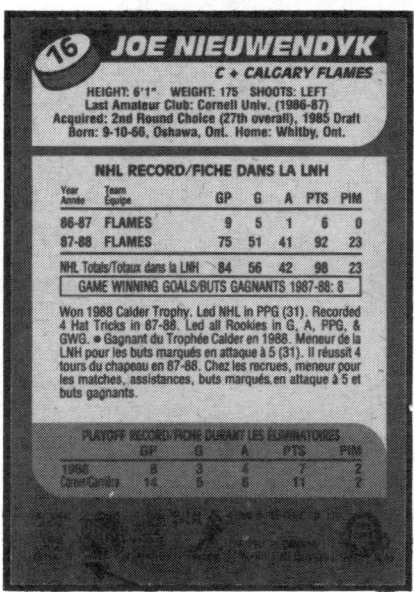

FACE

There is a series of black dots under the player's name on the face of the card intended to look like a shadow. These dots run into the top left corner of the player's picture. On the original the dots remain solid in colour and round, whereas on the forgery the dots have ragged edges and appear to be made from a cluster of smaller dots. Magnification is required to see this difference.

On the original the word O-Pee-Chee appears on the front of the card in black. This type is solid with well defined letters. On the fake the type is made up of dots and has a fuzzy appearance. A magnifying or printer's glass should be used to see this.

BACK

The edges of the original are slightly ragged due to the slitting operation they are put through. The fake card has cleaner edges and also shows traces of the orange ink from the backs. The fakes were probably guillotine cut and may have been slightly wet resulting in the orange edges and traces of offsetting. The orange edges are visible to the naked eye but magnification is required to see the other differences.

Note: Due to printing variations that occur over a long run of card sheets it's a good rule of thumb to have confirmation of two or more of the above points before a card is classified as counterfeit.

O-Pee-Chee 1988-89
CARD #66

BRETT HULL

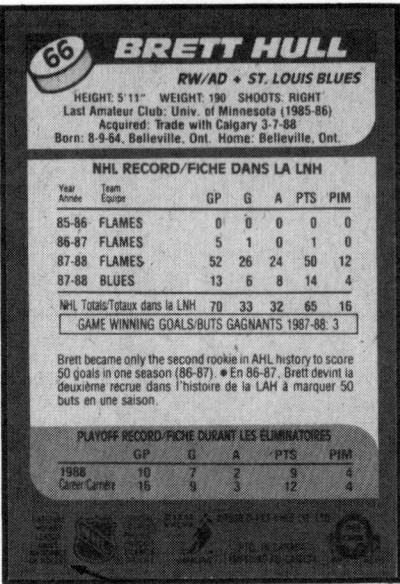

FACE

The push pin which holds the player's name plate has a small yellow dot on the original. This was caused by a small particle of dust during contacting of the final film and is therefore on all cards. The counterfeit cards do not have this yellow dot.
On the face of the card there is a series of black dots under the player's name plate intended to look like a shadow. These black dots run into the top part of the player's picture. On the original the dots remain solid and roundish in shape whereas the dots become greyish and fuzzy in appearance on the fake reproduction. This is visible to the naked eye, but becomes much more obvious using a magnifying glass. To the left of Hull's ear on the light coloured area is a net or mesh effect caused by the lithographic dots starting to align with one another in the reproduction process. Naturally this happens only on the original.

BACK

On the back of the cards, the type on the original is clear, even and consistent. On the fake the type is ragged and sometimes broken. For instance, in the playoff record area the word "career" has broken type in the "C" and the second "r". This is not the case on the original. Magnification is required to detect the difference.

O-Pee-Chee 1988-89
CARD #120

WAYNE GRETZKY

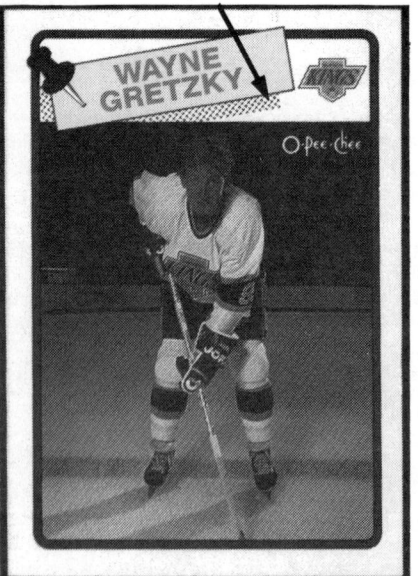

FACE

There's a series of black dots under the player's name on the face of the card intended to look like a shadow. These dots run into the top left corner of the player's picture. On the original the dots remain solid in colour and round, whereas on the forgery the dots have ragged edges and appear to be made from a cluster of smaller dots. Magnification is required to see this difference.
The edges of the original card are slightly ragged due to the slitting operation they are put through. The fake card has cleaner edges and also shows traces of the orange ink from the backs. The fakes were probably guillotine cut and may have been slightly wet resulting in the orange edges and traces of offsetting. The orange edges are visible to the naked eye.

BACK

The puck on the back of the card where the card number appears has a blue screen (blue dots) to give it dimension. On the original this screen is much lighter than the counterfeit. By looking through a magnifying glass this difference becomes more obvious.

Note: Due to printing variations that occur over a long run of card sheets it's a good rule of thumb to have confirmation of two or more of the above points before a card is classified as counterfeit.

• xxxi

O-Pee-Chee 1988-89
CARD #194

PIERRE TURGEON

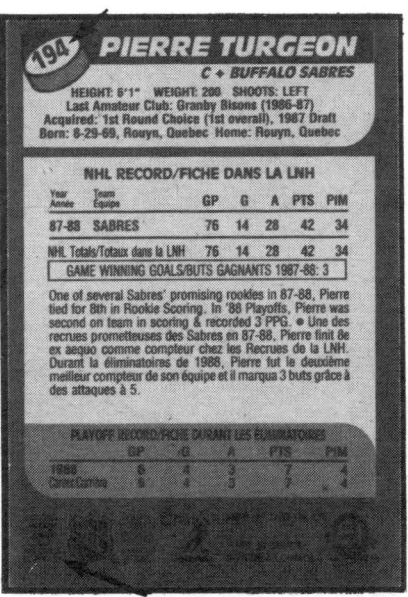

FACE

There's a series of black dots under the player's name on the face of the card intended to look like a shadow. These dots run into the top left corner of the player's picture. On the original the dots remain solid in colour and round, whereas on the forgery the dots have ragged edges and appear to be made from a cluster of smaller dots. Magnification is required to see this difference.

The edges of the original are slightly ragged due to the slitting operation they are put through. The fake card has cleaner edges and also shows traces of the orange ink from the backs. The fakes were probably guillotine cut and may have been slightly wet resulting in the orange edges and traces of offsetting. The orange edges are visible to the naked eye.

BACK

The puck on the back of the card where the card number appears has a blue screen (blue dots) to give it dimension. On the original this screen is much lighter than the counterfeit. By looking through a magnifying glass this difference becomes more obvious.

O-Pee-Chee
Premier 1990-91
CARD #30

SERGEI FEDOROV

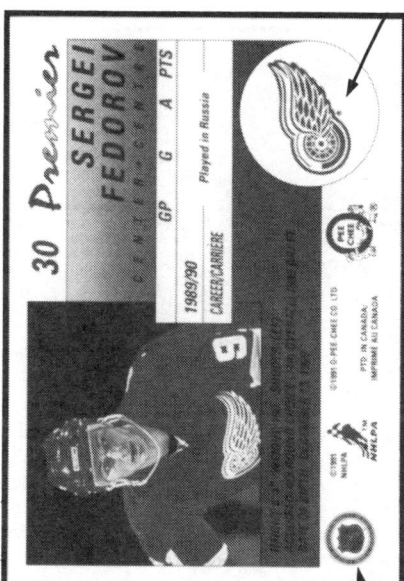

FACE

The borders on the face of the card are wider on the counterfeit than on the original.

The gold bar across the top on the face of the card holding "O-Pee-Chee" and "Premier" is flatter in appearance and has a greenish tint on the counterfeit.

The portrait on the face of the counterfeit card is not clear, with very little contrast and an overall reddish tint.

The "CCM" logo and the word "Detroit" are clear and white on the original while on the counterfeit card they are blurred and reddish in colour.

BACK

The portrait on the back of the counterfeit is mottled with little or no contrast and clarity. The originals are very crisp, with clean lines and sharp highlights.

The NHL logo and the type forming a ring around the logo is illegible while on the original it is very clear.

The registered symbol next to the "Red Wings" logo is fuzzy on the original while on counterfeit it is sharp and

Note: Due to printing variations that occur over a long run of card sheets it's a good rule of thumb to have confirmation of two or more of the above points before a card is classified as counterfeit.

xxxii •

O-Pee-Chee
Premier 1990-91
CARD #50

JAROMIR JAGR

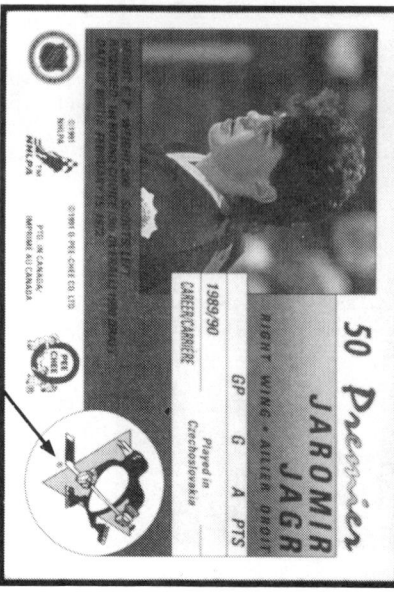

FACE

The borders on the face of the card are wider on the counterfeit card than on the original.
The gold bar across the top on the face of the card holding "O-Pee-Chee" and "Premier" is flatter in appearance and has a greenish tint on the counterfeit.
The portrait on the face of the counterfeit card is not clear, with very little contrast and an overall reddish tint.

BACK

The portrait on the back of the counterfeit is mottled with little or no contrast and clarity. The originals are very crisp, with clean lines and sharp hoghlights.
The NHL logo and the type forming a ring around the logo is illegible while on the original it is very clear.
The registered symbol next to the "Penguins" logo is fuzzy on the original while on counterfeit it is sharp and clear

O-Pee-Chee 1990-9
Premier
CARD #100

JEREMY ROENICK

FACE

The borders on the face of the card are wider on the counterfeit card than on the original.
The gold bar across the top on the face of the card holding "O-Pee-Chee" and "Premier" is flatter in appearance and has a greenish tint on the counterfeit
The portrait on the face of the counterfeit card is not clear, with very little contrast and an overall reddish tint.

BACK

The portrait on the back of the counterfeit is mottled with little or no contrast and clarity. The originals are very crisp, with clean lines and sharp highlights.
The NHL logo and the type forming a ring around the logo is illegible while on the original it is very clear.
The registered symbol next to the "Black Hawks" logo is fuzzy on the original while on the counterfeit it is sharp and clear

Note: Due to printing variations that occur over a long run of card sheets it's a good rule of thumb to have confirmation of two or more of the above points before a card is classified as counterfeit.

Durham Regional
Police 1989-90
CARD #31

ERIC LINDROS

AUTHENTIC SHEET

The Eric Lindros Durham Regional Police Card is in contention for first place — for hockey's most counterfeited card.

At press time, a second counterfeit card has surfaced.

To help collectors better understand the situation regarding this card, we have reproduced, on this page, the authentic sheet containing the Lindors card which was produced in January / February of 1990 by Magill Business Forms of Oshawa, Ontario.

The first sheet of this series, produced in September / October 1989 contained 30 cards. This sheet did not contain a Lindros card. The second sheet was acutally an update subset sheet and was numbered 31 to 35. On this second sheet, there are 8 Lindros cards (#31), 2 Armstrong cards (#32), 2 Vanclief cards (#33), 2 Luik cards (#34) and 2 Brathwaite cards (#35). There were a total of 16 cards on this second sheet.

In the previous edition of this catalouge we mistakenly stated that one of the conditions for the Lindros counterfeit card was the 'trimmed-off' second 'T' in Titan on Lindros' stick. It has come to our attention that this is not a reliable method of identifying the counterfeit card.

This method is no longer a vaild one for assessing the card's authenticity for a very simple reason. On close examination of the authentic sheet containing the Lindros card, one can see that the position of the 'T' in question varies in all 8 Lindros cards.

Since counterfeiting is done using photographic reproduction of authentic cards, the second 'T' method cannot be used. Collectors are warned to be cautious when buying this particular card.

xxxiv •

Durham Regional
Police 1989-90
CARD #31
— FIRST COUNTERFEIT

ERIC LINDROS

P.L.A.Y. Card #31
POLICE LAWS AND YOUTH
DRUG TIPS
from
DURHAM REGIONAL POLICE

Join the Generals in their fight against drug abuse.
Drugs are for healing not dealing.

NATIONAL Sports Centre
Five Points Mall
Ritson & Taunton.

Board of Police Commissioners
for the Regional Municipality
of Durham.

Whitby Lions Club.

Magill Business Forms
95 Athol St. Oshawa

FACE

The face of the card, from the ice surface to the card top, has a greenish tinge throughout the background. This can be seen clearly when comparing any parts of the background that were white on the original (the boards, the back drop on the stands and ice in the foreground) for example.
As with all photo reproductions you lose clairity when not producing from the orginal art. Facial expression, sweater folds, red sweater stripe and printing surface edges are all soft and lack sharp detail.
The "OSHAWA GENERALS" is clear and crisp. The type has fewer screen dots visible.

BACK

Another characteristic of photo reproduction is shrinkage and overall loss of detail. When a counterfeit is produced from an original you can expect a 5% loss of all detail across the newly reproduced card.
The dots on the "i" in Municipality are joined to the bottom

Durham Regional
Police 1989-90
CARD #31
— SECOND COUNTERFEIT

ERIC LINDROS

P.L.A.Y. Card #31
POLICE LAWS AND YOUTH
DRUG TIPS
from
DURHAM REGIONAL POLICE

Join the Generals in their fight against drug abuse.
Drugs are for healing not dealing.

NATIONAL Sports Centre
Five Points Mall
Ritson & Taunton.

Board of Police Commissioners
for the Regional Municipality
of Durham.

Whitby Lions Club.

Magill Business Forms
95 Athol St. Oshawa

FACE

Unlike the first counterfeit card, the second does not have the obvious green tinge. However, the detail on the counterfeit is not sharp and the type and the Oshawa Generals logo in the upper right corner are slightly blurred. The border of the card and the words "OSHAWA GENERALS" at the bottom are browner than the authentic card and screen dots are more in evidence.
The flesh tones on the counterfeit are deeper due to the fact that more yellow or red are present. In the counterfeit copy there is a small green dot just below the word 'Centre' at the top of the card. This would seem to indicate that the card was counterfeited from the card found second from the left and two down on the original sheet as this card also has this green dot. (See photo of sheet above).

BACK

The detail of the type on this counterfeit has been improved. The logos of National Sports Centre, Durham Regional Police, The Lions Club and Magill Business Forms are as sharp as those on the authentic card. However, the overal finish of the counterfeit has a slightly less glossy appearance than the authentic issue.

Note: Due to printing variations that occur over a long run of card sheets it's a good rule of thumb to have confirmation of two or more of the above points before a card is classified as counterfeit.

Score 1990-91
American
CARD #440

ERIC LINDROS

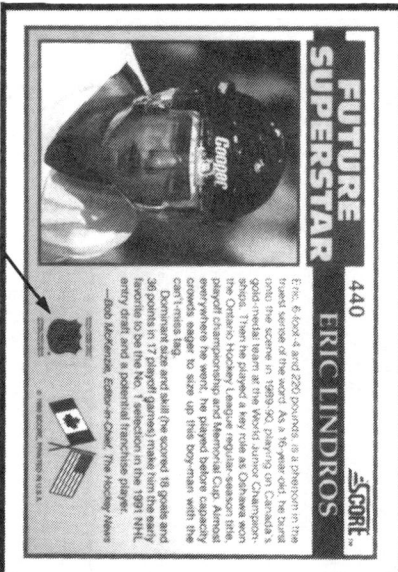

FACE

The overall colour of the counterfeit card is darker and more intense, the red of the Generals uniform is a reddish-maroon while the orginal is a bright red. The blues and yellows turn dark blue and orange respectively on the counterfeit.

An easy indentification point is the two red dots on the bottom blue stripe carrying "Eric Lindros." These dots are located to the right but in line with the top of the "S" in Lindros.

The ice surface on the counterfeit card has a blueish tinge, while the orginal ice surface has various shades of grey. The marks on the boards are more pronounced. They are blue in colour, larger and give the appearance of being a great many more than on the orginal.

BACK

Again, as with all counterfeits, there is a loss of clarity across the back portrait. The facial features are fuzzy with a reddish tinge.

The copy above and below the NHL logo cannot be read under even magnification. The type has completely broken down and is illegible.

7th Inning Sketch
1990-91 Regular Issue
CARD #96

ERIC LINDROS

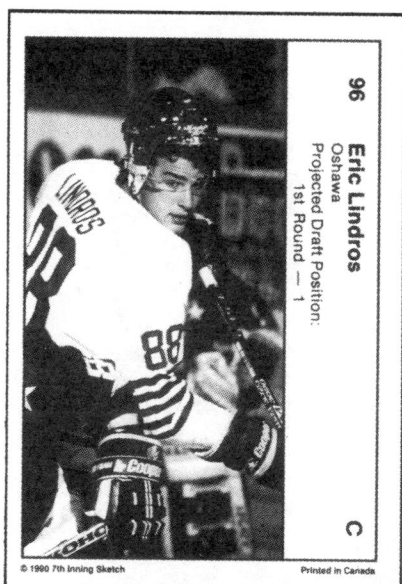

FACE

The simplest and easiest way to distinguish the counterfeit from the authentic card is to examine the top edge of the photograph of Lindros. On the genuine card the edge of the photo is straight and sharp to the naked eye. However, all other aspects of the counterfeit, including design, colours, photographic reproduction and positioning are virtually the same as the original.

BACK

The back of the counterfeit card is virtually indistinguishable from the genuine cardback.

Note: Due to printing variations that occur over a long run of card sheets it's a good rule of thumb to have confirmation of two or more of the above points before a card is classified as counterfeit.

Bowman
1992-93
CARD #442

ERIC LINDROS

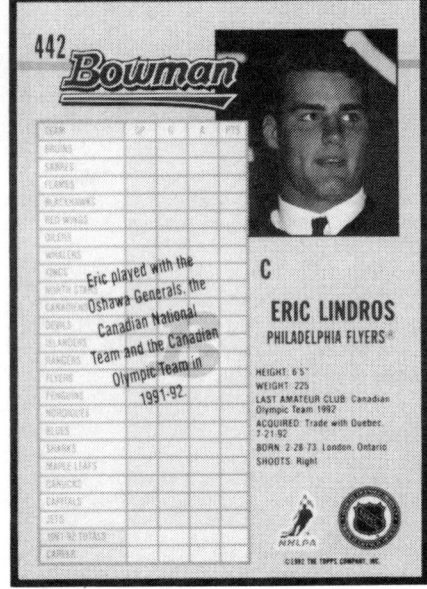

ORIGINAL

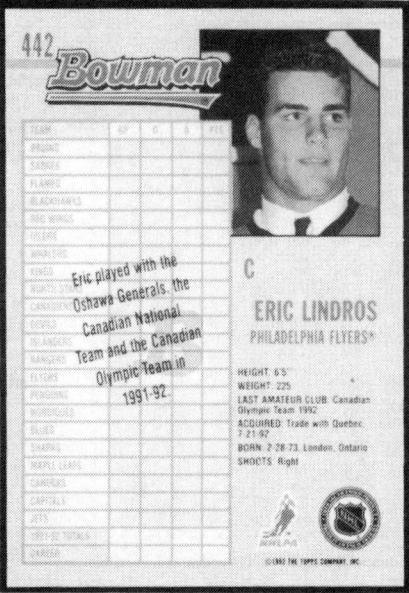

COUNTERFEIT

FACE

The genuine card face has high gloss and colours that are deep and rich in tone. The counterfeit card, however, has much less gloss and the colours are nowhere near as rich.

BACK

All of the colours on the back of the counterfeit, including the photo and the loops are distinctly paler. Also, there is the same lack of gloss when compared to the genuine card.

Score
Team Pinnacle Insert Set 1991-92
CARD #B-1

PATRICK ROY

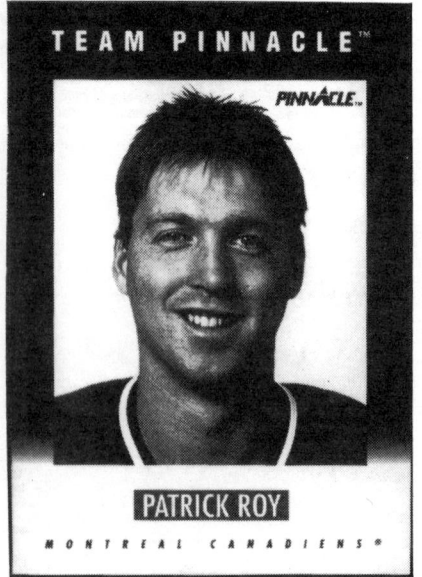

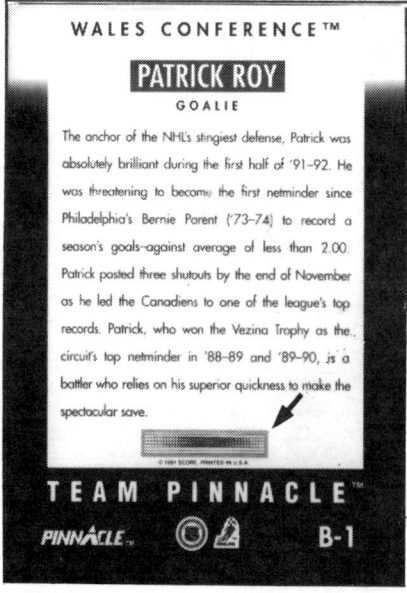

FACE

The black and white photograph on the back of the counterfeit card has a graining appearance whereas the genuine card is sharp and detailed.
This is a very good piece of counterfeiting and collectors should be careful.

BACK

The greyish box placed by Score to prove authenticity does not function as intended on the counterfeit card when viewed through a decoder.

Note: Due to printing variations that occur over a long run of card sheets it's a good rule of thumb to have confirmation of two or more of the above points before a card is classified as counterfeit.

**CHAPTER ONE
ADVERTISING
TRADE CARDS**

ALPHABETICAL LISTING OF MANUFACTUERS
ADVERTISING TRADE CARDS

Bufford Litho	3	Gottmann & Kretchmer	5
F. Mayer Boot & Shoe Co.	4	Great Atlantic and Pacific Tea Co.	4

ADVERTISING TRADE CARDS

Trade cards were produced predominantly between 1860 and 1920. They are usually 3" x 5" and promote an issuer's product, service or special event. While most trade cards are were produced in a generic format called "stock cards" many were designed for specific companies and have illustrations tailored for their specific products.

Stock cards were printed with general scenes and space was left on the card face or back to add an advertisement by the purchaser. Stock cards were printed by lithographers who usually marketed them to small businesses. Trade cards were the predecessor of the present day business card and probably are the first hockey cards ever produced. These cards may or may not be issued as part of a set or series.

BUFFORD LITHO

— 1879 - 1882 ISSUE —

Produced by Bufford Litho of Boston, Massachusetts as "stock cards". The cards were overprinted for various advertisers. The number of cards in the set is unknown. Only two cards are known to involve hockey or can be considered to contain hockey related scenes.
The "Race For the Cup" has four skaters carrying sticks.
Other cards in this series portray other sports or non-sport subjects.

Face of Card No. 431
"Hockey On The Ice"
Size: 2 11/16" x 4 1/2"

Back of Card No. 431

Face of Card No. 434
"Race For The Cup"
Size: 2 11/16" x 4 1/2"

Face: Pastel colourised print, beige border, cardstock
Back: Left blank for addition of advertisement
Imprint: Bufford Boston
ACC: H-820
Complete Set No.: Unknown
Complete Set Price: Unknown

No.	Scene	VG	EX
431	Hockey on the Ice	125.00	250.00
434	Race for the Cup	35.00	70.00

4 • THE GREAT ATLANTIC AND PACIFIC TEA CO. — 1888 ISSUE —

THE GREAT ATLANTIC AND PACIFIC TEA CO.
— 1888 ISSUE —

This set of advertising trade cards was printed by Bufford Litho in 1888 to promote A & P's Thea-Nectar tea. The number in the set is unknown and only one hockey scene has been recorded.

Card No. 517 Face
Hockey

Card No. 517 - Back

Card Size: 3 3/8" x 5 1/8"
Face: Six colour, yellow border print
Back: Back and white
Imprint: None
ACC: H-820
Complete Set No.: Unknown
Complete Set Price: Unknown

No.	Scene	VG	EX
517	Hockey	125.00	250.00

F. MAYER BOOT & SHOE CO.
— 1890 ISSUE —

Printed circa 1890 by Forbes Litho for the F. Mayer Boot & Shoe Co., this advertising card was used to promote their line of children's shoes. Two of the children are shown with hockey sticks.

"Children On Ice" Face

"Children On Ice" - Back

Card Size: 3 1/4" x 5 1/2"
Face: Colourised print on white stock
Back: Black and white on card stock
Imprint: Forbes, New York, Boston, Chicago
ACC: HP-3h
Complete Set No.: 1

No.	Scene	VG	EX
—	Children on Ice	45.00	90.00

GOTTMANN & KRETCHMER

— Circa 1900 ISSUE —

This set was issued by the candy manufacturer Gottmann & Kretchmer of Chicago, possibly with "Upon Honor" sweets or "Surinam" chocolates. The 12-card set, one for each month of the year, could be obtained by mailing in 10¢ in stamps. The printer is unknown.

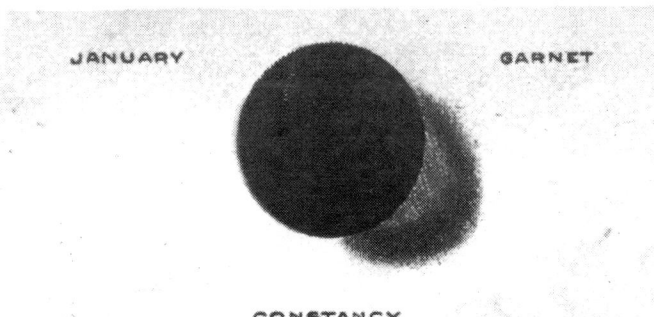

Face of Card No. 1
January

Birthday Horoscopes

January 1, 2, 3, 4, 5, 6.
You have much executive ability, like to be the leader in everything. You have much determination of character. Are a deep lover of your own family. You do not trouble about the highway if there is a shorter cut. You are dearly loved by a large circle of friends, in spite of your tendency to abruptness in speech.

January 7, 8, 9, 10, 11, 12.
You possess much mechanical ability, are a good financier, careful and watchful of your own interests, affectionate, just, when the exercise of this virtue is not detrimental to your own interests. You are stubborn, retaliative, have a fondness for giving advice, mysterious in your designs and movements, and capable of low cunning and trickery.

January 13, 14, 15, 16, 17.
Your mind is generally well balanced, and judgment accurate, careful and sound. Money maknig is your aim. You have the reputation of being close, sharp, shrewd. People growl about you behind your back, but continue to patronize you. Are sympathetic. You are a shrewd buyer and seller; prefer to go it alone. Devoted to your family; fond of sports.

January 19, 20, 21, 22, 23, 24.
You have marked executive talent; are positive, honest, earnest. Your higher spiritual faculties are capable of phenomenal development. You have an unbounded ability to see through everything—men and things. Have an artistic, poetic nature. Your strong trait is an inflexible love of justice, and you move slowly in new undertakings. Charitable in judgment.

January 25, 26, 27, 28, 29, 30, 31.
You are cool, cautious in some degree, active, restless. Generally truthful, though you lack frankness. You paint your own side of the question a vividly pronounced rose color. Are an adept at worming out of a scrape. You do not always let one know what you are driving at until you have worked yourself into his or her confidence. Sometimes original in ideas.
To keep in good health eat "UPON HONOR" SWEETS and "SURINAM" BRAND OF CHOCOLATES made only by GOTTMANN & KRETCHMER, Chicago, Ill.
A full set of 12 Horoscope Cards, one for each month, sent post-paid on receipt of 10 cents in stamps.
GOTTMANN & KRETCHMER
317 SO. PEORIA ST., CHICAGO, ILL.

Back Card No. 1

Card Size: 2 1/2" x 5 1/8"
Face: Colourised print on card stock
Back: Blue and white
Imprint: GOTTMANN & KRETCHMER, 317 SO. PEORIA ST., CHICAGO, ILL.
ACC.: HD-8f
Complete Set No.: 12
Complete Set Price: Unknown

No.	Month	VG	EX	
1	January	35.00	70.00	☐

TOPPS 1954 - 55

TOPPS 1954 - 55

**CHAPTER TWO
POSTCARDS**

ALPHABETICAL LISTING OF MANUFACTURERS OF POSTCARDS

Calumet Hockey Club of Laurium	10	Northern Hardware Company	9
A. R. Clarke & Co. Limited	10	Warwick Bros, & Rutter Ltd.	9

WARWICK BRO'S. & RUTTER LTD

— CIRCA 1896 ISSUE —

Face of Card No. 3247
New Liskeard's Hockey Team

Card Size: 5 9/16" X 3 5/8"
Face: Black and white photo on card stock
Back: Brown and white
Imprint: Warwick Bro's & Rutter, Limited, Publishers, Toronto

No.	Team	VG	EX
3247	New Liskeard's Hockey Team	90.00	150.00

NORTHERN HARDWARE COMPANY

— 1907 - 08 ISSUE —

Northern Hdw. Co. Hockey Team
Duluth, 1907-1908 - Face

Card Size: 5 1/2" x 3 11/16"
Face: Black and white photo om white card stock
Back: Black and white
Imprint: None

No.	Team	VG	EX
—	Northern Hdw. Co. Hockey Team, Duluth, 1907-1908	40.00	75.00

CALUMET HOCKEY CLUB OF LAURIUM
— 1912 - 13 ISSUE —

A. R. CLARKE & CO. LIMITED
— 1912 - 13 ISSUE —

Calumet Hockey Club of Laurium - 1912-13
Northwestern Intermediate Hockey Champions - Face

A. R. Clarke & Co. Limited, Hockey Team
Champions Riverdale Manufacturers' Hockey League, 1912-13 - Face

Card Size: 5 5/16" x 3 9/16"
Face: Black and white photo on card stock
Back: Sepia and white
Imprint: AZO

No.	Team	VG	EX
—	Calumet Hockey Club of Laurium 1912-13 Northwestern Intermediate Hockey Champions	30.00	55.00

Card Size: 5 9/16" X 3 7/16"
Face: Black and white photo on card stock
Back: Sepia and white
Imprint: AZO

No.	Team	VG	EX
—	Champions Riverdale Manufacturers' Hockey League, 1912-13	50.00	80.00

Available in April !

THE CHARLTON STANDARD CATALOGUE OF CANADIAN
BASEBALL & FOOTBALL CARDS

- Fourth Edition -

BASEBALL CARDS FROM 1912 — FOOTBALL CARDS FROM 1949

For Canadian Baseball and Football Card Collectors this Catalogue has it all!

IMPERIAL TOBACCO * MAPLE CRISPETTE * PARKHURST * O-PEE-CHEE * CANADA STARCH * STUART POST
TOPPS * WORLD WIDE GUM * NALLEYS * DONRUSS - LEAF * EDDIE SARGENT * PROVIGO
WILLARD * NABISCO * TORONTO BLUE JAYS * STANDARD OIL * BLUE RIBBON TEA * PANINI
GENERAL MILLS * SCORE * EXHIBITS * HOSTESS * PURITAN MEATS * GULF CANADA * JOGO * VACHON
ROYAL STUDIOS * NEILSON'S * BEN'S AULT FOODS * COCA-COLA * BAZOOKA * KFC
And All Other Major Manufacturers...

Complete price listings for all Major League Baseball and Canadian Football League cards!
Comprehensive baseball and football minor league card listings!
Regular issues, stickers, inserts, subsets, transfers and much, much more!
All major manufacturers!
Current Pricing for all cards in up to three grades of condition - VG, EX, and NRMT!
All rookie, last, pitcher, quarterback, error and variation cards identified and priced!
Plus Charlton's Fabulous Alphabetical Index!

OVER 300 PAGES * 60,000 PRICES * NEW, LARGER 8 1/2 x 11" FORMAT
RESERVE YOUR COPY TODAY DIRECTLY FROM THE PUBLISHER...

The Charlton Press

2010 YONGE STREET, TORONTO, ONTARIO M4S 1Z9
FOR TOLL FREE ORDERING PHONE 1-800-442-6042   FAX 1-800-442-1542 from anywhere in Canada or the U.S.

**CHAPTER THREE
TOBACCO CARDS,
FLANNELS AND
SILKS**

ALPHABETICAL LISTING OF MANUFACTURERS OF TOBACCO CARDS, FLANNELS AND SILK

Champ's Cigarettes	20	Imperial Tobacco	17
Hamilton Kings Cigarettes	13	Murad Cigarettes	13

— 1902 ISSUE — HAMILTON KINGS CIGARETTES • 13

AMERICAN TOBACCO COMPANY
(S. ANARGYROS CORPORATION)

HAMILTON KINGS CIGARETTES

— 1902 ISSUE —

Issued as a redeemable premium. Each card is issued on different coloured card stock. Artwork portrays ladies engaged in various activities.

Card No. 6 Hockey - Face

Card Size: 5 15/16" x 8"
Face: Black and blue with white print on beige stock
Back: Blank
Imprint: TURKISH TROPHIES COPYRIGHT, 1902, BY S. ANARGYROS
ACC: T-7
Complete Set No.: 12
Complete Set Price: 2,200.00   3,600.00

No.	Scene	VG	EX
6	Hockey	175.00	300.00

MURAD CIGARETTES COLLEGE SERIES

— 1908 FLANNEL ISSUE —

The sports portrayed are baseball, basketball, fencing, football, hockey, hurdles, rowing, shotput, swimming, tennis and track. Each college is portrayed in every sport.
The imprint varies with each cigarette brand and there may be more than the three listed here.
Two sizes were issued. One is 3 1/8" x 5 3/8" with fringes and the other approximately 7 1/2" x 11" but without fringes. Eleven flannels were issued for each college for each sport making a set totalling 297. The following colleges are known at this time.

Flannel No. 14 Oregon

Size: 3 1/8" x 5 3/8" with fringe
7 1/2" x 11" without fringe
Material: Flannel
Face: Colour print on flannel
Back: Factory stamp in magenta may be present
Imprint: 1. Factory No. 2163, 3rd Dist. N.Y.
2. Factory No. 30, 2nd Dist., N.Y
3. Egyptienne Luxury
ACC: B-33
Complete Set No.: 297
Complete Set Price: Unknown

	VG	EX
Hockey Flanels Small	70.00	100.00
Hockey Flanels Large	90.00	125.00

No.	College	No.	College
1	Amherst	15	Pennsylvania
2	Army	16	Princeton
3	Brown	17	Rutgers
4	Chicago	18	St. Louis
5	Colgate	19	Stanford
6	Colorado	20	Syracuse
7	Columbia	21	Trinity
8	Cornell	22	Tufts
9	Dartmouth	23	Utah
10	Harvard	24	Vermont
11	Johns Hopkins	25	Williams
12	Knox	26	Wisconsin
13	Navy	27	Yale
14	Oregon		

1909-10 COLLEGE SERIES - CARDS

There are six series of 25 cards each. The first two series exist in a 2nd edition with minor graphics changes. A few unfinished errors without printing are known. The cigarette packer number is hand-stamped on the back.

While the cards were issued in series they are unnumbered and listed below in alphabetical order by college. Exactly how many college cards display hockey scenes is not known.

Card No. 121 Rochester

Card Size: 2 1/8" x 2 11/16"
Face: Colour print on white card stock
Back: Black and white
ACC: T-51
Imprint: Murad Cigarettes S. Anargyros, New York.
A Corporation Factory No. 7, 3rd Dist. N.Y.
Complete Set No.: 150
Complete Set Price: VG   EX
                                                        Unknown
Hockey Card Price: 20.00   35.00

No.	College	No.	College
1	Adelphi	13	Berea
2	Adrian	14	Bethany
3	Albright	15	Blackburn
4	Alleghany	16	Boston College
5	Alfred	17	Barton University
6	Alma	18	Bowdoin
7	Amherst	19	Brooklyn Poly
8	Amity	20	Brown
9	Antiosh	21	Bucknell
10	Armour	22	Buchtel
11	Baker	23	C.C.N.Y.
12	Bates	24	C.U.A.

No.	College	No.	College
25	C.U. Kentucky	88	Lombard
26	California	89	Louisiana or L.S.U.
27	Canisius	90	Loyola
28	Carthage	91	Luther
29	Case	92	McGill
30	Cedarville	93	Marietta
31	Central College	94	Marquette
32	Chattanooga	95	Massachusetts Tech
33	Chicago	96	Michigan Agri.
34	Cincinatti	97	Michigan
35	Clark	98	Millsaps
36	Clarkson	99	Minnesota
37	Coe	100	Missouri
38	Colgate	101	Montana
39	Colorado	102	Mt. Union
40	Columbia	103	N.Y.U.
41	Cornell	104	Navy
42	Cotner	105	North Dakota
43	Dartmouth	106	North Western College
44	Davidson	107	North Western University
45	Denison	108	Notre Dame
46	Denver	109	O.S.U.
47	DePauw	110	O.W.U.
48	Dickinson	111	Occidental
49	Drake	112	Ohio
50	Fordham	113	Oklahoma
51	Franklin	114	Pennsylvania College
52	Furman	115	Penn. State
53	Geneva	116	Pennsylvania
54	Georgetown	117	Pratt
55	George Washington	118	Princeton
56	Greer	119	Purdue
57	Grove City	120	Rensselaer
58	Guilford	121	Rochester
59	Gustavas Adolphus	122	Rutgers
60	Hamilton	123	S.U. Kentucky
61	Hampden Sidney	124	St. Lawrence
62	Hampton	125	St. Louis
63	Harvard	126	South Carolina
64	Hastings	127	Stanford
65	Haverford	128	Stephens
66	Heidelberg	129	Swarthmore
67	Hendrix	130	Syracuse
68	Hiram	131	Tennessee
69	Hiwassww	132	Texas
70	Hobart	133	Toronto
71	Holy Cross	134	Trinity
72	Huron	135	Tufts
73	Illinois	136	Vanderbilt
74	Illinois College	137	Vermont
75	Indiana	138	Virginia
76	Iowa	139	W. & J.
77	Johns Hopkins	140	W.V.U.
78	Juniata	141	Washington and Lee
79	K.W.C.	142	Wesleyan
80	Kansas	143	Western R.U.
81	Kenyon	144	West Point
82	Knox	145	Whitman
83	Lafayette	146	Williams
84	Lawrence	147	Wisconsin
85	Lebanon	148	Worcester P.I.
86	Lehigh	149	Xavier
87	Lenox	150	Yale

MURAD CIGARETTES COLLEGE SERIES • 15

— 1910 - 11 COLLEGE SERIES PREMIUMS - CARDS —

Issued as a premium in exchange for 15 coupons from Murad Cigarettes. Each college portrays a different sports scene. This series exists with a 2nd edition with minor graphics changes. The cards are unnumbered and listed below alphabetically by college.

Card No. 12 Rochester (Hockey) - Face
1st Edition

Card No. 12 Rochester (Hockey) - Face
2nd Edition

Card Size: 8" x 5"
Face: Colour print on white card stock
Back: Black and white
Imprint: "Murad" Picture Dept. Drawer S. Jersey City, N.J.
This offer expires June 30th, 1911.
ACC: T-6
Complete Set No.: 25
Complete Set Price: Unknown

	VG	EX
Hockey Singles:	225.00	375.00

No.	College	No.	College
1	Amherst College (hammer)	13	Swarthmore College (unknown)
2	Brown University (discus)	14	Syracuse College (long jump)
3	Columbia (shot)	15	Texas University (rowing)
4	Cornell (rowing)	16	University of California (track)
5	College of the City of New York (pole)	17	University of Illinois (unknown)
		18	University of Michigan (football)
6	Dartmouth College (unknown)	19	Univeristy of Missouri (unknown)
7	Fordham University (baseball)	20	University of Pennsylvania (unknown)
8	Harvard (football)	21	University of Kansas (hammer)
9	New York University (unknown)	22	University of Denver (unknown)
10	Pennsylvania State College (unknown)	23	Washington and Jefferson (unknown)
		24	Williams College (unknown)
11	Princeton (hammer)	25	Yale (rowing)
12	Rochester (hockey)		

— 1912 - 15 COLLEGE SEAL SERIES —
LARGE SILKS

Issued as a redeemable premium. These silks are found with or without an impressed floral design and paper backing sheet. The back is blank and there are 25 colleges as listed below Each is found in the same ten designs: baseball pitcher, baseball batter, football, golf, hammer throwing, ice hockey, hurdles, rowing, running and putting the shot.

Silk No. 1 Annapolis

Size: 5" x 7"
Face: Colour print on white silk
Back: Blank or may come with paper backing sheet
Material: Silk
ACC: S-21
Imprint: Factory No. 7 3rd Dist. N.Y.
Complete Set No.: 250
Complete Hockey Set No.: 25

	VG	EX
Complete Set Price:	12,500.00	20,000.00
Complete Hockey Set Price:	1,500.00	2,500.00
Hockey Singles	75.00	125.00

No.	College	No.	College
1	Annapolis	14	Missouri
2	Brown	15	Ohio
3	California	16	Pennsylvania
4	Chicago	17	Princeton
5	Colorado	18	Purdue
6	Columbia	19	Stanford
7	Cornell	20	Texas
8	Dartmouth	21	Syracuse
9	Georgetown	22	West Point
10	Harvard	23	Wisconsin
11	Illinois	24	Virginia
12	Michigan	25	Yale
13	Minnesota		

16 • MURAD CIGARETTES COLLEGE SERIES

— 1912 - 15 COLLEGE SEAL SERIES —
SMALL SILKS

Issued as an insert in tobacco tins. These silks are found with and without an impressed floral design. The silks were folded twice and placed in a paper envelope in the tobacco tin. There are 25 colleges as listed below and each is found in the same 10 designs: baseball pitcher, baseball batter, football, golf, hammer throwing, ice hockey, hurdles, rowing, running and putting the shot.

Size: 3 1/2" x 5 1/2"
Face: Colour print on white silk
Back: Blank
Material: Silk
Imprint: Murad Cigarettes Factory No. 7 - 3rd Dist. N.Y.
ACC: S-22
Complete Set No.: 250
Complete Hockey Set No.: 25

	VG	EX
Complete Set Price:	7,500.00	12,500.00
Complete Hockey Set Price:	850.00	1,375.00
Hockey Singles:	37.50	75.00

No.	College	No.	College
1	Annapolis	14	Missouri
2	Brown	15	Ohio
3	California	16	Pennsylvania
4	Chicago	17	Princeton
5	Colorado	18	Purdue
6	Columbia	19	Stanford
7	Cornell	20	Texas
8	Dartmouth	21	Syracuse
9	Georgetown	22	West Point
10	Harvard	23	Wisconsin
11	Illinois	24	Virginia
12	Michigan	25	Yale
13	Minnesota		

Silk No. 1 Annapolis

THE CHARLTON STANDARD CATALOGUE OF CANADIAN
BASEBALL & FOOTBALL CARDS
- Fourth Edition -
BASEBALL CARDS FROM 1912 — FOOTBALL CARDS FROM 1949
For Canadian Baseball and Football Card Collectors this Catalogue has it all!

IMPERIAL TOBACCO * MAPLE CRISPETTE * PARKHURST * O-PEE-CHEE * CANADA STARCH * STUART POST *
TOPPS * WORLD WIDE GUM * NALLEYS * DONRUSS - LEAF * EDDIE SARGENT * PROVIGO *
WILLARD * NABISCO * TORONTO BLUE * JAYS * STANDARD OIL * BLUE RIBBON TEA * PANINI
GENERAL MILLS * SCORE * EXHIBITS * HOSTESS * PURITAN MEATS * GULF CANADA * JOGO * VACHON *
ROYAL STUDIOS * NEILSON'S * BEN'S AULT FOODS * COCA-COLA * BAZOOKA * KFC
And All Other Major Manufacturers...

Complete price listings for all Major League Baseball and Canadian Football League cards!
Comprehensive baseball and football minor league card listings!
Regular issues, stickers, inserts, subsets, transfers and much, much more!
All major manufacturers!
Current Pricing for all cards in up to three grades of condition - VG, EX, and NRMT!
All rookie, last, pitcher, quarterback, error and variation cards identified and priced!
Plus Charlton's Fabulous Alphabetical Index!
OVER 300 PAGES * 60,000 PRICES, NEW, LARGER 8 1/2 x 11" FORMAT
RESERVE YOUR COPY TODAY DIRECTLY FROM THE PUBLISHER...

The Charlton Press
2010 YONGE STREET, TORONTO, ONTARIO M4S 1Z9
FOR TOLL FREE ORDERING PHONE 1-800-442-6042 FAX 1-800-442-1542 from anywhere in Canada or the U.S.

IMPERIAL TOBACCO

— 1910 - 11 REGULAR ISSUE —

All these cards are considered rookie cards. Cards are numbered on the upper left corner. The player's name and team appear on the bottom border. The name of the series, "Hockey Series", appears on the back with a picture of two inverted crossed hockey sticks with a puck below them.

PRICE MOVEMENT OF EX SETS

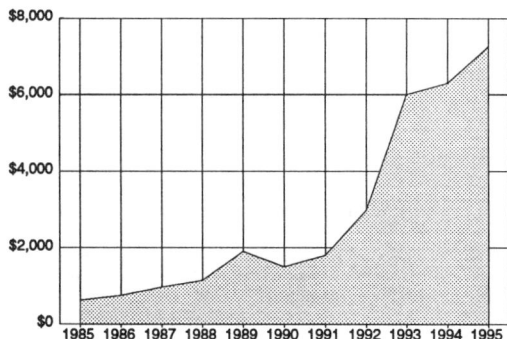

Imperial Tobacco
1910-11 Issue
Card No. 19,
J. Jones

Card Size: 1 1/2" X 2 1/2"
Face: Four colour; Name, Number, Team
Back: Black on card stock; Name, Resume
Imprint: None
ACC No.: C56
Complete Set No.: 36
Complete Set Price: 1,825.00 3,650.00 7,250.00
Common Card: 30.00 65.00 125.00

No.	Player	G	VG	EX
1	Frank Patrick, Ren., RC	80.00	175.00	350.00
2	Percy Lesueur, Goalie, Ott., RC	30.00	65.00	125.00
3	Gordon Roberts, Ott., RC	30.00	65.00	125.00
4	Barney Holden, Sha., RC	30.00	65.00	125.00
5	Frank Glass, Mon.W, RC	30.00	65.00	125.00
6	Edgar Dey, Hab., RC	30.00	65.00	125.00
7	Marty Walsh, Cob., RC	30.00	65.00	125.00
8	Art Ross, Hab., RC	150.00	300.00	600.00
9	Angus Campbell, Cob., RC	30.00	65.00	125.00
10	Harry Hyland, Mon.W, RC	30.00	65.00	125.00
11	Herb Clarke, Cob., RC	40.00	80.00	160.00
12	Art Ross, Hab., RC	150.00	300.00	600.00
13	Ed Decarie, Mtl. Can., RC	60.00	115.00	125.00
14	Tommy Dunderdale, Sha., RC	50.00	100.00	225.00
15	Fred Taylor, Ren., RC	175.00	350.00	700.00
16	Joseph Cattarinich, Goalie, Mon.C, RC	30.00	65.00	125.00
17	Bruce Stuart, Ott., RC	30.00	65.00	125.00
18	Nick Bawlf, Hab., RC	30.00	65.00	125.00
19	J. Jones, Cob., Goalie, RC	30.00	65.00	125.00
20	Ernest Russell, Mon.W, RC	50.00	100.00	200.00
21	Jack Laviolette, Mon.C, RC	30.00	65.00	125.00
22	Riley Hern, Goalie, Mon.W, RC	30.00	65.00	125.00
23	Didier Pitre, Mon.C, RC	30.00	65.00	125.00
24	George Poulin, Mon.C, RC	30.00	65.00	125.00
25	Art Bernier, Mon.C, RC	30.00	65.00	125.00
26	Lester Patrick, Ren., RC	120.00	235.00	475.00
27	Fred Lake, Ott., RC	30.00	65.00	125.00
28	Paddy Moran, Goalie, Hab., RC	50.00	100.00	200.00
29	C. Toms, Cob., RC	30.00	65.00	125.00
30	Ernie Johnson, Mon.W, RC	30.00	65.00	125.00
31	Horace Gaul, Hab., RC	30.00	65.00	125.00
32	Harold McNamara, Cob., RC	30.00	65.00	125.00
33	Jack Marshall, Mon.W, RC	30.00	65.00	125.00
34	Bruce Ridpath, Ott., RC	30.00	65.00	125.00
35	Jack Marshall, Sha., RC	30.00	65.00	125.00
36	Edouard Lalonde, Ren., RC	100.00	200.00	400.00

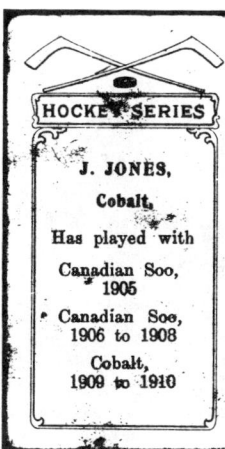

Imperial Tobacco
1910-11 Issue
Card No. 19,
J. Jones

Imperial Tobacco
1910-11 Issue
Card No. 34,
Bruce Ridpath

— 1910 - 11 POSTCARD ISSUE —

Printed in England by BAT for Imperial Tobacco of Canada, this postcard size hockey card was issued in tin boxes containing 50 Sweet Caporal "Flats" cigarettes. The photographs of this set were used as the basis to generate the drawings for the 1911-12 regular issue.

Card Size: 2 7/8" x 4 5/8"
Face: Black and white on card stock; Name, Team, Number
Back: Plain
Imprint: Printed in Britain.
Complete Set No.: 45
Complete Set Price: 3,000.00 6,000.00 12,000.00
Common Card: 50.00 100.00 200.00

QUEBEC BULLDOGS

No.	Player	G	VG	EX
1	Paddy Moran, Goalie	80.00	175.00	350.00
2	Joe Hall	50.00	100.00	200.00
3	Barney Holden	50.00	100.00	200.00
4	Joe Malone	80.00	175.00	350.00
5	Ed Oatman	50.00	100.00	200.00
6	Tommy Dunderdale	70.00	140.00	275.00
7	Ken Mallen	50.00	100.00	200.00
8	Jack McDonald	50.00	100.00	200.00

OTTAWA SENATORS

No.	Player	G	VG	EX
9	Fred Lake	50.00	100.00	200.00
10	Albert Kerr	50.00	100.00	200.00
11	Marty Walsh	50.00	100.00	200.00
12	Hamby Shore	50.00	100.00	200.00
13	Alex Currie	50.00	100.00	200.00
14	Bruce Ridpath	50.00	100.00	200.00
15	Bruce Stuart	50.00	100.00	200.00
16	Percy Lesueur, Goalie	60.00	125.00	250.00
17	Jack Darragh	60.00	125.00	250.00

RENFREW MILLIONAIRES

No.	Player	G	VG	EX
18	Steve Vair	50.00	100.00	200.00
19	Don Smith	50.00	100.00	200.00
20	Fred Taylor	130.00	260.00	525.00
21	Bert Lindsay, Goalie	50.00	100.00	200.00
22	Larry Gilmour	50.00	100.00	200.00
23	Bobby Rowe	50.00	100.00	200.00
24	Sprague Cleghorn	105.00	215.00	425.00
25	Odie Cleghorn	50.00	100.00	200.00
26	Skein Ronan, Error	50.00	100.00	200.00

MONTREAL WANDERERS

No.	Player	G	VG	EX
27	Walter Smaill	80.00	175.00	350.00
28	Ernie Johnson	50.00	100.00	200.00
29	Jack Marshall	50.00	100.00	200.00
30	Harry Hyland	50.00	100.00	200.00
31	Art Ross	200.00	400.00	800.00
32	Riley Hern, Goalie	50.00	100.00	200.00
33	Gordon Roberts	50.00	100.00	200.00
34	Frank Glass	50.00	100.00	200.00
35	Ernest Russell	50.00	100.00	200.00
36	James Gardiner	60.00	125.00	250.00

MONTREAL CANADIENS

No.	Player	G	VG	EX
37	Art Bernier	50.00	100.00	200.00
38	Georges Vezina, Goalie	460.00	925.00	1,850.00
39	Henri Dellaire	50.00	100.00	200.00
40	Rocket Power	50.00	100.00	200.00
41	Didier Pitre	50.00	100.00	200.00
42	Edouard Lalonde	145.00	290.00	575.00
43	Eugene Payan	50.00	100.00	200.00
44	George Poulin	50.00	100.00	200.00
45	Jack Laviolette	80.00	175.00	350.00

18 • IMPERIAL TOBACCO — 1911-12 REGULAR ISSUE —

— 1911-12 REGULAR ISSUE —

Players on the 1911-12 set are exact duplicates of those on the 1910-11 postcard issue. The player photos appear to form the models for the drawings used on this set. The colour portrait is framed by two hockey sticks. Both the front and back of the card are numbered.

PRICE MOVEMENT OF EX SETS

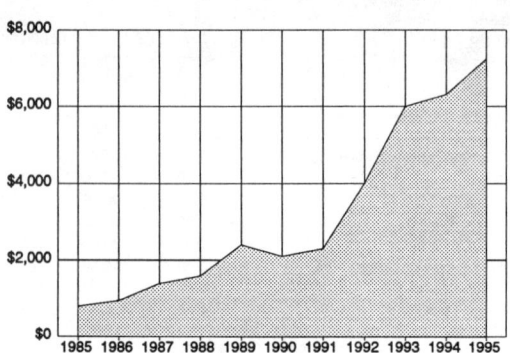

Imperial Tobacco
1911-12 Issue
Card No. 1,
Paddy Moran

Card Size: 1 1/2" X 2 1/2"
Face: Four colour; Name, Number
Back: Black on card stock; Name, Team, Number, Resume
Imprint: None
ACC No.: C55
Complete Set No.: 45

Complete Set Price:		1,825.00	3,650.00	7,250.00
Common Card:		30.00	65.00	125.00

QUEBEC BULLDOGS

No.	Player	G	VG	EX
1	Paddy Moran, Goalie	50.00	100.00	200.00
2	Joe Hall	30.00	65.00	125.00
3	Barney Holden	30.00	65.00	125.00
4	Joe Malone	50.00	100.00	200.00
5	Ed Oatman	30.00	65.00	125.00
6	Tommy Dunderdale	30.00	65.00	125.00
7	Ken Mallen	30.00	65.00	125.00
8	Jack McDonald	30.00	65.00	125.00

OTTAWA SENATORS

No.	Player	G	VG	EX
9	Fred Lake	30.00	65.00	125.00
10	Albert Kerr, RC	30.00	65.00	125.00
11	Marty Walsh	30.00	65.00	125.00
12	Hamby Shore, RC	30.00	65.00	125.00
13	Alex Currie, RC	30.00	65.00	125.00
14	Bruce Ridpath	30.00	65.00	125.00
15	Bruce Stuart, LC	30.00	65.00	125.00
16	Percy Lesueur, Goalie	30.00	65.00	125.00
17	Jack Darragh, RC	30.00	65.00	125.00

RENFREW MILLIONAIRES

No.	Player	G	VG	EX
18	Steve Vair	30.00	65.00	125.00
19	Don Smith	30.00	65.00	125.00
20	Fred Taylor	60.00	115.00	225.00
21	Bert Lindsay, Goalie	30.00	65.00	125.00
22	Larry Gilmour	30.00	65.00	125.00
23	Bobby Rowe	30.00	65.00	125.00
24	Sprague Cleghorn, RC	75.00	150.00	300.00
25	Odie Cleghorn, RC	30.00	65.00	125.00
26	Skein Ronan, RC	30.00	65.00	125.00

MONTREAL WANDERERS

No.	Player	G	VG	EX
27A	Walter Smaill, (With Stick)	60.00	115.00	225.00
27B	Walter Smaill, (Without Stick)	60.00	115.00	225.00
28	Ernie Johnson	30.00	65.00	125.00
29	Jack Marshall	30.00	65.00	125.00
30	Harry Hyland	30.00	65.00	125.00
31	Art Ross	75.00	150.00	300.00
32	Riley Hern, Goalie	30.00	65.00	125.00
33	Gordon Roberts	30.00	65.00	125.00
34	Frank Glass	30.00	65.00	125.00

Imperial Tobacco
1911-12 Issue
Card No. 24,
Sprague Cleghorn

Imperial Tobacco
1911-12 Issue
Card No. 38,
Georges Vezina

No.	Player	G	VG	EX
35	Ernest Russell	30.00	65.00	125.00
36	James Gardiner	40.00	75.00	150.00

MONTREAL CANADIENS

No.	Player	G	VG	EX
37	Art Bernier	30.00	65.00	125.00
38	Georges Vezina, Goalie	230.00	460.00	925.00
39	Henri Dellaire	30.00	65.00	125.00
40	Rocket Power	30.00	65.00	125.00
41	Didier Pitre	30.00	65.00	125.00
42	Edouard Lalonde	60.00	125.00	250.00
43	Eugene Payan	30.00	65.00	125.00
44	Georges Poulin	30.00	65.00	125.00
45	Jack Laviolette	50.00	100.00	200.00

Note: Cards must be graded accurately before they can be priced.

— 1912-13 REGULAR ISSUE —

These black and white cards have the player and team name on the border below the picture. The card number is found on the back to the right of the phrase, "Series of 50". The same crossed hockey sticks and puck design over the series' name "Hockey Series", is found on the C56 series, suggesting that the same producer issued the C56 and C57 issues.

PRICE MOVEMENT OF EX SETS

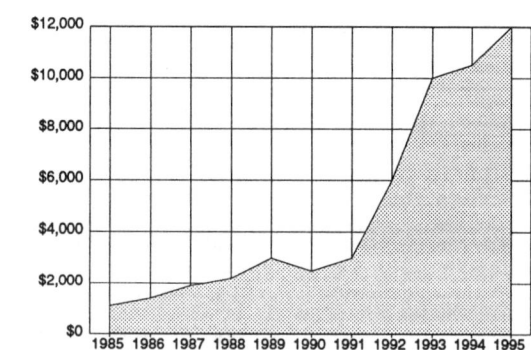

Card Size: 1 1/2" X 2 1/2"
Face: Black and white; Name, Team
Back: Black on card stock; Name, Team, Number, Resume
Imprint: None
ACC No.: C57
Complete Set No.: 50

Complete Set Price:		3,000.00	6,000.00	12,000.00
Common Card:		50.00	100.00	200.00

No.	Player	G	VG	EX
1	Georges Vezina, Goalie, Mon.C	230.00	460.00	925.00
2	Harry Broadbent, Ott., RC	75.00	145.00	290.00
3	Clint Benedict, Goalie, Ott, RC	70.00	140.00	275.00
4	A. Atchinson, NE, RC	50.00	100.00	200.00
5	Tommy Dunderdale, Que.B	65.00	125.00	250.00
6	Art Bernier, Mon.W	50.00	100.00	200.00
7	Henri Dellaire, Mon.C	50.00	100.00	200.00
8	George Poulin, Mon.C	50.00	100.00	200.00
9	Eugene Payan, Mon.C	50.00	100.00	200.00
10	Steve Vair, Ren.	50.00	100.00	200.00
11	Bobby Rowe, Ren.	50.00	100.00	200.00
12	Don Smith, Ren.	50.00	100.00	200.00
13	Bert Lindsay, Goalie, Ren.	50.00	100.00	200.00
14	Skein Ronan, Ott., LC	50.00	100.00	200.00
15	Sprague Cleghorn, Ren.	70.00	140.00	275.00
16	Joe Hall, Que.B	65.00	125.00	250.00
17	Jack McDonald, Que.B	50.00	100.00	200.00
18	Paddy Moran, Goalie, Que.B	65.00	125.00	250.00
19	Harry Hyland, Mon.W	65.00	125.00	250.00
20	Art Ross, Mon.W	125.00	250.00	500.00
21	Frank Glass, Mon.W	50.00	100.00	200.00
22	Walter Smaill, Mon.W	50.00	100.00	200.00
23	Gordon Roberts, Mon.W, LC	65.00	125.00	250.00
24	James Gardiner, Mon.W	65.00	125.00	250.00
25	Ernie Johnson, Mon.W	65.00	125.00	250.00

— 1912 - 13 REGULAR ISSUE — IMPERIAL TOBACCO • 19

No.	Player	G	VG	EX
26	Ernest Russell, Mon.W	75.00	150.00	300.00
27	Percy Lesueur, Goalie, Ott., LC	65.00	125.00	250.00
28	Bruce Ridpath, Ott., LC	50.00	100.00	200.00
29	Jack Darragh, Ott.	75.00	150.00	300.00
30	Hamby Shore, Ott., LC	50.00	100.00	200.00
31	Fred Lake, Ott., LC	50.00	100.00	200.00
32	Alex Currie, Ott., LC	50.00	100.00	200.00
33	Albert Kerr, Ott., LC	50.00	100.00	200.00
34	Eddie Gerard, NE, RC	65.00	125.00	250.00
35	Carl Kendall, RC	50.00	100.00	200.00
36	Jack Fournier, RC	50.00	100.00	200.00
37	Goldie Prodgers, Vic., RC	50.00	100.00	200.00
38	Jack Marks, Que., RC	50.00	100.00	200.00
39	George Broughton, Goalie, Mon. W, RC	50.00	100.00	200.00
40	Arthur Boyce, Goalie, Mon.W, RC	50.00	100.00	200.00
41	Lester Patrick	125.00	250.00	500.00
42	Joe Dennison, RC	50.00	100.00	200.00
43	Fred Taylor	155.00	310.00	625.00
44	Edouard Lalonde, Mon.C	115.00	225.00	450.00
45	Didier Pitre, Mon.C	65.00	125.00	250.00
46	Jack Laviolette, Mon.C	50.00	100.00	200.00
47	Ed Oatman, Vic.	50.00	100.00	200.00
48	Joe Malone, Que.B	65.00	125.00	250.00
49	Marty Walsh, Ott., LC	50.00	100.00	200.00
50	Odie Cleghorn, Mon.C	65.00	125.00	250.00

Note: Your cards must be accurately graded before they can be priced.

Imperial Tobacco
1912-13 Issue
Card No. 6,
Art Bernier

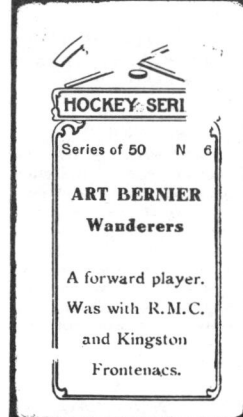

Imperial Tobacco
1912-13 Issue
Card No. 6,
Art Bernier

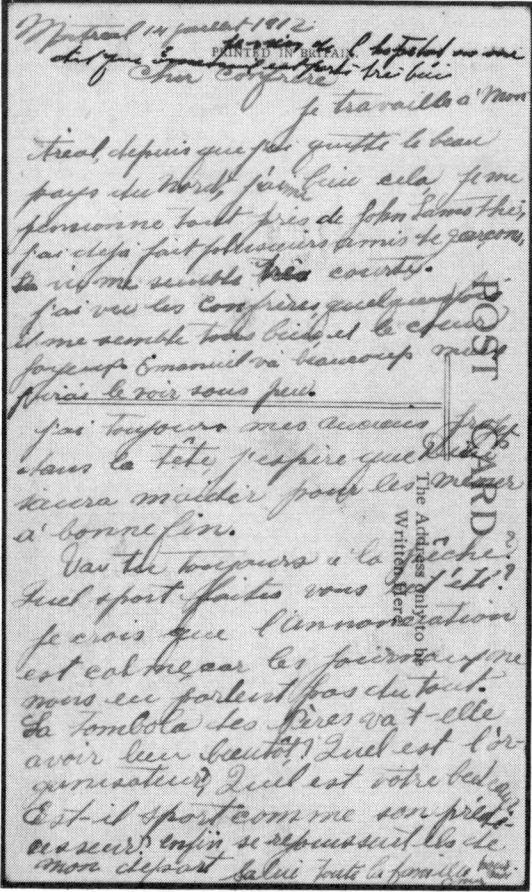

Imperial Tobacco 1910-11 Postcard Issue
Card No. 16, Percy Lesueur

CHAMP'S CIGARETTE CARDS

— 1924 - 25 REGULAR ISSUE —

Cards in this unnumbered set are presented below first alphabetically by team and then alphabetically by player within the team. The sepia-toned cards contain a short player biography in English on the back.

PRICE MOVEMENT OF EX SETS

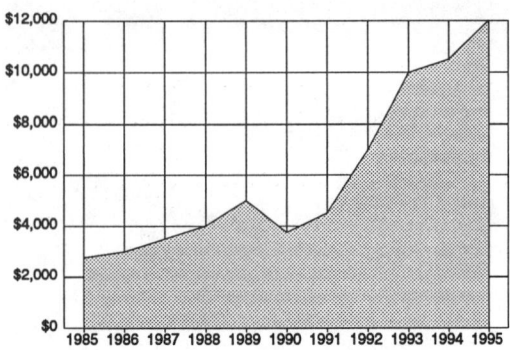

Card Size: 1 1/2" X 2 1/2"
Face: Sepia; Name
Back: Black on card stock; Name, Resume
Imprint: TOBACCO PRODUCTS CORPORATION OF CANADA, LTD.
ACC No.: C144
Complete Set No.: 60
Complete Set Price: 3,000.00   6,000.00   12,000.00
Common Card: 30.00   65.00   125.00

BOSTON

No.	Player	G	VG	EX
1	Carson Cooper, RC	40.00	75.00	150.00
2	Hec Fowler, Goalie, RC	30.00	65.00	125.00
3	Fern Headley, RC	30.00	65.00	125.00
4	James Herberts, RC	30.00	65.00	125.00
5	Herb Mitchell, RC	30.00	65.00	125.00
6	George Redding, RC	30.00	65.00	125.00
7	Werner Schnarr, RC	30.00	65.00	125.00
8	Alfred Skinner, RC	40.00	75.00	150.00

HAMILTON TIGERS

No.	Player	G	VG	EX
9	Edmond Bouchard	30.00	65.00	125.00
10	Billy Burch	45.00	85.00	175.00
11	Vernon Forbes, Goalie	30.00	65.00	125.00
12	Red (Redvers) Green	30.00	65.00	125.00
13	Wilf (Shorty) Green	45.00	85.00	175.00
14	Charlie Langlois, RC	30.00	65.00	125.00
15	Alex McKinnon, RC	30.00	65.00	125.00
16	Goldie Prodgers	30.00	65.00	125.00
17	Ken Randall	30.00	65.00	125.00
18	Mickey Roach	30.00	65.00	125.00
19	Jesse Spring	30.00	65.00	125.00

MONTREAL CANADIENS

No.	Player	G	VG	EX
20	Billy Boucher	30.00	65.00	125.00
21	Odie Cleghorn	40.00	75.00	150.00
22	Sprague Cleghorn	75.00	150.00	300.00
23	Billy Couture	30.00	65.00	125.00
24	Aurel Joliat	215.00	430.00	865.00
25	Sylvio Mantha	40.00	75.00	150.00
26	Howie Morenz	460.00	925.00	1,850.00
27	Georges Vezina, Goalie	225.00	450.00	900.00

MONTREAL MAROONS

No.	Player	G	VG	EX
28	Clint Benedict, Goalie, LC	45.00	85.00	175.00
29	Louis Berlinquette, RC	30.00	65.00	125.00
30	Harry Broadbent, LC	45.00	85.00	175.00
31	Jim Cain, RC	30.00	65.00	125.00
32	George Carroll, RC	30.00	65.00	125.00
33	Chuck Dinsmore, RC	30.00	65.00	125.00
34	Fred Lowrey, RC	30.00	65.00	125.00

Champ's Cigarette Cards
1924-25 Issue
Card No. 23,
Billy Couture
nicknamed Wilfrid Coutu

Champ's Cigarette Cards
1924-25 Issue
Card No. 23,
Billy Couture
nicknamed Wilfrid Coutu

Champ's Cigarette Cards
1924-25 Issue
Card No. 47,
Hooley Smith

No.	Player	G	VG	EX
35	Dunc Munro, RC	30.00	65.00	125.00
36	Gerry Munro, RC	30.00	65.00	125.00
37	Sam Rothschild, RC	30.00	65.00	125.00
38	Ganton Scott, RC	30.00	65.00	125.00

OTTAWA SENATORS

No.	Player	G	VG	EX
39	Robert Boucher, RC, LC	30.00	65.00	125.00
40	Spiff (Earl) Campbell, RC, LC	30.00	65.00	125.00
41	Francis Clancy	230.00	460.00	925.00
42	Alex Connell, Goalie, RC	30.00	65.00	125.00
43	Cy Denneny, LC	50.00	100.00	200.00
44	Frank Finnigan, RC	40.00	75.00	150.00
45	Lionel Hitchman	40.00	75.00	150.00
46	Frank Nighbor, LC	55.00	110.00	225.00
47	Hooley Smith, RC	55.00	110.00	225.00

TORONTO SAINT PATRICKS

No.	Player	G	VG	EX
48	Jack (Jock) Adams	55.00	110.00	225.00
49	Lloyd Andrews	30.00	65.00	125.00
50	Bert Corbeau	30.00	65.00	125.00
51	Hap Day, RC	130.00	260.00	525.00
52	Babe Dye	45.00	85.00	175.00
53	Albert Holway, RC	30.00	65.00	125.00
54	Stan Jackson, RC	30.00	65.00	125.00
55	Bert McCaffrey, RC	30.00	65.00	125.00
56	Reg Noble	55.00	110.00	225.00
57	Mickey O'Leary, RC	30.00	65.00	125.00
58	John Roach, Goalie	30.00	65.00	125.00
59	Chris Speyers, RC	30.00	65.00	125.00

THE STANLEY CUP

No.	Player	G	VG	EX
60	The Stanley Cup	100.00	200.00	400.00

SWEET CAPORAL

— 1934 - 35 PHOTO ISSUE —

These photos were inserts in the Montreal Forum game programs. A photo was inserted in the home game programs of the Canadiens and the Maroons. The photos are unnumbered and the players are listed below in alphabetical order within their respective teams.

Photo Size: 6 7/8" X 9 1/2"
Face: Four colour
Back: Blank
Imprint: None
Complete Set No.: 48
Complete Set Price: 625.00   1,250.00   2,500.00
Common Player: 7.50   15.00   30.00

BOSTON BRUINS

No.	Player	VG	EX	NRMT
1	Eddie Shore	50.00	100.00	200.00
2	Babe Siebert	7.50	15.00	30.00
3	Nels Stewart	22.50	45.00	90.00
4	Tiny Thompson, Goalie	15.00	30.00	60.00

CHICAGO BLACK HAWKS

No.	Player	VG	EX	NRMT
5	Lorne Chabot, Goalie	7.50	15.00	30.00
6	Mush March	7.50	15.00	30.00
7	Howie Morenz	85.00	175.00	350.00

DETROIT RED WINGS

No.	Player	VG	EX	NRMT
8	Larry Aurie	7.50	15.00	30.00
9	Ebbie Goodfellow	16.25	32.50	65.00
10	Herbie Lewis	7.50	15.00	30.00
11	Ralph Weiland	15.00	30.00	60.00

MONTREAL CANADIENS

No.	Player	VG	EX	NRMT
12	Gerry Carson, Error	7.50	15.00	30.00
13	Nels Crutchfield	7.50	15.00	30.00
14	Wilf Cude, Goalie	7.50	15.00	30.00

No.	Player	VG	EX	NRMT
15	Roger Jenkins	7.50	15.00	30.00
16	Aurel Joliat	55.00	110.00	225.00
17	Joe Lamb	7.50	15.00	30.00
18	Wildor Larochelle, Error	7.50	15.00	30.00
19	Pete Lepine	7.50	15.00	30.00
20	Georges Mantha	7.50	15.00	30.00
21	Sylvio Mantha	16.25	32.50	65.00
22	Jack McGill	7.50	15.00	30.00
23	Armand Mondou	7.50	15.00	30.00
24	Paul Raymond	7.50	15.00	30.00
25	Jack Riley	7.50	15.00	30.00

MONTREAL MAROONS

No.	Player	VG	EX	NRMT
26	Russ Blinco	7.50	15.00	30.00
27	Herbert Cain	7.50	15.00	30.00
28	Lionel Conacher	15.00	30.00	60.00
29	Alex Connell, Goalie	15.00	30.00	60.00
30	Stewart Evans	7.50	15.00	30.00
31	Dutch Gainor	7.50	15.00	30.00
32	Paul Haynes	7.50	15.00	30.00
33	Gus Marker	7.50	15.00	30.00
34	Baldy Northcott	7.50	15.00	30.00
35	Earl Robinson	7.50	15.00	30.00
36	Hooley Smith	17.50	35.00	70.00
37	Dave Trottier	7.50	15.00	30.00
38	Jimmy Ward	7.50	15.00	30.00
39	Cy Wentworth	7.50	15.00	30.00

NEW YORK RANGERS

No.	Player	VG	EX	NRMT
40	Bill Cook	10.00	20.00	40.00
41	Bun Cook	15.00	30.00	60.00
42	Ivan (Ching) Johnson	16.25	32.50	65.00
43	Dave Kerr, Goalie	7.50	15.00	30.00

TORONTO MAPLE LEAFS

No.	Player	VG	EX	NRMT
44	Francis Clancy	55.00	110.00	225.00
45	Charlie Conacher	55.00	110.00	225.00
46	Red Horner	15.00	30.00	60.00
47	Harvey Jackson	16.25	32.50	65.00
48	Joe Primeau	16.25	32.50	65.00

Sweet Caporal 1934-35 Photo Issue
Photo No. 45, Charlie Conacher

Sweet Caporal 1934-35 Photo Issue
Photo No. 45, Charlie Conacher

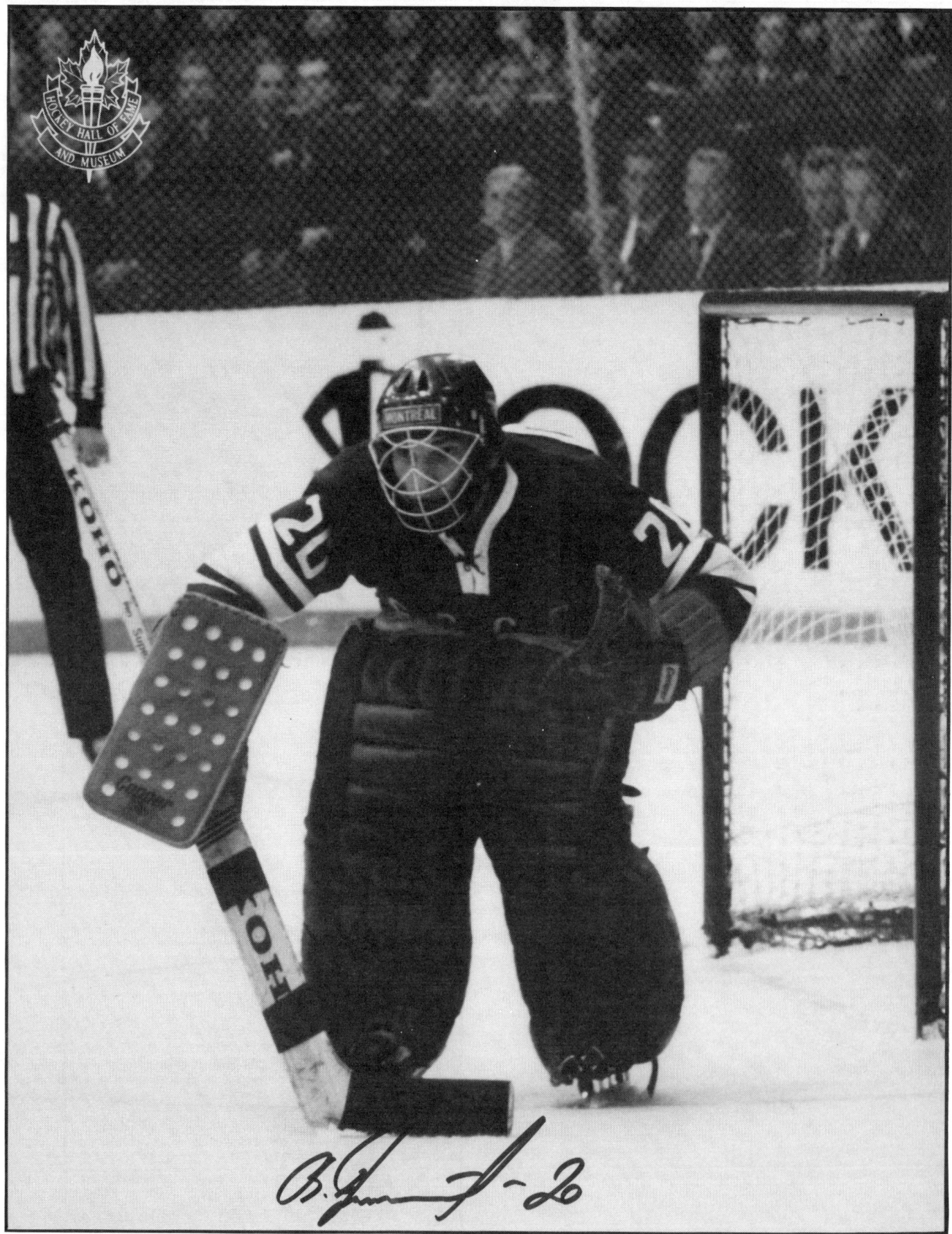

Vladislav Tretiak

CHAPTER FOUR
NATIONAL HOCKEY LEAGUE
1923-1995

ALPHABETICAL LISTING OF MANUFACTURERS

NATIONAL HOCKEY LEAGUE

Abalene Sales and Promotions Ltd.	419	La Patrie	187
Action Packed	339	La Presse	28
Adventure Gum	269	Leaf	447
Alphabetical Player Index	455	Letraset	301
Amalgamated Press	153	Lipton Soup	302
Anonymous	26	Loblaws	302
Bazooka	293	Mac's Milk	302
Bauer Skates	282	Maple Crispette	26
Bee Hive Variations	144	McDonald's Restaurants	308
Berk Ross	157	Nabisco	268
Bowman	340	O'Keefe Beverages	28
Canada Starch	152	O-Pee-Chee	33
Canadian Chewing Gum Sales Ltd.	29	Panini	324
Canadian Cycle and Motor Co.	29	Parkhurst	157
Celebrity Watch Inc.	339	PepsiCo	306
Chex	275	Popsicle	305
CHLP / CKAC / CKVL Radio	156	Post Cereal	278
Coca-Cola	276	Pro Set	346
Colgate	289	Quaker Oats	153
Dad's Cookies	290	Royal Desserts	187
Diamond Match Company	30	St. Lawrence Starch Company	143
Dimanche / Derniere Heure	298	Score	364
Dominion Chocolate	27	Season's	438
Donruss	440	Sega - E M Sports	445
Durivage	420	7-Eleven	317
Eaton's	278	Shirriff	269
Eddie Sargent Promotions Ltd.	283	Sportscaster Cards	305
El Producto	275	TCMA	307
Esso	291	Topps	188
Fleer	420	The Toronto Star	265
Frito-Lay	339	Toronto Sun	296
Funmate Canada Ltd.	314	Towers / Bonimart	301
Gillette	419	Ultimate Trading Card Company	438
Goudey Gum Co.	33	Upper Deck	398
Hamilton Gum	33	V129 Anonymous	141
Highliner	436	Vachon Foods	316
Hockey Hall of Fame	309	Willards Chocolate	28
Hockey Hall of Fame and Museum	437	William Paterson	25
Hockey Wit	444	Wonder Bread	273
Humpty Dumpty	437	World Wide Gum	140
Kellogg's	294	York Peanut Butter	273
Kenner	444	Zellers	439'
Kraft	318		

WILLIAM PATERSON LTD

— 1923 - 24 REGULAR ISSUE —

This set is very similar to the subsequent V145-2 set except for its sepia (dark brown) colour and size. The card number is located on the front lower left corner. The name of the player and team appear on the bottom border along with "National Hockey League". The card backs are blank.

PRICE MOVEMENT OF EX SETS

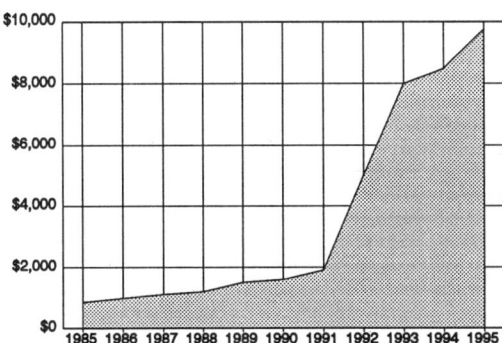

Card Size: 2" X 3 1/4"
Face: Sepia; Name, Team, Number, League
Back: Blank
Imprint: None
ACC No.: V145-1
Complete Set No.: 40
Complete Set Price: 2,450.00   4,875.00   9,750.00
Common Card: 30.00   65.00   125.00

OTTAWA SENATORS

No.	Player	G	VG	EX
1	Eddie Gerard, LC	60.00	115.00	225.00
2	Frank Nighbor, RC	95.00	190.00	375.00
3	Francis (King) Clancy, RC	350.00	700.00	1,400.00
4	Jack Darragh, LC	35.00	75.00	150.00
5	Harry Helman, RC, LC	40.00	75.00	150.00
6	George Boucher, RC	60.00	115.00	225.00
7	Clint Benedict, Goalie	60.00	115.00	225.00
8	Lionel Hitchman, RC	30.00	65.00	125.00
9	Harry Broadbent	40.00	75.00	150.00
10	Cy Denneny, RC	65.00	125.00	250.00

MONTREAL CANADIENS

No.	Player	G	VG	EX
11	Sprague Cleghorn	40.00	75.00	150.00
12	Sylvio Mantha, RC	40.00	75.00	150.00
13	Joe Malone	65.00	125.00	250.00
14	Aurel Joliat, RC	315.00	625.00	1,250.00
15	Howie Morenz, RC	565.00	1,125.00	2,250.00
16	Billy Boucher, RC	30.00	65.00	125.00
17	Billy Coutu, RC	30.00	65.00	125.00
18	Odie Cleghorn	30.00	65.00	125.00
19	Georges Vezina, Goalie	190.00	375.00	750.00

TORONTO SAINT PATRICKS

No.	Player	G	VG	EX
20	Amos Arbour, RC	30.00	65.00	125.00
21	Lloyd Andrews, RC	30.00	65.00	125.00
22	Billy Stuart, RC	45.00	85.00	175.00
23	Cecil (Babe) Dye, RC	60.00	115.00	225.00
24	Jack J. Adams, RC	60.00	115.00	225.00
25	Bert Corbeau, RC		Extremely Rare	
26	Reg Noble, RC	45.00	85.00	175.00
27	Stan Jackson, RC	30.00	65.00	125.00
28	John Roach, Goalie, RC	30.00	65.00	125.00

HAMILTON TIGERS

No.	Player	G	VG	EX
29	Vernon Forbes, Goalie, RC	30.00	65.00	125.00
30	Wilf (Shorty) Green, RC	45.00	85.00	175.00
31	Red (Redvers) Green, RC	30.00	65.00	125.00
32	Goldie Prodgers	30.00	65.00	125.00
33	Leo Reise, Sr., RC	30.00	65.00	125.00
34	Ken Randall, RC	40.00	75.00	150.00

William Paterson Ltd.
1924-25 Issue
Card No. 3,
Francis Clancy

William Paterson Ltd.
1924-25 Issue
Card No. 20, Error,
Name misspelled
Jess on face

William Paterson Ltd.
1924-25 Issue
Card No. 38,
Ganton Scott

No.	Player	G	VG	EX
35	Billy Burch, RC	45.00	85.00	175.00
36	Jesse Spring, RC	30.00	65.00	125.00
37	Edmond Bouchard, RC	30.00	65.00	125.00
38	Mickey Roach, RC	30.00	65.00	125.00
39	Charles Fraser, RC	30.00	65.00	125.00
40	Corbett Denneny, RC	60.00	115.00	225.00

— 1924 - 25 REGULAR ISSUE —

The cards are slightly smaller than the otherwise very similar V145-1 series and have a greenish black tone. Card no.3, Francis Clancy, is the only card numbered the same as the V145-1 series.

PRICE MOVEMENT OF EX SETS

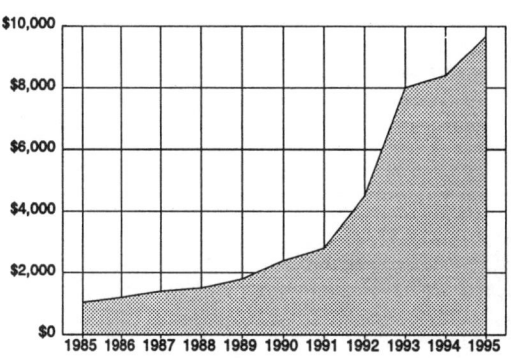

Card Size: 1 1/16" X 3 1/4"
Face: Green, Black and white; Name, Team, Number, League
Back: Blank
Imprint: None
ACC No.: V145-2
Complete Set No.: 60
Complete Set Price: 2,410.00   4,825.00   9,650.00
Common Card: 25.00   50.00   100.00

OTTAWA SENATORS

No.	Player	G	VG	EX
1	Joe Ironstone, Goalie, RC, LC	60.00	115.00	225.00
2	George Boucher, LC	60.00	115.00	225.00
3	Francis (King) Clancy	190.00	375.00	750.00
4	Lionel Hitchman	25.00	50.00	100.00
5	Hooley Smith, RC	40.00	75.00	150.00
6	Frank Nighbor, LC	40.00	75.00	150.00
7	Cy Denneny, LC, Error	30.00	65.00	125.00
8	Spiff Campbell, RC, LC	25.00	50.00	100.00
9	Frank Finnigan, RC	25.00	50.00	100.00
10	Alex Connell, Goalie, RC	30.00	65.00	125.00

HAMILTON TIGERS

No.	Player	G	VG	EX
11	Vernon Forbes, Goalie	25.00	50.00	100.00
12	Ken Randall	25.00	50.00	100.00
13	Billy Burch	30.00	65.00	125.00
14	Wilf (Shorty) Green	30.00	65.00	125.00
15	Red (Redvers) Green	25.00	50.00	100.00
16	Alex McKinnon, RC	25.00	50.00	100.00
17	Charlie Langlois, RC	25.00	50.00	100.00
18	Mickey Roach	25.00	50.00	100.00
19	Edmond Bouchard	25.00	50.00	100.00
20	Jesse Spring, Error	25.00	50.00	100.00

BOSTON

No.	Player	G	VG	EX
21	Carson Cooper, RC	25.00	50.00	100.00
22	Smokey Harris, RC	25.00	50.00	100.00
23	Fern Headley, RC	25.00	50.00	100.00
24	Bill Cook, RC	70.00	140.00	285.00
25	James Herberts, RC	25.00	50.00	100.00
26	Werner Schnarr, RC	25.00	50.00	100.00
27	Alf Skinner, RC	25.00	50.00	100.00
28	George Redding, RC	25.00	50.00	100.00
29	Herb Mitchell, RC	25.00	50.00	100.00
30	Hec Fowler, Goalie, RC	25.00	50.00	100.00
31	Billy Stuart	25.00	50.00	100.00

MAPLE CRISPETTE — 1924 - 25 REGULAR ISSUE

MONTREAL MAROONS

No.	Player	G	VG	EX
32	Clint Benedict, Goalie, LC	40.00	75.00	150.00
33	Gerry Munro, RC	25.00	50.00	100.00
34	Dunc Munro, RC	25.00	50.00	100.00
35	Jim Cain	25.00	50.00	100.00
36	Fred Lowrey, RC	25.00	50.00	100.00
37	Sam Rothschild, RC	25.00	50.00	100.00
38	Ganton Scott, RC	25.00	50.00	100.00
39	Harry Broadbent, LC	40.00	75.00	150.00
40	Chuck Dinsmore, RC	25.00	50.00	100.00
41	Louis Berlinquette, RC	25.00	50.00	100.00
42	George Carroll, RC	25.00	50.00	100.00

MONTREAL CANADIENS

No.	Player	G	VG	EX
43	Georges Vezina, Goalie	190.00	375.00	750.00
44	Billy Couture	25.00	50.00	100.00
45	Odie Cleghorn	25.00	50.00	100.00
46	Billy Boucher	25.00	50.00	100.00
47	Howie Morenz	350.00	700.00	1,400.00
48	Auriel Joliat	145.00	290.00	575.00
49	Sprague Cleghorn	30.00	65.00	125.00
50	Billy Mantha, RC	25.00	50.00	100.00

TORONTO SAINT PATRICKS

No.	Player	G	VG	EX
51	Reg Noble	30.00	65.00	125.00
52	John Roach, Goalie	25.00	50.00	100.00
53	Jack J. Adams	40.00	75.00	150.00
54	Babe Dye	40.00	75.00	150.00
55	Reg Reid, RC	25.00	50.00	100.00
56	Albert Holway, RC	25.00	50.00	100.00
57	Bert McCaffery, RC	25.00	50.00	100.00
58	Bert Corbeau	40.00	75.00	150.00
59	Lloyd Andrews	25.00	50.00	100.00
60	Stan Jackson	50.00	100.00	200.00

MAPLE CRISPETTE
— 1924 - 25 REGULAR ISSUE —

These black and white cards are numbered in the lower right corner and show the player's name in the opposite corner. The backs contain promotional information. Card No. 15, Sprague Cleghorn, is not included in the set price.

PRICE MOVEMENT OF EX SETS

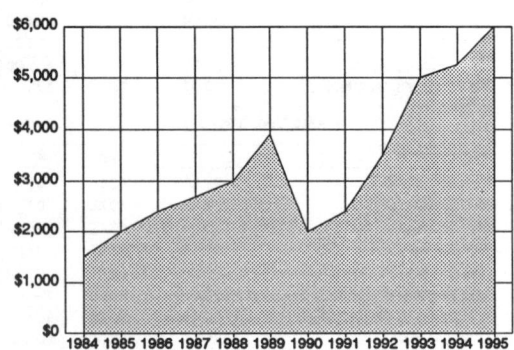

Card Size: 1 3/8" X 2 3/8"
Face: Black and white; Name, Number
Back: Black on card stock; Promotional Offer
Imprint: MAPLE CRISPETTE CO, LIMITED
ACC No.: V130
Complete Set No.: 30
Complete Set Price: 1,500.00 3,000.00 6,000.00
Common Card: 30.00 65.00 125.00

MONTREAL MAROONS

No.	Player	G	VG	EX
1	Dunc Munro, RC	55.00	110.00	225.00
2	Clint Benedict, Goalie, LC	50.00	100.00	200.00

Maple Crispette, 1924-25 Issue Card No. 2, Clint Benedict

Maple Crispette 1924-25 Issue Card No. 22, Wilf (Shorty) Green

Anonymous, 1925-26 "Borderless" Issue Card No. 22, Hooley Smith

BOSTON

No.	Player	G	VG	EX
3	Hec Fowler, Goalie, RC	30.00	65.00	125.00
4	Fern Headley, RC	30.00	65.00	125.00
5	Alf Skinner, RC	30.00	65.00	125.00
6	Lloyd Cook, RC	50.00	100.00	200.00
7	Smokey Harris, RC	30.00	65.00	125.00
8	James Herberts, RC	30.00	65.00	125.00
9	Carson Cooper, RC	30.00	65.00	125.00

HAMILTON TIGERS

No.	Player	G	VG	EX
10	Red (Redvers) Green	30.00	65.00	125.00

MONTREAL CANADIENS

No.	Player	G	VG	EX
11	Billy Boucher	30.00	65.00	125.00
12	Howie Morenz	300.00	600.00	1,200.00
13	Georges Vezina, Goalie	145.00	290.00	575.00
14	Aurel Joliat	125.00	250.00	500.00
15	Sprague Cleghorn		Extremely Rare	

MONTREAL MAROONS

No.	Player	G	VG	EX
16	Jim Cain, RC	30.00	65.00	125.00
17	Chuck Dinsmore, RC	30.00	65.00	125.00
18	Harry Broadbent, LC	50.00	100.00	200.00
19	Sam Rothschild, RC	30.00	65.00	125.00
20	George Carroll, RC	30.00	65.00	125.00

HAMILTON TIGERS

No.	Player	G	VG	EX
21	Billy Burch	55.00	110.00	225.00
22	Wilf (Shorty) Green	55.00	110.00	225.00
23	Mickey Roach	30.00	65.00	125.00
24	Ken Randall	30.00	65.00	125.00
25	Vernon Forbes, Goalie	30.00	65.00	125.00
26	Charlie Langlois, RC	30.00	65.00	125.00

MONTREAL CANADIENS

No.	Player	G	VG	EX
27	Edouard Lalonde	120.00	235.00	475.00

MONTREAL MAROONS

No.	Player	G	VG	EX
28	Fred Lowrey, RC	30.00	65.00	125.00
29	Ganton Scott, RC	30.00	65.00	125.00
30	Louis Berlinquette, RC	30.00	65.00	125.00

Note: For NRMT prices add 100% to the EX prices listed.

ANONYMOUS
—1925 - 26 "BORDERLESS" ISSUE —

Card Size: 1 3/8" x 2 3/8"
Face: Black and white photo, borderless; Name
Back: Black on card stock; Premium offer, Bilingual
Imprint: None
Complete Set No.: Unknown
Complete Set Price: Unknown
Common Card: 50.00 100.00 200.00

No.	Player	G	VG	EX
7	Wildor Larochelle, Mon.C.	100.00	200.00	400.00
12	Herb Rheaume, Goalie, Mon.C.	50.00	100.00	200.00
18	Francis (King) Clancy, Ott.	450.00	900.00	1,750.00
22	Hooley Smith, Ott.	145.00	290.00	575.00
39	Herb Mitchell, Bos.	50.00	100.00	200.00
41	Sprague Cleghorn, Bos., Error	65.00	125.00	250.00
46	Odie Cleghorn, Mon.C.	65.00	125.00	250.00
52	Hib (Hibbert) Milks, Pit.	65.00	125.00	250.00
91	Dutch Cain, Bos.	90.00	180.00	360.00
92	Duncan Munro, Mon.M.	125.00	250.00	500.00

—1926-27 "BORDERS" ISSUE —

Card Size: 1 1/2" x 2 3/8"
Face: Black and white photo, white border; Name
Back: Black on card stock; Premium offer, Bilingual
Imprint: None
Complete Set No.: Unknown
Complete Set Price: Unknown
Common Card: 65.00 125.00 250.00

MONTREAL CANADIENS

No.	Player	G	VG	EX
1	Billy Boucher	160.00	325.00	650.00
2	Billy Coutu	315.00	625.00	1,250.00
3	Georges Vezina, Goalie	325.00	650.00	1,300.00
4	Silvio Mantha	160.00	325.00	650.00
5	Roland Paulhus	80.00	160.00	325.00
6	Albert Leduc, Error	50.00	100.00	200.00
7	Wildor Larochelle, Error	100.00	200.00	400.00
8	Aurel Joliat	325.00	650.00	1,300.00
9	Howie Morenz	2,000.00	4,200.00	6,000.00
10	Hector Lepine	100.00	200.00	400.00
11	Alphonse Lacroix, Goalie	100.00	200.00	400.00
12	Art Gagne	100.00	200.00	400.00
14	Bill Holmes	65.00	125.00	250.00
15	Leo Dandurand, Director	200.00	400.00	800.00

OTTAWA SENATORS

No.	Player	G	VG	EX
16	Alex Connell, Goalie	135.00	275.00	550.00
17	Francis (King) Clancy	400.00	800.00	1,600.00
19	Hec Kilrea, RC	70.00	135.00	270.00
21	Hooley Smith	145.00	290.00	575.00
22	Alex Smith, RC	125.00	250.00	500.00

BOSTON BRUINS

No.	PLayer	G	VG	EX
31	Sprague Cleghorn	225.00	450.00	900.00
32	Carson Cooper	75.00	150.00	300.00
36	Hugo Harrington	125.00	250.00	500.00
38	Herb Mitchell	75.00	150.00	300.00
39	Charles Stewart, Goalie	85.00	175.00	350.00
40	Red Stuart	75.00	150.00	300.00
41	Lloyd Cook	65.00	125.00	250.00

PITTSBURGH PIRATES

No.	Player	G	VG	EX
46	Odie Cleghorn	100.00	200.00	400.00
47	Louis Berlinquette, Error	100.00	200.00	400.00
48	Hib (Hibbert) Milks	100.00	200.00	400.00

TORONTO SAINT PATRICKS

No.	Player	G	VG	EX
61	Pete Bellefeuille	290.00	575.00	1,150.00
62	Gerry Munro, (Mon.M. Jersey)	65.00	125.00	250.00

NEW YORK AMERICANS

No.	Player	G	VG	EX
76	Charlie Langlois	65.00	125.00	250.00
77	Jake Forbes, Goalie	100.00	200.00	400.00
79	Billy Burch	65.00	125.00	250.00
82	Joe Simpson	75.00	150.00	300.00

MONTREAL MAROONS

No.	Player	G	VG	EX
91	D. Munro	90.00	180.00	360.00
95	Clint Benedict, Goalie	75.00	150.00	300.00
96	Reg Noble	155.00	310.00	625.00
97	Nels Stewart	185.00	390.00	775.00
100	Sam Rothschild, Error	80.00	160.00	320.00

DETROIT COUGARS

No.	Player	G	VG	EX
121	Harry Holmes, Goalie	240.00	475.00	950.00
127	Clem Loughlin	105.00	215.00	425.00
129	Johnny Sheppard	65.00	125.00	250.00

CHICAGO BLACK HAWKS

No.	Player	G	VG	EX
136	Gord Fraser	100.00	200.00	400.00
138	Dick Irvin	180.00	360.00	725.00

Note: These sets are not complete. We would appreciate hearing from anyone who could help us complete this set.

Anonymous
1926-27" Borders" Issue
Card No. 7, Error,
Name shown as Victor

Dominion Chocolate
1925 Dominion Athletic Stars
Card No. 81
William Fraser

Dominion Chocolate
1926 Dominion Athletic Stars
Card No. 29,
Bud Fisher

DOMINION CHOCOLATE

— 1925 DOMINION ATHLETIC STARS —

This 120-card set, issued in 1925 to commemorate Canada's 1924 Olympic athletes, contains a selection of cards from various sports. Only 32 are hockey. The cards include a bottom tab used to claim a prize. This tab must be attached for these prices to apply.

Card Size: 2 7/8" x 1 1/4"
Face: Black and white, white border; Number, Name
Back: Black on card stock; Name, Resume
Imprint: Dominion Chocolate Co., Limited
   72 Duchess Street, Toronto, Canada
Complete Set No.: 120 / 32 Hockey
Complete Set Price: 13,750.00
Set Price - Hockey : 4,000.00
Common Hockey Card: 25.00 50.00 100.00

No.	Player	G	VG	EX
13	Granite Club, Olympic Champs	65.00	125.00	250.00
28	North Toronto, O.H.A.	40.00	75.00	150.00
35	Peterborough, O.H.A.	40.00	75.00	150.00
49	Owen Sound Jrs., O.H.A.	25.00	50.00	100.00
55	E.J. Collett, Granite	25.00	50.00	100.00
56	Hughie J. Fox, Granite	25.00	50.00	100.00
57	Dunc Munro, Granite	40.00	75.00	150.00
58	M. Rutherford, Granite	25.00	50.00	100.00
59	Beattie Ramsay, Granite	25.00	50.00	100.00
60	Bert McCaffery, Tor.	25.00	50.00	100.00
61	Soo Greyhounds	40.00	75.00	150.00
68	J.P. Aggatts	25.00	50.00	100.00
69	Hooley Smith, Granite, Error	50.00	100.00	200.00
70	J. Cameron, Goalie, Granite	25.00	50.00	100.00
81	William Fraser, Nova Scotia	25.00	50.00	100.00
82	Vernon Forbes, Goalie, Hamilton	25.00	50.00	100.00
83	Wilf (Shorty) Green, Hamilton	40.00	75.00	150.00
84	Red (Redvers) Green, Hamilton	25.00	50.00	100.00
86	Jack Langtry	25.00	50.00	100.00
89	Billy Coutu, Mon.C	40.00	75.00	150.00
92	J. Hughes	25.00	50.00	100.00
95	Edouard Lalonde	115.00	230.00	460.00
101	Bill Brydge, Port Arthur	25.00	50.00	100.00
103	Cecil Browne, Selkirk	25.00	50.00	100.00
106	J.C. "Red" Porter, Tor.	25.00	50.00	100.00
112	North Bay Hockey Team	25.00	50.00	100.00
113	Ross Somerville, Tor. Univ.	25.00	50.00	100.00
114	Harry Watson, Granite	60.00	115.00	225.00
117	Odie Cleghorn, Error	25.00	50.00	100.00
118	Lionel Conacher, Tor.	40.00	75.00	150.00
119	Aurel Joliat, Mon.	120.00	235.00	475.00
120	Georges Vezina, Goalie, Mon.	155.00	310.00	625.00

—1926 DOMINION ATHLETIC STARS —
NEW SERIES

Issued by Dominion Chocolates c1926 this 60-card set features Canadian athletes from several different sports. This set had a premium tab along the bottom of the card. There were two series of this set, both of which are identical except the second set was printed on a lighter weight stock. Only the five hockey cards are listed and priced here.

Photograph Size: 1 1/16" x 2 3/8"
Face: Black and white photo, white border; Name, Number, Promotional offer
Back: Black and white; Name, Number, Resume
Imprint: Dominion Chocolate Co., Limited
Complete Set Price: Unknown
Complete Set No.: 60

No.	Player	G	VG	EX
18	Ernie Williams	25.00	50.00	100.00
23	Douglas Young	25.00	50.00	100.00
26	George Clarke	25.00	50.00	100.00
28	Ken Doraty	25.00	50.00	100.00
29	Bud Fisher, Goalie	25.00	50.00	100.00

Note: For a listing of other cards in this set see the appendix at the back of this book. This set is not complete. We would appreciate hearing from anyone who could help us complete this set.

WILLARDS CHOCOLATE

—1925 SPORTING CHAMPIONS —

This set was made in the United States and inserted in Willard's "Sports" Nut Bar. It is uncertain if a Canadian version was produced. The set contains 56 cards featuring athletes of various sports including running, tennis, golf, skiing, rowing, swimming, speed boating, trap shooting, billiards, pole vaulting, fishing, lacrosse, horse racing, bowling, wrestling, shot put, cricket, skating, boxing, football, soccer, baseball and basketball. Only the hockey segment of the set is priced here.
For a listing of the complete set see the Appendix at the back of this book.

Photograph Size: 1 3/8" x 3 1/8"
Face: Black and white; Name, Number
Back: Blank
Imprint: None
ACC. No.: V-122
Complete Set No.: 56
Complete Set Price: 2,000.00 4,000.00 8,000.00 ☐
Wrapper Price: 200.00 400.00 600.00

CANADIAN OLYMPIC HOCKEY TEAM

No.	Player	G	VG	EX
43	Harry Watson	120.00	200.00	400.00 ☐
45	Ernie Collett, Goalie	120.00	200.00	400.00 ☐
47	Hooley Smith	120.00	200.00	400.00 ☐
52	Dunc Munro	120.00	200.00	400.00 ☐

La PATRIE 1927 - 28

This is a Montreal Canadiens team set. See page no. 612.

LA PRESSE

— 1927 - 1932 ISSUE —

This set was issued by the French Canadian newspaper in Montreal.

Photograph Size: 10" x 16 1/2"
Face: Four colour; Name
Back: Newspaper
Imprint: None
Complete Set No.: 70
Complete Set Price: 1,125.00 2,250.00 ☐
Common Hockey Player: 12.50 25.00

1927

No.	Player \ Date Issued	VG	EX
1	Howie Morenz, Mon.C., December 10	30.00	60.00 ☐
2	Aurel Joliat, Mon.C., December 17	30.00	60.00 ☐
3	Sylvio Mantha, Mon.C., December 24	22.50	45.00 ☐
4	Pit Lepine, Mon.C., December 31	12.50	25.00 ☐

1928

No.	Player \ Date Issued	VG	EX
5	George Hainsworth, Goalie, Mon.C., January 7	22.50	45.00 ☐
6	Art Gagne, Mon.C., January 14	15.00	30.00 ☐
7	Herb Gardiner, Mon.C., January 21	17.50	35.00 ☐
8	Albert Leduc, Mon.C., January 28	20.00	40.00 ☐
9	Wildor Larochelle, Mon.C., February 4	12.50	25.00 ☐
10	Leonard Gaudreault, Mon.C., February 11	12.50	25.00 ☐
11	Gizzy Hart, Mon.C., February 18	12.50	25.00 ☐
12	Charles Langlois, Mon.C., February 25	17.50	35.00 ☐
13	Georges Vezina, Goalie, Mon.C., March 3	30.00	60.00 ☐
14	Cattarinich, Hart, Dandurand, Letourmeau, Mon.C., March 31	12.50	25.00 ☐
15	Eddie Shore, Bos., April 7	30.00	60.00 ☐
16	Lionel Conacher, NYA, April 14	17.50	35.00 ☐
17	Red Porter, Tor. Grad., April 21	12.50	25.00 ☐
18	George Patterson, Mon.C., April 28	12.50	25.00 ☐
19	Martin Burke, Mon.C., December 15	12.50	25.00 ☐
20	Nels Stewart, Mon.M., December 22	22.50	45.00 ☐

Note: For a card to grade higher than EX it must have no wear, no creases, full colour and four square corners.

Willards Chocolate
1925 Sporting Champions
Card No. 45, Ernie Collett

Willards Chocolate
1925 Sporting Champions
Card No. 47, Hooley Smith

Willards Chocolate
1925 Sporting Champions
Card No. 52, Dunc Munro

1929 ISSUE

No.	Player \ Date Issued	VG	EX
21	Babe Siebert, Mon.M., January 5	22.50	45.00 ☐
22	Happy Day, Tor., January 12	22.50	45.00 ☐
23	Clint Benedict, Goalie, Mon.M., January 19	15.00	30.00 ☐
24	Red Dutton, Mon.M., January 26	15.00	30.00 ☐
25	Jimmy Ward, Mon.M., February 2	12.50	25.00 ☐
26	Bill Phillips, Mon.M., February 9	12.50	25.00 ☐
27	Frank Boucher, NYR, February 16	15.00	30.00 ☐
28	Lucien Brunet, Local League, February 23	12.50	25.00 ☐
29	George Boucher, Ott., March 2	12.50	25.00 ☐
30	Armand Mondou, Mon. C., March 16	12.50	25.00 ☐
31	Bun Cook, NYR, March 23	17.50	35.00 ☐
32	Georges Mantha, Mon.C., April 6	17.50	35.00 ☐
33	Gordon Fraser, Mon.C., November 30	12.50	25.00 ☐
34	Bert McCaffrey, Mon.C., December 7	12.50	25.00 ☐
35	Hec Kilrea, Ott., December 28	12.50	25.00 ☐

1930 ISSUE

No.	Player \ Date Issued	VG	EX
36	Andy Blair, Tor., January 4	12.50	25.00 ☐
37	Francis (King) Clancy, Ott., January 11	25.00	50.00 ☐
38	John Ross Roach, Goalie, Tor., January 18	12.50	25.00 ☐
39	Leo Bourgeault, NYR, January 25	12.50	25.00 ☐
40	Raymond Belanger, Club, Champtre, February 1	12.50	25.00 ☐
41	Lionel Hitchman, Bos., February 8	12.50	25.00 ☐
42	Joe Primeau, Tor., February 15	20.00	40.00 ☐
43	Dutch Gainor, Bos., February 22	12.50	25.00 ☐
44	Tiny Thompson, Goalie, Bos., March 1	15.00	30.00 ☐
45	Gus Rivers, Mon.C., March 8	12.50	25.00 ☐
46	Hooley Smith, Mon.C., March 29	17.50	35.00 ☐
47	Flat Walsh, Mon.M., April 5	12.50	25.00 ☐
48	Montreal Canadiens Team, April 26	20.00	40.00 ☐
49	Earl Miller, Chi., December 13	12.50	25.00 ☐
50	Johnny Gagnon, Mon.C., December 20	12.50	25.00 ☐
51	Art Sommers, Chi., December 27	12.50	25.00 ☐

1931 ISSUE

No.	Player \ Date Issued	VG	EX
52	Johnny Gottselig, Chi., January 3	12.50	25.00 ☐
53	Johnny Gallagher, Mon.M., January 17	12.50	25.00 ☐
54	Earl Roche, Mon.M., January 24	15.00	30.00 ☐
55	Jack McVicar, Mon.M., January 31	12.50	25.00 ☐
56	Dave Kerr, Goalie, Mon.M., February 7	12.50	25.00 ☐
57	Desse Roche, Mon.M., February 14	12.50	25.00 ☐
58	Al Huggins, Mon.M., February 28	12.50	25.00 ☐
59	Harvey Jackson, Tor., March 21	17.50	35.00 ☐
60	Charlie Conacher, Tor., March 28	17.50	35.00 ☐
61	Ralph Saint Germain, McGill, April 4	12.50	25.00 ☐
62	Ebbie Goodfellow, Falcons, April 11	15.00	30.00 ☐
63	Normie Himes, NYA, December 19	15.00	30.00 ☐
64	Rosario (Lolo) Couture, Chi., December 26	12.50	25.00 ☐

1932 ISSUE

No.	Player \ Date Issued	VG	EX
65	George Owen, Bos., January 2	12.50	25.00 ☐
66	Chuck Gardiner, Goalie, Chi., January 9	15.00	30.00 ☐
67	Tommy Cook, Chi., January 16	12.50	25.00 ☐
68	Frank Finnigan, March 12	17.50	35.00 ☐
69	William Cockburn, Win., March 19	12.50	25.00 ☐
70	Arthur Alexandre, Mon., April 16	12.50	25.00 ☐

O'KEEFE BEVERAGES

— 1932 - 33 ISSUE —

This is a Toronto Maple Leafs team set. See page no. 638.

Note: *The Charlton Standard Catalogue of Hockey Cards* arranges cards in their issue date order. This means the first date a manufacturer issues a card set determines the sequence of the manufacturer in the Standard Catalogue. In this manner the historical importance of early cards is maintained. See the last page of this catalogue for an alphabetical index of issuers.

All classical sets are extremely rare in NRMT and Mint condition.

CANADIAN CHEWING GUM SALES LTD

— 1933 - 34 REGULAR ISSUE —

The black and white pictures are framed in a red border with the top title phrase, "Hockey Picture Gum". A premium tab attached to the bottom of the card displays a large single letter in the middle. The back information is written in both French and English. Cards with the tabs removed are worth 50% less.

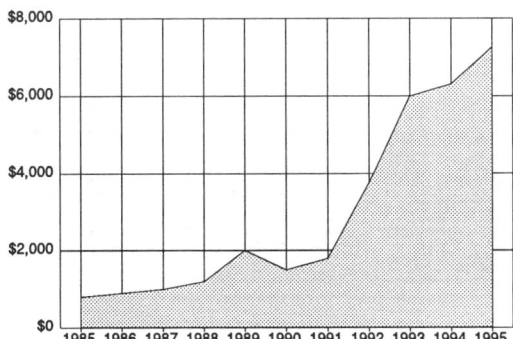

This set is unnumbered and is listed here in alphabetical order.

PRICE MOVEMENT OF EX SETS

Card Size: 2 1/2" X 3 1/4"
Face: Black and white in red frame, white border; Name, "Letter" and premium offer
Back: Black on card stock; Name, Team, Resume, Bilingual
Imprint: CANADIAN CHEWING GUM SALES LTD.
DEPT. A-1, 14 DICKENS ST., TORONTO, ONT.
ACC.No.: V252
Complete Set No.: 50
Complete Set Price: 1,810.00   3,625.00   7,250.00
Common Card: 20.00   37.50   75.00

No.	Player	G	VG	EX
1	Clarence Abel, Chi., RC	40.00	75.00	150.00
2	Larry Aurie, Det., RC	20.00	37.50	75.00
3	Ace Bailey, Tor., RC	80.00	175.00	350.00
4	Helge Bostrom, Chi., RC	20.00	37.50	75.00
5	Bill Brydge, NYA, RC	20.00	37.50	75.00
6	Glenn Brydson, Mon.M, RC	20.00	37.50	75.00
7	Marty Burke, Mon.C, RC	20.00	37.50	75.00
8	Gerry Carson, Mon.C, RC	20.00	37.50	75.00
9	Lorne Chabot, Goalie, Mon.C, RC	30.00	60.00	125.00
10	Francis (King) Clancy, Tor.	145.00	290.00	575.00
11	Dit Clapper, Bos., RC	50.00	100.00	200.00
12	Charlie Conacher, Tor., RC	145.00	290.00	575.00
13	Lionel Conacher, Chi., RC	60.00	115.00	225.00
14	Alex Connell, Goalie, Ott. LC	25.00	45.00	90.00
15	Bun Cook, NYR, RC	25.00	50.00	100.00
16	Danny Cox, Ott., RC, LC	20.00	37.50	75.00
17	Hap Day, Tor.	50.00	100.00	200.00
18	Cecil Dillon, NYR, RC	20.00	37.50	75.00
19	Lorne Duguid, Mon.M, RC	25.00	45.00	90.00
20	Duke Dutkowski, NYA, RC	20.00	37.50	75.00
21	Red Dutton, NYA, RC	40.00	75.00	150.00
22	Hap Emms, Det., RC	20.00	37.50	75.00
23	Frank Finnigan, Ott., LC	25.00	45.00	90.00
24	Chuck Gardiner, Goalie, Chi., RC	45.00	85.00	175.00
25	Ebbie Goodfellow, Det., RC	25.00	45.00	90.00
26	Johnny Gottselig, Chi., RC	25.00	45.00	90.00
27	Bob Gracie, Bos., RC	20.00	37.50	75.00
28	George Hainsworth, Goalie, Tor., RC	50.00	100.00	200.00
29	Ott Heller, NYR, RC	20.00	37.50	75.00
30	Normie Himes, NYA, RC	20.00	37.50	75.00
31	Red Horner, Tor., RC	45.00	90.00	175.00
32	Harvey Jackson, Tor., RC	60.00	115.00	225.00
33	Walt Jackson, NYA, RC	20.00	37.50	75.00
34	Aurel Joliat, Mon.C	115.00	225.00	450.00
35	Dave Kerr, Goalie, Mon.M, RC	20.00	37.50	75.00
36	Pit Lepine, Mon.C, RC	20.00	37.50	75.00
37	Georges Mantha, Mon.C, RC	25.00	45.00	90.00
38	Howie Morenz, Mon.C	275.00	550.00	1,100.00
39	Murray Murdoch, NYR, RC	20.00	37.50	75.00
40	Baldy Northcott, Mon.M, RC	20.00	37.50	75.00
41	John Roach, Goalie, Det.	20.00	37.50	75.00
42	Johnny Sheppard, Bos., RC	20.00	37.50	75.00
43	Babe Siebert, NYR, RC	70.00	140.00	275.00
44	Alex Smith, Bos.	20.00	37.50	75.00
45	John Sorrell, Det., RC	20.00	37.50	75.00
46	Nels Stewart, Bos., RC	85.00	165.00	325.00
47	Dave Trottier, Mon.M, RC	20.00	37.50	75.00
48	Bill Touhey, Ott., RC, LC	20.00	37.50	75.00
49	Jimmy Ward, Mon.M, RC	20.00	37.50	75.00
50	Nick Wasnie, Mon.C, RC	20.00	37.50	75.00

Canadian Chewing Gum
1933-34 Issue
Card No. 5
Bill Brydge

Canadian Chewing Gum
1933-34 Issue
Card No. 19,
Lorne Duguid

Canadian Chewing Gum
1933-34 Issue
Card No. 34,
Aurel Joliat

CCM 1933-36 Issue
Photo No. 9,
Kimberley Dynamiters, Winners
of the Allan Cup, 1936

CANADIAN CYCLE AND MOTOR COMPANY (CCM)

— 1933 - 36 ISSUE —

This series of photos was issued over a three year period promoting CCM skates. Different border designs were utilized depending on the type of photo.
For group photos the decorative border may be wine red, blue or grey. For the individual photos the single line border was green. The photos were available from CCM on a mail order basis with the collector receiving the current photos with matching coloured borders.

Photograph Size:
Individual: 8 1/4" x 10 1/2"
Group: 11 1/4" x 8 7/8"
Face: Black and white with coloured border; Name, Team
Back: Blank
Imprint: C.C.M. SKATES CHAMPIONS EVERYWHERE
Complete Set No.: Unknown
Common Set Price: Unknown

1933 - 34 TEAM PHOTOS

No.	Player	G	VG	EX
1	All Star Team 1934; Ace Bailey Benefit Game	35.00	75.00	150.00
2	Boston Bruins	18.00	37.50	75.00
3	Chicago Black Hawks; Stanley Cup Champions	40.00	75.00	150.00
4	Detroit Red Wings	18.00	37.50	75.00
5	Montreal Canadiens	30.00	65.00	125.00
6	Moncton Hawks, Allan Cup Winners	10.00	20.00	40.00
7	Montreal Maroons	18.00	37.50	75.00
8	New York Americans	18.00	37.50	75.00
9	New York Rangers	18.00	37.50	75.00
10	Providence Can-Am League Winners	12.50	25.00	50.00
11	St. Michael's College, Memorial Cup	10.00	20.00	40.00
12	Toronto Maple Leafs	25.00	50.00	100.00

1933 - 36 ISSUE

No.	Player	G	VG	EX
1	Boston Bruins, Winners American Section 1934-35	18.00	37.50	75.00
2	Boston Cubs, Winners Canadian American Hockey League 1935	10.00	20.00	40.00
3	Frank Boucher	12.50	25.00	50.00
4	Lorne Chabot, Goalie	12.50	25.00	50.00
5	Charlie Conacher	12.50	25.00	50.00
6	Detroit Red Wings Cup Winners 1935 - 36	12.50	25.00	50.00
7	Halifax Wolverines, Winners Allan Cup 1935	10.00	20.00	40.00
8	Foster Hewitt	12.50	25.00	50.00
9	Kimberley Dynamiters, Winners Allan Cup, 1936	10.00	20.00	40.00
10	Montreal Maroons; Stanley Cup Winners 1934-35	35.00	65.00	125.00
11	Toronto Maple Leafs, Winners Canadian Section 1934-35	15.00	30.00	60.00
12	Toronto Maple Leafs 1935 - 36	15.00	30.00	60.00
13	West Toronto Nationals,	10.00	20.00	40.00
14	Winnipeg Monarchs, Winners Memorial Cup 1935	10.00	20.00	40.00

Note: This set is not complete. We would appreciate your help in gathering further information on this set.

THE DIAMOND MATCH COMPANY

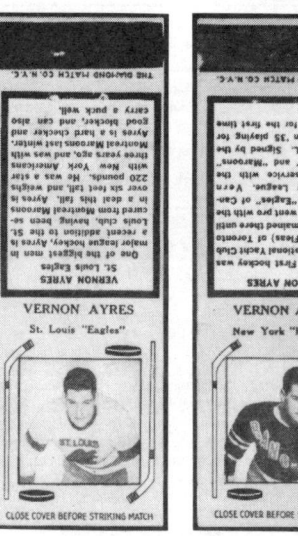
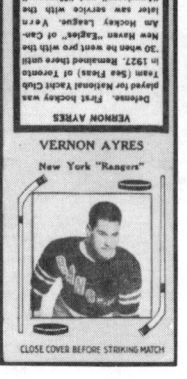

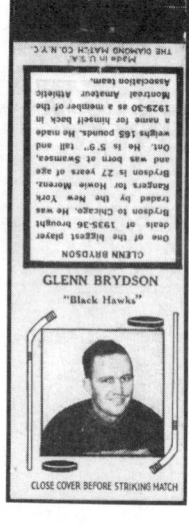

1933 - 35 "Silver" Issue | Type I | Type II | 1936 - 39 "Tan" Issue / Type III | Type IV | Type V | Type VI

SILVER HOCKEY SET (60). The first issue has a silver finish with green and black stripes running vertically on the left side of the cover. The book cover has a player's portrait with the back giving the player's resume. The back cover is black on green.

TAN ISSUE: The design of the book was modified with the cover being redesigned and the cover colour changing to tan. This basic design continued until the end of the issue in 1939.

However the second issue can be broken down into six different types issued over the years 1934 to 1939.

TYPE 1 (Tan Issue): At the top of the resume (back) is the player's name and the name of the team or the player's position. The imprint "The Diamond Match Co. NYC." is on one line.

TYPE 2 (Tan Issue): The team name, or team position has been removed from the top of the resume. The imprint is still on one line as in Type 1.

TYPE 3 (Tan Issue): The imprint is now on two lines "Made in U.S.A. / The Diamond Match Co. N.Y.C."

TYPE 4 (Tan Issue): All the remaining books (Type 4 to 6) will portray only Chicago Black Hawks players. They are now basically team sets. The team name reappears below the player's name but above the resume on the back of the book. The imprint is on two lines differentiating this type from Type 1.

TYPE 5 (Tan Issue): On the back, above the resume, the team name again disappears as does the "Chicago" of the Chicago Black Hawks on the front cover. The imprint is on two lines. The tan background colour covers the complete book with the striker pad being overlaid on the tan.

TYPE 6 (Tan Issue): The Type 6 variety differs from the Type 5 only in the background colour on which the striker is overlaid. This area is dark brown or black giving the appearance that the tip is black instead of tan. The imprint is on two lines.

— 1933 - 35 "SILVER" HOCKEY ISSUE —

Card Size: 1 1/16" x 4 1/2"
Face: Black and white with various two colour borders; Name; Team; Picture
Back: Black and white; Black script on light sketched hockey scene on thick card stock
Imprint: THE DIAMOND MATCH CO. N.Y.C.
Complete Set No.: 60
Complete Set Price: 650. 1,300. 2,600.
Common Card: 7.50 15.00 30.00

No.	Player	G	VG	EX
1	Clarence Abel, Chi.	7.50	15.00	30.00
2	Marty Barry, Bos.	12.50	25.00	50.00
3	Jack Beattie, Bos.	10.00	20.00	40.00
4	Frank Boucher, NYR	15.00	30.00	60.00
5	Doug Brennan, NYR	7.50	15.00	30.00
6	Bill Brydge, NYR	7.50	15.00	30.00
7	Eddie Burke, NYR	7.50	15.00	30.00
8	Marty Burke, Mon.	7.50	15.00	30.00
9	Gerry Carson, Mon.	7.50	15.00	30.00
10	Lorne Chabot, Goalie, Mon.	10.00	20.00	40.00
11	Art Chapman, Bos.	7.50	15.00	30.00
12	Dit Clapper, Bos.	18.50	37.50	75.00
13	Lionel Conacher, Chi.	7.50	15.00	30.00
14	Hugh (Red) Conn, NYA	7.50	15.00	30.00
15	Bill Cook, NYR	12.50	25.00	50.00
16	Bun (Fred) Cook, NYR	7.50	15.00	30.00
17	Tom Cook, Chi.	7.50	15.00	30.00
18	Rosario (Lolo) Couture, Chi.	7.50	15.00	30.00
19	Bob Davie, Bos.	7.50	15.00	30.00
20	Cecil Dillon, NYR	7.50	15.00	30.00
21	Duke Dutkowski, NYA	7.50	15.00	30.00
22	Red (Mervin) Dutton, NYA	12.50	25.00	50.00
23	Johnny Gagnon, Mon.	7.50	15.00	30.00
24	Chuck Gardiner, Goalie, Chi.	15.00	30.00	60.00
25	John Gottselig, Chi.	7.50	15.00	30.00

Diamond Match Co.
1933-35 "Silver" Issue
Card No. 2,
Marty Barry

No.	Player	G	VG	EX
26	Bob Gracie, Bos.	7.50	15.00	30.00
27	Lloyd Gross, NYA	7.50	15.00	30.00
28	Otto Heller, NYR	7.50	15.00	30.00
29	Normie Himes, NYA	7.50	15.00	30.00
30	Lional Hitchman, Bos.	7.50	15.00	30.00
31	Walter (Red) Jackson, NYA	7.50	15.00	30.00
32	Roger Jenkins, Chi.	7.50	15.00	30.00
33	Aurel Joliat, Mon.	40.00	85.00	175.00
34	Butch (Melville) Keeling, Chi.	7.50	15.00	30.00
35	William Kendall, Chi.	7.50	15.00	30.00
36	Lloyd Klein, NYA	7.50	15.00	30.00
37	Joe Lamb, Bos.	7.50	15.00	30.00
38	Wildor Larochelle, Mon.	7.50	15.00	30.00
39	Pit Lepine, Mon.	7.50	15.00	30.00
40	Jack Leswick, Chi.	7.50	15.00	30.00
41	Georges Mantha, Mon.	7.50	15.00	30.00
42	Sylvio Mantha, Mon.	12.50	25.00	50.00
43	Mush March, Chi.	7.50	15.00	30.00
44	Ron Martin, NYA	7.50	15.00	30.00
45	Charley McVeigh, NYA	7.50	15.00	30.00
46	Howie Morenz, Mon.	125.00	250.00	500.00
47	John Murray Murdoch, NYR	7.50	15.00	30.00
48	Harry Oliver, Bos.	12.50	25.00	50.00
49	George Patterson, NYA	7.50	15.00	30.00
50	Hal Picketts, NYA	7.50	15.00	30.00
51	Vic Ripley, Bos.	7.50	15.00	30.00
52	Doc Romnes, Chi.	7.50	15.00	30.00
53	Johnny Sheppard, Bos.	7.50	15.00	30.00
54	Eddie Shore, Bos.	60.00	115.00	225.00
55	Art Somers, NYR	7.50	15.00	30.00
56	Chris Speyers, NYA	7.50	15.00	30.00
57	Nels Stewart, Bos.	12.50	25.00	50.00
58	Tiny Thompson, Goalie, Bos.	15.00	30.00	60.00
59	Louis Trudel, Chi.	7.50	15.00	30.00
60	Roy Worters, Goalie, NYA	15.00	30.00	60.00

— 1936 - 39 "TAN" HOCKEY ISSUE —

— TYPE I —

Card Size: 1 1/16" x 4 1/2"
Face: Black and white photograph on tan coloured template with cream coloured border
Back: Black print on tan coloured thick card stock
Imprint: THE DIAMOND MATCH COMPANY, N.Y.C.
Complete Set No.: 70
Complete Set Price: 450.00 900.00 1,800.00
Common Card: 5.00 10.00 20.00

No.	Player	G	VG	EX
1	Andy Aitkenhead, Goalie, NYR	5.00	10.00	20.00
2	Vern Ayres, St.L E	5.00	10.00	20.00
3	Bill Beveridge, Goalie, ST.L E	5.00	10.00	20.00
4	Ralph Bowman, St.L E	5.00	10.00	20.00
5	Bill Brydge, NYA	5.00	10.00	20.00
6	Glenn Brydson, St.L E	5.00	10.00	20.00
7	Eddie Burke, NYA	5.00	10.00	20.00
8	Marty Burke, Chi.	5.00	10.00	20.00
9	Lorne Carr, NYA	5.00	10.00	20.00
10	Gerry Carson, Mon.	5.00	10.00	20.00
11	Lorne Chabot, Goalie, Chi.	6.00	12.50	25.00
12	Art Chapman, NYA	5.00	10.00	20.00
13	Hugh (Red) Conn, NYA	5.00	10.00	20.00
14	Bert Connolly, NYR	5.00	10.00	20.00
15	Bun (Fred) Cook, NYR	6.00	12.50	25.00
16	Tom Cook, Chi.	5.00	10.00	20.00
17	Art Coulter, Chi.	12.00	22.50	45.00
18	Rosario (Lolo) Couture, Chi.	5.00	10.00	20.00
19	Bill Cowley, St.L E	6.00	12.50	25.00
20	Wilf Cude, Goalie, Mon.	5.00	10.00	20.00
21	Red (Mervin) Dutton, NYA	10.00	20.00	40.00
22	Frank Finnigan, St.L E	6.00	12.50	25.00
23	Irvin Frew, St.L E	5.00	10.00	20.00
24	Leroy Goldsworthy, Chi.	5.00	10.00	20.00
25	Johnny Gottselig, Chi.	5.00	10.00	20.00
26	Bob Gracie, NYA	5.00	10.00	20.00
27	Otto Heller, NYR	5.00	10.00	20.00
28	Normie Himes, NYA	5.00	10.00	20.00
29	Syd Howe, St.L E	12.00	22.50	45.00
30	Roger Jenkins, Mon.	5.00	10.00	20.00
31	Ivan (Ching) Johnson, NYR	14.00	27.50	55.00
32	Aurel Joliat, Mon.	37.50	75.00	150.00
33	Max Kaminsky, St.L. E	5.00	10.00	20.00
34	Butch (Melville) Keeling, Chi.	5.00	10.00	20.00
35	William Kendall, Chi.	5.00	10.00	20.00
36	Lloyd Klein, NYA	5.00	10.00	20.00
37	Joe Lamb, Mon.	5.00	10.00	20.00
38	Wild0r Larochelle, Mon.	5.00	10.00	20.00
39	Pit Lepine, Mon.	5.00	10.00	20.00
40	Norman Locking, Chi.	5.00	10.00	20.00
41	Georges Mantha, Mon.	5.00	10.00	20.00
42	Sylvio Mantha, Mon.	10.00	20.00	40.00
43	Mush March, Chi.	5.00	10.00	20.00
44	Charley Mason, NYR	5.00	10.00	20.00
45	Donnie McFayden, Chi.	5.00	10.00	20.00
46	Jack McGill, Mon.	5.00	10.00	20.00
47	Charley McVeigh, NYA	5.00	10.00	20.00
48	Armand Mondou, Mon.	5.00	10.00	20.00
49	Howie Morenz, Chi.	85.00	175.00	350.00
50	John Murray Murdoch, NYR	5.00	10.00	20.00
51	Allan Murray, NYA	5.00	10.00	20.00
52	Harry Oliver, NYA	7.50	15.00	30.00
53	Jean Pusie, Bos.	5.00	10.00	20.00
54	Paul Raymond, Mon.	5.00	10.00	20.00
55	Jack Riley, Mon.	5.00	10.00	20.00
56	Vic Ripley, St.L E	5.00	10.00	20.00
57	Desse Roche, St.L E	5.00	10.00	20.00
58	Earl Roche, St.L E	5.00	10.00	20.00
59	Doc Romnes, Chi.	5.00	10.00	20.00
60	Sweeney Schriner, NYA	10.00	20.00	40.00
61	Earl Seibert, NYR	12.00	22.50	45.00
62	Gerry Shannon, St.L E	5.00	10.00	20.00
63	Alex Smith, NYA	5.00	10.00	20.00
64	Joe Starke, Chi.	5.00	10.00	20.00
65	Nels Stewart, Bos.	12.00	22.50	45.00
66	Paul Thompson, Chi.	5.00	10.00	20.00
67	Louis Trudel, Chi.	5.00	10.00	20.00
68	Carl Voss, St.L E	5.00	10.00	20.00
69	Art Wiebe, Chi.	5.00	10.00	20.00
70	Roy Worters, Goalie, NYA	10.00	20.00	40.00

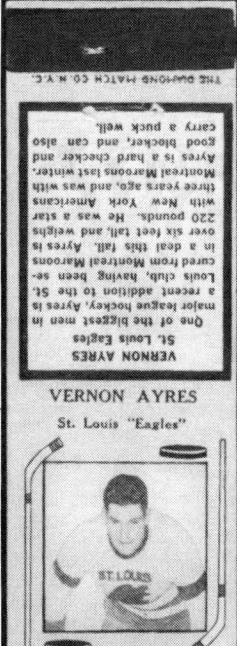

Diamond Match Co.
1936-39 "Tan" Issue
Type I
Card No. 2,
Vern Ayres

— TYPE II —

Card Size: 1 1/16" x 4 1/2"
Face: Black and white photograph on tan coloured template with cream coloured border
Back: Black print on tan coloured thick card stock
Imprint: THE DIAMOND MATCH CO., N.Y.C.
Complete Set No.: 65
Complete Set Price: 500.00 1,000.00 2,000.00
Common Card: 5.00 10.00 20.00

No.	Player	G	VG	EX
1	Tom Anderson, NYA	5.00	10.00	20.00
2	Vern Ayres, NYR	5.00	10.00	20.00
3	Frank Boucher, NYR	6.00	12.50	25.00
4	Frank Boucher, NYR	6.00	12.50	25.00
5	Bill Brydge, NYA	5.00	10.00	20.00
6	Marty Burke, Mon.	5.00	10.00	20.00
7	Lorne Carr, NYA	5.00	10.00	20.00
8	Lorne Chabot, Goalie	6.00	12.50	25.00
9	Art Chapman, NYA	5.00	10.00	20.00
10	Bert Connolly, NYR	5.00	10.00	20.00
11	Bill Cook, NYR	12.00	22.50	45.00
12	Bill Cook, NYR	12.00	22.50	45.00
13	Bun (Fred) Cook, NYR	5.00	10.00	20.00
14	Tom Cook, Chi.	5.00	10.00	20.00
15	Art Coulter, Chi.	6.00	12.50	25.00
16	Rosario (Lolo) Couture, Mon.	5.00	10.00	20.00
17	Wilf Cude, Goalie, Mon.	5.00	10.00	20.00
18	Cecil Dillon, NYR	5.00	10.00	20.00
19	Cecil Dillon, NYR	5.00	10.00	20.00
20	Red (Mervin) Dutton, NYA	12.50	25.00	50.00
21	Hap Emms, NYA	5.00	10.00	20.00
22	Irvin Frew, Mon.	5.00	10.00	20.00
23	Johnny Gagnon, Mon.	5.00	10.00	20.00
24	Leroy Goldsworthy, Mon.	5.00	10.00	20.00
25	Johnny Gottselig, Chi.	5.00	10.00	20.00
26	William Paul Haynes, Mon.	5.00	10.00	20.00
27	Otto Heller, NYR	5.00	10.00	20.00
28	Irving Jaffes	5.00	10.00	20.00
29	Joe Jerwa, NYA	5.00	10.00	20.00
30	Ivan (Ching) Johnson, NYR	15.00	30.00	60.00
31	Aurel Joliat, Mon.	37.50	75.00	150.00
32	Butch (Melville) Keeling, NYR	5.00	10.00	20.00
33	William Kendall, Chi.	5.00	10.00	20.00
34	Dave Kerr, Goalie, NYR	5.00	10.00	20.00
35	Lloyd Klein, NYA	5.00	10.00	20.00
36	Wildor Larochelle, Mon.	5.00	10.00	20.00
37	Pit Lepine, Mon.	5.00	10.00	20.00
38	Art Lesieur, Mon.	5.00	10.00	20.00
39	Alex Levinsky, NYR	6.00	12.50	25.00
40	Alex Levinsky, NYR	6.00	12.50	25.00
41	Norman Locking, Chi.	5.00	10.00	20.00
42	George Mantha, Mon.	5.00	10.00	20.00
43	Sylvio Mantha, Mon.	10.00	20.00	40.00
44	Mush March, Chi.	5.00	10.00	20.00
45	Charley Mason, NYR	5.00	10.00	20.00
46	Donnie McFaydon, Chi.	5.00	10.00	20.00
47	Jack McGill, Mon.	5.00	10.00	20.00
48	Armand Mondou, Mon.	5.00	10.00	20.00
49	Howie Morenz, Chi.	87.50	175.00	350.00
50	John Murray Murdoch, NYR	5.00	10.00	20.00
51	Allan Murray, NYA	5.00	10.00	20.00
52	Harry Oliver, NYA	10.00	20.00	40.00
53	Adelard Ouellette, Chi.	5.00	10.00	20.00
54	Lynn Patrick, NYR	25.00	50.00	100.00
55	Lynn Patrick, NYR	25.00	50.00	100.00
56	Paul Runge, Mon.	5.00	10.00	20.00
57	Sweeney Schriner, NYA	10.00	20.00	40.00
58	Art Somers, NYR	5.00	10.00	20.00
59	Harold Starr, NYR	5.00	10.00	20.00
60	Nels Stewart, NYA	10.00	20.00	40.00
61	Paul Thompson, Chi.	5.00	10.00	20.00
62	Louis Trudel, Chi.	5.00	10.00	20.00
63	Carl Voss, NYA	5.00	10.00	20.00
64	Art Wiebe, Chi.	5.00	10.00	20.00
65	Roy Worters, Goalie, NYA	10.00	20.00	40.00

Diamond Match Co.
1936-39 "Tan" Issue
Type II
Card No. 2,
Vern Ayres

32 • DIAMOND MATCH COMPANY 1936-39 "TAN" ISSUE

— TYPE III —

Card Size: 1 1/16" x 4 1/2"
Face: Black and white photograph on tan coloured template with cream coloured border
Back: Black print on tan coloured thick card stock
Imprint: Made in U.S.A. THE DIAMOND MATCH CO. N.Y.C.
Complete Set No.: 60

Complete Set Price:		450.00	900.00	1,800.00
Common Card:		5.00	10.00	20.00

No.	Player	G	VG	EX
1	Tom Anderson, NYA	5.00	10.00	20.00
2	Vern Ayres, NYR	5.00	10.00	20.00
3	Frank Boucher, NYR	10.00	20.00	40.00
4	Bill Brydge, NYA	5.00	10.00	20.00
5	Marty Burke, Chi.	5.00	10.00	20.00
6	Walt Buswell, Mon.	5.00	10.00	20.00
7	Lorne Carr, NYA	5.00	10.00	20.00
8	Lorne Chabot, Goalie, Mon.	5.00	10.00	20.00
9	Art Chapman, NYA	5.00	10.00	20.00
10	Bert Connolly, NYR	5.00	10.00	20.00
11	Bill Cook, NYR	12.00	22.50	45.00
12	Bun (Fred) Cook, NYR	6.00	12.50	25.00
13	Tom Cook, Chi.	5.00	10.00	20.00
14	Art Coulter, Chi.	6.00	12.50	25.00
15	Rosario (Lolo) Couture, Mon.	5.00	10.00	20.00
16	Wilf Cude, Goalie, Mon.	5.00	10.00	20.00
17	Cecil Dillon, NYR	5.00	10.00	20.00
18	Red (Mervin) Dutton, NYA	6.00	12.50	25.00
19	Hap Emms, NYA	5.00	10.00	20.00
20	Irvin Frew, Mon.	5.00	10.00	20.00
21	Johnny Gagnon, Mon.	5.00	10.00	20.00
22	Leroy Goldsworthy, Mon.	5.00	10.00	20.00
23	Johnny Gottselig, Chi.	5.00	10.00	20.00
24	Paul Haynes, Mon.	5.00	10.00	20.00
25	Otto Heller, NYR	5.00	10.00	20.00
26	Joe Jerwa, NYA	5.00	10.00	20.00
27	Ivan (Ching) Johnson, NYR	5.00	10.00	20.00
28	Aurel Joliat, Mon.	37.50	75.00	150.00
29	Mike Karakas, Goalie, Chi.	5.00	10.00	20.00
30	Butch (Melville) Keeling, NYR	5.00	10.00	20.00
31	Dave Kerr, Goalie, NYR	5.00	10.00	20.00
32	Lloyd Klein, NYA	5.00	10.00	20.00
33	Wildoer Larochelle, Mon.	5.00	10.00	20.00
34	Pit Lepine, Mon.	5.00	10.00	20.00
35	Art Lesieur, Mon.	5.00	10.00	20.00
36	Alex Levinsky, Chi.	5.00	10.00	20.00
37	Norman Locking, Chi.	5.00	10.00	20.00
38	Georges Mantha, Mon.	5.00	10.00	20.00
39	Sylvio Mantha, Mon.	5.00	10.00	20.00
40	Mush March, Chi.	5.00	10.00	20.00
41	Charlie Mason, NYR	5.00	10.00	20.00
42	Charlie Mason, NYR	5.00	10.00	20.00
43	Donnie McFayden, Chi.	5.00	10.00	20.00
44	Jack McGill, Mon.	5.00	10.00	20.00
45	Armand Mondou, Mon.	5.00	10.00	20.00
46	Howie Morenz, Chi.	87.50	175.00	350.00
47	John Murray Murdoch, NYR	5.00	10.00	20.00
48	Allan Murray, NYA	5.00	10.00	20.00
49	Harry Oliver, NYA	10.00	20.00	40.00
50	Adelard Ouellette, Chi.	5.00	10.00	20.00
51	Lynn Patrick, NYR	15.00	32.50	65.00
52	Paul Runge, Mon.	5.00	10.00	20.00
53	Sweeney Schriner, NYA	10.00	20.00	40.00
54	Harold Starr, NYR	5.00	10.00	20.00
55	Nels Stewart, NYA	10.00	20.00	40.00
56	Paul Thompson, Chi.	5.00	10.00	20.00
57	Louis Trudel, Chi.	5.00	10.00	20.00
58	Carl Voss, NYA	5.00	10.00	20.00
59	Art Wiebe, Chi.	5.00	10.00	20.00
60	Roy Worters, Goalie, NYA	10.00	20.00	40.00

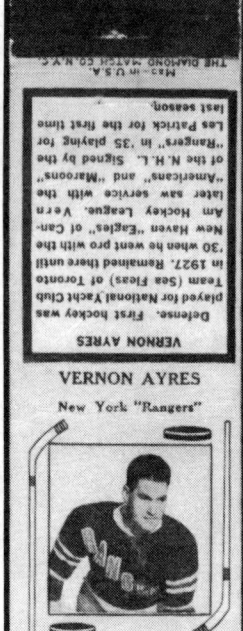

Diamond Match Co.
1936-39 "Tan" Issue
Type III
Card No. 2,
Vern Ayres

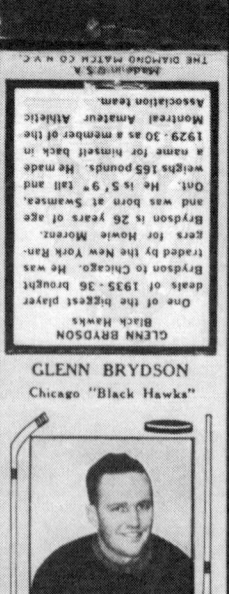

Diamond Match Co.
1936-39 "Tan" Issue
Type IV
Card No. 2,
Glenn Brydson

— TYPE IV —

Card Size: 1 1/16" x 4 1/2"
Face: Black and white photograph on tan coloured template with cream coloured border.
Back: Black print on tan coloured thick card stock
Imprint: Made in U.S.A. THE DIAMOND MATCH CO. N.Y.C.
Complete Set No.: 15

Complete Set Price:		95.00	185.00	375.00
Common Card:		6.00	12.50	25.00

CHICAGO BLACK HAWKS

No.	Player	G	VG	EX
1	Andy Blair	6.00	12.50	25.00
2	Glenn Brydson	6.00	12.50	25.00
3	Marty Burke	6.00	12.50	25.00
4	Tom Cook	6.00	12.50	25.00
5	Johnny Gottselig	6.00	12.50	25.00
6	Hal Jackson	6.00	12.50	25.00
7	Mike Karakas, Goalie	6.00	12.50	25.00
8	Wildor Larochelle	6.00	12.50	25.00
9	Alex Levinsky	7.50	15.00	30.00
10	Clem Loughlin	6.00	12.50	25.00
11	Mush March	6.00	12.50	25.00
12	Earl Seibert	10.00	20.00	40.00
13	Paul Thompson	6.00	12.50	25.00
14	Louis Trudel	6.00	12.50	25.00
15	Art Wiebe	8.75	17.50	35.00

— TYPE V —

Card Size: 1 1/16" x 4 1/2"
Face: Black and white photograph on tan coloured template with cream coloured border
Back: Black print on tan coloured thick card stock
Imprint: Made in U.S.A. THE DIAMOND MATCH CO. N.Y.C.
Complete Set No.: 14

Complete Set Price:		85.00	175.00	350.00
Common Card:		6.00	12.50	25.00

CHICAGO BLACK HAWKS

No.	Player	G	VG	EX
1	Glenn Brydson	6.00	12.50	25.00
2	Marty Burke	6.00	12.50	25.00
3	Tom Cook	7.50	15.00	30.00
4	Cully Dahlstrom	6.00	12.50	25.00
5	Johnny Gottselig	6.00	12.50	25.00
6	Vic Heyliger	6.00	12.50	25.00
7	Mike Karakas, Goalie	6.00	12.50	25.00
8	Alex Levinsky	7.50	15.00	30.00
9	Mush March	6.00	12.50	25.00
10	Earl Seibert	7.50	15.00	30.00
11	Bill Stewart, Manager	8.75	17.50	35.00
12	Paul Thompson	6.00	12.50	25.00
13	Louis Trudel	6.00	12.50	25.00
14	Art Wiebe	7.50	15.00	30.00

— TYPE VI —

Card Size: 1 1/16" x 4 1/2"
Face: Black and white photograph on tan coloured template cream coloured border
Back: Black print on tan coloured thick card stock
Imprint: Made in U.S.A. THE DIAMOND MATCH CO. N.Y.C.
Complete Set No.: 14

Complete Set Price:		70.00	140.00	280.00
Common Card:		5.00	10.00	20.00

CHICAGO BLACK HAWKS

No.	Player	G	VG	EX
1	Glenn Brydson	5.00	10.00	20.00
2	Marty Burke	5.00	10.00	20.00
3	Tom Cook	6.00	12.50	25.00
4	Cully Dahlstrom	5.00	10.00	20.00
5	Johnny Gottselig	5.00	10.00	20.00
6	Vic Heyliger	5.00	10.00	20.00
7	Mike Karakas, Goalie	5.00	10.00	20.00
8	Alex Levinsky	6.00	12.50	25.00
9	Mush March	5.00	10.00	20.00
10	Earl Seibert	9.00	17.50	35.00
11	Bill Stewart, Manager	5.00	10.00	20.00
12	Paul Thompson	5.00	10.00	20.00
13	Louis Trudel	5.00	10.00	20.00
14	Art Wiebe	6.00	12.50	25.00

GOUDEY GUM CO.

— 1933 SPORT KINGS —

This 48-card set features 18 different sports. Listed and priced here are the hockey cards from the set. For a complete listing of this set see the appendix at the back of this book.

Card Size: 2 3/8" x 2 7/8"
Face: Four colour, white bordered
Back: Black on white card stock
Imprint: Printed in Canada
Complete Set No.: 48 (4 hockey)
Complete Set Price: Unknown
Set Price - Hockey: 375.00   750.00   1,500.00

No.	Player	G	VG	EX
19	Eddie Shore	75.00	150.00	300.00
24	Howie Morenz	160.00	325.00	650.00
29	Ace Bailey	105.00	215.00	425.00
30	Ivan (Ching) Johnson	105.00	215.00	425.00

HAMILTON GUM

— 1933 - 34 REGULAR ISSUE —

The pictures are black and white and could appear with one of four background colours of beige, blue, green or orange. This skip-numbered set contains 21 cards with the backs written in French and English. It is doubtful that missing numbers exist.

PRICE MOVEMENT OF EX SETS

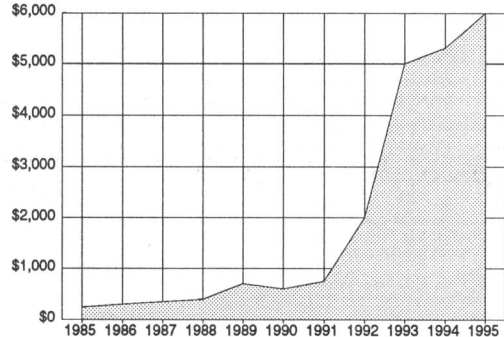

Card Size: 2 3/8" X 3"
Face: Black and white photo on coloured background; Name
 Background colours: Blue, Lime green, Beige or Orange
Back: Black on card stock; Name, Number, Team, Position, Bilingual
Imprint: HAMILTON CHEWING GUM, LTD.
ACC No.: V288
Complete Set No.: 21
Complete Set Price: 1,500.00   3,000.00   6,000.00
Common Card: 25.00   50.00   100.00

No.	Player	G	VG	EX
1	Nick Wasnie, Mon.C, RC	30.00	60.00	125.00
2	Joe Primeau, Tor., RC	70.00	140.00	275.00
3	Marty Burke, Mon.C, RC	25.00	50.00	100.00
7	Bill Thoms, Tor., RC	25.00	50.00	100.00
8	Howie Morenz, Mon.C	325.00	650.00	1,300.00
9	Andy Blair, Tor., RC	25.00	50.00	100.00
11	Ace Bailey, Tor., RC	100.00	200.00	400.00
14	Wildor Larochelle, Mon.C, RC	25.00	50.00	100.00
17	Francis Clancy, Tor.	150.00	300.00	600.00
18	Sylvio Mantha, Mon.C	25.00	50.00	100.00
21	Red Horner, Tor., RC	55.00	115.00	225.00
23	Pit Lepine, Mon.C, RC	25.00	50.00	100.00
27	Aurel Joliat, Mon.C	155.00	312.50	625.00
29	Harvey Jackson, Tor., RC	80.00	175.00	350.00
30	Lorne Chabot, Goalie, Mon.C, RC	40.00	75.00	150.00
33	Hap Day, Tor.	50.00	100.00	200.00
36	Alex Levinsky, Tor., RC	45.00	85.00	175.00
39	Baldy Cotton, Tor., RC	25.00	50.00	100.00
42	Ebbie Goodfellow, Det., RC	37.50	75.00	150.00
44	Larry Aurie, Det., RC	25.00	50.00	100.00
49	Charlie Conacher, Tor., RC	190.00	375.00	750.00

Hamilton Gum
1933-34 Issue
Card No. 23,
Pit Lepine

Hamilton Gum
1933-34 Series A
Card No. 30,
Lorne Chabot

O-Pee-Chee
1933-34 Series A
Card No. 6,
Nels Stewart

O-Pee-Chee
1933-34 Series A
Card No. 14,
George Patterson

O-PEE-CHEE

— 1933 - 34 REGULAR ISSUE —
SERIES A

PRICE MOVEMENT OF EX SETS

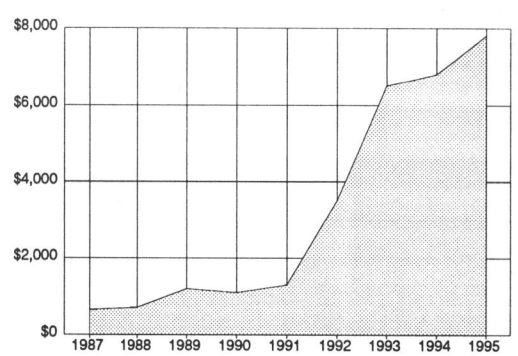

Card Size: 2 5/16" x 3 9/16"
Face: Black and white photo on coloured background; Name
 Background colours: Blue, Green, Red or Orange
Back: Black on card stock; Name, Number, Resume, Bilingual
Imprint: None
ACC No.: V304A
Complete Set No.: 48
Complete Set Price: 1,950.00   3,900.00   7,800.00
Common Card: 20.00   40.00   80.00

No.	Player	G	VG	EX
1	Danny Cox, Ott., RC, LC	25.00	50.00	100.00
2	Joe Lamb, Bos., RC	20.00	40.00	80.00
3	Eddie Shore, Bos., RC	180.00	360.00	725.00
4	Ken Doraty, Tor., RC	20.00	40.00	80.00
5	Lionel Hitchman, Bos., LC	20.00	40.00	80.00
6	Nels Stewart, Bos., RC	125.00	250.00	500.00
7	Walter Galbraith, Ott., RC, LC	20.00	40.00	80.00
8	Dit Clapper, Bos., RC	50.00	100.00	200.00
9	Harry Oliver, Bos., RC	20.00	40.00	80.00
10	Red Horner, Tor., RC	37.50	75.00	150.00
11	Alex Levinsky, Tor., RC	37.50	75.00	150.00
12	Joe Primeau, Tor., RC	40.00	75.00	150.00
13	Ace Bailey, Tor., RC	60.00	125.00	250.00
14	George Patterson, NYA, RC	20.00	40.00	80.00
15	George Hainsworth, Goalie, Tor., RC	30.00	65.00	125.00
16	Ott Heller, NYR, RC	20.00	40.00	80.00
17	Art Somers, NYR, RC	20.00	40.00	80.00
18	Lorne Chabot, Goalie, Mon.C, RC	25.00	45.00	90.00
19	Johnny Gagnon, Mon.C, RC	20.00	40.00	80.00
20	Alfred Lepine, Mon.C, RC	20.00	40.00	80.00
21	Wildor Larochelle, Mon.C, RC	20.00	40.00	80.00
22	Georges Mantha, Mon.C, RC	20.00	40.00	80.00
23	Howie Morenz, Mon.C	275.00	550.00	1,100.00
24	Syd Howe, Ott., RC	50.00	100.00	200.00
25	Frank Finnigan, Ott., LC	25.00	50.00	100.00
26	Bill Touhey, Ott., RC, LC	20.00	40.00	80.00
27	Cooney Weiland, Ott., RC	20.00	40.00	80.00
28	Leo Bourgeault, Ott., RC, LC	20.00	40.00	80.00
29	Normie Himes, NYA, RC	20.00	40.00	80.00
30	Johnny Sheppard, Bos., RC	20.00	40.00	80.00
31	Francis Clancy, Tor.	135.00	275.00	550.00
32	Hap Day, Tor.	40.00	75.00	150.00
33	Harvey Jackson, Tor., RC	75.00	150.00	300.00
34	Charlie Conacher, Tor., RC	120.00	235.00	475.00
35	Baldy Cotton, Tor., RC	20.00	40.00	80.00
36	Butch Keeling, NYR, RC	20.00	40.00	80.00
37	Murray Murdoch, NYR, RC	20.00	40.00	80.00
38	Bill Cook, NYR	30.00	60.00	120.00
39	Ivan (Ching) Johnson, NYR, RC	100.00	200.00	400.00
40	Hap Emms, Det.RW, RC	20.00	40.00	80.00
41	Bert McInenly, Det.F, RC	20.00	40.00	80.00
42	John Sorrell, Det.F, RC	20.00	40.00	80.00
43	Bill Phillips, NYA, RC	20.00	40.00	80.00
44	Charley McVeigh, NYA, RC	20.00	40.00	80.00
45	Roy Worters, Goalie, NYA, RC	30.00	60.00	120.00
46	Albert LeDuc, Mon.C, RC	20.00	40.00	80.00
47	Nick Wasnie, Mon.C, RC	20.00	40.00	80.00
48	Armand Mondou, Mon.C, RC	25.00	50.00	100.00

— 1934 - 35 REGULAR ISSUE —
SERIES B

A "Hockey Star Picture Album" was issued to hold the 72 cards of Series A and B. Each page was cut to hold six cards.

PRICE MOVEMENT OF EX SETS

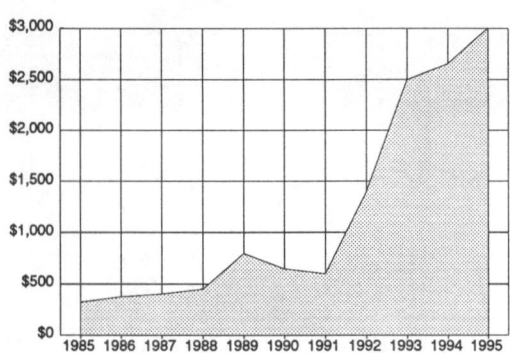

Card Size: 2 5/16" X 2 7/16"
Face: Black and white with either red, orange, turquoise or green background; Name
Back: Black on card stock; Name, Number, Resume, Bilingual
Imprint: None
ACC No.: V304B
Complete Set No.: 24
Complete Set Price: 750.00   1,500.00   3,000.00 ☐
Common Card: 20.00   40.00   80.00 ☐
Album: 150.00 ☐

No.	Player	G	VG	EX
49	Babe Siebert, NYR	45.00	85.00	175.00 ☐
50	Aurel Joliat, Mon.C	150.00	300.00	600.00 ☐
51	Larry Aurie, Det., RC, Error	20.00	40.00	80.00 ☐
52	Ebbie Goodfellow, Det.	40.00	75.00	150.00 ☐
53	John Roach, Goalie, Det.	20.00	40.00	80.00 ☐
54	Bill Beveridge, Goalie, Ott., RC	20.00	40.00	80.00 ☐
55	Earl Robinson, Mon.M, RC	20.00	40.00	80.00 ☐
56	Jimmy Ward, Mon.M	20.00	40.00	80.00 ☐
57	Archie Wilcox, Mon.M, RC	20.00	40.00	80.00 ☐
58	Lorne Duguid, Mon.M	20.00	40.00	80.00 ☐
59	Dave Kerr, Goalie, Mon.M	20.00	40.00	80.00 ☐
60	Baldy Northcott, Mon.M	20.00	40.00	80.00 ☐
61	Cy Wentworth, Mon.M, RC	25.00	50.00	100.00 ☐
62	Dave Trottier, Mon.M	20.00	40.00	80.00 ☐
63	Wally Kilrea, Mon.M, RC	20.00	40.00	80.00 ☐
64	Glenn Brydson, Mon.M	20.00	40.00	80.00 ☐
65	Vernon Ayers, Mon.M, RC	20.00	40.00	80.00 ☐
66	Robert Gracie, Bos.	20.00	40.00	80.00 ☐
67	Vic Ripley, Bos., RC	20.00	40.00	80.00 ☐
68	Tiny Thompson, Goalie, Bos., RC	45.00	85.00	175.00 ☐
69	Hooley Smith, Mon.M	30.00	65.00	125.00 ☐
70	Andy Blair, Tor.	20.00	40.00	80.00 ☐
71	Cecil Dillon, NYR	20.00	40.00	80.00 ☐
72	Bun Cook, NYR	37.50	75.00	150.00 ☐

O-Pee-Chee
1934-35 Series B
Card No. 50,
Aurel Joliat

O-Pee-Chee
1934-35 Series B
Card No. 72,
Bun Cook

O-Pee-Chee
1935-36 Series C
Card No. 84,
Nick Metz

O-Pee-Chee
1935-36 Series C
Card No. 94,
Art Chapman

— 1935 - 36 REGULAR ISSUE —
SERIES C

This series shows the player's surname on the face of the card and may or may not show the initial to the player's Christian name.

PRICE MOVEMENT OF EX SETS

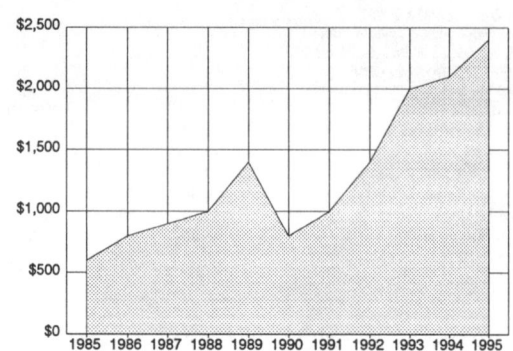

Card Size: 2 3/8" x 2 7/8"
Face: Black and white colour background, green, orange, yellow, pink, borderless; Name
Back: Black on card stock; Name, Resume, Bilingual
Imprint: None
ACC No.: V304C
Complete Set No.: 24
Complete Set Price: 600.00   1,200.00   2,400.00 ☐
Common Card: 20.00   45.00   90.00 ☐

No.	Player	G	VG	EX
73	Wilf Cude, Goalie, Mon.C, RC	35.00	70.00	140.00 ☐
74	Jack McGill, Mon.C, RC	20.00	45.00	90.00 ☐
75	Russ Blinco, Mon.M, RC	20.00	45.00	90.00 ☐
76	Hooley Smith, Mon.M	40.00	80.00	160.00 ☐
77	Herbert Cain, Mon.M, RC	20.00	45.00	90.00 ☐
78	Gus Marker, Mon.M, RC	20.00	45.00	90.00 ☐
79	Lynn Patrick, NYR, RC	50.00	100.00	200.00 ☐
80	Johnny Gottselig, Chi.	20.00	45.00	90.00 ☐
81	Marty Barry, Det.	45.00	85.00	175.00 ☐
82	Sylvio Mantha, Mon.C	35.00	70.00	140.00 ☐
83	Bill Hollett, Tor., RC	20.00	45.00	90.00 ☐
84	Nick Metz, Tor., RC	20.00	45.00	90.00 ☐
85	Bill Thoms, Tor.	20.00	45.00	90.00 ☐
86	Hec Kilrea, Det.	20.00	45.00	90.00 ☐
87	Reg Kelly, Tor., RC	30.00	65.00	125.00 ☐
88	Art Jackson, Tor., RC	25.00	50.00	100.00 ☐
89	Al Shields, Mon.M, RC	20.00	45.00	90.00 ☐
90	Buzz Boll, Tor.	25.00	50.00	100.00 ☐
91	Jean Pusie, Mon.C, RC	20.00	45.00	90.00 ☐
92	Roger Jenkins, Bos., RC, Error	20.00	45.00	90.00 ☐
93	Art Coulter, Chi., RC	35.00	70.00	140.00 ☐
94	Art Chapman, NYA	20.00	45.00	90.00 ☐
95	Paul Haynes, Mon.C	20.00	45.00	90.00 ☐
96	Leroy Goldsworthy, Mon.C, RC	35.00	70.00	140.00 ☐

— 1936 - 37 REGULAR ISSUE —
SERIES D

The cards in the fourth series are die-cut, allowing the cards to be folded so they could stand on end. The cards are black and white with a drawing of a mock game in the background. These cards show only the player's surname on the face of the card. This is the most valuable set of the series because the cards are very difficult to find without their backs missing.

PRICE MOVEMENT OF EX SETS

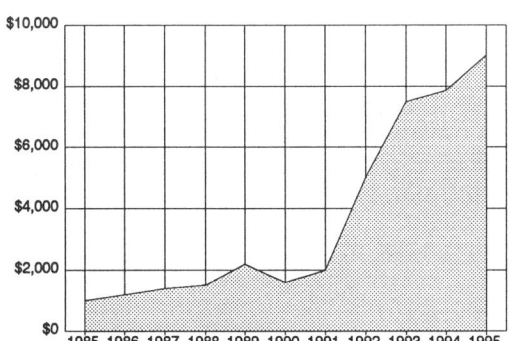

Card Size: 2 3/8" x 3"
Face: Die Cut, Black and white; Name
Back: Black on white card stock; Number, Resume, Bilingual
Imprint: None
ACC No.: V304D
Complete Set No.: 36
Complete Set Price: 2,250.00   4,500.00   9,000.00
Common Card: 30.00   60.00   120.00

No.	Player	G	VG	EX
97	Turk Broda, Goalie, Tor., RC	155.00	310.00	625.00
98	Sweeney Schriner, NYA, RC	45.00	85.00	175.00
99	Jack Shill, Tor., RC, LC	30.00	60.00	120.00
100	Bob Davidson, Tor., RC	30.00	60.00	120.00
101	Syl Apps, Sr., Tor., RC	105.00	215.00	425.00
102	Lionel Conacher, Mon.M	37.50	75.00	150.00
103	Jimmy Fowler, Tor., RC	30.00	60.00	120.00
104	Allan Murray, NYA, RC	30.00	60.00	120.00
105	Neil Colville, NYR, RC	37.50	75.00	150.00
106	Paul Runge, Mon.M, RC	30.00	60.00	120.00
107	Mike Karakas, Goalie, Chi. RC	30.00	60.00	120.00
108	John Gallagher, NYA, RC	30.00	60.00	120.00
109	Alex Shibicky, NYR, RC	30.00	60.00	120.00
110	Herbert Cain, Mon.M	30.00	60.00	120.00
111	Bill MacKenzie, Mon.C	30.00	60.00	120.00
112	Hal Jackson, Chi., RC, LC	30.00	60.00	120.00
113	Art Wiebe, Chi., RC, Error	45.00	85.00	175.00
114	Joffre Desilets, Mon.C., RC	30.00	60.00	120.00
115	Earl Robinson, Mon.M	30.00	60.00	120.00
116	Cy Wentworth, Mon.M	37.50	75.00	150.00
117	Ebbie Goodfellow, Det.	37.50	75.00	150.00
118	Eddie Shore, Bos.	225.00	450.00	900.00
119	Buzz Boll, Tor.	30.00	60.00	120.00
120	Wilf Cude, Goalie, Mon.C	30.00	60.00	120.00
121	Howie Morenz, Mon.C	375.00	750.00	1,500.00
122	Red Horner, Tor.	85.00	165.00	325.00
123	Charlie Conacher, Tor.	155.00	310.00	625.00
124	Harvey Jackson, Tor.	85.00	165.00	325.00
125	Francis Clancy, Tor., LC	170.00	340.00	675.00
126	Dave Trottier, Mon.M	30.00	60.00	120.00
127	Russ Blinco, Mon.M	30.00	60.00	120.00
128	Lynn Patrick, NYR	50.00	100.00	200.00
129	Aurel Joliat, Mon.C	150.00	300.00	600.00
130	Baldy Northcott, Mon.M	30.00	60.00	120.00
131	Larry Aurie, Det.	30.00	60.00	120.00
132	Hooley Smith, Mon.M	60.00	115.00	225.00

O-Pee-Chee
1936-37 Series D
Card No. 100,
Bob Davidson

O-Pee-Chee
1936-37 Series D
Card No. 113, Error,
Name misspelled
Weibe on face

O-Pee-Chee
1937-38 Series E
Card No. 134,
Red Horner

O-Pee-Chee
1937-38 Series E
Card No. 138, Charlie Conacher

— 1937 - 38 REGULAR ISSUE —
SERIES E

Cards can be found with either purple or blue borders.

PRICE MOVEMENT OF EX SETS

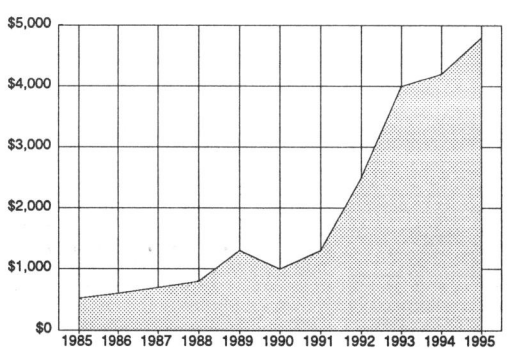

Card Size: 2 3/8" x 3 7/8"
Face: Black and white, white border, blue or purple frame
Back: Black on card stock; Name, Team, Bilingual, Resume, Number
Imprint: None
ACC No.: V304E
Complete Set No.: 48
Complete Set Price: 1,200.00   2,400.00   4,800.00
Common Card: 15.00   30.00   60.00

TORONTO MAPLE LEAFS

No.	Player	G	VG	EX
133	Turk Broda, Goalie	75.00	150.00	300.00
134	Red Horner	37.50	75.00	150.00
135	Jimmy Fowler	15.00	30.00	60.00
136	Bob Davidson	15.00	30.00	60.00
137	Reg Hamilton, RC	15.00	30.00	60.00
138	Charlie Conacher	105.00	215.00	425.00
139	Harvey Jackson	50.00	100.00	200.00
140	Buzz Boll	15.00	30.00	60.00
141	Syl Apps, Sr.	40.00	85.00	165.00
142	Gordie Drillon, RC	50.00	100.00	200.00
143	Bill Thoms	15.00	30.00	60.00
144	Nick Metz	15.00	30.00	60.00
145	Reg Kelly	15.00	30.00	60.00
146	Murray Armstrong, RC	15.00	30.00	60.00
147	Murph Chamberlain, RC	15.00	30.00	60.00

MONTREAL MAROONS

No.	Player	G	VG	EX
148	Des Smith, RC	15.00	30.00	60.00

MONTREAL CANADIENS

No.	Player	G	VG	EX
149	Wilf Cude, Goalie	15.00	30.00	60.00
150	Babe Siebert	40.00	80.00	165.00
151	Bill MacKenzie, Error	15.00	30.00	60.00
152	Aurel Joliat	115.00	225.00	450.00
153	Georges Mantha	15.00	30.00	60.00
154	Johnny Gagnon	15.00	30.00	60.00
155	Paul Haynes	15.00	30.00	60.00
156	Joffre Desilets	15.00	30.00	60.00
157	George Brown, RC	15.00	30.00	60.00
158	Polly Drouin	15.00	30.00	60.00
159	Pit Lepine	15.00	30.00	60.00
160	Toe Blake, RC	125.00	250.00	500.00

MONTREAL MAROONS

No.	Player	G	VG	EX
161	Bill Beveridge, Goalie, LC	15.00	30.00	60.00
162	Al Shields	15.00	30.00	60.00
163	Cy Wentworth	15.00	32.50	65.00
164	Stewart Evans	15.00	30.00	60.00
165	Earl Robinson, LC, Error	15.00	30.00	60.00
166	Baldy Northcott, LC	15.00	30.00	60.00
167	Paul Runge	15.00	30.00	60.00
168	Dave Trottier	15.00	30.00	60.00

36 • O-PEE-CHEE — 1939-40 REGULAR ISSUE

No.	Player	G	VG	EX
169	Russ Blinco	15.00	30.00	60.00
170	Jimmy Ward	15.00	30.00	60.00
171	Bob Gracie	15.00	30.00	60.00
172	Herbert Cain	15.00	30.00	60.00
173	Gus Marker	15.00	30.00	60.00

MONTREAL CANADIENS

No.	Player	G	VG	EX
174	Walt Buswell	15.00	30.00	60.00

MONTREAL MAROONS

No.	Player	G	VG	EX
175	Carl Voss	15.00	30.00	60.00

MONTREAL CANADIENS

No.	Player	G	VG	EX
176	Rod Lorraine, RC, Error	15.00	30.00	60.00
177	Armand Mondou	15.00	30.00	60.00
178	Red Goupille, RC	15.00	30.00	60.00
179	Gerry Shannon, RC, Error	15.00	30.00	60.00
180	Tom Cook	32.50	65.00	130.00

— 1939-40 REGULAR ISSUE —

These black and white cards have blank backs and are larger than the previous issues of the '30s. The player's name, team and position are shown beneath the photo with the card number to the right.

PRICE MOVEMENT OF EX SETS

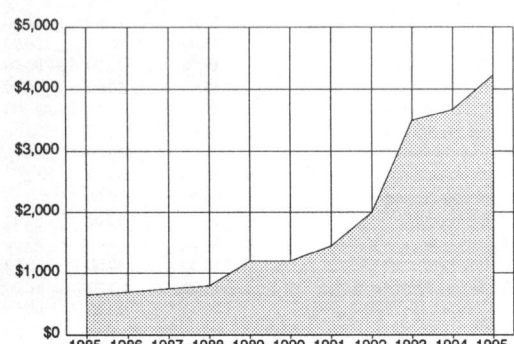

Card Size: 5" X 7"
Face: Black and white; Name, Number, Team, Position
Back: Blank
Imprint: LITHOGRAPHED IN CANADA
ACC No.: V301-1
Complete Set No.: 100
Complete Set Price: 1060.00 2,115.00 4,225.00
Common Card: 7.50 15.00 30.00

TORONTO MAPLE LEAFS

No.	Player	G	VG	EX
1	Reg Hamilton	12.50	25.00	50.00
2	Turk Broda, Goalie	30.00	65.00	125.00
3	Bingo Kampman, RC	7.50	15.00	30.00
4	Gordie Drillon	20.00	40.00	80.00
5	Bob Davidson	7.50	15.00	30.00
6	Syl Apps, Sr.	30.00	65.00	125.00
7	Pete Langelle, RC	7.50	15.00	30.00
8	Don Metz, RC	7.50	15.00	30.00
9	Reg Kelly	7.50	15.00	30.00
10	Red Horner	22.50	45.00	90.00
11	Wally Stanowski, RC, Error	7.50	15.00	30.00
12	Murph Chamberlain	7.50	15.00	30.00
13	Bucko McDonald	7.50	15.00	30.00
14	Sweeny Schriner	10.00	20.00	40.00
15	Billy Taylor, RC	7.50	15.00	30.00
16	Gus Marker	7.50	15.00	30.00

O-Pee-Chee
1937-38 Series E
Card No. 150,
Babe Siebert

O-Pee-Chee
1937-38 Series E
Card No. 165, Error,
Name misspelled Earle
in Facsimile signature

O-Pee-Chee
1939-40 Issue
Card No. 11, Error,
Name misspelled
Stanowsky on face

O-Pee-Chee
1939-40 Issue
Card No. 32,
Walt Buswell

BOSTON

No.	Player	G	VG	EX
17	Hooley Smith, LC	17.50	35.00	70.00
18	Art Chapman	7.50	15.00	30.00
19	Murray Armstrong	7.50	15.00	30.00
20	Harvey Jackson	25.00	50.00	100.00
21	Buzz Boll	7.50	15.00	30.00

MONTREAL CANADIENS

No.	Player	G	VG	EX
22	Red Goupille	7.50	15.00	30.00
23	Rod Lorraine	7.50	15.00	30.00
24	Polly Drouin	7.50	15.00	30.00
25	Johnny Gagnon	7.50	15.00	30.00
26	Georges Mantha	7.50	15.00	30.00
27	Armand Mondou	7.50	15.00	30.00
28	Claude Bourque, Goalie, RC	7.50	15.00	30.00
29	Ray Getliffe, RC	7.50	15.00	30.00
30	Cy Wentworth	8.50	17.50	35.00
31	Paul Haynes	7.50	15.00	30.00
32	Walt Buswell	7.50	15.00	30.00

NEW YORK RANGERS

No.	Player	G	VG	EX
33	Ott Heller	7.50	15.00	30.00
34	Art Coulter	8.50	17.50	35.00
35	Clint Smith, RC	10.00	20.00	40.00
36	Lynn Patrick	15.00	30.00	60.00
37	Dave Kerr, Goalie	7.50	15.00	30.00
38	Murray Patrick, RC	7.50	15.00	30.00
39	Neil Colville	15.00	30.00	60.00
40	Jack Portland, RC	7.50	15.00	30.00
41	Bill Hollett,	7.50	15.00	30.00
42	Herbert Cain	7.50	15.00	30.00

DETROIT

No.	Player	G	VG	EX
43	Mud Bruneteau, RC	7.50	15.00	30.00

CHICAGO

No.	Player	G	VG	EX
44	Joffre Desilets	7.50	15.00	30.00
45	Mush March	7.50	15.00	30.00
46	Cully Dahlstrom, RC	7.50	15.00	30.00
47	Mike Karakas, Goalie	7.50	15.00	30.00
48	Bill Thoms	7.50	15.00	30.00
49	Art Wiebe	7.50	15.00	30.00
50	Johnny Gottselig	7.50	15.00	30.00

TORONTO MAPLE LEAFS

No.	Player	G	VG	EX
51	Nick Metz	7.50	15.00	30.00
52	Jack Church, RC	7.50	15.00	30.00
53	Red Heron, RC	7.50	15.00	30.00
54	Hank Goldup, RC	7.50	15.00	30.00
55	Jimmy Fowler, Tor.	7.50	15.00	30.00

MONTREAL CANADIENS

No.	Player	G	VG	EX
56	Charlie Sands	7.50	15.00	30.00
57	Marty Barry	15.00	30.00	60.00
58	Douglas Young, RC	7.50	15.00	30.00

NEW YORK AMERICANS

No.	Player	G	VG	EX
59	Charlie Conacher	60.00	115.00	225.00
60	John Sorrell	7.50	15.00	30.00
61	Tom Anderson, RC	7.50	15.00	30.00
62	Lorne Carr	7.50	15.00	30.00
63	Earl Robertson, Goalie, RC, LC	7.50	15.00	30.00
64	Wilf Field, RC	7.50	15.00	30.00

DETROIT

No.	Player	G	VG	EX
65	Jimmy Orlando, Det., RC	7.50	15.00	30.00
66	Ebbie Goodfellow, Det.	15.00	30.00	60.00
67	Jack Keating, RC	7.50	15.00	30.00
68	Sid Abel, Det., RC	50.00	100.00	200.00
69	Gus Giesebrecht, Det., RC	7.50	15.00	30.00
70	Don Deacon, Det., RC	7.50	15.00	30.00

— 1940 - 41 REGULAR ISSUE — O-PEE-CHEE • 37

No.	Player	G	VG	EX
71	Hec Kilrea	7.50	15.00	30.00
72	Syd Howe, LC	15.00	30.00	60.00
73	Eddie Wares, RC	7.50	15.00	30.00
74	Carl Liscombe, Det., RC	7.50	15.00	30.00
75	Tiny Thompson, Goalie, Det.	18.00	35.50	75.00

CHICAGO

No.	Player	G	VG	EX
76	Earl Siebert	18.00	35.50	75.00
77	Des Smith	7.50	15.00	30.00
78	Les Cunningham, RC	7.50	15.00	30.00
79	George Allen, RC	7.50	15.00	30.00
80	Bill Carse, RC	7.50	15.00	30.00
81	Bill MacKenzie	7.50	15.00	30.00
82	Ab DeMarco, RC	7.50	15.00	30.00
83	Phil Watson, RC	7.50	15.00	30.00

NEW YORK RANGERS

No.	Player	G	VG	EX
84	Alf Pike, NYR, RC	7.50	15.00	30.00
85	Babe Pratt, RC	20.00	42.50	85.00
86	Bryan Hextall, Sr., NYR, RC	18.00	35.50	75.00
87	Kilby MacDonald, NYR, RC	7.50	15.00	30.00
88	Alex Shibicky, NYR	7.50	15.00	30.00
89	Dutch Hiller, RC	7.50	15.00	30.00
90	Mac Colville, NYR, RC	7.50	15.00	30.00

BOSTON

No.	Player	G	VG	EX
91	Roy Conacher, RC	7.50	15.00	30.00
92	Cooney Weiland, LC	7.50	15.00	30.00
93	Art Jackson	7.50	15.00	30.00
94	Woodie Dumart, Bos., RC	7.50	15.00	30.00
95	Dit Clapper, Bos.	20.00	42.50	85.00
96	Mel Hill, RC	7.50	15.00	30.00
97	Frank Brimsek, Goalie, RC	20.00	42.50	85.00
98	Bill Cowley, RC	15.00	30.00	60.00
99	Bobby Bauer, Bos., RC	7.50	15.00	30.00
100	Eddie Shore	70.00	140.00	280.00

— 1940 - 41 REGULAR ISSUE —

This set continues the sequential numbering from the V301-1 issue and follows the same format except for the sepia-toned photos.

PRICE MOVEMENT OF EX SETS

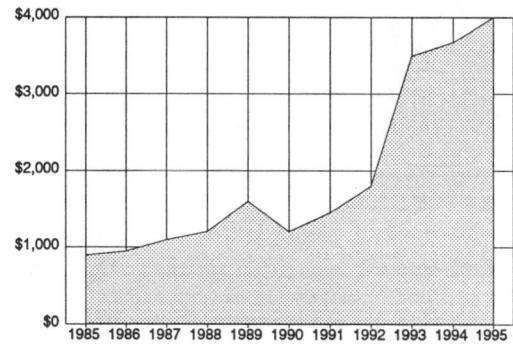

Card Size: 5" X 7"
Face: Sepia; Name, Cream border; Team, Position, Number
Back: Blank
Imprint: LITHOGRAPHED IN CANADA
ACC No.: V301-2
Complete Set No.: 50
Complete Set Price: 1,000.00   2,000.00   4,000.00
Common Card: (101 to 125)   7.50   15.00   30.00
Common Card: (126 to 150)   15.00   30.00   60.00

O-Pee-Chee
1939-40 Issue
Card No. 63,
Earl Robertson

O-Pee-Chee
1940-41 Issue
Card No. 120,
Red Goupille

O-Pee-Chee
1940-41 Issue
Card No. 122,
Sweeny Schriner

O-Pee-Chee
1940-41 Issue
Card No. 124,
Jack Stewart

No.	Player	G	VG	EX
101	Toe Blake, Mon.	45.00	85.00	175.00
102	Charlie Sands, LC	7.50	15.00	30.00
103	Wally Stanowski, LC	7.50	15.00	30.00
104	Jack E. Adams, Mon.C, RC	7.50	15.00	30.00
105	Johnny Mowers, Goalie, RC, LC	7.50	15.00	30.00
106	John Quilty, RC, LC	7.50	15.00	30.00
107	Billy Taylor, LC	7.50	15.00	30.00
108	Turk Broda, Goalie, Tor.	37.50	75.00	150.00
109	Bingo Kampman, Tor.	7.50	15.00	30.00
110	Gordie Drillon, LC	10.00	20.00	40.00
111	Don Metz, Tor.	7.50	15.00	30.00
112	Paul Haynes	7.50	15.00	30.00
113	Gus Marker	7.50	15.00	30.00
114	Alex Singbush, Mon.C, RC	7.50	15.00	30.00
115	Alex Motter, RC	7.50	15.00	30.00
116	Ken Reardon, Mon.C, RC	7.50	15.00	30.00
117	Pete Langelle, Tor.	7.50	15.00	30.00
118	Syl Apps, Sr., Tor.	30.00	65.00	125.00
119	Reg Hamilton	7.50	15.00	30.00
120	Red Goupille, Mon.C	7.50	15.00	30.00
121	Joe Benoit, RC	7.50	15.00	30.00
122	Sweeny Schriner, Tor.	7.50	15.00	30.00
123	Joe Carveth, RC	7.50	15.00	30.00
124	Jack Stewart, RC	7.50	15.00	30.00
125	Elmer Lach, Mon.C, RC	37.50	75.00	150.00
126	Jack Schewchuk, RC	15.00	30.00	60.00
127	Norman Larson, RC	15.00	30.00	60.00
128	Don Grosso, RC	15.00	30.00	60.00
129	Les Douglas, Det., RC	15.00	30.00	60.00
130	Turk Broda, Goalie, Tor.	75.00	150.00	300.00
131	Max Bentley, RC	60.00	115.00	225.00
132	Milt Schmidt, Bos., RC	70.00	140.00	275.00
133	Nick Metz, Tor.	15.00	30.00	60.00
134	John Crawford, Bos., RC	15.00	30.00	60.00
135	Bill Benson, RC	15.00	30.00	60.00
136	Lynn Patrick, NYR	30.00	65.00	125.00
137	Cully Dahlstrom, Chi.	15.00	30.00	60.00
138	Mud Bruneteau, Det.	15.00	30.00	60.00
139	Dave Kerr, Goalie, LC	15.00	30.00	60.00
140	Red Heron	15.00	30.00	60.00
141	Nick Metz, Tor.	15.00	30.00	60.00
142	Ott Heller, NYR	15.00	30.00	60.00
143	Philip Hergesheimer, RC	15.00	30.00	60.00
144	Tony DeMeres, RC	15.00	30.00	60.00
145	Arch Wilder, Det., RC	15.00	30.00	60.00
146	Syl Apps, Sr., Tor.	60.00	125.00	250.00
147	Ray Getliffe	15.00	30.00	60.00
148	Lex Chisholm, Tor., RC	15.00	30.00	60.00
149	Eddie Wiseman, RC	15.00	30.00	60.00
150	Paul Goodman, Goalie, Chi., RC	30.00	65.00	125.00

— 1968 - 69 REGULAR ISSUE —

Centering was a problem with this set. Well centered cards command a price premium over the normal issue either in NRMT or mint. Card number 193 may be unnumbered.

Mint cards command a 50% price premium over NRMT cards.

PRICE MOVEMENT OF EX SETS

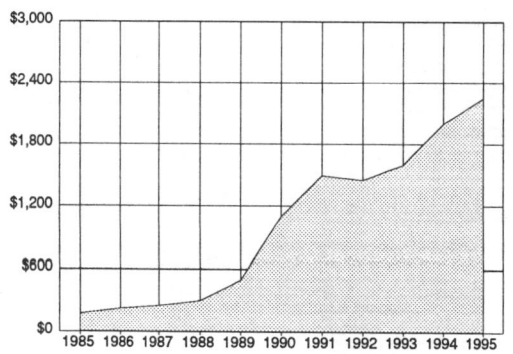

38 • O-PEE-CHEE — 1968 - 69 REGULAR ISSUE

Card Size: 2 1/2" X 3 1/2"
Face: Four colour, white border, Team logo, Position
Back: Black and red on grey card stock, Resume, Number,
Cartoon, Bilingual
Imprint: © T.C.G. PTD. IN CANADA
Complete Set No.: 216
Complete Set Price: 600.00 1,125.00 2,250.00
Common Card: 1.25 2.50 5.00

ST. LOUIS BLUES

No.	Player	VG	EX	NRMT
1	Doug Harvey, LC	5.50	11.00	22.00

BOSTON BRUINS

No.	Player	VG	EX	NRMT
2	Bobby Orr	100.00	200.00	400.00
3	Don Awrey, Error	1.25	2.50	5.00
4	Ted Green	1.25	2.50	5.00
5	John Bucyk	2.50	5.00	10.00
6	Derek Sanderson	5.00	10.00	20.00
7	Phil Esposito	15.00	27.50	55.00
8	Ken Hodge	1.25	.250	5.00
9	John McKenzie	1.25	2.50	5.00
10	Fred Stanfield	1.25	2.50	5.00
11	Tom Williams	1.25	2.50	5.00

CHICAGO BLACK HAWKS

No.	Player	VG	EX	NRMT
12	Denis DeJordy, Goalie	1.25	2.50	5.00
13	Doug Jarrett	1.25	2.50	5.00
14	Gilles Marotte	1.25	2.50	5.00
15	Pat Stapleton	1.25	2.50	5.00
16	Bobby Hull	30.00	65.00	125.00
17	Chico Maki	1.25	2.50	5.00
18	Pit Martin	1.25	2.50	5.00
19	Doug Mohns	1.25	2.50	5.00

MONTREAL CANADIENS

No.	Player	VG	EX	NRMT
20	John Ferguson, Sr.	1.25	2.50	5.00

CHICAGO BLACK HAWKS

No.	Player	VG	EX	NRMT
21	Jim Pappin	1.25	2.50	5.00
22	Kenny Wharram	1.25	2.50	5.00

DETROIT RED WINGS

No.	Player	VG	EX	NRMT
23	Roger Crozier, Goalie	1.25	2.50	5.00
24	Bob Baun	1.25	2.50	5.00
25	Gary Bergman	1.25	2.50	5.00
26	Kent Douglas, LC	1.25	2.50	5.00
27	Ron Harris, RC	1.25	2.50	5.00
28	Alex Delvecchio	2.50	5.00	10.00
29	Gordie Howe	40.00	80.00	160.00
30	Bruce MacGregor	1.25	2.50	5.00
31	Frank Mahovlich	4.50	9.00	18.00
32	Dean Prentice	1.25	2.50	5.00
33	Pete Stemkowski	1.25	2.50	5.00
34	Terry Sawchuk, Goalie	12.50	25.00	50.00

LOS ANGELES KINGS

No.	Player	VG	EX	NRMT
35	Larry Cahan	1.25	2.50	5.00
36	Real Lemieux, RC	1.25	2.50	5.00
37	Bill White, RC	2.00	4.00	8.00
38	Gord Labossiere, RC	1.25	2.50	5.00
39	Ted Irvine, RC	1.25	2.50	5.00
40	Eddie Joyal	1.25	2.50	5.00
41	Dale Rolfe, RC	1.25	2.50	5.00
42	Lowell MacDonald, RC	2.00	4.00	8.00
43	Skip Krake, Error	1.25	2.50	5.00
44	Terry Gray, LC	1.25	2.50	5.00

MINNESOTA NORTH STARS

No.	Player	VG	EX	NRMT
45	Cesare Maniago, Goalie	1.25	2.50	5.00
46	Mike McMahon	1.25	2.50	5.00
47	Wayne Hillman	1.25	2.50	5.00

O-Pee-Chee
1968-69 Issue
Card No. 14,
Gilles Marotte

O-Pee-Chee
1968-69 Issue
Card No. 77,
Jean Ratelle

O-Pee-Chee
1968-69 Issue
Card No. 84,
Gerry Ehman

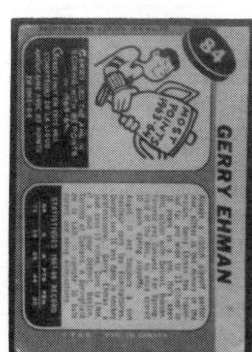

O-Pee-Chee
1968-69 Issue
Card No. 84,
Gerry Ehman

MONTREAL CANADIENS

No.	Player	VG	EX	NRMT
48	Larry Hillman	1.25	2.50	5.00

MINNESOTA NORTH STARS

No.	Player	VG	EX	NRMT
49	Bob Woytowich	1.25	2.50	5.00
50	Wayne Connelly	1.25	2.50	5.00
51	Claude Larose	1.25	2.50	5.00
52	Danny Grant, RC	2.50	5.00	10.00
53	Andre Boudrias, RC	1.25	2.50	5.00
54	Ray Cullen, RC	2.00	4.00	8.00
55	Parker MacDonald, Error, LC	1.25	2.50	5.00

MONTREAL CANADIENS

No.	Player	VG	EX	NRMT
56	Lorne Worsley, Goalie	3.50	7.00	14.00
57	Terry Harper	1.25	2.50	5.00
58	Jacques Laperriere	1.25	2.50	5.00
59	J.C. Tremblay	1.25	2.50	5.00
60	Ralph Backstrom	1.25	2.50	5.00

CHECKLIST

No.	Checklist	VG	EX	NRMT
61	Checklist I	45.00	85.00	175.00

MONTREAL CANADIENS

No.	Player	VG	EX	NRMT
62	Yvan Cournoyer	4.50	9.00	18.00
63	Jacques Lemaire	5.00	10.00	20.00
64	Mickey Redmond, RC	7.50	15.00	30.00
65	Bobby Rousseau	1.25	2.50	5.00
66	Gilles Tremblay	1.25	2.50	5.00

NEW YORK RANGERS

No.	Player	VG	EX	NRMT
67	Ed Giacomin, Goalie	5.00	10.00	20.00
68	Arnie Brown	1.25	2.50	5.00
69	Harry Howell	1.50	3.00	6.00
70	Al Hamilton, RC	1.25	2.50	5.00
71	Rod Seiling	1.25	2.50	5.00
72	Rod Gilbert	3.75	7.50	15.00
73	Phil Goyette	1.25	2.50	5.00
74	Larry Jeffrey	1.25	2.50	5.00
75	Don Marshall	1.25	2.50	5.00
76	Bob Nevin	1.25	2.50	5.00
77	Jean Ratelle	3.50	7.00	14.00

OAKLAND SEALS

No.	Player	VG	EX	NRMT
78	Charlie Hodge, Goalie	1.25	2.50	5.00
79	Bert Marshall	1.25	2.50	5.00
80	Billy Harris, LC	1.25	2.50	5.00
81	Carol Vadnais	1.25	2.50	5.00

CHICAGO BLACK HAWKS

No.	Player	VG	EX	NRMT
82	Howie Young, LC	1.25	2.50	5.00

OAKLAND SEALS

No.	Player	VG	EX	NRMT
83	John Brenneman, RC, LC	1.25	2.50	5.00
84	Gerry Ehman	1.25	2.50	5.00
85	Ted Hampson	1.25	2.50	5.00
86	Bill Hicke	1.25	2.50	5.00
87	Gary Jarrett	1.25	2.50	5.00
88	Doug Roberts	1.25	2.50	5.00

PHILADELPHIA FLYERS

No.	Player	VG	EX	NRMT
89	Bernie Parent, Goalie, RC	30.00	65.00	125.00
90	Joe Watson	1.25	2.50	5.00
91	Ed Van Impe	1.25	2.50	5.00
92	Larry Zeidel, LC	1.25	2.50	5.00
93	John Miszuk, RC	1.25	2.50	5.00
94	Gary Dornhoefer	1.25	2.50	5.00
95	Leon Rochefort, RC	1.25	2.50	5.00
96	Brit Selby	1.25	2.50	5.00
97	Forbes Kennedy, LC	1.25	2.50	5.00

1968-69 REGULAR ISSUE — O-PEE-CHEE

No.	Player	VG	EX	NRMT
98	Ed Hoekstra, RC, LC	1.25	2.50	5.00
99	Garry Peters	1.25	2.50	5.00

PITTSBURGH PENGUINS

No.	Player	VG	EX	NRMT
100	Les Binkley, Goalie, RC	2.50	5.00	10.00
101	Leo Boivin	1.25	2.50	5.00
102	Earl Ingarfield	1.25	2.50	5.00
103	Lou Angotti	1.25	2.50	5.00
104	Andy Bathgate	1.25	2.50	5.00
105	Wally Boyer	1.25	2.50	5.00
106	Ken Schinkel	1.25	2.50	5.00

ST. LOUIS BLUES

No.	Player	VG	EX	NRMT
107	Ab McDonald	1.25	2.50	5.00

PITTSBURGH PENGUINS

No.	Player	VG	EX	NRMT
108	Charlie Burns	1.25	2.50	5.00
109	Val Fonteyne	1.25	2.50	5.00
110	Noel Price	1.25	2.50	5.00

ST. LOUIS BLUES

No.	Player	VG	EX	NRMT
111	Glenn Hall, Goalie	3.75	7.50	15.00
112	Bob Plager, RC	3.00	6.00	12.00
113	Jim Roberts	1.25	2.50	5.00
114	Red Berenson	1.25	2.50	5.00
115	Larry Keenan	1.25	2.50	5.00
116	Camille Henry	1.25	2.50	5.00
117	Gary Sabourin, RC	1.25	2.50	5.00
118	Ron Schock	1.25	2.50	5.00
119	Gary Veneruzzo, RC	1.25	2.50	5.00
120	Gerry Melnyk, LC	1.25	2.50	5.00

CHECKLIST

No.	Checklist	VG	EX	NRMT
121	Checklist II	50.00	100.00	200.00

TORONTO MAPLE LEAFS

No.	Player	VG	EX	NRMT
122	Johnny Bower, Goalie	2.50	5.00	10.00
123	Tim Horton	3.75	7.50	15.00
124	Pierre Pilote, LC	1.25	2.50	5.00
125	Marcel Pronovost, LC	1.25	2.50	5.00
126	Ron Ellis	1.25	2.50	5.00
127	Paul Henderson	1.25	2.50	5.00

ST. LOUIS BLUES

No.	Player	VG	EX	NRMT
128	Al Arbour	1.25	2.50	5.00

TORONTO MAPLE LEAFS

No.	Player	VG	EX	NRMT
129	Bob Pulford	1.25	2.50	5.00
130	Floyd Smith	1.25	2.50	5.00
131	Norm Ullman	2.00	4.00	8.00
132	Mike Walton	1.25	2.50	5.00

BOSTON BRUINS

No.	Player	VG	EX	NRMT
133	Eddie Johnston, Goalie	1.25	2.50	5.00
134	Glen Sather	3.00	6.00	12.00
135	Ed Westfall	1.25	2.50	5.00
136	Dallas Smith	1.25	2.50	5.00
137	Eddie Shack	2.50	5.00	10.00
138	Gary Doak	1.25	2.50	5.00
139	Ron Murphy	1.25	2.50	5.00
140	Gerry Cheevers, Goalie	3.50	7.00	14.00

DETROIT RED WINGS

No.	Player	VG	EX	NRMT
141	Bob Falkenberg, RC	1.25	2.50	5.00
142	Garry Unger, RC	5.00	10.00	20.00
143	Pete Mahovlich	1.25	2.50	5.00
144	Roy Edwards, Goalie	1.25	2.50	5.00

O-Pee-Chee 1968-69 Issue Card No. 86, Bill Hicke

O-Pee-Chee 1968-69 Issue Card No. 117, Gary Sabourin

O-Pee-Chee 1968-69 Issue Card No. 145, Gary Bauman

O-Pee-Chee 1968-69 Issue Card No. 204, Bobby Hull

MINNESOTA NORTH STARS

No.	Player	VG	EX	NRMT
145	Gary Bauman, Goalie, RC, LC	1.25	2.50	5.00
146	Bob McCord	1.25	2.50	5.00
147	Elmer Vasko, LC	1.25	2.50	5.00
148	Bill Goldsworthy, RC	3.00	6.00	12.00
149	Jean-Paul Parise, RC	2.00	4.00	8.00

CHICAGO BLACK HAWKS

No.	Player	VG	EX	NRMT
150	Dave Dryden, Goalie	1.25	2.50	5.00
151	Howie Young, LC	1.25	2.50	5.00
152	Matt Ravlich	1.25	2.50	5.00
153	Dennis Hull	1.50	3.00	6.00
154	Eric Nesterenko	1.25	2.50	5.00
155	Stan Mikita	7.50	14.00	28.00

LOS ANGELES KINGS

No.	Player	VG	EX	NRMT
156	Bob Wall	1.25	2.50	5.00
157	Dave Amadio, RC	1.25	2.50	5.00
158	Howie Hughes, RC	1.25	2.50	5.00
159	Bill Flett, RC	1.25	2.50	5.00
160	Doug Robinson, LC	1.25	2.50	5.00

MINNESOTA NORTH STARS

No.	Player	VG	EX	NRMT
161	Dick Duff	1.25	2.50	5.00

MONTREAL CANADIENS

No.	Player	VG	EX	NRMT
162	Ted Harris	1.25	2.50	5.00
163	Claude Provost	1.25	2.50	5.00
164	Rogatien Vachon, Goalie	6.25	12.50	25.00
165	Henri Richard	3.75	7.50	15.00
166	Jean Beliveau	5.75	11.50	23.00

NEW YORK RANGERS

No.	Player	VG	EX	NRMT
167	Reggie Fleming	1.25	2.50	5.00
168	Ron Stewart	1.25	2.50	5.00
169	Dave Balon	1.25	2.50	5.00
170	Orland Kurtenbach	1.25	2.50	5.00
171	Vic Hadfield	1.25	2.50	5.00
172	Jim Neilson	1.25	2.50	5.00

OAKLAND SEALS

No.	Player	VG	EX	NRMT
173	Bryan Watson	1.25	2.50	5.00
174	George Swarbrick, RC	1.25	2.50	5.00
175	Joe Szura, RC	1.25	2.50	5.00
176	Gary Smith, Goalie, RC	2.00	4.00	8.00

ST. LOUIS BLUES

No.	Player	VG	EX	NRMT
177	Barclay Plager, Error	2.50	5.00	10.00
178	Tim Ecclestone, RC	1.25	2.50	5.00
179	Jean Guy Talbot	1.25	2.50	5.00
180	Ab McDonald	1.25	2.50	5.00
181	Jacques Plante, Goalie	11.25	22.50	45.00
182	Bill E. McCreary, RC	1.25	2.50	5.00

PHILADELPHIA FLYERS

No.	Player	VG	EX	NRMT
183	Allan Stanley, LC, Error	1.25	2.50	5.00
184	Andre Lacroix, RC	2.00	4.00	8.00
185	Jean Guy Gendron	1.25	2.50	5.00
186	Jim Johnson, RC	1.25	2.50	5.00
187	Simon Nolet, RC	1.25	2.50	5.00

PITTSBURG PENGUINS

No.	Player	VG	EX	NRMT
188	Joe Daley, Goalie, RC	2.00	4.00	8.00
189	John Arbour, RC	1.25	2.50	5.00
190	Billy Dea	1.25	2.50	5.00
191	Bob Dillabough	1.25	2.50	5.00
192	Bob Woytowich	1.25	2.50	5.00
193	Keith McCreary, RC, Error	1.75	3.50	7.00
193	Keith McCreary, RC, Corrected	1.25	2.50	5.00

O-PEE-CHEE — 1968-69 PUCK STICKERS —

TORONTO MAPLE LEAFS

No.	Player	VG	EX	NRMT
194	Murray Oliver	1.25	2.50	5.00
195	Larry Mickey, RC	1.25	2.50	5.00
196	Bill Sutherland, RC	1.25	2.50	5.00
197	Bruce Gamble, Goalie	1.25	2.50	5.00
198	Dave Keon	3.00	6.00	12.00

ALL STARS
First Team

No.	Player	VG	EX	NRMT
199	Gump Worsley, Goalie, Mon.	2.00	4.00	8.00
200	Bobby Orr, Bos.	37.50	75.00	150.00
201	Tim Horton, Tor.	2.50	5.00	10.00
202	Stan Mikita, Chi.	4.50	9.00	18.00
203	Gordie Howe, Det.	22.50	45.00	90.00
204	Bobby Hull, Chi.	17.50	35.00	70.00

Second Team

No.	Player	VG	EX	NRMT
205	Ed Giacomin, Goalie, NYR	3.00	6.00	12.00
206	J.C. Tremblay, Mon.	1.25	2.50	5.00
207	Jim Neilson, NYR	1.25	2.50	5.00
208	Phil Esposito, Bos.	11.25	22.50	25.00
209	Rod Gilbert, NYR	1.75	3.50	7.00
210	John Bucyk, Bos.	1.75	3.50	7.00

TROPHY WINNERS

No.	Trophy/Player	VG	EX	NRMT
211	The Art Ross Trophy, The Lady Byng Memorial Trophy, The Hart Memorial Trophy: Stan Mikita	6.25	12.50	25.00
212	The Vezina Trophy: Worsley & Vachon, Goalies	4.50	9.00	18.00
213	The Calder Memorial Trophy: Derek Sanderson	2.50	5.00	10.00
214	The James Norris Memorial Trophy: Bobby Orr	37.50	75.00	150.00
215	The Conn Smythe Trophy: Glenn Hall, Goalie	2.25	4.50	9.00
216	The Bill Masterton Memorial Trophy: Claude Provost	2.50	5.00	10.00

O-Pee-Chee
1968-69 Issue
Card No. 214,
James Norris Trophy, Bobby Orr

— 1968-69 PUCK STICKERS —

Sticker Size: 2 1/2" X 3 1/2"
Face: Four colour; Number, Name, Position, Team, Sticker application instructions
Back: Blank
Imprint: PRINTED IN CANADA
Complete Set No: 22

		VG	EX	NRMT
Complete Set Price:		80.00	175.00	350.00
Common Card:		1.00	2.00	4.00

No.	Player	VG	EX	NRMT
1	Stan Mikita, Chi.	3.25	6.50	13.00
2	Frank Mahovlich, Det.	3.25	6.50	13.00
3	Bobby Hull, Chi.	10.00	20.00	40.00
4	Bobby Orr, Bos.	15.00	30.00	60.00
5	Phil Esposito, Bos.	4.50	9.00	18.00
6	Gump Worsley, Goalie, Mon.	3.25	6.50	13.00
7	Jean Beliveau, Mon.	5.00	10.00	20.00
8	Elmer Vasko, Min.	1.00	2.00	4.00
9	Rod Gilbert, NYR	2.50	5.00	10.00
10	Roger Crozier, Goalie, Det.	1.00	2.00	4.00
11	Lou Angotti, Pit.	1.00	2.00	4.00
12	Charlie Hodge, Goalie, Oak.	1.00	2.00	4.00
13	Glenn Hall, Goalie, St.L., Error	3.25	6.50	13.00
14	Doug Harvey, St.L.	3.75	6.50	13.00
15	Jacques Plante, Goalie, St.L.	4.50	9.00	18.00
16	Allan Stanley, Phi.	1.75	3.50	7.00
17	Johnny Bower, Goalie, Tor.	3.00	6.00	12.00
18	Tim Horton, Tor.	3.50	7.00	14.00
19	Dave Keon, Tor.	4.50	9.00	18.00
20	Terry Sawchuk, Goalie, Det.	4.00	8.00	16.00
21	Henri Richard, Mon.	3.00	6.00	12.00
22	Gordie Howe, Det. 700th Goal	17.50	35.00	70.00

O-Pee-Chee
1968-69 Puck Sticker
Sticker No. 13, Error,
Name misspelled Glen on face

O-Pee-Chee
1969-70 Issue
Card No. 1,
Gump Worsley

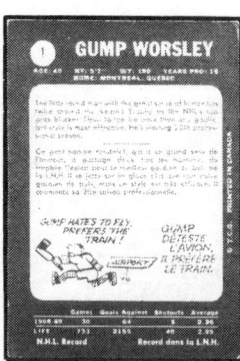

O-Pee-Chee
1969-70 Issue
Card No. 1,
Gump Worsley

— 1969-70 REGULAR ISSUE —

The backs were printed in navy blue ink resulting in the possible image transfer to the face of the card below if cards have been stored in stacks. This transferring of images on the face results in loss of value.

The backs of card nos. 206, 208, 209, 210, 212, 213, 218, 225, 226, 230 and 231 form a picture puzzle of Bobby Orr. The backs of card nos. 205, 207, 211, 214, 215, 216, 217, 220, 221, 222, 223, 224, 227, 228 and 229 form a picture puzzle of Phil Exposito.

Mint cards command a 50% price premium over NRMT cards.

PRICE MOVEMENT OF NRMT SETS

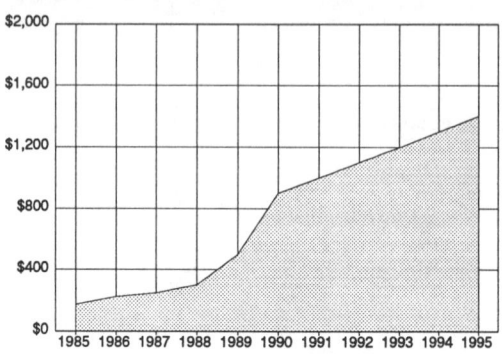

Card Size: 2 1/2" X 3 1/2"
Face: Four colour, white border, Team logo
Back: Blue and yellow on card stock, Resume, Number, Hockey trivia, Bilingual
Imprint: © T.C.G. PRINTED IN CANADA
Complete Set No.: 231

Complete Set Price:	350.00	700.00	1,400.00
Common Card:	.90	1.75	3.50

MONTREAL CANADIENS

No.	Player	VG	EX	NRMT
1	Gump Worsley, Goalie	5.50	11.00	22.00
2	Ted Harris	.90	1.75	3.50
3	Jacques Laperriere	.90	1.75	3.50
4	Serge Savard, RC	11.25	22.50	45.00
5	J. C. Tremblay	.90	1.75	3.50
6	Yvan Cournoyer	3.00	6.00	12.00
7	John Ferguson, Sr.	.90	1.75	3.50
8	Jacques Lemaire	3.00	6.00	12.00
9	Bobby Rousseau	.90	1.75	3.50
10	Jean Beliveau	5.00	10.00	20.00
11	Dick Duff	.90	1.75	3.50

ST. LOUIS BLUES

No.	Player	VG	EX	NRMT
12	Glenn Hall, Goalie	3.00	6.00	12.00
13	Bob Plager	.90	1.75	3.50
14	Ron C. Anderson, RC	.90	1.75	3.50
15	Jean-Guy Talbot	.90	1.75	3.50
16	Andre Boudrias	.90	1.75	3.50
17	Camille Henry, LC	.90	1.75	3.50
18	Ab McDonald	.90	1.75	3.50
19	Gary Sabourin	.90	1.75	3.50
20	Red Berenson	.90	1.75	3.50
21	Phil Goyette	.90	1.75	3.50

BOSTON BRUINS

No.	Player	VG	EX	NRMT
22	Gerry Cheevers, Goalie	4.50	9.00	18.00
23	Ted Green	.90	1.75	3.50
24	Bobby Orr	50.00	100.00	200.00
25	Dallas Smith	.90	1.75	3.50
26	John Bucyk	2.50	5.00	10.00
27	Ken Hodge, Sr.	.90	1.75	3.50
28	John McKenzie	.90	1.75	3.50
29	Ed Westfall	.90	1.75	3.50
30	Phil Esposito	8.75	17.50	35.00

— 1969 - 70 REGULAR ISSUE — O-PEE-CHEE • 41

CHECKLIST

No.	Checklist	VG	EX	NRMT
31	Checklist 2 (133 - 231)	30.00	60.00	120.00 ☐

BOSTON BRUINS

No.	Player	VG	EX	NRMT
32	Fred Stanfield	.90	1.75	3.50 ☐

NEW YORK RANGERS

No.	Player	VG	EX	NRMT
33	Ed Giacomin, Goalie	4.50	9.00	18.00 ☐
34	Arnie Brown	.90	1.75	3.50 ☐
35	Jim Neilson	.90	1.75	3.50 ☐
36	Rod Seiling	.90	1.75	3.50 ☐
37	Rod Gilbert	2.00	4.00	8.00 ☐
38	Vic Hadfield	.90	1.75	3.50 ☐
39	Don Marshall	.90	1.75	3.50 ☐
40	Bob Nevin	.90	1.75	3.50 ☐
41	Ron Stewart	.90	1.75	3.50 ☐
42	Jean Ratelle	2.00	4.00	8.00 ☐
43	**Walt Tkaczuk, RC**	2.00	4.00	8.00 ☐

TORONTO MAPLE LEAFS

No.	Player	VG	EX	NRMT
44	Bruce Gamble, Goalie	.90	1.75	3.50 ☐
45	**Jim Dorey, RC**	.90	1.75	3.50 ☐
46	Ron Ellis	.90	1.75	3.50 ☐
47	Paul Henderson	.90	1.75	3.50 ☐
48	Brit Selby	.90	1.75	3.50 ☐
49	Floyd Smith	.90	1.75	3.50 ☐
50	Mike Walton	.90	1.75	3.50 ☐
51	Dave Keon	2.25	4.50	9.00 ☐
52	Murray Oliver	.90	1.75	3.50 ☐
53	Bob Pulford	1.00	2.00	4.00 ☐
54	Norm Ullman	1.50	3.00	6.00 ☐

DETROIT RED WINGS

No.	Player	VG	EX	NRMT
55	Roger Crozier, Goalie	.90	1.75	3.50 ☐
56	Roy Edwards, Goalie	.90	1.75	3.50 ☐
57	Bob Baun	.90	1.75	3.50 ☐
58	Gary Bergman	.90	1.75	3.50 ☐
59	Carl Brewer	.90	1.75	3.50 ☐
60	Wayne Connelly	.90	1.75	3.50 ☐
61	Gordie Howe	25.00	50.00	100.00 ☐
62	Frank Mahovlich	3.75	7.50	15.00 ☐
63	Bruce MacGregor	.90	1.75	3.50 ☐
64	Ron Harris	.90	1.75	3.50 ☐
65	Pete Stemkowski	.90	1.75	3.50 ☐

CHICAGO BLACK HAWKS

No.	Player	VG	EX	NRMT
66	Denis DeJordy, Goalie	.90	1.75	3.50 ☐
67	Doug Jarrett	.90	1.75	3.50 ☐
68	Gilles Marotte	.90	1.75	3.50 ☐
69	Pat Stapleton	.90	1.75	3.50 ☐
70	Bobby Hull	18.75	37.50	75.00 ☐
71	Dennis Hull	.90	1.75	3.50 ☐
72	Doug Mohns	.90	1.75	3.50 ☐
73	**Howie Menard, RC**	.90	1.75	3.50 ☐
74	Kenny Wharram, LC	.90	1.75	3.50 ☐
75	Pit Martin	.90	1.75	3.50 ☐
76	Stan Mikita	5.00	10.00	20.00 ☐

CALIFORNIA GOLDEN SEALS

No.	Player	VG	EX	NRMT
77	Charlie Hodge, Goalie	.90	1.75	3.50 ☐
78	Gary Smith, Goalie	.90	1.75	3.50 ☐
79	Harry Howell	1.00	2.00	4.00 ☐
80	Bert Marshall	.90	1.75	3.50 ☐
81	Doug Roberts	.90	1.75	3.50 ☐
82	Carol Vadnais	.90	1.75	3.50 ☐
83	Gerry Ehman	.90	1.75	3.50 ☐
84	**Brian Perry, RC, LC**	.90	1.75	3.50 ☐
85	Gary Jarrett	.90	1.75	3.50 ☐
86	Ted Hampson	.90	1.75	3.50 ☐
87	Earl Ingarfield	.90	1.75	3.50 ☐

O-Pee-Chee
1969-70 Issue
Card No. 26,
John Bucyk

O-Pee-Chee
1969-70 Issue
Card No. 57,
Bob Baun

O-Pee-Chee
1969-70 Issue
Card No. 121,
Cesare Maniago

O-Pee-Chee
1969-70 Issue
Card No. 134,
Lou Angotti

PHILADELPHIA FLYERS

No.	Player	VG	EX	NRMT
88	Doug Favell, Goalie, RC	3.00	6.00	12.00 ☐
89	Bernie Parent, Goalie	11.25	22.50	45.00 ☐
90	Larry Hillman	.90	1.75	3.50 ☐
91	Wayne Hillman	.90	1.75	3.50 ☐
92	Ed Van Impe	.90	1.75	3.50 ☐
93	Joe Watson	.90	1.75	3.50 ☐
94	Gary Dornhoefer	.90	1.75	3.50 ☐
95	Reggie Fleming	.90	1.75	3.50 ☐
96	**Ralph MacSweyn, RC, LC**	.90	1.75	3.50 ☐
97	Jim Johnson	.90	1.75	3.50 ☐
98	Andre Lacroix	.90	1.75	3.50 ☐

LOS ANGELES KINGS

No.	Player	VG	EX	NRMT
99	**Gerry Desjardins, Goalie, RC**	1.75	3.50	7.00 ☐
100	Dale Rolfe	.90	1.75	3.50 ☐
101	Bill White	.90	1.75	3.50 ☐
102	Bill Flett	.90	1.75	3.50 ☐
103	Ted Irvine	.90	1.75	3.50 ☐
104	Ross Lonsberry	.90	1.75	3.50 ☐
105	Leon Rochefort	.90	1.75	3.50 ☐
106	**Brian Campbell, RC**	.90	1.75	3.50 ☐
107	**Dennis Hextall, RC**	1.25	2.50	5.00 ☐
108	Eddie Joyal	.90	1.75	3.50 ☐
109	Gord Labossiere	.90	1.75	3.50 ☐

PITTSBURGH PENGUINS

No.	Player	VG	EX	NRMT
110	Les Binkley, Goalie	.90	1.75	3.50 ☐
111	**Tracy Pratt, RC**	.90	1.75	3.50 ☐
112	Bryan Watson	.90	1.75	3.50 ☐
113	**Bob Blackburn, RC, LC**	.90	1.75	3.50 ☐
114	Keith McCreary	.90	1.75	3.50 ☐
115	Dean Prentice	.90	1.75	3.50 ☐
116	Glen Sather	1.25	2.50	5.00 ☐
117	Ken Schinkel	.90	1.75	3.50 ☐
118	Wally Boyer	.90	1.75	3.50 ☐
119	Val Fonteyne	.90	1.75	3.50 ☐
120	Ron Schock	.90	1.75	3.50 ☐

MINNESOTA NORTH STARS

No.	Player	VG	EX	NRMT
121	Cesare Maniago, Goalie	.90	1.75	3.50 ☐
122	Leo Boivin	1.00	2.00	4.00 ☐
123	Bob McCord	.90	1.75	3.50 ☐
124	John Miszuk	.90	1.75	3.50 ☐
125	Danny Grant	.90	1.75	3.50 ☐
126	**Bill Collins, RC**	.90	1.75	3.50 ☐
127	J. P. Parise	.90	1.75	3.50 ☐
128	Tom Williams	.90	1.75	3.50 ☐
129	Charlie Burns	.90	1.75	3.50 ☐
130	Ray Cullen	.90	1.75	3.50 ☐
131	**Danny O'Shea, RC**	.90	1.75	3.50 ☐

CHECKLIST

No.	Checklist	VG	EX	NRMT
132	Checklist 1 (1 - 132)	37.50	75.00	150.00 ☐

CHICAGO BLACK HAWKS

No.	Player	VG	EX	NRMT
133	Jim Pappin	.90	1.75	3.50 ☐
134	Lou Angotti	.90	1.75	3.50 ☐
135	**Terry Caffery, RC, LC**	.90	1.75	3.50 ☐
136	Eric Nesterenko	.90	1.75	3.50 ☐
137	Chico Maki	.90	1.75	3.50 ☐
138	**Tony Esposito, Goalie, RC**	31.25	62.50	125.00 ☐

LOS ANGELES KINGS

No.	Player	VG	EX	NRMT
139	Eddie Shack	1.25	2.50	5.00 ☐
140	Bob Wall	.90	1.75	3.50 ☐
141	**Skip Krake, RC**	.90	1.75	3.50 ☐
142	Howie Hughes, LC	.90	1.75	3.50 ☐
143	**Jimmy Peters, RC**	.90	1.75	3.50 ☐
144	**Brent Hughes, RC**	.90	1.75	3.50 ☐

O-PEE-CHEE — 1969-70 REGULAR ISSUE

CALIFORNIA GOLDEN SEALS

No.	Player	VG	EX	NRMT
145	Bill Hicke	.90	1.75	3.50
146	Norm Ferguson, RC	.90	1.75	3.50
147	Dick Mattiussi, RC	.90	1.75	3.50
148	Mike Laughton, RC	.90	1.75	3.50
149	Gene Ubriaco, RC, LC	1.00	2.00	4.00
150	Bob Dillabough, LC	.90	1.75	3.50

PITTSBURGH PENGUINS

No.	Player	VG	EX	NRMT
151	Bob Woytowich	.90	1.75	3.50
152	Joe Daley, Goalie	.90	1.75	3.50
153	Duane Rupp	.90	1.75	3.50
154	Bryan Hextall, Jr., RC	1.50	3.00	6.00
155	Jean Pronovost, RC	1.25	2.50	5.00
156	Jim Morrison	.90	1.75	3.50

DETROIT RED WINGS

No.	Player	VG	EX	NRMT
157	Alex Delvecchio	2.00	4.00	8.00
158	Poul Popiel	.90	1.75	3.50
159	Garry Unger	1.50	3.00	6.00
160	Garry Monahan	.90	1.75	3.50
161	Matt Ravlich	.90	1.75	3.50
162	Nick Libett, RC, Error	.90	1.75	3.50

MONTREAL CANADIENS

No.	Player	VG	EX	NRMT
163	Henri Richard	2.50	5.00	10.00
164	Terry Harper	.90	1.75	3.50
165	Rogatien Vachon, Goalie	3.00	6.00	12.00
166	Ralph Backstrom	.90	1.75	3.50
167	Claude Provost	.90	1.75	3.50
168	Gilles Tremblay, LC	.90	1.75	3.50

PHILADELPHIA FLYERS

No.	Player	VG	EX	NRMT
169	Jean-Guy Gendron	.90	1.75	3.50
170	Earl Heiskala, RC	.90	1.75	3.50
171	Garry Peters	.90	1.75	3.50
172	Bill Sutherland	.90	1.75	3.50
173	Dick Cherry, RC, LC	.90	1.75	3.50

ST. LOUIS BLUES

No.	Player	VG	EX	NRMT
174	Jim Roberts	.90	1.75	3.50
175	Noel Picard, RC	.90	1.75	3.50
176	Barclay Plager, RC	1.00	2.00	4.00
177	Frank St. Marseille, RC	.90	1.75	3.50
178	Al Arbour, LC	1.25	2.50	5.00
179	Tim Ecclestone	.90	1.75	3.50
180	Jacques Plante, Goalie	8.75	17.50	35.00
181	Billy McCreary, LC	.90	1.75	3.50

TORONTO MAPLE LEAFS

No.	Player	VG	EX	NRMT
182	Tim Horton	3.50	7.00	14.00
183	Rick Ley, RC	2.00	4.00	6.00
184	Wayne Carleton	.90	1.75	3.50
185	Marv Edwards, Goalie, RC, LC	.90	1.75	3.50
186	Pat Quinn, RC	3.00	6.00	12.00
187	Johnny Bower, Goalie, LC	2.00	4.00	8.00

NEW YORK RANGERS

No.	Player	VG	EX	NRMT
188	Orland Kurtenbach	.90	1.75	3.50
189	Terry Sawchuk, Goalie, LC	10.00	20.00	40.00
190	Real Lemieux	.90	1.75	3.50
191	Dave Balon	.90	1.75	3.50
192	Al Hamilton	.90	1.75	3.50

MR HOCKEY

No.	Player	VG	EX	NRMT
193A	Gordie Howe, Without "No."	35.00	75.00	150.00
193B	Gordie Howe, With "No."	30.00	60.00	125.00

MINNESOTA NORTH STARS

No.	Player	VG	EX	NRMT
194	Claude Larose	.90	1.75	3.50

O-Pee-Chee
1969-70 Issue
Card No.162, Error,
Name misspelled Libbett
on face and back

O-Pee-Chee
1969-70 Issue
Card No. 163,
Henri Richard

O-Pee-Chee
1969-70 Issue
Card No. 205A, Error
Card Numbered 214 on back

O-Pee-Chee
1969-70 Issue
Card No. 214, Phil Esposito

No.	Player	VG	EX	NRMT
195	Bill Goldsworthy	.90	1.75	3.50
196	Bob Barlow, RC	.90	1.75	3.50
197	Ken Broderick, Goalie, RC	.90	1.75	3.50
198	Lou Nanne, RC	1.25	2.50	5.00
199	Tom Polonic, RC, LC	.90	1.75	3.50

BOSTON BRUINS

No.	Player	VG	EX	NRMT
200	Eddie Johnston, Goalie	.90	1.75	3.50
201	Derek Sanderson	1.00	2.00	4.00
202	Gary Doak	.90	1.75	3.50
203	Don Awrey	.90	1.75	3.50
204	Ron Murphy, LC	.90	1.75	3.50

TROPHY WINNERS

No.	Trophy/Player	VG	EX	NRMT
205A	Art Ross Trophy, Hart Trophy: Phil Esposito, Bos., Error	6.25	12.50	25.00
205B	Phil Esposito, Bos., Corrected	5.00	10.00	20.00
206	Lady Byng Trophy: Alex Delvecchio	1.50	3.00	6.00
207	Vezina Trophy Winners: J. Plante, G. Hall, St. L.	7.50	15.00	30.00
208	Calder Trophy: Danny Grant, Min.	.90	1.75	3.50
209	James Norris Trophy: Bobby Orr, Bos.	20.00	40.00	80.00
210	Conn Smythe Trophy: Serge Savard, Mon.	2.50	5.00	10.00

1968 - 69 NHL ALL STARS
First Team

No.	Player	VG	EX	NRMT
211	Glenn Hall, Goalie, St. L.	2.00	4.00	8.00
212	Bobby Orr, Bos.	20.00	40.00	80.00
213	Tim Horton, Tor.	1.75	3.50	7.00
214	Phil Esposito, Bos.	5.00	10.00	20.00
215	Gordie Howe, Det.	15.00	30.00	60.00
216	Bobby Hull, Chi.	10.00	20.00	40.00

Second Team

No.	Player	VG	EX	NRMT
217	Ed Giacomin, Goalie, NYR	2.00	4.00	8.00
218	Ted Green, Bos.	.90	1.75	3.50
219	Ted Harris, Mon.	.90	1.75	3.50
220	Jean Beliveau, Mon.	3.00	6.00	12.00
221	Yvan Cournoyer, Mon.	1.50	3.00	6.00
222	Frank Mahovlich, Det.	2.50	5.00	10.00

TROPHY CARDS

No.	Trophy	VG	EX	NRMT
223	The Art Ross Trophy: Highest Scoring Points in League	.95	1.85	3.75
224	The Hart Memorial Trophy: Most Valuable on Team	.95	1.85	3.75
225	The Lady Byng Trophy: Sportsmanship and Gentlemanly Conduct	.95	1.85	3.75
226	The Vezina Trophy: Goalkeeper with Least Goals in 25 Games	.95	1.85	3.75
227	The Calder Memorial Trophy: Most Proficient in First Year	.95	1.85	3.75
228	The James Norris Memorial Trophy: Best All-Round Defense Player	.95	1.85	3.75
229	The Conn Smythe Trophy: Most Valuable Player To Team in Playoffs	.95	1.85	3.75
230	The Prince of Wales Trophy: First Place Winners -East Division	.95	1.85	3.75
231	The Stanley Cup: Winner of N.H.L. Playoffs	12.50	25.00	50.00

Note: Cards in this catalogue are listed in issue date order and then alphabetically by manufacturer. See the last page of this catalogue for an alphabetical index of issuers.

— 1969 - 70 STAMPS —

The stamps were included as inserts with the regular first series set of the same year and were intended to be applied to the backs of the respective cards in that set. The Card numbers are 6, 10, 12, 20, 24, 27, 30, 33, 37, 42, 51, 54, 61, 62, 70, 76, 82, 86, 89, 98, 99, 108, 110, 114, 125, 130. However, applying the stamps will decrease the value of both items and is discouraged among collectors. The stamps are unnumbered and are listed in alphabetical order.

Card Size: 2 1/2" X 1 1/4"
Face: Two colour, black and white photo; Red cartoon hockey player
Back: Blank
Complete Set No.: 26

Complete set price:	18.75	37.50	75.00
Common Card:	.25	.50	1.00

No.	Player	VG	EX	NRMT
1	Jean Beliveau, Mon.	2.00	4.00	8.00
2	Red Berenson, St.L.	.25	.50	1.00
3	Les Binkley, Goalie, Pit.	.25	.50	1.00
4	Yvan Cournoyer, Mon.	1.50	3.00	6.00
5	Ray Cullen, Min.	.25	.50	1.00
6	Gerry Desjardins, Goalie, LA	.25	.50	1.00
7	Phil Esposito, Bos.	2.00	4.00	8.00
8	Ed Giacomin, Goalie, NYR	1.00	2.00	4.00
9	Rod Gilbert, NYR	1.00	2.00	4.00
10	Danny Grant, Min.	.25	.50	1.00
11	Glenn Hall, Goalie, St.L.	2.00	4.00	8.00
12	Ted Hampson, Cal.	.25	.50	1.00
13	Ken Hodge, Sr., Bos.	.30	.60	1.25
14	Gordie Howe, Det.	5.00	10.00	20.00
15	Bobby Hull, Chi.	3.00	6.00	12.00
16	Eddie Joyal, LA	.25	.50	1.00
17	Dave Keon, Tor.	1.50	3.00	6.00
18	Andre Lacroix, Phi.	.25	.50	1.00
19	Frank Mahovlich, Det.	2.00	4.00	8.00
20	Keith McCreary, Pit.	.25	.50	1.00
21	Stan Mikita, Chi.	1.70	3.25	6.50
22	Bobby Orr, Bos.	7.50	15.00	30.00
23	Bernie Parent, Goalie, Phi.	1.75	3.50	7.00
24	Jean Ratelle, NYR	1.00	2.00	4.00
25	Norm Ullman, Tor.	1.00	2.00	4.00
26	Carol Vadnais, Cal.	.25	.50	1.00

— 1969 - 70 QUAD MINISTICKER CARDS —

The standard size card in this set contains four ministickers, each measuring 1" X 1 1/2". Distributed as an insert with the regular second series 1969-70 O-Pee-Chee set, the player stickers were meant to be separated and placed in the team booklet described next. However, detaching the minicards will greatly devalue them. Since the cards are unnumbered, the checklist is arranged alphabetically according to the name of the player in the upper left corner.

Card Size: 2 1/2" X 3 1/2"
Face: Four colour; Name, Team, Position
Back: Blank
Imprint: TCG PRINTED IN CANADA
Complete Set No.: 72

Complete Set Price:	225.00	450.00	900.00
Common Card:	8.75	17.50	35.00

No.	Player	VG	EX	NRMT
1	Bob Baun, Det.; Ken Schinkel, Pit.; Tim Horton, Tor.; Bernie Parent, Goalie, Phi.	11.25	22.50	45.00
2	Les Binkley, Goalie, Pit.; Ken Hodge, Sr., Bos.; Reggie Fleming, Phi.; Jacques Laperriere, Mon.	8.75	17.50	35.00
3	Yvan Cournoyer, Mon.; Jim Neilson, NYR; Gary Sabourin, St.L.; John Miszuk, Min.	8.75	17.50	35.00
4	Bruce Gamble, Goalie, Tor.; Carol Vadnais, Oak.; Frank Mahovlich, Det.; Larry Hillman, Phi.	12.50	25.00	50.00
5	Ed Giacomin, Goalie, NYR; Jean Beliveau, Mon.; Eddie Joyal, LA; Leo Boivin, Min.	12.50	25.00	50.00
6	Phil Goyette, St.L.; Doug Jarrett, Chi.; Ted Green, Bos.; Bill Hicke, Oak.	8.75	17.50	35.00
7	Ted Hampson, Oak.; Carl Brewer, Det.,; Denis DeJordy, Goalie, Chi.; Leon Rochefort, LA	8.75	17.50	35.00
8	Charlie Hodge, Goalie, Oak.; Pat Quinn, Tor.; Derek Sanderson, Bos.; Duane Rupp, Pit.	8.75	17.50	35.00

O-Pee-Chee
1969-70 Stamps
Stamp No. 1,
Jean Beliveau

O-Pee-Chee
1969-70 Stamps
Stamp No. 7,
Phil Esposito

O-Pee-Chee
1969-70 Stamps
Stamp No. 9,
Rod Gilbert

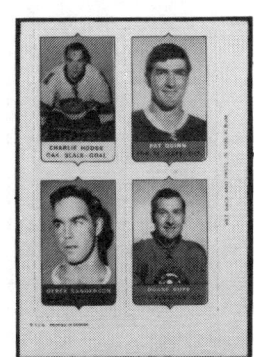

O-Pee-Chee
1969-70 Quad Ministickers
Card No. 8
Oakland Seals
C. Hodge, P. Quinn,
D. Sanderson, D. Rupp

O-Pee-Chee
1969-70 Mini-Card Albums
Album No. 1,
Boston Bruins

No.	Player	VG	EX	NRMT
9	Earl Ingarfield, Oak.; Jim Roberts, St.L.; Gump Worsley, Goalie, Mon.; Bobby Hull, Chi.	25.00	50.00	100.00
10	Andre Lacroix, Phi.; Bob Wall, LA; Serge Savard, Mon.; Roger Crozier, Goalie, Det.	8.75	17.50	35.00
11	Cesare Maniago, Goalie, Mon.; Bobby Orr, Bos.; Dave Keon, Tor.; Jean-Guy Gendron, Phi.	62.50	125.00	250.00
12	Keith McCreary, Pit.; Claude Larose, Min.; Rod Gilbert, NYR; Gerry Cheevers, Goalie, Bos.	12.50	25.00	50.00
13	Stan Mikita, Chi.; Al Arbour, St.L.; Rod Seiling, NYR; Ron Schock, Pit.	12.50	25.00	50.00
14	Doug Mohns, Chi.; Bob Woytowich, Pit.; Gordie Howe, Det.; Gerry Desjardins, Goalie, LA	37.50	75.00	150.00
15	Bob Nevin, NYR; Jacques Plante, Goalie, St.L.; Mike Walton, Tor.; Ray Cullen, Min.	12.50	25.00	50.00
16	Bob Pulford, Tor.; Henri Richard, Mon.; Red Berenson, St.L.; Eddie Shack, LA	12.50	25.00	50.00
17	Pat Stapleton, Chi.; Danny Grant, Min.; Bert Marshall, Oak.; Jean Ratelle, NYR	8.75	17.50	35.00
18	Ed Van Impe, Phi.; Dale Rolfe, LA; Alex Delvecchio, Det.; Phil Esposito, Bos.	20.00	40.00	80.00

— 1969 - 70 MINI-CARD ALBUMS —

The booklets were issued to hold the ministickers distributed as inserts with the regular second series 1969-70 O-Pee-Chee set. Each team booklet, measuring 2 3/8" X 3 1/2", contains four pages and holds six stickers.

Album Size: 2 3/8" X 3 1/2"
Face: Two colour, green and black
Back: Black on card stock
Complete Set No.: 12

Complete Set Price:	15.00	30.00	60.00
Common Card:	1.50	3.00	6.00

No.	Player	VG	EX	NRMT
1	Boston Bruins	1.50	3.00	6.00
2	Chicago Black Hawks	1.50	3.00	6.00
3	Detroit Red Wings	1.50	3.00	6.00
4	Los Angeles Kings	1.50	3.00	6.00
5	Minnesota North Stars	1.50	3.00	6.00
6	Montreal Canadiens	1.50	3.00	6.00
7	New York Rangers	1.50	3.00	6.00
8	Oakland Seals	1.50	3.00	6.00
9	Philadelphia Flyers	1.50	3.00	6.00
10	Pittsburgh Penguins	1.50	3.00	6.00
11	St. Louis Blues	1.50	3.00	6.00
12	Toronto Maple Leafs	1.50	3.00	6.00

— 1970 - 71 REGULAR ISSUE —

This was the first issue of modern hockey cards to carry the O-Pee-Chee imprint. Mint cards command a 50% price premium over NRMT cards.

PRICE MOVEMENT OF NRMT SETS

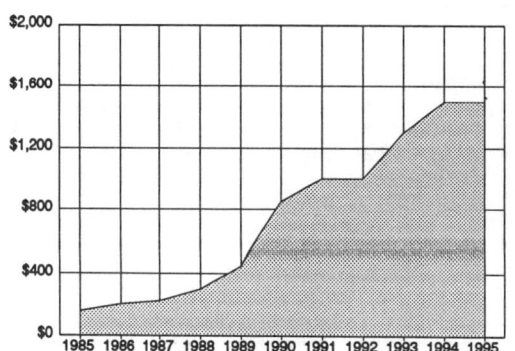

44 • O-PEE-CHEE — 1970 - 71 REGULAR ISSUE —

Card Size: 2 1/2" X 3 1/2"
Face: Four colour, white border, Position
Back: Green and black on card stock; Number, Resume, Player sketch, Bilingual
Imprint: © OPEECHEE PRINTED IN CANADA
Complet Set No.: 264

		VG	EX	NRMT
Complet Set Price:		375.00	750.00	1,500.00
Common Card:		.75	1.50	3.00

BOSTON BRUINS

No.	Player	VG	EX	NRMT
1	Gerry Cheevers, Goalie	5.00	10.00	20.00
2	John Bucyk	2.00	4.00	8.00
3	Bobby Orr	28.75	57.50	115.00
4	Don Awrey	.75	1.50	3.00
5	Fred Stanfield	.75	1.50	3.00
6	John McKenzie	.75	1.50	3.00
7	Wayne Cashman, RC	3.75	7.50	15.00
8	Ken Hodge	.75	1.50	3.00
9	Wayne Carleton	.75	1.50	3.00
10	Garnet Bailey, RC	.75	1.50	3.00
11	Phil Esposito	6.25	12.50	25.00

CHICAGO BLACK HAWKS

No.	Player	VG	EX	NRMT
12	Lou Angotti	.75	1.50	3.00
13	Jim Pappin	.75	1.50	3.00
14	Dennis Hull	.75	1.50	3.00
15	Bobby Hull	15.00	30.00	60.00
16	Doug Mohns	.75	1.50	3.00
17	Pat Stapleton	.75	1.50	3.00
18	Pit Martin	.75	1.50	3.00
19	Eric Nesterenko	.75	1.50	3.00
20	Stan Mikita	5.00	10.00	20.00

DETROIT RED WINGS

No.	Player	VG	EX	NRMT
21	Roy Edwards, Goalie	.75	1.50	3.00
22	Frank Mahovlich	3.75	7.50	15.00
23	Ron Harris	.75	1.50	3.00

CHECKLIST

No.	Checklist	VG	EX	NRMT
24	Checklist	25.00	50.00	100.00

DETROIT RED WINGS

No.	Player	VG	EX	NRMT
25	Pete Stemkowski	.75	1.50	3.00
26	Garry Unger	1.00	2.00	4.00
27	Bruce MacGregor	.75	1.50	3.00
28	Larry Jeffrey, LC	.75	1.50	3.00
29	Gordie Howe	17.50	35.00	75.00
30	Billy Dea, LC	.75	1.50	3.00

LOS ANGELES KINGS

No.	Player	VG	EX	NRMT
31	Denis DeJordy, Goalie	.75	1.50	3.00
32	Matt Ravlich, LC	.75	1.50	3.00
33	Dave Amadio, LC	.75	1.50	3.00
34	Gilles Marotte	.75	1.50	3.00
35	Eddie Shack	1.00	2.00	4.00
36	Bob Pulford	.75	1.50	3.00
37	Ross Lonsberry	.75	1.50	3.00
38	Gord Labossiere	.75	1.50	3.00
39	Eddie Joyal	.75	1.50	3.00

MINNESOTA NORTH STARS

No.	Player	VG	EX	NRMT
40	Gump Worsley, Goalie	2.50	5.00	10.00
41	Bob McCord, LC	.75	1.50	3.00
42	Leo Boivin, LC	.75	1.50	3.00
43	Tom Reid, RC	.75	1.50	3.00
44	Charlie Burns	.75	1.50	3.00
45	Bob Barlow, LC	.75	1.50	3.00
46	Bill Goldsworthy	.75	1.50	3.00
47	Danny Grant	.75	1.50	3.00
48	Norm Beaudin, RC	.75	1.50	3.00

MONTREAL CANADIENS

No.	Player	VG	EX	NRMT
49	Rogatien Vachon, Goalie	2.50	5.00	10.00
50	Yvan Cournoyer	2.50	5.00	10.00
51	Serge Savard	3.00	6.00	12.00

O-Pee-Chee
1970-71 Issue
Card No. 15,
Bobby Hull

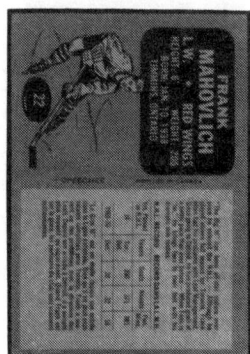

O-Pee-Chee
1970-71 Issue
Card No. 22,
Frank Mahovlich

O-Pee-Chee
1970-71 Issue
Card No. 29,
Gordie Howe

O-Pee-Chee
1970-71 Issue
Card No. 50,
Yvan Cournoyer

No.	Player	VG	EX	NRMT
52	Jacques Laperriere	.75	1.50	3.00
53	Terry Harper	.75	1.50	3.00
54	Ralph Backstrom	.75	1.50	3.00
55	Jean Beliveau, LC	4.50	9.00	18.00
56	Claude Larose	.75	1.50	3.00
57	Jacques Lemaire	1.50	3.00	6.00
58	Pete Mahovlich	.75	1.50	3.00

NEW YORK RANGERS

No.	Player	VG	EX	NRMT
59	Tim Horton	2.00	4.00	8.00
60	Bob Nevin	.75	1.50	3.00
61	Dave Balon	.75	1.50	3.00
62	Vic Hadfield	.75	1.50	3.00
63	Rod Gilbert	1.50	3.00	6.00
64	Ron Stewart	.75	1.50	3.00
65	Ted Irvine	.75	1.50	3.00
66	Arnie Brown	.75	1.50	3.00
67	Brad Park, RC	15.00	30.00	60.00
68	Ed Giacomin, Goalie	3.00	6.00	12.00

CALIFORNIA GOLDEN SEALS

No.	Player	VG	EX	NRMT
69	Gary Smith, Goalie	.75	1.50	3.00
70	Carol Vadnais	.75	1.50	3.00
71	Doug Roberts	.75	1.50	3.00
72	Harry Howell	.75	1.50	3.00
73	Joe Szura	.75	1.50	3.00
74	Mike Laughton, LC	.75	1.50	3.00
75	Gary Jarrett	.75	1.50	3.00
76	Bill Hicke	.75	1.50	3.00

PHILADELPHIA FLYERS

No.	Player	VG	EX	NRMT
77	Paul Andrea, RC, LC	.75	1.50	3.00
78	Bernie Parent, Goalie	5.00	10.00	20.00
79	Joe Watson	.75	1.50	3.00
80	Ed Van Impe	.75	1.50	3.00
81	Larry Hillman	.75	1.50	3.00
82	George Swarbrick, LC	.75	1.50	3.00

ST. LOUIS BLUES

No.	Player	VG	EX	NRMT
83	Bill Sutherland	.75	1.50	3.00

PHILADELPHIA FLYERS

No.	Player	VG	EX	NRMT
84	Andre Lacroix	.75	1.50	3.00
85	Gary Dornhoefer	.75	1.50	3.00
86	Jean Guy Gendron	.75	1.50	3.00

PITTSBURGH PENGUINS

No.	Player	VG	EX	NRMT
87	Al Smith, Goalie, RC	.75	1.50	3.00
88	Bob Woytowich	.75	1.50	3.00
89	Duane Rupp	.75	1.50	3.00
90	Jim Morrison, LC	.75	1.50	3.00
91	Ron Schock	.75	1.50	3.00
92	Ken Schinkel	.75	1.50	3.00
93	Keith McCreary	.75	1.50	3.00
94	Bryan Hextall	.75	1.50	3.00
95	Wayne Hicks, Jr., RC, LC	.75	1.50	3.00

ST. LOUIS BLUES

No.	Player	VG	EX	NRMT
96	Gary Sabourin	.75	1.50	3.00
97	Ernie Wakely, Goalie, RC	.75	1.50	3.00
98	Bob Wall	.75	1.50	3.00
99	Barclay Plager	.75	1.50	3.00
100	Jean-Guy Talbot, LC	.75	1.50	3.00
101	Gary Veneruzzo	.75	1.50	3.00
102	Tim Ecclestone	.75	1.50	3.00
103	Red Berenson	.75	1.50	3.00
104	Larry Keenan, LC	.75	1.50	3.00

TORONTO MAPLE LEAFS

No.	Player	VG	EX	NRMT
105	Bruce Gamble, Goalie	.75	1.50	3.00
106	Jim Dorey	.75	1.50	3.00

1970-71 REGULAR ISSUE — O-PEE-CHEE • 45

No.	Player	VG	EX	NRMT
107	**Mike Pelyk, RC**	.75	1.50	3.00
108	Rick Ley	.75	1.50	3.00
109	Mike Walton	.75	1.50	3.00
110	Norm Ullman	1.50	3.00	4.50

ST. LOUIS BLUES

No.	Player	VG	EX	NRMT
111a	Brit Selby "Traded to"	.75	1.50	3.00
111b	Brit Selby "No Trade"	2.00	4.00	8.00

TORONTO MAPLE LEAFS

No.	Player	VG	EX	NRMT
112	Garry Monahan	.75	1.50	3.00
113	George Armstrong, LC	1.10	2.25	3.50

VANCOUVER CANUCKS

No.	Player	VG	EX	NRMT
114	Gary Doak	.75	1.50	3.00
115	**Darryl Sly, RC, LC**	.75	1.50	3.00
116	Wayne Maki	.75	1.50	3.00
117	Orland Kurtenbach	.75	1.50	3.00
118	Murray Hall	.75	1.50	3.00
119	Marc Reaume, LC	.75	1.50	3.00
120	Pat Quinn	.75	1.50	3.00
121	Andre Boudrias	.75	1.50	3.00
122	Poul Popiel	.75	1.50	3.00

BUFFALO SABRES

No.	Player	VG	EX	NRMT
123	Paul Terbenche	.75	1.50	3.00
124	Howie Menard, LC	.75	1.50	3.00
125	**Gerry Meehan, RC**	1.00	2.00	4.00
126	Skip Krake, LC	.75	1.50	3.00
127	Phil Goyette	.75	1.50	3.00
128	Reggie Fleming	.75	1.50	3.00
129	Don Marshall	.75	1.50	3.00
130	**Bill Inglis RC, LC**	.75	1.50	3.00
131	**Gilbert Perreault, RC**	25.00	50.00	100.00

CHECKLIST

No.	Checklist	VG	EX	NRMT
132	Checklist 2	25.00	50.00	100.00

BOSTON BRUINS

No.	Player	VG	EX	NRMT
133	Eddie Johnston, Goalie	.75	1.50	3.00
134	Ted Green	.75	1.50	3.00
135	**Rick Smith, RC**	.75	1.50	3.00
136	Derek Sanderson	1.00	2.00	4.00
137	Dallas Smith	.75	1.50	3.00
138	**Don Marcotte, RC**	1.25	2.50	4.00
139	Ed Westfall	.75	1.50	3.00

BUFFALO SABRES

No.	Player	VG	EX	NRMT
140	Floyd Smith	.75	1.50	3.00
141	**Randy Wyrozub, RC, LC**	.75	1.50	3.00
142	**Cliff Schmautz, RC, LC**	.75	1.50	3.00
143	Mike McMahon	.75	1.50	3.00
144	Jim Watson	.75	1.50	3.00
145	Roger Crozier, Goalie	.75	1.50	3.00
146	Tracy Pratt	.75	1.50	3.00

CHICAGO BLACK HAWKS

No.	Player	VG	EX	NRMT
147	**Cliff Koroll, RC**	.75	1.50	3.00
148	**Gerry Pinder, RC**	.75	1.50	3.00
149	Chico Maki	.75	1.50	3.00
150	Doug Jarrett	.75	1.50	3.00
151	**Keith Magnuson, RC**	1.50	3.00	6.00
152	Gerry Desjardins, Goalie	.75	1.50	3.00
153	Tony Esposito, Goalie	15.00	30.00	60.00

DETROIT RED WINGS

No.	Player	VG	EX	NRMT
154	Gary Bergman	.75	1.50	3.00
155	**Tom Webster, RC**	1.25	2.50	5.00
156	Dale Rolfe	.75	1.50	3.00
157	Alex Delvecchio	1.50	3.00	6.00

O-Pee-Chee
1970-71 Issue
Card No. 110,
Norm Ullman

O-Pee-Chee
1970-71 Issue
Card No. 138,
Don Marcotte

O-Pee-Chee
1970-71 Issue
Card No. 145,
Roger Crozier

O-Pee-Chee
1970-71 Issue
Card No. 157,
Alex Delvecchio

No.	Player	VG	EX	NRMT
158	Nick Libett	.75	1.50	3.00
159	Wayne Connelly	.75	1.50	3.00

LOS ANGELES KINGS

No.	Player	VG	EX	NRMT
160	**Mike Byers, RC**	.75	1.50	3.00
161	Bill Flett	.75	1.50	3.00
162	Larry Mickey	.75	1.50	3.00
163	Noel Price	.75	1.50	3.00
164	Larry Cahan	.75	1.50	3.00
165	**Jack Norris, Goalie, RC**	.75	1.50	3.00

MINNESOTA NORTH STARS

No.	Player	VG	EX	NRMT
166	Ted Harris	.75	1.50	3.00
167	Murray Oliver	.75	1.50	3.00
168	J.P. Parise	.75	1.50	3.00
169	Tom Williams	.75	1.50	3.00
170	Bobby Rousseau	.75	1.50	3.00
171	**Jude Drouin, RC**	.75	1.50	3.00
172	**Walt McKechnie, RC**	.75	1.50	3.00
173	Cesare Maniago, Goalie	.75	1.50	3.00

MONTREAL CANADIENS

No.	Player	VG	EX	NRMT
174	**Rejean Houle, RC**	1.25	2.50	5.00
175	Mickey Redmond	.75	1.50	3.00
176	Henri Richard	2.00	4.00	8.00
177	**Guy Lapointe, RC**	6.00	12.00	24.00
178	J.C. Tremblay	.75	1.50	3.00
179	**Marc Tardif, RC**	1.25	2.50	5.00

NEW YORK RANGERS

No.	Player	VG	EX	NRMT
180	Walt Tkaczuk	.75	1.50	3.00
181	Jean Ratelle	1.50	3.00	6.00
182	Pete Stemkowski	.75	1.50	3.00
183	Gilles Villemure, Goalie	.75	1.50	3.00
184	Rod Seiling	.75	1.50	3.00
185	Jim Neilson	.75	1.50	3.00

CALIFORNIA GOLDEN SEALS

No.	Player	VG	EX	NRMT
186	Dennis Hextall	.75	1.50	3.00
187	Gerry Ehman, LC	.75	1.50	3.00
188	Bert Marshall	.75	1.50	3.00
189	**Gary Croteau, RC**	.75	1.50	3.00
190	Ted Hampson	.75	1.50	3.00
191	Earl Ingarfield, LC	.75	1.50	3.00
192	Dick Mattiussi, LC	.75	1.50	3.00

PHILADELPHIA FLYERS

No.	Player	VG	EX	NRMT
193	Earl Heiskala, LC	.75	1.50	3.00
194	Simon Nolet	.75	1.50	3.00
195	**Bobby Clarke, RC**	35.00	70.00	140.00
196	Garry Peters, LC	.75	1.50	3.00
197	**Lew Morrison, RC**	.75	1.50	3.00
198	Wayne Hillman	.75	1.50	3.00
199	Doug Favell, Goalie	.75	1.50	3.00

PITTSBURGH PENGUINS

No.	Player	VG	EX	NRMT
200	Les Binkley, Goalie	.75	1.50	3.00
201	Dean Prentice	.75	1.50	3.00
202	Jean Pronovost	.75	1.50	3.00
203	Wally Boyer	.75	1.50	3.00
204	Bryan Watson	.75	1.50	3.00
205	Glen Sather	.75	1.50	3.00
206	Lowell MacDonald	.75	1.50	3.00
207	Andy Bathgate, LC	1.35	1.75	3.50
208	Val Fonteyne	.75	1.50	3.00

ST. LOUIS BLUES

No.	Player	VG	EX	NRMT
209	**Jim Lorentz, RC**	.75	1.50	3.00
210	Glenn Hall, Goalie, LC	2.50	5.00	10.00
211	Bob Plager	.75	1.50	3.00
212	Noel Picard	.75	1.50	3.00

46 • O-PEE-CHEE — 1970 - 71 DECKLE EDGE —

No.	Player	VG	EX	NRMT
213	Jim Roberts	.75	1.50	3.00
214	Frank St. Marseille	.75	1.50	3.00
215	Ab McDonald	.75	1.50	3.00

TORONTO MAPLE LEAFS

No.	Player	VG	EX	NRMT
216	Brian Glennie, RC	.75	1.50	3.00
217	Paul Henderson	.75	1.50	3.00
218	Darryl Sittler, RC	31.25	62.50	125.00
219	Dave Keon	2.00	4.00	8.00
220	Jim Harrison, RC	.75	1.50	3.00
221	Ron Ellis	.75	1.50	.3.00
222	Jacques Plante, Goalie	7.50	15.00	30.00
223	Bob Baun	.75	1.50	3.00

VANCOUVER CANUCKS

No.	Player	VG	EX	NRMT
224	George Gardner, Goalie, RC	.75	1.50	3.00
225	Dale Tallon RC	1.00	2.00	4.00
226	Rosaire Paiement, RC	.75	1.50	3.00
227	Mike Corrigan, RC	.75	1.50	3.00
228	Ray Cullen, LC	.75	1.50	3.00
229	Charlie Hodge, Goalie, LC	.75	1.50	3.00
230	Len Lunde, LC	.75	1.50	3.00

SPECIAL CARDS

No.	Player	VG	EX	NRMT
231	**Special Memorial:** Terry Sawchuk, Goalie,	15.00	30.00	60.00
232	**Boston Bruins Team:** Stanley Cup Champions	3.00	6.00	12.00
233	**Esposito Line:** Hodge, Esposito, Cashman	6.25	12.50	25.00

ALL STARS
First Team

No.	Player	VG	EX	NRMT
234	Tony Esposito, Goalie, Chi.	4.50	9.00	18.00
235	Bobby Hull, Chi.	7.50	15.00	30.00
236	Bobby Orr, Bos.	15.00	30.00	60.00
237	Phil Esposito, Bos.	3.50	7.00	14.00
238	Gordie Howe, Det.	10.00	20.00	40.00
239	Brad Park, NYR	3.75	7.50	15.00

Second Team

No.	Player	VG	EX	NRMT
240	Stan Mikita, Chi.	2.00	4.00	8.00
241	John McKenzie, Bos.	.75	1.50	3.00
242	Frank Mahovlich, Det.	1.75	3.50	7.00
243	Carl Brewer, Det.	.75	1.50	3.00
244	Ed Giacomin, Goalie, NYR	1.25	2.50	4.00
245A	Jacques Laperriere, Mon. Printed on back "Gilbert Perreault Outstanding Rookie"	.75	1.50	3.00
245B	Jacques Laperriere, Mon., Plain back	.75	1.50	3.00

TROPHY WINNERS

No.	Trophy/Player	VG	EX	NRMT
246	**The Hart Memorial Trophy:** Bobby Orr	15.00	30.00	60.00
247	**The Calder Memorial Trophy:** Tony Esposito	3.00	6.00	12.00
248A	**The James Norris Memorial Trophy:** Bobby Orr, Error	15.00	30.00	60.00
248B	**The James Norris Memorial Trophy:** Bobby Orr, Corrected	15.00	30.00	60.00
249	**The Art Ross Trophy:** Bobby Orr	15.00	30.00	60.00
250	**The Vezina Trophy:** Tony Esposito	2.50	5.00	10.00
251	**The Lady Byng Memorial Trophy:** Phil Goyette	.75	1.50	3.00
252	**The Conn Smythe Trophy:** Bobby Orr	15.00	30.00	60.00
253	**The Bill Masterton Memorial Trophy:** Pit Martin	.75	1.50	3.00

TROPHY CARDS

No.	Trophy	VG	EX	NRMT
254	The Stanley Cup	1.40	2.75	5.50
255	The Prince of Wales Trophy	.85	1.75	3.50
256	The Conn Smythe Trophy	.85	1.75	3.50
257	The James Norris Memorial Trophy	.85	1.75	3.50
258	The Calder Memorial Trophy	.85	1.75	3.50

O-Pee-Chee 1970-71 Issue Card No. 233, Esposito Line Hodge, Esposito, Cashman

O-Pee-Chee 1970-71 Deckle Edge Card No. 1, Pat Quinn

O-Pee-Chee 1970-71 Deckle Edge Card No. 19, Jacques Lemaire

O-Pee-Chee 1970-71 Deckle Edge Card No. 37, Harry Howell

No.	Player	VG	EX	NRMT
259	The Vezina Trophy	.85	1.75	3.50
260	The Lady Byng Trophy	.85	1.75	3.50
261	The Hart Memorial Trophy	.85	1.75	3.50
262	The Art Ross Trophy	.85	1.75	3.50
263	The Clarence S. Campbell Bowl	.85	1.75	3.50

REGULAR ISSUE

No.	Player	VG	EX	NRMT
264	John Ferguson, Sr., LC	2.50	5.00	10.00

— 1970 - 71 DECKLE EDGE —

Issued as an insert, the black and white photographs have rough (deckle) edges.

Card Size: 2 1/4" X 3 1/4"
Face: Black and white; Facsimile autograph
Back: Number
Imprint: PRINTED IN CANADA
Complete Set No: 48
Complete Set Price: 75.00 150.00 300.00
Common Card: .50 1.00 2.00

No.	Player	VG	EX	NRMT
1	Pat Quinn, Van.	.75	1.50	3.00
2	Eddie Shack, LA	.75	1.50	3.00
3	Eddie Joyal, LA	.50	1.00	2.00
4	Bobby Orr, Bos.	12.50	25.00	50.00
5	Derek Sanderson, Bos.	.75	1.50	3.00
6	Phil Esposito, Bos.	3.75	7.50	15.00
7	Fred Stanfield, Bos.	.50	1.00	2.00
8	Bob Woytowich, Pit.	.50	1.00	2.00
9	Ron Schock, Pit.	.50	1.00	2.00
10	Les Binkley, Goalie, Pit.	.75	1.50	3.00
11	Roger Crozier, Goalie, Buf.	.75	1.50	3.00
12	Reggie Fleming, Buf.	.50	1.00	2.00
13	Charlie Burns, Min.	.50	1.00	2.00
14	Bobby Rousseau, Min.	.50	1.00	2.00
15	Leo Boivin, Min.	1.00	2.00	4.00
16	Garry Unger, Det.	.75	1.50	3.00
17	Frank Mahovlich, Det.	3.00	6.00	12.00
18	Gordie Howe, Det.	11.25	22.50	45.00
19	Jacques Lemaire, Mon.	1.25	2.50	5.00
20	Jacques Laperriere, Mon.	1.00	2.00	4.00
21	Jean Beliveau, Mon.	3.75	7.50	15.00
22	Rogatien Vachon, Goalie, Mon.	1.25	2.50	5.00
23	Yvan Cournoyer, Mon.	1.25	2.50	5.00
24	Henri Richard, Mon.	1.25	2.50	5.00
25	Red Berenson, St.L.	.75	1.50	3.00
26	Frank St. Marseille, St.L.	.50	1.00	2.00
27	Glenn Hall, Goalie, St.L.	1.75	3.50	7.00
28	Gary Sabourin, St.L.	.50	1.00	2.00
29	Doug Mohns, Chi.	.50	1.00	2.00
30	Bobby Hull, Chi.	6.25	12.50	25.00
31	Ray Cullen, Van.	.50	1.00	2.00
32	Tony Esposito, Goalie, Chi.	2.50	5.00	10.00
33	Gary Dornhoefer, Phi.	.50	1.00	2.00
34	Ed Van Impe, Phi.	.50	1.00	2.00
35	Doug Favell, Goalie, Phi.	.75	1.50	3.00
36	Carol Vadnais, Cal.	.50	1.00	2.00
37	Harry Howell, Cal.	1.00	2.00	4.00
38	Bill Hicke, Cal.	.50	1.00	2.00
39	Rod Gilbert, NYR	1.25	2.50	5.00
40	Jean Ratelle, NYR	1.25	2.50	5.00
41	Walt Tkaczuk, NYR	.75	1.50	3.00
42	Ed Giacomin, Goalie, NYR	1.75	3.50	7.00
43	Brad Park, NYR	1.75	3.50	7.00
44	Bruce Gamble, Goalie, Tor.	.50	1.00	2.00
45	Orland Kurtenbach, Van.	.75	1.50	3.00
46	Ron Ellis, Tor.	.50	1.00	2.00
47	Dave Keon, Tor.	1.50	3.00	6.00
48	Norm Ullman, Tor.	1.25	2.50	5.00

Note: Your cards must be accurately graded before they can be priced.

— 1970 - 71 STICKER STAMPS —

Issued in 1970-71 as an insert set. The peel-off sticker-like stamps are unnumbered and are listed alphabetically.

Sticker Size: 2 1/2" X 3 1/2"
Face: Four colour; Team name
Back: Blank
Imprint: ©T.C.G. PRTD. IN U.S.A.
Complete Set No.: 33

Complete Set Price:	75.00	150.00	300.00
Common Card:	.75	1.50	3.00

No.	Player	VG	EX	NRMT
1	Jean Beliveau	5.00	10.00	20.00
2	Red Berenson	.75	1.50	3.00
3	Wayne Carleton	.75	1.50	3.00
4	Tim Ecclestone	.75	1.50	3.00
5	Ron Ellis	.75	1.50	3.00
6	Phil Esposito	4.00	8.00	16.00
7	Tony Esposito, Goalie	2.50	5.00	10.00
8	Bill Flett	1.00	2.00	4.00
9	Ed Giacomin, Goalie	1.75	3.50	7.00
10	Rod Gilbert	1.25	2.50	5.00
11	Danny Grant	.75	1.50	3.00
12	Bill Hicke	.75	1.50	3.00
13	Gordie Howe	11.25	22.50	45.00
14	Bobby Hull	8.75	17.50	35.00
15	Earl Ingarfield	1.00	2.00	4.00
16	Eddie Joyal	.75	1.50	3.00
17	Dave Keon	1.50	3.00	6.00
18	Andre Lacroix	.75	1.50	3.00
19	Jacques Laperriere	1.00	2.00	4.00
20	Jacques Lemaire	1.25	2.50	5.00
21	Frank Mahovlich	3.00	6.00	12.00
22	Keith McCreary	.75	1.50	3.00
23	Stan Mikita	2.50	5.00	10.00
24	Bobby Orr	13.75	27.50	55.00
25	Jean Paul Parise	1.25	2.50	5.00
26	Jean Ratelle	1.25	2.50	5.00
27	Derek Sanderson	.75	1.50	3.00
28	Frank St. Marseille	.75	1.50	3.00
29	Ron Schock	.75	1.50	3.00
30	Garry Unger	.75	1.50	3.00
31	Carol Vadnais	.75	1.50	3.00
32	Ed Van Impe	.75	1.50	3.00
33	Bob Woytowich	.75	1.50	3.00

— 1971 - 72 REGULAR ISSUE —

Mint cards command a 50% price premium over NRMT cards.

PRICE MOVEMENT OF NRMT SETS

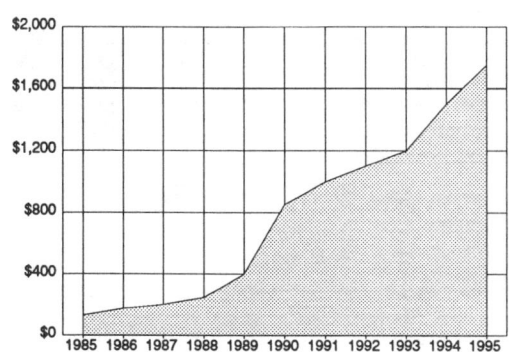

Card Size: 2 1/2" X 3 1/2"
Face: Four colour, white border, Team logo, Position
Back: Green and black on card stock, Number, Resume; Hockey trivia, Bilingual
Imprint: © OPEECHEE PRINTED IN CANADA
Complete Set No.: 264

Complete Set Price:	400.00	800.00	1,750.00
Common Card:	.75	1.50	3.00

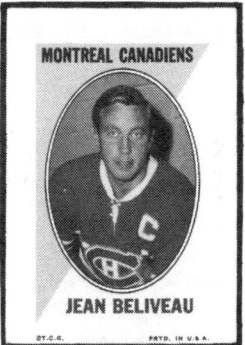

O-Pee-Chee
1970-71 Sticker Stamps
Stamp No. 1,
Jean Beliveau

O-Pee-Chee
1971-72 Issue
Card No. 1,
Poul Popiel

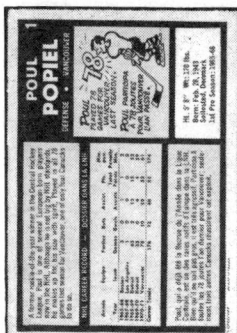

O-Pee-Chee
1971-72 Issue
Card No. 1,
Poul Popiel

O-Pee-Chee
1971-72 Issue
Card No. 5,
Guy Trottier

— 1970 - 71 STICKER STAMPS — O-PEE-CHEE • 47

No.	Player	VG	EX	NRMT
1	Poul Popiel, Van.	1.00	2.00	4.00
2	**Pierre Bouchard, Mon., RC**	**1.25**	**2.50**	**5.00**
3	Don Awrey, Bos.	.75	1.50	3.00
4	**Paul Curtis, LA, RC**	**.75**	**1.50**	**3.00**
5	**Guy Trottier, Tor., RC**	**.75**	**1.50**	**3.00**
6	**Paul Shmyr, CA, RC**	**.75**	**1.50**	**3.00**
7	Fred Stanfield, Bos.	.75	1.50	3.00
8	**Mike Robitaille, Buf., RC**	**.75**	**1.50**	**3.00**
9	Vic Hadfield, NYR	.75	1.50	3.00
10	Jim Harrison, Tor.	.75	1.50	3.00
11	Bill White, Chi.	.75	1.50	3.00
12	Andre Boudrias, Van.	.75	1.50	3.00
13	Gary Sabourin, St. L.	.75	1.50	3.00
14	Arnie Brown, Det.	.75	1.50	3.00
15	Yvan Cournoyer, Mon.	2.00	4.00	8.00
16	Bryan Hextall, Jr., Pit.	.75	1.50	3.00
17	Gary Croteau, Ca.	.75	1.50	3.00
18	Gilles Villemure, Goalie, NYR	.75	1.50	3.00
19	**Serge Bernier, Phi., RC**	**.75**	**1.50**	**3.00**
20	Phil Esposito, Bos.	5.00	10.00	20.00
21	Tom Reid, Min.	.75	1.50	3.00
22	**Doug Barrie, Buf., RC**	**.75**	**1.50**	**3.00**
23	Eddie Joyal, LA	.75	1.50	3.00
24	**Dunc Wilson, Goalie, Van., RC**	**.75**	**1.50**	**3.00**
25	Pat Stapleton, Chi.	.75	1.50	3.00
26	Garry Unger, St. L., Error	.75	1.50	3.00
27	Al Smith, Goalie, Det.	.75	1.50	3.00
28	Bob Woytowich, Pit.	.75	1.50	3.00
29	Marc Tardif, Mon., Error	.75	1.50	3.00
30	Norm Ullman, Tor.	.85	1.75	3.50
31	Tom Williams, Ca.	.75	1.50	3.00
32	Ted Harris, Min.	.75	1.50	3.00
33	Andre Lacroix, Phi.	.75	1.50	3.00
34	Mike Byers, LA, LC	.75	1.50	3.00
35	John Bucyk, Bos	1.50	3.00	6.00
36	Roger Crozier, Goalie, Buf.	.75	1.50	3.00
37	Alex Delvecchio, Det.	1.50	3.00	6.00
38	Frank St. Marseille, St. L.	.75	1.50	3.00
39	Pit Martin, Chi.	.75	1.50	3.00
40	Brad Park, NYR	5.00	10.00	20.00
41	**Greg Polis, Pit., RC**	**.75**	**1.50**	**3.00**
42	Orland Kurtenbach, Van.	.75	1.50	3.00
43	**Jim McKenny, Tor., RC**	**.75**	**1.50**	**3.00**
44	Bob Nevin, Min.	.75	1.50	3.00
45	**Ken Dryden, Goalie, Mon., RC**	**80.00**	**175.00**	**350.00**
46	Carol Vadnais, Ca.	.75	1.50	3.00
47	Bill Flett, LA	.75	1.50	3.00
48	Jim Johnson, Phi., LC	.75	1.50	3.00
49	Al Hamilton, Buf.	.75	1.50	3.00
50	Bobby Hull, Chi.	12.50	25.00	50.00
51	**Chris Bordeleau, St. L., RC**	**.75**	**1.50**	**3.00**
52	Tim Ecclestone, Det.	.75	1.50	3.00
53	Rod Seiling, NYR	.75	1.50	3.00
54	Gerry Cheevers, Goalie, Bos.	2.00	4.00	8.00
55	Bill Goldsworthy, Min.	.75	1.50	3.00
56	Ron Schock, Pit.	.75	1.50	3.00
57	Jim Dorey, Tor.	.75	1.50	3.00
58	Wayne Maki, Van.	.75	1.50	3.00
59	Terry Harper, Mon.	.75	1.50	3.00
60	Gilbert Perreault, Buf.	7.50	15.00	30.00
61	**Ernie Hicke, Ca., RC**	**.75**	**1.50**	**3.00**
62	Wayne Hillman, Phi.	.75	1.50	3.00
63	Denis DeJordy, Goalie, LA	.75	1.50	3.00
64	Ken Schinkel, Pit.	.75	1.50	3.00
65	Derek Sanderson, Bos.	.75	1.50	3.00
66	Barclay Plager, St. L.	.75	1.50	3.00
67	Paul Henderson, Tor.	.75	1.50	3.00
68	Jude Drouin, Min.	.75	1.50	3.00
69	Keith Magnuson, Chi.	.75	1.50	3.00
70	Ron Harris, Det.	.75	1.50	3.00
71	Jacques Lemaire, Mon.	1.00	2.00	4.00
72	Doug Favell, Goalie, Phi.	.75	1.50	3.00
73	Bert Marshall, Ca.	.75	1.50	3.00
74	Ted Irvine, NYR	.75	1.50	3.00
75	Walt Tkaczuk, NYR	.75	1.50	3.00
76	**Bob Berry, LA, RC**	**.75**	**1.50**	**3.00**
77	**Syl Apps, Jr., Pit., RC**	**.75**	**1.50**	**3.00**
78	Tom Webster, Det.	.75	1.50	3.00
79	Danny Grant, Min.	.75	1.50	3.00
80	Dave Keon, Tor.	1.00	2.00	4.00
81	Ernie Wakely, Goalie, St. L.	.75	1.50	3.00
82	John McKenzie, Bos.	.75	1.50	3.00
83	**Ron Stackhouse, Ca., RC**	**.75**	**1.50**	**3.00**

48 • O-PEE-CHEE — 1971-72 REGULAR ISSUE —

No.	Player	VG	EX	NRMT
84	Pete Mahovlich, Mon.	.75	1.50	3.00
85	Dennis Hull, Chi.	.75	1.50	3.00
86	**Juha Widing, LA, RC**	**.75**	**1.50**	**3.00**
87	Gary Doak, Van.	.75	1.50	3.00
88	Phil Goyette, Buf., LC	.75	1.50	3.00
89	Lew Morrison, Phi.	.75	1.50	3.00
90	**Ab DeMarco, NYR, RC**	**.75**	**1.50**	**3.00**
91	Red Berenson, Det.	.75	1.50	3.00
92	Mike Pelyk, Tor.	.75	1.50	3.00
93	Gary Jarrett, Ca.	.75	1.50	3.00
94	Bob Pulford, LA, LC	.75	1.50	3.00
95	**Danny Johnson, Van., RC, LC**	**.75**	**1.50**	**3.00**
96	Eddie Shack, Buf.	.75	1.50	3.00
97	Jean Ratelle, NYR	1.25	2.50	5.00
98	Jim Pappin, Chi.	.75	1.50	3.00
99	Roy Edwards, Goalie, Pit.	.75	1.50	3.00
100	Bobby Orr, Bos.	22.50	45.00	90.00
101	Ted Hampson, Min., LC	.75	1.50	3.00
102	Mickey Redmond, Det.	1.00	2.00	4.00
103	Bob Plager, St. L.	.75	1.50	3.00
104	**Barry Ashbee, Phi., RC**	**1.00**	**2.00**	**4.00**
105	Frank Mahovlich, Mon.	3.00	6.00	12.00
106	**Dick Redmond, Ca., RC**	**.75**	**1.50**	**3.00**
107	Tracy Pratt, Buf.	.75	1.50	3.00
108	Ralph Backstrom, LA	.75	1.50	3.00
109	Murray Hall, Van.	.75	1.50	3.00
110	Tony Esposito, Goalie, Chi.	7.50	12.50	25.00
111	Checklist 1 (1 - 132)	95.00	190.00	375.00
112	Jim Neilson, NYR	.75	1.50	3.00
113	Ron Ellis, Tor.	.75	1.50	3.00
114	Bobby Clarke, Phi.	10.00	20.00	40.00
115	Ken Hodge, Sr., Bos.	.75	1.50	3.00
116	Jim Roberts, St. L.	.75	1.50	3.00
117	Cesare Maniago, Goalie, Min.	.75	1.50	3.00
118	Jean Pronovost, Pit.	.75	1.50	3.00
119	Gary Bergman, Det.	.75	1.50	3.00
120	Henri Richard, Mon.	1.25	2.50	5.00
121	Ross Lonsberry, LA	.75	1.50	3.00
122	Pat Quinn, Van.	.75	1.50	3.00
123	Rod Gilbert, NYR	1.25	2.50	5.00
124	Walt McKechnie, Ca.	.75	1.50	3.00
125	Stan Mikita, Chi.	3.75	7.50	15.00
126	Ed Van Impe, Phi.	.75	1.50	3.00
127	**Terry Crisp, St. L., RC**	**1.75**	**3.50**	**7.00**
128	**Fred Barrett, Min., RC**	**.75**	**1.50**	**3.00**
129	Wayne Cashman, Bos.	.85	1.75	3.50
130	J. C. Tremblay, Mon.	.75	1.50	3.00
131	Bernie Parent, Goalie, Tor.	3.00	6.00	12.00
132	Bryan Watson, Pit.	.75	1.50	3.00

DETROIT RED WINGS

No.	Player	VG	EX	NRMT
133	**Marcel Dionne, RC**	**31.25**	**62.50**	**125.00**
134	Ab McDonald	.75	1.50	3.00
135	Leon Rochefort	.75	1.50	3.00
136	**Serge Lajeunesse, RC, LC**	**.75**	**1.50**	**3.00**
137	Joe Daley, Goalie	.75	1.50	3.00
138	Brian Conacher, LC	.75	1.50	3.00
139	Bill Collins	.75	1.50	3.00
140	Nick Libett	.75	1.50	3.00
141	Bill Sutherland, LC	.75	1.50	3.00
142	Bill Hicke	.75	1.50	3.00

MONTREAL CANADIENS

No.	Player	VG	EX	NRMT
143	Serge Savard	1.00	2.00	4.00
144	Jacques Laperriere	.75	1.50	3.00
145	Guy Lapointe, Error	1.00	2.00	4.00
146	Claude Larose, Error	.75	1.50	3.00
147	Rejean Houle	.75	1.50	3.00
148	**Guy Lafleur, RC, Error**	**50.00**	**100.00**	**200.00**
149	**Dale Hoganson, RC**	**.75**	**1.50**	**3.00**

LOS ANGELES KINGS

No.	Player	VG	EX	NRMT
150	**Al McDonough, RC**	**.75**	**1.50**	**3.00**
151	Gilles Marotte	.75	1.50	3.00
152	**Butch Goring, RC**	**3.75**	**7.50**	**15.00**
153	Harry Howell	.75	1.50	3.00
154	Real Lemieux	.75	1.50	3.00
155	**Gary Edwards, Goalie, RC**	**.75**	**1.50**	**3.00**
156	Rogatien Vachon, Goalie	1.50	3.00	6.00

O-Pee-Chee
1971-72 Issue
Card No. 148, Error, Name misspelled
LaFleur on face and back

O-Pee-Chee
1971-72 Issue
Card No. 186,
Tim Horton

O-Pee-Chee
1971-72 Issue
Card No. 193,
Darryl Sittler

O-Pee-Chee
1971-72 Issue
Card No. 195,
Jacques Plante

No.	Player	VG	EX	NRMT
157	Mike Corrigan	.75	1.50	3.00

BUFFALO SABRES

No.	Player	VG	EX	NRMT
158	Floyd Smith	.75	1.50	3.00
159	Dave Dryden, Goalie	.75	1.50	3.00
160	Gerry Meehan	.75	1.50	3.00
161	**Rick Martin, RC**	**5.00**	**10.00**	**20.00**
162	**Steve Atkinson, RC**	**.75**	**1.50**	**3.00**
163	Ron C. Anderson	.75	1.50	3.00
164	Dick Duff, LC	.75	1.50	3.00
165	Jim Watson, LC	.75	1.50	3.00
166	**Don Luce, RC**	**.75**	**1.50**	**3.00**
167	Larry Mickey, LC	.75	1.50	3.00
168	Larry Hillman	.75	1.50	3.00

BOSTON BRUINS

No.	Player	VG	EX	NRMT
169	Ed Westfall	.75	1.50	3.00
170	Dallas Smith	.75	1.50	3.00
171	Mike Walton	.75	1.50	3.00
172	Eddie Johnston, Goalie	.75	1.50	3.00
173	Ted Green	.75	1.50	3.00
174	Rick Smith	.75	1.50	3.00
175	**Reggie Leach, RC**	**4.00**	**8.00**	**16.00**
176	Don Marcotte	.75	1.50	3.00

CALIFORNIA GOLDEN SEALS

No.	Player	VG	EX	NRMT
177	**Bobby Sheehan, RC**	**.75**	**1.50**	**3.00**
178	Wayne Carleton	.75	1.50	3.00
179	Norm Ferguson	.75	1.50	3.00
180	**Don O'Donoghue, RC, LC**	**.75**	**1.50**	**3.00**
181	**Gary Kurt, Goalie, RC**	**.75**	**1.50**	**3.00**
182	**Joey Johnston, RC**	**.75**	**1.50**	**3.00**
183	**Stan Gilbertson, RC**	**.75**	**1.50**	**3.00**
184	**Craig Patrick, RC**	**1.25**	**2.50**	**5.00**
185	Gerry Pinder	.75	1.50	3.00

PITTSBURGH PENGUINS

No.	Player	VG	EX	NRMT
186	Tim Horton	1.25	2.50	5.00
187	**Darryl Edestrand, RC**	**.75**	**1.50**	**3.00**
188	Keith McCreary	.75	1.50	3.00
189	Val Fonteyne	.75	1.50	3.00
190	**Sheldon Kannegiesser, RC**	**.75**	**1.50**	**3.00**
191	**Nick Harbaruk, RC**	**.75**	**1.50**	**3.00**
192	Les Binkley, Goalie	.75	1.50	3.00

TORONTO MAPLE LEAFS

No.	Player	VG	EX	NRMT
193	**Darryl Sittler**	**11.25**	**22.50**	**45.00**
194	Rick Ley	.75	1.50	3.00
195	Jacques Plante, Goalie	5.50	11.00	22.00
196	Bobby Baun	.75	1.50	3.00
197	Brian Glennie	.75	1.50	3.00
198	**Brian Spencer, RC**	**.75**	**1.50**	**3.00**
199	Don Marshall, LC	.75	1.50	3.00
200	**Denis Dupere, RC**	**.75**	**1.50**	**3.00**

PHILADELPHIA FLYERS

No.	Player	VG	EX	NRMT
201	Bruce Gamble, Goalie, LC	.75	1.50	3.00
202	Gary Dornhoefer	.75	1.50	3.00
203	**Bob Kelly, RC**	**1.00**	**2.00**	**4.00**
204	Jean-Guy Gendron	.75	1.50	3.00
205	Brent Hughes	.75	1.50	3.00
206	Simon Nolet	.75	1.50	3.00
207	**Rick MacLeish, RC**	**5.00**	**10.00**	**20.00**

CHICAGO BLACK HAWKS

No.	Player	VG	EX	NRMT
208	Doug Jarrett	.75	1.50	3.00
209	Cliff Koroll	.75	1.50	3.00
210	Chico Maki	.75	1.50	3.00
211	Danny O'Shea	.75	1.50	3.00
212	Lou Angotti	.75	1.50	3.00
213	Eric Nesterenko, LC	.75	1.50	3.00
214	Bryan Campbell	.75	1.50	3.00

NEW YORK RANGERS

No.	Player	VG	EX	NRMT
215	Bill Fairbairn, RC	.75	1.50	3.00
216	Bruce MacGregor	.75	1.50	3.00
217	Pete Stemkowski	.75	1.50	3.00
218	Bobby Rousseau	.75	1.50	3.00
219	Dale Rolfe	.75	1.50	3.00
220	Ed Giacomin, Goalie	2.50	5.00	10.00
221	Glen Sather	1.25	2.50	5.00

ST. LOUIS BLUES

No.	Player	VG	EX	NRMT
222	Carl Brewer, LC	.75	1.50	3.00
223	George Morrison, RC	.75	1.50	3.00
224	Noel Picard	.75	1.50	3.00
225	Pete McDuffe, Goalie, RC, Error	.75	1.50	3.00
226	Brit Selby, LC	.75	1.50	3.00
227	Jim Lorentz	.75	1.50	3.00
228	Phil Roberto, RC	.75	1.50	3.00

VANCOUVER CANUCKS

No.	Player	VG	EX	NRMT
229	Dave Balon	.75	1.50	3.00
230	Barry Wilkins, RC	.75	1.50	3.00
231	Dennis Kearns, RC	.75	1.50	3.00
232	Jocelyn Guevremont, RC	1.00	2.00	4.00
233	Rosaire Paiement	.75	1.50	3.00
234	Dale Tallon	.75	1.50	3.00
235	George Gardner, Goalie, LC	.75	1.50	3.00
236	Ron Stewart, LC	.75	1.50	3.00
237	Wayne Connelly	.75	1.50	3.00

MINNESOTA NORTH STARS

No.	Player	VG	EX	NRMT
238	Charlie Burns	.75	1.50	3.00
239	Murray Oliver	.75	1.50	3.00
240	Lou Nanne	.75	1.50	3.00
241	Gump Worsley, Goalie	2.00	4.00	8.00
242	Doug Mohns	.75	1.50	3.00
243	J. P. Parise	.75	1.50	3.00
244	Dennis Hextall	.75	1.50	3.00

TROPHY WINNERS

No.	Trophy/Player	VG	EX	NRMT
245	**James Norris Memorial Trophy, The Hart Memorial Trophy:** Bobby Orr, Bos.	12.50	25.00	50.00
246	**The Calder Memorial Trophy:** Gilbert Perreault, Buf.	3.00	6.00	12.00
247	**The Art Ross Trophy:** Phil Esposito, Bos.	2.50	5.00	10.00
248	**The Vezina Trophy:** E. Giacomin, G. Villemure, NYR	1.25	2.50	5.00
249	**The Lady Byng Memorial Trophy:** John Bucyk Bos.	1.00	2.00	4.00

1970 - 71 ALL STARS
First Team

No.	Player	VG	EX	NRMT
250	Ed Giacomin, Goalie, NYR	1.50	3.00	6.00
251	Bobby Orr, Bos.	13.75	27.50	55.00
252	J. C. Tremblay, Mon.	.75	1.50	3.00
253	Phil Esposito, Bos.	2.50	5.00	10.00
254	Ken Hodge, Sr., Bos.	.75	1.50	3.00
255	John Bucyk, Bos.	.85	1.75	3.50

Second Team

No.	Player	VG	EX	NRMT
256	Jacques Plante, Goalie, Tor., Error	2.00	4.00	8.00
257	Brad Park, NYR	1.25	2.50	5.00
258	Pat Stapleton, Chi.	.75	1.50	3.00
259	Dave Keon, Tor.	1.25	2.50	5.00
260	Yvan Cournoyer, Mon.	1.25	2.50	5.00
261	Bobby Hull, Chi.	6.25	12.50	25.00

SPECIAL COLLECTOR'S CARD

No.	Player	VG	EX	NRMT
262	Gordie Howe, Mr. Hockey	20.00	40.00	80.00
263	Jean Beliveau, Le Gros Bill	8.75	17.50	35.00

O-Pee-Chee 1971-72 Issue Card No. 245, James Norris Trophy Hart Memorial Trophy Bobby Orr

O-Pee-Chee 1971-72 Issue Card No. 262, Gordie Howe, Mr. Hockey

O-Pee-Chee 1971-72 Booklets Booklet No. 10, The Bobby Clarke Story

O-Pee-Chee 1971-72 Booklets Booklet No. 17, The Ken Dryden Story

— 1971 - 72 BOOKLETS — O-PEE-CHEE • 49

CHECKLIST

No.	Checklist	VG	EX	NRMT
264	Checklist 2 (133 - 264)	37.50	75.00	150.00

— 1971 - 72 BOOKLETS —

These eight-page comic style booklets were issued as inserts with the regular 1971-72 O-Pee-Chee set. The back cover is a checklist. The inside story is a brief history of the player.

Booklet Size: 2 1/2" X 3 1/2"
Face: Four colour on paper stock; Name, Number
Back: Four colour; Checklist
Imprint: O-PEE-CHEE Printed in Canada
Complete Set No.: 24

Complete Set Price:	17.50	35.00	75.00
Common Card:	.30	.60	1.25

No.	Player	VG	EX	NRMT
1	Bobby Hull, Chi.	2.50	5.00	10.00
2	Phil Esposito, Bos.	1.50	3.00	6.00
3	Dale Tallon, Van.	.30	.60	1.25
4	Jacques Plante, Goalie, Tor.	1.25	2.50	5.00
5	Roger Crozier, Goalie, Buf.	.30	.60	1.25
6	Henri Richard, Mon.	.60	1.25	2.50
7	Ed Giacomin, Goalie, NYR	.75	1.50	3.00
8	Gilbert Perreault, Buf.	.75	1.50	3.00
9	Greg Polis, Pit.	.30	.60	1.25
10	Bobby Clarke, Phi.	.75	1.50	3.00
11	Danny Grant, Min.	.30	.60	1.25
12	Alex Delvecchio, Det.	.50	1.00	2.00
13	Tony Esposito, Goalie, Chi.	.60	1.25	2.50
14	Garry Unger, St.L.	.30	.60	1.25
15	Frank St. Marseille, St.L.	.30	.60	1.25
16	Dave Keon, Tor.	.75	1.50	3.00
17	Ken Dryden, Goalie, Mon.	3.00	6.00	12.00
18	Rod Gilbert, NYR	.50	1.00	2.00
19	Juha Widing, LA	.30	.60	1.25
20	Orland Kurtenbach, Van.	.30	.60	1.25
21	Jude Drouin, Min.	.30	.60	1.25
22	Gary Smith, Goalie, Ca.	.30	.60	1.25
23	Gordie Howe, Det.	3.25	6.50	13.00
24	Bobby Orr, Bos.	3.75	7.50	15.00

— 1971 - 72 POSTERS —

Posters are numbered _ of 24. Most posters have the player's facsimile autograph. The numbered posters were issued on their own, without cards, packaged folded with two to a wax pack.

Poster Size: 9 15/16" X 17 7/8"
Face: Four colour on coated newsprint; Bilingual
Back: Blank
Imprint: © O.P.C. PRINTED IN CANADA
Complete Set No.: 24

Complete Set Price:	150.00	300.00	600.00
Common Card:	3.00	6.00	12.00

No.	Player	VG	EX	NRMT
1	Bobby Orr, Bos.	27.50	55.00	110.00
2	Bob Pulford, LA	5.00	10.00	20.00
3	Dave Keon, Tor.	6.25	12.50	25.00
4	Yvan Cournoyer, Mon.	6.25	12.50	25.00
5	Dale Tallon, Van.	2.50	5.00	10.00
6	Richard Martin, Buf.	3.00	6.00	12.00
7	Rod Gilbert, NYR	6.25	12.50	25.00
8	Tony Esposito, Goalie, Chi.	8.75	17.50	35.00
9	Bobby Hull, Chi.	12.50	25.00	50.00
10	Red Berenson, Det.	3.75	7.50	15.00
11	Norm Ullman, Tor.	5.00	10.00	20.00
12	Orland Kurtenbach, Van.	3.75	7.50	15.00
13	Guy Lafleur, Mon.	10.00	21.00	42.00
14	Gilbert Perreault, Buf.	6.25	12.50	25.00
15	Jacques Plante, Goalie, Tor.	8.75	17.50	35.00
16	Bruce Gamble, Goalie, Phi.	2.50	5.00	10.00
17	Walt McKechnie, Ca.	2.50	5.00	10.00
18	Tim Horton, Pit.	7.50	15.00	30.00
19	Jean Ratelle, NYR	6.25	12.50	25.00
20	Garry Unger, St.L.	3.75	7.50	15.00
21	Phil Esposito, Bos.	7.50	15.00	30.00
22	Ken Dryden, Goalie, Mon.	8.75	17.50	35.00
23	Gump Worsley, Goalie, Min.	6.25	12.50	25.00
24	Club de Hockey Canadien 1970-71	5.00	10.00	20.00

For an illustration of the 1971-72 Posters see page no. 71.

— 1972 - 73 REGULAR ISSUE —

Card numbers 1 to 289 are NHL. Card number 208 was not issued. Card numbers 290 to 341 are WHA.
Mint cards, due to their coloured borders, command a 50% to 75% price premium over NRMT cards.

PRICE MOVEMENT OF NRMT SETS

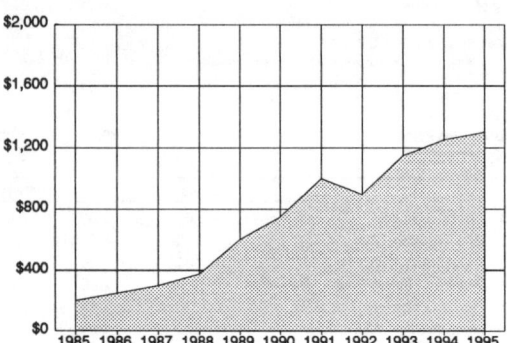

Card Size: 2 1/2" X 3 1/2"
Face: Four colour, beige border, Team logo
Back: Orange and black on card stock; Number, Resume, Hockey trivia, Bilingual
Imprint: © O.P.C. PRINTED IN CANADA
Complete Set No.: 341

Complete Set Price:	325.00	650.00	1,300.00
Common (1 - 110):	.35	.75	1.50
Common (111 - 209):	.50	1.00	2.00
Common (210 - 289):	.65	1.25	2.50
Common (290 - 341):	2.00	4.00	8.00

NATIONAL HOCKEY LEAGUE

No.	Player	VG	EX	NRMT
1	John Bucyk, Bos.	2.00	4.00	8.00
2	**Rene Robert, Buf., RC**	1.25	2.50	5.00
3	Gary Croteau, Ca.	.35	.75	1.50
4	Pat Stapleton, Chi.	.35	.75	1.50
5	Ron Harris, Atl.	.35	.75	1.50
6	Checklist 1(1 - 110)	8.75	17.50	35.00
7	1971 - 72 NHL Playoffs: Game 1 at Boston	.35	.75	1.50
8	Marcel Dionne, Det.	10.00	20.00	40.00
9	Bob Berry, LA	.35	.75	1.50
10	Lou Nanne, Min.	.35	.75	1.50
11	Marc Tardif, Mon.	.35	.75	1.50
12	Jean Ratelle, NYR	1.00	2.00	4.00
13	**Craig Cameron, NYI, RC**	.35	.75	1.50
14	Bobby Clarke, Phi.	5.00	10.00	20.00
15	**Jim Rutherford, Goalie, Pit., RC**	1.75	3.50	7.00
16	**Andre Dupont, St. L., RC**	.75	1.50	3.00
17	Mike Pelyk, Tor.	.35	.75	1.50
18	Dunc Wilson, Goalie, Van.	.35	.75	1.50
19	Checklist, Error	8.75	17.50	35.00
20	1971 - 72 NHL Playoffs: Game 2 at Boston	.35	.75	1.50
21	Dallas Smith, Bos.	.35	.75	1.50
22	Gerry Meehan, Buf.	.35	.75	1.50
23	Rick Smith, Ca., Error	.35	.75	1.50
24	Pit Martin, Chi.	.35	.75	1.50
25	Keith McCreary, Atl.	.35	.75	1.50
26	Alex Delvecchio, Det.	1.00	2.00	4.00
27	Gilles Marotte, LA	.35	.75	1.50
28	Gump Worsley, Goalie, Min.	1.25	2.50	5.00
29	Yvan Cournoyer, Mon.	1.25	2.50	5.00
30	1971 - 72 NHL Playoffs: Game 3 at New York	.35	.75	1.50
31	Vic Hadfield, NYR	.35	.75	1.50
32	**Tom Miller, NYI, RC**	.35	.75	1.50
33	Ed Van Impe, Phi.	.35	.75	1.50
34	Greg Polis, Pit.	.35	.75	1.50
35	Barclay Plager, St. L.	.35	.75	1.50
36	Ron Ellis, Tor.	.35	.75	1.50
37	Jocelyn Guevremont, Van.	.35	.75	1.50

O-Pee-Chee
1972-73 Issue
Card No. 1,
John Bucyk

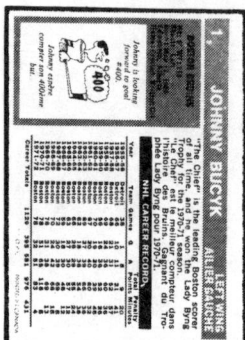

O-Pee-Chee
1972-73 Issue
Card No. 1,
John Bucyk

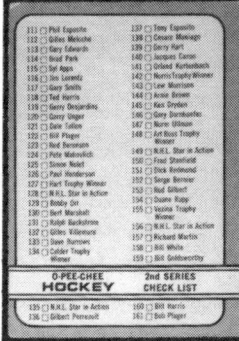

O-Pee-Chee
1972-73 Issue
Card No. 19, Error,
Same as Card No. 190

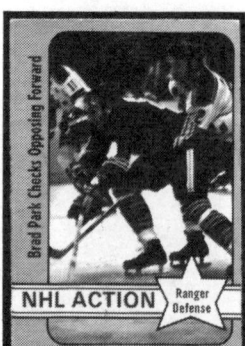

O-Pee-Chee
1972-73 Issue
Card No. 85B, Corrected
Brad Park as Defense

No.	Player	VG	EX	NRMT
38	1971 - 72 NHL Playoffs: Game 4 at New York	.35	.75	1.50
39	Carol Vadnais, Bos.	.35	.75	1.50
40	Steve Atkinson, Buf.	.35	.75	1.50
41	**Ivan Boldirev, Ca., RC**	.75	1.50	3.00
42	Jim Pappin, Chi.	.35	.75	1.50
43	Phil Myre, Goalie, Atl., RC	1.25	2.50	5.00
44	NHL Action: Yvan Cournoyer Sidesteps the Defence	.75	1.50	3.00
45	Nick Libett, Det.	.35	.75	1.50
46	Juha Widing, LA	.35	.75	1.50
47	Jude Drouin, Min.	.35	.75	1.50
48A	NHL Action: Jean Ratelle Digs For The Puck., (Defence), Error	1.50	3.00	6.00
48B	NHL Action: Jean Ratelle Digs For The Puck, (Centre), Corrected	.75	1.50	3.00
49	Ken Hodge, Sr., Bos.	.35	.75	1.50
50	Roger Crozier, Goalie, Buf.	.50	1.00	2.00
51	Reggie Leach, Ca.	1.00	2.00	4.00
52	Dennis Hull, Chi.	.35	.75	1.50
53	**Larry Hale, Atl., RC, LC**	.35	.75	1.50
54	1971 - 72 NHL Playoffs: Game 5 at Boston	.35	.75	1.50
55	Tim Ecclestone, Det.	.35	.75	1.50
56	Butch Goring, LA	1.00	2.00	4.00
57	Danny Grant, Min.	.35	.75	1.50
58	NHL Action: Bobby Orr On The Offensive	7.50	15.00	30.00
59	Guy Lafleur, Mon.	12.50	25.00	50.00
60	Jim Neilson, NYR	.35	.75	1.50
61	Brian Spencer, NYI	.35	.75	1.50
62	Joe Watson, Phi.	.35	.75	1.50
63	1971 - 72 NHL Playoffs: Game 6 at New York	.50	1.00	2.00
64	Jean Pronovost, Pit.	.35	.75	1.50
65	Frank St. Marseille, St. L.	.35	.75	1.50
66	Bob Baun, Tor., LC	.35	.75	1.50
67	Poul Popiel, Van.	.35	.75	1.50
68	Wayne Cashman, Bos.	.50	1.00	2.00
69	Tracy Pratt, Buf.	.35	.75	1.50
70	Stan Gilbertson, Ca.	.35	.75	1.50
71	Keith Magnuson, Chi.	.35	.75	1.50
72	Ernie Hicke, Atl.	.35	.75	1.50
73	Gary Doak, Det.	.35	.75	1.50
74	Mike Corrigan, LA	.35	.75	1.50
75	Doug Mohns, Min.	.35	.75	1.50
76	NHL Action: Phil Esposito Standing In The "Slot"	1.75	3.50	7.00
77	Jacques Lemaire, Mon.	1.00	2.00	4.00
78	Pete Stemkowski, NYR	.35	.75	1.50
79	**Bill Mikkelson, NYI, RC**	.35	.75	1.50
80	**Rick Foley, Phi., RC, LC**	.35	.75	1.50
81	Ron Schock, Pit.	.35	.75	1.50
82	Phil Roberto, St. L.	.35	.75	1.50
83	Jim McKenny, Tor.	.35	.75	1.50
84	Wayne Maki, Van., LC	.35	.75	1.50
85A	NHL Action: Brad Park Checks Opposing Forward, Error	2.00	4.00	8.00
85B	NHL Action: Brad Park Checks Opposing Forward, Corrected	1.00	2.00	4.00
86	Guy Lapointe, Mon.	.65	1.25	2.50
87	Bill Fairbairn, NYR	.35	.75	1.50
88	Terry Crisp, NYI	.50	1.00	2.00
89	Doug Favell, Goalie, Phi.	.35	.75	1.50
90	Bryan Watson, Pit.	.35	.75	1.50
91	Gary Sabourin, St. L.	.35	.75	1.50
92	Jacques Plante, Goalie, Tor.	3.75	7.50	15.00
93	Andre Boudrias, Van.	.35	.75	1.50
94	Mike Walton, Bos.	.35	.75	1.50
95	Don Luce, NYR	.35	.75	1.50
96	Joey Johnston, Ca.	.35	.75	1.50
97	Doug Jarrett, Chi.	.35	.75	1.50
98	**Billy MacMillan, Atl., RC**	.35	.75	1.50
99	Mickey Redmond, Det.	.65	1.25	2.50
100	Rogatien Vachon, Goalie, LA, Error	1.00	2.00	4.00
101	**Barry Gibbs, Min., RC**	.35	.75	1.50
102	Frank Mahovlich, Mon.	2.00	4.00	8.00
103	Bruce MacGregor, NYR	.35	.75	1.50
104	Ed Westfall, NYI	.35	.75	1.50
105	Rick MacLeish, Phi.	1.75	3.50	7.00
106	Nick Harbaruk, Pit.	.35	.75	1.50
107	**Jack Egers, St. L., RC**	.35	.75	1.50
108	Dave Keon, Tor.	.85	1.75	3.50
109	Barry Wilkins, Van.	.35	.75	1.50

— 1972 - 73 REGULAR ISSUE — O-PEE-CHEE • 51

No.	Player	VG	EX	NRMT
110	**NHL Action:** Walt Tkaczuk In On Boston Goal	.35	.75	1.50 ☐
111	Phil Esposito, Bos.	3.50	7.00	14.00 ☐
112	**Gilles Meloche, Goalie, Ca., RC**	**2.00**	**4.00**	**8.00** ☐
113	Gary Edwards, Goalie, LA	.50	1.00	2.00 ☐
114	Brad Park, NYR	2.50	5.00	10.00 ☐
115	Syl Apps, Jr., Pit.	.50	1.00	2.00 ☐
116	Jim Lorentz, Buf.	.50	1.00	2.00 ☐
117	Gary Smith, Goalie, Chi.	.50	1.00	2.00 ☐
118	Ted Harris, Min.	.50	1.00	2.00 ☐
119	Gerry Desjardins, Goalie, NYI	.50	1.00	2.00 ☐
120	Garry Unger, St. L.	.50	1.00	2.00 ☐
121	Dale Tallon, Van.	.50	1.00	2.00 ☐
122	**William Plager, Atl., RC, LC**	**.50**	**1.00**	**2.00** ☐
123	Red Berenson, Det.	.50	1.00	2.00 ☐
124	Pete Mahovlich, Mon.	.50	1.00	2.00 ☐
125	Simon Nolet, Phi.	.50	1.00	2.00 ☐
126	Paul Henderson, Tor.	.50	1.00	2.00 ☐
127	**Hart Memorial Trophy:** Bobby Orr, Bos.	.75	1.50	3.00 ☐
128	**NHL Action:** Montreal Vs. Toronto	1.25	2.50	5.00 ☐
129	Bobby Orr, Bos.	15.00	30.00	60.00 ☐
130	Bert Marshall, Ca.	.50	1.00	2.00 ☐
131	Ralph Backstrom, LA	.50	1.00	2.00 ☐
132	Gilles Villemure, Goalie, NYR	.50	1.00	2.00 ☐
133	**Dave Burrows, Pit., RC**	**.50**	**1.00**	**2.00** ☐
134	**Calder Trophy:** Ken Dryden, Mon.	.75	1.50	3.00 ☐
135	**NHL Action:** Boston vs. Toronto	.50	1.00	2.00 ☐
136	Gilbert Perreault, Buf.	3.75	7.50	15.00 ☐
137	Tony Esposito, Goalie, Chi.	3.75	7.50	15.00 ☐
138	Cesare Maniago, Goalie, Min.	.50	1.00	2.00 ☐
139	**Gerry Hart, NYI, RC**	**.50**	**1.00**	**2.00** ☐
140	**Jacques Caron, Goalie, St. L., RC, LC**	**.50**	**1.00**	**2.00** ☐
141	Orland Kurtenbach, Van.	.50	1.00	2.00 ☐
142	**James Norris Trophy:** Bobby Orr, Bos.	.75	1.50	3.00 ☐
143	Lew Morrison, Atl.	.50	1.00	2.00 ☐
144	Arnie Brown, NYI	.50	1.00	2.00 ☐
145	Ken Dryden, Goalie, Mon.	13.75	27.50	55.00 ☐
146	Gary Dornhoefer, Phi.	.50	1.00	2.00 ☐
147	Norm Ullman, Tor.	.80	1.60	3.25 ☐
148	**Art Ross Trophy:** Phil Esposito, Bos.	.85	1.75	3.50 ☐
149	**NHL Action:** Vancouver vs. Toronto	.50	1.00	2.00 ☐
150	Fred Stanfield, Bos.	.50	1.00	2.00 ☐
151	Dick Redmond, Ca.	.50	1.00	2.00 ☐
152	Serge Bernier, LA	.50	1.00	2.00 ☐
153	Rod Gilbert, NYR	1.00	2.00	4.00 ☐
154	Duane Rupp, Pit.	.50	1.00	2.00 ☐
155	**Vezina Trophy:** T. Esposito, G. Smith, Chi.	.75	1.50	3.00 ☐
156	**NHL Action:** Chicago vs. Toronto	1.25	2.50	5.00 ☐
157	Rick Martin, Buf.	1.00	2.00	4.00 ☐
158	Bill White, Chi.	.50	1.00	2.00 ☐
159	Bill Goldsworthy, Min.	.50	1.00	2.00 ☐
160	**Jack Lynch, Pit., RC**	**.50**	**1.00**	**2.00** ☐
161	Bob Plager, St. L.	.50	1.00	2.00 ☐
162	Dave Balon, Van., LC, Error	.50	1.00	2.00 ☐
163	Noel Price, Atl.	.50	1.00	2.00 ☐
164	Gary Bergman, Det.	.50	1.00	2.00 ☐
165	Pierre Bouchard, Mon.	.50	1.00	2.00 ☐
166	Ross Lonsberry, Phi.	.50	1.00	2.00 ☐
167	Denis Dupere, Tor.	.50	1.00	2.00 ☐
168	**Lady Byng Trophy:** Jean Ratelle, NYR	.75	1.50	3.00 ☐
169	**NHL Action:** Boston vs. Toronto	.50	1.00	2.00 ☐
170	Don Awrey, Bos.	.50	1.00	2.00 ☐
171	**Marshall Johnston, Ca., RC**	**.50**	**1.00**	**2.00** ☐
172	Terry Harper, LA	.50	1.00	2.00 ☐
173	Ed Giacomin, Goalie, NYR	1.25	2.50	5.00 ☐
174	Bryan Hextall, Jr., Pit.	.50	1.00	2.00 ☐
175	**Conn Smythe Trophy:** Bobby Orr, Bos.	.75	1.50	3.00 ☐
176	Larry Hillman, Buf., LC	.50	1.00	2.00 ☐
177	Stan Mikita, Chi.	3.00	6.00	12.00 ☐
178	Charlie Burns, Min., LC	.50	1.00	2.00 ☐
179	**Brian Marchinko, NYI, RC, LC**	**.50**	**1.00**	**2.00** ☐
180	Noel Picard, St. L.	.50	1.00	2.00 ☐
181	**Bobby Schmautz, Van., RC**	**1.00**	**2.00**	**4.00** ☐
182	**NHL Action:** Buffalo vs. Toronto, Error	.75	1.50	3.00 ☐
183	Pat Quinn, Atl.	.50	1.00	2.00 ☐
184	Denis DeJordy, Goalie, Det., LC, Error	.50	1.00	2.00 ☐
185	Serge Savard, Mon.	.85	1.75	3.50 ☐
186	**NHL Action:** Pittsburgh vs. Toronto	.50	1.00	2.00 ☐
187	Bill Flett, Phi.	.50	1.00	2.00 ☐
188	Darryl Sittler, Tor.	5.00	10.00	20.00 ☐
189	**NHL Action:** Minnesota vs. Toronto	1.00	2.00	4.00 ☐
190	Checklist	8.75	17.50	35.00 ☐

O-Pee-Chee, 1972-73 Issue Card No. 100, Error, Name misspelled Ragatien on back

O-Pee-Chee, 1972-73 Issue Card No. 162, Error, Name misspelled Ballon on back

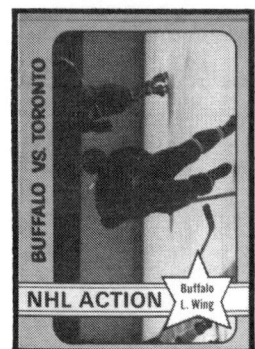

O-Pee-Chee, 1972-73 Issue Card No. 182, Error, NHL Action card shows Gilbert Perreault should be Rick Martin

O-Pee-Chee, 1972-73 Issue Card No. 227, Bobby Orr, Brad Park

No.	Player	VG	EX	NRMT
191	Garnet Bailey, Bos.	.50	1.00	2.00 ☐
192	Walt McKechnie, Ca.	.50	1.00	2.00 ☐
193	Harry Howell, LA, LC	.65	1.25	2.50 ☐
194	Rod Seiling, NYR	.50	1.00	2.00 ☐
195	Darryl Edestrand, Pit.	.50	1.00	2.00 ☐
196	**NHL Action:** Chicago vs. Toronto	1.50	3.00	6.00 ☐
197	Tim Horton, Buf.	1.00	2.00	4.00 ☐
198	Chico Maki, Chi.	.50	1.00	2.00 ☐
199	J. P. Parise, Min.	.50	1.00	2.00 ☐
200	**Germaine Gagnon, NYI, RC**	**.50**	**1.00**	**2.00** ☐
201	Danny O'Shea, St. L., LC	.50	1.00	2.00 ☐
202	**Richard Lemieux, Van., RC**	**.50**	**1.00**	**2.00** ☐
203	**Dan Bouchard, Goalie, Atl., RC**	**1.00**	**2.00**	**4.00** ☐
204	Leon Rochefort, Det.	.50	1.00	2.00 ☐
205	Jacques Laperriere, Mon.	.65	1.25	2.50 ☐
206	Barry Ashbee, Phi., LC	.50	1.00	2.00 ☐
207	Garry Monahan, Tor.	.35	.75	1.50 ☐
208	Not issued			
209	**NHL Action:** Toronto vs. Chicago	.75	1.50	3.00 ☐
210	Rejean Houle, Mon.	.65	1.25	2.50 ☐
211	**Dave Hudson, NYI, RC**	**.65**	**1.25**	**2.50** ☐
212	Ted Irvine, NYR	.65	1.25	2.50 ☐
213	**Don Saleski, Phi., RC**	**1.50**	**3.00**	**6.00** ☐
214	Lowell MacDonald, Pit.	.65	1.25	2.50 ☐
215	**Mike Murphy, St. L., RC**	**.65**	**1.25**	**2.50** ☐
216	Brian Glennie, Tor.	.65	1.25	2.50 ☐
217	**Bobby Lalonde, Van., RC**	**.65**	**1.25**	**2.50** ☐
218	**Bobby Leiter, Atl., RC**	**.65**	**1.25**	**2.50** ☐
219	Don Marcotte, Bos.	.65	1.25	2.50 ☐
220	**Jim Schoenfeld, Buf., RC**	**2.50**	**5.00**	**10.00** ☐
221	Craig Patrick, Ca.	1.25	2.50	5.00 ☐
222	Cliff Koroll, Chi.	.65	1.25	2.50 ☐
223	**Guy Charron, Det., RC**	**.65**	**1.25**	**2.50** ☐
224	Jimmy Peters, LA	.65	1.25	2.50 ☐
225	Dennis Hextall, Min.	.65	1.25	2.50 ☐

1971 - 72 NHL ALL STARS
First Team

No.	Player	VG	EX	NRMT
226	Tony Esposito, Goalie, Chi.	2.00	4.00	8.00 ☐
227	B. Orr, Bos.; B. Park, NYR	9.50	19.00	38.00 ☐
228	Bobby Hull, Chi.	6.00	12.00	24.00 ☐
229	Rod Gilbert, NYR	1.00	2.00	4.00 ☐
230	Phil Esposito, Bos.	2.50	5.00	10.00 ☐

REGULAR ISSUE

No.	Player	VG	EX	NRMT
231	Claude Larose, Mon., LC, Error	.65	1.25	2.50 ☐
232	**Jim Mair, NYI, RC, LC**	**.65**	**1.25**	**2.50** ☐
233	Bobby Rousseau, NYR	.65	1.25	2.50 ☐
234	Brent Hughes, St. L.	.65	1.25	2.50 ☐
235	Al McDonough, Pit.	.65	1.25	2.50 ☐
236	**Chris Evans, St. L., RC**	**.65**	**1.25**	**2.50** ☐
237	Pierre Jarry, Tor., RC	.65	1.25	2.50 ☐
238	**Don Tannahill, Van., RC**	**.65**	**1.25**	**2.50** ☐
239	**Rey Comeau, Atl., RC**	**.65**	**1.25**	**2.50** ☐
240	**Gregg Sheppard, Bos., RC, Error**	**.65**	**1.25**	**2.50** ☐
241	Dave Dryden, Goalie, Buf.	.65	1.25	2.50 ☐
242	**Ed McAneeley, Ca., RC**	**.65**	**1.25**	**2.50** ☐
243	Lou Angotti, Chi.	.65	1.25	2.50 ☐
244	**Len Fontaine, Det., RC, LC**	**.65**	**1.25**	**2.50** ☐
245	**Bill Lesuk, LA, RC**	**.65**	**1.25**	**2.50** ☐
246	Fred (Buster) Harvey, Min.	.65	1.25	2.50 ☐

1971-72 NHL ALL STARS
Second Team

No.	Player	VG	EX	NRMT
247	Ken Dryden, Goalie, Mon.	7.50	15.00	30.00 ☐
248	Bill White, Chi.	.65	1.25	2.50 ☐
249	Pat Stapleton, Chi.	.65	1.25	2.50 ☐
250	V. Hadfield, NYR, J. Ratelle, NYR, Y. Cournoyer, Mon.	1.75	3.50	7.00 ☐

REGULAR ISSUE

No.	Player	VG	EX	NRMT
251	Henri Richard, Mon.	1.75	3.50	7.00 ☐
252	**Bryan Lefley, NYI, RC**	**.65**	**1.25**	**2.50** ☐
253	**Stanley Cup Trophy:** Boston Bruins	2.00	4.00	8.00 ☐
254	**Steve Vickers, NYR, RC**	**1.75**	**3.50**	**7.00** ☐
255	Wayne Hillman, Phi., LC	.65	1.25	2.50 ☐
256	Ken Schinkel, Pit., LC, Error	.65	1.25	2.50 ☐
257	**Kevin O'Shea, St. L., RC, LC**	**.65**	**1.25**	**2.50** ☐

52 • O-PEE-CHEE — 1972-73 PLAYER CREST STICKERS —

No.	Player	VG	EX	NRMT
258	Ron Low, Tor., Goalie, RC	1.25	2.50	5.00
259	Don Lever, Van., RC	1.25	2.50	5.00
260	Randy Manery, Atl., RC	.75	1.25	2.50
261	Eddie Johnston, Goalie, Bos.	.65	1.25	2.50
262	Craig Ramsay, Buf., RC	1.50	3.00	6.00
263	Pete Laframboise, Ca., RC	.75	1.25	2.50
264	Dan Maloney, Chi., RC	1.00	2.00	4.00
265	Bill Collins, Det.	.65	1.25	2.50
266	Paul Curtis, LA, LC	.65	1.25	2.50
267	Bob Nevin, Min.	.65	1.25	2.50
268	1971/2 NHL Penalty Mins. Leaders: B. Watson, Pit., K. Magnuson, Chi. G. Dornhoefer, Phi.	.65	1.25	2.50
269	Jim Roberts, Mon.	.65	1.25	2.50
270	Brian Lavender, NYI, RC, LC	.65	1.25	2.50
271	Dale Rolfe, NYR	.65	1.25	2.50
272	1971/2 NHL Goals Leaders: P. Esposito, Bos., V. Hadfield, NYR, B. Hull, Chi.	3.75	7.50	15.00
273	Michel Belhumeur, Goalie, Phi., RC	1.00	2.00	4.00
274	Eddie Shack, Pit.	1.00	2.00	4.00
275	Wayne Stephenson, Goalie, St. L., RC	1.25	2.50	5.00
276	1971-72 Stanley Cup Champions: Boston Bruins	2.00	4.00	8.00
277	Rick Kehoe, Tor., RC	2.50	5.00	10.00
278	Gerry O'Flaherty, Van., RC, Error	.75	1.25	2.50
279	Jacques Richard, Atl., RC	.75	1.25	2.50
280	1971/2 NHL Scoring Leaders: P. Esposito, Bos., B. Orr, Bos., J. Ratelle, NYR	6.25	12.50	25.00
281	Nick Beverley, Bos., RC	1.50	3.00	6.00
282	Larry Carriere, Buf., RC	1.00	2.00	4.00
283	1971/2 NHL Assist Leaders: B. Orr, Bos., P. Esposito, Bos., J. Ratelle, NYR	6.25	12.50	25.00
284	Rick Smith, Ca., Error	.75	1.25	2.50
285	Jerry Korab, Chi., RC	1.25	2.50	5.00
286	1971/72 Goals Against Avg. Leaders: T. Esposito, Chi., G. Villemure, NYR, G. Worsley, Min.	2.00	4.00	8.00
287	Ron Stackhouse, Det.	.75	1.25	2.50
288	Barry Long, LA, RC	1.00	2.00	4.00
289	Dean Prentice, Min., LC	.75	1.25	2.50

WORLD HOCKEY ASSOCIATION

No.	Player	VG	EX	NRMT
290	Norm Beaudin, WiN.	2.00	4.00	8.00
291	Mike Amodeo, OtN, RC	2.00	4.00	8.00
292	Jim Harrison, AlO	2.00	4.00	8.00
293	J. C. Tremblay, QuN.	2.00	4.00	8.00
294	Murray Hall, HoA., LC	2.00	4.00	8.00
295	Bart Crashley, LAS, LC	2.00	4.00	8.00
296	Wayne Connelly, MFS.	2.00	4.00	8.00
297	Bobby Sheehan, NeR	2.00	4.00	8.00
298	Ron C. Anderson, ChC., RC	2.00	4.00	8.00
299	Chris Bordeleau, WiN.	2.00	4.00	8.00
300	Les Binkley, Goalie, OtN., LC	2.00	4.00	8.00
301	Ron Walters, AlO., RC, LC	2.00	4.00	8.00
302	Jean-Guy Gendron, QuN., LC	2.00	4.00	8.00
303	Gord Labossiere, HoA.	2.00	4.00	8.00
304	Gerry Odrowski, LAS	2.00	4.00	8.00
305	Mike McMahon, MFS., LC	2.00	4.00	8.00
306	Gary Kurt, Goalie, NeR	2.00	4.00	8.00
307	Larry Cahan, ChC., LC	2.00	4.00	8.00
308	Wally Boyer, WiN., LC	2.00	4.00	8.00
309	Bob Charlebois, OtN., RC, LC	2.00	4.00	8.00
310	Bob Falkenberg, AlO., LC	2.00	4.00	8.00
311	Jean Payette, QuN., RC, LC	2.00	4.00	8.00
312	Ted Taylor, HoA., LC	2.00	4.00	8.00
313	Joe Szura, LAS, LC	2.00	4.00	8.00
314	George Morrison, MFS., LC	2.00	4.00	8.00
315	Wayne Rivers, NeR	2.00	4.00	8.00
316	Reggie Fleming, ChC., LC	2.00	4.00	8.00
317	Larry Hornung, WiN., RC, LC	2.00	4.00	8.00
318	Ron Climie, OtN., RC	2.00	4.00	8.00
319	Val Fonteyne, AlO., LC	2.00	4.00	8.00
320	Michel Archambault, QuN., RC, LC	2.00	4.00	8.00
321	Ab McDonald, WiN., LC	2.00	4.00	8.00
322	Bob Leduc, OtN., RC, LC	2.00	4.00	8.00
323	Bob Wall, AlO., LC	2.00	4.00	8.00
324	Alain Caron, QuN., RC, LC	2.00	4.00	8.00
325	Bob Woytowich, WiN.	2.00	4.00	8.00
326	Guy Trottier, OtN., LC	2.00	4.00	8.00
327	Bill Hicke, AlO., LC	2.00	4.00	8.00

O-Pee-Chee
1972-73 Issue
Card No. 337, Error,
Name misspelled
Carlton on face

O-Pee-Chee
1972-73 Player Crest Stickers
Sticker No. 22, Orland Kurtenbach

O-Pee-Chee
1972-73 Team Logo Stickers
Sticker No. 4, Buffalo Sabres

O-Pee-Chee
1972-73 Team Logo Stickers
Sticker No. 7, Detroit Red Wings

No.	Player	VG	EX	NRMT
328	Guy Dufour, QuN., RC, LC	2.00	4.00	8.00
329	Wayne Rutledge, HoA., Goalie, RC	2.00	4.00	8.00
330	Gary Veneruzzo, LAS	2.00	4.00	8.00
331	Fred Speck, MFS., RC, LC	2.00	4.00	8.00
332	Ron Ward, NeR, RC	2.00	4.00	8.00
333	Rosaire Paiement, ChC.	2.00	4.00	8.00
334A	Checklist 3, (210-341) Error	12.50	25.00	50.00
334B	Checklist 3, Corrected	12.50	25.00	50.00
335	Michel Parizeau, QuN., RC	2.00	4.00	8.00
336	Bobby Hull, WiN.	17.50	35.00	70.00
337	Wayne Carleton, OtN., Error	2.00	4.00	8.00
338	John McKenzie, PhB.	2.00	4.00	8.00
339	Jim Dorey, NEW	2.00	4.00	8.00
340	Gerry Cheevers, Goalie, CIC.	7.50	15.00	30.00
341	Gerry Pinder, CIC.	3.00	6.00	12.00

— 1972-73 PLAYER CREST STICKERS —

The player crest stickers were issued as an insert with the regular first series set of the same year. Removing the pop-out crests from the cards is not recommended. Stickers are numbered _ of 22

Sticker Size: 2 1/2" X 3 1/2"
Face: Four colour on card stock; Name, Number, Postion, Team
Back: Blank
Imprint: None
Complete Set No.: 22
Complete Set Price: 17.50   35.00   70.00
Common Card: .55   1.15   2.25

No.	Player	VG	EX	NRMT
1	Pat Quinn, Atl.	.55	1.15	2.25
2	Phil Esposito, Bos.	2.50	5.00	10.00
3	Bobby Orr, Bos.	8.75	17.50	35.00
4	Richard Martin, Buf.	.55	1.15	2.25
5	Stan Mikita, Chi.	2.00	4.00	8.00
6	Bill White, Chi.	.55	1.15	2.25
7	Red Berenson, Det.	.55	1.15	2.25
8	Gary Bergman, Det.	.55	1.15	2.25
9	Gary Edwards, Goalie, LA	.55	1.15	2.25
10	Bill Goldsworthy, Min.	.55	1.15	2.25
11	Jacques Laperriere, Mon.	.75	1.50	3.00
12	Ken Dryden, Goalie, Mon.	4.00	8.00	16.00
13	Ed Westfall, NYI	.55	1.15	2.25
14	Walt Tkaczuk, NYR	.55	1.15	2.25
15	Brad Park, NYR	1.25	2.50	5.00
16	Doug Favell, Goalie, Phi.	.55	1.15	2.25
17	Eddie Shack, Pit.	.60	1.25	2.50
18	Jacques Caron, Goalie, St.L.	.55	1.15	2.25
19	Paul Henderson, Tor.	.55	1.15	2.25
20	Jim Harrison, AlO	.55	1.15	2.25
21	Dale Tallon, Van.	.55	1.15	2.25
22	Orland Kurtenbach, Van.	.55	1.15	2.25

— 1972-73 TEAM LOGO STICKERS —

The 1972-73 stickers have application instructions on the face distinguishing them from the 1973-74 Team Logo Stickers. Removing the pop-out logo from the card is not recommended.

Sticker Size: 2 1/2" X 3 1/2"
Face: Four colour
Back: Blank
Imprint: None
Complete Set No.: 30
Complete Set Price: 8.75   17.50   35.00
Common NHL: .30   .60   1.25
Common WHA   .35   .75   1.50

No.	Player	VG	EX	NRMT
1	NHL Logo	.30	.60	1.25
2	Atlanta Flames	.30	.60	1.25
3	Boston Bruins	.30	.60	1.25
4	Buffalo Sabres	.30	.60	1.25
5	California Golden Seals	.30	.60	1.25
6	Chicago Black Hawks	.30	.60	1.25
7	Detroit Red Wings	.30	.60	1.25
8	Los Angeles Kings	.30	.60	1.25
9	Minnesota North Stars	.30	.60	1.25
10	Montreal Canadiens	.30	.60	1.25
11	New York Islanders	.30	.60	1.25
12	New York Rangers	.30	.60	1.25

No.	Team	VG	EX	NRMT
13	Philadelphia Flyers	.30	.60	1.25 ☐
14	Pittsburgh Penguins	.30	.60	1.25 ☐
15	St. Louis Blues	.30	.60	1.25 ☐
16	Toronto Maple Leafs	.30	.60	1.25 ☐
17	Vancouver Canucks	.30	.60	1.25 ☐
18	WHA Logo	.35	.75	1.50 ☐
19	Chicago Cougars	.35	.75	1.50 ☐
20	Cleveland Crusaders	.35	.75	1.50 ☐
21	Edmonton Oilers	.35	.75	1.50 ☐
22	Houston Aeros	.35	.75	1.50 ☐
23	Los Angeles Sharks	.35	.75	1.50 ☐
24	Minnesota Fighting Saints	.35	.75	1.50 ☐
25	New England Whalers	.35	.75	1.50 ☐
26	New York Raiders	.35	.75	1.50 ☐
27	Ottawa Nationals	.35	.75	1.50 ☐
28	Philadelphia Blazers	.35	.75	1.50 ☐
29	Quebec Nordiques	.35	.75	1.50 ☐
30	Winnipeg Jets	.35	.75	1.50 ☐

— 1973 - 74 REGULAR ISSUE —

This set was produced from two different card stocks; one light beige and the other grey. Cards 1 to 132 have a red border while cards 133 to 264 were printed with a green border. These full colour borders mark easily, making mint cards difficult to find.

The set price listed below is for a set with mixed card stocks. A set printed on uniform card stock would command a premium over this price. Mint cards will command a price premium of 50 to 75% over NRMT cards.

PRICE MOVEMENT OF NRMT SETS

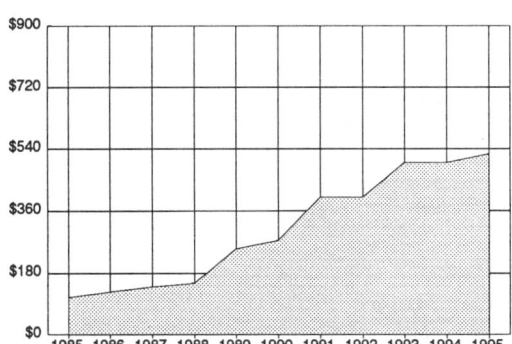

Card Size: 2 1/2" X 3 1/2"
Face: Four colour, red or green border, Position
Back: Dark and light brown on light beige or grey card stock, Number, Resume, Hockey trivia, Bilingual
Imprint: © O.P.C. PRINTED IN CANADA
Complete Set No.: 264

Complete Set Price:		130.00	260.00	525.00 ☐
Common Card:		.25	.50	1.00

No.	Player	VG	EX	NRMT
1	Alex Delvecchio, Det., LC	1.50	3.00	6.00 ☐
2	Gilles Meloche, Ca., Goalie	.35	.75	1.50 ☐
3	Phil Roberto, St. L.	.25	.50	1.00 ☐
4	Orland Kurtenbach, Van., LC	.25	.50	1.00 ☐
5	Gilles Marotte, LA	.25	.50	1.00 ☐
6	Stan Mikita, Chi.	2.00	4.00	8.00 ☐
7	Paul Henderson, Tor.	.25	.50	1.00 ☐
8	Gregg Sheppard, Bos., Error	.25	.50	1.00 ☐
9	Rod Seiling, NYR	.25	.50	1.00 ☐
10	Red Berenson, Det.	.25	.50	1.00 ☐
11	Jean Pronovost, Pit.	.25	.50	1.00 ☐
12	Dick Redmond, Chi.	.25	.50	1.00 ☐
13	Keith McCreary, Atl.	.25	.50	1.00 ☐
14	Bryan Watson, Pit.	.25	.50	1.00 ☐
15	Garry Unger, St. L.	.35	.75	1.50 ☐
16	**Neil Komadoski, LA, RC**	**.25**	**.50**	**1.00** ☐
17	Marcel Dionne, Det.	5.00	10.00	20.00 ☐
18	Ernie Hicke, NYI	.25	.50	1.00 ☐
19	Andre Boudrias, Van.	.25	.50	1.00 ☐
20	'72-73 NHL All-Stars, West: Bill Flett, Phi.	.25	.50	1.00 ☐
21	Marshall Johnston, Ca., LC	.25	.50	1.00 ☐

O-Pee-Chee
1973-74 Issue
Card No. 1,
Alex Delvecchio

O-Pee-Chee
1973-74 Issue
Card No. 1,
Alex Delvecchio

O-Pee-Chee, 1973-74 Issue
Card No. 8, Error,
Name misspelled
Greg on face and back

O-Pee-Chee
1973-74 Issue
Card No. 50,
Bobby Clarke

No.	Player	VG	EX	NRMT
22	Gerry Meehan, Buf.	.25	.50	1.00 ☐
23	Eddie Johnston, Goalie, Tor.	.35	.75	1.50 ☐
24	Serge Savard, Mon.	.65	1.25	2.50 ☐
25	Walt Tkaczuk, NYR	.25	.50	1.00 ☐
26	Ken Hodge, Bos.	.25	.50	1.00 ☐
27	Norm Ullman, Tor.	.65	1.25	2.50 ☐
28	Cliff Koroll, Chi.	.25	.50	1.00 ☐
29	Rey Comeau, Alt.	.25	.50	1.00 ☐
30	'72-73 NHL All-Stars, East: Bobby Orr, Bos.	12.50	25.00	50.00 ☐
31	Wayne Stephenson, Goalie, St. L.	.35	.75	1.50 ☐
32	Dan Maloney, LA	.25	.50	1.00 ☐
33	**Henry Boucha, Det., RC**	**.25**	**.50**	**1.00** ☐
34	Gerry Hart, NYI	.25	.50	1.00 ☐
35	Bobby Schmautz, Van.	.25	.50	1.00 ☐
36	Ross Lonsberry, Phi.	.25	.50	1.00 ☐
37	Ted McAneeley, Ca.	.25	.50	1.00 ☐
38	Don Luce, Buf.	.25	.50	1.00 ☐
39	Jim McKenny, Tor.	.25	.50	1.00 ☐
40	Jacques Laperriere, Mon.	.40	.85	1.75 ☐
41	Bill Fairbairn, NYR	.25	.50	1.00 ☐
42	Craig Cameron, NYI	.25	.50	1.00 ☐
43	Bryan Hextall, Jr., Pit.	.25	.50	1.00 ☐
44	**Chuck Lefley, Mon., RC**	**.25**	**.50**	**1.00** ☐
45	Dan Bouchard, Goalie, Atl.	.35	.75	1.50 ☐
46	J. P. Parise, Min.	.25	.50	1.00 ☐
47	Barclay Plager, St. L.	.25	.50	1.00 ☐
48	Mike Corrigan, LA	.25	.50	1.00 ☐
49	Nick Libett, Det.	.25	.50	1.00 ☐
50	'72-73 NHL All-Stars, West: Bobby Clarke, Phi.	4.50	9.00	18.00 ☐
51	Bert Marshall, NYI	.25	.50	1.00 ☐
52	Craig Patrick, Ca.	.25	.50	1.00 ☐
53	Richard Lemieux, Van.	.25	.50	1.00 ☐
54	Tracy Pratt, Buf.	.25	.50	1.00 ☐
55	Ron Ellis, Tor.	.25	.50	1.00 ☐
56	Jacques Lemaire, Mon.	.75	1.50	3.00 ☐
57	Steve Vickers, NYR	.25	.50	1.00 ☐
58	Carol Vadnais, Bos.	.25	.50	1.00 ☐
59	Jim Rutherford, Goalie, Pit.	.35	.75	1.50 ☐
60	Rick Kehoe, Tor.	.25	.50	1.00 ☐
61	Pat Quinn, Atl.	.25	.50	1.00 ☐
62	Bill Goldsworthy, Min.	.25	.50	1.00 ☐
63	Dave Dryden, Goalie, Buf.	.35	.75	1.50 ☐
64	Rogatien Vachon, Goalie, LA	.75	1.50	3.00 ☐
65	Gary Bergman, Det.	.25	.50	1.00 ☐
66	Bernie Parent, Goalie, Phi.	1.75	3.50	7.00 ☐
67	Ed Westfall, NYI	.25	.50	1.00 ☐
68	Ivan Boldirev, Ca.	.25	.50	1.00 ☐
69	Don Tannahill, Van., LC	.25	.50	1.00 ☐
70	Gilbert Perreault, Buf.	2.50	5.00	10.00 ☐
71	Mike Pelyk, Tor.	.25	.50	1.00 ☐
72	Guy Lafleur, Mon.	7.50	15.00	30.00 ☐
73	Pit Martin, Chi.	.25	.50	1.00 ☐
74	**Gilles Gilbert, Goalie, Bos., RC**	**1.25**	**2.50**	**5.00** ☐
75	Jim Lorentz, Buf.	.25	.50	1.00 ☐
76	Syl Apps, Jr., Pit.	.25	.50	1.00 ☐
77	Phil Myre, Goalie, Atl.	.35	.75	1.50 ☐
78	'72-73 NHL All-Stars, West: Bill White, Chi.	.25	.50	1.00 ☐
79	Jack Egers, St. L.	.25	.50	1.00 ☐
80	Terry Harper, LA	.25	.50	1.00 ☐
81	**Bill Barber, Phi., RC**	**7.50**	**15.00**	**30.00** ☐
82	Roy Edwards, Goalie, Det., LC	.35	.75	1.50 ☐
83	Brian Spencer, NYI	.25	.50	1.00 ☐
84	Reggie Leach, Ca.	.50	1.00	2.00 ☐
85	Wayne Cashman, Bos.	.25	.50	1.00 ☐
86	Jim Schoenfeld, Buf.	.25	.50	1.00 ☐
87	Henri Richard, Mon.	1.00	2.00	4.00 ☐
88	**Dennis O'Brien, Min., RC**	**.25**	**.50**	**1.00** ☐
89	Al McDonough, Pit.	.25	.50	1.00 ☐
90	'72-73 NHL All-Stars, West: Tony Esposito, Goalie, Chi.	2.75	5.50	11.00 ☐
91	Joe Watson, Phi.	.25	.50	1.00 ☐

TEAM CARDS

No.	Team	VG	EX	NRMT
92	Atlanta Flames	.65	1.35	2.75 ☐
93	Boston Bruins	.65	1.35	2.75 ☐
94	Buffalo Sabres	.65	1.35	2.75 ☐
95	California Golden Seals	.65	1.35	2.75 ☐
96	Chicago Black Hawks	.65	1.35	2.75 ☐
97	Detroit Red Wings	.65	1.35	2.75 ☐

54 • O-PEE-CHEE — 1973-74 REGULAR ISSUE —

No.	Player	VG	EX	NRMT
98	Los Angeles Kings	.65	1.35	2.75 ☐
99	Minnesota North Stars	.65	1.35	2.75 ☐
100	Montreal Canadiens	.65	1.35	2.75 ☐
101	New York Islanders	.65	1.35	2.75 ☐
102	New York Rangers	.65	1.35	2.75 ☐
103	Philadelphia Flyers	.65	1.35	2.75 ☐
104	Pittsburgh Penguins	.65	1.35	2.75 ☐
105	St. Louis Blues	.65	1.35	2.75 ☐
106	Toronto Maple Leafs	.65	1.35	2.75 ☐
107	Vancouver Canucks	.65	1.35	2.75 ☐

REGULAR ISSUE

No.	Player	VG	EX	NRMT
108	Vic Hadfield, NYR	.25	.50	1.00 ☐
109	Tom Reid, Min.	.25	.50	1.00 ☐
110	**Hilliard Graves, Ca., RC**	**.25**	**.50**	**1.00** ☐
111	Don Lever, Van.	.25	.50	1.00 ☐
112	Jim Pappin, Chi.	.25	.50	1.00 ☐
113	Andre Dupont, Phi.	.25	.50	1.00 ☐
114	**'72-73 NHL All-Stars, East:** Guy Lapointe, Mon.	**.50**	**1.00**	**2.00** ☐
115	Dennis Hextall, Min.	.25	.50	1.00 ☐
116	Checklist 1 (1 - 132)	8.75	17.50	35.00 ☐
117	Bobby Leiter, Atl.	.25	.50	1.00 ☐
118	Ab DeMarco, St. L.	.25	.50	1.00 ☐
119	Gilles Villemure, Goalie, NYR	.35	.75	1.50 ☐
120	**'72-73 NHL All-Stars, East:** Phil Esposito, Bos.	**2.50**	**5.00**	**10.00** ☐
121	Mike Robitaille, Buf.	.25	.50	1.00 ☐
122	Real Lemieux, LA, LC	.25	.50	1.00 ☐
123	Jim Neilson, NYR	.25	.50	1.00 ☐
124	**Steve Durbano, St. L., RC**	**.35**	**.75**	**1.50** ☐
125	Jude Drouin, Min.	.25	.50	1.00 ☐
126	Gary Smith, Goalie, Van.	.35	.75	1.50 ☐
127	Cesare Maniago, Goalie, Min.	.35	.75	1.50 ☐
128	Lowell MacDonald, Pit.	.25	.50	1.00 ☐
129	Checklist, Error	8.75	17.50	35.00 ☐
130	**Billy Harris, NYI, RC**	**.25**	**.50**	**1.00** ☐
131	Randy Manery, Atl.	.25	.50	1.00 ☐
132	Darryl Sittler, Tor.	4.50	9.00	18.00 ☐

1972-73 LEAGUE LEADERS

No.	Player	VG	EX	NRMT
133	**Goal Leaders:** P. Esposito, Bos., R. MacLeish, Phi.	1.12	2.25	4.50 ☐
134	**Assist Leaders:** P. Esposito, Bos., B. Clarke, Phi.	1.75	3.50	7.00 ☐
135	**Scoring Leaders:** P. Esposito, Bos., B. Clarke, Phi.	1.75	3.50	7.00 ☐
136	**Goals Against Avg. Leaders:** K. Dryden, Mon., T. Esposito, Chi.	3.00	6.00	12.00 ☐
137	**Penalty Minute Leaders:** J. Schoenfeld, Buf., D. Schultz, Phi.	.45	.85	1.75 ☐
138	**Power Play Goal Leaders:** P. Esposito, Bos., R. MacLeish, Phi.	1.00	2.00	4.00 ☐

REGULAR ISSUE

No.	Player	VG	EX	NRMT
139	Rene Robert, Buf.	.25	.50	1.00 ☐
140	Dave Burrows, Pit.	.25	.50	1.00 ☐
141	Jean Ratelle, NYR	.75	1.50	3.00 ☐
142	**Billy Smith, Goalie, NYI, RC**	**11.25**	**22.50**	**45.00** ☐
143	Jocelyn Guevremont, Van.	.25	.50	1.00 ☐
144	Tim Ecclestone, Tor.	.25	.50	1.00 ☐
145	**'72-73 NHL All-Stars, East:** Frank Mahovlich, Mon.	**2.00**	**4.00**	**8.00** ☐
146	Rick MacLeish, Phi.	.65	1.25	2.50 ☐
147	John Bucyk, Bos.	1.00	2.00	4.00 ☐
148	Bob Plager, St. L.	.25	.50	1.00 ☐
149	**Curt Bennett, Atl., RC**	**.25**	**.50**	**1.00** ☐
150	Dave Keon, Tor.	.75	1.50	3.00 ☐
151	Keith Magnuson, Chi.	.25	.50	1.00 ☐
152	Walt McKechnie, Ca.	.25	.50	1.00 ☐
153	Roger Crozier, Goalie, Buf.	.35	.75	1.50 ☐
154	Ted Harris, Det., LC	.25	.50	1.00 ☐
155	Butch Goring, LA	.35	.75	1.50 ☐
156	Rod Gilbert, NYR	.85	1.75	3.50 ☐
157	Yvan Cournoyer, Mon.	1.00	2.00	4.00 ☐
158	Doug Favell, Goalie, Tor.	.35	.75	1.50 ☐
159	Juha Widing, LA	.25	.50	1.00 ☐
160	Ed Giacomin, Goalie, NYR	1.00	2.00	4.00 ☐
161	Germaine Gagnon, NYI	.25	.50	1.00 ☐
162	Dennis Kearns, Van.	.25	.50	1.00 ☐

O-Pee-Chee 1973-74 Issue Card No. 157, Yvan Cournoyer

O-Pee-Chee, 1973-74 Issue Card No. 198, Montreal Canadiens, 1972-73 Stanley Cup Champions

O-Pee-Chee 1973-74 Issue Card No. 217, Pete Stemkowski

O-Pee-Chee 1973-74 Issue Card No. 230, Gump Worsley

No.	Player	VG	EX	NRMT
163	Bill Collins, Det.	.25	.50	1.00 ☐
164	Pete Mahovlich, Mon.	.25	.50	1.00 ☐
165	Brad Park, NYR	1.50	3.00	6.00 ☐
166	**Dave Schultz, Phi., RC**	**3.00**	**6.00**	**12.00** ☐
167	Dallas Smith, Bos.	.25	.50	1.00 ☐
168	Gary Sabourin, St. L.	.25	.50	1.00 ☐
169	Jacques Richard, Atl.	.25	.50	1.00 ☐
170	Brian Glennie, Tor.	.25	.50	1.00 ☐
171	**'72-73 NHL All-Stars, West:** Dennis Hull, Chi.	.25	.50	1.00 ☐
172	Joey Johnston, Ca.	.25	.50	1.00 ☐
173	Rick Martin, Buf.	.65	1.25	2.50 ☐
174	**'72-73 NHL All-Stars, West:** Barry Gibbs, Min.	.25	.50	1.00 ☐
175	Bob Berry, LA	.25	.50	1.00 ☐
176	Greg Polis, Pit.	.25	.50	1.00 ☐
177	Dale Rolfe, NYR	.25	.50	1.00 ☐
178	Gerry Desjardins, Goalie, NYI	.35	.75	1.50 ☐
179	Bobby Lalonde, Van.	.25	.50	1.00 ☐
180	**'72-73 NHL All Stars, East:** Mickey Redmond, Det.	.25	.50	1.00 ☐
181	Jim Roberts, Mon.	.25	.50	1.00 ☐
182	Gary Dornhoefer, Phi.	.25	.50	1.00 ☐
183	Derek Sanderson, Bos.	.25	.50	1.00 ☐
184	Brent Hughes, Det.	.25	.50	1.00 ☐
185	**Larry Romanchych, Atl., RC**	**.25**	**.50**	**1.00** ☐
186	Pierre Jarry, Det.	.25	.50	1.00 ☐
187	Doug Jarrett, Chi.	.25	.50	1.00 ☐
188	**Bob Stewart, Ca., RC**	**.25**	**.50**	**1.00** ☐
189	Tim Horton, Buf., LC	1.25	2.50	5.00 ☐
190	Fred (Buster) Harvey, Min.	.25	.50	1.00 ☐

1972-73 STANLEY CUP

No.	Games	VG	EX	NRMT
191	**NHL Quarter-Finals:** Games: Canadiens 4 Sabres 2	.45	.85	1.75 ☐
192	**NHL Quarter-Finals:** Games: Flyers 4 North Stars 2	.45	.85	1.75 ☐
193	**NHL Quarter-Finals:** Games: Black Hawks 4 Blues 1	.45	.85	1.75 ☐
194	**NHL Quarter-Finals:** Games: Rangers 4 Bruins 1	.45	.85	1.75 ☐
195	**NHL Semi-finals:** Games: Canadiens 4 Flyers 1	.45	.85	1.75 ☐
196	**NHL Semi-finals:** Games: Black Hawks 4 Rangers 1	.45	.85	1.75 ☐
197	**NHL Finals:** Games: Canadiens 4 Black Hawks 2	.55	1.12	2.25 ☐
198	**NHL Stanley Cup Champions:** Montreal Canadiens	.85	1.75	3.50 ☐

REGULAR ISSUE

No.	Player	VG	EX	NRMT
199	Gary Edwards, Goalie, LA	.35	.75	1.50 ☐
200	Ron Schock, Pit.	.25	.50	1.00 ☐
201	Bruce MacGregor, NYR	.25	.50	1.00 ☐
202	**Bob Nystrom, NYI, RC**	**1.75**	**3.50**	**7.00** ☐
203	Jerry Korab, Van.	.25	.50	1.00 ☐
204	**Thommie Bergman, Det., RC**	**.30**	**.65**	**1.25** ☐
205	Bill Lesuk, LA	.25	.50	1.00 ☐
206	Ed Van Impe, Phi.	.25	.50	1.00 ☐
207	Doug Roberts, Det.	.25	.50	1.00 ☐
208	Chris Evans, St. L.	.25	.50	1.00 ☐
209	**Lynn Powis, Chi., RC**	**.25**	**.50**	**1.00** ☐
210	Denis Dupere, Tor.	.25	.50	1.00 ☐
211	Dale Tallon, Chi.	.25	.50	1.00 ☐
212	Stan Gilbertson, Ca.	.25	.50	1.00 ☐
213	Craig Ramsay, Buf.	.25	.50	1.00 ☐
214	Danny Grant, Min.	.25	.50	1.00 ☐
215	**Doug Volmar, LA, RC, LC**	**.25**	**.50**	**1.00** ☐
216	Darryl Edestrand, Bos.	.25	.50	1.00 ☐
217	Pete Stemkowski, NYR	.25	.50	1.00 ☐
218	**Lorne Henning, NYI, RC**	**.25**	**.50**	**1.00** ☐
219	**Bryan McSheffrey, Van., RC, LC**	**.25**	**.50**	**1.00** ☐
220	Guy Charron, Det.	.25	.50	1.00 ☐
221	**Wayne Thomas, Goalie, Mon., RC**	**.75**	**1.50**	**3.00** ☐
222	Simon Nolet, Phi.	.25	.50	1.00 ☐
223	**Fred O'Donnell, Bos., RC, LC**	**.25**	**.50**	**1.00** ☐
224	Lou Angotti, St. L.	.25	.50	1.00 ☐
225	Arnie Brown, Atl., LC	.25	.50	1.00 ☐
226	Garry Monahan, Tor.	.25	.50	1.00 ☐
227	Chico Maki, Chi.	.25	.50	1.00 ☐
228	Gary Croteau, Ca.	.25	.50	1.00 ☐
229	Paul Terbenche, Buf.	.25	.50	1.00 ☐

No.	Player	VG	EX	NRMT
230	Gump Worsley, Goalie, Min., LC	1.25	2.50	5.00
231	Jimmy Peters, LA, LC	.25	.50	1.00
232	Jack Lynch, Pit.	.25	.50	1.00
233	Bobby Rousseau, NYR	.25	.50	1.00
234	Dave Hudson, NYI	.25	.50	1.00
235	Gregg Boddy, Van., RC, Error	.25	.50	1.00
236	Ron Stackhouse, Det.	.25	.50	1.00
237	Larry Robinson, Mon., RC	17.50	35.00	70.00
238	Bobby Taylor, Goalie, Phi., RC, LC	.35	.75	1.50
239	Nick Beverley, Pit.	.25	.50	1.00
240	Don Awrey, St. L.	.25	.50	1.00
241	Doug Mohns, Atl.	.25	.50	1.00
242	Eddie Shack, Tor., LC	.50	1.00	2.00
243	Phil Russell, Chi., RC	.50	1.00	2.00
244	Pete Laframboise, Ca.	.25	.50	1.00
245	Steve Atkinson, Buf.	.25	.50	1.00
246	Lou Nanne, Min.	.25	.50	1.00
247	Yvon Labre, Pit., RC	.25	.50	1.00
248	Ted Irvine, NYR	.25	.50	1.00
249	Tom Miller, NYI, LC	.25	.50	1.00
250	Gerry O'Flaherty, Van.	.25	.50	1.00
251	Larry Johnston, Det., RC	.25	.50	1.00
252	Michel Plasse, Goalie, Mon., RC	.35	.75	1.50
253	Bob Kelly, Phi.	.25	.50	1.00
254	Terry O'Reilly, Bos., RC	3.00	6.00	12.00
255	Pierre Plante, St. L., RC	.35	.75	1.50
256	Noel Price, Atl.	.25	.50	1.00
257	Dunc Wilson, Goalie, Tor.	.35	.75	1.50
258	J. P. Bordeleau, Chi., RC	.25	.50	1.00
259	Terry Murray, Ca., RC	.50	1.00	2.00
260	Larry Carriere, Buf.	.25	.50	1.00
261	Pierre Bouchard, Mon.	.25	.50	1.00
262	Frank St. Marseille, LA	.25	.50	1.00
263	Checklist	8.75	17.50	35.00
264	Fred Barrett, Min.	.60	1.25	2.50

— 1973 - 74 TEAM LOGO STICKERS —

Team logo stickers were inserted one per pack with the regular set of the same year. The unnumbered, colour logos without application instructions and with blank adhesive backs are listed alphabetically.

Sticker Size: 2 1/2" X 3 1/2"
Face: Four colour
Back: Blank
Imprint: None
Complete Set No.: 17
Complete Set Price: 5.00 10.00 20.00
Common Card: .35 .75 1.50

No.	Player	VG	EX	NRMT
1	NHL Logo	.35	.75	1.50
2	Atlanta Flames	.35	.75	1.50
3	Boston Bruins	.35	.75	1.50
4	Buffalo Sabres	.35	.75	1.50
5	California Golden Seals	.35	.75	1.50
6	Chicago Black Hawks	.35	.75	1.50
7	Detroit Red Wings	.35	.75	1.50
8	Los Angeles Kings	.35	.75	1.50
9	Minnesota North Stars	.35	.75	1.50
10	Montreal Canadiens	.35	.75	1.50
11	New York Islanders	.35	.75	1.50
12	New York Rangers	.35	.75	1.50
13	Philadelphia Flyers	.35	.75	1.50
14	Pittsburgh Penguins	.35	.75	1.50
15	Saint Louis Blues	.35	.75	1.50
16	Toronto Maple Leafs	.35	.75	1.50
17	Vancouver Canucks	.35	.75	1.50

Note: *The Charlton Standard Catalogue of Hockey Cards* arranges cards in their issue date order. This means the first date a manufacturer issues a card set determines the sequence of the manufacturer in the Standard Catalogue. In this manner the historical importance of early cards is maintained. See the last page of this catalogue for an alphabetical index of issuers.

O-Pee-Chee
1973-74 Team Logo Stickers
Sticker No. 7,
Detroit Red Wings

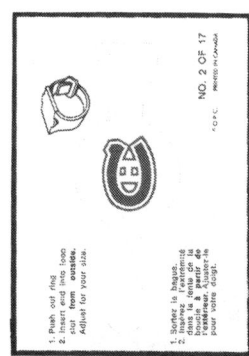

O-Pee-Chee
1973-74 Rings
Card No. 2,
Montreal Canadiens

O-Pee-Chee
1974-75 Issue
Card No. 1,
Goal Leaders

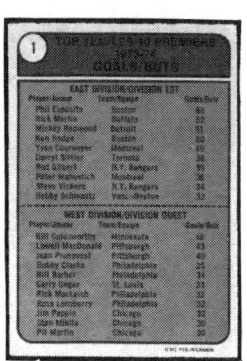

O-Pee-Chee
1974-75 Issue
Card No. 1,
Goal Leaders

— 1973 - 74 RINGS —

Cards are numbered _ of 17. Numbered cards contain a punch-out ring with assembly instructions.

Card Size: 2 1/2" X 3 1/2"
Face: Four colour
Back: Blank
Imprint: © O.P.C. PRINTED IN CANADA
Complete Set No.: 17
Complete Set Price: 9.00 18.00 38.00
Common Card: .75 1.50 3.00

No.	Player	VG	EX	NRMT
1	Vancouver Canucks	.75	1.50	3.00
2	Montreal Canadiens	.75	1.50	3.00
3	Toronto Maple Leafs	.75	1.50	3.00
4	NHL Logo	.75	1.50	3.00
5	Minnesota North Stars	.75	1.50	3.00
6	New York Rangers	.75	1.50	3.00
7	California Golden Seals	.75	1.50	3.00
8	Pittsburgh Penguins	.75	1.50	3.00
9	Philadelphia Flyers	.75	1.50	3.00
10	Chicago Blackhawks	.75	1.50	3.00
11	Boston Bruins	.75	1.50	3.00
12	Los Angeles Kings	.75	1.50	3.00
13	Detroit Red Wings	.75	1.50	3.00
14	St. Louis Blues	.75	1.50	3.00
15	Buffalo Sabres	.75	1.50	3.00
16	Atlanta Flames	.75	1.50	3.00
17	New York Islanders	.75	1.50	3.00

— 1974 - 75 REGULAR ISSUE —

Mint cards command a price premium of 50% over NRMT cards.

PRICE MOVEMENT OF NRMT SETS

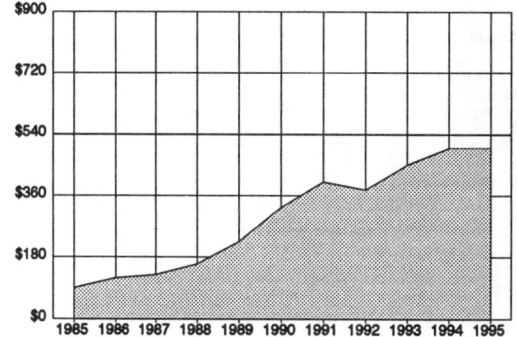

Card Size: 2 1/2" X 3 1/2"
Face: Four colour, white border, Team logo
Back: Two colour, brown and blue on card stock, Number, Resume, Hockey trivia, Bilingual
Imprint: O.P.C. PTD. IN CANADA
Complete Set No.: 396
Complete Set Price: 130.00 265.50 525.00
Common Card: .15 .35 .75

1973 - 74 LEAGUE LEADERS

No.	Player	VG	EX	NRMT
1	Goal Leaders: P. Esposito, Bos., East; B. Goldsworthy, Min., West	1.25	2.50	5.00
2	Assist Leaders: B. Orr, Bos., East; D. Hextall, Min., West	1.75	3.50	7.00
3	Scoring Leaders: P. Esposito, Bos., East,; B. Clarke, Phi., West	1.25	2.50	5.00
4	Goals Against Avg. Leaders: D. Favell, Tor., East; B. Parent, Phi., West	.65	1.25	2.50
5	Penalty Minute Leaders: B. Watson, Det., East; D. Schultz, Phi., West	.25	.50	1.00
6	Power Play Goal Leaders: M. Redmond, Det., East; R. MacLeish, Phi., West	.25	.50	1.00

56 • O-PEE-CHEE — 1974 - 75 REGULAR ISSUE

REGULAR ISSUE

No.	Player	VG	EX	NRMT
7	Gary Bromley, Goalie, Buf., RC	.25	.50	1.00
8	Bill Barber, Phi.	2.00	4.00	8.00
9	Emile Francis, Coach, NYR	.25	.50	1.00
10	Gilles Gilbert, Goalie, Bos.	.25	.50	1.00
11	John Davidson, Goalie, St. L., RC	2.00	4.00	8.00
12	Ron Ellis, Tor.	.15	.35	.75
13	Syl Apps, Jr., Pit.	.15	.35	.75
14	**Atlanta Flames Team Leaders:**	.65	1.25	2.50
	J. Richard, Goals; T. Lysiak, Assists, Points; K. McCreary, Scoring Pct.			
15	Dan Bouchard, Goalie, Atl.	.25	.50	1.00
16	Ivan Boldirev, Chi.	.15	.35	.75
17	**Gary Coalter, KC., RC**	.15	.35	.75
18	Bob Berry, LA	.15	.35	.75
19	Red Berenson, Det.	.15	.35	.75
20	Stan Mikita, Chi.	1.50	3.00	6.00
21	Fred Shero, Coach, Phi.	1.75	2.50	5.00
22	Gary Smith, Goalie, Van.	.25	.50	1.00
23	Bill Mikkelson, Wash.	.15	.35	.75
24	**Jacques Lemaire, Mon., Error**	.65	1.25	2.50
25	Gilbert Perreault, Buf.	2.00	4.00	8.00
26	Cesare Maniago, Goalie, Min.	.25	.50	1.00
27	Bobby Schmautz, Bos.	.15	.35	.75
28	**Boston Bruins Team Leaders:**	2.50	5.00	10.00
	P. Esposito, Goals, Points; B. Orr, Assists; Error, J. Bucyk, Scoring Pct.			
29	Steve Vickers, NYR	.15	.35	.75
30	Lowell MacDonald, Pit.	.15	.35	.75
31	Fred Stanfield, Min.	.15	.35	.75
32	Ed Westfall, NYI	.15	.35	.75
33	Curt Bennett, Atl.	.15	.35	.75
34	Bep Guidolin, Coach, KC	.15	.35	.75
35	Cliff Koroll, Chi.	.15	.35	.75
36	Gary Croteau, KC	.15	.35	.75
37	Mike Corrigan, LA	.15	.35	.75
38	Henry Boucha, Det.	.15	.35	.75
39	Ron Low, Goalie, Wash.	.25	.50	1.00
40	Darryl Sittler, Tor.	2.50	5.00	10.00
41	Tracy Pratt, Van.	.15	.35	.75
42	**Buffalo Sabres Team Leaders:**	.65	1.25	2.50
	R. Martin, Goals, Points, Scoring Pct.; R. Robert, Assists			
43	Larry Carriere, Buf.	.15	.35	.75
44	Gary Dornhoefer, Phi.	.15	.35	.75
45	**Denis Herron, Goalie, Pit., RC**	.75	1.50	3.00
46	Doug Favell, Goalie, Tor.	.25	.50	1.00
47	**Dave Gardner, St. L., RC**	.15	.35	.75
48	**Morris Mott, Ca., RC, LC**	.15	.35	.75
49	Marc Boileau, Coach, Pit.	.15	.35	.75
50	Brad Park, NYR	1.25	2.50	5.00
51	Bobby Leiter, Atl.	.15	.35	.75
52	Tom Reid, Min.	.15	.35	.75
53	Serge Savard, Mon.	.50	1.00	2.00
54	**Checklist 1 (1 - 132), Error**	5.50	11.00	22.00
55	Terry Harper, LA	.15	.35	.75
56	**California Golden Seals Team**	.65	1.25	2.50
	Leaders: J. Johnston, Goals, Assists, Points; W. McKechnie, Scoring Pct.			
57	Guy Charron, Det.	.15	.35	.75
58	Pit Martin, Chi.	.15	.35	.75
59	Chris Evans, KC	.15	.35	.75
60	Bernie Parent, Goalie, Phi.	1.25	2.50	5.00
61	Jim Lorentz, Buf.	.15	.35	.75
62	**Dave Kryskow, Wash., RC**	.15	.35	.75
63	Lou Angotti, St. L., LC	.15	.35	.75
64	Bill Flett, Tor.	.15	.35	.75
65	Vic Hadfield, Pit.	.15	.35	.75
66	**Wayne Merrick, St. L., RC**	.15	.35	.75
67	Andre Dupont, Phi.	.15	.35	.75
68	**Tom Lysiak, Atl., RC**	.35	.75	1.50
69	**Chicago Black Hawks Team**	.65	1.25	2.50
	Leaders: J. Pappin, Goals; S. Mikita, Assists, Points; J. P. Bordeleau, Scoring Pct.			
70	Guy Lapointe, Mon.	.50	1.00	2.00
71	Gerry O'Flaherty, Van.	.15	.35	.75
72	Marcel Dionne, Det.	3.00	6.00	12.00
73	**Butch Deadmarsh, KC, RC**	.15	.35	.75
74	Butch Goring, LA	.15	.35	.75
75	Keith Magnuson, Chi.	.15	.35	.75
76	Red Kelly, Coach, Tor.	.50	1.00	2.00
77	Pete Stemkowski, NYR	.15	.35	.75
78	Jim Roberts, Mon.	.15	.35	.75

O-Pee-Chee, 1974-75 Issue Card No. 24, Error, Jacques Lemaire in Buffalo Sabres uniform, should be Montreal Canadiens uniform

O-Pee-Chee 1974-75 Issue Card No. 100, Bobby Orr

O-Pee-Chee 1974-75 Issue Card No. 107, Error, Shows Barclay Plager

O-Pee-Chee, 1974-75 Issue Card No. 124, Montreal Canadien Team Leaders

No.	Player	VG	EX	NRMT
79	Don Luce, Buf.	.15	.35	.75
80	Don Awrey, St. L.	.15	.35	.75
81	Rick Kehoe, Tor.	.15	.35	.75
82	Billy Smith, Goalie, NYI	3.00	6.00	12.00
83	J. P. Parise, Min.	.15	.35	.75
84	**Detroit Red Wings Team**	.65	1.25	2.50
	Leaders: M. Redmond, Goals; M. Dionne, Assists, Points; B. Hogaboom, Scoring Pct.			
85	Ed Van Impe, Phi.	.15	.35	.75
86	Randy Manery, Atl.	.15	.35	.75
87	Barclay Plager, St. L.	.15	.35	.75
88	**Inge Hammarstrom, Tor., RC**	.15	.35	.75
89	Ab DeMarco, Pit.	.15	.35	.75
90	Bill White, Chi.	.15	.35	.75
91	Al Arbour, Coach, NYI	.75	1.50	3.00
92	Bob Stewart, Ca.	.15	.35	.75
93	Jack Egers, Wash.	.15	.35	.75
94	Don Lever, Van.	.15	.35	.75
95	Reggie Leach, Phi.	.15	.35	.75
96	Dennis O'Brien, Min.	.15	.35	.75
97	Pete Mahovlich, Mon.	.15	.35	.75
98	**Los Angeles Kings Team**	.65	1.25	2.50
	Leaders: B. Goring, Goals, Points; F. St. Marseille, Assists; D. Kozak, Scoring Pct.			
99	Gerry Meehan, Buf.	.15	.35	.75
100	Bobby Orr, Bos.	11.25	22.50	45.00
101	**Jean Potvin, NYI, RC**	.25	.50	1.00
102	Rod Seiling, NYR	.15	.35	.75
103	Keith McCreary, Atl., LC	.15	.35	.75
104	Phil Maloney, Coach, Van.	.15	.35	.75
105	Denis Dupere, Wash.	.15	.35	.75
106	Steve Durbano, Pit.	.15	.35	.75
107	Bob Plager, St. L., Error	.15	.35	.75
108	**Chris Oddleifson, Van., RC**	.15	.35	.75
109	Jim Neilson, Ca.	.15	.35	.75
110	Jean Pronovost, Pit.	.15	.35	.75
111	**Don Kozak, LA, RC**	.15	.35	.75
112	**Minnesota North Stars**	.65	1.25	2.50
	Team Leaders: B. Goldsworthy, Goals; D. Hextall, Assists, Points; D. Grant, Scoring Pct.			
113	Jim Pappin, Chi.	.15	.35	.75
114	Richard Lemieux, KC	.15	.35	.75
115	Dennis Hextall, Min.	.15	.35	.75
116	**Bill Hogaboam, Det., RC**	.15	.35	.75
117	**Vancouver Canucks Team**	.65	1.25	2.50
	Leaders: D. Ververgaert, B. Schmautz, Goals; A. Boudrias, Assists, Points; Dan Tannahill, Scoring Pct.			
118	Jim Anderson, Coach, Wash.	.15	.35	.75
119	Walt Tkaczuk, NYR	.15	.35	.75
120	Mickey Redmond, Det.	.15	.35	.75
121	Jim Schoenfeld, Buf.	.15	.35	.75
122	Jocelyn Guevremont, Van.	.15	.35	.75
123	Bob Nystrom, NYI	.50	1.00	2.00
124	**Montreal Canadiens Team**	.75	1.50	3.00
	Leaders: Y. Cournoyer, Goals; F. Mahovlich, Assists, Points; C. Larose, Scoring Pct.			
125	Lew Morrison, Wash.	.15	.35	.75
126	Terry Murray, Ca., LC	.25	.50	1.00

1973 - 74 ALL STARS
NHL East

No.	Player	VG	EX	NRMT
127	Rick Martin, Buf.	.15	.35	.75
128	Ken Hodge, Sr., Bos.	.15	.35	.75
129	Phil Esposito, Bos.	1.25	2.50	5.00
130	Bobby Orr, Bos.	5.00	10.00	20.00
131	Brad Park, NYR	.65	1.25	2.50
132	Gilles Gilbert, Goalie Bos.	.25	.50	1.00

NHL West

No.	Player	VG	EX	NRMT
133	Lowell MacDonald, Pit.	.15	.35	.75
134	Bill Goldsworthy, Min.	.15	.35	.75
135	Bobby Clarke, Phi.	1.25	2.50	5.00
136	Bill White, Chi.	.15	.35	.75
137	Dave Burrows, Pit.	.15	.35	.75
138	Bernie Parent, Goalie Phi.	.75	1.50	3.00

1974 - 75 REGULAR ISSUE — O-PEE-CHEE • 57

REGULAR ISSUE

No.	Player	VG	EX	NRMT
139	Jacques Richard, Atl.	.15	.35	.75
140	Yvan Cournoyer, Mon.	1.00	2.00	4.00
141	New York Rangers Team Leaders: R. Gilbert, Goals, Scoring Pct.; B. Park, Assists, Points	.65	1.25	2.50
142	Rene Robert, Buf.	.15	.35	.75
143	J. Bob Kelly, Pit., RC	.15	.35	.75
144	Ross Lonsberry, Phi.	.15	.35	.75
145	Jean Ratelle, NYR	.65	1.25	2.50
146	Dallas Smith, Bos.	.15	.35	.75
147	Bernie Geoffrion, Coach, Atl.	.75	1.50	3.00
148	Ted McAneeley, Ca., LC	.15	.35	.75
149	Pierre Plante, St. L.	.15	.35	.75
150	Dennis Hull, Chi.	.15	.35	.75
151	Dave Keon, Tor.	.50	1.00	2.00
152	Dave Dunn, Van., RC	.15	.35	.75
153	Michel Belhumeur, Goalie, Wash.	.25	.50	1.00
154	Philadelphia Flyers Team Leaders: B. Clarke, Goals, Assists, Points; D. Schultz, Scoring Pct	.75	1.50	3.00
155	Ken Dryden, Goalie, Mon.	6.25	12.50	25.00
156	John Wright, KC, RC, LC, Error	.15	.35	.75
157	Larry Romanchych, Atl.	.15	.35	.75
158	Ralph Stewart, NYI, RC	.15	.35	.75
159	Mike Robitaille, Buf.	.15	.35	.75
160	Ed Giacomin, Goalie, NYR	.65	1.25	2.50
161	Don Cherry, Coach, Bos.	8.75	17.50	35.00
162	Checklist 2 (133 - 264)	5.50	11.00	22.00
163	Rick MacLeish, Phi.	.50	1.00	2.00
164	Greg Polis, St. L.	.15	.35	.75
165	Carol Vadnais, Bos.	.15	.35	.75
166	Pete Laframboise, Wash.	.15	.35	.75
167	Ron Schock, Pit.	.15	.35	.75
168	Lanny McDonald, Tor., RC	11.25	22.50	45.00
169	Kansas City Scouts Emblem : Entered NHL, 1974	.65	1.25	2.50
170	Tony Esposito, Goalie, Chi.	1.50	3.00	6.00
171	Pierre Jarry, Det.	.15	.35	.75
172	Dan Maloney, LA	.15	.35	.75
173	Pete McDuffe, Goalie, KC	.25	.50	1.00
174	Danny Grant, Min.	.15	.35	.75
175	John Stewart, Ca., RC, LC	.15	.35	.75
176	Floyd Smith, Buf., LC	.15	.35	.75
177	Bert Marshall, NYI	.15	.35	.75
178	Chuck Lefley, Mon., Error	.15	.35	.75
179	Gilles Villemure, Goalie, NYR	.25	.50	1.00
180	Borje Salming, Tor., RC	5.50	11.00	22.00
181	Doug Mohns, Wash., LC	.15	.35	.75
182	Barry Wilkins, Van.	.15	.35	.75
183	Pittsburgh Penguins Team Leaders: L. MacDonald, Goals, Scoring Pct., Syl Apps, Assists, Points	.65	1.25	2.50
184	Gregg Sheppard, Bos.	.15	.35	.75
185	Joey Johnston, Ca.	.15	.35	.75
186	Dick Redmond, Chi.	.15	.35	.75
187	Simon Nolet, KC	.15	.35	.75
188	Ron Stackhouse, Pit.	.15	.35	.75
189	Marshall Johnston, Coach, Ca.	.15	.35	.75
190	Rick Martin, Buf.	.15	.35	.75
191	Andre Boudrias, Van.	.15	.35	.75
192	Steve Atkinson, Wash., LC	.15	.35	.75
193	Nick Libett, Det.	.15	.35	.75
194	Bob J. Murdoch, LA, RC	.15	.35	.75
195	Denis Potvin, NYI, RC	12.50	25.00	50.00
196	Dave Schultz, Phi.	1.00	2.00	4.00
197	St. Louis Blues Team Leaders: G. Unger, Goals, Assists, Points; P. Plante, Scoring Pct.	.65	1.25	2.50
198	Jim McKenny, Tor.	.15	.35	.75
199	Gerry Hart, NYI	.15	.35	.75
200	Phil Esposito, Bos.	1.75	3.50	7.00
201	Rod Gilbert, NYR	.75	1.50	3.00
202	Jacques Laperriere, Mon., LC	.25	.50	1.00
203	Barry Gibbs, Min.	.15	.35	.75
204	Billy Reay, Coach, Chi.	.15	.35	.75
205	Gilles Meloche, Goalie, Ca.	.25	.50	1.00
206	Wayne Cashman, Bos.	.15	.35	.75
207	Dennis Ververgaert, Van., RC	.15	.35	.75
208	Phil Roberto, St. L.	.15	.35	.75

O-Pee-Chee 1974-75 Issue Card No. 168, Lanny McDonald

O-Pee-Chee 1974-75 Issue Card No. 178, Error, Shows Pierre Bouchard

O-Pee-Chee 1974-75 Issue Card No. 201, Rod Gilbert

O-Pee-Chee 1974-75 Issue Card No. 228, Billy Harris

1973 - 74 STANLEY CUP PLAYOFFS

No.	Games	VG	EX	NRMT
209	Quarter-Finals: Flyers vs. Flames	.30	.60	1.25
210	Quarter-Finals: Rangers vs. Canadiens	.30	.60	1.25
211	Quarter-Finals: Bruins vs. Maple Leafs	.30	.60	1.25
212	Quarter-Finals: Black Hawks vs. Kings	.30	.60	1.25
213	Semi-Finals: Flyers vs. Rangers	.30	.60	1.25
214	Semi-Finals: Black Hawks vs. Bruins	.30	.60	1.25
215	Finals: Flyers vs. Bruins	.30	.60	1.25
216	Stanley Cup Champions: Philadelphia Flyers	.75	1.50	3.00

REGULAR ISSUE

No.	Player	VG	EX	NRMT
217	Joe Watson, Phi.	.15	.35	.75
218	Wayne Stephenson, Goalie, St. L	.25	.50	1.00
219	Toronto Maple Leafs Team Leaders: D. Sittler, Goals, Points; N. Ullman, Assists; P. Henderson, D. Dupere, Scoring Pct	.75	1.50	3.00
220	Bill Goldsworthy, Min.	.15	.35	.75
221	Don Marcotte, Bos.	.15	.35	.75
222	Alex Delvecchio, Coach, Det.	.65	1.25	2.50
223	Stan Gilbertson, Ca.	.15	.35	.75
224	Mike Murphy, LA	.15	.35	.75
225	Jim Rutherford, Goalie, Det.	.25	.50	1.00
226	Phil Russell, Chi.	.15	.35	.75
227	Lynn Powis, KC	.15	.35	.75
228	Billy Harris, NYI	.15	.35	.75
229	Bob Pulford, Coach, LA	.50	1.00	2.00
230	Ken Hodge, Bos.	.15	.35	.75
231	Bill Fairbairn, NYR	.15	.35	.75
232	Guy Lafleur, Mon.	5.00	10.00	20.00
233	New York Islanders Team Leaders: B. Harris & R. Stewart, Goals D. Potvin, Assists, Points; R. Stewart; Scoring Pct., Error	1.00	2.00	4.00
234	Fred Barrett, Min.	.15	.35	.75
235	Rogatien Vachon, Goalie, LA	.65	1.25	2.50
236	Norm Ullman, Tor.	.50	1.00	2.00
237	Garry Unger, St. L.	.25	.50	1.00
238	Jackie Gordon, Coach, Min.	.15	.35	.75
239	John Bucyk, Bos.	.75	1.50	3.00
240	Bob Dailey, Van., RC	.15	.35	.75
241	Dave Burrows, Pit.	.15	.35	.75
242	Len Frig, Ca., RC	.15	.35	.75

1973 - 74 TROPHY WINNERS

No.	Trophy	VG	EX	NRMT
243	Masterton Memorial Trophy: Henri Richard, Mon.	.50	1.00	2.00
244	Hart Memorial Trophy: Phil Esposito, Bos.	1.25	2.50	5.00
245	Lady Byng Memorial Trophy: John Bucyk, Bos.	.35	.75	1.50
246	Art Ross Trophy: Phil Esposito, Bos.	1.25	2.50	5.00
247	Prince of Wales Trophy: Boston Bruins	.25	.50	1.00
248	James Norris Memorial Trophy: Bobby Orr, Bos.	5.00	10.00	20.00
249	Vezina Trophy: Bernie Parent, Goalie, Phi.	.75	1.50	3.00
250	Stanley Cup: Philadelphia Flyers	.75	1.50	3.00
251	Conn Smythe Trophy: Bernie Parent, Goalie, Phi.	.75	1.50	3.00
252	Calder Memorial Trophy: Denis Potvin, NYI	3.00	6.00	12.00
253	Clarence Campbell Trophy: Philadelphia Flyers	.25	.50	1.00

REGULAR ISSUE

No.	Player	VG	EX	NRMT
254	Pierre Bouchard, Mon.	.15	.35	.75
255	Jude Drouin, Min.	.15	.35	.75
256	Washington Capitals Emblem: Entered NHL, 1974	.65	1.25	2.50
257	Michel Plasse, Goalie, KC	.25	.50	1.00
258	Juha Widing, LA	.15	.35	.75
259	Bryan Watson, Det.	.15	.35	.75
260	Bobby Clarke, Phi.	3.00	6.00	12.00
261	Scotty Bowman, Coach, Mon.	3.75	7.50	15.00
262	Craig Patrick, Ca.	.15	.35	.75

58 • O-PEE-CHEE — 1975 - 76 REGULAR ISSUE —

No.	Player	VG	EX	NRMT
263	Craig Cameron, NYI	.15	.35	.75
264	Ted Irvine, NYR	.15	.35	.75
265	Eddie Johnston, Goalie, St. L.	.25	.50	1.00
266	Dave Forbes, Bos., RC	.15	.35	.75
267	Detroit Red Wings Checklist	.65	1.25	2.50
268	Rick Dudley, Buf., RC	.25	.50	1.00
269	Darcy Rota, Chi., RC	.15	.35	.75
270	Phil Myre, Goalie, Atl.	.25	.50	1.00
271	Larry Brown, LA, RC	.15	.35	.75
272	Bob Neely, Tor., RC	.15	.35	.75
273	Jerry Byers, Atl., RC, LC	.15	.35	.75
274	Pittsburgh Penguins Checklist	.65	1.25	2.50
275	Glenn Goldup, Mon., RC, Error	.15	.35	.75
276	Ron Harris, NYR, LC	.15	.35	.75
277	Joe Lundrigan, Wash., RC, LC	.15	.35	.75
278	Mike Christie, Ca., RC	.15	.35	.75
279	Doug Rombough, NYI, RC	.15	.35	.75
280	Larry Robinson, Mon.	6.00	12.00	24.00
281	St. Louis Blues Checklist	.65	1.25	2.50
282	John Marks, Chi., RC	.15	.35	.75
283	Don Saleski, Phi.	.15	.35	.75
284	Rick Wilson, St. L., RC	.15	.35	.75
285	Andre Savard, Bos., RC	.15	.35	.75
286	Pat Quinn, Atl.	.15	.35	.75
287	Los Angeles Kings Checklist	.65	1.25	2.50
288	Norm Gratton, Buf., RC	.15	.35	.75
289	Ian Turnbull, Tor., RC	.35	.75	1.50
290	Derek Sanderson, NYR	.50	1.00	2.00
291	Murray Oliver, Min.	.15	.35	.75
292	Wilf Paiement, KC, RC, Error	.75	1.50	3.00
293	Nelson Debenedet, Pit., RC, LC	.15	.35	.75
294	Greg Joly, Wash., RC	.15	.35	.75
295	Terry O'Reilly, Bos.	.85	1.75	3.50
296	Rey Comeau, Atl.	.15	.35	.75
297	Michel Larocque, Goalie, Mon., RC	1.25	2.50	5.00
298	Floyd Thomson, St. L., RC, Error	.15	.35	.75
299	Jean-Guy Lagace, Pit., RC	.15	.35	.75
300	Philadelphia Flyers Checklist	.65	1.25	2.50
301	Al MacAdam, Ca., RC	1.25	2.50	3.00
302	George Ferguson, Tor., RC	.15	.35	.75
303	Jimmy Watson, Phi., RC	.75	1.50	3.00
304	Rick Middleton, NYR, RC	5.00	10.00	20.00
305	Craig Ramsay, Buf.	.15	.35	.75
306	Hilliard Graves, Atl.	.15	.35	.75
307	New York Islanders Checklist	.65	1.25	2.50
308	Blake Dunlop, Min., RC	.15	.35	.75
309	J. P. Bordeleau, Chi.	.15	.35	.75
310	Brian Glennie, Tor.	.15	.35	.75
311	Checklist 3 (265 - 396), Error	5.50	11.00	22.00
312	Doug Roberts, Det., LC	.15	.35	.75
313	Darryl Edestrand, Bos.	.15	.35	.75
314	Ron H. Anderson, Wash., RC, LC	.15	.35	.75
315	Chicago Black Hawks Checklist	.65	1.25	2.50
316	Steve Shutt, Mon., RC	6.25	12.50	25.00
317	Doug Horbul, KC., RC, LC	.15	.35	.75
318	Bill Lochead, Det., RC	.15	.35	.75
319	Fred (Buster) Harvey, Atl.	.15	.35	.75
320	Gene Carr, LA, RC	.15	.35	.75
321	Henri Richard, Mon., LC, Error	.75	1.50	3.00
322	Vancouver Canucks Checklist	.65	1.25	2.50
323	Tim Ecclestone, Tor.	.15	.35	.75
324	Dave Lewis, NYI, RC	.25	.50	1.00
325	Lou Nanne, Min.	.15	.35	.75
326	Bobby Rousseau, NYR, LC	.15	.35	.75
327	Dunc Wilson, Goalie, Tor.	.25	.50	1.00
328	Brian Spencer, Buf.	.15	.35	.75
329	Rick Hampton, Ca., RC	.15	.35	.75
330	Montreal Canadiens Checklist, Error	.65	1.25	2.50
331	Jack Lynch, Det.	.15	.35	.75
332	Garnet Bailey, St. L.	.15	.35	.75
333	Al Sims, Bos., RC	.15	.35	.75
334	Orest Kindrachuk, Phi., RC	.50	1.00	2.00
335	Dave Hudson, KC	.15	.35	.75
336	Bob Murray, Atl., RC	.15	.35	.75
337	Buffalo Sabres Checklist	.65	1.25	2.50
338	Sheldon Kannegiesser, LA	.15	.35	.75
339	Billy MacMillan, NYI	.15	.35	.75
340	Paulin Bordeleau, Van., RC	.15	.35	.75
341	Dale Rolfe, NYR, LC	.15	.35	.75
342	Yvon Lambert, Mon., RC	.15	.35	.75
343	Bob Paradise, Pit., RC	.15	.35	.75
344	Germain Gagnon, Chi.	.15	.35	.75
345	Yvon Labre, Wash.	.15	.35	.75

O-Pee-Chee
1974-75 Issue
Card No. 275, Error,
Name misspelled Glen
on face

O-Pee-Chee
1974-75 Issue
Card No. 292, Error,
Name misspelled
Paiemont on face

O-Pee-Chee
1974-75 Issue
Card No. 353, Error, Name
misspelled Glen on face

O-Pee-Chee
1974-75 Issue
Card No. 360, Error, Name
misspelled Talon on face

No.	Player	VG	EX	NRMT
346	Chris Ahrens, Min., RC	.15	.35	.75
347	Doug Grant, Goalie, Det., RC	.25	.50	1.00
348	Blaine Stoughton, Tor., RC	1.25	2.50	5.00
349	Gregg Boddy, Van. Error	.15	.35	.75
350	Boston Bruins Checklist	.65	1.25	2.50
351	Doug Jarrett, Chi.	.15	.35	.75
352	Terry Crisp, Phi.	.15	.35	.75
353	Glenn Resch, Goalie, NYI, RC, Error	4.50	9.00	18.00
354	Jerry Korab, Buf.	.15	.35	.75
355	Stan Weir, Ca., RC	.15	.35	.75
356	Noel Price, Atl.	.15	.35	.75
357	Bill Clement, Phi., RC	1.25	2.50	5.00
358	Neil Komadoski, LA	.15	.35	.75
359	Murray Wilson, Mon., RC	.15	.35	.75
360	Dale Tallon, Chi., Error	.15	.35	.75
361	Gary Doak, Bos.	.15	.35	.75
362	Randy Rota, KC, RC	.15	.35	.75
363	Minnesota North Stars Checklist	.65	1.25	2.50
364	Bill Collins, St. L., LC	.15	.35	.75
365	Thommie Bergman, Det., Error	.15	.35	.75
366	Dennis Kearns, Van.	.15	.35	.75
367	Lorne Henning, NYI	.15	.35	.75
368	Gary Sabourin, Tor.	.15	.35	.75
369	Mike Bloom, Wash., RC	.15	.35	.75
370	New York Rangers Checklist	.65	1.25	2.50
371	Gary Simmons, Goalie, Ca., RC	.50	1.00	2.00
372	Dwight Bialowas, Atl., RC	.15	.35	.75
373	Gilles Marotte, NYR	.15	.35	.75
374	Frank St. Marseille, LA	.15	.35	.75
375	Garry Howatt, NYI, RC	.18	.35	.75
376	Ross Brooks, Goalie, Bos., RC, LC	.35	.75	1.50
377	Atlanta Flames Checklist	.65	1.25	2.50
378	Bob Nevin, LA	.15	.35	.75
379	Lyle Moffat, Tor., RC	.15	.35	.75
380	Bob Kelly, Phi.	.15	.35	.75
381	John Gould, Van., RC	.15	.35	.75
382	Dave Fortier, NYI, RC	.15	.35	.75
383	Jean Hamel, Det., RC	.15	.35	.75
384	Bert Wilson, NYR, RC	.15	.35	.75
385	Chuck Arnason, Pit., RC	.15	.35	.75
386	Bruce Cowick, Wash., RC, LC	.15	.35	.75
387	Ernie Hicke, NYI	.15	.35	.75
388	Bob Gainey, Mon., RC	6.25	12.50	25.00
389	Vic Venasky, LA, RC	.15	.35	.75
390	Toronto Maple Leafs Checklist	.65	1.25	2.50
391	Eric Vail, Atl., RC	.50	1.00	2.00
392	Bobby Lalonde, Van.	.15	.35	.75
393	Jerry Butler, NYR, RC	.15	.35	.75
394	Tommy Williams, LA, RC	.15	.35	.75
395	Chico Maki, Chi., LC	.15	.35	.75
396	Tom Bladon, Phi., RC	.85	1.75	3.50

— 1975 - 76 REGULAR ISSUE —

The face of cards 1-330 are for the most part identical to those issued by Topps for this year. Checklist card number 395 was not issued, but two different checklist cards, both numbered 267, were produced. Team photo cards (81-90) have a checklist of players included on the back.

Mint cards command a 50% price premium over NRMT cards.

PRICE MOVEMENT OF NRMT SETS

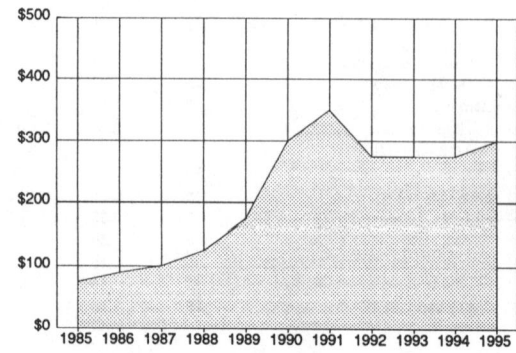

— 1975 - 76 REGULAR ISSUE — O-PEE-CHEE • 59

Card Size: 2 1/2" X 3 1/2"
Face: Four colour, white border, Position
Back: Two colour, brown on card stock, Number, Resume, Hockey trivia, Bilingual
Imprint: O.P.C. PTD. IN CANADA
Complete Set No.: 396
Complete Set Price: 75.00   150.00   300.00 ☐
Common Card: .15   .35   .75

1974 - 75 STANLEY CUP PLAYOFFS

No.	Team	VG	EX	NRMT
1	**Finals:** Philadelphia vs. Buffalo	.85	1.75	3.50 ☐
2	**Semi-finals:** Philadelphia vs. N.Y. Islanders	.15	.35	.75 ☐
3	**Semi-finals:** Buffalo vs. Montreal	.15	.35	.75 ☐
4	**Quarter Finals:** N.Y. Islanders vs. Pittsburgh	.15	.35	.75 ☐
5	**Quarter Finals:** Montreal vs. Vancouver	.15	.35	.75 ☐
6	**Quarter Finals:** Buffalo vs. Chicago	.15	.35	.75 ☐
7	**Quarter Finals:** Philadelphia vs. Toronto	.15	.35	.75 ☐

REGULAR ISSUE

No.	Player	VG	EX	NRMT
8	Curt Bennett, Atl.	.10	.25	.50 ☐
9	John Bucyk, Bos.	.55	1.12	2.25 ☐
10	Gilbert Perreault, Buf.	1.25	2.50	5.00 ☐
11	Darryl Edestrand, Bos.	.15	.35	.75 ☐
12	Ivan Boldirev, Chi.	.15	.35	.75 ☐
13	Nick Libett, Det.	.15	.35	.75 ☐
14	**Jim McElmury, KC, RC**	**.15**	**.35**	**.75** ☐
15	Frank St. Marseille, LA	.15	.35	.75 ☐
16	Blake Dunlop, Min.	.15	.35	.75 ☐
17	Yvon Lambert, Mon.	.15	.35	.75 ☐
18	Gerry Hart, NYI	.15	.35	.75 ☐
19	Steve Vickers, NYR	.15	.35	.75 ☐
20	Rick MacLeish, Phi.	.15	.35	.75 ☐
21	Bob Paradise, Pit.	.15	.35	.75 ☐
22	Red Berenson, St. L.	.15	.35	.75 ☐
23	Lanny McDonald, Tor.	3.00	6.00	12.00 ☐
24	Mike Robitaille, Van.	.15	.35	.75 ☐
25	Ron Low, Goalie, Wash.	.15	.35	.75 ☐
26	Bryan Hextall, Jr., Det.	.15	.35	.75 ☐
27	Carol Vadnais, Bos.	.15	.35	.75 ☐
28	Jim Lorentz, Buf.	.15	.35	.75 ☐
29	Gary Simmons, Goalie, Ca.	.15	.35	.75 ☐
30	Stan Mikita, Chi.	1.25	2.50	5.00 ☐
31	Bryan Watson, Det.	.15	.35	.75 ☐
32	Guy Charron, KC	.15	.35	.75 ☐
33	Bob J. Murdoch, LA	.15	.35	.75 ☐
34	Norm Gratton, Min., LC	.15	.35	.75 ☐
35	Ken Dryden, Goalie, Mon.	5.00	10.00	20.00 ☐
36	Jean Potvin, NYI	.15	.35	.75 ☐
37	Rick Middleton, NYR	1.50	3.00	6.00 ☐
38	Ed Van Impe, Phi.	.15	.35	.75 ☐
39	Rick Kehoe, Pit.	.15	.35	.75 ☐
40	Garry Unger, St. L.	.15	.35	.75 ☐
41	Ian Turnbull, Tor.	.15	.35	.75 ☐
42	Dennis Ververgaert, Van.	.15	.35	.75 ☐
43	**Mike Marson, Wash., RC, LC**	**.15**	**.35**	**.75** ☐
44	Randy Manery, Atl.	.15	.35	.75 ☐
45	Gilles Gilbert, Goalie, Bos.	.15	.35	.75 ☐
46	Rene Robert, Buf.	.15	.35	.75 ☐
47	Bob Stewart, Ca.	.15	.35	.75 ☐
48	Pit Martin, Chi.	.15	.35	.75 ☐
49	Danny Grant, Det.	.15	.35	.75 ☐
50	Pete Mahovlich, Mon.	.15	.35	.75 ☐
51	**Dennis Patterson, KC, RC, LC**	**.15**	**.35**	**.75** ☐
52	Mike Murphy, LA	.15	.35	.75 ☐
53	Dennis O'Brien, Min.	.15	.35	.75 ☐
54	Garry Howatt, NYI	.15	.35	.75 ☐
55	Ed Giacomin, Goalie, NYR (Sold to Detroit Oct. 31.)	.75	1.50	3.00 ☐
56	Andre Dupont, Phi.	.15	.35	.75 ☐
57	Chuck Arnason, Pit.	.15	.35	.75 ☐
58	**Bob Gassoff, St. L., RC**	**.15**	**.35**	**.75** ☐
59	Ron Ellis, Tor. (Retired before 1975-76 season.)	.15	.35	.75 ☐
60	Andre Boudrias, Van.	.15	.35	.75 ☐
61	Yvon Labre, Wash.	.15	.35	.75 ☐
62	Hilliard Graves, Atl.	.15	.35	.75 ☐
63	Wayne Cashman, Bos.	.15	.35	.75 ☐
64	**Danny Gare, Buf., RC**	**.85**	**1.75**	**3.50** ☐
65	Rick Hampton, Ca.	.15	.35	.75 ☐

O-Pee-Chee
1975-76 Issue
Card No. 1, Finals
Philadelphia vs Buffalo

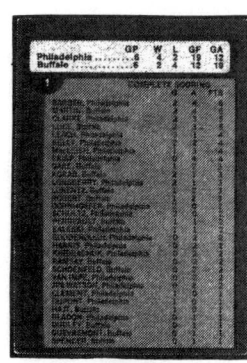

O-Pee-Chee
1975-76 Issue
Card No. 1, Finals
Philadelphia vs Buffalo

O-Pee-Chee
1975-76 Issue
Card No. 7, Quarter Finals
Philadelphia vs. Toronto

O-Pee-Chee
1975-76 Issue
Card No. 126, Error, Shows
position played as defense

No.	Player	VG	EX	NRMT
66	Darcy Rota, Chi.	.15	.35	.75 ☐
67	Bill Hogaboam, Det.	.15	.35	.75 ☐
68	Denis Herron, Goalie, KC	.15	.35	.75 ☐
69	Sheldon Kannegiesser, LA	.15	.35	.75 ☐
70	Yvan Cournoyer, Mon., Error	.75	1.50	3.00 ☐
71	Ernie Hicke, Min.	.15	.35	.75 ☐
72	Bert Marshall, NYI	.15	.35	.75 ☐
73	Derek Sanderson, NYR (Traded to St. Louis Oct. 30)	.15	.35	.75 ☐
74	Tom Bladon, Phi.	.15	.35	.75 ☐
75	Ron Schock, Pit.	.15	.35	.75 ☐
76	**Larry Sacharuk, St. L., RC, LC** (Traded to Rangers Sept. 21st.)	**.15**	**.35**	**.75** ☐
77	George Ferguson, Tor.	.15	.35	.75 ☐
78	Ab DeMarco, Van.	.15	.35	.75 ☐
79	Tom Williams, Wash., LC	.15	.35	.75 ☐
80	Phil Roberto, Det.	.15	.35	.75 ☐

TEAM CHECKLIST CARDS

No.	Team	VG	EX	NRMT
81	Boston Bruins	.50	1.00	2.00 ☐
82	California Golden Seals	.50	1.00	2.00 ☐
83	Buffalo Sabres	.50	1.00	2.00 ☐
84	Chicago Black Hawks	.50	1.00	2.00 ☐
85	Atlanta Flames	.50	1.00	2.00 ☐
86	Los Angeles Kings	.50	1.00	2.00 ☐
87	Detroit Red Wings	.50	1.00	2.00 ☐
88	Kansas City Scouts	.50	1.00	2.00 ☐
89	Minnesota North Stars	.50	1.00	2.00 ☐
90	Montreal Canadiens	.50	1.00	2.00 ☐
91	Toronto Maple Leafs	.50	1.00	2.00 ☐
92	New York Islanders	.50	1.00	2.00 ☐
93	Pittsburgh Penguins	.50	1.00	2.00 ☐
94	New York Rangers	.50	1.00	2.00 ☐
95	Philadelphia Flyers	.50	1.00	2.00 ☐
96	St. Louis Blues	.50	1.00	2.00 ☐
97	Vancouver Canucks	.50	1.00	2.00 ☐
98	Washington Capitals	.50	1.00	2.00 ☐

REGULAR ISSUE

No.	Player	VG	EX	NRMT
99	Checklist 1 (1 - 110), Error	3.75	7.50	15.00 ☐
100	Bobby Orr, Bos.	8.75	17.50	35.00 ☐
101	Germain Gagnon, Chi., LC (Traded to Kansas City Oct. 28)	.15	.35	.75 ☐
102	Phil Russell, Chi.	.15	.35	.75 ☐
103	Bill Lochead, Det.	.15	.35	.75 ☐
104	**Robin Burns, KC, RC, LC**	**.15**	**.35**	**.75** ☐
105	Gary Edwards, Goalie, LA	.15	.35	.75 ☐
106	Dwight Bialowas, Min.	.15	.35	.75 ☐
107	Doug Risebrough, Mon., Error	1.00	2.00	4.00 ☐
108	Dave Lewis, NYI	.15	.35	.75 ☐
109	Bill Fairbairn, NYR	.15	.35	.75 ☐
110	Ross Lonsberry, Phi.	.15	.35	.75 ☐
111	Ron Stackhouse, Pit.	.15	.35	.75 ☐
112	Claude Larose, St. L.	.15	.35	.75 ☐
113	Don Luce, Buf.	.15	.35	.75 ☐
114	**Errol Thompson, Tor., RC**	**.15**	**.35**	**.75** ☐
115	Gary Smith, Goalie, Van.	.15	.35	.75 ☐
116	Jack Lynch, Wash.	.15	.35	.75 ☐
117	Jacques Richard, Atl. (Traded to Buffalo Oct. 1)	.15	.35	.75 ☐
118	Dallas Smith, Bos.	.15	.35	.75 ☐
119	Dave Gardner, Ca.	.15	.35	.75 ☐
120	Mickey Redmond, Det.	.15	.35	.75 ☐
121	John Marks, Chi.	.15	.35	.75 ☐
122	Dave Hudson, KC	.15	.35	.75 ☐
123	Bob Nevin, LA	.15	.35	.75 ☐
124	Fred Barrett, Min.	.15	.35	.75 ☐
125	Gerry Desjardins, Goalie, Buf.	.15	.35	.75 ☐
126	Guy Lafleur, Mon., Error	3.75	7.50	15.00 ☐
127	J. P. Parise, NYI	.15	.35	.75 ☐
128	Walt Tkaczuk, NYR	.15	.35	.75 ☐
129	Gary Dornhoefer, Phi.	.15	.35	.75 ☐
130	Syl Apps, Jr., Pit.	.15	.35	.75 ☐
131	Bob Plager, St. L.	.15	.35	.75 ☐
132	Stan Weir, Tor.	.15	.35	.75 ☐
133	Tracy Pratt, Van.	.15	.35	.75 ☐
134	Jack Egers, Wash., LC	.15	.35	.75 ☐
135	Eric Vail, Atl.	.15	.35	.75 ☐
136	Al Sims, Bos.	.15	.35	.75 ☐
137	**Larry Patey, Ca., RC**	**.15**	**.35**	**.75** ☐
138	Jim Schoenfeld, Buf.	.15	.35	.75 ☐

60 • O-PEE-CHEE — 1975-76 REGULAR ISSUE

No.	Player	VG	EX	NRMT
139	Cliff Koroll, Chi.	.15	.35	.75
140	Marcel Dionne, LA	2.50	5.00	10.00
141	Jean-Guy Lagace, KC, LC	.15	.35	.75
142	Juha Widing, LA	.15	.35	.75
143	Lou Nanne, Min.	.15	.35	.75
144	Serge Savard, Mon.	.50	1.00	2.00
145	Glenn Resch, Goalie, NYI	1.25	2.50	5.00
146	**Ronald Greschner, NYR, RC**	.75	1.50	3.00
147	Dave Schultz, Phi.	.50	1.00	2.00
148	Barry Wilkins, Pit.	.15	.35	.75
149	Floyd Thomson, St. L.	.15	.35	.75
150	Darryl Sittler, Tor.	1.75	3.50	7.00
151	Paulin Bordeleau, Van.	.15	.35	.75
152	**Ron Lalonde, Wash., RC**	.15	.35	.75
153	Larry Romanchych, Atl.	.15	.35	.75
154	Larry Carriere, Buf. (Traded to Atlanta Oct. 1st.)	.15	.35	.75
155	Andre Savard, Bos.	.15	.35	.75
156	**Dave Hrechkosy, Ca., RC**	.15	.35	.75
157	Bill White, Chi.	.15	.35	.75
158	Dave Kryskow, Atl., LC	.15	.35	.75
159	Denis Dupere, KC	.15	.35	.75
160	Rogatien Vachon, Goalie, LA	.50	1.00	2.00
161	Doug Rombough, Min., LC	.15	.35	.75
162	Murray Wilson, Mon.	.15	.35	.75
163	**Bob Bourne, NYI, RC**	1.00	2.00	4.00
164	Gilles Marotte, NYR	.15	.35	.75
165	Vic Hadfield, Pit.	.15	.35	.75
166	Reggie Leach, Phi.	.15	.35	.75
167	Jerry Butler, St. L.	.15	.35	.75
168	Inge Hammarstrom, Tor.	.15	.35	.75
169	Chris Oddleifson, Van.	.15	.35	.75
170	Greg Joly, Wash.	.15	.35	.75
171	Checklist 2 (111 - 220)	3.75	7.50	15.00
172	Pat Quinn, Atl.	.15	.35	.75
173	Dave Forbes, Bos.	.15	.35	.75
174	Len Frig, Ca.	.15	.35	.75
175	Rick Martin, Buf.	.15	.35	.75
176	Keith Magnuson, Chi.	.15	.35	.75
177	Dan Maloney, Det.	.15	.35	.75
178	Craig Patrick, KC	.15	.35	.75
179	Tommy Williams, LA	.15	.35	.75
180	Bill Goldsworthy, Min.	.15	.35	.75
181	Steve Shutt, Mon.	1.50	3.00	6.00
182	Ralph Stewart, NYI	.15	.35	.75
183	John Davidson, Goalie, NYR	.75	1.50	3.00
184	Bob Kelly, Phi.	.15	.35	.75
185	Eddie Johnston, Goalie, St. L.	.25	.50	1.00
186	Dave Burrows, Pit.	.15	.35	.75
187	Dave Dunn, Tor., LC	.15	.35	.75
188	Dennis Kearns, Van.	.15	.35	.75
189	Bill Clement, Wash.	.50	1.00	2.00
190	Gilles Meloche, Goalie, Ca.	.15	.35	.75
191	Bobby Leiter, Atl., LC	.15	.35	.75
192	Jerry Korab, Buf.	.15	.35	.75
193	Joey Johnston, Chi.	.15	.35	.75
194	Walt McKechnie, Det.	.15	.35	.75
195	Wilf Paiement, KC	.15	.35	.75
196	Bob Berry, LA	.15	.35	.75
197	**Dean Talafous, Min., RC**	.15	.35	.75
198	Guy Lapointe, Mon.	.35	.75	1.50
199	**Clark Gillies, NYI, RC**	2.00	4.00	8.00
200a	Phil Esposito, "Traded" Bos.	2.00	4.00	8.00
200b	Phil Esposito, "Not Traded", Bos.	2.00	4.00	8.00
201	Greg Polis, NYR	.15	.35	.75
202	Jimmy Watson, Phi.	.15	.35	.75
203	**Gord McRae, Goalie, Tor., RC**	.25	.50	1.00
204	Lowell MacDonald, Pit.	.15	.35	.75
205	Barclay Plager, St. L., LC	.15	.35	.75
206	Don Lever, Van.	.15	.35	.75
207	Bill Mikkelson, Wash., LC	.15	.35	.75

1974 - 75 LEAGUE LEADERS

No.	Player	VG	EX	NRMT
208	**Goal Leaders:** P. Esposito, Bos., G. Lafleur, Mon., R. Martin, Buf.	1.25	2.50	5.00
209	**Assist Leaders:** B. Orr, Bos., B. Clarke, Phi., P. Mahovlich, Mon.	2.25	4.50	9.00
210	**Scoring Leaders:** B. Orr, Bos., P. Esposito, Bos., M. Dionne, LA	2.25	4.50	9.00
211	**Penalty Minute Leaders:** D. Schultz, Phi., A. Dupont, Phi., P. Russell, Chi.	.15	.35	.75
212	**Power Play Goal Leaders:**	1.25	2.50	5.00

O-Pee-Chee
1975-76 Issue
Card No. 173,
Dave Forbes

O-Pee-Chee
1975-76 Issue
Card No. 244, Error
Shows Ted Harris

O-Pee-Chee
1975-76 Issue
Card No. 258,
Jacques Lemaire

O-Pee-Chee, 1975-76 Issue
Card No. 267B, Error,
#362 Name misspelled Laroque
#396 Name misspelled Snepts

No.	Player	VG	EX	NRMT
	P. Esposito, Bos., R. Martin, Buf., D. Grant, Det.			
213	**Goals Against Avg Leaders:** B. Parent, Phi., R. Vachon, LA, K. Dryden, Mon.	1.50	3.00	6.00

REGULAR ISSUE

No.	Player	VG	EX	NRMT
214	Barry Gibbs, Atl.	.15	.35	.75
215	Ken Hodge, Sr., Bos.	.15	.35	.75
216	Jocelyn Guevremont, Buf.	.15	.35	.75
217	**Warren Williams, Ca., RC, LC**	.15	.35	.75
218	Dick Redmond, Chi.	.15	.35	.75
219	Jim Rutherford, Goalie, Det.	.15	.35	.75
220	Simon Nolet, KC	.15	.35	.75
221	Butch Goring, LA	.15	.35	.75
222	Glen Sather, Min.	.25	.50	1.00
223	**Mario Tremblay, Mon., RC, Error**	1.00	2.00	4.00
224	Jude Drouin, NYI	.15	.35	.75
225	Rod Gilbert, NYR	.50	1.00	2.00
226	Bill Barber, Phi	1.25	2.50	5.00
227	**Gary Inness, Goalie, Pit., RC**	.15	.35	.75
228	Wayne Merrick, St. L.	.15	.35	.75
229	Rod Seiling, Tor.	.15	.35	.75
230	Tom Lysiak, Atl.	.15	.35	.75
231	Bob Dailey, Van.	.15	.35	.75
232	Michel Belhumeur, Goalie, Wash.	.15	.35	.75
233	**Bill Hajt, Buf., RC**	.15	.35	.75
234	Jim Pappin, Ca., LC	.15	.35	.75
235	Gregg Sheppard, Bos.	.15	.35	.75
236	Gary Bergman, Det.	.15	.35	.75
237	Randy Rota, KC	.15	.35	.75
238	Neil Komadoski, LA	.15	.35	.75
239	Craig Cameron, Min.	.15	.35	.75
240	Tony Esposito, Goalie, Chi.	1.00	2.00	4.00
241	Larry Robinson, Mon.	3.50	7.00	14.00
242	Billy Harris, NYI	.15	.35	.75
243	Jean Ratelle, NYR	.50	1.00	2.00
244	Ted Irvine, St. L., Error	.15	.35	.75
245	Bob Neely, Tor.	.15	.35	.75
246	Bobby Lalonde, Van.	.15	.35	.75
247	**Ron Jones, Wash., RC, LC**	.15	.35	.75
248	Rey Comeau, Atl.	.15	.35	.75
249	Michel Plasse, Goalie, Pit.	.15	.35	.75
250	Bobby Clarke, Phi.	2.50	5.00	10.00
251	Bobby Schmautz, Bos.	.15	.35	.75
252	**Peter McNab, Buf., RC**	1.00	2.00	4.00
253	Al MacAdam, Ca.	.15	.35	.75
254	Dennis Hull, Chi.	.15	.35	.75
255	Terry Harper, Det.	.15	.35	.75
256	Pete McDuffe, Goalie, KC, LC (Traded to Detroit Aug. 22nd.)	.15	.35	.75
257	Jean Hamel, Det.	.15	.35	.75
258	Jacques Lemaire, Mon.	.50	1.00	2.00
259	Bob Nystrom, NYI	.15	.35	.75
260a	Brad Park, "Traded", NYR	1.00	2.00	4.00
260b	Brad Park, "Not Traded", NYR	1.00	2.00	4.00
261	Cesare Maniago, Goalie, Min.	.15	.35	.75
262	Don Saleski, Phi.	.15	.35	.75
263	J. Bob Kelly, Pit.	.15	.35	.75
264	**Bob Hess, St. L., RC**	.15	.35	.75
265	Blaine Stoughton, Tor.	.25	.50	1.00
266	John Gould, Van.	.15	.35	.75
267A	Checklist 3 (221-330)	3.75	7.50	15.00
267B	Checklist 4 (331-396), Error	3.75	7.50	15.00
268	Dan Bouchard, Goalie, Atl.	.15	.35	.75
269	Don Marcotte, Bos.	.15	.35	.75
270	Jim Neilson, Ca.	.15	.35	.75
271	Craig Ramsay, Buf.	.15	.35	.75
272	**Grant Mulvey, Chi., RC**	.35	.75	1.50
273	**Larry Giroux, Det., RC, LC**	.15	.35	.75
274	Richard Lemieux, KC (Traded to Atlanta Oct. 13th.)	.15	.35	.75
275	Denis Potvin, NYI	4.00	8.00	16.00
276	Don Kozak, NYI	.15	.35	.75
277	Tom Reid, Min.	.15	.35	.75
278	Bob Gainey, Mon.	2.00	4.00	8.00
279	Nick Beverley, NYR	.15	.35	.75
280	Jean Pronovost, Pit.	.15	.35	.75
281	Joe Watson, Phi.	.15	.35	.75
282	Chuck Lefley, St. L.	.15	.35	.75
283	Borje Salming, Tor.	1.75	3.50	7.00
284	Garnet Bailey, Wash.	.15	.35	.75
285	Gregg Boddy, Van., LC	.15	.35	.75

— 1975 - 76 REGULAR ISSUE — O-PEE-CHEE • 61

1974 - 75 ALL STARS
First Team

No.	Player	VG	EX	NRMT
286	Bobby Clarke, Phi.	1.00	2.00	4.00
287	Denis Potvin, NYI	1.75	3.50	7.00
288	Bobby Orr, Bos.	3.75	7.50	15.00
289	Rick Martin, Buf.	.15	.35	.75
290	Guy Lafleur, Mon.	1.35	2.75	5.50
291	Bernie Parent, Goalie, Phi.	.60	1.25	2.50

Second Team

No.	Player	VG	EX	NRMT
292	Phil Esposito, Bos.	.75	1.50	3.00
293	Guy Lapointe, Mon.	.15	.35	.75
294	Borje Salming, Tor.	.35	.75	1.50
295	Steve Vickers, NYR	.15	.35	.75
296	Rene Robert, Buf.	.15	.35	.75
297	Rogatien Vachon, Goalie, LA	.35	.75	1.50

REGULAR ISSUE

No.	Player	VG	EX	NRMT
298	Fred (Buster) Harvey, Atl. (Traded to Kansas City Oct. 13)	.15	.35	.75
299	Gary Sabourin, Ca.	.15	.35	.75
300	Bernie Parent, Goalie, Phi.	1.00	2.00	4.00
301	Terry O'Reilly, Bos.	.50	1.00	2.00
302	Ed Westfall, NYI	.15	.35	.75
303	Pete Stemkowski, NYR	.15	.35	.75
304	Pierre Bouchard, Mon.	.15	.35	.75
305	**Pierre Larouche, Pit., RC**	**2.00**	**4.00**	**8.00**
306	**Lee Fogolin, Buf., RC**	**.15**	**.35**	**.75**
307	Gerry O'Flaherty, Van.	.15	.35	.75
308	Phil Myre, Goalie, Atl.	.15	.35	.75
309	Pierre Plante, St. L.	.15	.35	.75
310	Dennis Hextall, Min.	.15	.35	.75
311	Jim McKenny, Tor.	.15	.35	.75
312	Vic Venasky, LA	.15	.35	.75

TEAM LEADERS

No.	Team	VG	EX	NRMT
313	**Atlanta Flames:** E. Vail, Goals; T. Lysiak, Assists, Points, Power Play Goals	.25	.50	1.00
314	**Boston Bruins:** P. Esposito, Goals, Power Play Goals; B. Orr, Assists, Points	2.00	4.00	8.00
315	**Buffalo Sabres:** R. Martin, Goals, Power Play Goals; R. Robert, Assists, Points	.25	.50	1.00
316	**California Golden Seals:** D. Hrechkosy, Goals; L. Patey/S. Weir, Points; S. Weir, Assists; L. Patey/ D. Hrechkosy, Power Play Goals	.25	.50	1.00
317	**Chicago Black Hawks:** S. Mikita/ J. Pappin, Goals; S. Mikita, Assists, Points, Power Play Goals	.50	1.00	2.00
318	**Detroit Red Wings:** D. Grant, Goals, Power Play Goals; M. Dionne, Points, Power Play Goals	.60	1.25	2.50
319	**Kansas City Scouts:** S. Nolet/ W. Paiement, Goals; G. Charron, Assists; S. Nolet,Points, Power Play Goals	.25	.50	1.00
320	**Los Angeles Kings:** B. Nevin, Goals, Assists, Points; B. Nevin/J. Widing/ B. Berry, Power Play Goals	.25	.50	1.00
321	**Minnesota North Stars:** B. Goldsworthy, Goals, Power Play Goals; D. Hextall, Assists,Points	.25	.50	1.00
322	**Montreal Canadiens:** G. Lafleur, Goals, Points, Power Play Goals; P. Mahovlich;, Assists	.60	1.25	2.50
323	**New York Islanders:** B. Nystrom, Goals; D. Potvin, Assists, Points, C. Gilles, Power Play Goals	.75	1.50	3.00
324	**New York Rangers:** S. Vickers, Goals; R. Gilbert, Assists, Points; J. Ratelle/S. VIckers, Power Play Goals	.50	1.00	2.00
325	**Philadelphia Flyers:** R. Leach, Goals, Power Play Goals; B. Clarke, Assists, Points	.75	1.50	3.00
326	**Pittsburgh Penguins:** J. Pronovost, Goals, Power Play Goals, R. Schock,	.25	.50	1.00
327	**St. Louis Blues:** G. Unger, Goals, Assists, Points; G. Unger/L. Sacharuk, Power Play Goals	.25	.50	1.00

O-Pee-Chee
1975-76 Issue
Card No. 288,
Bobby Orr

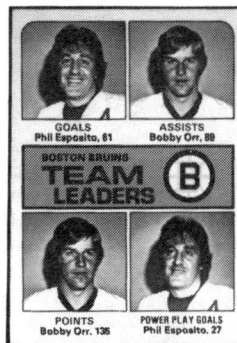

O-Pee-Chee
1975-76 Issue
Card No. 314,
Boston Bruins

O-Pee-Chee
1975-76 Issue
Card No. 333,
Doug Jarrett

O-Pee-Chee
1975-76 Issue
Card No. 382, Error,
Shows Denis Dupere

No.	Team	VG	EX	NRMT
328	**Toronto Maple Leafs:** D. Sittler, Goals, Assists, Points, Power Play Goals	.50	1.00	2.00
329	**Vancouver Canucks:** D. Lever, Goals, Power Play Goals; A. Boudria, Assists, Points	.25	.50	1.00
330	**Washington Capitals:** T. Williams, Goals, Power Play Goals; G. Bailey, Assists; T. Williams/G. Bailey, Points	.25	.50	1.00

REGULAR ISSUE

No.	Player	VG	EX	NRMT
331	Noel Price, Atl., LC (Retired before 1975-76 season.)	.15	.35	.75
332	Fred Stanfield, Buf.	.15	.35	.75
333	Doug Jarrett, Chi., LC (Traded to N.Y. Rangers Oct. 28)	.15	.35	.75
334	Gary Coalter, KC, LC	.15	.35	.75
335	Murray Oliver, Min., LC (Retired before 1975-76 season.)	.15	.35	.75
336	Dave Fortier, NYI	.15	.35	.75
337	Terry Crisp, Phi., LC, Error	.15	.35	.75
338	Bert Wilson, St. L.	.15	.35	.75
339	**John Grisdale, Van., RC**	**.15**	**.35**	**.75**
340	Ken Broderick, Goalie, Bos.	.15	.35	.75
341	**Frank Spring, Ca., RC, LC**	**.15**	**.35**	**.75**
342	**Mike Korney, Det., RC, LC**	**.15**	**.35**	**.75**
343	Gene Carr, LA	.15	.35	.75
344	Don Awrey, Mon.	.15	.35	.75
345	Pat Hickey, NYR	.15	.35	.75
346	**Colin Campbell, Pit., RC**	**.15**	**.35**	**.75**
347	Wayne Thomas, Goalie, Tor.	.15	.35	.75
348	**Bob Gryp, Wash., RC, LC**	**.15**	**.35**	**.75**
349	Bill Flett, Atl.	.15	.35	.75
350	Roger Crozier, Goalie, Buf., LC	.15	.35	.75
351	Dale Tallon, Chi.	.15	.35	.75
352	Larry Johnston, KC, LC	.15	.35	.75
353	**John Flesch, Min., RC, LC**	**.15**	**.35**	**.75**
354	Lorne Henning, NYI	.15	.35	.75
355	Wayne Stephenson, Goalie, Phi.	.15	.35	.75
356	Rick Wilson, St. L.	.15	.35	.75
357	Garry Monahan, Van.	.15	.35	.75
358	Gary Doak, Bos.	.15	.35	.75
359A	Pierre Jarry, Det., Error	.15	.35	.75
359B	Pierre Jarry, Det., Corrected (Traded to Minnesota Nov. 25)	.15	.35	.75
360	**George Pesut, Ca., RC, LC**	**.15**	**.35**	**.75**
361	Mike Corrigan, LA	.15	.35	.75
362	Michel Larocque, Goalie, Mon.	.15	.35	.75
363	Wayne Dillon, NYR	.15	.35	.75
364	Pete Laframboise, Pit., LC	.15	.35	.75
365	Brian Glennie, Tor.	.15	.35	.75
366	Mike Christie, Ca.	.15	.35	.75
367	**Jean Lemieux, Atl., RC**	**.15**	**.35**	**.75**
368	Gary Bromley, Goalie, Buf.	.25	.50	1.00
369	J.P. Bordeleau, Chi.	.15	.35	.75
370	**Ed Gilbert, KC, RC**	**.15**	**.35**	**.75**
371	Chris Ahrens, Min., LC	.15	.35	.75
372	Billy Smith, Goalie, NYI	1.50	3.00	6.00
373	**Larry Goodenough, Phi., RC**	**.15**	**.35**	**.75**
374	Leon Rochefort, Van., LC	.15	.35	.75
375	**Doug Gibson, Bos., RC, LC**	**.15**	**.35**	**.75**
376	Mike Bloom, Det.	.15	.35	.75
377	Larry Brown, LA	.15	.35	.75
378	Jim Roberts, Mon.	.15	.35	.75
379	Gilles Villemure, Goalie, NYR (Traded to Chicago Oct. 28)	.15	.35	.75
380	**Dennis Owchar, Pit., RC**	**.15**	**.35**	**.75**
381	Doug Favell, Goalie, Tor.	.15	.35	.75
382	Stan Gilbertson, Wash., Error	.15	.35	.75
383	**Ed Kea, Atl., RC**	**.15**	**.35**	**.75**
384	Brian Spencer, Buf.	.15	.35	.75
385	**Mike Veisor, Goalie, Chi., RC**	**.15**	**.35**	**.75**
386	Bob Murray, Van.	.15	.35	.75
387	**Andre St. Laurent, NYI, RC**	**.15**	**.35**	**.75**
388	**Rick Chartraw, Mon., RC**	**.15**	**.35**	**.75**
389	Orest Kindrachuk, Phi.	.15	.35	.75
390	**Dave Hutchison, LA, RC**	**.15**	**.35**	**.75**
391	Glenn Goldup, Mon.	.15	.35	.75
392	**Jerry Holland, NYR, RC**	**.15**	**.35**	**.75**
393	**Peter Sturgeon, Bos., RC, LC**	**.15**	**.35**	**.75**
394	**Alain Daigle, Chi., RC**	**.15**	**.35**	**.75**
395	No card issued; Should be Checklist 4 (331 - 396) See Card No. 267B			
396	**Harold Snepsts, Van., RC**	**3.75**	**7.50**	**15.00**

62 • O-PEE-CHEE — 1974 - 75 REGULAR ISSUE

— 1976 - 77 REGULAR ISSUE —

The card faces are similar to the Topps set for the same year. Team cards (132-149) have a checklist on the back for all players in the set. The set features four "record breaking" cards Nos. 65-68.
Mint cards command a 50% price premium over NRMT cards.

PRICE MOVEMENT OF NRMT SETS

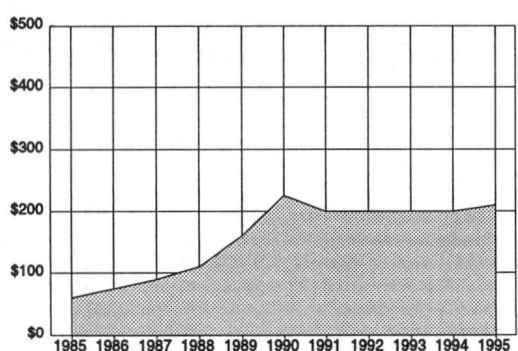

Card Size: 2 1/2" X 3 1/2"
Face: Four colour, white border, Team logo, Position
Back: Blue and green on card stock, Number, Resume, Hockey trivia, Bilingual
Imprint: © O-PEE-CHEE PRINTED IN CANADA. and © 1976 NHL PLAYERS ASSOCIATION
Complete Set No.: 396

Complete Set Price:	50.00	105.00	210.00
Common Card:	.10	.25	.45

'75 - 76 LEAGUE LEADERS

No.	Player	VG	EX	NRMT
1	**Goal Leaders:** R. Leach, Phi., G. Lafleur, Mon., P. Larouche, Pit.	.85	1.75	3.50
2	**Assist Leaders:** B. Clarke, Phi., P. Mahovlich, Mon., G. Lafleur, Mon., G. Perrault, Buf., J. Ratelle, Bos.	.75	1.50	3.00
3	**Scoring Leaders:** G. Lafleur, Mon., B. Clarke, Phi., G. Perrault, Buf.;	.75	1.50	3.00
4	**Penalty Minute Leaders:** S. Durbano, KC; B. Watson, Det., D. Schultz, Phi.	.10	.25	.50
5	**Power Play Goal Leaders:** P. Esposito, NYR; G. Lafleur, Mon., R. Martin, Buf., P. Larouche, Pit.; D. Potvin, NYI	.75	1.50	3.00
6	**Goals Against Avg Leaders:** K. Dryden, Mon., G. Resch, NYI, M. Larocque, Goalie, Mon	.60	1.25	2.50

REGULAR ISSUE

No.	Player	VG	EX	NRMT
7	Gary Doak, Bos.	.10	.25	.45
8	Jacques Richard, Buf.	.10	.25	.45
9	Wayne Dillon, NYR	.10	.25	.45
10	Bernie Parent, Goalie, Phi.	.80	1.65	3.25
11	Ed Westfall, NYI	.10	.25	.45
12	Dick Redmond, Chi.	.10	.25	.45
13	Bryan Hextall, Jr., Min., LC	.10	.25	.45
14	Jean Pronovost, Pit.	.10	.25	.45
15	Pete Mahovlich, Mon.	.10	.25	.45
16	Danny Grant, Det.	.10	.25	.45
17	Phil Myre, Goalie, Atl.	.12	.25	.45
18	Wayne Merrick, Cle.	.10	.25	.45
19	Steve Durbano, Col., LC	.10	.25	.45
20	Derek Sanderson, St. L.	.10	.25	.45
21	Mike Murphy, LA	.10	.25	.45
22	Borje Salming, Tor., 2nd Team All Star	.50	1.00	2.00
23	Mike Walton, Van.	.10	.25	.45
24	Randy Manery, Atl.	.10	.25	.45
25	Ken Hodge, Sr., NYR	.10	.25	.45
26	**Mel Bridgman, Phi., RC**	.60	1.25	2.50
27	Jerry Korab, Buf.	.10	.25	.45
28	Gilles Gratton, Goalie, NYR	.12	.25	.45
29	Andre St. Laurent, NYI	.10	.25	.45
30	Yvan Cournoyer, Mon.	.50	1.00	2.00
31	Phil Russell, Chi.	.10	.25	.45
32	Dennis Hextall, Det.	.10	.25	.45
33	Lowell MacDonald, Pit.	.10	.25	.45
34	Dennis O'Brien, Min.	.10	.25	.45

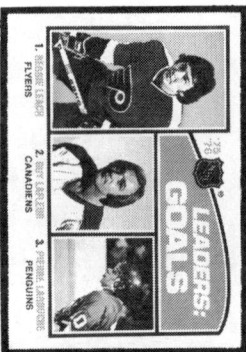

O-Pee-Chee 1976-77 Issue Card No. 1, Goal Leaders

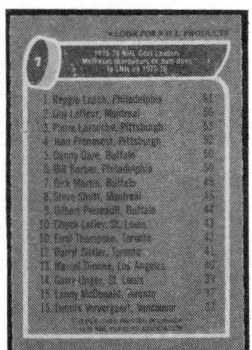

O-Pee-Chee 1976-77 Issue Card No. 1, Goal Leaders

O-Pee-Chee 1976-77 Issue Card No. 36, Gilles Meloche

O-Pee-Chee 1976-77 Issue Card No. 67, Bryan Trottier

No.	Player	VG	EX	NRMT
35	Gerry Meehan, Wash.	.10	.25	.45
36	Gilles Meloche, Goalie, Cle. (Team transferred to Cleveland)	.12	.25	.45
37	Wilf Paiement, Col. (Team Transferred to Colorado)	.10	.25	.45
38	**Bob MacMillan, St. L., RC**	.10	.25	.45
39	Ian Turnbull, Tor.	.10	.25	.45
40	Rogatien Vachon, Goalie, LA	.40	.85	1.75
41	Nick Beverley, NYR	.10	.25	.45
42	Rene Robert, Buf.	.10	.25	.45
43	Andre Savard, Buf.	.10	.25	.45
44	Bob Gainey, Mon.	.50	1.00	2.00
45	Joe Watson, Phi.	.10	.25	.45
46	Billy Smith, Goalie, NYI	.75	1.50	3.00
47	Darcy Rota, Chi.	.10	.25	.45
48	**Rick Lapointe, Det., RC**	.10	.25	.45
49	Pierre Jarry, Min.	.10	.25	.45
50	Syl Apps, Jr., Pit.	.10	.25	.45
51	Eric Vail, Atl.	.10	.25	.45
52	Greg Joly, Wash.	.10	.25	.45
53	Don Lever, Van.	.10	.25	.45
54	**Bob L. Murdoch, Cle., RC** (Team transferred to Cleveland)	.10	.25	.45
55	Denis Herron, Goalie, Pit. (Now with Penguins)	.10	.25	.45
56	Mike Bloom, Det.	.10	.25	.45
57	Bill Fairbairn, NYR	.10	.25	.45
58	Fred Stanfield, Buf.	.10	.25	.45
59	Steve Shutt, Mon.	.75	1.50	3.00
60	Brad Park, Bos., 1st Team All Star	.60	1.25	2.50
61	Gilles Villemure, Goalie, Chi., LC	.12	.25	.45
62	Bert Marshall, NYI	.10	.25	.45
63	Chuck Lefley, St. L.	.10	.25	.45
64	Simon Nolet, Col., LC	.10	.25	.45

75 - 76 RECORD BREAKERS

No.	Player	VG	EX	NRMT
65	**Most Goals, Playoffs:** Reggie Leach, Phi.,	.10	.25	.50
66	**Most Points, Game:** Darryl Sittler, Tor.,	.40	.85	1.75
67	**Most Points, Season, Rookie:** Bryan Trottier, NYI,	2.00	4.00	8.00
68	**Most Consecutive Games, Lifetime:** Garry Unger, St. L.,	.10	.25	.50

REGULAR ISSUE

No.	Player	VG	EX	NRMT
69	Ron Low, Goalie, Wash.	.12	.25	.45
70	Bobby Clarke, Phi., 1st Team All Star	1.50	3.00	6.00
71	**Michel Bergeron, Det., RC**	.50	1.00	2.00
72	Ron Stackhouse, Pit.	.10	.25	.45
73	Bill Hogaboam, Min.	.10	.25	.45
74	Bob J. Murdoch, LA	.10	.25	.45
75	Steve Vickers, NYR	.10	.25	.45
76	Pit Martin, Chi.	.10	.25	.45
77	Gerry Hart, NYI	.10	.25	.45
78	Craig Ramsay, Buf.	.10	.25	.45
79	Michel Larocque, Goalie, Mon.	.12	.25	.45
80	Jean Ratelle, Bos.	.40	.85	1.75
81	Don Saleski, Phi.	.10	.25	.45
82	Bill Clement, Atl.	.10	.25	.45
83	Dave Burrows, Pit.	.10	.25	.45
84	Wayne Thomas, Goalie, Tor.	.12	.25	.45
85	John Gould, Van.	.10	.25	.45
86	**Dennis Maruk, Cle., RC,** (Team transferred to Cleveland)	1.00	2.00	4.00
87	Ernie Hicke, Min.	.10	.25	.45
88	Jim Rutherford, Goalie, Det.	.12	.25	.45
89	Dale Tallon, Chi.	.10	.25	.45
90	Rod Gilbert, NYR	.50	1.00	2.00
91	Marcel Dionne, LA	2.00	4.00	8.00
92	Chuck Arnason, Col.	.10	.25	.45
93	Jean Potvin, NYI	.10	.25	.45
94	Don Luce, Buf.	.10	.25	.45
95	John Bucyk, Bos.	.40	1.00	2.00
96	Larry Goodenough, Phi.	.10	.25	.45
97	Mario Tremblay, Mon.	.10	.25	.45
98	**Nelson Pyatt, Col., RC** (Now with Rockies)	.10	.25	.45
99	Brian Glennie, Tor.	.10	.25	.45
100	Tony Esposito, Goalie, Chi.	.85	1.75	3.50
101	Dan Maloney, Det.	.10	.25	.45
102	Dunc Wilson, Goalie, Pit.	.12	.25	.45

1976-77 REGULAR ISSUE — O-PEE-CHEE

No.	Player	VG	EX	NRMT
103	Dean Talafous, Min.	.10	.25	.45
104	**Ed Staniowski, Goalie, St. L., RC**	.15	.35	.75
105	Dallas Smith, Bos., LC	.10	.25	.45
106	Jude Drouin, NYI	.10	.25	.45
107	Pat Hickey, NYR	.10	.25	.45
108	Jocelyn Guevremont, Buf.	.10	.25	.45
109	**Doug Risebrough, Mon., RC**	.10	.25	.45
110	Reggie Leach, Phi., 2nd Team All Star	.10	.25	.45
111	Dan Bouchard, Goalie, Atl.	.12	.25	.45
112	Chris Oddleifson, Van.	.10	.25	.45
113	Rick Hampton, Cle. (Team transferred to Cleveland)	.10	.25	.45
114	John Marks, Chi.	.10	.25	.45
115	**Bryan Trottier, NYI, RC**	18.75	37.50	65.00
116	Checklist 1 (1 - 132)	3.00	6.00	12.00
117	Greg Polis, NYR	.10	.25	.45
118	Peter McNab, Bos.	.10	.25	.45
119	Jim Roberts, Mon.	.10	.25	.45
120	Gerry Cheevers, Goalie, Bos.	.75	1.50	3.00
121	Rick MacLeish, Phi.	.10	.25	.45
122	Bill Lochead, Det.	.10	.25	.45
123	Tom Reid, Min.	.10	.25	.45
124	Rick Kehoe, Pit.	.10	.25	.45
125	Keith Magnuson, Chi.	.10	.25	.45
126	Clark Gillies, NYI	.50	1.00	2.00
127	Rick Middleton, Bos.	.75	1.50	3.00
128	Bill Hajt, Buf.	.10	.25	.45
129	Jacques Lemaire, Mon.	.35	.75	1.50
130	Terry O'Reilly, Bos.	.25	.50	1.00
131	Andre Dupont, Phi.	.10	.25	.45

TEAM CHECKLIST CARDS

No.	Team	VG	EX	NRMT
132	Atlanta Flames	.35	.75	1.50
133	Bruins, Adams Division	.35	.75	1.50
134	Sabres, Adams Division	.35	.75	1.50
135	Seals, Adams Division, (Team tranferred to Cleveland)	.35	.75	1.50
136	Black Hawks, Smythe Division	.35	.75	1.50
137	Red Wings, Norris Division	.35	.75	1.50
138	Scouts, Smythe Division, (Team transferred to Colorado)	.35	.75	1.50
139	Kings, Norris Division	.35	.75	1.50
140	North Stars, Smythe Division	.35	.75	1.50
141	Canadiens, Norris Division	.35	.75	1.50
142	Islanders, Patrick Division	.35	.75	1.50
143	Rangers, Patrick Division	.35	.75	1.50
144	Flyers, Patrick Division	.35	.75	1.50
145	Penguins, Norris Division	.35	.75	1.50
146	Blues, Smythe Division	.35	.75	1.50
147	Maple Leafs, Adams Division	.35	.75	1.50
148	Canucks, Smythe Division	.35	.75	1.50
149	Capitals, Norris Division	.35	.75	1.50

REGULAR ISSUE

No.	Player	VG	EX	NRMT
150	Dave Schultz, LA (Now with Kings)	.10	.25	.45
151	Larry Robinson, Mon.	2.00	4.00	8.00
152	Al Smith, Goalie, Buf.	.12	.25	.45
153	Bob Nystrom, NYI	.10	.25	.45
154	Ronald Greschner, NYR	.25	.50	1.00
155	Gregg Sheppard, Bos.	.10	.25	.45
156	Alain Daigle, Chi.	.10	.25	.45
157	Ed Van Impe, Pit., LC	.10	.25	.45
158	**Tim Young, Min., RC**	.15	.30	.60
159	Bryan Lefley, Col.	.10	.25	.45
160	Ed Giacomin, Goalie, Det.	.50	1.00	2.00
161	Yvon Labre, Wash.	.10	.25	.45
162	Jim Lorentz, Buf.	.10	.25	.45
163	Guy Lafleur, Mon., 1st Team All Star	3.00	6.00	12.00
164	Tom Bladon, Phi.	.10	.25	.45
165	Wayne Cashman, Bos.	.10	.25	.45
166	Pete Stemkowski, NYR	.10	.25	.45
167	Grant Mulvey, Chi.	.10	.25	.45
168	**Yves Belanger, Goalie, St. L., RC**	.15	.30	.60
169	Bill Goldsworthy, Min.	.10	.25	.45
170	Denis Potvin, NYI, 1st Team All Star	2.00	4.00	8.00
171	Nick Libett, Det.	.10	.25	.45
172	Michel Plasse, Goalie, Col.	.12	.25	.45
173	Lou Nanne, Min.	.10	.25	.45
174	Tom Lysiak, Atl.	.10	.25	.45
175	Dennis Ververgaert, Van.	.10	.25	.45
176	Gary Simmons, Goalie, Cle.	.12	.25	.45

O-Pee-Chee 1976-77 Issue Card No. 168, Yves Belanger

O-Pee-Chee 1976-77 Issue Card No. 170, Denis Potvin

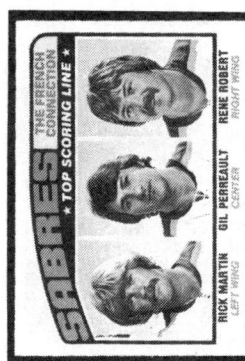

O-Pee-Chee 1976-77 Issue Card No. 214, The French Connection

O-Pee-Chee 1976-77 Issue Card No. 243, Scott Garland

No.	Player	VG	EX	NRMT
177	Pierre Bouchard, Mon.	.10	.25	.45
178	Bill Barber, Phi., 1st Team All Star	.75	1.50	3.00
179	Darryl Edestrand, Bos.	.10	.25	.45
180	Gilbert Perreault, Buf., 2nd Team All Star	.85	1.75	3.50
181	Dave Maloney, NYR, RC	.25	.50	1.00
182	J. P. Parise, NYI	.10	.25	.45
183	Jim Harrison, Chi.	.10	.25	.45
184	**Pete LoPresti, Goalie, Min., RC**	.12	.25	.45
185	Don Kozak, LA	.10	.25	.45
186	Guy Charron, Wash., (Now with Capitals)	.10	.25	.45
187	Stan Gilbertson, Pit.	.10	.25	.45
188	**Bill Nyrop, Mon., RC**	.17	.35	.75
189	Bobby Schmautz, Bos.	.10	.25	.45
190	Wayne Stephenson, Goalie, Phi.	.12	.25	.45
191	Brian Spencer, Buf.	.10	.25	.45
192	Gilles Marotte, St. L., LC (Now with Blues)	.10	.25	.45
193	Lorne Henning, NYI	.10	.25	.45
194	Bob Neely, Tor.	.10	.25	.45
195	Dennis Hull, Chi.	.10	.25	.45
196	Walt McKechnie, Det.	.10	.25	.45
197	**Curt Ridley, Goalie, Van., RC**	.12	.25	.45
198	Dwight Bialowas, Min.	.10	.25	.45
199	Pierre Larouche, Pit.	.60	1.25	2.50
200	Ken Dryden, Goalie, Mon., 1st Team All Star	4.50	9.00	18.00
201	Ross Lonsberry, Phi.	.10	.25	.45
202	Curt Bennett, Atl.	.10	.25	.45
203	**Hartland Monahan, Wash., RC**	.10	.25	.45
204	John Davidson, Goalie, NYR	.12	.25	.45
205	Serge Savard, Mon.	.30	.65	1.25
206	Garry Howatt, NYI	.10	.25	.45
207	Darryl Sittler, Tor.	1.50	3.00	6.00
208	J. P. Bordeleau, Chi.	.10	.25	.45
209	Henry Boucha, Col., LC (Team transferred to Colorado)	.10	.25	.45
210	Rick Martin, Buf., 2nd Team All Star	.10	.25	.45
211	Vic Venasky, LA	.10	25	.45
212	Fred (Buster) Harvey, Det.	.10	.25	.45
213	Bobby Orr, Chi.	6.75	13.50	27.00

TOP SCORING LINE

No.	Player	VG	EX	NRMT
214	**The French Connection:** Martin, Perreault, Robert, Buf.	.60	1.25	2.50
215	**LCB Line:** Barber, Clarke, Leach, Phi.	.75	1.50	3.00
216	**Long Island Lightning Co.:** Gillies, Trottier, Harris, NYI	1.10	2.25	4.50
217	**Checking Line:** Gainey, Jarvis, Roberts, Mon.	.30	.65	1.25
218	**Bicentennial Line:** MacDonald, Apps, Pronovost, Pit.	.15	.35	.75

REGULAR ISSUE

No.	Player	VG	EX	NRMT
219	Bob Kelly, Phi.	.10	.25	.45
220	Walt Tkaczuk, NYR	.10	.25	.45
221	Dave Lewis, NYI	.10	.25	.45
222	Danny Gare, Buf.	.10	.25	.45
223	Guy Lapointe, Mon., 2nd Team All Star	.10	.25	.50
224	**Hank Nowak, Bos., RC, LC**	.10	.25	.45
225	Stan Mikita, Chi.	1.00	2.00	4.00
226	Vic Hadfield, Pit., LC	.10	.25	.45
227	**Bernie Wolfe, Goalie, Wash., RC**	.07	.25	50
228	Bryan Watson, Det.	.10	.25	.45
229	Ralph Stewart, Van. (Now with Canucks)	.10	.25	.45
230	Gerry Desjardins, Goalie, Buf.	.12	.25	.45
231	**John Bednarski, NYR, RC, LC**	.10	.25	.45
232	Yvon Lambert, Mon.	.10	.25	.45
233	Orest Kindrachuk, Phi.	.10	.25	.45
234	Don Marcotte, Bos.	.10	.25	.45
235	Bill White, Chi., LC	.10	.25	.45
236	Red Berenson, St.L.	.10	.25	.45
237	Al MacAdam, Cle. (Team transferred to Cleveland)	.10	.25	.45
238	**Rick Blight, Van., RC**	.10	.25	.45
239	Butch Goring, LA	.10	.25	.45
240	Cesare Maniago, Goalie, Van.	.12	.25	.45
241	Jim Schoenfeld, Buf.	.10	.25	.45
242	Cliff Koroll, Chi.	.10	.25	.45
243	**Scott Garland, Tor., RC**	.10	.25	.45
244	Rick Chartraw, Mon.	.10	.25	.45

64 • O-PEE-CHEE — 1976 - 77 REGULAR ISSUE —

No.	Player	VG	EX	NRMT
245	Phil Esposito, NYR	1.00	2.00	4.00
246	Dave Forbes, Bos.	.10	.25	.45
247	Jimmy Watson, Phi.	.10	.25	.45
248	Ron Schock, Pit.	.10	.25	.45
249	Fred Barrett, Min.	.10	.25	.45
250	Glenn Resch, Goalie, NYI, 2nd Team All Star	.50	1.00	2.00
251	Ivan Boldirev, Chi.	.10	.25	.45
252	Billy Harris, NYI	.10	.25	.45
253	Lee Fogolin, Buf.	.10	.25	.45
254	Murray Wilson, Mon.	.10	.25	.45
255	Gilles Gilbert, Goalie, Bos.	.12	.25	.45
256	Gary Dornhoefer, Phi.	.10	.25	.45
257	Carol Vadnais, NYR	.10	.25	.45
258	Checklist 2 (133 - 264)	3.00	6.00	12.00
259	Errol Thompson, Tor.	.10	.25	.45
260	Garry Unger, St. L.	.10	.25	.45
261	J. Bob Kelly, Pit.	.10	.25	.45
262	Terry Harper, Det.	.10	.25	.45
263	Blake Dunlop, Min.	.10	.25	.45
264	'75-76 Stanley Cup Champions: Canadiens Sweep Flyers in 4	.60	1.25	2.50
265	Richard Mulhern, Atl., RC	.10	.25	.45
266	Gary Sabourin, Cle., LC	.10	.25	.45
267	Bill McKenzie, Goalie, Col., RC, Error	.12	.25	.45
268	Mike Corrigan, Pit.	.10	.25	.45
269	Rick Smith, St. L.	.10	.25	.45
270	Stan Weir, Tor.	.10	.25	.45
271	Ron Sedlbauer, Van., RC	.10	.25	.45
272	Jean Lemieux, Wash., LC	.10	.25	.45
273	Hilliard Graves, Atl.	.10	.25	.45
274	Dave Gardner, Cle.	.10	.25	.45
275	Tracy Pratt, Col., LC	.10	.25	.45
276	Frank St. Marseille, LA, LC	.10	.25	.45
277	Bob Hess, St. L.	.10	.25	.45
278	Bobby Lalonde, Van.	.10	.25	.45
279	Tony White, Wash., RC	.10	.25	.45
280	Rod Seiling, St. L.	.10	.25	.45
281	Larry Romanchych, Atl., LC	.10	.25	.45
282	Ralph Klassen, Cle., RC	.10	.25	.45
283	Gary Croteau, Col.	.10	.25	.45
284	Neil Komadoski, LA	.10	.25	.45
285	Eddie Johnston, Goalie, St. L.	.12	.25	.45
286	George Ferguson, Tor.	.10	.25	.45
287	Gerry O'Flaherty, Van.	.10	.25	.45
288	Jack Lynch, Wash.	.10	.25	.45
289	Pat Quinn, Atl., LC	.10	.25	.45
290	Gene Carr, LA	.10	.25	.45
291	Bob Stewart, Cle.	.10	.25	.45
292	Doug Favell, Goalie, Col.	.12	.25	.45
293	Rick Wilson, Det.	.10	.25	.45
294	Jack Valiquette, Tor., RC	.10	.25	.45
295	Garry Monahan, Van.	.10	.25	.45
296	Michel Belhumeur, Goalie, Atl., LC	.12	.25	.45
297	Larry Carriere, Atl.	.10	.25	.45
298	Fred Ahern, Cle., RC	.10	.25	.45
299	Dave Hudson, Col.	.10	.25	.45
300	Bob Berry, LA	.10	.25	.45
301	Bob Gassoff, St. L., LC	.10	.25	.45
302	Jim McKenny, Tor.	.10	.25	.45
303	Gord Smith, Wash., RC	.10	.25	.45
304	Garnet Bailey, Wash.	.10	.25	.45
305	Bruce Affleck, St. L., RC	.15	.30	.60
306	Doug Halward, Bos., RC	.10	.25	.45
307	Lew Morrison, Pit.	.10	.25	.45
308	Bob Sauve, Goalie, Buf., RC	.30	.65	1.25
309	Bob Murray, Chi.	.15	.35	.75
310	Claude Larose, St. L.	.10	.25	.45
311	Don Awrey, Pit.	.10	.25	.45
312	Billy MacMillan, NYI, LC	.10	.25	.45
313	Doug Jarvis, Mon., RC	.75	1.50	3.00
314	Dennis Owchar, Pit.	.10	.25	.45
315	Jerry Holland, NYR, LC	.10	.25	.45
316	Guy Chouinard, Atl., RC	.15	.35	.75
317	Gary Smith, Goalie, Min.	.12	.25	.45
318	Pat Price, NYI, RC	.10	.25	.45
319	Tommy Williams, LA	.10	.25	.45
320	Larry Patey, St. L.	.10	.25	.45
321	Claire Alexander, Tor., RC, LC	.10	.25	.45
322	Larry Bolonchuk, Wash., RC	.10	.25	.45
323	Bob Sirois, Wash., LC	.10	.25	.45
324	Joe Zanussi, Bos., RC, LC	.10	.25	.45
325	Joey Johnston, Chi., LC	.10	.25	.45

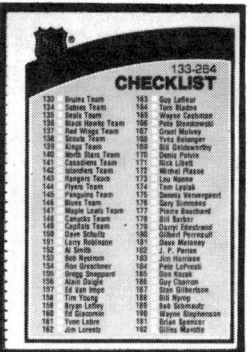

O-Pee-Chee 1976-77 Issue Card No. 258, Checklist 2 (133-264)

O-Pee-Chee, 1976-77 Issue Card No. 267, Error, Name misspelled KcKenzie on face

O-Pee-Chee, 1976-77 Issue Card No. 348, Error, Name misspelled MacDonald on face and back

O-Pee-Chee 1976-77 Issue Card No. 373, David Williams

No.	Player	VG	EX	NRMT
326	J. P. LeBlanc, Det., Error	.10	.25	.45
327	Craig Cameron, Min., LC	.10	.25	.45
328	Dave Fortier, Van., LC	.10	.25	.45
329	Ed Gilbert, Pit., LC	.10	.25	.45
330	John Van Boxmeer, Mon., RC	.12	.25	.50
331	Gary Inness, Goalie, Phi.	.12	.25	.50
332	Bill Flett, Atl.	.10	.25	.45
333	Mike Christie, Cle.	.10	.25	.45
334	Denis Dupere, Col.	.10	.25	.45
335	Sheldon Kannegiesser, LA	.10	.25	.45
336	Jerry Butler, St. L.	.10	.25	.45
337	Gord McRae, Goalie, Tor.	.12	.25	.45
338	Dennis Kearns, Van.	.10	.25	.45
339	Ron Lalonde, Wash.	.10	.25	.45
340	Jean Hamel, Det.	.10	.25	.45
341	Barry Gibbs, Atl.	.10	.25	.45
342	Mike Pelyk, Tor., LC	.10	.25	.45
343	Rey Comeau, Atl.	.10	.25	.45
344	Jim Neilson, Cle.	.10	.25	.45
345	Phil Roberto, Col., LC	.10	.25	.45
346	Dave Hutchison, LA	.10	.25	.45
347	Ted Irvine, St. L., LC	.10	.25	.45
348	Lanny McDonald, Tor., Error	1.75	3.50	7.00
349	Jim Moxey, Cle., RC, LC	.10	.25	.45
350	Bob Dailey, Van.	.10	.25	.45
351	Tim Ecclestone, Atl.	.10	.25	.45
352	Len Frig, Cle.	.10	.25	.45
353	Randy Rota, Col., LC	.10	.25	.45
354	Juha Widing, LA	.10	.25	.45
355	Larry Brown, LA	.10	.25	.45
356	Floyd Thomson, St. L.	.10	.25	.45
357	Richard Nantais, Min., RC, LC	.10	.25	.45
358	Inge Hammarstrom, Tor.	.10	.25	.45
359	Mike Robitaille, Van., LC	.10	.25	.45
360	Rejean Houle, Mon.	.10	.25	.45
361	Ed Kea, Atl.	.10	.25	.45
362	Bob Girard, Cle., RC	.10	.25	.45
363	Bob Murray, Van.	.10	.25	.45
364	Dave Hrechkosy, St. L., LC	.10	.25	.45
365	Gary Edwards, Goalie, LA	.12	.25	.45
366	Harold Snepsts, Van.	.50	1.00	2.00
367	Pat Boutette, Tor., RC	.25	.50	1.00
368	Bob Paradise, Wash.	.10	.25	.45
369	Bob Plager, St. L., LC	.10	.25	.45
370	Tim Jacobs, Cle., RC, LC	.10	.25	.45
371	Pierre Plante, St. L.	.10	.25	.45
372	Colin Campbell, Col.	.10	.25	.45
373	David Williams, Tor., RC	3.00	6.00	12.00
374	Ab DeMarco, LA	.10	.25	.45
375	Mike Lampman, Wash., RC	.10	.25	.45
376	Mark Heaslip, NYR, RC	.10	.25	.45
377	Checklist 3 (265 - 396)	2.50	5.00	10.00
378	Bert Wilson, LA	.10	.25	.45

1975 - 76 TEAM LEADERS

No.	Team	VG	EX	NRMT
379	**Atlanta Flames:** C. Bennett, Goals; T. Lysiak, Assists; P. Quinn, Penalty Mins.; C. St. Sauveur, Power Play Goals	.15	.35	.75
380	**Buffalo Sabres:** D. Gare, Goals, Penalty Mins.; G. Perreault, Assists; R. Martin, Power Play Goals	.35	.75	1.50
381	**Boston Bruins:** J. Bucyk/J. Ratelle, Goals; J. Ratelle, Assists, Power Play Goals; T. O'Reilly, Penalty Mins.	.40	.85	1.75
382	**Chicago Black Hawks:** P. Martin, Goals; D. Tallon, Assists; P. Russell, Penalty Mins.; C. Koroll, Power Play Goals	.15	.35	.75
383	**California Golden Seals:** W. Merrick/A. MacAdam, Goals; R. Hampton, Assists; M. Christie, Penalty Mins.; B. Murdoch, Power Play Goals	.15	.35	.75
384	**Kansas City Scouts:** G. Charron, Goals, Assists, Power Play Goals; S. Durbano, Penalty Mins.	.15	.35	.75
385	**Detroit Red Wings:** M. Bergeron, Goals, Power Play Goals; W. McKechnie, Assists; B. Watson, Penalty Mins.	.15	.35	.75
386	**Los Angeles Kings:** M. Dionne, Goals, Assists; D. Hutchison, Penalty Mins. M. Corrigan, Power Play Goals	.40	.85	1.75

— 1977 - 78 REGULAR ISSUE — O-PEE-CHEE • 65

No.	Team	VG	EX	NRMT
387	**Minnesota North Stars:** B. Hogaboam, Goals, Power Play Goals; T. Young, Assists; D. O'Brien, Penalty Mins.	.15	.35	.75 □
388	**Montreal Canadiens:** G. Lafleur, Goals, Power Play Goals, P. Mahovlich, Assists; D. Risebrough, Penalty Mins.	.50	1.00	2.00 □
389	**New York Islanders:** C. Gilles, Goals; D. Potvin, Assists, Power Play Goals; G. Howatt, Penalty Mins.	.50	1.00	2.00 □
390	**New York Rangers:** R. Gilbert, Goals; S. Vickers, Assists; C. Vadnais, Penalty Mins.; P. Esposito, Power Play Goals	.40	.85	1.75 □
391	**Philadelphia Flyers:** R. Leach, Goals; B. Clarke, Assists; D. Schultz, Penalty Mins.; B. Barber, Power Play Goals	.50	1.00	2.00 □
392	**Pittsburgh Penguins:** P. Larouche, Goals, Power Play Goals; S. Apps, Jr. Assists; R. Shock, Penalty Mins.	.15	.35	.75 □
393	**St. Louis Blues:** C. Lefley, Goals; G. Unger, Assists, Power Play Goals; B. Gassoff, Penalty Mins.	.15	.35	.75 □
394	**Toronto Maple Leafs:** E. Thompson, Goals, Power Play Goals; D. Sittler, Assists; D. Williams, Penalty Mins.	.15	.35	.75 □
395	**Vancouver Canucks:** D. Ververgaert; Goals, Power Play Goals; C. Oddleifson/ D. Kearns, Assists; H. Snepsts, Penalty Mins.	.15	.35	.75 □
396	**Washington Capitals:** N. Pyatt, Goals; G. Meehan, Assists; Y. Labre, Penalty Mins.; T. White, Power Play Goals	.25	.50	1.00 □

— 1977 - 78 REGULAR ISSUE —

Cards 322-339 show the team emblem on the front and player records on the back. The set features all-star and record breaking players. Mint cards command a price premium of 50% over NRMT cards.

PRICE MOVEMENT OF NRMT SETS

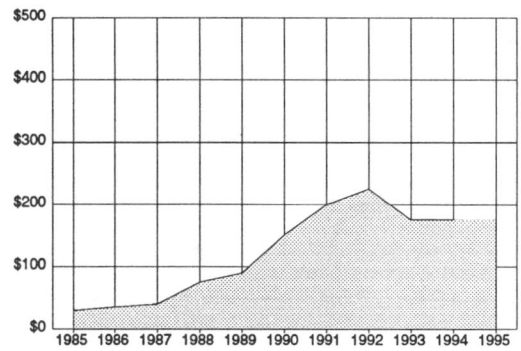

Card Size: 2 1/2" X 3 1/2"
Face: Four colour, white border, Team logo, Position
Back: Brown and blue on card stock, Number, Resume, Hockey trivia, Bilingual
Imprint: ** © 1977 O-PEE-CHEE PRINTED IN CANADA
Complete Set No.: 396
Complete Set Price: 45.00 85.00 175.00 □
Card: .07 .15 .30

1976 - 77 NHL LEAGUE LEADERS

No.	Player	VG	EX	NRMT
1	**Goal Leaders:** S. Shutt, Mon.; G. Lafleur, Mon.; M. Dionne, LA	.85	1.75	3.50 □
2	**Assist Leaders:** G. Lafleur, Mon.; M. Dionne, LA; L. Robinson, Mon.; B. Salming, Tor.; T. Young, Min.	.55	1.12	2.25 □
3	**Scoring Leaders:** G. Lafleur, Mon.; M. Dionne, LA; S. Shutt, Mon.	.55	1.12	2.25 □
4	**Penalty Minute Leaders:** D. Williams, Tor.; D. Polonich,Det.; B. Gassoff, St. L	.25	.50	1.00 □

O-Pee-Chee 1977-78 Issue Card No. 1, Goal Leaders

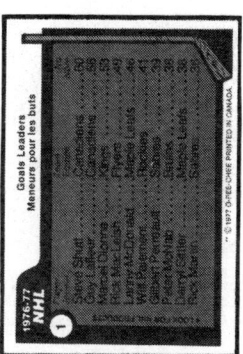

O-Pee-Chee 1977-78 Issue Card No. 1, Goal Leaders

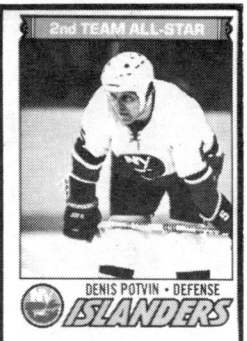

O-Pee-Chee 1977-78 Issue Card No. 10, Denis Potvin

O-Pee-Chee 1977-78 Issue Card No. 65, Bernie Parent

No.	Player	VG	EX	NRMT
5	**Power Play Goal Leaders:** L. McDonald, Tor.; P. Esposito, NYR; T. Williams, LA	.25	.50	1.00 □
6	**Goals Against Avg Leaders:** M. Larocque, Mon.; K. Dryden, Mon.; G. Resch, NYI	.50	1.00	2.00 □
7	**Game Winning Goal Leaders:** G. Perreault, Buf.; S, Shutt, Mon; G. Lafleur, Mon.; R. MacLeish, Phi.; P. McNab, Bos.	.55	1.15	2.25 □
8	**Shutout Leaders:** K. Dryden, Mon.; R. Vachon, LA; B. Parent, Phi.; D. Wilson, Pit.	.50	1.00	2.00 □

REGULAR ISSUE

No.	Player	VG	EX	NRMT
9	Brian Spencer, Pit. (Now with Penguins)	.07	.15	.30 □
10	Denis Potvin, NYI, 2nd Team All-Star	1.25	2.50	5.00 □
11	Nick Fotiu, NYR	.15	.30	.60 □
12	Bob Murray, Chi.	.07	.15	.30 □
13	Pete LoPresti, Goalie, Min.	.07	.15	.30 □
14	J. Bob Kelly, Chi. (Now with Black Hawks)	.07	.15	.30 □
15	Rick MacLeish, Phi.	.07	.15	.30 □
16	Terry Harper, Det.	.07	.15	.30 □
17	**Willi Plett, Atl., RC**	.50	1.00	2.00 □
18	Peter McNab, Bos.	.07	.15	.30 □
19	Wayne Thomas, Goalie, NYR, (Now with Rangers)	.07	.15	.30 □
20	Pierre Bouchard, Mon.	.07	.15	.30 □
21	Dennis Maruk, Cle.	.25	.50	1.00 □
22	Mike Murphy, LA	.07	.15	.30 □
23	Cesare Maniago, Goalie, Van., LC	.07	.15	.30 □
24	**Paul Gardner, Col., RC**	.15	.25	.50 □
25	Rod Gilbert, NYR, LC	.35	.75	1.50 □
26	Orest Kindrachuk, Phi.	.07	.15	.30 □
27	Bill Hajt, Buf.	.07	.15	.30 □
28	John Davidson, Goalie, NYR	.07	.15	.30 □
29	J. P. Parise, NYI	.07	.15	.30 □
30	Larry Robinson, Mon., 1st Team All-Star	1.25	2.50	5.00 □
31	Yvon Labre, Wash.	.07	.15	.30 □
32	Walt McKechnie, Wash. (Now with Capitals)	.07	.15	.30 □
33	Rick Kehoe, Pit.	.07	.15	.30 □
34	**Randy Holt, Chi., RC**	.07	.15	.30 □
35	Garry Unger, St. L.	.07	.15	.30 □
36	Lou Nanne, Min., LC	.07	.15	.30 □
37	Dan Bouchard, Goalie, Atl.	.07	.15	.30 □
38	Darryl Sittler, Tor.	1.15	2.25	4.50 □
39	Bob L. Murdoch, Cle.	.07	.15	.30 □
40	Jean Ratelle, Bos.	.50	1.00	2.00 □
41	Dave Maloney, NYR	.07	.15	.30 □
42	Danny Gare, Buf.	.07	.15	.30 □
43	Jimmy Watson, Phi.	.07	.15	.30 □
44	Tommy Williams, LA	.07	.15	.30 □
45	Serge Savard, Mon.	.25	.50	1.00 □
46	Derek Sanderson, Van., LC	.15	.30	.60 □
47	John Marks, Chi.	.07	.15	.30 □
48	**Al Cameron, Det., RC**	.07	.15	.30 □
49	Dean Talafous, Min.	.07	.15	.30 □
50	Glenn Resch, Goalie, NYI	.25	.50	1.00 □
51	Ron Schock, Buf., (Now with Sabres)	.07	.15	.30 □
52	Gary Croteau, Col.	.07	.15	.30 □
53	Gerry Meehan, Wash.	.07	.15	.30 □
54	Ed Staniowski, Goalie, St. L.	.07	.15	.30 □
55	Phil Esposito, NYR	1.15	2.25	4.50 □
56	Dennis Ververgaert, Van.	.07	.15	.30 □
57	Rick Wilson, Det., LC	.07	.15	.30 □
58	Jim Lorentz, Buf.	.07	.15	.30 □
59	Bobby Schmautz, Bos.	.07	.15	.30 □
60	Guy Lapointe, Mon., 2nd Team All-Star	.07	.15	.30 □
61	Ivan Boldirev, Chi.	.07	.15	.30 □
62	Bob Nystrom, NYI	.07	.15	.30 □
63	Rick Hampton, Cle.	.07	.15	.30 □
64	Jack Valiquette, Tor.	.07	.15	.30 □
65	Bernie Parent, Goalie, Phi.	.60	1.25	2.50 □
66	Dave Burrows, Pit.	.07	.15	.30 □
67	Butch Goring, LA	.07	.15	.30 □
68	Checklist 1 (1 - 132)	2.00	4.00	8.00 □
69	Murray Wilson, Mon., LC	.07	.15	.30 □
70	Ed Giacomin, Goalie, Det., LC	.30	.65	1.25 □

66 • O-PEE-CHEE — 1977 - 78 REGULAR ISSUE —

TEAM CHECKLIST CARDS

No.	Team	VG	EX	NRMT
71	Atlanta Flames	.25	.50	1.00
72	Boston Bruins	.25	.50	1.00
73	Buffalo Sabres	.25	.50	1.00
74	Chicago Black Hawks	.25	.50	1.00
75	Cleveland Barons	.25	.50	1.00
76	Colorado Rockies	.25	.50	1.00
77	Detroit Red Wings	.25	.50	1.00
78	Los Angeles Kings	.25	.50	1.00
79	Minnesota North Stars	.25	.50	1.00
80	Montreal Canadiens	.25	.50	1.00
81	New York Islanders	.25	.50	1.00
82	New York Rangers	.25	.50	1.00
83	Philadelphia Flyers	.25	.50	1.00
84	Pittsburgh Penguins	.25	.50	1.00
85	St. Louis Blues	.25	.50	1.00
86	Toronto Maple Leafs	.25	.50	1.00
87	Vancouver Canucks	.25	.50	1.00
88	Washington Capitals	.25	.50	1.00

REGULAR ISSUE

No.	Player	VG	EX	NRMT
89	Keith Magnuson, Chi.	.07	.15	.30
90	Walt Tkaczuk, NYR	.07	.15	.30
91	Bill Nyrop, Mon.	.07	.15	.30
92	Michel Plasse, Goalie, Col.	.07	.15	.30
93	Bob Bourne, NYI	.07	.15	.30
94	Lee Fogolin, Buf.	.07	.15	.30
95	Gregg Sheppard, Bos.	.07	.15	.30
96	Hartland Monahan, LA, (Now with Kings)	.07	.15	.30
97	Curt Bennett, Atl.	.07	.15	.30
98	Bob Dailey, Phi.	.07	.15	.30
99	Bill Goldsworthy, NYR, LC	.07	.15	.30
100	Ken Dryden, Mon., Goalie, 1st Team All-Star	3.50	7.00	14.00
101	Grant Mulvey, Chi.	.07	.15	.30
102	Pierre Larouche, Pit.	.07	.15	.30
103	Nick Libett, Det.	.07	.15	.30
104	Rick Smith, Bos.	.07	.15	.30
105	Bryan Trottier, NYI	5.00	10.00	20.00
106	Pierre Jarry, Min., LC	.07	.15	.30
107	Red Berenson, St. L.	.07	.15	.30
108	Jim Schoenfeld, Buf.	.07	.15	.30
109	Gilles Meloche, Goalie, Cle.	.07	.15	.30
110	Lanny McDonald, Tor., 2nd Team All-Star	.85	1.75	3.50
111	Don Lever, Van.	.07	.15	.30
112	Greg Polis, NYR	.07	.15	.30
113	**Gary Sargent, LA, RC**	.15	.35	.75
114	**Earl Anderson, Bos., RC, LC**	.07	.15	.30
115	Bobby Clarke, Phi.	1.15	2.25	4.50
116	Dave Lewis, NYI	.07	.15	.30
117	Darcy Rota, Chi.	.07	.15	.30
118	Andre Savard, Buf.	.07	.15	.30
119	Denis Herron, Goalie, Pit.	.07	.15	.30
120	Steve Shutt, Mon., 1st Team All-Star	.50	1.00	2.00
121	Mel Bridgman, Phi.	.07	.15	.30
122	Fred (Buster) Harvey, Det., LC	.07	.15	.30
123	**Rolie Eriksson, Min., RC**	.07	.15	.30
124	Dale Tallon, Chi.	.07	.15	.30
125	Gilles Gilbert, Goalie, Bos.	.07	.15	.30
126	Billy Harris, NYI	.07	.15	.30
127	Tom Lysiak, Atl.	.07	.15	.30
128	Jerry Korab, Buf.	.07	.15	.30
129	Bob Gainey, Mon.	.50	1.00	2.00
130	Wilf Paiement, Col.	.07	.15	.30
131	Tom Bladon, Phi.	.07	.15	.30
132	Ernie Hicke, LA, LC, (Now with Kings)	.07	.15	.30
133	J. P. LeBlanc, Det., LC, Error	.07	.15	.30
134	**Mike Milbury, Bos., RC**	.50	1.00	2.00
135	Pit Martin, Van. (Now with Vancouver)	.07	.15	.30
136	Steve Vickers, NYR	.07	.15	.30
137	Don Awrey, NYR (Now with Rangers)	.07	.15	.30
138	Bernie Wolfe, Goalie, Wash.	.07	.15	.30
139	Doug Jarvis, Mon.	.15	.35	.75
140	Borje Salming, Tor., 1st Team All-Star	.35	.75	1.50
141	Bob MacMillan, St. L.	.07	.15	.30
142	Wayne Stephenson, Goalie, Phi.	.07	.15	.30
143	Dave Forbes, Wash. (Now with Capitals)	.07	.15	.30
144	Jean Potvin, NYI	.07	.15	.30
145	Guy Charron, Wash.	.07	.15	.30
146	Cliff Koroll, Chi.	.07	.15	.30
147	Danny Grant, Det.	.07	.15	.30

O-Pee-Chee
1977-78 Issue
Card No. 105,
Bryan Trottier

O-Pee-Chee
1977-78 Issue
Card No. 123,
Rolie Eriksson

O-Pee-Chee
1977-78 Issue
Card No. 158,
Glen Sharpley

No.	Player	VG	EX	NRMT
148	Bill Hogaboam, Min.	.07	.15	.30
149	Al MacAdam, Cle.	.07	.15	.30
150	Gerry Desjardins, Goalie, Buf., LC	.07	.15	.30
151	Yvon Lambert, Mon.	.07	.15	.30
152	Rick Lapointe, Phi.	.07	.15	.30
153	Ed Westfall, NYI	.07	.15	.30
154	Carol Vadnais, NYR	.07	.15	.30
155	John Bucyk, Bos., LC	.40	.85	1.75
156	J. P. Bordeleau, Chi.	.07	.15	.30
157	Ron Stackhouse, Pit.	.07	.15	.30
158	**Glen Sharpley, Min., RC**	.07	.15	.30
159	Michel Bergeron, NYI (Now with Islanders)	.07	.15	.30
160	Rogatien Vachon, Goalie, LA, 2nd Team All-Star	.30	.65	1.25
161	Fred Stanfield, Buf.	.07	.15	.30
162	Gerry Hart, NYI	.07	.15	.30
163	Mario Tremblay, Mon.	.07	.15	.30
164	Andre Dupont, Phi.	.07	.15	.30
165	Don Marcotte, Bos.	.07	.15	.30
166	Wayne Dillon, NYR	.07	.15	.30
167	Claude Larose, St. L., LC	.07	.15	.30
168	Eric Vail, Atl.	.07	.15	.30
169	**Tom Edur, Col., RC**	.07	.15	.30
170	Tony Esposito, Goalie, Chi.	.60	1.25	2.50
171	Andre St. Laurent, Det. (Now with Red Wings)	.07	.15	.30
172	Dan Maloney, Det.	.07	.15	.30
173	Dennis O'Brien, Min.	.07	.15	.30
174	**Blair Chapman, Pit., RC**	.07	.15	.30
175	Dennis Kearns, Van.	.07	.15	.30
176	Wayne Merrick, Cle.	.07	.15	.30
177	Michel Larocque, Goalie, Mon.	.07	.15	.30
178	Bob Kelly, Phi.	.07	.15	.30
179	**Dave Farrish, NYR, RC**	.07	.15	.30
180	Rick Martin, Buf., 2nd Team All-Star	.07	.15	.30
181	Gary Doak, Bos.	.07	.15	.30
182	Jude Drouin, NYI	.07	.15	.30
183	**Barry Dean, Phi., RC, (Now with Flyers)**	.07	.15	.30
184	Gary Smith, Goalie, Wash., (Now with Capitals)	.07	.15	.30
185	Reggie Leach, Phi.	.07	.15	.30
186	Ian Turnbull, Tor.	.07	.15	.30
187	Vic Venasky, LA	.07	.15	.30
188	**Wayne Bianchin, Pit., RC**	.07	.15	.30
189	Doug Risebrough, Mon.	.07	.15	.30
190	Brad Park, Bos.	.50	1.00	2.00
191	Craig Ramsay, Buf.	.07	.15	.30
192	Ken Hodge, Sr., NYR, LC	.07	.15	.30
193	Phil Myre, Goalie, Atl.	.07	.15	.30
194	Garry Howatt, NYI	.07	.15	.30
195	Stan Mikita, Chi.	1.00	2.00	4.00
196	Garnet Bailey, Wash., LC	.07	.15	.30
197	Dennis Hextall, Det.	.07	.15	.30
198	Nick Beverley, Min.	.07	.15	.30
199	Larry Patey, St. L.	.07	.15	.30
200	Guy Lafleur, Mon., 1st Team All-Star	2.50	5.00	10.00
201	**Don Edwards, Goalie, Buf., RC**	.30	.60	1.25
202	Gary Dornhoefer, Phi., LC	.07	.15	.30
203	Bob Paradise, Pit.	.07	.15	.30
204	**Alex Pirus, Min., RC, LC**	.07	.15	.30
205	Pete Mahovlich, Mon.	.07	.15	.30
206	Bert Marshall, NYI	.07	.15	.30
207	Gilles Gratton, Goalie, NYR, LC	.12	.25	.50
208	Alain Daigle, Chi.	.07	.15	.30
209	Chris Oddleifson, Van.	.07	.15	.30
210	Gilbert Perreault, Buf., 2nd Team All-Star	.55	1.10	2.25
211	**Mike Palmateer, Goalie, Tor., RC**	1.50	3.00	6.00
212	Bill Lochead, Det.	.07	.15	.30
213	Dick Redmond, St. L. (Now with Blues)	.07	.15	.30

1976 - 66 RECORD BREAKERS

No.	Player	VG	EX	NRMT
214	Guy Lafleur, Mon., Most Points, Season, Right Wing	.65	1.35	2.75
215	Ian Turnbull, Tor., Most Goals Game, Defenceman	.12	.25	.50
216	Guy Lafleur, Mon., Longest Point-Scoring Streak	.65	1.35	2.75
217	Steve Shutt, Mon., Most Goals Season, Left Wing	.12	.25	.50
218	Guy Lafleur, Mon., Most Assists, Season, Right Wing	.65	1.35	2.75

O-Pee-Chee
1977-78 Issue
Card No. 201,
Don Edwards

— 1977 - 78 REGULAR ISSUE — O-PEE-CHEE • 67

REGULAR ISSUE

No.	Player	VG	EX	NRMT
219	Lorne Henning, NYI	.07	.15	.30
220	Terry O'Reilly, Bos.	.10	.25	.50
221	Pat Hickey, NYR	.07	.15	.30
222	Rene Robert, Buf.	.07	.15	.30
223	Tim Young, Min.	.07	.15	.30
224	Dunc Wilson, Goalie, Pit., LC	.07	.15	.30
225	Dennis Hull, Chi., LC	.07	.15	.30
226	Rod Seiling, St. L.	.07	.15	.30
227	Bill Barber, Phi.	.50	1.00	2.00
228	**Dennis Polonich, Det., RC**	.07	.15	.30
229	Billy Smith, Goalie, NYI	.50	1.00	2.00
230	Yvan Cournoyer, Mon.	.50	1.00	2.00
231	Don Luce, Buf.	.07	.15	.30
232	**Mike McEwen, NYR, RC**	.15	.30	.60
233	Don Saleski, Phi.	.07	.15	.30
234	Wayne Cashman, Bos.	.07	.15	.30
235	Phil Russell, Chi.	.07	.15	.30
236	Mike Corrigan, Pit., LC	.07	.15	.30
237	Guy Chouinard, Atl.	.07	.15	.30
238	**Steve Jensen, Min., RC**	.07	.15	.30
239	Jim Rutherford, Goalie, Det.	.07	.15	.30
240	Marcel Dionne, LA, 1st Team All-Star	1.75	3.50	7.00
241	Rejean Houle, Mon.	.07	.15	.30
242	Jocelyn Guevremont, Buf.	.07	.15	.30
243	Jim Harrison, Chi., LC	.07	.15	.30
244	**Don Murdoch, NYR, RC**	.07	.15	.30
245	**Richard Green, Wash., RC**	.25	.50	1.00
246	Rick Middleton, Bos.	.50	1.00	2.00
247	Joe Watson, Phi.	.07	.15	.30
248	Syl Apps, Jr., LA (Now with Kings)	.07	.15	.30
249	Checklist 2 (133 - 264), Error	2.00	4.00	8.00
250	Clark Gillies, NYI	.07	.15	.30
251	Bobby Orr, Chi., LC	6.25	12.50	25.00
252	Nelson Pyatt, Col.	.07	.15	.30
253	**Gary McAdam, Buf., RC**	.10	.25	.50
254	Jacques Lemaire, Mon.	.30	.65	1.25
255	Bob Girard, Cle.	.07	.15	.30
256	Ronald Greschner, NYR	.07	.15	.30
257	Ross Lonsberry, Phi.	.07	.15	.30
258	Dave Gardner, Cle.	.07	.15	.30
259	Rick Blight, Van.	.07	.15	.30
260	Gerry Cheevers, Goalie, Bos.	.55	1.10	2.25
261	Jean Pronovost, Pit.	.07	.15	.30

1976 - 77 STANLEY CUP PLAYOFFS

No.	Team	VG	EX	NRMT
262	**Semi-finals:** Canadiens Skate Past Islanders	.10	.25	.50
263	**Semi-finals:** Bruins Advance to Finals	.10	.25	.50
264	**Finals:** Canadiens Win 20th Stanley Cup	.35	.75	1.50

REGULAR ISSUE

No.	Player	VG	EX	NRMT
265	**Rick Bowness, Det., RC** (Now with Red Wings)	.35	.75	1.50
266	George Ferguson, Tor.	.07	.15	.30
267	**Mike Kitchen, Col., RC**	.07	.15	.30
268	Bob Berry, LA, LC	.07	.15	.30
269	**Greg Smith, Cle., RC**	.07	.15	.30
270	**Stan Jonathan, Bos., RC**	.25	.50	1.00
271	Dwight Bialowas, Min., LC	.07	.15	.30
272	Pete Stemkowski, LA (Now with Kings)	.07	.15	.30
273	Greg Joly, Det.	.07	.15	.30
274	**Ken Houston, Atl., RC**	.07	.15	.30
275	Brian Glennie, Tor.	.07	.15	.30
276	Eddie Johnston, Goalie, St. L., LC	.07	.15	.30
277	John Grisdale, Van.	.07	.15	.30
278	Craig Patrick, Wash., LC	.07	.15	.30
279	**Ken Breitenbach, Buf., RC, LC**	.07	.15	.30
280	Fred Ahern, Cle., (Now with Barons)	.07	.15	.30
281	Jim Roberts, St. L., LC (Traded from Montreal 8/18/77)	.07	.15	.30
282	**Harvey Bennett, Phi., RC**	.07	.15	.30
283	Ab DeMarco, Atl., LC (Traded from LA 5/24/77)	.07	.15	.30
284	Pat Boutette, Tor.	.07	.15	.30
285	Bob Plager, St. L., (Now Coaching St. Louis Minor Team)	.07	.15	.30
286	Hilliard Graves, Van.	.07	.15	.30
287	**Gordie Lane, Wash., RC**	.07	.15	.30
288	**Ron Andruff, Col., RC**	.07	.15	.30

O-Pee-Chee
1977-78 Issue
Card No. 263, Semi-Finals
Bruins Advance to Finals

O-Pee-Chee
1977-78 Issue
Card No. 270,
Stan Jonathan

O-Pee-Chee
1977-78 Issue
Card No. 325,
Chicago Black Hawks

O-Pee-Chee
1977-78 Issue
Card No. 354,
Doug Palazzari

No.	Player	VG	EX	NRMT
289	Larry Brown, LA	.07	.15	.30
290	**Mike Fidler, Cle., RC**	.07	.15	.30
291	Fred Barrett, Min.	.07	.15	.30
292	Bill Clement, Atl.	.07	.15	.30
293	Errol Thompson, Tor.	.07	.15	.30
294	Doug Grant, Goalie, St. L.	.07	.15	.30
295	Harold Snepsts, Van.	.07	.15	.30
296	**Rick Bragnalo, Wash., RC**	.25	.50	1.00
297	Bryan Lefley, Col.	.07	.15	.30
298	Gene Carr, Pit. (Now with Penguins)	.07	.15	.30
299	Bob Stewart, Cle.	.07	.15	.30
300	Lew Morrison, Pit., LC	.07	.15	.30
301	Ed Kea, Atl.	.07	.15	.30
302	Scott Garland, Tor.	.07	.15	.30
303	Bill Fairbairn, St. L. (Now with Blues)	.07	.15	.30
304	Larry Carriere, Van.	.07	.15	.30
305	Ron Low, Goalie, Det. (Traded from Washington 8/17/77)	.07	.15	.30
306	Tom Reid, Min., LC	.07	.15	.30
307	**Paul Holmgren, Phi., RC**	.50	1.00	2.00
308	Pat Price, NYI	.07	.15	.30
309	**Kirk Bowman, Chi., RC**	.07	.15	.30
310	**Bobby Simpson, Atl., RC**	.07	.15	.30
311	Ron Ellis, Tor.	.07	.15	.30
312	Rick Bourbonnais, St. L., Error	.35	.75	1.50
313	Bobby Lalonde, Atl., (Now with Flames)	.07	.15	.30
314	Tony White, Wash., LC	.07	.15	.30
315	John Van Boxmeer, Col.	.07	.15	.30
316	Don Kozak, LA	.07	.15	.30
317	Jim Neilson, Cle., LC (Drafted from Rangers 6/10/74)	.07	.15	.30
318	**Terry Martin, Buf., RC**	.07	.15	.30
319	Barry Gibbs, Atl.	.07	.15	.30
320	Inge Hammarstrom, St. L. (Now with Blues)	.07	.15	.30
321	Darryl Edestrand, Bos.	.07	.15	.30

TEAM RECORD CARDS

No.	Team	VG	EX	NRMT
322	Atlanta Flames	.25	.50	1.00
323	Boston Bruins	.25	.50	1.00
324	Buffalo Sabres	.25	.50	1.00
325	Chicago Black Hawks	.25	.50	1.00
326	Cleveland Barons	.25	.50	1.00
327	Colorado Rockies	.25	.50	1.00
328	Detroit Red Wings	.25	.50	1.00
329	Los Angeles Kings	.25	.50	1.00
330	Minnesota North Stars	.25	.50	1.00
331	Montreal Canadiens	.25	.50	1.00
332	New York Islanders	.25	.50	1.00
333	New York Rangers	.25	.50	1.00
334	Philadelphia Flyers	.25	.50	1.00
335	Pittsburgh Penguins	.25	.50	1.00
336	St. Louis Blues	.25	.50	1.00
337	Toronto Maple Leafs	.25	.50	1.00
338	Vancouver Canucks	.25	.50	1.00
339	Washington Capitals	.25	.50	1.00

REGULAR ISSUE

No.	Player	VG	EX	NRMT
340	Chuck Lefley, St. L.	.07	.15	.30
341	Garry Monahan, Van.	.07	.15	.30
342	Bryan Watson, Wash.	.07	.15	.30
343	Dave Hudson, Col.	.07	.15	.30
344	Neil Komadoski, LA	.07	.15	.30
345	Gary Edwards, Goalie, Cle. (Traded from LA 1/21/77)	.07	.15	.30
346	Rey Comeau, Atl.	.07	.15	.30
347	Bob Neely, Tor., LC	.07	.15	.30
348	Jean Hamel, Det.	.07	.15	.30
349	Jerry Butler, Tor. (Now with Toronto)	.07	.15	.30
350	Mike Walton, Van.	.07	.15	.30
351	Bob Sirois, Wash.	.07	.15	.30
352	Jim McElmury, Col., LC	.07	.15	.30
353	Dave Schultz, Pit. (Now with Penguins)	.07	.15	.30
354	**Doug Palazzari, St. L., RC, LC**	.07	.15	.30
355	**Dave Shand, Atl., RC**	.07	.15	.30
356	Stan Weir, Tor.	.07	.15	.30
357	Mike Christie, Cle.	.07	.15	.30
358	Floyd Thomson, St. L, LC	.07	.15	.30
359	Larry Goodenough, Van. (Traded from Phil. 1/20/77)	.07	.15	.30
360	**Bill Riley, Wash., RC**	.15	.30	.60

68 • O-PEE-CHEE — 1977 - 78 GLOSSY PHOTOS —

No.	Player	VG	EX	NRMT
361	Doug Hicks, Min., RC	.07	.15	.30
362	Dan Newman, NYR, RC	.07	.15	.30
363	Rick Chartraw, Mon.	.07	.15	.30
364	Tim Ecclestone, Atl., LC	.07	.15	.30
365	Don Ashby, Tor., RC	.07	.15	.30
366	Jacques Richard, Buf.	.07	.15	.30
367	Yves Belanger, Goalie, St. L.	.07	.15	.30
368	Ron Sedlbauer, Van.	.07	.15	.30
369	Jack Lynch, Wash., LC, Error	.07	.15	.30
370	Doug Favell, Goalie, Col.	.07	.15	.30
371	Bob Murdoch, LA	.07	.15	.30
372	Ralph Klassen, Cle.	.07	.15	.30
373	Richard Mulhern, Atl.	.07	.15	.30
374	Jim McKenny, Tor., LC	.07	.15	.30
375	Mike Bloom, Det., LC	.07	.15	.30
376	Bruce Affleck, St. L.	.07	.15	.30
377	Gerry O'Flaherty, Van.	.07	.15	.30
378	Ron Lalonde, Wash.	.07	.15	.30
379	Chuck Arnason, Col.	.07	.15	.30
380	Dave Hutchison, LA	.07	.15	.30
381	Checklist 3 (265 - 396)	2.00	4.00	8.00
382	John Gould, Atl.	.07	.15	.30
383	Dave Williams, Tor.	.35	.75	1.50
384	Len Frig, St. L., LC	.07	.15	.30
	(Traded from Cle. 8/18/77)			
385	Pierre Plante, Chi.,	.07	.15	.30
	(Traded from St. Louis 8/6/77)			
386	Ralph Stewart, Van., LC	.07	.15	.30
387	Gord Smith, Wash.	.07	.15	.30
388	Denis Dupere, Col.	.07	.15	.30
389	Randy Manery, LA	.07	.15	.30
	(Traded from Atlanta 5/24/77)			
390	Lowell MacDonald, Pit., LC	.07	.15	.30
391	Dennis Owchar, Pit.	.07	.15	.30
392	Jimmy Roberts, Min., RC	.07	.15	.30
393	Mike Veisor, Goalie, Chi.	.07	.15	.30
394	Bob Hess, St. L.	.07	.15	.30
395	Curt Ridley, Goalie, Van.	.07	.15	.30
396	Mike Lampman, Wash., LC	.15	.30	.60

— 1977 - 78 GLOSSY PHOTOS —

The glossy colour photos come with square or rounded corners. Photos are numbered _ of 22.

Photo Size: 2 1/2" X 3 1/2"
Face: Four colour, borderless; Player's facsimile autograph
Back: Dark blue on card stock; Name, Team, Position, Number
Imprint: **© 1977 O-PEE-CHEE PRINTED IN CANADA.
Complete Set No: 22

Complete Set Price:		3.75	7.50	15.00
Common Card:		.12	.25	.50

No.	Player	VG	EX	NRMT
1	Wayne Cashman, Bos.	.12	.25	.50
2	Gerry Cheevers, Goalie, Bos.	.30	.60	1.25
3	Bobby Clarke, Phi.	.30	.60	1.25
4	Marcel Dionne, LA	.30	.60	1.25
5	Ken Dryden, Goalie, Mon.	.50	1.00	2.00
6	Clark Gillies, NYI	.12	.25	.50
7	Guy Lafleur, Mon.	.30	.60	1.25
8	Reggie Leach, Phi.	.12	.25	.50
9	Rick MacLeish, Phi.	.12	.25	.50
10	Dave Maloney, NYR	.12	.25	.50
11	Richard Martin, Buf.	.12	.25	.50
12	Don Murdoch, NYR	.12	.25	.50
13	Brad Park, Bos.	.12	.25	.50
14	Gilbert Perreault, Buf.	.12	.25	.50
15	Denis Potvin, NYI	.30	.60	1.25
16	Jean Ratelle, Bos.	.12	.25	.50
17	Glenn Resch, Goalie, NYI	.12	.25	.50
18	Larry Robinson, Mon.	.12	.25	.50
19	Steve Shutt, Mon.	.12	.25	.50
20	Darryl Sittler, Tor.	.25	.50	1.00
21	Rogatien Vachon, Goalie, LA	.12	.25	.50
22	Tim Young, Min.	.12	.25	.50

O-Pee-Chee
1977-78 Issue
Card No. 369, Error,
Shows Bill Collins

O-Pee-Chee
1977-78 Glossy Photos
Photo No. 5,
Ken Dryden

O-Pee-Chee
1978-79 Issue
Card No. 1,
Mike Bossy Sets Record

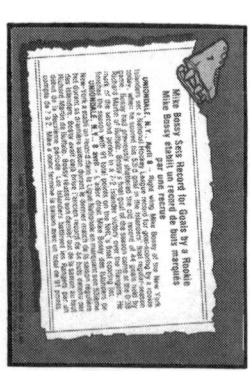

O-Pee-Chee
1978-79 Issue
Card No. 1,
Mike Bossy Sets Record

— 1978 - 79 REGULAR ISSUE —

Card number 300 commemorates the early retirement of Bobby Orr. The first five cards feature the previous season's highlights. Poor centering and poor cutting thoughout this set place a premium on well centered cards.
For mint prices an additional premium of 50% must be added to NRMT prices.

PRICE MOVEMENT OF NRMT SETS

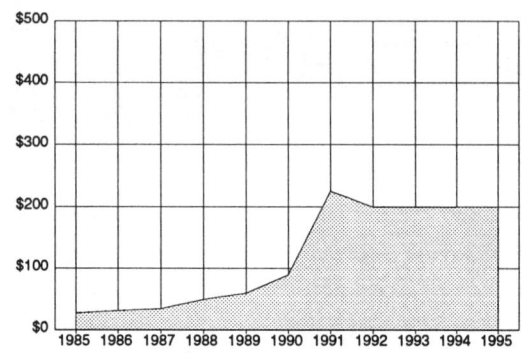

Card Size: 2 1/2" X 3 1/2"
Face: Four colour, white border, Team Logo, Position
Back: Two colour, brown and green on card stock, Number, Resume, Player's authograph, Bilingual
Imprint: © 1978 O-PEE-CHEE PRINTED IN CANADA.
Complete Set No.: 396

Complete Set Price:	50.00	100.00	200.00
Common Card:	.06	.12	.25
Wax Pack:			12.00
Wax Box: (48 Packs)			475.00
Wax Case: (16 Boxex)			7,000.00

1977-78 HIGHLIGHTS

No.	Player	VG	EX	NMRT
1	Mike Bossy Sets Record for Goals by a Rookie	2.00	4.00	8.00
2	Phil Esposito Tops Mark with 29th Hat Trick	.40	.85	1.75
3	Guy Lafleur Scores vs. Every Team in League	.50	1.00	2.00
4	Darryl Sittler Finds Net in 9 Straight Games	.15	.35	.70
5	Garry Unger Plays in 803rd Consecutive Game	.09	.18	.35

REGULAR ISSUE

No.	Player	VG	EX	NRMT
6	Gary Edwards, Goalie, Min.	.07	.15	.30
7	Rick Blight, Van.	.06	.12	.25
8	Larry Patey, St. L.	.06	.12	.25
9	Craig Ramsay, Buf.	.06	.12	.25
10	Bryan Trottier, NYI	2.50	5.00	10.00
11	Don Murdoch, NYR	.06	.12	.25
12	Phil Russell, Chi.	.06	.12	.25
13	Doug Jarvis, Mon.	.06	.12	.25
14	Gene Carr, Atl., LC	.06	.12	.25
15	Bernie Parent, Goalie, Phi., LC	.50	1.00	2.00
16	Perry Miller, Det.	.06	.12	.25
17	Kent-Erik Andersson, Min., RC	.06	.12	.25
18	Gregg Sheppard, Pit.	.06	.12	.25
19	Dennis Owchar, Col., LC	.06	.12	.25
20	Rogatien Vachon, Goalie, Det. (Now with Red Wings)	.25	.50	1.00
21	Dan Maloney, Tor.	.06	.12	.25
22	Guy Charron, Wash.	.06	.12	.25
23	Dick Redmond, Bos.	.06	.12	.25
24	Checklist 1 (1 - 132)	1.50	3.00	6.00
25	Anders Hedberg, NYR	.06	.12	.25
26	Mel Bridgman, Phi.	.06	.12	.25
27	Lee Fogolin, Buf.	.06	.12	.25
28	Gilles Meloche, Goalie, Min.	.07	.15	.30
29	Garry Howatt, NYI	.06	.12	.25
30	Darryl Sittler, Tor.	.75	1.50	3.00
31	Curt Bennett, St. L.	.06	.12	.25
32	Andre St. Laurent, Det.	.06	.12	.25
33	Blair Chapman, Pit.	.06	.12	.25
34	Keith Magnuson, Chi., LC	.06	.12	.25
35	Pierre Larouche, Mon.	.06	.12	.25

— 1978 - 79 REGULAR ISSUE — O-PEE-CHEE • 69

No.	Player	VG	EX	NRMT
36	Michel Plasse, Goalie, Col.	.07	.15	.30
37	Gary Sargent, Min.	.06	.12	.25
38	Mike Walton, St. L.	.06	.12	.25
39	**Robert Picard, Wash., RC**	**.12**	**.25**	**.50**
40	Terry O'Reilly, Bos.	.07	.15	.30
41	Dave Farrish, NYR	.06	.12	.25
42	Gary McAdam, Buf.	.06	.12	.25
43	Joe Watson, Col., LC (Now with Rockies)	.06	.12	.25
44	Yves Belanger, Goalie, Atl., LC	.07	.15	.30
45	Steve Jensen, LA (Now with Kings)	.06	.12	.25
46	Bob Stewart, St. L.	.06	.12	.25
47	Darcy Rota, Chi.	.06	.12	.25
48	Dennis Hextall, Det.	.06	.12	.25
49	Bert Marshall, NYI, LC	.06	.12	.25
50	Ken Dryden, Goalie, Mon.	2.50	5.00	10.00
51	Pete Mahovlich, Pit.	.06	.12	.25
52	Dennis Ververgaert, Van.	.06	.12	.25
53	Inge Hammarstrom, St. L., LC	.06	.12	.25
54	Doug Favell, Goalie, Col.	.07	.15	.30
55	Steve Vickers, NYR	.06	.12	.25
56	Syl Apps, Jr., LA	.06	.12	.25
57	Errol Thompson, Det.	.06	.12	.25
58	Don Luce, Buf.	.06	.12	.25
59	Mike Milbury, Bos.	.15	.30	.60
60	Yvan Cournoyer, Mon., LC	.30	.65	1.25
61	Kirk Bowman, Chi., LC	.06	.12	.25
62	Billy Smith, Goalie, NYI	.35	.75	1.50

1977 - 78 LEAGUE LEADERS

No.	Player	VG	EX	NRMT
63	**Goal Leaders:** G. Lafleur, Mon.; M. Bossy, NYI; S. Shutt, Mon.	.40	.85	1.75
64	**Assist Leaderss:** B. Trottier, NYI; G. Lafleur, Mon.,; D. Sittler, Tor.	.35	.75	1.50
65	**Scoring Leaders:** G. Lafleur, Mon.; B. Trottier, NYI; D. Sittler, Tor.	.35	.75	1.50
66	**Penalty Minute Leaders:** D. Schultz, Pit.; D. Williams, Tor.; D. Polonich, Det.	.12	.25	.50
67	**Power Play Goal Leaders:** M. Bossy, NYI; P. Esposito, NYR; S. Shutt, Mon.	.75	1.50	3.00
68	**Goals Against Avg Leaders:** K. Dryden, Mon.; B. Parent, Phi.; G. Gilbert, Bos.	.75	1.50	3.00
69	**Game Winning Goal Leaders:** G. Lafleur, Mon.; B. Barber, Phi.; D. Sittler, Tor.; B. Bourne, NYI	.75	1.50	3.00
70	**Shutout Leaders:** B. Parent, Phi.; K. Dryden, Mon.; D. Edwards, Buf.; T. Esposito, Chi.; M. Palmateer, Tor.	.75	1.50	3.00

REGULAR ISSUE

No.	Player	VG	EX	NRMT
71	Bob Kelly, Phi.	.06	.12	.25
72	Ron Stackhouse, Pit.	.06	.12	.25
73	Wayne Dillon, NYR	.06	.12	.25
74	Jim Rutherford, Goalie, Det.	.07	.15	.30
75	Stan Mikita, Chi.	.65	1.35	2.75
76	Bob Gainey, Mon.	.25	.50	1.00
77	Gerry Hart, NYI	.06	.12	.25
78	Lanny McDonald, Tor.	.35	.75	1.50
79	Brad Park, Bos.	.35	.75	1.50
80	Rick Martin, Buf.	.06	.12	.25
81	Bernie Wolfe, Goalie, Wash., LC	.07	.15	.30
82	Bob MacMillan, Atl.	.06	.12	.25
83	**Brad Maxwell, Min., RC**	**.06**	**.12**	**.25**
84	Mike Fidler, Min.	.06	.12	.25
85	Carol Vadnais, NYR	.06	.12	.25
86	Don Lever, Van.	.06	.12	.25
87	Phil Myre, Goalie, St. L.	.07	.15	.30
88	Paul Gardner, Col.	.06	.12	.25
89	Bob Murray, Chi.	.06	.12	.25
90	Guy Lafleur, Mon.	1.50	3.00	6.00
91	Bob J. Murdoch, LA	.06	.12	.25
92	Ron Ellis, Tor.	.06	.12	.25
93	Jude Drouin, NYI, (As of 11/15/78 unsigned free agent)	.06	.12	.25
94	Jocelyn Guevremont, Buf.	.06	.12	.25
95	Gilles Gilbert, Goalie, Bos.	.07	.15	.30
96	Bob Sirois, Wash.	.06	.12	.25
97	Tom Lysiak, Atl.	.06	.12	.25
98	Andre Dupont, Phi.	.06	.12	.25
99	**Per-Olov Brasar, Min., RC**	**.06**	**.12**	**.25**
100	Phil Esposito, NYR	.75	1.50	3.00

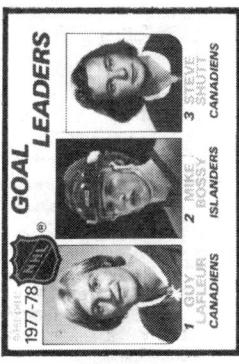

O-Pee-Chee
1978-79 Issue
Card No. 63,
Goal Leaders

O-Pee-Chee
1978-79 Issue
Card No. 115,
Mike Bossy

O-Pee-Chee
1978-79 Issue
Card No. 121,
Barry Beck

O-Pee-Chee
1978-79 Issue
Card No. 168,
Douglas Wilson

No.	Player	VG	EX	NRMT
101	J. P. Bordeleau, Chi.	.06	.12	.25
102	**Pierre Mondou, Mon., RC**	**.25**	**.50**	**1.00**
103	Wayne Bianchin, Pit.	.06	.12	.25
104	Dennis O'Brien, Bos.	.06	.12	.25
105	Glenn Resch, Goalie, NYI	.25	.65	1.25
106	Dennis Polonich, Det.	.06	.12	.25
107	**Kris Manery, Min., RC**	**.06**	**.12**	**.25**
108	Bill Hajt, Buf.	.06	.12	.25
109	**Jere Gillis, Van., RC**	**.06**	**.12**	**.25**
110	Garry Unger, St. L.	.06	.12	.25
111	Nick Beverley, LA, (Now with Kings) LC	.06	.12	.25
112	Pat Hickey, NYR	.06	.12	.25
113	Rick Middleton, Bos.	.25	.50	1.00
114	Orest Kindrachuk, Pit.	.06	.12	.25
115	**Mike Bossy, NYI, RC**	**15.00**	**30.00**	**60.00**
116	Pierre Bouchard, Mon., (Retired from active playing)	.06	.12	.25
117	Alain Daigle, Chi.	.06	.12	.25
118	Terry Martin, Buf.	.06	.12	.25
119	Tom Edur, St. L., (Now with Blues) LC (Retired from active playing)	.06	.12	.25
120	Marcel Dionne, LA	.75	1.50	3.00
121	**Barry Beck, Col., RC**	**.35**	**.75**	**1.50**
122	Bill Lochead, Det.	.06	.12	.25
123	**Paul Harrison, Goalie, Tor., RC**	**.07**	**.15**	**.30**
124	Wayne Cashman, Bos.	.06	.12	.25
125	Rick MacLeish, Phi.	.06	.12	.25
126	Bob Bourne, NYI	.06	.12	.25
127	Ian Turnbull, Tor.	.06	.12	.25
128	Gerry Meehan, Wash., LC	.06	.12	.25
129	Eric Vail, Atl.	.06	.12	.25
130	Gilbert Perreault, Buf.	.40	.85	1.75
131	Bob Dailey, Phi.	.06	.12	.25
132	**Dale McCourt, Det., RC**	**.15**	**.30**	**.60**
133	**John Wensink, Bos., RC**	**.15**	**.35**	**.75**
134	Bill Nyrop, Mon., LC	.06	.12	.25
135	Ivan Boldirev, Chi.	.06	.12	.25
136	**Lucien Deblois, NYR, RC**	**.15**	**.30**	**.60**
137	Brian Spencer, Pit., LC	.06	.12	.25
138	Tim Young, Min.	.06	.12	.25
139	Ron Sedlbauer, Van.	.06	.12	.25
140	Gerry Cheevers, Goalie, Bos.	.40	.85	1.75
141	Dennis Maruk, Wash., (Now with Capitals)	.06	.12	.25
142	Barry Dean, Phi.	.06	.12	.25
143	**Bernie Federko, St. L., RC**	**4.50**	**9.00**	**18.00**
144	**Stefan Persson, NYI, RC**	**.12**	**.25**	**.50**
145	Wilf Paiement, Col.	.06	.12	.25
146	Dale Tallon, Pit., LC, (Now with Penguins)	.06	.12	.25
147	Yvon Lambert, Mon.	.06	.12	.25
148	Greg Joly, Det.	.06	.12	.25
149	Dean Talafous, NYR, (Now with Rangers)	.06	.12	.25
150	Don Edwards, Goalie, Buf.	.07	.15	.30
151	Butch Goring, LA	.06	.12	.25
152	Tom Bladon, Pit.	.06	.12	.25
153	Bob Nystrom, NYI	.06	.12	.25
154	Ronald Greschner, NYR	.06	.12	.25
155	Jean Ratelle, Bos.	.30	.65	1.25
156	**Russ Anderson, Pit., RC**	**.06**	**.12**	**.25**
157	John Marks, Chi.	.06	.12	.25
158	Michel Larocque, Goalie, Mon.	.07	.15	.30
159	**Paul Woods, Det., RC**	**.06**	**.12**	**.25**
160	Mike Palmateer, Goalie, Tor.	.07	.15	.30
161	Jim Lorentz, Buf., LC, (Retired from active playing)	.06	.12	.25
162	Dave Lewis, NYI	.06	.12	.25
163	Harvey Bennett, St. L., LC, (Now with Blues)	.06	.12	.25
164	Rick Smith, Bos.	.06	.12	.25
165	Reggie Leach, Phi.	.06	.12	.25
166	Wayne Thomas, Goalie, NYR	.07	.15	.30
167	Dave Forbes, Wash., LC	.06	.12	.25
168	**Douglas Wilson, Chi., RC**	**4.50**	**9.00**	**18.00**
169	Dan Bouchard, Goalie, Atl.	.07	.15	.30
170	Steve Shutt, Mon.	.25	.50	1.00
171	**Mike Kaszycki, NYI, RC**	**.06**	**.12**	**.25**
172	Denis Herron, Goalie, Pit.	.07	.15	.30
173	Rick Bowness, St. L., (Now with Blues)	.06	.12	.25
174	Rick Hampton, LA, (Now with Kings)	.06	.12	.25
175	Glen Sharpley, Min.	.06	.12	.25
176	Bill Barber, Phi.	.35	.75	1.50
177	**Ron Duguay, NYR, RC**	**1.00**	**2.00**	**4.00**
178	Jim Schoenfeld, Buf.	.06	.12	.25
179	Pierre Plante, NYR, (Now with Rangers)	.06	.12	.25

70 • O-PEE-CHEE — 1978-79 REGULAR ISSUE

No.	Player	VG	EX	NRMT
180	Jacques Lemaire, Mon., LC	.25	.50	1.00
181	Stan Jonathan, Bos.	.06	.12	.25
182	Billy Harris, NYI	.06	.12	.25
183	Chris Oddleifson, Van.	.06	.12	.25
184	Jean Pronovost, Atl., (Now with Flames)	.06	.12	.25
185	Fred Barrett, Min.	.06	.12	.25
186	Ross Lonsberry, Pit.	.06	.12	.25
187	Mike McEwen, NYR	.06	.12	.25
188	Rene Robert, Buf.	.06	.12	.25
189	J. Bob Kelly, Chi.	.06	.12	.25
190	Serge Savard, Mon.	.25	.50	1.00
191	Dennis Kearns, Van.	.06	.12	.25

TEAM CHECKLIST CARDS

No.	Team	VG	EX	NRMT
192	Atlanta Flames	.15	.35	.75
193	Boston Bruins	.15	.55	.75
194	Buffalo Sabres	.15	.35	.75
195	Chicago Black Hawks	.15	.35	.75
196	Colorado Rockies	.15	.35	.75
197	Detroit Red Wings	.15	.35	.75
198	Los Angeles Kings	.15	.35	.75
199	Minnesota North Stars	.15	.35	.75
200	Montreal Canadiens	.15	.35	.75
201	New York Islanders	.15	.35	.75
202	New York Rangers	.15	.35	.75
203	Philadelphia Flyers	.15	.35	.75
204	Pittsburgh Penguins	.15	.35	.75
205	St. Louis Blues	.15	.35	.75
206	Toronto Maple Leafs	.15	.35	.75
207	Vancouver Canucks	.15	.35	.75
208	Washington Capitals	.15	.35	.75

REGULAR ISSUE

No.	Player	VG	EX	NRMT
209	Danny Gare, Buf.	.06	.12	.25
210	Larry Robinson, Mon.	.60	1.25	2.50
211	John Davidson, Goalie, NYR	.07	.15	.30
212	Peter McNab, Bos.	.06	.12	.25
213	Rick Kehoe, Pit.	.06	.12	.25
214	Terry Harper, Det., LC	.06	.12	.25
215	Bobby Clarke, Phi.	.75	1.50	3.00
216	Bryan Maxwell, Min., Error	.06	.12	.25
217	Ted Bulley, Chi., RC	.06	.12	.25
218	Red Berenson, St. L., LC, (Retired from active playing)	.06	.12	.25
219	Ron Grahame, Goalie, LA, LC, (Now with Kings)	.07	.15	.30
220	Clark Gillies, NYI	.06	.12	.25
221	Dave Maloney, NYR	.06	.12	.25
222	Derek Smith, Buf., RC	.12	.25	.50
223	Wayne Stephenson, Goalie, Phi.	.07	.15	.30
224	John Van Boxmeer, Col.	.06	.12	.25
225	Dave Schultz, Pit.	.06	.12	.25
226	Reed Larson, Det., RC	.15	.35	.75
227	Rejean Houle, Mon.	.06	.12	.25
228	Doug Hicks, Chi.	.06	.12	.25
229	Mike Murphy, LA	.06	.12	.25
230	Pete LoPresti, Goalie, Min.	.07	.15	.30
231	Jerry Korab, Buf.	.06	.12	.25
232	Ed Westfall, NYI, LC	.06	.12	.25
233	Greg Malone, Pit., RC	.10	.20	.40
234	Paul Holmgren, Phi.	.15	.30	.60
235	Walt Tkaczuk, NYR	.06	.12	.25
236	Don Marcotte, Bos.	.06	.12	.25
237	Ron Low, Goalie, Det.	.07	.15	.30
238	Rick Chartraw, Mon.	.06	.12	.25
239	Cliff Koroll, Chi.	.06	.12	.25
240	Borje Salming, Tor.	.25	.50	1.00
241	Rolie Eriksson, Van.	.06	.12	.25
242	Ric Seiling, Buf., RC	.06	.12	.25
243	Jim Bedard, Goalie, Wash., RC	.07	.15	.30
244	Peter Lee, Pit., RC	.06	.12	.25
245	Denis Potvin, NYI	.85	1.75	3.50
246	Greg Polis, NYR	.06	.12	.25
247	Jimmy Watson, Phi.	.06	.12	.25
248	Bobby Schmautz, Bos.	.06	.12	.25
249	Doug Risebrough, Mon.	.06	.12	.25
250	Tony Esposito, Goalie, Chi.	.50	1.00	2.00
251	Nick Libett, Det.	.06	.12	.25
252	Ron Zanussi, Min., RC	.07	.15	.30
253	Andre Savard, Buf.	.06	.12	.25

O-Pee-Chee
1978-79 Issue
Card No. 196,
Colorado Rockies

O-Pee-Chee
1978-79 Issue
Card No. 216, Error,
Shows Brad Maxwell

O-Pee-Chee
1978-79 Issue
Card No. 276,
Garnet Bailey

O-Pee-Chee
1978-79 Issue
Card No. 300,
Bobby Orr

No.	Player	VG	EX	NRMT
254	Dave Burrows, Tor.	.06	.12	.25
255	Ulf Nilsson, NYR	.15	.30	.60
256	Richard Mulhern, Atl.	.06	.12	.25
257	Don Saleski, Phi., LC	.06	.12	.25
258	Wayne Merrick, NYI	.06	.12	.25
259	Checklist 2 (133 - 264)	1.50	3.00	6.00
260	Guy Lapointe, Mon.	.10	.20	.40
261	Grant Mulvey, Chi.	.06	.12	.25

1977 - 78 STANLEY CUP PLAYOFFS

No.	Teams	VG	EX	NRMT
262	Semi-Finals, Canadiens sweep Maple Leafs	.07	.15	.30
263	Semi-Finals, Bruins skate past the Flyers	.07	.15	.30
264	Finals, Canadiens win 3rd straight cup.	.25	.50	1.00

REGULAR ISSUE

No.	Player	VG	EX	NRMT
265	Bob Sauve, Goalie, Buf.	.07	.15	.30
266	Randy Manery, LA	.06	.12	.25
267	Bill Fairbairn, St. L., LC	.06	.12	.25
268	Garry Monahan, Tor., LC	.06	.12	.25
269	Colin Campbell, Pit., (Now with Penguins)	.06	.12	.25
270	Dan Newman, Mon., LC, (Now with Canadiens)	.06	.12	.25
271	Dwight Foster, Bos., RC	.07	.15	.30
272	Larry Carriere, Buf., LC, (Retired from active playing)	.06	.12	.25
273	Michel Bergeron, Wash., LC, (Now with Capitals)	.06	.12	.25
274	Scott Garland, LA, LC, (Now with Kings)	.06	.12	.25
275	Bill McKenzie, Goalie, Col., LC	.07	.15	.30
276	Garnet Bailey, Wash., LC, (As of 11/15/78 Unsigned Free Agent)	.06	.12	.25
277	Ed Kea, Atl.	.06	.12	.25
278	Dave Gardner, LA, LC, (Now with Kings)	.06	.12	.25
279	Bruce Affleck, St. L., LC	.06	.12	.25
280	Bruce Boudreau, Tor., RC	.07	.15	.30
281	Jean Hamel, Det.	.06	.12	.25
282	Kurt Walker, LA, RC, LC, (Now with Kings)	.06	.12	.25
283	Denis Dupere, Col., LC	.06	.12	.25
284	Gordie Lane, Wash.	.06	.12	.25
285	Bobby Lalonde, Atl.	.06	.12	.25
286	Pit Martin, Van., LC	.06	.12	.25
287	Jean Potvin, Min., (Now with North Stars)	.06	.12	.25
288	Jimmy Jones, Tor., RC	.07	.15	.30
289	Dave Hutchison, Tor.	.06	.12	.25
290	Pete Stemkowski, LA, LC	.06	.12	.25
291	Mike Christie, Col.	.06	.12	.25
292	Bill Riley, Wash.	.06	.12	.25
293	Rey Comeau, Col., (Now with Rockies)	.06	.12	.25
294	Jack McIlhargey, Van., RC	.06	.12	.25
295	Tom Younghans, Min., RC	.06	.12	.25
296	Mario Faubert, Pit., RC	.06	.12	.25
297	Checklist 3 (265 - 396)	1.50	3.00	6.00
298	Rob Palmer, LA, RC	.06	.12	.25
299	Dave Hudson, Col., LC	.06	.12	.25

SPECIAL COLLECTOR'S CARD

No.	Player	VG	EX	NRMT
300	Bobby Orr, Bos.	8.75	17.50	35.00

REGULAR ISSUE

No.	Player	VG	EX	NRMT
301	Lorne Stamler, Tor., RC, LC	.06	.12	.25
302	Curt Ridley, Goalie, Van., LC	.07	.15	.30
303	Greg Smith, Min., (Now with North Stars)	.06	.12	.25
304	Jerry Butler, Tor.	.06	.12	.25
305	Gary Doak, Bos.	.06	.12	.25
306	Danny Grant, LA, LC, (Now with Kings)	.06	.12	.25
307	Mark Suzor, Bos., RC, LC, (Now with Bruins)	.06	.12	.25
308	Rick Bragnalo, Wash., LC	.06	.12	.25
309	John Gould, Atl.	.06	.12	.25
310	Sheldon Kannegiesser, Van., LC	.06	.12	.25

1978 - 79 REGULAR ISSUE — O-PEE-CHEE

No.	Player	VG	EX	NRMT
311	Bobby Sheehan, Min., LC, (Now with North Stars)	.06	.12	.25
312	**Randy Carlyle, Pit., RC,** (Now with Penguins)	1.75	3.50	7.00
313	Lorne Henning, NYI	.06	.12	.25
314	Tommy Williams, LA, LC	.06	.12	.25
315	Ron Andruff, Col., LC	.06	.12	.25
316	Bryan Watson, Wash., LC	.06	.12	.25
317	Willi Plett, Atl.	.06	.12	.25
318	John Grisdale, Van., LC	.06	.12	.25
319	**Brian Sutter, St. L., RC**	2.50	5.00	10.00
320	**Trevor Johansen, Tor., RC, LC**	.12	.25	.50
321	Vic Venasky, LA	.06	.12	.25
322	Rick Lapointe, Phi.	.06	.12	.25
323	**Ron Delorme, Col., RC**	.07	.15	.30
324	Yvon Labre, Wash.	.06	.12	.25

1977 - 78 ALL STARS
First Team

No.	Player	VG	EX	NRMT
325	Bryan Trottier, NYI	.75	1.50	3.00
326	Guy Lafleur, Mon.	.75	1.50	3.00
327	Clark Gillies, NYI	.07	.15	.30
328	Borje Salming, Tor.	.15	.35	.75
329	Larry Robinson, Mon.	.25	.50	1.00
330	Ken Dryden, Goalie, Mon.	.75	1.50	3.00

Second Team

No.	Player	VG	EX	NRMT
331	Darryl Sittler, Tor.	.17	.35	.75
332	Terry O'Reilly, Bos.	.10	.25	.50
333	Steve Shutt, Mon.	.10	.25	.50
334	Denis Potvin, NYI	.35	.75	1.50
335	Serge Savard, Mon.	.12	.25	.50
336	Don Edwards, Goalie, Buf.	.07	.15	.30

REGULAR ISSUE

No.	Player	VG	EX	NRMT
337	Glenn Goldup, LA	.06	.12	.25
338	Mike Kitchen, Col.	.06	.12	.25
339	Bob Girard, Wash., LC	.06	.12	.25
340	Guy Chouinard, Atl.	.06	.12	.25
341	Randy Holt, Van.	.06	.12	.25
342	Jimmy Roberts, Min., LC	.06	.12	.25
343	**Dave Logan, Chi., RC, LC**	.06	.12	.25
344	Walt McKechnie, Tor.	.06	.12	.25
345	Brian Glennie, LA, (Now with Kings)	.06	.12	.25
346	Ralph Klassen, Col., LC	.06	.12	.25
347	Gord Smith, Wash.	.06	.12	.25
348	Ken Houston, Atl.	.06	.12	.25
349	**Bob Manno, Van., RC**	.06	.12	.25
350	J. P. Parise, Min., (Now with North Stars)	.06	.12	.25
351	Don Ashby, Tor., LC	.06	.12	.25
352	Fred Stanfield, Buf., LC	.06	.12	.25
353	**David Taylor, LA, RC**	4.50	9.00	18.00
354	Nelson Pyatt, Col., LC	.06	.12	.25
355	**Blair Stewart, Wash., RC**	.06	.12	.25
356	Dave Shand, Atl.	.06	.12	.25
357	Hilliard Graves, Van.	.06	.12	.25
358	Bob Hess, St. L., LC	.06	.12	.25
359	David Williams, Tor.	.06	.12	.25
360	**Larry Wright, Det., RC, LC**	.06	.12	.25
361	Larry Brown, LA	.06	.12	.25
362	Gary Croteau, Col.	.06	.12	.25
363	Richard Green, Wash.	.06	.12	.25
364	Bill Clement, Atl.	.06	.12	.25
365	Gerry O'Flaherty, Atl., LC	.06	.12	.25
366	**John Baby, Min., RC,** (Now with North Stars)	.06	.12	.25
367	Nick Fotiu, NYR	.06	.12	.25
368	Pat Price, NYI	.06	.12	.25
369	Bert Wilson, LA, LC	.06	.12	.25
370	Bryan Lefley, Col., LC, (Now retired from active playing)	.06	.12	.25
371	Ron Lalonde, Wash., LC	.06	.12	.25
372	Bobby Simpson, Atl.	.06	.12	.25
373	Doug Grant, Goalie, St. L., LC	.07	.15	.30
374	Pat Boutette, Tor.	.06	.12	.25
375	Bob Paradise, Pit., LC	.06	.12	.25
376	Mario Tremblay, Mon.	.06	.12	.25
377	Darryl Edestrand, LA, (Now with Kings)	.06	.12	.25
378	**Andy Spruce, Col., RC, LC**	.06	.12	.25

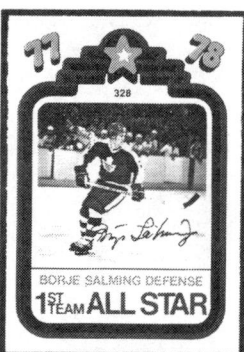

O-Pee-Chee 1978-79 Issue Card No. 328, Borje Salming

No.	Player	VG	EX	NRMT
379	Jack Brownschidle, St. L., RC	.06	.12	.25
380	Harold Snepsts, Van.	.06	.12	.25
381	Al MacAdam, Min. (Now with North Stars)	.06	.12	.25
382	Neil Komadoski, St. L., LC, (Now with Blues)	.06	.12	.25
383	Don Awrey, Col., (Now with Rockies) LC	.06	.12	.25
384	Ron Schock, Buf.(Now with Sabres) LC	.06	.12	.25
385	Gary Simmons, Goalie, LA, LC	.07	.15	.30
386	Fred Ahern, Min. LC (Now with North Stars)	.06	.12	.25
387	Larry Bolonchuk, Wash., LC	.06	.12	.25
388	**Brad Gassoff, Van., RC**	.06	.12	.25
389	Chuck Arnason, Min., LC, (Now with North Stars)	.06	.12	.25
390	Barry Gibbs, St. L., (Now with Blues)	.06	.12	.25
391	Jack Valiquette, Col. (Now with Rockies)	.06	.12	.25
392	Doug Halward, LA, (Now with Kings)	.06	.12	.25
393	Hartland Monahan, LA, LC	.06	.12	.25
394	Rod Seiling, Atl. (Now with Flames) LC	.06	.12	.25
395	George Ferguson, Pit., (Now with Penguins)	.06	.12	.25
396	Al Cameron, Det., LC	.07	.15	.30

O-Pee-Chee 1971-72 Posters, Poster No. 1, Bobby Orr

O-PEE-CHEE — 1979-80 REGULAR ISSUE —

— 1979 - 80 REGULAR ISSUE —

The blue border printed to the edge of the cards highlights wear and edge damage. The rookie card of Wayne Gretzky was illegally reprinted. The majority of these copies have been destroyed or marked, however, some are still in existence. See page XXII in the counterfeit section for details on card no. 18, Wayne Gretzky. Mint cards, due to the printed borders, command a price premium of 50 - 75% over NRMT cards.

PRICE MOVEMENT OF NRMT SETS

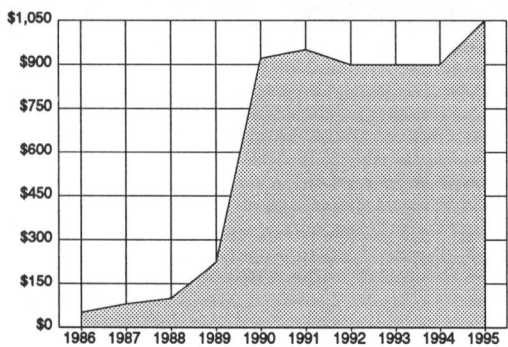

Card Size: 2 1/2" X 3 1/2"
Face: Four colour, blue border, Team logo, Position
Back: Two colour, blue and brown on card stock, Number, Resume Hockey trivia, Bilingual
Imprint: © 1979 O-PEE-CHEE PRINTED IN CANADA
Complete Set No.: 396

Complete Set Price:	250.00	500.00	1,050.00
Common Card:	.10	.20	.40
Wax Pack:			125.00
Wax Box: (48 Packs)			4,000.00
Wax Case: (16 Boxes)			60,000.00

LEAGUE LEADERS

No.	Player	VG	EX	NRMT
1	Goal Leaders: M. Bossy, NYI; M. Dionne, LA; G.Lafleur, Mon.	.85	1.75	3.50
2	Assist Leaders: B. Trottier, NYI; G. Lafleur, Mon.; M. Dionne, LA; B. MacMillan, Atl.	.35	.75	1.50
3	Scoring Leaders: B. Trottier, NYI; M. Dionne, LA; G. Lafleur, Mon.	.35	.75	1.50
4	Penalty Minute Leaders: D. Williams, Tor.; R. Holt, LA; D. Schultz, Buf.	.15	.35	.75
5	Power Play Goal Leaders: M. Bossy, NYI; M. Dionne, LA; L. McDonald, Tor.; P. Gardner, Tor.	.35	.75	1.50
6	Goals Against Average: K. Dryden, Mon.; G. Resch, NYI; B. Parent, Phi.	.35	.75	1.50
7	Game Winning Goals: G. Lafleur, Mon.; M. Bossy, NYI; B. Trottier, NYI; J. Pronovost, Atl.; T. Bulley, Chi.	.35	.75	1.50
8	Shutouts: K. Dryden, Mon.; T. Esposito, Chi.; M. Palmateer, Tor.; M. Lessard, LA; B. Parent, Phi.	.35	.75	1.50

REGULAR ISSUE

No.	Player	VG	EX	NRMT
9	Greg Malone, Pit.	.10	.20	.40
10	Rick Middleton, Bos.	.25	.50	1.00
11	Greg Smith, Min.	.10	.20	.40
12	Rene Robert, Col., "Now With Rockies"	.10	.20	.40
13	Doug Risebrough, Mon.	.10	.20	.40
14	Bob Kelly, Phi.	.10	.20	.40
15	Walt Tkaczuk, NYR	.10	.20	.40
16	John Marks, Chi.	.10	.20	.40
17	Willie Huber, Det., RC	.10	.20	.40
18	Wayne Gretzky, Edm., RC	275.00	450.00	900.00
19	Ron Sedlbauer, Van.	.10	.20	.40
20	Glenn Resch, Goalie, NYI, 2nd Team All*Star	.15	.35	.75
21	Blair Chapman, Pit.	.10	.20	.40
22	Ron Zanussi, Min.	.10	.20	.40
23	Brad Park, Bos.	.30	.65	1.25
24	Yvon Lambert, Mon.	.10	.20	.40

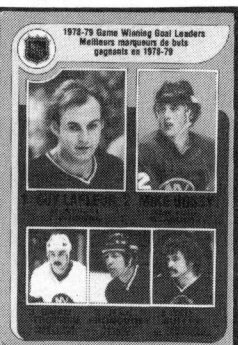

O-Pee-Chee 1979-80 Issue Card No. 1, Goal Leaders

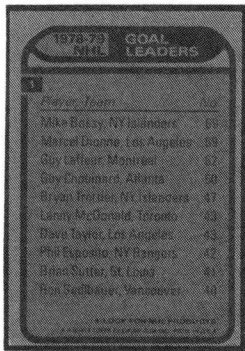

O-Pee-Chee 1979-80 Issue Card No. 1, Goal Leaders

O-Pee-Chee, 1979-80 Issue Card No. 59, Error, Kingston misspelled Kinston on back

O-Pee-Chee 1979-80 Issue Card No. 82, Edmonton Oilers Logo

No.	Player	VG	EX	NRMT
25	Andre Savard, Buf.	.10	.20	.40
26	Jimmy Watson, Phi.	.10	.20	.40
27	Harold Phillipoff, Chi., RC, LC	.10	.20	.40
28	Dan Bouchard, Goalie, Atl.	.10	.20	.40
29	Bob Sirois, Wash.	.10	.20	.40
30	Ulf Nilsson, NYR	.10	.20	.40
31	Mike Murphy, LA	.10	.20	.40
32	Stefan Persson, NYI	.10	.20	.40
33	Garry Unger, Atl., "Now With Flames"	.10	.20	.40
34	Rejean Houle, Mon.	.10	.20	.40
35	Barry Beck, NYR	.10	.20	.40
36	Tim Young, Min.	.10	.20	.40
37	Rick Dudley, Buf.	.10	.20	.40
38	Wayne Stephenson, Goalie, Wash., "Now With Capitals"	.10	.20	.40
39	Peter McNab, Bos.	.10	.20	.40
40	Borje Salming, Tor., 2nd Team All*Star	.15	.35	.75
41	Tom Lysiak, Chi.	.10	.20	.40
42	Donald Maloney, NYR, RC	.30	.65	1.25
43	Mike Rogers, Har.	.10	.20	.40
44	Dave Lewis, NYI	.10	.20	.40
45	Peter Lee, Pit.	.10	.20	.40
46	Marty Howe, Har.	.10	.20	.40
47	Serge Bernier, Que.	.10	.20	.40
48	Paul Woods, Det.	.10	.20	.40
49	Bob Sauve, Goalie, Buf.	.10	.20	.40
50	Larry Robinson, Mon., 1st Team All*Star	.65	1.35	2.75
51	Tom Gorence, Phi., RC	.10	.20	.40
52	Gary Sargent, Min.	.10	.20	.40
53	Thomas Gradin, Van., RC	.50	1.00	2.00
54	Dean Talafous, NYR	.10	.20	.40
55	Bob Murray, Chi.	.10	.20	.40
56	Bob Bourne, NYI	.10	.20	.40
57	Larry Patey, St. L.	.10	.20	.40
58	Ross Lonsberry, Buf.	.10	.20	.40
59	Rick Smith, Bos., LC, Error	.10	.20	.40
60	Guy Chouinard, Atl.	.10	.20	.40
61	Danny Gare, Buf.	.10	.20	.40
62	Jim Bedard, Goalie, Wash., LC	.10	.20	.40
63	Dale McCourt, Det.	.10	.20	.40
64	Steve Payne, Min., RC	.12	.25	.50
65	Pat Hughes, Pit., RC, "Now With Penguins"	.10	.20	.40
66	Mike McEwen, NYR, "Now With Rockies"	.10	.20	.40
67	Reg Kerr, Chi., RC	.10	.20	.40
68	Walt McKechnie, Tor.	.10	.20	.40
69	Michel Plasse, Goalie, Col.	.10	.20	.40
70	Denis Potvin, NYI, 1st Team All*Star	.50	1.00	2.00
71	Dave Dryden, Goalie, Edm., LC	.10	.20	.40
72	Gary McAdam, Pit.	.10	.20	.40
73	Andre St. Laurent, LA, "Now With Kings"	.10	.20	.40
74	Jerry Korab, Buf.	.10	.20	.40
75	Rick MacLeish, Phi.	.10	.20	.40
76	Dennis Kearns, Van.	.10	.20	.40
77	Jean Pronovost, Atl.	.10	.20	.40
78	Ronald Greschner, NYR	.10	.20	.40
79	Wayne Cashman, Bos.	.10	.20	.40
80	Tony Esposito, Goalie, Chi.	.50	1.00	2.00

TEAM LOGO CARDS

No.	Team	VG	EX	NRMT
81	Winnipeg Jets	.75	1.50	3.00
82	Edmonton Oilers	1.50	3.00	6.00

STANLEY CUP PLAYOFFS

No.	Team	VG	EX	NRMT
83	Stanley Cup Finals: Montreal vs. New York Rangers	.15	.35	.75

REGULAR ISSUE

No.	Player	VG	EX	NRMT
84	Brian Sutter, St. L.	1.00	2.00	4.00
85	Gerry Cheevers, Goalie, Bos.,LC	.35	.75	1.50
86	Pat Hickey, Col., "Now With Rockies"	.10	.20	.40
87	Mike Kaszycki, NYI	.10	.20	.40
88	Grant Mulvey, Chi.	.10	.20	.40
89	Derek Smith, Buf.	.10	.20	.40
90	Steve Shutt, Mon.	.25	.50	1.00
91	Robert Picard, Wash.	.10	.20	.40
92	Dan Labraaten, Det.	.10	.20	.40
93	Glen Sharpley, Min.	.10	.20	.40

— 1979 - 80 REGULAR ISSUE — O-PEE-CHEE • 73

No.	Player	VG	EX	NRMT
94	Denis Herron, Goalie, Mon., "Now With Canadiens"	.10	.20	.40
95	Reggie Leach, Phi.	.10	.20	.40
96	John Van Boxmeer, Buf., "Now With Sabres"	.10	.20	.40
97	David Williams, Tor.	.10	.20	.40
98	Butch Goring, LA	.10	.20	.40
99	Don Marcotte, Bos.	.10	.20	.40
100	Bryan Trottier, NYI, 1st Team All*Star	.90	1.75	3.75
101	Serge Savard, Mon., 2nd Team All*Star	.20	.40	.80
102	Cliff Koroll, Chi., LC	.10	.20	.40
103	Gary Smith, Goalie, Win., LC	.10	.20	.40
104	Al MacAdam, Min.	.10	.20	.40
105	Don Edwards, Goalie, Buf.	.10	.20	.40
106	Errol Thompson, Det.	.10	.20	.40
107	Andre Lacroix, Har., LC	.10	.20	.40
108	Marc Tardif, Que.	.10	.20	.40
109	Rick Kehoe, Pit.	.10	.20	.40
110	John Davidson, Goalie, NYR	.10	.20	.40
111	**Behn Wilson, Phi., RC**	.12	.25	.50
112	Doug Jarvis, Mon.	.10	.20	.40
113	**Tom Rowe, Wash., RC**	.10	.20	.40
114	•Mike Milbury, Bos.	.10	.20	.40
115	Billy Harris, NYI	.10	.20	.40
116	**Greg Fox, Chi., RC**	.10	.20	.40
117	Curt Fraser, Van., RC	.10	.20	.40
118	J. P. Parise, Min., LC	.10	.20	.40
119	Ric Seiling, Buf.	.10	.20	.40
120	Darryl Sittler, Tor.	.65	1.25	2.50
121	Rick Lapointe, St. L.	.10	.20	.40
122	Jim Rutherford, Goalie, Det.	.10	.20	.40
123	Mario Tremblay, Mon.	.10	.20	.40
124	Randy Carlyle, Pit.	.50	1.00	2.00
125	Bobby Clarke, Phi.	.75	1.50	3.00
126	Wayne Thomas, NYR, Goalie, LC	.10	.20	.40
127	Ivan Boldirev, Atl.	.10	.20	.40
128	Ted Bulley, Chi.	.10	.20	.40
129	Dick Redmond, Bos.	.10	.20	.40
130	Clark Gillies, NYI, 1st Team All*Star	.10	.20	.40
131	Checklist 1 (1 - 132)	2.00	4.00	8.00
132	Vaclav Nedomansky, Det.	.10	.20	.40
133	Richard Mulhern, LA	.10	.20	.40
134	Dave Schultz, Buf., LC	.10	.20	.40
135	Guy Lapointe, Mon.	.10	.20	.40
136	Gilles Meloche, Goalie, Min.	.10	.20	.40
137	Randy Pierce, Col., Error	.10	.20	.40
138	Cam Connor, Edm.	.10	.20	.40
139	George Ferguson, Pit.	.10	.20	.40
140	Bill Barber, Phi., 2nd Team All*Star	.30	.65	1.25
141	Terry Ruskowski, Chi., Error	.10	.20	.40
142	**Wayne Babych, St. L., RC**	.10	.25	.50
143	Phil Russell, Atl.	.10	.20	.40
144	Bobby Schmautz, Bos., LC	.10	.20	.40
145	Carol Vadnais, NYR	.10	.20	.40
146	**John Tonelli, NYI, RC**	2.25	4.50	9.00
147	**Peter Marsh, Win., RC, Error**	.10	.20	.40
148	Thommie Bergman, Det., LC	.10	.20	.40
149	Rick Martin, Buf.	.10	.20	.40
150	Ken Dryden, Goalie, Mon., LC (Now Retired) 1st Team All*Star	2.25	4.50	9.00
151	Kris Manery, Min.	.10	.20	.40
152	Guy Charron, Wash.	.10	.20	.40
153	Lanny McDonald, Tor.	.30	.65	1.25
154	Ron Stackhouse, Pit.	.10	.20	.40
155	Stan Mikita, Chi., LC	.55	1.15	2.25
156	Paul Holmgren, Phi.	.10	.20	.40
157	Perry Miller, Det.	.10	.20	.40
158	Gary Croteau, Col., LC, Error	.10	.20	.40
159	Dave Maloney, NYR	.10	.20	.40
160	Marcel Dionne, LA, 2nd Team All*Star	.85	1.75	3.50

RECORD BREAKERS

No.	Player	VG	EX	NRMT
161	Mike Bossy, NYI	1.00	2.00	4.00
162	Donald Maloney, NYR	.10	.20	.40

TEAM LOGO CARDS

No.	Team	VG	EX	NRMT
163	Hartford Whalers	.75	1.50	3.00

O-Pee-Chee 1979-80 Issue Card No. 137, Error, Shows Ron Delorme

O-Pee-Chee, 1979-80 Issue Card No. 141, Error, Name misspelled Ruskousky on face and back

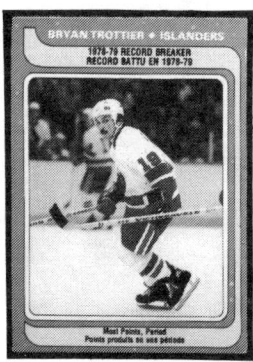

O-Pee-Chee 1979-80 Issue Card No. 165, Bryan Trottier

O-Pee-Chee 1979-80 Issue Card No. 185, Bobby Hull

RECORD BREAKERS

No.	Player	VG	EX	NRMT
164	Brad Park, Bos.	.15	.35	.75
165	Bryan Trottier, NYI	.30	.65	1.25

REGULAR ISSUE

No.	Player	VG	EX	NRMT
166	**Al Hill, Phi., RC**	.10	.20	.40
167	Gary Bromley, Goalie, Van.	.10	.20	.40
168	Don Murdoch, NYR	.10	.20	.40
169	Wayne Merrick, NYI	.10	.20	.40
170	Bob Gainey, Mon.	.25	.50	1.00
171	Jim Schoenfeld, Buf.	.10	.20	.40
172	Gregg Sheppard, Pit.	.10	.20	.40
173	**Dan Bolduc, Det., RC, LC**	.10	.20	.40
174	Blake Dunlop, St. L.	.10	.20	.40
175	Gordie Howe, Har., LC	8.75	17.50	35.00
176	Richard Brodeur, Goalie, NYI, "Now With Islanders"	.25	.50	1.00
177	Tom Younghans, Min.	.10	.20	.40
178	Andre Dupont, Phi.	.10	.20	.40
179	**Eddie Johnstone, NYR, RC**	.10	.20	.40
180	Gilbert Perreault, Buf.	.40	.85	1.75
181	**Bob Lorimer, NYI, RC**	.10	.20	.40
182	John Wensink, Bos.	.10	.20	.40
183	Lee Fogolin, Edm.	.10	.20	.40
184	**Greg Carroll, Har., RC, LC, "Now With Whalers"**	.10	.20	.40
185	Bobby Hull, Win., "Now With Jets" LC	7.50	15.00	30.00
186	Harold Snepsts, Van.	.10	.20	.40
187	Pete Mahovlich, Det., "Now With Red Wings"	.10	.20	.40
188	Eric Vail, Atl.	.10	.20	.40
189	Phil Myre, Goalie, Phi.	.10	.20	.40
190	Wilf Paiement, Col.	.10	.20	.40
191	**Charlie Simmer, LA, RC**	1.50	3.00	6.00
192	Per-Olov Brasar, Min.	.10	.20	.40
193	Lorne Henning, NYI, LC	.10	.20	.40
194	Don Luce, Buf.	.10	.20	.40
195	Steve Vickers, NYR	.10	.20	.40
196	**Bob Miller, Bos., RC**	.10	.20	.40
197	Mike Palmateer, Goalie, Tor.	.10	.20	.40
198	Nick Libett, Pit., "Now With Penguins" LC	.10	.20	.40
199	**Pat Ribble, Chi., RC**	.10	.20	.40
200	Guy Lafleur, Mon., 1st Team All*Star	1.25	2.50	5.00
201	Mel Bridgman, Phi.	.10	.20	.40
202	**Morris Lukowich, Win., RC**	.10	.20	.40
203	Don Lever, Van.	.10	.20	.40
204	Tom Bladon, Pit.	.10	.20	.40
205	Garry Howatt, NYI	.10	.20	.40
206	**Robert Smith, Min., RC**	2.50	5.00	10.00
207	Craig Ramsay, Buf.	.10	.20	.40
208	Ron Duguay, NYR	.10	.20	.40
209	Gilles Gilbert, Goalie, Bos.	.10	.20	.40
210	Bob MacMillan, Atl.	.10	.20	.40
211	Pierre Mondou, Mon.	.10	.20	.40
212	J. P. Bordeleau, Chi.	.10	.20	.40
213	Reed Larson, Det.	.10	.20	.40
214	Dennis Ververgaert, Phi.	.10	.20	.40
215	Bernie Federko, St. L.	1.00	2.00	4.00
216	Mark Howe, Har.	.85	1.75	3.50
217	Bob Nystrom, NYI	.10	.20	.40
218	Orest Kindrachuk, Pit.	.10	.20	.40
219	Mike Fidler, Min.	.10	.20	.40
220	Phil Esposito, NYR	.75	1.50	3.00
221	Bill Hajt, Buf.	.10	.20	.40
222	Mark Napier, Mon.	.10	.20	.40
223	Dennis Maruk, Wash.	.10	.20	.40
224	Dennis Polonich, Det.	.10	.20	.40
225	Jean Ratelle, Bos.	.25	.50	1.00
226	Bob Dailey, Phi.	.10	.20	.40
227	Alain Daigle, Chi., LC	.10	.20	.40
228	Ian Turnbull, Tor.	.10	.20	.40
229	Jack Valiquette, Col.	.10	.20	.40
230	Mike Bossy, NYI, 2nd Team All*Star	3.75	7.50	15.00
231	Brad Maxwell, Min.	.10	.20	.40
232	David Taylor, LA	1.85	3.75	7.50
233	Pierre Larouche, Mon.	.10	.20	.40
234	**Rod Schutt, Pit., RC**	.10	.20	.40
235	Rogatien Vachon, Goalie, Det.	.35	.75	1.50
236	**Ryan Walter, Wash., RC**	.35	.75	1.50
237	Checklist 2 (133 - 264), Error	2.00	4.00	8.00
238	Terry O'Reilly, Bos.	.10	.20	.40
239	Real Cloutier, Que.	.10	.20	.40

74 • O-PEE-CHEE — 1979-80 REGULAR ISSUE

No.	Player	VG	EX	NRMT
240	Anders Hedberg, NYR	.10	.20	.40
241	Ken Linseman, Phi., RC	1.25	2.50	5.00
242	Billy Smith, Goalie, NYI	.25	.50	1.00
243	Rick Chartraw, Mon.	.10	.20	.40

TEAM CHECKLIST CARDS

No.	Team	VG	EX	NRMT
244	Atlanta Flames	.40	.85	1.75
245	Boston Bruins	.40	.85	1.75
246	Buffalo Sabres	.40	.85	1.75
247	Chicago Black Hawks	.40	.85	1.75
248	Colorado Rockies	.40	.85	1.75
249	Detroit Red Wings	.40	.85	1.75
250	Los Angeles Kings	.40	.85	1.75
251	Minnesota North Stars	.40	.85	1.75
252	Montreal Canadiens	.40	.85	1.75
253	New York Islanders	.40	.85	1.75
254	New York Rangers	.40	.85	1.75
255	Philadelphia Flyers	.40	.85	1.75
256	Pittsburgh Penguins	.40	.85	1.75
257	St. Louis Blues	.40	.85	1.75
258	Toronto Maple Leafs	.40	.85	1.75
259	Vancouver Canucks	.40	.85	1.75
260	Washington Capitals	.40	.85	1.75
261	Quebec Nordiques	.40	.85	1.75

REGULAR ISSUE

No.	Player	VG	EX	NRMT
262	Jean Hamel, Det.	.10	.20	.40
263	Stan Jonathan, Bos.	.10	.20	.40
264	Russ Anderson, Pit., LC	.10	.20	.40
265	Gordon Roberts, Har., RC	.75	1.50	3.00
266	Bill Flett, Edm., LC	.10	.20	.40
267	Robbie Ftorek, Que.	.06	.15	.30
268	Mike Amodeo, Win., LC	.10	.20	.40
269	Vic Venasky, LA	.10	.20	.40
270	Bob Manno, Van.	.10	.20	.40
271	Dan Maloney, Tor.	.10	.20	.40
272	Al Sims, Har.	.10	.20	.40
273	Greg Polis, Wash., LC	.10	.20	.40
274	Doug Favell, Goalie, Edm., LC	.10	.20	.40
275	Pierre Plante, Que.	.10	.20	.40
276	Bob J. Murdoch, Atl.	.10	.20	.40
277	Lyle Moffat, Win., LC	.10	.20	.40
278	Jack Brownschidle, St. L.	.10	.20	.40
279	Dave Keon, Har.	.35	.75	1.50
280	Darryl Edestrand, LA, LC	.10	.20	.40
281	Greg Millen, Goalie, Pit., RC	1.25	2.50	5.00
282	John Gould, Buf., LC	.10	.20	.40
283	Rich LeDuc, Que.	.10	.20	.40
284	Ron Delorme, Col.	.10	.20	.40
285	Gord Smith, Win., LC	.10	.20	.40
286	Nick Fotiu, Har.	.10	.20	.40
287	Kevin McCarthy, Van., RC, "Now With Canucks"	.10	.20	.40
288	Jimmy Jones, Tor., LC	.10	.20	.40
289	Pierre Bouchard, Wash., "Now With Capitals"	.10	.20	.40
290	Wayne Bianchin, Edm.,LC, "Now With Oilers"	.10	.20	.40
291	Garry Lariviere, Que.	.10	.20	.40
292	Steve Jensen, LA	.10	.20	.40
293	John Garrett, Goalie, Har.	.10	.20	.40
294	Hilliard Graves, Win.,LC	.10	.20	.40
295	Bill Clement, Atl.	.10	.20	.40
296	Michel Larocque, Goalie, Mon.	.10	.20	.40
297	Bob Stewart, St. L., LC	.10	.20	.40
298	Doug Patey, Edm., RC, LC, "Now With Oilers"	.10	.20	.40
299	Dave Farrish, Que.	.10	.20	.40
300	Al Smith, Goalie, Har.	.10	.20	.40
301	Bill Lochead, NYR, LC, "Now With Rangers"	.10	.20	.40
302	Dave Hutchison, Tor.	.10	.20	.40
303	Bill Riley, Win., LC	.10	.20	.40
304	Barry Gibbs, LA, "Now With Kings"	.10	.20	.40
305	Chris Oddleifson, Van.	.10	.20	.40
306	J. Bob Kelly, Edm., LC, Error "Now With Oilers"	.10	.20	.40
307	Al Hangsleben, Har., RC	.10	.20	.40
308	Curt Brackenbury, Que., RC	.10	.20	.40
309	Richard Green, Wash.	.10	.20	.40
310	Ken Houston, Atl.	.10	.20	.40

O-Pee-Chee
1979-80 Issue
Card No. 241,
Ken Linseman

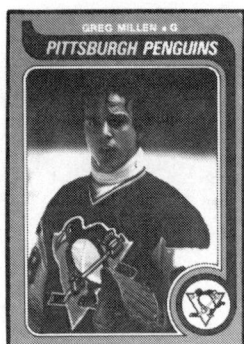

O-Pee-Chee
1979-80 Issue
Card No. 281,
Greg Millen

O-Pee-Chee
1979-80 Issue
Card No. 306, Error,
Shows Bob Kelly

O-Pee-Chee
1979-80 Issue
Card No. 308,
Curt Brackenbury

No.	Player	VG	EX	NRMT
311	Greg Joly, Det.	.10	.20	.40
312	Bill Lesuk, Win., LC	.10	.20	.40
313	Bill Stewart, Buf., RC, LC	.10	.20	.40
314	Rick Ley, Har.	.10	.20	.40
315	Brett Callighen, Edm., RC	.10	.20	.40
316	Michel Dion, Goalie, Que.	.10	.20	.40
317	Randy Manery, LA	.10	.20	.40
318	Barry Dean, Phi., LC	.10	.20	.40
319	Pat Boutette, Tor.	.10	.20	.40
320	Mark Heaslip, Win., LC, "Now With Jets",	.10	.20	.40
321	Dave Inkpen, Har., LC	.10	.20	.40
322	Jere Gillis, Van.	.10	.20	.40
323	Larry Brown, Edm., LC "Now With Oilers"	.10	.20	.40
324	Alain Cote, Que., RC	.10	.20	.40
325	Gordie Lane, Wash.	.10	.20	.40
326	Bobby Lalonde, Bos., "Now With Bruins"	.10	.20	.40
327	Ed Staniowski, Goalie, St. L.	.10	.20	.40
328	Ron Plumb, Har., LC, "Now With Whalers"	.10	.20	.40
329	Jude Drouin, Win.	.10	.20	.40
330	Rick Hampton, LA	.10	.20	.40
331	Stan Weir, Edm.	.10	.20	.40
332	Blair Stewart, Que., LC, "Now With Nordiques"	.10	.20	.40
333	Mike Polich, Min., RC	.10	.20	.40
334	Jean Potvin, NYI, LC	.10	.20	.40
335	Jordy Douglas, Har., RC	.10	.20	.40
336	Joel Quenneville, Tor., RC	.10	.20	.40
337	Glen Hanlon, Goalie, Van., RC	.60	1.25	2.50
338	Dave Hoyda, Win., RC	.10	.20	.40
339	Colin Campbell, Edm., "Now With Oilers"	.10	.20	.40
340	John Smrke, Que., RC, LC	.10	.20	.40
341	Brian Glennie, LA	.10	.20	.40
342	Don Kozak, Har., LC	.10	.20	.40
343	Yvon Labre, Wash., LC	.10	.20	.40
344	Curt Bennett, Atl., LC	.10	.20	.40
345	Mike Christie, Col.	.10	.20	.40
346	Checklist 3 (265 - 396)	2.00	4.00	8.00
347	Pat Price, Edm., "Now With Oilers"	.10	.20	.40
348	Ron Low, Goalie, Que., "Now With Nordiques"	.10	.20	.40
349	Mike Antonovich, Har., LC	.10	.20	.40
350	Rolie Eriksson, Win., LC, "Now With Jets"	.10	.20	.40
351	Bob L. Murdoch, St. L., LC, "Now With Blues"	.10	.20	.40
352	Rob Palmer, LA	.10	.20	.40
353	Brad Gassoff, Van., LC	.10	.20	.40
354	Bruce Boudreau, Tor., LC	.10	.20	.40
355	Al Hamilton, Edm., LC	.10	.20	.40
356	Blaine Stoughton, Har.	.10	.20	.40
357	John Baby, Que., LC	.10	.20	.40
358	Gary Inness, Goalie, Wash., LC	.10	.20	.40
359	Wayne Dillon, Win., LC	.10	.20	.40
360	Darcy Rota, Atl.	.10	.20	.40
361	Brian Engblom, Mon., RC	.10	.20	.40
362	Bill Hogaboam, Det., LC	.10	.20	.40
363	Dave Debol, Har., RC	.10	.20	.40
364	Pete LoPresti, Goalie, Edm., LC	.10	.20	.40
365	Gerry Hart, Que.	.10	.20	.40
366	Syl Apps, Jr., LA	.10	.20	.40
367	Jack McIlhargey, Van., LC	.10	.20	.40
368	Willy Lindstrom, Win.	.10	.20	.40
369	Don Laurence, St. L., RC, LC, "Now With Blues"	.10	.20	.40
370	Chuck Luksa, Har., RC, LC	.10	.20	.40
371	Dave Semenko, Edm., RC	1.00	2.00	4.00
372	Paul Baxter, Que., RC, LC	.10	.20	.40
373	Ron Ellis, Tor.	.10	.20	.40
374	Leif Svensson, Wash., RC, LC	.10	.20	.40
375	Dennis O'Brien, Bos., LC, "Now With Bruins"	.10	.20	.40
376	Glenn Goldup, LA	.10	.20	.40
377	Terry Richardson, Goalie, Har., RC, LC	.10	.20	.40
378	Peter Sullivan, Win.	.10	.20	.40
379	Doug Hicks, Edm., "Now With Oilers"	.10	.20	.40
380	Jamie Hislop, Que.	.10	.20	.40
381	Jocelyn Guevremont, NYR, LC, "Now With Rangers"	.10	.20	.40
382	Willi Plett, Atl.	.10	.20	.40
383	Larry Goodenough, Van., LC	.10	.20	.40

No.	Player	VG	EX	NRMT
384	Jim Warner, Har., RC, LC	.10	.20	.40
385	Rey Comeau, Col., LC	.10	.20	.40
386	Barry Melrose, Win., RC	.15	.30	.60
387	Dave Hunter, Edm., RC	.25	.50	1.00
388	Wally Weir, Que., LC	.10	.20	.40
389	Mario Lessard, Goalie, LA., RC	.18	.35	.75
390	Ed Kea, St. L., "Now With Blues"	.10	.20	.40
391	Bob Stephenson, Har., RC, LC	.10	.20	.40
392	Dennis Hextall, Wash., LC	.10	.20	.40
393	Jerry Butler, Tor.	.10	.20	.40
394	Dave Shand, Atl.	.10	.20	.40
395	Rick Blight, Van.	.10	.20	.40
396	Lars-Erik Sjoberg, Win., LC	.15	.35	.75

— 1980 - 81 REGULAR ISSUE —

Cards with an American flag on the face designate the player as a member of the Gold Medal USA Olympic team (9, 22, 69, 103, 127, 232). The first five cards of the set are record breaking achievements of the previous NHL season.
Mint cards command a 50% price premium over NRMT cards.

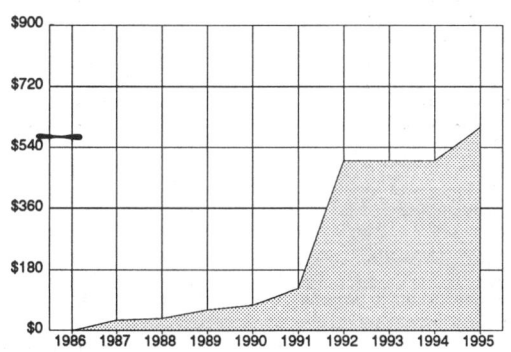

Card Size: 2 1/2" X 3 1/2"
Face: Four colour, white border, Position
Back: Green and yellow on card stock, Number, Resume, Hockey trivia, Bilingual
Imprint: © 1980 O-PEE-CHEE PRINTED IN CANADA and © NHLPA
Complete Set No.: 396
Complete Set Price: 170.00 340.00 675.00
Common Card: .08 .17 .35
Wax Pack: 50.00
Wax Box: (48 Packs) 2,000.00
Wax Case: (16 Boxes) 28,500.00

1979-80 RECORD BREAKERS

No.	Player	VG	EX	NRMT
1	Philadelphia Flyers go to 35 games without a loss	.25	.50	1.00
2	Ray Bourque sets mark for rookie Defenseman	3.00	6.00	12.00
3	Wayne Gretzky is youngest to score 50 goals	8.75	17.50	35.00
4	Charlie Simmer scores in 13 straight games	.12	.25	.50
5	Billy Smith becomes 1st Goalie to score a goal	.12	.25	.50

REGULAR ISSUE

No.	Player	VG	EX	NRMT
6	Jean Ratelle, Bos., LC	.25	.50	1.00
7	Dave Maloney, NYR	.08	.17	.35
8	Phil Myre, Goalie, Phi., LC	.08	.17	.35
9	Ken Morrow, NYI, RC	.35	.75	1.50
10	Guy Lafleur, Mon.	.85	1.75	3.50
11	Bill Derlago, Tor., RC	.08	.17	.35
12	Douglas Wilson, Chi.	1.00	2.00	4.00
13	Craig Ramsay, Buf.	.08	.17	.35
14	Pat Boutette, Har.	.08	.17	.35
15	Eric Vail, Cal.	.08	.17	.35
16	Red Wings Team Leader: Mike Foligno	.08	.17	.35

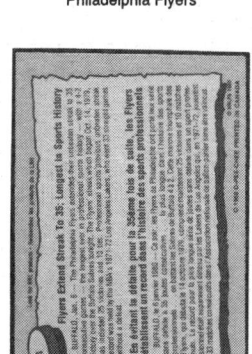
O-Pee-Chee 1980-81 Issue Card No. 1, Philadelphia Flyers

O-Pee-Chee 1980-81 Issue Card No. 6, Jean Ratelle

O-Pee-Chee 1980-81 Issue Card No. 31, Mike Liut

No.	Player	VG	EX	NRMT
17	Robert Smith, Min.	.75	1.50	3.00
18	Rick Kehoe, Pit.	.08	.17	.35
19	Joel Quenneville, Col.	.08	.17	.35
20	Marcel Dionne, LA	.75	1.50	3.00
21	Kevin McCarthy, Van.	.08	.17	.35
22	Jim Craig, Goalie, Bos., RC, LC	.25	.50	1.00
23	Steve Vickers, NYR, LC	.08	.17	.35
24	Ken Linseman, Phi.	.18	.35	.75
25	Mike Bossy, NYI	2.50	5.00	10.00
26	Serge Savard, Mon.	.18	.35	.75
27	Black Hawks Team Leader: Grant Mulvey	.08	.17	.35
28	Pat Hickey, Tor.	.08	.17	.35
29	Peter Sullivan, Win., LC	.08	.17	.35
30	Blaine Stoughton, Har.	.08	.17	.35
31	Michael Liut, Goalie, St. L., RC	2.50	5.00	10.00
32	Blair MacDonald, Edm.	.08	.17	.35
33	Richard Green, Wash.	.08	.17	.35
34	Al MacAdam, Min.	.08	.17	.35
35	Robbie Ftorek, Que.	.08	.17	.35
36	Dick Redmond, Bos.	.08	.17	.35
37	Ron Duguay, NYR	.08	.17	.35
38	Sabres Team Leader: Danny Gare	.08	.17	.35
39	Brian Propp, Phi., RC	2.50	5.00	10.00
40	Bryan Trottier, NYI	1.00	2.00	4.00
41	Rich Preston, Chi.	.08	.17	.35
42	Pierre Mondou, Mon.	.08	.17	.35
43	Reed Larson, Det.	.08	.17	.35
44	George Ferguson, Pit.	.08	.17	.35
45	Guy Chouinard, Cal.	.08	.17	.35
46	Billy Harris, LA	.08	.17	.35
47	Gilles Meloche, Goalie, Min.	.08	.17	.35
48	Blair Chapman, St. L.	.08	.17	.35
49	Capitals Team Leader: Michael Gartner	1.50	3.00	6.00
50	Darryl Sittler, Tor.	.50	1.00	2.00
51	Rick Martin, Buf., LC	.08	.17	.35
52	Ivan Boldirev, Van.	.08	.17	.35
53	Craig Norwich, St. L., RC, LC	.08	.17	.35
54	Dennis Polonich, Det., LC	.08	.17	.35
55	Bobby Clarke, Phi.	.75	1.50	3.00
56	Terry O'Reilly, Bos.	.10	.20	.40
57	Carol Vadnais, NYR	.08	.17	.35
58	Bob Gainey, Mon.	.18	.35	.75
59	Whalers Team Leader: Blaine Stoughton	.08	.17	.35
60	Billy Smith, Goalie, NYI	.18	.35	.75
61	Michael O'Connell, Chi., RC	.12	.25	.50
62	Lanny McDonald, Col.	.25	.50	1.00
63	Lee Fogolin, Edm.	.08	.17	.35
64	Rocky Saganiuk, Tor., RC	.08	.17	.35
65	Rolf Edberg, Wash., RC, LC	.08	.17	.35
66	Paul Shmyr, Min., LC	.08	.17	.35
67	Michel Goulet, Que., RC	6.50	11.00	22.00
68	Dan Bouchard, Goalie, Cal.	.08	.17	.35
69	Mark Johnson, Pit., RC	.25	.50	1.00
70	Reggie Leach, Phi.	.08	.17	.35
71	Blues Team Leader: Bernie Federko	.08	.17	.35
72	Pete Mahovlich, Det., LC	.08	.17	.35
73	Anders Hedberg, NYR	.08	.17	.35
74	Brad Park, Bos.	.25	.50	1.00
75	Clark Gillies, NYI	.08	.17	.35
76	Doug Jarvis, Mon.	.08	.17	.35
77	John Garrett, Goalie, Har.	.08	.17	.35
78	Dave Hutchison, Chi., LC	.08	.17	.35
79	John Anderson, Tor., RC	.10	.20	.40
80	Gilbert Perreault, Buf.	.30	.65	1.25

ALL STARS

First Team

No.	Player	VG	EX	NRMT
81	Marcel Dionne, LA	.35	.75	1.50
82	Guy Lafleur, Mon.	.35	.75	1.50
83	Charlie Simmer, LA	.10	.20	.40
84	Larry Robinson, Mon.	.25	.50	1.00
85	Borje Salming, Tor.	.10	.20	.40
86	Tony Esposito, Goalie, Chi.	.25	.50	1.00

76 • O-PEE-CHEE — 1980-81 REGULAR ISSUE

Second Team

No.	Player	VG	EX	NRMT
87	Wayne Gretzky, Edm.	5.00	25.00	50.00
88	Danny Gare, Buf.	.08	.17	.35
89	Steve Shutt, Mon.	.08	.17	.35
90	Barry Beck, NYR	.08	.17	.35
91	Mark Howe, Har.	.10	.20	.40
92	Don Edwards, Goalie, Buf.	.08	.17	.35

REGULAR ISSUE

No.	Player	VG	EX	NRMT
93	Tom McCarthy, Min., RC	.08	.17	.35
94	Bruins Team Leaders: P. McNab/R. Middleton	.08	.17	.35
95	Mike Palmateer, Goalie, Wash.	.08	.17	.35
96	Jim Schoenfeld, Buf.	.08	.17	.35
97	Jordy Douglas, Har.	.08	.17	.35
98	Keith Brown, Chi., RC	.15	.30	.60
99	Dennis Ververgaert, Wash., (Now with Capitals)	.08	.17	.35
100	Phil Esposito, NYR, LC	.75	1.50	3.00
101	Jack Brownschidle, St. L.	.08	.17	.35
102	Bob Nystrom, NYI	.08	.17	.35
103	Steve Christoff, Min., RC	.10	.20	.40
104	Rob Palmer, LA, LC	.08	.17	.35
105	David Williams, Van.	.08	.17	.35
106	Flames Team Leader: Kent Nilsson	.08	.17	.35
107	Morris Lukowich, Win.	.08	.17	.35
108	Jack Valiquette, Col., LC	.08	.17	.35
109	Richard Dunn, Buf., RC	.08	.17	.35
110	Rogatien Vachon, Goalie, Bos.	.18	.35	.75
111	Mark Napier, Mon.	.08	.17	.35
112	Gordon Roberts, Har.	.08	.17	.35
113	Stan Jonathan, Bos.	.08	.17	.35
114	Brett Callighen, Edm.	.08	.17	.35
115	Rick MacLeish, Phi.	.08	.17	.35
116	Ulf Nilsson, NYR	.08	.17	.35
117	Penguins Team Leader: Rick Kehoe	.08	.17	.35
118	Dan Maloney, Tor.	.08	.17	.35
119	Terry Ruskowski, Chi.	.08	.17	.35
120	Denis Potvin, NYI	.60	1.25	2.50
121	Wayne Stephenson, Goalie, Wash., LC	.08	.17	.35
122	Rich LeDuc, Que., LC	.08	.17	.35
123	Checklist 1 (1 - 132)	1.50	3.00	6.00
124	Don Lever, Cal.	.08	.17	.35
125	Jim Rutherford, Goalie, Det., LC	.08	.17	.35
126	Ray Allison, Har., RC, LC	.08	.17	.35
127	Michael Ramsey, Buf., RC	.75	1.50	3.00
128	Canucks Team Leader: Stan Smyl	.08	.17	.35
129	Al Secord, Bos., RC	1.00	2.00	4.00
130	Denis Herron, Goalie, Mon.	.08	.17	.35
131	Bob Dailey, Phi.	.08	.17	.35
132	Dean Talafous, NYR	.08	.17	.35
133	Ian Turnbull, Tor.	.08	.17	.35
134	Ron Sedlbauer, Chi.	.08	.17	.35
135	Tom Bladon, Edm., LC, (Now with Oilers)	.08	.17	.35
136	Bernie Federko, St. L.	.75	1.50	3.00
137	David Taylor, LA	.60	1.25	2.50
138	Bob Lorimer, NYI	.08	.17	.35
139	North Stars Team Leaders: A. MacAdam/S. Payne	.08	.17	.35
140	Raymond Bourque, Bos., RC	30.00	65.00	125.00
141	Glen Hanlon, Goalie, Van.	.15	.30	.60
142	Willy Lindstrom, Win.	.08	.17	.35
143	Mike Rogers, Har.	.08	.17	.35
144	Anthony McKegney, Buf., RC	.15	.30	.60
145	Behn Wilson, Phi.	.08	.17	.35
146	Lucien DeBlois, Col.	.08	.17	.35
147	Dave Burrows, Pit., LC, (Now with Pittsburgh)	.08	.17	.35
148	Paul Woods, Det.	.08	.17	.35
149	Rangers Team Leader: Phil Esposito	.25	.50	1.00
150	Tony Esposito, Goalie, Chi.	.50	1.00	2.00
151	Pierre Larouche, Mon.	.08	.17	.35
152	Brad Maxwell, Min.	.08	.17	.35
153	Stan Weir, Edm.	.08	.17	.35
154	Ryan Walter, Wash.	.08	.17	.35
155	Dale Hoganson, Que.	.08	.17	.35
156	Anders Kallur, NYI, RC	.08	.17	.35
157	Paul Reinhart, Cal., RC	.60	1.25	2.50

O-Pee-Chee
1980-81 Issue
Card No. 67,
Michel Goulet

O-Pee-Chee
1980-81 Issue
Card No. 127,
Michael Ramsey

O-Pee-Chee
1980-81 Issue
Card No. 140,
Raymond Bourque

O-Pee-Chee
1980-81 Issue
Card No. 195,
Michael Gartner

No.	Player	VG	EX	NRMT
158	Greg Millen, Goalie, Pit.	.35	.75	1.50
159	Ric Seiling, Buf.	.08	.17	.35
160	Mark Howe, Har.	.18	.35	.75

1979-80 LEAGUE LEADERS

No.	Player	VG	EX	NRMT
161	Goal Leaders: D. Gare, Buf.; C. Simmer, LA; B. Stoughton, Har.	.30	.65	1.25
162	Assist Leaders: W. Gretzky, Edm.; M. Dionne, LA; G. Lafleur, Mon.	3.75	7.50	15.00
163	Scoring Leaders: M. Dionne, LA; W. Gretzky, Edm.; G. Lafleur, Mon.	3.75	7.50	15.00
164	Penalty Minute Leaders: J. Mann, Win.; D. Williams, Van.; P. Holmgren, Phi.	.18	.35	.75
165	Power Play Goal Leaders: C. Simmer, LA; M. Dionne, LA; D. Gare, Buf.; S. Shutt, Mon.; D. Sittler, Tor.	.30	.65	1.25
166	Goals Against Ave Leaders: B. Sauve, Buf.; D. Herron, Mon.; D. Edwards, Buf.	.30	.65	1.25
167	Game Winning Goal Leaders: D. Gare, Buf.; P. McNab, Bos.; B. Stoughton, Har.	.30	.65	1.25
168	Shutout Leaders: T. Esposito, Chi.; G. Cheevers, Bos.; B. Sauve, Buf.; R. Vachon, Det.	.25	.50	1.00

REGULAR ISSUE

No.	Player	VG	EX	NRMT
169	Perry Turnbull, St. L., RC	.10	.20	.40
170	Barry Beck, NYR	.08	.17	.35
171	Kings Team Leader: Charlie Simmer	.08	.17	.35
172	Paul Holmgren, Phi.	.08	.17	.35
173	Willie Huber, Det.	.08	.17	.35
174	Tim Young, Min.	.08	.17	.35
175	Gilles Gilbert, Goalie, Det.	.08	.17	.35
176	Dave Christian, Win., RC	1.00	2.00	4.00
177	Lars Lindgren, Van., RC	.08	.17	.35
178	Real Cloutier, Que.	.08	.17	.35
179	Laurie Boschman, Tor., RC	.25	.50	1.00
180	Steve Shutt, Mon.	.15	.30	.60
181	Bob Murray, Chi.	.08	.17	.35
182	Oilers Team Leader: Wayne Gretzky	5.00	10.00	20.00
183	John Van Boxmeer, Buf.	.08	.17	.35
184	Nick Fotiu, Har.	.08	.17	.35
185	Mike McEwen, Col.	.08	.17	.35
186	Greg Malone, Pit.	.08	.17	.35
187	Mike Foligno, Det., RC	1.75	3.50	7.00
188	Dave Langevin, NYI, RC	.10	.20	.40
189	Mel Bridgman, Phi.	.08	.17	.35
190	John Davidson, Goalie, NYR	.08	.17	.35
191	Mike Milbury, Bos.	.08	.17	.35
192	Ron Zanussi, Min.	.08	.17	.35
193	Maple Leafs Team Leader: Darryl Sittler	.18	.35	.75
194	John Marks, Chi.	.08	.17	.35
195	Michael Gartner, Wash., RC	20.00	40.00	80.00
196	Dave Lewis, LA	.08	.17	.35
197	Kent Nilsson, Cal., RC	.75	1.50	3.00
198	Rick Ley, Har., LC	.08	.17	.35
199	Derek Smith, Buf.	.08	.17	.35
200	Bill Barber, Phi.	.20	.40	.80
201	Guy Lapointe, Mon.	.12	.25	.50
202	Vaclav Nedomansky, Det.	.08	.17	.35
203	Don Murdoch, Edm., LC	.08	.17	.35
204	Islanders Team Leader: Mike Bossy	.50	1.00	2.00
205	Pierre Hamel, Win., Goalie, RC	.08	.17	.35
206	Mike Eaves, Min., RC	.08	.17	.35
207	Doug Halward, LA	.08	.17	.35
208	Stanley Smyl, Van., RC	.25	.50	1.00
209	Mike Zuke, St. L., RC	.08	.17	.35
210	Borje Salming, Tor.	.15	.30	.60
211	Walt Tkaczuk, NYR, LC	.08	.17	.35
212	Grant Mulvey, Chi.	.08	.17	.35
213	George (Rob) Ramage, Col., RC	1.00	2.00	4.00
214	Tom Rowe, Har.	.08	.17	.35
215	Don Edwards, Goalie, Buf.	.08	.17	.35
216	Canadiens Team Leaders: G. Lafleur/P Larouche	.30	.65	1.25
217	Dan Labraaten, Det.	.08	.17	.35
218	Glen Sharpley, Min.	.08	.17	.35
219	Stefan Persson, NYI	.08	.17	.35
220	Peter McNab, Bos.	.08	.17	.35

— 1980 - 81 REGULAR ISSUE — O-PEE-CHEE • 77

No.	Player	VG	EX	NRMT
221	Doug Hicks, Edm.	.08	.17	.35
222	**Bengt-Ake Gustafsson, Wash., RC**	**.12**	**.25**	**.50**
223	Michel Dion, Goalie, Que.	.08	.17	.35
224	Jimmy Watson, Phi.	.08	.17	.35
225	Wilf Paiement, Tor.	.08	.17	.35
226	Phil Russell, Cal.	.08	.17	.35
227	**Jets Team Leader:** Morris Lukowich	.08	.17	.35
228	Ron Stackhouse, Pit.	.08	.17	.35
229	Ted Bulley, Chi.	.08	.17	.35
230	Larry Robinson, Mon.	.30	.65	1.25
231	Donald Maloney, NYR	.08	.17	.35
232	**Rob McClanahan, Buf., RC**	**.12**	**.25**	**.50**
233	Al Sims, Har.	.08	.17	.35
234	Errol Thompson, Det., LC	.08	.17	.35
235	Glenn Resch, Goalie, NYI	.15	.30	.60
236	Bob Miller, Bos., LC	.08	.17	.35
237	Gary Sargent, Min., LC	.08	.17	.35
238	**Nordiques Team Leader:** Real Cloutier	.08	.17	.35
239	Rene Robert, Col.	.08	.17	.35
240	Charlie Simmer, LA	.50	1.00	2.00
241	Thomas Gradin, Van.	.08	.17	.35
242	**Richard Vaive, Tor., RC**	**1.20**	**2.40**	**4.75**
243	**Ronald Wilson, Win., RC**	**.25**	**.50**	**1.00**
244	Brian Sutter, St. L.	.35	.75	1.50
245	Dale McCourt, Det.	.08	.17	.35
246	Yvon Lambert, Mon.	.08	.17	.35
247	Tom Lysiak, Chi.	.08	.17	.35
248	Ronald Greschner, NYR	.08	.17	.35
249	**Flyers Team Leader:** Reggie Leach	.08	.17	.35
250	Wayne Gretzky, Edm.	35.00	75.00	150.00
251	Rick Middleton, Bos.	.15	.30	.60
252	Al Smith, Goalie, Col., LC, (Now with Rockies)	.08	.17	.35
253	Fred Barrett, Min., LC	.08	.17	.35
254	Butch Goring, NYI	.08	.17	.35
255	Robert Picard, Tor.	.08	.17	.35
256	Marc Tardif, Que.	.08	.17	.35
257	Checklist 2 (133 - 264)	1.50	3.00	6.00
258	Barry Long, Win., (Now with Jets)	.08	.17	.35
259	**Rookies Team Leader:** Rene Robert	.08	.17	.35
260	Danny Gare, Buf.	.08	.17	.35
261	Rejean Houle, Mon.	.08	.17	.35

1979 - 80 STANLEY CUP PLAYOFFS

No.	Teams	VG	EX	NRMT
262	**Semi-Finals:** Islanders defeat Sabres in six	.08	.17	.35
263	**Semi-Finals:** Flyers skate past North Stars	.08	.17	.35
264	**Finals:** Islanders win their first Stanley Cup	.12	.25	.50

REGULAR ISSUE

No.	Player	VG	EX	NRMT
265	Bobby Lalonde, Bos., LC, (Now with Bruins)	.08	.17	.35
266	Bob Sauve, Goalie, Buf.	.08	.17	.35
267	Bob MacMillan, Cal.	.08	.17	.35
268	Greg Fox, Chi.	.08	.17	.35
269	**Hardy Astrom, Col., Goalie, RC, LC**	**.10**	**.20**	**.40**
270	Greg Joly, Det.	.08	.17	.35
271	**Dave Lumley, Edm., RC**	**.08**	**.17**	**.35**
272	Dave Keon, Har.	.18	.35	.75
273	Garry Unger, LA,, (Now with Kings)	.08	.17	.35
274	Steve Payne, Min.	.08	.17	.35
275	Doug Risebrough, Mon., Error	.08	.17	.35
276	Bob Bourne, NYI	.08	.17	.35
277	Eddie Johnstone, NYR	.08	.17	.35
278	Peter Lee, Pit.	.08	.17	.35
279	**Peter Peeters, Goalie, Phi., RC**	**2.00**	**4.00**	**8.00**
280	Ron Chipperfield, Que., LC	.08	.17	.35
281	Wayne Babych, St. L.	.08	.17	.35
282	Dave Shand, Tor., LC	.08	.17	.35
283	Jere Gillis, NYR, (Now with Rangers)	.08	.17	.35
284	Dennis Maruk, Wash.	.08	.17	.35
285	Jude Drouin, Win., LC, (Now with Jets)	.08	.17	.35
286	Mike Murphy, LA	.08	.17	.35
287	Curt Fraser, Van.	.08	.17	.35
288	Gary McAdam, Pit.	.08	.17	.35
289	**Mark Messier, Edm., RC**	**35.00**	**75.00**	**150.00**
290	Vic Venasky, LA, LC	.08	.17	.35

O-Pee-Chee
1980-81 Issue
Card No. 232,
Rob McClanahan

O-Pee-Chee
1980-81 Issue
Card No. 263,
Semi-Finals

O-Pee-Chee
1980-81 Issue
Card No. 275, Error,
Shows Serge Savard

O-Pee-Chee
1980-81 Issue
Card No. 289,
Mark Messier

No.	Player	VG	EX	NRMT
291	Per-Olov Brasar, Van., LC	.08	.17	.35
292	Orest Kindrachuk, Pit., LC	.08	.17	.35
293	Dave Hunter, Edm.	.08	.17	.35
294	Steve Jensen, LA	.08	.17	.35
295	Chris Oddleifson, Van., LC	.08	.17	.35
296	**Larry Playfair, Buf., RC**	**.08**	**.17**	**.35**
297	Mario Tremblay, Mon.	.08	.17	.35
298	**Gilles Lupien, Pit., RC, LC**	**.08**	**.17**	**.35**
299	Pat Price, Edm.	.08	.17	.35
300	Jerry Korab, LA, (Now with Kings)	.08	.17	.35
301	Darcy Rota, Van.	.08	.17	.35
302	Don Luce, Buf.	.08	.17	.35
303	Ken Houston, Cal.	.08	.17	.35
304	Brian Engblom, Mon.	.08	.17	.35
305	John Tonelli, NYI	.60	1.25	2.50
306	**Douglas Sulliman, NYR, RC**	**.08**	**.17**	**.35**
307	Rod Schutt, Pit.	.08	.17	.35
308	**Norm Barnes, Phi., RC, LC**	**.08**	**.17**	**.35**
309	Serge Bernier, Que., LC	.08	.17	.35
310	Larry Patey, St. L.	.08	.17	.35
311	Dave Farrish, Tor., (Now with Maple Leafs)	.08	.17	.35
312	Harold Snepsts, Van.	.08	.17	.35
313	Bob Sirois, Wash., LC	.08	.17	.35
314	Peter Marsh, Win.	.08	.17	.35
315	**Risto Siltanen, Edm., RC**	**.10**	**.20**	**.40**
316	Andre St. Laurent, LA	.08	.17	.35
317	**Craig Hartsburg, Min., RC**	**.18**	**.35**	**.75**
318	Wayne Cashman, Bos.	.08	.17	.35
319	**Lindy Ruff, Buf., RC**	**.10**	**.20**	**.40**
320	Willi Plett, Cal.	.08	.17	.35
321	Ron Delorme, Col.	.08	.17	.35
322	**Gaston Gingras, Mon., RC**	**.10**	**.20**	**.40**
323	Gordie Lane, NYI	.08	.17	.35
324	**Doug Soetaert, Goalie, NYR, RC**	**.10**	**.20**	**.40**
325	Gregg Sheppard, Pit.,LC, (Now with Penguins)	.08	.17	.35
326	**Mike Busniuk, Phi., RC**	**.08**	**.17**	**.35**
327	Jamie Hislop, Que.	.08	.17	.35
328	Ed Staniowski, Goalie, St. L.	.08	.17	.35
329	Ron Ellis, Tor., LC	.08	.17	.35
330	Gary Bromley, Goalie, Van., LC	.08	.17	.35
331	**Mark Lofthouse, Wash., RC, LC**	**.08**	**.17**	**.35**
332	Dave Hoyda, Win., LC	.08	.17	.35
333	Ron Low, Goalie, Edm., (Now with Oilers)	.08	.17	.35
334	Barry Gibbs, LA, LC	.08	.17	.35
335	Gary Edwards, Goalie, Min., LC	.08	.17	.35
336	Don Marcotte, Bos.	.08	.17	.35
337	Bill Hajt, Buf.	.08	.17	.35
338	**Bradley Marsh, Cal., RC**	**2.50**	**5.00**	**10.00**
339	J. P. Bordeleau, Chi., LC	.08	.17	.35
340	**Randy Pierce, Col., RC, LC**	**.08**	**.17**	**.35**
341	**Ed Mio, Edm., Goalie, RC**	**.12**	**.25**	**.50**
342	Randy Manery, LA, LC	.08	.17	.35
343	Tom Younghans, Min.	.08	.17	.35
344	**Rod Langway, Mon., RC**	**3.75**	**7.50**	**15.00**
345	Wayne Merrick, NYI	.08	.17	.35
346	**Steve Baker, Goalie, NYR, RC**	**.08**	**.17**	**.35**
347	Pat Hughes, Pit.	.08	.17	.35
348	Al Hill, Phi., LC	.08	.17	.35
349	Gerry Hart, St. L., (Now with Blues) LC	.08	.17	.35
350	Richard Mulhern, Tor., LC, (Now with Maple Leafs)	.08	.17	.35
351	Jerry Butler, Van., Now with Cannucks	.08	.17	.35
352	Guy Charron, Wash., LC	.08	.17	.35
353	**Jimmy Mann, Win., RC**	**.10**	**.20**	**.40**
354	**Byron (Brad) McCrimmon, Bos., RC**	**1.25**	**2.50**	**5.00**
355	Rick Dudley, Buf.	.08	.17	.35
356	Pekka Rautakallio, Cal.	.08	.17	.35
357	**Tim Trimper, Chi., RC**	**.08**	**.17**	**.35**
358	Mike Christie, Col., LC	.08	.17	.35
359	**John Ogrodnick, Det., RC**	**1.00**	**2.00**	**4.00**
360	Dave Semenko, Edm.	.08	.17	.35
361	Mike Veisor, Goalie, Har., LC, (Now with Whalers)	.08	.17	.35
362	Syl Apps, Jr., LA, (Now Retired) LC	.08	.17	.35
363	Mike Polich, Min.	.08	.17	.35
364	Rick Chartraw, Mon., LC	.08	.17	.35
365	**Steve Tambellini, NYI, RC**	**.10**	**.20**	**.40**
366	**Ed Hospodar, NYR, RC**	**.08**	**.17**	**.35**
367	Randy Carlyle, Pit.	.08	.17	.35
368	Tom Gorence, Phi.	.08	.17	.35

78 • O-PEE-CHEE — 1981-82 REGULAR ISSUE

No.	Player	VG	EX	NRMT
369	Pierre Plante, Que., LC, (Now with Nordiques)	.08	.17	.35
370	Blake Dunlop, St. L., (Now with Blues)	.08	.17	.35
371	Mike Kaszycki, Tor., LC, (Now with Maple Leafs)	.08	.17	.35
372	Rick Blight, Van., LC	.08	.17	.35
373	Pierre Bouchard, Wash., LC	.08	.17	.35
374	Gary Doak, Bos., LC	.08	.17	.35
375	Andre Savard, Buf.	.08	.17	.35
376	Bill Clement, Cal.	.08	.17	.35
377	Reg Kerr, Chi.	.08	.17	.35
378	Walt McKechnie, Col., (Now with Rockies)	.08	.17	.35
379	George Lyle, Det., RC	.08	.17	.35
380	Colin Campbell, Edm.	.08	.17	.35
381	Dave Debol, Har., LC	.08	.17	.35
382	Glenn Goldup, LA, LC	.08	.17	.35
383	Kent-Erik Andersson, Min.	.08	.17	.35
384	Tony Currie, St. L., RC	.08	.17	.35
385	Richard Sevigny, Goalie, Mon., RC	.15	.30	.60
386	Garry Howatt, NYI	.08	.17	.35
387	Cam Connor, NYR, LC	.08	.17	.35
388	Ross Lonsberry, Pit.	.08	.17	.35
389	Frank Bathe, Phi., RC, LC	.08	.17	.35
390	John Wensink, Que., LC, (Now with Nordiques)	.08	.17	.35
391	Paul Harrison, Goalie, Tor., LC	.08	.17	.35
392	Dennis Kearns, Van.	.08	.17	.35
393	Pat Ribble, Wash., (Now with Capitals)	.08	.17	.35
394	Markus Mattson, Goalie, Win., RC	.08	.17	.35
395	Chuck Lefley, St. L., LC	.08	.17	.35
396	Checklist 3 (265 - 396)	2.00	4.00	8.00

U.S.A. OLYMPIC TEAM GOLD MEDAL
U.S. Flag on Face

- 9 Ken Morrow, New York Islanders
- 22 Jim Craig, Boston Bruins
- 69 Mark Johnson, Pittsburgh Penguins
- 103 Steve Christoff, Minnesota North Stars
- 127 Mike Ramsey, Buffalo Sabres
- 232 Rob McClanahan, Buffalo Sabres

— 1981 - 82 REGULAR ISSUE —

The set features special 'super action' and 'record breaking' cards. Mint cards command a 25% price premium over NRMT cards.

PRICE MOVEMENT OF NRMT SETS

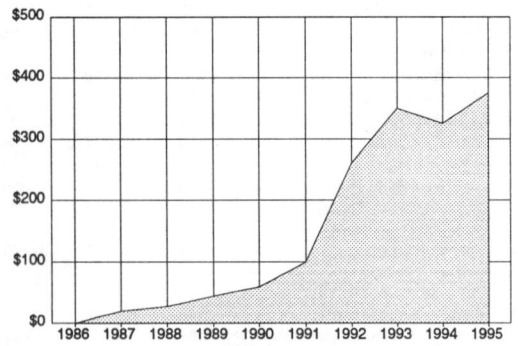

Card Size: 2 1/2" X 3 1/2"
Face: Four colour, white border, Team logo, Position
Back: Blue and black on card stock, Number, Resume, Bilingual
Imprint: © 1981 O-Pee-Chee Ptd. In Canada/Imprimé au Canada and
 © 1981 NHLPA
Complete Set No.: 396

	VG	EX	NRMT
Complete Set Price:	110.00	225.00	450.00
Common Card:	.07	.15	.30
Wax Pack:			35.00
Wax Box: (48 Packs)			1,500.00
Wax Case: (16 Boxes)			22,000.00

O-Pee-Chee
1981-82 Issue
Card No. 1,
Raymond Bourque

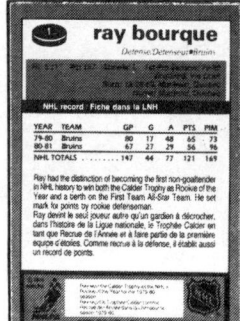

O-Pee-Chee
1981-82 Issue
Card No. 1,
Raymond Bourque

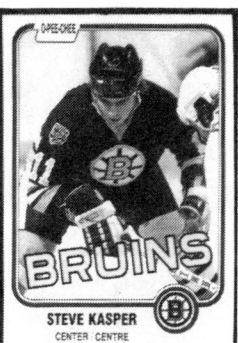

O-Pee-Chee
1981-82 Issue
Card No. 4,
Stephen Kasper

O-Pee-Chee
1981-82 Issue
Card No. 44,
Rejean Lemelin

BOSTON BRUINS

No.	Player	VG	EX	NRMT
1	Raymond Bourque	7.50	15.00	30.00
2	Rick Middleton	.10	.20	.40

COLORADO ROCKIES

No.	Player	VG	EX	NRMT
3	Dwight Foster, (Now with Rockies)	.07	.15	.30

BOSTON BRUINS

No.	Player	VG	EX	NRMT
4	Stephen Kasper, RC	.50	1.00	2.00
5	Peter McNab	.07	.15	.30
6	Michael O'Connell	.07	.15	.30
7	Terry O'Reilly	.10	.20	.40
8	Brad Park	.18	.35	.70
9	Dick Redmond, LC	.07	.15	.30
10	Rogatien Vachon, Goalie	.15	.30	.60
11	Wayne Cashman	.07	.15	.30
12	Mike Gillis, RC, LC	.07	.15	.30
13	Stan Jonathan, LC	.07	.15	.30
14	Don Marcotte	.07	.15	.30
15	Byron (Brad) McCrimmon	.15	.30	.60
16	Mike Milbury	.07	.15	.30
17	Super Action: Ray Bourque	1.75	3.50	7.00
18	Super Action: Rick Middleton	.07	.15	.30
19	Bruins Team Leader: Rick Middleton	.10	.20	.40

BUFFALO SABRES

No.	Player	VG	EX	NRMT
20	Danny Gare, (Traded to Red Wings, 12/2/81)	.07	.15	.30
21	Don Edwards, Goalie	.07	.15	.30
22	Anthony McKegney	.07	.15	.30
23	Bob Sauve, Goalie, (Now with Red Wings)	.07	.15	.30
24	Andre Savard	.07	.15	.30
25	Derek Smith, (Traded to Red Wings, 12/2/81)	.07	.15	.30
26	John Van Boxmeer	.07	.15	.30
27	Super Action: Danny Gare, (Traded to Red Wings, 12/2/81)	.07	.15	.30
28	Buffalo Sabres Team Leader: Danny Gare			
29	Richard Dunn	.07	.15	.30
30	Gilbert Perreault	.25	.50	1.00
31	Craig Ramsay	.07	.15	.30
32	Ric Seiling	.07	.15	.30

CALGARY FLAMES

No.	Player	VG	EX	NRMT
33	Guy Chouinard	.07	.15	.30
34	Kent Nilsson	.07	.15	.30
35	Willi Plett	.07	.15	.30
36	Paul Reinhart	.07	.15	.30
37	Pat Riggin, Goalie, RC	.12	.25	.50

DETROIT RED WINGS

No.	Player	VG	EX	NRMT
38	Eric Vail, (Now with Red Wings)	.07	.15	.30

CALGARY FLAMES

No.	Player	VG	EX	NRMT
39	Bill Clement	.07	.15	.30
40	Jamie Hislop	.07	.15	.30

WASHINGTON CAPITALS

No.	Player	VG	EX	NRMT
41	Randy Holt, LC (Now with Capitals)	.07	.15	.30

CALGARY FLAMES

No.	Player	VG	EX	NRMT
42	Dan Labraaten, LC	.07	.15	.30
43	Kevin LaVallee, RC	.07	.15	.30
44	Rejean Lemelin, Goalie, RC	1.50	3.00	6.00

1981-82 REGULAR ISSUE — O-PEE-CHEE • 79

COLORADO ROCKIES

No.	Player	VG	EX	NRMT
45	Don Lever, (Now with Rockies)	.07	.15	.30 ☐
46	Bob MacMillan, (Now with Rockies)	.07	.15	.30 ☐

PHILADELPHIA FLYERS

No.	Player	VG	EX	NRMT
47	Bradley Marsh, (Now with Flyers)	.07	.15	.30 ☐

CALGARY FLAMES

No.	Player	VG	EX	NRMT
48	Bob J. Murdoch	.07	.15	.30 ☐
49	**James (Jim) Peplinski, RC**	**.75**	**1.50**	**3.00 ☐**
50	Pekka Rautakallio, LC	.07	.15	.30 ☐
51	Phil Russell	.07	.15	.30 ☐
52	**Super Action:** Kent Nilsson	.07	.15	.30 ☐
53	**Calgary Flames Team Leader:** Kent Nilsson	.07	.15	.30 ☐

CHICAGO BLACK HAWKS

No.	Player	VG	EX	NRMT
54	Tony Esposito, Goalie	.25	.50	1.00 ☐
55	Keith Brown	.07	.15	.30 ☐
56	Ted Bulley	.07	.15	.30 ☐
57	**Tim Higgins, RC**	**.07**	**.15**	**.30 ☐**
58	Reg Kerr	.07	.15	.30 ☐
59	Tom Lysiak	.07	.15	.30 ☐
60	Grant Mulvey	.07	.15	.30 ☐
61	Bob Murray	.07	.15	.30 ☐
62	Terry Ruskowski	.07	.15	.30 ☐
63	**Denis Savard, RC**	**6.00**	**12.50**	**25.00 ☐**
64	Glen Sharpley	.07	.15	.30 ☐
65	**Darryl Sutter, RC**	**.50**	**1.00**	**2.00 ☐**
66	Douglas Wilson	.50	1.00	2.00 ☐
67	**Super Action:** Tony Esposito	.18	.35	.75 ☐
68	**Murray Bannerman, Goalie, RC**	**.20**	**.40**	**.80 ☐**
69	Greg Fox	.07	.15	.30 ☐
70	John Marks, LC	.07	.15	.30 ☐
71	Peter Marsh, LC	.07	.15	.30 ☐
72	Al Secord	.18	.35	.75 ☐
73	**Chicago Black Hawks Team Leader:** Tom Lysiak	.07	.15	.30 ☐

WINNIPEG JETS

No.	Player	VG	EX	NRMT
74	Lucien DeBlois	.07	.15	.30 ☐

COLORADO ROCKIES

No.	Player	VG	EX	NRMT
75	**Paul Gagne, RC**	**.07**	**.15**	**.30 ☐**
76	**Merlin Malinowski, RC**	**.07**	**.15**	**.30 ☐**

CALGARY FLAMES

No.	Player	VG	EX	NRMT
77	Lanny McDonald, (Now with Flames)	.18	.35	.75 ☐

COLORADO ROCKIES

No.	Player	VG	EX	NRMT
78	Joel Quenneville	.07	.15	.30 ☐
79	George (Rob) Ramage	.12	.25	.50 ☐
80	Glenn Resch, Goalie	.10	.20	.40 ☐
81	Steve Tambellini	.07	.15	.30 ☐

VANCOUVER CANUCKS

No.	Player	VG	EX	NRMT
82	Ron Delorme, (Now with Canucks)	.07	.15	.30 ☐

COLORADO ROCKIES

No.	Player	VG	EX	NRMT
83	Mike Kitchen, LC	.07	.15	.30 ☐
84	**Yvon Vautour, RC, LC**	**.07**	**.15**	**.30 ☐**
85	**Colorado Rockies Team Leader:** Lanny McDonald	.10	.20	.40 ☐

BUFFALO SABRES

No.	Player	VG	EX	NRMT
86	Dale McCourt, (Now with Sabres)	.07	.15	.30 ☐

O-Pee-Chee
1981-82 Issue
Card No. 63,
Denis Savard

O-Pee-Chee
1981-82 Issue
Card No. 75,
Paul Gagne

O-Pee-Chee
1981-82 Issue
Card No. 106,
Wayne Gretzky

O-Pee-Chee
1981-82 Issue
Card No. 111,
Paul Coffey

DETROIT RED WINGS

No.	Player	VG	EX	NRMT
87	Mike Foligno, (Traded to Buffalo 12/2/81)	.07	.15	.30 ☐
88	Gilles Gilbert, Goalie	.07	.15	.30 ☐
89	Willie Huber	.07	.15	.30 ☐
90	**Mark Kirton, RC**	**.07**	**.15**	**.30 ☐**
91	**James Korn, RC**	**.07**	**.15**	**.30 ☐**
92	Reed Larson	.07	.15	.30 ☐

CALGARY FLAMES

No.	Player	VG	EX	NRMT
93	Gary McAdam, (Now with Flames)	.07	.15	.30 ☐

DETROIT RED WINGS

No.	Player	VG	EX	NRMT
94	Vaclav Nedomansky, LC	.07	.15	.30 ☐
95	John Ogrodnick	.18	.35	.75 ☐
96	**Super Action:** Dale McCourt, (Traded to Buffalo 12/2/81)	.07	.15	.30 ☐

REGULAR ISSUE

No.	Player	VG	EX	NRMT
97	Jean Hamel, Que., (Now with Nordiques)	.07	.15	.30 ☐
98	**Glenn Hicks, Win., RC, LC, (Now with Jets)**	**.07**	**.15**	**.30 ☐**
99	**Larry Lozinski, Det., Goalie, RC, LC**	**.07**	**.15**	**.30 ☐**
100	George Lyle, Har., (Now with Whalers) LC	.07	.15	.30 ☐
101	Perry Miller, Det., LC	.07	.15	.30 ☐
102	Brad Maxwell, Min.	.07	.15	.30 ☐
103	**Brad Smith, Det., RC, LC, (Now with Red Wings)**	**.07**	**.15**	**.30 ☐**
104	Paul Woods, Det.	.07	.15	.30 ☐
105	**Detroit Red Wings Team Leader:** Dale McCourt	.07	.15	.30 ☐

EDMONTON OILERS

No.	Player	VG	EX	NRMT
106	Wayne Gretzky	13.75	27.50	55.00 ☐
107	**Jari Kurri, RC**	**10.00**	**20.00**	**40.00 ☐**
108	**Glenn Anderson, RC**	**3.75**	**7.50**	**15.00 ☐**
109	Curt Brackenbury, LC	.07	.15	.30 ☐
110	Brett Callighen	.07	.15	.30 ☐
111	**Paul Coffey, RC**	**24.00**	**48.00**	**95.00 ☐**
112	Lee Fogolin	.07	.15	.30 ☐
113	**Matti Hagman, RC**	**.07**	**.15**	**.30 ☐**
114	Doug Hicks	.07	.15	.30 ☐
115	Dave Hunter	.07	.15	.30 ☐
116	Garry Lariviere, (Now with Oilers)	.07	.15	.30 ☐
117	**Kevin Lowe, RC**	**2.50**	**5.00**	**10.00 ☐**
118	Mark Messier	10.00	20.00	40.00 ☐
119	Ed Mio, Goalie	.07	.15	.30 ☐
120	**Andrew Moog, Goalie, RC**	**7.00**	**14.00**	**28.00 ☐**
121	Dave Semenko	.07	.15	.30 ☐
122	Risto Siltanen	.07	.15	.30 ☐
123	Garry Unger, (Now with Oilers)	.07	.15	.30 ☐
124	Stan Weir, LC	.07	.15	.30 ☐
125	**Super Action:** Wayne Gretzky	6.00	12.50	25.00 ☐
126	**Edmonton Oilers Team Leader:** Wayne Gretzky	2.50	5.00	10.00 ☐

NEW YORK RANGERS

No.	Player	VG	EX	NRMT
127	Mike Rogers, (Now with Rangers)	.07	.15	.30 ☐

HARTFORD WHALERS

No.	Player	VG	EX	NRMT
128	Mark Howe	.10	.20	.40 ☐
129	Dave Keon, LC	.15	.30	.60 ☐
130	**Warren Miller, RC**	**.07**	**.15**	**.30 ☐**

LOS ANGELES KINGS

No.	Player	VG	EX	NRMT
131	Al Sims, LC, (Now with Kings)	.07	.15	.30 ☐

80 • O-PEE-CHEE — 1981-82 REGULAR ISSUE

HARTFORD WHALERS

No.	Player	VG	EX	NRMT
132	Blaine Stoughton	.07	.15	.30
133	Rick MacLeish	.07	.15	.30
134	Greg Millen, Goalie	.07	.15	.30
135	**Super Action:** Mike Rogers	.07	.15	.30
136	Mike Fidler, LC	.07	.15	.30
137	John Garrett, Goalie	.07	.15	.30
138	**Donald Nachbauer, RC, LC**	.07	.15	.30
139	Tom Rowe, LC	.07	.15	.30
140	**Hartford Whalers Team** Leader: Mike Rogers	.07	.15	.30

LOS ANGELES KINGS

No.	Player	VG	EX	NRMT
141	Marcel Dionne	.50	1.00	2.00
142	Charlie Simmer	.25	.50	1.00
143	David Taylor	.25	.50	1.00

TORONTO MAPLE LEAFS

No.	Player	VG	EX	NRMT
144	Billy Harris, (Now with Maple Leafs)	.07	.15	.30

LOS ANGELES KINGS

No.	Player	VG	EX	NRMT
145	Jerry Korab, LC	.07	.15	.30
146	Mario Lessard, Goalie	.07	.15	.30

TORONTO MAPLE LEAFS

No.	Player	VG	EX	NRMT
147	Don Luce, LC	.07	.15	.30

LOS ANGELES KINGS

No.	Player	VG	EX	NRMT
148	**Lawrence Murphy, RC**	3.75	7.50	15.00
149	Mike Murphy, LC	.07	.15	.30
150	**Super Action:** Marcel Dionne	.25	.50	1.00
151	**Super Action:** Charlie Simmer	.10	.20	.40
152	**Super Action:** David Taylor	.10	.20	.40
153	**Jim Fox, RC**	.07	.15	.30
154	Steve Jensen, LC	.07	.15	.30
155	**Greg Terrion, RC**	.07	.15	.30
156	**Los Angeles Kings Team** Leader: Marcel Dionne	.18	.35	.75

MINNESOTA NORTH STARS

No.	Player	VG	EX	NRMT
157	Robert Smith	.25	.50	1.00
158	Kent-Erik Andersson	.07	.15	.30
159	**Donald Beaupre, Goalie, RC**	2.00	4.00	8.00
160	Steve Christoff	.07	.15	.30
161	**Dino Ciccarelli, RC**	6.00	12.50	25.00
162	Craig Hartsburg	.07	.15	.30
163	Al MacAdam	.07	.15	.30
164	Tom McCarthy	.07	.15	.30
165	Gilles Meloche, Goalie	.07	.15	.30
166	Steve Payne	.07	.15	.30
167	Gordon Roberts	.07	.15	.30

DETROIT RED WINGS

No.	Player	VG	EX	NRMT
168	Greg Smith, (Now with Red Wings)	.07	.15	.30

MINNESOTA NORTH STARS

No.	Player	VG	EX	NRMT
169	Tim Young	.07	.15	.30
170	**Super Action:** Robert Smith	.12	.25	.50
171	Mike Eaves	.07	.15	.30
172	Mike Polich, LC	.07	.15	.30

NEW YORK RANGERS

No.	Player	VG	EX	NRMT
173	Tom Younghans, (Now with Rangers) LC	.07	.15	.30

MINNESOTA NORTH STARS

No.	Player	VG	EX	NRMT
174	**Minnesota North Stars** Team Leader: Robert Smith	.07	.15	.30

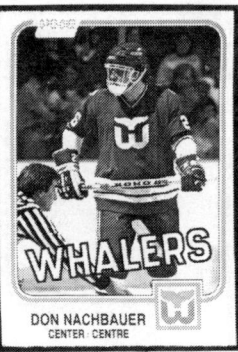

O-Pee-Chee
1981-82 Issue
Card No. 138,
Donald Nachbauer

O-Pee-Chee
1981-82 Issue
Card No. 141,
Marcel Dionne

O-Pee-Chee
1981-82 Issue
Card No. 161,
Dino Ciccarelli

O-Pee-Chee
1981-82 Issue
Card No. 193,
Douglas Wickenheiser

MONTREAL CANADIENS

No.	Player	VG	EX	NRMT
175	Brian Engblom	.07	.15	.30
176	Bob Gainey	.12	.25	.50
177	Guy Lafleur	.70	1.40	2.75
178	Mark Napier	.07	.15	.30
179	Larry Robinson	.25	.50	1.00
180	Steve Shutt	.10	.20	.40
181	**Keith Acton, RC**	.07	.15	.30
182	Gaston Gingras	.07	.15	.30
183	Rejean Houle	.07	.15	.30
184	Doug Jarvis	.07	.15	.30

BUFFALO SABRES

No.	Player	VG	EX	NRMT
185	Yvon Lambert, (Now with Sabres)	.07	.15	.30

MONTREAL CANADIENS

No.	Player	VG	EX	NRMT
186	Rod Langway	.75	1.50	3.00
187	Pierre Larouche	.07	.15	.30
188	Pierre Mondou	.07	.15	.30
189	Robert Picard	.07	.15	.30
190	Doug Risebrough	.07	.15	.30
191	Richard Sevigny, Goalie	.07	.15	.30
192	Mario Tremblay	.07	.15	.30
193	**Douglas Wickenheiser, RC**	.12	.25	.50
194	**Super Action:** Bob Gainey	.10	.20	.40
195	**Super Action:** Guy Lafleur	.30	.60	1.20
196	**Super Action:** Larry Robinson	.10	.20	.40
197	**Montreal Canadiens Team** Leader: Steve Shutt	.10	.20	.40

NEW YORK ISLANDERS

No.	Player	VG	EX	NRMT
198	Mike Bossy	1.12	2.25	4.50
199	Denis Potvin	.35	.75	1.50
200	Bryan Trottier	.50	1.00	2.00
201	Bob Bourne	.07	.15	.30
202	Clark Gillies	.07	.15	.30
203	Butch Goring	.07	.15	.30
204	Anders Kallur	.07	.15	.30
205	Ken Morrow	.07	.15	.30
206	Stefan Persson	.07	.15	.30
207	Billy Smith, Goalie	.12	.25	.50
208	**Super Action:** Mike Bossy	.35	.75	1.50
209	**Super Action:** Denis Potvin	.18	.35	.75
210	**Super Action:** Bryan Trottier	.25	.50	1.00
211	**Duane Sutter, RC**	.35	.75	1.50
212	Gord Lane, LC	.07	.15	.30
213	Dave Langevin	.07	.15	.30

COLORADO ROCKIES

No.	Player	VG	EX	NRMT
214	Bob Lorimer, (Now with Rockies)	.07	.15	.30

NEW YORK ISLANDERS

No.	Player	VG	EX	NRMT
215	Mike McEwen, (Now with Islanders)	.07	.15	.30
216	Wayne Merrick	.07	.15	.30
217	Bob Nystrom	.07	.15	.30
218	John Tonelli	.25	.50	1.00
219	**New York Islanders Team** Leader: Mike Bossy	.18	.35	.75

NEW YORK RANGERS

No.	Player	VG	EX	NRMT
220	Barry Beck	.07	.15	.30
221	**Mike Allison, RC**	.07	.15	.30
222	John Davidson, Goalie, LC	.07	.15	.30
223	Ron Duguay	.07	.15	.30
224	Ronald Greschner	.07	.15	.30
225	Anders Hedberg	.07	.15	.30
226	Eddie Johnstone	.07	.15	.30
227	Dave Maloney	.07	.15	.30
228	Donald Maloney	.07	.15	.30
229	Ulf Nilsson, LC	.07	.15	.30
230	**Super Action:** Barry Beck	.07	.15	.30
231	Steve Baker, Goalie, LC	.07	.15	.30
232	Jere Gillis, (Now with Rangers)	.07	.15	.30
233	Ed Hospodar, LC	.07	.15	.30

— 1981-82 REGULAR ISSUE — O-PEE-CHEE • 81

No.	Player	VG	EX	NRMT
234	Thomas Laidlaw, RC	.07	.15	.30
235	Dean Talafous, LC	.07	.15	.30
236	Carol Vadnais	.07	.15	.30
237	New York Rangers Team Leader: Anders Hedberg	.07	.15	.30

PHILADELPHIA FLYERS

No.	Player	VG	EX	NRMT
238	Bill Barber	.18	.35	.70
239	Behn Wilson	.07	.15	.30
240	Bobby Clarke	.40	.85	1.75
241	Bob Dailey, LC	.07	.15	.30
242	Paul Holmgren	.07	.15	.30
243	Reggie Leach	.07	.15	.30
244	Ken Linseman	.07	.15	.30
245	Peter Peeters, Goalie	.40	.85	1.75
246	Brian Propp	.50	1.00	2.00
247	Super Action: Bill Barber	.07	.15	.30

CALGARY FLAMES

No.	Player	VG	EX	NRMT
248	Mel Bridgman, (Now with Flames)	.07	.15	.30

PHILADELPHIA FLYERS

No.	Player	VG	EX	NRMT
249	Mike Busniuk, LC	.07	.15	.30
250	Tom Gorence	.07	.15	.30
251	Tim Kerr, RC	.75	3.50	7.00
252	Rick St. Croix, Goalie, RC	.07	.15	.30
253	Philadelphia Flyers Team Leader: Bill Barber	.07	.15	.30

PITTSBURGH PENGUINS

No.	Player	VG	EX	NRMT
254	Rick Kehoe	.07	.15	.30
255	Pat Boutette	.07	.15	.30
256	Randy Carlyle	.07	.15	.30
257	Paul Gardner	.07	.15	.30
258	Peter Lee, LC	.07	.15	.30
259	Rod Schutt, LC	.07	.15	.30
260	Super Action: Rick Kehoe	.07	.15	.30
261	Mario Faubert, LC	.07	.15	.30
262	George Ferguson	.07	.15	.30
263	Ross Lonsberry, (Now Retired), LC	.07	.15	.30
264	Greg Malone	.07	.15	.30
265	Pat Price, (Now with Penguins)	.07	.15	.30
266	Ron Stackhouse	.07	.15	.30
267	Pittsburgh Penguins Team Leader: Rick Kehoe	.07	.15	.30

QUEBEC NORDIQUES

No.	Player	VG	EX	NRMT
268	Jacques Richard	.07	.15	.30
269	Peter Stastny, RC	6.25	12.50	25.00
270	Dan Bouchard, Goalie	.07	.15	.30

TORONTO MAPLE LEAFS

No.	Player	VG	EX	NRMT
271	Kim Clackson, RC, LC, (Now with Maple Leafs)	.07	.15	.30

QUEBEC NORDIQUES

No.	Player	VG	EX	NRMT
272	Alain Cote	.07	.15	.30
273	Andre Dupont	.07	.15	.30
274	Robbie Ftorek	.07	.15	.30
275	Michel Goulet	1.25	2.50	5.00
276	Dale Hoganson, LC	.07	.15	.30
277	Dale Hunter, RC	3.00	6.00	12.00
278	Pierre Lacroix, RC	.07	.15	.30
279	Mario Marois, RC, (Now with Nordiques)	.12	.25	.50
280	Dave Pichette, RC	.07	.15	.30
281	Michel Plasse, Goalie, LC	.07	.15	.30
282	Anton Stastny, RC	.18	.35	.75
283	Marc Tardif	.07	.15	.30
284	Wally Weir	.07	.15	.30
285	Super Action: Jacques Richard	.07	.15	.30
286	Super Action: Peter Stastny	1.25	2.50	5.00
287	Quebec Nordiques Team Leader: Peter Stastny	.50	1.00	2.00

O-Pee-Chee
1981-82 Issue
Card No. 251,
Tim Kerr

O-Pee-Chee
1981-82 Issue
Card No. 269,
Peter Stastny

O-Pee-Chee
1981-82 Issue
Card No. 279,
Mario Marois

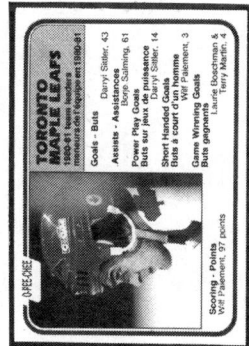

O-Pee-Chee
1981-82 Issue
Card No. 326,
Toronto Maple Leafs

ST. LOUIS BLUES

No.	Player	VG	EX	NRMT
288	Bernie Federko	.35	.75	1.50
289	Michael Liut, Goalie	.50	1.00	2.00
290	Wayne Babych	.07	.15	.30
291	Blair Chapman, LC	.07	.15	.30
292	Tony Currie	.07	.15	.30
293	Blake Dunlop	.07	.15	.30
294	Ed Kea, LC	.07	.15	.30
295	Rick Lapointe	.07	.15	.30
296	Jorgen Pettersson, RC	.10	.20	.40
297	Brian Sutter	.07	.15	.30
298	Perry Turnbull	.07	.15	.30
299	Mike Zuke	.07	.15	.30
300	Super Action: Bernie Federko	.12	.25	.50
301	Super Action: Michael Liut	.07	.15	.30
302	Jack Brownschidle	.07	.15	.30
303	Larry Patey	.07	.15	.30
304	St. Louis Blues Team Leader: Bernie Federko	.07	.15	.30

TORONTO MAPLE LEAFS

No.	Player	VG	EX	NRMT
305	Bill Derlago	.07	.15	.30
306	Wilf Paiement	.07	.15	.30
307	Borje Salming	.07	.15	.30
308	Darryl Sittler	.18	.35	.75

LOS ANGELES KINGS

No.	Player	VG	EX	NRMT
309	Ian Turnbull, (Now with Kings), LC	.07	.15	.30

TORONTO MAPLE LEAFS

No.	Player	VG	EX	NRMT
310	Richard Vaive	.25	.50	1.00
311	Super Action: Wilf Paiement	.07	.15	.30
312	Super Action: Darryl Sittler	.10	.20	.40
313	John Anderson	.07	.15	.30
314	Laurie Boschman	.07	.15	.30
315	Jiri Crha, Goalie, RC, LC	.07	.15	.30
316	Vitezslav Duris, RC, LC	.07	.15	.30
317	Dave Farrish	.07	.15	.30

NEW YORK RANGERS

No.	Player	VG	EX	NRMT
318	Pat Hickey, (Now with Rangers)	.07	.15	.30

TORONTO MAPLE LEAFS

No.	Player	VG	EX	NRMT
319	Michel Larocque, Goalie, (Now with Maple Leafs)	.07	.15	.30
320	Dan Maloney	.07	.15	.30
321	Terry Martin, (Now with Maple Leafs)	.07	.15	.30
322	Rene Robert	.07	.15	.30
323	Rocky Saganiuk	.07	.15	.30
324	Ron Sedlbauer, LC (Now with Maple Leafs)	.07	.15	.30
325	Ron Zanussi, LC (Now with Maple Leafs)	.07	.15	.30
326	Toronto Maple Leafs Team Leader: Wilf Paiement	.07	.15	.30

VANCOUVER CANUCKS

No.	Player	VG	EX	NRMT
327	Thomas Gradin	.07	.15	.30
328	Stanley Smyl	.07	.15	.30
329	Ivan Boldirev	.07	.15	.30
330	Per-Olov Brasar, Error	.07	.15	.30
331	Richard Brodeur, Goalie	.07	.15	.30
332	Jerry Butler, LC	.07	.15	.30
333	Colin Campbell	.07	.15	.30
334	Curt Fraser	.07	.15	.30
335	Doug Halward	.07	.15	.30
336	Glen Hanlon, Goalie	.07	.15	.30
337	Dennis Kearns, LC	.07	.15	.30
338	Rick Lanz, Error	.07	.15	.30

WASHINGTON CAPITALS

No.	Player	VG	EX	NRMT
339	Pat Ribble, LC	.07	.15	.30

82 • O-PEE-CHEE — 1982 - 83 REGULAR ISSUE

VANCOUVER CANUCKS

No.	Player	VG	EX	NRMT
340	Blair MacDonald	.07	.15	.30
341	Kevin McCarthy	.07	.15	.30
342	**Gerry Minor, RC**	**.07**	**.15**	**.30**
343	Darcy Rota	.07	.15	.30
344	Harold Snepsts	.07	.15	.30
345	David Williams	.07	.15	.30
346	**Vancouver Canucks Team Leader:** Thomas Gradin	.07	.15	.30

WASHINGTON CAPITALS

No.	Player	VG	EX	NRMT
347	Michael Gartner	4.50	9.00	18.00
348	Richard Green	.07	.15	.30
349	Bob Kelly, LC	.07	.15	.30
350	Dennis Maruk	.07	.15	.30
351	Mike Palmateer, Goalie	.07	.15	.30
352	Ryan Walter	.07	.15	.30
353	Bengt-ake Gustafsson	.07	.15	.30
354	Al Hangsleben, LC	.07	.15	.30
355	Jean Pronovost, LC	.07	.15	.30
356	Dennis Ververgaert, LC	.07	.15	.30
357	**Washington Capitals Team Leader:** Dennis Maruk	.07	.15	.30

WINNIPEG JETS

No.	Player	VG	EX	NRMT
358	**Dave Babych, RC**	**.18**	**.35**	**.75**
359	Dave Christian	.25	.50	1.00
360	Super Action: Dave Christian	.07	.15	.30
361	Rick Bowness, LC	.07	.15	.30
362	Rick Dudley, LC	.07	.15	.30
363	**Norm Dupont, RC**	**.07**	**.15**	**.30**
364	**Danny Geoffrion, RC, LC**	**.07**	**.15**	**.30**
365	Pierre Hamel, Goalie, LC	.07	.15	.30
366	Dave Hoyda, Error	.07	.15	.30
367	**Doug Lecuyer, RC, LC**	**.07**	**.15**	**.30**
368	Willy Lindstrom	.07	.15	.30
369	Barry Long, LC	.07	.15	.30
370	Morris Lukowich	.07	.15	.30
371	Kris Manery, LC	.07	.15	.30
372	Jimmy Mann, LC	.07	.15	.30
373	**Maurice Mantha, RC**	**.20**	**.40**	**.80**
374	Markus Mattson, Goalie, LC, Error	.07	.15	.30
375	**Don Spring, RC**	**.07**	**.15**	**.30**
376	Tim Trimper	.07	.15	.30
377	Ronald Wilson	.07	.15	.30
378	**Winnipeg Jets Team Leader:** Dave Christian	.07	.15	.30

CHECKLISTS

No.	Checklist	VG	EX	NRMT
379	Checklist 1 (1 - 132)	1.50	3.00	6.00
380	Checklist 2 (133 - 264)	1.50	3.00	6.00
381	Checklist 3 (265 - 396)	1.50	3.00	6.00

LEAGUE LEADERS

No.	Player	VG	EX	NRMT
382	**Goal Leader:** Mike Bossy, NYI	.35	.75	1.50
383	**Assists Leader:** Wayne Gretzky, Edm.	2.50	5.00	10.00
384	**Scoring Leader:** Wayne Gretzky	2.50	5.00	10.00
385	**Penalty Minute Leader:** Dave Williams, Van.	.12	.25	.50
386	**Power Play Goal Leader:** Mike Bossy, NYI	.30	.60	1.25
387	**Goals Against Average Leader:** Richard Sevigny, Mon.	.07	.15	.30
388	**Game Winning Goal Leader:** Mike Bossy, NYI	.30	.60	1.25
389	**Shutout Leader:** Don Edwards, Buf.	.10	.20	.40

RECORD BREAKERS

No.	Player	VG	EX	NRMT
390	Mike Bossy, NYI	.30	.60	1.25
391	Dionne Simmer, Taylor, LA	.35	.75	1.50
392	Wayne Gretzky, Edm.	2.50	5.00	10.00
393	Lawrence Murphy, LA	.25	.50	1.00
394	Mike Palmateer, Goalie, Wash.	.07	.15	.30
395	Peter Stastny, Que.	1.00	2.00	4.00

REGULAR ISSUE

No.	Player	VG	Ex	NRMT
396	Bob Manno, Tor.	.15	.30	.60

O-Pee-Chee
1982-83 Issue
Card No. 1,
Wayne Gretzky

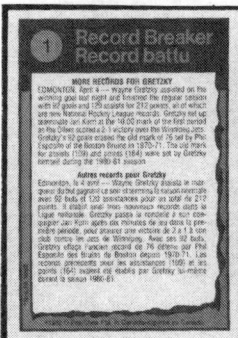

O-Pee-Chee
1982-83 Issue
Card No. 1,
Wayne Gretzky

O-Pee-Chee
1982-83 Issue
Card No. 11,
Tom Fergus

O-Pee-Chee
1982-83 Issue
Card No. 19,
Brad Park

— 1982 - 83 REGULAR ISSUE —

The set features record breaking, in-action and team scoring leader cards. Mint cards command a 25% price premium over NRMT cards.

PRICE MOVEMENT OF NRMT SETS

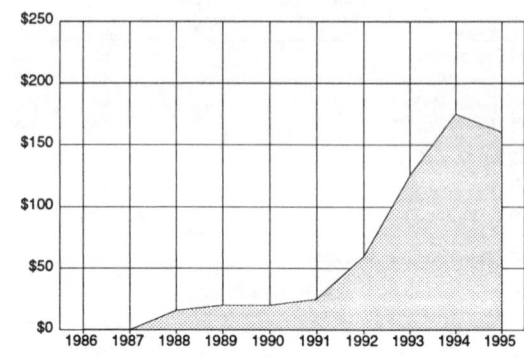

Card Size: 2 1/2" X 3 1/2"
Face: Four colour, white border, Team logo, Position
Back: Purple on card stock, Number, Resume, Bilingual
Imprint: © 1982 O-Pee-Chee Ptd. In Canada • Imprimé au Canada
Complete Set No.: 396
Complete Set Price: 40.00 80.00 160.00
Common Card: .05 .10 .20
Wax Pack: 9.00
Wax Box: (48 Packs) 350.00
Wax Case: (16 Boxes) 4,500.00

RECORD BREAKERS

No.	Player	VG	Ex	NRMT
1	Wayne Gretzky, Edm.	2.50	5.00	10.00
2	Mike Bossy, NYI	.30	.60	1.25
3	**Dale Hawerchuk, Win., RC**	**1.25**	**2.50**	**5.00**
4	**Mikko Leinonen, NYR, RC**	**.05**	**.10**	**.20**
5	Bryan Trottier, NYI	.18	.35	.75

BOSTON BRUINS

No.	Player	VG	EX	NRMT
6	**Boston Bruins Team Leader:** Rick Middleton	.05	.10	.20
7	Ray Bourque	2.00	4.00	8.00
8	Wayne Cashman, LC	.05	.10	.20
9	**Bruce Crowder, RC**	**.05**	**.10**	**.20**
10	**Keith Crowder, RC**	**.07**	**.15**	**.30**
11	**Tom Fergus, RC**	**.50**	**1.00**	**2.00**
12	Stephen Kasper	.05	.10	.20
13	**Normand Leveille, RC, LC**	**.05**	**.10**	**.20**
14	Don Marcotte, LC	.05	.10	.20
15	Rick Middleton	.10	.20	.35
16	Peter McNab	.05	.10	.20
17	Michael O'Connell	.05	.10	.20
18	Terry O'Reilly	.15	.30	.60
19	Brad Park	.18	.35	.75
20	**Barry Pederson, RC**	**.10**	**.20**	**.40**
21	**Brad Palmer, RC, LC**	**.05**	**.10**	**.20**
22	Peter Peeters, Goalie	.15	.30	.60
23	Rogatien Vachon, Goalie, LC (Free agent as of Nov. 9/82)	.10	.20	.40
24	**In Action:** Ray Bourque	.70	1.40	2.75

BUFFALO SABRES

No.	Player	VG	EX	NRMT
25	**Buffalo Sabres Team Leader:** Gilbert Perreault	.07	.15	.30
26	Mike Foligno	.05	.10	.20
27	Yvon Lambert, LC	.05	.10	.20
28	Dale McCourt	.05	.10	.20
29	Anthony McKegney	.05	.10	.20
30	Gilbert Perreault	.25	.50	1.00
31	Lindy Ruff	.10	.20	.40
32	Michael Ramsey	.05	.10	.20
33	**Jean F. Sauvé, RC, LC**	**.05**	**.10**	**.20**
34	Bob Sauve, Goalie	.05	.10	.20
35	Ric Seiling	.05	.10	.20
36	John Van Boxmeer	.05	.10	.20
37	**In Action:** John Van Boxmeer	.05	.10	.20

1982 - 83 REGULAR ISSUE — O-PEE-CHEE • 83

CALGARY FLAMES

No.	Player	VG	EX	NRMT
38	**Calgary Flames Team**	.07	.15	.30
	Leader: Lanny McDonald			
39	Mel Bridgman	.05	.10	.20
40	In Action: Mel Bridgman	.05	.10	.20
41	Guy Chouinard	.05	.10	.20
42	Steve Christoff	.05	.10	.20
43	**Denis Cyr, RC, LC**	**.05**	**.10**	**.20**
44	Bill Clement, LC	.05	.10	.20
	(Free agent as of Nov. 9/82)			
45	Richard Dunn	.05	.10	.20
46	Don Edwards, Goalie	.05	.10	.20
47	Jamie Hislop	.05	.10	.20
48	**Stephen Konroyd, RC**	**.10**	**.20**	**.40**
49	Kevin LaVallee	.05	.10	.20
50	Rejean Lemelin, Goalie	.18	.35	.75
51	Lanny McDonald	.18	.35	.75
52	In Action: Lanny McDonald	.07	.15	.30
53	Bob J. Murdoch, LC	.05	.10	.20
54	Kent Nilsson	.05	.10	.20
55	James Peplinski	.05	.10	.20
56	Paul Reinhart	.05	.10	.20
57	Doug Risebrough	.05	.10	.20
58	Phil Russell	.05	.10	.20
59	**Howard Walker, RC, LC**	**.05**	**.10**	**.20**

CHICAGO BLACK HAWKS

No.	Player	VG	EX	NRMT
60	**Chicago Black Hawks Team**	.05	.10	.20
	Leader: Al Secord			
61	Murray Bannerman, Goalie	.05	.10	.20
62	Keith Brown	.05	.10	.20
63	**Doug Crossman, RC**	**.18**	**.35**	**.75**
64	Tony Esposito, Goalie	.25	.50	1.00
65	Greg Fox	.05	.10	.20
66	Tim Higgins	.05	.10	.20
67	Reg Kerr, LC	.05	.10	.20
68	Tom Lysiak	.05	.10	.20
69	Grant Mulvey, LC	.05	.10	.20
70	Bob Murray	.05	.10	.20
71	Rich Preston	.05	.10	.20

LOS ANGELES KINGS

No.	Player	VG	EX	NRMT
72	Terry Ruskowski, (Now with Kings)	.05	.10	.20

CHICAGO BLACK HAWKS

No.	Player	VG	EX	NRMT
73	Denis Savard	1.50	3.00	6.00
74	Al Secord	.05	.10	.20
75	Glen Sharpley, LC	.05	.10	.20
76	Darryl Sutter	.05	.10	.20
77	Douglas Wilson	.25	.50	1.00
78	In Action: Douglas Wilson	.05	.10	.20

DETROIT RED WINGS

No.	Player	VG	EX	NRMT
79	**Detroit Red Wings Team**	.05	.10	.20
	Leader: John Ogrodnick			
80	**John Barrett, RC**	**.05**	**.10**	**.20**
81	**Michael Blaisdell, RC**	**.05**	**.10**	**.20**
82	Colin Campbell	.05	.10	.20
83	Danny Gare	.05	.10	.20
84	Gilles Gilbert, Goalie, LC	.05	.10	.20
85	Willie Huber	.05	.10	.20
86	Greg Joly, LC	.05	.10	.20
87	Mark Kirton	.05	.10	.20
88	Reed Larson	.05	.10	.20
89	In Action: Reed Larson	.05	.10	.20
90	Reggie Leach, LC	.05	.10	.20
91	Walt McKechnie, LC	.05	.10	.20
92	John Ogrodnick	.05	.10	.20
93	**Mark Osborne, RC**	**.25**	**.50**	**1.00**
94	Jim Schoenfeld	.05	.10	.20
95	Derek Smith, LC	.05	.10	.20
96	Greg Smith	.05	.10	.20
97	Eric Vail, LC	.05	.10	.20
98	Paul Woods	.05	.10	.20

O-Pee-Chee
1982-83 Issue
Card No. 64,
Tony Esposito

O-Pee-Chee
1982-83 Issue
Card No. 105,
Grant Fuhr

O-Pee-Chee
1982-83 Issue
Card No. 123,
Ron Francis

O-Pee-Chee
1982-83 Issue
Card No. 164,
Neal Broten

EDMONTON OILERS

No.	Player	VG	EX	NRMT
99	**Edmonton Oilers Team Leader:**	1.50	3.00	6.00
	Wayne Gretzky			
100	Glenn Anderson	.75	1.50	3.00
101	Paul Coffey	4.50	9.00	18.00
102	In Action: Paul Coffey	1.50	3.00	6.00
103	Brett Callighen, LC	.05	.10	.20
	(Free agent as of Nov. 9/82)			
104	Lee Fogolin	.05	.10	.20
105	**Grant Fuhr, Goalie, RC**	**6.00**	**12.00**	**24.00**
106	Wayne Gretzky	8.75	17.50	35.00
107	In Action: Wayne Gretzky	3.25	6.50	13.00
108	Matti Hagman, LC	.05	.10	.20
109	Pat Hughes	.05	.10	.20
110	Dave Hunter	.05	.10	.20
111	Jari Kurri	1.75	3.50	7.00
112	Ron Low, Goalie	.05	.10	.20
113	Kevin Lowe	.50	1.00	2.00
114	Dave Lumley	.05	.10	.20
115	Ken Linseman	.05	.10	.20
116	Garry Lariviere, LC	.05	.10	.20
117	Mark Messier	3.75	7.50	15.00
118	**Tom Roulston, RC**	**.05**	**.10**	**.20**
119	Dave Semenko, LC	.05	.10	.20
120	Garry Unger, LC	.05	.10	.20

CHECKLIST

No.	Checklist	VG	EX	NRMT
121	Checklist 1(1 - 132)	1.20	2.40	4.75

HARTFORD WHALERS

No.	Player	VG	EX	NRMT
122	**Hartford Whalers Team Leader:**	.05	.10	.20
	Blaine Stoughton			
123	**Ron Francis, RC**	**4.50**	**9.00**	**18.00**
124	**Christopher Kotsopoulos, RC**	**.05**	**.10**	**.20**
125	Pierre Larouche	.05	.10	.20
126	Greg Millen, Goalie	.05	.10	.20
127	Warren Miller, LC	.05	.10	.20
128	Merlin Malinowski (Now with Whalers)	.05	.10	.20
129	Risto Siltanen	.05	.10	.20
130	Blaine Stoughton	.05	.10	.20
131	In Action: Blaine Stoughton	.05	.10	.20
132	Douglas Sulliman	.05	.10	.20
133	**Blake Wesley, RC**	**.05**	**.10**	**.20**

NEW JERSEY DEVILS

No.	Player	VG	EX	NRMT
134	**New Jersey Devils Team**	.05	.10	.20
	Leader: Steve Tambellini			
135	**Brent Ashton, RC**	**.05**	**.10**	**.20**
136	**Aaron Broten, RC**	**.07**	**.15**	**.30**
137	**Joe Cirella, RC**	**.07**	**.15**	**.30**

DETROIT RED WINGS

No.	Player	VG	EX	NRMT
138	Dwight Foster (Now with Red Wings)	.05	.10	.20

NEW JERSEY DEVILS

No.	Player	VG	EX	NRMT
139	Paul Gagne	.05	.10	.20
140	Garry Howatt (Now with Devils)	.05	.10	.20
141	Don Lever	.05	.10	.20
142	Bob Lorimer	.05	.10	.20
143	Bob MacMillan	.05	.10	.20
144	**Richard Meagher, RC**	**.25**	**.50**	**1.00**
	(Now with Devils)			
145	Glenn Resch, Goalie	.25	.50	1.00
146	In Action: Glenn Resch, Goalie	.10	.20	.40
147	Steve Tambellini, LC	.05	.10	.20
148	Carol Vadnais, LC	.05	.10	.20

LOS ANGELES KINGS

No.	Player	VG	EX	NRMT
149	**Los Angeles Kings Team Leader:**	.12	.25	.50
	Marcel Dionne			
150	**Dan Bonar, RC, LC**	**.05**	**.10**	**.20**
151	**Steve Bozek, RC**	**.07**	**.15**	**.30**
152	Marcel Dionne	.25	.50	1.00
153	In Action: Marcel Dionne	.18	.35	.75
154	Jim Fox	.05	.10	.20

84 • O-PEE-CHEE — 1982 - 83 REGULAR ISSUE

No.	Player	VG	EX	NRMT
155	**Mark Hardy, RC**	.05	.10	.20
156	Mario Lessard, Goalie, LC	.05	.10	.20
157	Dave Lewis	.05	.10	.20
158	Lawrence Murphy	.05	.10	.20
159	Charlie Simmer	.12	.25	.50
160	**Douglas Smith, RC**	.05	.10	.20
161	David Taylor	.12	.25	.50

MINNESOTA NORTH STARS

No.	Player	VG	EX	NRMT
162	**Minnesota North Stars Team** Leader: Dino Ciccarelli	.10	.20	.40
163	Donald Beaupre, Goalie	.05	.10	.20
164	**Neal Broten, RC**	1.10	2.25	4.50
165	Dino Ciccarelli	.75	1.50	3.00
166	**Curt Giles, RC**	.10	.20	.40
167	Craig Hartsburg	.05	.10	.20
168	Brad Maxwell	.05	.10	.20
169	Tom McCarthy	.05	.10	.20
170	Gilles Meloche, Goalie	.05	.10	.20
171	Al MacAdam	.05	.10	.20
172	Steve Payne	.05	.10	.20
173	Willi Plett	.05	.10	.20
174	Gordon Roberts	.05	.10	.20
175	Robert Smith	.12	.25	.50
176	In Action: Robert Smith	.05	.10	.20
177	Tim Young	.05	.10	.20

MONTREAL CANADIENS

No.	Player	VG	EX	NRMT
178	**Montreal Canadiens Team** Leader: Mark Napier	.05	.10	.20
179	Keith Acton	.05	.10	.20
180	In Action: Keith Acton	.05	.10	.20
181	Bob Gainey	.12	.25	.50
182	Gaston Gingras	.05	.10	.20
183	Richard Green	.05	.10	.20
184	Rejean Houle, LC (Now with Canadiens)	.05	.10	.20
185	**Mark Hunter, RC**	.25	.50	1.00
186	Guy Lafleur	.35	.75	1.50
187	In Action: Guy Lafleur	.25	.50	1.00
188	Pierre Mondou	.05	.10	.20
189	Mark Napier	.05	.10	.20
190	Robert Picard	.05	.10	.20
191	Larry Robinson	.18	.35	.75
192	Steve Shutt	.10	.20	.40
193	Mario Tremblay	.05	.10	.20
194	Ryan Walter	.05	.10	.20
195	**Richard Wamsley, Goalie, RC**	.35	.75	1.50
196	Douglas Wickenheiser	.05	.10	.20

NEW YORK ISLANDERS

No.	Player	VG	EX	NRMT
197	**New York Islanders Team** Leader: Mike Bossy	.25	.50	1.00
198	Bob Bourne	.05	.10	.20
199	Mike Bossy	.50	1.00	2.00
200	Butch Goring	.05	.10	.20
201	Clark Gillies	.05	.10	.20
202	**Tomas Jonsson, RC**	.07	.15	.30
203	Anders Kallur, LC	.05	.10	.20
204	Dave Langevin	.05	.10	.20
205	Wayne Merrick, LC	.05	.10	.20
206	Ken Morrow	.05	.10	.20
207	Mike McEwen, LC	.05	.10	.20
208	Bob Nystrom	.05	.10	.20
209	Stefan Persson	.05	.10	.20
210	Denis Potvin	.25	.50	1.00
211	Billy Smith, Goalie	.10	.20	.40
212	Duane Sutter	.05	.10	.20
213	John Tonelli	.10	.20	.40
214	Bryan Trottier	.35	.75	1.50
215	In Action: Bryan Trottier	.12	.25	.50
216	**Brent Sutter, RC**	1.00	2.00	4.00

NEW YORK RANGERS

No.	Player	VG	EX	NRMT
217	**New York Rangers Team** Leader: Ron Duguay	.05	.10	.20
218	Kent-Erik Andersson, LC (Now with Rangers)	.05	.10	.20

O-Pee-Chee
1982-83 Issue
Card No. 216,
Brent Sutter

O-Pee-Chee, 1982-83 Issue
Card No. 235,
1981-1982 Goal Leader
Wayne Gretzky

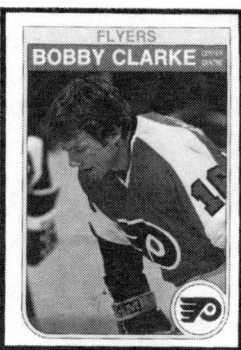

O-Pee-Chee
1982-83 Issue
Card No. 248,
Bobby Clarke

O-Pee-Chee
1982-83 Issue
Card No. 264,
Mike Bullard

No.	Player	VG	EX	NRMT
219	Barry Beck	.05	.10	.20
220	In Action: Barry Beck	.05	.10	.20
221	Ronald Duguay	.05	.10	.20
222	Nick Fotiu	.05	.10	.20
223	Robbie Ftorek	.05	.10	.20
224	Ronald Greschner	.05	.10	.20
225	Anders Hedberg	.05	.10	.20
226	Eddie Johnstone	.05	.10	.20
227	Thomas Laidlaw	.05	.10	.20
228	Dave Maloney	.05	.10	.20
229	Donald Maloney	.05	.10	.20
230	Ed Mio, Goalie	.05	.10	.20
231	**Mark Pavelich, RC**	.07	.15	.30
232	Mike Rogers	.05	.10	.20
233	**Reijo Ruotsalainen, RC**	.15	.30	.60
234	**Stephen Weeks, Goalie, RC**	.12	.25	.50

1981-82 LEAGUE LEADERS

No.	Player	VG	EX	NRMT
235	Goal Leader: Wayne Gretzky, Edm.	1.50	3.00	6.00
236	Power Play Goal Leader: Paul Gardner, Pit.	.07	.15	.30
237	Shorthanded Goal Leaders: Wayne Gretzky, Edm. Michael Goulet, Que.	1.50	3.00	6.00
238	Penalty Minute Leader: Paul Baxter, Pit.	.07	.15	.30
239	Goals Against Avg. Leader: Denis Herron, Mon.	.07	.15	.30
240	Assist Leader: Wayne Gretzky, Edm.	1.50	3.00	6.00
241	Shutout Leader: Denis Herron, Mon. Game Winning Go	.07	.15	.30
242	al Leader: Wayne Gretzky, Edm.	1.50	3.00	6.00
243	Scoring Leader: Wayne Gretzky, Edm.	1.50	3.00	6.00

PHILADELPHIA FLYERS

No.	Player	VG	EX	NRMT
244	**Philadelphia Flyers Team** Leader: Bill Barber	.05	.10	.20
245	**Fred Arthur, RC, LC**	.05	.10	.20
246	Bill Barber	.12	.25	.50
247	In Action: Bill Barber	.05	.10	.20
248	Bobby Clarke	.30	.65	1.25
249	**Ron Flockhart, RC**	.05	.10	.20
250	Tom Gorence, LC	.05	.10	.20
251	Paul Holmgren	.05	.10	.20
252	Mark Howe	.10	.20	.40
253	Tim Kerr	.30	.60	1.25
254	Bradley Marsh	.05	.10	.20
255	Byron (Brad) McCrimmon	.05	.10	.20
256	Brian Propp	.25	.50	1.00
257	Darryl Sittler	.15	.30	.60
258	Rick St. Croix, Goalie	.05	.10	.20
259	Jimmy Watson, LC	.05	.10	.20
260	Behn Wilson, LC	.05	.10	.20

CHECKLIST

No.	Checklist	VG	EX	NRMT
261	Checklist 2 (133 - 264)	1.00	2.00	4.00

PITTSBURGH PENGUINS

No.	Player	VG	EX	NRMT
262	**Pittsburgh Penguins Team** Leader: Mike Bullard	.05	.10	.20
263	Pat Boutette	.05	.10	.20
264	**Mike Bullard, RC**	.35	.75	1.50
265	Randy Carlyle	.05	.10	.20
266	In Action: Randy Carlyle	.05	.10	.20
267	Michel Dion, Goalie	.05	.10	.20

MINNESOTA NORTH STARS

No.	Player	VG	EX	NRMT
268	George Ferguson	.05	.10	.20

PITTSBURGH PENGUINS

No.	Player	VG	EX	NRMT
269	Paul Gardner	.05	.10	.20
270	Denis Herron, Goalie	.05	.10	.20
271	Rick Kehoe	.05	.10	.20
272	Greg Malone	.05	.10	.20
273	Rick MacLeish, LC	.05	.10	.20
274	Pat Price	.05	.10	.20
275	Ron Stackhouse, LC	.05	.10	.20

QUEBEC NORDIQUES

No.	Player	VG	EX	NRMT
276	**Quebec Nordiques Team** Leader: Peter Stastny	.12	.25	.50
277	**Pierre Aubry, RC**	**.05**	**.10**	**.20**
278	Dan Bouchard, Goalie	.05	.10	.20
279	Real Cloutier	.05	.10	.20
280	In Action: Real Cloutier	.05	.10	.20
281	Alain Cote	.05	.10	.20
282	Andre Dupont, LC	.05	.10	.20
283	John Garrett, Goalie	.05	.10	.20
284	Michel Goulet	.75	1.50	3.00
285	Dale Hunter	.75	1.50	3.00
286	Pierre Lacroix, LC	.05	.10	.20
287	Mario Marois	.05	.10	.20
288	Wilf Paiement	.05	.10	.20
289	Dave Pichette	.05	.10	.20
290	Jacques Richard, LC	.05	.10	.20
291	**Normand Rochefort, RC**	**.10**	**.20**	**.40**
292	Peter Stastny	1.50	3.00	6.00
293	In Action: Peter Stastny	.35	.75	1.50
294	Anton Stastny	.05	.10	.20
295	**Marian Stastny, RC**	**.07**	**.15**	**.30**
296	Marc Tardif	.05	.10	.20
297	Wally Weir	.05	.10	.20

ST. LOUIS BLUES

No.	Player	VG	EX	NRMT
298	**St. Louis Blues Team** Leader: Brian Sutter	.05	.10	.20
299	Wayne Babych	.05	.10	.20
300	Jack Brownschidle	.05	.10	.20
301	Blake Dunlop	.05	.10	.20
302	Bernie Federko	.05	.10	.20
303	In Action: Bernie Federko	.05	.10	.20
304	Pat Hickey, LC	.05	.10	.20
305	Guy Lapointe, LC	.05	.10	.20
306	Michael Liut, Goalie	.25	.50	1.00
307	**Joe Mullen, RC**	**4.50**	**9.00**	**18.00**
308	Larry Patey	.05	.10	.20
309	Jorgen Pettersson	.05	.10	.20
310	George (Rob) Ramage	.05	.10	.20
311	Brian Sutter	.05	.10	.20
312	Perry Turnbull	.05	.10	.20
313	Mike Zuke	.05	.10	.20

TORONTO MAPLE LEAFS

No.	Player	VG	EX	NRMT
314	**Toronto Maple Leafs Team** Leader: Richard Vaive	.05	.10	.20
315	John Anderson	.05	.10	.20
316	**Normand Aubin, RC, LC**	**.05**	**.10**	**.20**
317	**Jim Benning, RC**	**.07**	**.15**	**.30**
318	**Fred Bolmistruck, RC, LC**	**.05**	**.10**	**.20**
319	Bill Derlago	.05	.10	.20
320	In Action: Bill Derlago	.05	.10	.20
321	**Miroslav Frycer, RC**	**.05**	**.10**	**.20**
322	Billy Harris	.05	.10	.20
323	James Korn	.05	.10	.20
324	Michel Larocque, Goalie, LC	.05	.10	.20
325	Bob Manno	.05	.10	.20
326	Dan Maloney, LC	.05	.10	.20
327	**Robert McGill, RC**	**.10**	**.20**	**.40**
328	Barry Melrose, LC	.05	.10	.20
329	Terry Martin	.05	.10	.20
330	Rene Robert, LC (Free agent as of Nov. 9/82)	.05	.10	.20
331	Rocky Saganiuk, LC	.05	.10	.20
332	Borje Salming	.05	.10	.20
333	Greg Terrion (Now with Maple Leafs)	.05	.10	.20
334	**Vincent Tremblay, Goalie, RC, LC**	**.05**	**.10**	**.20**
335	Richard Vaive	.10	.20	.40
336	In Action: Richard Vaive	.05	.10	.20

VANCOUVER CANUCKS

No.	Player	VG	EX	NRMT
337	**Vancouver Canucks Team** Leader: Thomas Gradin	.05	.10	.20
338	Ivan Boldirev	.05	.10	.20
339	Richard Brodeur, Goalie	.05	.10	.20
340	In Action: Richard Brodeur, Goalie	.05	.10	.20
341	Tony Currie, LC	.05	.10	.20
342	**Marc Crawford, RC, LC**	**.05**	**.10**	**.20**
343	Curt Fraser	.05	.10	.20

O-Pee-Chee
1982-83 Issue
Card No. 284,
Michel Goulet

O-Pee-Chee
1982-83 Issue
Card No. 307,
Joe Mullen

O-Pee-Chee
1982-83 Issue
Card No. 346, Error,
Shows Jiri Bubla

O-Pee-Chee
1982-83 Issue
Card No. 361,
Robert Carpenter

No.	Player	VG	EX	NRMT
344	Thomas Gradin	.05	.10	.20
345	In Action: Thomas Gradin	.05	.10	.20
346	**Ivan Hlinka, RC, LC, Error**	**.07**	**.15**	**.30**
347	Ron Delorme	.05	.10	.20
348	Rick Lanz	.05	.10	.20
349	Lars Lindgren	.05	.10	.20
350	Blair MacDonald, LC	.05	.10	.20
351	Kevin McCarthy	.05	.10	.20
352	Gerry Minor, LC	.05	.10	.20
353	**Lars Molin, RC, LC**	**.05**	**.10**	**.20**
354	**Gary Lupul, RC**	**.05**	**.10**	**.20**
355	Darcy Rota	.05	.10	.20
356	Stanley Smyl	.05	.10	.20
357	Harold Snepsts	.05	.10	.20
358	David Williams	.05	.10	.20

WASHINGTON CAPITALS

No.	Player	VG	EX	NRMT
359	**Washington Capitals Team** Leader: Dennis Maruk	.05	.10	.20
360	Ted Bulley, (Now with Capitals), LC	.05	.10	.20
361	**Robert Carpenter, RC**	**.50**	**1.00**	**2.00**
362	Brian Engblom	.05	.10	.20
363	Michael Gartner	2.00	4.00	8.00
364	Bengt-ake Gustafsson	.05	.10	.20
365	Doug Hicks, LC	.05	.10	.20
366	Ken Houston	.05	.10	.20
367	Doug Jarvis (Now with Capitals)	.05	.10	.20
368	Rod Langway (Now with Capitals)	.25	.50	1.00
369	Dennis Maruk	.05	.10	.20
370	In Action: Dennis Maruk	.05	.10	.20
371	**Dave Parro, Goalie, RC, LC**	**.05**	**.10**	**.20**
372	Pat Riggin, Goalie	.05	.10	.20
373	**Chris Valentine, RC, LC**	**.05**	**.10**	**.20**

WINNIPEG JETS

No.	Player	VG	EX	NRMT
374	**Winnipeg Jets Team Leader:** Dale Hawerchuk	.60	1.25	2.50
375	David Babych	.05	.10	.20
376	In Action: David Babych	.05	.10	.20
377	Dave Christian	.10	.20	.40
378	Norm Dupont, LC	.05	.10	.20
379	Lucien DeBlois	.05	.10	.20
380	**Dale Hawerchuk, RC**	**5.00**	**10.00**	**20.00**
381	In Action: Dale Hawerchuk	1.25	2.50	5.00
382	**Craig Levie, RC, LC**	**.05**	**.10**	**.20**
383	Morris Lukowich	.05	.10	.20
384	Willy Lindstrom	.05	.10	.20
385	**Bengt Lundholm, RC**	**.05**	**.10**	**.20**
386	**Paul MacLean, RC**	**.18**	**.35**	**.75**
387	Bryan Maxwell, LC	.05	.10	.20
388	**Doug Smail, RC**	**.15**	**.30**	**.60**
389	Douglas Soetaert, Goalie	.05	.10	.20
390	Serge Savard, LC	.12	.25	.50
391	**Thomas Steen, RC**	**1.25**	**2.50**	**5.00**
392	Don Spring	.05	.10	.20
393	Ed Staniowski, Goalie, LC	.05	.10	.20
394	Tim Trimper, LC	.05	.10	.20
395	**Timothy Watters, RC**	**.05**	**.10**	**.20**

CHECKLIST

No.	Checklist	VG	EX	NRMT
396	Checklist 3 (265 - 396)	1.00	2.00	4.00

Note: *The Charlton Standard Catalogue of Hockey Cards* arranges cards in their issue date order. This means the first date a manufacturer issues a card set determines the sequence of the manufacturer in the Standard Catalogue. In this manner the historical importance of early cards is maintained. See the last page of this catalogue for an alphabetical index of issuers.

86 • O-PEE-CHEE — 1983 - 84 REGULAR ISSUE

— 1983 - 84 REGULAR ISSUE —

The set features in-action and scoring leader cards for each team as well as record breaking and cup winner cards.
Mint cards command a 25% price premium over NRMT cards.

PRICE MOVEMENT OF NRMT SETS

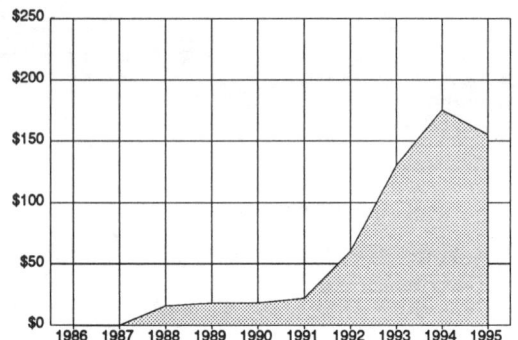

Card Size: 2 1/2" X 3 1/2"
Face: Four colour, white border, Team logo
Back: Green and blue on card stock, Number, Resume, Bilingual
Imprint © 1983 O-Pee-Chee Ptd. In Canada-Imprimé au Canada
© 1983 NHLPA
Complete Set No.: 396

Complete Set Price:	40.00	80.00	160.00
Common Card:	.05	.10	.20
Wax Pack:			9.00
Wax Box: (48 Packs)			325.00
Wax Case: (16 Boxes)			4,500.00

NEW YORK ISLANDERS

No.	Player	VG	EX	NRMT
1	New York Islanders Goal Leader: Mike Bossy	.25	.50	1.00
2	**Highlight:** Denis Potvin	.18	.35	.75
3	Mike Bossy	.50	1.00	2.00
4	Bob Bourne	.05	.10	.20
5	**Billy Carroll, RC**	.05	.10	.20
6	Clark Gillies	.05	.10	.20
7	Butch Goring	.05	.10	.20
8	**Mats Hallin, RC, LC**	.05	.10	.20
9	Tomas Jonsson	.05	.10	.20
10	Gord Lane, LC	.05	.10	.20
11	Dave Langevin	.05	.10	.20
12	**Roland Melanson, Goalie, RC**	.18	.35	.75
13	Ken Morrow	.05	.10	.20
14	Bob Nystrom	.05	.10	.20
15	Stefan Persson	.05	.10	.20
16	Denis Potvin	.18	.35	.75
17	Billy Smith, Goalie	.10	.20	.40
18	**Brent Sutter**	.12	.25	.50
19	Duane Sutter	.05	.10	.20
20	John Tonelli	.07	.15	.30
21	Bryan Trottier	.25	.50	1.00

EDMONTON OILERS

No.	Player	VG	EX	NRMT
22	Edmonton Oilers Goal Leader: Wayne Gretzky	1.50	3.00	6.00
23	**Highlight:** Messier & Gretzky	5.00	10.00	20.00
24	Glenn Anderson	.60	1.25	2.50
25	Paul Coffey	2.50	5.00	10.00
26	Lee Fogolin	.05	.10	.20
27	Grant Fuhr, Goalie	1.50	3.00	6.00
28	**Randall Gregg, RC**	.35	.75	1.50
29	Wayne Gretzky	7.00	14.00	28.00
30	**Charles Huddy, RC**	.50	1.00	2.00
31	Pat Hughes	.05	.10	.20
32	Dave Hunter	.05	.10	.20
33	**Don Jackson, RC**	.05	.10	.20
34	Jari Kurri	1.25	2.50	5.00
35	Willy Lindstrom	.05	.10	.20
36	Ken Linseman	.05	.10	.20
37	Kevin Lowe	.35	.75	1.50
38	Dave Lumley	.05	.10	.20
39	**Mark Messier**	2.50	5.00	10.00
40	Andrew Moog, Goalie	1.50	3.00	6.00

O-Pee-Chee, 1983-84 Issue
Card No. 1,
New York Islanders Goal Leader, Mike Bossy

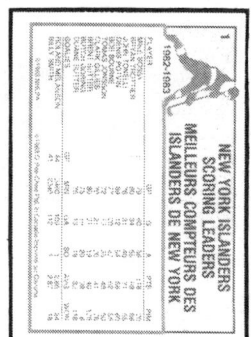

O-Pee-Chee, 1983-84 Issue
Card No. 1,
New York Islanders Goal Leader, Mike Bossy

O-Pee-Chee
1983-84 Issue
Card No. 39,
Mark Messier

O-Pee-Chee
1983-84 Issue
Card No. 65,
Phil Housley

No.	Player	VG	EX	NRMT
41	**Jaroslav Pouzar, RC**	.05	.10	.20
42	Tom Roulston	.05	.10	.20

BOSTON BRUINS

No.	Player	VG	EX	NRMT
43	**Boston Bruins Goal Leader:** Rick Middleton	.05	.10	.20
44	**Highlight:** Peter Peeters, Goalie	.05	.10	.20
45	Ray Bourque	1.50	3.00	6.00
46	Bruce Crowder, LC	.05	.10	.20
47	Keith Crowder	.05	.10	.20
48	**Luc Dufour, RC**	.07	.15	.30
49	Tom Fergus	.05	.10	.20
50	Stephen Kasper	.05	.10	.20
51	**Gordon Kluzak, RC**	.12	.25	.50
52	**Michael Krushelnyski, RC**	.50	1.00	2.00
53	Peter McNab	.05	.10	.20
54	Rick Middleton	.07	.15	.30
55	Mike Milbury	.05	.10	.20
56	Michael O'Connell	.05	.10	.20
57	Barry Pederson	.05	.10	.20
58	Peter Peeters, Goalie	.07	.15	.30
59	Jim Schoenfeld, LC	.05	.10	.20

BUFFALO SABRES

No.	Player	VG	EX	NRMT
60	**Buffalo Sabres Goal Leader:** Anthony McKegney	.05	.10	.20
61	**Highlight:** Bob Sauve, Goalie	.05	.10	.20
62	Real Cloutier	.05	.10	.20
63	Mike Foligno	.05	.10	.20
64	Bill Hajt	.05	.10	.20
65	**Phil Housley, RC**	3.25	6.50	13.00

TORONTO MAPLE LEAFS

No.	Player	VG	EX	NRMT
66	Dale McCourt, LC	.05	.10	.20

BUFFALO SABRES

No.	Player	VG	EX	NRMT
67	Gilbert Perreault	.18	.35	.75
68	**Brent Peterson, RC**	.05	.10	.20
69	Craig Ramsay	.05	.10	.20
70	Michael Ramsey	.05	.10	.20
71	Bob Sauve, Goalie	.05	.10	.20
72	Ric Seiling	.05	.10	.20

QUEBEC NORDIQUES

No.	Player	VG	EX	NRMT
73	John Van Boxmeer, LC (Now with Quebec)	.05	.10	.20

CALGARY FLAMES

No.	Player	VG	EX	NRMT
74	**Calgary Flames Goal Leader:** Lanny McDonald	.07	.15	.30
75	**Highlight:** Lanny McDonald	.05	.10	.20
76	**Ed Beers, RC**	.07	.15	.30
77	Steve Bozek	.05	.10	.20

ST. LOUIS BLUES

No.	Player	VG	EX	NRMT
78	Guy Chouinard, LC	.05	.10	.20

CALGARY FLAMES

No.	Player	VG	EX	NRMT
79	Mike Eaves	.05	.10	.20
80	Don Edwards, Goalie	.05	.10	.20
81	**Kari Eloranta, RC**	.05	.10	.20
82	**Dave Hindmarch, RC**	.05	.10	.20
83	Jamie Hislop, LC	.05	.10	.20
84	**James Jackson, RC**	.05	.10	.20
85	Stephen Konroyd	.05	.10	.20
86	Rejean Lemelin, Goalie	.07	.15	.30
87	Lanny McDonald	.15	.30	.60
88	**Greg Meredith, RC, LC**	.05	.10	.20
89	Kent Nilsson	.05	.10	.20
90	James Peplinski	.05	.10	.20
91	Paul Reinhart	.05	.10	.20
92	Doug Risebrough	.05	.10	.20
93	Steve Tambellini	.05	.10	.20
94	**Mickey Volcan, RC, LC**	.05	.10	.20

— 1983 - 84 REGULAR ISSUE — O-PEE-CHEE • 87

CHICAGO BLACK HAWKS

No.	Player	VG	EX	NRMT
95	**Chicago Black Hawks Goal Leader:** Al Secord	.05	.10	.20 ☐
96	**Highlight:** Denis Savard	.18	.35	.75 ☐
97	Murray Bannerman, Goalie	.05	.10	.20 ☐
98	Keith Brown	.05	.10	.20 ☐
99	Tony Esposito, Goalie, LC	.20	.45	.90 ☐
100	Dave Feamster, RC, LC	.05	.10	.20 ☐
101	Greg Fox	.05	.10	.20 ☐
102	Curt Fraser	.05	.10	.20 ☐
103	**Bill Gardner, RC**	.05	.10	.20 ☐
104	Tim Higgins	.05	.10	.20 ☐
105	**Steve Larmer, RC, Error,**	4.50	9.00	18.00 ☐
106	**Steve Ludzik, RC, Error,**	1.25	2.50	5.00 ☐
107	Tom Lysiak	.05	.10	.20 ☐
108	Bob Murray	.05	.10	.20 ☐
109	**Rick Paterson, RC**	.05	.10	.20 ☐
110	Rich Preston	.05	.10	.20 ☐
111	Denis Savard	.60	1.25	2.50 ☐
112	Al Secord	.05	.10	.20 ☐
113	Darryl Sutter	.05	.10	.20 ☐
114	Douglas Wilson	.18	.35	.70 ☐

DETROIT RED WINGS

No.	Player	VG	EX	NRMT
115	**Detroit Red Wings Goal Leader:** John Ogrodnick	.05	.10	.20 ☐
116	**Highlight:** Corrado Micalef, Goalie	.05	.10	.20 ☐
117	John Barrett	.05	.10	.20 ☐
118	Ivan Boldirev	.05	.10	.20 ☐
119	Colin Campbell	.05	.10	.20 ☐
120	**Murray Craven, RC**	.75	1.50	3.00 ☐
121	Ron Duguay	.05	.10	.20 ☐
122	Dwight Foster	.05	.10	.20 ☐
123	Danny Gare	.05	.10	.20 ☐
124	Eddie Johnstone	.05	.10	.20 ☐
125	Reed Larson	.05	.10	.20 ☐
126	**Corrado Micalef, Goalie, RC, Error**	.07	.15	.30 ☐
127	Ed Mio, Goalie	.05	.10	.20 ☐
128	John Ogrodnick	.05	.10	.20 ☐
129	Brad Park	.18	.35	.75 ☐
130	Greg Smith	.05	.10	.20 ☐

MINNESOTA NORTH STARS

No.	Player	VG	EX	NRMT
131	**Ken Solheim, RC, LC**	.10	.20	.40 ☐

DETROIT RED WINGS

No.	Player	VG	EX	NRMT
132	Bob Manno	.10	.20	.40 ☐
133	Paul Woods	.10	.20	.40 ☐

CHECKLIST

No.	Checklist	VG	EX	NRMT
134	Checklist 1 (1 - 132)	1.00	2.00	4.00 ☐

HARTFORD WHALERS

No.	Player	VG	EX	NRMT
135	**Hartford Whalers Goal Leader:** Blaine Stoughton	.05	.10	.20 ☐
136	**Highlight:** Blaine Stoughton	.05	.10	.20 ☐
137	Richard Dunn	.05	.10	.20 ☐
138	Ron Francis	1.25	2.50	5.00 ☐
139	Marty Howe	.05	.10	.20 ☐
140	Mark Johnson	.05	.10	.20 ☐
141	**Paul Lawless, RC, LC**	.05	.10	.20 ☐
142	Merlin Malinowski (Playing in Europe) LC	.05	.10	.20 ☐
143	Greg Millen, Goalie	.05	.10	.20 ☐
144	**Ray Neufeld, RC**	.05	.10	.20 ☐
145	Joel Quenneville	.05	.10	.20 ☐
146	Risto Siltanen	.05	.10	.20 ☐
147	Blaine Stoughton	.05	.10	.20 ☐
148	Douglas Sulliman	.05	.10	.20 ☐
149	**Bob Sullivan, RC, LC**	.05	.10	.20 ☐

LOS ANGELES KINGS

No.	Player	VG	EX	NRMT
150	**Los Angeles Kings Goal Leader:** Marcel Dionne	.12	.25	.50 ☐
151	**Highlight:** Marcel Dionne	.12	.25	.50 ☐

O-Pee-Chee
1983-84 Issue
Card No. 105, Error,
Shows Steve Ludzik

O-Pee-Chee
1983-84 Issue
Card No. 106, Error,
Shows Steve Larmer

O-Pee-Chee, 1983-84 Issue
Card No. 126, Error,
Name misspelled
Carrado on face

O-Pee-Chee
1983-84 Issue
Card No. 160,
Bernie Nicholls

No.	Player	VG	EX	NRMT
152	**Marcel Dionne**	.18	.35	.75 ☐
153	**Daryl Evans, RC, LC**	.05	.10	.20 ☐
154	Jim Fox	.05	.10	.20 ☐
155	Mark Hardy	.05	.10	.20 ☐
156	**Gary Laskoski, Goalie, RC, LC**	.05	.10	.20 ☐
157	Kevin Lavallee	.05	.10	.20 ☐

NEW JERSEY DEVILS

No.	Player	VG	EX	NRMT
158	Dave Lewis (Now with New Jersey)	.05	.10	.20 ☐

WASHINGTON CAPITALS

No.	Player	VG	EX	NRMT
159	Larry Murphy	.50	1.00	2.00 ☐

LOS ANGELES KINGS

No.	Player	VG	EX	NRMT
160	**Bernie Nicholls, RC**	3.25	6.50	13.00 ☐
161	Terry Ruskowski	.05	.10	.20 ☐
162	Charlie Simmer	.05	.10	.20 ☐
163	David Taylor	.12	.25	.50 ☐

MINNESOTA NORTH STARS

No.	Player	VG	EX	NRMT
164	**Minnesota North Stars Goal Leader:** Dino Ciccarelli	.07	.15	.30 ☐
165	**Highlight:** Brian Bellows	.60	1.25	2.50 ☐
166	Don Beaupre, Goalie	.05	.10	.20 ☐
167	**Brian Bellows, RC**	4.50	9.00	18.00 ☐
168	Neal Broten	.25	.50	1.00 ☐

LOS ANGELES KINGS

No.	Player	VG	EX	NRMT
169	Steve Christoff (Now with Los Angeles)	.05	.10	.20 ☐

MINNESOTA NORTH STARS

No.	Player	VG	EX	NRMT
170	Dino Ciccarelli	.60	1.25	2.50 ☐
171	George Ferguson, LC	.05	.10	.20 ☐
172	Craig Hartsburg	.05	.10	.20 ☐
173	Al MacAdam	.05	.10	.20 ☐
174	Dennis Maruk	.05	.10	.20 ☐
175	Brad Maxwell	.05	.10	.20 ☐
176	Tom McCarthy	.05	.10	.20 ☐
177	Gilles Meloche, Goalie	.05	.10	.20 ☐
178	Steve Payne	.05	.10	.20 ☐
179	Willi Plett, LC	.05	.10	.20 ☐
180	Gordon Roberts	.05	.10	.20 ☐

MONTREAL CANADIENS

No.	Player	VG	EX	NRMT
181	Robert Smith (Now with Montreal)	.10	.20	.40 ☐
182	**Montreal Canadiens Goal Leader:** Mark Napier	.05	.10	.20 ☐
183	**Highlight:** Guy Lafleur	.20	.40	.80 ☐

MINNESOTA NORTH STARS

No.	Player	VG	EX	NRMT
184	Keith Acton (Now with Minnesota)	.05	.10	.20 ☐

MONTREAL CANADIENS

No.	Player	VG	EX	NRMT
185	**Guy Carbonneau, RC**	1.75	3.50	7.00 ☐
186	**Gilbert Delorme, RC**	.05	.10	.20 ☐
187	Bob Gainey	.07	.15	.30 ☐
188	Richard Green	.05	.10	.20 ☐
189	Guy Lafleur	.30	.60	1.25 ☐
190	**Craig Ludwig, RC**	.12	.25	.50 ☐
191	Pierre Mondou	.05	.10	.20 ☐

MINNESOTA NORTH STARS

No.	Player	VG	EX	NRMT
192	Mark Napier (Now with Minnesota)	.05	.10	.20 ☐

MONTREAL CANADIENS

No.	Player	VG	EX	NRMT
193	**Mats Naslund, RC**	.60	1.25	2.50 ☐
194	**Christopher Nilan, RC**	.50	1.00	2.00 ☐

88 • O-PEE-CHEE — 1983-84 REGULAR ISSUE

No.	Player	VG	EX	NRMT
195	Larry Robinson	.12	.25	.50
196	**William Root, RC**	**.05**	**.10**	**.20**
197	Richard Sevigny, Goalie	.05	.10	.20
198	Steve Shutt	.05	.10	.20
199	Mario Tremblay	.05	.10	.20
200	Ryan Walter	.05	.10	.20
201	Richard Wamsley, Goalie	.05	.10	.20
202	Douglas Wickenheiser	.05	.10	.20

TROPHY CARDS

No.	Player	VG	EX	NRMT
203	The Hart Memorial Trophy: Wayne Gretzky	1.50	3.00	6.00
204	The Art Ross Trophy: Wayne Gretzky	1.50	3.00	6.00
205	The Lady Byng Memorial Trophy: Mike Bossy	.25	.50	1.00
206	The Calder Memorial Trophy: Steve Larmer	1.00	2.00	4.00
207	The James Norris Memorial Trophy: Rod Langway	.07	.15	.30
208	The Bill Masterton Memorial Trophy: Lanny McDonald	.07	.15	.30
209	The Vezina Trophy: Peter Peeters	.07	.15	.30

RECORD BREAKERS

No.	Player	VG	EX	NRMT
210	Mike Bossy, NYI	.25	.50	1.00
211	Marcel Dionne, LA	.18	.35	.75
212	Wayne Gretzky, Edm.	1.50	3.00	6.00
213	Pat Hughes, Edm.	.05	.10	.20
214	Rick Middleton, Bos.	.05	.10	.20

LEAGUE LEADERS

No.	Player	VG	EX	NRMT
215	Goal Leader: Wayne Gretzky, Edm.	1.50	3.00	6.00
216	Assist Leader: Wayne Gretzky, Edm.	1.50	3.00	6.00
217	Scoring Leader: Wayne Gretzky, Edm.	1.50	3.00	6.00
218	Game Winning Goal Leader: Brian Propp, Phi.	.05	.10	.20
219	Power Play Goal Leader: Paul Gardner and Al Secord	.05	.10	.20
220	Penalty Minute Leader: Randy Holt, Wash.	.05	.10	.20
221	Goals Against Avg Leader: Peter Peeters, Goalie, Bos.	.05	.10	.20
222	Shutout Leader: Peter Peeters, Goalie, Bos.	.05	.10	.20

NEW JERSEY DEVILS

No.	Player	VG	EX	NRMT
223	New Jersey Devils Goal Leader: Steve Tambellini	.05	.10	.20
224	Highlight: Don Lever	.05	.10	.20

MINNESOTA NORTH STARS

No.	Player	VG	EX	NRMT
225	Brent Ashton	.05	.10	.20

NEW JERSEY DEVILS

No.	Player	VG	EX	NRMT
226	Mel Bridgman	.05	.10	.20
227	Aaron Broten	.05	.10	.20
228	**James (Murray) Brumwell, RC, LC**	**.05**	**.10**	**.20**
229	Garry Howatt, LC	.05	.10	.20
230	**Jeff Larmer, RC**	**.05**	**.10**	**.20**
231	Don Lever	.05	.10	.20
232	Bob Lorimer	.05	.10	.20
233	Ron Low, Goalie	.05	.10	.20
234	Bob MacMillan	.05	.10	.20
235	**Hector Marini, RC, LC**	**.05**	**.10**	**.20**
236	Glenn Resch, Goalie	.07	.15	.30
237	Phil Russell	.05	.10	.20

NEW YORK RANGERS

No.	Player	VG	EX	NRMT
238	New York Rangers Goal Leader: Mark Pavelich	.05	.10	.20
239	Highlight: Mark Pavelich	.05	.10	.20
240	**Bill Baker, RC, LC**	**.05**	**.10**	**.20**
241	Barry Beck	.05	.10	.20
242	Michael Blaisdell, LC	.05	.10	.20

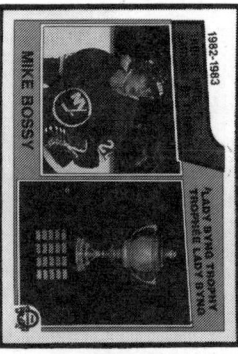

O-Pee-Chee, 1983-84 Issue
Card No. 205,
Lady Byng Trophy,
Mike Bossy

O-Pee-Chee, 1983-84 Issue
Card No. 211,
Record Breaker,
Marcel Dionne

O-Pee-Chee
1983-84 Issue
Card No. 268,
Pelle Lindbergh

O-Pee-Chee
1983-84 Issue
Card No. 281,
David Hannan

No.	Player	VG	EX	NRMT
243	Nick Fotiu	.05	.10	.20
244	Robbie Ftorek, LC	.05	.10	.20
245	Anders Hedberg	.05	.10	.20
246	Willie Huber	.05	.10	.20
247	Thomas Laidlaw	.05	.10	.20
248	Mikko Leinonen, LC	.05	.10	.20
249	Dave Maloney	.05	.10	.20
250	Donald Maloney	.05	.10	.20
251	Rob McClanahan	.05	.10	.20
252	Mark Osborne	.05	.10	.20
253	Mark Pavelich	.05	.10	.20
254	Mike Rogers	.05	.10	.20
255	Reijo Ruotsalainen	.05	.10	.20

CHECKLIST

No.	Checklist	VG	EX	NRMT
256	Checklist 2 (133 - 264)	1.00	2.00	4.00

PHILADELPHIA FLYERS

No.	Player	VG	EX	NRMT
257	Philadelphia Flyers Goal Leader: Darryl Sittler	.07	.15	.30
258	Highlight: Darryl Sittler	.07	.15	.30
259	Ray Allison, LC	.05	.10	.20
260	Bill Barber	.12	.25	.50
261	**Lindsay Carson, RC, LC**	**.05**	**.10**	**.20**
262	Bobby Clarke, LC	.30	.65	1.25
263	Doug Crossman	.05	.10	.20
264	Ron Flockhart	.05	.10	.20
265	**Robert Froese, Goalie, RC**	**.35**	**.75**	**1.50**
266	Paul Holmgren	.05	.10	.20
267	Mark Howe	.07	.15	.30
268	**Pelle Lindbergh, Goalie, RC**	**4.50**	**9.00**	**18.00**
269	Bradley Marsh	.05	.10	.20
270	Byron (Brad) McCrimmon	.05	.10	.20
271	Brian Propp	.07	.35	.75
272	Darryl Sittler	.12	.25	.50
273	**Mark Taylor, RC**	**.05**	**.10**	**.20**

PITTSBURGH PENGUINS

No.	Player	VG	EX	NRMT
274	Pittsburgh Penguins Goal Leader: Rick Kehoe	.05	.10	.20
275	Highlight: Paul Gardner	.05	.10	.20
276	Pat Boutette	.05	.10	.20
277	Mike Bullard	.05	.10	.20
278	Randy Carlyle	.05	.10	.20
279	Michel Dion, Goalie	.05	.10	.20
280	Paul Gardner, LC	.05	.10	.20
281	**David Hannan, RC**	**.10**	**.20**	**.40**
282	Rick Kehoe	.05	.10	.20
283	**Randy Boyd, RC, LC**	**.05**	**.10**	**.20**

HARTFORD WHALERS

No.	Player	VG	EX	NRMT
284	Greg Malone (Now with Hartford)	.05	.10	.20

PITTSBURGH PENGUINS

No.	Player	VG	EX	NRMT
285	**Douglas Shedden, RC**	**.07**	**.15**	**.30**
286	Andre St. Laurent, LC	.05	.10	.20

QUEBEC NORDIQUES

No.	Player	VG	EX	NRMT
287	Quebec Nordiques Goal Leader: Michel Goulet	.07	.15	.30
288	Highlight: Michel Goulet	.07	.15	.30
289	Pierre Aubry, LC	.05	.10	.20
290	Dan Bouchard, Goalie	.05	.10	.20
291	Alain Cote	.05	.10	.20
292	Michel Goulet	.30	.60	1.25
293	Dale Hunter	.12	.25	.50
294	Rick Lapointe, LC	.05	.10	.20
295	Mario Marois	.05	.10	.20
296	Anthony McKegney	.05	.10	.20
297	**Randy Moller, RC**	**.07**	**.15**	**.30**
298	Wilf Paiement	.05	.10	.20
299	Dave Pichette	.05	.10	.20
300	Normand Rochefort	.05	.10	.20
301	**Louis Sleigher, RC**	**.05**	**.10**	**.20**
302	Anton Stastny	.05	.10	.20

1983 - 84 REGULAR ISSUE — O-PEE-CHEE • 89

No.	Player	VG	EX	NRTM
303	Marian Stastny	.05	.10	.20
304	Peter Stastny	.85	1.75	3.50
305	Marc Tardif, LC	.05	.10	.20
306	Wally Weir, LC	.05	.10	.20
307	Blake Wesley	.05	.10	.20

ST. LOUIS BLUES

No.	Player	VG	EX	NRTM
308	**St. Louis Blues Goal Leader:** Brian Sutter	.05	.10	.20
309	**Highlight:** Michael Liut, Goalie	.05	.10	.20
310	Wayne Babych	.05	.10	.20
311	Jack Brownschidle, LC	.05	.10	.20

HARTFORD WHALERS

No.	Player	VG	EX	NRTM
312	**Mike Crombeen, RC, LC** (Now with Hartford)	.05	.10	.20

ST. LOUIS BLUES

No.	Player	VG	EX	NRTM
313	**Andre Dore, RC**	.05	.10	.20
314	Blake Dunlop, LC	.05	.10	.20
315	Bernie Federko	.05	.10	.20
316	Michael Liut, Goalie	.12	.25	.50
317	Joe Mullen	1.25	2.50	5.00
318	Jorgen Pettersson	.05	.10	.20
319	George (Rob) Ramage	.05	.10	.20
320	Brian Sutter	.05	.10	.20
321	Perry Turnbull	.05	.10	.20

HARTFORD WHALERS

No.	Player	VG	EX	NRTM
322	Mike Zuke	.05	.10	.20

TORONTO MAPLE LEAFS

No.	Player	VG	EX	NRTM
323	**Toronto Maple Leafs Goal Leader:** Richard Vaive	.05	.10	.20
324	**Highlight:** Richard Vaive	.05	.10	.20
325	John Anderson	.05	.10	.20
326	Jim Benning	.05	.10	.20
327	Bill Derlago	.05	.10	.20
328	**Dan Daoust, RC**	.05	.10	.20
329	Dave Farrish	.05	.10	.20
330	Miroslav Frycer	.05	.10	.20
331	**Robert (Stewart) Gavin, RC**	.10	.20	.40
332	Gaston Gingras	.05	.10	.20
333	Billy Harris, LC	.05	.10	.20
334	**Peter Ihnacak, RC, LC**	.05	.10	.20
335	James Korn	.05	.10	.20
336	Terry Martin	.05	.10	.20
337	**Frank Nigro, RC, LC**	.05	.10	.20
338	Mike Palmateer, Goalie	.05	.10	.20
339	**Walter Poddubny, RC**	.25	.50	1.00
340	Rick St. Croix, Goalie	.05	.10	.20
341	Borje Salming	.07	.15	.30
342	Greg Terrion	.05	.10	.20
343	Richard Vaive	.07	.15	.30

VANCOUVER CANUCKS

No.	Player	VG	EX	NRTM
344	**Vancouver Canucks Goal Leader:** Darcy Rota	.05	.10	.20
345	**Highlight:** Darcy Rota	.05	.10	.20
346	Richard Brodeur, Goalie	.05	.10	.20
347	**Jiri Bubla, RC**	.07	.15	.30
348	Ron Delorme	.05	.10	.20
349	John Garrett, Goalie	.05	.10	.20
350	Thomas Gradin	.05	.10	.20
351	Doug Halward	.05	.10	.20
352	Mark Kirton, LC	.05	.10	.20
353	Rick Lanz	.05	.10	.20

MINNESOTA NORTH STARS

No.	Player	VG	EX	NRTM
354	Lars Lindgren, LC	.05	.10	.20

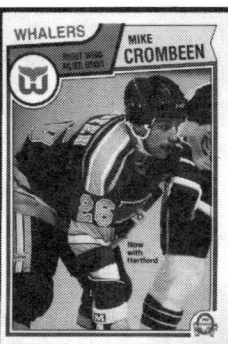

O-Pee-Chee 1983-84 Issue Card No. 312, Mike Crombeen

O-Pee-Chee 1983-84 Issue Card No. 371, Ken Houston

O-Pee-Chee 1983-84 Issue Card No. 376, Scott Stevens

O-Pee-Chee 1983-84 Issue Card No. 384, Murray Eaves

VANCOUVER CANUCKS

No.	Player	VG	EX	NRTM
355	Gary Lupul	.05	.10	.20
356	Kevin McCarthy	.05	.10	.20
357	**James Nill, RC**	.05	.10	.20
358	Darcy Rota	.05	.10	.20
359	Stanley Smyl	.05	.10	.20
360	Harold Snepsts	.05	.10	.20
361	**Patrik Sundstrom, RC**	.25	.50	1.00
362	**Tony Tantl, RC**	.35	.75	1.50
363	David Williams	.05	.10	.20

WASHINGTON CAPITALS

No.	Player	VG	EX	NRTM
364	**Washington Capitals Goal Leader:** Michael Gartner	.15	.30	.60
365	**Highlight:** Rod Langway	.07	.15	.30
366	Robert Carpenter	.20	.40	.80
367	Dave Christian	.10	.20	.40

LOS ANGELES KINGS

No.	Player	VG	EX	NRTM
368	Brian Engblom	.05	.10	.20

WASHINGTON CAPITALS

No.	Player	VG	EX	NRTM
369	Michael Gartner	1.25	2.50	5.00
370	Bengt-ake Gustafsson	.05	.10	.20

LOS ANGELES KINGS

No.	Player	VG	EX	NRTM
371	Ken Houston, LC (Now with Los Angeles)	.05	.10	.20

WASHINGTON CAPITALS

No.	Player	VG	EX	NRTM
372	Doug Jarvis	.05	.10	.20
373	**Al Jensen, Goalie, RC**	.12	.25	.50
374	Rod Langway	.07	.15	.30
375	**Craig Laughlin, RC**	.05	.10	.20
376	**Scott Stevens, RC**	3.75	7.50	15.00

WINNIPEG JETS

No.	Player	VG	EX	NRTM
377	**Winnipeg Jets Goal Leader:** Dale Hawerchuk	.12	.25	.50
378	**Highlight:** Lucien DeBlois	.05	.10	.20
379	**Scott Arniel, RC**	.12	.25	.50
380	Dave Babych	.05	.10	.20
381	Laurie Boschman	.05	.10	.20
382	Wade Campbell, LC	.05	.10	.20
383	Lucien DeBlois	.05	.10	.20
384	**Murray Eaves, RC, LC**	.05	.10	.20
385	Dale Hawerchuk	1.50	3.00	6.00
386	Morris Lukowich	.05	.10	.20
387	Bengt Lundholm	.05	.10	.20
388	Paul Maclean	.07	.15	.30
389	**Brian Mullen, RC**	.60	1.25	2.50
390	Douglas Smail	.05	.10	.20
391	Doug Soetaert, Goalie	.05	.10	.20
392	Don Spring, LC	.05	.10	.20
393	Thomas Steen	.12	.25	.50
394	Timothy Watters	.05	.10	.20
395	Tim Young	.05	.10	.20

CHECKLIST

No.	Checklist	VG	EX	NRTM
396	Checklist 3 (265 - 396)	1.00	2.00	4.00

Note: *The Charlton Standard Catalogue of Hockey Cards* arranges cards in their issue date order. This means the first date a manufacturer issues a card set determines the sequence of the manufacturer in the Standard Catalogue. In this manner the historical importance of early cards is maintained. See the last page of this catalogue for an alphabetical index of issuers.

90 • O-PEE-CHEE — 1984-85 REGULAR ISSUE

— 1984-85 REGULAR ISSUE —

This set features all-star players and each team's scoring leader. Mint cards command a price premium of 25% over NRMT cards.

PRICE MOVEMENT OF NRMT SETS

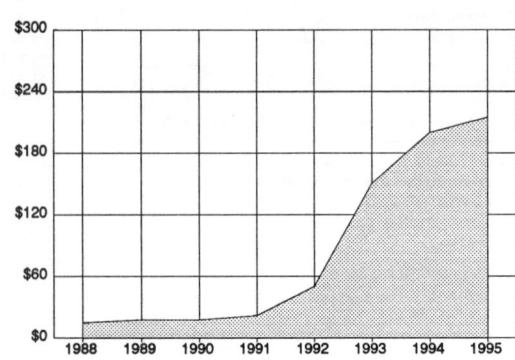

Card Size: 2 1/2" X 3 1/2"
Face: Four colour, white border; Position
Back: Pink and blue on card stock; Number, Resume, Bilingual
Imprint: Ptd. in Canada Imprimé au Canada © 1984 O-Pee-Chee
© 1984 NHLPA
Complete Set No.: 396

Complete Set Price:	70.00	140.00	280.00 ☐
Common Card:	.05	.10	.20
Wax Pack: (10 Cards)			22.00
Wax Box: (48 Packs)			825.00
Wax Case: (20 Boxes)			14,000.00

BOSTON BRUINS

No.	Player	VG	EX	NRMT
1	Raymond Bourque	1.50	3.00	6.00 ☐
2	Keith Crowder	.05	.10	.20 ☐
3	Luc Dufour, LC	.05	.10	.20 ☐
4	Tom Fergus	.05	.10	.20 ☐
5	**Doug Keans, Goalie, RC**	**.07**	**.15**	**.30** ☐
6	Gordon Kluzak	.05	.10	.20 ☐
7	Ken Linseman	.05	.10	.20 ☐
8	**Nevin Markwart, RC**	**.05**	**.10**	**.20** ☐
9	Rick Middleton	.07	.15	.25 ☐
10	Mike Milbury, LC	.05	.10	.20 ☐
11	James Nill	.05	.10	.20 ☐
12	Michael O'Connell	.05	.10	.20 ☐
13	Terry O'Reilly, LC	.05	.10	.20 ☐
14	Barry Pederson	.05	.10	.20 ☐
15	Peter Peeters, Goalie	.07	.15	.30 ☐
16	Dave Silk, RC, LC	.05	.10	.20 ☐

BUFFALO SABRES

No.	Player	VG	EX	NRMT
17	**Dave Andreychuk, RC**	**7.50**	**15.00**	**30.00** ☐
18	**Tom Barrasso, Goalie, RC**	**3.00**	**6.00**	**12.00** ☐
19	Real Cloutier, LC	.05	.10	.20 ☐
20	Mike Foligno	.05	.10	.20 ☐
21	Bill Hajt	.05	.10	.20 ☐
22	**Gilles Hamel, RC**	**.05**	**.10**	**.20** ☐
23	Phil Housley	.60	1.25	2.50 ☐
24	Gilbert Perreault	.18	.35	.75 ☐
25	Brent Peterson	.05	.10	.20 ☐
26	Larry Playfair	.05	.10	.20 ☐
27	Craig Ramsay	.05	.10	.20 ☐
28	Michael Ramsey	.05	.10	.20 ☐
29	Lindy Ruff	.05	.10	.20 ☐
30	Bob Sauve, Goalie	.07	.15	.30 ☐
31	Ric Seiling	.05	.10	.20 ☐

CHICAGO BLACK HAWKS

No.	Player	VG	EX	NRMT
32	Murray Bannerman, Goalie	.05	.10	.20 ☐
33	Keith Brown	.05	.10	.20 ☐
34	Curt Fraser	.05	.10	.20 ☐
35	Bill Gardner, LC	.05	.10	.20 ☐
36	Jeff Larmer, LC	.05	.10	.20 ☐
37	Steve Larmer	1.25	2.50	5.00 ☐

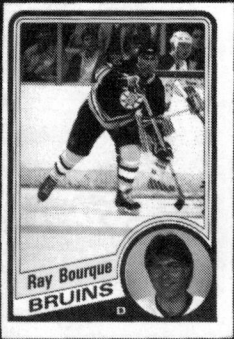

O-Pee-Chee
1984-85 Issue
Card No. 1,
Raymond Bourque

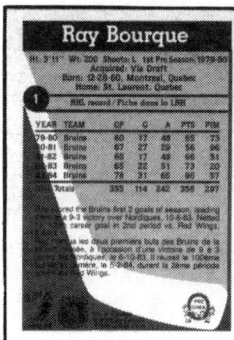

O-Pee-Chee
1984-85 Issue
Card No. 1,
Raymond Bourque

O-Pee-Chee
1984-85 Issue
Card No. 17,
Dave Andreychuk

O-Pee-Chee
1984-85 Issue
Card No. 79,
Sylvain Turgeon

No.	Player	VG	EX	NRMT
38	Steve Ludzik, LC	.05	.10	.20 ☐
39	Tom Lysiak	.05	.10	.20 ☐
40	Bob MacMillan	.05	.10	.20 ☐
41	•Bob Murray	.05	.10	.20 ☐
42	**Troy Murray, RC**	**.50**	**1.00**	**2.00** ☐
43	**Jack O'Callahan, RC**	**.05**	**.10**	**.20** ☐
44	Rick Paterson, LC	.05	.10	.20 ☐
45	Denis Savard	.50	1.00	2.00 ☐
46	Alan Secord	.05	.10	.20 ☐
47	Darryl Sutter	.05	.10	.20 ☐
48	Douglas Wilson	.12	.25	.50 ☐

DETROIT RED WINGS

No.	Player	VG	EX	NRMT
49	John Barrett, LC	.05	.10	.20 ☐
50	Ivan Boldirev	.05	.10	.20 ☐
51	Colin Campbell, LC	.05	.10	.20 ☐
52	Ron Duguay	.05	.10	.20 ☐
53	Dwight Foster	.05	.10	.20 ☐
54	Danny Gare	.05	.10	.20 ☐
55	Eddie Johnstone, LC	.05	.10	.20 ☐
56	**Kelly Kisio, RC**	**.35**	**.75**	**1.50** ☐
57	**Lane Lambert, RC**	**.05**	**.10**	**.20** ☐
58	Reed Larson	.05	.10	.20 ☐
59	Bob Manno	.05	.10	.20 ☐
60	**Randy Ladouceur, RC**	**.05**	**.10**	**.20** ☐
61	Ed Mio, Goalie, LC	.05	.10	.20 ☐
62	John Ogrodnick	.05	.10	.20 ☐
63	Brad Park, LC	.12	.25	.50 ☐
64	Greg Smith, LC	.05	.10	.20 ☐
65	**Gregory Stefan, Goalie, RC**	**.15**	**.30**	**.60** ☐
66	Paul Woods, LC	.05	.10	.20 ☐
67	**Steve Yzerman, RC**	**17.00**	**34.00**	**68.00** ☐

HARTFORD WHALERS

No.	Player	VG	EX	NRMT
68	**Bob Crawford, RC**	**.07**	**.15**	**.30** ☐
69	Richard Dunn, LC	.05	.10	.20 ☐
70	Ron Francis	.50	1.00	2.00 ☐
71	Marty Howe, LC	.05	.10	.20 ☐
72	Mark Johnson	.05	.10	.20 ☐
73	Christopher Kotsopoulos	.05	.10	.20 ☐
74	Greg Malone	.05	.10	.20 ☐
75	Greg Millen, Goalie	.05	.10	.20 ☐
76	Ray Neufeld	.05	.10	.20 ☐
77	Joel Quenneville	.05	.10	.20 ☐
78	Risto Siltanen	.05	.10	.20 ☐
79	**Sylvain Turgeon, RC**	**.25**	**.50**	**1.00** ☐
80	Mike Zuke	.05	.10	.20 ☐

LOS ANGELES KINGS

No.	Player	VG	EX	NRMT
81	Steve Christoff, LC	.05	.10	.20 ☐
82	Marcel Dionne	.25	.50	1.00 ☐
83	Brian Engblom	.05	.10	.20 ☐
84	Jim Fox	.05	.10	.20 ☐
85	**Anders Hakansson, RC, LC**	**.05**	**.10**	**.20** ☐
86	Mark Hardy	.05	.10	.20 ☐
87	**Brian MacLellan, RC**	**.07**	**.15**	**.30** ☐
88	Bernie Nicholls	.75	1.50	3.00 ☐
89	Terry Ruskowski	.05	.10	.20 ☐

BOSTON BRUINS

No.	Player	VG	EX	NRMT
90	Charlie Simmer (Now with Bruins)	.05	.10	.20 ☐

LOS ANGELES KINGS

No.	Player	VG	EX	NRMT
91	Douglas Smith	.05	.10	.20 ☐
92	David Taylor	.05	.10	.20 ☐

MINNESOTA NORTH STARS

No.	Player	VG	EX	NRMT
93	Keith Acton	.05	.10	.20 ☐
94	Donald Beaupre, Goalie	.05	.10	.20 ☐
95	Brian Bellows	.75	1.50	3.00 ☐
96	Neal Broten	.12	.25	.50 ☐
97	Dino Ciccarelli	.25	.50	1.00 ☐
98	Craig Hartsburg	.05	.10	.20 ☐
99	**Tom Hirsch, RC, LC**	**.05**	**.10**	**.20** ☐

— 1984 - 85 REGULAR ISSUE — O-PEE-CHEE • 91

No.	Player	VG	EX	NRMT
100	Paul Holmgren, LC	.05	.10	.20 ☐
101	Dennis Maruk	.05	.10	.20 ☐
102	Brad Maxwell	.05	.10	.20 ☐
103	Tom McCarthy	.05	.10	.20 ☐
104	Gilles Meloche, Goalie	.05	.10	.20 ☐
105	Mark Napier	.05	.10	.20 ☐
106	Steve Payne	.05	.10	.20 ☐
107	Gordon Roberts	.05	.10	.20 ☐
108	Harold Snepsts	.05	.10	.20 ☐

NEW JERSEY DEVILS

No.	Player	VG	EX	NRMT
109	Mel Bridgman	.05	.10	.20 ☐
110	Joe Cirella	.05	.10	.20 ☐
111	Tim Higgins	.05	.10	.20 ☐
112	Don Lever	.05	.10	.20 ☐
113	Dave Lewis	.05	.10	.20 ☐
114	Bob Lorimer, LC	.05	.10	.20 ☐
115	Ron Low, Goalie, LC	.05	.10	.20 ☐
116	**Jan Ludvig, RC, LC**	.05	.10	.20 ☐
117	Gary McAdam, LC	.05	.10	.20 ☐
118	Rich Preston (Now with Devils)	.05	.10	.20 ☐
119	Glenn Resch, Goalie	.07	.15	.30 ☐
120	Phil Russell	.05	.10	.20 ☐
121	**Patrick Verbeek, RC**	1.50	3.00	6.00 ☐

NEW YORK ISLANDERS

No.	Player	VG	EX	NRMT
122	Mike Bossy	.30	.60	1.25 ☐
123	Bob Bourne	.05	.10	.20 ☐
124	**Patrick Flatley, RC**	.25	.50	1.00 ☐
125	**Gregory Gilbert, RC**	.15	.30	.60 ☐
126	Clark Gillies	.05	.10	.20 ☐
127	Butch Goring, LC	.05	.10	.20 ☐
128	Tomas Jonsson	.05	.10	.20 ☐
129	**Pat LaFontaine, RC**	11.25	22.50	45.00 ☐
130	Roland Melanson, Goalie	.05	.10	.20 ☐
131	Ken Morrow	.05	.10	.20 ☐
132	Bob Nystrom	.05	.10	.20 ☐
133	Stefan Persson, LC	.05	.10	.20 ☐
134	Denis Potvin	.18	.35	.75 ☐
135	Billy Smith, Goalie	.07	.15	.35 ☐
136	Brent Sutter	.15	.30	.60 ☐
137	Duane Sutter	.05	.10	.20 ☐
138	John Tonelli	.05	.10	.20 ☐
139	Bryan Trottier	.25	.50	1.00 ☐

NEW YORK RANGERS

No.	Player	VG	EX	NRMT
140	Barry Beck	.05	.10	.20 ☐
141	Ronald Greschner	.05	.10	.20 ☐
142	Glen Hanlon, Goalie	.05	.10	.20 ☐
143	Anders Hedberg, LC	.05	.10	.20 ☐
144	Thomas Laidlaw	.05	.10	.20 ☐
145	Pierre Larouche	.05	.10	.20 ☐
146	Dave Maloney	.05	.10	.20 ☐
147	Donald Maloney	.05	.10	.20 ☐
148	Mark Osborne	.05	.10	.20 ☐
149	Larry Patey, LC	.05	.10	.20 ☐
150	**James Patrick, RC**	.60	1.25	2.50 ☐
151	Mark Pavelich	.05	.10	.20 ☐
152	Mike Rogers	.05	.10	.20 ☐
153	Reijo Ruotsalainen	.05	.10	.20 ☐
154	Blaine Stoughton, LC	.05	.10	.20 ☐
155	**Peter Sundstrom, RC, LC**	.12	.25	.50 ☐

PHILADELPHIA FLYERS

No.	Player	VG	EX	NRMT
156	Bill Barber, LC	.10	.20	.40 ☐
157	Doug Crossman	.05	.10	.20 ☐
158	**Thomas Eriksson, RC, LC**	.05	.10	.20 ☐
159	Robert Froese, Goalie	.07	.15	.30 ☐
160	**Paul Guay, RC, LC**	.05	.10	.20 ☐
161	Mark Howe	.10	.20	.40 ☐
162	Tim Kerr	.07	.15	.30 ☐
163	Bradley Marsh	.07	.15	.30 ☐
164	Byron (Brad) McCrimmon	.05	.10	.20 ☐
165	**David Poulin, RC**	.85	1.75	3.50 ☐
166	Brian Propp	.10	.20	.40 ☐
167	**Ilkka Sinisalo, RC**	.15	.30	.60 ☐

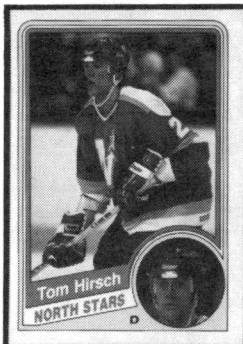

O-Pee-Chee
1984-85 Issue
Card No. 99,
Tom Hirsch

O-Pee-Chee
1984-85 Issue
Card No. 116,
Jan Ludvig

O-Pee-Chee
1984-85 Issue
Card No. 170,
Ronald Sutter

O-Pee-Chee
1984-85 Issue
Card No. 185,
Douglas Gilmour

DETROIT RED WINGS

No.	Player	VG	EX	NRMT
168	Darryl Sittler, LC (Traded to Detroit October 1984)	.12	.25	.50 ☐

PHILADELPHIA FLYERS

No.	Player	VG	EX	NRMT
169	**Richard Sutter, RC**	.25	.50	1.00 ☐
170	**Ronald Sutter, RC**	.25	.50	1.00 ☐

PITTSBURGH PENGUINS

No.	Player	VG	EX	NRMT
171	Pat Boutette, LC	.05	.10	.20 ☐
172	Mike Bullard	.05	.10	.20 ☐
173	Michel Dion, Goalie, LC	.05	.10	.20 ☐
174	Ron Flockhart	.05	.10	.20 ☐
175	Greg Fox, LC	.05	.10	.20 ☐
176	Denis Herron, Goalie	.05	.10	.20 ☐
177	Rick Kehoe, LC	.05	.10	.20 ☐
178	Kevin McCarthy, LC	.05	.10	.20 ☐
179	Tom Roulston, LC	.05	.10	.20 ☐
180	Mark Taylor, LC	.05	.10	.20 ☐
181	Wayne Babych (Drafted to Pittsburgh October 1984)	.05	.10	.20 ☐

ST. LOUIS BLUES

No.	Player	VG	EX	NRMT
182	**Tim Bothwell, RC**	.05	.10	.20 ☐
183	Kevin LaVallee, LC	.05	.10	.20 ☐
184	Bernie Federko	.05	.10	.20 ☐
185	**Douglas Gilmour, RC**	15.00	30.00	60.00 ☐
186	**Terry Johnson, RC, LC**	.05	.10	.20 ☐
187	Michael Liut, Goalie	.12	.25	.50 ☐
188	Joe Mullen	.75	1.50	3.00 ☐
189	Jorgen Pettersson, LC	.05	.10	.20 ☐
190	George (Rob) Ramage	.05	.10	.20 ☐
191	**Dwight Schofield, RC, LC**	.05	.10	.20 ☐
192	Brian Sutter	.05	.10	.20 ☐
193	Douglas Wickenheiser	.05	.10	.20 ☐

WASHINGTON CAPITALS

No.	Player	VG	EX	NRMT
194	Robert Carpenter	.05	.10	.20 ☐
195	Dave Christian	.05	.10	.20 ☐
196	**Robert Gould, RC**	.05	.10	.20 ☐
197	Michael Gartner	.75	1.50	3.00 ☐
198	Bengt-ake Gustafsson	.05	.10	.20 ☐
199	**Alan Haworth, RC**	.05	.10	.20 ☐
200	Doug Jarvis	.05	.10	.20 ☐
201	Al Jensen, Goalie	.05	.10	.20 ☐
202	Rod Langway	.10	.20	.40 ☐
203	Craig Laughlin	.05	.10	.20 ☐
204	Lawrence Murphy	.05	.10	.20 ☐
205	Pat Riggin, Goalie	.05	.10	.20 ☐
206	Scott Stevens	1.00	2.00	4.00 ☐

ALL STARS
First Team

No.	Player	VG	EX	NRMT
207	Michel Goulet, Que.	.12	.25	.50 ☐
208	Wayne Gretzky, Edm.	1.25	2.50	5.00 ☐
209	Mike Bossy, NYI	.25	.50	1.00 ☐
210	Rod Langway, Wash.	.05	.10	.20 ☐
211	Raymond Bourque, Bos.	.40	.85	1.75 ☐
212	Tom Barrasso, Goalie, Buf.	.50	1.00	2.00 ☐

Second Team

No.	Player	VG	EX	NRMT
213	Mark Messier, Edm.	.75	1.50	3.00 ☐
214	Bryan Trottier, NYI	.10	.20	.40 ☐
215	Jari Kurri, Edm.	.18	.35	.75 ☐
216	Denis Potvin, NYI	.10	.30	.60 ☐
217	Paul Coffey, Edm.	.35	.75	1.50 ☐
218	Pat Riggin, Goalie, Wash.	.07	.15	.25 ☐

CALGARY FLAMES

No.	Player	VG	EX	NRMT
219	Ed Beers	.05	.10	.20 ☐
220	Steve Bozek	.05	.10	.20 ☐
221	Mike Eaves	.05	.10	.20 ☐

92 • O-PEE-CHEE — 1984-85 REGULAR ISSUE —

No.	Player	VG	EX	NRMT
222	Don Edwards, Goalie	.05	.10	.20
223	Kari Eloranta, LC	.05	.10	.20
224	Dave Hindmarch, LC	.05	.10	.20
225	James Jackson, LC	.05	.10	.20
226	Stephen Konroyd	.05	.10	.20
227	**Richard Kromm, RC**	.05	.10	.20
228	Rejean Lemelin, Goalie	.07	.15	.30
229	**Hakan Loob, RC**	.35	.75	1.50
230	**Jamie Macoun, RC**	.35	.75	1.50
231	Lanny McDonald	.10	.20	.40
232	Kent Nilsson, LC	.05	.10	.20
233	James Peplinski	.05	.10	.20
234	**Dan Quinn, RC**	.12	.25	.50
235	Paul Reinhart	.05	.10	.20
236	Doug Risebrough	.05	.10	.20
237	Steve Tambellini	.05	.10	.20

EDMONTON OILERS

No.	Player	VG	EX	NRMT
238	Glenn Anderson	.25	.50	1.00
239	Paul Coffey	1.10	2.25	4.50
240	Lee Fogolin	.05	.10	.20
241	Grant Fuhr, Goalie	1.00	2.00	4.00
242	Randall Gregg	.05	.10	.20
243	Wayne Gretzky	5.00	10.00	20.00
244	Charles Huddy	.05	.10	.20
245	Pat Hughes, LC	.05	.10	.20
246	Dave Hunter	.05	.10	.20
247	Don Jackson, LC	.05	.10	.20
248	Michael Krushelnyski (Now with Oilers)	.05	.10	.20
249	Jari Kurri	.75	1.50	3.00
250	Willy Lindstrom	.05	.10	.20
251	Kevin Lowe	.12	.25	.50
252	Dave Lumley, LC (Drafted to Hartford October 1984)	.05	.10	.20
253	**Kevin McClelland, RC**	.05	.10	.20
254	Mark Messier	1.75	3.50	7.00
255	Andrew Moog, Goalie	1.00	2.00	4.00
256	Jaroslav Pouzar, LC	.05	.10	.20

MONTREAL CANADIENS

No.	Player	VG	EX	NRMT
257	Guy Carbonneau	.60	1.25	2.50
258	**John Chabot, RC**	.05	.10	.20
259	**Chris Chelios, RC**	3.75	7.50	15.00
260	Lucien DeBlois, Error	.05	.10	.20
261	Bob Gainey	.07	.15	.30
262	Richard Green	.05	.10	.20
263	Jean Hamel, LC	.05	.10	.20
264	Guy Lafleur	.25	.50	1.00
265	Craig Ludwig	.05	.10	.20
266	Pierre Mondou	.05	.10	.20
267	Mats Naslund	.18	.35	.75
268	Christopher Nilan	.06	.12	.25
269	**Steve Penney, Goalie, RC**	.07	.15	.30
270	Larry Robinson	.10	.20	.40

TORONTO MAPLE LEAFS

No.	Player	VG	EX	NRMT
271	William Root, LC (Traded to Toronto Summer 1984)	.05	.10	.20

MONTREAL CANADIENS

No.	Player	VG	EX	NRMT
272	Steve Shutt, LC	.07	.15	.30
273	Robert Smith	.07	.15	.30
274	Mario Tremblay	.05	.10	.20
275	Ryan Walter	.05	.10	.20

QUEBEC NORDIQUES

No.	Player	VG	EX	NRMT
276	**Bo Berglund, RC, LC**	.05	.10	.20
277	Dan Bouchard, Goalie	.05	.10	.20
278	Alain Coté	.05	.10	.20

NEW YORK RANGERS

No.	Player	VG	EX	NRMT
279	André Doré, LC (Drafted to New York Rangers October 1984)	.05	.10	.20

O-Pee-Chee
1984-85 Issue
Card No. 229,
Hakan Loob

O-Pee-Chee
1984-85 Issue
Card No. 258,
John Chabot

O-Pee-Chee
1984-85 Issue
Card No. 259,
Chris Chelios

O-Pee-Chee
1984-85 Issue
Card No. 307,
Gary Nylund

QUEBEC NORDIQUES

No.	Player	VG	EX	NRMT
280	Michel Goulet	.25	.50	1.00
281	Dale Hunter	.05	.10	.20
282	Mario Marois	.05	.10	.20
283	Anthony McKegney	.05	.10	.20
284	Randy Moller	.05	.10	.20
285	Wilf Paiement	.05	.10	.20
286	Pat Price, LC	.05	.10	.20
287	Normand Rochefort	.05	.10	.20
288	Andre Savard, LC	.05	.10	.20
289	Richard Sevigny, Goalie, LC	.05	.10	.20

BOSTON BRUINS

No.	Player	VG	EX	NRMT
290	Louis Sleigher, (Now with Bruins), LC	.05	.10	.20

QUEBEC NORDIQUES

No.	Player	VG	EX	NRMT
291	Anton Stastny	.05	.10	.20
292	Marian Stastny, LC	.05	.10	.20
293	Peter Stastny	.60	1.25	2.50
294	Blake Wesley, LC	.05	.10	.20

TORONTO MAPLE LEAFS

No.	Player	VG	EX	NRMT
295	John Anderson	.05	.10	.20
296	Jim Benning	.05	.10	.20
297	**Allan Bester, Goalie, RC, Error**	.12	.25	.50
298	**Rich Costello, RC, LC**	.05	.10	.20
299	Dan Daoust	.05	.10	.20
300	Bill Derlago	.05	.10	.20
301	Dave Farrish, LC	.05	.10	.20
302	Robert (Stewart) Gavin	.05	.10	.20
303	Gaston Gingras	.05	.10	.20
304	James Korn	.05	.10	.20
305	**Gary Leeman, RC**	.25	.50	1.00

EDMONTON OILERS

No.	Player	VG	EX	NRMT
306	Terry Martin, LC (Drafted to Edmonton October 1984)	.05	.10	.20

TORONTO MAPLE LEAFS

No.	Player	VG	EX	NRMT
307	**Gary Nylund, RC**	.07	.15	.30
308	Mike Palmateer, Goalie, LC	.05	.10	.20
309	Walter Poddubny	.05	.10	.20
310	Rick St. Croix, Goalie, LC	.05	.10	.20
311	Borje Salming	.10	.20	.40
312	Greg Terrion	.05	.10	.20
313	Richard Vaive	.07	.15	.30

VANCOUVER CANUCKS

No.	Player	VG	EX	NRMT
314	Richard Brodeur, Goalie	.05	.10	.20
315	Jiri Bubla, LC	.05	.10	.20
316	Ron Delorme, LC	.05	.10	.20
317	John Garrett, Goalie, LC	.05	.10	.20
318	Jere Gillis, LC	.05	.10	.20
319	Thomas Gradin	.05	.10	.20
320	Doug Halward	.05	.10	.20
321	Rick Lanz	.05	.10	.20
322	**Moe Lemay, RC**	.05	.10	.20
323	Gary Lupul, LC	.05	.10	.20
324	Al MacAdam (Now with Canucks)	.05	.10	.20
325	Rob McClanahan, LC	.05	.10	.20
326	Peter McNab, LC	.05	.10	.20
327	**Cam Neely, RC**	8.75	17.50	35.00
328	Darcy Rota, LC	.05	.10	.20
329	**Andy Schliebener, RC, LC**	.05	.10	.20
330	Stanley Smyl	.05	.10	.20
331	Patrik Sundstrom	.05	.10	.20
332	Tony Tanti	.05	.10	.20

WINNIPEG JETS

No.	Player	VG	EX	NRMT
333	Scott Arniel	.05	.10	.20
334	Dave Babych	.05	.10	.20
335	Laurie Boschman	.05	.10	.20
336	Wade Campbell, LC	.05	.10	.20

— 1985 - 86 REGULAR ISSUE — O-PEE-CHEE • 93

No.	Player	VG	EX	NRMT
337	Randy Carlyle	.05	.10	.20
338	Jordy Douglas, LC	.05	.10	.20
339	Dale Hawerchuk	.75	1.50	3.00
340	Morris Lukowich	.05	.10	.20
341	Bengt Lundholm, LC	.05	.10	.20
342	Paul MacLean	.05	.10	.20
343	**Andrew McBain, RC**	**.05**	**.10**	**.20**
344	Brian Mullen	.05	.10	.20
345	Robert Picard	.05	.10	.20
346	Douglas Smail	.05	.10	.20

MONTREAL CANADIENS

No.	Player	VG	EX	NRMT
347	Doug Soetaert, Goalie, LC (Traded to Montreal October 1984)	.06	.12	.25

WINNIPEG JETS

No.	Player	VG	EX	NRMT
348	Thomas Steen	.05	.10	.20
349	Perry Turnbull	.05	.10	.20
350	Timothy Watters	.05	.10	.20
351	Tim Young, LC	.05	.10	.20

TEAM LEADERS

No.	Player	VG	EX	NRMT
352	**Boston Bruins:** Rick Middleton	.05	.10	.20
353	**Buffalo Sabres:** Dave Andreychuk	.50	1.00	2.00
354	**Calgary Flames:** Ed Beers	.05	.10	.20
355	**Chicago Black Hawks:** Denis Savard	.12	.25	.50
356	**Detroit Red Wings:** John Ogrodnick	.06	.12	.25
357	**Edmonton Oilers Leader:** Wayne Gretzky	1.25	2.50	5.00
358	**Los AngelesKings Leader:** Charlie Simmer	.05	.10	.20
359	**Minnesota North Stars:** Brian Bellows	.12	.25	.50
360	**Montreal Canadiens:** Guy Lafleur	.18	.35	.75
361	**New Jersey Devils:** Mel Bridgman	.05	.10	.20
362	**New York Islanders:** Mike Bossy	.18	.35	.75
363	**New York Rangers:** Pierre Larouche	.05	.10	.20
364	**Philadelphia Flyers:** Tim Kerr	.05	.10	.20
365	**Pittsburgh Penguins:** Mike Bullard	.05	.10	.20
366	**Quebec Nordiques:** Michel Goulet	.12	.25	.50
367	**St. Louis Blues:** B. Federko & J. Mullen	.07	.15	.30
368	**Toronto Maple Leafs:** Richard Vaive	.05	.10	.20
369	**Vancouver Canucks:** Tony Tanti	.05	.10	.20
370	**Washington Capitals:** Michael Gartner	.07	.15	.30
371	**Winnipeg Jets:** Paul MacLean	.05	.10	.20
372	**Hartford Whalers:** Sylvain Turgeon	.05	.10	.20

TROPHY WINNERS

No.	Player	VG	EX	NRMT
373	**Art Ross Trophy:** Wayne Gretzky	1.25	2.50	5.00
374	**Hart Trophy:** Wayne Gretzky	1.25	2.50	5.00
375	**Calder Trophy:** Tom Barrasso	.50	1.00	2.00
376	**Lady Byng Trophy:** Mike Bossy	.18	.35	.75
377	**Norris Trophy:** Rod Langway	.05	.10	.20
378	**Masterton Trophy:** Brad Park	.07	.15	.30
379	**Vezina Trophy:** Tom Barrasso	.25	.50	1.00

LEAGUE LEADERS

No.	Player	VG	EX	NRMT
380	**Scoring:** Wayne Gretzky, Edm.	1.25	2.50	5.00
381	**Goals:** Wayne Gretzky, Edm.	1.25	2.50	5.00
382	**Assists:** Wayne Gretzky, Edm.	1.25	2.50	5.00
383	**Power Play Goals:** Wayne Gretzky, Edm.	1.25	2.50	5.00
384	**Game Winning Goals:** Michel Goulet, Que.	.12	.25	.50
385	**Rookie Scorer:** Stever Yzerman, Det.	1.75	3.50	7.00
386	**Goals Against Average:** Pat Riggin, Wash.	.05	.10	.20
387	**Save Percentage:** Roland Melanson, NYI	.05	.10	.20

RECORD BREAKERS

No.	Player	VG	EX	NRMT
388	Wayne Gretzky, Edm.	1.25	2.50	5.00
389	Denis Potvin, NYI	.18	.35	.75
390	Brad Park, Det., LC	.10	.20	.40
391	Michel Goulet, Que.	.12	.25	.50
392	Pat LaFontaine, NYI	1.50	3.00	6.00
393	Dale Hawerchuk, Win.	.25	.50	1.00

O-Pee-Chee 1985-86 Issue Card No. 1, Lanny McDonald

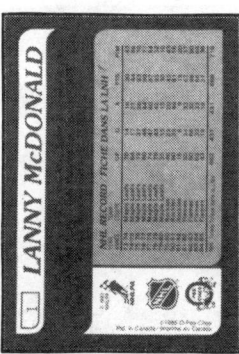

O-Pee-Chee 1985-86 Issue Card No. 1, Lanny McDonald

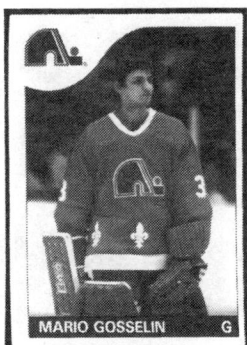

O-Pee-Chee 1985-86 Issue Card No. 18, Mario Gosselin

O-Pee-Chee 1985-86 Issue Card No. 34, Kevin Dineen

CHECKLIST

No.	Player	VG	EX	NRMT
394	Checklist 1 (1 - 132)	.75	1.50	3.00
395	Checklist 2 (133 -264)	.75	1.50	3.00
396	Checklist 3 (264 - 396)	.75	1.50	3.00

— 1985 - 86 REGULAR ISSUE —

Mint cards command a price premium of 25% over NRMT cards.

PRICE MOVEMENT OF NRMT SETS

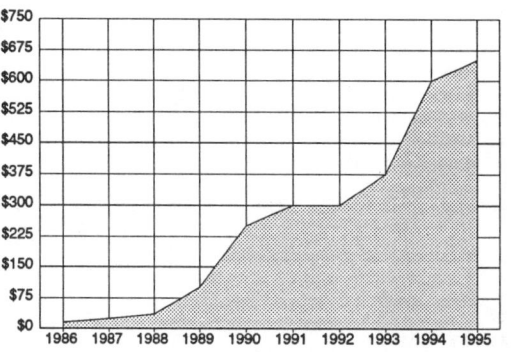

Card Size: 2 1/2" X 3 1/2"
Face: Four colour, white border, Team logo, Position
Back: Rust and blue on card stock, Number, Resume, Bilingual
Imprint: © 1985 O-Pee-Chee Ptd. in Canada/Imprimé au Canada
© 1985 NHLPA
Complete Set No.: 264

Complete Set Price:	160.00	325.00	650.00
Common Card:	.07	.15	.30
Wax Pack: (10 Cards)			50.00
Wax Box: (48 Packs)			22,000.00
Wax Case: (16 Boxes)			

No.	Player	VG	EX	NRMT
1	Lanny McDonald, Cal.	.15	.30	.60
2	Michael O'Connell, Bos.	.07	.15	.30
3	Curt Fraser, Chi.	.07	.15	.30
4	Steve Penney, Goalie, Mon.	.07	.15	.30
5	Brian Engblom, LA	.07	.15	.30
6	Ronald Sutter, Phi.	.07	.15	.30
7	Joe Mullen, St. L.	.35	.75	1.50
8	Rod Langway, Wash.	.07	.15	.30
9	**Mario Lemieux, Pit., RC**	**115.00**	**225.00**	**450.00**
10	David Babych, Win.	.07	.15	.30
11	Bob Nystrom, NYI	.07	.15	.30
12	Andrew Moog, Goalie, Edm.	.75	1.50	3.00
13	Dino Ciccarelli, Min.	.15	.30	.60
14	Dwight Foster, Det., LC	.07	.15	.30
15	James Patrick, NYR	.15	.30	.60
16	Thomas Gradin, Van., LC	.07	.15	.30
17	Mike Foligno, Buf.	.07	.15	.30
18	**Mario Gosselin, Goalie, Que., RC**	**.15**	**.30**	**.60**
19	Mike Zuke, Har., LC	.07	.15	.30
20	John Anderson, Que. (Now with Nordiques)	.07	.15	.30
21	Dave Pichette, NJ, LC	.07	.15	.30
22	Nick Fotiu, NYR, LC	.07	.15	.30
23	Tom Lysiak, Chi., LC	.07	.15	.30
24	**Peter Zezel, Phi., RC**	**1.25**	**2.50**	**5.00**
25	Denis Potvin, NYI	.18	.35	.75
26	Robert Carpenter, Wash.	.07	.15	.30
27	Murray Bannerman, Goalie, Chi.	.07	.15	.30
28	Gordon Roberts, Min.	.07	.15	.30
29	Steve Yzerman, Det.	6.25	12.50	25.00
30	Phil Russell, NJ	.07	.15	.30
31	Peter Stastny, Que.	.40	.85	1.75
32	Craig Ramsay, Buf., LC	.07	.15	.30
33	Terry Ruskowski, Pit.	.07	.15	.30
34	**Kevin Dineen, Har., RC**	**2.00**	**4.00**	**8.00**
35	Mark Howe, Phi.	.07	.15	.30
36	Glenn Resch, Goalie, NJ	.07	.15	.30
37	Danny Gare, Det.	.07	.15	.30
38	**Doug Bodger, Pit., RC**	**.18**	**.35**	**.75**

94 • O-PEE-CHEE — 1985 - 86 REGULAR ISSUE —

No.	Player	VG	EX	NRMT
39	Mike Rogers, NYR, LC	.07	.15	.30
40	Raymond Bourque, Bos.	1.25	2.50	5.00
41	John Tonelli, NYI	.07	.15	.30
42	Mel Bridgman, NJ	.07	.15	.30
43	Sylvain Turgeon, Har.	.07	.15	.30
44	Mark Johnson, St. L.	.07	.15	.30
45	Douglas Wilson, Chi.	.10	.20	.40
46	Michael Gartner, Wash.	.1.00	2.00	4.00
47	Brent Peterson, Buf.	.07	.15	.30
48	Paul Reinhart, Cal.	.07	.15	.30
49	Michael Krushelnyski, Edm.	.07	.15	.30
50	Brian Bellows, Min.	.30	.65	1.25
51	Chris Chelios, Mon.	.85	1.75	3.50
52	Barry Pederson, Bos.	.07	.15	.30
53	Murray Craven, Phi.	.07	.15	.30
54	Pierre Larouche, NYR, LC	.07	.15	.30
55	Reed Larson, Det.	.07	.15	.30
56	Patrick Verbeek, NJ	.25	.50	1.00
57	Randy Carlyle, Win.	.07	.15	.30
58	Ray Neufeld, Har.	.07	.15	.30
59	Keith Brown, Chi.	.07	.15	.30
60	Bryan Trottier, NYI	.18	.35	.75
61	Jim Fox, LA	.07	.15	.30
62	Scott Stevens, Wash.	.85	1.75	3.50
63	Phil Housley, Buf.	.50	1.00	2.00
64	Rick Middleton, Bos.	.07	.15	.30
65	Steve Payne, Min.	.07	.15	.30
66	Dave Lewis, NJ	.07	.15	.30
67	Mike Bullard, Pit.	.07	.15	.30
68	Stanley Smyl, Van.	.07	.15	.30
69	Mark Pavelich, NYR, LC	.07	.15	.30
70	John Ogrodnick, Det.	.07	.15	.30
71	Bill Derlago, Bos. (Now with Bruins)	.07	.15	.30
72	Bradley Marsh, Phi.	.07	.15	.30
73	Denis Savard, Chi.	.40	.85	1.75
74	Mark Fusco, Har., RC, LC	.07	.15	.30
75	Peter Peeters, Goalie, Wash. (Now with Capitals)	.07	.15	.30
76	Douglas Gilmour, St. L.	7.50	15.00	30.00
77	Michael Ramsey, Buf.	.07	.15	.30
78	Anton Stastny, Que.	.07	.15	.30
79	Stephen Kasper, Bos.	.07	.15	.30
80	Bryan Erickson, Wash., RC	.07	.15	.30
81	Clark Gillies, NYI	.07	.15	.30
82	Keith Acton, Min.	.07	.15	.30
83	Patrick Flatley, NYI	.07	.15	.30
84	Kirk Muller, NJ, RC	4.50	9.00	18.00
85	Paul Coffey, Edm.	1.00	2.00	4.00
86	Ed Olczyk, Chi., RC	.75	1.50	3.00
87	Charlie Simmer, Bos.	.07	.15	.30
88	Michael Liut, Goalie, Har.	.07	.15	.30
89	Dave Maloney, Buf., LC (Retired July 1985)	.07	.15	.30
90	Marcel Dionne, LA	.25	.50	1.00
91	Tim Kerr, Phi.	.07	.15	.30
92	Ivan Boldirev, Det., LC	.07	.15	.30
93	Ken Morrow, NYI	.07	.15	.30
94	Donald Maloney, NYR	.07	.15	.30
95	Rejean Lemelin, Goalie, Cal.	.07	.15	.30
96	Curt Giles, Min.	.07	.15	.30
97	Bob Bourne, NYI	.07	.15	.30
98	Joe Cirella, NJ	.07	.15	.30
99	Dave Christian, Wash.	.07	.15	.30
100	Darryl Sutter, Chi.	.07	.15	.30
101	Kelly Kisio, Det.	.12	.25	.50
102	Mats Naslund, Mon.	.10	.20	.40
103	Joel Quenneville, Har.	.07	.15	.30
104	Bernie Federko, St. L.	.07	.15	.30
105	Tom Barrasso, Goalie, Buf.	1.25	2.50	5.00
106	Richard Vaive, Tor.	.07	.15	.30
107	Brent Sutter, NYI	.10	.20	.40
108	Wayne Babych, Que. (Now with Nordiques)	.07	.15	.30
109	Dale Hawerchuk, Win.	.75	1.50	3.00
110	Pelle Lindbergh, Goalie, Phi., LC	3.75	7.50	15.00
111	Dennis Maruk, Min.	.07	.15	.30
112	Reijo Ruotsalainen, NYR	.07	.15	.30
113	Tom Fergus, Tor. (Now with Maple Leafs)	.07	.15	.30
114	Bob Murray, Chi.	.07	.15	.30
115	Patrik Sundstrom, Van.	.07	.15	.30
116	Ron Duguay, Det.	.07	.15	.30
117	Alan Haworth, Wash.	.07	.15	.30
118	Greg Malone, Har., LC	.07	.15	.30
119	Bill Hajt, Buf.	.07	.15	.30

O-Pee-Chee
1985-86 Issue
Card No. 51,
Chris Chelios

O-Pee-Chee
1985-86 Issue
Card No. 80,
Bryan Erickson

O-Pee-Chee
1985-86 Issue
Card No. 122,
Kelly Hrudey

O-Pee-Chee
1985-86 Issue
Card No. 137,
Pat LaFontaine

No.	Player	VG	EX	NRMT
120	Wayne Gretzky, Edm.	6.25	12.50	25.00
121	Craig Redmond, LA, RC, LC	.07	.15	.30
122	Kelly Hrudey, Goalie, NYI, RC	2.50	5.00	10.00
123	Tomas Sandstrom, NYR, RC	2.50	5.00	10.00
124	Neal Broten, Min.	.07	.15	.30
125	Maurice Mantha, Pit.	.07	.15	.30
126	Gregory Gilbert, NYI	.07	.15	.30
127	Bruce Driver, NJ, RC	.40	.85	1.75
128	David Poulin, Phi.	.07	.15	.30
129	Morris Lukowich, Bos., LC	.07	.15	.30
130	Mike Bossy, NYI	.30	.65	1.25
131	Larry Playfair, Buf.	.07	.15	.30
132	Steve Larmer, Chi.	1.00	2.00	4.00
133	Doug Keans, Goalie, Bos.	.07	.15	.30
134	Bob Manno, Det., (Free agent, now playing with team in Italy), LC	.07	.15	.30
135	Brian Sutter, St. L.	.07	.15	.30
136	Pat Riggin, Goalie, Bos., LC (Now with Bruins)	.07	.15	.30
137	Pat LaFontaine, NYI	5.00	10.00	20.00
138	Barry Beck, NYR, LC	.07	.15	.30
139	Rich Preston, NJ	.07	.15	.30
140	Ron Francis, Har.	.25	.50	1.00
141	Brian Propp, Phi.	.03	.15	.30
142	Donald Beaupre, Goalie, Min.	.07	.15	.30
143	Dave Andreychuk, Buf.	3.00	6.00	12.00
144	Ed Beers, Cal.	.07	.15	.30
145	Paul MacLean, Win.	.07	.15	.30
146	Troy Murray, Chi.	.07	.15	.30
147	Larry Robinson, Mon.	.12	.25	.50
148	Bernie Nicholls, LA	.40	.85	1.75
149	Glen Hanlon, Goalie, NYR	.07	.15	.30
150	Michel Goulet, Que.	.25	.50	1.00
151	Doug Jarvis, Wash.	.07	.15	.30
152	Warren Young, Det., RC (Now with Detroit)	.10	.20	.40
153	Tony Tanti, Van.	.07	.15	.30
154	Tomas Jonsson, NYI	.07	.15	.30
155	Jari Kurri, Edm.	.60	1.25	2.50
156	Anthony McKegney, Min.	.07	.15	.30
157	Gregory Stefan, Goalie, Det.	.07	.15	.30
158	Byron (Brad) McCrimmon, Phi.	.07	.15	.30
159	Keith Crowder, Bos.	.07	.15	.30
160	Gilbert Perreault, Buf.	.12	.25	.50
161	Tim Bothwell, Har. (Now with Whalers)	.07	.15	.30
162	Bob Crawford, Har., LC	.07	.15	.30
163	Paul Gagne, NJ, LC	.07	.15	.30
164	Dan Daoust, Tor.	.07	.15	.30
165	Checklist 1 (1 - 132)	1.50	3.00	6.00
166	Tim Bernhardt, Goalie, Tor., RC	.07	.15	.30
167	Gordon Kluzak, Bos.	.07	.15	.30
168	Glenn Anderson, Edm.	.15	.30	.60
169	Bob Gainey, Mon.	.07	.15	.30
170	Brent Ashton, Que.	.07	.15	.30
171	Ron Flockhart, St. L.	.07	.15	.30
172	Gary Nylund, Tor.	.07	.15	.30
173	Moe Lemay, Van.	.07	.15	.30
174	Bob Sauve, Goalie, Chi.	.07	.15	.30
175	Douglas Smail, Win.	.07	.15	.30
176	Dan Quinn, Cal.	.07	.15	.30
177	Mark Messier, Edm.	1.75	3.50	7.00
178	Gordon (Jay) Wells, LA, RC	.07	.15	.30
179	Dale Hunter, Que.	.07	.15	.30
180	Richard Brodeur, Goalie, Van.	.07	.15	.30
181	Robert Smith, Mon.	.07	.15	.30
182	Ronald Greschner, NYR	.07	.15	.30
183	Don Edwards, Goalie, Tor., LC	.07	.15	.30
184	Hakan Loob, Cal.	.07	.15	.30
185	Dave Ellett, Win., RC	1.85	3.75	7.50
186	Denis Herron, Goalie, Pit., LC	.07	.15	.30
187	Charles Huddy, Edm.	.07	.15	.30
188	Ilkka Sinisalo, Phi.	.07	.15	.30
189	Doug Halward, Van.	.07	.15	.30
190	Craig Laughlin, Wash.	.07	.15	.30
191	Carey Wilson, Cal., RC	.15	.30	.60
192	Craig Ludwig, Mon.	.07	.15	.30
193	Bob MacMillan, Chi., LC	.07	.15	.30
194	Mario Marois, Que.	.07	.15	.30
195	Brian Mullen, Win.	.07	.15	.30
196	George (Rob) Ramage, St. L.	.07	.15	.30
197	Rick Lanz, Van.	.07	.15	.30
198	Miroslav Frycer, Tor.	.07	.15	.30
199	Randall Gregg, Edm.	.07	.15	.30

1986 - 87 REGULAR ISSUE — O-PEE-CHEE

Mint cards command a price premium of 25% over NRMT cards.

PRICE MOVEMENT OF NRMT SETS

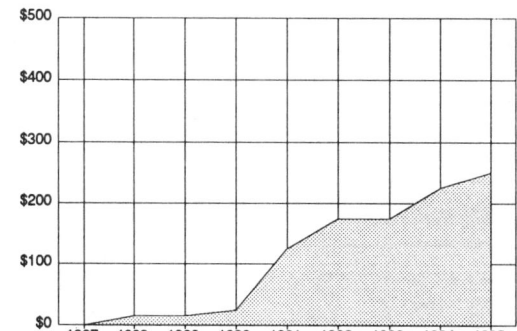

Card Size: 2 1/2" X 3 1/2"
Face: Four colour, white border, Team Logo, Position
Back: Blue and black on card stock, Number, Resume, Bilingual
Imprint: © 1986 O-Pee-Chee Ptd. in Canada/Imprimé au Canada
© 1986 NHLPA
Complete Set No.: 264

	VG	EX	NRMT
Complete Set Price:	70.00	140.00	275.00
Common Card:		.03	.07	.15
Wax Pack: (7 Cards)			18.00
Wax Box: (48 Packs)			1,000.00
Wax Case: (16 Boxes)			14,500.00

No.	Player	VG	EX	NRMT
1	Raymond Bourque, Bos.	.85	1.75	3.50
2	Pat LaFontaine, NYI	2.00	4.00	8.00
3	Wayne Gretzky, Edm.	4.50	9.00	18.00
4	Lindy Ruff, Buf.	.03	.07	.15
5	Byron (Brad) McCrimmon, Phi.	.03	.07	.15
6	David Williams, LA, LC	.03	.07	.15
7	Denis Savard, Chi.	.30	.60	1.25
8	Lanny McDonald, Cal.	.12	.25	.50
9	John Vanbiesbrouck, Goalie, NYR, RC	3.75	7.50	15.00
10	Greg Adams, NJ, RC	.50	1.00	2.00
11	Steve Yzerman, Det.	3.25	6.50	13.00
12	Craig Hartsburg, Min.	.03	.07	.15
13	John Anderson, Har.	.03	.07	.15
14	Bob Bourne, LA (Now with Kings)	.03	.07	.15
15	Kjell Dahlin, Mon., RC, LC	.15	.30	.60
16	David Andreychuk, Buf.	1.75	3.50	7.00
17	George (Rob) Ramage, St. L.	.03	.07	.15
18	Ronald Greschner, NYR	.03	.07	.15
19	Bruce Driver, NJ	.03	.07	.15
20	Peter Stastny, Que.	.35	.75	1.50
21	Dave Christian, Wash.	.03	.07	.15
22	Doug Keans, Goalie, Bos.	.05	.10	.20
23	Scott Bjugstad, Min., RC	.07	.15	.30
24	Doug Bodger, Pit.	.03	.07	.15
25	Troy Murray, Chi.	.03	.07	.15
26	Al Iafrate, Tor.	1.35	2.75	5.50
27	Kelly Hrudey, Goalie, NYI	.50	1.00	2.00
28	Doug Jarvis, Har.	.03	.07	.15
29	Richard Sutter, Van.	.03	.07	.15
30	Marcel Dionne, LA	.20	.40	.80
31	Curt Fraser, Chi., LC	.03	.07	.15
32	Doug Lidster, Van.	.03	.07	.15
33	Brian MacLellan, Min. (Now with Northstars)	.03	.07	.15
34	Barry Pederson, Van.	.03	.07	.15
35	Craig Laughlin, Wash.	.03	.07	.15
36	Ilkka Sinisalo, Phi.	.03	.07	.15
37	John MacLean, NJ, RC	1.75	3.50	7.00
38	Brian Mullen, Win.	.03	.07	.15
39	Duane Sutter, NYI	.03	.07	.15
40	Brian Engblom, Cal., LC (Now with Flames)	.03	.07	.15
41	Chris Cichocki, Det., RC, LC	.03	.07	.15
42	Gordon Roberts, Min.	.03	.07	.15
43	Ron Francis, Har.	.25	.50	1.00
44	Joe Mullen, Cal.	.25	.50	1.00
45	Maurice Mantha, Pit.	.03	.07	.15

No.	Player	VG	EX	NRMT
200	Corrado Micalef, Goalie, Det., LC	.07	.15	.30
201	Jamie Macoun, Cal.	.07	.15	.30
202	Bob Brooke, NYR, RC	.07	.15	.30
203	Billy Carroll, Edm., LC	.07	.15	.30
204	Brian MacLellan, LA	.07	.15	.30
205	Alain Coté, Que.	.07	.15	.30
206	Thomas Steen, Win.	.07	.15	.30
207	Grant Fuhr, Goalie, Edm.	.75	1.50	3.00
208	Richard Sutter, Phi.	.07	.15	.30
209	Al MacAdam, Van., LC	.07	.15	.30
210	Al Iafrate, Tor., RC	5.50	11.00	22.00
211	Pierre Mondou, Mon., (Now Retired) LC	.07	.15	.30
212	Randy Hillier, Pit., RC	.07	.15	.30
213	Mike Eaves, Cal., (Now Retired) LC	.07	.15	.30
214	David Taylor, LA	.07	.15	.30
215	Robert Picard, Win.	.07	.15	.30
216	Randy Ladouceur, Det.	.07	.15	.30
217	Willy Lindstrom, Pit.	.07	.15	.30
218	Torrie Robertson, Har., RC	.07	.15	.30
219	Tom Kurvers, Mon., RC	.18	.35	.75
220	John Garrett, Van. (Now Assistant General Manager)	.07	.15	.30
221	Greg Millen, Goalie, St. L.	.07	.15	.30
222	Richard Kromm, Cal.	.07	.15	.30
223	Bob Janecyk, Goalie, LA, RC	.15	.30	.60
224	Brad Maxwell, Tor.	.07	.15	.30
225	Michael McPhee, Mon., RC	.75	1.50	3.00
226	Brian Hayward, Goalie, Win., RC	.75	1.50	3.00
227	Duane Sutter, NYI	.07	.15	.30
228	Cam Neely, Van.	3.75	7.50	15.00
229	Douglas Wickenheiser, St. L.	.07	.15	.30
230	Roland Melanson, Goalie, Min.	.07	.15	.30
231	Bruce Bell, St. L., RC, LC	.07	.15	.30
232	Harold Snepsts, Det.	.07	.15	.30
233	Guy Carbonneau, Mon.	.12	.25	.50
234	Douglas Sulliman, NJ	.07	.15	.30
235	Lee Fogolin, Edm.	.07	.15	.30
236	Lawrence Murphy, Wash.	.07	.15	.30
237	Allan MacInnis, Cal., RC	8.75	17.50	35.00
238	Don Lever, Buf., LC	.07	.15	.30
239	Kevin Lowe, Edm.	.12	.25	.50
240	Randy Moller, Que.	.07	.15	.30
241	Doug Lidster, Van., RC	.25	.50	1.00
242	Craig Hartsburg, Min.	.07	.15	.30
243	Doug Risebrough, Cal.	.07	.15	.30
244	John Chabot, Pit.	.07	.15	.30
245	Mario Tremblay, Que.	.07	.15	.30
246	Dan Bouchard, Goalie, Win., LC	.07	.15	.30
247	Douglas Shedden, Pit.	.07	.15	.30
248	Borje Salming, Tor.	.07	.15	.30
249	Aaron Broten, NJ	.07	.15	.30
250	Jim Benning, Tor.	.07	.15	.30
251	Laurie Boschman, Win.	.07	.15	.30
252	George McPhee, NYR, RC, LC	.03	.15	.30
253	Mark Napier, Edm.	.07	.15	.30
254	Perry Turnbull, Win.	.07	.15	.30
255	Warren Skorodenski, Goalie, Chi., RC, LC	.03	.15	.30
256	Checklist 2 (133 - 264)	.75	1.50	3.00

LEAGUE LEADERS

No.	Player	VG	EX	NRMT
257	**Goals:** Wayne Gretzky, Edm.	1.50	3.00	6.00
258	**Assists:** Wayne Gretzky, Edm.	1.50	3.00	6.00
259	**Scoring:** Wayne Gretzky, Edm.	1.50	3.00	6.00
260	**Power Play Goals:** Tim Kerr, Phi.	.07	.15	.30
261	**Game Winning Goals:** Jari Kurri, Edm.	.25	.50	1.00
262	**Rookie Scorer:** Mario Lemieux, Pit.	10.00	20.00	45.00
263	**Goals Against Average:** Tom Barrasso, Goalie, Buf.	.07	.15	.30
264	**Save Percentage:** Warren Skorodenski, Goalie, Chi.	.10	.20	.40

Note: *The Charlton Standard Catalogue of Hockey Cards* arranges cards in their issue date order. This means the first date a manufacturer issues a card set determines the sequence of the manufacturer in the Standard Catalogue. In this manner the historical importance of early cards is maintained. See the last page of this catalogue for an alphabetical index of issuers.

O-Pee-Chee
1986-87 Issue
Card No. 1,
Raymond Bourque

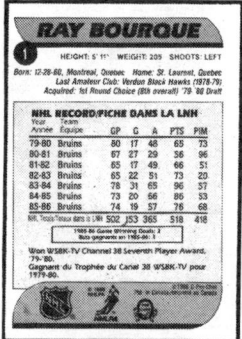

O-Pee-Chee
1986-87 Issue
Card No. 1,
Raymond Bourque

O-Pee-Chee
1986-87 Issue
Card No. 9,
John Vanbiesbrouck

O-Pee-Chee
1986-87 Issue
Card No. 37,
John MacLean

96 • O-PEE-CHEE — 1986-87 REGULAR ISSUE —

No.	Player	VG	EX	NRMT
46	Patrick Verbeek, NJ	.18	.35	.75
47	**Clint Malarchuk, Goalie, Que., RC**	**.25**	**.50**	**1.00**
48	Bob Brooke, NYR	.03	.07	.15
49	Darryl Sutter, Chi., LC	.03	.07	.15
50	Stanley Smyl, Van.	.03	.07	.15
51	Gregory Stefan, Goalie, Det.	.05	.10	.20
52	Bill Hajt, Buf., LC	.03	.07	.15
53	**Patrick Roy, Goalie, Mon., RC**	**35.00**	**70.00**	**145.00**
54	Gordon Kluzak, Bos.	.03	.07	.15
55	Robert Froese, Goalie, Phi.	.05	.10	.20
56	Grant Fuhr, Goalie, Edm.	.35	.75	1.50
57	Mark Hunter, St. L.	.03	.07	.15
58	**Dana Murzyn, Har., RC**	**.07**	**.15**	**.30**
59	Michael Gartner, Wash.	.25	.50	1.00
60	Dennis Maruk, Min.	.03	.07	.15
61	Rich Preston, Chi., LC (Now with Black Hawks)	.03	.07	.15
62	Larry Robinson, Mon.	.10	.20	.40
63	David Taylor, LA	.03	.07	.15
64	Bob Murray, Chi.	.03	.07	.15
65	Ken Morrow, NYI	.03	.07	.15
66	**Mike Ridley, NYR, RC**	**1.00**	**2.00**	**4.00**
67	**John Tucker, Buf., RC**	**.12**	**.25**	**.50**
68	Miroslav Frycer, Tor., LC	.03	.07	.15
69	Danny Gare, Edm., (Now with Oilers) LC	.03	.07	.15
70	**Randy Burridge, Bos., RC**	**.50**	**1.00**	**2.00**
71	David Poulin, Phi.	.03	.07	.15
72	Brian Sutter, St. L., LC	.03	.07	.15
73	Dave Babych, Har.	.03	.07	.15
74	Dale Hawerchuk, Win.	.35	.75	1.50
75	Brian Bellows, Min.	.18	.35	.75
76	**Dave Pasin, Bos., RC, LC**	**.03**	**.07**	**.15**
77	Peter Peeters, Goalie, Wash.	.07	.15	.30
78	Tomas Jonsson, NYI	.03	.07	.15
79	Gilbert Perreault, Buf., LC	.12	.25	.50
80	Glenn Anderson, Edm.	.25	.50	1.00
81	Donald Maloney, NYR	.03	.07	.15
82	Ed Olczyk, Chi.	.12	.25	.50
83	Mike Bullard, Pit	.03	.07	.15
84	Tom Fergus, Tor.	.03	.07	.15
85	Dave Lewis, Det. (Now with Red Wings)	.03	.07	.15
86	Brian Propp, Phi.	.07	.15	.30
87	John Ogrodnick, Det.	.03	.07	.15
88	Kevin Dineen, Har.	.30	.60	1.25
89	Don Beaupre, Goalie, Min.	.05	.10	.20
90	Mike Bossy, NYI	.25	.50	1.00
91	Tom Barrasso, Goalie, Buf.	.50	1.00	2.00
92	Michel Goulet, Que.	.10	.20	.40
93	Douglas Gilmour, St. L.	3.75	7.50	15.00
94	Kirk Muller, NJ	1.00	2.00	4.00
95	**Larry Melnyk, NYR, RC**	**.03**	**.07**	**.15**
96	Bob Gainey, Mon.	.07	.15	.30
97	Stephen Kasper, Bos.	.03	.07	.15
98	**Petr Klima, Det., RC**	**.75**	**1.50**	**3.00**
99	Neal Broten, Min.	.03	.07	.15
100	Al Secord, Chi.	.03	.07	.15
101	Bryan Erickson, LA	.03	.07	.15
102	Rejean Lemelin, Goalie, Cal.	.05	.10	.20
103	Sylvain Turgeon, Har.	.03	.07	.15
104	Bob Nystrom, NYI, (Now Assistant Coach with Islanders) LC	.03	.07	.15
105	Bernie Federko, St. L.	.03	.07	.15
106	Doug Wilson, Chi.	.10	.20	.40
107	Alan Haworth, Wash.	.03	.07	.15
108	Jari Kurri, Edm.	.25	.50	1.00
109	Ronald Sutter, Phi.	.03	.07	.15
110	Reed Larson, Bos.	.03	.07	.15
111	Terry Ruskowski, Pit.	.03	.07	.15
112	Mark Johnson, NJ	.03	.07	.15
113	James Patrick, NYR	.03	.07	.15
114	Paul MacLean, Win.	.03	.07	.15
115	Michael Ramsey, Buf.	.03	.07	.15
116	Kelly Kisio, NYR (Now with Rangers)	.03	.07	.15
117	Brent Sutter, NYI	.03	.07	.15
118	Joel Quenneville, Har.	.03	.07	.15
119	Curt Giles, Min.	.03	.07	.15
120	Tony Tanti, Van.	.03	.07	.15
121	Douglas Sulliman, NJ	.03	.07	.15
122	Mario Lemieux, Pit.	17.50	35.00	70.00
123	Mark Howe, Phi.	.07	.15	.25
124	Bob Sauve, Goalie, Chi.	.05	.10	.20
125	Anton Stastny, Que.	.03	.07	.15
126	Scott Stevens, Wash.	.35	.75	1.50
127	Mike Foligno, Buf.	.03	.07	.15

O-Pee-Chee
1986-87 Issue
Card No. 53,
Patrick Roy

O-Pee-Chee
1986-87 Issue
Card No. 95,
Larry Melnyk

O-Pee-Chee
1986-87 Issue
Card No. 122,
Mario Lemieux

O-Pee-Chee
1986-87 Issue
Card No. 149,
Wendel Clark

No.	Player	VG	EX	NRMT
128	Reijo Ruotsalainen, NYR, LC (Free agent presently in Finland)	.03	.07	.15
129	Denis Potvin, NYI	.12	.25	.50
130	Keith Crowder, Bos.	.03	.07	.15
131	Bob Janecyk, Goalie, LA, LC	.05	.10	.20
132	John Tonelli, Cal.	.03	.07	.15
133	Michael Liut, Goalie, Har.	.07	.15	.30
134	Tim Kerr, Phi.	.05	.10	.20
135	Al Jensen, Goalie, Wash., LC	.05	.10	.20
136	Mel Bridgman, NJ	.03	.07	.15
137	Paul Coffey, Edm.	.50	1.00	2.00
138	Dino Ciccarelli, Min.	.10	.20	.40
139	Steve Larmer, Chi.	.35	.75	1.50
140	Michael O'Connell, Det.	.03	.07	.15
141	Clark Gillies, Buf. (Now with Sabres)	.03	.07	.15
142	Phil Russell, Buf., LC	.03	.07	.15
143	**Dirk Graham, Min., RC**	**.75**	**1.50**	**3.00**
144	Randy Carlyle, Win.	.03	.07	.15
145	Charlie Simmer, Bos.	.03	.07	.15
146	Ron Flockhart, St. L.	.03	.07	.15
147	Thomas Laidlaw, NYR	.03	.07	.15
148	**Dave Tippett, Har., RC**	**.10**	**.20**	**.40**
149	**Wendel Clark, Tor., RC**	**8.75**	**17.50**	**35.00**
150	Robert Carpenter, Wash.	.03	.07	.15
151	**Bill Watson, Chi., RC, LC**	**.03**	**.07**	**.15**
152	**Roberto Romano, Goalie, Pit., RC, LC**	**.07**	**.15**	**.30**
153	Douglas Shedden, Det.	.03	.07	.15
154	Phil Housley, Buf.	.25	.50	1.00
155	Bryan Trottier, NYI	.15	.30	.60
156	Patrik Sundstrom, Van.	.03	.07	.15
157	Rick Middleton, Bos.	.03	.07	.15
158	Glenn Resch, Goalie, Phi., LC	.07	.15	.30
159	Bernie Nicholls, LA	.30	.65	1.25
160	**Ray Ferraro, Har., RC**	**.85**	**1.75**	**3.50**
161	Mats Naslund, Mon.	.07	.15	.30
162	Patrick Flatley, NYI	.03	.07	.15
163	Joe Cirella, NJ	.03	.07	.15
164	Rod Langway, Wash.	.05	.10	.20
165	Checklist 1 (1 - 132)	1.00	2.00	4.00
166	Carey Wilson, Cal.	.03	.07	.15
167	Murray Craven, Phi.	.03	.07	.15
168	**Paul Gillis, Que., RC**	**.03**	**.07**	**.15**
169	Borje Salming, Tor.	.05	.10	.20
170	Perry Turnbull, Win., LC	.03	.07	.15
171	Chris Chelios, Mon.	.75	1.50	3.00
172	Keith Acton, Min.	.03	.07	.15
173	Allan MacInnis, Cal.	2.50	5.00	10.00
174	**Russ Courtnall, Tor., RC**	**1.75**	**3.50**	**7.00**
175	Bradley Marsh, Phi.	.03	.07	.15
176	Guy Carbonneau, Mon.	.10	.20	.40
177	Ray Neufeld, Win.	.03	.07	.15
178	**Craig MacTavish, Edm., RC**	**.50**	**1.00**	**2.00**
179	Rick Lanz, Van.	.03	.07	.15
180	Murray Bannerman, Goalie, Chi., LC	.05	.10	.20
181	Brent Ashton, Que.	.03	.07	.15
182	James Peplinski, Cal.	.03	.07	.15
183	Mark Napier, Edm., LC	.03	.07	.15
184	Laurie Boschman, Win.	.03	.07	.15
185	Lawrence Murphy, Wash.	.03	.07	.15
186	Mark Messier, Edm.	1.00	2.00	4.00
187	Risto Siltanen, Que., LC	.03	.07	.15
188	Robert Smith, Mon.	.05	.10	.20
189	**Gary Suter, Cal., RC**	**1.00**	**2.00**	**4.00**
190	Peter Zezel, Phi.	.03	.07	.15
191	Richard Vaive, Tor.	.03	.07	.15
192	Dale Hunter, Que.	.03	.07	.15
193	Michael Krushelnyski, Edm.	.03	.07	.15
194	Scott Arniel, Buf. (Now with Sabres)	.03	.07	.15
195	Larry Playfair, LA	.03	.07	.15
196	Doug Risebrough, Cal., LC	.03	.07	.15
197	Kevin Lowe, Edm.	.10	.20	.40
198	Checklist 2 (133 - 264)	1.00	2.00	4.00
199	Christopher Nilan, Mon.	.03	.07	.15
200	**Paul Cyr, Buf., RC**	**.03**	**.07**	**.15**
201	Ric Seiling, Det., LC	.03	.07	.15
202	Douglas Smith, Buf., LC	.03	.07	.15
203	Jamie Macoun, Cal.	.03	.07	.15
204	Dan Quinn, Cal.	.03	.07	.15
205	Paul Reinhart, Cal.	.03	.07	.15
206	Keith Brown, Chi.	.03	.07	.15
207	Jack O'Callahan, Chi., LC	.03	.07	.15
208	**Steve Richmond, NJ, RC, LC**	**.03**	**.07**	**.15**
209	Warren Young, Pit., LC	.03	.07	.15

— 1987 - 88 REGULAR ISSUE — O-PEE-CHEE

No.	Player	VG	EX	NRMT
210	Lee Fogolin, Edm., LC	.03	.07	.15
211	Charles Huddy, Edm.	.03	.07	.15
212	Andrew Moog, Goalie, Edm.	.50	1.00	2.00
213	Wayne Babych, Har., LC	.03	.07	.15
214	Torrie Robertson, Har.	.03	.07	.15
215	Jim Fox, LA	.03	.07	.15
216	**Phil Sykes, LA, RC**	**.03**	**.07**	**.15**
217	Gordon (Jay) Wells, LA	.03	.07	.15
218	Dave Langevin, Min., LC	.03	.07	.15
219	Steve Payne, Min., LC	.03	.07	.15
220	Craig Ludwig, Mon.	.03	.07	.15
221	Micheal McPhee, Mon.	.12	.25	.50
222	Steve Penney, Goalie, Win., LC	.05	.10	.20
223	Mario Tremblay, Mon., LC (Now retired from NHL)	.03	.07	.15
224	Ryan Walter, Mon.	.03	.07	.15
225	**Alain Chevrier, Goalie, NJ, RC**	**.15**	**.30**	**.60**
226	**Ullie Hiemer, NJ, RC, LC, Error**	**.03**	**.07**	**.15**
227	Tim Higgins, De*., LC	.03	.07	.15
228	Billy Smith, Goalie, NYI	.05	.15	.30
229	Richard Kromm, NYI, LC	.03	.07	.15
230	Tomas Sandstrom, NYR	1.00	2.00	4.00
231	**Jim Johnson, Pit., RC**	**.07**	**.15**	**.30**
232	Willy Lindstrom, Pit., LC	.03	.07	.15
233	Alain Cote, Que.	.03	.07	.15
234	Gilbert Delorme, Que.	.03	.07	.15
235	Mario Gosselin, Goalie, Que.	.05	.10	.20
236	**David Shaw, Que., RC**	**.07**	**.15**	**.30**
237	**Dave Barr, Har., RC**	**.10**	**.20**	**.40**
238	Ed Beers, St. L., LC	.03	.07	.15
239	**Charlie Bourgeois, St. L., RC, LC**	**.03**	**.07**	**.15**
240	Richard Wamsley, Goalie, St. L..	.05	.10	.20
241	Dan Daoust, Tor.	.03	.07	.15
242	Brad Maxwell, Van., LC	.03	.07	.15
243	Gary Nylund, Chi.	.03	.07	.15
244	Greg Terrion, Tor.	.03	.07	.15
245	**Steve Thomas, Tor., RC**	**1.00**	**2.00**	**4.00**
246	Richard Brodeur, Goalie, Van.	.05	.10	.20
247	**Joel Otto, RC, Error**	**.60**	**1.25**	**2.50**
248	Doug Halward, Van.	.03	.07	.15
249	Moe Lemay, (Now with Canucks) LC, Error	.07	.15	.30
250	Cam Neely, Bos.	1.75	3.50	7.00
251	Brent Peterson, Van.	.03	.07	.15
252	**Petri Skriko, Van., RC**	**.12**	**.25**	**.50**
253	**Greg Adams, Wash., RC**	**.03**	**.07**	**.15**
254	Bill Derlago, Win., LC	.03	.07	.15
255	Brian Hayward, Goalie, Mon.	.07	.15	.30
256	Douglas Smail, Win.	.03	.07	.15
257	Thomas Steen, Win.	.03	.07	.15

LEAGUE LEADERS

No.	Player	VG	EX	NRMT
258	**Goals:** Jari Kurri, Edm.	.25	.50	1.00
259	**Assists:** Wayne Gretzky, Edm.	1.25	2.50	5.00
260	**Scoring:** Wayne Gretzky, Edm.	1.25	2.50	5.00
261	**Power Play Goals:** Tim Kerr, Phi.	.05	.10	.20
262	**Rookie Scorer:** Kjell Dahlin, Mon.	.05	.10	.20
263	**Goals Against Average:** Robert Froese, Phi.	.05	.10	.20
264	**Save Percentage:** Robert Froese, Phi.	.12	.25	.50

Note: *The Charlton Standard Catalogue of Hockey Cards* arranges cards in their issue date order. This means the first date a manufacturer issues a card set determines the sequence of the manufacturer in the Standard Catalogue. In this manner the historical importance of early cards is maintained. See the last page of this catalogue for an alphabetical index of issuers.

O-Pee-Chee
1987-88 Issue
Card No. 1,
Denis Potvin

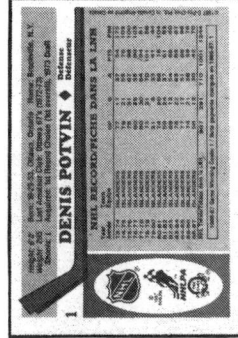

O-Pee-Chee
1987-88 Issue
Card No. 1,
Denis Potvin

O-Pee-Chee, 1987-88 Issue
Card No. 9, Error,
Name misspelled Calryle
on face and back

O-Pee-Chee
1987-88 Issue
Card No. 42,
Luc Robitaille

— 1987 - 88 REGULAR ISSUE —

Mint cards command a price premium of 25% over NRMT cards.

PRICE MOVEMENT OF NRMT SETS

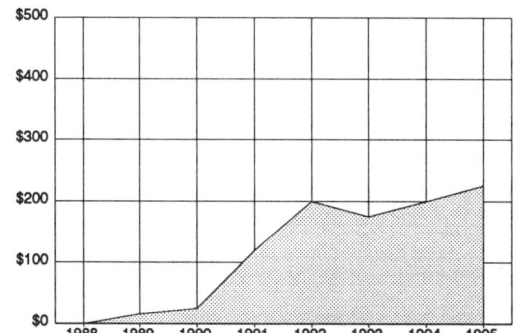

Card Size: 2 1/2" X 3 1/2"
Face: Four colour, white border, Team name, Position
Back: Pink and black on card stock, Number, Resume, Bilingual
Imprint: ©1987 O-Pee-Chee Ptd. in Canada/Imprimé au Canada
©1987 NHLPA
Complete Set No.: 264

Complete Set Price:	60.00	125.00	250.00
Common Goalie:	.03	.07	.15
Common Player:	.03	.07	.15
Wax Pack:			15.00
Wax Box: (48 Packs)			650.00
Wax Case: (16 Boxes)			9,000.00

No.	Player	VG	EX	NRMT
1	Denis Potvin, NYI, LC	.15	.30	.60
2	**Rick Tocchet, Phi., RC**	**4.50**	**9.00**	**18.00**
3	David Andreychuk, Buf.	.85	1.75	3.50
4	Stanley Smyl, Van.	.03	.07	.15
5	David Babych, Har.	.03	.07	.15
6	Patrick Verbeek, NJ	.07	.15	.30
7	**Esa Tikkanen, Edm., RC**	**2.50**	**5.00**	**10.00**
8	Mike Ridley, Wash.	.10	.20	.40
9	Randy Carlyle, Win., Error	.03	.07	.15
10	**Greg Paslawski, St. L., RC**	**.07**	**.15**	**.30**
11	Neal Broten, Min.	.03	.07	.15
12	Wendel Clark, Tor.	1.50	3.00	6.00
13	**Bill Ranford, Goalie, Bos., RC**	**3.75**	**7.50**	**15.00**
14	Douglas Wilson, Chi.	.07	.15	.30
15	Mario Lemieux, Pit.	8.75	17.50	35.00
16	Mats Naslund, Mon.	.07	.15	.30
17	Mel Bridgman, Det., LC	.03	.07	.15
18	James Patrick, NYR	.03	.07	.15
19	Roland Melanson, Goalie, LA	.03	.07	.15
20	Lanny McDonald, Cal.	.07	.15	.30
21	Peter Stastny, Que.	.18	.35	.75
22	Murray Craven, Phi.	.03	.07	.15
23	**Ulf Samuelsson, Har., RC**	**1.75**	**2.50**	**5.00**
24	**Michael Thelven, Bos., RC, LC, Error**	**.07**	**.15**	**.30**
25	Scott Stevens, Wash.	.25	.50	1.00
26	Petr Klima, Det.	.12	.25	.50
27	Brent Sutter, NYI	.03	.07	.15
28	Tomas Sandstrom, NYR	1.00	2.00	4.00
29	Tim Bothwell, St. L., LC	.03	.07	.15
30	Robert Carpenter, LA	.03	.07	.15
31	Brian MacLellan, Min.	.03	.07	.15
32	John Chabot, Pit.	.03	.07	.15
33	Phil Housley, Buf.	.15	.30	.60
34	Patrik Sundstrom, Van.	.03	.07	.15
35	David Ellett, Win.	.25	.50	1.00
36	John Vanbiesbrouck, Goalie, NYR	1.00	2.00	4.00
37	Dave Lewis, Det., LC	.03	.07	.15
38	Tom McCarthy, Bos., LC	.03	.07	.15
39	David Poulin, Phi.	.03	.07	.15
40	Mike Foligno, Buf.	.03	.07	.15
41	Gordon Roberts, Min.	.03	.07	.15
42	**Luc Robitaille, LA, RC**	**12.50**	**25.00**	**50.00**
43	Duane Sutter, NYI	.03	.07	.15
44	Peter Peeters, Goalie, Wash.	.03	.07	.15
45	John Anderson, Har.	.03	.07	.15
46	Aaron Broten, NJ	.03	.07	.15

98 • O-PEE-CHEE — 1987-88 REGULAR ISSUE —

No.	Player	VG	EX	NRMT
47	Keith Brown, Chi.	.03	.07	.15
48	Robert Smith, Mon.	.05	.10	.20
49	Donald Maloney, NYR	.03	.07	.15
50	Mark Hunter, St. L.	.03	.07	.15
51	Maurice Mantha, Pit.	.03	.07	.15
52	Charlie Simmer, Bos.	.03	.07	.15
53	Wayne Gretzky, Edm.	4.35	8.75	17.50
54	Mark Howe, Phi.	.07	.15	.30
55	Robert Gould, Wash.	.03	.07	.15
56	Steve Yzerman, Det.	1.75	3.50	7.00
57	Larry Playfair, LA, LC	.03	.07	.15
58	Alain Chevrier, Goalie, NJ	.03	.07	.15
59	Steve Larmer, Chi.	.20	.40	.80
60	Bryan Trottier, NYI	.12	.25	.50
61	Robert (Stewart) Gavin, Har.	.03	.07	.15
62	Russ Courtnall, Tor.	.35	.75	1.50
63	Michael Ramsey, Buf.	.03	.07	.15
64	Bob Brooke, Min.	.03	.07	.15
65	Richard Wamsley, Goalie, St. L.	.03	.07	.15
66	Ken Morrow, NYI	.03	.07	.15
67	**Gerard Gallant, Det., RC, Error**	.35	.75	1.50
68	**Kevin Hatcher, Wash., RC**	2.50	5.00	10.00
69	Cam Neely, Bos.	1.25	2.50	5.00
70	Sylvain Turgeon, Har.	.03	.07	.15
71	Peter Zezel, Phi.	.03	.07	.15
72	Al MacInnis, Cal.	.85	1.75	3.50
73	Terry Ruskowski, Pit., LC	.03	.07	.15
74	Troy Murray, Chi.	.03	.07	.15
75	Jim Fox, LA	.03	.07	.15
76	Kelly Kisio, NYR	.03	.07	.15
77	Michel Goulet, Que.	.07	.15	.30
78	Tom Barrasso, Goalie, Buf.	.07	.15	.30
79	Bruce Driver, NJ	.03	.07	.15
80	**Craig Simpson, Pit., RC**	.75	1.50	3.00
81	Dino Ciccarelli, Min.	.07	.15	.30
82	Gary Nylund, Chi.	.03	.07	.15
83	Bernie Federko, St. L.	.03	.07	.15
84	John Tonelli, Cal.	.03	.07	.15
85	Byron (Brad) McCrimmon, Phi.	.03	.07	.15
86	Dave Tippett, Har.	.03	.07	.15
87	Raymond Bourque, Bos.	.35	.75	1.50
88	Dave Christian, Wash.	.03	.07	.15
89	Glen Hanlon, Goalie, Det.	.03	.07	.15
90	**Brian Curran, NYI, RC**	.03	.07	.15
91	Paul MacLean, Win.	.03	.07	.15
92	**Jimmy Carson, LA, RC**	.75	1.50	3.00
93	Willie Huber, Van., LC (Now with Vancouver Canucks)	.03	.07	.15
94	Brian Bellows, Min.	.07	.15	.30
95	Doug Jarvis, Har., LC	.03	.07	.15
96	Clark Gillies, Buf.	.03	.07	.15
97	Tony Tanti, Van.	.03	.07	.15
98	**Per-Erik Eklund, Phi., RC**	.30	.60	1.25
99	Paul Coffey, Edm.	.35	.75	1.50
100	Brent Ashton, Det.	.03	.07	.15
101	Mark Johnson, NJ	.03	.07	.15
102	**Greg Johnston, Bos., RC, LC**	.03	.07	.15
103	Ron Flockhart, St. L., LC	.03	.07	.15
104	Ed Olczyk, Tor. (Now with Toronto Maple Leafs)	.15	.30	.60
105	Mike Bossy, NYI, LC	.12	.35	.75
106	Chris Chelios, Mon.	.25	.50	1.00
107	Gilles Meloche, Goalie, Pit.	.03	.07	.15
108	Rod Langway, Wash.	.03	.07	.15
109	Ray Ferraro, Har.	.18	.35	.75
110	Ron Duguay, NYR, LC	.03	.07	.15
111	Al Secord, Tor. (Now with Toronto Maple Leafs)	.03	.07	.15
112	**Mark Messier, Edm.**	.75	1.50	3.00
113	Ronald Sutter, Phi.	.03	.07	.15
114	**Darren Veitch, Det., RC**	.05	.10	.20
115	Rick Middleton, Bos.	.03	.07	.15
116	Douglas Sulliman, NJ	.03	.07	.15
117	Dennis Maruk, Min., LC	.03	.07	.15
118	David Taylor, LA	.03	.07	.15
119	Kelly Hrudey, Goalie, NYI	.12	.25	.50
120	Tom Fergus, Tor.	.03	.07	.15
121	**Christian Ruuttu, Buf., RC**	.18	.35	.75
122	Brian Benning, St. L., RC	.12	.25	.50
123	**Adam Oates, Det., RC**	10.00	20.00	40.00
124	Kevin Dineen, Har.	.25	.50	1.00
125	Doug Bodger, Pit.	.03	.07	.15
126	Joe Mullen, Cal.	.07	.15	.30
127	Denis Savard, Chi.	.18	.35	.75

O-Pee-Chee
1987-88 Issue
Card No. 80,
Craig Simpson

O-Pee-Chee
1987-88 Issue
Card No. 123,
Adam Oates

O-Pee-Chee
1987-88 Issue
Card No. 169,
Ron Hextall

O-Pee-Chee
1987-88 Issue
Card No. 205,
Martin McSorely

No.	Player	VG	EX	NRMT
128	Bradley Marsh, Phi.	.03	.07	.15
129	Marcel Dionne, NYR	.18	.35	.75
130	Bryan Erickson, LA, LC	.03	.07	.15
131	Reed Larson, Bos.	.03	.07	.15
132	Don Beaupre, Goalie, Min.	.03	.07	.15
133	Lawrence Murphy, Wash.	.03	.07	.15
134	John Ogrodnick, Que.	.03	.07	.15
135	Greg Adams, NJ	.03	.07	.15
136	Patrick Flatley, NYI	.03	.07	.15
137	Scott Arniel, Buf.	.03	.07	.15
138	Dana Murzyn, Har.	.03	.07	.15
139	Greg Adams, Wash.	.03	.07	.15
140	Bob Sauve, Goalie, NJ, LC	.03	.07	.15
141	Michael O'Connell, Det.	.03	.07	.15
142	Walter Poddubny, NYR	.03	.07	.15
143	Paul Reinhart, Cal.	.03	.07	.15
144	Tim Kerr, Phi.	.03	.07	.15
145	**Brian Lawton, Min., RC**	.10	.20	.40
146	**Gino Cavallini , St. L., RC**	.10	.20	.40
147	Doug Keans, Goalie, Bos., LC	.03	.07	.15
148	Jari Kurri, Edm.	.20	.40	.80
149	Dale Hawerchuk, Win.	.25	.50	1.00
150	**Randy Cunneyworth, Pit., RC**	.10	.20	.40
151	Gordon (Jay) Wells, LA	.03	.07	.15
152	Michael Liut, Goalie, Har.	.05	.10	.20
153	Stephen Konroyd, NYI	.03	.07	.15
154	John Tucker, Buf.	.03	.07	.15
155	Richard Vaive, Chi. (Now with Chicago Black Hawks)	.03	.07	.15
156	Bob Murray, Chi.	.03	.07	.15
157	Kirk Muller, NJ	.25	.50	1.00
158	Brian Propp, Phi.	.05	.10	.20
159	Ronald Greschner, NYR	.03	.07	.15
160	George (Rob) Ramage, St. L.	.03	.07	.15
161	Craig Laughlin, Wash.	.03	.07	.15
162	Stephen Kasper, Bos.	.03	.07	.15
163	Patrick Roy, Goalie, Mon.	8.75	17.50	35.00
164	**Shawn Burr, Det., RC**	.12	.25	.50
165	Craig Hartsburg, Min.	.03	.07	.15
166	**Dean Evason, Har., RC**	.10	.20	.40
167	Bob Bourne, LA	.03	.07	.15
168	Michael Gartner, Wash.	.25	.50	1.00
169	**Ron Hextall, Goalie, Phi., RC**	2.00	4.00	8.00
170	Joe Cirella, NJ	.03	.07	.15
171	Dan Quinn, Pit.	.03	.07	.15
172	Anthony McKegney, St. L.	.03	.07	.15
173	Pat LaFontaine, NYI	1.00	2.00	4.00
174	**Allen Pedersen, Bos., RC**	.03	.07	.15
175	Douglas Gilmour, St. L.	.10	.20	.40
176	Gary Suter, Cal.	.12	.25	.50
177	Barry Pederson, Van.	.03	.07	.15
178	Grant Fuhr, Goalie, Edm.	.25	.50	1.00
179	**Wayne Presley, Chi., RC**	.12	.25	.50
180	Wilf Paiement, Pit., LC	.03	.07	.15
181	Douglas Smail, Win.	.03	.07	.15
182	Doug Crossman, Phi.	.03	.07	.15
183	Bernie Nicholls, LA, Error	.15	.30	.60
184	Dirk Graham, Min., Error	.03	.07	.15
185	Anton Stastny, Que.	.03	.07	.15
186	Gregory Stefan, Goalie, Det.	.03	.07	.15
187	Ron Francis, Har.	.12	.25	.50
188	Steve Thomas, Chi. (Now with Chicago Black Hawks)	.25	.50	1.00
189	**Kelly Miller, Wash., RC**	.25	.50	1.00
190	Tomas Jonsson, NYI	.03	.07	.15
191	John MacLean, NJ	.25	.50	1.00
192	Larry Robinson, Mon.	.07	.15	.30
193	Douglas Wickenheiser, St. L.	.03	.07	.15
194	Keith Crowder, Bos.	.03	.07	.15
195	Robert Froese, Goalie, NYR, LC	.03	.07	.15
196	Jim Johnson, Pit.	.03	.07	.15
197	Checklist 1 (1 - 132)	.75	1.50	3.00
198	Checklist 2 (133 - 264)	.75	1.50	3.00

EDMONTON OILERS

No.	Player	VG	EX	NRMT
199	Glenn Anderson	.07	.15	.30
200	Kevin Lowe	.05	.10	.20
201	Kevin McClelland	.03	.07	.15
202	Michael Krushelnyski	.03	.07	.15
203	Craig MacTavish	.03	.07	.15
204	Andrew Moog, Goalie	.15	.30	.60
205	**Martin McSorley, RC**	3.00	6.00	12.00

— 1988 - 89 REGULAR ISSUE — O-PEE-CHEE • 99

No.	Player	VG	EX	NRMT
206	Craig Muni, RC	.07	.15	.30
207	Charles Huddy	.03	.07	.15

CALGARY FLAMES

No.	Player	VG	EX	NRMT
208	Hakan Loob	.03	.07	.15
209	James Peplinski	.03	.07	.15
210	Mike Bullard	.03	.07	.15
211	Carey Wilson	.03	.07	.15
212	Joel Otto	.03	.07	.15
213	Neil Sheehy, RC	.07	.15	.30
214	Jamie Macoun	.03	.07	.15
215	Michael Vernon, Goalie, RC	2.00	4.00	8.00
216	Steve Bozek	.03	.07	.15

WINNIPEG JETS

No.	Player	VG	EX	NRMT
217	Daniel Berthiaume, Goalie, RC	.50	1.00	2.00
218	Gilles Hamel, LC	.03	.07	.15
219	Timothy Watters	.03	.07	.15
220	Mario Marois, Error	.03	.07	.15
221	Thomas Steen	.03	.07	.15
222	Laurie Boschman	.03	.07	.15
223	Steve Rooney, RC, LC	.05	.10	.20
224	Ronald Wilson	.03	.07	.15
225	Fredrik Olausson, RC	.50	1.00	2.00
226	James Kyte, RC	.07	.15	.30

MONTREAL CANADIENS

No.	Player	VG	EX	NRMT
227	Claude Lemieux, RC	3.00	6.00	12.00
228	Bob Gainey	.05	.10	.20

ST. LOUIS BLUES

No.	Player	VG	EX	NRMT
229	Gaston Gingras	.03	.07	.15

MONTREAL CANADIENS

No.	Player	VG	EX	NRMT
230	Brian Hayward, Goalie	.07	.15	.30
231	Ryan Walter	.03	.07	.15
232	Guy Carbonneau	.03	.07	.15
233	Stephane Richer, RC	3.00	6.00	12.00
234	Richard Green	.03	.07	.15
235	Brian Skrudland, RC	.25	.50	1.00

TORONTO MAPLE LEAFS

No.	Player	VG	EX	NRMT
236	Allan Bester, Goalie	.03	.07	.15
237	Borje Salming	.03	.07	.15
238	Al Iafrate	.15	.30	.60
239	Rick Lanz	.03	.07	.15
240	Gary Leeman	.10	.20	.40
241	Greg Terrion, LC	.03	.07	.15
242	Ken Wregget, RC, Goalie	.20	.40	.80
243	Vincent Damphousse, RC	4.50	9.00	18.00
244	Christopher Kotsopoulos	.03	.07	.15

WASHINGTON CAPITALS

No.	Player	VG	EX	NRMT
245	Dale Hunter	.03	.07	.15
246	Clint Malarchuk, Goalie	.07	.15	.30

QUEBEC NORDIQUES

No.	Player	VG	EX	NRMT
247	Paul Gillis	.03	.07	.15
248	Robert Picard	.03	.07	.15
249	Douglas Shedden	.03	.07	.15
250	Mario Gosselin, Goalie	.03	.07	.15
251	Randy Moller	.03	.07	.15
252	David Shaw	.03	.07	.15
253	Mike Eagles, RC	.12	.25	.50
254	Alain Coté	.03	.07	.15

VANCOUVER CANUCKS

No.	Player	VG	EX	NRMT
255	Petri Skriko	.03	.07	.15
256	Doug Lidster	.03	.07	.15
257	Richard Brodeur, Goalie, LC	.03	.07	.15

O-Pee-Chee
1987-88 Issue
Card No. 215,
Michael Vernon

O-Pee-Chee
1987-88 Issue
Card No. 263,
Brent Peterson

O-Pee-Chee
1988-89 Issue
Card No. 1,
Mario Lemieux

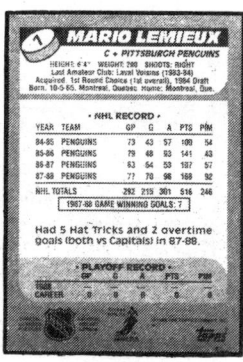

O-Pee-Chee
1988-89 Issue
Card No. 1,
Mario Lemieux

No.	Player	VG	EX	NRMT
258	Richard Sutter	.03	.07	.15
259	Steve Tambellini	.03	.07	.15
260	Jim Benning	.03	.07	.15
261	Dave Richter, RC, LC	.03	.07	.15

NEW YORK RANGERS

No.	Player	VG	EX	NRMT
262	Michel Petit, RC (Now with New York Rangers)	.07	.15	.30

VANCOUVER CANUCKS

No.	Player	VG	EX	NRMT
263	Brent Peterson, LC	.03	.07	.15
264	Jim Sandlak, RC	.25	.50	1.00

— 1988 - 89 REGULAR ISSUE —

Card numbers 1, 16, 66, 120 and 194 were counterfeited. Please refer to pages XXXI to XXXIII in the counterfeit section for details on how to recognize these cards. Mint cards command a price premium of 25% over NRMT cards.

PRICE MOVEMENT OF NRMT SETS

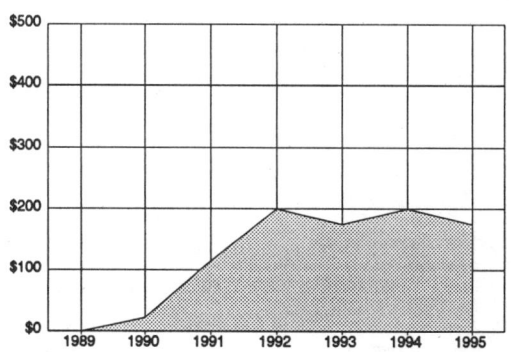

Card Size: 2 1/2" X 3 1/2"
Face: Four colour, white border, Team logo
Back: Orange and blue on card stock, Number, Resume, Bilingual
Imprint: © 1988 O-PEE-CHEE CO. LTD. PTD. IN CANADA/ IMPRIMÉ AU CANADA © 1988 NHLPA
Complete Set No.: 264
Complete Set Price: 40.00 80.00 160.00
Common Card: .03 .07 .15
Wax Pack: 13.00
Wax Box: (48 Packs) 425.00
Wax Case: (16 Boxes) 5,000.00

No.	Player	VG	EX	NRMT
1	Mario Lemieux, Pit.	2.50	5.00	10.00
2	Robert Joyce, Bos., RC	.12	.25	.50
3	Joel Quenneville, Har.	.03	.07	.15
4	Anthony McKegney, St. L.	.03	.07	.15
5	Stephane Richer, Mon.	.75	1.25	2.50
6	Mark Howe, Phi.	.06	.12	.25
7	Brent Sutter, NYI	.03	.07	.15
8	Gilles Meloche, Goalie, Pit., LC	.03	.07	.15
9	Jimmy Carson, Edm.	.18	.35	.75
10	John MacLean, NJ	.15	.30	.60
11	Gary Leeman, Tor.	.05	.10	.20
12	Gerard Gallant, Det.	.07	.15	.30
13	Marcel Dionne, NYR, LC	.10	.20	.40
14	Dave Christian, Wash.	.03	.07	.15
15	Gary Nylund, Chi.	.03	.07	.15
16	Joe Nieuwendyk, Cal., RC	3.50	7.00	14.00
17	Billy Smith, Goalie, NYI	.07	.15	.30
18	Christian Ruuttu, Buf.	.03	.07	.15
19	Randy Cunneyworth, Pit.	.03	.07	.15
20	Brian Lawton, Min.	.03	.07	.15
21	Scott Mellanby, Phi., RC	.35	.75	1.50
22	Peter Stastny, Que.	.12	.25	.50
23	Gordon Kluzak, Bos.	.03	.07	.15
24	Sylvain Turgeon, Har.	.03	.07	.15
25	Clint Malarchuk, Goalie, Wash.	.05	.10	.20
26	Denis Savard, Chi.	.12	.25	.50

100 • O-PEE-CHEE — 1988 - 89 REGULAR ISSUE —

No.	Player	VG	EX	NRMT
27	Craig Simpson, Edm.	.10	.20	.40
28	Petr Klima, Det.	.15	.30	.60
29	Patrick Verbeek, NJ	.07	.15	.30
30	Maurice Mantha, Min.	.03	.07	.15
31	Christopher Nilan, NYR	.03	.07	.15
32	Barry Pederson, Van.	.03	.07	.15
33	Randy Burridge, Bos.	.10	.20	.40
34	Ron Hextall, Goalie, Phi.	.30	.60	1.25
35	Gaston Gingras, St. L.	.03	.07	.15
36	Kevin Dineen, Har.	.05	.10	.20
37	Thomas Laidlaw, LA	.03	.07	.15
38	Paul MacLean, Det.	.03	.07	.15
39	John Chabot, Det.	.03	.07	.15
40	Lindy Ruff, Buf.	.03	.07	.15
41	Dan Quinn, Pit.	.03	.07	.15
42	Don Beaupre, Goalie, Min.	.03	.07	.15
43	Gary Suter, Cal.	.07	.15	.30
44	**Mikko Makela, NYI, RC**	**.03**	**.07**	**.15**
45	Mark Johnson, NJ	.03	.07	.15
46	David Taylor, LA	.03	.07	.15
47	**Ulf Dahlen, NYR, RC**	**.50**	**1.00**	**2.00**
48	**Jeff Sharples, Det., RC**	**.06**	**.12**	**.25**
49	Chris Chelios, Mon.	.15	.30	.60
50	Michael Gartner, Wash.	.12	.25	.50
51	**Darren Pang, Goalie, Chi., RC**	**.07**	**.15**	**.30**
52	Ron Francis, Har.	.07	.15	.35
53	Ken Morrow, NYI, LC	.07	.15	.30
54	Michel Goulet, Que.	.07	.15	.30
55	**Ray Sheppard, Buf., RC**	**2.00**	**4.00**	**8.00**
56	Douglas Gilmour, St. L. (Now with Flames 9-5-88)	1.25	2.50	5.00
57	David Shaw, NYR	.03	.07	.15
58	Cam Neely, Bos.	.35	.75	1.50
59	Grant Fuhr, Goalie, Edm.	.15	.30	.60
60	Scott Stevens, Wash.	.05	.10	.20
61	Bob Brooke, Min.	.03	.07	.15
62	Dave Hunter, Pit., LC (Now with Jets 10-3-88)	.03	.07	.15
63	**Alan Kerr, NYI, RC**	**.03**	**.07**	**.15**
64	Bradley Marsh, Phi. (Now with Leafs 10-3-88)	.03	.07	.15
65	Dale Hawerchuk, Win.	.18	.35	.75
66	**Brett Hull, St. L., RC**	**16.25**	**32.50**	**65.00**
67	Patrik Sundstrom, NJ	.03	.07	.15
68	Gregory Stefan, Goalie, Det.	.03	.07	.15
69	James Patrick, NYR	.03	.07	.15
70	Dale Hunter, Wash.	.03	.07	.15
71	Al Iafrate, Tor.	.18	.35	.75
72	Robert Carpenter, LA	.03	.07	.15
73	Raymond Bourque, Bos.	.25	.50	1.00
74	John Tucker, Buf.	.03	.07	.15
75	Carey Wilson, Har.	.03	.07	.15
76	Joe Mullen, Cal.	.07	.15	.30
77	Richard Vaive, Chi.	.03	.07	.15
78	Shawn Burr, Det.	.03	.07	.15
79	Murray Craven, Phi.	.03	.07	.15
80	Clark Gillies, Buf., LC	.03	.07	.15
81	Bernie Federko, St. L.	.03	.07	.15
82	Tony Tanti, Van.	.03	.07	.15
83	Gregory Gilbert, NYI	.03	.07	.15
84	Kirk Muller, NJ	.30	.60	1.25
85	Dave Tippett, Har.	.03	.07	.15
86	Kevin Hatcher, Wash.	.50	1.00	2.00
87	Rick Middleton, Bos., LC	.03	.07	.15
88	Robert Smith, Mon.	.05	.10	.20
89	Douglas Wilson, Chi.	.07	.15	.30
90	Scott Arniel. Buf.	.03	.07	.15
91	Brian Mullen, NYR	.03	.07	.15
92	Michael O'Connell, Det.	.03	.07	.15
93	Mark Messier, Edm.	.35	.75	1.50
94	**Sean Burke, Goalie, NJ, RC**	**.60**	**1.25**	**2.50**
95	Brian Bellows, Min.	.07	.15	.30
96	Doug Bodger, Pit.	.03	.07	.15
97	Bryan Trottier, NYI	.10	.20	.40
98	Anton Stastny, Que.	.03	.07	.15
99A	Checklist 1, (1 - 99), Error	1.00	2.00	4.00
99B	Checklist 1, (1 - 132), Corrected	.75	1.50	3.00
100	David Poulin, Phi.	.03	.07	.15
101	Bob Bourne, LA, LC	.03	.07	.15
102	John Vanbiesbrouck, Goalie, NYR	.18	.35	1.75
103	Allen Pedersen, Bos.	.03	.07	.15
104	Mike Ridley, Wash.	.03	.07	.15
105	Andrew McBain, Win.	.03	.07	.15
106	Troy Murray, Chi.	.03	.07	.15

O-Pee-Chee
1988-89 Issue
Card No. 56,
Douglas Gilmore

O-Pee-Chee
1988-89 Issue
Card No. 66,
Brett Hull

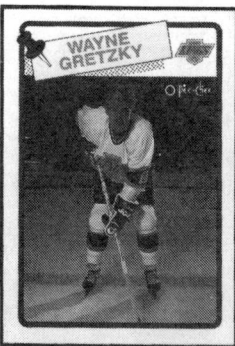

O-Pee-Chee, 1988-89 Issue
Card No. 120, Error,
"C" for position missing
from top left corner

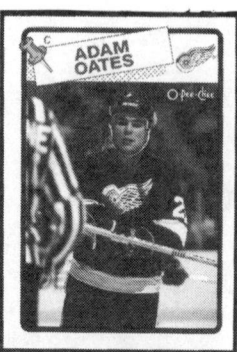

O-Pee-Chee
1988-89 Issue
Card No. 161,
Adam Oates

No.	Player	VG	EX	NRMT
107	Tom Barrasso, Goalie, Buf.	.07	.15	.30
108	Tomas Jonsson, NYI, LC	.03	.07	.15
109	**Rob Brown, Pit., RC**	**.18**	**.35**	**.75**
110	Hakan Loob, Cal., LC	.03	.07	.15
111	Ilkka Sinisalo, Phi.	.03	.07	.15
112	**Dave Archibald, Min., RC**	**.10**	**.20**	**.40**
113	Doug Halward, Det., LC	.03	.07	.15
114	Ray Ferraro, Har.	.03	.07	.15
115	Doug Brown, NJ	.05	.10	.20
116	Patrick Roy, Goalie, Mon.	2.00	4.00	8.00
117	Greg Millen, Goalie, St. L..	.03	.07	.15
118	Ken Linseman, Bos.	.03	.07	.15
119	Phil Housley, Buf.	.12	.25	.50
120	Wayne Gretzky, LA, Error	3.75	7.50	15.00
121	Tomas Sandstrom, NYR	.15	.30	.60
122	**Brendan Shanahan, NJ, RC**	**5.00**	**10.00**	**20.00**
123	Pat LaFontaine, NYI	.50	1.00	2.00
124	Luc Robitaille, LA	2.10	4.25	8.50
125	Ed Olczyk, Tor.	.07	.15	.30
126	Ronald Sutter, Phi.	.03	.07	.15
127	Michael Liut, Goalie, Har.	.07	.15	.30
128	Brent Ashton, Win.	.03	.07	.15
129	**Anthony Hrkac, St. L., RC**	**.15**	**.30**	**.60**
130	Kelly Miller, Wash.	.03	.07	.15
131	Alan Haworth, Que.	.03	.07	.15
132	**Dave McLlwain, Pit., RC**	**.07**	**.15**	**.30**
133	Michael Ramsey, Buf.	.03	.07	.15
134	**Robert Sweeney, Bos., RC**	**.07**	**.15**	**.30**
135	Dirk Graham, Chi.	.03	.07	.15
136	Ulf Samuelsson, Har.	.18	.35	.75
137	Petri Skriko, Van.	.03	.07	.15
138	Aaron Broten, NJ	.03	.07	.15
139	Jim Fox, LA	.03	.07	.15
140	**Randy Wood, NYI, RC**	**.12**	**.25**	**.50**
141	Lawrence Murphy, Wash.	.03	.07	.15
142	Daniel Berthiaume, Goalie, Win.	.07	.15	.35
143	Kelly Kisio, NYR	.03	.07	.15
144	Neal Broten, Min.	.03	.07	.15
145	Reed Larson, Bos.	.03	.07	.15
146	Peter Zezel, Phi.	.03	.07	.15
147	Jari Kurri, Edm.	.15	.30	.60
148	Jim Johnson, Pit.	.03	.07	.15
149	Gino Cavallini, St. L.	.03	.07	.15
150	Glen Hanlon, Goalie, Det.	.03	.07	.15
151	Bengt-ake Gustafsson, Wash.	.03	.07	.15
152	Mike Bullard, Cal. (Now with Blues 9-5-88)	.03	.07	.15
153	John Ogrodnick, NYR	.03	.07	.15
154	Steve Larmer, Chi.	.12	.25	.50
155	Kelly Hrudey, Goalie, NYI	.07	.15	.30
156	Mats Naslund, Mon.	.07	.15	.30
157	Bruce Driver, NJ	.03	.07	.15
158	Randy Hillier, Pit.	.03	.07	.15
159	Craig Hartsburg, Min., LC	.03	.07	.15
160	Roland Melanson, Goalie, LA, LC	.03	.07	.15
161	Adam Oates, Det.	1.75	3.50	7.00
162	Greg Adams, Van.	.03	.07	.15
163	Dave Andreychuk, Buf.	.03	.07	.15
164	Dave Babych, Har.	.03	.07	.15
165	**Brian Noonan, Chi., RC**	**.18**	**.35**	**.75**
166	**Glen Wesley, Bos., RC**	**.50**	**1.00**	**2.00**
167	Dave Ellett, Win.	.03	.07	.15
168	Brian Propp, Phi.	.05	.10	.20
169	Bernie Nicholls, LA	.07	.15	.30
170	Walter Poddubny, NYR (Now with Nordiques 8-1-88)	.03	.07	.15
171	Stephen Konroyd, NYI	.03	.07	.15
172	Douglas Sulliman, NJ (Now with Flyers 10-3-88)	.03	.07	.15
173	Mario Gosselin, Goalie, Que.	.03	.07	.15
174	Brian Benning, St. L.	.03	.07	.15
175	Dino Ciccarelli, Min.	.07	.15	.30
176	Stephen Kasper, Bos.	.03	.07	.15
177	Rick Tocchet, Phi.	1.25	2.50	5.00
178	Byron (Brad) McCrimmon, Cal.	.03	.07	.15
179	Paul Coffey, Pit.	.18	.35	.75
180	Peter Peeters, Goalie, Wash.	.03	.07	.15
181	**Bob Probert, Det., RC**	**2.00**	**4.00**	**8.00**
182	**Steve Duchesne, LA, RC**	**1.50**	**3.00**	**6.00**
183	Russ Courtnall, Tor.	.07	.15	.30
184	Mike Foligno, Buf.	.03	.07	.15
185	Wayne Presley, Chi.	.03	.07	.15
186	Rejean Lemelin, Goalie, Bos.	.03	.07	.15

No.	Player	VG	EX	NRMT
187	Mark Hunter, St. L. (Now with Flames 9-5-88)	.03	.07	.15
188	Joe Cirella, NJ	.03	.07	.15
189	Glenn Anderson, Edm.	.06	.12	.25
190	John Anderson, Har.	.03	.07	.15
191	Patrick Flatley, NYI	.03	.07	.15
192	Rod Langway, Wash.	.03	.07	.15
193	Brian MacLellan, Min	.03	.07	.15
194	Pierre Turgeon, Buf., RC	7.50	15.00	30.00
195	Brian Hayward, Goalie, Mon.	.03	.07	.15
196	Steve Yzerman, Det.	1.00	2.00	4.00
197	Doug Crossman, Phi.	.03	.07	.15
198A	Checklist 2, Error, (100 - 198)	.50	1.00	2.00
198B	Checklist 2, Corrected, (133 - 264)	.50	1.00	2.00
199	Greg Adams, Wash. (Now with Oilers 7-22-88)	.03	.07	.15
200	Laurie Boschman, Win.	.03	.07	.15
201	Jeff Brown, Que., RC	1.25	2.50	5.00
202	Garth Butcher, Van., RC	.25	.50	1.00
203	Guy Carbonneau, Mon.	.03	.07	.15
204	Randy Carlyle, Win.	.03	.07	.15
205	Alain Cote, Que.	.03	.07	.15
206	Keith Crowder, Bos.	.03	.07	.15
207	Vincent Damphousse, Tor.	1.75	3.50	7.00
208	Gaetan Duchesne, Que., RC	.10	.20	.40
209	Iain Duncan, Win., RC	.03	.07	.15
210	Tommy Albelin, Que., RC	.02	.07	.15
211	Per-Erik Eklund, Phi.	.03	.07	.15
212	Jan Erixon, NYR, RC	.05	.10	.20
213	Paul Fenton, LA, RC	.05	.10	.20
214	Tom Fergus, Tor.	.03	.07	.15
215	Dave Gagner, Min., RC	.75	1.50	3.00
216	Bob Gainey, Mon., LC	.03	.07	.15
217	Robert (Stewart) Gavin, Har. (Now with North Stars 10-3-88)	.03	.07	.15
218	Charles Huddy, Edm.	.03	.07	.15
219	Jeff Jackson, Que., RC	.05	.10	.20
220	Uwe Krupp, Buf., RC	.12	.25	.50
221	Michael Krushelnyski, Edm (Traded to Kings 8-9-88)	.03	.07	.15
222	Tom Kurvers, NJ	.03	.07	.15
223	Jason Lafreniere, Que., RC	.03	.07	.15
224	Lane Lambert, Que.	.03	.07	.15
225	Rick Lanz, Tor.	.03	.07	.15
226	Brad Lauer, NYI, RC	.05	.10	.20
227	Claude Lemieux, Mon.	.50	1.00	2.00
228	Doug Lidster, Van.	.03	.07	.15
229	Kevin Lowe, Edm., Error	.05	.10	.20
230	Craig Ludwig, Mon.	.03	.07	.15
231	Al MacInnis, Cal.	.50	1.00	2.00
232	Craig MacTavish, Edm.	.03	.07	.15
233	Mario Marois, Win., Error	.03	.07	.15
234	Lanny McDonald, Cal.	.06	.12	.25
235	Rickard Meagher, St. L.	.03	.07	.15
236	Craig Muni, Edm.	.03	.07	.15
237	Michael McPhee, Mon.	.03	.07	.15
238	Eric Nattress, Cal., RC	.03	.07	.15
239	Ray Neufeld, Win.	.03	.07	.15
240	Lee Norwood, Det., RC	.03	.07	.15
241	Mark Osborne, Tor., Error	.03	.07	.15
242	Joel Otto, Cal.	.03	.07	.15
243	James Peplinski, Cal.	.03	.07	.15
244	George (Rob) Ramage, Cal.	.03	.07	.15
245	Luke Richardson, Tor., RC	.10	.20	.40
246	Larry Robinson, Mon.	.03	.07	.15
247	Borje Salming, Tor.	.03	.07	.15
248	David Saunders, Van., RC, LC	.03	.07	.15
249	Al Secord, Tor.	.03	.07	.15
250	Charlie Simmer, Pit., LC	.03	.07	.15
251	Douglas Smail, Win.	.03	.07	.15
252	Steve Smith, Edm., RC (Now with Sabres 10-3-88)	1.25	2.50	5.00
253	Stanley Smyl, Van.	.03	.07	.15
254	Thomas Steen, Win.	.03	.07	.15
255	Richard Sutter, Van.	.03	.07	.15
256	Petr Svoboda, Mon., RC	.25	.50	1.00
257	Peter Taglianetti, Win., RC	.12	.25	.50
258	Stephen Tambellini, Van.	.03	.07	.15
259	Steve Thomas, Chi.	.03	.07	.15
260	Esa Tikkanen, Edm.	.50	1.00	2.00
261	Michael Vernon, Goalie, Cal.	.15	.30	.60
262	Ryan Walter, Mon.	.03	.07	.15
263	Douglas Wickenheiser, Van. (Now with Rangers 7-14-88)	.03	.07	.15
264	Ken Wregget, Goalie, Tor.	.06	.12	.25

Available in April!

THE CHARLTON STANDARD CATALOGUE OF CANADIAN
BASEBALL & FOOTBALL CARDS

- Fourth Edition -

BASEBALL CARDS FROM 1912
FOOTBALL CARDS FROM 1949

For Canadian Baseball and Football Card Collectors this Catalogue has it all!

IMPERIAL TOBACCO * MAPLE CRISPETTE
PARKHURST * O-PEE-CHEE * CANADA STARCH
STUART * POST * TOPPS * WORLD WIDE GUM
NALLEYS * DONRUSS - LEAF * EDDIE SARGENT
PROVIGO * WILLARD TORONTO BLUE JAYS
STANDARD OIL * NABISCO * BLUE RIBBON TEA
PANINI * GENERAL MILLS * SCORE EXHIBITS
HOSTESS * PURITAN MEATS * GULF CANADA JOGO
VACHON * ROYAL STUDIOS * NEILSON'S
BEN'S AULT FOODS * COCA-COLA * BAZOOKA * KFC
And All Other Major Manufacturers...

Complete price listings for all Major League Baseball and Canadian Football League cards! Comprehensive baseball and football minor league card listings! Regular issues, stickers, inserts, subsets, transfers and much, much more! All major manufacturers! Current Pricing for all cards in up to three grades of condition - VG, EX, and NRMT! All rookie, last, pitcher, quarterback, error and variation cards identified and priced! Plus Charlton's Fabulous Alphabetical Index!

OVER 300 PAGES * 60,000 PRICES
NEW, LARGER 8 1/2 x 11" FORMAT
RESERVE YOUR COPY TODAY DIRECTLY
FROM THE PUBLISHER...

The Charlton Press

2010 YONGE STREET, TORONTO, ONTARIO M4S 1Z9
FOR TOLL FREE ORDERING PHONE 1-800-442-6042
FAX 1-800-442-1542 from anywhere in Canada or the U.S.

102 • O-PEE-CHEE — 1989-90 REGULAR ISSUE —

— 1989 - 90 REGULAR ISSUE —

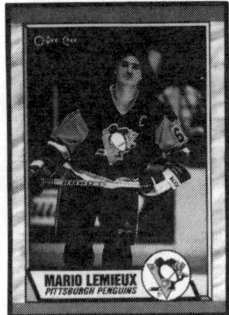 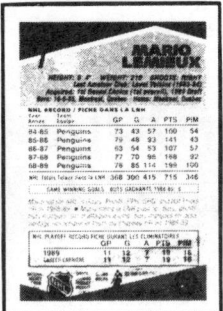

1989-90 Regular Issue
Card No. 1, Mario Lemieux

Card Size: 2 1/2" x 3 1/2"
Face: Four colour, blue and marble border, Team Logo
Back: Red and black on card stock, Number, Resume, Bilingual
Imprint: © 1989 O-PEE-CHEE CO. LTD. PTD. IN CANADA/IMPRIMÉ AU CANADA © 1989 NHLPA
Complete Set No.: 330

		EX	NRMT
Complete Set Price:		9.00	18.00
Common Card:		.03	.05
Wax Pack: (9 Cards)			1.00
Wax Box: (48 Packs)			40.00
Wax Case: (16 Boxes)			600.00

No.	Player	EX	NRMT
1	Mario Lemieux, Pit.	.50	1.00
2	Ulf Dahlen, NYR	.03	.05
3	**Terry Carkner, Phi., RC**	.07	.15
4	Anthony McKegney, Det.	.03	.05
5	Denis Savard, Chi.	.15	.30
6	**Derek King, NYI, RC**	.35	.75
7	Lanny McDonald, Cal., LC (Retired 2-28-89)	.10	.20
8	John Tonelli, LA	.03	.05
9	Tom Kurvers, NJ (Now with Maple Leafs 10-16-89)	.03	.05
10	Dave Archibald, Min.	.03	.05
11	**Peter Sidorkiewicz, Goalie, Har., RC**	.19	.20
12	Esa Tikkanen, Edm.	.12	.25
13	Dave Barr, Det.	.03	.05
14	Brent Sutter, NYI	.03	.05
15	Cam Neely, Bos.	.10	.20
16	**Calle Johansson, Wash., RC**	.10	.20
17	Patrick Roy, Goalie, Mon.	.35	.75
18	**Dale DeGray, LA, RC**	.03	.05
19	**Phil Bourque, Pit., RC**	.07	.15
20	Kevin Dineen, Har.	.03	.05
21	Mike Bullard, Phi.	.03	.05
22	Gary Leeman, Tor.	.03	.05
23	Gregory Stefan, Goalie, Det.	.03	.05
24	Brian Mullen, NYR	.03	.05
25	Pierre Turgeon, Buf.	.40	.80
26	**Robert Rouse, Wash., RC**	.05	.10
27	Peter Zezel, St. L.	.03	.05
28	Jeff Brown, Que.	.10	.20
29	**Andy Brickley, Bos., RC**	.07	.15
30	Michael Gartner, Min.	.07	.15
31	Darren Pang, Goalie, Chi.	.03	.05
32	Patrick Verbeek, Har.	.03	.05
33	Petri Skriko, Van.	.03	.05
34	Tom Laidlaw, LA	.03	.05
35	Randy Wood, NYI	.03	.05
36	Thomas Barrasso, Goalie, Pit.	.03	.05
37	John Tucker, Buf.	.03	.05
38	Andrew McBain, Pit.	.03	.05
39	David Shaw, NYR	.03	.05
40	Rejean Lemelin, Goalie, Bos.	.03	.05
41	Dino Ciccarelli, Wash.	.03	.05
42	Jeff Sharples, Det.	.03	.05
43	Jari Kurri, Edm.	.12	.25
44	Murray Craven, Phi.	.03	.05
45	**Cliff Ronning, St. L., RC**	.50	1.00
46	Dave Babych, Har.	.03	.05
47	Bernie Nicholls, LA	.10	.20
48	**Jon Casey, Goalie, Min., RC**	.35	.75
49	Al MacInnis, Cal.	.07	.15
50	**Bob Errey, Pit., RC**	.15	.30
51	Glen Wesley, Bos.	.03	.05
52	Dirk Graham, Chi.	.03	.05
53	Guy Carbonneau, Mon.	.03	.05
54	Tomas Sandstrom, NYR	.07	.15
55	Rod Langway, Wash.	.03	.05
56	Patrik Sundstrom, NJ	.03	.05
57	Michel Goulet, Que.	.07	.15
58	David Taylor, LA	.03	.05
59	Phil Housley, Buf.	.10	.20
60	Pat LaFontaine, NYI	.20	.40
61	**Kirk McLean, Goalie, Van., RC**	.50	1.00
62	Ken Linseman, Bos.	.03	.05
63	Randy Cunneyworth, Win.	.03	.05
64	Anthony Hrkac, St. L.	.03	.05
65	Mark Messier, Edm.	.25	.50
66	Carey Wilson, NYR	.03	.05
67	**Stephen Leach, Wash., RC**	.15	.30
68	Christian Ruuttu, Buf.	.03	.05
69	Dave Ellett, Win.	.03	.05
70	Ray Ferraro, Har.	.03	.05
71	**Colin Patterson, Cal., RC**	.03	.05
72	Tim Kerr, Phi.	.03	.05
73	Robert Joyce, Bos.	.03	.05
74	Douglas Gilmour, Cal.	.25	.50
75	Lee Norwood, Det.	.03	.05
76	Dale Hunter, Wash.	.03	.05
77	Jim Johnson, Pit.	.03	.05
78	Mike Foligno, Buf.	.03	.05
79	Al Iafrate, Tor.	.05	.10
80	Rick Tocchet, Phi.	.10	.20
81	**Greg Hawgood, Bos., RC**	.07	.15
82	Steve Thomas, Chi.	.03	.05
83	Steve Yzerman, Det.	.15	.30
84	Michael McPhee, Mon.	.03	.05
85	**David Volek, NYI, RC**	.12	.25
86	Brian Benning, St. L.	.03	.05
87	Neal Broten, Min.	.03	.05
88	Luc Robitaille, LA	.25	.50
89	**Trevor Linden, Van., RC**	.75	1.50
90	James Patrick, NYR	.03	.05
91	Brian Lawton, Har.	.03	.05
92	Sean Burke, Goalie, NJ	.03	.05
93	Scott Stevens, Wash.	.05	.10
94	**Pat Elynuik, Win., RC**	.12	.25
95	Paul Coffey, Pit.	.10	.20
96	Jan Erixon, NYR	.03	.05
97	Michael Liut, Goalie, Har.	.03	.05
98	Wayne Presley, Chi.	.03	.05
99	Craig Simpson, Edm.	.07	.15
100	**Kjell Samuelsson, Phi., RC**	.07	.15
101	Shawn Burr, Det.	.03	.05
102	John MacLean, NJ	.03	.05
103	Tom Fergus, Tor	.03	.05
104	Michael Krushelnyski, LA	.03	.05
105	Gary Nylund, NYI	.03	.05
106	Dave Andreychuk, Buf.	.10	.20
107	Bernie Federko, Det.	.03	.05
108	Gary Suter, Cal.	.07	.15
109	Dave Gagner, Min.	.15	.30
110	Raymond Bourque, Bos.	.12	25
111	**Geoff Courtnall, Wash., RC**	.35	.75
112	Douglas Wilson, Chi.	.03	.05
113	**Joe Sakic, Que., RC**	2.50	5.00
114	John Vanbiesbrouck, Goalie, NYR	.10	.20
115	David Poulin, Phi.	.03	.05
116	Richard Meagher, St. L.	.05	.10
117	Kirk Muller, NJ	.03	.05
118	Mats Naslund, Mon.	.03	.05
119	Ray Sheppard, Buf.	.12	.25
120	**Jeff Norton, NYI, RC**	.10	.20
121	Randy Burridge, Bos.	.03	.05
122	Dale Hawerchuk, Win.	.05	.10
123	Steve Duchesne, LA	.10	.20
124	John Anderson, Har., LC	.03	.05
125	Richard Vaive, Buf.	.03	.05
126	Randy Hillier, Pit.	.03	.05
127	Jimmy Carson, Edm.	.03	.05
128	Lawrence Murphy, Min.	.03	.05
129	Paul MacLean, St. L.	.03	.05
130	Joe Cirella, Que.	.03	.05
131	Kelly Miller, Wash.	.03	.05
132	Alain Chevrier, Goalie, Chi.	.03	.05
133	Ed Olczyk, Tor.	.03	.05
134	Dave Tippett, Har.	.03	.05
135	Robert Sweeney, Bos.	.03	.05
136	**Brian Leetch, NYR, RC**	2.50	5.00
137	Greg Millen, Goalie, St. L.	.03	.05
138	Joe Nieuwendyk, Cal.	.12	.25
139	Brian Propp, Phi.	.03	.05
140	Michael Ramsey, Buf.	.03	.05
141	Mike Allison, LA	.03	.05
142	**Shawn Chambers, Min., RC**	.07	.15
143	Peter Stastny, Que.	.10	.20
144	Glen Hanlon, Goalie, Det.	.03	.05
145	**John Cullen, Pit., RC**	.20	.40
146	Kevin Hatcher, Wash.	.10	.20
147	Brendan Shanahan, NJ	.35	.75
148	Paul Reinhart, Van.	.03	.05
149	Bryan Trottier, NYI	.10	.20
150	**Dave Manson, Chi., RC**	.20	.40
151	**Mark Habscheid, Det., RC**	.03	.05
152	Dan Quinn, Pit.	.03	.05
153	Stephane J. J. Richer, Mon.	.10	.20
154	Doug Bodger, Buf.	.03	.05
155	Ron Hextall, Goalie, Phi.	.12	.25
156	Wayne Gretzky, LA	.75	1.50
157	**Steve Tuttle, St. L., RC**	.07	.15
158	Charles Huddy, Edm.	.03	.05
159	Dave Christian, Wash.	.03	.05
160	Andrew Moog, Goalie, Bos.	.07	.15
161	**Tony Granato, NYR, RC**	.25	.50
162	Sylvain Cote, Har., RC	.03	.05
163	Michael Vernon, Goalie, Cal.	.10	.20
164	**Steve Chiasson, Det., RC**	.15	.30
165	Mike Ridley, Wash.	.03	.05
166	Kelly Hrudey, Goalie, LA	.03	.05
167	Robert Carpenter, Bos.	.03	.05
168	**Zarley Zalapski, Pit., RC**	.15	.30
169	**Derek Laxdal, Tor., RC**	.03	.05
170	Clint Malarchuk, Goalie, Buf.	.03	.05
171	Kelly Kisio, NYR	.03	.05
172	Gerard Gallant, Det.	.03	.05
173	Ronald Sutter, Phi.	.03	.05
174	Chris Chelios, Mon.	.10	.20
175	Ron Francis, Har.	.10	.20
176	Gino Cavallini, St. L.	.03	.05
177	Brian Bellows, Min.	.07	.15
178	Greg Adams, Van.	.03	.05
179	Steve Larmer, Chi.	.10	.20
180	Aaron Broten, NJ	.03	.05
181	Brent Ashton, Win.	.03	.05
182	**Gerald Diduck, NYI, RC**	.03	.05
183	**Paul MacDermid, Har., RC**	.03	.05
184	Walter Poddubny, NJ	.03	.05
185	Adam Oates, St. L.	.30	.60
186	Brett Hull, St. L.	1.25	2.50
187	Scott Arniel, Buf.	.03	.05
188	Robert Smith, Mon.	.03	.05
189	Guy Lafleur, NYR	.05	.10
190	**Craig Janney, Bos., RC**	.85	1.75
191	Mark Howe, Phi.	.03	.05
192	Grant Fuhr, Goalie, Edm.	.07	.15
193	Rob Brown, Pit.	.03	.05
194	Stephen Kasper, LA	.03	.05
195	Peter Peeters, Goalie, Phi.	.03	.05
196	Joe Mullen, Cal.	.10	.20
197	Checklist 1 (1 - 110)	.10	.20
198	Checklist 2 (111 - 220)	.10	.20
199	Keith Crowder, LA	.03	.05
200	Daren Puppa, Goalie, Buf., RC	.30	.60
201	Benoit Hogue, Buf., RC	.30	.60

CALGARY FLAMES

No.	Player	EX	NRMT
202	**Gary Roberts, RC**	.75	1.50
203	Byron (Brad) McCrimmon	.03	.05
204	Richard Wamsley, Goalie	.03	.05
205	Joel Otto	.03	.05
206	James Peplinski	.03	.05
207	Jamie Macoun	.03	.05
208	Brian MacLellan	.03	.05

— 1989 - 90 REGULAR ISSUE — O-PEE-CHEE • 103

HARTFORD WHALERS

No.	Player	EX	NRMT
209	**Scott Young, RC**	**.12**	**.25**
210	Ulf Samuelsson	.03	.05
211	Joel Quenneville	.03	.05

LOS ANGELES KINGS

No.	Player	EX	NRMT
212	Timothy Watters, LA	.03	.05

MINNESOTA NORTH STARS

No.	Player	EX	NRMT
213	Curt Giles	.03	.05
214	Robert (Stewart) Gavin	.03	.05
215	Bob Brooke	.03	.05
216	**Basil McRae, RC**	**.15**	**.30**
217	**Frantisek Musil, RC**	**.10**	**.20**

CHICAGO BLACK HAWKS

No.	Player	EX	NRMT
218	**Adam Creighton, RC**	**.12**	**.25**
219	Troy Murray	.03	.05
220	Stephen Konroyd	.03	.05
221	Duane Sutter	.03	.05
222	**Trent Yawney, RC**	**.03**	**.05**

DETROIT RED WINGS

No.	Player	EX	NRMT
223	Michael O'Connell	.03	.05
224	James Nill, LC	.03	.05
225	John Chabot	.03	.05

EDMONTON OILERS

No.	Player	EX	NRMT
226	Glenn Anderson	.03	.05
227	Kevin Lowe	.03	.05
228	Steve Smith	.10	.20
229	Randall Gregg	.03	.05
230	Craig MacTavish	.03	.05
231	Craig Muni	.03	.05

CALGARY FLAMES

No.	Player	EX	NRMT
232	**Theoren Fleury, RC**	**2.00**	**4.00**

EDMONTON OILERS

No.	Player	EX	NRMT
233	Bill Ranford, Goalie	.20	.40

MONTREAL CANADIENS

No.	Player	EX	NRMT
234	Claude Lemieux	.15	.30

LOS ANGELES KINGS

No.	Player	EX	NRMT
235	Larry Robinson	.03	.05

MONTREAL CANADIENS

No.	Player	EX	NRMT
236	Craig Ludwig	.03	.05
237	Brian Hayward, Goalie	.03	.05
238	Petr Svoboda	.03	.05
239	Russ Courtnall	.03	.05
240	Ryan Walter	.03	.05

NEW JERSEY DEVILS

No.	Player	EX	NRMT
241	Tommy Albelin	.03	.05
242	Doug Brown	.03	.05
243	**Kenneth Daneyko, RC**	**.10**	**.20**
244	Mark Johnson	.02.	.05
245	**Randy Velischek, RC**	**.07**	**.15**

NEW YORK ISLANDERS

No.	Player	EX	NRMT
246	**Brad Dalgarno, RC**	**.03**	**.05**
247	Mikko Makela	.03	.05

MONTREAL CANADIENS

No.	Player	EX	NRMT
248	**Shayne Corson, RC**	**.25**	**.50**

NEW YORK ISLANDERS

No.	Player	EX	NRMT
249	**Marc Bergevin, RC**	**.05**	**.10**
250	Patrick Flatley	.03	.05

NEW YORK RANGERS

No.	Player	EX	NRMT
251	Michel Petit (Now with Nordiques 10-5-89)	.03	.05
252	Mark Hardy	.03	.05

PHILADELPHIA FLYERS

No.	Player	EX	NRMT
253	Scott Mellanby	.03	.05
254	Keith Acton	.03	.05
255	Ken Wregget, Goalie	.03	.05

PITTSBURGH PENGUINS

No.	Player	EX	NRMT
256	**Gord Dineen, RC**	**.07**	**.15**
257	David Hannan (Now with Maple Leafs 10-2-89)	.03	.05

LOS ANGELES KINGS

No.	Player	EX	NRMT
258	Mario Gosselin, Goalie	.03	.05

QUEBEC NORDIQUES

No.	Player	EX	NRMT
259	Randy Moller (Now with Rangers 10-5-89)	.03	.05
260	Mario Marois	.03	.05
261	Robert Picard	.03	.05
262	**Marc Fortier, RC**	**.03**	**.05**
263	**Ron Tugnutt, Goalie RC**	**.25**	**.50**
264	**Iiro Jarvi, RC**	**.03**	**.05**
265	Paul Gillis	.03	.05
266	**Mike Hough, RC**	**.03**	**.05**

VANCOUVER CANUCKS

No.	Player	EX	NRMT
267	Jim Sandlak	.03	.05

WINNIPEG JETS

No.	Player	EX	NRMT
268	Greg Paslawski	.03	.05

ST. LOUIS BLUES

No.	Player	EX	NRMT
269	**Paul Cavallini, RC**	**.15**	**.30**
270	Gaston Gingras	.03	.05

TORONTO MAPLE LEAFS

No.	Player	EX	NRMT
271	Allan Bester, Goalie	.03	.05
272	Vincent Damphousse	.25	.50
273	**Daniel Marois, RC**	**.12**	**.25**
274	Mark Osborne, Error	.03	.05
275	Craig Laughlin, LC	.03	.05
276	Bradley Marsh	.03	.05
277	Dan Daoust	.03	.05

DETROIT RED WINGS

No.	Player	EX	NRMT
278	Borje Salming	.03	.05
279	Christopher Kotsopoulos	.03	.05

VANCOUVER CANUCKS

No.	Player	EX	NRMT
280	Tony Tanti	.03	.05
281	Barry Pederson	.03	.05
282	Richard Sutter	.03	.05
283	Stanley Smyl	.03	.05
284	Doug Lidster	.03	.05
285	Stephen Weeks, Goalie	.03	.05
286	Harold Snepsts	.03	.05
287	**Brian Bradley, RC**	**.50**	**1.00**
288	Larry Melnyk	.03	.05

WASHINGTON CAPITALS

No.	Player	EX	NRMT
289	Robert Gould (Now with Bruins 9-28-89)	.03	.05

WINNIPEG JETS

No.	Player	EX	NRMT
290	Thomas Steen	.03	.05
291	Randy Carlyle	.03	.05
292	**Hannu Jarvenpaa, RC, Error**	**.03**	**.05**
293	Iain Duncan	.03	.05
294	Douglas Smail	.03	.05

PITTSBURGH PENGUINS

No.	Player	EX	NRMT
295	James Kyte	.03	.05

WINNIPEG JETS

No.	Player	EX	NRMT
296	Daniel Berthiaume, Goalie	.03	.05
297	Peter Taglianetti	.03	.05

TEAM CARDS

No.	Team	EX	NRMT
298	Boston Bruins	.03	.05
299	Buffalo Sabres	.03	.05
300	Calgary Flames	.03	.05
301	Chicago Black Hawks	.03	.05
302	Detroit Red Wings	.03	.05
303	Edmonton Oilers	.03	.05
304	Hartford Whalers	.03	.05
305	Los Angeles Kings	.03	.05
306	Minnesota North Stars	.03	.05
307	Montreal Canadiens	.03	.05
308	New Jersey Devils	.03	.05
309	New York Islanders	.03	.05
310	New York Rangers	.03	.05
311	Philadelphia Flyers	.03	.05
312	Pittsburgh Penguins	.03	.05
313	Quebec Nordiques	.03	.05
314	St. Louis Blues	.03	.05
315	Toronto Maple Leafs	.03	.05
316	Vancouver Canucks	.03	.05
317	Washington Capitals	.03	.05
318	Winnipeg Jets	.03	.05

TROPHY WINNERS

No.	Player	EX	NRMT
319	**The Art Ross Trophy:** Mario Lemieux	**.15**	**.30**
320	**The Hart Trophy:** Wayne Gretzky	**.25**	**.50**
321	**The Calder Memorial Trophy:** Brian Leetch	**.30**	**.60**
322	**The Vezina Trophy:** Patrick Roy	**.20**	**.45**
323	**The James Norris Memorial Trophy:** Chris Chelios	**.10**	**.20**
324	**The Lady Byng Memorial Trophy:** Joe Mullen	**.12**	**.25**

1988-89 HIGHLIGHTS

No.	Player	EX	NRMT
325	Wayne Gretzky	.20	.40
326	Brian Leetch, Error	.20	.40
327	Mario Lemieux	.20	.40
328	Esa Tikkanen	.03	.05
329	**Stanley Cup Champions:** Calgary Flames	**.03**	**.05**
330	Checklist 3 (221 - 330)	.05	.10

104 • O-PEE-CHEE — 1990 - 91 REGULAR ISSUE —

— 1990 - 91 REGULAR ISSUE —

 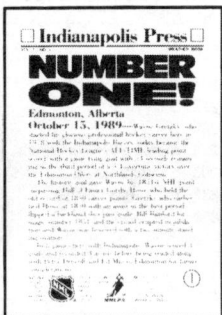

1990 - 91 Regular Issue
Card No. 1, Wayne Gretzky
Indianapolis Press

Card Size: 2 1/2" X 3 1/2"
Face: Four colour, white border, Team name, Position
Back: Green and blue on white card, Number, Resume, Bilingual
Imprint: © 1990 O-PEE-CHEE CO. LTD. PTD. IN CANADA
IMPRIMÉ AU CANADA © 1990 NHLPA
Complete Set No.: 528

Complete Set Price:	10.00	20.00
Common Card:	.03	.05
Wax Pack: (9 Cards)		.75
Wax Box: (36 Packs)		20.00
Wax Case: (24 Boxes)		275.00

TRIBUTE TO GRETZKY

No.	Player	EX	NRMT
1	Wayne Gretzky, Indianapolis Press	.25	.50
2	Wayne Gretzky, Edmonton Times	.25	.50
3	Wayne Gretzky, Los Angeles News	.25	.50

1989-90 HIGHLIGHTS

No.	Player	EX	NRMT
4	Brett Hull, St. L.	.10	.20
5	Jari Kurri, Edm., Error	.03	.05
6	Bryan Trottier, NYI	.03	.05

REGULAR ISSUE

No.	Player	EX	NRMT
7	Jeremy Roenick, Chi., RC	1.00	2.00
8	Brian Propp, Bos.	.03	.05
9	Top Prospect: Jim Hrivnak, Goalie, Wash., RC	.12	.25
10	Mick Vukota, NYI, RC	.03	.05
11	Tom Kurvers, Tor.	.03	.05
12	Ulf Dahlen, Min.	.03	.05
13	Bernie Nicholls, NYR	.08	.15
14	Peter Sidorkiewicz, Goalie, Har.	.03	.06
15	Peter Zezel, St. L. (Now with Capitals)	.03	.05
16	Mike Hartman, Buf., RC	.03	.05
17	Los Angeles Kings	.03	.05
18	Jim Sandlak, Van.	.03	.05
19	Rob Brown, Pit.	.03	.05
20	Paul Ranheim, Cal., RC	.10	.20
21	Richard Zombo, Det., RC	.03	.05
22	Paul Gillis, Que.	.03	.05
23	Brian Hayward, Goalie, Mon.	.03	.06
24	Brent Ashton, Win.	.03	.05
25	Mark Lamb, Edm., RC	.03	.05
26	Rick Tocchet, Phi.	.08	.15
27	Vlacheslav Fetisov, NJ, RC	.12	.25
28	Denis Savard, Chi. (Now with Canadiens)	.08	.15
29	Chris Chelios, Mon. (Now with Blackhawks)	.08	.15
30	Janne Ojanen, NJ, RC	.03	.05
31	Donald Maloney, NYI	.03	.05
32	Allan Bester, Goalie, Tor.	.03	.06
33	Geoff Smith, Edm., RC	.03	.05
34	Daniel Shank, Det., RC	.03	.05
35	Bo Mikael Andersson, Har., RC	.05	.10
36	Gino Cavallini, St. L.	.03	.05
37	Top Prospect: Rob Murphy, Van., RC	.03	.05
38	Calgary Flames	.03	.05
39	Laurie Boschman, Win.	.03	.05
40	Craig Wolanin, Que., RC	.03	.05
41	Phil Bourque, Pit.	.03	.05
42	Alexander Mogilny, Buf., RC	.75	1.50
43	Raymond Bourque, Bos.	.12	.25
44	Michael Liut, Goalie, Wash.	.03	.06
45	Ronald Sutter, Phi.	.03	.05
46	Bob Kudelski, LA, RC	.20	.40
47	Lawrence Murphy, Min.	.03	.05
48	Darren Turcotte, NYR, RC	.12	.25
49	Top Prospect: Paul Ysebaert, NJ, RC	.12	.25
50	Alan Kerr, NYI	.03	.05
51	Randy Carlyle, Win.	.03	.05
52	Iiro Jarvi, Que.	.03	.05
53	Don Barber, Min., RC	.10	.20
54	Carey Wilson, Har., Error	.03	.05
55	Joey Kocur, Det., RC	.08	.15
56	Steve Larmer, Chi.	.03	.05
57	Paul Cavallini, St. L.	.03	.05
58	Shayne Corson, Mon.	.03	.05
59	Vancouver Canucks	.03	.05
60	Sergei Makarov, Cal., RC	.25	.50
61	Kjell Samuelsson, Phi.	.03	.05
62	Tony Granato, LA	.10	.20
63	Tom Fergus, Tor.	.03	.05
64	Martin Gelinas, Edm., RC	.07	.15
65	Tom Barrasso, Goalie, Pit.	.03	.06
66	Pierre Turgeon, Buf.	.15	.30
67	Randy Cunneyworth, Har.	.03	.05
68	Michal Pivonka, Wash., RC	.15	.30
69	Cam Neely, Bos.	.15	.30
70	Brian Bellows, Min.	.03	.05
71	Pat Elynuik, Win.	.03	.05
72	Doug Crossman, NYI	.03	.05
73	Sylvain Turgeon, NJ	.03	.05
74	Shawn Burr, Det.	.03	.05
75	John Vanbiesbrouck, Goalie, NYR	.10	.20
76	Steve Bozek, Van.	.03	.05
77	Brett Hull, St. L.	.30	.60
78	Zarley Zalapski, Pit.	.03	.05
79	Wendel Clark, Tor.	.03	.05
80	Philadelphia Flyers	.03	.05
81	Kelly Miller, Wash.	.03	.05
82	Top Prospect: Mark Pederson, Mon., RC	.03	.05
83	Adam Creighton, Chi.	.03	.05
84	Scott Young, Har.	.03	.05
85	Petr Klima, Edm.	.03	.05
86	Steve Duchesne, LA	.03	.05
87	Joe Nieuwendyk, Cal.	.07	.15
88	Andy Brickley, Bos.	.03	.05
89	Phil Housley, Buf. (Now with Jets)	.03	.05
90	Neal Broten, Min.	.03	.05
91	Al Iafrate, Tor.	.03	.05
92	Steve Thomas, Chi.	.03	.05
93	Guy Carbonneau, Mon.	.03	.05
94	Steve Chiasson, Det.	.03	.05
95	Mike Tomlak, Har., RC	.03	.05
96	Top Prospect: Roger Johansson, Cal., RC	.03	.05
97	Randy Wood, NYI	.03	.05
98	Jim Johnson, Pit.	.03	.05
99	Bob Sweeney, Bos.	.03	.05
100	Dino Ciccarelli, Wash.	.03	.05
101	New York Rangers	.03	.05
102	Michael Ramsey, Buf.	.03	.05
103	Kelly Hrudey, Goalie, LA	.03	.06
104	Dave Ellett, Win.	.03	.05
105	Bob Brooke, NJ	.03	.05
106	Greg Adams, Van.	.03	.05
107	Joe Cirella, Que.	.03	.05
108	Jari Kurri, Edm.	.03	.05
109	Peter Peeters, Goalie, Phi.	.03	.06
110	Paul MacLean, St. L.	.03	.05
111	Douglas Wilson, Chi.	.03	.05
112	Patrick Verbeek, Har.	.03	.05
113	Top Prospect: Bob Beers, Bos., RC	.07	.15
114	Michael O'Connell, Det.	.03	.05
115	Brian Bradley, Van.	.03	.05
116	Paul Coffey, Pit.	.10	.20
117	Doug Brown, NJ	.03	.05
118	Aaron Broten, Min.	.03	.05
119	Bob Essensa, Goalie, Win., RC	.25	.50
120	Wayne Gretzky, LA, Error	.75	1.50
121	Vincent Damphousse, Tor.	.03	.05
122	Quebec Nordiques	.03	.05
123	Mike Foligno, Buf.	.03	.05
124	Russ Courtnall, Mon.	.03	.05
125	Richard Meagher, St. L.	.03	.05
126	Top Prospect: Craig Fisher, Phi., RC	.03	.05
127	Al MacInnis, Cal.	.15	.25
128	Derek King, NYI	.03	.05
129	Dale Hunter, Wash.	.03	.05
130	Mark Messier, Edm.	.20	.35
131	James Patrick, NYR, Error	.03	.05
132	Checklist 1 (1 - 132)	.08	.15
133	Detroit Red Wings	.03	.05
134	Barry Pederson, Pit.	.03	.05
135	Gary Leeman, Tor.	.03	.05
136	Douglas Gilmour, Cal.	.12	.25
137	Michael McPhee, Mon.	.03	.05
138	Bob Murray, Chi., LC	.03	.05
139	Robert Carpenter, Bos.	.03	.05
140	Sean Burke, Goalie, NJ	.03	.06
141	Dale Hawerchuk, Win. (Now with Sabres)	.08	.15
142	Guy Lafleur, Que.	.10	.20
143	Lindy Ruff, NYR	.03	.05
144	Hartford Whalers	.03	.05
145	Glenn Anderson, Edm.	.03	.05
146	Top Prospect: Dave Chyzowski, NYI, RC	.03	.05
147	Kevin Hatcher, Wash.	.03	.05
148	Richard Vaive, Buf.	.03	.05
149	Adam Oates, St. L.	.12	.25
150	Garth Butcher, Van.	.03	.05
151	Basil McRae, Min.	.03	.05
152	Ilkka Sinisalo, Phi. (Now with North Stars)	.03	.05
153	Stephen Kasper, LA	.03	.05
154	Greg Paslawski, Win.	.03	.05
155	Bradley Marsh, Tor.	.03	.05
156	Esa Tikkanen, Edm.	.03	.05
157	Tony Tanti, Pit.	.03	.05
158	Mario Marois, Que.	.03	.05
159	Sylvain Lefebvre, Mon., RC	.08	.15
160	Troy Murray, Chi.	.03	.05
161	Gary Roberts, Cal.	.03	.05
162	Randy Ladouceur, Har.	.03	.05
163	John Chabot, Det.	.03	.05
164	Calle Johansson, Wash.	.03	.05
165	Boston Bruins	.03	.05
166	Jeff Norton, NYI	.03	.05
167	Michael Krushelnyski, LA	.03	.05
168	Dave Gagner, Min.	.03	.05
169	Dave Andreychuk, Buf.	.03	.05
170	Dave Capuano, Van., RC	.03	.05
171	Top Prospect: Curtis Joseph, Goalie, St. L., RC	.50	1.00
172	Bruce Driver, NJ	.03	.05
173	Scott Mellanby, Phi.	.03	.05
174	John Ogrodnick, NYR	.03	.05
175	Mario Lemieux, Pit.	.50	1.00
176	Mark Fortier, Que.	.03	.05
177	Vincent Riendeau, Goalie, St. L., RC	.10	.20
178	Mark Johnson, NJ	.03	.05
179	Dirk Graham, Chi.	.03	.05
180	Winnipeg Jets	.03	.05
181	Top Prospect: Robb Stauber, Goalie, LA, RC	.12	.25
182	Christian Ruuttu, Buf.	.03	.05
183	Dave Tippett, Har.	.03	.05
184	Pat LaFontaine, NYI	.10	.20
185	Mark Howe, Phi.	.03	.05
186	Stephane Richer, Mon.	.05	.10
187	Jan Erixon, NYR	.03	.05
188	Neil Sheehy, Wash.	.03	.05
189	Craig MacTavish, Edm.	.03	.05
190	Randy Burridge, Bos.	.03	.05
191	Bernie Federko, Det.	.03	.05
192	Shawn Chambers, Min.	.03	.05

ALL STARS
First Team

No.	Player	EX	NRMT
193	Mark Messier, Edm.	.10	.20
194	Luc Robitaille, LA	.10	.20
195	Brett Hull, St. L.	.15	.30
196	Raymond Bourque, Bos.	.07	.15
197	Al MacInnis, Cal.	.10	.20
198	Patrick Roy, Goalie, Mon.	.25	.50

— 1990 - 91 REGULAR ISSUE — O-PEE-CHEE • 105

Second Team

No.	Player	EX	NRMT
199	Wayne Gretzky, LA	.20	.40
200	Brian Bellows, Min.	.03	.05
201	Cam Neely, Bos.	.03	.05
202	Paul Coffey, Pit.	.03	.05
203	Douglas Wilson, Chi.	.03	.05
204	Daren Puppa, Goalie, Buf.	.03	.06

REGULAR ISSUE

No.	Player	EX	NRMT
205	Gary Suter, Cal.	.03	.05
206	Ed Olczyk, Tor.	.03	.05
207	Doug Lidster, Van.	.03	.05
208	John Cullen, Pit.	.03	.05
209	Luc Robitaille, LA	.20	.40
210	Tim Kerr, Phi.	.03	.05
211	Scott Stevens, Wash. (Now with Blues)	.03	.05
212	Craig Janney, Bos.	.10	.20
213	Kevin Dineen, Har.	.03	.05
214	**Top Prospect: Jimmy Waite, Goalie, Chi., RC**	.12	.25
215	Benoit Hogue, Buf.	.03	.05
216	**Curtis Leschyshyn, Que., RC**	.03	.05
217	Brad Lauer, NYI	.03	.05
218	Joe Mullen, Cal. (Now with Penguins)	.03	.05
219	Patrick Roy, Goalie, Mon.	.15	.30
220	St. Louis Blues	.03	.05
221	Brian Leetch, NYR	.12	.25
222	Steve Yzerman, Det.	.20	.40
223	**Top Prospect: Stephane Beauregard, Goalie, Win., RC**	.10	.20
224	John MacLean, NJ	.03	.05
225	Trevor Linden, Van.	.12	.25
226	Bill Ranford, Goalie, Edm.	.08	.15
227	Mark Osborne, Tor.	.03	.05
228	Curt Giles, Min.	.03	.05
229	Mikko Makela, LA	.03	.05
230	Bob Errey, Pit.	.03	.05
231	Jimmy Carson, Det.	.03	.05
232	**Top Prospect: Kay Whitmore, Goalie, Har., RC**	.15	.25
233	Gary Nylund, NYI	.03	.05
234	**Jiri Hrdina, Cal., RC**	.05	.10
235	Stephen Leach, Wash., Error	.03	.05
236	Greg Hawgood, Bos.	.03	.05
237	**Jocelyn Lemieux, Chi., RC**	.08	.15
238	Daren Puppa, Goalie, Buf.	.03	.06
239	Kelly Kisio, NYR	.03	.05
240	Craig Simpson, Edm.	.03	.05
241	Toronto Maple Leafs	.03	.05
242	Fredrik Olausson, Win.	.03	.05
243	Ron Hextall, Goalie, Phi.	.03	.06
244	**Sergio Momesso, St. L., RC**	.13	.25
245	Kirk Muller, NJ	.03	.05
246	Petr Svoboda, Mon.	.03	.05
247	Daniel Berthiaume, Goalie, Min.	.03	.06
248	Andrew McBain, Van.	.03	.05
249	Jeff Jackson, Que.	.03	.05
250	**Randy Gilhen, Pit., RC**	.03	.05
251	Edmonton Oilers	.03	.05
252	**Top Prospect: Eric Bennet, NYR, RC**	.03	.05
253	Don Beaupre, Goalie, Wash.	.03	.06
254	Per-Eirk Eklund, Phi.	.03	.05
255	Gregory Gilbert, Chi.	.03	.05
256	Gordon Roberts, St. L.	.03	.05
257	Kirk McLean, Goalie, Van.	.08	.15
258	Brent Sutter, NYI	.03	.05
259	Brendan Shanahan, NJ	.08	.15
260	**Todd Krygier, Har., RC**	.08	.15
261	Larry Robinson, LA	.03	.05
262	Buffalo Sabres	.03	.05
263	Dave Christian, Bos.	.03	.05
264	Checklist 2 (133 - 264)	.08	.15
265	Jamie Macoun, Cal.	.03	.05
266	Glen Hanlon, Goalie, Det.	.03	.06
267	Daniel Marois, Tor.	.10	.20
268	Douglas Smail, Win.	.03	.05
269	Jon Casey, Goalie, Min.	.03	.06
270	Brian Skrudland, Mon.	.03	.05
271	Michel Petit, Que.	.03	.05
272	Dan Quinn, Van.	.03	.05
273	Geoff Courtnall, Wash. (Now with Blues)	.03	.05
274	Mike Bullard, Phi.	.03	.05

No.	Player	EX	NRMT
275	Randall Gregg, Edm.	.03	.05
276	Keith Brown, Chi.	.03	.05
277	**Troy Mallette, NYR, RC**	.03	.05
278	Steve Tuttle, St. L.	.03	.05
279	**Brad Shaw, Har., RC**	.08	.15
280	**Mark Recchi, Pit., RC**	.60	1.25
281	John Tonelli, LA	.03	.05
282	Doug Bodger, Buf.	.03	.05
283	Thomas Steen, Win.	.03	.05
284	New Jersey Devils	.03	.05
285	Lee Norwood, Det.	.03	.05
286	Brian MacLellan, Cal.	.03	.05
287	Robert Smith, Mon.	.03	.05
288	**Robert Cimetta, Bos., RC**	.03	.05
289	**Top Prospect: Rob Zettler, Min., RC**	.03	.05
290	**David Reid, Tor., RC**	.03	.05
291	Bryan Trottier, NYI (Now with Penguins)	.03	.05
292	Brian Mullen, NYR	.03	.05
293	Paul Reinhart, Van.	.03	.05
294	Andrew Moog, Goalie, Bos.	.03	.05
295	Jeff Brown, St. L.	.03	.05
296	Ryan Walter, Mon.	.03	.05
297	Trent Yawney, Chi.	.03	.05
298	**John Druce, Wash., RC**	.03	.05
299	Dave McIlwain, Win.	.03	.05
300	David Volek, NYI	.03	.05
301	Tomas Sandstrom, LA	.03	.05
302	**Gordon Murphy, Phi., RC**	.03	.05
303	**Lou Franceschetti, Tor., RC**	.03	.05
304	Dana Murzyn, Cal	.03	.05
305	Minnesota North Stars	.03	.05
306	Patrik Sundstrom, NJ	.03	.05
307	Kevin Lowe, Edm	.03	.05
308	Dave Barr, Det.	.03	.05
309	Wendell Young, Goalie, Pit., RC	.07	.15
310	**Top Prospect: Darrin Shannon, Buf., RC**	.08	.15
311	Ron Francis, Har.	.03	.05
312	**Top Prospect: Stephane Fiset, Goalie, Que., RC**	.20	.40
313	Paul Fenton, Win.	.03	.05
314	David Taylor, LA	.03	.05
315	New York Islanders	.03	.05
316	Petri Skriko, Van.	.03	.05
317	George (Rob) Ramage, Tor.	.03	.05
318	Murray Craven, Phi.	.03	.05
319	Gaetan Duchesne, Min.	.03	.05
320	Byron (Brad) McCrimmon, Cal. (Now with Red Wings)	.03	.05
321	Grant Fuhr, Goalie, Edm.	.08	.15
322	Gerard Gallant, Det.	.03	.05
323	Tommy Albelin, NJ	.03	.05
324	Scott Arniel, Buf. (Now with Jets)	.03	.05
325	**Mike Keane, Mon., RC**	.12	.25
326	Pittsburgh Penguins	.03	.05
327	Mike Ridley, Wash.	.03	.05
328	Dave Babych, Har.	.03	.05
329	Michel Goulet, Chi.	.03	.05
330	**Mike Richter, Goalie, NYR, RC**	.50	1.00
331	Garry Galley, Bos., RC	.03	.05
332	**Rod Brind'Amour, St. L., RC**	.40	.80
333	Anthony McKegney, Que.	.03	.05
334	Peter Stastny, NJ	.03	.05
335	Greg Millen, Goalie, Chi.	.03	.06
336	Ray Ferraro, Har,	.03	.05
337	**Miloslav Horava, NYR, RC**	.03	.05
338	Paul MacDermid, Win.	.03	.05
339	**Craig Coxe, Van., RC**	.03	.05
340	**Dave Snuggerud, Buf., RC**	.03	.05
341	**Mike Lalor, St. L., RC** (Now with Capitals)	.03	.05
342	Marc Habscheid, Det.	.03	.05
343	Rejean Lemelin, Goalie, Bos.	.03	.06
344	Charles Huddy, Edm.	.03	.05
345	Ken Linseman, Phi.	.03	.05
346	Montreal Canadiens	.03	.05
347	Troy Loney, Pit., RC	.03	.05
348	**Michael Modano, Min., RC**	.60	1.25
349	**Top Prospect: Jeff Reese, Goalie, Tor., RC**	.08	.15
350	Patrick Flatley, NYI	.03	.05
351	Michael Vernon, Goalie, Cal.	.08	.15
352	**Todd Elik, LA, RC**	.12	.25
353	Rod Langway, Wash.	.03	.05

No.	Player	EX	NRMT
354	Maurice Mantha, Win.	.03	.05
355	Keith Acton, Phi.	.03	.05
356	**Scott Pearson, Tor., RC**	.25	.50
357	**Perry Berezan, Min., RC**	.03	.05
358	**Alexei Kasatonov, NJ, RC**	.10	.20
359	**Igor Larionov, Van., RC**	.15	.30
360	**Kevin Stevens, Pit., RC**	.60	1.25
361	**Top Prospect: Yves Racine, Det., RC**	.03	.05
362	David Poulin, Bos.	.03	.05
363	Chicago Blackhawks	.03	.05
364	**Yvon Corriveau, Har., RC**	.03	.05
365	Brian Benning, LA	.03	.05
366	**Huble McDonough, NYI, RC**	.03	.05
367	Ron Tugnutt, Goalie, Que.	.03	.06
368	Steve Smith, Edm.	.03	.05
369	Joel Otto, Cal.	.03	.05
370	**Dave Lowry, St. L., RC**	.03	.05
371	Clint Malarchuk, Goalie, Buf.	.03	.06
372	**Mathieu Schneider, Mon., RC**	.18	.35
373	Michael Gartner, NYR	.03	.05
374	John Tucker, Wash. (Now with Sabres)	.03	.05
375	**Chris Terreri, Goalie, NJ, RC**	.20	.40
376	Dean Evason, Har.	.03	.05
377	**Top Prospect: Jamie Leach, Pit., RC**	.03	.05
378	**Jacques Cloutier, Goalie, Chi., RC**	.05	.10
379	Glen Wesley, Bos.	.03	.05
380	Vladimir Krutov, Van.	.08	.15
381	Terry Carkner, Phi.	.03	.05
382	John McIntyre, Tor., RC	.08	.15
383	**Ville Siren, Min., RC**	.03	.05
384	Joe Sakic, Que.	.30	.60
385	**Teppo Numminen, Win., RC**	.13	.25
386	Theoren Fleury, Cal.	.20	.40
387	**Glen Featherstone, St. L., RC**	.03	.05
388	**Stephan Lebeau, Mon., RC**	.20	.40
389	Kevin McClelland, Det.	.03	.05
390	Uwe Krupp, Buf.	.03	.05
391	**Mark Janssens, NYR, RC**	.03	.05
392	Martin McSorley, LA	.03	.05
393	**Top Prospect: Vladimir Ruzicka, Edm., RC**	.12	.25
394	Washington Capitals	.03	.05
395	**Mark Fitzpatrick, Goalie, NYI, RC**	.05	.10
396	Checklist 3 (265 - 396)	.08	.15
397	Dave Manson, Chi.	.03	.05
398	Robert Gould, Bos.	.03	.05
399	**Bill Houlder, Wash., RC**	.03	.05
400	Glenn Healy, Goalie, NYI, RC	.08	.15
401	**John Kordic, Tor., RC, Error**	.13	.25
402	Robert (Stewart) Gavin, Min.	.03	.05
403	David Shaw, NYR	.03	.05
404	**Edward Kastelic, Har., RC**	.03	.05
405	Richard Sutter, St. L.	.03	.05
406	**Grant Ledyard, Buf., RC**	.03	.05
407	Stephen Weeks, Goalie, Van.	.03	.06
408	Randy Hillier, Pit.	.03	.05
409	Richard Wamsley, Goalie, Cal.	.03	.06
410	Doug Houda, Det., RC	.03	.05
411	Ken McRae, Que., RC	.03	.05
412	Craig Ludwig, Mon.	.03	.05
413	**Doug Evans, Win., RC**	.03	.05
414	**Ken Baumgartner, NYI, RC**	.03	.05
415	Ken Wregget, Goalie, Phi.	.03	.06
416	**Eric Weinrich, NJ, RC**	.10	.20
417	Mike Allison, LA	.03	.05
418	Joel Quenneville, Har.	.03	.05
419	Larry Melnyk, Van.	.03	.05
420	Colin Patterson, Cal.	.03	.05
421	Gerald Diduck, NYI	.03	.05
422	**Brent Gilchrist, Mon., RC**	.07	.15
423	Craig Muni, Edm.	.03	.05
424	**Mike Hudson, Chi., RC**	.08	.15
425	**Eric Desjardins, Mon., RC**	.12	.25
426	Walter Poddubny, NJ	.03	.05
427	Mike Hough, Que.	.03	.05
428	Luke Richardson, Tor.	.03	.05
429	**Joe Murphy, Edm., RC**	.15	.30
430	**Tim Cheveldae, Goalie, Det., RC**	.15	.30
431	**Adam Burt, Har., RC**	.03	.05
432	**Kelly Chase, St. L., RC**	.03	.05
433	**Robert Nordmark, Van., RC**	.03	.05
434	**Timothy Hunter, Cal., RC**	.10	.20
435	Peter Taglianetti, Win.,	.03	.05

106 • O-PEE-CHEE — 1990 - 91 INSERT SET —

No.	Player	EX	NRMT
436	Alain Chevrier, Goalie, Pit.	.03	.06
437	**Darin Kimble**, Que., RC	.07	.15
438	**David Maley**, NJ, RC	.03	.05
439	**James Wiemer**, Bos., RC, LC	.03	.05
440	**Nicholas Kypreos**, Wash., RC	.03	.05
441	Lucien DeBlois, Que.	.03	.05
442	Mario Gosselin, Goalie, LA	.03	.06
443	**Neil Wilkinson**, Min., RC	.05	.10
444	**Mark Kumpel**, Win., RC	.03	.05
445	**Sergei Mylnikov**, Goalie, Que., RC, Error	.10	.20
446	Ray Sheppard, Buf. (Now with Rangers)	.03	.05
447	Ronald Greschner, NYR (Released 7/17/90)	.03	.05
448	**Craig Berube**, Phi., RC	.03	.05
449	David Hannan, Tor.	.03	.05
450	James Korn, Cal.	.03	.05
451	Claude Lemieux, Mon.	.03	.05
452	**Eldon Reddick**, Goalie, Edm., RC	.03	.05
453	Randy Velischek, NJ	.03	.05
454	Christopher Nilan, NYR (Now with Bruins)	.03	.05
455	Jim Benning, Van.	.03	.05
456	Wayne Presley, Chi.	.03	.05
457	Jon Morris, NJ., RC	.03	.05
458	**Clark Donatelli**, Min., RC	.03	.05
459	Eric Nattress, Cal.	.03	.05
460	**Rob Murray**, Wash., RC	.03	.05
461	Timothy Watters, LA	.03	.05
462	Checklist 4 (397 - 528)	.08	.15
463	**Derrick Smith**, Phi., RC	.03	.05
464	**Lyndon Byers**, Bos., RC	.03	.05
465	**Jeff Chychrun**, Phi., RC	.03	.05
466	Duane Sutter, Chi.	.03	.05
467	**The Conn Smythe Trophy:** Bill Ranford, Goalie	.03	.06
468	Anatoli Semenov, Dynamo Riga	.20	.40
469	Konstantin Kurashov, Soviet Wings	.08	.15
470	Gord Dineen, Pit.	.03	.05
471	**Jeff Beukeboom**, Edm., RC	.08	.15
472	Andrei Lomakin, Dynamo Riga	.15	.30
473	Douglas Sulliman, Phi.	.03	.05
474	Alexander Kerch, Dynamo Riga	.03	.05
475	**The James Norris Memorial Trophy:** Ray Bourque	.03	.05
476	Keith Crowder, LA	.03	.05
477	Oleg Znarok, Dynamo Riga	.03	.05
478	Dimitri Zinovjev, Dynamo Riga	.03	.05
479	Igor Esmantovich, Soviet Wings	.03	.05
480	**Adam Graves**, Edm., RC	.75	1.50
481	**Petr Prajsler**, LA, RC	.08	.15
482	Sergei Yashin, Dynamo Riga	.03	.05
483	**Jeff Bloemberg**, NYR, RC	.03	.05
484	Yuri Strakhov, Soviet Wings	.03	.05
485	Sergei B. Makarov, Soviet Wings	.03	.05
486	**The William J. Jennings Trophy:** R. Lemelin / A. Moog	.03	.05
487	Sergei Zaitsev, Soviet Wings	.03	.05
488	**The Frank J. Selke Trophy:** Richard Meagher	.03	.05
489	Yuri Kusnetsov, Soviet Wings	.08	.15
490	**Tom Chorske**, Mon., RC	.03	.05
491	Igor Akulinin, Dynamo Riga	.03	.05
492	Mikhail Panin, Soviet Wings	.03	.05
493	Sergei Nemchinov, Soviet Wings	.35	.75
494	Vladimir Yurzinov, Coach, Dynamo Riga	.03	.05
495	Gordon Kluzak, Bos.	.03	.05
496	Sergei Skosyrev, Dynamo Riga	.03	.05
497	**Jeff Parker**, Buf., RC, (Now with Jets)	.03	.05
498	Tom Tilley, St. L., RC	.03	.05
499	Alexander Smirnov, Dynamo Riga	.10	.20
500	Alexander Lysenko, Soviet Wings	.10	.20
501	Arturs Irbe, Goalie, Dynamo Riga, Error	1.85	3.75
502	Alexei Frolikov, Dynamo Riga	.03	.05
503	**The Calder Memorial Trophy:** Sergei Makarov, RC	.03	.05
504	Nikolai Varjanov, Dynamo Riga	.03	.05
505	Allen Pedersen, Bos.	.03	.05
506	Vladimir Shashov, Dynamo Riga	.03	.05
507	**Tim Bergland**, Wash., RC	.03	.05
508	Gennady Lebedev, Soviet Wings	.03	.05
509	**Rod Buskas**, Pit., RC	.03	.05
510	**Grant Jennings**, Har., RC	.03	.05
511	Ulf Samuelsson, Har.	.03	.05
512	**The Vezina Trophy:** Patrick Roy	.12	.25
513	**The Lady Byng Trophy:** Brett Hull	.10	.20
514	Dimitri Mironov, Soviet Wings	.25	.50
515	Randy Moller, NYR	.03	.05
516	**Kerry Huffman**, Phi., RC	.03	.05
517	Gilbert Delorme, Pit.	.03	.05
518	Greg C. Adams, Det.	.03	.05
519	**The Hart Trophy:** Mark Messier	.08	.15
520	**Sheldon Kennedy**, Det., RC	.15	.30
521	Harijs Vitolinsh, Dynamo Riga	.03	.05
522	**The Art Ross Trophy:** Wayne Gretzky	.25	.50
523	Dmitri Frolov, Dynamo Riga	.03	.05
524	Thomas Laidlaw, LA	.03	.05
525	Oleg Bratash, Soviet Wings, Goalie	.05	.10
526	**Kris King**, NYR, RC	.05	.10
527	**Wayne Van Dorp**, Chi., RC	.03	.05
528	**Chris Dahlquist**, Pit., RC	.08	.15

— 1990 - 91 REGULAR ISSUE —
INSERT SET - CENTRAL RED ARMY

This set was available only in wax packs and was not included in regular factory sets.

1990 - 91 Insert Set - Central Red Army
Card No. 1R, Ilya Byalsin

Card Size: 2 1/2" X 3 1/2"
Face: Four colour, white border
Back: Two colour, green and blue on card stock, Number, Resume, Position
Imprint: © 1990 SOVIET ICE HOCKEY FEDERATION
© 1990 O-PEE-CHEE CO. LTD.
PTD. IN CANADA/IMPRIMÉ AU CANADA
Complete Set No.: 22
Complete Set Price: 7.00 14.00
Common Player: .05 .10

No.	Player	EX	NRMT
1R	Ilya Byalsin	.05	.10
2R	Vladimir Malakhov	.50	1.000
3R	Andrei Khomutov	.20	.40
4R	Valeri Kamensky	1.00	2.00
5R	Dimitri Motkov	.20	.45
6R	Evgeny Shastin	.12	.25
7R	Arturs Irbe, Goalie	2.00	4.00
8R	Igor Chibirev	.35	.75
9R	Maxim Mikhailovsky, Goalie	.20	.40
10R	Vyacheslav Bykov	.25	.50
11R	Super Series A (1976; 1980; 1986)	.15	.30
12R	Super Series B (1989; 1990)	.15	.30
13R	Valeri Shiryev	.15	.30
14R	Igor Maslennikov	.15	.30
15R	Igor Malykhin	.18	.35
16R	Dimitri Khristich	.75	1.50
17R	Viktor Tikhonov, Coach	.18	.35
18R	Evgeny Davydov, Error	.35	.75
19R	Sergei Fedorov	2.50	5.00
20R	Pavel Kostichkin	.20	.40
21R	Vladimir Konstantinov	.50	1.00
22R	Checklist (1R - 22R)	.20	.40

— 1990 - 91 PREMIER ISSUE —

Keeping with the trend of improving card quality, O-Pee-Chee issued a premium card set for the 1990-91 season. This first issue had a low print run and was the top set for this year. Beware of counterfeits of Fedorov, Jagr and Roenick. Details are in the front of this book.

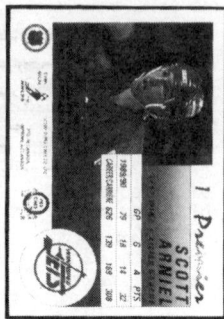

1990 - 91 Premier Issue
Card No. 1, Scott Arniel

Card Size: 2 1/2" X 3 1/2"
Face: Four colour, white border, Position, Bilingual
Back: Four colour, Team Logo, Number, Resume, Bilingual
Imprint: © 1991 O-PEE-CHEE CO. LTD. PTD IN CANADA/
IMPRIMÉ AU CANADA © 1991 NHLPA
Complete Set No.: 132
Complete Set Price: 35.00 75.00
Common Card: .10 .20
Wax Pack: (7 Cards) 6.00
Wax Box: (36 Packs) 175.00
Wax Case: (24 Boxes) 3,600.00

No.	Player	EX	NRMT
1	**Scott Arniel**, Win.	.10	.20
2	**Jergus Baca**, Har., RC	.10	.20
3	Brian Bellows, Min.	.10	.20
4	**Jean-Claude Bergeron**, Goalie, Mon., RC	.25	.50
5	Daniel Berthiaume, Goalie, LA	.20	.40
6	**Robert Blake**, LA, RC	2.00	4.00
7	**Peter Bondra**, Wash., RC	1.25	2.50
8	Laurie Boschman, NJ	.10	.20
9	Ray Bourque, Bos.	.25	.50
10	Aaron Broten, Que. (Now with Maple Leafs)	.10	.20
11	**Greg Brown**, Buf., RC	.20	.40
12	Jimmy Carson, Det.	.20	.40
13	Chris Chelios, Chi.	.30	.60
14	Dino Ciccarelli, Wash.	.10	.20
15	**Zdeno Ciger**, NJ, RC	.20	.40
16	Paul Coffey, Pit.	.45	.90
17	**Danton Cole**, Win., RC	.20	.40
18	Geoff Courtnall, St. L.	.10	.20
19	**Mike Craig**, Min., RC, Error	.20	.40
20	John Cullen, Pit.	.10	.20
21	Vincent Damphousse, Tor.	.25	.50
22	Gerald Diduck, Mon.	.10	.20
23	Kevin Dineen, Har.	.10	.20
24	**Per Olav Djoos**, Det., RC, Error	.10	.20
25	**Tahir Domi**, NYR, RC	.50	1.00
26	**Peter Douris**, Bos., RC	.10	.20
27	**Rob DiMaio**, NYI, RC	.10	.20
28	Pat Elynuik, Win.	.10	.20
29	**Bob Essensa**, Goalie, Win., RC	.50	1.00
30	**Sergei Fedorov**, Det., RC	8.00	16.00
31	**Brent Fedyk**, Det., RC	.35	.70
32	Ronald Francis, Har.	.10	.20
33	**Link Gaetz**, Min., RC	.15	.30
34	**Troy Gamble**, Goalie, Van, RC	.10	.20
35	**Johan Garpenlov**, Det., RC	.40	.85
36	Michael Gartner, NYR	.10	.20
37	Richard Green, Det.	.10	.20
38	Wayne Gretzky, LA	2.50	5.00
39	**Jeff Hackett**, Goalie, NYI, RC	.25	.50
40	Dale Hawerchuk, Buf., Error	.10	.20
41	Ron Hextall, Goalie, Phi.	.10	.20
42	**Bruce Hoffort**, Goalie, Phi., RC	.10	.20
43	**Robert Holik**, Har., RC	.85	1.75
44	**Martin Hostak**, Phi., RC	.10	.20
45	Phil Housley, Win.	.10	.20
46	**Jody Hull**, NYR, RC	.10	.20

— 1991 - 92 REGULAR ISSUE — O-PEE-CHEE • 107

No.	Player	EX	NRMT
47	Brett Hull, St. L.	1.50	3.00
48	Al Iafrate, Tor.	.12	.25
49	Peter Ing, Goalie, Tor., RC	.10	.20
50	Jaromir Jagr, Pit., RC	8.50	17.00
51	Curtis Joseph, Goalie, St.L., RC	3.25	6.50
52	Robert Kron, Van., RC	.10	.20
53	Frantisek Kucera, Chi., RC	.10	.20
54	Dale Kushner, Phi., RC	.10	.20
55	Guy Lafleur, Que.	.10	.20
56	Pat LaFontaine, NYI	.75	1.50
57	Mike Lalor, Wash., RC	.10	.20
58	Steve Larmer, Chi.	.10	.20
59	Jiri Latal, Phi., RC	.10	.20
60	Jamie Leach, Pit., RC	.10	.40
61	Brian Leetch, NYR	1.00	2.00
62	Claude Lemieux, NJ	.10	.20
63	Mario Lemieux, Pit.	3.00	6.00
64	Craig Ludwig, NYI	.10	.20
65	Al MacInnis, Cal.	.25	.50
66	Mikko Makela, Buf.	.10	.20
67	David Marcinyshyn, NJ, RC	.10	.20
68	Stephane Matteau, Cal., RC	.35	.75
69	Byron (Brad) McCrimmon, Det.	.10	.20
70	Kirk McLean, Goalie, Van.	.50	1.00
71	Mark Messier, Edm.	.50	1.00
72	Kelly Miller, Wash.	.10	.20
73	Kevin Miller, NYR, RC	.50	1.00
74	Michael Modano, Min., RC	4.00	8.00
75	Alexander Mogilny, Buf., RC	6.50	13.00
76	Andrew Moog, Goalie, Bos.	.20	.40
77	Joe Mullen, Pit.	.10	.20
78	Kirk Muller, NJ	.10	.20
79	Pat Murray, Phi., RC	.10	.20
80	Jarmo Myllys, Goalie, Min., RC	.20	.40
81	Petr Nedved, Van., RC	2.00	4.00
82	Cam Neely, Bos.	.30	.60
83	Bernie Nicholls, NYR	.10	.20
84	Joe Nieuwendyk, Cal.	.25	.50
85	Christopher Nilan, Bos.	.10	.20
86	Owen Nolan, Que., RC	1.50	3.00
87	Brian Noonan, Chi.	.10	.20
88	Adam Oates, St. L.	.35	.75
89	Greg Parks, NYI, RC	.10	.20
90	Adrien Plavsic, Van., RC	.10	.20
91	Keith Primeau, Det., RC	.85	1.75
92	Brian Propp, Min.	.10	.20
93	Dan Quinn, Van.	.10	.20
94	Bill Ranford, Goalie, Edm.	.25	.50
95	Robert Reichel, Cal., RC	1.50	3.00
96	Mike Ricci, Phi., RC, Error	1.25	2.50
97	Steven Rice, NYR RC	.25	.50
98	Stephane Richer, Mon.	.10	.20
99	Luc Robitaille, LA	.50	1.00
100	Jeremy Roenick, Chi., RC	8.00	16.00
101	Patrick Roy, Goalie, Mon.	1.50	3.00
102	Joe Sakic, Que.	1.00	2.00
103	Denis Savard, Mon.	.10	.20
104	Anatoli Semenov, Edm., RC	.35	.75
105	Brendan Shanahan, NJ	.60	1.25
106	Ray Sheppard, NYR	.25	.50
107	Mike Sillinger, Det., RC	.25	.50
108	Ilkka Sinisalo, Min.	.10	.20
109	Robert Smith, Min.	.10	.20
110	Paul Stanton, Pit., RC	.10	.20
111	Kevin Stevens, Pit., RC	3.00	6.00
112	Scott Stevens, St. L.	.20	.40
113	Allan Stewart, NJ, RC	.10	.20
114	Mats Sundin, Que., RC	4.50	9.00
115	Brent Sutter, NYI	.10	.20
116	Tim Sweeney, Cal., RC	.12	.25
117	Peter Taglianetti, Min.	.10	.20
118	John Tanner, Goalie, Que., RC	.10	.20
119	Dave Tippett, Wash.	.10	.20
120	Rick Tocchet, Phi.	.20	.40
121	Bryan Trottier, Pit.	.10	.20
122	John Tucker, Buf.	.10	.20
123	Darren Turcotte, NYR, RC	.75	1.50
124	Pierre Turgeon, Buf.	.60	1.25
125	Randy Velischek, Que.	.15	.30
126	Michael Vernon, Goalie, Cal.	.10	.20
127	Wes Walz, Bos., RC	.25	.50
128	Carey Wilson, Har.	.10	.20
129	Douglas Wilson, Chi.	.10	20

No.	Player	EX	NRMT
130	Steve Yzerman, Det.	.85	1.75
131	Peter Zezel, Wash.	.10	.20
132	Checklist (1 - 132)	.25	.50

— 1991 - 92 REGULAR ISSUE —

This set of has the largest number of cards ever issued for an O-PEE-CHEE hockey set. Included in the wax packs is an insert set divided between the new NHL franchise San Jose Sharks and a set showing three Russian teams.

The O-PEE-CHEE 1991-92 regular issue set has the same photographs as the Topps set.

 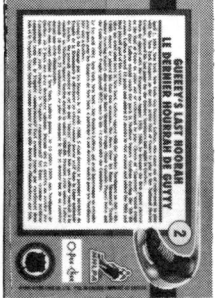

1991 - 92 Regular Issue
Card No. 2, Gueeey's Last Hoorah

Card Size: 2 1/2" X 3 1/2"
Face: Four colour, white border
Back: Blue, red and yellow on white card, Number, Resume, Bilingual
Imprint: © 1992 O-PEE-CHEE CO. LTD. PTD. IN CANADA IMPRIMÉ AU CANADA © 1992 NHLPA
Complete Set No.: 528
Complete Set Price: 6.50 13.00
Common Card: .03 .05
Wax Pack: (9 Cards) .50
Wax Box: (36 Packs) 7.00
Wax Case: (24 Boxes) 150.00

TRIBUTE TO LAFLEUR

No.	Player	EX	NRMT
1	Goodbye Guy!!	.05	.10
2	Gueeey's Last Hoorah	.05	.10
3	Guy Bids Farewell	.05	.10

SUPER ROOKIE

No.	Player	EX	NRMT
4	Ed Belfour, Goalie, Chi., Rookie Goals Against Average Leader	.10	.20
5	Kenneth Hodge, Jr., Bos., Rookie Power Play Goal Leader	.03	.05
6	Robert Blake, LA, Rookie Defenseman Points Leader	.05	.10
7	Robert Holik, Har., Rookie Left Wing Goal Leader	.05	.10
8	Sergei Fedorov, Det., Error Rookie Scoring Leader	.15	.30
9	Jaromir Jagr, Pit., Rookie Right Wing Goal Scoring Leader	.15	.30
10	Eric Weinrich, NJD Games Played by Rookie Defenseman	.03	.05
11	Mike Richter, Goalie, NYR, Rookie Save Percentage Leader	.08	.15
12	Mats Sundin, Que., Rookie Right Wing Points Leader	.13	.25
13	Mike Ricci, Phi., Rookie Power Play Goal Leader	.07	.15

REGULAR ISSUE

No.	Player	EX	NRMT
14	Eric Desjardins, Mon.	.03	.05
15	Paul Ranheim, Cal.	.03	.05
16	Joe Sakic, Que.	.15	.30
17	Curt Giles, Min.	.03	.05
18	Mike Foligno, Tor.	.03	.05
19	Bradley Marsh, Det.	.03	.05
20	Ed Belfour, Goalie, Chi.	.15	.30
21	James (Steve) Smith, Edm.	.03	.05

No.	Player	EX	NRMT
22	Kirk Muller, NJD	.03	.05
23	Kelly Chase, St. L.	.03	.05
24	Jim McKenzie, Har., RC	.05	.10
25	Mick Vukota, NYI	.03	.05
26	Top Prospect: Anthony Amonte, NYR, RC	.25	.50
27	Danton Cole, Win.	.03	.05
28	Jay Mazur, Van., RC	.03	.05
29	Peter Peeters, Goalie, Phi.	.03	.05
30	Petri Skriko, Bos.	.03	.05
31	Steve Duchesne, Phi., (Now With Flyers)	.03	.05
32	1990-91 Final Standings: Buffalo Sabres	.03	.05
33	Phil Bourque, Pit.	.03	.05
34	Tim Bergland, Was.	.03	.05
35	Tim Cheveldae, Goalie, Det.	.10	.20
36	Top Prospect: Bill Armstrong, Phi., RC	.03	.05
37	John McIntyre, LA	.03	.05
38	David Andreychuk, Buf.	.05	.10
39	Curtis Leschyshyn, Que.	.03	.05
40	Jaromir Jagr, Pit.	.40	.80
41	Craig Janney, Bos.	.07	.15
42	Doug Brown, NJD	.03	.05
43	Ken Sabourin, Was.	.03	.05
44	90-91 Final Standings: Minnesota North Stars	.03	.05
45	Fredrik Olausson, Win., Error	.03	.05
46	Michael Gartner, NYR	.05	.10
47	Mark Fitzpatrick, Goalie, NYI	.03	.05
48	Joe Murphy, Edm.	.03	.05
49	Douglas Wilson, Chi.	.03	.05
50	Brian MacLellan, Det. (Now With Red Wings)	.03	.05
51	Bob Bassen, St. L.	.03	.05
52	Robert Kron, Van.	.05	.10
53	Roger Johansson, Cal.	.05	.10
54	Guy Carbonneau, Mon.	.05	.10
55	George (Rob) Ramage, Min. (Now With North Stars)	.03	.05
56	Robert Holik, Har.	.10	.20
57	Alan May, Was.	.03	.05
58	Richard Meagher, St. L.	.03	.05
59	Cliff Ronning, Van.	.03	.05
60	90-91 Final Standings: Detroit Red Wings	.03	.05
61	Bob Kudelski, LA	.03	.05
62	Wayne McBean, NYI	.03	.05
63	Craig MacTavish, Edm.	.03	.05
64	Owen Nolan, Que.	.10	.20
65	Dale Hawerchuk, Buf.	.05	.10
66	Raymond Bourque, Bos.	.05	.10
67	Sean Burke, Goalie, NJD	.03	.05
68	Frantisek Musil, Cal.	.03	.05
69	Joe Mullen, Pit.	.05	.10
70	Top Prospect: Drake Berehowsky, Tor.	.05	.10
71	Darren Turcotte, NYR	.03	.05
72	Randy Carlyle, Win.	.03	.05
73	Paul Cyr, Har.	.03	.05
74	Dave Gagner, Min.	.03	.05
75	Steve Larmer, Chi.	.03	.05
76	Petr Svoboda, Mon.	.03	.05
77	Keith Acton, Phi.	.03	.05
78	Dmitri Khristich, Wash.	.03	.05
79	Byron (Brad) McCrimmon, Det.	.03	.05
80	Pat LaFontaine, NYI, Error	.15	.30
81	Jeff Reese, Goalie, Tor.	.03	.05
82	Mario Marois, St. L.	.03	.05
83	Rob Brown, Har.	.05	.10
84	Grant Fuhr, Goalie, Edm.	.03	.05
85	Carey Wilson, Cal.	.03	.05
86	Garry Galley, Bos.	.03	.05
87	Troy Murray, Win., (Now With Jets)	.03	.05
88	Tony Granato, LA	.03	.05
89	Gordon Murphy, Phi.	.03	.05
90	Brent Gilchrist, Mon.	.03	.05
91	Michael Richter, Goalie, NYR	.12	.25
92	Eric Weinrich, NJD	.03	.05
93	Marc Bureau, Min.	.03	.05
94	Bob Errey, Pit.	.03	.05
95	Dave McIlwain, Win.	.03	.05
96	90-91 Final Standings: Quebec Nordiques	.03	.05
97	Clint Malarchuk, Goalie, Buf.	.03	.05

No.	Player	EX	NRMT
98	**Top Prospect:** Shawn Antoski, Van.	.05	.10
99	Robert Sweeney, Bos.	.03	.05
100	Stephen Leach, Bos., (Now With Bruins)	.03	.05
101	Gary Nylund, NYI	.03	.05
102	Lucien DeBlois, Tor.	.03	.05
103	**90-91 Final Standings:** Edmonton Oilers	.03	.05
104	Jimmy Carson, Det.	.03	.05
105	Rod Langway, Was.	.03	.05
106	Jeremy Roenick, Chi.	.30	.60
107	Mike Vernon, Goalie, Cal.	.03	.05
108	Brian Leetch, NYR	.15	.30
109	Mark Hunter, Har.	.03	.05
110	Brian Bellows, Min.	.03	.05
111	Per-erik Eklund, Phi.	.03	.05
112	Robert Blake, LA	.08	.15
113	Mike Hough, Que.	.03	.05
114	Frank Pietrangelo, Goalie, Pit.	.03	.05
115	Christian Ruuttu, Buf.	.03	.05
116	**Top Prospect:** Bryan Marchment, Win., RC	.05	.10
117	Garry Valk, Van.	.03	.05
118	Ken Daneyko, NJD	.03	.05
119	Russell Courtnall, Mon.	.03	.05
120	Ronald Wilson, St. L.	.03	.05
121	**Top Prospect:** Shayne Stevenson, Bos.	.03	.05
122	Bill Berg, NYI, RC	.03	.05
123	**90-91 Final Standings:** Toronto Maple Leafs	.03	.05
124	Glenn Anderson, Edm.	.05	.10
125	Kevin Miller, Det.	.03	.05
126	Calle Johansson, Was.	.03	.05
127	Jim Waite, Goalie, Chi.	.03	.05
128	Allen Pedersen, Min., (Now With North Stars)	.03	.05
129	Brian Mullen, SJ	.03	.05
130	Ronald Francis, Pit.	.03	.05
131	**Top Prospect:** Jergus Baca, Har.	.03	.05
132	Checklist 1 (1 to 132)	.03	.05
133	Tony Tanti, Buf.	.03	.05
134	Wes Walz, Bos.	.03	.05
135	Stephan Lebeau, Mon.	.10	.20
136	Ken Wregget, Goalie, Phi.	.03	.05
137	Scott Arniel, Win.	.03	.05
138	David Taylor, LA	.03	.05
139	Steven Finn, Que.	.03	.05
140	Brendan Shanahan, St. L., (Now With Blues)	.05	.10
141	Petr Nedved, Van.	.13	.25
142	Chris Dahlquist, Min.	.03	.05
143	Richard Sutter, St. L.	.03	.05
144	Joe Reekie, NYI	.03	.05
145	Peter Ing, Goalie, Tor.	.03	.05
146	Ken Linseman, Edm.	.03	.05
147	David Barr, Det.	.03	.05
148	Al Iafrate, Was.	.03	.05
149	Gregory Gilbert, Chi.	.03	.05
150	Craig Ludwig, Min., (Now With North Stars)	.03	.05
151	Gary Suter, Cal.	.03	.05
152	Jan Erixon, NYR	.03	.05
153	Mario Lemieux, Pit.	.35	.70
154	Michael Liut, Goalie, Was.	.03	.05
155	Uwe Krupp, Buf.	.03	.05
156	Darin Kimble, St. L.	.03	.05
157	Shayne Corson, Mon.	.03	.05
158	**90-91 Final Standings:** Winnipeg Jets	.03	.05
159	Stephane Morin, Que.	.05	.10
160	Rick Tocchet, Phi.	.03	.05
161	John Tonelli, LA	.03	.05
162	Adrien Plavsic, Van.	.03	.05
163	**Top Prospect:** Jason Miller, NJD	.03	.05
164	Tim Kerr, NYR, (Now With Rangers)	.03	.05
165	Brent Sutter, NYI	.03	.05
166	Michel Petit, Tor.	.03	.05
167	Adam Graves, Edm.	.03	.05
168	Jamie Macoun, Cal.	.03	.05
169	Terry Yake, Har.	.03	.05
170	**90-91 Final Standings:** Boston Bruins	.03	.05
171	Alexander Mogilny, Buf.	.20	.40
172	**Top Prospect:** Karl Dykhuis, Chi.	.03	.05
173	Tomas Sandstrom, LA	.03	.05
174	Bernie Nicholls, NYR	.03	.05
175	Viacheslav Fetisov, NJD	.03	.05
176	Andrew Cassels, Mon.	.03	.05
177	Ulf Dahlen, Min.	.03	.05
178	Brian Hayward, Goalie, SJ	.03	.05
179	Doug Lidster, Van.	.03	.05
180	Dave Lowry, St. L.	.03	.05
181	Ron Tugnutt, Goalie, Que.	.03	.05
182	Ed Olczyk, Win.	.03	.05
183	Paul Coffey, Pit.	.05	.10
184	Shawn Burr, Det.	.03	.05
185	**90-91 Final Standings:** Hartford Whalers	.03	.05
186	Mark Janssens, NYR	.03	.05
187	**Top Prospect:** Mike Craig, Min.	.03	.05
188	Gary Leeman, Tor.	.03	.05
189	Phil Sykes, Win.	.03	.05
190	**Goal Scoring Leaders:** Brett Hull, St. L.	.12	.25
191	**90-91 Final Standings:** New Jersey Devils	.03	.05
192	Cam Neely, Bos.	.05	.10
193	Petr Klima, Edm.	.03	.05
194	Mike Ricci, Phi.	.12	.25
195	Kelly Hrudey, Goalie, LA	.03	.05
196	Mark Recchi, Pit.	.15	.30
197	Mikael Andersson, Har.	.03	.05
198	Bob Probert, Det.	.03	.05
199	Craig Wolanin, Que.	.03	.05
200	Scott Mellanby, Edm. (Now With Oilers)	.03	.05
201	**Hockey Highlights 1991:** Gretzky Scores 2000th Point	.13	.25
202	Laurie Boschman, NJD	.03	.05
203	Gino Odjick, Van.	.03	.05
204	Garth Butcher, St. L.	.03	.05
205	Randy Wood, NYI	.03	.05
206	John Druce, Was.	.03	.05
207	Doug Bodger, Buf.	.03	.05
208	Douglas Gilmour, Cal.	.10	.20
209	**Top Prospect:** John LeClair, Mon., RC	.12	.25
210	Steve Thomas, Chi.	.03	.05
211	Kjell Samuelsson, Phi.	.03	.05
212	Daniel Marois, Tor.	.03	.05
213	Jiri Hrdina, Pit.	.03	.05
214	Darrin Shannon, Buf.	.03	.05
215	**90-91 Final Standings:** New York Rangers	.03	.05
216	Robert McGill, SJ	.03	.05
217	Dirk Graham, Chi.	.03	.05
218	Thomas Steen, Win.	.03	.05
219	Mats Sundin, Que.	.12	.25
220	Kevin Lowe, Edm.	.03	.05
221	Kirk McLean, Goalie, Van.	.03	.05
222	Jeff Brown, St. L.	.03	.05
223	Joe Nieuwendyk, Cal.	.08	.15
224	**Assist Leader:** Wayne Gretzky, LA	.15	.30
225	Martin McSorley, LA	.03	.05
226	John Cullen, Har.	.03	.05
227	Brian Propp, Min.	.03	.05
228	Yves Racine, Det.	.03	.05
229	Dale Hunter, Was.	.03	.05
230	**Top Prospect:** Dennis Vaske, NYI, RC	.03	.05
231	Sylvain Turgeon, Pit.	.03	.05
232	Ronalda Sutter, Phi.	.03	.05
233	Chris Chelios, Chi.	.03	.05
234	Brian Bradley, Tor.	.03	.05
235	Scott Young, Pit.	.03	.05
236	Michael Ramsey, Buf.	.03	.05
237	Jon Casey, Goalie, Min.	.03	.05
238	Nevin Markwart, Bos.	.03	.05
239	John MacLean, NJD	.03	.05
240	Brent Ashton, Win.	.03	.05
241	Anthony Hrkac, SJ	.03	.05
242	**90-91 Final Standings:** Vancouver Canucks	.03	.05
243	Jeff Norton, NYI	.03	.05
244	Martin Gelinas, Edm.	.03	.05
245	Mike Ridley, Was.	.03	.05
246	**Top Prospect:** Pat Jablonski, Goalie, St. L.	.03	.05
247	**90-91 Final Standings:** Calgary Flames	.03	.05
248	Paul Ysebaert, Det.	.03	.05
249	Sylvain Coté, Har.	.03	.05
250	Marc Habscheid, Cal. (Now With Flames)	.03	.05
251	Todd Elik, Min., (Now With North Stars)	.03	.05
252	Michael McPhee, Mon.	.03	.05
253	James Patrick, NYR	.03	.05
254	Murray Craven, Phi.	.03	.05
255	Trent Yawney, Chi.	.03	.05
256	Robert Cimetta, Tor.	.03	.05
257	**League Leaders Point:** Wayne Gretzky	.12	.25

1ST TEAM NHL ALL STAR

No.	Player	EX	NRMT
258	Wayne Gretzky, LA	.10	.20
259	Brett Hull, St. L.	.10	.20
260	Luc Robitaille, LA	.03	.05
261	Raymond Bourque, Bos.	.08	.15
262	Allan MacInnis, Cal.	.03	.05
263	Ed Belfour, Goalie, Chi.	.08	.15

CHECKLIST

No.	Checklist	EX	NRMT
264	Checklist 2 (133 to 264)	.03	.05

2ND TEAM NHL ALL STAR

No.	Player	EX	NRMT
265	Adam Oates, St. L.	.03	.05
266	Cam Neely, Bos.	.03	.05
267	Kevin Stevens, Pit.	.08	.15
268	Chris Chelios, Chi.	.03	.05
269	Brian Leetch, NYR	.03	.05
270	Patrick Roy, Goalie, Mon.	.12	.25

REGULAR ISSUE

No.	Player	EX	NRMT
271	**League Leader Wins:** Ed Belfour, Goalie, Chi.	.10	.20
272	Rob Zettler, SJ	.03	.05
273	**Top Prospect:** Donald Audette, Buf.	.03	.05
274	Teppo Numminen, Win.	.10	.20
275	Peter Stastny, NJD	.03	.05
276	David Christian, Bos.	.03	.05
277	Lawrence Murphy, Pit.	.03	.05
278	Johan Garpenlov, Det.	.03	.05
279	Tom Fitzgerald, NYI	.03	.05
280	Gerald Diduck, Van.	.03	.05
281	Gino Cavallini, St. L.	.03	.05
282	Theoren Fleury, Cal.	.10	.20
283	**90-91 Final Standings:** Los Angeles Kings	.03	.05
284	Jeff Beukeboom, Edm.	.03	.05
285	Kevin Dineen, Har.	.03	.05
286	Jacques Cloutier, Goalie, Que.	.03	.05
287	Tom Chorske, Mon.	.03	.05
288	**League Leader Save Pct:** Ed Belfour, Chi.	.10	.20
289	Ray Sheppard, NYR	.03	.05
290	**Top Prospect:** Olaf Kolzig, Goalie, Wash.	.03	.05
291	Terry Carkner, Phi.	.03	.05
292	Benoit Hogue, Buf.	.03	.05
293	Mike Peluso, Chi.	.03	.05
294	Bruce Driver, NJD	.03	.05
295	Jari Kurri, LA, (Now With Kings)	.03	.05
296	Peter Sidorkiewicz, Goalie, Har.	.03	.05
297	Scott Pearson, Que.	.03	.05
298	**90-91 Final Standings:** Montreal Canadiens	.03	.05
299	Vincent Damphousse, Tor.	.03	.05
300	John Carter, Bos.	.03	.05
301	Geoff Smith, Edm.	.03	.05
302	Stephen Kasper, Phi. (Now With Flyers)	.03	.05
303	Brett Hull, St. L.	.25	.50
304	Ray Ferraro, NYI	.03	.05
305	Geoff Courtnall, Van.	.03	.05
306	David Shaw, NYR	.03	.05
307	Bob Essensa, Goalie, Win.	.03	.05
308	Mark Tinordi, Min.	.03	.05
309	Keith Primeau, Det.	.03	.05
310	Kevin Hatcher, Was.	.03	.05
311	Christopher Nilan, Bos.	.03	.05
312	**Top Prospect:** Trevor Kidd, Goalie, Cal., RC	.03	.05
313	Daniel Berthiaume, Goalie, LA	.03	.05
314	Adam Creighton, Chi.	.03	.05
315	Everett Sanipass, Que.	.03	.05
316	Ken Baumgartner, NYI	.03	.05
317	**Top Prospect:** Sheldon Kennedy, Det.	.03	.05
318	Dave Capuano, Van.	.03	.05

— 1991 - 92 REGULAR ISSUE — O-PEE-CHEE • 109

No.	Player	EX	NRMT
319	Don Sweeney, Bos.	.03	.05
320	Gary Roberts, Cal.	.03	.05
321	Wayne Gretzky, LA	.50	1.00
322	League Leaders Plus/Minus: T. Fleury, Cal., M. McSorley, LA, Error	.03	.05
323	Ulf Samuelsson, Pit.	.03	.05
324	Michael Krushelnyski, Tor.	.03	.05
325	Dean Evason, Har.	.03	.05
326	Pat Elynuik, Win.	.03	.05
327	Michal Pivonka, Was.	.03	.05
328	Paul Cavallini, St. L.	.03	.05
329	90-91 Final Standings: Philadelphia Flyers	.03	.05
330	Denis Savard, Mon.	.03	.05
331	Paul Fenton, Cal.	.03	.05
332	Jon Morris, NJD	.03	.05
333	Daren Puppa, Goalie, Buf.	.03	.05
334	Douglas Smail, Min.	.03	.05
335	Kelly Kisio, SJ	.03	.05
336	Michel Goulet, Chi.	.03	.05
337	Mike Sillinger, Det.	.03	.05
338	Andrew Moog, Goalie, Bos.	.03	.05
339	Paul Stanton, Pit.	.03	.05
340	Greg Adams, Van.	.03	.05
341	Douglas Crossman, Det.	.03	.05
342	Kelly Miller, Was.	.03	.05
343	Patrick Flatley, NYI	.03	.05
344	Zarley Zalapski, Har.	.03	.05
345	Mark Osborne, Win.	.03	.05
346	Mark Messier, Edm.	.10	.20
347	90-91 Final Standings: St. Louis Blues	.03	.05
348	Neil Wilkinson, SJ	.03	.05
349	Brian Skrudland, Mon.	.03	.05
350	Lyle Odelein, Mon.	.03	.05
351	Luke Richardson, Tor.	.03	.05
352	Zdeno Ciger, NJD	.03	.05
353	John Vanbiesbrouck, Goalie, NYR	.03	.05
354	Lou Franceschetti, Buf.	.03	.05
355	Alexei Gusarov, Que.	.03	.05
356	Bill Ranford, Goalie, Edm.	.03	.05
357	Normand Lacombe, Phi., Error	.03	.05
358	Randy Burridge, Wash., (Now With Capitals)	.03	.05
359	Brian Benning, LA	.03	.05
360	David Hannan, Tor.	.03	.05
361	Todd Gill, Tor.	.03	.05
362	Peter Bondra, Was.	.03	.05
363	Mike Hartman, Buf.	.03	.05
364	Trevor Linden, Van.	.03	.05
365	John Ogrodnick, NYR	.03	.05
366	Stephen Konroyd, Chi.	.03	.05
367	Michael Modano, Min.	.18	.35
368	Glenn Healy, Goalie, NYI	.03	.05
369	Stephane Richer, Mon.	.03	.05
370	Vincent Riendeau, Goalie, St. L.	.03	.05
371	Randy Moller, NYR	.03	.05
372	90-91 Final Standings: Pittsburgh Penguins	.03	.05
373	Murray Baron, Phi.	.03	.05
374	Troy Crowder, NJD	.03	.05
375	Richard Tabaracci, Goalie, Win.	.03	.05
376	Brent Fedyk, Det.	.03	.05
377	Randy Velischek, Que.	.03	.05
378	Esa Tikkanen, Edm.	.03	.05
379	Richard Pilon, NYI	.03	.05
380	Jeff Lazaro, Bos., RC	.03	.05
381	David Ellett, Tor.	.03	.05
382	Jeff Hackett, Goalie, SJ	.03	.05
383	Stephane Matteau, Cal.	.03	.05
384	90-91 Final Standings: Washington Capitals	.03	.05
385	Wayne Presley, Chi.	.03	.05
386	Grant Ledyard, Buf.	.03	.05
387	Top Prospect: Kip Miller, Que.	.03	.05
388	Edward (Dean) Kennedy, Buf.	.03	.05
389	Hubie McDonough, NYI	.03	.05
390	Anatoli Semenov, Edm.	.03	.05
391	Daryl Reaugh, Goalie, Har.	.03	.05
392	Mathieu Schneider, Mon.	.03	.05
393	Dan Quinn, St L	.03	.05
394	Claude Lemieux, NJD	.03	.05
395	Phil Housley, Win.	.03	.05
396	Checklist 3 (265 - 396)	.03	.05
397	Steven Bozek, Van.	.03	.05

No.	Player	EX	NRMT
398	Robert Smith, Min.	.03	.05
399	Mark Pederson, Phi.	.03	.05
400	Kevin Todd, NJD	.12	.25
401	Sergei Fedorov, Cal.	.30	.60
402	Tom Barrasso, Goalie, Pit.	.03	.05
403	Hockey Highlights 1991: Brett Hull, St. L.	.10	.20
404	Robert Carpenter, Bos.	.03	.05
405	Luc Robitaille, LA	.10	.20
406	Mark Hardy, NYR	.03	.05
407	Neil Sheehy, Was.	.03	.05
408	Michael McNeill, Que.	.03	.05
409	Dave Manson, Chi.	.03	.05
410	Mike Tomlak, Har.	.03	.05
411	Robert Reichel, Cal.	.13	.25
412	90-91 Final Standings: New York Islanders	.03	.05
413	Patrick Roy, Goalie, Mon.	.10	.20
414	Top Prospect: Shaun Van Allen, Edm., RC	.08	.15
415	Dale Kushner, Phi.	.03	.05
416	Pierre Turgeon, Buf.	.03	.05
417	Curtis Joseph, Goalie, St. L.	.03	.05
418	Randy Gilhen, LA (Now With Kings)	.03	.05
419	Jyrki Lumme, Van.	.03	.05
420	Neal Broten, Min.	.03	.05
421	Kevin Stevens, Pit.	.12	.25
422	Chris Terreri, Goalie, NJD	.05	.10
423	David Reid, Tor.	.03	.05
424	Steve Yzerman, Det.	.15	.30
425	League Leader G.A.A.: Ed Belfour, Chi.	.10	.20
426	Jim Johnson, Min.	.03	.05
427	Joey Kocur, NYR	.03	.05
428	Joel Otto, Cal.	.03	.05
429	Dino Ciccarelli, Was.	.03	.05
430	90-91 Final Standings: Chicago Black Hawks	.03	.05
431	Claude Lapointe, Que., Error	.03	.05
432	Chris Joseph, Edm.	.03	.05
433	Gaetan Duchesne, Min.	.03	.05
434	Mike Keane, Mon.	.03	.05
435	David Chyzowski, NYI	.03	.05
436	Glen Featherstone, St. L.	.03	.05
437	Top Prospect: Jim Paek, Pit., RC	.08	.15
438	Doug Evans, Win.	.03	.05
439	Alexei Kasatonov, NJD, Error	.03	.05
440	Kenneth Hodge, Jr., Bos.	.03	.05
441	Dave Snuggerud, St. L.	.03	.05
442	Brad Shaw, Har.	.03	.05
443	Gerard Gallant, Det.	.03	.05
444	Jiri Latal, Phi.	.03	.05
445	Peter Zezel, Tor.	.03	.05
446	Troy Gamble, Goalie, Van.	.03	.05
447	Craig Coxe, SJ	.03	.05
448	Adam Oates, St. L.	.12	.25
449	Todd Krygier, Har.	.03	.05
450	Andre Racicot, Goalie, Mon., RC	.08	.15
451	Patrik Sundstrom, NJD	.03	.05
452	Glen Wesley, Bos.	.03	.05
453	Jocelyn Lemieux, Chi.	.03	.05
454	Rick Zombo, Det.	.03	.05
455	Derek King, NYI	.03	.05
456	Jean-Jacques Daigneault, Mon.	.03	.05
457	Richard Vaive, Buf.	.03	.05
458	Larry Robinson, LA	.03	.05
459	Richard Wamsley, Goalie, Cal.	.03	.05
460	Craig Simpson, Edm.	.03	.05
461	Corey Millen, NYR, RC	.13	.25
462	Sergio Momesso, Van.	.03	.05
463	Paul MacDermid, Win.	.03	.05
464	Wendel Clark, Tor.	.03	.05
465	Mikhail Tatarinov, Que., (Now With Nordiques)	.03	.05
466	Mark Howe, Phi.	.03	.05
467	Jay Miller, LA	.03	.05
468	Grant Jennings, Pit.	.03	.05
469	Paul Gillis, Chi.	.03	.05
470	Ron Hextall, Goalie, Phi.	.03	.05
471	Alexander Godynyuk, Tor., RC, Error	.03	.05
472	Bryan Trottier, Pit.	.03	.05
473	Kevin Haller, Buf., RC	.07	.15
474	Troy Mallette, NYR	.03	.05
475	James Wiemer, Bos.	.03	.05

No.	Player	EX	NRMT
476	David Maley, NJD	.03	.05
477	Maurice Mantha, Win.	.03	.05
478	Brad Jones, LA, RC	.03	.05
479	Craig Muni, Edm.	.03	.05
480	Igor Larionov, Van.	.03	.05
481	Scott Stevens, St. L.	.03	.05
482	Sergei Makarov, Cal.	.03	.05
483	Mike Lalor, Was.	.03	.05
484	Anthony McKegney, Chi.	.03	.05
485	Perry Berezan, Min.	.03	.05
486	Derrick Smith, Phi.	.03	.05
487	Jim Hrivnak, Goalie, Was.	.03	.05
488	David Volek, NYI	.03	.05
489	Sylvain Lefebvre, Mon.	.03	.05
490	Rod Brind'Amour, St. L.	.03	.05
491	Allan MacInnis, Cal.	.03	.05
492	Jamie Leach, Pit.	.03	.05
493	Robert Dirk, Van.	.03	.05
494	Gordon Roberts, Pit.	.03	.05
495	Mike Hudson, Chi.	.03	.05
496	Top Prospect: Francois Breault, LA	.03	.05
497	Rejean Lemelin, Goalie, Bos.	.03	.05
498	Kris King, NYR	.03	.05
499	Patrick Verbeek, Har.	.03	.05
500	Bryan Fogarty, Que.	.03	.05
501	Perry Anderson, SJ, RC	.03	.05
502	Joe Cirella, NYR	.03	.05
503	Mikko Makela, Buf.	.03	.05
504	Hockey Highlights 1991: Coffey Scores 1000th Point	.03	.05
505	Donald Beaupre, Goalie, Was.	.03	.05
506	Brian Glynn, Min.	.03	.05
507	David Poulin, Bos.	.03	.05
508	Steve Chiasson, Det.	.03	.05
509	Myles O'Connor, NJD, RC	.03	.05
510	Ilkka Sinisalo, LA	.03	.05
511	Nicholas Kypreos, Was.	.03	.05
512	Doug Houda, Har.	.03	.05

FUTURE NHLER

No.	Player	EX	NRMT
513	Valeri Kamensky, Que.	.25	.50
514	Sergei Nemchinov, NYR	.10	.20
515	Dimitri Mironov, Tor.	.10	.20

TROPHY WINNERS

No.	Player	EX	NRMT
516	Hart Trophy: Brett Hull, St. L.	.13	.25
517	Norris Trophy: Raymond Bourque, Bos.	.03	.05
518	Calder Trophy: Ed Belfour, Chi.	.05	.10
519	Vezina Trophy: Ed Belfour, Chi.	.05	.10
520	Lady Bing Trophy: Wayne Gretzky, LA	.13	.25
521	Selke Trophy: Dirk Graham, Chi.	.03	.05
522	Art Ross Trophy: Wayne Gretzky, LA	.13	.25
523	Conn Smythe Trophy: Mario Lemieux, Pit.	.13	.25

REGULAR ISSUE

No.	Player	EX	NRMT
524	Hockey Highlights 1991: Gretzky Joins the 700 Club	.13	.25
525	San Jose Sharks Roster	.18	.35
526	Tampa Bay Lightning	.13	.25
527	Ottawa Senators	.13	.25
528	Checklist 4 (397 to 528)	.03	.05

110 • O-PEE-CHEE — 1991 - 92 PREMIER ISSUE —

—1991 - 92 REGULAR ISSUE—
INSERT SET - SAN JOSE/RUSSIA

The set was available only in wax packs and was not included in regular factory sets.

 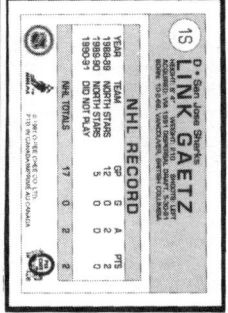

1991 - 92 Insert Set - San Jose / Russia
Card No. 1S Link Gaetz

Card: 2 1/2" X 3 1/2"
Face: Four colour, white border
Back - San Jose Sharks:
  Blue and red on white card stock Number, NHL Record
Back - Russian Insert Set:
  Two colour, red on card white stock, Blue star with hammer and sickle, Number, Soviets vs. NHL Record
Imprint - San Jose Sharks:
  © 1991 O-PEE-CHEE CO. LTD. PTD. IN CANADA/
  IMPRIMÉ AU CANADA
Imprint - Russian Insert Set:
  © 1991 SOVIET ICE HOCKEY FEDERATION
  © 1991 O-PEE-CHEE CO. LTD. PTD. IN CANADA/
  IMPRIMÉ AU CANADA
Complete Set No.: 66
Complete Set Price: 7.50 15.00
Common Card: .05 .10

SAN JOSE SHARKS

No.	Player	EX	NRMT
1S	Link Gaetz	.05	.10
2S	Bengt-ake Gustafsson	.05	.10
3S	Dan Keczmer	.07	.15
4S	Dean Kolstad	.05	.10
5S	Peter Lappin	.05	.10
6S	Jeff Madill	.05	.10
7S	Michael McHugh	.05	.10
8S	Jarmo Myllys, Goalie, Error	.05	.10
9S	Doug Zmolek	.07	.15
10S	San Jose Sharks Checklist	.05	.10

CENTRAL RED ARMY

No.	Player	EX	NRMT
11R	Vadim Brezgunov	.05	.10
12R	Vyacheslav Butsayev	.25	.50
13R	Ilya Byakin	.20	.40
14R	Igor Chibirev	.15	.30
15R	Viktor Gordijuk, Error	.12	.25
16R	Yuri Khmylev, Error	.20	.45
17R	Pavel Kostichkin	.05	.10
18R	Andrei Kovalenko	.35	.75
19R	Igor Kravchuk	.25	.50
20R	Igor Malykhin	.13	.25
21R	Igor Maslennikov	.05	.10
22R	Maxim Mikhailovsky	.10	.20
23R	Dimitri Mironov	.35	.75
24R	Sergei Nemchinov	.25	.50
25R	Alexander Prokopjev	.05	.10
26R	Igor Stelnov	.05	.10
27R	Sergei Vostrikov	.05	.10
28R	Sergei Zubov	1.50	3.00
29R	1990-91 Super Series: Central Red Army vs. NHL	.05	.10
30R	1990-91 Super Series: Central Red Army Team	.05	.10

DYNAMO MOSCOW

No.	Player	EX	NRMT
31R	Alexander Andreivsky	.10	.20
32R	Igor Dorofeyev	.05	.10
33R	Alexander Galchenyuk	.05	.10
34R	Roman Ilyin	.05	.10
35R	Alexander Karpovtsev	.20	.40

No.	Player	EX	NRMT
36R	Ravil Khaidarov	.05	.10
37R	Igor Korolev, Error	.05	.10
38R	Andrei Kovalyov	.05	.10
39R	Yuri Leonov	.05	.10
40R	Andrei Lomakin, Error	.18	.35
41R	Evgeny Popikhin	.05	.10
42R	Alexander Semak	.35	.75
43R	Mikhail Shtalenkov, Goalie	.25	.50
44R	Sergei Sorokin, Error	.05	.10
45R	Andrei Trefilov, Goalie	.25	.50
46R	Ravil Yakubov	.05	.10
47R	Alexander Yudin	.05	.10
48R	Alexei Zhamnov	1.25	2.50

KHIMIK

No.	Player	EX	NRMT
49R	Andrei Basalgin	.05	.10
50R	Lev Berdichevsky	.05	.10
51R	Konstantin Kapkaikin, Goalie	.05	.10
52R	Konstantin Kurashov	.05	.10
53R	Andrei Kvartalnov	.20	.45
54R	Albert Malgin	.05	.10
55R	Nikolai Maslov	.05	.10
56R	Anatoli Naida	.05	.10
57R	Roman Oksyuta	.15	.30
58R	Sergei Selyanin	.05	.10
59R	Valeri Shiryev	.05	.10
60R	Alexander Smirnov	.05	.10
61R	Leonid Trukhno	.05	.10
62R	Igor Ulanov, Error	.20	.40
63R	Andrei Yakovenko	.05	.10
64R	Oleg Yashin	.05	.10
65R	Valeri Zelepukin	.50	1.00
66R	Checklist, Error	.13	.25

— 1991 - 92 PREMIER ISSUE —

1991 - 92 Premier Issue
Card No. 1, Dale Hawerchuk

Card: 2 1/2" X 3 1/2"
Face: Four colour, white border, gold band across top of photograph; Position
Back: Four colour on white card, Number, Resume, Team logo
Imprint: © 1992 O-PEE-CHEE CO. LTD. PTD IN CANADA
  IMPRIMÉ AU CANADA © 1992 NHLPA
Complete Set No.: 198
Complete Set Price: 7.50 15.00
Common Card: .03 .05
Wax Pack: (8 Cards) .50
Wax Box: (36 Packs) 10.00
Wax Case: (24 Boxes) 175.00

No.	Player	EX	NRMT
1	Dale Hawerchuk, Buf.	.03	.05
2	Ray Sheppard, Det.	.05	.10
3	Wayne Gretzky, LA	.60	1.25
4	John MacLean, NJD	.05	.10
5	Patrick Verbeek, Har.	.05	.10
6	Douglas Wilson, SJ	.05	.10
7	Adam Oates, St. L.	.10	.20
8	Robert McGill, SJ	.05	.10
9	Mike Vernon, Cal.	.05	.10
10	Glenn Anderson, Tor.	.05	.10
11	**Anthony Amonte, NYR, RC**	.35	.75
12	Stephen Leach, Bos.	.05	.10
13	Steve Duchesne, Phi.	.05	.10

No.	Player	EX	NRMT
14	Patrick Roy, Goalie, Mon.	.25	.50
15	Jarmo Myllys, Goalie, SJ	.03	.05
16	**Yanic Dupre, Phi., RC**	.03	.05
17	Chris Chelios, Chi.	.03	.05
18	Bill Ranford, Goalie, Edm.	.03	.05
19	Ed Belfour, Goalie, Chi.	.20	.40
20	**Michel Picard, Har., RC**	.03	.05
21	Rob Zettler, SJ	.05	.10
22	**Kevin Todd, NJ, RC**	.07	.15
23	Mike Ricci, Phi.	.12	.25
24	Jaromir Jagr, Pit.	.35	.75
25	Sergei Nemchinov, NYR	.12	.25
26	Kevin Stevens, Pit.	.30	.60
27	Dan Quinn, Phi.	.05	.10
28	Adam Graves, NYR	.05	.10
29	**Pat Jablonski, Goalie, St. L., RC**		.03
30	Scott Mellanby, Edm.	.05	.10
31	Tomas Forslund, Cal.	.25	.50
32	**Doug Weight, NYR, RC**	.20	.40
33	Peter Ing, Goalie, Edm.	.03	.05
34	Luc Robitaille, LA	.15	.30
35	**Scott Niedermayer, NJD, RC**	.30	.65
36	Dean Evason, SJ	.05	.10
37	John Tonelli, Chi.	.05	.10
38	Ron Hextall, Goalie, Phi.	.03	.05
39	Troy Mallette, Edm.	.05	.10
40	Anthony Hrkac, SJ	.05	.10
41	Kenneth Hodge, Jr., Bos.	.03	.05
42	Kip Miller, Que.	.05	.10
43	Randy Burridge, Was.	.05	.10
44	Robert Blake, LA	.12	.25
45	Sergei Makarov, Cal.	.05	.10
46	Luke Richardson, Edm.	.05	.10
47	Craig Berube, Tor.	.05	.10
48	Joe Nieuwendyk, Cal.	.03	.05
49	Brett Hull, St. L.	.35	.75
50	Phil Housley, Win.	.03	.05
51	Mark Messier, NYR	.15	.30
52	Jeremy Roenick, Chi.	.60	1.25
53	David Christian, St. L.	.05	.10
54	David Barr, NJD	.05	.10
55	Sergio Momesso, Van.	.05	.10
56	**Pat Falloon, SJ, RC**	.60	1.25
57	Brian Leetch, NYR	.20	.40
58	Russell Courtnall, Mon.	.05	.10
59	Pierre Turgeon, NYI	.12	.25
60	Steve Larmer, Chi.	.03	.05
61	Petr Klima, Edm.	.05	.10
62	Mikhail Tatarinov, Que.	.03	.05
63	Rick Tocchet, Phi.	.05	.10
64	Pat LaFontaine, Buf.	.20	.40
65	**Rob Pearson, Tor., RC**	.20	.40
66	Glen Featherstone, Bos.	.05	.10
67	**Pavel Bure, Van., RC**	1.25	2.50
68	**Sergei Fedorov, Det., RC**	1.00	2.00
69	Kelly Kisio, SJ	.05	.10
70	Joe Sakic, Que.	.15	.30
71	Denis Savard, Mon.	.03	.05
72	Andrew Cassels, Har.	.05	.10
73	Steve Yzerman, Det.	.18	.35
74	Todd Elik, Min.	.05	.10
75	Troy Murray, Win.	.05	.10
76	George (Rob) Ramage, Min.	.05	.10
77	Trevor Linden, Van.	.12	.25
78	Michael Richter, Goalie, NYR	.12	.25
79	Paul Coffey, Pit.	.15	.25
80	Craig Ludwig, Min.	.05	.10
81	Allan MacInnis, Cal.	.03	.05
82	Tomas Sandstrom, LA	.05	.10
83	Tim Kerr, NYR	.05	.10
84	Scott Stevens, NJ	.05	.10
85	Stephen Kasper, Phi.	.05	.10
86	Kirk Muller, Mon.	.05	.10
87	**Pat MacLeod, SJ, RC**	.03	.05
88	Kevin Hatcher, Was.	.05	.10
89	Wayne Presley, SJ	.05	.10
90	Darryl Sydor, LA	.03	.05
91	Tom Chorske, NJD	.05	.10
92	Theoren Fleury, Cal.	.10	.20
93	Craig Janney, Bos.	.10	.20
94	Rod Brind'Amour, Phi.	.10	.20
95	Ronald Sutter, St. L.	.05	.10
96	**Matt DelGuidice, Goalie, Bos., RC**	.03	.05

1992 PROMOTIONAL SHEET — O-PEE-CHEE

No.	Player	EX	NRMT
97	Rollie Melanson, Goalie, Mon.	.03	.05
98	Tom Kurvers, NYI	.05	.10
99	**Bryan Marchment, Chi., RC**	.05	.10
100	Grant Fuhr, Goalie, Tor.	.03	.05
101	Geoff Courtnall, Van.	.05	.10
102	Joel Otto, Cal.	.05	.10
103	Tom Barrasso, Goalie, Pit.	.03	.05
104	Vincent Damphousse, Edm.	.03	.05
105	**John LeClair, Mon., RC**	.20	.40
106	Gary Leeman, Tor.	.05	.10
107	Cam Neely, Bos.	.10	.20
108	Jeff Hackett, Goalie, SJ	.03	.05
109	Stu Barnes, Win.	.05	.10
110	Neil Wilkinson, SJ	.05	.10
111	Jari Kurri, LA	.03	.05
112	Jon Casey, Goalie, Min.	.03	.05
113	Stephane Richer, NJD	.05	.10
114	Mario Lemieux, Pit.	.60	1.25
115	**Brad Jones, Phi., RC**	.05	.10
116	Wendel Clark, Tor.	.10	.20
117	**Nicklas Lidstrom, Det., RC**	.35	.75
118A	**Vladimir Konstantinov, Det., RC, Error**	7.50	15.00
118B	**Vladimir Konstantinov, Det., RC, Corrected**	.40	.80
119	Raymond Bourque, Bos.	.12	.25
120	Ronald Francis, Pit.	.05	.10
121	Esa Tikkanen, Edm.	.05	.10
122	Randy Hillier, Buf.	.05	.10
123	Randy Gilhen, Har.	.05	.10
124	Barry Pederson, Har.	.05	.10
125	Charles Huddy, LA	.05	.10
126	Gary Roberts, Cal.	.05	.10
127	John Cullen, Har.	.03	.05
128	Dave Gagner, Min.	.05	.10
129	Bob Kudelski, LA	.05	.10
130	Brendan Shanahan, St. L.	.15	.30
131	Dirk Graham, Chi.	.05	.10
132	Checklist 1 (1 to 99)	.10	.20
133	Andrew Moog, Goalie, Bos.	.03	.05
134	Toronto Maple Leafs: Gary Leeman	.05	.10
135	Chicago Black Hawks: Steve Larmer	.05	.10
136	James (Steve) Smith, Chi.	.05	.10
137	Dave Manson, Edm.	.05	.10
138	Nelson Emerson, St. L.	.20	.40
139	New York Rangers: Doug Weight	.03	.05
140	Uwe Krupp, NYI	.05	.10
141	Boston Bruins: Peter Douris	.05	.10
142	Detroit Red Wings: Steve Yzerman	.10	.20
143	Derian Hatcher, Min.	.03	.05
144	Boston Bruins: Vladimir Ruzicka	.03	.05
145	Montreal Canadiens: Kirk Muller	.05	.10
146	Darrin Shannon, Win.	.05	.10
147	New York Rangers: Michael Gartner	.05	.10
148	Boston Bruins: Robert Carpenter	.05	.10
149	**Josef Beranek, Edm., RC**	.35	.75
150	Chicago Black Hawks:	.05	.10
151	Toronto Maple Leafs: Robert Rouse	.05	.10
152	**Montreal Canadiens:** Guy Carbonneau	.05	.10
153	Joe Mullen, Pit.	.05	.10
154	Boston Bruins: Kenneth Hodge, Jr.	.05	.10
155	Detroit Red Wings: Vladimir Konstantinov	.10	.20
156	Brent Sutter, Chi.	.05	.10
157	Montreal Canadiens: Eric Desjardins	.05	.10
158	Kirk McLean, Goalie, Van.	.10	.20
159	Chicago Blackhawks: John Tonelli	.05	.10
160	Toronto Maple Leafs: Robert Cimetta	.05	.10
161	Shayne Corson, Mon.	.05	.10
162	**Russ Romaniuk, Win., RC**	.10	.20
163	Detroit Red Wings: Nicklas Lidstrom	.12	.25
164	Michael Gartner, NYR	.05	.10
165	Curtis Joseph, Goalie, St. L	.20	.40
166	Brian Mullen, SJ	.05	.10
167	Jimmy Carson, Det.	.03	.05
168	Montreal Canadiens: Petr Svoboda	.05	.10
169	Troy Crowder, Det.	.05	.10
170	Montreal Canadiens: Patrick Roy, Goalie	.25	.50
171	Adam Creighton, NYI	.05	.10
172	New York Rangers: James Patrick	.05	.10
173	Detroit Red Wings: Sergei Fedorov	.30	.60
174	Chicago Black Hawks: Jeremy Roenick	.30	.60

No.	Player	EX	NRMT
175	**Detoirt Red Wings:** Tim Cheveldae, Goalie	.03	.05
176	Dimitri Khristich, Wash.	.03	.05
177	Toronto Maple Leafs: Wendel Clark	.03	.05
178	Andrei Lomakin, Phi.	.03	.05
179	Benoit Hogue, NYI	.05	.10
180	Toronto Maple Leafs: David Ellett	.05	.10
181	Montreal Canadiens: Mathieu Schneider	.05	.10
182	Kay Whitmore, Goalie, Har.	.03	.05
183	New York Rangers: Brian Leetch	.10	.20
184	**Montreal Canadiens:** Sylvain Turgeon	.05	.10
185	Toronto Maple Leafs: Brian Bradley	.05	.10
186	Montreal Canadiens: John LeClair	.03	.05
187	Paul Fenton, SJ	.05	.10
188	Montreal Canadiens: Alain Coté	.05	.10
189	Toronto Maple Leafs: Michael Krushelnyski, Error	.05	.10
190	Brian Bradley, Tor.	.05	.10
191	Toronto Maple Leafs: Grant Fuhr, Goalie	.03	.05
192	Boston Bruins: Raymond Bourque	.03	.05
193	Owen Nolan, Que.	.12	.25
194	**Montreal Canadiens:** Russell Courtnall	.05	.10
195	Steve Thomas, NYI	.05	.10
196	Ed Olczyk, Win.	.05	.10
197	Chris Terreri, Goalie, NJD	.03	.05
198	Checklist 2 (100 to 198)	.05	.10

— 1992 PROMOTIONAL SHEET —

These nine cards are printed on a 7 3/4" x 10 3/4" paper mini-sheet comprising seven cards from the 1992-93 regular issue and two cards from the 25th Anniversary insert set.

Sheet Size: 7 3/4" X 10 3/4"
Card Size: 2 1/2" X 3 1/2"
Face: Four colour, white border
Back: Four colour on paper stock; "1992 PRE-PRODUCTION SAMPLE Échantillon De Présérie De 1992
Imprint: © 1992 O-PEE-CHEE CO. LTD. PTD. IN CANADA \IMPRIMÉ AU CANADA
Sheet Price: 15.00 30.00

No.	Player	EX	NRMT
1	Donald Beaupre, Goalie, Wash.	1.50	3.00
2	Marcel Dionne, Det.	1.50	3.00
3	Sergei Fedorov, Det.	2.50	5.00
4	Ron Francis, Pit.	1.50	3.00
5	Grant Fuhr,, Goalie, Tor.	2.00	4.00
6	Brett Hull, St.L.	2.50	5.00
7	Darren Turcotte, NYR	1.50	3.00
8	Darryl Sittler, Tor.,	1.50	3.00
9	Checklist: 25th Anniversary Series	1.00	2.00

— 1992 - 93 REGULAR ISSUE —

The 1992-93 season was the 25th Anniversary of continuous hockey card production by O-Pee-Chee. While cards were first issued in 1933-34, the longest continuous run began in 1968-69. This is also the first wax of the regular issue cards to be released without gum.

1992- 93 Regular Issue
Card No. 1, Kevin Todd

Card Size: 2 /12" X 3 1/2"
Face: Four colour, white border; Name, Team
Back: Four colour on card stock; Name, Number, Resume, Bilingual
Imprint: © 1992 O-PEE-CHEE CO. LTD. PTD. IN CANADA /IMPRIMÉ AU CANADA © 1992 NHLPA
Complete Set No.: 396
Complete Set Price: 10.00 20.00
Factory Set Price: 12.50 25.00
25th Anniversary Factory Set 85.00
Common Card: .03 .05
Wax Pack: (9 Cards) 1.00
Wax Box: (36 Packs) 20.00
Wax Case: (24 Boxes) 500.00

No.	Player	EX	NRMT
1	Kevin Todd, NJD	.03	.05
2	Robert Kron, Van.	.03	.05
3	David Volek, NYI	.03	.05
4	Teppo Numminen, Win.	.03	.05
5	Paul Coffey, LA	.03	.05
6	Luc Robitaille, LA	.10	.20
7	Steven Finn, Que.	.03	.05
8	**Gord Hynes, Bos., RC**	.08	.15
9	Dave Ellett, Tor.	.03	.05
10	Alexander Godynyuk, Cal.	.03	.05
11	Darryl Sydor, LA	.03	.05
12	Randy Carlyle, Win.	.03	.05
13	Chris Chelios, Chi.	.03	.05
14	Kent Manderville, Tor.	.03	.05
15	Wayne Gretzky, LA	.60	1.25
16	Jon Casey, Goalie, Min.	.03	.05
17	Mark Tinordi, Min.	.03	.05
18	Dale Hunter, Wash.	.03	.05
19	Martin Gelinas, Edm.	.03	.05
20	Todd Elik, Min.	.03	.05
21	Robert Sweeney, Bos.	.03	.05
22	Chris Dahlquist, Min.	.03	.05
23	Joe Mullen, Pit.	.03	.05
24	Shawn Burr, Det.	.03	.05
25	Pavel Bure, Van.	.60	1.25
26	Randy Gilhen, NYR	.03	.05
27	Brian Bradley, TB, (Now with Lightning)	.03	.05
28	Donald Beaupre, Goalie, Wash.	.03	.05
29	Kevin Stevens, Pit.	.03	.05
30	Michal Pivonka, Wash.	.03	.05
31	Grant Fuhr, Goalie, Tor.	.03	.05
32	Steve Larmer, Chi.	.03	.05
33	Gary Leeman, Cal.	.03	.05
34	Tony Tanti, Buf.	.03	.05
35	Denis Savard, Mon.	.03	.05
36	Paul Ranheim, Cal.	.03	.05
37	Andrei Lomakin, Phi.	.03	.05
38	Perry Anderson, SJ	.03	.05
39	Stu Barnes, Win.	.03	.05
40	Don Sweeney, Bos.	.03	.05
41	Jamie Baker, Que.	.03	.05
42	Ray Ferraro, NYI	.03	.05
43	Bobby Clarke, (1970 Style)	.20	.40
44	Kelly Hrudey, Goalie, LA	.03	.05
45	Brian Skrudland, Mon.	.03	.05
46	Paul Ysebaert, Det.	.03	.05
47	Pierre Turgeon, NYI	.03	.05
48	Keith Brown, Chi.	.03	.05
49	Rod Brind'Amour, Phi.	.03	.05
50	Wayne McBean, NYI	.03	.05
51	Doug Lidster, Van.	.03	.05
52	Bernie Nicholls, Edm.	.03	.05
53	Daren Puppa, Goalie, Buf.	.03	.05
54	Joe Sakic, Que.	.03	.05
55	Joe Sakic, (1989 Style)	.12	.25
56	Dave Manson, Edm.	.03	.05
57	Denis Potvin, NYI (1974 Style)	.12	.25
58	Daniel Marois, Mon.	.03	.05
59	Martin Brodeur, Goalie, NJD	.25	.50
60	Brent Sutter, Chi.	.03	.05
61	Steve Yzerman, Det.	.10	.20
62	Neal Broten, Min.	.03	.05
63	Darcy Wakaluk, Goalie, Min.	.03	.05
64	Troy Murray, Win.	.03	.05
65	Tony Granato, LA	.03	.05
66	Frantisek Musil, Cal.	.03	.05
67	Claude Lemieux, NJD	.03	.05
68	Brian Benning, Phi.	.03	.05
69	Stephane Matteau, Chi.	.03	.05
70	Tomas Forslund, Cal.	.03	.05

112 • O-PEE-CHEE — 1992 - 93 REGULAR ISSUE —

No.	Player	EX	NRMT
71	Dimitri Mironov, Tor.	.03	.05
72	Gary Roberts, Cal.	.03	.05
73	Felix Potvin, Goalie, Tor.	.60	1.25
74	Glenn Murray, Bos.	.03	.05
75	Stephane Fiset, Goalie, Que.	.03	.05
76	Stephane J.J. Richer, NJD	.03	.05
77	Jeff Reese, Goalie, Cal.	.03	.05
78	Marc Bureau, Min.	.03	.05
79	Derek King, NYI	.03	.05
80	Dave Gagner, Min.	.03	.05
81	Ed Belfour, Goalie, Chi.	.12	.25
82	Joel Otto, Cal.	.03	.05
83	Anatoli Semenov, TB (Now with Lightning)	.03	.05
84	Ron Hextall, Goalie, Que.	.03	.05
85	Adam Creighton, NYI	.03	.05
86	Kris King, NYR	.03	.05
87	Brett Hull, St.L.	.25	.50
88	Zdeno Ciger, NJD	.03	.05
89	Petr Nedved, Van.	.03	.05
90	Sergei Makarov, Cal.	.03	.05
91	Tomas Sandstrom, LA	.03	.05
92	**Steve Heinze, Bos., RC**	**.03**	**.05**
93	Robert Reichel, Cal.	.03	.05
94	Cliff Ronning, Van.	.03	.05
95	Eric Weinrich, NJD	.03	.05
96	Wendel Clark, Tor.	.03	.05
97	Richard Zombo, St.L.	.03	.05
98	Eric Nattress, Tor.	.03	.05
99	Theoren Fleury, Cal.	.03	.05
100	Joe Murphy, Edm.	.03	.05
101	Gordon Murphy, Bos.	.03	.05
102	Jaromir Jagr, Pit.	.20	.40
103	Mike Craig, Min.	.03	.05
104	John Cullen, Har.	.03	.05
105	John Druce, Wash.	.03	.05
106	Peter Bondra, Wash.	.03	.05
107	Bryan Trottier, (1976 Style)	.12	.25
108	James (Steve) Smith, Chi.	.03	.05
109	Petr Svoboda, Buf.	.03	.05
110	Mats Sundin, Que.	.12	.25
111	Patrick Roy, Goalie, (1986 Style)	.75	1.50
112	Stephen Leach, Bos.	.03	.05
113	Jacques Cloutier, Goalie, Que.	.03	.05
114	Doug Weight, NYR	.03	.05
115	Frank Pietrangelo, Goalie, Har.	.03	.05
116	**Guy Hebert, Goalie, St.L., RC**	**.25**	**.50**
117	Donald Audette, Buf.	.03	.05
118	Craig MacTavish, Edm.	.03	.05
119	Grant Fuhr, Goalie, (1982 Style)	.12	.25
120	Trevor Linden, Van.	.05	.10
121	Fredrick Olausson, Win.	.03	.05
122	Geoff Sanderson, Har.	.03	.05
123	Derian Hatcher, Min.	.03	.05
124	Brett Hull, (1988 Style)	.50	1.00
125	Kelly Buchberger, Edm.	.03	.05
126	Raymond Bourque, Bos.	.10	.20
127	Murray Craven, Har.	.03	.05
128	Tim Cheveldae, Goalie, Det.	.03	.05
129	Ulf Dahlen, Min.	.03	.05
130	Bryan Trottier, Pit.	.03	.05
131	Robert Carpenter, Wash. (Now with Capitals)	.03	.05
132	Benoit Hogue, NYI	.03	.05
133	Claude Vilgrain, NJD	.03	.05
134	Glenn Anderson, Tor.	.03	.05
135	**Marty McInnis, NYI, RC**	**.03**	**.05**
136	Rob Pearson, Tor.	.03	.05
137	Bill Ranford, Goalie, Edm.	.03	.05
138	Mario Lemieux, Pit.	.35	.75
139	Bob Bassen, St.L.	.03	.05
140	Scott Mellanby, Edm.	.03	.05
141	David Andreychuk, Buf.	.05	.10
142	Kelly Miller, Wash.	.03	.05
143	Gaetan Duchesne, Min.	.03	.05
144	**Mike Sullivan, SJ, RC**	**.03**	**.05**
145	Kevin Hatcher, Wash.	.03	.05
146	Doug Bodger, Buf.	.03	.05
147	Craig Berube, Cal.	.03	.05
148	Rick Tocchet, Pit.	.03	.05
149	Luciano Borsato, Win.	.03	.05
150	Glen Wesley, Bos.	.03	.05
151	Mike Donnelly, LA	.03	.05
152	Jimmy Carson, Det.	.03	.05
153	Jocelyn Lemieux, Chi.	.03	.05

No.	Player	EX	NRMT
154	Ray Sheppard, Det.	.03	.05
155	Anthony Amonte, NYR	.12	.25
156	Adrien Plavsic, Van.	.03	.05
157	Mark Pederson, Phi.	.03	.05
158	Adam Graves, NYR	.03	.05
159	Igor Larionov, Van.	.03	.05
160	Steve Chiasson, Det.	.03	.05
161	Igor Kravchuk, Chi.	.03	.05
162	Viacheslav Fetisov, NJD	.03	.05
163	Gerard Gallant, Det.	.03	.05
164	Patrick Roy, Goalie, Mon.	.25	.50
165	Kenneth Sutton, Buf.	.03	.05
166	Mathieu Schneider, Mon.	.03	.05
167	Larry Robinson, (1973 Style)	.12	.25
168	Jim Sandlak, Van.	.03	.05
169	Joey Kocur, NYR	.03	.05
170	Rob Brown, Chi.	.03	.05
171	Luke Richardson, Edm.	.03	.05
172	Adam Oates, (1987 Style)	.12	.25
173	Uwe Krupp, NYI	.03	.05
174	Cam Neely, Bos.	.03	.05
175	Peter Sidorkiewicz, Goalie, Ott.	.03	.05
176	Geoff Courtnall, Van.	.03	.05
177	Douglas Gilmour, Tor.	.18	.35
178	Josef Beranek, Edm.	.10	.20
179	Michel Picard, Har.	.03	.05
180	Terry Carkner, Phi.	.03	.05
181	Nelson Emerson, St.L.	.05	.10
182	Perry Berezan, SJ	.03	.05
183	Checklist C	.05	.10
184	Andrew Moog, Goalie, Bos.	.03	.05
185	Michel Petit, Cal.	.03	.05
186	Mark Greig, Har.	.03	.05
187	Paul Coffey, (1981 Style)	.18	.35
188	Ron Francis, Pit.	.08	.15
189	Joseph Juneau, Bos.	.75	1.50
190	Jeff Odgers, SJ	.03	.05
191	Darry Sittler, (1975 Style)	.20	.40
192	Vincent Damphousse, Edm.	.03	.05
193	Gregory Paslawski, Que.	.03	.05
194	Tony Esposito, Goalie, (1969 Style)	.18	.35
195	Sergei Fedorov, Det.	.35	.75
196	Douglas Smail, Que.	.03	.05
197	Patrick Verbeek, Har.	.03	.05
198	Dominic Roussel, Goalie, Phi.	.10	.20
199	Michael McPhee, Mon.	.03	.05
200	Kevin Dineen, Phi.	.03	.05
201	Pat Elynuik, Win.	.03	.05
202	Tom Kurvers, NYI	.03	.05
203	Chris Joseph, Edm.	.03	.05
204	Mark Fitzpatrick, Goalie, NYI	.03	.05
205	Jari Kurri, LA	.03	.05
206	Guy Carbonneau, Mon.	.03	.05
207	Jan Erixon, NYR	.03	.05
208	Mark Messier, NYR	.07	.15
209	Lawrence Murphy, Pit.	.03	.05
210	Dirk Graham, Chi.	.03	.05
211	Ron Tugnutt, Goalie, Edm.	.03	.05
212	Dale Hawerchuk, Buf.	.03	.05
213	David Babych, Van.	.03	.05
214	Bo Mikael Andersson, Har.	.03	.05
215	James Patrick, NYR	.03	.05
216	Peter Stastny, NJD	.03	.05
217	Bernie Parent, Goalie, (1968 Style)	.25	.50
218	Jeff Hackett, Goalie, SJ	.03	.05
219	Dave Lowry, St.L.	.03	.05
220	Wayne Gretzky, (1979 Style)	1.50	3.00
221	Brent Gilchrist, Mon.	.03	.05
222	Andrew Cassels, Har.	.03	.05
223	Calle Johansson, Wash.	.03	.05
224	Joe Reekie, TB (Now with Lightning)	.03	.05
225	Craig Simpson, Edm.	.03	.05
226	Bob Essensa, Goalie, Win.	.03	.05
227	Pat Falloon, SJ	.12	.25
228	Vladimir Ruzicka, Bos.	.03	.05
229	Igor Ulanov, Win.	.03	.05
230	Kjell Samuelsson, Pit.	.03	.05
231	Shayne Corson, Mon.	.03	.05
232	Kelly Kisio, SJ	.03	.05
233	Gordon Roberts, Bos. (Now with Bruins)	.03	.05
234	Brian Noonan, Chi.	.03	.05
235	Viacheslav Kozlov, Det.	.35	.75
236	Checklist B	.03	.05

No.	Player	EX	NRMT
237	Jeff Beukeboom, NYR	.03	.05
238	Stephen Konroyd, Har.	.03	.05
239	Patrice Brisebois, Mon.	.03	.05
240	MVP: Mario Lemieux, Pit.	.12	.25
241	Dana Murzyn, Van.	.03	.05
242	Per-Erik Eklund, Phi.	.03	.05
243	Rob Blake, LA	.03	.05
244	Brendan Shanahan, St.L.	.03	.05
245	**500 Career Goals:** Michael Gartner, NYR	.03	.05
246	David Bruce, SJ	.03	.05
247	Michael Vernon, Goalie, Cal.	.03	.05
248	Zarley Zalapski, Har.	.03	.05
249	Dino Ciccarelli, Det. (Now with Red Wings)	.03	.05
250	David Williams, SJ,	.03	.05
251	Scott Stevens, (1983 Style)	.07	.15
252	Bob Probert, Det.	.03	.05
253	Mikhail Tatarinov, Que.	.03	.05
254	Robert Holik, Har.	.03	.05
255	Anthony Amonte, (1991 Style)	.05	.10
256	Brad May, Buf.	.03	.05
257	Philippe Bozon, St.L.	.03	.05
258	Mark Messier, (1980 Style)	.35	.75
259	Mike Richter, Goalie, NYR	.10	.20
260	Brian Mullen, SJ	.03	.05
261	Marin McSorley, LA	.03	.05
262	Glenn Healy, Goalie, NYI	.03	.05
263	Russell Romaniuk, Win.	.03	.05
264	Dan Quinn, Phi.	.03	.05
265	Jyrki Lumme, Van.	.03	.05
266	Valeri Kamensky, Que.	.12	.25
267	Vladimir Konstantinov, Det.	.03	.05
268	Peter Ahola, LA	.03	.05
269	**Guy Larose, Tor., RC**	**.03**	**.05**
270	Ulf Samuelsson, Pit.	.03	.05
271	Dale Craigwell, SJ	.03	.05
272	Adam Oates, Bos.	.10	.20
273	Pat MacLeod, SJ	.03	.05
274	Mike Keane, Mon.	.03	.05
275	John Vanbiesbrouck, Goalie, NYR	.07	.15
276	Brian Lawton, SJ	.03	.05
277	Sylvain Cote, Wash.	.03	.05
278	Gary Suter, Cal.	.03	.05
279	Alexander Mogilny, Buf.	.25	.50
280	Garth Butcher, St.L.	.03	.05
281	Douglas Wilson, Jr., SJ	.03	.05
282	Chris Terreri, Goalie, NJD	.03	.05
283	Phil Esposito, (1977 Style)	.12	.25
284	Russ Courtnall, Mon.	.03	.05
285	Pat LaFontaine, Buf.	.07	.15
286	Dimitri Khristich, Wash.	.03	.05
287	**John LeBlanc, Win., RC**	**.03**	**.05**
288	Randy Velischek, Que.	.03	.05
289	Dave Christian, St.L.	.03	.05
290	Kevin Haller, Mon.	.03	.05
291	Kevin Miller, Wash. (Now with Capitals)	.03	.05
292	Mario Lemieux, (1985 Style)	1.50	3.00
293	Stephan Lebeau, Mon.	.03	.05
294	Marcel Dionne, (1971 Style)	.15	.30
295	Barry Pederson, Bos.	.03	.05
296	Steve Duchesne, Que., (Now with Nordiques)	.03	.05
297	Yves Racine, Det.	.03	.05
298	Phil Housley, Win.	.03	.05
299	Randy Ladouceur, Har.	.03	.05
300	Michael Gartner, NYR	.03	.05
301	**Dominik Hasek, Goalie, Chi., RC**	**.25**	**.50**
302	Kevin Lowe, Edm.	.03	.05
303	Sylvain Lefebvre, Mon.	.03	.05
304	Jean-Jacques Daigneault, Mon.	.03	.05
305	Mike Ridley, Wash.	.03	.05
306	Curtis Leschyshyn, Que.	.03	.05
307	Gilbert Dionne, Mon.,	.03	.05
308	**Bill Guerin, NJD, RC**	**.10**	**.20**
309	Gerald Diduck, Van.	.03	.05
310	Rick Wamsley, Goalie, Tor.	.03	.05
311	Pat Jablonski, Goalie, Ott., (Now with Senators)	.03	.05
312	Jayson More, SJ, RC	.03	.05
313	Michael Modano, Min.	.03	.05
314	Checklist A	.05	.10
315	Sylvain Turgeon, Ott. (Now with Senators)	.03	.05
316	Sergei Nemchinov, NYR	.03	.05
317	Garry Galley, Phi.	.03	.05
318	#1 Defenseman: Paul Coffey, Pit.	.03	.05
319	Esa Tikkanen, Edm.	.03	.05

No.	Player	EX	NRMT
320	Claude Lapointe, Que.	.03	.05
321	Steve Yzerman, (1984 Style)	.25	.50
322	Mark Lamb, Ott., (Now with Senators)	.03	.05
323	Bob Errey, Pit.	.03	.05
324	Pavel Bure, (1992 Premier Style)	.15	.30
325	Craig Janney, St.L.	.03	.05
326	Bob Kudelski, LA	.03	.05
327	Kirk Muller, Mon.	.03	.05
328	Jim Paek, Pit.	.03	.05
329	Mike Ricci, Que. (Now with Nordiques)	.03	.05
330	Allan MacInnis, Cal.	.03	.05
331	Mike Hudson, Chi.	.03	.05
332	Darrin Shannon, Win.	.03	.05
333	Doug Brown, NJD	.03	.05
334	Corey Mullen, LA	.03	.05
335	Michael Krushelnyski, Tor.	.03	.05
336	Scott Stevens, NJD	.03	.05
337	Peter Zezel, Tor.	.03	.05
338	Geoff Smith, Edm.	.03	.05
339	Curtis Joseph, Goalie, St.L.	.03	.05
340	Tom Barrasso, Goalie, Pit.	.07	.15
341	Al Iafrate, Wash.	.03	.05
342	Patrick Flatley, NYI	.03	.05
343	Gerry Cheevers, Goalie, (1972 Style)	.12	.25
344	Norm Maciver, Edm.	.03	.05
345	Jeremy Roenick, Chi.	.25	.50
346	**Keith Tkachuk, Win., RC**	**.20**	**.40**
347	Rod Langway, Wash.	.03	.05
348	1,000 Points: Raymond Bourque, Bos.	.03	.05
349	Kirk McLean, Goalie, Van.	.03	.05
350	Brian Propp, Min.	.03	.05
351	John Ogrodnick, NYR	.03	.05
352	Benoit Brunet, Mon.	.03	.05
353	Alexei Kasatonov, NJD	.03	.05
354	Joseph Nieuwendyk, Cal.	.03	.05
355	Joe Sacco, Tor.	.03	.05
356	Tom Fergus, Van.	.03	.05
357	Dan Lambert, Que.	.03	.05
358	Michel Goulet, Chi.	.03	.05
359	Shawn McEachern, Pit.	.15	.30
360	Eric Desjardins, Mon.	.03	.05
361	Paul Stanton, Pit.	.03	.05
362	Ronald Sutter, St.L.	.03	.05
363	Derrick Smith, Min.	.03	.05
364	Paul Broten, NYR	.03	.05
365	Gregory Adams, Van.	.03	.05
366	Rob Zettler, SJ	.03	.05
367	David Poulin, Bos.	.03	.05
368	Keith Acton, Phi.	.03	.05
369	Nicklas Lidstrom, Det.	.03	.05
370	Randy Burridge, Wash.	.03	.05
371	Jamie Macoun, Tor.	.03	.05
372	Craig Billington, Goalie, NJ	.03	.05
373	Mark Recchi, Phi.	.07	.15
374	Kris Draper, Win.	.03	.05
375	Ed Olczyk, Win.	.03	.05
376	Tom Draper, Goalie, Buf.	.03	.05
377	Sergio Momesso, Van.	.03	.05
378	Brian Leetch, NYR	.03	.05
379	Paul Cavallini, St.L.	.03	.05
380	Paul Fenton, SJ	.03	.05
381	Dean Evason, SJ	.03	.05
382	Owen Nolan, Que.	.03	.05
383	Jeremy Roenick, (1990 Style)	.20	.40
384	Brian Bellows, Min.	.03	.05
385	Thomas Steen, Win.	.03	.05
386	John LeClair, Mon.	.03	.05
387	Darren Turcotte, NYR	.03	.05
388	James Black, Har.	.03	.05
389	Alexei Gusarov, Que.	.03	.05
390	Scott Lachance, NYI	.03	.05
391	Mike Bossy, (1978 Style)	.15	.30
392	Mike Hough, Que.	.03	.05
393	Grant Ledyard, Buf.	.03	.05
394	**Tom Fitzgerald, NYI**	**.03**	**.05**
395	Steve Thomas, NYI	.03	.05
396	Robert Smith, Min.	.03	.05

— 1992 - 93 REGULAR ISSUE —
INSERT SET - 25TH ANNIVERSARY

These 25 cards commemorate each of the past 25 years commencing with the 1968-69 issue plus one checklist. Each card features a reproduction of the face and back of the actual card design from each of the last 25 years. Card faces are bordered in silver metallic ink with a 'watermark' mat varnish "25th" logo to commemorate the Anniversary.

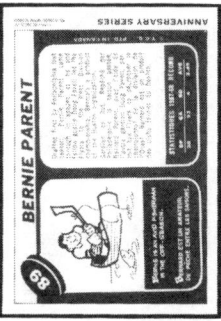 

1992 - 93 25th Anniversary Insert Set
Card No. 1, Bernie Parent

Card Size: 2 1/2" X 3 1/2"
Face: Four colour, white border; Name, Team
Back: Four colour on card stock; Name, Number, Resume, Bilingual
Imprint: © 1992 O-PEE-CHEE CO. LTD. PTD. IN CANADA /IMPRIMÉ AU CANADA © 1992 NHLPA
Complete Set No.: 26
Complete Set Price: 5.00 10.00
Common Card: .10 .20

No.	Player	EX	NRMT
1	Bernie Parent, Goalie, Phi.	.25	.50
2	Tony Esposito, Goalie, Chi.	.25	.50
3	Bobby Clarke, Phi.	.15	.30
4	Marcel Dionne, Det.	.15	.30
5	Gerry Cheevers, Goalie, CIC	.10	.20
6	Larry Robinson, Mon.	.10	.20
7	Denis Potvin, NYI	.15	.30
8	Darryl Sittler, Tor.	.10	.20
9	Bryan Trottier, NYI	.10	.20
10	Phil Esposito, NYR	.15	.30
11	Mike Bossy, NYI	.20	.40
12	Wayne Gretzky, Edm.	1.50	2.00
13	Mark Messier, Edm.	.20	.40
14	Paul Coffey, Edm.	.10	.20
15	Grant Fuhr, Goalie, Edm.	.10	.20
16	Scott Stevens, Wash.	.10	.20
17	Steve Yzerman, Det.	.10	.20
18	Mario Lemieux, Pit.	1.00	2.00
19	Patrick Roy, Goalie, Mon.	.50	1.00
20	Adam Oates, Det.	.10	.20
21	Brett Hull, St.L.	.25	.50
22	Joe Sakic, Que.	.10	.20
23	Jeremy Roenick, Chi., TP	.25	.50
24	Anthony Amonte, NYR, TP	.12	.25
25	Pavel Bure, Van., TP	.50	1.00
—	Checklist: 25th Anniversary Series	.10	.20

THE CHARLTON STANDARD CATALOGUE OF CANADIAN BASEBALL AND FOOTBALL CARDS
- Fourth Edition -
Coming in April!

— 1992 - 93 PREMIER ISSUE —

This 132-card set was O-Pee-Chee's way of marketing the premium stars and rookies through a small, low production premium set.

1992 - 93 25th Premier Issue
Card No. 1, Dave Christian

Card Size: 2.1/2" c 3.1/2"
Face: Four colour, white border; Name
Back: Four colour, white border on card stock; Name; Resume; Team logo;
Imprint: © 1993 O-PEE-CHEE CO. LTD. PRINTED IN CANADA /IMPRIME AU CANADA
Complete Set No.: 132
Complete Set Price: 9.00 18.00
Common Card: .03 .05
Foil Pack: (8 cards) .35
Foil Box: (36 packs) 10.00 20.00

No.	Player	EX	NRMT
1	Dave Christian, Chi.	.03	.05
2	Christian Ruuttu, Chi.	.03	.05
3	Vincent Damphousse, Mon.	.03	.05
4	Chris Lindberg, Cal.	.07	.15
5	**Bill Lindsay, Que., RC**	**.07**	**.15**
6	**Dmitri Kvartalnov, Bos., RC**	**.15**	**.30**
7	**Darcy Loewen, Ott., RC**	**.03**	**.05**
8	**Ed Courtenay, SJ, RC**	**.03**	**.05**
9	**Sergei Krivokrasov, Chi., RC**	**.12**	**.25**
10	Shawn Antoski, Van.	.03	.05
11	Andre Racicot, Goalie, Mon.	.03	.05
12	Marty McInnis, NYI	.03	.05
13	Alexei Zhamnov, Win.	.35	.75
14	**Keith Jones, Wash., RC**	**.10**	**.20**
15	**Steve Konowalchuk, Wash., RC**	**.10**	**.20**
16	Darryl Sydor, LA	.03	.05
17	Janne Ojanen, NJ	.03	.05
18	**Doug Zmolek, SJ, RC**	**.12**	**.25**
19	**Mikael Nylander, Hart., RC**	**.25**	**.50**
20	Russell Courtnall, Min.	.03	.05
21	**Martin Straka, Pit., RC**	**.75**	**1.50**
22	**Kevin Dahl, Cal., RC**	**.03**	**.05**
23	Kent Manderville, Tor.	.10	.20
24	Steve Heinze, Bos.	.03	.05
25	Philippe Bozon, St.L	.03	.05
26	Brent Fedyk, Phi.	.03	.05
27	Kris Draper, Win.	.03	.05
28	Brad Schlegel, Wash.	.03	.05
29	**Patrik Kjellberg, Mon., RC, Error**	**.03**	**.05**
30	Ted Donato, Bos.	.03	.05
31	**Vjateslav Butsayev, Phi., RC**	**.12**	**.25**
32	Tyler Wright, Edm.	.03	.05
33	**Tom Pederson, SJ, RC**	**.03**	**.05**
34	**Jim Hiller, LA, RC**	**.03**	**.05**
35	**Chris Luongo, Ott., RC**	**.03**	**.05**
36	**Robert Petrovicky, Hart., RC**	**.12**	**.25**
37	**Jean-Francois Quintin, SJ, RC**	**.03**	**.05**
38	Chris Dahlquist, Cal.	.03	.05
39	**Daniel LaPerriere, St.L, RC**	**.03**	**.05**
40	**Guy Hebert, Goalie, St.L, RC**	**.07**	**.15**
41	**Ed Ronan, Mon., RC**	**.07**	**.15**
42	Shawn Cronin, Phi.	.03	.05
43	Keith Tkachuk, Win.	.03	.05
44	Dino Ciccarelli, Det.	.03	.05
45	Doug Evans, Phi.	.03	.05
46	**Roman Hamrlik, TB, RC**	**.25**	**.50**
47	**Robert Lang, LA, RC**	**.12**	**.25**
48	Kerry Huffman, Que.	.03	.05
49	Patrick Conacher, LA	.03	.05

114 • O-PEE-CHEE — 1992 - 93 PREMIER INSERT SETS

No.	Player	EX	NRMT
50	Dominik Hasek, Goalie, Buf.	.18	.35
51	Dominic Roussel, Goalie, Phi.	.12	.25
52	Glen Murray, Bos.	.03	.05
53	Igar Korolev, St.L, RC	.10	.20
54	Jiri Slegr, Van.	.03	.05
55	Bo Mikael Andersson, TB	.03	.05
56	Bob Babcock, Wash., RC	.03	.05
57	Ron Hextall, Goalie, Que.	.03	.05
58	Jeff Daniels, Pit.	.03	.05
59	Douglas Crossman, TB	.03	.05
60	Viktor Gordijuk, Buf., RC	.12	.25
61	Adam Creighton, TB	.03	.05
62	Robert DiMaio, TB	.03	.05
63	Eric Weinrich, Hart.	.03	.05
64	Vitali Prokhorov, St.L, RC	.12	.25
65	Dimitri Yushkevich, Phi., RC	.12	.25
66	Eugeny Davydov, Win. Error	.03	.05
67	Dixon Ward, Van., RC	.12	.25
68	Teemu Selanne, Win., RC	1.50	3.00
69	Rob Zamuner, TB, RC	.07	.15
70	Joe Reekie, TB	.03	.05
71	Viacheslav Kozlov, Det.	.50	1.00
72	Philippe Boucher, Buf.	.03	.05
73	Phillippe Bourque, NYR	.03	.05
74	Yvon Corriveau, SJ	.03	.05
75	Brian Bellows. Mon.	.03	.05
76	Wendell Young, Goalie, TB	.03	.05
77	Robert Holik, NJ	.07	.15
78	Robert Carpenter, Wash.	.03	.05
79	Scott Lachance, NYI	.03	.05
80	John Druce, Win.	.03	.05
81	Keith Carney, Buf., RC	.07	.15
82	Neil Brady, Ott.	.03	.05
83	Richard Matvichuk, Min., RC	.10	.20
84	Sergei Bautin, Win., RC	.12	.25
85	Patrick Poulin, Hart.	.03	.05
86	Gordon Roberts, Bos.	.03	.05
87	Kay Whitmore, Goalie, Van.	.03	.05
88	Stephane Beauregard, Goalie, Phi.	.03	.05
89	Vladimir Malakhov, NYI	.12	.25
90	Richard Smehilk, Buf., RC	.12	.25
91	Mike Ricci, Que.	.03	.05
92	Sean Burke, Goalie, Hart.	.03	.05
93	Andrei Kovalenko, Que., RC	.45	.90
94	Shawn McEachern, Pit.	.50	1.00
95	Pat Jablonski, Goalie, TB	.03	.05
96	Oleg Petrov, Mon., RC	.30	.65
97	Glenn Mulvenna, Phi., RC	.03	.05
98	Jason Woolley, Wash., RC	.07	.15
99	Mark Greig, Hart., RC	.03	.05
100	Nikolai Borschevsky, Tor., RC	.30	.60
101	Joseph Juneau, Bos.	1.25	2.50
102	Eric Lindros, Phi.	3.00	6.00
103	Darius Kasparaitis, NYI	.12	.25
104	Sandis Ozolinsh, SJ, RC, Error	.35	.75
105	Stan Drulla, TB, RC	.03	.05
106	Mike Needham, Pit., RC	.10	.20
107	Norm Maciver, Ott.	.03	.05
108	Sylvain Lefebvre, Tor.	.03	.05
109	Tommy Sjodin, Min., RC	.10	.20
110	Robert Sweeney, Buf.	.03	.05
111	Brian Mullen, NYI	.03	.05
112	Peter Sidorkiewicz, Goalie, Ott.	.03	.05
113	Scott Niedermayer, NJ	.18	.35
114	Felix Potvin, Goalie, Tor.	.85	1.75
115	Robb Stauber, Goalie, LA	.03	.05
116	Sylvain Turgeon, Ott.	.03	.05
117	Mark Janssens, Hart.	.03	.05
118	Darren Banks, Bos., RC	.03	.05
119	Pat Elynuik, Wash.	.03	.05
120	Bill Guerin, NJ	.10	.20
121	Reginald Savage, Wash.	.03	.05
122	Enrico Ciccone, Min.	.03	.05
123	Chris Kontos, TB, RC	.10	.20
124	Martin Rucinsky, Que.	.03	.05
125	Alexei Zhitnik, LA	.25	.50
126	Alexei Kovalev, NYR	.35	.75
127	Tim Kerr, Hart.	.03	.05
128	Guy Larose, Tor., RC	.03	.05
129	Brent Gilchrist, Edm.	.03	.05
130	Steve Duchesne, Que.	.03	.05
131	Drake Berehowsky, Tor.	.03	.05
132	Checklist	.03	.05

— 1992 - 93 PREMIER INSERT SETS —
STAR PERFORMERS

This 22-card set was inserted one card per foil pack in Premier foil.

1992-93 Star Performers
Card No. 10, Pavel Bure

Card Size: 2 1/2" x 3 1/2"
Face: Four colour, white border; Name
Back: Four colour on white card stock; Name, Resume, Team logo
Imprint: © 1993 O-PEE-CHEE CO. LTD. PRINTED IN CANADA /IMPRIME AU CANADA
Complete Set No.: 22
Complete Set Price: 6.00 12.00
Common Card: .07 .15

No.	Player	EX	NRMT
1	Ray Ferraro, NYI	.07	.15
2	Dale Hunter, Wash.	.07	.15
3	Murray Craven, Hart.	.07	.15
4	Paul Coffey, LA	.18	.35
5	Jeremy Roenick, Chi.	.60	1.25
6	Denis Savard, Mon.	.12	.25
7	Jon Casey, Goalie,Min.	.07	.15
8	Douglas Gilmour, Tor.	.35	.75
9	Rod Brind'Amour Phi.	.07	.15
10	Pavel Bure, Van.	1.25	2.50
11	Joe Sakic, Que.	.25	.50
12	Pat Falloon, SJ	.20	.40
13	Adam Oates, Bos.	.20	.40
14	Gary Roberts, Cal.	.07	.15
15	Mark Messier, NYR	.10.	.20
16	Phil Housley, Win.	.12	.25
17	Pat LaFontaine, Buf.	.25	.50
18	Stephane J. J. Richer, NJ	.07	.15
19	Bill Ranford, Goalie, Edm.	.07	.15
20	Sergei Fedorov, Det.	.50	1.00
21	Brett Hull, St.L	.50	1.00
22	Mario Lemieux, Pit.	1.00	2.00

TOP ROOKIES

The cards from this 4-card set were randomly inserted into the premier foil packs as chase cards

1992-93 Top Rookies
Card No. 3, Dominic Roussel

Card Size: 2 1/2" x 3 1/2"
Face: Four colour, white border; Name
Back: Four colour with white border on card stock; Name, Resume, Team logo
Imprint: © 1993 O-PEE-CHEE CO. LTD. PRINTED IN CANDA / IMPRIME AU CANADA
Complete Set No.: 4
Complete Set Price: 7.50 15.00
Common Card: 1.50 3.00

No.	Player	EX	NRMT
1	Eric Lindros, Phi.	4.00	8.00
2	Roman Hamrlik, TB	1.50	3.00
3	Dominic Roussel, Goalie, Phi.	1.50	3.00
4	Felix Potvin, Goalie, Tor.	3.50	7.00

— 1993 HOCKEY FANFEST —
PROMOTIONAL SHEET
— MONTREAL CANADIENS —

In 1993 O-Pee-Chee produced a 1993 Hockeyfest Montreal Canadiens Commemorative Sheet and set. These are listed in the Team Set section. See page No. 656.

— 1993 - 94 PREMIER ISSUE —

This 528-card set was printed by TOPPS in the United States, the only difference between the O-Pee-Chee Issue and Topps is the addition of "PTD IN U.S.A." to the imprint. The set is divided into two series with a Gold and other insert cards randomly inserted into Series One and Two foil packs.

1993-94 Premier 1993-94 Gold
No. 1, Patrick Roy   No. 337, Geoff Courtnall

Card Size: 2 1/2" x 3 1/2"
Face: Four colour, white border; Name, Position
Back: Four colour, white border; Name, Number, Team, Position, Resume
Imprint: ©1994 THE TOPPS COMPANY, INC. PTD IN U.S.A.
Complete Set No.: 528
Series One 264
Series Two 264

	Regular	Gold
Complete Set Price:	40.00	250.00
Series One Price:	20.00	125.00
Series Two Price:	20.00	125.00
Common Card:	.05	.40

— SERIES ONE —

No.	Player	Regular NRMT	Gold NRMT
1	Patrick Roy, Goalie, Mon.	.50	4.00
2	Alexei Zhitnik, LA	.10	.70
3	Uwe Krupp, NYI	.05	.40
4	Todd Gill, Tor.	.05	.40
5	Paul Stanton, Pit.	.05	.40
6	Sergio Momesso, Van.	.05	.40
7	Dale Hawerchuck, Buf.	.05	.40
8	Kevin Miller, St. L	.05	.40
9	Nicklas Lidstrom, Det.	.05	.40
10	Joe Sakic, Que.	.20	1.00
11	Thomas Steen, Win.	.05	.40
12	Peter Bondra, Wash.	.05	.40
13	Brian Noonan, Chi.	.05	.40
14	Glen Featherstone, Bos.	.05	.40

1993 - 94 PREMIER ISSUE — O-PEE-CHEE • 115

No.	Player	Regular NRMT	Gold NRMT
15	Michael Vernon, Goalie, Cal.	.05	.40
16	Janne Ojanen, NJ	.05	.40
17	Neil Brady, Ott.	.05	.40
18	Dimitri Yushkievich, Phi.	.05	.40
19	Rob Zamuner, TB	.05	.40
20	Zarley Zalapski, Hart.	.05	.40
21	Mike Sullivan, SJ	.05	.40
22	Jamie Baker, Ott.	.05	.40
23	Craig MacTavish, Edm.	.05	.40
24	Mark Tinordi	.05	.40
25	Brian Leetch, NYR	.25	1.25
26	Brian Skrudland, Fl.	.05	.40
27	Keith Tkachuk, Win.	.20	1.00
28	Patrick Flatley, NYI	.05	.40
29	Doug Bodger, Buf.	.05	.40
30	Felix Potvin, Goalie, Tor.	.65	5.00
31	Shawn Antoski, Van.	.05	.40
32	Eric Desjardins, Mon.	.05	.40
33	Mike Donnelley, LA	.05	.40
34	Kjell Samuelsson, Pit.	.05	.40
35	Nelson Emerson, St. L	.05	.40
36	Phil Housley, Win.	.05	.40
37	**Plus/Minus Leader:** Mario Lemieux, Pit.	.25	1.50
38	Shayne Corson, Edm.	.05	.40
39	James (Steve) Smith, Chi.	.05	.40
40	Bob Kudelski, Ott.	.05	.40
41	Joe Cirella, Fl.	.05	.40
42	Sergei Nemchinov, NYR	.05	.40
43	Kerry Huffman, Que.	.05	.40
44	Bob Beers, TB	.05	.40
45	Al Iafrate, Wash.	.20	1.25
46	Michael Modano, Dal.	.05	.40
47	Patrick Verbeek, Hart.	.05	.40
48	Joel Otto, Cal.	.05	.40
49	Dino Ciccarelli, Det.	.05	.40
50	Adam Oates, Bos.	.15	1.00
51	Pat Elynuik, Wash.	.05	.40
52	Robert Holik, NJ	.05	.40
53	Johan Garpenlov, SJ	.05	.40
54	Jeff Beukeboom, NYR	.05	.40
55	Tommy Soderstrom, Goalie, Phi.	.15	1.00
56	Robert Blake, LA	.05	.40
57	Martin McInnis, NYI	.05	.40
58	Dixon Ward, Van.	.05	.40
59	Patrice Brisebois, Mon.	.05	.40
60	Ed Belfour, Goalie, Chi.	.15	1.00
61	Donald Audette, Buf.	.05	.40
62	Mike Ricci, Que.	.05	.40
63	Frederik Olausson, Win.	.05	.40
64	Norm Maciver, Ott.	.05	.40
65	Andrew Cassels, Hart.	.05	.40
66	Tim Cheveldae, Goalie, Det.	.05	.40
67	David Reid, Bos.	.05	.40
68	Philippe Bozon, St.L	.05	.40
69	Drake Berehowsky, Tor.	.05	.40
70	Anthony Amonte, NYR	.05	.40
71	Dave Manson, Edm.	.05	.40
72	Rick Tocchet, Pit.	.05	.40
73	Stephen Kasper, TB	.05	.40
74	Assist leader: Adam Oates, Bos.	.05	.40
75	Ulf Dahlen, Dal.	.05	.40
76	Chris Lindberg, Cal.	.05	.40
77	Douglas Jr. Wilson	.05	.40
78	Mike Ridley, Wash.	.05	.40
79	Vjateslav Butsayev, Phi.	.05	.40
80	Scott Stevens, NJ	.05	.40
81	Cliff Ronning, Van.	.05	.40
82	Andrei Lomakin, Fl.	.05	.40
83	Shawn Burr, Det.	.05	.40
84	Benoit Brunet, Mon.	.05	.40
85	Valeri Kamensky, Que.	.20	1.25
86	Randy Carlyle, Win.	.05	.40
87	Chris Joseph, Edm.	.05	.40
88	Dirk Graham, Chi.	.05	.40
89	Kenneth Sutton, Buf.	.05	.40

NHL FIRST TEAM ALL-STAR

No.	Player	Regualr NRMT	Gold NRMT
90	Luc Robitaille, LA	.05	.40
91	Mario Lemieux, Pit.	.25	1.50
92	Temmu Selanne, Win.	.35	2.00
93	Raymond Bourque, Bos.	.05	.40
94	Chris Chelios, Chi.	.05	.40
95	Ed Belfour, Goalie, Chi.	.15	1.00

REGULAR ISSUE

No.	Player	Regular NRMT	Gold NRMT
96	Keith Jones, Wash.	.05	.40
97	Sylvain Turgeon, Ott.	.05	.40
98	Jim Johnson, DAl.	.05	.40
99	Mikael Nylander, Hart.	.15	1.00
100	Theoren Fleury, Cal.	.05	.40
101	Shawn Chambers, TB	.05	.40
102	Alexander Semak, NJ	.05	.40
103	Ronald Sutter, St.L	.05	.40
104	Glenn Anderson, Tor.	.05	.40
105	Jaromir Jagr, Pit.	.05	.40
106	Adam Graves, NYR	.15	1.00
107	Nikolai Borschevsky, Tor.	.15	1.00
108	Vladimir Konstantinov, Det.	.05	.40
109	Robb Stauber, Goalie, LA	.05	.40
110	Arturs Irbe, Goalie, SJ	.20	1.50
111	**Goals Against Average:** Felix Potvin, Goalie, Tor.	.35	2.00
112	Darius Kasparaitis, NYI	.05	.40
113	Kirk McLean, Goalie, Van.	.05	.40
114	Glen Wesley, Bos.	.05	.40
115	Rod Brind'Amour, Phi.	.05	.40
116	Mike Eagles, Win.	.05	.40
117	Brian Bradley, TB	.05	.40
118	Dave Christian, Chi.	.05	.40
119	Randy Wood, Buf.	.05	.40
120	Craig Janney, St.L	.05	.40

SUPER ROOKIE

No.	Player	Regular NRMT	Gold NRMT
121	Eric Lindros, Phi.	1.00	7.00
122	Tommy Soderstrom, Goalie, Phi.	.10	.75
123	Shawn McEachern, Pit.	.10	.75
124	Andrew Kovalenko, Que.	.10	.75
125	Joseph Juneau, Bos.	.25	1.50
126	Felix Potvin, Goalie, Tor.	.25	1.50
127	Dixon Ward, Van.	.05	.40
128	Alexei Zhamnov, Win.	.20	1.25
129	Vladimir Malakhov, NYI	.05	.40
130	Teemu Selanne, Win.	.70	4.50

REGULAR ISSUE

No.	Player	Regular NRMT	Gold NRMT
131	Neal Broten, Dal.	.05	.40
132	Ulf Samuelsson, Pit.	.05	.40
133	Mark Janssens, Hart.	.05	.40
134	Claude Lemieux, Edm.	.05	.40
135	Mike Richter, Goalie, NYR	.10	.75
136	Doug Weight, NYR	.05	.40
137	Rob Pearson, Tor.	.05	.40
138	Sylvain Cote, Wash.	.05	.40
139	Mike Keane, Mon.	.05	.40
140	Benoit Hogue, NYI	.05	.40
141	Michel Petit, Cal.	.05	.40
142	Mark Freer, Ott.	.05	.40
143	Doug Zmolek, SJ	.05	.40
144	Tony Granato, LA	.05	.40
145	Paul Coffey, Det.	.10	.75
146	Ted Donato, Bos.	.05	.40
147	Brent Sutter, Chi.	.05	.40
148	**Goal Scoring Leader:** Temmu Selanne, Win.; Alexander Mogilny, Buf.	.25	1.50
149	James Patrick, NYI	.05	.40
150	Mikael Andersson, TB	.05	.40
151	Steve Duchesne, Que.	.05	.40
152	Terry Carkner, Phi.	.05	.40
153	Russell Courtnall, Dal.	.05	.40
154	Brian Mullen, NYI	.05	.40
155	Martin Straka, Pit.	.30	1.75
156	Geoff Sanderson, Hart.	.30	1.75
157	Mark Howe, Det.	.05	.40
158	Stephane J. J. Richer, NJ	.05	.40
159	Doug Crossman, St.L	.05	.40
160	John Vanbiesbrouck, Goalie, Fl.	.10	.75
161	Bob Essensa, Goalie, Win.	.05	.40
162	Wayne Presley, Buf.	.05	.40
163	Mathieu Schneider, Mon.	.05	.40
164	Jiri Slegr, Van.	.05	.40
165	Stephane Fiset, Goalie, Que.	.05	.40
166	Wendell Young, Goalie, TB	.05	.40
167	Kevin Dineen, Phi.	.05	.40
168	Sandis Ozolinsh, SJ	.15	1.00
169	Michael Krushelnyski, Tor.	.05	.40

NHL SECOND TEAM ALL-STAR

No.	Player	Regular NRMT	Gold NRMT
170	Kevin Stevens, Pit.	.10	1.00
171	Pat LaFontaine, Buf.	.10	1.00
172	Alexander Mogilny, Buf.	.25	1.50
173	Lawrence Murphy, Pit.	.05	.40
174	Al Iafrate, Wash.	.05	.40
175	Tom Barrasso, Goalie, Pit.	.10	.75

REGULAR ISSUE

No.	Player	Regular NRMT	Gold NRMT
176	Derek King, NYI	.05	.40
177	Bob Probert, Det.	.05	.40
178	Gary Suter, Cal.	.05	.40
179	David Shaw, Bos.	.05	.40
180	Luc Robitaille, LA	.10	.75
181	John LeClair, Mon.	.05	.40
182	Troy Murray, Chi.	.05	.40
183	Dave Gagner, Dal.	.05	.40
184	Darcy Loewen, Ott.	.05	.40
185	**Points Leader:** Mario Lemieux, Pit.	.25	1.50
186	Pat Jablonsky, Goalie, TB	.05	.40
187	Alexei Kovalev, NYR	.25	1.50
188	Todd Krygier, Wash.	.05	.40
189	Lawrence Murphy, Pit.	.05	.40
190	Pierre Turgeon, NYI	.10	.75
191	Craig Ludwig, Dal.	.05	.40
192	Brad May, Buf.	.05	.40
193	John MacLean, NJ	.05	.40
194	Ronald Wilson, St.L	.05	.40
195	Eric Wienrich, Hart.	.05	.40
196	Steve Chiasson, Det.	.05	.40
197	Dmitri Kvartalnov, Bos.	.05	.40
198	Andrei Kovalenko, Que.	.10	.75
199	Rob Gaudreau, SJ	.30	1.50
200	Evgeny Davydov, Win.	.05	.40
201	Adrien Plavsic, Van.	.05	.40
202	Brian Bellows, Mon.	.05	.40
203	Doug Evans, Phi.	.05	.40
204	**Win Leader:** Tom Barrasso, Goalie,	.05	.40
205	Joe Nieuwendyk, Cal.	.05	.40
206	Jari Kurri, LA	.05	.40
207	Robert Rouse, Tor.	.05	.40
208	Yvon Corriveau, Hart.	.05	.40
209	John Blue, Goalie, Bos.	.05	.40
210	Dimitri Khristich, Wash.	.05	.40
211	Brent Fedyk, Phi.	.05	.40
212	Jody Hull, Ott.	.05	.40
213	Chris Terreri, Goalie, NJ	.05	.40
214	Michael McPhee, Dal.	.05	.40
215	Chris Kontos, TB	.05	.40
216	Greg Gilbert, Chi.	.05	.40
217	Sergei Zubov, NYR	.35	2.00
218	Grant Fuhr, Goalie, Buf.	.05	.40
219	Charlie Huddy, LA	.05	.40
220	Marlo Lemieux, Pit.	.75	5.00
221	Sheldon Kennedy, Det.	.05	.40
222	**Save Percentage:** Curtis Joseph, Goalie, St.L	.05	.40
223	Brad Dalgarno, NYI	.05	.40
224	Bret Hedican, St.L	.05	.40
225	Trevor Linden, Van.	.05	.40
226	Darryl Sydor, LA	.05	.40
227	Jayson More, SJ	.05	.40
228	David Poulin, Bos.	.05	.40
229	Frantisek Musil, Cal.	.05	.40
230	Mark Recchi, Phi.	.10	.75
231	Craig Simpson, Edm.	.05	.40
232	Gino Cavallini, Que.	.05	.40

O-PEE-CHEE — 1993-94 PREMIER ISSUE

No.	Player	Regular NRMT	Gold NRMT
233	Vincent Damphousse, Mon.	.05	.40
234	Luciano Borsato, Win.	.05	.40
235	David Andreychuk, Tor.	.10	.75
236	Ken Daneyko, NJ	.05	.40
237	Chris Chelios, Chi.	.05	.40
238	Andrew McBain, Ott.	.05	.40
239	Rick Tabaracci, Goalie, Wash.	.05	.40
240	Steve Larmer, Chi.	.05	.40
241	Sean Burke, Goalie, Hart.	.05	.40
242	Robert DiMaio, TB	.05	.40
243	Jim Paek, Pit.	.05	.40
244	Dave Lowry, Fl.	.05	.40
245	Alexander Mogilny, Buf.	.25	1.50
246	Darren Turcotte, NYR	.05	.40
247	Brendan Shanahan, St.L	.15	1.00
248	Peter Taglianetti, Pit.	.05	.40
249	Scott Mellanby, Fl.	.05	.40
250	Guy Carbonneau, Mon.	.05	.40
251	Claude LaPointe, Que.	.05	.40
252	Pat Conacher, LA	.05	.40
253	Roger Johansson, Cal..	.05	.40
254	Cam Neely, Bos.	.05	.40
255	Garry Galley, Phi.	.05	.40
256	Keith Primeau, Det.	.05	.40
257	Scott Lachance, NYI	.05	.40
258	Bill Ranford, Goalie, Edm.	.05	.40
259	Pat Falloon, SJ	.10	.75
260	Pavel Bure, Van.	.75	5.00
261	Darrin Shannon, Win.	.05	.40
262	Michael Foligno, Tor.	.05	.40
263	Checklist 1-132, Martin Lapointe, Det.	.05	.40
264	Checklist 133-264, Kevin Miehn, St.L	.05	.40

— SERIES TWO —

No.	Player	Regular NRMT	Gold NRMT
265	Peter Douris, SJ	.05	.40
266	Warren Rychel, LA	.05	.40
267	Owen Nolan, Que.	.05	.40
268	Mark Osborne, Tor.	.05	.40
269	Teppo Numminen, Win.	.05	.40
270	Rob Niedermayer, Fl.	.50	3.00
271	Mark Lamb, Ott.	.05	.40
272	Curtis Joseph, Goalie, St.L	.10	.75
273	Joe Murphy, Chi.	.05	.40
274	Bernie Nicholls, NJ	.05	.40
275	Gordon Roberts, Bos.	.05	.40
276	Allan MacInnis, Cal.	.05	.40
277	Ken Wregget, Goalie, Pit.	.05	.40
278	Calle Johansson, Wash.	.05	.40
279	Tom Kurvers, NYI	.05	.40
280	Steve Yzerman, Det.	.15	1.00
281	Roman Hamrlik, TB	.10	.75
282	Esa Tikkanen, NYR	.05	.40
283	**Darrin Madeley, Goalie, Ott, RC**	.10	.75
284	Robert Dirk, Van.	.05	.40
285	**Derek Plante, Buf., RC**	.70	4.00
286	Ron Tugnutt, Goalie, MDA	.05	.40
287	Frank Pietrangelo, Goalie, Hart.	.05	.40
288	Paul DiPietro, Mon.	.05	.40
289	Alexander Godynyuk, Fl.	.05	.40
290	**Kirk Maltby, Edm., RC**	.10	.75
291	Olaf Kolzig, Goalie, Wash.	.05	.40
292	Vitali Karamnov, St.L	.05	.40
293	Alexei Gusarov, Que.	.05	.40
294	Bryan Erikson, Win.	.05	.40
295	Jocelyn Lemieux, Chi.	.05	.40
296	Bryan Trottier, Pit.	.05	.40
297	David Ellett, Tor.	.05	.40
298	Tim Watters, LA	.05	.40
299	Joseph Juneau, Bos.	.40	3.25
300	James (Steve) Thomas, NYI	.05	.40
301	Mark Greig, Hart.	.05	.40
302	Jeff Reese, Goalie, Cal.	.05	.40
303	Steven King, MDA	.05	.40
304	Donald Beaupre, Goalie, Wash.	.05	.40
305	Denis Savard, TB	.05	.40
306	Greg Smyth, Fl.	.05	.40
307	**Jaroslav Modry, NJ, RC**	.10	.75
308	Petr Svoboda, Buf.	.05	.40

No.	Player	Regular NRMT	Gold NRMT
309	Mike Craig, Dal.	.05	.40
310	Eric Lindros, Phi.	2.00	15.00
311	Dana Murzyn, Van.	.05	.40
312	Sean Hill, MDA	.05	.40
313	Andre Racicot, Goalie, Mon.	.05	.40
314	John Vanbiesbrouck, Goalie, Fl.	.10	.75
315	Doug Lidster, NYR	.05	.40
316	Garth Butcher, St.L	.05	.40
317	**Alexei Yashin, Ott., RC**	1.00	7.00
318	Sergei Fedorov, Det.	.05	.40
319	Louie DeBrusk, Edm.	.05	.40
320	Dominik Hasek, Goalie, Buf.	.10	.75
321	Michal Pivonka, Wash.	.05	.40
322	Robert Holik, NJ	.05	.40
323	Roman Hamrlik, TB	.10	.75
324	Petr Svoboda, Buf.	.05	.40
325	Jaromir Jagr, Pit.	.30	2.00
326	Steven Finn, Que.	.05	.40
327	Stephane J. J. Richer, NJ	.05	.40
328	Claude Loiselle, NYI	.05	.40
329	Joseph Sacco, MDA	.05	.40
330	Wayne Gretzky, LA	.75	5.00
331	Sylvain Lefebvre, Tor.	.05	.40
332	Sergei Bautin, Win.	.05	.40
333	Craig Simpson, Buf.	.05	.40
334	Don Sweeney, Bos.	.05	.40
335	Dominic Roussel, Goalie, Phi.	.10	.75
336	**Scott Thomas, Buf., RC**	.10	.75
337	Geoff Courtnall, Van.	.05	.40
338	Tom Fitzgerald, Fl.	.05	.40
339	Kevin Haller, Mon.	.05	.40
340	Troy Loney, MDA	.05	.40
341	Ronald Stern, Cal.	.05	.40
342	**Mark Astley, Buf., RC**	.10	.75
343	Jeff Daniels, Pit.	.05	.40
344	Marc Bureau, TB	.05	.40
345	**Micah Alvazoff, Det., RC**	.10	.75
346	Matthew Barnaby, Buf.	.10	.75
347	C.J. Young, Fl.	.05	.40
348	Dale Craigwell, SJ	.05	.40
349	Ray Ferraro, NYI	.05	.40
350	Raymond Bourque, Bos.	.10	.75
351	Stu Barnes, Win.	.05	.40
352	**Allan Conroy, Phi., RC**	.10	.75
353	Shawn McEachern, LA	.10	.75
354	Garry Valk, MDA	.05	.40
355	Christian Ruuttu, Chi.	.05	.40
356	Darren Rumble, Ott.	.05	.40
357	Stu Grimson, MDA	.05	.40
358	Alexander Karpovtsev, NYR	.10	.75
359	Wendel Clark, Tor.	.10	.75
360	Michal Pivonka, Wash.	.05	.40
361	**Peter Popovic, Mon., RC**	.10	.75
362	Kevin Dahl, Cal.	.05	.40
363	Jeff Brown, St.L	.05	.40
364	Darren Puppa, Goalie, TB	.05	.40
365	**Dallas Drake, Det., RC**	.20	1.50
366	Dean McAmmond, Edm.	.05	.40
367	Martin Rucinsky, Que.	.05	.40
368	Shane Churla, Dal.	.05	.40
369	Todd Ewen, MDA	.05	.40
370	Kevin Stevens, Pit.	.15	1.75
371	David Volek, NYI	.05	.40
372	Jean-Jaques Daigneault, Mon.	.05	.40
373	Marc Bergevin, TB	.05	.40
374	Craig Billington, Goalie, Ott.	.05	.40
375	Michael Gartner, NYR	.05	.40
376	Jimmy Carson, LA	.05	.40
377	Bruce Driver, NJ	.05	.40
378	Steve Heinze, Bos.	.05	.40
379	Patrick Carnback, MDA	.10	.75

CANADA

No.	Player	Regular NRMT	Gold NRMT
380	Wayne Gretzky, LA	.75	5.00
381	Jeff Brown, St.L	.05	.40
382	Gary Roberts, Cal.	.05	.40
383	Raymond Bourque, Bos.	.10	.75
384	Michael Gartner, NYR	.10	.75
385	Felix Potvin, Goalie, Tor.	.50	3.50

REGULAR ISSUE

No.	Player	Regular NRMT	Gold NRMT
386	Michel Goulet, Chi.	.05	.40
387	Dave Tippett, Phi.	.05	.40
388	Jim Waite, Goalie, SJ	.05	.40
389	Yuri Khmylev, Buf.	.05	.40
390	Douglas Gilmour, Tor.	.25	2.00
391	Brad McCrimmon, Hart.	.05	.40
392	Brent Severyn, Fl., RC	.10	.75
393	**Jocelyn Thibault, Goalie, Que., RC**	.75	5.00
394	Boris Mironov, Win.	.05	.40
395	Martin McSorley, Pit.	.05	.40
396	Shaun Van Allen, MDA	.05	.40
397	Gary Leeman, Mon.	.05	.40
398	Ed Olczyk, NYR	.05	.40
399	Darcy Wakaluk, Goalie, Dal.	.05	.40
400	Murray Craven, Van.	.05	.40
401	Martin Brodeur, Goalie, NJ	.25	2.00
402	Paul Laus, Fl.	.05	.40
403	Bill Houlder, MDA	.05	.40
404	Robert Reichel, Cal.	.05	.40
405	Alexandre Daigle, Ott., RC	1.00	7.00
406	Brent Thompson, LA	.05	.40
407	Keith Acton, NYI	.05	.40
408	Dave Karpa, Que.	.05	.40
409	Igor Korolev, St.L	.05	.40
410	Chris Gratton, TB	.05	.40
411	Vincent Riendeau, Goalie, Det.	.05	.40
412	Darren McCarty, Det.	.05	.40
413	Robert Carpenter, NJ	.05	.40
414	Joe Cirella, Fl.	.05	.40
415	Stephane Matteau, Chi.	.05	.40
416	Josef Stumpel, Bos.	.05	.40
417	Richard Pilon, NYI	.05	.40
418	**Mattias Norstrom, NYR, RC**	.10	.75
419	Dmitri Mironov, Tor.	.05	.40
420	Alexei Zhamnov, Win.	.30	2.25
421	Bill Guerin, NJ	.05	.40
422	Greg Hawgood, Phi.	.05	.40
423	Randy Cunneyworth, Hart.	.05	.40
424	Ronald Francis, Pit.	.05	.40
425	Brett Hull, St.L	.25	2.00
426	Tim Sweeney, MDA	.05	.40
427	Mike Rathje, SJ	.05	.40
428	David Babych, Van.	.05	.40
429	**Chris Tancill, Dal., RC**	.10	.75
430	Mark Messier, NYR	.15	1.00
431	Bob Sweeney, Buf.	.05	.40
432	Terry Yake, MDA	.05	.40
433	Joe Reekie, TB	.05	.40
434	Tomas Sandstrom, LA	.05	.40
435	Kevin Hatcher, Wash.	.05	.40
436	Bill Lindsay, Fl.	.05	.40
437	Jon Casey, Goalie, Bos.	.05	.40
438	Dennis Vaske, NYI	.05	.40
439	Allen Pedersen, Hart.	.05	.40
440	Pavel Bure, Van.	.75	5.00
441	Sergei Fedorov, Det.	.40	2.50
442	Arturs Irbe, Goalie, SJ	.15	1.00
443	Darius Kasparaitis, NYI	.05	.40
444	Evgeny Davydov, Fl.	.05	.40
445	Vladimir Malakhov, NYI	.05	.40
446	Tom Barrasso, Goalie, Pit.	.05	.40
447	Jeff Norton, SJ	.05	.40
448	David Emma, NJ	.05	.40
449	Per-Erik Eklund, Phi.	.05	.40
450	Jeremy Roenick, Chi.	.25	1.75
451	Jesse Belanger, Fl.	.25	1.75
452	Vitali Prokhorov, St.L	.05	.40
453	Arto Blomsten, Win.	.05	.40
454	Peter Zezel, Tor.	.05	.40
455	Kelly Kisio, Cal.	.05	.40
456	Zdeno Ciger, Edm.	.05	.40
457	Greg Johnson, Det.	.05	.40
458	Dave Archibald, Ott.	.05	.40
459	Vladimir Vujtek, Edm.	.05	.40
460	Mats Sundin, Que.	.15	1.00
461	Dan Keczmer, Hart.	.05	.40
462	Stephan Lebeau, Mon.	.05	.40
463	Dominik Hasek, Goalie, Buf.	.10	.75
464	Kevin Lowe, NYR	.05	.40
465	Gordon Murphy, Fl.	.05	.40
466	Bryan Smolinski, Bos.	.35	2.50

— 1993 - 94 INSERT SETS — O-PEE-CHEE • 117

No.	Player	Regular NRMT	Gold NRMT
467	Josef Beranek, Phi.	.10	.75
468	Ron Hextall, Goalie, NYI	.05	.40
469	Randy Ladouceur, MDA	.05	.40
470	Scott Niedermayer, NJ	.15	1.00
471	Kelly Hrudey, Goalie, LA	.05	.40
472	Mike Needham, Pit.	.05	.40
473	John Tucker, TB	.05	.40
474	Kelly Miller, Wash.	.05	.40
475	Jyrki Lumme, Van.	.05	.40
476	Andrew Moog, Goalie, Dal.	.05	.40
477	Glen Murray, Bos.	.05	.40
478	Mark Ferner, MDA, RC	.10	.75
479	John Cullen, Tor.	.05	.40
480	Gilbert Dionne, Mon.	.05	.40
481	Paul Ranheim, Cal.	.05	.40
482	Mike Hough, Fl.	.05	.40
483	Teemu Selanne, Win.	1.25	10.00
484	**Aaron Ward, Det., RC**	.10	.75
485	Chris Pronger, Hart.	.35	2.50
486	Glenn Healy, Goalie, NYR	.05	.40
487	Curtis Leschyshyn, Que.	.05	.40
488	**Jim Montgomery, St.L, RC**	.15	1.00
489	Travis Green, NYI	.05	.40
490	Pat LaFontaine, Buf.	.20	1.50
491	**Bobby Dollas, MDA, RC**	.10	.75
492	Alexei Kasatonov	.05	.40
493	Corey Millen, NJ	.05	.40
494	Viacheslav Kozlov, Det.	.20	1.75
495	Igor Kravchuk, Edm.	.05	.40
496	Dimitri Filimonov, Ott.	.05	.40
497	Jeff Odgers, SJ	.05	.40
498	Joe Mullen, Pit.	.05	.40
499	Gary Shuchuk, LA	.05	.40

AMERICA

No.	Player	Regular NRMT	Gold NRMT
500	Jeremy Roenick, Chi.	.35	2.50
501	Tom Barrasso, Goalie, Pit.	.05	.40
502	Keith Tkachuk, Win.	.05	.40
503	Phil Housley, St.L	.05	.40
504	Anthony Granato, LA	.05	.40
505	Brian Leetch, NYR	.20	1.50

REGULAR ISSUE

No.	Player	Regular NRMT	Gold NRMT
506	Anatoli Semenov, MDA	.05	.40
507	Stephen Leach, Bos.	.05	.40
508	Brian Skrudland, Fl.	.05	.40
509	Kirk Muller, Mon.	.05	.40
510	Gary Roberts, Cal.	.05	.40
511	Gerard Gallant, TB	.05	.40
512	Joey Kocur, NYR	.05	.40
513	Tahir Domi, Win.	.05	.40
514	Kay Whitmore, Goalie, Van.	.05	.40
515	Vladimir Malakhov, NYI	.05	.40
516	**Stewart Malgunas, Phl., RC**	.10	.75
517	Jamie Macoun, Tor.	.05	.40
518	Alan May, Wash.	.05	.40
519	Guy Hebert, Goalie, St.L	.05	.40
520	Derian Hatcher, Dal.	.05	.40
521	Richard Smehlik, Buf.	.05	.40
522	**Joby Messier, NYR, rc**	.10	.75
523	Trent Klatt, Dal.	.05	.40
524	Tom Chorske, NJ	.05	.40
525	**Iain Fraser, Que., RC**	.10	.75
526	Daniel Laperriere, St.L	.05	.40
527	Checklist (265-396)	.05	.40
528	Checklist (397-528)	.05	.40

— 1993 - 94 INSERT SETS —

BLACK GOLD

This 24-card set consists of 12 randomly inserted cards in both Series One and Two foil packs.

 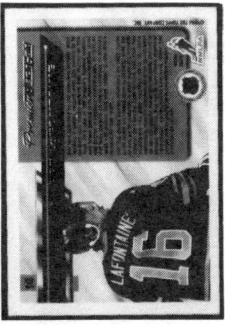

1993-94 Black Gold
Card No. 16, Pat LaFontaine

Size: 2 1/2" x 3 1/2"
Face: Four colour, white border; Gold foil on black background, Black gold logo, Name
Back: Four colour, white border; Gold foil, Team, Name, Resume
Imprint: © 1994 THE TOPPS COMPANY, INC. PTD IN U.S.A.
Complete Set No.: 24
  Series One No.: 12
  Series Two No.: 12
Complete Set Price: 135.00 275.00
  Series One Price: 75.00 150.00
  Series Two Price: 62.50 125.00
Common Card: 3.50 7.00

SERIES ONE

No.	Player	EX	NRMT
1	Wayne Gretzky, LA	20.00	40.00
2	Vincent Damphousse, Mon.	3.50	7.00
3	Adam Oates, Bos.	5.00	10.00
4	Phil Housley, Win.	3.50	7.00
5	Michael Vernon, Goalie, Cal.	3.50	7.00
6	Mats Sundin, Que.	5.00	10.00
7	Pavel Bure, Van.	12.50	25.00
8	Patrick Roy, Goalie, Mon.	12.50	25.00
9	Tom Barrasso, Goalie, Pit.	3.50	7.00
10	Alecander Mogilny, Buf.	7.50	15.00
11	Douglas Gilmour, Tor.	7.50	15.00
12	Eric Lindros, Phi.	22.50	45.00

SERIES TWO

No.	Player	EX	NRMT
13	Theoren Fleury, Cal.	3.50	7.00
14	Pat LaFontaine, Buf.	5.00	10.00
15	Joe Sakic, Que.	5.00	10.00
16	Ed Belfour, Goalie, Chi.	5.00	10.00
17	Felix Potvin, Goalie, Tor.	12.50	25.00
18	Mario Lemieux, Pit.	17.50	35.00
19	Jaromir Jagr, Pit.	7.50	15.00
20	Teemu Selanne, Win.	7.50	15.00
21	Raymond Bourque, Bos.	5.00	10.00
22	Brett Hull, St.L	6.00	12.00
23	Steve Yzerman, Det.	7.50	15.00
24	Kirk Muller, Mon.	3.50	7.00

FINEST HOCKEY ROSTER

This 12-card insert set was randomly inserted into the Series Two O-Pee-Chee foil packs. The player selection only includes players selected first overall in their draft year.

1993-94 Finest Hockey Roster
Card No. 9, Wendel Clark

Size: 2 1/2" x 3 1/2"
Face: Four colour, blue marble border; Name, Position
Back: Four colour, borderless; Name, Resume
Imprint: © THE TOPPS COMPANY, INC. PTD IN U.S.A.
Complete Set No.: 12
Complete Set Price: 37.50 75.00
Common Player: 1.75 3.00

No.	Player	EX	NRMT
1	Alexandre Daigle, Ott.	6.00	12.00
2	Roman Hamrlik, TB	1.50	3.00
3	Eric Lindros, Phi.	12.50	25.00
4	Owen Nolan, Que.	1.50	3.00
5	Mats Sundin, Que.	3.50	7.00
6	Michael (Mike) Modano, Dal.	3.50	7.00
7	Pierre Turgeon, NYI	3.50	7.00
8	Joe Murphy, Det.	1.50	3.00
9	Wendel Clark, Tor.	3.50	7.00
10	Mario Lemieux, Pit.	10.00	20.00
11	Dale Hawerchuk, Buf.	1.50	3.00
12	Rob Ramage, Phi.	1.50	3.00

FINEST REDEMPTION CARD

These cards were randomly inserted into the Series Two foil packs and could be redeemed for the entire set of O-Pee-Chee Finest if redeemed during 1994.

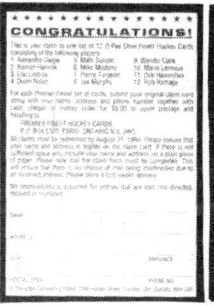 

Finest Redemption Card

Size: 2 1/2" x 3 1/2"
Face: Four colour foil, blue marble border; Redemption Logo
Back: Black on white card stock; Instructions on redemption
Imprint: © 1994 The TOPPS COMPANY, INC. PTD IN U.S.A.
Complete Set No.: 2
Complete Set Price: 30.00 60.00

No.	Player	EX	NRMT
—	Redemption Card (Single)	2.50	5.00
—	Redemption Card (Set)	30.00	60.00

TEAM CANADA

This 19-card set was randomly inserted into Series Two foil packs. The set depicts the young players who represented their country in the 1994 Olympic Games in Norway.

1993-94 Team Canada
Card No. 17, Paul Kariya

Size: 2 1/2" x 3 1/2"
Face: Four colour, borderless; Hockey Canada Logo, Name
Back: Four colour, borderless; Hockey Canada Logo, Name, Resume on white card stock
Imprint: © 1994 THE TOPPS COMPANY, INC. PTD IN U.S.A.
Complete Set No.: 19
Complete Set Price: 30.00 / 60.00
Common Card: 1.50 / 3.00

No.	Player	EX	NRMT
1	Brett Lindros	5.00	10.00
2	Manny Legace, Goalie	2.00	4.00
3	Adrian Aucoin	1.50	3.00
4	Ken Lovsin	1.50	3.00
5	Craig Woodcroft	1.50	3.00
6	Derek Mayer	1.50	3.00
7	Fabian Joseph	1.50	3.00
8	Todd Brost	1.50	3.00
9	Chris Therien	1.50	3.00
10	Brad Turner	1.50	3.00
11	Trevor Sim	1.50	3.00
12	Todd Hlushko	2.50	5.00
13	Dwayne Norris	1.50	3.00
14	Chris Kontos	2.50	5.00
15	Petr Nedved	2.50	5.00
16	Brian Savage	1.50	3.00
17	Paul Kariya	5.00	10.00
18	Corey Hirsch, Goalie	3.00	6.00
19	Todd Warriner	4.00	8.00

— 1993 - 94 STADIUM CLUB and FIRST DAY PRODUCTION —

This 250-card set is identical to Topps Stadium Club with the only difference being the addition of "PTD IN U.S.A." being added to the imprint.

1993-94 Stadium Club
Card No. 200A, Wayne Gretzky

1993-94 First Day Production
Wayne Gretzky
Card No. 200A   Card No. 200B

Card Size: 2 1/2" x 3 1/2"
Face: Four colour, borderless; Name
Back: Four colour, borderless; Name, Resume on white card stock
Imprint: © 1993 THE TOPPS COMPANY, INC. PTD IN U.S.A.
Complete Set No.: 250
Complete Set Price: 20.00 / 1,750.00
Common Player: .10 / 5.00
Common Goalie: .10 / 5.00

SERIES ONE

No.	Player	Stadium NRMT	First Day NRMT
1	Guy Carbonneau, Mon., Error	.10	5.00
2	Joe Cirella, Fl.	.10	5.00
3	Laurie Boschman, Ott.	.10	5.00
4	Arturs Irbe, Goalie, SJ	.10	5.00
5	Adam Creighton, TB	.10	5.00
6	Michael McPhee, Dal.	.10	5.00
7	Jeff Beukeboom, NYR	.10	5.00
8	Kevin Todd, Edm.	.10	5.00
9	Yvon Corriveau, Hart.	.10	5.00
10	Eric Lindros, Phi.	3.00	250.00
11	Martin Rucinsky, Que.	.10	5.00
12	Michel Goulet, Chi.	.10	5.00
13	Scott Pellerin, NJ	.10	5.00
14	Mike Eagles, Win.	.10	5.00
15	Steve Heinze, Bos.	.10	5.00
16	Gerard Gallant, Det.	.10	5.00
17	Kelly Miller, Wash.	.10	5.00
18	Petr Nedved, Van.	.10	5.00
19	Joe Mullen, Pit	.10	5.00
20	Pat LaFontaine, Buf.	.30	30.00
21	Garth Butcher, St.L	.10	5.00
22	Jeff Reese, Goalie, Cal.	.10	5.00
23	David Andreychuk, Tor.	.15	10.00
24	Patrick Flatley, NYI	.10	5.00
25	Tomas Sandstrom, LA	.15	15.00
26	Andre Racicot, Goalie, Mon.	.10	5.00
27	Patrice Brisebois, Mon.	.10	5.00
28	Neal Broten, Dal.	.10	5.00
29	Mark Freer, Ott.	.10	5.00
30	Kelly Kisio, SJ	.10	5.00
31	Scott Mellanby, Fl.	.10	5.00
32	Joe Sakic, Que.	.20	15.00
33	Kerry Huffman, Que.	.10	5.00
34	Evgeny Davydov, Win.	.10	5.00
35	Mark Messier, NYR	.30	20.00
36	Pat Verbeek, Hart.	.10	5.00
37	Gregory Gilbert, NYR	.10	5.00
38	John Tucker, TB	.10	5.00
39	Claude Lemieux, NJ	.10	5.00
40	Shayne Corson, Edm.	.10	5.00
41	Gordon Roberts, Bos.	.10	5.00
42	Jiri Slegr, Van.	.10	5.00
43	Kevin Dineen, Phi.	.10	5.00
44	Johan Garpenlov, SJ	.10	5.00
45	Sergei Fedorov, Det.	.30	75.00
46	Richard Sutter, St.L	.10	5.00
47	David Hannan, Buf.	.10	5.00
48	Sylvain Lefebvre, Tor.	.10	5.00
49	Pat Elynuik, Wash.	.10	5.00
50	Ray Ferraro, NYI	.10	5.00
51	Brent Ashton, Cal.	.10	5.00

No.	Player	Stadium NRMT	First Day NRMT
52	Paul Stanton, Pit.	.10	5.00
53	Kevin Haller, Mon.	.10	5.00
54	Kelly Hrudey, Goalie, LA	.10	5.00
55	Russell Courtnall, Dal.	.10	5.00
56	Alexei Zhamnov, Win.	.15	10.00
57	Andrei Lomakin, Fl.	.10	5.00
58	Keith Brown, Chi.	.10	5.00
59	Glenn Murray, Bos.	.10	5.00
60	Kay Whitmore, Goalie, Van.	.10	5.00
61	Stephane J. J. Richer, NJ	.10	5.00
62	Todd Gill, Tor.	.10	5.00
63	Bob Sweeney, Buf.	.10	5.00
64	Mike Richter, Goalie, NYR	.10	5.00
65	Brett Hull, St.L	.25	50.00
66	Sylvain Cote, Wash.	.10	5.00
67	Kirk Muller, Mon.	.10	5.00
68	Ronald Stern, Cal.	.10	5.00
69	Josef Beranek, Phi.	.20	15.00
70	Steve Yzerman, Det.	.20	40.00
71	Donald Beaupre, Goalie, Wash.	.10	5.00
72	Ed Courtenay, SJ	.10	5.00
73	Zdeno Ciger, Edm.	.10	5.00
74	Andrew Cassels, Hart.	.10	5.00
75	Roman Hamrlik, TB	.10	5.00
76	Benoit Hogue, NYI	.10	5.00
77	Andrei Kovalenko, Que.	.10	5.00
78	Rod Brind'amour, Phi.	.10	5.00
79	Tom Barrasso, Goalie, Pit.	.15	10.00
80	Al Iafrate, Wash.	.10	5.00
81	Bret Hedican, Ch.	.10	5.00
82	Peter Bondra, Wash.	.10	5.00
83	Ted Donato, Bos.	.10	5.00
84	Chris Lindberg, Cal.	.10	5.00
85	John Vanbiesbrouk, Goalie, Fl.	.15	10.00
86	Ronald Sutter, St.L	.10	5.00
87A	Luc Robitaille, LA	.30	20.00
87B	Luc Robitaille, LA, Variation	.30	25.00
88	Brian Leetch, NYR	.10	5.00
89	Randy Wood, Buf.	.10	5.00
90	Dirk Graham, Chi.	.10	5.00
91	Alexander Mogilny, Buf.	.25	40.00
92	Mike Keane, Mon.	.10	5.00
93	Adam Oates, Bos.	.15	10.00
94	Vjateslav Butsayev, Phi. Error	.10	5.00
95	John LeClair, Mon.	.10	5.00
96	Joe Nieuwendyk, Cal.	.10	5.00
97	Bo Mikael Andersson, TB	.10	5.00
98	Jaromir Jagr, Pit.	.25	50.00
99	Ed. Belfour, Goalie, Chi.	.25	35.00
100	David Reid, Bos.	.10	5.00
101	Darius Kasparaitis, NYI	.10	5.00
102	Zarley Zalapski, Hart.	.10	5.00
103	Christian Ruuttu, Chi.	.10	5.00
104	Phil Housley, Win.	.10	5.00
105	Al MacInnis, Cal.	.10	5.00
106	Tommy Sjodin, Dal.	.10	5.00
107	Richard Smehlik, Buf.	.10	5.00
108	Jyrki Lumme, Van.	.10	5.00
109	Dominic Roussel, Goalie, Phi.	.10	5.00
110	Michael Gartner, NYR	.20	15.00
111	Bernie Nicholls, NJ	.10	5.00
112	Mark Howe, Det.	.10	5.00
113	Richard Pilon, NYI	.10	5.00
114	Jeff Odgers, SJ	.10	5.00
115	Gilbert Dionne, Mon.	.10	5.00
116	Peter Zezel, Tor.	.10	5.00
117	Don Sweeney, Bos.	.10	5.00
118	Jimmy Carson, LA	.10	5.00
119	Igor Korolev, St.L	.10	5.00
120	Bob Kudelski, Ott.	.10	5.00
121	Dave Lowry, Fl.	.10	5.00
122	Stephen Kasper, TB	.10	5.00
123	Mike Ridley, Wash.	.10	5.00
124	Dave Tippett, Pit.	.10	5.00
125	Cliff Ronning, Van.	.10	5.00
126	Bruce Driver, NJ	.10	5.00
127	Stephane Matteau, Chi.	.10	5.00
128	Joel Otto, Cal.	.10	5.00
129	Alexei Kovalev, NYR	.10	5.00
130	Michael Modano, Dal.	.20	35.00

— 1994 - 95 REGULAR ISSUE — O-PEE-CHEE • 119

No.	Player	Stadium NRMT	First Day NRMT
131	Bill Ranford, Goalie, Edm.	.10	5.00
132	Petr Svoboda, Buf.	.10	5.00
133	Roger Johansson, Cal.	.10	5.00
134	Marc Bureau, TB	.10	5.00
135	Keith Tkachuk, Win.	.15	10.00
136	Mark Recchi, Phi.	.10	5.00
137	Bob Probert, Det.	.10	5.00
138	Uwe Krupp. NYI	.10	5.00
139	Mike Sullivan, SJ	.10	5.00
140	Douglas Gilmour, Tor.	.35	55.00

CALDER TROPHY WINNER

No.	Player	Stadium NRMT	First Day NRMT
141	**Rookie of the Year:** Teemu Selanne, Win.	.40	30.00
142	**Clancy Trophy Winner:** Dave Poulin, Bos.	.10	5.00
143	**Hart Trophy Winner:** Mario Lemieux, Pit.	.30	60.00
144	**Jennings Trophy Winner:** Ed. Belfour, Goalie, Chi.	.20	20.00
145	**Lady Byng Trophy Winner:** Pierre Turgeon, NYI	.10	5.00
146	**Masterton Trophy Winner:** Mario Lemieux, Pit	.15	60.00
147	**Norris Trophy Winner:** Chris Chelios, Chi.	.10	5.00
148	**Art Ross Trophy Winner:** Mario Lemieux, Pit.	.30	60.00
149	**Selke Trophy Winner:** Douglas Gilmour, Tor.	.25	20.00
150	**Vezina Trophy Winner:** Ed Belfour, Goalie, Chi.	.20	20.00
151	Paul Ranheim, Cal.	.10	5.00
152	Gino Cavallini, Que.	.10	5.00
153	Kevin Hatcher, Wash.	.10	5.00
154	Marc Bergevin, TB	.10	5.00
155	Martin McSorly, LA	.10	5.00
156	Brian Bellows, Mon.	.10	5.00
157	Patrick Poulin, Hart.	.10	5.00
158	Kevin Stevens, Pit.	.10	5.00
159	Robert Holik, NJ	.10	5.00
160	Raymond Bourque, Bos.	.10	5.00
161	Bryan Marchment Chi.	.10	5.00
162	Curtis Joseph, Goalie, St.L	.10	5.00
163	Kirk McLean, Goalie, Van.	.10	5.00
164	Teppo Numminen, Win.	.10	5.00
165	Kevin Lowe, NYR	.10	5.00
166	Tim Cheveldae, Goalie, Det.	.10	5.00
167	Brad Dalgarno, NYI	.10	5.00
168	Glenn Anderson, Tor.	.10	5.00
169	Frantisek Musil, Cal.	.10	5.00
170	Eric Desjardins, Mon.	.10	5.00
171	Douglas Zmolek, SJ	.10	5.00
172	Mark Lamb, Ott.	.10	5.00
173	Craig Ludwig, Dal.	.10	5.00
174	Rob Gaudreau, SJ	.10	5.00
175	Robert Carpenter, Wash.	.10	5.00
176	Mike Recci, Que.	.10	5.00
177	Brian Skrudland, Fl.	.10	5.00
178	Dominik Hasek, Goalie, Buf.	.10	5.00
179	Pat Conacher, LA	.10	5.00
180	Mark Janssens, Hart.	.10	5.00
181	Brent Fedyk, Phi.	.10	5.00
182	Robert DiMaio, TB	.10	5.00
183	Dave Manson, Edm.	.10	5.00
184	Janne Ojanen, NJ	.10	5.00
185	Ryan Walter, Van.	.10	5.00
186	Mikael Nylander, Hart.	.10	5.00
187	Stephen Leach, Bos.	.10	5.00
188	Jeff Brown, St.L	.10	5.00
189	Shawn McEachern, Pit.	.10	5.00
190	Jeremy Roenick, Chi.	.25	50.00
191	Darrin Shannon, Win.	.10	5.00
192	Wendel Clark, Tor.	.20	20.00
193	Kevin Miller, St.L	.10	5.00
194	Paul DiPietro, Mon.	.10	5.00
195	Steve Thomas, NYI	.10	5.00
196	Niklas Lidstrom, Det.	.10	5.00
197	Ed Olczyk, NYR	.10	5.00
198	Robert Reichel, Cal.	.10	5.00
199	Neil Brady, Ott.	.10	5.00
200A	Wayne Gretzky, LA	1.50	275.00
200B	Wayne Gretzky, LA, Variation	N/A	275.00

No.	Player	Stadium NRMT	First Day NRMT
201	Adrien Plavsic, Van.	.10	5.00
202	Joseph Juneau, Bos.	.60	60.00
203	Brad May, Buf.	.10	5.00
204	Igor Kravchuk, Edm.	.10	5.00
205	Keith Acton, Phi.	.10	5.00
206	Ken Daneyko, NJ	.10	5.00
207	Sean Burke, Goalie, Hart.	.10	5.00
208	Jayson More, SJ	.10	5.00
209	John Cullen, Tor.	.10	5.00
210	Teemu Selanne, Win.	.75	60.00
211	Brent Sutter, Chi.	.10	5.00
212	Brian Bradley, TB	.10	5.00
213	Donald Audette, Buf.	.10	5.00
214	Philippe Bozon, St.L	.10	5.00
215	Derek King, NYI	.10	5.00
216	Cam Neely, Bos.	.10	5.00
217	Keith Primeau, Det.	.10	5.00
218	James (Steve) Smith, Chi.	.10	5.00
219	Kenneth Sutton, Buf.	.10	5.00
220	Dale Hawerchuk, Buf.	.10	5.00
221	Alexei Zhitnik, LA	.10	5.00
222	Glen Wesley, Bos.	.10	5.00
223	Nelson Emerson, St.L	.10	5.00
224	Pat Falloon, SJ	.10	5.00
225	Darryl Sydor, LA	.10	5.00
226	Anthony Amonte, NYR	.10	5.00
227	Brian Mullen, NYI	.10	5.00
228	Gary Suter, Cal.	.10	5.00
229	David Shaw, Bos.	.10	5.00
230	Troy Murray, Chi.	.10	5.00
231	Patrick Roy, Goalie, Mon.	.75	125.00
232	Michel Petit, Cal.	.10	5.00
233A	Wayne Presley, Buf.	.10	5.00
233B	Wayne Presley, Buf. Variation	.10	5.00
234	Keith Jones, Wash.	.10	5.00
235	Gary Roberts, Cal.	.10	5.00
236	Steve Larmer, Chi.	.10	5.00
237	Valeri Kamensky, Que.	.10	5.00
238	Ulf Dahlen, Dal.	.10	5.00
239	Danton Cole, TB	.10	5.00
240A	Vincent Damphousse, Mon.	.15	10.00
240B	Vincent Damphousse, Mon. Variation	.15	10.00
241	Yuri Khmylev, Buf.	.10	5.00
242	Stephane Quintal, St.L	.10	5.00
243	Peter Taglianetti, Pit.	.10	5.00
244	Gary Leeman, Mon.	.10	5.00
245	Sergei Nemchinov, NYR	.10	5.00
246	Robert Blake, LA	.10	5.00
247	Steve Chiasson, Det.	.10	5.00
248	Vladimir Malakhov, NYI	.10	5.00
249	Checklist One (1-125)	5.00	10.00
250	Checklist Two (126-250)	5.00	10.00

— 1993 - 94 STADIUM CLUB INSERT SET —
NHL ALL STAR 1992-1993

This 23-card set has two face portraits. The cards were randomly inserted into Series One foil packs of O-Pee-Chee Stadium Club hockey. The cards depict All Star teams from both the Wales and Campbell Conferences. One player from each team playing the same position is illustrated per card.
Card Size: 2 1/2" x 3 1/2"

1993-94 NHL All Star 1992-93
Card No. 1, Ed Belfour, Patrick Roy

Face: Four colour, black background; Name
Back: Four colour, white card stock; Name, Resume
Imprint: © 1993 THE TOPPS COMPANY, INC.
Complete Set No.: 23
Complete Set Price: 75.00   150.00
Common Card: 1.50   3.00

No.	Player	EX	NRMT
1	Ed. Belfour, Patrick Roy, Goalies	12.50	25.00
2	Craig Billington, Jon Casey, Goalies	1.50	3.00
3	Peter Bondra, Kelly Kisio	1.50	3.00
4	Raymond Bourque, Paul Coffey	1.75	3.50
5	Brian Bradley, Adam Oates	2.00	4.00
6	Pavel Bure, Kevin Stevens	7.50	15.00
7	Garth Butcher, Kevin Lowe	1.50	3.00
8	Randy Carlyle, Brad Marsh	1.50	3.00
9	Chris Chelios, Al Iafrate	1.50	3.00
10	Steve Chiasson, Steve Duchesne	1.50	3.00
11	Michael Gartner, Teemu Selanne	6.00	12.00
12	Douglas Gilmour, Joe Sakic	6.00	12.00
13	Phil Housley, Scott Stevens	1.50	3.00
14	Brett Hull, Jaromir Jagr	6.00	12.00
15	Jari Kurri, Alexander Mogilny	3.50	7.00
16	Pat LaFontaine, Steve Yzerman	6.00	12.00
17	Mario Lemieux, Wayne Gretzky	30.00	60.00
18	Dave Manson, Zarley Zalapski	1.50	3.00
19	Michael Modano, Pierre Turgeon	5.00	10.00
20	Kirk Muller, Gary Roberts	1.50	3.00
21	Mark Recchi, Luc Robitaille	4.00	8.00
22	Jeremy Roenick, Rick Tocchet		3.50
23	Peter Sidorkiewicz, Michael Vernon, Goalies	1.50	3.00

— 1994 - 95 REGULAR ISSUE —

Again the O-Pee-Chee issue was printed by Topps in the U.S.A.

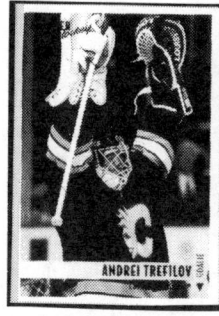

1994-95 Regular Issue
Card No. 166, Andrei Trefilov

Card Size: 3 1/2" x 2 1/2"
Face: Four colour, white border; Name, Team, Position
Back: Four colour with black border on card stock; Name, Number, Team, Resume
Imprint: © 1994 THE TOPPS COMPANY, INC. PTD IN U.S.A.
Complete Set No.: 275
Complete Set Price: 7.50   15.00
Common Card: .05   .10

— SERIES ONE —

No.	Player	EX	NRMT
1	Mark Messier, NYR	.10	.20
2	Darren Turcotte, Har.	.05	.10
3	Mikhail Shtalenkov, Goalie, MDA	.05	.10
4	Robert Gaudreau, SJ	.05	.10
5	Anthony Amonte, Chi.	.05	.10
6	Stephane Quintal, Win.	.05	.10
7	Iain Fraser, Que.	.05	.10
8	Doug Weight, Edm.	.05	.10
9	German Titov, Cal.	.05	.10
10	Lawrence Murphy, Pit.	.05	.10
11	Danton Cole, TB	.05	.10
12	Pat Peake, Wash.	.05	.10
13	Chris Terreri, Goalie, NJ	.05	.10
14	Yuri Khmylev, Buf.	.05	.10
15	Paul Coffey, Det.	.05	.10
16	Brian Savage, Mon.	.05	.10

O-PEE-CHEE — 1994-95 REGULAR ISSUE

No.	Player	EX	NRMT
17	Rod Brind'Amour, Phi.	.05	.10
18	Nathan Lafayette, Van., RC	.12	.25
19	Gordon Murphy, Fl.	.05	.10
20	Al Iafrate, Bos.	.05	.10
21	Kevin Miller, St.L	.05	.10
22	Peter Zezel, Tor.	.05	.10
23	Sylvain Turgeon, Ott.	.05	.10
24	Mark Tinordi, Dal.	.05	.10
25	Jari Kurri, LA	.05	.10
26	Benoit Hogue, NYI	.05	.10
27	Jeff Reese, Goalie, Har.	.05	.10
28	Brian Noonan, NYR	.05	.10
29	Denis Tsygurov, Buf., RC	.07	.15
30	James Patrick, Cal.	.05	.10
31	Robert Corkum, MDA	.05	.10
32	Valeri Kamensky, Que.	.05	.10
33	Ray Whitney, SJ	.05	.10
34	Joe Murphy, Chi.	.05	.10

1ST TEAM ALL-STAR

No.	Player	EX	NRMT
35	Dominik Hasek, Goalie, Buf.	.10	.20
36	Raymond Bourque, Bos.	.07	.15
37	Brian Leetch, NYR	.10	.20
38	David Andreychuk, Tor.	.07	.15
39	Pavel Bure, Van.	.15	.30
40	Sergei Fedorov, Det.	.15	.30

REGULAR ISSUE

No.	Player	EX	NRMT
41	Bob Beers, Edm.	.05	.10
42	Byron DaFoe, Wash., RC	.07	.15
43	Lyle Odelein, Mon.	.05	.10
44	Markus Naslund, Pit.	.05	.10
45	Dean Chynoweth, NYI	.05	.10
46	Trent Klatt, Dal.	.05	.10
47	Murray Craven, Van.	.05	.10
48	David Mackey, St.L	.05	.10
49	Norm Maciver, Ott.	.05	.10
50	Alexander Mogilny, Buf.	.05	.10
51	David Reid, Bos.	.05	.10
52	Nicklas Lidstrom, Det.	.05	.10
53	Tom Fitzgerald, Fl.	.05	.10
54	Roman Hamrlik, TB	.05	.10
55	Wendel Clark, Tor.	.07	.15
56	Dominic Roussel, Goalie, Phi.	.05	.10
57	Alexei Zhitnik, LA	.07	.15
58	Valeri Zelepukin, NJ	.05	.10
59	Calle Johanson, Wash.	.05	.10
60	Craig Janney, St.L	.05	.10
61	Randy Wood, Buf.	.05	.10
62	Curtis Leschyshyn, Que.	.05	.10
63	Stephan Lebeau, MDA	.05	.10
64	Dallas Drake, Win.	.05	.10
65	Vincent Damphousse, Mon.	.05	.10
66	Scott Lachance, NYI	.05	.10
67	Dirk Graham, Chi.	.05	.10
68	Kevin Smyth, Har.	.05	.10
69	Denis Savard, TB	.05	.10
70	Mike Richter, Goalie, NYR	.07	.15
71	Ronald Stern, Cal.	.05	.10
72	Kirk Maltby, Edm.	.05	.10
73	Kjell Samuelsson, Pit.	.05	.10
74	Neal Broten, Dal.	.05	.10
75	Trevor Linden, Van.	.07	.15
76	Todd Elik, SJ	.05	.10
77	Andrew McBain, Ott.	.05	.10
78	Alexei Kudashov, Tor.	.05	.10
79	Kenneth Daneyko, NJ	.05	.10

GOAL-TENDING DUOS

No.	Player	EX	NRMT
80	Dominik Hasek/Grant Fuhr	.07	.15
81	Andrew Moog/Darcy Wakaluk	.05	.10
82	John Vanbiesbrouck/Mark Fitzpatrick	.05	.10
83	Martin Brodeur/Chris Terreri	.07	.15
84	Tom Barrasso/Ken Wregget	.05	.10
85	Kirk McLean/Kay Whitmore	.05	.10

REGULAR ISSUE

No.	Player	EX	NRMT
86	Darryl Sydor, LA	.05	.10
87	Chris Osgood, Goalie, Det.	.05	.10
88	Edward Donato, Bos.	.05	.10
89	Dave Lowry, Fl.	.05	.10
90	Mark Recchi, Phi.	.07	.15
91	Jim Montgomery, St.L	.05	.10
92	Bill Houlder, MDA	.05	.10
93	Richard Smehlik, Buf.	.05	.10
94	Benoit Brunet, Mon.	.05	.10
95	Teemu Selanne, Win.	.12	.25
96	Paul Ranheim, Har.	.05	.10
97	Andrei Kovalenko, Que.	.07	.15
98	Grant Ledyard, Dal.	.05	.10
99	Brent Grieve, Edm.	.05	.10
100	Joseph Juneau, Wash.	.10	.20
101	Martin Gelinas, Van.	.05	.10
102	Jamie Macoun, Tor.	.05	.10
103	Craig MacTavish, NYR	.05	.10
104	Micah Aivazoff, Det.	.05	.10
105	Stephane J.J. Richer, NJ	.05	.10
106	Eric Weinrich, Chi.	.05	.10
107	Pat Elynuik, TB	.05	.10
108	Tomas Sandstrom, Pit.	.05	.10
109	Darrin Madeley, Goalie, Ott.	.05	.10
110	Allan MacInnis, Cal.	.05	.10
111	Cam Stewart, Bos.	.05	.10
112	Dixon Ward, LA	.05	.10
113	Vlastimil Kroupa, SJ	.05	.10
114	Robert DiMaio, Phi.	.05	.10
115	Pierre Turgeon, NYI	.05	.10
116	Mike Hough, Fl.	.05	.10
117	John LeClair, Mon.	.05	.10
118	David Hannan, Buf.	.05	.10
119	Todd Ewen, MDA	.05	.10
120	Team Card: New York Rangers - Stanley Cup	.05	.10
121	Dave Manson, Win.	.05	.10
122	Jocelyn Lemieux, Har.	.05	.10
123	Jocelyn Thibault, Goalie, Que.	.05	.10
124	Scott Pearson, Edm.	.05	.10

2ND TEAM ALL-STAR

No.	Player	EX	NRMT
125	Patrick Roy, Goalie, Mon.	.07	.15
126	Scott Stevens, NJ	.05	.10
127	Allan MacInnis, Cal.	.05	.10
128	Adam Graves, NYR	.07	.15
129	Cam Neely, Bos.	.05	.10
130	Wayne Gretzky, LA	.12	.25

REGULAR ISSUE

No.	Player	NRMT	Mint
131	Tom Chorske, NJ	.05	.10
132	John Tucker, TB	.05	.10
133	James (Steve) Smith, Chi.	.05	.10
134	Kay Whitmore, Goalie, Van.	.05	.10
135	Adam Oates, Bos.	.05	.10
136	Bill Berg, Tor.	.05	.10
137	Wes Walz, Cal.	.05	.10
138	Jeff Beukeboom, NYR	.05	.10
139	Ronald Francis, Pit.	.05	.10
140	Alexandre Daigle, Ott.	.12	.25
141	Josef Beranek, Phi.	.05	.10
142	Tom Pederson, SJ	.05	.10
143	Jamie McLennan, NYI	.05	.10
144	Scott Mellanby, Fl.	.05	.10
145	Vyacheslav Kozlov, Det.	.12	.25
146	Martin McSorley, LA	.05	.10
147	Tim Sweeney, MDA	.05	.10
148	Luciano Borsato, Win.	.05	.10
149	Jason Dawe, Buf.	.05	.10

LEAGUE LEADERS

No.	Player	EX	NRMT
150	Wayne Gretzky, Point Leader	.12	.25
151	Pavel Bure, Goal Scoring Leader	.07	.15
152	Dominik Hasek, Goalie, G.A.A. Leader	.07	.15
153	Scott Stevens, +/- Leader	.05	.10
154	Wayne Gretzky, Asst. Leader	.12	.25
155	Mike Richter, Goalie, Win Leader	.07	.15
156	Dominik Hasek, Save Pct. Leader	.10	.20

REGULAR ISSUE

No.	Player	EX	NRMT
157	Edward Drury, Har.	.05	.10
158	Peter Popovic, Mon.	.07	.15
159	Alexei Kasatonov, St.L	.07	.15
160	Mats Sundin, Que.	.05	.10
161	Brad Shaw, Ott.	.05	.10
162	Bret Hedican, Van.	.05	.10
163	Michael McPhee, Dal.	.05	.10
164	Martin Straka, Pit.	.05	.10
165	Dmitri Mironov, Tor.	.05	.10
166	Andrei Trefilov, Goalie, Cal.	.05	.10
167	Joe Reekie, Wash.	.05	.10
168	Gary Suter, Chi.	.05	.10
169	Gregory Gilbert, NYR	.05	.10
170	Igor Larionov, SJ	.05	.10
171	Mike Sillinger, Det.	.05	.10
172	Igor Kravchuk, Edm.	.05	.10
173	Glen Murray, Bos.	.05	.10
174	Shawn Chambers, TB	.05	.10
175	John MacLean, NJ	.05	.10
176	Yves Racine, Phi.	.05	.10
177	Andrei Lomakin, Fl.	.05	.10
178	Patrick Flatley, NYI	.05	.10
179	Igor Ulanov, Win.	.05	.10
180	Pat LaFontaine, Buf.	.05	.10
181	Mathieu Schneider, Mon.	.05	.10
182	Peter Stastny, St.L	.05	.10
183	Tony Granato, LA	.05	.10
184	Peter Douris, MDA	.05	.10
185	Alexei Kovalev, NYR	.10	.20
186	Geoff Courtnall, Van.	.05	.10
187	Richard Matvichuk, Dal.	.05	.10
188	Troy Murray, Ott.	.05	.10
189	Todd Gill, Tor.	.05	.10

ROOKIE SENSATIONS

No.	Player	EX	NRMT
190	Martin Brodeur, Goalie, NJ	.10	.20
191	Mikael Renberg, Phi.	.15	.30
192	Alexei Yashin, Ott.	.25	.50
193	Jason Arnott, Edm.	.50	1.00
194	Derek Plante, Buf.	.12	.25
195	Alexandre Daigle, Ott.	.12	.25
196	Bryan Smolinski, Bos.	.10	.20
197	Jesse Belanger, Fl.	.05	.10
198	Chris Pronger, Har.	.05	.10
199	Chris Osgood, Goalie, Det.	.07	.15

REGULAR ISSUE

No.	Player	EX	NRMT
200	Jeremy Roenick, Chi.	.15	.30
201	Johan Garpenlov, SJ	.05	.10
202	Dave Karpa, Que.	.05	.10
203	Darren McCarty, Det.	.05	.10
204	Claude Lemieux, NJ	.05	.10
205	Geoff Sanderson, Har.	.05	.10
206	Tom Barrasso, Goalie, Pit.	.05	.10
207	Kevin Dineen, Phi.	.05	.10
208	Sylvain Cote, Wash.	.05	.10
209	Brent Gretzky, TB	.05	.10
210	Shayne Corson, Edm.	.05	.10
211	Darius Kasparaitis, NYI	.05	.10
212	Peter Andersson, Fl.	.05	.10
213	Robert Reichel, Cal.	.05	.10
214	Jozef Stumpel, Bos.	.05	.10
215	Brendan Shanahan, St.L	.05	.10
216	Craig Muni, Buf.	.05	.10
217	Alexei Zhamnov, Win.	.10	.20
218	Robert Lang, LA	.05	.10
219	Brian Bellows, Mon.	.05	.10
220	Steven King, MDA	.05	.10
221	Sergei Zubov, NYR	.15	.30
222	Kelly Miller, Wash.	.05	.10
223	Ilya Byakin, Edm.	.05	.10
224	Chris Tamer, Pit.	.05	.10
225	Douglas Gilmour, Tor.	.15	.30
226	Shawn Antoski, Van.	.05	.10
227	Andrew Cassels, Har.	.05	.10
228	Craig Wolanin, Que.	.05	.10
229	Jon Casey, Goalie, Bos.	.05	.10
230	Michael Modano, Dal.	.10	.20
231	Bill Guerin, NJ	.05	.10

No.	Player	EX	NRMT
232	Gaetan Duchesne, SJ	.05	.10
233	Steve Dubinsky, Chi.	.05	.10
234	Jason Bowen, Phi.	.05	.10
235	Steve Yzerman, Det.	.15	.30
236	David Poulin, Wash.	.05	.10
237	Mikael Nylander, Cal.	.05	.10

TEAM OF THE FUTURE

No.	Player	EX	NRMT
238	Felix Potvin, Goalie, Tor.	.25	.50
239	Sandis Ozolinch, SJ	.05	.10
240	Scott Niedermayer, NJ	.05	.10
241	Eric Lindros, Phi.	.75	1.50
242	Keith Tkachuk, Win.	.12	.25
243	Teemu Selanne, Win.	.12	.25

REGULAR ISSUE

No.	Player	EX	NRMT
244	Martin McInnis, NYI	.05	.10
245	Bob Kudelski, Fl.	.05	.10
246	Paul Cavallini, TB	.05	.10
247	Brian Bradley, TB	.05	.10
248	Robb Stauber, LA	.05	.10
249	Jay Wells, NYR	.05	.10
250	Mario Lemieux, Pit.	.35	.75

No.	Player	EX	NRMT
251	Tommy Albelin, NJ	.05	.10
252	Paul DiPietro, Mon.	.05	.10
253	Michael Gartner, Tor.	.07	.15
254	Darrin Shannon, Win.	.05	.10
255	Alexander Karpovtsev, NYR	.05	.10
256	Dave Babych, Van.	.05	.10
257	Greg Johnson, Det.	.05	.10
258	Frantisek Musil, Cal.	.05	.10
259	Michal Pivonka, Wash.	.05	.10
260	Arturs Irbe, Goalie, SJ	.10	.20
261	Paul Broten, Dal.	.05	.10
262	Don Sweeney, Bos.	.05	.10
263	Doug Brown, Pit.	.05	.10
264	Bobby Dollas, MDA	.05	.10
265	Brian Skrudland, Fl.	.05	.10
266	Dan Plante, NYI, RC	.10	.20
267	Chad Penney, Ott., RC	.10	.20
268	Stephen Leach, Bos.	.05	.10
269	Damian Rhodes, Goalie, Tor.	.05	.10
270	Glenn Anderson, NYR	.05	.10
271	Randy McKay, NJ	.05	.10
272	Jeff Brown, Van.	.05	.10
273	Steve Konowalchuk, Wash.	.05	.10
274A	Checklist (1 - 136)	.05	.10
274B	Rudy Poeschek, TB	.05	.10
275A	Checklist (137 - 275)	.05	.10
275B	Michael Peca, Van.	.05	.10

— 1994 - 95 INSERT SET—

Card Size: 3 1/2" x 2 1/2"
Face: Four colour, white border; Name, Team, Position
Back: Four colour on card stock; Name, Number, Team, Resume
Imprint: © 1994 THE TOPPS COMPANY, INC.
Complete Set No.: 23
Complete Set Price: 115.00
Common Card: 2.50 5.00

No.	Player	EX	NRMT
1	Patrik Carnback, MDA	2.50	5.00
2	Bryan Smolinski, Bos.	5.00	10.00
3	Derek Plante, Buf.	5.00	10.00
4	Alexander Karpovtsev, Que.	2.50	5.00
5	Trevor Kidd, Goalie, Cal.	3.50	7.00
6	Iain Fraser, Que.	2.50	5.00
7	Alexandre Daigle, Ott.	5.00	10.00
8	Chris Osgood, Goalie, Det.	5.00	10.00
9	Rob Niedermayer, Fl.	3.50	7.00
10	Jason Arnott, Edm.	9.00	18.00
11	Chris Pronger, Har.	3.50	7.00
12	Jesse Belanger, Fl.	2.50	5.00
13	Oleg Petrov, Mon.	3.00	6.00
14	Martin Brodeur, Goalie, NJ	5.00	10.00
15	Alexei Yashin, Ott.	5.00	10.00
16	Mikael Renberg, Phi.	4.50	9.00
17	Boris Mironov, Win.	2.50	5.00
18	Damian Rhodes, Goalie, Tor.	2.50	5.00
19	Darren McCarty, Det.	2.50	5.00
20	Chris Gratton, TB	3.50	7.00
21	Jamie McLennan, NYI	2.50	5.00
22	Nathan Lafayette, Van.	3.50	7.00
23	Jeff Shantz, Chi.	2.50	5.00

Available in April !
THE CHARLTON STANDARD CATALOGUE OF CANADIAN
BASEBALL & FOOTBALL CARDS
- Fourth Edition -

BASEBALL CARDS FROM 1912 — FOOTBALL CARDS FROM 1949

For Canadian Baseball and Football Card Collectors this Catalogue has it all!

IMPERIAL TOBACCO * MAPLE CRISPETTE * PARKHURST * O-PEE-CHEE * CANADA STARCH * STUART POST
TOPPS * WORLD WIDE GUM * NALLEYS * DONRUSS - LEAF * EDDIE SARGENT * PROVIGO
WILLARD * NABISCO * TORONTO BLUE JAYS * STANDARD OIL * BLUE RIBBON TEA * PANINI
GENERAL MILLS * SCORE * EXHIBITS * HOSTESS * PURITAN MEATS * GULF CANADA * JOGO * VACHON
ROYAL STUDIOS * NEILSON'S * BEN'S AULT FOODS * COCA-COLA * BAZOOKA * KFC
And All Other Major Manufacturers...

Complete price listings for all Major League Baseball and Canadian Football League cards!
Comprehensive baseball and football minor league card listings!
Regular issues, stickers, inserts, subsets, transfers and much, much more!
All major manufacturers!
Current Pricing for all cards in up to three grades of condition - VG, EX, and NRMT!
All rookie, last, pitcher, quarterback, error and variation cards identified and priced!
Plus Charlton's Fabulous Alphabetical Index!

OVER 300 PAGES * 60,000 PRICES * NEW, LARGER 8 1/2 x 11" FORMAT
RESERVE YOUR COPY TODAY DIRECTLY FROM THE PUBLISHER...

The Charlton Press
2010 YONGE STREET, TORONTO, ONTARIO M4S 1Z9
FOR TOLL FREE ORDERING PHONE 1-800-442-6042 FAX 1-800-442-1542 from anywhere in Canada or the U.S.

122 • O-PEE-CHEE — 1980 - 81 PHOTOS

O-PEE-CHEE MISCELLANEOUS ISSUES

— 1980 - 81 PHOTOS —

The colour photographs are printed on thick cardboard stock and were distributed unwrapped. Photos are numberd _ of 24.

1980-81 Photos
Photo No. 2, Gilbert Perreault
Photo No. 7, Wayne Gretzky

Photo Size: 5" X 7"
Face: Four colour, white border; Name
Back: Black and grey on card stock; Name, Team, Position, Number
Imprint: © 1981 O-Pee-Chee Co. Ltd. London, Ontario Printed in Canada - Imprimé au Canada
Complete Set No.: 24
Complete Set Price: 16.00 32.00
Common Player: .25 .50

No.	Player	EX	NRMT
1	Brad Park, Bos.	.50	1.00
2	Gilbert Perreault, Buf.	.50	1.00
3	Kent Nilsson, Ca.	.25	.50
4	Tony Esposito, Goalie, Chi.	1.00	2.00
5	Lanny McDonald, Col.	.50	1.00
6	Pete Mahovlich, Det.	.25	.50
7	Wayne Gretzky, Edm.	7.50	15.00
8	Marcel Dionne, LA	1.50	3.00
9	Bob Gainey, Mon.	.50	1.00
10	Guy Lafleur, Mon.	1.50	3.00
11	Larry Robinson, Mon.	.75	1.50
12	Mike Bossy, NYI	1.50	3.00
13	Denis Potvin, NYI	1.00	2.00
14	Phil Esposito, NYR	1.50	3.00
15	Anders Hedberg, NYR	.25	.50
16	Bobby Clarke, Phi.	1.00	2.00
17	Marc Tardif, Que.	.25	.50
18	Bernie Federko, St.L.	.25	.50
19	Borje Salming, Tor.	.25	.50
20	Darryl Sittler, Tor.	1.00	2.00
21	Ian Turnbull, Tor.	.25	.50
22	Glen Hanlon, Van.	.25	.50
23	Mike Palmateer, Goalie, Wash.	.25	.50
24	Morris Lukowich, Win.	.25	.50

— 1981 - 82 STICKERS —

An album was issued to hold these stickers. This issue is now popular more by player than by set.

1981-82 Stickers
Sticker No. 22, Steve Payne
Sticker No. 29, Guy Lafleur

Sticker Size: 2" X 2 1/2"
Face: Four colour; Number
Back: Black and white; Number, Name, Team, Instructions, Bilingual
Imprint: © 1981 O-PEE-CHEE CO. LTD.
Complete Set No.: 269
Complete Set Price: 11.00 22.00
Common Player: .03 .05
Album: 5.00

THE STANLEY CUP

No.	Player	EX	NRMT
1	The Stanley Cup	.10	.20
2	The Stanley Cup	.10	.20
3	The Stanley Cup	.10	.20
4	The Stanley Cup	.10	.20
5	The Stanley Cup	.10	.20
6	The Stanley Cup	.10	.20

1981 STANLEY CUP PLAYOFFS

No.	Player	EX	NRMT
7	Oiler vs. Islanders	.03	.05
8	Oiler vs. Islanders	.03	.05
9	Oiler vs. Islanders	.03	.05
10	Oiler vs. Islanders	.03	.05
11	Jari Kurri, Edm.	.25	.50
12	Pat Riggin, Goalie	.05	.10
13	Flames vs. Flyers	.03	.05
14	Flames vs. Flyers	.03	.05
15	Flames vs. Flyers	.03	.05
16	Flames vs. Flyers	.03	.05

1981 STANLEY CUP FINALS

No.	Player	EX	NRMT
17	Stanley Cup Winners 1980/81 N.Y. Islanders	.03	.05
18	Stanley Cup Winners 1980/81 N.Y. Islanders	.03	.05
19	Conn Smythe, Trophy MVP - Finals	.03	.05
20	Butch Goring, Most Valuable Player	.03	.05
21	North Stars vs. Islanders	.03	.05
22	Steve Payne	.03	.05
23	North Stars vs. Islanders	.03	.05
24	North Stars vs. Islanders	.03	.05
25	North Stars vs. Islanders	.03	.05
26	North Stars vs. Islanders	.03	.05

MONTREAL CANADIENS

No.	Player	EX	NRMT
27	Prince of Wales Trophy	.10	.20
28	Prince of Wales Trophy	.10	.20
29	Guy Lafleur	.10	.20
30	Bob Gainey	.05	.10
31	Larry Robinson	.07	.15
32	Steve Shutt	.03	.05
33	Brian Engblom	.03	.05
34	Doug Jarvis	.03	.05
35	Yvon Lambert	.03	.05
36	Mark Napier	.03	.05
37	Rejean Houle	.03	.05
38	Pierre Larouche	.03	.05
39	Rod Langway	.03	.05
40	Richard Sevigny, Goalie	.03	.05
41	Guy Lafleur	.10	.20
42	Larry Robinson	.07	.15
43	Bob Gainey	.03	.05
44	Steve Shutt	.05	.10

BOSTON BRUINS

No.	Player	EX	NRMT
45	Rick Middleton	.03	.05
46	Peter McNab	.03	.05
47	Rogatien Vachon, Goalie	.03	.05
48	Brad Park	.03	.05
49	Raymond Bourque	1.00	2.00
50	Terry O'Reilly	.03	.05
51	Stephen Kasper	.03	.05
52	Dwight Foster	.03	.05

BUFFALO SABRES

No.	Player	EX	NRMT
53	Danny Gare	.03	.05
54	Andre Savard	.03	.05
55	Don Edwards, Goalie	.03	.05
56	Bob Sauve, Goalie	.03	.05
57	Anthony McKegney	.03	.05
58	John Van Boxmeer	.03	.05
59	Derek Smith	.03	.05
60	Gilbert Perreault	.03	.05

HARTFORD WHALERS

No.	Player	EX	NRMT
61	Mike Rogers	.03	.05
62	Mark Howe	.03	.05
63	Blaine Stoughton	.03	.05
64	Rick Ley	.03	.05
65	Jordy Douglas	.03	.05
66	Al Sims	.03	.05
67	Norm Barnes	.03	.05
68	John Garrett, Goalie	.03	.05

QUEBEC NORDIQUES

No.	Player	EX	NRMT
69	Peter Stastny	.07	.15
70	Anton Stastny	.03	.05
71	Jacques Richard	.03	.05
72	Robbie Ftorek	.03	.05
73	Dan Bouchard, Goalie	.03	.05
74	Real Cloutier	.03	.05
75	Michel Goulet	.03	.05
76	Marc Tardif	.03	.05

SUPER ACTION

No.	Player	EX	NRMT
77	Capitals vs. Maple Leafs	.03	.05
78	Capitals vs. Maple Leafs	.03	.05
79	Capitals vs. Maple Leafs	.03	.05
80	Capitals vs. Maple Leafs	.03	.05
81	Whalers vs. Capitals	.03	.05
82	Whalers vs. Capitals	.03	.05
83	Canadiens vs. Capitals	.03	.05
84	Dan Bouchard, Goalie, Que.	.03	.05
85	North Stars vs. Capitals	.03	.05
86	North Stars vs. Capitals	.03	.05
87	Bruins vs. Capitals	.03	.05

1981-82 STICKERS — O-PEE-CHEE • 123

MINNESOTA NORTH STARS

No.	Player	EX	NRMT
88	Robert Smith	.03	.05
89	Donald Beaupre, Goalie	.03	.05
90	Al MacAdam	.03	.05
91	Craig Hartsburg	.03	.05
92	Steve Payne	.03	.05
93	Gilles Meloche, Goalie	.03	.05
94	Tim Young	.03	.05
95	Tom McCarthy	.03	.05

TORONTO MAPLE LEAFS

No.	Player	EX	NRMT
96	Wilf Paiement	.03	.05
97	Darryl Sittler	.35	.75
98	Borje Salming	.12	.25
99	Bill Derlago	.03	.05
100	Ian Turnbull	.03	.05
101	Richard Vaive	.03	.05
102	Dan Maloney	.03	.05
103	Laurie Boschman	.03	.05
104	Pat Hickey	.03	.05
105	Michel Larocque, Goalie	.03	.05
106	Jiri Crha, Goalie	.03	.05
107	John Anderson	.03	.05
108	Bill Derlago	.03	.05
109	Darryl Sittler	.35	.75
110	Wilf Paiement	.03	.05
111	Borje Salming	.12	.25

CHICAGO BLACK HAWKS

No.	Player	EX	NRMT
112	Denis Savard	1.00	2.00
113	Tony Esposito, Goalie	.05	.10
114	Tom Lysiak	.03	.05
115	Keith Brown	.03	.05
116	Glen Sharpley	.03	.05
117	Terry Ruskowski	.03	.05
118	Reg Kerr	.03	.05
119	Bob Murray	.03	.05

DETROIT RED WINGS

No.	Player	EX	NRMT
120	Dale McCourt	.03	.05
121	John Ogrodnick	.03	.05
122	Mike Foligno	.15	.30
123	Gilles Gilbert, Goalie	.03	.05
124	Reed Larson	.03	.05
125	Vaclav Nedomansky	.03	.05
126	Willie Huber	.03	.05
127	James Korn	.03	.05

ST. LOUIS BLUES

No.	Player	EX	NRMT
128	Bernie Federko	.05	.10
129	Michael Liut, Goalie	.03	.05
130	Wayne Babych	.03	.05
131	Blake Dunlop	.03	.05
132	Mike Zuke	.03	.05
133	Brian Sutter	.05	.10
134	Rick Lapointe	.03	.05
135	Jorgen Pettersson	.03	.05

WINNIPEG JETS

No.	Player	EX	NRMT
136	Dave Christian	.05	.10
137	David Babych	.03	.05
138	Morris Lukowich	.03	.05
139	Norm Dupont	.03	.05
140	Ronald Wilson	.03	.05
141	Danny Geoffrion	.03	.05
142	Barry Long	.03	.05
143	Pierre Hamel, Goalie	.03	.05

WALES CONFERENCE ALL STARS

No.	Player	EX	NRMT
144	Charlie Simmer	.03	.05
145	Mark Howe	.12	.25
146	Donald Beaupre, Goalie	.03	.05
147	Marcel Dionne	.12	.25
148	Larry Robinson	.35	.75
149	David Taylor	.12	.25

CAMPBELL CONFERENCE ALL STARS

No.	Player	EX	NRMT
150	Mike Bossy	.20	.40
151	Denis Potvin	.10	.20
152	Bryan Trottier	.10	.20
153	Michael Liut, Goalie	.03	.05
154	George (Rob) Ramage	.10	.20
155	Bill Barber	.03	.05

NEW YORK ISLANDERS

No.	Player	EX	NRMT
156	Campbell Bowl	.03	.05
157	Campbell Bowl	.03	.05
158	Mike Bossy	.50	1.00
159	Denis Potvin	.25	.50
160	Bryan Trottier	.25	.50
161	Billy Smith, Goalie	.03	.05
162	Anders Kallur	.03	.05
163	Bob Bourne	.03	.05
164	Clark Gillies	.03	.05
165	Ken Morrow	.03	.05

NEW YORK RANGERS

No.	Player	EX	NRMT
166	Anders Hedberg	.03	.05
167	Ronald Greschner	.03	.05
168	Barry Beck	.03	.05
169	Eddie Johnstone, Goalie	.03	.05
170	Donald Maloney	.03	.05
171	Ron Duguay	.03	.05
172	Ulf Nilsson	.03	.05
173	Dave Maloney	.03	.05

PHILADELPHIA FLYERS

No.	Player	EX	NRMT
174	Bill Barber	.03	.05
175	Behn Wilson	.03	.05
176	Ken Linseman	.03	.05
177	Peter Peeters, Goalie	.03	.05
178	Bobby Clarke	.03	.05
179	Paul Holmgren	.03	.05
180	Brian Propp	.05	.10
181	Reggie Leach	.03	.05

PITTSBURGH PENGUINS

No.	Player	EX	NRMT
182	Rick Kehoe	.03	.05
183	Randy Carlyle	.03	.05
184	George Ferguson	.03	.05
185	Peter Lee	.03	.05
186	Rod Schutt	.03	.05
187	Paul Gardner	.03	.05
188	Ron Stackhouse	.03	.05
189	Mario Faubert	.03	.05

WASHINGTON CAPITALS

No.	Player	EX	NRMT
190	Michael Gartner	.50	1.00
191	Dennis Maruk	.03	.05
192	Ryan Walter	.03	.05
193	Richard Green	.03	.05
194	Mike Palmateer, Goalie	.03	.05
195	Bob Kelly	.03	.05
196	Jean Pronovost	.03	.05
197	Al Hangsleben	.03	.05

SUPER ACTION

No.	Player	EX	NRMT
198	Flames vs. Capitals	.03	.05
199	Oilers vs. Islanders	.03	.05
200	Oilers vs. Islanders	.03	.05
201	Oilers vs. Islanders	.03	.05
202	Oilers vs. Islanders	.03	.05
203	Rangers vs. Islanders	.03	.05
204	Rangers vs. Islanders	.03	.05
205	Flyers vs. Capitals	.03	.05
206	Flyers vs. Capitals	.03	.05
207	Rangers vs. Capitals	.03	.05
208	Canadiens vs. Capitals	.03	.05

EDMONTON OILERS

No.	Player	EX	NRMT
209	Wayne Gretzky	2.00	4.00
210	Mark Messier	1.00	2.00
211	Jari Kurri	.25	.50
212	Brett Callighen	.03	.05
213	Matti Hagman	.03	.05
214	Risto Siltanen	.03	.05
215	Lee Fogolin	.03	.05
216	Ed Mio, Goalie	.03	.05
217	Glenn Anderson	.25	.50

CALGARY FLAMES

No.	Player	EX	NRMT
218	Kent Nilsson	.03	.05
219	Guy Chouinard	.03	.05
220	Eric Vail	.03	.05
221	Pat Riggin, Goalie	.03	.05
222	Willi Plett	.03	.05
223	Pekka Rautakallio	.03	.05
224	Paul Reinhart	.03	.05
225	Bradley Marsh	.10	.20
226	Phil Russell	.03	.05

COLORADO ROCKIES

No.	Player	EX	NRMT
227	Lanny McDonald	.25	.50
228	Merlin Malinowski	.03	.05
229	George (Rob) Ramage	.12	.25
230	Glenn Resch, Goalie	.03	.05
231	Ron Delorme	.03	.05
232	Lucien DeBlois	.03	.05
233	Paul Gagne	.03	.05
234	Joel Quenneville	.03	.05

LOS ANGELES KINGS

No.	Player	EX	NRMT
235	Marcel Dionne	.10	.20
236	Charlie Simmer	.03	.05
237	David Taylor	.03	.05
238	Mario Lessard, Goalie	.03	.05
239	Lawrence Murphy	.50	1.00
240	Jerry Korab	.03	.05
241	Mike Murphy	.03	.05
242	Billy Harris	.03	.05

VANCOUVER CANUCKS

No.	Player	EX	NRMT
243	Thomas Gradin	.03	.05
244	Per-Olov Brasar	.03	.05
245	Glen Hanlon, Goalie	.03	.05
246	Chris Oddleifson	.03	.05
247	David Williams	.03	.05
248	Kevin McCarthy	.03	.05
249	Dennis Kearns	.03	.05
250	Harold Snepsts	.03	.05

1980/81 LEADERS

No.	Player	EX	NRMT
251	Art Ross Trophy, Most Points	.03	.05
252	**Art Ross Trophy Winner:** Wayne Gretzky, Edm.	1.50	3.00
253	**Most Goals:** Mike Bossy, NYI	.75	1.50
254	Norris Trophy, Best Defenseman	.03	.05
255	**James Norris Trophy Winner:** Randy Carlyle, Pit.	.03	.05
256	**Vezina Trophy Winner:** Richard Sevigny, Mon.	.03	.05
257	Vezina Trophy Goal Tending - Team	.03	.05
258	**Vezina Trophy Winner:** Denis Herron, Mon.	.10	.20
259	**Vezina Trophy Winner:** Michel Larocque, Mon.	.03	.05
260	Lady Byng Trophy, Sportsmanship	.03	.05
261	**Lady Byng Trophy Winner:** Rick Kehoe, Pit.	.03	.05
262	Calder Trophy, Rookie of the Year	.03	.05
263	**Calder Trophy Winner:** Peter Stastny, Que.	.25	.50
264	**Hart Trophy Winner:** Wayne Gretzky, Edm.	1.50	3.00
265	Hart Trophy, Most Valuable Player	.03	.05

KINGS "TRIPLE CROWN LINE"

No.	Player	EX	NRMT
266	Charlie Simmer	.05	.10
267	Marcel Dionne	.10	.20
268	David Taylor	.05	.10

1980/81 LEADERS

No.	Player	EX	NRMT
269	Bob Gainey, Mon.	.05	.10

— 1982 - 83 STICKERS —

An album was issued to hold these stickers.

1982-83 Stickers
Sticker No. 1, Mike Bossy
Sticker No. 95, Grant Fuhr

Sticker Size: 2" X 2 1/2"
Face: Four colour, white border
Back: Black on buff; Number, Name, Team, Bilingual
Imprint: © 1982 TOPPS CHEWING GUM, INC.
Complete Set No.: 263
Complete Set Price: 16.00 / 32.00
Common Player: .03 / .05
Album: 5.00

1982 STANLEY CUP FINALS

No.	Player	EX	NRMT
1	**Conn Smythe Trophy:** Mike Bossy, NYI	.15	.30
2	Conn Smythe Trophy	.10	.20
3	**1981/82 Stanley Cup Winners:** NY Islanders	.03	.05
4	**1981/82 Stanley Cup Winners:** NY Islanders	.03	.05
5	Stanley Cup Finals	.03	.05
6	Stanley Cup Finals	.03	.05
7	Richard Brodeur, Goalie	.03	.05
8	Victory	.03	.05
9	Stanley Cup Finals	.03	.05
10	Stanley Cup Finals	.03	.05

1982 STANLEY CUP PLAYOFFS

No.	Player	EX	NRMT
11	Stanley Cup Playoffs	.03	.05
12	Stanley Cup Playoffs	.03	.05
13	Stanley Cup Playoffs	.03	.05
14	Tom Lysiak	.03	.05
15	Peter Stastny	.25	.50
16	Stanley Cup Playoffs	.03	.05
17	Stanley Cup Playoffs	.03	.05
18	Stanley Cup Playoffs	.03	.05

QUEBEC NORDIQUES

No.	Player	EX	NRMT
19	Peter Stastny	.25	.50
20	Marian Stastny	.05	.10
21	Marc Tardif	.05	.10
22	Wilf Paiement	.05	.10
23	Real Cloutier	.05	.10
24	Anton Stastny	.05	.10
25	Michel Goulet	.05	.10
26	Dale Hunter	.05	.10
27	Dan Bouchard, Goalie	.05	.10

MONTREAL CANADIENS

No.	Player	EX	NRMT
28	Guy Lafleur	.25	.50
29	Guy Lafleur	.25	.50
30	Mario Tremblay	.03	.05
31	Larry Robinson	.25	.50
32	Steve Shutt	.03	.05
33	Steve Shutt	.03	.05
34	Rod Langway	.03	.05
35	Pierre Mondou	.03	.05
36	Bob Gainey	.03	.05
37	Rick Wamsley, Goalie	.03	.05
38	Mark Napier	.03	.05
39	Mark Napier	.03	.05
40	Doug Jarvis	.03	.05
41	Denis Herron, Goalie	.03	.05
42	Keith Acton	.03	.05
43	Keith Acton	.03	.05

NEW YORK ISLANDERS

No.	Player	EX	NRMT
44	Prince of Wales Trophy	.05	.10
45	Prince of Wales Trophy	.05	.10
46	Denis Potvin	.10	.20
47	Bryan Trottier	.25	.50
48	Bryan Trottier	.25	.50
49	John Tonelli	.03	.05
50	Mike Bossy	.25	.50
51	Mike Bossy	.25	.50
52	Duane Sutter	.03	.05
53	Bob Bourne	.03	.05
54	Clark Gillies	.03	.05
55	Clark Gillies	.03	.05
56	Brent Sutter	.03	.05
57	Anders Kallur	.03	.05
58	Ken Morrow	.03	.05
59	Bob Nystrom	.03	.05
60	Billy Smith, Goalie	.10	.20
61	Billy Smith, Goalie	.10	.20

TORONTO MAPLE LEAFS

No.	Player	EX	NRMT
62	Richard Vaive	.03	.05
63	Richard Vaive	.03	.05
64	Jim Benning	.03	.05
65	Miroslav Frycer	.03	.05
66	Terry Martin	.03	.05
67	Bill Derlago	.03	.05
68	Bill Derlago	.03	.05
69	Rocky Saganiuk	.03	.05
70	Vince Tremblay, Goalie	.03	.05
71	Bob Manno	.03	.05
72	Dan Maloney	.03	.05
73	John Anderson	.03	.05
74	John Anderson	.03	.05
75	Borje Salming	.12	.25
76	Borje Salming	.12	.25
77	Michel Larocque, Goalie	.03	.05

BOSTON BRUINS

No.	Player	EX	NRMT
78	Rick Middleton	.03	.05
79	Rick Middleton	.05	.10
80	Keith Crowder	.05	.10
81	Stephen Kasper	.05	.10
82	Brad Park	.03	.05
83	Peter McNab	.03	.05
84	Peter McNab	.03	.05
85	Terry O'Reilly	.03	.05
86	Raymond Bourque	.50	1.00
87	Raymond Bourque	.50	1.00
88	Tom Fergus	.03	.05
89	Michael O'Connell	.03	.05
90	Byron (Brad) McCrimmon	.03	.05
91	Don Marcotte	.03	.05
92	Barry Pederson	.03	.05
93	Barry Pederson	.03	.05

EDMONTON OILERS

No.	Player	EX	NRMT
94	Mark Messier	.50	1.00
95	Grant Fuhr, Goalie	.50	1.00
96	Kevin Lowe	.03	.05
97	Wayne Gretzky	2.00	4.00
98	Wayne Gretzky	2.00	4.00
99	Glenn Anderson	.03	.05
100	Glenn Anderson	.03	.05
101	Dave Lumley	.03	.05
102	Dave Hunter	.03	.05
103	Matti Hagman	.03	.05
104	Paul Coffey	.25	.50
105	Paul Coffey	.25	.50
106	Lee Fogolin	.03	.05
107	Ron Low, Goalie	.03	.05
108	Jari Kurri	.15	.30
109	Jari Kurri	.15	.30

PHILADELPHIA FLYERS

No.	Player	EX	NRMT
110	Bill Barber	.10	.20
111	Brian Propp	.05	.10
112	Ken Linseman	.03	.05
113	Ron Flockhart	.03	.05
114	Darryl Sittler	.12	.25
115	Bobby Clarke	.18	.35
116	Paul Holmgren	.03	.05
117	Peter Peeters, Goalie	.03	.05

BUFFALO SABRES

No.	Player	EX	NRMT
118	Gilbert Perreault	.12	.25
119	Dale McCourt	.03	.05
120	Mike Foligno	.03	.05
121	John Van Boxmeer	.03	.05
122	Anthony McKegney	.03	.05
123	Ric Seiling	.03	.05
124	Don Edwards, Goalie	.03	.05
125	Yvon Lambert	.03	.05

HARTFORD WHALERS

No.	Player	EX	NRMT
126	Blaine Stoughton	.03	.05
127	Pierre Larouche	.03	.05
128	Douglas Sulliman	.03	.05
129	Ron Francis	.20	.40
130	Greg Millen, Goalie	.03	.05
131	Mark Howe	.10	.20
132	Christopher Kotsopoulos	.03	.05
133	Garry Howatt	.03	.05

NEW YORK RANGERS

No.	Player	EX	NRMT
134	Ron Duguay	.03	.05
135	Barry Beck	.03	.05
136	Mike Rogers	.03	.05
137	Donald Maloney	.03	.05
138	Mark Pavelich	.03	.05
139	Eddie Johnstone, Goalie	.03	.05
140	Dave Maloney	.03	.05
141	Stephan Weeks, Goalie	.03	.05
142	Ed Mio, Goalie	.03	.05

PITTSBURGH PENGUINS

No.	Player	EX	NRMT
143	Rick Kehoe	.03	.05
144	Randy Carlyle	.03	.05
145	Paul Gardner	.03	.05
146	Michel Dion, Goalie	.03	.05
147	Rick MacLeish	.03	.05
148	Pat Boutette	.03	.05
149	Mike Bullard	.03	.05
150	George Ferguson	.03	.05

WASHINGTON CAPITALS

No.	Player	EX	NRMT
151	Dennis Maruk	.03	.05
152	Ryan Walter	.03	.05
153	Michael Gartner	.25	.50
154	Robert Carpenter	.03	.05
155	Chris Valentine	.03	.05
156	Richard Green	.03	.05
157	Bengt-Aka Gustafsson	.03	.05
158	Dave Parro, Goalie	.03	.05

CAMPBELL CONFERENCE ALL STARS

No.	Player	EX	NRMT
159	Mark Messier, Edm.	1.00	2.00
160	Paul Coffey, Edm.	.25	.50
161	Grant Fuhr, Goalie, Edm.	.75	1.50
162	Wayne Gretzky, Edm.	2.00	4.00
163	Douglas Wilson, Jr., Chi.	.15	.30
164	David Taylor, LA	.15	.30

WALES CONFERENCE ALL STARS

No.	Player	EX	NRMT
165	Mike Bossy, NYI	.50	1.00
166	Raymond Bourque, Bos.	.50	1.00
167	Peter Stastny, Que.	.25	.50
168	Michel Dion, Goalie, Pit.	.20	.40
169	Larry Robinson, Mon.	.15	.30
170	Bill Barber, Phi.	.15	.30

CHICAGO BLACK HAWKS

No.	Player	EX	NRMT
171	Denis Savard	.25	.50
172	Douglas Wilson, Jr.	.03	.05
173	Grant Mulvey	.03	.05
174	Tom Lysiak	.03	.05
175	Alan Secord	.03	.05
176	Reg Kerr	.03	.05
177	Tim Higgins	.03	.05
178	Terry Ruskowski	.03	.05

DETROIT RED WINGS

No.	Player	EX	NRMT
179	John Ogrodnick	.03	.05
180	Reed Larson	.03	.05
181	Bob Sauve, Goalie	.03	.05
182	Mark Osborne	.03	.05
183	Jim Schoenfeld	.03	.05
184	Danny Gare	.03	.05
185	Willie Huber	.03	.05
186	Walt McKechnie	.03	.05
187	Paul Woods	.03	.05

MINNESOTA NORTH STARS

No.	Player	EX	NRMT
188	Robert Smith	.10	.20
189	Dino Ciccarelli	.10	.20
190	Neal Broten	.15	.30
191	Steve Payne	.03	.05
192	Craig Hartsburg	.03	.05
193	Donald Beaupre, Goalie	.03	.05
194	Steve Christoff	.03	.05
195	Gilles Meloche, Goalie	.03	.05

ST. LOUIS BLUES

No.	Player	EX	NRMT
196	Michael Liut, Goalie	.03	.05
197	Bernie Federko	.03	.05
198	Brian Sutter	.03	.05
199	Blake Dunlop	.03	.05
200	Joe Mullen	.03	.05
201	Wayne Babych	.03	.05
202	Jorgen Pettersson	.03	.05
203	Perry Turnbull	.03	.05

WINNIPEG JETS

No.	Player	EX	NRMT
204	Dale Hawerchuk	.50	1.00
205	Morris Lukowich	.03	.05
206	Dave Christian	.03	.05
207	David Babych	.03	.05
208	Paul MacLean	.03	.05
209	Willy Lindstrom	.03	.05
210	Ed Staniowski, Goalie	.03	.05
211	Doug Soetaert, Goalie	.03	.05
212	Lucien DeBlois	.03	.05

CALGARY FLAMES

No.	Player	EX	NRMT
213	Mel Bridgman	.03	.05
214	Lanny McDonald	.25	.50
215	Guy Chouinard	.03	.05
216	James Peplinski	.03	.05

No.	Player	EX	NRMT
217	Kent Nilsson	.03	.05
218	Pekka Rautakallio	.03	.05
219	Paul Reinhart	.03	.05
220	Kevin LaVallee	.03	.05
221	Ken Houston	.03	.05

COLORADO ROCKIES

No.	Player	EX	NRMT
222	Glenn Resch, Goalie	.10	.20
223	George (Rob) Ramage	.03	.05
224	Don Lever	.03	.05
225	Bob MacMillan	.03	.05
226	Steve Tambellini	.03	.05
227	Brent Ashton	.03	.05
228	Bob Lorimer	.03	.05
229	Merlin Malinowski	.03	.05

LOS ANGELES KINGS

No.	Player	EX	NRMT
230	Marcel Dionne	.25	.50
231	David Taylor	.03	.05
232	Lawrence Murphy	.20	.40
233	Steve Bozek	.03	.05
234	Greg Terrion	.03	.05
235	Jim Fox	.03	.05
236	Mario Lessard, Goalie	.03	.05
237	Charlie Simmer	.03	.05

VANCOUVER CANUCKS

No.	Player	EX	NRMT
238	Campbell Bowl	.05	.10
239	Campbell Bowl	.05	.10
240	Thomas Gradin	.03	.05
241	Ivan Boldirev	.03	.05
242	Stanley Smyl	.03	.05
243	Harold Snepsts	.03	.05
244	Curt Fraser	.03	.05
245	Lars Molin	.03	.05
246	Kevin McCarthy	.03	.05
247	Richard Brodeur, Goalie	.03	.05

1981-82 LEADERS

No.	Player	EX	NRMT
248	Calder Trophy	.03	.05
249	**Calder Trophy Winner:** Rookie of the Year Dale Hawerchuk, Win.	.25	.50
250	Vezina Trophy	.03	.05
251	**Vezina Trophy Winner:** Most Valuable Goalie Billy Smith, NYI	.12	.25
252	**William Jennings Trophy Winners:** Goal Tending - Team Denis Herron, Mon.; Rick Wamsley, Mon.	.03	.05
253	**Frank J. Selke Trophy Winner:** Best Defensive Forward Stephen Kasper, Bos.	.03	.05
254	**Norris Trophy Winner:** Best Defenseman Douglas Wilson, Jr., Chi.	.03	.05
255	Norris Trophy	.10	.20

No.	Player	EX	NRMT
256	**Art Ross Trophy Winner:** 212 Points; **Hart Trophy Winner:** Most Valuable Player Wayne Gretzky, Edm.	1.50	3.00
257	Wayne Gretzky	1.50	3.00
258	Wayne Gretzky	1.50	3.00
259	Wayne Gretzky	1.50	3.00
260	Hart Trophy	.10	.20
261	Art Ross Trophy	.10	.20
262	**Lady Byng Trophy Winner:** Sportsmanship Rick Middleton, Bos.	.10	.20
263	Lady Byng Trophy	.10	.20

— 1983 - 84 STICKERS —

An album was issued to hold these stickers.

1983-84 Stickers
Stickers Nos. 58 and 59, Guy Lafleur

Sticker Size: 1 15/16" X 2 9/16"
Face: Four colour, white or foil border; Number
Back: Blue on card stock; Name, Number, Bilingual
Imprint: ©1983 O-PEE-CHEE CO. LTD.
Complete Set No.: 330
Complete Set Price: 16.00 32.00
Common Player: .03 .05
Album: 5.00

RECORD HOLDERS

No.	Player	EX	NRMT
1	Marcel Dionne, LA	.25	.50
2	Guy Lafleur, Mon.	.25	.50
3	Darryl Sittler, Phi.	.25	.50
4	Gilbert Perreault, Buf.	.12	.25
5	Bill Barber, Phi.	.05	.10
6	Steve Shutt, Mon.	.05	.10
7	Wayne Gretzky, Edm.	2.00	4.00
8	Lanny McDonald, Ca.	.12	.25
9	Reggie Leach, Det.	.03	.05
10	Mike Bossy, NYI	.12	.25
11	Rick Kehoe, Pit.	.03	.05
12	Bobby Clarke, Phi.	.10	.20
13	Butch Goring, NYI	.03	.05
14	Rick Middleton, Bos.	.03	.05

1983 STANLEY CUP FINALS

No.	Player	EX	NRMT
15	Conn Smythe Trophy	.10	.20
16	**Conn Smythe Trophy Winner:** MVP - Finals, Billy Smith, Goalie, NYI	.03	.05
17	Lee Fogolin, Edm.	.03	.05
18	Stanley Cup Finals	.03	.05
19	Stanley Cup Finals	.03	.05
20	Stanley Cup Finals	.03	.05
21	Stanley Cup Finals	.03	.05
22	Stanley Cup	.10	.20
23	Stanley Cup	.10	.20
24	Stanley Cup	.10	.20

TORONTO MAPLE LEAFS

No.	Player	EX	NRMT
25	Richard Vaive	.03	.05
26	Richard Vaive	.03	.05
27	Billy Harris	.03	.05
28	Dan Daoust	.03	.05
29	Dan Daoust	.03	.05
30	John Anderson	.03	.05
31	John Anderson	.03	.05
32	Peter Ihnacak	.03	.05
33	Borje Salming	.12	.25
34	Borje Salming	.12	.25
35	Bill Derlago	.03	.05
36	Rick St. Croix, Goalie	.03	.05
37	Greg Terrion	.03	.05
38	Miroslav Frycer	.03	.05
39	Mike Palmateer, Goalie	.03	.05
40	Gaston Gingras	.03	.05

O-PEE-CHEE — 1983-84 STICKERS

BOSTON BRUINS

No.	Player	EX	NRMT
41	Peter Peeters, Goalie	.03	.05
42	Peter Peeters, Goalie	.03	.05
43	Michael Krushelnyski	.03	.05
44	Rick Middleton	.05	.10
45	Rick Middleton	.05	.10
46	Raymond Bourque	.25	.50
47	Raymond Bourque	.25	.50
48	Brad Park	.03	.05
49	Barry Pederson	.03	.05
50	Barry Pederson	.03	.05
51	Peter McNab	.03	.05
52	Michael O'Connell	.03	.05
53	Stephen Kasper	.03	.05
54	Marty Howe	.03	.05
55	Tom Fergus	.03	.05
56	Keith Crowder	.03	.05

MONTREAL CANADIENS

No.	Player	EX	NRMT
57	Steve Shutt	.03	.05
58	Guy Lafleur	.25	.50
59	Guy Lafleur	.25	.50
60	Larry Robinson	.12	.25
61	Larry Robinson	.12	.25
62	Ryan Walter	.03	.05
63	Ryan Walter	.03	.05
64	Mark Napier	.03	.05
65	Mark Napier	.03	.05
66	Bob Gainey	.03	.05
67	Douglas Wickenheiser	.03	.05
68	Pierre Mondou	.03	.05
69	Mario Tremblay	.03	.05
70	Gilbert Delorme	.03	.05
71	Mats Naslund	.03	.05
72	Rick Wamsley, Goalie	.03	.05

NEW YORK ISLANDERS

No.	Player	EX	NRMT
73	Ken Morrow	.03	.05
74	John Tonelli	.05	.10
75	John Tonelli	.05	.10
76	Bryan Trottier	.07	.15
77	Bryan Trottier	.07	.15
78	Mike Bossy	.20	.40
79	Mike Bossy	.20	.40
80	Bob Bourne	.03	.05
81	Denis Potvin	.12	.25
82	Denis Potvin	.12	.25
83	Dave Langevin	.03	.05
84	Clark Gillies	.03	.05
85	Bob Nystrom	.03	.05
86	Billy Smith	.03	.05
87	Tomas Jonsson	.03	.05
88	Rolland Melanson, Goalie	.03	.05

EDMONTON OILERS

No.	Player	EX	NRMT
89	Wayne Gretzky	2.00	4.00
90	Wayne Gretzky	2.00	4.00
91	Willy Lindstrom	.03	.05
92	Glenn Anderson	.10	.20
93	Glenn Anderson	.10	.20
94	Paul Coffey	.12	.25
95	Paul Coffey	.12	.25
96	Charles Huddy	.03	.05
97	Mark Messier	.50	1.00
98	Mark Messier	.50	1.00
99	Andrew Moog, Goalie	.15	.30
100	Lee Fogolin	.03	.05
101	Kevin Lowe	.20	.40
102	Ken Linseman	.03	.05
103	Tom Roulston	.03	.05
104	Jari Kurri	.12	.25

CHICAGO BLACK HAWKS

No.	Player	EX	NRMT
105	Darryl Sutter	.05	.10
106	Denis Savard	.12	.25
107	Denis Savard	.12	.25
108	Steve Larmer	.25	.50
109	Bob Murray	.03	.05
110	Tom Lysiak	.03	.05
111	Alan Secord	.03	.05
112	Douglas Wilson, Jr.	.03	.05
113	Murray Bannerman, Goalie	.03	.05

MINNESOTA NORTH STARS

No.	Player	EX	NRMT
114	Gordon Roberts	.03	.05
115	Tom McCarthy	.03	.05
116	Robert Smith	.03	.05
117	Craig Hartsburg	.03	.05
118	Dino Ciccarelli	.10	.20
119	Dino Ciccarelli	.10	.20
120	Neal Broten	.03	.05
121	Steve Payne	.03	.05
122	Donald Beaupre, Goalie	.03	.05

ST. LOUIS BLUES

No.	Player	EX	NRMT
123	Jorgen Pettersson	.03	.05
124	Perry Turnbull	.03	.05
125	Bernie Federko	.03	.05
126	Mike Crombeen	.03	.05
127	Brian Sutter	.03	.05
128	Brian Sutter	.03	.05
129	Michael Liut, Goalie	.03	.05
130	George (Rob) Ramage	.03	.05
131	Blake Dunlop	.03	.05

DETROIT RED WINGS

No.	Player	EX	NRMT
132	Ivan Boldirev	.03	.05
133	Dwight Foster	.03	.05
134	Reed Larson	.03	.05
135	Danny Gare	.03	.05
136	Jim Schoenfeld	.03	.05
137	John Ogrodnick	.03	.05
138	John Ogrodnick	.03	.05
139	Willie Huber	.03	.05
140	Greg Smith	.03	.05

STARS OF THE FUTURE CAMPBELL CONFERENCE

No.	Player	EX	NRMT
141	Eddy Beers, Cal.	.03	.05
142	Brian Bellows, Min.	.35	.75
143	Jiri Bubla, Van.	.03	.05
144	Daryl Evans, LA	.03	.05
145	Randall Gregg, Edm.	.12	.25
146	James Jackson, Cal.	.03	.05
147	Corrado Micalef, Goalie, Det.	.03	.05
148	Brian Mullen, Win.	.03	.05
149	Frank Nigro, Tor.	.03	.05
150	Walter Poddubny, Tor.	.03	.05
151	Jaroslav Pouzar, Edm.	.03	.05
152	Patrik Sundstrom, Van.	.03	.05

CAMPBELL CONFERENCE CHAMPIONSHIP

No.	Player	EX	NRMT
153	Denis Savard, Chi.	.07	.15
154	Dave Hunter, Edm.	.03	.05
155	Andrew Moog, Goalie, Edm.	.15	.30
156	Alan Secord, Chi.	.03	.05
157	Mark Messier, Edm.	.50	1.00
158	Glenn Anderson, Edm.	.12	.25
159	Jaroslav Pouzar, Edm.	.03	.05

CAMPBELL CONFERENCE ALL STARS

No.	Player	EX	NRMT
160	Alan Secord, Chi.	.03	.05
161	Wayne Gretzky, Edm.	1.50	3.00
162	Lanny McDonald, Cal.	.05	.10
163	David Babych, Win.	.03	.05
164	Murray Bannerman, Goalie, Chi.	.03	.05
165	Douglas Wilson, Jr., Chi.	.03	.05

WALES CONFERENCE ALL STARS

No.	Player	EX	NRMT
166	Michel Goulet, Que.	.03	.05
167	Peter Stastny, Que.	.10	.20
168	Marian Stastny, Que.	.03	.05
169	Denis Potvin, NYI	.10	.20
170	Peter Peeters, Goalie, Bos.	.03	.05
171	Mark Howe, Phi.	.03	.05

WALES CONFERENCE CHAMPIONSHIP

No.	Player	EX	NRMT
172	Luc Dufour, Bos.	.03	.05
173	Raymond Bourque, Bos.	.35	.75
174	Bob Bourne, NYI	.03	.05
175	Denis Potvin, NYI	.03	.05
176	Mike Bossy, NYI	.10	.20
177	Butch Goring, NYI	.03	.05
178	Brad Park, Bos.	.03	.05

STARS OF THE FUTURE WALES CONFERENCE

No.	Player	EX	NRMT
179	James (Murray) Brumwell, NJD	.03	.05
180	Guy Carbonneau, Mon.	.35	.75
181	Lindsay Carson, Phi.	.03	.05
182	Luc Dufour, Bos.	.03	.05
183	Robert Froese, Goalie, Phi.	.03	.05
184	Mats Hallin, NYI	.03	.05
185	Gordon Kluzak, Bos.	.10	.20
186	Jeff Larmer, NJD	.03	.05
187	Milan Novy, Wash.	.03	.05
188	Scott Stevens, Wash.	.35	.75
189	Bob Sullivan, Har.	.03	.05
190	Mark Taylor, Phi.	.03	.05

PHILADELPHIA FLYERS

No.	Player	EX	NRMT
191	Darryl Sittler	.12	.25
192	Ron Flockhart	.03	.05
193	Byron (Brad) McCrimmon	.03	.05
194	Bill Barber	.03	.05
195	Mark Howe	.12	.25
196	Mark Howe	.12	.25
197	Pelle Lindbergh, Goalie	.75	1.50
198	Bobby Clarke	.18	.35
199	Brian Propp	.03	.05

WASHINGTON CAPITALS

No.	Player	EX	NRMT
200	Ken Houston	.03	.05
201	Rod Langway	.03	.05
202	Al Jensen, Goalie	.03	.05
203	Brian Engblom	.03	.05
204	Dennis Maruk	.03	.05
205	Dennis Maruk	.03	.05
206	Robert Carpenter	.03	.05
207	Michael Gartner	.25	.50
208	Doug Jarvis	.03	.05

NEW YORK RANGERS

No.	Player	EX	NRMT
209	Ed Mio, Goalie	.03	.05
210	Barry Beck	.03	.05
211	Dave Maloney	.03	.05
212	Donald Maloney	.03	.05
213	Mark Pavelich	.03	.05
214	Mark Pavelich	.03	.05
215	Anders Hedberg	.03	.05
216	Reijo Ruotsalainen	.03	.05
217	Mike Rogers	.03	.05

NEW JERSEY DEVILS

No.	Player	EX	NRMT
218	Don Lever	.03	.05
219	Steve Tambellini	.03	.05
220	Bob MacMillan	.03	.05
221	Hector Marini	.03	.05
222	Glenn Resch, Goalie	.03	.05
223	Glenn Resch, Goalie	.03	.05
224	Carol Vadnais	.03	.05
225	Joel Quenneville	.03	.05
226	Aaron Broten	.03	.05

1984 - 85 STICKERS — O-PEE-CHEE

Sticker Size: 1 7/8" x 2 15/16"
Face: Four colour, white on foil border; Number
Back: Black on card stock; Name, Number, Bilingual
Imprint: © 1984 O-PEE-CHEE CO. LTD.
Complete Set No.: 292
Complete Set Price: 16.00   32.00
Common Player: .03   .05
Album: 5.00

PITTSBURGH PENGUINS

No.	Player	EX	NRMT
227	Randy Carlyle	.03	.05
228	Douglas Shedden	.03	.05
229	Greg Malone	.03	.05
230	Paul Gardner	.03	.05
231	Rick Kehoe	.03	.05
232	Rick Kehoe	.03	.05
233	Pat Boutette	.03	.05
234	Michel Dion, Goalie	.03	.05
235	Mike Bullard	.03	.05

BUFFALO SABRES

No.	Player	EX	NRMT
236	Dale McCourt	.03	.05
237	Mike Foligno	.03	.05
238	Phil Housley	.20	.40
239	Anthony McKegney	.03	.05
240	Gilbert Perreault	.07	.15
241	Gilbert Perreault	.07	.15
242	Bob Sauve, Goalie	.03	.05
243	Michael Ramsey	.03	.05
244	John Van Boxmeer	.03	.05

QUEBEC NORDIQUES

No.	Player	EX	NRMT
245	Dan Bouchard, Goalie	.03	.05
246	Real Cloutier	.03	.05
247	Marc Tardif	.03	.05
248	Randy Moller	.03	.05
249	Michel Goulet	.03	.05
250	Michel Goulet	.07	.15
251	Marian Stastny	.07	.15
252	Anton Stastny	.03	.05
253	Peter Stastny	.10	.20

HARTFORD WHALERS

No.	Player	EX	NRMT
254	Mark Johnson	.03	.05
255	Ron Francis	.07	.15
256	Douglas Sulliman	.03	.05
257	Risto Siltanen	.03	.05
258	Blaine Stoughton	.03	.05
259	Blaine Stoughton	.03	.05
260	Ray Neufeld	.03	.05
261	Pierre Lacroix	.03	.05
262	Greg Millen, Goalie	.03	.05

CALGARY FLAMES

No.	Player	EX	NRMT
263	Lanny McDonald	.05	.10
264	Paul Reinhart	.03	.05
265	Mel Bridgman	.03	.05
266	Rejean Lemelin, Goalie	.10	.20
267	Kent Nilsson	.03	.05
268	Kent Nilsson	.03	.05
269	Doug Risebrough	.03	.05
270	Kari Eloranta	.03	.05
271	Phil Russell	.03	.05

VANCOUVER CANUCKS

No.	Player	EX	NRMT
272	Darcy Rota	.03	.05
273	Thomas Gradin	.03	.05
274	Stanley Smyl	.03	.05
275	John Garrett	.03	.05
276	Richard Brodeur, Goalie	.03	.05
277	Richard Brodeur, Goalie	.03	.05
278	Doug Halward	.03	.05
279	Kevin McCarthy	.03	.05
280	Rick Lanz	.03	.05

WINNIPEG JETS

No.	Player	EX	NRMT
281	Morris Lukowich	.03	.05
282	Dale Hawerchuk	.20	.40
283	Paul MacLean	.03	.05
284	Lucien DeBlois	.03	.05
285	David Babych	.03	.05
286	David Babych	.03	.05
287	Douglas Smail	.03	.05
288	Doug Soetaert, Goalie	.03	.05
289	Thomas Steen	.03	.05

LOS ANGELES KINGS

No.	Player	EX	NRMT
290	Charlie Simmer	.03	.05
291	Terry Ruskowski	.03	.05
292	Bernie Nicholls	.25	.50
293	Jim Fox	.03	.05
294	Marcel Dionne	.10	.20
295	Marcel Dionne	.10	.20
296	Gary Laskoski, Goalie	.03	.05
297	Jerry Korab	.03	.05
298	Lawrence Murphy	.12	.25

1982 - 1983 LEADERS

No.	Player	EX	NRMT
299	Hart Trophy	.10	.20
300	Hart Trophy	.10	.20
301	**Hart Trophy Winner:** Most Valuable Player, Wayne Gretzky, Edm.	1.50	3.00
302	**Frank J. Selke Trophy Winner:** Best Defensive Forward, Bobby Clarke, Phi.	.05	.10
303	**Bill Masterton Trophy Winner:** For Perseverance, Sportsmanship and Dedication, Lanny McDonald, Cal.	.05	.10
304	Lady Byng Trophy	.10	.20
305	Lady Byng Trophy	.10	.20
306	**Lady Byng Trophy Winner:** Sportsmanship, Mike Bossy, NYI	.10	.20
307	**Art Ross Trophy Winner:** 196 Points, Wayne Gretzky, Edm.	1.50	3.00
308	Art Ross Trophy	.10	.20
309	Art Ross Trophy	.10	.20
310	Calder Trophy	.10	.20
311	Calder Trophy	.10	.20
312	**Calder Trophy Winner:** Rookie of the Year, Steve Larmer, Chi.	.20	.40
313	**Norris Trophy Winner:** Best Defenseman, Rod Langway, Wash.	.05	.10
314	Norris Trophy	.10	.20
315	Norris Trophy	.10	.20
316	**William Jennings Trophy Winner:** Goal Tending - Team, Billy Smith, NYI	.05	.10
317	**William Jennings Trophy Winner:** Goal Tending - Team, Roland Melanson, NYI	.03	.05
318	**Vezina Trophy Winnder:** Most Valuable Goalie, Peter Peeters, Bos.	.03	.05
319	Vezina Trophy	.10	.20
320	Vezina Trophy	.10	.20

1982 - 83 RECORD BREAKERS

No.	Player	EX	NRMT
321	Mike Bossy, NYI	.20	.40
322	Mike Bossy, NYI	.20	.40
323	Marcel Dionne, St.L.	.20	.40
324	Marcel Dionne, St.L.	.20	.40
325	Wayne Gretzky, Edm.	1.50	3.00
326	Wayne Gretzky, Edm.	1.50	3.00
327	Pat Hughes, Edm.	.10	.20
328	Pat Hughes, Edm.	.10	.20
329	Rick Middleton, Bos.	.10	.20
330	Rick Middleton, Bos.	.15	.30

— 1984 - 85 STICKERS —

1984-85 Stickers

Sticker No. 10, Dan Daoust

Sticker No. 79, Denis Potvin

1984 STANLEY CUP

No.	Player	EX	NRMT
1	Islanders vs. Oilers	.05	.10
2	Islanders vs. Oilers	.05	.10
3	Islanders vs. Oilers	.05	.10
4	Islanders vs. Oilers	.05	.10
5	**Conn Smythe Trophy Winner:** MVP - Finals: Mark Messier, Edm.	.15	.30

TORONTO MAPLE LEAFS

No.	Player	EX	NRMT
6	Toronto Maple Leafs Team Logo	.05	.10
7	Borje Salming	.10	.20
8	Borje Salming	.10	.20
9	Dan Daoust	.03	.05
10	Dan Daoust	.03	.05
11	Richard Vaive	.03	.05
12	Richard Vaive	.03	.05
13	Dale McCourt	.03	.05
14	Bill Derlago	.03	.05
15	Gary Nylund	.03	.05
16	Gary Nylund	.03	.05
17	James Korn	.03	.05
18	John Anderson	.03	.05
19	Greg Terrion	.03	.05
20	Allan Bester, Goalie	.03	.05
21	Jim Benning	.03	.05
22	Mike Palmateer, Goalie	.03	.05

CHICAGO BLACK HAWKS

No.	Player	EX	NRMT
23	Chicago Blackhawks Team Logo	.05	.10
24	Denis Savard	.12	.25
25	Denis Savard	.12	.25
26	Bob Murray	.03	.05
27	Douglas Wilson, Jr.	.03	.05
28	Keith Brown	.03	.05
29	Steve Larmer	.10	.20
30	Darryl Sutter	.03	.05
31	Tom Lysiak	.03	.05
32	Murray Bannerman, Goalie	.03	.05

DETROIT RED WINGS

No.	Player	EX	NRMT
33	Detroit Red Wings Team Logo	.05	.10
34	John Ogrodnick	.03	.05
35	John Ogrodnick	.03	.05
36	Reed Larson	.03	.05
37	Steve Yzerman	1.50	3.00
38	Brad Park	.12	.25
39	Ivan Boldirev	.03	.05
40	Kelly Kisio	.03	.05
41	Gregory Stefan, Goalie	.03	.05
42	Ron Duguay	.03	.05

MINNESOTA NORTH STARS

No.	Player	EX	NRMT
43	Minnesota North Stars Team Logo	.05	.10
44	Brian Bellows	.10	.20
45	Brian Bellows	.10	.20
46	Neal Broten	.03	.05
47	Dino Ciccarelli	.10	.20
48	Dennis Maruk	.03	.05
49	Steve Payne	.03	.05
50	Brad Maxwell	.03	.05
51	Gilles Meloche, Goalie	.03	.05
52	Tom McCarthy	.03	.05

ST. LOUIS BLUES

No.	Player	EX	NRMT
53	St. Louis Blues Team Logo	.05	.10
54	Bernie Federko	.12	.25
55	Bernie Federko	.12	.25
56	Brian Sutter	.03	.05
57	Michael Liut, Goalie	.03	.05

128 • O-PEE-CHEE — 1984-85 STICKERS —

No.	Player	EX	NRMT
58	Douglas Wickenheiser	.03	.05
59	Jorgen Pettersson	.03	.05
60	Douglas Gilmour	1.00	2.00
61	Joe Mullen	.03	.05
62	George (Rob) Ramage	.03	.05

1983-84 LEAGUE LEADERS

No.	Player	EX	NRMT
63	Wayne Gretzky, Edm. Goals, Power Play Goals, Assists, Total Points Shorthanded Goals	1.50	3.00
64	Michel Goulet, Game Winning Goals	.03	.05
65	Pat Riggin, Goals Against Average	.03	.05
66	Denis Potvin, Leading Defenceman	.03	.05

NEW JERSEY DEVILS

No.	Player	EX	NRMT
67	New Jersey Devils Team Logo	.05	.10
68	Glenn Resch, Goalie	.03	.05
69	Glenn Resch, Goalie	.03	.05
70	Don Lever	.03	.05
71	Mel Bridgman	.03	.05
72	Bob MacMillan	.03	.05
73	Patrick Verbeek	.15	.30
74	Joe Cirella	.03	.05
75	Phil Russell	.35	.75
76	Jan Ludvig	.03	.05

NEW YORK ISLANDERS

No.	Player	EX	NRMT
77	New York Islanders Team Logo	.05	.10
78	Denis Potvin	.03	.05
79	Denis Potvin	.03	.05
80	John Tonelli	.03	.05
81	John Tonelli	.03	.05
82	Mike Bossy	.12	.25
83	Mike Bossy	.12	.25
84	Butch Goring	.03	.05
85	Bob Nystrom	.03	.05
86	Bryan Trottier	.10	.20
87	Bryan Trottier	.10	.20
88	Brent Sutter	.03	.05
89	Bob Bourne	.03	.05
90	Gregory Gilbert	.03	.05
91	Billy Smith, Goalie	.05	.10
92	Roland Melanson, Goalie	.03	.05
93	Ken Morrow	.03	.05

NEW YORK RANGERS

No.	Player	EX	NRMT
94	New York Rangers Team Logo	.05	.10
95	Donald Maloney	.03	.05
96	Donald Maloney	.03	.05
97	Mark Pavelich	.03	.05
98	Glen Hanlon, Goalie	.03	.05
99	Mike Rogers	.03	.05
100	Barry Beck	.03	.05
101	Reijo Ruotsalainen	.03	.05
102	Anders Hedberg	.03	.05
103	Pierre Larouche	.03	.05

PHILADELPHIA FLYERS

No.	Player	EX	NRMT
104	Philadelphia Flyers Team Logo	.05	.10
105	Tim Kerr	.03	.05
106	Tim Kerr	.03	.05
107	Ronald Sutter	.03	.05
108	Darryl Sittler	.12	.25
109	Mark Howe	.07	.15
110	David Poulin	.05	.10
111	Richard Sutter	.03	.05
112	Brian Propp	.03	.05
113	Robert Froese, Goalie	.03	.05

PITTSBURGH PENGUINS

No.	Player	EX	NRMT
114	Pittsburgh Penguins Team Logo	.05	.10
115	Ron Flockhart	.03	.05
116	Ron Flockhart	.03	.05
117	Rick Kehoe	.03	.05
118	Mike Bullard	.03	.05
119	Kevin McCarthy	.03	.05
120	Douglas Shedden	.03	.05
121	Mark Taylor	.03	.05
122	Denis Herron, Goalie	.03	.05
123	Tom Roulston	.03	.05

WASHINGTON CAPITALS

No.	Player	EX	NRMT
124	Washington Capitals Team Logo	.05	.10
125	Rod Langway	.03	.05
126	Rod Langway	.03	.05
127	Lawrence Murphy	.12	.25
128	Al Jensen, Goalie	.03	.05
129	Doug Jarvis	.03	.05
130	Bengt-aka Gustafsson	.03	.05
131	Michael Gartner	.12	.25
132	Robert Carpenter	.03	.05
133	Dave Christian	.03	.05

ALL STARS CAMPBELL CONFERENCE

No.	Player	EX	NRMT
134	Paul Coffey, Edm.	.25	.50
135	Murray Bannerman, Goalie, Chi.	.10	.20
136	George (Rob) Ramage, St.L.	.10	.20
137	John Ogrodnick, Det.	.10	.20
138	Wayne Gretzky, Edm.	1.50	3.00
139	Richard Vaive, Tor.	.10	.20
140	Michel Goulet, Que.	.10	.20
141	Peter Stastny, Que.	.10	.20
142	Rick Middleton, Bos.	.10	.20
143	Raymond Bourque, Bos.	.35	.75
144	Peter Peeters, Goalie, Bos.	.10	.20
145	Denis Potvin, NYI	.10	.20

MONTREAL CANADIENS

No.	Player	EX	NRMT
146	Montreal Canadiens Team Logo	.05	.10
147	Larry Robinson	.15	.30
148	Larry Robinson	.15	.30
149	Guy Lafleur	.20	.40
150	Guy Lafleur	.20	.40
151	Robert Smith	.10	.20
152	Robert Smith	.10	.20
153	Bob Gainey	.03	.05
154	Craig Ludwig	.03	.05
155	Mats Naslund	.03	.05
156	Mats Naslund	.03	.05
157	Rick Wamsley, Goalie	.03	.05
158	Jean Hamel	.03	.05
159	Ryan Walter	.03	.05
160	Guy Carbonneau	.20	.40
161	Mario Tremblay	.03	.05
162	Pierre Mondou	.03	.05

QUEBEC NORDIQUES

No.	Player	EX	NRMT
163	Quebec Nordiques Team Logo	.05	.10
164	Peter Stastny	.20	.40
165	Peter Stastny	.20	.40
166	Mario Marois	.03	.05
167	Mario Marois	.03	.05
168	Michel Goulet	.12	.25
169	Michel Goulet	.12	.25
170	Andre Savard	.03	.05
171	Anthony McKegney	.03	.05
172	Dan Bouchard, Goalie	.03	.05
173	Dan Bouchard, Goalie	.03	.05
174	Randy Moller	.03	.05
175	Wilf Paiement	.03	.05
176	Normand Rochefort	.03	.05
177	Marian Stastny	.03	.05
178	Anton Stastny	.03	.05
179	Dale Hunter	.05	.10

BOSTON BRUINS

No.	Player	EX	NRMT
180	Boston Bruins Team Logo	.05	.10
181	Rick Middleton	.10	.20
182	Rick Middleton	.10	.20
183	Raymond Bourque	.25	.50
184	Peter Peeters, Goalie	.03	.05
185	Michael O'Connell	.03	.05
186	Gord Kluzak	.03	.05
187	Barry Pederson	.03	.05
188	Michael Krushelnyski	.03	.05
189	Tom Fergus	.03	.05

HARTFORD WHALERS

No.	Player	EX	NRMT
190	Hartford Whalers Team Logo	.05	.10
191	Sylvain Turgeon	.03	.05
192	Sylvain Turgeon	.03	.05
193	Mark Johnson	.03	.05
194	Greg Malone	.03	.05
195	Mike Zuke	.03	.05
196	Ron Francis	.15	.30
197	Bob Crawford	.03	.05
198	Greg Millen, Goalie	.03	.05
199	Ray Neufeld	.03	.05

BUFFALO SABRES

No.	Player	EX	NRMT
200	Buffalo Sabres Team Logo	.05	.10
201	Gilbert Perreault	.07	.15
202	Gilbert Perreault	.07	.15
203	Phil Housley	.07	.15
204	Phil Housley	.07	.15
205	Tom Barrasso, Goalie	.75	1.50
206	Tom Barrasso, Goalie	.75	1.50
207	Larry Playfair	.03	.05
208	Bob Sauve, Goalie	.03	.05
209	David Andreychuk	1.00	2.00
210	David Andreychuk	1.00	2.00
211	Michael Ramsey	.03	.05
212	Mike Foligno	.03	.05
213	Lindy Ruff	.03	.05
214	Bill Hajt	.03	.05
215	Craig Ramsay	.03	.05
216	Ric Seiling	.03	.05

1983-84 LEAGUE LEADERS

No.	Player	EX	NRMT
217	Hart Trophy	.05	.10
218	Vezina Trophy	.05	.10
219	Jennings Trophy	.05	.10
220	Calder Trophy	.05	.10
221	Art Ross Trophy	.05	.10
222	Norris Trophy	.05	.10
223	Masterton Trophy	.05	.10
224	Selke Trophy	.05	.10
225	Lady Byng Trophy	.05	.10
226	Hart Trophy Winner: Wayne Gretzky, Edm.	1.50	3.00
227	Vezina Trophy Winner: Tom Barrasso, Buf.	.25	.50
228	Calder Trophy Winner: Tom Barrasso, Buf.	.25	.50
229	Art Ross Trophy Winner: Wayne Gretzky, Edm.	1.50	3.00
230	Norris Trophy Winner: Rod Langway, Wash.	.03	.05
231	Bill Masterton Trophy Winner: Brad Park, Det.	.03	.05
232	William Jennings Trophy Winner: Al Jensen, Wash.	.03	.05
233	William Jennings Trophy Winner: Pat Riggin, Wash.	.03	.05
234	Frank J. Selke Trophy Winner: Doug Jarvis, Wash.	.03	.05
235	Lady Byng Trophy Winner: Mike Bossy, NYI	.12	.25

CALGARY FLAMES

No.	Player	EX	NRMT
236	Calgary Flames Team Logo	.05	.10
237	Lanny McDonald	.25	.30
238	Lanny McDonald	.25	.30
239	Steve Tambellini	.03	.05
240	Rejean Lemelin, Goalie	.03	.05
241	Doug Risebrough	.03	.05
242	Hakan Loob	.03	.05
243	Eddy Beers	.03	.05
244	Mike Eaves	.03	.05
245	Kent Nilsson	.03	.05

1985 - 86 BOX BOTTOMS — O-PEE-CHEE • 129

EDMONTON OILERS

No.	Player	EX	NRMT
246	Edmonton Oilers Team Logo	.05	.10
247	Glenn Anderson	.10	.20
248	Glenn Anderson	.10	.20
249	Jari Kurri	.15	.30
250	Jari Kurri	.15	.30
251	Paul Coffey	.25	.50
252	Paul Coffey	.25	.50
253	Kevin Lowe	.03	.05
254	Lee Fogolin	.03	.05
255	Wayne Gretzky	2.00	4.00
256	Wayne Gretzky	2.00	4.00
257	Randall Gregg	.03	.05
258	Charles Huddy	.03	.05
259	Grant Fuhr, Goalie	.25	.50
260	Willy Lindstrom	.03	.05
261	Mark Messier	.50	1.00
262	Andrew Moog, Goalie	.10	.20

LOS ANGELES KINGS

No.	Player	EX	NRMT
263	Los Angeles Kings Team Logo	.05	.10
264	Marcel Dionne	.20	.40
265	Marcel Dionne	.20	.40
266	Charlie Simmer	.03	.05
267	David Taylor	.03	.05
268	Jim Fox	.03	.05
269	Bernie Nicholls	.03	.05
270	Terry Ruskowski	.03	.05
271	Brian Engblom	.03	.05
272	Mark Hardy	.03	.05

VANCOUVER CANUCKS

No.	Player	EX	NRMT
273	Vancouver Canucks Team Logo	.05	.10
274	Tony Tanti	.03	.05
275	Tony Tanti	.03	.05
276	Rick Lanz	.03	.05
277	Richard Brodeur, Goalie	.03	.05
278	Doug Halward	.03	.05
279	Patrik Sundstrom	.03	.05
280	Darcy Rota	.03	.05
281	Stanley Smyl	.03	.05
282	Thomas Gradin	.03	.05

WINNIPEG JETS

No.	Player	EX	NRMT
283	Winnipeg Jets Team Logo	.05	.10
284	Dale Hawerchuk	.10	.20
285	Dale Hawerchuk	.10	.20
286	Scott Arniel	.03	.05
287	David Babych	.03	.05
288	Laurie Boschman	.03	.05
289	Paul MacLean	.03	.05
290	Lucien DeBlois	.03	.05
291	Randy Carlyle	.03	.05
292	Thomas Steen	.03	.05

— 1985 - 86 BOX BOTTOMS —

The cards were issued as the bottom wax box panel, with four cards per panel. The set features team scoring leaders.

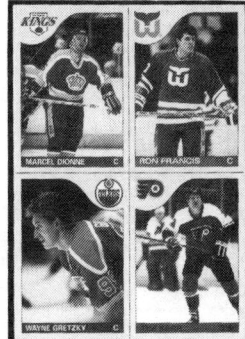

1985-86 Box Bottom, Panel No. 2
Marcel Dionne, Ron Francis
Wayne Gretsky, Tim Kerr

Panel Size: 5 1/16" x 7"
Face: Four colour, yellow border; Name, Position, Team logo
Back: Two colour, maroon and purple on card stock; Name, Letter, Resume, Bilingual
Imprint: ©1985 O-Pee-Chee Ptd. in Canada/Imprimé au Canada
Complete Set No.: 4 Panels
Complete Set Price: 50.00 100.00
Common Panel: .50 .50
Common Card: .20 .20

No.	Player	EX	NRMT
	Panel 1	1.00	2.00
A	Brian Bellows, Min.	.25	.50
B	Raymond Bourque, Bos.	.50	1.00
C	Robert Carpenter, Wash.	.12	.25
D	Chris Chelios, Mon.	.35	.75
	Panel 2	5.00	10.00
E	Marcel Dionne, LA	.50	1.00
F	Ron Francis, Har.	.35	.75
G	Wayne Gretzky, Edm.	5.00	10.00
H	Tim Kerr, Phi.	.10	.20
	Panel 3	42.50	85.00
I	Mario Lemieux, Pit.	42.50	85.00
J	John Ogrodnick, Det.	.10	.20
K	Gilbert Perreault, Buf.	.25	.50
L	Glenn Resch, Goalie, NJD	.12	.25
	Panel 4	.25	.50
M	Reijo Ruotsalainen, NYR	.10	.20
N	Brian Sutter, St.L.	.10	.20
O	John Tonelli, NYI	.10	.20
P	Douglas Wilson, Jr., Chi.	.10	.20

— 1985 - 86 STICKERS —

An album was issued to hold these stickers. The set comes in both English and French editions. These stickers are price in NRMT.

1985-86 Stickers
No.5, Wayne Gretsky

Sticker Size: 2 1/8" X 2 15/16" or 1 7/8" X 2 1/8"
Face: Four colour, white border; Number
Back: Blue on stock; Name, Number, Hockey Offer, French and English
Imprint: ©1985 O-PEE-CHEE CO. LTD MADE IN ITALY or
©1985 O-PEE-CHEE LTÉE FABRIQUÉ EN ITALIE
Complete Set No.: 255
Complete Set Price: 17.50 35.00
Common Player: .03 .05
Album: 5.00

1985 STANLEY CUP

No.	Player	English	French
1	Stanley Cup Final	.03	.05
2	Stanley Cup Final	.03	.05
3	Stanley Cup Final	.03	.05
4	Stanley Cup Final	.03	.05
5	Wayne Gretzky, Edm. Conn Smythe Troyphy Winner	.50	1.00

TORONTO MAPLE LEAFS

No.	Player	English	French
6	Richard Vaive	.03	.05
7	Bill Derlago	.03	.05
8	Rick St. Croix, Goalie	.03	.05
9	Tim Bernhardt, Goalie	.03	.05
10	John Anderson	.03	.05
11	Dan Daoust	.03	.05
12	Borje Salming	.10	.20
13	Al Iafrate	.35	.75
14	Gary Nylund	.03	.05
15	Robert McGill	.03	.05
16	Jim Benning	.03	.05
17	Robert (Stewart) Gavin	.03	.05
18	Greg Terrion	.03	.05
19	Peter Ihnacak	.03	.05
20	Russell Courtnall	.35	.75
21	Miroslav Frycer	.03	.05

CHICAGO BLACK HAWKS

No.	Player	English	French
22	Denis Savard	.12	.25
23	Darryl Sutter	.03	.05
24	Curt Fraser	.03	.05
25	Douglas Wilson, Jr.	.03	.05
26	Ed Olczyk	.12	.25
27	Murray Bannerman, Goalie	.03	.05
28	Steve Larmer	.12	.25
29	Troy Murray	.03	.05

DETROIT RED WINGS

No.	Player	English	French
30	Steve Yzerman	.50	1.00
31	Gregory Stefan, Goalie	.03	.05
32	Ron Duguay	.03	.05
33	Reed Larson	.03	.05
34	Ivan Boldirev	.03	.05
35	Danny Gare	.03	.05
36	Darryl Sittler	.12	.25
37	John Ogrodnick	.03	.05

MINNESOTA NORTH STARS

No.	Player	English	French
38	Keith Acton	.03	.05
39	Dino Ciccarelli	.12	.25
40	Neal Broten	.03	.05
41	Brian Bellows	.05	.10
42	Steve Payne	.03	.05
43	Gordon Roberts	.03	.05
44	Harold Snepsts	.03	.05
45	Anthony McKegney	.03	.05

ST. LOUIS BLUES

No.	Player	English	French
46	Brian Sutter	.03	.05
47	Joe Mullen	.03	.05
48	Douglas Gilmour	1.00	2.00
49	Tim Bothwell	.03	.05
50	Mark Johnson	.03	.05
51	Greg Millen, Goalie	.03	.05
52	Douglas Wickenheiser	.03	.05
53	Bernie Federko	.15	.30

1984-85 LEAGUE LEADERS

No.	Player	English	French
54	Wayne Gretzky, Edm., Goals, Assists, Total Points, Shorthanded Goals	1.00	2.00
55	Tom Barrasso, Buf. Goals Against Average	.10	.20
56	Paul Coffey, Edm. Leading Defenceman	.15	.30

NEW JERSEY DEVILS

No.	Player	English	French
57	Mel Bridgman	.03	.05
58	Phil Russell	.03	.05
59	Dave Lewis	.03	.05
60	Paul Gagne	.03	.05
61	Glenn Resch, Goalie	.03	.05
62	Aaron Broten	.03	.05
63	Dave Pichette	.03	.05
64	Kirk Muller	.50	1.00

NEW YORK ISLANDERS

No.	Player	English	French
65	Bryan Trottier	.20	.40
66	Mike Bossy	.25	.50
67	Bob Bourne	.03	.05
68	Clark Gillies	.03	.05
69	Bob Nystrom	.03	.05

130 • O-PEE-CHEE — 1985-86 STICKERS —

No.	Player	English	French
70	Denis Potvin	.10	.20
71	Brent Sutter	.03	.05
72	Duane Sutter	.03	.05
73	Patrick Flatley	.03	.05
74	Pat LaFontaine	.50	1.00
75	Gregory Gilbert	.03	.05
76	Billy Smith, Goalie	.03	.05
77	Gord Lane	.03	.05
78	Tomas Jonsson	.03	.05
79	Kelly Hrudey, Goalie	.10	.20
80	John Tonelli	.03	.05

NEW YORK RANGERS

No.	Player	English	French
81	Reijo Ruotsalainen	.03	.05
82	Barry Beck	.03	.05
83	James Patrick	.03	.05
84	Mark Pavelich	.03	.05
85	Pierre Larouche	.03	.05
86	Mike Rogers	.03	.05
87	Glen Hanlon, Goalie	.03	.05
88	John Vanbiesbrouck, Goalie	.35	.75

PHILADELPHIA FLYERS

No.	Player	English	French
89	David Poulin	.03	.05
90	Brian Propp	.03	.05
91	Pelle Lindbergh, Goalie	.50	1.00
92	Byron (Brad) McCrimmon	.03	.05
93	Mark Howe	.15	.30
94	Peter Zezel	.03	.05
95	Murray Craven	.03	.05
96	Tim Kerr	.03	.05

PITTSBURGH PENGUINS

No.	Player	English	French
97	Mario Lemieux	3.50	7.00
98	Maurice Mantha	.03	.05
99	Doug Bodger	.03	.05
100	Warren Young	.03	.05
101	John Chabot	.03	.05
102	Douglas Shedden	.03	.05
103	Wayne Babych	.03	.05
104	Mike Bullard	.03	.05

WASHINGTON CAPITALS

No.	Player	English	French
105	Rod Langway	.03	.05
106	Pat Riggin, Goalie	.03	.05
107	Scott Stevens	.35	.75
108	Alan Haworth	.03	.05
109	Doug Jarvis	.03	.05
110	Dave Christian	.03	.05
111	Michael Gartner	.20	.40
112	Robert Carpenter	.03	.05

ALL STARS CAMPBELL CONFERENCE

No.	Player	English	French
113	Rod Langway, Wash.	.10	.20
114	Tom Barrasso, Goalie, Buf.	.25	.50
115	Raymond Bourque, Bos.	.25	.50
116	John Tonelli, NYI	.10	.20
117	Brent Sutter, NYI	.10	.20
118	Mike Bossy, NYI	.25	.50
119	John Ogrodnick, Det.	.10	.20
120	Wayne Gretzky, Edm.	1.00	2.00
121	Jari Kurri, Edm.	.20	.40
122	Douglas Wilson, Jr., Chi.	.15	.30
123	Andrew Moog, Goalie, Edm.	.20	.40
124	Paul Coffey, Edm.	.20	.40

MONTREAL CANADIENS

No.	Player	English	French
125	Chris Chelios	.10	.20
126	Steve Penney, Goalie	.03	.05
127	Christopher Nilan	.03	.05
128	Ron Flockhart	.03	.05
129	Tom Kurvers	.03	.05
130	Craig Ludwig	.03	.05
131	Mats Naslund	.03	.05
132	Robert Smith	.03	.05
133	Pierre Mondou	.03	.05
134	Mario Tremblay	.03	.05
135	Guy Carbonneau	.03	.05
136	Doug Soetaert, Goalie	.03	.05
137	Mark Hunter	.03	.05
138	Bob Gainey	.03	.05
139	Petr Svoboda	.03	.05
140	Larry Robinson	.12	.25

QUEBEC NORDIQUES

No.	Player	English	French
141	Michel Goulet	.10	.20
142	Bruce Bell	.03	.05
143	Dan Bouchard, Goalie	.03	.05
144	Mario Marois	.03	.05
145	Randy Moller	.03	.05
146	Mario Gosselin, Goalie	.03	.05
147	Anton Stastny	.03	.05
148	Normand Rochefort	.03	.05
149	Alain Cote	.03	.05
150	Paul Gillis	.03	.05
151	Dale Hunter	.05	.10
152	Wilf Paiement	.03	.05
153	Brent Ashton	.03	.05
154	Brad Maxwell	.03	.05
155	Jenn F. Sauve	.07	.15
156	Peter Stastny	.20	.40

BOSTON BRUINS

No.	Player	English	French
157	Raymond Bourque	.25	.50
158	Charlie Simmer	.03	.05
159	Rick Middleton	.03	.05
160	Peter Peeters, Goalie	.03	.05
161	Michael O'Connell	.03	.05
162	Terry O'Reilly	.05	.10
163	Keith Crowder	.03	.05
164	Tom Fergus	.03	.05

HARTFORD WHALERS

No.	Player	English	French
165	Sylvain Turgeon	.03	.05
166	Greg Malone	.03	.05
167	Bob Crawford	.03	.05
168	Kevin Dineen	.10	.20
169	Michael Liut, Goalie	.03	.05
170	Joel Quenneville	.03	.05
171	Ray Neufeld	.03	.05
172	Ron Francis	.10	.20

BUFFALO SABRES

No.	Player	English	French
173	Phil Housley	.05	.10
174	Mike Foligno	.03	.05
175	Craig Ramsay	.03	.05
176	Bill Hajt	.03	.05
177	Dave Maloney	.03	.05
178	Brent Peterson	.03	.05
179	Tom Barrasso, Goalie	.15	.30
180	Michael Ramsey	.03	.05
181	Bob Sauve, Goalie	.03	.05
182	Ric Seiling	.03	.05
183	Paul Cyr	.03	.05
184	John Tucker	.03	.05
185	Gilles Hamel	.03	.05
186	Mal Davis	.03	.05
187	David Andreychuk	.20	.40
188	Gilbert Perreault	.03	.05

1984-85 LEADERS & TROPHIES

No.	Player	English	French
189	William Jennings Trophy Winner: Tom Barrasso, Goalie, Buf.	.10	.20
190	William Jennings Trophy Winner: Bob Sauve, Goalie, Buf.	.03	.05
191	Norris Trophy Winner: Paul Coffey, Edm.	.15	.30
192	Frank J. Selke Trophy Winner: Craig Ramsay, Buf.	.03	.05
193	Vezina Trophy Winner: Pelle Lindbergh, Goalie, Phi.	.35	.75
194	Jennings Trophy	.05	.10
195	Norris Trophy	.05	.10
196	Selke Trophy	.05	.10
197	Vezina Trophy	.05	.10
198	**Hart Trophy Winner:** Wayne Gretzky, Edm.	1.00	2.00
199	**Calder Trophy Winner:** Mario Lemieux, Pit.	2.00	4.00
200	**Bill Masterton Trophy Winner:** Anders Hedberg, NYR	.03	.05
201	**Lady Byng Trophy Winner:** Jari Kurri, Edm.	.07	.15
202	**Art Ross Trophy Winner:** Wayne Gretzky, Edm.	1.00	2.00
203	Hart Trophy	.05	.10
204	Calder Trophy	.05	.10
205	Masterton Trophy	.05	.10
206	Lady Byng Trophy	.05	.10
207	Art Ross Trophy	.05	.10

CALGARY FLAMES

No.	Player	English	French
208	Kent Nilsson	.03	.05
209	Paul Reinhart	.03	.05
210	Rejean Lemelin, Goalie	.03	.05
211	Allan MacInnis	.50	1.00
212	Jamie Macoun	.03	.05
213	Carey Wilson	.03	.05
214	Eddy Beers	.03	.05
215	Lanny McDonald	.15	.30

EDMONTON OILERS

No.	Player	English	French
216	Charles Huddy	.03	.05
217	Paul Coffey	.25	.50
218	Lee Fogolin	.03	.05
219	Kevin Lowe	.10	.20
220	Andrew Moog, Goalie	.07	.15
221	Grant Fuhr, Goalie	.10	.20
222	Wayne Gretzky	1.50	3.00
223	Michael Krushelnyski	.03	.05
224	Billy Carroll	.03	.05
225	Randall Gregg	.03	.05
226	Willy Lindstrom	.03	.05
227	Glenn Anderson	.07	.15
228	Mark Messier	.50	1.00
229	Pat Hughes	.03	.05
230	Kevin McClelland	.03	.05
231	Jari Kurri	.10	.20

LOS ANGELES KINGS

No.	Player	English	French
232	Bernie Nicholls	.10	.20
233	Brian Engblom	.03	.05
234	Mark Hardy	.03	.05
235	Marcel Dionne	.10	.20
236	Jim Fox	.03	.05
237	Terry Ruskowski	.03	.05
238	David Taylor	.03	.05
239	Bob Janecyk, Goalie	.03	.05

VANCOUVER CANUCKS

No.	Player	English	French
240	Thomas Gradin	.03	.05
241	Patrik Sundstrom	.03	.05
242	Al MacAdam	.03	.05
243	Doug Halward	.03	.05
244	Peter McNab	.03	.05
245	Tony Tanti	.03	.05
246	Moe Lemay	.03	.05
247	Stanley Smyl	.03	.05

WINNIPEG JETS

No.	Player	English	French
248	Dale Hawerchuk	.10	.20
249	David Babych	.03	.05
250	Paul MacLean	.03	.05
251	Randy Carlyle	.05	.10
252	Robert Picard	.03	.05
253	Thomas Steen	.03	.05
254	Laurie Boschman	.05	.10
255	Douglas Smail	.03	.05

— 1986 - 87 BOX BOTTOMS —

These cards were issued as the bottom wax box panel with four cards per panel. The set features team scoring leaders and each card is lettered.

1986-87 Box Bottoms, Panel No. 3
Mario Lemieux, Lanny McDonald
Bernie Nicholls, Mike Ridley

Panel Size: 5" X 7"
Face: Four colour; Name, Position, Team, Letter
Back: Blank
Imprint:
Complete Set No.: 4 Panels / 16 Cards
Complete Set: 12.50 / 25.00
Common Panel: .50 / 1.00
Common Card: .07 / .15

No.	Player	EX	NRMT
	Panel 1	.50	1.00
A	Gregory Adams, NJD	.07	.15
B	Mike Bossy, NYI	.50	1.00
C	Dave Christian, Wash.	.07	.15
D	Mike Foligno, Buf.	.07	.15
	Panel 2	.50	1.00
E	Michel Goulet, Que.	.25	.50
F	Wayne Gretzky, Edm.	.50	1.00
G	Tim Kerr, Phi.	.12	.25
H	Jari Kurri, Edm.	.35	.75
	Panel 3	7.50	15.00
I	Mario Lemieux, Pit.	7.50	15.00
J	Lanny McDonald, Cal.	.20	.40
K	Bernie Nicholls, LA	.20	.40
L	Mike Ridley, NYR	.07	.15
	Panel 4	.50	1.00
M	Larry Robinson, Mon.	.20	.40
N	Denis Savard, Chi.	.20	.40
O	Brian Sutter, St.L.	.07	.15
P	Bryan Trottier, NYI	.35	.75

— 1986 - 87 STICKERS —

An album was issued to hold these stickers. These stickers are issued in English only.

1986-87 Stickers
Sticker No. 19, Patrick Roy

Sticker Size: 2 1/8" X 3" or 1 1/2" X 2 1/8"
Face: Four colour, white border; Number
Back: Black on card stock; Name, Number
Imprint: © 1986 O-PEE-CHEE CO. LTD
Complete Set No.: 255
Complete Set Price: 17.50 / 35.00
Common Player: .03 / .05
Album: 5.00

1986 STANLEY CUP

No.	Player	EX	NRMT
1	Stanley Cup Finals	.03	.05
2	Stanley Cup Finals	.03	.05
3	Stanley Cup Finals	.03	.05
4	Stanley Cup Finals	.03	.05
5	Patrick Roy, Goalie, Mon. Conn Smythe Trophy Winner, M.V.P.	2.50	5.00

MONTREAL CANADIENS

No.	Player	EX	NRMT
6	Chris Chelios	.03	.05
7	Guy Carbonneau	.03	.05
8	Larry Robinson	.05	.10
9	Mario Tremblay	.03	.05
10	Tom Kurvers	.03	.05
11	Mats Naslund	.03	.05
12	Bob Gainey	.03	.05
13	Robert Smith	.03	.05
14	Craig Ludwig	.03	.05
15	Michael McPhee	.03	.05
16	Doug Soetaert, Goalie	.03	.05
17	Petr Svoboda	.03	.05
18	Kjell Dahlin	.03	.05
19	Patrick Roy, Goalie	2.50	5.00

QUEBEC NORDIQUES

No.	Player	EX	NRMT
20	Alain Cote	.03	.05
21	Mario Gosselin, Goalie	.03	.05
22	Michel Goulet	.05	.10
23	Jenn F. Sauve	.03	.05
24	Paul Gillis	.03	.05
25	Brent Ashton	.03	.05
26	Peter Stastny	.12	.25
27	Anton Stastny	.03	.05
28	Gilbert Delorme	.03	.05
29	Risto Siltanen	.03	.05
30	Robert Picard	.03	.05
31	David Shaw	.03	.05
32	Dale Hunter	.03	.05
33	Clint Malarchuk, Goalie	.03	.05

BOSTON BRUINS

No.	Player	EX	NRMT
34	Raymond Bourque	.25	.50
35	Rick Middleton	.03	.05
36	Charlie Simmer	.03	.05
37	Keith Crowder	.03	.05
38	Barry Pederson	.03	.05
39	Reed Larson	.03	.05
40	Stephen Kasper	.03	.05
41	Pat Riggin, Goalie	.03	.05

BUFFALO SABRES

No.	Player	EX	NRMT
42	Mike Foligno	.03	.05
43	Gilbert Perreault	.03	.05
44	Michael Ramsey	.03	.05
45	Tom Barrasso, Goalie	.05	.10
46	Brian Engblom	.03	.05
47	Phil Housley	.03	.05
48	John Tucker	.03	.05
49	David Andreychuk	.10	.20

HARTFORD WHALERS

No.	Player	EX	NRMT
50	David Babych	.03	.05
51	Ronald Francis	.07	.15
52	Michael Liut, Goalie	.03	.05
53	Sylvain Turgeon	.03	.05
54	John Anderson	.03	.05
55	Joel Quenneville	.03	.05
56	Kevin Dineen	.03	.05
57	Ray Ferraro	.05	.10

1985-86 ACTION

No.	Player	EX	NRMT
58	Action	.03	.05
59	Action	.03	.05
60	Action	.03	.05
61	Action	.03	.05
62	Action	.03	.05
63	Action	.03	.05
64	Action	.03	.05
65	Action	.03	.05

EDMONTON OILERS

No.	Player	EX	NRMT
66	Andrew Moog, Goalie	.10	.20
67	Grant Fuhr, Goalie	.12	.25
68	Paul Coffey	.20	.40
69	Charles Huddy	.03	.05
70	Kevin Lowe	.03	.05
71	Lee Fogolin	.03	.05
72	Wayne Gretzky	1.50	3.00
73	Jari Kurri	.10	.20
74	Michael Krushelnyski	.03	.05
75	Mark Napier	.03	.05
76	Craig MacTavish	.03	.05
77	Kevin McClelland	.03	.05
78	Glenn Anderson	.07	.15
79	Mark Messier	.35	.75

CALGARY FLAMES

No.	Player	EX	NRMT
80	Lanny McDonald	.05	.10
81	John Tonelli	.03	.05
82	Joe Mullen	.03	.05
83	Rejean Lemelin, Goalie	.03	.05
84	James Peplinski	.03	.05
85	Jamie Macoun	.03	.05
86	Allan MacInnis	.15	.30
87	Dan Quinn	.03	.05

LOS ANGELES KINGS

No.	Player	EX	NRMT
88	Marcel Dionne	.10	.20
89	Jim Fox	.03	.05
90	David Taylor	.03	.05
91	Bob Janecyk, Goalie	.03	.05
92	Gordon (Jay) Wells	.03	.05
93	Bryan Erikson	.03	.05
94	David Williams	.03	.05
95	Bernie Nicholls	.10	.20

VANCOUVER CANUCKS

No.	Player	EX	NRMT
96	Stanley Smyl	.03	.05
97	Doug Halward	.03	.05
98	Richard Brodeur, Goalie	.03	.05
99	Tony Tanti	.03	.05
100	Brent Peterson	.03	.05
101	Patrik Sundstrom	.03	.05
102	Doug Lidster	.03	.05
103	Petri Skriko	.03	.05

WINNIPEG JETS

No.	Player	EX	NRMT
104	Dale Hawerchuk	.10	.20
105	Bill Derlago	.03	.05
106	Ray Neufeld	.03	.05
107	Randy Carlyle	.03	.05
108	Paul MacLean	.03	.05
109	Brian Mullen	.03	.05
110	Thomas Steen	.03	.05
111	Laurie Boschman	.03	.05

ALL STARS FIRST TEAM

No.	Player	EX	NRMT
112	Paul Coffey, Edm.	.15	.30
113	Michel Goulet, Que.	.10	.20
114	John Vanbiesbrouck, Goalie, NYR	.10	.20
115	Wayne Gretzky, Edm.	1.25	2.50
116	Mark Howe, Phi.	.05	.10
117	Mike Bossy, NYI	.10	.20

ALL STARS SECOND TEAM

No.	Player	EX	NRMT
118	Jari Kurri, Edm.	.10	.20
119	Raymond Bourque, Bos.	.12	.25
120	Mario Lemieux, Pit.	.75	1.50

132 • O-PEE-CHEE — 1987-88 HOCKEY LEADERS

No.	Player	EX	NRMT
121	Grant Fuhr, Goalie, Edm.	.10	.20
122	Mats Naslund, Mon.	.05	.10
123	Larry Robinson, Mon.	.05	.10

1985-86 TOP ROOKIES

No.	Player	EX	NRMT
124	Chris Cichocki, Det.	.05	.10
125	Wendel Clark, Tor.	.50	1.00
126	Kjell Dahlin, Mon.	.05	.10
127	Per-Erik Eklund, Phi.	.05	.10
128	Jim Johnson, Pit.	.05	.10
129	Petr Klima, Det.	.25	.50
130	Joel Otto, Cal.	.05	.10
131	Mike Ridley, NYR	.05	.10
132	Patrick Roy, Goalie, Mon.	1.50	3.00
133	David Shaw, Que.	.05	.10
134	Gary Suter, Cal.	.05	.10
135	Steve Thomas, Tor.	.05	.10

TORONTO MAPLE LEAFS

No.	Player	EX	NRMT
136	Borje Salming	.05	.10
137	Gary Nylund	.03	.05
138	Richard Vaive	.03	.05
139	Don Edwards, Goalie	.03	.05
140	Steve Thomas	.03	.05
141	Wendel Clark	1.00	2.00
142	Miroslav Frycer	.03	.05
143	Tom Fergus	.03	.05
144	Marian Stastny	.03	.05
145	Brad Maxwell	.03	.05
146	Dan Daoust	.03	.05
147	Greg Terrion	.03	.05
148	Al Iafrate	.15	.30
149	Russell Courtnall	.35	.75

CHICAGO BLACK HAWKS

No.	Player	EX	NRMT
150	Denis Savard	.05	.10
151	Darryl Sutter	.03	.05
152	Bob Sauve, Goalie	.03	.05
153	Douglas Wilson, Jr.	.03	.05
154	Troy Murray	.03	.05
155	Alan Secord	.03	.05
156	Ed Olczyk	.03	.05
157	Steve Larmer	.05	.10

DETROIT RED WINGS

No.	Player	EX	NRMT
158	John Ogrodnick	.03	.05
159	Danny Gare	.03	.05
160	Michael O'Connell	.03	.05
161	Steve Yzerman	.25	.50
162	Petr Klima	.15	.30
163	Kelly Kisio	.03	.05
164	Douglas Shedden	.03	.05
165	Gregory Stefan, Goalie	.03	.05

MINNESOTA NORTH STARS

No.	Player	EX	NRMT
166	Neal Broten	.03	.05
167	Brian Bellows	.03	.05
168	Scott Bjugstad	.03	.05
169	Dino Ciccarelli	.07	.15
170	Dennis Maruk	.03	.05
171	Dirk Graham	.03	.05
172	Curt Giles	.03	.05
173	Craig Hartsburg	.03	.05

ST. LOUIS BLUES

No.	Player	EX	NRMT
174	Bernie Federko	.03	.05
175	Brian Sutter	.03	.05
176	Ron Flockhart	.03	.05
177	Douglas Gilmour	1.00	2.00
178	Charlie Bourgeois	.03	.05
179	Rick Wamsley, Goalie	.03	.05
180	George (Rob) Ramage	.03	.05
181	Mark Hunter	.03	.05

1985-86 LEAGUE LEADERS

No.	Player	EX	NRMT
182	Robert Froese, Goalie, Phi.	.03	.05
183	Wayne Gretzky, Edm.	1.25	2.50
184	Mark Howe, Phi.	.07	.15
185	Jari Kurri, Edm.	.10	.20

TROPHY WINNERS

No.	Player	EX	NRMT
186	William Jennings Trophy: Robert Froese, Goalie, Phi.	.03	.05
187	William Jennings Trophy: Darren Jensen, Phi.	.03	.05
188	Norris Trophy: Paul Coffey, Edm.	.10	.20
189	Frank J. Selke Trophy: Troy Murray, Chi.	.03	.05
190	Vezina Trophy: John Vanbiesbrouck, Goalie, NYR	.03	.05
191	Art Ross Trophy: Wayne Gretzky, Edm.	1.25	2.50
192	Calder Trohpy: Gary Suter, Cal.	.03	.05
193	Bill Masterton Trophy: Robert Froese, Goalie, Phi.	.03	.05
194	Lady Byng Trophy: Mike Bossy, NYI	.10	.20
195	Art Ross Trophy: Wayne Gretzky, Edm.	1.25	2.50

NEW JERSEY DEVILS

No.	Player	EX	NRMT
196	Gregory Adams	.03	.05
197	Dave Lewis	.03	.05
198	Joe Cirella	.03	.05
199	Rich Preston	.03	.05
200	Mark Johnson	.03	.05
201	Kirk Muller	.35	.75
202	Patrick Verbeek	.07	.15
203	Mel Bridgman	.03	.05

NEW YORK ISLANDERS

No.	Player	EX	NRMT
204	Bob Nystrom	.03	.05
205	Clark Gillies	.03	.05
206	Pat LaFontaine	.10	.20
207	Patrick Flatley	.03	.05
208	Bob Bourne	.03	.05
209	Denis Potvin	.12	.25
210	Duane Sutter	.03	.05
211	Brent Sutter	.03	.05
212	Kelly Hrudey, Goalie	.03	.05
213	Billy Smith, Goalie	.03	.05
214	Tomas Jonsson	.03	.05
215	Ken Morrow	.03	.05
216	Bryan Trottier	.10	.20
217	Mike Bossy	.15	.30

NEW YORK RANGERS

No.	Player	EX	NRMT
218	John Vanbiesbrouck, Goalie	.10	.20
219	Bob Brooke	.03	.05
220	James Patrick	.03	.05
221	Mike Ridley	.07	.15
222	Ronald Greschner	.03	.05
223	Thomas Laidlaw	.03	.05
224	Larry Melnyk	.03	.05
225	Reijo Ruotsalainen	.03	.05

PITTSBURGH PENGUINS

No.	Player	EX	NRMT
226	Terry Ruskowski	.03	.05
227	Willy Lindstrom	.03	.05
228	Mike Bullard	.03	.05
229	Roberto Romano, Goalie	.03	.05
230	John Chabot	.03	.05
231	Maurice Mantha	.03	.05
232	Doug Bodger	.03	.05
233	Mario Lemieux	1.50	3.00

PHILADELPHIA FLYERS

No.	Player	EX	NRMT
234	Glenn Resch, Goalie	.03	.05
235	Bradley Marsh	.03	.05
236	Robert Froese, Goalie	.03	.05
237	Doug Crossman	.03	.05
238	Ilkka Sinisalo	.03	.05
239	Brian Propp	.03	.05
240	Tim Kerr	.05	.10
241	David Poulin	.05	.10
242	Richard Sutter	.05	.10
243	Ronald Sutter	.05	.10
244	Murray Craven	.03	.05
245	Peter Zezel	.03	.05
246	Mark Howe	.07	.15
247	Byron (Brad) McCrimmon	.03	.05

WASHINGTON CAPITALS

No.	Player	EX	NRMT
248	Dave Christian	.03	.05
249	Rod Langway	.03	.05
250	Robert Carpenter	.03	.05
251	Michael Gartner	.12	.25
252	Al Jensen, Goalie	.03	.05
253	Craig Laughlin	.03	.05
254	Scott Stevens	.12	.25
255	Alan Haworth	.03	.05

— 1987-88 HOCKEY LEADERS —

Issued in five card cello packs, these minicards feature players who finished in the top five of any statistical category, won trophies or selected as all-stars.

1987-88 Hockey Leaders
Card No. 1, Glenn Anderson

Card Size: 2 1/8" X 3"
Face: Four colour, white border; Name
Back: Two colour, blue and pink on white card stock; Name, Number, Resume, Bilingual
Imprint: ©1987 O-Pee-Chee Co. Ltd. Made in Canada /Fabriqué au Canada
Complete Set No.: 42
Complete Set Price: 9.00 / 18.00
Common Player: .03 / .05
Wax Pack: (6 Cards): .60
Wax Box: (48 Packs): 25.00
Case: (24 Boxes): 450.00

No.	Player	EX	NRMT
1	Glenn Anderson, Edm.	.10	.20
2	Brian Benning, St.L.	.03	.05
3	Daniel Berthiaume, Goalie, Win.	.07	.15
4	Raymond Bourque, Bos.	.75	1.50
5	Shawn Burr, Det.	.05	.10
6	Jimmy Carson, LA	.20	.40
7	Dino Ciccarelli, Min.	.07	.15
8	Paul Coffey, Edm.	.35	.75
9	Per-Erik Eklund, Phi.	.05	.10
10	Ron Francis, Har.	.15	.30
11	Douglas Gilmour, St.L.	1.00	2.00
12	Michel Goulet, Que.	.10	.20
13	Wayne Gretzky, Edm.	3.00	6.00
14	Glen Hanlon, Goalie, Det.	.05	.10
15	Brian Hayward, Goalie, Mon.	.05	.10
16	Ron Hextall, Goalie, Phi.	.20	.40
17	Phil Housley, Buf.	.05	.10
18	Mark Howe, Phi.	.05	.10
19	Doug Jarvis, Har.	.03	.05
20	Tim Kerr, Phi.	.05	.10
21	Jari Kurri, Edm.	.20	.40
22	Pat LaFontaine, NYI	.15	.30
23	Mario Lemieux, Pit.	3.00	6.00

1987-88 BOX BOTTOMS — O-PEE-CHEE • 133

No.	Player	EX	NRMT
24	Michael Liut, Goalie, Har.	.05	.10
25	Kevin Lowe, Edm.	.05	.10
26	Al MacInnis, Cal.	.25	.50
27	Byron (Brad) McCrimmon, Phi.	.05	.10
28	Mark Messier, Edm.	1.00	2.00
29	Joe Mullen, Cal.	.10	.20
30	Craig Muni, Edm.	.03	.05
31	Lawrence Murphy, Wash.	.12	.25
32	David Poulin, Phi.	.05	.10
33	Brian Propp, Phi.	.15	.30
34	Paul Reinhart, Cal.	.05	.10
35	Luc Robitaille, LA	1.25	2.50
36	Patrick Roy, Goalie, Mon.	2.50	5.00
37	Christian Ruuttu, Buf.	.07	.15
38	Tomas Sandstrom, NYR	.15	.30
39	Denis Savard, Chi.	.15	.30
40	Petri Skriko, Van.	.05	.10
41	Bryan Trottier, NYI	.15	.30
42	Checklist (1-42)	.03	.05

— 1987-88 BOX BOTTOMS —

The cards were issued on box bottoms. The panel has four cards. The set features team scoring leaders.

1987-88 Box Bottoms, Panel No. 1,
Wayne Gretzky, Tim Kerr,
Steve Yzerman, Luc Robitaille

Panel Size: 5" X 7"
Face: Four colour, yellow border; Name, Team, Position
Back: Two colour, purple and black on card stock; Name, Position, Letter, Resume, Bilingual
Imprint: ©1987 O-Pee-Chee Ptd. in Canada/Imprimé au Canada
Complete Set No.: 4 Panels / 16 Cards
Complete Set Price: 7.50 15.00
Common Panel: .25 .50
Common Player: .05 .10

No.	Player	EX	NRMT
	Panel 1	5.00	10.00
A	Wayne Gretzky, Edm.	3.00	6.00
B	Tim Kerr, Phi.	.05	.10
C	Steve Yzerman, Det.	1.25	2.50
D	Luc Robitaille, LA	1.50	3.00
	Panel 2	1.50	3.00
E	Douglas Gilmour, St.L.	1.00	2.00
F	Raymond Bourque, Bos.	.50	1.00
G	Joe Mullen, Cal.	.10	.20
H	Lawrence Murphy, Wash.	.10	.20
	Panel 3	.50	1.00
I	Dale Hawerchuk, Win.	.20	.40
J	Ronald Francis, Har.	.20	.40
K	Walter Poddubny, NYR	.05	.10
L	Mats Naslund, Mon.	.05	.10
	Panel 4	1.00	2.00
M	Michel Goulet, Que.	.25	.50
N	Denis Savard, Chi.	.25	.50
O	Bryan Trottier, NYI	.35	.75
P	Russell Courtnall, Tor.	.35	.75

— 1987-88 STICKERS —

1987-88 Stickers
Sticker No. 6,   Sticker No. 43
Mats Naslund   Lanny McDonald

Card Size: 2 1/8" X 3"
Face: Four colour, white border; Name
Back: Two colour, blue and red on white card stock; Name, Number, Promotional offer, Bilingual
Imprint: © 1987 O-Pee-Chee Co. Ltd. Made In Canada and © 1987 O-PEE-CHEE LTEÉ FABRIQUÉ EN CANADA
Complete Set No.: 255
Complete Set Price: 16.00 32.00
Common Player: .03 .05
Album: 5.00

STANLEY CUP

No.	Player	EX	NRMT
1	Ron Hextall, Goalie, Phi., M.V.P.	.05	.10
2	Stanley Cup Action	.03	.05
3	Stanley Cup Action	.03	.05
4	Stanley Cup Action	.03	.05
5	Stanley Cup Action	.03	.05

MONTREAL CANADIENS

No.	Player	EX	NRMT
6	Mats Naslund	.03	.05
7	Guy Carbonneau	.10	.20
8	Gaston Gingras	.03	.05
9	Chris Chelios	.03	.05
10	Robert Smith	.03	.05
11	Richard Green	.03	.05
12	Bob Gainey	.03	.05
13	Patrick Roy, Goalie	1.25	2.50
14	Kjell Dahlin	.03	.05
15	Christopher Nilan	.03	.05
16	Larry Robinson	.03	.05
17	Ryan Walter	.03	.05
18	Petr Svoboda	.03	.05
19	Claude Lemieux	.50	1.00

ST. LOUIS BLUES

No.	Player	EX	NRMT
20	George (Rob) Ramage	.03	.05
21	Mark Hunter	.03	.05
22	Rick Wamsley, Goalie	.03	.05
23	Greg Palawski	.03	.05
24	Bernie Federko	.03	.05
25	Ron Flockhart	.03	.05
26	Tim Bothwell	.03	.05
27	Douglas Gilmour	.50	1.00
28	Kelly Kisio	.03	.05
29	Donald Maloney	.03	.05
30	James Patrick	.03	.05
31	Willie Huber	.03	.05
32	Walter Poddubny	.03	.05
33	John Vanbiesbrouck, Goalie	.07	.15
34	Marcel Dionne	.05	.10
35	Tomas Sandstrom	.07	.15

CALGARY FLAMES

No.	Player	EX	NRMT
36	Joe Mullen	.03	.05
37	Mike Bullard	.03	.05
38	Neil Sheehy	.03	.05
39	Paul Reinhart	.03	.05
40	Allan MacInnis	.12	.25
41	Michael Vernon, Goalie	.07	.15
42	Joel Otto	.10	.20
43	Lanny McDonald	.10	.20
44	Hakan Loob	.03	.05
45	Carey Wilson	.03	.05
46	James Peplinski	.03	.05
47	John Tonelli	.03	.05
48	Jamie Macoun	.03	.05
49	Gary Suter	.35	.75

MINNESOTA NORTH STARS

No.	Player	EX	NRMT
50	Dennis Maruk	.03	.05
51	Donald Beaupre, Goalie	.03	.05
52	Neal Broten	.03	.05
53	Brian Bellows	.03	.05
54	Craig Hartsburg	.03	.05
55	Gordon Roberts	.03	.05
56	Steve Payne	.03	.05
57	Dino Ciccarelli	.10	.20

NEW JERSEY DEVILS

No.	Player	EX	NRMT
58	Patrick Verbeek	.05	.10
59	Douglas Sulliman	.03	.05
60	Bruce Driver	.03	.05
61	Joe Cirella	.03	.05
62	Aaron Broten	.03	.05
63	Alain Chevrier, Goalie	.03	.05
64	Mark Johnson	.03	.05
65	Kirk Muller	.07	.15

ACTION STICKERS

No.	Player	EX	NRMT
66A	Face-off: Jim Sandlak, Van.	.03	.05
66B	Face-off: Stephen Kasper, Bos.	.03	.05
67	Raymond Bourque, Bos.; Tim Kerr, Phi.	.10	.20
68	Calgary vs Boston	.03	.05
69	Murray Craven, Phi.	.03	.05
70	Boston Bruins	.03	.05
71	New York Islanders	.03	.05
72	Sean Burke, Goalie, NJD	.03	.05
73	Patrick Roy, Goalie	.75	1.50

CHICAGO BLACK HAWKS

No.	Player	EX	NRMT
74	Alan Secord	.03	.05
75	Bob Sauve, Goalie	.03	.05
76	Ed Olczyk	.03	.05
77	Douglas Wilson, Jr.	.03	.05
78	Denis Savard	.05	.10
79	Troy Murray	.03	.05
80	Gary Nylund	.03	.05
81	Steve Larmer	.07	.15

EDMONTON OILERS

No.	Player	EX	NRMT
82	Jari Kurri	.10	.20
83	Esa Tikkanen	.05	.10
84	Kevin Lowe	.07	.15
85	Grant Fuhr, Goalie	.12	.25
86	Wayne Gretzky	1.50	3.00
87	Charles Huddy	.03	.05
88	Kent Nilsson	.03	.05
89	Paul Coffey	.12	.25
90	Michael Krushelnyski	.03	.05
91	Craig MacTavish	.03	.05
92	Mark Messier	.35	.75
93	Andrew Moog, Goalie	.07	.15
94	Randall Gregg	.03	.05
95	Glenn Anderson	.12	.25

PHILADELPHIA FLYERS

No.	Player	EX	NRMT
96	Peter Zezel	.03	.05
97	Brian Propp	.03	.05
98	David Poulin	.03	.05
99	Byron (Brad) McCrimmon	.03	.05
100	Mark Howe	.03	.05
101	Ron Hextall, Goalie	.05	.10
102	Ronald Sutter	.03	.05
103	Tim Kerr	.03	.05

134 • O-PEE-CHEE — 1988 - 89 NHL STARS —

DETROIT RED WINGS

No.	Player	EX	NRMT
104	Petr Klima	.03	.05
105	Adam Oates	.35	.75
106	Gerard Gallant	.03	.05
107	Michael O'Connell	.03	.05
108	Brent Ashton	.03	.05
109	Glen Hanlon, Goalie	.03	.05
110	Harold Snepsts	.03	.05
111	Steve Yzerman	.25	.50

ALL STARS

No.	Player	EX	NRMT
112	Mark Howe, Phi.	.03	.05
113	Michel Goulet, Que.	.07	.15
114	Ron Hextall, Goalie, Phi.	.05	.10
115	Wayne Gretzky, Edm.	.75	1.50
116	Raymond Bourque, Bos.	.25	.50
117	Jari Kurri, Edm.	.10	.20
118	Dino Ciccarelli, Min.	.03	.05
119	Lawrence Murphy, Wash.	.07	.15
120	Mario Lemieux, Phi.	.75	1.50
121	Michael Liut, Goalie, Har.	.05	.10
122	Luc Robitaille, LA	.20	.40
123	Al MacInnis, Cal.	.10	.20

ROOKIES

No.	Player	EX	NRMT
124	Brian Benning, St.L.	.03	.05
125	Shawn Burr, Det.	.03	.05
126	Jimmy Carson, LA	.15	.30
127	Shayne Corson, Mon.	.10	.20
128	Vincent Damphousse, Tor.	.35	.75
129	Ron Hextall, Goalie, Phi.	.03	.05
130	Jason Lafreniere, Que.	.03	.05
131	Ken Leiter, NYI	.03	.05
132	Allen Pedersen, Bos.	.03	.05
133	Luc Robitaille, LA	.25	.50
134	Christian Ruuttu, Buf.	.03	.05
135	Jim Sandlak, Van.	.03	.05

BOSTON BRUINS

No.	Player	EX	NRMT
136	Keith Crowder	.03	.05
137	Charlie Simmer	.03	.05
138	Rick Middleton	.03	.05
139	Doug Keans, Goalie	.03	.05
140	Raymond Bourque	.25	.50
141	Tom McCarthy	.03	.05
142	Reed Larson	.03	.05
143	Cam Neely	.20	.40

BUFFALO SABRES

No.	Player	EX	NRMT
144	Christian Ruuttu	.03	.05
145	John Tucker	.03	.05
146	Steve Dykstra	.03	.05
147	David Andreychuk	.10	.20
148	Tom Barrasso, Goalie	.10	.20
149	Michael Ramsey	.03	.05
150	Mike Foligno	.03	.05
151	Phil Housley	.07	.15

TORONTO MAPLE LEAFS

No.	Player	EX	NRMT
152	Wendel Clark	.50	1.00
153	Greg Terrion	.03	.05
154	Steve Thomas	.03	.05
155	Richard Vaive	.03	.05
156	Russell Courtnall	.25	.50
157	Rick Lanz	.03	.05
158	Miroslav Frycer	.03	.05
159	Tom Fergus	.03	.05
160	Al Iafrate	.03	.05
161	Gary Leeman	.03	.05
162	Allan Bester, Goalie	.03	.05
163	Todd Gill	.03	.05
164	Ken Wregget, Goalie	.03	.05
165	Borje Salming	.10	.20

PITTSBURGH PENGUINS

No.	Player	EX	NRMT
166	Craig Simpson	.10	.20
167	Terry Ruskowski	.03	.05
168	Gilles Meloche, Goalie	.03	.05
169	John Chabot	.03	.05
170	Mario Lemieux	1.50	3.00
171	Maurice Mantha	.03	.05
172	Jim Johnson	.03	.05
173	Dan Quinn	.03	.05

1987-88 LEAGUE LEADERS

No.	Player	EX	NRMT
174	Wayne Gretzky, Edm.	.75	1.50
175	Brian Hayward, Goalie, Mon.	.03	.05
176	Mark Howe, Phi.	.03	.05
177	Luc Robitaille, LA	.25	.50
178	Raymond Bourque, Bos.	.12	.25
179	David Poulin, Phi.	.03	.05
180	**Hart Trophy Winner:** Wayne Gretzky, Edm.	.75	1.50
181	**Ross Trophy Winner:** Wayne Gretzky, Edm.	.75	1.50
182	Ron Hextall, Goalie, Phi.	.07	.15
183	Doug Jarvis, Har.	.03	.05
184	Brian Hayward, Goalie, Tor., Mon.	.03	.05
185	Patrick Roy, Goalie, Mon.	1.00	2.00
186	Joe Mullen, Cal.	.03	.05
187	Luc Robitaille, LA	.25	.50

VANCOUVER CANUCKS

No.	Player	EX	NRMT
188	Barry Pederson	.03	.05
189	Richard Brodeur, Goalie	.03	.05
190	Dave Richter	.03	.05
191	Doug Lidster	.03	.05
192	Petri Skriko	.03	.05
193	Richard Sutter	.03	.05
194	Jim Sandlak	.03	.05
195	Tony Tanti	.03	.05
196	Michel Petit	.03	.05
197	Jim Benning	.03	.05
198	Stanley Smyl	.03	.05
199	Brent Peterson	.03	.05
200	Garth Butcher	.03	.05
201	Patrik Sundstrom	.03	.05

HARTFORD WHALERS

No.	Player	EX	NRMT
202	Kevin Dineen	.03	.05
203	Sylvain Turgeon	.03	.05
204	John Anderson	.03	.05
205	Ulf Samuelsson	.03	.05
206	Ronald Francis	.07	.15
207	Doug Jarvis	.03	.05
208	David Babych	.03	.05
209	Michael Liut, Goalie	.03	.05

LOS ANGELES KINGS

No.	Player	EX	NRMT
210	Jimmy Carson	.12	.25
211	Larry Playfair	.03	.05
212	Gordon (Jay) Wells	.03	.05
213	Roland Melanson, Goalie	.03	.05
214	Bernie Nicholls	.03	.05
215	David Taylor	.03	.05
216	Jim Fox	.03	.05
217	Luc Robitaille	.50	1.00

QUEBEC NORDIQUES

No.	Player	EX	NRMT
218	John Ogrodnick	.03	.05
219	Jason Lafreniere	.03	.05
220	Mike Hough	.03	.05
221	Paul Gillis	.03	.05
222	Peter Stastny	.07	.15
223	David Shaw	.03	.05
224	Bill Derlago	.03	.05
225	Michel Goulet	.05	.10
226	Douglas Shedden	.03	.05
227	Basil McRae	.03	.05
228	Anton Stastny	.03	.05

No.	Player	EX	NRMT
229	Randy Moller	.03	.05
230	Robert Picard	.03	.05
231	Mario Gosselin, Goalie	.03	.05

WASHINGTON CAPITALS

No.	Player	EX	NRMT
232	Lawrence Murphy	.07	.15
233	Scott Stevens	.10	.20
234	Mike Ridley	.03	.05
235	Dave Christian	.03	.05
236	Rod Langway	.05	.10
237	Robert Gould	.03	.05
238	Bob Mason, Goalie	.03	.05
239	Michael Gartner	.12	.25

NEW YORK ISLANDERS

No.	Player	EX	NRMT
240	Bryan Trottier	.07	.15
241	Brent Sutter	.03	.05
242	Kelly Hrudey, Goalie	.03	.05
243	Pat LaFontaine	.15	.30
244	Mike Bossy	.15	.30
245	Patrick Flatley	.03	.05
246	Ken Morrow	.03	.05
247	Denis Potvin	.07	.15

WINNIPEG JETS

No.	Player	EX	NRMT
248	Randy Carlyle	.03	.05
249	Daniel Berthiaume, Goalie	.03	.05
250	Mario Marois	.03	.05
251	Dave Ellett	.03	.05
252	Paul MacLean	.03	.05
253	Gilles Hamel	.03	.05
254	Douglas Smail	.03	.05
255	Dale Hawerchuk	.07	.15

— 1988 - 89 NHL STARS —

Issued in five-card cello packs this set of minicards features players who finished in the top five of any statistical category, won trophies or selected as all-stars.

1988-89 NHL Stars
Card No. 1, Tom Barrasso

Card Size: 2 1/8" X 3"
Face: Four colour, white border; Name
Back: Two colour, pink and purple on white card stock; Name, Number, Resume, Bilingual
Imprint: ©1988 O-PEE-CHEE CO. LTD. PTD. IN CANADA/ IMPRIMÉ AU CANADA
Complete Set No.: 46
Complete Set Price: 7.50 15.00
Common Player: .03 .05
Wax Pack: (6 Cards) .75
Wax Box: (48 Packs) 25.00
Case: (24 Boxes) 500.00

No.	Player	EX	NRMT
1	Tom Barrasso, Goalie, Buf.	.15	.30
2	Bob Bourne, LA	.03	.05
3	Raymond Bourque, Bos.	.50	1.00
4	Guy Carbonneau, Mon.	.05	.10
5	Jimmy Carson, Edm.	.15	.30
6	Paul Coffey, Pit.	.25	.50

1988-89 BOX BOTTOMS — O-PEE-CHEE • 135

No.	Player	EX	NRMT
7	Ulf Dahlen, NYR	.05	.10
8	Marcel Dionne, NYR	.25	.50
9	Grant Fuhr, Goalie, Edm.	.25	.50
10	Michel Goulet, Que.	.10	.20
11	Wayne Gretzky, LA	2.00	4.00
12	Dale Hawerchuk, Win.	.12	.25
13	Brian Hayward, Goalie, Mon.	.05	.10
14	Ron Hextall, Goalie, Phi.	.12	.25
15	Anthony Hrkac, St.L.	.05	.10
16	Brett Hull, St.L.	3.50	7.00
17	Steve Larmer, Chi.	.10	.20
18	Rejean Lemelin, Goalie, Bos.	.05	.10
19	Mario Lemieux, Pit.	2.00	4.00
20	Michael Liut, Goalie, Har.	.05	.10
21	Hakan Loob, Cal.	.05	.10
22	Al MacInnis, Cal.	.15	.30
23	Paul MacLean, Win.	.05	.10
24	Byron (Brad) McCrimmon, Cal.	.05	.10
25	Mark Messier, Edm.	.50	1.00
26	Mats Naslund, Mon.	.10	.20
27	Cam Neely, Bos.	.25	.50
28	Bernie Nicholls, LA	.15	.30
29	Joe Nieuwendyk, Cal.	.50	1.00
30	Pete Peeters, Goalie, Wash.	.05	.10
31	Stephane J.J. Richer, Mon.	.15	.30
32	Luc Robitaille, LA	.50	1.00
33	Patrick Roy, Goalie, Mon.	2.00	4.00
34	Denis Savard, Chi.	.15	.30
35	Ray Sheppard, Buf.	.03	.05
36	Craig Simpson, Edm.	.15	.30
37	Peter Stastny, Que.	.15	.30
38	Gregory Stefan, Goalie, Det.	.05	.10
39	Scott Stevens, Wash.	.10	.20
40	Gary Suter, Cal.	.10	.20
41	Petr Svoboda, Mon.	.03	.05
42	John Vanbiesbrouck, Goalie, NYR	.35	.75
43	Patrick Verbeek, NJD	.10	.20
44	Michael Vernon, Goalie, Cal.	.15	.30
45	Carey Wilson, Har.	.03	.05
46	Checklist (1-46)	.03	.05

— 1988-89 BOX BOTTOMS —

These cards were issued as the bottom wax box panel with four cards per panel. The set features team scoring leaders.

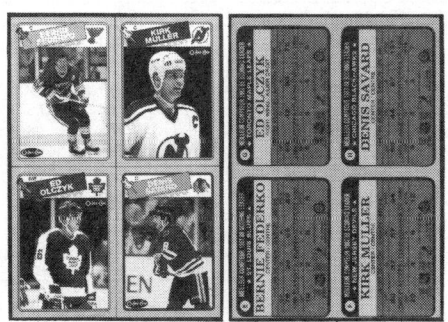

1988-89 Box Bottoms, Panel No. 2
B. Federko, K. Muller, E. Olczyk, D. Savard

Panel Size: 5" X 7"
Face: Four colour, grey border; Name, Position, Team logo
Back: Two colour, black and yellow on card stock; Name, Letter, Resume, Bilingual
Imprint: © O-PEE-CHEE CO. LTD. PTD IN CANADA /IMPRIMÉ AU CANADA
Complete Set No.: 4 Panels / 16 Cards
Complete Set: 4.00 8.00
Common Panel: .50 1.00
Common Player: .05 .10

No.	Player	EX	NRMT
	Panel 1	2.50	5.00
A	Ronald Francis, Har.	.10	.20
B	Wayne Gretzky, LA	2.50	5.00
C	Pat LaFontaine, NYI	.15	.30
D	Bobby Smith, Mon.	.15	.30
	Panel 2	.50	1.00
E	Bernie Federko, St.L.	.10	.20
F	Kirk Muller, NJD	.10	.20
G	Ed Olczyk, Tor.	.10	.20
H	Denis Savard, Chi.	.25	.50
	Panel 3	1.00	2.00
I	Raymond Bourque, Bos.	.50	1.00
J	Murray Craven, Phi.	.10	.20
	Brian Propp, Phi.		
K	Dale Hawerchuk, Win.	.15	.30
L	Steve Yzerman, Det.	.50	1.00
	Panel 4	1.00	2.00
M	Dave Andreychuk, Buf.	.25	.50
N	Mike Gartner, Wash.	.25	.50
O	Hakan Loob, Cal.	.05	.10
P	Luc Robitaille, LA	.50	1.00

— 1988-89 STICKERS —

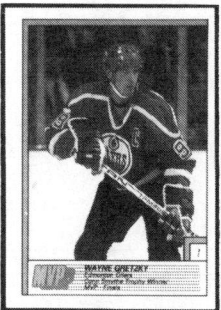 

1988-89 Stickers
Sticker No. 1, Wayne Gretzky
Sticker No. 103, Ron Hextall

Sticker Size: 2 1/2" X 3 1/2"
Face: Four colour, white border; Number
Back: Two colour, either blue and black or red and black or black on white card stock; Bilingual, Promotional offer
Imprint: © 1988 O-PEE-CHEE CO. LTD. PTD. IN CANADA/ IMPRIMÉ AU CANADA or
©1988 O-PEE-CHEE CO. LTD. MADE IN CANADA or
©1988 O-PEE-CHEE CIE LTÉE FABRIQUÉ AU CANADA
Complete Set No.: 270
Complete Set Price: 16.00 32.00
Common Player: .03 .05
Album: 5.00

1988 STANLEY CUP CHAMPIONSHIP

No.	Player	EX	NRMT
1	Wayne Gretzky, LA, Conn Smythe Trophy Winner, M.V.P.	1.00	2.00
2	Oilers vs Bruins	.03	.05
3	Oilers vs Bruins	.03	.05
4	Oilers vs Bruins	.03	.05
5	Oilers vs Bruins	.03	.05

CHICAGO BLACK HAWKS

No.	Player	EX	NRMT
6	Douglas Wilson, Jr.	.03	.05
7	Dirk Graham	.03	.05
8	Darren Pang, Goalie	.03	.05
9	Richard Vaive	.03	.05
10	Troy Murray	.03	.05
11	Brian Noonan	.03	.05
12	Steve Larmer	.05	.10
13	Denis Savard	.07	.15

ST. LOUIS BLUES

No.	Player	EX	NRMT
14	Mark Hunter	.03	.05
15	Brian Sutter	.03	.05
16	Brett Hull	1.00	2.00
17	Anthony McKegney	.03	.05
18	Brian Benning	.03	.05
19	Anthony Hrkac	.03	.05
20	Douglas Gilmour	.50	1.00
21	Bernie Federko	.03	.05

BOSTON BRUINS

No.	Player	EX	NRMT
22	Cam Neely	.10	.20
23	Raymond Bourque	.10	.20
24	Rejean Lemelin, Goalie	.03	.05
25	Gordon Kluzak	.03	.05
26	Rick Middleton	.03	.05
27	Stephen Kasper	.03	.05
28	Robert Sweeney	.03	.05
29	Randy Burridge	.03	.05

1987-88 NHL ACTION

No.	Player	EX	NRMT
30	Whalers vs Bruins	.03	.05
31	Canadiens vs Bruins	.03	.05
32	Canadiens vs Bruins	.03	.05
33	Blues vs Devils	.03	.05
34	Canadiens vs Bruins	.03	.05
35	Canadiens vs Bruins	.03	.05
36	Canadiens vs Bruins	.03	.05
37	Canadiens vs Bruins	.03	.05
38	Canadiens vs Bruins	.03	.05

MONTREAL CANADIENS

No.	Player	EX	NRMT
39	Larry Robinson	.03	.05
40	Ryan Walter	.03	.05
41	Guy Carbonneau	.07	.25
42	Bob Gainey	.03	.05
43	Claude Lemieux	.05	.10
44	Petr Svoboda	.03	.05
45	Patrick Roy, Goalie	1.25	2.50
46	Robert Smith	.03	.05
47	Michael McPhee	.03	.05
48	Craig Ludwig	.03	.05
49	Stephane J.J. Richer	.10	.20
50	Mats Naslund	.03	.05
51	Chris Chelios	.10	.20
52	Brian Hayward, Goalie	.03	.05

VANCOUVER CANUCKS

No.	Player	EX	NRMT
53	Larry Melnyk	.03	.05
54	Garth Butcher	.03	.05
55	Kirk McLean, Goalie	.05	.10
56	Douglas Wickenheiser	.03	.05
57	Richard Sutter	.03	.05
58	Jim Benning	.03	.05
59	Tony Tanti	.03	.05
60	Stanley Smyl	.03	.05
61	David Saunders	.03	.05
62	Steve Tambellini	.03	.05
63	Doug Lidster	.03	.05
64	Petri Skriko	.03	.05
65	Barry Pederson	.03	.05
66	Gregory Adams	.03	.05

WASHINGTON CAPITALS

No.	Player	EX	NRMT
67	Michael Gartner	.12	.25
68	Scott Stevens	.10	.20
69	Rod Langway	.03	.05
70	Dave Christian	.03	.05
71	Lawrence Murphy	.10	.20
72	Clint Malarchuk, Goalie	.03	.05
73	Dale Hunter	.03	.05
74	Mike Ridley	.05	.10

NEW JERSEY DEVILS

No.	Player	EX	NRMT
75	Kirk Muller	.20	.40
76	Aaron Broten	.03	.05
77	Bruce Driver	.03	.05
78	John MacLean	.03	.05
79	Joe Cirella	.03	.05
80	Doug Brown	.03	.05
81	Patrick Verbeek	.07	.15
82	Sean Burke, Goalie	.03	.05

O-PEE-CHEE — 1989-90 STICKERS

CALGARY FLAMES

No.	Player	EX	NRMT
83	Joel Otto	.03	.05
84	George (Rob) Ramage	.03	.05
85	Lanny McDonald	.07	.15
86	Michael Vernon, Goalie	.05	.10
87	John Tonelli	.03	.05
88	James Peplinski	.03	.05
89	Gary Suter	.03	.05
90	Joe Nieuwendyk	.20	.40
91	Eric Nattress	.03	.05
92	Al MacInnis	.05	.10
93	Mike Bullard	.03	.05
94	Hakan Loob	.03	.05
95	Joe Mullen	.07	.15
96	Byron (Brad) McCrimmon	.03	.05

PHILADELPHIA FLYERS

No.	Player	EX	NRMT
97	Brian Propp	.03	.05
98	Murray Craven	.03	.05
99	Rick Tocchet	.07	.15
100	Doug Crossman	.03	.05
101	Bradley Marsh	.03	.05
102	Peter Zezel	.03	.05
103	Ron Hextall, Goalie	.05	.10
104	Mark Howe	.05	.10

NEW YORK ISLANDERS

No.	Player	EX	NRMT
105	Brent Sutter	.03	.05
106	Alan Kerr	.03	.05
107	Randy Wood	.03	.05
108	Mikko Makela	.03	.05
109	Kelly Hrudey, Goalie	.03	.05
110	Steve Konroyd	.03	.05
111	Pat LaFontaine	.25	.50
112	Bryan Trottier	.10	.20

ALL STARS FIRST TEAM

No.	Player	EX	NRMT
113	Gary Suter, Cal.	.10	.20
114	Luc Robitaille, LA	.15	.30
115	Patrick Roy, Goalie, Mon.	1.00	2.00
116	Mario Lemieux, Pit.	1.00	2.00
117	Raymond Bourque, Bos.	.05	.10
118	Hakan Loob, Cal.	.03	.05

ALL STARS SECOND TEAM

No.	Player	EX	NRMT
119	Mike Bullard, Cal.	.03	.05
120	Byron (Brad) McCrimmon, Cal.	.03	.05
121	Wayne Gretzky, LA	1.00	2.00
122	Grant Fuhr, Goalie, Edm.	.05	.10
123	Craig Simpson, Edm.	.03	.05
124	Mark Howe, Phi.	.03	.05

1987-88 TOP ROOKIES

No.	Player	EX	NRMT
125	Joe Nieuwendyk, Cal.	.20	.40
126	Ray Sheppard, Buf.	.03	.05
127	Brett Hull, St.L.	.75	1.50
128	Ulf Dahlen, NYR	.03	.05
129	Anthony Hrkac, St.L.	.03	.05
130	Robert Sweeney, Bos.	.03	.05
131	Rob Brown, Pit.	.10	.20
132	Iain Duncan, Win.	.03	.05
133	Pierre Turgeon, Buf.	.50	1.00
134	Calle Johansson, Buf.	.03	.05
135	Darren Pang, Goalie, Chi.	.03	.05
136	Kirk McLean, Goalie, Van.	.25	.50

WINNIPEG JETS

No.	Player	EX	NRMT
137	Douglas Smail	.03	.05
138	Thomas Steen	.03	.05
139	Laurie Boschman	.03	.05
140	Iain Duncan	.03	.05
141	Ray Neufeld	.03	.05
142	Mario Marois	.03	.05
143	Dale Hawerchuk	.05	.10
144	Paul MacLean	.03	.05
145	James Kyte	.03	.05
146	Eldon Reddick, Goalie	.03	.05
147	Andrew McBain	.03	.05
148	Randy Carlyle	.03	.05
149	Daniel Berthiaume, Goalie	.03	.05
150	Dave Ellett	.03	.05

LOS ANGELES KINGS

No.	Player	EX	NRMT
151	Roland Melanson, Goalie	.03	.05
152	Steve Duchesne	.05	.10
153	Robert Carpenter	.03	.05
154	Jim Fox	.03	.05
155	David Taylor	.03	.05
156	Bernie Nicholls	.10	.20
157	Luc Robitaille	.25	.50
158	Jimmy Carson	.03	.05

1987-88 ACTION

No.	Player	EX	NRMT
159	Bruins vs Canadiens	.03	.05
160	Nordiques vs Devils	.03	.05
161	Nordiques vs Devils	.03	.05
162	North Stars vs Devils	.03	.05
163	Oilers vs Devils	.03	.05
164	Oilers vs Devils	.03	.05
165	Oilers vs Devils	.03	.05
166	Oilers vs Devils	.03	.05
167	Bruins vs Canadiens	.03	.05

TORONTO MAPLE LEAFS

No.	Player	EX	NRMT
168	Mark Osborne	.03	.05
169	Dan Daoust	.03	.05
170	Tom Fergus	.03	.05
171	Vincent Damphousse	.12	.25
172	Wendel Clark	.25	.50
173	Luke Richardson	.03	.05
174	Borje Salming	.10	.20
175	Russell Courtnall	.07	.15
176	Rick Lanz	.03	.05
177	Ken Wregget, Goalie	.03	.05
178	Gary Leeman	.03	.05
179	Alan Secord	.03	.05
180	Al Iafrate	.07	.15
181	Ed Olczyk	.03	.05

QUEBEC NORDIQUES

No.	Player	EX	NRMT
182	Normand Rochefort	.03	.05
183	Lane Lambert	.03	.05
184	Tommy Albelin	.03	.05
185	Jason Lafreniere	.03	.05
186	Alain Cote	.03	.05
187	Gaetan Duchesne	.03	.05
188	Michel Goulet	.07	.15
189	Peter Stastny	.12	.25
190	Jeff Jackson	.03	.05
191	Mike Eagles	.03	.05
192	Jeff Brown	.07	.15
193	Mario Gosselin, Goalie	.03	.05
194	Anton Stastny	.03	.05
195	Alan Haworth	.03	.05

MINNESOTA NORTH STARS

No.	Player	EX	NRMT
196	Donald Beaupre, Goalie	.03	.05
197	Brian MacLellan	.03	.05
198	Brian Lawton	.03	.05
199	Craig Hartsburg	.03	.05
200	Maurice Mantha	.03	.05
201	Neal Broten	.03	.05
202	Dino Ciccarelli	.10	.20
203	Brian Bellows	.10	.20

1987-88 LEAGUE LEADERS

No.	Player	EX	NRMT
204	Mario Lemieux, Pit.	.75	1.50
205	Joe Nieuwendyk, Cal.	.20	.40
206	Byron (Brad) McCrimmon, Cal.	.20	.40
207	Peter Peeters, Goalie, Wash.	.03	.05
208	Norris Trophy Winner: Raymond Bourque, Bos.	.07	.15
209	Frank J. Selke Trophy Winner: Guy Carbonneau, Mon.	.07	.15
210	Hart Trophy Winner: Mario Lemieux, Pit.	.75	1.50
211	Art Ross Trophy Winner: Mario Lemieux, Pit.	.75	1.50
212	Vezina Trophy Winner: Grant Fuhr, Goalie, Edm.	.10	.20
213	Bill Masterton Trophy Winner: Bob Bourne	.03	.05
214	William Jennings Trophy Winners: Brian Hayward; Patrick Roy, Goalie, Mon.	.75	1.50
215	Lady Byng Trophy Winner: Mats Naslund, Mon.	.03	.05
216	Calder Trophy Winner: Joe Nieuwendyk, Cal	.12	.25

EDMONTON OILERS

No.	Player	EX	NRMT
217	Craig MacTavish	.03	.05
218	Chris Joseph	.03	.05
219	Kevin Lowe	.03	.05
220	Esa Tikkanen	.03	.05
221	Charles Huddy	.03	.05
222	Geoff Courtnall	.10	.20
223	Grant Fuhr, Goalie	.10	.20
224	Wayne Gretzky	1.25	2.50
225	James (Steve) Smith	.05	.10
226	Michael Krushelnyski	.03	.05
227	Jari Kurri	.07	.15
228	Craig Simpson	.03	.05
229	Glenn Anderson	.03	.05
230	Mark Messier	.35	.75

PITTSBURGH PENGUINS

No.	Player	EX	NRMT
231	Randy Cunneyworth	.03	.05
232	Mario Lemieux	1.25	2.50
233	Paul Coffey	.03	.05
234	Doug Bodger	.03	.05
235	Dave Hunter	.03	.05
236	Dan Quinn	.03	.05
237	Rob Brown	.10	.20
238	Gilles Meloche, Goalie	.03	.05

NEW YORK RANGERS

No.	Player	EX	NRMT
239	Kelly Kisio	.03	.05
240	Walter Poddubny	.03	.05
241	John Vanbiesbrouck, Goalie	.25	.50
242	Tomas Sandstrom	.03	.05
243	David Shaw	.03	.05
244	Marcel Dionne	.05	.10
245	Christopher Nilan	.03	.05
246	James Patrick	.03	.05

DETROIT RED WINGS

No.	Player	EX	NRMT
247	Bob Probert	.15	.30
248	Michael O'Connell	.03	.05
249	Jeff Sharples	.03	.05
250	Brent Ashton	.03	.05
251	Petr Klima	.03	.05
252	Gregory Stefan, Goalie	.03	.05
253	Steve Yzerman	.25	.50
254	Gerald Gallant	.03	.05

BUFFALO SABRES

No.	Player	EX	NRMT
255	Phil Housley	.03	.05
256	Christian Ruuttu	.03	.05
257	Mike Foligno	.03	.05
258	Scott Arniel	.03	.05
259	Tom Barrasso, Goalie	.12	.25
260	Michael Ramsey	.03	.05
261	David Andreychuk	.12	.25
262	Ray Sheppard	.03	.05

HARTFORD WHALERS

No.	Player	EX	NRMT
263	Michael Liut, Goalie	.03	.05
264	Ron Francis	.05	.10
265	Ulf Samuelsson	.03	.05
266	Carey Wilson	.03	.05
267	Dave Babych	.03	.05
268	Ray Ferraro	.03	.05
269	Kevin Dineen	.03	.05
270	John Anderson	.03	.05

— 1988 - 89 FUTURE STARS —

These "Future Stars" insert cards appear on the back of sticker nos. 53/184, 23, 63, 158, 126/258, 108/238, 123/255, 36, 81/210, 90, 254, 189, 11/140, 134/270, 147, 18/151, 74/205, 161, 68, 69/198, 85/215, 202. After the sticker has been removed you are left with the insert card.

1988-89 Future Stars
Card No. 9, Brett Hull
Card No. 19, Robert Sweeney

Card Size: 2 1/8" X 3"
Face: Four colour, white border; Number
Back: Four colour on card stock; Name, Number, Position, Team
Imprint: ©O-PEE-CHEE PTD IN CANADA/IMPRIMÉ AU CANADA
Complete Set No.: 22
Complete Set Price: 5.00 10.00
Common Player: .05 .10

No.	Player	EX	NRMT
1	Dave Archibald, Min.	.05	.10
2	Doug Brown, NJD	.05	.10
3	Rob Brown, Pit.	.25	.50
4	Sean Burke, Goalie, NJD	.15	.30
5	Ulf Dahlen, NYR	.10	.20
6	Iain Duncan, Win.	.05	.10
7	Glenn Healy, Goalie, LA	.05	.10
8	Anthony Hrkac, St.L.	.05	.10
9	Brett Hull, St.L.	2.50	5.00
10	Craig Janney, Bos.	.50	1.00
11	Calle Johansson, Buf.	.05	.10
12	Brian Leetch, NYR	1.50	3.00
13	Kirk McLean, Goalie, Van.	.10	.20
14	Joe Nieuwendyk, Cal.	.50	1.00
15	Brian Noonan, Chi.	.05	.10
16	Darren Pang, Goalie, Chi.	.10	.20
17	Jeff Sharples, Det.	.05	.10
18	Ray Sheppard, Buf.	.75	1.50
19	Robert Sweeney, Bos.	.05	.10
20	Pierre Turgeon, Buf.	1.00	2.00
21	Glen Wesley, Bos.	.10	.20
22	Randy Wood, NYI	.05	.10

— 1989 - 90 BOX BOTTOMS —

These box bottom cards feature the 1988-89 scoring leaders.

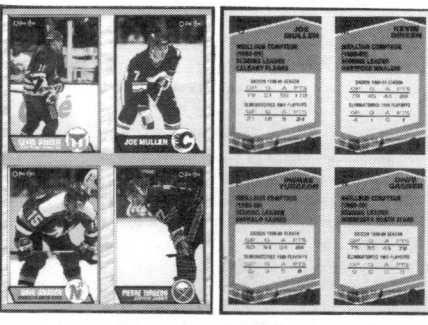

1989-90 Box Bottoms, Panel 4,
K. Dineen, D. Gagner, J. Mullen, P. Turgeon

Panel Size: 5" x 7"
Face: Four colour, blue and marble border, Name, Team, Logo
Back: Red and black on card stock, Name, Letter, Resume, Bilingual
Imprint: © 1989 O-PEE-CHEE CO. LTD. PTD. IN CANADA/ IMPRIMÉ AU CANADA © 1989 NHLPA
Complete Set No.: 4 Panels / 16 Cards
Complete Set Price: 2.50 5.00
Common Panel: .25 .50
Common Player: .05 .10

No.	Player	EX	NRMT
	Panel 1	.50	1.00
A	Mario Lemieux, Pit.	.50	1.00
B	Mike Ridley, Wash.	.05	.10
C	Tomas Sandstrom, NYR	.05	.10
D	Petri Skriko, Van.	.05	.10
	Panel 2	1.00	2.00
E	Wayne Gretzky, LA	.75	1.50
F	Brett Hull, St.L.	.35	.75
G	Tim Kerr, Phi.	.05	.10
H	Mats Naslund, Mon.	.05	.10
	Panel 3		
I	Jari Kurri, Edm.	.15	.30
J	Steve Larmer, Chi.	.10	.20
K	Cam Neely, Bos.	.20	.40
L	Steve Yzerman, Det.	.20	.40
	Panel 4	.25	.50
M	Kevin Dineen, Har.	.10	.20
N	Dave Gagner, Min.	.10	.20
O	Joe Mullen, Cal.	.10	.20
P	Pierre Turgeon, Buf.	.15	.30

— 1989 - 90 STICKERS —

1989-90 Stickers
Sticker No. 81, Mike Riley

Sticker Size: 2 1/8" x 3" or 1 1/2" x 2 1/8"
Face: Four colour, coloured frame, white border; Number
Back: 1: Blue and black on card stock; Premium offer; Bilingual
2: Green and black on card stock; Hockey trivia; Bilingual
3: 1989-90 Future Stars Set
Imprint: ©1989 O-PEE-CHEE CO. LTD. MADE IN CANADA or ©1989 O-PEE-CHEE CIE LTÉE FABRIQUÉ AU CANADA or ©1989 O-PEE-CHEE PTD. IN CANADA/IMPRIMÉ AU CANADA

Complete Set No.: 270
Complete Set Price: 11.00 22.00
Common Player: .03 .05
Album: 5.00

1989 STANLEY CUP CHAMPIONSHIP

No.	Player	EX	NRMT
1	Calgary Flames vs Montreal Canadiens	.03	.05
2	Calgary Flames vs Montreal Canadiens	.03	.05
3	Calgary Flames vs Montreal Canadiens	.03	.05
4	Calgary Flames vs Montreal Canadiens	.03	.05
5	Al MacInnis, Cal. Conn Smythe Trophy Winner, M.V.P.	.05	.10
6	Calgary Flames vs Montreal Canadiens	.03	.05
7	Calgary Flames vs Montreal Canadiens	.03	.05
8	Calgary Flames vs Montreal Canadiens	.03	.05
9	Calgary Flames vs Montreal Canadiens	.03	.05

CHICAGO BLACK HAWKS

No.	Player	EX	NRMT
10	Darren Pang, Goalie	.03	.05
11	Troy Murray	.03	.05
12	Dirk Graham	.03	.05
13	Dave Manson	.03	.05
14	Douglas Wilson, Jr.	.03	.05
15	Steve Thomas	.03	.05
16	Denis Savard	.05	.10
17	Steve Larmer	.05	.10

ST. LOUIS BLUES

No.	Player	EX	NRMT
18	Paul MacLean	.03	.05
19	Paul Cavallini	.03	.05
20	Cliff Ronning	.03	.05
21	Gaston Gingras	.03	.05
22	Brett Hull	.25	.50
23	Peter Zezel	.03	.05
24	Brian Benning	.03	.05
25	Anthony Hrkac	.03	.05

BOSTON BRUINS

No.	Player	EX	NRMT
26	Ken Linseman	.03	.05
27	Glen Wesley	.03	.05
28	Randy Burridge	.03	.05
29	Craig Janney	.15	.30
30	Andrew Moog, Goalie	.05	.10
31	Robert Joyce	.03	.05
32	Raymond Bourque	.10	.20
33	Cam Neely	.10	.20

1988 - 89 TOP ROOKIES

No.	Player	EX	NRMT
34	Sean Burke, Goalie, NJD	.03	.05
35	Pat Elynuik, Win.	.10	.20
36	Tony Granato, NYR	.05	.10
37	Benoit Hogue, Buf.	.03	.05
38	Craig Janney, Bos.	.20	.40
39	Brian Leetch, NYR	.15	.30
40	Trevor Linden, Van.	.10	.20
41	Joe Sakic, Que.	.50	1.00
42	Peter Sidorkiewicz, Goalie, Har.	.03	.05
43	David Volek, NYI	.05	.10
44	Scott Young, Har.	.03	.05
45	Zarley Zalapski, Pit.	.03	.05

MONTREAL CANADIENS

No.	Player	EX	NRMT
46	Mats Naslund	.03	.05
47	Robert Smith	.03	.05
48	Guy Carbonneau	.03	.05
49	Shayne Corson	.03	.05
50	Brian Hayward, Goalie	.03	.05
51	Stephane J.J. Richer	.05	.10
52	Claude Lemieux	.03	.05
53	Russ Courtnall	.03	.05
54	Petr Svoboda	.03	.05
55	Larry Robinson	.03	.05
56	Chris Chelios	.03	.05
57	Patrick Roy, Goalie	.50	1.00
58	Bob Gainey	.07	.15
59	Michael McPhee	.03	.05

138 • O-PEE-CHEE — 1989-90 STICKERS

VANCOUVER CANUCKS

No.	Player	EX	NRMT
60	Barry Pederson	.03	.05
61	Trevor Linden	.35	.75
62	Richard Sutter	.03	.05
63	Brian Bradley	.03	.05
64	Kirk McLean, Goalie	.03	.05
65	Paul Reinhart	.03	.05
66	Robert Nordmark	.03	.05
67	Steve Bozek	.03	.05
68	Stanley Smyl	.03	.05
69	Doug Lidster	.03	.05
70	Petri Skriko	.03	.05
71	Tony Tanti	.03	.05
72	Garth Butcher	.03	.05
73	Larry Melnyk	.03	.05

WASHINGTON CAPITALS

No.	Player	EX	NRMT
74	Kelly Miller	.03	.05
75	Dino Ciccarelli	.03	.05
76	Scott Stevens	.03	.05
77	Rod Langway	.03	.05
78	Dave Christian	.03	.05
79	Stephen Leach	.03	.05
80	Geoff Courtnall	.10	.20
81	Mike Ridley	.03	.05

NEW JERSEY DEVILS

No.	Player	EX	NRMT
82	Patrik Sundstrom	.03	.05
83	Kirk Muller	.07	.15
84	Tom Kurvers	.03	.05
85	Walter Poddubny	.03	.05
86	Sean Burke, Goalie	.03	.05
87	John MacLean	.05	.10
88	Aaron Broten	.03	.05
89	Brendan Shanahan	.03	.05

CALGARY FLAMES

No.	Player	EX	NRMT
90	Joe Mullen	.05	.10
91	Byron (Brad) McCrimmon	.03	.05
92	Lanny McDonald	.05	.10
93	Rick Wamsley, Goalie	.03	.05
94	Michael Vernon, Goalie	.05	.10
95	Al MacInnis	.07	.15
96	Joel Otto	.03	.05
97	Jiri Hrdina	.03	.05
98	Gary Roberts	.12	.25
99	James Peplinski	.03	.05
100	Gary Suter	.03	.05
101	Joe Nieuwendyk	.12	.25
102	Colin Patterson	.03	.05
103	Douglas Gilmour	.03	.05

PHILADELPHIA FLYERS

No.	Player	EX	NRMT
104	Mike Bullard	.03	.05
105	Per-Erik Eklund	.03	.05
106	Brian Propp	.03	.05
107	Ronald Sutter	.03	.05
108	Rick Tocchet	.07	.15
109	Mark Howe	.03	.05
110	Tim Kerr	.03	.05
111	Ron Hextall, Goalie	.05	.10

NEW YORK ISLANDERS

No.	Player	EX	NRMT
112	Mikko Makela	.03	.05
113	David Volek	.03	.05
114	Gary Nylund	.03	.05
115	Brent Sutter	.03	.05
116	Derek King	.03	.05
117	Gerald Diduck	.03	.05
118	Bryan Trottier	.10	.20
119	Pat LaFontaine	.10	.20

1988-89 ACTION

No.	Player	EX	NRMT
120	St. Louis Blues vs Boston Bruins	.03	.05
121	St. Louis Blues vs Boston Bruins	.03	.05
122	New York Rangers vs Boston Bruins	.03	.05
123	New York Rangers vs Boston Bruins	.03	.05
124	Chicago Black Hawks	.03	.05
125	Boston Bruins vs Montreal Canadiens	.03	.05
126	New Jersey Devils vs Boston Bruins	.03	.05
127	Calgary Flames vs New Jersey Devils	.03	.05
128	Montreal Canadiens vs Philadelphia Flyers	.03	.05
129	Philadelphia Flyers vs Edmonton Oilers	.03	.05
130	Vancouver Canucks vs Boston Bruins	.03	.05
131	Vancouver Canucks vs Boston Bruins	.03	.05
132	Minnesota North Stars vs Boston Bruins	.03	.05
133	Minnesota North Stars vs Boston Bruins	.03	.05

WINNIPEG JETS

No.	Player	EX	NRMT
134	Dale Hawerchuk	.05	.10
135	Andrew McBain	.03	.05
136	Iain Duncan	.03	.05
137	Eldon Reddick, Goalie	.03	.05
138	Brent Ashton	.03	.05
139	Dave Ellett	.03	.05
140	James Kyte	.03	.05
141	Douglas Smail	.03	.05
142	Pat Elynuik	.03	.05
143	Randy Carlyle	.03	.05
144	Thomas Steen	.03	.05
145	Hannu Jarvenpaa	.03	.05
146	Peter Taglianetti	.03	.05
147	Laurie Boschman	.03	.05

LOS ANGELES KINGS

No.	Player	EX	NRMT
148	Luc Robitaille	.07	.15
149	Kelly Hrudey, Goalie	.03	.05
150	Steve Duchesne	.03	.05
151	David Taylor	.03	.05
152	Stephen Kasper	.03	.05
153	Michael Krushelnyski	.03	.05
154	Wayne Gretzky	1.00	2.00
155	Bernie Nicholls	.05	.10

1988-89 ALL STARS FIRST TEAM

No.	Player	EX	NRMT
156	Chris Chelios, Mon.	.03	.05
157	Gerard Gallant, Det.	.03	.05
158	Mario Lemieux, Pit.	.50	1.00
159	Allan MacInnis, Cal.	.05	.10
160	Joe Mullen, Cal.	.03	.05
161	Patrick Roy, Goalie, Mon.	.50	1.00

1988-89 ALL STARS SECOND TEAM

No.	Player	EX	NRMT
162	Raymond Bourque, Bos.	.07	.15
163	Rob Brown, Pit.	.05	.10
164	Geoff Courtnall, Wash.	.03	.05
165	Steve Duchesne, LA	.03	.05
166	Wayne Gretzky, LA	.50	1.00
167	Michael Vernon, Goalie, Cal.	.03	.05

TORONTO MAPLE LEAFS

No.	Player	EX	NRMT
168	Gary Leeman	.03	.05
169	Allan Bester, Goalie	.03	.05
170	David Reid	.03	.05
171	Craig Laughlin	.03	.05
172	Ed Olczyk	.03	.05
173	Tom Fergus	.03	.05
174	Mark Osborne	.03	.05
175	Bradley Marsh	.03	.05
176	Daniel Marois	.03	.05
177	Dan Daoust	.03	.05
178	Al Iafrate	.05	.10
179	Vincent Damphousse	.05	.10
180	Christopher Kotsopoulos	.03	.05
181	Derek Laxdal	.03	.05

QUEBEC NORDIQUES

No.	Player	EX	NRMT
182	Peter Stastny	.05	.10
183	Paul Gillis	.03	.05
184	Jeff Jackson	.03	.05
185	Mario Marois	.03	.05
186	Michel Goulet	.05	.10
187	Joe Sakic	.50	1.00
188	Bob Mason, Goalie	.03	.05
189	Marc Fortier	.03	.05
190	Robert Picard	.03	.05
191	Steven Finn	.03	.05
192	Iiro Jarvi	.03	.05
193	Jeff Brown	.03	.05
194	Gaetan Duchesne	.03	.05
195	Randy Moller	.03	.05

MINNESOTA NORTH STARS

No.	Player	EX	NRMT
196	Michael Gartner	.07	.15
197	Jon Casey, Goalie	.10	.20
198	Marc Habscheid	.03	.05
199	Lawrence Murphy	.05	.10
200	Brian Bellows	.05	.10
201	Dave Archibald	.03	.05
202	Neal Broten	.03	.05
203	Dave Gagner	.10	.20

1988-1989 LEAGUE LEADERS

No.	Player	EX	NRMT
204	Vezina Trophy	.03	.05
205	Jennings Trophy	.03	.05
206	Selke Trophy	.03	.05
207	Masterton Trophy	.03	.05

TROPHY WINNERS

No.	Player	EX	NRMT
208	Art Ross Trophy: Mario Lemieux, Pit.	.10	.20
209	Hart Trophy: Wayne Gretzky, LA	.50	1.00
210	Vezina Trophy: Patrick Roy, Mon.	.50	1.00
211	William Jennings Trophy: Patrick Roy, Mon.; Brian Hayward, Mon.	.20	.40
212	Norris Trophy: Chris Chelios, Mon.	.03	.05
213	Frank J. Selke Trophy: Guy Carbonneau, Mon.	.03	.05
214	Lady Byng Trophy: Joe Mullen, Cal.	.03	.05
215	Calder Trophy: Brian Leetch, NYR	.35	.75
216	Masterton Trophy: Tim Kerr, Phi.	.03	.05

EDMONTON OILERS

No.	Player	EX	NRMT
217	Craig Simpson	.03	.05
218	Glenn Anderson	.05	.10
219	Esa Tikkanen	.03	.05
220	Charles Huddy	.03	.05
221	Jari Kurri	.07	.15
222	Jimmy Carson	.05	.10
223	James (Steve) Smith	.03	.05
224	Kevin Lowe	.03	.05
225	Chris Joseph	.03	.05
226	Craig MacTavish	.03	.05
227	Mark Messier	.35	.75
228	Grant Fuhr, Goalie	.05	.10
229	Craig Muni	.03	.05
230	Bill Ranford, Goalie	.05	.10

PITTSBURGH PENGUINS

No.	Player	EX	NRMT
231	John Cullen	.07	.15
232	Zarley Zalapski	.03	.05
233	Bob Errey	.03	.05
234	Dan Quinn	.03	.05
235	Tom Barrasso, Goalie	.03	.05
236	Rob Brown	.05	.10
237	Paul Coffey	.03	.05
238	Mario Lemieux	1.00	2.00

NEW YORK RANGERS

No.	Player	EX	NRMT
239	Carey Wilson	.03	.05
240	Brian Leetch	.75	1.50
241	Tony Granato	.05	.10
242	James Patrick	.03	.05
243	Brian Mullen	.03	.05
244	Tomas Sandstrom	.03	.05
245	Guy Lafleur	.05	.10
246	John Vanbiesbrouck, Goalie	.10	.20

DETROIT RED WINGS

No.	Player	EX	NRMT
247	Bernie Federko	.03	.05
248	Gregory Stefan, Goalie	.03	.05
249	Michael O'Connell	.03	.05
250	David Barr	.03	.05
251	Lee Norwood	.03	.05
252	Shawn Burr	.03	.05
253	Gerard Gallant	.03	.05
254	Steve Yzerman	.25	.50

BUFFALO SABRES

No.	Player	EX	NRMT
255	Christian Ruuttu	.03	.05
256	Richard Vaive	.03	.05
257	Doug Bodger	.03	.05
258	David Andreychuk	.05	.10
259	Ray Sheppard	.10	.20
260	Mike Foligno	.03	.05
261	Phil Housley	.03	.05
262	Pierre Turgeon	.10	.20

HARTFORD WHALERS

No.	Player	EX	NRMT
263	Ray Ferraro	.03	.05
264	Scott Young	.03	.05
265	David Babych	.03	.05
266	Paul MacDermid	.03	.05
267	Michael Liut, Goalie	.03	.05
268	Dave Tippett	.03	.05
269	Ron Francis	.03	.05
270	Kevin Dineen	.03	.05

— 1989 - 90 FUTURE STARS —

The "Future Stars" insert cards appear on the backs of sticker nos. 2, 4, 7, 10/150, 14/156, 18, 21/161, 32, 47, 54/198, 55/199, 60, 61, 63/205, 64, 65, 66/206, 67/207, 72/210, 76/215, 77/216, 88/229, 91, 96/233, 102/239, 107/246, 112/249, 117/256, 146/265, 175/35, 185/41, 187, 184/40, 203. After the sticker has been removed you are left with the insert card.

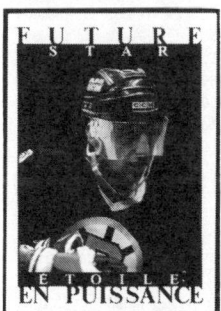 

1989-90 Future Stars
Sticker No. 1, Greg Hawgood, Sticker No. 8, Sean Burke

Card Size: 2 1/2" x 3"
Face: Four colour, coloured background white border; Number, Name, Position, Team
Back: 1989-90 Sticker Set
Imprint: © 1989 O-PEE-CHEE CO. LTD. PTD. IN CANADA/ IMPRIMÉ AU CANADA
Complete Set No.: 34
Complete Set Price: 2.50 / 5.00
Common Player: .03 / .05

No.	Player	EX	NRMT
1	Greg Hawgood, Bos.	.05	.10
2	Craig Janney, Bos.	.15	.30
3	Robert Joyce, Bos.	.05	.10
4	Benoit Hogue, Buf.	.05	.10
5	Jiri Hrdina, Cal.	.03	.05
6	Peter Sidorkiewicz, Goalie, Har.	.03	.05
7	Scott Young, Har.	.05	.10
8	Sean Burke, Goalie, NJD	.03	.05
9	David Volek, NYI	.03	.05
10	Tony Granato, NYR	.03	.05
11	Brian Leetch, NYR	.15	.30
12	Gordon Murphy, Phi.	.03	.05
13	John Cullen, Pit.	.12	.25
14	Zarley Zalapski, Pit.	.07	.15
15	Iiro Jarvi, Que.	.05	.10
16	Joe Sakic, Que.	.25	.50
17	Vincent Riendeau, Goalie, St.L.	.03	.05
18	Daniel Marois, Tor.	.03	.05
19	Trevor Linden, Van.	.03	.05
20	Pat Elynuik, Win.	.05	.10
21	Bob Essensa, Goalie, Win.	.15	.30
22	Checklist (1-34)	.12	.25
23	Joe Mullen, Cal.	.35	.75
24	Mario Lemieux, Pit.	.25	.50
25	Gerard Gallant, Cal.	.15	.30
26	Chris Chelios, Mon.	.15	.30
27	Al MacInnis, Cal.	.25	.50
28	Patrick Roy, Goalie, Mon.	.50	1.00
29	Geoff Courtnall, Wash.	.03	.05
30	Wayne Gretzky, LA	.25	.50
31	Rob Brown, Pit.	.10	.20
32	Steve Duchesne, LA	.03	.05
33	Raymond Bourque, Bos.	.20	.40
34	Michael Vernon, Goalie, Cal.	.05	.10

— 1990 - 91 BOX BOTTOMS —

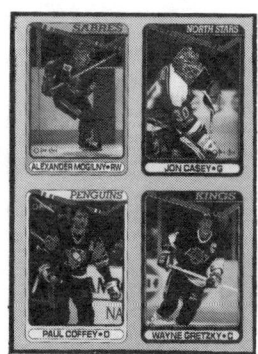

1990-91 Box Bottoms, Panel No. 1, Alexander Mogilny, Jon Casey, Paul Coffey, Wayne Gretzky

Panel Size: 5" X 7"
Face: Four colour, turquoise border; Name, Team, Position
Back: Blue and yellow on cardstock; Letter Divison, Name, Leaders, Logos, Bilingual
Imprint: © 1990 O-PEE-CHEE CO. LTD. PRINTED IN CANADA/IMPRIMÉ AU CANADA © 1990 NHLPA
Complete Set No.: 16
Complete Set Price: 2.50 / 5.00
Common Panel: .12 / .25
Common Player: .07 / .15

No.	Player	EX	NRMT
	Panel 1	1.00	2.00
A	Alexander Mogilny, Buf.	.25	.50
B	Jon Casey, Goalie, Min.	.05	.10
C	Paul Coffey, Pit.	.10	.20
D	Wayne Gretzky, LA	.75	1.50
	Panel 2	1.50	3.00
E	Patrick Roy, Goalie, Mon.	.75	1.50
F	Michael Modano, Min.	.05	.10
G	Mario Lemieux, Pit.	.75	1.50
H	Al MacInnis, Cal.	.07	.15
	Panel 3	.50	1.00
I	Raymond Bourque, Bos.	.25	.50
J	Steve Yzerman, Det.	.25	.50
K	Darren Turcotte, NYR	.05	.10
L	Michael Vernon, Goalie, Cal.	.05	.10
	Panel 4	.25	.50
M	Pierre Turgeon, Buf.	.12	.25
N	Douglas Wilson, Jr., Chi.	.05	.10
O	Donald Beaupre, Goalie, Wash.	.10	.20
P	Sergei Makarov, Cal.	.12	.25

— 1992 - 93 BOX BOTTOMS —

Panels are listed alphabetically by player as they are unnumbered.

1992-93 Box Bottoms
No. 1, Pavel Bure

Card Size: 5" X 6 3/4"
Face: Four colour, white border; Name, Team
Back: Blue on card stock; Name, Resume, Bilingual
Imprint: © 1992 O-PEE-CHEE CO. LTD. PTD. IN CANADA /IMPRIMÉ AU CANADA
Complete Set No.: 4
Complete Set Price: 5.00 / 10.00
Common Player: 1.25 / 2.50

No.	Player	NRMT	Mint
1	1992 Calder Trophy Winner: Pavel Bure, Van.	1.25	2.50
2	1992 James Norris Trophy Winner: Brian Leetch, NYR	1.25	2.50
3	1992 Hart Trophy Winner: Mark Messier, NYR	1.25	2.50
4	1992 Vezina Trophy Winner: Patrick Roy, Goalie, Mon	1.25	2.50

WORLD WIDE GUM

— 1933 - 34 ICE KINGS —

Photos are black and white with the player's face tinted with flesh tones. The player's name is shown on the front of the card. Player biographies appear on the back in either French and English or English only.

Card Size: 2 3/8" x 2 7/8"
Face: Brown on card stock; Name
Back: Green, Name, Number, Resume, English or Bilingual
Imprint: ICE KINGS, World Wide Gum Co., Ltd. Montreal, Printed in Canada
ACC No.: V357
Complete Set No.: 72

	G	VG	EX
Complete Set Price:	3,375.00	6,750.00	13,500.00
Common Player: (1-48)	22.50	45.00	90.00
Common Player: (49-72)	32.50	65.00	130.00

No.	Player	G	VG	EX
1	Dit Clapper, Bos., RC	80.00	160.00	325.00
2	Bill Brydge, NYA, RC	22.50	45.00	90.00
3	Aurel Joliat, Can., Error	162.50	325.00	650.00
4	Andy Blair, Tor., RC	22.50	45.00	90.00
5	Earl Robinson, Mon.M, RC	22.50	45.00	90.00
6	Paul Haynes, Mon.M, RC	22.50	45.00	90.00
7	Ron Martin, NYA, RC	22.50	45.00	90.00
8	Babe Siebert, NYR, RC, Error	50.00	100.00	200.00
9	Archie Wilcox, Mon.M, RC	22.50	45.00	90.00
10	Hap Day, Tor.	50.00	100.00	200.00
11	Roy Worters, Goalie, NYA, RC	55.00	110.00	225.00
12	Nels Stewart, Bos., RC	100.00	200.00	400.00
13	Francis (King) Clancy, Tor.	155.00	310.00	625.00
14	Marty Burke, Mon., RC	22.50	45.00	90.00
15	Cecil Dillon, NYR, RC	22.50	45.00	90.00
16	Red Horner, Tor., RC	50.00	100.00	200.00
17	Armand Mondou, Mon., RC	22.50	45.00	90.00
18	Paul Raymond, Mon., RC	22.50	45.00	90.00
19	Dave Kerr, Goalie, Mon.M, RC	22.50	45.00	90.00
20	Butch Keeling, NYR, RC	22.50	45.00	90.00
21	Johnny Gagnon, Mon., RC	22.50	45.00	90.00
22	Ace Bailey, Tor., RC	80.00	160.00	325.00
23	Harry Oliver, Bos.	22.50	45.00	90.00
24	Gerry Carson, Mon., RC	22.50	45.00	90.00
25	Red Dutton, NYA	22.50	45.00	90.00
26	Georges Mantha, Mon., RC	22.50	45.00	90.00
27	Marty Barry, Bos., RC	30.00	60.00	125.00
28	Wildor Larochelle, Mon., RC	22.50	45.00	90.00
29	Red Beattie, Bos.	22.50	45.00	90.00
30	Bill Cook, NYR	55.00	110.00	225.00
31	Hooley Smith, Mon.M	45.00	85.00	175.00
32	Art Chapman, Bos., RC	22.50	45.00	90.00
33	Baldy Cotton, Tor., RC	22.50	45.00	90.00
34	Lionel Hitchman, Bos., LC	22.50	45.00	90.00
35	George Patterson, NYA, RC	22.50	45.00	90.00
36	Howie Morenz, Mon.	410.00	825.00	1,650.00
37	Jimmy Ward, Mon.M, RC	22.50	45.00	90.00
38	Charley McVeigh, NYA, RC	22.50	45.00	90.00
39	Glenn Brydson, Mon.M, RC, Error	22.50	45.00	90.00
40	Joe Primeau, Tor., RC	70.00	140.00	275.00
41	Joe Lamb, Bos., RC	22.50	45.00	90.00
42	Sylvio Mantha, Mon.	22.50	45.00	90.00
43	Cy Wentworth, Mon.M, RC	22.50	45.00	90.00
44	Normie Himes, NYA, RC	22.50	45.00	90.00
45	Doug Brennan, NYR, RC	22.50	45.00	90.00
46	Pit Lepine, Mon., RC	22.50	45.00	90.00
47	Alex Levinsky, Tor., RC	30.00	60.00	125.00
48	Baldy Northcott, Mon.M, RC	22.50	45.00	90.00
49	Ken Doraty, NYA, RC	32.50	65.00	130.00
50	Bill Thoms, Tor., RC	32.50	65.00	130.00
51	Vern Ayers, Mon.M, RC	32.50	65.00	130.00
52	Lorne Duguid, Mon.M, RC	32.50	65.00	130.00
53	Wally Kilrea, Mon.M, RC	32.50	65.00	130.00
54	Vic Ripley, Bos., RC	32.50	65.00	130.00
55	Hap Emms, Det., RC	32.50	65.00	130.00
56	Duke Dutkowski, NYR, RC	32.50	65.00	130.00
57	Tiny Thompson, Goalie, Bos., RC	45.00	85.00	175.00
58	Charlie Sands, Tor., RC	32.50	65.00	130.00
59	Larry Aurie, Det., RC	32.50	65.00	130.00
60	Bill Beveridge, Goalie, Ott., RC	32.50	65.00	130.00
61	Bill MacKenzie, Mon.C, RC	32.50	65.00	130.00
62	Earl Roche, Ott., RC	32.50	65.00	130.00
63	Bob Gracie, Bos., RC	32.50	65.00	130.00
64	Hec Kilrea, Det.	32.50	65.00	130.00
65	Cooney Weiland, Ott., RC	75.00	150.00	300.00
66	Bun Cook, NYR, RC	55.00	110.00	225.00
67	John Roach, Goalie, Det.	32.50	65.00	130.00
68	Murray Murdock, NYR	32.50	65.00	130.00
69	Danny Cox, Ott., R.C., LC	32.50	65.00	130.00
70	Desse Roche, Mon.M, RC, LC	32.50	65.00	130.00
71	Lorne Chabot, Goalie, Mon.	50.00	100.00	200.00
72	Syd Howe, Ott., RC	65.00	125.00	250.00

World Wide Gum 1933-34 Ice Kings Card No. 1, Dit Clapper

World Wide Gum 1933-34 Ice Kings Card No. 3, Error, Aurel Joliat

World Wide Gum 1933-34 Ice Kings, Card No. 65, Cooney Weiland

World Wide Gum 1936-37 Issue Card No. 20, Hooley Smith

— 1933 - 34 ICE KINGS PREMIUM —

The following six cards are write-in offers from the Ice Kings wrappers.

Card Size: 8" X 10"
Face: Black and white; Name
Back: Blank
Imprint: None
Complete Set No.: 6

	G	VG	EX
Complete Set Price:	150.00	300.00	600.00
Common Player:	12.50	25.00	50.00

No.	Player	G	VG	EX
1	Francis Clancy, Tor.	30.00	60.00	125.00
2	Hap Day, Tor.	20.00	40.00	80.00
3	Aurel Joliat, Mon.C	45.00	85.00	175.00
4	Howie Morenz, Mon.C	75.00	150.00	300.00
5	Al Shields, Ott.	12.50	25.00	50.00
6	Hooley Smith, Mon.M	20.00	40.00	80.00

— 1936 - 37 REGULAR ISSUE —

The greenish-gray cards show the card number and player's name in a box under the picture. The card number and player information appear on the back in both French and English.

Card Size: 2 3/8" x 2 7/8"
Face: Green-grey, white border; Number
Back: Black and white; Number, Resume, Bilingual, Name
Imprint: Printed in Canada / Imprimé au Canada
ACC No.: V356
Complete Set No.: 135

	G	VG	EX
Complete Set Price:	6,750.	13,500.	27,000.
Common Player:	37.50	75.00	150.00

No.	Player	G	VG	EX
1	Charlie Conacher, Tor.	205.00	410.00	825.00
2	Jimmy Ward, Mon.M	37.50	75.00	150.00
3	Babe Siebert, Mon.C	70.00	140.00	275.00
4	Marty Barry, Det.	70.00	140.00	250.00
5	Eddie Shore, Bos.	220.00	440.00	875.00
6	Paul Thompson, Chi.	37.50	75.00	150.00
7	Roy Worters, Goalie, NYA	70.00	140.00	275.00
8	Red Horner, Tor.	70.00	140.00	275.00
9	Wilf Cude, Goalie, Mon.	37.50	75.00	150.00
10	Lionel Conacher, Mon.M	70.00	140.00	275.00
11	Ebbie Goodfellow, Det.	50.00	100.00	200.00
12	Tiny Thompson, Goalie, Bos.	37.50	75.00	150.00
13	Mush March, Chi., RC	37.50	75.00	150.00
14	Red Dutton, NYA	37.50	75.00	150.00
15	Butch Keeling, NYR	37.50	75.00	150.00
16	Frank Boucher, NYR	65.00	125.00	250.00
17	Tommy Gorman, Mgr., Mon.M	37.50	75.00	150.00
18	Howie Morenz, NYR	550.00	1,100.00	2,200.00
19	Cy Wentworth, Mon.M	37.50	75.00	150.00
20	Hooley Smith, Bos.	55.00	110.00	225.00
21	Ivan (Ching) Johnson, NYR	70.00	140.00	275.00
22	Baldy Northcott	37.50	75.00	150.00
23	Syl Apps, Sr., Tor.	115.00	225.00	450.00
24	Hec Kilrea, Tor.	37.50	75.00	150.00
25	John Sorrell, Det.	37.50	75.00	150.00
26	Lorne Carr, NYA, RC	37.50	75.00	150.00
27	Charlie Sands, Bos.	37.50	75.00	150.00
28	Nick Metz, Tor.	37.50	75.00	150.00
29	Francis Clancy, Tor., LC	200.00	400.00	800.00
30	Russ Blinco, Mon.M	37.50	75.00	150.00
31	Pete Martin, RC, LC	37.50	75.00	150.00
32	Walt Buswell, Mon.C, RC	37.50	75.00	150.00
33	Paul Haynes, Mon.C	37.50	75.00	150.00
34	Wildor Larochelle, Chi.	37.50	75.00	150.00
35	Baldy Cotton, Tor.	37.50	75.00	150.00
36	Dit Clapper, Bos.	70.00	140.00	275.00
37	Joe Lamb, NYA	37.50	75.00	150.00

— 1933 - 34 ISSUE — V129 ANONYMOUS • 141

No.	Player	G	VG	EX
38	Bob Gracie, Mon.M	37.50	75.00	150.00
39	Jack Shill, Tor., LC	37.50	75.00	150.00
40	Buzz Boll, Tor.	37.50	75.00	150.00
41	John Gallagher, NYA	37.50	75.00	150.00
42	Art Chapman, NYA	37.50	75.00	150.00
43	**Tom Cook, Chi., RC**	**37.50**	**75.00**	**150.00**
44	Bill MacKenzie, Mon.C	37.50	75.00	150.00
45	Georges Mantha, Mon.	37.50	75.00	150.00
46	Herbert Cain, Mon.M	37.50	75.00	150.00
47	Mud Bruneteau, Det.	37.50	75.00	150.00
48	Bob Davidson, Tor.	37.50	75.00	150.00
49	**Douglas Young, Det., RC**	**37.50**	**75.00**	**150.00**
50	**Polly Drouin, Mon., RC**	**37.50**	**75.00**	**150.00**
51	Harvey Jackson, Tor.	85.00	175.00	350.00
52	Hap Day, Tor.	70.00	140.00	275.00
53	Dave Kerr, Goalie	37.50	75.00	150.00
54	Allan Murray, NYA	37.50	75.00	150.00
55	Johnny Gottselig, Chi.	37.50	75.00	150.00
56	Andy Blair, Chi.	37.50	75.00	150.00
57	Lynn Patrick, NYR	70.00	140.00	275.00
58	**Sweeney Schriner, NYA, RC**	**50.00**	**100.00**	**200.00**
59	Hap Emms, NYA	37.50	75.00	150.00
60	Al Shields, NYA	37.50	75.00	150.00
61	Alex Levinsky, Tor.	37.50	75.00	150.00
62	Frank Hollett, Bos.	37.50	75.00	150.00
63	Peggy O'Neil, Bos.	37.50	75.00	150.00
64	Herbie Lewis, Det.	37.50	75.00	150.00
65	Aurel Joliat, Mon.	195.00	390.00	775.00
66	**Carl Voss, Mon.M, RC**	**37.50**	**75.00**	**150.00**
67	**Stewart Evans, Mon.M, RC**	**37.50**	**75.00**	**150.00**
68	Bun Cook, Bos.	45.00	85.00	175.00
69	Cooney Weiland, Bos.	45.00	90.00	175.00
70	Dave Trottier, Mon.M	37.50	75.00	150.00
71	Louis Trudel, Chi.	37.50	75.00	150.00
72	Marty Burke, Chi.	37.50	75.00	150.00
73	Leroy Goldsworthy, Bos.	37.50	75.00	150.00
74	Norman Smith, Goalie, Det.	37.50	75.00	150.00
75	Syd Howe, Det.	50.00	100.00	200.00
76	Gord Pettinger, Det.	37.50	75.00	150.00
77	Jack McGill, Mon.	37.50	75.00	150.00
78	Pit Lepine, Mon.	37.50	75.00	150.00
79	Sammy McManus, Bos.	37.50	75.00	150.00
80	Phil Watson, NYR	37.50	75.00	150.00
81	Paul Runge, Mon.M	37.50	75.00	150.00
82	Bill Beveridge, Goalie, Mon.M	37.50	75.00	150.00
83	Johnny Gagnon, Mon.C	37.50	75.00	150.00
84	Bucko McDonald, Det.	37.50	75.00	150.00
85	Earl Robinson, Mon.M	37.50	75.00	150.00
86	Pep (Regis) Kelly, Tor.	37.50	75.00	150.00
87	Ott Heller, NYR	37.50	75.00	150.00
88	Murray Murdock, NYR	37.50	75.00	150.00
89	Mac Colville, NYR	37.50	75.00	150.00
90	Alex Shibicky, NYR	37.50	75.00	150.00
91	Neil Colville, NYR	50.00	100.00	200.00
92	Normie Himes, NYA	37.50	75.00	150.00
93	Charley McVeigh, NYA	37.50	75.00	150.00
94	Lester Patrick, Coach, NYR	95.00	190.00	375.00
95	**Conn Smythe, Mgr. Tor.**	**105.00**	**210.00**	**425.00**
96	**Art Ross, Coach, Bos.**	**100.00**	**200.00**	**400.00**
97	Cecil M. Hart, Coach, Mon.	90.00	175.00	350.00
98	Dutch Gainor, Mon.M	37.50	75.00	150.00
99	Jack J. Adams, Coach, Det.	80.00	160.00	325.00
100	Howie Morenz, Jr., Mascot, Mon.C	80.00	160.00	325.00
101	**Buster Mundy, RC, LC**	**37.50**	**75.00**	**150.00**
102	**Johnny Wing, Rc, LC**	**37.50**	**75.00**	**150.00**
103	Maurice Croghan, Mon.M	37.50	75.00	150.00
104	**Pete Jotkus, RC, LC**	**37.50**	**75.00**	**150.00**
105	**Doug MacQuisten, RC, LC**	**37.50**	**75.00**	**150.00**
106	**Lester Brennan, Rc, LC**	**37.50**	**75.00**	**150.00**
107	**Jack O'Connell, RC, LC**	**37.50**	**75.00**	**150.00**
108	**Ray Malenfant, RC, LC**	**37.50**	**75.00**	**150.00**
109	**Ken Murray, Mon.R, RC**	**37.50**	**75.00**	**150.00**
110	**Frank Stangle, RC, LC**	**37.50**	**75.00**	**150.00**
111	**Dave Neville, RC, LC**	**37.50**	**75.00**	**150.00**
112	**Claude Burke, RC, Lc**	**37.50**	**75.00**	**150.00**
113	**Herman Murray, RC, LC**	**37.50**	**75.00**	**150.00**
114	**Buddy O'Connor, RC, LC**	**37.50**	**75.00**	**150.00**
115	**Albert Perreault, RC, LC**	**37.50**	**75.00**	**150.00**
116	**Johnny Taugher, RC, LC**	**37.50**	**75.00**	**150.00**
117	**Rene Boudreau, RC, LC**	**37.50**	**75.00**	**150.00**
118	**Kenny McKinnon, Goalie, Que.A, RC**	**37.50**	**75.00**	**150.00**
119	**Alex Bolduc, RC, LC**	**37.50**	**75.00**	**150.00**

No.	Player	G	VG	EX
120	**Jimmy Keiller, RC, LC**	**37.50**	**75.00**	**150.00**
121	**Lloyd McIntyre, RC, LC**	**37.50**	**75.00**	**150.00**
122	**Emile Fortin, RC, LC**	**37.50**	**75.00**	**150.00**
123	**Mike Karakas, RC, LC**	**37.50**	**75.00**	**150.00**
124	Art Wiebe, Chi.	37.50	75.00	150.00
125	**Lulu Denis, RC, LC**	**37.50**	**75.00**	**150.00**
126	**Stan Pratt, RC, LC**	**37.50**	**75.00**	**150.00**
127	**Jules Cholette, RC ,LC**	**37.50**	**75.00**	**150.00**
128	**Jimmy Muir, RC, LC**	**37.50**	**75.00**	**150.00**
129	**Pete Morin, RC, LC**	**37.50**	**75.00**	**150.00**
130	**Jimmy Heffernan, RC, LC**	**37.50**	**75.00**	**150.00**
131	**Morris Bastien, RC, LC**	**37.50**	**75.00**	**150.00**
132	**Tuffy Griffiths, RC, LC**	**37.50**	**75.00**	**150.00**
133	**John Mahaffy, RC, LC**	**37.50**	**75.00**	**150.00**
134	**Truman Donnelly, RC, LC**	**37.50**	**75.00**	**150.00**
135	**Bill Stewart , RC, LC**	**50.00**	**100.00**	**200.00**

World Wide Gum
1936-37 Issue
Card No. 45,
Georges Mantha

World Wide Gum
1936-37 Issue
Card No. 109
Ken Murray

V129 Anonymous
1933-34 Issue
Card No. 28, Error,
Name misspelled
Seibert on face

V129 ANONYMOUS

— 1933 - 34 ISSUE —

These sepia-toned cards are numbered on the back along with a short biography in French and English. The player's name appears on the front bottom border. It is believed that card no.39 was purposefully held back by the issuer.

Card Size: 1 5/8" X 2 7/8"
Face: Brown on white card stock, white border; Name
Back: Number, Name, Resume, Bilingual
Imprint: None
ACC No.: V129
Complete Set No.: 50
Complete Set Price: 2,875.   5,750.   11,500.
Common Player: 37.50   75.00   150.00

TORONTO

No.	Player	G	VG	EX
1	Red Horner, RC	110.00	225.00	450.00
2	Hap Day	80.00	160.00	325.00
3	Ace Bailey, RC	100.00	200.00	400.00
4	Buzz Boll, RC	37.50	75.00	150.00
5	Charlie Conacher, RC	170.00	340.00	675.00
6	Harvey Jackson, RC	95.00	190.00	375.00
7	Joe Primeau, RC	90.00	175.00	350.00
8	Francis Clancy	170.00	340.00	675.00
9	Alex Levinsky, RC	55.00	110.00	225.00
10	Bill Thoms, RC	37.50	75.00	150.00
11	Andy Blair, RC	37.50	75.00	150.00
12	Baldy Cotton, RC	37.50	75.00	150.00
13	George Hainsworth, Goalie	80.00	160.00	325.00
14	Ken Doraty, RC	37.50	75.00	150.00

DETROIT

No.	Player	G	VG	EX
15	Fred Robertson, RC	37.50	75.00	150.00
16	Charlie Sands, RC	37.50	75.00	150.00
17	Hec Kilrea	37.50	75.00	150.00
18	John Roach, Goalie	37.50	75.00	150.00
19	Larry Aurie, RC	37.50	75.00	150.00
20	Ebbie Goodfellow, RC	60.00	125.00	250.00

NEW YORK AMERICANS

No.	Player	G	VG	EX
21	Normie Himes, RC	37.50	75.00	150.00
22	Bill Brydge, RC	37.50	75.00	150.00
23	Red Dutton	55.00	110.00	225.00

OTTAWA

No.	Player	G	VG	EX
24	Cooney Weiland, RC	55.00	110.00	225.00
25	Bill Beveridge, Goalie, RC	37.50	75.00	150.00
26	Frank Finnigan, LC	37.50	75.00	150.00

MONTREAL

No.	Player	G	VG	EX
27	Albert Leduc, RC	45.00	85.00	175.00

142 • V129 ANONYMOUS — 1933 - 34 ISSUE —

NEW YORK RANGERS

No.	Player	G	VG	EX
28	Babe Siebert, RC, Error	75.00	150.00	300.00
29	Murray Murdock	37.50	75.00	150.00
30	Butch Keeling, RC	37.50	75.00	150.00
31	Bill Cook	70.00	140.00	275.00
32	Cecil Dillon, RC	37.50	75.00	150.00
33	Ivan (Ching) Johnson, RC	95.00	190.00	375.00
34	Ott Heller, RC	37.50	75.00	150.00

BOSTON

No.	Player	G	VG	EX
35	Red Beattie, Error	37.50	75.00	150.00
36	Dit Clapper, RC	75.00	150.00	300.00
37	Eddie Shore, RC	345.00	690.00	1,375.00
38	Marty Barry, RC	45.00	85.00	175.00
39	Harry Oliver		Extremely Rare	
40	Bob Gracie, RC	37.50	75.00	150.00

MONTREAL

No.	Player	G	VG	EX
41	Howie Morenz	425.00	850.00	1,700.00
42	Pit Lepine, RC	37.50	75.00	150.00
43	Johnny Gagnon, RC	37.50	75.00	150.00
44	Armand Mondou, RC	37.50	75.00	150.00
45	Lorne Chabot, Goalie	55.00	110.00	225.00

REGULAR ISSUE

No.	Player	G	VG	EX
46	Bun Cook, NYR, RC	70.00	140.00	275.00
47	Alex Smith	37.50	75.00	150.00
48	Danny Cox, Ott., RC, LC	37.50	75.00	150.00
49	Baldy Northcott, Mon.M, RC	37.50	75.00	150.00
50	Paul Thompson, NY, RC	80.00	160.00	325.00

Note: All classical sets are extremely rare in NRMT and Mint condition.

"RED" BEATTY

V129 Anonymous
1933-34 Issue
Card No. 35, Error,
Name misspelled Beatty on face

V129 Anonymous
1933-34 Issue
Card No. 35, Error,
Name misspelled
Beatty on face

INTERFERENCE

Available in April!

THE CHARLTON STANDARD CATALOGUE OF CANADIAN

BASEBALL & FOOTBALL CARDS

- Fourth Edition -

BASEBALL CARDS FROM 1912
FOOTBALL CARDS FROM 1949

For Canadian Baseball and Football Card Collectors this Catalogue has it all!

IMPERIAL TOBACCO * MAPLE CRISPETTE
BAZOOKA *PARKHURST * O-PEE-CHEE
CANADA STARCH * STUART * POST
TOPPS * WORLD WIDE GUM * NALLEYS
DONRUSS - LEAF * EDDIE SARGENT
WILLARD * TORONTO BLUE JAYS
STANDARD OIL * NABISCO * VACHON
BLUE RIBBON TEA * PANINI * PROVIGO
GENERAL MILLS * SCORE * EXHIBITS
HOSTESS * PURITAN MEATS * JOGO
GULF CANADA * ROYAL STUDIOS
BEN'S AULT FOODS * COCA-COLA * KFC
And All Other Major Manufacturers...

Complete price listings for all Major League Baseball and Canadian Football League cards!
Comprehensive baseball and football minor league card listings!
Regular issues, stickers, inserts, subsets, transfers and much, much more!
All major manufacturers!
Current Pricing for all cards in up to three grades of condition - VG, EX, and NRMT!
All rookie, last, pitcher, quarterback, error and variation cards identified and priced!
Plus Charlton's Fabulous Alphabetical Index!

OVER 300 PAGES * 60,000 PRICES
NEW, LARGER 8 1/2 x 11" FORMAT
RESERVE YOUR COPY TODAY
DIRECTLY FROM THE PUBLISHER...

The Charlton Press

**2010 YONGE STREET,
TORONTO, ONTARIO M4S 1Z9**
FOR TOLL FREE ORDERING PHONE
1-800-442-6042 FAX 1-800-442-1542
from anywhere in Canada or the U.S.

ST. LAWRENCE STARCH COMPANY

— BEE HIVE PHOTOS —

PLANT OF
ST. LAWRENCE STARCH COMPANY LIMITED
PORT CREDIT, ONT.

The photos were produced by the St. Lawrence Starch Company of Port Credit, Ontario. They were obtained by sending complete labels from St. Lawrence Starch products to the company. The name Bee Hive became associated with the photos because the majority of labels submitted were from Bee Hive Corn Syrup. Collectors were allowed to select the photo of their choice from player lists published each year. Because of this, photos of the favourite players are easier to find. Photos of the less popular players are the hardest to find and are valued higher due to their scarcity. The issuing of these player lists, however, still did not guarantee photo distribution. Some player's names appeared on the lists, but their actual photos remain unconfirmed.

The mat colours the photos were mounted on vary and may be beige, red, or blue. All photographs are unnumbered and are listed alphabetically by team and then by player name. In some cases a number of photographic variations of the same player exist. These variations are included in the listings with brief descriptions indicating the major identifying feature.

The photos are divided into three groups according to their autographs. The information below will help the collector identify the different groups and assign photos to the right era. Over the years, the method used to print the players name on the photo varied. The groupings below are not 100% fool proof but will prove extremely helpful to collectors.

Player's List For 1940 - 1941

1934 TO 1943 GROUP I

Facsimile Autograph

Block Letter Autograph

Script Letter Autograph
Black Type   White Type

1944 TO 1963 GROUP II   1964 TO 1967 GROUP III

1944 - 1945
Facsimile Autograph

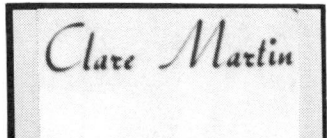

Script Letter Autograph
Thin Type   Thick Type

Woodgrain Border

BEE HIVE VARIATIONS

One of the interesting aspects of the Bee Hive series is the many variations that exist and it seems that more are found each year. We have divided the variations into four major categories. Many of the players have more than one photo issued.

UNIFORM VARIATIONS	PHOTOGRAPH VARIATIONS		NAME VARIATIONS	STICK VARIATIONS
"A" on sweater	White background	Full length pose	White Script	Blade of stick visible
Away, Light uniform	Light background	Horizontal photo	Black Script	Blade of stick not visible
Home, Dark uniform	Dark background	Vertical photo	Name away from skate	
"C" on sweater	White border around photo	Negative reversed	Name near skate	
Helmet	Action shot	Bee Hive promotion	Name overlaps stick	
No Helmet	Posed on ice		Name overlaps skate	
Number on sleeve	Posed in dressing room		Name printed diagonally	
No number on sleeve	Portrait pose		Name parallel to bottom	
Plain sleeve				

UNIFORM VARIATIONS

No Helmet

Helmet

PHOTOGRAPH VARIATIONS

Posed in Dressing Room

Posed on Ice

Action Photo

Number on Sleeve

No Number on Sleeve

NAME VARIATIONS

Name Diagonally

Name Parallel

Black Script

Name Overlaps Stick

Home, Dark Uniform

Away, Light Uniform

STICK VARIATIONS

Stick Visible

Stick Not Visible

BEEHIVE PHOTOS ST. LAWRENCE STARCH COMPANY • 145

GROUP ONE PHOTOS

— 1934 TO 1944 —

The first group has three main varieties of player names printed on the photos as follows:
1. Facsimile Autograph
2. Block Autorgraph
3. Script Autograph

One or two other name styles exist but their use is minimal and cannot be used as an identifying feature.

Photo Size: 4 1/4" X 6 3/4"
Mat Size: 5 1/2" X 8"
Face: Black and white
Mat: Red, blue or beige
Back: pt for trophies
Imprint: None
Complete Set No.: Unknown
Common Player: 2.50 5.00 10.00

BOSTON BRUINS

No.	Player	VG	EX	NRMT
1	Bobby Bauer	2.50	5.00	10.00
2	Red Beattie	3.75	7.50	15.00
3	Buzz Boll		Unconfirmed	
4	Yank Boyd	20.00	37.50	75.00
5A	Frankie Brimsek, Goalie, With Net	2.50	5.00	10.00
5B	Frankie Brimsek, Goalie, Without Net	7.50	15.00	30.00
6	Herbert Cain		Unconfirmed	
7	Murph Chamberlain		Unconfirmed	
8	Dit Clapper	2.50	5.00	10.00
9	Roy Conacher	3.00	6.00	12.00
10	Bun Cook	3.75	7.50	15.00
11	Bill Cowley	2.50	5.00	10.00
12	John Crawford, Jersey No. 19	3.00	6.00	12.00
13	Woody Dumart	5.00	10.00	20.00
14	Don Gallinger	25.00	50.00	100.00
15	Ray Getliffe	3.00	6.00	12.00
16	Leroy Goldsworthy		Unconfirmed	
17	Bep Guidolin	25.00	50.00	100.00
18	Red Hamill	6.25	12.50	25.00
19	Mel Hill	3.00	6.00	12.00
20	Frank Hollett		Unconfirmed	
21	Art Jackson		Unconfirmed	
22	Harvey Jackson		Unconfirmed	
23	Bill Jennings		Unconfirmed	
24	Pat McReavy		Unconfirmed	
25	Alex Motter	6.25	12.50	25.00
26	Peggy O'Neil	5.00	10.00	20.00
27	Gord Pettinger		Unconfirmed	
28	Jack Portland		Unconfirmed	
29	Charlie Sands	3.75	7.50	15.00
30	Jackie Schmidt	25.00	50.00	100.00
31	Milt Schmidt	5.00	10.00	20.00
32	Jack Shewchuk	3.00	6.00	12.00
33	Eddie Shore	7.50	15.00	30.00
34	Des Smith		Unconfirmed	
35	Tiny Thompson, Goalie	5.00	10.00	20.00
36	Cooney Weiland	3.75	7.50	15.00
37	Eddie Wiseman		Unconfirmed	

CHICAGO BLACK HAWKS

No.	Player	VG	EX	NRMT
38	George Allen	4.50	9.00	18.00
39	Doug Bentley	3.75	7.50	15.00
40	Max Bentley	3.75	7.50	15.00
41	Russ Blinco		Unconfirmed	
42	Glenn Brydson	25.00	50.00	100.00
43	Marty Burke	3.00	6.00	12.00
44	Bill Carse	3.00	6.00	12.00
45	Bob Carse	3.00	6.00	12.00
46	Lorne Chabot, Goalie	5.00	10.00	20.00
47	John Chad	6.25	12.50	25.00
48	Joe Cooper		Unconfirmed	
49	Les Cunningham	5.00	10.00	20.00
50	Cully Dahlstrom	3.75	7.50	15.00
51	Joffre Desilets		Unconfirmed	
52	Bert Gardiner, Goalie		Unconfirmed	
53	Leroy Goldsworthy	6.25	12.50	25.00
54	Paul Goodman, Goalie	6.25	12.50	25.00
55	Johnny Gottselig	4.50	9.00	18.00
56	Philip Hergesheimer	3.00	6.00	12.00
57	Roger Jenkins		Unconfirmed	

Bee Hive Group One
1934-44 Issue
Card No. 11,
Bill Cowley

Bee Hive Group One
1934-44 Issue
Card No. 70, Error, Name
misspelled Mitchel on face

Bee Hive Group One
1934-44 Issue
Card No. 83, Error, Name
misspelled Trudell on face

Bee Hive Group One
1934-44 Issue
Card No. 100, Error, Name
misspelled Geisebrecht on face

No.	Player	VG	EX	NRMT
58	George (Wingy) Johnston	30.00	60.00	125.00
59	Alex Kaleta	6.25	12.50	25.00
60	Mike Karakas, Goalie	3.00	6.00	12.00
61	Pep (Regis) Kelly		Unconfirmed	
62	William Kendall		Unconfirmed	
63	Alex Levinsky	3.75	7.50	15.00
64	Sam LoPresti, Goalie	6.25	12.50	25.00
65	Dave Mackay	50.00	100.00	200.00
66	Bill MacKenzie		Unconfirmed	
67	Mush March	3.00	6.00	12.00
68	John Mariucci	12.50	25.00	50.00
69	Joe Matte	30.00	60.00	125.00
70	Red Mitchell, Error	30.00	60.00	125.00
71	Baldy Northcott		Unconfirmed	
72	Peter Palangio	17.50	35.00	70.00
73	Joe Papike	17.50	35.00	70.00
74	Jack Portland		Unconfirmed	
75	Cliff Purpur	30.00	60.00	125.00
76	Earl Robinson		Unconfirmed	
77	Doc Romnes	7.50	15.00	30.00
78	Earl Seibert	5.00	10.00	20.00
79	Jack Shill		Unconfirmed	
80	Des Smith		Unconfirmed	
81	Paul Thompson	4.50	9.00	18.00
82	Bill Thoms		Unconfirmed	
83	Louis Trudel, Error	7.50	15.00	30.00
84	Audley Tuten	30.00	60.00	125.00
85	Art Wiebe	4.00	8.00	16.00

DETROIT RED WINGS

No.	Player	VG	EX	NRMT
86	Sid Abel	5.00	10.00	20.00
87	Larry Aurie	3.00	6.00	12.00
88	Marty J. Barry	5.00	10.00	20.00
89	Ralph Bowman	5.00	10.00	20.00
90	Adam Brown	12.50	25.00	50.00
91	Connie Brown	12.50	25.00	50.00
92	Jerry Brown	50.00	100.00	200.00
93	Modere Bruneteau	3.00	6.00	12.00
94	Eddie Bush	40.00	85.00	165.00
95	Joe Carveth	3.00	6.00	12.00
96	Charlie Conacher		Unconfirmed	
97	Doug Deacon		Unconfirmed	
98	Cecil Dillon		Unconfirmed	
99	Les Douglas	12.50	25.00	50.00
100	Gus Giesebrecht, Error	3.75	7.50	15.00
101	Ebbie Goodfellow	4.00	8.00	16.00
102	Don Grosso	3.00	6.00	12.00
103	Dutch Hiller		Unconfirmed	
104	Syd H. Howe	3.00	6.00	12.00
105	Bill Jennings	12.50	25.00	50.00
106	Jack Keating	7.50	15.00	30.00
107	Pete Kelly	3.00	6.00	12.00
108	Hec Kilrea	3.00	6.00	12.00
109	Ken Kilrea	5.00	10.00	20.00
110	Wally Kilrea	3.00	6.00	12.00
111	Herbert A. Lewis	3.75	7.50	15.00
112	Carl Liscombe	3.75	7.50	15.00
113	Charley Mason		Unconfirmed	
114	Douglas McCaig	12.50	25.00	50.00
115A	Bucko McDonald, Ice Photo	15.00	30.00	60.00
115B	Bucko McDonald, Dressing Room Photo	15.00	30.00	60.00
116	Pat McReavy	10.00	20.00	40.00
117	Alex Motter		Unconfirmed	
118	Johnny Mowers, Goalie	3.75	7.50	15.00
119	Jimmy Orlando	3.00	6.00	12.00
120	Gord Pettinger	4.50	9.00	18.00
121	John Sherf	10.00	20.00	40.00
122	Cully Simon		Unconfirmed	
123	Norman Smith, Goalie	5.00	10.00	20.00
124	Johnn Sorrell	5.00	10.00	20.00
125	Jack Stewart	3.75	7.50	15.00
126	Harvey Teno, Goalie		Unconfirmed	
127	Tiny Thompson, Goalie		Unconfirmed	
128	Carl Voss	12.50	25.00	50.00
129	Eddie Wares	7.50	15.00	30.00
130	Harry Watson		Unconfirmed	
131	Arch Wilder	5.00	10.00	20.00
132	Douglas Young	5.00	10.00	20.00

146 • ST. LAWRENCE STARCH COMPANY BEEHIVE PHOTOS

MONTREAL CANADIENS

No.	Player	VG	EX	NRMT
133	Jack J. Adams	3.75	7.50	15.00
134	Marty Barry	68.75	137.50	275.00
135	Joe Benoit	3.75	7.50	15.00
136	Paul Bibeault, Goalie	6.25	12.50	25.00
137	Toe Blake	4.50	9.00	18.00
138	Emile (Butch) Bouchard	4.50	9.00	18.00
139	Claude Bourque, Goalie	4.50	9.00	18.00
140	George Allan Brown	20.00	45.00	90.00
141	Walt Buswell	10.00	20.00	40.00
142	Herbert Cain		Unconfirmed	
143	Murph Chamberlain	5.00	10.00	20.00
144	Wilf Cude, Goalie	4.50	9.00	18.00
145	Bunny Dame	10.00	20.00	40.00
146	Tony DeMers, Error	3.75	7.50	15.00
147	Joffre Desilets	5.00	10.00	20.00
148	Gordie Drillon	125.00	250.00	500.00
149	Polly Drouin	3.75	7.50	15.00
150	Stewart Evans		Unconfirmed	
151	Johnny Gagnon	3.00	6.00	12.00
152	Bert Gardiner, Goalie	5.00	10.00	20.00
153	Ray Getliffe	20.00	40.00	80.00
154	Red Goupille	5.00	10.00	20.00
155	Tony Graboski	3.75	7.50	15.00
156	Bob Gracie		Unconfirmed	
157	Paul Haynes	3.00	6.00	12.00
158	Gerry Heffernan	30.00	60.00	120.00
159	Dutch Hiller		Unconfirmed	
160	Roger Jenkins	7.50	15.00	30.00
161	Aurel Joliat	10.00	20.00	40.00
162	Elmer Lach, Ice Photo	7.50	15.00	30.00
163	Leo Lamoureux, Error	30.00	60.00	120.00
164	Pit Lepine	3.00	6.00	12.00
165	Rod Lorraine	5.00	10.00	20.00
166	Georges Mantha	3.00	6.00	12.00
167	Sylvio Mantha	5.00	10.00	20.00
168	Bill McKenzie		Unconfirmed	
169	Armand Mondou	3.00	6.00	12.00
170	Howie Morenz	125.00	250.00	500.00
171	Pete Morin	30.00	60.00	120.00
172	Buddy O'Connor	30.00	60.00	120.00
173	Peggy O'Neil		Unconfirmed	
174	Charles Phillippe		Unconfirmed	
175	Jack Portland	5.00	10.00	20.00
176	John Quilty	3.75	7.50	15.00
177	Ken Reardon	7.00	14.00	28.00
178	Terry Reardon	30.00	60.00	120.00
179	Maurice Richard	68.75	137.50	275.00
180	Earl Robinson	60.00	112.50	225.00
181	Charlie Sands	20.00	40.00	80.00
182	Babe Siebert	7.50	15.00	30.00
183	Alex Singbush	17.50	35.00	70.00
184	Bill Summerhill	30.00	60.00	120.00
185	Louis Trudel	20.00	42.50	85.00
186	Jimmy Ward		Unconfirmed	
187	Cy Wentworth		Extremely Rare	
188	Douglas Young	20.00	42.50	85.00

MONTREAL MAROONS

No.	Player	VG	EX	NRMT
189	Bill Beveridge, Goalie	15.00	30.00	60.00
190	Russ Blinco	15.00	30.00	60.00
191	Herbert Cain	15.00	30.00	60.00
192	Gerry Carson, Error	33.75	67.50	135.00
193	Francis Clancy		Unconfirmed	
194	Alex Connell, Goalie	10.00	20.00	40.00
195	Tom Cook	10.00	20.00	40.00
196	Stewart Evans	10.00	20.00	40.00
197	Bob Gracie	12.50	25.00	50.00
198	Max Kaminsky	40.00	80.00	160.00
199	Bill MacKenzie	33.75	67.50	135.00
200	Gus Marker	33.75	67.50	135.00
201	Baldy Northcott	15.00	30.00	60.00
202	Earl Robinson	12.50	25.00	50.00
203	Paul Runge	33.75	67.50	135.00
204	Gerry Shannon, Error	33.75	67.50	135.00
205	Al Shields		Unconfirmed	
206	Des Smith	10.00	20.00	40.00
207	Hooley Smith	10.00	20.00	40.00
208	Dave Trottier	15.00	30.00	60.00
209	Jimmy Ward	15.00	30.00	60.00
210	Cy Wentworth	15.00	30.00	60.00

Bee Hive Group One
1933-34 Issue
Card No. 146, Error, Name misspelled Demers on face

Bee Hive Group One
1933-34 Issue
Card No. 163, Error, Name misspelled Lamoureaux on face

Bee Hive Group One
1933-34 Issue
Card No. 192, Error, Name misspelled Jerry on face

Bee Hive Group One
1933-34 Issue
Card No. 318, Name misspelled Jimmie on face

NEW YORK AMERICANS

No.	Player	VG	EX	NRMT
211	V. (Squee) Allen	15.00	30.00	60.00
212	Tom Anderson	7.50	15.00	30.00
213	Murray Armstrong		Unconfirmed	
214	Red Beattie		Unconfirmed	
215	Bill Benson	12.50	25.00	50.00
216	Buzz Boll		Unconfirmed	
217	Andy Brannigan		Unconfirmed	
218	Lorne Carr	7.50	15.00	30.00
219	Art Chapman	7.50	15.00	30.00
220	Charlie Conacher		Unconfirmed	
221	Hap Day		Unconfirmed	
222	Red Dutton	7.50	15.00	30.00
223	Pat Egan	15.00	30.00	60.00
224	Hap Emms	15.00	30.00	60.00
225	Wilf Field	7.50	15.00	30.00
226	John Gallagher	7.50	15.00	30.00
227	Leroy Goldsworthy		Unconfirmed	
228	Red Heron		Unconfirmed	
229	Mel Hill		Unconfirmed	
230	Art Jackson		Unconfirmed	
231	Harvey Jackson		Unconfirmed	
232	Joe Jerwa	12.50	25.00	50.00
233	Pete Kelly		Unconfirmed	
234	Jim Klein	15.00	30.00	60.00
235	Nick Knott		Unconfirmed	
236	Joe Krol		Extremely Rare	
237	Joe Lamb	15.00	30.00	60.00
238	Norman Larson	15.00	30.00	60.00
239	Gus Marker		Unconfirmed	
240	Ron Martin		Unconfirmed	
241	Hazen McAndrew		Extremely Rare	
242	Charley McVeigh		Unconfirmed	
243	Kenny Mosdell	68.75	137.50	275.00
244	Al Murray	7.50	15.00	30.00
245	John O'Flaherty	12.50	25.00	50.00
246	Chuck Rayner, Goalie	35.00	70.00	140.00
247	Earl Robertson, Goalie	7.50	15.00	30.00
248	Doc Romnes		Unconfirmed	
249	Sweeny Schriner	7.50	15.00	30.00
250	Al Shields	12.50	25.00	50.00
251	Jack Shill		Unconfirmed	
252	Pete Slobodzian, Error	12.50	25.00	50.00
253	Hooley Smith		Unconfirmed	
254	John Sorrell		Unconfirmed	
255	Nells Stewart	7.50	15.00	30.00
256	Fred Thurier	17.50	35.00	75.00
257	Harry Watson	45.00	90.00	180.00
258	Eddie Wiseman	7.50	15.00	30.00
259	Roy Worters, Goalie	7.50	15.00	30.00
260	Ralph Wycherly	15.00	30.00	60.00

NEW YORK RANGERS

No.	Player	VG	EX	NRMT
261	Frank Boucher	3.00	6.00	12.00
262	Doug Brennan		Unconfirmed	
263	Norm Burns	15.00	30.00	60.00
264	Angus Cameron		Unconfirmed	
265	Mac Colville	2.50	5.00	10.00
266	Neil Colville	2.50	5.00	10.00
267	Bill Cook	3.00	6.00	12.00
268	Joe Cooper	3.00	6.00	12.00
269	Art Coulter	2.50	5.00	10.00
270	Gord Davidson	12.50	25.00	50.00
271	Cecil Dillon	3.75	7.50	15.00
272	Jim Franks, Goalie	33.75	67.50	135.00
273	Red Garrett	33.75	67.50	135.00
274	Hank Goldup		Unconfirmed	
275	Ott Heller	3.00	6.00	12.00
276A	Jim Henry, Goalie, Vertical Photo	17.50	35.00	70.00
276B	Jim Henry, Goalie, Horizontal Photo	20.00	42.50	85.00
277	Bryan Hextall, Sr.	3.00	6.00	12.00
278	Dutch Hiller	3.75	7.50	15.00
279	Ivan (Ching) Johnson	3.00	6.00	12.00
280	Bill Juzda	5.00	10.00	20.00
281	Butch Keeling	3.75	7.50	15.00
282	David Kerr, Goalie	3.00	6.00	12.00
283	Bobby Kirk	5.00	10.00	20.00
284	Bob Kirkpatrick	5.00	10.00	20.00
285	Kilby MacDonald	3.75	7.50	15.00
286	Larry Molyneaux	3.75	7.50	15.00

BEEHIVE PHOTOS ST. LAWRENCE STARCH COMPANY • 147

No.	Player	VG	EX	NRMT
287	John Murray Murdoch	3.75	7.50	15.00
288	Vic Myles	30.00	65.00	135.00
289	Lynn Patrick	3.00	6.00	12.00
290	Murray Patrick	3.00	6.00	12.00
291	Alf Pike	3.00	6.00	12.00
292	Babe Pratt	3.00	6.00	12.00
293	Alex Shibicky	3.00	6.00	12.00
294	Clint Smith	3.00	6.00	12.00
295	Norman Tustin	20.00	42.50	85.00
296	Grant Warwick	6.25	12.50	25.00
297	Phil Watson	2.50	5.00	10.00

MAPLE LEAFS

No.	Player	VG	EX	NRMT
298	Syl Apps, Sr., Photo on Ice	5.00	10.00	20.00
299	Murray Armstrong	3.00	6.00	12.00
300	Andy Blair	3.00	6.00	12.00
301	Buzz Boll	3.00	6.00	12.00
302	George Boothman	33.75	67.50	135.00
303	Turk Broda, Goalie	3.75	7.50	15.00
304	Lorne Carr	12.50	25.00	50.00
305	Murph Chamberlain	3.75	7.50	15.00
306	Lex Chisholm	6.25	12.50	25.00
307	Jack Church	6.25	12.50	25.00
308	Francis Clancy	3.00	6.00	12.00
309	Charlie Conacher	3.00	6.00	12.00
310	Bob Copp	12.50	25.00	50.00
311	Baldy Cotton	3.00	6.00	12.00
312	Bob Davidson	3.00	6.00	12.00
313	Hap Day	3.00	6.00	12.00
314	Ernie Dickens	33.75	67.50	135.00
315	Gordie Drillon	3.00	6.00	12.00
316	Frank Finnigan	3.75	7.50	15.00
317	Jack Forsey	33.50	67.50	135.00
318	Jimmy Fowler, Error	3.00	6.00	12.00
319	Bob Goldham	35.00	70.00	140.00
320	Hank Goldup	3.75	7.50	15.00
321	George Hainsworth, Goalie	3.75	7.50	15.00
322	Reg Hamilton	3.00	6.00	12.00
323	Red Heron	3.75	7.50	15.00
324	Mel Hill	33.75	67.50	135.00
325	Frank Hollett	3.00	6.00	12.00
326	Red Horner	3.00	6.00	12.00
327	Art Jackson	3.00	6.00	12.00
328	Harvey Jackson	3.00	6.00	12.00
329	Bingo Kampman	3.00	6.00	12.00
330	Pep (Regis) Kelly	3.00	6.00	12.00
331	William Kendall	15.00	30.00	60.00
332	Hec Kilrea	15.00	30.00	60.00
333	Pete Langelle	3.75	7.50	15.00
334	Bucko McDonald	6.25	12.50	25.00
335A	Norm Mann, Name Clear	3.75	7.50	15.00
335B	Norm Mann, Name Overlaps Stick	37.50	75.00	150.00
336	Gus Marker	3.75	7.50	15.00
337	Johnny McCreedy	6.25	12.50	25.00
338	Jack McLean	20.00	40.00	80.00
339	Don Metz, Young Photo	3.00	6.00	12.00
340	Nick Metz, Young Photo	3.00	6.00	12.00
341	George Parsons	3.75	7.50	15.00
342	Bud (Norman) Poile	33.75	67.50	135.00
343	Babe Pratt	43.75	87.50	175.00
344	Joe Primeau	3.75	7.50	15.00
345	Doc Romnes	12.50	25.00	50.00
346	Sweeny Schriner	3.75	7.50	15.00
347	Jack Shill	3.75	7.50	15.00
348	Wally Stanowski, Error	3.00	6.00	12.00
349	Phil Stein, Goalie	6.25	12.50	25.00
350A	Gaye Stewart, Home	43.75	87.50	175.00
350B	Gaye Stewart, Away	40.00	80.00	160.00
351	Billy Taylor	3.75	7.50	15.00
352	Rhys Thompson	50.00	100.00	200.00
353	Bill Thoms	3.00	6.00	12.00
354	1944-45 Team Picture	43.75	87.50	175.00

MISCELLANEOUS PHOTOS

No.	Player	VG	EX	NRMT
355	1937 Winnipeg Monarchs	25.00	50.00	100.00
356	Foster Hewitt	12.50	25.00	50.00
357	Wes McKnight	25.00	50.00	100.00

Bee Hive Group One
1933-34 Issue
Card No. 348, Error, Name misspelled
Stanowsky on face

Bee Hive Group One
1933-34 Issue
Card No. 359,
Byng Trophy

Bee Hive Group One
1933-34 Issue
Card No. 361,
Hart Trophy

Bee Hive Group Two
1945-63 Issue
Card No. 16,
Woody Dumart

TROPHIES
DATED ON THE BACK
LAST WINNER 1938-39 SEASON

No.	Player	VG	EX	NRMT
358	Allan Cup	12.50	25.00	50.00
359	Byng Trophy	12.50	25.00	50.00
360	Calder Trophy	12.50	25.00	50.00
361	Hart Trophy	12.50	25.00	50.00
362	Memorial Cup	12.50	25.00	50.00
363	Prince of Wales Trophy	12.50	25.00	50.00
364	Stanley Cup	12.50	25.00	50.00
365	Georges Vezina Trophy	12.50	25.00	50.00

NOT DATED
BLANK BACK

No.	Player	VG	EX	NRMT
366	Allan Cup	37.50	75.00	150.00
367	Byng Trophy	37.50	75.00	150.00
368	Calder Trophy	37.50	75.00	150.00
369	Hart Trophy	37.50	75.00	150.00
370	Memorial Cup	37.50	75.00	150.00
371	Prince of Wales Trophy	37.50	75.00	150.00
372A	Stanley Cup, Name Horizontal	37.50	75.00	150.00
372B	Stanley Cup, Name Diagonal	37.50	75.00	100.00
373	Georges Vezina Trophy	37.50	75.00	150.00

GROUP TWO PHOTOS

— 1944 TO 1963 —

Photographs were updated starting with the Toronto Maple Leafs team of 1944-45. These photos were issued with the player's facsimile autograph. A team photo of the 1944-45 Stanley Cup Champions was also issued. After 1945 the Maple Leaf photos were issued with a new large-size script for the players' names which is now characteristic of Group II. New photos with the new script were gradually added year by year until 1948, when the complete series was available. In some cases, although a player's name may appear on the company photo list, proof of actual photo distribution remains unconfirmed.

Photo Size: 4 1/4" x 6 3/4"
Mat Size: 5 1/2" X 8"
Face: Black and white; Name
Mat: Red, blue or beige
Back: Blank
Imprint: None
Complete Set No.: Unknown
Common Player: 1.25 2.50 5.00

BOSTON BRUINS

No.	Player	VG	EX	NRMT
1	Bob Armstrong	1.25	2.50	5.00
2	Pete Babando	10.00	20.00	40.00
3	Ray Barry	12.50	25.00	50.00
4	Gus Bodnar	10.00	20.00	40.00
5	Leo Boivin	2.50	5.00	10.00
6	Frankie Brimsek, Goalie	3.75	7.50	15.00
7	Adam Brown, With Net		Unconfirmed	
8	John Bucyk	2.50	5.00	10.00
9	Charlie Burns	1.25	2.50	5.00
10	Jack Caffrey	10.00	20.00	40.00
11	Real Chevrefils	1.25	2.50	5.00
12A	Wayne Connelly	3.75	7.50	15.00
12B	Wayne Connelly, Name Overlaps Skate	12.50	25.00	50.00
13	Murray Costello	3.00	6.00	12.00
14	John Crawford, Jersey No 6	3.75	7.50	15.00
15A	Dave Creighton, White	2.50	5.00	10.00
15B	Dave Creighton, Photo on Ice	10.00	20.00	40.00
16	Woody Dumart	3.00	6.00	12.00
17	Pat Eagan	3.75	7.50	15.00
18	Bill Ezinicki		Unconfirmed	
19	Lorne Ferguson	3.00	6.00	12.00
20A	Fern Flaman	3.00	6.00	12.00
20B	Fern Flaman	1.25	2.50	5.00
21	Bruce Gamble, Goalie	1.25	2.50	5.00
22	Cal Gardner	2.50	5.00	10.00
23	Ray Gariepy	3.75	7.50	15.00
24	Jack Gelineau, Goalie	3.75	7.50	15.00
25	Guy Gendron	1.25	2.50	5.00
26A	Warren Godfrey, Ass't Captain	2.00	4.00	8.00
26B	Warren Godfrey, Jersey No 25 With Puck	12.50	25.00	50.00
26C	Warren Godfrey, Jersey No 25 Without Puck	17.50	35.00	75.00

148 • ST. LAWRENCE STARCH COMPANY BEEHIVE PHOTOS

No.	Player	VG	EX	NRMT
27	Ed Harrison	2.00	4.00	8.00
28	Don Head, Goalie	1.50	3.00	6.00
29	Andy Hebenton	2.00	4.00	8.00
30	Murray Henderson	2.50	5.00	10.00
31	Jim Henry, Goalie	3.75	7.50	15.00
32	Larry Hillman	10.00	20.00	40.00
33	Pete Horeck	3.75	7.50	15.00
34	Bronco Horvath	1.25	2.50	5.00
35	Tom Johnson	1.50	3.00	6.00
36	Eddie Johnston, Goalie	2.50	5.00	10.00
37	Forbes Kennedy		Unconfirmed	
38	Joe Klukay	35.00	70.00	140.00
39	Edward Kryznowski	2.50	5.00	10.00
40	Orland Kurtenbach	3.75	7.50	15.00
41	Leo Labine	1.25	2.50	5.00
42	Hal Laycoe	2.00	4.00	8.00
43	Harry Lumley, Goalie	2.00	4.00	8.00
44	Pentti Lund		Unconfirmed	
45	Fleming Mackell	1.25	2.50	5.00
46	Phi. Maloney	2.50	5.00	10.00
47	Frank Martin	2.50	5.00	10.00
48	Jack McIntyre	2.50	5.00	10.00
49	Don McKenney	1.25	2.50	5.00
50	Dick Meissner	1.50	3.00	6.00
51	Doug Mohns	1.25	2.50	5.00
52	Murray Oliver	1.25	2.50	5.00
53	Willie O'Ree	1.50	3.00	6.00
54A	John Peirson	2.50	5.00	10.00
54B	Johnny Peirson	22.50	45.00	90.00
55A	Cliff Pennington, Name Far From Skate	2.00	10.00	20.00
55B	Cliff Pennington, Name Near Skate	15.00	30.00	60.00
56A	Robert Perreault, Goalie	2.00	10.00	20.00
56B	Robert Perreault, Goalie Name Overlaps Skate	15.00	30.00	60.00
57	Jim Peters	7.50	15.00	30.00
58	Dean Prentice	2.00	4.00	8.00
59	Andre Pronovost	2.00	4.00	8.00
60	Bill Quackenbush	2.50	5.00	10.00
61	Larry Regan	10.00	20.00	40.00
62	Earl Reibel	10.00	20.00	40.00
63	Paul Ronty	2.00	4.00	8.00
64	Ed Sanford	2.00	4.00	8.00
65	Terry Sawchuk	18.75	37.50	75.00
66A	Don Simmons, Goalie	1.25	2.50	5.00
66B	Don Simmons, Goalie, Error, Photo of Norm Defelice	35.00	70.00	140.00
67	Kenny Smith	3.75	7.50	15.00
68A	Pat Stapleton, Name Far From Skate	2.00	10.00	20.00
68B	Pat Stapleton, Name Near Skate	15.00	30.00	60.00
69	Vic Stasiuk	2.00	4.00	8.00
70	George (Red) Sullivan	3.75	7.50	15.00
71	Jerry Toppazzini	1.25	2.50	5.00
72	Zellio Toppazzini	1.25	2.50	5.00
73	Grant Warwick	7.50	15.00	30.00
74	Tom Williams	2.00	4.00	8.00

CHICAGO BLACK HAWKS

No.	Player	VG	EX	NRMT
75	Al Arbour	3.75	7.50	15.00
76	Pete Babando	6.25	12.50	25.00
77	Earl Balfour	1.25	2.50	5.00
78	Murray Balfour	1.25	2.50	5.00
79	Jim Bedard	3.00	6.00	12.00
80	Doug Bentley, Ass't Captain	3.00	6.00	12.00
81	Gus Bodnar	3.00	6.00	12.00
82	Frankie Brimsek, Goalie	3.50	7.00	14.00
83	Adam Brown	4.50	9.00	18.00
84	Hank Ciesla	7.50	15.00	30.00
85	Jim Conacher	3.00	6.00	12.00
86	Pete Conacher	1.75	3.50	7.00
87	Roy Conacher	1.75	3.50	7.00
88	Joe Conn	8.75	17.50	35.00
89	Murray Costello	12.50	25.00	50.00
90	Gerry Couture	3.00	6.00	12.00
91	Al Dewsbury	3.00	6.00	12.00
92	Ernie Dickens	3.00	6.00	12.00
93	Jack Evans	1.25	2.50	5.00
94	Reggie Fleming	2.50	5.00	10.00
95	Lidio (Lee) Fogolin	3.00	6.00	12.00
96	Bill Gadsby	1.25	2.50	5.00
97	George Gee	3.00	6.00	12.00
98	Bob Goldham	3.00	6.00	12.00
99	Bep Guidolin	3.00	6.00	12.00

Bee Hive Group Two
1945-63 Issue
Card No. 38,
Joe Klukay

Bee Hive Group Two
1945-63 Issue
Card No. 54A,
John Peirson

Bee Hive Group Two
1945-63 Issue
Card No. 94,
Reggie Fleming

Bee Hive Group Two
1945-63 Issue
Card No. 124, Error, Name
misspelled Jerry on face

No.	Player	VG	EX	NRMT
100	Glenn Hall, Goalie	1.25	2.50	5.00
101	Murray Hall	5.00	10.00	20.00
102	Red Hamill	3.00	6.00	12.00
103	Billy Hay	1.25	2.50	5.00
104	Jim Henry, Goalie	5.00	10.00	20.00
105	Wayne Hillman	4.50	9.00	18.00
106	Pete Horeck		Unconfirmed	
107	Bronco Horvath	1.75	3.50	7.00
108	Fred Hucul	4.50	9.00	18.00
109A	Bobby Hull, Jersey No. 9	40.00	80.00	160.00
109B	Bobby Hull, Jersey No. 16	2.50	5.00	10.00
110	Lou Jankowski	6.25	12.50	25.00
111	Forbes Kennedy	10.00	20.00	40.00
112	Ted Lindsay	2.50	5.00	10.00
113	Ed Litzenberger	1.25	2.50	5.00
114	Harry Lumley, Goalie	2.50	5.00	10.00
115A	Len Lunde	10.00	20.00	40.00
115B	Len Lunde, Name Overlaps Stick	4.50	9.00	18.00
116	Pat Lundy	3.00	6.00	12.00
117	Vic Lynn		Unconfirmed	
118A	Al MacNeil, Name Ovelaps Stick and Skate	10.00	20.00	40.00
118B	Al MacNeil, Name Overlaps Stick	4.50	9.00	18.00
119A	Chico Maki	6.25	12.50	25.00
119B	Chico Maki, Name Overlaps Stick	4.50	9.00	18.00
120	Douglas McCaig	3.00	6.00	12.00
121	Ab McDonald	1.25	2.50	5.00
122	Jim McFadden	10.00	20.00	40.00
123	Max McNab		Unconfirmed	
124	Gerry Melnyk, Error	1.75	3.50	7.00
125	Stan Mikita	1.25	2.50	5.00
126	Don Morrison		Unconfirmed	
127	Gus Mortson	3.00	6.00	12.00
128	Bill Mosienko	1.25	2.50	5.00
129	Ron Murphy	1.25	2.50	5.00
130	Ralph Nattrass	3.00	6.00	12.00
131	Eric Nesterenko	1.25	2.50	5.00
132	Bert Olmstead	3.00	6.00	12.00
133	Jim Peters	10.00	20.00	40.00
134	Pierre Pilote	1.25	2.50	5.00
135	Metro Prystai	3.00	6.00	12.00
136	Max Quackenbush		Unconfirmed	
137	Clare Raglan	3.00	6.00	12.00
138A	Al Rollins, Goalie, Vertical Photo	15.00	30.00	60.00
138B	Al Rollins, Goalie, Horizontal Photo	10.00	20.00	40.00
139	Tod Sloan	1.25	2.50	5.00
140	Dollard St. Laurent	1.25	2.50	5.00
141	Gaye Stewart	3.00	6.00	12.00
142	Jack Stewart	7.50	15.00	30.00
143A	Bob Turner	12.50	25.00	50.00
143B	Bob Turner, Name Overlaps Stick	2.00	10.00	20.00
144	Elmer Vasko	1.25	2.50	5.00
145	Kenny Wharram	1.25	2.50	5.00
146	Larry Wilson	3.50	7.00	14.00
147	Howie Young	6.25	12.50	25.00
148	Larry Zeidel		Unconfirmed	

DETROIT RED WINGS

No.	Player	VG	EX	NRMT
149	Syd Abel, Captain	3.75	7.50	15.00
150	Al Arbour	7.50	15.00	30.00
151	Pete Babando	3.50	7.00	14.00
152A	Doug Barkley, Partial Blade	8.75	17.50	35.00
152B	Doug Barkley, No Blade	4.50	9.00	18.00
153	Hank Bassen, Goalie	1.25	2.50	5.00
154	Stephen Black	4.50	9.00	18.00
155	Marcel Bonin	3.50	7.00	14.00
156	John Bucyk	7.50	15.00	30.00
157	John Conacher	27.50	55.00	110.00
158	Gerry Couture, Error	5.00	10.00	20.00
159	Billy Dea	4.50	9.00	18.00
160	Alex Delvecchio	2.50	5.00	10.00
161	Bill Delvecchio	2.50	5.00	10.00
162	Al Dewsbury		Unconfirmed	
163	Bill Dineen	1.75	3.50	7.00
164	Jim Enio	7.50	15.00	30.00
165	Alex Faulkner	1.75	3.50	7.00
166	Lidio (Lee) Fogolin	3.50	7.00	14.00
167	Val Fonteyne	1.25	2.50	5.00
168A	Bill Gadsby, Low Name	3.00	6.00	12.00
168B	Bill Gadsby, High Name	3.00	6.00	12.00
169A	Fern Gauthier	5.00	10.00	20.00

BEEHIVE PHOTOS ST. LAWRENCE STARCH COMPANY • 149

No.	Player	VG	EX	NRMT
169B	Fern Gauthier, Error	40.00	80.00	160.00
170	George Gee	1.75	3.50	7.00
171	Fred Glover	1.75	3.50	7.00
172	Howie Glover	1.25	2.50	5.00
173	Warren Godfrey	1.25	2.50	5.00
174	Peter Goegan	1.25	2.50	5.00
175	Bob Goldham	1.75	3.50	7.00
176	Glenn Hall, Goalie	10.00	20.00	40.00
177	Larry Hillman	12.50	25.00	50.00
178	Pete Horeck	10.00	20.00	40.00
179A	Gordie Howe	6.25	12.50	25.00
179B	Gordie Howe, Captain	7.50	15.00	30.00
180	Ron Ingram	3.00	6.00	12.00
181	Larry Jeffrey	8.75	17.50	35.00
182	Al Johnson	1.25	2.50	5.00
183	Red Kelly	1.25	2.50	5.00
184	Forbes Kennedy	1.25	2.50	5.00
185	Leo Labine	1.25	2.50	5.00
186	Tony Leswick	1.25	2.50	5.00
187	Ted Lindsay	2.50	5.00	10.00
188	Ed Litzenberger	8.75	17.50	35.00
189	Harry Lumley, Goalie	2.50	5.00	10.00
190	Len Lunde	1.25	2.50	5.00
191	Parker MacDonald	1.25	2.50	5.00
192	Bruce MacGregor	1.75	3.50	7.00
193	Clare Martin	3.75	7.50	15.00
194	Jim McFadden	3.75	7.50	15.00
195	Max McNab	3.75	7.50	15.00
196	Gerry Melnyk, Error	1.75	3.50	7.00
197	Don Morrison	6.25	12.50	25.00
198	Roderick Morrison	10.00	20.00	40.00
199	Gerry Odrowski	1.25	2.50	5.00
200	Murray Oliver	1.25	2.50	5.00
201	Marty Pavelich	1.25	2.50	5.00
202	Jim Peters	12.50	25.00	50.00
203	Bud (Norman) Poile	17.50	35.00	70.00
204	Andre Pronovost	2.50	5.00	10.00
205	Marcel Pronovost	2.50	5.00	10.00
206	Metro Prystai	1.25	2.50	5.00
207	Bill Quackenbush, Ass't Captain	12.50	25.00	50.00
208	Earl Reibel	1.25	2.50	5.00
209	Leo Reise, Jr.	1.75	3.50	7.00
210A	Terry Sawchuk, Goalie	3.75	7.50	15.00
210B	Terry Sawchuk, Goalie, Partial Stick	2.00	10.00	20.00
211	Glen Skov	1.25	2.50	5.00
212	Floyd Smith	1.75	3.50	7.00
213A	Vic Stasiuk, Home, Full Stick	4.50	9.00	18.00
213B	Vic Stasiuk, Home, Partial Stick	12.50	25.00	50.00
213C	Vic Stasiuk, Away	1.75	3.50	7.00
214	Gaye Stewart	5.00	10.00	20.00
215	Jack Stewart, Ass't Captian	1.75	3.50	7.00
216	Norm Ullman	1.25	2.50	5.00
217	Johnny Wilson	1.25	2.50	5.00
218	Benny Woit	1.75	3.50	7.00
219	Howie Young	3.75	7.50	15.00
220	Larry Zeidel	4.50	9.00	18.00

MONTREAL CANADIENS

No.	Player	VG	EX	NRMT
221	Ralph Backstrom	1.25	2.50	5.00
223	Dave Balon	1.25	2.50	5.00
223	Jean Beliveau	3.75	7.50	15.00
224A	Red Berenson, White Script	7.50	15.00	30.00
224B	Red Berenson, Black Script	57.50	115.00	230.00
225	Marcel Bonin	1.25	2.50	5.00
226	Emile (Butch) Bouchard	2.50	5.00	10.00
227	Tod Campeau	10.00	20.00	40.00
228	Joe Carveth	3.00	6.00	12.00
229	Murph Chamberlain, Ass't Captain	17.50	25.00	50.00
230	Doc Couture	7.50	15.00	30.00
231	Floyd Curry, Error	1.25	2.50	5.00
232	Ian Cushenan	2.50	5.00	10.00
233	Lorne Davis	3.00	6.00	12.00
234	Eddie Dorohoy	4.50	9.00	18.00
235	Gilles Dube	10.00	20.00	40.00
236	Bill Durnan, Goalie	4.50	9.00	18.00
237	Norm Dussault	3.75	7.50	15.00
238	John Ferguson	2.50	5.00	10.00
239	Bob Fillion	3.00	6.00	12.00
240	Louie Fontinato	1.25	2.50	5.00
241	Dick Gamble	3.00	6.00	12.00
242	Bernard Geoffrion	3.00	6.00	12.00
243	Phil Goyette	1.25	2.50	5.00

Bee Hive Group Two
1945-63 Issue
Card No. 231, Error, Name
misspelled Currie on face

Bee Hive Group Two
1945-63 Issue
Card No. 245,
John Hanna

Bee Hive Group Two
1945-63 Issue
Card No. 252A,
Charlie Hodge, White Script

Bee Hive Group Two
1945-63 Issue
Card No. 252AB
Charlie Hodge, Black Script

No.	Player	VG	EX	NRMT
244	Leo Gravelle	4.50	9.00	18.00
245	John Hanna	12.50	25.00	50.00
246	Glen Harmon	3.00	6.00	12.00
247	Terry Harper	1.25	2.50	5.00
248	Doug Harvey	2.50	5.00	10.00
249	Bill Hicke	1.25	2.50	5.00
250	Ike Hildebrand		Unconfirmed	
251	Bert Hirschfeld		Unconfirmed	
252A	Charlie Hodge, Goalie, White Script	12.50	25.00	50.00
252B	Charlie Hodge, Goalie, Black Script	2.50	5.00	10.00
253	Tom Johnson	1.00	2.00	4.00
254	Vern Kaiser	4.50	9.00	18.00
255	Frank King	7.50	15.00	30.00
256	Elmer Lach, White Background	2.50	5.00	10.00
257	Al Langlois	1.25	2.50	5.00
258	Jacques Laperriere	1.25	2.50	5.00
259	Hal Laycoe	3.00	6.00	12.00
260	Jackie Leclair	1.25	2.50	5.00
261	Roger Leger	1.80	6.00	12.00
262	Ed Litzenberger	5.00	10.00	20.00
263	Ross Lowe	7.50	15.00	30.00
264	Al MacNeil	1.25	2.50	5.00
265	Bud MacPherson	1.25	2.50	5.00
266	Cesare Maniago, Goalie	1.25	2.50	5.00
267	Don Marshall	1.25	2.50	5.00
268	Paul Masnick	3.00	6.00	12.00
269	Eddie Mazur	3.00	6.00	12.00
270	John McCormack	3.00	6.00	12.00
271	Alvin McDonald	1.25	2.50	5.00
272	Callum McKay	3.00	6.00	12.00
273	Gerry McNeil, Goalie	2.50	5.00	10.00
274	Paul Meger	3.00	6.00	12.00
275	Dickie Moore	2.50	5.00	10.00
276	Kenny Mosdell	6.25	12.50	25.00
277	Bert Olmstead	1.25	2.50	5.00
278	Gerry Plamondon	4.50	9.00	18.00
279	Jacques Plante, Goalie	3.75	7.50	15.00
280	Andre Pronovost	1.25	2.50	5.00
281	Claude Provost	1.25	2.50	5.00
282	Ken Reardon	2.50	5.00	10.00
283	Billy Reay	1.25	2.50	5.00
284	Henri Richard	3.75	7.50	15.00
285	Maurice Richard, White Background	4.50	9.00	18.00
286	Rip Riopelle	4.50	9.00	18.00
287	George Robertson	10.00	20.00	40.00
288	Bobby Rousseau	1.25	2.50	5.00
289	Dollard St. Laurent	1.25	2.50	5.00
290	Jean-Guy Talbot	1.25	2.50	5.00
291A	Gilles Tremblay	1.25	2.50	5.00
291B	Gilles Tremblay, Light Background	27.50	55.00	110.00
292A	J.C. Tremblay	1.25	2.50	5.00
292B	J.C. Tremblay, Light Background	27.50	55.00	110.00
293	Bob Turner	1.25	2.50	5.00
294	Grant Warwick	8.75	17.50	35.00
295	Gump Worsley, Goalie	2.50	5.00	10.00

NEW YORK RANGERS

No.	Player	VG	EX	NRMT
296	Clint Albright	3.50	7.00	14.00
297A	Dave Balon, Name High	2.50	5.00	10.00
297B	Dave Balon, Name Low	2.50	5.00	10.00
298A	Andy Bathgate, Home	3.75	7.50	15.00
298B	Andy Bathgate, Away	5.00	10.00	20.00
299	Max Bentley	10.00	20.00	40.00
300	Johnny Bower, Goalie	10.00	20.00	40.00
301	Hyman Buller	4.50	9.00	18.00
302A	Larry Cahan, Home	2.50	5.00	10.00
302B	Larry Cahan, Away, Name Overlaps Both Skates	3.75	7.50	15.00
302C	Larry Cahan, Away, Name Overlaps Right Skate	18.75	37.50	75.00
303	Bob Crystal	4.50	9.00	18.00
304	Jim Conacher		Unconfirmed	
305	Brian Cullen	1.25	2.50	5.00
306	Ian Cushenan	1.25	2.50	5.00
307	Billy Dea	4.50	9.00	18.00
308	Frank Eddolls	2.50	5.00	10.00
309	Pat Egan	4.50	9.00	18.00
310A	Jack Evans, Name Parallel To Bottom	1.25	2.50	5.00
310B	Jack Evans, Name Printed Diagonally	6.25	12.50	25.00
311	Dunc Fisher	3.00	6.00	12.00
312	Louie Fontinato	1.25	2.50	5.00
313	Bill Gadsby	2.00	4.00	8.00

150 • ST. LAWRENCE STARCH COMPANY BEEHIVE PHOTOS

No.	Player	VG	EX	NRMT
314	Guy Gendron	1.25	2.50	5.00
315	Rod Gilbert	2.00	4.00	8.00
316	Howie Glover	12.50	25.00	50.00
317	Jackie Gordon		Unconfirmed	
318	Phil Goyette	1.25	2.50	5.00
319	Aldo Guidolin	4.50	9.00	18.00
320	Vic Hadfield	1.25	2.50	5.00
321	Ted Hampson	1.25	2.50	5.00
322	Doug Harvey	1.25	2.50	5.00
323	Andy Hebenton	3.00	6.00	12.00
324	Camille Henry	1.25	2.50	5.00
325	Wally Hergesheimer	1.25	2.50	5.00
326	Ike Hildebrand	7.50	15.00	30.00
327	Bronco Horvath	2.50	5.00	10.00
328	Harry Howell	2.50	5.00	10.00
329A	Earl Ingarfield, Sr., Name Near Stick	2.50	5.00	10.00
329B	Earl Ingarfield, Sr., Name Far From Stick	2.50	5.00	10.00
330	Bing (Winston) Juckes	8.75	17.50	35.00
331	Alex Kaleta	3.00	6.00	12.00
332	Stephen Kraftcheck	7.50	15.00	30.00
333	Eddie Kullman	3.00	6.00	12.00
334	Gus Kyle	3.00	6.00	12.00
335	Gord Labossiere	6.00	12.50	25.00
336	Al Langlois	1.25	2.50	5.00
337	Edgar Laprade	3.00	6.00	12.00
338	Tony Leswick	2.50	5.00	10.00
339	Danny Lewicki	2.50	5.00	10.00
340	Pentti Lund	3.00	6.00	12.00
341	Don Marshall	1.25	2.50	5.00
342	Jack McCartan, Goalie	1.25	2.50	5.00
343	Bill McDonagh	4.00	10.00	20.00
344	Don McKenney	3.00	6.00	12.00
345	Jackie McLeod	2.50	5.00	10.00
346	Nick Mickoski	2.50	5.00	10.00
347	Billy Moe	3.50	7.00	14.00
348	Elwyn Morris		Unconfirmed	
349	Ron Murphy	1.25	2.50	5.00
350	Buddy O'Connor	3.00	6.00	12.00
351	Marcel Paille, Goalie	17.50	35.00	70.00
352	Jacques Plante, Goalie	12.50	25.00	50.00
353	Bud (Norman) Poile	7.50	15.00	30.00
354	Larry Popein	4.00	8.00	16.00
355A	Dean Prentice, Home	1.25	2.50	5.00
355B	Dean Prentice, Away, Name High	3.00	6.00	12.00
355C	Dean Prentice, Away, Name High	5.00	10.00	20.00
356	Don Raleigh	2.50	5.00	10.00
357A	Jean Ratelle	5.00	10.00	20.00
357B	Jean Ratelle, Error	7.50	15.00	30.00
358	Chuck Rayner, Goalie	2.50	5.00	10.00
359	Leo Reise, Jr.	2.50	5.00	10.00
360	Paul Ronty	2.50	5.00	10.00
361	Ken Schinkel	1.25	2.50	5.00
362	Eddie Shack	1.25	2.50	5.00
363	Fred Shero	3.50	7.00	14.00
364	Reg Sinclair	4.50	9.00	18.00
365	Eddie Slowinski	3.50	7.00	14.00
366	Allan Stanley	1.25	2.50	5.00
367	Wally Stanowski	3.00	6.00	12.00
368	George (Red) Sullivan	1.25	2.50	5.00
369	Zellio Toppazzini		Unconfirmed	
370	Gump Worsley, Goalie	1.25	2.50	5.00

TORONTO MAPLE LEAFS

No.	Player	VG	EX	NRMT
371	Garry Aldcorn	3.50	7.00	14.00
372	Syl Apps, Sr., Posed Near Boards	37.50	75.00	150.00
373	Al Arbour	2.50	5.00	10.00
374A	George Armstrong	2.50	5.00	10.00
374B	George Armstrong, Captain	3.50	7.00	14.00
374C	George Armstrong, Captain, Light Background	40.00	82.50	165.00
375	Bob Bailey	4.50	9.00	18.00
376	Earl Balfour	3.00	6.00	12.00
377	Bill Barilko	4.50	9.00	18.00
378	Andy Bathgate	6.25	12.50	25.00
379	Bob Baun	1.25	2.50	5.00
380	Max Bentley	2.50	5.00	10.00
381	Jack Bionda	25.00	50.00	100.00
382	Garth Boesch	1.75	3.50	7.00
383	Leo Boivin	3.00	6.00	12.00
384	Hugh Bolton	4.50	9.00	18.00
385	Johnny Bower, Goalie	2.50	5.00	10.00

Bee Hive Group Two
1945-63 Issue
Card No. 357B, Error, Name misspelled John on face

Bee Hive Group Two
1945-63 Issue
Card No. 447, David Reid

Bee Hive Group Two
1945-63 Issue
Card No. 454A, Error, Name misspelled Alan on face
(Dark Background)

Bee Hive Group Two
1945-63 Issue
Card No. 454A, Allan Stanley
(Light background)

No.	Player	VG	EX	NRMT
386	Carl Brewer	1.25	2.50	5.00
387	Turk Broda, Goalie	2.50	5.00	10.00
388	Larry Cahan	3.00	6.00	12.00
389	Ray Ceresino	7.50	15.00	30.00
390	Ed Chadwick, Goalie	2.50	5.00	10.00
391	Pete Conacher	15.00	30.00	60.00
392	Les Costello	4.50	9.00	18.00
393	Dave Creighton	3.50	7.00	14.00
394A	Barry Cullen	4.50	9.00	18.00
394B	Barry Cullen, Error	12.50	25.00	50.00
395	Brian Cullen	3.00	6.00	12.00
396	Robert Dawes	4.50	9.00	18.00
397	Kent Douglas	1.25	2.50	5.00
398	Dick Duff	1.25	2.50	5.00
399	Garry Edmundson	1.25	2.50	5.00
400	Gerry Ehman	1.25	2.50	5.00
401	Bill Ezinicki	2.50	5.00	10.00
402	Fern Flaman	10.00	20.00	40.00
403	Cal Gardner	3.00	6.00	12.00
404	Ted Hampson	1.25	2.50	5.00
405	Gord Hannigan	3.50	7.00	14.00
406	Billy Harris	1.25	2.50	5.00
407	Bob Hassard	12.50	25.00	50.00
408	Larry Hillman	1.25	2.50	5.00
409	Tim Horton	3.00	6.00	12.00
410	Bronco Horvath	3.00	6.00	12.00
411	Ron Hurst	25.00	50.00	100.00
412	Gerry James, Error	5.00	10.00	20.00
413	Bill Juzda	3.00	6.00	12.00
414A	Red Kelly	2.50	5.00	10.00
414B	Red Kelly, Helmet	5.00	10.00	20.00
415	Ted Kennedy	2.50	5.00	10.00
416	Dave Keon	2.50	5.00	10.00
417	Joe Klukay	1.75	3.50	7.00
418	Stephen Kraftcheck	7.50	15.00	30.00
419	Danny Lewicki	3.00	6.00	12.00
420	Ed Litzenberger	1.75	3.50	7.00
421	Harry Lumley, Goalie	3.00	6.00	12.00
422	Vic Lynn	2.50	5.00	10.00
423	Fleming MacKell	3.00	6.00	12.00
424	John MacMillan	1.25	2.50	5.00
425	Al MacNeil	3.00	6.00	12.00
426	Frank Mahovlich	3.00	6.00	12.00
427	Phi. Maloney	25.00	50.00	100.00
428	Cesare Maniago, Goalie	1.25	2.50	5.00
429	Frank Mathers	4.50	9.00	18.00
430	John McCormack	6.25	12.50	25.00
431	Parker McDonald	3.00	6.00	12.00
432	Don McKenney	6.25	12.50	25.00
433	Howie Meeker	2.50	5.00	10.00
434	Don Metz, Group One Photo With Scrip	50.00	105.00	210.00
435	Nick Metz, Group One Photo With Scrip	50.00	105.00	210.00
436	Rudy Migay	1.25	2.50	5.00
437	Jim Mikol	1.25	2.50	5.00
438	Jim Morrison	3.00	6.00	12.00
439	Gus Mortson	1.75	3.50	7.00
440	Eric Nesterenko	3.00	6.00	12.00
441	Bob Nevin	1.25	2.50	5.00
442	Mike Nykoluk	7.50	15.00	30.00
443	Bert Olmstead	2.50	5.00	10.00
444	Bob Pulford	2.50	5.00	10.00
445	Marc Reaume	2.50	5.00	10.00
446	Larry Regan	1.25	2.50	5.00
447	David Reid	20.00	40.00	80.00
448	Al Rollins, Goalie	3.00	6.00	12.00
449A	Eddie Shack	2.50	5.00	10.00
449B	Eddie Shack, Group Two Photo, Light Background	37.50	75.00	150.00
450	Don Simmons, Goalie	1.75	3.50	7.00
451	Tod Sloan	1.75	3.50	7.00
452	Sid Smith	1.75	3.50	7.00
453	Bob Solinger	10.00	20.00	40.00
454A	Allan Stanley, Dark Background, Error	2.50	5.00	10.00
454B	Allan Stanley, Light Background	3.75	7.50	15.00
455	Wally Stanowski	60.00	125.00	250.00
456	Ron Stewart	1.25	2.50	5.00
457	Harry Taylor	5.00	10.00	20.00
458	Jim Thomson	1.75	3.50	7.00
459	Ray Timgren	3.00	6.00	12.00
460	Harry Watson	1.75	3.50	7.00
461	Johnny Wilson	1.25	2.50	5.00
462	1962-63 Team Picture	112.50	225.00	450.00

FOUR WHITE BORDERS

No.	Player	VG	EX	NRMT
463	Allan Cup		Unconfirmed	
464	Byng Trophy	37.50	75.00	150.00
465	Calder Memorial Trophy	37.50	75.00	150.00
466	Hart Trophy	37.50	75.00	150.00
467	Memorial Cup		Unconfirmed	
468	James Norris Memorial Trophy	37.50	75.00	150.00
469	Prince of Wales Trophy	37.50	75.00	150.00
470	Art Ross Trophy	37.50	75.00	150.00
471	Stanley Cup	37.50	75.00	150.00
472	Georges Vezina Trophy	37.50	75.00	150.00

BOTTOM WHITE BORDER

No.	Player	VG	EX	NRMT
473	Allan Cup		Unconfirmed	
474	Byng Trophy	17.50	35.00	75.00
475	Calder Memorial Trophy	17.50	35.00	75.00
476	Hart Trophy	17.50	35.00	75.00
477	Memorial Cup Inc.		Unconfirmed	
478	James Norris Memorial Trophy	17.50	35.00	75.00
479	Prince of Wales Trophy	17.50	35.00	75.00
480	Art Ross Trophy	17.50	35.00	75.00
481	Stanley Cup	17.50	35.00	75.00
482	Georges Vezina Trophy	17.50	35.00	75.00

GROUP THREE

— 1964 TO 67 —

These unnumbered black and white photographs feature a woodgrain border. They were issued between 1964 and 1967. The players' names appear inscribed in a nameplate at the bottom centre of the border. They were not numbered and are listed alphabetically by team and then alphabetically within the team. As with all Beehive groups, it is not known if the listings are complete.

Card Size: 5 1/2" X 8"
Face: Black and white, wood grain border on paper stock; Name
Back: Blank
Imprint: None
Complete Set No.: Unknown due to unconfirmed photos
Common Player: 3.00 6.00 12.00

BOSTON BRUINS

No.	Player	VG	EX	NRMT
1	Murray Balfour	3.00	6.00	12.00
2	Leo Boivin	3.00	6.00	12.00
3	John Bucyk	3.00	6.00	12.00
4	Wayne Connelly	30.00	60.00	120.00
5	Bob Dillabough	3.00	6.00	12.00
6	Gary Dornhoefer	3.00	6.00	12.00
7	Reggie Fleming	3.00	6.00	12.00
8	Guy Gendron	25.00	50.00	100.00
9	Warren Godfrey	45.00	87.50	175.00
10	Ted Green	3.00	6.00	12.00
11	Andy Hebenton	25.00	50.00	100.00
12	Eddie Johnston, Goalie	3.00	6.00	12.00
13	Tom Johnson	3.00	6.00	12.00
14	Forbes Kennedy	3.00	6.00	12.00
15	Orland Kurtenbach	4.50	9.00	18.00
16	Bobby Leiter	3.00	6.00	12.00
17	Parker MacDonald	3.00	6.00	12.00
18	Bob McCord	3.00	6.00	12.00
19	Ab McDonald	3.00	6.00	12.00
20	Murray Oliver	3.00	6.00	12.00
21	Bernie Parent, Goalie	10.00	20.00	40.00
22	Cliff Pennington	37.50	75.00	150.00
23	Robert Perreault, Goalie	50.00	100.00	200.00
24	Dean Prentice	3.00	6.00	12.00
25	Ron Schock, Error	3.00	6.00	12.00
26	Pat Stapleton	15.00	30.00	60.00
27	Ron Stewart	3.00	6.00	12.00
28	Ed Westfall	3.00	6.00	12.00
29	Tom Williams	3.00	6.00	12.00

CHICAGO BLACK HAWKS

No.	Players	VG	EX	NRMT
30	Lou Angotti	3.00	6.00	12.00
31	Wally Boyer	3.00	6.00	12.00
32	Denis DeJordy, Goalie	3.00	6.00	12.00
33	Dave Dryden, Goalie	3.00	6.00	12.00

Bee Hive Group Three
1964-67 Issue
Card No. 4,
Wayne Connelly

Bee Hive Group Three
1964-67 Issue
Card No. 25, Error,
Name misspelled
Shock on face

Bee Hive Group Three
1964-67 Issue
Card No. 35, Error,
Name misspelled
Glen on face

No.	Player	VG	EX	NRMT
34A	Phil Esposito, With Blade	7.50	15.00	30.00
34B	Phil Esposito, Without Blade	3.00	6.00	12.00
35	Glenn Hall, Goalie, Error	3.00	6.00	12.00
36	Murray Hall	37.50	75.00	150.00
37	Billy Hay	3.00	6.00	12.00
38	Camille Henry	5.50	11.00	22.00
39	Wayne Hillman	25.00	50.00	100.00
40	Ken Hodge, Sr.	3.00	6.00	12.00
41A	Bobby Hull, Home	32.50	65.00	130.00
41B	Bobby Hull, Home, Negative Reversed	50.00	100.00	200.00
41C	Bobby Hull, Away, with Blade	5.00	10.00	20.00
41D	Bobby Hull, Away, without Blade	5.00	10.00	20.00
41E	Bobby Hull, Home Portrait	65.00	130.00	260.00
41F	Bobby Hull, Promotional Portrait	5.00	10.00	20.00
42	Dennis Hull	3.00	6.00	12.00
43	Doug Jarrett	3.00	6.00	12.00
44	Len Lunde	3.00	6.00	12.00
45	Al MacNeil	3.00	6.00	12.00
46A	Chico Maki	18.75	37.50	75.00
46B	Chico Maki, Portrait	3.00	6.00	12.00
47	John McKenzie	3.00	6.00	12.00
48	Gerry Melnyk		Unconfirmed	
49	Stan Mikita	3.00	6.00	12.00
50	Doug Mohns	3.00	6.00	12.00
51A	Eric Nesterenko, Light Background	45.00	85.00	175.00
51B	Eric Nesterenko, Dark Background	3.00	6.00	12.00
52A	Pierre Pilote, Home	45.00	85.00	175.00
52B	Pierre Pilote, Away	3.00	6.00	12.00
53	Matt Ravlich	3.00	6.00	12.00
54	Dollard St. Laurent		Unconfirmed	
55A	Fred Stanfield	25.00	50.00	100.00
55B	Fred Stanfield, Reversed Negative	25.00	50.00	100.00
56	Pat Stapleton	3.00	6.00	12.00
57	Bob Turner	40.00	80.00	160.00
58	Ed Van Impe	3.00	6.00	12.00
59	Elmer Vasko	3.00	6.00	12.00
60	Kenny Wharram	3.00	6.00	12.00

DETROIT RED WINGS

No.	Player	VG	EX	NRMT
61	Doug Barkley	3.00	6.00	12.00
62	Hank Bassen, Goalie	3.00	6.00	12.00
63A	Andy Bathgate, Total number on sleeve	3.00	6.00	12.00
63B	Andy Bathgate, Partial number on sleeve	3.00	6.00	12.00
64	Gary Bergman	3.00	6.00	12.00
65	Leo Boivin	3.00	6.00	12.00
66	Roger Crozier, Goalie	3.00	6.00	12.00
67A	Alex Delvecchio, Home	3.00	6.00	12.00
67B	Alex Delvecchio, Away	45.00	90.00	180.00
68	Alex Faulkner	40.00	80.00	160.00
69	Val Fonteyne	3.00	6.00	12.00
70	Bill Gadsby	3.75	7.50	15.00
71	Warren Godfrey	3.75	7.50	15.00
72	Pete Goegan	3.75	7.50	15.00
73	Murray Hall	3.00	6.00	12.00
74	Ted Hampson	3.00	6.00	12.00
75	Billy Harris	5.00	10.00	20.00
76	Paul Henderson	3.00	6.00	12.00
77A	Gordie Howe	5.00	10.00	20.00
77B	Gordie Howe, Captain	25.00	50.00	100.00
78	Ron Ingram	33.75	67.50	135.00
79A	Larry Jeffrey, Home	12.50	25.00	50.00
79B	Larry Jeffrey, Away	12.50	25.00	50.00
80A	Eddie Joyal	3.00	6.00	12.00
80B	Eddie Joyal, Reversed Negative	30.00	62.50	125.00
81	Al Langlois	3.00	6.00	12.00
82	Ted Lindsay	3.00	6.00	12.00
83	Parker MacDonald	3.00	6.00	12.00
84A	Bruce MacGregor, Home	5.00	10.00	20.00
84B	Bruce MacGregor, Away	12.50	25.00	50.00
85	Pete Mahovlich	3.00	6.00	12.00
86	Bert Marshall	3.00	6.00	12.00
87	Pit Martin	3.00	6.00	12.00
88	Bob McCord		Unconfirmed	
89	Ab McDonald	3.00	6.00	12.00
90	Ron Murphy	3.00	6.00	12.00
91	Dean Prentice	3.00	6.00	12.00
92	Andre Pronovost	6.00	12.50	25.00
93	Marcel Pronovost		Unconfirmed	
94A	Floyd Smith, Home	5.00	10.00	20.00

152 • ST. LAWRENCE STARCH COMPANY BEEHIVE PHOTOS

No.	Player	VG	EX	NRMT
94B	Floyd Smith, Home, Reversed Negative	45.00	90.00	180.00
94C	Floyd Smith, Away	32.50	65.00	130.00
95	Norm Ullman	3.00	6.00	12.00
96	Bob Wall	3.00	6.00	12.00

MONTREAL CANADIENS

No.	Player	VG	EX	NRMT
97	Ralph Backstrom	3.00	6.00	12.00
98	Dave Balon	3.00	6.00	12.00
99	Jean Beliveau	4.50	9.00	18.00
100	Red Berenson	3.00	6.00	12.00
101	Yvan Cournoyer	3.00	6.00	12.00
102	Dick Duff	3.00	6.00	12.00
103	John Ferguson	3.00	6.00	12.00
104	John Hanna	32.50	65.00	130.00
105A	Terry Harper, Posed in Dressing Room	32.50	65.00	130.00
105B	Terry Harper, Action	3.50	7.00	14.00
106	Ted Harris	3.00	6.00	12.00
107	Bill Hicke	3.00	6.00	12.00
108	Charlie Hodge, Goalie	3.00	6.00	12.00
109	Jacques Laperriere	3.00	6.00	12.00
110A	Claude Larose	3.00	6.00	12.00
110B	Claude Larose, Reversed Negative	30.00	62.50	125.00
111	Claude Provost	3.00	6.00	12.00
112	Henri Richard	3.75	7.50	15.00
113	Maurice Richard	7.50	15.00	30.00
114	Jim Roberts	3.00	6.00	12.00
115	Bobby Rousseau	3.00	6.00	12.00
116	Jean-Guy Talbot	3.00	6.00	12.00
117A	Gilles Tremblay, Jersey No. 21	3.00	6.00	12.00
117B	Gilles Tremblay, Jersey No. 24	25.00	50.00	100.00
118	J.C. Tremblay	3.00	6.00	12.00
119	Gump Worsley, Goalie	3.00	6.00	12.00

NEW YORK RANGERS

No.	Player	VG	EX	NRMT
120	Lou Angotti	3.00	6.00	12.00
121	Arnie Brown	3.00	6.00	12.00
122	Larry Cahan	35.00	70.00	140.00
123	Dick Duff		Unconfirmed	
124	Reggie Fleming	3.00	6.00	12.00
125	Bernie Geoffrion	3.00	6.00	12.00
126	Ed Giacomin, Goalie	3.00	6.00	12.00
127	Rod Gilbert	3.00	6.00	12.00
128	Phil Goyette	3.00	6.00	12.00
129	Vic Hadfield	3.00	6.00	12.00
130	Doug Harvey		Unconfirmed	
131	Camille Henry	25.00	50.00	100.00
132	Bill Hicke	3.00	6.00	12.00
133	Wayne Hillman	3.00	6.00	12.00
134	Harry Howell	3.00	6.00	12.00
135	Earl Ingarfield, Sr.	3.00	6.00	12.00
136	Don Johns		Unconfirmed	
137	Orland Kurtenbach	3.00	6.00	12.00
138	Gord Labossiere	20.00	40.00	80.00
139	Al MacNeil	3.00	6.00	12.00
140	Cesare Maniago, Goalie	3.00	6.00	12.00
141	Don Marshall	3.00	6.00	12.00
142	Jim Mikol		Unconfirmed	
143	Jim Neilson	3.00	6.00	12.00
144	Bob Nevin	3.00	6.00	12.00
145	Marcel Paille, Goalie	5.00	10.00	20.00
146	Jacques Plante, Goalie	10.00	20.00	40.00
147	Jean Ratelle	3.75	7.50	15.00
148	Rod Seiling	3.00	6.00	12.00
149	George (Red) Sullivan		Unconfirmed	

TORONTO MAPLE LEAFS

No.	Player	VG	EX	NRMT
150	Al Arbour		Unconfirmed	
151	George Armstrong	3.00	6.00	12.00
152	Andy Bathgate	3.00	6.00	12.00
153A	Bob Baun, Number 21	3.00	6.00	12.00
153B	Bob Baun, No Number	15.00	32.50	65.00
154A	Johnny Bower, Goalie, Number 1	27.50	55.00	110.00
154B	Johnny Bower, Goalie, No Number	3.00	6.00	12.00
155	Wally Boyer	5.00	10.00	20.00
156	John Brenneman	5.00	10.00	20.00
157	Carl Brewer	3.00	6.00	12.00
158	Turk Broda, Goalie	5.00	10.00	20.00

No.	Player	VG	EX	NRMT
159	Brian Conacher	3.00	6.00	12.00
160	Kent Douglas	3.00	6.00	12.00
161	Ron Ellis	3.00	6.00	12.00
162	Bruce Gamble, Goalie	3.00	6.00	12.00
163A	Billy Harris, Number 15	15.00	30.00	60.00
163B	Billy Harris, No Number	43.75	37.50	75.00
164	Larry Hillman	5.00	10.00	20.00
165A	Tim Horton, Number 7	22.50	45.00	90.00
165B	Tim Horton, No Number	3.00	6.00	12.00
166	Bronco Horvath	25.00	50.00	100.00
167	Larry Jeffrey	7.50	15.00	30.00
168	Eddie Joyal	5.00	10.00	20.00
169	Red Kelly	3.00	6.00	12.00
170	Ted Kennedy	3.00	6.00	12.00
171A	Dave Keon, Number 14	20.00	42.50	85.00
171B	Dave Keon, No Number	3.75	7.50	15.00
172	Orland Kurtenbach	3.75	7.50	15.00
173	Ed Litzenberger	20.00	42.50	85.00
174A	Frank Mahovlich, Number 27	22.50	45.00	90.00
174B	Frank Mahovlich, No Number	3.00	6.00	12.00
175A	Don McKenney, Small Photo Image	15.00	30.00	60.00
175B	Don McKenney, Large	3.00	6.00	12.00
176	Dickie Moore	3.00	6.00	12.00
177	Jim Pappin	3.00	6.00	12.00
178A	Marcel Pronovost, With Blade	3.00	6.00	12.00
179B	Marcel Pronovost, Without Blade	6.00	12.50	25.00
180A	Bob Pulford, Number 20	20.00	42.50	85.00
180B	Bob Pulford, No Number	3.00	6.00	12.00
181	Terry Sawchuk, Goalie	3.00	6.00	12.00
182	Brit Selby	3.00	6.00	12.00
183	Eddie Shack	3.00	6.00	12.00
184	Don Simmons, Goalie	3.00	6.00	12.00
185	Allan Stanley	3.00	6.00	12.00
186	Pete Stemkowski	3.00	6.00	12.00
187A	Ron Stewart, Number 12	22.50	45.00	90.00
187B	Ron Stewart, No Number	7.50	15.00	30.00
188	Mike Walton	3.00	6.00	12.00

TROPHIES AND MISCELLANEOUS

No.	Player	VG	EX	NRMT
189	Bernie Geoffrion	15.00	30.00	60.00
190	Byng Trophy	20.00	37.50	75.00
191	Calder Memorial Trophy	20.00	37.50	75.00
192	Hart Trophy	20.00	37.50	75.00
193	Prince of Wales Trophy	20.00	37.50	75.00
194	James Norris Memorial Trophy	20.00	37.50	75.00
195	Art Ross Trophy	20.00	37.50	75.00
196	Stanley Cup	20.00	37.50	75.00
197	Vezina Trophy	20.00	37.50	75.00

Bee Hive Group Three
1964-67 Issue
Card No. 119,
Gump Worsley

Bee Hive Group Three
1964-67 Issue
Card No. 146,
Jacques Plante

Canada Starch
1935-40 Crown Brand
Card No. 57,
Howie Morenz

CANADA STARCH

— 1935 - 1940 CROWN BRAND —

With the success of the Beehive promotion Canada Starch was prompted into action. They soon joined the write-in redemption coupon game. The photos issued by Canada Starch are all "Rice" or "Rice Copyrighted" from the Rice Studios of Montreal.

Card Size: Player Photos: 4 1/2" x 7 3/4"
Player Photos with mat: 6 3/4" x 8 3/4"
Team Photos: 9 1/2" x 4 3/4"
Team Photos with mat: 10 3/4" x 6 1/2"
Also: 7 3/4" x 5"
with mat: 8 3/4" x 6 1/2"
Face: Black and white on sepia; Facsimile autograph, Number, Write-in premium redeemable with proof of purchase?
Back: Blank
Imprint: None
Complete Set No.: Unknown
Complete Set Price: Unknown
Common Player: 5.00 10.00 20.00

No.	Player	VG	EX	NRMT
49	Montreal Maroons 1936-37	7.50	15.00	30.00
50	Montreal Les Canadiens 1936-37	7.50	15.00	30.00
51	Baldy Northcott	5.00	10.00	20.00
52	Dave Trottier	5.00	10.00	20.00
53	Russ Blinco	5.00	10.00	20.00

AMALGAMATED PRESS

— 1935 - 36 CHAMPION MAGAZINE —

POSTCARD ISSUE

Issued as inserts in a magazine published in Great Britain and distributed in Canada during 1935 and 1936. The cards are unnumbered and are listed below in alphabetical order. Paper storage pouches were available from the magazine.

Postcard Size: 4" x 6"
Face: Sepia
Back: Postcard back
Imprint: None
Complete Set No.: 10

Complete Set Price:		575.00	1,150.00	2,300.00
Common Player:		37.50	75.00	150.00

No.	Player	VG	EX	NRMT
1	Marty Barry, Bos.	45.00	85.00	175.00
2	Francis Clancy, Tor.	125.00	250.00	500.00
3	Charlie Conacher, Tor.	75.00	150.00	300.00
4	Bun Cook, NYR	40.00	85.00	175.00
5	Bill Cook, NYR	40.00	85.00	175.00
6	Aurel Joliat, Mon.	150.00	300.00	600.00
7	Pep Kelly, Tor.	37.50	75.00	150.00
8	Mush March, Chi.	37.50	75.00	150.00
9	Sweeney Schriner, NYA	37.50	75.00	150.00
10	Hooley Smith, Mon.	40.00	85.00	175.00

— 1935 - 36 TRIUMPH MAGAZINE —

POSTCARD ISSUE

Issued as inserts in a magazine published in Great Britain and distributed in Canada during 1935 and 1936. The cards are unnumbered and are listed below in alphabetical order. Paper storage pouches were available from the magazine.

Postcard Size: 4" x 6"
Face: Sepia
Back: Postcard back
Imprint: None
Complete Set No.: 10

Complete Set Price:		525.00	1,050.00	2,100.00
Common Player:		37.50	75.00	150.00

No.	Player	VG	EX	NRMT
1	Lionel Conacher, Mon.	75.00	150.00	300.00
2	Harvey Jackson, Tor.	70.00	140.00	275.00
3	Ivan (Ching) Johnson, NYR	62.50	125.00	250.00
4	Herbie Lewis, Det.	37.50	75.00	150.00
5	Sylvio Mantha, Mon.	50.00	100.00	200.00
6	Nick Metz, Tor.	37.50	75.00	150.00
7	Baldy Northcott, Mon.M	37.50	75.00	150.00
8	Eddie Shore, Bos.	110.00	225.00	450.00
9	Paul Thomson, Chi.	37.50	75.00	150.00
10	Roy Worters, Goalie, NYA	40.00	85.00	175.00

QUAKER OATS

— 1938 - 39 PHOTO ISSUE —

Photo Size: 6 1/4" x 7 1/2"
Face: Black and white on card stock
Back: Blank
Imprint: None
Complete Set No.: 30

Complete Set Price:		200.00	400.00	800.00
Common Player:		5.00	10.00	20.00

MONTREAL

No.	Player	VG	EX	NRMT
1	Toe Blake	30.00	60.00	120.00
2	Walt Buswell	5.00	10.00	20.00
3	Herbert Cain	5.00	10.00	20.00
4	Wilf Cude, Goalie	5.00	10.00	20.00
5	Polly Drouin	5.00	10.00	20.00
6	Stewart Evans	5.00	10.00	20.00
7	Johnny Gagnon	5.00	10.00	20.00
8	Bob Gracie	5.00	10.00	20.00
9	Paul Haynes	5.00	10.00	20.00
10	Rod Lorraine	5.00	10.00	20.00
11	Georges Mantha	5.00	10.00	20.00
12	Babe Siebert	15.00	30.00	60.00

No.	Player	VG	EX	NRMT
54	Earl Robinson	5.00	10.00	20.00
55	Bob Gracie	5.00	10.00	20.00
56	Gus Marker	5.00	10.00	20.00
57	Howie Morenz	35.00	75.00	150.00
58	Johnny Gagnon	5.00	10.00	20.00
59	Wilf Cude, Goalie	5.00	10.00	20.00
60	Georges Mantha	5.00	10.00	20.00
61	Paul Haynes	5.00	10.00	20.00
62	Marty Barry	7.50	15.00	30.00
63	Pete Kelly	5.00	10.00	20.00
64	Dave Kerr, Goalie	5.00	10.00	20.00
65	Roy Worters, Goalie	7.50	15.00	30.00
66	Ace Bailey	20.00	40.00	80.00
67	Art Lesieur	5.00	10.00	20.00
68	Frank Boucher	7.50	15.00	30.00
69	Marty Burke	5.00	10.00	20.00
70	Alex Levinsky	5.00	10.00	20.00
71	The Maple Leaf Team of "Father Levesque's Pewee Hockey Club"	55.00	110.00	225.00
72	Six Stars of "Father Levesque's PeeWee Hockey Club"	55.00	110.00	225.00
76	The "Canadien" team of "Father Levesque's Peewee Hockey Club	55.00	110.00	225.00
77	Stewart Evans	5.00	10.00	20.00
78	Herbert Cain	5.00	10.00	20.00
79	Carl Voss	5.00	10.00	20.00
80	Roger Jenkins	5.00	10.00	20.00
81	Jack McGill	5.00	10.00	20.00
82	Mush March	5.00	10.00	20.00
106	Montreal Maroons 1937-38	17.50	35.00	70.00
107	Montreal Les Canadiens 1937-38	17.50	35.00	70.00
108	Toe Blake	15.00	30.00	60.00
109	Joffre Desilets	7.50	15.00	30.00
110	Babe Siebert	12.50	25.00	50.00
111	Francis Clancy	17.50	35.00	70.00
112	Aurel Joliat, Error	35.00	75.00	150.00
113	Walt Buswell	7.50	15.00	30.00
114	Bill MacKenzie	7.50	15.00	30.00
115	Pit Lepine	7.50	15.00	30.00
116	Red Goupille	7.50	15.00	30.00
117	Rod Lorraine	7.50	15.00	30.00
118	Polly Drouin	7.50	15.00	30.00
119	Cy Wentworth	7.50	15.00	30.00
120	Al Shields	7.50	15.00	30.00
121	Jimmy Ward	7.50	15.00	30.00
122	Bill Beveridge, Goalie	7.50	15.00	30.00
123	Gerry Shannon	7.50	15.00	30.00
124	Des Smith	7.50	15.00	30.00
125	Armand Mondou	7.50	15.00	30.00
151	Montreal Les Canadiens 1938-39	10.00	50.00	100.00
152	Herbert Cain	12.50	25.00	50.00
153	Bob Gracie	12.50	25.00	50.00
154	Jimmy Ward	12.50	25.00	50.00
155	Stewart Evans	12.50	25.00	50.00
156	Louis Trudel	12.50	25.00	50.00
157	Cy Wentworth	12.50	25.00	50.00
195	Marty Barry	17.50	35.00	75.00
196	Earl Robinson	12.50	25.00	50.00
197	Ray Getliffe	12.50	25.00	50.00
198	Charlie Sands	12.50	25.00	50.00
199	Claude Bourque, Goalie	12.50	25.00	50.00
200	Douglas Young	12.50	25.00	50.00
201	Montreal Les Canadiens 1939-40	20.00	50.00	100.00

UNNUMBERED

No.	Player	VG	EX	NRMT
—	1936 - 37 Montreal Maroons	22.50	45.00	90.00
—	1935 - 36 Montreal Canadiens	22.50	45.00	90.00
—	1936 Canadian Olympic Team	41.25	42.50	85.00

Note: Your cards must be accurately graded before they can be priced.

Note: All classical sets are extremely rare in NRMT and Mint condition.

Canada Starch 1935-40 Crown Brand Card No. 58, Johnny Gagnon

Canada Starch 1935-40 Crown Brand Card No. 112, Error, Name misspelled Aurele on face

Quaker Oats, 1938-39 Photo Issue Photo No. 11, Georges Mantha

Quaker Oats, 1938-39 Photo Issue Photo No. 12, Babe Siebert

154 • QUAKER OATS — 1945 - 54 PHOTO ISSUE —

No.	Player	VG	EX	NRMT
13	Jimmy Ward	5.00	10.00	20.00
14	Cy Wentworth	5.00	10.00	20.00

TORONTO

No.	Player	VG	EX	NRMT
15	Syl Apps, Sr.	20.00	40.00	80.00
16	Buzz Boll	5.00	10.00	20.00
17	Turk Broda, Goalie	20.00	40.00	80.00
18	Murph Chamberlain	5.00	10.00	20.00
19	Bob Davidson	5.00	10.00	20.00
20	Gordie Drillon	15.00	30.00	55.00
21	Jimmy Fowler	5.00	10.00	20.00
22	Reg Hamilton	5.00	10.00	20.00
23	Red Horner	20.00	40.00	80.00
24	Harvey Jackson	10.00	20.00	40.00
25	Bingo Kampman	5.00	10.00	20.00
26	Pep (Regis) Kelly	5.00	10.00	20.00
27	Nick Metz	5.00	10.00	20.00
28	George Parsons	5.00	10.00	20.00
29	Bill Thoms	6.00	12.50	25.00

THE VOICE OF HOCKEY

No.	Player	VG	EX	NRMT
30	Foster Hewitt	25.00	50.00	100.00

— 1945 - 54 PHOTO ISSUE —

Card Size: 8" X 10"
Face: Black and whtie photo, white border; Facsimile autograph
Back: Blank
Imprint: None
Complete Set No.: Unknown
Complete Set Price: Unknown
Common Player: 8.00

MONTREAL CANADIENS

No.	Player	EX
1	George Allen	8.00
2	Jean Beliveau	30.00
3	Joe Benoit	8.00
4A	Toe Blake, Signed Hector Blake	14.00
4B	Toe Blake, Signed Toe Blake	14.00
4C	Toe Blake, Retouched Photo	30.00
5A	Emile (Butch) Bouchard, Still-Skates Visible	10.00
5B	Emile (Butch) Bouchard, Still, Skates Cropped	10.00
5C	Emile (Butch) Bouchard, Action	15.00
6	Tod Campeau	30.00
7	Bob Carse	15.00
8	Joe Carveth	15.00
9A	Murph Chamberlain, Still, Facing Forward	30.00
9B	Murph Chamberlain, Still, Side View	30.00
9C	Murph Chamberlain, Still, Side View-Skates Cropped	30.00
10	Gerry Couture	30.00
11A	Floyd Curry, Still	10.00
11B	Floyd Curry, Action	10.00
12	Eddie Dorohoy	15.00
13A	Bill Durnan, Goalie, Still	18.00
13B	Bill Durnan, Goalie, Action	18.00
14A	Norm Dussault, Portrait	15.00
14B	Norm Dussault, Action	15.00
15	Frank Eddolls	20.00
16A	Bob Fillion, Still On Ice	12.00
16B	Bob Fillion, As A) Larger Image	15.00
16C	Bob Fillion, As A) Background Airbrushed	15.00
16D	Bob Fillion, Action	15.00
17	Dick Gamble	12.00
18	Bernie Geoffrion	12.00
19A	Leo Gravelle, Still-home Uniform	15.00
19B	Leo Gravelle, Still-away Uniform	15.00
19C	Leo Gravelle, Action	15.00
20A	Glen Harmon, Still-with Puck	10.00
20B	Glen Harmon, Still-no Puck	10.00
20C	Glen Harmon, Action	10.00
21A	Doug Harvey, Still	18.00
21B	Doug Harvey, Action	18.00
22	Dutch Hiller	20.00
23	Bert Hirschfeld	20.00
24	Tom Johnson	8.00
25	Vern Kaiser	20.00
26A	Elmer Lach, Still-stick Cropped	12.00

Quaker Oats
1938-39 Photo Issue
Photo No. 15,
Syl Apps, Sr.

Quaker Oats
1938-39 Photo Issue
Photo No. 30,
Foster Hewitt

Quaker Oats
1945-54 Photo Issue
Photo No. 5C,
Emile Bouchard

Quaker Oats
1945-54 Photo Issue
Photo No. 19C
Leo Gravelle

No.	Player	EX
26B	Elmer Lach, Still-stick in Corner	12.00
26C	Elmer Lach, Still-stick 1/2" From Corner	12.00
26D	Elmer Lach, Action	15.00
27A	Leo Lamoureux, Still-entire Blade	15.00
27B	Leo Lamoureux, Still-blade Cropped	15.00
28A	Hal Laycoe, Action	12.00
28B	Hal Laycoe, Portrait	12.00
29A	Roger Leger, Still-light Background, Error	15.00
29B	Roger Leger, Still-dark Background, Error	15.00
29C	Roger Leger, Action, Error	20.00
30	Jacques Locas	20.00
31	Ross Lowe	20.00
32	Calum MacKay	12.00
33	Murdo MacKay	15.00
34	Paul Masnick	10.00
35A	John McCormack, Horizontal	10.00
35B	John McCormack, Vertical	10.00
36	Mike McMahon	20.00
37	Gerry McNeil, Goalie	10.00
38	Jim McPherson	10.00
39	Paul Meger	10.00
40	Dickie Moore	18.00
41A	Kenny Mosdell, Still-small Image	20.00
41B	Kenny Mosdell, Still-large Image	20.00
41C	Kenny Mosdell, Action	25.00
42A	Buddy O'Connor, Still With Blade	15.00
42B	Buddy O'Connor, Still Blade Cropped	15.00
43	Bert Olmstead	10.00
44A	Jim Peters, Still With Blade	15.00
44B	Jim Peters, Still Blade Cropped	15.00
45	Gerry Plamondon	15.00
46	John Quilty	20.00
47A	Ken Reardon, Still Small Image	12.00
47B	Ken Reardon, Still Large Image	12.00
47C	Ken Reardon, Action	15.00
48A	Billy Reay, Still Blade On Border	8.00
48B	Billy Reay, Still Blade Away From Border	8.00
48C	Billy Reay, Action	10.00
49A	Maurice Richard, Still	30.00
49B	Maurice Richard, Still Photographed From Above	30.00
49C	Maurice Richard, As B) Larger Image Auto. Cropped	30.00
49D	Maurice Richard, Action	35.00
50A	Howard Riopelle, Still	20.00
50B	Howard Riopelle, Action	20.00
51	George Robertson	30.00
52	Dollard St. Laurent	10.00
53	Grant Warwick	20.00

TORONTO MAPLE LEAFS

No.	Player	EX
54	1947-48-49 Team Picture	20.00
55A	Syl Apps, Sr., Still Auto. C.J.S. Apps	25.00
55B	Syl Apps, Sr., Still Auto. Syl Apps	25.00
55C	Syl Apps, Sr., With Stanley Cup	25.00
56	George Armstrong	15.00
57	Doug Baldwin	15.00
58A	Bill Barilko, Home Uniform	20.00
58B	Bill Barilko, Away Uniform	20.00
59	Baz Bastien, Goalie	20.00
60	Gordie Bell, Goalie	20.00
61A	Max Bentley, Home Uniform	14.00
61B	Max Bentley, Away Uniform	14.00
61C	Max Bentley, In Front Of Locker	14.00
62	Gus Bodnar	20.00
63A	Garth Boesch, Home Closed "B" In Auto	10.00
63B	Garth Boesch, Home Open "B" In Auto	10.00
63C	Garth Boesch, Away	10.00
64	Leo Boivin	12.00
65	Hugh Bolton	8.00
66A	Turk Broda, Goalie, Splits Auto. W.E. Broda	18.00
66B	Turk Broda, Goalie, Splits Auto. Turk Broda	18.00
66C	Turk Broda, Goalie, Action	18.00
67	Lorne Carr	15.00
68	Les Costello	20.00
69	Bob Davidson	20.00
70A	Bill Ezinicki, Still Auto. William Ezinicki	10.00
70B	Bill Ezinicki, As A) Larger Image	10.00
70C	Bill Ezinicki, Still Auto. Bill Ezinicki	10.00
70D	Bill Ezinicki, Action	15.00
71	Fern Flaman	25.00
72A	Cal Gardner, Home Uniform	12.00
72B	Cal Gardner, Away Uniform	12.00
73A	Bob Goldham, Sweeping "G" Auto.	15.00

1955 - 56 REGULAR ISSUE — QUAKER OATS

— 1955 - 56 REGULAR ISSUE —

No.	Player	EX
73B	Bob Goldham, Normal "G" Auto.	15.00
74	Gord Hannigan	12.00
75	Bob Hassard	30.00
76	Mel Hill	10.00
77	Tim Horton	25.00
78A	Bill Juzda, Home Uniform	15.00
78B	Bill Juzda, Away Uniform	15.00
79A	Ted Kennedy, Home Posed At Right	15.00
79B	Ted Kennedy, Home as A) Centred	15.00
79C	Ted Kennedy, "C" On Uniform	15.00
79D	Ted Kennedy, With Stanley Cup	18.00
79E	Ted Kennedy, Away Uniform	15.00
80A	Joe Klukay, Home Uniform	8.00
80B	Joe Klukay, Away Uniform	8.00
81	Danny Lewicki	15.00
82	Harry Lumley, Goalie	15.00
83A	Vic Lynn, Home Uniform	10.00
83B	Vic Lynn, Away Uniform	10.00
84A	Fleming Mackell, Home Uniform	10.00
84B	Fleming Mackell, Away Uniform	10.00
85	Phi. Maloney	40.00
86	Frank Mathers	20.00
87	Frank McCool, Goalie	20.00
88	John McCormack	30.00
89A	Howie Meeker, Home Uniform	12.00
89B	Howie Meeker, As A) Larger Image	12.00
89C	Howie Meeker, Away Uniform	12.00
90A	Don Metz, Still Posed At Left	10.00
90B	Don Metz, As A) Centered	10.00
91A	Nick Metz, Still	10.00
91B	Nick Metz, As A) Stick Retouched	10.00
92	Rudy Migay	10.00
93	Elwyn Morris	15.00
94	Jim Morrison	10.00
95A	Gus Mortson, Home Uniform	8.00
95B	Gus Mortson, Away Uniform	8.00
96	Eric Nesterenko	15.00
97	Bud (Norman) Poile	15.00
98	Babe Pratt	20.00
99	Al Rollins, Goalie	12.00
100	Sweeny Schriner	20.00
101A	Tod Sloan, Home Uniform	10.00
101B	Tod Sloan, Away Uniform	10.00
102A	Sid Smith, Home Uniform	10.00
102B	Sid Smith, Away Uniform	10.00
103	Bob Solinger	40.00
104A	Wally Stanowski, Entire Blade	40.00
104B	Wally Stanowski, Blade Cropped	40.00
105	Gaye Stewart	10.00
106	Ron Stewart	8.00
107	Harry Taylor	20.00
108	W.J. Taylor	20.00
109	Cy Thomas	15.00
110A	Jim Thomson, Home Uniform	8.00
110B	Jim Thomson, Away Uniform	8.00
111A	Ray Timgren, Home Uniform	10.00
111B	Ray Timgren, Away Uniform	10.00
112A	Harry Watson, Home Uniform	10.00
112B	Harry Watson, Higher Image	10.00
112C	Harry Watson, Away Uniform	10.00

ACTION

No.	Player	EX
113	Gardner, Watson, Meeker Attack McNeil	8.00
114	Gardner Coming In On Harvey	8.00
115	Juzda And Rollins Stop Curry	8.00
116	McNeil Saves On Gardner	8.00

Note: For a card to grade higher than EX it must have no wear, no creases, full colour and four square corners.

Quaker Oats
1945-54 Photos
Card No. 29C, Error,
Name misspelled Liger on face

Quaker Oats
1945-54 Photos
Card No. 107,
Harry Taylor

Quaker Oats
1955-56 Issue
Card No. 11,
Jim Thomson

Quaker Oats
1955-56 Issue
Card No. 11,
Jim Thomson

Quaker Oats issued a set virtually identical to the Parkhurst set of the same year. The only difference is the distinctive green backs. A Quaker Oats advertisement is in place of the "Did You Know" tip on the back of the card. The "green-backs" are rare. As with all strong coloured borders the bottom red border marks easily. Mint cards command price premiums of 50% over NRMT cards. For the corresponding Parkhurst issue see page no. 161.

Card Size: 2 1/2" X 3 9/16"
Face: Four colour, red border along bottom, Team logo, Number
Back: Green on card stock; Resume, Hockey trivia, Bilingual
Imprint: Quaker Hockey Trading Card.
Complete Set No.: 79
Complete Set Price: 3,750. 7,500. 15,000.
Common Player: 20.00 40.00 80.00

TORONTO MAPLE LEAFS

No.	Player	VG	EX	NRMT
1	Harry Lumley, Goalie, LC	100.00	200.00	400.00
2	Sid Smith	20.00	40.00	80.00
3	Tim Horton	110.00	225.00	450.00
4	George Armstrong	40.00	85.00	175.00
5	Ron Stewart	20.00	40.00	80.00
6	Joe Klukay, LC	20.00	40.00	80.00
7	Marc Reaume, RC	22.50	45.00	90.00
8	Jim Morrison	20.00	40.00	80.00
9	Parker MacDonald, RC	22.50	45.00	90.00
10	Tod Sloan	20.00	40.00	80.00
11	Jim Thomson	20.00	40.00	80.00
12	Rudy Migay	20.00	40.00	80.00
13	Brian Cullen, RC	20.00	40.00	80.00
14	Hugh Bolton	20.00	40.00	80.00
15	Eric Nesterenko	22.50	45.00	90.00
16	Larry Cahan, RC	20.00	40.00	80.00
17	Willie Marshall, RC	20.00	40.00	80.00
18	Dick Duff, RC	40.00	85.00	175.00
19	Jack Caffery, RC	20.00	40.00	80.00
20	Billy Harris, RC	40.00	80.00	160.00

TORONTO MAPLE LEAFS OLDTIME GREATS

No.	Player	VG	EX	NRMT
21	Lorne Chabot, Goalie	20.00	40.00	80.00
22	Harvey Jackson	30.00	62.50	125.00
23	Turk Broda, Goalie	40.00	85.00	175.00
24	Joe Primeau	30.00	60.00	120.00
25	Gordie Drillon	20.00	40.00	80.00
26	Charlie Conacher	25.00	50.00	100.00
27	Sweeny Schriner	20.00	40.00	80.00
28	Syl Apps, Sr.	20.00	40.00	80.00
29	Ted Kennedy	35.00	75.00	150.00
30	Ace Bailey	40.00	85.00	175.00
31	Babe Pratt	20.00	40.00	80.00
32	Baldy Cotton	20.00	40.00	80.00

TORONTO MAPLE LEAFS MANAGEMENT

No.	Player	VG	EX	NRMT
33	Francis Clancy, Coach	40.00	85.00	175.00
34	Hap Day, Manager	20.00	40.00	80.00

MONTREAL CANADIENS

No.	Player	VG	EX	NRMT
35	Don Marshall, RC	20.00	40.00	80.00
36	Jackie Leclair, RC, LC	20.00	40.00	80.00
37	Maurice Richard	425.00	850.00	1,700.00
38	Dickie Moore	40.00	85.00	175.00
39	Kenny Mosdell, LC	20.00	40.00	80.00
40	Floyd Curry	20.00	40.00	80.00
41	Calum MacKay, LC	20.00	40.00	80.00
42	Bert Olmstead	20.00	40.00	80.00
43	Bernie Geoffrion	90.00	180.00	375.00
44	Jean Beliveau	250.00	500.00	1,000.00
45	Doug Harvey	60.00	125.00	250.00
46	Emile (Butch) Bouchard, LC	25.00	50.00	100.00
47	Bud MacPherson, LC	20.00	40.00	80.00
48	Dollard St. Laurent	20.00	40.00	80.00
49	Tom Johnson	20.00	40.00	80.00
50	Jacques Plante, Goalie, RC	750.00	1,500.00	3,000.00
51	Paul Meger	20.00	40.00	80.00
52	Gerry McNeil, Goalie, LC	25.00	50.00	100.00
53	Jean-Guy Talbot, RC	22.50	45.00	90.00
54	Bob Turner, RC	20.00	40.00	80.00

156 • CHLP / CKAC / CKVL RADIO — 1943 - 47 PARADE SPORTIVE COVERS —

MONTREAL CANADIENS OLDTIME GREATS

No.	Player	VG	EX	NRMT
55	Edouard Lalonde	40.00	85.00	175.00
56	Georges Vezina, Goalie	75.00	150.00	300.00
57	Howie Morenz	75.00	150.00	300.00
58	Aurel Joliat	35.00	75.00	150.00
59	George Hainsworth, Goalie	35.00	75.00	150.00
60	Sylvio Mantha	22.50	45.00	90.00
61	Albert Leduc	30.00	60.00	120.00
62	Babe Siebert, Error	30.00	60.00	120.00
63	Bill Durnan, Goalie, RC, LC	28.75	57.50	115.00
64	Ken Reardon	25.00	50.00	100.00
65	Johnny Gagnon	20.00	40.00	80.00
66	Billy Reay	20.00	40.00	80.00

MONTREAL CANADIENS MANAGERMENT

No.	Player	VG	EX	NRMT
67	Toe Blake, Coach	25.00	50.00	100.00
68	Frank Selke, Manager	28.75	57.50	115.00

ACTION CARDS

No.	Player	VG	EX	NRMT
69	Hugh Beats Hodge	20.00	40.00	80.00
70	Lum Stops Boom-Boom	45.00	85.00	175.00
71	Plante Is Protected	70.00	140.00	280.00
72	Rocket Roars Through	75.00	150.00	300.00
73	Richard Tests Lumley	75.00	150.00	300.00
74	Beliveau Bats Puck	55.00	110.00	225.00
75	Leaf Speedster Attack	55.00	110.00	225.00
76	Curry Scores Again	20.00	40.00	80.00
77	Jammed On The Boards	55.00	110.00	225.00

STADIUMS

No.	Stadium	VG	EX	NRMT
78	The Montreal Forum	160.00	325.00	650.00
79	Maple Leaf Gardens	187.50	375.00	750.00

CHLP / CKAC / CKVL RADIO

— 1943 - 47 PARADE SPORTIVE COVERS —

Issued on semi-glossy paper stock these items were available at a nominal cost from three radio stations that aired this popular show during the 1943 to 1947 era. Most photos are black and white but blue, brown, green and red tints have been seen. Size varies from 4 3/4" x 8 3/8" to 6 3/4" x 10". Variations of the same poses are plentiful. Different sizes, tints, script, etc. exist. No variation of a specific pose is scarce or valuable. Other athletes and sports were included but this listing is limited to hockey. It is possible that three different sets one for each of the three radio stations exist.

Photo Size: 4 3/4" X 8 3/8" to 6 3/4" X 10"
Face: Black and white; Name, Facsimile autograph
Back: Blank
Imprint: PHOTO, PARADE SPORTIVE
Complete Set No.: Unknown
Complete Set Price: Unknown
Common Player: 1.25 2.50 5.00

BOSTON BRUINS

No.	Player	VG	EX	NRMT
1	Bauer; Schmidt; Dumart	1.25	2.50	5.00
2	Frankie Brimsek, Goalie	1.25	2.50	5.00
3	Bill Cowley	1.75	3.50	7.00
4	Armand Gaudreault	1.25	2.50	5.00
5	Jean Gladu	1.25	2.50	5.00
6	Jean Gladu	1.25	2.50	5.00

CHICAGO BLACK HAWKS

No.	Player	VG	EX	NRMT
7	Mike Karakas, Goalie	1.25	2.50	5.00
8	B. Mosienko; M. Bentley; D. Bentley	1.75	3.50	7.00

DETROIT RED WINGS

No.	Player	VG	EX	NRMT
9	Eddie Bruneteau	1.25	2.50	5.00
10	Modere Bruneteau	1.25	2.50	5.00
11	Harry Lumley	1.75	3.50	7.00

CKAC Radio
1943-47 Parade Sportive
Cover No. 51,
Fern Gauthier

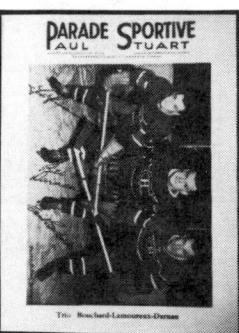

CHLP Radio
1943-47 Parade Sportive
Cover No. 62,
Bouchard; Lamoureux;
Durnan

CHLP Radio
1943-47 Parade Sportive
Cover No. 77A,
Maurice Richard

NEW YORK RANGERS

No.	Player	VG	EX	NRMT
12	Edgar Laprade	1.25	2.50	5.00
13	Phil Watson	1.25	2.50	5.00

TORONTO MAPLE LEAFS

No.	Player	VG	EX	NRMT
14	Baz Bastien, Goalie	1.25	2.50	5.00
15	Turk Broda, Goalie	3.00	6.00	12.00
16	Gaye Stewart	1.25	2.50	5.00

MINORS

No.	Player	VG	EX	NRMT
17	Lionel Bouvrette, Goalie	1.25	2.50	5.00
18	Denys Casavant	1.25	2.50	5.00
19	Connie Dion, Goalie	1.25	2.50	5.00
20	Jim Henry	1.75	3.50	7.00
21	Ernie Laforce	1.25	2.50	5.00
22	Jean Marois, Goalie	1.25	2.50	5.00
23	Gerry McNeil, Goalie	1.75	3.50	7.00
24	Robert Pepin	1.25	2.50	5.00
25	Gerry Plamondon	1.25	2.50	5.00

MONTREAL CANADIENS

No.	Player	VG	EX	NRMT
26	1943 - 44 Team Photo	2.50	5.00	10.00
27	1944 - 45 Team Photo	2.50	5.00	10.00
28	1945 - 46 Team Photo	2.50	5.00	10.00
29	1946 - 47 Team Photo	2.50	5.00	10.00
30	George Allen	1.25	2.50	5.00
31	Joe Benoit	1.25	2.50	5.00
32	Paul Bibeault, Goalie	1.25	2.50	5.00
33	Toe Blake	1.75	3.50	7.00
34	Emile (Butch) Bouchard	1.85	3.75	7.50
35	Emile (Butch) Bouchard	1.85	3.75	7.50
36	Jean-Claude Campeau	1.25	2.50	5.00
37	J.P. Campeau	1.25	2.50	5.00
38	Bob Carse	1.25	2.50	5.00
39	Joe Carveth	1.25	2.50	5.00
40	Murph Chamberlain	1.25	2.50	5.00
41	Floyd Curry	1.25	2.50	5.00
42	Tony DeMers, Error	1.25	2.50	5.00
43	Bill Durnan, Goalie, Full Crest	1.25	2.50	5.00
44	Bill Durnan, Goalie, Partial Crest	1.25	2.50	5.00
45	Norm Dussault	1.25	2.50	5.00
46	Frank Eddolls	1.25	2.50	5.00
47	Bob Fillion	1.25	2.50	5.00
48	Bob Fillion, Portrait	1.25	2.50	5.00
49	Johnny Gagnon	1.25	2.50	5.00
50	Gagnon; Joliat; Howie Morenz	2.00	4.00	8.00
51	Fern Gauthier	1.25	2.50	5.00
52	Gauthier; O'Connor; Hiller	1.25	2.50	5.00
53	Leo Gravelle	1.25	2.50	5.00
54	Glen Harmon	1.25	2.50	5.00
55	Glen Harmon, Portrait	1.25	2.50	5.00
56	Doug Harvey	2.50	5.00	10.00
57	Heffernan; O'Connor; Morin	1.25	2.50	5.00
58	Dutch Hiller	1.25	2.50	5.00
59	Rosairo Joanette	1.25	2.50	5.00
60	Elmer Lach	2.50	5.00	10.00
61	Leo Lamoreaux	1.25	2.50	5.00
62	Bouchard; Lamoureux; Durnan	1.25	2.50	5.00
63	Hal Laycoe	1.25	2.50	5.00
64	Roger Leger	1.25	2.50	5.00
65	Jacques Locas	1.25	2.50	5.00
66	Fern Majeau	1.25	2.50	5.00
67	Georges Mantha	1.85	3.75	7.50
68	Georges Mantha	1.85	3.75	7.50
69	Mike McMahon	1.25	2.50	5.00
70	Kenny Mosdell	1.85	3.75	7.50
71	Buddy O'Connor	1.25	2.50	5.00
72	Jim Peters	1.25	2.50	5.00
73	John Quilty	1.25	2.50	5.00
74	Paul Raymond	1.25	2.50	5.00
75	Ken Reardon	1.25	2.50	5.00
76	Billy Reay	2.50	5.00	10.00
77A	Maurice Richard, Autograph on Photo	3.75	7.50	15.00
77B	Maurice Richard, Autograph on Border	3.75	7.50	15.00
78	Howard Riopellie	1.25	2.50	5.00

Note: This listing is not complete. We would appreciate hearing from anyone who could help us complete this set.

BERK ROSS

— 1951 HIT PARADE OF CHAMPIONS —

This is an all-sport set of 72 cards. They were issued in panels of two cards and numbered in four series of subsets, one to eighteen, two to eighteen, etc. Centering of this set is poor.

Card Size: 2 1/16" x 2 1/2"
Face: Four colour, white border
Back: Black on card stock; Name, Number, Position, Team
Imprint: © Berk Ross Inc. New York, N.Y.
Complete Set No.: 72

		VG	EX	NRMT
Common Goalie		25.00	50.00	100.00
Common Player:		25.00	50.00	100.00

No.	Player	VG	EX	NRMT
—	Sid Abel, Det.	25.00	50.00	100.00
—	Jack Stewart, Det.	25.00	50.00	100.00
1-17	Bill Durnan, Goalie, Mon.	25.00	50.00	100.00
1-18	Bill Quackenbush, Bos.	25.00	50.00	100.00

PAIRS

	Bill Quackenbush and Bill Durnan, Goalie		50.00	100.00

Berk Ross
1951 Hit Parade of Champions
Cards No. 1-17 / 1-18
B. Durnan / B. Quackenbush

PARKHURST

— 1951 - 52 REGULAR ISSUE —

This is the first set of modern cards. This set is almost impossible to find in the higher grades. Mint cards will command a 50% to 75% price premium over NRMT cards.

Aging causes discolouration (browning) of the cards. This is a natural process with the card stock and cannot be easily stopped or reversed. There are counterfeits. Please see Section C at the front of this book.

PRICE MOVEMENT OF NRMT SETS

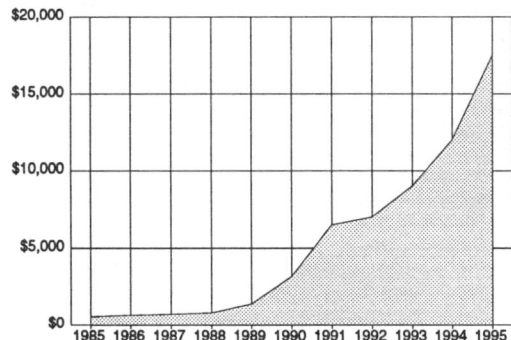

Card Size: 1 3/4" X 2 1/2"
Face: Four colour, Number, Resume
Back: Blank
Imprint: None
Complete Set No.: 105

	VG	EX	NRMT
Complete Set Price:	4,375.00	8,750.00	17,500.00
Common Player:	8.75	17.50	35.00

MONTREAL CANADIENS

No.	Player	VG	EX	NRMT
1	Elmer Lach	125.00	250.00	500.00
2	Paul Meger, RC	12.50	25.00	50.00
3	Emile (Butch) Bouchard	18.75	37.50	75.00
4	Maurice Richard, RC	500.00	1,000.00	2,000.00
5	Bert Olmstead, RC	25.00	50.00	100.00
6	Bud MacPherson, RC	12.50	25.00	50.00
7	Tom Johnson, RC	18.75	37.50	75.00
8	Paul Masnick, RC	12.50	25.00	50.00
9	Calum MacKay, RC	12.50	25.00	50.00
10	Doug Harvey, RC	100.00	200.00	400.00
11	Kenny Mosdell, RC	12.50	25.00	50.00
12	Floyd Curry, RC	12.50	25.00	50.00
13	Billy Reay, RC	12.50	25.00	50.00
14	Bernie Geoffrion, RC	150.00	300.00	600.00

Berk Ross
1951 Hit Parade of Champions
Cards No. 1-17 / 1-18
B. Durnan / B. Quackenbush

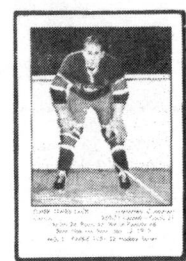

Parkhurst 1951-52 Issue
Card No. 1,
Elmer Lach

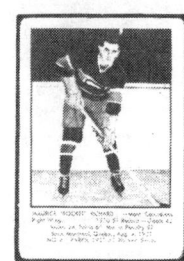

Parkhurst 1951-52 Issue
Card No. 4,
Maurice Richard

— 1951 HIT PARADE OF CHAMPIONS — BERK ROSS • 157

No.	Player	VG	EX	NRMT
15	Gerry McNeil, Goalie, RC	25.00	50.00	100.00
16	Dick Gamble, RC	12.50	25.00	50.00
17	Gerald Couture, RC	12.50	25.00	50.00
18	Ross Lowe, RC, LC	12.50	25.00	50.00

BOSTON BRUINS

No.	Player	VG	EX	NRMT
19	Jim Henry, Goalie, RC	18.75	37.50	75.00
20	Vic Lynn, RC, LC	12.50	25.00	50.00
21	Walter Kyle, RC, LC	12.50	25.00	50.00
22	Ed Sandford, RC	12.50	25.00	50.00
23	John Henderson, RC, LC	12.50	25.00	50.00
24	Robert Fisher, RC, LC	12.50	25.00	50.00
25	Hal Laycoe, RC	12.50	25.00	50.00
26	Bill Quackenbush, RC	25.00	50.00	100.00
27	George Sullivan, RC	12.50	25.00	50.00
28	Woody Dumart	12.50	25.00	50.00
29	Milt Schmidt	35.00	75.00	150.00
30	Adam Brown, RC, LC	12.50	25.00	50.00
31	Pentti Lund, RC	12.50	25.00	50.00
32	Ray Barry, RC, LC	12.50	25.00	50.00
33	Edward Kryznowski, RC, Error	12.50	25.00	50.00
34	Johnny Peirson, RC	12.50	25.00	50.00
35	Lorne Ferguson, RC	12.50	25.00	50.00
36	Clare Raglan, RC	12.50	25.00	50.00

CHICAGO BLACK HAWKS

No.	Player	VG	EX	NRMT
37	Bill Gadsby, RC	25.00	50.00	100.00
38	Al Dewsbury, RC	12.50	25.00	50.00
39	George Martin, RC, LC	12.50	25.00	50.00
40	Gus Bodnar, RC	12.50	25.00	50.00
41	Jim Peters	12.50	25.00	50.00
42	Bep Guidolin, RC, LC	12.50	25.00	50.00
43	George Gee, RC	12.50	25.00	50.00
44	Jim McFadden, RC	12.50	25.00	50.00
45	Fred Hucul, RC	12.50	25.00	50.00
46	Lidio (Lee) Fogolin, RC, Error	12.50	25.00	50.00
47	Harry Lumley, Goalie, RC	50.00	100.00	200.00
48	Doug Bentley, RC, LC	37.50	75.00	150.00
49	Bill Mosienko, RC	25.00	50.00	100.00
50	Roy Conacher, LC	12.50	25.00	50.00
51	Pete Babando, RC	12.50	25.00	50.00
52	The Winning Goal	100.00	200.00	400.00
53	Jack Stewart, LC	12.50	25.00	50.00
54	Marty Pavelich, RC	12.50	25.00	50.00

DETROIT RED WINGS

No.	Player	VG	EX	NRMT
55	Red Kelly, RC	100.00	200.00	400.00
56	Ted Lindsay, RC	100.00	200.00	400.00
57	Glen Skov, RC	12.50	25.00	50.00
58	Benny Woit, RC	12.50	25.00	50.00
59	Tony Leswick, RC	12.50	25.00	50.00
60	Fred Glover, RC	12.50	25.00	50.00
61	Terry Sawchuk, Goalie, RC	375.00	750.00	1,500.00
62	Vic Stasiuk, RC	12.50	25.00	50.00
63	Alex Delvecchio, RC	100.00	200.00	400.00
64	Sid Abel, LC	25.00	50.00	100.00
65	Metro Prystal, RC	12.50	25.00	50.00
66	Gordie Howe, RC	1,125.00	2,250.00	4,500.00
67	Bob Goldham, RC	12.50	25.00	50.00
68	Marcel Pronovost, RC	25.00	50.00	100.00
69	Leo Reise	12.50	25.00	50.00

TORONTO MAPLE LEAFS

No.	Player	VG	EX	NRMT
70	Harry Watson, RC	15.00	30.00	60.00
71	Danny Lewicki, RC	12.50	25.00	50.00
72	Howie Meeker, RC	40.00	85.00	175.00
73	Gus Mortson, RC	12.50	25.00	50.00
74	Joe Klukay, RC	12.50	25.00	50.00
75	Turk Broda, Goalie	75.00	150.00	300.00
76	Al Rollins, Goalie, RC	25.00	50.00	100.00
77	Bill Juzda, RC, LC	12.50	25.00	50.00
78	Ray Timgren, RC	12.50	25.00	50.00
79	Hugh Bolton, RC	12.50	25.00	50.00
80	Fern Flaman, RC	15.00	30.00	60.00
81	Max Bentley	37.50	75.00	150.00
82	Jim Thomson, RC	12.50	25.00	50.00
83	Fleming Mackell	12.50	25.00	50.00

PARKHURST — 1952-53 REGULAR ISSUE

No.	Player	VG	EX	NRMT
84	Sid Smith, RC	15.00	30.00	60.00
85	Cal Gardner, RC	12.50	25.00	50.00
86	Ted Kennedy, RC	50.00	100.00	200.00
87	Tod Sloan, RC	12.50	25.00	50.00
88	Bob Solinger, RC	12.50	25.00	50.00
89	Frank Eddolls, RC, LC	12.50	25.00	50.00

NEW YORK RANGERS

No.	Player	VG	EX	NRMT
90	Jack Evans, RC	12.50	25.00	50.00
91	Hyman Buller, RC	12.50	25.00	50.00
92	Stephen Kraftcheck, RC	12.50	25.00	50.00
93	Don Raleigh, RC	12.50	25.00	50.00
94	Allan Stanley, RC	35.00	75.00	150.00
95	Paul Ronty, RC	12.50	25.00	50.00
96	Edgar LaPrade, RC	12.50	25.00	50.00
97	Nick Mickoski, RC	12.50	25.00	50.00
98	Jackie McLeod, RC	12.50	25.00	50.00
99	Gaye Stewart, RC	12.50	25.00	50.00
100	Wally Hergesheimer, RC	12.50	25.00	50.00
101	Eddie Kullman, RC	12.50	25.00	50.00
102	Eddie Slowinski, RC	12.50	25.00	50.00
103	Reg Sinclair, RC	12.50	25.00	50.00
104	Chuck Rayner, Goalie, RC	35.00	75.00	150.00
105	Jim Conacher, RC	75.00	150.00	300.00

— 1952-53 REGULAR ISSUE —

This set is almost impossible to find in the high grade. Mint cards will command a 50% to 75% price premium over NRMT cards.

As with the first year of issue this set does not age well and centering is a problem. The "Parkie" 25¢ NHL album was introduced this year.

PRICE MOVEMENT OF NRMT SETS

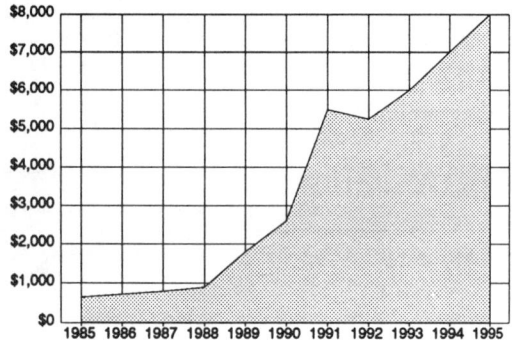

Card Size: 1 15/16" X 2 15/16"
Face: Four colour, white border, Signature
Back: Black on card stock, Number
Imprint: None
Complete Set No.: 105

	VG	EX	NRMT
Complete Set Price:	2,000.00	4,000.00	8,000.00
Common Player:	8.75	17.50	35.00
Album:	25.00	50.00	100.00

No.	Player	VG	EX	NRMT
1	Maurice Richard, Mon.	375.00	750.00	1500.00
2	Billy Reay, Mon., LC	8.75	17.50	35.00
3	Bernie Geoffrion, Mon., Error	75.00	150.00	300.00
4	Paul Meger, Mon.	8.75	17.50	35.00
5	Dick Gamble, Mon.	8.75	17.50	35.00
6	Elmer Lach, Mon.	15.00	30.00	60.00
7	Floyd Curry, Mon.	8.75	17.50	35.00
8	Kenny Mosdell, Mon.	8.75	17.50	35.00
9	Tom Johnson, Mon.	10.00	20.00	40.00
10	Dickie Moore, Mon, RC	37.50	75.00	150.00
11	Bud MacPherson, Mon.	8.75	17.50	35.00
12	Gerry McNeil, Goalie, Mon.	15.00	30.00	60.00
13	Emile (Butch) Bouchard, Mon.	10.00	20.00	40.00
14	Doug Harvey, Mon.	45.00	90.00	175.00
15	John McCormack, Mon., RC	8.75	17.50	35.00
16	Pete Babando, Chi., LC	8.75	17.50	35.00
17	Al Dewsbury, Chi.	8.75	17.50	35.00
18	Eddie Kullman, NYR	8.75	17.50	35.00

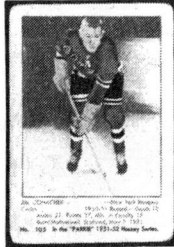

Parkhurst
1951-52 Issue
Card No. 105,
Jim Conacher

Parkhurst
1952-53 Issue
Card No. 1,
Maurice Richard

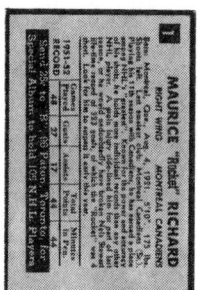

Parkhurst
1952-53 Issue
Card No. 1,
Maurice Richard

Parkhurst
1952-53 Issue
Card No. 3, Error,
Name misspelled
Gioffrion on back

No.	Player	VG	EX	NRMT
19	Eddie Slowinski, NYR	8.75	17.50	35.00
20	Wally Hergesheimer, NYR	8.75	17.50	35.00
21	Allan Stanley, NYR	11.00	22.50	45.00
22	Chuck Rayner, Goalie, NYR	15.00	30.00	60.00
23	Stephen Kraftcheck, NYR	8.75	17.50	35.00
24	Paul Ronty, NYR	8.75	17.50	35.00
25	Gaye Stewart, NYR, LC	8.75	17.50	35.00
26	Fred Hucul, Chi.	8.75	17.50	35.00
27	Bill Mosienko, Chi.	11.00	22.50	45.00
28	Jim Morrison, Tor., RC	8.75	17.50	35.00
29	Edward Kryznowski, Chi., LC, Error	8.75	17.50	35.00
30	Cal Gardner, Chi.	8.75	17.50	35.00
31	Al Rollins, Goalie, Chi.	12.50	25.00	50.00
32	Enio Sclisizzi, Chi., RC, LC	8.75	17.50	35.00
33	Pete Conacher, Chi., RC	8.75	17.50	35.00
34	Leo Boivin, Tor., RC	15.00	30.00	60.00
35	Jim Peters, Chi.	8.75	17.50	35.00
36	George Gee, Chi.	8.75	17.50	35.00
37	Gus Bodnar, Chi.	8.75	17.50	35.00
38	Jim McFadden, Chi.	8.75	17.50	35.00
39	Gus Mortson, Chi.	8.75	17.50	35.00
40	Fred Glover, Chi., LC	8.75	17.50	35.00
41	Gerry Couture, Chi.	8.75	17.50	35.00
42	Howie Meeker, Tor., LC	15.00	30.00	60.00
43	Jim Thomson, Tor.	8.75	17.50	35.00
44	Ted Kennedy, Tor.	17.50	35.00	70.00
45	Sid Smith, Tor.	8.75	17.50	35.00
46	Harry Watson, Tor.	8.75	17.50	35.00
47	Fern Flaman, Tor.	10.00	20.00	40.00
48	Tod Sloan, Tor.	8.75	17.50	35.00
49	Leo Reise, NYR	8.75	17.50	35.00
50	Bob Solinger, Tor.	8.75	17.50	35.00
51	George Armstrong, Tor., RC	50.00	100.00	200.00
52	Dollard St. Laurent, Mon., RC	8.75	17.50	35.00
53	Alex Delvecchio, Det.	37.50	75.00	150.00
54	Gordon Hannigan, Tor., RC	8.75	17.50	35.00
55	Lidio (Lee) Fogolin, Chi.	8.75	17.50	35.00
56	Bill Gadsby, Chi.	15.00	30.00	60.00
57	Herb Dickenson, NYR, RC, LC	8.75	17.50	35.00
58	Tim Horton, Tor., RC	150.00	300.00	600.00
59	Harry Lumley, Goalie, Tor.	12.50	25.00	50.00
60	Metro Prystai, Det.	8.75	17.50	35.00
61	Marcel Pronovost, Det.	11.00	22.50	45.00
62	Benny Woit, Det.	8.75	17.50	35.00
63	Glen Skov, Det.	8.75	17.50	35.00
64	Bob Goldham, Det.	8.75	17.50	35.00
65	Tony Leswick, Det.	8.75	17.50	35.00
66	Marty Pavelich, Det.	8.75	17.50	35.00
67	Red Kelly, Det.	37.50	75.00	150.00
68	Bill Quackenbush, Bos.	11.00	22.50	45.00
69	Ed Sandford, Bos.	8.75	17.50	35.00
70	Milt Schmidt, Bos.	12.50	25.00	50.00
71	Hal Laycoe, Bos.	8.75	17.50	35.00
72	Woody Dumart, Bos.	8.75	17.50	35.00
73	Zellio Toppazzini, Bos., RC, LC	8.75	17.50	35.00
74	Jim Henry, Goalie, Bos.	8.75	17.50	35.00
75	Joe Klukay, Bos.	8.75	17.50	35.00
76	Dave Creighton, Bos., RC	8.75	17.50	35.00
77	Jack McIntyre, Bos., RC	8.75	17.50	35.00
78	Johnny Peirson, Bos.	8.75	17.50	35.00
79	George Sullivan, Bos.	8.75	17.50	35.00
80	Real Chevrefils, Bos., RC	8.75	17.50	35.00
81	Leo Labine, Bos., RC	8.75	17.50	35.00
82	Fleming Mackell, Bos.	8.75	17.50	35.00
83	Pentti Lund, Bos. LC	8.75	17.50	35.00
84	Bob Armstrong, Bos., RC	8.75	17.50	35.00
85	Warren Godfrey, Bos., RC	8.75	17.50	35.00
86	Terry Sawchuk, Goalie, Det.	250.00	500.00	1,000.00
87	Ted Lindsay, Det.	43.75	87.50	175.00
88	Gordie Howe, Det.	500.00	1,000.00	2,000.00
89	Johnny Wilson, Det., RC	8.75	17.50	35.00
90	Vic Stasiuk, Det.	8.75	17.50	35.00
91	Larry Zeidel, Det., RC	8.75	17.50	35.00
92	Larry Wilson, Det., RC	8.75	17.50	35.00
93	Bert Olmstead, Mon.	10.00	20.00	40.00
94	Ron Stewart, Tor., RC	8.75	17.50	35.00
95	Max Bentley, Tor.	10.00	20.00	40.00
96	Rudy Migay, Tor., RC	8.75	17.50	35.00
97	Jack Stoddard, NYR, RC	8.75	17.50	35.00
98	Hyman Buller, NYR	8.75	17.50	35.00
99	James Donald Raleigh, NYR	8.75	17.50	35.00
100	Edgar Laprade, NYR	8.75	17.50	35.00

— 1953 - 54 REGULAR ISSUE — PARKHURST • 159

No.	Player	VG	EX	NRMT
101	Nick Mickoski, NYR	8.75	17.50	35.00
102	Jackie (Robert) McLeod, NYR, LC	8.75	17.50	35.00
103	Jim Conacher, NYR, LC	8.75	17.50	35.00
104	Reg Sinclair, Det., LC	8.75	17.50	35.00
105	Bob Hassard, Tor., RC	50.00	100.00	200.00

— 1953 - 54 REGULAR ISSUE —

The card stock used for this set ages very poorly, the white face portion turning an uneven light brown across the card face. Beware of cards that do not have this discolouration. It would be unnatural for it not to appear. "Parkies" NHL Hockey Albums were available for this set.
Mint condition cards will command a price premium of 50% to 100% over NRMT cards.

PRICE MOVEMENT OF NRMT SETS

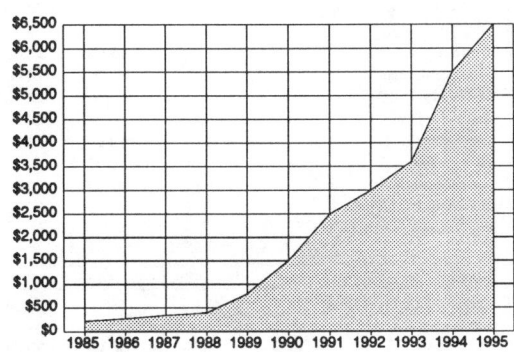

Card Size: 2 1/2" X 3 5/8"
Face: Four colour, white border
Back: Black on card stock, Number, Resume, Bilingual
Imprint: Printed In Canada
Complete Set No.: 100
Complete Set Price: 1,625.00   3,250.00   6,500.00
Common Player: 7.50   15.00   30.00
Album: 25.00   50.00   100.00

TORONTO MAPLE LEAFS

No.	Player	VG	EX	NRMT
1	Harry Lumley, Goalie	75.00	150.00	300.00
2	Sid Smith	7.50	15.00	30.00
3	Gord Hannigan	7.50	15.00	30.00
4	Bob Hassard, LC	7.50	15.00	30.00
5	Tod Sloan	7.50	15.00	30.00
6	Leo Boivin	7.50	15.00	30.00
7	Ted Kennedy	25.00	50.00	100.00
8	Jim Thomson	7.50	15.00	30.00
9	Ron Stewart	7.50	15.00	30.00
10	Eric Nesterenko, RC	8.75	17.50	35.00
11	George Armstrong	25.00	50.00	100.00
12	Harry Watson	7.50	15.00	30.00
13	Tim Horton	50.00	100.00	200.00
14	Fern Flaman	7.50	15.00	30.00
15	Jim Morrison	7.50	15.00	30.00
16	Bob Solinger, LC	7.50	15.00	30.00
17	Rudy Migay	7.50	15.00	30.00

MONTREAL CANADIENS

No.	Player	VG	EX	NRMT
18	Dick Gamble	7.50	15.00	30.00
19	Bert Olmstead	7.50	15.00	30.00
20	Eddie Mazur, RC	7.50	15.00	30.00
21	Paul Meger	7.50	15.00	30.00
22	Bud MacPherson	7.50	15.00	30.00
23	Dollard St. Laurent	7.50	15.00	30.00
24	Maurice Richard	112.50	225.00	650.00
25	Gerry McNeil, Goalie	10.00	20.00	40.00
26	Doug Harvey	25.00	50.00	100.00
27	Jean Beliveau, RC	200.00	400.00	800.00
28	Dickie Moore	15.00	30.00	60.00
29	Bernie Geoffrion	62.50	125.00	250.00
30	Lach & Richard	75.00	150.00	300.00
31	Elmer Lach, LC	7.50	15.00	30.00
32	Emile (Butch) Bouchard	7.50	15.00	30.00
33	Kenny Mosdell	7.50	15.00	30.00

Parkhurst 1952-53 Issue Card No. 102, Jackie (Robert) McLeod

Parkhurst 1953-54 Issue Card No. 1, Harry Lumley

Parkhurst 1953-54 Issue Card No. 38, Errror, Photo shows Al Arbour

Parkhurst 1953-54 Issue Card No. 88, Error, Name misspelled Pierson on back

No.	Player	VG	EX	NRMT
34	John McCormack	7.50	15.00	30.00
35	Floyd Curry	7.50	15.00	30.00

DETROIT RED WINGS

No.	Player	VG	EX	NRMT
36	Earl Reibel, RC	7.50	15.00	30.00
37	Al Arbour, Error	15.00	30.00	60.00
38	Bill Dineen, Error	15.00	30.00	60.00
39	Vic Stasiuk	7.50	15.00	30.00
40	Red Kelly	25.00	50.00	100.00
41	Marcel Pronovost	7.50	15.00	30.00
42	Metro Prystai	7.50	15.00	30.00
43	Tony Leswick	7.50	15.00	30.00
44	Marty Pavelich	7.50	15.00	30.00
45	Benny Woit	7.50	15.00	30.00
46	Terry Sawchuk, Goalie	85.00	175.00	350.00
47	Alex Delvecchio	25.00	50.00	100.00
48	Glen Skov	7.50	15.00	30.00
49	Bob Goldham	7.50	15.00	30.00
50	Gordie Howe	300.00	600.00	1,200.00
51	Johnny Wilson	7.50	15.00	30.00
52	Ted Lindsay	18.75	37.50	75.00

NEW YORK RANGERS

No.	Player	VG	EX	NRMT
53	Gump Worsley, Goalie, RC	100.00	200.00	400.00
54	Jack Evans	7.50	15.00	30.00
55	Max Bentley, LC	7.50	15.00	30.00
56	Andy Bathgate, RC	43.75	87.50	175.00
57	Harry Howell, RC	43.75	87.50	175.00
58	Hyman Buller, LC	7.50	15.00	30.00
59	Chuck Rayner, Goalie, LC	7.50	15.00	30.00
60	Jack Stoddard, LC	7.50	15.00	30.00
61	Eddie Kullman, LC	7.50	15.00	30.00
62	Nick Mickoski	7.50	15.00	30.00
63	Paul Ronty	7.50	15.00	30.00
64	Allan Stanley	7.50	15.00	30.00
65	Leo Reise	7.50	15.00	30.00
66	Aldo Guidolin, RC, LC	7.50	15.00	30.00
67	Wally Hergesheimer	7.50	15.00	30.00
68	Don Raleigh	7.50	15.00	30.00

CHICAGO BLACK HAWKS

No.	Player	VG	EX	NRMT
69	Jim Peters, LC	7.50	15.00	30.00
70	Pete Conacher	7.50	15.00	30.00
71	Fred Hucul, LC	7.50	15.00	30.00
72	Lidio (Lee) Fogolin	7.50	15.00	30.00
73	Larry Zeidel	7.50	15.00	30.00
74	Larry Wilson	7.50	15.00	30.00
75	Gus Bodnar	7.50	15.00	30.00
76	Bill Gadsby	12.50	25.00	50.00
77	Jim McFadden, LC	7.50	15.00	30.00
78	Al Dewsbury	7.50	15.00	30.00
79	Clare Raglan, LC	7.50	15.00	30.00
80	Bill Mosienko	12.50	25.00	50.00
81	Gus Mortson	7.50	15.00	30.00
82	Al Rollins, Goalie	7.50	15.00	30.00
83	George Gee	7.50	15.00	30.00
84	Gerald Couture, LC	7.50	15.00	30.00

BOSTON BRUINS

No.	Player	VG	EX	NRMT
85	Dave Creighton	7.50	15.00	30.00
86	Jim Henry, Goalie	7.50	15.00	30.00
87	Hal Laycoe	7.50	15.00	30.00
88	Johnny Peirson, Error	7.50	15.00	30.00
89	Real Chevrefils	7.50	15.00	30.00
90	Ed Sandford	7.50	15.00	30.00
91A	Fleming Mackell, With "biography" on back	7.50	15.00	30.00
91B	Fleming Mackell, Without "biography" on back	7.50	15.00	30.00
92	Milt Schmidt	7.50	15.00	30.00
93	Leo Labine	7.50	15.00	30.00
94	Joe Klukay	7.50	15.00	30.00
95	Warren Godfrey	7.50	15.00	30.00
96	Woody Dumart, LC	7.50	15.00	30.00
97	Frank Martin, RC	7.50	15.00	30.00
98	Jerry Toppazzini, RC	7.50	15.00	30.00
99	Cal Gardner	7.50	15.00	30.00
100	Bill Quackenbush	35.00	75.00	150.00

PARKHURST — 1954-55 REGULAR ISSUE

— 1954-55 REGULAR ISSUE —

This set has the "Lucky Premium Card" backs. Mint condition cards will command a price premium of 50% over NRMT cards.

PRICE MOVEMENT OF NRMT SETS

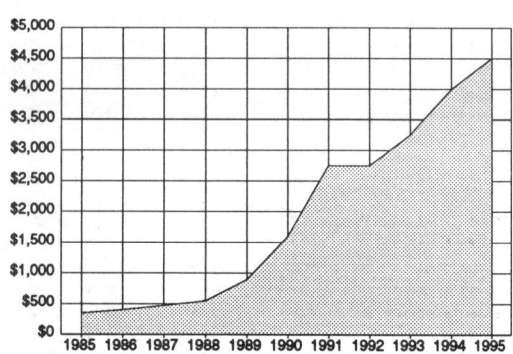

Card Size: 2 1/2" X 3 5/8"
Face: Four colour, white border, Number, Signature
Back: Black on card stock, Resume, Bilingual
Imprint: Printed In Canada
Complete Set No.: 100

	VG	EX	NRMT
Complete Set Price:	1,125.00	2,250.00	4,500.00
Common Player:	5.00	10.00	20.00
Album:	25.00	50.00	100.00

MONTREAL CANADIENS

No.	Player	VG	EX	NRMT
1	Gerry McNeil, Goalie	17.50	35.00	75.00
2	Dickie Moore	7.50	15.00	30.00
3	Jean Beliveau	75.00	150.00	300.00
4	Eddie Mazur, LC	5.00	10.00	20.00
5	Bert Olmstead	6.50	13.00	26.00
6	Emile (Butch) Bouchard	6.00	12.00	24.00
7	Maurice Richard	125.00	250.00	500.00
8	Bernie Geoffrion	22.50	45.00	90.00
9	John McCormack, LC	5.00	10.00	20.00
10	Tom Johnson	6.25	12.50	25.00
11	Calum MacKay	5.00	10.00	20.00
12	Kenny Mosdell	5.00	10.00	20.00
13	Paul Masnick, LC	5.00	10.00	20.00
14	Doug Harvey	25.00	50.00	100.00
15	Floyd Curry	5.00	10.00	20.00

TORONTO MAPLE LEAFS

No.	Player	VG	EX	NRMT
16	Harry Lumley, Goalie	15.00	30.00	60.00
17	Harry Watson, LC	5.00	10.00	20.00
18	Jim Morrison	5.00	10.00	20.00
19	Eric Nesterenko	5.00	10.00	20.00
20	Fernie Flaman	6.25	12.50	25.00
21	Rudy Migay	5.00	10.00	20.00
22	Sid Smith	5.00	10.00	20.00
23	Ron Stewart	5.00	10.00	20.00
24	George Armstrong	10.00	20.00	40.00
25	Earl Balfour, RC	5.00	10.00	20.00
26	Leo Boivin	6.00	12.00	24.00
27	Gord Hannigan, LC	5.00	10.00	20.00
28	Bob Bailey, RC	5.00	10.00	20.00
29	Ted Kennedy	12.50	25.00	50.00
30	Tod Sloan	5.00	10.00	20.00
31	Tim Horton	37.50	75.00	150.00
32	Jim Thomson, Error	5.00	10.00	20.00

DETROIT RED WINGS

No.	Player	VG	EX	NRMT
33	Terry Sawchuk, Goalie	75.00	150.00	300.00
34	Marcel Pronovost	6.00	12.00	24.00
35	Metro Prystai, LC	5.00	10.00	20.00
36	Alex Delvecchio	17.50	35.00	70.00
37	Earl Reibel	5.00	10.00	20.00
38	Benny Woit, LC	5.00	10.00	20.00
39	Bob Goldham, LC	5.00	10.00	20.00
40	Glen Skov	5.00	10.00	20.00

Parkhurst 1954-55 Issue Card No. 1, Gerry McNeil

Parkhurst 1954-55 Issue Card No.12, Kenny Mosdell

Parkhurst 1954-55 Issue Card No.100, Sawchuk Stops Boom Boom

No.	Player	VG	EX	NRMT
41	Gordie Howe	200.00	400.00	800.00
42	Red Kelly	11.00	22.50	45.00
43	Marty Pavelich, LC	5.00	10.00	20.00
44	Johnny Wilson	5.00	10.00	20.00
45	Tony Leswick, LC	5.00	10.00	20.00
46	Ted Lindsay	15.00	30.00	60.00
47	Keith Allen, RC, LC	5.00	10.00	20.00
48	Bill Dineen, RC	5.00	10.00	20.00

BOSTON BRUINS

No.	Player	VG	EX	NRMT
49	Jim Henry, Goalie, LC	6.00	12.00	24.00
50	Fleming Mackell	5.00	10.00	20.00
51	Bill Quackenbush, LC	6.00	12.00	24.00
52	Hal Laycoe, LC	5.00	10.00	20.00
53	Cal Gardner, LC	5.00	10.00	20.00
54	Joe Klukay	5.00	10.00	20.00
55	Bob Armstrong	5.00	10.00	20.00
56	Warren Godfrey	5.00	10.00	20.00
57	Doug Mohns, RC	6.00	12.50	25.00
58	Dave Creighton	5.00	10.00	20.00
59	Milt Schmidt, LC	6.00	12.50	25.00
60	Johnny Peirson, LC	5.00	10.00	20.00
61	Leo Labine	5.00	10.00	20.00
62	Gus Bodnar, LC	5.00	10.00	20.00
63	Real Chevrefils	5.00	10.00	20.00
64	Ed Sandford, LC	5.00	10.00	20.00

NEW YORK RANGERS

No.	Player	VG	EX	NRMT
65	Johnny Bower, Goalie, RC, Error	85.00	175.00	350.00
66	Paul Ronty, LC	5.00	10.00	20.00
67	Leo Reise, LC	5.00	10.00	20.00
68	Don Raleigh, LC	5.00	10.00	20.00
69	Bob Chrystal, RC, LC	5.00	10.00	20.00
70	Harry Howell	15.00	30.00	60.00
71	Wally Hergesheimer	5.00	10.00	20.00
72	Jack Evans	5.00	10.00	20.00
73	Camille Henry, RC	8.75	17.50	35.00
74	Dean Prentice, RC	10.00	20.00	40.00
75	Nick Mickoski	5.00	10.00	20.00
76	Ron Murphy, RC	5.00	10.00	20.00

CHICAGO BLACK HAWKS

No.	Player	VG	EX	NRMT
77	Al Rollins, Goalie, LC	5.00	10.00	20.00
78	Al Dewsbury, LC	5.00	10.00	20.00
79	Lou Jankowski, RC, LC	5.00	10.00	20.00
80	George Gee, LC	5.00	10.00	20.00
81	Gus Mortson	5.00	10.00	20.00
82	Fred Sasakamoose, RC, LC	5.00	10.00	20.00
83	Ike Hildebrand, RC, LC	5.00	10.00	20.00
84	Lidio (Lee) Fogolin, LC	5.00	10.00	20.00
85	Larry Wilson, LC	5.00	10.00	20.00
86	Pete Conacher	5.00	10.00	20.00
87	Bill Gadsby	6.00	12.00	24.00
88	Jack McIntyre	5.00	10.00	20.00

ACTION CARDS

No.	Player	VG	EX	NRMT
89	Busher Curry Goes Up-And-Over	5.00	10.00	20.00
90	Delvecchio Finds Leaf Defense Hard to Crack	7.50	15.00	30.00
91	The Battle of the All-Stars	7.00	14.00	28.00
92	Lum Stops Howe With Help of Stewart's Stick	30.00	60.00	125.00
93	Netminder's Nightmare	6.00	12.50	25.00
94	Meger Goes Down And Under	5.00	10.00	20.00
95	Harvey Takes a Nose-Dive	6.00	12.50	25.00
96	Terry Boots Out Teeder's Blast	25.00	50.00	100.00
97	Dutch Reibel Tests Habs' Rookie "Mr. Zero"	25.00	50.00	100.00
98	Plante Protects Against Slippery Sloan	25.00	50.00	100.00
99	Placid Plante Foils Tireless Teeder	25.00	50.00	100.00
100	Sawchuk Stops Boom Boom	37.50	75.00	150.00

— 1955 - 56 REGULAR ISSUE —

Features "Oldtime Great" cards—Nos.21-32 and 55-66. The "Oldtime Great" subset contains the first and last card of Bill Durnan (#63). The Parkhurst/Quaker Oats issue of 1955/56 is his only appearance on a card. As with all strong coloured borders the bottom red border marks easily. Mint cards command price premiums of 50% to 100% over NRMT cards.

PRICE MOVEMENT OF NRMT SETS

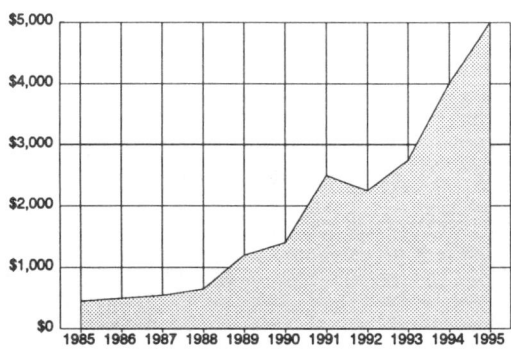

Card Size: 2 1/2" X 3 9/16"
Face: Four colour, red borber along bottom, Team logo, Number
Back: Red on card stock; Resume, Hockey trivia, Bilingual
Imprint: Printed In Canada
Complete Set No.: 79
Complete Set Price: 1,125.00   2,500.00   5,000.00
Common Player: 7.50   15.00   30.00

TORONTO MAPLE LEAFS

No.	Player	VG	EX	NRMT
1	Harry Lumley, Goalie, LC	87.50	175.00	350.00
2	Sid Smith	7.50	15.00	30.00
3A	Tim Horton	25.00	50.00	100.00
3B	Tim Horton (Reverse "N" in "Defense")	200.00	400.00	800.00
4	George Armstrong	12.50	25.00	50.00
5	Ron Stewart	7.50	15.00	30.00
6	Joe Klukay, LC	7.50	15.00	30.00
7	Marc Reaume, RC	7.50	15.00	30.00
8	Jim Morrison	7.50	15.00	30.00
9	Parker MacDonald, RC	7.50	15.00	30.00
10	Tod Sloan	7.50	15.00	30.00
11	Jim Thomson	7.50	15.00	30.00
12	Rudy Migay	7.50	15.00	30.00
13	Brian Cullen, RC	7.50	15.00	30.00
14	Hugh Bolton	7.50	15.00	30.00
15	Eric Nesterenko	7.50	15.00	30.00
16	Larry Cahan, RC	7.50	15.00	30.00
17	Willie Marshall, RC	7.50	15.00	30.00
18	Dick Duff, RC	12.50	25.00	50.00
19	Jack Caffery, RC	7.50	15.00	30.00
20	Billy Harris, RC	10.00	20.00	40.00

TORONTO MAPLE LEAFS OLDTIME GREATS

No.	Player	VG	EX	NRMT
21	Lorne Chabot, Goalie	12.50	25.00	50.00
22	Harvey Jackson	12.50	25.00	50.00
23	Turk Broda, Goalie	25.00	50.00	100.00
24	Joe Primeau	17.50	35.00	75.00
25	Gordie Drillon	10.00	20.00	40.00
26	Charlie Conacher	12.50	25.00	50.00
27	Sweeney Schriner	10.00	20.00	40.00
28	Syl Apps Sr.	10.00	20.00	40.00
29	Ted Kennedy	17.50	35.00	75.00
30	Ace I. Bailey	17.50	35.00	75.00
31	Babe Pratt	10.00	20.00	40.00
32	Harold Cotton	10.00	20.00	40.00

TORONTO MAPLE LEAFS MANAGEMENT

No.	Player	VG	EX	NRMT
33	Francis (King) Clancy, Coach	25.00	50.00	100.00
34	Hap Day, Manager	7.50	15.00	30.00

Parkhurst 1955-56 Issue Card No. 1, Harry Lumley

Parkhurst 1955-56 Issue Card No. 3B, Tim Horton

Parkhurst 1955-56 Issue Card No. 23, Turk Broda

MONTREAL CANADIENS

No.	Player	VG	EX	NRMT
35	Don Marshall, RC	7.50	15.00	30.00
36	Jackie LeClair, RC, LC	7.50	15.00	30.00
37	Maurice Richard	150.00	300.00	600.00
38	Dickie Moore	8.75	17.50	35.00
39	Kenny Mosdell, LC	7.50	15.00	30.00
40	Floyd Curry	7.50	15.00	30.00
41	Calum MacKay, LC	7.50	15.00	30.00
42	Bert Olmstead	7.50	15.00	30.00
43	Bernie Geoffrion	37.50	75.00	150.00
44	Jean Beliveau	60.00	125.00	250.00
45	Doug Harvey	11.00	22.50	45.00
46	Emile (Butch) Bouchard, LC	7.50	15.00	30.00
47	Bud MacPherson, LC	7.50	15.00	30.00
48	Dollard St. Laurent	7.50	15.00	30.00
49	Tom Johnson	7.50	15.00	30.00
50	Jacques Plante, Goalie, RC	250.00	500.00	1,000.00
51	Paul Meger, LC	7.50	15.00	30.00
52	Gerry McNeil, Goalie, LC	7.50	15.00	30.00
53	Jean-Guy Talbot, RC	7.50	15.00	30.00
54	Bob Turner, RC	7.50	15.00	30.00

MONTREAL CANADIENS OLDTIME GREATS

No.	Player	VG	EX	NRMT
55	Newsy Lalonde	10.00	20.00	40.00
56	Georges Vezina, Goalie	31.25	62.50	125.00
57	Howie Morenz	31.25	62.50	125.00
58	Aurel Joliat	17.50	35.00	75.00
59	George Hainsworth, Goalie	10.00	20.00	40.00
60	Sylvio Mantha	10.00	20.00	40.00
61	Albert Leduc	10.00	20.00	40.00
62	Babe Siebert, Error	10.00	20.00	40.00
63	Bill Durnan, Goalie	10.00	20.00	40.00
64	Ken Reardon	10.00	20.00	40.00
65	Johnny Gagnon	10.00	20.00	40.00
66	Billy Reay	10.00	20.00	40.00

MONTREAL CANADIENS MANAGEMENT

No.	Player	VG	EX	NRMT
67	Toe Blake, Coach	15.00	30.00	60.00
68	Frank Selke, Manager	15.00	30.00	60.00

ACTION CARDS

No.	Player	VG	EX	NRMT
69	Hugh Beats Hodge	7.50	15.00	30.00
70	Lum Stops Boom-Boom	15.00	30.00	60.00
71	Plante Is Protected	25.00	50.00	100.00
72	Rocket Roars Through	25.00	50.00	100.00
73	Richard Tests Lumley	25.00	50.00	100.00
74	Beliveau Bats Puck	18.75	37.50	75.00
75	Leaf Speedster Attack	7.50	15.00	30.00
76	Curry Scores Agains	7.50	15.00	30.00
77	Jammed On The Boards	7.50	15.00	30.00

STADIUMS

No.	Stadium	VG	EX	NRMT
78	The Montreal Forum	50.00	100.00	200.00
79	Maple Leaf Gardens	62.50	125.00	250.00

Note: Parkhurst did not issue a 1956-57 set of cards.
Note: For the Quaker Oats Issue see page no. 155.

THE CHARLTON STANDARD CATALOGUE OF CANADIAN BASEBALL AND FOOTBALL CARDS

- Fourth Edition -

Coming in April!

1957 - 58 REGULAR ISSUE —

The NHL Album offer no longer appeared on the Parkhurst cards. Mint condition cards will command a 50% premium over the NRMT prices.

PRICE MOVEMENT OF NRMT SETS

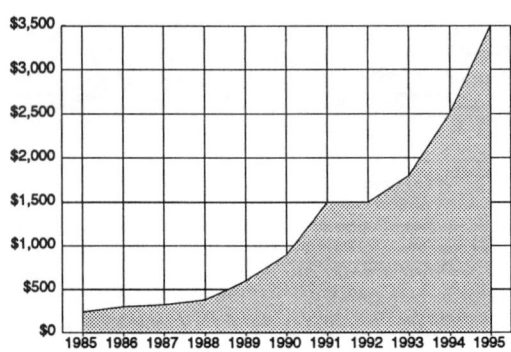

Card Size: 2 7/16" X 3 5/8"
Face: Four colour, white border, Number, Team logo
Back: Blue on card stock, Resume, Bilingual
Imprint: None
Complete Set No.: 50

Complete Set Price:	875.00	1,750.00	3,500.00
Common Player:	7.50	15.00	30.00

MONTREAL

No.	Player	VG	EX	NRMT
1	Doug Harvey, SP	75.00	150.00	300.00
2	Bernie Geoffrion, SP	50.00	100.00	200.00
3	Jean Beliveau, SP	75.00	150.00	300.00
4	Henri Richard, RC, SP	125.00	250.00	500.00
5	Maurice Richard, SP	125.00	250.00	500.00
6	Tom Johnson	7.50	15.00	30.00
7	Andre Pronovost, RC	7.50	15.00	30.00
8	Don Marshall	7.50	15.00	30.00
9	Jean-Guy Talbot	7.50	15.00	30.00
10	Dollard St. Laurent	7.50	15.00	30.00
11	Phil Goyette, RC	7.50	15.00	30.00
12	Claude Provost, RC	7.50	15.00	30.00
13	Bob Turner	7.50	15.00	30.00
14	Dickie Moore	7.50	15.00	30.00
15	Jacques Plante, Goalie	112.50	225.00	450.00
16	Toe (Hector) Blake, Coach	7.50	15.00	30.00
17	Charlie Hodge, Goalie, RC	7.50	15.00	30.00
18	Marcel Bonin	7.50	15.00	30.00
19	Bert Olmstead	7.50	15.00	30.00
20	Floyd Curry, LC	7.50	15.00	30.00

ACTION CARDS

No.	Player	VG	EX	NRMT
21	Canadiens on Guard	10.00	20.00	40.00
22	Barry Cullen Scores	10.00	20.00	40.00
23	Puck and Sticks High	10.00	20.00	40.00
24	Geoffrion Sidesteps Chadwick	10.00	20.00	40.00
25	Olmstead Beats Chadwick	10.00	20.00	40.00

TORONTO

No.	Player	VG	EX	NRMT
1	George Armstrong, SP	62.50	125.00	250.00
2	Ed Chadwick, Goalie, RC, SP	17.50	35.00	75.00
3	Dick Duff, SP	15.00	30.00	60.00
4	Bob Pulford, RC, SP	25.00	50.00	100.00
5	Tod Sloan, SP	15.00	30.00	60.00
6	Rudy Migay, LC	7.50	15.00	30.00
7	Ron Stewart	7.50	15.00	30.00
8	Gerry James, RC	7.50	15.00	30.00
9	Brian Cullen	7.50	15.00	30.00
10	Sid Smith, LC	7.50	15.00	30.00
11	Jim Morrison	7.50	15.00	30.00
12	Marc Reaume	7.50	15.00	30.00
13	Hugh Bolton, LC	7.50	15.00	30.00
14	Pete Conacher, LC	7.50	15.00	30.00
15	Billy Harris	7.50	15.00	30.00
16	Mike Nykoluk, RC, LC	7.50	15.00	30.00

Parkhurst 1957-58 Issue
Card No. 5,
Maurice Richard

Parkhurst 1958-59 Issue
Card No. 1,
Pulford Comes Close

No.	Player	VG	EX	NRMT
17	Frank Mahovlich, RC	140.00	275.00	550.00
18	Kenny Girard, RC, LC	7.50	15.00	30.00
19	Al MacNeil, RC, Error	7.50	15.00	30.00
20	Bob Baun, RC	7.50	15.00	30.00
21	Barry Cullen, RC	7.50	15.00	30.00
22	Tim Horton	22.50	45.00	90.00
23	Gary Collins, RC, LC	7.50	15.00	30.00
24	Gary Aldcorn, RC	7.50	15.00	30.00
25	Billy Reay, Coach	7.50	15.00	30.00

— 1958 - 59 REGULAR ISSUE —

Cards in mint condition will command a 50% price premium over NRMT cards.

PRICE MOVEMENT OF NRMT SETS

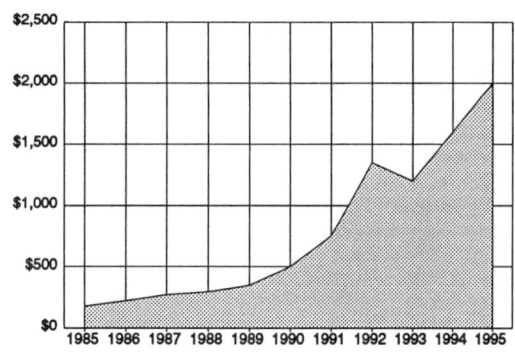

Card Size: 2 7/16" X 3 5/8"
Face: Four colour, white border, Team logo, Number, Position
Back: Black on card stock, Resume, Bilingual
Imprint: None
Complete Set No.: 50

Complete Set Price:	500.00	1000.00	2,000.00
Common Player:	4.50	9.00	18.00

No.	Player	VG	EX	NRMT
1	Pulford Comes Close	15.00	30.00	60.00
2	Henri Richard, Mon.	30.00	60.00	125.00
3	Andre Pronovost, Mon.	4.50	9.00	18.00
4	Billy Harris, Tor.	4.50	9.00	18.00
5	Al Langlois, Mon., RC	4.50	9.00	18.00
6	Noel Price, Tor., RC	4.50	9.00	18.00
7	Armstrong Breaks Through	5.00	10.00	20.00
8	Dickie Moore, Mon.	6.25	12.50	25.00
9	Toe Blake, Coach, Mon.	5.00	10.00	20.00
10	Tom Johnson, Mon.	5.00	10.00	20.00
11	An Object of Interest	10.00	20.00	40.00
12	Ed Chadwick, Goalie, Tor.	4.50	9.00	18.00
13	Bob Nevin, Tor., RC	5.00	10.00	20.00
14	Ron Stewart, Tor.	4.50	9.00	18.00
15	Bob Baun, Tor.	4.50	9.00	18.00
16	Ralph Backstrom, Mon., RC	6.25	12.50	25.00
17	Charlie Hodge, Goalie, Mon.	4.50	9.00	18.00
18	Gary Aldcorn, Tor.	4.50	9.00	18.00
19	Willie Marshall, Tor., LC	4.50	9.00	18.00
20	Marc Reaume, Tor	4.50	9.00	18.00
21	All Eyes on The Puck	10.00	20.00	40.00
22	Jacques Plante, Goalie, Mon.	55.00	110.00	225.00
23	Allan Stanley, Tor., Error	5.50	11.00	22.00
24	Ian Cushenan, Mon., RC	4.50	9.00	18.00
25	Billy Reay, Coach, Tor.	4.50	9.00	18.00
26	Plante Catches a Shot	10.00	20.00	40.00
27	Bert Olmstead, Tor.	5.00	10.00	20.00
28	Bernie Geoffrion, Mon.	25.00	50.00	100.00
29	Dick Duff, Tor.	4.50	9.00	18.00
30	Ab McDonald, Mon., RC	4.50	9.00	18.00
31	Barry Cullen, Tor.	4.50	9.00	18.00
32	Marcel Bonin, Mon.	4.50	9.00	18.00
33	Frank Mahovlich, Tor.	50.00	100.00	200.00
34	Jean Beliveau, Mon.	45.00	85.00	175.00
35	Canadiens on Guard	7.50	15.00	30.00
36	Barry Cullen Shoots	4.50	9.00	18.00

— 1959 - 60 REGULAR ISSUE — PARKHURST • 163

No.	Player	VG	EX	NRMT
37	Stephen Kraftcheck, Tor.	4.50	9.00	18.00
38	Maurice Richard, Mon.	85.00	175.00	350.00
39	Action Around the Net	10.00	20.00	40.00
40	Bob Turner, Mon.	4.50	9.00	18.00
41	Jean-Guy Talbot, Mon.	4.50	9.00	18.00
42	Tim Horton, Tor.	15.00	30.00	60.00
43	Claude Provost, Mon.	4.50	9.00	18.00
44	Don Marshall, Mon.	4.50	9.00	18.00
45	Bob Pulford, Tor.	4.50	9.00	18.00
46	Johnny Bower, Goalie, Tor. Error	15.00	30.00	60.00
47	Phil Goyette, Mon.	4.50	9.00	18.00
48	George Armstrong, Tor.	5.50	11.00	22.00
49	Doug Harvey, Mon.	8.75	17.50	35.00
50	Brian Cullen, Tor.	7.00	14.00	28.00

— 1959 - 60 REGULAR ISSUE —

Mint condition cards will command a 50% premium over NRMT cards.

PRICE MOVEMENT OF NRMT SETS

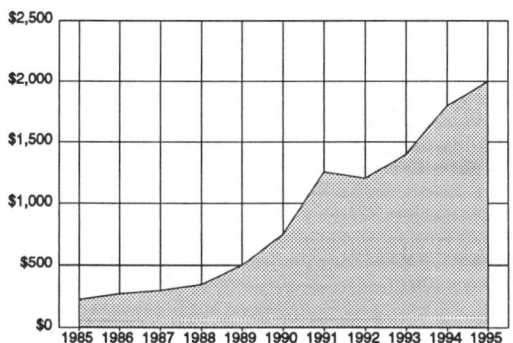

Card Size: 2 7/16" X 3 5/8"
Face: Four colour, white border, Team logo, Mixed Formats, Number
Back: Two colour, red and black on card stock; Resume, Bilingual
Imprint: None
Complete Set No.: 50

Complete Set Price:	500.00	1,000.00	2,000.00
Common Player:	4.00	8.00	16.00

No.	Player	VG	EX	NRMT
1	Canadiens on Guard	25.00	50.00	100.00
2	Maurice Richard, Mon.	85.00	175.00	350.00
3	Carl Brewer, Tor., RC	8.75	17.50	35.00
4	Phil Goyette, Mon.	4.00	8.00	16.00
5	Ed Chadwick, Goalie, Tor., LC	4.00	8.00	16.00
6	Jean Beliveau, Mon.	37.50	75.00	150.00
7	George Armstrong, Tor.	6.00	12.00	24.00
8	Doug Harvey, Mon.	6.25	12.50	25.00
9	Billy Harris, Tor.	4.00	8.00	16.00
10	Tom Johnson, Mon.	5.00	10.00	20.00
11	Marc Reaume, Tor.	4.00	8.00	16.00
12	Marcel Bonin, Mon.	4.00	8.00	16.00
13	Johnny Wilson, Tor.	4.00	8.00	16.00
14	Dickie Moore, Mon.	5.50	11.00	22.00
15	Punch Imlach, Tor., Manager & Coach	5.00	10.00	20.00
16	Charlie Hodge, Goalie, Mon.	4.00	8.00	16.00
17	Larry Regan, Tor.	4.00	8.00	16.00
18	Claude Provost, Mon.	4.00	8.00	16.00
19	Gerry Ehman, Tor., RC	4.00	8.00	16.00
20	Ab McDonald, Mon.	4.00	8.00	16.00
21	Bob Baun, Tor.	4.00	8.00	16.00
22	Ken Reardon, Mon., Vice President	4.50	9.00	18.00
23	Tim Horton, Tor.	10.00	20.00	40.00
24	Frank Mahovlich, Tor.	30.00	60.00	125.00
25	Bower In Action	5.00	10.00	20.00
26	Ron Stewart, Tor.	4.00	8.00	16.00
27	Toe Blake, Coach, Mon.	5.00	10.00	20.00
28	Bob Pulford, Tor.	4.00	9.50	16.00
29	Ralph Backstrom, Mon.	4.00	8.00	16.00
30	Action Around the Net	4.00	8.00	16.00

Parkhurst 1959-60 Issue Card No. 1, Canadiens on Guard

Parkhurst 1959-60 Issue Card No. 1, Canadiens on Guard

Parkhurst 1960-61 Issue Card No. 1, Tim Horton

Parkhurst 1960-61 Issue Card No. 1, Tim Horton

No.	Player	VG	EX	NRMT
31	Bill Hicke, Mon., RC	4.50	9.00	18.00
32	Johnny Bower, Goalie, Tor.	8.75	17.50	35.00
33	Bernie Geoffrion, Mon.	18.75	37.50	75.00
34	Ted Hampson, Tor., RC	3.75	7.50	15.00
35	Andre Pronovost, Mon.	4.00	8.00	16.00
36	Stafford Smythe, Chairman, Hockey Committee, Tor.	5.00	10.00	20.00
37	Don Marshall, Mon.	4.00	8.00	16.00
38	Dick Duff, Tor.	4.00	8.00	16.00
39	Henri Richard, Mon.	15.00	30.00	60.00
40	Bert Olmstead, Tor.	5.00	10.00	20.00
41	Jacques Plante, Goalie, Mon.	40.00	80.00	160.00
42	Noel Price, Tor.	4.00	8.00	16.00
43	Bob Turner, Mon.	4.00	8.00	16.00
44	Allan Stanley, Tor.	5.00	10.00	20.00
45	Al Langlois, Mon.	4.00	8.00	16.00
46	Officials Intervene	4.00	8.00	16.00
47	Frank Selke, Mon., Managing Director	4.00	8.00	16.00
48	Gary Edmundson, Tor., RC	4.00	8.00	16.00
49	Jean-Guy Talbot, Mon.	4.00	8.00	16.00
50	Francis (King) Clancy, Assistant General Manager, Tor.	25.00	50.00	100.00

— 1960 - 61 REGULAR ISSUE —

Mint condition cards will command a 50% price premium over NRMT cards.

PRICE MOVEMENT OF NRMT SETS

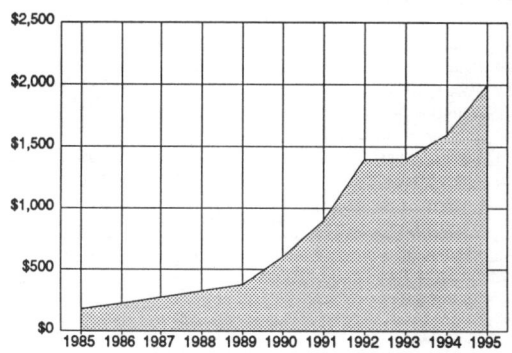

Card Size: 2 7/16" X 3 5/8"
Face: Four colour, white border, black and yellow banner; Number
Back: Resume, Bilingual
  Toronto: Red on card stock with blue overprint logo
  Detroit and Montreal: Blue on card stock with red overprint logo
Imprint: None
Complete Set No.: 61

Complete Set Price:	500.00	1,000.00	2,000.00
Common Player:	3.75	7.50	15.00

TORONTO MAPLE LEAFS

No.	Player	VG	EX	NRMT
1	Tim Horton	25.00	50.00	100.00
2	Frank Mahovlich	22.50	45.00	90.00
3	Johnny Bower, Goalie	15.00	30.00	60.00
4	Bert Olmstead	5.00	10.00	20.00
5	Gary Edmundson, LC	3.75	7.50	15.00
6	Ron Stewart	3.75	7.50	15.00
7	Gerry James, LC	3.75	7.50	15.00
8	Gerry Ehman	3.75	7.50	15.00
9	Red Kelly	6.25	12.50	25.00
10	Dave Creighton, LC	3.75	7.50	15.00
11	Bob Baun	3.75	7.50	15.00
12	Dick Duff	3.75	7.50	15.00
13	Larry Regan, LC	3.75	7.50	15.00
14	Johnny Wilson, LC	3.75	7.50	15.00
15	Billy Harris	3.75	7.50	15.00
16	Allan Stanley	4.50	9.00	18.00
17	George Armstrong	4.50	9.00	18.00
18	Carl Brewer	3.75	7.50	15.00
19	Bob Pulford	4.00	8.00	16.00

164 • PARKHURST — 1961-62 REGULAR ISSUE —

DETROIT RED WINGS

No.	Player	VG	EX	NRMT
20	Gordie Howe	100.00	200.00	400.00
21	Val Fonteyne, RC	3.75	7.50	15.00
22	Murray Oliver, RC	3.75	7.50	15.00
23	Sid Abel, Coach	3.75	7.50	15.00
24	Jack McIntyre, LC	3.75	7.50	15.00
25	Marc Reaume	3.75	7.50	15.00
26	Norm Ullman	7.50	15.00	30.00
27	Brian S. Smith, RC, LC	3.75	7.50	15.00
28	Gerry Melnyk, RC, Error	3.75	7.50	15.00
29	Marcel Pronovost	4.50	9.00	18.00
30	Warren Godfrey	3.75	7.50	15.00
31	Terry Sawchuk, Goalie	37.50	75.00	150.00
32	Barry Cullen, LC	3.75	7.50	15.00
33	Gary Aldcorn, LC	3.75	7.50	15.00
34	Peter Goegan	3.75	7.50	15.00
35	Len Lunde	3.75	7.50	15.00
36	Alex Delvecchio	6.25	12.50	25.00
37	John McKenzie, RC	4.50	9.00	18.00

MONTREAL CANADIENS

No.	Player	VG	EX	NRMT
38	Dickie Moore	5.50	11.00	22.00
39	Al Langlois	3.75	7.50	15.00
40	Bill Hicke	3.75	7.50	15.00
41	Ralph Backstrom	3.75	7.50	15.00
42	Don Marshall	3.75	7.50	15.00
43	Bob Turner	3.75	7.50	15.00
44	Tom Johnson	4.00	8.00	16.00
45	Maurice Richard, LC	50.00	100.00	200.00
46	Bernie Geoffrion	12.50	25.00	50.00
47	Henri Richard	10.00	20.00	40.00
48	Doug Harvey	7.50	15.00	30.00
49	Jean Beliveau	37.50	75.00	150.00
50	Phil Goyette	3.75	7.50	15.00
51	Marcel Bonin	3.75	7.50	15.00
52	Jean-Guy Talbot	3.75	7.50	15.00
53	Jacques Plante, Goalie	37.50	75.00	150.00
54	Claude Provost	3.75	7.50	15.00
55	Andre Pronovost	3.75	7.50	15.00

LINE CARDS

No.	Players	VG	EX	NRMT
56	Bill Hicke, Ralph Backstrom, Ab McDonald	3.75	7.50	15.00
57	Don Marshall, Henri Richard, Dickie Moore	7.50	15.00	30.00
58	Claude Provost, Phil Goyette, Andre Pronovost	3.75	7.50	15.00
59	Bernie Geoffrion, Jean Beliveau, Don Marshall	15.00	30.00	60.00

REGULAR ISSUE

No.	Player	VG	EX	NRMT
60	Ab McDonald, Mon.	3.75	7.50	15.00
61	Jim Morrison, Det.	6.25	12.50	25.00

— 1961 - 62 REGULAR ISSUE —

Mint condition cards will command a 50% price premium over NRMT cards.

PRICE MOVEMENT OF NRMT SETS

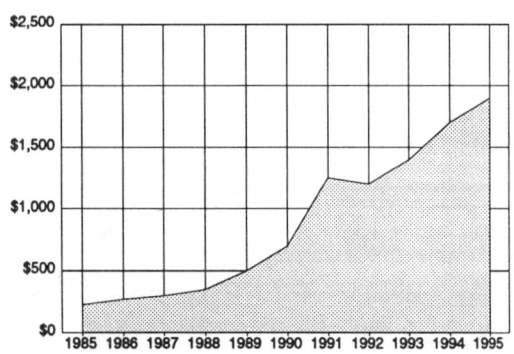

Parkhurst
1961-62 Issue
Card No. 1,
Tim Horton

Parkhurst
1961-62 Issue
Card No. 1,
Tim Horton

Parkhurst
1961-62 Issue
Card No. 25,
Alex Delvecchio

Parkhurst
1961-62 Issue
Card No. 45,
Jean Beliveau

Card Size: 2 7/16" X 3 5/8"
Face: Four colour, white border, Team logo, Number
Back: Black on card stock, Resume, Cartoon quiz
Imprint: None
Complete Set No.: 51

Complete Set Price:	475.00	950.00	1,900.00
Common Player:	3.50	7.00	14.00

TORONTO MAPLE LEAFS

No.	Player	VG	EX	NRMT
1	Tim Horton	22.50	45.00	90.00
2	Frank Mahovlich	22.50	45.00	90.00
3	Johnny Bower, Goalie	12.50	25.00	50.00
4	Bert Olmstead	4.50	9.00	18.00
5	Dave Keon, RC	100.00	200.00	400.00
6	Ron Stewart	3.50	7.00	14.00
7	Eddie Shack	5.00	10.00	20.00
8	Bob Pulford	3.50	7.00	14.00
9	Red Kelly	7.50	15.00	30.00
10	Bob Nevin	3.50	7.00	14.00
11	Bob Baun	3.50	7.00	14.00
12	Dick Duff	3.75	7.50	15.00
13	Larry Keenan, RC	3.50	7.00	14.00
14	Larry Hillman	3.50	7.00	14.00
15	Billy Harris	3.50	7.00	14.00
16	Allan Stanley	4.00	8.00	16.00
17	George Armstrong	7.50	15.00	30.00
18	Carl Brewer	3.50	7.00	14.00

DETROIT RED WINGS

No.	Player	VG	EX	NRMT
19	Howie Glover, RC	3.50	7.00	14.00
20	Gordie Howe	100.00	200.00	400.00
21	Val Fonteyne	3.50	7.00	14.00
22	Al Johnson, RC, LC	3.50	7.00	14.00
23	Peter Goegan	3.50	7.00	14.00
24	Len Lunde	3.50	7.00	14.00
25	Alex Delvecchio	7.50	15.00	30.00
26	Norm Ullman	4.00	8.00	16.00
27	Bill Gadsby	4.00	8.00	16.00
28	Ed Litzenberger	3.50	7.00	14.00
29	Marcel Pronovost	4.00	8.00	16.00
30	Warren Godfrey	3.50	7.00	14.00
31	Terry Sawchuk, Goalie	30.00	60.00	125.00
32	Vic Stasiuk	3.50	7.00	14.00
33	Leo Labine	3.50	7.00	14.00
34	John McKenzie	3.50	7.00	14.00

MONTREAL CANADIENS

No.	Player	VG	EX	NRMT
35	Bernie Geoffrion	15.00	30.00	60.00
36	Dickie Moore	5.00	10.00	20.00
37	Al Langlois	3.50	7.00	14.00
38	Bill Hicke	3.50	7.00	14.00
39	Ralph Backstrom	3.50	7.00	14.00
40	Don Marshall	3.50	7.00	14.00
41	Bob Turner	3.50	7.00	14.00
42	Tom Johnson	4.00	8.00	16.00
43	Henri Richard	10.00	20.00	40.00
44	Wayne Connelly, RC, Error	3.50	7.00	14.00
45	Jean Beliveau	25.00	50.00	100.00
46	Phil Goyette	3.50	7.00	14.00
47	Marcel Bonin	3.50	7.00	14.00
48	Jean-Guy Talbot	3.50	7.00	14.00
49	Jacques Plante, Goalie	37.50	75.00	150.00
50	Claude Provost	3.50	7.00	14.00
51	Andre Pronovost	10.00	20.00	40.00

Note: Cards are listed in this catalogue chronologically by manufacturer's first date of issue. For all manufacturers, subsequent cards appear in issue date order following that manufacturer's first listing. See the last page of this catalogue for an alphabetical index of issuers.

— 1962 - 63 REGULAR ISSUE —

Mint condition cards will command a 50% premium over NRMT prices.

PRICE MOVEMENT OF NRMT SETS

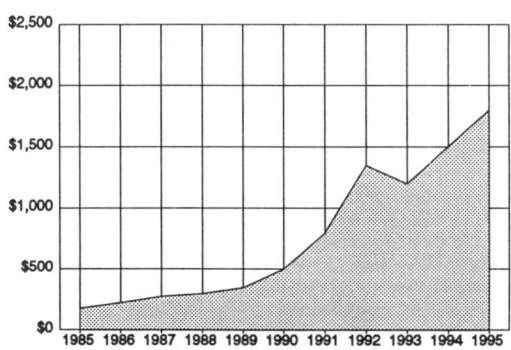

Card Size: 2 7/16" X 3 5/8"
Face: Four colour, white border, Signature, Number
Back: Black on card stock, Resume, Bilingual
Imprint: None
Complete Set No.: 55
Complete Set Price: 450.00 900.00 1,800.00
Common Player: 2.50 5.00 10.00

TORONTO MAPLE LEAFS

No.	Player	VG	EX	NRMT
1	Billy Harris	5.00	10.00	20.00
2	Dick Duff	2.50	5.00	10.00
3	Bob Baun	2.75	5.50	11.00
4	Frank Mahovlich	18.75	37.50	75.00
5	Red Kelly	5.00	10.00	20.00
6	Ron Stewart	2.50	5.00	10.00
7	Tim Horton	6.25	12.50	25.00
8	Carl Brewer	2.50	5.00	10.00
9	Allan Stanley	3.50	7.00	14.00
10	Bob Nevin	2.50	5.00	10.00
11	Bob Pulford	3.00	6.00	12.00
12	Ed Litzenberger	2.50	5.00	10.00
13	George Armstrong	4.00	8.00	16.00
14	Eddie Shack	4.00	8.00	16.00
15	Dave Keon	10.00	20.00	40.00
16	Johnny Bower, Goalie	7.00	14.00	28.00
17	Larry Hillman	2.50	5.00	10.00
18	Frank Mahovlich	18.75	37.50	75.00

DETROIT RED WINGS

No	Player	VG	EX	NRMT
19	Hank Bassen, Goalie, RC	2.50	5.00	10.00
20	Gerry Odrowski, RC	2.50	5.00	10.00
21	Norm Ullman	4.50	9.00	18.00
22	Vic Stasiuk	2.50	5.00	10.00
23	Bruce MacGregor, RC	2.25	5.50	11.00
24	Claude Laforge, LC	2.50	5.00	10.00
25	Bill Gadsby	3.50	7.00	14.00
26	Leo Labine, LC	2.50	5.00	10.00
27	Val Fonteyne	2.50	5.00	10.00
28	Howie Glover, LC	2.50	5.00	10.00
29	Marc Boileau, RC, LC	2.50	5.00	10.00
30	Gordie Howe	87.50	175.00	350.00
31	Gordie Howe	87.50	175.00	350.00
32	Alex Delvecchio	5.00	10.00	20.00
33	Marcel Pronovost	3.50	7.00	14.00
34	Sid Abel, Coach	3.50	7.00	14.00
35	Len Lunde	2.50	5.00	10.00
36	Warren Godfrey, LC	2.50	5.00	10.00

MONTREAL CANADIENS

No.	Player	VG	EX	NRMT
37	Phil Goyette	2.50	5.00	10.00
38	Henri Richard	4.50	9.00	18.00
39	Jean Beliveau	22.50	45.00	90.00
40	Bill Hicke	2.50	5.00	10.00
41	Claude Provost	2.50	5.00	10.00
42	Dickie Moore, LC	4.50	9.00	18.00

Parkhurst
1962-63 Issue
Card No. 1,
Billy Harris

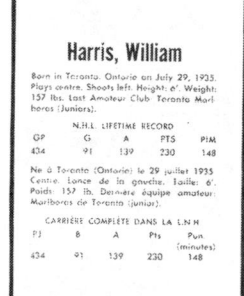

Parkhurst
1962-63 Issue
Card No. 1,
Billy Harris

Parkhurst
1963-64 Issue
Card No. 34,
Toe Blake

Parkhurst
1963-64 Issue
Card No. 34,
Toe Blake

No.	Player	VG	EX	NRMT
43	Don Marshall	2.50	5.00	10.00
44	Ralph Backstrom	2.50	5.00	10.00
45	Marcel Bonin, LC	2.50	5.00	10.00
46	Gilles Tremblay, RC	3.50	7.00	14.00
47	Bobby Rousseau, RC	3.50	7.00	14.00
48	Bernie Geoffrion	15.00	30.00	60.00
49	Jacques Plante, Goalie	30.00	60.00	125.00
50	Tom Johnson	3.50	7.00	14.00
51	Jean-Guy Talbot	2.50	5.00	10.00
52	Louie Fontinato, LC	2.50	5.00	10.00
53	Bernie Geoffrion	15.00	30.00	60.00
54	J.C. Tremblay, RC	5.00	10.00	20.00
—	Tally Card (Checklist)	75.00	150.00	300.00
—	Zip Card	10.00	20.00	40.00

— 1963 - 64 REGULAR ISSUE —

Mint condition cards will command a 50% premium over NRMT prices.

PRICE MOVEMENT OF NRMT SETS

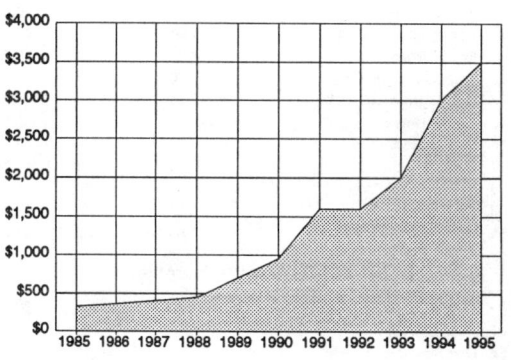

Card Size: 2 7/16" X 3 5/8"
Face: Four colour, white border, mixed backgrounds
Back: Black on card stock, Resume, Number, Bilingual
Imprint: None
Complete Set No.: 99
Complete Set Price: 875.00 1,750.00 3,500.00
Common Player: 4.50 9.00 18.00

TORONTO MAPLE LEAFS

No.	Player	VG	EX	NRMT
1	Allan Stanley	15.00	30.00	60.00
2	Don Simmons, Goalie	4.50	9.00	18.00
3	Red Kelly	7.50	15.00	30.00
4	Dick Duff	4.50	9.00	18.00
5	Johnny Bower, Goalie	12.50	25.00	50.00
6	Ed Litzenberger, LC	4.50	9.00	18.00
7	Kent Douglas, RC	4.50	9.00	18.00
8	Carl Brewer	4.50	9.00	18.00
9	Eddie Shack	5.00	10.00	20.00
10	Bob Nevin	4.50	9.00	18.00
11	Billy Harris	4.50	9.00	18.00
12	Bob Pulford	4.50	9.00	18.00
13	George Armstrong	5.00	10.00	20.00
14	Ron Stewart	4.50	9.00	18.00
15	John MacMillan, RC, LC	4.50	9.00	18.00
16	Tim Horton	12.50	25.00	50.00
17	Frank Mahovlich	22.50	45.00	90.00
18	Bob Baun	4.50	9.00	18.00
19	Punch Imlach, Manager & Coach	4.50	9.00	18.00
20	Francis (King) Clancy, Assistant General Manager	7.50	15.00	30.00

MONTREAL CANADIENS

No.	Player	VG	EX	NRMT
21	Gilles Tremblay	4.50	9.00	18.00
22	Jean-Guy Talbot	4.50	9.00	18.00
23	Henri Richard	10.00	20.00	40.00
24	Ralph Backstrom	4.50	9.00	18.00
25	Bill Hicke	4.50	9.00	18.00
26	Red Berenson, RC	4.50	9.00	18.00
27	Jacques Laperriere, RC	10.00	20.00	40.00

166 • PARKHURST — 1963-64 REGULAR ISSUE

No.	Player	VG	EX	NRMT
28	Jean Gauthier, RC, LC	4.50	9.00	18.00
29	Bernie Geoffrion	17.50	35.00	70.00
30	Jean Beliveau	22.50	45.00	90.00
31	J.C. Tremblay	4.50	9.00	18.00
32	Terry Harper, RC	4.50	9.00	18.00
33	John Ferguson Sr., RC	10.00	20.00	40.00
34	Toe Blake, Coach	4.50	9.00	18.00
35	Bobby Rousseau	7.50	15.00	30.00
36	Claude Provost	4.50	9.00	18.00
37	Marc Reaume	4.50	9.00	18.00
38	Dave Balon	4.50	9.00	18.00
39	Gump Worsley, Goalie	12.50	25.00	50.00
40	Cesare Maniago, Goalie, RC	5.50	15.00	30.00

DETROIT RED WINGS

No.	Player	VG	EX	NRMT
41	Bruce MacGregor	4.50	9.00	18.00
42	Alex Faulkner, RC, LC	4.50	9.00	18.00
43	Peter Goegan, LC	4.50	9.00	18.00
44	Parker MacDonald	4.50	9.00	18.00
45	Andre Pronovost, LC	4.50	9.00	18.00
46	Marcel Pronovost	4.50	9.00	18.00
47	Bob Dillabough, RC	4.50	9.00	18.00
48	Larry Jeffrey, RC	4.50	9.00	18.00
49	Ian Cushenan, LC	4.50	9.00	18.00
50	Alex Delvecchio	10.00	20.00	40.00
51	Hank Ciesla, LC	4.50	9.00	18.00
52	Norm Ullman	4.50	9.00	18.00
53	Terry Sawchuk, Goalie	37.50	75.00	150.00
54	Ron Ingram, RC, LC	4.50	9.00	18.00
55	Gordie Howe	125.00	250.00	500.00
56	Billy McNeill, LC	4.50	9.00	18.00
57	Floyd Smith, RC	4.50	9.00	18.00
58	Vic Stasiuk, LC	4.50	9.00	18.00
59	Bill Gadsby	4.50	9.00	18.00
60	Doug Barkley, RC	4.50	9.00	18.00

TORONTO MAPLE LEAFS

No.	Player	VG	EX	NRMT
61	Allan Stanley	4.50	9.00	18.00
62	Don Simmons, Goalie	4.50	9.00	18.00
63	Red Kelly	7.50	15.00	30.00
64	Dick Duff	4.50	9.00	18.00
65	Johnny Bower, Goalie	12.50	25.00	50.00
66	Ed Litzenberger, LC	4.50	9.00	18.00
67	Kent Douglas, RC	4.50	9.00	18.00
68	Carl Brewer	4.50	9.00	18.00
69	Eddie Shack	5.00	10.00	20.00
70	Bob Nevin	4.50	9.00	18.00
71	Billy Harris	4.50	9.00	18.00
72	Bob Pulford	4.50	9.00	18.00
73	George Armstrong	5.00	10.00	20.00
74	Ron Stewart	4.50	9.00	18.00
75	Dave Keon	12.50	25.00	50.00
76	Tim Horton	12.50	25.00	50.00
77	Frank Mahovlich	17.50	35.00	70.00
78	Bob Baun	4.50	9.00	18.00
79	Punch Imlach, Manager & Coach	4.50	9.00	18.00

MONTREAL CANADIENS

No.	Player	VG	EX	NRMT
80	Gilles Tremblay	4.50	9.00	18.00
81	Jean-Guy Talbot	4.50	9.00	18.00
82	Henri Richard	10.00	20.00	40.00
83	Ralph Backstrom	4.50	9.00	18.00
84	Bill Hicke	4.50	9.00	18.00
85	Red Berenson, RC	4.50	9.00	18.00
86	Jacques Laperriere, RC	10.00	20.00	40.00
87	Jean Gauthier, RC, LC	4.50	9.00	18.00
88	Bernie Geoffrion	17.50	35.00	70.00
89	Jean Beliveau	22.50	45.00	90.00
90	J.C. Tremblay	4.50	9.00	18.00
91	Terry Harper, RC	4.50	9.00	18.00
92	John Ferguson Sr., RC	10.00	20.00	40.00
93	Toe Blake, Coach	4.50	9.00	18.00
94	Bobby Rousseau	4.50	9.00	18.00
95	Claude Provost	4.50	9.00	18.00
96	Marc Reaume	4.50	9.00	18.00
97	Dave Balon	4.50	9.00	18.00
98	Gump Worsley, Goalie	5.50	11.00	22.00
99	Cesare Maniago, Goalie, RC	37.50	75.00	150.00

Parkhurst 1963-64 Issue Card No. 35, Bobby Rousseau

Parkhurst 1963-64 Issue Card No. 47, Bob Dillabough

Parkhurst 1963-64 Issue Card No. 79, Punch Imlach

Parkhurst 1963-64 Issue Card No. 88, Bernie Geoffrion

Available in April!

THE CHARLTON STANDARD CATALOGUE OF CANADIAN BASEBALL & FOOTBALL CARDS

- Fourth Edition -

BASEBALL CARDS FROM 1912
FOOTBALL CARDS FROM 1949

For Canadian Baseball and Football Card Collectors this Catalogue has it all!

IMPERIAL TOBACCO * MAPLE CRISPETTE
BAZOOKA * PARKHURST * O-PEE-CHEE
CANADA STARCH * STUART * POST
TOPPS * WORLD WIDE GUM * NALLEYS
DONRUSS - LEAF * EDDIE SARGENT
WILLARD * TORONTO BLUE JAYS
STANDARD OIL * NABISCO * VACHON
BLUE RIBBON TEA * PANINI * PROVIGO
GENERAL MILLS * SCORE * EXHIBITS
HOSTESS * PURITAN MEATS * JOGO
GULF CANADA * ROYAL STUDIOS
BEN'S AULT FOODS * COCA-COLA * KFC
And All Other Major Manufacturers...

Complete price listings for all Major League Baseball and Canadian Football League cards!
Comprehensive baseball and football minor league card listings!
Regular issues, stickers, inserts, subsets, transfers and much, much more!
All major manufacturers!
Current Pricing for all cards in up to three grades of condition - VG, EX, and NRMT!
All rookie, last, pitcher, quarterback, error and variation cards identified and priced!
Plus Charlton's Fabulous Alphabetical Index!

OVER 300 PAGES * 60,000 PRICES
NEW, LARGER 8 1/2 x 11" FORMAT
RESERVE YOUR COPY TODAY
DIRECTLY FROM THE PUBLISHER...

The Charlton Press

**2010 YONGE STREET,
TORONTO, ONTARIO M4S 1Z9**
FOR TOLL FREE ORDERING PHONE
1-800-442-6042 FAX 1-800-442-1542
from anywhere in Canada or the U.S.

— 1991 - 92 PROMOTIONAL CARDS —

This two-card set has printed on the back "PROTOTYPE FOR REVIEW ONLY". The cards are unnumbered. Except for the missing number and the "Prototype for Review Only" the cards are identical to the Gilmour and Reichel in Series One.

1991-92 Parkhurst Promotional Card
Douglas Gilmore

Card Size: 2 1/2" x 3 1/2"
Face: Four colour, motted brown border on left side
Back: Four colour; Name; Resume on card stock
Imprint: Pro Set Inc. ©NHL 1991 ©NHLPA 1991
Complete Set No. 2
Complete Set Price: 100.00   200.00

CALGARY FLAMES

No.	Player	EX	NRMT
—	Douglas Gilmour	90.00	175.00
—	Robert Reichel	25.00	50.00

— 1991 - 92 REGULAR ISSUE—

SERIES ONE

This is the first issue of a Parkhurst set after a span of nearly thirty years. The Parkhurst Company was re-instated in 1990 and licensed Pro Set to produce and market Parkhurst cards. This set is available only in foil packs. Factory sealed cases are numbered 1 to 2,500 for the French issue and 2,501 to 15,000 for the English issue. Thirty-five to forty per cent of the cases were allocated to the Canadian market and the balance to the U.S.A. market.

1991-92 Series One French
Card No. 1, Matt DelGuidice

Card Size: 2 1/2" X 3 1/2"
Face: Four colour, mottled brown border on left side
Back: Four colour, Resume, Number
Imprint: Pro Set Inc. © NHL 1991 © NHLPA 1991
Complete Set No.: 225
Complete Set Price: 12.50   25.00
Common Player: .05   .10
Common Goalie: .05   .10
Foil Pack: (12 Cards)   1.25
Foil Box: (36 Packs)   30.00
Foil Case: (20 Boxes)   550.00
Production:
Factory Sealed Cases: 12,500

BOSTON BRUINS

No.	Player	English NRMT	French NRMT
1	Matt DelGuidice, Goalie, RC	.10	.20
2	Kenneth Hodge, Jr.	.07	.15
3	Vladimir Ruzicka, Error	.12	.25
4	Craig Janney	.10	.20
5	Glen Wesley	.05	.10
6	Stephen Leach	.05	.10
7	Garry Galley	.05	.10
8	Andrew Moog, Goalie	.07	.15
9	Raymond Bourque	.10	.20

BUFFALO SABRES

No.	Player	English NRMT	French NRMT
10	Brad May, RC	.10	.20
11	Donald Audette, RC	.10	.20
12	Alexander Mogilny	.75	1.50
13	Randy Wood	.05	.10
14	Daren Puppa, Goalie	.05	.10
15	Doug Bodger	.05	.10
16	Pat LaFontaine	.25	.50
17	David Andreychuk	.05	.10
18	Dale Hawerchuk	.07	.15
19	Michael Ramsey	.05	.10

CALGARY FLAMES

No.	Player	English NRMT	French NRMT
20	Tomas Forslund, RC, Error	.17	.35
21	Robert Reichel	.15	.30
22	Theoren Fleury	.10	.20
23	Joe Nieuwendyk	.10	.20
24	Gary Roberts	.05	.10
25	Gary Suter	.05	.10
26	Douglas Gilmour	.12	.25
27	Michael Vernon, Goalie	.05	.10
28	Allan MacInnis	.07	.15

CHICAGO BLACK HAWKS

No.	Player	English NRMT	French NRMT
29	Jeremy Roenick	.75	1.50
30	Ed Belfour, Goalie	.50	1.00
31	James (Steve) Smith	.05	.10
32	Chris Chelios	.05	.10
33	Dirk Graham	.05	.10
34	Steve Larmer	.07	.15
35	Brent Sutter	.05	.10
36	Michel Goulet	.07	.15

DETROIT RED WINGS

No.	Player	English NRMT	French NRMT
37	Nicklas Lidstrom, RC, Error	.50	1.00
38	Sergei Fedorov	.60	1.25
39	Tim Cheveldae, Goalie	.12	.25
40	Kevin Miller	.07	.15
41	Ray Sheppard	.05	.10
42	Paul Ysebaert	.12	.25
43	Jimmy Carson	.05	.10
44	Steve Yzerman	.12	.25
45	Shawn Burr	.05	.10
46	Vladimir Konstantinov, RC	.25	.50

EDMONTON OILERS

No.	Player	English NRMT	French NRMT
47	Josef Beranek, RC	.17	.35
48	Vincent Damphousse	.07	.15
49	Dave Manson	.05	.10
50	Scott Mellanby	.05	.10
51	Kevin Lowe	.05	.10
52	Joe Murphy	.07	.15
53	Bill Ranford, Goalie	.07	.15
54	Craig Simpson	.05	.10
55	Esa Tikkanen	.05	.10

HARTFORD WHALERS

No.	Player	English NRMT	French NRMT
56	Michel Picard, RC	.07	.15
57	Geoff Sanderson, RC	1.00	2.00
58	Kay Whitmore, Goalie	.05	.10
59	John Cullen	.07	.15
60	Rob Brown	.05	.10
61	Zarley Zalapski	.05	.10
62	Brad Shaw	.05	.10
63	Bo Mikael Andersson	.05	.10
64	Patrick Verbeek	.05	.10

LOS ANGELES KINGS

No.	Player	English NRMT	French NRMT
65	Peter Ahola, RC	.10	.20
66	Tony Granato	.05	.10
67	David Taylor	.05	.10
68	Luc Robitaille	.15	.30
69	Martin McSorley	.05	.10
70	Tomas Sandstrom	.05	.10
71	Kelly Hrudey, Goalie	.05	.10
72	Jari Kurri	.10	.20
73	Wayne Gretzky	.65	1.25
74	Larry Robinson	.05	.10

MINNESOTA NORTH STARS

No.	Player	English NRMT	French NRMT
75	Derian Hatcher, RC	.12	.25
76	Ulf Dahlen	.05	.10
77	Jon Casey, Goalie	.05	.10
78	Dave Gagner	.05	.10
79	Brian Bellows	.05	.10
80	Neal Broten	.05	.10
81	Michael Modano	.17	.35
82	Brian Propp	.05	.10
83	Robert Smith	.05	.10

MONTREAL CANADIENS

No.	Player	English NRMT	French NRMT
84	John LeClair, RC	.25	.50
85	Éric Desjardins	.07	.15
86	Shayne Corson	.05	.10
87	Stephan Lebeau	.25	.50
88	Mathieu Schneider	.05	.10
89	Kirk Muller	.07	.15
90	Patrick Roy, Goalie	.30	.60
91	Sylvain Turgeon	.05	.10
92	Guy Carbonneau	.05	.10
93	Denis Savard	.05	.10

NEW JERSEY DEVILS

No.	Player	English NRMT	French NRMT
94	Scott Niedermayer, RC	.50	1.00
95	Tom Chorske	.05	.10
96	Viacheslav Fetisov	.05	.10
97	Kevin Todd, RC	.15	.30
98	Chris Terreri, Goalie	.07	.15
99	David Maley	.05	.10
100	Stéphane Richer	.05	.10
101	Claude Lemieux	.05	.10
102	Scott Stevens	.05	.10
103	Peter Stastny	.05	.10

NEW YORK ISLANDERS

No.	Player	English NRMT	French NRMT
104	David Volek	.05	.10
105	Steve Thomas	.05	.10
106	Pierre Turgeon	.25	.50
107	Glenn Healy, Goalie, Error	.05	.10
108	Derek King	.05	.10
109	Uwe Krupp	.05	.10
110	Ray Ferraro	.05	.10
111	Patrick Flatley	.05	.10
112	Tom Kurvers	.05	.10
113	Adam Creighton	.05	.10

NEW YORK RANGERS

No.	Player	English NRMT	French NRMT
114	Anthony Amonte, RC	1.00	2.00
115	John Ogrodnick	.05	.10
116	Doug Weight, RC	.20	.40
117	Mike Richter, Goalie	.12	.35
118	Darren Turcotte	.07	.15

PARKHURST — 1991-92 REGULAR ISSUE

No.	Player	English NRMT	French NRMT
119	Brian Leetch	.20	.40
120	James Patrick	.05	.10
121	Mark Messier	.17	.35
122	Michael Gartner	.05	.10

PHILADELPHIA FLYERS

No.	Player	English NRMT	French NRMT
123	Mike Ricci	.17	.35
124	Rod Brind'Amour	.17	.35
125	Steve Duchesne	.05	.10
126	Ron Hextall, Goalie	.05	.10
127	Brad Jones, RC	.07	.15
128	Per-Erik Eklund	.05	.10
129	Rick Tocchet	.05	.10
130	Mark Howe	.05	.10
131	Andrei Lomakin	.12	.25

PITTSBURGH PENGUINS

No.	Player	English NRMT	French NRMT
132	Jaromir Jagr	.85	1.75
133	Jim Paek, RC	.10	.20
134	Mark Recchi	.35	.70
135	Kevin Stevens	.50	1.00
136	Phillippe Bourque	.07	.15
137	Mario Lemieux	.85	1.75
138	Bob Errey	.05	.10
139	Tom Barrasso, Goalie	.05	.10
140	Paul Coffey	.10	.20
141	Joe Mullen	.05	.10

QUEBEC NORDIQUES

No.	Player	English NRMT	French NRMT
142	Kip Miller, RC	.07	.15
143	Owen Nolan	.25	.50
144	Mats Sundin	.25	.50
145	Mikhail Tatarinov	.12	.25
146	Bryan Fogarty	.05	.10
147	Stéphane Morin	.06	.12
148	Joe Sakic	.30	.60
149	Ron Tugnutt, Goalie	.05	.10
150	Mike Hough	.05	.10

ST. LOUIS BLUES

No.	Player	English NRMT	French NRMT
151	Nelson Emerson, RC	.35	.75
152	Curtis Joseph, Goalie	.05	.10
153	Brendan Shanahan	.07	.15
154	Paul Cavallini	.05	.10
155	Adam Oates	.12	.25
156	Jeff Brown	.05	.10
157	Brett Hull	.50	1.00
158	Ronald Sutter	.05	.10
159	Dave Christian	.05	.10

SAN JOSE SHARKS

No.	Player	English NRMT	French NRMT
160	Pat Falloon, RC	.75	1.50
161	Pat MacLeod, RC	.10	.20
162	Jarmo Myllys, Goalie	.05	.10
163	Wayne Presley	.05	.10
164	Perry Anderson, RC	.05	.10
165	Kelly Kisio	.05	.10
166	Brian Mullen	.05	.10
167	Brian Lawton	.05	.10
168	Douglas Wilson	.05	.10

TORONTO MAPLE LEAFS

No.	Player	English NRMT	French NRMT
169	Rob Pearson, RC	.50	1.00
170	Wendel Clark	.05	.10
171	Brian Bradley	.05	.10
172	David Ellett	.05	.10
173	Gary Leeman	.05	.10
174	Peter Zezel	.05	.10
175	Grant Fuhr, Goalie	.10	.20
176	Robert Rouse	.05	.10

No.	Player	English NRMT	French NRMT
177	Glenn Anderson	.05	.10

VANCOUVER CANUCKS

No.	Player	English NRMT	French NRMT
178	Petr Nedved	.17	.35
179	Trevor Linden	.17	.35
180	Jyrki Lumme	.05	.10
181	Kirk McLean, Goalie	.10	.20
182	Cliff Ronning	.05	.10
183	Greg Adams	.05	.10
184	Doug Lidster	.05	.10
185	Sergio Momesso	.05	.10
186	Geoff Courtnall	.05	.10
187	David Babych	.05	.10

WASHINGTON CAPITALS

No.	Player	English NRMT	French NRMT
188	Peter Bondra	.12	.25
189	Dimitri Khristich	.12	.25
190	Randy Burridge	.05	.10
191	Kevin Hatcher	.05	.10
192	Mike Ridley	.05	.10
193	Dino Ciccarelli	.05	.10
194	Al Iafrate	.05	.10
195	Dale Hunter	.05	.10
196	Michael Liut, Goalie	.05	.10

WINNIPEG JETS

No.	Player	English NRMT	French NRMT
198	Russell Romaniuk, RC	.07	.15
199	Bob Essensa, Goalie	.10	.20
200	Teppo Numminen	.05	.10
201	Darrin Shannon	.05	.10
202	Pat Elynuik	.05	.10
203	Fredrik Olausson	.05	.10
204	Ed Olczyk	.05	.10
205	Phil Housley	.07	.15
206	Troy Murray	.05	.10

1,000 POINT CLUB

No.	Player	English NRMT	French NRMT
207	Wayne Gretzky, LA	.25	.50
208	Bryan Trottier, Pit.	.05	.10
209	Peter Stastny, NJD	.05	.10
210	Jari Kurri, LA	.05	.10
211	Denis Savard, Mon.	.10	.20
212	Paul Coffey, Pit.	.12	.25
213	Mark Messier, NYR	.07	.15
214	David Taylor, LA	.05	.10
215	Michel Goulet, Chi.	.05	.10
216	Dale Hawerchuk, Buf.	.05	.10
217	Robert Smith, Min.	.05	.10

LEADERS

No.	Player	English NRMT	French NRMT
218	Save Percentage Leader: Ed Belfour, Goalie, Chi.,	.15	.30
219	Power Play Goal Leader: Brett Hull, St. L.,	.25	.50

FREQUENT ALL-STAR

No.	Player	English NRMT	French NRMT
220	Patrick Roy, Goalie, Mon.	.12	.25
221	Raymond Bourque, Bos.	.07	.15
222	Wayne Gretzky, St. L.	.25	.50
223	Jari Kurri, LA	.07	.15
224	Luc Robitaille, LA	.10	.20
225	Paul Coffey, Pit.	.07	.15

— 1991-92 REGULAR ISSUE —

SERIES TWO

1991-92 Series Two English
Card No. 404, Pavel Bure

Face: Four colour, mottled brown border on left side
Back: Four colour; Resume, Number
Imprint: Pro Set Inc. © NHL 1992 © NHLPA 1992
Complete Set No.: 225

Complete Set Price:	12.50	25.00
Common Player:	.05	.10
Common Goalie:	.05	.10
Foil Pack: (12 Cards)		.75
Foil Box: (36 Packs)		25.00
Foil Case: (20 Boxes)		375.00

BOSTON BRUINS

No.	Player	English NRMT	French NRMT
226	Robert Carpenter	.05	.10
227	Gordon Murphy	.05	.10
228	Don Sweeney	.05	.10
229	Glen Murray, RC	.25	.50
230	Ted Donato, RC	.25	.50
231	Josef Stumpel, RC	.15	.30
232	Stephen Heinze, RC	.35	.70
233	Adam Oates	.10	.20
234	Joseph Juneau, RC	3.00	6.00
235	Rookie: Gord Hynes, RC	.07	.15

BUFFALO SABRES

No.	Player	English NRMT	French NRMT
236	Tony Tanti	.05	.10
237	Petr Svoboda	.05	.10
238	Bob Corkum	.05	.10
239	Kenneth Sutton, RC	.10	.20
240	Tom Draper, Goalie, RC	.12	.25
241	Grant Ledyard	.05	.10
242	Christian Ruuttu	.05	.10
243	Brad Miller	.05	.10
244	Clint Malarchuk, Goalie	.05	.10

CALGARY FLAMES

No.	Player	English NRMT	French NRMT
245	Trent Yawney	.05	.10
246	Craig Berube	.05	.10
247	Sergei Makarov	.05	.10
248	Alexander Godynyuk	.07	.15
249	Paul Ranheim	.05	.10
250	Jeff Reese, Goalie	.05	.10
251	Chris Lindberg, RC	.10	.20
252	Michel Petit	.05	.10
253	Joel Otto	.05	.10
254	Gary Leeman	.05	.10

CHICAGO BLACK HAWKS

No.	Player	English NRMT	French NRMT
255	Raymond LeBlanc, Goalie, RC	.12	.25
256	Jocelyn Lemieux	.05	.10
257	Igor Kravchuk, RC	.25	.50
258	Rob Brown	.05	.10
259	Stephane Matteau	.05	.10
260	Mike Hudson	.05	.10
261	Keith Brown	.05	.10
262	Karl Dykhuis	.07	.15
263	Dominik Hasek, Goalie, RC	.30	.60
264	Brian Noonan	.05	.10

1991 - 92 REGULAR ISSUE — PARKHURST • 169

DETROIT RED WINGS

No.	Player	English NRMT	French NRMT
265	Yves Racine	.05	.10
266	**Viacheslav Kozlov, Error, RC**	**.75**	**1.50**
267	Martin Lapointe	.15	.30
268	Steve Chiasson	.05	.10
269	Gerard Gallant	.05	.10
270	Brent Fedyk	.05	.10
271	Byron (Brad) McCrimmon	.05	.10
272	Bob Probert	.07	.15
273	Alan Kerr	.05	.10

EDMONTON OILERS

No.	Player	English NRMT	French NRMT
274	Luke Richardson	.05	.10
275	Kelly Buchberger	.05	.10
276	Craig MacTavish	.05	.10
277	Ron Tugnutt, Goalie	.05	.10
278	Bernie Nicholls	.05	.10
279	Anatoli Semenov	.05	.10
280	Petr Klima	.05	.10
281	**Louie DeBrusk, RC**	**.07**	**.15**
282	**Norm MacIver, RC**	**.07**	**.15**
283	Martin Gelinas	.07	.15

HARTFORD WHALERS

No.	Player	English NRMT	French NRMT
284	Randy Cunneyworth	.05	.10
285	Andrew Cassels	.05	.10
286	Peter Sidorkiewicz, Goalie	.05	.10
287	Stephen Konroyd	.05	.10
288	Murray Craven	.05	.10
289	Randy Ladouceur	.05	.10
290	Robert Holik	.15	.30
291	Adam Burt	.05	.10

LOS ANGELES KINGS

No.	Player	English NRMT	French NRMT
292	**Corey Millen, RC**	**.20**	**.45**
293	Robert Blake	.15	.30
294	**Mike Donnelly, RC**	**.15**	**.30**
295	**Kyosti Karjalainen, RC**	**.10**	**.20**
296	John McIntyre	.05	.10
297	Paul Coffey	.10	.20
298	Charles Huddy	.05	.10
299	Bob Kudelski	.05	.10

MINNESOTA NORTH STARS

No.	Player	English NRMT	French NRMT
300	Todd Elik	.05	.10
301	Mike Craig	.07	.15
302	Marc Bureau	.05	.10
303	Jim Johnson	.05	.10
304	Mark Tinordi	.05	.10
305	Gaetan Duchesne	.05	.10
306	**Darcy Wakaluk, Goalie, RC**	**.07**	**.15**

MONTREAL CANADIENS

No.	Player	English NRMT	French NRMT
307	Sylvain Lefebvre	.05	.10
308	Russ Courtnall	.05	.10
309	Patrice Brisebois	.12	.25
310	Michael McPhee	.05	.10
311	Michael Keane	.05	.10
312	Jean-Jacques Daigneault	.05	.10
313	**Gilbert Dionne, RC**	**.75**	**1.50**
314	Brian Skrudland	.05	.10
315	Brent Gilchrist	.05	.10

NEW JERSEY DEVILS

No.	Player	English NRMT	French NRMT
316	Laurie Boschman	.05	.10
317	Ken Daneyko	.05	.10
318	Eric Weinrich	.05	.10
319	Alexei Kasatonov	.05	.10
320	**Craig Billington, Goalie, RC**	**.30**	**.60**
321	Claude Vilgrain	.05	.10
322	Bruce Driver	.05	.10
323	**Alexander Semak, RC**	**.45**	**.90**
324	**Valeri Zelepukin, RC**	**.45**	**.90**

NEW YORK ISLANDERS

No.	Player	English NRMT	French NRMT
325	Rob DiMaio	.05	.10
326	**Scott Lachance, RC**	**.45**	**.90**
327	**Marty McInnis, RC**	**.12**	**.25**
328	Joe Reekie	.05	.10
329	Daniel Marois	.05	.10
330	Wayne McBean	.05	.10
331	Jeff Norton	.05	.10
332	Benoit Hogue	.05	.10

NEW YORK RANGERS

No.	Player	English NRMT	French NRMT
333	Tahir (Tie) Domi	.07	.15
334	Sergei Nemchinov	.30	.60
335	Randy Gilhen	.05	.10
336	Paul Broten	.05	.10
337	Kris King	.05	.10
338	John Vanbiesbrouck, Goalie	.05	.10
339	Adam Graves	.07	.15
340	Joe Cirella	.05	.10
341	Jeff Beukeboom	.05	.10

PHILADELPHIA FLYERS

No.	Player	English NRMT	French NRMT
342	Terry Carkner	.05	.10
343	**Mark Freer, RC**	**.07**	**.15**
344	**Corey Foster, RC**	**.07**	**.15**
345	Mark Pederson	.05	.10
346	Kimbi Daniels	.10	.20
347	Mark Recchi	.35	.75
348	Kevin Dineen	.05	.10
349	Kerry Huffman	.05	.10
350	Garry Galley	.05	.10
351	Dan Quinn	.05	.10

PITTSBURGH PENGUINS

No.	Player	English NRMT	French NRMT
352	Troy Loney	.05	.10
353	Ron Francis	.10	.20
354	Rick Tocchet	.10	.20
355	**Shawn McEachern, RC**	**2.00**	**4.00**
356	Kjell Samuelsson	.05	.10
357	Ken Wregget, Goalie	.05	.10
358	Lawrence Murphy	.05	.10
359	Ken Priestlay	.07	.15
360	Bryan Trottier	.07	.15
361	Ulf Samuelsson	.05	.10

QUEBEC NORDIQUES

No.	Player	English NRMT	French NRMT
362	**Valeri Kamensky, RC**	**.75**	**1.50**
363	Stephane Fiset, Goalie	.05	.10
364	**Alexei Gusarov, RC**	**.05**	**.10**
365	Gregory Paslawski	.05	.10
366	**Martin Rucinsky, RC**	**.25**	**.50**
367	Curtis Leschyshyn	.05	.10
368	Jacques Cloutier, Goalie	.05	.10
369	Craig Wolanin	.05	.10
370	Rookie: Claude Lapointe, RC	.10	.20
371	**Adam Foote, RC**	**.07**	**.15**

ST. LOUIS BLUES

No.	Player	English NRMT	French NRMT
372	Richard Sutter	.05	.10
373	Lee Norwood	.05	.10
374	Garth Butcher	.05	.10
375	**Philippe Bozon, RC**	**.12**	**.25**
376	Dave Lowry	.05	.10
377	Darin Kimble	.05	.10
378	Craig Janney	.07	.15
379	Bob Bassen	.05	.10
380	Richard Zombo	.05	.10

SAN JOSE SHARKS

No.	Player	English NRMT	French NRMT
381	Perry Berezan	.05	.10
382	Neil Wilkinson	.05	.10
383	**Michael Sullivan, RC**	**.07**	**.15**
384	**David Bruce, RC**	**.07**	**.15**
385	Johan Garpenlov	.05	.10
386	**Jeff Odgers, RC**	**.05**	**.10**
387	**Jayson More, RC**	**.07**	**.15**
388	Dean Evason	.12	.25
389	Dale Craigwell	.15	.30

TORONTO MAPLE LEAFS

No.	Player	English NRMT	French NRMT
390	**Darryl Shannon, RC**	**.07**	**.15**
391	Dimitri Mironov	.15	.30
392	Kent Manderville,	.17	.35
393	Todd Gill	.05	.10
394	Richard Wamsley, Goalie	.05	.10
395	**Joseph Sacco, RC**	**.15**	**.30**
396	Douglas Gilmour	.12	.25
397	Mike Bullard	.05	.10
398	Felix Potvin, Goalie	1.00	2.00
399	**Guy Larose, RC**	**.07**	**.15**

VANCOUVER CANUCKS

No.	Player	English NRMT	French NRMT
400	Tom Fergus	.05	.10
401	Ryan Walter	.05	.10
402	Troy Gamble, Goalie	.05	.10
403	Robert Dirk	.05	.10
404	Pavel Bure	1.75	3.50
405	Jim Sandlak	.05	.10
406	Igor Larionov	.05	.10
407	Gerald Diduck	.05	.10

WASHINGTON CAPITALS

No.	Player	English NRMT	French NRMT
408	Todd Krygier	.05	.10
409	Tim Bergland	.05	.10
410	Calle Johansson	.05	.10
411	Nicholas Kypreos	.05	.10
412	Michal Pivonka	.10	.20
413	**Brad Schlegel, RC**	**.07**	**.15**
414	Kelly Miller	.05	.10
415	John Druce	.05	.10
416	Donald Beaupre, Goalie	.05	.10
417	Alan May	.05	.10

WINNIPEG JETS

No.	Player	English NRMT	French NRMT
418	Randy Carlyle	.05	.10
419	Stu Barnes	.07	.15
420	Mike Eagles	.05	.10
421	**Igor Ulanov, RC**	**.25**	**.50**
422	**Evgeny Davydov, RC**	**.35**	**.75**
423	Shawn Cronin	.05	.10
424	**Keith Tkachuk, RC**	**.75**	**1.50**
425	**Luciano Borsato, RC**	**.15**	**.30**
426	Stephane Beauregard, Goalie	.05	.10
427	Mike Lalor	.05	.10

500-GOAL CLUB

No.	Player	English NRMT	French NRMT
428	Michel Goulet, Chi.	.07	.15
429	Wayne Gretzky, LA	.25	.50
430	Michael Gartner, NYR	.07	.15
431	Bryan Trottier, NYI	.05	.10

PARKHURST — 1991 - 92 INSERT SET —

LEAGUE LEADERS

No.	Player	English NRMT	French NRMT
432	Goal: Brett Hull, St. L.	.20	.40
433	Assists: Wayne Gretzky, LA	.25	.50
434	Shorthanded-Goal: Steve Yzerman, Det.	.10	.20
435	Plus/Minus: Paul Ysebaert, Det.	.07	.15
436	Shooting Percentage: Gary Roberts, Cal.	.05	.10
437	Power-Play Goal: David Andreychuk, Buf.	.07	.15
438	Defenseman Scoring: Brian Leetch, NYR	.07	.15
439	Game-Winning Goals: Jeremy Roenick, Chi.	.15	.30
440	Goalie Wins: Kirk McLean, Goalie, Van.	.05	.10
441	Goalie Wins: Tim Chevaldae, Goalie, Det.	.07	.15
442	Goals-Against Average: Patrick Roy, Goalie, Mon.	.12	.25

ROOKIE LEADERS

No.	Player	English NRMT	French NRMT
443	Right Wing Scoring: Anthony Amonte, NYR	.20	.40
444	Center Scoring: Kevin Todd, NJ	.07	.15
445	Defenseman Scoring: Nicklas Lidstrom, Det.	.20	.40
446	Left Wing Scoring: Pavel Bure, Van.	.60	1.25
447	Shooting Pct.: Gilbert Dionne, Mon.	.17	.35
448	Goalie Win: Tom Draper, Goalie, Buf.	.07	.15
449	Goalie Win: Dominik Hasek, Goalie, Chi.	.10	.20
450	Save Pct.: Dominic Roussel, Goalie, Phi.	.25	.50

— 1991 - 92 INSERT SET —

These cards were randomly inserted into foil packs of Series One and Two.

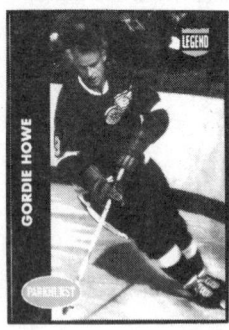 

1992 Insert Set
Card No. PHC1, Gordie Howe

Card Size: 2 1/2" X 3 1/2"
Face: Four colour, mottled brown border on left side
Back: Four colour, brown background; Resume, Number
Imprint: Pro Set Inc. © NHL 1992
Complete Set No.: 225
Complete Set Price: 12.50 25.00

HAPPY HOLIDAYS

No.	Player	English NRMT	French NRMT
---	Happy Holidays	1.50	3.00

LEGENDS

No.	Player	English NRMT	French NRMT
PHC1	Gordie Howe	2.50	5.00
PHC2	Alex Delvecchio	1.25	2.50

LEADERS

No.	Player	English NRMT	French NRMT
PHC3	Rookie Shooting Accuracy Leader: Kenneth Hodge, Jr.	.75	1.50
PHC4	Rookie Shorthanded Goals Leader: Robert Kron,	.75	1.50
PHC5	Rookie Shorthanded Goals Leader: Sergei Fedorov,	2.00	4.00
PHC6	Brett Hull	2.00	4.00
PHC7	Mario Lemieux	3.50	7.00
PHC8	Award Winner: New York Rangers	.75	1.50
PHC9	Terry Sawchuk	1.50	3.00

— 1991 - 92 FINAL UPDATE —

This 25-card set is perhaps the most limited of current issued sets for Pro-Set.
Pro Set was going through financial difficulties and decided to print enough sets to fulfil paid orders. Issued only as complete sets they were wrapped in a clear cello pack. There was no French version

 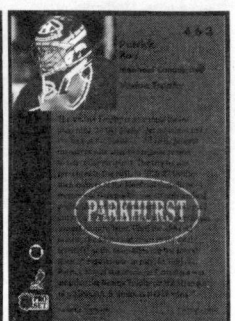

1991-92 Final Update
Card No. 463, Patrick Roy

of this set.

Card Size: 2 1/2" x 3 1/2"
Face: Four colour, mottled brown border on left side; Name
Back: Four colour; Name, Number, Team, Resume
Imprint: Pro Set Inc. © NHL, 1992; ©NHLPA 1992
Complete Set No.: 25
Complete Set Price: 22.50 45.00
Common Goalie: 50 1.00
Common Player: 50 1.00

REGULAR ISSUE

No.	Player	EX	NRMT
451	Checklist: Parkhurst Cover card	.50	1.00
452	Rookie: Trent Klatt, Min., RC	.75	1.50
453	Rookie: Bill Guerin, NJ, RC	.75	1.50
454	Rookie: Ray Whitney, SJ, RC	1.25	2.50
455	Boston Wins Adams Division	.50	1.00
456	Pittsburgh Wins Patrick Division	.75	1.50
457	Chicago Wins Norris Division	.50	1.00
458	Edmonton Wins Smythe Division	.50	1.00
459	Pittsburgh Wins Wales Conference	.75	1.50
460	Chicago Wins Campbell Conference	.50	1.00
461	Pittsburgh Wins Stanley Cup	1.00	2.00

AWARD WINNERS

No.	Player	EX	NRMT
462	Calder Memorial Trophy: Pavel Bure, Van.	4.00	8.00
463	Vezina Trophy: Patrick Roy, Goalie, Mon.	3.00	6.00
464	James Norris Memorial Trophy: Brian Leetch, NYR	1.50	3.00
465	Lady Byng Memorial Trophy: Wayne Gretzky, LA	4.00	8.00
466	Frank J. Selke Trophy: Guy Carbonneau, Mon.	1.50	3.00
467	Conn Smythe Trophy: Mario Lemieux, Pit.	4.00	8.00
468	Lester B. Pearson Award: Mark Messier, NYR	2.50	5.00
469	King Clancy Memorial Trophy: Raymond Bourque, Bos.	1.50	3.00

ALL STAR TEAM

No.	Player	EX	NRMT
470	Patrick Roy, Goalie, Mon.	4.00	8.00
471	Brian Leetch, NYR	1.50	3.00
472	Raymond Bourque, Bos.	1.50	3.00
473	Kevin Stevens, Pit.	1.50	3.00
474	Brett Hull, St.L	2.50	5.00
475	Mark Messier, NYR	2.50	5.00

1992 - 93 PARKHURST PROMO CARDS

Note: For a listing of thes cards see the Pro Set section page no.

— 1992 - 93 REGULAR ISSUE —

and EMERALD ICE

This Parkhurst set has the most up to date photography of all the card sets for the 1992-93 season. The majority of cards carry photos taken during the 1992-93 season.

 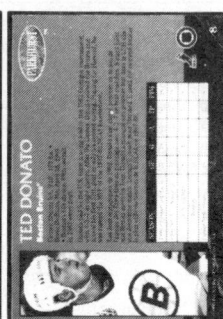

1992-93 Regular Issue Series One
Card No. 8, Ted Donato

Card Size: 2 1/2" x 3 1/2"
Face: Four colour, turquoise marble left border; Name
Back: Four colour; Name, Number, Team, Resume, Bilingual
Imprint: © 1993 Pro Set Inc. / Printed in the U.S.A.
Complete Set No.: 240
Complete Set Price: 12.50 25.00
Common Goalie: .05 .10
Common Player: .05 .10
Foil Pack: (13 Cards) .75 1.50
Foil Box: (36 Packs) 45.00
Jumbo Pack: (25 Cards) 3.00
Jumbo Foil Box: (25 Packs) 70.00

SERIES ONE

BOSTON BRUINS

No.	Player	Regular NRMT	Emerald NRMT
1	Raymond Bourque	.10	.20
2	Calder Candidate: Joseph Juneau	1.25	2.50
3	Andrew Moog, Goalie	.05	.10
4	Adam Oates	.07	.15
5	Vladimir Ruzicka	.05	.10
6	Glen Wesley	.05	.10
7	Dmitri Kvartalnov, RC	1.00	2.00
8	Calder Candidate: Ted Donato	.12	.25
9	Calder Candidate: Glen Murray	.15	.30

BUFFALO SABRES

No.	Player	Regular NRMT	Emerald NRMT
10	David Andreychuk	.05	.10
11	Dale Hawerchuk	.05	.10
12	Pat LaFontaine	.15	.30
13	Alexander Mogilny	.35	.75
14	Calder Candidate: Richard Smehlik, RC	.25	.50
15	Calder Candidate: Keith Carney, RC	.12	.25
16	Calder Candidate: Philippe Boucher	.05	.10

1992 - 93 REGULAR ISSUE — PARKHURST • 171

No.	Player	Regular NRMT	Emerald NRMT
17	**Calder Candidate:** Viktor Gordijuk, RC	.12	.25
18	Donald Audette	.05	.10

CALGARY FLAMES

No.	Player	Regular NRMT	Emerald NRMT
19	Theoren Fleury	.10	.20
20	Allan MacInnis	.05	.10
21	Joe Nieuwendyk	.05	.10
22	Gary Roberts	.05	.10
23	Gary Suter	.05	.10
24	Michael Vernon, Goalie	.05	.10
25	Sergei Makarov	.05	.10
26	Robert Reichel	.05	.10
27	**Calder Candidate:** Chris Lindberg	.10	.20

CHICAGO BLACK HAWKS

No.	Player	Regular NRMT	Emerald NRMT
28	Ed Belfour, Goalie	.25	.50
29	Chris Chelios	.05	.10
30	Steve Larmer	.05	.10
31	Jeremy Roenick	.50	1.00
32	James (Steve) Smith	.05	.10
33	Brent Sutter	.05	.10
34	Christian Ruuttu	.05	.10
35	Igor Kravchuk	.07	.15
36	**Calder Candidate:** Sergei Krivokrasov	.25	.50

DETROIT RED WINGS

No.	Player	Regular NRMT	Emerald NRMT
37	Tim Cheveldae, Goalie	.05	.10
38	**Calder Candidate:** Mike Sillinger	.05	.10
39	Sergei Fedorov	.50	1.00
40	**Calder Candidate:** Vyacheslav Kozlov	.50	1.00
41	Bob Probert	.05	.10
42	Nicklas Lidstrom	.07	.15
43	Paul Ysebaert	.05	.10
44	Steve Yzerman	.12	.25
45	Dino Ciccarelli	.05	.10

EDMONTON OILERS

No.	Player	Regular NRMT	Emerald NRMT
46	Esa Tikkanen	.05	.10
47	Dave Manson	.05	.10
48	Craig MacTavish	.05	.10
49	Bernie Nicholls	.05	.10
50	Bill Ranford, Goalie	.05	.10
51	Craig Simpson	.05	.10
52	Scott Mellanby	.05	.10
53	Shayne Corson	.05	.10
54	Petr Klima	.05	.10

HARTFORD WHALERS

No.	Player	Regular NRMT	Emerald NRMT
55	Murray Craven	.05	.10
56	Eric Weinrich	.05	.10
57	Sean Burke, Goalie	.05	.10
58	Patrick Verbeek	.05	.10
59	Zarley Zalapski	.05	.10
60	**Calder Candidate:** Patrick Poulin	.25	.50
61	**Calder Candidate:** Robert Petrovicky	.20	.40
62	Geoff Sanderson	.25	.50

LOS ANGELES KINGS

No.	Player	Regular NRMT	Emerald NRMT
63	Paul Coffey	.07	.15
64	**Calder Candidate:** Robert Lang, RC	.25	.50
65	Wayne Gretzky	.75	1.50
66	Kelly Hrudey, Goalie	.05	.10
67	Jari Kurri	.05	.10
68	Luc Robitaille	.12	.25
69	**Calder Candidate:** Darryl Sydor	.05	.10
70	**Calder Candidate:** Jim Hiller, RC	.15	.30
71	**Calder Candidate:** Alexei Zhitnik	.35	.75

MINNESOTA NORTH STARS

No.	Player	Regular NRMT	Emerald NRMT
72	Derian Hatcher	.05	.10
73	Jon Casey, Goalie	.05	.10
74	**Calder Candidate:** Richard Matvichuk, RC	.12	.25
75	Michael Modano	.10	.20
76	Mark Tinordi	.05	.10
77	Todd Elik	.05	.10
78	Russell Courtnall	.05	.10
79	Tommy Sjodin, RC	.25	.50

MONTREAL CANADIENS

No.	Player	Regular NRMT	Emerald NRMT
80	Eric Desjardins	.05	.10
81	Gilbert Dionne	.12	.25
82	Stephan Lebeau	.10	.20
83	Kirk Muller	.05	.10
84	Patrick Roy, Goalie	.35	.75
85	Denis Savard	.05	.10
86	Vincent Damphousse	.05	.10
87	Brian Bellows	.05	.10
88	**Calder Candidate:** Ed Ronan, RC	.12	.25

NEW JERSEY DEVILS

No.	Player	Regular NRMT	Emerald NRMT
89	Claude Lemieux	.05	.10
90	John MacLean	.05	.10
91	Stephane Richer	.05	.10
92	Scott Stevens	.05	.10
93	Chris Terreri, Goalie	.05	.10
94	Kevin Todd	.05	.10
95	**Calder Candidate:** Scott Niedermayer	.15	.30
96	Robert Holik	.10	.20
97	**Calder Candidate:** Bill Guerin, RC	.17	.35

NEW YORK ISLANDERS

No.	Player	Regular NRMT	Emerald NRMT
98	Ray Ferraro	.05	.10
99	Mark Fitzpatrick, Goalie	.05	.10
100	Derek King	.05	.10
101	Uwe Krupp	.05	.10
102	**Calder Candidate:** Darius Kasparaitis	.25	.50
103	Pierre Turgeon	.17	.35
104	Benoit Hogue	.05	.10
105	**Calder Candidate:** Scott Lachance	.25	.50
106	**Calder Candidate:** Marty McInnis	.07	.15

NEW YORK RANGERS

No.	Player	Regular NRMT	Emerald NRMT
107	Anthony Amonte	.20	.40
108	Michael Gartner	.05	.10
109	**Calder Candidate:** Alexei Kovalev	1.25	2.50
110	Brian Leetch	.12	.25
111	Mark Messier	.20	.40
112	Mike Richter, Goalie	.05	.10
113	James Patrick	.05	.10
114	Sergei Nemchinov	.10	.20
115	Doug Weight	.05	.10

OTTAWA SENATORS

No.	Player	Regular NRMT	Emerald NRMT
116	Mark Lamb	.05	.10
117	Norm Maciver	.05	.10
118	Mike Peluso	.05	.10
119	Jody Hull	.05	.10
120	Peter Sidorkiewicz, Goalie	.05	.10
121	Sylvain Turgeon	.05	.10
122	Laurie Boschman	.05	.10
123	Bradley Marsh	.05	.10
124	Neil Brady	.05	.10

PHILADELPHIA FLYERS

No.	Player	Regular NRMT	Emerald NRMT
125	Brian Benning	.05	.10
126	Rod Brind'Amour	.10	.20
127	Kevin Dineen	.05	.10
128	**Calder Candidate:** Eric Lindros	3.50	7.00
129	**Calder Candidate:** Dominic Roussel, Goalie	.20	.40
130	Mark Recchi	.20	.40
131	Brent Fedyk	.05	.10
132	Gregory Paslawski	.05	.10
133	**Calder Candidate:** Dimitri Yushkevich, RC	.25	.50

PITTSBURGH PENGUINS

No.	Player	Regular NRMT	Emerald NRMT
134	Tom Barrasso, Goalie	.05	.10
135	Jaromir Jagr	.50	1.00
136	Mario Lemieux	.75	1.50
137	Lawrence Murphy	.05	.10
138	Kevin Stevens	.20	.40
139	Rick Tocchet	.05	.10
140	**Calder Candidate:** Martin Straka, RC	.35	.75
141	Ronald Francis	.05	.10
142	**Calder Candidate:** Shawn McEachern	.60	1.25

QUEBEC NORDIQUES

No.	Player	Regular NRMT	Emerald NRMT
143	Steve Duchesne	.05	.10
144	Ron Hextall, Goalie	.05	.10
145	Owen Nolan	.12	.25
146	Mike Ricci	.12	.25
147	Joe Sakic	.17	.35
148	Mats Sundin	.12	.25
149	**Calder Candidate:** Martin Rucinsky	.05	.10
150	**Calder Candidate:** Andrei Kovalenko, RC	.50	1.00
151	**Calder Candidate:** Dave Karpa, RC	.10	.20

ST. LOUIS BLUES

No.	Player	Regular NRMT	Emerald NRMT
152	Nelson Emerson	.12	.25
153	Brett Hull	.35	.75
154	Craig Janney	.05	.10
155	Curtis Joseph, Goalie	.10	.20
156	Brendan Shanahan	.05	.10
157	**Calder Candidate:** Vitali Prokhorov, RC	.12	.25
158	**Calder Candidate:** Igor Korolev, RC	.25	.50
159	**Calder Candidate:** Philippe Bozon	.05	.10

SAN JOSE SHARKS

No.	Player	Regular NRMT	Emerald NRMT
160	Ray Whitney, RC	.25	.50
161	Pat Falloon	.25	.50
162	Jeff Hackett, Goalie	.05	.10
163	Brian Lawton	.05	.10
164	**Calder Candidate:** Sandis Ozolinsh	.15	.30
165	Neil Wilkinson	.05	.10
166	Kelly Kisio	.05	.10
167	Douglas Wilson	.05	.10
168	Dale Craigwell	.05	.10

TAMPA BAY LIGHTNING

No.	Player	Regular NRMT	Emerald NRMT
169	Bo Mikael Andersson	.05	.10
170	Wendell Young, Goalie	.05	.10
171	**Calder Candidate:** Rob Zamuner, RC	.15	.30
172	Adam Creighton	.05	.10
173	**Calder Candidate:** Roman Hamrlik, RC	1.00	2.00
174	Brian Bradley	.05	.10
175	George (Rob) Ramage	.05	.10
176	Chris Kontos, RC	.25	.50
177	**Calder Candidate:** Stan Drulia, RC	.07	.15

TORONTO MAPLE LEAFS

No.	Player	Regular NRMT	Emerald NRMT
178	Glenn Anderson	.05	.10
179	Wendel Clark	.07	.15
180	John Cullen	.05	.10

172 • PARKHURST — 1992-93 REGULAR ISSUE —

No.	Player	Regular NRMT	Emerald NRMT
181	David Ellett	.05	.10
182	Grant Fuhr, Goalie	.07	.15
183	Douglas Gilmour	.12	.25
184	**Calder Candidate:** Kent Manderville	.07	.15
185	Joseph Sacco	.10	.20
186	Nikolai Borschevsky, RC	**.60**	**1.25**
187	**Calder Candidate:** Felix Potvin, Goalie	.60	1.25

VANCOUVER CANUCKS

No.	Player	Regular NRMT	Emerald NRMT
188	Pavel Bure	1.50	3.00
189	Geoff Courtnall	.05	.10
190	Trevor Linden	.10	.20
191	Jyrki Lumme	.05	.10
192	Kirk McLean, Goalie	.05	.10
193	Cliff Ronning	.05	.10
194	**Calder Candidate:** Dixon Ward, RC	.35	.75
195	**Calder Candidate:** Jiri Slegr	.05	.10

WASHINGTON CAPITALS

No.	Player	Regular NRMT	Emerald NRMT
197	Donald Beaupre, Goalie	.05	.10
198	Kevin Hatcher	.05	.10
199	**Calder Candidate:** Brad Schlegel	.05	.10
200	Mike Ridley	.05	.10
201	Calle Johansson	.05	.10
202	**Calder Candidate:** Steve Konowalchuk, RC	.12	.25
203	Al Iafrate	.05	.10
204	Peter Bondra	.05	.10
205	Pat Elynuik	.05	.10

WINNIPEG JETS

No.	Player	Regular NRMT	Emerald NRMT
206	Keith Tkachuk	.20	.40
207	Bob Essensa, Goalie	.05	.10
208	Phil Housley	.05	.10
209	**Calder Candidate:** Teemu Selanne	3.00	6.00
210	**Calder Candidate:** Alexei Zhamnov	.35	.75
211	**Calder Candidate:** Eugeny Davydov, Error	.25	.50
212	Fredrik Olausson	.05	.10
213	Ed Olczyk	.05	.10
214	Thomas Steen	.05	.10

INTERNATIONAL RISING STARS

No.	Player	Regular NRMT	Emerald NRMT
215	Darius Kasparaitis, NYI	.05	.10
216	Nikolai Borschevsky, Tor.	.35	.75
217	Teemu Selanne, Win.	2.00	4.00
218	Alexander Mogilny, Buf.	.25	.50
219	Sergei Fedorov, Det.	.15	.30
220	Jaromir Jagr, Pit.	.20	.40
221	Mats Sundin, Que.	.10	.20
222	Dmitri Kvartalnov, Bos.	.35	.75
223	Andrei Kovalenko, Que.	.20	.40
224	Tommy Sjodin, Min.	.05	.10
225	Alexei Kovalev, NYR	.50	1.00
226	Evgeny Davydov, Win.	.05	.10
227	Robert Lang, LA	.12	.25

SENSATIONAL SOPHOMORE

No.	Player	Regular NRMT	Emerald NRMT
228	Valeri Zelepukin, NJ	.05	.10
229	Doug Weight, NYR	.05	.10
230	Valeri Kamensky, Que.	.12	.25
231	Donald Audette, Buf.	.05	.10
232	Nelson Emerson, St.L	.10	.20
233	Pat Falloon, SJ	.15	.30
234	Pavel Bure, Van.	1.00	2.00
235	Anthony Amonte, NYR	.10	.20
236	Sergei Nemchinov, NYR	.05	.10
237	Gilbert Dionne, Mon.	.10	.20
238	Kevin Todd, NJ	.05	.10
239	Nicklas Lidstrom, Det.	.12	.25
240	Brad May, Buf.	.05	.10

— 1992-93 REGULAR ISSUE —

and EMERALD ICE

Series Two was issued early 1993 and serves as an update set with new pictures of the high point players not involved in Series One.

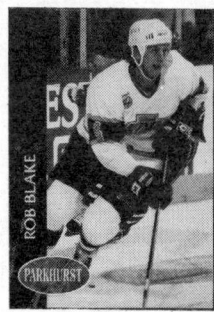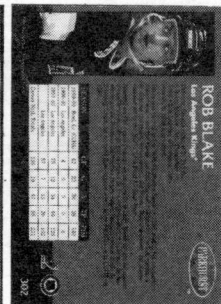

1992-93 Emerald Ice Series Two
Card No. 302, Robert Blake

Card Size: 2-1/2" x 3-1/2"
Face: Four colour, turquoise marble border; Name
Back: Four colour; Name, Number, Team, Resume, Bilingual
Imprint: © 1993 Pro Set Inc. / Printed in the U.S.A.

Complete Set No.:		240
Complete Set Price:	12.50	25.00
Common Goalie:	.05	.10
Common Player:	.05	.10
Foil Pack:(13 Cards)	.75	1.50
Foil Box:(36 Packs)	22.50	45.00
Jumbo Pack:(25 cards)		3.00
Jumbo Foil Box:(25 Packs)		70.00

SERIES TWO

BOSTON BRUINS

No.	Player	Regular NRMT	Emerald NRMT
241	Stephen Leach	.05	.10
242	David Poulin	.05	.10
243	**Calder Candidate:** Grigori Panteleyev, RC	.25	.50
244	Don Sweeney	.05	.10
245	John Blue, Goalie, RC	.12	.25
246	**Calder Candidate:** C.J. Young, RC	.12	.25
247	**Calder Candidate:** Stephen Heinze	.12	.25
248	Cam Neely	.07	.15
249	David Reid	.05	.10

BUFFALO SABRES

No.	Player	Regular NRMT	Emerald NRMT
250	Grant Fuhr, Goalie	.07	.15
251	Robert Sweeney	.05	.10
252	Robert Ray	.05	.10
253	Doug Bodger	.05	.10
254	Kenneth Sutton	.05	.10
255	Yuri Khmylev, RC	.25	.50
256	Michael Ramsey	.05	.10
257	Brad May	.05	.10

CALGARY FLAMES

No.	Player	Regular NRMT	Emerald NRMT
258	Brent Ashton	.05	.10
259	Joel Otto	.05	.10
260	Paul Ranheim	.05	.10
261	**Calder Candidate:** Kevin Dahl, RC	.07	.15
262	Trent Yawney	.05	.10
263	Roger Johansson	.05	.10
264	Jeff Reese, Goalie	.05	.10
265	Ronald Stern	.05	.10
266	Brian Skrudland	.05	.10

CHICAGO BLACKHAWKS

No.	Player	Regular NRMT	Emerald NRMT
267	Bryan Marchment	.05	.10
268	Stephane Matteau	.05	.10
269	Frantisek Kucera	.05	.10
270	Jimmy Waite, Goalie	.05	.10

No.	Player	Regular NRMT	Emerald NRMT
271	Dirk Graham	.05	.10
272	Michel Goulet	.05	.10
273	Joe Murphy	.05	.10
274	Keith Brown	.05	.10
275	Jocelyn Lemieux	.05	.10

DETROIT RED WINGS

No.	Player	Regular NRMT	Emerald NRMT
276	Paul Coffey	.07	.15
277	Keith Primeau	.05	.10
278	Vincent Riendeau, Goalie	.05	.10
279	Mark Howe	.05	.10
280	Ray Sheppard	.05	.10
281	**Calder Candidate:** Jim Hiller, RC	.12	.25
282	Steve Chiasson	.05	.10
283	Vladimir Konstantinov	.10	.20

EDMONTON OILERS

No.	Player	Regular NRMT	Emerald NRMT
284	Brian Benning	.05	.10
285	Kevin Todd	.05	.10
286	Zdenco Ciger	.05	.10
287	Brian Glynn	.05	.10
288	Shaun Van Allen	.05	.10
289	**Calder Candidate:** Brad Werenka, RC	.10	.20
290	Ron Tugnutt, Goalie	.05	.10
291	Igor Kravchuk	.05	.10
292	Todd Elik	.05	.10

HARTFORD WHALERS

No.	Player	Regular NRMT	Emerald NRMT
293	Terry Yake	.05	.10
294	**Calder Candidate:** Mikael Nylander, RC	.25	.50
295	Yvon Corriveau	.07	.15
296	Frank Pietrangelo, Goalie	.05	.10
297	Nicholas Kypreos	.05	.10
298	Andrew Cassels	.05	.10
299	Stephen Konroyd	.05	.10
300	Allen Pedersen	.05	.10

LOS ANGELES KINGS

No.	Player	Regular NRMT	Emerald NRMT
301	Tony Granato	.05	.10
302	Robert Blake	.10	.20
303	**Calder Candidate:** Robb Stauber, Goalie	.05	.10
304	Martin McSorley	.05	.10
305	**Calder Candidate:** Lonnie Loach, RC	.07	.15
306	Corey Millen	.05	.10
307	David Taylor	.05	.10
308	Jimmy Carson	.05	.10
309	Warren Rychel, RC	.25	.50

MINNESOTA NORTH STARS

No.	Player	Regular NRMT	Emerald NRMT
310	Ulf Dahlen	.05	.10
311	Dave Gagner	.05	.10
312	Brad Berry, RC	.07	.15
313	Neal Broten	.05	.10
314	Mike Craig	.05	.10
315	Darcy Wakaluk, Goalie	.05	.10
316	Shane Churla	.05	.10
317	**Calder Candidate:** Trent Klatt, RC	.10	.20

MONTREAL CANADIENS

No.	Player	Regular NRMT	Emerald NRMT
318	Mike Keane	.05	.10
319	Mathieu Schneider	.07	.15
320	Patrice Brisebois	.05	.10
321	Andre Racicot, Goalie	.05	.10
322	Mario Roberge, RC	.07	.15
323	Gary Leeman	.05	.10
324	Jean-Jacques Daigneault	.05	.10
325	Lyle Odelein	.05	.10

1992-93 REGULAR ISSUE — PARKHURST • 173

No.	Player	Regular NRMT	Emerald NRMT
326	John LeClair	.07	.15

NEW JERSEY DEVILS

No.	Player	Regular NRMT	Emerald NRMT
327	Valeri Zelepukin	.12	.25
328	Bernie Nicholls	.12	.25
329	Alexander Semak	.05	.10
330	Craig Billington, Goalie	.05	.10
331	Randy McKay	.05	.10
332	Kenneth Daneyko	.05	.10
333	Bruce Driver	.05	.10
334	Viacheslav Fetisov	.05	.10

NEW YORK ISLANDERS

No.	Player	Regular NRMT	Emerald NRMT
335	Dennis Vaske	.05	.10
336	Brad Dalgarno	.05	.10
337	Jeff Norton	.05	.10
338	Steve Thomas	.05	.10
339	Calder Candidate: Vladimir Malakhov	.15	.30
340	David Volek	.05	.10
341	Glenn Healy, Goalie	.05	.10
342	Patrick Flatley	.05	.10
343	Calder Candidate: Travis Green, RC	.12	.25

NEW YORK RANGERS

No.	Player	Regular NRMT	Emerald NRMT
344	Calder Candidate: Corey Hirsch, Goalie, RC	.35	.75
345	Darren Turcotte	.05	.10
346	Adam Graves	.05	.10
347	Steven King, RC	.25	.50
348	Kevin Lowe	.05	.10
349	John Vanbiesbrouck, Goalie	.05	.10
350	Ed Olczyk	.05	.10
351	Calder Candidate: Sergei Zubov, RC	.30	.60

OTTAWA SENATORS

No.	Player	Regular NRMT	Emerald NRMT
352	Brad Shaw	.05	.10
353	Jamie Baker	.05	.10
354	Mark Freer, RC	.07	.15
355	Calder Candidate: Darcy Loewen, RC	.07	.15
356	Darren Rumble, RC	.07	.15
357	Bob Kudelski	.05	.10
358	Ken Hammond	.05	.10
359	Daniel Berthiaume, Goalie	.05	.10

PHILADELPHIA FLYERS

No.	Player	Regular NRMT	Emerald NRMT
360	Josef Beranek	.05	.10
361	Greg Hawgood	.05	.10
362	Terry Carkner	.05	.10
363	Calder Candidate: Vjateslav Butsayev, RC	.20	.40
364	Garry Galley	.05	.10
365	Calder Candidate: Andre Faust, RC	.07	.15
366	Calder Candidate: Ryan McGill, RC	.07	.15
367	Calder Candidate: Tommy Soderstrom, Goalie, RC	1.00	2.00

PITTSBURGH PENGUINS

No.	Player	Regular NRMT	Emerald NRMT
368	Joe Mullen	.05	.10
369	Ulf Samuelsson	.05	.10
370	Calder Candidate: Mike Needham, RC	.12	.25
371	Ken Wregget, Goalie	.05	.10
372	Dave Tippett	.05	.10
373	Kjell Samuelsson	.05	.10
374	Bob Errey	.05	.10
375	Jim Paek	.05	.10

QUEBEC NORDIQUES

No.	Player	Regular NRMT	Emerald NRMT
376	Calder Candidate: Bill Lindsay, RC	.07	.15
377	Valeri Kamensky	.25	.50
378	Stephane Fiset, Goalie	.05	.10
379	Steven Finn	.05	.10
380	Mike Hough	.05	.10
381	Scott Pearson	.05	.10
382	Kerry Huffman	.05	.10
383	Scott Young	.05	.10

ST. LOUIS BLUES

No.	Player	Regular NRMT	Emerald NRMT
384	Stephane Quintal	.05	.10
385	Calder Candidate: Bret Hedican, RC	.20	.40
386	Calder Candidate: Guy Hebert, Goalie, RC	.15	.30
387	Calder Candidate: Vitali Karamnov, RC	.20	.40
388	Douglas Crossman	.05	.10
389	Ronald Sutter	.05	.10
390	Garth Butcher	.05	.10
391	Basil McRae	.05	.10

SAN JOSE SHARKS

No.	Player	Regular NRMT	Emerald NRMT
392	Dean Evason	.05	.10
393	Calder Candidate: Doug Zmolek, RC	.12	.25
394	Jayson More	.05	.10
395	Mike Sullivan	.05	.10
396	Calder Candidate: Arturs Irbe, Goalie	.05	.10
397	Johan Garpenlov	.05	.10
398	Jeff Odgers	.05	.10
399	Calder Candidate: Jaroslav Otevrel, RC	.07	.15

TAMPA BAY LIGHTNING

No.	Player	Regular NRMT	Emerald NRMT
400	Marc Bureau	.05	.10
401	Bob Beers	.05	.10
402	Robert DiMaio	.05	.10
403	Steven Kasper	.05	.10
404	Pat Jablonski, Goalie	.05	.10
405	John Tucker	.05	.10
406	Shawn Chambers	.05	.10
407	Mike Hartman	.05	.10
408	Danton Cole	.05	.10

TORONTO MAPLE LEAFS

No.	Player	Regular NRMT	Emerald NRMT
409	David Andreychuk	.07	.15
410	Peter Zezel	.05	.10
411	Michael Krushelnyski	.05	.10
412	Daren Puppa, Goalie	.05	.10
413	Ken Baumgartner	.05	.10
414	Rob Pearson	.12	.25
415	Mike Foligno	.05	.10
416	Sylvain Lefebvre	.05	.10
417	Dimitri Mironov, RC	.10	.20

VANCOUVER CANUCKS

No.	Player	Regular NRMT	Emerald NRMT
418	Petr Nedved	.07	.15
419	Gerald Diduck	.05	.10
420	Anatoli Semenov	.05	.10
421	Sergio Momesso	.05	.10
422	Gino Odjick	.05	.10
423	Kay Whitmore, Goalie	.05	.10
424	David Babych	.05	.10
425	Robert Dirk	.05	.10

WASHINGTON CAPITALS

No.	Player	Regular NRMT	Emerald NRMT
426	Calder Candidate: Reginald Savage	.05	.10
427	Calder Candidate: Keith Jones, RC	.10	.20
428	Dimitri Khristich	.05	.10
429	Calder Candidate: Jason Woolley, RC	.07	.15
430	Jim Hrivnak, Goalie	.05	.10
431	Sylvain Cote	.05	.10
432	Michal Pivonka	.05	.10

WINNIPEG JETS

No.	Player	Regular NRMT	Emerald NRMT
434	Tahir Domi	.05	.10
435	Calder Candidate: Sergei Bautin, RC	.20	.40
436	Darrin Shannon	.05	.10
437	John Druce	.05	.10
438	Teppo Numminen	.05	.10
439	Luciano Borsato	.05	.10
440	Igor Ulanov	.05	.10
441	Calder Candidate: Michael O'Neill, Goalie, RC	.07	.15
442	Kris King	.05	.10

INTERNATIONAL RISING STARS

No.	Player	Regular NRMT	Emerald NRMT
443	Roman Hamrlik, TB	.50	1.00
444	James (Steve) Smith, Chi.	.05	.10
445	Jari Kurri, LA	.05	.10
446	Ulf Samuelsson, Pit.	.05	.10
447	Sergei Nemchinov, NYR	.10	.20
448	Tommy Soderstrom, Goalie, Phi., RC	.50	1.00
449	Petr Nedved, Van.	.07	.15
450	Peter Sidorkiewicz, Goalie, Ott.	.05	.10
451	Nicklas Lidstrom, Det.	.12	.25
452	Philippe Bozon, St.L	.05	.10
453	Uwe Krupp, NYI	.05	.10
454	Steve Thomas, NYI	.05	.10
455	Owen Nolan, Que.	.10	.20

ALL STARS

No.	Player	Regular NRMT	Emerald NRMT
456	Steve Yzerman, Det.	.10	.20
457	Chris Chelios, Chi.	.05	.10
458	Paul Coffey, Det.	.10	.20
459	Brett Hull, St. L	.25	.50
460	Pavel Bure, Van.	.75	1.50
461	Ed. Belfour, Goalie, Chi.	.12	.25
462	Mario Lemieux, Pit.	.50	1.00
463	Patrick Roy, Goalie, Mon.	.25	.50
464	Raymond Bourque, Bos.	.05	.10
465	Jaromir Jagr, Pit.	.25	.50
466	Kevin Stevens, Pit.	.12	.25
467	Brian Leetch, NYR	.12	.25

BROAD ST. NORTH - DYNASTY

No.	Player	Regular NRMT	Emerald NRMT
468	Bobby Clarke	.12	.25
469	Bill Barber	.07	.15
470	Bernie Parent, Goalie	.07	.15
471	Reginald Leach	.05	.10
472	Rick MacLeish	.05	.10
473	Dave Schultz	.05	.10
474	Joe Watson	.05	.10
475	Bobby Taylor, Goalie	.05	.10
476	Orest Kindrachuk	.05	.10
477	Bob Kelly	.05	.10
478	Bill Clement	.05	.10
479	Ed Van Impe	.05	.10
480	Fred Shero, Coach	.05	.10

PARKHURST — 1992-93 INSERT SETS

—1992-93 INSERT SETS—

Besides the Emerald Ice insert set the regular and jumbo packs carried their normal share of typical inserts.

PARKHURST REPRINT CARDS

This 36-card set was randomly inserted in the regular and jumbo foil packs of Series One and Two as follows:
  Series One Regular Foil: The goalies plus the first checklist (PR1-PR8)
  Series One Jumbo Foil: The defenceman series and the second checklist (PR9-PR16).
  Series Two Regular Foil: The first forward set, plus the third checklist (PR17-PR24).
  Series Two Jumbo Foil: The second forward set, plus the fourth checklist. (PR25 - 32)

1992-93 Parkhurst Reprint Cards
Card No. PR-3, Johnny Bower

Card Size: 2 1/2" x 3 1/2"
Face: Four colour, various borders
Back: Black, blue or red on white card stock, Name, Resume, Bilingual
Imprint: OFFERS NO LONGER VALID. PRINTED IN CANADA © 1993 PRO SET INC.
Complete Set No.: 36
Complete Set Price: 425.00 / 850.00
Common Player: 12.50 / 25.00
Common Goalie: 12.50 / 25.00

INSERTED IN SERIES ONE REGULAR FOIL

No.	Player	EX	NRMT
—	Checklist #1	17.50	35.00
PR-1	Jacques Plante, Goalie, Mon	17.50	35.00
PR-2	Terry Sawchuk, Goalie, Det.	17.50	35.00
PR-3	Johnny Bower, Goalie, Tor.	17.50	35.00
PR-4	Lorne "Gump" Worsley, Goalie, NYR	15.00	30.00
PR-5	Harry Lumley, Goalie, Tor.	12.50	25.00
PR-6	Turk Broda, Goalie, Tor.	12.50	25.00
PR-8	Al Rollins, Goalie, Chi.	12.50	25.00

INSERTED IN SERIES ONE JUMBO FOIL

No.	Player	EX	NRMT
—	Checklist #2	17.50	35.00
PR-9	Bill Gadsby, Chi.	12.50	25.00
PR-10	Red Kelly, Det.	15.00	30.00
PR-11	Allan Stanley, NYR	14.00	28.00
PR-12	Bobby Baun, Tor.	13.50	27.00
PR-13	Carl Thomas Brewer, Tor.	12.50	25.00
PR-14	Doug Harvey, Mon.	17.50	35.00
PR-15	Harry Howell, NYR	12.50	25.00
PR-16	Tim Horton, Tor.	20.00	40.00

INSERTED IN SERIES TWO REGULAR FOIL

Checklist No. 3 and the following eight cards are also available overprinted "Promo" on the back. They were used as promotional hand-outs during the 1992-93 season. The promo cards command a price of 1.5 times the regular catalogue price listed below.

No.	Player	EX	NRMT
—	Checklist #3	17.50	35.00
PR-17	George Armstrong, Tor.	14.00	28.00
PR-18	Ralph Backstrom, Mon.	12.50	25.00
PR-19	Alex Peter Delvecchio, Det.	12.50	25.00
PR-20	Bill Mosienko, Chi.	12.50	25.00
PR-21	Dave Keon, Tor.	12.50	25.00
PR-22	Andy Bathgate, NYR	13.50	27.00
PR-23	Milton Schmidt, Bos.	12.50	25.00
PR-24	Dick Duff, Tor.	12.50	25.00

INSERTED IN SERIES TWO JUMBO FOIL

No.	Player	EX	NRMT
—	Checklist	17.50	35.00
PR-25	Norm Ullman, Det.	13.50	27.00
PR-26	Dickie Moore, Mon.	13.50	27.00
PR-27	Jerry Toppazzini, Bos.	12.50	25.00
PR-28	Henri Richard, Mon	15.00	30.00
PR-29	Frank Mahovlich, Tor.	20.00	40.00
PR-30	Jean Beliveau, Mon.	20.00	40.00
PR-31	Ted Lindsay, Det.	17.50	35.00
PR-32	Bernard (Boom Boom) Geoffrion, Mon.	17.50	35.00

DON CHERRY REPRINT CARD

The Don Cherry card is a reprint of the 1954-55 Parkhurst card no. 56 of Warren Godfrey. The reprint has Don Cherry's portrait superimposed on Godfrey's and the card number changed to 101. The cards are found only in Canadian distributed Series Two regular and jumbo foils. They were inserted approximately one per case and are thus scarce. There are also 300 signed Don Cherry Reprint cards.

Card Size: 2 1/2" x 3 1/2"
Face: Four colour, white border; Number
Back: Two colour black, on white card stock; Name; Resume
Imprint: OFFERS NO LONGER VALID. PRINTED IN CANADA. © 1993 PRO SET INC.

No.	Player	NRMT	Mint
101	Don Cherry	40.00	80.00
101	Don Cherry, Autographed	150.00	300.00

CHERRY PICKS

This 21-card set was randomly inserted in the Series Two regular and jumbo foil packs. The Don Cherry "Thumbs Up" autographed card was inserted only in jumbo Foil Series Two foil packs. The players were selectected by Don Cherry as his Dream Team.

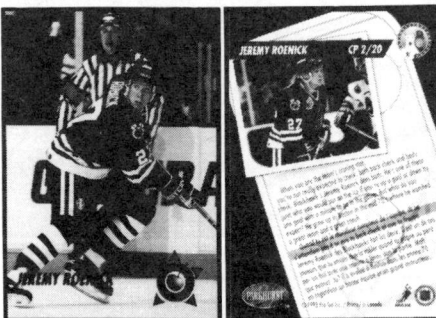

1992-93 Cherry Picks
Card No. CP2, Jeremy Roenick

Card Size: 2 1/2" x 3 1/2"
Face: Four colour, borderless; Name
Back: Four colour; Name, Number, Biography, Bilingual
Imprint: © 1993 Pro Set Inc. / Printed in Canada
Complete Set No.: 21
Complete Set Price: 87.50 / 175.00
Common Goalie: 4.00 / 8.00
Common Player: 4.00 / 8.00

No.	Player	EX	NRMT
—	Don Cherry "Thumbs Up" / Checklist	12.50	25.00
—	Don Cherry "Thumbs Up" / Checklist, Autographed	150.00	300.00
CP1	Douglas Gilmour, Tor.	6.00	12.00
CP2	Jeremy Roenick, Chi.	6.00	12.00
CP3	Brent Sutter, Chi.	4.00	8.00
CP4	Mark Messier, NYR	4.50	9.00
CP5	Kirk Muller, Mon.	5.00	10.00
CP6	Eric Lindros, Phi.	20.00	40.00
CP7	Dale Hunter, Wash.	4.00	8.00
CP8	Gary Roberts, Cal.	4.00	8.00
CP9	Bob Probert, Det.	5.00	10.00
CP10	Brendan Shanahan, St.L	4.00	8.00
CP11	Wendel Clark, Tor.	5.00	10.00
CP12	Rick Tocchet, Pit.	4.50	9.00
CP13	Owen Nolan, Que.	4.50	9.00
CP14	Cam Neely, Bos.	4.50	9.00
CP15	Dave Manson, Edm.	4.00	8.00
CP16	Chris Chelios, Chi.	4.50	9.00
CP17	Marty McSorely, LA	4.50	9.00
CP18	Scott Stevens, NJ	4.50	9.00
CP19	John Blue, Goalie, Bos.	4.00	8.00
CP20	Ron Hextall, Goalie, Que.	4.00	8.00

DON CHERRY REDEMPTION CARD

Inserted in jumbo Series Two foil four of these cards were required to obtain a 1993 Cherry Pick's Limited Edition Sheet encased in a lucite holder. This sheet was available by mail.

Card Size: 2 1/2" x 3 1/2"
Face: Four colour, borderless; Gold embossed redemption card
Back: Black on white card stock
Imprint: Printed in Canada © 1993 Pro Set Inc.

No.	Player	EX	NRMT
—	Cherry/Redemption card	12.50	25.00

—1992-93 FINAL UPDATE— REGULAR and EMERALD ICE

This set of cards was issued in a regular box. The card numbering system is carried forward from the regular issue Series Two.

Emerald Ice   Final Update
Card No. 483   Card No. 487
M. Barnaby   Sean Hill

Card Size: 2 1/2" x 3 1/2"
Face: Four colour, turquoise marble left border; Name
Back: Four colour; Name, Team, Resume, Bilingual
Imprint: © 1993 Pro Set Inc. / Printed in Canada
Complete Set No. 30
Factory Set Price: 9.00 / 18.00
Common Player: .10 / .20

REGULAR ISSUE

No.	Player	Regular NRMT	Emerald NRMT
481	Bryan Smolinski, Bos., RC	.35	.75
482	Sergei Zholtok, Bos., RC	.35	.75
483	Matthew Barnaby, Buf., RC	.25	.50
484	Gary Shuchuk, LA, RC	.35	.75
485	Guy Carbonneau, Mon.	.10	.20
486	Oleg Petrov, Mon., RC	.35	.75
487	Sean Hill, Mon., RC	.25	.50
488	Jesse Belanger, Mon., RC	.25	.50
489	Paul Di Pietro, Mon.	.25	.50
490	Richard Pilon, NYI	.10	.20
491	Greg Parks, NYI, RC	.20	.40
492	Jeff Daniels, Pit., RC	.20	.40
493	Denny Felsner, St.L., RC	.25	.50
494	Michael Eastwood, Tor., RC	.35	.75
495	Murray Craven, Van.	.10	.20

1993 STANLEY CUP PLAYOFFS

No.	Player	Regular NRMT	Emerald NRMT
496	Vincent Damphousse, Mon.	.15	.30
497	Grant Fuhr, Goalie, Buf.	.15	.30
498	Mario Lemieux, Pit.	.50	1.00
499	Ray Ferraro, NYI	.10	.20
500	Teemu Selanne, Win.	1.00	2.00
501	Luc Robitaille, LA	.25	.50
502	Douglas Gilmour, Tor.	.35	.75
503	Curtis Joseph, Goalie, St. L.	.35	.75
504	Kirk Muller, Mon.	.25	.50
505	Glenn Healy, Goalie, NYI	.10	.20
506	Pavel Bure, Van.	.85	1.75
507	Felix Potvin, Goalie, Tor.	1.00	2.00
508	Guy Carbonneau, Mon.	.10	.20
509	Wayne Gretzky, LA	.50	1.00
510	Patrick Roy, Goalie, Mon.	.75	1.50

— 1992 - 93 FINAL UPDATE INSERT CARD —

One chase card was inserted in the Final Update set, the Doug Gilmour "Cherry's Pick of the Year."

1992-93 Cherry's Pick of the Year
Douglas Gilmore

Card Size: 2 1/2" x 3 1/2"
Face: Four colour, borderless
Back: Four colour
Imprint: © 1993 PRO SET INC. / PRINTED IN CANADA

No.	Player	EX	NRMT
----	Cherry's Pick of the Year: Douglas Gilmour	12.50	25.00

— 1992 - 93 COMMEMORATIVE SHEETS —

These five different commemorative sheets were issued during the 1992-93 season, first as "promos" and then as regular issue in regular and jumbo foil cases.

PROMO SHEETS

The oval at the bottom right of the sheet carries the word "promo".

Sheet Size: 8 1/2" x 11"
Face: Four colour; green marble background; Name, Number
Back: Blank
Imprint: © 1993 Pro Set Inc.
Complete Set No.: 5
Complete Set Price: 60.00

No.	Player	EX	NRMT
1	Goalies	7.50	15.00
2	Defense	7.50	15.00
3	Forwards # 1	7.50	15.00
4	Forwards # 2	7.50	15.00
5	The Stanley Cup Update Sheet	7.50	15.00

REGULAR SHEETS

The oval at the bottom right of the sheet carries the sheet number _ of _. See below for the number issued of each sheet.

Sheet Size: 8 1/2" x 11"
Face: Four colour; green marble background; Name, Number
Back: Blank
Imprint: © 1993 Pro Set Inc.
Complete Set No.: 5
Complete Set Price: 25.00 50.00

No.	Player	EX	NRMT
1	Goalies (7,000)	6.25	12.50
2	Defense (3,000)	6.25	12.50
3	Forwards #1 (7,000)	6.25	12.50
4	Forwards #2 (3,000)	6.25	12.50
5	The Stanley Cup Update Sheet (7,000)	6.25	12.50

MAPLE LEAFS ALUMNI GAME SHEET

Designed for the Alumni Game on April 4th, 1993, this sheet was issued at the game and was only available in promo form. Ten thousand sheets were issued.

Sheet Size: 8 1/2" x 11"
Face: Four colour, green marble background
Back: Blank
Imprint: ©1993 Pro Set Inc.

No.	Player	EX	NRMT
----	Toronto Maple Leafs vs. Montreal Canadiens April 4, 1993 Maple Leaf Gardens	7.50	15.00

LIMITED EDITION CANADIAN TOUR SHEETS

These sheets were handed out to fans at the home stadium in question on the date printed on the face of the sheet. The Montreal sheet, however, was not allowed to be distributed as it was not bilingual.

Sheet Size: 8 1/2" x 11"
Face: Four colour, numbered sheet of 22,000
Back: Blank
Imprint: © 1993 Pro Set Inc.
Complete Set No.: 8
Complete Set Price: 35.00 70.00

No.	Sheet	EX	NRMT
1	Calgary Flames, Olympic Saddledome, April 1, 1993	2.50	5.00
2	Edmonton Oilers, Northlands Coliseum, April 3, 1993	2.50	5.00
3	Quebec Nordiques, Colisee De Quebec, April 6, 1993	2.50	5.00
4	Vancouver Canucks, Pacific Coliseum, April 11, 1993	2.50	5.00
5	Montreal Canadiens, The Forum, April 12, 1993	17.50	35.00
6	Toronto Maple Leafs, Maple Leaf Gardens, April 13, 1993	2.50	5.00
7	Ottawa Senators, Ottawa Civic Centre, April 14, 1993	2.50	5.00
8	Winnipeg Jets, Winnipeg Arena, April 15, 1993	2.50	5.00

CHERRY PICKS SHEETS

This sheet was produced as a promo and then as a regular issue. The regular issue was obtainable from Pro Set in the U.S.A. or PHC Distribution in Canada by sending four Don Cherry redemption cards to either address. The regular issue sheet came in a lucite holder. For redemption card listing see page no. 194. This issue was limited to 1993 sheets and numbered _ of 1993.

Sheet Size: 8 1/2" x 11"
Face: Four colour, borderless; Cherry Pick cards pictured
Back: Blank
Imprint: ©1993 Pro Set Inc. / Printed in Canada

No.	Player	EX	NRMT
----	Promo Issue	50.00	100.00
----	Regular Issue	50.00	100.00

Coming in April!

THE CHARLTON STANDARD CATALOGUE OF CANADIAN BASEBALL AND FOOTBALL CARDS

- Fourth Edition -

1993 CHERRY PICKS

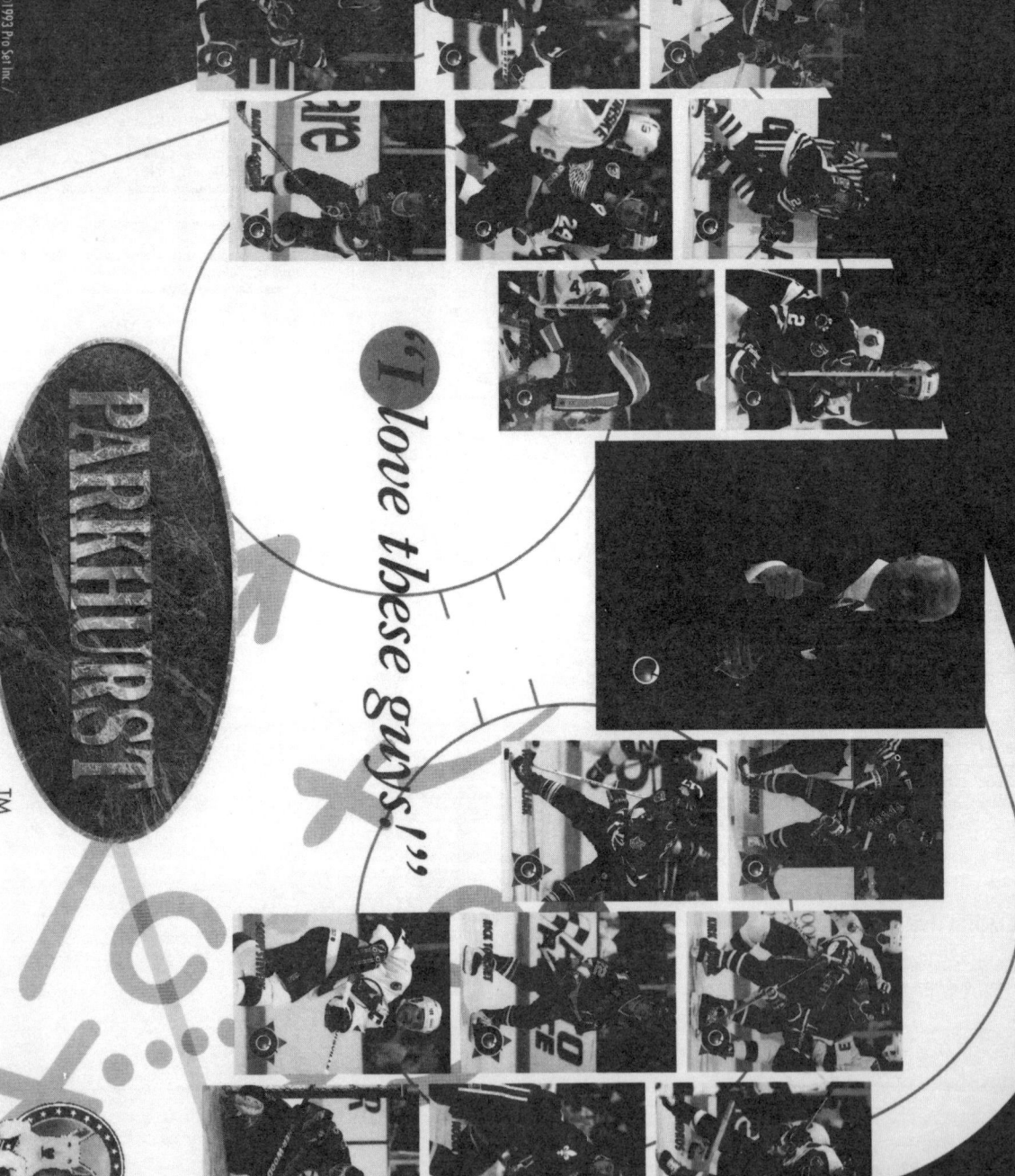

"I love these guys!"

PARKHURST

— 1993 - 94 REGULAR ISSUE —

and EMERALD ICE

This 540-card set was divided into two series of 270 cards each. The Emerald Ice cards were inserted one per pack and two per jumbo pack in both Series One and Series Two regular foils.

There are three different foil packs in the 1993-94 issues, American Hobby, American Retail and Canadian Foils.

1993-94 Regular Issue,
Card No. 1, Stephen King

Size: 2 1/2" x 3 1/2"
Face: Four colour, borderless; Name, Silver foil stamped logo
Back: Four colour, borderless; Name, Number, Position, Resume on card stock
Imprint: PARKHURST™, PARKHURST™ and Design, EMERALD ICE™ and PARKIE™ are trademarks of Parkhurst Products Inc., used under license by The Upper Deck Company. Upper Deck and the card/hologram combination are trademarks of The Upper Deck Company.
© 1993 The Upper Deck Company. All Rights Reserved.
Printed in the U.S.A.

		Regular	Emerald Ice
Complete Set No.:	540		
Series One:	270		
Series Two:	270		
Complete Set Price:		60.00	350.00
Series One:		30.00	175.00
Series Two:		30.00	175.00
Common Card:		.10	.50
Foil Pack Series 1 or 2: (12 Cards)			1.75
Foil Box Series 1 or 2: (36 Packs)			65.00
Jumbo Pack Series 1 or 2: (18 Cards)			3.00
Jumbo Box Series 1 or 2: (24 Packs)			68.00

SERIES ONE

MIGHTY DUCKS OF ANAHEIM

No.	Player	Regular NRMT	Emerald NRMT
1	Steven King	.10	.50
2	Sean Hill	.10	.50
3	Anatoli Semenov	.10	.50
4	Garry Valk	.10	.50
5	Todd Ewen	.10	.50
6	Bob Corkum	.10	.50
7	Tim Sweeney	.10	.50
8	**Patrik Carnback, RC**	**.15**	**.75**
9	Troy Loney	.10	.50

BOSTON BRUINS

No.	Player	Regular NRMT	Emerald NRMT
10	Cam Neely	.15	.75
11	Adam Oates	.20	1.00
12	Jon Casey, Goalie	.10	.50
13	Don Sweeney	.10	.50
14	Raymond Bourque	.20	1.00
15	Jozef Stumpel	.10	.50
16	Glen Murray	.10	.50
17	Glen Wesley	.10	.50
18	**Fred Knipscheer, RC**	**.25**	**1.25**

BUFFALO SABRES

No.	Player	Regular NRMT	Emerald NRMT
19	Craig Simpson	.10	.50
20	Richard Smehlik	.10	.50
21	Alexander Mogilny	.50	2.50
22	Grant Fuhr, Goalie	.10	.50
23	Dale Hawerchuk	.10	.50
24	Philippe Boucher	.10	.50
25	**Scott Thomas, RC**	**.15**	**.75**
26	Donald Audette	.10	.50
27	Brad May	.10	.50

CALGARY FLAMES

No.	Player	Regular NRMT	Emerald NRMT
28	Theoren Fleury	.10	.50
29	Andrei Trefilov, Goalie	.30	1.50
30	**Sandy McCarthy, RC**	**.15**	**.75**
31	Joe Nieuwendyk	.10	.50
32	Paul Ranheim	.10	.50
33	Kelly Kisio	.10	.50
34	Joel Otto	.10	.50
35	Ted Drury	.10	.50
36	Allan MacInnis	.10	.50

CHICAGO BLACK HAWKS

No.	Player	Regular NRMT	Emerald NRMT
37	Kevin Todd	.10	.50
38	Joe Murphy	.10	.50
39	Christian Ruuttu	.10	.50
40	**Steve Dubinsky, RC**	**.20**	**1.00**
41	Stephane Matteau	.10	.50
42	**Ivan Droppa, RC**	**.15**	**.75**
43	Jocelyn Lemieux	.10	.50
44	Ed Belfour, Goalie	.25	1.25
45	Chris Chelios	.15	.75

DALLAS STARS

No.	Player	Regular NRMT	Emerald NRMT
46	Derian Hatcher	.10	.50
47	Andrew Moog, Goalie	.10	.50
48	Trent Klatt	.10	.50
49	Michael Modano	.30	1.50
50	Paul Cavallini	.10	.50
51	Michael McPhee	.10	.50
52	Brent Gilchrist	.10	.50
53	Russell Courtnall	.10	.50
54	Neal Broten	.10	.50

DETROIT RED WINGS

No.	Player	Regular NRMT	Emerald NRMT
55	Steve Chiasson	.10	.50
56	Paul Coffey	.10	.50
57	Vyacheslav Kozlov	.75	3.75
58	Sergei Fedorov	1.00	5.00
59	Tim Cheveldae, Goalie	.10	.50
60	Dino Ciccarelli	.15	.75
61	**Dallas Drake, RC**	**.25**	**1.25**
62	Nicklas Lidstrom	.10	.50
63	Martin Lapointe	.10	.50

EDMONTON OILERS

No.	Player	Regular NRMT	Emerald NRMT
64	Dean McAmmond	.10	.50
65	Igor Kravchuk	.10	.50
66	**Shjon Podein, RC**	**.20**	**1.00**
67	Bill Ranford, Goalie	.15	.75
68	Brad Werenka	.10	.50
69	Doug Weight	.10	.50
70	**Ian Herbers, RC**	**.15**	**.75**
71	Todd Elik	.10	.50
72	Steve Rice	.10	.50

FLORIDA PANTHERS

No.	Player	Regular NRMT	Emerald NRMT
73	John Vanbiesbrouck, Goalie	.20	1.00
74	Alexander Godynyuk	.10	.50
75	Brian Skrudland	.10	.50
76	Jody Hull	.10	.50
77	**Brent Severyn, RC**	**.15**	**.75**
78	Evgeny Davydov	.10	.50
79	Dave Lowry	.10	.50
80	**Scott Levins, RC**	**.20**	**1.00**
81	Scott Mellanby	.10	.50

HARTFORD WHALERS

No.	Player	Regular NRMT	Emerald NRMT
82	Dan Keczmer	.10	.50
83	Michael Nylander	.20	1.00
84	Jim Sandlak	.10	.50
85	Brian Propp	.10	.50
86	Geoff Sanderson	.30	1.50
87	**Mike Lenarduzzi, Goalie, RC**		**.15**
88	Zarley Zalapski	.10	.50
89	Robert Petrovicky	.10	.50
90	Robert Kron	.10	.50

LOS ANGELES KINGS

No.	Player	Regular NRMT	Emerald NRMT
91	Luc Robitaille	.20	1.00
92	Alexei Zhitnik	.20	1.00
93	Tony Granato	.10	.50
94	Robert Blake	.10	.50
95	Gary Shuchuk	.10	.50
96	Darryl Sydor	.10	.50
97	Kelly Hrudey, Goalie	.10	.50
98	Warren Rychel	.10	.50
99	Wayne Gretzky	2.00	10.00

MONTREAL CANADIENS

No.	Player	Regular NRMT	Emerald NRMT
100	Patrick Roy, Goalie	1.00	5.00
101	Gilbert Dionne	.10	.50
102	Eric Desjardins	.10	.50
103	**Peter Popovic, RC**	**.25**	**1.25**
104	Vincent Damphousse	.10	.50
105	Patrice Brisebois	.10	.50
106	Pierre Sevigny	.10	.50
107	John LeClair	.10	.50
108	Paul DiPietro	.10	.50

NEW JERSEY DEVILS

No.	Player	Regular NRMT	Emerald NRMT
109	Alexander Semak	.10	.50
110	Claude Lemieux	.10	.50
111	Scott Niedermayer	.20	1.00
112	Chris Terreri, Goalie	.10	.50
113	Stephane J. J. Richer	.15	.75
114	Scott Stevens	.15	.75
115	John MacLean	.10	.50
116	**Scott Pellerin, RC**	**.20**	**1.00**
117	Bernie Nicholls	.10	.50

NEW YORK ISLANDERS

No.	Player	Regular NRMT	Emerald NRMT
118	Ron Hextall, Goalie	.10	.50
119	Derek King	.10	.50
120	Scott Lachance	.10	.50
121	Scott Scissons	.10	.50
122	Darius Kasparaitis	.10	.50
123	Ray Ferraro	.10	.50
124	Steve Thomas	.10	.50
125	Vladimir Malakhov	.20	1.00
126	Travis Green	.10	.50

NEW YORK RANGERS

No.	Player	Regular NRMT	Emerald NRMT
127	Mark Messier	.20	1.00
128	Sergei Nemchinov	.10	.50
129	Mike Richter, Goalie	.20	1.00
130	Alexei Kovalev	.60	3.00
131	Brian Leetch	.30	1.50
132	Anthony Amonte	.10	.50
133	Sergei Zubov	.60	3.00
134	Adam Graves	.30	1.50
135	Esa Tikkanen	.10	.50

178 • PARKHURST — 1993-94 REGULAR ISSUE —

OTTAWA SENATORS

No.	Player	Regular NRMT	Emerald NRMT
136	Sylvain Turgeon	.10	.50
137	Norm Maciver	.10	.50
138	Craig Billington, Goalie	.10	.50
139	Dmitri Filimonov	.10	.50
140	Pavol Demitra	.15	.75
141	Brian Glynn	.10	.50
142	Darrin Madeley, Goalie, RC	.20	1.00
143	Rader Hamr, RC	.20	1.00
144	Robert Burakovsky, RC	.15	.75

PHILADELPHIA FLYERS

No.	Player	Regular NRMT	Emerald NRMT
145	Dimitri Yushkevich	.10	.50
146	Claude Boivin	.10	.50
147	Per-Erik Eklund	.10	.50
148	Brent Fedyk	.10	.50
149	Mark Recchi	.25	1.25
150	Tommy Soderstrom, Goalie	.20	1.00
151	Vyacheslav Butsayev	.10	.50
152	Rod Brind'Amour	.20	1.00
153	Josef Beranek	.15	.75

PITTSBURGH PENGUINS

No.	Player	Regular NRMT	Emerald NRMT
154	Jaromir Jagr	.50	2.50
155	Ulf Samuelsson	.10	.50
156	Martin Straka	.50	2.50
157	Tom Barrasso, Goalie	.10	.50
158	Kevin Stevens	.20	1.00
159	Joe Mullen	.10	.50
160	Ronald Francis	.10	.50
161	Martin McSorley	.10	.50
162	Lawrence Murphy	.10	.50

QUEBEC NORDIQUES

No.	Player	Regular NRMT	Emerald NRMT
163	Owen Nolan	.15	.75
164	Stephane Fiset, Goalie	.20	1.00
165	Dave Karpa	.10	.50
166	Martin Gelinas	.10	.50
167	Andrei Kovalenko	.20	1.00
168	Steve Duchesne	.10	.50
169	Joe Sakic	.25	1.25
170	Martin Rucinsky	.10	.50
171	Chris Simon, RC	.20	1.00

ST. LOUIS BLUES

No.	Player	Regular NRMT	Emerald NRMT
172	Brendan Shanahan	.20	1.00
173	Jeff Brown	.10	.50
174	Phil Housley	.10	.50
175	Curtis Joseph, Goalie	.25	1.25
176	Jim Montgomery, RC	.20	1.00
177	Bret Hedican	.10	.50
178	Kevin Miller	.10	.50
179	Philippe Bozon	.10	.50
180	Brett Hull	.60	3.00

SAN JOSE SHARKS

No.	Player	Regular NRMT	Emerald NRMT
181	Jimmy Waite, Goalie	.10	.50
182	Ray Whitney	.10	.50
183	Pat Falloon	.10	.50
184	Tom Pederson	.10	.50
185	Igor Larionov	.10	.50
186	Dody Wood, RC	.15	.75
187	Sandis Ozolinch	.25	1.25
188	Sergei Makarov	.10	.50
189	Rob Gaudreau, RC	.25	1.25

TAMPA BAY LIGHTNING

No.	Player	Regular NRMT	Emerald NRMT
190	Roman Hamrlik	.20	1.00
191	Stan Drulia	.10	.50
192	Pat Jablonski, Goalie	.10	.50
193	Denis Savard	.15	.75
194	Rob Zamuner	.10	.50
195	Petr Klima	.10	.50
196	Robert Dimaio	.10	.50
197	Chris Kontos	.10	.50
198	Bo Mikael Andersson	.10	.50

TORONTO MAPLE LEAFS

No.	Player	Regular NRMT	Emerald NRMT
199	Drake Berehowsky	.15	.75
200	David Andreychuk	.20	1.00
201	Glenn Anderson	.10	.50
202	Felix Potvin, Goalie	1.00	5.00
203	Nikolai Borschevsky	.20	1.00
204	Kent Manderville	.10	.50
205	David Ellett	.10	.50
206	Peter Zezel	.10	.50
207	Ken Baumgartner	.10	.50

VANCOUVER CANUCKS

No.	Player	Regular NRMT	Emerald NRMT
208	Murray Craven	.10	.50
209	Dixon Ward	.10	.50
210	Cliff Ronning	.10	.50
211	Pavel Bure	1.25	7.00
212	Sergio Momesso	.10	.50
213	Kirk McLean, Goalie	.20	1.00
214	Jiri Slegr	.10	.50
215	Trevor Linden	.20	1.00
216	Geoff Courtnall	.10	.50

WASHINGTON CAPITALS

No.	Player	Regular NRMT	Emerald NRMT
217	Al Iafrate	.10	.50
218	Mike Ridley	.10	.50
219	Enrico Ciccone	.10	.50
220	Dimitri Khristich	.10	.50
221	Kevin Hatcher	.10	.50
222	Peter Bondra	.10	.50
223	Steve Konowalchuk	.10	.50
224	Pat Elynuik	.10	.50
225	Donald Beaupre, Goalie	.10	.50

WINNIPEG JETS

No.	Player	Regular NRMT	Emerald NRMT
226	Stu Barnes	.10	.50
227	Fredrik Olausson	.10	.50
228	Keith Tkachuk	.10	.50
229	Mike Eagles	.10	.50
230	Tahir Domi	.10	.50
231	Teppo Numminen	.10	.50
232	Arto Blomsten, RC	.15	.75
233	Teemu Selanne	1.00	5.00
234	Bob Essensa, Goalie	.10	.50

SENSATIONAL SOPHOMORES

No.	Player	Regular NRMT	Emerald NRMT
235	Teemu Selanne, Win.	.60	3.00
236	Eric Lindros, Phi.	2.00	10.00
237	Felix Potvin, Goalie, Tor.	.50	2.50
238	Alexei Kovalev, NYR	.30	1.50
239	Vladimir Malakhov, NYI	.10	.50
240	Scott Niedermayer, NJ	.10	.50
241	Joseph Juneau, Bos.	.25	1.25
242	Shawn McEachern, LA	.10	.50
243	Alexei Zhamnov, Win.	.10	.50

PARKHURST PROSPECTS

No.	Player	Regular NRMT	Emerald NRMT
244	Alexandre Daigle, Ott., RC	1.00	5.00
245	Markus Naslund, Pit., RC	.20	1.00
246	Rob Niedermayer, Fl., RC	.75	4.00
247	Jocelyn Thibault, Goalie, Que., RC	.75	5.00
248	Brent Gretzky, TB, RC	.10	.50
249	Chris Pronger, Hart., RC	.40	2.00
250	Chris Gratton, TB, RC	.75	4.00
251	Mikael Renberg, Phi., RC	1.00	5.00
252	Jarkko Varvio, Dal., RC	.20	1.00
253	Micah Alvazoff, Det., RC	.20	1.00
254	Alexei Yashin, Ott., RC	1.50	7.50
255	German Titov, Goalie, Cal., RC	.50	2.50
256	Mattias Norstrom, NYR, RC	.15	.75
257	Michal Sykora, SJ, RC	.20	1.00
258	Roman Oksyuta, Edm., RC	.15	.75
259	Bryan Smolinski, Bos., RC	.60	3.00
260	Alexei Kudashov, Tor., RC	.30	1.50
261	Jason Arnott, Edm., RC	3.00	15.00
262	Aaron Ward, Det., RC	.10	.50
263	Vesa Viitakoski, Cal., RC	.10	.50
264	Boris Mironov, Win., RC	.10	.50
265	Darren McCarty, Det., RC	.25	1.25
266	Vlastimil Kroupa, SJ, RC	.25	1.25
267	Denny Felsner, St.L, RC	.10	.50
268	Milos Holan, Phi., RC	.10	.50
269	Alexander Karpovtsev, NYR, RC	.10	.50
270	Greg Johnson, Det., RC	.10	.50

SERIES TWO

1993-94 Emerald Ice,
Card No. 471, Matt Martin

MIGHTY DUCKS OF ANAHEIM

No.	Player	Regular NRMT	Emerald NRMT
271	Terry Yake	.10	.50
272	Bill Houlder	.10	.50
273	Joseph Sacco	.10	.50
274	Myles O'Connor	.10	.50
275	Mark Ferner, RC	.15	.75
276	Alexei Kasatonov	.10	.50
277	Stu Grimson	.10	.50
278	Shaun Van Allen	.10	.50
279	Guy Hebert, Goalie	.15	.75

BOSTON BRUINS

No.	Player	Regular NRMT	Emerald NRMT
280	Joseph Juneau	.50	2.50
281	Sergei Zholtok	.10	.50
282	Daniel Marois	.10	.50
283	Ted Donato	.10	.50
284	Cam Stewart, RC	.15	.75
285	Stephen Leach	.10	.50
286	Darren Banks	.10	.50
287	Dmitri Kvartalnov	.10	.50
288	Paul Stanton	.10	.50

BUFFALO SABRES

No.	Player	Regular NRMT	Emerald NRMT
289	Pat LaFontaine	.25	1.25
290	Bob Sweeney	.10	.50
291	Craig Muni	.10	.50
292	Sergei Petrenko	.10	.50
293	Derek Plante, RC	1.00	5.00
294	Wayne Presley	.10	.50

PARKURST — 1993-94 REGULAR ISSUE — 179

No.	Player	Regular NRMT	Emerald NRMT
295	**Mark Astley, RC**	**.15**	**.75**
296	Matthew Barnaby	.20	1.00
297	Randy Wood	.10	.50

CALGARY FLAMES

No.	Player	Regular NRMT	Emerald NRMT
298	Kevin Dahl	.10	.50
299	Gary Suter	.10	.50
300	Robert Reichel	.20	1.00
301	Michael Vernon, Goalie	.10	.50
302	Gary Roberts	.15	.75
303	Ronald Stern	.10	.50
304	Michel Petit	.10	.50
305	Wes Walz	.10	.50
306	Brad Miller	.10	.50

CHICAGO BLACKHAWKS

No.	Player	Regular NRMT	Emerald NRMT
307	Patrick Poulin	.10	.50
308	Brent Sutter	.10	.50
309	Jeremy Roenick	.75	4.00
310	James (Steve) Smith	.10	.50
311	Eric Weinrich	.10	.50
312	Jeff Hackett, Goalie	.10	.50
313	Michel Goulet	.10	.50
314	**Jeff Shantz, RC**	**.15**	**.75**
315	Neil Wilkinson	.10	.50

DALLAS STARS

No.	Player	Regular NRMT	Emerald NRMT
316	Shane Churla	.10	.50
317	Dave Gagner	.10	.50
318	Chris Tancill	.10	.50
319	Dean Evason	.10	.50
320	Mark Tinordi	.10	.50
321	Grant Ledyard	.10	.50
322	Ulf Dahlen	.10	.50
323	Mike Craig	.10	.50
324	Paul Broten	.10	.50

DETROIT RED WINGS

No.	Player	Regular NRMT	Emerald NRMT
325	Vladimir Konstantinov	.10	.50
326	Steve Yzerman	.30	1.50
327	Keith Primeau	.10	.50
328	Shawn Burr	.10	.50
329	**Chris Osgood, Goalie, RC**	**1.00**	**5.00**
330	Ray Sheppard	.20	1.00
331	Mike Sillinger	.10	.50
332	Terry Carkner	.10	.50
333	Bob Probert	.10	.50

EDMONTON OILERS

No.	Player	Regular NRMT	Emerald NRMT
334	Adam Bennett	.10	.50
335	Dave Manson	.10	.50
336	Zdeno Ciger	.10	.50
337	Louie DeBrusk	.10	.50
338	Shayne Corson	.10	.50
339	Vladimir Vujtek	.10	.50
340	Tyler Wright	.10	.50
341	**Ilya Byakin, RC**	**.15**	**.75**
342	Craig MacTavish	.10	.50

FLORIDA PANTHERS

No.	Player	Regular NRMT	Emerald NRMT
343	Brian Benning	.10	.50
344	Mark Fitzpatrick, Goalie	.10	.50
345	Gordon Murphy	.10	.50
346	Jesse Belanger	.10	.50
347	Joe Cirella	.10	.50
348	Tom Fitzgerald	.10	.50
349	Anrei Lomakin	.10	.50
350	Bill Lindsay	.10	.50
451	Len Barrie	.10	.50

HARTFORD WHALERS

No.	Player	Regular NRMT	Emerald NRMT
352	Frank Pietrangelo, Goalie	.10	.50
353	Patrick Verbeek	.10	.50
354	Jim Storm	.10	.50
355	Mark Janssens	.10	.50
356	Darren Turcotte	.10	.50
357	Jim McKenzie	.10	.50
358	Brad McCrimmon	.10	.50
359	Andrew Cassels	.10	.50
360	James Patrick	.10	.50

LOS ANGELES KINGS

No.	Player	Regular NRMT	Emerald NRMT
361	**Bob Jay, RC**	**.15**	**.75**
362	Tomas Sandstrom	.10	.50
363	Pat Conacher	.10	.50
364	Shawn McEachern	.10	.50
365	Jari Kurri	.10	.50
366	Dominic Lavoie	.10	.50
367	David Taylor	.10	.50
368	Jimmy Carson	.10	.50
369	Mike Donnelley	.10	.50

MONTREAL CANADIENS

No.	Player	Regular NRMT	Emerald NRMT
370	Lyle Odelein	.10	.50
371	Brian Bellows	.10	.50
372	Guy Carbonneau	.10	.50
373	Mathieu Schneider	.10	.50
374	Stephan Lebeau	.10	.50
375	Benoit Brunet	.10	.50
376	Kevin Haller	.10	.50
377	Jean-Jacques Daigneault	.10	.50
378	Kirk Muller	.10	.50

NEW JERSEY DEVILS

No.	Player	Regular NRMT	Emerald NRMT
79	**Jason Smith, RC**	**.15**	**.75**
380	Martin Brodeur, Goalie	.50	2.50
381	Corey Millen	.10	.50
382	Bill Guerin	.10	.50
383	Valeri Zelepukin	.10	.50
384	Tom Chorske	.10	.50
385	Robert Holik	.10	.50
386	Jaroslav Modry, RC	.20	1.00
387	Kenneth Daneyko	.10	.50

NEW YORK ISLANDERS

No.	Player	Regular NRMT	Emerald NRMT
388	Uwe Krupp	.10	.50
389	Pierre Turgeon	.25	1.25
390	Marty McInnis	.10	.50
391	Patrick Flatley	.10	.50
392	Tom Kurvers	.10	.50
393	Brad Dalgarno	.10	.50
394	**Steve Junker, RC**	**.15**	**.75**
395	David Volek	.10	.50
396	Benoit Hogue	.10	.50
397	Zigmund Palffy	.10	.50

NEW YORK RANGERS

No.	Player	Regular NRMT	Emerald NRMT
398	Does not exist should be Steve Larmer		
399	**Joby Messier, RC**	**.15**	**.75**
400	Michael Gartner	.15	.75
401	Joey Kocur	.10	.50
402	Ed Olczyk	.10	.50
403	Doug Lidster	.10	.50
404A	Gregory Gilbert	.10	.50
404B	Steve Larmer	.10	.50
405	Glenn Healy, Goalie	.10	.50

OTTAWA SENATORS

No.	Player	Regular NRMT	Emerald NRMT
406	Dennis Vial	.10	.50
407	Darcy Loewen	.10	.50
408	Bob Kudelski	.10	.50
409	**Hank Lammens, RC**	**.15**	**.75**
410	Jarmo Kekalainen	.10	.50
411	Darren Rumble	.10	.50
412	Francois Leroux	.10	.50
413	Troy Mallette	.10	.50
414	**Bill Huard, RC**	**.15**	**.75**

PHILADELPHIA FLYERS

No.	Player	Regular NRMT	Emerald NRMT
415	Ryan McGill	.10	.50
416	Eric Lindros	3.00	15.00
417	Dominic Roussel, Goalie	.25	1.25
418	**Jason Bowen, RC**	**.15**	**.75**
419	Andre Faust	.10	.50
420	**Stewart Malgunas, RC**	**.15**	**.75**
421	Kevin Dineen	.10	.50
422	Yves Racine	.10	.50
423	Garry Galley	.10	.50

PITTSBURGH PENGUINS

No.	Player	Regular NRMT	Emerald NRMT
424	Doug Brown	.10	.50
425	Mario Lemieux	1.50	7.50
426	Ladislav Karabin	.10	.50
427	Grant Jennings	.10	.50
428	Rick Tocchet	.10	.50
429	Jeff Daniels	.10	.50
430	Peter Taglianetti	.10	.50
431	Bryan Trottier	.10	.50
432	Kjell Samuelsson	.10	.50

QUEBEC NORDIQUES

No.	Player	Regular NRMT	Emerald NRMT
433	**Rene Corbet, RC**	**.15**	**.75**
434	**Iain Fraser, RC**	**.20**	**1.00**
435	Mats Sundin	.20	1.00
436	Curtis Leschyshyn	.10	.50
437	Claude Lapointe	.10	.50
438	Valeri Kamensky	.20	1.00
439	Mike Ricci	.15	.75
440	Chris Lindberg	.10	.50
441	Alexei Gusarov	.10	.50

ST. LOUIS BLUES

No.	Player	Regular NRMT	Emerald NRMT
442	Tom Tilley	.10	.50
443	Craig Janney	.10	.50
444	Vitali Karamnov	.20	1.00
445	Bob Bassen	.10	.50
446	Igor Korolev	.20	1.00
447	**Kevin Miehm, RC**	**.15**	**.75**
448	Tony Hrkac	.10	.50
449	Garth Butcher	.10	.50
450	**Vitali Prokhorov, RC**	**.15**	**.75**

SAM JOSE SHARKS

No.	Player	Regular NRMT	Emerald NRMT
451	Arturs Irbe, Goalie	.40	2.00
452	Jayson More	.10	.50
453	Bob Errey	.10	.50
454	Mike Sullivan	.10	.50
455	Jeff Norton	.10	.50
456	Gaetan Duchesne	.10	.50
457	Doug Zmolek	.10	.50
458	**Mike Rathje, RC**	**.15**	**.75**
459	Jamie Baker	.10	.50

TAMPA BAY LIGHTNING

No.	Player	Regular NRMT	Emerald NRMT
460	Joe Reekie	.10	.50
461	Marc Bureau	.10	.50
462	John Tucker	.10	.50
463	**Bill McDougall, RC**	**.15**	**.75**

180 • PARKHURST — 1993-94 INSERT SETS

No.	Player	Regular NRMT	Emerald NRMT
464	Danton Cole	.10	.50
465	Brian Bradley	.10	.50
466	Jason Lafreniere	.10	.50
467	Donald Dufresne	.10	.50
468	Daren Puppa, Goalie	.10	.50

TORONTO MAPLE LEAFS

No.	Player	Regular NRMT	Emerald NRMT
469	Douglas Gilmour	.50	2.50
470	Damian Rhodes, Goalie	.30	1.50
471	Matt Martin, RC	.10	.50
472	Bill Berg	.10	.50
473	John Cullen	.10	.50
474	Rob Pearson	.10	.50
475	Wendel Clark	.20	1.00
476	Mark Osborne	.10	.50
477	Dmitri Mironov	.15	.75

VANCOUVER CANUCKS

No.	Player	Regular NRMT	Emerald NRMT
478A	Kay Whitmore, Goalie	.10	.50
478B	Kris King, Win.	.10	.50
479	Shawn Antoski	.10	.50
480	Greg Adams	.10	.50
481	David Babych	.10	.50
482	John McIntyre	.10	.50
483	Jyrki Lumme	.10	.50
484	Jose Charbonneau	.10	.50
485	Gino Odjick	.10	.50
486	Dana Murzyn	.10	.50

WASHINGTON CAPITALS

No.	Player	Regular NRMT	Emerald NRMT
487	Michal Pivonka	.10	.50
488	David Poulin	.10	.50
489	Sylvain Cote	.10	.50
490	Pat Peake	.15	.75
491	Kelly Miller	.10	.50
492	Randy Burridge	.10	.50
493	Kevin Kaminski, RC	.20	1.00
494	John Slaney	.10	.50
495	Keith Jones	.10	.50

WINNIPEG JETS

No.	Player	Regular NRMT	Emerald NRMT
496	Harijs Vitolinsh	.15	.75
497	Nelson Emerson	.10	.50
498	Does not exsit Should be Kris King	.10	.50
499	Darrin Shannon	.10	.50
500	Stephane Quintal	.10	.50
501	Luciano Borsato	.10	.50
502	Thomas Steen	.10	.50
503	Alexei Zhamnov	.40	2.00
504	Paul Ysebaert	.10	.50

WORLD JUNIOR

No.	Player	Regular NRMT	Emerald NRMT
505	Jeff Friesen	1.50	7.50
506	Niklas Sundstrom	.40	2.00
507	Nick Stajduhar	.40	2.00
508	Jamie Storr, Goalie	2.50	12.50
509	Valeri Bure	1.50	7.50
510	Jason Bonsignore	2.00	10.00
511	Mats Lindgren	.40	2.00
512	Yanick Dube	.50	2.50
513	Todd Harvey	.75	4.00

EURO JUNIORS

No.	Player	Regular NRMT	Emerald NRMT
514	Ladislav Prokupek	.25	1.25
515	Tomas Vlasak	.20	1.00
516	Josef Marha	.20	1.00
517	Tomas Blazek	.20	1.00
518	Zdenek Nedved	.30	1.50
519	Jaroslav Miklenda	.25	1.25
520	Janne Niinimaa	.25	1.25
521	Saku Koivu	.75	3.75
522	Tommi Miettinen	.15	.75
523	Tuomas Gronman	.10	.50
524	Jani Nikko	.15	.75
525	Jonni Vauhkonen	.10	.50
526	Nikolai Tsulygin	.10	.50
527	Vadim Sharifjanov	.50	2.50
528	Valeri Bure	1.25	6.75
529	Alexander Kharlamov	1.00	5.00
530	Nikolai Zavarukhin	.20	1.00
531	Oleg Tverdovski	1.25	6.25
532	Sergei Kondrashkin	.20	1.00
533	Evgeni Riabchikov	.40	2.00
534	Mats Lindgren	.40	2.00
535	Kenny Jonsson	.40	2.00
536	Edvin Frylen	.25	1.25
537	Mathias Johansson	.15	.75
538	Johan Davidsson	.15	.75
539	Mikael Hakansson	.15	.75
540	Anders Eriksson	.15	.75

— 1993 - 94 INSERT SETS —

EAST / WEST STARS

Randomly inserted in American Hobby Series Two foil packs.

1993-94 East / West Stars
Card No. W1, Wayne Gretzky

Card Size: 2 1/2" x 3 1/2"
Face: Four colour; Name, Logo, Silver foil logo
Back: Four colour, card stock; Name, Number, Resume
Imprint: © 1993 THE UPPER DECK COMPANY
Complete Set No.: 20
Complete Set Price: 200.00   400.00
Common Card: 7.50   15.00

No.	Player	EX	NRMT
E1	Eric Lindros, Phi.	25.00	50.00
E2	Mario Lemieux, Pit.	15.00	30.00
E3	Alexandre Daigle, Ott.	7.50	15.00
E4	Patrick Roy, Goalie, Mon.	14.00	28.00
E5	Rob Niedermayer, Fl.	7.50	15.00
E6	Chris Gratton	7.50	15.00
E7	Alexei Yashin, Ott.	10.00	20.00
E8	Pat LaFontaine, Buf.	7.50	15.00
E9	Joe Sakic, Que.	7.50	15.00
E10	Pierre Turgeon, NYI	7.50	15.00
W1	Wayne Gretzky, LA	25.00	50.00
W2	Pavel Bure, Van.	17.50	35.00
W3	Teemu Selanne, Win.	10.00	20.00
W4	Douglas Gilmour, Tor.	10.00	20.00
W5	Steve Yzerman, Det.	9.00	18.00
W6	Jeremy Roenick, Chi.	9.00	18.00
W7	Brett Hull, St.L	7.50	15.00
W8	Jason Arnott, Edm.	12.50	25.00
W9	Felix Potvin, Goalie, Tor.	10.00	20.00
W10	Sergei Federov, Det.	10.00	20.00

CALDER CANDIDATES

Randomly inserted in American Series Two Retail Foil packs.

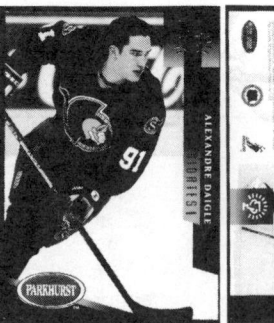 

1993-94 Calder Candidates
Card No. C1, Alexandre Daigle

Card Size: 2 1/2" x 3 1/2"
Face: Four colour
Back: Four colour
Imprint: © THE UPPER DECK COMPANY
Complete Set No.: 20
Complete Set Price: Silver 125.00   Gold 175.00
Common Card: 5.00   7.00

No.	Player	Silver	Gold
C1	Alexandre Daigle, Ott.	10.00	13.00
C2	Chris Pronger, Hart.	10.00	13.00
C3	Chris Gratton, TB	10.00	13.00
C4	Rob Niedermayer, Fl.	10.00	13.00
C5	Markus Naslund, Pit.	5.00	7.00
C6	Jason Arnott, Edm.	25.00	35.00
C7	Pierre Sevigny, Mon.	5.00	7.00
C8	Jarkko Varvio, Dal.	5.00	7.00
C9	Dean McAmmond, Edm.	5.00	7.00
C10	Alexei Yashin, Ott.	18.00	25.00
C11	Phillippe Boucher, Buf.	5.00	7.00
C12	Mikael Renberg, Phi.	15.00	25.00
C13	Chris Simon, Que.	5.00	7.00
C14	Brent Gretzky, TB	7.00	10.00
C15	Jesse Belanger, Fl.	7.00	10.00
C16	Jocelyn Thibault, Goalie, Que.	12.00	18.00
C17	Chris Osgood, Goalie, Det.	10.00	15.00
C18	Derek Plante, Buf.	10.00	15.00
C19	Iain Fraser, Que.	5.00	7.00
C20	Vesa Viitakoski, Cal.	5.00	7.00
---	Silver Trade Card	5.00	—
---	Gold Trade Card	—	10.00

Trade cards expired August 31, 1994

CHERRY'S PLAYOFF HEROES

Randomly inserted in Canadian Series Two foil packs.

1993-94 Cherry's Playoff Heroes
Card No. D1, Wayne Gretzky

Card Size: 2 1/2" x 3 1/2"
Face: Four colour
Back: Four colour
Imprint: © 1993 THE UPPER DECK COMPANY
Complete Set No.: 20
Complete Set Price: 250.00   500.00
Common Card: 7.50   15.00

PARKURST USA AND CANADA GOLD FOIL 181

No.	Player	EX	NRMT
D1	Wayne Gretzky, LA	45.00	95.00
D2	Mario Lemieux, Pit.	30.00	60.00
D3	Al MacInnis, Cal.	7.50	15.00
D4	Mark Messier, NYR	12.50	25.00
D5	Dino Ciccarelli, Det.	6.00	12.00
D6	Dale Hunter, Wash.	6.00	12.00
D7	Grant Fuhr, Goalie, Buf.	6.00	12.00
D8	Paul Coffey, Det.	7.50	15.00
D9	Douglas Gilmour, Tor.	20.00	40.00
D10	Patrick Roy, Goalie, Mon.	30.00	65.00
D11	Alexandre Daigle, Ott.	10.00	20.00
D12	Chris Gratton	10.00	20.00
D13	Chris Pronger, Hart.	10.00	20.00
D14	Felix Potvin, Goalie, Tor.	25.00	50.00
D15	Eric Lindros, Phi.	45.00	90.00
D16	Maurice Richard, Mon.	15.00	30.00
D17	Gordie Howe, Det.	20.00	40.00
D18	Henri Richard, Mon.	7.50	15.00
D19	Reggie Leach, Phi.	6.00	12.00
D20	Don Cherry Checklist	15.00	30.00

FIRSTS OVERALL

Randomly inserted in Canadian Series One foil packs.

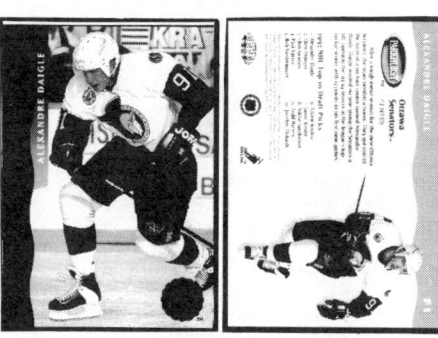

1993-94 Firsts Overall
Card No. F1, Alexandre Daigle

Card Size: 2 1/2" x 3 1/2"
Face: Four colour; Name
Back: Four colour; Name, Number, Team, Resume
Imprint: © 1993 THE UPPER DECK COMPANY
Complete Set No.: 10
Complete Set Price: 50.00 100.00
Common Card: 2.50 5.00

No.	Player	EX	NRMT
F1	Alexandre Daigle, Ott.	5.00	10.00
F2	Roman Hamrlik, TB	2.50	5.00
F3	Eric Lindros, Phi.	25.00	50.00
F4	Owen Nolan, Que.	3.50	7.00
F5	Mats Sundin, Que.	5.00	10.00
F6	Michael Modano, Dal.	5.00	10.00
F7	Pierre Turgeon, NYI	5.00	10.00
F8	Joe Murphy, Chi.	2.50	5.00
F9	Wendel Clark, Tor.	5.00	10.00
F10	Mario Lemieux, Pitt.	12.50	25.00

PARKIE REPRINTS

This set is a continuation of the Parkie Reprints that began in the 1992-93 season. The numbers are continuous. The cards were randomly inserted in all foil packs as listed below.

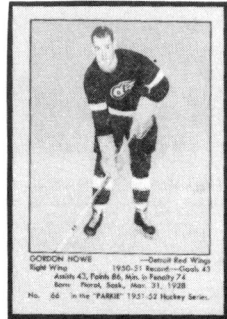 

1993-94 Parkie Reprints
Card No. PR33, Gordie Howe

Card Size: 2 1/2" x 3 1/2"
Face: Four colour; Name, Team, Position, Resume
Back: Four colour; Name, Number
Imprint: © PARKHURST™ PRINTED IN CANAA
Complete Set No.: 40
Complete Set Price: 300.00 600.00
Common Card: 5.00 10.00

SERIES ONE AMERICAN AND CANADIAN FOIL

No.	Player	EX	NRMT
PR33	Gordie Howe	17.50	35.00
PR34	Tim Horton	12.50	25.00
PR35	Bill Barilko	10.00	20.00
PR36	Elmer Lach, Maurice Richard	10.00	20.00
PR37	Terry Sawchuk	10.00	20.00
PR38	Camille Henry	5.00	10.00
PR39	Doug Harvey	7.50	15.00
PR40	Maurice Richard	12.50	25.00
PR41	Ted Kennedy	5.00	10.00
---	Checklist No. 5	17.50	35.00

SERIES ONE AMERICAN AND CANADIAN JUMBO

No.	Player	EX	NRMT
PR42	Gordie Howe, '51-52	17.50	35.00
PR43	Jacques Plante	12.50	25.00
PR44	Boom Boom Geoffrion	7.50	15.00
PR45	Gump Worsley	7.50	15.00
PR46	Billy Harris	7.50	15.00
PR47	Ted Lindsay	5.00	10.00
PR48	George Armstrong	5.00	10.00
PR49	Fern Flaman	5.00	10.00
PR50	Frank Mahovlich	10.00	20.00
---	Checklist No. 6	17.50	35.00

SERIES TWO AMERICAN AND CANADIAN FOIL

No.	Player	EX	NRMT
PR51	Gordie Howe	17.50	35.00
PR52	Jean Guy Talbot	5.00	10.00
PR53	Terry Sawchuk, Goalie	10.00	20.00
PR54	Warren Godfrey	5.00	10.00
PR55	Tom Johnson	5.00	10.00
PR56	Bert Olmstead	5.00	10.00
PR57	Cal Gardner	5.00	10.00
PR58	Red Kelly	5.00	10.00
PR59	Phil Goyette	5.00	10.00
---	Checklist No. 7	17.50	35.00

SERIES TWO AMERICAN AND CANADIAN JUMBO

No.	Player	EX	NRMT
PR60	Gordie Howe	17.50	35.00
PR61	Lou Fontinato	5.00	10.00
PR62	Bill Dineen	5.00	10.00
PR63	Maurice Richard	12.50	25.00
PR64	Vic Stasiuk	5.00	10.00
PR65	Marcel Pronovost	5.00	10.00
PR66	Ed Litzenberger	5.00	10.00
PR67	Dave Keon	7.50	15.00
PR68	Dollard St. Laurent	17.50	35.00
---	Checklist No. 7	17.50	35.00

PARKIE CASE INSERTS

Inserted into every case were six cards. Series One had DPR1 to DPR6 inserted while DPR7 to DPR12 was inserted in Series Two cases.

1993-94 Parkie Case Inserts
Card No. DPR1, Gordie Howe

Card Size: 2 1/2" X 3 1/2"
Face: Four Colour, white border
Back: Black or red on white card stock; Name, Number, Resume, Bilingual
Imprint: PARKHURST™ PRINTED IN CANADA
Complete Set No.: 12
Complete Set Price: 17.50 35.00

No.	Player	EX	NRMT
DPR1	Gordie Howe	3.70	7.00
DPR2	Milt Schmidt	1.00	2.00
DPR3	Tim Horton	2.00	4.00
DPR4	Al Rollins, Goalie	1.00	2.00
DPR5	Maurice Richard	2.50	5.00
DPR6	Harry Howell	1.00	2.00
DPR7	Gordie Howe	3.50	7.00
DPR8	Johnny Bower, Goalie	1.00	2.00
DPR9	Dean Prentice	1.00	2.00
DPR10	Leo Labine	1.00	2.00
DPR11	Harry Watson	1.00	2.00
DPR12	Dickie Moore	1.50	3.00

USA AND CANADA GOLD FOIL

Randomly inserted in American Series One Hobby and Retail foil packs.

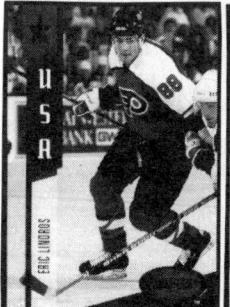 

1993-94 USA and Canada Gold Foil
Card No. 3, Eric Lindros

Card Size: 2 1/2" x 3 1/2"
Face: Four colour; Name, Gold foil
Back: Four colour; Name, Number, Team, Resume
Imprint: ©
Complete Set No.: 10
Complete Set Price: 75.00 150.00
Common Card: 5.00 10.00

No.	Player	EX	NRMT
1	Wayne Gretzky, LA	25.00	50.00
2	Mario Lemieux, Pit.	15.00	30.00
3	Eric Lindros, Phi.	20.00	40.00
4	Brett Hull, St.L	6.00	12.00
5	Rob Niedermayer, TB	5.00	10.00
6	Alexandre Daigle, Ott.	6.00	12.00
7	Pavel Bure, Van.	15.00	30.00
8	Teemu Selanne, Win.	7.50	15.00
9	Patrick Roy, Mon.	12.50	25.00
10	Doug Gilmour, Tor.	7.50	15.00

PARKHURST — 1993-94 ISSUES

— 1993-94 ISSUES —

THE MISSING LINK 1956-57

PROMOTIONAL CARDS

Issued at the Sportscard and Memorabilia Expo during the Spring of 1994. The regular issue cards listed below were overprinted in black "Promotional"

 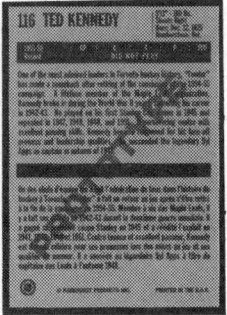

1993-94 Missing Link Promotional Card
Ted Kennedy

Card Size: 2 1/2" x 3 1/2"
Face: Four colour
Back: Four colour
Imprint: © PARKHURST PRODUCTS INC. PRINTED IN U.S.A.
Complete Set No.: 3
Complete Set Price: 7.50   15.00

No.	Player	EX	NRMT
	Doug Harvey	2.50	5.00
	Ted Kennedy	2.50	5.00
	Ed Chadwick	2.50	5.00

PROMOTIONAL SHEET

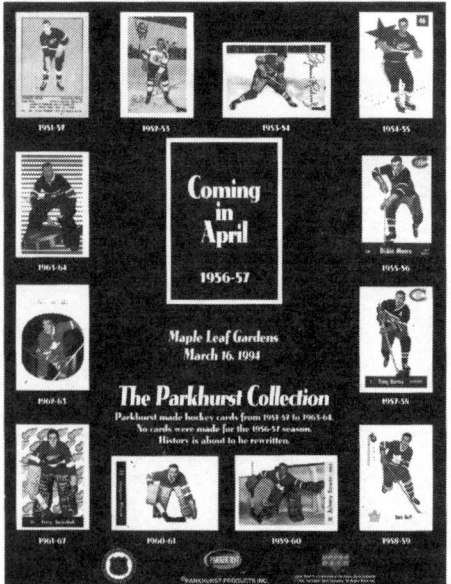

1993-94 Missing Link
Promotional Sheet

Card Size: 8 1/2" X 11"
Face: Four colour, black border
Back: Blank
Imprint: © PARKHURST PRODUCTS INC. PRINTED IN U.S.A.

No.	Player	EX	NRMT
	Sheet	7.50	15.00

— 1956-57 MISSING LINK —

In 1994 Parkhurst began filling in the missing years by issuing cards which may be considered comparable to cards of the period. Style, format and packaging design were reproduced.

 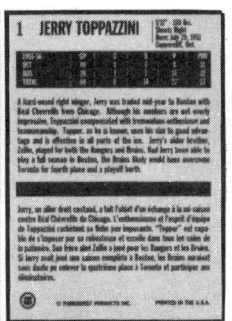

1994-95 Issue
Card No. 1, Jerry Toppazzini

Card Size: 2 1/2" x 3 1/2"
Face: Four colour; Name, Team logo
Back: Four colour, card stock; Name, Number, Resume
Imprint: © PARKHURST PRODUCTS INC. PRINTED IN U.S.A.
Complete Set No.: 180
Complete Set Price: 25.00   50.00
Common Player: .12   .25
Wax Pack: (10 Cards) 1.50   3.00
Wax Box: (24 Wax Packs) 35.00   70.00

BOSTON BRUINS

No.	Player	EX	NRMT
1	Jerry Toppazzini	.12	.25
2	Fern Flaman	.12	.25
3	Fleming MacKell	.12	.25
4	Leo Labine	.12	.25
5	John Peirson	.12	.25
6	Don McKenney	.12	.25
7	Bob Armstrong	.12	.25
8	Real Chevrefils	.12	.25
9	Vic Stasiuk	.12	.25
10	Cal Gardner	.12	.25
11	Leo Boivin	.12	.25
12	Jack Caffery	.12	.25
13	Bob Beckett	.12	.25
14	Jack Bionda	.12	.25
15	Claude Pronovost	.12	.25
16	Larry Regan	.12	.25
17	Terry Sawchuk, Goalie	1.00	2.00
18	Doug Mohns	.12	.25
19	Marcel Bonin	.12	.25
20	Allan Stanley	.25	.50
21	Milt Schmidt, Coach	.25	.50

CHICAGO BLACK HAWKS

No.	Player	EX	NRMT
22	Al Dewsbury	.12	.25
23	Glen Skov	.12	.25
24	Ed Litzenberger	.12	.25
25	Nick Mickoski	.12	.25
26	Wally Hergesheimer	.12	.25
27	Jack McIntyre	.12	.25
28	Al Rollins, Goalie	.12	.25
29	Hank Ciesla	.12	.25
30	Gus Mortson	.12	.25
31	Elmer Vasko	.12	.25
32	Pierre Pilote	.25	.50
33	Ron Ingram	.12	.25
34	Frank Martin	.12	.25
35	Forbes Kennedy	.12	.25
36	Harry Watson	.12	.25
37	Eddie Kachur	.12	.25
38	Hec Lalande	.12	.25
39	Eric Nesterenko	.12	.25
40	Ben Woit	.12	.25
41	Ken Mosdell	.12	.25
42	Tommy Ivan, Coach	.12	.25

DETROIT RED WINGS

No.	Player	EX	NRMT
43	Gordie Howe	2.00	4.00
44	Ted Lindsay	.50	1.00
45	Norm Ullman	.50	1.00
46	Glenn Hall, Goalie	.12	.25
47	Billy Dea	.12	.25
48	Bill McNeill	.12	.25
49	Earl Reibel	.12	.25
50	Bill Dineen	.12	.25
51	Warren Godfrey	.12	.25
52	Red Kelly	.50	1.00
53	Marty Pavelich	.12	.25
54	Lorne Ferguson	.12	.25
55	Larry Hillman	.12	.25
56	John Bucyk	.25	.50
57	Metro Prystai	.12	.25
58	Marcel Pronovost	.25	.50
59	Alex Delvecchio	.50	1.00
60	Murray Costello	.12	.25
61	Al Arbour	.25	.50
62	Bucky Hollingworth	.12	.25
63	Jim Skinner, Coach	.12	.25

MONTREAL CANADIENS

No.	Player	EX	NRMT
64	Jean Beliveau	1.50	3.00
65	Maurice Richard	2.00	4.00
66	Henri Richard	.35	.75
67	Doug Harvey	.35	.75
68	Bernie Geoffrion	.35	.75
69	Dollard St. Laurent	.12	.25
70	Dickie Moore	.25	.50
71	Bert Olmstead	.25	.50
72	Jacques Plante, Goalie	1.50	3.00
73	Claude Provost	.12	.25
74	Phil Goyette	.12	.25
75	Andre Pronovost	.12	.25
76	Don Marshall	.12	.25
77	Ralph Backstrom	.12	.25
78	Floyd Curry	.12	.25
79	Tom Johnson	.12	.25
80	Jean-Guy Talbot	.12	.25
81	Bob Turner	.12	.25
82	Connie Broden	.12	.25
83	Jackie Leclair	.12	.25
84	Toe Blake	.12	.25
85	Frank Selke, Coach	.12	.25

NEW YORK RANGERS

No.	Player	EX	NRMT
86	George Sullivan	.12	.25
87	Larry Cahan	.12	.25
88	Jean Guy Gendron	.12	.25
89	Bill Gadsby	.25	.50
90	Andy Bathgate	.25	.50
91	Dean Prentice	.12	.25
92	Lorne (Gump) Worsley, Goalie	.50	1.00
93	Lou Fontinato	.12	.25
94	Gerry Foley	.12	.25
95	Larry Popein	.12	.25
96	Harry Howell	.35	.75
97	Andy Hebenton	.12	.25
98	Danny Lewicki	.12	.25
99	Dave Creighton	.12	.25
100	Camille Henry	.12	.25
101	Jack Evans	.12	.25
102	Ron Murphy	.12	.25
103	Johnny Bower, Goalie	.50	1.00
104	Parker MacDonald	.12	.25
105	Bronco Horvath	.12	.25
106	Bruce Cline	.12	.25
107	Ivan Irwin	.12	.25
108	Phil Watson, Coach	.12	.25

TORONTO MAPLE LEAFS

No.	Player	EX	NRMT
109	Sid Smith	.12	.25
110	Ron Stewart	.12	.25
111	Rudy Migay	.12	.25
112	Tod Sloan	.12	.25
113	Bob Pulford	.12	.25
114	Marc Reaume	.12	.25

PARKURST US AND CANADIAN POP UP GREATS 183

No.	Player	EX	NRMT
115	Jim Morrison	.12	.25
116	Ted Kennedy	.25	.50
117	Gerry James	.12	.25
118	Brian Cullen	.12	.25
119	Jim Thomson	.12	.25
120	Barry Cullen	.12	.25
121	Al MacNeil	.12	.25
122	Gary Aldcorn	.12	.25
123	Bob Baun	.12	.25
124	Hugh Bolton	.12	.25
125	George Armstrong	.25	.50
126	Dick Duff	.12	.25
127	Tim Horton	1.00	2.00
128	Ed Chadwick, Goalie	.12	.25
129	Billy Harris	.12	.25
130	Mike Nykoluk	.12	.25
131	Noel Price	.12	.25
132	Ken Girard	.12	.25
133	Howie Meeker	.25	.50
134	Hap Day, Coach	.12	.25

FIRST TEAM ALL STAR

No.	Player	EX	NRMT
135	Jacques Plante, Goalie, Mon.	.50	1.00
136	Doug Harvey, Mon.	.12	.25
137	Bill Gadsby, NYR	.12	.25
138	Jean Beliveau, Mon.	.50	1.00
139	Maurice Richard, Mon.	1.00	2.00
140	Ted Lindsay, Det.	.12	.25

SECOND TEAM ALL STAR

No.	Player	EX	NRMT
141	Glenn Hall, Goalie, Det.	.25	.50
142	Red Kelly, Det.	.12	.25
143	Tom Johnson, Mon.	.12	.25
144	Tod Sloan, Tor.	.12	.25
145	Gordie Howe, Det.	1.00	2.00
146	Bert Olmstead, Mon.	.12	.25
147	Earl Reibel, Det.	.12	.25
148	Doug Harvey, Mon.	.12	.25
149	Jean Beliveau, Mon.	.50	1.00

TROPHY WINNERS

No.	Player	EX	NRMT
150	Art Ross Trophy: Jean Beliveau	.50	1.00
151	Vezina Trophy: Jacques Plante	.75	1.50
152	Calder Trophy: Glenn Hall	.25	.50
153	Sawchuk Picks Pocket	.50	1.00
154	Opening Nights Face-Off	.12	.25
155	Lindsay Loses Battle	.12	.25
156	Beliveau Draws Crowd	.50	1.00
157	Beliveau In Close	.50	1.00
158	Leafs Besiege Hall	.25	.50
159	Hall Makes The Save	.25	.50
160	Howe Notches Another	1.00	2.00
161	Plante Stands Guard	.50	1.00
162	Howe Outhustles Habs	1.00	2.00
163	Plante's Flying Save	.50	1.00
164	Canadien's Big Line	.50	1.00
165	Gump Stops Leafs	.25	.50
166	Rollins Eyes Teeder	.12	.25
167	Sawchuk Foils Duff	.35	.75
168	Sawchuk In Action	.35	.75

SCORING LEADERS 1955/1956

No.	Player	EX	NRMT
169	Vic Stasiuk, Bos.	.12	.25
170	George Sullivan, Chi.	.12	.25
171	Gordie Howe, Det.	1.00	2.00
172	Jean Beliveau, Mon.	.50	1.00
173	Andy Bathgate, NYR	.25	.50
174	Tod Sloan, Tor.	.12	.25

1956 STANLEY CUP FINAL

No.	Player	EX	NRMT
175	1955-56 Semi-Finals: Montreal 4 - New York 1	.12	.25
176	1955-56 Semi-Finals: Detroit 4 - Toronto 1	.12	.25
177	1955-56 Semi-Finals: Montreal 4 - Detroit 1	.12	.25
178	Stanley Cup Champions: Montreal Canadiens	.12	.25
179	Tally Card #1 (1/90)	.12	.25
180	Tally Card #2 (91/180)	.12	.25

— 1993 - 94 INSERT SETS —

AUTOGRAPHED CARDS

Six different players signed 956 cards. all are hand numbered and hand signed. These were randomly inserted into all packs.

1993-94 Parkhurst Missing Link
Autographed Cards
Card No. A-6, Frank Mahovlich

Card Size: 2 1/2" X 3 1/2"
Face: Four colour, white border; Autograph
Back: Black on card stock; Name, Number
Imprint: © PARKHURST PRODUCTS INC.
PRINTED IN THE U.S.A.
Complete Set No.: 6
Complete Set Price: 425.00 850.00

No.	Player	EX	NRMT
A-1	Gordie Howe, Det.	150.00	300.00
A-2	Maurice Richard, Mon.	125.00	250.00
A-3	Bernie Geoffrion, Mon.	75.00	150.00
A-4	Lorne (Gump) Worsley, NYR	75.00	150.00
A-5	Jean Beliveau, Mon.	100.00	200.00
A-6	Frank Mahovlich, Tor.	100.00	200.00

FUTURE STARS

Randomly inserted in Canadian and American wax boxes at the rate of one card per box.

Future Stars
Card No. FS-1, Carl Brewer

Card Size: 2 1/2" X 3 1/2"
Face: Four colour, borderless; Name
Back: Black on brown card stock; Name, Number, Resume
Imprint: © PARKHURST PRODUCTS INC. PRINTED IN THE U.S.A.
Complete Set No.: 6
Complete Set Price: 50.00 100.00

No.	Player	EX	NRMT
FS-1	Carl Brewer	7.50	15.00
FS-2	Dave Keon	12.50	25.00
FS-3	Stan Mikita	15.00	30.00
FS-4	Eddie Shack	10.00	20.00
FS-5	Frank Mahovlich	15.00	30.00
FS-6	Charlie Hodge, Goalie	10.00	20.00

US AND CANADIAN POP UP GREATS

Cards P1 to P6 were randomly inserted in Canadian wax packs. Cards P7 to P12 were randomly inserted in American wax packs.

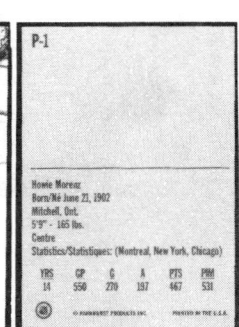

US and Canadian Pop-up Greats
Card No. P-1, Howie Morenz

Card Size: 2 1/2" x 3 1/2"
Face: Four colour; Name
Back: Black and white, Name, Resume
Imprint: PARKHURST PRODUCTS INC.
PRINTED IN THE U.S.A.
Complete Set No.: 12
Complete Set Price: 275.00 550.00

No.	Player	EX	NRMT
P-1	Howie Morenz, Mon.	35.00	75.00
P-2	George Hainsworth, Goalie, Mon.	20.00	40.00
P-3	Georges Vezina, Goalie, Mon.	35.00	70.00
P-4	King Clancy, Tor.	25.00	50.00
P-5	Syl Apps, Tor.	20.00	40.00
P-6	Turk Broda, Goalie, Tor.	20.00	40.00
P-7	Eddie Shore, Bos.	30.00	60.00
P-8	Bill Cook, NYR	20.00	40.00
P-9	Woody Dumart, Bos.	20.00	40.00
P10	Lester Patrick, NYR	25.00	50.00
P11	Doug Bentley, Chi.	20.00	40.00
P12	Earl Seibert, NYR	20.00	40.00

NHL ALL-STAR REDEMPTION SHEET

For ten wax wrappers and $19.95 you could obtain the redemption sheet which featured the 1956-57 All-Star team.

NHL All-Star Redemption Sheet

Card Size: 8 1/2" x 11"
Face: Four colour, white border
Back: Blank
Imprint: © 1994 PARKHURST PRODUCTS INC. PRINTED IN THE U.S.A.

No.	Player	EX	NRMT
	1956-57 All-star Team	12.50	25.00

1994 - 95 ISSUES

GOLD AND SILVER PARKIES

The first series of 315 cards was silver foil-stamped on the face with a small hockey player in the lower right corner. An insert card, gold foil-stamped with the same small player, was inserted one per 48 packs.

1994-95 Regular Issue
Card No. 1, Anatoli Semenov

Card Size: 2 1/2" x 3 1/2"
Face: Four colour, borderless; Name, Logo, Silver foil logo
Back: Four colour
Imprint: © 1994 THE UPPER DECK COMPANY

	Regular	Gold
Complete Set No.: 315		
Complete Set Price:	12.50	2500.00
Common Card:	.10	5.00
Wax Pack: (10 Cards)		1.25
Wax Box: (48 Packs)		55.00

SERIES ONE

MIGHTY DUCKS OF ANAHEIM

No.	Player	Regular NRMT	Gold NRMT
1	Anatoli Semenov	.10	5.00
2	Stephan Lebeau	.10	5.00
3	Stu Grimson	.10	5.00
4	Mikhail Shtalenkov, Goalie	.15	7.50
5	Troy Loney	.10	5.00
6	Sean Hill	.10	5.00
7	Patrick Carnback	.10	5.00
8	John Lilley	.10	5.00
9	Tim Sweeney	.10	5.00
10	Maxim Bets	.10	5.00

BOSTON BRUINS

No.	Player	Regular NRMT	Gold NRMT
11	Cam Neely	.20	10.00
12	Bryan Smolinski	.40	20.00
13	Raymond Bourque	.20	10.00
14	Vincent Riendeau, Goalie	.10	5.00
15	Al Iafrate	.15	7.50
16	Andrew McKim	.10	5.00
17	Glen Wesley	.10	5.00
18	Daniel Marois	.10	5.00
19	Jozef Stumpel	.20	10.00

BUFFALO SABRES

No.	Player	Regular EX	Gold NRMT
20	**Mariusz Czerkawski, RC**	.15	7.50
21	Alexander Mogilny	.25	12.00
22	Yuri Khmylev	.10	5.00
23	**Denis Tsygurov, RC**	.15	7.50
24	Dominik Hasek, Goalie	.20	10.00
25	Derek Plante	.40	20.00
26	Brad May	.10	5.00
27	Wayne Presley	.10	5.00
28	Richard Smehlik	.10	5.00
29	Dale Hawerchuk	.10	5.00
30	Robert Ray	.10	5.00

CALGARY FLAMES

No.	Player	Regular EX	Gold NRMT
31	Zarley Zalapski	.10	5.00
32	Michael Nylander	.20	10.00
33	Joe Nieuwendyk	.10	5.00
34	Robert Reichel	.10	5.00
35	Allan MacInnis	.10	5.00
36	Andrei Trefilov, Goalie	.20	10.00
37	**Leonard Esau, RC**	.15	7.50
38	Wes Walz	.10	5.00
39	Michel Petit	.10	5.00
40	James Patrick	.10	5.00

CHICAGO BLACK HAWKS

No.	Player	Regular NRMT	Gold NRMT
41	Ed Belfour, Goalie	.20	10.00
42	Christian Ruuttu	.10	5.00
43	Eric Weinrich	.10	5.00
44	Joe Murphy	.10	5.00
45	Chris Chelios	.10	5.00
46	Jeff Shantz	.10	5.00
47	Gary Suter	.10	5.00
48	Paul Ysebaert	.10	5.00
49	Ivan Droppa	.10	5.00
50	Sergei Krivokrasov	.10	5.00

DALLAS STARS

No.	Player	Regular NRMT	Gold NRMT
51	Andrew Moog, Goalie	.10	5.00
52	Russell Courtnall	.10	5.00
53	Neal Broten	.10	5.00
54	Mike Craig	.10	5.00
55	Brent Gilchrist	.10	5.00
56	Per-Erik Eklund	.10	5.00
57	Richard Matvichuk	.10	5.00
58	Dave Gagner	.10	5.00
59	Derrick Smith	.10	5.00
60	Paul Broten	.10	5.00

DETROIT RED WINGS

No.	Player	Regular NRMT	Gold NRMT
61	Nicklas Lidstrom	.10	5.00
62	Shawn Burr	.10	5.00
63	Paul Coffey	.15	7.50
64	Bob Essensa, Goalie	.10	5.00
65	Dino Ciccarelli	.10	5.00
66	Vyacheslav Kozlov	.40	20.00
67	Keith Primeau	.10	5.00
68	Steve Chiasson	.10	5.00
69	Terry Carkner	.10	5.00
70	Martin Lapointe	.10	5.00
71	Bob Probert	.10	5.00

EDMONTON OILERS

No.	Player	Regular NRMT	Gold NRMT
72	Bill Ranford, Goalie	.10	5.00
73	Illya Byakin	.10	5.00
74	Doug Weight	.10	5.00
75	Shayne Corson	.10	5.00
76	Zdeno Ciger	.10	5.00
77	Todd Marchant	.10	5.00
78	Scott Pearson	.10	5.00
79	Brent Grieve	.10	5.00
80	**Alexander Kerch, RC**	.15	7.50
81	Shjon Podein	.10	5.00
82	Geoff Smith	.10	5.00

FLORIDA PANTHERS

No.	Player	Regular NRMT	Gold NRMT
83	Bob Kudelski	.10	5.00
84	Andrei Lomakin	.10	5.00
85	Scott Mellanby	.10	5.00
86	Jesse Belanger	.10	5.00
87	Mark Fitzpatrick, Goalie	.10	5.00
88	Peter Andersson	.10	5.00
89	Jody Hull	.10	5.00
90	Brent Severyn	.10	5.00
91	Jocelyn Lemieux	.10	5.00

HARTFORD WHALERS

No.	Player	Regular NRMT	Gold NRMT
92	Patrick Verbeek	.10	5.00
93	Ted Crowley	.10	5.00
94	Paul Ranheim	.10	5.00
95	Geoff Sanderson	.20	10.00
96	Jeff Reese, Goalie	.10	5.00
97	Andrew Cassels	.10	5.00
98	Igor Chibirev	.10	5.00
99	Kevin Smyth	.10	5.00
100	John Stevens	.10	5.00

LOS ANGELES KINGS

No.	Player	Regular NRMT	Gold NRMT
101	Alexei Zhitnik	.10	5.00
102	**Justin Hocking, RC**	.15	7.50
103	Wayne Gretzky	1.50	150.00
104	Jari Kurri	.10	5.00
105	Robert Blake	.10	5.00
106	Martin McSorley	.10	5.00
107	Pat Conacher	.10	5.00
108	Kevin Todd	.10	5.00
109	Robb Stauber, Goalie	.10	5.00
110	Keith Redmond	.10	5.00

MONTREAL CANADIENS

No.	Player	Regular NRMT	Gold NRMT
111	John LeClair	.10	5.00
112	Brian Bellows	.10	5.00
113	Patrick Roy, Goalie	.75	125.00
114	Lindsay Vallis	.10	5.00
115	Vincent Damphousse	.10	5.00
116	Patrice Brisebois	.10	5.00
117	Gerry Fleming	.10	5.00
118	Eric Desjardins	.10	5.00
119	Donald Brashear	.10	5.00
120	Kevin Haller	.10	5.00
121	Brian Savage	.10	5.00

NEW JERSEY DEVILS

No.	Player	Regular NRMT	Gold NRMT
122	Corey Millen	.10	5.00
123	Jaroslav Modry	.10	5.00
124	Valeri Zelepukin	.10	5.00
125	John MacLean	.10	5.00
126	Martin Brodeur, Goalie	.40	20.00
127	Bill Guerin	.10	5.00
128	Robert Holik	.10	5.00
129	Claude Lemieux	.10	5.00
130	Jason Smith	.10	5.00
131	Kenneth Daneyko	.10	5.00

NEW YORK ISLANDERS

No.	Player	Regular NRMT	Gold NRMT
132	Derek King	.10	5.00
133	Darius Kasparaitis	.10	5.00
134	Ray Ferraro	.10	5.00
135	Pierre Turgeon	.10	5.00
136	Ron Hextall, Goalie	.10	5.00
137	Zigmund Palffy	.10	5.00
138	Joseph Day	.10	5.00
139	David Volek	.10	5.00
140	Scott Lachance	.10	5.00
141	Dennis Vaske	.10	5.00

NEW YORK RANGERS

No.	Player	Regular NRMT	Gold NRMT
142	Alexei Kovalev	.40	20.00
143	Brian Noonan	.10	5.00
144	Sergei Zubov	.20	10.00
145	Craig MacTavish	.10	5.00
146	Steve Larmer	.10	5.00
147	Adam Graves	.25	15.00
148	Daniel Lacroix	.10	5.00
149	Corey Hirsch, Goalie	.10	5.00
150	Stephane Matteau	.10	5.00
151	Brian Leetch	.25	5.00

PARKURST — 1994-95 ISSUES — 185

OTTAWA SENATORS

No.	Player	NRMT
152	**Mattias Norstrom, RC**	.15 / 7.50
153	Sylvain Turgeon	.10 / 5.00
154	Norm Maciver	.10 / 5.00
155	Scott Levins	.10 / 5.00
156	Derek Mayer	.10 / 5.00
157	Dave McLlwain	.10 / 5.00
158	Craig Billington, Goalie	.10 / 5.00
159	Claude Boivin	.10 / 5.00
160	Kevin MacDonald	.10 / 5.00
161	Evgeny Davydov	.10 / 5.00
162	Dimitri Filimonov	.10 / 5.00

PHILADELPHIA FLYERS

No.	Player	Regular NRMT	Gold NRMT
163	Dimitri Yushkevich	.10	5.00
164	Todd Hlushko	.10	5.00
165	Mark Recchi	.20	10.00
166	Josef Beranek	.10	5.00
167	Rod Brind'Amour	.20	10.00
168	Yves Racine	.10	5.00
169	Frederic Chabot, Goalie	.10	5.00
170	Brent Fedyk	.10	5.00
171	Bob Wilkie	.10	5.00
172	Kevin Dineen	.10	5.00

PITTSBURGH PENGUINS

No.	Player	Regular EX	Gold NRMT
173	Shawn McEachern	.10	5.00
174	Jaromir Jagr	.30	15.00
175	Tomas Sandstrom	.10	5.00
176	Ronald Francis	.10	5.00
177	Kevin Stevens	.10	5.00
178	Chris Tamer	.10	5.00
179	Lawrence Murphy	.10	5.00
180	Joe Mullen	.10	5.00
181	Justin Duberman	.10	5.00
182	Tom Barraso, Goalie	.10	5.00
183	Ulf Samuelsson	.10	5.00

QUEBEC NORDIQUES

No.	Player	Regular NRMT	Gold NRMT
184	Bob Bassen	.10	5.00
185	Mats Sundin	.20	10.00
186	Mike Ricci	.10	5.00
187	Iain Fraser	.10	5.00
188	Garth Butcher	.10	5.00
189	Jocelyn Thibault, Goalie	.25	12.50
190	Valeri Kamensky	.10	5.00
191	Garth Snow, Goalie	.10	5.00
192	Dwayne Norris	.10	5.00
193	Rene Corbet	.10	5.00
194	Jon Klemm	.10	5.00

ST. LOUIS BLUES

No.	Player	Regular NRMT	Gold NRMT
195	Alexei Kasatonov	.10	5.00
196	Brendan Shanahan	.20	10.00
197	Phil Housley	.10	5.00
198	Jim Montgomery	.10	5.00
199	Curtis Joseph, Goalie	.25	12.50
200	Craig Janney	.10	5.00
201	Ian Laperriere	.10	5.00
202	Dave Mackey	.10	5.00
203	Peter Stastny	.10	5.00
204	**Terry Hollinger, RC**	.15	7.50
205	Steve Duchesne	.10	5.00
206	Vitali Prokhorov	.10	5.00

SAN JOSE SHARKS

No.	Player	Regular NRMT	Gold NRMT
207	Rob Gaudreau	.10	5.00
208	Sandis Ozolinsh	.20	10.00
209	Johan Garpenlov	.10	5.00
210	Todd Elik	.10	5.00
211	Sergei Makarov	.10	5.00

No.	Player	Regular EX	Gold NRMT
212	Jean-Francois Quintin	.10	5.00
213	Vyacheslav Butsayev	.10	5.00
214	Jimmy Waite, Goalie	.10	5.00
215	Ulf Dahlen	.10	5.00
216	Andrei Nazarov	.10	5.00

TAMPA BAT LIGHTNING

No.	Player	Regular NRMT	Gold NRMT
217	Denis Savard	.10	5.00
218	Brent Gretzky	.10	5.00
219	Petr Klima	.10	5.00
220	Chris Gratton	.30	15.00
221	Brian Bradley	.10	5.00
222	Adam Creighton	.10	5.00
223	Eric Charron	.10	5.00
224	Rob Zamuner	.10	5.00
225	Daren Puppa, Goalie	.10	5.00
226	Bo Mikael Andersson	.10	5.00

TORONTO MAPLE LEAFS

No.	Player	Regular NRMT	Gold NRMT
227	David Ellett	.10	5.00
228	Michael Gartner	.10	5.00
229	Felix Potvin, Goalie	.50	25.00
230	Yanic Perreault	.10	5.00
231	Nikolai Borschevsky	.10	5.00
232	John Cullen	.10	5.00
233	David Harlock	.10	5.00
234	Eric Lacroix	.10	5.00
235	Kent Manderville	.10	5.00
236	David Sacco	.10	5.00
237	Frank Bialowas	.10	5.00

VANCOUVER CANUCKS

No.	Player	Regular NRMT	Gold NRMT
238	Kirk McLean, Goalie	.20	10.00
239	Jimmy Carson	.10	5.00
240	Geoff Courtnall	.10	5.00
241	Trevor Linden	.20	10.00
242	Murray Craven	.10	5.00
243	Brent Hedican	.10	5.00
244	Jeff Brown	.10	5.00
245	Mike Peca	.10	5.00
246	Yevgeny Namestnikov	.10	5.00
247	Nathan Lafayette	.10	5.00
248	Shawn Antoski	.10	5.00
249	Sergio Momesso	.10	5.00

WASHINGTON CAPITALS

No.	Player	Regular NRMT	Gold NRMT
250	Mike Ridley	.10	5.00
251	Peter Bondra	.10	5.00
252	Dimitri Khristich	.10	5.00
253	Joseph Juneau	.30	15.00
254	Dale Hunter	.10	5.00
255	Byron Dafoe, Goalie	.10	5.00
256	Kelly Miller	.10	5.00
257	John Slaney	.10	5.00
258	Todd Krygier	.10	5.00
259	Jason Wolley	.10	5.00

WINNIPEG JETS

No.	Player	Regular NRMT	Gold NRMT
260	Alexei Zhamnov	.25	12.50
261	Dallas Drake	.15	7.50
262	Dave Manson	.10	5.00
263	Thomas Steen	.10	5.00
264	Keith Tkachuk	.25	12.50
265	Craig Fisher	.10	5.00
266	Kevin McClelland	.10	5.00
267	Nelson Emerson	.10	5.00
268	**Michael O'Neill, Goalie, RC**	.15	7.50
269	Kris King	.10	5.00
270	Teppo Numminen	.10	5.00

1993-94 ROOKIE STANDOUTS

No.	Player	Regular NRMT	Gold NRMT
271	Jason Arnott, Edm.	1.00	50.00
272	Mikael Renberg, Phi.	.30	15.00
273	Alexei Yashin, Ott.	.60	30.00
274	Chris Pronger, Hart.	.30	15.00
275	Jocelyn Thibault, Goalie, Que.	.20	10.00
276	Bryan Smolinski, Bos.	.20	10.00

No.	Player	Regular NRMT	Gold NRMT
277	Derek Plante, Buf.	.50	25.00
278	Martin Brodeur, Goalie, NJ	.40	20.00
279	Boris Mironov, Win.	.15	7.50
280	Iain Fraser, Que.	.10	5.00
281	Pat Peake, Wash.	.10	5.00
282	Chris Gratton, TB	.30	15.00
283	Chris Osgood, Goalie, Det.	.30	15.00
284	Jesse Belanger, Fl.	.15	7.50
285	Alexandre Daigle, Ott.	.40	20.00
286	Robert Lang, LA	.10	5.00
287	Markus Naslund, Pit.	.10	5.00
288	Trevor Kidd, Goalie, Cal.	.10	5.00
289	Jeff Shantz, Chi.	.10	5.00
290	Jaroslav Modry, NJ	.10	5.00
291	Oleg Petrov, Mon.	.10	5.00
292	Scott Levins, Win.	.10	5.00
293	Jozef Stumpel, Bos.	.10	5.00
294	Rob Niedermayer, FL.	.30	15.00
295	Brent Gretzky, TB	.15	7.50

1993-94 STARS

No.	Player	Regular NRMT	Gold NRMT
296	Mario Lemieux, Pit.	1.00	75.00
297	Pavel Bure, Van.	1.00	75.00
298	Brendan Shanahan, St.L	.20	10.00
299	Steve Yzerman, Det.	.25	12.50
300	Teemu Selanne, Win.	.30	15.00
301	Eric Lindros, Phi.	1.00	150.00
302	Jeremy Roenick, Chi.	.40	25.00
303	David Andreychuk, Tor.	.15	7.50
304	Raymond Bourque, Bos.	.20	10.00
305	Sergei Fedorov, Det.	1.00	75.00
306	Wayne Gretzky, LA	1.00	75.00
307	Adam Graves, NYR	.30	15.00
308	Michael Modano, Dal.	.20	10.00
309	Brett Hull, St.L	.25	12.50
310	Pat LaFontaine, Buf.	.20	10.00
311	Adam Oates, Bos.	.20	10.00
312	Patrick Roy, Goalie, Mon.	.50	35.00
313	Douglas Gilmour, Tor.	.40	25.00
314	Jaromir Jagr. Pit.	.40	25.00
315	Mark Recchi, Phi.	.25	12.50

THE CHARLTON STANDARD CATALOGUE OF CANADIAN BASEBALL AND FOOTBALL CARDS

- Fourth Edition -

Coming in April!

186 • PARKHURST — 1994 - 95 INSERT SETS —

— 1994 - 95 INSERT SETS —

"CRASH THE GAME"

With the winning of certain games (as listed on the back of the card) the card became redeemable for either a Silver or Gold foil set of "Crash the Game".

These contest cards are randomly inserted into Series One Hobby packs as listed below.

1994-95 "Crash the Game"
Card No. C17, Eric Lindros

Card Size: 2 1/2" x 3 1/2"
Face: Four colour, borderless; Name, Red foil logo
Back: Four colour, Black small print explaining contest
Imprint: © 1994 THE UPPER DECK COMPANY

American Hobby Set - 28 Cards	300.00
American Retail Set - 28 Cards	300.00
Canadian Set - 28 Cards	300.00
Complete Set No.: 84	900.00
Common Card:	7.00

AMERICAN HOBBY FOIL

No.	Player	NRMT
H1	Stephen Lebeau, MDA	7.00
H2	Raymond Bourque, Bos.	14.00
H3	Pat LaFontaine, Buf.	14.00
H4	Joe Nieuwendyk, Cal.	7.00
H5	Jeremy Roenick, Chi.	15.00
H6	Michael Modano, Dal.	10.00
H7	Sergei Fedorov, Det.	20.00
H8	Jason Arnott, Edm.	20.00
H9	John Vanbiesbrouck, Goalie, Fl.	7.00
H10	Geoff Sanderson, Har.	10.00
H11	Wayne Gretzky, L.A.	40.00
H12	Patrick Roy, Goalie, Mon.	30.00
H13	Scott Stevens, N.J.	7.00
H14	Pierre Turgeon, NYI	7.00
H15	Adam Graves, NYR	15.00
H16	Alexei Yashin, Ott.	15.00
H17	Eric Lindros, Phi.	40.00
H18	Mario Lemieux, Pit.	30.00
H19	Mats Sundin, Que.	10.00
H20	Brett Hull, St.L	12.00
H21	Sandis Ozolinsh, S.J.	7.00
H22	Chris Gratton, T.B.	10.00
H23	Douglas Gilmour, Tor.	15.00
H24	Pavel Bure, Van.	20.00
H25	Joseph Juneau, Wash.	12.00
H26	Teemu Selanne, Win.	15.00
H27	Eastern Conf. All-Star	15.00
H28	Western Conf. All-Star	15.00

AMERICAN RETAIL FOIL

No.	Player	NRMT
R1	Stephen Lebeau, MDA	7.00
R2	Raymond Bourque, Bos.	14.00
R3	Pat LaFontaine, Buf.	14.00
R4	Joe Nieuwendyk, Cal.	7.00
R5	Jeremy Roenick, Chi.	15.00
R6	Michael Modano, Dal.	10.00
R7	Sergei Fedorov, Det.	20.00
R8	Jason Arnott, Edm.	20.00
R9	John Vanbiesbrouck, Goalie, Fl.	7.00
R10	Geoff Sanderson, Har.	10.00
R11	Wayne Gretzky, L.A.	40.00
R12	Patrick Roy, Goalie, Mon.	30.00
R13	Scott Stevens, N.J.	7.00
R14	Pierre Turgeon, NYI	7.00
R15	Adam Graves, NYR	15.00
R16	Alexei Yashin, Ott.	15.00
R17	Eric Lindros, Phi.	40.00
R18	Mario Lemieux, Pit.	30.00
R19	Mats Sundin, Que.	10.00
R20	Brett Hull, St.L	12.00
R21	Sandis Ozolinsh, S.J.	7.00
R22	Chris Gratton, T.B.	10.00
R23	Douglas Gilmour, Tor.	15.00
R24	Pavel Bure, Van.	20.00
R25	Joseph Juneau, Wash.	12.00
R26	Teemu Selanne, Win.	15.00
R27	Eastern Conf. All-Star	15.00
R28	Western Conf. All-Star	15.00

CANADIAN FOIL

No.	Player	NRMT
C1	Stephan Lebeau, MDA	7.00
C2	Raymond Bourque, Bos.	14.00
C3	Pat LaFontaine, Buf.	14.00
C4	Joe Nieuwendyk, Cal.	7.00
C5	Jeremy Roenick, Chi.	15.00
C6	Michael Modano, Dal.	10.00
C7	Sergei Fedorov, Det.	20.00
C8	Jason Arnott, Edm.	20.00
C9	John Vanbiesbrouck, Goalie, Fl.	7.00
C10	Geoff Sanderson, Har.	10.00
C11	Wayne Gretzky, L.A.	40.00
C12	Patrick Roy, Goalie, Mon.	30.00
C13	Scott Stevens, N.J.	7.00
C14	Pierre Turgeon, NYI	7.00
C15	Adam Graves, NYR	15.00
C16	Alexei Yashin, Ott.	15.00
C17	Eric Lindros, Phil.	40.00
C18	Mario Lemieux, Pit.	30.00
C19	Mats Sundin, Que.	10.00
C20	Brett Hull, St.L	12.00
C21	Sandis Ozolinsh, S.J.	7.00
C22	Chris Gratton, T.B.	10.00
C23	Douglas Gilmour, Tor.	15.00
C24	Pavel Bure, Van.	20.00
C25	Joseph Juneau, Wash.	12.00
C26	Teemu Selanne, Win.	15.00
C27	Eastern Conf. All-Stars	15.00
C28	Western Conf. All-Stars	15.00

VINTAGE PARKHURST

Inserted in all foil packs, American and Canadian, one per pack.

 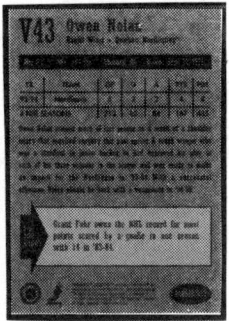

Vintage Parkhurst
Card No. V43, Owen Nolan

Card Size: 2 1/2" x 3 1/2"
Face: Four colour
Back: Four colour
Imprint: © 1994 THE UPPER DECK COMPANY
Complete Set No.: 90

Complete Set Price:	20.00	40.00
Common Card:	.12	.25

No.	Player	EX	NRMT
V1	Dominik Hasek, Goalie, Buf.	.50	1.00
V2	Michael Modano, Dal.	.50	1.00
V3	Shayne Corson, Edm.	.12	.25
V4	Kirk Muller, Mon.	.12	.25
V5	Michael Richter, Goalie, NYR	.50	1.00
V6	Mario Lemieux, Pit.	2.00	4.00
V7	Sandis Ozolinsh, SJ	.50	1.00
V8	David Ellett, Tor.	.12	.25
V9	Dave Manson, Edm.	.12	.25
V10	Terry Yake, Hart.	.12	.25
V11	Craig Simpson, Van.	.12	.25
V12	Paul Cavallini, Dal.	.12	.25
V13	John Vanbiesbrouck, Goalie, Fl.	.35	.75
V14	Gilbert Dionne, Mon.	.12	.25
V15	Brian Leetch, NYR	.50	1.00
V16	Martin Straka, Pit.	.75	1.50
V17	Curtis Joseph, Goalie, St.L	1.00	2.00
V18	Pavel Bure, Van.	2.00	4.00
V19	Garry Valk, MDA	.12	.25
V20	Theoren Fleury, Cal.	.12	.25
V21	Brent Gilchrist, Dal.	.12	.25
V22	Rob Niedermayer, Fl.	.50	1.00
V23	Vincent Damphousse, Mon.	.12	.25
V24	Alexei Kovalev, NYR	.50	1.00
V25	Rick Tocchet, Pit.	.12	.25
V26	Steve Duchesne, St.L	.12	.25
V27	Jiri Slegr, Van.	.12	.25
V28	Patrik Carnback, MDA	.12	.25
V29	Gary Roberts, Cal.	.12	.25
V30	Derian Hatcher, Dal.	.12	.25
V31	Jesse Belanger, Fl.	.50	1.00
V32	Mathieu Schneider, Mon.	.12	.25
V33	Mark Messier, NYR	.75	1.50
V34	Joe Sakic, Que.	.50	1.00
V35	Brett Hull, St.L	1.00	2.00
V36	Martin Gelinas, Van.	.12	.25
V37	Maxim Bets, MDA	.12	.25
V38	Michael Nylander, Cal.	.35	.75
V39	Sergei Fedorov, Det.	1.25	2.50
V40	Chris Pronger, Hart.	.50	1.00
V41	Scott Stevens, NJ	.25	.50
V42	Alexandre Daigle, Ott.	1.00	2.00
V43	Owen Nolan, Que.	.12	.25
V44	Petr Nedved, St.L	.12	.25
V45	Jeff Brown, Van.	.12	.25
V46	Adam Oates, Bos.	.25	.50
V47	Robert Reichel, Cal.	.12	.25
V48	Vyacheslav Kozlov, Det.	.50	1.00
V49	Geoff Sanderson, Hart.	.50	1.00
V50	Stephane J.J. Richer, NJ	.12	.25
V51	Sylvain Turgeon, Ott.	.12	.25
V52	Mats Sundin, Que.	.50	1.00
V53	Roman Hamrlik, TB	.12	.25
V54	Kevin Hatcher, Wash.	.12	.25
V55	Jon Casey, Goalie, Bos	.12	.25
V56	Anthony Amonte, Chi.	.50	1.00
V57	Steve Yzerman, Det.	.12	.25
V58	Andrew Cassels, Hart.	.12	.25
V59	Claude Lemieux, NJ	.12	.25
V60	Derek Mayer, ??	.12	.25
V61	Jocelyn Thibault, Goalie, Que.	.85	1.75
V62	Brent Gretzky, TB	.25	.50
V63	Pat Peake, Wash.	.25	.50
V64	Cam Neely, Bos.	.35	.75
V65	Jeremy Roenick, Chi.	.75	1.50
V66	Keith Primeau, Det.	.12	.25
V67	Luc Robitaille, LA	.75	1.50
V68	Steve Thomas, NYI	.12	.25
V69	Eric Lindros, Phi.	2.00	4.00
V70	Pat Falloon, SJ	.12	.25
V71	Brian Bradley, TB	.12	.25
V72	Mike Ridley, Wash.	.12	.25
V73	Pat LaFontaine, Buf.	.75	1.50
V74	Gary Suter, Cal.	.12	.25
V75	Bill Ranford, Goalie, Edm.	.25	.50
V76	Tony Granato, LA	.12	.25
V77	Vladimir Malakhov, NYI	.25	.50
V78	Mikael Renberg, Phi.	.75	1.50
V79	Arturs Irbe, Goalie, SJ	.75	1.50
V80	Douglas Gilmour, Tor.	1.25	2.50
V81	Teemu Selanne, Win.	1.25	2.50
V82	Derek Plante, Buf.	1.00	2.00
V83	Eric Weinrich, Hart.	.12	.25
V84	Jason Arnott, Edm.	1.25	2.50
V85	Robert Blake, La	.12	.25
V86	Ray Ferraro, NYI	.12	.25
V87	Garry Galley, Phi.	.12	.25
V88	Igor Larionov, SJ	.12	.25
V89	David Andreychuk, Tor.	.25	.50
V90	Dallas Drake, Det.	.25	.50

LA PATRIE

— 1951 - 54 ISSUES —

Card Size: 2 5/8" x 3 1/4"
Face: Four colour
Back: Newspaper
Imprint: None
Complete Set No.: 44
Complete Set Price: 500.00 1,000.00 ☐

1951 ISSUE - CANADIENS

No.	Player / Date Issued	VG	EX
1	Maurice Richard, December 2	12.00	25.00 ☐
2	Butch Bouchard, December 9	12.00	25.00 ☐
3	Elmer Lach, December 16	12.00	25.00 ☐
4	Gerry McNeil, December 23	12.00	25.00 ☐
5	Bernie Geoffrion, December 31	12.00	25.00 ☐

1952 ISSUE

No.	Player / Date Issued	VG	EX
6	Doug Harvey, Mon., January 6	12.00	25.00 ☐
7	Jean Beliveau, Quebec Aces, January 15	12.00	25.00 ☐
8	Kenny Mosdell, Mon., January 20	12.00	25.00 ☐
9	Dick Gamble, Mon., January 27	12.00	25.00 ☐
10	Paul Meger, February 3	12.00	25.00 ☐
11	Billy Reay, Mon., February 10	12.00	25.00 ☐
12	Floyd Curry, Mon., February 17	12.00	25.00 ☐
13	Dollard St. Laurent, Mon., February 24	12.00	25.00 ☐
14	Jean Guy Talbot, Trois Rivieres, March 2	12.00	25.00 ☐
15	Dickie Moore, Mon., March 9	12.00	25.00 ☐
16	Bert Olmstead, Mon., March 16	12.00	25.00 ☐
17	Andre Corriveau, Valleyfield, March 23	12.00	25.00 ☐
18	Marcel Pelletier, Les Saguenees, March 30	12.00	25.00 ☐
19	Tom Johnson, Mon., April 8	12.00	25.00 ☐
20	Bud MacPherson, Mon., April 13	12.00	25.00 ☐
21	John McCormack, Mon., April 20	12.00	25.00 ☐

1953 ISSUE

No.	Player / Date Issued	VG	EX
22	Roger Leger, RHC, January 11	12.00	25.00 ☐
23	Henri Richard, Mon., January 18	12.00	25.00 ☐
24	Camille Henry, Quebec Cit., January 25	12.00	25.00 ☐
25	Jean Paul Lamirande, Les Saguenees, February 1	12.00	25.00 ☐
26	Eddie Litzenberger, RHC, February 8	12.00	25.00 ☐
27	Skippy Burchell, RHC, February 15	12.00	25.00 ☐
28	Herbie Carnegie, Quebec Aces, March 1	12.00	25.00 ☐
29	Jean Marois, Quebec Aces, March 8	12.00	25.00 ☐
30	Don Raleigh, NYR, March 15	12.00	25.00 ☐
31	Wally Hergesheimer, NYR, March 22	12.00	25.00 ☐
32	Tod Campeau, Sherbrooke Saints, March 29	12.00	25.00 ☐
33	Guy Rousseau, Jr. Canadiens, April 5	12.00	25.00 ☐
34	Sherman White, Les Saguenees November 29	12.00	25.00 ☐
35	Claude Provost, Mon., December 13	12.00	25.00 ☐
36	Gaetan Dessureault, Mon., December 20	12.00	25.00 ☐
37	Del Topoll, Frontenac Que., December 27	12.00	25.00 ☐

1954 ISSUE

No.	Player / Date Issued	VG	EX
38	Claude Pronovost, RHC, January 3	12.00	25.00 ☐
39	Herve Lalonde, Trois Rivieres, January 10	12.00	25.00 ☐
40	Guy Rousseau, Frontenac Que., January 17	12.00	25.00 ☐
41	Jean Guy Gendron, Trois Rivieres, January 24	12.00	25.00 ☐
42	Claude Dufour, Trois Rivieres, January 31	12.00	25.00 ☐
43	Jacques Marcotte, Frontenac Que., February 7	12.00	25.00 ☐
44	Calum Mackay, Mon., February 14	12.00	25.00 ☐

ROYAL DESSERTS

— 1952 ROYAL STARS OF HOCKEY —

The complete set of this issue features hockey, baseball and basketball players, soldiers, aeroplanes and movie stars. Cards were obtained by cutting the backs from Royal Desserts packages. Many of these cards, as a result, will have rough edges. An album with eight clear envelopes could be obtained from, Royal Desserts by mail for displaying the cards.

Card Size: 2 5/8" x 3 1/4"
Face: Four colour, red border at top, white border at bottom; Name, Number, Resume, Facsimile autograph
Back: Blank
Imprint: None
Complete Set No.: 8
Common Set Price: 425.00 850.00 1,700.00 ☐
Common Player: 25.00 50.00 100.00
Album: 100.00 ☐

No.	Player	VG	EX	NRMT
1	Tony Leswick, Det.	25.00	50.00	100.00 ☐
2	Chuck Rayner, Goalie, NYR	25.00	50.00	100.00 ☐
3	Edgar Laprade, NYR	25.00	50.00	100.00 ☐
4	Sid Abel, Det.	35.00	75.00	150.00 ☐
5	Ted Lindsay, Det.	35.00	75.00	150.00 ☐
6	Leo Reise, Det.	25.00	50.00	100.00 ☐
7	Red Kelly, Det.	35.00	75.00	150.00 ☐
8	Gordie Howe, Det.	250.00	500.00	1,000.00 ☐

Royal Desserts
1952 Royal Stars of Hockey
Card No. 3, Edgar Laprade

HOLDING

TOPPS

— 1954 - 55 REGULAR ISSUE —

The bottom border, which is printed in blue, scuffs easily. This compounds the problem of finding NRMT to mint cards. Mint condition cards will command price premiums of 50% to 75% over NRMT cards. The first issue of Topps was not bilingual.

PRICE MOVEMENT OF NRMT SETS

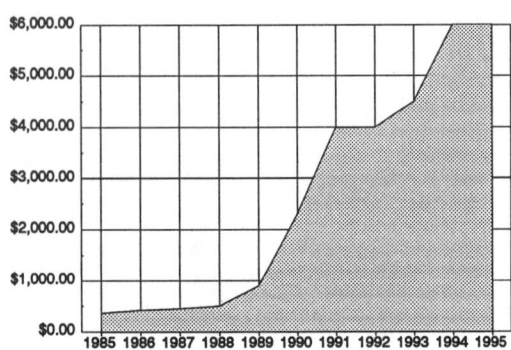

Card Size: 2 5/8" X 3 3/4"
Face: Four colour, blue and red border along bottom, Team logo
Back: Red and blue on card stock; Number, Resume, Hockey tip
Imprint: © T.C.G. printed in U.S.A.
Complete Set No.: 60

Complete Set Price:	1,500.00	3,000.00	6,000.00
Common Player:	11.25	22.50	45.00

No.	Player	VG	EX	NRMT
1	Dick Gamble, Chi., LC	35.00	75.00	150.00
2	**Bob Chrystal, NYR, RC, LC**	11.25	22.50	45.00
3	Harry Howell, NYR	35.00	75.00	150.00
4	Johnny Wilson, Det.	11.25	22.50	45.00
5	Red Kelly, Det.	40.00	85.00	175.00
6	Real Chevrefils, Bos.	11.25	22.50	45.00
7	Bob Armstrong, Bos.	11.25	22.50	45.00
8	Gordie Howe, Det.	625.00	1,250.00	2,500.00
9	Benny Woit, Det., LC	11.25	22.50	45.00
10	Gump Worsley, Goalie, NYR	70.00	140.00	275.00
11	Andy Bathgate, NYR	35.00	75.00	150.00
12	**Bucky Hollingworth, Chi., RC, LC**	11.25	22.50	45.00
13	Ray Timgren, Chi., LC	11.25	22.50	45.00
14	Jack Evans, NYR	11.25	22.50	45.00
15	Paul Ronty, NYR, LC	11.25	22.50	45.00
16	Glen Skov, Det.	11.25	22.50	45.00
17	Gus Mortson, Chi.	11.25	22.50	45.00
18	**Doug Mohns, Bos., RC**	20.00	42.50	85.00
19	Leo LaBine, Bos.	11.25	22.50	45.00
20	Bill Gadsby, Chi.	20.00	42.50	85.00
21	Jerry Toppazzini, Chi.	11.25	22.50	45.00
22	Wally Hergesheimer, NYR	11.25	22.50	45.00
23	Danny Lewicki, NYR	11.25	22.50	45.00
24	Metro Prystai, Chi., LC	11.25	22.50	45.00
25	Fern Flaman, Bos.	17.50	35.00	75.00
26	Al Rollins, Goalie, Chi., LC	17.50	35.00	75.00
27	Marcel Pronovost, Det.	17.50	35.00	75.00
28	**Lou Jankowski, Chi., RC, LC**	11.25	22.50	45.00
29	Nick Mickoski, NYR	11.25	22.50	45.00
30	Frank Martin, Chi., LC	11.25	22.50	45.00
31	Lorne Ferguson, Bos.	11.25	22.50	45.00
32	**Camille Henry, NYR, RC**	11.25	22.50	45.00
33	Pete Conacher, Chi.	11.25	22.50	45.00
34	Marty Pavelich, Det., LC	11.25	22.50	45.00
35	**Don McKenney, Bos., RC**	17.50	35.00	70.00
36	Fleming Mackell, Bos.	11.25	22.50	45.00
37	Jim Henry, Goalie, Bos., LC	17.50	35.00	75.00
38	Hal Laycoe, Bos., LC	11.25	22.50	45.00
39	Alex Delvecchio, Det.	40.00	85.00	175.00
40	Larry Wilson, Chi., LC	11.25	22.50	45.00
41	Allan Stanley, NYR	25.00	50.00	100.00
42	**Red Sullivan, Chi., RC**	11.25	22.50	45.00
43	Jack McIntyre, Chi.	11.25	22.50	45.00
44	**Ivan Irwin, NYR, RC, LC**	11.25	22.50	45.00
45	Tony Leswick, Det., LC	11.25	22.50	45.00
46	Bob Goldham, Det., LC	15.00	30.00	60.00
47	Cal Gardner, Bos., LC	11.25	22.50	45.00
48	Ed Sandford, Bos., LC	11.25	22.50	45.00
49	Bill Quackenbush, Bos., LC	20.00	37.50	75.00
50	Warren Godfrey, Bos.	11.25	22.50	45.00
51	Ted Lindsay, Det.	40.00	85.00	175.00
52	Earl Reibel, Det.	11.25	22.50	45.00
53	Don Raleigh, NYR, LC	11.25	22.50	45.00
54	Bill Mosienko, Chi., LC	17.50	35.00	70.00
55	**Larry Popein, NYR, RC**	11.25	22.50	45.00
56	Edgar Laprade, NYR, LC	11.25	22.50	45.00
57	Bill Dineen, Det.	11.25	22.50	45.00
58	Terry Sawchuk, Goalie, Det.	162.50	325.00	650.00
59	**Marcel Bonin, Det., RC**	11.25	22.50	45.00
60	Milt Schmidt, Bos., LC	62.50	125.00	250.00

Note: Topps did not produce hockey cards for the years 1955-56 and 1956-57.

Topps
1954-55 Issue
Card No. 1,
Dick Gamble

Topps
1954-55 Issue
Card No. 1,
Dick Gamble

Topps
1957-58 Issue
Card No. 1
Real Chevrefils

Topps
1957-58 Issue
Card No. 1,
Real Chevrefils

— 1957 - 58 REGULAR ISSUE —

The quality of the card stock continued to create problems with card appearance. A loss of gloss from the card surface occurs as the card ages. Mint cards command a premium of 50% to 75% over NRMT cards.

PRICE MOVEMENT OF NRMT SETS

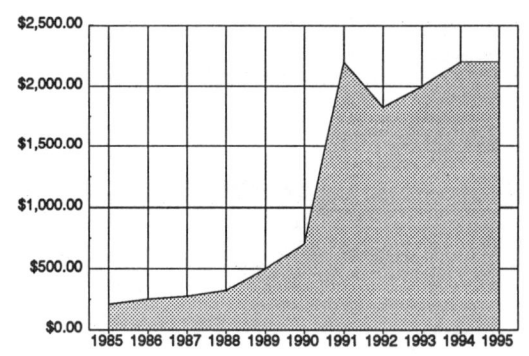

Card Size: 2 1/2" X 3 1/2"
Face: Four colour, white border, Team logo
Back: Red and blue on card stock, Hockey trivia, Number, Resume, Bilingual
Imprint: © T.C.G. PRINTED IN U.S.A.
Complete Set No.: 66

Complete Set Price:	550.00	1,100.00	2,200.00
Common Player:	4.50	9.00	18.00

BOSTON BRUINS

No.	Player	VG	EX	NRMT
1	Real Chevrefils, LC	10.00	20.00	45.00
2	**Jack Bionda, RC, LC**	4.50	9.00	18.00
3	Bob Armstrong	4.50	9.00	18.00
4	Fern Flaman	5.00	10.00	20.00
5	Jerry Toppazzini	4.50	9.00	18.00
6	**Larry Regan, RC**	4.50	9.00	18.00
7	**Bronco Horvath, RC**	4.50	9.00	18.00
8	Jack Caffery, LC	4.50	9.00	18.00
9	Leo Labine	4.50	9.00	18.00
10	**John Bucyk, RC**	55.00	110.00	225.00
11	Vic Stasiuk	4.50	9.00	18.00
12	Doug Mohns	4.50	9.00	18.00
13	Don McKenney	4.50	9.00	18.00
14	**Don Simmons, Goalie, RC**	7.50	15.00	30.00
15	Allan Stanley	5.00	10.00	20.00
16	Fleming Mackell	4.50	9.00	18.00
17	**Larry Hillman, RC**	4.50	9.00	18.00
18	Leo Boivin	4.50	9.00	18.00

1958 - 59 REGULAR ISSUE — TOPPS • 189

CHICAGO BLACK HAWKS

No.	Player	VG	EX	NRMT
19	Bob Bailey, LC	4.50	9.00	18.00
20	Glenn Hall, Goalie, RC	75.00	150.00	300.00
21	Ted Lindsay	7.50	15.00	30.00
22	Pierre Pilote, RC	30.00	60.00	125.00
23	Jim Thomson, LC	4.50	9.00	18.00
24	Eric Nesterenko	4.50	9.00	18.00
25	Gus Mortson	4.50	9.00	18.00
26	Ed Litzenberger, RC	4.50	9.00	18.00
27	Elmer Vasko, RC	4.50	9.00	18.00
28	Jack McIntyre	4.50	9.00	18.00
29	Ron Murphy	4.50	9.00	18.00
30	Glen Skov	4.50	9.00	18.00
31	Hec Lalande, RC, LC	4.50	9.00	18.00
32	Nick Mickoski	4.50	9.00	18.00
33	Wally Hergesheimer, LC	4.50	9.00	18.00

DETROIT RED WINGS

No.	Player	VG	EX	NRMT
34	Alex Delvecchio	17.50	35.00	70.00
35	Terry Sawchuk, Goalie, Error	55.00	110.00	225.00
36	Guyle Fielder, RC, LC	4.50	9.00	18.00
37	Tom McCarthy, RC, LC	4.50	9.00	18.00
38	Al Arbour	10.00	20.00	40.00
39	Billy Dea, RC	4.50	9.00	18.00
40	Lorne Ferguson	4.50	9.00	18.00
41	Warren Godfrey	4.50	9.00	18.00
42	Gordie Howe	150.00	300.00	600.00
43	Marcel Pronovost	5.00	10.00	20.00
44	Billy McNeill, RC	4.50	9.00	18.00
45	Earl Reibel	4.50	9.00	18.00
46	Norm Ullman, RC	50.00	100.00	200.00
47	Johnny Wilson	4.50	9.00	18.00
48	Red Kelly	15.00	30.00	60.00
49	Bill Dineen, LC	4.50	9.00	18.00
50	Forbes Kennedy, RC	6.00	12.50	25.00

NEW YORK RANGERS

No.	Player	VG	EX	NRMT
51	Harry Howell	10.00	20.00	45.00
52	Jean-Guy Gendron, RC	4.50	9.00	18.00
53	Gump Worsley, Goalie	30.00	60.00	125.00
54	Larry Popein	4.50	9.00	18.00
55	Jack Evans	4.50	9.00	18.00
56	George Sullivan	4.50	9.00	18.00
57	Gerry Foley, RC, LC	4.50	9.00	18.00
58	Andy Hebenton, RC	4.50	9.00	18.00
59	Larry Cahan	4.50	9.00	18.00
60	Andy Bathgate	10.00	20.00	40.00
61	Danny Lewicki	4.50	9.00	18.00
62	Dean Prentice	5.00	10.00	20.00
63	Camille Henry	6.00	12.50	25.00
64	Louie Fontinato, RC	7.50	15.00	30.00
65	Bill Gadsby	7.50	15.00	30.00
66	Dave Creighton	10.00	20.00	40.00

— 1958 - 59 REGULAR ISSUE —

Centering of the cards was a problem. Well centered NRMT and mint cards will command a premium of 50% over those prices listed below.

PRICE MOVEMENT OF NRMT SETS

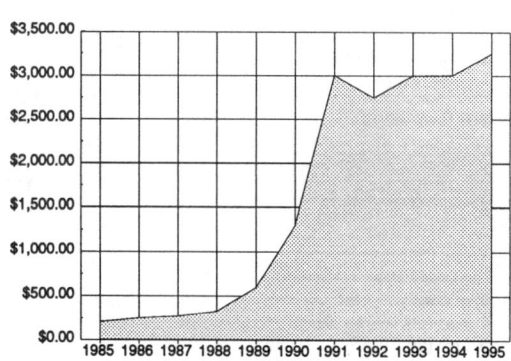

Topps, 1957-58 Issue
Card No. 35, Error,
Name misspelled
Sawchuck on face

Topps
1958-59 Issue
Card No. 1,
Bob Armstrong

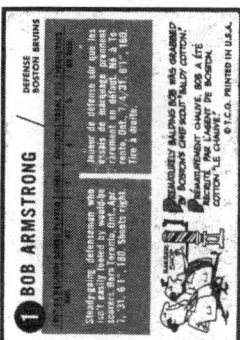

Topps
1958-59 Issue
Card No. 1,
Bob Armstrong

Topps, 1958-59 Issue
Card No. 8, Error,
Name misspelled
Gordy on face

Card Size: 2 1/2" X 3 1/2"
Face: Four colour, white border
Back: Black and green on card stock, Number, Resume, Bilingual
Imprint: © T.C.G. PRINTED IN U.S.A.
Complete Set No.: 66
Complete Set Price: 810.00 1,625.00 3,250.00
Common Player: 3.75 7.50 15.00

No.	Player	VG	EX	NRMT
1	Bob Armstrong, Bos.	7.50	15.00	30.00
2	Terry Sawchuk, Goalie, Det.	45.00	85.00	175.00
3	Glen Skov, Chi.	3.75	7.50	15.00
4	Leo Labine, Bos.	3.75	7.50	15.00
5	Dollard St. Laurent, Chi.	3.75	7.50	15.00
6	Danny Lewicki, Chi., LC	3.75	7.50	15.00
7	John Hanna, NYR, RC	3.75	7.50	15.00
8	Gordie Howe, Det., Error	125.00	250.00	500.00
9	Vic Stasiuk, Bos.	3.75	7.50	15.00
10	Larry Regan, Bos.	3.75	7.50	15.00
11	Forbes Kennedy, Det.	3.75	7.50	15.00
12	Elmer Vasko, Chi.	3.75	7.50	15.00
13	Glenn Hall, Goalie, Chi.	35.00	75.00	150.00
14	Kenny Wharram, Chi., RC	5.00	10.00	20.00
15	Len Lunde, Det., RC	3.75	7.50	15.00
16	Ed Litzenberger, Chi.	3.75	7.50	15.00
17	Norm Johnson, Bos., RC, LC	3.75	7.50	15.00
18	Earl Ingarfield, NYR, RC	3.75	7.50	15.00
19	Les Colwill, NYR, RC, LC	3.75	7.50	15.00
20	Leo Boivin, Bos.	4.00	8.00	16.00
21	Andy Bathgate, NYR	8.75	17.50	35.00
22	Johnny Wilson, Det.	3.75	7.50	15.00
23	Larry Cahan, NYR	3.75	7.50	15.00
24	Marcel Pronovost, Det.	5.00	10.00	20.00
25	Larry Hillman, Bos.	3.75	7.50	15.00
26	Jim Bartlett, NYR, RC	3.75	7.50	15.00
27	Nick Mickoski, Det.	3.75	7.50	15.00
28	Larry Popein, NYR	3.75	7.50	15.00
29	Fleming Mackell, Bos.	3.75	7.50	15.00
30	Eddie Shack, NYR, RC	30.00	62.50	125.00
31	Jack Evans, Chi.	3.75	7.50	15.00
32	Dean Prentice, NYR	3.75	7.50	15.00
33	Claude Laforge, Det., RC	3.75	7.50	15.00
34	Bill Gadsby, NYR	5.00	10.00	20.00
35	Bronco Horvath, Bos.	3.75	7.50	15.00
36	Pierre Pilote, Chi.	15.00	30.00	60.00
37	Earl Balfour, Chi.	3.75	7.50	15.00
38	Gus Mortson, Det., LC	3.75	7.50	15.00
39	Gump Worsley, Goalie, NYR	15.00	30.00	60.00
40	John Bucyk, Bos.	20.00	45.00	90.00
41	Louie Fontinato, NYR	3.75	7.50	15.00
42	Tod Sloan, Chi.	3.75	7.50	15.00
43	Charlie Burns, Det., RC	3.75	7.50	15.00
44	Don Simmons, Goalie, Bos.	3.75	7.50	15.00
45	Jerry Toppazzini, Bos., Error	3.75	7.50	15.00
46	Andy Hebenton, NYR	3.75	7.50	15.00
47	Peter Goegan, Det., RC, Error	3.75	7.50	15.00
48	George Sullivan, NYR	3.75	7.50	15.00
49	Hank Ciesla, NYR, RC	3.75	7.50	15.00
50	Doug Mohns, Bos.	3.75	7.50	15.00
51	Jean-Guy Gendron, Bos.	3.75	7.50	15.00
52	Alex Delvecchio, Det.	7.50	15.00	30.00
53	Eric Nesterenko, Chi.	3.75	7.50	15.00
54	Camille Henry, NYR	3.75	7.50	15.00
55	Lorne Ferguson, Chi., LC	3.75	7.50	15.00
56	Fern Flaman, Bos.	5.00	10.00	20.00
57	Earl Reibel, Bos., LC	3.75	7.50	15.00
58	Warren Godfrey, Det.	3.75	7.50	15.00
59	Ron Murphy, Chi.	3.75	7.50	15.00
60	Harry Howell, NYR	7.50	15.00	30.00
61	Red Kelly, Det.	8.75	17.50	35.00
62	Don McKenney, Bos.	3.75	7.50	15.00
63	Ted Lindsay, Chi.	8.75	17.50	35.00
64	Al Arbour, Chi.	6.25	12.50	25.00
65	Norm Ullman, Det.	17.50	35.00	75.00
66	Bobby Hull, Chi., RC	625.00	1,250.00	2,500.00

Note: For a card to grade higher than EX it must have no wear, no creases, full colour and four square corners.

TOPPS — 1959-60 REGULAR ISSUE

— 1959-60 REGULAR ISSUE —

Of all the Topps sets this one could be their most "off-centred" set. Well centered NRMT and mint cards are very scarce and have high price premiums. Mint cards will command a premium of 50% over NRMT cards.

PRICE MOVEMENT OF NRMT SETS

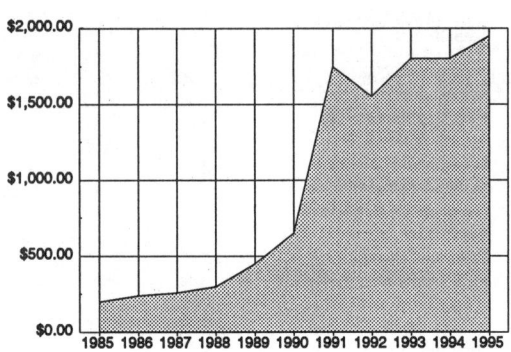

Card Size: 2 1/2" X 3 1/2"
Face: Four colour, white border, Team logo
Back: Two colour, red and black on card stock, Number, Resume, Hockey trivia, Bilingual
Imprint: © T.C.G. PRINTED IN U.S.A.
Complete Set No.: 66

		VG	EX	NRMT
Complete Set Price:		490.00	975.00	1,950.00
Common Player:		3.75	7.50	15.00

No.	Player	VG	EX	NRMT
1	Eric Nesterenko, Chi.	7.50	15.00	30.00
2	Pierre Pilote, Chi.	7.50	15.00	30.00
3	Elmer Vasko, Chi.	3.75	7.50	15.00
4	Peter Goegan, Det.	3.75	7.50	15.00
5	Louie Fontinato, NYR	3.75	7.50	15.00
6	Ted Lindsay, Chi.	7.50	15.00	30.00
7	Leo Labine, Bos.	3.75	7.50	15.00
8	Alex Delvecchio, Det., Error	7.50	15.00	30.00
9	Don McKenney, Bos., Error	3.75	7.50	15.00
10	Earl Ingarfield, NYR	3.75	7.50	15.00
11	Don Simmons, Goalie, Bos.	3.75	7.50	15.00
12	Glen Skov, Chi., LC	3.75	7.50	15.00
13	Tod Sloan, Chi.	3.75	7.50	15.00
14	Vic Stasiuk, Bos.	3.75	7.50	15.00
15	Gump Worsley, Goalie, NYR	8.75	17.50	35.00
16	Andy Hebenton, NYR	3.75	7.50	15.00
17	Dean Prentice, NYR	3.75	7.50	15.00
18	Oops! Pardon My Stick! Strickly Accidental	3.75	7.50	15.00
19	Fleming Mackell, Bos., LC	3.75	7.50	15.00
20	Harry Howell, NYR	4.00	8.00	16.00
21	Larry Popein, NYR, LC	3.75	7.50	15.00
22	Len Lunde, Det.	3.75	7.50	15.00
23	John Bucyk, Bos.	10.00	20.00	40.00
24	Jean-Guy Gendron, Bos.	3.75	7.50	15.00
25	Barry Cullen, Det., Error	3.75	7.50	15.00
26	Leo Boivin, Bos.	4.00	8.00	16.00
27	Warren Godfrey, Det.	3.75	7.50	15.00
28	This Looks Like A Sure Goal - But Is It?	4.00	8.00	16.00
29	Fern Flaman, Bos.	3.75	7.50	15.00
30	Jack Evans, Chi.	3.75	7.50	15.00
31	John Hanna, NYR, LC	3.75	7.50	15.00
32	Glenn Hall, Goalie, Chi.	12.50	25.00	50.00
33	Murray Balfour, Chi., RC	3.75	7.50	15.00
34	Andy Bathgate, NYR	4.50	9.00	18.00
35	Al Arbour, Chi.	5.00	10.00	20.00
36	Jim Morrison, Det.	3.75	7.50	15.00
37	Nick Mickoski, Bos., LC	3.75	7.50	15.00
38	Jerry Toppazzini, Bos.	3.75	7.50	15.00
39	Bob Armstrong, Bos.	3.75	7.50	15.00
40	Charlie Burns, Bos., Error	3.75	7.50	15.00
41	Billy McNeill, Det.	3.75	7.50	15.00
42	Terry Sawchuk, Goalie, Det.	30.00	60.00	120.00
43	Dollard St. Laurent, Chi.	3.75	7.50	15.00
44	Marcel Pronovost, Det.	3.75	7.50	15.00
45	Norm Ullman, Det.	8.75	17.50	35.00
46	Camille Henry, NYR	3.75	7.50	15.00

Topps 1959-60 Issue
Card No. 1,
Eric Nesterenko

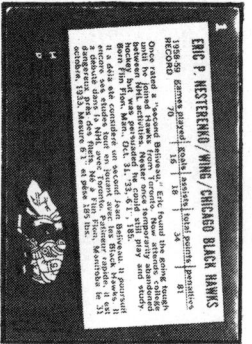

Topps 1959-60 Issue
Card No. 1,
Eric Nesterenko

Topps 1960-61 Issue
Card No. 1,
Lester Patrick

Topps 1960-61 Issue
Card No. 1,
Lester Patrick

No.	Player	VG	EX	NRMT
47	Bobby Hull, Chi., Error	135.00	275.00	550.00
48	Hockey's Strong Man In Action	25.00	60.00	100.00
49	Lou Marcon, Det., RC, LC	3.75	7.50	15.00
50	Earl Balfour, Chi.	3.75	7.50	15.00
51	Jim Bartlett, NYR, LC	3.75	7.50	15.00
52	Forbes Kennedy, Det.	3.75	7.50	15.00
53	Looks Like a Perfect Three Point Landing	3.75	7.50	15.00
54	Trying to Score a Goal, The Hard Way	3.75	7.50	15.00
55	Brian Cullen, NYR, LC	3.75	7.50	15.00
56	Bronco Horvath, Bos.	3.75	7.50	15.00
57	Eddie Shack, NYR	6.25	12.50	25.00
58	Doug Mohns, Bos.	3.75	7.50	15.00
59	George Sullivan, NYR	3.75	7.50	15.00
60	So Near and Yet So Far	3.75	7.50	15.00
61	Ed Litzenberger, Chi.	3.75	7.50	15.00
62	Bill Gadsby, NYR	3.75	7.50	15.00
63	Gordie Howe, Det.	110.00	225.00	450.00
64	Claude LaForge, Det.	3.75	7.50	15.00
65	Red Kelly, Det.	7.50	15.00	30.00
66	Ron Murphy, Chi.	6.25	12.50	25.00

Note: Your cards must be accurately graded before they can be priced.

— 1960-61 REGULAR ISSUE —

The set includes All-Time Great cards as well as players from Boston, Chicago and New York. In the "All-Time Great" subset the cards for Dickie Boon (#17), Hugh Lehman (#38), Herb Gardiner (#44) and Francis Goheen (#63) are first and last cards. They were never before portrayed on a card, even in the classic era of 1900 to 1945. Mint Cards command a price premium of 50% over NRMT cards.

PRICE MOVEMENT OF NRMT SETS

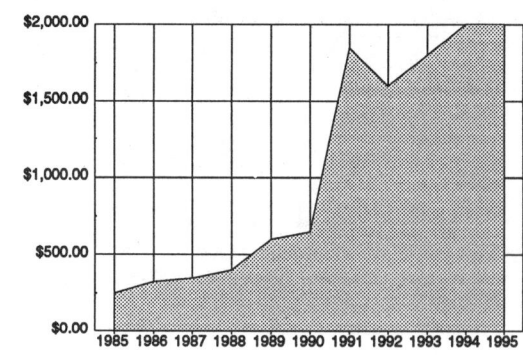

Card Size: 2 1/2" X 3 1/2"
Face: Four colour, white border
Back: Orange on card stock, Number, Resume, Quiz, Bilingual
Imprint: © T.C.G. PRINTED IN U.S.A.
Complete Set No.: 66

		VG	EX	NRMT
Complete Set Price:		500.00	1,000.00	2,000.00
Common Player:		3.25	6.50	13.00

No.	Player	VG	EX	NRMT
1	Lester Patrick, All-Time Great	15.00	30.00	60.00
2	Paddy Moran, Goalie, All-Time Great	4.50	9.00	18.00
3	Joe Malone, All-Time Great	6.25	12.50	25.00
4	Ernest (Moose) Johnson, All-Time Great	3.00	6.00	12.00
5	Nels Stewart, All-Time Great	5.00	10.00	20.00
6	Billy Hay, Chi., RC	4.50	9.00	18.00
7	Eddie Shack, NYR	10.00	20.00	40.00
8	Cy Denneny, All-Time Great	3.00	6.00	12.00
9	Jim Morrison, NYR	3.25	6.50	13.00
10	Bill Cook, All-Time Great	3.00	6.00	12.00
11	John Bucyk, Bos.	10.00	20.00	40.00
12	Murray Balfour, Chi.	3.25	6.50	13.00
13	Leo Labine, Bos.	3.25	6.50	13.00
14	Stan Mikita, Chi., RC	110.00	225.00	450.00
15	George Hay, All-Time Great	3.00	6.00	12.00
16	Mervyn (Red) Dutton, All-Time Great	3.00	6.00	12.00
17	Richard (Dickie) Boon, All-Time Great	3.50	7.00	14.00
18	George Sullivan, NYR	3.25	6.50	13.00

1961 - 62 REGULAR ISSUE — TOPPS • 191

No.	Player	VG	EX	NRMT
19	Georges Vezina, Goalie, All-Time Great	17.50	35.00	70.00
20	Eddie Shore, All-Time Great	17.50	35.00	70.00
21	Ed Litzenberger, Chi.	3.25	6.50	13.00
22	Bill Gadsby, NYR	3.75	7.50	15.00
23	Elmer Vasko, Chi.	3.25	6.50	13.00
24	Charlie Burns, Bos.	3.25	6.50	13.00
25	Glenn Hall, Goalie, Chi.	17.50	35.00	70.00
26	Dit Clapper, All-Time Great	7.50	15.00	30.00
27	Art Ross, All-Time Great	10.00	20.00	40.00
28	Jerry Toppazzini, Bos.	3.25	6.50	13.00
29	Frank Boucher, All-TimeGreat	3.00	6.00	12.00
30	Jack Evans, Chi.	3.25	6.50	13.00
31	Jean Guy Gendron, Bos.	3.25	6.50	13.00
32	Chuck Gardiner, Goalie, All-Time Great	7.50	15.00	30.00
33	Ab McDonald, Chi.	3.25	6.50	13.00
34	Frank Frederickson, All-Time Great, Error	3.00	6.00	12.00
35	Frank Nighbor, All-Time Great	3.50	7.00	14.00
36	Gump Worsley, Goalie, NYR	12.50	25.00	50.00
37	Dean Prentice, NYR	3.00	6.00	12.00
38	Hugh Lehman, Goalie, All-Time Great	3.00	6.00	12.00
39	**Jack McCartan, Goalie, NYR, RC, LC**	**3.75**	**7.50**	**15.00**
40	Don McKenney, Bos., Error	3.25	6.50	13.00
41	Ron Murphy, Chi.	3.25	6.50	13.00
42	Andy Hebenton, NYR	3.25	6.50	13.00
43	Don Simmons, Goalie, Bos.	3.25	6.50	13.00
44	Herb Gardiner, All-Time Great	3.00	6.00	12.00
45	Andy Bathgate, NYR	6.25	12.50	25.00
46	Fred (Cyclone) Taylor, All-Time Great	7.50	15.00	30.00
47	Francis (King) Clancy, All-Time Great	15.00	30.00	60.00
48	Edward (Newsy) Lalonde, All-Time Great	7.50	15.00	30.00
49	Harry Howell, NYR	5.50	11.00	22.00
50	**Ken Schinkel, NYR, RC**	**3.00**	**6.00**	**12.00**
51	Tod Sloan, Chi., LC	3.25	6.50	13.00
52	Doug Mohns, Bos.	3.25	6.50	13.00
53	Camille Henry, NYR	3.25	6.50	13.00
54	Bronco Horvath, Bos.	3.25	6.50	13.00
55	Tiny Thompson, Goalie, All-Time Great	5.00	10.00	20.00
56	Bob Armstrong, Bos.	3.25	6.50	13.00
57	Fern Flaman, Bos., LC	3.50	7.00	14.00
58	Bobby Hull, Chi.	110.00	225.00	450.00
59	Howie Morenz, All-Time Great	15.00	30.00	65.00
60	Dick Irvin, All-Time Great	7.50	15.00	30.00
61	Louie Fontinato, NYR, LC	3.25	6.50	13.00
62	Leo Boivin, Bos.	3.75	7.50	15.00
63	Francis (Moose) Goheen, All-Time Great	3.00	6.00	12.00
64	Al Arbour, Chi.	5.00	10.00	20.00
65	Pierre Pilote, Chi.	7.50	15.00	30.00
66	Vic Stasiuk, Bos.	7.00	14.00	28.00

— 1961 - 62 REGULAR ISSUE —

Mint cards will command a 50% price premium over NRMT cards.

PRICE MOVEMENT OF NRMT SETS

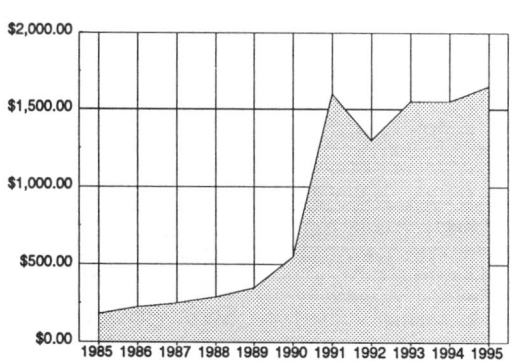

Topps 1960-61 Issue, Card No. 40, Error, Name misspelled McKenny on face

Topps 1960-61 Issue, Card No. 61, Louie Fontinato

Topps 1961-62 Issue Card No. 1, Phil Watson

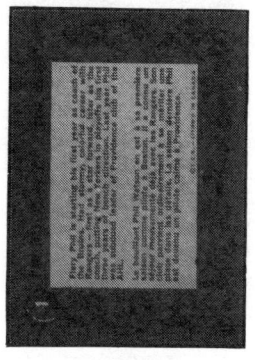

Topps 1961-62 Issue Card No. 1, Phil Watson

Card Size: 2 1/2" X 3 1/2"
Face: Four colour, white border
Back: Orange and black on card stock; Number, Resume, Bilingual
Imprint: © T.C.G. — LITHO'D IN CANADA
Complete Set No.: 66
Complete Set Price: 410.00 825.00 1,650.00
Common Player: 3.00 6.00 12.00

BOSTON BRUINS

No.	Player	VG	EX	NRMT
1	Phil Watson, Coach	6.25	12.50	25.00
2	**Ted Green, RC**	**10.00**	**20.00**	**40.00**
3	Earl Balfour, LC	3.00	6.00	12.00
4	**Dallas Smith, RC, Error**	**7.50**	**15.00**	**30.00**
5	Andre Pronovost	3.00	6.00	12.00
6	**Dick Meissner, RC**	**3.00**	**6.00**	**12.00**
7	Leo Boivin	3.00	6.00	12.00
8	John Bucyk	10.00	20.00	40.00
9	Jerry Toppazzini	3.00	6.00	12.00
10	Doug Mohns	3.00	6.00	12.00
11	Charlie Burns	3.00	6.00	12.00
12	Don McKenney	3.00	6.00	12.00
13	Bob Armstrong, LC	3.00	6.00	12.00
14	Murray Oliver	3.00	6.00	12.00
15	**Orland Kurtenbach, RC**	**5.00**	**10.00**	**20.00**
16	**Terry Gray, RC**	**3.00**	**6.00**	**12.00**
17	**Don Head, Goalie, RC, LC**	**3.00**	**6.00**	**12.00**
18	**Pat Stapleton, RC**	**7.50**	**15.00**	**30.00**
19	**Cliff Pennington, RC**	**3.00**	**6.00**	**12.00**
20	1961 Boston Bruins	7.50	15.00	30.00

HOCKEY HIGHLIGHTS

No.	Highlights	VG	EX	NRMT
21	Action Near The Cage	3.00	6.00	12.00
22	Bathgate Bangs One In	6.25	12.50	25.00

CHICAGO BLACK HAWKS

No.	Player	VG	EX	NRMT
23	Rudy Pilous, Coach	4.50	9.00	18.00
24	Pierre Pilote	5.50	11.00	22.00
25	Elmer Vasko	3.00	6.00	12.00
26	**Reggie Fleming, RC**	**3.75**	**7.50**	**15.00**
27	Ab McDonald	3.00	6.00	12.00
28	Eric Nesterenko	3.00	6.00	12.00
29	Bobby Hull	85.00	175.00	350.00
30	Kenny Wharram	3.00	6.00	12.00
31	Dollard St.Laurent	3.00	6.00	12.00
32	Glenn Hall, Goalie	12.50	25.00	50.00
33	Murray Balfour	3.00	6.00	12.00
34	Ron Murphy	3.00	6.00	12.00
35	Red Hay	3.00	6.00	12.00
36	Stan Mikita	45.00	85.00	175.00
37	**Denis DeJordy, Goalie, RC**	**7.50**	**15.00**	**30.00**
38	**Wayne Hillman, RC**	**3.00**	**6.00**	**12.00**
39	**Rino Robazza, RC, LC**	**3.00**	**6.00**	**12.00**
40	Bronco Horvath	3.00	6.00	12.00
41	Bob Turner	3.00	6.00	12.00
42	1961 Chicago Black Hawks	7.50	15.00	30.00

HOCKEY HIGHLIGHTS

No.	Highlights	VG	EX	NRMT
43	A Scramble at the Net	3.00	6.00	12.00
44	Dollard Doubles as Goalie	3.00	6.00	12.00

NEW YORK RANGERS

No.	Player	VG	EX	NRMT
45	Doug Harvey	8.75	17.50	35.00
46	Al Langlois	3.00	6.00	12.00
47	**Irv Spencer, RC**	**3.00**	**6.00**	**12.00**
48	Red Sullivan	3.00	6.00	12.00
49	Earl Ingarfield	3.00	6.00	12.00
50	Gump Worsley, Goalie	10.00	20.00	40.00
51	Harry Howell	5.50	11.00	22.00
52	Larry Cahan	3.00	6.00	12.00
53	Andy Bathgate	5.50	11.00	22.00
54	Dean Prentice	3.00	6.00	12.00
55	Andy Hebenton	3.00	6.00	12.00
56	Camille Henry	3.00	6.00	12.00
57	Jean Guy Gendron	3.00	6.00	12.00
58	**Pat Hannigan, RC**	**3.00**	**6.00**	**12.00**
59	Ted Hampson	3.00	6.00	12.00
60	**Jean Ratelle, RC**	**30.00**	**62.50**	**125.00**
61	**Al LeBrun, RC**	**3.00**	**6.00**	**12.00**

192 • TOPPS — 1961-62 STAMPS

No.	Player	VG	EX	NRMT
62	Rod Gilbert, RC	35.00	75.00	150.00
63	1961 New York Rangers	7.50	15.00	30.00

HOCKEY HIGHLIGHTS

No.	Highlights	VG	EX	NRMT
64	Going, Going, Goal!!	5.00	10.00	20.00
65	Gump Makes Important Save	5.00	10.00	20.00

CHECKLIST

No.	Checklist	VG	EX	NRMT
66	Checklist (1 - 66)	85.00	165.00	325.00

— 1961 - 62 STAMPS —

Issued in pairs in 1961-62 these "stamp" inserts are extremely difficult to find in NRMT. The stamps are not numbered and are listed here alphabetically by team and then by player within teams.

Stamp Size: 1 3/8" X 1 7/8"
Face: Blue and white; Name, Team, Position
Back: Blank (Gum)
Imprint: None
Complete Set No.: 52
Complete Set Price: 300.00   600.00   1,200.00
Common Player: 5.00   10.00   20.00

BOSTON BRUINS

No.	Player	VG	EX	NRMT
1	Leo Boivin	10.00	20.00	40.00
2	John Bucyk	11.00	22.50	45.00
3	Charlie Burns	5.00	10.00	20.00
4	Don McKenney	5.00	10.00	20.00
5	Doug Mohns	5.00	10.00	20.00
6	Murray Oliver	5.00	10.00	20.00
7	Andre Pronovost	5.00	10.00	20.00
8	Dallas Smith	5.00	10.00	20.00

NEW YORK RANGERS

No.	Player	VG	EX	NRMT
9	Andy Bathgate	11.00	22.50	45.00
10	Doug Harvey	12.50	25.00	50.00
11	Andy Hebenton	5.00	10.00	20.00
12	Camille Henry	5.00	10.00	20.00
13	Harry Howell	11.00	22.50	45.00
14	Al Langlois	5.00	10.00	20.00
15	Dean Prentice	6.25	12.50	25.00
16	Gump Worsley, Goalie	16.25	32.50	65.00

CHICAGO BLACK HAWKS

No.	Player	VG	EX	NRMT
17	Murray Balfour	5.00	10.00	20.00
18	Jack Evans	5.00	10.00	20.00
19	Glenn Hall, Goalie	12.50	25.00	50.00
20	Billy Hay	5.00	10.00	20.00
21	Bronco Horvath	5.00	10.00	20.00
22	Bobby Hull	50.00	100.00	210.00
23	Stan Mikita	20.00	37.50	75.00
24	Ron Murphy	5.00	10.00	20.00
25	Pierre Pilote	10.00	20.00	40.00
26	Elmer Vasko	5.00	10.00	20.00

ALL TIME GREATS

No.	Player	VG	EX	NRMT
27	Richard Boon	6.25	12.50	25.00
28	Frank Boucher	6.25	12.50	25.00
29	Francis (King) Clancy	11.00	22.50	45.00
30	Dit Clapper	7.50	15.00	30.00
31	Spague Cleghorn	5.00	10.00	20.00
32	Alex Connell, Goalie	5.00	10.00	20.00
33	Bill Cook	5.00	10.00	20.00
34	Cy Denneny	6.25	12.50	25.00
35	Frank Frederickson	5.00	10.00	20.00
36	Chuck Gardiner, Goalie	6.25	12.50	25.00
37	Herb Gardiner	5.00	10.00	20.00
38	Eddie Gerard	5.00	10.00	20.00
39	Frank (Moose) Goheen	5.00	10.00	20.00
40	George Hay	6.25	12.50	25.00
41	Dick Irvin	10.00	20.00	40.00
42	Ernest (Moose) Johnson	5.00	10.00	20.00

Topps
1961-62 Stamps
Stamp Nos. 16 & 3,
Gump Worsley; Charlie Burns

Topps
1962-63 Issue
Card No. 1,
Phil Watson

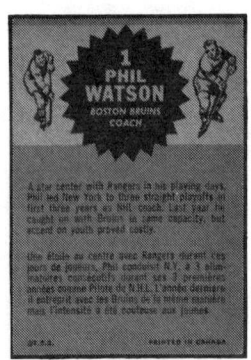

Topps
1962-63 Issue
Card No. 1,
Phil Watson

No.	Player	VG	EX	NRMT
43	Edouard Lalonde	7.50	15.00	30.00
44	Hugh Lehman	5.00	10.00	20.00
45	Joe Malone	8.00	17.50	35.00
46	Paddy Moran, Goalie	7.50	15.00	30.00
47	Howie Morenz	20.00	40.00	80.00
48	Frank Nighbor	5.00	10.00	20.00
49	Art Ross	11.00	22.50	45.00
50	Nels Stewart	10.00	20.00	40.00
51	Fred Taylor	14.00	27.50	55.00
52	Georges Vezina, Goalie	11.00	22.50	45.00

— 1962 - 63 REGULAR ISSUE —

The blue borders have made mint cards of this set difficult to locate. Mint cards will command a price premium of 50% over NRMT cards.

PRICE MOVEMENT OF NRMT SETS

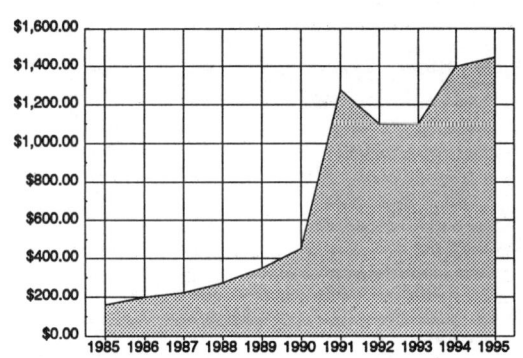

Card Size: 2 1/2" X 3 1/2"
Face: Four colour, blue border, Team logo, Position
Back: Black and blue on card stock, Number, Resume, Bilingual
Imprint: PRINTED IN CANADA © T.C.G.
Complete Set No.: 66
Complete Set Price: 360.00   725.00   1,450.00
Common Player: 3.00   6.00   12.00

BOSTON BRUINS

No.	Player	VG	EX	NRMT
1	Phil Watson, Coach	6.00	12.00	24.00
2	Robert Perreault, Goalie, RC, LC	3.00	6.00	12.00
3	Bruce Gamble, Goalie, RC	3.00	6.00	12.00
4	Warren Godfrey, LC	3.00	6.00	12.00
5	Leo Boivin	3.00	7.00	12.00
6	Doug Mohns	3.00	6.00	12.00
7	Ted Green	3.00	6.00	12.00
8	Pat Stapleton	3.00	6.00	12.00
9	Dallas Smith, Error	3.00	6.00	12.00
10	Don McKenney	3.00	6.00	12.00
11	John Bucyk	7.50	15.00	30.00
12	Murray Oliver	3.00	6.00	12.00
13	Jerry Toppazzini	3.00	6.00	12.00
14	Cliff Pennington, LC	3.00	6.00	12.00
15	Charlie Burns	3.00	6.00	12.00
16	Jean-Guy Gendron	3.00	6.00	12.00
17	Irv Spencer, LC	3.00	6.00	12.00
18	Wayne Connelly	3.00	6.00	12.00
19	Andre Pronovost	3.00	6.00	12.00
20	Terry Gray	3.00	6.00	12.00
21	Tom Williams, RC	3.75	7.50	15.00
22	Boston Bruins	7.50	15.00	30.00

CHICAGO BLACK HAWKS

No.	Player	VG	EX	NRMT
23	Rudy Pilous, Coach	3.00	6.00	12.00
24	Glenn Hall, Goalie	11.25	22.50	45.00
25	Denis DeJordy, Goalie	3.00	6.00	12.00
26	Jack Evans, LC	3.00	6.00	12.00
27	Elmer Vasko	3.00	6.00	12.00
28	Pierre Pilote	5.00	10.00	20.00
29	Bob Turner	3.00	6.00	12.00
30	Dollard St. Laurent, LC	3.00	6.00	12.00

1962 - 63 HOCKEY BUCKS — TOPPS • 193

No.	Player	VG	EX	NRMT
31	Wayne Hillman	3.00	6.00	12.00
32	Al MacNeil	3.00	6.00	12.00
33	Bobby Hull	75.00	150.00	300.00
34	Stan Mikita	31.25	62.50	125.00
35	Red Hay	3.00	6.00	12.00
36	Murray Balfour	3.00	6.00	12.00
37	**Chico Maki, RC**	**5.00**	**10.00**	**20.00**
38	Ab McDonald, Error	3.00	6.00	12.00
39	Kenny Wharram	3.00	6.00	12.00
40	Ron Murphy	3.00	6.00	12.00
41	Eric Nesterenko	3.00	6.00	12.00
42	Reggie Fleming	3.00	6.00	12.00
43	**Murray Hall, RC**	**3.00**	**6.00**	**12.00**
44	Chicago Black Hawks	7.50	15.00	30.00

NEW YORK RANGERS

No.	Player	VG	EX	NRMT
45	Gump Worsley, Goalie	8.75	17.50	35.00
46	Harry Howell	4.50	9.00	18.00
47	Al Langlois	3.00	6.00	12.00
48	Larry Cahan	3.00	6.00	12.00
49	**Jim Neilson, RC**	**4.50**	**9.00**	**18.00**
50	Al LeBrun, LC	3.00	6.00	12.00
51	Earl Ingarfield	3.00	6.00	12.00
52	Andy Bathgate	4.50	9.00	18.00
53	Dean Prentice	3.00	6.00	12.00
54	Andy Hebenton	3.00	6.00	12.00
55	Ted Hampson	3.00	6.00	12.00
56	**Dave Balon, RC**	**3.75**	**7.50**	**15.00**
57	Bert Olmstead, LC	3.50	7.00	14.00
58	Jean Ratelle	11.25	22.50	45.00
59	Rod Gilbert	11.25	22.50	45.00
60	**Vic Hadfield, RC**	**8.75**	**17.50**	**35.00**
61	Frank Paice, Trainer	3.00	6.00	12.00
62	Camille Henry	3.00	6.00	12.00
63	Bronco Horvath, LC	3.00	6.00	12.00
64	Pat Hannigan, LC, Error	3.00	6.00	12.00
65	New York Rangers	7.50	15.00	30.00

CHECKLIST

No.	Checklist	VG	EX	NRMT
66	Checklist (1 - 66)	80.00	160.00	325.00

— 1962 - 63 HOCKEY BUCKS —

Unnumbered bucks came folded, one per pack.

Buck Size: 4 1/8" X 1 3/4"
Face: Green on paper stock; Name, Team, Facsimile autograph
Back: Patterned green
Imprint: None
Complete Set No.: 24

		VG	EX	NRMT
Complete Set Price:		230.00	460.00	925.00
Common Player:		6.25	12.50	25.00

BOSTON BRUINS

No.	Player	VG	EX	NRMT
1	Leo Boivin	10.00	20.00	40.00
2	John Bucyk	10.00	20.00	40.00
3	Warren Godfrey	6.25	12.50	25.00
4	Ted Green	8.75	17.50	35.00
5	Don McKenney	6.25	12.50	25.00
6	Doug Mohns	6.25	12.50	25.00
7	Murray Oliver	6.25	12.50	25.00
8	Jerry Toppazzini	6.25	12.50	25.00

CHICAGO BLACK HAWKS

No.	Player	VG	EX	NRMT
9	Reggie Fleming	6.25	12.50	25.00
10	Glenn Hall, Goalie	10.00	20.00	40.00
11	Billy Hay	6.25	12.50	25.00
12	Bobby Hull	55.00	110.00	225.00
13	Ab McDonald, Error	6.25	12.50	25.00
14	Stan Mikita	27.50	55.00	110.00
15	Pierre Pilote	8.75	17.50	35.00
16	Elmer Vasko	6.25	12.50	25.00

NEW YORK RANGERS

No.	Player	VG	EX	NRMT
17	Dave Balon	6.25	12.50	25.00

Topps
1962-63 Hockey Bucks
Buck No. 13, Error, Name
Misspelled MacDonald on face

Topps
1963-64 Issue
Card No. 1,
Milt Schmidt

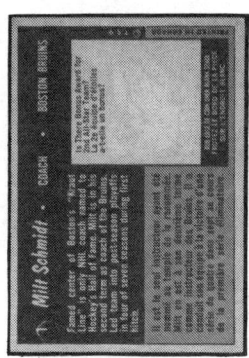

Topps
1963-64 Issue
Card No. 1,
Milt Schmidt

No.	Player	VG	EX	NRMT
18	Andy Bathgate	11.25	22.50	45.00
19	Andy Hebenton	6.25	12.50	25.00
20	Harry Howell	8.75	17.50	35.00
21	Earl Ingarfield	6.25	12.50	25.00
22	Al Langlois	6.25	12.50	25.00
23	Dean Prentice	6.25	12.50	25.00
24	Gump Worsley, Goalie	13.75	27.50	55.00

— 1963 - 64 REGULAR ISSUE —

Mint cards will command a price premium of 50% over NRMT cards.

PRICE MOVEMENT OF NRMT SETS

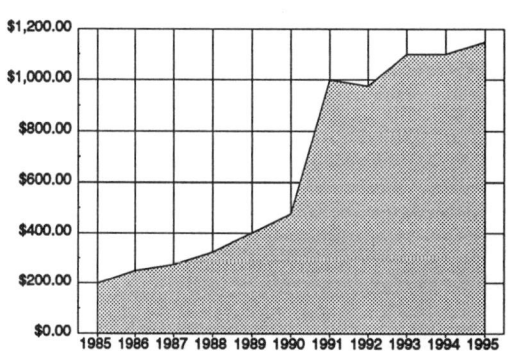

Card Size: 2 1/2" X 3 1/2"
Face: Four colour, black and white action photo at right side
Back: Blue on card stock, Number, Resume, Hockey trivia, Bilingual
Imprint: © T.C.G. PRINTED IN CANADA
Complete Set No.: 66

	VG	EX	NRMT
Complete Set Price:	295.00	590.00	1,150.00
Common Player:	2.25	4.50	9.00

BOSTON BRUINS

No.	Player	VG	EX	NRMT
1	Milt Schmidt, Coach	6.25	12.50	25.00
2	**Ed Johnston, Goalie, RC**	**7.50**	**15.00**	**30.00**
3	Doug Mohns	2.25	4.50	9.00
4	Tom Johnson	3.00	6.00	12.00
5	Leo Boivin	3.00	6.00	12.00
6	**Bob McCord, RC**	**2.25**	**4.50**	**9.00**
7	Ted Green	2.50	5.00	10.00
8	**Ed Westfall, RC**	**7.50**	**15.00**	**30.00**
9	Charlie Burns	2.25	4.50	9.00
10	Murray Oliver	2.25	4.50	9.00
11	John Bucyk	5.50	11.00	22.00
12	Tom Williams	2.25	4.50	9.00
13	Dean Prentice	2.75	5.50	11.00
14	**Bobby Leiter, RC**	**2.25**	**4.50**	**9.00**
15	Andy Hebenton, LC	2.25	4.50	9.00
16	Jean-Guy Gendron	2.25	4.50	9.00
17	**Wayne Rivers, RC**	**2.25**	**4.50**	**9.00**
18	Jerry Toppazzini, LC	2.25	4.50	9.00
19	Forbes Kennedy	2.25	4.50	9.00
20	Orland Kurtenbach	2.25	4.50	9.00
21	Boston Bruins Team Picture	7.50	15.00	30.00

CHICAGO BLACK HAWKS

No.	Player	VGV	EX	NRMT
22	Billy Reay, Coach	2.50	5.00	10.00
23	Glenn Hall, Goalie	8.75	17.50	35.00
24	Denis DeJordy, Goalie	2.25	4.50	9.00
25	Pierre Pilote	3.75	7.50	15.00
26	Elmer Vasko	2.25	4.50	9.00
27	Wayne Hillman	2.25	4.50	9.00
28	Al MacNeil	2.25	4.50	9.00
29	**Howie Young, RC**	**3.00**	**6.00**	**12.00**
30	**Ed Van Impe, RC**	**2.75**	**5.50**	**11.00**
31	Reggie Fleming	2.25	4.50	9.00
32	Bob Turner, LC	2.25	4.50	9.00
33	**Bobby Hull**	**50.00**	**100.00**	**200.00**
34	Red Hay	2.25	4.50	9.00

194 • TOPPS — 1964-65 REGULAR ISSUE

No.	Player	VG	EX	NRMT
35	Murray Balfour	2.25	4.50	9.00
36	Stan Mikita	25.00	50.00	100.00
37	Ab McDonald, Error	2.25	4.50	9.00
38	Kenny Wharram	2.25	4.50	9.00
39	Eric Nesterenko	2.25	4.50	9.00
40	Ron Murphy	2.25	4.50	9.00
41	Chico Maki	2.50	5.00	10.00
42	John McKenzie	2.50	5.00	10.00
43	Chicago Black Hawks, Team Picture	7.50	15.00	30.00

NEW YORK RANGERS

No.	Player	VG	EX	NRMT
44	George Sullivan	2.50	5.00	10.00
45	Jacques Plante, Goalie	31.25	62.50	125.00
46	Gilles Villemure, Goalie, RC	5.50	11.00	22.00
47	Doug Harvey, LC	7.50	15.00	30.00
48	Harry Howell	3.75	7.50	15.00
49	Al Langlois	2.25	4.50	9.00
50	Jim Neilson	2.25	4.50	9.00
51	Larry Cahan	2.25	4.50	9.00
52	Andy Bathgate	3.75	7.50	15.00
53	Don McKenney	2.25	4.50	9.00
54	Vic Hadfield	3.75	7.50	15.00
55	Earl Ingarfield	2.25	4.50	9.00
56	Camille Henry	2.25	4.50	9.00
57	Rod Gilbert	7.50	15.00	30.00
58	Phil Goyette	2.25	4.50	9.00
59	Don Marshall	2.25	4.50	9.00
60	Dick Meissner, LC	2.25	4.50	9.00
61	Val Fonteyne	2.25	4.50	9.00
62	Ken Schinkel	2.25	4.50	9.00
63	Jean Ratelle	7.50	15.00	30.00
64	Don Johns, RC, LC	2.25	4.50	9.00
65	New York Rangers, Team Picture	7.50	15.00	30.00

CHECKLIST

No.	Checklist	VG	EX	NRMT
66	Checklist (1 - 66)	75.00	150.00	300.00

— 1964 - 65 REGULAR ISSUE —

This issue features players from all six NHL teams. The card is larger than previous years and some of the second series' higher numbers were short-printed. Mint cards will command a 50% price premium over NRMT cards.

PRICE MOVEMENT OF NRMT SETS

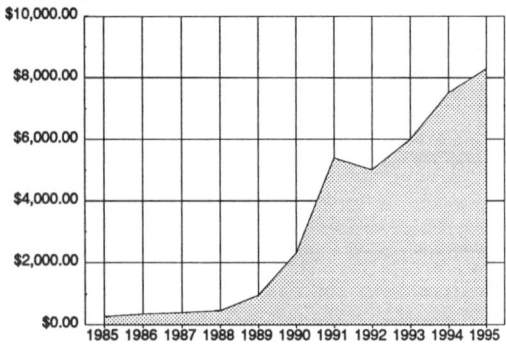

Card Size: 2 1/2" X 4 11/16"
Face: Four colour, white border, Position
Back: Black and red on card stock, Number, Resume, Cartoon, Bilingual
Imprint: © T.C.G. PRINTED IN CANADA
Complete Set No.: 110
Complete Set Price: 2,075.00 4,150.00 8,300.00
Common Player (1 - 55): 5.00 10.00 20.00
Common Player (56 - 110): 2.50 25.00 50.00

No.	Player	VG	EX	NRMT
1	Pit Martin, Det., RC	15.00	30.00	60.00
2	Gilles Tremblay, Mon.	5.00	10.00	20.00
3	Terry Harper, Mon.	5.00	10.00	20.00
4	John Ferguson Sr., Mon.	10.00	20.00	40.00

Topps 1964-65 Issue Card No. 20, Bobby Hull

Topps 1964-65 Issue Card No. 20, Bobby Hull

Topps 1964-65 Issue Card No. 89, Gordie Howe

No.	Player	VG	EX	NRMT
5	Elmer Vasko, Chi.	5.00	10.00	20.00
6	Terry Sawchuk, Goalie, Tor.	31.25	62.50	125.00
7	Billy Hay, Chi.	5.00	10.00	20.00
8	Gary Bergman, Det., RC	7.50	15.00	30.00
9	Doug Barkley, Det.	5.00	10.00	20.00
10	Bob McCord, Bos.	5.00	10.00	20.00
11	Parker MacDonald, Det.	5.00	10.00	20.00
12	Glenn Hall, Goalie, Chi.	15.00	30.00	60.00
13	Al Langlois, Det.	5.00	10.00	20.00
14	Camille Henry, NYR	5.00	10.00	20.00
15	Norm Ullman, Det.	7.50	15.00	30.00
16	Ab McDonald, Bos.	5.00	10.00	20.00
17	Charlie Hodge, Goalie, Mon.	5.00	10.00	20.00
18	Orland Kurtenbach, Bos.	5.00	10.00	20.00
19	Dean Prentice, Bos.	5.00	10.00	20.00
20	Bobby Hull, Chi.	87.50	175.00	350.00
21	Ed Johnston, Goalie, Bos.	6.25	12.50	25.00
22	Denis DeJordy, Goalie, Chi.	5.00	10.00	20.00
23	Claude Provost, Mon.	5.00	10.00	20.00
24	Rod Gilbert, NYR	12.50	25.00	50.00
25	Doug Mohns, Chi.	5.00	10.00	20.00
26	Al MacNeil, Chi.	5.00	10.00	20.00
27	Billy Harris, Tor.	5.00	10.00	20.00
28	Kenny Wharram, Chi.	5.00	10.00	20.00
29	George (Red) Sullivan, NYR, LC	5.00	10.00	20.00
30	John McKenzie, Chi.	5.00	10.00	20.00
31	Stan Mikita, Chi.	31.25	62.50	125.00
32	Ted Green, Bos.	5.00	10.00	20.00
33	Jean Beliveau, Mon.	30.00	60.00	125.00
34	Arnie Brown, NYR, RC	5.00	10.00	20.00
35	Reggie Fleming, Bos.	5.00	10.00	20.00
36	Jim Mikol, NYR, RC, LC	5.00	10.00	20.00
37	Dave Balon, Mon.	5.00	10.00	20.00
38	Billy Reay, Chi., Coach	5.00	10.00	20.00
39	Marcel Pronovost, Det.	5.00	10.00	20.00
40	Johnny Bower, Goalie, Tor.	12.50	25.00	50.00
41	Wayne Hillman, Chi.	5.00	10.00	20.00
42	Floyd Smith, Det.	5.00	10.00	20.00
43	Toe Blake, Mon., Coach	5.00	10.00	20.00
44	Red Kelly, Tor.	7.00	14.00	28.00
45	Punch Imlach, Tor., Coach	7.50	15.00	30.00
46	Dick Duff, NYR	5.00	10.00	20.00
47	Roger Crozier, Goalie, Det., RC	15.00	30.00	60.00
48	Henri Richard, Mon.	20.00	40.00	80.00
49	Larry Jeffrey, Det.	5.00	10.00	20.00
50	Leo Boivin, Bos.	5.00	10.00	20.00
51	Ed Westfall, Bos.	5.00	10.00	20.00
52	Jean-Guy Talbot, Mon.	5.00	10.00	20.00
53	Jacques Laperriere, Mon.	5.00	10.00	20.00
54	Checklist 1 (1 - 54)	100.00	200.00	400.00
55	Checklist 2 (55 - 110)	100.00	200.00	400.00
56	Ron Murphy, Det.	12.50	25.00	50.00
57	Bob Baun, Tor.	12.50	25.00	50.00
58	Tom Williams, Bos., SP	45.00	90.00	180.00
59	Pierre Pilote, Chi., SP	62.50	125.00	250.00
60	Bob Pulford, Tor.	12.50	25.00	50.00
61	Red Berenson, Mon.	12.50	25.00	50.00
62	Vic Hadfield, NYR	12.50	25.00	50.00
63	Bobby Leiter, Bos.	12.50	25.00	50.00
64	Jim Pappin, Tor., RC	15.00	30.00	60.00
65	Earl Ingarfield, NYR	12.50	25.00	50.00
66	Lou Angotti, NYR, RC	12.50	25.00	50.00
67	Rod Seiling, NYR, RC	12.50	25.00	50.00
68	Jacques Plante, Goalie, NYR	45.00	85.00	175.00
69	George Armstrong, Tor.	16.25	32.50	65.00
70	Milt Schmidt, Bos., Coach	15.00	30.00	60.00
71	Eddie Shack, Tor.	20.00	40.00	80.00
72	Gary Dornhoefer, Bos., RC, SP	70.00	140.00	275.00
73	Chico Maki, Chi., SP	62.50	125.00	250.00
74	Gilles Villemure, Goalie, NYR, SP	50.00	100.00	200.00
75	Carl Brewer, Tor.	12.50	25.00	50.00
76	Bruce MacGregor, Det.	12.50	25.00	50.00
77	Bob Nevin, NYR	12.50	25.00	50.00
78	Ralph Backstrom, Mon.	12.50	25.00	50.00
79	Murray Oliver, Bos.	12.50	25.00	50.00
80	Bobby Rousseau, Mon., SP	50.00	100.00	200.00
81	Don McKenney, Tor.	12.50	25.00	50.00
82	Ted Lindsay, Det., LC	20.00	40.00	80.00
83	Harry Howell, NYR	16.25	32.50	65.00
84	Doug Robinson, Chi., RC	12.50	25.00	50.00
85	Frank Mahovlich, Tor.	40.00	80.00	160.00
86	Andy Bathgate, Tor.	15.00	30.00	60.00
87	Phil Goyette, NYR	12.50	25.00	50.00

1965 - 66 REGULAR ISSUE — TOPPS • 195

No.	Player	VG	EX	NRMT
88	J.C. Tremblay, Mon.	12.50	25.00	50.00
89	Gordie Howe, Det.	150.00	300.00	600.00
90	Murray Balfour, Bos., LC	12.50	25.00	50.00
91	Eric Nesterenko, Chi., SP	50.00	100.00	200.00
92	**Marcel Paille, Goalie, NYR, RC, LC**	70.00	140.00	275.00
93	Sid Abel, Det., Coach, SP	12.50	25.00	50.00
94	Dave Keon, Tor.	25.00	50.00	100.00
95	Alex Delvecchio, Det.	20.00	40.00	80.00
96	Bill Gadsby, Det.	15.00	30.00	60.00
97	Don Marshall, NYR	12.50	25.00	50.00
98	Bill Hicke, Mon., SP	50.00	100.00	200.00
99	Ron Stewart, Tor.	12.50	25.00	50.00
100	John Bucyk, Bos.	22.50	45.00	90.00
101	Tom Johnson, Bos.	12.50	25.00	50.00
102	Tim Horton, Tor.	31.25	62.50	125.00
103	Jim Neilson, NYR	12.50	25.00	50.00
104	Allan Stanley, Tor.	15.00	30.00	60.00

ALL STARS

No.	Player	VG	EX	NRMT
105	Tim Horton, Tor., SP	75.00	150.00	300.00
106	Stan Mikita, Chi., SP	75.00	150.00	300.00
107	Bobby Hull, Chi.	50.00	100.00	200.00
108	Kenny Wharram, Chi.	12.50	25.00	50.00
109	Pierre Pilote, Chi.	15.00	30.00	60.00
110	Glenn Hall, Goalie, Chi.	37.50	75.00	150.00

— 1965 - 66 REGULAR ISSUE —

Card nos. 122-128 are more difficult to find and are not even listed on the checklist card No. 121. Mint cards command a price premium of 50% over NRMT cards.

PRICE MOVEMENT OF NRMT SETS

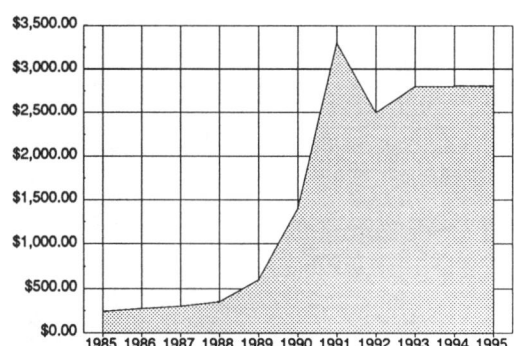

Card Size: 2 1/2" X 3 1/2"
Face: Four colour, white border
Team Cards - Two colour, black and white photograph
Back: Black on card stock; Number, Resume, Hockey trivia, Bilingual
Imprint: © T.C.G. PRINTED IN CANADA
Complete Set No.: 128
Complete Set Price: 700.00   1,400.00   2,800.00
Common Player: 2.25   4.50   9.00

MONTREAL CANADIENS

No.	Player	VG	EX	NRMT
1	Toe Blake, Coach	5.50	11.00	22.00
2	Gump Worsley, Goalie	5.00	10.00	20.00
3	Jacques Laperriere	3.75	7.50	15.00
4	Jean-Guy Talbot	2.25	4.50	9.00
5	**Ted Harris, RC**	2.25	4.50	9.00
6	Jean Beliveau	13.75	27.50	55.00
7	Dick Duff	2.25	4.50	9.00
8	Claude Provost	2.25	4.50	9.00
9	Red Berenson	2.25	4.50	9.00
10	John Ferguson, Sr.	2.25	4.50	9.00

TORONTO MAPLE LEAFS

No.	Player	VG	EX	NRMT
11	Punch Imlach, Coach	2.50	5.00	10.00
12	Terry Sawchuk, Goalie	17.50	35.00	70.00
13	Bob Baun	2.25	4.50	9.00

Topps
1965-66 Issue
Card No. 1,
Toe Blake

Topps
1965-66 Issue
Card No. 1,
Toe Blake

Topps, 1965-66
Card No. 28, Error,
Name misspelled
Gary on face

Topps, 1965-66
Card No. 76, Error,
Name misspelled Yvon
on face and back

No.	Player	VG	EX	NRMT
14	Kent Douglas	2.25	4.50	9.00
15	Red Kelly	4.50	9.00	18.00
16	Jim Pappin	2.25	4.50	9.00
17	Dave Keon	7.50	15.00	30.00
18	Bob Pulford	2.25	4.50	9.00
19	George Armstrong	2.75	5.50	11.00
20	Orland Kurtenbach	2.25	4.50	9.00

NEW YORK RANGERS

No.	Player	VG	EX	NRMT
21	**Ed Giacomin, Goalie, RC**	30.00	60.00	125.00
22	Harry Howell	2.75	5.50	11.00
23	Rod Seiling	2.25	4.50	9.00
24	**Mike McMahon, RC**	2.25	4.50	9.00
25	Jean Ratelle	6.25	12.50	25.00
26	Doug Robinson	2.25	4.50	9.00
27	Vic Hadfield	2.50	5.00	10.00
28	**Garry Peters, RC, Error**	2.25	4.50	9.00
29	Don Marshall	2.25	4.50	9.00
30	Bill Hicke	2.25	4.50	9.00

BOSTON BRUINS

No.	Player	VG	EX	NRMT
31	**Gerry Cheevers, Goalie, RC**	30.00	60.00	125.00
32	Leo Boivin	2.25	4.50	9.00
33	Al Langlois, LC	2.25	4.50	9.00
34	Murray Oliver	2.25	4.50	9.00
35	Tom Williams	2.25	4.50	9.00
36	**Ron Schock, RC**	2.25	4.50	9.00
37	Ed Westfall	2.50	5.00	10.00
38	Gary Dornhoefer	2.25	4.50	9.00
39	Bob Dillabough	2.25	4.50	9.00
40	**Poul Popiel, RC, Error**	2.25	4.50	9.00

DETROIT RED WINGS

No.	Player	VG	EX	NRMT
41	Sid Abel, Coach	2.75	5.50	11.00
42	Roger Crozier, Goalie	3.25	6.50	13.00
43	Doug Barkley, LC	2.25	4.50	9.00
44	Bill Gadsby, LC	2.75	5.50	11.00
45	**Bryan Watson, RC**	3.75	7.50	15.00
46	Bob McCord	2.25	4.50	9.00
47	Alex Delvecchio	3.75	7.50	15.00
48	Andy Bathgate	3.00	6.00	12.00
49	Norm Ullman	3.00	6.00	12.00
50	Ab McDonald	2.25	4.50	9.00
51	**Paul Henderson, RC**	12.50	25.00	50.00
52	Pit Martin	2.25	4.50	9.00
53	Billy Harris	2.25	4.50	9.00

CHICAGO BLACK HAWKS

No.	Player	VG	EX	NRMT
54	Billy Reay, Coach	2.75	5.50	11.00
55	Glenn Hall, Goalie	8.75	17.50	35.00
56	Pierre Pilote	2.50	5.00	10.00
57	Al MacNeil	2.25	4.50	9.00
58	Camille Henry	2.25	4.50	9.00
59	Bobby Hull	50.00	100.00	200.00
60	Stan Mikita	15.00	30.00	60.00
61	Kenny Wharram	2.25	4.50	9.00
62	Billy Hay, LC	2.25	4.50	9.00
63	**Fred Stanfield, RC**	2.50	5.00	10.00
64	**Dennis Hull, RC**	6.50	13.00	26.00
65	**Ken Hodge, RC**	7.50	15.00	30.00

CHECKLIST

No.	Checklist	VG	EX	NRMT
66	Checklist (1 - 66)	56.25	112.50	225.00

MONTREAL CANADIENS

No.	Player	VG	EX	NRMT
67	Charlie Hodge, Goalie	2.25	4.50	9.00
68	Terry Harper	2.25	4.50	9.00
69	J.C. Tremblay	2.25	4.50	9.00
70	Bobby Rousseau	2.25	4.50	9.00
71	Henri Richard	6.25	12.50	25.00
72	Dave Balon	2.25	4.50	9.00
73	Ralph Backstrom	2.25	4.50	9.00
74	**Jim Roberts, RC**	2.75	5.50	11.00
75	**Claude Larose, RC**	2.50	5.00	10.00
76	**Yvan Cournoyer, RC, Error**	31.25	62.50	125.00

196 • TOPPS — 1966 - 67 REGULAR ISSUE

TORONTO MAPLE LEAFS

No.	Player	VG	EX	NRMT
77	Johnny Bower, Goalie	3.75	7.50	15.00
78	Carl Brewer	2.50	5.00	10.00
79	Tim Horton	8.75	17.50	35.00
80	Marcel Pronovost	3.00	6.00	12.00
81	Frank Mahovlich	10.00	20.00	40.00
82	Ron Ellis, RC	8.75	17.50	35.00
83	Larry Jeffrey	2.25	4.50	9.00
84	Pete Stemkowski, RC	3.00	6.00	12.00
85	Eddie Joyal, RC	2.25	4.50	9.00
86	Mike Walton, RC	3.00	6.00	12.00

NEW YORK RANGERS

No.	Player	VG	EX	NRMT
87	George Sullivan, LC	2.25	4.50	9.00
88	Don Simmons, Goalie, LC	2.25	4.50	9.00
89	Jim Neilson	2.25	4.50	9.00
90	Arnie Brown	2.25	4.50	9.00
91	Rod Gilbert	5.50	11.00	22.00
92	Phil Goyette	2.25	4.50	9.00
93	Bob Nevin	2.25	4.50	9.00
94	John McKenzie	2.25	4.50	9.00
95	Ted Taylor, RC	2.25	4.50	9.00

BOSTON BRUINS

No.	Player	VG	EX	NRMT
96	Milt Schmidt, Coach	3.00	6.00	12.00
97	Ed Johnston, Goalie	2.50	5.00	10.00
98	Ted Green	2.25	4.50	9.00
99	Don Awrey, RC	2.50	5.00	10.00
100	Bob Woytowich, RC	2.25	4.50	9.00
101	John Bucyk	5.00	10.00	20.00
102	Dean Prentice	2.50	5.00	10.00
103	Ron Stewart	2.25	4.50	9.00
104	Reggie Fleming	2.25	4.50	9.00
105	Parker MacDonald	2.25	4.50	9.00

DETROIT RED WINGS

No.	Player	VG	EX	NRMT
106	Hank Bassen, Goalie	2.25	4.50	9.00
107	Gary Bergman	2.25	4.50	9.00
108	Gordie Howe	50.00	100.00	200.00
109	Floyd Smith	2.25	4.50	9.00
110	Bruce MacGregor	2.25	4.50	9.00
111	Ron Murphy	2.25	4.50	9.00
112	Don McKenney, LC	2.25	4.50	9.00

CHICAGO BLACK HAWKS

No.	Player	VG	EX	NRMT
113	Denis DeJordy, Goalie	2.25	4.50	9.00
114	Elmer Vasko	2.25	4.50	9.00
115	Matt Ravlich, RC	2.25	4.50	9.00
116	Phil Esposito, RC	85.00	175.00	350.00
117	Chico Maki	2.25	4.50	9.00
118	Doug Mohns	2.25	4.50	9.00
119	Eric Nesterenko	2.25	4.50	9.00
120	Pat Stapleton	2.25	4.50	9.00

CHECKLIST

No.	Checklist	VG	EX	NRMT
121	Checklist (67 - 128)	56.25	112.50	225.00

HOWE'S 600TH GOAL

No.	Player	VG	EX	NRMT
122	Gordie Howe, SP "First N.H.L. 600 Goal Scorer"	85.00	175.00	350.00

TEAM CARDS

No.	Team	VG	EX	NRMT
123	Toronto Maple Leafs	20.00	40.00	80.00
124	Chicago Black Hawks	20.00	40.00	80.00
125	Detroit Red Wings	20.00	40.00	80.00
126	Montreal Canadiens	20.00	40.00	80.00
127	New York Rangers	20.00	40.00	80.00
128	Boston Bruins	45.00	90.00	180.00

Topps 1966-67 Issue Card No. 1, Toe Blake

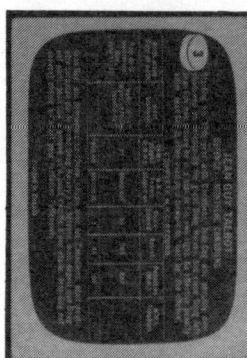

Topps 1966-67 Issue Card No. 3, Jean-Guy Talbot

Topps 1966-67 Issue Card No. 13, Terry Sawchuk

Topps 1966-67 Issue Card No. 32, Ed Westfall

— 1966 - 67 REGULAR ISSUE —

The unique format of this issue simulates a television screen with a wood grain border. The key card in this issue is Bobby Orr's rookie card. The card backs summarize the player's entire NHL record. The wood grain border printed to the card edge makes these cards difficult to obtain in mint. Mint cards will bring premiums of 50% to 75% over NRMT cards.

PRICE MOVEMENT OF NRMT SETS

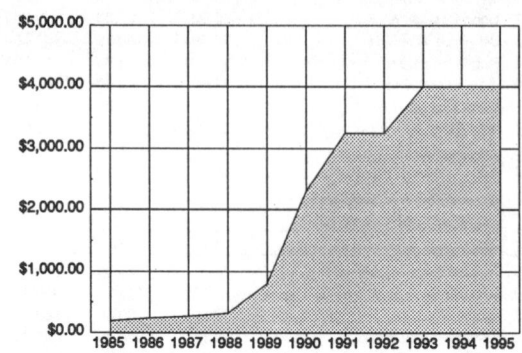

Card Size: 2 1/2" X 3 1/2"
Face: Four colour, woodgrain border, Position
Back: Black on card stock, Number, Resume, Bilingual
Imprint: Printed in Canada
Complete Set No.: 132

Complete Set Price:	1,000.00	2,000.00	4,000.00
Common Player:	2.00	4.00	8.00

MONTREAL CANADIENS

No.	Player	VG	EX	NRMT
1	Toe Blake, Coach	4.50	9.00	18.00
2	Gump Worsley, Goalie	6.00	12.50	25.00
3	Jean-Guy Talbot	2.00	4.00	8.00
4	Gilles Tremblay	2.00	4.00	8.00
5	J.C. Tremblay	2.00	4.00	8.00
6	Jim Roberts	2.00	4.00	8.00
7	Bobby Rousseau	2.00	4.00	8.00
8	Henri Richard	6.00	12.50	25.00
9	Claude Provost	2.00	4.00	8.00
10	Claude Larose	2.00	4.00	8.00

TORONTO MAPLE LEAFS

No.	Player	VG	EX	NRMT
11	Punch Imlach, Coach	2.25	4.50	9.00
12	Johnny Bower, Goalie	4.00	8.00	16.00
13	Terry Sawchuk, Goalie	11.25	22.50	55.00
14	Mike Walton	2.00	4.00	8.00
15	Pete Stemkowski	2.00	4.00	8.00
16	Allan Stanley	2.50	5.00	10.00
17	Eddie Shack	2.25	4.50	9.00
18	Brit Selby, RC	2.00	4.00	8.00
19	Bob Pulford	2.25	4.50	9.00
20	Marcel Pronovost	2.25	4.50	9.00

NEW YORK RANGERS

No.	Player	VG	EX	NRMT
21	Emile Francis, Coach	6.00	12.00	24.00
22	Rod Seiling	2.00	4.00	8.00
23	Ed Giacomin, Goalie	10.00	20.00	40.00
24	Don Marshall	2.00	4.00	8.00
25	Orland Kurtenbach	2.00	4.00	8.00
26	Rod Gilbert	5.00	10.00	20.00
27	Bob Nevin	2.00	4.00	8.00
28	Phil Goyette	2.00	4.00	8.00
29	Jean Ratelle	5.00	10.00	20.00
30	Earl Ingarfield	2.00	4.00	8.00

BOSTON BRUINS

No.	Player	VG	EX	NRMT
31	Harry Sinden, Coach	5.75	11.50	23.00
32	Ed Westfall	2.00	4.00	8.00
33	Joe Watson, RC	2.00	4.00	8.00
34	Bob Woytowich	2.00	4.00	8.00
35	Bobby Orr, RC	550.00	1,100.00	2,200.00

— 1966-67 REGULAR ISSUE — TOPPS • 197

No.	Player	VG	EX	NRMT
36	Gilles Marotte, RC	2.25	4.50	9.00
37	Ted Green	2.00	4.00	8.00
38	Tom Williams	2.00	4.00	8.00
39	John Bucyk	4.50	9.00	18.00
40	Wayne Connelly	2.00	4.00	8.00
41	Pit Martin	2.00	4.00	8.00

DETROIT RED WINGS

No.	Player	VG	EX	NRMT
42	Sid Abel, Coach	2.25	4.50	9.00
43	Roger Crozier, Goalie	2.25	4.50	9.00
44	Andy Bathgate	3.50	7.00	14.00
45	Dean Prentice	2.25	4.50	9.00
46	Paul Henderson	3.50	7.00	14.00
47	Gary Bergman	2.00	4.00	8.00
48	Bryan Watson	2.00	4.00	8.00
49	Bob Wall, RC	2.00	4.00	8.00
50	Leo Boivin	2.25	4.50	9.00
51	Bert Marshall, RC	2.00	4.00	8.00
52	Norm Ullman	3.50	7.00	14.00

CHICAGO BLACK HAWKS

No.	Player	VG	EX	NRMT
53	Billy Reay, Coach	2.00	4.00	8.00
54	Glenn Hall, Goalie	7.50	15.00	30.00
55	Wally Boyer, RC	2.00	4.00	8.00
56	Fred Stanfield	2.00	4.00	8.00
57	Pat Stapleton	2.00	4.00	8.00
58	Matt Ravlich	2.00	4.00	8.00
59	Pierre Pilote	2.25	4.50	9.00
60	Eric Nesterenko	2.00	4.00	8.00
61	Doug Mohns	2.00	4.00	8.00
62	Stan Mikita	12.50	25.00	50.00
63	Phil Esposito	35.00	75.00	150.00
64	Bobby Hull, Scoring Leader	17.50	35.00	70.00

TROPHY CARDS

No.	Trophy	VG	EX	NRMT
65	The Vezina Trophy: Hodge & Worsley	3.75	7.50	15.00

CHECKLIST

No.	Checklist	VG	EX	NRMT
66	Checklist 1 (1 - 66)	55.00	110.00	225.00

MONTREAL CANADIENS

No.	Player	VG	EX	NRMT
67	Jacques Laperriere	3.00	6.00	12.00
68	Terry Harper	2.00	4.00	8.00
69	Ted Harris	2.00	4.00	8.00
70	John Ferguson, Sr.	2.00	4.00	8.00
71	Dick Duff	2.00	4.00	8.00
72	Yvan Cournoyer	11.00	22.50	45.00
73	Jean Beliveau	12.50	25.00	50.00
74	Dave Balon	2.00	4.00	8.00
75	Ralph Backstrom	2.00	4.00	8.00

TORONTO MAPLE LEAFS

No.	Player	VG	EX	NRMT
76	Jim Pappin	2.00	4.00	8.00
77	Frank Mahovlich	10.00	20.00	40.00
78	Dave Keon	6.25	12.50	25.00
79	Red Kelly, LC	3.75	7.50	15.00
80	Tim Horton	8.75	17.50	35.00
81	Ron Ellis	2.00	4.00	8.00
82	Kent Douglas	2.00	4.00	8.00
83	Bob Baun	2.00	4.00	8.00
84	George Armstrong	3.00	6.00	12.00

NEW YORK RANGERS

No.	Player	VG	EX	NRMT
85	Bernie Geoffrion	7.00	14.00	28.00
86	Vic Hadfield	2.00	4.00	8.00
87	Wayne Hillman	2.00	4.00	8.00
88	Jim Neilson	2.00	4.00	8.00
89	Al MacNeil, LC	2.00	4.00	8.00
90	Arnie Brown	2.00	4.00	8.00
91	Harry Howell	2.50	5.00	10.00
92	Red Berenson	2.00	4.00	8.00
93	Reggie Fleming	2.00	4.00	8.00

Topps 1966-67 Issue Card No. 47, Gary Bergman

Topps 1966-67 Issue Card No. 59, Pierre Pilote

Topps 1966-67 Issue Card No. 106, Floyd Smith

Topps 1966-67 Issue Card No. 116, Lou Angotti

BOSTON BRUINS

No.	Player	VG	EX	NRMT
94	Ron Stewart	2.00	4.00	8.00
95	Murray Oliver	2.00	4.00	8.00
96	Ron Murphy	2.00	4.00	8.00
97	John McKenzie	2.00	4.00	8.00
98	Bob Dillabough	2.00	4.00	8.00
99	Ed Johnston, Goalie	2.00	4.00	8.00
100	Ron Schock	2.00	4.00	8.00
101	Dallas Smith	2.00	4.00	8.00

DETROIT RED WINGS

No.	Player	VG	EX	NRMT
102	Alex Delvecchio	4.00	8.00	16.00
103	Pete Mahovlich, RC	6.25	12.50	25.00
104	Bruce MacGregor	2.00	4.00	8.00
105	Murray Hall	2.00	4.00	8.00
106	Floyd Smith	2.00	4.00	8.00
107	Hank Bassen, Goalie, LC	2.00	4.00	8.00
108	Val Fonteyne	2.00	4.00	8.00
109	Gordie Howe	50.00	100.00	200.00

CHICAGO BLACK HAWKS

No.	Player	VG	EX	NRMT
110	Chico Maki	2.00	4.00	8.00
111	Doug Jarrett, RC	2.25	4.50	9.00
112	Bobby Hull	37.50	75.00	150.00
113	Dennis Hull	2.75	5.50	11.00
114	Ken Hodge	2.75	5.50	11.00
115	Denis DeJordy, Goalie	2.00	4.00	8.00
116	Lou Angotti	2.00	4.00	8.00
117	Kenny Wharram	2.00	4.00	8.00

TEAM CARDS

No.	Team	VG	EX	NRMT
118	Montreal Canadiens	6.25	12.50	25.00
119	Detroit Red Wings	6.25	12.50	25.00

CHECKLIST

No.	Checklist	VG	EX	NRMT
120	Checklist 2 (67 - 132)	55.00	110.00	225.00

ALL STARS

First Team

No.	Player	VG	EX	NRMT
121	Gordie Howe, Det.	30.00	60.00	120.00
122	Jacques Laperriere, Mon.	2.75	5.50	9.00
123	Pierre Pilote, Chi.	2.75	5.50	9.00
124	Stan Mikita, Chi.	7.50	15.00	30.00
125	Bobby Hull, Chi.	20.00	40.00	85.00
126	Glenn Hall, Goalie, Chi.	4.50	9.00	18.00

Second Team

No.	Player	VG	EX	NRMT
127	Jean Beliveau, Mon.	5.00	10.00	20.00
128	Allan Stanley, Tor.	2.25	4.50	9.00
129	Pat Stapleton, Chi.	2.00	4.00	8.00
130	Gump Worsley, Goalie, Mon.	5.00	10.00	20.00
131	Frank Mahovlich, Mon.	4.50	9.00	18.00
132	Bobby Rousseau, Mon.	4.50	9.00	18.00

Note: Your cards must be accurately graded before they can be priced.

— 1966 - 67 USA TEST —

Thought to be a market test, this issue is very rare because of its limited distribution. The card format is very similar to that of the regular 1966-67 Topps series, except the card backs are printed in English only. The television screen wood grain border is a lighter shade than the regular issue. These cards are very scarce. The prices below are indications only since so few cards trade hands. There are three known uncut sheets of this issue.

PRICE MOVEMENT OF NRMT SETS

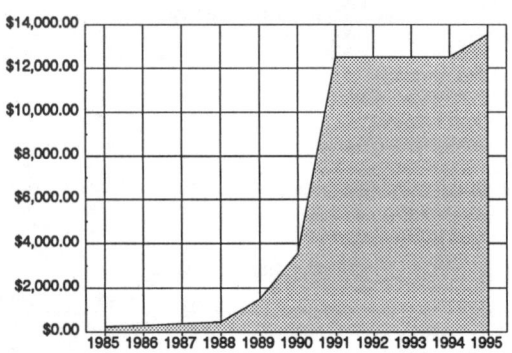

Card Size: 2 1/2" X 3 1/2"
Face: Four colour, woodgrain border, Position
Back: Black on card stock, Number, Resume
Imprint: © T.C.G. PRTD. IN U.S.A.
Complete Set No.: 66
Complete Set Price: 3,375.00 6,750.00 13,500.00
Common Player: 12.50 25.00 50.00

No.	Player	VG	EX	NRMT
1	Dennis Hull, Chi.	17.00	35.00	75.00
2	Gump Worsley, Goalie, Mon.	30.00	60.00	125.00
3	Dallas Smith, Bos.	12.50	25.00	50.00
4	Gilles Tremblay, Mon.	12.50	25.00	50.00
5	J.C. Tremblay, Mon.	12.50	25.00	50.00
6	Ralph Backstrom, Mon.	12.50	25.00	50.00
7	Bobby Rousseau, Mon.	12.50	25.00	50.00
8	Henri Richard, Mon.	17.00	35.00	75.00
9	Claude Provost, Mon.	12.50	25.00	50.00
10	Red Berenson, NYR	12.50	25.00	50.00
11	Punch Imlach, Coach, Tor.	12.50	25.00	50.00
12	Johnny Bower, Goalie, Tor.	25.00	50.00	100.00
13	Yvan Cournoyer, Mon.	35.00	75.00	150.00
14	Mike Walton, Tor.	12.50	25.00	50.00
15	Pete Stemkowski, Tor.	12.50	25.00	50.00
16	Allan Stanley, Tor.	17.00	35.00	75.00
17	George Armstrong, Tor.	17.00	35.00	75.00
18	Harry Howell, NYR	12.50	25.00	50.00
19	Vic Hadfield, NYR	12.50	25.00	50.00
20	Marcel Pronovost, Tor.	17.00	35.00	75.00
21	Pete Mahovlich, Det., RC	17.00	35.00	75.00
22	Rod Seiling, NYR	12.50	25.00	50.00
23	Gordie Howe, Det.	300.00	625.00	1,250.00
24	Don Marshall, NYR	12.50	25.00	50.00
25	Orland Kurtenbach, NYR	12.50	25.00	50.00
26	Rod Gilbert, NYR	30.00	60.00	125.00
27	Bob Nevin, NYR	12.50	25.00	50.00
28	Phil Goyette, NYR	12.50	25.00	50.00
29	Jean Ratelle, NYR	25.00	50.00	100.00
30	Dave Keon, Tor.	17.00	35.00	75.00
31	Jean Beliveau, Mon.	35.00	75.00	150.00
32	Ed Westfall, Bos.	12.50	25.00	50.00
33	Ron Murphy, Bos.	12.50	25.00	50.00
34	Wayne Hillman, NYR	12.50	25.00	50.00
35	Bobby Orr, Bos., RC	2,500.	5,000.	10,000.
36	Bernie Geoffrion, NYR	12.50	25.00	50.00
37	Ted Green, Bos.	12.50	25.00	50.00
38	Tom Williams, Bos.	12.50	25.00	50.00
39	John Bucyk, Bos.	25.00	50.00	100.00
40	Bobby Hull, Bos.	125.00	250.00	500.00
41	Ted Harris, Mon.	12.50	25.00	50.00
42	Red Kelly, Tor., LC	17.00	35.00	75.00
43	Roger Crozier, Goalie, Det.	17.00	35.00	75.00
44	Kenny Wharram, Chi.	12.50	25.00	50.00
45	Dean Prentice, Det.	12.50	25.00	50.00
46	Paul Henderson, Det.	17.00	35.00	75.00
47	Gary Bergman, Det.	12.50	25.00	50.00
48	Arnie Brown, NYR	12.50	25.00	50.00
49	Jim Pappin, Tor.	12.50	25.00	50.00
50	Denis DeJordy, Goalie, Chi.	12.50	25.00	50.00
51	Frank Mahovlich, Mon.	25.00	50.00	100.00
52	Norm Ullman, Det.	17.00	35.00	75.00
53	Chico Maki, Chi.	12.50	25.00	50.00
54	Reggie Fleming, NYR	12.50	25.00	50.00
55	Jim Neilson, NYR	12.50	25.00	50.00
56	Bruce MacGregor, Det.	12.50	25.00	50.00
57	Pat Stapleton, Chi.	12.50	25.00	50.00
58	Matt Ravlich, Chi.	12.50	25.00	50.00
59	Pierre Pilote, Chi.	20.00	40.00	80.00
60	Eric Nesterenko, Chi.	17.00	35.00	75.00
61	Doug Mohns, Chi.	12.50	25.00	50.00
62	Stan Mikita, Chi.	50.00	100.00	200.00
63	Alex Delvecchio, Det.	17.00	35.00	75.00
64	Ed Johnston, Goalie, Bos.	12.50	25.00	50.00
65	John Ferguson, Sr., Mon.	12.50	25.00	50.00
66	John McKenzie, Bos.	12.50	25.00	50.00

Note: Card No. 35, Bobby Orr in NRMT/Mint sold in 1991 to a Florida collector for $10,000.00. Prices for these rare cards are indications only and cards may trade higher or lower depending on demand.

Topps
1966-67 USA Test
Card No. 23,
Gordie Howe

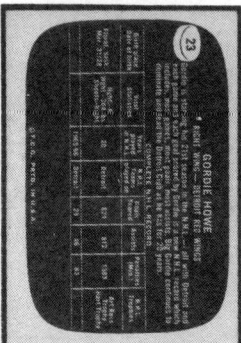

Topps
1966-67 USA Test
Card No. 23,
Gordie Howe

Topps
1967-68 Issue
Card No. 31,
Jean Ratelle

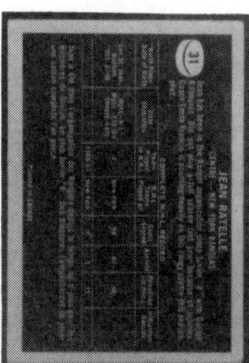

Topps
1967-68 Issue
Card No. 31,
Jean Ratelle

— 1967 - 68 REGULAR ISSUE —

Mint condition cards will command a price premium of 50% to 75% over NRMT cards.

PRICE MOVEMENT OF NRMT SETS

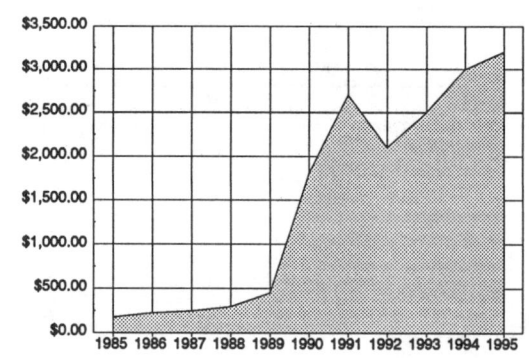

Card Size: 2 1/2" X 3 1/2"
Face: Four colour, white border, Position
Back: Black on card stock, Number, Resume, Bilingual
Imprint: Printed in Canada
Complete Set No.: 132
Complete Set Price: 800.00 1,600.00 3,200.00
Common Player: 2.50 5.00 10.00

MONTREAL CANADIENS

No.	Player	VG	EX	NRMT
1	Gump Worsley, Goalie	10.00	20.00	40.00
2	Dick Duff	2.50	5.00	10.00
3	**Jacques Lemaire, RC**	**16.25**	**32.50**	**65.00**
4	Claude Larose	2.50	5.00	10.00
5	Gilles Tremblay	2.50	5.00	10.00
6	Terry Harper	2.50	5.00	10.00
7	Jacques Laperriere	2.50	5.00	10.00
8	**Garry Monahan, RC**	**2.50**	**5.00**	**10.00**
9	**Carol Vadnais, RC**	**3.75**	**7.50**	**15.00**
10	Ted Harris	2.50	5.00	10.00

TORONTO MAPLE LEAFS

No.	Player	VG	EX	NRMT
11	Dave Keon	5.00	10.00	20.00
12	Pete Stemkowski	2.50	5.00	10.00
13	Allan Stanley	2.50	5.00	10.00
14	Ron Ellis	2.50	5.00	10.00
15	Mike Walton	2.50	5.00	10.00
16	Tim Horton	7.50	15.00	30.00
17	**Brian Conacher, RC**	**2.50**	**5.00**	**10.00**
18	Bruce Gamble, Goalie	2.50	5.00	10.00

1967 - 68 REGULAR ISSUE — TOPPS • 199

No.	Player	VG	EX	NRMT
19	Bob Pulford	2.50	5.00	10.00
20	**Duane Rupp, RC**	**2.50**	**5.00**	**10.00**

NEW YORK RANGERS

No.	Player	VG	EX	NRMT
21	Larry Jeffrey	2.50	5.00	10.00
22	Wayne Hillman	2.50	5.00	10.00
23	Don Marshall	2.50	5.00	10.00
24	Red Berenson	2.50	5.00	10.00
25	Phil Goyette	2.50	5.00	10.00
26	Camille Henry	2.50	5.00	10.00
27	Rod Seiling	2.50	5.00	10.00
28	Bob Nevin	2.50	5.00	10.00
29	Bernie Geoffrion, LC	5.50	11.00	22.00
30	Reggie Fleming	2.50	5.00	10.00
31	Jean Ratelle	5.00	10.00	20.00

BOSTON BRUINS

No.	Player	VG	EX	NRMT
32	Phil Esposito	25.00	50.00	100.00
33	**Derek Sanderson, RC**	**15.00**	**30.00**	**60.00**
34	Eddie Shack	3.25	6.50	13.00
35	**Ross Lonsberry, RC**	**2.50**	**5.00**	**10.00**
36	Fred Stanfield	2.50	5.00	10.00
37	Don Awrey, Error	2.50	5.00	10.00
38	**Glen Sather, RC**	**7.50**	**15.00**	**30.00**
39	John McKenzie	2.50	5.00	10.00
40	Tom Williams	2.50	5.00	10.00
41	Dallas Smith	2.50	5.00	10.00
42	John Bucyk	3.50	7.00	14.00

DETROIT RED WINGS

No.	Player	VG	EX	NRMT
43	Gordie Howe	40.00	85.00	175.00
44	**Gary Jarrett, RC**	**2.50**	**5.00**	**10.00**
45	Bert Marshall	2.50	5.00	10.00
46	Dean Prentice	2.50	5.00	10.00
47	Gary Bergman	2.50	5.00	10.00
48	Roger Crozier, Goalie	2.50	5.00	10.00
49	Howie Young	2.50	5.00	10.00
50	**Doug Roberts, RC**	**2.50**	**5.00**	**10.00**
51	Alex Delvecchio	4.50	9.00	18.00
52	Floyd Smith	2.50	5.00	10.00

CHICAGO BLACK HAWKS

No.	Player	VG	EX	NRMT
53	**Doug Shelton, RC, LC**	**2.50**	**5.00**	**10.00**
54	**Gerry Goyer, RC, LC**	**2.50**	**5.00**	**10.00**
55	**Wayne Maki, RC**	**2.50**	**5.00**	**10.00**
56	Dennis Hull	2.50	5.00	10.00
57	**Dave Dryden, Goalie, RC**	**3.75**	**7.50**	**15.00**
58	**Paul Terbenche, RC**	**2.50**	**5.00**	**10.00**
59	Gilles Marotte	2.50	5.00	10.00
60	Eric Nesterenko	2.50	5.00	10.00
61	Pat Stapleton	2.50	5.00	10.00
62	Pierre Pilote	2.50	6.00	10.00
63	Doug Mohns	2.50	5.00	10.00

TROPHY WINNERS

No.	Trophy	VG	EX	NRMT
64	**Art Ross Trophy, Hart Trophy, Lady Byng Trophy:** Stan Mikita	**8.75**	**17.50**	**35.00**
65	**The Vezina Trophy:** Hall & DeJordy	4.50	9.00	18.00

CHECKLIST

No.	Checklist	VG	EX	NRMT
66	Checklist 1 (1 - 66)	50.00	100.00	200.00

MONTREAL CANADIENS

No.	Player	VG	EX	NRMT
67	Ralph Backstrom	2.50	5.00	10.00
68	Bobby Rousseau	2.50	5.00	10.00
69	John Ferguson, Sr.	2.50	5.00	10.00
70	Yvan Cournoyer	7.00	14.00	28.00
71	Claude Provost	2.50	5.00	10.00
72	Henri Richard	3.75	7.50	15.00
73	J.C. Tremblay	2.50	5.00	10.00
74	Jean Beliveau	10.00	20.00	40.00
75	**Rogatien Vachon, Goalie, RC**	**22.50**	**45.00**	**90.00**

Topps 1967-68 Issue Card No. 20, Duane Rupp

Topps 1967-68 Issue Card No. 45, Bert Marshall

Topps 1967-68 Issue Card No. 105, Bart Crashley

Topps 1967-68 Issue Card No. 113, Bobby Hull

TORONTO MAPLE LEAFS

No.	Player	VG	EX	NRMT
76	Johnny Bower, Goalie	3.75	7.50	15.00
77	**Wayne Carleton, RC**	**2.50**	**5.00**	**10.00**
78	Jim Pappin	2.50	5.00	10.00
79	Frank Mahovlich	7.50	15.00	30.00
80	Larry Hillman	2.50	5.00	10.00
81	Marcel Pronovost	2.50	5.00	10.00
82	Murray Oliver	2.50	5.00	10.00
83	George Armstrong	2.50	5.00	10.00

NEW YORK RANGERS

No.	Player	VG	EX	NRMT
84	Harry Howell	2.50	5.00	10.00
85	Ed Giacomin, Goalie	7.50	15.00	30.00
86	Gilles Villemure, Goalie	2.50	5.00	10.00
87	Orland Kurtenbach	2.50	5.00	10.00
88	Vic Hadfield	2.50	5.00	10.00
89	Arnie Brown	2.50	5.00	10.00
90	Rod Gilbert	4.50	9.00	18.00
91	Jim Neilson	2.50	5.00	10.00

BOSTON BRUINS

No.	Player	VG	EX	NRMT
92	Bobby Orr	185.00	375.00	750.00
93	Skip Krake, Error	2.50	5.00	10.00
94	Ted Green	2.50	5.00	10.00
95	Ed Westfall	2.50	5.00	10.00
96	Ed Johnston, Goalie	2.50	5.00	10.00
97	**Gary Doak, RC**	**2.50**	**5.00**	**10.00**
98	Ken Hodge	2.50	5.00	10.00
99	Gerry Cheevers, Goalie	12.50	25.00	50.00
100	Ron Murphy	2.50	5.00	10.00

DETROIT RED WINGS

No.	Player	VG	EX	NRMT
101	Norm Ullman	2.50	5.00	10.00
102	Bruce MacGregor	2.50	5.00	10.00
103	Paul Henderson	2.50	5.00	10.00
104	Jean Guy Talbot	2.50	5.00	10.00
105	**Bart Crashley RC**	**2.50**	**5.00**	**10.00**
106	**Roy Edwards, Goalie, RC**	**2.50**	**5.00**	**10.00**
107	**Jim Watson, RC**	**2.50**	**5.00**	**10.00**
108	Ted Hampson	2.50	5.00	10.00

CHICAGO BLACK HAWKS

No.	Player	VG	EX	NRMT
109	**Bill Orban, RC, LC**	**2.50**	**5.00**	**10.00**
110	**Jeff Powis, RC, LC**	**2.50**	**5.00**	**10.00**
111	Chico Maki	2.50	5.00	10.00
112	Doug Jarrett	2.50	5.00	10.00
113	Bobby Hull	35.00	75.00	150.00
114	Stan Mikita	11.25	22.50	45.00
115	Denis DeJordy, Goalie	2.50	5.00	10.00
116	Pit Martin	2.50	5.00	10.00
117	Kenny Wharram	2.50	5.00	10.00

TROPHY WINNERS

No.	Player	VG	EX	NRMT
118	**Calder Trophy:** Bobby Orr	75.00	150.00	300.00
119	**Norris Trophy:** Harry Howell	2.50	5.00	10.00

CHECKLIST

No.	Checklist	VG	EX	NRMT
120	Checklist 2 (67 - 132)	50.00	100.00	200.00

ALL STARS

First Team

No.	Player	VG	EX	NRMT
121	Harry Howell, NYR	2.50	5.00	10.00
122	Pierre Pilote, Chi.	2.50	5.00	10.00
123	Ed Giacomin, Goalie, NYR	3.75	7.50	15.00
124	Bobby Hull, Chi.	20.00	37.50	75.00
125	Kenny Wharram, Chi.	2.50	5.00	10.00
126	Stan Mikita, Chi.	5.50	11.00	22.00

Second Team

No.	Player	VG	EX	NRMT
127	Tim Horton, Tor.	2.50	5.00	10.00
128	Bobby Orr, Bos.	75.00	150.00	300.00

200 • TOPPS — 1968 - 69 REGULAR ISSUE

No.	Player	VG	EX	NRMT
129	Glenn Hall, Goalie, Chi.	3.50	8.50	14.00
130	Don Marshall, NYR	2.50	5.00	10.00
131	Gordie Howe, Det.	31.25	62.50	125.00
132	Norm Ullman, Det.	5.00	10.00	20.00

— 1968 - 69 REGULAR ISSUE —

Topps did not issue bilingual backs this year. They did, however, plug the sport with the caption "Watch NHL Hockey on CBS Network". Mint cards will command a price premium of 50% over NRMT cards.

PRICE MOVEMENT OF NRMT SETS

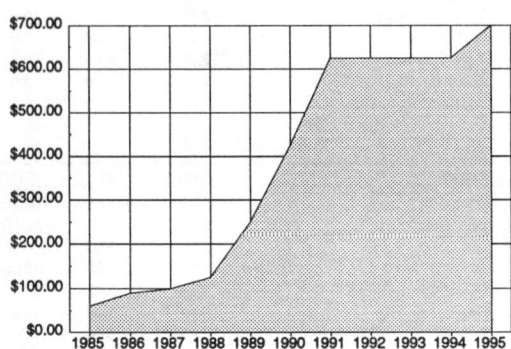

Card Size: 2 1/2" X 3 1/2"
Face: Four colour, white border, Team logo, Position
Back: Red and blue on card stock, Number, Resume, Hockey facts
Imprint: © T.C.G. PRINTED IN U.S.A.
Complete Set No.: 132
Complete Set Price: 175.00 350.00 700.00
Common Card: .85 1.75 3.50

BOSTON BRUINS

No.	Player	VG	EX	NRMT
1	Gerry Cheevers, Goalie	5.00	10.00	20.00
2	Bobby Orr	55.00	110.00	225.00
3	Don Awrey, Error	.85	1.75	3.50
4	Ted Green	.85	1.75	3.50
5	John Bucyk	2.00	4.00	8.00
6	Derek Sanderson	2.50	5.00	10.00
7	Phil Esposito	8.75	17.50	35.00
8	Ken Hodge	.85	1.75	3.50
9	John McKenzie	.85	1.75	3.50
10	Fred Stanfield	.85	1.75	3.50
11	Tom Williams	.85	1.75	3.50

CHICAGO BLACK HAWKS

No.	Player	VG	EX	NRMT
12	Denis DeJordy, Goalie	.85	1.75	3.50
13	Doug Jarrett	.85	1.75	3.50
14	Gilles Marotte	.85	1.75	3.50
15	Pat Stapleton	.85	1.75	3.50
16	Bobby Hull	15.00	30.00	60.00
17	Chico Maki	.85	1.75	3.50
18	Pit Martin	.85	1.75	3.50
19	Doug Mohns	.85	1.75	3.50
20	Stan Mikita	4.50	9.00	18.00
21	Jim Pappin	.85	1.75	3.50
22	Kenny Wharram	.85	1.75	3.50

DETROIT RED WINGS

No.	Player	VG	EX	NRMT
23	Roger Crozier, Goalie	.85	1.75	3.50
24	Bob Baun	.85	1.75	3.50
25	Gary Bergman	.85	1.75	3.50
26	Kent Douglas, LC	.85	1.75	3.50
27	Ron Harris, RC	.85	1.75	3.50
28	Alex Delvecchio	2.00	4.00	8.00
29	Gordie Howe	27.50	55.00	110.00
30	Bruce MacGregor	.85	1.75	3.50
31	Frank Mahovlich	3.75	7.50	15.00
32	Dean Prentice	.85	1.75	3.50
33	Pete Stemkowski	.85	1.75	3.50

Topps 1968-69 Issue Card No. 1, Gerry Cheevers

Topps 1968-69 Issue Card No. 1, Gerry Cheevers

Topps 1968-69 Issue Card No. 3, Error, Card shows Skip Krake

Topps 1968-69 Issue Card No. 43, Error, Card shows Don Awrey

LOS ANGELES KINGS

No.	Player	VG	EX	NRMT
34	Terry Sawchuk, Goalie	8.75	17.50	35.00
35	Larry Cahan	.85	1.75	3.50
36	Real Lemieux, RC	.85	1.75	3.50
37	Bill White, RC	1.00	2.00	4.00
38	Gord Labossiere, RC	.85	1.75	3.50
39	Ted Irvine, RC	.85	1.75	3.50
40	Eddie Joyal	.85	1.75	3.50
41	Dale Rolfe, RC	.85	1.75	3.50
42	Lowell MacDonald, RC	.85	1.75	3.50
43	Skip Krake, Error	.85	1.75	3.50
44	Terry Gray, LC	.85	1.75	3.50

MINNESOTA NORTH STARS

No.	Player	VG	EX	NRMT
45	Cesare Maniago, Goalie	.85	1.75	3.50
46	Mike McMahon	.85	1.75	3.50
47	Wayne Hillman	.85	1.75	3.50
48	Larry Hillman	.85	1.75	3.50
49	Bob Woytowich	.85	1.75	3.50
50	Wayne Connelly	.85	1.75	3.50
51	Claude Larose	.85	1.75	3.50
52	Danny Grant, RC	1.25	2.50	5.00
53	Andre Boudrias, RC	.85	1.75	3.50
54	Ray Cullen, RC	1.00	2.00	4.00
55	Parker MacDonald, LC	.85	1.75	3.50

MONTREAL CANADIENS

No.	Player	VG	EX	NRMT
56	Gump Worsley, Goalie	2.00	4.00	8.00
57	Terry Harper	.85	1.75	3.50
58	Jacques Laperriere	1.00	2.00	4.00
59	J.C. Tremblay	.85	1.75	3.50
60	Ralph Backstrom	.85	1.75	3.50
61	Jean Beliveau	4.50	9.00	18.00
62	Yvan Cournoyer	2.00	4.00	8.00
63	Jacques Lemaire	3.00	6.00	12.00
64	Henri Richard	2.00	4.00	8.00
65	Bobby Rousseau	.85	1.75	3.50
66	Gilles Tremblay	.85	1.75	3.50

NEW YORK RANGERS

No.	Player	VG	EX	NRMT
67	Ed Giacomin, Goalie	3.00	6.00	12.00
68	Arnie Brown	.85	1.75	3.50
69	Harry Howell	1.00	2.25	4.50
70	Jim Neilson	.85	1.75	3.50
71	Rod Seiling	.85	1.75	3.50
72	Rod Gilbert	2.00	4.00	8.00
73	Phil Goyette	.85	1.75	3.50
74	Vic Hadfield	.85	1.75	3.50
75	Don Marshall	.85	1.75	3.50
76	Bob Nevin	.85	1.75	3.50
77	Jean Ratelle	2.00	4.00	8.00

OAKLAND SEALS

No.	Player	VG	EX	NRMT
78	Charlie Hodge, Goalie	.85	1.75	3.50
79	Bert Marshall	.85	1.75	3.50
80	Billy Harris, LC	.85	1.75	3.50
81	Carol Vadnais	.85	1.75	3.50
82	Howie Young, LC	.85	1.75	3.50
83	John Brenneman, RC, LC	.85	1.75	3.50
84	Gerry Ehman	.85	1.75	3.50
85	Ted Hampson	.85	1.75	3.50
86	Bill Hicke	.85	1.75	3.50
87	Gary Jarrett	.85	1.75	3.50
88	Doug Roberts	.85	1.75	3.50

PHILADELPHIA FLYERS

No.	Player	VG	EX	NRMT
89	Bernie Parent, Goalie, RC	20.00	40.00	85.00
90	Joe Watson	.85	1.75	3.50
91	Ed Van Impe	.85	1.75	3.50
92	Larry Zeidel, LC	.85	1.75	3.50
93	John Miszuk, RC	.85	1.75	3.50
94	Gary Dornhoefer	.85	1.75	3.50
95	Leon Rochefort, RC	.85	1.75	3.50
96	Brit Selby	.85	1.75	3.50
97	Forbes Kennedy, LC	.85	1.75	3.50
98	Ed Hoekstra, RC, LC	.85	1.75	3.50

1969 - 70 REGULAR ISSUE — TOPPS • 201

No.	Checklist	VG	EX	NRMT
99	Garry Peters	.85	1.75	3.50

PITTSBURGH PENGUINS

No.	Player	VG	EX	NRMT
100	Les Binkley, Goalie, RC	1.25	2.50	5.00
101	Leo Boivin	1.00	2.00	4.00
102	Earl Ingarfield	.85	1.75	3.50
103	Lou Angotti	.85	1.75	3.50
104	Andy Bathgate	1.00	2.00	4.00
105	Wally Boyer	.85	1.75	3.50
106	Ken Schinkel	.85	1.75	3.50
107	Ab McDonald	.85	1.75	3.50
108	Charlie Burns	.85	1.75	3.50
109	Val Fonteyne	.85	1.75	3.50
110	Noel Price	.85	1.75	3.50

ST. LOUIS BLUES

No.	Player	VG	EX	NRMT
111	Glenn Hall, Goalie	2.75	5.50	11.00
112	Bob Plager, RC	1.00	2.00	4.00
113	Jim Roberts	.85	1.75	3.50
114	Red Berenson	.85	1.75	3.50
115	Larry Keenan	.85	1.75	3.50
116	Camille Henry	.85	1.75	3.50
117	Gary Sabourin RC	.85	1.75	3.50
118	Ron Schock	.85	1.75	3.50
119	Gary Veneruzzo RC	.85	1.75	3.50
120	Gerry Melnyk, LC	.85	1.75	3.50

CHECKLIST

No.	Checklist	VG	EX	NRMT
121	Checklist (1 - 132)	20.00	42.50	85.00

TORONTO MAPLE LEAFS

No.	Player	VG	EX	NRMT
122	Johnny Bower, Goalie	2.00	4.00	8.00
123	Tim Horton	3.00	6.00	12.00
124	Pierre Pilote, LC	1.00	2.00	4.00
125	Marcel Pronovost, LC	1.00	2.00	4.00
126	Ron Ellis	.85	1.75	3.50
127	Paul Henderson	.85	1.75	3.50
128	Dave Keon	2.00	4.00	8.00
129	Bob Pulford	.85	1.75	3.50
130	Floyd Smith	.85	1.75	3.50
131	Norm Ullman	1.00	2.00	4.00
132	Mike Walton	2.00	4.00	8.00

— 1969 - 70 REGULAR ISSUE —

Again, Topps continued the policy of not issuing bilingual cards. Mint cards command a price premium of 25% over NRMT cards.

PRICE MOVEMENT OF NRMT SETS

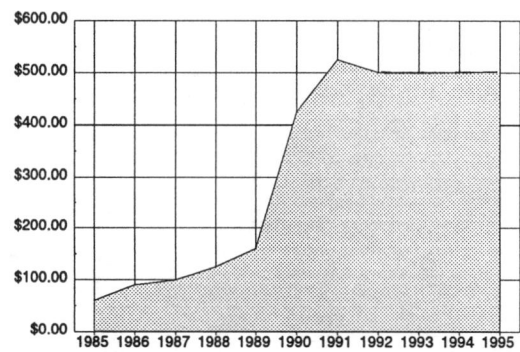

Card Size: 2 1/2" X 3 1/2"
Face: Four colour, white border, Team logo, Position
Back: Yellow and blue on card stock, Number, Resume, Hockey trivia / stamps
Imprint: © T.C.G. PRINTED IN U.S.A.
Complete Set No.: 132
Complete Set Price: 125.00 250.00 500.00
Common Card: .50 1.00 2.00

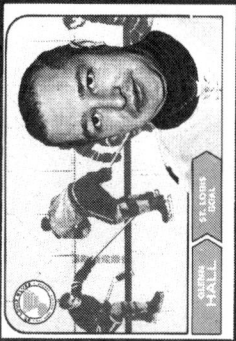

Topps 1968-69 Issue
Card No. 111,
Glenn Hall

Topps 1969-70 Issue
Card No. 1,
Gump Worsley

Topps 1969-70 Issue
Card No. 1,
Gump Worsley

Topps 1969-70 Issue
Card No. 24,
Bobby Orr

MONTREAL CANADIENS

No.	Player	VG	EX	NRMT
1	Gump Worsley, Goalie	4.50	9.00	18.00
2	Ted Harris	.50	1.00	2.00
3	Jacques Laperriere	.75	1.50	3.00
4	Serge Savard, RC	7.50	15.00	30.00
5	J.C. Tremblay	.50	1.00	2.00
6	Yvan Cournoyer	2.00	4.00	8.00
7	John Ferguson, Sr.	.50	1.00	2.00
8	Jacques Lemaire	2.00	4.00	8.00
9	Bobby Rousseau	.50	1.00	2.00
10	Jean Beliveau	3.75	7.50	15.00
11	Henri Richard	2.00	4.00	8.00

ST. LOUIS BLUES

No.	Player	VG	EX	NRMT
12	Glenn Hall, Goalie	2.00	4.00	8.00
13	Bob Plager	.50	1.00	2.00
14	Jim Roberts	.50	1.00	2.00
15	Jean-Guy Talbot	.50	1.00	2.00
16	Andre Boudrias	.50	1.00	2.00
17	Camille Henry, LC	.50	1.00	2.00
18	Ab McDonald	.50	1.00	2.00
19	Gary Sabourin	.50	1.00	2.00
20	Red Berenson	.50	1.00	2.00
21	Phil Goyette	.50	1.00	2.00

BOSTON BRUINS

No.	Player	VG	EX	NRMT
22	Gerry Cheevers, Goalie	2.50	5.00	10.00
23	Ted Green	.50	1.00	2.00
24	Bobby Orr	30.00	60.00	125.00
25	Dallas Smith	.50	1.00	2.00
26	John Bucyk	1.25	2.50	5.00
27	Ken Hodge, Sr.	.50	1.00	2.00
28	John McKenzie	.50	1.00	2.00
29	Ed Westfall	.50	1.00	2.00
30	Phil Esposito	6.00	12.50	25.00
31	Derek Sanderson	1.50	3.00	6.00
32	Fred Stanfield	.50	1.00	2.00

NEW YORK RANGERS

No.	Player	VG	EX	NRMT
33	Ed Giacomin, Goalie	2.50	5.00	10.00
34	Arnie Brown	.50	1.00	2.00
35	Jim Neilson	.50	1.00	2.00
36	Rod Seiling	.50	1.00	2.00
37	Rod Gilbert	1.25	2.50	5.00
38	Vic Hadfield	.50	1.00	2.00
39	Don Marshall	.50	1.00	2.00
40	Bob Nevin	.50	1.00	2.00
41	Ron Stewart	.50	1.00	2.00
42	Jean Ratelle	1.25	2.50	5.00
43	Walt Tkaczuk, RC	1.75	3.50	7.00

TORONTO MAPLE LEAFS

No.	Player	VG	EX	NRMT
44	Bruce Gamble, Goalie	.75	1.50	3.00
45	Tim Horton	2.00	4.00	8.00
46	Ron Ellis	.50	1.00	2.00
47	Paul Henderson	.50	1.00	2.00
48	Brit Selby	.50	1.00	2.00
49	Floyd Smith	.50	1.00	2.00
50	Mike Walton	.50	1.00	2.00
51	Dave Keon	1.50	3.00	6.00
52	Murray Oliver	.50	1.00	2.00
53	Bob Pulford	.65	1.25	2.50
54	Norm Ullman	1.00	2.00	4.00

DETROIT RED WINGS

No.	Player	VG	EX	NRMT
55	Roger Crozier, Goalie	.75	1.50	3.00
56	Roy Edwards, Goalie	.75	1.50	3.00
57	Bob Baun	.50	1.00	2.00
58	Gary Bergman	.50	1.00	2.00
59	Carl Brewer	.50	1.00	2.00
60	Wayne Connelly	.50	1.00	2.00
61	Gordie Howe	20.00	37.50	75.00
62	Frank Mahovlich	3.00	6.00	12.00
63	Bruce MacGregor	.50	1.00	2.00
64	Alex Delvecchio	1.50	3.00	6.00
65	Pete Stemkowski	.50	1.00	2.00

202 • TOPPS — 1970-71 REGULAR ISSUE

CHICAGO BLACK HAWKS

No.	Player	VG	EX	NRMT
66	Denis DeJordy, Goalie	.75	1.50	3.00
67	Doug Jarrett	.50	1.00	2.00
68	Gilles Marotte	.50	1.00	2.00
69	Pat Stapleton	.50	1.00	2.00
70	Bobby Hull	17.50	35.00	70.00
71	Dennis Hull	.50	1.00	2.00
72	Doug Mohns	.50	1.00	2.00
73	Jim Pappin	.50	1.00	2.00
74	Kenny Wharram, LC	.50	1.00	2.00
75	Pit Martin	.50	1.00	2.00
76	Stan Mikita	3.75	7.50	15.00

OAKLAND SEALS

No.	Player	VG	EX	NRMT
77	Charlie Hodge, Goalie	.75	1.50	3.00
78	Gary Smith, Goalie	.75	1.50	3.00
79	Harry Howell	1.00	2.00	4.00
80	Bert Marshall	.50	1.00	2.00
81	Doug Roberts	.50	1.00	2.00
82	Carol Vadnais	.50	1.00	2.00
83	Gerry Ehman	.50	1.00	2.00
84	Bill Hicke	.50	1.00	2.00
85	Gary Jarrett	.50	1.00	2.00
86	Ted Hampson	.50	1.00	2.00
87	Earl Ingarfield	.50	1.00	2.00

PHILADELPHIA FLYERS

No.	Player	VG	EX	NRMT
88	Doug Favell, Goalie, RC	1.00	2.00	4.00
89	Bernie Parent, Goalie	6.00	12.50	25.00
90	Larry Hillman	.50	1.00	2.00
91	Wayne Hillman	.50	1.00	2.00
92	Ed Van Impe	.50	1.00	2.00
93	Joe Watson	.50	1.00	2.00
94	Gary Dornhoefer	.50	1.00	2.00
95	Reggie Fleming	.50	1.00	2.00
96	Jean Guy Gendron	.50	1.00	2.00
97	Jim Johnson	.50	1.00	2.00
98	Andre Lacroix	.50	1.00	2.00

LOS ANGELES KINGS

No.	Player	VG	EX	NRMT
99	Gerry Desjardins, Goalie, RC	1.00	2.00	4.00
100	Dale Rolfe	.50	1.00	2.00
101	Bill White	.50	1.00	2.00
102	Bill Flett	.50	1.00	2.00
103	Ted Irvine	.50	1.00	2.00
104	Ross Lonsberry	.50	1.00	2.00
105	Leon Rochefort	.50	1.00	2.00
106	Eddie Shack	1.00	2.00	4.00
107	Dennis Hextall, RC	.75	1.50	3.00
108	Eddie Joyal	.50	1.00	2.00
109	Gord Labossiere	.50	1.00	2.00

PITTSBURGH PENGUINS

No.	Player	VG	EX	NRMT
110	Les Binkley, Goalie	.75	1.50	3.00
111	Tracy Pratt, RC	.50	1.00	2.00
112	Bryan Watson	.50	1.00	2.00
113	Bob Woytowich	.50	1.00	2.00
114	Keith McCreary	.50	1.00	2.00
115	Dean Prentice	.50	1.00	2.00
116	Glen Sather	1.00	2.00	4.00
117	Ken Schinkel	.50	1.00	2.00
118	Wally Boyer	.50	1.00	2.00
119	Val Fonteyne	.50	1.00	2.00
120	Ron Schock	.50	1.00	2.00

MINNESOTA NORTH STARS

No.	Player	VG	EX	NRMT
121	Cesare Maniago, Goalie	.75	1.50	3.00
122	Leo Boivin	.75	1.50	3.00
123	Bob McCord	.50	1.00	2.00
124	John Miszuk	.50	1.00	2.00
125	Danny Grant	.50	1.00	2.00
126	Claude Larose	.50	1.00	2.00
127	Jean Paul Parise	.50	1.00	2.00
128	Tom Williams	.50	1.00	2.00
129	Charlie Burns	.50	1.00	2.00
130	Ray Cullen	.50	1.00	2.00

Topps
1970-71 Issue
Card No. 1,
Gerry Cheevers

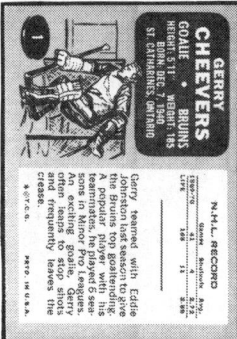

Topps
1970-71 Issue
Card No. 1,
Gerry Cheevers

Topps
1970-71 Issue
Card No. 3,
Bobby Orr

Topps
1970-71 Issue
Card No. 22,
Frank Mahovlich

No.	Checklist	VG	EX	NRMT
131	Danny O'Shea, RC	.50	1.00	2.00

CHECKLIST

No.	Checklist	VG	EX	NRMT
132	Checklist (1 - 132)	20.00	40.00	80.00

— 1970 - 71 REGULAR ISSUE —

Mint cards command a price premium of 25% over NRMT cards.

PRICE MOVEMENT OF NRMT SETS

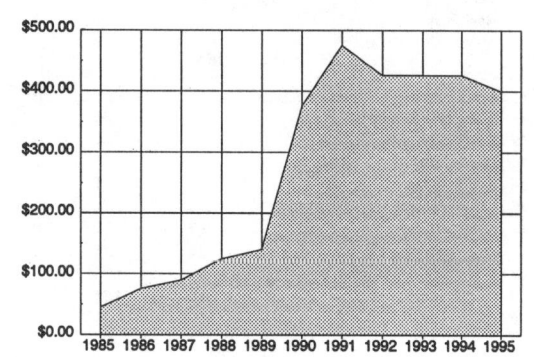

Card Size: 2 1/2" X 3 1/2"
Face: Four colour, white border, Position
Back: Black and green on card stock, Number, Resume
Imprint: *©T.C.G. PRTD. IN U.S.A.
Complete Set No.: 132

	VG	EX	NRMT
Complete Set Price:	100.00	200.00	400.00
Common Card:	.40	.85	1.75

BOSTON BRUINS

No.	Player	VG	EX	NRMT
1	Gerry Cheevers, Goalie	3.75	7.50	15.00
2	John Bucyk	.75	1.50	3.00
3	Bobby Orr	17.50	35.00	70.00
4	Don Awrey	.40	.85	1.75
5	Fred Stanfield	.40	.85	1.75
6	John McKenzie	.40	.85	1.75
7	Wayne Cashman, RC	1.75	3.50	7.00
8	Ken Hodge, Sr.	.40	.85	1.75
9	Wayne Carleton	.40	.85	1.75
10	Garnet Bailey, RC	.40	.85	1.75
11	Phil Esposito	3.50	7.00	14.00

CHICAGO BLACK HAWKS

No.	Player	VG	EX	NRMT
12	Lou Angotti	.40	.85	1.75
13	Jim Pappin	.40	.85	1.75
14	Dennis Hull	.40	.85	1.75
15	Bobby Hull	7.50	15.00	30.00
16	Doug Mohns	.40	.85	1.75
17	Pat Stapleton	.40	.85	1.75
18	Pit Martin	.40	.85	1.75
19	Eric Nesterenko	.40	.85	1.75
20	Stan Mikita	2.00	4.00	8.00

DETROIT RED WINGS

No.	Player	VG	EX	NRMT
21	Roy Edwards, Goalie	.65	1.35	2.75
22	Frank Mahovlich	2.00	4.00	8.00
23	Ron Harris	.40	.85	1.75

BUFFALO SABRES

No.	Player	VG	EX	NRMT
24	Bob Baun	.40	.85	1.75

DETROIT RED WINGS

No.	Player	VG	EX	NRMT
25	Pete Stemkowski	.40	.85	1.75
26	Garry Unger	.75	1.50	3.00
27	Bruce MacGregor	.40	.85	1.75
28	Larry Jeffrey, LC	.40	.85	1.75

1970-71 REGULAR ISSUE — TOPPS • 203

No.	Player	VG	EX	NRMT
29	Gordie Howe	10.00	20.00	40.00
30	Billy Dea, LC	.40	.85	1.75

LOS ANGELES KINGS

No.	Player	VG	EX	NRMT
31	Denis DeJordy, Goalie	.65	1.35	2.75
32	Matt Ravlich, LC	.40	.85	1.75
33	Dave Amadio, LC	.40	.85	1.75
34	Gilles Marotte	.40	.85	1.75
35	Eddie Shack	.75	1.50	3.00
36	Bob Pulford	.40	.85	1.75
37	Ross Lonsberry	.40	.85	1.75
38	Gord Labossiere	.40	.85	1.75
39	Eddie Joyal	.40	.85	1.75

MINNESOTA NORTH STARS

No.	Player	VG	EX	NRMT
40	Gump Worsley, Goalie	1.50	3.00	6.00
41	Bob McCord, LC	.40	.85	1.75
42	Leo Boivin, LC	.40	.85	1.75
43	Tom Reid, RC	.50	1.00	2.00
44	Charlie Burns	.40	.85	1.75
45	Bob Barlow, LC	.40	.85	1.75
46	Bill Goldsworthy	.40	.85	1.75
47	Danny Grant	.40	.85	1.75
48	Norm Beaudin, RC	.40	.85	1.75

MONTREAL CANADIENS

No.	Player	VG	EX	NRMT
49	Rogatien Vachon, Goalie	1.50	3.00	6.00
50	Yvan Cournoyer	1.35	2.25	5.50
51	Serge Savard	1.75	3.50	7.00
52	Jacques Laperriere	.75	1.50	3.00
53	Terry Harper	.40	.85	1.75
54	Ralph Backstrom	.40	.85	1.75
55	Jean Beliveau, LC	2.50	5.00	10.00
56	Claude Larose, Error	.40	.85	1.75
57	Jacques Lemaire	1.50	3.00	6.00
58	Pete Mahovlich	.40	.85	1.75

NEW YORK RANGERS

No.	Player	VG	EX	NRMT
59	Tim Horton	1.50	3.00	6.00
60	Bob Nevin	.40	.85	1.75
61	Dave Balon	.40	.85	1.75
62	Vic Hadfield	.40	.85	1.75
63	Rod Gilbert	1.25	2.50	5.00
64	Ron Stewart	.40	.85	1.75
65	Ted Irvine	.40	.85	1.75
66	Arnie Brown	.40	.85	1.75
67	Brad Park, RC	7.50	15.00	30.00
68	Ed Giacomin, Goalie	1.50	3.00	6.00

CALIFORNIA GOLDEN SEALS

No.	Player	VG	EX	NRMT
69	Gary Smith, Goalie	.65	1.35	2.75
70	Carol Vadnais	.40	.85	1.75
71	Doug Roberts	.40	.85	1.75
72	Harry Howell	.75	1.50	3.00
73	Joe Szura	.40	.85	1.75
74	Mike Laughton, LC	.40	.85	1.75
75	Gary Jarrett	.40	.85	1.75
76	Bill Hicke	.40	.85	1.75

BUFFALO SABRES

No.	Player	VG	EX	NRMT
77	Paul Andrea, RC, LC	.40	.85	1.75

PHILADELPHIA FLYERS

No.	Player	VG	EX	NRMT
78	Bernie Parent, Goalie	3.00	6.00	12.00
79	Joe Watson	.40	.85	1.75
80	Ed Van Impe	.40	.85	1.75
81	Larry Hillman	.40	.85	1.75
82	George Swarbrick, LC	.40	.85	1.75

Topps, 1970-71 Issue
Card No. 56, Error,
Name misspelled
LaRose on face and back

Topps
1970-71 Issue
Card No. 67,
Brad Park

Topps
1970-71 Issue
Card No. 87,
Al Smith

Topps, 1970-71 Issue
Card No. 122, Error,
Name misspelled
Paul on face and back

ST. LOUIS BLUES

No.	Player	VG	EX	NRMT
83	Bill Sutherland	.40	.85	1.75

PHILADELPHIA FLYERS

No.	Player	VG	EX	NRMT
84	Andre Lacroix	.40	.85	1.75
85	Gary Dornhoefer	.40	.85	1.75
86	Jean-Guy Gendron	.40	.85	1.75

PITTSBURGH PENGUINS

No.	Player	VG	EX	NRMT
87	Al Smith, Goalie, RC	.40	.85	1.75
88	Bob Woytowich	.40	.85	1.75
89	Duane Rupp	.40	.85	1.75
90	Jim Morrison, LC	.40	.85	1.75
91	Ron Schock	.40	.85	1.75
92	Ken Schinkel	.40	.85	1.75
93	Keith McCreary	.40	.85	1.75
94	Bryan Hextall	.40	.85	1.75
95	Wayne Hicks, Jr., RC, LC	.40	.85	1.75

ST. LOUIS BLUES

No.	Player	VG	EX	NRMT
96	Gary Sabourin	.40	.85	1.75
97	Ernie Wakely, Goalie, RC	.40	.85	1.75
98	Bob Wall	.40	.85	1.75
99	Barclay Plager	.75	1.50	3.00
100	Jean-Guy Talbot, LC	.40	.85	1.75
101	Gary Veneruzzo	.40	.85	1.75
102	Tim Ecclestone	.40	.85	1.75
103	Red Berenson	.40	.85	1.75
104	Larry Keenan, LC	.40	.85	1.75

TORONTO MAPLE LEAFS

No.	Player	VG	EX	NRMT
105	Bruce Gamble, Goalie	.40	.85	1.75
106	Jim Dorey	.40	.85	1.75
107	Mike Pelyk, RC	.60	1.25	2.50
108	Rick Ley	.40	.85	1.75
109	Mike Walton	.40	.85	1.75
110	Norm Ullman	.75	1.50	3.00

ST. LOUIS BLUES

No.	Player	VG	EX	NRMT
111	Brit Selby	.40	.85	1.75

TORONTO MAPLE LEAFS

No.	Player	VG	EX	NRMT
112	Garry Monahan	.40	.85	1.75
113	George Armstrong, LC	.75	1.50	3.00

VANCOUVER CANUCKS

No.	Player	VG	EX	NRMT
114	Gary Doak	.40	.85	1.75
115	Darryl Sly, RC, LC	.40	.85	1.75
116	Wayne Maki	.40	.85	1.75
117	Orland Kurtenbach	.40	.85	1.75
118	Murray Hall	.40	.85	1.75
119	Marc Reaume, LC	.40	.85	1.75
120	Pat Quinn	.55	1.15	2.25
121	Andre Boudrias	.40	.85	1.75

BUFFALO SALBRES

No.	Player	VG	EX	NRMT
122	Poul Popiel, Error	.40	.85	1.75
123	Paul Terbenche	.40	.85	1.75
124	Howie Menard, LC	.40	.85	1.75
125	Gerry Meehan, RC	.60	1.25	2.50
126	Skip Krake, LC	.40	.85	1.75
127	Phil Goyette	.40	.85	1.75
128	Reggie Fleming	.40	.85	1.75
129	Don Marshall	.40	.85	1.75
130	Bill Inglis, RC, LC	.40	.85	1.75
131	Gilbert Perreault, RC	11.00	22.50	45.00

CHECKLIST

No.	Checklist	VG	EX	NRMT
132	Checklist (1 - 132)	16.00	32.50	65.00

— 1970 - 71 DECKLE EDGE —

Issued as an insert, the black and white photographs have rough (deckle) edges.

Card Size: 2 1/4" X 3 1/4"
Face: Black and white; Facsimile autograph
Back: Number
Imprint: None
Complete Set No: 48

		VG	EX	NRMT
Complete Set Price:		60.00	125.00	250.00 ☐
Common Player:		.55	1.10	2.25

No.	Player	VG	EX	NRMT
1	Pat Quinn, Van.	.60	1.25	2.50 ☐
2	Eddie Shack, LA	.85	1.75	3.50 ☐
3	Eddie Joyal, LA	.55	1.10	2.25 ☐
4	Bobby Orr, Bos.	11.00	22.50	45.00 ☐
5	Derek Sanderson, Bos.	.60	1.25	2.50 ☐
6	Phil Esposito, Bos.	3.75	7.50	15.00 ☐
7	Fred Stanfield, Bos.	.55	1.10	2.25 ☐
8	Bob Woytowich, Pit.	.55	1.10	2.25 ☐
9	Ron Schock, Pit.	.55	1.10	2.25 ☐
10	Les Binkley, Goalie, Pit.	.60	1.25	2.50 ☐
11	Roger Crozier, Goalie, Buf.	.60	1.25	2.50 ☐
12	Reggie Fleming, Buf.	.55	1.10	2.25 ☐
13	Charlie Burns, Min.	.55	1.10	2.25 ☐
14	Bobby Rousseau, Min.	.55	1.10	2.25 ☐
15	Leo Boivin, Min.	.80	1.60	3.25 ☐
16	Garry Unger, Det.	.60	1.25	2.50 ☐
17	Frank Mahovlich, Det.	2.00	4.00	8.00 ☐
18	Gordie Howe, Det.	12.50	25.00	50.00 ☐
19	Jacques Lemaire, Mon.	1.00	2.00	4.00 ☐
20	Jacques Laperriere, Mon.	.80	1.60	3.25 ☐
21	Jean Beliveau, Mon.	2.50	4.75	9.50 ☐
22	Rogatien Vachon, Goalie, Mon.	1.25	2.50	5.00 ☐
23	Yvan Cournoyer, Mon.	1.25	2.50	5.00 ☐
24	Henri Richard, Mon.	1.25	2.50	5.00 ☐
25	Red Berenson, St.L.	.60	1.25	2.50 ☐
26	Frank St. Marseille, St.L.	.55	1.10	2.25 ☐
27	Glenn Hall, Goalie, St.L.	1.35	2.75	5.50 ☐
28	Gary Sabourin, St.L.	.55	1.10	2.25 ☐
29	Doug Mohns, Chi.	.55	1.10	2.25 ☐
30	Bobby Hull, Chi.	5.00	10.00	20.00 ☐
31	Ray Cullen, Van.	.55	1.10	2.25 ☐
32	Tony Esposito, Goalie, Chi.	2.50	5.00	10.00 ☐
33	Gary Dornhoefer, Phi.	.55	1.10	2.25 ☐
34	Ed Van Impe, Phi.	.55	1.10	2.25 ☐
35	Doug Favell, Goalie, Phi., Error	.60	1.25	2.50 ☐
36	Carol Vadnais, Cal.	.55	1.10	2.25 ☐
37	Harry Howell, Cal.	.80	1.60	3.25 ☐
38	Bill Hicke, Cal.	.55	1.10	2.25 ☐
39	Rod Gilbert, NYR	1.00	2.00	4.00 ☐
40	Jean Ratelle, NYR	1.00	2.00	4.00 ☐
41	Walt Tkaczuk, NYR	.60	1.25	2.50 ☐
42	Ed Giacomin, Goalie, NYR	1.00	2.00	4.00 ☐
43	Brad Park, NYR	1.75	3.50	7.00 ☐
44	Bruce Gamble, Goalie, Tor.	.55	1.10	2.25 ☐
45	Orland Kurtenbach, Van.	.60	1.25	2.50 ☐
46	Ron Ellis, Tor.	.55	1.10	2.25 ☐
47	Dave Keon, Tor.	1.35	2.75	5.50 ☐
48	Norm Ullman, Tor.	1.00	2.00	4.00 ☐

— 1970 - 71 STICKER STAMPS —

The unnumbered colour sticker inserts are listed alphabetically.

Sticker Size 2 1/2" X 3 1/2"
Face: Four colour, cream border on card stock; Name, Team
Back: Blank
Imprint: © T.C.G. PRTD. IN U.S.A.
Complete Set No.: 33

	VG	EX	NRMT
Complete Set Price:	55.00	112.00	225.00 ☐
Common Goalie:	.75	1.50	3.00
Common Player:	.75	1.50	3.00

No.	Player	VG	EX	NRMT
1	Jean Beliveau, Mon.	6.00	12.50	25.00 ☐
2	Red Berenson, St.L.	1.00	2.00	4.00 ☐
3	Wayne Carleton, Bos.	.75	1.50	3.00 ☐
4	Tim Ecclestone, St.L.	.75	1.50	3.00 ☐
5	Ron Ellis, Tor.	.75	1.50	3.00 ☐
6	Phil Esposito, Bos.	7.00	14.00	28.00 ☐
7	Tony Esposito, Goalie, Chi.	3.75	7.50	15.00 ☐
8	Bill Flett, LA	.75	1.50	3.00 ☐
9	Ed Giacomin, Goalie, NYR	1.85	3.75	7.50 ☐

Topps
1970-71 Deckle Edge
Card No. 45,
Orland Kurtenbach

Topps
1970-71 Sticker Stamps
Sticker No. 10,
Rod Gilbert

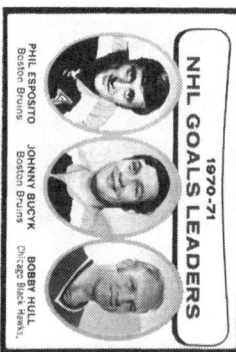

Topps
1971-72 Issue
Card No. 1,
NHL Goals Leaders

No.	Player	VG	EX	NRMT
10	Rod Gilbert, NYR	1.85	3.75	7.50 ☐
11	Danny Grant, Min.	.75	1.50	3.00 ☐
12	Bill Hicke, Oak.	.75	1.50	3.00 ☐
13	Gordie Howe, Det.	14.00	27.50	55.00 ☐
14	Bobby Hull, Chi.	8.00	16.50	33.00 ☐
15	Earl Ingarfield, Oak.	.75	1.50	3.00 ☐
16	Eddie Joyal, LA	.75	1.50	3.00 ☐
17	Dave Keon, Tor.	1.85	3.75	7.50 ☐
18	Andre Lacroix, Phi.	.75	1.50	3.00 ☐
19	Jacques Laperriere, Mon.	1.00	2.00	4.00 ☐
20	Jacques Lemaire, Mon.	1.85	3.75	7.50 ☐
21	Frank Mahovlich, Det.	3.50	7.00	14.00 ☐
22	Keith McCreary, Pit.	.75	1.50	3.00 ☐
23	Stan Mikita, Chi.	3.50	7.00	14.00 ☐
24	Bobby Orr, Bos.	11.00	22.50	45.00 ☐
25	Jean Paul Parise, Min.	.75	1.50	3.00 ☐
26	Jean Ratelle, NYR	1.85	3.75	7.50 ☐
27	Frank St. Marseille, St.L.	1.00	2.00	4.00 ☐
28	Derek Sanderson, Bos.	.75	1.50	3.00 ☐
29	Ron Schock, Pit.	.75	1.50	3.00 ☐
30	Garry Unger, Det.	1.00	2.00	4.00 ☐
31	Carol Vadnais, Oak.	.75	1.50	3.00 ☐
32	Ed Van Impe, Phi.	.75	1.50	3.00 ☐
33	Bob Woytowich, Pit.	.75	1.50	3.00 ☐

— 1971 - 72 REGULAR ISSUE —

Mint cards command a price premium of 25% over NRMT cards.

PRICE MOVEMENT OF NRMT SETS

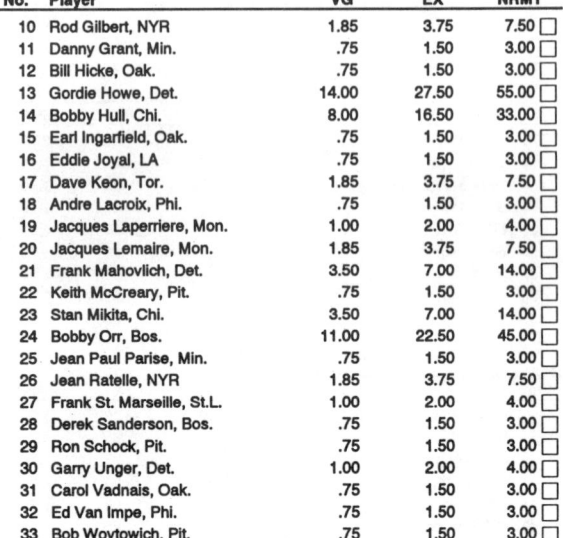

Card Size: 2 1/2" X 3 1/2"
Face: Four colour, white border, Team logo, Position
Back: Yellow and green on card stock, Number, Resume, Hockey trivia
Imprint: *© T.C.G. PRTD. IN U.S.A. or
**© T.C.G. PRTD. IN U.S.A.
Complete Set No.: 132

	VG	EX	NRMT
Complete Set Price:	90.00	180.00	375.00 ☐
Common Card:	.30	.60	1.25

1970 - 71 LEAGUE LEADERS

No.	League Leaders	VG	EX	NRMT
1	**NHL Goals Leaders:** P. Esposito, Bos., J. Bucyk, Bos., B. Hull, Chi.	3.50	7.00	14.00 ☐
2	**NHL Assists Leaders:** B. Orr, Bos., P. Esposito, Bos., J. Bucyk, Bos.	3.50	7.00	14.00 ☐
3	**NHL Scoring Leaders:** P. Esposito, Bos., B. Orr, Bos., J. Bucyk, Bos.	3.50	7.00	14.00 ☐
4	**NHL Goalies Wins Leaders:** T. Esposito, Chi., E. Johnston, Bos., G. Cheevers, Bos., E. Giacomin, NYR	1.75	3.50	7.00 ☐
5	**NHL Shutouts Leaders:** E. Giacomin, NYR, T. Esposito, Chi., C. Maniago, Min.	1.10	2.25	4.50 ☐
6	**NHL Goals-Against Average Leaders:** J. Plante, Tor., E. Giacomin, NYR, T. Esposito, Chi.	1.75	3.50	7.00 ☐

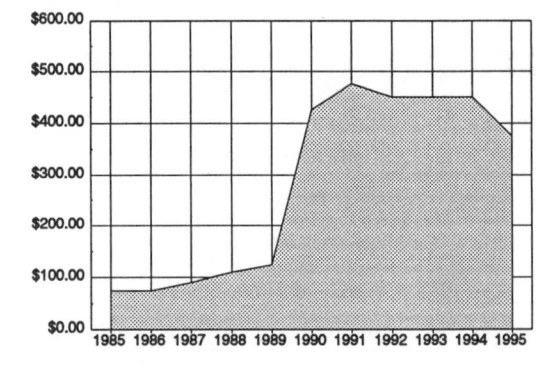

Topps
1971-72 Issue
Card No. 1,
NHL Goals Leaders

— 1971 - 72 BOOKLETS — TOPPS • 205

REGULAR ISSUE

No.	Player	VG	EX	NRMT
7	Fred Stanfield, Bos.	.30	.60	1.25
8	**Mike Robitaille, Buf., RC**	**.30**	**.60**	**1.25**
9	Vic Hadfield, NYR	.30	.60	1.25
10	Jacques Plante, Goalie, Tor.	3.00	6.00	12.00
11	Bill White, Chi.	.30	.60	1.25
12	Andre Boudrias, Van.	.30	.60	1.25
13	Jim Lorentz, St. L.	.30	.60	1.25
14	Arnie Brown, Det.	.30	.60	1.25
15	Yvan Cournoyer, Mon.	.75	1.50	3.00
16	Bryan Hextall, Jr., Pit.	.30	.60	1.25
17	Gary Croteau, Ca.	.30	.60	1.25
18	Gilles Villemure, Goalie, NYR	.50	1.00	2.00
19	**Serge Bernier, Phi., RC**	**.30**	**.60**	**1.25**
20	Phil Esposito, Bos.	3.00	6.00	12.00
21	Charlie Burns, Min.	.30	.60	1.25
22	**Doug Barrie, Buf., RC**	**.30**	**.60**	**1.25**
23	Eddie Joyal, LA	.30	.60	1.25
24	Rosaire Paiement, Van.	.30	.60	1.25
25	Pat Stapleton, Chi.	.30	.60	1.25
26	Garry Unger, St. L.	.50	1.00	2.00
27	Al Smith, Goalie, Det.	.50	1.00	2.00
28	Bob Woytowich, Pit.	.30	.60	1.25
29	Marc Tardif, Mon.	.40	.85	1.75
30	Norm Ullman, Tor.	.50	1.00	2.00
31	Tom Williams, Ca.	.30	.60	1.25
32	Ted Harris, Min.	.30	.60	1.25
33	Andre Lacroix, Phi.	.30	.60	1.25
34	Mike Byers, LA, LC	.30	.60	1.25
35	John Bucyk, Bos.	.75	1.50	3.00
36	Roger Crozier, Goalie, Buf.	.60	1.25	2.50
37	Alex Delvecchio, Det.	.75	1.50	3.00
38	Frank St. Marseille, St. L.	.30	.60	1.25
39	Pit Martin, Chi.	.30	.60	1.25
40	Brad Park, NYR	3.00	6.00	12.00
41	**Greg Polis, Pit., RC**	**.30**	**.60**	**1.25**
42	Orland Kurtenbach, Van.	.30	.60	1.25
43	**Jim McKenny, Tor., RC**	**.30**	**.60**	**1.25**
44	Bob Nevin, Min.	.30	.60	1.25
45	**Ken Dryden, Goalie, Mon., RC**	**25.00**	**47.50**	**95.00**
46	Carol Vadnais, Ca.	.30	.60	1.25
47	Bill Flett, LA	.30	.60	1.25
48	Jim Johnson, Phi., LC	.30	.60	1.25
49	Allan Hamilton, Buf.	.30	.60	1.25
50	Bobby Hull, Chi.	5.00	10.00	20.00
51	**Chris Bordeleau, St. L., RC**	**.30**	**.60**	**1.25**
52	Tim Ecclestone, Det.	.30	.60	1.25
53	Rod Seiling, NYR	.30	.60	1.25
54	Gerry Cheevers, Goalie, Bos.	1.10	2.25	4.50
55	Bill Goldsworthy, Min.	.30	.60	1.25
56	Ron Schock, Pit.	.30	.60	1.25
57	Jim Dorey, Tor.	.30	.60	1.25
58	Wayne Maki, Van.	.30	.60	1.25
59	Terry Harper, Mon.	.30	.60	1.25
60	Gilbert Perreault, Buf.	4.00	8.00	16.00
61	**Ernie Hicke, Ca., RC**	**.40**	**.85**	**1.75**
62	Wayne Hillman, Phi.	.30	.60	1.25
63	Denis DeJordy, Goalie, LA	.50	1.00	2.00
64	Ken Schinkel, Pit.	.30	.60	1.25
65	Derek Sanderson, Bos.	.75	1.50	3.00
66	Barclay Plager, St. L.	.30	.60	1.25
67	Paul Henderson, Tor.	.30	.60	1.25
68	Jude Drouin, Min.	.30	.60	1.25
69	Keith Magnuson, Chi.	.35	.85	1.75
70	Gordie Howe, Det.	12.50	25.00	50.00
71	Jacques Lemaire, Mon.	.75	1.50	3.00
72	Doug Favell, Goalie, Phi.	.50	1.00	2.00
73	Bert Marshall, Ca.	.30	.60	1.25
74	Gerry Meehan, Buf.	.30	.60	1.25
75	Walt Tkaczuk, NYR	.30	.60	1.25
76	**Bob Berry, LA, RC**	**.40**	**.85**	**1.75**
77	**Syl Apps, Jr., Pit., RC**	**.40**	**.85**	**1.75**
78	Tom Webster, Det.	.50	1.00	2.00
79	Danny Grant, Min.	.30	.60	1.25
80	Dave Keon, Tor.	.85	1.75	3.50
81	Ernie Wakely, Goalie, St. L.	.50	1.00	2.00
82	John McKenzie, Bos.	.30	.60	1.25
83	Doug Roberts, Det.	.30	.60	1.25
84	Peter Mahovlich, Mon.	.30	.60	1.25
85	Dennis Hull, Chi.	.30	.60	1.25
86	**Juha Widing, LA, RC**	**.40**	**.85**	**1.75**
87	Gary Doak, Van.	.30	.60	1.25
88	Phil Goyette, Buf., LC	.30	.60	1.25

No.	Player	VG	EX	NRMT
89	Gary Dornhoefer, Phi.	.30	.60	1.25
90	Ed Giacomin, Goalie, NYR	1.25	2.50	5.00
91	Red Berenson, Det.	.30	.60	1.25
92	Mike Pelyk, Tor.	.30	.60	1.25
93	Gary Jarrett, Ca.	.30	.60	1.25
94	Bob Pulford, LA, LC	.30	.60	1.25
95	Dale Tallon, Van.	.30	.60	1.25
96	Eddie Shack, Buf.	.75	1.50	3.00
97	Jean Ratelle, NYR	.75	1.50	3.00
98	Jim Pappin, Chi.	.30	.60	1.25
99	Roy Edwards, Goalie, Pit.	.50	1.00	2.00
100	Bobby Orr, Bos.	11.00	22.50	45.00
101	Ted Hampson, Min., LC	.30	.60	1.25
102	Mickey Redmond, Det.	.50	1.00	2.00
103	Bob Plager, St. L.	.30	.60	1.25
104	Bruce Gamble, Goalie, Phi., LC	.50	1.00	2.00
105	Frank Mahovlich, Mon.	1.50	3.00	6.00
106	**Tony Featherstone, Ca., RC**	**.30**	**.60**	**1.25**
107	Tracy Pratt, Buf.	.30	.60	1.25
108	Ralph Backstrom, LA	.30	.60	1.25
109	Murray Hall, Van.	.30	.60	1.25
110	Tony Esposito, Goalie, Chi.	4.00	8.50	17.00
111	Checklist (1 - 132)	11.00	22.50	45.00
112	Jim Neilson, NYR	.30	.60	1.25
113	Ron Ellis, Tor.	.30	.60	1.25
114	Bobby Clarke, Phi.	6.25	12.50	25.00
115	Ken Hodge, Bos.	.30	.60	1.25
116	Jim Roberts, St. L.	.30	.60	1.25
117	Cesare Maniago, Goalie, Min.	.50	1.00	2.00
118	Jean Pronovost, Pit.	.60	1.25	2.50
119	Gary Bergman, Det.	.30	.60	1.25
120	Henri Richard, Mon.	.80	1.75	3.50
121	Ross Lonsberry, LA	.30	.60	1.25
122	Pat Quinn, Van.	.30	.60	1.25
123	Rod Gilbert, NYR	.75	1.50	3.00
124	Gary Smith, Goalie, Ca.	.50	1.00	2.00
125	Stan Mikita, Chi.	2.00	4.00	8.00
126	Ed Van Impe, Phi.	.30	.60	1.25
127	Wayne Connelly, St. L.	.30	.60	1.25
128	Dennis Hextall, Min.	.30	.60	1.25
129	Wayne Cashman, Bos.	.50	1.00	2.00
130	J.C. Tremblay, Mon.	.30	.60	1.25
131	Bernie Parent, Goalie, Tor.	2.00	4.00	8.00
132	**Dunc McCallum, Pit., RC, LC**	**.75**	**1.50**	**3.00**

Topps
1971-72 Issue
Card No. 45,
Ken Dryden

Topps
1971-72 Issue
Card No. 125,
Stan Mikita

Topps
1971-72 Issue
Card No. 132,
Dunc McCallum

Topps
1971-72 Booklets
Booklet No.6,
The Henri Richard Story

— 1971 - 72 BOOKLETS —

Six inside pages of comics the tell story of the player listed on the cover. The back cover is a checklist. These eight page comic style booklets were issued as inserts with the regular 1971-72 Topps set.

Booklet Size: 2 1/2" X 3 1/2"
Face: Four colour; Name, Number, English
Back: Four colour on buff paper stock; Checklist
Imprint: ©T.C.G. PRINTED IN U.S.A.
Complete Set No.: 24
Complete Set Price: 8.50 | 17.50 | 35.00
Common Player: .25 | .50 | 1.00

No.	Player	VG	EX	NRMT
1	Bobby Hull, Chi.	1.75	3.50	7.00
2	Phil Esposito, Bos.	1.00	2.00	4.00
3	Dale Tallon, Van.	.25	.50	1.00
4	Jacques Plante, Goalie, Tor.	.75	1.50	3.00
5	Roger Crozier, Goalie, Buf.	.25	.50	1.00
6	Henri Richard, Mon.	.35	.75	1.50
7	Ed Giacomin, Goalie, NYR	.35	.75	1.50
8	Gilbert Perreault, Buf.	.35	.75	1.50
9	Greg Polis, Pit.	.25	.50	1.00
10	Bobby Clarke, Phi.	.50	1.00	2.00
11	Danny Grant, Min.	.25	.50	1.00
12	Alex Delvecchio, Det.	.50	1.00	2.00
13	Tony Esposito, Goalie, Chi.	.25	.50	1.00
14	Garry Unger, St.L.	.25	.50	1.00
15	Frank St. Marseille, St.L.	.35	.75	1.50
16	Dave Keon, Tor.	.75	1.50	3.00
17	Ken Dryden, Goalie, Mon.	1.25	2.50	5.00
18	Rod Gilbert, NYR	.25	.50	1.00
19	Juha Widing, LA	.25	.50	1.00
20	Orland Kurtenbach, Van.	.25	.50	1.00
21	Jude Drouin, Min.	.25	.50	1.00
22	Gary Smith, Goalie, Ca.	.25	.50	1.00
23	Gordie Howe, Det.	3.25	6.50	13.00
24	Bobby Orr, Bos.	3.25	6.50	13.00

TOPPS — 1972-73 REGULAR ISSUE

— 1972-73 REGULAR ISSUE —

This year Topps carried the message to watch hockey on "NBC." Mint cards command a price premium of 25% over NRMT cards.

PRICE MOVEMENT OF NRMT SETS

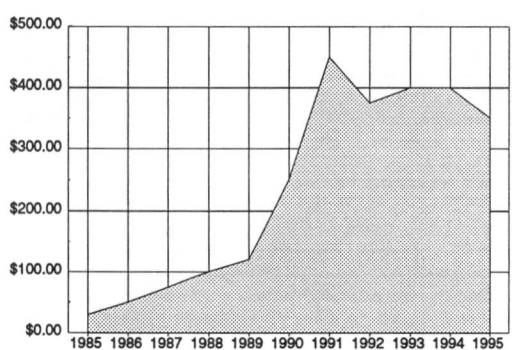

Card Size: 2 1/2" X 3 1/2"
Face: Four colour, beige border, Team logo
Back: Orange and black on card stock, Number, Resume, Hockey trivia
Imprint: * © TCG PRTD. IN U.S.A. or
** © TCG PRTD. IN U.S.A.
Complete Set No.: 176
Complete Set Price: 85.00 175.00 350.00
Common Card: .25 .50 1.00

1971-72 STANLEY CUP CHAMPS

No.	Team	VG	EX	NRMT
1	Boston Bruins	1.00	2.00	4.00

1971-72 NHL PLAYOFFS

No.	Game	VG	EX	NRMT
2	Game 1 at Boston	.25	.50	1.00
3	Game 2 at Boston	.25	.50	1.00
4	Game 3 at New York	.25	.50	1.00
5	Game 4 at New York	.25	.50	1.00
6	Game 5 at Boston	.25	.50	1.00
7	Game 6 at New York	.25	.50	1.00
8	Stanley Cup Trophy	.75	1.50	3.00

REGULAR ISSUE

No.	Player	VG	EX	NRMT
9	Ed Van Impe, Phi.	.25	.50	1.00
10	Yvan Cournoyer, Mon.	.50	1.00	2.00
11	Syl Apps, Jr., Pit.	.25	.50	1.00
12	**William Plager, Atl., RC, LC**	**.40**	**.85**	**1.75**
13	Ed Johnston, Goalie, Bos.	.50	1.00	2.00
14	Walt Tkaczuk, NYR	.25	.50	1.00
15	Dale Tallon, Van.	.25	.50	1.00
16	Gerry Meehan, Buf.	.25	.50	1.00
17	Reggie Leach, Ca.	.60	1.25	2.50
18	Marcel Dionne, Det.	4.50	8.75	17.00
19	**Andre Dupont, St. L., RC**	**.40**	**.85**	**1.75**
20	Tony Esposito, Goalie, Chi.	2.00	4.00	8.00
21	Bob Berry, LA	.25	.50	1.00
22	**Craig Cameron, NYI, RC**	**.25**	**.50**	**1.00**
23	Ted Harris, Min.	.25	.50	1.00
24	Jacques Plante, Goalie, Tor.	2.50	5.00	10.00
25	Jacques Lemaire, Mon.	.50	1.00	2.00
26	Simon Nolet, Phi.	.25	.50	1.00
27	Keith McCreary, Atl.	.25	.50	1.00
28	Duane Rupp, Pit.	.25	.50	1.00
29	Wayne Cashman, Bos.	.25	.50	1.00
30	Brad Park, NYR	1.25	2.50	5.00
31	Roger Crozier, Goalie, Buf.	.50	1.00	2.00
32	**Wayne Maki, Van., LC**	.25	.50	1.00
33	Tim Ecclestone, Det.	.25	.50	1.00
34	Rick Smith, Ca.	.25	.50	1.00
35	Garry Unger, St. L.	.30	.60	1.25
36	Serge Bernier, LA	.25	.50	1.00
37	Brian Glennie, Tor.	.25	.50	1.00
38	Gerry Desjardins, Goalie, NYI	.25	.50	1.00
39	Danny Grant, Min.	.25	.50	1.00
40	Bill White, Chi.	.25	.50	1.00

Topps 1972-73 Issue Card No. 1, Boston Bruins

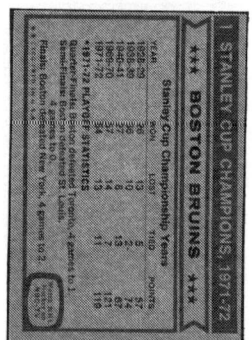

Topps 1972-73 Issue Card No. 1, Boston Bruins

Topps 1972-73 Issue Card No. 14, Walt Tkaczuk

Topps 1972-73 Issue Card No. 18, Marcel Dionne

No.	Player	VG	EX	NRMT
41	Gary Dornhoefer, Phi.	.25	.50	1.00
42	Pete Mahovlich, Mon.	.25	.50	1.00
43	Greg Polis, Pit.	.25	.50	1.00
44	**Larry Hale, Atl., RC, LC**	**.25**	**.50**	**1.00**
45	Dallas Smith, Bos.	.25	.50	1.00
46	Orland Kurtenbach, Van.	.25	.50	1.00
47	Steve Atkinson, Buf.	.25	.50	1.00
48	Joey Johnston, Ca.	.25	.50	1.00
49	Gary Bergman, Det.	.25	.50	1.00
50	Jean Ratelle, NYR	.75	1.50	3.00
51	Rogatien Vachon, Goalie, LA	.75	1.50	3.00
52	Phil Roberto, St. L.	.25	.50	1.00
53	Brian Spencer, NYI	.25	.50	1.00
54	Jim McKenny, Tor.	.25	.50	1.00
55	Gump Worsley, Goalie, Min.	.75	1.50	3.00
56	Stan Mikita, Chi.	1.25	2.50	5.00
57	Guy Lapointe, Mon.	.50	1.00	2.00
58	Lew Morrison, Atl.	.25	.50	1.00
59	Ron Schock, Pit	.25	.50	1.00
60	John Bucyk, Bos.	.50	1.00	2.00

NHL 1971-72 LEAGUE LEADERS

No.	Player	VG	EX	NRMT
61	**Goals Leaders:** P. Esposito, Bos., V. Hadfield, NYR, B. Hull, Chi.	2.00	4.00	8.00
62	**Assist Leaders:** B. Orr, Bos., P. Esposito, Bos., J. Ratelle, NYR	2.50	5.00	10.00
63	**Scoring Leaders:** P. Esposito, Bos., B. Orr, Bos., J. Ratelle, NYR;	2.50	5.00	10.00
64	**Goals Against Avg. Leaders:** T. Esposito, Chi., G. Villemure, NYR, G. Worsley, Min.	1.10	2.25	4.50
65	**Penalty Minute Leaders:** B. Watson, Pit., K. Magnuson, Chi., G. Dornhoefer, Phi.	.25	.50	1.00

REGULAR ISSUE

No.	Player	VG	EX	NRMT
66	Jim Neilson, NYR	.25	.50	1.00
67	Nick Libett, Det.	.25	.50	1.00
68	Jim Lorentz, Buf.	.25	.50	1.00
69	**Gilles Meloche, Goalie, Ca., RC**	**1.00**	**2.00**	**4.00**
70	Pat Stapleton, Chi.	.25	.50	1.00
71	Frank St. Marseille, St. L.	.25	.50	1.00
72	Butch Goring, LA	.75	1.50	3.00
73	Paul Henderson, Tor.	.25	.50	1.00
74	Doug Favell, Goalie, Phi.	.50	1.00	2.00
75	Jocelyn Guevremont, Van.	.25	.50	1.00
76	**Tom Miller, NYI, RC**	**.25**	**.50**	**1.00**
77	**Billy MacMillan, Atl., RC**	**.25**	**.50**	**1.00**
78	Doug Mohns, Min.	.25	.50	1.00
79	Guy Lafleur, Mon.	5.00	10.00	20.00
80	Rod Gilbert, NYR	.75	1.50	3.00
81	Gary Doak, Det.	.25	.50	1.00
82	**Dave Burrows, Pit., RC**	**.25**	**.50**	**1.00**
83	Gary Croteau, Ca.	.25	.50	1.00
84	Tracy Pratt, Buf.	.25	.50	1.00
85	Carol Vadnais, Bos.	.25	.50	1.00
86	**Jacques Caron, Goalie, St. L., RC, LC**	**.50**	**1.00**	**2.00**
87	Keith Magnuson, Chi.	.25	.50	1.00
88	Dave Keon, Tor.	.85	1.75	3.50
89	Mike Corrigan, LA	.25	.50	1.00
90	Bobby Clarke, Phi.	3.00	6.50	13.00
91	Dunc Wilson, Goalie, Van.	.50	1.00	2.00
92	**Gerry Hart, NYI, RC**	**.25**	**.50**	**1.00**
93	Lou Nanne, Min.	.25	.50	1.00
94	Checklist (1-176)	6.25	12.50	25.00
95	Red Berenson, Det.	.25	.50	1.00
96	Bob Plager, St. L.	.25	.50	1.00
97	**Jim Rutherford, Goalie, Pit., RC**	**.85**	**1.75**	**3.50**
98	**Rick Foley, Phi., RC, LC**	**.25**	**.50**	**1.00**
99	Pit Martin, Chi.	.25	.50	1.00
100	Bobby Orr, Bos.	7.50	15.00	30.00
101	Stan Gilbertson, Ca.	.25	.50	1.00
102	Barry Wilkins, Van.	.25	.50	1.00
103	Terry Crisp, NYI	.25	.60	1.25
104	Cesare Maniago, Goalie, Min.	.50	1.00	2.00

REGULAR ISSUE

No.	Player	VG	EX	NRMT
105	Marc Tardif, Mon.	.25	.50	1.00
106	Don Luce, Buf.	.25	.50	1.00
107	Mike Pelyk, Tor.	.25	.50	1.00

1973 - 74 REGULAR ISSUE — TOPPS • 207

No.	Player	VG	EX	NRMT
108	Juha Widing, LA	.25	.50	1.00
109	**Phil Myre, Goalie, Atl., RC**	.50	1.00	2.00
110	Vic Hadfield, NYR	.25	.50	1.00
111	Arnie Brown, Det.	.25	.50	1.00
112	Ross Lonsberry, Phi.	.25	.50	1.00
113	Dick Redmond, Ca.	.25	.50	1.00
114	Gary Smith, Goalie, Chi.	.50	1.00	2.00
115	Bill Goldsworthy, Min.	.25	.50	1.00
116	Bryan Watson, Pit.	.25	.50	1.00
117	Dave Balon, Van., LC	.25	.50	1.00
118	**Bill Mikkelson, NYI, RC**	.25	.50	1.00
119	Terry Harper, Mon.	.25	.50	1.00
120	Gilbert Perreault, Buf.	1.25	2.50	5.00

1971-72 NHL ALL STAR
First Team

No.	Player	VG	EX	NRMT
121	Tony Esposito, Goalie, Chi.	1.25	2.50	5.00
122	Bobby Orr, Bos.	3.75	7.50	15.00
123	Brad Park, NYR	1.00	2.00	4.00
124	Phil Esposito, Bos.	2.00	4.25	8.50
125	Rod Gilbert, NYR	.75	1.50	3.00
126	Bobby Hull, Chi.	3.75	7.50	15.00

Second Team

No.	Player	VG	EX	NRMT
127	Ken Dryden, Goalie, Mon.	3.75	7.50	15.00
128	Bill White, Chi.	.25	.50	1.00
129	Pat Stapleton, Chi.	.25	.50	1.00
130	Jean Ratelle, NYR	.35	.75	1.50
131	Yvan Cournoyer, Mon.	.35	.75	1.50
132	Vic Hadfield, NYR	.25	.50	1.00

REGULAR ISSUE

No.	Player	VG	EX	NRMT
133	Ralph Backstrom, LA	.25	.50	1.00
134	Bob Baun, Tor.	.25	.50	1.00
135	Fred Stanfield, Bos.	.25	.50	1.00
136	Barclay Plager, St. L.	.25	.50	1.00
137	Gilles Villemure, Goalie, NYR	.25	.50	1.00
138	Ron Harris, Atl.	.25	.50	1.00
139	Bill Flett, Phi.	.25	.50	1.00
140	Frank Mahovlich, Mon.	1.00	2.00	4.00
141	Alex Delvecchio, Det.	.60	1.25	2.50
142	Poul Popiel, Van.	.25	.50	1.00
143	Jean Pronovost, Pit.	.25	.50	1.00
144	Denis DeJordy, Goalie, Atl., LC	.50	1.00	2.00
145	Rick Martin, Buf.	.60	1.25	2.50
146	**Ivan Boldirev, Ca., RC**	.50	1.00	2.00
147	**Jack Egers, St. L., RC**	.25	.50	1.00
148	Jim Pappin, Chi.	.25	.50	1.00
149	Rod Seiling, NYR	.25	.50	1.00
150	Phil Esposito, Bos.	2.00	4.00	8.00
151	Gary Edwards, Goalie, LA	.50	1.00	2.00
152	Ron Ellis, Tor.	.25	.50	1.00
153	Jude Drouin, Min.	.25	.50	1.00
154	Ernie Hicke, Atl.	.25	.50	1.00
155	Mickey Redmond, Det.	.30	.60	1.25
156	Joe Watson, Phi.	.25	.50	1.00
157	Bryan Hextall, Jr., Pit.	.25	.50	1.00
158	Andre Boudrias, Van.	.25	.50	1.00
159	Ed Westfall, NYI	.25	.50	1.00
160	Ken Dryden, Goalie, Mon.	8.75	17.50	35.00
161	**Rene Robert, Buf., RC**	.50	1.00	2.00
162	Bert Marshall, Ca.	.25	.50	1.00
163	Gary Sabourin, St. L.	.25	.50	1.00
164	Dennis Hull, Chi.	.25	.50	1.00
165	Ed Giacomin, Goalie, NYR	.50	1.00	2.00
166	Ken Hodge, Bos.	.25	.50	1.00
167	Gilles Marotte, LA	.25	.50	1.00
168	Norm Ullman, Tor.	.35	.75	1.50
169	**Barry Gibbs, Min., RC**	.25	.50	1.00

TROPHY CARDS

No.	Trophy	VG	EX	NRMT
170	**The Art Ross Trophy:** Phil Esposito	.35	.75	1.50
171	**The Hart Memorial Trophy:** Bobby Orr	.35	.75	1.50
172	**The James Norris Memorial Trophy:** Bobby Orr	.35	.75	1.50

Topps 1972-73 Issue Card No. 118, Bill Mikkelson

Topps 1972-73 Issue Card No. 146, Ivan Boldirev

Topps 1973-74 Issue Card No. 1, Goal Leaders

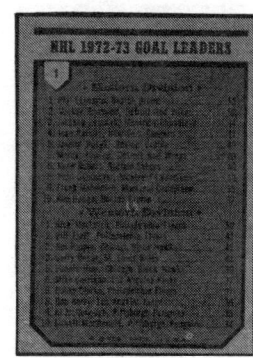

Topps 1973-74 Issue Card No. 1, Goal Leaders

No.	Trophy	VG	EX	NRMT
173	**The Vezina Trophy:** Tony Esposito, Gary Smith	.35	.75	1.50
174	**The Calder Memorial Trophy:** Ken Dryden	.35	.75	1.50
175	**The Lady Byng Memorial Trophy:** Jean Ratelle	.35	.75	1.50
176	**The Conn Smythe Trophy:** Bobby Orr	.75	1.50	3.00

— 1973 - 74 REGULAR ISSUE —

The team cards show team and player records on the back. Blue, green, red and yellow were used as border colours. This was a test by Topps to increase the number of combinations. Sets with identical borders command price premiums. Mint cards are difficult to find due to the coloured borders and will command a price premium of 50% over NRMT cards.

PRICE MOVEMENT OF NRMT SETS

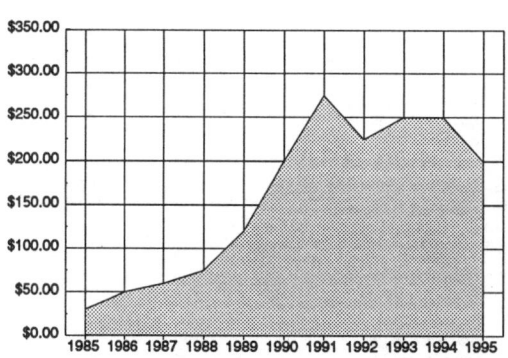

Card Size: 2 1/2" X 3 1/2"
Face: Four colour, red, green, yellow and blue borders, Position
Back: Brown and orange on card stock, Number, Resume, Hockey Trivia
Imprint: * © TCG PRTD. IN U.S.A. or
** © TCG PRTD. IN U.S.A.
Complete Set No.: 198
Complete Set Price: 50.00   100.00   200.00
Common Card: .15   .35   .75

1972 - 73 LEAGUE LEADERS

No.	Player	VG	EX	NRMT
1	**Goal Leaders:** P. Esposito, Bos., NHL East R. MacLeish, Phi., NHL West	1.25	2.50	5.00
2	**Assist Leaders:** P. Esposito, Bos., NHL East B. Clarke, Phi., NHL West	1.25	2.50	5.00
3	**Scoring Leaders:** P. Esposito, Bos., NHL East B. Clarke, Phi., NHL West	1.25	2.50	5.00
4	**Goals Against Avg. Leaders:** K. Dryden, Mon., NHL East T. Esposito, Chi., NHL West	1.25	2.50	5.00
5	**Penalty Minute Leaders** J. Schoenfeld, Buf., NHL East D. Schultz, Mon., NHL West	.40	.85	1.75
6	**Power Play Goal Leaders:** P. Esposito, Bos., NHL East R. MacLeish, Phi., NHL West	.75	1.50	3.00

REGULAR ISSUE

No.	Player	VG	EX	NRMT
7	Paul Henderson, Tor.	.15	.35	.75
8	Gregg Sheppard, Bos., Error	.15	.35	.75
9	Rod Seiling, NYR	.15	.35	.75
10	Ken Dryden, Goalie, Mon., '72-73 NHL All-Stars, East	8.75	17.50	35.00
11	Jean Pronovost, Pit.	.15	.35	.75
12	Dick Redmond, Chi.	.15	.35	.75
13	Keith McCreary, Atl.	.15	.35	.75
14	Ted Harris, Min., LC	.15	.35	.75
15	Garry Unger, St. L.	.30	.60	1.25
16	**Neil Komadoski, LA, RC**	.15	.35	.75
17	Marcel Dionne, Det.	2.50	5.00	10.00
18	Ernie Hicke, NYI	.15	.35	.75

TOPPS — 1973-74 REGULAR ISSUE

No.	Player	VG	EX	NRMT
19	Andre Boudrias, Van.	.15	.35	.75
20	Bill Flett, Phi., '72-73 NHL All-Stars, West	.15	.35	.75
21	Marshall Johnston, Ca., LC	.15	.35	.75
22	Gerry Meehan, Buf.	.15	.35	.75
23	Ed Johnston, Goalie, Tor.	.25	.50	1.00
24	Serge Savard, Mon.	.35	.75	1.50
25	Walt Tkaczuk, NYR	.15	.35	.75
26	John Bucyk, Bos.	.50	1.00	2.00
27	Dave Burrows, Pit.	.15	.35	.75
28	Cliff Koroll, Chi.	.15	.35	.75
29	Rey Comeau, Atl.	.15	.35	.75
30	Barry Gibbs, Min., '72-73 NHL All-Stars, West	.15	.35	.75
31	Wayne Stephenson, Goalie, St. L.	.15	.35	.75
32	Dan Maloney, LA	.15	.35	.75
33	Henry Boucha, Det., RC	.15	.35	.75
34	Gerry Hart, NYI	.15	.35	.75
35	Bobby Schmautz, Van.	.15	.35	.75
36	Ross Lonsberry, Phi.	.15	.35	.75
37	Ted McAneeley, Ca.	.15	.35	.75
38	Don Luce, Buf.	.15	.35	.75
39	Jim McKenny, Tor.	.15	.35	.75
40	Frank Mahovlich, Mon., '72-73 NHL All-Stars, East	.75	1.50	3.00
41	Bill Fairbairn, NYR	.15	.35	.75
42	Dallas Smith, Bos.	.15	.35	.75
43	Bryan Hextall, Jr., Pit.	.15	.35	.75
44	Keith Magnuson, Chi.	.15	.35	.75
45	Dan Bouchard, Goalie, Atl.	.15	.35	.75
46	Jean Paul Parise, Min.	.15	.35	.75
47	Barclay Plager, St. L.	.15	.35	.75
48	Mike Corrigan, LA	.15	.35	.75
49	Nick Libett, Det.	.15	.35	.75
50	Bobby Clarke, Phi., '72-73 NHL All-Stars, West	2.50	5.00	10.00
51	Bert Marshall, NYI	.15	.35	.75
52	Craig Patrick, Ca.	.30	.60	1.25
53	Richard Lemieux, Van.	.15	.35	.75
54	Tracy Pratt, Buf.	.15	.35	.75
55	Ron Ellis, Tor.	.15	.35	.75
56	Jacques Lemaire, Mon.	.40	.80	1.75
57	Steve Vickers, NYR	.15	.35	.75
58	Carol Vadnais, Bos.	.15	.35	.75
59	Jim Rutherford, Goalie, Pit.	.15	.35	.75
60	Dennis Hull, Chi., '72-73 NHL All-Stars, West	.15	.35	.75
61	Pat Quinn, St. L.	.15	.35	.75
62	Bill Goldsworthy, Min.	.15	.35	.75
63	Frank Huck, St. L., RC	.15	.35	.75
64	Rogatien Vachon, Goalie, LA	.35	.75	1.50
65	Gary Bergman, Det.	.15	.35	.75
66	Bernie Parent, Goalie, Phi.	1.00	2.00	4.00
67	Ed Westfall, NYI	.15	.35	.75
68	Ivan Boldirev, Ca.	.15	.35	.75
69	Don Tannahill, Van., LC	.15	.35	.75
70	Gilbert Perreault, Buf.	1.25	2.50	5.00
71	Mike Pelyk, Tor.	.15	.35	.75
72	Guy Lafleur, Mon.	3.00	6.00	12.00
73	Jean Ratelle, NYR	.50	1.00	2.00
74	Gilles Gilbert, Goalie, Bos., RC	.50	1.00	2.00
75	Greg Polis, Pit.	.15	.35	.75
76	Doug Jarrett, Chi.	.15	.35	.75
77	Phil Myre, Goalie, Atl.	.15	.35	.75
78	Buster Harvey, Min.	.15	.35	.75
79	Jack Egers, St. L.	.15	.35	.75
80	Terry Harper, LA	.15	.35	.75
81	Bill Barber, Phi., RC	3.00	6.50	13.00
82	Roy Edwards, Goalie, Det., LC	.15	.35	.75
83	Brian Spencer, NYI	.15	.35	.75
84	Reggie Leach, Ca.	.15	.35	.75
85	Dave Keon, Tor.	.35	.75	1.50
86	Jim Schoenfeld, Buf.	.35	.75	1.50
87	Henri Richard, Mon.	.35	.75	1.50
88	Rod Gilbert, NYR	.35	.75	1.50
89	Don Marcotte, Bos.	.15	.35	.75
90	Tony Esposito, Goalie, Chi., '72-73 NHL All-Stars, West	1.50	3.00	6.00
91	Joe Watson, Phi.	.15	.35	.75

Topps 1973-74 Issue Card No. 32, Dan Maloney

Topps 1973-74 Issue Card No. 50, Bobby Clarke

Topps 1973-74 Issue Card No. 96, Chicago Black Hawks

Topps 1973-74 Issue Card No. 149 Dave Schultz

TEAM CARDS

No.	Team	VG	EX	NRMT
92	Atlanta Flames	.35	.75	1.50
93	Boston Bruins	.35	.75	1.50
94	Buffalo Sabres	.35	.75	1.50
95	California Golden Seals	.35	.75	1.50
96	Chicago Black Hawks	.35	.75	1.50
97	Detroit Red Wings	.35	.75	1.50
98	Los Angeles Kings	.35	.75	1.50
99	Minnesota North Stars	.35	.75	1.50
100	Montreal Canadiens	.35	.75	1.50
101	New York Islanders	.35	.75	1.50
102	New York Rangers	.35	.75	1.50
103	Philadelphia Flyers	.35	.75	1.50
104	Pittsburgh Penguins	.35	.75	1.50
105	St. Louis Blues	.35	.75	1.50
106	Toronto Maple Leafs	.35	.75	1.50
107	Vancouver Canucks	.35	.75	1.50

REGULAR ISSUE

No.	Player	VG	EX	NRMT
108	Roger Crozier, Goalie, Buf.	.15	.35	.75
109	Tom Reid, Min.	.15	.35	.75
110	Hilliard Graves, Ca., RC	.15	.35	.75
111	Don Lever, Van.	.15	.35	.75
112	Jim Pappin, Chi.	.15	.35	.75
113	Ron Schock, Pit.	.15	.35	.75
114	Gerry Desjardins, Goalie, NYI	.15	.35	.75
115	Yvan Cournoyer, Mon.	.50	1.00	2.00
116	Checklist (1 - 198)	5.00	10.00	20.00
117	Bobby Leiter, Atl.	.15	.35	.75
118	Ab DeMarco, St. L.	.15	.35	.75
119	Doug Favell, Goalie, Tor.	.15	.35	.75
120	Phil Esposito, Bos., '72-73 NHL All-Stars, East	1.25	2.50	5.00
121	Mike Robitaille, Buf.	.15	.35	.75
122	Real Lemieux, LA, LC	.15	.35	.75
123	Jim Neilson, NYR	.15	.35	.75
124	Tim Ecclestone, Det.	.15	.35	.75
125	Jude Drouin, Min.	.15	.35	.75
126	Gary Smith, Goalie, Van.	.15	.35	.75
127	Walt McKechnie, Ca.	.15	.35	.75
128	Lowell MacDonald, Pit.	.15	.35	.75
129	Dale Tallon, Chi.	.15	.35	.75
130	Billy Harris, NYI, RC	.15	.35	.75
131	Randy Manery, Atl.	.15	.35	.75
132	Darryl Sittler, Tor.	1.75	3.50	7.00
133	Ken Hodge, Bos.	.15	.35	.75
134	Bob Plager, St. L.	.15	.35	.75
135	Rick MacLeish, Phi.	.50	1.00	2.00
136	Dennis Hextall, Min.	.15	.35	.75
137	Jacques Laperriere, Mon.	.15	.35	.75
138	Butch Goring, LA	.25	.50	1.00
139	Rene Robert, Buf.	.15	.35	.75
140	Ed Giacomin, Goalie, NYR	.60	1.25	2.50
141	Alex Delvecchio, Det., LC	.35	.75	1.50
142	Jocelyn Guevremont, Van.	.15	.35	.75
143	Joey Johnston, Ca.	.15	.35	.75
144	Bryan Watson, Pit.	.15	.35	.75
145	Stan Mikita, Chi.	1.25	2.50	5.00
146	Cesare Maniago, Goalie, Min.	.15	.35	.75
147	Craig Cameron, NYI	.15	.35	.75
148	Norm Ullman, Tor.	.25	.50	1.00
149	Dave Schultz, Phi., RC	1.75	3.50	7.00
150	Bobby Orr, Bos., '72-73 NHL All-Stars, East	6.00	12.50	25.00
151	Phil Roberto, St. L.	.15	.35	.75
152	Curt Bennett, Atl., RC	.15	.35	.75
153	Gilles Villemure, Goalie, NYR	.15	.35	.75
154	Chuck Lefley, Mon., RC	.15	.35	.75
155	Rick Martin, Buf.	.50	1.00	2.00
156	Juha Widing, LA	.15	.35	.75
157	Orland Kurtenbach, Van., LC	.15	.35	.75
158	Bill Collins, Det.	.15	.35	.75
159	Bob Stewart, Ca., RC	.15	.35	.75
160	Syl Apps, Jr., Pit.	.15	.35	.75
161	Danny Grant, Min.	.15	.35	.75
162	Billy Smith, Goalie, NYI, RC	5.50	11.00	22.00
163	Brian Glennie, Tor.	.15	.35	.75
164	Pit Martin, Chi.	.15	.35	.75
165	Brad Park, NYR	.75	1.50	3.00
166	Wayne Cashman, Bos.	.15	.35	.75
167	Gary Dornhoefer, Phi.	.15	.35	.75
168	Steve Durbano, St. L., RC	.15	.35	.75

1974 - 75 REGULAR ISSUE — TOPPS • 209

No.	Player	VG	EX	NRMT
169	Jacques Richard, Atl.	.15	.35	.75
170	Guy Lapointe, Mon.,'72-73 NHL All-Stars, East	.25	.50	1.00
171	Jim Lorentz, Buf.	.15	.35	.75
172	Bob Berry, LA	.15	.35	.75
173	Dennis Kearns, Van.	.15	.35	.75
174	Red Berenson, Det.	.15	.35	.75
175	Gilles Meloche, Goalie, Ca.	.15	.35	.75
176	Al McDonough, Pit.	.15	.35	.75
177	**Dennis O'Brien, Min., RC**	**.15**	**.35**	**.75**
178	Germaine Gagnon, NYI	.15	.35	.75
179	Rick Kehoe, Tor.	.15	.35	.75
180	Bill White, Chi., '72-73 NHL All-Stars, West	.15	.35	.75
181	Vic Hadfield, NYR	.15	.35	.75
182	Derek Sanderson, Bos.	.15	.35	.75
183	Andre Dupont, Phi.	.15	.35	.75
184	Gary Sabourin, St. L.	.15	.35	.75
185	**Larry Romanchych, Atl., RC**	**.15**	**.35**	**.75**
186	Pete Mahovlich, Mon.	.15	.35	.75
187	Dave Dryden, Goalie, Buf.	.15	.35	.75
188	Gilles Marotte, LA	.15	.35	.75
189	Bobby Lalonde, Van.	.15	.35	.75
190	Mickey Redmond, Det., '72-73 NHL All-Stars, East	.15	.35	.75

1972 - 73 STANLEY CUP PLAYOFFS

No.	Team	VG	EX	NRMT
191	**NHL Quarter Finals:** Games: Canadiens 4 Sabres 2	.25	.50	1.00
192	**NHL Quarter Finals:** Games: Flyers 4 North Stars 2	.25	.50	1.00
193	**NHL Quarter Finals:** Games: Black Hawks 4 Blues 1	.25	.50	1.00
194	**NHL Quarter Finals:** Games: Rangers 4 Bruins 1	.25	.50	1.00
195	**NHL Semi-Finals:** Games: Canadiens 4 Flyers 1	.25	.50	1.00
196	**NHL Semi-Finals:** Games: Black Hawks 4 Rangers 1	.25	.50	1.00
197	**NHL Finals:** Games: Canadiens 4 Black Hawks 2	.25	.50	1.00
198	**Stanley Cup Champions:** Montreal Canadiens	.75	1.50	3.00

— 1974 - 75 REGULAR ISSUE —

Mint cards command a price premium of 25% over NRMT cards.

PRICE MOVEMENT OF NRMT SETS

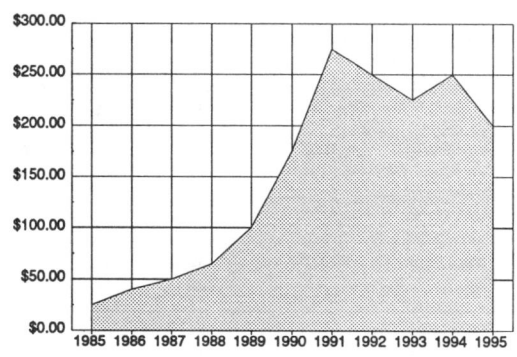

Card Size: 2 1/2" X 3 1/2"
Face: Four colour, white border, Team logo
Back: Brown and blue on card stock, Number, Resume, Hockey trivia
Imprint: * © TOPPS CHEWING GUM, INC. PRTD IN U.S.A. or
** © TOPPS CHEWING GUM, INC. PRTD. IN U.S.A.
Complete Set No.: 264
Complete Set Price: 50.00 100.00 200.00
Common Card: .10 .25 .50

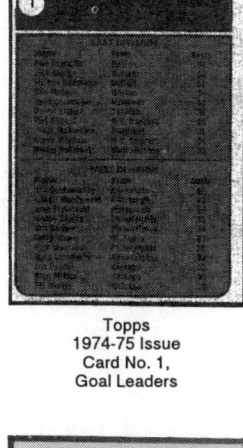

Topps
1974-75 Issue
Card No.1,
Goal Leaders

Topps
1974-75 Issue
Card No. 1,
Goal Leaders

Topps
1974-75 Issue
Card No. 19,
Red Berenson

Topps
1974-75 Issue
Card No. 50,
Brad Park

1973 - 1974 LEAGUE LEADERS

No.	Player	VG	EX	NRMT
1	**Goal Leaders:** P. Esposito, Bos.,, NHL East B. Goldsworthy, Min., NHL West	.60	1.25	2.50
2	**Assist Leaders:** B. Orr, Bos., NHL East D. Hextall, Min., NHL West	1.25	2.50	5.00
3	**Scoring Leaders:** P. Esposito, Bos., NHL East B. Clarke, Phi., NHL West	.85	1.75	3.50
4	**Goals Against Avg. Leaders:** D. Favell, Tor., NHL East B. Parent, Phi., NHL West	.25	.50	1.00
5	**Penalty Minute Leaders:** B. Watson, Det., NHL East D. Schultz, Phi., NHL West	.15	.35	.75
6	**Power Play Goal Leaders:** M. Redmond, Det., NHL East R. MacLeish, Phi., NHL West	.15	.35	.75

REGULAR ISSUE

No.	Player	VG	EX	NRMT
7	**Gary Bromley, Goalie, Buf., RC**	**.12**	**.25**	**.50**
8	Bill Barber, Phi.	2.00	4.00	8.00
9	Emile Francis, Coach, NYR	.12	.25	.50
10	Gilles Gilbert, Goalie, Bos.	.12	.25	.50
11	**John Davidson, Goalie, St. L., RC**	**1.50**	**3.00**	**6.00**
12	Ron Ellis, Tor.	.12	.25	.50
13	Syl Apps, Jr., Pit.	.12	.25	.50
14	**Atlanta Flames Team Leaders:** J. Richard, Goals; T. Lysiak, Assists, Points; K. McCreary, Scoring pct.	.12	.25	.50
15	Dan Bouchard, Goalie, Atl.	.12	.25	.50
16	Ivan Boldirev, Chi.	.12	.25	.50
17	**Gary Coalter, KC, RC**	**.12**	**.25**	**.50**
18	Bob Berry, LA	.12	.25	.50
19	Red Berenson, Det.	.12	.25	.50
20	Stan Mikita, Chi.	1.25	2.50	5.00
21	Fred Shero, Coach, Phi.,	.75	1.50	3.00
22	Gary Smith, Goalie, Van.	.12	.25	.50
23	Bill Mikkelson, Wash.	.12	.25	.50
24	Jacques Lemaire, Mon., Error	.50	1.00	2.00
25	Gilbert Perreault, Buf.	1.25	2.50	5.00
26	Cesare Maniago, Goalie, Min.	.12	.25	.50
27	Bobby Schmautz, Bos.	.12	.25	.50
28	**Boston Bruins Team Leaders:** P. Esposito, Goals, Points; B. Orr, Assists; J. Bucyk, Scoring Pct.	1.85	3.75	7.50
29	Steve Vickers, NYR	.12	.25	.50
30	Lowell MacDonald, Pit.	.12	.25	.50
31	Fred Stanfield, Min.	.12	.25	.50
32	Ed Westfall, NYI	.12	.25	.50
33	Curt Bennett, Atl.	.12	.25	.50
34	Bep Guidolin, Coach, KC	.12	.25	.50
35	Cliff Koroll, Chi.	.12	.25	.50
36	Gary Croteau, KC	.12	.25	.50
37	Mike Corrigan, LA	.12	.25	.50
38	Henry Boucha, Det.	.12	.25	.50
39	Ron Low, Goalie, Wash.	.12	.25	.50
40	Darryl Sittler, Tor.	1.50	3.00	6.00
41	Tracy Pratt, Van.	.12	.25	.50
42	**Buffalo Sabres Team Leaders:** R. Martin, Goals, Points, Scoring Pct.; R. Robert, Assists	.15	.35	.75
43	Larry Carriere, Buf.	.12	.25	.50
44	Gary Dornhoefer, Phi., Error	.12	.25	.50
45	**Denis Herron, Goalie, Pit., RC**	**.50**	**1.00**	**2.00**
46	Doug Favell, Goalie, Tor.	.12	.25	.50
47	**Dave Gardner, St. L., RC**	**.12**	**.25**	**.50**
48	**Morris Mott, Ca., RC, LC**	**.12**	**.25**	**.50**
49	Marc Boileau, Coach, Pit.,	.12	.25	.50
50	Brad Park, NYR	.75	1.50	3.00
51	Bobby Leiter, Atl.	.12	.25	.50
52	Tom Reid, Min.	.12	.25	.50
53	Serge Savard, Mon.	.30	.60	1.25
54	**Checklist 1 (1 - 132)**	**3.00**	**6.00**	**12.00**
55	Terry Harper, LA	.12	.25	.50
56	**California Golden Seals Team Leaders:** J. Johnston, Goals, Assists, Points; W. McKechnie, Scoring Pct.	.12	.25	.50
57	Guy Charron, Det.	.12	.25	.50
58	Pit Martin, Chi.	.12	.25	.50
59	Chris Evans, KC	.12	.25	.50
60	Bernie Parent, Goalie, Phi.	.75	1.50	3.00
61	Jim Lorentz, Buf.	.12	.25	.50

210 • TOPPS — 1974-75 REGULAR ISSUE

No.	Player	VG	EX	NRMT
62	**Dave Kryskow, Wash., RC**	.12	.25	.50
63	Lou Angotti, St. L., LC	.12	.25	.50
64	Bill Flett, Tor.	.12	.25	.50
65	Vic Hadfield, Pit.	.12	.25	.50
66	**Wayne Merrick, St. L., RC**	.12	.25	.50
67	Andre Dupont, Phi.	.12	.25	.50
68	**Tom Lysiak, Atl., RC**	.25	.50	1.00
69	**Chicago Black Hawks Team**	.25	.50	1.00
	Leaders: J. Pappin, Goals; S. Mikita, Assists, Points; J. P. Bordelaeau, Scoring Pct.			
70	Guy Lapointe, Mon.	.25	.50	1.00
71	Gerry O'Flaherty, Van.	.12	.25	.50
72	Marcel Dionne, Det.	1.80	3.75	7.50
73	**Butch Deadmarsh, KC, RC**	.12	.25	.50
74	Butch Goring, LA	.12	.25	.50
75	Keith Magnuson, Chi.	.12	.25	.50
76	Red Kelly, Coach, Tor.	.25	.50	1.00
77	Pete Stemkowski, NYR	.12	.25	.50
78	Jim Roberts, Mon.	.12	.25	.50
79	Don Luce, Buf.	.12	.25	.50
80	Don Awrey, St. L.	.12	.25	.50
81	Rick Kehoe, Tor.	.12	.25	.50
82	Billy Smith, Goalie, NYI	1.75	3.50	7.00
83	J. P. Parise, Min.	.12	.25	.50
84	**Detroit Red Wings Team**	.35	.75	1.50
	Leaders: M. Redmond, Goals; M. Dionne, Assists, Points; B. Hogaboam, Scoring Pct.			
85	Ed Van Impe, Phi.	.12	.25	.50
86	Randy Manery, Atl.	.12	.25	.50
87	Barclay Plager, St. L.	.12	.25	.50
88	**Inge Hammarstrom, Tor., RC**	.12	.25	.50
89	Ab DeMarco, Pit.	.12	.25	.50
90	Bill White, Chi.	.12	.25	.50
91	Al Arbour, Coach, NYI	.50	1.00	2.00
92	Bob Stewart, Ca.	.12	.25	.50
93	Jack Egers, Wash.	.12	.25	.50
94	Don Lever, Van.	.12	.25	.50
95	Reggie Leach, Phi.	.12	.25	.50
96	Dennis O'Brien, Min.	.12	.25	.50
97	Pete Mahovlich, Mon.	.12	.25	.50
98	**Los Angeles Kings Team Leaders:**	.12	.25	.50
	B. Goring, Goals, Points; F. St. Marseille, Assists; D. Kozak, Scoring Pct.			
99	Gerry Meehan, Buf.	.12	.25	.50
100	Bobby Orr, Bos.	5.50	11.00	22.00
101	**Jean Potvin, NYI, RC**	.25	.50	1.00
102	Rod Seiling, NYR	.12	.25	.50
103	Keith McCreary, Atl., LC	.12	.25	.50
104	Phil Maloney, Coach, Van.	.12	.25	.50
105	Denis Dupere, Wash.	.12	.25	.50
106	Steve Durbano, Pit.	.12	.25	.50
107	**Bob Plager, St.L., Error**	.12	.25	.50
108	**Chris Oddleifson, Van., RC**	.12	.25	.50
109	Jim Neilson, Ca.	.12	.25	.50
110	Jean Pronovost, Pit.	.12	.25	.50
111	**Don Kozak, LA, RC**	.12	.25	.50
112	**Minnesota North Stars Team Leaders:**	.12	.25	.50
	B. Goldsworthy, Goals; D. Hextall, Assists, Points; D. Grant, Scoring Pct.			
113	Jim Pappin, Chi.	.12	.25	.50
114	Richard Lemieux, KC	.12	.25	.50
115	Dennis Hextall, Min.	.12	.25	.50
116	**Bill Hogaboam, Det., RC**	.12	.25	.50
117	**Vancouver Canucks Team**	.12	.25	.50
	Leaders: D. Ververgaert and B. Schmautz, Goals; A. Boudrias, Assists, Points; D. Tannahill, Scoring Pct.			
118	Jim Anderson, Coach, Wash.	.12	.25	.50
119	Walt Tkaczuk, NYR	.12	.25	.50
120	Mickey Redmond, Det.	.12	.25	.50
121	Jim Schoenfeld, Buf.	.25	.50	1.00
122	Jocelyn Guevremont, Van.	.12	.25	.50
123	Bob Nystrom, NYI	.25	.50	1.00
124	**Montreal Canadiens Team**	.60	1.25	2.50
	Leaders: Y. Cournoyer, Goals; F. Mahovlich, Assists, Points; C. Larose, Scoring Pct.			
125	Lew Morrison, Wash.	.12	.25	.50
126	Terry Murray, Ca., LC	.25	.50	1.00

Topps, 1974-75 Issue
Card No.84,
Detroit Red Wings
Team Leaders

Topps
1974-75 Issue
Card No.91,
Al Arbour

Topps
1974-75 Issue
Card No.107, Error,
Card shows Barclay Plager

Topps
1974-75 Issue
Card No.168,
Lanny McDonald

1973 - 74 ALL STARS

NHL East

No.	Player	VG	EX	NRMT
127	Rick Martin, Buf.	.12	.25	.50
128	Ken Hodge, Bos.	.12	.25	.50
129	Phil Esposito, Bos.	1.00	2.00	4.00
130	Bobby Orr, Bos.	3.00	6.00	12.00
131	Brad Park, NYR	.25	.50	1.00
132	Gilles Gilbert, Goalie, Bos.	.12	.25	.50

NHL West

No.	Player	VG	EX	NRMT
133	Lowell MacDonald, Pit.	.12	.25	.50
134	Bill Goldsworthy, Min.	.12	.25	.50
135	Bobby Clarke, Phi.	1.00	2.00	4.00
136	Bill White, Chi.	.12	.25	.50
137	Dave Burrows, Pit.	.12	.25	.50
138	Bernie Parent, Goalie, Phi.	.50	1.00	2.00

REGULAR ISSUE

No.	Player	VG	EX	NRMT
139	Jacques Richard, Atl.	.12	.25	.50
140	Yvan Cournoyer, Mon.	.75	1.50	3.00
141	**New York Rangers Team**	.55	1.10	2.25
	Leaders: R. Gilbert, Goals, Scoring Pct. B. Park, Assists, Points			
142	Rene Robert, Buf.	.12	.25	.50
143	**J. Bob Kelly, Pit., RC**	.12	.25	.50
144	Ross Lonsberry, Phi.	.12	.25	.50
145	Jean Ratelle, NYR	.35	.75	1.50
146	Dallas Smith, Bos.	.12	.25	.50
147	Bernie Geoffrion, Coach, Atl.	.55	1.10	2.25
148	Ted McAneeley, Ca., LC	.12	.25	.50
149	Pierre Plante, St. L.	.12	.25	.50
150	Dennis Hull, Chi.	.12	.25	.50
151	Dave Keon, Tor.	.35	.75	1.50
152	**Dave Dunn, Van., RC**	.12	.25	.50
153	Michel Belhumeur, Goalie, Wash.	.12	.25	.50
154	**Philadelphia Flyers Team**	.50	1.00	2.00
	Leaders: B. Clarke, Goals, Assists, Points; D. Schultz, Scoring Pct.			
155	Ken Dryden, Goalie, Mon.	4.50	9.00	18.00
156	**John Wright, KC, RC, LC**	.12	.25	.50
157	Larry Romanchych, Atl.	.12	.25	.50
158	**Ralph Stewart, NYI, RC**	.12	.25	.50
159	Mike Robitaille, Buf.	.12	.25	.50
160	Ed Giacomin, Goalie, NYR	.50	1.00	2.00
161	Don Cherry, Coach, Bos.	4.25	8.50	17.00
162	Checklist 2 (133 - 264)	3.00	6.00	12.00
163	Rick MacLeish, Phi.	.25	.50	1.00
164	Greg Polis, St. L.	.12	.25	.50
165	Carol Vadnais, Bos.	.12	.25	.50
166	Pete Laframboise, Wash.	.12	.25	.50
167	Ron Schock, Pit.	.12	.25	.50
168	**Lanny McDonald, Tor., RC**	6.00	12.00	24.00
169	Kansas City Scouts Emblem Entered NHL, 1974	.35	.75	1.50
170	Tony Esposito, Goalie, Chi.	1.25	2.50	5.00
171	Pierre Jarry, Det.	.12	.25	.50
172	Dan Maloney, LA	.12	.25	.50
173	Pete McDuffe, Goalie ,KC	.12	.25	.50
174	Danny Grant, Min.	.12	.25	.50
175	**John Stewart, Ca., RC, LC**	.12	.25	.50
176	Floyd Smith, Buf., LC	.12	.25	.50
177	Bert Marshall, NYI	.12	.25	.50
178	Chuck Lefley, Error,	.12	.25	.50
179	Gilles Villemure, Goalie, NYR	.12	.25	.50
180	**Borje Salming, Tor., RC**	2.50	5.00	10.00
181	Doug Mohns, Wash., LC	.12	.25	.50
182	Barry Wilkins, Van.	.12	.25	.50
183	**Pittsburgh Penguins Team**	.12	.25	.50
	Leaders: L. MacDonald, Goals, Scoring Oct.; S. Apps, Jr., Assists, Points			
184	Gregg Sheppard, Bos.	.12	.25	.50
185	Joey Johnston, Ca.	.12	.25	.50
186	Dick Redmond, Chi.	.12	.25	.50
187	Simon Nolet, KC	.12	.25	.50
188	Ron Stackhouse, Pit.	.12	.25	.50
189	Marshall Johnston, Coach, Ca.	.12	.25	.50
190	Rick Martin, Buf.	.12	.25	.50
191	Andre Boudrias, Van.	.12	.25	.50
192	Steve Atkinson, Wash., LC	.12	.25	.50

1975 - 76 REGULAR ISSUE — TOPPS • 211

No.	Player	VG	EX	NRMT
193	Nick Libett, Det.	.12	.25	.50
194	Bob J. Murdoch, LA, RC	.12	.25	.50
195	Denis Potvin, NYI, RC	7.50	15.00	30.00
196	Dave Schultz, Phi.	.35	.75	1.50
197	St. Louis Blues Team Leaders: G. Unger, Goals, Assists, Points; P. Plante, Scoring Pct.	.12	.25	.50
198	Jim McKenny, Tor.	.12	.25	.50
199	Gerry Hart, NYI	.12	.25	.50
200	Phil Esposito, Bos.	1.10	2.25	4.50
201	Rod Gilbert, NYR	.60	1.25	1.50
202	Jacques Laperriere, Mon., LC	.12	.25	.50
203	Barry Gibbs, Min.	.12	.25	.50
204	Billy Reay, Coach, Chi.	.12	.25	.50
205	Gilles Meloche, Goalie, Ca.	.12	.25	.50
206	Wayne Cashman, Bos.	.12	.25	.50
207	Dennis Ververgaert, Van., RC	.12	.25	.50
208	Phil Roberto, St. L.	.12	.25	.50

1973 - 74 STANLEY CUP PLAYOFFS

No.	Teams	VG	EX	NRMT
209	Quarter-Finals: Flyers vs. Flames	.15	.35	.75
210	Quarter-Finals,: Rangers vs. Canadiens	.15	.35	.75
211	Quarter-Finals,: Bruins vs. Maple Leafs	.15	.35	.75
212	Quarter-Finals: Black Hawks vs. Kings	.15	.35	.75
213	Semi-Finals: Flyers vs. Rangers	.15	.35	.75
214	Semi-Finals: Black Hawks vs. Bruins	.15	.35	.75
215	Finals: Flyers vs. Bruins	.15	.35	.75
216	Stanley Cup Champions: Philadelphia Flyers	.50	1.00	2.00

REGULAR ISSUE

No.	Player	VG	EX	NRMT
217	Joe Watson, Phi.	.12	.25	.50
218	Wayne Stephenson, Goalie, St. L.	.12	.25	.50
219	Toronto Maple Leafs Team Leaders: D. Sittler, Goals, Points; N. Ullman, Assists; P. Henderson & D. Dupere, Scoring Pct.	.40	.85	1.75
220	Bill Goldsworthy, Min.	.12	.25	.50
221	Don Marcotte, Bos.	.12	.35	.50
222	Alex Delvecchio, Coach, Det.	.25	.50	1.00
223	Stan Gilbertson, Ca.	.12	.25	.50
224	Mike Murphy, LA	.12	.25	.50
225	Jim Rutherford, Goalie, Det.	.12	.25	.50
226	Phil Russell, Chi.	.12	.25	.50
227	Lynn Powis, KC	.12	.25	.50
228	Billy Harris, NYI	.12	.25	.50
229	Bob Pulford, Coach, LA	.12	.25	.50
230	Ken Hodge, Bos.	.12	.25	.50
231	Bill Fairbairn, NYR	.12	.25	.50
232	Guy Lafleur, Mon.	3.75	7.50	15.00
233	New York Islanders Team Leaders: B. Harris & R. Stewart, Goals; D. Potvin, Assists, Points; R. Steward, Scoring Pct.	.75	1.50	3.00
234	Fred Barrett, Min.	.12	.25	.50
235	Rogatien Vachon, Goalie, LA	.35	.75	1.50
236	Norm Ullman, Tor.	.25	.50	1.00
237	Garry Unger, St. L.	.25	.50	1.00
238	Jackie Gordon, Coach, Min.	.12	.25	.50
239	John Bucyk, Bos.	.50	1.00	2.00
240	Bob Dailey, Van., RC	.12	.25	.50
241	Dave Burrows, Pit.	.12	.25	.50
242	Len Frig, Ca., RC	.12	.25	.50

1973 - 74 TROPHY WINNERS

No.	Trophy	VG	EX	NRMT
243	Masterton Memorial Trophy: Henri Richard, Canadiens	.30	.60	1.25
244	Hart Memorial Trophy: Phil Esposito, Bruins	.75	1.50	3.00
245	Lady Byng Memorial Trophy: John Bucyk, Bruins	.25	.50	1.00
246	Art Ross Trophy: Phil Esposito, Bruins	.75	1.50	3.00
247	Prince of Wales Trophy: Boston Bruins	.12	.25	.50
248	James Norris Trophy: Bobby Orr, Bruins	2.50	5.00	10.00

Topps
1974-75 Issue
Card No.195,
Denis Potvin

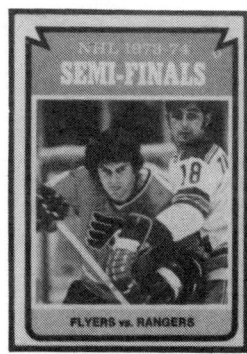

Topps, 1974-75 Issue
Card No.213,
Semi-Finals,
Flyers vs. Rangers

Topps
1975-76 Issue
Card No.1,
Stanley Cup Finals

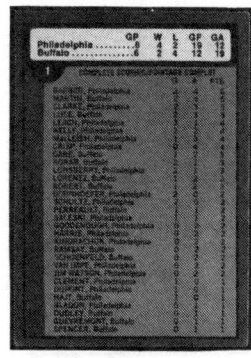

Topps
1975-76 Issue
Card No.1,
Stanley Cup Finals

No.	Trophy	VG	EX	NRMT
249	Vezina Trophy: Bernie Parent, Goalie, Flyers	.35	.75	1.50
250	Stanley Cup, 1973-74 Winner: Philadelphia Flyers	.35	.75	1.50
251	Conn Smythe Trophy: Bernie Parent, Goalie,Flyers	.35	.75	1.50
252	Calder Memorial Trophy: Denis Potvin, Islanders	2.00	4.00	8.00
253	Clarence Campbell Trophy: Philadelphia Flyers	.12	.25	.50

REGULAR ISSUE

No.	Player	VG	EX	NRMT
254	Pierre Bouchard, Mon.	.12	.25	.50
255	Jude Drouin, Min.	.12	.25	.50
256	Washington Capitals Entered NHL, 1974	.12	.25	.50
257	Michel Plasse, Goalie, KC	.20	.40	.80
258	Juha Widing, LA	.12	.25	.50
259	Bryan Watson, Det.	.12	.25	.50
260	Bobby Clarke, Phi.	1.80	3.75	7.50
261	Scotty Bowman, Coach, Mon.	2.50	5.00	10.00
262	Craig Patrick, Ca.	.12	.25	.50
263	Craig Cameron, NYI	.12	.25	.50
264	Ted Irvine, NYR	.30	.65	1.25

— 1975 - 76 REGULAR ISSUE —

The fronts of cards 1-330 are for the most part identical to those issued by O-Pee-Chee the same year. Team photo cards (81-90) have a checklist of players on the reverse side.

PRICE MOVEMENT OF NRMT SETS

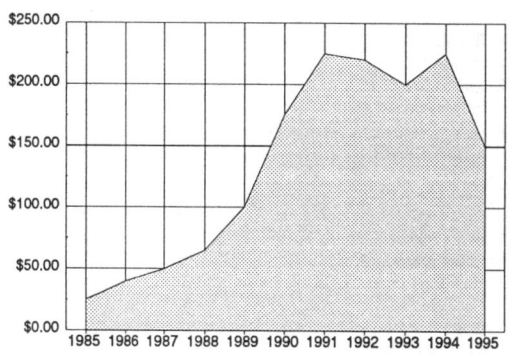

Card Size: 2 1/2" X 3 1/2"
Face: Four colour, white border, Position
Back: Brown and black on card stock; Number, Resume, Hockey trivia
Imprint: © 1975 NHL Players Association.
 * © 1975 TOPPS CHEWING GUM, INC. PRTD. IN U.S.A. or
 * © 1975 NHL Players Association.
 ** © 1975 TOPPS CHEWING GUM, INC. PRTD. IN U.S.A.
Complete Set No.: 330
Complete Set Price: 37.50 75.00 150.00
Common Card: .10 .20 .40

1974 - 75 STANLEY CUP PLAYOFFS

No.	Teams	VG	EX	NRMT
1	Finals: Philadelphia vs. Buffalo	.50	1.00	2.00
2	Semi-finals: Philadelphia vs. NY Islanders	.12	.25	.50
3	Semi-finals: Buffalo vs. Montreal	.12	.25	.50
4	Quarter Finals: NY Islanders vs. Pittsburgh	.12	.25	.50
5	Quarter Finals: Montreal vs. Vancouver	.12	.25	.50
6	Quarter Finals: Buffalo vs. Chicago	.12	.25	.50
7	Quarter Finals: Philadelphia vs. Toronto	.12	.25	.50

REGULAR ISSUE

No.	Player	VG	EX	NRMT
8	Curt Bennett, Atl.	.10	.20	.40
9	John Bucyk, Bos.	.30	.60	1.25

212 • TOPPS — 1975-76 REGULAR ISSUE

No.	Player	VG	EX	NRMT
10	Gilbert Perreault, Buf.	.75	1.50	3.00
11	Darryl Edestrand, Bos.	.10	.20	.40
12	Ivan Boldirev, Chi.	.10	.20	.40
13	Nick Libett, Det.	.10	.20	.40
14	**Jim McElmury, KC, RC**	**.10**	**.20**	**.40**
15	Frank St. Marseille, LA	.10	.20	.40
16	Blake Dunlop, Min.	.10	.20	.40
17	Yvon Lambert, Mon.	.10	.20	.40
18	Gerry Hart, NYI	.10	.20	.40
19	Steve Vickers, NYR	.10	.20	.40
20	Rick MacLeish, Phi.	.10	.20	.40
21	Bob Paradise, Pit.	.10	.20	.40
22	Red Berenson, St. L.	.10	.20	.40
23	Lanny McDonald, Tor.	1.75	3.50	7.00
24	Mike Robitaille, Van.	.10	.20	.40
25	Ron Low, Goalie, Wash.	.10	.20	.40
26	Bryan Hextall, Jr., Det.	.10	.20	.40
27	Carol Vadnais, Bos.	.10	.20	.40
28	Jim Lorentz, Buf.	.10	.20	.40
29	Gary Simmons, Goalie, Ca.	.10	.20	.40
30	Stan Mikita, Chi.	.85	1.75	3.50
31	Bryan Watson, Det.	.10	.20	.40
32	Guy Charron, KC	.10	.20	.40
33	Bob J. Murdoch, LA	.10	.20	.40
34	Norm Gratton, Min., LC	.10	.20	.40
35	Ken Dryden, Goalie, Mon.	3.75	7.50	15.00
36	Jean Potvin, NYI	.10	.20	.40
37	Rick Middleton, NYR	1.00	2.00	4.00
38	Ed Van Impe, Phi.	.10	.20	.40
39	Rick Kehoe, Pit.	.10	.20	.40
40	Garry Unger, St. L.	.10	.20	.40
41	Ian Turnbull, Tor.	.10	.20	.40
42	Dennis Ververgaert, Van.	.10	.20	.40
43	**Mike Marson, Wash., RC, LC**	**.10**	**.20**	**.40**
44	Randy Manery, Atl.	.10	.20	.40
45	Gilles Gilbert, Goalie, Bos.	.10	.20	.40
46	Rene Robert, Buf.	.10	.20	.40
47	Bob Stewart, Ca.	.10	.20	.40
48	Pit Martin, Chi.	.10	.20	.40
49	Danny Grant, Det.	.10	.20	.40
50	Pete Mahovlich, Mon.	.10	.20	.40
51	**Dennis Patterson, KC, RC, LC**	**.10**	**.20**	**.40**
52	Mike Murphy, LA	.10	.20	.40
53	Dennis O'Brien, Min.	.10	.20	.40
54	Garry Howatt, NYI	.10	.20	.40
55	Ed Giacomin, Goalie, NYR	.50	1.00	2.00
56	Andre Dupont, Phi.	.10	.20	.40
57	Chuck Arnason, Pit.	.10	.20	.40
58	**Bob Gassoff, St. L., RC**	**.10**	**.20**	**.40**
59	Ron Ellis, Tor.	.10	.20	.40
60	Andre Boudrias, Van.	.10	.20	.40
61	Yvon Labre, Wash.	.10	.20	.40
62	Hilliard Graves, Atl.	.10	.20	.40
63	Wayne Cashman, Bos.	.10	.20	.40
64	**Danny Gare, Buf., RC**	**.50**	**1.00**	**2.00**
65	Rick Hampton, Ca.	.10	.20	.40
66	Darcy Rota, Chi.	.10	.20	.40
67	Bill Hogaboam, Det.	.10	.20	.40
68	Denis Herron, Goalie, KC	.10	.20	.40
69	Sheldon Kannegiesser, LA	.10	.20	.40
70	Yvan Cournoyer, Mon., Error	.40	.85	1.75
71	Ernie Hicke, Min.	.10	.20	.40
72	Bert Marshall, NYI	.10	.20	.40
73	Derek Sanderson, NYR	.10	.20	.40
74	Tom Bladon, Phi.	.10	.20	.40
75	Ron Schock, Pit.	.10	.20	.40
76	**Larry Sacharuk, St. L., RC, LC**	**.10**	**.20**	**.40**
77	George Ferguson, Tor.	.10	.20	.40
78	Ab DeMarco, Van.	.10	.20	.40
79	Tom Williams, Wash., LC	.10	.20	.40
80	Phil Roberto, Det.	.10	.20	.40

1974 - 75 TEAM - CHECKLIST CARDS

No.	Team Checklist	VG	EX	NRMT
81	Boston Bruins	.35	.75	1.50
82	California Golden Seals	.35	.75	1.50
83	Buffalo Sabres, Error	.35	.75	1.50
84	Chicago Black Hawks, Error	.35	.75	1.50
85	Atlanta Flames	.35	.75	1.50
86	Los Angeles Kings	.35	.75	1.50
87	Detroit Red Wings	.35	.75	1.50
88	Kansas City Scouts, Error	.35	.75	1.50
89	Minnesota North Stars	.35	.75	1.50
90	Montreal Canadiens	.35	.75	1.50
91	Toronto Maple Leafs	.35	.75	1.50
92	New York Islanders	.35	.75	1.50
93	Pittsburgh Penguins	.35	.75	1.50
94	New York Rangers	.35	.75	1.50
95	Philadelphia Flyers, Error	.35	.75	1.50
96	St. Louis Blues	.35	.75	1.50
97	Vancouver Canucks, Error	.35	.75	1.50
98	Washington Capitals	.35	.75	1.50

REGULAR ISSUE

No.	Player	VG	EX	NRMT
99	Checklist 1 (1 - 110)	2.50	5.00	10.00
100	Bobby Orr, Bos.	5.00	10.00	20.00
101	Germaine Gagnon, Chi., LC, Error	.10	.20	.40
102	Phil Russell, Chi.	.10	.20	.40
103	Bill Lochead, Det.	.10	.20	.40
104	**Robin Burns, KC, RC, LC**	**.10**	**.20**	**.40**
105	Gary Edwards, Goalie, LA	.10	.20	.40
106	Dwight Bialowas, Min.	.10	.20	.40
107	Doug Risebrough, Mon., Error	.50	1.00	2.00
108	Dave Lewis, NYI	.10	.20	.40
109	Bill Fairbairn, NYR	.10	.20	.40
110	Ross Lonsberry, Phi.	.10	.20	.40
111	Ron Stackhouse, Pit.	.10	.20	.40
112	Claude Larose, St. L.	.10	.20	.40
113	Don Luce, Buf.	.10	.20	.40
114	**Errol Thompson, Tor., RC**	**.10**	**.20**	**.40**
115	Gary Smith, Goalie, Van.	.10	.20	.40
116	Jack Lynch, Wash.	.10	.20	.40
117	Jacques Richard, Atl.	.10	.20	.40
118	Dallas Smith, Bos.	.10	.20	.40
119	Dave Gardner, Ca.	.10	.20	.40
120	Mickey Redmond, Det.	.10	.20	.40
121	John Marks, Chi.	.10	.20	.40
122	Dave Hudson, KC	.10	.20	.40
123	Bob Nevin, LA	.10	.20	.40
124	Fred Barrett, Min.	.10	.20	.40
125	Gerry Desjardins, Goalie, Buf.	.10	.20	.40
126	Guy Lafleur, Mon., Error	2.50	5.00	10.00
127	J. P. Parise, NYI	.10	.20	.40
128	Walt Tkaczuk, NYR	.10	.20	.40
129	Gary Dornhoefer, Phi.	.10	.20	.40
130	Syl Apps, Jr., Pit.	.10	.20	.40
131	Bob Plager, St. L.	.10	.20	.40
132	Stan Weir, Tor.	.10	.20	.40
133	Tracy Pratt, Van.	.10	.20	.40
134	Jack Egers, Wash., LC	.10	.20	.40
135	Eric Vail, Atl.	.10	.20	.40
136	Al Sims, Bos.	.10	.20	.40
137	**Larry Patey, Ca., RC**	**.10**	**.20**	**.40**
138	Jim Schoenfeld, Buf.	.10	.20	.40
139	Cliff Koroll, Chi.	.10	.20	.40
140	Marcel Dionne, LA	1.50	3.00	6.00
141	Jean-Guy Lagace, KC, LC	.10	.20	.40
142	Juha Widing, LA	.10	.20	.40
143	Lou Nanne, Min.	.10	.20	.40
144	Serge Savard, Mon.	.25	.50	1.00
145	Glenn Resch, Goalie, NYI	.75	1.50	3.00
146	**Ronald Greschner, NYR, RC**	**.60**	**1.25**	**2.50**
147	Dave Schultz, Phi.	.15	.35	.75
148	Barry Wilkins, Pit.	.10	.20	.40
149	Floyd Thomson, St. L.	.10	.20	.40
150	Darryl Sittler, Tor.	1.10	2.25	4.50
151	Paulin Bordeleau, Van.	.10	.20	.40
152	**Ron Lalonde, Wash., RC**	**.10**	**.20**	**.40**
153	Larry Romanchych, Atl.	.10	.20	.40
154	Larry Carriere, Buf.	.10	.20	.40
155	Andre Savard, Bos.	.10	.20	.40
156	**Dave Hrechkosy, Ca., RC**	**.10**	**.20**	**.40**
157	Bill White, Chi.	.10	.20	.40
158	Dave Kryskow, Atl., LC	.10	.20	.40
159	Denis Dupere, KC	.10	.20	.40
160	Rogatien Vachon, Goalie, LA	.30	.60	1.25
161	Doug Rombough, Min., LC	.10	.20	.40
162	Murray Wilson, Mon.	.10	.20	.40
163	**Bob Bourne, NYI, RC**	**.35**	**.75**	**1.50**
164	Gilles Marotte, NYR	.10	.20	.40
165	Vic Hadfield, Pit., LC	.10	.20	.40
166	Reggie Leach, Phi.	.10	.20	.40
167	Jerry Butler, St. L.	.10	.20	.40
168	Inge Hammarstrom, Tor.	.10	.20	.40
169	Chris Oddleifson, Van.	.10	.20	.40

Topps
1975-76 Issue
Card No. 43,
Mike Marson

Topps
1975-76 Issue
Card No. 51,
Dennis Patterson

Topps
1975-76 Issue
Card No. 145,
Glenn Resch

Topps
1975-76 Issue
Card No. 150,
Darryl Sittler

1975 - 76 REGULAR ISSUE — TOPPS • 213

No.	Player	VG	EX	NRMT
170	Greg Joly, Wash.	.10	.20	.40
171	Checklist 2 (111 - 220)	2.50	5.00	10.00
172	Pat Quinn, Atl.	.10	.20	.40
173	Dave Forbes, Bos.	.10	.20	.40
174	Len Frig, Ca.	.10	.20	.40
175	Rick Martin, Buf.	.10	.20	.40
176	Keith Magnuson, Chi.	.10	.20	.40
177	Dan Maloney, Det.	.10	.20	.40
178	Craig Patrick, KC	.10	.20	.40
179	Tommy Williams, LA	.10	.20	.40
180	Bill Goldsworthy, Min.	.10	.20	.40
181	Steve Shutt, Mon.	1.00	2.00	4.00
182	Ralph Stewart, NYI	.10	.20	.40
183	John Davidson, Goalie, NYR	.25	.50	1.00
184	Bob Kelly, Phi.	.10	.20	.40
185	Ed Johnston, Goalie, St. L.	.10	.20	.40
186	Dave Burrows, Pit.	.10	.20	.40
187	Dave Dunn, Tor., LC	.10	.20	.40
188	Dennis Kearns, Van.	.10	.20	.40
189	Bill Clement, Wash.	.10	.20	.40
190	Gilles Meloche, Goalie, CA	.10	.20	.40
191	Bobby Leiter, Atl., LC	.10	.20	.40
192	Jerry Korab, Buf.	.10	.20	.40
193	Joey Johnston, Chi.	.10	.20	.40
194	Walt McKechnie, Det.	.10	.20	.40
195	Wilf Paiement, KC	.10	.20	.40
196	Bob Berry, LA	.10	.20	.40
197	**Dean Talafous, Min., RC**	.10	.20	.40
198	Guy Lapointe, Mon.	.10	.20	.40
199	**Clark Gillies, NYI, RC**	1.25	2.50	5.00
200	Phil Esposito, Bos.	1.25	2.50	5.00
201	Greg Polis, NYR	.10	.20	.40
202	Jimmy Watson, Phi.	.10	.20	.40
203	**Gord McRae, Goalie, Tor., RC**	.10	.20	.40
204	Lowell MacDonald, Pit.	.10	.20	.40
205	Barclay Plager, St. L., LC	.10	.20	.40
206	Don Lever, Van.	.10	.20	.40
207	Bill Mikkelson, Wash., LC	.10	.20	.40

LEAGUE LEADERS

No.	Player	VG	EX	NRMT
208	**Goal Leaders:** P. Esposito, Bos., G. Lafleur, Mon., R. Martin, Buf.	.85	1.75	3.50
209	**Assist Leaders:** B. Orr, Bos., B. Clarke, Phi., P. Mahovlich, Mon.	1.25	2.50	5.00
210	**Scoring Leaders:** B. Orr, Bos., P. Esposito, Bos., M. Dionne, Det.	1.75	3.50	7.00
211	**Penalty Minute Leaders:** D. Schultz, Phi., A. Dupont, Phi., P. Russel, Chi.	.35	.75	1.50
212	**Power Play Goal Leaders:** P. Esposito, Bos.,R. Martin, Buf., D. Grant, Det.	.50	1.00	2.00
213	**Goals Against Average: Leaders:** B. Parent, Phi., R. Vachon, LA, K. Dryden, Mon.	1.50	3.00	6.00

REGULAR ISSUE

No.	Player	VG	EX	NRMT
214	Barry Gibbs, Alt.	.10	.20	.40
215	Ken Hodge, Bos.	.10	.20	.40
216	Jocelyn Guevremont, Buf.	.10	.20	.40
217	**Warren Williams, Ca., RC, LC**	.10	.20	.40
218	Dick Redmond, Chi.	.10	.20	.40
219	Jim Rutherford, Goalie, Det.	.10	.20	.40
220	Simon Nolet, KC	.10	.20	.40
221	Butch Goring, LA	.10	.20	.40
222	Glen Sather, Min.	.25	.50	1.00
223	**Mario Tremblay, Mon., RC**	.35	.75	1.50
224	Jude Drouin, NYI	.10	.20	.40
225	Rod Gilbert, NYR	.35	.75	1.50
226	Bill Barber, Phi.	.75	1.50	3.00
227	**Gary Inness, Goalie, Pit., RC**	.10	.20	.40
228	Wayne Merrick, St. L.	.10	.20	.40
229	Rod Seiling, Tor.	.10	.20	.40
230	Tom Lysiak, Atl.	.10	.20	.40
231	Bob Dailey, Van.	.10	.20	.40
232	Michel Belhumeur, Goalie, Wash.	.10	.20	.40
233	**Bill Hajt, Buf., RC**	.10	.20	.40
234	Jim Pappin, Ca., LC	.10	.20	.40
235	Gregg Sheppard, Bos.	.10	.20	.40
236	Gary Bergman, Det.	.10	.20	.40
237	Randy Rota, KC	.10	.20	.40
238	Neil Komadoski, LA	.10	.20	.40

Topps
1975-76 Issue
Card No. 203,
Gord McRae

Topps
1975-76 Issue
Card No. 244, Error,
Card shows Ted Harris

Topps
1975-76 Issue
Card No. 275,
Denis Potvin

Topps
1975-76 Issue
Card No. 305,
Pierre Larouche

No.	Player	VG	EX	NRMT
239	Craig Cameron, Min.	.10	.20	.40
240	Tony Esposito, Goalie, Chi.	.85	1.75	3.50
241	Larry Robinson, Mon.	2.00	4.00	8.00
242	Billy Harris, NYI	.10	.20	.40
243	Jean Ratelle, NYR	.35	.75	1.50
244	Ted Irvine, St. L., Error	.10	.20	.40
245	Bob Neely, Tor.	.10	.20	.40
246	Bobby Lalonde, Van.	.10	.20	.40
247	**Ron Jones, Wash., RC, LC**	.10	.20	.40
248	Rey Comeau, Atl.	.10	.20	.40
249	Michel Plasse, Goalie, Pit.	.10	.20	.40
250	Bobby Clarke, Phi.	1.45	2.90	5.75
251	Bobby Schmautz, Bos.	.10	.20	.40
252	**Peter McNab, Buf., RC**	.60	1.25	2.50
253	Al MacAdam, Ca.	.10	.20	.40
254	Dennis Hull, Chi.	.10	.20	.40
255	Terry Harper, Det.	.10	.20	.40
256	Peter McDuffe, Goalie, KC, LC	.10	.20	.40
257	Jean Hamel, Det.	.10	.20	.40
258	Jacques Lemaire, Mon.	.30	.60	1.25
259	Bob Nystrom, NYI	.10	.20	.40
260	Brad Park, NYR	.50	1.00	2.00
261	Cesare Maniago, Goalie, Min.	.10	.20	.40
262	Don Saleski, Phi.	.10	.20	.40
263	J. Bob Kelly, Pit.	.10	.20	.40
264	**Bob Hess, St. L., RC**	.10	.20	.40
265	Blaine Stoughton, Tor.	.25	.50	1.00
266	John Gould, Van.	.10	.20	.40
267	Checklist 3 (221 - 330)	2.50	5.00	10.00
268	Dan Bouchard, Goalie, Atl.	.10	.20	.40
269	Don Marcotte, Bos.	.10	.20	.40
270	Jim Neilson, Ca.	.10	.20	.40
271	Craig Ramsay, Buf.	.10	.20	.40
272	**Grant Mulvey, Chi., RC**	.25	.50	1.00
273	**Larry Giroux, Det., RC, LC**	.10	.20	.40
274	Richard Lemieux, KC	.10	.20	.40
275	Denis Potvin, NYI	2.00	4.00	8.00
276	Don Kozak, LA	.10	.20	.40
277	Tom Reid, Min.	.10	.20	.40
278	Bob Gainey, Mon.	1.00	2.00	4.00
279	Nick Beverley, NYR	.10	.20	.40
280	Jean Pronovost, Pit.	.10	.20	.40
281	Joe Watson, Phi.	.10	.20	.40
282	Chuck Lefley, St. L.	.10	.20	.40
283	Borje Salming, Tor.	.75	1.50	3.00
284	Garnet Bailey, Wash.	.10	.20	.40
285	Gregg Boddy, Van., LC	.10	.20	.40

1974 - 75 ALL-STARS

First Team

No.	Player	VG	EX	NRMT
286	Bobby Clarke, Phi.	.50	1.00	2.00
287	Denis Potvin, NYI	.75	1.50	3.00
288	Bobby Orr, Bos.	2.00	4.00	8.00
289	Rick Martin, Buf.	.10	.20	.40
290	Guy Lafleur, Mon.	.75	1.50	3.00
291	Bernie Parent, Goalie, Phi.	.25	.50	1.00

Second Team

No.	Player	VG	EX	NRMT
292	Phil Esposito, Bos.	.50	1.00	2.00
293	Guy Lapointe, Mon.	.12	.25	.50
294	Borje Salming, Tor.	.25	.50	1.00
295	Steve Vickers, NYR	.12	.25	.50
296	Rene Robert, Buf.	.12	.25	.50
297	Rogatien Vachon, Goalie, LA	.18	.35	.75

REGULAR ISSUE

No.	Player	VG	EX	NRMT
298	Buster Harvey, Atl.	.10	.20	.40
299	Gary Sabourin, Ca.	.10	.20	.40
300	Bernie Parent, Goalie, Phi.	.50	1.00	2.00
301	Terry O'Reilly, Bos.	.25	.50	1.00
302	Ed Westfall, NYI	.10	.20	.40
303	Pete Stemkowski, NYR	.10	.20	.40
304	Pierre Bouchard, Mon.	.10	.20	.40
305	**Pierre Larouche, Pit., RC**	1.25	2.50	5.00
306	**Lee Fogolin, Buf., RC**	.10	.25	.50
307	Gerry O'Flaherty, Van.	.10	.20	.40
308	Phil Myre, Goalie, Atl.	.10	.20	.40
309	Pierre Plante, St. L.	.10	.20	.40

214 • TOPPS — 1976-77 REGULAR ISSUE

No.	Player	VG	EX	NRMT
310	Dennis Hextall, Min.	.10	.20	.40
311	Jim McKenny, Tor.	.10	.20	.40
312	Vic Venasky, LA	.10	.20	.40

TEAM LEADERS

No.	Team/Player	VG	EX	NRMT
313	**Atlanta Flames:** E. Vail, Goals; T. Lysiak, Assists, Points and Power Play Goals	.12	.25	.50
314	**Boston Bruins:** P. Esposito, Goals and Power Play Goals; B. Orr, Assists and Points	1.25	2.50	5.00
315	**Buffalo Sabres:** R. Martin, Goals and Power Play Goals; R. Robert, Assists and Points	.12	.25	.50
316	**California Golden Seals:** D. Hrechkosy, Goals; L. Patey and S. Weir, Points; S. Weir, Assists; L. Patey and D. Hrechkosy, Power Play Goals	.12	.25	.50
317	**Chicago Black Hawks:** S. Mikita and J. Pappin, Goals; S. Mikita, Assists, Points and Power Play Goals	.30	.60	1.25
318	**Detroit Red Wings:** D. Grant, Goals and Power Play Goals; M. Dionne, Assists and Points	.30	.60	1.25
319	**Kansas City Scouts:** S. Nolet and W. Paiement, Goals; G. Charron, Assists; S. Nolet, Points and Power Play Goals	.35	.75	1.50
320	**Los Angeles Kings:** B. Nevin, Goals Assists and Points; B. Nevin, J. Widing and B. Berry, Power Play Goals	.12	.25	.50
321	**Minnesota North Stars:** B. Goldsworthy, Goals, and Power Play Goals; D. Hextall, Assists and Points	.12	.25	.50
322	**Montreal Canadiens:** G. Lafleur, Goals, Points and Power Play Goals; P. Mahovlich, Assists;	.35	.75	1.50
323	**New York Islanders:** B. Nystrom, Goals; D. Potvin, Assists and Points; C. Gilles, Power Play Goals	.40	.85	1.75
324	**New York Rangers:** S. Vickers, Goals; R. Gilbert, Assists and Points; J. Rattelle and S. Vickers, Power Play Goals;	.12	.25	.50
325	**Philadelphia Flyers:** R. Leach, Goals and Power Play Goals; B. Clarke, Assists and Points;	.30	.60	1.25
326	**Pittsburgh Penguins:** J. Pronovost, Goals and Power Play Goals; R. Schock, Assists and Points	.12	.25	.50
327	**St. Louis Blues:** G. Unger, Goals, Assists and Points; G. Unger, and L. Sacharuk, Power Play Goals;	.12	.25	.50
328	**Toronto Maple Leafs:** D. Sittler, Goals, Assists, Points and Power Play Goals	.50	1.00	2.00
329	**Vancouver Canucks:** D. Lever, Goals and Power Play Goals; A. Boudrias, Assists and Points	.12	.25	.50
330	**Washington Capitals:** T. Williams, Goals and Power Play Goals; G. Bailey, Assists; T. Williams and G. Bailey, Points	.12	.25	.50

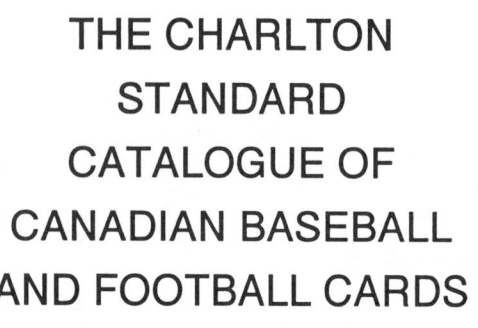

THE CHARLTON STANDARD CATALOGUE OF CANADIAN BASEBALL AND FOOTBALL CARDS
- Fourth Edition -
Coming in April!

Topps 1976-77 Issue Card No. 1, Goal Leaders

Topps 1976-77 Issue Card No. 1, Goal Leaders

Topps 1976-77 Issue Card No. 3, Scoring Leaders

Topps 1976-77 Issue Card No. 15, Pete Mahovlich

— 1976 - 77 REGULAR ISSUE —

The card faces are very similar to the O-Pee-Chee set for the same year. The only exceptions are Nos. 102, 159, 183, and 243. Team cards 132 to 149 have a checklist on the back for all players in the set. The set features four "record breaking" cards 65 to 68. Mint cards command a price premium of 25% over NRMT cards.

PRICE MOVEMENT OF NRMT SETS

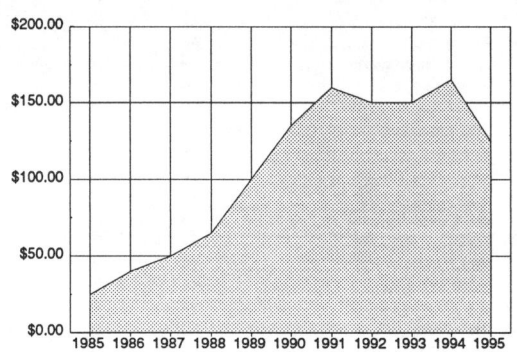

Card Size: 2 1/2" X 3 1/2"
Face: Four colour, white border, Team logo, Position
Back: Green and blue on card stock, Number, Resume, Hockey trivia
Imprint: * © 1976 TOPPS CHEWING GUM, INC. PRTD. IN U.S.A.
  © 1976 NHL PLAYERS ASSOCIATION
or ** © 1976 TOPPS CHEWING GUM, INC. PRTD. IN U.S.A.
  © 1976 NHL PLAYERS ASSOCIATION
Complete Set No.: 264

Complete Set Price:		30.00	60.00	125.00
Common Card:		.07	.15	.30

1975-76 - LEAGUE LEADERS

No.	Player	VG	EX	NRMT
1	**Goal Leaders:** R. Leach, Phi.; G. Lafleur, Mon.; P. Larouche, Pit.	.50	1.00	2.00
2	**Assist Leaders:** B. Clarke, Phi.; P. Mahovlich, Mon.; G. Lafleur, Mon.; G. Perreault, Buf.; J. Ratelle, NYR	.50	1.00	2.00
3	**Scoring Leaders:** G. Lafleur, Mon.; B. Clarke, Phi.; G. Perreault, Buf.	.50	1.00	2.00
4	**Penalty Minute Leaders:** Steve Durbano, KC; Bryan Watson, Det.; Dave Schultz, Phi.	.12	.25	.50
5	**Power Play Goal Leaders:** P. Esposito, NYR; G. Lafleur, Mon.; R. Martin, Buf.; P. Larouche, Pit.; D. Potvin, NYI	.50	1.00	2.00
6	**Goals Against Avg Leaders:** K. Dryden, Mon.; G. Resch, NYI; M. Larocque, Mon.	.60	1.25	2.50

REGULAR ISSUE

No.	Player	VG	EX	NRMT
7	Gary Doak, Bos.	.07	.15	.30
8	Jacques Richard, Buf.	.07	.15	.30
9	Wayne Dillon, NYR	.07	.15	.30
10	Bernie Parent, Goalie, Phi.	.50	1.00	2.00
11	Ed Westfall, NYI	.07	.15	.30
12	Dick Redmond, Chi.	.07	.15	.30
13	Bryan Hextall, Jr., Min., LC	.07	.15	.30
14	Jean Pronovost, Pit.	.07	.15	.30
15	Pete Mahovlich, Mon.	.07	.15	.30
16	Danny Grant, Det.	.07	.15	.30
17	Phil Myre, Goalie, Atl.	.09	.18	.35
18	Wayne Merrick, Ca.	.07	.15	.30
19	Steve Durbano, KC, LC	.07	.15	.30
20	Derek Sanderson, St. L.	.07	.15	.30
21	Mike Murphy, LA	.07	.15	.30
22	Borje Salming, Tor., 2nd Team All Star	.35	.75	1.50
23	Mike Walton, Van.	.07	.15	.30
24	Randy Manery, Atl.	.07	.15	.30
25	Ken Hodge, Sr., NYR	.07	.15	.30
26	Mel Bridgman, Phi., RC	.50	1.00	2.00
27	Jerry Korab, Buf.	.07	.15	.30
28	Gilles Gratton, Goalie, NYR	.07	.15	.30
29	Andre St. Laurent, NYI	.07	.15	.30
30	Yvan Cournoyer, Mon.	.35	.75	1.50
31	Phil Russell, Chi.	.07	.15	.30

1976 - 77 REGULAR ISSUE — TOPPS • 215

No.	Player	VG	EX	NRMT
32	Dennis Hextall, Det.	.07	.15	.30
33	Lowell MacDonald, Pit.	.07	.15	.30
34	Dennis O'Brien, Min.	.07	.15	.30
35	Gerry Meehan, Wash.	.07	.15	.30
36	Gilles Meloche, Goalie, Ca.	.09	.18	.35
37	Wilf Paiement, KC	.07	.15	.30
38	**Bob MacMillan, St. L., RC**	**.07**	**.15**	**.30**
39	Ian Turnbull, Tor.	.07	.15	.30
40	Rogatien Vachon, Goalie, LA	.25	.50	1.00
41	Nick Beverley, NYR	.07	.15	.30
42	Rene Robert, Buf.	.07	.15	.30
43	Andre Savard, Buf.	.07	.15	.30
44	Bob Gainey, Mon.	.50	1.00	2.00
45	Joe Watson, Phi.	.07	.15	.30
46	Billy Smith, Goalie, NYI	.40	.85	1.75
47	Darcy Rota, Chi.	.07	.15	.30
48	**Rick Lapointe, Det., RC**	**.07**	**.15**	**.30**
49	Pierre Jarry, Min.	.07	.15	.30
50	Syl Apps, Jr., Pit.	.07	.15	.30
51	Eric Vail, Atl.	.07	.15	.30
52	Greg Joly, Wash.	.07	.15	.30
53	Don Lever, Van.	.07	.15	.30
54	**Bob L. Murdoch, Ca., RC**	**.07**	**.15**	**.30**
55	Denis Herron, Goalie, KC	.07	.15	.30
56	Mike Bloom, Det.	.07	.15	.30
57	Bill Fairbairn, NYR	.07	.15	.30
58	Fred Stanfield, Buf.	.07	.15	.30
59	Steve Shutt, Mon.	.50	1.00	2.00
60	Brad Park, Bos., 1st Team All Star	.40	.85	1.75
61	Gilles Villemure, Goalie, Chi., LC	.07	.15	.30
62	Bert Marshall, NYI	.07	.15	.30
63	Chuck Lefley, St. L.	.07	.15	.30
64	Simon Nolet, Pit., LC	.07	.15	.30

'75 - 76 - RECORD BREAKERS

No.	Player	VG	EX	NRMT
65	**Most Goals, Playoffs:** Reggie Leach, Phi.	.07	.15	.30
66	**Most Points, Game:** Darryl Sittler, Tor.	.25	.50	1.00
67	**Most Points, Season, Rookie:** Bryan Trottier, NYI	1.25	2.50	5.00
68	**Most Consecutive Games, Lifetime:** Garry Unger, St. L.	.07	.15	.30

REGULAR ISSUE

No.	Player	VG	EX	NRMT
69	Ron Low, Goalie, Wash.	.09	.18	.35
70	Bobby Clarke, Phi., 1st Team All Star	.60	1.25	2.50
71	**Michel Bergeron, Det., RC**	**.07**	**.15**	**.30**
72	Ron Stackhouse, Pit.	.07	.15	.30
73	Bill Hogaboam, Min.	.07	.15	.30
74	Bob J. Murdoch, LA	.07	.15	.30
75	Steve Vickers, NYR	.07	.15	.30
76	Pit Martin, Chi.	.07	.15	.30
77	Gerry Hart, NYI	.07	.15	.30
78	Craig Ramsay, Buf.	.07	.15	.30
79	Michel Larocque, Goalie, Mon.	.07	.15	.30
80	Jean Ratelle, Bos.	.35	.75	1.50
81	Don Saleski, Phi.	.07	.15	.30
82	Bill Clement, Atl.	.07	.15	.30
83	Dave Burrows, Pit.	.07	.15	.30
84	Wayne Thomas, Goalie, Tor.	.10	.25	.50
85	John Gould, Van.	.07	.15	.30
86	**Dennis Maruk, Ca., RC**	**.75**	**1.50**	**3.00**
87	Ernie Hicke, Min.	.07	.15	.30
88	Jim Rutherford, Goalie, Det.	.07	.15	.30
89	Dale Tallon, Chi.	.07	.15	.30
90	Rod Gilbert, NYR	.30	.60	1.25
91	Marcel Dionne, LA	1.25	2.50	5.00
92	Chuck Arnason, KC	.07	.15	.30
93	Jean Potvin, NYI	.07	.15	.30
94	Don Luce, Buf.	.07	.15	.30
95	John Bucyk, Bos.	.25	.50	1.00
96	Larry Goodenough, Phi.	.07	.15	.30
97	Mario Tremblay, Mon.	.07	.15	.30
98	**Nelson Pyatt, Wash., RC**	**.07**	**.15**	**.30**
99	Brian Glennie, Tor.	.07	.15	.30
100	Tony Esposito, Goalie, Chi.	.60	1.25	2.50
101	Dan Maloney, Det.	.07	.15	.30
102	Barry Wilkins, Pit., LC	.07	.15	.30

Topps
1976-77 Issue
Card No. 39,
Ian Turnbull

Topps
1976-77 Issue
Card No. 91,
Marcel Dionne

Topps
1976-77 Issue
Card No.115,
Bryan Trottier

Topps
1976-77 Issue
Card No.120,
Gerry Cheevers

No.	Player	VG	EX	NRMT
103	Dean Talafous, Min.	.07	.15	.30
104	**Ed Staniowski, Goalie, St. L., RC**	**.07**	**.15**	**.30**
105	Dallas Smith, Bos., LC	.07	.15	.30
106	Jude Drouin, NYI	.07	.15	.30
107	Pat Hickey, NYR	.07	.15	.30
108	Jocelyn Guevremont, Buf.	.07	.15	.30
109	**Doug Risebrough, Mon., RC**	**.07**	**.15**	**.30**
110	Reggie Leach, Phi., 2nd Team All Star	.07	.15	.30
111	Dan Bouchard, Goalie, Atl.	.07	.15	.30
112	Chris Oddleifson, Van.	.07	.15	.30
113	Rick Hampton, Ca.	.07	.15	.30
114	John Marks, Chi.	.07	.15	.30
115	**Bryan Trottier, NYI, RC**	**7.50**	**15.00**	**30.00**
116	Checklist 1 (1 - 132)	2.00	4.00	8.00
117	Greg Polis, NYR	.07	.15	.30
118	Peter McNab, Bos.	.07	.15	.30
119	Jim Roberts, Mon.	.07	.15	.30
120	Gerry Cheevers, Goalie, Bos.	.50	1.00	2.00
121	Rick MacLeish, Phi.	.07	.15	.30
122	Bill Lochead, Det.	.07	.15	.30
123	Tom Reid, Min.	.07	.15	.30
124	Rick Kehoe, Pit.	.07	.15	.30
125	Keith Magnuson, Chi.	.07	.15	.30
126	Clark Gillies, NYI	.20	.50	1.00
127	Rick Middleton, Bos.	.50	1.00	2.00
128	Bill Hajt, Buf.	.07	.15	.30
129	Jacques Lemaire, Mon.	.25	.50	1.00
130	Terry O'Reilly, Bos.	.15	.30	.60
131	Andre Dupont, Phi.	.07	.15	.30

TEAM CHECKLIST CARDS

No.	Team	VG	EX	NRMT
132	Flames, Patrick Division	.30	.65	1.25
133	Bruins, Adams Division	.30	.65	1.25
134	Sabres, Adams Division	.30	.65	1.25
135	Seals, Adams Division	.30	.65	1.25
136	Black Hawks, Smythe Division	.30	.65	1.25
137	Red Wings, Norris Division	.30	.65	1.25
138	Scouts, Smythe Division	.30	.65	1.25
139	Kings, Norris Division	.30	.65	1.25
140	North Stars, Smythe Division	.30	.65	1.25
141	Canadiens, Norris Division	.30	.65	1.25
142	Islanders, Patrick Division	.30	.65	1.25
143	Rangers, Patrick Division	.30	.65	1.25
144	Flyers, Patrick Division	.30	.65	1.25
145	Penguins, Norris Division	.30	.65	1.25
146	Blues, Smythe Division	.30	.65	1.25
147	Maple Leafs, Adams Division	.30	.65	1.25
148	Canucks, Smythe Division	.30	.65	1.25
149	Capitals, Norris Division	.30	.65	1.25

REGULAR ISSUE

No.	Player	VG	EX	NRMT
150	Dave Schultz, Phi.	.15	.30	.60
151	Larry Robinson, Mon.	.85	1.75	3.50
152	Al Smith, Goalie, Buf.	.07	.15	.30
153	Bob Nystrom, NYI	.07	.15	.30
154	Ronald Greschner, NYR	.20	.35	.75
155	Gregg Sheppard, Bos.	.07	.15	.30
156	Alain Daigle, Chi.	.07	.15	.30
157	Ed Van Impe, Pit., LC	.07	.15	.30
158	**Tim Young, Min., RC**	**.10**	**.20**	**.40**
159	Gary Bergman, KC, LC	.07	.15	.30
160	Ed Giacomin, Goalie, Det.	.35	.75	1.50
161	Yvon Labre, Wash.	.07	.15	.30
162	Jim Lorentz, Buf.	.07	.15	.30
163	Guy Lafleur, Mon., 1st Team All Star	2.25	4.50	9.00
164	Tom Bladon, Phi.	.07	.15	.30
165	Wayne Cashman, Bos.	.07	.15	.30
166	Pete Stemkowski, NYR	.07	.15	.30
167	Grant Mulvey, Chi.	.07	.15	.30
168	**Yves Belanger, Goalie, St. L., RC**	**.07**	**.15**	**.30**
169	Bill Goldsworthy, Min.	.07	.15	.30
170	Denis Potvin, NYI, 1st Team All Star	1.25	2.50	5.00
171	Nick Libett, Det.	.07	.15	.30
172	Michel Plasse, Goalie, Pit.	.07	.15	.30
173	Lou Nanne, Min.	.07	.15	.30
174	Tom Lysiak, Atl.	.07	.15	.30
175	Dennis Ververgaert, Van.	.07	.15	.30
176	Gary Simmons, Goalie, Ca.	.07	.15	.30
177	Pierre Bouchard, Mon.	.07	.15	.30

216 • TOPPS — 1976 - 77 GLOSSY INSERT SET

No.	Player	VG	EX	NRMT
177	Pierre Bouchard, Mon.	.07	.15	.30
178	Bill Barber, Phi., 1st Team All Star	.35	.75	1.50
179	Darryl Edestrand, Bos.	.07	.15	.30
180	Gilbert Perreault, Buf., 2nd Team All Star	.40	.85	1.75
181	**Dave Maloney, NYR, RC**	.12	.25	.50
182	J. P. Parise, NYI	.07	.15	.30
183	Bobby Sheehan, Chi.	.07	.15	.30
184	**Pete LoPresti, Goalie, Min., RC**	.07	.15	.30
185	Don Kozak, LA	.07	.15	.30
186	Guy Charron, KC	.07	.15	.30
187	Stan Gilbertson, Pit.	.07	.15	.30
188	**Bill Nyrop, Mon., RC**	.07	.15	.30
189	Bobby Schmautz, Bos.	.07	.15	.30
190	Wayne Stephenson, Goalie, Phi.	.09	.18	.35
191	Brian Spencer, Buf.	.07	.15	.30
192	Gilles Marotte, NYR, LC	.07	.15	.30
193	Lorne Henning, NYI	.07	.15	.30
194	Bob Neely, Tor.	.07	.15	.30
195	Dennis Hull, Chi.	.07	.15	.30
196	Walt McKechnie, Det.	.07	.15	.30
197	**Curt Ridley, Goalie, Van., RC**	.07	.15	.30
198	Dwight Bialowas, Min.	.07	.15	.30
199	Pierre Larouche, Pit.	.35	.75	1.50
200	Ken Dryden, Goalie, Mon., 1st Team All Star	3.00	6.00	12.00
201	Ross Lonsberry, Phi.	.07	.15	.30
202	Curt Bennett, Atl.	.07	.15	.30
203	**Hartland Monahan, Wash., RC**	.07	.15	.30
204	John Davidson, Goalie, NYR	.07	.15	.30
205	Serge Savard, Mon.	.12	.25	.50
206	Garry Howatt, NYI	.07	.15	.30
207	Darryl Sittler, Tor.	.85	1.75	3.50
208	J.P. Bordeleau, Chi.	.07	.15	.30
209	Henry Boucha, KC	.07	.15	.30
210	Rick Martin, Buf., 2nd Team All Star	.07	.15	.30
211	Vic Venasky, LA	.07	.15	.30
212	Fred (Buster) Harvey, Det.	.07	.15	.30
213	Bobby Orr, Bos.	4.25	8.50	17.00

TOP SCORING LINE

No.	Players	VG	EX	NRMT
214	The French Connection Martin, Perreault, Robert, Buf.	.50	1.00	2.00
215	LCB Line Barber, Clarke, Leach, Phi.	.55	1.10	2.25
216	Long Island Lightning Co. Gillies, Trottier, Harris, NYI	.75	1.50	3.00
217	Checking Line Gainey, Jarvis, Roberts, Mon.	.20	.35	.75
218	Bicentennial Line MacDonald, Apps, Pronovost, Pit.	.20	.35	.75

REGULAR ISSUE

No.	Player	VG	EX	NRMT
219	Bob Kelly, Phi.	.07	.15	.30
220	Walt Tkaczuk, NYR	.07	.15	.30
221	Dave Lewis, NYI	.07	.15	.30
222	Danny Gare, Buf.	.12	.25	.50
223	Guy Lapointe, Mon., 2nd Team All Star	.10	.25	.50
224	**Hank Nowak, Bos., RC, LC**	.07	.15	.30
225	Stan Mikita, Chi.	.75	1.50	3.00
226	Vic Hadfield, Pit., LC	.07	.15	.30
227	**Bernie Wolfe, Goalie, Wash., RC**	.07	.15	.30
228	Bryan Watson, Det.	.07	.15	.30
229	Ralph Stewart, NYI	.07	.15	.30
230	Gerry Desjardins, Goalie, Buf.	.07	.15	.30
231	**John Bednarski, NYR, RC, LC**	.07	.15	.30
232	Yvon Lambert, Mon.	.07	.15	.30
233	Orest Kindrachuk, Phi.	.07	.15	.30
234	Don Marcotte, Bos.	.07	.15	.30
235	Bill White, Chi., LC	.07	.15	.30
236	Red Berenson, St. L.	.07	.15	.30
237	Al MacAdam, Ca.	.07	.15	.30
238	**Rick Blight, Van., RC**	.07	.15	.30
239	Butch Goring, LA	.07	.15	.30
240	Cesare Maniago, Goalie, Min.	.07	.15	.30
241	Jim Schoenfeld, Buf.	.07	.15	.30
242	Cliff Koroll, Chi.	.07	.15	.30
243	Mickey Redmond, Det., LC	.07	.15	.30
244	Rick Chartraw, Mon.	.07	.15	.30
245	Phil Esposito, NYR	.75	1.50	3.00
246	Dave Forbes, Bos.	.07	.15	.30

Topps 1976-77 Issue Card No.200, Ken Dryden

Topps 1976-77 Issue Card No.238, Rick Blight

Topps 1977-78 Issue Card No. 1, Goal Leaders

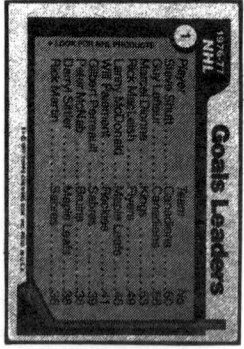
Topps 1976-77 Issue Card No. 1, Goal Leaders

No.	Player	VG	EX	NRMT
247	Jimmy Watson, Phi.	.07	.15	.30
248	Ron Schock, Pit.	.07	.15	.30
249	Fred Barrett, Min.	.07	.15	.30
250	Glenn Resch, Goalie, NYI, 2nd Team All Star	.30	.60	1.25
251	Ivan Boldirev, Chi.	.07	.15	.30
252	Billy Harris, NYI	.07	.15	.30
253	Lee Fogolin, Buf	.07	.15	.30
254	Murray Wilson, Mon.	.07	.15	.30
255	Gilles Gilbert, Goalie, Bos.	.07	.15	.30
256	Gary Dornhoefer, Phi.	.07	.15	.30
257	Carol Vadnais, NYR	.07	.15	.30
258	Checklist 2 (133 - 264)	2.00	4.00	8.00
259	Errol Thompson, Tor.	.07	.15	.30
260	Garry Unger, St. L.	.07	.15	.30
261	J. Bob Kelly, Pit.	.07	.15	.30
262	Terry Harper, Det.	.07	.15	.30
263	Blake Dunlop, Min.	.07	.15	.30
264	'75-76 Stanley Cup Champions 'Canadiens Sweep Flyers in 4'	.50	1.00	2.00

— 1976 - 77 GLOSSY INSERT SET —

This 22-card insert set was randomly inserted in the 1976-77 regular issue wax packs. The cards are numbered _ of 22.

Card Size: 2 1/4" x 3 1/4"
Face: Four colour, borderless; Facsimile autograph
Back: Blue on card stock; Name, Team, Position, Number
Imprint: * © 1976 TOPPS CHEWING GUM, INC. PRTD IN U.S.A.
© 1976 NHL PLAYERS ASSOCIATION
Complete Set No.: 22

Complete Set Price:		8.75	17.50	35.00
Common Card:		.25	.50	1.00

No.	Player	VG	EX	NRMT
1	Bobby Clarke, Phi.	.35	.75	1.50
2	Brad Park, Bos.	.25	.50	1.00
3	Tony Esposito, Goalie, Chi.	.35	.75	1.50
4	Marcel Dionne, LA	.50	1.00	2.00
5	Ken Dryden, Goalie, Mon.	1.00	2.00	4.00
6	Glenn Resch, Goalie, NYI	.25	.50	1.00
7	Phil Esposito, NYR	.50	1.00	2.00
8	Darryl Sittler, Tor.	.50	1.00	2.00
9	Gilbert Perreault, Buf.	.35	.75	1.50
10	Denis Potvin, NYI	.35	.75	1.50
11	Guy Lafleur, Mon.	.75	1.50	3.00
12	Bill Barber, Phi.	.25	.50	1.00
13	Syl Apps, Jr., Pit.	.25	.50	1.00
14	John Bucyk, Bos.	.25	.50	1.00
15	Bryan Trottier, NYI	.75	1.50	3.00
16	Dennis Hull, Chi.	.25	.50	1.00
17	Guy Lapointe, Mon.	.25	.50	1.00
18	Rod Gilbert, NYR	.25	.50	1.00
19	Richard Martin, Buf.	.25	.50	1.00
20	Bobby Orr, Chi.	1.25	2.50	5.00
21	Reggie Leach, Phi.	.25	.50	1.00
22	Jean Ratelle, NYR	.25	.50	1.00

— 1977 - 78 REGULAR ISSUE —

Only cards 203 and 255 show different players than the O-Pee-Chee set of the same year. Mint cards command a price premium of 25% over NRMT cards.

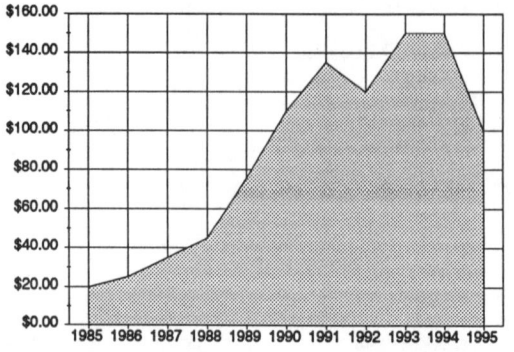
PRICE MOVEMENT OF NRMT SETS

1977 - 78 REGULAR ISSUE — TOPPS • 217

Card Size: 2 1/2" X 3 1/2"
Face: Four colour, white border, Team logo, Position
Back: Brown and blue on card stock, Number, Resume, Hockey trivia
Imprint: A * © 1977 TOPPS CHEWING GUM, INC. PRTD. IN U.S.A. or
B * © 1977 TOPPS CHEWING GUM, INC. PRTD. IN U.S.A.
Complete Set No.: 264
Complete Set Price: 25.00 50.00 100.00 ☐
Common Card: .06 .13 .25

1976-77 NHL LEADERS

No.	Player	VG	EX	NRMT
1	Goal Leaders: S. Shutt, Mon.; G. Lafleur, Mon.; M. Dionne, LA	.50	1.00	2.00 ☐
2	Assist Leaders: G. Lafleur, Mon.; M. Dionne, LA; L. Robinson, Mon.; B. Salming, Tor.; T. Young, Min.	.35	.75	1.50 ☐
3	Scoring Leaders: G. Lafleur, Mon.; M. Dionne, LA; S. Shutt, Mon.	.40	.85	1.75 ☐
4	Penalty Minute Leaders: D. Williams, Tor.; D. Polonich, Det.; B. Gassoff, St. L.	.12	.25	.50 ☐
5	Power Play Goal Leaders: L. McDonald, Tor.; P. Esposito, NYR; T. Williams, LA	.25	.50	1.00 ☐
6	Goals Against Avg Leaders: M. Larocque, Mon.; K. Dryden, Mon.; G. Resch, NYI	.35	.75	1.50 ☐
7	Game Winning Goal Leaders: G. Perreault, Buf.; S. Shutt, Mon.; G. Lafleur, Mon.; R. MacLeish, Phi.; P. McNab, Bos.	.50	1.00	2.00 ☐
8	Shutout Leaders: K. Dryden, Mon.; R. Vachon, LA; B. Parent, Phi.; D. Wilson, Pit.	.50	1.00	2.00 ☐

REGULAR ISSUE

No.	Player	VG	EX	NRMT
9	Brian Spencer, Buf.	.06	.13	.25 ☐
10	Denis Potvin, NYI, 2nd Team All-Star	.60	1.25	2.50 ☐
11	Nick Fotiu, NYR	.06	.13	.25 ☐
12	Bob Murray, Chi.	.06	.13	.25 ☐
13	Pete LoPresti, Goalie, Min.	.06	.13	.25 ☐
14	J. Bob Kelly, Pit.	.06	.13	.25 ☐
15	Rick MacLeish, Phi.	.06	.13	.25 ☐
16	Terry Harper, Det.	.06	.13	.25 ☐
17	**Willi Plett, Atl., RC**	**.35**	**.75**	**.1.50** ☐
18	Peter McNab, Bos.	.06	.13	.25 ☐
19	Wayne Thomas, Goalie, Tor.	.06	.13	.25 ☐
20	Pierre Bouchard, Mon.	.06	.13	.25 ☐
21	Dennis Maruk, Cle.	.20	.35	.75 ☐
22	Mike Murphy, LA	.06	.13	.25 ☐
23	Cesare Maniago, Goalie, Van., LC	.06	.13	.25 ☐
24	**Paul Gardner, Col., RC**	**.06**	**.15**	**.30** ☐
25	Rod Gilbert, NYR, LC	.25	.50	1.00 ☐
26	Orest Kindrachuk, Phi.	.06	.13	.25 ☐
27	Bill Hajt, Buf.	.06	.13	.25 ☐
28	John Davidson, Goalie, NYR	.06	.13	.25 ☐
29	J. P. Parise, NYI	.06	.13	.25 ☐
30	Larry Robinson, Mon., 1st Team All-Star	.75	1.50	3.00 ☐
31	Yvon Labre, Wash.	.06	.13	.25 ☐
32	Walt McKechnie, Det.	.06	.13	.25 ☐
33	Rick Kehoe, Pit.	.06	.13	.25 ☐
34	**Randy Holt, Chi., RC**	**.06**	**.13**	**.25** ☐
35	Garry Unger, St. L.	.06	.13	.25 ☐
36	Lou Nanne, Min., LC	.06	.13	.25 ☐
37	Dan Bouchard, Goalie, Atl.	.06	.13	.25 ☐
38	Darryl Sittler, Tor.	.60	1.25	2.50 ☐
39	Bob L. Murdoch, Cle.	.06	.13	.25 ☐
40	Jean Ratelle, Bos.	.25	.50	1.00 ☐
41	Dave Maloney, NYR	.06	.13	.25 ☐
42	Danny Gare, Buf.	.06	.13	.25 ☐
43	Jimmy Watson, Phi.	.06	.13	.25 ☐
44	Tommy Williams, LA	.06	.13	.25 ☐
45	Serge Savard, Mon.	.10	.20	.40 ☐
46	Derek Sanderson, Van., LC	.06	.13	.25 ☐
47	John Marks, Chi.	.06	.13	.25 ☐
48	**Al Cameron, Det., RC**	**.06**	**.13**	**.25** ☐
49	Dean Talafous, Min.	.06	.13	.25 ☐
50	Glenn Resch, Goalie, NYI	.25	.50	1.00 ☐
51	Ron Schock, Pit.	.06	.13	.25 ☐
52	Gary Croteau, Col.	.06	.13	.25 ☐
53	Gerry Meehan, Wash.	.06	.13	.25 ☐
54	Ed Staniowski, Goalie, St. L.	.09	.18	.35 ☐
55	Phil Esposito, NYR	.50	1.00	2.00 ☐
56	Dennis Ververgaert, Van.	.06	.13	.25 ☐
57	Rick Wilson, Det., LC	.06	.13	.25 ☐

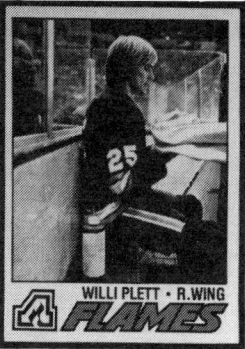

Topps 1977-78 Issue
Card No. 17,
Willi Plett

Topps 1977-78 Issue
Card No. 34,
Randy Holt

Topps 1977-78 Issue
Card No. 65,
Bernie Parent

Topps, 1977-78 Issue
Card No. 86,
Toronto Maple Leafs
Team Checklist

No.	Player	VG	EX	NRMT
58	Jim Lorentz, Buf.	.06	.13	.25 ☐
59	Bobby Schmautz, Bos.	.06	.13	.25 ☐
60	Guy Lapointe, Mon., 2nd Team All-Star	.06	.13	.25 ☐
61	Ivan Boldirev, Chi.	.06	.13	.25 ☐
62	Bob Nystrom, NYI	.06	.13	.25 ☐
63	Rick Hampton, Cle.	.06	.13	.25 ☐
64	Jack Valiquette, Tor.	.06	.13	.25 ☐
65	Bernie Parent, Goalie, Phi.	.30	.60	1.25 ☐
66	Dave Burrows, Pit.	.06	.13	.25 ☐
67	Butch Goring, LA	.06	.13	.25 ☐
68	Checklist 1 (1 - 132)	1.25	2.50	5.00 ☐
69	Murray Wilson, Mon., LC	.06	.13	.25 ☐
70	Ed Giacomin, Goalie, Det., LC	.25	.50	1.00 ☐

TEAM CHECKLIST CARDS

No.	Team	VG	EX	NRMT
71	Atlanta Flames	.18	.35	.75 ☐
72	Boston Bruins	.18	.35	.75 ☐
73	Buffalo Sabres	.18	.35	.75 ☐
74	Chicago Black Hawks	.18	.35	.75 ☐
75	Cleveland Barons	.18	.35	.75 ☐
76	Colorado Rockies	.18	.35	.75 ☐
77	Detroit Red Wings	.18	.35	.75 ☐
78	Los Angeles Kings	.18	.35	.75 ☐
79	Minnesota North Stars	.18	.35	.75 ☐
80	Montreal Canadiens	.18	.35	.75 ☐
81	New York Islanders	.18	.35	.75 ☐
82	New York Rangers	.18	.35	.75 ☐
83	Philadelphia Flyers	.18	.35	.75 ☐
84	Pittsburgh Penguins	.18	.35	.75 ☐
85	St. Louis Blues	.18	.35	.75 ☐
86	Toronto Maple Leafs	.18	.35	.75 ☐
87	Vancouver Canucks	.18	.35	.75 ☐
88	Washington Capitals	.18	.35	.75 ☐

REGULAR ISSUE

No.	Player	VG	EX	NRMT
89	Keith Magnuson, Chi.	.06	.13	.25 ☐
90	Walt Tkaczuk, NYR	.06	.13	.25 ☐
91	Bill Nyrop, Mon.	.06	.13	.25 ☐
92	Michel Plasse, Goalie, Col.	.06	.13	.25 ☐
93	Bob Bourne, NYI	.06	.13	.25 ☐
94	Lee Fogolin, Buf.	.06	.13	.25 ☐
95	Gregg Sheppard, Bos.	.06	.13	.25 ☐
96	Hartland Monahan, Wash.	.06	.13	.25 ☐
97	Curt Bennett, Atl.	.06	.13	.25 ☐
98	Bob Dailey, Phi.	.06	.13	.25 ☐
99	Bill Goldsworthy, NYR, LC	.06	.13	.25 ☐
100	Ken Dryden, Goalie, Mon., 1st Team All-Star	2.25	4.50	9.00 ☐
101	Grant Mulvey, Chi.	.06	.13	.25 ☐
102	Pierre Larouche, Pit.	.12	.25	.50 ☐
103	Nick Libett, Det.	.06	.13	.25 ☐
104	Rick Smith, Bos.	.06	.13	.25 ☐
105	Bryan Trottier, NYI	2.50	5.00	10.00 ☐
106	Pierre Jarry, Min., LC	.06	.13	.25 ☐
107	Red Berenson, St. L.	.06	.13	.25 ☐
108	Jim Schoenfeld, Buf.	.06	.13	.25 ☐
109	Gilles Meloche, Goalie, Cle.	.06	.13	.25 ☐
110	Lanny McDonald, Tor., 2nd Team All-Star	.50	1.00	2.00 ☐
111	Don Lever, Van.	.06	.13	.25 ☐
112	Greg Polis, NYR	.06	.13	.25 ☐
113	**Gary Sargent, LA, RC**	**.10**	**.25**	**.50** ☐
114	Earl Anderson, Bos., RC, LC	.06	.13	.25 ☐
115	Bobby Clarke, Phi.	.75	1.50	3.00 ☐
116	Dave Lewis, NYI	.06	.13	.25 ☐
117	Darcy Rota, Chi.	.06	.13	.25 ☐
118	Andre Savard, Buf.	.06	.13	.25 ☐
119	Denis Herron, Goalie, Pit.	.07	.13	.25 ☐
120	Steve Shutt, Mon., 1st Team All-Star	.35	.75	1.50 ☐
121	Mel Bridgman, Phi.	.06	.13	.25 ☐
122	Buster Harvey, Det., LC	.06	.13	.25 ☐
123	**Rolie Eriksson, Min., RC**	**.06**	**.13**	**.25** ☐
124	Dale Tallon, Chi.	.06	.13	.25 ☐
125	Gilles Gilbert, Goalie, Bos.	.07	.13	.25 ☐
126	Billy Harris, NYI	.06	.13	.25 ☐
127	Tom Lysiak, Atl.	.06	.13	.25 ☐
128	Jerry Korab, Buf.	.06	.13	.25 ☐
129	Bob Gainey, Mon.	.30	.60	1.25 ☐
130	Wilf Paiement, Col.	.06	.13	.25 ☐

TOPPS — 1977-78 REGULAR ISSUE

No.	Player	VG	EX	NRMT
131A	Tom Bladon, Phi., Error Card Shows Bob Daily	.06	.13	.25
131B	Tom Bladon, Phi., Corrected	.06	.13	.25
132	Ernie Hicke, Min., LC	.06	.13	.25
133	J. P. LeBlanc, Det., LC	.06	.13	.25
134	**Mike Milbury, Bos., RC**	.35	.75	1.50
135	Pit Martin, Chi.	.06	.13	.25
136	Steve Vickers, NYR	.06	.13	.25
137	Don Awrey, Pit.	.06	.13	.25
138A	Bernie Wolfe MacAdam, Goalie, Wash., Error	.50	1.00	2.00
138B	Bernie Wolfe, Goalie, Wash., Corrected	.06	.13	.25
139	Doug Jarvis, Mon.	.10	.25	.50
140	Borje Salming, Tor., 1st Team All-Star	.25	.50	1.00
141	Bob MacMillan, St. L.	.06	.13	.25
142	Wayne Stephenson, Goalie, Phi.	.09	.18	.35
143	Dave Forbes, Bos.	.06	.13	.25
144	Jean Potvin, NYI	.06	.13	.25
145	Guy Charron, Wash.	.06	.13	.25
146	Cliff Koroll, Chi.	.06	.13	.25
147	Danny Grant, Det.	.06	.13	.25
148	Bill Hogaboam, Min.	.06	.13	.25
149	Al MacAdam, Cle.	.06	.13	.25
150	Gerry Desjardins, Goalie, Buf., LC	.06	.13	.25
151	Yvon Lambert, Mon.	.06	.13	.25
152A	Rick Lapointe, Phi., Without mustache	.50	1.00	2.00
152B	Rick Lapointe, Phi., With mustache	.06	.13	.25
153	Ed Westfall, NYI	.06	.13	.25
154	Carol Vadnais, NYR	.06	.13	.25
155	John Bucyk, Bos., LC	.18	.35	.75
156	J. P. Bordeleau, Chi.	.06	.13	.25
157	Ron Stackhouse, Pit.	.06	.13	.25
158	**Glen Sharpley, Min., RC**	.06	.13	.25
159	Michel Bergeron, Det.	.06	.13	.25
160	Rogatien Vachon, Goalie, LA, 2nd Team All-Star	.18	.35	.75
161	Fred Stanfield, Buf.	.06	.13	.25
162	Gerry Hart, NYI	.06	.13	.25
163	Mario Tremblay, Mon.	.06	.13	.25
164	Andre Dupont, Phi.	.06	.13	.25
165	Don Marcotte, Bos.	.06	.13	.25
166	Wayne Dillon, NYR	.06	.13	.25
167	Claude Larose, St. L., LC	.06	.13	.25
168	Eric Vail, Atl.	.06	.13	.25
169	**Tom Edur, Col., RC**	.06	.13	.25
170	Tony Esposito, Goalie, Chi.	.35	.75	1.50
171	Andre St. Laurent, NYI	.06	.13	.25
172	Dan Maloney, Det.	.06	.13	.25
173	Dennis O'Brien, Min.	.06	.13	.25
174	Blair Chapman, Pit., RC	.06	.13	.25
175	Dennis Kearns, Van.	.06	.13	.25
176	Wayne Merrick, Cle.	.06	.13	.25
177	Michel Larocque, Goalie, Mon.	.06	.13	.25
178	Bob Kelly, Phi.	.06	.13	.25
179	**Dave Farrish, NYR, RC**	.06	.13	.25
180	Rick Martin, Buf., 2nd Team All-Star	.06	.13	.25
181	Gary Doak, Bos.	.06	.13	.25
182	Jude Drouin, NYI	.06	.13	.25
183	**Barry Dean, Col., RC**	.06	.13	.25
184	Gary Smith, Goalie, Min.	.09	.18	.35
185	Reggie Leach, Phi.	.06	.13	.25
186	Ian Turnbull, Tor.	.06	.13	.25
187	Vic Venasky, LA	.06	.13	.25
188	**Wayne Bianchin, Pit., RC**	.06	.13	.25
189	Doug Risebrough, Mon.	.06	.13	.25
190	Brad Park, Bos.	.25	.50	1.00
191	Craig Ramsay, Buf.	.06	.13	.25
192	Ken Hodge, Sr., NYR, LC	.06	.13	.25
193	Phil Myre, Goalie, Atl.	.06	.13	.25
194	Garry Howatt, NYI	.06	.13	.25
195	Stan Mikita, Chi.	.60	1.25	2.50
196	Garnet Bailey, Wash., LC	.06	.13	.25
197	Dennis Hextall, Det.	.06	.13	.25
198	Nick Beverley, Min.	.06	.13	.25
199	Larry Patey, St. L.	.06	.13	.25
200	Guy Lafleur, Mon., 1st Team All-Star	1.50	3.00	6.00
201	**Don Edwards, Goalie, Buf., RC**	.35	.75	1.50
202	Gary Dornhoefer, Phi., LC	.06	.13	.25
203	Stan Gilbertson, Pit., LC	.06	.13	.25
204	**Alex Pirus, Min., RC, LC**	.06	.13	.25
205	Peter Mahovlich, Mon.	.06	.13	.25
206	Bert Marshall, NYI	.06	.13	.25
207	Gilles Gratton, Goalie, NYR, LC	.06	.13	.25

Topps, 1977-78 Issue Card No. 160, Rogatien Vachon, 2nd Team All Star

Topps 1977-78 Issue Card No. 201, Don Edwards

Topps 1977-78 Issue Card No. 232, Mike McEwen

Topps, 1977-78 Issue Card No. 264, Canadiens Win 20th Stanley Cup

No.	Player	VG	EX	NRMT
208	Alain Daigle, Chi.	.06	.13	.25
209	Chris Oddleifson, Van.	.06	.13	.25
210	Gilbert Perreault, Buf., 2nd Team All-Star	.35	.75	1.50
211	**Mike Palmateer, Goalie, Tor., RC**	.50	1.00	2.00
212	Bill Lochead, Det.	.06	.13	.25
213	Dick Redmond, Chi.	.06	.13	.25

1976-77 RECORD BREAKERS

No.	Player	VG	EX	NRMT
214	**Most Points, Season, Right ing:** Guy Lafleur, Mon.	.50	1.00	2.00
215	**Most Goals, Game, Defenseman:** Ian Turnbull, Tor.	.10	.25	.50
216	**Longest Point-Scoring Streak:** Guy Lafleur, Mon.	.50	1.00	2.00
217	**Most Goals, Season, Left Wing:** Steve Shutt, Mon.	.10	.25	.50
218	**Most Assists, Season, Right Wing:** Guy Lafleur, Mon.	.50	1.00	2.00

REGULAR ISSUE

No.	Player	VG	EX	NRMT
219	Lorne Henning, NYI	.06	.13	.25
220	Terry O'Reilly, Bos.	.10	.20	.40
221	Pat Hickey, NYR	.06	.13	.25
222	Rene Robert, Buf.	.06	.13	.25
223	Tim Young, Min.	.06	.13	.25
224	Dunc Wilson, Goalie, Pit., LC	.06	.13	.25
225	Dennis Hull, Chi., LC	.06	.13	.25
226	Rod Seiling, St. L.	.06	.13	.25
227	Bill Barber, Phi.	.30	.60	1.25
228	**Dennis Polonich, Det., RC**	.06	.13	.25
229	Billy Smith, Goalie, NYI	.30	.60	1.25
230	Yvan Cournoyer, Mon.	.25	.50	1.00
231	Don Luce, Buf.	.06	.13	.25
232	**Mike McEwen, NYR, RC**	.10	.20	.40
233	Don Saleski, Phi.	.06	.13	.25
234	Wayne Cashman, Bos.	.06	.13	.25
235	Phil Russell, Chi.	.06	.13	.25
236	Mike Corrigan, Pit., LC	.06	.13	.25
237	Guy Chouinard, Atl.	.10	.20	.40
238	**Steve Jensen, Min., RC**	.06	.13	.25
239	Jim Rutherford, Goalie, Det.	.06	.13	.25
240	Marcel Dionne, LA, 1st Team All-Star	1.00	2.00	4.00
241	Rejean Houle, Mon.	.06	.13	.25
242	Jocelyn Guevremont, Buf.	.06	.13	.25
243	Jim Harrison, Chi., LC	.06	.13	.25
244	**Don Murdoch, NYR, RC**	.06	.13	.25
245	**Richard Green, Wash., RC**	.20	.40	.80
246	Rick Middleton, Bos.	.25	.50	1.00
247	Joe Watson, Phi.	.06	.13	.25
248	Syl Apps, Jr., Pit.	.06	.13	.25
249	Checklist 2 (133 - 264)	1.25	2.50	5.00
250	Clark Gillies, NYI	.06	.13	.25
251	Bobby Orr, Chi., LC	3.75	7.50	15.00
252	Nelson Pyatt, Col.	.06	.13	.25
253	**Gary McAdam, Buf., RC**	.06	.13	.25
254	Jacques Lemaire, Mon.	.25	.50	1.00
255	Bill Fairbairn, Min.	.06	.13	.25
256	Ronald Greschner, NYR	.06	.13	.25
257	Ross Lonsberry, Phi.	.06	.13	.25
258	Dave Gardner, Cle.	.06	.13	.25
259	Rick Blight, Van.	.06	.13	.25
260	Gerry Cheevers, Goalie, Bos.	.30	.60	1.25
261	Jean Pronovost, Pit.	.06	.13	.25

1976 - 1977 STANLEY CUP

No.	Team	VG	EX	NRMT
262	Semi-finals: Canadiens Skate Past Islanders	.10	.25	.50
263	Semi-finals: Bruins Advance to Finals	.10	.25	.50
264	Finals: Canadiens Win 20th Stanley Cup	.25	.50	1.00

—1977 - 78 GLOSSY PHOTOS —

These glossy colour photos come with square or rounded corners. The two varieties appear to have been issued in equal quantities and there is no price differential. The only difference between the O-Pee-Chee and the Topps inserts is the imprint. These photos are numbered _ of 22.

Photo Size: Square Corners: 2 1/2" X 3 1/2"
             Round Corners: 2 1/4" X 3 1/4"
Face: Four colour, borderless; Facsimile autograph
Back: Blue on card stock; Name, Team, Position, Number
Imprint: * © 1977 TOPPS CHEWING GUM, INC. PRTD. IN U.S.A.
Complete Set No.: 22
Complete Set Price: 3.00   6.00   12.00
Common Player: .06   .12   .25

No.	Player	VG	EX	NRMT
1	Wayne Cashman, Bos.	.06	.12	.25
2	Gerry Cheevers, Goalie, Bos.	.18	.35	.75
3	Bobby Clarke, Phi.	.25	.50	1.00
4	Marcel Dionne, LA	.25	.50	1.00
5	Ken Dryden, Goalie, Mon.	1.00	2.00	4.00
6	Clark Gillies, NYI	.06	.12	.25
7	Guy Lafleur, Mon.	.50	1.00	2.00
8	Reggie Leach, Phi.	.06	.12	.25
9	Rick MacLeish, Phi.	.06	.12	.25
10	Dave Maloney, NYR	.06	.12	.25
11	Richard Martin, Buf.	.12	.25	.50
12	Don Murdoch, NYR	.06	.12	.25
13	Brad Park, Bos.	.25	.50	1.00
14	Gilbert Perreault, Buf.	.25	.50	1.00
15	Denis Potvin, NYI	.25	.50	1.00
16	Jean Ratelle, Bos.	.12	.25	.50
17	Glenn Resch, Goalie, NYI	.12	.25	.50
18	Larry Robinson, Mon.	.25	.50	1.00
19	Steve Shutt, Mon.	.12	.25	.50
20	Darryl Sittler, Tor.	.35	.75	1.50
21	Rogatien Vachon, Goalie, LA	.20	.35	.75
22	Tim Young, Min.	.06	.12	.25

— 1978 - 79 REGULAR ISSUE —

The first five cards feature the previous season's highlights. Mint cards command a price premium of 25% over NRMT cards.

PRICE MOVEMENT OF NRMT SETS

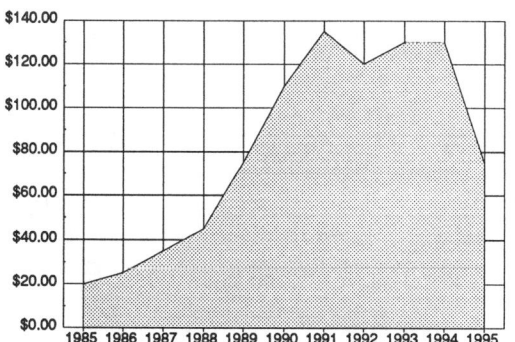

Card Size: 2 1/2" X 3 1/2"
Face: Four colour, white border, Team logo, Position
Back: Orange and green on card stock, Number, Resume, Player's signature
Imprint: A* © 1978 TOPPS CHEWING GUM, INC. PRTD IN U.S.A. or
         B © 1978 TOPPS CHEWING GUM, INC. PRTD. IN U.S.A.
Complete Set No.: 264
Complete set Price: 17.50   35.00   75.00
Common Card: .05   .10   .20
Wax Pack: (12 Cards)   10.00
Wax Box: (48 Packs)   300.00
Wax Case: (16 Boxes)   2,850.00

1977 - 78 HIGHLIGHTS

No.	Highlights	VG	EX	NRMT
1	Mike Bossy Sets Record for Goals by a Rookie.	1.10	2.25	4.50
2	Phil Esposito Tops Mark with 29th Hat Trick.	.25	.50	1.00
3	Guy Lafleur Scores vs. Every Team in League.	.25	.50	1.00

Topps
1977-78 Glossy Photos
Photo No. 1 Wayne Cashman
Square Corners

Topps
1977-78 Glossy Photos
Photo No. 1 Wayne Cashman
Round Corners

Topps
1978-79 Issue
Card No.1,
Mike Bossy Sets Record
for Goals by a Rookie

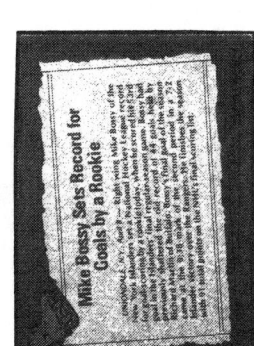

Topps
1978-79 Issue
Card No.1,
Mike Bossy Sets Record
for Goals by a Rookie

No.	Player	VG	EX	NRMT
4	Darryl Sittler Finds Net in 9 Straight Games.	.20	.35	.75
5	Garry Unger Plays in 803rd Consecutive Game.	.05	.10	.20

REGULAR ISSUE

No.	Player	VG	EX	NRMT
6	Gary Edwards, Goalie, Min.	.05	.10	.20
7	Rick Blight, Van.	.05	.10	.20
8	Larry Patey, St. L.	.05	.10	.20
9	Craig Ramsay, Buf.	.05	.10	.20
10	Bryan Trottier, NYI, 1st Team All-Star	1.00	2.00	4.00
11	Don Murdoch, NYR	.05	.10	.20
12	Phil Russell, Chi.	.05	.10	.20
13	Doug Jarvis, Mon.	.05	.10	.20
14	Gene Carr, Pit., LC	.05	.10	.20
15	Bernie Parent, Goalie, Phi., LC	.25	.50	1.00
16	Perry Miller, Det.	.05	.10	.20
17	Kent-Erik Andersson, Min., RC	.05	.10	.20
18	Gregg Sheppard, Bos.	.05	.10	.20
19	Dennis Owchar, Col., LC	.05	.10	.20
20	Rogatien Vachon, Goalie, LA	.10	.25	.50
21	Dan Maloney, Tor.	.05	.10	.20
22	Guy Charron, Wash.	.05	.10	.20
23	Dick Redmond, Atl.	.05	.10	.20
24	Checklist 1 (1 - 132)	1.00	2.00	4.00
25	Anders Hedberg, NYR	.05	.10	.20
26	Mel Bridgman, Phi.	.05	.10	.20
27	Lee Fogolin, Buf.	.05	.10	.20
28	Gilles Meloche, Goalie, Min.	.05	.10	.20
29	Garry Howatt, NYI	.05	.10	.20
30	Darryl Sittler, Tor., 2nd Team All-Star	.35	.75	1.50
31	Curt Bennett, St. L.	.05	.10	.20
32	Andre St. Laurent, Det.	.05	.10	.20
33	Blair Chapman, Pit.	.05	.10	.20
34	Keith Magnuson, Chi., LC	.05	.10	.20
35	Pierre Larouche, Mon.	.05	.10	.20
36	Michel Plasse, Goalie, Col.	.05	.10	.20
37	Gary Sargent, LA	.05	.10	.20
38	Mike Walton, St. L.	.05	.10	.20
39	Robert Picard, Wash., RC	.07	.15	.30
40	Terry O'Reilly, Bos., 2nd Team All-Star	.10	.20	.40
41	Dave Farrish, NYR	.05	.10	.20
42	Gary McAdam, Buf.	.05	.10	.20
43	Joe Watson., Phi., LC	.05	.10	.20
44	Yves Belanger, Goalie, Atl., LC	.05	.10	.20
45	Steve Jensen, Min.	.05	.10	.20
46	Bob Stewart, Min.	.05	.10	.20
47	Darcy Rota, Chi.	.05	.10	.20
48	Dennis Hextall, Det.	.05	.10	.20
49	Bert Marshall, NYI, LC	.05	.10	.20
50	Ken Dryden, Goalie, Mon., 1st Team All-Star	1.25	2.50	5.00
51	Pete Mahovlich, Pit.	.05	.10	.20
52	Dennis Ververgaert, Van.	.05	.10	.20
53	Inge Hammarstrom, St. L., LC	.05	.10	.20
54	Doug Favell, Goalie, Col.	.05	.10	.20
55	Steve Vickers, NYR	.05	.10	.20
56	Syl Apps, Jr., LA	.05	.10	.20
57	Errol Thompson, Det.	.05	.10	.20
58	Don Luce, Buf.	.05	.10	.20
59	Mike Milbury, Bos.	.10	.20	.40
60	Yvan Cournoyer, Mon., LC	.18	.35	.75
61	Kirk Bowman, Chi., LC	.05	.10	.20
62	Billy Smith, Goalie, NYI	.25	.50	1.00

1977 - 78 LEAGUE LEADERS

No.	Player	VG	EX	NRMT
63	**Goal Leaders:** G. Lafleur, Mon.; M. Bossy, NYI; S. Shutt, Mon.	.50	1.00	2.00
64	**Assist Leaders:** B. Trottier, NYI; G. Lafleur, Mon.; D. Sittler, Tor.	.35	.75	1.50
65	**Scoring Leaders:** G. Lafleur, Mon.; B. Trottier, NYI; D. Sittler, Tor.	.35	.75	1.50
66	**Penalty Min. Leaders:** D. Schultz, Pit.; D. Williams, Tor.; D. Polonich, Det.	.10	.25	.50
67	**Power Play Goal Leaders:** M. Bossy, NYI; P. Esposito, NYR; S. Shutt, Mon.	.35	.75	1.50
68	**Goals Against Average Leaders:** K. Dryden, Mon.; B. Parent, Phi.; G. Gilbert, Bos.;	.40	.85	1.75

220 • TOPPS — 1978-79 REGULAR ISSUE

No.	Player	VG	EX	NRMT
69	**Game Winning Goal Leaders:** G. Lafleur, Mon.; B. Barber, Phi.; D. Sittler, Tor.; B. Bourne, NYI	.35	.75	1.50 ☐
70	**Shutout Leaders:** B. Parent, Phi.; K. Dryden, Mon.; D. Edwards, Buf.; T. Esposito, Chi.; M. Palmateer, Tor.	.40	.85	1.75 ☐

REGULAR ISSUE

No.	Player	VG	EX	NRMT
71	Bob Kelly, Phi.	.05	.10	.20 ☐
72	Ron Stackhouse, Pit.	.05	.10	.20 ☐
73	Wayne Dillon, NYR	.05	.10	.20 ☐
74	Jim Rutherford, Goalie, Det.	.07	.15	.30 ☐
75	Stan Mikita, Chi.	.50	1.00	2.00 ☐
76	Bob Gainey, Mon.	.25	.50	1.00 ☐
77	Gerry Hart, NYI	.05	.10	.20 ☐
78	Lanny McDonald, Tor.	.25	.50	1.00 ☐
79	Brad Park, Bos.	.25	.50	1.00 ☐
80	Rick Martin, Buf.	.05	.10	.20 ☐
81	Bernie Wolfe, Goalie, Wash., LC	.05	.10	.20 ☐
82	Bob MacMillan, Atl.	.05	.10	.20 ☐
83	**Brad Maxwell, Min., RC**	**.05**	**.10**	**.20** ☐
84	Mike Fidler, Min.	.05	.10	.20 ☐
85	Carol Vadnais, NYR	.05	.10	.20 ☐
86	Don Lever, Van.	.05	.10	.20 ☐
87	Phil Myre, Goalie, St. L.	.05	.10	.20 ☐
88	Paul Gardner, Col.	.05	.10	.20 ☐
89	Bob Murray, Chi.	.05	.10	.20 ☐
90	Guy Lafleur, Mon., 1st Team All-Star	1.00	2.00	4.00 ☐
91	Bob J. Murdoch, LA	.05	.10	.20 ☐
92	Ron Ellis, Tor.	.05	.10	.20 ☐
93	Jude Drouin, NYI	.05	.10	.20 ☐
94	Jocelyn Guevremont, Buf.	.05	.10	.20 ☐
95	Gilles Gilbert, Goalie, Bos.	.05	.10	.20 ☐
96	Bob Sirois, Wash.	.05	.10	.20 ☐
97	Tom Lysiak, Atl.	.05	.10	.20 ☐
98	Andre Dupont, Phi.	.05	.10	.20 ☐
99	**Per-Olov Brasar, Min., RC**	.05	.10	.20 ☐
100	Phil Esposito, NYR	.50	1.00	2.00 ☐
101	J. P. Bordeleau, Chi.	.05	.10	.20 ☐
102	**Pierre Mondou, Mon., RC**	**.12**	**.25**	**.50** ☐
103	Wayne Bianchin, Pit.	.05	.10	.20 ☐
104	Dennis O'Brien, Bos.	.05	.10	.20 ☐
105	Glenn Resch, Goalie, NYI	.12	.25	.50 ☐
106	Dennis Polonich, Det.	.05	.10	.20 ☐
107	**Kris Manery, Min., RC**	.05	.10	.20 ☐
108	Bill Hajt, Buf.	.05	.10	.20 ☐
109	**Jere Gillis, Van., RC**	.05	.10	.20 ☐
110	Garry Unger, St. L.	.05	.10	.20 ☐
111	Nick Beverley, Min., LC	.05	.10	.20 ☐
112	Pat Hickey, NYR	.05	.10	.20 ☐
113	Rick Middleton, Bos.	.25	.50	1.00 ☐
114	Orest Kindrachuk, Pit.	.05	.10	.20 ☐
115	**Mike Bossy, NYI, RC**	**6.00**	**12.00**	**24.00** ☐
116	Pierre Bouchard, Mon.	.05	.10	.20 ☐
117	Alain Daigle, Chi.	.05	.10	.20 ☐
118	Terry Martin, Buf.	.05	.10	.20 ☐
119	Tom Edur, Pit., LC	.05	.10	.20 ☐
120	Marcel Dionne, LA	.75	1.50	3.00 ☐
121	**Barry Beck, Col., RC**	.25	.50	1.00 ☐
122	Bill Lochead, Det.	.05	.10	.20 ☐
123	**Paul Harrison, Goalie, Tor., RC**	.05	.10	.20 ☐
124	Wayne Cashman, Bos.	.05	.10	.20 ☐
125	Rick MacLeish, Phi.	.05	.10	.20 ☐
126	Bob Bourne, NYI	.05	.10	.20 ☐
127	Ian Turnbull, Tor.	.05	.10	.20 ☐
128	Gerry Meehan, Wash., LC	.05	.10	.20 ☐
129	Eric Vail, Atl.	.05	.10	.20 ☐
130	Gilbert Perreault, Buf.	.25	.50	1.00 ☐
131	Bob Dailey, Phi.	.05	.10	.20 ☐
132	**Dale McCourt, Det., RC**	**.10**	**.25**	**.50** ☐
133	**John Wensink, Bos., RC**	.10	.25	.50 ☐
134	Bill Nyrop, Mon., LC	.05	.10	.20 ☐
135	Ivan Boldirev, Chi.	.05	.10	.20 ☐
136	**Lucien DeBlois, NYR, RC**	.10	.25	.50 ☐
137	Brian Spencer, Pit., LC	.05	.10	.20 ☐
138	Tim Young, Min.	.05	.10	.20 ☐
139	Ron Sedlbauer, Van.	.05	.10	.20 ☐
140	Gerry Cheevers, Goalie, Bos.	.18	.35	.75 ☐
141	Dennis Maruk, Min.	.05	.10	.20 ☐
142	Barry Dean, Phi.	.05	.10	.20 ☐
143	**Bernie Federko, St. L., RC**	**2.00**	**4.00**	**8.00** ☐

Topps
1978-79 Issue
Card No. 102,
Pierre Mondou

Topps
1978-79 Issue
Card No. 115,
Mike Bossy

Topps
1978-79 Issue
Card No. 177,
Ron Duguay

Topps
1978-79 Issue
Card No. 216, Error,
Card shows Brad Maxwell

No.	Player	VG	EX	NRMT
144	**Stefan Persson, NYI, RC**	.10	.25	.50 ☐
145	Wilf Paiement, Col.	.05	.10	.20 ☐
146	Dale Tallon, Chi., LC	.05	.10	.20 ☐
147	Yvon Lambert, Mon.	.05	.10	.20 ☐
148	Greg Joly, Det.	.05	.10	.20 ☐
149	Dean Talafous, Min.	.05	.10	.20 ☐
150	Don Edwards, Goalie, Buf., 2nd Team All-Star	.07	.15	.30 ☐
151	Butch Goring, LA	.05	.10	.20 ☐
152	Tom Bladon, Pit.	.05	.10	.20 ☐
153	Bob Nystrom, NYI	.05	.10	.20 ☐
154	Ronald Greschner, NYR	.05	.10	.20 ☐
155	Jean Ratelle, Bos.	.18	.35	.75 ☐
156	**Russ Anderson, Pit., RC**	.05	.10	.20 ☐
157	John Marks, Chi.	.05	.10	.20 ☐
158	Michel Larocque, Goalie, Mon.	.05	.10	.20 ☐
159	**Paul Woods, Det., RC**	.05	.10	.20 ☐
160	Mike Palmateer, Goalie, Tor.	.05	.10	.20 ☐
161	Jim Lorentz, Buf., LC	.05	.10	.20 ☐
162	Dave Lewis, NYI	.05	.10	.20 ☐
163	Harvey Bennet, Min., LC	.05	.10	.20 ☐
164	Rick Smith, Bos.	.05	.10	.20 ☐
165	Reggie Leach, Phi.	.05	.10	.20 ☐
166	Wayne Thomas, Goalie, NYR	.07	.15	.30 ☐
167	Dave Forbes, Wash., LC	.05	.10	.20 ☐
168	**Douglas Wilson, Chi., RC**	1.75	3.50	7.00 ☐
169	Dan Bouchard, Goalie, Atl.	.07	.15	.30 ☐
170	Steve Shutt, Mon., 2nd Team All-Star	.25	.50	1.00 ☐
171	**Mike Kaszycki, NYI, RC**	.05	.10	.20 ☐
172	Denis Herron, Goalie, Pit.	.05	.10	.20 ☐
173	Rick Bowness, Det.	.05	.10	.20 ☐
174	Rick Hampton, Min.	.05	.10	.20 ☐
175	Glen Sharpley, Min.	.05	.10	.20 ☐
176	Bill Barber, Phi.	.18	.35	.75 ☐
177	**Ron Duguay, NYR, RC**	**.35**	**.75**	**1.50** ☐
178	Jim Schoenfeld, Buf.	.05	.10	.20 ☐
179	Pierre Plante, Chi.	.05	.10	.20 ☐
180	Jacques Lemaire, Mon., LC	.12	.25	.50 ☐
181	Stan Jonathan, Bos.	.05	.10	.20 ☐
182	Billy Harris, NYI	.05	.10	.20 ☐
183	Chris Oddleifson, Van.	.05	.10	.20 ☐
184	Jean Pronovost, Pit.	.05	.10	.20 ☐
185	Fred Barrett, Min.	.05	.10	.20 ☐
186	Ross Lonsberry, Pit.	.05	.10	.20 ☐
187	Mike McEwen, NYR	.05	.10	.20 ☐
188	Rene Robert, Buf.	.05	.10	.20 ☐
189	J. Bob Kelly, Chi.	.05	.10	.20 ☐
190	Serge Savard, Mon., 2nd Team All-Star	.06	.12	.25 ☐
191	Dennis Kearns, Van.	.05	.10	.20 ☐

1978 - 78 TEAM CHECKLIST CARDS

No.	Team	VG	EX	NRMT
192	Atlanta Flames	.12	.25	.50 ☐
193	Boston Bruins	.12	.25	.50 ☐
194	Buffalo Sabres	.12	.25	.50 ☐
195	Chicago Black Hawks	.12	.25	.50 ☐
196	Colorado Rockies	.12	.25	.50 ☐
197	Detroit Red Wings	.12	.25	.50 ☐
198	Los Angeles Kings	.12	.25	.50 ☐
199	Minnesota North Stars	.12	.25	.50 ☐
200	Montreal Canadiens	.12	.25	.50 ☐
201	New York Islanders	.12	.25	.50 ☐
202	New York Rangers	.12	.25	.50 ☐
203	Philadelphia Flyers	.12	.25	.50 ☐
204	Pittsburgh Penguins	.12	.25	.50 ☐
205	St. Louis Blues	.12	.25	.50 ☐
206	Toronto Maple Leafs	.12	.25	.50 ☐
207	Vancouver Canucks	.12	.25	.50 ☐
208	Washington Capitals	.12	.25	.50 ☐

REGULAR ISSUE

No.	Player	VG	EX	NRMT
209	Danny Gare, Buf.	.05	.10	.20 ☐
210	Larry Robinson, Mon., 1st Team All-Star	.40	.85	1.75 ☐
211	John Davidson, Goalie, NYR	.05	.10	.20 ☐
212	Peter McNab, Bos.	.05	.10	.20 ☐
213	Rick Kehoe, Pit.	.05	.10	.20 ☐
214	Terry Harper, Det., LC	.05	.10	.20 ☐
215	Bobby Clarke, Phi.	.40	.85	1.75 ☐
216	Bryan Maxwell, Min., Error	.05	.10	.20 ☐

1978-79 TEAM INSERTS TOPPS • 221

No.	Player	VG	EX	NRMT
217	Ted Bulley, Chi., RC	.05	.10	.20
218	Red Berenson, St. L., LC	.05	.10	.20
219	Ron Grahame, Goalie, Bos., LC	.05	.10	.20
220	Clark Gillies, NYI, 1st Team All-Star	.05	.10	.20
221	Dave Maloney, NYR	.05	.10	.20
222	**Derek Smith, Buf., RC**	.05	.10	.20
223	Wayne Stephenson, Goalie, Phi.	.05	.10	.20
224	John Van Boxmeer, Col.	.05	.10	.20
225	Dave Schultz, Pit.	.05	.10	.20
226	**Reed Larson, Det., RC**	.10	.25	.50
227	Rejean Houle, Mon.	.05	.10	.20
228	Doug Hicks, Chi.	.05	.10	.20
229	Mike Murphy, LA	.05	.10	.20
230	Pete LoPresti, Goalie, Min.	.05	.10	.20
231	Jerry Korab, Buf.	.05	.10	.20
232	Ed Westfall, NYI, LC	.05	.10	.20
233	**Greg Malone, Pit., RC**	.05	.10	.20
234	Paul Holmgren, Phi.	.10	.20	.40
235	Walt Tkaczuk, NYR	.05	.10	.20
236	Don Marcotte, Bos.	.05	.10	.20
237	Ron Low, Goalie, Det.	.05	.10	.20
238	Rick Chartraw, Mon.	.05	.10	.20
239	Cliff Koroll, Chi	.05	.10	.20
240	Borje Salming, Tor., 1st Team All-Star	.18	.35	.75
241	Roland Eriksson, Min.	.05	.10	.20
242	**Ric Seiling, Buf., RC**	.05	.10	.20
243	**Jim Bedard, Goalie, Wash., RC**	.05	.10	.20
244	**Peter Lee, Pit., RC**	.05	.10	.20
245	Denis Potvin, NYI, 2nd Team All-Star	.60	1.25	2.50
246	Greg Polis, NYR	.05	.10	.20
247	Jimmy Watson, Phi.	.05	.10	.20
248	Bobby Schmautz, Bos.	.05	.10	.20
249	Doug Risebrough, Mon.	.05	.10	.20
250	Tony Esposito, Goalie, Chi.	.25	.50	1.00
251	Nick Libett, Det.	.05	.10	.20
252	**Ron Zanussi, Min., RC**	.05	.10	.20
253	Andre Savard, Buf.	.05	.10	.20
254	Dave Burrows, Tor.	.05	.10	.20
255	Ulf Nilsson, NYR	.10	.20	.40
256	Richard Mulhern, Atl.	.05	.10	.20
257	Don Saleski, Phi., LC	.05	.10	.20
258	Wayne Merrick, NYI	.05	.10	.20
259	Checklist 2 (133 - 264)	1.00	2.00	4.00
260	Guy Lapointe, Mon.	.10	.20	.40
261	Grant Mulvey, Chi.	.05	.10	.20

1977-78 STANLEY CUP PLAYOFFS

No.	Team	VG	EX	NRMT
262	**Semi-finals** Canadiens sweep Maple Leafs.	.07	.15	.35
263	**Semi-finals** Bruins skate past the Flyers.	.07	.15	.35
264	**Finals** Canadiens win 3rd straight cup.	.25	.50	1.00

1978 - 79 TEAM INSERTS

This 22-card sticker insert set features team logos, numbers, sticks, pucks and various words. They were intended as helmet stickers for young hockey players and collectors.

Card Size: 2 1/2" x 3 1/2"
Face: Logo, words and numbers
Back: Blank
Imprint: © 1978 TOPPS CHEWING GUM, INC. PRTD IN U.S.A.
Complete Set No.: 22
Complete Set Price: 15.00 30.00
Common Team: .35 .75 1.50

No.	Player	VG	EX	NRMT
1	Altanta Flames	.35	.75	1.50
2	Boston Bruins/Hockey stick/3	.35	.75	1.50
3	Boston Bruins/Puck/1	.35	.75	1.50
4	Buffalo Sabres	.35	.75	1.50
5	Chicago Black Hawks	.35	.75	1.50
6	Colorado Rockies	.35	.75	1.50
7	Detroit Red Wings	.35	.75	1.50
8	Los Angeles Kings	.35	.75	1.50
9	Minnesota North Stars	.35	.75	1.50
10	Montreal Canadiens/Mask/5	.35	.75	1.50
11	Montreal Canadiens/Puck/0	.35	.75	1.50
12	New York Islanders/Crossed sticks/7	.35	.75	1.50

Topps
1978-79 Issue
Card No. 222,
Derek Smith

Topps
1978-79 Issue
Card No. 264,
Canadiens win 3rd straight cup

Topps
1979-80 Issue
Card No.1,
Goal Leaders

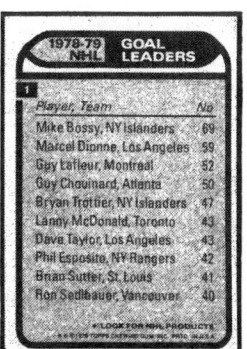

Topps
1979-80 Issue
Card No.1,
Goal Leaders

No.	Player	VG	EX	NRMT
13	New York Islanders/Hockey Stick/2	.35	.75	1.50
14	New York Rangers/Mask/1	.35	.75	1.50
15	New York Rangers/Crossed Sticks/9	.35	.75	1.50
16	Philadelphia Flyers/Mask/6	.35	.75	1.50
17	Philadelphia Flyers/Crossed Sticks/8	.35	.75	1.50
18	Pittsburgh Penguins	.35	.75	1.50
19	St. Louis Blues	.35	.75	1.50
20	Toronto Maple Leafs	.35	.75	1.50
21	Vancouver Canucks	.35	.75	1.50
22	Washington Capitals	.35	.75	1.50

— 1979 - 80 REGULAR ISSUE —

The team photo cards have a checklist on the back. The set includes the rookie card of Wayne Gretzky. Mint cards command a price premium of 25% over NRMT cards.

PRICE MOVEMENT OF NRMT SETS

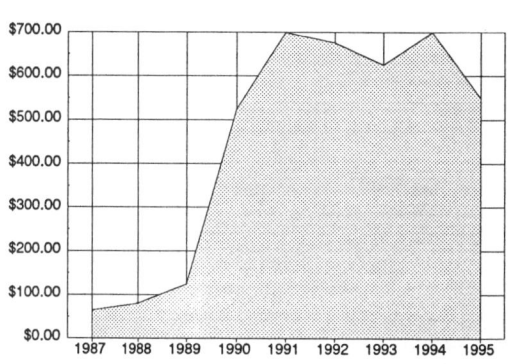

Card Size: 2 1/2" X 3 1/2"
Face: Four colour, blue border, Team logo, Position
Back: Blue and black on card stock; Number, Resume, Hockey trivia
Imprint: * © 1979 TOPPS CHEWING GUM, INC. PRTD. IN U.S.A. or
** © 1979 TOPPS CHEWING GUM, INC. PRTD IN U.S.A.
Complete Set No.: 264
Complete Set Price: 125.00 275.00 550.00
Common Card: .06 .12 .25
Wax Pack: (12 Cards) 60.00
Wax Box: (48 Packs) 1,800.00
Wax Case: (16 Boxes) 25,000.00

1978 - 79 LEAGUE LEADERS

No.	Player	VG	EX	NRMT
1	**Goal Leaders:** M. Bossy, NYI; M. Dionne, LA; G. Lafleur, Mon.	.50	1.00	2.00
2	**Assist Leaders:** B. Trottier, NYI; G. Lafleur, Mon.; M. Dionne, LA; B. MacMillan, Atl.	.35	.75	1.50
3	**Scoring Leaders:** B. Trottier, NYI; M. Dionne, LA; G. Lafleur, Mon.	.35	.75	1.50
4	**Penalty Minute Leaders:** D. Williams, Tor.; R. Holt, LA; D. Schultz, Buf.	.20	.35	.75
5	**Power Play Goal Leaders:** M. Bossy, NYI; M. Dionne, LA L. McDonald, Tor.; P. Gardner,Tor.	.35	.75	1.50
6	**Goals Against Avg. Leaders:** K. Dryden, Mon.; G. Resch, NYI; B. Parent, Phi.	.55	1.10	2.25
7	**Game Winning Goal Leaders:** G. Lafleur, Mon.; M. Bossy, NYI; B. Trottier, NYI; . Pronovost, Atl.; JT. Bulley, Chi.	.35	.75	1.50
8A	**Shutouts:** Error, K. Dryden, Mon; T. Esposito, Chi.; M. Palmateer, Tor.; M. Lessard, LA; B. Parent, Phi.	2.50	5.00	10.00
8B	**Shutouts:** Corrected, Palmateer and Lessard reversed	.35	.75	1.50

REGULAR ISSUE

No.	Player	VG	EX	NRMT
9	Greg Malone, Pit.	.06	.12	.25
10	Rick Middleton, Bos.	.15	.30	.60
11	Greg Smith, Min.	.06	.12	.25

222 • TOPPS — 1979 - 80 REGULAR ISSUE

No.	Player	VG	EX	NRMT
12	Rene Robert, Buf.	.06	.12	.25
13	Doug Risebrough, Mon.	.06	.12	.25
14	Bob Kelly, Phi.	.06	.12	.25
15	Walt Tkaczuk, NYR	.06	.12	.25
16	John Marks, Chi.	.06	.12	.25
17	Willie Huber, Det., RC	.06	.12	.25
18	Wayne Gretzky, Edm., RC	110.00	225.00	450.00
19	Ron Sedlbauer, Van.	.06	.12	.25
20	Glenn Resch, Goalie, NYI, 2nd Team All-Star	.09	.18	.35
21	Blair Chapman, Pit.	.06	.12	.25
22	Ron Zanussi, Min.	.06	.12	.25
23	Brad Park, Bos.	.15	.30	.60
24	Yvon Lambert, Mon.	.06	.12	.25
25	Andre Savard, Buf.	.06	.12	.25
26	Jimmy Watson, Phi.	.06	.12	.25
27	Harold Phillipoff, Chi., RC, LC	.06	.12	.25
28	Dan Bouchard, Goalie, Atl.	.06	.12	.25
29	Bob Sirois, Wash.	.06	.12	.25
30	Ulf Nilsson, NYR	.06	.12	.25
31	Mike Murphy, LA	.06	.12	.25
32	Stefan Persson, NYI	.06	.12	.25
33	Garry Unger, St. L.	.06	.12	.25
34	Rejean Houle, Mon.	.06	.12	.25
35	Barry Beck, Col.	.06	.12	.25
36	Tim Young, Min.	.06	.12	.25
37	Rick Dudley, Buf.	.06	.12	.25
38	Wayne Stephenson, Goalie, Phi.	.06	.12	.25
39	Peter McNab, Bos.	.06	.12	.25
40	Borje Salming, Tor., 2nd Team All-Star	.10	.25	.50
41	Tom Lysiak, Chi.	.06	.12	.25
42	Donald Maloney, NYR, RC	.25	.50	1.00
43	Mike Rogers, Har.	.06	.13	.25
44	Dave Lewis, NYI	.06	.12	.25
45	Peter Lee, Pit.	.06	.12	.25
46	Marty Howe, Har.	.06	.12	.25
47	Serge Bernier, Que.	.06	.12	.25
48	Paul Woods, Det.	.06	.12	.25
49	Bob Sauve, Goalie, Buf.	.06	.12	.25
50	Larry Robinson, Mon., 1st Team All-Star	.35	.75	1.50
51	Tom Gorence, Phi., RC	.06	.12	.25
52	Gary Sargent, Min.	.06	.12	.25
53	Thomas Gradin, Van., RC	.25	.50	1.00
54	Dean Talafous, NYR	.06	.12	.25
55	Bob Murray, Chi.	.06	.12	.25
56	Bob Bourne, NYI	.06	.12	.25
57	Larry Patey, St. L.	.06	.12	.25
58	Ross Lonsberry, Pit.	.06	.12	.25
59	Rick Smith, Bos.	.06	.12	.25
60	Guy Chouinard, Atl.	.06	.12	.25
61	Danny Gare, Buf.	.06	.12	.25
62	Jim Bedard, Goalie, Wash., LC	.06	.12	.25
63	Dale McCourt, LA	.06	.12	.25
64	Steve Payne, Min., RC	.10	.20	.40
65	Pat Hughes, Mon., RC	.06	.12	.25
66	Mike McEwen, NYR	.06	.12	.25
67	Reg Kerr, Chi., RC	.06	.12	.25
68	Walt McKechnie, Tor.	.06	.12	.25
69	Michel Plasse, Goalie, Col.	.06	.12	.25
70	Denis Potvin, NYI, 1st Team All-Star	.30	.60	1.25
71	Dave Dryden, Goalie, Edm., LC	.06	.12	.25
72	Gary McAdam, Pit.	.06	.12	.25
73	Andre St. Laurent, Det.	.06	.12	.25
74	Jerry Korab, Buf.	.06	.12	.25
75	Rick MacLeish, Phi.	.06	.12	.25
76	Dennis Kearns, Van.	.06	.12	.25
77	Jean Pronovost, Atl.	.06	.12	.25
78	Ronald Greschner, NYR	.06	.12	.25
79	Wayne Cashman, Bos.	.06	.12	.25
80	Tony Esposito, Goalie, Chi.	.30	.60	1.25

1978 - 79 STANLEY CUP PLAYOFFS

No.	Teams	VG	EX	NRMT
81	Semi-finals: Canadiens Squeak Past Bruins	.12	.25	.50
82	Semi-finals: Rangers Upset Islanders in 6	.12	.25	.50
83	Finals: Canadiens Make it 4 Straight Cups	.12	.25	.50

Topps 1979-80 Issue
Card No. 65,
Pat Hughes

Topps 1979-80 Issue
Card No. 100,
Bryan Trottier

Topps 1979-80 Issue
Card No. 131,
Checklist 1 (1-132)

Topps 1979-80 Issue
Card No. 153,
Lanny McDonald

REGULAR ISSUE

No.	Player	VG	EX	NRMT
84	Brian Sutter, St. L.	.75	1.50	3.00
85	Gerry Cheevers, Goalie, Bos., LC	.12	.25	.50
86	Pat Hickey, NYR	.06	.12	.25
87	Mike Kaszycki, NYI	.06	.12	.25
88	Grant Mulvey, Chi.	.06	.12	.25
89	Derek Smith, Buf.	.06	.12	.25
90	Steve Shutt, Mon.	.20	.35	.75
91	Robert Picard, Wash.	.06	.12	.25
92	Dan Labraaten, Det.,	.06	.12	.25
93	Glen Sharpley, Min.	.06	.12	.25
94	Denis Herron, Goalie, Pit.	.06	.12	.25
95	Reggie Leach, Phi.	.06	.12	.25
96	John Van Boxmeer, Col.	.06	.12	.25
97	David Williams, Tor.	.10	.25	.50
98	Butch Goring, LA	.06	.12	.25
99	Don Marcotte, Bos.	.06	.12	.25
100	Bryan Trottier, NYI, 1st Team All-Star	.85	1.75	2.50
101	Serge Savard, Mon., 2nd Team All-Star	.06	.12	.25
102	Cliff Koroll, Chi., LC	.06	.12	.25
103	Gary Smith, Goalie, Win., LC	.06	.12	.25
104	Al MacAdam, Min.	.06	.12	.25
105	Don Edwards, Goalie, Buf.	.06	.12	.25
106	Errol Thompson, Det.	.06	.12	.25
107	Andre Lacroix, Har., LC	.06	.12	.25
108	Marc Tardif, Que.	.06	.12	.25
109	Rick Kehoe, Pit.	.06	.12	.25
110	John Davidson, Goalie, NYR	.06	.12	.25
111	Behn Wilson, Phi., RC	.09	.18	.35
112	Doug Jarvis, Mon.	.06	.12	.25
113	Tom Rowe, Wash., RC	.06	.12	.25
114	Mike Milbury, Bos.	.06	.12	.25
115	Billy Harris, NYI	.06	.12	.25
116	Greg Fox, Chi., RC	.06	.12	.25
117	Curt Fraser, Van., RC	.12	.25	.50
118	J. P. Parise, Min., LC	.06	.12	.25
119	Ric Seiling, Buf.	.06	.12	.25
120	Darryl Sittler, Tor.	.35	.75	1.50
121	Rick Lapointe, St. L.	.06	.12	.25
122	Jim Rutherford, Goalie, Det.	.06	.12	.25
123	Mario Tremblay, Mon.	.06	.12	.25
124	Randy Carlyle, Pit.	.25	.50	1.00
125	Bobby Clarke, Phi.	.35	.75	1.50
126	Wayne Thomas, Goalie, NYR, LC	.06	.12	.25
127	Ivan Boldirev, Atl.	.06	.12	.25
128	Ted Bulley, Chi.	.06	.12	.25
129	Dick Redmond, Bos.	.06	.12	.25
130	Clark Gillies, NYI, 1st Team All-Star	.06	.12	.25
131	Checklist 1 (1 - 132)	1.25	2.50	5.00
132	Vaclav Nedomansky, Det.	.06	.12	.25
133	Richard Mulhern, LA	.06	.12	.25
134	Dave Schultz, Buf., LC	.06	.12	.25
135	Guy Lapointe, Mon.	.06	.12	.25
136	Gilles Meloche, Goalie, Min.	.06	.12	.25
137	Randy Pierce, Col., Error	.06	.12	.25
138	Cam Connor, Edm.	.06	.12	.25
139	George Ferguson, Pit.	.06	.12	.25
140	Bill Barber, Phi., 2nd Team All-Star	.12	.25	.50
141	Mike Walton, Chi., LC	.06	.12	.25
142	Wayne Babych, St. L., RC	.12	.25	.50
143	Phil Russell, Atl.	.06	.12	.25
144	Bobby Schmautz, Bos., LC	.06	.12	.25
145	Carol Vadnais, NYR	.06	.12	.25
146	John Tonelli, NYI, RC	1.25	2.50	5.00
147	Peter Marsh, Win., RC	.06	.12	.25
148	Thommie Bergman, Det., LC	.06	.12	.25
149	Rick Martin, Buf.	.06	.12	.25
150	Ken Dryden, Goalie, Mon., 1st Team All-Star, LC	1.00	2.00	4.00
151	Kris Manery, Min.	.06	.12	.25
152	Guy Charron, Wash.	.06	.12	.25
153	Lanny McDonald, Tor.	.25	.50	1.00
154	Ron Stackhouse, Pit.	.06	.12	.25
155	Stan Mikita, Chi., LC	.35	.75	1.50
156	Paul Holmgren, Phi.	.06	.12	.25
157	Perry Miller, Det.	.06	.12	.25
158	Gary Croteau, Col., LC	.06	.12	.25
159	Dave Maloney, NYR	.06	.12	.25
160	Marcel Dionne, LA, 2nd Team All-Star	.60	1.25	2.50

1978 - 79 RECORD BREAKERS

No.	Player	VG	EX	NRMT
161	**Most Goals, Right Wing, Season:** Mike Bossy, NYI	.50	1.00	2.00
162	**Most Points, Rookie, Playoff Series:** Donald Maloney, NYR	.12	.25	.50
163	**Highest Scoring Percentage, Season:** Ulf Nilsson, NYR	.12	.25	.50
164	**Most Career Playoff Goals, Defenceman:** Brad Park, Bos.	.10	.25	.50
165	**Most Points, Period:** Bryan Trottier, NYI	.25	.50	1.00

REGULAR ISSUE

No.	Player	VG	EX	NRMT
166	**Al Hill, Phil., RC**	.06	.12	.25
167	Gary Bromley, Goalie, Van.	.06	.12	.25
168	Don Murdoch, NYR	.06	.12	.25
169	Wayne Merrick, NYI	.06	.12	.25
170	Bob Gainey, Mon.	.20	.35	.75
171	Jim Schoenfeld, Buf.	.06	.12	.25
172	Gregg Sheppard, Pit.	.06	.12	.25
173	**Dan Bolduc, Det., RC, LC**	.06	.12	.25
174	Blake Dunlop, St. L.	.06	.12	.25
175	Gordie Howe, Har., LC	5.50	11.00	22.00
176	Richard Brodeur, Goalie, Que.	.18	.35	.75
177	Tom Younghans, Min.	.06	.12	.25
178	Andre Dupont, Phi.	.06	.12	.25
179	**Eddie Johnstone, NYR, RC**	.06	.12	.25
180	Gilbert Perreault, Buf.	.25	.50	1.00
181	**Bob Lorimer, NYI, RC**	.06	.12	.25
182	John Wensink, Bos.	.06	.12	.25
183	Lee Fogolin, Edm.	.06	.12	.25
184	**Greg Carroll, Det., RC, LC**	.06	.12	.25
185	Bobby Hull, Chi., LC	4.50	9.00	18.00
186	Harold Snepsts, Van.	.10	.25	.50
187	Pete Mahovlich, Pit.	.06	.12	.25
188	Eric Vail, Atl.	.06	.12	.25
189	Phil Myre, Goalie, Phi.	.06	.12	.25
190	Wilf Paiement, Col.	.06	.12	.25
191	**Charlie Simmer, LA, RC**	1.00	2.00	4.00
192	Per-Olov Brasar, Min.	.06	.12	.25
193	Lorne Henning, NYI, LC	.06	.12	.25
194	Don Luce, Buf.	.06	.12	.25
195	Steve Vickers, NYR	.06	.12	.25
196	**Bob Miller, Bos., RC**	.06	.12	.25
197	Mike Palmateer, Goalie, Tor.	.06	.12	.25
198	Nick Libett, Det., LC	.06	.12	.25
199	**Pat Ribble, Chi., RC**	.06	.12	.25
200	Guy Lafleur, Mon., 1st Team All Star	.85	1.75	3.50
201	Mel Bridgman, Phi.	.06	.12	.25
202	**Morris Lukowich, Win., RC**	.06	.12	.25
203	Don Lever, Van.	.06	.12	.25
204	Tom Bladon, Pit.	.06	.12	.25
205	Garry Howatt, NYI	.06	.12	.25
206	**Robert Smith, Min., RC**	1.25	2.50	5.00
207	Craig Ramsay, Buf.	.06	.12	.25
208	Ron Duguay, NYR	.06	.12	.25
209	Gilles Gilbert, Goalie, Bos.	.06	.12	.25
210	Bob MacMillan, Atl.	.06	.12	.25
211	Pierre Mondou, Mon.	.06	.12	.25
212	J. P. Bordeleau, Chi.	.06	.12	.25
213	Reed Larson, Det.	.06	.12	.25
214	Dennis Ververgaert, Phi.	.06	.12	.25
215	Bernie Federko, St. L.	.60	1.25	2.50
216	Mark Howe, Har.	.40	.85	1.75
217	Bob Nystrom, NYI	.06	.12	.25
218	Orest Kindrachuk, Pit.	.06	.12	.25
219	Mike Fidler, Min.	.06	.12	.25
220	Phil Esposito, NYR	.50	1.00	2.00
221	Bill Hajt, Buf.	.06	.12	.25
222	Mark Napier, Mon.	.06	.12	.25
223	Dennis Maruk, Wash.	.06	.12	.25
224	Dennis Polonich, Det.	.06	.12	.25
225	Jean Ratelle, Bos.	.18	.35	.75
226	Bob Dailey, Phi.	.06	.12	.25
227	Alain Daigle, Chi., LC	.06	.12	.25
228	Ian Turnbull, Tor.	.06	.12	.25
229	Jack Valiquette, Col.	.06	.12	.25
230	Mike Bossy, NYI, 2nd Team All-Star	2.25	4.50	9.00
231	Brad Maxwell, Min.	.06	.12	.25
232	David Taylor, LA	1.25	2.50	5.00
233	Pierre Larouche, Mon.	.06	.12	.25
234	**Rod Schutt, Pit., RC**	.06	.12	.25

Topps 1979-80 Issue Card No. 175, Gordie Howe

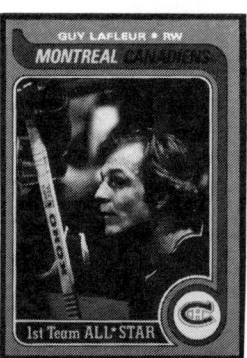

Topps 1979-80 Issue Card No. 200, Guy Lafleur

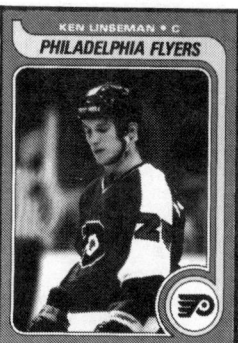

Topps 1979-80 Issue Card No. 241, Ken Linseman

Topps 1979-80 Helmet and Stick Decals Card No. 14 Philadelphia Flyers

1979 - 80 HELMET AND STICK DECALS INSERTS — TOPPS • 223

No.	Player	VG	EX	NRMT
235	Rogatien Vachon, Goalie, Det.	.12	.25	.50
236	**Ryan Walter, Wash., RC**	.30	.60	1.25
237	Checklist 2 (133 - 264)	1.25	2.50	5.00
238	Terry O'Reilly, Bos.	.60	.12	.25
239	Real Cloutier, Que.	.06	.12	.25
240	Anders Hedberg, NYR	.06	.12	.25
241	**Ken Linseman, Phi., RC**	.60	1.25	2.50
242	Billy Smith, Goalie, NYI	.12	.25	.50
243	Rick Chartraw, Mon.	.06	.12	.25

TEAM CARD CHECKLISTS

No.	Team	VG	EX	NRMT
244	Atlanta Flames	.25	.50	1.00
245	Boston Bruins	.25	.50	1.00
246	Buffalo Sabres	.25	.50	1.00
247	Chicago Black Hawks	.25	.50	1.00
248	Colorado Rockies	.25	.50	1.00
249	Detroit Red Wings	.25	.50	1.00
250	Los Angeles Kings	.25	.50	1.00
251	Minnesota North Stars	.25	.50	1.00
252	Montreal Canadiens	.25	.50	1.00
253	New York Islanders	.25	.50	1.00
254	New York Rangers	.25	.50	1.00
255	Philadelphia Flyers	.25	.50	1.00
256	Pittsburgh Penguins	.25	.50	1.00
257	St. Louis Blues	.25	.50	1.00
258	Toronto Maple Leafs	.25	.50	1.00
259	Vancouver Canucks	.25	.50	1.00
260	Washington Capitals	.25	.50	1.00
261	1979 - 80 Entries Edmonton Oilers, Hartford Whalers, Winnipeg Jets, Quebec Nordiques Logos	1.60	3.25	6.50

REGULAR ISSUE

No.	Player	VG	EX	NRMT
262	Jean Hamel, Det.	.06	.12	.25
263	Stan Jonathan, Bos.	.06	.12	.25
264	Russ Anderson, Pit., LC	.10	.25	.50

— 1979 - 80 HELMET AND STICK DECALS INSERTS —

The one card per pack insert contains one team decal and three assorted decals.

Card Size: 2 1/2" X 3 1/2"
Face: Four colour, white border, Team, Name
Back: Four colour on white card stock; Promotional offer
Imprint: * © 1979 TOPPS CHEWING GUM, INC. PRTD IN U.S.A.
Complete Set No.: 21
Complete set Price: 2.50 5.00 10.00
Common Player: .12 .25 .50

No.	Team	VG	EX	NRMT
1	Atlanta Flames	.12	.25	.50
2	Boston Bruins	.12	.25	.50
3	Buffalo Sabres	.12	.25	.50
4	Chicago Black Hawks	.12	.25	.50
5	Colorado Rockies	.12	.25	.50
6	Detroit Red Wings	.12	.25	.50
7	Edmonton Oilers	.12	.25	.50
8	Hartford Whalers	.12	.25	.50
9	Los Angeles Kings	.12	.25	.50
10	Minnesota North Stars	.12	.25	.50
11	Montreal Canadiens	.12	.25	.50
12	New York Islanders	.12	.25	.50
13	New York Rangers	.12	.25	.50
14	Philadelphia Flyers	.12	.25	.50
15	Pittsburgh Penguins	.12	.25	.50
16	Quebec Nordiques	.12	.25	.50
17	St. Louis Blues	.12	.25	.50
18	Toronto Maple Leafs	.12	.25	.50
19	Vancouver Canucks	.12	.25	.50
20	Washington Capitals	.12	.25	.50
21	Winnipeg Jets	.12	.25	.50

Note: For a card to grade higher than EX it must have no wear, no creases, full colour and four square corners.

224 • TOPPS — 1980 - 81 REGULAR ISSUE —
— 1980 - 81 REGULAR ISSUE —

Cards with an American flag on the front designate the player as a member of the Gold Medal winning USA Olympic team (9, 22, 69, 103, 127, 232). The first five cards of the set are record-breaking achievements of the previous season. The face design includes a black scratch section in the form of a puck that reveals the player's name. If the overprint has been removed the card must be graded VG or less. Mint and NRMT cards must have this area intact. Mint cards command a 25% price premium over NRMT cards.

PRICE MOVEMENT OF NRMT SETS

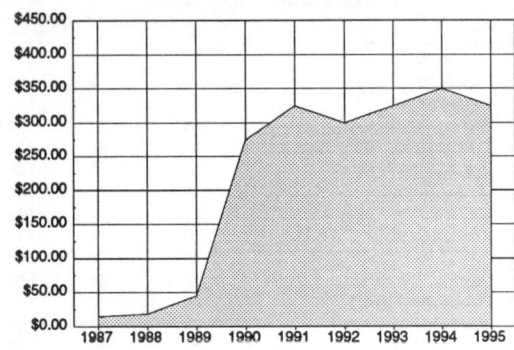

Card Size: 2 1/2" X 3 1/2"
Face: Four colour, white border, Position
Back: Green and yellow on card stock; Number, Resume, Hockey trivia
Imprint: * © 1980 TOPPS CHEWING GUM, INC. PRTD. IN U.S.A. and © NHLPA 1980
or ** © 1980 TOPPS CHEWING GUM. INC. PRTD. IN U.S.A. and © NHLPA 1980

Complete Set No.:	264		
Complete Set Price:	80.00	160.00	325.00
Common Card:	.05	.10	.20
Wax Pack:			25.00
Wax Box: (48 Packs)			800.00
Wax Case: (16 Boxes)			12,500.00

1979-80 RECORD BREAKERS

No.	Player	VG	EX	NRMT
1	Flyers Extend Streak to 35; Longest in Sports History	.12	.25	.50
2	65 Points for Bourque, Record for Rookie Defenseman	1.50	3.00	6.00
3	Wayne Gretzky; Youngest Ever 50-Goal Scorer	5.00	10.00	20.00
4	Simmer Scores in 13th Straight Game, an NHL Record	.10	.20	.40
5	Billy Smith Becomes First Goalie to Score a Goal	.10	.20	.40

REGULAR ISSUE

No.	Player	VG	EX	NRMT
6	Jean Ratelle, Bos., LC	.18	.35	.75
7	Dave Maloney, NYR	.05	.10	.20
8	Phil Myre, Goalie, Phi., LC	.07	.15	.30
9	**Ken Morrow, NYI, RC**	.25	.50	1.00
10	Guy Lafleur, Mon.	.70	1.40	2.75
11	**Bill Derlago, Tor., RC**	.07	.15	.30
12	Douglas Wilson, Chi.	.50	1.00	2.00
13	Craig Ramsay, Buf.	.05	.10	.20
14	Pat Boutette, Har.	.05	.10	.20
15	Eric Vail, Cal.	.05	.10	.20
16	**Red Wings Team Leaders:** Mike Foligno, Goals; D. McCourt, Assists; V. Nedomansky, Power Play Goals, Game Winning Goals	.05	.10	.20
17	Robert Smith, Min.	.25	.50	1.00
18	Rick Kehoe, Pit.	.05	.10	.20
19	Joel Quenneville, Col.	.05	.10	.20
20	Marcel Dionne, LA	.40	.85	1.75
21	Kevin McCarthy, Van.	.05	.10	.20
22	**Jim Craig, Goalie, Bos., RC, LC**	.18	.35	.75
23	Steve Vickers, NYR, LC	.05	.10	.20
24	Ken Linseman, Phi.	.12	.25	.50
25	Mike Bossy, NYI	1.10	2.35	4.75
26	Serge Savard, Mon.	.18	.35	.75
27	**Black Hawks Team Leader:** Grant Mulvey, Goals & Power Play Goals; T. Ruskowski, Assists; T. Lysiak and G. Mulvey, Game Winning Goals	.05	.10	.20

Topps
1980-81 Issue
Card No. 1,
Flyers Extend Streak to 35

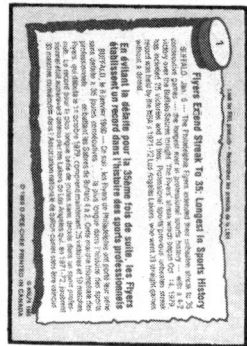

Topps
1980-81 Issue
Card No. 1,
Flyers Extend Streak to 35

Topps
1980-81 Issue
Card No. 3,
Wayne Gretzky

Topps
1980-81 Issue
Card No. 31,
Michael Liut

No.	Player	VG	EX	NRMT
28	Pat Hickey, Tor.	.05	.10	.20
29	Peter Sullivan, Win., LC	.05	.10	.20
30	Blaine Stoughton, Har.	.05	.10	.20
31	**Michael Liut, Goalie, St. L., RC**	1.25	2.50	5.00
32	Blair MacDonald, Edm.	.05	.10	.20
33	Richard Green, Wash.	.05	:10	.20
34	Al MacAdam, Min.	.05	.10	.20
35	Robbie Ftorek, Que.	.05	.10	.20
36	Dick Redmond, Bos.	.05	.10	.20
37	Ron Duguay, NYR	.05	.10	.20
38	**Buffalo Sabres Team Leader:** Danny Gare, Goals, Power Play Goals, Game Winning Goals; G. Perreault, Assists	.05	.10	.20
39	**Brian Propp, Phi., RC**	.50	2.50	5.00
40	Bryan Trottier, NYI	.50	1.00	2.00
41	Rich Preston, Chi.	.05	.10	.20
42	Pierre Mondou, Mon.	.05	.10	.20
43	Reed Larson, Det.	.05	.10	.20
44	George Ferguson, Pit.	.05	.10	.20
45	Guy Chouinard, Atl.	.05	.10	.20
46	Billy Harris, LA	.05	.10	.20
47	Gilles Meloche, Goalie, Min.	.05	.10	.20
48	Blair Chapman, St. L.	.05	.10	.20
49	**Washington Capitals Team Leaders:** Mike Gartner, Goals; R. Picard, Assists; R. Walter; Power Play Goals; R. Edberg, Game Winning Goals	1.00	2.00	4.00
50	Darryl Sittler, Tor.	.25	.50	1.00
51	Rick Martin, Buf., LC	.05	.10	.20
52	Ivan Boldirev, Van.	.05	.10	.20
53	**Craig Norwich, St. L., RC, LC**	.05	.10	.20
54	Dennis Polonich, Det., LC	.05	.10	.20
55	Bobby Clarke, Phi.	.25	.50	1.00
56	Terry O'Reilly, Bos.	.05	.10	.20
57	Carol Vadnais, NYR	.05	.10	.20
58	Bob Gainey, Mon.	.12	.25	.50
59	**Hartford Whalers Team Leaders:** Blaine Stoughton, Goals	.05	.10	.20
60	Billy Smith, Goalie, NYI	.10	.25	.50
61	**Michael O'Connell, Chi., RC**	.07	.15	.30
62	Lanny McDonald, Col.	.25	.50	1.00
63	Lee Fogolin, Edm.	.05	.10	.20
64	**Rocky Saganiuk, Tor., RC**	.05	.10	.20
65	**Rolf Edberg, Wash., RC, LC**	.05	.10	.20
66	Paul Shmyr, Min., LC	.05	.10	.20
67	**Michel Goulet, Que., RC**	3.75	7.50	15.00
68	Dan Bouchard, Goalie, Cal.	.07	.15	.30
69	**Mark Johnson, Pit., RC**	.12	.25	.50
70	Reggie Leach, Phi.	.05	.10	.20
71	**St. Louis Blues Team Leaders:** Bernie Federko, Goals	.07	.15	.30
72	Pete Mahovlich, Det., LC	.05	.10	.20
73	Anders Hedberg, NYR	.05	.10	.20
74	Brad Park, Bos.	.12	.25	.50
75	Clark Gillies, NYI	.05	.10	.20
76	Doug Jarvis, Mon.	.05	.10	.20
77	John Garrett, Goalie, Har.	.05	.10	.20
78	Dave Hutchison, Chi., LC	.05	.10	.20
79	**John Anderson, Tor., RC**	.12	.25	.50
80	Gilbert Perreault, Buf.	.18	.35	.75

ALL STARS
First Team

No.	Player	VG	EX	NRMT
81	Marcel Dionne, LA	.12	.25	.50
82	Guy Lafleur, Mon.	.18	.35	.75
83	Charlie Simmer, LA	.06	.12	.25
84	Larry Robinson, Mon.	.10	.20	.35
85	Borje Salming, Tor.	.07	.15	.30
86	Tony Esposito, Goalie, Chi.	.12	.25	.50

Second Team

No.	Player	VG	EX	NRMT
87	Wayne Gretzky, Edm.	6.00	12.50	25.00
88	Danny Gare, Buf.	.05	.10	.20
89	Steve Shutt, Mon.	.05	.10	.20
90	Barry Beck, NYR	.05	.10	.20
91	Mark Howe, Har.	.07	.15	.30
92	Don Edwards, Goalie, Buf.	.07	.15	.30

1980-81 REGULAR ISSUE — TOPPS • 225

REGULAR ISSUE

No.	Player	VG	EX	NRMT
93	Tom McCarthy, Min., RC	.10	.20	.40
94	**Boston Bruins Team Leaders:** P. McNab & R. Middleton, Goals; R. Middleton, Assists; J. Ratelle, Power Play Goals; P. McNab, Game Winning Goals	.07	.15	.30
95	Mike Palmateer, Goalie, Wash.	.07	.15	.30
96	Jim Schoenfeld, Buf.	.05	.10	.20
97	Jordy Douglas, Har.	.05	.10	.20
98	**Keith Brown, , Chi., RC**	.12	.25	.50
99	Dennis Ververgaert, Phi.	.05	.10	.20
100	Phil Esposito, NYR, LC	.35	.75	1.50
101	Jack Brownschidle, St. L.	.05	.10	.20
102	Bob Nystrom, NYI	.05	.10	.20
103	**Steve Christoff, Min., RC**	.07	.15	.30
104	Rob Palmer, LA, LC	.05	.10	.20
105	David Williams, Van.	.05	.10	.20
106	**Calgary Flames Team Leaders:** Kent Nilsson, Goals	.05	.10	.20
107	Morris Lukowich, Win.	.05	.10	.20
108	Jack Valiquette, Col., LC	.05	.10	.20
109	**Richard Dunn, Buf., RC**	.05	.10	.20
110	Rogatien Vachon, Goalie, Bos.	.10	.20	.35
111	Mark Napier, Mon.	.05	.10	.20
112	Gordon Roberts, Har.	.05	.10	.20
113	Stan Jonathan, Bos.	.05	.10	.20
114	Brett Callighen, Edm.	.05	.10	.20
115	Rick MacLeish, Phi.	.05	.10	.20
116	Ulf Nilsson, NYR	.05	.10	.20
117	**Pittsburgh Penguins Team Leaders:** Rick Kehoe, Goals	.05	.10	.20
118	Dan Maloney, Tor.	.05	.10	.20
119	Terry Ruskowski, Chi.	.05	.10	.20
120	Denis Potvin, NYI	.25	.50	1.00
121	Wayne Stephenson, Goalie, Wash., LC	.07	.15	.30
122	Rich LeDuc, Que., LC	.05	.10	.20
123	Checklist 1 (1 - 132)	.75	1.50	3.00
124	Don Lever, Ca.	.05	.10	.20
125	Jim Rutherford, Goalie, Det., LC	.07	.15	.30
126	**Ray Allison, Har., RC**	.05	.10	.20
127	**Michael Ramsey, Buf., RC**	.50	1.00	2.00
128	**Vancouver Canucks Team Leaders:** Stanley Smyl	.05	.10	.20
129	**Alan Secord, Bos., RC**	.20	1.00	2.00
130	Denis Herron, Goalie, Mon.	.10	.20	.40
131	Bob Dailey, Phi.	.05	.10	.20
132	Dean Talafous, NYR	.05	.10	.20
133	Ian Turnbull, Tor.	.05	.10	.20
134	Ron Sedlbauer, Chi.	.05	.10	.20
135	Tom Bladon, Pit., LC	.05	.10	.20
136	Bernie Federko, St. L.	.30	.60	1.25
137	David Taylor, LA	.35	.75	1.50
138	Bob Lorimer, NYI	.05	.10	.20
139	**Minnesota North Stars Team Leaders:** MacAdam and Payne, Goals	.07	.15	.30
140	**Raymond Bourque, Bos., RC**	16.00	32.50	65.00
141	Glen Hanlon, Goalie, Van.	.10	.20	.35
142	Willy Lindstrom, Win.	.05	.10	.20
143	Mike Rogers, Har.	.05	.10	.20
144	**Anthony McKegney, Buf., RC**	.12	.25	.50
145	Behn Wilson, Phi.	.05	.10	.20
146	Lucien DeBlois, Col.	.05	.10	.20
147	Dave Burrows, Tor., LC	.05	.10	.20
148	Paul Woods, Det.	.05	.10	.20
149	**New York Rangers Team Leaders:** Phil Esposito, Goals	.18	.35	.75
150	Tony Esposito, Goalie, Chi.	.25	.50	1.00
151	Pierre Larouche, Mon.	.05	.10	.20
152	Brad Maxwell, Min.	.05	.10	.20
153	Stan Weir, Edm.	.05	.10	.20
154	Ryan Walter, Wash.	.07	.15	.30
155	Dale Hoganson, Que.	.05	.10	.20
156	**Anders Kallur, NYI, RC**	.07	.15	.30
157	**Paul Reinhart, Cal., RC**	.35	.75	1.50
158	Greg Millen, Goalie, Pit.	.25	.50	1.00
159	Ric Seiling, Buf.	.05	.10	.20
160	Mark Howe, Har.	.18	.35	.75

Topps 1980-81 Issue Card No.86, Tony Esposito

Topps 1980-81 Issue Card No.127, Michael Ramsey

Topps 1980-81 Issue Card No.140, Raymond Bourque

Topps 1980-81 Issue Card No.161, Goal Leaders

1979-80 LEAGUE LEADERS

No.	Players	VG	EX	NRMT
161	**Goal Leaders:** D. Gare, Buf.; C. Simmer, LA; B. Stoughton, Har.	.12	.25	.50
162	**Assist Leaders:** W. Gretzky, Edm.; M. Dionne, LA; G. Lafleur, Mon.	2.50	5.00	10.00
163	**Scoring Leaders:** M. Dionne, LA; W. Gretzky, Edm.; G. Lafleur, Mon.	2.50	5.00	10.00
164	**Penalty Minute Leaders:** J. Mann, Win.; D. Williams, Tor./Van.; P. Holmgren, Phi.	.12	.25	.50
165	**Power Play Goal Leaders:** C. Simmer, LA; M. Dionne, LA; D. Gare, Buf; S. Shutt, Mon.; D. Sittler, Tor.	.12	.25	.50
166	**Goals Against Avg. Leaders:** B. Sauve, Buf.; D. Herron, Mon.; D. Edwards, Buf.	.10	.20	.40
167	**Game-Winning Goal Leaders:** D. Gare, Buf.; P. McNab, Bos.; B. Stoughton, Har.	.10	.20	.40
168	**Shutout Leaders:** T. Esposito, Chi.; G. Cheevers, Bos.; B. Sauve, Buf.; R. Vachon, Det.	.25	.50	1.00

REGULAR ISSUE

No.	Player	VG	EX	NRMT
169	**Perry Turnbull, St. L., RC**	.07	.15	.30
170	Barry Beck, NYR	.05	.10	.20
171	**Los Angeles Kings Team Leaders:** Charlie Simmer, Goals	.10	.20	.40
172	Paul Holmgren, Phi.	.05	.10	.20
173	Willie Huber, Det.	.05	.10	.20
174	Tim Young, Min.	.05	.10	.20
175	Gilles Gilbert, Goalie, Det.	.07	.15	.30
176	**Dave Christian, Win., RC**	.75	1.50	3.00
177	**Lars Lindgren, Van., RC**	.05	.10	.20
178	Real Cloutier, Que.	.05	.10	.20
179	**Laurie Boschman, Tor., RC**	.15	.30	.60
180	Steve Shutt, Mon.	.05	.10	.20
181	Bob Murray, Chi.	.05	.10	.20
182	**Edmonton Oilers Team Leaders:** Wayne Gretzky, Goals	3.75	7.50	15.00
183	John Van Boxmeer, Buf.	.05	.10	.20
184	Nick Fotiu, NYR	.05	.10	.20
185	Mike McEwen, Col.	.05	.10	.20
186	Greg Malone, Pit.	.05	.10	.20
187	**Mike Foligno, Det., RC**	1.00	2.00	4.00
188	**Dave Langevin, NYI, RC**	.05	.10	.20
189	Mel Bridgman, Phi.	.05	.10	.20
190	John Davidson, Goalie, NYR	.07	.15	.30
191	Mike Milbury, Bos.	.05	.10	.20
192	Ron Zanussi, Min.	.05	.10	.20
193	**Toronto Maple Leafs Team Leaders:** Darryl Sittler, Goals	.10	.20	.40
194	John Marks, Chi.	.05	.10	.20
195	**Mike Gartner, Wash., RC**	10.00	20.00	40.00
196	Dave Lewis, LA	.05	.10	.20
197	**Kent Nilsson, Cal., RC**	.50	1.00	2.00
198	Rick Ley, Har., LC	.05	.10	.20
199	Derek Smith, Buf.	.05	.10	.20
200	Bill Barber, Phi.	.10	.20	.35
201	Guy Lapointe, Mon.	.05	.10	.20
202	Vaclav Nedomansky, Det.	.05	.10	.20
203	Don Murdoch, Edm., LC	.05	.10	.20
204	**New York Islanders Team Leaders:** Mike Bossy, Goals	.25	.50	1.00
205	Pierre Hamel, Goalie, Win.	.05	.10	.20
206	**Mike Eaves, Min., RC**	.05	.10	.20
207	Doug Halward, LA	.05	.10	.20
208	**Stanley Smyl, Van., RC**	.18	.35	.75
209	**Mike Zuke, St. L., RC**	.05	.10	.20
210	Borje Salming, Tor.	.10	.20	.40
211	Walt Tkaczuk, NYR, LC	.05	.10	.20
212	Grant Mulvey, Chi.	.05	.10	.20
213	**George (Rob) Ramage, Col., RC**	.50	1.00	2.00
214	Tom Rowe, Har.	.05	.10	.20
215	Don Edwards, Goalie, Buf.	.07	.15	.30
216	**Montreal Canadiens Team Leaders:** Leaders: Lafleur and Larouche, Goals; G. Lafleur, Assists; S. Shutt, Power Play Goals; G. Lafleur, Y. Lambert, P. Larouche, Game Win. Goals	.25	.50	1.00
217	Dan Labraaten, Det.	.05	.10	.20
218	Glen Sharpley, Min.	.05	.10	.20
219	Stefan Persson, NYI	.05	.10	.20

226 • TOPPS — 1980 - 81 TEAM POSTERS —

No.	Player	VG	EX	NRMT
220	Peter McNab, Bos.	.05	.10	.20
221	Doug Hicks, Edm.	.05	.10	.20
222	**Bengt-ake Gustafsson, Wash., RC**	.10	.20	.35
223	Michel Dion, Goalie, Que.	.05	.10	.20
224	Jimmy Watson, Phi.	.05	.10	.20
225	Wilf Paiement, Tor.	.05	.10	.20
226	Phil Russell, Cal.	.05	.10	.20
227	**Winnipeg Jets Team Leaders:** Morris Lukowich, Goals	.05	.10	.20
228	Ron Stackhouse, Pit.	.05	.10	.20
229	Ted Bulley, Chi.	.05	.10	.20
230	Larry Robinson, Mon.	.18	.35	.75
231	Donald Maloney, NYR	.05	.10	.20
232	**Rob McClanahan, Buf., RC**	.05	.10	.20
233	Al Sims, Har.	.05	.10	.20
234	Errol Thompson, Det., LC	.05	.10	.20
235	Glenn Resch, Goalie, NYI	.05	.10	.20
236	Bob Miller, Bos., LC	.05	.10	.20
237	Gary Sargent, Min., LC	.05	.10	.20
238	**Quebec Nordiques Team Leaders:** Real Cloutier, Goals	.15	.30	.60
239	Rene Robert, Col.	.05	.10	.20
240	Charlie Simmer, LA	.35	.75	1.50
241	Thomas Gradin, Van.	.06	.12	.25
242	**Richard Vaive, Tor., RC**	.60	1.25	2.50
243	**Ronald Wilson, Win., RC**	.12	.25	.50
244	Brian Sutter, St. L.	.25	.50	1.00
245	Dale McCourt, Det.	.05	.10	.20
246	Yvon Lambert, Mon.	.05	.10	.20
247	Tom Lysiak, Chi.	.05	.10	.20
248	Ronald Greschner, NYR	.05	.10	.20
249	Flyers Leader, Reggie Leach	.15	.30	.60
250	Wayne Gretzky, Edm.	27.50	55.00	110.00
251	Rick Middleton, Bos.	.10	.20	.40
252	Al Smith, Goalie, Har., LC	.07	.15	.30
253	Fred Barrett, Min., LC	.05	.10	.20
254	Butch Goring, NYI	.05	.10	.20
255	Robert Picard, Tor.	.05	.10	.20
256	Marc Tardif, Que.	.05	.10	.20
257	Checklist 2 (133 - 264)	.75	1.50	3.00
258	Barry Long, Det.	.05	.10	.20
259	**Colorado Rockies Team Leaders:** Rene Robert, Goals	.05	.10	.20
260	Danny Gare, Buf.	.05	.10	.20
261	Rejean Houle, Mon.	.05	.10	.20

1979-80 STANLEY CUP PLAYOFFS

No.	Teams	VG	EX	NRMT
262	**Semi-finals:** Islanders defeat Sabres in Six	.10	.20	.40
263	**Semi-finals:** Flyers Skate Past North Stars	.10	.20	.40
264	**Stanley Cup Finals:** Islanders Win Their 1st Stanley Cup	.18	.35	.75

U.S.A. OLYMPIC TEAM GOLD MEDAL WINNERS

U.S. Flag on Face of Card

- 9 Ken Morrow, New York Islanders
- 22 Jim Craig, Boston Bruins
- 69 Mark Johnson, Pittsburgh Penguins
- 103 Steve Christoff, Minnesota North Stars
- 127 Mike Ramsey, Buffalo Sabres
- 176 Dave Christian, Winnipeg Jets
- 232 Rob McClanahan, Buffalo Sabres

Note: *The Charlton Standard Catalogue of Hockey Cards* arranges cards in their issue date order. This means the first date a manufacturer issues a card set determines the sequence of the manufacturer in the Standard Catalogue. In this manner the historical importance of early cards is maintained. See the last page of this catalogue for an alphabetical index of issuers.

Topps
1980-81 Team Posters
Poster No. 4,
Boston Bruins

Topps
1980-81 Team Posters
Poster No. 9,
Minnesota North Stars

Topps
1981-82 Issue
Card No.1,
Dave Babych

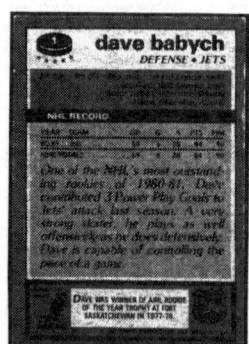

Topps
1981-82 Issue
Card No.1,
Dave Babych

— 1980 - 81 TEAM POSTERS —

The team posters were folded twice and inserted into the Topps wax of 1981-82. Each NHL team for the 1979-80 season is featured. Posters are numbered _ of 16.

Poster Size:
Face: Four colour, white border on paper stock; Team name, Number
Back: Blank
Imprint: © 1980 TOPPS CHEWING GUM, INC. PRTD. IN U.S.A.
and © 1980 NHLPA
Complete Set No.: 16
Complete Set Price: 1.00 5.00 10.00
Common Team: .08 .35 .75

No.	Team	VG	EX	NRMT
1	New York Islanders	.08	.35	.75
2	New York Rangers	.08	.35	.75
3	Philadelphia Flyers	.08	.35	.75
4	Boston Bruins	.08	.35	.75
5	Hartford Whalers	.08	.35	.75
6	Buffalo Sabres	.08	.35	.75
7	Chicago Blackhawks	.08	.35	.75
8	Detroit Red Wings	.08	.35	.75
9	Minnesota North Stars	.08	.35	.75
10	Toronto Maple Leafs	.08	.35	.75
11	Montreal Canadiens	.08	.35	.75
12	Colorado Rockies	.08	.35	.75
13	Los Angeles Kings	.08	.35	.75
14	Vancouver Canucks	.08	.35	.75
15	St. Louis Blues	.08	.35	.75
16	Washington Captials	.08	.35	.75

Note: Cards in this catalogue are listed in issue date order and then alphabetically by manufacturer. See the last page of this catalogue for an alphabetical index of issuers.

— 1981 - 82 REGULAR ISSUE —

The distribution concept of this set was to test the regional preferences of cards. Cards 1-66 were distributed normally, but two regional sub-sets ("east" and "west") were produced, with the cards in the sub-sets favouring the region where they were distributed. Cards 1 to 66 are double printed. Mint cards will command a price premium of 25% over NRMT cards.

PRICE MOVEMENT OF NRMT SETS

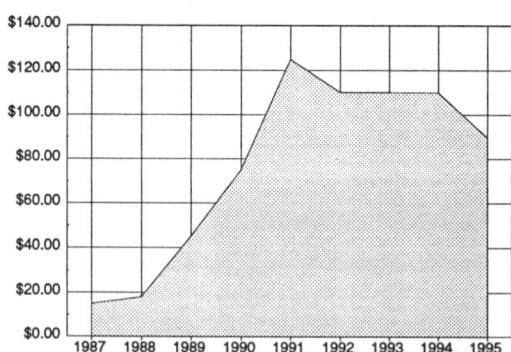

Card Size: 2 1/2" X 3 1/2"
Front: Four colour, white border; Team logo
Back: Blue and black on card stock; Number, Resume, Hockey trivia
Imprint: A © 1981 TOPPS CHEWING GUM, INC. PRTD. IN U.S.A.
and © 1981 NHLPA or
E * © 1981 TOPPS CHEWING GUM, INC. PRTD. IN U.S.A.
and © 1981 NHLPA or
W * © 1981 TOPPS CHEWING GUM, INC. PRTD. IN U.S.A.
and © 1981 NHLPA
Complete Set No.: 198
Complete Set Price: 20.00 45.00 90.00
Cards 1 to 66
Common Player: Cards 67E to 132E .02 .05 .10
Common Player: Cards 67W to 132W .04 .08 .15
Common Player: .06 .12 .25
Wax Pack: (13 Cards) 9.00
Wax Box: (36 Packs) 250.00
Wax Case: (16 Boxes) 3,750.00

No.	Player	VG	EX	NRMT
1	Dave Babych, Win., RC	.12	.25	.50

1981-82 REGULAR ISSUE — TOPPS

No.	Player	VG	EX	NRMT
2	Bill Barber, Phi.	.05	.10	.20
3	Barry Beck, NYR	.02	.05	.10
4	Mike Bossy, NYI	.35	.75	1.50
5	Ray Bourque, Bos.	1.00	2.00	4.00
6	Guy Chouinard, Cal.	.02	.05	.10
7	Dave Christian, Win.	.02	.05	.10
8	Bill Derlago, Tor.	.02	.05	.10
9	Marcel Dionne, LA	.18	.35	.75
10	Brian Engblom, Mon.	.02	.05	.10
11	Tony Esposito, Goalie, Chi.	.15	.30	.60
12	Bernie Federko, St. L.	.10	.20	.35
13	Bob Gainey, Mon.	.02	.05	.10
14	Danny Gare, Buf.	.02	.05	.10
15	Thomas Gradin, Van.	.02	.05	.10
16	Wayne Gretzky, Edm.	3.50	7.00	14.00
17	Rick Kehoe, Pit.	.02	.05	.10
18	**Jari Kurri, Edm., RC**	**1.25**	**2.50**	**5.00**
19	Guy Lafleur, Mon.	.25	.50	1.00
20	Michael Liut, Goalie, St. L.	.10	.20	.40
21	Dale McCourt, Det.	.02	.05	.10
22	Rick Middleton, Bos.	.06	.12	.25
23	Mark Napier, Mon.	.02	.05	.10
24	Kent Nilsson, Cal.	.02	.05	.10
25	Wilf Paiement, Tor.	.02	.05	.10
26	Willi Plett, Cal.	.02	.05	.10
27	Denis Potvin, NYI	.12	.25	.50
28	Paul Reinhart, Cal.	.02	.05	.10
29	Jacques Richard, Que.	.02	.05	.10
30	**Pat Riggin, Goalie, Cal., RC**	**.06**	**.12**	**.25**
31	Larry Robinson, Mon.	.10	.20	.35
32	Mike Rogers, Har.	.02	.05	.10
33	Borje Salming, Tor.	.07	.15	.25
34	Steve Shutt, Mon.	.07	.15	.25
35	Charlie Simmer, LA	.07	.15	.25
36	Darryl Sittler, Tor.	.12	.25	.50
37	Robert Smith, Min.	.07	.15	.25
38	Stanley Smyl, Van.	.02	.05	.10
39	**Peter Stastny, Que., RC**	**1.00**	**2.00**	**4.00**
40	David Taylor, LA	.12	.25	.50
41	Bryan Trottier, NYI	.18	.35	.75
42	Ian Turnbull, Tor., LC	.02	.05	.10
43	Eric Vail, Cal.	.02	.05	.10
44	Richard Vaive, Tor.	.10	.20	.40
45	Behn Wilson, Phi.	.02	.05	.10

1980-81 TEAM LEADERS

No.	Team/Player	VG	EX	NRMT
46	**Boston Bruins:** Rick Middleton	.03	.07	.15
47	**Buffalo Sabres:** Danny Gare	.05	.10	.20
48	**Calgary Flames:** Kent Nilsson	.05	.10	.20
49	**Chicago Black Hawks:** Ton Lysiak	.05	.10	.20
50	**Colorado Rockies:** Lanny McDonald	.05	.15	.25
51	**Detroit Red Wings:** Dale McCourt	.05	.10	.20
52	**Edmonton Oilers:** Wayne Gretzky	.75	1.50	3.00
53	**Hartford Whalers:** Mike Rogers	.05	.10	.20
54	**Los Angeles Kings:** Marcel Dionne	.07	.15	.30
55	**Minnesota North Stars:** Robert Smith	.05	.10	.20
56	**Montreal Canadiens:** Steve Shutt	.07	.15	.30
57	**New York Islanders:** Mike Bossy	.07	.15	.30
58	**New York Rangers:** Anders Hedberg	.05	.10	.20
59	**Philadelphia Flyers:** Bill Barber	.05	.10	.20
60	**Pittsburgh Penguins:** Rick Kehoe	.05	.10	.20
61	**Quebec Nordiques:** Peter Stastny	.07	.15	.30
62	**St. Louis Blues:** Bernie Federko	.05	.10	.20
63	**Toronto Maple Leafs:** Wilf Paiement	.05	.10	.20
64	**Vancouver Canucks:** Thomas Gradin	.05	.10	.20
65	**Washington Capitals:** Dennis Maruk	.05	.10	.20
66	**Winnipeg Jets:** Dave Christian	.05	.10	.20

EASTERN DISTRIBUTION
BOSTON BRUINS

No.	Player	VG	EX	NRMT
67	Dwight Foster	.04	.08	.15
68	**Stephen Kasper, RC**	**.25**	**.50**	**1.00**
69	Peter McNab	.04	.08	.15
70	Michael O'Connell	.04	.08	.15
71	Terry O'Reilly	.05	.10	.20
72	Brad Park	.10	.20	.35
73	Dick Redmond, LC	.04	.08	.15
74	Rogatien Vachon, Goalie	.10	.20	.40

Topps
1981-82 Issue
Card No. 18,
Jari Kurri

Topps
1981-82 Issue
Card No. 39,
Peter Stastny

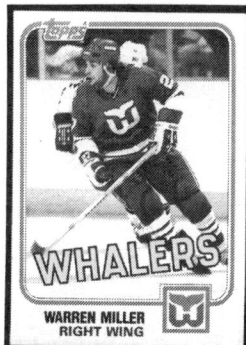

Topps
1981-82 Issue
Eastern Distribution,
Card No. 84, Warren Miller

Topps
1981-82 Issue
Eastern Distribution
Card No. 113, Paul Gardner

BUFFALO SABRES

No.	Player	VG	EX	NRMT
75	Don Edwards, Goalie	.04	.08	.15
76	Anthony McKegney	.04	.08	.15
77	Bob Sauve, Goalie	.04	.08	.15
78	Andre Savard	.04	.08	.15
79	Derek Smith	.04	.08	.15
80	John Van Boxmeer	.04	.08	.15

PITTSBURGH PENGUINS

No.	Player	VG	EX	NRMT
81	Pat Boutette	.04	.08	.15

HARTFORD WHALERS

No.	Player	VG	EX	NRMT
82	Mark Howe	.05	.20	.40
83	Dave Keon, LC	.06	.12	.25
84	**Warren Miller, RC**	**.04**	**.08**	**.15**
85	Al Sims, LC	.04	.08	.15
86	Blaine Stoughton	.04	.08	.15

NEW YORK ISLANDERS

No.	Player	VG	EX	NRMT
87	Bob Bourne	.04	.08	.15
88	Clark Gillies	.04	.08	.15
89	Butch Goring	.04	.08	.15
90	Anders Kallur	.04	.08	.15
91	Ken Morrow	.04	.08	.15
92	Stefan Persson	.04	.08	.15
93	Billy Smith, Goalie	.06	.12	.25

NEW YORK RANGERS

No.	Player	VG	EX	NRMT
94	**Michael Allison, RC**	**.04**	**.08**	**.15**
95	John Davidson, Goalie, LC	.04	.08	.15
96	Ron Duguay	.04	.08	.15
97	Ronald Greschner	.04	.08	.15
98	Anders Hedberg	.04	.08	.15
99	Eddie Johnstone	.04	.08	.15
100	Dave Maloney	.04	.08	.15
101	Donald Maloney	.04	.08	.15
102	Ulf Nilsson, LC	.04	.08	.15

PHILADELPHIA FLYERS

No.	Player	VG	EX	NRMT
103	Bobby Clarke	.05	.10	.20
104	Bob Dailey, LC	.04	.08	.15
105	Paul Holmgren	.04	.08	.15
106	Reggie Leach	.04	.08	.15
107	Ken Linseman	.04	.08	.15

HARTFORD WHALERS

No.	Player	VG	EX	NRMT
108	Rick MacLeish	.04	.08	.15

PHILADELPHIA FLYERS

No.	Player	VG	EX	NRMT
109	Peter Peeters, Goalie	.18	.35	.75
110	Brian Propp	.18	.35	.75

CHECKLIST

No.	Checklist	VG	EX	NRMT
111	Checklist 1 (1 - 132)	.50	1.00	2.00

PITTSBURGH PENGUINS

No.	Player	VG	EX	NRMT
112	Randy Carlyle	.04	.08	.15
113	Paul Gardner	.04	.08	.15
114	Peter Lee, LC	.04	.08	.15

HARTFORD WHALERS

No.	Player	VG	EX	NRMT
115	Greg Millen, Goalie	.07	.15	.25

PITTSBURGH PENGUINS

No.	Player	VG	EX	NRMT
116	Rod Schutt, LC	.04	.08	.15

TOPPS — 1984-85 REGULAR ISSUE

WASHINGTON CAPITALS

No.	Player	VG	EX	NRMT
117	Michael Gartner	1.25	2.50	5.00
118	Richard Green	.04	.08	.15
119	Bob Kelly, LC	.04	.08	.15
120	Dennis Maruk	.04	.08	.15
121	Mike Palmateer, Goalie	.06	.12	.25
122	Ryan Walter	.04	.08	.15

SUPER ACTION

No.	Player	VG	EX	NRMT
123	Bill Barber, Phi.	.04	.08	.15
124	Barry Beck, NYR	.04	.08	.15
125	Mike Bossy, NYI	.25	.50	1.00
126	Ray Bourque, Bos.	.50	1.00	2.00
127	Danny Gare, Buf.	.04	.08	.15
128	Rick Kehoe, Pit.	.04	.08	.15
129	Rick Middleton, Bos.	.04	.08	.15
130	Denis Potvin, NYI	.10	.20	.40
131	Mike Rogers, Har.	.04	.08	.15
132	Bryan Trottier, NYI	.12	.25	.50

WESTERN DISTRIBUTION
CHICAGO BLACK HAWKS

No.	Player	VG	EX	NRMT
67	Keith Brown	.06	.12	.25
68	Ted Bulley	.06	.12	.25
69	Tim Higgins, RC	.06	.12	.25
70	Reg Kerr	.06	.12	.25
71	Tom Lysiak	.06	.12	.25
72	Grant Mulvey	.06	.12	.25
73	Bob Murray	.06	.12	.25
74	Terry Ruskowski	.06	.12	.25
75	Denis Savard, RC	3.75	7.50	15.00
76	Glen Sharpley	.06	.12	.25
77	Darryl Sutter, RC	.25	.50	1.00
78	Douglas Wilson	.25	.50	1.00

WINNIPEG JETS

No.	Player	VG	EX	NRMT
79	Lucien DeBlois	.06	.12	.25

COLORADO ROCKIES

No.	Player	VG	EX	NRMT
80	Paul Gagne, RC	.06	.12	.25
81	Merlin Malinowski, RC	.06	.12	.25
82	Lanny McDonald	.12	.25	.50
83	Joel Quenneville	.06	.12	.25
84	George (Rob) Ramage	.09	.18	.35
85	Glenn Resch, Goalie	.06	.12	.25
86	Steve Tambellini	.06	.12	.25

DETROIT RED WINGS

No.	Player	VG	EX	NRMT
87	Mike Foligno	.10	.20	.40
88	Gilles Gilbert, Goalie	.06	.12	.25
89	Willie Huber	.06	.12	.25
90	Mark Kirton, RC	.06	.12	.25
91	James Korn RC	.06	.12	.25
92	Reed Larson	.06	.12	.25
93	Gary McAdam	.06	.12	.25
94	Vaclav Nedomansky, LC	.06	.12	.25
95	John Ogrodnick	.15	.30	.60

LOS ANGELES KINGS

No.	Player	VG	EX	NRMT
96	Billy Harris	.06	.12	.25
97	Jerry Korab, LC	.06	.12	.25
98	Mario Lessard, Goalie	.07	.15	.30

TORONTO MAPLE LEAFS

No.	Player	VG	EX	NRMT
99	Don Luce, LC	.06	.12	.25

LOS ANGELES KINGS

No.	Player	VG	EX	NRMT
100	Lawrence Murphy, RC	1.75	3.50	7.00
101	Mike Murphy, LC	.06	.12	.25

Topps
1981-82 Issue
Western Distribution
Card No. 75, Denis Savard

Topps
1981-82 Issue
Western Distribution
Card No. 81, Merlin Malinowski

Topps
1984-85 Issue
Card No. 1,
Raymond Bourque

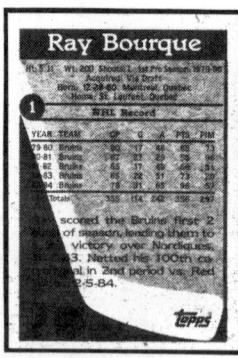

Topps
1984-85 Issue
Card No. 1,
Raymond Bourque

MINNESOTA NORTH STARS

No.	Player	VG	EX	NRMT
102	Kent-Erik Andersson	.06	.12	.25
103	Don Beaupre, RC, Goalie	.75	1.50	3.00
104	Steve Christoff	.06	.12	.25
105	Dino Ciccarelli, RC	2.50	5.00	10.00
106	Craig Hartsburg	.06	.12	.25
107	Al MacAdam	.06	.12	.25
108	Tom McCarthy	.06	.12	.25
109	Gilles Meloche, Goalie	.07	.15	.25
110	Steve Payne	.06	.12	.25
111	Gordon Roberts	.06	.12	.25
112	Greg Smith	.06	.12	.25
113	Tim Young	.06	.12	.25

ST. LOUIS BLUES

No.	Player	VG	EX	NRMT
114	Wayne Babych	.06	.12	.25
115	Blair Chapman, LC	.06	.12	.25
116	Tony Currie	.06	.12	.25
117	Blake Dunlop	.06	.12	.25
118	Ed Kea, LC	.06	.12	.25
119	Rick Lapointe	.06	.12	.25

CHECKLIST

No.	Checklist	VG	EX	NRMT
120	Checklist 2 (1 - 132)	.75	1.50	3.00

ST. LOUIS BLUES

No.	Player	VG	EX	NRMT
121	Jorgen Pettersson, RC	.06	.12	.25
122	Brian Sutter	.12	.25	.50
123	Perry Turnbull	.06	.12	.25
124	Mike Zuke	.06	.12	.25

SUPER ACTION

No.	Player	VG	EX	NRMT
125	Marcel Dionne, LA	.12	.25	.50
126	Tony Esposito, Goalie, Chi.	.12	.25	.50
127	Bernie Federko, St. L.	.10	.20	.40
128	Michael Liut, Goalie, St. L.	.10	.20	.40
129	Dale McCourt, Det.	.06	.12	.25
130	Charlie Simmer, LA	.05	.10	.15
131	Robert Smith, Min.	.07	.15	.30
132	David Taylor, LA	.15	.30	.60

— 1982 TO 1984 —

Topps did not issue regular cards during the 1982-83 and 1983-84 seasons.

— 1984 - 85 REGULAR ISSUE —

After missing two seasons, Topps resumed with a 165-card set focusing primarily on American teams. The set features all-star selections for the season. One third of the cards were single printed. These are marked, SP.

PRICE MOVEMENT OF NRMT SETS

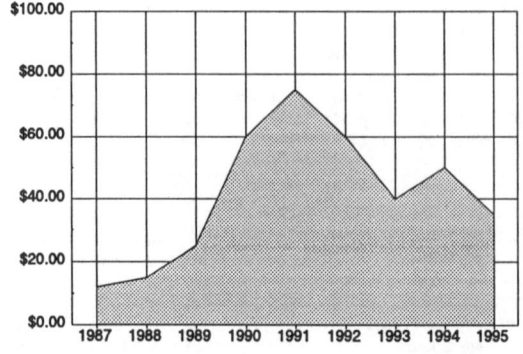

1984 - 85 REGULAR ISSUE — TOPPS • 229

Card Size: 2 1/2" X 3 1/2"
Face: Four colour, white border, Position
Back: Purple and mauve on card stock; Number, Resume
Imprint: PRINTED IN U.S.A. * © 1984 TOPPS CHEWING GUM, INC.
and © 1984 NHLPA or
PRINTED IN U.S.A. * * © 1984 TOPPS CHEWING GUM, INC.
and © 1984 NHLPA

Complete Set No.: 165
Complete Set Price: 10.00 20.00 35.00
Common Card: .02 .05 .10
Wax Pack: (12 Cards) 8.00
Wax Box: (36 Packs) 250.00
Wax Case: (16 Boxes) 3,750.00

BOSTON BRUINS

No.	Player	VG	EX	NRMT
1	Raymond Bourque	.25	.50	1.00
2	Keith Crowder, SP	.02	.10	.15
3	Tom Fergus	.02	.05	.10
4	**Doug Keans, Goalie, RC**	**.02**	**.05**	**.10**
5	Gordon Kluzak, SP	.03	.07	.15
6	Michael Krushelnyski, SP	.06	.12	.25
7	**Nevin Markwart, RC**	**.02**	**.05**	**.10**
8	Rick Middleton	.02	.05	.10
9	Michael O'Connell	.02	.05	.10
10	Terry O'Reilly, LC, SP	.03	.07	.15
11	Barry Pederson	.02	.05	.10
12	Peter Peeters, Goalie	.02	.05	.10

BUFFALO SABRES

No.	Player	VG	EX	NRMT
13	**David Andreychuk, RC, SP**	**2.00**	**4.00**	**8.00**
14	**Tom Barrasso, Goalie, RC**	**1.00**	**2.00**	**4.00**
15	Real Cloutier, LC, SP	.02	.10	.15
16	Mike Foligno	.02	.05	.10
17	Bill Hajt, SP	.02	.10	.15
18	Phil Housley, SP	.50	1.00	2.00
19	Gilbert Perreault	.06	.12	.25
20	Larry Playfair, SP	.03	.07	.15
21	Craig Ramsay, SP	.03	.07	.15
22	Michael Ramsey, SP	.03	.07	.15
23	Lindy Ruff, SP	.03	.07	.15

CALGARY FLAMES

No.	Player	VG	EX	NRMT
24	Ed Beers	.02	.05	.10
25	Rejean Lemelin, Goalie, SP	.05	.10	.20
26	Lanny McDonald	.05	.10	.20

CHICAGO BLACK HAWKS

No.	Player	VG	EX	NRMT
27	Murray Bannerman, Goalie	.02	.05	.10
28	Keith Brown, SP	.03	.07	.15
29	Curt Fraser	.02	.05	.10
30	Steve Larmer	.35	.75	1.50
31	Tom Lysiak	.02	.05	.10
32	Bob Murray	.02	.05	.10
33	**Jack O'Callahan, RC, SP**	**.03**	**.07**	**.15**
34	Rich Preston	.02	.05	.10
35	Denis Savard	.15	.30	.60
36	Darryl Sutter	.02	.05	.10
37	Douglas Wilson	.02	.05	.10

DETROIT RED WINGS

No.	Player	VG	EX	NRMT
38	Ivan Boldirev	.02	.05	.10
39	Colin Campbell, LC, SP	.03	.07	.15
40	Ron Duguay, SP	.03	.07	.15
41	Dwight Foster, SP	.03	.07	.15
42	Danny Gare, SP	.03	.07	.15
43	Eddie Johnstone, LC	.02	.05	.10
44	Reed Larson, SP	.03	.07	.15
45	Ed Mio, Goalie, LC, SP	.03	.07	.15
46	John Ogrodnick	.02	.05	.10
47	Brad Park, LC	.03	.07	.15
48	**Gregory Stefan, Goalie, RC, SP**	**.06**	**.12**	**.25**
49	**Steve Yzerman, RC**	**3.50**	**7.00**	**14.00**

EDMONTON OILERS

No.	Player	VG	EX	NRMT
50	Paul Coffey	.50	1.00	2.00
51	Wayne Gretzky	3.00	6.00	12.00
52	Jari Kurri	.25	.50	1.00

Topps
1984-85 Issue
Card No. 13,
David Andreychuk

Topps
1984-85 Issue
Card No. 49,
Steve Yzerman

Topps
1984-85 Issue
Card No. 88,
Jan Ludvig

Topps
1984-85 Issue
Card No. 96,
Pat LaFontaine

HARTFORD WHALERS

No.	Player	VG	EX	NRMT
53	Bob Crawford, RC	.02	.05	.10
54	Ron Francis	.20	.40	.80
55	Marty Howe, LC	.02	.05	.10
56	Mark Johnson, SP	.03	.07	.15
57	Greg Malone, SP	.03	.07	.15
58	Greg Millen, Goalie, SP	.03	.07	.15
59	Ray Neufeld	.02	.05	.10
60	Joel Quenneville, SP	.03	.07	.15
61	Risto Siltanen	.02	.05	.10
62	**Sylvain Turgeon, RC**	**.15**	**.30**	**.60**
63	Mike Zuke, SP	.03	.07	.15

LOS ANGELES KINGS

No.	Player	VG	EX	NRMT
64	Marcel Dionne	.07	.15	.30
65	Brian Engblom, SP	.03	.07	.15
66	Jim Fox, SP	.03	.07	.15
67	Bernie Nicholls	.25	.50	1.00
68	Terry Ruskowski, SP	.03	.07	.15
69	Charlie Simmer	.02	.05	.10

MINNESOTA NORTH STARS

No.	Player	VG	EX	NRMT
70	Don Beaupre, Goalie	.02	.05	.10
71	Brian Bellows	.10	.50	1.00
72	Neal Broten, SP	.06	.30	.60
73	Dino Ciccarelli	.10	.20	.35
74	Paul Holmgren, SP, LC	.03	.07	.15
75	Al MacAdam, SP	.03	.07	.15
76	Dennis Maruk	.02	.05	.10
77	Brad Maxwell, SP	.03	.07	.15
78	Tom McCarthy, SP	.03	.07	.15
79	Gilles Meloche, Goalie, SP	.03	.07	.15
80	Steve Payne	.02	.05	.10

MONTREAL CANADIENS

No.	Player	VG	EX	NRMT
81	Guy Lafleur	.12	.25	.50
82	Larry Robinson	.03	.07	.15
83	Robert Smith	.03	.07	.15

NEW JERSEY DEVILS

No.	Player	VG	EX	NRMT
84	Mel Bridgman	.02	.05	.10
85	Joe Cirella	.02	.05	.10
86	Don Lever	.02	.05	.10
87	Dave Lewis	.02	.05	.10
88	**Jan Ludvig RC, LC**	**.02**	**.05**	**.10**
89	Glenn Resch, Goalie	.02	.05	.10
90	**Patrick Verbeek, RC**	**.50**	**1.00**	**2.00**

NEW YORK ISLANDERS

No.	Player	VG	EX	NRMT
91	Mike Bossy	.18	.35	.75
92	Bob Bourne	.02	.05	.10
93	**Gregory Gilbert, RC**	**.06**	**.12**	**.25**
94	Clark Gillies, SP	.03	.07	.15
95	Butch Goring, LC, SP	.03	.07	.15
96	**Pat LaFontaine, RC, SP**	**3.50**	**7.00**	**14.00**
97	Ken Morrow	.02	.05	.10
98	Bob Nystrom, SP	.03	.07	.15
99	Stefan Persson, LC, SP	.03	.07	.15
100	Denis Potvin	.18	.35	.75
101	Billy Smith, Goalie, SP	.07	.15	.30
102	Brent Sutter, SP	.07	.15	.30
103	John Tonelli	.02	.05	.10
104	Bryan Trottier	.12	.25	.50

NEW YORK RANGERS

No.	Player	VG	EX	NRMT
105	Barry Beck	.02	.05	.10
106	Glen Hanlon, Goalie, SP	.03	.07	.15
107	Anders Hedberg, LC, SP	.03	.07	.15
108	Pierre Larouche, SP	.03	.07	.15
109	Donald Maloney, SP	.03	.07	.15
110	Mark Osborne, SP	.03	.07	.15
111	Larry Patey, LC	.02	.05	.10
112	**James Patrick, RC**	**.25**	**.50**	**1.00**
113	Mark Pavelich, SP	.03	.07	.15

230 • TOPPS — 1985-86 REGULAR ISSUE

No.	Player	VG	EX	NRMT
114	Mike Rogers, SP	.03	.07	.15
115	Reijo Ruotsalainen, SP	.03	.07	.15
116	Peter Sundstrom, RC, LC, SP	.06	.12	.25

PHILADELPHIA FLYERS

No.	Player	VG	EX	NRMT
117	Robert Froese, Goalie	.05	.10	.20
118	Mark Howe	.05	.15	.25
119	Tim Kerr, SP	.07	.15	.30
120	David Poulin, RC	.25	.50	1.00
121	Darryl Sittler, LC, SP	.10	.20	.40
122	Ronald Sutter	.10	.20	.40

PITTSBURGH PENGUINS

No.	Player	VG	EX	NRMT
123	Mike Bullard, SP	.03	.07	.15
124	Ron Flockhart, SP	.03	.07	.15
125	Rick Kehoe, LC	.02	.05	.10
126	Kevin McCarthy, LC, SP	.03	.07	.15
127	Mark Taylor, LC	.02	.05	.10

QUEBEC NORDIQUES

No.	Player	VG	EX	NRMT
128	Dan Bouchard, Goalie	.02	.05	.10
129	Michel Goulet	.12	.25	.50
130	Peter Stastny, SP	.35	.75	1.50

ST. LOUIS BLUES

No.	Player	VG	EX	NRMT
131	Bernie Federko	.05	.10	.20
132	Michael Liut, Goalie	.02	.05	.10
133	Joe Mullen, SP	.35	.75	1.50
134	George (Rob) Ramage	.02	.05	.10
135	Brian Sutter	.03	.07	.15

TORONTO MAPLE LEAFS

No.	Player	VG	EX	NRMT
136	John Anderson, SP	.03	.07	.15
137	Dan Daoust	.02	.05	.10
138	Richard Vaive	.02	.05	.10

VANCOUVER CANUCKS

No.	Player	VG	EX	NRMT
139	Darcy Rota, LC, SP	.03	.07	.15
140	Stanley Smyl, SP	.03	.07	.15
141	Tony Tanti	.02	.05	.10

WASHINGTON CAPITALS

No.	Player	VG	EX	NRMT
142	Dave Christian, SP	.03	.07	.15
143	Michael Gartner, SP	.40	.85	1.75
144	Bengt-ake Gustafsson, SP	.03	.07	.15
145	Doug Jarvis	.02	.05	.10
146	Al Jensen, Goalie	.02	.05	.10
147	Rod Langway	.07	.15	.30
148	Pat Riggin, Goalie, SP	.07	.15	.20
149	Scott Stevens	.75	1.50	3.00

WINNIPEG JETS

No.	Player	VG	EX	NRMT
150	Dave Babych	.02	.05	.10
151	Laurie Boschman	.02	.05	.10
152	Dale Hawerchuk	.25	.50	1.00

ALL STARS
First Team

No.	Player	VG	EX	NRMT
153	Michel Goulet, Que.	.03	.07	.15
154	Wayne Gretzky, Edm.	.75	1.50	3.00
155	Mike Bossy, NYI	.06	.12	.25
156	Rod Langway, Wash.	.02	.05	.10
157	Raymond Bourque, Bos.	.12	.25	.50
158	Tom Barrasso, Goalie, Buf.	.12	.25	.50

Second Team

No.	Player	VG	EX	NRMT
159	Mark Messier, Edm.	.35	.75	1.50
160	Bryan Trottier, NYI	.05	.10	.20

Topps 1984-85 Issue Card No. 158, Tom Barrasso

Topps 1985-86 Issue Card No. 1, Lanny McDonald

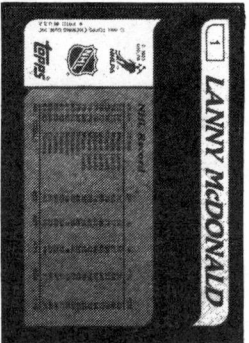

Topps 1985-86 Issue Card No. 1, Lanny McDonald

Topps 1985-86 Issue Card No. 9, Mario Lemieux

No.	Player	VG	EX	NRMT
161	Jari Kurri, Edm.	.06	.12	.25
162	Denis Potvin, NYI	.02	.05	.10
163	Paul Coffey, Edm.	.10	.20	.35
164	Pat Riggin, Goalie, Wash.	.02	.05	.10

CHECKLIST

No.	Checklist	VG	EX	NRMT
165	Checklist, SP (1-165)	.60	1.25	2.50

— 1985-86 REGULAR ISSUE —

Again in the 1985-86 season Topps single printed a third of the year's cards. Mint cards command a 25% price premium over NRMT cards.

PRICE MOVEMENT OF NRMT SETS

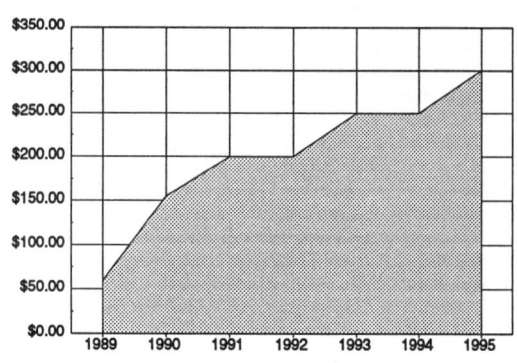

Card Size: 2 1/2" X 3 1/2"
Face: Four colour, white border, Team logo, Name, Position
Back: Red and blue on card stock; Number, Resume
Imprint: © 1985 TOPPS CHEWING GUM, INC. * PRTD. IN U.S.A. and © 1985 NHLPA or
© 1985 TOPPS CHEWING GUM, INC. ** PRTD IN U.S.A. and © 1985 NHLPA

Complete Set No.: 165

	VG	EX	NRMT
Complete Set Price:	75.00	150.00	300.00
Common Card:	.05	.10	.20
Wax Pack: (12 Cards)			26.00
Wax Box: (36 Packs)			900.00
Wax Case: (16 Boxes)			14,000.00

No.	Player	VG	EX	NRMT
1	Lanny McDonald, Cal.	.12	.25	.50
2	Michael O'Connell, Bos., SP	.10	.20	.35
3	Curt Fraser, Chi., SP	.10	.20	.35
4	Steve Penney, Mon., Goalie	.05	.10	.20
5	Brian Engblom, LA	.05	.10	.20
6	Ronald Sutter, Phi.	.05	.10	.20
7	Joe Mullen, St. L.	.20	.40	.80
8	Rod Langway, Wash.	.05	.10	.20
9	Mario Lemieux, Pit., RC	55.00	110.00	225.00
10	Dave Babych, Win.	.05	.10	.20
11	Bob Nystrom, NYI	.05	.10	.20
12	Andrew Moog, Goalie, Edm., SP	.60	1.25	2.50
13	Dino Ciccarelli, Min.	.12	.25	.50
14	Dwight Foster, Det., LC, SP	.10	.20	.35
15	James Patrick, NYR, SP	.10	.20	.35
16	Thomas Gradin, Van., LC, SP	.10	.20	.35
17	Mike Foligno, Buf.	.05	.10	.20
18	Mario Gosselin, Goalie, Que., RC	.10	.20	.35
19	Mike Zuke, Har., LC, SP	.10	.20	.35
20	John Anderson, Tor., SP	.10	.20	.35
21	Dave Pichette, NJ, LC	.05	.10	.20
22	Nick Fotiu, NYR, LC, SP	.10	.20	.35
23	Tom Lysiak, LC, Chi.	.05	.10	.20
24	Peter Zezel, Phi., RC	.75	1.50	3.00
25	Denis Potvin, NYI	.15	.30	.60
26	Robert Carpenter, Wash.	.05	.10	.20
27	Murray Bannerman, Goalie, Chi., SP	.10	.20	.35
28	Gordon Roberts, Min., SP	.10	.20	.35
29	Steve Yzerman, Det.	3.75	7.50	15.00
30	Phil Russell, NJ	.05	.10	.20
31	Peter Stastny, Que.	.18	.35	.75
32	Craig Ramsay, Buf., LC, SP	.10	.20	.35

1985-86 STICKER INSERTS — TOPPS

No.	Player	VG	EX	NRMT
33	Terry Ruskowski, LA, SP	.10	.20	.35
34	**Kevin Dineen, Har., RC, SP**	**1.25**	**2.50**	**5.00**
35	Mark Howe, Phi.	.07	.15	.30
36	Glenn Resch, NJ, Goalie	.05	.10	.20
37	Danny Gare, Det., SP	.10	.20	.35
38	**Doug Bodger, Pit., RC**	**.15**	**.30**	**.60**
39	Mike Rogers, NYR, LC	.05	.10	.20
40	Raymond Bourque, Bos.	.60	1.25	2.50
41	John Tonelli, NYI	.05	.10	.20
42	Mel Bridgman, NJ	.05	.10	.20
43	Sylvain Turgeon, Har., SP	.10	.20	.35
44	Mark Johnson, St. L.	.05	.10	.20
45	Douglas Wilson, Chi.	.05	.10	.20
46	Michael Gartner, Wash.	.40	.85	1.75
47	Brent Peterson, Buf.	.05	.10	.20
48	Paul Reinhart, Cal., SP	.10	.20	.35
49	Michael Krushelnyski, Edm.	.05	.10	.20
50	Brian Bellows, Min.	.40	.85	1.75
51	Chris Chelios, Mon.	.75	1.50	3.00
52	Barry Pederson, Bos., SP	.10	.20	.35
53	Murray Craven, Phi., SP	.12	.25	.50
54	Pierre Larouche, NYR, LC, SP	.10	.20	.35
55	Reed Larson, Det.	.05	.10	.20
56	Patrick Verbeek, NJ, SP	.25	.50	1.00
57	Randy Carlyle, Win.	.05	.10	.20
58	Ray Neufeld, Har., SP	.10	.20	.35
59	Keith Brown, Chi., SP	.10	.20	.35
60	Bryan Trottier, NYI	.10	.20	.40
61	Jim Fox, LA, SP	.10	.20	.35
62	Scott Stevens, Wash.	.50	1.00	2.00
63	Phil Housley, Buf.	.25	.50	1.00
64	Rick Middleton, Bos.	.05	.10	.20
65	Steve Payne, Min.	.05	.10	.20
66	Dave Lewis, NJ	.05	.10	.20
67	Mike Bullard, Pit.	.05	.10	.20
68	Stanley Smyl, Van., SP	.10	.20	.35
69	Mark Pavelich, NYR, LC, SP	.10	.20	.35
70	John Ogrodnick, Det.	.05	.10	.20
71	Bill Derlago, Tor., SP	.10	.20	.35
72	Bradley Marsh, Phi., SP	.10	.20	.35
73	Denis Savard, Chi.	.18	.35	.75
74	**Mark Fusco, Har., RC. LC**	**.02**	**.10**	**.20**
75	Peter Peeters, Goalie, Bos.	.05	.10	.20
76	Douglas Gilmour, St. L.	4.50	9.00	18.00
77	Michael Ramsey, Buf.	.05	.10	.20
78	Anton Stastny, Que., SP	.10	.20	.35
79	Stephen Kasper, Bos., SP	.10	.20	.35
80	**Bryan Erickson, Wash., RC, SP**	**.10**	**.20**	**.35**
81	Clark Gillies, NYI	.05	.10	.20
82	Keith Acton, Min.	.05	.10	.20
83	Patrick Flatley, NYI	.05	.10	.20
84	**Kirk Muller, NJ, RC**	**2.50**	**5.00**	**10.00**
85	Paul Coffey, Edm.	.50	1.00	2.00
86	**Ed Olczyk, Chi., RC**	**.35**	**.75**	**1.50**
87	Charlie Simmer, Bos.	.05	.10	.20
88	Michael Liut, Goalie, Har.	.05	.10	.20
89	Dave Maloney, Buf., LC	.05	.10	.20
90	Marcel Dionne, LA	.12	.25	.50
91	Tim Kerr, Phi.	.05	.10	.20
92	Ivan Boldirev, Det., LC, SP	.10	.20	.35
93	Ken Morrow, NYI, SP	.10	.20	.35
94	Donald Maloney, NYR, SP	.10	.20	.35
95	Rejean Lemelin, Goalie, Cal.	.05	.10	.20
96	Curt Giles, Min.	.05	.10	.20
97	Bob Bourne, NYI	.05	.10	.20
98	Joe Cirella, NJ	.05	.10	.20
99	Dave Christian, Wash., SP	.10	.20	.35
100	Darryl Sutter, Chi.	.05	.10	.20
101	Kelly Kisio, Det.	.10	.20	.40
102	Mats Naslund, Mon.	.05	.10	.20
103	Joel Quenneville, Har., SP	.10	.20	.35
104	Bernie Federko, St. L.	.05	.10	.20
105	Tom Barrasso, Goalie, Buf.	.80	1.60	3.25
106	Richard Vaive, Tor.	.05	.10	.20
107	Brent Sutter, NYI	.07	.15	.30
108	Wayne Babych, Pit.	.05	.10	.20
109	Dale Hawerchuk, Win.	.35	.75	1.50
110	Pelle Lindbergh, Goalie, Phi., LC, SP	3.75	7.50	15.00
111	Dennis Maruk, Min., SP	.10	.20	.35
112	Reijo Ruotsalainen, NYR, SP	.10	.20	.35
113	Tom Fergus, Bos., SP	.10	.20	.35
114	Bob Murray, Chi., SP	.10	.20	.35
115	Patrik Sundstrom, Van.	.05	.10	.20

Topps
1985-86 Issue
Card No. 84,
Kirk Muller

Topps
1985-86 Issue
Card No. 123,
Tomas Sandstrom

Topps, 1985-86
Sticker Inserts
Sticker No. 1,
John Ogrodnick

Topps, 1985-86
Sticker Inserts
Sticker No. 1,
John Ogrodnick

No.	Player	VG	EX	NRMT
116	Ron Duguay, Det., SP	.10	.20	.35
117	Alan Haworth, Wash., SP	.10	.20	.35
118	Greg Malone, Har., LC	.05	.10	.20
119	Bill Hajt, Buf.	.05	.10	.20
120	Wayne Gretzky, Edm.	5.00	10.00	20.00
121	**Craig Redmond, LA, RC, LC**	**.05**	**.10**	**.20**
122	**Kelly Hrudey, Goalie, NYI, RC**	**1.50**	**3.00**	**6.00**
123	**Tomas Sandstrom, NYR, RC**	**2.25**	**4.50**	**9.00**
124	Neal Broten, Min.	.05	.10	.20
125	Maurice Mantha, Pit., SP	.10	.20	.35
126	Gregory Gilbert, NYI, SP	.10	.20	.35
127	**Bruce Driver, NJ, RC**	**.25**	**.50**	**1.00**
128	David Poulin, Phi.	.05	.10	.20
129	Morris Lukowich, Bos., LC	.05	.10	.20
130	Mike Bossy, NYI	.18	.35	.75
131	Larry Playfair, Buf., SP	.10	.20	.35
132	Steve Larmer, Chi.	.50	1.00	2.00
133	Doug Keans, Goalie, Bos., SP	.10	.20	.35
134	Bob Manno, Det., LC	.05	.10	.20
135	Brian Sutter, St. L.	.05	.10	.20
136	Pat Riggin, Goalie, Wash., LC	.05	.10	.20
137	Pat LaFontaine, NYI	3.00	6.00	12.00
138	Barry Beck, NYR, LC, SP	.10	.20	.35
139	Rich Preston, NJ, SP	.10	.20	.35
140	Ron Francis, Har.	.25	.50	1.00
141	Brian Propp, Phi., SP	.10	.20	.35
142	Don Beaupre, Goalie, Min.	.05	.10	.20
143	David Andreychuk, Buf., SP	1.50	3.00	6.00
144	Ed Beers, Cal.	.05	.10	.20
145	Paul MacLean, Win.	.05	.10	.20
146	Troy Murray, Chi., SP	.18	.35	.75
147	Larry Robinson, Mon.	.05	.10	.20
148	Bernie Nicholls, LA	.25	.50	1.00
149	Glen Hanlon, Goalie, NYR, SP	.10	.20	.35
150	Michel Goulet, Que.	.12	.25	.50
151	Doug Jarvis, Wash., SP	.10	.20	.35
152	**Warren Young, Pit., RC**	**.05**	**.10**	**.20**
153	Tony Tanti, Van.	.05	.10	.20
154	Tomas Jonsson, NYI, SP	.10	.20	.35
155	Jari Kurri, Edm.	.35	.75	1.50
156	Anthony McKegney, Min.	.05	.10	.20
157	Gregory Stefan, Goalie, Det., SP	.10	.20	.35
158	Bryon (Brad) McCrimmon, Phi., SP	.10	.20	.35
159	Keith Crowder, Bos., SP	.10	.20	.35
160	Gilbert Perreault, Buf.	.07	.15	.30
161	Tim Bothwell, St. L., SP	.10	.20	.35
162	Bob Crawford, Har., LC, SP	.10	.20	.35
163	Paul Gagne, NJ, LC, SP	.10	.20	.35
164	Dan Daoust, Tor., SP	.10	.20	.35
165	Checklist, SP (1 - 165)	.75	1.50	3.00

— 1985 - 86 STICKER INSERTS —

Card Size: 2 1/2" X 3 1/2"
All Star:
Face: Four colour, white border, Name
Back: Two colour, blue and red on card stock; Name, Number, Position, Resume
Stickers:
Face: Four colour, white background; Team logo, Number, Hockey pucks
Back: Two colour, blue and red on card stock; Promotional offer
Imprint: * or ** © 1985 TOPPS CHEWING GUM, INC.
PRTD. IN U.S.A. © 1985 NHLPA
Complete Set No.: 33
Complete Set Price: 10.00 20.00
Common Player: .12 .25
Common Team: .10 .20

ALL STARS

No.	Player	NRMT	Mint
1	John Ogrodnick, Det.	.15	.30
2	Wayne Gretzky, Edm.	5.00	10.00
3	Jari Kurri, Edm.	.25	.50
4	Paul Coffey, Edm.	.35	.75
5	Raymond Bourque, Bos.	.35	.75
6	Pelle Lindbergh, Goalie, Phi.	2.50	5.00
7	John Tonelli, NYI	.12	.25
8	Dale Hawerchuk, Win.	.20	.40
9	Mike Bossy, NYI	.50	1.00
10	Rod Langway, Wash.	.12	.25
11	Douglas Wilson, Chi.	.20	.40
12	Tom Barrasso, Goalie, Buf.	.35	.75

232 • TOPPS — 1986-87 REGULAR ISSUE —

TEAM HELMET STICKERS

No.	Team	VG	EX	NRMT
13	Toronto Maple Leafs	.05	.10	.20
14	Buffalo Sabres	.05	.10	.20
15	Detroit Red Wings	.05	.10	.20
16	Pittsburgh Penguins	.05	.10	.20
17	New York Rangers	.05	.10	.20
18	Calgary Flames	.05	.10	.20
19	Winnpeg Jets	.05	.10	.20
20	Quebec Nordiques	.05	.10	.20
21	Chicago Black Hawks	.05	.10	.20
22	Los Angeles Kings	.05	.10	.20
23	Montreal Canadiens	.05	.10	.20
24	Vancouver Canucks	.05	.10	.20
25	Hartford Whalers	.05	.10	.20
26	Philadelphia Flyers	.05	.10	.20
27	New Jersey Devils	.05	.10	.20
28	St. Louis Blues	.05	.10	.20
29	Minnesota North Stars	.05	.10	.20
30	Washington Capitals	.05	.10	.20
31	Boston Bruins	.05	.10	.20
32	New York Islanders	.05	.10	.20
33	Edmonton Oilers	.05	.10	.20

— 1986-87 REGULAR ISSUE —

With the increase in card count to 198 for 1986-87, Topps still had production problems. However, only a third of this issue was double-printed. The cards which were double-printed are marked DP. Mint cards command a price premium of 25% over NRMT cards.

PRICE MOVEMENT OF NRMT SETS

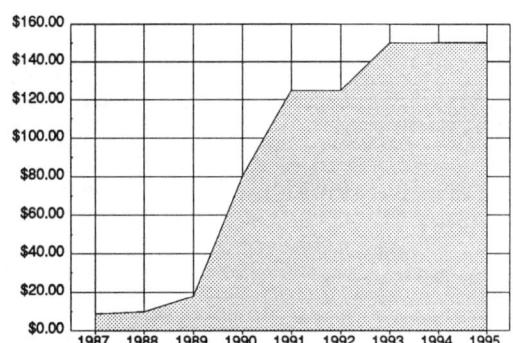

Card Size: 2 1/2" X 3 1/2"
Face: Four colour, white border, Team logo, Position
Back: Blue and black on card stock, Number, Resume, Hockey trivia
Imprint: © 1986 TOPPS CHEWING GUM, INC. * PRTD. IN U.S.A. and © 1986 NHLPA or
© 1986 TOPPS CHEWING GUM, INC. ** PRTD. IN U.S.A. and © 1986 NHLPA

Complete Set No.:	198			
Complete Set Price:		40.00	75.00	150.00
Common Card:		.02	.05	.10
Wax Pack: (12 Cards)				17.50
Wax Box: (36 Packs)				500.00
Wax Case: (20 Boxes)				9,500.00

No.	Player	VG	EX	NRMT
1	Raymond Bourque, Bos.	.50	1.00	2.00
2	Pat LaFontaine, NYI, DP	.85	1.75	3.50
3	Wayne Gretzky, Edm.	4.50	9.00	18.00
4	Lindy Ruff, Buf.	.02	.05	.10
5	Bryon (Brad) McCrimmon, Phi.	.02	.05	.10
6	David Williams, LA, LC	.02	.05	.10
7	Denis Savard, Chi., DP	.15	.30	.60
8	Lanny McDonald, Cal.	.05	.10	.20
9	John Vanbiesbrouck, Goalie, NYR RC, DP	1.50	3.00	6.00
10	Greg Adams, NJ, RC	.35	.75	1.50
11	Steve Yzerman, Det.	2.00	4.00	8.00
12	Craig Hartsburg, Min.	.02	.05	.10
13	John Anderson, Har., DP	.02	.05	.10
14	Bob Bourne, NYI, DP	.02	.05	.10
15	Kjell Dahlin, Mon., RC, LC	.07	.15	.30

Topps
1985-86 Stickers
Sticker No. 21,
Chicago Black Hawks

Topps
1986-87 Issue
Card No. 1,
Raymond Bourque

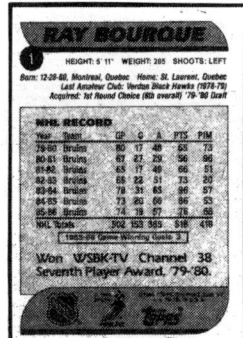

Topps
1986-87 Issue
Card No. 1,
Raymond Bourque

Topps
1986-87 Issue
Card No. 95,
Larry Melnyk

No.	Player	VG	EX	NRMT
16	David Andreychuk, Buf.	1.00	2.00	4.00
17	George (Rob) Ramage, St. L., DP	.02	.05	.10
18	Ronald Greschner, NYR, DP	.02	.05	.10
19	Bruce Driver, NJ	.02	.05	.10
20	Peter Stastny, Que.	.18	.35	.75
21	Dave Christian, Wash.	.02	.05	.10
22	Doug Keans, Goalie, Bos.	.02	.05	.10
23	Scott Bjugstad, Min., RC	.02	.05	.10
24	Doug Bodger, Pit., DP	.02	.05	.10
25	Troy Murray, Chi., DP	.02	.05	.10
26	Al Iafrate, Tor.	.85	1.75	3.50
27	Kelly Hrudey, Goalie, NYI	.30	.60	1.25
28	Doug Jarvis, Har.	.02	.05	.10
29	Richard Sutter, Van.	.02	.05	.10
30	Marcel Dionne, LA	.07	.15	.30
31	Curt Fraser, Chi., LC	.02	.05	.10
32	Doug Lidster, Van.	.02	.05	.10
33	Brian MacLellan, NYR	.02	.05	.10
34	Barry Pederson, Van.	.02	.05	.10
35	Craig Laughlin, Wash.	.02	.05	.10
36	Ilkka Sinisalo, Phi., DP	.02	.05	.10
37	John MacLean, NJ, RC	.60	1.25	4.50
38	Brian Mullen, Win.	.02	.05	.10
39	Duane Sutter, NYI, DP	.02	.05	.10
40	Brian Engblom, Buf., DP	.02	.05	.10
41	Chris Cichocki, Det., RC, LC	.02	.05	.10
42	Gordon Roberts, Min.	.02	.05	.10
43	Ron Francis, Har.	.12	.25	.50
44	Joe Mullen, Cal.	.12	.25	.50
45	Maurice Mantha, Pit., DP	.02	.05	.10
46	Patrick Verbeek, NJ	.07	.15	.30
47	Clint Malarchuk, Goalie, Que., RC	.20	.45	.90
48	Bob Brooke, NYR, DP	.02	.05	.10
49	Darryl Sutter, Chi., LC, DP	.02	.05	.10
50	Stanley Smyl, Van., DP	.02	.05	.10
51	Gregory Stefan, Goalie, Det.	.02	.05	.10
52	Bill Hajt, Buf., LC, DP	.02	.05	.10
53	Patrick Roy, Goalie, Mon., RC	17.50	35.00	75.00
54	Gordon Kluzak, Bos.	.02	.05	.10
55	Robert Froese, Goalie, Phi., DP	.02	.05	.10
56	Grant Fuhr, Goalie, Edm.	.30	.65	1.25
57	Mark Hunter, St. L., DP	.02	.05	.10
58	Dana Murzyn, Har., RC	.02	.05	.10
59	Michael Gartner, Wash.	.20	.45	.90
60	Dennis Maruk, Min.	.02	.05	.10
61	Rich Preston, NJ, LC	.02	.05	.10
62	Larry Robinson, Mon., DP	.05	.10	.20
63	David Taylor, LA, DP	.02	.05	.10
64	Bob Murray, Chi., DP	.02	.05	.10
65	Ken Morrow, NYI	.02	.05	.10
66	Mike Ridley, NYR, RC	.60	1.25	2.50
67	John Tucker, Buf., RC	.02	.05	.10
68	Miroslav Frycer, Tor., LC	.02	.05	.10
69	Danny Gare, Det., LC	.02	.05	.10
70	Randy Burridge, Bos., RC	.25	.50	1.00
71	David Poulin, Phi.	.02	.05	.10
72	Brian Sutter, St. L., LC	.02	.05	.10
73	Dave Babych, Har.	.02	.05	.10
74	Dale Hawerchuk, Win., DP	.18	.35	.75
75	Brian Bellows, Min.	.18	.35	.75
76	Dave Pasin, Bos., RC, LC	.02	.05	.10
77	Peter Peeters, Goalie, Wash., DP	.02	.05	.10
78	Tomas Jonsson, NYI, DP	.02	.05	.10
79	Gilbert Perreault, Buf., LC, DP	.02	.05	.10
80	Glenn Anderson, Edm., DP	.10	.20	.35
81	Donald Maloney, NYR	.02	.05	.10
82	Ed Olczyk, Chi., DP	.06	.12	.25
83	Mike Bullard, Pit.	.02	.05	.10
84	Tom Fergus, Tor.	.02	.05	.10
85	Dave Lewis, NJ	.02	.05	.10
86	Brian Propp, Phi.	.02	.05	.10
87	John Ogrodnick, Det.	.02	.05	.10
88	Kevin Dineen, Har., DP	.12	.25	.50
89	Don Beaupre, Goalie, Min.	.02	.05	.10
90	Mike Bossy, NYI, DP	.12	.25	.50
91	Tom Barrasso, Goalie, Buf., DP	.18	.35	.75
92	Michel Goulet, Que., DP	.07	.15	.30
93	Douglas Gilmour, St. L.	2.00	4.00	8.00
94	Kirk Muller, NJ	.75	1.50	3.00
95	Larry Melnyk, NYR, RC, DP	.02	.05	.10
96	Bob Gainey, Mon., DP	.02	.05	.10
97	Stephen Kasper, Bos.	.02	.05	.10
98	Petr Klima, Det., RC	.50	1.00	2.00

No.	Player	NRMT	Mint
99	Neal Broten, Min., DP	.02	.05	.10
100	Alan Secord, Chi., DP	.02	.05	.10
101	Bryan Erickson, LA, DP	.02	.05	.10
102	Rejean Lemelin, Goalie, Cal.	.02	.05	.10
103	Sylvain Turgeon, Har.	.02	.05	.10
104	Bob Nystrom, NYI, LC	.02	.05	.10
105	Bernie Federko, St. L.	.02	.05	.10
106	Douglas Wilson, Chi., DP	.03	.07	.15
107	Alan Haworth, Wash.	.02	.05	.10
108	Jari Kurri, Edm.	.18	.35	.75
109	Ronald Sutter, Phi.	.02	.05	.10
110	Reed Larson, Bos., DP	.02	.05	.10
111	Terry Ruskowski, Pit., DP	.02	.05	.10
112	Mark Johnson, NJ, DP	.02	.05	.10
113	James Patrick, NYR	.02	.05	.10
114	Paul MacLean, Win.	.02	.05	.10
115	Michael Ramsey, Buf., DP	.02	.05	.10
116	Kelly Kisio, Det., DP	.02	.05	.10
117	Brent Sutter, NYI	.02	.05	.10
118	Joel Quenneville, Har.	.02	.05	.10
119	Curt Giles, Min., DP	.02	.05	.10
120	Tony Tanti, Van., DP	.02	.05	.10
121	Douglas Sulliman, NJ, DP	.02	.05	.10
122	Mario Lemieux, Pit.	10.00	20.00	40.00
123	Mark Howe, Phi., DP	.02	.05	.10
124	Bob Sauve, Goalie, Chi.	.02	.05	.10
125	Anton Stastny, Que.	.02	.05	.10
126	Scott Stevens, Wash., DP	.12	.25	.50
127	Mike Foligno, Buf.	.02	.05	.10
128	Reijo Ruotsalainen, NYR, LC, DP	.02	.05	.10
129	Denis Potvin, NYI	.06	.12	.25
130	Keith Crowder, Bos.	.02	.05	.10
131	Bob Janecyk, Goalie, LA, LC, DP	.02	.05	.10
132	John Tonelli, Cal.	.02	.05	.10
133	Michael Liut, Goalie, Har., DP	.02	.05	.10
134	Tim Kerr, Phi., DP	.02	.05	.10
135	Al Jensen, Goalie, Wash., LC	.02	.05	.10
136	Mel Bridgman, NJ	.02	.05	.10
137	Paul Coffey, Edm., DP	.25	.50	1.00
138	Dino Ciccarelli, Min., DP	.06	.12	.25
139	Steve Larmer, Chi.	.18	.35	.75
140	Michael O'Connell, Det.	.02	.05	.10
141	Clark Gillies, NYI	.02	.05	.10
142	Phil Russell, Buf., LC, DP	.02	.05	.10
143	**Dirk Graham, Min., RC, DP**	.35	.75	1.50
144	Randy Carlyle, Win.	.02	.05	.10
145	Charlie Simmer, Bos.	.02	.05	.10
146	Ron Flockhart, St. L., DP	.02	.05	.10
147	Thomas Laidlaw, NYR	.02	.05	.10
148	**Dave Tippett, Har., RC**	.12	.25	.50
149	**Wendel Clark, Tor., RC, DP**	3.50	7.00	14.00
150	Robert Carpenter, Wash., DP	.02	.05	.10
151	**Bill Watson, Chi., RC, LC**	.02	.05	.10
152	**Roberto Romano, Goalie, Pit., RC, LC, DP**	.02	.05	.10
153	Douglas Shedden, Det.	.02	.05	.10
154	Phil Housley, Buf.	.15	.30	.60
155	Bryan Trottier, NYI	.10	.20	.35
156	Patrik Sundstrom, Van., DP	.02	.05	.10
157	Rick Middleton, Bos., DP	.02	.05	.10
158	Glenn Resch, Goalie, Phi., LC	.02	.05	.10
159	Bernie Nicholls, LA, DP	.10	.20	.40
160	**Ray Ferraro, Har., RC**	.50	1.00	2.00
161	Mats Naslund, Mon., DP	.02	.05	.10
162	Patrick Flatley, NYI, DP	.02	.05	.10
163	Joe Cirella, NJ	.02	.05	.10
164	Rod Langway, Wash., DP	.02	.05	.10
165	Checklist 1 (1 - 99)	.50	1.00	2.00
166	Carey Wilson, Cal.	.02	.05	.10
167	Murray Craven, Phi.	.02	.05	.10
168	**Paul Gillis, Que., RC**	.02	.05	.10
169	Borje Salming, Tor.	.02	.05	.10
170	Perry Turnbull, Win., LC	.02	.05	.10
171	Chris Chelios, Mon.	.35	.75	1.50
172	Keith Acton, Min.	.02	.05	.10
173	Al MacInnis, Cal.	1.75	3.50	7.00
174	**Russell Courtnall, Tor., RC**	1.00	2.00	4.00
175	Bradley Marsh, Phi.	.02	.05	.10
176	Guy Carbonneau, Mon.	.12	.25	.50
177	Ray Neufeld, Win.	.02	.05	.10
178	**Craig MacTavish, Edm., RC**	.18	.35	.75
179	Rick Lanz, Van.	.02	.05	.10
180	Murray Bannerman, Goalie, Chi., LC	.02	.05	.10

Topps
1986-87 Issue
Card No. 122,
Mario Lemieux

Topps
1986-87 Issue
Card No. 152,
Roberto Romano

Topps
1986-87 Stickers
Sticker No. 1,
John Vanbiesbrouck

Topps
1986-87 Stickers
Sticker No. 1,
John Vanbiesbrouck

No.	Player	VG	EX	NRMT
181	Brent Ashton, Que.	.02	.05	.10
182	James Peplinski, Cal.	.02	.05	.10
183	Mark Napier, Edm., LC	.02	.05	.10
184	Laurie Boschman, Win.	.02	.05	.10
185	Lawrence Murphy, Wash.	.02	.05	.10
186	Mark Messier, Edm.	.75	1.50	3.00
187	Risto Siltanen, Que., LC	.02	.05	.10
188	Robert Smith, Mon.	.02	.05	.10
189	**Gary Suter, Cal., RC**	.75	1.50	3.00
190	Peter Zezel, Phi.	.05	.10	.20
191	Richard Vaive, Tor.	.02	.05	.10
192	Dale Hunter, Que.	.02	.05	.10
193	Michael Krushelnyski, Edm.	.02	.05	.10
194	Scott Arniel, Win.	.02	.05	.10
195	Larry Playfair, LA	.02	.05	.10
196	Doug Risebrough, Cal., LC	.02	.05	.10
197	Kevin Lowe, Edm.	.12	.25	.50
198	Checklist 2 (100 - 198)	.50	1.00	2.00

— 1986 - 87 STICKER INSERTS —

Colour inserts were issued one per pack and featured 12 All-Star players and 21 team logo stickers.

Sticker Size: 2 1/2" X 3 1/2"
All Star Stickers:
Face: Four colour, white border, Name, Position
Back: Two colour, blue and red on card stock; Name, Number, Position, Resume
Team Helmet Stickers:
Face: Four colour, white background; Team logo, Number, Hockey pucks
Back: Two colour, blue and red on card stock; Promotional offer
Imprint: * or ** © 1986 TOPPS CHEWING GUM, INC. PRTD. IN U.S.A. © 1986 NHLPA
Complete Set No.: 33

Complete Set Price:		4.25	8.50	17.00
Common Player:		.06	.12	.25
Common Team:		.05	.10	.20

ALL STAR FIRST TEAM

No.	Player	VG	EX	NRMT
1	John Vanbiesbrouck, Goalie, NYR	.10	.20	.40
2	Michel Goulet, Que.	.10	.20	.40
3	Wayne Gretzky, Edm.	2.00	4.00	8.00
4	Mike Bossy, NYI	.18	.35	.75
5	Paul Coffey, Edm.	.18	.35	.75
6	Mark Howe, Phi.	.06	.12	.25

ALL STAR SECOND TEAM

No.	Player	VG	EX	NRMT
7	Bob Froese, Goalie, Phi.	.06	.12	.25
8	Mats Naslund, Mon.	.06	.12	.25
9	Mario Lemieux, Pit.	2.00	4.00	8.00
10	Jari Kurri, Edm.	.10	.20	.40
11	Raymond Bourque, Bos.	.25	.50	1.00
12	Larry Robinson, Mon.	.10	.20	.40

TEAM HELMET STICKERS

No.	Team	VG	EX	NRMT
13	Toronto Maple Leafs	.05	.10	.20
14	Buffalo Sabres	.05	.10	.20
15	Detroit Red Wings	.05	.10	.20
16	Pittsburgh Penguins	.05	.10	.20
17	New York Rangers	.05	.10	.20
18	Calgary Flames	.05	.10	.20
19	Winnipeg Jets	.05	.10	.20
20	Quebec Nordiques	.05	.10	.20
21	Chicago Blackhawks	.05	.10	.20
22	Los Angeles Kings	.05	.10	.20
23	Montreal Canadiens	.05	.10	.20
24	Vancouver Canucks	.05	.10	.20
25	Hartford Whalers	.05	.10	.20
26	Philadelphia Flyers	.05	.10	.20
27	New Jersey Devils	.05	.10	.20
28	St. Louis Blues	.05	.10	.20
29	Minnesota North Stars	.05	.10	.20
30	Washington Capitals	.05	.10	.20
31	Boston Bruins	.05	.10	.20
32	New York Islanders	.05	.10	.20
33	Edmonton Oilers	.05	.10	.20

234 • TOPPS — 1987-88 REGULAR ISSUE

— 1987-88 REGULAR ISSUE —

As with the previous season Topps produced a 198-card set with one third of the cards double printed. Mint cards will command a 25% price premium over NRMT cards.

PRICE MOVEMENT OF NRMT SETS

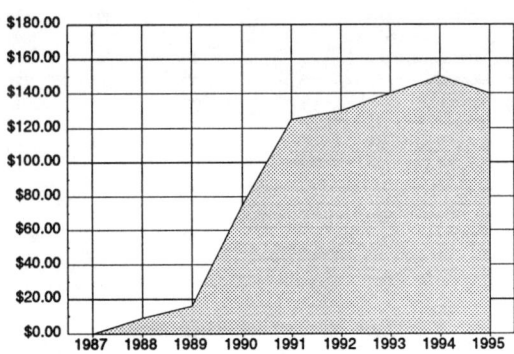

Card Size: 2 1/2" X 3 1/2"
Face: Four colour, white border, Position
Back: Purple and black on card stock, Number, Resume, Hockey trivia
Imprint: * © TOPPS CHEWING GUM, INC. PRTD. IN U.S.A.
and © 1987 NHLPA or
** © TOPPS CHEWING GUM, INC. PRTD. IN U.S.A.
and © 1987 NHLPA

Complete Set No.:	198		
Complete Price Set:	30.00	70.00	140.00
Common Goalie, SP:	.05	.10	.20
Common Goalie, DP:	.02	.08	.15
Common Player, SP:	.02	.08	.15
Common Card:	.02	.05	.10
Wax Pack: (12 Cards)			12.00
Wax Box: (36 Packs)			375.00
Wax Case: (20 Boxes)			7,000.00

Topps 1987-88 Issue Card No. 1, Dennis Potvin

Topps 1987-88 Issue Card No. 1, Dennis Potvin

Topps 1987-88 Issue Card No. 2, Rick Rocchet

Topps 1987-88 Issue Card No. 80, Craig Simpson

No.	Player	VG	EX	NRMT
1	Denis Potvin, NYI, LC, DP	.05	.15	.35
2	**Rick Tocchet, Phi., RC**	**2.50**	**5.00**	**10.00**
3	David Andreychuk, Buf.	.35	.75	1.50
4	Stanley Smyl, Van.	.02	.05	.10
5	Dave Babych, Har., DP	.02	.05	.10
6	Patrick Verbeek, NJ	.06	.12	.25
7	**Esa Tikkanen, Edm., RC**	**1.25**	**2.50**	**5.00**
8	Mike Ridley, Wash.	.12	.25	.50
9	Randy Carlyle, Win.	.02	.05	.10
10	**Gregory Paslawski, St. L., RC**	.05	.10	.20
11	Neal Broten, Min.	.02	.05	.10
12	Wendel Clark, Tor., DP	.70	1.40	2.75
13	**Bill Ranford, Goalie, Bos., RC, DP**	**1.25**	**2.50**	**5.00**
14	Douglas Wilson, Chi.	.02	.05	.10
15	Mario Lemieux, Pit.	5.00	10.00	20.00
16	Mats Naslund, Mon.	.02	.05	.10
17	Mel Bridgman, Det., LC	.02	.05	.10
18	James Patrick, NYR, DP	.02	.05	.10
19	Roland Melanson, Goalie, LA	.02	.05	.10
20	Lanny McDonald, Cal.	.02	.05	.10
21	Peter Stastny, Que.	.12	.25	.50
22	Murray Craven, Phi.	.02	.05	.10
23	**Ulf Samuelsson, Har., RC, DP**	.75	1.50	3.00
24	**Michael Thelven, Bos., RC, LC, DP, Error**	.02	.05	.10
25	Scott Stevens, Wash.	.15	.30	.65
26	Petr Klima, Det.	.07	.15	.35
27	Brent Sutter, NYI, DP	.02	.05	.10
28	Tomas Sandstrom, NYR	.25	.50	1.00
29	Tim Bothwell, St. L., LC	.02	.05	.10
30	Robert Carpenter, LA, DP	.02	.05	.10
31	Brian MacLellan, Min., DP	.02	.05	.10
32	John Chabot, Pit.	.02	.05	.10
33	Phil Housley, Buf., DP	.07	.15	.25
34	Patrik Sundstrom, Van., DP	.02	.05	.10
35	Dave Ellett, Win.	.12	.25	.50
36	John Vanbiesbrouck, Goalie, NYR	.60	1.25	2.50
37	Dave Lewis, Det., LC	.02	.05	.10
38	Tom McCarthy, Bos., LC, DP	.02	.05	.10
39	David Poulin, Phi.	.02	.05	.10
40	Mike Foligno, Buf.	.02	.05	.10
41	Gordon Roberts, Min.	.02	.05	.10
42	**Luc Robitaille, LA, RC**	**7.50**	**15.00**	**30.00**
43	Duane Sutter, NYI	.02	.05	.10
44	Peter Peeters, Goalie, Wash.	.02	.05	.10
45	John Anderson, Har.	.02	.05	.10
46	Aaron Broten, NJ	.02	.05	.10
47	Keith Brown, Chi.	.02	.05	.10
48	Robert Smith, Mon.	.02	.05	.10
49	Donald Maloney, NYR	.02	.05	.10
50	Mark Hunter, St. L.	.02	.05	.10
51	Maurice Mantha, Pit.	.02	.05	.10
52	Charlie Simmer, Bos.	.02	.05	.10
53	Wayne Gretzky, Edm.	3.75	7.50	15.00
54	Mark Howe, Phi.	.02	.05	.10
55	Robert Gould, Wash.	.02	.05	.10
56	Steve Yzerman, Det., DP	.75	1.50	3.00
57	Larry Playfair, LA, LC	.02	.05	.10
58	Alain Chevrier, Goalie, NJ	.02	.05	.10
59	Steve Larmer, Chi.	.10	.20	.40
60	Bryan Trottier, NYI	.06	.12	.25
61	Robert (Stewart) Gavin, Har., DP	.02	.05	.10
62	Russell Courtnall, Tor., DP	.18	.35	.75
63	Michael Ramsey, Buf., DP	.02	.05	.10
64	Bob Brooke, Min.	.02	.05	.10
65	Richard Wamsley, Goalie, St. L., DP	.02	.05	.10
66	Ken Morrow, NYI	.02	.05	.10
67	**Gerard Gallant, Det., RC, Error**	.10	.20	.35
68	**Kevin Hatcher, Wash., RC**	**1.50**	**3.00**	**6.00**
69	Cam Neely, Bos.	.75	1.50	3.00
70	Sylvain Turgeon, Har., DP	.02	.05	.10
71	Peter Zezel, Phi.	.02	.05	.10
72	Allan MacInnis, Cal.	.75	1.50	3.00
73	Terry Ruskowski, Pit., LC, DP	.02	.05	.10
74	Troy Murray, Chi.	.02	.05	.10
75	Jim Fox, LA, DP	.02	.05	.10
76	Kelly Kisio, NYR	.02	.05	.10
77	Michel Goulet, Que., DP	.05	.10	.20
78	Tom Barrasso, Goalie, Buf., DP	.10	.20	.40
79	Bruce Driver, NJ, DP	.02	.05	.10
80	**Craig Simpson, Pit., RC, DP**	**.25**	**.50**	**1.00**
81	Dino Ciccarelli, Min.	.05	.10	.20
82	Gary Nylund, Chi., DP	.02	.05	.10
83	Bernie Federko, St. L.	.02	.05	.10
84	John Tonelli, Cal., DP	.02	.05	.10
85	Byron (Brad) McCrimmon, Phi., DP	.02	.05	.10
86	Dave Tippett, Har., DP	.02	.05	.10
87	Ray Bourque, Bos., DP	.25	.50	1.00
88	Dave Christian, Wash.	.02	.05	.10
89	Glen Hanlon, Goalie, Det.	.02	.05	.10
90	**Brian Curran, NYI, RC**	.02	.05	.10
91	Paul MacLean, Win.	.02	.05	.10
92	**Jimmy Carson, LA, RC**	.35	.75	1.50
93	Willie Huber, NYR, LC	.02	.05	.10
94	Brian Bellows, Min	.12	.25	.50
95	Doug Jarvis, Har., LC, DP	.02	.05	.10
96	Clark Gillies, Buf.	.02	.05	.10
97	Tony Tanti, Van.	.02	.05	.10
98	**Per-Erik Eklund, Phi., RC, DP**	.12	.25	.50
99	Paul Coffey, Edm.	.25	.50	1.00
100	Brent Ashton, Det., DP	.02	.05	.10
101	Mark Johnson, NJ	.02	.05	.10
102	**Greg Johnston, Bos., RC, LC**	.02	.05	.10
103	Ron Flockhart, St. L., LC	.02	.05	.10
104	Ed Olczyk, Chi.	.02	.05	.10
105	Mike Bossy, NYI, LC	.12	.25	.50
106	Chris Chelios, Mon.	.20	.40	.80
107	Gilles Meloche, Goalie, Pit.	.05	.10	.20
108	Rod Langway, Wash.	.02	.05	.10
109	Ray Ferraro, Har., DP	.05	.10	.20
110	Ron Duguay, NYR, LC, DP	.02	.05	.10
111	Alan Secord, Chi., DP	.02	.05	.10
112	Mark Messier, Edm.	.40	.85	1.75
113	Ronald Sutter, Phi.	.02	.05	.10
114	**Darren Veitch, Det., RC**	.02	.05	.10
115	Rick Middleton, Bos., LC	.02	.05	.10
116	Douglas Sulliman, NJ	.02	.05	.10
117	Dennis Maruk, Min., LC, DP	.02	.05	.10
118	David Taylor, LA	.02	.05	.10
119	Kelly Hrudey, Goalie, NYI	.10	.20	.40
120	Tom Fergus, Tor.	.02	.05	.10
121	**Christian Ruuttu, Buf., RC**	.18	.35	.75
122	**Brian Benning, St. L., RC**	.06	.12	.25
123	**Adam Oates, Det., RC**	**6.25**	**12.50**	**25.00**
124	Kevin Dineen, Har.	.07	.15	.30

No.	Player	VG	EX	NRMT
125	Doug Bodger, Pit., DP	.02	.05	.10
126	Joe Mullen, Cal.	.07	.15	.30
127	Denis Savard, Chi.	.12	.25	.50
128	Bradley Marsh, Phi.	.02	.05	.10
129	Marcel Dionne, NYR, DP	.07	.15	.30
130	Bryan Erickson, LA, LC	.02	.05	.10
131	Reed Larson, Bos., DP	.02	.05	.10
132	Don Beaupre, Goalie, Min.	.02	.05	.10
133	Lawrence Murphy, Wash., DP	.06	.12	.25
134	John Ogrodnick, Que., DP	.02	.05	.10
135	Greg Adams, NJ, DP	.02	.05	.10
136	Patrick Flatley, NYI, DP	.02	.05	.10
137	Scott Arniel, Buf.	.02	.05	.10
138	Dana Murzyn, Har.	.02	.05	.10
139	Greg Adams, Wash.	.02	.05	.10
140	Bob Sauve, Goalie, NJ, LC	.02	.05	.10
141	Michael O'Connell, Det.	.02	.05	.10
142	Walter Poddubny, NYR, DP	.02	.05	.10
143	Paul Reinhart, Cal.	.02	.05	.10
144	Tim Kerr, Phi., DP	.02	.05	.10
145	**Brian Lawton, Min., RC**	.02	.05	.10
146	**Gino Cavallini, St. L., RC**	.06	.12	.25
147	Doug Keans, Goalie, Bos., LC, DP	.02	.05	.10
148	Jari Kurri, Edm.	.15	.30	.60
149	Dale Hawerchuk, Win.	.18	.35	.75
150	**Randy Cunneyworth, Pit., RC**	.06	.12	.25
151	Gordon (Jay) Wells, LA	.02	.05	.10
152	Michael Liut, Goalie, Har., DP	.02	.05	.10
153	Stephen Konroyd, NYI	.02	.05	.10
154	John Tucker, Buf.	.02	.05	.10
155	Richard Vaive, Tor., DP	.02	.05	.10
156	Bob Murray, Chi.	.02	.05	.10
157	Kirk Muller, NJ, DP	.18	.35	.75
158	Brian Propp, Phi.	.02	.05	.10
159	Ronald Greschner, NYR	.02	.05	.10
160	George (Rob) Ramage, St. L.	.02	.05	.10
161	Craig Laughlin, Wash.	.02	.05	.10
162	Stephen Kasper, Bos., DP	.02	.05	.10
163	Patrick Roy, Goalie, Mon.	6.25	12.50	25.00
164	**Shawn Burr, Det., RC, DP**	.10	.20	.35
165	Craig Hartsburg, Min., DP	.02	.05	.10
166	**Dean Evason, Har., RC**	.10	.20	.35
167	Bob Bourne, LA	.02	.05	.10
168	Michael Gartner, Wash.	.10	.20	.40
169	**Ron Hextall, Goalie, Phi., RC**	1.25	2.50	5.00
170	Joe Cirella, NJ	.02	.05	.10
171	Dan Quinn, Pit., DP	.02	.05	.10
172	Anthony McKegney, St. L.	.02	.05	.10
173	Pat LaFontaine, NYI, DP	.50	1.00	2.00
174	**Allen Pedersen, Bos., RC, DP**	.02	.05	.10
175	Douglas Gilmour, St. L.	1.00	2.00	4.00
176	Gary Suter, Cal., DP	.10	.20	.40
177	Barry Pederson, Van., DP	.02	.05	.10
178	Grant Fuhr, Goalie, Edm., DP	.07	.25	.50
179	**Wayne Presley, Chi., RC**	.07	.25	.50
180	Wilf Paiement, Pit., LC	.02	.05	.10
181	Douglas Smail, Win.	.02	.05	.10
182	Doug Crossman, Phi., DP	.02	.05	.10
183	Bernie Nicholls, LA, Error	.06	.12	.25
184	Dirk Graham, Min., Error	.02	.05	.10
185	Anton Stastny, Que.	.02	.05	.10
186	Gregory Stefan, Goalie, Det.	.02	.05	.10
187	Ron Francis, Har.	.10	.20	.40
188	Steve Thomas, Tor., DP	.12	.25	.50
189	**Kelly Miller, Wash., RC**	.20	.45	.90
190	Tomas Jonsson, NYI	.02	.05	.10
191	John MacLean, NJ	.12	.25	.50
192	Larry Robinson, Mon., DP	.02	.05	.10
193	Douglas Wickenheiser, St. L., DP	.02	.05	.10
194	Keith Crowder, Bos., DP	.02	.05	.10
195	Robert Froese, Goalie, NYR, LC	.02	.05	.10
196	Jim Johnson, Pit.	.02	.05	.10
197	Checklist 1 (1 - 99)	.60	1.25	2.50
198	Checklist 2 (100 - 198)	.60	1.25	2.50

Note: Cards are listed in this catalogue chronologically by manufacturer's first date of issue. For all manufacturers, subsequent cards appear in issue date order following that manufacturer's first listing. See the last page of this catalogue for an alphabetical index of issuers.

Topps
1987-88 Issue
Card No. 150,
Randy Cunneyworth

Topps
1987-88 Issue
Card No. 189,
Kelly Miller

Topps
1987-88 Sticker Inserts
Sticker No. 13,
Toronto Maple Leafs

Topps
1987-88 Issue
Sticker No. 31,
Boston Bruins

— 1987 - 88 STICKER INSERTS —

Colour inserts were issued one per pack and featured 12 All-Star players and 21 team logo stickers.

Sticker Size: 2 1/2" X 3 1/2"
All Star Stickers:
Face: Four colour, white border, Name, Position
Back: Two colour, blue and red on card stock; Name, Number, Position, Resume
Team Helmet Stickers
Face: Four colour, white background; Team logo, Number, Hockey pucks
Back: Two colour, blue and red on card stock; Promotional offer
Imprint: * or ** © 1987 TOPPS CHEWING GUM, INC.
PRTD. IN U.S.A. © 1987 NHLPA
Complete Set No.: 33

Complete Set Price:	3.50	7.00	14.00
Common Card:	.05	.10	.20
Common Team:	.05	.10	.20

ALL STAR FIRST TEAM

No.	Player	VG	EX	NRMT
1	Raymond Bourque, Bos.	.18	.35	.75
2	Ron Hextall, Goalie	.12	.25	.50
3	Mark Howe	.06	.12	.25
4	Jari Kurri, Edm.	.12	.25	.50
5	Wayne Gretzky, Edm.	1.25	2.50	5.00
6	Michel Goulet	.25	.50	1.00

ALL STAR SECOND TEAM

No.	Player	VG	EX	NRMT
7	Lawrence Murphy	.12	.25	.50
8	Michael Liut, Goalie	.12	.25	.50
9	Al MacInnis	.12	.25	.50
10	Tim Kerr	.05	.10	.20
11	Mario Lemieux	1.50	3.00	6.00
12	Luc Robitaille	1.25	2.50	5.00

TEAM HELMET STICKERS

No.	Team	VG	EX	NRMT
13	Toronto Maple Leafs	.05	.10	.20
14	Buffalo Sabres	.05	.10	.20
15	Detroit Red Wings	.05	.10	.20
16	Pittsburgh Penguins	.05	.10	.20
17	New York Rangers	.05	.10	.20
18	Calgary Flames	.05	.10	.20
19	Winnipeg Jets	.05	.10	.20
20	Quebec Nordiques	.05	.10	.20
21	Chicago Blackhawks	.05	.10	.20
22	Los Angeles Kings	.05	.10	.20
23	Montreal Canadiens	.05	.10	.20
24	Vancouver Canucks	.05	.10	.20
25	Hartford Whalers	.05	.10	.20
26	Philadelphia Flyers	.05	.10	.20
27	New Jersey Devils	.05	.10	.20
28	St. Louis Blues	.05	.10	.20
29	Minnesota North Stars	.05	.10	.20
30	Washington Capitals	.05	.10	.20
31	Boston Bruins	.05	.10	.20
32	New York Islanders	.05	.10	.20
33	Edmonton Oilers	.05	.10	.20

— 1988 - 89 REGULAR ISSUE —

PRICE MOVEMENT OF MINT SETS

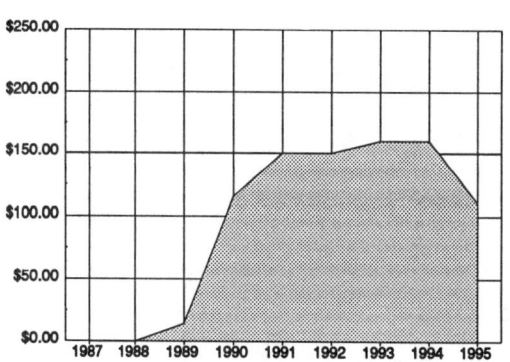

236 • TOPPS — 1988 - 89 REGULAR ISSUE

Card Size: 2 1/2" X 3 1/2"
Face: Four colour, white Border, Team logo, Position
Back: Orange and purple on card stock, Number, Resume
Imprint: * © 1988 THE TOPPS COMPANY, INC. © 1988 NHLPA
Complete Set No.: 198

Complete Set Price:		25.00	55.00	110.00
Common Card:		.01	.03	.06
Wax Pack: (12 Cards)				6.00
Wax Box: (36 Packs)				200.00
Wax Case: (20 Boxes)				3,500.00

No.	Player	VG	EX	NRMT
1	Mario Lemieux, Pit., DP	1.75	3.50	7.00
2	Robert Joyce, Bos., RC, DP	.02	.05	.10
3	Joel Quenneville, Har., DP	.01	.03	.06
4	Anthony McKegney, St. L.	.01	.03	.06
5	Stephane J.J. Richer, Mon., DP	.25	.50	1.00
6	Mark Howe, Phi., DP	.01	.03	.06
7	Brent Sutter, NYI, DP	.01	.03	.06
8	Gilles Meloche, Goalie, Pit., LC, DP	.01	.03	.06
9	Jimmy Carson, Edm., DP	.06	.12	.25
10	John MacLean, NJ	.07	.15	.30
11	Gary Leeman, Tor.	.01	.03	.06
12	Gerard Gallant, Det., DP	.01	.03	.06
13	Marcel Dionne, NYR, LC	.06	.12	.25
14	Dave Christian, Wash., DP	.01	.03	.06
15	Gary Nylund, Chi.	.01	.03	.06
16	**Joe Nieuwendyk, Cal., RC**	**1.75**	**3.50**	**7.00**
17	Billy Smith, Goalie, NYI, LC, DP	.01	.03	.06
18	Christian Ruuttu, Buf.	.01	.03	.06
19	Randy Cunneyworth, Pit.	.01	.03	.06
20	Brian Lawton, Min.	.01	.03	.06
21	**Scott Mellanby, Phi., RC, DP**	**.10**	**.20**	**.40**
22	Peter Stastny, Que., DP	.06	.12	.25
23	Gordon Kluzak, Bos.	.01	.03	.06
24	Sylvain Turgeon, Har.	.01	.03	.06
25	Clint Malarchuk, Goalie, Wash.	.01	.03	.06
26	Denis Savard, Chi.	.08	.17	.35
27	Craig Simpson, Edm.	.06	.12	.25
28	Petr Klima, Det.	.01	.03	.06
29	Patrick Verbeek, NJ	.06	.12	.25
30	Maurice Mantha, Min.	.01	.03	.06
31	Christopher Nilan, NYR	.01	.03	.06
32	Barry Pederson, Van.	.01	.03	.06
33	Randy Burridge, Bos.	.01	.03	.06
34	Ron Hextall, Goalie, Phi.	.18	.35	.75
35	Gaston Gingras, St. L.	.01	.03	.06
36	Kevin Dineen, Har.	.01	.03	.06
37	Thomas Laidlaw, LA	.01	.03	.06
38	Paul MacLean, Det., DP	.01	.03	.06
39	John Chabot, Det., DP	.01	.03	.06
40	Lindy Ruff, Buf.	.01	.03	.06
41	Dan Quinn, Pit., DP	.01	.03	.06
42	Donald Beaupre, Goalie, Min.	.01	.03	.06
43	Gary Suter, Cal.	.06	.12	.25
44	**Mikko Makela, NYI, RC, DP**	**.01**	**.03**	**.06**
45	Mark Johnson, NJ, DP	.01	.03	.06
46	David Taylor, LA, DP	.01	.03	.06
47	Ulf Dahlen, NYR, RC	.15	.30	.60
48	**Jeff Sharples, Det., RC**	**.01**	**.03**	**.06**
49	Chris Chelios, Mon.	.10	.20	.40
50	Michael Gartner, Wash., DP	.07	.15	.25
51	**Darren Pang, Goalie, Chi., RC, DP**	**.01**	**.03**	**.06**
52	Ronald Francis, Har.	.07	.15	.30
53	Ken Morrow, NYI, LC	.01	.03	.06
54	Michel Goulet, Que.	.01	.03	.06
55	**Ray Sheppard, Buf., RC**	**1.00**	**2.00**	**4.00**
56	Douglas Gilmour, St. L.	.60	1.25	2.50
57	David Shaw, NYR, DP	.01	.03	.06
58	Cam Neely, Bos., DP	.20	.40	.80
59	Grant Fuhr, Goalie, Edm., DP	.10	.20	.40
60	Scott Stevens, Wash.	.09	.18	.35
61	Bob Brooke, Min.	.01	.03	.06
62	Dave Hunter, Pit.	.01	.03	.06
63	**Alan Kerr, NYI, RC**	**.01**	**.03**	**.06**
64	Bradley Marsh, Phi.	.01	.03	.06
65	Dale Hawerchuk, Win., DP	.10	.20	.40
66	**Brett Hull, St. L., RC, DP**	**7.50**	**15.00**	**30.00**
67	Patrik Sundstrom, NJ, DP	.01	.03	.06
68	Gregory Stefan, Goalie, Det.	.01	.03	.06
69	James Patrick, NYR	.01	.03	.06
70	Dale Hunter, Wash., DP	.01	.03	.06
71	Al Iafrate, Tor.	.10	.20	.40
72	Robert Carpenter, LA	.01	.03	.06
73	Ray Bourque, Bos., DP	.12	.25	.50
74	John Tucker, Buf., DP	.01	.03	.06

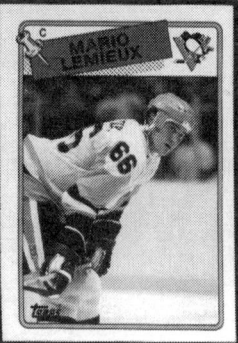

Topps
1988-89 Issue
Card No. 1,
Mario Lemieux

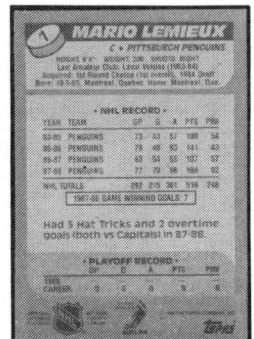

Topps
1988-89 Issue
Card No. 1,
Mario Lemieux

Topps
1988-89 Issue
Card No. 66,
Brett Hull

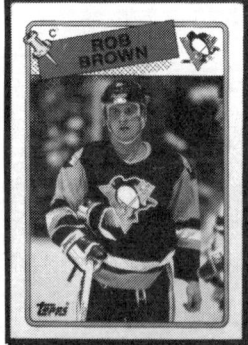

Topps
1988-89 Issue
Card No. 109,
Rob Brown

No.	Player	VG	EX	NRMT
75	Carey Wilson, Har.	.01	.03	.06
76	Joe Mullen, Cal.	.09	.18	.35
77	Richard Vaive, Chi.	.01	.03	.06
78	Shawn Burr, Det., DP	.01	.03	.06
79	Murray Craven, Phi.	.01	.03	.06
80	Clark Gillies, Buf., LC	.01	.03	.06
81	Bernie Federko, St. L.	.01	.03	.06
82	Tony Tanti, Van.	.01	.03	.06
83	Gregory Gilbert, NYI	.01	.03	.06
84	Kirk Muller, NJ	.12	.25	.50
85	Dave Tippett, Har.	.01	.03	.06
86	Kevin Hatcher, Wash., DP	.25	.50	1.00
87	Rick Middleton, Bos., LC, DP	.01	.03	.06
88	Robert Smith, Mon.	.01	.03	.06
89	Douglas Wilson, Chi., DP	.01	.03	.06
90	Scott Arniel, Buf.	.01	.03	.06
91	Brian Mullen, NYR	.01	.03	.06
92	Michael O'Connell, Det., DP	.01	.03	.06
93	Mark Messier, Edm., DP	.20	.40	.85
94	**Sean Burke, Goalie, NJ, RC**	**.25**	**.50**	**1.00**
95	Brian Bellows, Min., DP	.06	.12	.25
96	Doug Bodger, Pit.	.01	.03	.06
97	Bryan Trottier, NYI	.05	.10	.20
98	Anton Stastny, Que.	.02	.05	.10
99	Checklist 1 (1 - 99)	.25	.50	1.00
100	David Poulin, Phi., DP	.01	.03	.06
101	Bob Bourne, LA, DP	.01	.03	.06
102	John Vanbiesbrouck, Goalie, NYR	.25	.50	1.00
103	Allen Pedersen, Bos.	.01	.03	.06
104	Mike Ridley, Wash.	.01	.03	.06
105	Andrew McBain, Win.	.01	.03	.06
106	Troy Murray, Chi., DP	.01	.03	.06
107	Tom Barrasso, Goalie, Buf.	.07	.15	.30
108	Tomas Jonsson, NYI, LC	.01	.03	.06
109	**Rob Brown, Pit., RC**	**.12**	**.25**	**.50**
110	Hakan Loob, Cal., LC, DP	.01	.03	.06
111	Ilkka Sinisalo, Phi., DP	.01	.03	.06
112	**Dave Archibald, Min., RC**	**.05**	**.10**	**.20**
113	Doug Halward, Det., LC	.01	.03	.06
114	Ray Ferraro, Har.	.01	.03	.06
115	**Doug Brown, NJ, RC**	**.10**	**.20**	**.40**
116	Patrick Roy, Goalie, Mon., DP	1.10	2.25	4.50
117	Greg Millen, Goalie, St. L.	.01	.03	.06
118	Ken Linseman, Bos.	.01	.03	.06
119	Phil Housley, Buf., DP	.09	.18	.35
120	Wayne Gretzky, LA	8.75	17.50	35.00
121	Tomas Sandstrom, NYR	.07	.15	.30
122	**Brendan Shanahan, NJ, RC**	**2.50**	**5.00**	**10.00**
123	Pat LaFontaine, NYI	.30	.60	1.25
124	Luc Robitaille, LA, DP	1.00	2.00	4.00
125	Ed Olczyk, Tor., DP	.01	.03	.06
126	Ronald Sutter, Phi.	.01	.03	.06
127	Michael Liut, Goalie, Har.	.01	.03	.06
128	Brent Ashton, Win., DP	.01	.03	.06
129	**Anthony Hrkac, St. L., RC**	**.06**	**.12**	**.25**
130	Kelly Miller, Wash.	.01	.03	.06
131	Alan Haworth, Que.	.01	.03	.06
132	**Dave McIlwain, Pit., RC**	**.05**	**.10**	**.20**
133	Michael Ramsey, Buf.	.01	.03	.06
134	**Robert Sweeney, Bos., RC**	**.05**	**.10**	**.20**
135	Dirk Graham, Chi., DP	.01	.03	.06
136	Ulf Samuelsson, Har.	.10	.20	.40
137	Petri Skriko, Van.	.01	.03	.06
138	Aaron Broten, NJ, DP	.01	.03	.06
139	Jim Fox, LA	.01	.03	.06
140	**Randy Wood, NYI, RC, DP**	**.07**	**.15**	**.30**
141	Lawrence Murphy, Wash.	.01	.03	.06
142	Daniel Berthiaume, Goalie, Win., DP	.01	.03	.06
143	Kelly Kisio, NYR	.01	.03	.06
144	Neal Broten, Min.	.01	.03	.06
145	Reed Larson, Bos.	.01	.03	.06
146	Peter Zezel, Phi., DP	.01	.03	.06
147	Jari Kurri, Edm.	.10	.20	.40
148	Jim Johnson, Pit.	.01	.03	.06
149	Gino Cavallini, St. L., DP	.01	.03	.06
150	Glen Hanlon, Goalie, Det., DP	.01	.03	.06
151	Bengt-ake Gustafsson, Was. LC	.01	.03	.06
152	Mike Bullard, Phi.	.01	.03	.06
153	John Ogrodnick, NYR	.01	.03	.06
154	Steve Larmer, Chi.	.09	.18	.35
155	Kelly Hrudey, Goalie, NYI	.07	.15	.30
156	Mats Naslund, Mon.	.01	.03	.06
157	Bruce Driver, NJ	.01	.03	.06

1988 - 89 STICKER INSERTS — TOPPS • 237

No.	Player	VG	EX	NRMT
158	Randy Hillier, Pit.	.01	.03	.06
159	Craig Hartsburg, Min., LC	.01	.03	.06
160	Roland Melanson, Goalie, LA, LC	.01	.03	.06
161	Adam Oates, Det.	.75	1.50	3.00
162	Greg Adams, Van.	.01	.03	.06
163	David Andreychuk, Buf.	.15	.30	.65
164	Dave Babych, Har.	.01	.03	.06
165	**Brian Noonan, Chi., RC**	.12	.25	.50
166	**Glen Wesley, Bos., RC**	.30	.60	1.25
167	Dave Ellett, Win.	.01	.03	.06
168	Brian Propp, Phi.	.01	.03	.06
169	Bernie Nicholls, LA	.06	.12	.25
170	Walter Poddubny, NYR	.01	.03	.06
171	Stephen Konroyd, NYI	.01	.03	.06
172	Douglas Sulliman, NJ, DP	.01	.03	.06
173	Mario Gosselin, Goalie, Que.	.01	.03	.06
174	Brian Benning, St. L.	.01	.03	.06
175	Dino Ciccarelli, Min.	.01	.03	.06
176	Stephen Kasper, Bos.	.01	.03	.06
177	Rick Tocchet, Phi.	.50	1.00	2.00
178	Byron (Brad) McCrimmon, Cal.	.01	.03	.06
179	Paul Coffey, Pit.	.18	.35	.75
180	Peter Peeters, Goalie, Wash.	.01	.03	.06
181	**Bob Probert, Det., RC, DP**	.75	1.50	3.00
182	**Steve Duchesne, LA, RC, DP**	.50	1.00	2.00
183	Russell Courtnall, Tor.	.10	.20	.40
184	Mike Foligno, Buf., DP	.01	.03	.06
185	Wayne Presley, Chi., DP	.01	.03	.06
186	Rejean Lemelin, Goalie, Bos.	.01	.03	.06
187	Mark Hunter, St. L.	.01	.03	.06
188	Joe Cirella, NJ	.01	.03	.06
189	Glenn Anderson, Edm., DP	.03	.07	.15
190	John Anderson, Har.	.01	.03	.06
191	Patrick Flatley, NYI	.01	.03	.06
192	Rod Langway, Wash.	.01	.03	.06
193	Brian MacLellan, Min.	.01	.03	.06
194	**Pierre Turgeon, Buf., RC**	4.50	9.00	18.00
195	Brian Hayward, Goalie, Mon.	.01	.03	.06
196	Steve Yzerman, Det., DP	.40	.85	1.75
197	Doug Crossman, Phi.	.01	.03	.06
198	Checklist 2 (100 - 198)	.25	.50	1.00

— 1988 - 89 STICKER INSERTS —

Colour inserts were issued one per pack and featured 12 All-Star players and 21 team logo stickers.

Sticker Size: 2 1/2" X 3 1/2"
All Star Stickers:
Face: Four colour, white border, Name, Position
Back: Two colour, blue and red on card stock; Name, Number, Position, Resume
Team Helmet Stickers
Face: Four colour, white background; Team logo, Number, Hockey pucks
Back: Two colour, blue and red on card stock; Promotional offer
Imprint: * or ** © 1988 TOPPS CHEWING GUM, INC.
PRTD. IN U.S.A. © 1988 NHLPA
Complete Set No.: 33
Complete Set Price: 3.75 7.50 15.00
Common Card: .02 .05 .10
Common Team: .02 .05 .10

ALL STAR FIRST TEAM

No.	Player		NRMT	Mint
1	Luc Robitaille, LA	.25	.50	1.00
2	Mario Lemieux, Pit.	1.25	2.50	5.00
3	Hakan Loob, Ca.	.05	.10	.20
4	Scott Stevens, Wash.	.05	.10	.20
5	Raymond Bourque, Bos.	.25	.50	1.00
6	Grant Fuhr, Goalie, Edm..	.25	.50	1.00

ALL STAR SECOND TEAM

No.	Player		NRMT	Mint
7	Michel Goulet, Que.	.05	.50	1.00
8	Wayne Gretzky, Edm.	.75	1.50	3.00
9	Cam Neely, Bos.	.25	.50	1.00
10	Byron (Brad) McCrimmon, Phi.	.05	.10	.20
11	Gary Suter, Cal.	.05	.10	.20
12	Patrick Roy, Goalie, Mon.	.75	1.50	3.00

TEAM HELMET STICKERS

No.	Team	VG	EX	NRMT
13	Toronto Maple Leafs	.02	.05	.10
14	Buffalo Sabres	.02	.05	.10
15	Detroit Red Wings	.02	.05	.10
16	Pittsburgh Penguins	.02	.05	.10
17	New York Rangers	.02	.05	.10
18	Calgary Flames	.02	.05	.10
19	Winnipeg Jets	.02	.05	.10
20	Quebec Nordiques	.02	.05	.10
21	Chicago Blackhawks	.02	.05	.10
22	Los Angeles Kings	.02	.05	.10
23	Montreal Canadiens	.02	.05	.10
24	Vancouver Canucks	.02	.05	.10
25	Hartford Whalers	.02	.05	.10
26	Philadelphia Flyers	.02	.05	.10
27	New Jersey Devils	.02	.05	.10
28	St. Louis Blues	.02	.05	.10
29	Minnesota North Stars	.02	.05	.10
30	Washington Capitals	.02	.05	.10
31	Boston Bruins	.02	.05	.10
32	New York Islanders	.02	.05	.10
33	Edmonton Oilers	.02	.05	.10

Topps
1988-89 Issue
Card No. 169,
Bernie Nicholls

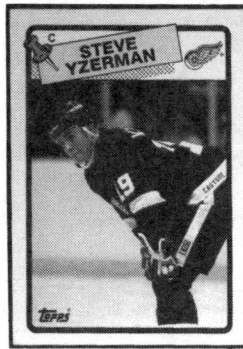

Topps
1988-89 Issue
Card No. 196,
Steve Yzerman

Topps
1988-89 Sticker
Sticker No. 1,
Luc Robitaille

Topps
1988-89 Sticker
Sticker No. 1,
Luc Robitaille

Available in April !

THE CHARLTON STANDARD CATALOGUE OF CANADIAN

BASEBALL & FOOTBALL CARDS

- *Fourth Edition* -
BASEBALL CARDS FROM 1912
FOOTBALL CARDS FROM 1949

For Canadian Baseball and Football Card Collectors this Catalogue has it all!

IMPERIAL TOBACCO * MAPLE CRISPETTE * BAZOOKA
*PARKHURST * O-PEE-CHEE * CANADA STARCH
STUART * POST * TOPPS * WORLD WIDE GUM * NALLEYS
DONRUSS - LEAF * EDDIE SARGENT * WILLARD
TORONTO BLUE JAYS * STANDARD OIL * NABISCO
VACHON BLUE RIBBON TEA * PANINI * PROVIGO
GENERAL MILLS * SCORE * EXHIBITS * HOSTESS
PURITAN MEATS * JOGO * GULF CANADA * KFC
ROYAL STUDIOS * BEN'S AULT FOODS * COCA-COLA
And All Other Major Manufacturers...

Complete price listings for all Major League
Baseball and Canadian Football League cards!
Comprehensive baseball and football
minor league card listings!
Regular issues, stickers, inserts, subsets, transfers
and much, much more!
All major manufacturers!
Current Pricing for all cards in up to three grades of
condition - VG, EX, and NRMT!
All rookie, last, pitcher, quarterback, error
and variation cards identified and priced!
Plus Charlton's Fabulous Alphabetical Index!
OVER 300 PAGES * 60,000 PRICES
NEW, LARGER 8 1/2 x 11" FORMAT
RESERVE YOUR COPY TODAY
DIRECTLY FROM THE PUBLISHER...

The Charlton Press

2010 YONGE STREET, TORONTO, ONTARIO M4S 1Z9
FOR TOLL FREE ORDERING PHONE 1-800-442-6042
FAX 1-800-442-1542 from anywhere in Canada or the U.S.

238 • TOPPS — 1989-90 REGULAR ISSUE

— 1989-90 REGULAR ISSUE —

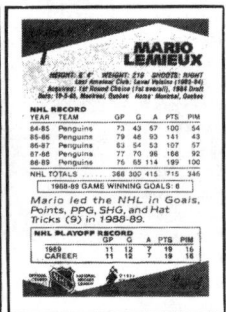

1989-90 Issue
Card No. 1, Mario Lemieux

Card Size: 2 1/2" x 3 1/2"
Face: Four colour, blue and marble border, Team logo
Back: Red and black on card stock; Number, Resume
Imprint: ** © 1989 THE TOPPS COMPANY, INC. © 1989 NHLPA
Complete Set No.: 198

	EX	NRMT
Complete Set Price:	25.00	45.00
Common Player:	.03	.06
Wax Pack: (13 Cards; 12 + Insert)		2.50
Wax Box: (36 Packs)		85.00
Wax Case: (20 Packs)		1,500.00

No.	Player	EX	NRMT
1	Mario Lemieux, Pit.	1.25	2.50
2	Ulf Dahlen, NYR	.03	.06
3	**Terry Carkner, Phi., RC**	**.10**	**.15**
4	Anthony McKegney, Det.	.03	.06
5	Denis Savard, Chi.	.12	.25
6	**Derek King, NYI, RC, DP**	**.35**	**.75**
7	Lanny McDonald, Cal.	.10	.15
8	John Tonelli, LA	.03	.06
9	Tom Kurvers, NJ, DP	.03	.06
10	Dave Archibald, Min., LC	.03	.06
11	**Peter Sidorkiewicz, Goalie, Har., RC**	**.12**	**.25**
12	Esa Tikkanen, Edm.	.15	.30
13	Dave Barr, Det.	.03	.06
14	Brent Sutter, NYI	.03	.06
15	Cam Neely, Bos.	.17	.35
16	**Calle Johansson, Wash., RC**	**.15**	**.30**
17	Patrick Roy, Goalie, Mon., DP	.60	1.25
18	Dale DeGray, LA, DP	.03	.06
19	**Phil Bourque, Pit., RC**	**.15**	**.30**
20	Kevin Dineen, Har.	.03	.06
21	Mike Bullard, Phi.	.03	.06
22	Gary Leeman, Tor.	.03	.06
23	Gregory Stefan, Goalie, Det.	.03	.06
24	Brian Mullen, NYR	.03	.06
25	Pierre Turgeon, Buf., DP	.50	1.00
26	**Robert Rouse, Wash., RC, DP**	**.03**	**.06**
27	Peter Zezel, St. L.	.03	.06
28	Jeff Brown, Que., DP	.15	.30
29	**Andy Brickley, Bos., RC, DP**	**.10**	**.20**
30	Michael Gartner, Min.	.20	.40
31	Darren Pang, Goalie, Chi.	.04	.08
32	Patrick Verbeek, Har.	.03	.06
33	Petri Skriko, Van.	.03	.06
34	Thomas Laidlaw, LA	.03	.06
35	Randy Wood, NYI	.03	.06
36	Tom Barrasso, Goalie, Pit., DP	.03	.06
37	John Tucker, Buf.	.03	.06
38	Andrew McBain, Pit.	.03	.06
39	David Shaw, NYR	.03	.06
40	Rejean Lemelin, Goalie, Bos.	.03	.06
41	Dino Ciccarelli, Wash., DP	.03	.06
42	Jeff Sharples, Det.	.03	.06
43	Jari Kurri, Edm.	.10	.20
44	Murray Craven, Phi.	.03	.06
45	**Cliff Ronning, St. L., RC, DP**	**.60**	**1.25**
46	Dave Babych, Har.	.03	.06
47	Bernie Nicholls, LA, DP	.03	.06
48	**Jon Casey, Goalie, Min., RC**	**.60**	**1.25**
49	Allan MacInnis, Cal.	.10	.20
50	**Bob Errey, Pit., RC, DP**	**.10**	**.20**
51	Glen Wesley, Bos.	.03	.06
52	Dirk Graham, Chi.	.03	.06
53	Guy Carbonneau, Mon.	.03	.06
54	Tomas Sandstrom, NYR	.03	.06

No.	Player	EX	NRMT
55	Rod Langway, Wash., DP	.03	.06
56	Patrik Sundstrom, NJ	.03	.06
57	Michel Goulet, Que.	.03	.06
58	David Taylor, LA	.03	.06
59	Phil Housley, Buf.	.03	.06
60	Pat LaFontaine, NYI, DP	.20	.40
61	**Kirk McLean, Goalie, Van., RC, DP**	**.75**	**1.50**
62	Ken Linseman, Bos.	.03	.06
63	Randy Cunneyworth, Win.	.03	.06
64	Anthony Hrkac, St. L.	.03	.06
65	Mark Messier, Edm., DP	.35	.75
66	Carey Wilson, NYR	.03	.06
67	**Stephen Leach, Wash., RC**	**.25**	**.50**
68	Christian Ruuttu, Buf.	.03	.06
69	Dave Ellett, Win.	.03	.06
70	Ray Ferraro, Har.	.03	.06
71	**Colin Patterson, Cal., RC**	**.03**	**.06**
72	Tim Kerr, Phi.	.03	.06
73	Robert Joyce, Bos.	.03	.06
74	Douglas Gilmour, Cal., DP	.35	.75
75	Lee Norwood, Det., DP	.03	.06
76	Dale Hunter, Wash.	.03	.06
77	Jim Johnson, Pit.	.03	.06
78	Mike Foligno, Buf.	.03	.06
79	Al Iafrate, Tor.	.12	.25
80	Rick Tocchet, Phi., DP	.12	.25
81	**Greg Hawgood, Bos., RC, DP**	**.10**	**.20**
82	Steve Thomas, Chi.	.03	.06
83	Steve Yzerman, Det., DP	.25	.50
84	Michael McPhee, Mon.	.03	.06
85	**David Volek, NYI, RC, DP**	**.12**	**.25**
86	Brian Benning, St. L.	.03	.06
87	Neal Broten, Min.	.03	.06
88	Luc Robitaille, LA, DP	.50	1.00
89	**Trevor Linden, Van., RC, D**	**2.00**	**4.00**
90	James Patrick, NYR	.03	.06
91	Brian Lawton, Har.	.03	.06
92	Sean Burke, Goalie, NJ, DP	.03	.06
93	Scott Stevens, Wash.	.03	.06
94	**Pat Elynuik, Win., RC, DP**	**.20**	**.40**
95	Paul Coffey, Pit.	.15	.30
96	Jan Erixon, NYR, DP	.03	.06
97	Michael Liut, Goalie, Har.	.03	.06
98	Wayne Presley, Chi.	.03	.06
99	Craig Simpson, Edm.	.03	.06
100	**Kjell Samuelsson, Phi., RC**	**.20**	**.40**
101	Shawn Burr, Det.	.03	.06
102	John MacLean, NJ	.03	.06
103	Tom Fergus, Tor.	.03	.06
104	Michael Krushelnyski, LA	.03	.06
105	Gary Nylund, NYI	.03	.06
106	David Andreychuk, Buf.	.15	.30
107	Bernie Federko, Det.	.03	.06
108	Gary Suter, Cal.	.03	.06
109	Dave Gagner, Min., DP	.20	.40
110	Raymond Bourque, Bos.	.25	.50
111	**Geoff Courtnall, Wash., RC**	**.60**	**1.25**
112	Douglas Wilson, Chi.	.10	.15
113	**Joe Sakic, Que., RC**	**4.00**	**8.00**
114	John Vanbiesbrouck, Goalie, NYR	.12	.25
115	David Poulin, Phi.	.03	.06
116	Richard Meagher, St. L.	.03	.06
117	Kirk Muller, NJ, DP	.07	.15
118	Mats Naslund, Mon.	.03	.06
119	Ray Sheppard, Buf.	.25	.50
120	**Jeff Norton, NYI, RC**	**.15**	**.30**
121	Randy Burridge, Bos.	.03	.06
122	Dale Hawerchuk, Win., DP	.05	.10
123	Steve Duchesne, LA	.12	.25
124	John Anderson, Har., LC	.03	.06
125	Richard Vaive, Buf.	.03	.06
126	Randy Hillier, Pit.	.03	.06
127	Jimmy Carson, Edm.	.03	.06
128	Lawrence Murphy, Min.	.05	.10
129	Paul MacLean, St. L.	.03	.06
130	Joe Cirella, Que.	.03	.06
131	Kelly Miller, Wash.	.03	.06
132	Alain Chevrier, Goalie, Chi.	.04	.08
133	Ed Olczyk, Tor.	.05	10
134	Dave Tippett, Har.	.03	.06
135	Robert Sweeney, Bos.	.03	.06
136	**Brian Leetch, NYR, RC**	**5.00**	**10.00**
137	Greg Millen, Goalie, St. L..	.04	.08

No.	Player	EX	NRMT
138	Joe Nieuwendyk, Cal.	.25	.50
139	Brian Propp, Phi.	.03	.06
140	Michael Ramsey, Buf.	.03	.06
141	Mike Allison, LA	.03	.06
142	**Shawn Chambers, Min., RC**	**.08**	**.15**
143	Peter Stastny, Que., DP	.03	.06
144	Glen Hanlon, Goalie, Det.	.04	.08
145	**John Cullen, Pit., RC**	**.25**	**.50**
146	Kevin Hatcher, Wash.	.10	.20
147	Brendan Shanahan, NJ	.85	1.75
148	Paul Reinhart, Van.	.03	.06
149	Bryan Trottier, NYI	.10	.20
150	**Dave Manson, Chi., RC**	**.35**	**.75**
151	**Marc Habscheid, Det., RC, DP**	**.03**	**.06**
152	Dan Quinn, Pit.	.03	.06
153	Stephane J. J. Richer, Mon., DP	.15	.30
154	Doug Bodger, Buf.	.03	.06
155	Ron Hextall, Goalie, Phi.	.10	.20
156	Wayne Gretzky, LA	1.50	3.00
157	**Steve Tuttle, St. L., RC, DP**	**.03**	**.06**
158	Charles Huddy, Edm.	.03	.06
159	Dave Christian, Wash.	.03	.06
160	Andrew Moog, Goalie, Bos.	.08	.15
161	**Tony Granato, NYR, RC**	**.35**	**.75**
162	**Sylvain Cote, Har., RC**	**.03**	**.06**
163	Michael Vernon, Goalie, Cal.	.15	.25
164	**Steve Chiasson, Det., RC**	**.20**	**.45**
165	Mike Ridley, Wash.	.03	.06
166	Kelly Hrudey, Goalie, LA	.04	.08
167	Robert Carpenter, Bos.	.03	.06
168	**Zarley Zalapski, Pit., RC**	**.17**	**.35**
169	**Derek Laxdal, Tor., RC**	**.03**	**.06**
170	Clint Malarchuk, Goalie, Buf.	.04	.08
171	Kelly Kisio, NYR	.03	.06
172	Gerard Gallant, Det.	.03	.06
173	Ronald Sutter, Phi.	.03	.06
174	Chris Chelios, Mon.	.10	.20
175	Ron Francis, Har.	.08	.15
176	Gino Cavallini, St. L.	.03	.06
177	Brian Bellows, Min., DP	.08	.15
178	Greg Adams, Van.	.03	.06
179	Steve Larmer, Chi.	.08	.15
180	Aaron Broten, NJ	.03	.06
181	Brent Ashton, Win.	.03	.06
182	**Gerald Diduck, NYI, RC, DP**	**.03**	**.06**
183	**Paul MacDermid, Har., RC**	**.03**	**.06**
184	Walter Poddubny, NJ	.03	.06
185	Adam Oates, St. L.	.40	.80
186	Brett Hull, St. L.	2.25	4.50
187	Scott Arniel, Buf.	.03	.06
188	Robert Smith, Mon.	.03	.06
189	Guy Lafleur, NYR	.15	.30
190	**Craig Janney, Bos., RC**	**1.50**	**3.00**
191	Mark Howe, Phi.	.03	.06
192	Grant Fuhr, Goalie, Edm., DP	.07	.15
193	Rob Brown, Pit.	.03	.06
194	Stephen Kasper, LA	.03	.06
195	Peter Peeters, Goalie, Phi.	.04	.08
196	Joe Mullen, Cal.	.08	.15
197	Checklist 1 (1 - 99)	.25	.50
198	Checklist 2 (100 - 198)	.25	.50

— 1989-90 STICKER INSERTS —

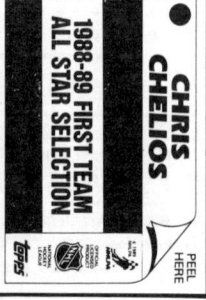

1989-90 Sticker Inserts
Sticker No. 1, Chris Chelios

— 1990 - 91 REGULAR ISSUE — TOPPS • 239

Sticker Size: 2 1/2" X 3 1/2"
All Star:
Face: Four colour, white border, Name, Position
Back: Two colour, blue and red on card stock; Name, Number, Position, Resume
Stickers:
Face: Four colour, white background; Team logo, Number, Hockey pucks
Back: Two colour, blue and red on card stock; Promotional offer
Imprint: * or ** © 1989 TOPPS CHEWING GUM, INC.
PRTD. IN U.S.A. © 1989 NHLPA
Complete Set No.: 33
Complete Set Price: 3.50 / 7.00
Common Player: .04 / .08
Common Team: .05 / .10

ALL STAR FIRST TEAM

No.	Player	EX	NRMT
1	Chris Chelios, Mon.	.20	.40
2	Gerard Gallant, Det.	.04	.08
3	Mario Lemieux, Pit.	1.50	3.00
4	Allan MacInnis, Cal.	.15	.30
5	Joe Mullen, Cal.	.07	.15
6	Patrick Roy, Goalie, Mon.	.75	1.50

ALL STAR SECOND TEAM

No.	Player	EX	NRMT
7	Raymond Bourque, Bos.	.30	.60
8	Rob Brown, Pit.	.12	.25
9	Geoff Courtnall, Wash.	.04	.08
10	Steve Duchesne, LA	.04	.08
11	Wayne Gretzky, LA	1.50	3.00
12	Michael Vernon, Goalie, Cal.	.12	.25

TEAM HELMET STICKERS

No.	Team	EX	NRMT
13	Toronto Maple Leafs	.05	.10
14	Buffalo Sabres	.05	.10
15	Detroit Red Wings	.05	.10
16	Pittsburgh Penguins	.05	.10
17	New York Rangers	.05	.10
18	Calgary Flames	.05	.10
19	Winnpeg Jets	.05	.10
20	Quebec Nordiques	.05	.10
21	Chicago Black Hawks	.05	.10
22	Los Angeles Kings	.05	.10
23	Montreal Canadiens	.05	.10
24	Vancouver Canucks	.05	.10
25	Hartford Whalers	.05	.10
26	Philadelphia Flyers	.05	.10
27	New Jersey Devils	.05	.10
28	St. Louis Blues	.05	.10
29	Minnesota North Stars	.05	.10
30	Washington Capitals	.05	.10
31	Boston Bruins	.05	.10
32	New York Islanders	.05	.10
33	Edmonton Oilers	.05	.10

— 1990 - 91 REGULAR ISSUE —

Topps produced a high quality limited edition set in 1990 called "Tiffany". This set, with 396 cards plus a 21-card scoring leader subset, came in a special serial numbered box. Three thousand sets were issued.

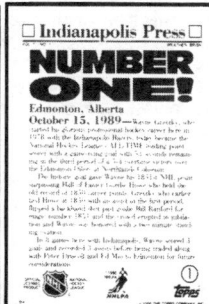

1990-91 Issue
Card No. 1, Wayne Gretsky
Indianapolis Press

Card Size: 2 1/2" X 3 1/2"
Face: Four colour, white border, Position
Back: Two colour, green and blue on card stock, Number, Resume
Imprint: A*, B* or C* © 1990 THE TOPPS COMPANY, INC.
Complete Set No.: 396
Complete Set Price:
  Regular: 7.50 / 15.00
  Tiffany: 37.50 / 75.00
Common Card: .02 / .05
Wax Pack: (15 Cards) .75
Wax Box: (36 Packs) 15.00
Wax Case: (20 Boxes): 200.00

TRIBUTE TO GRETZKY

No.	Player	EX	NRMT
1	Wayne Gretzky, Indianapolis Press	.15	.30
2	Wayne Gretzky, Edmonton Times	.15	.30
3	Wayne Gretzky, Los Angeles News	.15	.30

1990 HIGHLIGHTS

No.	Player	EX	NRMT
4	Brett Hull, St. L.	.10	.20
5	Jari Kurri, Edm., Error	.02	.05
6	Bryan Trottier, NYI	.02	.05

REGULAR ISSUE

No.	Player	EX	NRMT
7	Jeremy Roenick, Chi., RC	.75	1.50
8	Brian Propp, Bos.	.02	.05
9	Top Prospect: Jim Hrivnak, Goalie, Wash., RC	.08	.15
10	Mick Vukota, NYI, RC	.02	.05
11	Tom Kurvers, Tor.	.02	.05
12	Ulf Dahlen, Min.	.02	.05
13	Bernie Nicholls, NYR	.02	.05
14	Peter Sidorkiewicz, Goalie, Har.	.03	.06
15	Peter Zezel, St. L.	.02	.05
16	Mike Hartman, Buf., RC	.02	.05
17	Los Angeles Kings	.02	.05
18	Jim Sandlak, Van.	.02	.05
N9	Rob Brown, Pit.	.02	.05
20	Paul Ranheim, Cal., RC	.08	.15
21	Richard Zombo, Det., RC	.02	.05
22	Paul Gillis, Que.	.02	.05
23	Brian Hayward, Goalie, Mon.	.02	.05
24	Brent Ashton, Win.	.02	.05
25	Mark Lamb, Edm., RC	.02	.05
26	Rick Tocchet, Phi.	.02	.05
27	Viacheslav Fetisov, NJ, RC	.10	.20
28	Denis Savard, Chi.	.02	.05
29	Chris Chelios, Mon.	.02	.05
30	Janne Ojanen, NJ, RC	.02	.05
31	Donald Maloney, NYI	.02	.05
32	Allan Bester, Goalie, Tor.	.02	.05
33	Geoff Smith, Edm., RC	.02	.05
34	Daniel Shank, Det., RC	.02	.05
35	Mikael Andersson, Har., RC	.02	.05
36	Gino Cavallini, St. L.	.02	.05
37	Top Prospect: Rob Murphy, Van., RC	.02	.05
38	Calgary Flames	.02	.05
39	Laurie Boschman, Win.	.02	.05
40	Craig Wolanin, Que., RC	.02	.05
41	Phil Bourque, Pit.	.02	.05
42	Alexander Mogilny, Buf., RC	.60	1.25
43	Raymond Bourque, Bos.	.07	.15
44	Michael Liut, Goalie, Wash.	.02	.05
45	Ronald Sutter, Phi.	.02	.05
46	Bob Kudelski, LA, RC	.10	.20
47	Lawrence Murphy, Min.	.02	.05
48	Darren Turcotte, NYR, RC	.12	.25
49	Top Prospect: Paul Ysebaert, NJ, RC	.12	.25
50	Alan Kerr, NYI	.02	.05
51	Randy Carlyle, Win.	.02	.05
52	Iiro Jarvi, Que.	.02	.05
53	Don Barber, Min., RC	.02	.05
54	Carey Wilson, NYR, Error	.02	.05
55	Joey Kocur, Det., RC	.02	.05
56	Steve Larmer, Chi.	.02	.05
57	Paul Cavallini, St. L.	.02	.05
58	Shayne Corson, Mon.	.02	.05
59	Vancouver Canucks	.02	.05
60	Sergei Makarov, Cal., RC	.15	.30
61	Kjell Samuelsson, Phi.	.02	.05

No.	Player	EX	NRMT
62	Tony Granato, LA	.05	.10
63	Tom Fergus, Tor.	.02	.05
64	Martin Gelinas, Edm., RC	.08	.15
65	Tom Barrasso, Goalie, Pit.	.02	.05
66	Pierre Turgeon, Buf.	.15	.30
67	Randy Cunneyworth, Har.	.02	.05
68	Michal Pivonka, Wash., RC	.12	.25
69	Cam Neely, Bos.	.05	.10
70	Brian Bellows, Min.	.02	.05
71	Pat Elynuik, Win.	.02	.05
72	Doug Crossman, NYI	.02	.05
73	Sylvain Turgeon, NJ	.02	.05
74	Shawn Burr, Det.	.02	.05
75	John Vanbiesbrouck, Goalie, NYR	.07	.15
76	Steven Bozek, Van., RC	.02	.05
77	Brett Hull, St. L.	.30	.60
78	Zarley Zalapski, Pit.	.02	.05
79	Wendel Clark, Tor.	.07	.15
80	Philadelphia Flyers	.02	.05
81	Kelly Miller, Wash.	.02	.05
82	Mark Pederson, Mon., RC	.02	.05
83	Adam Creighton, Chi.	.02	.05
84	Scott Young, Har.	.02	.05
85	Petr Klima, Edm.	.02	.05
86	Steve Duchesne, LA	.02	.05
87	Joe Nieuwendyk, Cal.	.05	.10
88	Andy Brickley, Bos.	.02	.05
89	Phil Housley, Win.	.02	.05
90	Neal Broten, Min.	.02	.05
91	Al Iafrate, Tor.	.02	.05
92	Steve Thomas, Chi.	.02	.05
93	Guy Carbonneau, Mon.	.02	.05
94	Steve Chiasson, Det.	.02	.05
95	Mike Tomlak, Har., RC	.02	.05
96	Top Prospect: Roger Johansson, Cal., RC	.02	.05
97	Randy Wood, NYI	.02	.05
98	Jim Johnson, Pit.	.02	.05
99	Robert Sweeney, Bos.	.02	.05
100	Dino Ciccarelli, Wash.	.02	.05
101	New York Rangers	.02	.05
102	Michael Ramsey, Buf.	.02	.05
103	Kelly Hrudey, Goalie, LA	.02	.05
104	Dave Ellett, Win.	.02	.05
105	Bob Brooke, NJ	.02	.05
106	Greg Adams, Van.	.02	.05
107	Joe Cirella, Que.	.02	.05
108	Jari Kurri, Edm.	.02	.05
109	Peter Peeters, Goalie, Phi.	.02	.05
110	Paul MacLean, St. L.	.02	.05
111	Douglas Wilson, Chi.	.02	.05
112	Patrick Verbeek, Har.	.02	.05
113	Bob Beers, Bos., RC	.05	.10
114	Michael O'Connell, Det.	.02	.05
115	Brian Bradley, Van.	.02	.05
116	Paul Coffey, Pit.	.08	.15
117	Doug Brown, NJ	.02	.05
118	Aaron Broten, Min.	.02	.05
119	Bob Essensa, Goalie, Win., RC	.15	.30
120	Wayne Gretzky, LA, Error	.60	1.25
121	Vincent Damphousse, Tor.	.08	.15
122	Quebec Nordiques	.02	.05
123	Mike Foligno, Buf.	.02	.05
124	Russ Courtnall, Mon.	.02	.05
125	Richard Meagher, St. L.	.02	.05
126	Craig Fisher, Phi., RC	.02	.05
127	Al MacInnis, Cal.	.05	.10
128	Derek King, NYI	.02	.05
129	Dale Hunter, Wash.	.02	.05
130	Mark Messier, Edm.	.18	.35
131	James Patrick, NYR, Error	.02	.05
132	Checklist 1 (1 - 132)	.05	.10
133	Detroit Red Wings	.02	.05
134	Barry Pederson, Pit.	.02	.05
135	Gary Leeman, Tor.	.02	.05
136	Douglas Gilmour, Cal.	.02	.05
137	Michael McPhee, Mon.	.02	.05
138	Bob Murray, Chi., LC	.02	.05
139	Robert Carpenter, Bos.	.02	.05
140	Sean Burke, NJ, Goalie	.03	.06
141	Dale Hawerchuk, Buf.	.08	.06
142	Guy Lafleur, Que.	.05	.10
143	Lindy Ruff, NYR	.02	.05

TOPPS — 1990-91 REGULAR ISSUE

No.	Player	EX	NRMT
144	Hartford Whalers	.02	.05
145	Glenn Anderson, Edm.	.02	.05
146	Top Prospect: Dave Chyzowski, NYI, RC	.02	.05
147	Kevin Hatcher, Wash.	.02	.05
148	Richard Vaive, Buf.	.02	.05
149	Adam Oates, St. L.	.05	.10
150	Garth Butcher, Van.	.02	.05
151	Basil McRae, Min.	.02	.05
152	Ilkka Sinisalo, Phi.	.02	.05
153	Stephen Kasper, LA	.02	.05
154	Greg Paslawski, Win.	.02	.05
155	Bradley Marsh, Tor.	.02	.05
156	Esa Tikkanen, Edm.	.02	.05
157	Tony Tanti, Pit.	.02	.05
158	Mario Marois, Que.	.02	.05
159	Sylvain Lefebvre, Mon., RC	.05	.10
160	Troy Murray, Chi.	.02	.05
161	Gary Roberts, Cal.	.08	.15
162	Randy Ladouceur, Har.	.02	.05
163	John Chabot, Det.	.02	.05
164	Calle Johansson, Wash.	.02	.05
165	Boston Bruins	.02	.05
166	Jeff Norton, NYI	.02	.05
167	Michael Krushelnyski, LA	.02	.05
168	Dave Gagner, Min.	.02	.05
169	David Andreychuk, Buf.	.05	.10
170	Dave Capuano, Van., RC	.02	.05
171	Top Prospect: Curtis Joseph, Goalie, St. L., RC	.40	.85
172	Bruce Driver, NJ	.02	.05
173	Scott Mellanby, Phi.	.02	.05
174	John Ogrodnick, NYR, LC	.02	.05
175	Mario Lemieux, Pit.	.50	1.00
176	Marc Fortier, Que.	.02	.05
177	Vincent Riendeau, Goalie, St. L., RC	.10	.20
178	Mark Johnson, NJ	.02	.05
179	Dirk Graham, Chi.	.02	.05
180	Winnipeg Jets	.02	.05
181	Top Prospect: Robb Stauber, Goalie, LA, RC	.15	.30
182	Christian Ruuttu, Buf.	.02	.05
183	Dave Tippett, Har.	.02	.05
184	Pat LaFontaine, NYI	.15	.30
185	Mark Howe, Phi.	.02	.05
186	Stephane J. J. Richer, Mon.	.02	.05
187	Jan Erixon, NYR	.02	.05
188	Neil Sheehy, Wash.	.02	.05
189	Craig MacTavish, Edm.	.02	.05
190	Randy Burridge, Bos.	.02	.05
191	Bernie Federko, Det.	.02	.05
192	Shawn Chambers, Min.	.02	.05

ALL STARS
First Team

No.	Player	EX	NRMT
193	Mark Messier, Edm.	.05	.10
194	Luc Robitaille, LA	.04	.08
195	Brett Hull, St. L.	.10	.20
196	Ray Bourque, Bos.	.04	.08
197	Al MacInnis, Cal.	.04	.08
198	Patrick Roy, Goalie, Mon.	.12	.25

Second Team

No.	Player	EX	NRMT
199	Wayne Gretzky, LA	.18	.35
200	Brian Bellows, Min.	.02	.05
201	Cam Neely, Bos.	.04	.08
202	Paul Coffey, Pit.	.04	.08
203	Douglas Wilson, Chi.	.02	.05
204	Daren Puppa, Goalie, Buf., Error	.03	.06

REGULAR ISSUE

No.	Player	EX	NRMT
205	Gary Suter, Cal.	.02	.05
206	Ed Olczyk, Tor.	.02	.05
207	Doug Lidster, Van.	.02	.05
208	John Cullen, Pit.	.02	.05
209	Luc Robitaille, LA	.10	.20
210	Tim Kerr, Phi.	.02	.05
211	Scott Stevens, Wash.	.02	.05
212	Craig Janney, Bos.	.08	.15

No.	Player	EX	NRMT
213	Kevin Dineen, Har.	.02	.05
214	Top Prospect: Jimmy Waite, Goalie, Chi., RC	.12	.25
215	Benoit Hogue, Buf.	.02	.05
216	Curtis Leschyshyn, Que., RC	.02	.05
217	Brad Lauer, NYI	.02	.05
218	Joe Mullen, Pit.	.02	.05
219	Patrick Roy, Goalie, Mon.	.25	.50
220	St. Louis Blues	.02	.05
221	Brian Leetch, NYR	.12	.25
222	Steve Yzerman, Det.	.12	.25
223	Top Prospect: Steph Beauregard, Goalie, Win., RC	.10	.20
224	John MacLean, NJ	.02	.05
225	Trevor Linden, Van.	.12	.25
226	Bill Ranford, Goalie, Edm.	.04	.08
227	Mark Osborne, Tor.	.02	.05
228	Curt Giles, Min.	.02	.05
229	Mikko Makela, LA	.02	.05
230	Bob Errey, Pit.	.02	.05
231	Jimmy Carson, Det.	.04	.08
232	Kay Whitmore, Goalie, Har., RC	.07	.15
233	Gary Nylund, NYI	.02	.05
234	Jiri Hrdina, Cal., RC	.02	.05
235	Stephen Leach, Wash., Error	.02	.05
236	Greg Hawgood, Bos.	.02	.05
237	Jocelyn Lemieux, Chi., RC	.08	.15
238	Daren Puppa, Buf., Goalie	.02	.05
239	Kelly Kisio, NYR	.02	.05
240	Craig Simpson, Edm.	.02	.05
241	Toronto Maple Leafs	.02	.05
242	Fredrik Olausson, Win.	.02	.05
243	Ron Hextall, Goalie, Phi.	.02	.05
244	Sergio Momesso, St. L., RC	.07	.15
245	Kirk Muller, NJ	.02	.05
246	Petr Svoboda, Mon.	.02	.05
247	Daniel Berthiaume, Goalie, Min.	.03	.06
248	Andrew McBain, Van.	.02	.05
249	Jeff Jackson, Que.	.02	.05
250	Randy Gilhen, Pit., RC	.02	.05
251	Edmonton Oilers	.02	.05
252	Top Prospect: Rick Bennett, NYR	.02	.05
253	Don Beaupre, Goalie, Wash.	.03	.06
254	Per-Erik Eklund, Phi.	.02	.05
255	Gregory Gilbert, Chi.	.02	.05
256	Gordon Roberts, St. L.	.02	.05
257	Kirk McLean, Goalie, Van.	.05	.10
258	Brent Sutter, NYI	.02	.05
259	Brendan Shanahan, NJ	.10	.20
260	Todd Krygier, Har., RC	.05	.10
261	Larry Robinson, LA	.02	.05
262	Buffalo Sabres	.02	.05
263	Dave Christian, Bos.	.02	.05
264	Checklist 2 (133 - 264)	.05	.10
265	Jamie Macoun, Cal.	.02	.05
266	Glen Hanlon, Goalie, Det.	.02	.05
267	Daniel Marois, Tor.	.02	.05
268	Douglas Smail, Win.	.02	.05
269	Jon Casey, Goalie, Min.	.02	.05
270	Brian Skrudland, Mon.	.02	.05
271	Michel Petit, Que.	.02	.05
272	Dan Quinn, Van.	.02	.05
273	Geoff Courtnall, Wash.	.02	.05
274	Mike Bullard, Phi.	.02	.05
275	Randall Gregg, Edm.	.02	.05
276	Keith Brown, Chi.	.02	.05
277	Troy Mallette, NYR, RC	.02	.05
278	Steve Tuttle, St. L.	.02	.05
279	Brad Shaw, Har., RC	.02	.05
280	Mark Recchi, Pit., RC	.50	1.00
281	John Tonelli, LA	.02	.05
282	Doug Bodger, Buf.	.02	.05
283	Thomas Steen, Win.	.02	.05
284	New Jersey Devils	.02	.05
285	Lee Norwood, Det.	.02	.05
286	Brian MacLellan, Cal.	.02	.05
287	Robert Smith, Mon.	.02	.05
288	Robert Cimetta, Bos., RC	.02	.05
289	Top Prospect: Rob Zettler, Min., RC	.05	.10
290	David Reid, Tor., RC	.02	.05
291	Bryan Trottier, NYI	.02	.05
292	Brian Mullen, NYR	.02	.05
293	Paul Reinhart, Van.	.02	.05

No.	Player	EX	NRMT
294	Andrew Moog, Goalie, Bos.	.02	.05
295	Jeff Brown, St. L.	.02	.05
296	Ryan Walter, Mon.	.02	.05
297	Trent Yawney, Chi.	.02	.05
298	John Druce, Wash., RC	.04	.08
299	Dave McLlwain, Win., Error	.02	.05
300	David Volek, NYI	.02	.05
301	Tomas Sandstrom, LA	.02	.05
302	Gordon Murphy, Phi., RC	.02	.05
303	Lou Franceschetti, Tor., RC	.02	.05
304	Dana Murzyn, Cal.	.02	.05
305	Minnesota North Stars	.02	.05
306	Patrik Sundstrom, NJ	.02	.05
307	Kevin Lowe, Edm.	.02	.05
308	Dave Barr, Det.	.02	.05
309	Wendell Young, Goalie, Pit., RC	.04	.08
310	Top Prospect: Darrin Shannon, Buf., RC	.08	.15
311	Ronald Francis, Har.	.02	.05
312	Top Prospect: Stephane Fiset, Goalie, Que., RC	.15	.30
313	Paul Fenton, Win.	.02	.05
314	David Taylor, LA	.02	.05
315	New York Islanders	.02	.05
316	Petri Skriko, Van.	.02	.05
317	George (Rob) Ramage, Tor.	.02	.05
318	Murray Craven, Phi.	.02	.05
319	Gaetan Duchesne, Min.	.02	.05
320	Byron (Brad) McCrimmon, Det.	.02	.05
321	Grant Fuhr, Goalie, Edm.	.02	.05
322	Gerard Gallant, Det.	.02	.05
323	Tommy Albelin, NJ	.02	.05
324	Scott Arniel, Buf.	.02	.05
325	Mike Keane, Mon., RC	.12	.25
326	Pittsburgh Penguins	.02	.05
327	Mike Ridley, Wash.	.02	.05
328	Dave Babych, Har.	.02	.05
329	Michel Goulet, Chi.	.02	.05
330	Mike Richter, Goalie, NYR, RC	.35	.75
331	Garry Galley, Bos., RC	.05	.10
332	Rod Brind'Amour, St. L., RC	.25	.50
333	Anthony McKegney, Que.	.02	.05
334	Peter Stastny, NJ	.04	.08
335	Greg Millen, Goalie, Chi.	.03	.06
336	Ray Ferraro, Har.	.02	.05
337	Miloslav Horava, NYR, RC	.02	.05
338	Paul MacDermid, Win.	.02	.05
339	Craig Coxe, Van.	.02	.05
340	Dave Snuggerud, Buf., RC	.02	.05
341	Mike Lalor, St. L., RC	.02	.05
342	Marc Habscheid, Det.	.02	.05
343	Rejean Lemelin, Goalie, Bos.	.02	.05
344	Charles Huddy, Edm.	.02	.05
345	Ken Linseman, Phi.	.02	.05
346	Montreal Canadiens	.02	.05
347	Troy Loney, Pit., RC	.02	.05
348	Michael Modano, Min., RC	.50	1.00
349	Top Prosepct: Jeff Reese, Goalie, Tor., RC	.05	.10
350	Patrick Flatley, NYI	.02	.05
351	Michael Vernon, Goalie, Cal.	.08	.15
352	Todd Elik, LA, RC	.12	.25
353	Rod Langway, Wash.	.02	.05
354	Maurice Mantha, Win.	.02	.05
355	Keith Acton, Phi.	.02	.05
356	Scott Pearson, Tor., RC	.05	.10
357	Perry Berezan, Min., RC	.02	.05
358	Alexei Kasatonov, NJ, RC	.10	.20
359	Igor Larionov, Van., RC	.18	.35
360	Kevin Stevens, Pit., RC	.50	1.00
361	Top Prospect: Yves Racine, Det., RC	.08	.15
362	David Poulin, Bos.	.02	.05
363	Chicago Black Hawks	.02	.05
364	Yvon Corriveau, Har., RC	.02	.05
365	Brian Benning, LA	.02	.05
366	Hubie McDonough, NYI, RC	.05	.10
367	Ron Tugnutt, Goalie, Que.	.02	.05
368	Steve Smith, Edm.	.02	.05
369	Joel Otto, Cal.	.02	.05
370	Dave Lowry, St. L., RC	.02	.05
371	Clint Malarchuk, Goalie, Buf.	.02	.05
372	Mathieu Schneider, Mon., RC	.15	.35
373	Michael Gartner, NYR	.02	.05

No.	Player	EX	NRMT
374	John Tucker, Wash.	.02	.05
375	Chris Terreri, Goalie, NJ, RC	.12	.25
376	Dean Evason, Har.	.02	.05
377	Top Prospect: Jamie Leach, Pit., RC	.02	.05
378	Jacques Cloutier, Goalie, Chi., RC	.02	.05
379	Glen Wesley, Bos.	.02	.05
380	Vladimir Krutov, Van., RC	.02	.05
381	Terry Carkner, Phi.	.02	.05
382	John McIntyre, Tor., RC	.02	.05
383	Ville Siren, Min., RC	.02	.05
384	Joe Sakic, Que.	.35	.70
385	Teppo Numminen, Win., RC	.25	.50
386	Theoren Fleury, Cal.	.10	.20
387	Glen Featherstone, St. L., RC	.02	.05
388	Stephan Lebeau, Mon., RC	.20	.40
389	Kevin McClelland, Det.	.02	.05
390	Uwe Krupp, Buf.	.02	.05
391	Mark Janssens, NYR, RC	.02	.05
392	Martin McSorley, LA	.04	.08
393	Vladimir Ruzicka, Edm., RC	.12	.25
394	Washington Capitals	.02	.05
395	Mark Fitzpatrick, Goalie, NYI, RC	.04	.08
396	Checklist 3 (265 - 396)	.05	.10

— 1990 - 91 INSERT SET —
1989 - 90 TEAM SCORING LEADERS

This insert set shows the top scoring leader on each team for the 1989-90 season. This insert set was available only in wax packs and not in factory sets.

1990-91 Insert Set
Card No. 1, Steve Larmer

Card Size: 2 1/2" X 3 1/2"
Face: Four colour, white border
Back: Two colour, green and blue on card stock; Number
Imprint: ** © 1990 THE TOPPS COMPANY, INC. and © 1990 NHLPA
Complete Set No.: 21
Complete Set Price: 3.00 6.00
Common Player: .08 .15

No.	Player	EX	NRMT
1	**Chicago Black Hawks:** Steve Larmer	.08	.15
2	**St. Louis Blues:** Brett Hull	.60	1.25
3	**Boston Bruins:** Cam Neely	.08	.15
4	**Montreal Canadiens:** Stephane Richer	.08	.15
5	**Vancouver Canucks:** Paul Reinhart	.08	.15
6	**Washington Capitals:** Dino Ciccarelli	.08	.15
7	**New Jersey Devils:** Kirk Muller	.08	.15
8	**Calgary Falmes:** Joe Nieuwendyk	.08	.15
9	**Philadelphia Flyers:** Rick Tocchet	.08	.15
10	**New York Islanders:** Pat LaFontaine	.20	.40
11	**Winnipeg Jets:** Dale Hawerchuk	.08	.15
12	**Los Angeles Kings:** Wayne Gretzky	1.00	2.00
13	**Toronto Maple Leafs:** Gary Leeman	.08	.15
14	**Quebec Nordiques:** Joe Sakic	.12	.25
15	**Minnesota North Stars:** Brian Bellows	.08	.15
16	**Edmonton Oilers:** Mark Messier	.35	.75
17	**Pittsburgh Penguins:** Mario Lemieux	.85	1.75
18	**New York Rangers:** John Ogrodnick	.25	.50
19	**Detroit Red Wings:** Steve Yzerman	.35	.75
20	**Buffalo Sabres:** Pierre Turgeon	.20	.40
21	**Hartford Whalers:** Ron Francis	.08	.15

— 1991 PROMOTIONAL CARDS —

The 1991-92 promotional cards were issued in a nine-card minisheet with five Topps and four Bowman cards. The Bowman promotional cards are listed on page number ??? The cards are not numbered and are listed alphabetically.

1991 Promotional Card
Ed Belfour

Card Size: 2 1/2" X 3 1/2"
Face: Four colour, white border, Position
Back: Blue on white card stock
Imprint: *©1991 THE TOPPS COMPANY, INC.

No.	Player	EX	NRMT
—	Ed Belfour, Goalie, Chi.	1.50	3.00
—	Brett Hull, St. L.	1.50	3.00
—	Pat LaFontaine, NYI	1.50	3.00
—	Mario Lemieux, Pit.	1.50	3.00
—	Joe Sakic, Que.	1.50	3.00

— 1991 - 92 REGULAR ISSUE —

This Topps 528-card set utilizes the same photographs and layout as O-Pee-Chee, right down to identical errors exist in both sets. The back resume is in English only and the wax packs contained a twenty-one card insert set.

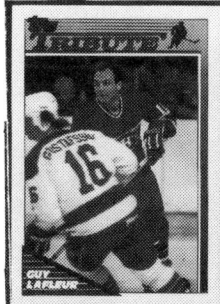 

1991-92 Issue
Card No. 1, Goodbye Guy!!!

Card Size: 2 1/2" X 3 1/2"
Face: Four colour, white border, Position
Back: Four colour, yellow, red and blue on card stock; Number, Resume
Imprint: A, B, C or D *©1991 THE TOPPS COMPANY, INC.
Complete Set No.: 528
Complete Set Price: 6.50 13.00
Common Card: .02 .05
Wax Pack: (15 Cards) .50
Wax Box: (36 Packs) 7.00
Wax Case: (20 Boxes) 150.00
Jumbo Pack: (34 Cards) .75
Jumbo Box: (24 Packs) 8.00

TRIBUTE TO LAFLEUR

No.	Player	EX	NRMT
1	Goodbye Guy!!	.05	.10
2	Gueeey's Last Hoorah	.05	.10
3	Guy Bids Farewell	.05	.10

SUPER ROOKIE

No.	Player	EX	NRMT
4	Ed Belfour, Goalie, Chi., Rookie Goals Against Average Leader	.10	.20
5	Kenneth Hodge, Jr., Bos., Rookie Power Play Goal Leader	.03	.06
6	Robert Blake, LA, Rookie Defenseman Points Leader	.05	.10
7	Robert Holik, Har., Rookie Left Wing Goal Leader	.05	.10
8	Sergei Fedorov, Det., Rookie Scoring Leader, Error	.15	.30
9	Jaromir Jagr, Pit., Rookie Right Wing Goal Scoring Leader	.15	.30
10	Eric Weinrich, NJD, Games Played by Rookie Defensemen	.03	.06
11	Mike Richter, NYR, Goalie Rookie Save Percentage Leader	.07	.15
12	Mats Sundin, Que., Rookie Right Wing Points Leader	.12	.25
13	Mike Ricci, Phi., Rookie Power Play Goal Leader	.08	.15

REGULAR ISSUE

No.	Player	EX	NRMT
14	Eric Desjardins, Mon.	.02	.05
15	Paul Ranheim, Cal.	.02	.05
16	Joe Sakic, Que.	.15	.30
17	Curt Giles, Min.	.02	.05
18	Mike Foligno, Tor.	.02	.05
19	Bradley Marsh, Det.	.02	.05
20	Ed Belfour, Chi., Goalie	.15	.30
21	James (Steve) Smith, Edm.	.02	.05
22	Kirk Muller, NJD	.02	.05
23	Kelly Chase, St. L.	.02	.05
24	Jim McKenzie, Har., RC	.05	.10
25	Mick Vukota, NYI	.02	.05
26	Top Prospect: Anthony Amonte, NYR, RC	.25	.50
27	Danton Cole, Win.	.02	.05
28	Jay Mazur, Van., RC	.02	.05
29	Peter Peeters, Goalie, Phi.	.02	.05
30	Petri Skriko, Bos.	.02	.05
31	Steve Duchesne, Phi., (Now With Flyers)	.02	.05
32	1990-91 Final Standings: Buffalo Sabres		
33	Phillippe Bourque, Pit.	.02	.05
34	Tim Bergland, Wash.	.02	.05
35	Tim Cheveldae, Goalie, Det.	.10	.20
36	Top Prospect: William Armstrong, Phi.	.02	.05
37	John McIntyre, LA	.02	.05
38	David Andreychuk, Buf.	.05	.10
39	Curtis Leschyshyn, Que.	.02	.05
40	Jaromir Jagr, Pit.	.40	.80
41	Craig Janney, Bos.	.08	.15
42	Doug Brown, NJD	.02	.05
43	Ken Sabourin, Wash.	.02	.05
44	1990-91 Final Standings: Minnesota North Stars	.02	.05
45	Fredrik Olausson, Win., Error	.02	.05
46	Michael Gartner, NYR	.02	.05
47	Mark Fitzpatrick, Goalie, NYI	.02	.05
48	Joe Murphy, Edm.	.02	.05
49	Douglas Wilson Jr., Chi.	.02	.05
50	Brian MacLellan, Det., (Now With Red Wings)	.02	.05
51	Bob Bassen, St. L.	.02	.05
52	Robert Kron, Van.	.05	.10
53	Roger Johansson, Cal.	.02	.05
54	Guy Carbonneau, Mon.	.05	.10
55	George (Rob) Ramage, Min., (Now With North Stars)	.02	.05
56	Robert Holik, Har.	.10	.20
57	Alan May, Wash.	.02	.05
58	Richard Meagher, St. L.	.02	.05
59	Cliff Ronning, Van.	.02	.05
60	1990-91 Final Standings: Detroit Red Wings	.02	.05
61	Bob Kudelski, LA	.02	.05
62	Wayne McBean, NYI	.02	.05
63	Craig MacTavish, Edm.	.02	.05
64	Owen Nolan, Que.	.10	.20
65	Dale Hawerchuk, Buf.	.05	.10
66	Raymond Bourque, Bos.	.10	.20
67	Sean Burke, Goalie, NJD	.02	.05
68	Frantisek Musil, Cal.	.02	.05

TOPPS — 1991-92 REGULAR ISSUE

No.	Player	EX	NRMT
69	Joe Mullen, Pit.	.02	.05
70	Top Prospect: Drake Berehowsky, Tor., RC	.05	.10
71	Darren Turcotte, NYR	.02	.05
72	Randy Carlyle, Win.	.02	.05
73	Paul Cyr, Har.	.02	.05
74	Dave Gagner, Min.	.02	.05
75	Steve Larmer, Chi.	.02	.05
76	Petr Svoboda, Mon.	.02	.05
77	Keith Acton, Phi.	.02	.05
78	Dimitri Khristich, Wash., Error	.02	.05
79	Byron (Brad) McCrimmon, Det.	.02	.05
80	Pat LaFontaine, NYI	.15	.30
81	Jeff Reese, Goalie, Tor.	.02	.05
82	Mario Marois, St. L.	.02	.05
83	Rob Brown, Har.	.05	.10
84	Grant Fuhr, Goalie, Edm.	.02	.05
85	Carey Wilson, Cal.	.02	.05
86	Garry Galley, Bos.	.02	.05
87	Troy Murray, Win. (Now With Jets)	.02	.05
88	Tony Granato, LA	.02	.05
89	Gordon Murphy, Phi.	.02	.05
90	Brent Gilchrist, Mon.	.02	.05
91	Mike Richter, Goalie, NYR	.12	.25
92	Eric Weinrich, NJD	.02	.05
93	Marc Bureau, Min.	.02	.05
94	Bob Errey, Pit.	.02	.05
95	Dave McLlwain, Win.	.02	.05
96	1990-91 Final Standings: Quebec Nordiques	.02	.05
97	Clint Malarchuk, Goalie, Buf.	.02	.05
98	Top Prospect: Shawn Antoski, Van., RC	.05	.10
99	Robert Sweeney, Bos.	.02	.05
100	Stephen Leach, Bos., (Now With Bruins)	.02	.05
101	Gary Nylund, NYI	.02	.05
102	Lucien DeBlois, Tor.	.02	.05
103	1990-91 Final Standings: Edmonton Oilers	.02	.05
104	Jimmy Carson, Det.	.02	.05
105	Rod Langway, Wash.	.02	.05
106	Jeremy Roenick, Chi.	.30	.60
107	Mike Vernon, Goalie, Cal.	.02	.05
108	Brian Leetch, NYR	.15	.30
109	Mark Hunter, Har.	.02	.05
110	Brian Bellows, Min.	.02	.05
111	Per-erik Eklund, Phi.	.02	.05
112	Robert Blake, LA	.08	.15
113	Mike Hough, Que.	.02	.05
114	Frank Pietrangelo, Goalie, Pit.	.02	.05
115	Christian Ruuttu, Buf.	.02	.05
116	Top Prospect: Bryan Marchment, Win., RC	.05	.10
117	Garry Valk, Van.	.02	.05
118	Kenneth Daneyko, NJD	.02	.05
119	Russell Courtnall, Mon.	.02	.05
120	Ronald Wilson, St. L.	.02	.05
121	Top Prospect: Shayne Stevenson, Bos.	.02	.05
122	Bill Berg, NYI, RC	.02	.05
123	1990-91 Final Standings: Toronto Maple Leafs	.02	.05
124	Glenn Anderson, Edm.	.05	.10
125	Kevin Miller, Det.	.02	.05
126	Calle Johansson, Wash.	.02	.05
127	Jimmy Waite, Goalie, Chi.	.02	.05
128	Allen Pedersen, Min., (Now With North Stars)	.02	.05
129	Brian Mullen, SJ	.02	.05
130	Ronald Francis, Pit.	.02	.05
131	Top Prospect: Jergus Baca, Har.	.02	.05
132	Checklist 1 (1 to 132)		
133	Tony Tanti, Buf.	.02	.05
134	Wes Walz, Bos.	.02	.05
135	Stephan Lebeau, Mon.	.10	.20
136	Ken Wregget, Goalie, Phi.	.02	.05
137	Scott Arniel, Win.	.02	.05
138	David Taylor, LA	.02	.05
139	Steven Finn, Que.	.05	.10
140	Brendan Shanahan, St. L., (Now With Blues)	.05	.10
141	Petr Nedved, Van.	.12	.25
142	Chris Dahlquist, Min.	.02	.05
143	Richard Sutter, St. L.	.02	.05
144	Joe Reekie, NYI	.02	.05

No.	Player	EX	NRMT
145	Peter Ing, Goalie, Tor.	.02	.05
146	Ken Linseman, Edm.	.02	.05
147	David Barr, Det.	.02	.05
148	Al Iafrate, Wash.	.02	.05
149	Gregory Gilbert, Chi.	.02	.05
150	Craig Ludwig, Min., (Now With North Stars)	.02	.05
151	Gary Suter, Cal.	.02	.05
152	Jan Erixon, NYR	.02	.05
153	Mario Lemieux, Pit.	.35	.70
154	Michael Liut, Goalie, Wash.	.02	.05
155	Uwe Krupp, Buf.	.02	.05
156	Darin Kimble, St. L.	.02	.05
157	Shayne Corson, Mon.	.02	.05
158	1990-91 Final Standings: Winnipeg Jets	.02	.05
159	Stephane Morin, Que.	.05	.10
160	Rick Tocchet, Phi.	.02	.05
161	John Tonelli, LA	.02	.05
162	Adrien Plavsic, Van.	.02	.05
163	Top Prospect: Jason Miller, NJD, RC	.02	.05
164	Tim Kerr, NYR, (Now With Rangers)	.02	.05
165	Brent Sutter, NYI	.02	.05
166	Michel Petit, Tor.	.02	.05
167	Adam Graves, Edm.	.02	.05
168	Jamie Macoun, Cal.	.02	.05
169	Terry Yake, Har.	.02	.05
170	1990-91 Final Standings: Boston Bruins	.02	.05
171	Alexander Mogilny, Buf.	.20	.40
172	Top Prospect: Karl Dykhuis, Chi.	.02	.05
173	Tomas Sandstrom, LA	.02	.05
174	Bernie Nicholls, NYR	.02	.05
175	Viacheslav Fetisov, NJD	.02	.05
176	Andrew Cassels, Mon.	.02	.05
177	Ulf Dahlen, Min.	.02	.05
178	Brian Hayward, Goalie, SJ	.02	.05
179	Doug Lidster, Van.	.02	.05
180	Dave Lowry, St. L.	.02	.05
181	Ron Tugnutt, Goalie, Que.	.02	.05
182	Ed Olczyk, Win.	.02	.05
183	Paul Coffey, Pit.	.05	.10
184	Shawn Burr, Det.	.02	.05
185	1990-91 Final Standings: Hartford Whalers	.02	.05
186	Mark Janssens, NYR	.02	.05
187	Top Prospect: Mike Craig, Min.	.02	.05
188	Gary Leeman, Tor.	.02	.05
189	Phil Sykes, Win.	.02	.05
190	Goal Scoring Leader: Brett Hull, St. L.	.12	.25
191	1990-91 Final Standings: New Jersey Devils	.02	.05
192	Cam Neely, Bos.	.05	.10
193	Petr Klima, Edm.	.02	.05
194	Mike Ricci, Phi.	.13	.25
195	Kelly Hrudey, Goalie, LA	.02	.05
196	Mark Recchi, Pit.	.15	.30
197	Mikael Andersson, Har.	.02	.05
198	Bob Probert, Det.	.02	.05
199	Craig Wolanin, Que.	.02	.05
200	Scott Mellanby, Edm. (Now With Oilers)	.02	.05
201	Hockey Highlights 1991: Gretzky Scores 2000th Point	.13	.25
202	Laurie Boschman, NJD	.02	.05
203	Gino Odjick, Van.	.02	.05
204	Garth Butcher, St. L.	.02	.05
205	Randy Wood, NYI	.02	.05
206	John Druce, Wash.	.02	.05
207	Doug Bodger, Buf.	.02	.05
208	Douglas Gilmour, Cal.	.10	.20
209	Top Prospect: John LeClair, Mon., RC	.13	.25
210	Steve Thomas, Chi.	.02	.05
211	Kjell Samuelsson, Phi.	.02	.05
212	Daniel Marois, Tor.	.02	.05
213	Jiri Hrdina, Pit.	.02	.05
214	Darrin Shannon, Buf.	.02	.05
215	1990-91 Final Standings: New York Rangers	.02	.05
216	Robert McGill, SJ	.02	.05
217	Dirk Graham, Chi.	.02	.05
218	Thomas Steen, Win.	.02	.05
219	Mats Sundin, Que.	.12	.25
220	Kevin Lowe, Edm.	.02	.05

No.	Player	EX	NRMT
221	Kirk McLean, Goalie, Van.	.02	.05
222	Jeff Brown, St. L.	.02	.05
223	Joe Nieuwendyk, Cal.	.08	.15
224	Assist Leader: Wayne Gretzky, LA	.15	.30
225	Martin McSorley, LA	.02	.05
226	John Cullen, Har.	.02	.05
227	Brian Propp, Min.	.02	.05
228	Yves Racine, Det.	.02	.05
229	Dale Hunter, Wash.	.02	.05
230	Top Prospect: Dennis Vaske, NYI, RC	.02	.05
231	Sylvain Turgeon, Mon.		.05
232	Ronald Sutter, Phi.	.02	.05
233	Chris Chelios, Chi.	.02	.05
234	Brian Bradley, Tor.	.02	.05
235	Scott Young, Pit.	.02	.05
236	Michael Ramsey, Buf.	.02	.05
237	Jon Casey, Goalie, Min.	.02	.05
238	Nevin Markwart, Bos.	.02	.05
239	John MacLean, NJD	.02	.05
240	Brent Ashton, Win.	.02	.05
241	Anthony Hrkac, SJ	.02	.05
242	1990-91 Final Standings: Vancouver Canucks	.02	.05
243	Jeff Norton, NYI	.02	.05
244	Martin Gelinas, Edm.	.02	.05
245	Mike Ridley, Wash.	.02	.05
246	Top Prospect: Pat Jablonski, Goalie, St. L., RC	.02	.05
247	1990-91 Final Standings: Calgary Flames	.02	.05
248	Paul Ysebaert, Det.	.02	.05
249	Sylvain Coté, Har.	.02	.05
250	Marc Habscheid, Cal., (Now With Flames)	.02	.05
251	Todd Elik, Min., (Now With North Stars)	.02	.05
252	Michael McPhee, Mon.	.02	.05
253	James Patrick, NYR	.02	.05
254	Murray Craven, Phi.	.02	.05
255	Trent Yawney, Chi.	.02	.05
256	Robert Cimetta, Tor.	.02	.05
257	League Leaders Point: Wayne Gretzky, LA	.15	.30

1ST TEAM NHL ALL STARS

No.	Player	EX	NRMT
258	Wayne Gretzky, LA	.10	.20
259	Brett Hull, St. L.	.10	.20
260	Luc Robitaille, LA	.02	.05
261	Raymond Bourque, Bos.	.08	.15
262	Allan MacInnis, Cal.	.02	.05
263	Ed Belfour, Goalie, Chi.	.07	.15

CHECKLIST

No.	Checklist	EX	NRMT
264	Checklist 2 (133 to 264)	.02	.05

2ND TEAM NHL ALL STAR

No.	Player	EX	NRMT
265	Adam Oates, St. L.	.02	.05
266	Cam Neely, Bos.	.02	.05
267	Kevin Stevens, Pit.	.07	.15
268	Chris Chelios, Chi.	.02	.05
269	Brian Leetch, NYR	.02	.05
270	Patrick Roy, Goalie, Mon.	.12	.25

REGULAR ISSUE

No.	Player	EX	NRMT
271	League Leader Wins: Ed Belfour, Goalie, Chi.	.10	.20
272	Rob Zettler, SJ	.02	.05
273	Top Prospect: Donald Audette, Buf., RC	.02	.05
274	Teppo Numminen, Win.	.10	.20
275	Peter Stastny, NJD	.02	.05
276	David Christian, Bos.	.02	.05
277	Lawrence Murphy, Pit.	.02	.05
278	Johan Garpenlov, Det.	.02	.05
279	Tom Fitzgerald, NYI	.02	.05
280	Gerald Diduck, Van.	.02	.05
281	Gino Cavallini, St. L.	.02	.05
282	Theoren Fleury, Cal.	.10	.20

… 1991 - 92 REGULAR ISSUE — TOPPS • 243

No.	Player	EX	NRMT
283	1990-91 Final Standings: Los Angeles Kings	.02	.05
284	Jeff Beukeboom, Edm.	.02	.05
285	Kevin Dineen, Har.	.02	.05
286	Jacques Cloutier, Goalie, Que.	.02	.05
287	Tom Chorske, Mon.	.02	.05
288	League Leader Save Pct: Ed Belfour, Chi., Goalie	.10	.20
289	Ray Sheppard, NYR	.02	.05
290	Top Prospect: Olaf Kolzig, Goalie, Wash.	.02	.05
291	Terry Carkner, Phi.	.02	.05
292	Benoit Hogue, Buf.	.02	.05
293	Mike Peluso, Chi.	.02	.05
294	Bruce Driver, NJD	.02	.05
295	Jari Kurri, LA, (Now With Kings)	.02	.05
296	Peter Sidorkiewicz, Goalie, Har.	.02	.05
297	Scott Pearson, Que.	.02	.05
298	1990-91 Final Standings: Montreal Canadiens	.02	.05
299	Vincent Damphousse, Tor.	.02	.05
300	John Carter, Bos.	.02	.05
301	Geoff Smith, Edm.	.02	.05
302	Stephen Kasper, Phi. (Now With Flyers)	.02	.05
303	Brett Hull, St. L.	.25	.50
304	Ray Ferraro, NYI	.02	.05
305	Geoff Courtnall, Van.	.02	.05
306	David Shaw, NYR	.02	.05
307	Bob Essensa, Goalie, Win.	.02	.05
308	Mark Tinordi, Min.	.02	.05
309	Keith Primeau, Det.	.02	.05
310	Kevin Hatcher, Wash.	.02	.05
311	Christopher Nilan, Bos.	.02	.05
312	Top Prospect: Trevor Kidd, Goalie, Cal.	.02	.05
313	Daniel Berthiaume, Goalie, LA	.02	.05
314	Adam Creighton, Chi.	.02	.05
315	Everett Sanipass, Que.	.02	.05
316	Ken Baumgartner, NYI	.02	.05
317	Top Prospect: Sheldon Kennedy, Det.	.02	.05
318	Dave Capuano, Van.	.02	.05
319	Don Sweeney, Bos.	.02	.05
320	Gary Roberts, Cal.	.02	.05
321	Wayne Gretzky, LA	.50	1.00
322	League Leaders Plus/Minus: T. Fleury, Cal., M. McSorley, LA, Error	.02	.05
323	Ulf Samuelsson, Pit.	.02	.05
324	Michael Krushelnyski, Tor.	.02	.05
325	Dean Evason, Har.	.02	.05
326	Pat Elynuik, Win.	.02	.05
327	Michal Pivonka, Wash.	.02	.05
328	Paul Cavallini, St. L.	.02	.05
329	1990-91 Final Standings: Philadelphia Flyers	.02	.05
330	Denis Savard, Mon.	.02	.05
331	Paul Fenton, Cal.	.02	.05
332	Jon Morris, NJD	.02	.05
333	Daren Puppa, Goalie, St. L.	.02	.05
334	Douglas Smail, Min.	.02	.05
335	Kelly Kisio, SJ	.02	.05
336	Michel Goulet, Chi.	.02	.05
337	Mike Sillinger, Det.	.02	.05
338	Andrew Moog, Goalie, Bos.	.02	.05
339	Paul Stanton, Pit.	.02	.05
340	Greg Adams, Van.	.02	.05
341	Douglas Crossman, Det.	.02	.05
342	Kelly Miller, Wash.	.02	.05
343	Patrick Flatley, NYI	.02	.05
344	Zarley Zalapski, Har.	.02	.05
345	Mark Osborne, Win.	.02	.05
346	Mark Messier, Edm.	.10	.20
347	1990-91 Final Standings: St. Louis Blues	.02	.05
348	Neil Wilkinson, SJ	.02	.05
349	Brian Skrudland, Mon.	.02	.05
350	Lyle Odelein, Mon.	.02	.05
351	Luke Richardson, Tor.	.02	.05
352	Zdeno Ciger, NJD	.02	.05
353	John Vanbiesbrouck, Goalie, NYR	.02	.05
354	Lou Franceschetti, Buf.	.02	.05
355	Alexei Gusarov, Que., RC	.02	.05
356	Bill Ranford, Goalie, Edm.	.02	.05
357	Normand Lacombe, Phi., Error	.02	.05
358	Randy Burridge, Wash. (Now With Capitals)	.02	.05

No.	Player	EX	NRMT
359	Brian Benning, LA	.02	.05
360	David Hannan, Tor.	.02	.05
361	Todd Gill, Tor.	.02	.05
362	Peter Bondra, Wash.	.02	.05
363	Mike Hartman, Buf.	.02	.05
364	Trevor Linden, Van.	.02	.05
365	John Ogrodnick, NYR	.02	.05
366	Stephen Konroyd, Chi.	.02	.05
367	Michael Modano, Min.	.18	.35
368	Glenn Healy, Goalie, NYI	.02	.05
369	Stephane J. J. Richer, Mon.	.02	.05
370	Vincent Riendeau, Goalie, St. L.	.02	.05
371	Randy Moller, NYR	.02	.05
372	1990-91 Final Standings: Pittsburgh Penguins	.02	.05
373	Murray Baron, Phi.	.02	.05
374	Troy Crowder, NJD	.02	.05
375	Richard Tabaracci, Goalie, Win.	.02	.05
376	Brent Fedyk, Det.	.02	.05
377	Randy Velischek, Que.	.02	.05
378	Esa Tikkanen, Edm.	.02	.05
379	Richard Pilon, NYI	.02	.05
380	Jeff Lazaro, Bos., RC	.02	.05
381	David Ellett, Tor.	.02	.05
382	Jeff Hackett, Goalie, SJ	.02	.05
383	Stephane Matteau, Cal.	.02	.05
384	1990-91 Final Standings: Washington Capitals	.02	.05
385	Wayne Presley, Chi.	.02	.05
386	Grant Ledyard, Buf.	.02	.05
387	Top Prospect: Kip Miller, Que.	.02	.05
388	Edward (Dean) Kennedy, Buf.	.02	.05
389	Hubie McDonough, NYI	.02	.05
390	Anatoli Semenov, Edm.	.02	.05
391	Daryl Reaugh, Goalie, Har.	.02	.05
392	Mathieu Schneider, Mon.	.02	.05
393	Dan Quinn, St L.	.02	.05
394	Claude Lemieux, NJD	.02	.05
395	Phil Housley, Win.	.02	.05
396	Checklist 3 (265 - 396)	.02	.05
397	Steven Bozek, Van.	.02	.05
398	Robert Smith, Min.	.02	.05
399	Mark Pederson, Phi.	.02	.05
400	Kevin Todd, NJD, RC	.12	.25
401	Sergei Fedorov, Cal.	.30	.60
402	Tom Barrasso, Goalie, Pit.	.02	.05
403	Hockey Highlights 1991: Brett Hull, St. L.	.10	.20
404	Robert Carpenter, Bos.	.02	.05
405	Luc Robitaille, LA	.10	.20
406	Mark Hardy, NYR	.02	.05
407	Neil Sheehy, Wash.	.02	.05
408	Michael McNeill, Que.	.02	.05
409	Dave Manson, Chi.	.02	.05
410	Mike Tomlak, Har.	.02	.05
411	Robert Reichel, Cal.	.12	.25
412	1990-91 Final Standings: New York Islanders	.02	.05
413	Patrick Roy, Goalie, Mon.	.10	.20
414	Top Prospect: Shaun Van Allen, Edm., RC	.08	.15
415	Dale Kushner, Phi.	.02	.05
416	Pierre Turgeon, Buf.	.02	.05
417	Curtis Joseph, Goalie, St. L.	.02	.05
418	Randy Gilhen, Pit., (Now With Kings)	.02	.05
419	Jyrki Lumme, Van.	.02	.05
420	Neal Broten, Min.	.02	.05
421	Kevin Stevens, Pit.	.12	.25
422	Chris Terreri, Goalie, NJD	.05	.10
423	David Reid, Tor.	.02	.05
424	Steve Yzerman, Det.	.15	.30
425	League Leader G.A.A.: Ed Belfour, Chi., Goalie	.10	.20
426	Jim Johnson, Min.	.02	.05
427	Joey Kocur, NYR	.02	.05
428	Joel Otto, Cal.	.02	.05
429	Dino Ciccarelli, Wash.	.02	.05
430	1990-91 Final Standings: Chicago Black Hawks	.02	.05
431	Claude Lapointe, Que., RC, Error	.02	.05
432	Chris Joseph, Edm.	.02	.05
433	Gaetan Duchesne, Min.	.02	.05
434	Mike Keane, Mon.	.02	.05
435	David Chyzowski, NYI	.02	.05

No.	Player	EX	NRMT
436	Glen Featherstone, St. L.	.02	.05
437	Top Prospect: Jim Paek, Pit., RC	.08	.15
438	Doug Evans, Win.	.05	.10
439	Alexei Kasatonov, NJD, Error	.02	.05
440	Kenneth Hodge, Jr., Bos.	.02	.05
441	Dave Snuggerud, St. L.	.02	.05
442	Brad Shaw, Har.	.02	.05
443	Gerard Gallant, Det.	.02	.05
444	Jiri Latal, Phi.	.02	.05
445	Peter Zezel, Tor.	.02	.05
446	Troy Gamble, Goalie, Van.	.02	.05
447	Craig Coxe, SJ	.02	.05
448	Adam Oates, St. L.	.12	.25
449	Todd Krygier, Har.	.02	.05
450	Andre Racicot, Goalie, Mon., RC	.07	.15
451	Patrik Sundstrom, NJD	.02	.05
452	Glen Wesley, Bos.	.02	.05
453	Jocelyn Lemieux, Chi.	.02	.05
454	Rick Zombo, Det.	.02	.05
455	Derek King, NYI	.02	.05
456	Jean-Jacques Daigneault, Mon.	.02	.05
457	Richard Vaive, Buf.	.02	.05
458	Larry Robinson, LA	.02	.05
459	Richard Wamsley, Goalie, Cal.	.02	.05
460	Craig Simpson, Edm.	.02	.05
461	Corey Millen, NYR, RC	.12	.25
462	Sergio Momesso, Van.	.02	.05
463	Paul MacDermid, Win.	.02	.05
464	Wendel Clark, Tor.	.02	.05
465	Mikhail Tatarinov, Que.	.02	.05
466	Mark Howe, Phi.	.02	.05
467	Jay Miller, LA	.02	.05
468	Grant Jennings, Pit.	.02	.05
469	Paul Gillis, Chi.	.02	.05
470	Ron Hextall, Goalie, Phi.	.02	.05
471	Alexander Godynyuk, Tor., RC, Error	.02	.05
472	Bryan Trottier, Pit.	.02	.05
473	Kevin Haller, Buf., RC	.08	.15
474	Troy Mallette, NYR	.02	.05
475	James Wiemer, Bos.	.02	.05
476	David Maley, NJD	.02	.05
477	Maurice Mantha, Win.	.02	.05
478	Brad Jones, LA, RC	.02	.05
479	Craig Muni	.02	.05
480	Igor Larionov, Van.	.02	.05
481	Scott Stevens, St. L.	.02	.05
482	Sergei Makarov, Cal.	.02	.05
483	Mike Lalor, Wash.	.02	.05
484	Anthony McKegney, Chi.	.02	.05
485	Perry Berezan, Min.	.02	.05
486	Derrick Smith, Phi.	.02	.05
487	Jim Hrivnak, Goalie, Wash.	.02	.05
488	David Volek, NYI	.02	.05
489	Sylvain Lefebvre, Mon.	.02	.05
490	Rod Brind'Amour, St. L.	.02	.05
491	Allan MacInnis, Cal.	.02	.05
492	Jamie Leach, Pit.	.02	.05
493	Robert Dirk, Van.	.02	.05
494	Gordon Roberts, Pit.	.02	.05
495	Mike Hudson, Chi.	.02	.05
496	Top Prospect: Francois Breault, LA	.02	.05
497	Rejean Lemelin, Goalie, Bos.	.02	.05
498	Kris King, NYR	.02	.05
499	Patrick Verbeek, Har.	.02	.05
500	Bryan Fogarty, Que.	.02	.05
501	Perry Anderson, SJ, RC	.02	.05
502	Joe Cirella, NYR	.02	.05
503	Mikko Makela, Buf.	.02	.05
504	Hockey Highlights 1991: Coffey Scores 1000th Point	.02	.05
505	Donald Beaupre, Goalie, Wash.	.02	.05
506	Brian Glynn, Min., RC	.02	.05
507	David Poulin, Bos.	.02	.05
508	Steve Chiasson, Det.	.02	.05
509	Myles O'Connor, NJD, RC	.02	.05
510	Ilkka Sinisalo, LA	.02	.05
511	Nicholas Kypreos, Wash.	.02	.05
512	Doug Houda, Har.	.02	.05

FUTURE NHLER

No.	Player	EX	NRMT
513	Valeri Kamensky, Que.	.25	.50
514	Sergei Nemchinov, NYR	.10	.20

TOPPS — 1991-92 STADIUM CLUB

No.	Player	EX	NRMT
515	Dimitri Mironov, Tor.	.10	.20

TROPHY WINNERS

No.	Player	EX	NRMT
516	**Hart Trophy Winner:** Brett Hull, St.L.	.13	.25
517	**Norris Trophy Winner:** Raymond Bourque, Bos.	.02	.05
518	**Calder Trophy Winner:** Ed Belfour, Goalie, Chi.	.05	.10
519	**Vezina Trophy Winner:** Ed Belfour, Goalie, Chi.	.05	.10
520	**Lady Bing Trophy Winner:** Wayne Gretzky, LA	.13	.25
521	**Selke Trophy Winner:** Dirk Graham, Chi.	.02	.05
522	**Art Ross Trophy Winner:** Wayne Gretzky, LA	.13	.25
523	**Conn Smythe Trophy Winner:** Mario Lemieux, Pit.	.13	.25

REGULAR ISSUE

No.	Player	EX	NRMT
524	**Hockey Highlights 1991:** Gretzky Joins the 700 Club	.13	.25
525	San Jose Sharks Roster	.18	.35
526	Tampa Bay Lightning	.12	.25
527	Ottawa Senators	.12	.25
528	Checklist 4 (397 to 528)	.02	.05

— 1991-92 INSERT SET —
'90-'91 TEAM SCORING LEADERS

This insert set illustrates the twenty-one team scoring leaders for the 1990-91 season.

1991-92 Insert Set
Card No. 6, Esa Tikkanen

Card Size: 2 1/2" X 3 1/2"
Face: Four colour, white border, blue and yellow stripes at lower part of picture
Back: Four colour, red, blue and black on card stock, Number, Resume
Imprint: B* © 1991 THE TOPPS COMPANY, INC.
Complete Set No.: 21
Complete Set Price: 3.00 6.00
Common Player: .08 .15

No.	Player	EX	NRMT
1	**Hartford Whalers:** Patrick Verbeek	.08	.15
2	**Buffalo Sabres:** Dale Hawerchuk	.08	.15
3	**Detroit Red Wings:** Steve Yzerman	.30	.60
4	**New York Rangers:** Brian Leetch	.25	.50
5	**Pittsburgh Penguins:** Mark Recchi	.08	.15
6	**Edmonton Oilers:** Esa Tikkanen	.08	.15
7	**Minnesota North Stars:** Dave Gagne	.08	.15
8	**Quebec Nordiques:** Joe Sakic, Que	.15	.30
9	**Toronto Maple Leafs:** Vincent Damphousse	.08	.15
10	**Los Angeles Kings:** Wayne Gretzky	.60	1.25
11	**Winnipeg Jets:** Phil Housley	.08	.15
12	**New York Islanders:** Pat LaFontaine	.08	.15
13	**Philadelphia Flyers:** Rick Tocchet	.08	.15
14	**Calgary Flames:** Theoren Fleury, Error	.15	.30
15	**New Jersey Devils:** John MacLean	.08	.15
16	**Washington Capitals:** Kevin Hatcher	.08	.15
17	**Vancouver Canucks:** Trevor Linden	.10	.20
18	**Montreal Canadiens:** Russell Courtnall	.08	.15
19	**Boston Bruins:** Raymond Bourque	.30	.60
20	**St. Louis Blues:** Brett Hull	.50	1.00
21	**Chicago Black Hawks:** Steve Larmer	.08	.15

— 1991-92 STADIUM CLUB —

These 12-card foil packs were released in November 1991. The borderless face photographs were printed by Kodak utilizing their high-gloss finishing process. The back carries a miniature reproduction of the player's "Topps Rookie Card".

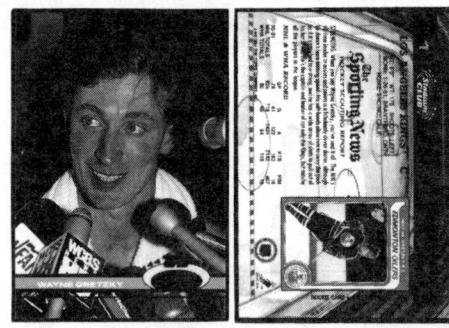

1991-92 Stadium Club
Card No. 1, Wayne Gretzky

Card Size: 2 1/2" X 3 1/2"
Face: Four colour, borderless
Back: Four colour, Number, Resume
Complete Set No.: 400
Complete Set Price: 20.00 40.00
Common Card: .08 .15
Foil Pack: (12 Cards) 1.25
Foil Box: (36 Packs) 35.00
Foil Case: (12 Boxes): 450.00

TEAM SCORING LEADERS

No.	Player	EX	NRMT
1	Wayne Gretzky, LA	2.00	4.00
2	Randy Moller, NYR	.08	.15
3	Ray Ferraro, NYI	.08	.15
4	Craig Wolanin, Que.	.08	.15
5	Shayne Corson, Mon.	.08	.15
6	Chris Chelios, Chi.	.08	.15
7	Joe Mullen, Pit.	.08	.15
8	Ken Wregget, Goalie, Phi.	.08	.15
9	Robert Cimetta, Tor.	.08	.15
10	Michael Liut, Goalie, Wash.	.08	.15
11	Martin Gelinas, Edm.	.08	.15
12	Mario Marois, St. L.	.08	.15
13	Richard Vaive, Buf.	.08	.15
14	Byron (Brad) McCrimmon, Det.	.08	.15
15	Mark Hunter, Har.	.08	.15
16	James Wiemer, Bos.	.08	.15
17	Sergio Momesso, Van.	.08	.15
18	Claude Lemieux, NJD	.08	.15
19	Brian Hayward, Goalie, SJ, (Now With Sharks)	.08	.15
20	Patrick Flatley,	.08	.15
21	Mark Osborne, Win.	.08	.15
22	Mike Hudson, Chi.	.08	.15
23	Rejean Lemelin, Goalie, Bos.	.08	.15
24	Viacheslav Fetisov, NJD	.08	.15
25	Robert Smith, Min.	.08	.15
26	Kris King, NYR	.08	.15
27	Randy Velischek, Que.	.08	.15
28	Steven Bozek, SJ (Now With Sharks)	.08	.15
29	Mike Foligno, Tor.	.08	.15
30	Scott Arniel, Win.	.08	.15
31	Sergei Makarov, Cal.	.12	.25
32	Rick Zombo, Det.	.08	.15
33	Christian Ruuttu, Buf.	.08	.15
34	Gino Cavallini, St. L.	.08	.15
35	Rick Tocchet, Phi.	.08	.15
36	Jiri Hrdina, Pit.	.08	.15
37	Peter Bondra, Wash.	.12	.25
38	Craig Ludwig, Min. (Now With North Stars)	.08	.15
39	Mikael Andersson, Har.	.08	.15
40	Bob Kudelski, LA	.12	.25
41	Guy Carbonneau, Mon.	.08	.15
42	Geoff Smith, Edm.	.08	.15
43	Russell Courtnall, Mon.	.08	.15
44	Michal Pivonka, Wash.	.08	.15
45	Todd Krygier, Har.	.08	.15
46	Jeremy Roenick, Chi.	1.50	3.00
47	Doug Brown, NJD	.08	.15
48	Paul Cavallini, St. L.	.08	.15
49	Ronald Sutter, Phi.	.08	.15
50	Paul Ranheim, Cal.	.08	.15
51	Michael Gartner, NYR	.12	.25
52	Greg Adams, Van.	.08	.15
53	Dave Capuano, Van.	.08	.15
54	Michael Krushelnyski, Tor.	.08	.15
55	Ulf Dahlen, Min.	.08	.15
56	Steven Finn, Que.	.08	.15
57	Ed Olczyk, Win.	.08	.15
58	Steve Duchesne, Phi., (Now With Flyers)	.08	.15
59	Bob Probert, Det.	.08	.15
60	Joe Nieuwendyk, Cal.	.12	.25
61	Petr Klima, Edm.	.08	.15
62	Uwe Krupp, Buf.	.08	.15
63	Jay Miller, LA	.08	.15
64	Cam Neely, Bos.	.13	.25
65	Phil Housley, Win.	.08	.15
66	Michel Goulet, Chi.	.08	.15
67	Brett Hull, St. L.	1.00	2.00
68	Mike Ridley, Wash.	.08	.15
69	Esa Tikkanen, Edm.	.08	.15
70	Kjell Samuelsson, Phi.	.08	.15
71	**Corey Millen, NYR, RC**	**.30**	**.65**
72	Doug Lidster, Van.	.08	.15
73	Ronald Francis, Pit.	.08	.15
74	Scott Young, Pit.	.08	.15
75	Robert Sweeney, Bos.	.08	.15
76	Sean Burke, Goalie, NJD	.08	.15
77	Pierre Turgeon, Buf.	.50	1.00
78	David Reid, Tor.	.08	.15
79	Allan MacInnis, Cal.	.12	.25
80	Mike Hough, Que.	.08	.15
81	Steve Yzerman, Det.	.50	1.00
82	Derek King, NYI	.08	.15
83	Brad Shaw, Har.	.08	.15
84	Trevor Linden, Van.	.25	.50
85	Richard Meagher, St. L.	.08	.15
86	Stephane J. J. Richer, Mon.	.08	.15
87	Brian Bellows, Min.	.08	.15
88	Peter Peeters, Goalie, Phi.	.08	.15
89	Adam Creighton, Chi.	.08	.15
90	Brent Ashton, Pit.	.08	.15
91	Bryan Trottier, Pit.	.08	.15
92	Michael Richter, Goalie, NYR	.35	.75
93	David Andreychuk, Buf.	.12	.25
94	Randy Carlyle,	.08	.15
95	David Christian, St. L., (Now With Blues)	.08	.15
96	Douglas Gilmour, Cal.	.50	1.00
97	Tony Granato, LA	.08	.15
98	Jeff Norton, NYI	.08	.15
99	Neal Broten, Min	.08	.15
100	Jody Hull, NYR	.08	.15
101	Shawn Burr, Det.	.08	.15
102	Patrick Verbeek, Har., Error	.08	.15
103	Kenneth Daneyko, NJD	.08	.15
104	Peter Zezel, Tor.	.08	.15
105	Kirk McLean, Goalie, Van.	.12	.25
106	Kelly Miller, Wash.	.08	.15
107	Patrick Roy, Goalie, Mon.	1.00	2.00
108	Adam Oates, St. L.	.25	.50
109	Steve Thomas, Chi.	.08	.15
110	Scott Mellanby, Edm., (Now With Oilers)	.08	.15
111	Mark Messier, Edm.	.35	.75

1991-92 STADIUM CLUB — TOPPS • 245

No.	Player	EX	NRMT
112	Lawrence Murphy, Pit.	.12	.25
113	Mark Janssens, NYR	.08	.15
114	Doug Bodger, Buf.	.08	.15
115	Ron Tugnutt, Goalie, Que.	.08	.15
116	Glenn Anderson, Edm.	.08	.15
117	Dave Gagner, Min.	.08	.15
118	Dino Ciccarelli, Wash.	.08	.15
119	Randy Burridge, Wash., (Now With Capitals)	.08	.15
120	Kelly Hrudey, Goalie, LA	.08	.15
121	Jimmy Carson, Det.	.08	.15
122	Bruce Driver, NJD	.08	.15
123	Pat LaFontaine, NYI	.50	1.00
124	Wendel Clark, Tor.	.12	.25
125	Peter Sidorkiewicz, Goalie, Har.	.08	.15
126	Gary Roberts, Cal.	.08	.15
127	Petr Svoboda, Mon.	.08	.15
128	Vincent Riendeau, Goalie, St. L.	.08	.15
129	Brian Skrudland, Mon.	.08	.15
130	Tim Kerr, NYR	.08	.15
131	Douglas Wilson Jr., SJ, (Now With Sharks)	.08	.15
132	Pat Elynuik, Win.	.08	.15
133	Craig MacTavish, Edm.	.08	.15
134	Troy Mallette, NYR	.08	.15
135	Michael Ramsey, Buf.	.08	.15
136	Anthony Hrkac, SJ, (Now With Sharks)	.08	.15
137	Craig Simpson, Edm.	.08	.15
138	Jon Casey, Goalie, Min.	.08	.15
139	Steven Kasper, Phi., (Now With Flyers)	.08	.15
140	Kevin Hatcher, Wash.	.08	.15
141	David Barr, NJD, (Now With Devils)	.08	.15
142	Brad Lauer, NYI	.08	.15
143	Gary Suter, Cal.	.08	.15
144	John MacLean, NJD	.08	.15
145	Dean Evason, Har.	.08	.15
146	Vincent Damphousse, Tor.	.12	.25
147	Craig Janney, Bos.	.12	.25
148	Jeff Brown, St. L.	.08	.15
149	Geoff Courtnall, Van.	.08	.15
150	Igor Larionov, Van.	.12	.25
151	Jan Erixon, NYR	.08	.15
152	Bob Essensa, Goalie, Win.	.08	.15
153	Gaetan Duchesne, Min.	.08	.15
154	Jyrki Lumme, Van.	.08	.15
155	Tom Barrasso, Goalie, Pit.	.08	.15
156	Curtis Leschyshyn, Que.	.08	.15
157	Benoit Hogue, Buf.	.08	.15
158	Gary Leeman, Tor.	.08	.15
159	Luc Robitaille, LA	.35	.75
160	Jamie Macoun, Cal.	.08	.15
161	Robert Carpenter, Bos.	.08	.15
162	Kevin Dineen, Har.	.08	.15
163	Gary Nylund, NYI	.08	.15
164	Dale Hunter, Wash.	.08	.15
165	Gerard Gallant, Det.	.08	.15
166	Jacques Cloutier, Goalie, Que.	.08	.15
167	Troy Murray, Win., (Now With Jets)	.08	.15
168	Phillippe Bourque, Pit.	.08	.15
169	Grant Ledyard, Buf.	.08	.15
170	Joel Otto, Cal.	.08	.15
171	Paul Ysebaert, Det.	.08	.15
172	Luke Richardson, Tor.	.08	.15
173	Ron Hextall, Goalie, Phi.	.08	.15
174	Mario Lemieux, Pit.	2.00	4.00
175	Garry Galley, Bos.	.08	.15
176	Murray Craven, Phi.	.08	.15
177	Walter Poddubny, NJD	.08	.15
178	Scott Pearson, Que.	.08	.15
179	Kevin Lowe, Edm.	.08	.15
180	Brent Sutter, NYI	.08	.15
181	Dirk Graham, Chi.	.08	.15
182	Per-erik Eklund, Phi.	.08	.15
183	Sylvain Coté, Wash., (Now With Capitals)	.08	.15
184	Rod Brind'Amour, St. L.	.30	.60
185	Fredrik Olausson, Win.	.08	.15
186	Kelly Kisio, SJ	.08	.15
187	Michael Modano, Min.	.50	1.00
188	Calle Johansson, Wash.	.08	.15
189	John Tonelli, Chi., (Now With Black Hawks)	.08	.15
190	Glen Wesley, Bos.	.08	.15
191	Bob Errey, Pit.	.08	.15
192	Richard Sutter, St. L.	.08	.15
193	Kirk Muller, NJD	.12	.25
194	Rob Zettler, SJ	.08	.15
195	Alexander Mogilny, Buf.	1.50	3.00
196	Adrien Plavsic, Van.	.08	.15
197	Daniel Marois, Tor.	.08	.15
198	Yves Racine, Det.	.08	.15
199	Brendan Shanahan, St. L., (Now With Blues)	.30	.65
200	Rob Brown, Har.	.08	.15
201	Brian Leetch, NYR	.50	1.00
202	Dave McLlwain, Win.	.08	.15
203	Charles Huddy, LA, (Now With Kings)	.08	.15
204	David Volek, NYI	.08	.15
205	Trent Yawney, Chi.	.08	.15
206	Brian MacLellan, Det., (Now With Red Wings)	.08	.15
207	Thomas Steen, Win.	.08	.15
208	Sylvain Lefebvre, Mon.	.08	.15
209	Tomas Sandstrom, LA	.08	.15
210	Michael McPhee, Mon.	.08	.15
211	Andrew Moog, Goalie, Bos.	.08	.15
212	Paul Coffey, Pit.	.15	.35
213	Denis Savard, Mon.	.08	.15
214	Eric Desjardins, Mon.	.08	.15
215	Wayne Presley, Chi.	.08	.15
216	Stephane Morin, Que.	.08	.15
217	Eric Nattress, Cal.	.08	.15
218	Troy Gamble, Goalie, Van.	.08	.15
219	Terry Carkner, Phi.	.08	.15
220	David Hannan, Tor.	.08	.15
221	Randy Wood, NYI	.08	.15
222	Brian Mullen, SJ, (Now With Sharks)	.08	.15
223	Garth Butcher, St. L.	.08	.15
224	Tim Cheveldae, Goalie, Det.	.08	.15
225	Rod Langway, Wash.	.08	.15
226	Stephen Leach, Bos., (Now With Bruins)	.08	.15
227	Perry Berezan, Min.	.08	.15
228	Zarley Zalapski, Har.	.08	.15
229	Patrik Sundstrom, NJD	.08	.15
230	James (Steve) Smith, Edm.	.08	.15
231	Daren Puppa, Goalie, Buf.	.08	.15
232	David Taylor, LA	.08	.15
233	Raymond Bourque, Bos.	.25	.50
234	Kevin Stevens, Pit.	.50	1.00
235	Frantisek Musil, Cal.	.08	.15
236	Mike Keane, Mon.	.08	.15
237	Brian Propp, Min.	.08	.15
238	Brent Fedyk, Det.	.08	.15
239	George (Rob) Ramage, Min., (Now With North Stars)	.08	.15
240	Robert Kron, Van.	.08	.15
241	Michael McNeill, Que.	.08	.15
242	Gregory Gilbert, Chi.	.08	.15
243	Dan Quinn, St. L.	.08	.15
244	Christopher Nilan, Bos.	.08	.15
245	Bernie Nicholls, NYR	.08	.15
246	Donald Beaupre, Goalie, Wash.	.08	.15
247	Keith Acton, Phi.	.08	.15
248	Gordon Murphy, Phi.	.08	.15
249	Bill Ranford, Goalie, Edm.	.08	.15
250	David Chyzowski, NYI	.08	.15
251	Clint Malarchuk, Goalie, Buf.	.08	.15
252	Larry Robinson, LA	.08	.15
253	David Poulin, Bos.	.08	.15
254	Paul MacDermid, Win.	.08	.15
255	Douglas Smail, Que., (Now With Nordiques)	.08	.15
256	Mark Recchi, Pit.	.85	1.75
257	Brian Bradley, Tor.	.08	.15
258	Grant Fuhr, Goalie, Edm.	.08	.15
259	Owen Nolan, Que.	.25	.50
260	Hubie McDonough, NYI	.08	.15
261	Mikko Makela, Buf.	.08	.15
262	Mathieu Schneider, Mon.	.12	.25
263	Peter Stastny, NJD	.12	.25
264	Jim Hrivnak, Goalie, Wash.	.08	.15
265	Scott Stevens, St. L.	.08	.15
266	Mike Tomlak, Har.	.08	.15
267	Martin McSorley, LA	.08	.15
268	Johan Garpenlov, Det.	.08	.15
269	Mike Vernon, Goalie, Cal.	.08	.15
270	Steve Larmer, Chi.	.08	.15
271	Phil Sykes, Win.	.08	.15
272	**Jay Mazur, Van., RC**	**.08**	**.15**
273	John Ogrodnick, NYR	.08	.15
274	David Ellett, Tor.	.08	.15
275	Randy Gilhen, LA, (Now With Kings)	.08	.15
276	Tom Chorske, Mon.	.08	.15
277	James Patrick, NYR	.08	.15
278	Darin Kimble, St. L.	.08	.15
279	Paul Cyr, Har.	.08	.15
280	Petr Nedved, Van.	.25	.50
281	Anthony McKegney, Chi.	.08	.15
282	Alexei Kasatonov, NJD	.08	.15
283	Stephan Lebeau, Mon.	.20	.45
284	Everett Sanipass, Que.	.08	.15
285	Tony Tanti, Buf.	.08	.15
286	Kevin Miller, Det.	.88	.15
287	Maurice Mantha, Win.	.08	.15
288	Alan May, Wash.	.08	.15
289	John Cullen, Har.	.08	.15
290	Daniel Berthiaume, Goalie, LA	.08	.15
291	Mark Pederson, Phi.	.08	.15
292	Laurie Boschman, NJD	.08	.15
293	Neil Wilkinson, SJ	.08	.15
294	Richard Wamsley, Goalie, Cal.	.08	.15
295	Ken Linseman, Edm.	.08	.15
296	Jamie Leach, Pit.	.08	.15
297	Chris Terreri, Goalie, NJD	.08	.15
298	Cliff Ronning, Van.	.08	.15
299	Robert Holik, Har.	.08	.15
300	Mats Sundin, Que.	.50	1.00
301	Carey Wilson, Cal.	.08	.15
302	Teppo Numminen, Win.	.08	.15
303	Dave Lowry, St. L.	.08	.15
304	Joe Reekie, NYI	.08	.15
305	Keith Primeau, Det.	.25	.50
306	David Shaw, NYR	.08	.15
307	Nicholas Kypreos, Wash.	.08	.15
308	Dave Manson, Chi.	.08	.15
309	Mick Vukota, NYI	.08	.15
310	Todd Elik, Min., (Now With North Stars)	.08	.15
311	Michel Petit, Tor.	.08	.15
312	Dale Hawerchuk, Buf.	.12	.25
313	Joe Murphy, Edm.	.08	.15
314	Chris Dahlquist, Min.	.08	.15
315	Petri Skriko, Bos.	.08	.15
316	Sergei Fedorov, Det.	2.00	4.00
317	Lee Norwood, NJD	.08	.15
318	Garry Valk, Van.	.08	.15
319	Glen Featherstone, Bos., (Now With Bruins)	.08	.15
320	Dave Snuggerud, Buf.	.08	.15
321	Doug Evans, Win.	.08	.15
322	Marc Bureau, Min.	.08	.15
323	John Vanbiesbrouck, Goalie, NYR	.20	.45
324	John McIntyre, LA	.08	.15
325	Wes Walz, Bos.	.08	.15
326	Daryl Reaugh, Goalie, Har.	.08	.15
327	Paul Fenton, Har., (Now With Whalers)	.08	.15
328	Ulf Samuelsson, Pit.	.08	.15
329	Andrew Cassels, Mon.	.08	.15
330	**Alexei Gusarov, Que., RC**	**.12**	**.25**
331	John Druce, Wash.	.08	.15
332	Adam Graves, NYR, (Now With Rangers)	.50	1.00
333	Ed Belfour, Goalie, Chi.	.75	1.50
334	Murray Baron, Phi.	.08	.15
335	John Tucker, NYI	.08	.15
336	Todd Gill, Tor.	.08	.15
337	Martin Hostak, Phi.	.08	.15
338	Gino Odjick, Van.	.08	.15
339	Eric Weinrich, NJD	.08	.15
340	Todd Ewen, Mon.	.08	.15
341	Mike Hartman, Buf.	.08	.15
342	Danton Cole, Win.	.08	.15
343	Jaromir Jagr, Pit.	1.50	3.00
344	Mike Craig, Min.	.25	.50
345	Mark Fitzpatrick, Goalie, NYI	.08	.15
346	Darren Turcotte, NYR	.08	.15
347	Ronald Wilson, St. L.	.08	.15
348	Robert Blake, LA	.25	.50
349	Dale Kushner, Phi.	.08	.15
350	Jeff Beukeboom, Edm.	.08	.15
351	Tim Bergland, Wash.	.08	.15

TOPPS — 1992-93 REGULAR ISSUE

No.	Player	EX	NRMT
352	Peter Ing, Goalie, Tor.	.08	.15
353	Wayne McBean, NYI	.08	.15
354	**Jim McKenzie, Har., RC**	**.08**	**.15**
355	Theoren Fleury, Cal.	.25	.50
356	Jocelyn Lemieux, Chi.	.08	.15
357	Kenneth Hodge, Jr., Bos.	.08	.15
358	Shawn Anderson, Que.	.08	.15
359	Dimitri Khristich, Wash., Error	.08	.15
360	Jon Morris, NJD	.08	.15
361	Darrin Shannon, Buf.	.08	.15
362	Chris Joseph, Edm.	.08	.15
363	Normand Lacombe, Phi., Error	.08	.15
364	Frank Pietrangelo, Goalie, Pit.	.08	.15
365	Joey Kocur, NYR	.08	.15
366	Anatoli Semenov, Edm.	.08	.15
367	Bob Bassen, St. L.	.08	.15
368	**Brad Jones, Phi., RC** (Now With Flyers)	**.08**	**.15**
369	Glenn Healy, Goalie, NYI	.08	.15
370	Don Sweeney, Bos.	.08	.15
371	Brad Dalgarno, NYI	.08	.15
372	Al Iafrate, Wash.	.08	.15
373	**Patrick Lebeau, Mon., RC**	**.15**	**.30**
374	Terry Yake, Har.	.08	.15
375	Roger Johansson, Cal.	.08	.15
376	Paul Broten, NYR	.08	.15
377	**Andre Racicot, Goalie, Mon., RC**	**.12**	**.25**
378	Scott Thornton, Tor.	.08	.15
379	Zdeno Ciger, NJD	.08	.15
380	Paul Stanton, Pit.	.08	.15
381	Ray Sheppard, Det., (Now With Red Wings)	.12	.25
382	**Kevin Haller, Buf., RC**	**.12**	**.25**
383	Vladimir Ruzicka, Bos.	.08	.15
384	**Bryan Marchment, Chi., RC** (Now With Blackhawks)	**.12**	**.25**
385	**Bill Berg, NYI, RC**	**.12**	**.25**
386	Mike Ricci, Phi.	.25	.50
387	Patrick Conacher, NJD	.08	.15
388	**Brian Glynn, Min., RC**	**.08**	**.15**
389	Joe Sakic, Que.	.50	1.00
390	Mikhail Tatarinov, Que., (Now With Nordiques)	.07	.15
391	Stephane Matteau, Cal.	.08	.15
392	Mark Tinordi, Min.	.08	.15
393	Robert Reichel, Cal.	.25	.50
394	Tim Sweeney, Cal.	.08	.15
395	Richard Tabaracci, Goalie, Win.	.08	.15
396	Ken Sabourin, Wash.	.08	.15
397	**Jeff Lazaro, Bos., RC**	**.13**	**.25**

CHECKLISTS

No.	Checklist	EX	NRMT
398	Checklist 1 (1 to 133)	.08	.15
399	Checklist 2 (134 to 266)	.08	.15
400	Checklist 3 (267 to 400)	.08	.15

— 1991-92 STADIUM CLUB — CHARTER MEMBER SET

This Charter Member set was available only through Topps by direct subscription to the Stadium Club. Each set of fifty cards was issued in a custom, black and gold box stamped "Charter Member Limited Edition Cards". The face of the card has "Charter Member" stamped in gold foil. Each set depicts thirty-two baseball, nine football and nine hockey players.

1991-92 Charter Member Set
Card No. 21, Ray Owns The Norris

Card Size: 2 1/2" X 3 1/2"
Face: Four colour, borderless
Back: Two colour, black and tan on card stock, Resume
Imprint: © 1991 THE TOPPS COMPANY, INC.
Complete Set No.: 100
Complete Set No. - Hockey: 22
Complete Set Price: 65.00 125.00
Complete Set Price - Hockey: 25.00 50.00
Common Player: .10 .20

No.	Player	EX	NRMT
1	Always A Gentleman (Gretzky)	3.00	6.00
2	Belfour Cops The Vezina	1.00	2.00
3	Belfour Is Top Goalie	1.00	2.00
4	Brett's All Hart	1.25	2.50
5	Brett Does It Again	1.25	2.50
6	Carbonneau Wins Selke Trophy	.25	.50
7	Coffey Nets No. 1000	.75	1.50
8	Coffey's The Best	.75	1.50
9	Goulet Joins the Club	.25	.50
10	Gretzky Takes No. 2000	3.00	6.00
11	Hull Joins 50-50 Club	1.25	2.50
12	Leetch is The Best	.50	1.00
13	Lemieux Takes 3rd Ross Trophy	2.50	5.00
14	Mario Repeats as MVP	2.50	5.00
15	Mario Takes Club MVP	2.00	4.00
16	Mark Takes Hart	.75	1.50
17	Mike Makes it 500	.75	1.50
18	Mike Makes it Two	.75	1.50
19	Patrick is Still the Best	1.25	2.50
20	Pavel Cops Calder	2.00	4.00
21	Ray Owns The Norris	.75	1.50
22	The 700 Club (Gretzky)	3.00	6.00

Note: Only the hockey cards of the 1992-93 StadiumClub Charter Member Set are listed here. For a complete listing of this set see the appendix at the back of this catalogue.

— 1992-93 REGULAR ISSUE —

This 529-card set is an improvement over Topps' sets of previous years. A stiffer card stock and better picture quality have made this set one of the more desirable for the '92-93 season.

The 529 gold card set is similar to the regular Topps issue with the following exceptions. The name plate on the face of the card has a raised gold embossed plate and the back of the card has the Topps Gold logo faintly printed under the player's career stats. The four checklists are replaced by players that are not in the regular set. These cards were inserted in wax packs, one per pack, in jumbo packs three per pack and in the factory sets twenty cards per set. There are some cards that are short printed. They are denoted with "SP".

 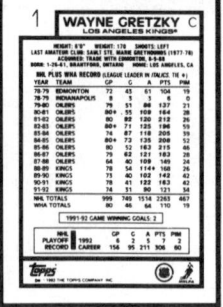

1992-93 Issue
Card No. 1, Wayne Gretzky

Card Size: 2-1/2" x 3-1/2"
Face: **Reg:** Four colour, white border; Name, Team
Gold: Four colour, white border, gold embossed name plate; Name, Team
Back: **Reg:** Four colour with white border on card stock; Name, Resume
Gold: Four colour; Name, Number, Position, Resume, Topps logo
Imprint: A*, B*, C*, D* or blank © 1992 THE TOPPS COMPANY, INC.

		REG	GOLD
Complete Set No.:	529		
Complete Set Price:		20.00	450.00
Common Card:		.10	.50
Wax Pack: (15 Cards)			2.50
Wax Box: (36 Packs)			70.00
Jumbo Pack: (24 cards)			3.00
Jumbo Box: (24 packs)			70.00
Factory Set:			25.00

REGULAR ISSUE

No.	Player	Regular NRMT	Gold NRMT
1	Wayne Gretzky, LA	1.00	50.00
2	Brett Hull, St.L	.50	20.00
3	Felix Potvin, Goalie, Tor.	.50	20.00
4	Mark Tinordi, Min.	.10	.50
5	**Highlight:** Paul Coffey, LA	.10	.50

SUPER ROOKIE

No.	Player	Regular NRMT	Gold NRMT
6	Anthony Amonte, NYR	.20	.75
7	Pat Falloon, SJ	.20	.75
8	Pavel Bure, Van.	.50	5.00
9	Nicklas Lidstrom, Det.	.10	.75
10	Dominic Roussel, Goalie Phi.	.20	2.00
11	Nelson Emerson, St.L	.10	.75
12	Donald Audette, Buf.	.10	.75
13	Gilbert Dionne, Mon.	.10	.75
14	Vladimir Konstantinov, Det.	.10	.75
15	Kevin Todd, NJ	.10	.75

REGULAR ISSUE

No.	Player	Regular NRMT	Gold NRMT
16	Stephen Leach, Bos.	.10	.50
17	Ed Olczyk, Win.	.10	.50
18	Jim Hrivnak, Goalie, Wash.	.10	.50
19	Gilbert Dionne, Mon.	.10	.75
20	Michael Vernon, Goalie, Cal.	.10	.50
21	Dave Christian, St.L	.10	.50
22	Ed Belfour, Goalie, Chi.	.25	2.50
23	Andrew Cassels, Hart.	.10	.50
24	Jaromir Jagr, Pit.	.50	5.00
25	Arturs Irbe, Goalie, SJ	.30	3.00
26	Petr Klima, Ed	.10	.50
27	Randy Gilhen, NYR	.10	.50
28	Ulf Dahlen, Min.	.10	.50
29	Kelly Hrudey, Goalie, LA	.10	.50
30	David Ellett, Tor.	.10	.50
31	Tom Fitzgerald, NYI	.10	.50
32	Cam Neely, Bos.	.15	2.00
33	Gregory Paslawski, Que.	.10	.50
34	Brad May, Buf.	.10	.50
35	Viacheslav Kozlov, Det.	.50	5.00
36	Mark Hunter, Wash.	.10	.50
37	Steve Chiasson, Det.	.10	.50
38	Joe Murphy, Edm.	.10	.50
39	Darryl Sydor, LA	.10	.50
40	Ron Hextall, Goalie, Que.	.10	.50
41	Jim Sandlak, Van.	.10	.50
42	Dave Lowry, St.L	.10	.50
43	Claude Lemieux, NJ	.10	.50
44	Gerald Diduck, Van.	.10	.50
45	Michael McPhee, Mon.	.10	.50
46	Rod Langway, Wash.	.10	.50
47	Guy Larose, Tor.	.10	.50
48	Craig Billington, Goalie, NJ	.10	.50
49	Daniel Marois, NYI	.10	.50
50	**Todd Nelson, Pit., RC**	**.10**	**.50**
51	Jari Kurri, LA	.10	.50
52	Keith Brown, Chi.	.10	.50
53	Valeri Kamensky, Que.	.25	2.50
54	Jim Johnson, Min.	.10	.50
55	Vincent Damphousse, Edm.	.10	.75
56	Pat Elynuik, Win.	.10	.50
57	Jeff Beukeboom, NYR	.10	.50
58	Paul Ysebaert, Det.	.10	.50
59	Kenneth Sutton, Buf.	.10	.50
60	Dale Craigwell, SJ	.10	.50
61	Marc Bergevin, TB	.10	.50
62	Stephane Beauregard, Goalie, Win.	.10	.50
63	Bob Probert, Det.	.10	1.50
64	Jergus Baca, Hart.	.10	.50
65	Brian Propp, Min.	.10	.50
66	Jacques Cloutier, Goalie, Que.	.10	.50
67	**Jim Thomson, Ott., RC**	**.10**	**.50**
68	Anatoli Semenov, TB	.10	.50
69	Stephan Lebeau, Mon.	.10	.50
70	Rick Tocchet, Pit.	.10	.50
71	James Patrick, NYR	.10	.50
72	Rob Brown, Chi.	.10	.50

1992-93 REGULAR ISSUE — TOPPS

No.	Player	Regular NRMT	Gold NRMT
73	Peter Ahola, LA	.10	.50
74	Bob Corkum, Buf.	.10	.50
75	Brent Sutter, Chi.	.10	.50
76	Neil Wilkinson, SJ	.10	.50
77	Mark Osborne, Tor.	.10	.50
78	Ronald Wilson, St.L	.10	.50
79	Todd Richards, Hart	.10	.50
80	Robert Kron, Van.	.10	.50
81	Cliff Ronning, Van.	.10	.50
82	Zarley Zalapski, Hart.	.10	.50
83	Randy Burridge, Wash.	.10	.50
84	Jarrod Skalde, NJ	.10	.50
85	Gary Leeman, Cal.	.10	.50
86	Mike Ricci, Que.	.10	1.50
87	Dennis Vaske, NYI	.10	.50
88	**John LeBlanc, Win., RC**	**.10**	**.50**
89	Brad Shaw, Ott.	.10	.50
90	Rod Brind'amour, Phi.	.20	10.00
91	Colin Patterson, Buf.	.10	.50
92	Gerard Gallant, Det.	.10	.50
93	**Per-Olav Djoos, NYR, RC**	**.10**	**.50**
94	Claude LaPointe, Que.	.10	.50
95	Bob Errey, Pit.	.10	.50
96	Norm Maciver, Edm.	.10	.50
97	Todd Elik, Min.	.10	.50
98	Chris Chelios, Chi.	.10	.50
99	Keith Primeau, Det.	.10	.50
100	Jimmy Waite, Goalie, Chi.	.10	.50
101	Luc Robitaille, LA	.15	.50
102	Keith Tkachuk, Win.	.40	4.00
103	Benoit Hogue, NYI	.10	.50
104	Brian Mullen, SJ	.10	.50
105	Joe Nieuwendyk, Cal.	.10	.50
106	Randy McKay, NJ	.10	.50
107	Michal Pivonka, Wash.	.10	.50
108	Darcy Wakaluk, Goalie, Min.	.10	.50
109	Andy Brickley, Bos.	.10	.50
110	League Leader Goals Against Average: Patrick Roy, Goalie, Mon.	.25	10.00
111	Robert Sweeney, Bos.	.10	.50
112	**Guy Hebert, Goalie, St.L, RC**	**.50**	**.50**
113	Joe Mullen, Pit.	.10	.50
114	Gordon Murphy, Bos.	.10	.50
115	Eugeny Davydov, Win., Error	.10	.50
116	Gary Roberts, Cal.	.10	.50
117	Per-Erik Eklund, Phi.	.10	.50
118	Tom Kurvers, NYI	.10	.50
119	John Tonelli, Que.	.10	.50
120	Fredrik Olausson, Win.	.10	.50
121	Mike Donnelly, LA	.10	.50
122	Douglas Gilmour, Tor.	.25	10.00
123	League Leader Assists: Wayne Gretzky, LA	.30	10.00
124	Curtis Leschyshyn, Que.	.10	.50
125	Guy Carbonneau, Mon.	.10	.50
126	Bill Ranford, Goalie, Edm.	.10	.50
127	Ulf Samuelsson, Pit.	.10	.50
128	Joey Kocur, NYR	.10	.50
129	Kevin Miller, Wash.	.10	.50
130	Kirk McLean, Goalie, Van.	.10	.50
131	Kevin Dineen, Phi.	.10	.50
132	John Cullen, Hart.	.10	.50
133	Al Iafrate, Wash.	.10	.50
134	Craig Janney, St.L	.10	.50
135	Patrick Flatley, NYI	.10	.50
136	Dominik Hasek, Goalie, Chi.	.25	2.50
137	Benoit Brunet, Mon.	.10	.50
138	David Babych, Van.	.10	.50
139	Doug Brown, NJ	.10	.50
140	Mike Lalor, Win.	.10	.50
141	Thomas Steen, Win.	.10	.50
142	Frantisek Musil, Cal.	.10	.50
143	Dan Quinn, Phi.	.10	.50
144	Dmitri Mironov, Tor.	.10	8.00
145	Bob Kudelski, LA	.10	.50
146	Michael Bullard, Tor.	.10	.50
147	Randy Carlyle, Win.	.10	.50
148	Kent Manderville, Tor.	.10	.50
149	Kevin Hatcher, Wash.	.10	.50
150	Stephen Kasper, Phi.	.10	.50
151	Bo Mikael Andersson, TB	.10	.50
152	Alexei Kasatonov, NJ	.10	.50

No.	Player	Regular NRMT	Gold NRMT
153	Jan Erixon, NYR	.10	.50
154	Craig Ludwig, Min.	.10	.50
155	David Poulin, Bos.	.10	.50
156	Scott Stevens, NJ	.10	.50
157	Robert Reichel, Cal.	.10	.50
158	Uwe Krupp, NYI	.10	.50
159	Brian Noonan, Chi.	.10	.50
160	Stephane J. J. Richer, NJ	.10	.50
161	Brent Thompson, LA	.10	.50
162	Glenn Anderson, Tor.	.10	.50
163	Joe Cirella, NYR	.10	.50
164	David Andreychuk, Buf.	.20	15.00
165	Vladimir Konstantinov, Det.	.10	.50
166	Michael McNeill, Que.	.10	.50
167	Darrin Shannon, Win.	.10	.50
168	Rob Pearson, Tor.	.10	.50
169	John Vanbiesbrouck, Goalie, NYR	.20	2.00
170	Randy Wood, Buf.	.10	.50
171	Martin McSorley, LA	.10	.50
172	Mike Hudson, Chi.	.10	.50
173	Paul Fenton, SJ	.10	.50
174	Jeff Brown, St.L	.10	.50
175	Mark Greig, Hart.	.10	.50
176	Gordon Roberts, Bos.	.10	.50
177	Josef Beranek, Edm.	.20	2.00
178	Shawn Burr, Det.	.10	.50
179	Marc Bureau, Min.	.10	.50
180	Mikhail Tatarinov, Que.	.10	.50
181	Robert Cimetta, Tor.	.10	.50
182	Paul Coffey, LA	.20	2.00
183	Bob Essense, Goalie, Win.	.10	.50
184	Joe Reekie, TB	.10	.50
185	Jeff Hackett, Goalie, SJ	.10	.50
186	Tomas Forslund, Cal.	.10	.50
187	Claude Vilgrain, NJ	.10	.50
188	John Druce, Wash.	.10	.50
189	Patrice Brisebois, Mon.	.10	.50
190	Peter Douris, Bos.	.10	.50
191	Brent Ashton, Bos.	.10	.50
192	Eric Desjardins, Mon.	.10	.50
193	Nicholas Kypreos, Hart.	.10	.50
194	Dana Murzyn, Van.	.10	.50
195	Donald Beaupre, Goalie, Wash.	.10	8.00
196	Jeff Chychrun, Pit.	.10	.50
197	David Barr, NJ	.10	.50
198	Brian Glynn, Edm.	.10	.50
199	Keith Acton, Phi.	.10	.50
200	Igor Kravchuk, Chi.	.10	.50
201	Shayne Corson, Mon.	.10	.50
202	Curt Giles, St.L	.10	.50
203	Darren Turcotte, NYR	.10	.50
204	David Volek, NYI	.10	.50
205	**Ray Whitney, SJ, RC**	**.25**	**2.50**
206	Donald Audette, Buf.	.10	.50
207	Steve Yzerman, Det.	.25	7.00
208	Craig Berube, Cal.	.10	.50
209	Robert McGill, TB	.10	.50
210	Stu Barnes, Win.	.10	.50
211	Robert Blake, LA	.10	.50
212	Mario Lemieux, Pit.	.75	35.00
213	Dominic Roussel, Goalie, Phi.	.30	3.00
214	Sergio Momesso, Van.	.10	.50
215	Bradley Marsh, Ott.	.10	.50
216	Mark Fitzpatrick, Goalie, NYI	.10	.50
217	Ken Baumgartner, Tor.	.10	.50
218	Gregory Gilbert, Chi.	.10	.50
219	Eric Nattress, Phi.	.10	.50
220	Theoren Fleury, Cal.	.10	.50
221	Raymond Bourque, Bos.	.15	1.50
222	Steve Thomas, NYI	.10	8.00
223	Scott Niedermayer, NJ	.40	.50
224	Jeff Lazaro, Ott.	.10	.50
225	League Leader Wins: Kirk McLean, Goalie, Van.	.10	8.00
225	League Leader Wins: Tim Cheveldae, Goalie, Det.	.10	8.00
226	Marc Fortier, Que.	.10	.50
227	Rob Zettler, SJ	.10	.50
228	Kevin Todd, NJ	.10	.50
229	Anthony Amonte, NYR	.20	4.00
230	Mark Lamb, Ott.	.10	.50
231	Chris Dahlquist, Min.	.10	.50

No.	Player	Regular NRMT	Gold NRMT
232	James Black, Hart.	.10	.50
233	Paul Cavallini, St.L	.10	.50
234	Gino Cavallini, Que.	.10	.50
235	Tony Tanti, Buf.	.10	.50
236	Mike Ridley, Wash.	.10	.50
237	Curtis Joseph, Goalie, St.L	.15	1.75
238	Mike Craig, Min.	.10	.50
239	Luciano Borsato, Win.	.10	.50
240	Brian Bellows, Min.	.10	.50
241	Barry Pederson, Bos.	.10	.50
242	Tony Granato, LA	.10	.50
243	Jim Paek, Pit.	.10	.50
244	Tim Bergland, TB	.10	.50
245	Jayson More, SJ	.10	.50
246	Laurie Boschman, Ott.	.10	.50
247	Doug Bodger, Buf.	.10	.50
248	Murray Craven, Hart.	.10	.50
249	Kris Draper, Win.	.10	.50
250	Brian Benning, Phi.	.10	.50
251	Jarmo Myllys, Goalie, Tor.	.10	.50
252	Sergei Fedorov, Det.	.50	5.00
253	Mathieu Schneider, Mon.	.10	.50
254	Dave Gagner, Min.	.10	.50
255	Michel Goulet, Chi.	.10	.50
256	Alexander Godynyuk, Cal.	.10	.50
257	Ray Sheppard, Det.	.10	.50

1992 ALL STAR

No.	Player	Regular	Gold
258	Mark Messier, NYR	.10	1.00
259	Kevin Stevens, Pit.	.10	2.00
260	Brett Hull, St.L	.20	3.00
261	Brian Leetch, NYR	.10	1.00
262	Raymond Bourque, Bos.	.10	1.00
263	Patrick Roy, Goalie, Mon.	.25	10.00
264	Michael Gartner, NYR	.10	.75
265	Mario Lemieux, Pit.	.25	10.00
266	Luc Robitaille, LA	.20	1.00
267	Mark Recchi, Phi.	.10	1.00
268	Phil Housley, Win.	.10	.50
269	Scott Stevens, NJ	.10	.50
270	Kirk McLean, Goalie, Van.	.10	1.00

REGULAR ISSUE

No.	Player	Regular NRMT	Gold NRMT
271	Steve Duchesne, Que.	.10	.50
272	Jiri Hrdina, Pit.	.10	8.00
273	John MacLean, NJ	.10	.50
274	Mark Messier, NYR	.20	8.00
275	Geoff Smith, Edm.	.10	.50
276	Russell Courtnall, Mon.	.10	.50
277	Yves Racine, Det.	.10	.50
278	Tom Draper, Goalie, Buf.	.10	.50
279	Charles Huddy, LA	.10	.50
280	Trevor Kidd, Goalie, Cal.	.10	.50
281	Garth Butcher, St.L	.10	.50
282	Mike Sullivan, SJ	.10	.50
283	Adam Burt, Hart.	.10	.50
284	Troy Murray, Win.	.10	.50
285	Stephane Fiset, Goalie, Que.	.10	.50
286	Perry Anderson, SJ	.10	.50
287	Sergei Nemchinov, NYR	.10	.75
288	Richard Zombo, St.L	.10	.50
289	Pierre Turgeon, NYI	.20	2.00
290	Kevin Lowe, Edm.	.10	.50
291	Brian Bradley, TB	.10	.50
292	Martin Gelinas, Edm.	.10	.50
293	Brian Leetch, NYR	.20	2.50
294	Peter Bondra, Wash.	.10	.50
295	Brendan Shanahan, St.L	.20	1.50
296	Dale Hawerchuk, Buf.	.10	1.50
297	Mike Hough, Que.	.10	.50
298	Roland Melanson, Goalie, Mon.	.10	.50
299	Brad Jones, Phi.	.10	8.00
300	Jocelyn Lemieux, Chi.	.10	.50
301	Byron McCrimmon, Det.	.10	.50
302	Marty McInnis, NYI	.10	.50
303	Chris Terreri, Goalie, NJ	.10	.50
304	Dean Evason, SJ	.10	.50
305	Glenn Healy, Goalie, NYI	.10	.50

TOPPS — 1992-93 REGULAR ISSUE

No.	Player	Regular NRMT	Gold NRMT
306	Kenneth Hodge Jr., Bos.	.10	.50
307	Michael Liut, Goalie, Wash.	.10	8.00
308	Gary Suter, Cal.	.10	.50
309	Neal Broten, Min.	.10	.50
310	Tim Cheveldae, Goalie, Det.	.10	.50
311	Thomas Fergus, Van.	.10	.50
312	Petr Svoboda, Buf.	.10	.50
313	Tom Chorske, NJ	.10	.50
314	**League Leader Plus/Minus:** Paul Ysebaert, Det.	.10	.50
315	James (Steve) Smith, Chi.	.10	.50
316	Stephane Morin, Que.	.10	.50
317	Pat MacLeod, SJ	.10	.50
318	Dino Ciccarelli, Det.	.10	.50
319	Peter Zezel, Tor.	.10	.50
320	Chris Lindberg, Cal.	.10	.50
321	Grant Ledyard, Buf.	.10	.50
322	Ronald Francis, Pit.	.10	.50
323	Adrien Plavsic, Van.	.10	.50
324	Ray Ferraro, NYI	.10	8.00
325	Wendel Clark, Tor.	.10	1.75
326	Corey Millen, LA	.10	.50
327	Mark Pederson, Phi.	.10	.50
328	Patrick Poulin, Hart.	.10	.50
329	Adam Graves, NYR	.25	2.50
330	Robert Holik, Hart.	.10	.50
331	Kelly Kisio, SJ	.10	.50
332	Peter Sidorkiewicz, Goalie, Ott.	.10	.50
333	Vladimir Ruzicka, Bos.	.10	.50
334	Jean-Jacques Daigneault, Mon.	.10	.50
335	Troy Mallette, NJ	.10	.50
336	Craig MacTavish, Edm.	.10	.50
337	Michel Petit, Cal.	.10	.50
338	Claude Loiselle, NYI	.10	.50
339	Teppo Numminen, Win.	.10	.50
340	**League Leader Goals:** Brett Hull, St.L	.20	2.00
341	Sylvain Lefebvre, Mon.	.10	.50
342	Perry Berezan, SJ	.10	.50
343	Kevin Stevens, Pit.	.20	2.00
344	Randy Ladouceur, Hart.	.10	.50
345	Pat LaFontaine, Buf.	.20	5.00
346	Glen Wesley, Bos.	.10	.50
347	**Highlight:** Michel Goulet, Chi.	.10	.50
348	Jamie Macoun, Tor.	.10	.50
349	Owen Nolan, Que.	.15	.50
350	Grant Fuhr, Goalie, Tor.	.10	8.00
351	Tim Kerr, Hart.	.10	.50
352	Kjell Samuelsson, Pit.	.10	.50
353	Pavel Bure, Van.	1.25	18.00
354	Murray Baron, St.L	.10	.50
355	Paul Broten, NYR	.10	.50
356	Craig Simpson, Edm.	.10	.50
357	Kenneth Daneyko NJ	.10	.50
358	Greg Hawgood, Edm.	.10	.50
359	Johan Garpenlov, SJ	.10	.50
360	Garry Galley, Phi.	.10	.50
361	Paul Di Pietro, Mon.	.10	.50
362	Jamie Leach, Pit.	.10	.50
363	Clint Malarchuk, Goalie, Buf.	.10	.50
364	Dan Lambert, Que.	.10	.50
365	Joseph Juneau, Bos.	1.50	18.00
366	Scott Lachance, NYI	.10	12.00
367	Mike Richter, Goalie, NYR	.20	.50
368	Sheldon Kennedy, Det.	.10	.50
369	John McIntyre, LA	.10	.50
370	Glen Murray, Bos.	.10	.50
371	Ronald Sutter, St.L	.10	.50
372	**David Williams, SJ, RC**	.10	.50
373	**Bill Lindsay, Que., RC**	.10	.50
374	Todd Gill, Tor.	.10	.50
375	Sylvain Turgeon, Ott.	.10	.50
376	Dirk Graham, Chi.	.10	.50
377	Brad Schlegel, Wash.	.10	.50
378	Robert Carpenter, Wash.	.10	.50
379	Jon Casey, Goalie, Min.	.10	.50
380	Andrei Lomakin, Phi.	.10	.50
381	Kay Whitmore, Goalie, Hart.	.10	.50
382	Alexander Mogilny, Buf.	.50	7.00
383	Garry Valk, Van.	.10	.50
384	Bruce Driver, NJ	.10	.50
385	Jeff Reese, Goalie, Cal.	.10	.50
386	Brent Gilchrist, Mon.	.10	.50

No.	Player	Regular NRMT	Gold NRMT
387	Kerry Huffman, Que.	.10	.50
388	Robert (Bobby) Smith, Min.	.10	.50
389	Dave Manson, Edm.	.10	.50
390	Russell Romaniuk, Win.	.10	.50
391	Paul MacDermid, Wash.	.10	.50
392	Louie DeBrusk, Edm.	.10	.50
393	Dave McLlwain, Tor.	.10	.50
394	Andrew Moog, Goalie, Bos.	.10	.50
395	Tahir (Tie) Domi, NYR	.10	.50
396	Pat Jablonski, Goalie, TB	.10	.50
397	Troy Loney, Pit.	.10	.50
398	Jimmy Carson, Det.	.10	.50
399	Eric Weinrich, NJ	.10	.50
400	Jeremy Roenick, Chi.	.50	.50
401	Brent Fedyk, Det.	.10	.50
402	Geoff Sanderson, Hart.	.50	5.00
403	Doug Lidster, Van.	.10	.50
404	Michael Gartner, NYR	.10	2.00
405	Derian Hatcher, Min.	.10	.50
406	Gaetan Duchesne, Min.	.10	.50
407	Randy Moller, Buf.	.10	.50
408	Brian Skrudland, Mon.	.10	.50
409	Luke Richardson, Edm.	.10	.50
410	Mark Recchi, Phi.	.25	3.00
411	Stephen Konroyd, Hart.	.10	.50
412	Troy Gamble, Goalie, Van.	.10	.50
413	Greg Johnston, Tor.	.10	8.00
414	Denis Savard, Mon.	.10	.50
415	Mats Sundin, Que.	.25	4.00
416	Bryan Trottier, Pit.	.10	.50
417	Don Sweeney, Bos.	.10	.50
418	Pat Falloon, SJ	.20	2.50
419	Alexander Semak, NJ	.10	1.00
420	David Shaw, Min.	.10	8.00
421	Tomas Sandstrom, LA	.10	.50
422	Petr Nedved, Van.	.10	8.00
423	Peter Ing, Goalie, Edm.	.10	.50
424	Wayne Presley, Buf.	.10	8.00
425	Richard Wamsley, Goalie, Tor.	.10	.50
426	**Rob Zamuner, TB, RC**	.20	.50
427	Claude Boivin, Phi.	.10	.50
428	Sylvain Cote, Wash.	.10	.50
429	**Highlight:** Kevin Stevens, Pit.	.10	1.50
430	Randy Velischek, Que.	.10	.50
431	Derek King, NYI	.10	.50
432	Terry Yake, Hart.	.10	.50
433	Phillipe Bozon, St.L	.10	.50
434	Richard Sutter, St.L	.10	.50
435	Brian Lawton, Hart.	.10	.50
436	Brian Hayward, Goalie, SJ	.10	.50
437	Robert Dirk, Van.	.10	.50
438	Bernie Nicholls, Edm.	.10	.50
439	Michel Picard, Hart.	.10	.50
440	Nicklas Lidstrom, Det.	.10	2.00
441	Michael Modano, Min.	.40	5.00
442	Phillippe Bourque, Pit.	.10	.50
443	Wayne McBean, NYI	.10	.50
444	Scott Mellanby, Edm.	.10	.50
445	Kevin Haller, Mon.	.10	.50
446	David Taylor, LA	.10	.50
447	Lawrence Murphy, Pit.	.10	.50
448	David Bruce, SJ	.10	.50
449	Steven Finn, Que.	.10	.50
450	Michael Krushelnyski, Tor.	.10	.50
451	Adam Creighton, NYI	.10	.50
452	Allan MacInnis, Cal.	.10	.50
453	Richard Tabaracci, Win.	.10	.50
454	Bob Bassen, NYI	.10	.50
455	Kelly Buchberger, Edm.	.10	.50
456	Phil Housley, Win.	.10	.50
457	Daren Puppa, Goalie, Buf.	.10	.50
458	Viacheslav Fetisov, NJ	.10	.50
459	Douglas Smail, Que.	.10	.50
460	Paul Stanton, Pit.	.10	.50
461	Stephen Weeks, Goalie, Wash.	.10	.50
462	Valeri Zelepukin, NJ	.20	1.00
463	Stephane Matteau, Chi.	.10	.50
464	Dale Hunter, Wash.	.10	.50
465	Terry Carkner, Phi.	.10	.50
466	Vincent Riendeau, Goalie, Det.	.10	.50
467	Sergei Makarov, Cal.	.10	.50
468	Igor Ulanov, Win.	.10	1.50

No.	Player	Regular NRMT	Gold NRMT
469	Peter Stastny, NJ	.10	.50
470	Dimitri Khristich, Wash.	.10	.50
471	Joel Otto, Cal.	.10	.50
472	Geoff Courtnall, Van.	.10	.50
473	Michael Ramsey, Buf.	.10	.50
474	Yvon Corriveau, Hart.	.10	.50
475	Adam Oates, Bos.	.20	.50
476	Esa Tikkanen, Edm.	.10	.50
477	Doug Weight, NYR	.10	1.00
478	Mike Keane, Mon	.10	.50
479	Kelly Miller, Wash.	.10	.50
480	Nelson Emerson, St.L	.20	.50
481	Shawn McEachern, Pit.	.25	2.50
482	Douglas Wilson, SJ	.10	.50
483	Jeff Odgers, SJ	.10	.50
484	Stephane Quintal, St.L	.10	.50
485	Christian Ruuttu, Win.	.10	.50
486	Paul Ranheim, Cal.	.10	.50
487	Craig Wolanin, Que.	.10	.50
488	Robert DiMaio, TB	.10	.50
489	Shawn Cronin, Win.	.10	.50
490	Kirk Muller, Mon.	.10	.50
491	**League Leader Save PCT:** Patrick Roy, Goalie, Mon.	.25	10.00
492	Richard Pilon, NYI	.10	.50
493	Patrick Verbeek, Hart.	.10	.50
494	Ken Wregget, Goalie, Pit.	.10	.50
495	Joe Sakic, Que.	.20	2.50
496	Zdeno Ciger, NJ	.10	.50
497	Steve Larmer, Chi.	.10	8.00
498	Calle Johansson, Wash.	.10	.50
499	Trevor Linden, Van.	.20	.50
500	John LeClair, Mon.	.10	.50
501	Bryan Marchment, Chi.	.10	.50
502	Todd Krygier, Wash.	.10	.50
503	Tom Barrasso, Goalie, Pit.	.10	1.50
504	**League Leader Points:** Mario Lemieux, Pit.	.30	10.00
505	Daniel Berthiaume, Goalie, Win.	.10	.50
506	Jamie Baker, Que.	.10	.50
507	Greg Adams, Van.	.10	.50
508	Patrick Roy, Goalie, Mon.	.50	30.00
509	Kris King, NYR	.10	.50
510	Jurki Lumme, Van.	.10	.50
511	Darin Kimble, TB	.10	.50
512	Igor Larionov, Van.	.10	.50
513	Martin Brodeur, Goalie, NJ	.10	8.00
514	**Denny Felsner, St.L, RC**	.20	4.00
515	Yanic Dupre, Phi.	.10	2.00
516	**Bill Guerin, NJ, RC**	.30	.50
517	**Brett Hedican, St.L, RC**	.20	.50
518	Mike Hartman, TB	.10	.50
519	Stephen Heinze, Bos.	.10	.50
520	Frantisek Kucera, Chi.	.10	.50
521	David Reid, Bos.	.10	.50
522	Frank Pietrangelo, Goalie, Hart.	.10	.50
523	Martin Rucinsky, Que.	.20	.50
524	Anthony Hrkac, Chi.	.10	.50
525	Checklist 1 (1 - 132)	.10	---
526	Checklist 2 (133 - 264)	.10	---
527	Checklist 3 (265 - 396)	.10	---
528	Checklist 4 (397 - 528)	.10	---
529	Eric Lindros, Phi.	5.00	50.00
525	Allan Conroy, Phi.	---	1.50
526	Jeff Norton, NYI	---	1.50
527	Rob Robinson, TB	---	1.50
528	Adam Foote, Que.	---	1.50

Note: The checklist cards were replaced in the Gold Series with player cards.

— 1992 - 93 STADIUM CLUB —

The 1992 - 93 Stadium Club Set is a continuation of the previous year's. This is Topps premium set.

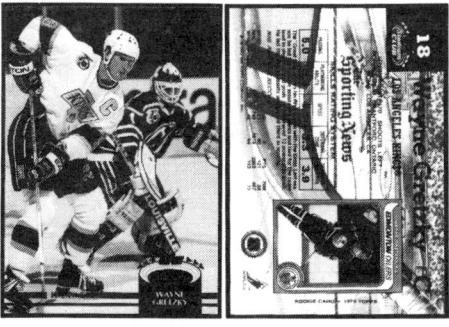

1992-93 Stadium Club
Card No. 18, Wayne Gretzky

Card Size: 2 1/2" x 3 1/2"
Face: Four colour, borderless; Name, Team, Topps Stadium Logo
Back: Four colour, card stock, borderless; Name, Team, Resume
Imprint: A, B, C, D, E, or F © 1992 THE TOPPS COMPANY, INC
Complete Set No.: 501

Complete Set Price:	25.00	50.00
Series One:	12.50	25.00
Series Two:	15.00	30.00
Common Player:	.05	.10
Cellophane Packs: (15 Cards)		1.75
Boxes: (36 Packs)		50.00

SERIES ONE

No.	Players	EX	NRMT
1	Brett Hull, St.L	.50	1.00
2	Theoren Fleury, Cal.	.07	.15
3	Joseph Sakic, Que.	.17	.35
4	Michael Modano, Min.	.25	.50
5	Dmitri Mironov, Tor.	.05	.10
6	Yves Racine, Det.	.05	.10
7	Igor Kravchuk, Chi.	.05	.10
8	Philippe Bozon, St.L	.05	.10
9	Stephane J. J. Richer, NJ	.05	.10
10	David Lowry, St.L	.05	.10
11	Dean Evason, SJ	.05	.10
12	Mark Fitzpatrick, Goalie, NYI	.05	.10
13	David Poulin, Bos.	.05	.10
14	Phil Housley, Win.	.05	.10
15	Adrien Plavsic, Van.	.05	.10
16	Claude Boivin, Phil.	.05	.10
17	**Bill Guerin, NJ, RC**	**.20**	**.40**
18	Wayne Gretzky, LA	.75	1.50
19	Steve Yzerman, Det.	.25	.50
20	Joe Mullen, Pit.	.05	.10
21	Byron (Brad) McCrimmon, Det.	.05	.10
22	Dan Quinn, Phil.	.05	.10
23	Robert Blake, LA	.05	.10
24	Wayne Presley, Buf.	.05	.10
25	Zarley Zalapski, Har.	.05	.10
26	Bryan Trottier, Pit.	.05	.10
27	Peter Sidorkiewicz, Goalie, Ott.	.05	.10
28	John MacLean, NJ	.05	.10
29	Brad Schlegel, Wash.	.05	.10
30	Marc Bureau, Min.	.05	.10
31	Troy Murray, Win.	.05	.10
32	Anthony Amonte, NYR	.15	.30
33	Robert DiMaio, TB	.05	.10
34	Joe Murphy, Edm.	.05	.10
35	Jimmy Waite, Goalie, Chi.	.05	.10
36	Ronald Sutter, St.L	.05	.10
37	Joe Nieuwendyk, Cal.	.05	.10
38	Kevin Haller, Mon.	.05	.10
39	Andrew Cassels, Har.	.05	.10
40	Dale Hunter, Wash.	.05	.10
41	Craig Janney, St.L	.12	.25
42	Sergio Momesso, Van.	.05	.10
43	Nicklas Lidstrom, Det.	.15	.30
44	Luc Robitaille, LA	.15	.30
45	Adam Creighton, NYI	.05	.10
46	Norm Maciver, Edm.	.05	.10
47	Mikhail Tatarinov, Que.	.05	.10
48	Gary Roberts, Cal.	.05	.10

No.	Players	EX	NRMT
49	Gord Hynes, Bos.	.05	.10
50	Claude Lemieux, NJ	.05	.10
51	Brad May, Buf.	.05	.10
52	Paul Stanton, Pit.	.05	.10
53	Richard Wamsley, Goalie, Tor.	.05	.10
54	Steve Larmer, Chi.	.05	.10
55	Darrin Shannon, Win.	.05	.10
56	Pat Falloon, SJ	.12	.25
57	Chris Dahlquist, Min.	.05	.10
58	John Vanbiesbrouck, Goalie, NYR	.05	.10
59	Sylvain Turgeon, Ott.	.05	.10
60	Jayson More, SJ	.05	.10
61	Randy Burridge, Wash.	.05	.10
62	Viacheslav Kozlov, Det.	.75	1.50
63	Daniel Marois, NYI	.05	.10
64	Curt Giles, St.L	.05	.10
65	Brad Shaw, Ott.	.05	.10
66	Bill Ranford, Goalie, Edm.	.05	.10
67	Frantisek Musil, Cal.	.05	.10
68	Stephen Leach, Bos.	.05	.10
69	Michel Goulet, Chi.	.05	.10
70	Mathieu Schneider, Mon.	.05	.10
71	Stephen Kasper, Phi.	.05	.10
72	Darryl Sydor, LA	.05	.10
73	Brian Leetch, NYR	.20	.40
74	Chris Terreri, Goalie, NJ	.05	.10
75	Jim Johnson, Min.	.05	.10
76	Rick Tocchet, Pit.	.05	.10
77	Teppo Numminen, Win.	.05	.10
78	Owen Nolan, Que.	.05	.10
79	Grant Ledyard, Buf.	.05	.10
80	Trevor Linden, Van.	.15	.30
81	Luciano Borsato, Win.	.05	.10
82	Derek King, NYI	.05	.10
83	Robert Cimetta, Tor.	.05	.10
84	Geoff Smith, Edm.	.05	.10
85	Ray Sheppard, Det.	.05	.10
86	Dimitri Khristich, Wash.	.05	.10
87	Chris Chelios, Chi.	.05	.10
88	Alexander Godynyuk, Cal.	.05	.10
89	Perry Anderson, SJ	.05	.10
90	Neal Broten, Min.	.05	.10
91	Brian Benning, Phil.	.05	.10
92	Brent Thompson, LA	.05	.10
93	Claude LaPointe, Que.	.05	.10
94	Mario Lemieux, Pit.	.75	1.50
95	Pat LaFontaine, Buf.	.25	.50
96	Frank Pietrangelo, Goalie, Har.	.05	.10
97	Gerald Diduck, Van.	.05	.10
98	Paul DiPietro, Mon.	.05	.10
99	Valeri Zelepukin, NJ	.12	.25
100	Richard Zombo, St.L	.05	.10
101	Daniel Berthiaume, Goalie, Win.	.05	.10
102	Tom Fitzgerald, NYI	.05	.10
103	Ken Baumgartner, Tor.	.05	.10
104	Esa Tikkanen, Edm.	.05	.10
105	Steve Chiasson, Det.	.05	.10
106	Robert Holik, Har.	.35	.75
107	Dominik Hasek, Goalie, Chi.	.05	.10
108	Jeff Hackett, Goalie, SJ	.05	.10
109	Paul Broten, NYR	.05	.10
110	Kevin Stevens, Pit.	.30	.60
111	Geoff Sanderson, Har.	.05	.10
112	Donald Audette, Buf.	.05	.10
113	Jarmo Myllys, Goalie, Tor.	.05	.10
114	Brian Skrudland, Mon.	.05	.10
115	Andrei Lomakin, Phi.	.05	.10
116	Keith Tkachuk, Win.	.20	.40
117	John McIntyre, LA	.05	.10
118	Jacques Cloutier, Goalie, Que.	.05	.10
119	Michel Picard, Har.	.05	.10
120	David Babych, Van.	.05	.10
121	Dave Gagner, Min.	.05	.10
122	Robert Carpenter, Wash.	.05	.10
123	Ray Ferraro, NYI	.05	.10
124	Glenn Anderson, Tor.	.05	.10
125	Craig MacTavish, Edm.	.05	.10
126	Shawn Burr, Det.	.05	.10
127	Tim Bergland, TB	.05	.10
128	Allan MacInnis, Cal.	.05	.10
129	Jeff Beukeboom, NYR	.05	.10
130	Ken Wregget, Goalie, Pit.	.05	.10
131	Arturs Irbe, Goalie, SJ	.30	.60

No.	Players	EX	NRMT
132	David Andreychuk, Buf.	.05	.10
133	Patrick Roy, Goalie, Mon.	.35	.75
134	Benoit Brunet, Mon.	.05	.10
135	Richard Tabaracci, Goalie, Win.	.05	.10
136	Jamie Baker, Que.	.05	.10
137	Yanic Dupre, Phi.	.05	.10
138	Jari Kurri, LA	.05	.10
139	Adam Burt, Har.	.05	.10
140	Peter Stastny, NJ	.05	.10
141	Brad Jones	.05	.10
142	Jeff Odgers, SJ	.05	.10
143	Anatoli Semenov, TB	.05	.10
144	Paul Ranheim, Cal.	.05	.10
145	Sylvain Cote, Wash.	.05	.10
146	Brent Ashton, Bos.	.05	.10
147	Doug Bodger, Buf.	.05	.10
148	Bryan Marchment, Chi.	.05	.10
149	Bob Kudelski, LA	.05	.10
150	Adam Graves, NYR	.20	.40
151	Scott Stevens, NJ	.05	.10
152	Russell Courtnall, Mon.	.05	.10
153	Darcy Wakaluk, Goalie, Min.	.05	.10
154	Per-Erik Eklund, Phil.	.05	.10
155	Robert Kron, Van.	.05	.10
156	Randy Ladouceur, Har.	.05	.10
157	Ed Olczyk, Win.	.05	.10
158	Jiri Hrdina, Pit.	.05	.10
159	John Tonelli, Que.	.05	.10
160	John Cullen, Har.	.05	.10
161	Jan Erixon, Har.	.05	.10
162	David Shaw, Min.	.05	.10
163	Brian Bradley, TB	.05	.10
164	Russell Romaniuk, Win.	.05	.10
165	Eric Weinrich, NJ	.05	.10
166	Stephen Heinze, Bos.	.05	.10
167	Jeremy Roenick, Chi.	.50	1.25
168	Mark Pederson, Phi.	.05	.10
169	Paul Coffey, LA	.05	.10
170	Bob Errey, Pit.	.05	.10
171	Brian Lawton, SJ	.05	.10
172	Vincent Riendeau, Goalie, Det.	.05	.10
173	Marc Fortier, Que.	.05	.10
174	Marc Bergevin, TB	.05	.10
175	Jim Sandlak, Van.	.05	.10
176	Bob Bassen, St.L	.05	.10
177	Uwe Krupp, NYI	.05	.10
178	Paul MacDermid, Wash.	.05	.10
179	Bob Corkum, Buf.	.05	.10
180	Robert Reichel, Cal.	.05	.10
181	John LeClair, Mon.	.05	.10
182	Mike Hudson, Chi.	.05	.10
183	Mark Recchi, Phi.	.25	.50
184	Roland Melanson, Goalie, Mon.	.05	.10
185	Gordon Roberts, Bos.	.05	.10
186	Clint Malarchuk, Goalie, Buf.	.05	.10
187	Kris King, NYR	.05	.10
188	Adam Oates, Bos.	.12	.25
189	Jarrod Skalde, NJ	.05	.10
190	Mike Lalor, Win.	.05	.10
191	Vincent Damphousse, Edm.	.05	.10
192	Peter Ahola, LA, Error,	.05	.10
193	Kirk McLean, Goalie, Van.	.05	.10
194	Murray Baron, St.L	.05	.10
195	Michel Petit, Cal.	.05	.10
196	Stephane Fiset, Goalie, Que.	.05	.10
197	Patrick Verbeek, Har.	.05	.10
198	Jon Casey, Goalie, Min.	.05	.10
199	Tim Cheveldae, Goalie, Det.	.05	.10
200	Mike Ridley, Wash.	.05	.10
201	Scott Lachance, NYI	.05	.10
202	Rod Brind'Amour, Phi.	.12	.25
203	**Brett Hedican, St.L, RC**	**.20**	**.40**
204	Wendel Clark, Tor.	.05	.10
205	Shawn McEachern, Pit.	.20	.40
206	Randy Wood, Buf.	.05	.10
207	Ulf Dahlen, Min.	.05	.10
208	Andy Brickley, Bos.	.05	.10
209	Scott Niedermayer, NJ	.25	.50
210	Bob Essensa, Goalie, Win.	.05	.10
211	Patrick Poulin, Har.	.05	.10
212	Johan Garpenlov, SJ	.05	.10
213	Marty McInnis, NYI	.05	.10
214	Josef Beranek, Edm.	.12	.25

TOPPS — 1992-93 STADIUM CLUB

No.	Player	EX	NRMT
215	Rod Langway, Wash.	.05	.10
216	Dave Christian, St.L	.05	.10
217	Sergei Makarov, Cal.	.05	.10
218	Gerard Gallant, Det.	.05	.10
219	Neil Wilkinson, SJ	.05	.10
220	Tomas Sandstrom, LA	.05	.10
221	Shayne Corson, Mon.	.05	.10
222	John Ogrodnick, NYR	.05	.10
223	Keith Acton, Phi.	.05	.10
224	Paul Fenton, SJ	.05	.10
225	Rob Zettler, SJ	.05	.10
226	Todd Elik, Min.	.05	.10
227	Petr Svoboda, Buf.	.05	.10
228	Zdeno Ciger, NJ	.05	.10
229	Kevin Miller, Wash.	.05	.10
230	Richard Pilon, NYI	.05	.10
231	Pat Jablonski, Goalie, TB	.05	.10
232	Greg Adams, Van.	.05	.10
233	Martin Brodeur, Goalie, NJ	.35	.75
234	David Taylor, LA	.05	.10
235	Kelly Buchberger, Edm.	.05	.10
236	Stephen Konroyd, Har.	.05	.10
237	Guy Larose, Tor.	.05	.10
238	Patrice Brisebois, Mon.	.05	.10
239	1992 Hockey Checklist (1-125)	.05	.10
240	1992 Hockey Checklist (126-25)	.05	.10

MEMBERS CHOICE

No.	Player	EX	NRMT
241	Mark Messier, NYR	.12	.25
242	Mike Richter, Goalie, NYR	.05	.10
243	Ed Belfour, Goalie, Chi.	.25	.50
244	Sergei Fedorov, Det.	.50	1.00
245	Adam Oates, Bos.	.12	.25
246	Pavel Bure, Van.	1.00	2.00
247	Luc Robitaille, LA	.12	.25
248	Brian Leetch, NYR	.05	.10
249	Raymond Bourque, Bos.	.05	.10
250	Anthony Amonte, NYR	.20	.40

SERIES TWO

MEMBERS CHOICE

No.	Player	EX	NRMT
251	Mario Lemieux, Pit.	.75	1.50
252	Patrick Roy, Goalie, Mon.	.25	.50
253	Nicklas Lidstrom, Det.	.12	.25
254	Steve Yzerman, Det.	.12	.25
255	Jeremy Roenick, Chi.	.50	1.00
256	Wayne Gretzky, LA	.75	1.50
257	Kevin Stevens, Pit.	.25	.50
258	Brett Hull, St.L	.35	.75
259	Pat Falloon, SJ	.15	.30
260	Guy Carbonneau, Mon.	.05	.10

REGULAR ISSUE

No.	Player	EX	NRMT
261	Todd Gill, Tor.	.05	.10
262	Mike Sullivan, SJ	.05	.10
263	Jeff Brown, St.L	.05	.10
264	Joe Reekie, TB, Error	.05	.10
265	Geoff Courtnall, Van.	.05	.10
266	Mike Richter, Goalie, NYR	.15	.30
267	Raymond Bourque, Bos.	.12	.25
268	Mike Craig, Min.	.05	.10
269	Scott King, Goalie, Det.	.05	.10
270	Donald Beaupre, Goalie, Wash.	.05	.10
271	Ted Donato, Bos.	.12	.25
272	Gary Leeman, Cal.	.05	.10
273	Stephen Weeks, Goalie, Wash.	.05	.10
274	Keith Brown, Chi.	.05	.10
275	Gregory Paslawski, Que.	.05	.10
276	Pierre Turgeon, NYI	.25	.50
277	Jimmy Carson, Det.	.05	.10
278	Thomas Fergus, Van.	.05	.10
279	Glen Wesley, Bos.	.05	.10
280	Tomas Forslund, Cal.	.05	.10
281	Tony Granato, LA	.05	.10

No.	Player	EX	NRMT
282	Phillippe Bourque, Pit.	.05	.10
283	David Ellet, Tor.	.05	.10
284	David Bruce, SJ	.05	.10
285	Stu Barnes, Win.	.05	.10
286	Peter Bondra, Wash.	.05	.10
287	Garth Butcher, St.L	.05	.10
288	Ron Hextall, Goalie, Que.	.05	.10
289	Guy Carbonneau, Mon.	.05	.10
290	Louie DeBrusk, Edm.	.05	.10
291	David Barr, NJ	.05	.10
292	Kenneth Sutton, Buf.	.05	.10
293	Brian Bellows, Min.	.05	.10
294	Michael McNeill, Que.	.05	.10
295	Rob Brown, Chi.	.05	.10
296	Corey Millen, LA	.05	.10
297	Joseph Juneau, Bos.	1.50	3.00
298	Jeff Chychrun, Pit. Error	.05	.10
299	Igor Larionov, Van.	.05	.10
300	Sergei Fedorov, Det.	.50	1.00
301	Kevin Hatcher, Wash.	.05	.10
302	Al Iafrate, Wash.	.05	.10
303	James Black, Har.	.05	.10
304	Stephane Beauregard, Goalie, Buf.	.05	.10
305	Joel Otto, Cal.	.05	.10
306	Nelson Emerson, St.L	.20	.40
307	Gaeton Duchesne, Min.	.05	.10
308	Jean-Jacques Daigneault, Mon.	.05	.10
309	Jamie Macoun, Tor.	.05	.10
310	Laurie Boschman, Ott.	.05	.10
311	Michael Gartner, NYR	.05	.10
312	Tony Tanti, Buf.	.05	.10
313	Steve Duchesne, Que.	.05	.10
314	Martin Gelinas, Edm.	.05	.10
315	Dominic Roussel, Goalie, Phi.	.15	.30
316	Cam Neely, Bos.	.05	.10
317	Craig Walanin, Que.	.05	.10
318	Randy Gilhen, NYR	.05	.10
319	David Volek, NYI	.05	.10
320	Alexander Mogilny, Buf.	.50	1.00
321	Jyrki Lumme, Van.	.05	.10
322	Jeff Reese, Goalie, Cal.	.05	.10
323	Gregory Gilbert, Chi.	.05	.10
324	Jeff Norton, NYI	.05	.10
325	Jim Hrivnak, Goalie, Wash.	.05	.10
326	Eric Desjardins, Mon.	.05	.10
327	Curtis Joseph, Goalie, St.L	.12	.25
328	Eric Nattress, Tor.	.05	.10
329	Jamie Leach, Pit.	.05	.10
330	Christian Ruuttu, Win.	.05	.10
331	Doug Brown, NJ	.05	.10
332	Randy Carlyle, Win.	.05	.10
333	Ed Belfour, Goalie, Chi.	.20	.40
334	Douglas Smail, Que.	.05	.10
335	Hubie McDonough, NYI	.05	.10
336	Pat MacLeod, SJ	.05	.10
337	Don Sweeney, Bos.	.05	.10
338	Felix Potvin, Goalie, Tor.	1.25	2.50
339	Kent Manderville, Tor.	.05	.10
340	Sergei Nemchinov, NYR	.05	.10
341	Calle Johansson, Wash.	.05	.10
342	Dirk Graham, Chi.	.05	.10
343	Craig Billington, Goalie, NJ	.05	.10
344	Valeri Kamensky, Que.	.25	.50
345	Michael Vernon, Goalie, Cal.	.05	.10
346	Fredrik Olausson, Win.	.05	.10
347	Peter Ing, Goalie, Edm.	.05	.10
348	Bo Mikael Andersson, TB	.05	.10
349	Mike Keane, Mon.	.05	.10
350	Stephane Quintal, St.L	.05	.10
351	Tom Chorske, NJ	.05	.10
352	Ronald Francis, Pit.	.05	.10
353	Dana Murzyn, Van.	.05	.10
354	Craig Ludwig, Min.	.05	.10
355	Bob Probert, Det.	.05	.10
356	Glenn Healy, Goalie, NYI	.05	.10
357	Troy Loney, Pit.	.05	.10
358	Vladimir Ruzicka, Bos.	.05	.10
359	Douglas Gilmour, Tor.	.25	.50
360	Darren Turcotte, NYR	.05	.10
361	Kelly Miller, Wash.	.05	.10
362	Dennis Vaske, NYI	.05	.10
363	Stephane Matteau, Chi.	.05	.10
364	Brian Hayward, Goalie, SJ	.05	.10

No.	Player	EX	NRMT
365	Kevin Dineen, Phi.	.05	.10
366	Igor Ulanov, Win.	.05	.10
367	Sylvain Lefebvre, Mon.	.05	.10
368	Petr Klima, Edm.	.05	.10
369	Steve Thomas, NYI	.05	.10
370	Daren Puppa, Goalie, Buf.	.05	.10
371	Brendan Shanahan, St.L	.12	.25
372	Charles Huddy, LA	.05	.10
373	Cliff Ronning, Van.	.05	.10
374	Brian Propp, Min.	.05	.10
375	Lawrence Murphy, Pit.	.05	.10
376	Bruce Driver, NJ	.05	.10
377	Rob Pearson, Tor.	.05	.10
378	Paul Yserbaert, Det.	.05	.10
379	Mark Osborne, Tor.	.05	.10
380	Doug Weight, NYR	.05	.10
381	Kerry Huffman, Phi.	.05	.10
382	Michal Pivonka, Wash.	.05	.10
383	James (Steve) Smith, Chi.	.05	.10
384	Steven Finn, Que.	.05	.10
385	Kevin Lowe, Edm.	.05	.10
386	Michael Ramsey, Buf.	.05	.10
387	Kirk Muller, Mon.	.05	.10
388	**John LeBlanc, Win., RC**	**.05**	**.10**
389	Richard Sutter, St.L	.05	.10
390	Brent Fedyk, Det.	.05	.10
391	Kelly Hrudey, Goalie, LA	.05	.10
392	Viacheslav Fetisov, NJ	.05	.10
393	Glenn Murray, Bos.	.05	.10
394	James Patrick, NYR	.05	.10
395	Tom Draper, Goalie, Buf.	.05	.10
396	Mark Hunter, Wash.	.05	.10
397	Wayne McBean, NYI	.05	.10
398	Joseph Sacco, Tor.	.07	.15
399	Dino Ciccarelli, Det.	.05	.10
400	Brian Noonan, Chi.	.05	.10
401	**Guy Hebert, Goalie, St.L, RC**	**.35**	**.75**
402	Peter Douris, Bos.	.05	.10
403	Gilbert Dionne, Mon.	.05	.10
404	Doug Lidster, Van.	.05	.10
405	John Druce, Win.	.05	.10
406	Alexei Kasatonov, NJ	.05	.10
407	Chris Lindberg, Cal.	.05	.10
408	Mike Ricci, Que.	.05	.10
409	Tom Kurvers, NYI	.05	.10
410	Pat Elynuik, Win.	.05	.10
411	Mike Donnelly, LA	.05	.10
412	Grant Fuhr, Goalie, Tor.	.05	.10
413	Curtis Leschyshyn,	.05	.10
414	Derian Hatcher, Min.	.05	.10
415	Michel Mongeau, TB	.05	.10
416	Tom Barrasso, Goalie, Pit.	.05	.10
417	Joey Kocur, NYR	.05	.10
418	Vladimir Konstantinov, Det.	.05	.10
419	Dale Hawerchuk, Buf	.05	.10
420	Brian Mullen, SJ	.05	.10
421	Mark Greig, Har.	.05	.10
422	Claude Vilgrain, NJ	.05	.10
423	Gary Suter, Cal.	.05	.10
424	Garry Galley, Phi.	.05	.10
425	Benoit Hogue, NYI	.05	.10
426	**Jeff Finley, NYI, RC**	**.05**	**.10**
427	Robert Smith, Min.	.05	.10
428	Brent Sutter, Chi.	.05	.10
429	Ronald Wilson, St.L	.05	.10
430	Andrew Moog, Goalie, Bos.	.05	.10
431	Stephan Lebeau, Mon.	.05	.10
432	Troy Mallette, NJ	.05	.10
433	Peter Zezel, Tor.	.05	.10
434	Mike Hough, Que.	.05	.10
435	Mark Tinordi, Min.	.05	.10
436	Dave Manson, Edm.	.05	.10
437	Jim Paek, Pit.	.05	.10
438	Frantisek Kucera, Chi.	.05	.10
439	**Rob Zamuner, TB, RC**	**.05**	**.10**
440	Ulf Samuelsson, Pit.	.05	.10
441	Perry Berezan, SJ	.05	.10
442	Murray Craven, Har.	.05	.10
443	Mark Messier, NYR	.20	.40
444	Alexander Semak, NJ	.05	.10
445	Gordon Murphy, Bos.	.05	.10
446	Jocelyn Lemieux, Chi.	.05	.10
447	Paul Cavallini, St.L	.05	.10

No.	Player	EX	NRMT
448	Bernie Nicholls, Edm.	.05	.10
449	Brent Gilchrist, Mon.	.05	.10
450	Randy McKay, NJ	.05	.10
451	Alexei Gusarov, Que.	.05	.10
452	Michael McPhee, Mon.	.05	.10
453	Kimbi Daniels, Phi.	.05	.10
454	Kelly Kisio, SJ	.05	.10
455	Robert Sweeney, Bos.	.05	.10
456	Luke Richardson, Edm.	.05	.10
457	Petr Nedved, Van.	.12	.25
458	Craig Berube, Cal.	.05	.10
459	Kay Whitmore, Goalie, Har.	.05	.10
460	Randy Velischek, Que.	.05	.10
461	**David Williams, SJ, RC**	**.05**	**.10**
462	Scott Mellanby, Edm.	.05	.10
463	Terry Carkner, Phi.	.05	.10
464	Dale Craigwell, SJ	.05	.10
465	Kevin Todd, NJ	.05	.10
466	Kjell Samuelsson, Pit.	.05	.10
467	Denis Savard, Mon.	.05	.10
468	Adam Foote, Que.	.05	.10
469	Stephane Morin, Que.	.05	.10
470	Douglas Wilson, SJ	.05	.10
471	Shawn Cronin, Win.	.05	.10
472	Brian Glynn, Edm.	.05	.10
473	Craig Simpson, Edm.	.05	.10
474	Todd Krygier, Wash.	.05	.10
475	Brad Miller, Ott.	.05	.10
476	Yvon Corriveau, Har.	.05	.10
477	Patrick Flatley, NYI	.05	.10
478	Mats Sundin, Que.	.15	.30
479	Joe Cirella, NYR	.05	.10
480	Gino Cavallini, Que.	.05	.10
481	Martin McSorely, LA	.05	.10
482	Bradley Marsh, Ott.	.05	.10
483	Robert McGill, TB	.05	.10
484	Randy Moller, Buf.	.05	.10
485	Keith Primeau, Det.	.05	.10
486	Darin Kimble, TB	.05	.10
487	Michael Krushelnyski, Tor.	.05	.10
488	Sutter Brothers, St.L	.05	.10
489	Pavel Bure, Van.	1.75	3.50
490	**Ray Whitney, SJ, RC**	**.20**	**.40**
491	Dave McLlwain, Tor.	.05	.10
492	**Per Djoos, NYR, RC**	**.05**	**.10**
493	Garry Valk, Van.	.05	.10
494	Michael Bullard, Tor.	.05	.10
495	Greg Hawgood, Edm.	.05	.10
496	Terry Yake, Har.	.05	.10
497	Mike Hartman, TB	.05	.10
498	Jaromir Jagr, Pit.	.50	1.00
499	1992 Hockey Checklist, cards 251-384	.05	.10
500	1992 Hockey Checklist, cards 385-500	.05	.10
501	Eric Lindros, Phil.	3.00	6.00

— 1992 - 93 STADIUM CLUB MEMBERS ONLY —

The 5 hockey cards in this send-away set commemorate important events during the 1992-93 NHL season. The cards are similar to the regular issue but have a distinct gold embossed bar that says MEMBERS ONLY.

1992-93 Stadium Club Members Only
Card No. 4, Eric Lindros

Card Size: 2 1/2 x 3 1/2
Face: Four colour, borderless; Name
Back: Four colour on card stock, borderless; Resume
Imprint: **©1992 THE TOPPS COMPANY, INC.
Complete Set No.: 5
Complete Price Set: 5.00 10.00
Common Player: .25 .50

No.	Player	NRMT	Mint
1	**Neil Nets 1st:** Neil Brady, Ott.	.25	.50
2	**Lightning Has Struck:** Chris Kontos, TB	.35	.75
3	**Kurri Joins 500 Club:** Jari Kurri, LA	.35	.75
4	**Lindros Makes Debut:** Eric Lindros, Phi.	4.25	8.50
5	**Reggie Makes History:** Reggie Savage, Was.	.25	.50

— 1993 - 94 PROMOTIONAL SHEET —

This 9-card sheet was sent to the dealers to promote their upcoming set.

Card Size: 7 1/2" x 10 1/2"
Face: Four Colour, white border; Name, Logo
Back: Four Colour on card stock;, Name, Resume
Imprint: 1994 THE TOPPS COMPANY INC.
Complete Set No.: 1
Complete Price Set: 5.00 10.00

No.	Player
—	Dave Lowrey, Fl.
—	Mark Messier, NYR
—	Mark Lamb, Ott.
—	Mike Vernon, Goalie, Cal.
—	Patrick Roy, Goalie, Mon.
—	Theoren Fluery, Cal.
—	Scott Lachance, NYI
—	Geoff Sanderson, Hart.
—	Raymond Bourque, Bos.

— 1993 - 94 PREMIER ISSUE —

This 528-card set is divided into two equal series, available through foil packs and has an insert gold card in every pack. Other randomly inserted sets also appear in both Series One and Two foil packs.

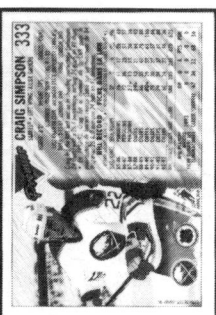

1993-94 Premier Issue
Card No. 333, Craig Simpson

Card Size: 2 1/2" x 3 1/2"
Face: Four Colour, white border; Name, Logo
Back: Four Colour; Name, Number, Team, Position, Resume
Imprint© 1993 THE TOPPS COMPANY, INC.
Complete Set No.: 528
Series One No.: 264
Series Two No.: 264

	Regular	Gold
Complete Price Set:	40.00	250.00
Series One Price:	20.00	125.00
Series Two Price:	20.00	125.00
Common Card:	.05	.40

Foil Pack: (12 Cards)
Boxes: (36 Packs)

SERIES ONE

No.	Player	Regular NRMT	Gold NRMT
1	Patrick Roy, Goalie, Mon.	.50	4.00
2	Alexei Zhitnik, LA	.10	.70
3	Uwe Krupp, NYI	.05	.40
4	Todd Gill, Tor.	.05	.40
5	Paul Stanton, Pit.	.05	.40
6	Petr Nedved, Van.	.05	.40
7	Dale Hawerchuk, Buf.	.05	.40
8	Kevin Miller, St.L	.05	.40
9	Nicklas Lidstrom, Det.	.05	.40
10	Joe Sakic, Que.	.20	1.00
11	Thomas Steen, Win.	.05	.40
12	Peter Bondra, Wash.	.05	.40
13	Brian Noonan, Chi.	.05	.40
14	Glen Featherstone, Bos.	.05	.40
15	Michael Vernon, Goalie, Cal.	.05	.40
16	Janne Ojanen, NJ	.05	.40
17	Neil Brady, Ott.	.05	.40
18	Dimitri Yushkevich, Phi.	.05	.40
19	Rob Zamuner, TB	.05	.40
20	Zarley Zalapski, Hart.	.05	.40
21	Mike Sullivan, SJ	.05	.40
22	Jamie Baker, Ott.	.05	.40
23	Craig MacTavish, Edm.	.05	.40
24	Mark Tinordi, Dal.	.05	.40
25	Brian Leetch, NYR	.25	1.25
26	Brian Skrudland, Fl.	.05	.40
27	Keith Tkachuk, Win.	.20	1.00
28	Patrick Flatley, NYI	.05	.40
29	Doug Bodger, Buf.	.05	.40
30	Felix Potvin, Goalie, Tor.	.65	5.00
31	Shawn Antoski, Van.	.05	.40
32	Eric Desjardins, Mon.	.05	.40
33	Mike Donnelly, LA	.05	.40
34	Kjell Samuelsson, Pit.	.05	.40
35	Nelson Emerson, St.L	.05	.40
36	Phil Housley, Win.	.05	.40
37	**Plus/Minus Leader:** Mario Lemieux, Pit.	.25	1.50
38	Shayne Corson, Edm.	.05	.40
39	James (Steve) Smith, Chi.	.05	.40
40	Bob Kudelski, Ott.	.05	.40
41	Joe Cirella, Fl.	.05	.40
42	Sergei Nemchinov, NYR	.05	.40
43	Kerry Huffman, Que.	.05	.40
44	Bob Beers, TB	.05	.40
45	Al Iafrate, Wash.	.05	.40
46	Michael Modano, Dal.	.20	1.25
47	Patrick Verbeek, Hart.	.05	.40
48	Joel Otto, Cal.	.05	.40
49	Dino Ciccarelli, Det.	.05	.40
50	Adam Oates, Bos.	.15	1.00
51	Pat Elynuik, Wash.	.05	.40
52	Robert Holik, NJ	.05	.40
53	Johan Garpenlov, SJ	.05	.40
54	Jeff Beukeboom, NYR	.05	.40
55	Tommy Soderstrom, Goalie, Phi.	.15	1.00
56	Robert Blake, LA	.05	.40
57	Martin McInnes, NYI	.05	.40
58	Dixon Ward, Van.	.05	.40
59	Patrice Brisebois, Mon.	.05	.40
60	Ed Belfour, Goalie, Chi.	.15	1.00
61	Donald Audette, Buf.	.05	.40
62	Mike Ricci, Que.	.05	.40
63	Fredrick Olausson, Win.	.05	.40
64	Norm Maciver, Ott.	.05	.40
65	Andrew Cassels, Hart.	.05	.40
66	Tim Cheveldae, Goalie, Det.	.05	.40
67	David Reid, Bos.	.05	.40
68	Philippe Bozon, St.L	.05	.40
69	Drake Berehowsky, Tor.	.05	.40
70	Anthony Amonte, NYR	.05	.40
71	Dave Manson, Edm.	.05	.40
72	Rick Tocchet, Pit.	.05	.40
73	Stephen Kasper, TB	.05	.40
74	Assist Leader: Adam Oates, Bos.	.05	.40
75	Ulf Dahlen, Dal.	.05	.40
76	Chris Lindberg, Cal.	.05	.40
77	Douglas Jr. Wilson, SJ	.05	.40
78	Mike Ridley, Wash.	.05	.40
79	Vjateslav Butsayev, Phi.	.05	.40

252 • TOPPS — 1982-83 STICKERS —

No.	Player	Regular NRMT	Gold NRMT
80	Scott Stevens, NJ	.05	.40
81	Cliff Ronning, Van.	.05	.40
82	Andrei Lomakin, Fl.	.05	.40
83	Shawn Burr, Det.	.05	.40
84	Benoit Brunet, Mon.	.05	.40
85	Valeri Kamensky, Que.	.20	1.25
86	Randy Carlyle, Win.	.05	.40
87	Chris Joseph, Edm.	.05	.40
88	Dirk Graham, Chi.	.05	.40
89	Kenneth Sutton, Buf.	.05	.40

NHL FIRST TEAM ALL STAR

No.	Player	Regular NRMT	Gold NRMT
90	Luc Robitaille, LA	.05	.40
91	Mario Lemieux, Pit	.25	1.50
92	Teemu Selanne, Win.	.35	2.00
93	Raymond Bourque, Bos.	.05	.40
94	Chris Chelios, Chi.	.05	.40
95	Ed Belfour, Goalie, Chi.	.15	1.00

REGULAR ISSUE

No.	Player	Regular NRMT	Gold NRMT
96	Keith Jones, Wash.	.05	.40
97	Sylvain Turgeon, Ott.	.05	.40
98	Jim Johnson, Dal.	.05	.40
99	Mikael Nylander, Hart.	.15	1.00
100	Theoren Fleury, Cal.	.05	.40
101	Shawn Chambers, TB	.05	.40
102	Alexander Semak, NJ	.05	.40
103	Ronald Sutter, St.L	.05	.40
104	Glenn Anderson, Tor.	.05	.40
105	Jaromir Jagr, Pit.	.05	.40
106	Adam Graves, NYR	.15	1.00
107	Nikolai Borschevsky, Tor.	.15	1.00
108	Vladimir Konstantinov, Det.	.05	.40
109	Robb Stauber, LA, Goalie	.05	.40
110	Arturs Irbe, Goalie, SJ	.05	.40
111	Goals-Against Average Leader: Felix Potvin, Goalie, Tor.	.35	2.00
112	Darius Kasparaitis, NYI	.05	.40
113	Kirk McLean, Goalie, Van.	.05	.40
114	Glen Wesley, Bos.	.05	.40
115	Rod Brind'Amour, Phi.	.05	.40
116	Mike Eagles, Win.	.05	.40
117	Brian Bradley, TB	.05	.40
118	Dave Christian, Chi.	.05	.40
119	Randy Wood, Buf.	.05	.40
120	Craig Janney, St.L	.05	.40

SUPER ROOKIE

No.	Player	Regular NRMT	Gold NRMT
121	Eric Lindros, Phi.	1.00	7.00
122	Tommy Soderstrom, Goalie, Phi.	.10	.75
123	Shawn McEachern, Pit.	.10	.75
124	Andrei Kovalenko, Que.	.10	.75
125	Joseph Juneau, Bos.	.25	1.50
126	Felix Potvin, Goalie, Tor.	.25	1.50
127	Dixon Ward, Van.	.05	.40
128	Alexei Zhamnov, Win.	.20	1.25
129	Vladimir Malakhov, NYI	.05	.40
130	Teemu Selanne, Win.	.70	4.50

REGULAR ISSUE

No.	Player	Regular NRMT	Gold NRMT
131	Neal Broten, Dal.	.05	.40
132	Ulf Samuelsson, Bos.	.05	.40
133	Mark Janssens, Hart.	.05	.40
134	Claude Lemieux, NJ	.05	.40
135	Mike Richter, Goalie, NYR	.10	.75
136	Doug Weight, Edm.	.05	.40
137	Rob Pearson, Tor.	.05	.40
138	Sylvain Cote, Wash.	.05	.40
139	Mike Keane, Mon.	.05	.40
140	Benoit Hogue, NYI	.05	.40
141	Michel Petit, Cal.	.05	.40
142	Mark Freer, Ott.	.05	.40
143	Doug Zmolek, SJ	.05	.40
144	Tony Granato, LA	.05	.40
145	Paul Coffey, Det.	.10	.75
146	Ted Donato, Bos.	.05	.40
147	Brent Sutter, Chi.	.05	.40
148	Goal Scoring Leaders: Teemu Selanne, Win. Alexander Mogilny, Buf.	.25	1.50
149	James Patrick, NYR	.05	.40
150	Bo Mikael Andersson, TB	.05	.40
151	Steve Duchesne Que.	.05	.40
152	Terry Carkner, Phi.	.05	.40
153	Russell Courtnall, Dal.	.05	.40
154	Brian Mullen, NYI	.05	.40
155	Martin Straka, Pit.	.30	1.75
156	Geoff Sanderson, Hart.	.30	1.75
157	Mark Howe, Det.	.05	.40
158	Stephane J. J. Richer, NJ	.05	.40
159	Douglas Crossman, St.L	.05	.40
160	John Vanbiesbrouck, Goalie, Fl.	.10	.75
161	Bob Essensa, Goalie, Win.	.05	.40
162	Wayne Presley, Buf.	.05	.40
163	Mathieu Schneider, Mon.	.05	.40
164	Jiri Slegr, Van.	.05	.40
165	Stephane Fiset, Goalie, Que.	.05	.40
166	Wendell Young, Goalie, TB	.05	.40
167	Kevin Dineen, Phi.	.05	.40
168	Sandis Ozolinch, TB	.15	1.00
169	Michael Krushelnyski, Tor.	.05	.40

NHL SECOND TEAM ALL STAR

No.	Player	Regular NRMT	Gold NRMT
170	Kevin Stevens, Pit.	.10	1.00
171	Pat LaFontaine, Buf.	.10	1.00
172	Alexander Mogilny, Buf.	.25	.150
173	Lawrence Murphy, Pit.	.05	.40
174	Al Iafrate, Wash.	.05	.40
175	Tom Barrasso, Goalie, Pit.	.10	.75

REGULAR ISSUE

No.	Player	Regular NRMT	Gold NRMT
176	Derek King, NYI	.05	.40
177	Bob Probert, Det.	.05	.40
178	Gary Suter, Cal.	.05	.40
179	David Shaw, Bos.	.05	.40
180	Luc Robitaille, LA	.10	.75
181	John LeClair, Mon.	.05	.40
182	Troy Murray, Chi.	.05	.40
183	Dave Gagner, Dal.	.05	.40
184	Darcy Loewen, Ott.	.05	.40
185	Point Leader: Mario Lemieux, Pit.	.25	1.50
186	Pat Jablonski, Goalie, TB	.05	.40
187	Alexei Kovalev, NYR	.25	1.50
188	Todd Krygier, Wash.	.05	.40
189	Lawrence Murphy, Pit.	.05	.40
190	Pierre Turgeon, NYI	.10	.75
191	Craig Ludwig, Dal.	.05	.40
192	Brad May, Buf.	.05	.40
193	John MacLean, NJ	.05	.40
194	Ronald Wilson, St.L	.05	.40
195	Eric Weinrich, Hart.	.05	.40
196	Steve Chiasson, Det.	.05	.40
197	Dmitri Kvartalnov, Bos.	.05	.40
198	Andrei Kovalenko, Que.	.10	.75
199	**Rob Gaudreau, SJ, RC**	.30	1.75
200	Eugeny Davydov, Win.	.05	.40
201	Adrien Plavsic, Van.	.05	.40
202	Brian Bellows, Mon.	.05	.40
203	Doug Evans, Phi.	.05	.40
204	Win Leader: Tom Barrasso, Goalie, Pit.	.05	.40
205	Joe Nieuwendyk, Cal.	.05	.40
206	Jari Kurri, LA	.05	.40
207	Robert Rouse, Tor.	.05	.40
208	Yvon Corriveau, Hart.	.05	.40
209	John Blue, Goalie, Bos.	.05	.40
210	Dimitri Khristich, Wash.	.05	.40
211	Brent Fedyk, Phi.	.05	.40
212	Jody Hull, Ott.	.05	.40
213	Chris Terreri, Goalie, NJ	.05	.40
214	Michael McPhee, Dal.	.05	.40
215	Chris Kontos, TB	.05	.40
216	Gregory Gilbert, Chi.	.05	.40
217	Sergei Zubov, NYR	.35	2.00
218	Grant Fuhr, Goalie, Buf.	.05	.40
219	Charles Huddy, LA	.05	.40
220	Mario Lemieux, Pit.	.75	5.00
221	Sheldon Kennedy, Det.	.05	.40
222	Curtis Joseph, Goalie, St.L	.05	.40
223	Brad Dalgarno, NYI	.05	.40
224	Bret Hedican, St.L	.05	.40
225	Trevor Linden, Van.	.05	.40
226	Darryl Sydor, LA	.05	.40
227	Jayson More, SJ	.05	.40
228	David Poulin, Bos.	.05	.40
229	Frantisek Musil, Cal.	.05	.40
230	Mark Recchi, Phi.	.10	.75
231	Craig Simpson, Edm.	.05	.40
232	Gino Cavallini, Que.	.05	.40
233	Vincent Damphousse, Mon.	.05	.40
234	Luciano Borsato, Win.	.05	.40
235	David Andreychuk, Tor.	.10	.75
236	Kenneth Daneyko, NJ	.05	.40
237	Chris Chelios, Chi.	.05	.40
238	Andrew McBain Ott.	.05	.40
239	Richard Tabaracci, Goalie, Wash.	.05	.40
240	Steve Larmer, Chi.	.05	.40
241	Sean Burke, Goalie, Hart.	.05	.40
242	Robert DiMaio, TB	.05	.40
243	Jim Paek, Pit.	.05	.40
244	Dave Lowry, Fl.	.05	.40
245	Alexander Mogilny, Buf.	.25	1.50
246	Darren Turcotte, NYR	.05	.40
247	Brendan Shanahan, St.L	.15	1.00
248	Peter Taglianetti, Pit.	.05	.40
249	Scott Mellanby, Fl.	.05	.40
250	Guy Carbonneau, Mon.	.05	.40
251	Claude Lapointe, Que.	.05	.40
252	Patrick Conacher, LA	.05	.40
253	Roger Johansson, Cal.	.05	.40
254	Cam Neely, Bos.	.05	.40
255	Garry Galley Phi.	.05	.40
256	Keith Primeau, Det.	.05	.40
257	Scott Lachance, NYI	.05	.40
258	Bill Ranford, Goalie, Edm.	.05	.40
259	Pat Falloon, SJ	.10	.75
260	Pavel Bure, Van.	.75	5.00
261	Darrin Shannon, Win.	.05	.40
262	Mike Foligno, Tor.	.05	.40
263	Checklist 1, Martin Lapointe(1-132)	.05	.40
264	Checklist 2, Kevin Miehm(133-264)	.05	.40

SERIES TWO

No.	Player	Regular NRMT	Gold NRMT
265	Peter Douris, MDA	.05	.40
266	Warren Rychel, LA	.05	.40
267	Owen Nolan, Que.	.05	.40
268	Mark Osborne, Tor.	.05	.40
269	Teppo Numminen, Win.	.05	.40
270	Rob Niedermayer, Fl.	.50	3.00
271	Mark Lamb, Ott.	.05	.40
272	Curtis Joseph, Goalie, St.L	.10	.75
273	Joe Murphy, Chi.	.05	.40
274	Bernie Nicholls, NJ	.05	.40
275	Gordon Roberts, Bos.	.05	.40
276	Allan MacInnis, Cal.	.05	.40
277	Ken Wregget, Goalie, Pit.	.05	.40
278	Calle Johansson, Wash.	.05	.40
279	Tom Kurvers, NYI	.05	.40
280	Steve Yzerman, Det.	.15	1.00
281	Roman Hamrlik, TB	.10	.75
282	Esa Tikkanen, NYR	.05	.40
283	**Darrin Madeley, Ott., RC**	.10	.75
284	Robert Dirk, Van.	.05	.40
285	**Derek Plante, Buf., RC**	.70	4.00
286	Ron Tugnutt, Goalie, MDA	.05	.40
287	Frank Pietrangelo, Goalie, Hart.	.05	.40
288	Paul Di Pietro, Mon.	.05	.40
289	Alexander Godynyuk, Fl.	.05	.40
290	Kirk Maltby, Edm.	.10	.75

… 1993-94 PREMIER ISSUE — TOPPS • 253

No.	Player	Regular NRMT	Gold NRMT
291	Olaf Kolzig, Goalie, Wash.	.05	.40
292	Vitali Karamnov, St.L	.05	.40
293	Alexei Gusarov, Que.	.05	.40
294	Bryan Erickson, Win.	.05	.40
295	Jocelyn Lemieux, Chi.	.05	.40
296	Bryan Trottier, Pit.	.05	.40
297	David Ellett, Tor.	.05	.40
298	Timothy Watters, LA	.05	.40
299	Joseph Juneau, Bos.	.40	3.25
300	Steve Thomas, NYI	.05	.40
301	Mark Greig, Hart.	.05	.40
302	Jeff Reese, Goalie, Cal.	.05	.40
303	Steven King, MDA	.05	.40
304	Donald Beaupre, Goalie, Wash.	.05	.40
305	Denis Savard, TB	.05	.40
306	Greg Smyth, Fl.	.05	.40
307	**Jaroslav Modry, NJ, RC**	**.10**	**.75**
308	Petr Svoboda, Buf.	.05	.40
309	Mike Craig, Dal.	.05	.40
310	Eric Lindros, Phi.	2.00	15.00
311	Dana Murzyn, Van.	.05	.40
312	Sean Hill, MDA	.05	.40
313	Andre Racicot, Goalie, Mon.	.05	.40
314	John Vanbiesbrouck, Goalie, Fl.	.10	.75
315	Doug Lidster, NYR	.05	.40
316	Garth Butcher, St.L	.05	.40
317	**Alexei Yashin, Ott., RC**	**1.00**	**7.00**
318	Sergei Fedorov, Det.	.05	.40
319	Louie DeBrusk, Edm.	.05	.40
320	Dominik Hasek, Goalie, Buf.	.10	.75
321	Michal Pivonka, Wash.	.05	.40
322	Robert Holik, NJ	.05	.40
323	Roman Hamrlik, TB	.10	.75
324	Petr Svoboda, Buf.	.05	.40
325	Jaromir Jagr, Pit.	.30	2.00
326	Steven Finn, Que.	.05	.40
327	Stephane J. J. Richer, Fl.	.05	.40
328	Claude Loiselle, NYI	.05	.40
329	Joe Sacco, MDA	.05	.40
330	Wayne Gretzky, LA	.75	5.00
331	Sylvain Lefebvre, Tor.	.05	.40
332	Sergei Bautin, Win.	.05	.40
333	Craig Simpson, Buf.	.05	.40
334	Don Sweeney, Dos.	.05	.40
335	Dominic Roussel, Goalie, Phi.	.10	.75
336	**Scott Thomas, Buf., RC**	**.10**	**.75**
337	Geoff Courtnall, Van.	.05	.40
338	Tom Fitzgerald, Fl.	.05	.40
339	Kevin Haller, Mon.	.05	.40
340	Troy Loney, MDA	.05	.40
341	Ronald Stern, Cal.	.05	.40
342	**Mark Astley, Buf., RC**	**.10**	**.75**
343	Jeff Daniels, Pit.	.05	.40
344	Marc Bureau, TB	.05	.40
345	**Micah Aivazoff, Det., RC**	**.10**	**.75**
346	**Matthew Barnaby, Buf., RC**	**.10**	**.75**
347	C.J. Young, Fl.	.05	.40
348	Dale Craigwell. SJ	.05	.40
349	Ray Ferraro, NYI	.05	.40
350	Raymond Bourque, Bos.	.10	.75
351	Stu Barnes, Win.	.05	.40
352	**Allan Conroy, Phi., RC**	**.10**	**.75**
353	Shawn McEachern, LA,	.10	.75
354	Garry Valk, MDA	.05	.40
355	Christian Ruuttu.Chi.	.05	.40
356	Darren Rumble, Ott.	.05	.40
357	Stu Grimson, MDA	.05	.40
358	Alexander Karpovtsev, NYR	.10	.75
359	Wendel Clark, Tor.	.10	.75
360	Michal Pivonka, Wash.	.05	.40
361	**Peter Popovic, Mon., RC**	**.10**	**.75**
362	Kevin Dahl, Cal.	.05	.40
363	Jeff Brown, St.L	.05	.40
364	Daren Puppa, Goalie, TB	.05	.40
365	**Dallas Drake, Det., RC**	**.20**	**1.50**
366	Dean McAmmond, Edm.	.05	.40
367	Martin Rucinsky, Que.	.05	.40
368	Shane Churla, Dal.	.05	.40
369	Todd Ewen, MDA	.05	.40
370	Kevin Stevens, Pit.	.15	1.75
371	David Volek, NYI	.05	.40
372	Jean-Jacques Daigneault, Mon.	.05	.40

No.	Player	Regular NRMT	Gold NRMT
373	Marc Bergevin, TB	.05	.40
374	Craig Billington, Goalie, Ott.	.05	.40
375	Michael Gartner, NYR	.05	.40
376	Jimmy Carson, LA	.05	.40
377	Bruce Driver, NJ	.05	.40
378	Stephen Heinze, Bos.	.05	.40
379	Patrik Carnback. MDA	.10	.75

CANADA

No.	Player	Regular NRMT	Gold NRMT
380	Wayne Gretzky, LA	.75	5.00
381	Jeff Brown, St.L	.05	.40
382	Gary Roberts, Cal.	.05	.40
383	Raymond Bourque, Bos.	.10	.75
384	Michael Gartner, NYR	.10	.75
385	Felix Potvin, Goalie, Tor.	.50	3.50

REGULAR ISSUE

No.	Player	Regular NRMT	Gold NRMT
386	Michel Goulet, Chi.	.05	.40
387	Dave Tippett, Phi.	.05	.40
388	Jimmy Waite, Goalie, SJ	.05	.40
389	Yuri Khmylev, Buf.	.05	.40
390	Douglas Gilmour, Tor.	.25	2.00
391	Byron (Brad) McCrimmon, Hart.	.05	.40
392	**Brent Severyn, Fl., RC**	**.10**	**.75**
393	**Jocelyn Thibault, Goalie, Que., RC**	**.75**	**5.00**
394	Boris Mironov, Win.	.05	.40
395	Martin McSorley, Pit.	.05	.40
396	Shaun Van Allen, MDA	.05	.40
397	Gary Leeman, Mon.	.05	.40
398	Ed Olczyk, NYR	.05	.40
399	Darcy Wakaluk. Goalie, Dal.	.05	.40
400	Murray Craven, Van.	.05	.40
401	Martin Brodeur, Goalie, NJ	.25	2.00
402	Paul Laus, Fl.	.05	.40
403	Bill Houlder, Fl.	.05	.40
404	Robert Reichel, Cal	.05	.40
405	**Alexandre Daigle, Ott., RC**	**1.00**	**7.00**
406	Brent Thompson, LA	.05	.40
407	Keith Acton, NYI	.05	.40
408	Dave Karpa, Que.	.05	.40
409	Igor Korolev, St.L	.05	.40
410	Chris Gratton, TB	.05	.40
411	Vincent Riendeau, Goalie, Det.	.05	.40
412	Darren McCarty, Det.	.05	.40
413	Robert Carpenter, NJ	.05	.40
414	Joe Cirella, Fl.	.05	.40
415	Stephane Matteau, Chi.	.05	.40
416	Josef Stumpel, Bos.	.05	.40
417	Richard Pilon, NYI	.05	.40
418	**Mattias Norstrom, NYR, RC**	**.10**	**.75**
419	Dmitri Mironov, Tor.	.05	.40
420	Alexei Zhamnov, Win.	.30	2.25
421	Bill Guerin. NJ	.05	.40
422	Greg Hawgood, Phi.	.05	.40
423	Randy Cunneyworth, Hart.	.05	.40
424	Ronald Francis, Pit.	.05	.40
425	Brett Hull, St.L	.25	2.00
426	Tim Sweeney, MDA	.05	.40
427	Mike Rathje, SJ	.05	.40
428	David Babych, Van.	.05	.40
429	**Chris Tancill, Dal., RC**	**.10**	**.75**
430	Mark Messier, NYR	.15	1.00
431	Robert Sweeney, Buf.	.05	.40
432	Terry Yake, MDA	.05	.40
433	Joe Reekie, TB	.05	.40
434	Tomas Sandstrom, LA	.05	.40
435	Kevin Hatcher, Wash.	.05	.40
436	Bill Lindsay, Fl.	.05	.40
437	Jon Casey, Goalie, Bos.	.05	.40
438	Dennis Vaske, NYI	.05	.40
439	Allen Pedersen, Hart.	.05	.40
440	Pavel Bure, Van.	.75	5.00
441	Sergei Fedorov, Det.	.40	2.50
442	Arturs Irbe, Goalie, SJ	.15	1.00
443	Darius Kasparaitis, NYI	.05	.40
444	Eugeny Davydov, Fl.	.05	.40
445	Vladimir Malakhov, NYI	.05	.40
446	Tom Barrasso, Goalie, Pit.	.05	.40

No.	Player	Regular NRMT	Gold NRMT
447	Jeff Norton, SJ	.05	.40
448	David Emma, NJ	.05	.40
449	Per-Erik Eklund, Phi.	.05	.40
450	Jeremy Roenick, Chi.	.25	1.75
451	Jesse Belanger, Fl.	.25	1.75
452	Vitali Prokhorov, St.L	.05	.40
453	Arto Blomsten, Win.	.05	.40
454	Peter Zezel, Tor.	.05	.40
455	Kelly Kisio, Cal.	.05	.40
456	Zdeno Ciger, Edm.	.05	.40
457	Greg Johnson, Det.	.05	.40
458	Dave Archibald, Ott.	.05	.40
459	Vladimir Vujtek, Edm.	.05	.40
460	Mats Sundin, Que.	.15	1.00
461	Dan Keczmer, Hart.	.05	.40
462	Stephan Lebeau, Mon.	.05	.40
463	Dominik Hasek, Goalie, Buf.	.10	.75
464	Kevin Lowe, NYR	.05	.40
465	Gordon Murphy, Fl.	.05	.40
466	Bryan Smolinski, Bos.	.35	2.50
467	Josef Beranek, Phi.	.10	.75
468	Ron Hextall, Goalie, NYI	.05	.40
469	Randy Ladouceur, MDA	.05	.40
470	Scott Niedermayer, NJ	.15	.100
471	Kelly Hrudey, Goalie, LA	.05	.40
472	Mike Needham, Pit.	.05	.40
473	John Tucker, TB	.05	.40
474	Kelly Miller, Wash.	.05	.40
475	Jyrki Lumme, Van.	.05	.40
476	Andrew Moog, Goalie, Dal.	.05	.40
477	Glen Murray, Bos.	.05	.40
478	**Mark Ferner, MDA, RC**	**.10**	**.75**
479	John Cullen, Tor.	.05	.40
480	Gilbert Dionne, Mon.	.05	.40
481	Paul Ranheim, Cal.	.05	.40
482	Mike Hough, Fl.	.05	.40
483	Teemu Selanne, Win.	1.25	10.00
484	**Aaron Ward, Det., RC**	**.10**	**.75**
485	Chris Pronger, Hart.	.35	2.50
486	Glenn Healy, Goalie, NYR	.05	.40
487	Curtis Leschyshyn, Que.	.05	.40
488	**Jim Montgomery, St.L, RC**	**.15**	**1.00**
489	Travis Green, NYI	.05	.40
490	Pat LaFontaine, Buf.	.20	1.50
491	**Bobby Dollas, MDA, RC**	**.10**	**.75**
492	Alexei Kasatonov, MDA	.05	.40
493	Corey Millen, NJ	.05	.40
494	Viacheslav Kozlov, Det.	.20	1.75
495	Igor Kravchuk, Edm.	.05	.40
496	Dimitri Filimonov, Ott.	.05	.40
497	Jeff Odgers, SJ	.05	.40
498	Joe Mullen, Pit.	.05	.40
499	Gary Shuchuk, LA	.05	.40

AMERICA

No.	Player	Regular NRMT	Gold NRMT
500	Jeremy Roenick, Chi.	.35	2.50
501	Tom Barrasso, Goalie, Pit.	.05	.40
502	Keith Tkachuk, Win.	.10	.75
503	Phil Housley, St.L	.05	.40
504	Tony Granato, LA	.05	.40
505	Brian Leetch, NYR	.20	1.50

REGULAR ISSUE

No.	Player	Regular NRMT	Gold NRMT
506	Anatoli Semenov, MDA	.05	.40
507	Stephen Leach, Bos.	.05	.40
508	Brian Skrudland, Fl.	.05	.40
509	Kirk Muller, Mon.	.05	.40
510	Gary Roberts, Cal.	.05	.40
511	Gerard Gallant, TB	.05	.40
512	Joey Kocur, NYR	.05	.40
513	Tahir (Tie) Domi, Win.	.05	.40
514	Kay Whitmore, Goalie, Van.	.05	.40
515	Valdimir Malakhov, NYI	.05	.40
516	**Stewart Malgunas, Phi., RC**	**.10**	**.75**
517	Jamie Macoun, Tor.	.05	.40
518	Alan May, Wash.	.05	.40
519	Guy Hebert, Goalie, MDA	.05	.40
520	Derian Hatcher, Dal.	.05	.40

254 • TOPPS — 1982-83 STICKERS —

No.	Player	Regular NRMT	Gold NRMT
521	Richard Smehlik, Buf.	.05	.40
522	Joby Messier, NYR, RC	.10	.75
523	Trent Klatt, Dal.	.05	.40
524	Tom Chorske, NJ	.05	.40
525	Iain Fraser, Que., RC	.10	.75
526	Daniel Laperriere, St.L	.05	.40
527	Checklist No.1 (265-396)	.05	.40
528	Checklist No.2 (397-528)	.05	.40

—1993-94 INSERT SETS—
BLACK GOLD

This 24-card set consists of twelve cards randomly inserted in Series One and Two foil packs. Cards 1-12 were issued in Series One and 13-24 were issued in Series Two

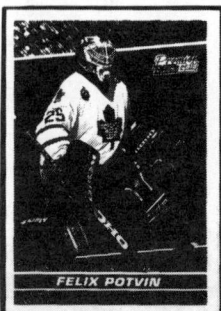 

1993-94 Black Gold
Card No. 3, Felix Potvin

Card Size: 2 1/2" x 3 1/2"
Face: Four colour, white border; Name
Back: Four colour, white border; Name, Resume
Imprint © 1994 THE TOPPS COMPANY, INC.
Complete Set No.: 24
Complete Price Set: 30.00 60.00
Common Card: 1.00 2.00

No.	Player	EX	NRMT
1	Teemu Selanne, Win.	2.50	5.00
2	Steve Duchesne, Que.	1.00	2.00
3	Felix Potvin, Goalie, Tor.	3.00	6.00
4	Shawn McEachern, Pit.	1.00	2.00
5	Adam Oates, Bos.	1.75	3.50
6	Paul Coffey, Det.	1.00	2.00
7	Wayne Gretzky, LA	5.00	10.00
8	Alexei Zhamnov, Win.	1.50	3.00
9	Mario Lemieux, Pit.	3.50	7.00
10	Gary Suter, Cal.	1.00	2.00
11	Tom Barrasso, Goalie, Pit.	1.25	2.50
12	Joseph Juneau, Bos.	1.50	3.00
13	Eric Lindros, Phi.	5.00	10.00
14	Ed. Belfour, Goalie, Chi.	2.00	4.00
15	Raymond Bourque, Bos.	1.00	2.00
16	Steve Yzerman, Det.	1.50	3.00
17	Andrei Kovalenko	1.00	2.00
18	Curtis Joseph, Goalie, St.L	1.50	3.00
19	Phil Housley, St.L	1.00	2.00
20	Pierre Turgeon, NYI	1.50	3.00
21	Brett Hull, St.L	1.50	3.00
22	Patrick Roy, Goalie, Mon.	4.00	8.00
23	Lawrence Murphy, Pit.	1.00	2.00
24	Pat LaFontaine, Buf.	1.50	3.00

BLACK GOLD REDEMPTION CARDS

This 2-card set allows the owners to redeem them for Black Gold cards from Topps. There are two different cards that can be redeemed for either Series One (1-12) or Series Two (13-24). These cards were randomly inserted in both Series Foil packs. These cards had to be redeemed by May 31, 1994.

Card Size: 2 1/2" x 3 1/2"
Face: Four Colour, white border; Winner card "A" or "B" Logo.
Back: Black on white card stock; Redemption directions
Imprint © 1994 THE TOPPS COMPANY, INC.
Complete Set No.: 3
Complete Price Set: 5.00 10.00

Black Gold Redemption Card

No.	Player	EX	NRMT
—	Winner A (1-12), Now Expired	.25	2.50
—	Winner B (13-24), Now Expired	1.25	2.50
—	Winner A and B (1-24) Now Expired	2.50	5.00

PREMIER FINEST

This 12-card set was randomly inserted into the Series Two foil packs. The players included in this set were all picked first overall in their first draft year.

1993-94 Premier Finest
Card No. 10, Mario Lemieux

Size: 2 1/2" x 3 1/2"
Face: Four colour, blue marble border; Name, Position
Back: Four colour on card stock; Name, Resume
Imprint: © 1994 The TOPPS COMPANY, Inc.
Complete Set No.: 12
Complete Price Set: 27.50 55.00
Common Player: 1.25 2.50

No.	Player	EX	NRMT
1	Alexandre Daigle, Ott.	4.00	8.00
2	Roman Hamrlik, TB	1.25	2.50
3	Eric Lindros, Phi.	12.50	25.00
4	Owen Nolan, Que.	1.25	2.50
5	Mats Sundin, Que.	2.50	5.00
6	Michael Modano, Dal.	2.50	5.00
7	Pierre Turgeon, NYI	2.50	5.00
8	Joe Murphy, Chi.	1.25	2.50
9	Wendel Clark, Tor.	2.50	5.00
10	Mario Lemieux, Pit.	7.50	15.00
11	Dale Hawerchuk, Buf.	1.25	2.50
12	Rob Ramage, Phi.	1.25	2.50

FINEST REDEMPTION CARD

This card was randomly inserted into the Series Two foil packs and could be redeemed for the entire set of Topps Finest if redeemed by May 31, 1994.

Card Size: 2 1/2" x 3 1/2"
Face: Four Colour, blue marble border; Redemption Logo.
Back: Black on white card stock; Instructions on redemption
Imprint © 1994 The TOPPS Company, Inc.
Complete Set No.: 1
Complete Price Set: 2.50 5.00

No.	Player	EX	NRMT
—	Redemption card (Single), Expired	.50	1.00
—	Redemption card (Set), Expired	2.00	4.00

TEAM U.S.A.

This 23-card set was randomly inserted into Series Two foil packs. The set depicts the players who represented their country in the 1994 Olympic Games in Norway.

1993-94 Team U.S.A.
Card No. 11, Chris Imes

Card Size: 2 1/2" x 3 1/2"
Face: Four colour, borderless; Name, USA Team logo
Back: Four colour on card stock; Name, Resume, USA Flag, USA logo
Imprint © 1994 THE TOPPS COMPANY, INC.
Complete Set No.: 23
Complete Price Set: 25.00 50.00
Common Player: 1.50 3.00

No.	Player	EX	NRMT
1	Mike Dunham, Goalie	1.50	3.00
2	Ian Moran	1.50	3.00
3	Peter Laviolette	1.50	3.00
4	Darby Hendrickson	1.50	3.00
5	Brian Rolston	2.00	4.00
6	Mark Beaufait	1.50	3.00
7	Travis Richards	1.50	3.00
8	John Lilley	1.50	3.00
9	Chris Ferraro	1.50	3.00
10	Jon Hillebrandt, Goalie	1.50	3.00
11	Chris Imes	1.50	3.00
12	Ted Crowley	1.50	3.00
13	David Sacco	2.00	4.00
14	Todd Marchant	1.50	3.00
15	Peter Ferraro	2.00	4.00
16	David Roberts	1.50	3.00
17	Jim Campbell	1.50	3.00
18	Barry Richter	1.50	3.00
19	Craig Johnson	1.50	3.00
20	Brett Hauer	1.50	3.00
21	Jeff Lazaro	1.50	3.00
22	Jim Storm	1.50	3.00
23	Matt Martin	2.00	4.00

—1993-94 STADIUM CLUB—
—1993-94 FIRST DAY PRODUCTION—

This 500-card set was issued in two series of 250 cards each. A small number of cards was stamped with a small rectangular silver foil box stating "First Day Production Set". These stamped cards were randomly inserted into the foil packs at the rate of one per 24 packs.

1993-93 Stadium Club   1993-94 First Day Prod.
Card No. 35, Mark Messier   Card No. 45, Sergei Fedorov

1993 - 94 Stadium Club — TOPPS

Card Size: 2 1/2" x 3 1/2"
Face: Four colour, borderless; Name
Back: Four colour on white card stock; Name, Number, Team, Resume
Imprint: © 1993 THE TOPPS COMPANY, INC.
Complete Card No.: 500
 Series One: 250
 Series Two: 250

	Regular	First Day
Complete Set Price:	40.00	3,500.00
Series One:	20.00	1,750.00
Series Two:	20.00	1,750.00
Common Player	.10	5.00
Foil Pack: (10 Cards)		1.00
Box: (24 Packs)		20.00

— SERIES ONE —

No.	Players	Regular NRMT	First Day NRMT
1	Guy Carbonneau, Mon., Error	.10	5.00
2	Joe Cirella, Fl.	.10	5.00
3	Laurie Boschman, Ott.	.10	5.00
4	Arturs Irbe, Goalie, SJ	.10	5.00
5	Adam Creighton, TB	.10	5.00
6	Michael McPhee, Dal.	.10	5.00
7	Jeff Beukeboom, NYR	.10	5.00
8	Kevin Todd, Edm.	.10	5.00
9	Yvon Corriveau, Hart.	.10	5.00
10	Eric Lindros, Phi.	3.00	250.00
11	Martin Rucinsky, Que.	.10	5.00
12	Michel Goulet, Chi.	.10	5.00
13	Scott Pellerin, NJ	.10	5.00
14	Mike Eagles, Win.	.10	5.00
15	Steve Heinze, Bos.	.10	5.00
16	Gerard Gallant, Det.	.10	5.00
17	Kelly Miller, Wash.	.10	5.00
18	Petr Nedved, Van.	.10	5.00
19	Joe Mullen, Pit	.10	5.00
20	Pat LaFontaine, Buf.	.35	30.00
21	Garth Butcher, St.L	.10	5.00
22	Jeff Reese, Goalie, Cal.	.10	5.00
23	David Andreychuk, Tor.	.15	10.00
24	Patrick Flatley, NYI	.10	5.00
25	Tomas Sandstrom, LA	.15	10.00
26	Andre Racicot, Goalie, Mon.	.10	5.00
27	Patrice Brisebois, Mon.	.10	5.00
28	Neal Broten, Dal.	.10	5.00
29	Mark Freer, Ott.	.10	5.00
30	Kelly Kisio, SJ	.10	5.00
31	Scott Mellanby, Fl.	.10	5.00
32	Joe Sakic, Que.	.20	15.00
33	Kerry Huffman, Que.	.10	5.00
34	Eugeny Davydov, Win.	.10	5.00
35	Mark Messier, NYR	.30	20.00
36	Pat Verbeek, Hart.	.10	5.00
37	Gregory Gilbert, NYR (Chi. shirt)	.10	5.00
38	John Tucker, TB	.10	5.00
39	Claude Lemieux, NJ	.10	5.00
40	Shayne Corson, Edm.	.10	5.00
41	Gordon Roberts, Bos.	.10	5.00
42	Jiri Slegr, Van.	.10	5.00
43	Kevin Dineen, Phi.	.10	5.00
44	Johan Garpenlov, SJ	.10	5.00
45	Sergei Fedorov, Det.	.50	75.00
46	Richard Sutter, St.L	.10	5.00
47	David Hannan, Buf.	.10	5.00
48	Sylvain Lefebvre, Tor.	.10	5.00
49	Pat Elynuik, Wash.	.10	5.00
50	Ray Ferraro, NYI	.10	5.00
51	Brent Ashton, Cal.	.10	5.00
52	Paul Stanton, Pit.	.10	5.00
53	Kevin Haller, Mon.	.10	5.00
54	Kelly Hrudey, Goalie, LA	.10	5.00
55	Russell Courtnall, Dal.	.10	5.00
56	Alexei Zhamnov, Win.	.15	10.00
57	Andrei Lomakin, Fl.	.10	5.00
58	Keith Brown, Chi.	.10	5.00
59	Glenn Murray, Bos.	.10	5.00
60	Kay Whitmore, Goalie, Van.	.10	5.00
61	Stephane J. J. Richer, NJ	.10	5.00
62	Todd Gill, Tor.	.10	5.00
63	Bob Sweeney, Buf.	.10	5.00
64	Mike Richter, Goalie, NYR	.10	5.00
65	Brett Hull, St.L	.30	50.00
66	Sylvain Cote, Wash.	.10	5.00
67	Kirk Muller, Mon.	.10	5.00
68	Ronald Stern, Cal.	.20	15.00
69	Josef Beranek, Phi.	.20	15.00
70	Steve Yzerman, Det.	.25	40.00
71	Donald Beaupre, Goalie, Wash.	.10	5.00
72	Ed Courtenay, SJ	.10	5.00
73	Zdeno Ciger, Edm.	.10	5.00
74	Andrew Cassels, Hart.	.10	5.00
75	Roman Hamrlik, TB	.10	5.00
76	Benoit Hogue, NYI	.10	5.00
77	Andrei Kovalenko, Que.	.10	5.00
78	Rod Brind'amour, Phi.	.10	5.00
79	Tom Barrasso, Goalie, Pit.	.15	10.00
80	Al Iafrate, Wash.	.10	5.00
81	Bret Hedican, St.L	.10	5.00
82	Peter Bondra, Wash.	.10	5.00
83	Ted Donato, Bos.	.10	5.00
84	Chris Lindberg, Cal.	.10	5.00
85	John Vanbiesbrouk, Goalie, Fl.	.15	10.00
86	Ronald Sutter, St.L	.10	5.00
87A	Luc Robitaille, LA	.30	20.00
87B	Luc Robitaille, LA, Variation	.30	25.00
88	Brian Leetch, NYR	.30	25.00
89	Randy Wood, Buf.	.10	5.00
90	Dirk Graham, Chi.	.10	5.00
91	Alexander Mogilny, Buf.	.25	40.00
92	Mike Keane, Mon.	.10	5.00
93	Adam Oates, Bos.	.15	10.00
94	Vjateslav Butsayev, Phi. Error	.10	5.00
95	John LeClair, Mon.	.10	5.00
96	Joe Nieuwendyk, Cal.	.10	5.00
97	Bo Mikael Andersson, TB	.10	5.00
98	Jaromir Jagr, Pit.	.45	50.00
99	Ed. Belfour, Goalie, Chi.	.30	35.00
100	David Reid, Bos.	.10	5.00
101	Darius Kasparaitis, NYI	.10	5.00
102	Zarley Zalapski, Hart.	.10	5.00
103	Christian Ruuttu, Chi.	.10	5.00
104	Phil Housley, Win.	.10	5.00
105	Allan MacInnis, Cal.	.10	5.00
106	Tommy Sjodin, Dal.	.10	5.00
107	Richard Smehlik, Buf.	.10	5.00
108	Jyrki Lumme, Van.	.10	5.00
109	Dominic Roussel, Goalie, Phi.	.10	5.00
110	Michael Gartner, NYR	.20	15.00
111	Bernie Nicholls, NJ	.10	5.00
112	Mark Howe, Det.	.10	5.00
113	Richard Pilon, NYI	.10	5.00
114	Jeff Odgers, SJ	.10	5.00
115	Gilbert Dionne, Mon.	.10	5.00
116	Peter Zezel, Tor.	.10	5.00
117	Don Sweeney, Bos.	.10	5.00
118	Jimmy Carson, LA	.10	5.00
119	Igor Korolev, St.L	.10	5.00
120	Bob Kudelski, Ott.	.10	5.00
121	Dave Lowry, Fl.	.10	5.00
122	Stephen Kasper, TB	.10	5.00
123	Mike Ridley, Wash.	.10	5.00
124	Dave Tippett, Pit.	.10	5.00
125	Cliff Ronning, Van.	.10	5.00
126	Bruce Driver, NJ	.10	5.00
127	Stephane Matteau, Chi.	.10	5.00
128	Joel Otto, Cal.	.10	5.00
129	Alexei Kovalev, NYR	.10	5.00
130	Michael Modano, Dal.	.40	35.00
131	Bill Ranford, Goalie, Edm.	.10	5.00
132	Petr Svoboda, Buf.	.10	5.00
133	Roger Johansson, Cal.	.10	5.00
134	Marc Bureau, TB	.10	5.00
135	Keith Tkachuk, Win.	.15	10.00
136	Mark Recchi, Phi.	.10	5.00
137	Bob Probert, Det.	.10	5.00
138	Uwe Krupp. NYI	.10	5.00
139	Mike Sullivan, SJ	.10	5.00
140	Douglas Gilmour, Tor.	.40	55.00

CALDER TROPHY WINNER

No.	Players	Regular NRMT	First Day NRMT
141	Rookie of the Year: Teemu Selanne, Win.	.25	30.00
142	Clancy Trophy Winner: Dave Poulin	.10	5.00
143	Hart Trophy Winner: Mario Lemieux, Pit	.50	60.00
144	Jennings Trophy Winner: Ed. Belfour, Goalie, Chi.	.20	20.00
145	Lady Byng Trophy Winner: Pierre Turgeon, NYI	.10	5.00
146	Masterton Trophy Winner: Mario Lemieux, Pit	.50	60.00
147	Norris Trophy Winner: Chris Chelios, Chi.	.10	5.00
148	Art Ross Trophy Winner: Mario Lemieux, Pit.	.50	60.00
149	Selke Trophy Winner: Douglas Gilmour, Tor.	.20	20.00
150	Vezina Trophy Winner: Ed Belfour, Goalie, Chi.	.20	20.00

REGULAR ISSUE

No.	Players	Regular NRMT	First Day NRMT
151	Paul Ranheim, Cal.	.10	5.00
152	Gino Cavallini, Que.	.10	5.00
153	Kevin Hatcher, Wash.	.10	5.00
154	Marc Bergevin, TB	.10	5.00
155	Martin McSorly, LA	.10	5.00
156	Brian Bellows, Mon.	.10	5.00
157	Patrick Poulin, Hart.	.10	5.00
158	Kevin Stevens, Pit.	.10	5.00
159	Robert Holik, NJ	.10	5.00
160	Raymond Bourque, Bos.	.10	5.00
161	Bryan Marchment Chi.	.10	5.00
162	Curtis Joseph, Goalie, St.L	.10	5.00
163	Kirk McLean, Goalie, Van.	.10	5.00
164	Teppo Numminen, Win.	.10	5.00
165	Kevin Lowe, NYR	.10	5.00
166	Tim Cheveldae, Goalie, Det.	.10	5.00
167	Brad Dalgarno, NYI	.10	5.00
168	Glenn Anderson, Tor.	.10	5.00
169	Frantisek Musil, Cal.	.10	5.00
170	Eric Desjardins, Mon.	.10	5.00
171	Douglas Zmolek, SJ	.10	5.00
172	Mark Lamb, Ott.	.10	5.00
173	Craig Ludwig, Dal.	.10	5.00
174	Rob Gaudreau, SJ	.10	5.00
175	Robert Carpenter, Wash.	.10	5.00
176	Mike Recci, Que.	.10	5.00
177	Brian Skrudland, Fl.	.10	5.00
178	Dominik Hasek, Goalie, Buf.	.10	5.00
179	Pat Conacher, LA	.10	5.00
180	Mark Janssens, Hart.	.10	5.00
181	Brent Fedyk, Phi.	.10	5.00
182	Robert DiMaio, TB	.10	5.00
183	Dave Manson, Edm.	.10	5.00
184	Janne Ojanen, NJ	.10	5.00
185	Ryan Walter, Van.	.10	5.00
186	Mikael Nylander, Hart.	.10	5.00
187	Stephen Leach, Bos.	.10	5.00
188	Jeff Brown, St.L	.10	5.00
189	Shawn McEachern, Pit.	.10	5.00
190	Jeremy Roenick, Chi.	.45	50.00
191	Darrin Shannon, Win.	.10	5.00
192	Wendel Clark, Tor.	.15	20.00
193	Kevin Miller, St.L	.10	5.00
194	Paul DiPietro, Mon.	.10	5.00
195	Steve Thomas, NYI	.10	5.00
196	Niklas Lidstrom, Det.	.10	5.00
197	Ed Olczyk, NYR	.10	5.00
198	Robert Reichel, Cal.	.10	5.00
199	Neil Brady, Ott.	.10	5.00
200A	Wayne Gretzky, LA	1.50	275.00
200B	Wayne Gretzky, LA, Variation	1.50	275.00
201	Adrien Plavsic, Van.	.10	5.00
202	Joseph Juneau, Bos.	.50	60.00
203	Brad May, Buf.	.10	5.00
204	Igor Kravchuk, Edm.	.10	5.00
205	Keith Acton, Phi.	.10	5.00
206	Kenneth Daneyko, NJ	.10	5.00
207	Sean Burke, Goalie, Hart.	.10	5.00
208	Jayson More, SJ	.10	5.00
209	John Cullen, Tor.	.10	5.00
210	Teemu Selanne, Win.	.50	60.00
211	Brent Sutter, Chi.	.10	5.00
212	Brian Bradley, TB	.10	5.00
213	Donald Audette, Buf.	.10	5.00

256 • TOPPS — 1993-94 STADIUM CLUB

No.	Player	Regular NRMT	First Day NRMT
214	Philippe Bozon, St.L	.10	5.00
215	Derek King, NYI	.10	5.00
216	Cam Neely, Bos.	.10	5.00
217	Keith Primeau, Det.	.10	5.00
218	James (Steve) Smith, Chi.	.10	5.00
219	Kenneth Sutton, Buf.	.10	5.00
220	Dale Hawerchuk, Buf.	.10	5.00
221	Alexei Zhitnik, LA	.10	5.00
222	Glen Wesley, Bos.	.10	5.00
223	Nelson Emerson, St.L	.10	5.00
224	Pat Falloon, SJ	.10	5.00
225	Darryl Sydor, LA	.10	5.00
226	Anthony Amonte, NYR	.10	5.00
227	Brian Mullen, NYI	.10	5.00
228	Gary Suter, Cal.	.10	5.00
229	David Shaw, Bos.	.10	5.00
230	Troy Murray, Chi.	.10	5.00
231	Patrick Roy, Goalie, Mon.	1.00	125.00
232	Michel Petit, Cal.	.10	5.00
233A	Wayne Presley, Buf.	.10	5.00
233B	Wayne Presley, Buf., Variation	.10	5.00
234	Keith Jones, Wash.	.10	5.00
235	Gary Roberts, Cal.	.10	5.00
236	Steve Larmer, Chi.	.10	5.00
237	Valeri Kamensky, Que.	.10	5.00
238	Ulf Dahlen, Dal.	.10	5.00
239	Danton Cole, TB	.10	5.00
240A	Vincent Damphousse, Mon.	.15	10.00
240B	Vincent Damphousse, Mon., Variation	.15	10.00
241	Yuri Khmylev, Buf.	.10	5.00
242	Stephane Quintal, St.L	.10	5.00
243	Peter Taglianetti, Pit.	.10	5.00
244	Gary Leeman, Mon.	.10	5.00
245	Sergei Nemchinov, NYR	.10	5.00
246	Robert Blake, LA	.10	5.00
247	Steve Chiasson, Det.	.10	5.00
248	Vladimir Malakhov, NYI	.10	5.00
249	Checklist 1 (1 - 125)	.15	10.00
250	Checklist 2 (126 - 250)	.15	10.00

— SERIES TWO —

1993-94 Stadium Club
Card No. 350, Chris Osgood   Card No. 455, Al Iafrate

No.	Players	Regular NRMT	First Day NRMT
251	Kjell Samuelsson, Pit.	.10	5.00
252	Terry Carkner, Det.	.10	5.00
253	Bill Lindsay, Fl.	.10	5.00
254	Bob Essensa, Goalie, Win.	.10	5.00
255	Jocelyn Lemieux, Chi.	.10	5.00
256	Joseph Sacco, MDA	.10	5.00
257	Marty McInnis, NYI	.10	5.00
258	Warren Rychel, LA	.10	5.00
259	David Maley, SJ	.10	5.00
260	Grant Fuhr, Goalie, Buf.	.10	5.00
261	Scott Young, Que.	.10	5.00
262	Ed Ronan, Que.	.10	5.00
263	Micah Alvazoff, Det., RC	.15	7.50
264	Murray Craven, Van.	.10	5.00
265	Viacheslav Fetisov, NJ	.10	5.00
266	Chris Dahlquist, Cal.	.10	5.00
267	Norm Maciver, Ott.	.10	5.00
268	Alexander Godynyuk, Fl.	.10	5.00
269	Mikael Renberg, Phi., RC	.75	60.00
270	Adam Graves, NYR	.25	20.00
271	Randy Ladouceur, MDA	.10	5.00
272	Frank Pietrangelo, Goalie, MDA	.10	5.00

No.	Player	Regular NRMT	First Day NRMT
273	Basil McRae, St.L	.10	5.00
274	Bryan Smolinski, Bos., RC	.50	40.00
275	Daren Puppa, Goalie, TB	.10	5.00
276	Darcy Wakaluk, Goalie, Dal.	.10	5.00
277	Dimitri Khristich, Wash.	.10	5.00
278	Vladimir Vujtek, Edm.	.10	5.00
279	Tom Kurvers, NYI	.10	5.00
280	Felix Potvin, Goalie, Tor.	1.00	100.00
281	Keith Brown, Fl.	.10	5.00
282	Thomas Steen, Win.	.10	5.00
283	Lawrence Murphy, Pit.	.10	5.00
284	Bob Corkum, MDA	.10	5.00
285	Tony Granato, LA	.10	5.00
286	Cam Russel, Chi., RC	.15	7.50
287	John MacLean, NJ	.10	5.00
288	Shawn Antoski, Van.	.10	5.00
289	Per-Erik Eklund, Phi.	.10	5.00
290	NHL Debut 10/6/93: Chris Pronger, Hart., RC	.60	45.00
291	NHL Debut 10/9/93: Alexander Karpovtsev, NYR, RC	.15	7.50
292	NHL Debut 10/14/93: Paul Laus, Fl., RC	.10	5.00
293	Jaroslav Otevrel, SJ, RC	.15	7.50
294	Dino Ciccarelli, Det.	.10	5.00
295	Guy Hebert, Goalie, MDA	.20	10.00
296	Dave Karpa, Que.	.10	5.00
297	Denis Savard, TB	.10	5.00
298	Jim Johnson, Dal.	.10	5.00
299	NHL Debut 10/8/93: Kirk Maltby, Edm., RC	.15	7.50
300	NHL Debut 10/6/93: Alexandre Daigle, Ott., RC	.75	50.00
301	David Poulin, Wash.	.10	5.00
302	James Patrick, Hart.	.10	5.00
303	Jon Casey, Goalie, Bos.	.10	5.00
304	Yves Racine, Phi.	.10	5.00
305	Craig Simpson, Buf.	.10	5.00
306	Michael Krushelnyski, Tor.	.10	5.00
307	Mark Fitzpatrick, Goalie, Fl.	.10	5.00
308	Charles Huddy, LA	.10	5.00
309	Todd Ewen, MDA	.10	5.00
310	Mario Lemieux, Pit.	1.00	140.00
311	NHL Debut 10/12/93: Mark Astley, Buf., RC	.15	7.50
312	Sergei Zubov, NYR	.50	35.00
313	Shawn Burr, Det.	.10	5.00
314	Valeri Zelepukin, NJ	.10	5.00
315	Stephane Fiset, Goalie, Que.	.20	10.00
316	C.J. Young, Fl.	.10	5.00
317	Luciano Borsato, Win.	.10	5.00
318	Darcy Loewen, Ott.	.10	5.00
319	Michael Vernon, Goalie, Cal.	.10	5.00
320	NHL Debut 10/6/93: Chris Gratton, TB, RC	.60	45.00
321	Matthew Barnaby, Buf.	.10	5.00
322	NHL Debut 10/6/93: Mike Rathje, SJ, RC	.15	7.50
323	Sergio Momesso, Van.	.10	5.00
324	David Volek, NYR	.10	5.00
325	Ron Tugnutt, Goalie, Ott.	.10	5.00
326	Jeff Hackett, Goalie, Chi.	.10	5.00
327	Robb Stauber, Goalie, LA	.10	5.00
328	Chris Terreri, Goalie, NJ	.10	5.00
329	Rick Tocchet, Pit.	.10	5.00
330	John Vanbiesbrouck, Goalie, Fl.	.15	7.50
331	Drake Berehowsky, Tor.	.15	7.50
332	Alexei Kasatonov, MDA	.10	5.00
333	Vladimir Konstantinov, Det.	.10	5.00
334	John Blue, Goalie, Bos.	.10	5.00
335	Craig Janney, St.L	.10	5.00
336	Curtis Leschyshyn, Que.	.10	5.00
337	Todd Krygier, Wash.	.10	5.00
338	NHL Debut 10/6/93: Boris Mironov, Win., RC	.15	7.50
339	Joby Messier, NYR, RC	.15	7.50
340	Tommy Soderstrom, Goalie, Phi.	.20	10.00
341	Randy Cunneyworth, Har.	.10	5.00
342	Mark Ferner, MDA, RC	.15	7.50
343	Stephan Lebeau, Mon.	.10	5.00
344	Jody Hull, Fl.	.10	5.00
345	NHL Debut 10/5/93: Jason Arnott, Edm., RC	2.50	100.00
346	Gerard Gallant, TB	.10	5.00
347	Stephane J.J. Richer, Fl.	.10	5.00

No.	Player	Regular NRMT	First Day NRMT
348	NHL Debut 10/18/93: Jeff Shantz, Chi., RC	.15	7.50
349	Brian Skrudland, Fl.	.10	5.00
350	NHL Debut 10/15/93: Chris Osgood, Goalie, Det., RC	.75	50.00
351	Gary Shuchuk, LA	.10	5.00
352	Martin Brodeur, Goalie, NJ	.40	30.00
353	Robert Rouse, Tor.	.10	5.00
354	Doug Bodger, Buf.	.10	5.00
355	Mike Craig, Dal.	.10	5.00
356	Ulf Samuelsson, Pit.	.10	5.00
357	Trevor Linden, Van.	.20	10.00
358	Dennis Vaske, NYI	.10	5.00
359	NHL Debut 10/6/93: Alexei Yashin, Ott., RC	1.00	75.00
360	Paul Ysebaert, Win.	.10	5.00
361	Shaun Van Allen, MDA	.10	5.00
362	Sandis Ozolinch, SJ	.20	10.00
363	Todd Elik, SJ	.10	5.00
364	NHL Debut 10/5/93: German Titov, Cal., RC	.40	20.00
365	Alexander Semak, NJ	.10	5.00
366	Allen Pedersen, Har.	.10	5.00
367	NHL Debut 10/5/93: Greg Johnson, Det., RC	.20	10.00
368	Anatoli Semenov, MDA	.10	5.00
369	Scott Mellanby, Fl.	.10	5.00
370	Mats Sundin, Que.	.20	10.00
371	NHL Debut 10/11/93: Mattias Norstrom, NYR, RC	.20	10.00
372	Glen Featherstone, Bos.	.10	5.00
373	NHL Debut 10/10/93: Sergei Petrenko, Buf., RC	.20	10.00
374	Mike Donnelly, LA	.10	5.00
375	Nikolai Borschevsky, Tor.	.10	5.00
376	Rob Zamuner, TB	.10	5.00
377	Steven King, MDA	.10	5.00
378	Richard Tabaracci, Goalie, Wash.	.10	5.00
379	Dave Lowry, Fl.	.10	5.00
380	Pierre Trugeon, NYI	.10	5.00
381	Garry Galley, Phi.	.10	5.00
382	Doug Weight, Edm.	.10	5.00
383	Scott Stevens, NJ	.20	10.00
384	Mark Tinordi, Dal.	.10	5.00
385	Ronald Francis, Pit.	.10	5.00
386	Mark Greig, Har.	.10	5.00
387	Sean Hill, MDA	.10	5.00
388	Vyacheslav Kozlov, Det.	.50	35.00
389	Brendan Shanahan, St.L	.20	10.00
390	Theoren Fleury, Cal.	.10	5.00
391	Mathieu Schneider, Mon.	.10	5.00
392	Tom Fitzgerald, Fl.	.10	5.00
393	NHL Debut 10/5/93: Markus Naslund, Pit., RC	.20	10.00
394	Travis Green, NYI	.10	5.00
395	Troy Loney, MDA	.10	5.00
396	Gordon Donnelly, Buf.	.10	5.00
397	Owen Nolan, Que.	.20	10.00
398	Steve Larmer, NYR	.10	5.00
399	Dave Archibald, Ott.	.10	5.00
400	Jari Kurri, LA	.10	5.00
401	Jim Paek, Pit.	.10	5.00
402	Andrei Lomakin, Fl.	.10	5.00
403	Scott Niedermayer, NJ	.20	10.00
404	Bob Errey, SJ	.10	5.00
405	Michal Pivonka, Wash.	.10	5.00
406	Doug Lidster, NYR	.10	5.00
407	Garry Valk, MDA	.10	5.00
408	Geoff Sanderson, Har.	.30	15.00
409	NHL Debut 10/5/93: Stewart Malgunas, Phi., RC	.20	10.00
410	Craig MacTavish, Edm.	.10	5.00
411	NHL Debut 10/6/93: Jaroslav Modry, NJ, RC	.20	10.00
412	Shawn Chambers, TB	.10	5.00
413	Geoff Courtnall, Van.	.10	5.00
414	Mark Hardy, LA	.10	5.00
415	Martin Straka, Pit.	.40	20.00
416	Randy Burridge, Wash.	.10	5.00
417	Kent Manderville, Tor.	.10	5.00
418	Darren Rumble, Ott.	.10	5.00
419	Bill Houlder, MDA	.10	5.00
420	Chris Chelios, Chi.	.10	5.00
421	Jim Hrivnak, Goalie, St.L	.10	5.00

1993 - 94 INSERT SETS — TOPPS • 257

No.	Players	Regular NRMT	First Day NRMT
422	Benoit Brunet, Mon.	.10	5.00
423	NHL Debut 10/5/93: Aaron Ward, Det., RC	.20	10.00
424	Alexei Gusarov, Que.	.10	5.00

TEAM SWEDEN

No.	Players	Regular NRMT	First Day NRMT
425	Mats Sundin, Que.	.20	10.00
426	Kjell Samuelsson, Pit.	.10	5.00
427	Bo Mikael Anderssson, TB	.10	5.00
428	Ulf Dahlen, Dal.	.10	5.00
429	Nicklas Lidstrom, Det.	.10	5.00
430	Tommy Soderstrom, Goalie, Phi.	.15	7.50

REGULAR ISSUE

No.	Players	Regular NRMT	First Day NRMT
431	Darrin Madeley, Goalie, Ott., RC	.20	10.00
432	Kevin Dahl, Cal.	.10	5.00
433	Ron Hextall, Goalie, NYI	.10	5.00
434	Patrik Carnback, MDA, RC	.15	7.50
435	Randy Moller, Buf.	.10	5.00
436	Dave Gagner, Dal.	.10	5.00
437	Corey Millen, NJ	.10	5.00
438	Olaf Kolzig, Goalie, Wash.	.10	5.00
439	Gordon Murphy, Fl.	.10	5.00
440	NHL Debut 10/5/93: Cam Stewart, Bos., RC	.20	7.50
441	NHL Debut 10/5/93: Darren McCarty, Det., RC	.20	7.50
442	Frantisek Kucera, Chi.	.10	5.00
443	NHL Debut 10/5/93: Ted Drury, Cal., RC	.20	7.50
444	Troy Mallette, Ott.	.10	5.00
445	Robin Bawa, MDA, RC	.15	7.50
446	Steven Rice, Edm.	.10	5.00
447	Pat Elynuik, TB	.10	5.00
448	Jim Cummins, Phi., RC	.15	7.50
449	NHL Debut 10/6/93: Rob Niedermayer, Fl., RC	.60	30.00
450	Paul Coffey, Det.	.20	10.00
451	Calle Johansson, Wash.	.10	5.00
452	Mike Needham, Pit.	.10	5.00
453	Glenn Healy, Goalie, NYR	.10	5.00
454	Dixon Ward, Van.	.10	5.00

TEAM U.S.A.

No.	Players	Regular NRMT	First Day NRMT
455	Al Iafrate, Wash.	.10	5.00
456	Jon Casey, Goalie, Bos.	.10	5.00
457	Kevin Stevens, Pit.	.15	7.50
458	Anthony Amonte, NYR	.10	5.00
459	Chris Chelios, Chi.	.10	5.00
460	Pat LaFontaine, Buf.	.15	7.50

REGULAR ISSUE

No.	Players	Regular EX	First Day NRMT
461	Jamie Baker, SJ	.10	5.00
462	Andre Faust, Phi.	.10	5.00
463	Bobby Dollas, MDA	.10	5.00
464	Steven Finn, Que.	.10	5.00
465	Scott Lachance, NYI	.10	5.00
466	Mike Hough, Fl.	.10	5.00
467	Bill Guerin, NJ	.10	5.00
468	NHL Debut 10/6/93: Dmitri Filimonov, Ott., RC	.15	7.50
469	David Ellett, Tor.	.10	5.00
470	Andrew Moog, Goalie, Dal.	.10	5.00
471	Scott Thomas, Buf., RC	.15	7.50
472	Trent Yawney, Cal.	.10	5.00
473	Tim Sweeney, MDA	.10	5.00
474	Shjon Podein, Edm., RC	.15	7.50
475	Jean-Jacques Daigneault, Mon.	.10	5.00
476	Darren Turcotte, Har.	.10	5.00
477	Esa Tikkanen, NYR	.10	5.00
478	Vitali Karamnov, St.L	.10	5.00
479	NHL Debut 10/9/93: Jocelyn Thibault, Goalie, Que., RC	.60	35.00
480	Pavel Bure, Van.	1.00	140.00
481	Steve Konowalchuk, Wash.	.10	5.00
482	Sylvain Turgeon, Ott.	.10	5.00
483	Jeff Daniels, Pit.	.10	5.00
484	Dallas Drake, Det., RC	.20	10.00
485	Iain Fraser, Que., RC	.15	7.50
486	Joe Reekie, TB	.10	5.00
487	Evgeny Davydov, Fl.	.10	5.00
488	Jozef Stumpel, Bos.	.10	5.00
489	Brent Thompson, LA	.10	5.00
490	Terry Yake, MDA	.10	5.00
491	NHL Debut 10/7/93: Derek Plante, Buf., RC	.75	30.00
492	Dimitri Yushkevich, Phi.	.10	5.00
493	Wayne McBean, NYI	.10	5.00
494	Derian Hatcher, Dal.	.10	5.00
495	Jeff Norton, SJ	.10	5.00
496	Adam Foote, Que.	.10	5.00
497	Mike Peluso, NJ	.10	5.00
498	Rob Pearson, Tor.	.10	5.00
499	1994-95 Checklist 251-375	.15	10.00
500	1994-95 Checklist 376-500	.15	10.00

— 1993 - 94 INSERT SETS —

MASTER PHOTOS

This 5" x 7" 24-photo set was inserted in the bottom of foil boxes and also available through redemption cards. The photos are numbered - of 24.

1993-94 Master Photos
Card No. 3, Raymond Bourque

Card Size: 5" x 7"
Face: Four colour, on white card stock, Name, Stadium Club logo
Back: Four colour, white border; Name, Number, Resume
Imprint: © 1993 THE TOPPS COMPANY, INC.
Complete Set No.: 24
  Series One: 12
  Series Two: 12
Complete Set Price: 13.00 / 28.00
  Series One: 9.00 / 18.00
  Series Two: 9.00 / 18.00
Common Card: .50 / 1.00

SERIES ONE

No.	Player	EX	NRMT
1	Pat LaFontaine, Buf.	1.00	2.00
2	Douglas Gilmour, Tor.	1.00	2.00
3	Raymond Bourque, Bos.	.75	1.50
4	Teemu Selanne, Win.	1.25	2.50
5	Eric Lindros, Phi.	2.50	5.00
6	Ray Ferraro, NYI	.50	1.00
7	Patrick Roy, Goalie, Mon.	2.50	5.00
8	Wayne Gretzky, LA	3.00	6.00
9	Brett Hull, St.L	1.00	2.00
10	John Vanbiesbrouck, Goalie, Fl.	.50	1.00
11	Adam Oates, Bos.	.50	1.00
12	Tom Barrasso, Goalie, Pit.	.50	1.00

SERIES TWO

No.	Player	EX	NRMT
13	Jari Kurri, LA	.50	1.00
14	Esa Tikkanen, Edm.	.50	1.00
15	Grant Fuhr, Goalie, Buf.	.50	1.00
16	Scott Lachance, NYI	.50	1.00
17	Theoren Fluery, Cal.	.50	1.00
18	Adam Graves, NYR	1.00	2.00
19	Richard Tabaracci, Goalie, Wash.	.50	1.00
20	Pierre Turgeon, NYI	.75	1.50
21	Steven Finn, Que.	.50	1.00
22	Craig Janney, St.L	.50	1.00
23	Matthias Schneider, Mon.	.60	1.25
24	Felix Potvin, Goalie, Tor.	2.00	4.00

NHL ALL STAR 1992 - 1993

This 23-card set that has two fronts was randomly inserted into Series One foil packs of Topps Stadium Club hockey. The cards depict the All-Star teams for both the Wales and Campbell Conferences. One player from each team in the same position per card.

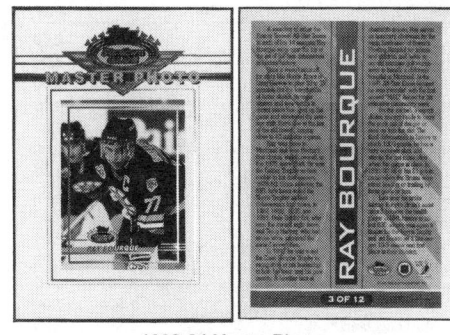

1993-94 NHL All Star 1992-93
Card No. 17, Mario Lemieux, Wayne Gretzky

Card Size: 2 1/2" x 3 1/2"
Face: Four colour, black background; Name
Back: Four colour, white card stock; Name, Number, Resume
Imprint: © 1993 THE TOPPS COMPANY, INC.
Complete Set No.: 23
Complete Set Price: 75.00 / 150.00
Common Player: 1.50 / 3.00

No.	Player	EX	NRMT
1	Ed Belfour, Patrick Roy, Goalies	12.50	25.00
2	Craig Billington, Jon Casey, Goalies	1.50	3.00
3	Peter Bondra, Kelly Kisio	1.50	3.00
4	Raymond Bourque, Paul Coffey	1.75	3.50
5	Brian Bradley, Adam Oates	2.00	4.00
6	Pavel Bure, Kevin Stevens	7.50	15.00
7	Garth Butcher, Kevin Lowe	1.50	3.00
8	Randy Carlyle, Brad Marsh	1.50	3.00
9	Chris Chelios, Al Iafrate	1.50	3.00
10	Steve Chiasson, Steve Duchesne	1.50	3.00
11	Miichael Gartner, Teemu Selanne	6.00	12.00
12	Douglas Gilmour, Joe Sakic	6.00	12.00
13	Phil Housley, Scott Stevens	1.50	3.00
14	Brett Hull, Jaromir Jagr	6.00	12.00
15	Jari Kurri, Alexander Mogilny	3.50	7.00
16	Pat LaFontaine, Steve Yzerman	6.00	12.00
17	Mario Lemieux, Wayne Gretzky	30.00	60.00
18	Dave Manson, Zarley Zalapski	1.50	3.00
19	Michael Modano, Pierre Turgeon	5.00	10.00
20	Kirk Muller, Gary Roberts	1.50	3.00
21	Mark Recchi, Luc Robitaille	4.00	8.00
22	Jeremy Roenick, Rick Tocchet	3.50	7.00
23	Peter Sidorkiewicz, Michael Vernon, Goalies	1.50	3.00

STADIUM CLUB FINEST

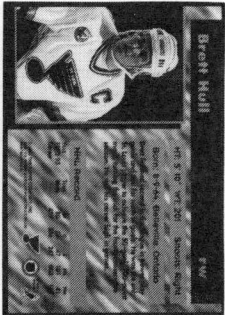

1993-94 Stadium Club Finest
Card No. 3, Brett Hull

258 • TOPPS — 1994-95 REGULAR ISSUE

This 12-card set could be found randomly inserted in Series Two Topps Stadium Club foil packs.

Card Size: 2 1/2" x 3 1/2"
Face: Four colour, foil embossed and coated; Name
Back: Four colour on white card stock; Name, Number, Resume
Imprint: © 1994 THE TOPPS COMPANY, INC.
Complete Set No.: 12
Complete Set Price: 42.50 85.00
Common Player: 2.00 4.00

No.	Players	EX	NRMT
1	Wayne Gretzky, LA	10.00	20.00
2	Jeff Brown, St.L	2.00	4.00
3	Brett Hull, St.L	4.00	8.00
4	Paul Coffey, Det.	2.50	5.00
5	Felix Potvin, Goalie, Tor.	7.50	15.00
6	Michael Gartner, NYR	2.50	5.00
7	Luc Robitaille, LA	3.00	6.00
8	Martin McSorley, Pit.	2.00	4.00
9	Gary Roberts, Cal.	2.00	4.00
19	Mario Lemieux, Pit.	7.50	15.00
11	Patrick Roy, Goalie, Mon.	7.50	15.00
12	Raymond Bourque, Bos.	2.50	5.00

MASTER PHOTO WINNER CARDS

These cards are randomly into the foil packs of both Series One and Two. Each winner card entitles the bearer to three Master Photos, the one on the front of the card plus two others listed on the back. These winner cards must be redeemed by June 1, 1994.

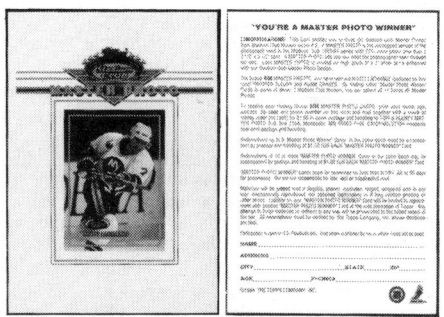

Master Photo Winner Cards
Card No. 16, Scott Lachance

Card Size: 2 1/2" x 3 1/2"
Face: Four colour, white border
Back: Black on white card stock; Name, Number
Imprint: © 1994 THE TOPPS COMPANY, INC.
Complete Set No.: 24
Complete Set Price: 10.00 20.00
Common Player: .50 1.00

No.	Players	EX	NRMT
1	Pat LaFontaine, Buf.	.50	1.00
2	Douglas Gilmour, Tor.	.50	1.00
3	Raymond Bourque, Bos.	.50	1.00
4	Teemu Selanne, Win.	.50	1.00
5	Eric Lindros, Phi.	.50	1.00
6	Ray Ferraro, NYI	.50	1.00
7	Patrick Roy, Goalie, Mon.	.50	1.00
8	Wayne Gretzky, LA	.50	1.00
9	Brett Hull, St.L	.50	1.00
10	John Vanbiesbrouck, Goalie, Fl.	.50	1.00
11	Adam Oates, Bos.	.50	1.00
12	Tom Barrasso, Goalie, Pit.	.50	1.00
13	Jarri Kurri, LA	.50	1.00
14	Esa Tikkanen, Edm.	.50	1.00
15	Grant Fuhr, Goalie, Buf.	.50	1.00
16	Scott Lachance, NYI	.50	1.00
17	Theoren Fleury, Cal.	.50	1.00
18	Adam Graves, NYR	.50	1.00
19	Richard Tabaracci, Goalie, Wash.	.50	1.00
20	Pierre Turgeon, NYI	.50	1.00
21	Steve Finn, Que.	.50	1.00
22	Craig Janney, St.L	.50	1.00
23	Mattieu Schneider, Mon.	.50	1.00
24	Felix Potvin, Goalie, Tor.	.50	1.00

STADIUM CLUB TEAM U.S.A.

This 23-card set was randomly inserted in the Stadium Club Series Two foil packs. The cards are of the U.S.A. Olympic hockey team that represented their country in Norway February 1994. Cards are numbered - of 23

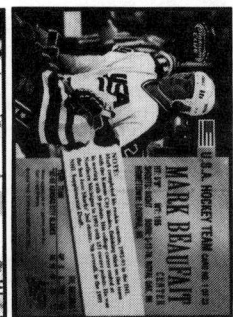

1993-94 Stadium Club Team U.S.A.
Card No. 1, Mark Beaufait

Card Size: 2 1/2" x 3 1/2"
Face: Four colour, borderless; Name
Back: Four colour, borderless; Name, Number, Resume, Team U.S.A. logo
Imprint: © 1994 THE TOPPS COMPANY, INC.
Complete Set No.: 23
Complete Set Price: 27.50 55.00
Common Card: 1.00 2.00

No.	Players	EX	NRMT
1	Mark Beaufait	1.00	2.00
2	Jim Campbell	1.50	3.00
3	Ted Crowley	1.50	3.00
4	Mike Dunham, Goalie	2.00	4.00
5	Chris Ferraro	1.00	2.00
6	Peter Ferraro	2.50	5.00
7	Brett Hauer	1.00	2.00
8	Darby Hendrickson	1.50	3.00
9	Jon Hillebrandt	1.00	2.00
10	Chris Imes	1.00	2.00
11	Craig Johnson	1.00	2.00
12	Peter Laviolette	1.00	2.00
13	John Lilley	1.50	3.00
14	Todd Marchant	1.50	3.00
15	Matt Martin	2.00	4.00
16	Ian Moran	1.00	2.00
17	Travis Richards	1.00	2.00
18	Barry Richter	1.50	3.00
19	David Roberts	1.50	3.00
20	Brian Rolston	2.50	5.00
21	David Sacco	1.00	2.00
22	Jim Storm, Goalie	1.50	3.00
23	Jeff Lazaro	1.00	2.00

— 1994 - 95 REGULAR ISSUE —

1994 - 95 Issue
Card No. Andrei Trefilov

Card Size: 2 1/2" x 3 1/2"
Face: Four colour, white border, silver foil logo; Name, Position
Back: Four colour, black border; Name, Number, Resume
Imprint: © 1994 THE TOPPS COMPANY, INC.
Complete Set No.: 275
Complete Set Price: 7.50 20.00
Common Card: .05 .10
Foil Pack: N/A
Foil Box: N/A

No.	Player	EX	NRMT
1	Mark Messier, NYR	.10	.20
2	Darren Turcotte, Har.	.05	.10
3	Mikhail Shtalenkov, Goalie, MDA	.05	.10
4	Robert Gaudreau, SJ	.05	.10
5	Anthony Amonte, Chi.	.05	.10
6	Stephane Quintal, Win.	.05	.10
7	Iain Fraser, Que.	.05	.10
8	Doug Weight, Edm.	.05	.10
9	German Titov, Cal.	.05	.10
10	Lawrence Murphy, Pit.	.05	.10
11	Danton Cole, TB	.05	.10
12	Pat Peake, Wash.	.05	.10
13	Chris Terreri, Goalie, NJ	.05	.10
14	Yuri Khmylev, Buf.	.05	.10
15	Paul Coffey, Det.	.05	.10
16	Brian Savage, Mon.	.05	.10
17	Rod Brind'Amour, Phi.	.05	.10
18	Nathan Lafayette, Van., RC	.12	.25
19	Gordon Murphy, Fl.	.05	.10
20	Al Iafrate, Bos.	.05	.10
21	Kevin Miller, St.L	.05	.10
22	Peter Zezel, Tor.	.05	.10
23	Sylvain Turgeon, Ott.	.05	.10
24	Mark Tinordi, Dal.	.05	.10
25	Jari Kurri, LA	.05	.10
26	Benoit Hogue, NYI	.05	.10
27	Jeff Reese, Goalie, Har.	.05	.10
28	Brian Noonan, NYR	.05	.10
29	Denis Tsygurov, Buf., RC	.07	.15
30	James Patrick, Cal.	.05	.10
31	Robert Corkum, MDA	.05	.10
32	Valeri Kamensky, Que.	.05	.10
33	Ray Whitney, SJ	.05	.10
34	Joe Murphy, Chi.	.05	.10

1ST TEAM ALL-STAR

No.	Player	EX	NRMT
35	Dominik Hasek, Goalie, Buf.	.10	.20
36	Raymond Bourque, Bos.	.07	.15
37	Brian Leetch, NYR	.10	.20
38	David Andreychuk, Tor.	.07	.15
39	Pavel Bure, Van.	.15	.30
40	Sergei Fedorov, Det.	.15	.30

REGULAR ISSUE

No.	Player	EX	NRMT
41	Bob Beers, Edm.	.05	.10
42	Byron Dafoe, Wash., RC	.07	.15
43	Lyle Odelein, Mon.	.05	.10
44	Markus Naslund, Pit.	.05	.10
45	Dean Chynoweth, NYI	.05	.10
46	Trent Klatt, Dal.	.05	.10
47	Murray Craven, Van.	.05	.10
48	David Mackey, St.L	.05	.10
49	Norm Maciver, Ott.	.05	.10
50	Alexander Mogilny, Buf.	.05	.10
51	David Reid, Bos.	.05	.10
52	Nicklas Lidstrom, Det.	.05	.10
53	Tom Fitzgerald, Fl.	.05	.10
54	Roman Hamrlik, TB	.05	.10
55	Wendel Clark, Tor.	.07	.15
56	Dominic Roussel, Goalie, Phi.	.05	.10
57	Alexei Zhitnik, LA	.07	.15
58	Valeri Zelepukin, NJ	.05	.10
59	Calle Johanson, Wash.	.05	.10
60	Craig Janney, St.L	.05	.10
61	Randy Wood, Buf.	.05	.10
62	Curtis Leschyshyn, Que.	.05	.10
63	Stephan Lebeau, MDA	.05	.10
64	Dallas Drake, Win.	.05	.10
65	Vincent Damphousse, Mon.	.05	.10
66	Scott Lachance, NYI	.05	.10
67	Dirk Graham, Chi.	.05	.10
68	Kevin Smyth, Har.	.05	.10

1994-95 REGULAR ISSUE — TOPPS

No.	Player	EX	NRMT
69	Denis Savard, TB	.05	.10
70	Mike Richter, Goalie, NYR	.07	.15
71	Ronald Stern, Cal.	.05	.10
72	Kirk Maltby, Edm.	.05	.10
73	Kjell Samuelsson, Pit.	.05	.10
74	Neal Broten, Dal.	.05	.10
75	Trevor Linden, Van.	.07	.15
76	Todd Elik, SJ	.05	.10
77	Andrew McBain, Ott.	.05	.10
78	Alexei Kudashov, Tor.	.05	.10
79	Kenneth Daneyko, NJ	.05	.10

GOAL-TENDING DUOS

No.	Player	EX	NRMT
80	Dominik Hasek/Grant Fuhr	.07	.15
81	Andrew Mood/Darcy Wakaluk	.05	.10
82	John Vanbiesbrouck/Mark Fitzpatrick	.05	.10
83	Martin Brodeur/Chris Terreri	.07	.15
84	Tom Barrasso/Ken Wregget	.05	.10
85	Kirk McLean/Kay Whitmore	.05	.10

REGULAR ISSUE

No.	Player	EX	NRMT
86	Darryl Sydor, LA	.05	.10
87	Chris Osgood, Goalie, Det.	.05	.10
88	Edward Donato, Bos.	.05	.10
89	Dave Lowry, Fl.	.05	.10
90	Mark Recchi, Phi.	.07	.15
91	Jim Montgomery, St.L	.05	.10
92	Bill Houlder, MDA	.05	.10
93	Richard Smehlik, Buf.	.05	.10
94	Benoit Brunet, Mon.	.05	.10
95	Teemu Selanne, Win.	.12	.25
96	Paul Ranheim, Har.	.05	.10
97	Andrei Kovalenko, Que.	.07	.15
98	Grant Ledyard, Dal.	.05	.10
99	Brent Grieve, Edm.	.05	.10
100	Joseph Juneau, Wash.	.10	.20
101	Martin Gelinas, Van.	.05	.10
102	Jamie Macoun, Tor.	.05	.10
103	Craig MacTavish, NYR	.05	.10
104	Micah Aivazoff, Det.	.05	.10
105	Stephane J.J. Richer, NJ	.05	.10
106	Eric Weinrich, Chi.	.05	.10
107	Pat Elynuik, TB	.05	.10
108	Tomas Sandstrom, Pit.	.05	.10
109	Darrin Madeley, Goalie, Ott.	.05	.10
110	Allan MacInnis, Cal.	.05	.10
111	Cam Stewart, Bos.	.05	.10
112	Dixon Ward, LA	.05	.10
113	Vlastimil Kroupa, SJ	.05	.10
114	Robert DiMaio, Phi.	.05	.10
115	Pierre Turgeon, NYI	.05	.10
116	Mike Hough, Fl.	.05	.10
117	John LeClair, Mon.	.05	.10
118	David Hannan, Buf.	.05	.10
119	Todd Ewen, MDA	.05	.10
120	**Team Card:** New York Rangers, Stanley Cup	.05	.10
121	Dave Manson, Win.	.05	.10
122	Jocelyn Lemieux, Har.	.05	.10
123	Jocelyn Thibault, Goalie, Que.	.05	.10
124	Scott Pearson, Edm.	.05	.10

2ND TEAM ALL-STAR

No.	Player	EX	NRMT
125	Patrick Roy, Goalie, Mon.	.07	.15
126	Scott Stevens, NJ	.05	.10
127	Allan MacInnis, Cal.	.05	.10
128	Adam Graves, NYR	.07	.15
129	Cam Neely, Bos.	.05	.10
130	Wayne Gretzky, LA	.12	.25

REGULAR ISSUE

No.	Player	EX	NRMT
131	Tom Chorske, NJ	.05	.10
132	John Tucker, TB	.05	.10
133	James (Steve) Smith, Chi.	.05	.10
134	Kay Whitmore, Goalie, Van.	.05	.10
135	Adam Oates, Bos.	.05	.10
136	Bill Berg, Tor.	.05	.10
137	Wes Walz, Cal.	.05	.10
138	Jeff Beukeboom, NYR	.05	.10
139	Ronald Francis, Pit.	.05	.10
140	Alexandre Daigle, Ott.	.12	.25
141	Josef Beranek, Phi.	.05	.10
142	Tom Pederson, SJ	.05	.10
143	Jamie McLennan, NYI	.05	.10
144	Scott Mellanby, Fl.	.05	.10
145	Vyacheslav Kozlov, Det.	.12	.25
146	Martin McSorley, LA	.05	.10
147	Tim Sweeney, MDA	.05	.10
148	Luciano Borsato, Win.	.05	.10
149	Jason Dawe, Buf.	.05	.10

LEAGUE LEADERS

No.	Player	EX	NRMT
150	Wayne Gretzky, Point Leader	.12	.25
151	Pavel Bure, Goal Scoring Leader	.07	.15
152	Dominik Hasek, Goalie, G.A.A. Leader	.07	.15
153	Scott Stevens, +/- Leader	.05	.10
154	Wayne Gretzky, Asst. Leader	.12	.25
155	Mike Richter, Goalie, Win Leader	.07	.15
156	Dominik Hasek, Save Pct. Leader	.10	.20

REGULAR ISSUE

No.	Player	EX	NRMT
157	Edward Drury, Har.	.05	.10
158	Peter Popovic, Mon.	.07	.15
159	Alexei Kasatonov, St.L	.07	.15
160	Mats Sundin, Que.	.05	.10
161	Brad Shaw, Ott.	.05	.10
162	Bret Hedican, Van.	.05	.10
163	Michael McPhee, Dal.	.05	.10
164	Martin Straka, Pit.	.05	.10
165	Dmitri Mironov, Tor.	.05	.10
166	Andrei Trefilov, Goalie, Cal.	.05	.10
167	Joe Reekie, Wash.	.05	.10
168	Gary Suter, Chi.	.05	.10
169	Gregory Gilbert, NYR	.05	.10
170	Igor Larionov, SJ	.05	.10
171	Mike Sillinger, Det.	.05	.10
172	Igor Kravchuk, Edm.	.05	.10
173	Glen Murray, Bos.	.05	.10
174	Shawn Chambers, TB	.05	.10
175	John MacLean, NJ	.05	.10
176	Yves Racine, Phi.	.05	.10
177	Andrei Lomakin, Fl.	.05	.10
178	Patrick Flatley, NYI	.05	.10
179	Igor Ulanov, Win.	.05	.10
180	Pat LaFontaine, Buf.	.05	.10
181	Mathieu Schneider, Mon.	.05	.10
182	Peter Stastny, St.L	.05	.10
183	Tony Granato, LA	.05	.10
184	Peter Douris, MDA	.05	.10
185	Alexei Kovalev, NYR	.10	.20
186	Geoff Courtnall, Van.	.05	.10
187	Richard Matvichuk, Dal.	.05	.10
188	Troy Murray, Ott.	.05	.10
189	Todd Gill, Tor.	.05	.10

ROOKIE SENSATIONS

No.	Player	EX	NRMT
190	Martin Brodeur, Goalie, NJ	.10	.20
191	Mikael Renberg, Phi.	.15	.30
192	Alexei Yashin, Ott.	.25	.50
193	Jason Arnott, Edm.	.50	1.00
194	Derek Plante, Buf.	.12	.25
195	Alexandre Daigle, Ott.	.12	.25
196	Bryan Smolinski, Bos.	.10	.20
197	Jesse Belanger, Fl.	.05	.10
198	Chris Pronger, Har.	.05	.10
199	Chris Osgood, Goalie, Det.	.07	.15

REGULAR ISSUE

No.	Player	EX	NRMT
200	Jeremy Roenick, Chi.	.15	.30
201	Johan Garpenlov, SJ	.05	.10
202	Dave Karpa, Que.	.05	.10
203	Darren McCarty, Det.	.05	.10
204	Claude Lemieux, NJ	.05	.10
205	Geoff Sanderson, Har.	.05	.10
206	Tom Barrasso, Goalie, Pit.	.05	.10
207	Kevin Dineen, Phi.	.05	.10
208	Sylvain Cote, Wash.	.05	.10
209	Brent Gretzky, TB	.05	.10
210	Shayne Corson, Edm.	.05	.10
211	Darius Kasparaitis, NYI	.05	.10
212	Peter Andersson, Fl.	.05	.10
213	Robert Reichel, Cal.	.05	.10
214	Jozef Stumpel, Bos.	.05	.10
215	Brendan Shanahan, St.L	.05	.10
216	Craig Muni, Buf.	.05	.10
217	Alexei Zhamnov, Win.	.10	.20
218	Robert Lang, LA	.05	.10
219	Brian Bellows, Mon.	.05	.10
220	Steven King, MDA	.05	.10
221	Sergei Zubov, NYR	.15	.30
222	Kelly Miller, Wash.	.05	.10
223	Ilya Byakin, Edm.	.05	.10
224	Chris Tamer, Pit.	.05	.10
225	Douglas Gilmour, Tor.	.15	.30
226	Shawn Antoski, Van.	.05	.10
227	Andrew Cassels, Har.	.05	.10
228	Craig Wolanin, Que.	.05	.10
229	Jon Casey, Goalie, Bos.	.05	.10
230	Michael Modano, Dal.	.10	.20
231	Bill Guerin, NJ	.05	.10
232	Gaetan Duchesne, SJ	.05	.10
233	Steve Dubinsky, Chi.	.15	.30
234	Jason Bowen, Phi.	.05	.10
235	Steve Yzerman, Det.	.05	.10
236	David Poulin, Wash.	.05	.10
237	Mikael Nylander, Cal.	.05	.10

TEAM OF THE FUTURE

No.	Player	EX	NRMT
238	Felix Potvin, Goalie, Tor.	.25	.50
240	Scott Niedermayer, NJ	.05	.10
241	Eric Lindros, Phi.	.75	1.50
242	Keith Tkachuk, Win.	.12	.25
243	Teemu Selanne, Win.	.12	.25

REGULAR ISSUE

No.	Player	EX	NRMT
244	Marty McInnis, NYI	.05	.10
245	Bob Kudelski, Fl.	.05	.10
246	Paul Cavallini, TB	.05	.10
247	Brian Bradley, TB	.05	.10
248	Robb Stauber, LA	.05	.10
249	Jay Wells, NYR	.05	.10
250	Mario Lemieux, Pit.	.35	.75
251	Tommy Albelin, NJ	.05	.10
252	Paul DiPietro, Mon.	.05	.10
253	Michael Gartner, Tor.	.07	.15
254	Darrin Shannon, Win.	.05	.10
255	Alexander Karpovtsev, NYR	.05	.10
256	Dave Babych, Van.	.05	.10
257	Greg Johnson, Det.	.05	.10
258	Frantisek Musil, Cal.	.05	.10
259	Michal Pivonka, Wash.	.05	.10
260	Arturs Irbe, Goalie, SJ	.10	.20
261	Paul Broten, Dal.	.05	.10
262	Don Sweeney, Bos.	.05	.10
263	Doug Brown, Pit.	.05	.10
264	Bobby Dollas, MDA	.05	.10
265	Brian Skrudland, Fl.	.05	.10
266	Dan Plante, NYI, RC	.10	.20
267	Chad Penney, Ott., RC	.10	.20
268	Stephen Leach, Bos.	.05	.10
269	Damian Rhodes, Goalie, Tor.	.05	.10
270	Glenn Anderson, NYR	.05	.10
271	Randy McKay, NJ	.05	.10
272	Jeff Brown, Van.	.05	.10
273	Steve Konowalchuk, Wash.	.05	.10
274A	Checklist (1 - 136)	.05	.10
274B	Rudy Poeschek, TB	.05	.10
275A	Checklist (137 - 275)	.05	.10
275B	Michael Peca, Van.	.05	.10

260 • TOPPS — 1982-83 STICKERS

— 1994-95 INSERT SET —

Card Size: 2 1/2" x 3 1/2"
Face: N/A
Back: N/A
Imprint: ©
Complete Set No.: 23
Complete Set Price: 35.00 / 75.00
Common Card: 2.00 / 4.00

No.	Player	EX	NRMT
1	Pavel Bure, Van.	7.50	15.00
2	Brett Hull, St.L	3.50	7.00
3	Sergei Fedorov, Det.	7.50	15.00
4	David Andreychuk, Tor.	2.00	4.00
5	Brendan Shanahan, St.L	2.00	4.00
6	Ray Sheppard, Det.	2.00	4.00
7	Adam Graves, NYR	3.50	7.00
8	Cam Neely, Bos.	2.50	5.00
9	Michael Modano, Dal.	2.00	4.00
10	Wendel Clark, Tor.	3.00	6.00
11	Jeremy Roenick, Chi.	3.50	7.00
12	Eric Lindros, Phi.	7.50	15.00
13	Luc Robitaille, LA	2.50	5.00
14	Steve Thomas, NYI	2.00	4.00
15	Geoff Sanderson, Hart.	2.00	4.00
16	Gary Roberts, Cal.	2.00	4.00
17	Kevin Stevens, Pit.	2.00	4.00
18	Keith Tkachuk, Win.	2.50	5.00
19	Theoren Fleury, Cal.	2.00	4.00
20	Robert Reichel, Cal.	2.00	4.00
21	Mark Recchi, Phi.	2.50	5.00
22	Vincent Damphousse, Mon.	2.00	4.00
23	Bob Kudelski, Fl.	2.00	4.00

TOPPS MISCELLANEOUS ISSUES

— 1982-83 STICKERS —

This set was issued by Topps and O-Pee-Chee. The sets are identical with the exception of the backs. The O-Pee-Chee is bilingual. An album was available to hold the stickers.

1982-83 Stickers
Sticker No. 2, Conn Smythe Trophy

Sticker Size: 2" X 2 1/2"
Face: Four colour, white border; Number
Back: Black on buff card stock; Number
Imprint: © 1982 TOPPS CHEWING GUM, INC. MADE IN ITALY
Complete Set No.: 263
Complete Set Price: 15.00 / 30.00
Common Player: .03 / .05
Album: — / 5.00

1982 STANLEY CUP FINALS

No.	Player	EX	NRMT
1	Conn Smythe Trophy: Mike Bossy, NYI	.15	.30
2	Conn Smythe Trophy	.03	.05
3	1981/82 Stanley Cup Winners: NY Islanders	.03	.05
4	1981/82 Stanley Cup Winners: NY Islanders	.03	.05
5	Stanley Cup Finals	.03	.05
6	Stanley Cup Finals	.03	.05
7	Richard Brodeur, Goalie	.03	.05
8	Victory	.03	.05
9	Stanley Cup Finals	.03	.05
10	Stanley Cup Finals	.03	.05

1982 STANLEY CUP PLAYOFFS

No.	Player	EX	NRMT
11	Stanley Cup Playoffs	.03	.05
12	Stanley Cup Playoffs	.03	.05
13	Stanley Cup Playoffs	.03	.05
14	Tom Lysiak	.03	.05
15	Peter Stastny	.10	.20
16	Stanley Cup Playoffs	.03	.05
17	Stanley Cup Playoffs	.03	.05
18	Stanley Cup Playoffs	.03	.05

QUEBEC NORDIQUES

No.	Player	EX	NRMT
19	Peter Stastny	.12	.25
20	Marian Stastny	.05	.10
21	Marc Tardif	.05	.10
22	Wilf Paiement	.05	.10
23	Real Cloutier	.05	.10
24	Anton Stastny	.05	.10
25	Michel Goulet	.12	.25
26	Dale Hunter	.05	.10
27	Dan Bouchard, Goalie	.05	.10

MONTREAL CANADIENS

No.	Player	EX	NRMT
28	Guy Lafleur	.20	.40
29	Guy Lafleur	.20	.40
30	Mario Tremblay	.03	.05
31	Larry Robinson	.03	.05
32	Steve Shutt	.03	.05
33	Steve Shutt	.03	.05
34	Rod Langway	.03	.05
35	Pierre Mondou	.03	.05
36	Bob Gainey	.03	.05
37	Rick Wamsley, Goalie	.03	.05
38	Mark Napier	.03	.05
39	Mark Napier	.03	.05
40	Doug Jarvis	.03	.05
41	Denis Herron, Goalie	.03	.05
42	Keith Acton	.03	.05
43	Keith Acton	.03	.05

NEW YORK ISLANDERS

No.	Player	EX	NRMT
44	Prince of Wales Trophy	.05	.10
45	Prince of Wales Trophy	.05	.10
46	Denis Potvin	.10	.20
47	Bryan Trottier	.10	.20
48	Bryan Trottier	.10	.20
49	John Tonelli	.03	.05
50	Mike Bossy	.12	.25
51	Mike Bossy	.12	.25
52	Duane Sutter	.03	.05
53	Bob Bourne	.03	.05
54	Clark Gillies	.03	.05
55	Clark Gillies	.03	.05
56	Brent Sutter	.03	.05
57	Anders Kallur	.03	.05
58	Ken Morrow	.03	.05
59	Bob Nystrom	.03	.05
60	Billy Smith, Goalie	.10	.20
61	Billy Smith, Goalie	.10	.20

TORONTO MAPLE LEAFS

No.	Player	EX	NRMT
62	Richard Vaive	.03	.05
63	Richard Vaive	.03	.05
64	Jim Benning	.03	.05
65	Miroslav Frycer	.03	.05
66	Terry Martin	.03	.05
67	Bill Derlago	.03	.05
68	Bill Derlago	.03	.05
69	Rocky Saganiuk	.03	.05
70	Vince Tremblay, Goalie	.03	.05
71	Bob Manno	.03	.05
72	Dan Maloney	.03	.05
73	John Anderson	.03	.05
74	John Anderson	.03	.05
75	Borje Salming	.07	.15
76	Borje Salming	.07	.15
77	Michel Larocque, Goalie	.03	.05

BOSTON BRUINS

No.	Player	EX	NRMT
78	Rick Middleton	.03	.05
79	Rick Middleton	.03	.05
80	Keith Crowder	.03	.05
81	Stephen Kasper	.03	.05
82	Brad Park	.03	.05
83	Peter McNab	.03	.05
84	Peter McNab	.03	.05
85	Terry O'Reilly	.03	.05
86	Raymond Bourque	.50	1.00
87	Raymond Bourque	.50	1.00
88	Tom Fergus	.03	.05
89	Michael O'Connell	.03	.05
90	Byron (Brad) McCrimmon	.03	.05
91	Don Marcotte	.03	.05
92	Barry Pederson	.03	.05
93	Barry Pederson	.03	.05

EDMONTON OILERS

No.	Player	EX	NRMT
94	Mark Messier	.50	1.00
95	Grant Fuhr, Goalie	.50	1.00
96	Kevin Lowe	.03	.05
97	Wayne Gretzky	2.50	5.00
98	Wayne Gretzky	2.50	5.00
99	Glenn Anderson	.03	.05
100	Glenn Anderson	.03	.05
101	Dave Lumley	.03	.05
102	Dave Hunter	.03	.05
103	Matti Hagman	.03	.05
104	Paul Coffey	.25	.50
105	Paul Coffey	.25	.50
106	Lee Fogolin	.03	.05
107	Ron Low, Goalie	.03	.05
108	Jari Kurri	.15	.30
109	Jari Kurri	.15	.30

1983-84 STICKERS — TOPPS • 261

PHILADELPHIA FLYERS

No.	Player	EX	NRMT
110	Bill Barber	.03	.05
111	Brian Propp	.05	.10
112	Ken Linseman	.03	.05
113	Ron Flockhart	.03	.05
114	Darryl Sittler	.15	.30
115	Bobby Clarke	.15	.30
116	Paul Holmgren	.03	.05
117	Peter Peeters, Goalie	.03	.05

BUFFALO SABRES

No.	Player	EX	NRMT
118	Gilbert Perreault	.03	.05
119	Dale McCourt	.03	.05
120	Mike Foligno	.07	.15
121	John Van Boxmeer	.03	.05
122	Anthony McKegney	.03	.05
123	Ric Seiling	.03	.05
124	Don Edwards, Goalie	.03	.05
125	Yvon Lambert	.03	.05

HARTFORD WHALERS

No.	Player	EX	NRMT
126	Blaine Stoughton	.03	.05
127	Pierre Larouche	.03	.05
128	Douglas Sulliman	.03	.05
129	Ron Francis	.15	.30
130	Greg Millen, Goalie	.03	.05
131	Mark Howe	.10	.20
132	Christopher Kotsopoulos	.03	.05
133	Garry Howatt	.03	.05

NEW YORK RANGERS

No.	Player	EX	NRMT
134	Ron Duguay	.03	.05
135	Barry Beck	.03	.05
136	Mike Rogers	.03	.05
137	Donald Maloney	.03	.05
138	Mark Pavelich	.03	.05
139	Eddie Johnstone, Goalie	.03	.05
140	Dave Maloney	.03	.05
141	Stephan Weeks, Goalie	.03	.05
142	Ed Mio, Goalie	.03	.05

PITTSBURGH PENGUINS

No.	Player	EX	NRMT
143	Rick Kehoe	.03	.05
144	Randy Carlyle	.10	.20
145	Paul Gardner	.03	.05
146	Michel Dion, Goalie	.03	.05
147	Rick MacLeish	.03	.05
148	Pat Boutette	.03	.05
149	Mike Bullard	.03	.05
150	George Ferguson	.03	.05

WASHINGTON CAPITALS

No.	Player	EX	NRMT
151	Dennis Maruk	.03	.05
152	Ryan Walter	.03	.05
153	Michael Gartner	.35	.75
154	Robert Carpenter	.03	.05
155	Chris Valentine	.03	.05
156	Richard Green	.03	.05
157	Bengt-Aka Gustafsson	.03	.05
158	Dave Parro, Goalie	.03	.05

CAMPBELL CONFERENCE ALL STARS

No.	Player	EX	NRMT
159	Mark Messier, Edm.	.35	.75
160	Paul Coffey, Edm.	.25	.50
161	Grant Fuhr, Goalie, Edm.	.35	.75
162	Wayne Gretzky, Edm.	1.75	3.50
163	Douglas Wilson, Jr., Chi.	.15	.30
164	David Taylor, LA	.15	.30

WALES CONFERENCE ALL STARS

No.	Player	EX	NRMT
165	Mike Bossy, NYI	.35	.75
166	Raymond Bourque, Bos.	.35	.75
167	Peter Stastny, Que.	.25	.50
168	Michel Dion, Goalie, Pit.	.07	.15
169	Larry Robinson, Mon.	.10	.20

No.	Player	EX	NRMT
170	Bill Barber, Phi.	.07	.15

CHICAGO BLACK HAWKS

No.	Player	EX	NRMT
171	Denis Savard	.50	1.00
172	Douglas Wilson, Jr.	.03	.05
173	Grant Mulvey	.03	.05
174	Tom Lysiak	.03	.05
175	Alan Secord	.03	.05
176	Reg Kerr	.03	.05
177	Tim Higgins	.03	.05
178	Terry Ruskowski	.03	.05

DETROIT RED WINGS

No.	Player	EX	NRMT
179	John Ogrodnick	.03	.05
180	Reed Larson	.03	.05
181	Bob Sauve, Goalie	.03	.05
182	Mark Osborne	.03	.05
183	Jim Schoenfeld	.03	.05
184	Danny Gare	.03	.05
185	Willie Huber	.03	.05
186	Walt McKechnie	.03	.05
187	Paul Woods	.03	.05

MINNESOTA NORTH STARS

No.	Player	EX	NRMT
188	Robert Smith	.20	.40
189	Dino Ciccarelli	.20	.40
190	Neal Broten	.15	.30
191	Steve Payne	.03	.05
192	Craig Hartsburg	.03	.05
193	Donald Beaupre, Goalie	.03	.05
194	Steve Christoff	.03	.05
195	Gilles Meloche, Goalie	.03	.05

ST. LOUIS BLUES

No.	Player	EX	NRMT
196	Michael Liut, Goalie	.07	.15
197	Bernie Federko	.10	.20
198	Brian Sutter	.03	.05
199	Blake Dunlop	.03	.05
200	Joe Mullen	.35	.75
201	Wayne Babych	.03	.05
202	Jorgen Pettersson	.03	.05
203	Perry Turnbull	.03	.05

WINNIPEG JETS

No.	Player	EX	NRMT
204	Dale Hawerchuk	.25	.50
205	Morris Lukowich	.03	.05
206	Dave Christian	.03	.05
207	David Babych	.03	.05
208	Paul MacLean	.03	.05
209	Willy Lindstrom	.03	.05
210	Ed Staniowski, Goalie	.03	.05
211	Doug Soetaert, Goalie	.03	.05
212	Lucien DeBlois	.03	.05

CALGARY FLAMES

No.	Player	EX	NRMT
213	Mel Bridgman	.03	.05
214	Lanny McDonald	.15	.30
215	Guy Chouinard	.03	.05
216	James Peplinski	.03	.05
217	Kent Nilsson	.03	.05
218	Pekka Rautakallio	.03	.05
219	Paul Reinhart	.03	.05
220	Kevin LaVallee	.03	.05
221	Ken Houston	.03	.05

COLORADO ROCKIES

No.	Player	EX	NRMT
222	Glenn Resch, Goalie	.05	.10
223	George (Rob) Ramage	.05	.10
224	Don Lever	.05	.10
225	Bob MacMillan	.05	.10
226	Steve Tambellini	.05	.10
227	Brent Ashton	.05	.10
228	Bob Lorimer	.05	.10
229	Merlin Malinowski	.05	.10

LOS ANGELES KINGS

No.	Player	EX	NRMT
230	Marcel Dionne	.15	.30
231	David Taylor	.05	.10
232	Lawrence Murphy	.15	.30
233	Steve Bozek	.03	.05
234	Greg Terrion	.03	.05
235	Jim Fox	.03	.05
236	Mario Lessard, Goalie	.03	.05
237	Charlie Simmer	.03	.05

VANCOUVER CANUCKS

No.	Player	EX	NRMT
238	Campbell Bowl	.05	.10
239	Campbell Bowl	.05	.10
240	Thomas Gradin	.03	.05
241	Ivan Boldirev	.03	.05
242	Stanley Smyl	.03	.05
243	Harold Snepsts	.03	.05
244	Curt Fraser	.03	.05
245	Lars Molin	.03	.05
246	Kevin McCarthy	.03	.05
247	Richard Brodeur, Goalie	.03	.05

1981-82 LEADERS

No.	Player	EX	NRMT
248	Calder Trophy	.03	.05
249	**Calder Trophy Winner:** Rookie of the Year, Dale Hawerchuk, Win.	.15	.30
250	Vezina Trophy	.03	.05
251	**Vezina Trophy Winner:** Most Valuable Goalie, Billy Smith, NYI	.03	.05
252	**William Jennings Trophy Winners:** Goal Tending - Team: Denis Herron, Mon.; Rick Wamsley, Mon.	.03	.05
253	**Frank J. Selke Trophy Winner:** Best Defensive Forward Stephen Kasper, Bos.	.03	.05
254	**Norris Trophy Winner:** Best Defenseman, Douglas Wilson, Jr., Chi.	.03	.05
255	Norris Trophy	.10	.20
256	**Art Ross Trophy Winner:** **Hart Trophy Winner:** Wayne Gretzky, Edm.	1.75	3.50
257	Wayne Gretzky	1.75	3.50
258	Wayne Gretzky	1.75	3.50
259	Wayne Gretzky	1.75	3.50
260	Hart Trophy	.10	.20
261	Art Ross Trophy	.10	.20
262	**Lady Byng Trophy Winner:** Sportsmanship, Rick Middleton, Bos.	.10	.20
263	Lady Byng Trophy	.10	.20

— 1983 - 84 STICKERS —

As with the first issue in 1982-83 Topps and O-Pee-Chee stickers are identical with the exception of their backs. An album was available to hold the stickers.

1983-84 Stickers
Sticker No. 1, Marcel Dionne

Sticker Size: 1 15/16" X 2 9/16"
Face: Four colour, white border; Number
Back: Blue on card stock; Name, Number
Imprint: © TOPPS CHEWING GUM, INC.
Complete Set No.: 330
Complete Set Price: 15.00 30.00
Common Player: .03 .05
Album: 5.00

262 • TOPPS — 1983-84 STICKERS —

RECORD HOLDERS

No.	Player	EX	NRMT
1	Marcel Dionne, LA	.15	.30
2	Guy Lafleur, Mon.	.15	.30
3	Darryl Sittler, Phi.	.12	.25
4	Gilbert Perreault, Buf.	.12	.25
5	Bill Barber, Phi.	.05	.10
6	Steve Shutt, Mon.	.05	.10
7	Wayne Gretzky, Edm.	1.75	3.50
8	Lanny McDonald, Ca.	.05	.10
9	Reggie Leach, Det.	.03	.05
10	Mike Bossy, NYI	.12	.25
11	Rick Kehoe, Pit.	.03	.05
12	Bobby Clarke, Phi.	.10	.20
13	Butch Goring, NYI	.03	.05
14	Rick Middleton, Bos.	.03	.05

1983 STANLEY CUP FINALS

No.	Player	EX	NRMT
15	Conn Smythe Trophy	.10	.20
16	Conn Smythe Trophy Winner: MVP - Finals, Billy Smith, Goalie, NYI	.03	.05
17	Lee Fogolin, Edm.	.03	.05
18	Stanley Cup Finals	.03	.05
19	Stanley Cup Finals	.03	.05
20	Stanley Cup Finals	.03	.05
21	Stanley Cup Finals	.03	.05
22	Stanley Cup	.10	.20
23	Stanley Cup	.10	.20
24	Stanley Cup	.10	.20

TORONTO MAPLE LEAFS

No.	Player	EX	NRMT
25	Richard Vaive	.03	.05
26	Richard Vaive	.03	.05
27	Billy Harris	.03	.05
28	Dan Daoust	.03	.05
29	Dan Daoust	.03	.05
30	John Anderson	.03	.05
31	John Anderson	.03	.05
32	Peter Ihnacak	.03	.05
33	Borje Salming	.07	.15
34	Borje Salming	.07	.15
35	Bill Derlago	.03	.05
36	Rick St. Croix, Goalie	.03	.05
37	Greg Terrion	.03	.05
38	Miroslav Frycer	.03	.05
39	Mike Palmateer, Goalie	.03	.05
40	Gaston Gingras	.03	.05

BOSTON BRUINS

No.	Player	EX	NRMT
41	Peter Peeters, Goalie	.03	.05
42	Peter Peeters, Goalie	.03	.05
43	Michael Krushelnyski	.03	.05
44	Rick Middleton	.03	.05
45	Rick Middleton	.03	.05
46	Raymond Bourque	.35	.75
47	Raymond Bourque	.35	.75
48	Brad Park	.03	.05
49	Barry Pederson	.03	.05
50	Barry Pederson	.03	.05
51	Peter McNab	.03	.05
52	Michael O'Connell	.03	.05
53	Stephen Kasper	.03	.05
54	Marty Howe	.03	.05
55	Tom Fergus	.03	.05
56	Keith Crowder	.03	.05

MONTREAL CANADIENS

No.	Player	EX	NRMT
57	Steve Shutt	.03	.05
58	Guy Lafleur	.15	.30
59	Guy Lafleur	.15	.30
60	Larry Robinson	.07	.15
61	Larry Robinson	.07	.15
62	Ryan Walter	.03	.05
63	Ryan Walter	.03	.05
64	Mark Napier	.03	.05
65	Mark Napier	.03	.05
66	Bob Gainey	.10	.20
67	Douglas Wickenheiser	.03	.05
68	Pierre Mondou	.03	.05
69	Mario Tremblay	.03	.05
70	Gilbert Delorme	.03	.05
71	Mats Naslund	.10	.20
72	Rick Wamsley, Goalie	.03	.05

NEW YORK ISLANDERS

No.	Player	EX	NRMT
73	Ken Morrow	.03	.05
74	John Tonelli	.05	.10
75	John Tonelli	.05	.10
76	Bryan Trottier	.07	.15
77	Bryan Trottier	.07	.15
78	Mike Bossy	.20	.40
79	Mike Bossy	.20	.40
80	Bob Bourne	.03	.05
81	Denis Potvin	.15	.30
82	Denis Potvin	.15	.30
83	Dave Langevin	.03	.05
84	Clark Gillies	.03	.05
85	Bob Nystrom	.03	.05
86	Billy Smith	.07	.15
87	Tomas Jonsson	.03	.05
88	Rolland Melanson, Goalie	.03	.05

EDMONTON OILERS

No.	Player	EX	NRMT
89	Wayne Gretzky	2.50	5.00
90	Wayne Gretzky	2.50	5.00
91	Willy Lindstrom	.03	.05
92	Glenn Anderson	.10	.20
93	Glenn Anderson	.10	.20
94	Paul Coffey	.15	.30
95	Paul Coffey	.15	.30
96	Charles Huddy	.03	.05
97	Mark Messier	.50	1.00
98	Mark Messier	.50	1.00
99	Andrew Moog, Goalie	.25	.50
100	Lee Fogolin, Edm.	.03	.05
101	Kevin Lowe	.03	.05
102	Ken Linseman	.03	.05
103	Tom Roulston	.03	.05
104	Jari Kurri	.12	.25

CHICAGO BLACK HAWKS

No.	Player	EX	NRMT
105	Darryl Sutter	.05	.10
106	Denis Savard	.12	.25
107	Denis Savard	.12	.25
108	Steve Larmer	.25	.50
109	Bob Murray	.03	.05
110	Tom Lysiak	.03	.05
111	Alan Secord	.03	.05
112	Douglas Wilson, Jr.	.03	.05
113	Murray Bannerman, Goalie	.03	.05

MINNESOTA NORTH STARS

No.	Player	EX	NRMT
114	Gordon Roberts	.03	.05
115	Tom McCarthy	.03	.05
116	Robert Smith	.03	.05
117	Craig Hartsburg	.03	.05
118	Dino Ciccarelli	.07	.15
119	Dino Ciccarelli	.07	.15
120	Neal Broten	.03	.05
121	Steve Payne	.03	.05
122	Donald Beaupre, Goalie	.03	.05

ST. LOUIS BLUES

No.	Player	EX	NRMT
123	Jorgen Pettersson	.03	.05
124	Perry Turnbull	.03	.05
125	Bernie Federko	.05	.10
126	Mike Crombeen	.03	.05
127	Brian Sutter	.03	.05
128	Brian Sutter	.03	.05
129	Michael Liut, Goalie	.03	.05
130	George (Rob) Ramage	.03	.05
131	Blake Dunlop	.03	.05

DETROIT RED WINGS

No.	Player	EX	NRMT
132	Ivan Boldirev	.03	.05
133	Dwight Foster	.03	.05
134	Reed Larson	.03	.05
135	Danny Gare	.03	.05
136	Jim Schoenfeld	.03	.05
137	John Ogrodnick	.03	.05
138	John Ogrodnick	.03	.05
139	Willie Huber	.03	.05
140	Greg Smith	.03	.05

STARS OF THE FUTURE CAMPBELL CONFERENCE

No.	Player	EX	NRMT
141	Eddy Beers, Cal.	.03	.05
142	Brian Bellows, Min.	.25	.50
143	Jiri Bubla, Van.	.03	.05
144	Daryl Evans, LA	.03	.05
145	Randall Gregg, Edm.	.03	.05
146	James Jackson, Cal.	.03	.05
147	Corrado Micalef, Goalie, Det.	.03	.05
148	Brian Mullen, Win.	.03	.05
149	Frank Nigro, Tor.	.03	.05
150	Walter Poddubny, Tor.	.03	.05
151	Jaroslav Pouzar, Edm.	.03	.05
152	Patrik Sundstrom, Van.	.07	.15

CAMPBELL CONFERENCE CHAMPIONSHIP

No.	Player	EX	NRMT
153	Denis Savard, Chi.	.10	.20
154	Dave Hunter, Edm.	.03	.05
155	Andrew Moog, Goalie, Edm.	.15	.30
156	Alan Secord, Chi.	.03	.05
157	Mark Messier, Edm.	.25	.50
158	Glenn Anderson, Edm.	.07	.15
159	Jaroslav Pouzar, Edm.	.03	.05

CAMPBELL CONFERENCE ALL STARS

No.	Player	EX	NRMT
160	Alan Secord, Chi.	.03	.05
161	Wayne Gretzky, Edm.	1.75	3.50
162	Lanny McDonald, Cal.	.05	.10
163	David Babych, Win.	.03	.05
164	Murray Bannerman, Goalie, Chi.	.03	.05
165	Douglas Wilson, Jr., Chi.	.03	.05

WALES CONFERENCE ALL STARS

No.	Player	EX	NRMT
166	Michel Goulet, Que.	.03	.05
167	Peter Stastny, Que.	.10	.20
168	Marian Stastny, Que.	.03	.05
169	Denis Potvin, NYI	.10	.20
170	Peter Peeters, Goalie, Bos.	.03	.05
171	Mark Howe, Phi.	.10	.20

WALES CONFERENCE CHAMPIONSHIP

No.	Player	EX	NRMT
172	Luc Dufour, Bos.	.03	.05
173	Raymond Bourque, Bos.	.25	.50
174	Bob Bourne, NYI	.03	.05
175	Denis Potvin, NYI	.03	.05
176	Mike Bossy, NYI	.10	.20
177	Butch Goring, NYI	.03	.05
178	Brad Park, Bos.	.07	.15

STARS OF THE FUTURE WALES CONFERENCE

No.	Player	EX	NRMT
179	James (Murray) Brumwell, NJD	.03	.05
180	Guy Carbonneau, Mon.	.03	.05
181	Lindsay Carson, Phi.	.03	.05
182	Luc Dufour, Bos.	.03	.05
183	Robert Froese, Goalie, Phi.	.03	.05
184	Mats Hallin, NYI	.03	.05
185	Gordon Kluzak, Bos.	.03	.05
186	Jeff Larmer, NJD	.03	.05
187	Milan Novy, Wash.	.03	.05
188	Scott Stevens, Wash.	.25	.50
189	Bob Sullivan, Har.	.03	.05
190	Mark Taylor, Phi.	.03	.05

1985 - 86 BOX BOTTOMS — TOPPS • 263

PHILADELPHIA FLYERS

No.	Player	EX	NRMT
191	Darryl Sittler	.07	.15
192	Ron Flockhart	.03	.05
193	Byron (Brad) McCrimmon	.03	.05
194	Bill Barber	.03	.05
195	Mark Howe	.07	.15
196	Mark Howe	.07	.15
197	Pelle Lindbergh, Goalie	.75	1.50
198	Bobby Clarke	.10	.20
199	Brian Propp	.03	.05

WASHINGTON CAPITALS

No.	Player	EX	NRMT
200	Ken Houston	.03	.05
201	Rod Langway	.03	.05
202	Al Jensen, Goalie	.03	.05
203	Brian Engblom	.03	.05
204	Dennis Maruk	.03	.05
205	Dennis Maruk	.03	.05
206	Robert Carpenter	.03	.05
207	Michael Gartner	.20	.40
208	Doug Jarvis	.03	.05

NEW YORK RANGERS

No.	Player	EX	NRMT
209	Ed Mio, Goalie	.03	.05
210	Barry Beck	.03	.05
211	Dave Maloney	.03	.05
212	Donald Maloney	.03	.05
213	Mark Pavelich	.03	.05
214	Mark Pavelich	.03	.05
215	Anders Hedberg	.03	.05
216	Reijo Ruotsalainen	.03	.05
217	Mike Rogers	.03	.05

NEW JERSEY DEVILS

No.	Player	EX	NRMT
218	Don Lever	.03	.05
219	Steve Tambellini	.03	.05
220	Bob MacMillan	.03	.05
221	Hector Marini	.03	.05
222	Glenn Resch, Goalie	.03	.05
223	Glenn Resch, Goalie	.03	.05
224	Carol Vadnais	.03	.05
225	Joel Quenneville	.03	.05
226	Aaron Broten	.03	.05

PITTSBURGH PENGUINS

No.	Player	EX	NRMT
227	Randy Carlyle	.05	.10
228	Douglas Shedden	.03	.05
229	Greg Malone	.03	.05
230	Paul Gardner	.03	.05
231	Rick Kehoe	.03	.05
232	Rick Kehoe	.03	.05
233	Pat Boutette	.03	.05
234	Michel Dion, Goalie	.03	.05
235	Mike Bullard	.05	.10

BUFFALO SABRES

No.	Player	EX	NRMT
236	Dale McCourt	.03	.05
237	Mike Foligno	.05	.10
238	Phil Housley	.25	.50
239	Anthony McKegney	.03	.05
240	Gilbert Perreault	.07	.15
241	Gilbert Perreault	.07	.15
242	Bob Sauve, Goalie	.03	.05
243	Michael Ramsey	.03	.05
244	John Van Boxmeer	.03	.05

QUEBEC NORDIQUES

No.	Player	EX	NRMT
245	Dan Bouchard, Goalie	.03	.05
246	Real Cloutier	.03	.05
247	Marc Tardif	.03	.05
248	Randy Moller	.03	.05
249	Michel Goulet	.03	.05
250	Michel Goulet	.07	.15
251	Marian Stastny	.07	.15
252	Anton Stastny	.03	.05
253	Peter Stastny	.10	.20

HARTFORD WHALERS

No.	Player	EX	NRMT
254	Mark Johnson	.03	.05
255	Ron Francis	.10	.20
256	Douglas Sulliman	.03	.05
257	Risto Siltanen	.03	.05
258	Blaine Stoughton	.03	.05
259	Blaine Stoughton	.03	.05
260	Ray Neufeld	.03	.05
261	Pierre Lacroix	.03	.05
262	Greg Millen, Goalie	.03	.05

CALGARY FLAMES

No.	Player	EX	NRMT
263	Lanny McDonald	.10	.20
264	Paul Reinhart	.03	.05
265	Mel Bridgman	.03	.05
266	Rejean Lemelin, Goalie	.03	.05
267	Kent Nilsson	.03	.05
268	Kent Nilsson	.03	.05
269	Doug Risebrough	.03	.05
270	Kari Eloranta	.03	.05
271	Phil Russell	.03	.05

VANCOUVER CANUCKS

No.	Player	EX	NRMT
272	Darcy Rota	.03	.05
273	Thomas Gradin	.03	.05
274	Stanley Smyl	.03	.05
275	John Garrett	.03	.05
276	Richard Brodeur, Goalie	.03	.05
277	Richard Brodeur, Goalie	.03	.05
278	Doug Halward	.03	.05
279	Kevin McCarthy	.03	.05
280	Rick Lanz	.03	.05

WINNIPEG JETS

No.	Player	EX	NRMT
281	Morris Lukowich	.03	.05
282	Dale Hawerchuk	.10	.20
283	Paul MacLean	.03	.05
284	Lucien DeBlois	.03	.05
285	David Babych	.03	.05
286	David Babych	.03	.05
287	Douglas Smail	.03	.05
288	Doug Soetaert, Goalie	.03	.05
289	Thomas Steen	.03	.05

LOS ANGELES KINGS

No.	Player	EX	NRMT
290	Charlie Simmer	.03	.05
291	Terry Ruskowski	.03	.05
292	Bernie Nicholls	.15	.30
293	Jim Fox	.03	.05
294	Marcel Dionne	.10	.20
295	Marcel Dionne	.10	.20
296	Gary Laskoski, Goalie	.03	.05
297	Jerry Korab	.03	.05
298	Lawrence Murphy	.12	.25

1982 - 1983 LEADERS

No.	Player	EX	NRMT
299	Hart Trophy	.10	.20
300	Hart Trophy	.10	.20
301	**Hart Trophy Winner:** Most Valuable Player, Wayne Gretzky, Edm.	1.75	3.50
302	**Frank J. Selke Trophy Winner:** Best Defensive Forward, Bobby Clarke, Phi.	.05	.10
303	**Bill Masterton Trophy Winner:** For Perserverance, Sportsmanship and Dedication, Lanny McDonald, Cal.	.07	.15
304	Lady Byng Trophy	.05	.10
305	Lady Byng Trophy	.05	.10
306	**Lady Byng Trophy Winner:** Sportsmanship, Mike Bossy, NYI	.10	.20
307	**Art Ross Trophy Winner:** 196 Points, Wayne Gretzky, Edm.	1.75	3.50
308	Art Ross Trophy	.05	.10
309	Art Ross Trophy	.05	.10
310	Calder Trophy	.05	.10
311	Calder Trophy	.05	.10
312	**Calder Trophy Winner:** Rookie of the Year, Steve Larmer, Chi.	.20	.40
313	**Norris Trophy Winner:** Best Defenseman, Rod Langway, Wash.	.05	.10
314	Norris Trophy	.05	.10
315	Norris Trophy	.05	.10
316	**William Jennings Trophy Winner:** Goal Tending Team, Billy Smith, NYI	.05	.10
317	**William Jennings Trophy Winner:** Goal Tending Team, Roland Melanson, NYI	.03	.05
318	**Vezina Trophy Winner:** Most Valuable Goalie, Peter Peeters, Bos.	.03	.05
319	Vezina Trophy	.05	.10
320	Vezina Trophy	.05	.10

1982 - 83 RECORD BREAKERS

No.	Player	EX	NRMT
321	Mike Bossy, NYI	.20	.40
322	Mike Bossy, NYI	.20	.40
323	Marcel Dionne, St.L.	.20	.40
324	Marcel Dionne, St.L.	.20	.40
325	Wayne Gretzky, Edm.	2.50	5.00
326	Wayne Gretzky, Edm.	2.50	5.00
327	Pat Hughes, Edm.	.10	.20
328	Pat Hughes, Edm.	.10	.20
329	Rick Middleton, Bos.	.10	.20
330	Rick Middleton, Bos.	.15	.30

— 1985 - 86 BOX BOTTOMS —

1985-86 Box Bottom Panel No. 4
Reijo Ruotsalainen, Brian Sutter
John Tonelli, Douglas Wilson

Panel Size: 5" X 7"
Face: Four colour, white border; Team logo, Name, Position
Back: Red and blue on card stock; Letter, Resume
Imprint: © 1985 TOPPS CHEWING GUM, INC. PRTD. IN U.S.A.
Complete Set No.: 4 Panels / 16 Cards
Complete Set Price: 35.00 75.00
Common Panel: .50 1.00
Common Card: .12 .25

No.	Player	EX	NRMT
	Panel 1	1.25	2.50
A	Brian Bellows, Min.	.50	1.00
B	Raymond Bourque, Bos.	1.00	2.00
C	Robert Carpenter, Wash.	.12	.25
D	Chris Chelios, Mon.	.50	1.00
	Panel 2	3.00	6.00
E	Marcel Dionne, LA	.35	.75
F	Ron Francis, Har.	.35	.75
G	Wayne Gretzky, Edm.	2.50	5.00
H	Tim Kerr, Phi.	.12	.25
	Panel 3	30.00	60.00
I	Mario Lemieux, Pit.	30.00	60.00
J	John Ogrodnick, Det.	.12	.25
K	Gilbert Perreault, Buf.	.30	.60
L	Glenn Resch, Goalie, NJD	.25	.50
	Panel 4	.50	1.00
M	Reijo Ruotsalainen, NYR	.12	.25
N	Brian Sutter, St.L.	.12	.25
O	John Tonelli, NYI	.12	.25
P	Douglas Wilson, Chi.	.12	.25

— 1986 - 87 BOX BOTTOMS —

The cards were issued as the bottom wax box panel with four cards per panel. The set features team scoring leaders.

Panel Size: 5" X 7"
Face: Four colour, white border; Name, Position, Team logo
Back: Blue and black on card stock; Number, Resume
Imprint: © TOPPS CHEWING GUM, INC. PRTD. IN U.S.A.
Complete Set No.: 4 Panels / 16 Cards

Complete Set (4 panels):		15.00	30.00
Common Panel:		.50	1.00
Common Player:		.12	.25

No.	Player	EX	NRMT
	Panel 1	.50	1.00
A	Gregory Adams, NJD	.12	.25
B	Mike Bossy, NYI	.50	1.00
C	Dave Christian, Wash.	.12	.25
D	Mike Foligno, Buf.	.12	.25
	Panel 2	7.50	15.00
E	Michel Goulet, Que.	.20	.40
F	Wayné Gretzky, Edm.	.75	1.50
G	Tim Kerr, Phi.	.12	.25
H	Jari Kurri, Edm.	.35	.75
	Panel 3	10.00	20.00
I	Mario Lemieux, Pit.	10.00	20.00
J	Lanny McDonald, Cal.	.35	.75
K	Bernie Nicholls, LA	.20	.40
L	Mike Ridley, NYR	.12	.25
	Panel 4	.60	1.25
M	Larry Robinson, Mon.	.20	.40
N	Denis Savard, Chi.	.30	.60
O	Brian Sutter, St.L.	.12	.25
P	Bryan Trottier, NYI	.35	.75

— 1987 - 88 BOX BOTTOMS —

The cards were issued as the bottom wax box panel with four cards per panel. The set features team scoring leaders.

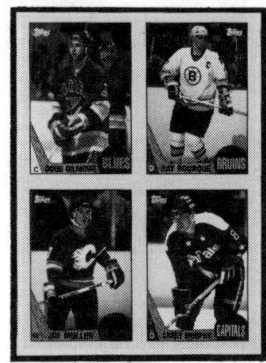

1987-88 Box Bottoms, Panel No. 2,
D. Gilmore, R. Bourque, J. Mullen, L. Murphy

Panel Size: 5" X 7"
Face: Four colour, yellow border; Name, Team, Position
Back: Two colour, purple and black on card stock; Name, Position, Initial, Resume, Bilingual
Imprint: © TOPPS CHEWING GUM, INC. PRTD. IN U.S.A.
Complete Set No.: 4 Panels / 16 Cards

Complete Set Price:		11.50	23.00
Common Panel:		.50	1.00
Common Player:		.10	.20

No.	Player	EX	NRMT
	Panel 1	10.00	20.00
A	Wayne Gretzky, Edm.	4.50	9.00
B	Tim Kerr, Phi.	.12	.25
C	Steve Yzerman, Det.	1.00	2.00
D	Luc Robitaille, LA	5.00	10.00
	Panel 2	2.00	4.00
E	Douglas Gilmour, St.L.	1.00	2.00
F	Raymond Bourque, Bos.	.50	1.00
G	Joe Mullen, Cal.	.25	.50
H	Lawrence Murphy, Wash.	.25	.50
	Panel 3	1.00	2.00
I	Dale Hawerchuk, Win.	.35	.75
J	Ron Francis, Har.	.35	.75
K	Walter Poddubny, NYR	.10	.20
L	Mats Naslund, Mon.	.20	.40
	Panel 4	1.00	2.00
M	Michel Goulet, Que.	.35	.75
N	Denis Savard, Chi.	.15	.30
O	Bryan Trottier, NYI	.35	.75
P	Russ Courtnall, Tor.	.35	.75

— 1988 - 89 BOX BOTTOMS —

The cards were issued as the bottom wax box panel with four cards per panel. The set features the 1987-88 team scoring leaders.

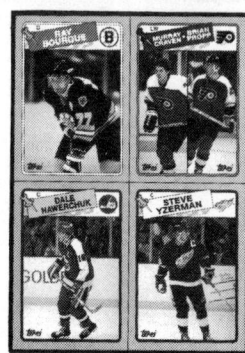

1988-89 Box Bottom Panel No. 3
Raymond Bourque, Murray Craven/Brian Propp,
Dale Hawerchuk, Steve Yzerman

Panel Size: 5" X 7"
Face: Four colour, grey border; Name, Team logo
Back: Two colour, blue and orange on card stock; Name, Letter, Team, Resume
Imprint: © 1988 THE TOPPS COMPANY. INC. © 1988 NHLPA
Complete Set No.: 4 Panels / 16 Cards

Complete Set Price:		5.00	10.00
Common Panel:		.50	1.00
Common Player:		.10	.20

No.	Player	EX	NRMT
	Panel 1	3.00	6.00
A	Ron Francis, Har.	.25	.50
B	Wayne Gretzky, LA	2.50	5.00
C	Pat LaFontaine, NYI	.50	1.00
D	Bobby Smith, Mon.	.10	.20
	Panel 2	.75	1.50
E	Bernie Federko, St.L.	.25	.50
F	Kirk Muller, NJD	.50	1.00
G	Ed Olczyk, Tor.	.20	.40
H	Denis Savard, Chi.	.25	.50
	Panel 3	.50	1.00
I	Raymond Bourque, Bos.	.35	.75
J	Murray Craven, Phi.; Brian Propp, Phi.	.10	.20
K	Dale Hawerchuk, Win.	.25	.50
L	Steve Yzerman, Det.	.35	.75
	Panel 4	1.00	2.00
M	David Andreychuk, Buf.	.25	.50
N	Michael Gartner, Wash.	.50	1.00
O	Hakan Loob, Cal.	.10	.20
P	Luc Robitaille, LA	.50	1.00

— 1989 - 90 BOX BOTTOMS —

The 1989-90 box bottoms feature the 1988-89 scoring leaders.
Panel Size: 5" x 7"

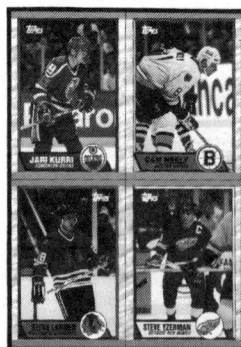

1989-90 Box Bottoms, Panel No. 3,
J. Kurri, S. Larmer, C. Neely, S. Yzerman

Face: Four colour, blue and marble border, Name, Team, Logo
Back: Two colour, black and red on card stock; Name, Letter, Resume
Imprint: ** © 1989 THE TOPPS COMPANY. INC. © 1989 NHLPA
Complete Set No.: 4 Panels / 16 Cards

Complete Set Price:		4.00	8.00
Common Panel:		.75	1.50
Common Card:		.08	.15

No.	Player	EX	NRMT
	Panel 1	1.50	3.00
A	Mario Lemieux, Pit.	1.25	2.50
B	Mike Ridley, Wash.	.08	.15
C	Tomas Sandstrom, NYR	.12	.25
D	Petri Skriko, Van.	.08	.15
	Panel 2	2.00	4.00
E	Wayne Gretzky, LA	1.25	2.50
F	Brett Hull, St.L.	.75	1.50
G	Tim Kerr, Phi.	.12	.25
H	Mats Naslund, Mon.	.12	.25
	Panel 3	.85	1.75
I	Jari Kurri, Edm.	.25	.50
J	Steve Larmer, Chi.	.17	.35
K	Cam Neely, Bos.	.30	.60
L	Steve Yzerman, Det.	.30	.60
	Panel 4	.75	1.50
M	Kevin Dineen, Har.	.12	.25
N	Dave Gagner, Min.	.17	.35
O	Joe Mullen, Cal.	.12	.25
P	Pierre Turgeon, Buf.	.50	1.00

— 1990 - 91 BOX BOTTOMS —

The 1990-91 box bottoms feature the 1989-90 league leaders.

1990-91 Box Bottoms, Panel No. 3,
Ray Bourque, Steve Yzerman
Darrent Turcotte, Michael Vernon

Panel Size: 5" X 7"
Face: Four colour, turquoise border; Name, Position, Team
Back: Two colour, green and blue on cardstock; Name, Letter, Resume
Imprint: © 1990 THE TOPPS COMPANY, INC. © 1990 NHLPA
Complete Set No.: 4 Panels / 16 Cards

Complete Set Price:		2.00	4.00
Common Panel:		.12	.25
Common Card:		.05	.10

No.	Player	EX	NRMT
	Panel 1	.75	1.50
A	Alexander Mogilny, Buf.	.25	.50
B	Jon Casey, Goalie, Min.	.05	.10
C	Paul Coffey, Pit.	.12	.15
D	Wayne Gretzky, LA	.50	1.00
	Panel 2	.75	1.50
E	Patrick Roy, Goalie, Mon.	.25	.50
F	Michael Modano, Min.	.25	.50
G	Mario Lemieux, Pit.	.35	.75
H	Allan MacInnis, Cal.	.07	.15
	Panel 3	.25	.50
I	Raymond Bourque, Bos.	.12	.25
J	Steve Yzerman, Det.	.12	.25
K	Darren Turcotte, NYR	.05	.10
L	Mike Vernon, Goalie, Cal.	.05	.10
	Panel 4	.12	.25
M	Pierre Turgeon, Buf.	.12	.25
N	Doug Wilson, Chi.	.05	.10
O	Donald Beaupre, Goalie, Wash.	.07	.15
P	Sergei Makarov, Cal.	.12	.25

THE TORONTO STAR

— 1954 - 67 WEEKEND MAGAZINE ISSUE —

These photos appeared in the Star Weekend Magazine between 1958 and 1967 to help boost sales. No photos appeared during 1964-65.

Card Size: 5 1/2" x 6 1/2"
Face: Four colour
Back: Newsprint
Imprint: None
Complete Set No.: Unknown
Complete Set Price: Unknown
Common Photo   5.00   10.00

1954 ISSUE

No.	Player	VG	EX
1	Ted Kennedy, Tor., (Vol. No. 4)	7.50	15.00
2	Elmer Lach, Mon., (Vol. No. 6)	5.00	10.00
3	Gus Mortson, Chi., (Vol. No. 7)	5.00	10.00
4	Ted Lindsay, Det., (Vol. No. *)	7.50	15.00
5	Milt Schmidt, Bos., (Vol. No. 9)	6.00	12.00
6	Ed Sandford, Bos., Vol. No. 10)	5.00	10.00
7	Wally Hergesheimer, NYR, (Vol. No. 11)	5.00	10.00

1955 ISSUE

No.	Player	VG	EX
8	Harry Lumley, Goalie, Tor.	6.00	12.00
9	Fleming Mackell, Bos.	5.00	10.00
10	Harry Watson, Chi.	6.00	12.00
11	Earl Reibel, Det.	5.00	10.00
12	Bill Quackenbush, Bos.	5.00	10.00
13	Bill Gadsby, NYR	5.00	10.00
14	Jimmy Thomson, Tor.	5.00	10.00

1958 - 59 ISSUE

No.	Player	VG	EX
15	Dickie Moore, Mon.	7.50	15.00
16	Glenn Hall, Goalie, Chi.	7.50	15.00
17	Frank Mahovlich, Tor.	10.00	20.00
18	Henri Richard, Mon.	7.50	15.00
19	Camille Henry, NYR	5.00	10.00
20	Marcel Pronovost , Det.	5.00	10.00
21	Eddie Litzenberger, Chi.	5.00	10.00
22	Bob Pulford, Tor.	5.00	10.00
23	Andy Bathgate, NYR	7.50	15.00
24	Fern Flaman, Bos.	5.00	10.00
25	Doug Harvey, Mon.	7.50	15.00
26	Vic Stasiuk, Bos.	5.00	10.00
27	Alex Delvecchio, Det.	5.00	10.00

1959 - 60 ISSUE

No.	Player	VG	EX
28	Tom Johnson, Mon.	5.00	10.00
29	Dick Duff , Tor.	7.50	15.00
30	Norm Ullman, Det.	7.50	15.00
31	Jacques Plante, Goalie, Mon.	12.50	25.00
32	Bobby Hull, Chi.	15.00	30.00
33	Bronco Horvath, Bos.	5.00	10.00
34	Andy Hebenton, NYR	5.00	10.00
35	Leo Boivin, Bos.	5.00	10.00
36	Terry Sawchuk, Goalie, Det.	12.50	25.00
37	Billy Harris, Tor.	5.00	10.00
38	Tod Sloan, Chi.	5.00	10.00
39	Ralph Backstrom, Mon.	5.00	10.00
40	Goerge (Red) Sullivan, NYR	5.00	10.00
41	Carl Brewer, Tor.	5.00	10.00

1960 - 61 ISSUE

No.	Player	VG	EX
42	Gordie Howe, Det.	20.00	40.00
43	Jean Beliveau, Mon.	17.50	35.00
44	George Armstrong, Tor.	15.00	30.00
45	Billy Hay, Chi.	5.00	10.00
46	Lou Fontinato, NYR	5.00	10.00
47	Jerry Toppazzini, Bos.	5.00	10.00
48	Bernie Geoffrion. Mon.	10.00	20.00
49	Red Kelly. Tor.	7.50	15.00
50	John Bucyk. Bos.	7.50	15.00
51	Dean Prentice, NYR	5.00	10.00
52	Pierre Pilote, Chi.	5.00	10.00
53	Ron Stewart, Tor.	5.00	10.00
54	Don Marshall, Mon.	5.00	10.00

PHOTOGRAPH NOT AVAILABLE AT PRESS TIME

1961 - 62 ISSUE

No.	Player	VG	EX
55	Claude Provost, Mon,	5.00	10.00
56	Elmer Vasko, Chi.	5.00	10.00
57	Dave Keon, Tor.	7.50	15.00
58	Warren Godfrey, Det.	5.00	10.00
59	Gump Worsley, Goalie, NYR	10.00	20.00
60	Doug Mohns, Bos.	5.00	10.00
61	Marcel Bonin, Mon.	5.00	10.00
62	Alan Stanley, Tor.	7.50	15.00
63	Johnny Bower, Goalie, Tor.	7.50	15.00
64	Stan Mikita, Chi.	7.50	15.00
65	Don McKenney, Bos.	5.00	10.00
66	Doug Harvey, NYR	7.50	15.00
67	Jean Guy Talbot, Mon,	5.00	10.00

1962 - 63 ISSUE

No.	Player	VG	EX
68	Frank Mahovlich, Tor.	7.50	15.00
69	Gilles Tremblay, Mon.	5.00	10.00
70	Ab McDonald, Chi.	5.00	10.00
71	Alex Delvecchio, Det.	5.00	10.00
72	Earl Ingarfield, NYR	5.00	10.00
73	Tim Horton, Tor.	7.50	15.00
74	Glen Hall, Goalie, Chi.	7.50	15.00
75	Murray Oliver, Bos.	5.00	10.00
76	Marcel Pronovost, Det.	5.00	10.00
77	Henri Richard, Mon.	7.50	15.00
78	Andy Bathgate, NYR	7.50	15.00

1963 - 64 ISSUE

No.	Player	VG	EX
79	Bobby Rousseau, Mon.	5.00	10.00
80	Bob Pulford, Tor.	5.00	10.00
81	Parker MacDonald, Det.	5.00	10.00
82	Jacques Plante, Goalie, NYR	10.00	20.00
83	Kenny Wharram, Chi.	5.00	10.00
84	Tom Williams, Bos.	5.00	10.00
85	Gordie Howe, Det..	12.50	25.00
86	Dave Balon, Mon.	5.00	10.00
87	Phil Goyette, NYR	5.00	10.00
88	Carl Brewer, Tor.	5.00	10.00
89	Terry Sawchuk, Goalie, Det.	10.00	20.00
90	Bobby Hull, Chi.	10.00	20.00
91	John Ferguson, Mon.	5.00	10.00

1965 - 66 ALL STAR TEAM

No.	Player	VG	EX
92	Glenn Hall, Goalie, Chi.	7.50	15.00
93	Jacques Laperriere, Mon.	5.00	10.00
94	Pierre Pilote, Chi.	5.00	10.00
95	Gordie Howe, Det.	12.50	25.00
96	Stan Mikita, Chicago	7.50	15.00
97	Bobby Hull, Chi.	10.00	20.00

1966 - 67 ISSUE

No.	Player	VG	EX
98	Frank Mahovlich, Tor.	7.50	15.00
99	Bobby Rousseau, Mon.	5.00	10.00
100	Pat Stapleton, Chi.	5.00	10.00
101	Roger Crozier, Goalie, Det.	5.00	10.00
102	Don Marshall, NYR	5.00	10.00
103	Terry Sawchuk, Goalie, Tor.	10.00	20.00
104	Jean Beliveau, Mon.	10.00	20.00
105	Doug Mohns, Chi.	5.00	10.00
106	Bob Nevin New York	5.00	10.00
107	Pit Martin, Bos.	5.00	10.00
108	Allan Stanley, Tor.	5.00	10.00
109	Harry Howell, NYR	5.00	10.00

266 • THE TORONTO STAR — 1956 - 67 DAILY STAR HOCKEY PHOTOS —

— 1956 - 67 DAILY STAR HOCKEY PHOTOS —

Photograph Size: Unknown
Face: Four colour, white border; Name
Back: Newsprint
Imprint: None
Complete Set No.: Unknown
Complete Set Price: Unknown
Common Photo: 5.00   10.00

1956 ISSUE

No.	Players / Date Issued	VG	EX
1	Team photo Kitchener-Waterloo Olympic Team, Feb. 25, 1956	5.00	10.00
2	Team photo, Chicago Black Hawks, March 10, 1956	5.00	10.00
3	Team photo New York Rangers, March 24, 1956	5.00	10.00

1957 ISSUE

No.	Players / Date Issued	VG	EX
4	E. Chadwick, Goalie; T. Horton, Tor. Nov. 2	12.50	25.00
5	S. Smith; B. Pulford, Tor., Nov. 9	5.00	10.00
6	D. Duff; J. Morrison, Tor., Nov. 16	5.00	10.00
7	G. Mortson; J. Thompson, Chi., Nov. 23	5.00	10.00
8	T. Lindsay; E. Nesterenko, Chi., Nov. 30	7.50	15.00
9	Toronto Maple Leafs Team Photo, Dec. 7	10.00	20.00
10	M. Richard; H. Richard, Mon., Dec. 14	15.00	30.00
11	B. Geoffrion; D. Harvey, Mon., Dec. 21	12.50	25.00
12	A. Hebenton; L. Worsley, Goalie, NYR, Dec. 28	7.50	15.00

1958 ISSUE

No.	Players / Date Issued	VG	EX
13	Montreal Canadiens Team Photo, Jan. 4	10.00	20.00
14	F. Flaman; D. Simmons, Goalie, Bos., Jan. 11	5.00	10.00
15	B. Gadsby; C. Henry, NYR, Jan. 18	5.00	10.00
16	D. McKenney; R. Chevrefils, Bos., Jan. 25	5.00	10.00
17	G. Howe; R. Kelly, Det., Feb. 1	22.50	45.00
18	Detroit Red Wings Team Photo, Feb. 8	10.00	20.00
19	J. Plante; J. Beliveau, Mon., Feb. 15	15.00	30.00
20	New York Rangers Team Photo, Feb. 22	10.00	20.00
21	Whitby Dunlops Team Photo, Mar. 1	7.50	15.00
22	A. Delvecchio; T. Sawchuk, Goalie, Det., Mar. 8	15.00	30.00
23	G. Armstrong; B. Cullen, Tor., Mar. 15	10.00	20.00
24	R. Stewart; F. Mahovlich, Mar. 22	12.50	25.00

STARS OF THE WORLDS FASTEST GAME
1958 ISSUE

No.	Players / Date Issued	VG	EX
25	G. Armstrong; B. Olmstead; F. Mahovlich, Tor., Nov. 29	10.00	20.00
26	D. Duff; B. Harris; R. Stewart, Tor., Dec. 6	7.50	15.00
27	G. Howe; N. Ullman; A. Delvecchio, Det., Dec. 13	22.50	45.00
28	Montreal Canadiens Team Photo, Dec. 20	10.00	20.00
29	K. Wharram; D. Lewicki; T. Lindsay, Chi., Dec. 27	10.00	20.00

1959 ISSUE

No.	PlayerS / Date Issued	VG	EX
30	H. Richard; M. Richard, Mon., Jan. 3	15.00	30.00
31	E. Litzenberger; T. Sloan; L. Ferguson, Chi., Jan. 10	7.50	15.00
32	Boston Bruins Team Photo, Jan. 17	10.00	20.00
33	Minor Hockey Picture of Boys on Ice, Double Page, Jan. 24	7.50	15.00
34	D. Moore; J. Beliveau; A. McDonald, Mon., Jan. 31	12.50	25.00
35	New York Rangers Team Photo, Feb. 7	10.00	20.00
36	F. Flaman; D. Simmons, Goalie; J. Morrison, Bos., Feb. 14	5.00	10.00
37	Detroit Red Wings Team Photo, Feb. 21	10.00	20.00
38	A. Bathgate; L. Popein; D. Prentice, NYR, Feb. 28	7.50	15.00
39	Toronto Maple Leafs Team Photo, Mar. 7	10.00	20.00
40	Belleville McFarlands Canada's Hockey Champions, Mar. 14	7.50	15.00
41	J. G. Talbot; T. Johnston; B. Turner, Mon., Mar. 21	5.00	10.00

CARDS NOT AVAILABLE AT PRESSTIME

1959 ACTION SHOTS

No.	Player / Date Issued	VG	EX
42	Harry Lumley, Goalie, Bos., Dec. 15	7.50	15.00
43	Bert Olmstead, Tor., Dec. 26	5.00	10.00

1960 ACTION SHOTS

No.	Player / Date Issued	VG	EX
44	Henri Richard, Mon., Jan. 2	7.50	15.00
45	Gordie Howe, Det., Jan. 9	20.00	40.00
46	Johnny Bower, Goalie, Tor., Jan. 16	12.50	25.00
47	George (Red) Sullivan, NYR, Jan. 23	5.00	10.00
48	Tod Sloan, Chi., Jan. 30	5.00	10.00
49	Bob Armstrong, Bos., Feb. 6	5.00	10.00
50	Jacques Plante, Goalie, Mon., Feb. 13	17.50	35.00
51	Tom Johnson, Mon., Feb. 20	5.00	10.00
52	Glenn Hall, Goalie, Chi., Feb. 27	10.00	20.00
53	Bill Gadsby, NYR, Mar. 5	5.00	10.00

STARS OF THE WORLDS FASTEST GAME
1960 ACTION SHOTS

No.	Player / Date Issued	VG	EX
54	Bobby Hull, Chi., Dec. 10	20.00	40.00
55	Frank Mahovlich, Tor, Dec. 17	15.00	30.00
56	Terry Sawchuk, Goalie Det., Dec. 24	17.50	35.00

1961 ACTION SHOTS

No.	Player / Date Issued	VG	EX
57	Elmer Vasko, Chi., Jan. 7	5.00	10.00
58	Andy Bathgate, NYR, Jan. 14	7.50	15.00
59	Ralph Backstrom, Mon., Jan. 28	7.50	15.00
60	Fern Flaman, Bos., Feb. 4	5.00	10.00
61	Allan Stanley, Tor., Feb. 11	7.50	15.00
62	Gump Worsley, Goalie, NYR, Feb. 18	10.00	20.00
63	Not issued		
64	Marcel Pronovost, Det., Mar. 4	5.00	10.00
65	Don Marshall, Mon., Mar. 11	5.00	10.00

1961 - 62 N.H.L. STARS IN ACTION
ACTION SHOTS

No.	Player / Date Issued	VG	EX
66	Elmer Vasko, Chi., Jan. 6	5.00	10.00
67	Gump Worsley, Goalie, NYR, Jan. 13	10.00	20.00
68	Don McKenney, Bos., Jan. 20	5.00	10.00
69	Eddie Shack, Tor., Jan. 27	7.50	15.00
70	Claude Provost, Mon., Feb. 3	5.00	10.00
71	Gordie Howe, Det., Feb. 10	17.50	35.00
72	Glenn Hall, Goalie, Chi., Feb. 17	7.50	15.00
73	Doug Harvey, NYR, Feb. 24	7.50	15.00
74	Jacques Plante, Goalie, Mon., Mar. 3	12.50	25.00
75	Carl Brewer, Tor., Mar. 10	5.00	10.00
76	Dave Keon, Tor., Mar. 17	7.50	15.00
77	Bill Gadsby, NYR, Mar. 24	5.00	10.00

STARS OF THE WORLDS FASTEST GAME
1962 ACTION SHOTS

No.	Player / Date Issued	VG	EX
78	Ron Stewart, Tor., Dec. 8	5.00	10.00
79	Robert Perreault, Goalie, Bos., Dec. 15, (2 pages)	5.00	10.00
80	Dean Prentice, NYR, Dec. 22	5.00	10.00
81	Terry Sawchuk, Goalie Det., Dec. 29, (2 Pages)	10.00	20.00
82	Bobby Hull, Chi., Dec. 29	15.00	30.00

1963 ACTION SHOTS

No.	Player / Date Issued	VG	EX
83	Louie Fontinato, Mon., Jan. 5, (2 Pages.)	5.00	10.00
84	Frank Mahovlich, Tor., Jan. 12	10.00	20.00
85	Bill Hay, Chi., Jan. 19	5.00	10.00
86	Charlie Burns, Bos., Jan. 26	5.00	10.00
87	Rod Gilbert, NYR, Feb. 2	5.00	10.00
88	Henri Richard, Mon., Feb. 9	7.50	15.00
89	Camill Henry, NYR, Feb. 16	5.00	10.00
90	Leo Boivin, Bos., Feb. 23	5.00	10.00
91	Dickie Moore, Mon., Mar. 2	7.50	15.00
92	Parker MacDonald, Det., Mar. 9	5.00	10.00
93	Kenny Wharram, Chi., Mar. 16	5.00	10.00
94	Kent Douglas, Tor., Mar. 23	5.00	10.00

STARS OF THE WORLDS FASTEST GAME
1963 ISSUE

No.	Player / Date Issued	VG	EX
95	John Bucyk, Bos., Dec. 7	7.50	15.00
96	Bob Pulford, Tor., Dec. 14	5.00	10.00
97	Stan Mikita, Chi., Dec. 21	7.50	15.00
98	Henri Richard, Mon., Dec. 28	7.50	15.00

1964 ACTION SHOTS

No.	Player / Date Issued	VG	EX
99	Bobby Hull, Chi., Jan. 4	12.50	25.00
100	Bobby Rousseau, Mon., Jan. 11	5.00	10.00
101	Tim Horton, Tor., Jan. 18	10.00	20.00
102	Andy Bathgate, NYR, Jan. 25	7.50	15.00
103	Bob Baun, Tor., Feb. 1	5.00	10.00
104	Glenn Hall, Goalie, Chi., Feb. 8	7.50	15.00
105	Alan Stanley, Tor., Feb. 15	5.00	10.00
106	Vic Hadfield, NYR, Feb. 22	5.00	10.00
107	Kenny Wharram, Chi., Feb. 29	5.00	10.00
108	Gordie Howe, Det., Mar. 7	15.00	30.00
109	Charlie Hodge, Goalie, Mon., Mar. 14	5.00	10.00
110	Marcel Pronovost, Det., Mar. 21	5.00	10.00
111	George Armstrong, Tor., Mar. 28	7.50	15.00
112	Jean Beliveau, Mon., Apr. 4	10.00	20.00

STARS OF THE WORLDS FASTEST GAME
1964 MULTI-PHOTO PAGES

No.	Player / Date Issued	VG	EX
113	Stan Mikita, Chi., Dec. 5	7.50	15.00
114	Bobby Hull, Chi., Dec. 12	12.50	25.00
115	Tim Horton, Tor., Dec. 19	10.00	20.00
116	John Beliveau, Mon., Dec. 26	10.00	20.00

1965 MULTI-PHOTO PAGES

No.	Player / Date Issued	VG	EX
117	Bob Pulford, Tor., Jan. 2	5.00	10.00
118	Dean Prentice, NYR, Jan. 9	5.00	10.00
119	Ron Ellis, Tor., Jan. 16	7.50	15.00
120	Rod Gilbert, NYR, Jan. 23	5.00	10.00
121	Jacques Lapierrer, Mon., Jan. 30	5.00	10.00
122	Terry Sawchuk, Goalie, Tor., Feb. 6	10.00	20.00
123	February 13, Not Issue		
124	Charlie Hodge, Goalie, Mon., Feb. 20	5.00	10.00
125	Vic Hadfield, NYR, Feb. 27	5.00	10.00
126	Frank Mahovlich, Tor., Mar. 6	7.50	15.00
127	Glenn Hall, Goalie, Chi., Mar. 13	7.50	15.00
128	Ken Wharram, Chi., Mar. 20	5.00	10.00
129	Norm Ullman, Det., Mar. 27	5.00	10.00

HOCKEY'S HOTTEST
1965 ACTION SHOTS

No.	Player / Date Issued	VG	EX
130	Marcel Pronovost, Tor., Dec. 18	5.00	10.00
131	Henri Richard, Mon., Dec. 25	7.50	15.00

1966 ACTION SHOTS

No.	Player / Date Issued	VG	EX
132	Norm Ullman, Det., Jan. 1	5.00	10.00
133	Frank Mahovlich, Tor., Jan. 8	10.00	20.00
134	Ed Giacomin, Goalie, NYR, Jan. 15	7.50	15.00
135	Jean Beliveau, Mon., Jan. 22	10.00	20.00
136	Doug Mohns, Chi., Jan. 29	5.00	10.00
137	Eddie Shack, Tor., Feb. 5	7.50	15.00
138	Claude Provost, Mon., Feb. 12	5.00	10.00
139	Ted Green, Bos., Feb. 19	5.00	10.00
140	Tim Horton, Tor., Feb. 26	10.00	20.00
141	Jacques Lapierrer, Mon., Mar. 5	5.00	10.00
142	Bill Hay, Chi., Mar. 12	5.00	10.00
143	Dave Keon, Tor., Mar. 19	7.50	15.00
144	J. C. Tremblay, Mon., Mar. 26	5.00	10.00
145	Bob Baun, Tor., Apr. 2	5.00	10.00

The Toronto Star
1963-64 Hockey Stars in Action
Photo No. 33,
Kent Douglas

The Toronto Star
1963-64 Hockey Stars in Action
Photo No. 35,
Tim Horton

1963 - 64 HOCKEY STARS IN ACTION

These photos are unnumbered and are listed below alphabetically by team and then by player within the team.

Coin Size: 4 3/4"X 6 11/16"
Face: Four colour, white border
Back: Black on paper stock; Name, Team, Player history
Imprint: None
Complete Set No.: 42
Complete Set Price: 90.00 185.00 365.00
Common Player: 1.50 3.00 6.00

BOSTON BRUINS

No.	Player	VG	EX	NRMT
1	Leo Boivin	2.25	4.50	9.00
2	John Bucyk	2.75	5.50	11.00
3	Jean-Guy Gendron	1.50	3.00	6.00

CHICAGO BLACK HAWKS

No.	Player	VG	EX	NRMT
4	Glenn Hall, Goalie	3.25	6.50	13.00
5	Billy Hay	1.50	3.00	6.00
6	Bobby Hull	7.50	15.00	30.00
7	Stan Mikita	3.75	7.50	15.00
8	Eric Nesterenko	1.50	3.00	6.00
9	Elmer Vasko	1.50	3.00	6.00
10	Kenny Wharram	1.50	3.00	6.00

DETROIT RED WINGS

No.	Player	VG	EX	NRMT
11	Alex Delvecchio, Error	2.75	5.50	11.00
12	Bill Gadsby	2.00	4.00	8.00
13	Gordie Howe	15.00	27.50	55.00
14	Parker MacDonald	1.50	3.00	6.00
15	Marcel Pronovost	2.00	4.00	8.00
16	Terry Sawchuk, Goalie	5.50	11.00	22.00
17	Norm Ullman	2.75	5.50	11.00

MONTREAL CANADIENS

No.	Player	VG	EX	NRMT
18	Jean Beliveau	4.50	9.00	18.00
19	Bernie Geoffrion	3.50	7.00	14.00
20	Dickie Moore	2.75	5.50	11.00
21	Claude Provost	1.50	3.00	6.00
22	Henri Richard	2.75	5.50	11.00
23	Jean-Guy Talbot	1.50	3.00	6.00
24	Gilles Tremblay	1.50	3.00	6.00
25	J.C. Tremblay	1.50	3.00	6.00

NEW YORK RANGERS

No.	Player	VG	EX	NRMT
26	Andy Bathgate	2.25	4.50	9.00
27	Doug Harvey	3.50	7.00	14.00
28	Camille Henry	1.50	3.00	6.00

TORONTO MAPLE LEAFS

No.	Player	VG	EX	NRMT
29	George Armstrong	2.25	4.50	9.00
30	Bob Baun	1.50	3.00	6.00
31	John Bower, Goalie	3.25	6.50	13.00
32	Carl Brewer	1.50	3.00	6.00
33	Kent Douglas	1.50	3.00	6.00
34	Dick Duff	1.50	3.00	6.00
35	Tim Horton	3.25	6.50	13.00
36	Red Kelly	2.75	5.50	11.00
37	Dave Keon	2.00	4.00	8.00
38	Frank Mahovlich	4.00	8.00	16.00
39	Bob Pulford	2.00	4.00	8.00
40	Eddie Shack	2.50	5.00	10.00
41	Allan Stanley	2.00	4.00	8.00
42	Ron Stewart	1.50	3.00	6.00

TRIPPING

— 1964 - 65 REGULAR ISSUE —

Card Size: 4 1/8" X 5 1/8"
Face: Four colour, white strip at bottom on paper stock; Name, Jersey number, Team, Play-by-play action
Back: Blank
Imprint: None
Complete Set No.: 48
Complete Set Price: 95.00 190.00 375.00
Common Player: 1.50 3.00 6.00
Album: 12.50 25.00 50.00

BOSTON BRUINS

No.	Player	VG	EX	NRMT
1	Leo Boivin	2.00	4.00	8.00
2	Ted Green	1.50	3.00	6.00
3	Tom Johnson	2.00	4.00	8.00
4	Forbes Kennedy	1.50	3.00	6.00
5	Orland Kurtenbach	1.75	3.50	7.00
6	Wayne Rivers	1.50	3.00	6.00

CHICAGO BLACK HAWKS

No.	Player	VG	EX	NRMT
7	Glenn Hall, Goalie	3.00	6.00	12.00
8	Billy Hay	1.50	3.00	6.00
9	Wayne Hillman	1.50	3.00	6.00
10	Bobby Hull	7.00	14.00	28.00
11	Al MacNeil	1.50	3.00	6.00
12	Chico Maki	1.50	3.00	6.00
13	John McKenzie	1.50	3.00	6.00
14	Stan Mikita	3.50	7.00	14.00
15	Pierre Pilote	2.00	4.00	8.00
16	Elmer Vasko	1.50	3.00	6.00

DETROIT RED WINGS

No.	Player	VG	EX	NRMT
17	Alex Delvecchio	2.50	5.00	10.00
18	Paul Henderson	2.25	4.50	9.00
19	Gordie Howe	12.50	25.00	50.00
20	Larry Jeffrey	1.50	3.00	6.00
21	Parker MacDonald	2.00	4.00	8.00
22	Marcel Pronovost, Error	2.00	4.00	8.00
23	Floyd Smith	1.50	3.00	6.00
24	Norm Ullman	2.50	5.00	10.00

MONTREAL CANADIENS

No.	Player	VG	EX	NRMT
25	Dave Balon	1.50	3.00	6.00
26	Jean Beliveau	5.00	10.00	20.00
27	Red Berenson	1.50	3.00	6.00
28	Charlie Hodge, Goalie	1.75	3.50	7.00
29	Jacques Laperriere	2.00	4.00	8.00
30	Claude Provost	1.50	3.00	6.00
31	Henri Richard	2.50	5.00	10.00
32	J.C. Tremblay	1.50	3.00	6.00

NEW YORK RANGERS

No.	Player	VG	EX	NRMT
33	Rod Gilbert	2.50	5.00	10.00
34	Harry Howell	2.00	4.00	8.00
35	Jim Neilson	1.50	3.00	6.00
36	Jacques Plante, Goalie	3.50	7.00	14.00

TORONTO MAPLE LEAFS

No.	Player	VG	EX	NRMT
37	Andy Bathgate	2.00	4.00	8.00
38	Bob Baun	1.50	3.00	6.00
39	Carl Brewer	1.50	3.00	6.00
40	Billy Harris	1.50	3.00	6.00
41	Tim Horton	3.75	7.50	15.00
42	Dave Keon	2.50	5.00	10.00
43	Frank Mahovlich	3.25	7.50	15.00
44	Don McKenney	1.50	3.00	6.00
45	Jim Pappin	1.50	3.00	6.00
46	Bob Pulford	2.00	4.00	8.00
47	Allan Stanley	2.00	4.00	8.00
48	Ron Stewart	1.50	3.00	6.00

The Toronto Star
1964-65 Issue
Card No. 1,
Leo Boivin

The Toronto Star
1964-65 Issue
Card No. 22, Error, Name misspelled Provost on face

NABISCO

— 1955 - 56 ISSUE —

This set is not complete. We would appreciate hearing from anyone would could supply further information.

Coin Size: 1 15/16" x 2 7/8"
Face: Four colour print; Number
Back: Black and white; Name, Number, Resume, Bilingual
Imprint: The Canadian Shredded Wheat Company Ltd. Niagara Falls, Ont.
ACC: FC-26-3
Complete Set No.: 70
Complete Set Price: Unknown

No.	Player	VG	EX	NRMT
62	Ted Reeve, Stick Handling	2.50	.500	10.00

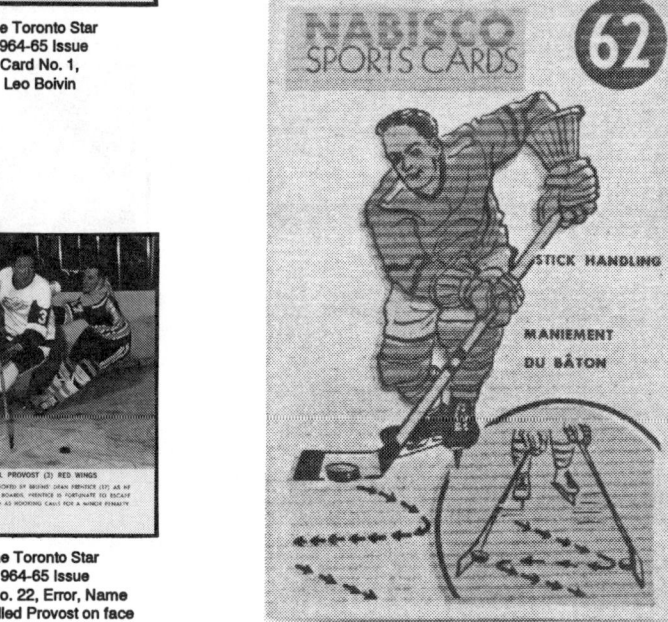

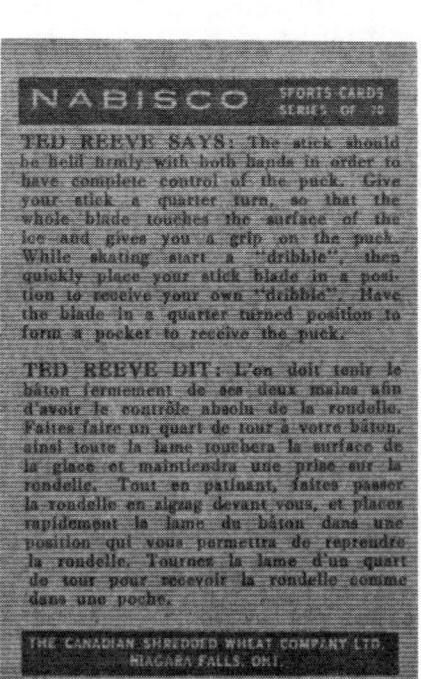

Nabisco
1955-56 Issue
Card No. 62, Ted Reeves

ADVENTURE GUM

— 1956 ISSUE —

This is a sport and non-sport action series. We would appreciate hearing from anyone who could help with further information.

Card Size: 2 1/2" x 3/12"
Face: Four colour print
Back: Blue and grey; Name, Number, Resume
Imprint: Printed in U.S.A. Gum Products Inc 1956
ACC: R-749
Complete Set No.: Unknown
Complete Set Price: Unknown
Common Player:

No.	Player	VG	EX	NRMT
63	Hockey's Hardy Perennials Gordie Howe, Chuck Raynor	12.50	25.00	50.00

SHIRRIFF

— 1960 - 61 HOCKEY COINS —

This is the first year of issue for Shirriff Foods. These hockey coins were used as premiums in Shirriff's desserts. There is a clear plastic crystal on each coin. The paper was loose under the crystal.

Coin Size: 1 9/16" Diameter
Face: Four colour; Name, Number
Back: "SAVE 120 'HOCKEY COINS' COLLECTIONNEZ LEZ 120 PIÉCES DE HOCKEY"
Imprint: Shirriff Lushus Jelly & Puddings Pat. Pend.
Complete Set No.: 120
Complete Set Price: 120.00 240.00 475.00
Common Player: .85 1.75 3.50

TORONTO MAPLE LEAFS

No.	Player	VG	EX	NRMT
1	Johnny Bower, Goalie	3.00	6.00	12.00
2	Dick Duff	.85	1.75	3.50
3	Carl Brewer	.85	1.75	3.50
4	Red Kelly	2.00	4.00	8.00
5	Tim Horton	4.25	8.50	17.00
6	Allan Stanley	1.25	2.50	5.00
7	Bob Baun	.85	1.75	3.50
8	Billy Harris	.85	1.75	3.50
9	George Armstrong	1.75	3.50	7.00
10	Ron Stewart	.85	1.75	3.50
11	Bert Olmstead	1.25	2.50	5.00
12	Frank Mahovlich	4.25	8.50	17.00
13	Bob Pulford	1.25	2.50	5.00
14	Garry Edmundson	.85	1.75	3.50
15	Johnny Wilson	.85	1.75	3.50
16	Larry Regan	.85	1.75	3.50
17	Gerry James	.85	1.75	3.50
18	Rudy Migay	.85	1.75	3.50
19	Gerry Ehman	.85	1.75	3.50
20	Punch Imlach, Coach	1.50	3.00	6.00

MONTREAL CANADIENS

No.	Player	VG	EX	NRMT
21	Jacques Plante, Goalie	5.00	10.00	20.00
22	Dickie Moore	2.75	5.50	11.00
23	Don Marshall	.85	1.75	3.50
24	Al Langlois	.85	1.75	3.50
25	Tom Johnson	1.25	2.50	5.00
26	Doug Harvey	2.75	5.50	11.00
27	Phil Goyette	.85	1.75	3.50
28	Bernie Geoffrion	4.00	8.00	16.00
29	Marcel Bonin	.85	1.75	3.50
30	Jean Beliveau	6.75	13.50	27.00
31	Ralph Backstrom	.85	1.75	3.50
32	Andre Pronovost	.85	1.75	3.50
33	Claude Provost	.85	1.75	3.50
34	Henri Richard	2.25	4.50	9.00
35	Jean-Guy Talbot	.85	1.75	3.50
36	J.C. Tremblay	.85	1.75	3.50
37	Bob Turner	.85	1.75	3.50
38	Bill Hicke	.85	1.75	3.50
39	Charlie Hodge, Goalie	1.25	2.50	5.00
40	Toe Blake, Coach	1.25	2.50	5.00

Adventure Gum
1956 Issue, Coin No. 63,
Hockey's Hardy Perennials
G. Howe, C. Raynor

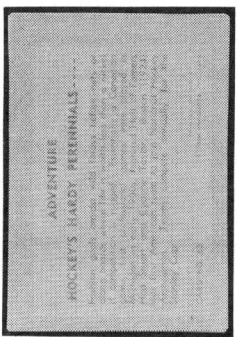

Adventure Gum
1956 Issue, Coin No. 63,
Hockey's Hardy Perennials
G. Howe, C. Raynor

Shirriff
1960-61 Hockey Coins
Coin No. 28,
Bernie Geoffrion

Shirriff
1960-61 Hockey Coins
Coin No. 63,
Bobby Hull

DETROIT RED WINGS

No.	Player	VG	EX	NRMT
41	Terry Sawchuk, Goalie	6.00	12.00	24.00
42	Gordie Howe	12.50	25.00	50.00
43	John McKenzie	.85	1.75	3.50
44	Alex Delvecchio	2.50	5.00	10.00
45	Norm Ullman	2.00	4.00	8.00
46	Jack McIntyre	.85	1.75	3.50
47	Barry Cullen	.85	1.75	3.50
48	Val Fonteyne	.85	1.75	3.50
49	Warren Godfrey	.85	1.75	3.50
50	Peter Goegan	.85	1.75	3.50
51	Gerry Melnyk, Error	.85	1.75	3.50
52	Marc Reaume	.85	1.75	3.50
53	Gary Aldcorn	.85	1.75	3.50
54	Len Lunde	.85	1.75	3.50
55	Murray Oliver	.85	1.75	3.50
56	Marcel Pronovost	1.50	3.00	6.00
57	Howie Glover	.85	1.75	3.50
58	Gerry Odrowski	.85	1.75	3.50
59	Parker MacDonald	.85	1.75	3.50
60	Sid Abel, Coach	1.25	2.50	5.00

CHICAGO BLACK HAWKS

No.	Player	VG	EX	NRMT
61	Glenn Hall, Goalie	4.00	8.00	16.00
62	Ed Litzenberger	.85	1.75	3.50
63	Bobby Hull	8.50	17.00	34.00
64	Tod Sloan	.85	1.75	3.50
65	Murray Balfour	1.00	2.00	4.00
66	Pierre Pilote	1.50	3.00	6.00
67	Al Arbour	1.50	3.00	6.00
68	Earl Balfour	.85	1.75	3.50
69	Eric Nesterenko	1.00	2.00	4.00
70	Kenny Wharram	.85	1.75	3.50
71	Stan Mikita	3.75	7.50	15.00
72	Ab McDonald	.85	1.75	3.50
73	Elmer Vasko	.85	1.75	3.50
74	Dollard St. Laurent	.85	1.75	3.50
75	Ron Murphy	.85	1.75	3.50
76	Jack Evans	.85	1.75	3.50
77	Billy Hay	.85	1.75	3.50
78	Reggie Fleming	.85	1.75	3.50
79	Cecil Hoekstra	.85	1.75	3.50
80	Tommy Ivan, Coach	.85	1.75	3.50

NEW YORK RANGERS

No.	Player	VG	EX	NRMT
81	Jack McCartan, Goalie	.85	1.75	3.50
82	Red Sullivan	.85	1.75	3.50
83	Camille Henry	.85	1.75	3.50
84	Larry Popein	.85	1.75	3.50
85	John Hanna	.85	1.75	3.50
86	Harry Howell	2.00	4.00	8.00
87	Eddie Shack	2.00	4.00	8.00
88	Irv Spencer	.85	1.75	3.50
89	Andy Bathgate	2.00	4.00	8.00
90	Bill Gadsby	1.25	2.50	5.00
91	Andy Hebenton	.85	1.75	3.50
92	Earl Ingarfield, Sr.	.85	1.75	3.50
93	Don Johns	.85	1.75	3.50
94	Dave Balon	.85	1.75	3.50
95	Jim Morrison	.85	1.75	3.50
96	Ken Schinkel	.85	1.75	3.50
97	Louie Fontinato	.85	1.75	3.50
98	Ted Hampson	.85	1.75	3.50
99	Brian Cullen	.85	1.75	3.50
100	Alf Pike, Coach	.85	1.75	3.50

BOSTON BRUINS

No.	Player	VG	EX	NRMT
101	Don Simmons, Goalie	.85	1.75	3.50
102	Fern Flaman	1.25	2.50	5.00
103	Vic Stasiuk	.85	1.75	3.50
104	John Bucyk	2.25	4.50	9.00
105	Bronco Horvath	.85	1.75	3.50
106	Doug Mohns	.85	1.75	3.50
107	Leo Boivin	1.25	2.50	5.00
108	Don McKenney	.85	1.75	3.50
109	John-Guy Gendron	1.00	2.00	4.00
110	Jerry Toppazzini	.85	1.75	3.50
111	Dick Meissner	.85	1.75	3.50
112	Aut Erickson	.85	1.75	3.50

270 • SHIRRIFF — 1961 - 62 SHIRRIFF / SALADA

No.	Player	VG	EX	NRMT
113	Jim Bartlett	.85	1.75	3.50
114	Orval Tessier	.85	1.75	3.50
115	Billy Carter	.85	1.75	3.50
116	Dallas Smith	.85	1.75	3.50
117	Leo Labine	.85	1.75	3.50
118	Bob Armstrong	.85	1.75	3.50
119	Bruce Gamble, Goalie	.85	1.75	3.50
120	Milt Schmidt, Coach	2.25	4.50	9.00

— 1961 - 62 SHIRRIFF / SALADA —

HOCKEY COINS

The hockey coins for the 1961-62 season were produced for both Shirriff and Salada. The only difference is the maker's name. Team shield holders were abailable for this issue.

Coin Size: 1 7/8" Diameter
Face: Four colour; Name, Number, Year
Back: "SAVE 120 'HOCKEY COINS' COLLECTIONNEZ LEZ 120 PIÉCES DE HOCKEY"
Imprint: Shirriff Lushus Jelly & Puddings Pat. Pend.
Complete Set No.: 120
Complete Set Price: 85.00   175.00   350.00
Common Player: .75   1.50   3.00

BOSTON BRUINS

No.	Player	VG	EX	NRMT
1	Cliff Pennington	.75	1.50	3.00
2	Dallas Smith	.75	1.50	3.00
3	Andre Pronovost	.75	1.50	3.00
4	Charlie Burns	.75	1.50	3.00
5	Leo Boivin	1.25	2.50	5.00
6	Don McKenney	.75	1.50	3.00
7	John Bucyk	2.00	4.00	8.00
8	Murray Oliver	.75	1.50	3.00
9	Jerry Toppazzini	.75	1.50	3.00
10	Doug Mohns	.75	1.50	3.00
11	Don Head, Goalie	.75	1.50	3.00
12	Bob Armstrong	.75	1.50	3.00
13	Pat Stapleton	.75	1.50	3.00
14	Orland Kurtenbach	.75	1.50	3.00
15	Dick Meissner	.75	1.50	3.00
16	Ted Green	.75	1.50	3.00
17	Tom Williams	.75	1.50	3.00
18	Aut Erickson	.75	1.50	3.00
19	Phil Watson, Coach	.75	1.50	3.00
20	Ed Chadwick, Goalie	.75	1.50	3.00
—	Team Shield (Brown)	12.50	25.00	50.00

CHICAGO BLACK HAWKS

No.	Player	VG	EX	NRMT
21	Wayne Hillman	.75	1.50	3.00
22	Stan Mikita	2.25	4.50	9.00
23	Eric Nesterenko	.75	1.50	3.00
24	Reggie Fleming	.75	1.50	3.00
25	Bobby Hull	6.25	12.50	25.00
26	Elmer Vasko	.75	1.50	3.00
27	Pierre Pilote	1.00	2.00	4.00
28	Chico Maki	.75	1.50	3.00
29	Glenn Hall, Goalie	2.50	5.00	10.00
30	Murray Balfour	.75	1.50	3.00
31	Bronco Horvath	.75	1.50	3.00
32	Kenny Wharram	.75	1.50	3.00
33	Ab McDonald	.75	1.50	3.00
34	Billy Hay	.75	1.50	3.00
35	Dollard St. Laurent	.75	1.50	3.00
36	Ron Murphy	.75	1.50	3.00
37	Bob Turner	.75	1.50	3.00
38	Gerry Melnyk, Error	.75	1.50	3.00
39	Jack Evans	.75	1.50	3.00
40	Rudy Pilous, Coach	1.00	2.00	4.00
—	Team Shield (Yellow)	12.50	25.00	50.00

TORONTO MAPLE LEAFS

No.	Player	VG	EX	NRMT
41	Johnny Bower, Goalie	2.50	5.00	10.00
42	Allan Stanley	1.00	2.00	4.00
43	Frank Mahovlich	3.50	7.00	14.00
44	Tim Horton	3.50	7.00	14.00
45	Carl Brewer	.75	1.50	3.00

Shirriff/Salada
1961-62 Hockey Coins
Coin No. 25,
Bobby Hull

Shirriff/Salada
1961-62 Hockey Coins
Coin No. 41,
Johnny Bower

Shirriff/Salada
1961-62 Hockey Coins
Coin No. 49,
Red Kelly

Shirriff/Salada
1961-62 Hockey Coins
Coin No. 77,
Terry Sawchuk

No.	Player	VG	EX	NRMT
46	Bob Pulford	1.25	2.50	5.00
47	Bob Nevin	.75	1.50	3.00
48	Eddie Shack	2.00	4.00	8.00
49	Red Kelly	2.00	4.00	8.00
50	Bob Baun	.75	1.50	3.00
51	George Armstrong	1.35	2.75	5.50
52	Bert Olmstead	1.00	2.00	4.00
53	Dick Duff	.75	1.50	3.00
54	Billy Harris	.75	1.50	3.00
55	Larry Keenan	.75	1.50	3.00
56	John MacMillan	.75	1.50	3.00
57	Punch Imlach, Coach	.75	1.50	3.00
58	Dave Keon	3.50	7.00	14.00
59	Larry Hillman	.75	1.50	3.00
60	Al Arbour	1.50	2.50	5.00
—	Team Shield (Light Blue)	12.50	25.00	50.00

DETROIT RED WINGS

No.	Player	VG	EX	NRMT
61	Sid Abel, Coach	1.00	2.00	4.00
62	Warren Godfrey	.75	1.50	3.00
63	Vic Stasiuk	.75	1.50	3.00
64	Leo Labine	.75	1.50	3.00
65	Howie Glover	.75	1.50	3.00
66	Gordie Howe	11.00	22.00	44.00
67	Val Fonteyne	.75	1.50	3.00
68	Marcel Pronovost	1.00	2.00	4.00
69	Parker MacDonald	.75	1.50	3.00
70	Alex Delvecchio	2.00	4.00	8.00
71	Ed Litzenberger	.75	1.50	3.00
72	Al Johnson	.75	1.50	3.00
73	Bruce MacGregor	.75	1.50	3.00
74	Howie Young	.75	1.50	3.00
75	Peter Goegan	.75	1.50	3.00
76	Norm Ullman	1.75	3.50	7.00
77	Terry Sawchuk, Goalie	6.00	12.00	24.00
78	Gerry Odrowski	.75	1.50	3.00
79	Bill Gadsby	1.00	2.00	4.00
80	Hank Bassen, Goalie	.75	1.50	3.00
—	Team Shield (Red)	12.50	25.00	50.00

NEW YORK RANGERS

No.	Player	VG	EX	NRMT
81	Doug Harvey, Coach	2.00	4.00	8.00
82	Earl Ingarfield, Sr.	.75	1.50	3.00
83	Pat Hannigan	.75	1.50	3.00
84	Dean Prentice	.75	1.50	3.00
85	Gump Worsley, Goalie	2.50	5.00	10.00
86	Irv Spencer	.75	1.50	3.00
87	Camille Henry	.75	1.50	3.00
88	Andy Bathgate	2.00	4.00	8.00
89	Harry Howell	2.00	4.00	8.00
90	Andy Hebenton	.75	1.50	3.00
91	George (Red) Sullivan	.75	1.50	3.00
92	Ted Hampson	.75	1.50	3.00
93	Jean-Guy Gendron	.75	1.50	3.00
94	Al Langlois	.75	1.50	3.00
95	Larry Cahan	.75	1.50	3.00
96	Bob Cunningham	.75	1.50	3.00
97	Vic Hadfield	1.25	2.50	5.00
98	Jean Ratelle	2.00	4.00	8.00
99	Ken Schinkel	.75	1.50	3.00
100	Johnny Wilson	.75	1.50	3.00
—	Team Shield (Dark Blue)	12.50	25.00	50.00

MONTREAL CANADIENS

No.	Player	VG	EX	NRMT
101	Toe Blake, Coach	1.25	2.50	5.00
102	Jean Beliveau	4.25	8.50	17.00
103	Don Marshall	.75	1.50	3.00
104	Bernie Geoffrion	4.25	8.50	17.00
105	Claude Provost	.75	1.50	3.00
106	Tom Johnson	1.00	2.00	4.00
107	Dickie Moore	2.00	4.00	8.00
108	Bill Hicke	.75	1.50	3.00
109	Jean-Guy Talbot	.75	1.50	3.00
110	Henri Richard	2.00	4.00	8.00
111	Louie Fontinato	.75	1.50	3.00
112	Gilles Tremblay	.75	1.50	3.00
113	Jacques Plante, Goalie	5.50	11.00	22.00
114	Ralph Backstrom	.75	1.50	3.00
115	Marcel Bonin	.75	1.50	3.00

No.	Player	VG	EX	NRMT
116	Phil Goyette	.75	1.50	3.00
117	Bobby Rousseau	.75	1.50	3.00
118	J.C. Tremblay	.75	1.50	3.00
119	Al MacNeil	.75	1.50	3.00
120	Jean Gauthier	.75	1.50	3.00
—	Team Shield (White)	12.50	25.00	50.00

— 1962 - 63 HOCKEY COINS —

The 1962-63 issue of hockey coins are metal, unlike the previous years' which were plastic. Coins are hard to find unscratched and well centered.

Coin Size: 1 1/2" Diameter
Face: Four colour; Name, Number
Back: Black on tin; Name, Resume, Bilingual
Imprint: SHIRRIFF HOCKEY COIN PIECE DE HOCKEY SHIRRIFF MADE IN U.S.A.
Complete Set No.: 60
Complete Set Price: 125.00 250.00 500.00
Common Player: 1.25 2.50 5.00

TORONTO MAPLE LEAFS STANLEY CUP CHAMPIONS

No.	Player	VG	EX	NRMT
1	Johnny Bower, Goalie	3.75	7.50	15.00
2	Allan Stanley	1.50	3.00	6.00
3	Frank Mahovlich	4.50	9.00	18.00
4	Tim Horton	4.50	9.00	18.00
5	Carl Brewer	1.25	2.50	5.00
6	Bob Pulford	1.50	3.00	6.00
7	Bob Nevin	1.25	2.50	5.00
8	Eddie Shack	3.00	6.00	12.00
9	Red Kelly	2.00	4.00	8.00
10	George Armstrong	1.75	3.50	7.00
11	Bert Olmstead	1.25	2.50	5.00
12	Dick Duff	1.25	2.50	5.00
13	Billy Harris	1.25	2.50	5.00
14	John MacMillan	1.25	2.50	5.00
15	Punch Imlach, Coach	1.25	2.50	5.00
16	Dave Keon	4.25	8.50	17.00
17	Larry Hillman	1.25	2.50	5.00
18	Ed Litzenberger	1.25	2.50	5.00
19	Bob Baun	1.25	2.50	5.00
20	Al Arbour	1.75	3.50	7.00
21	Ron Stewart	1.25	2.50	5.00
22	Don Simmons, Goalie	1.25	2.50	5.00

MONTREAL CANADIENS LEAGUE CHAMPIONS 1961-62

No.	Player	VG	EX	NRMT
23	Louie Fontinato	1.25	2.50	5.00
24	Gilles Tremblay	1.25	2.50	5.00
25	Jacques Plante, Goalie	7.50	15.00	30.00
26	Ralph Backstrom	1.25	2.50	5.00
27	Marcel Bonin	1.25	2.50	5.00
28	Phil Goyette	1.25	2.50	5.00
29	Bobby Rousseau	1.25	2.50	5.00
30	J.C. Tremblay	1.25	2.50	5.00
31	Toe Blake, Coach	1.85	3.75	7.50
32	Jean Beliveau	5.50	11.00	22.00
33	Don Marshall	1.25	2.50	5.00
34	Bernie Geoffrion	4.50	9.00	18.00
35	Claude Provost	1.25	2.50	5.00
36	Tom Johnson	1.50	3.00	6.00
37	Dickie Moore	2.00	4.00	8.00
38	Bill Hicke	1.50	3.00	6.00
39	Jean-Guy Talbot	1.25	2.50	5.00
40	Al MacNeil	1.25	2.50	5.00
41	Henri Richard	2.00	4.00	8.00
42	Red Berenson	1.25	2.50	5.00

ALL STARS

No.	Player	VG	EX	NRMT
43	Jacques Plante, Goalie	7.50	15.00	30.00
44	Jean-Guy Talbot	1.25	2.50	5.00
45	Doug Harvey	2.50	5.00	10.00
46	Stan Mikita	3.50	7.00	14.00
47	Bobby Hull	8.75	17.50	35.00
48	Andy Bathgate	1.50	3.00	6.00
49	Glenn Hall, Goalie	2.50	5.00	10.00
50	Pierre Pilote	1.75	3.50	6.00

Shirriff
1962-63 Hockey Coins
Coin No. 20,
Al Arbour

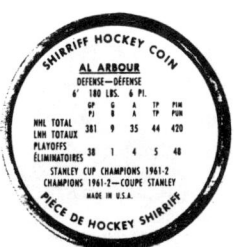

Shirriff
1962-63 Hockey Coins
Coin No. 20,
Al Arbour

Shirriff
1968-69 Hockey Coins
Coin No. A-1,
Eddie Shack

Shirriff
1968-69 Hockey Coins
Coin No. C-12,
Frank Mahovlich

— 1962 - 63 HOCKEY COINS — SHIRRIFF • 271

No.	Player	VG	EX	NRMT
51	Carl Brewer	1.25	2.50	5.00
52	Dave Keon	3.75	7.50	15.00
53	Frank Mahovlich	3.75	7.50	15.00
54	Gordie Howe	12.50	25.00	50.00

1961-62 TROPHY WINNERS

No.	Player	VG	EX	NRMT
55	**Byng Trophy:** Dave Keon, Tor.	2.50	5.00	10.00
56	**Calder Trophy:** Bobby Rousseau, Mon.	1.25	2.50	5.00
57	**Art Ross Trophy:** Bobby Hull, Chi.	7.00	14.00	28.00
58	**Vezina Trophy; Hart Trophy:** Jacques Plante, Goalie, Mon., with mask	5.50	11.00	22.00
59	**Vezina Trophy; Hart Trophy:** Jacques Plante, Goalie, Mon., without mask	5.50	11.00	22.00
60	**Norris Trophy:** Doug Harvey, NYR	2.50	5.00	10.00

— 1968 - 69 HOCKEY COINS —

The numbering on this set is a little different than the previous coins. The coins are numbered within the teams. Some coins were short-issued and are scarce.

Coin Size: 1 3/8" Diameter
Face: Four colour; Name, Number
Back: Unknown
Imprint: Unknown
Complete Set No.: 176
Complete Set Price: 1,575.00 3,150.00 6,300.00
Common Player: (Original Six) 1.50 3.00 6.00
Common Player: (Expansion) 2.00 4.00 8.00

BOSTON BRUINS — A

No.	Player	VG	EX	NRMT
1	Eddie Shack	3.00	6.00	12.00
2	Ed Westfall	1.50	3.00	6.00
3	Don Awrey	1.50	3.00	6.00
4	Gerry Cheevers, Goalie	4.50	9.00	18.00
5	Bobby Orr	40.00	85.00	175.00
6	John Bucyk	5.00	10.00	20.00
7	Derek Sanderson	3.00	6.00	12.00
8	Phil Esposito	10.00	20.00	40.00
9	Fred Stanfield	1.50	3.00	6.00
10	Ken Hodge, Sr.	2.00	4.00	8.00
11	John McKenzie	1.50	3.00	6.00
12	Ted Green	2.00	4.00	8.00
13	Dallas Smith, SP	22.50	45.00	90.00
14	Gary Doak, SP	22.50	45.00	90.00
15	Glen Sather, SP	35.00	70.00	140.00
16	Tom Williams, SP	22.50	45.00	90.00

CHICAGO BLACK HAWKS — B

No.	Player	VG	EX	NRMT
1	Bobby Hull	17.50	35.00	75.00
2	Pat Stapleton	1.50	3.00	6.00
3	Wayne Maki	1.50	3.00	6.00
4	Denis DeJordy, Goalie	2.50	5.00	10.00
5	Kenny Wharram	1.50	3.00	6.00
6	Pit Martin	1.50	3.00	6.00
7	Chico Maki	1.50	3.00	6.00
8	Doug Mohns	1.50	3.00	6.00
9	Stan Mikita	7.50	15.00	30.00
10	Doug Jarrett	1.50	3.00	6.00
11A	Dennis Hull, Small Portrait	45.00	90.00	175.00
11B	Dennis Hull, Large Portrait	10.00	20.00	40.00
12	Matt Ravlich	1.50	3.00	6.00
13	Dave Dryden, Goalie, SP	27.50	55.00	110.00
14	Eric Nesterenko, SP	22.50	45.00	90.00
15	Gilles Marotte, SP	22.50	45.00	90.00
16	Jim Pappin, SP	25.00	50.00	100.00

DETROIT RED WINGS — C

No.	Player	VG	EX	NRMT
1	Gary Bergman	1.50	3.00	6.00
2	Roger Crozier, Goalie	3.00	6.25	12.50
3	Pete Mahovlich	1.50	3.00	6.00
4	Alex Delvecchio	5.00	10.00	20.00
5	Dean Prentice	1.50	3.00	6.00

272 • SHIRRIFF — 1968 - 69 HOCKEY COINS

No.	Player	VG	EX	NRMT
6	Kent Douglas	1.50	3.00	6.00
7	Roy Edwards, Goalie	2.50	5.00	10.00
8	Bruce MacGregor	1.50	3.00	6.00
9	Garry Unger	2.50	5.00	10.00
10	Pete Stemkowski	1.50	3.00	6.00
11	Gordie Howe	37.50	75.00	150.00
12	Frank Mahovlich	10.00	20.00	40.00
13	Bob Baun, SP	27.50	55.00	110.00
14	Brian Conacher, SP	22.50	45.00	90.00
15	Jimmy Watson, SP	22.50	45.00	90.00
16	Nick Libett, SP	22.50	45.00	90.00

LOS ANGELES KINGS — D

No.	Player	VG	EX	NRMT
1	Real Lemieux	2.00	4.00	8.00
2	Ted Irvine	2.00	4.00	8.00
3	Bob Wall	2.00	4.00	8.00
4	Bill White	3.00	6.00	12.00
5	Gord Labossiere	2.00	4.00	8.00
6	Eddie Joyal	2.00	4.00	8.00
7	Lowell MacDonald	2.00	4.00	8.00
8	Bill Flett	2.25	4.50	9.00
9	Wayne Rutledge, Goalie	2.00	4.00	8.00
10	Dave Amadio	2.00	4.00	8.00
11	Skip Krake, SP	27.50	55.00	110.00
12	Doug Robinson, SP	27.50	55.00	110.00

MINNESOTA NORTH STARS — E

No.	Player	VG	EX	NRMT
1	Wayne Connelly	2.00	4.00	8.00
2	Bob Woytowich	2.00	4.00	8.00
3	Andre Boudrias	2.00	4.00	8.00
4	Bill Goldsworthy	2.50	5.00	10.00
5	Cesare Maniago, Goalie	3.00	6.00	12.00
6	Milan Marcetta	2.00	4.00	8.00
7A	Bill Collins	10.00	20.00	40.00
7B	Claude Larose	45.00	90.00	175.00
8	Parker MacDonald	2.00	4.00	8.00
9	Ray Cullen	2.00	4.00	8.00
10	Mike McMahon	2.00	4.00	8.00
11	Bob McCord, SP	27.50	55.00	115.00
12	Larry Hillman, SP	30.00	60.00	120.00

MONTREAL CANADIENS — F

No.	Player	VG	EX	NRMT
1	Gump Worsley, Goalie	5.50	11.00	22.00
2	Rogatien Vachon, Goalie	5.50	11.00	22.00
3	Ted Harris	1.50	3.00	6.00
4	Jacques Laperriere	3.00	6.00	12.00
5	J.C. Tremblay	1.50	3.00	6.00
6	Jean Beliveau	12.50	25.00	50.00
7	Gilles Tremblay	1.50	3.00	6.00
8	Ralph Backstrom	1.50	3.00	6.00
9	Bobby Rousseau	1.50	3.00	6.00
10	John Ferguson	2.50	5.00	10.00
11	Dick Duff	1.50	3.00	6.00
12	Terry Harper	1.50	3.00	6.00
13	Yvan Cournoyer	6.00	12.50	25.00
14	Jacques Lemaire	5.00	10.00	20.00
15	Henri Richard	5.00	10.00	20.00
16	Claude Provost, SP	27.50	55.00	110.00
17	Serge Savard, SP	45.00	90.00	175.00
18	Mickey Redmond, SP	27.50	55.00	110.00

NEW YORK RANGERS — G

No.	Player	VG	EX	NRMT
1	Rod Seiling	1.50	3.00	6.00
2	Jean Ratelle	3.50	7.00	14.00
3	Ed Giacomin, Goalie	3.50	7.00	14.00
4	Reggie Fleming	1.50	3.00	6.00
5	Phil Goyette	1.50	3.00	6.00
6	Arnie Brown	1.50	3.00	6.00
7	Don Marshall	1.50	3.00	6.00
8	Orland Kurtenbach	1.50	3.00	6.00
9	Bob Nevin	1.50	3.00	6.00
10	Rod Gilbert	4.00	8.00	16.00
11	Harry Howell	3.00	6.00	12.00
12	Jim Neilson	1.50	3.00	6.00
13	Vic Hadfield, SP	27.50	55.00	110.00
14	Larry Jeffrey, SP	125.00	250.00	500.00
15	Dave Balon, SP	22.50	45.00	90.00
16	Ron Stewart, SP	27.50	55.00	110.00

Shirriff
1968-69 Hockey Coins
Coin No. D-1,
Real Lemieux

Shirriff
1968-69 Hockey Coins
Coin No. F-14,
Jacques Lemaire

Shirriff
1968-69 Hockey Coins
Coin No. J-4,
Gary Dornhoefer

Shirriff
1968-69 Hockey Coins
Coin No. M-13,
Marcel Pronovost

OAKLAND SEALS — H

No.	Player	VG	EX	NRMT
1	Gerry Ehman	2.00	4.00	8.00
2	John Brenneman	2.00	4.00	8.00
3	Ted Hampson	2.00	4.00	8.00
4	Billy Harris	2.00	4.00	8.00
5A	George Swarbrick	12.50	25.00	50.00
5B	Carol Vadnais, SP	190.00	375.00	750.00
6	Gary Smith, Goalie	2.50	5.00	10.00
7	Charlie Hodge, Goalie	2.50	5.00	10.00
8	Bert Marshall	2.00	4.00	8.00
9	Bill Hicke	2.00	4.00	8.00
10	Tracy Pratt	2.00	4.00	8.00
11	Gary Jarrett, SP	125.00	250.00	500.00
12	Howie Young, SP	125.00	250.00	500.00

PHILADELPHIA FLYERS — J

No.	Player	VG	EX	NRMT
1	Bernie Parent, Goalie	9.50	19.00	38.00
2	John Miszuk	2.00	4.00	8.00
3A	Ed Hoekstra	10.00	20.00	40.00
3B	Allan Stanley	40.00	80.00	160.00
4	Gary Dornhoefer	2.50	5.00	10.00
5	Doug Favell, Goalie	2.50	5.00	10.00
6	Andre Lacroix	2.00	4.00	8.00
7	Brit Selby	2.00	4.00	8.00
8	Don Blackburn	2.00	4.00	8.00
9	Leon Rochefort	2.00	4.00	8.00
10	Forbes Kennedy	2.00	4.00	8.00
11	Claude Laforge, SP	30.00	60.00	120.00
12	Pat Hannigan, SP	30.00	60.00	120.00

PITTSBURGH PENGUINS — K

No.	Player	VG	EX	NRMT
1	Ken Schinkel	2.00	4.00	8.00
2	Earl Ingarfield, Sr.	2.00	4.00	8.00
3	Val Fonteyne	2.00	4.00	8.00
4	Noel Price	2.00	4.00	8.00
5	Andy Bathgate	4.00	8.00	16.00
6	Les Binkley, Goalie	2.00	4.00	8.00
7	Leo Boivin	3.00	6.00	12.00
8	Paul Andrea	2.00	4.00	8.00
9	Dunc McCallum	2.00	4.00	8.00
10	Keith McCreary	2.00	4.00	8.00
11	Lou Angotti, SP	27.50	55.00	110.00
12	Wally Boyer, SP	27.50	55.00	110.00

ST. LOUIS BLUES — L

No.	Player	VG	EX	NRMT
1	Ron Schock	2.00	4.00	8.00
2	Bob Plager	2.50	5.00	10.00
3	Al Arbour	3.75	7.50	15.00
4	Red Berenson	2.00	4.00	8.00
5	Glenn Hall, Goalie	5.00	10.00	20.00
6	Jim Roberts	2.00	4.00	8.00
7	Noel Picard	2.00	4.00	8.00
8	Barclay Plager	2.50	5.00	10.00
9	Larry Keenan	2.00	4.00	8.00
10	Terry Crisp	2.50	5.00	10.00
11	Gary Sabourin, SP	27.50	55.00	110.00
12	Ab McDonald, SP	27.50	55.00	110.00

TORONTO MAPLE LEAFS — M

No.	Player	VG	EX	NRMT
1	George Armstrong	3.75	7.50	15.00
2	Wayne Carleton	1.50	3.00	6.00
3	Paul Henderson	5.00	10.00	20.00
4	Bob Pulford	3.75	7.50	15.00
5	Mike Walton	1.50	3.00	6.00
6	Johnny Bower, Goalie	5.00	10.00	20.00
7	Ron Ellis	2.50	5.00	10.00
8	Mike Pelyk	1.50	3.00	6.00
9	Murray Oliver	1.50	3.00	6.00
10	Norm Ullman	4.00	8.00	16.00
11	Dave Keon	6.00	12.50	25.00
12	Floyd Smith	1.50	3.00	6.00
13	Marcel Pronovost	3.00	6.00	12.00
14	Tim Horton	6.00	12.50	25.00
15	Bruce Gamble, Goalie	2.50	5.00	10.00
16	Jim McKenny, SP	30.00	60.00	125.00
17	Mike Byers, SP	25.00	50.00	100.00
18	Pierre Pilote, SP	30.00	60.00	125.00

WONDER BREAD

— 1960 WRAPPER ISSUE —

Single cards of this set came enclosed in plastic at the end of loaves of Wonder bread. There were two cards per loaf. There was a premium offered whereby customers could send in 25¢ and five cards to Wonder Sports Club for a black and white 5" x 7" photo of the player. This photo was printed on a heavier weight stock than the cards in the bread.

Card Size: 2 3/4" x 2 3/4"
Face: Red and black
Back: Blank
Imprint: None
Complete Set No.: 4

Complete Set Price:		185.00	375.00	750.00
Common Player:		35.00	75.00	150.00

No.	Player	VG	EX	NRMT
1	Gordie Howe, Det.	60.00	125.00	250.00
2	Bobby Hull, Chi.	50.00	100.00	200.00
3	Dave Keon, Tor.	35.00	75.00	150.00
4	Maurice Richard, Mon.	50.00	100.00	200.00

— 1960 PREMIUM PHOTOS —

These photos were available from Wonder Bread by sending 25¢ and five end wrappers to Wonder Sports Club in exchange for a black and white 5" x 7" photo of the player. This photo was printed on a heavier weight stock than the cards in the bread.

Card Size: 5" x 7"
Face: Black and white glossy on card stock
Back: Blank
Imprint: None
Complete Set No.: 4

Complete Set Price:		185.00	375.00	750.00
Common Player:		35.00	75.00	150.00

No.	Player	VG	EX	NRMT
1	Gordie Howe, Det.	60.00	125.00	250.00
2	Bobby Hull, Chi.	50.00	100.00	200.00
3	Dave Keon, Tor.	35.00	75.00	150.00
4	Maurice Richard, Mon.	50.00	100.00	200.00

YORK PEANUT BUTTER

— 1960 - 61 PREMIUMS —

These unnumbered photographs feature players of the Montreal Canadiens and the Toronto Maple Leafs. Player's names are presented in alphabetical order by team. The black and white cards show no indication of the issuer.

Photo Size: 5" X 7"
Face: Black and white; Facsimile autograph
Back: Blank
Imprint: None
Complete Set No.: 37

Complete Set Price:		800.00	1,600.00	3,300.00
Common Player:		17.50	35.00	70.00

MONTREAL CANADIENS

No.	Player	VG	EX	NRMT
1	Ralph Backstrom	17.50	35.00	70.00
2	Jean Beliveau	55.00	110.00	225.00
3	Marcel Bonin	17.50	35.00	70.00
4	Jean-Guy Gendron	17.50	35.00	70.00
5	Bernie Geoffrion	45.00	90.00	175.00
6	Phil Goyette	17.50	35.00	70.00
7	Doug Harvey	35.00	70.00	140.00
8	Bill Hicke	17.50	35.00	70.00
9	Charlie Hodge, Goalie	25.00	50.00	100.00
10	Tom Johnson	22.50	45.00	90.00
11	Al Langlois	17.50	35.00	70.00
12	Don Marshall	17.50	35.00	70.00
13	Dickie Moore	25.00	50.00	100.00
14	Jacques Plante, Goalie	50.00	100.00	200.00
15	Claude Provost	17.50	35.00	70.00
16	Henri Richard	35.00	70.00	140.00
17	Jean-Guy Talbot	17.50	35.00	70.00
18	Gilles Tremblay	17.50	35.00	70.00
19	Bob Turner	17.50	35.00	70.00

Wonder Bread, 1960 Wrapper Issue Wrapper No. 1, Gordie Howe

Wonder Bread 1960 Wrapper Issue Wrapper No. 4, Maurice Richard

York 1961-62 Yellow Backs Card No. 14, Bob Pulford

York 1961-62 Yellow Backs Card No. 27, Dave Keon

TORONTO MAPLE LEAFS

No.	Player	VG	EX	NRMT
20	George Armstrong	30.00	60.00	120.00
21	Bob Baun	17.50	35.00	70.00
22	Johnny Bower, Goalie	30.00	60.00	120.00
23	Carl Brewer	17.50	35.00	70.00
24	Dick Duff	17.50	35.00	70.00
25	Billy Harris	17.50	35.00	70.00
26	Larry Hillman	17.50	35.00	70.00
27	Tim Horton	35.00	75.00	150.00
28	Red Kelly	30.00	65.00	130.00
29	Dave Keon	35.00	75.00	150.00
30	Frank Mahovlich	40.00	80.00	160.00
31	Bob Nevin	17.50	35.00	70.00
32	Bert Olmstead	22.50	45.00	90.00
33	Bob Pulford	22.50	45.00	90.00
34	Larry Regan	17.50	35.00	70.00
35	Eddie Shack	25.00	50.00	100.00
36	Allan Stanley	22.50	45.00	90.00
37	Ron Stewart	17.50	35.00	70.00

— 1961 - 62 YELLOW BACKS —

Card Size: 2 1/2" X 2 1/2"
Face: Four colour, coloured background (yellow, green, red and pale blue)
Back: Black on yellow card stock; Number, Name, Resume, Album offer, Bilingual
Imprint: None
Complete Set No.: 42

Complete Set Price:		165.00	325.00	650.00
Common Player:		2.50	5.00	10.00
Album:		25.00	50.00	100.00

No.	Player	VG	EX	NRMT
1	Bob Baun, Tor.	2.50	5.00	10.00
2	Dick Duff, Tor.	2.50	5.00	10.00
3	Frank Mahovlich, Tor.	8.75	17.50	35.00
4	Gilles Tremblay, Mon.	2.50	5.00	10.00
5	Dickie Moore, Mon.	4.00	8.00	16.00
6	Don Marshall, Mon.	2.50	5.00	10.00
7	Tim Horton, Tor.	8.75	17.50	35.00
8	Johnny Bower, Goalie, Tor.	6.00	12.50	25.00
9	Allan Stanley, Tor.	4.00	8.00	16.00
10	Jean Beliveau, Mon.	8.75	17.50	35.00
11	Tom Johnson, Mon.	3.00	6.00	12.00
12	Jean-Guy Talbot, Mon.	2.50	5.00	10.00
13	Carl Brewer, Tor.	2.50	5.00	10.00
14	Bob Pulford, Tor.	3.75	7.50	15.00
15	Billy Harris, Tor.	2.50	5.00	10.00
16	Bill Hicke, Mon.	2.50	5.00	10.00
17	Claude Provost, Mon.	2.50	5.00	10.00
18	Henri Richard, Mon.	5.50	11.00	22.00
19	Bert Olmstead, Tor.	2.50	5.00	10.00
20	Ron Stewart, Tor.	2.50	5.00	10.00
21	Red Kelly, Tor.	5.50	11.00	22.00
22	Toe Blake, Coach, Mon.	3.75	7.50	15.00
23	Jacques Plante, Goalie, Mon.	7.50	15.00	35.00
24	Ralph Backstrom, Mon.	2.50	5.00	10.00
25	Eddie Shack, Tor.	5.50	11.00	22.00
26	Bob Nevin, Tor.	2.50	5.00	10.00
27	Dave Keon, Tor.	8.75	17.50	35.00
28	Bernie Geoffrion, Mon.	7.50	15.00	30.00
29	Marcel Bonin, Mon.	2.50	5.00	10.00
30	Phil Goyette, Mon.	2.50	5.00	10.00
31	Larry Hillman, Tor.	2.50	5.00	10.00
32	Larry Keenan, Tor.	2.50	5.00	10.00
33	Al Arbour, Tor.	3.75	7.50	15.00
34	J.C. Tremblay, Mon.	2.50	5.00	10.00
35	Bobby Rousseau, Mon.	2.50	5.00	10.00
36	Al MacNeil, Mon.	2.50	5.00	10.00
37	George Armstrong, Tor.	4.50	9.00	18.00
38	Punch Imlach, Manager & Coach, Tor.	3.00	6.00	12.00
39	Francis Clancy, Assistant General Manager, Tor.	5.50	11.00	22.00
40	Louie Fontinato, Mon.	2.50	5.00	10.00
41	Cesare Maniago, Goalie, Mon.	3.00	6.00	12.00
42	Jean Gauthier, Mon.	2.50	5.00	10.00

274 • YORK PEANUT BUTTER — 1962-63 IRON-ON TRANSFERS —

— 1962 - 63 IRON-ON TRANSFERS —

These iron-on transfers were inserted into jars of peanut butter and packages of salted peanuts. There were twelve players from each of the Toronto, Montreal and Detroit teams.

Card Size: 2 3/16" X 4 5/16"
Face: Blue wording on transfer, team colour; Instructions, Bilingual
Back: Blank
Imprint: None
Complete Set No.: 36

Complete Set Price:	600.00	1,200.00	2,400.00
Common Player:	12.50	25.00	50.00

No.	Player	VG	EX	NRMT
1	Johnny Bower, Goalie, Tor.	20.00	40.00	85.00
2	Jacques Plante, Goalie, Mon.	30.00	60.00	125.00
3	Tim Horton, Tor.	30.00	60.00	120.00
4	Jean-Guy Talbot, Mon.	12.50	25.00	50.00
5	Carl Brewer, Tor.	12.50	25.00	50.00
6	J.C. Tremblay, Mon.	12.50	25.00	50.00
7	Dick Duff, Mon.	12.50	25.00	50.00
8	Jean Beliveau, Mon.	30.00	60.00	115.00
9	Dave Keon, Tor.	20.00	42.50	85.00
10	Henri Richard, Mon.	20.00	42.50	85.00
11	Frank Mahovlich, Tor.	20.00	42.50	85.00
12	Bernie Geoffrion, Mon.	25.00	50.00	100.00
13	Kent Douglas, Tor.	12.50	25.00	50.00
14	Claude Provost, Mon.	12.50	25.00	50.00
15	Bob Pulford, Tor.	15.00	30.00	60.00
16	Ralph Backstrom, Mon.	12.50	25.00	50.00
17	George Armstrong, Tor.	20.00	42.50	85.00
18	Bobby Rousseau, Mon.	12.50	25.00	50.00
19	Gordie Howe, Det.	90.00	175.00	350.00
20	Red Kelly, Tor.	20.00	40.00	80.00
21	Alex Delvecchio, Det.	20.00	40.00	80.00
22	Dickie Moore, Mon.	20.00	40.00	80.00
23	Marcel Pronovost, Mon.	15.00	30.00	60.00
24	Doug Barkley, Det.	12.50	25.00	50.00
25	Terry Sawchuk, Goalie, Det.	30.00	60.00	125.00
26	Billy Harris, Tor.	12.50	25.00	50.00
27	Parker MacDonald, Det.	12.50	25.00	50.00
28	Don Marshall, Mon.	12.50	25.00	50.00
29	Norm Ullman, Tor.	20.00	40.00	80.00
30A	Andre Pronovost, Mon.	12.50	25.00	50.00
30B	Vic Stasiuk, Det.	12.50	25.00	50.00
31	Bill Gadsby, Det.	15.00	30.00	60.00
32	Eddie Shack, Tor.	17.50	35.00	70.00
33	Larry Jeffrey, Det.	12.50	25.00	50.00
34	Gilles Tremblay, Mon.	12.50	25.00	50.00
35	Howie Young, Det.	12.50	25.00	50.00
36	Bruce MacGregor, Det.	12.50	25.00	50.00

— 1963 - 64 WHITE BACKS —

This 54-card set was issued in York Peanut Butter and York Salted Nuts.

Card Size: 2 1/2" x 2 1/2"
Face: Four colour
Back: White card stock; Number, Name, Resume, Bilingual
Imprint: None
Complete Set No.: 54

Complete Set Price:	200.00	400.00	800.00
Common Player:	2.50	5.00	10.00
Album:	25.00	50.00	100.00

TORONTO MAPLE LEAFS

No.	Player	VG	EX	NRMT
1	Tim Horton	7.50	15.00	30.00
2	Johnny Bower	6.00	12.50	25.00
3	Ron Stewart	2.50	5.00	10.00
4	Eddie Shack	6.00	12.50	25.00
5	Frank Mahovlich	7.50	15.00	30.00
6	Dave Keon	7.50	15.00	30.00
7	Bob Baun	2.50	5.00	10.00
8	Bob Nevin	2.50	5.00	10.00
9	Dick Duff	2.50	5.00	10.00
10	Billy Harris	2.50	5.00	10.00
11	Larry Hillman	2.50	5.00	10.00
12	Red Kelly	4.50	9.00	18.00
13	Kent Douglas	2.50	5.00	10.00
14	Allan Stanley	4.00	8.00	16.00
15	Don Simmons, Goalie	3.00	6.00	12.00
16	George Armstrong	4.50	9.00	18.00
17	Carl Brewer	2.50	5.00	10.00
18	Bob Pulford	3.75	7.50	15.00

York
1962-63 Iron-On Transfers
Transfer No. 28,
Don Marshall

York
1963-64 White Backs
Card No. 27,
Ralph Backstrom

York
1963-64 White Backs
Card No. 46,
Doug Barkley

York
1967-68 Hockey Action
Card No. 33,
Terry Harper, Bobby
Rousseau, Marcel Pronovost

MONTREAL CANADIENS

No.	Player	VG	EX	NRMT
19	Henri Richard	5.00	10.00	20.00
20	Bernie Geoffrion	7.50	15.00	30.00
21	Gilles Tremblay	2.50	5.00	10.00
22	Gump Worsley, Goalie	6.00	12.50	25.00
23	Jean-Guy Talbot	2.50	5.00	10.00
24	J.C. Tremblay	3.00	6.00	12.00
25	Bobby Rousseau	2.50	5.00	10.00
26	Jean Beliveau	7.50	15.00	30.00
27	Ralph Backstrom	2.50	5.00	10.00
28	Claude Provost	2.50	5.00	10.00
29	Jean Gauthier	2.50	5.00	10.00
30	Bill Hicke	2.50	5.00	10.00
31	Terry Harper	2.50	5.00	10.00
32	Marc Reaume	2.50	5.00	10.00
33	Dave Balon	2.50	5.00	10.00
34	Jacques Laperriere	3.50	7.00	14.00
35	John Ferguson	3.75	7.50	15.00
36	Red Berenson	3.00	6.00	12.00

DETROIT RED WINGS

No.	Player	VG	EX	NRMT
37	Terry Sawchuk, Goalie	15.00	27.50	55.00
38	Marcel Pronovost	3.00	6.00	12.00
39	Bill Gadsby	3.00	6.00	12.00
40	Parker MacDonald	2.50	5.00	10.00
41	Larry Jeffrey	2.50	5.00	10.00
42	Floyd Smith	2.50	5.00	10.00
43	Andre Pronovost	2.50	5.00	10.00
44	Art Stratton	2.50	5.00	10.00
45	Gordie Howe	40.00	80.00	160.00
46	Doug Barkley	2.50	5.00	10.00
47	Norm Ullman	4.00	8.00	16.00
48	Eddie Joyal	2.50	5.00	10.00
49	Alex Faulkner	3.00	6.00	12.00
50	Alex Delvecchio	5.50	11.00	22.00
51	Bruce MacGregor	2.50	5.00	10.00
52	Ted Hampson	2.50	5.00	10.00
53	Peter Goegan	2.50	5.00	10.00
54	Ron Ingram	2.50	5.00	10.00

— 1967 - 68 HOCKEY ACTION —

This set was issued in York Peanut Butter. Each card displays two or three players in action. The first twelve cards are unnumbered. For simplicity these cards have been assigned numbers based on the alphabetical ordering of the last name of the first player recorded on the back of the card.

Card Size: 2 7/8" X 2 7/8"
Face: Four colour, white border; Number (13-36) or unnumbered, Name, Jersey Number
Back: Black on white card stock; Contest rules
Imprint: Weekend Magazine Photo
Complete Set No.: 36

Complete Set Price:	120.00	240.00	475.00
Common Player:	2.50	5.00	10.00

No.	Player	VG	EX	NRMT
1	B. Conacher, Tor.; A. Stanley, Tor.; L. Rochefort, Mon.	3.00	6.00	12.00
2	T. Harper, Mon.; G. Worsley, Goalie, Mon.; M. Walton, Tor.	3.00	6.00	12.00
3	T. Horton, Tor.; G. Armstrong; J. Beliveau, Mon.	7.50	15.00	30.00
4	D. Keon, Tor.; G. Armstrong; Tor. C. Provost, Mon.	6.00	12.00	25.00
5	J. Laperriere, Mon.; R. Vachon, Goalie, Mon.; B. Pulford, Tor.	3.00	6.00	12.00
6	B. Pulford, Tor.; B. Conacher, Tor.; C. Provost, Mon.	2.50	5.00	10.00
7	B. Pulford, Tor.; J. Pappin, Tor.; T. Harper, Mon.	2.50	5.00	10.00
8	P. Stemkowski, Tor.; J. Pappin, Tor.; T. Harris, Mon.	2.50	5.00	10.00
9	J.C. Tremblay, Mon.; R. Vachon, Goalie, Mon.; P. Stemkowski, Tor.	3.00	6.00	12.00
10	R. Vachon, Goalie, Mon.; R. Backstrom, Mon.; B. Pulford, Tor.	3.00	6.50	13.00
11	R. Vachon, Goalie, Mon.; J. Laperriere, Mon.; M. Walton, Tor.	3.00	6.50	13.00
12	M. Walton, Tor.; P. Stemkowski, Tor.; J.C. Tremblay, Mon.	2.50	5.00	10.00
13	D. Keon, Tor.; M. Walton, Tor.; J.C. Tremblay, Mon.	3.00	6.00	12.00
14	P. Stemkowski, Tor.; R. Backstrom, Mon.	2.50	5.00	10.00
15	R. Vachon, Goalie, Mon.; B. Pulford, Tor.	3.00	6.00	12.00

— 1962 - 63 ISSUE — EL PRODUCTO • 275

No.	Player	VG	EX	NRMT
16	J. Bower, Goalie, Tor.; R. Ellis, Tor.; J. Ferguson, Sr., Mon.	4.25	8.50	17.00 ☐
17	R. Ellis, Tor.; G. Worsley, Goalie, Mon.	3.50	7.00	14.00 ☐
18	G. Worsley, Goalie, Mon.; J. Laperriere, Mon.; F. Mahovlich, Tor.	5.50	11.00	22.00 ☐
19	J.C. Tremblay, Mon.; D. Keon, Tor.	4.50	9.00	18.00 ☐
20	C. Provost, Mon.; F. Mahovlich, Tor.	4.50	9.00	18.00 ☐
21	J. Ferguson, Sr., Mon.; T. Horton, Tor.	4.50	9.00	18.00 ☐
22	G. Worsley, Goalie, Mon.; R. Ellis, Tor.	3.75	7.50	15.00 ☐
23	J. Bower, Goalie, Tor.; M. Walton, Tor.; J. Beliveau, Mon.	5.00	10.00	20.00 ☐
24	J.C. Tremblay; G. Worsley, Goalie; B. Pulford	3.25	7.50	15.00 ☐
25	T. Horton, Tor.; J. Bower, Goalie, Tor.; J. Beliveau, Mon.	7.50	15.00	30.00 ☐
26	A. Stanley, Tor.; J. Bower, Goalie, Tor.; D. Duff, Mon.	3.25	7.50	15.00 ☐
27	R. Backstrom, Mon.; J. Bower, Tor.	3.50	7.00	14.00 ☐
28	Y. Cournoyer, Mon.; J. Beliveau, Mon.; F. Mahovlich, Tor.	6.25	12.50	25.00 ☐
29	J. Bower, Goalie, Tor.; L. Hillman, Tor.; Y. Cournoyer, Mon.	3.00	6.00	12.00 ☐
30	J. Bower, Tor.; Y. Cournoyer, Mon.	3.50	7.00	14.00 ☐
31	T. Horton, Tor.; R. Vachon, Goalie, Mon.	4.50	9.00	18.00 ☐
32	J. Pappin, Tor.; B. Pulford, Tor.; R. Vachon;, Goalie, Mon.	3.00	6.00	12.00 ☐
33	T. Harper, Mon.; B. . Rousseau, Mon.; M. Pronovost, Tor.	2.50	5.00	10.00 ☐
34	J. Bower, Goalie, Tor.; M. Pronovost, Tor.; R. Backstrom, Mon.	2.50	5.00	10.00 ☐
35	F. Mahovlich, Tor.; G. Worsley, Goalie, Mon.	4.25	8.50	17.00 ☐
36	C. Provost, Mon.; J. Bower, Goalie, Tor.	3.00	6.00	12.00 ☐

EL PRODUCTO

— 1962 - 63 ISSUE —

Obtained from small and large boxes of El Producto cigars, these cards had to be removed from the boxes. The condition of the card therefore is a function of how well it was removed. This set is not complete. We would appreciate hearing from anyone who could provide further information.

Card Size:
  Large Size: 5" x 9 1/2"
  Small Size: 3 1/2" x 6 1/2"
Face: Four colour
Back: Blank
Imprint: None
Complete Set No.:
  Large Size: Unknown
  Small Size: Unknown

LARGE SIZE

No.	Player	VG	EX	NRMT
1	Jean Beliveau	25.00	50.00	100.00 ☐
2	Glenn Hall, Goalie	25.00	50.00	100.00 ☐

SMALL SIZE

No.	Player	VG	EX	NRMT
1	Gordie Howe	75.00	150.00	300.00 ☐

— 1962 - 63 DISKS —

Issued in a strip of six, these unnumbered disks are listed as they appear in the strip.

Disk Size: 3" Diameter
Face: Four colour, white border
Back: Black on white card stock; Name, Position, Resume, Bilingual
Imprint: None
Complete Set No.: 6
Complete Set Price: 45.00 85.00 170.00 ☐
Common Player: 8.75 17.50 35.00

No.	Player	VG	EX	NRMT
1	Jean Beliveau, Mon.	12.50	25.00	45.00 ☐
2	Gordie Howe, Det.	15.00	30.00	60.00 ☐
3	Dave Keon, Tor.	8.75	17.50	35.00 ☐
4	Glenn Hall, Goalie, Chi.	10.00	20.00	40.00 ☐
5	Henri Richard, Mon.	8.75	17.50	35.00 ☐
6	Frank Mahovlich, Tor.	8.75	17.50	35.00 ☐

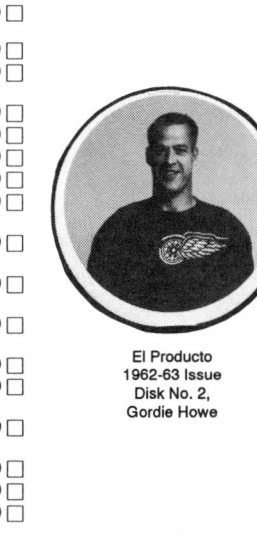
El Producto
1962-63 Issue
Disk No. 2,
Gordie Howe

El Producto
1962-63 Issue
Disk No. 3,
Dave Keon

Chex
1963-65 Photos
Photo No. 5,
Bobby Hull

Chex
1963-65 Photos
Photo No. 14,
Gordie Howe

CHEX

— 1963 - 65 PHOTOS —

There were two printings of this set. One is believed to have been issued in 1963/64 and the other in 1964/65. Colouring between the two printings vary slightly with the second printing having more of a reddish tint. The cards are unnumbered. The cards are listed below alphabetically by team and then by player.

Card Size: 5 1/16" X 7"
Face: Four colour, white border; Name
Back: Blank
Imprint: None
Complete Set No.: 58
Complete Set Price: 275.00 550.00 1,100.00 ☐
Common Player: 3.75 7.50 15.00

CHICAGO BLACK HAWKS

No.	Player	VG	EX	NRMT
1	Phil Esposito	16.00	32.50	65.00 ☐
2	Glenn Hall, Goalie	10.00	20.00	40.00 ☐
3	Billy Hay	3.75	7.50	15.00 ☐
4	Wayne Hillman	3.75	7.50	15.00 ☐
5	Bobby Hull	20.00	42.50	85.00 ☐
6	Chico Maki	3.75	7.50	15.00 ☐
7	Stan Mikita	12.00	22.50	45.00 ☐
8	Pierre Pilote	6.00	12.50	25.00 ☐
9	Elmer Vasko	3.75	7.50	15.00 ☐
10	Ken Wharram	3.75	7.50	15.00 ☐

DETROIT RED WINGS

No.	Player	VG	EX	NRMT
11	Alex Delvecchio	12.00	22.50	45.00 ☐
12	Bill Gadsby	7.50	15.00	30.00 ☐
13	Paul Henderson	5.00	10.00	20.00 ☐
14	Gordie Howe	37.50	75.00	150.00 ☐
15	Parker MacDonald	3.75	7.50	15.00 ☐
16	Bruce MacGregor	3.75	7.50	15.00 ☐
17	Pit Martin	3.75	7.50	15.00 ☐
18	Marcel Pronovost	5.00	10.00	20.00 ☐
19	Norm Ullman	8.75	17.50	35.00 ☐

MONTREAL CANADIENS

No.	Player	VG	EX	NRMT
20	Ralph Backstrom	3.75	7.50	15.00 ☐
21	Dave Balon	3.75	7.50	15.00 ☐
22A	Jean Beliveau, Front View	17.50	35.00	65.00 ☐
22B	Jean Beliveau, Side View	17.50	35.00	65.00 ☐
23	Red Berenson	4.50	9.00	18.00 ☐
24	Toe Blake, Coach	8.75	17.50	35.00 ☐
25	John Ferguson	4.50	9.00	18.00 ☐
26	Jean Gauthier	3.75	7.50	15.00 ☐
27	Bernie Geoffrion	12.50	25.00	50.00 ☐
28	Terry Harper	3.75	7.50	15.00 ☐
29	Bill Hicke	3.75	7.50	15.00 ☐
30	Charlie Hodge, Goalie	5.00	10.00	20.00 ☐
31	Jacques Laperriere	6.00	12.50	25.00 ☐
32	Claude Provost	3.75	7.50	15.00 ☐
33	Marc Reaume	3.75	7.50	15.00 ☐
34	Henri Richard	8.75	17.50	35.00 ☐
35A	Bobby Rousseau	4.50	9.00	18.00 ☐
35B	Bobby Rousseau (Bob Rousseau on card)	4.50	9.00	18.00 ☐
36	Jean Guy Talbot	3.75	7.50	15.00 ☐
37	Gilles Tremblay	3.75	7.50	15.00 ☐
38A	J.C. Tremblay	5.00	10.00	20.00 ☐
38B	J.C. Tremblay (Jean Claude on card)	5.00	10.00	20.00 ☐
39	Gump Worsley, Goalie	12.00	22.50	45.00 ☐

TORONTO MAPLE LEAFS

No.	Player	VG	EX	NRMT
40	George Armstrong	8.75	17.50	35.00 ☐
41	Bob Baun	3.75	7.50	15.00 ☐
42	Johnny Bower, Goalie	10.00	20.00	40.00 ☐
43	Kent Douglas	3.75	7.50	15.00 ☐
44	Dick Duff	3.75	7.50	15.00 ☐
45	Billy Harris	3.75	7.50	15.00 ☐
46	Tim Horton	10.00	20.00	40.00 ☐
47	Punch Imlach, Coach	5.00	10.00	20.00 ☐
48	Red Kelly	10.00	20.00	40.00 ☐
49	Dave Keon	8.75	17.50	35.00 ☐
50	Ed Litzenberger	3.75	7.50	15.00 ☐
51	John MacMillan	3.75	7.50	15.00 ☐

276 • COCA-COLA — 1964-65 CAPS

No.	Player	VG	EX	NRMT
52	Frank Mahovlich	15.00	27.50	55.00
53	Bob Nevin	3.75	7.50	15.00
54	Bob Pulford	6.00	12.50	25.00
55	Eddie Shack	6.00	12.50	25.00
56	Don Simmons, Goalie	3.75	7.50	15.00
57	Allan Stanley	6.00	12.50	25.00
58	Ron Stewart	3.75	7.50	15.00

COCA-COLA
— 1964 - 65 CAPS —

These caps were issued by both Coke and Sprite. The Sprite caps are more difficult to find and will command twice the value of the Coke caps. The caps are unnumbered except for a jersey number and are arranged here alphabetically by team and then by player.

Cap Size: 1 1/8" Diameter
Face: Player's image; Jersey number
Back: Plain
Imprint: None
Complete Set No.: 108
Complete Set Price: 175.00 350.00
Common Player: 1.25 2.50
Display Plastic Rink: 35.00 75.00
  (White with four coloured team logos)

BOSTON BRUINS

No.	Player	VG	EX
1	Murray Balfour	1.25	2.50
2	Leo Boivin	1.75	3.50
3	John Bucyk	3.00	6.00
4	Gary Dornhoefer	1.25	2.50
5	Reggie Fleming	1.25	2.50
6	Ted Green	1.25	2.50
7	Tom Johnson	1.25	2.50
8	Eddie Johnston, Goalie	1.25	2.50
9	Forbes Kennedy	1.25	2.50
10	Orland Kurtenbach	1.25	2.50
11	Bobby Leiter	1.25	2.50
12	Bob McCord	1.25	2.50
13	Ab McDonald	1.25	2.50
14	Murray Oliver	1.25	2.50
15	Dean Prentice	1.25	2.50
16	Ron Schock	1.25	2.50
17	Ed Westfall	1.75	3.50
18	Tom Williams	1.25	2.50

CHICAGO BLACK HAWKS

No.	Player	VG	EX
19	John Brenneman	1.25	2.50
20	Denis DeJordy, Goalie	1.25	2.50
21	Phil Esposito	12.50	25.00
22	Glenn Hall, Goalie	3.50	7.00
23	Billy Hay	1.25	2.50
24	Wayne Hillman	1.25	2.50
25	Bobby Hull	18.50	37.00
26	Al MacNeil	1.25	2.50
27	Chico Maki	1.25	2.50
28	John McKenzie	1.25	2.50
29	Stan Mikita	5.00	10.00
30	Doug Mohns	1.25	2.50
31	Eric Nesterenko	1.25	2.50
32	Pierre Pilote	1.75	3.50
33	Doug Robinson	1.25	2.50
34	Fred Stanfield	1.25	2.50
35	Elmer Vasko	1.25	2.50
36	Kenny Wharram	1.25	2.50

DETROIT RED WINGS

No.	Player	VG	EX
37	Doug Barkley	1.25	2.50
38	Gary Bergman	1.25	2.50
39	Roger Crozier, Goalie	1.75	3.50
40	Alex Delvecchio	5.00	10.00
41	Bill Gadsby	1.75	3.50
42	Paul Henderson	1.25	2.50
43A	Gordie Howe, #9	25.00	50.00
43B	Gordie Howe, #10	25.00	50.00
44	Larry Jeffrey	1.25	2.50

Coca-Cola
1964-65 Caps
Cap No. 38,
Gary Bergman

Coca-Cola
1964-65 Caps
Cap No. 51,
Ron Murphy

Coca-Cola
1964-65 Caps
Cap No. 56,
Dave Balon

Coca-Cola
1964-65 Caps
Cap No. 88,
Marcel Paille

No.	Player	VG	EX
45	Eddie Joyal	1.25	2.50
46	Al Langlois	1.25	2.50
47	Ted Lindsay	4.00	8.00
48	Parker MacDonald	1.25	2.50
49	Bruce MacGregor	1.25	2.50
50	Pit Martin	1.25	2.50
51	Ron Murphy	1.25	2.50
52	Marcel Pronovost	1.75	3.50
53	Floyd Smith	1.25	2.50
54	Norm Ullman	1.75	3.50

MONTREAL CANADIENS

No.	Player	VG	EX
55	Ralph Backstrom	1.25	2.50
56	Dave Balon	1.25	2.50
57	Jean Beliveau	7.50	15.00
58	Yvan Cournoyer	3.50	7.00
59	John Ferguson	1.25	2.50
60	Terry Harper	1.25	2.50
61	Ted Harris	1.25	2.50
62	Bill Hicke	1.25	2.50
63	Charlie Hodge, Goalie	1.75	3.50
64	Jacques Laperriere	1.75	3.50
65	Claude Larose	1.25	2.50
66	Claude Provost	1.25	2.50
67	Henri Richard	4.00	8.00
68	Jim Roberts	1.25	2.50
69	Bobby Rousseau	1.25	2.50
70	Jean-Guy Talbot	1.25	2.50
71	Gilles Tremblay	1.25	2.50
72	J.C. Tremblay	1.25	2.50

NEW YORK RANGERS

No.	Player	VG	EX
73	Lou Angotti	1.25	2.50
74	Arnie Brown	1.25	2.50
75	Dick Duff	1.25	2.50
76	Val Fonteyne	1.25	2.50
77	Rod Gilbert	2.75	5.50
78	Phil Goyette	1.25	2.50
79	Vic Hadfield	2.50	5.00
80	Camille Henry	1.25	2.50
81	Harry Howell	1.75	3.50
82	Earl Ingarfield, Sr.	1.25	2.50
83	Don Johns	1.25	2.50
84	Don Marshall	1.25	2.50
85	Jim Mikol	1.25	2.50
86	Jim Neilson	1.25	2.50
87	Bob Nevin	1.25	2.50
88	Marcel Paille, Goalie	1.25	2.50
89	Jacques Plante, Goalie	10.00	20.00
90	Rod Seiling	1.25	2.50

TORONTO MAPLE LEAFS

No.	Player	VG	EX
91	George Armstrong	5.00	10.00
92A	Andy Bathgate, #9	2.50	5.00
92B	Andy Bathgate, #10	2.50	5.00
93	Bob Baun	1.25	2.50
94	Johnny Bower, Goalie	4.00	8.00
95	Carl Brewer	1.25	2.50
96	Kent Douglas	1.25	2.50
97	Ron Ellis	1.25	2.50
98	Tim Horton	6.00	12.00
99	Red Kelly	3.00	6.00
100	Dave Keon	5.00	10.00
101	Frank Mahovlich	6.00	12.00
102	Don McKenney	1.25	2.50
103	Dickie Moore	2.50	5.00
104	Bob Pulford	1.75	3.50
105	Terry Sawchuk, Goalie	6.00	12.00
106	Eddie Shack	3.00	6.00
107	Allan Stanley	1.75	3.50
108	Ron Stewart	1.25	2.50

— 1965 - 66 REGULAR ISSUE —

Card Size: 2 3/4" X 3 1/2"
Face: Black and white; Name, Resume
Back: Black and white; Name, Bilingual
Imprint: None
Complete Set No.: 108

Complete Set Unperforated:	150.00	300.00	600.00
Complete Set Price:	95.00	190.00	375.00
Common Player:	.60	1.25	2.50
Album:	12.50	25.00	50.00

BOSTON BRUINS

No.	Player	VG	EX	NRMT
1	Barry Ashbee	3.75	7.50	15.00
2	Don Awrey	.60	1.25	2.50
3	Leo Boivin	1.50	3.00	6.00
4	John Bucyk	2.00	4.00	8.00
5	Gerry Cheevers, Goalie	2.00	4.00	8.00
6	Bob Dillabough	.60	1.25	2.50
7	Reggie Fleming	.60	1.25	2.50
8	Ted Green	.60	1.25	2.50
9	Forbes Kennedy	.60	1.25	2.50
10	Al Langlois	.60	1.25	2.50
11	Parker MacDonald	.60	1.25	2.50
12	Murray Oliver	.60	1.25	2.50
13	Bernie Parent, Goalie	3.50	7.00	14.00
14	Dean Prentice	.60	1.25	2.50
15	Ron Stewart	.60	1.25	2.50
16	Ed Westfall	.60	1.25	2.50
17	Tom Williams	.60	1.25	2.50
18	Bob Woytowich	.60	1.25	2.50
	Unperforated Team Set	25.00	50.00	100.00

CHICAGO BLACK HAWKS

No.	Player	VG	EX	NRMT
19	Dave Dryden, Goalie	.60	1.25	2.50
20	Phil Esposito	6.25	12.50	25.00
21	Glenn Hall, Goalie	4.00	8.00	16.00
22	Billy Hay	.60	1.25	2.50
23	Ken Hodge, Sr.	1.00	2.00	4.00
24	Bobby Hull	10.00	20.00	40.00
25	Dennis Hull	1.50	3.00	6.00
26	Doug Jarrett	.60	1.25	2.50
27	Al MacNeil	.60	1.25	2.50
28	Chico Maki	.60	1.25	2.50
29	John McKenzie	.60	1.25	2.50
30	Stan Mikita	3.00	6.00	12.00
31	Doug Mohns	.60	1.25	2.50
32	Eric Nesterenko	.60	1.25	2.50
33	Pierre Pilote	1.50	3.00	6.00
34	Matt Ravlich	.60	1.25	2.50
35	Fred Stanfield	.60	1.25	2.50
36	Elmer Vasko	.60	1.25	2.50
37	Kenny Wharram	.60	1.25	2.50
	Unperforated Team Set	35.00	75.00	150.00

DETROIT RED WINGS

No.	Player	VG	EX	NRMT
38	Hank Bassen, Goalie	.60	1.25	2.50
39	Doug Barkley	.60	1.25	2.50
40	Gary Bergman	.60	1.25	2.50
41	Roger Crozier, Goalie	1.00	2.00	4.00
42	Alex Delvecchio	2.50	5.00	10.00
43	Val Fonteyne	.60	1.25	2.50
44	Bill Gadsby	1.50	3.00	6.00
45	Warren Godfrey	.60	1.25	2.50
46	Billy Harris	.60	1.25	2.50
47	Paul Henderson	1.75	3.50	7.00
48	Gordie Howe	17.50	35.00	75.00
49	Bruce MacGregor	.60	1.25	2.50
50	Bert Marshall	.60	1.25	2.50
51	Ab McDonald	.60	1.25	2.50
52	Ron Murphy	.60	1.25	2.50
53	Floyd Smith	.60	1.25	2.50
54	Norm Ullman	1.75	3.50	7.00
	Unperforated Team Set	50.00	100.00	200.00

MONTREAL CANADIENS

No.	Player	VG	EX	NRMT
55	Ralph Backstrom	.60	1.25	2.50
56	Jean Beliveau	7.50	15.00	30.00
57	Yvan Cournoyer	2.00	4.00	8.00
58	Dick Duff	.60	1.25	2.50
59	John Ferguson	1.00	2.00	4.00
60	Terry Harper	.60	1.25	2.50
61	Ted Harris	.60	1.25	2.50
62	Charlie Hodge, Goalie	1.00	2.00	4.00
63	Jacques Laperriere	1.25	2.50	5.00
64	Claude Larose	.60	1.25	2.50
65	Garry Peters	.60	1.25	2.50
66	Claude Provost	.60	1.25	2.50
67	Henri Richard	2.00	4.00	8.00
68	Jim Roberts	.60	1.25	2.50
69	Bobby Rousseau	.60	1.25	2.50
70	Don Simmons, Goalie	.60	1.25	2.50
71	Jean-Guy Talbot	.60	1.25	2.50
72	Gilles Tremblay	.60	1.25	2.50
73	J.C. Tremblay	.60	1.25	2.50
74	Gump Worsley, Goalie	4.50	9.00	18.00
	Unperforated Team Set	35.00	75.00	150.00

NEW YORK RANGERS

No.	Player	VG	EX	NRMT
75	Arnie Brown	.60	1.25	2.50
76	Ed Giacomin, Goalie	4.00	8.00	16.00
77	Rod Gilbert	1.50	3.00	6.00
78	Phil Goyette	.60	1.25	2.50
79	Vic Hadfield	1.00	2.00	4.00
80	Bill Hicke	.60	1.25	2.50
81	Wayne Hillman	.60	1.25	2.50
82	Harry Howell	1.50	3.00	6.00
83	Earl Ingarfield, Sr.	.60	1.25	2.50
84	Don Marshall	.60	1.25	2.50
85	Mike McMahon	.60	1.25	2.50
86	Jim Neilson	.60	1.25	2.50
87	Bob Nevin	.60	1.25	2.50
88	Jean Ratelle	1.50	3.00	6.00
89	Doug Robinson	.60	1.25	2.50
	Unperforated Team Set	25.00	50.00	100.00

TORONTO MAPLE LEAFS

No.	Player	VG	EX	NRMT
90	George Armstrong	1.50	3.00	6.00
91	Andy Bathgate	1.75	3.50	7.00
92	Bob Baun	.60	1.25	2.50
93	Johnny Bower, Goalie	2.75	5.50	11.00
94	Kent Douglas	.60	1.25	2.50
95	Ron Ellis	.60	1.25	2.50
96	Tim Horton	3.75	7.50	15.00
97	Red Kelly	2.00	4.00	8.00
98	Dave Keon	2.00	4.00	8.00
99	Orland Kurtenbach	.60	1.25	2.50
100	Frank Mahovlich	3.75	7.50	15.00
101	Bob Pulford	1.00	2.00	4.00
102	Marcel Pronovost	1.50	3.00	6.00
103	Terry Sawchuk, Goalie	5.50	11.00	22.00
104	Brit Selby	.60	1.25	2.50
105	Eddie Shack	1.50	3.00	6.00
106	Allan Stanley	1.25	2.50	5.00
107	Pete Stemkowski	.60	1.25	2.50
108	Mike Walton	.60	1.25	2.50
	Unperforated Team Set	35.00	75.00	150.00

Coca-Cola
1965-66 Issue
Card No. 1,
Barry Ashbee

Coca-Cola
1965-66 Issue
Card No. 13,
Bernie Parent

Coca-Cola
1965-66 Issue
Card No. 61,
Ted Harris

Coca-Cola
1966 Booklets
Booklet No. "D",
Henri Richard

— 1966 BOOKLETS —

This is a 32-page instructional booklet called: "How to Play".

Booklet Size: 4 5/16" X 3 15/16"
Face: Four colour, blue background, black lettering
Back: Black on blue background
Imprint: None
Complete Set No.: 8

Complete Set Price:	50.00	100.00	200.00

ENGLISH ISSUE

No.	Player	VG	EX	NRMT
A	Johnny Bower, How to Play Goal	12.50	25.00	50.00
B	David Keon, How to Play Forward (Defensive)	12.50	25.00	50.00
C	Jacques Laperriere, How to Play Defence	12.50	25.00	50.00
D	Henri Richard, How to Play Forward (Offensive)	12.50	25.00	50.00

278 • EATON'S — 1977-78 MINI ISSUE

FRENCH ISSUE

No.	Player	VG	EX	NRMT
W	Johnny Bower, Comment les Buts	12.50	25.00	50.00
X	David Keon, Comment Jouer à l'àvant	12.50	25.00	50.00
Y	Jacques Laperriere, Comment Jouer à la défense	12.50	25.00	50.00
Z	Henri Richard, Comment Jouer à l'àvant	12.50	25.00	50.00

— 1977-78 MINI ISSUE —

The set is unnumbered and is listed alphabetically.

Card Size: 1 3/8" X 1 3/8"
Face: Four colour; Name, Team
Back: Resume
Imprint: © THE COCA-COLA COMPANY
Complete Set No.: 30
Complete Set Price: 7.00 / 14.00 / 28.00
Common Player: .12 / .25 / .50

No.	Player	VG	EX	NRMT
1	Syl Apps, Jr., Pit.	.12	.25	.50
2	Dave Burrows, Pit.	.12	.25	.50
3	Bobby Clarke, Phi.	.75	1.50	3.00
4	Yvan Cournoyer, Mon.	.50	1.00	2.00
5	John Davidson, Goalie, NYR	.18	.35	.75
6	Marcel Dionne, LA	.75	1.50	3.00
7	Doug Favell, Goalie	.12	.25	.50
8	Rod Gilbert, NYR	.35	.75	1.50
9	Brian Glennie, Tor.	.12	.25	.50
10	Butch Goring, LA	.12	.25	.50
11	Lorne Henning, NYI	.12	.25	.50
12	Cliff Koroll, Chi.	.12	.25	.50
13	Guy Lapointe, Mon.	.25	.50	1.00
14	Dave Maloney, NYR	.12	.25	.50
15	Pit Martin, Chi.	.12	.25	.50
16	Lou Nanne, Min.	.12	.25	.50
17	Bobby Orr, Chi.	3.00	6.00	12.00
18	Brad Park, Bos.	.35	.75	1.50
19	Craig Ramsey, Buf.	.12	.25	.50
20	Larry Robinson, Mon.	.35	.75	1.50
21	Jim Rutherford, Goalie, Det.	.12	.25	.50
22	Don Saleski, Phi.	.12	.25	.50
23	Steve Shutt, Mon.	.12	.25	.50
24	Darryl Sittler, Tor.	.75	1.50	3.00
25	Billy Smith, Goalie, NYI	.50	1.00	2.00
26	Bob Stewart, Cle.	.12	.25	.50
27	Rogatien Vachon, Goalie, LA	.50	1.00	2.00
28	Jimmy Watson, Phi.	.12	.25	.50
29	Joe Watson, Phi.	.12	.25	.50
30	Ed Westfall, NYI	.12	.25	.50

EATON'S

— 1964-67 GORDIE HOWE — "SPORTS ADVISER"

These cards were issued by Eaton's between 1964 and 1967 as promotional cards for their Truline Sports Equipment. During the summer months Howe toured Canada appearing at the Eaton stores to promote this line of equipment.

Card Size: 3 1/2" x 5 1/2"
Face: Four colour, white border
Back: Blue and black on white card stock; Facsimile autograph
Imprint: EATON'S
Complete Set No.: 3
Complete Set Price: 20.00 / 40.00 / 80.00

No.	Player	VG	EX	NRMT
1	1964-65 "All-Star" Uniform	7.50	15.00	30.00
2	1965-66 "Action" Pose	7.50	15.00	30.00
3	1966-67 "Standing Pose"	7.50	15.00	30.00

Eaton's
1964-67 Gordie Howe
Card No. 3,
1966-67 "Standing Pose"

Post Cereal
1966-67 Hockey Tips
Card No. 3,
Gordie Howe

Post Cereal
1966-67 Hockey Tips
Card No. 5,
Dave Keon

Post Cereal
1967-68 Issue
Card No. 2B,
Harry Howel

POST CEREAL

— 1966-67 HOCKEY TIPS — LARGE SIZE

Issued on the backs of Post cereal boxes, these cards are unnumbered and have blank backs. Two different photos of each player were issued.

Card Size: 6" X 9 1/4"
Face: Four colour; Name, Facsimile signature, Hockey tip, Bilingual
Back: Blank
Imprint: None
Complete Set No.: 18
Complete Set Price: 22.50 / 45.00 / 85.00
Common Player: .75 / 1.50 / 3.00

ALL-STARS

No.	Player	VG	EX	NRMT
1	Glenn Hall, Goalie, Chi.	1.75	3.50	7.00
2	Tim Horton, Tor.	1.75	3.50	7.00
3	Gordie Howe, Det.	6.00	12.00	24.00
4	Harry Howell, NYR	.75	1.50	3.00
5	Dave Keon, Tor.	1.50	3.00	6.00
6	Frank Mahovlich, Tor.	3.00	6.00	12.00
7	Stan Mikita, Chi.	1.25	2.50	5.00
8	Bob Nevin, NYR	.75	1.50	3.00
9	Murray Oliver, Bos.	.75	1.50	3.00
10	Pierre Pilote, Chi.	1.25	2.50	5.00
11	Bob Pulford, Tor.	1.00	2.00	4.00
12	Norm Ullman, Det.	1.25	2.50	5.00

MONTREAL

No.	Player	VG	EX	NRMT
13	Jacques Laperriere	.75	1.50	3.00
14	Henri Richard	1.25	2.50	5.00
15	Bobby Rousseau	.75	1.50	3.00
16	Gilles Tremblay	.75	1.50	3.00
17	J.C. Tremblay	.75	1.50	3.00
18	Gump Worsley, Goalie	4.50	9.00	18.00

— 1966-67 HOCKEY TIPS — SMALL SIZE

Card Size: 2 5/8" X 2 5/8"
Face: Four colour
Back: Blank
Imprint: None
Complete Set No.: 9
Complete Set Price: 10.00 / 20.00 / 40.00
Common Player: .75 / 1.50 / 3.00

ALL-STARS

No.	Player	VG	EX	NRMT
1	Glenn Hall, Goalie, Chi.	1.50	2.50	5.00
2	Gordie Howe, Det.	6.00	12.00	24.00
3	Dave Keon, Tor.	1.50	3.00	6.00
4	Frank Mahovlich, Tor.	3.00	6.00	12.00
5	Bob Nevin, NYR	.75	1.50	3.00
6	Bob Pulford, Tor.	.75	1.50	3.00

MONTREAL CANADIENS

No.	Player	VG	EX	NRMT
7	Bobby Rousseau	.75	1.50	3.00
8	J.C. Tremblay	.75	1.50	3.00
9	Gump Worsley, Goalie	2.00	4.00	8.00

Note: Cards are listed in this catalogue chronologically by manufacturer's first date of issue. For all manufacturers, subsequent cards appear in issue date order following that manufacturer's first listing. See the last page of this catalogue for an alphabetical index of issuers.

— 1967 - 68 ISSUE —

Issued on the backs of Post cereal boxes, these cards are unnumbered and have blank backs. Two different photos of each player were issued.

Card Size: 6 1/8" X 7 1/8"
Face: Four colour, Borderless; Facsimile autograph
Back: Blank
Imprint: None
Complete Set No.: 12
Complete Set Price: 17.50   35.00   75.00 ☐
Common Player: .75   1.50   3.00

No.	Player	VG	EX	NRMT
1A	Gordie Howe, Det. with net	5.50	11.00	22.00 ☐
1B	Gordie Howe, Det. without net	5.50	11.00	22.00 ☐
2A	Harry Howell, NYR, Passing	.75	1.50	3.00 ☐
2B	Harry Howell, NYR Blocking Shot	.75	1.50	3.00 ☐
3A	Jacques Laperrier, Mon. with net	.75	1.50	3.00 ☐
3B	Jacques Laperrier, Mon. without net	.75	1.50	3.00 ☐
4A	Stan Mikita, Chi.	2.00	4.00	8.00 ☐
4B	Stan Mikita, Chi.	2.00	4.00	8.00 ☐
5A	Bobby Orr, Bos., Still	5.50	11.00	22.00 ☐
5B	Bobby Orr, Bos., Action	5.50	11.00	22.00 ☐
6A	Henri Richard, Mon., Puck in skates	1.25	2.50	5.00 ☐
6B	Henri Richard, Mon.	1.25	2.50	5.00 ☐

— 1968 - 69 MARBLES —

A white plastic rink-shaped game board was available. The Montreal and Toronto team logos and the Post logo was displayed on the rink, and the wording was bilingual. There were perforations on the rink and in the penalty box to hold the marbles.

Marble Size: 3/4" Diameter
Rink Size: 30" x 18"
Face: Four colour; Name
Back: Team colours
Imprint: None
Complete Set No.: 30
Complete Set Price: 90.00   175.00 ☐
Common Player: 2.00   4.00
Rink: 30.00 ☐

MONTREAL CANADIENS

No.	Player	VG	EX
1	Ralph Backstrom	2.00	4.00 ☐
2	Jean Beliveau	11.00	22.00 ☐
3	Yvan Cournoyer	7.00	14.00 ☐
4	John Ferguson	2.00	4.00 ☐
5	Terry Harper	2.00	4.00 ☐
6	Ted Harris	2.00	4.00 ☐
7	Jacques Laperriere	5.00	10.00 ☐
8	Jacques Lemaire	5.00	10.00 ☐
9	Henri Richard	5.00	10.00 ☐
10	Bobby Rousseau	2.00	4.00 ☐
11	Serge Savard	4.00	8.00 ☐
12	Gilles Tremblay	2.00	4.00 ☐
13	J.C. Tremblay	2.00	4.00 ☐
14	Rogatien Vachon, Goalie	5.00	10.00 ☐
15	Gump Worsley, Goalie	7.00	14.00 ☐

TORONTO MAPLE LEAFS

No.	Player	VG	EX
16	Johnny Bower, Goalie	7.00	14.00 ☐
17	Wayne Carleton	2.00	4.00 ☐
18	Ron Ellis	3.00	6.00 ☐
19	Bruce Gamble, Goalie	2.00	4.00 ☐
20	Paul Henderson	2.50	5.00 ☐
21	Tim Horton	7.00	14.00 ☐
22	Dave Keon	5.00	10.00 ☐
23	Murray Oliver	2.00	4.00 ☐
24	Mike Pelyk	2.00	4.00 ☐
25	Pierre Pilote	4.50	9.00 ☐
26	Marcel Pronovost	4.50	9.00 ☐
27	Bob Pulford	4.50	9.00 ☐
28	Floyd Smith	2.00	4.00 ☐
29	Norm Ullman	4.50	9.00 ☐
30	Mike Walton	2.00	4.00 ☐

Post Cereal
1972-73 Hockey Action
Transfer No. 6,
Break away/Echappée

Post Cereal
1981-82 NHL Stars In Action
Card No. 1,
Raymond Bourque

Post Cereal
1981-82 NHL Stars In Action
Card No. 28,
Kent Nilsson

— 1972 - 73 HOCKEY ACTION TRANSFERS —

These transfers are numbered PR 146 - 1 of 12.

Booklet Size: 4 7/8" X 3"
Face: Four colour; Number, Post logo, Bilingual
Back: Four colour on blue background; Two players, Name, Resume, Bilingual
Imprint: © 1972 Letraset (Industrial) Limited, London S.E. 1 England.
© General Foods Ltd. / Phase III Promotions Ltd.
Transfer Size: 4 7/8" X 2 5/8"
Face: Four colour; Four transfers per sheet
Back: Transfer instructions, Bilingual
Imprint: PR146 — PATENTED PRINTED IN ENGLAND BY LETRASET
Complete Set No.: 30
Complete Set Price: 75.00   150.00   300.00 ☐
Common Player: 2.50   5.00   10.00

No.	Player	VG	EX	NRMT
1	Defense / Sur la Défensive: Garry Unger; Bobby Orr	6.25	12.50	25.00 ☐
4	Power save / Arrêt du gart: Jim McKenny; Ed Giacomin, Goalie	3.00	6.00	12.00 ☐
5	Power play goal / Jue de Puissance: P. Quinn; K. Magnuson	3.75	7.50	15.00 ☐
6	Break away / Echappée: Paul Shmyr; Rod Seiling	2.50	5.00	10.00 ☐
7	Rebound / Retour de lancer: Syl Apps Jr,; Serge Savard	2.50	5.00	10.00 ☐
9	Wrist shot / Lancer du poignet: Gump Worsley, Goalie; Gary Bergman	2.50	5.00	10.00 ☐
10	Last minute / Dernière minute: Roger Crozier, Goalie; Ed Westfall	2.50	5.00	10.00 ☐
11	Goalmouth scramble / Mêlée devant les buts: Dennis Hull; Orland Kurtenbach	2.50	5.00	10.00 ☐
12	Chest save / Arrêt de la poitrine: Rogatien Vachon, Goalie; Yvan Cournoyer	2.50	5.00	10.00 ☐

Note: This set is incomplete. We would appreciate hearing form anyone who can supply further information.

— 1981 - 82 NHL STARS IN ACTION — SALESMAN'S SAMPLE

Card Size: 2 3/16" X 3 3/16 (Booklet)
Face: Four colour standup, facsimile signature, "Pop-up" instructions, bilingual
Back: Blank
Imprint: General Foods Inc. Megaprint Canada Ltd.
Complete Set No.: Unknown
Complete Set Price: Unknown ☐

No.	Player	VG	EX	NRMT
—	Darryl Sittler	2.50	5.00	10.00 ☐

— 1981 - 82 NHL STARS IN ACTION —

This is a die cut stand-up set. Prices listed are for cards in original unfolded position.

Card Size: 2 3/16" X 3 3/16 (Booklet)
Face: Four colour standup, facsimile signature, "Pop-up" instructions, bilingual
Back: Blank
Imprint: General Foods Inc. Megaprint Canada Ltd.
Complete Set No.: 28
Complete Set Price: 25.00   50.00 ☐
Common Player: .50   1.00

No.	Player	EX	NRMT
1	Raymond Bourque, Bos.	5.00	10.00 ☐
2	Gilbert Perreault, Bos.	1.00	2.00 ☐
3	Denis Savard, Chi.	1.50	3.00 ☐
4	Dale McCourt, Det.	.50	1.00 ☐
5	Robert Smith, Min.	.75	1.50 ☐
6	Mike Bossy, NYI	2.50	5.00 ☐
7	Bobby Clarke, Phi.	1.25	2.50 ☐
8	Randy Carlyle, Pit.	.50	1.00 ☐
9	Mike Palmateer, Goalie, Wash.	.75	1.50 ☐
10	David Williams, Van.	.50	1.00 ☐
11	Mark Howe, Har.	1.50	3.00 ☐
12	Marcel Dionne, LA	1.50	3.00 ☐
13	Mike Liut, Goalie, St. L.	.75	1.50 ☐
14	Barry Beck, NYR	.50	1.00 ☐
15	Mark Messier, Edm.	5.00	10.00 ☐
16	Larry Robinson, Mon.	1.50	3.00 ☐

POST CEREAL — 1982-83 ISSUE

No.	Player	EX	NRMT
17	Real Cloutier, Que.	.50	1.00
18	Borje Salming, Tor.	.75	1.50
19	Morris Lukowich, Win.	.50	1.00
20	Brett Callighen, Edm.	.50	1.00
21	George (Rob) Ramage, Col.	1.00	2.00
22	Wilf Paiement, Tor.	.50	1.00
23	Mario Tremblay, Mon.	.50	1.00
24	Robbie Ftorek, Que.	.50	1.00
25	Stanley Smyl, Van.	.50	1.00
26	David Babych, Win.	.50	1.00
27	Willi Plett, Cal.	.50	1.00
28	Kent Nilsson, Cal.	.50	1.00

— 1982-83 ISSUE —

The sixteen mini-cards for each team, plus a hockey offer were issued in a strip format. Cards have either yellow, red, blue, gold or green bottom borders. Backs are either black, red, brown, blue or purple.

Strip: 13 1/4" X 4 1/8"
Card Size: 1 5/8" X 2 1/8"
Face: Four colour, cream border, Player's name and jersey number
Back: Blue, red and white on card stock; Team and sponsor logos
Imprint: None
Complete Set No.: 336
Complete Set Price: 20.00 40.00
Common Player: .05 .10

BOSTON BRUINS

No.	Player	EX	NRMT
1	Raymond Bourque	1.50	3.00
2	Wayne Cashman	.10	.20
3	Bruce Crowder	.05	.10
4	Tom Fergus	.05	.10
5	Mike Gillis	.05	.10
6	Stan Jonathan	.05	.10
7	Steven Kasper	.05	.10
8	Byron (Brad) McCrimmon	.05	.10
9	Peter McNab	.05	.10
10	Larry Melnyk	.05	.10
11	Rick Middleton	.05	.10
12	Mike Milbury	.05	.10
13	Mike O'Connell	.05	.10
14	Terry O'Reilly	.05	.10
15	Brad Park	.25	.50
16	Rogatien Vachon, Goalie	.12	.25

BUFFALO SABRES

No.	Player	EX	NRMT
17	Richie Dunn	.05	.10
18	Don Edwards, Goalie	.05	.10
19	Mike Foligno	.05	.10
20	Bill Hajt	.05	.10
21	Yvon Lambert	.05	.10
22	Dale McCourt	.05	.10
23	Anthony McKegney	.05	.10
24	Gilbert Perreault	.12	.25
25	Larry Playfair	.05	.10
26	Craig Ramsey	.05	.10
27	Micheal Ramsey	.05	.10
28	Lindy Ruff	.05	.10
29	Ric Seiling	.05	.10
30	Jenn F. Sauve	.05	.10
31	Andre Savard	.25	.50
32	John Van Boxmeer	.05	.10

CALGARY FLAMES

No.	Player	EX	NRMT
33	Mel Bridgman	.12	.25
34	Guy Chouinard	.05	.10
35	Denis Cyr	.05	.10
36	Jamie Hislop	.05	.10
37	Ken Houston	.05	.10
38	Kevin LaVallee	.05	.10
39	Gary McAdam	.05	.10
40	Lanny McDonald	.25	.50
41	Bob Murdoch	.05	.10
42	Kent Nilsson	.05	.10
43	James Peplinski	.07	.15
44	Willi Plett	.05	.10
45	Pekka Rautakallio	.05	.10
46	Paul Reinhart	.05	.10
47	Pat Riggin, Goalie	.05	.10
48	Phil Russell	.05	.10

CHICAGO BLACK HAWKS

No.	Player	EX	NRMT
49	Ted Bulley	.05	.10
50	Doug Crossman	.05	.10
51	Tony Esposito, Goalie	.25	.50
52	Greg Fox	.05	.10
53	Bill Gardner	.05	.10
54	Tim Higgins	.05	.10
55	Dave Hutchison	.05	.10
56	Reg Kerr	.05	.10
57	Tom Lysiak	.05	.10
58	Grant Mulvey	.05	.10
59	Rick Paterson	.05	.10
60	Rich Preston	.05	.10
61	Terry Ruskowski	.05	.10
62	Denis Savard	.10	.20
63	Allan Secord	.10	.20
64	Douglas Wilson	.05	.10

DETROIT RED WINGS

No.	Player	EX	NRMT
65	John Barrett	.05	.10
66	Michael Blaisdell	.05	.10
67	Danny Gare	.05	.10
68	Willie Huber	.05	.10
69	Greg Joly	.05	.10
70	Mark Kirton	.05	.10
71	Reed Larson	.05	.10
72	Walt McKechnie	.05	.10
73	Vaclav Nedomansky	.05	.10
74	John Ogrodnick	.05	.10
75	Mark Osborne	.05	.10
76	Bob Sauve, Goalie	.05	.10
77	Jim Schoenfeld	.05	.10
78	Derrek Smith	.05	.10
79	Greg Smith	.05	.10
80	Paul Woods	.05	.10

EDMONTON OILERS

No.	Player	EX	NRMT
81	Glenn Anderson	.25	.50
82	Brett Callighen	.05	.10
83	Paul Coffey	.50	1.00
84	Lee Fogolin	.05	.10
85	Grant Fuhr, Goalie	.50	1.00
86	Wayne Gretzky	4.00	8.00
87	Matti Hagman	.05	.10
88	Pat Hughes	.05	.10
89	Dave Hunter	.05	.10
90	Jari Kurri	.50	1.00
91	Garry Lariviere	.05	.10
92	Kevin Lowe	.05	.10
93	Dave Lumley	.05	.10
94	Mark Messier	1.00	2.00
95	Dave Semenko	.05	.10
96	Risto Siltanen	.05	.10

HARTFORD WHALERS

No.	Player	EX	NRMT
97	Jordy Douglas	.05	.10
98	Ron Francis	.13	.25
99	Garry Howatt	.05	.10
100	Mark Howe	.25	.50
101	Dave Keon	.35	.70
102	Christopher Kotsopoulos	.05	.10
103	Pierre Larouche	.05	.10
104	George Lyle	.05	.10
105	Jack McIlhargey	.05	.10
106	Greg Millen, Goalie	.05	.10
107	Warren Miller	.05	.10
108	Donald Nachbaur	.05	.10
109	Paul Shmyr	.05	.10
110	Blaine Stoughton	.05	.10
111	Douglas Sulliman	.05	.10
112	Blake Wesley	.05	.10

Post
1982-83 Issue
Card No. 52,
Greg Fox

Post
1982-83 Issue
Card No. 57,
Tom Lysiak

Post
1982-83 Issue
Card No. 58,
Grant Mulvey

— 1982 - 83 ISSUE — POST CEREAL • 281

LOS ANGELES KINGS

No.	Player	EX	NRMT
113	Steve Bozek	.05	.10
114	Rick Chartraw	.05	.10
115	Marcel Dionne	.10	.20
116	Jim Fox	.05	.10
117	Mark Hardy	.05	.10
118	Dean Hopkins	.05	.10
119	Steve Jensen	.05	.10
120	John Paul Kelly	.05	.10
121	Jerry Korab	.05	.10
122	Mario Lessard, Goalie	.05	.10
123	Dave Lewis	.05	.10
124	Lawrence Murphy	.12	.25
125	Charlie Simmer	.05	.10
126	Douglas Smith	.05	.10
127	David Taylor	.10	.20
128	Gordon (Jay) Wells	.05	.10

MINNESOTA NORTH STARS

No.	Player	EX	NRMT
129	Kent-Erik Andersson	.05	.10
130	Fred Barrett	.05	.10
131	Steve Christoff	.05	.10
132	Dino Ciccarelli	.50	1.00
133	Curt Giles	.05	.10
134	Craig Hartsburg	.05	.10
135	Brad Maxwell	.05	.10
136	Al MacAdam	.05	.10
137	Tom McCarthy	.05	.10
138	Gilles Meloche, Goalie	.05	.10
139	Brad Palmer	.05	.10
140	Steve Payne	.05	.10
141	Gordon Roberts	.10	.20
142	Gary Sargent	.05	.10
143	Robert Smith	.05	.10
144	Tim Young	.05	.10

MONTREAL CANADIENS

No.	Player	EX	NRMT
145	Keith Acton	.05	.10
146	Brian Engblom	.05	.10
147	Bob Gainey	.05	.10
148	Mark Hunter	.05	.10
149	Doug Jarvis	.05	.10
150	Guy Lafleur	.20	.40
151	Rod Langway	.05	.10
152	Craig Laughlin	.05	.10
153	Pierre Mondou	.05	.10
154	Mark Napier	.05	.10
155	Robert Picard	.05	.10
156	Doug Risebrough	.05	.10
157	Larry Robinson	.20	.40
158	Richard Sevigny, Goalie	.05	.10
159	Steve Shutt	.10	.20
160	Mario Tremblay	.05	.10

NEW JERSEY DEVILS

No.	Player	EX	NRMT
161	Brent Ashton	.05	.10
162	Dave Cameron	.05	.10
163	Joe Cirella	.05	.10
164	Dwight Foster	.05	.10
165	Mike Kitchen	.05	.10
166	Don Lever	.05	.10
167	Bob Lorimer	.05	.10
168	Merlin Malinowski	.05	.10
169	Bob MacMillan	.05	.10
170	Kevin Maxwell	.05	.10
171	Joe Micheletti	.05	.10
172	Bob Miller	.05	.10
173	George (Rob) Ramage	.05	.10
174	Glenn Resch, Goalie	.05	.10
175	Steve Tambellini	.05	.10
176	John Wensink	.05	.10

NEW YORK ISLANDERS

No.	Player	EX	NRMT
177	Mike Bossy	.35	.75
178	Bob Bourne	.05	.10
179	Clark Gillies	.05	.10
180	Butch Goring	.07	.15

Post
1982-83 Issue
Card No. 60,
Rich Preston

Post
1982-83 Issue
Card No. 63,
Allan Secord

Post
1982-83 Issue
Card No. 64,
Doug Wilson

No.	Player	EX	NRMT
181	Anders Kallur	.05	.10
182	Tomas Jonsson	.05	.10
183	Dave Langevin	.05	.10
184	Mike McEwen	.05	.10
185	Wayne Merrick	.05	.10
186	Ken Morrow	.05	.10
187	Bob Nystrom	.07	.15
188	Stefan Persson	.05	.10
189	Denis Potvin	.25	.50
190	Billy Smith, Goalie	.15	.30
191	John Tonelli	.05	.10
192	Bryan Trottier	.05	.10

NEW YORK RANGERS

No.	Player	EX	NRMT
193	Mike Allison	.05	.10
194	Barry Beck	.07	.15
195	Andre Dore	.05	.10
196	Ron Duguay	.07	.15
197	Nick Fotiu	.05	.10
198	Robbie Ftorek	.05	.10
199	Ronald Greschner	.05	.10
200	Ed Johnstone	.05	.10
201	Thomas Laidlaw	.05	.10
202	Dave Maloney	.05	.10
203	Donald Maloney	.05	.10
204	Mark Pavelich	.05	.10
205	Mike Rogers	.05	.10
206	Reijo Ruotsalainen	.05	.10
207	Stephen Weeks, Goalie	.05	.10
208	Steve Vickers	.05	.10

PHILADELPHIA FLYERS

No.	Player	EX	NRMT
209	Fred Arthur	.05	.10
210	Reid Bailey	.05	.10
211	Bill Barber	.10	.20
212	Bobby Clarke	.25	.50
213	Glen Cochrane	.05	.10
214	Paul Holmgren	.05	.10
215	Tim Kerr	.10	.20
216	Reggie Leach	.12	.25
217	Ken Linsemam	.05	.10
218	Bradley Marsh	.07	.15
219	Peter Peeters, Goalie	.05	.10
220	Ilkka Sinisalo	.05	.10
221	Darryl Sittler	.25	.50
222	Brian Propp	.10	.20
223	Jimmy Watson	.05	.10
224	Behn Wilson	.05	.10

PITTSBURGH PENGUINS

No.	Player	EX	NRMT
225	Paul Baxter	.05	.10
226	Pat Boutette	.05	.10
227	Mike Bullard	.05	.10
228	Randy Carlyle	.10	.20
229	Marc Chorney	.05	.10
230	Michel Dion, Goalie	.05	.10
231	George Ferguson	.05	.10
232	Paul Gardner	.05	.10
233	Pat Graham	.05	.10
234	Rick Kehoe	.05	.10
235	Peter Lee	.05	.10
236	Greg Malone	.05	.10
237	Pat Price	.05	.10
238	Douglas Shedden	.05	.10
239	Gregg Sheppard	.05	.10
240	Ron Stackhouse	.05	.10

QUEBEC NORDIQUES

No.	Player	EX	NRMT
241	Real Cloutier	.05	.10
242	Alain Cote	.05	.10
243	Andre Dupont	.05	.10
244	John Garrett, Goalie	.05	.10
245	Jere Gillis	.05	.10
246	Michel Goulet	.35	.75
247	Dale Hunter	.07	.15
248	Mario Marois	.05	.10
249	Wilf Paiement	.05	.10

282 • BAUER SKATES — 1968 - 69 ISSUE —

No.	Player	EX	NRMT
250	Jacques Richard	.05	.10
251	Normand Rochefort	.05	.10
252	Anton Stastny	.05	.10
253	Marion Stastny	.05	.10
254	Peter Stastny	.35	.75
255	Marc Tardif	.05	.10
256	Wally Weir	.05	.10

ST. LOUIS BLUES

No.	Player	EX	NRMT
257	Wayne Babych	.05	.10
258	Bill Baker	.05	.10
259	Jack Brownschidle	.05	.10
260	Mike Crombeen	.05	.10
261	Blake Dunlop	.05	.10
262	Bernie Federko	.05	.10
263	Ed Kea	.05	.10
264	Rick Lapointe	.05	.10
265	Guy Lapointe	.05	.10
266	Mike Liut, Goalie	.10	.20
267	Larry Patey	.05	.10
268	Jim Pavese	.05	.10
269	Jorgen Pettersson	.05	.10
270	Brian Sutter	.05	.10
271	Perry Turnbull	.05	.10
272	Mike Zuke	.05	.10

TORONTO MAPLE LEAFS

No.	Player	EX	NRMT
273	John Anderson	.05	.10
274	Normand Aubin	.05	.10
275	Jim Benning	.05	.10
276	Fred Boimistruck	.05	.10
277	Bill Derlago	.05	.10
278	Miroslav Frycer	.05	.10
279	Robert (Stewart) Gavin	.05	.10
280	Michel Larocque, Goalie	.05	.10
281	Bob Manno	.05	.10
282	Terry Martin	.05	.10
283	Robert McGill	.05	.10
284	Barry Melrose	.05	.10
285	Walter Poddubny	.05	.10
286	Rocky Saganiuk	.05	.10
287	Borje Salming	.12	.25
288	Richard Vaive	.05	.10

VANCOUVER CANUCKS

No.	Player	EX	NRMT
289	Ivan Boldirev	.05	.10
290	Richard Brodeur, Goalie	.10	.20
291	Marc Crawford	.05	.10
292	Ron Delorme, Goalie	.05	.10
293	Curt Fraser	.05	.10
294	Thomas Gradin	.05	.10
295	Doug Halward	.05	.10
296	Ivan Hlinka	.05	.10
297	Lars Lindgren	.05	.10
298	Gary Lupul	.05	.10
299	Kevin McCarthy	.05	.10
300	Lars Molin	.05	.10
301	Darcy Rota	.05	.10
302	Stanley Smyl	.05	.10
303	Harold Snepsts	.10	.20
304	David Williams	.10	.20

WASHINGTON CAPITALS

No.	Player	EX	NRMT
305	Robert Carpenter	.10	.20
306	Glen Currie	.05	.10
307	Gaetan Duchesne	.05	.10
308	Michael Gartner	.50	1.00
309	Robert Gould	.05	.10
310	Richard Green	.05	.10
311	Bengt-ake Gustafsson	.05	.10
312	Doug Hicks	.05	.10
313	Randy Holt	.05	.10
314	Al Jensen, Goalie	.05	.10
315	Dennis Maruk	.05	.10
316	Terry Murray	.05	.10
317	Greg Theberge	.05	.10
318	Chris Valentine	.05	.10

Post 1982-83 Issue
Card No. 177, Mike Bossy

Post 1982-83 Issue
Card No. 190, Billy Smith

Post 1982-83 Issue
Card No. 246, Michel Goulet

No.	Player	EX	NRMT
319	Darren Veitch	.05	.10
320	Ryan Walter	.05	.10

WINNIPEG JETS

No.	Player	EX	NRMT
321	Scott Arniel	.05	.10
322	David Babych	.05	.10
323	Dave Christian	.05	.10
324	Lucien DeBlois	.05	.10
325	Norm Dupont	.05	.10
326	Dale Hawerchuk	.75	1.50
327	Willy Lindstrom	.05	.10
328	Bengt Lundholm	.05	.10
329	Morris Lukowich	.05	.10
330	Paul MacLean	.05	.10
331	Bryan Maxwell	.05	.10
332	Serge Savard	.05	.10
333	Don Spring	.05	.10
334	Ed Staniowski, Goalie	.05	.10
335	Tim Trimper	.05	.10
336	Timothy Watters	.05	.10

BAUER SKATES

— 1968 - 69 ISSUE —

Photograph Size: 8" x 10"
Face: Four colour, white border
Back: Blank
Imprint: None
Complete Set No.: 22
Complete Set Price: 250.00 500.00
Common Player: 10.00 20.00

No.	Player	VG	EX
1	Andy Bathgate, Pit.	12.50	25.00
2	Gary Bergman, Det.	12.50	25.00
3	Charlie Burns, Pit.	10.00	20.00
4	Ray Cullen, Min.	10.00	20.00
5	Gary Dornhoefer, Phi.	10.00	20.00
6	Kent Douglas, Tor.	10.00	20.00
7	Tim Ecclestone, St.L.	10.00	20.00
8	Bill Flett, LA	10.00	20.00
9	Ed Giacomin, Goalie, NYR	17.50	35.00
10	Ted Harris, Mon.	10.00	20.00
11	Paul Henderson, Tor.	10.00	20.00
12	Ken Hodge, Bos.	10.00	20.00
13	Harry Howell, NYR	10.00	20.00
14	Earl Ingarfield, Pit.	10.00	20.00
15	Gilles Marotte, Chi.	12.50	25.00
16	Mike McMahon, Min.	10.00	20.00
17	Doug Mohns, Chi.	12.50	25.00
18	Bobby Orr, Bos.	25.00	50.00
19	Claude Provost, Mon.	10.00	20.00
20	Gary Sabourin, St.L.	12.50	25.00
21	Brian Smith, Det.	10.00	20.00
22	Bob Woytowich, Min.	12.50	25.00

ELBOWING

EDDIE SARGENT PROMOTIONS LTD

— 1969 STICKERS —

This set is incomplete. Any information collectors may have regarding this issue would be greatly appreciated.

Sticker Size: 1 7/8" X 2 1/2"
Face: Four colour, white border; Name, Team, Number
Back: Blank
Imprint: © 1971 NHLPA PRINTED IN USA
Complete Set No.: 224
Complete Set Price: Unknown
Common Player: .12   .25   .50
Album: 100.00

ALL-STARS

No.	Player	VG	EX	NRMT
10	Ken Hodge	.35	.75	1.50
16	Dallas Smith	.12	.25	.50
44	Pat Stapleton	.12	.25	.50
52	Ron Harris	.12	.25	.50
77	Jim Peters	.12	.25	.50
91	Barry Gibbs	.12	.25	.50
98	Henri Richard, Mon.	.75	1.50	3.00
109	Yvan Cournoyer, Mon.	1.25	2.50	5.00
123	Bill Fairbairn	.12	.25	.50
143	Billy Hicke	.12	.25	.50
146	Bernie Parent, Goalie	2.50	5.00	10.00
153	Jim Johnson	.12	.25	.50
160	Wayne Hillman	.12	.25	.50
166	Duane Rupp	.12	.25	.50
188	Tim Ecclestone	.12	.25	.50
195	Paul Henderson, Tor.	.25	.50	1.00
208	Dave Keon, Tor.	.75	1.50	3.00
217	Bob Dillabough	.12	.25	.50
219	Andre Boudrias	.12	.25	.50

— 1970 - 71 STICKERS —

Sticker Size: 1 7/8" X 2 1/2"
Face: Four colour, white border; Name, Team, Number
Back: Blank
Imprint: © 1971 NHLPA PRINTED IN USA
Complete Set No.: 224
Complete Set Price: 45.00   75.00   150.00
Common Player: .06   .13   .25
Album: 100.00

BOSTON BRIUNS

No.	Player	VG	EX	NRMT
1	Bobby Orr	5.00	10.00	20.00
2	Don Awrey	.06	.13	.25
3	Derek Sanderson	.06	.13	.25
4	Ted Green	.06	.13	.25
5	Ed. Johnston, Goalie	.06	.13	.25
6	Wayne Carleton	.06	.13	.25
7	Ed. Westfall	.25	.50	1.00
8	John Bucyk	.75	1.50	3.00
9	John McKenzie	.12	.25	.50
10	Ken Hodge	.25	.50	1.00
11	Rick Smith	.06	.13	.25
12	Fred Stanfield	.06	.13	.25
13	Garnet Bailey	.06	.13	.25
14	Phil Esposito	1.75	3.50	7.00
15	Gerry Cheevers, Goalie	1.25	2.50	5.00
16	Dallas Smith	.06	.13	.25

BUFFALO SABRES

No.	Player	VG	EX	NRMT
17	Joe Daley, Goalie	.06	.13	.25
18	Ron Anderson	.06	.13	.25
19	Tracy Pratt	.06	.13	.25
20	Gerry Meehan	.06	.13	.25
21	Reg Fleming	.06	.13	.25
22	Allan Hamilton	.06	.13	.25
23	Gilbert Perreault	1.25	2.50	5.00
24	Skip Krake	.06	.13	.25
25	Kevin O'Shea	.06	.13	.25
26	Roger Crozier, Goalie	.75	1.50	3.00
27	Bill Inglis	.06	.13	.25

Eddie Sargent
1970-71 Stickers
Sticker No. 1,
Bobby Orr

Eddie Sargent
1970-71 Stickers
Sticker No. 2,
Don Awrey

Eddie Sargent
1970-71 Stickers
Sticker No. 17,
Joe Daley

Eddie Sargent
1970-71 Stickers
Sticker No. 26
Roger Crozier

1969 STICKERS — EDDIE SARGENT PROMOTIONS LTD • 283

No.	Player	VG	EX	NRMT
28	Mike McMahon	.06	.13	.25
29	Cliff Shmautz	.06	.13	.25
30	Floyd Smith	.12	.25	.50
31	Randy Wyrozub	.06	.13	.25
32	Jim Watson	.06	.13	.25

CHICAGO BLACK HAWKS

No.	Player	VG	EX	NRMT
33	Tony Esposito, Goalie	1.25	2.50	5.00
34	Doug Jarrett	.06	.13	.25
35	Keith Magnuson	.06	.13	.25
36	Dennis Hull	.06	.13	.25
37	Cliff Koroll	.06	.13	.25
38	Eric Nesterenko	.06	.13	.25
39	Pit Martin	.12	.25	.50
40	Lou Angotti	.12	.25	.50
41	Jim Pappin	.18	.35	.75
42	Gerry Pinder	.06	.13	.25
43	Bobby Hull	3.50	7.00	14.00
44	Pat Stapleton	.06	.13	.25
45	Gerry Desjardins, Goalie	.50	1.00	2.00
46	Chico Maki	.12	.25	.50
47	Doug Mohns	.06	.13	.25
48	Stan Mikita	1.25	2.50	5.00

DETROIT RED WINGS

No.	Player	VG	EX	NRMT
49	Gary Bergman	.06	.13	.25
50	Pete Stemkowski	.06	.13	.25
51	Bruce MacGregor	.06	.13	.25
52	Ron Harris	.06	.13	.25
53	Billy Dea	.06	.13	.25
54	Wayne Connelly	.06	.13	.25
55	Dale Rolfe	.06	.13	.25
56	Gordie Howe	5.00	10.00	20.00
57	Tom Webster	.06	.13	.25
58	Al Karlander	.06	.13	.25
59	Alex Delvecchio	1.00	2.00	4.00
60	Nick Libett	.06	.13	.25
61	Garry Unger	.18	.35	.75
62	Roy Edwards, Goalie	.06	.13	.25
63	Frank Mahovlich	1.25	2.50	5.00
64	Bob Baun	.12	.25	.50

LOS ANGELES KINGS

No.	Player	VG	EX	NRMT
65	Dick Duff	.06	.13	.25
66	Ross Lonsberry	.06	.13	.25
67	Ed Joyal	.06	.13	.25
68	Dale Hoganson	.06	.13	.25
69	Ed Shack	.25	.50	1.00
70	Realm Lemieux	.06	.13	.25
71	Matt Ravlich	.06	.13	.25
72	Bob Pulford	.12	.25	.50
73	Denis Dejordy, Goalie	.06	.13	.25
74	Larry Mickey	.06	.13	.25
75	Bill Flett	.06	.13	.25
76	Juha Widing	.06	.13	.25
77	Jim Peters	.06	.13	.25
78	Gilles Marotte	.06	.13	.25
79	Larry Cahan	.06	.13	.25
80	Howie Hughes	.06	.13	.25

MINNESOTA NORTH STARS

No.	Player	VG	EX	NRMT
81	Cesare Maniago, Goalie	.50	1.00	2.00
82	Ted Harris	.06	.13	.25
83	Tom Williams	.06	.13	.25
84	Gump Worsley, Goalie	1.25	2.50	5.00
85	Tom Reid	.06	.13	.25
86	Murray Oliver	.06	.13	.25
87	Charlie Burns	.06	.13	.25
88	Jude Drouin	.06	.13	.25
89	Walt McKechnie	.06	.13	.25
90	Danny O'Shea	.06	.13	.25
91	Barry Gibbs	.06	.13	.25
92	Danny Grant	.06	.13	.25
93	Bob Barlow	.06	.13	.25
94	Jean Paul Parise	.06	.13	.25
95	Bill Goldsworthy	.06	.13	.25
96	Bob Rousseau	.06	.13	.25

284 • EDDIE SARGENT PROMOTIONS LTD — 1970 - 71 STICKERS

MONTREAL CANADIENS

No.	Player	VG	EX	NRMT
97	Jacques Laperriere	.12	.25	.50
98	Henri Richard	1.25	2.50	5.00
99	J.C. Tremblay	.12	.25	.50
100	Rogatien Vachon, Goalie	1.00	2.00	4.00
101	Claude Larose	.06	.13	.25
102	Peter Mahovlich	.50	1.00	2.00
103	Jacques Lemaire	.60	1.25	2.50
104	Bill Collins	.06	.13	.25
105	Guy Lapointe	.35	.75	1.50
106	Mickey Redmond	.35	.75	1.50
107	Larry Pleau	.06	.13	.25
108	Jean Beliveau	2.00	4.00	8.00
109	Yvan Cournoyer	1.50	3.00	6.00
110	Serge Savard	1.25	2.50	5.00
111	Terry Harper	.06	.13	.25
112	Phil Myre, Goalie	.25	.50	1.00

NEW YORK RANGERS

No.	Player	VG	EX	NRMT
113	Syl Apps	.25	.50	1.00
114	Ted Irvine	.06	.13	.25
115	Ed Giacomin, Goalie	1.00	2.00	4.00
116	Arnie Brown	.06	.13	.25
117	Walt Tkaczuk	.50	1.00	2.00
118	Jean Ratelle	.50	1.00	2.00
119	Dave Balon	.06	.13	.25
120	Ron Stewart	.06	.13	.25
121	Jim Neilson	.06	.13	.25
122	Rod Gilbert	.50	1.00	2.00
123	Bill Fairbairn	.06	.13	.25
124	Brad Park	1.00	2.00	4.00
125	Tim Horton	1.00	2.00	4.00
126	Vic Hadfield	.35	.75	1.50
127	Bob Nevin	.06	.13	.25
128	Rod Seiling	.12	.25	.50

CALIFORNIA GOLDEN SEALS

No.	Player	VG	EX	NRMT
129	Gary Smith, Goalie	.25	.50	1.00
130	Carol Vadnais	.12	.25	.50
131	Bert Marshall	.06	.13	.25
132	Earl Ingarfield	.06	.13	.25
133	Dennis Hextall	.06	.13	.25
134	Harry Howell	.18	.35	.75
135	Wayne Muloin	.06	.13	.25
136	Mike Laughton	.06	.13	.25
137	Ted Hampson	.06	.13	.25
138	Doug Roberts	.06	.13	.25
139	Dick Mattiussi	.06	.13	.25
140	Gary Jarrett	.06	.13	.25
141	Gary Croteau	.06	.13	.25
142	Norm Ferguson	.06	.13	.25
143	Bill Hicke	.06	.13	.25
144	Gerry Ehman	.06	.13	.25

PHILADELPHIA FLYERS

No.	Player	VG	EX	NRMT
145	Ralph MacSweyn	.06	.13	.25
146	Bernie Parent, Goalie	1.00	2.00	4.00
147	Brent Hughes	.06	.13	.25
148	Bob Clarke	2.50	5.00	10.00
149	Gary Dornhoefer	.50	1.00	2.00
150	Simon Nolet	.06	.13	.25
151	Garry Peters	.06	.13	.25
152	Doug Favell, Goalie	.12	.25	.50
153	Jim Johnson	.06	.13	.25
154	Andre Lacroix	.06	.13	.25
155	Larry Hale	.06	.13	.25
156	Joe Watson	.12	.25	.50
157	Jean-Guy Gendron	.06	.13	.25
158	Larry Hillman	.06	.13	.25
159	Ed Van Impe	.06	.13	.25
160	Wayne Hillman	.06	.13	.25

Eddie Sargent
1971-72 Stickers
Sticker No. 59,
Alex Delvecchio

Eddie Sargent
1971-72 Stickers
Sticker No. 115,
Ed Giacomin

Eddie Sargent
1971-72 Stickers
Sticker No. 126,
Vic Hadfield

Eddie Sargent
1971-72 Stickers
Sticker No. 143,
Bill Hicke

PITTSBURGH PENGUINS

No.	Player	VG	EX	NRMT
161	Al Smith, Goalie	.06	.13	.25
162	Jean Pronovost	.06	.13	.25
163	bob Woytowich	.06	.13	.25
164	Bryan Watson	.06	.13	.25
165	Dean Prentice	.06	.13	.25
166	Duane Rupp	.06	.13	.25
167	Glen Sather	.35	.75	1.50
168	Keith McCreary	.06	.13	.25
169	Jim Morrison	.06	.13	.25
170	Ron Schock	.06	.13	.25
171	Wally Boyer	.06	.13	.25
172	Nick Harbaruk	.06	.13	.25
173	Andy Bathgate	.35	.75	1.50
174	Ken Schinkel	.06	.13	.25
175	Les Binkley, Goalie	.06	.13	.25
176	Val Fonteyne	.06	.13	.25

ST. LOUIS BLUES

No.	Player	VG	EX	NRMT
177	Red Berenson	.06	.13	.25
178	Ab McDonald	.06	.13	.25
179	Jim Roberts	.25	.50	1.00
180	Frank Marseille	.06	.13	.25
181	Ernie Wakely, Goalie	.12	.25	.50
182	Terry Crisp	.25	.50	1.00
183	Bob Plager	.25	.50	1.00
184	Barclay Plager	.25	.50	1.00
185	Christian Bordeleau	.06	.13	.25
186	Gary Sabourin	.06	.13	.25
187	Bill Plager	.25	.50	1.00
188	Tim Ecclestone	.06	.13	.25
189	Jean-Guy Talbot	.06	.13	.25
190	Noel Picard	.06	.13	.25
191	Bob Wall	.06	.13	.25
192	Jim Lorentz	.06	.13	.25

TORONTO MAPLE LEAFS

No.	Player	VG	EX	NRMT
193	Bruce Gamble, Goalie	.06	.13	.25
194	Jim Harrison	.06	.13	.25
195	Paul Henderson	.25	.50	1.00
196	Brian Glennie	.12	.25	.50
196	Jim Dorey	.06	.13	.25
198	Rick Ley	.06	.13	.25
199	Jacques Plante, Goalie	1.25	2.50	5.00
200	Ron Ellis	.50	1.00	2.00
201	Jim McKenny	.06	.13	.25
202	Brit Selby	.06	.13	.25
203	Mike Pelyk	.06	.13	.25
204	Norm Ullman	.35	.75	1.50
205	Bill MacMillan	.06	.13	.25
206	Mike Walton	.06	.13	.25
207	Garry Monahan	.06	.13	.25
208	Dave Keon	.75	1.50	3.00

VANCOUVER CANUCKS

No.	Player	VG	EX	NRMT
209	Pat Quinn	.06	.13	.25
210	Wayne Maki	.06	.13	.25
211	Charlie Hodge, Goalie	.06	.13	.25
212	Orland Kurtenbach	.06	.13	.25
213	Paul Popiel	.06	.13	.25
214	Danny Johnson	.06	.13	.25
215	Dale Tallon	.06	.13	.25
216	Ray Cullen	.06	.13	.25
217	Bob Dillabough	.06	.13	.25
218	Gary Doak	.12	.25	.50
219	Andre Boudrias	.06	.13	.25
220	Rosaire Paiement	.06	.13	.25
221	Darryl Sly	.06	.13	.25
222	George Gardner, Goalie	.12	.25	.50
223	Jim Wiste	.06	.13	.25
224	Murray Hall	.06	.13	.25

— 1971 - 72 STICKERS —

These stickers were issued in a 7 3/4" x 9 3/4" sheet with 14 players and 2 series stickers per sheet. Each sheet contains one player from each of the 14 teams in the NHL during that season.

Sticker Size: 1 7/8" X 2 1/2"
Face: Four colour, white border; Name, Team, Number
Back: Blank
Imprint: © 1971 NHLPA PRINTED IN USA
Complete Set No.: 224

	VG	EX	NRMT
Complete Set Price:	45.00	75.00	150.00
Common Player:	.06	.13	.25
Album:			100.00

BOSTON BRUINS

No.	Player	VG	EX	NRMT
1	Fred Stanfield	.06	.13	.25
2	Ed Westfall	.25	.50	1.00
3	John McKenzie	.50	1.00	2.00
4	Derek Sanderson	.25	.50	1.00
5	Rick Smith	.06	.13	.25
6	Ted Green	.06	.13	.25
7	Phil Esposito	1.50	3.00	6.00
8	Ken Hodge	.25	.50	1.00
9	John Bucyk	.75	1.50	3.00
10	Bobby Orr	4.50	9.00	18.00
11	Dallas Smith	.06	.13	.25
12	Mike Walton	.06	.13	.25
13	Don Awrey	.06	.13	.25
14	Wayne Cashman	.25	.50	1.00
15	Ed Johnson, Goalie	.25	.50	1.00
16	Gerry Cheevers, Goalie	.50	1.00	2.00

BUFFALO SABRES

No.	Player	VG	EX	NRMT
17	Gerry Meehan	.12	.25	.50
18	Ron C. Anderson	.06	.13	.25
19	Gilbert Perreault	1.50	3.00	6.00
20	Eddie Shack	.35	.75	1.50
21	Jim Watson	.06	.13	.25
22	Kevin O'Shea	.06	.13	.25
23	Al Hamilton	.06	.13	.25
24	Dick Duff	.12	.25	.50
25	Tracy Pratt	.12	.25	.50
26	Don Luce	.12	.25	.50
27	Roger Crozier, Goalie	.50	1.00	2.00
28	Doug Barrie	.06	.13	.25
29	Mike Robitaille	.06	.13	.25
30	Phil Goyette	.06	.13	.25
31	Larry Keenan	.06	.13	.25
32	Dave Dryden, Goalie	.12	.25	.50

CHICAGO BLACKHAWKS

No.	Player	VG	EX	NRMT
33	Stan Mikita	2.00	4.00	8.00
34	Bobby Hull	3.00	6.00	12.00
35	Cliff Koroll	.06	.13	.25
36	Chico Maki	.06	.13	.25
37	Danny O'Shea	.06	.13	.25
38	Lou Angotti	.06	.13	.25
39	Andre Lacroix	.06	.13	.25
40	Jim Pappin	.06	.13	.25
41	Doug Jarrett	.06	.13	.25
42	Pit Martin	.06	.13	.25
43	Gary Smith, Goalie	.06	.13	.25
44	Tony Esposito, Goalie	.06	.13	.25
45	Pat Stapleton	.06	.13	.25
46	Dennis Hull	.06	.13	.25
47	Bill White	.06	.13	.25
48	Keith Magnuson	.06	.13	.25

DETROIT RED WINGS

No.	Player	VG	EX	NRMT
49	Bill Collins	.06	.13	.25
50	Bob Wall	.06	.13	.25
51	Red Berenson	.06	.13	.25
52	Mickey Redmond	.35	.75	1.50
53	Nick Libett	.12	.25	.50
54	Gary Bergman	.06	.13	.25
55	Alex Delvecchio	.06	.13	.25
56	Tim Ecclestone	.06	.13	.25
57	Arnie Brown	.06	.13	.25
58	Ron Harris	.06	.13	.25

Eddie Sargent
1971-72 Stickers
Sticker No. 2,
Ed Westfall

Eddie Sargent
1971-72 Stickers
Sticker No. 18,
Ron C. Anderson

Eddie Sargent
1971-72 Stickers
Sticker No. 19,
Gilbert Perreault

Eddie Sargent
1971-72 Stickers
Sticker No. 35,
Cliff Koroll

No.	Player	VG	EX	NRMT
59	Ab McDonald	.06	.13	.25
60	Guy Charron	.06	.13	.25
61	Al Smith, Goalie	.06	.13	.25
62	Joe Daley, Goalie	.12	.25	.50
63	Leon Rochefort	.06	.13	.25
64	Ron Stackhouse	.06	.13	.25

LOS ANGELES KINGS

No.	Player	VG	EX	NRMT
65	Juha Widing	.06	.13	.25
66	Bob Pulford	.25	.50	1.00
67	Bill Flett	.06	.13	.25
68	Rogatien Vachon, Goalie	.75	1.50	3.00
69	Ross Lonsberry	.25	.50	1.00
70	Gilles Marotte	.06	.13	.25
71	Harry Howell	.25	.50	1.00
72	Real Lemieux	.06	.13	.25
73	Butch Goring	.06	.13	.25
74	Ed Joyal	.06	.13	.25
75	Larry Hillman	.06	.13	.25
76	Lucien Grenier	.06	.13	.25
77	Paul Curtis	.06	.13	.25
78	Jim Stanfield	.06	.13	.25
79	Ralph Backstrom	.12	.25	.50
80	Mike Byers	.06	.13	.25

MINNESOTA NORTH STARS

No.	Player	VG	EX	NRMT
81	Tom Reid	.06	.13	.25
82	Jude Drouin, Min.	.06	.13	.25
83	Jean Paul Parise, Min.	.06	.13	.25
84	Doug Mohns	.06	.13	.25
85	Danny Grant	.12	.25	.50
86	Bill Goldsworthy	.06	.13	.25
87	Charlie Burns	.06	.13	.25
88	Murray Oliver	.06	.13	.25
89	Dean Prentice	.06	.13	.25
90	Bob Nevin	.06	.13	.25
91	Ted Harris	.06	.13	.25
92	Cesare Maniago, Goalie	.35	.75	1.50
93	Lou Nanne	.06	.13	.25
94	Ted Hampson	.06	.13	.25
95	Barry Gibbs	.06	.13	.25
96	Lorne "Gump" Worsley, Goalie	.75	1.50	3.00

MONTREAL CANADIENS

No.	Player	VG	EX	NRMT
97	J. C. Tremblay	.25	.50	1.00
98	Guy LaPointe	.25	.50	1.00
99	Peter Mahovlich	.35	.75	1.50
100	Larry Pleau	.06	.13	.25
101	Phil Myre, Goalie	.06	.13	.25
102	Yvan Cournoyer	.75	1.50	3.00
103	Henri Richard	.75	1.50	3.00
104	Frank Mahovlich	1.25	2.50	5.00
105	Jacques Lemaire	.50	1.00	2.00
106	Claude Larose	.06	.13	.25
107	Terry Harper	.06	.13	.25
108	Jacques Laperriere	.25	.50	1.00
109	Phil Roberto	.12	.25	.50
110	Serge Savard	1.00	2.00	4.00
111	Pierre Bouchard	.06	.13	.25
112	Marc Tardif	.06	.13	.25

NEW YORK RANGERS

No.	Player	VG	EX	NRMT
113	Rod Gilbert	.75	1.50	3.00
114	Jean Ratelle	.75	1.50	3.00
115	Peter Stemkowski	.25	.50	1.00
116	Brad Park	.75	1.50	3.00
117	Bobby Rousseau	.06	.13	.25
118	Dale Rolfe	.06	.13	.25
119	Rod Seiling	.06	.13	.25
120	Walt Tkachuk	.06	.13	.25
121	Vic Hadfield	.25	.50	1.00
122	Jim Neilson	.25	.50	1.00
123	Bill Fairbairn	.06	.13	.25
124	Bruce MacGregor	.06	.13	.25
125	Dave Balon	.06	.13	.25
126	Ted Irvine	.06	.13	.25
127	Gilles Villemure, Goalie	.18	.35	.75
128	Ed Giacomin, Goalie	.60	1.25	2.50

286 • EDDIE SARGENT PROMOTIONS LTD — 1972-73 STICKERS

CALIFORNIA SEALS

No.	Player	VG	EX	NRMT
129	Walt McKechnie	.12	.25	.50
130	Tommy Williams	.06	.13	.25
131	Wayne Carleton	.06	.13	.25
132	Gerry Pinder	.06	.13	.25
133	Gary Croteau	.06	.13	.25
134	Bert Marshall	.06	.13	.25
135	Tom Webster	.06	.13	.25
136	Norm Ferguson	.06	.13	.25
137	Carol Vadnais	.12	.25	.50
138	Gary Jarrett	.06	.13	.25
139	Ernest Hicke	.06	.13	.25
140	Paul Shmyr	.06	.13	.25
141	Marshall Johnston	.06	.13	.25
142	Don O'Donoghue	.06	.13	.25
143	Joey Johnston	.06	.13	.25
144	Dick Redmond	.06	.13	.25

PHILADELPHIA FLYERS

No.	Player	VG	EX	NRMT
145	Jim Johnson	.06	.13	.25
146	Wayne Hillman	.06	.13	.25
147	Brent Hughes	.06	.13	.25
148	Simon Nolet	.06	.13	.25
149	Larry Mickey	.06	.13	.25
150	Ed Van Impe	.06	.13	.25
151	Gary Dornhoefer	.12	.25	.50
152	Bob Clarke	1.50	3.00	6.00
153	Jean-Guy Gendron	.06	.13	.25
154	Larry Hale	.06	.13	.25
155	Serge Bernier	.06	.13	.25
156	Doug Favel, Goalie	.25	.50	1.00
157	Bob Kelly	.06	.13	.25
158	Joe Watson	.18	.35	.75
159	Larry Brown	.06	.13	.25
160	Bruce Gamble, Goalie	.12	.25	.50

PITTSBURGH PENGUINS

No.	Player	VG	EX	NRMT
161	Syl Apps	.12	.25	.50
162	Ken Schinkel	.06	.13	.25
163	Val Fonteyne	.06	.13	.25
164	Bryan Watson	.12	.25	.50
165	Bob Woytowich	.06	.13	.25
166	Les Binkley, Goalie	.06	.13	.25
167	Roy Edwards, Goalie	.06	.13	.25
168	Jean Pronovost	.12	.25	.50
169	Tim Horton	.85	1.75	3.50
170	Ron Schock	.06	.13	.25
171	Nick Harbaruk	.06	.13	.25
172	Greg Polis	.06	.13	.25
173	Bryan Hextall	.06	.13	.25
174	Keith McCreary	.06	.13	.25
175	Bill Hicke	.06	.13	.25
176	Jim Rutherford, Goalie	.12	.25	.50

ST. LOUIS BLUES

No.	Player	VG	EX	NRMT
177	Gary Sabourin	.06	.13	.25
178	Garry Unger	.06	.13	.25
179	Terry Crisp	.25	.50	1.00
180	Noel Picard	.06	.13	.25
181	Jim Roberts	.25	.50	1.00
182	Barclay Plager	.12	.25	.50
183	Brit Selby	.12	.25	.50
184	Frank St. Marseille	.06	.13	.25
185	Ernie Wakley, Goalie	.06	.13	.25
186	Wayne Connelly	.06	.13	.25
187	Christain Bordeleau	.06	.13	.25
188	Bill Sutherland	.06	.13	.25
189	Bob Plager	.12	.25	.50
190	Bill Plager	.12	.25	.50
191	George Morrison	.06	.13	.25
192	Jim Lorentz	.06	.13	.25

TORONTO MAPLE LEAFS

No.	Player	VG	EX	NRMT
193	Norm Ullman	.25	.50	1.00
194	Jim McKenny	.06	.13	.25
195	Rick Ley	.06	.13	.25
196	Bob Baun	.12	.25	.50
197	Mike Pelyk	.06	.13	.25
198	Bill MacMillan	.06	.13	.25
199	Garry Monahan	.06	.13	.25
200	Paul Henderson	.18	.35	.75
201	Jim Dorey	.06	.13	.25
202	Jim Harrison	.06	.13	.25
203	Ron Ellis	.50	1.00	2.00
204	Darryl Sittler	2.00	4.00	8.00
205	Bernie Parent, Goalie	1.00	2.00	4.00
206	Dave Keon	.75	1.50	3.00
207	Brad Selwood	.06	.13	.25
208	Don Marshall	.06	.13	.25

VANCOUVER CANUCKS

No.	Player	VG	EX	NRMT
209	Dale Tallon	.06	.13	.25
210	Danny Johnson	.06	.13	.25
211	Murray Hall	.06	.13	.25
212	Poul Popiel	.06	.13	.25
213	George Gardner, Goalie	.06	.13	.25
214	Gary Doak	.06	.13	.25
215	Andre Boudrais	.06	.13	.25
216	Orland Kurtenbach	.12	.25	.50
217	Wayne Make	.06	.13	.25
218	Rosaire Paiement	.06	.13	.25
219	Pat Quinn	.25	.50	1.00
220	Fred Speck	.06	.13	.25
221	Barry Wilkins	.06	.13	.25
222	Dunc Wilson, Goalie	.25	.50	1.00
223	Ted Taylor	.06	.13	.25
224	Mike Corrigan	.06	.13	.25

— 1972-73 STICKERS —

Issued one sheet per NHL team, the 16 stamp sheets had 14 players plus two series number stickers. Two different covered albums were available.

Sticker Size: 1 7/8" X 2 1/2"
Face: Four colour, white border; Name, Team, Number
Back: Blank
Imprint: © 1972 NATIONAL HOCKEY LEAGUE PLAYERS' ASSOCIATION, SPORTS ALBUM INC., EDDIE SARGENT PROMOTIONS LTD
Complete Set No.: 224

	VG	EX	NRMT
Complete Set Price:	45.00	75.00	150.00
Common Player:	.07	.12	.25
Album: (Henderson)	25.00	50.00	100.00
Album: (Orr)	15.00	25.00	50.00

ATLANTA FLAMES

No.	Player	VG	EX	NRMT
1	Lucien Grenier	.07	.12	.25
2	Phil Myre, Goalie	.07	.12	.25
3	Ernie Hicke	.07	.12	.25
4	Keith McCreary	.07	.12	.25
5	Billy MacMillan	.07	.12	.25
6	Pat Quinn	.25	.50	1.00
7	William Plager	.07	.12	.25
8	Noel Price	.07	.12	.25
9	Bobby Leiter	.07	.12	.25
10	Randy Manery	.07	.12	.25
11	Bob Paradise	.07	.12	.25
12	Larry Romanchych	.07	.12	.25
13	Lew Morrison	.07	.12	.25
14	Dan Bouchard, Goalie	.08	.13	.25

BOSTON BRUINS

No.	Player	VG	EX	NRMT
15	Fred Stanfield	.07	.12	.25
16	John Bucyk	.50	1.00	2.00
17	Bobby Orr	3.75	7.50	15.00
18	Wayne Cashman	.07	.12	.25
19	Dallas Smith	.07	.12	.25
20	Eddie Johnston, Goalie	.07	.12	.25
21	Phil Esposito	1.25	2.50	5.00
22	Ken Hodge, Sr.	.12	.25	.50
23	Don Awrey	.07	.12	.25
24	Mike Walton	.07	.12	.25
25	Carol Vadnais	.07	.12	.25
26	Doug Roberts	.07	.12	.25
27	Don Marcotte	.07	.12	.25
28	Garnet Bailey	.07	.12	.25

Eddie Sargent
1971-72 Stickers
Sticker No. 134,
Bert Marshall

Eddie Sargent
1971-72 Stickers
Sticker No. 150,
Ed Van Impe

Eddie Sargent
1971-72 Stickers
Sticker No. 178,
Gary Unger

Eddie Sargent
1971-72 Stickers
Sticker No. 211,
Murray Hall

1972-73 STICKERS — EDDIE SARGENT PROMOTIONS LTD • 287

BUFFALO SABRES

No.	Player	VG	EX	NRMT
29	Gerry Meehan	.07	.12	.25
30	Tracy Pratt	.07	.12	.25
31	Gilbert Perreault	.75	1.50	3.00
32	Roger Crozier, Goalie	.07	.12	.25
33	Don Luce	.07	.12	.25
34	Dave Dryden, Goalie	.07	.12	.25
35	Richard Martin	.07	.12	.25
36	Jim Lorentz	.07	.12	.25
37	Tim Horton	1.10	2.25	4.50
38	Craig Ramsey	.07	.12	.25
39	Larry Hillman	.07	.12	.25
40	Steve Atkinson	.07	.12	.25
41	Jim Schoenfeld	.07	.12	.25
42	Rene Robert	.07	.12	.25

CALIFORNIA GOLDEN SEALS

No.	Player	VG	EX	NRMT
43	Walt McKechnie	.07	.12	.25
44	Marshall Johnston	.07	.12	.25
45	Joey Johnston	.07	.12	.25
46	Dick Redmond	.07	.12	.25
47	Bert Marshall	.07	.12	.25
48	Gary Croteau	.07	.12	.25
49	Marv Edwards, Goalie	.07	.12	.25
50	Gilles Meloche, Goalie	.07	.12	.25
51	Ivan Boldirev	.07	.12	.25
52	Stan Gilbertson	.07	.12	.25
53	Pete Laframboise	.07	.12	.25
54	Reggie Leach	.12	.25	.50
55	Craig Patrick	.07	.12	.25
56	Bob Stewart	.07	.12	.25

CHICAGO BLACK HAWKS

No.	Player	VG	EX	NRMT
57	Keith Magnuson	.07	.12	.25
58	Doug Jarrett.	.07	.12	.25
59	Cliff Koroll	.07	.12	.25
60	Chico Maki	.07	.12	.25
61	Gary Smith, Goalie	.07	.12	.25
62	Bill White	.07	.12	.25
63	Stan Mikita	.75	1.50	3.00
64	Jim Pappin	.07	.12	.25
65	Lou Angotti	.07	.12	.25
66	Tony Esposito, Goalie	.75	1.50	3.00
67	Dennis Hull	.25	.50	1.00
68	Pit Martin	.07	.12	.25
69	Pat Stapleton	.07	.12	.25
70	Dan Maloney	.07	.12	.25

DETROIT RED WINGS

No.	Player	VG	EX	NRMT
71	Bill Collins	.07	.12	.25
72	Arnie Brown	.07	.12	.25
73	Red Berenson	.07	.12	.25
74	Mickey Redmond	.07	.12	.25
75	Nick Libett	.07	.12	.25
76	Alex Delvecchio	.50	1.00	2.00
77	Ron Stackhouse	.07	.12	.25
78	Tim Ecclestone	.07	.12	.25
79	Gary Bergman	.07	.12	.25
80	Guy Charron	.07	.12	.25
81	Leon Rochefort	.07	.12	.25
82	Larry Johnston	.07	.12	.25
83	Andy Brown, Goalie	.07	.12	.25
84	Henry Boucha	.07	.12	.25

LOS ANGELES KINGS

No.	Player	VG	EX	NRMT
85	Paul Curtis	.07	.12	.25
86	Jim Stanfield	.07	.12	.25
87	Rogatien Vachon, Goalie	.50	1.00	2.00
88	Ralph Backstrom	.07	.12	.25
89	Gilles Marotte	.07	.12	.25
90	Harry Howell	.35	.75	1.50
91	Real Lemieux	.07	.12	.25
92	Butch Goring	.07	.12	.25
93	Juha Widing	.07	.12	.25
94	Mike Corrigan	.07	.12	.25
95	Larry Brown	.07	.12	.25
96	Terry Harper	.07	.12	.25

Eddie Sargent 1972-73 Stickers Sticker No. 6, Pat Quinn

Eddie Sargent 1972-73 Stickers Sticker No. 41, Jim Schoenfeld

Eddie Sargent 1972-73 Stickers Sticker No. 68, Pit Martin

Eddie Sargent 1972-73 Stickers Sticker No. 91, Real Lemieux

No.	Player	VG	EX	NRMT
97	Serge Bernier	.07	.12	.25
98	Bob Berry	.07	.12	.25

MINNESOTA NORTH STARS

No.	Player	VG	EX	NRMT
99	Tom Reid	.07	.12	.25
100	Jude Drouin	.07	.12	.25
101	Jean Paul Parise	.07	.12	.25
102	Doug Mohns	.07	.12	.25
103	Danny Grant	.07	.12	.25
104	Bill Goldsworthy	.07	.12	.25
105	Gump Worsley, Goalie	.75	1.50	3.00
106	Charlie Burns	.07	.12	.25
107	Murray Oliver	.07	.12	.25
108	Barry Gibbs	.07	.12	.25
109	Ted Harris	.07	.12	.25
110	Cesare Maniago, Goalie	.07	.12	.25
111	Lou Nanne	.10	.20	.40
112	Bob Nevin	.07	.12	.25

MONTREAL CANADIENS

No.	Player	VG	EX	NRMT
113	Guy Lapointe	.25	.50	1.00
114	Pete Mahovlich	.07	.12	.25
115	Jacques Lemaire	.35	.75	1.50
116	Pierre Bouchard	.07	.12	.25
117	Yvan Cournoyer	.50	1.00	2.00
118	Marc Tardif	.07	.12	.25
119	Henri Richard	.50	1.00	2.00
120	Frank Mahovlich	1.00	2.00	4.00
121	Jacques Laperriere	.25	.50	1.00
122	Claude Larose	.07	.12	.25
123	Serge Savard	.25	.50	1.00
124	Ken Dryden, Goalie	2.00	4.00	8.00
125	Rejean Houle	.07	.12	.25
126	Jim Roberts	.07	.12	.25

NEW YORK ISLANDERS

No.	Player	VG	EX	NRMT
127	Ed Westfall	.07	.12	.25
128	Terry Crisp	.07	.12	.25
129	Gerry Desjardins, Goalie	.07	.12	.25
130	Denis DeJordy, Goalie, Error	.07	.12	.25
131	Billy Harris	.07	.12	.25
132	Brian Spencer	.07	.12	.25
133	Germain Gagnon	.07	.12	.25
134	Dave Hudson	.07	.12	.25
135	Lorne Henning	.07	.12	.25
136	Brian Marchinko	.07	.12	.25
137	Tom Miller	.07	.12	.25
138	Gerry Hart	.07	.12	.25
139	Bryan Lefley	.07	.12	.25
140	Jim Mair	.07	.12	.25

NEW YORK RANGERS

No.	Player	VG	EX	NRMT
141	Rod Gilbert	.50	1.00	2.00
142	Jean Ratelle	.50	1.00	2.00
143	Pete Stemkowski	.07	.12	.25
144	Brad Park	.50	1.00	2.00
145	Bobby Rousseau	.07	.12	.25
146	Dale Rolfe	.07	.12	.25
147	Ed Giacomin, Goalie	.50	1.00	2.00
148	Rod Seiling	.07	.12	.25
149	Walt Tkaczuk	.10	.20	.40
150	Bill Fairbairn	.07	.12	.25
151	Vic Hadfield	.10	.20	.40
152	Ted Irvine	.07	.12	.25
153	Bruce MacGregor	.07	.12	.25
154	Jim Neilson	.07	.12	.25

PHILADELPHIA FLYERS

No.	Player	VG	EX	NRMT
155	Brent Hughes	.07	.12	.25
156	Wayne Hillman	.07	.12	.25
157	Doug Favell, Goalie	.07	.12	.25
158	Simon Nolet	.07	.12	.25
159	Joe Watson	.07	.12	.25
160	Ed Van Impe	.07	.12	.25
161	Gary Dornhoefer	.07	.12	.25
162	Bobby Clarke	.75	1.50	3.00

288 • EDDIE SARGENT PROMOTIONS LTD — 1972-73 STICKERS

No.	Player	VG	EX	NRMT
163	Bob Kelly	.05	.13	.25
164	Bill Flett	.05	.13	.25
165	Rick Foley	.05	.13	.25
166	Ross Lonsberry	.05	.13	.25
167	Rick MacLeish	.25	.50	1.00
168	Bill Clement	.07	.12	.25

PITTSBURGH PENGUINS

No.	Player	VG	EX	NRMT
169	Syl Apps, Jr.	.07	.12	.25
170	Ken Schinkel	.07	.12	.25
171	Nick Harbaruk	.07	.12	.25
172	Bryan Watson	.07	.12	.25
173	Bryan Hextall, Jr.	.07	.12	.25
174	Roy Edwards, Goalie	.07	.12	.25
175	Jim Rutherford, Goalie	.07	.12	.25
176	Jean Pronovost	.07	.12	.25
177	Rick Kessell	.07	.12	.25
178	Greg Polis	.07	.12	.25
179	Ron Schock	.07	.12	.25
180	Duane Rupp	.07	.12	.25
181	Darryl Edestrand	.07	.12	.25
182	Dave Burrows	.07	.12	.25

ST. LOUIS BLUES

No.	Player	VG	EX	NRMT
183	Gary Sabourin	.07	.12	.25
184	Garry Unger	.10	.20	.40
185	Noel Picard	.07	.12	.25
186	Bob Plager	.07	.12	.25
187	Barclay Plager	.07	.12	.25
188	Frank St. Marseille	.07	.12	.25
189	Danny O'Shea	.07	.12	.25
190	Kevin O'Shea	.07	.12	.25
191	Wayne Stephenson, Goalie	.07	.12	.25
192	Chris Evans	.07	.12	.25
193	Jacques Caron, Goalie	.07	.12	.25

Eddie Sargent
1972-73 Stickers
Sticker No. 204,
Darryl Sittler

No.	Player	VG	EX	NRMT
194	Andre Dupont	.07	.12	.25
195	Mike Murphy	.07	.12	.25
196	Jack Egers	.07	.12	.25

TORONTO MAPLE LEAFS

No.	Player	VG	EX	NRMT
197	Norm Ullman	.35	.75	1.50
198	Jim McKenny	.07	.12	.25
199	Bob Baun	.07	.12	.25
200	Mike Pelyk	.07	.12	.25
201	Ron Ellis	.12	.25	.50
202	Garry Monahan	.07	.12	.25
203	Paul Henderson	.35	.75	1.50
204	Darryl Sittler	.75	1.50	3.00
205	Brian Glennie	.07	.12	.25
206	Dave Keon	.50	1.00	2.00
207	Jacques Plante, Goalie	1.00	2.00	4.00
208	Pierre Jarry	.07	.12	.25
209	Rick Kehoe	.07	.12	.25
210	Denis Dupere	.07	.12	.25

VANCOUVER CANUCKS

No.	Player	VG	EX	NRMT
211	Dale Tallon	.07	.12	.25
212	Murray Hall, Goalie	.07	.12	.25
213	Dunc Wilson, Goalie	.07	.12	.25
214	Andre Boudrias	.07	.12	.25
215	Orland Kurtenbach	.07	.12	.25
216	Wayne Maki	.07	.12	.25
217	Barry Wilkins	.07	.12	.25
218	Richard Lemieux	.07	.12	.25
219	Bobby Schmautz	.07	.12	.25
220	Dave Balon	.07	.12	.25
221	Bobby Lalonde	.07	.12	.25
222	Jocelyn Guevremont	.07	.12	.25
223	Gregg Boddy	.07	.12	.25
224	Dennis Kearns	.07	.12	.25

Eddie Sargent
1972-73 Stickers
Sticker No. 207,
Jacques Plante

Available in April!

THE CHARLTON STANDARD CATALOGUE OF CANADIAN
BASEBALL & FOOTBALL CARDS

- Fourth Edition -

BASEBALL CARDS FROM 1912 — FOOTBALL CARDS FROM 1949
For Canadian Baseball and Football Card Collectors this Catalogue has it all!

IMPERIAL TOBACCO * MAPLE CRISPETTE * PARKHURST * O-PEE-CHEE * CANADA STARCH * STUART POST * TOPPS
WORLD WIDE GUM * NALLEYS * DONRUSS - LEAF * EDDIE SARGENT * PROVIGO * WILLARD * NABISCO * BAZOOKA * KFC
TORONTO BLUE JAYS * STANDARD OIL * BLUE RIBBON TEA * PANINI * GENERAL MILLS * SCORE * EXHIBITS * HOSTESS
PURITAN MEATS * GULF CANADA * JOGO * VACHON * ROYAL STUDIOS * NEILSON'S * BEN'S AULT FOODS * COCA-COLA
And All Other Major Manufacturers...

Complete price listings for all Major League Baseball and Canadian Football League cards!
Comprehensive baseball and football minor league card listings!
Regular issues, stickers, inserts, subsets, transfers and much, much more! All major manufacturers!
Current Pricing for all cards in up to three grades of condition - VG, EX, and NRMT!
All rookie, last, pitcher, quarterback, error and variation cards identified and priced!
Plus Charlton's Fabulous Alphabetical Index!

OVER 300 PAGES * 60,000 PRICES * NEW, LARGER 8 1/2 x 11" FORMAT
RESERVE YOUR COPY TODAY DIRECTLY FROM THE PUBLISHER...

The Charlton Press
2010 YONGE STREET, TORONTO, ONTARIO M4S 1Z9
FOR TOLL FREE ORDERING PHONE 1-800-442-6042 FAX 1-800-442-1542 from anywhere in Canada or the U.S.

COLGATE

— 1970 - 71 STAMPS —

Sheets of 31 stamps were offered as premiums with various size tubes of toothpaste.

Stamp Size: 1" X 1 1/4"
Face: Four colour, whtie border; Name, Number, Facsimile autograph
Back: Blank
Imprint: None
Complete Set No.: 93
Complete Set Price: 25.00 50.00 100.00
Common Player: .12 .25 .50

No.	Player	VG	EX	NRMT
1	Walt McKechnie, Min.	.12	.25	.50
2	Bob Pulford, LA	.35	.75	1.50
3	Mike Walton, Tor.	.12	.25	.50
4	Alex Delvecchio, Det.	.60	1.25	2.50
5	Tom Williams, Min.	.12	.25	.50
6	Derek Sanderson, Bos.	.17	.35	.75
7	Garry Unger, Det.	.12	.25	.50
8	Lou Angotti, Chi.	.12	.25	.50
9	Ted Hampson, Cal.	.12	.25	.50
10	Phil Goyette, Buf.	.12	.25	.50
11	Juha Widing, LA	.12	.25	.50
12	Norm Ullman, Tor.	.50	1.00	2.00
13	Garry Monahan, Tor.	.12	.25	.50
14	Henri Richard, Mon.	.60	1.25	2.50
15	Ray Cullen, Van.	.12	.25	.50
16	Danny O'Shea, Chi.	.12	.25	.50
17	Marc Tardif, Mon., Error	.12	.25	.50
18	Jude Drouin, Min.	.12	.25	.50
19	Charlie Burns, Min.	.12	.25	.50
20	Gerry Meehan, Buf.	.12	.25	.50
21	Ralph Backstrom, Mon.	.12	.25	.50
22	Frank St. Marseille, St.L.	.12	.25	.50
23	Orland Kurtenbach, Van.	.12	.25	.50
24	Red Berenson, St.L.	.12	.25	.50
25	Jean Ratelle, NYR	.50	1.00	2.00
26	Syl Apps, Jr., Pit.	.12	.25	.50
27	Don Marshall, Buf.	.12	.25	.50
28	Gilbert Perreault, Buf.	.50	1.00	2.00
29	Andre Lacroix, Phi.	.12	.25	.50
30	Jacques Lemaire, Mon.	.50	1.00	2.00
31	Pit Martin, Chi.	.12	.25	.50
32	Dennis Hull, Chi.	.25	.50	1.00
33	Dave Balon, NYR	.12	.25	.50
34	Keith McCreary, Pit.	.12	.25	.50
35	Bobby Rousseau, Min.	.12	.25	.50
36	Danny Grant, Min.	.12	.25	.50
37	Brit Selby, St.L.	.12	.25	.50
38	Bob Nevin, NYR	.12	.25	.50
39	Rosaire Paiement, Van.	.12	.25	.50
40	Gary Dornhoefer, Phi.	.12	.25	.50
41	Eddie Shack, LA	.25	.50	1.00
42	Ron Schock, Pit.	.12	.25	.50
43	Jim Pappin, Chi.	.12	.25	.50
44	Mickey Redmond, Mon.	.12	.25	.50
45	Vic Hadfield, NYR	.12	.25	.50
46	John Bucyk, Bos.	.50	1.00	2.00
47	Gordie Howe, Det.	3.75	7.50	15.00
48	Ron C. Anderson, Buf.	.12	.25	.50
49	Gary Jarrett, Cal.	.12	.25	.50
50	Jean Pronovost, Pit.	.12	.25	.50
51	Simon Nolet, Phi.	.12	.25	.50
52	Bill Goldsworthy, Min.	.12	.25	.50
53	Rod Gilbert, NYR	.50	1.00	2.00
54	Ron Ellis, Tor.	.25	.50	1.00
55	Mike Byers, LA	.12	.25	.50
56	Norm Ferguson, Cal.	.12	.25	.50
57	Gary Sabourin, St.L.	.12	.25	.50
58	Tim Ecclestone, St.L.	.12	.25	.50
59	John McKenzie, Bos.	.12	.25	.50
60	Yvan Cournoyer, Mon.	.50	1.00	2.00
61	Ken Schinkel, Pit.	.12	.25	.50
62	Ken Hodge, Sr., Bos.	.25	.50	1.00
63	Cesare Maniago, Goalie, Min.	.12	.25	.50
64	J.C. Tremblay, Mon.	.12	.25	.50
65	Gilles Marotte, LA	.12	.25	.50
66	Bob Baun, Tor.	.12	.25	.50
67	Gerry Desjardins, Goalie, Chi.	.12	.25	.50
68	Charlie Hodge, Goalie, Van.	.17	.35	.75
69	Matt Ravlich, LA	.12	.25	.50
70	Ed Giacomin, Goalie, NYR	.50	1.00	2.00
71	Gerry Cheevers, Goalie, Bos.	.50	1.00	2.00
72	Pat Quinn, Van.	.12	.25	.50
73	Gary Bergman, Det.	.12	.25	.50
74	Serge Savard, Mon.	.35	.75	1.50
75	Les Binkley, Goalie, Pit.	.12	.25	.50
76	Arnie Brown, NYR	.12	.25	.50
77	Pat Stapleton, Chi.	.12	.25	.50
78	Ed Van Impe, Phi.	.12	.25	.50
79	Jim Dorey, Tor.	.12	.25	.50
80	Dave Dryden, Goalie, Buf.	.12	.25	.50
81	Dale Tallon, Van.	.12	.25	.50
82	Bruce Gamble, Goalie, Tor.	.12	.25	.50
83	Roger Crozier, Goalie, Buf.	.12	.25	.50
84	Denis DeJordy, Goalie, LA	.12	.25	.50
85	Rogatien Vachon, Goalie, Mon.	.50	1.00	2.00
86	Carol Vadnais, Cal.	.12	.25	.50
87	Bobby Orr, Bos.	3.75	7.50	15.00
88	Noel Picard, St.L.	.12	.25	.50
89	Gilles Villemure, Goalie, NYR	.12	.25	.50
90	Gary Smith, Goalie, Cal.	.12	.25	.50
91	Doug Favell, Goalie, Phi.	.12	.25	.50
92	Ernie Wakely, Goalie, St.L.	.12	.25	.50
93	Bernie Parent, Goalie, Phi.	.50	1.00	2.00

Colgate 1970-71 Stamps Stamp No. 1, Walt McKechnie

Colgate 1970-71 Stamps Stamp No. 7, Garry Unger

Colgate 1970-71 Stamps Stamp No. 10, Phil Goyette

Colgate 1970-71 Stamps Stamp No. 17, Error, Name misspelled Tardiff on face

— 1971 - 72 HEADS —

These heads are unnumbered and are listed below in alphabetical order.

Head Size: 1 1/4" Height
Head: Moulded beige plastic; Name on back
Imprint: None
Complete Set No.: 16
Complete Set Price: 125.00
Common Player: 3.00

No.	Player	NRMT
1	Yvan Cournoyer, Mtl.	6.00
2	Marcel Dionne, Det.	10.00
3	Ken Dryden, Goalie, Mtl.	12.00
4	Paul Henderson, Tor.	3.00
5	Guy Lafleur, Mon.	10.00
6	Frank Mahovlich, Mon.	13.00
7	Richard Martin, Buf.	6.00
8	Bobby Orr, Bos.	12.00
9	Brad Park, NYR	6.00
10	Jacques Plante, Goalie, Tor.	8.00
11	Jean Ratelle, NYR	3.00
12	Derek Sanderson, Bos.	8.00
13	Dale Tallon, Van.	3.00
14	Walter Tkaczuk, NYR	4.00
15a	Norm Ullman, Tor.	6.00
15b	Norm Ullman, Tor. Error	3.00
16	Garry Unger, St. L.	4.00

MISCONDUCT

290 • DAD'S COOKIES — 1970-71 ISSUE —

DAD'S COOKIES

— 1970 - 71 ISSUE —

Players are listed alphabetically for this unnumbered set. Each player is photographed wearing an "NHL Players" jersey.

Card Size: 1 7/8" x 5 3/8"
Face: Four colour; Name, Team, Resume
Back: Black on card stock; Promotional offer, Bilingual
Imprint: ©1969 N.H.L. PLAYERS ASSOCIATION
Complete Set No.: 144
Complete Set Price: 25.00   50.00   100.00
Common Player: .12   .25   .50

BOSTON BRUINS

No.	Player	VG	EX	NRMT
1	Don Awrey	.12	.25	.50
2	John Bucyk	.50	1.00	2.00
3	Gerry Cheevers, Goalie	.75	1.50	3.00
4	Phil Esposito	1.25	2.50	5.00
5	Ted Green	.12	.25	.50
6	Ken Hodge, Sr.	.12	.25	.50
7	Eddie Johnston	.12	.25	.50
8	John McKenzie	.12	.25	.50
9	Bobby Orr	3.75	7.50	15.00
10	Derek Sanderson	.12	.25	.50
11	Fred Stanfield	.12	.25	.50

BUFFALO SABRES

No.	Player	VG	EX	NRMT
12	Roger Crozier, Goalie	.12	.25	.50
13	Dick Duff	.12	.25	.50
14	Reggie Fleming	.12	.25	.50
15	Phil Goyette	.12	.25	.50
16	Al Hamilton	.12	.25	.50
17	Skip Krake	.12	.25	.50
18	Don Marshall	.12	.25	.50
19	Mike McMahon	.12	.25	.50
20	Gilbert Perreault	.12	.25	.50
21	Tracy Pratt	.12	.25	.50
22	Eddie Shack	.12	.25	.50
23	Floyd Smith	.12	.25	.50

CALIFORNIA GOLDEN SEALS

No.	Player	VG	EX	NRMT
24	Gerry Ehman	.12	.25	.50
25	Norm Ferguson	.12	.25	.50
26	Ted Hampson	.12	.25	.50
27	Bill Hicke	.12	.25	.50
28	Harry Howell	.50	1.00	2.00
29	Earl Ingarfield, Sr.	.12	.25	.50
30	Gary Jarrett	.12	.25	.50
31	Bert Marshall	.12	.25	.50
32	Wayne Muloin	.12	.25	.50
33	Carol Vadnais	.12	.25	.50

CHICAGO BLACK HAWKS

No.	Player	VG	EX	NRMT
34	Lou Angotti	.12	.25	.50
35	Tony Esposito, Goalie	1.00	2.00	4.00
36	Bobby Hull	2.00	4.00	8.00
37	Dennis Hull	.30	.50	1.00
38	Doug Jarrett	.12	.25	.50
39	Keith Magnuson	.12	.25	.50
40	Chico Maki	.12	.25	.50
41	Pit Martin	.12	.25	.50
42	Stan Mikita	.75	1.50	3.00
43	Doug Mohns	.12	.25	.50
44	Pat Stapleton	.12	.25	.50

DETROIT RED WINGS

No.	Player	VG	EX	NRMT
45	Gary Bergman	.12	.25	.50
46	Wayne Connelly	.12	.25	.50
47	Alex Delvecchio	.50	1.00	2.00
48	Roy Edwards, Goalie	.12	.25	.50
49	Gordie Howe	3.75	7.50	15.00
50	Bruce MacGregor	.12	.25	.50
51	Frank Mahovlich	1.00	2.00	4.00
52	Dale Rolfe	.12	.25	.50
53	Garry Unger	.12	.25	.50
54	Tom Webster	.12	.25	.50

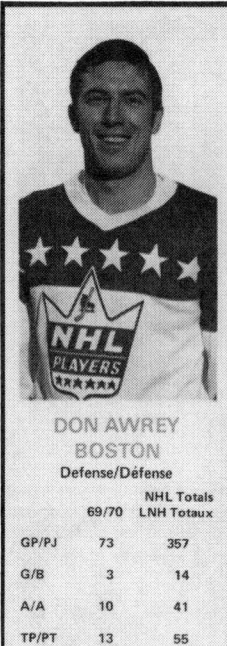

Dad's Cookies
1970-71 Issue
Card No. 1,
Don Awrey

Dad's Cookies
1970-71 Issue
Card No. 9,
Bobby Orr

LOS ANGELES KINGS

No.	Player	VG	EX	NRMT
55	Larry Cahan	.12	.25	.50
56	Denis DeJordy, Goalie	.12	.25	.50
57	Bill Flett	.12	.25	.50
58	Gilles Marotte	.12	.25	.50
59	Larry Mickey	.12	.25	.50
60	Bob Pulford	.12	.25	.50
61	Matt Ravlich	.12	.25	.50
62	Juha Widing	.12	.25	.50

MINNESOTA NORTH STARS

No.	Player	VG	EX	NRMT
63	Charlie Burns	.12	.25	.50
64	Bill Goldsworthy	.12	.25	.50
65	Danny Grant	.12	.25	.50
66	Ted Harris	.12	.25	.50
67	Murray Oliver	.12	.25	.50
68	Danny O'Shea	.12	.25	.50
69	Jean Paul Parise	.12	.25	.50
70	Bobby Rousseau	.12	.25	.50
71	Tom Williams	.12	.25	.50
72	Gump Worsley, Goalie	.75	1.50	3.00

MONTREAL CANADIENS

No.	Player	VG	EX	NRMT
73	Jean Beliveau	1.75	3.50	7.00
74	Yvan Cournoyer	.50	1.00	2.00
75	John Ferguson	.12	.25	.50
76	Terry Harper	.12	.25	.50
77	Jacques Laperriere	.12	.25	.50
78	Jacques Lemaire	.50	1.00	2.00
79	Mickey Redmond	.12	.25	.50
80	Henri Richard	.75	1.50	3.00
81	Serge Savard	.35	.75	1.50
82	J.C. Tremblay	.12	.25	.50
83	Rogatien Vachon, Goalie	.50	1.00	2.00

NEW YORK RANGERS

No.	Player	VG	EX	NRMT
84	Arnie Brown	.12	.25	.50
85	Ed Giacomin, Goalie	.35	.75	1.50
86	Rod Gilbert	.35	.75	1.50
87	Vic Hadfield	.12	.25	.50
88	Jim Neilson	.12	.25	.50
89	Bob Nevin	.12	.25	.50
90	Brad Park	.35	.75	1.50
91	Jean Ratelle	.35	.75	1.50
92	Rod Seiling	.12	.25	.50
93	Walt Tkaczuk	.12	.25	.50

PHILADELPHIA FLYERS

No.	Player	VG	EX	NRMT
94	Bobby Clarke	1.25	2.50	5.00
95	Gary Dornhoefer	.12	.25	.50
96	Doug Favell, Goalie	.12	.25	.50
97	Jean-Guy Gendron	.12	.25	.50
98	Larry Hillman	.12	.25	.50
99	Wayne Hillman	.12	.25	.50
100	Andre Lacroix	.12	.25	.50
101	Bernie Parent, Goalie	.50	1.00	2.00
102	Ed Van Impe	.12	.25	.50
103	Joe Watson	.12	.25	.50

PITTSBURGH PENGUINS

No.	Player	VG	EX	NRMT
104	Les Binkley, Goalie	.12	.25	.50
105	Wally Boyer	.12	.25	.50
106	Bryan Hextall, Jr.	.12	.25	.50
107	Keith McCreary	.12	.25	.50
108	Dean Prentice	.12	.25	.50
109	Jean Pronovost	.12	.25	.50
110	Glen Sather	.12	.25	.50
111	Ken Schinkel	.12	.25	.50
112	Bryan Watson	.12	.25	.50
113	Bob Woytowich	.12	.25	.50

ST. LOUIS BLUES

No.	Player	VG	EX	NRMT
114	Red Berenson	.12	.25	.50
115	Tim Ecclestone	.12	.25	.50

No.	Player	VG	EX	NRMT
116	Ab McDonald	.12	.25	.50
117	Noel Picard	.12	.25	.50
118	Barclay Plager	.12	.25	.50
119	Jim Roberts	.12	.25	.50
120	Gary Sabourin	.12	.25	.50
121	Brit Selby	.12	.25	.50
122	Frank St. Marseille	.12	.25	.50
123	Bob Wall	.12	.25	.50

TORONTO MAPLE LEAFS

No.	Player	VG	EX	NRMT
124	Bob Baun	.12	.25	.50
125	Ron Ellis	.12	.25	.50
126	Bruce Gamble, Goalie	.12	.25	.50
127	Paul Henderson	.12	.25	.50
128	Dave Keon	.75	1.50	3.00
129	Rick Ley	.12	.25	.50
130	Jim McKenny	.12	.25	.50
131	Mike Pelyk	.12	.25	.50
132	Jacques Plante, Goalie	1.20	2.00	4.00
133	Norm Ullman	.35	.75	1.50
134	Mike Walton	.12	.25	.50

VANCOUVER CANUCKS

No.	Player	VG	EX	NRMT
135	Andre Boudrias	.12	.25	.50
136	Ray Cullen	.12	.25	.50
137	Bob Dillabough	.12	.25	.50
138	Gary Doak	.12	.25	.50
139	Charlie Hodge, Goalie	.12	.25	.50
140	Orland Kurtenbach	.12	.25	.50
141	Rosaire Paiement	.12	.25	.50
142	Pat Quinn	.35	.75	1.50
-143	Dale Tallon	.12	.25	.50
144	Jim Wiste	.12	.25	.50

ESSO

— 1970 - 71 POWER PLAYERS —

This set is unnumbered except for the player's jersey number. It is arranged in alphabetical order by team and then by player within the team.

Card Size: 1 1/2 X 2 1/8
Face: Four colour, white border; Player's name and jersey number
Back: Blank
Imprint: None
Complete Set No.: 252
Complete Set Price: 30.00 60.00 115.00
Common Player: .05 .10 .20
Album: Hard Cover 7.50 15.00 25.00
Album: Soft Cover 50.00
Vinyl Wallet: 5.00

BOSTON BRUINS

No.	Player	VG	EX	NRMT
1	Don Awrey	.05	.10	.20
2	Garnet Bailey	.05	.10	.20
3	John Bucyk	.50	1.00	2.00
4	Wayne Carleton	.05	.10	.20
5	Wayne Cashman	.05	.10	.20
6	Gerry Cheevers, Goalie	.50	1.00	2.00
7	Phil Esposito	1.00	2.00	4.00
8	Ted Green	.05	.10	.20
9	Ken Hodge, Sr.	.05	.10	.20
10	Eddie Johnston, Goalie	.05	.10	.20
11	Don Marcotte	.05	.10	.20
12	John McKenzie	.05	.10	.20
13	Bobby Orr	3.75	7.50	15.00
14	Derek Sanderson	.25	.50	1.00
15	Dallas Smith	.05	.10	.20
16	Rick Smith	.05	.10	.20
17	Fred Stanfield	.05	.10	.20
18	Ed Westfall	.05	.10	.20

Esso
1970-71 Power Players
Card No. 6,
Gerry Cheevers

Esso
1970-71 Power Players
Card No. 8,
Ted Green

Esso
1970-71 Power Players
Card No. 63, Error, Name
misspelled Magnusson on face

Esso
1970-71 Power Players
Card No. 86,
Frank Mahovlich

BUFFALO SABRES

No.	Player	VG	EX	NRMT
19	Paul Andrea	.05	.10	.20
20	Ron C. Anderson	.05	.10	.20
21	Steve Atkinson	.05	.10	.20
22	Doug Barrie	.05	.10	.20
23	Roger Crozier, Goalie	.10	.20	.40
24	Reggie Fleming	.05	.10	.20
25	Phil Goyette	.05	.10	.20
26	Al Hamilton	.05	.10	.20
27	Larry Keenan	.05	.10	.20
28	Skip Krake	.05	.10	.20
29	Don Marshall	.05	.10	.20
30	Gerry Meehan	.05	.10	.20
31	Gilbert Perreault	.50	1.00	2.00
32	Tracy Pratt	.05	.10	.20
33	Cliff Schmautz	.05	.10	.20
34	Eddie Shack	.25	.50	1.00
35	Floyd Smith	.05	.10	.20
36	Jimmy Watson	.05	.10	.20

CALIFORNIA GOLDEN SEALS

No.	Player	VG	EX	NRMT
37	Gary Croteau	.05	.10	.20
38	Gerry Ehman	.05	.10	.20
39	Tony Featherstone	.05	.10	.20
40	Ted Hampson	.05	.10	.20
41	Joe Hardy	.05	.10	.20
42	Dennis Hextall	.05	.10	.20
43	Bill Hicke	.05	.10	.20
44	Ernie Hicke	.05	.10	.20
45	Harry Howell	.25	.50	1.00
46	Earl Ingarfield, Sr.	.05	.10	.20
47	Gary Jarrett	.05	.10	.20
48	Dick Mattiussi	.05	.10	.20
49	Wayne Muloin	.05	.10	.20
50	Doug Roberts	.05	.10	.20
51	Gary Smith, Goalie	.12	.25	.50
52	Bob Sneddon	.05	.10	.20
53	Ron Stackhouse	.05	.10	.20
54	Carol Vadnais	.10	.20	.40

CHICAGO BLACK HAWKS

No.	Player	VG	EX	NRMT
55	Lou Angotti	.05	.10	.20
56	Bryan Campbell	.05	.10	.20
57	Gerry Desjardins, Goalie	.05	.10	.20
58	Tony Esposito, Goalie	.75	1.50	3.00
59	Bobby Hull	2.25	4.50	9.00
60	Dennis Hull	.17	.35	.75
61	Doug Jarrett	.05	.10	.20
62	Cliff Koroll	.05	.10	.20
63	Keith Magnuson, Error	.05	.10	.20
64	Chico Maki	.05	.10	.20
65	Pit Martin	.05	.10	.20
66	Stan Mikita	.75	1.50	3.00
67	Doug Mohns	.05	.10	.20
68	Eric Nesterenko	.05	.10	.20
69	Jim Pappin	.05	.10	.20
70	Gerry Pinder	.05	.10	.20
71	Pat Stapleton	.05	.10	.20
72	Bill White	.05	.10	.20

DETROIT RED WINGS

No.	Player	VG	EX	NRMT
73	Gary Bergman	.05	.10	.20
74	Larry Brown	.05	.10	.20
75	Wayne Connelly	.05	.10	.20
76	Billy Dea	.05	.10	.20
77	Alex Delvecchio	.50	1.00	2.00
78	Roy Edwards, Goalie	.05	.10	.20
79	Ron Harris	.05	.10	.20
80	Gordie Howe	3.75	7.50	15.00
81	Al Karlander	.05	.10	.20
82	Serge Lajeunesse	.05	.10	.20
83	Nick Libett	.05	.10	.20
84	Don Luce	.05	.10	.20
85	Bruce MacGregor	.05	.10	.20
86	Frank Mahovlich	1.00	2.00	4.00
87	Dale Rolfe	.05	.10	.20
88	Jim Rutherford, Goalie	.05	.10	.20
89	Garry Unger	.05	.10	.20
90	Tom Webster	.05	.10	.20

292 • ESSO — 1970-71 POWER PLAYERS —

LOS ANGELES KINGS

No.	Player	VG	EX	NRMT
91	Bob Berry	.05	.10	.20
92	Mike Byers	.05	.10	.20
93	Larry Cahan	.05	.10	.20
94	Paul Curtis	.05	.10	.20
95	Denis DeJordy, Goalie	.05	.10	.20
96	Bill Flett	.05	.10	.20
97	Dale Hoganson	.05	.10	.20
98	Eddie Joyal	.05	.10	.20
99	Gord Labossiere	.05	.10	.20
100	Ross Lonsberry	.05	.10	.20
101	Gilles Marotte	.05	.10	.20
102	Larry Mickey	.05	.10	.20
103	Jack Norris	.05	.10	.20
104	Noel Price	.05	.10	.20
105	Bob Pulford	.50	1.00	2.00
106	Matt Ravlich	.05	.10	.20
107	Doug Robinson	.05	.10	.20
108	Juha Widing	.05	.10	.20

MINNESOTA NORTH STARS

No.	Player	VG	EX	NRMT
109	Fred Barrett	.05	.10	.20
110	Charlie Burns	.05	.10	.20
111	Barry Gibbs	.05	.10	.20
112	Bill Goldsworthy	.05	.10	.20
113	Danny Grant	.05	.10	.20
114	Ted Harris	.05	.10	.20
115	Fred (Buster) Harvey	.05	.10	.20
116	Danny Lawson	.05	.10	.20
117	Cesare Maniago, Goalie	.18	.35	.75
118	Walt McKechnie	.05	.10	.20
119	Lou Nanne	.07	.15	.30
120	Murray Oliver	.05	.10	.20
121	Danny O'Shea	.05	.10	.20
122	Jean Paul Parise	.05	.10	.20
123	Tom Reid	.05	.10	.20
124	Bobby Rousseau	.05	.10	.20
125	Tom Williams	.05	.10	.20
126	Gump Worsley, Goalie	1.00	2.00	4.00

MONTREAL CANADIENS

No.	Player	VG	EX	NRMT
127	Jean Beliveau	1.75	3.50	7.00
128	Bill Collins	.05	.10	.20
129	Yvan Cournoyer	.35	.75	1.50
130	John Ferguson	.05	.10	.20
131	Terry Harper	.05	.10	.20
132	Fran Huck	.05	.10	.20
133	Guy Lapointe	.10	.20	.40
134	Jacques Laperriere	.05	.10	.20
135	Claude Larose	.05	.10	.20
136	Jacques Lemaire	.50	1.00	2.00
137	Pete Mahovlich	.10	.20	.40
138	Phil Myre, Goalie	.05	.10	.20
139	Mickey Redmond	.05	.10	.20
140	Henri Richard	.75	1.50	3.00
141	Serge Savard	.50	1.00	2.00
142	Marc Tardif	.05	.10	.20
143	J.C. Tremblay	.05	.10	.20
144	Rogatien Vachon, Goalie	.50	1.00	2.00

NEW YORK RANGERS

No.	Player	VG	EX	NRMT
145	Dave Balon	.05	.10	.20
146	Arnie Brown	.05	.10	.20
147	Jack Egers	.05	.10	.20
148	Bill Fairbairn	.05	.10	.20
149	Ed Giacomin, Goalie	.50	1.00	2.00
150	Rod Gilbert	.35	.75	1.50
151	Vic Hadfield	.05	.10	.20
152	Tim Horton	.75	1.50	3.00
153	Ted Irvine	.05	.10	.20
154	Jim Neilson	.05	.10	.20
155	Bob Nevin	.05	.10	.20
156	Brad Park	.50	1.00	2.00
157	Jean Ratelle	.75	1.25	2.50
158	Rod Seiling	.05	.10	.20
159	Pete Stemkowski	.05	.10	.20
160	Ron Stewart	.05	.10	.20
161	Walt Tkaczuk	.05	.10	.20
162	Gilles Villemure, Goalie	.05	.10	.20

Esso
1970-71 Power Players
Card No. 119,
Lou Nanne

Esso
1970-71 Power Players
Card No. 132,
Fran Huck

Esso
1970-71 Power Players
Card No. 161,
Walt Tkaczuk

Esso
1970-71 Power Players
Card No. 167,
Doug Favell

PHILADELPHIA FLYERS

No.	Player	VG	EX	NRMT
163	Barry Ashbee	.05	.10	.20
164	Serge Bernier	.05	.10	.20
165	Bobby Clarke	.75	1.50	3.00
166	Gary Dornhoefer	.05	.10	.20
167	Doug Favell, Goalie	.05	.10	.20
168	Jean-Guy Gendron	.05	.10	.20
169	Larry Hale	.05	.10	.20
170	Earl Heiskala	.05	.10	.20
171	Larry Hillman	.05	.10	.20
172	Wayne Hillman	.05	.10	.20
173	Jim Johnson	.05	.10	.20
174	Bob Kelly	.05	.10	.20
175	Andre Lacroix	.05	.10	.20
176	Lew Morrison	.05	.10	.20
177	Bernie Parent, Goalie	.50	1.00	2.00
178	Garry Peters	.05	.10	.20
179	Ed Van Impe	.07	.15	.30
180	Joe Watson	.07	.15	.30

PITTSBURGH PENGUINS

No.	Player	VG	EX	NRMT
181	Andy Bathgate	.50	1.00	2.00
182	Les Binkley, Goalie	.05	.10	.20
183	Bob Blackburn	.05	.10	.20
184	Wally Boyer	.05	.10	.20
185	Nick Harbaruk	.05	.10	.20
186	Bryan Hextall, Jr.	.05	.10	.20
187	Dunc McCallum	.05	.10	.20
188	Keith McCreary	.05	.10	.20
189	Jim Morrison	.05	.10	.20
190	Dean Prentice	.05	.10	.20
191	Jean Pronovost	.05	.10	.20
192	Duane Rupp	.05	.10	.20
193	Glen Sather	.12	.25	.50
194	Ken Schinkel	.05	.10	.20
195	Ron Schock	.05	.10	.20
196	Al Smith, Goalie	.05	.10	.20
197	Bryan Watson	.05	.10	.20
198	Bob Woytowich	.05	.10	.20

ST. LOUIS BLUES

No.	Player	VG	EX	NRMT
199	Red Berenson	.05	.10	.20
200	Chris Bordeleau	.05	.10	.20
201	Terry Crisp	.12	.25	.50
202	Tim Ecclestone	.05	.10	.20
203	Glenn Hall, Goalie	1.00	2.00	4.00
204	Jim Lorentz	.05	.10	.20
205	Bill E. McCreary	.05	.10	.20
206	Ab McDonald	.05	.10	.20
207	George Morrison	.05	.10	.20
208	Noel Picard	.05	.10	.20
209	Bob Plager	.05	.10	.20
210	Barclay Plager	.05	.10	.20
211	Jim Roberts	.07	.15	.30
212	Gary Sabourin	.05	.10	.20
213	Brit Selby	.05	.10	.20
214	Frank St. Marseille	.05	.10	.20
215	Bob Wall	.05	.10	.20
216	Ernie Wakely, Goalie	.05	.10	.20

TORONTO MAPLE LEAFS

No.	Player	VG	EX	NRMT
217	Bob Baun	.05	.10	.20
218	Jim Dorey	.05	.10	.20
219	Ron Ellis	.18	.35	.75
220	Bruce Gamble, Goalie	.05	.10	.20
221	Brian Glennie	.05	.10	.20
222	Paul Henderson	.07	.15	.30
223	Jim Harrison	.05	.10	.20
224	Dave Keon	.75	1.50	3.00
225	Rick Ley	.05	.10	.20
226	Billy MacMillan	.05	.10	.20
227	Jim McKenny	.05	.10	.20
228	Garry Monahan	.05	.10	.20
229	Mike Pelyk	.05	.10	.20
230	Jacques Plante, Goalie	1.25	2.50	5.00
231	Darryl Sittler	.75	1.50	3.00
232	Guy Trottier	.05	.10	.20
233	Norm Ullman	.25	.50	1.00
234	Mike Walton	.05	.10	.20

VANCOUVER CANUCKS

No.	Player	VG	EX	NRMT
235	Andre Boudrias	.05	.10	.20
236	Mike Corrigan	.05	.10	.20
237	Ray Cullen	.05	.10	.20
238	Gary Doak	.05	.10	.20
239	Murray Hall	.05	.10	.20
240	Charlie Hodge, Goalie	.05	.10	.20
241	Danny Johnson	.05	.10	.20
242	Orland Kurtenbach	.05	.10	.20
243	Len Lunde	.05	.10	.20
244	Wayne Maki	.05	.10	.20
245	Rosaire Paiement	.05	.10	.20
246	Poul Popiel	.05	.10	.20
247	Pat Quinn	.05	.10	.20
248	Marc Reaume	.05	.10	.20
249	Darryl Sly	.05	.10	.20
250	Dale Tallon	.05	.10	.20
251	Barry Wilkins	.05	.10	.20
252	Dunk Wilson, Goalie	.05	.10	.20

— 1983 - 84 ISSUE —

This unnumbered set was issued as part of a lottery game, one in French and one in English. Actual player photographs measure 2" x 3" with statistics on the back. Distributed throughout Canada with the exception of Quebec.

Card Size: 2" X 3"
Face: Four colour, white border; Name
Back: Black on white card stock; Name, Resume
Imprint: Registered Trademark of the National Hockey League Players Association
Complete Set No.: 21
Complete Set Price: English 6.00 French 12.00
Common Player: .13 .18

No.	Player	English NRMT	French NRMT
1	Glenn Anderson, Edm.	.25	.35
2	John Anderson, Tor.	.13	.18
3	David Babych, Win.	.13	.18
4	Richard Brodeur, Goalie, Van.	.13	.18
5	Paul Coffey, Edm.	.75	1.00
6	Bill Derlago, Tor.	.13	.18
7	Bob Gainey, Mon.	.13	.18
8	Michel Goulet, Que.	.25	.35
9	Dale Hawerchuk, Win.	.50	.60
10	Dale Hunter, Que.	.13	.18
11	Morris Lukowich, Win.	.13	.18
12	Lanny McDonald, Cal.	.50	.60
13	Mark Messier, Edm.	1.25	1.50
14	James Peplinski, Cal.	.13	.18
15	Paul Reinhart, Cal.	.13	.18
16	Larry Robinson, Mon.	.50	.60
17	Stanley Smyl, Van.	.13	.18
18	Harold Snepsts, Van.	.13	.18
19	Marc Tardif, Que.	.13	.18
20	Mario Tremblay, Mon.	.13	.18
21	Richard Vaive, Tor.	.13	.18

— 1988 - 89 ALL STAR STICKERS —

A 32-page album was available in English or French to hold the stickers. The stickers are unnumbered, so the players are listed here alphabetically. On the back is a checklist of all cards to be collected. The title card says "Collect all 53 players in our NHL All-Star Album". However, five are photographs of players already in the album and not collectable.

Sticker Size: 2 1/8" X 3 1/4"
Face: Four colour, white border at bottom; Name, Team, Facsimile signature
Back: Black on card stock; Bilingual
Imprint: None
Complete Set No.: 48
Complete Set Price: 9.00 18.00
Common Player: .10 .20
Album: (English) 2.50 5.00
Album: (French) 2.50 5.00

Esso
1983-84 Issue
Card No. 5,
Paul Coffey

Esso
1983-84 Issue
Card No. 13,
Mark Messier

Esso
1988-89 All Star Stickers
Sticker No. 2,
Mike Bossy

— 1971 - 72 ISSUE — BAZOOKA • 293

No.	Player	NRMT	Mint
—	Title Card: Esso NHL All-Star Collection	.10	.20
1	Jean Beliveau, Mon.	.50	1.00
2	Mike Bossy, NYI	.35	.75
3	Raymond Bourque, Bos.	.50	1.00
4	Johnny Bower, Goalie	.13	.25
5	Bobby Clarke, Phi.	.13	.25
6	Paul Coffey, Pit.	.20	.40
7	Yvan Cournoyer, Mon.	.18	.35
8	Marcel Dionne, LA	.25	.50
9	Ken Dryden, Goalie, Mon.	.50	1.00
10	Phil Esposito, Bos.	.25	.50
11	Tony Esposito, Goalie	.15	.30
12	Grant Fuhr, Goalie, Edm.	.15	.30
13	Clark Gillies, NYI	.10	.20
14	Michel Goulet, Que.	.18	.35
15	Wayne Gretzky, Edm.	2.00	4.00
16	Dale Hawerchuk, Win.	.15	.30
17	Ron Hextall, Goalie, Phi.	.15	.30
18	Gordie Howe, Det.	1.50	3.00
19	Mark Howe, Phi.	.10	.20
20	Bobby Hull, Chi.	.50	1.00
21	Tim Kerr, Phi.	.10	.20
22	Jari Kurri, Edm.	.10	.20
23	Guy Lafleur, Mon.	.25	.50
24	Rod Langway, Wash.	.10	.20
25	Jacques Laperriere, Mon.	.10	.20
26	Guy Lapointe, Mon.	.10	.20
27	Mario Lemieux, Pit.	1.50	3.00
28	Frank Mahovlich, Mon.	.35	.75
29	Lanny McDonald, Cal.	.18	.35
30	Mark Messier, Edm.	.25	.50
31	Stan Mikita, Chi.	.15	.30
32	Mats Naslund, Mon.	.10	.20
33	Bobby Orr, Bos.	.50	1.00
34	Brad Park, NYR	.15	.30
35	Gilbert Perreault, Buf.	.15	.30
36	Denis Potvin, NYI	.15	.30
37	Larry Robinson, Mon.	.10	.20
38	Luc Robitaille, LA	.25	.50
39	Borje Salming, Tor.	.20	.40
40	Denis Savard, Chi.	.10	.20
41	Serge Savard, Mon.	.10	.20
42	Steve Shutt, Mon.	.10	.20
43	Darryl Sittler, Tor.	.10	.20
44	Billy Smith, Goalie, NYI	.10	.20
45	John Tonelli, NYI	.10	.20
46	Bryan Trottier, NYI	.15	.30
47	Norm Ullman, Tor.	.15	.30
48	Gump Worsley, Goalie, Mon.	.20	.40

BAZOOKA

— 1971 - 72 ISSUE —

Issued in twelve panels of three cards each on the bottom of Bazooka bubble gum boxes. The designs are identical to 1971-72 O-Pee-Chee and Topps regular issues.

Card Size: 2 1/2" X 3 1/2"
Face: Four colour, white border; Number, Team logo, Position
Back: Blank
Imprint: None
Complete Set No.: 12 Panels / 36 Cards
Complete Set Price: 300.00 600.00 1,200.00
Common Player: 3.00 6.00 12.00
Common Panel: 16.00 32.50 65.00

No.	Player	VG	EX	NRMT
—	Panel	60.00	115.00	235.00
1	Phil Esposito, Bos.	22.50	45.00	90.00
2	Frank Mahovlich, Mon.	17.50	35.00	75.00
3	Ed Van Impe, Phi.	3.00	6.00	12.00
—	Panel	60.00	125.00	250.00
4	Bobby Hull, Chi.	25.00	50.00	100.00
5	Henri Richard, Mon.	12.00	22.50	45.00
6	Gilbert Perreault, Buf.	17.50	35.00	65.00
—	Panel	25.00	50.00	100.00
7	Alex Delvecchio, Det.	10.00	20.00	40.00
8	Denis DeJordy, Goalie, LA	4.00	8.00	16.00
9	Ted Harris, Min.	3.00	6.00	12.00
—	Panel	35.00	75.00	150.00
10	Gilles Villemure, Goalie, NYR	4.00	8.00	16.00

294 • KELLOGG'S — 1971 IRON ON TRANSFERS —

No.	Player	VG	EX	NRMT
11	Dave Keon, Tor.	12.00	22.50	45.00
12	Derek Sanderson, Bos.	7.50	15.00	30.00
—	Panel	25.00	50.00	100.00
13	Orland Kurtenbach, Van.	4.00	8.00	16.00
14	Bob Nevin, Min.	3.00	6.00	12.00
15	Yvan Cournoyer, Mon.	9.00	18.00	35.00
—	Panel	20.00	40.00	80.00
16	Andre Boudrias, Van.	3.00	6.00	12.00
17	Frank St. Marseille, St.L.	3.00	6.00	12.00
18	Norm Ullman, Tor.	11.00	18.00	35.00
—	Panel	16.00	32.50	65.00
19	Garry Unger, St.L.	4.00	8.00	16.00
20	Pierre Bouchard, Mon.	3.00	6.00	12.00
21	Roy Edwards, Goalie, LA	4.00	8.00	16.00
—	Panel	17.00	35.00	75.00
22	Ralph Backstrom, LA	3.00	6.00	12.00
23	Guy Trottier, Tor.	3.00	6.00	12.00
24	Serge Bernier, Phi.	3.00	6.00	12.00
—	Panel	17.00	35.00	75.00
25	Bert Marshall, Ca.	3.00	6.00	12.00
26	Wayne Hillman, Phi.	3.00	6.00	12.00
27	Tim Ecclestone, Det.	3.00	6.00	12.00
—	Panel	50.00	100.00	200.00
28	Walt McKechnie, Ca.	3.00	6.00	12.00
29	Tony Esposito, Goalie, Chi.	22.50	45.00	90.00
30	Rod Gilbert, NYR	12.00	22.50	45.00
—	Panel	16.00	32.50	65.00
31	Walt Tkaczuk, NYR	4.00	8.00	16.00
32	Roger Crozier, Goalie, Det.	4.00	8.00	16.00
33	Ken Schinkel, Pit.	3.00	6.00	12.00
—	Panel	115.00	225.00	450.00
34	Ron Ellis, Tor.	3.00	6.00	12.00
35	Stan Mikita, Chi.	22.50	45.00	90.00
36	Bobby Orr, Bos.	70.00	140.00	275.00

KELLOGG'S

— 1971 IRON ON TRANSFERS —

Very little is known of this set and players are listed alphabetically. Additional information would be appreciated.

Size: 8 1/2" X 6 1/2"
Face: Four colour caricature on light paper stock
Back: Blank
Imprint: None
Complete Set No.: 6
Complete Set Price: 85.00   175.00

No.	Player	EX	NRMT
1	Ron Ellis, Tor.	12.50	25.00
2	Phil Esposito, Bos.	20.00	40.00
3	Rod Gilbert, NYR	12.50	25.00
4	Bobby Hull, Chi.	25.00	50.00
5	Frank Mahovlich, Tor.	20.00	40.00
6	Stan Mikita, Chi.	17.50	35.00

— 1984 PUCK ISSUE —

These player disks were issued in strips of six disks and the team logos individually. Both came inside a black or orange plastic puck with the NHL crest moulded on the top lid. The pucks in turn can be mounted in a display shield. The disks are arranged in alphabetical order by the first player of each strip.

Disk Size: 2 1/16" Diameter
Face: Four colour, white border
Back: Black on white card stock; Team logo, Name, Position, Resume, Bilingual, Facsimile autograph
Imprint: None
Complete Set No.: 64 (48 Hockey)
Sticker Size: 1 1/4" X 1 1/4"
Face: Four colour on white background
Back: Blank
Imprint: None
Complete Set No.: 22 (21 Hockey)
Complete Set No.: 8 Panels / 48 Disks; 21 Stickers
Complete Set Price: 17.50   35.00
Shield: 50.00

Kellogg's
1984 Puck Issue
Strip 1,
P. Coffey, M. Tremblay,
J. Anderson, D. Hawerchuk,
R. Kehoe, B. Beck

No.	Player	EX	NRMT
—	Strip 1	2.75	5.50
1	Paul Coffey, Edm.		
2	Mario Tremblay, Chi.		
3	John Anderson, Tor.		
4	Dale Hawerchuk, Win.		
5	Rick Kehoe, Pit.		
6	Barry Beck, NYR		
—	Strip 2	2.50	5.00
7	Bernie Federko, St.L.		
8	Ron Francis, Har.		
9	Stan Smyl, Van.		
10	Michael Gartner, Wash.		
11	David Babych, Win.		
12	Lanny McDonald, Cal.		
—	Strip 3	2.50	5.00
13	Paul Reinhart, Cal.		
14	Jari Kurri, Edm.		
15	Michel Goulet, Que.		
16	Richard Brodeur, Goalie, Van.		
17	Mike Bossy, NYI		
18	Dino Ciccarelli, Min.		
—	Strip 4	2.50	5.00
19	Larry Robinson, Mon.		
20	Doug Risebrough, Cal.		
21	Paul MacLean, Win.		
22	Peter Stastny, Que.		
23	Marcel Dionne, LA		
24	Reed Larson, Det.		
—	Strip 5	2.50	5.00
25	Borje Salming, Tor.		
26	Kevin Lowe, Edm.		
27	Guy Lafleur, Mon.		
28	Rick Middleton, Bos.		
29	Gilbert Perreault, Buf.		
30	The Stanley Cup		
—	Strip 6	2.50	5.00
31	Richard Vaive, Tor.		
32	Glenn Resch, Goalie, NJ		
33	Darryl Sittler, Phi.		
34	Douglas Wilson, Chi.		
35	Dale Hunter, Que.		
36	Thomas Gradin, Van.		
—	Strip 7	2.25	4.50
37	Tracy Austin		
38	Olga Korbut		
39	Rosi Mettermaier		
40	Angela Taylor		
41	Anne Ottenbrite		
42	Paul Martini, Barbara Underhill		
—	Strip 8	2.25	4.50
43	Tatiana Kolpakova		
44	Kay Thompson		
45	Kornelia Ender		
46	Melanie Smith		
47	Nadia Comaneci		
48	Carling Basset		

TEAM LOGO STICKERS

No.	Player	EX	NRMT
49	Boston Bruins	.03	.05
50	Buffalo Sabres	.03	.05
51	Calgary Flames	.03	.05
52	Chicago Black Hawks	.03	.05
53	Detroit Red Wings	.03	.05
54	Edmonton Oilers	.03	.05
55	Hartford Whalers	.03	.05
56	Los Angeles Kings	.03	.05
57	Minnesota North Stars	.03	.05
58	Montreal Canadiens	.03	.05
59	New Jersey Devils	.03	.05
60	New York Islanders	.03	.05
61	New York Rangers	.03	.05
62	Philadelphia Flyers	.03	.05
63	Pittsburgh Penguins	.03	.05
64	Quebec Nordiques	.03	.05
65	St. Louis Blues	.03	.05
66	Toronto Maple Leafs	.03	.05
67	Vancouver Canucks	.03	.05
68	Washington Capitals	.03	.05
69	Winnipeg Jets	.03	.05
70	World Games	.03	.05

KELLOGG'S 1971 IRON-ON TRANSFER
Transfer No. 4, Bobby Hull

— 1992 ISSUE —

These cards were issued as a premium in two card packs with each box of Kellogg's corn flakes during the early months of 1992. The complete set of 24 cards was also available, together with a card holder, by submitting three Kellogg's box tokens plus $5.99 to Kellogg's. The set was produced by Score under their NHL license. The set does not contain a checklist.

Card Size: 2 1/2" X 3 1/2"
Face: Four colour, purple border, Team and Score logo
Back: Four colour, red, purple and black on white card stock, Number, Resume, Position, Kellogg's and Score Logo, Bilingual
Imprint: © 1991 SCORE, PRINTED IN USA
Complete Set No.: 24

Set Price:	7.50	15.00
Common Goalie:	.13	.25
Common Player:	.13	.25

No.	Player	EX	NRMT
1	Patrick Roy, Goalie, Mon.	1.50	3.00
2	Rick Tocchet, Phi.	.25	.50
3	Wendel Clark, Tor.	.50	1.00
4	Michael Modano, Min.	.35	.75
5	Jeremy Roenick, Chi.	.85	1.75
6	Pierre Turgeon, Buf.	.40	.80
7	Kevin Hatcher, Wash.	.30	.60
8	Brian Leetch, NYR	.75	1.50
9	Mark Recchi, Pit.	.50	1.00
10	Andrew Moog, Goalie, Bos.	.20	.40
11	Kevin Dineen, Har.	.20	.40
12	Joe Sakic, Que.	.35	.75
13	John MacLean, NJD	.13	.25
14	Steve Yzerman, Det.	.35	.75
15	Pat LaFontaine, NYI	.35	.75
16	Al MacInnis, Cal.	.25	.50
17	Petr Klima, Edm.	.13	.25
18	Ed Olczyk, Win.	.13	.25
19	Douglas Wilson, SJ	.13	.25
20	Trevor Linden, Van.	.13	.25
21	Brett Hull, St. L.	.50	1.00
22	Rob Blake, LA	.25	.50
23	Dave Ellett, Tor.	.13	.25
24	Cornelius Rooster, Kelloggs	.13	.25

— 1992 RICE KRISPIES —

These limited edition cards were issued in two seres (cards 1-2-3 and 3-4-5), one series free inside 700g size of Rice Krispies, in the summer of 1992. There were one million issued.

Card Size: 2 1/2" x 3 1/2"
Face: Four colour, borderless; Trophy Name, Number
Back: White and black on red, Card stock; Trophy Name, Resume, Bilingual
Imprint: *Registered trademark of /*Marque deposee de KELLOGG'S CANADA INC. © 1992
Complete Set No. 8

Complete Set Price:	5.00	10.00

No.	Player	EX	NRMT
1	Stanley Cup	1.50	3.00
2	Art Ross Memorial Trophy	.50	1.00
3	Hart Memorial Trophy	.50	1.00
4	Conn Smythe Trophy	.50	1.00
5	Vezina Trophy	.50	1.00
6	James Norris Memorial Trophy	.50	1.00
7	Calder Memorial Trophy	.50	1.00
8	Frank J. Selke Trophy	.50	1.00

— 1992 - 93 POSTERS —

This 5-poster set was inserted in specially marked boxes of Kellogg's Corn Flakes of 525g and 675g sizes. The set has four NHL superstars and features Kellogg's Cornelius Rooster. The posters are bilingual, one side English the other French. There were 700,000 of each poster produced and distributed. The posters came in cellophane wrappers folded eight times and are unnumbered. They are listed here alphabetically.

Poster Size: 9 1/4" x 14 1/8"
Face: Four colour, borderless; Name; Kellogg's and NHL logos
Back: Four colour, Name, Kellogg's and NHL logos
Imprint: *Registered trademark of /*Marque deposee de KELLOGG'S CANADA INC. © 1992
Complete Set No. 5

Complete Set Price:	7.50	15.00
Common Poster:	1.50	3.00

Kellogg's 1992 Issue Card No. 1, Patrick Roy

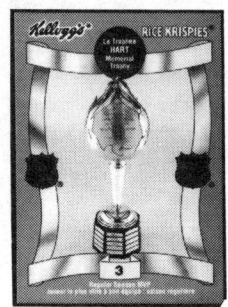

Kellogg's 1992 Rice Krispies Card No. 3, Hart Memorial Trophy

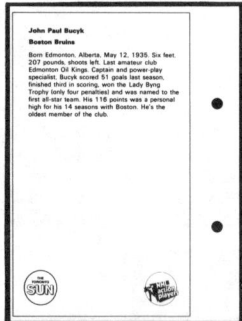

Toronto Sun 1971-72 Issue Card No. 5, John Bucyk

No.	Player	EX	NRMT
1	Mario Lemieux, "Man of Steel" / "L'Homme de Fer"	1.50	3.00
2	Mark Messier, "Power Broker" / "LA Super Star"	1.50	3.00
3	Luc Robitaille, "Robo Shot" / "Le Coupe De Maitre"	1.50	3.00
4	Patrick Roy, Goalie, "Road Block" / "Le Baraque"	1.50	3.00
5	Cornelius Rooster, "Frequent Flyer" / "Vol-Au-Vent"	1.50	3.00

— 1992 RICE KRISPIES —

Limited edition poster (1 million issed) free inside 700g size of Rice Krispies issued March to April 1993.

Card Size: 14" x 9 1/4"
Face: Four colour, white border, paper stock
Back: Blank
Imprint: *Registered trademark of /*Marque deposee de KELLOGG'S CANADA INC. © 1992
Complete Set No. 3

Complete Set Price:	5.00	10.00

No.	Player	EX	NRMT
1	Campbell Conference All Stars	2.50	5.00
2	Wales Conference All Stars	2.50	5.00
3	All Stars "Snap, Crackle, Pop"	2.50	5.00

TORONTO SUN

— 1971 - 72 ISSUE —

This unnumbered set is arranged below in alphabetical order by team and then by player within the team. It was also issued in the Vancouver area with the "Columbian" logo replacing the "Sun" logo, and in Moncton, NB "Les Etoiles, De la LNH en Action Presentees Le Progrès l'évangéline.

Card Size: 5 1/4" X 7"
Face: Four colour, cream border; Name, Facsimile autograph, Team logo
Back: Black on beige paper stock; Name, Team, Resume, Sponsor's logos
Imprint: THE TORONTO SUN; COLUMBIAN
Complete Set No.: 294

Complete Set Price:	75.00	150.00	300.00
Common Player:	.25	.50	1.00
Album:	20.00	35.00	75.00

TITLE CARD

No.	Player	VG	EX	NRMT
—	"Scott Young"	.25	.50	1.00

BOSTON BRUINS

No.	Player	VG	EX	NRMT
1	Bruins Team Crest	.25	.50	1.00
2	Don Awrey	.50	1.00	2.00
3	Garnet Bailey	.25	.50	1.00
4	Ivan Boldirev	.25	.50	1.00
5	John Bucyk	.75	1.50	3.00
6	Wayne Cashman	.25	.50	1.00
7	Gerry Cheevers, Goalie	1.25	2.50	5.00
8	Phil Esposito	2.00	4.00	8.00
9	Ted Green	.25	.50	1.00
10	Ken Hodge, Sr.	.50	1.00	2.00
11	Eddie Johnston, Goalie	.25	.50	1.00
12	Reggie Leach	.50	1.00	2.00
13	Don Marcotte	.25	.50	1.00
14	John McKenzie	.50	1.00	2.00
15	Bobby Orr	10.00	20.00	40.00
16	Derek Sanderson	.75	1.50	3.00
17	Dallas Smith	.25	.50	1.00
18	Rick Smith	.25	.50	1.00
19	Fred Stanfield	.25	.50	1.00
20	Mike Walton	.25	.50	1.00
21	Ed Westfall	.50	1.00	2.00

BUFFALO SABRES

No.	Player	VG	EX	NRMT
22	Sabres Team Crest	.25	.50	1.00
23	Doug Barrie	.25	.50	1.00
24	Roger Crozier, Goalie	.25	.50	1.00
25	Dave Dryden, Goalie	.25	.50	1.00
26	Dick Duff	.25	.50	1.00
27	Phil Goyette	.25	.50	1.00
28	Al Hamilton	.25	.50	1.00
29	Larry Keenan	.25	.50	1.00
30	Danny Lawson	.25	.50	1.00

— 1971 - 72 ISSUE — TORONTO SUN • 297

No.	Player	VG	EX	NRMT
31	Don Luce	.25	.50	1.00
32	Richard Martin	.50	1.00	2.00
33	Ray McKay	.25	.50	1.00
34	Gerry Meehan	.25	.50	1.00
35	Kevin O'Shea	.25	.50	1.00
36	Gilbert Perreault	1.00	2.00	4.00
37	Tracy Pratt	.25	.50	1.00
38	Mike Robitaille	.25	.50	1.00
39	Eddie Shack	.50	1.00	2.00
40	Jimmy Watson	.25	.50	1.00
41	Rod Zaine	.25	.50	1.00

CALIFORNIA GOLDEN SEALS

No.	Player	VG	EX	NRMT
42	California Team Crest	.50	1.00	2.00
43	Wayne Carleton	.25	.50	1.00
44	Lyle Carter, Goalie	.35	.75	1.50
45	Gary Croteau	.25	.50	1.00
46	Norm Ferguson	.25	.50	1.00
47	Stan Gilbertson	.25	.50	1.00
48	Ernie Hicke	.25	.50	1.00
49	Gary Jarrett	.25	.50	1.00
50	Joey Johnston	.25	.50	1.00
51	Marshall Johnston	.25	.50	1.00
52	Bert Marshall	.25	.50	1.00
53	Walt McKechnie	.25	.50	1.00
54	Don O'Donoghue	.25	.50	1.00
55	Gerry Pinder	.25	.50	1.00
56	Dick Redmond	.25	.50	1.00
57	Bobby Sheehan	.25	.50	1.00
58	Paul Shmyr	.25	.50	1.00
59	Ron Stackhouse	.25	.50	1.00
60	Carol Vadnais	.25	.50	1.00
61	Tom Williams	.25	.50	1.00

CHICAGO BLACK HAWKS

No.	Player	VG	EX	NRMT
62	Chicago Team Crest	.25	.50	1.00
63	Lou Angotti	.25	.50	1.00
64	Bryan Campbell	.25	.50	1.00
65	Tony Esposito, Goalie	1.25	2.50	5.00
66	Bobby Hull	5.00	10.00	20.00
67	Dennis Hull	.25	.50	1.00
68	Doug Jarrett	.25	.50	1.00
69	Jerry Korab	.25	.50	1.00
70	Cliff Koroll	.25	.50	1.00
71	Daryl Maggs	.25	.50	1.00
72	Keith Magnuson	.25	.50	1.00
73	Chico Maki	.25	.50	1.00
74	Dan Maloney	.25	.50	1.00
75	Pit Martin	.25	.50	1.00
76	Stan Mikita	1.25	2.50	5.00
77	Eric Nesterenko	.25	.50	1.00
78	Danny O'Shea	.25	.50	1.00
79	Jim Pappin	.25	.50	1.00
80	Gary Smith, Goalie	.25	.50	1.00
81	Pat Stapleton	.25	.50	1.00
82	Bill White	.25	.50	1.00

DETROIT RED WINGS

No.	Player	VG	EX	NRMT
83	Detroit Team Crest	.25	.50	1.00
84	Red Berenson	.25	.50	1.00
85	Gary Bergman	.25	.50	1.00
86	Arnie Brown	.25	.50	1.00
87	Guy Charron	.25	.50	1.00
88	Bill Collins	.25	.50	1.00
89	Brian Conacher	.25	.50	1.00
90	Joe Daley, Goalie	.35	.75	1.50
91	Alex Delvecchio	.75	1.50	3.00
92	Marcel Dionne	3.75	7.50	15.00
93	Tim Ecclestone	.25	.50	1.00
94	Ron Harris	.25	.50	1.00
95	Gerry Hart	.25	.50	1.00
96	Gordie Howe	10.00	20.00	40.00
97	Al Karlander	.25	.50	1.00
98	Nick Libett	.25	.50	1.00
99	Ab McDonald	.25	.50	1.00
100	Jim Niekamp	.25	.50	1.00
101	Mickey Redmond	.25	.50	1.00
102	Leon Rochefort	.25	.50	1.00
103	Al Smith, Goalie	.25	.50	1.00

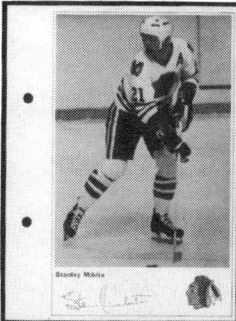

Toronto Sun
1971-72 Issue
Card No. 76,
Stan Mikita

Toronto Sun
1971-72 Issue
Card No. 161,
Henri Richard

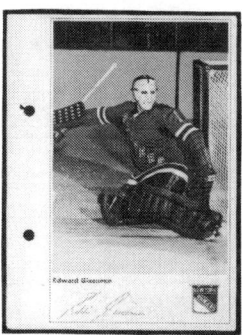

Toronto Sun
1971-72 Issue
Card No. 172,
Ed Giacomin

LOS ANGELES KINGS

No.	Player	VG	EX	NRMT
104	Kings Team Crest	.25	.50	1.00
105	Ralph Backstrom	.25	.50	1.00
106	Robert Perry	.25	.50	1.00
107	Mike Byers	.25	.50	1.00
108	Larry Cahan	.25	.50	1.00
109	Paul Curtis	.25	.50	1.00
110	Denis DeJordy, Goalie	.25	.50	1.00
111	Gary Edwards, Goalie	.25	.50	1.00
112	Bill Flett	.25	.50	1.00
113	Butch Goring	.25	.50	1.00
114	Lucien Grenier	.25	.50	1.00
115	Larry Hillman	.25	.50	1.00
116	Dale Hoganson	.25	.50	1.00
117	Harry Howell	.50	1.00	2.00
118	Eddie Joyal	.25	.50	1.00
119	Real Lemieux	.25	.50	1.00
120	Ross Lonsberry	.25	.50	1.00
121	Al McDonough	.25	.50	1.00
122	Jean Potvin	.25	.50	1.00
123	Bob Pulford	.35	.75	1.50
124	Juha Widing	.25	.50	1.00

MINNESOTA NORTH STARS

No.	Player	VG	EX	NRMT
125	Minnesota Team Crest	.25	.50	1.00
126	Fred Barrett	.25	.50	1.00
127	Charlie Burns	.25	.50	1.00
128	Jude Drouin	.25	.50	1.00
129	Barry Gibbs	.25	.50	1.00
130	Gilles Gilbert, Goalie	.35	.75	1.50
131	Bill Goldsworthy	.35	.75	1.50
132	Danny Grant	.50	1.00	2.00
133	Ted Hampson	.25	.50	1.00
134	Ted Harris	.25	.50	1.00
135	Buster (Fred) Harvey	.25	.50	1.00
136	Cesare Maniago, Goalie	.50	1.00	2.00
137	Doug Mohns	.25	.50	1.00
138	Lou Nanne	.35	.75	1.50
139	Bob Nevin	.25	.50	1.00
140	Dennis O'Brien	.25	.50	1.00
141	Murray Oliver	.25	.50	1.00
142	Jean Paul Parise	.35	.75	1.50
143	Dean Prentice	.25	.50	1.00
144	Tom Reid	.25	.50	1.00
145	Gump Worsley, Goalie	1.25	2.50	5.00

MONTREAL CANADIENS

No.	Player	VG	EX	NRMT
146	Montreal Team Crest	.25	.50	1.00
147	Pierre Bouchard	.25	.50	1.00
148	Yvan Cournoyer	1.00	2.00	4.00
149	Ken Dryden, Goalie	5.00	10.00	20.00
150	Terry Harper	.25	.50	1.00
151	Rejean Houle	.25	.50	1.00
152	Guy Lafleur	3.00	6.00	12.00
153	Jacques Laperriere	.50	1.00	2.00
154	Guy Lapointe	.50	1.00	2.00
155	Claude Larose	.25	.50	1.00
156	Jacques Lemaire	.50	1.00	2.00
157	Frank Mahovlich	2.50	5.00	10.00
158	Pete Mahovlich	.35	.75	1.50
159	Phil Myre	.35	.75	1.50
160	Larry Pleau	.25	.50	1.00
161	Henri Richard	1.25	2.50	5.00
162	Phil Roberto	.25	.50	1.00
163	Serge Savard	.50	1.00	2.00
164	Marc Tardif	.25	.50	1.00
165	J.C. Tremblay	.25	.50	1.00
166	Rogatien Vachon, Goalie	.75	1.50	3.00

NEW YORK RANGERS

No.	Player	VG	EX	NRMT
167	Rangers Team Crest	.25	.50	1.00
168	Dave Balon	.25	.50	1.00
169	Ab DeMarco	.25	.50	1.00
170	Jack Egers	.25	.50	1.00
171	Bill Fairbairn	.25	.50	1.00
172	Ed Giacomin, Goalie	1.00	2.00	4.00
173	Rod Gilbert	.75	1.50	3.00
174	Vic Hadfield	.50	1.00	2.00
175	Ted Irvine	.25	.50	1.00

298 • DIMANCHE / DERNIERE HEURE — 1972-84 ISSUES —

No.	Player	VG	EX	NRMT
176	Bruce MacGregor	.25	.50	1.00
177	Jim Neilson	.25	.50	1.00
178	Brad Park	.75	1.50	3.00
179	Jean Ratelle	.75	1.50	3.00
180	Dale Rolfe	.25	.50	1.00
181	Bobby Rousseau	.25	.50	1.00
182	Glen Sather	.50	1.00	2.00
183	Rod Seiling	.25	.50	1.00
184	Pete Stemkowski	.25	.50	1.00
185	Walt Tkaczuk	.25	.50	1.00
186	Gilles Villemure, Goalie	.45	.75	1.50

PHILADELPHIA FLYERS

No.	Player	VG	EX	NRMT
187	Flyers Team Crest	.25	.50	1.00
188	Barry Ashbee	.25	.50	1.00
189	Serge Bernier	.25	.50	1.00
190	Larry Brown	.25	.50	1.00
191	Bobby Clarke	1.25	2.50	5.00
192	Gary Dornhoefer	.25	.50	1.00
193	Doug Favell, Goalie	.50	1.00	2.00
194	Bruce Gamble, Goalie	.35	.75	1.50
195	Jean-Guy Gendron	.25	.50	1.00
196	Larry Hale	.25	.50	1.00
197	Wayne Hillman	.25	.50	1.00
198	Brent Hughes	.25	.50	1.00
199	Jim Johnson	.25	.50	1.00
200	Bob Kelly	.25	.50	1.00
201	Andre Lacroix	.25	.50	1.00
202	Bill Lesuk	.25	.50	1.00
203	Rick MacLeish	.50	1.00	2.00
204	Larry Mickey	.25	.50	1.00
205	Simon Nolet	.25	.50	1.00
206	Pierre Plante	.25	.50	1.00
207	Ed Van Impe	.25	.50	1.00
208	Joe Watson	.25	.50	1.00

PITTSBURGH PENGUINS

No.	Player	VG	EX	NRMT
209	Penguins Team Crest	.25	.50	1.00
210	Syl Apps, Sr.	.25	.50	1.00
211	Les Binkley, Goalie	.25	.50	1.00
212	Wally Boyer	.25	.50	1.00
213	Darryl Edestrand	.25	.50	1.00
214	Roy Edwards, Goalie	.25	.50	1.00
215	Nick Harbaruk	.25	.50	1.00
216	Bryan Hextall, Jr.	.25	.50	1.00
217	Bill Hicke	.25	.50	1.00
218	Tim Horton	1.25	2.50	5.00
219	Sheldon Kannegiesser	.25	.50	1.00
220	Bobby Leiter	.25	.50	1.00
221	Keith McCreary	.25	.50	1.00
222	Joe Noris	.25	.50	1.00
223	Greg Polis	.25	.50	1.00
224	Jean Pronovost	.25	.50	1.00
225	Rene Robert	.25	.50	1.00
226	Duane Rupp	.25	.50	1.00
227	Ken Schinkel	.25	.50	1.00
228	Ron Schock	.25	.50	1.00
229	Bryan Watson	.25	.50	1.00
230	Bob Woytowich	.25	.50	1.00

ST. LOUIS BLUES

No.	Player	VG	EX	NRMT
231	Blues Team Crest	.25	.50	1.00
232	Al Arbour	.75	1.50	3.00
233	John Arbour	.25	.50	1.00
234	Chris Bordeleau	.25	.50	1.00
235	Carl Brewer	.25	.50	1.00
236	Gene Carr	.25	.50	1.00
237	Wayne Connelly	.25	.50	1.00
238	Terry Crisp	.50	1.00	2.00
239	Jim Lorentz	.25	.50	1.00
240	Pete McDuffe	.25	.50	1.00
241	George Morrison	.25	.50	1.00
242	Michel Parizeau	.25	.50	1.00
243	Noel Picard	.25	.50	1.00
244	Barclay Plager	.25	.50	1.00
245	Bob Plager	.25	.50	1.00
246	Jim Roberts	.25	.50	1.00
247	Gary Sabourin	.25	.50	1.00
248	Jim Shires	.25	.50	1.00

Toronto Sun
1971-72 Issue
Card No. 193,
Doug Favell

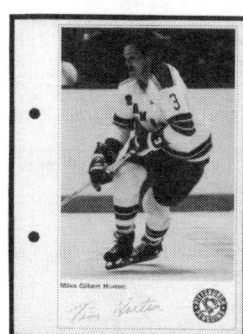

Toronto Sun
1971-72 Issue
Card No. 218,
Tim Horton

Toronto Sun
1971-72 Issue
Card No. 267,
Bernie Parent

Toronto Sun
1971-72 Issue
Card No. 269,
Jacques Plante

No.	Player	VG	EX	NRMT
249	Frank St. Marseille	.25	.50	1.00
250	Bill Sutherland	.25	.50	1.00
251	Garry Unger	.50	1.00	2.00
252	Ernie Wakely, Goalie	.25	.50	1.00

TORONTO MAPLE LEAFS

No.	Player	VG	EX	NRMT
253	Toronto Team Crest	.25	.50	1.00
254	Bob Baun	.25	.50	1.00
255	Jim Dorey	.25	.50	1.00
256	Denis Dupere	.25	.50	1.00
257	Ron Ellis	.50	1.00	2.00
258	Brian Glennie	.25	.50	1.00
259	Jim Harrison	.25	.50	1.00
260	Paul Henderson	.25	.50	1.00
261	Dave Keon	1.00	2.00	4.00
262	Rick Ley	.25	.50	1.00
263	Billy MacMillan	.25	.50	1.00
264	Don Marshall	.25	.50	1.00
265	Jim McKenny	.25	.50	1.00
266	Garry Monahan	.25	.50	1.00
267	Bernie Parent, Goalie	.75	1.50	3.00
268	Mike Pelyk	.25	.50	1.00
269	Jacques Plante, Goalie	1.60	3.25	6.50
270	Brad Selwood	.25	.50	1.00
271	Darryl Sittler	1.25	2.50	5.00
272	Brian Spencer	.25	.50	1.00
273	Guy Trottier	.25	.50	1.00
274	Norm Ullman	.50	1.00	2.00

VANCOUVER CANUCKS

No.	Player	VG	EX	NRMT
275	Canucks Team Crest	.25	.50	1.00
276	Andre Boudrias	.25	.50	1.00
277	George Gardner, Goalie	.25	.50	1.00
278	Jocelyn Guevremont	.25	.50	1.00
279	Murray Hall	.25	.50	1.00
280	Danny Johnson	.25	.50	1.00
281	Dennis Kearns	.25	.50	1.00
282	Orland Kurtenbach	.25	.50	1.00
283	Bobby Lalonde	.25	.50	1.00
284	Wayne Maki	.25	.50	1.00
285	Rosaire Paiement	.25	.50	1.00
286	Poul Popeil	.25	.50	1.00
287	Pat Quinn	.50	1.00	2.00
288	John Schella	.25	.50	1.00
289	Bobby Schmautz	.25	.50	1.00
290	Fred Speck	.25	.50	1.00
291	Dale Tallon	.25	.50	1.00
292	Ron Ward	.25	.50	1.00
293	Barry Wilkins	.25	.50	1.00
294	Dunc Wilson, Goalie	.35	.75	1.50

DIMANCHE / DERNIERE HEURE

— 1972 - 84 ISSUES —

These photos were inserted in the Derniere magazine. Three holes were punched on the left side to allow for storage in a binder. This set of photographs included hockey, baseball, football and soccer players, as well as wrestling, boxing, car racing and golf. Only the hockey photos are listed here.

Stamp Size: 8" X 10"
Face: Four colour, white border; Name, Jersey Number, Position, Resume, French
Back: Blank
Imprint: DIMANCHE / DERNIERE HEURE
Complete Set No.: Unknown
Complete Set Price: 550.00 1,100.00
Common Player: 1.50 3.00

1972 ISSUE

No.	Player / Date Issued	VG	EX
1	Ken Dryden, Goalie, October 15	7.50	15.00
2	Frank Mahovlich, October 22	6.00	12.00
3	Guy Lapointe, October 29	2.50	5.00
4	Serge Savard, November 5	2.50	5.00
5	Jacques Lemaire, November 12	2.50	5.00
6	Pierre Bouchard, November 19	1.50	3.00
7	Henri Richard, November 26	4.00	8.00

1972 - 84 ISSUES — DIMANCHE / DERNIERE HEURE

No.	Player / Date Issued	VG	EX
8	Guy Lafleur, December 3	6.00	12.00
9	Jacques Laperriere, December 10	2.00	4.00
10	Marc Tardif, December 17	1.50	3.00
11	Scotty Bowman, Coach, December 24	2.00	4.00
12	Pete Mahovlich, December 31	2.00	4.00

1973 ISSUE

No.	Player / Date Issued	VG	EX
13	Michel Plasse, Goalie, January 7	2.00	4.00
14	Chuck Lefley, January 14	1.50	3.00
15	Claude Larose, January 21	1.50	3.00
16	Jim Roberts, January 28	1.50	3.00
17	Bob Murdoch, February 4	1.50	3.00
18	Chuck Arnason, February 11	1.50	3.00
19	Murray Wilson, February 18	1.50	3.00
20	Wayne Thomas, February 25	2.00	4.00
21	Dale Hoganson, March 4	1.50	3.00
22	Larry Robinson, March 11	4.00	8.00
23	Rejean Houle, March 18	1.50	3.00
24	Steve Shutt, March 25	2.50	5.00
25	Yvan Cournoyer, April 1	4.00	8.00
26	Jean Beliveau, April 8	5.00	10.00
27	Henri Richard, November 18	2.50	5.00
28	Guy LaPointe, November 25	2.50	5.00
29	Chuck Lefley, December 2	1.50	3.00
30	Yvan Cournoyer, December 9	2.50	5.00
31	Guy Lafleur, December 16	4.00	8.00
32	Pierre Bouchard, December 23	1.50	3.00
33	Wayne Thomas, December 30	2.00	4.00

1974 ISSUE

No.	Player / Date Issued	VG	EX
34	Jacques Laperriere, January 6	2.00	4.00
35	Serge Savard, January 13	2.50	5.00
36	Frank Mahovlich, January 20	5.00	10.00
37	Claude Larose, January 27	1.50	3.00
38	Michel Plasse, Goalie, February 3	2.00	4.00
39	Michel Larocque, Goalie, February 10	2.50	5.00
40	Pete Mahovlich, February 17	2.00	4.00
41	Steve Shutt, February 24	2.50	5.00
42	Jim Roberts, March 3	1.50	3.00
43	Bob Gainey, March 10	2.50	5.00
44	Murray Wilson, March 17	1.50	3.00
45	Larry Robinson, March 24	3.00	6.00
46	Yvon Lambert, March 31	1.50	3.00
47	Jacques Lemaire, April 7	2.50	5.00

1977 ISSUE

No.	Player / Date Issued	VG	EX
48	Real Cloutier, March 13	1.50	3.00
49	Rogatien Vachon, Goalie, March 20	3.00	6.00
50	Bernard Parent, Goalie, March 27	4.00	8.00
51	Real Cloutier, April 3	1.50	3.00
52	Jean-Claude Tremblay, April 10	3.50	7.00
53	Serge Bernier, April 17	1.50	3.00
54	Denis Potvin, April 24	4.00	8.00

1978

No.	Player / Date Issued	VG	EX
55	Robert Picard, January 1	2.00	4.00
56	Lucien Deblois, January 8	1.50	3.00
57	Michael Bossy, January 15	5.00	10.00
58	Jean Savard, January 22	1.50	3.00
59	Jere Gillis, January 29	1.50	3.00
60	Maurice Richard, February 5	7.50	15.00
61	Toe (Hector) Blake, Coach, February 12	5.00	10.00
62	Elmer Lach, February 19	5.00	10.00
63	Jean Beliveau, February 26	5.00	10.00
64	Floyd Curry, March 5	3.00	6.00
65	Emile Bouchard, March 12	2.50	5.00
66	Tom Johnson, March 19	2.50	5.00
67	Bernard Geoffrion, March 26	4.00	8.00
68	Henri Richard, April 2	4.00	8.00
69	Dickie Moore, April 9	4.00	8.00
70	Claude Provost, April 16	3.50	7.00
71	Jean-Guy Talbot, April 23	3.00	6.00
72	Jacques Plante, Goalie, April 30	6.00	12.00
73	Jean-Claude Tremblay, December 10	2.50	5.00
74	Nordique Player, December 17	1.50	3.00
75	Danny Geoffrion, December 24	1.50	3.00
76	Paul Baxter, December 31	1.50	3.00

CARDS NOT AVAILABLE AT PRESSTIME

1979

No.	Player / Date Issued	VG	EX
77	Normand Dube, January 7	1.50	3.00
78	Jim Corsi, January 14	1.50	3.00
79	Jim Dorey, January 21	1.50	3.00
80	Marc Tardiff, January 28	2.00	4.00
81	Bob Fitchner, February 4	1.50	3.00
82	Alain Cote, February 11	1.50	3.00
83	Richard David, February 18	1.50	3.00
84	Jacques Demers, Coach, February 25	2.50	5.00
85	Francois Lacombe, March 4	1.50	3.00
86	Real Cloutier, March 11	2.00	4.00
87	Curt Brackenbury, March 18	1.50	3.00
88	Richard Brodeur, Goalie, March 25	2.50	5.00
89	Dale Hoganson, April 1	1.50	3.00
90	Wally Weir, April 8	1.50	3.00
91	Serge Bernier, April 15	1.50	3.00
92	Gary Lariviere, April 22	1.50	3.00
93	Paul Baxter, April 29	1.50	3.00
94	Jean Ratelle, December 2	3.50	7.00
95	Guy Chouinard, December 9	1.50	3.00
96	Raymond Bourque, December 16	7.50	15.00
97	Robert Picard, December 23	1.50	3.00
98	Carol Vadnais, December 30	2.50	5.00

1980

No.	Player / Date Issued	VG	EX
99	Marcel Dionne, January 6	6.00	12.00
100	Anders Hedberg, January 13	2.50	5.00
101	Bobby Hull, January 20	7.50	15.00
102	Wilf Paiement, January 27	2.00	4.00
103	Guy Charron, February 3	1.50	3.00
104	Phil Myre, Goalie, February 10	2.00	4.00
105	Rene Robert, February 17	2.00	4.00
106	Bobby Clarke, February 24	2.50	5.00
107	J.P. Bordeleau, March 2	1.50	3.00
108	Andre Dupont, March 9	1.50	3.00
109	Brad Park, March 16	3.50	7.00
110	Pierre Bouchard, March 23	1.50	3.00
111	Borje Salming, March 30	3.00	6.00
112	Dale McCourt, Aprril 6	1.50	3.00
113	Daniel Bouchard, Goalie, April 13	2.50	5.00
114	Serge Savard, November 30	2.50	5.00
115	Yvon Lambert, December 7	1.50	3.00
116	Bob Gainey, December 14	3.00	6.00
117	Rejean Houle, December 21	2.00	4.00
118	Claude Ruel, Coach, December 28	2.00	4.00

1981

No.	Player / Date Issued	VG	EX
119	Doug Jarvis, January 4	2.00	4.00
120	Michel Larocque, Goalie, January 11	1.50	3.00
121	Pierre Larouche, January 18	2.50	5.00
122	Larry Robinson, January 25	4.00	8.00
123	Mario Tremblay, February 1	2.00	4.00
124	Guy Lapointe, February 8	3.00	6.00
125	Gaston Gingras, February 15	1.50	3.00
126	Richard / Bossy, February 22	6.00	12.00
127	Brian Engblom, March 1	1.50	3.00
128	Doug Risebrough, March 8	2.00	4.00
129	Rod Langway, March 15	2.50	5.00
130	Guy Lafleur, March 22	4.00	8.00
131	Steve Shutt, March 29	2.50	5.00
132	Mark Napier, April 5	2.00	4.00
133	Richard Sevigny, Goalie, April 12	2.00	4.00
134	Chris Nilan, April 19	2.00	4.00
135	Pierre Mondou, April 26	1.50	3.00
136	Keith Acton, May 3	2.50	5.00
137	Denis Herron, Goalie, May 10	3.00	6.00
138	Marc Tardif, November 8	2.50	5.00
139	Michel Bergeron, November 15	2.50	5.00
140	Daniel Bouchard, Goalie, November 22	3.00	6.00
141	Jacques Richard, November 29	2.00	4.00
142	Marian Stastny, December 6	2.00	4.00
143	Michel Goulet, December 13	4.00	8.00
144	Andre Dupont, December 20	1.50	3.00
145	Robbie Ftorek, December 27	2.00	4.00

1982

No.	Player / Date Issued	VG	EX
146	Michel Plasse, Goalie, January 3	2.00	4.00
147	Pierre Lacroix, January 10	1.50	3.00
148	Dale Hoganson, January 17	2.00	4.00

DIMANCHE/DERNIERE HEURE, 28 janvier 1973

JIM ROBERTS (6) AVANT

Né le 9 avril 1940, à Toronto, Ontario... Demeure à Montréal, Québec... Défenseur et ailier droit... Il lance de la droite... Taille: 5'-10''... Poids: 185 lbs... Dernier club amateur: Petes de Peterborough... Il est marié et père d'un enfant.

Dimanche / Derniere Heure 1972 - 84 Issues
Photograph No. 16, Jim Roberts

— 1972 HOCKEY INSTRUCTION BOOKLETS — TOWERS/BONIMART • 301

No.	Player / Date Issued	VG	EX
149	Mario Marois, January 24	2.00	4.00
150	Normand Rochefort, January 31	2.00	4.00
151	Anton Stastny, February 7	2.50	5.00
152	Dale Hunter, February 14	3.00	6.00
153	Dave Pichette, February 21	1.50	3.00
154	Pierre Aubry, February 28	1.50	3.00
155	Real Cloutier, March 7	1.50	3.00
156	Alain Cote, March 14	2.00	4.00
157	Wally Weir, March 21	1.50	3.00
158	Peter Stastny, March 28	4.00	8.00
159	Miroslav Frycer, April 4	1.50	3.00
160	Wayne Gretzky, April 11	17.50	35.00
161	Raymond Bourque, November 14	5.00	10.00
162	Denis Savard, November 21	4.00	8.00
163	Serge Savard, November 28	3.00	6.00
164	Bryan Trottier, December 5	4.00	8.00
165	Wilf Paiement, December 12	2.50	5.00
166	Michael Bossy, December 19	5.00	10.00
167	Ron Duguay, December 26	2.00	4.00

1983

No.	Player / Date Issued	VG	EX
168	Bobby Clarke, January 2	5.00	10.00
169	Mike Rogers, January 9	2.00	4.00
170	Darryl Sittler, January 16	5.00	10.00
171	Carol Vadnais, January 23	3.00	6.00
172	Mark Howe, January 30	3.00	6.00
173	Vladislav Tretiak, Goalie, February 6	7.50	15.00
174	Pierre Larouche, February 13	3.00	6.00
175	Gilbert Perreault, February 20	5.00	10.00
176	Gaston Gingras, February 27	1.50	3.00
177	Richard Brodeur, Goalie, March 6	1.50	3.00
178	Dale Hawerchuk, March 13	4.00	8.00
179	Pat Lafontaine, March 20	10.00	20.00
180	Brian Engblom, March 27	2.00	4.00
181	Dan Daoust, April 3	1.50	3.00
182	Doug Risebrough, April 10	1.50	3.00
183	Rod Langway, April 17	2.50	5.00
184	Doug Jarvis, April 24	1.50	3.00
185	Superstar, November 20	1.50	3.00
186	Rick Wamsley, Goalie, November 27	1.50	3.00
187	Larry Robinson, December 4	3.00	6.00
188	Guy Lafleur, December 11	4.00	8.00
189	Mario Tremblay, December 18	1.50	3.00
190	Mats Naslund, December 25	2.50	5.00

1984

No.	Player / Date Issued	VG	EX
191	Chris Nilan, Jan.1	1.50	3.00
192	Les Canadiens, Jan.8	10.00	20.00
193	Gilbert Dionne, Jan.15	1.50	3.00
194	Pierre Mondou, Jan.22	1.50	3.00
195	Steve Shutt, Jan.29	3.50	7.00
196	Bill Root, Feb.5	1.50	3.00

DATES UNKNOWN

No.	Player	VG	EX
197	Marcel Dionne,	6.00	12.00
198	Real Cloutier	1.50	3.00
199	Pierre Larouche	3.50	7.00
200	Richard Martin	3.00	6.00
201	Gilbert Perreault	5.00	10.00
202	Jean Pronovost	3.50	7.00
203	Daniel Bouchard	3.50	7.00
204	Christian Bordeleau	2.00	4.00

Note: *The Charlton Standard Catalogue of Hockey Cards* arranges cards in their issue date order. This means the first date a manufacturer issues a card set determines the sequence of the manufacturer in the Standard Catalogue. In this manner the historical importance of early cards is maintained. See the last page of this catalogue for an alphabetical index of issuers.

Towers / Bonimart
1972 Instructional Booklet
Booklet No. 1,
Skating Skills

Letraset
1973 Action Replay Transfers
Transfer No.17,
Norm Ullman

Letraset
1973 Action Replay Transfers
Transfer No. 20,
Brad Park

TOWERS/BONIMART

— 1972 HOCKEY INSTRUCTION BOOKLETS —

These six booklets were a promotion from the two companies informing young children how to play hockey. Each booklet covered a different aspect of the game including skating skills, puck control, shooting, checking, goaltending and team play. Original cost of these booklets was .20¢.

Booklet Size: 5" x 7"
Face: Four colour; Number
Back: Black on newsprint
Imprint: Copyright 1972 Photo Pix Productions, Toronto.
Complete Set No.: 6
Complete Set Price: 20.00 40.00

No.	Player	NRMT	Mint
1	Skating Skills	3.50	7.00
2	Puck Control	3.50	7.00
3	Shooting	3.50	7.00
4	Checking	3.50	7.00
5	Goaltending	3.50	7.00
6	Team Play	3.50	7.00

LETRASET

— 1973 ACTION REPLAY TRANSFERS —

Issued in booklet form, the action transfers could be used on any part of the action rink illustrated in the booklet. Four transfers of hockey players in action, plus transfer of the centre player in the following listings.

Transfer Size: 4 7/8" X 2 3/8"
Face: Four colour
Back: Blank
Imprint: GK 121/ ---- Patented. Printed in England by Letraset Ltd.
Complete Set No.: 24
Complete Set Price: 65.00 125.00 250.00
Common Player: 2.50 5.00 10.00

No.	Player	VG	EX	NRMT
1	Rogatien Vachon, Goalie, LA	3.00	6.00	12.00
	David Keon, Tor., Gilles Marotte, LA			
2	Ken Dryden, Goalie, Mon.	6.25	12.50	25.00
	Chiko Maki, Chi., Jacques Laperriere, Mon.			
3	Gary Dornhoefer, Phi., Roger Crozier, Goalie, Buf., Tracy Pratt, Buf.	2.50	5.00	10.00
4	Walt Tkaczuk, NYR, Gump Worsley, Goalie, Min., Vic Hadfield, NYR	3.75	7.50	15.00
5	Dallas Smith, Bos., Bobby Orr, Bos., Walt McKechnie, Cal.	7.50	15.00	30.00
6	Ab MacDonald, Det., Gary Sabourin, St. L, Garry Unger, St. L	2.50	5.00	10.00
7	Jim Rutherford, Pit. Orland Kurtenbach, Van., Bob Woytowich, Pit	2.50	5.00	10.00
8	Gerry Cheevers, Goalie, Bos. Frank Mahovlich, Mon., Don Awrey, Bos.	3.50	7.00	14.00
9	Tim Ecclestone, Det., Bob Baun, Tor., Jacques Plante, Goalie, Tor.	3.00	6.00	12.00
10	Stan Mikita, Chi., Ed Giacomin, Goalie, NYR, Jim Pappin, Chi.	4.50	9.00	18.00
11	Doug Favell, Goalie, Phi. Danny Grant, Phi., Ed Van Impe, Phi.	2.50	5.00	10.00
12	Ernie Wakley. St. L, Barclay Plager, St. L, Gary Croteau, Cal.	2.50	5.00	10.00
13	Unknown			
14	Jean Ratelle, NYR, Rod Gilbert, NYR, Jim Roberts, St. L	3.75	7.50	15.00
15	Jacques Lemaire, Mon. Henri Richard, Mon., Yvan Cournoyer, Mon.	3.75	7.50	15.00
16	George Gardiner, Van., Dennis Hull, Chi., Lou Angotti, Chi.	2.50	5.00	10.00
17	Ed Johnston, Bos., Norm Ullman, Tor., Bobby Orr, Bos.	7.50	15.00	30.00
18	Gilles Meloche, Cal., Wayne Carleton, Cal., Dick Redmond, Cal.	2.50	5.00	10.00
19	Al Smith, Det., Gary Bergman, Det., Stan Gilbertson, Cal.	2.50	5.00	10.00
20	Dunc Wilson, Goalie, Van., Brad Park, NYR, Dale Tallon, Van.	2.50	5.00	10.00
21	Jude Drouin, Min., Doug Favell, Goalie, Phi., Barry Ashbee, Phi.	2.50	5.00	10.00
22	Ron Ellis, Tor., Ken Dryden, Goalie, Mon., Paul Henderson, Tor.	5.50	11.00	22.00

302 • MAC'S MILK — 1973-74 ISSUE —

No.	Player	VG	EX	NRMT
23	Gary Edwards, Goalie, LA	2.50	5.00	10.00
	Jean Pronovost, Mon., Ron Schock, Pit.			
24	Cesare Maniago, Goalie, Min.	2.50	5.00	10.00
	Chris Bordeleau, St. L, Ted Harris, Min.			

MAC'S MILK
— 1973 - 74 ISSUE —

These disks show caricatures of various players.

Disk Size: 3" diameter
Face: Four colour, red, purple, green, blue or black border; Name
Back: Blank
Imprint: NHLPA
Complete Set No.: 30

	VG	EX	NRMT
Complete Set Price:	35.00	65.00	130.00
Common Player:	.60	1.25	2.50

No.	Player	VG	EX	NRMT
1	Gary Bergman, Det.	.60	1.25	2.50
2	John Bucyk, Bos.	1.25	2.50	5.00
3	Wayne Cashman, Bos.	.60	1.25	2.50
4	Bobby Clarke, Phi.	2.25	4.50	9.00
5	Yvan Cournoyer, Mon.	.85	1.75	3.50
6	Ron Ellis, Tor.	.75	1.50	3.00
7	Rod Gilbert, NYR	.75	1.50	3.00
8	Brian Glennie, Tor.	.60	1.25	2.50
9	Paul Henderson, Tor.	1.25	2.50	5.00
10	Eddie Johnston, Goalie, Tor.	.60	1.25	2.50
11	Rick Kehoe, Tor.	.60	1.25	2.50
12	Orland Kurtenbach, Van.	.75	1.50	3.00
13	Guy Lapointe, Mon.	.60	1.25	2.50
14	Jacques Lemaire, Mon.	1.25	2.50	5.00
15	Frank Mahovlich, Mon.	3.75	7.50	15.00
16	Pete Mahovlich, Mon.	1.00	2.00	4.00
17	Richard Martin, Buf.	.60	1.25	2.50
18	Jim McKenny, Tor.	.60	1.25	2.50
19	Bobby Orr, Bos.	6.00	12.50	25.00
20	Jean Paul Parise, Min.	.60	1.25	2.50
21	Brad Park, NYR	1.00	2.00	4.00
22	Jacques Plante, Goalie, Tor.	3.75	7.50	15.00
23	Jean Ratelle, NYR	1.00	2.00	4.00
24	Mickey Redmond, Det.	.60	1.25	2.50
25	Serge Savard, Mon.	.60	1.25	2.50
26	Darryl Sittler, Tor.	2.25	4.50	9.00
27	Pat Stapleton, Chi.	.60	1.25	2.50
28	Dale Tallon, Chi.	.60	1.25	2.50
29	Norm Ullman, Tor.	1.25	2.50	5.00
30	Bill White, Chi.	.60	1.25	2.50

LIPTON SOUP
— 1974 - 75 ISSUE —

This set was issued as two-card panels on the backs of Lipton Soup packages.

Card Size: 2 1/4" X 3 3/8"
Face: Four colour, white border; Name, Team
Back: Black on buff card stock; name, Number, Team, Resume, Bilingual, Facsimile signature
Imprint: © NHL TM NATIONAL HOCKEY LEAGUE PLAYERS ASSOCIATION
Complete Set No.: 51

	VG	EX	NRMT
Complete Set Price:	75.00	150.00	300.00
Common Player:	.60	1.25	2.50

No.	Player	VG	EX	NRMT
1	Norm Ullman, Tor.	2.50	5.00	10.00
2	Gilbert Perreault, Buf.	2.50	5.00	10.00
3	Darryl Sittler, Tor.	2.50	5.00	10.00
4	Jean Paul Parise, Min.	.60	1.25	2.50
5	Garry Unger, St.L.	.60	1.25	2.50
6	Ron Ellis, Tor.	1.25	2.50	5.00
7	Rogatien Vachon, Goalie, LA	2.50	5.00	10.00
8	Bobby Orr, Bos.	12.50	25.00	50.00
9	Wayne Cashman, Bos.	.60	1.25	2.50
10	Brad Park, NYR	2.00	4.00	8.00
11	Serge Savard, Mon.	2.00	4.00	8.00

Mac's Milk
1973-74 Issue
Disk No. 20,
Jean-Paul Parise

Lipton Soup
1974-75 Issue
Card No. 36, Error,
Name misspelled Papin on face

Lipton Soup
1974-75 Issue
Card No. 41C, Error, Name
misspelled Bjore on face

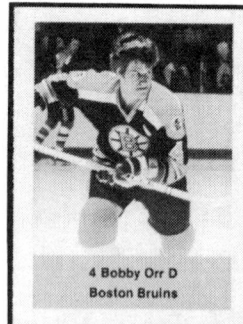

Loblaws
1974-75 NHL Action Players
Card No. 30,
Bobby Orr

No.	Player	VG	EX	NRMT
12	Walt Tkaczuk, NYR	.60	1.25	2.50
13	Yvan Cournoyer, Mon.	2.00	4.00	8.00
14	Andre Boudrias, Van.	.60	1.25	2.50
15	Gary Smith, Goalie, Van.	.60	1.25	2.50
16	Guy Lapointe, Mon.	.60	1.25	2.50
17	Dennis Hull, Chi.	.60	1.25	2.50
18	Bernie Parent, Goalie, Phi.	2.50	5.00	10.00
19	Ken Dryden, Goalie, Mon.	5.00	10.00	20.00
20	Rick MacLeish, Phi.	.60	1.25	2.50
21	Bobby Clarke, Phi.	2.50	5.00	10.00
22	Dale Tallon, Chi.	.60	1.25	2.50
23	Jim McKenny, Tor.	.60	1.25	2.50
24	Rene Robert, Buf.	.60	1.25	2.50
25	Red Berenson, Det.	.60	1.25	2.50
26	Ed Giacomin, Goalie, NYR	2.00	4.00	8.00
27	Cesare Maniago, Goalie, Min.	.60	1.25	2.50
28	Ken Hodge, Sr., Bos.	.60	1.25	2.50
29	Gregg Sheppard, Bos.	.60	1.25	2.50
30	Dave Schultz, Phi.	1.00	2.00	4.00
31	Bill Barber, Phi.	2.00	4.00	8.00
32	Henry Boucha, Det.	.60	1.25	2.50
33	Richard Martin, Buf.	.60	1.25	2.50
34	Steve Vickers, NYR	.60	1.25	2.50
35	Billy Harris, NYI	.60	1.25	2.50
36	Jim Pappin, Chi., Error	.60	1.25	2.50
37	Pit Martin, Chi.	.60	1.25	2.50
38	Jacques Lemaire, Mon.	2.00	4.00	8.00
39	Pete Mahovlich, Mon.	.60	1.25	2.50
40	Rod Gilbert, NYR	1.75	3.50	7.00
41A	Borje Salming, Tor., Vertical picture, Error, name misspelled Bjore on face	2.50	5.00	10.00
41B	Borje Salming, Tor., Vertical picture, Corrected	2.50	5.00	10.00
41C	Borje Salming, Tor., Horizontal picture, Error name misspelled Bjore on face	2.50	5.00	10.00
41D	Borje Salming, Tor., Horizontal picture, Corrected	2.50	5.00	10.00
42	Pete Stemkowski, NYR	.60	1.25	2.50
43	Ron Schock, Pit.	.60	1.25	2.50
44	Dan Bouchard, Goalie, Atl.	.60	1.25	2.50
45	Tony Esposito, Goalie, Chi.	3.00	6.00	12.00
46	Craig Patrick, Cal.	.60	1.25	2.50
47	Ed Westfall, NYI	.60	1.25	2.50
48	Jocelyn Guevremont, Van.	.60	1.25	2.50
49	Syl Apps, Jr., Pit.	2.50	5.00	10.00
50	Dave Keon, Tor.	1.50	3.00	6.00

LOBLAWS
— 1974 - 75 NHL ACTION PLAYERS —

Stamp Size: 1 11/16" X 2 1/4"
Face: Four colour, white border; Jersey number, Name, Position, Team
Back: 1. Black print on paper stock
2. Black with white print on paper stock; Loblaws logo
3. Blank
Imprint: Printed in U.S.A. or Printed in Canada
Complete Set No.: 324

	VG	EX	NRMT
Complete Set Price:	60.00	125.00	250.00
Common Player:	.07	.12	.25
Album:	6.00	12.50	25.00

ATLANTA FLAMES

No.	Player	VG	EX	NRMT
1	Curt Bennett	.07	.12	.25
2	Dan Bouchard, Goalie	.12	.25	.50
3	Arnie Brown	.07	.12	.25
4	Jerry Byers	.07	.12	.25
5	Rey Comeau	.07	.12	.25
6	Fred (Buster) Harvey	.07	.12	.25
7	Bobby Leiter	.07	.12	.25
8	Jean Lemieux	.07	.12	.25
9	Tom Lysiak	.12	.25	.50
10	Randy Manery	.07	.12	.25
11	Keith McCreary	.07	.12	.25
12	Bob J. Murray	.07	.12	.25
13	Phil Myre, Goalie	.10	.15	.30
14	Noel Price	.07	.12	.25
15	Pat Quinn	.12	.25	.50
16	Jacques Richard	.07	.12	.25
17	Larry Romanchych	.07	.12	.25
18	Eric Vail	.07	.12	.25

1974-75 NHL ACTION PLAYERS — LOBLAWS

BOSTON BRUINS

No.	Player	VG	EX	NRMT
19	Ross Brooks, Goalie	.07	.12	.25
20	John Bucyk	.25	.50	1.00
21	Wayne Cashman	.10	.20	.40
22	Darryl Edestrand	.07	.12	.25
23	Phil Esposito	.75	1.50	3.00
24	Dave Forbes	.07	.12	.25
25	Gilles Gilbert, Goalie	.12	.25	.50
26	Ken Hodge, Sr.	.07	.12	.25
27	Don Marcotte	.07	.12	.25
28	Walt McKechnie	.07	.12	.25
29	Terry O'Reilly	.25	.50	1.00
30	Bobby Orr	5.00	10.00	20.00
31	Andre Savard	.07	.12	.25
32	Bobby Schmautz	.07	.12	.25
33	Gregg Sheppard	.07	.12	.25
34	Al Sims	.07	.12	.25
35	Dallas Smith	.07	.12	.25
36	Carol Vadnais	.07	.12	.25

BUFFALO SABRES

No.	Player	VG	EX	NRMT
37	Gary Bromley, Goalie	.07	.12	.25
38	Larry Carriere	.07	.12	.25
39	Roger Crozier, Goalie	.12	.25	.50
40	Rick Dudley	.07	.12	.25
41	Lee Fogolin	.12	.25	.50
42	Norm Gratton	.07	.12	.25
43	Jerry Korab	.07	.12	.25
44	Jim Lorentz	.07	.12	.25
45	Don Luce	.10	.20	.40
46	Richard Martin	.18	.35	.75
47	Gerry Meehan	.07	.12	.25
48	Larry Mickey	.07	.12	.25
49	Gilbert Perreault	.75	1.50	3.00
50	Craig Ramsay	.07	.12	.25
51	Rene Robert	.07	.15	.30
52	Mike Robitaille	.07	.12	.25
53	Jim Schoenfeld	.25	.50	1.00
54	Brian Spencer	.07	.12	.25

CALIFORNIA GOLDEN SEALS

No.	Player	VG	EX	NRMT
55	Bruce Affleck	.07	.12	.25
56	Mike Christie	.07	.12	.25
57	Len Frig	.07	.12	.25
58	Stan Gilbertson	.07	.12	.25
59	Rick Hampton	.07	.12	.25
60	David Hrechkosy	.07	.12	.25
61	Ron Huston	.07	.12	.25
62	Joseph Johnston	.07	.12	.25
63	Wayne King	.07	.12	.25
64	Al MacAdam	.10	.20	.40
65	Ted McAneeley	.08	.15	.25
66	Gilles Meloche, Goalie	.12	.25	.50
67	Jim Neilson	.08	.15	.25
68	Larry Patey	.08	.15	.25
69	Craig Patrick	.10	.20	.40
70	Bob Stewart	.07	.12	.25
71	Stan Weir	.07	.12	.25
72	Larry Wright	.07	.12	.25

CHICAGO BLACK HAWKS

No.	Player	VG	EX	NRMT
73	Ivan Boldirev	.07	.12	.25
74	J.P. Bordeleau	.07	.12	.25
75	Tony Esposito, Goalie	.75	1.50	3.00
76	Germain Gagnon	.07	.12	.25
77	Dennis Hull	.07	.12	.25
78	Doug Jarrett	.07	.12	.25
79	Cliff Koroll	.07	.12	.25
80	Keith Magnuson	.07	.12	.25
81	Chico Maki	.07	.12	.25
82	John Marks	.07	.12	.25
83	Pit Martin	.07	.12	.25
84	Stan Mikita	1.00	2.00	4.00
85	Jim Pappin	.10	.20	.40
86	Dick Redmond	.07	.15	.30
87	Darcy Rota	.07	.12	.25
88	Phil Russell	.07	.12	.25
89	Dale Tallon	.07	.12	.25
90	Bill White	.07	.15	.30

Loblaws
1974-75 NHL Action Players
Card No. 49,
Gilbert Perreault

Loblaws
1974-75 NHL Action Players
Card No. 116,
Brent Hughes

Loblaws
1974-75 Issue
Card No. 137,
Dan Maloney

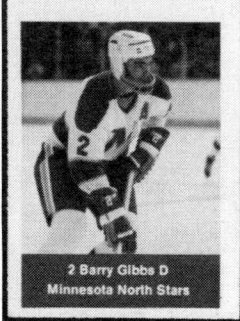

Loblaws
1974-75 Issue
Card No. 151,
Barry Gibbs

DETROIT RED WINGS

No.	Player	VG	EX	NRMT
91	Red Berenson	.07	.12	.25
92	Thommie Bergman	.07	.12	.25
93	Guy Charron	.07	.12	.25
94	Marcel Dionne	.75	1.50	3.00
95	Danny Grant	.07	.15	.30
96	Doug Grant, Goalie	.07	.12	.25
97	Jean Hamel	.07	.12	.25
98	Bill Hogaboam	.07	.12	.25
99	Pierre Jarry	.07	.12	.25
100	Nick Libett	.07	.12	.25
101	Bill Lochead	.07	.12	.25
102	Jack Lynch	.07	.12	.25
103	Hank Nowak	.07	.12	.25
104	Nelson Pyatt	.07	.12	.25
105	Mickey Redmond	.07	.15	.30
106	Doug Roberts	.07	.12	.25
107	Jim Rutherford, Goalie	.07	.12	.25
108	Bryan Watson	.07	.12	.25

KANSAS CITY SCOUTS

No.	Player	VG	EX	NRMT
109	Robin Burns	.07	.12	.25
110	Gary Coalter	.07	.12	.25
111	Gary Croteau	.07	.12	.25
112	Chris Evans	.07	.12	.25
113	Ed Gilbert	.07	.12	.25
114	Doug Horbul	.07	.12	.25
115	Dave Hudson	.07	.12	.25
116	Brent Hughes	.07	.12	.25
117	Bryan Lefley	.07	.12	.25
118	Richard Lemieux	.07	.12	.25
119	Pete McDuffe, Goalie	.07	.12	.25
120	Simon Nolet	.07	.12	.25
121	Dennis Patterson	.07	.12	.25
122	Michel Plasse, Goalie	.07	.12	.25
123	Lynn Powis	.07	.12	.25
124	Randy Rota	.07	.12	.25
125	Ted Snell	.07	.12	.25
126	John Wright	.07	.12	.25

LOS ANGELES KINGS

No.	Player	VG	EX	NRMT
127	Bob Berry	.07	.12	.25
128	Gene Carr	.07	.12	.25
129	Mike Corrigan	.07	.12	.25
130	Gary Edwards, Goalie	.12	.25	.50
131	Butch Goring	.25	.50	1.00
132	Terry Harper	.07	.12	.25
133	Dave Hutchison	.07	.12	.25
134	Sheldon Kannegiesser	.07	.12	.25
135	Neil Komadoski	.07	.12	.25
136	Don Kozak	.07	.12	.25
137	Dan Maloney	.07	.15	.30
138	Bob J. Murdoch	.07	.12	.25
139	Mike Murphy	.10	.20	.40
140	Bob Nevin	.07	.12	.25
141	Frank St. Marseille	.07	.12	.25
142	Rogatien Vachon, Goalie	.75	1.50	3.00
143	Juha Widing	.07	.12	.25
144	Tom Williams	.07	.12	.25

MINNESOTA NORTH STARS

No.	Player	VG	EX	NRMT
145	Chris Ahrens	.07	.12	.25
146	Fred Barrett	.07	.12	.25
147	Gary Bergman	.07	.12	.25
148	Henry Boucha	.07	.12	.25
149	Jude Drouin	.07	.12	.25
150	Blake Dunlop	.07	.12	.25
151	Barry Gibbs	.07	.12	.25
152	Bill Goldsworthy	.07	.12	.25
153	Dennis Hextall	.07	.12	.25
154	Cesare Maniago, Goalie	.35	.75	1.50
155	Don Martineau	.07	.12	.25
156	Lou Nanne	.10	.20	.40
157	Dennis O'Brien	.07	.12	.25
158	Murray Oliver	.07	.12	.25
159	Jean Paul Parise	.07	.12	.25
160	Tom Reid	.07	.12	.25
161	Fern Rivard, Goalie	.07	.12	.25
162	Fred Stanfield	.07	.12	.25

304 • LOBLAWS — 1974-75 NHL ACTION PLAYERS —

MONTREAL CANADIENS

No.	Player	VG	EX	NRMT
163	Pierre Bouchard	.07	.12	.25
164	Yvan Cournoyer	.75	1.50	3.00
165	Ken Dryden, Goalie	4.50	9.00	18.00
166	Guy Lafleur	2.00	4.00	8.00
167	Yvon Lambert	.07	.12	.25
168	Jacques Laperriere	.12	.25	.50
169	Guy Lapointe	.12	.25	.50
170	Michel Larocque, Goalie	.07	.12	.25
171	Claude Larose	.07	.12	.25
172	Chuck Lefley	.07	.12	.25
173	Jacques Lemaire	.12	.25	.50
174	Pete Mahovlich	.07	.12	.25
175	Henri Richard	.25	.50	1.00
176	Jim Roberts	.07	.12	.25
177	Larry Robinson	.50	1.00	2.00
178	Serge Savard	.12	.25	.50
179	Steve Shutt	.25	.50	1.00
180	Murray Wilson	.07	.12	.25

NEW YORK ISLANDERS

No.	Player	VG	EX	NRMT
181	Craig Cameron	.07	.12	.25
182	Clark Gillies	.12	.25	.50
183	Billy Harris	.07	.12	.25
184	Gerry Hart	.07	.12	.25
185	Lorne Henning	.07	.12	.25
186	Ernie Hicke	.07	.12	.25
187	Garry Howatt	.07	.12	.25
188	Dave Lewis	.07	.12	.25
189	Billy MacMillan	.07	.12	.25
190	Bert Marshall	.07	.12	.25
191	Bob Nystrom	.10	.20	.40
192	Denis Potvin	2.50	5.00	10.00
193	Jean Potvin	.07	.12	.25
194	Glenn Resch, Goalie	.35	.75	1.50
195	Doug Rombough	.07	.12	.25
196	Billy Smith, Goalie	.50	1.00	2.00
197	Ralph Stewart	.07	.12	.25
198	Ed Westfall	.07	.12	.25

NEW YORK RANGERS

No.	Player	VG	EX	NRMT
199	Jerry Butler	.07	.12	.25
200	Bill Fairbairn	.07	.12	.25
201	Ed Giacomin, Goalie	.60	1.00	2.00
202	Rod Gilbert	.10	.20	.40
203	Ron Harris	.07	.12	.25
204	Ted Irvine	.07	.12	.25
205	Gilles Marotte	.07	.12	.25
206	Brad Park	.50	1.00	2.00
207	Greg Polis	.07	.12	.25
208	Jean Ratelle	.25	.50	1.00
209	Dale Rolfe	.07	.12	.25
210	Bobby Rousseau	.07	.12	.25
211	Derek Sanderson	.35	.75	1.50
212	Rod Seiling	.07	.12	.25
213	Pete Stemkowski	.07	.15	.30
214	Walt Tkaczuk	.07	.15	.30
215	Steve Vickers	.07	.12	.25
216	Gilles Villemure, Goalie	.25	.50	1.00

PHILADELPHIA FLYERS

No.	Player	VG	EX	NRMT
217	Bill Barber	.25	.50	1.00
218	Tom Bladon	.07	.12	.25
219	Bobby Clarke	1.50	3.00	6.00
220	Bill Clement	.07	.12	.25
221	Terry Crisp	.07	.15	.30
222	Gary Dornhoefer	.07	.15	.30
223	Andre Dupont	.07	.12	.25
224	Bob Kelly	.07	.12	.25
225	Orest Kindrachuk	.07	.12	.25
226	Reggie Leach	.10	.20	.40
227	Ross Lonsberry	.07	.12	.25
228	Rick MacLeish	.18	.35	.75
229	Bernie Parent, Goalie	.75	1.50	3.00
230	Don Saleski	.07	.12	.25
231	Dave Schultz	.12	.25	.50
232	Ed Van Impe	.07	.12	.25
233	Jimmy Watson	.07	.15	.30
234	Joe Watson	.07	.15	.30

Loblaws 1974-75 Issue Card No. 170, Michel Laroque

Loblaws 1974-75 Issue Card No. 244, Bob Johnson

Loblaws 1974-75 Issue Card No. 270, Rick Wilson

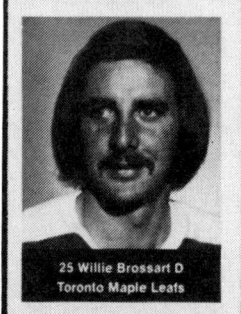

Loblaws 1974-75 Card No. 271 Willie Brossart

PITTSBURGH PENGUINS

No.	Player	VG	EX	NRMT
235	Syl Apps, Sr.	.07	.12	.25
236	Chuck Arnason	.07	.12	.25
237	Wayne Bianchin	.07	.12	.25
238	Dave Burrows	.07	.12	.25
239	Nelson Debenedet	.18	.30	.60
240	Ab DeMarco	.07	.12	.25
241	Steve Durbano	.07	.12	.25
242	Vic Hadfield	.07	.12	.25
243	Denis Herron	.07	.12	.25
244	Bob Johnson, Goalie	.12	.25	.50
245	Rick Kehoe	.07	.12	.25
246	Bob Kelly	.07	.15	.30
247	Bobby Lalonde	.07	.12	.25
248	Lowell MacDonald	.07	.12	.25
249	Bob Paradise	.07	.12	.25
250	Jean Pronovost	.07	.12	.25
251	Ron Schock	.07	.12	.25
252	Ron Stackhouse	.07	.12	.25

ST. LOUIS BLUES

No.	Player	VG	EX	NRMT
253	Don Awrey	.07	.12	.25
254	Ace Bailey	.07	.15	.30
255	Bill Collins	.07	.12	.25
256	John Davidson, Goalie	.25	.50	1.00
257	Dave Gardner	.07	.12	.25
258	Bob Gassoff	.07	.12	.25
259	Larry Giroux	.07	.12	.25
260	Eddie Johnston, Goalie	.35	.75	1.50
261	Wayne Merrick	.07	.12	.25
262	Brian Ogilvie	.07	.12	.25
263	Barclay Plager	.07	.12	.25
264	Bob Plager	.07	.12	.25
265	Pierre Plante	.07	.12	.25
266	Phil Roberto	.07	.12	.25
267	Larry Sacharuk	.07	.12	.25
268	Floyd Thomson	.07	.12	.25
269	Garry Unger	.12	.25	.50
270	Rick Wilson	.07	.12	.25

TORONTO MAPLE LEAFS

No.	Player	VG	EX	NRMT
271	Willie Brossart	.07	.12	.25
272	Tim Ecclestone	.07	.12	.25
273	Ron Ellis	.07	.15	.30
274	Doug Favell, Goalie	.18	.30	.60
275	Bill Flett	.07	.12	.25
276	Brian Glennie	.07	.12	.25
277	Inge Hammarstrom	.07	.15	.30
278	Dave Keon	.17	.35	.75
279	Lanny McDonald	.75	1.50	3.00
280	Jim McKenny	.07	.12	.25
281	Bob Neely	.07	.12	.25
282	Gary Sabourin	.07	.12	.25
283	Borje Salming	.25	.50	1.00
284	Darryl Sittler	1.50	3.00	6.00
285	Errol Thompson	.07	.12	.25
286	Ian Turnbull	.07	.12	.25
287	Norm Ullman	.25	.50	1.00
288	Dunc Wilson, Goalie	.07	.15	.25

VANCOUVER CANUCKS

No.	Player	VG	EX	NRMT
289	Gregg Boddy	.07	.12	.25
290	Paulin Bordeleau	.07	.12	.25
291	Andre Boudrias	.07	.12	.25
292	Bob Dailey	.07	.12	.25
293	Dave Dunn	.07	.12	.25
294	John Gould	.07	.12	.25
295	Jocelyn Guevremont	.07	.15	.30
296	Dennis Kearns	.12	.25	.50
297	Don Lever	.07	.12	.25
298	Ken Lockett, Goalie	.07	.12	.25
299	Bryan McSheffrey	.07	.12	.25
300	Chris Oddleifson	.07	.12	.25
301	Gerry O'Flaherty	.07	.12	.25
302	Tracy Pratt	.07	.12	.25
303	Gary Smith, Goalie	.07	.12	.25
304	Dennis Ververgaert	.07	.12	.25
305	Jim Wiley	.07	.12	.25
306	Barry Wilkins	.07	.12	.25

WASHINGTON CAPITALS

No.	Player	VG	EX	NRMT
307	Ron H. Anderson	.07	.12	.25
308	Steve Atkinson	.07	.12	.25
309	Mike Bloom	.07	.12	.25
310	Gord Brooks	.07	.12	.25
311	Bob Collyard	.07	.12	.25
312	Jack Egers	.07	.12	.25
313	Lawrence Fullan	.07	.12	.25
314	Bob Gryp	.07	.12	.25
315	Jim Hrycuik	.07	.12	.25
316	Greg Joly	.07	.15	.30
317	Dave Kryskow	.07	.12	.25
318	Peter Laframboise	.07	.12	.25
319	Ron Low, Goalie	.10	.20	.40
320	Joe Lundrigan	.07	.12	.25
321	Mike Marson	.07	.12	.25
322	Bill Mikkelson	.07	.12	.25
323	Doug Mohns	.07	.12	.25
324	Lew Morrison	.07	.12	.25

Loblaws
1974-75 Issue
Card No. 317,
Dave Kryskow

POPSICLE

— 1975 - 76 ISSUE —

This 18-card set is unnumbered and is listed alphabetically by team.

Card Size: 2 1/2" x 3 1/2"
Face: Four colour; Team name, history and logo
Back: Team resume, Bilingual
Imprint: None
Complete Set No.: 18
Complete Set Price: 5.50 11.00 22.00
Common Team: .35 .75 1.50

No.	Team	VG	EX	NRMT
1	Atlanta Flames	.35	.75	1.50
2	Boston Bruins	.35	.75	1.50
3	Buffalo Sabres	.35	.75	1.50
4	California Golden Seals	.35	.75	1.50
5	Chicago Blackhawks	.35	.75	1.50
6	Detroit Red Wings	.35	.75	1.50
7	Kansas City Scouts	.35	.75	1.50
8	Los Angeles Kings	.35	.75	1.50
9	Minnesota North Stars	.35	.75	1.50
10	Montreal Canadiens	.35	.75	1.50
11	New York Islanders	.35	.75	1.50
12	New York Rangers	.35	.75	1.50
13	Philadelphia Flyers	.35	.75	1.50
14	Pittsburgh Penguins	.35	.75	1.50
15	St. Louis Blues	.35	.75	1.50
16	Toronto Maple Leafs	.35	.75	1.50
17	Vancouver Canucks	.35	.75	1.50
18	Washington Capitals	.35	.75	1.50

— 1976 - 77 ISSUE —

The 18-card set is unnumbered and is listed alphabetically by team.

Cap Size: 2 1/2" x 3 1/2"
Face: Four colour; Name, Team, Team and NHL logos
Back: Black and white. Team history
Imprint: Printed in U.S.A.
Complete Set No.: 18
Complete Set Price: 5.50 11.00 22.00
Common Player: .35 .75 1.50

No.	Team	VG	EX	NRMT
1	Atlanta Flames	.35	.75	1.50
2	Boston Bruins	.35	.75	1.50
3	Buffalo Sabres	.35	.75	1.50
4	Chicago Blackhawks	.35	.75	1.50
5	Cleveland Barons	.35	.75	1.50
6	Colorado Rockies	.35	.75	1.50
7	Detroit Red Wings	.35	.75	1.50
8	Los Angeles Kings	.35	.75	1.50
9	Minnesota North Stars	.35	.75	1.50
10	Montreal Canadiens	.35	.75	1.50
11	New York Islanders	.35	.75	1.50
12	Philadelphia Flyers	.35	.75	1.50
13	St. Louis Blues	.35	.75	1.50

No.	Player	VG	EX	NRMT
14	Pittsburgh Penguins	.35	.75	1.50
15	New York Rangers	.35	.75	1.50
16	Toronto Maple Leafs	.35	.75	1.50
17	Vancouver Canucks	.35	.75	1.50
18	Washington Capitals	.35	.75	1.50

SPORTSCASTER CARDS

— 1977 - 79 ISSUE —

This set is made up of 150 different sports with 2,184 cards in all. Listed are only the hockey cards.

Card Size: 4 3/4" x 6 1/4"
Face: Four golour, top blue border; Name
Back: Black on white card stock; Name, Resume
Imprint: © 1978 Editions Recontre SA., Lausanne
Complete Set No.: 2184
Hockey: 65
Complete Set Price: 175.00 350.00 700.00
Common Card: 1.00 2.00 4.00

No.	Player	VG	EX	NRMT
103	Alexander Yakushev	4.50	9.00	18.00
67/21	Bill Chadwick	3.00	6.00	12.00
60/12	Bobby Clarke	5.50	11.00	23.00
05/20	Bobby Hull	1.75	3.50	7.00
01/02	Bobby Orr	1.75	3.50	7.00
07/17	Brad Park	1.50	9.00	18.00
46/21	Bryan Trottier	1.00	2.00	4.00
102/14	Charlamov-Petrov-Michailov	4.00	8.00	16.00
73/11	Czechoslovakia 1976	2.50	5.00	10.00
51/01	Czechoslovakia in 1977	1.25	2.50	5.00
47/18	Darryl Sittler	1.25	2.50	5.00
82/23	Dave Dryden	5.00	10.00	20.00
17/09	Dennis Potvin	1.00	2.00	4.00
77/24	Expansion (Whalers/Oilers)	3.00	6.00	12.00
50/04	Facemasks	1.00	2.00	4.00
18/23	Garry Unger	1.00	2.00	4.00
44/20	Gerry Cheevers, Goalie	1.25	2.50	5.00
02/06	Gordie Howe	1.75	3.50	7.00
06/07	Lorne "Gump" Worsley, Goalie	1.25	2.50	5.00
51/18	Guy Lafleur	1.75	3.50	7.00
70/06	Hall of Fame	3.75	6.50	13.00
11/19	Hat Trick (Bob Hodges)	1.00	2.00	4.00
71/12	Hedberg and Nilsson	3.25	6..50	13.00
45/14	In The Corners	1.00	2.00	4.00
81/19	Jacques Lemaire	6.00	12.00	24.00
44/03	Jaroslav Jirik	1.00	2.00	4.00
10/14	Jean Beliveau	1.00	2.00	4.00
55/14	Jiri and Jaroslav Holik	1.00	2.00	4.00
80/18	John Davidson, Goalie	5.00	10.00	20.00
14/23	Ken Dryden, Goalie	1.50	3.00	6.00
62/17	Lester Patrick	2.50	5.00	10.00
33/03	Lines in The Ice	1.00	2.00	4.00
61/03	Lingo (Wayne Giacomin)	3.00	6.00	12.00
43/04	Major and Minor Penalties	1.00	2.00	4.00
56/05	Montreal Forum	3.00	6.00	12.00
27/24	National Hockey League	1.00	2.00	4.00
76/03	NCAA Hockey Champions	3.50	7.00	14.00
31/03	Penalty Killing (Bobby Clarke)	1.50	3.00	6.00
03/19	Phil and Tony Esposito	1.00	2.00	4.00
78/04	Real Cloutier	1.00	2.00	4.00
43/06	Rogatien Vachon, Goalie	1.25	2.50	5.00
82/05	Scotty Bowman	8.00	16.00	32.00
12/22	Stan Mikita	1.50	3.00	6.00
45/13	Steve Shutt	1.50	3.00	6.00
50/03	Sticks (Bobby Hull)	2.50	5.00	10.00
64/16	Sudden Death (Pete Stemkowski)	2.50	5.00	10.00
74/17	The 1978 WCH (USSR)	3.50	7.00	14.00
71/04	Abrahamsson Brothers	4.00	8.00	16.00
21/12	The Equipment (Fussen WGE)	1.00	2.00	4.00
63/09	The Howe Family	5.50	11.00	22.00
29/08	The Power Play (Phil Esposito)	1.25	2.50	5.00
38/07	The Seven Prof. Trop. (Lefleur)	1.25	2.50	5.00
35/03	The Spenger Cup (Davos-Switz)	1.00	2.00	4.00
40/24	The Stanley Cup (Rangers/Blues)	1.25	2.50	5.00
02/13	The Stanley Cup (Cournoyer)	1.00	2.00	4.00
05/09	The USA vs Czechoslovakia	1.00	2.00	4.00
47/16	Trio Grande (Trott-Gill-Boss)	1.75	3.50	7.00
07/08	USSR-1976 Team	1.00	2.00	4.00
73/01	USSR vs NHL	3.50	7.00	14.00

Sportscaster Cards
1977-79 Issue
Card No. 17/09,
Dennis Potvin

306 • PEPSICO — 1980 - 81 CAPS —

No.	Player	VG	EX	NRMT
74/24	Vaclav Nedomansku	3.75	7.50	15.00
77/01	Wayne Gretzky (WHA)	65.00	130.00	260.00
12/15	World Champions (Czech/USSR)	1.00	2.00	4.00
19/15	World Champions (1977 Canada)	1.00	2.00	4.00
55/23	World Hockey Association	2.50	5.00	10.00
15/13	Yvan Cournover	1.00	2.00	4.00

PEPSICO

— 1980 - 81 CAPS —

This unnumbered 140-cap set is arranged alphabetically by team and then by player within the team.

Cap Size: 1 1/8" Diameter
Face: Black and white portrait; Name, Team
Back: Pepsi promotional information
Imprint: PEPSI
Complete Set No.: 140
Complete Set Price: 40.00   85.00
Common Player: .25   .50
Plastic Display: 25.00   50.00

CALGARY FLAMES

No.	Player	VG	EX
1	Dan Bouchard, Goalie	.35	.75
2	Guy Chouinard	.25	.50
3	Bill Clement	.25	.50
4	Randy Holt	.25	.50
5	Ken Houston	.25	.50
6	Kevin LaVallee, Error	.25	.50
7	Don Lever	.25	.50
8	Bob MacMillan	.25	.50
9	Bradley Marsh	.50	1.00
10	Bob Murdoch	.25	.50
11	Kent Nilsson	.35	.75
12	James Peplinski	.35	.75
13	Willi Plett	.25	.50
14	Pekka Rautakillio	.25	.50
15	Paul Reinhart	.25	.50
16	Pat Riggin, Goalie	.25	.50
17	Phil Russell	.25	.50
18	Brad Smith	.25	.50
19	Eric Vail	.25	.50
20	Bert Wilson	.25	.50

EDMONTON OILERS

No.	Player	VG	EX
21	Glenn Anderson	.50	1.00
22	Curt Brackenbury	.25	.50
23	Brett Callighen	.25	.50
24	Paul Coffey	2.00	4.00
25	Lee Fogolin	.25	.50
26	Matti Hagman	.25	.50
27	John Hughes	.25	.50
28	Dave Hunter	.25	.50
29	Jari Kurri	1.00	2.00
30	Ron Low, Goalie	.25	.50
31	Kevin Lowe	.50	1.00
32	Dave Lumley	.25	.50
33	Blair MacDonald	.25	.50
34	Mark Messier	2.50	5.00
35	Ed Mio, Goalie	.25	.50
36	Don Murdoch	.25	.50
37	Pat Price	.25	.50
38	Dave Semenko	.25	.50
39	Risto Siltanen	.25	.50
40	Stan Weir	.25	.50

MONTREAL CANADIENS

No.	Player	VG	EX
41	Keith Acton	.25	.50
42	Brian Engblom	.25	.50
43	Bob Gainey	.75	1.50
44	Gaston Gingras	.25	.50
45	Denis Herron, Goalie	.25	.50
46	Rejean Houle	.25	.50
47	Doug Jarvis	.25	.50
48	Yvon Lambert	.25	.50
49	Rod Langway	.50	1.00

PepsiCO
1980-81Caps
Cap No. 6, Error,
Name misspelled
Lavalee on face

PepsiCo
1980-81 Caps
Cap No. 29,
Jari Kurri

PepsiCo
1980-81 Caps
Cap No. 34,
Mark Messier

PepsiCo
1980-81 Caps
Cap No. 77,
Peter Stastny

No.	Player	VG	EX
50	Guy Lapointe	2.00	4.00
51	Pierre Larouche	.25	.50
52	Pierre Mondou	.25	.50
53	Mark Napier	.25	.50
54	Christopher Nilan	.25	.50
55	Doug Risebrough	.25	.50
56	Larry Robinson	1.50	3.00
57	Serge Savard	.75	1.50
58	Steve Shutt	.50	1.00
59	Mario Tremblay	.25	.50
60	Douglas Wickenheiser	.25	.50

QUEBEC NORDIQUES

No.	Player	VG	EX
61	Serge Bernier	.25	.50
62	Kim Clackson	.25	.50
63	Real Cloutier	.25	.50
64	Andre Dupont	.25	.50
65	Robbie Ftorek	.25	.50
66	Michel Goulet	1.50	3.00
67	Jamie Hislop	.25	.50
68	Dale Hoganson	.25	.50
69	Dale Hunter	.25	.50
70	Pierre Lacroix	.25	.50
71	Garry Lariviere	.25	.50
72	Rich Leduc	.25	.50
73	John Paddock	.25	.50
74	Michel Plasse, Goalie	.25	.50
75	Jacques Richard	.25	.50
76	Anton Stastny	.25	.50
77	Peter Stastny	1.50	3.00
78	Marc Tardif	.25	.50
79	Wally Weir	.25	.50
80	John Wensink	.25	.50

TORONTO MAPLE LEAFS

No.	Player	VG	EX
81	John Anderson	.25	.50
82	Laurie Boschman	.25	.50
83	Jiri Crha, Goalie	.25	.50
84	Bill Derlago	.25	.50
85	Vitezslav Duris	.25	.50
86	Ron Ellis	.35	.75
87	Dave Farrish	.25	.50
88	Robert (Stewart) Gavin	.25	.50
89	Pat Hickey	.25	.50
90	Dan Maloney	.25	.50
91	Terry Martin	.25	.50
92	Barry Melrose	.35	.75
93	Wilf Paiement	.25	.50
94	Robert Picard	.25	.50
95	Jim Rutherford, Goalie	.25	.50
96	Rocky Saganiuk	.25	.50
97	Borje Salming	1.00	2.00
98	Dave Shand	.25	.50
99	Ian Turnbull	.25	.50
100	Richard Vaive	.50	1.00

VANCOUVER CANUCKS

No.	Player	VG	EX
101	Brent Ashton	.25	.50
102	Ivan Boldirev	.25	.50
103	Per-Olov Brasar	.25	.50
104	Richard Brodeur, Goalie	.25	.50
105	Jerry Butler	.25	.50
106	Colin Campbell	.25	.50
107	Curt Fraser	.25	.50
108	Thomas Gradin	.25	.50
109	Dennis Kearns	.25	.50
110	Rick Lanz	.25	.50
111	Lars Lindgren	.25	.50
112	Dave Logan	.25	.50
113	Mario Marois	.25	.50
114	Kevin McCarthy	.25	.50
115	Gerry Minor	.25	.50
116	Darcy Rota	.25	.50
117	Bobby Schmautz	.25	.50
118	Stanley Smyl	.25	.50
119	Harold Snepsts	.25	.50
120	David Williams	.35	.75

WINNIPEG JETS

No.	Player	VG	EX
121	David Babych	.25	.50
122	Al Cameron	.25	.50
123	Scott Campbell	.25	.50
124	Dave Christian	.25	.50
125	Jude Drouin	.25	.50
126	Norm Dupont	.25	.50
127	Danny Geoffrion	.25	.50
128	Pierre Hamel, Goalie	.25	.50
129	Barry Legge	.25	.50
130	Willy Lindstrom	.25	.50
131	Barry Long	.25	.50
132	Kris Manery	.25	.50
133	Jimmy Mann	.25	.50
134	Maurice Mantha	.25	.50
135	Markus Mattsson, Goalie	.25	.50
136	Don Spring	.25	.50
137	Douglas Smail	.35	.75
138	Anders Steen	.35	.75
139	Peter Sullivan	.25	.50
140	Ronald Wilson	.25	.50

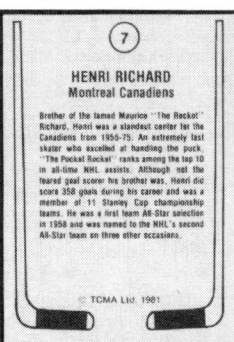

TCMA Ltd.
1981 Issue
Card No. 7,
Henri Richard

TCMA LTD

— 1981 ISSUE —

This 13-card set contains eleven Hall of Famers.

Card Size: 2 1/2" x 3 1/2"
Face: Four colour, white border
Back: Black and white on card stock; Two black hockey sticks on either side of the resume
Imprint: © TMCA Ltd. 1981
Complete Set No.: 13
Complete Set Price: 5.00 10.00
Common Goalie: .25 .50
Common Player: .25 .50

No.	Player	EX	NRMT
1	Norm Ullman, Det.	.25	.50
2	Lorne (Gump) Worsley, Goalie, NYR	.25	.50
3	J.C. Tremblay, Mon.	.25	.50
4	Louie Fontinato, NYR	.25	.50
5	John Bucyk, Bos.	.25	.50
6	Harry Howell, NYR	.35	.75
7	Henri Richard, Mon.	.50	1.00
8	Andy Bathgate, NYR	.25	.50
9	Bobby Orr, Bos.	1.00	2.00
10	Frank Mahovlich, Tor.	.50	1.00
11	Jean Beliveau, Mon.	.35	.75
12	Jacques Plante, Goalie, Mon.	.50	1.00
13	Stan Mikita, Chi.	.35	.75

Kellog's 1993 Rice Krispies Poster
Campbell Conference All Stars

McDONALD'S RESTAURANTS

— 1982 - 83 STICKERS —

The set was issued only in Quebec. It has a 12-page album.

Sticker Size: 1 15/16" X 2 9/16"
Face: Four colour, red border; Name, McDonald's logo
Back: Black on buff card stock; Name, Number, Position, Team, Bilingual
Imprint: © 1983 La corporation McDonald's/McDonald's Corporation
Complete Set No.: 36

Complete Set Price:		10.00	20.00
Common Player:		.10	.20
Album:		2.50	5.00

No.	Player	EX	NRMT
1	Dan Bouchard, Goalie, Que.	.10	.20
2	Richard Brodeur, Goalie, Van.	.10	.20
3	Gilles Meloche, Goalie, Min.	.10	.20
4	Billy Smith, Goalie, NYI	.10	.20
5	Richard Wamsley, Goalie, Mon.	.10	.20
6	Mike Bossy, NYI	.25	.50
7	Dino Ciccarelli, Min.	.35	.75
8	Guy Lafleur, Mon.	.50	1.00
9	Rick Middleton, Bos.	.10	.20
10	Marian Stastny, Que.	.10	.20
11	Bill Barber, Phi.	.10	.20
12	Bob Gainey, Mon.	.15	.30
13	Clark Gillies, NYI	.10	.20
14	Michel Goulet, Que.	.50	1.00
15	Mark Messier, Edm.	1.50	3.00

ALL STARS

No.	Player	EX	NRMT
16	Billy Smith, Goalie, NYI	.13	.25
17	Larry Robinson, Mon.	.35	.75
18	Denis Potvin, NYI	.25	.50
19	Michel Goulet, Que.	.25	.50
20	Wayne Gretzky, Edm.	3.00	6.00
21	Mike Bossy, NYI	.50	1.00

REGULAR ISSUE

No.	Player	EX	NRMT
22	Wayne Gretzky, Edm.	3.75	7.50
23	Denis Savard, Chi.	.25	.50
24	Peter Stastny, Que.	.50	1.00
25	Bryan Trottier, NYI	.25	.50
26	Douglas Wickenheiser, Mon.	.10	.20
27	Barry Beck, NYR	.10	.20
28	Raymond Bourque, Bos.	1.00	2.00
29	Brian Engblom, Wash.	.10	.20
30	Craig Hartsburg, Min.	.10	.20
31	Mark Howe, Phi.	.13	.25
32	Rod Langway, Wash.	.25	.50
33	Denis Potvin, NYI	.35	.75
34	Larry Robinson, Mon.	.50	1.00
35	Normand Rochefort, Que.	.10	.20
36	Douglas Wilson, Edm.	.10	.20

— 1991 - 92 ALL-STARS —

Issued in Canada by McDonald's. A foil pack was available as a promotional incentive when any size soft drink was purchased. The cards are bilingual.

Card Size: 2 1/2" X 3 1/2"
Face: Four colour, white border, Position, McDonald's and Upper Deck logo
Back: Four colour, Hologram, Number, Resume, Bilingual
Imprint: © 1991 The Upper Deck Co. All Rights Reserved Printed in the U.S.A.
Complete Set No.: 31

Complete Set Price:		10.00	20.00
Common Player		.25	.50
Foil Packs: (3 Cards plus Hologram)			

HOLOGRAMS

No.	Player	EX	NRMT
McH1	Wayne Gretzky. LA	2.00	4.00
McH2	Chris Chelios, Chi.	.75	1.50
McH3	Raymond Bourque, Bos.	.75	1.50
McH4	Brett Hull, St. L.	1.00	2.00
McH5	Cam Neely, Bos.	.75	1.50
McH6	Patrick Roy, Goalie, Mon.	2.00	4.00

McDonald's
1982-83 Stickers
Sticker No. 3,
Gilles Meloche

McDonald's
1982-83 Stickers
Sticker No. 3,
Gilles Meloche

McDonald's
1991-92 All-Stars
Card No. Mc 1,
Cam Neely

McDonald's
1991-92 All-Stars
Card No. Mc 1,
Cam Neely

REGULAR ISSUE

No.	Player	EX	NRMT
Mc 1	Cam Neely, Bos.	.35	.75
Mc 2	Rick Tocchet, Phi.	.25	.50
Mc 3	Kevin Stevens, Pit.	.35	.75
Mc 4	Mark Recchi, Pit.	.25	.50
Mc 5	Joe Sakic, Que.	.50	1.00
Mc 6	Pat LaFontaine, Buf.	.75	1.50
Mc 7	Darren Turcotte, NYR	.25	.50
Mc 8	Patrick Roy, Goalie, Mon.	1.00	2.00
Mc 9	Andrew Moog, Goalie, Bos.	.25	.50
Mc10	Raymond Bourque, Bos.	.25	.50
Mc11	Paul Coffey, Pit.	.25	.50
Mc12	Brian Leetch, NYR	.25	.50
Mc13	Brett Hull, St. L.	.50	1.00
Mc14	Luc Robitaille, LA	.25	.50
Mc15	Steve Larmer, Chi.	.25	.50
Mc16	Vincent Damphousse, Edm.	.25	.50
Mc17	Wayne Gretzky, LA	1.00	2.00
Mc18	Theoren Fleury, Cal.	.25	.50
Mc19	Steve Yzerman, Det.	.50	1.00
Mc20	Mike Vernon, Goalie, Cal.	.25	.50
Mc21	Bill Ranford, Goalie, Edm.	.25	.50
Mc22	Chris Chelios, Chi.	.25	.50
Mc23	Allan MacInnis, Cal.	.25	.50
Mc24	Scott Stevens, St. L	.25	.50
Mc25	Checklist	.25	.50

— 1992 - 93 ISSUE —

Card Size: 2 1/2" X 3 1/2"
Face: Four colour, white border, Position, McDonald's and Upper Deck logo
Back: Four colour, Hologram, Number, Resume, Bilingual
Imprint: © 1991 The Upper Deck Co. All Rights Reserved Printed in the U.S.A.
Complete Set No.: 34

Complete Set Price:		12.50	25.00
Common Player		.10	.20
Foil Packs: (3 Cards plus Hologram)			1.00

HOLOGRAMS

No.	Player	EX	NRMT
Mc01	Mark Messier, NYR	1.50	3.00
Mc02	Brett Hull, Sl.L	1.50	3.00
Mc03	Kevin Stevens, Pit.	1.50	3.00
Mc04	Raymond Bourque, Bos.	1.50	3.00
Mc05	Brian Leetch, NYR	2.50	5.00
Mc06	Patrick Roy, Goalie, Mon.	3.50	7.00

REGULAR ISSUE

No.	Player	EX	NRMT
---	Checklist, SP	1.00	2.00
Mc01	Ed Belfour, Goalie, Chi.	.25	.50
Mc02	Brian Bellows, Mon.	.10	.20
Mc03	Chris Chelios, Chi.	.12	.25
Mc04	Vincent Damphousse, Mon.	.10	.20
Mc05	David Ellet. Tor.	.10	.20
Mc06	Sergei Fedorov, Det.	.50	1.00
Mc07	Theoren Fleury, Cal.	.10	.20
Mc08	Phil Housley, Win.	.10	.20
Mc09	Trevor Lindon, Van.	.20	.40
Mc10	Allan MacInnis, Cal.	.10	.20
Mc11	Adam Oates, Bos	.20	.40
Mc12	Luc Robitaille, LA	.25	.50
Mc13	Jeremy Roenick, Chi.	.35	.75
Mc14	Steve Yzerman, Det.	.50	1.00
Mc15	Donald Beaupre, Goalie, Wash.	.10	.20
Mc16	Rod Brind'Amour, Phi.	.15	.30
Mc17	Paul Coffey, Det.	.15	.30
Mc18	John Cullen, Tor.	.10	.20
Mc19	Kevin Hatcher, Wash.	.10	.20
Mc20	Jaromir Jagr, Pit.	.25	.50
Mc21	Mario Lemieux, Pit.	.50	1.00
Mc22	Alexander Mogilny, Buf.	.25	.50
Mc23	Kirk Muller, Mon.	.10	.20
Mc24	Owen Nolan, Que.	.10	.20
Mc25	Mike Richter, Goalie, NYR	.15	.30
Mc26	Joe Sakic, Que.	.15	.30
Mc27	Scott Stevens, NJ	.10	.20

— 1993 - 94 ISSUE —

Card Size: 2 1/2" X 3 1/2"
Face: Four colour, white border; Name, Position,
McDonald's and Upper Deck logo
Back: Four colour, white border; Name, Hologram,
Number, Resume, Bilingual
Imprint: Upper Deck and the card/hologram combination are the trademarks of The Upper Deck Company © 1993 The Upper Deck Company. All Rights Reserved. Printed in the U.S.A.
Complete Set No.: 34
Complete Set Price: 15.00 30.00
Common Card: .12 .25
Foil Packs: (3 Cards plus Hologram) 1.00

HOLOGRAMS

No.	Player	EX	NRMT
McH-01	Mario Lemieux, Pit.	2.50	5.00
McH-02	Teeme Selane, Win.	2.00	4.00
McH-03	Luc Robitaille, LA	1.00	2.00
McH-04	Raymond Bourque, Bos.	1.00	2.00
McH-05	Chris Chelios, Chi.	.75	1.50
McH-06	Ed Belfour, Goalie, Chi.	1.50	3.00

REGULAR ISSUE

No.	Player	EX	NRMT
—	Checklist	1.00	2.00
McD-01	Brian Bradley, TB	.12	.25
McD-02	Pavel Bure, Van.	.50	1.00
McD-03	Jon Casey, Goalie, Min.	.12	.25
McD-04	Paul Coffey, Det.	.25	.50
McD-05	Douglas Gilmour, Tor.	.50	1.00
McD-06	Phil Housley, Win.	.12	.25
McD-07	Brett Hull, St.L	.25	.50
McD-08	Jarri Kurri, LA	.12	.25
McD-09	Dave Manson, Edm.	.12	.25
McD-10	Michael Modano, Min.	.25	.50
McD-11	Gary Roberts, Cal.	.12	.25
McD-12	Jeremy Roenick, Chi.	.35	.75
McD-13	Steve Yzerman, Det.	.35	.75
McD-14	Steve Duchesne, Que.	.12	.25
McD-15	Michael Gartner, NYR	.12	.25
McD-16	Al Iaftrate, Wash.	.12	.25
McD-17	Jaromir Jagr, Pit.	.25	.50
McD-18	Pat LaFontaine, Buf.	.25	.50
Mc-D19	Alexander Mogilny, Buf.	.25	.50
McD-20	Kirk Muller, Mon.	.12	.25
Mcd-21	Adam Oates, Bos.	.12	.25
McD-22	Mark Recchi, Phi.	.25	.50
McD-23	Patrick Roy, Goalie, Mon.	.35	.75
McD-24	Joe Sakic, Que.	.12	.25
McD-25	Kevin Stevens, Pit.	.12	.25
McD-26	Scott Stevens, NJ	.12	.25
McD-27	Pierre Turgeon, NYI	.12	.25

— REDEMPTION CARDS 1993 - 94 —

These were randomly inserted into McDonalds All-Star packs.

Card Size: 2 1/2" X 3 1/2"
Face: Four colour, white border, Position, McDonald's and Upper Deck logo
Back: Four colour
Imprint: © 1991 The Upper Deck Co. All Rights Reserved Printed in the U.S.A.
Complete Set No.: 14
Complete Set Price:
Common Player

No.	Player	EX	NRMT
1	Patrick Roy, 5 x 7 MVP Card	3.50	7.00
2	Complete Set Framed	50.00	100.00
3	Press Sheet	20.00	40.00
4	Official CCM All-Star Jersey	25.00	50.00
5	Autographed McDonalds Official All Star Cards	37.50	75.00
6	One on One Shooting with Patrick Roy	50.00	100.00
7	Skating Lessons from Pavel Bure	50.00	100.00
8	Trip for Two for One Game of the Stanley Cup Finals	200.00	400.00
9	Trip for Two to the 1995 All-Star Game	200.00	400.00
10	Trip for Two to watch your Favourite Team at Home	50.00	100.00
11	N.H.L. Fantasy Contract & Salary for a Day	250.00	500.00
12	N.H.L. Autographed Pucks	10.00	20.00
13	Easton Autographed Sticks	20.00	40.00
14	$200 Gift Certificate Redeemable for Hockey Equipment	75.00	150.00

McDonald's Restaurants
1993-94 Issue
Card No. McD-02,
Pavel Bure

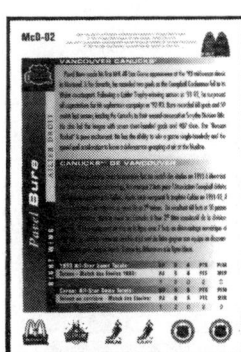

McDonald's Restaurants
1993-94 Issue
Card No. McD-02,
Pavel Bure

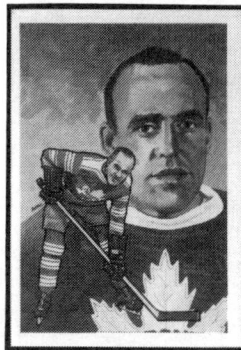

Hockey Hall of Fame
1983 Issue
Card No. 33,
Francis (King) Clancy

Hockey Hall of Fame
1983 Issue
Card No. 49, Error, Name
misspelled Fredrickson on back

HOCKEY HALL OF FAME

— 1983 REGULAR ISSUE —

Issued in 1983 for the Hall of Fame inductees for 1983.

Card Size: 2 1/2" X 3 1/2"
Face: Four colour, white border
Back: Black and white; Number, Resume, Bilingual
Imprint: © HOCKEY HALL OF FAME / C. McDIARMID / CARTOPHILIUM 1983
Printed in Canada / Imprimé au Canada
Complete Set No.: 240
Complete Set Price: 15.00 30.00
Common Player: .08 .15

No.	Player	EX	NRMT
1	Maurice Richard	.50	1.00
2	Sid Abel	.12	.25
3	Harry Broadbent	.08	.15
4	Clarence Campbell	.08	.15
5	Neil Colville	.08	.15
6	Charlie Conacher	.08	.15
7	Red Dutton	.08	.15
8	Foster Hewitt	.08	.15
9	Mickey Ion	.08	.15
10	Ernest (Moose) Johnson	.08	.15
11	Bill Mosienko	.12	.25
12	Russell (Barney) Stanley	.08	.15
13	Lord Stanley	.08	.15
14	Fred Taylor	.12	.25
15	Tiny Thompson, Goalie	.08	.15
16	Gordie Howe	.75	1.50
17	Hobey Baker	.08	.15
18	Frank Calder	.08	.15
19	Jim Hendy	.08	.15
20	Frank Foyston	.08	.15
21	Harry Lumley, Goalie	.08	.15
22	Reg Noble	.08	.15
23	Frank Patrick	.08	.15
24	Harvey Pulford	.08	.15
25	Ken Reardon	.08	.15
26	Joe Simpson	.08	.15
27	Conn Smythe	.08	.15
28	Red Storey	.08	.15
29	Lloyd Turner	.08	.15
30	Georges Vezina, Goalie	.08	.15
31	Jean Beliveau	.50	1.00
32	Max Bentley	.08	.15
33	Francis Clancy	.08	.15
34	Babe Dye	.08	.15
35	Ebbie Goodfellow	.08	.15
36	Charles Hay	.08	.15
37	Percy Lesueur, Goalie	.08	.15
38	Tommy Lockhart	.08	.15
39	Jack Marshall	.08	.15
40	Lester Patrick	.08	.15
41	Frank Selke	.08	.15
42	Cooper Smeaton	.08	.15
43	Hooley Smith	.08	.15
44	James T Sutherland	.08	.15
45	Fred Whitcroft	.08	.15
46	Terry Sawchuk, Goalie	.50	1.00
47	Charles Adams	.08	.15
48	Russell Bowie	.08	.15
49	Frank Frederickson, Error	.08	.15
50	Billy Gilmour	.08	.15
51	Ching (Ivan) Johnson	.08	.15
52	Tom Johnson	.08	.15
53	Aurel Joliat	.25	.50
54	Duke Keats	.08	.15
55	Red Kelly	.08	.15
56	Frank McGee	.08	.15
57	James D. Norris	.08	.15
58	Philip Ross	.08	.15
59	Babe Siebert	.08	.15
60	Roy Worters, Goalie	.08	.15
61	Bobby Orr	.50	1.00
62	T. Franklin Ahearn	.08	.15
63	Harold Ballard	.08	.15
64	Billy Burch	.08	.15
65	Bill Chadwick	.08	.15
66	Sprague Cleghorn	.08	.15
67	Rusty Crawford	.08	.15
68	George Dudley	.08	.15
69	Ted Kennedy	.12	.25

310 • HOCKEY HALL OF FAME — 1983 REGULAR ISSUE

No.	Player	EX	NRMT
70	Edouard Lalonde	.08	.15
71	Billy McGimsie	.08	.15
72	Frank Nighbor	.08	.15
73	Donat Raymond	.08	.15
74	Art Ross	.08	.15
75	Jack Walker	.08	.15
76	Jacques Plante, Goalie	.50	1.00
77	Doug Bentley	.08	.15
78	Walter Brown	.08	.15
79	Dit Clapper	.08	.15
80	Hap Day	.08	.15
81	Frank Dilio	.08	.15
82	Bobby Hewitson	.08	.15
83	Harry Howell	.08	.15
84	Sylvio Mantha	.08	.15
85	George Richardson	.08	.15
86	Nels Stewart	.08	.15
87	Hod Stuart	.08	.15
88	Harry Trihey	.08	.15
89	Marty Walsh	.08	.15
90	Arthur Wirtz	.08	.15
91	Henri Richard	.10	.20
92	Toe Blake	.08	.15
93	Frank Boucher	.08	.15
94	Turk Broda, Goalie	.08	.15
95	Harry Cameron	.08	.15
96	Leo Dandurand	.08	.15
97	Joe Hall	.08	.15
98	George Hay	.08	.15
99	William A. Hewitt	.08	.15
100	J.B. Hutton, Goalie	.08	.15
101	Dick Irvin	.08	.15
102	John Ross Robertson	.08	.15
103	Frank D. Smith	.08	.15
104	Norm Ullman	.08	.15
105	Harry Watson	.08	.15
106	Howie Morenz	.50	1.00
107	Clint Benedict, Goalie	.08	.15
108	Richard Boon	.08	.15
109	Gordie Drillon	.08	.15
110	Bill Gadsby	.08	.15
111	Rod Gilbert	.08	.15
112	Francis (Moose) Goheen	.08	.15
113	Tommy Gorman	.08	.15
114	Glenn Hall, Goalie	.12	.25
115	Red Horner	.08	.15
116	John Kilpatrick	.08	.15
117	Robert LeBel	.08	.15
118	Fred Scanlan	.08	.15
119	Fred C. Waghorne	.08	.15
120	Cooney Weiland	.08	.15
121	Frank Mahovlich	.35	.75
122	Weston W. Adams Sr.	.08	.15
123	Montagu Allan	.08	.15
124	Frankie Brimsek, Goalie	.08	.15
125	Angus Campbell	.08	.15
126	Bill Cook	.08	.15
127	Tommy Dunderdale	.08	.15
128	Chuck Gardiner, Goalie	.08	.15
129	Elmer Lach	.08	.15
130	Didier Pitre	.08	.15
131	Joe Primeau	.08	.15
132	Frank Rankin	.08	.15
133	Ernie Russell	.08	.15
134	W. Thayer Tutt	.08	.15
135	Harry Westwick	.08	.15
136	Yvan Cournoyer	.12	.25
137	Scotty Davidson	.08	.15
138	Cy Denneny	.08	.15
139	Bill Durnan, Goalie	.08	.15
140	Wilf (Shorty) Green	.08	.15
141	Bryan Hextall, Sr.	.08	.15
142	Bill Jennings	.08	.15
143	Gordon W. Juckes	.08	.15
144	Paddy Moran, Goalie	.08	.15
145	James D. Norris	.08	.15
146	Harry Oliver	.08	.15
147	Sam Pollock	.08	.15
148	Marcel Pronovost	.08	.15
149	Jack Ruttan	.08	.15
150	Earl Seibert	.08	.15
151	Ted Lindsay	.08	.15
152	George V. Brown	.08	.15

Hockey Hall of Fame
1983 Issue
Card No. 60,
Roy Worters

Hockey Hall of Fame
1983 Issue
Card No. 101,
Dick Irvin

Hockey Hall of Fame
1983 Issue
Card No. 144,
Paddy Moran

No.	Player	EX	NRMT
153	Arthur Farrell	.08	.15
154	Herb Gardiner	.08	.15
155	Si Griffis	.08	.15
156	Harry Holmes, Goalie	.08	.15
157	Harry Hyland	.08	.15
158	Tommy Ivan	.08	.15
159	Jack Laviolette	.08	.15
160	Francis Nelson	.08	.15
161	William Northey	.08	.15
162	Babe Pratt	.08	.15
163	Chuck Rayner, Goalie	.08	.15
164	Mike Rodden	.08	.15
165	Milt Schmidt	.08	.15
166	Bernie Geoffrion	.25	.50
167	Jack Butterfield	.08	.15
168	Joseph Cattarinich, Goalie	.08	.15
169	Alex Connell, Goalie	.08	.15
170	Bill Cowley	.08	.15
171	Chaucer Elliott	.08	.15
172	Jimmy Gardner	.08	.15
173	Tom Hooper	.08	.15
174	Syd Howe	.08	.15
175	Harvey Jackson	.08	.15
176	Al Leader	.08	.15
177	Fred Maxwell	.08	.15
178	Blair Russell	.08	.15
179	Bill Wirtz	.08	.15
180	Gump Worsley, Goalie	.25	.50
181	John Bucyk	.08	.15
182	Jack J. Adams	.08	.15
183	J. Frank Ahearne	.08	.15
184	J.P. Bickell	.08	.15
185	Art Coulter	.08	.15
186	Graham Drinkwater	.08	.15
187	George Hainsworth, Goalie	.08	.15
188	Tim Horton	.35	.75
189	Frederic McLaughlin	.08	.15
190	Dickie Moore	.12	.25
191	Pierre Pilote	.08	.15
192	Claude Robinson	.08	.15
193	Oliver Seibert	.08	.15
194	Alf Smith	.08	.15
195	Gord Wilson	.08	.15
196	Ken Dryden, Goalie	.50	1.00
197	George Armstrong	.08	.15
198	Ace Bailey	.08	.15
199	Jack Darragh	.08	.15
200	Eddie Gerard	.08	.15
201	Jack Gibson	.08	.15
202	Hugh Lehman, Goalie	.08	.15
203	Mickey MacKay	.08	.15
204	Joe Malone	.08	.15
205	Bruce Norris	.08	.15
206	J.A. O'Brien	.08	.15
207	Lynn Patrick	.08	.15
208	Tom Phillips	.08	.15
209	Allan Pickard	.08	.15
210	Jack Stewart	.08	.15
211	Johnny Bower, Goalie	.08	.15
212	Syl Apps, Sr.	.08	.15
213	John Ashley, Referee	.08	.15
214	Marty Barry	.08	.15
215	Andy Bathgate	.08	.15
216	Frank Buckland	.08	.15
217	James Dunn	.08	.15
218	Mike Grant	.08	.15
219	Doug Harvey	.12	.25
220	George McNamara	.08	.15
221	Hartland Molson	.08	.15
222	Gordon Roberts	.08	.15
223	Eddie Shore	.08	.15
224	Bruce Stuart	.08	.15
225	Carl Voss	.08	.15
226	Stan Mikita	.15	.30
227	Donald Bain	.08	.15
228	Emile (Butch) Bouchard	.08	.15
229	George Boucher	.08	.15
230	Alex Delvecchio	.12	.25
231	Emile Francis	.08	.15
232	Riley Hern, Goalie	.08	.15
233	Fred Hume	.08	.15
234	Paul Loicq	.08	.15
235	Bill Quackenbush	.08	.15

No.	Player	EX	NRMT
236	Sweeny Schriner, Error	.08	.15
237	Tommy Smith	.08	.15
238	Allan Stanley	.08	.15
239	Anatoli Tarasov	.08	.15
240	Frank Udvari	.08	.15

— 1983 POSTCARDS —

These cards were produced by Cartophilium with artwork by Carlton McDiarmid and write-ups by Lefty Reid of the Hockey Hall of Fame. This set consists of 15 subseries of 16 players elected to the Hockey Hall of Fame.

Card Size: 4" X 6"
Face: Four colour, white border; Name
Back: Black on white card stock; Name, Resume, Number, Bilingual
Imprint: © HOCKEY HALL OF FAME / C. McDIARMID / CARTOPHILIUM 1983 Printed in Canada / Imprimé au Canada
Complete Set No.: 240
Complete Set Price: 50.00 100.00
Common Player: .25 .50

No.	Player	EX	NRMT
A1	Sid Abel	.25	.50
A2	Harry Broadbent	.25	.50
A3	Clarence Campbell	.25	.50
A4	Neil Colville	.25	.50
A5	Charlie Conacher	.25	.50
A6	Red Dutton	.25	.50
A7	Foster Hewitt	.25	.50
A8	Fred Hume	.25	.50
A9	Mickey Ion	.25	.50
A10	Ernest (Moose) Johnson	.25	.50
A11	Bill Mosienko	.50	1.00
A12	Maurice Richard	.50	1.00
A13	Russell (Barney) Stanley	.25	.50
A14	Lord Stanley	.25	.50
A15	Fred Taylor	.25	.50
A16	Tiny Thompson, Goalie	.25	.50
B1	Donald Bain	.25	.50
B2	Hobey Baker	.25	.50
B3	Frank Calder	.25	.50
B4	Frank Foyston	.25	.50
B5	James Hendy	.25	.50
B6	Gordie Howe	.75	1.50
B7	Harry Lumley, Goalie	.25	.50
B8	Reg Noble	.25	.50
B9	Frank Patrick	.25	.50
B10	Harvey Pulford	.25	.50
B11	Ken Reardon	.25	.50
B12	Joe Simpson	.25	.50
B13	Conn Smythe	.25	.50
B14	Red Storey	.25	.50
B15	Lloyd Turner	.25	.50
B16	Georges Vezina, Goalie	.35	.75
C1	Jean Beliveau	.50	1.00
C2	Max Bentley	.25	.50
C3	Francis Clancy	.35	.75
C4	Babe Dye	.25	.50
C5	Ebbie Goodfellow	.25	.50
C6	Charles Hay	.25	.50
C7	Percy Lesueur, Goalie	.25	.50
C8	Tommy Lockhart	.25	.50
C9	Jack Marshall	.25	.50
C10	Lester Patrick	.25	.50
C11	Bill Quackenbush	.25	.50
C12	Frank Selke	.25	.50
C13	Cooper Smeaton	.25	.50
C14	Hooley Smith	.25	.50
C15	James T. Sutherland	.25	.50
C16	Fred Whitcroft	.25	.50
D1	Charles Adams	.25	.50
D2	Russell Bowie	.25	.50
D3	Frank Frederickson	.25	.50
D4	Billy Gilmour	.25	.50
D5	Ivan (Ching) Johnson	.25	.50
D6	Tom Johnson	.25	.50
D7	Aurel Joliat	.25	.50
D8	Duke Keats	.25	.50
D9	Red Kelly	.25	.50
D10	Frank McGee	.25	.50
D11	James D. Norris	.25	.50
D12	Philip Ross	.25	.50

Hockey Hall of Fame
1983 Postcards
Postcard No. B16,
Georges Vezina

Hockey Hall of Fame
1983 Postcards
Postcard No. B16,
Georges Vezina

Hockey Hall of Fame
1983 Postcards
Postcard No. C9,
Jack Marshall

Hockey Hall of Fame
1983 Postcards
Postcard No. I6,
Tommy Dunderdal

No.	Player	EX	NRMT
D13	Terry Sawchuk, Goalie	.50	1.00
D14	Babe Siebert	.25	.50
D15	Anatoli V. Tarasov	.25	.50
D16	Roy Worters, Goalie	.25	.50
E1	T. Franklin Ahearn	.25	.50
E2	Harold Ballard	.25	.50
E3	Billy Burch	.25	.50
E4	Bill Chadwick	.25	.50
E5	Sprague Cleghorn	.25	.50
E6	Rusty Crawford	.25	.50
E7	Alex Delvecchio	.35	.75
E8	George Dudley	.25	.50
E9	Ted Kennedy	.35	.75
E10	Edouard Lalonde	.25	.50
E11	Billy McGimsie	.25	.50
E12	Frank Nighbor	.25	.50
E13	Bobby Orr	1.00	2.00
E14	Sen. Donat Raymond	.25	.50
E15	Art Ross	.25	.50
E16	Jack Walker	.25	.50
F1	Doug Bentley	.25	.50
F2	Walter Brown	.25	.50
F3	Dit Clapper	.25	.50
F4	Hap Day	.25	.50
F5	Frank Dilio	.25	.50
F6	Bobby Hewitson	.25	.50
F7	Harry Howell	.25	.50
F8	Paul Loicq	.25	.50
F9	Sylvio Mantha	.25	.50
F10	Jacques Plante, Goalie	.50	1.00
F11	George Richardson	.25	.50
F12	Nels Stewart	.25	.50
F13	Hod Stuart	.25	.50
F14	Harry Trihey	.25	.50
F15	Marty Walsh	.25	.50
F16	Arthur Wirtz	.25	.50
G1	Toe Blake	.25	.50
G2	Frank Boucher	.25	.50
G3	Turk Broda, Goalie	.25	.50
G4	Harry Cameron	.25	.50
G5	Leo Dandurand	.25	.50
G6	Joe Hall	.25	.50
G7	George Hay	.25	.50
G8	William A. Hewitt	.25	.50
G9	Bouse Hutton	.25	.50
G10	Dick Irvin	.25	.50
G11	Henri Richard	.35	.75
G12	John Ross Robertson	.25	.50
G13	Frank D. Smith	.25	.50
G14	Allan Stanley	.25	.50
G15	Norm Ullman	.25	.50
G16	Harry Watson	.25	.50
H1	Clint Benedict, Goalie	.25	.50
H2	Richard Boon	.25	.50
H3	Gordie Drillon	.25	.50
H4	Bill Gadsby	.25	.50
H5	Rod Gilbert	.25	.50
H6	Francis (Moose) Goheen	.25	.50
H7	Tommy Gorman	.25	.50
H8	Glenn Hall, Goalie	.35	.75
H9	Red Horner	.25	.50
H10	John Kilpatrick	.25	.50
H11	Robert LeBel	.25	.50
H12	Howie Morenz	.50	1.00
H13	Fred Scanlan	.25	.50
H14	Tommy Smith	.25	.50
H15	Fred C. Waghorne	.25	.50
H16	Cooney Weiland	.25	.50
I1	Weston W. Adams	.25	.50
I2	Montagu Allan	.25	.50
I3	Frankie Brimsek, Goalie	.25	.50
I4	Angus Campbell	.25	.50
I5	Bill Cook	.25	.50
I6	Tommy Dunderdale	.25	.50
I7	Emile Francis	.25	.50
I8	Chuck Gardiner, Goalie	.25	.50
I9	Elmer Lach	.25	.50
I10	Frank Mahovlich	.50	1.00
I11	Didier Pitre	.25	.50
I12	Joe Primeau	.25	.50
I13	Frank Rankin	.25	.50
I14	Ernie Russell	.25	.50
I15	W. Thayer Tutt	.25	.50
I16	Harry Westwick	.25	.50
J1	Jack J. Adams	.25	.50

HOCKEY HALL OF FAME — 1987 REGULAR ISSUE

No.	Player	EX	NRMT
J2	J. Frank Ahearne	.25	.50
J3	J.P. Bickell	.25	.50
J4	John Bucyk	.25	.50
J5	Art Coulter	.25	.50
J6	Graham Drinkwater	.25	.50
J7	George Hainsworth, Goalie	.25	.50
J8	Tim Horton	.50	1.00
J9	Frederic McLaughlin	.25	.50
J10	Dickie Moore	.25	.50
J11	Pierre Pilote	.25	.50
J12	Claude Robinson	.25	.50
J13	Sweeny Schriner	.25	.50
J14	Oliver Seibert	.25	.50
J15	Albert Smith	.25	.50
J16	Phat Wilson	.25	.50
K1	Yvan Cournoyer	.25	.50
K2	Scotty Davidson	.25	.50
K3	Cy Denneny	.25	.50
K4	Bill Durnan, Goalie	.25	.50
K5	Wilf (Shorty) Green	.25	.50
K6	Riley Hern, Goalie	.25	.50
K7	Bryan Hextall, Sr.	.25	.50
K8	Bill Jennings	.25	.50
K9	Gordon W. Juckes	.25	.50
K10	Paddy Moran, Goalie	.25	.50
K11	James D. Norris	.25	.50
K12	Harry Oliver	.25	.50
K13	Sam Pollock	.25	.50
K14	Marcel Pronovost	.25	.50
K15	Jack Ruttan	.25	.50
K16	Earl Seibert	.25	.50
L1	Buck Boucher	.25	.50
L2	George V. Brown	.25	.50
L3	Arthur F. Farrell	.25	.50
L4	Herb Gardiner	.25	.50
L5	Si Griffis	.25	.50
L6	Harry Holmes, Goalie	.25	.50
L7	Harry Hyland	.25	.50
L8	Tommy Ivan	.25	.50
L9	Jack Laviolette	.25	.50
L10	Ted Lindsay	.25	.50
L11	Francis Nelson	.25	.50
L12	William Northey	.25	.50
L13	Babe Pratt	.25	.50
L14	Chuck Rayner, Goalie	.25	.50
L15	Mike Rodden	.25	.50
L16	Milt Schmidt	.25	.50
M1	Emile (Butch) Bouchard	.25	.50
M2	Jack Butterfield	.25	.50
M3	Joseph Cattarinich, Goalie	.25	.50
M4	Alex Connell, Goalie	.25	.50
M5	Bill Cowley	.25	.50
M6	Chaucer Elliott	.25	.50
M7	Jimmy Gardner	.25	.50
M8	Bernie Geoffrion	.25	.50
M9	Tom Hooper	.25	.50
M10	Syd Howe	.25	.50
M11	Harvey Jackson	.25	.50
M12	Al Leader	.25	.50
M13	Kevin Maxwell	.25	.50
M14	Blair Russell	.25	.50
M15	Bill Wirtz	.25	.50
M16	Gump Worsley, Goalie	.35	.75
N1	George Armstrong	.25	.50
N2	Ace Bailey	.25	.50
N3	Jack Darragh	.25	.50
N4	Ken Dryden, Goalie	.50	1.00
N5	Eddie Gerard	.25	.50
N6	Jack Gibson	.25	.50
N7	Hugh Lehman, Goalie	.25	.50
N8	Mickey MacKay	.25	.50
N9	Joe Malone	.25	.50
N10	Bruce A. Norris	.25	.50
N11	J.A. O'Brien	.25	.50
N12	Lynn Patrick	.25	.50
N13	Tommy Phillips	.25	.50
N14	Allan W. Pickard	.25	.50
N15	Jack Stewart	.25	.50
N16	Frank Udvari	.25	.50
O1	Syl Apps, Sr.	.25	.50
O2	John Ashley	.25	.50
O3	Marty Barry	.25	.50
O4	Andy Bathgate	.25	.50

Hockey Hall of Fame
1987 Issue
Card No. 1,
Maurice Richard

Hockey Hall of Fame
1987 Issue
Card No. 1,
Maurice Richard

No.	Player	EX	NRMT
O5	Johnny Bower, Goalie	.25	.50
O6	Frank Buckland	.25	.50
O7	James Dunn	.25	.50
O8	Mike Grant	.25	.50
O9	Doug Harvey	.35	.75
O10	George McNamara	.25	.50
O11	Stan Mikita	.35	.75
O12	Sen. H. de M. Molson	.25	.50
O13	Gordon Roberts	.25	.50
O14	Eddie Shore	.25	.50
O15	Bruce Stuart	.25	.50
O16	Carl P. Voss	.25	.50

— 1987 REGULAR ISSUE —

This set added another 21 cards to include HOF inductees selected after 1983. A total of 261 cards were issued. The two sets are distinguished by the copyright year marked on the backs of the cards. Colour artwork interpretations were supplied by Carlton McDiarmid.

Card Size: 2 1/2" X 3 1/2"
Face: Four colour
Back: Black and white; Name, Resume, Bilingual
Imprint: Printed in Canada / Imprimé au Canada © C. McDIARMID / CARTOPHILIUM INC. 1987
Complete Set No.: 261
Complete Set Price: 17.50 35.00
Common Player: .08 .15

No.	Player	EX	NRMT
1	Maurice Richard	.50	1.00
2	Sid Abel	.08	.15
3	Harry Broadbent	.08	.15
4	Clarence Campbell	.08	.15
5	Neil Colville	.08	.15
6	Charlie Conacher	.08	.15
7	Red Dutton	.08	.15
8	Foster Hewitt	.08	.15
9	Mickey Ion	.08	.15
10	Ernest (Moose) Johnson	.08	.15
11	Bill Mosienko	.08	.15
12	Russell (Barney) Stanley	.08	.15
13	Lord Stanley	.08	.15
14	Fred Taylor	.08	.15
15	Tiny Thompson, Goalie	.08	.15
16	Gordie Howe	.50	1.00
17	Hobey Baker	.08	.15
18	Frank Calder	.08	.15
19	Jim Hendy	.08	.15
20	Frank Foyston	.08	.15
21	Harry Lumley, Goalie	.08	.15
22	Reg Noble	.08	.15
23	Frank Patrick	.08	.15
24	Harvey Pulford	.08	.15
25	Ken Reardon	.08	.15
26	Joe Simpson	.08	.15
27	Conn Smythe	.08	.15
28	Red Storey	.08	.15
29	Lloyd Turner	.08	.15
30	Georges Vezina, Goalie	.08	.15
31	Jean Beliveau	.50	1.00
32	Max Bentley	.08	.15
33	Francis Clancy	.08	.15
34	Babe Dye	.08	.15
35	Ebbie Goodfellow	.08	.15
36	Charles Hay	.08	.15
37	Percy Lesueur, Goalie	.08	.15
38	Tommy Lockhart	.08	.15
39	Jack Marshall	.08	.15
40	Lester Patrick	.08	.15
41	Frank Selke	.08	.15
42	Cooper Smeaton	.08	.15
43	Hooley Smith	.08	.15
44	James T. Sutherland	.08	.15
45	Fred Whitcroft	.08	.15
46	Terry Sawchuk, Goalie	.50	1.00
47	Charles Adams	.08	.15
48	Russell Bowie	.08	.15
49	Frank Frederickson, Error		.15
50	Billy Gilmour	.08	.15
51	Ching (Ivan) Johnson	.08	.15
52	Tom Johnson	.08	.15
53	Aurel Joliat	.12	.25

Hockey Hall of Fame
1987 Issue
Card No. 6,
Charlie Conacher

1987 REGULAR ISSUE — HOCKEY HALL OF FAME • 313

No.	Player	EX	NRMT
54	Duke Keats	.08	.15
55	Red Kelly	.08	.15
56	Frank McGee	.08	.15
57	James D. Norris	.08	.15
58	Philip Ross	.08	.15
59	Babe Siebert	.08	.15
60	Roy Worters, Goalie	.08	.15
61	Bobby Orr	.50	1.00
62	T. Franklin Ahearn	.08	.15
63	Harold Ballard	.08	.15
64	Billy Burch	.08	.15
65	Bill Chadwick	.08	.15
66	Sprague Cleghorn	.08	.15
67	Rusty Crawford	.08	.15
68	George Dudley	.08	.15
69	Ted Kennedy	.12	.25
70	Edouard Lalonde	.08	.15
71	Billy McGimsie	.08	.15
72	Frank Nighbor	.08	.15
73	Donat Raymond	.08	.15
74	Art Ross	.08	.15
75	Jack Walker	.08	.15
76	Jacques Plante, Goalie	.50	1.00
77	Doug Bentley	.08	.15
78	Walter Brown	.08	.15
79	Dit Clapper	.08	.15
80	Hap Day	.08	.15
81	Frank Dilio	.08	.15
82	Bobby Hewitson	.08	.15
83	Harry Howell	.08	.15
84	Sylvio Mantha	.08	.15
85	George Richardson	.08	.15
86	Nels Stewart	.08	.15
87	Hod Stuart	.08	.15
88	Harry Trihey	.08	.15
89	Marty Walsh	.08	.15
90	Arthur Wirtz	.08	.15
91	Henri Richard	.12	.25
92	Toe Blake	.08	.15
93	Frank Boucher	.08	.15
94	Turk Broda, Goalie	.08	.15
95	Harry Cameron	.08	.15
96	Leo Dandurand	.08	.15
97	Joe Hall	.08	.15
98	George Hay	.08	.15
99	William A. Hewitt	.08	.15
100	J.B. Hutton, Goalie	.08	.15
101	Dick Irvin	.08	.15
102	John Ross Robertson	.08	.15
103	Frank D. Smith	.08	.15
104	Norm Ullman	.08	.15
105	Harry Watson	.08	.15
106	Howie Morenz	.50	1.00
107	Clint Benedict, Goalie	.08	.15
108	Richard Boon	.08	.15
109	Gordie Drillon	.08	.15
110	Bill Gadsby	.08	.15
111	Rod Gilbert	.08	.15
112	Francis (Moose) Goheen	.08	.15
113	Tommy Gorman	.08	.15
114	Glenn Hall, Goalie	.12	.25
115	Red Horner	.08	.15
116	John Kilpatrick	.08	.15
117	Robert LeBel	.08	.15
118	Fred Scanlan	.08	.15
119	Fred C. Waghorne	.08	.15
120	Cooney Weiland	.08	.15
121	Frank Mahovlich	.50	1.00
122	Weston W. Adams Sr.	.08	.15
123	Montagu Allan	.08	.15
124	Frankie Brimsek, Goalie	.08	.15
125	Angus Campbell	.08	.15
126	Bill Cook	.08	.15
127	Tommy Dunderdale	.08	.15
128	Chuck Gardiner, Goalie	.08	.15
129	Elmer Lach	.08	.15
130	Didier Pitre	.08	.15
131	Joe Primeau	.08	.15
132	Frank Rankin	.08	.15
133	Ernie Russell	.08	.15
134	W. Thayer Tutt	.08	.15
135	Harry Westwick	.08	.15
136	Yvan Cournoyer	.12	.25

Hockey Hall of Fame
1987 Issue
Card No. 155,
Si Griffis

Hockey Hall of Fame
1987 Issue
Card No. 228,
Emile (Butch) Bouchard

Hockey Hall of Fame
1987 Issue
Card No. 236, Error,
Name misspelled
Sweeney on back

No.	Player	EX	NRMT
137	Scotty Davidson	.08	.15
138	Cy Denneny	.08	.15
139	Bill Durnan, Goalie	.08	.15
140	Wilf (Shorty) Green	.08	.15
141	Bryan Hextall, Sr.	.08	.15
142	William Jennings	.08	.15
143	Gordon W. Juckes	.08	.15
144	Paddy Moran, Goalie	.08	.15
145	James D. Norris	.08	.15
146	Harry Oliver	.08	.15
147	Sam Pollock	.08	.15
148	Marcel Pronovost	.08	.15
149	Jack Ruttan	.08	.15
150	Earl Seibert	.08	.15
151	Ted Lindsay	.08	.15
152	George V. Brown	.08	.15
153	Arthur Farrell	.08	.15
154	Herb Gardiner	.08	.15
155	Si Griffis	.08	.15
156	Harry Holmes, Goalie	.08	.15
157	Harry Hyland	.08	.15
158	Tommy Ivan	.08	.15
159	Jack Laviolette	.08	.15
160	Francis Nelson	.08	.15
161	William Northey	.08	.15
162	Babe Pratt	.08	.15
163	Chuck Rayner, Goalie	.08	.15
164	Mike Rodden	.08	.15
165	Milt Schmidt	.08	.15
166	Bernie Geoffrion	.25	.50
167	Jack Butterfield	.08	.15
168	Joseph Cattarinich, Goalie	.08	.15
169	Alex Connell, Goalie	.08	.15
170	Bill Cowley	.08	.15
171	Chaucer Elliott	.08	.15
172	Jimmy Gardner	.08	.15
173	Tom Hooper	.08	.15
174	Syd Howe	.08	.15
175	Harvey (Busher) Jackson	.08	.15
176	Al Leader	.08	.15
177	Fred Maxwell	.08	.15
178	Blair Russell	.08	.15
179	Bill Wirtz	.08	.15
180	Gump Worsley, Goalie	.25	.50
181	John Bucyk	.08	.15
182	Jack J. Adams	.08	.15
183	J. Frank Ahearne	.08	.15
184	J.P. Bickell	.08	.15
185	Art Coulter	.08	.15
186	Graham Drinkwater	.08	.15
187	George Hainsworth, Goalie	.08	.15
188	Tim Horton	.35	.75
189	Frederic McLaughlin	.08	.15
190	Dickie Moore	.08	.15
191	Pierre Pilote	.08	.15
192	Claude Robinson	.08	.15
193	Oliver Seibert	.08	.15
194	Alf Smith	.08	.15
195	Gord Wilson	.08	.15
196	Ken Dryden, Goalie	.50	1.00
197	George Armstrong	.12	.25
198	Ace Bailey	.08	.15
199	Jack Darragh	.08	.15
200	Eddie Gerard	.08	.15
201	Jack Gibson	.08	.15
202	Hugh Lehman, Goalie	.08	.15
203	Mickey MacKay	.08	.15
204	Joe Malone	.08	.15
205	Bruce Norris	.08	.15
206	J.A. O'Brien	.08	.15
207	Lynn Patrick	.08	.15
208	Tom Phillips	.08	.15
209	Allan Pickard	.08	.15
210	Jack Stewart	.08	.15
211	Johnny Bower, Goalie	.08	.15
212	Syl Apps, Sr.	.08	.15
213	John Ashley, Referee	.08	.15
214	Marty Barry	.08	.15
215	Andy Bathgate	.08	.15
216	Frank Buckland	.08	.15
217	James Dunn	.08	.15
218	Mike Grant	.08	.15
219	Doug Harvey	.12	.25

314 • FUNMATE CANADA LTD — 1983-84 PUFFY STICKERS

No.	Player	EX	NRMT
220	George McNamara	.08	.15
221	Hartland Molson	.08	.15
222	Gordon Roberts	.08	.15
223	Eddie Shore	.08	.15
224	Bruce Stuart	.08	.15
225	Carl Voss	.08	.15
226	Stan Mikita	.25	.50
227	Donald Bain	.08	.15
228	Emile (Butch) Bouchard	.08	.15
229	George Boucher	.08	.15
230	Alex Delvecchio	.08	.15
231	Emile Francis	.08	.15
232	Riley Hern, Goalie	.08	.15
233	Fred Hume	.08	.15
234	Paul Loicq	.08	.15
235	Bill Quackenbush	.08	.15
236	Sweeny Schriner, Error	.08	.15
237	Tommy Smith	.08	.15
238	Allan Stanley	.08	.15
239	Anatoli Tarasov	.08	.15
240	Frank Udvari	.08	.15
241	Harry Sinden	.08	.15
242	Bobby Hull	.50	1.00
243	Punch Imlach	.08	.15
244	Phil Esposito	.35	.75
245	Jacques Lemaire	.07	.15
246	Bernard Marcel	.08	.15
247	Rudy Pilous	.08	.15
248	Bert Olmstead	.08	.15
249	Jean Ratelle	.08	.15
250	Gerry Cheevers, Goalie	.08	.15
251	Bill Hanley	.08	.15
252	Leo Boivin	.08	.15
253	Jake Milford	.08	.15
254	John Mariucci	.08	.15
255	Dave Keon	.25	.50
256	Serge Savard	.08	.15
257	John Ziegler	.08	.15
258	Bobby Clarke	.25	.50
259	Ed Giacomin, Goalie	.25	.50
260	Jacques Laperriere	.08	.15
261	Matt Pavelich	.08	.15

FUNMATE CANADA LTD

— 1983-84 PUFFY STICKERS —

These stickers were issued in cello packs of six stickers each. The 26 different packs are numbered Series 1 to 21. The last 5 packs are unnumbered. Since the stickers are unnumbered they are listed below in alphabetical order by team and then by player within the team.

Sticker Size: Oval 1 3/8" X 1 13/16"
Face: Four colour, woodgrain border; Team, Name
Back: Blank
Imprint: None
Complete Set No.: 25 Cello Packs / 156 Stickers
Complete Set Price: 15.00 30.00
Common Player: .05 .10
Album: 10.00 20.00

BOSTON BRUINS

No.	Player	EX	NRMT
1	Team Logo	.05	.10
2	Raymond Bourque	.75	1.50
3	Rick Middleton	.05	.10
4	Terry O'Reilly	.20	.40
5	Barry Pederson	.05	.10
6	Pete Peeters, Goalie	.05	.10
7	Jim Schoenfeld	.05	.10

BUFFALO SABRES

No.	Player	EX	NRMT
8	Team Logo	.05	.10
9	Real Cloutier	.05	.10
10	Mike Foligno	.05	.10
11	Phil Housley	.05	.10
12	Dale McCourt	.05	.10
13	Gilbert Perreault	.20	.40
14	John Van Boxmeer	.05	.10

Funmate Canada
1983-84 Puffy Stickers
Sticker No. 20,
Doug Risebrough

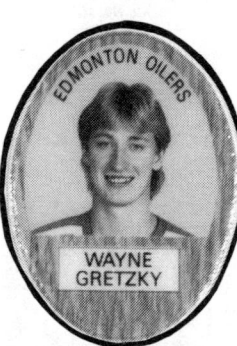

Funmate Canada
1983-84 Puffy Stickers
Sticker No. 39,
Wayne Gretzky

Funmate Canada
1983-84 Puffy Stickers
Sticker No. 42,
Mark Messier

Funmate Canada
1983-84 Puffy Stickers
Sticker No. 65,
Guy Lafleur

CALGARY FLAMES

No.	Player	EX	NRMT
15	Team Logo	.05	.10
16	Don Edwards, Goalie	.05	.10
17	Lanny McDonald	.35	.75
18	Kent Nilsson	.05	.10
19	Paul Reinhart	.05	.10
20	Doug Risebrough	.05	.10
21	Steve Tambellini	.05	.10

CHICAGO BLACKHAWKS

No.	Player	EX	NRMT
22	Team Logo	.05	.10
23	Tony Esposito, Goalie	.13	.25
24	Steve Larmer	.25	.50
25	Tom Lysiak	.05	.10
26	Denis Savard	.25	.50
27	Alan Secord	.05	.10
28	Douglas Wilson	.05	.10

DETROIT RED WINGS

No.	Player	EX	NRMT
29	Team Logo	.05	.10
30	Ron Duguay	.05	.10
31	Danny Gare	.05	.10
32	Reed Larson	.05	.10
33	Walt McKechnie	.05	.10
34	John Ogrodnick	.05	.10
35	Brad Park	.05	.10

EDMONTON OILERS

No.	Player	EX	NRMT
36	Team Logo	.05	.10
37	Glenn Anderson	.13	.25
38	Paul Coffey	.50	1.00
39	Wayne Gretzky	3.00	6.00
40	Jari Kurri	.25	.50
41	Ken Linseman	.05	.10
42	Mark Messier	1.00	2.00

HARTFORD WHALERS

No.	Player	EX	NRMT
43	Team logo	.05	.10
44	Ron Francis	.25	.50
45	Mark Johnson	.05	.10
46	Pierre Larouche	.05	.10
N47	Greg Millen, Goalie	.05	.10
48	Risto Siltanen	.05	.10
49	Blaine Stoughton	.05	.10

LOS ANGELES KINGS

No.	Player	EX	NRMT
50	Team Logo	.05	.10
51	Marcel Dionne	.25	.50
52	Jim Fox	.05	.10
53	Larry Murphy	.13	.25
54	Bernie Nichols	.13	.25
55	Charlie Simmer	.05	.10
56	Dave Taylor	.13	.25

MINNESOTA NORTH STARS

No.	Player	EX	NRMT
57	Team Logo	.05	.10
58	Brian Bellows	.13	.25
59	Neal Broten	.05	.10
60	Dino Ciccarelli	.20	.40
61	Craig Hartsburg	.05	.10
62	Dennis Maruk	.05	.10
63	Bobby Smith	.10	.20

MONTREAL CANADIENS

No.	Player	EX	NRMT
64	Team logo	.05	.10
65	Guy Lafleur	.25	.50
66	Mats Naslund	.05	.10
67	Larry Robinson	.25	.50
68	Steve Shutt	.10	.20
69	Mario Tremblay	.10	.20
70	Ryan Walter	.05	.10

1983-84 PUFFY STICKERS — FUNMATE CANADA LTD • 315

NEW JERSEY DEVILS

No.	Player	EX	NRMT
71	Team Logo	.05	.10
72	Don Lever	.05	.10
73	Tapio Levo	.05	.10
74	Bob MacMillan	.05	.10
75	Hector Marini	.05	.10
76	Glenn Resch, Goalie	.13	.25
77	Phil Russell	.05	.10

NEW YORK ISLANDERS

No.	Player	EX	NRMT
78	Team Logo	.05	.10
79	Mike Bossy	.25	.50
80	Clark Gillies	.05	.10
81	Denis Potvin	.25	.50
82	Billy Smith, Goalie	.13	.25
83	John Tonelli	.05	.10
84	Bryan Trottier	.13	.25

NEW YORK RANGERS

No.	Player	EX	NRMT
85	Team Logo	.05	.10
86	Barry Beck	.05	.10
87	Anders Hedberg	.05	.10
88	Willie Huber	.05	.10
89	Donald Maloney	.05	.10
90	Rob McClanahan	.05	.10
91	Reijo Ruotsalainen	.05	.10

PHILADELPHIA FLYERS

No.	Player	EX	NRMT
92	Team Logo	.05	.10
93	Bill Barber	.10	.20
94	Bobby Clarke	.50	1.00
95	Mark Howe	.13	.25
96	Brian Propp	.05	.10
97	Darryl Sittler	.50	1.00
98	Behn Wilson	.05	.10

PITTSBURGH PENGUINS

No.	Player	EX	NRMT
99	Team Logo	.05	.10
100	Mike Bullard	.05	.10
101	Randy Carlyle	.10	.20
102	Michel Dion, Goalie	.05	.10
103	Paul Gardner	.05	.10
104	Rick Kehoe	.05	.10
105	Greg Malone	.05	.10

QUEBEC NORDIQUES

No.	Player	EX	NRMT
106	Team Logo	.05	.10
107	Dan Bouchard, Goalie	.05	.10
108	Michel Goulet	.25	.50
109	Anthony McKegney	.05	.10
110	Anton Stastny	.05	.10
111	Marian Stastny	.05	.10
112	Peter Stastny	.25	.50

ST. LOUIS BLUES

No.	Player	EX	NRMT
113	Team Logo	.05	.10
114	Blake Dunlop	.05	.10
115	Bernie Federko	.05	.10
116	Mike Liut, Goalie	.13	.25
117	Jorgen Pettersson	.05	.10
118	George (Rob) Ramage	.05	.10
119	Brian Sutter	.13	.25

TORONTO MAPLE LEAFS

No.	Player	EX	NRMT
120	Team Logo	.05	.10
121	John Anderson	.10	.20
122	Bill Derlago	.05	.10
123	Peter Ihnacak	.05	.10
124	Mike Palmateer, Goalie	.10	.20
125	Borje Salming	.25	.50
126	Richard Vaive	.15	.30

Funmate Canada
1983-84 Puffy Stickers
Sticker No. 122,
Bill Derlago

Funmate Canada
1983-84 Puffy Stickers
Sticker No. 133,
David Williams

Funmate Canada
1983-84 Puffy Stickers
Sticker No. 143,
David Babych

VANCOUVER CANUCKS

No.	Player	EX	NRMT
127	Team Logo	.05	.10
128	Richard Brodeur, Goalie	.05	.10
129	Thomas Gradin	.05	.10
130	Kevin McCarthy	.05	.10
131	Darcy Rota	.05	.10
132	Stanley Smyl	.05	.10
133	David Williams	.10	.20

WASHINGTON CAPITALS

No.	Player	EX	NRMT
134	Team Logo	.05	.10
135	Robert Carpenter	.05	.10
136	Brian Engblom	.05	.10
137	Michael Gartner	.35	.75
138	Rod Langway	.05	.10
139	Milan Novy	.05	.10
140	Pat Riggin, Goalie	.05	.10

WINNIPEG JETS

No.	Player	EX	NRMT
141	Team Logo	.05	.10
142	Scott Arniel	.05	.10
143	David Babych	.05	.10
144	Dale Hawerchuk	.25	.50
145	Morris Lukowich	.05	.10
146	Paul MacLean	.05	.10
147	Brian Mullen	.05	.10

TROPHIES AND AWARDS

No.	Player	EX	NRMT
148	Calder Trophy	.10	.20
149	Conn Smythe Trophy	.10	.20
150	Hart Trophy	.10	.20
151	James Norris Trophy	.10	.20
152	Lady Byng Trophy	.10	.20
153	Vezina Trophy	.10	.20

LOGOS

No.	Player	EX	NRMT
154	NHL, Large	.05	.10
155	NHL, Small	.05	.10
156	NHLPA	.05	.10

CELLO PACKS

No.	Player	EX	NRMT
1	D. Risebrough; W. Gretzky; M. Naslund; B. Derlago; R. Brodeur; D. Babych	3.50	7.00
2	G. Anderson; L. Robinson; R. Vaive; S. Smyl; S. Arniel; D. Edwards	.75	1.50
3	R. Walter; P. Ihnacak; T. Gradin; M. Lukowich; K. Nilsson; P. Coffey	1.00	2.00
4	J. Anderson; D. Williams; B. Mullen; S. Tambellini; M. Messier; G. Lafleur	1.25	2.50
5	D. Rota; D. Hawerchuk; P. Reinhart; J. Kurri; M. Tremblay; M. Palmateer, Goalie	.75	1.50
6	P. MacLean; L. McDonald; K. Linseman; S. Shutt;; B. Salming; K. McCarthy	.50	1.00
7	B. Pederson; M. Foligno; J. Fox; D. Lever; B. Clarke; G. Malone	1.00	2.00
8	G. Perreault; C. Simmer; H. Marini; M. Howe; R. Kehoe; J. Schoenfeld	.75	1.50
9	L. Murphy; P. Russell; B. Barber; M. Bullard; P. Peeters, Goalie; J. Van Boxmeer	.50	1.00
10	T. Levo; D. Sittler; P. Gardner; R. Middleton; R. Cloutier; B. Nicholls	1.00	2.00
11	B. Propp; M. Dion; R. Bourque; D. McCourt; M. Dionne; B. MacMillan	.50	1.00
12	R. Carlyle; T. O'Reilly; P. Housley; D. Taylor; G. Resch, Goalie; B. Wilson	.50	1.00
13	T. Esposito, Goalie; R. Duguay; P. Larouche; N. Broten; P. Stastny; B. Dunlop	.50	1.00
14	W. McKechnie; R. Siltanen; B. Smith, Goalie; A. Stastny; M. Liut, Goalie; D. Wilson	.50	1.00
15	B. Stoughton; D. Ciccarelli; M. Goulet; J. Pettersson; T. Lysiak; B. Park	.75	1.50
16	C. Hartsburg; M. Stastny; R. Ramage; A. Secord; J. Ogrodnick; G. Millen	.50	1.00
17	T. McKegney; B. Sutter; S. Larmer; D. Gare; M. Johnson; B. Bellows	.50	1.00
18	B. Federko; D. Savard; R. Larson; R. Francis; D. Maruk; D. Bouchard	.50	1.00
19	M. Bossy; A. Hedberg; R. Langway; B. Smith, Goalie; R. Ruotsalainen; M. Novy	.50	1.00
20	B. Beck; B. Carpenter; C. Gillies; R. McClanahan; B. Engblom; D. Potvin	.50	1.00

No.	Player	EX	NRMT
21	M. Gartner; J. Tonelli; W. Huber; P. Riggin, Goalie; B. Trottier; D. Maloney	.75	1.50
—	**Norris Division:** Blackhawks; Red Wings; North Stars; Blues; Maple Leafs; NHL	.50	1.00
—	**Patrick Division:** Devils; Islanders; Rangers; Flyers; Penguins; Capitals	.50	1.00
—	**Adams Division:** Bruins; Sabres; Whalers; Canadiens; Nordiques; NHL	.50	1.00
—	**Smythe Division:** Flames; Oilers; Kings; Canucks; Jets; NHL	.50	1.00
—	**Trophies and Awards:** Hart Trophy; Calder Trophy; Lady Byng Trophy; Vezina Trophy; Conn Smythe Trophy; James Norris Trophy	.50	1.00

VACHON FOODS
— 1983 - 84 ISSUE —

The set was issued as a two-card panel on Vachon Food product packages. The error noted for card no.96 was corrected in the second series issue. Vachon also sold complete sets. Cards are numbered _ of 140.

Card Size: 2 9/16" X 3 9/16"
Face: Four colour, white border; Name, Number, Team and Sponsor logos
Back: Blue on buff card stock; Name, Number, Team, Resume, Bilingual
Imprint: PROMO MARKETING NHLPA
Complete Set No.: 140
Complete Set Price: 40.00 / 80.00
Common Player: .13 / .25

CALGARY FLAMES

No.	Player	EX	NRMT
1	Paul Baxter	.13	.25
2	Eddy Beers	.13	.25
3	Steve Bozek	.13	.25
4	Mike Eaves	.13	.25
5	Don Edwards, Goalie	.18	.35
6	Kari Eloranta	.13	.25
7	Dave Hindmarch	.13	.25
8	Jamie Hislop	.13	.25
9	Stephen Konroyd	.13	.25
10	Rejean Lemelin, Goalie	.25	.50
11	Hakan Loob	.18	.35
12	Jamie Macoun	.18	.35
13	Lanny McDonald	.50	1.00
14	Kent Nilsson	.25	.50
15	Colin Patterson	.13	.25
16	James Peplinski	.13	.25
17	Paul Reinhart	.13	.25
18	Doug Risebrough	.13	.25
19	Steve Tambellini	.13	.25
20	Mickey Volcan	.13	.25

EDMONTON OILERS

No.	Player	EX	NRMT
21	Glenn Anderson	.13	.25
22	Paul Coffey	1.00	2.00
23	Lee Fogolin	.20	.40
24	Grant Fuhr, Goalie	1.00	2.00
25	Randall Gregg	.20	.40
26	Wayne Gretzky	6.00	12.00
27	Charles Huddy	.20	.40
28	Pat Hughes	.13	.25
29	Dave Hunter	.13	.25
30	Don Jackson	.13	.25
31	Jari Kurri	.50	1.00
32	Willy Lindstrom	.13	.25
33	Ken Linseman	.13	.25
34	Kevin Lowe	.35	.75
35	Dave Lumley	.13	.25
36	Mark Messier	2.00	4.00
37	Andrew Moog, Goalie	.50	1.00
38	Jaroslav Pouzar	.13	.25
39	Tom Roulston	.13	.25
40	Dave Semenko	.13	.25

MONTREAL CANADIENS

No.	Player	EX	NRMT
41	Guy Carbonneau	.50	1.00
42	Kent Carlson	.13	.25
43	Gilbert Delorme	.13	.25
44	Bob Gainey	.20	.40

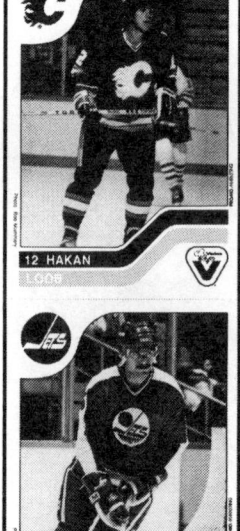

Vachon Foods
1983-84 Issue
Card No. 11, Hakan Loob;
Card No. 131, Paul McLean

Vachon Foods
1983-84 Issue
Card No. 24, Grant Fuhr
Card No. 104, Ron Delorme

No.	Player	EX	NRMT
45	Jean Hamel	.13	.25
46	Mark Hunter	.13	.25
47	Guy Lafleur	1.00	2.00
48	Craig Ludwig	.13	.25
49	Pierre Mondou	.13	.25
50	Mats Naslund	.50	1.00
51	Christopher Nilan	.13	.25
52	Gregory Paslawski	.13	.25
53	Larry Robinson	.50	1.00
54	Richard Sevigny, Goalie	.13	.25
55	Steve Shutt	.20	.40
56	Robert Smith	.13	.25
57	Mario Tremblay	.13	.25
58	Ryan Walter	.13	.25
59	Richard Wamsley, Goalie	.13	.25
60	Douglas Wickenheiser	.13	.25

QUEBEC NORDIQUES

No.	Player	EX	NRMT
61	Bo Berglund	.13	.25
62	Dan Bouchard, Goalie	.13	.25
63	Alain Cote	.13	.25
64	Brian Ford, Goalie	.13	.25
65	Michel Goulet	1.00	2.00
66	Dale Hunter	.13	.25
67	Mario Marois	.13	.25
68	Anthony McKegney	.13	.25
69	Randy Moller	.13	.25
70	Wilf Paiement	.13	.25
71	Pat Price	.13	.25
72	Normand Rochefort	.13	.25
73	Andre Savard	.13	.25
74	Louis Sleigher	.13	.25
75	Anton Stastny	.13	.25
76	Marian Stastny	.13	.25
77	Peter Stastny	1.00	2.00
78	John Van Boxmeer	.13	.25
79	Wally Weir	.13	.25
80	Blake Wesley	.13	.25

TORONTO MAPLE LEAFS

No.	Player	EX	NRMT
81	John Anderson	.13	.25
82	Jim Benning	.13	.25
83	Dan Daoust	.13	.25
84	Bill Derlago	.13	.25
85	Dave Farrish	.13	.25
86	Miroslav Frycer	.13	.25
87	Robert (Stewart) Gavin	.13	.25
88	Gaston Gingras	.13	.25
89	Billy Harris	.13	.25
90	Peter Ihnacak	.50	1.00
91	James Korn	.13	.25
92	Terry Martin	.13	.25
93	Dale McCourt	.13	.25
94	Gary Nylund	.13	.25
95	Mike Palmateer, Goalie	.13	.25
96A	Walter Poddubny, Error	.50	1.00
96B	Walter Poddubny, Corrected	.50	1.00
97	Borje Salming	.75	1.50
98	Rick St. Croix, Goalie	.13	.25
99	Greg Terrion	.13	.25
100	Richard Vaive	.20	.40

VANCOUVER CANUCKS

No.	Player	EX	NRMT
101	Richard Brodeur, Goalie	.25	.50
102	Jiri Bubla	.13	.25
103	Garth Butcher	.13	.25
104	Ron Delorme	.13	.25
105	John Garrett, Goalie	.13	.25
106	Jere Gillis	.13	.25
107	Thomas Gradin	.13	.25
108	Doug Halward	.13	.25
109	Mark Kirton	.13	.25
110	Rick Lanz	.13	.25
111	Gary Lupul	.13	.25
112	Kevin McCarthy	.13	.25
113	Lars Molin	.13	.25
114	James Nill	.13	.25
115	Darcy Rota	.13	.25
116	Stanley Smyl	.13	.25

No.	Player	EX	NRMT
117	Harold Snepsts	.20	.40
118	Patrik Sundstrom	.13	.25
119	Tony Tanti	.20	.40
120	David Williams	.20	.40

WINNIPEG JETS

No.	Player	EX	NRMT
121	Scott Arniel	.13	.25
122	David Babych	.13	.25
123	Laurie Boschman	.13	.25
124	Wade Campbell	.13	.25
125	Lucien DeBlois	.13	.25
126	Dale Hawerchuk	1.00	2.00
127	Brian Hayward, Goalie	.13	.25
128	James Kyte	.13	.25
129	Morris Lukowich	.13	.25
130	Bengt Lundholm	.13	.25
131	Paul MacLean	.20	.40
132	Maurice Mantha	.13	.25
133	Andrew McBain	.13	.25
134	Brian Mullen	.13	.25
135	Robert Picard	.13	.25
136	Douglas Smail	.13	.25
137	Doug Soetaert, Goalie	.13	.25
138	Thomas Steen	.13	.25
139	Timothy Watters	.13	.25
140	Tim Young	.13	.25

7-ELEVEN

— 1984 - 85 STICKER DISKS —

Disk Size: 2" Diameter
Face: Four colour, coloured border; Alternating photo/team logo, Jersey number, Name, Team logo
Back: Blank
Imprint: None
Complete Set No.: 60
Complete Set Price: 22.50 45.00
Common Player: .50 1.00

BOSTON BRUINS

No.	Player	EX	NRMT
1	Raymond Bourque	1.50	3.00
2	Rick Middleton	.50	1.00

BUFFALO SABRES

No.	Player	EX	NRMT
3	Tom Barrasso, Goalie	2.25	4.50
4	Gilbert Perreault	1.00	2.00

CALGARY FLAMES

No.	Player	EX	NRMT
5	Rejean Lemelin, Goalie	.50	1.00
6	Lanny McDonald	1.00	2.00
7	Paul Reinhart	.50	1.00
8	Doug Risebrough	.50	1.00

CHICAGO BLACK HAWKS

No.	Player	EX	NRMT
9	Denis Savard	1.00	2.00
10	Alan Secord	.50	1.00

DETROIT RED WINGS

No.	Player	EX	NRMT
11	Dave Williams	.50	1.00
12	Steve Yzerman	1.00	2.00

EDMONTON OILERS

No.	Player	EX	NRMT
13	Glenn Anderson	.75	1.50
14	Paul Coffey	1.00	2.00
15	Wayne Gretzky	4.00	8.00
16	Charles Huddy	.50	1.00
17	Pat Hughes	.50	1.00
18	Jari Kurri	1.00	2.00
19	Kevin Lowe	.50	1.00
20	Mark Messier	1.50	3.00

7-Eleven
1984-85 Sticker Disks
Sticker No. 1,
Raymond Bourque

7-Eleven
1984-85 Sticker Disks
Sticker No. 4,
Gilbert Perreault

7-Eleven
1984-85 Sticker Disks
Sticker No. 13,
Glenn Anderson

7-Eleven
1984-85 Sticker Disks
Sticker No. 28,
Bob Gainey

HARTFORD WHALERS

No.	Player	EX	NRMT
21	Ron Francis	.75	1.50
22	Sylvain Turgeon	.50	1.00

LOS ANGELES KINGS

No.	Player	EX	NRMT
23	Marcel Dionne	1.00	2.00
24	David Taylor	.50	1.00

MINNESOTA NORTH STARS

No.	Player	EX	NRMT
25	Brian Bellows	.85	1.75
26	Dino Ciccarelli	.85	1.75
27	Harold Snepsts	.50	1.00

MONTREAL CANADIENS

No.	Player	EX	NRMT
28	Bob Gainey	1.00	2.00
29	Larry Robinson	1.00	2.00

NEW JERSEY DEVILS

No.	Player	EX	NRMT
30	Mel Bridgman	.50	1.00
31	Glenn Resch, Goalie	.50	1.00

NEW YORK ISLANDERS

No.	Player	EX	NRMT
32	Mike Bossy	1.50	3.00
33	Bryan Trottier	1.00	2.00

NEW YORK RANGERS

No.	Player	EX	NRMT
34	Barry Beck	.50	1.00
35	Donald Maloney	.50	1.00

PHILADELPHIA FLYERS

No.	Player	EX	NRMT
36	Tim Kerr	.50	1.00
37	Darryl Sittler	1.50	3.00

PITTSBURGH PENGUINS

No.	Player	EX	NRMT
38	Mike Bullard	.50	1.00
39	Rick Kehoe	.50	1.00

QUEBEC NORDIQUES

No.	Player	EX	NRMT
40	Michel Goulet	1.00	2.00
41	Peter Stastny	1.50	3.00

ST. LOUIS BLUES

No.	Player	EX	NRMT
42	Bernie Federko	.50	1.00
43	Rob Ramage	.50	1.00

TORONTO MAPLE LEAFS

No.	Player	EX	NRMT
44	John Anderson	.50	1.00
45	Bill Derlago	.50	1.00
46	Gary Nylund	.50	1.00
47	Richard Vaive	.75	1.50

VANCOUVER CANUCKS

No.	Player	EX	NRMT
48	Richard Brodeur, Goalie	.50	1.00
49	Gary Lupul	.50	1.00
50	Darcy Rota	.50	1.00
51	Stanley Smyl	.50	1.00
52	Tony Tanti	.50	1.00

WASHINGTON CAPITALS

No.	Player	EX	NRMT
53	Michael Gartner	1.50	3.00
54	Rod Langway	.50	1.00

KRAFT — 1986-87 DRAWINGS

WINNIPEG JETS

No.	Player	EX	NRMT
55	Scott Arniel	.50	1.00
56	David Babych	.50	1.00
57	Laurie Boschman	.50	1.00
58	Dale Hawerchuk	1.00	2.00
59	Paul MacLean	.50	1.00
60	Brian Mullen	.50	1.00

— 1985 - 86 CREDIT CARDS —

Card Size: 2 1/8" X 3 3/8"
Face: Four colour, black border; Name Position, Jersey number
Back: Blue and red on plastic; Team, Numbered _ of 25, Resume, Team and sponsor logos
Imprint: © 1985 Super Star Sports. Printed in Canada.
Complete Set No.: 25

	EX	NRMT
Complete Set Price:	19.00	38.00
Common Player:	.50	1.00

No.	Player	EX	NRMT
1	Raymond Bourque, Bos.; Rick Middleton, Bos.	1.50	3.00
2	Tom Barrasso, Goalie, Buf.; Gilbert Perreault, Buf.	1.25	2.50
3	Paul Reinhart, Cal.; Lanny McDonald, Cal.	.50	1.00
4	Denis Savard, Chi.; Doug Wilson, Chi.	1.00	2.00
5	Ron Duguay, Det.; Steve Yzerman, Det	1.00	2.00
6	Paul Coffey, Edm.; Jari Kurri, Edm.	1.50	3.00
7	Ron Frances, Har.; Mike Liut, Goalie, Har.	.50	1.00
8	Marcel Dionne, LA; Dave Taylor, LA	.50	1.00
9	Brian Bellows, Min.; Dino Ciccarelli, Min.1	.50	3.00
10	Larry Robinson, Mon.; Guy Charbonneau, Mon.	.75	1.50
11	Mel Bridgman, NJ; Chico Resch, Goalie, NJ	.50	1.00
12	Mike Bossy, NYI; Bryan Trottier, NYI	1.00	2.00
13	Reijo Ruotsalainen, NYR; Barry Beck, NYR	.50	1.00
14	Tim Kerr, Phi.; Mark Howe, Phi.	.50	1.00
15	Mario Lemieux, Pit.; Mike Bullard, Pit.	5.00	10.00
16	Peter Stastny, Que.; Michel Goulet, Que.	.50	1.00
17	George (Rob) Ramage, St.L.; Brian Sutter, St.L.	.50	1.00
18	Rick Vaive, Tor.; Borje Salming, Tor.	.75	1.50
19	Patrik Sundstrom, Van.; Stan Smyl, Van.	.50	1.00
20	Rod Langway; Mike Gartner.	1.50	3.00
21	Dale Hawerchuk, Wash.; Paul MacLean, Wash.	.50	1.00
22	Stanley Cup Winners	.50	1.00
23	Prince of Wales; Trophy Winners	.50	1.00
24	Clarence S. Campbell; Bowl Winners	.50	1.00
25	Title Card: Superstar Collectors' Series	.50	1.00

KRAFT

— 1986 - 87 DRAWINGS —

DREAM TEAM COLLECTABLE CARDS

These Dream Team cards were issued in Kraft products and on Kraft packaging during 1986 and 1987. The cards come in two different card stock weights due to the different packaging. This set is unnumbered and is listed alphabetically and then by player within each team. Jerry Hersh drew 42 and Carleton McDiarmid drew 30 of the 81 black and white drawings.

Card Size: 2 1/2" X 3 5/16"
Face: Black and white; Name, Jersey number, Logos
Back: Black and white; Checklist, Offer
Imprint: © KRAFT LIMITED
Complete Set No.: 81

	EX	NRMT
Complete Set Price:	37.50	75.00
Common Player:	.25	.50
Album:	25.00	50.00

CALGARY FLAMES

No.	Player	EX	NRMT
1	Rejean Lemelin, Goalie	.50	1.00
2	Hakan Loob	.50	1.00
3	Lanny McDonald	1.00	2.00
4	Joe Mullen	1.00	2.00
5	James Peplinski	.25	.50
6	Paul Reinhart	.25	.50
7	Doug Risebrough	.25	.50
8	Gary Suter	.25	.50
9	Mike Vernon, Goalie	.75	1.50
10	Carey Wilson	.25	.50

7 - Eleven
1985-86 Credit Cards
Card No. 2,
T. Barrasso / G. Perreault

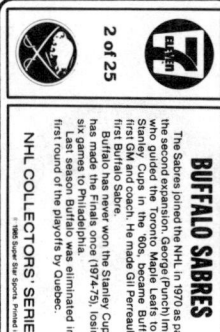

7 - Eleven
1985-86 Credit Cards
Card No. 2,
T. Barrasso / G. Perreault

Kraft
1986-87 Drawings
Card No. 1
Rejean Lemelin

Kraft
1986-87 Drawings
Card No. 1, Rejean Lemelin

EDMONTON OILERS

No.	Player	EX	NRMT
11	Glenn Anderson	.75	1.50
12	Paul Coffey	1.00	2.00
13	Grant Fuhr, Goalie	1.00	2.00
14	Wayne Gretzky	7.50	15.00
15	Michael Krushelnyski	.50	1.00
16	Jari Kurri	1.00	2.00
17	Kevin Lowe	.50	1.00
18	Mark Messier	2.50	5.00
19	Andrew Moog, Goalie	.75	1.50
20	Mark Napier	.50	1.00

MONTREAL CANADIENS

No.	Player	EX	NRMT
21	Guy Carbonneau	.75	1.50
22	Chris Chelios	.75	1.50
23	Kjell Dahlin	.25	.50
24	Bob Gainey	.25	.50
25	Gaston Gingras	.25	.50
26	Richard Green	.25	.50
27	Brian Hayward, Goalie	.25	.50
28	Mike Lalor	.25	.50
29	Claude Lemieux	.25	.50
30	Craig Ludwig	.25	.50
31	Michael McPhee	.25	.50
32	Sergio Momesso	.75	1.50
33	Mats Naslund	.50	1.00
34	Christopher Nilan	.25	.50
35	Stephane J.J. Richer	1.00	2.00
36	Larry Robinson	.75	1.50
37	Patrick Roy, Goalie	6.00	12.00
38	Brian Skrudland	.75	1.50
39	Robert Smith	.50	1.00
40	Petr Svoboda	.75	1.50
41	Ryan Walter	.25	.50

QUEBEC NORDIQUES

No.	Player	EX	NRMT
42	Brent Ashton	.25	.50
43	Alain Cote	.25	.50
44	Mario Gosselin, Goalie	.25	.50
45	Michel Goulet	.75	1.50
46	Dale Hunter	.25	.50
47	Clint Malarchuk, Goalie	.25	.50
48	Randy Moller	.25	.50
49	Pat Price	.25	.50
50	Anton Stastny	.25	.50
51	Peter Stastny	.75	1.50

TORONTO MAPLE LEAFS

No.	Player	EX	NRMT
52	Wendel Clark	1.50	3.00
53	Russ Courtnall	.75	1.50
54	Dan Daoust	.25	.50
55	Tom Fergus	.25	.50
56	Gary Leeman	.25	.50
57	Borje Salming	.50	1.00
58	Greg Terrion	.25	.50
59	Steve Thomas	.25	.50
60	Richard Vaive	.25	.50
61	Ken Wregget, Goalie	.25	.50

VANCOUVER CANUCKS

No.	Player	EX	NRMT
62	Richard Brodeur, Goalie	.25	.50
63	Glen Cochrane	.25	.50
64	Doug Halward	.25	.50
65	Doug Lidster	.25	.50
66	Barry Pederson	.25	.50
67	Brent Peterson	.25	.50
68	Petri Skriko	.25	.50
69	Stanley Smyl, Error	.25	.50
70	Patrik Sundstrom	.25	.50
71	Tony Tanti	.25	.50

WINNIPEG JETS

No.	Player	EX	NRMT
72	Laurie Boschman	.25	.50
73	Randy Carlyle	.35	.75
74	Bill Derlago	.25	.50

1986 - 87 POSTERS — KRAFT • 319

No.	Player	EX	NRMT
75	Dale Hawerchuk	1.50	3.00
76	Paul MacLean	.25	.50
77	Mario Marois	.25	.50
78	Brian Mullen	.25	.50
79	Steve Penney, Goalie	.25	.50
80	Thomas Steen	.25	.50
81	Perry Turnbull	.25	.50

— 1986 - 87 POSTERS —

The posters were a special Kraft offer on the backs of the 1986-87 cards. All 81 players were available in poster format.

Poster Size: 16" X 20"
Face: Charcoal Illustrations
Back: Blank
Imprint: None
Complete Set No.: 81

Complete Set Price:		125.00	250.00
Common Player:		1.50	3.00

CALGARY FLAMES

No.	Player	EX	NRMT
1	Rejean Lemelin, Goalie	1.50	3.00
2	Hakan Loob	1.50	3.00
3	Lanny McDonald	2.50	5.00
4	Joe Mullen	2.50	5.00
5	James Peplinski	1.50	3.00
6	Paul Reinhart	1.50	3.00
7	Doug Risebrough	1.50	3.00
8	Gary Suter	1.50	3.00
9	Mike Vernon, Goalie	2.50	5.00
10	Carey Wilson	1.50	3.00

EDMONTON OILERS

No.	Player	EX	NRMT
11	Glenn Anderson	2.50	5.00
12	Paul Coffey	2.50	5.00
13	Grant Fuhr, Goalie	2.50	5.00
14	Wayne Gretzky	15.00	30.00
15	Michael Krushelnyski	1.50	3.00
16	Jari Kurri	1.50	3.00
17	Kevin Lowe	1.50	3.00
18	Mark Messier	5.00	10.00
19	Andrew Moog, Goalie	2.50	5.00
20	Mark Napier	1.50	3.00

MONTREAL CANADIENS

No.	Player	EX	NRMT
21	Guy Carbonneau	2.50	5.00
22	Chris Chelios	3.50	7.00
23	Kjell Dahlin	1.50	3.00
24	Bob Gainey	1.50	3.00
25	Gaston Gingras	1.50	3.00
26	Richard Green	1.50	3.00
27	Brian Hayward, Goalie	1.50	3.00
28	Mike Lalor	1.50	3.00
29	Claude Lemieux	1.50	3.00
30	Craig Ludwig	1.50	3.00
31	Michael McPhee	1.50	3.00
32	Sergio Momesso	2.50	5.00
33	Mats Naslund	1.50	3.00
34	Christopher Nilan	1.50	3.00
35	Stephane J.J. Richer	2.50	5.00
36	Larry Robinson	3.50	7.00
37	Patrick Roy, Goalie	12.50	25.00
38	Brian Skrudland	2.50	5.00
39	Robert Smith	2.50	5.00
40	Petr Svoboda	2.50	5.00
41	Ryan Walter	1.50	3.00

QUEBEC NORDIQUES

No.	Player	EX	NRMT
42	Brent Ashton	1.50	3.00
43	Alain Cote	1.50	3.00
44	Mario Gosselin, Goalie	1.50	3.00
45	Michel Goulet	3.00	6.00
46	Dale Hunter	1.50	3.00
47	Clint Malarchuk, Goalie	1.50	3.00
48	Randy Moller	1.50	3.00

Kraft
1986-87 Drawings
Card No. 75,
Dale Hawerchuk

Kraft
1990 Issue
Card No. 1,
Douglas Gilmour

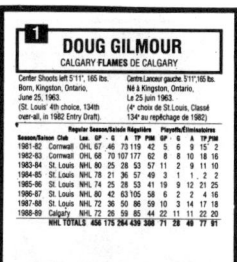

Kraft
1990 Issue
Card No. 1,
Douglas Gilmour

Kraft
1990 Issue
Card No. 2,
Theoren Fleury

No.	Player	EX	NRMT
49	Pat Price	1.50	3.00
50	Anton Stastny	1.50	3.00
51	Peter Stastny	3.00	6.00

TORONTO MAPLE LEAFS

No.	Player	EX	NRMT
52	Wendel Clark	5.00	10.00
53	Russell Courtnall	2.50	5.00
54	Dan Daoust	1.50	3.00
55	Tom Fergus	1.50	3.00
56	Gary Leeman	1.50	3.00
57	Borje Salming	1.50	3.00
58	Greg Terrion	1.50	3.00
59	Steve Thomas	1.50	3.00
60	Richard Vaive	1.50	3.00
61	Ken Wregget, Goalie	1.50	3.00

VANCOUVER CANUCKS

No.	Player	EX	NRMT
62	Richard Brodeur, Goalie	1.50	3.00
63	Glen Cochrane	1.50	3.00
64	Doug Halward	1.50	3.00
65	Doug Lidster	1.50	3.00
66	Barry Pederson	1.50	3.00
67	Brent Peterson	1.50	3.00
68	Petri Skriko	1.50	3.00
69	Stanley Smyl	1.50	3.00
70	Patrik Sundstrom	1.50	3.00
71	Tony Tanti	1.50	3.00

WINNIPEG JETS

No.	Player	EX	NRMT
72	Laurie Boschman	1.50	3.00
73	Randy Carlyle	2.50	5.00
74	Bill Derlago	1.50	3.00
75	Dale Hawerchuk	3.50	7.00
76	Paul MacLean	1.50	3.00
77	Mario Marois	1.50	3.00
78	Brian Mullen	1.50	3.00
79	Steve Penney, Goalie	1.50	3.00
80	Thomas Steen	1.50	3.00
81	Perry Turnbull	1.50	3.00

— 1990 REGULAR ISSUE —

Cards 1 to 51 and 64 were issued on the backs of Kraft Dinner, Rock-O-Rama, Spirals and Egg Noodles. Cards 52 to 63 were issued only in full cases of Kraft Dinner as six panels or two cards. Factory cut cards were also available by mail. The factory set commands a 200% price premium since the box panel cards were difficult to trim uniformly. Also included in the mail offering was a spiral bound album.

Card Size: 2 1/2" X 3 1/2"
Face: Four colour; Name, Jersey number, Logo
Back: Four colour; Number, Name, Resume
Imprint: KRAFT
Complete Set No.: 64

Complete Set Price:		30.00	60.00
Factory Set Price:		45.00	90.00
Common Player:		.13	.25
Album:		17.50	35.00

CALGARY FLAMES

No.	Player	EX	NRMT
1	Douglas Gilmour	1.50	3.00
2	Theoren Fleury	.50	1.00
3	Allan MacInnis	.75	1.50
4	Sergei Makarov	.25	.50
5	Joe Nieuwendyk	.75	1.50
6	Joel Otto	.13	.25
7	Colin Patterson	.13	.25
8	Sergei Priakin	.13	.25
9	Paul Ranheim	.13	.25

EDMONTON OILERS

No.	Player	EX	NRMT
10	Glenn Anderson	.35	.75
11	Grant Fuhr, Goalie	.75	1.50
12	Charles Huddy	.13	.25
13	Jari Kurri	.50	1.00
14	Kevin Lowe	.13	.25
15	Mark Messier	1.75	3.50

320 • KRAFT — 1990 STICKERS —

No.	Player	EX	NRMT
16	Craig Simpson	.13	.25
17	James (Steve) Smith	.25	.50
18	Esa Tikkanen	.25	.50

MONTREAL CANADIENS

No.	Player	EX	NRMT
19	Guy Carbonneau	.35	.75
20	Chris Chelios	.75	1.50
21	Shayne Corson	.13	.25
22	Russell Courtnall	.13	.25
23	Mats Naslund	.13	.25
24	Stephane J.J. Richer	.50	1.00
25	Patrick Roy, Goalie	2.50	5.00
26	Robert Smith	.35	.75
27	Petr Svoboda	.13	.25

QUEBEC NORDIQUES

No.	Player	EX	NRMT
28	Jeff Brown	.13	.25
29	Paul Gillis	.13	.25
30	Michel Goulet	.25	.50
31	Guy Lafleur	.50	1.00
32	Joe Sakic	1.25	2.50
33	Peter Stastny	.25	.50

TORONTO MAPLE LEAFS

No.	Player	EX	NRMT
34	Wendel Clark	.75	1.50
35	Vincent Damphousse	.50	1.00
36	Gary Leeman	.13	.25
37	Daniel Marois	.13	.25
38	Ed Olczyk	.13	.25
39	George (Rob) Ramage	.13	.25

VANCOUVER CANUCKS

No.	Player	EX	NRMT
40	Vladimir Krutov	.13	.25
41	Igor Larionov	.25	.50
42	Trevor Linden	1.00	2.00
43	Kirk McLean, Goalie	1.00	2.00
44	Paul Reinhart	.13	.25
45	Tony Tanti	.13	.25

WINNIPEG JETS

No.	Player	EX	NRMT
46	Brent Ashton	.13	.25
47	Randy Carlyle	.35	.75
48	Randy Cunneyworth	.13	.25
49	Dave Ellett	.13	.25
50	Dale Hawerchuk	.75	1.50
51	Fredrik Olausson	.25	.50

ALL STARS
PRINCE OF WALES CONFERENCE

No.	Player	EX	NRMT
52	Raymond Bourque	1.00	2.00
53	Sean Burke, Goalie	.25	.50
54	Paul Coffey	1.00	2.00
55	Mario Lemieux	4.00	8.00
56	Cam Neely	1.00	2.00
57	Rick Tocchet	.50	1.00

CAMPBELL CONFERENCE

No.	Player	EX	NRMT
58	Steve Duchesne	.50	1.00
59	Wayne Gretzky	4.00	8.00
60	Joey Mullen	.50	1.00
61	Gary Suter	.50	1.00
62	Mike Vernon, Goalie	.75	1.50
63	Steve Yzerman	1.00	2.00

CHECKLIST

No.	Checklist	EX	NRMT
64	Checklist	.50	1.00

Kraft
1990-91 Issue
Card No. 4,
Sean Burke

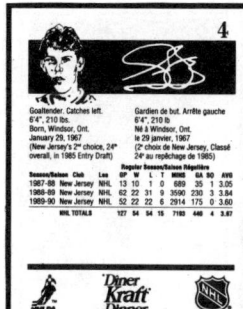

Kraft
1990-91 Issue
Card No. 4,
Sean Burke

Kraft
1990-91 Issue
Card No. 45,
Bill Ranford

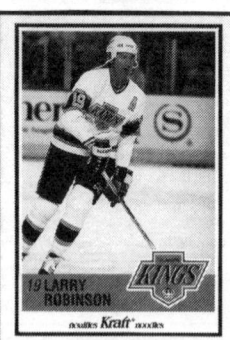

Kraft
1990-91 Issue
Card No. 47,
Larry Robinson

— 1990 STICKERS —

These stickers were issued in Kraft Cheese Slices and were designed to complement the Album issued for the regular cards of 1990. Panels of six stickers each, 2 players and 4 team logos were issued. The panels are numbered _ of 6.

Panel Size: 4 1/2" X 2 3/4"
Face: Four colour; Name, Numbered _ of 6
Back: Black on white paper stock; Premium offer
Imprint: KRAFT
Complete Set No.: 6 Panels / 36 Stickers
Complete Set Price: 6.00   12.00
Common Player: .25   .50

No.	Player	EX	NRMT
1	Paul Reinhart, Cal.; Mike McPhee; Montreal; Washington; Toronto; Vancouver	.25	.50
2	Wayne Gretzky, LA; Rick Tocchet; Los Angeles; Minnesota; Philadelphia; Quebec	2.50	5.00
3	Paul Coffey; Steve Yzerman; Detroit; Hartford; Rangers; Prince of Wales Conference	1.00	2.00
4	Mike Vernon, Goalie; Raymond Bourque; Clagary; St. Louis; Islanders; Boston	1.00	2.00
5	Jari Kurri, Edm.; Mario Lemieux; Pittsburgh; Buffalo; Winnipeg; NHL	2.50	5.00
6	Kevin Lowe, Edm.; Sean Burke, Goalie; Edmonton; Chicago; New Jersey; Clarence Campbell Conference	.25	.50

— 1990 - 91 REGULAR ISSUE —

Kraft issued cards for the 1990-91 season in much the same manner as the 1990 issues. The list below domiciles the cards to the different Kraft products:

Card Nos. 1 to 64: Red backs on box stock; Issued on Kraft Dinner, Spirals and Noodles boxes.
Card Nos. 65 to 91: Red backs on box stock; Issued on Jell-O boxes.
Card Nos. 92 to 112 Blue backs on box stock; Issued in Kraft Cheese Singles packages.

No stickers were issued in 1990-91. Again factory trimmed cards were available. These will command a price premium of twice the box cut cards.

Card Size: 2 1/2" X 3 1/2"
Face: Four colour; Name, Logo
Back: Number, Facsimile autograph, Resume, Bilingual
Imprint: KRAFT
Complete Set No.: 112
Complete Set Price: 37.50   75.00
Factory Set Price: 75.00   150.00
Common Player: .25   .50
Album: 17.50   35.00

No.	Player	EX	NRMT
1	David Babych, Har.	.25	.50
2	Brian Bellows, Min.	.75	1.50
3	Raymond Bourque, Bos.	1.00	2.00
4	Sean Burke, Goalie, NJ	.25	.50
5	Jimmy Carson, Det.	.25	.50
6	Chris Chelios, Chi.	.75	1.50
7	Dino Ciccarelli, Wash.	.50	1.00
8	Paul Coffey, Pit.	.75	1.50
9	Geoff Courtnall, St.L.	.50	1.00
10	Doug Crossman, NYI	.25	.50
11	Kevin Dineen, Har.	.25	.50
12	Pat Elynuik, Win.	.25	.50
13	Ron Francis, Har.	.25	.50
14	Gerard Gallant, Det.	.25	.50
15	Wayne Gretzky, LA	3.00	6.00
16	Dale Hawerchuk, Buf.	.75	1.50
17	Ron Hextall, Goalie, Phi.	.50	1.00
18	Phil Housley, Win.	.50	1.00
19	Mark Howe, Phi.	.50	1.00
20	Brett Hull, St.L.	1.50	3.00
21	Al Iafrate, Tor.	.50	1.00
22	Guy Lafleur, Que.	.50	1.00
23	Pat LaFontaine, NYI	1.50	3.00
24	Rod Langway, Wash.	.25	.50
25	Igor Larionov, Van.	.25	.50
26	Steve Larmer, Chi.	.35	.75
27	Gary Leeman, Tor.	.25	.50
28	Brian Leetch, NYR	1.00	2.00
29	Mario Lemieux, Pit.	3.00	6.00
30	Trevor Linden, Van.	1.00	2.00
31	Mike Liut, Goalie, Wash.	.25	.50
32	Mark Messier, Edm.	1.50	3.00
33	Al MacInnis, Cal.	.35	.75
34	Michael Modano, Min.	.75	1.50

No.	Player	EX	NRMT
35	Andrew Moog, Goalie, Bos.	.25	.50
36	Joe Mullen, Pit.	.25	.50
37	Kirk Muller, NJ	.25	.50
38	Petr Nedved, Van.	.50	1.00
39	Cam Neely, Bos.	.50	1.00
40	Bernie Nicholls, NYR	.25	.50
41	Joe Nieuwendyk, Cal.	.50	1.00
42	Mats Sundin, Que.	1.00	2.00
43	Daren Puppa, Goalie, Buf.	.25	.50
44	George (Rob) Ramage, Tor.	.25	.50
45	Bill Ranford, Goalie, Edm.	.35	.75
46	Stephane J.J Richer, Mon.	.25	.50
47	Larry Robinson, LA	.35	.75
48	Luc Robitaille, LA	.50	1.00
49	Patrick Roy, Goalie, Mon.	2.50	5.00
50	Joe Sakic, Que.	1.50	3.00
51	Denis Savard, Mon.	.50	1.00
52	Craig Simpson, Edm.	.25	.50
53	Robert Smith, Min.	.35	.75
54	Peter Stastny, NJ	.25	.50
55	Thomas Steen, Win.	.25	.50
56	Scott Stevens, St.L.	.35	.75
57	Brent Sutter, NYI	.25	.50
58	Rick Tocchet, Phi.	.35	.75
59	Pierre Turgeon, Buf.	1.00	2.00
60	John Vanbriesbrouck, Goalie, NYR	.75	1.50
61	Mike Vernon, Goalie, Cal.	.25	.50
62	Douglas Wilson, Chi.	.25	.50
63	Steve Yzerman, Det.	.75	1.50
64	Checklist	.25	.50

PRINCE OF WALES CONFERENCE

No.	Player	EX	NRMT
65	Steve Duchesne, LA	.35	.75
66	Brett Hull, St.L.	.75	1.50
67	Wayne Gretzky, LA	2.00	4.00
68	Jari Kurri, Edm.	.35	.75
69	Michael Gartner, NYR	.50	1.00
70	Kirk McLean, Goalie, Van.	.35	.75
71	Mark Messier, Edm.	1.00	2.00
72	Joe Mullen, Pit.	.25	.50
73	Bernie Nicholls, NYR	.25	.50
74	Joe Nieuwendyk, Cal.	.25	.50
75	Luc Robitaille, LA	.50	1.00
76	Mike Vernon, Goalie, Cal.	.25	.50
77	Douglas Wilson, Chi.	.25	.50
78	Steve Yzerman, Det.	.75	1.50

PRINCE OF WALES CONFERENCE

No.	Player	EX	NRMT
79	Joe Sakic, Que.	.75	1.50
80	Raymond Bourque, Bos.	.50	1.00
81	Chris Chelios, Chi.	.50	1.00
82	Paul Coffey, Pit.	.75	1.50
83	Ron Francis, Har.	.25	.50
84	Cam Neely, Bos.	.50	1.00
85	Phil Housley, Win.	.35	.75
86	Pat LaFontaine, NYI	1.25	2.50
87	Mario Lemieux, Pit.	2.00	4.00
88	Kirk Muller, NJ	.25	.50
89	Stephane J.J. Richer, Mon.	.25	.50
90	Patrick Roy, Goalie, Mon.	2.00	4.00
91	Pierre Turgeon, Buf.	.75	1.50

TEAM PICTURES

No.	Player	EX	NRMT
92	Boston Bruins	.25	.50
93	Buffalo Sabres	.25	.50
94	Calgary Flames	.25	.50
95	Chicago Blackhawks	.25	.50
96	Detroit Red Wings	.25	.50
97	Edmonton Oilers	.25	.50
98	Hartford Whalers	.25	.50
99	Los Angeles Kings	.25	.50
100	Minnesota North Stars	.25	.50
101	Montreal Canadiens	.25	.50
102	New Jersey Devils	.25	.50
103	New York Islanders	.25	.50
104	New York Rangers	.25	.50
105	Philadelphia Flyers	.25	.50
106	Pittsburgh Penguins	.25	.50
107	Quebec Nordiques	.25	.50

Kraft
1991-92 Special Edition
Card No. 1,
Mario Lemieux

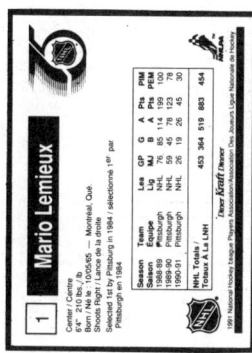

Kraft
1991-92 Special Edition
Card No. 1,
Mario Lemieux

Kraft
1991-92 Special Edition
Card No. 8,
Pat Falloon

No.	Player	EX	NRMT
108	St. Louis Blues	.25	.50
109	Toronto Maple Leafs	.25	.50
110	Vancouver Canucks	.25	.50
111	Washington Capitals	.25	.50
112	Winnipeg Jets	.25	.50
113	Chris Nilan, Bos. SP	7.50	15.00
114	Mike Hartman, Buf. SP	7.50	15.00

— 1991 - 92 SPECIAL EDITION —

75TH ANNIVERSARY OF THE NHL

As in previous years, Kraft issued a series of cards as premiums with their products. However, included in the 1991-92 set was the first issue of cards in disk format. The 24 disks were inserted under the lids of Kraft Peanut Butter jars.

Cards: 1 to 20; 20 to 40 and 64:
  Red backs; Issued on Kraft Dinner packages.
Cards: 41 to 56:
  Red backs; Issued on Kraft Spirals packages.
Cards: 21 and 57 to 63:
  Red backs; Issued on Kraft Noodles packages.
Disks: 67 to 88:
  Yellow backs; Issued in Kraft Peanut Butter.
Subset: Unnumbered:
  Maroon backs; Issued in the "Special Edition" album.

Factory-cut cards were available and command a 200% price premium over the cards cut from boxes. Three "Original Six" and one "Stanley Cup" unnumbered cards were issued with an album to hold the complete set.

Card Size: 2 1/2" X 3 1/2"
Face: Four colour; Name, Team, Logos, Bilingual
Back: Red on box stock; Number, Name, Resume, Logos, Bilingual
Imprint: KRAFT
Disk Size: 2 3/4" Diameter
Face: Four colour; Name, Team, Logos, Bilingual
Back: Black on yellow stock; Name, Number, Resume, Logos, Bilingual
Imprint: KRAFT
Complete Set No.: 92

Complete Set Price:	17.50	35.00
Factory Set Price:	35.00	70.00
Common Player:	.10	.20
Album:	12.50	25.00

No.	Player	EX	NRMT
1	Mario Lemieux, Pit.	1.50	3.00
2	Mark Recchi, Pit.	.50	1.00
3	Jaromir Jagr, Pit.	.50	1.00
4	Mats Sundin, Que.	.50	1.00
5	Adam Oates, St. L.	.35	.75
6	**Great Moments:** Rocket Richard; Jacques Plante, Goalie; Canadien Dynasty	.10	.20
7	Brendan Shanahan, St. L.	.10	.20
8	Pat Falloon, SJ	.25	.50
9	Grant Fuhr, Goalie, Tor.	.50	1.00
10	Gary Leeman, Tor.	.10	.20
11	Petr Nedved, Van.	.35	.75
12	Kirk Muller, Mon.	.50	1.00
13	Theoren Fleury, Cal.	.35	.75
14	Dino Ciccarelli, Wash.	.25	.50
15	Geoff Courtnall, Van.	.25	.50
16	Mark Messier, NYR	1.00	2.00
17	Ken Hodge, Jr., Bos.	.10	.20
18	Chris Chelios, Chi.	.50	1.00
19	Mike Vernon, Goalie, Cal.	.20	.40
20	Kevin Hatcher, Wash.	.25	.50
21	Stephane J.J. Richer, NJD	.10	.20
22	Mark Tinordi, Min.	.10	.20
23	Patrick Verbeek, Har.	.10	.20
24	John Cullen, Har.	.10	.20
25	Pat LaFontaine, Buf.	1.00	2.00
26	Stephan Lebeau, Mon.	.25	.50
27	Michael Gartner, NYR	.50	1.00
28	**Great Moments:** Bobby Baun, Last Leaf Dynasty	.10	.20
29	Shayne Corson, Mon.	.10	.20
30	Trevor Linden, Van.	.50	1.00
31	Craig Janney, Bos.	.25	.50
32	Al MacInnis, Cal.	.10	.20
33	Phil Housley, Win.	.20	.40
34	Douglas Wilson, SJ	.10	.20
35	Tony Granato, LA	.10	.20
36	Dale Hawerchuk, Buf.	.35	.75
37	**Great Moments:** Bill Durnan; Turk Broda, Goaltending Greats	.10	.20

322 • KRAFT — 1993 REGULAR ISSUE —

No.	Player	EX	NRMT
38	Brian Bellows, Min.	.35	.75
39	**Great Moments:** Bob Gainey, Number 23 with number 23	.10	.20
40	**Great Moments:** Darryl Sittler, A Night to Remember	.25	.50
41	Joe Sakic, Que.	.50	1.00
42	Wendel Clark, Tor.	.50	1.00
43	Brent Sutter, Chi.	.10	.20
44	Bill Ranford, Goalie, Edm.	.35	.75
45	Rick Tocchet, Phi.	.25	.50
46	Paul Ysebaert, Det.	.10	.20
47	Adam Creighton, NYI	.10	.20
48	Michael Modano, Min.	.35	.75
49	Russ Courtnall, Mon.	.10	.20
50	**Great Moments:** Syl Apps, Evolution of Stanley Cup	.10	.20
51	Sergei Fedorov, Det.	1.00	2.00
52	Mike Ricci, Phi.	.50	1.00
53	Scott Stevens, NJD	.35	.75
54	**Great Moments:** Bobby Clarke, The Ultimate Expansion	.10	.20
55	Owen Nolan, Que.	.50	1.00
56	Jeremy Roenick, Chi.	1.00	2.00
57	Raymond Bourque, Bos.	.50	1.00
58	Gerard Gallant, Det.	.10	.20
59	Andrew Moog, Goalie, Bos.	.10	.20
60	Alexander Mogilny, Buf.	.75	1.50
61	**Great Moments:** Denis Potvin, Islander Tradition	.10	.20
62	Ed Olczyk, Win.	.10	.20
63	Tomas Sandstrom	.20	.40
64	Checklist 1 (1-56)	.10	.20

1991 KRAFT DISKS

No.	Player	EX	NRMT
65	Wayne Gretzky, LA; Maurice Richard, Mon.	2.50	5.00
66	Brett Hull, St. L.; Guy Lafleur, Mon.	.50	1.00
67	Jari Kurri, LA; Bobby Clarke, Phi.	.35	.75
68	Steve Yzerman, Det.; Jean Beliveau, Mon.	1.00	2.00
69	Steve Larmer, Chi.; Pat Stapleton, Chi.	.35	.75
70	Luc Robitaille, LA; Ted Lindsay, Det.	.50	1.00
71	Larry Murphy, Phi.; Doug Harvey, Mon.	.50	1.00
72	Denis Potvin, NYI; Gary Suter, Cal.	.35	.75
73	Brian Leetch, NYR; Harry Howell, NYR	.75	1.50
74	Paul Coffey, Pit.; Bill Gadsby, Det.	.75	1.50
75	Jon Casey, Goalie, Min.; Terry Sawchuk, Goalie, Det.	.50	1.00
76	Patrick Roy, Goalie, Mon.; Jacques Plante, Goalie, Mon.	2.00	4.00
77	Denis Savard, Mon.; Serge Savard, Mon.	.50	1.00
78	Doug IasGilmour, Cal.; Bob Baun, Tor.	1.00	2.00
79	Guy Carbonneau, Mon.; Yvan Cournoyer, Mon.	.50	1.00
80	Gilbert Perreault, Buf.; Larry Robinson, LA	.35	.75
81	Red Kelly, Tor.; Craig Simpson, Edm.	.35	.75
82	Bobby Smith, Min.; Rod Gilbert, NYR	.75	1.50
83	Syl Apps, Tor.; Peter Stastny, NJD	.35	.75
84	Bernie Geoffrion, Mon.; Vince Damphousse, Edm.	.75	1.50
85	Marcel Dionne, LA; Steve Smith, Chi.	.35	.75
86	Tim Horton, Tor.; Kevin Dineen, Har.	.50	1.00
87	Michel Goulet, Chi.; Frank Mahovlich, Tor.	.50	1.00
88	Mike Richter, NYR; Henri Richard, Mon.	.50	1.00

ORIGINAL SIX TEAM LOGOS

No.	Player	EX	NRMT
—	Montreal Canadiens; Toronto Maple Leafs	.10	.20
—	Chicago Blackhawks; Detroit Red Wings	.10	.20
—	Boston Bruins; New York Rangers	.10	.20

STANLEY CUP

No.	Player	EX	NRMT
—	Stanley Cup	.10	.20

Note: *The Charlton Standard Catalogue of Hockey Cards* arranges cards in their issue date order. This means the first date a manufacturer issues a card set determines the sequence of the manufacturer in the Standard Catalogue. In this manner the historical importance of early cards is maintained. See the last page of this catalogue for an alphabetical index of issuers.

Kraft
1991-92 Special Edition
Disk No. 65,
W. Gretzky / M. Richard

Kraft
1993 Issue
Card No. 25,
Boston Bruins

Kraft
1993 Issue
Card No. 29,
Detroit Red Wings

— 1993 REGULAR ISSUE —

This 48-card set could be obtained through either the purchase of various Kraft products or by mail order from Kraft Foods Products in Woodbridge, Ontario.

Card Size: 3 1/2" x 5 1/4" (Dinner)
Disk Size: 2 1/2" Diameter (Peanut Butter)
Card Size: 1 3/4" x 2 1/2" (Cheese)
Card Nos.: 1 to 12   Issued in Kraft Peanut Butter
Card Nos.: 13 to 24   Issued in Kraft Singles
Card Nos.: 25 to 48   Red backs on box stock; issued on Kraft Dinner boxes
Imprint: © 1992 NATIONAL HOCKEY LEAGUE/LIGUE NATIONALE DE HOCKEY 1992. TM / © 1992 NATIONAL HOCKEY LEAGUE PLAYERS ASSOCIATION / ASSOCIATION DES JOUEURS LIGUE NATIONALE DE HOCKEY 1992
Complete Set No.: 48
Complete Set Price: 12.50   25.00
Common Goalie: .12   .25
Common Player: .12   .25

GOALIES

No.	Player	EX	NRMT
1	Andrew Moog, Bos.; Mark Fitzpatrick, NYI	.12	.25
2	Dominik Hasek, Buf.; Chris Terreri, NJ	.75	1.50
3	Mike Vernon, Cal.; Ed. Belfour, Chi.	.50	1.00
4	Tim Cheveldae, Det.; Sean Burke, Har.	.35	.75
5	Bill Ranford, Edm.; Kelly Hrudey, LA	.35	.75
6	Jon Casey, Min.; Dominic Roussel, Phi.	.12	.25
7	Patrick Roy, Mon.; John Vanbiesbrouk, NYR	1.50	3.00
8	Peter Sidorkiewicz, Ott.; Grant Fuhr, Tor.	.12	.25
9	Tom Barrasso, Pit.; Wendel Young, TB	.75	1.50
10	Ron Hextall, Que.; Curtis Joseph, St. L	.50	1.00
11	Jeff Hackett, SJ; Kirk McLean, Van.	.35	.75
12	Donald Beaupre, Wash.; Bob Essensa, Win.	.12	.25

CAMPBELL CONFERENCE

No.	Player	EX	NRMT
13	Chris Chelios, Chi.	.25	.50
14	Wayne Gretzky, LA	1.50	3.00
15	Brett Hull, St.L	.35	.75
16	Trevor Linden, Van.	.35	.75
17	Jeremy Roenick, Chi.	.50	1.00
18	Steve Yzerman, Det.	.35	.75

WALES CONFERENCE

No.	Player	EX	NRMT
19	Raymond Bourque, Bos.	.50	1.00
20	Paul Coffey, LA	.35	.75
21	Jaromir Jagr, Pit.	.50	1.00
22	Mario Lemieux, Pit.	1.00	2.00
23	Mark Messier, NYR	.50	1.00
24	Patrick Roy, Goalie, Mon.	1.00	2.00

TEAM PHOTOGRAPHS

No.	Player	EX	NRMT
25	Boston Bruins, 1924-1993	.20	.40
26	Buffalo Sabres, 1970-1993	.20	.40
27	Calgary Flames	.20	.40
28	Chicago Black Hawks, 1926-1993	.20	.40
29	Detroit Red Wings, 1926-1993	.20	.40
30	Edmonton Oilers	.20	.40
31	Hartford Whalers	.20	.40
32	Los Angeles Kings, 1967-1993	.20	.40
33	Minnesota North Stars, 1967-1993	.20	.40
34	Montreal Canadiens, 1917-1993	.20	.40
35	New Jersey Devils	.20	.40
36	New York Islander	.20	.40
37	New York Rangers, 1926-1993	.20	.40
38	Ottawa Senators, 1992-1993	.20	.40
39	Philadelphia Flyers	.20	.40
40	Pittsburgh Penguins	.20	.40
41	Quebec Nordiques, 1979-1993	.20	.40
42	St. Louis Blues	.20	.40
43	San Jose Sharks	.20	.40
44	Tampa Bay Lightning	.20	.40
45	Toronto Maple Leafs	.20	.40
46	Vancouver Canucks, 1970-1993	.20	.40
47	Washington Capitals	.20	.40
48	Winnipeg Jets	.20	.40

— 1994 REGULAR ISSUE —

This 68-card set could be obtained through either the purchase of various Kraft products or by mail order from Kraft Foods Products in Woodbridge, Ontario.

Card Size: 3 1/2" x 5 1/4"
Disk Size: 2 1/2" Diameter
Standups Size: 2 1/2" x 2 3/4"
Card Nos.: 1 to 23   Issued in Kraft Dinner boxes
Card Nos.: 30 to 52:   Issued in Kraft Peanut Butter
Card Nos.: 53 to 68   Issued in Kraft Jello Boxes
Imprint: © 1993 NATIONAL HOCKEY LEAGUE/LIGUE NATIONALE DE HOCKEY 1993. TM / © 1993 NATIONAL HOCKEY LEAGUE PLAYERS ASSOCIATION / ASSOCIATION DES JOUEURS LIGUE NATIONALE DE HOCKEY 1993
Complete Set No.: 68
Complete Set Price: 70.00   140.00
Common Card: .25   .50
Album: 50.00

No.	Player	EX	NRMT
1	Ed Belfour, Goalie, Chi.	1.25	2.50
2	Brian Bradley, TB	.25	.50
3	Pavel Bure, Van.	1.75	3.50
4	Paul Coffey, Det.	.25	.50
5	Alexandre Daigle, Ott.	.50	1.00
6	Pat Falloon, SJ	.25	.50
7	Theoren Fleury, Cal.	.25	.50
8	Douglas Gilmour, Tor.	1.00	2.00
9	Adam Graves, NYR	.50	1.00
10	Stu Grimson, MDA	.25	.50
11	Al Iafrate, Wash.	.25	.50
12	Jaromir Jagr, Pit.	1.00	2.00
13	Joseph Juneau, Bos.	.50	1.00
14	Eric Lindros, Phi.	1.50	3.00
15	Kirk Muller, Mon.	.25	.50
16	Bill Ranford, Goalie, Edm.	.25	.50
17	Mike Ricci, Que.	.25	.50
18	Luc Robitaille, LA	.50	1.00
19	Geoff Sanderson, Har.	.35	.75
20	Teemu Selanne, Win.	1.25	2.50
21	Pierre Turgeon, NYI	.50	1.00
22	John Vanbiesbrouck, Goalie, Fl.	.50	1.00
23	Valeri Zelepukin, NJ	.25	.50

GOLD EDITION

No.	Player	EX	NRMT
24	Jason Arnott, Edm.	1.50	3.00
25	Chris Chelios, Chi.	.25	.50
26	Mario Lemieux, Pit.	1.50	3.00
27	Rob Niedermayer, Fl.	.50	1.00
28	Chris Pronger, Har.	.50	1.00
29	Patrick Roy, Goalie, Mon.	1.50	3.00

Kraft
1994 Issue
Card No. 21,
Pierre Turgeon

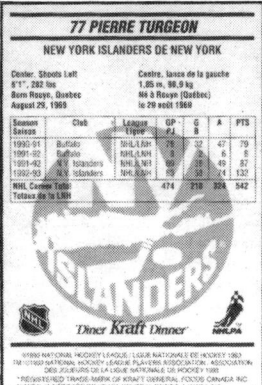

Kraft
1994 Issue
Card No. 21,
Pierre Turgeon

DISKS - CAPTAINS / COACHES

No.	Player	EX	NRMT
30	Al Arbour, Coach, NYI	.25	.50
31	Bob Berry, Coach, St.L	.25	.50
32	Raymond Bourque, Bos. / Patrick Flatley, NYI	1.00	2.00
33	Scott Bowman, Coach, Det.	.35	.75
34	Pat Burns, Coach, Tor.	.35	.75
35	Guy Carbonneau, Mon. / Jeremy Roenick, Chi.	1.00	2.00
36	Jacques Demers, Coach, Mon.	.25	.50
37	Kevin Dineen, Phi. / Kevin Hatcher, Wash.	.25	.50
38	Wayne Gretzky, LA / Wendel Clark, Tor.	2.50	5.00
39	Brett Hull, St.L / Brad Shaw, Ott.	1.00	2.00
40	Eddie Johnston, Coach, Pit.	.50	1.00
41	Dean Kennedy, Win. / Denis Savard, TB	.50	1.00
42	Dave King, Coach, Cal.	.25	.50
43	Pat LaFontaine, Buf. / Pat Verbeek, Har.	.75	1.50
44	Mike Lalor, SJ / Mark Tinordi, Dal.	.25	.50
45	Mario Lemieux, Pit. / Mark Messier, NYR	2.00	4.00
46	Trevor Linden, Van. / Troy Loney, MDA	.75	1.50
47	Craig MacTavish, Edm. / Brian Skrudland, Fl.	.25	.50
48	Barry Melrose, Coach, LA	.25	.50
49	John Muckler, Coach, Buf.	.25	.50
50	Joe Nieuwendyk, Cal. / Joe Sakic, Mon.	.75	1.50
51	Pierre Page, Coach, Que.	.25	.50
52	Scott Stevens, NJ / Steve Yzerman, Det.	1.00	2.00

STAND UPS

No.	Player	EX	NRMT
53	Tom Barrasso, Goalie, Pit.	.35	.75
54	Pavel Bure, Van.	1.50	3.00
55	Stephane Fiset, Goalie, Que.	.50	1.00
56	Douglas Gilmour, Toronto	1.00	2.00
57	Wayne Gretzky, LA	1.50	3.00
58	Kelly Hrudey, Goalie, LA	.25	.50
59	Mario Lemieux, Pit.	1.50	3.00
60	Eric Lindros, Phi.	1.50	3.00
61	Kirk McLean, Goalie, Van.	.50	1.00
62	Kirk Muller, Mon.	.25	.50
63	Joe Nieuwendyk, Cal.	.25	.50
64	Felix Potvin, Goalie, Tor.	1.50	3.00
65	Dominic Roussel, Goalie, Phi.	.25	.50
66	Patrick Roy, Goalie, Pit.	1.50	3.00
67	Joe Sakic, Que.	.75	1.50
68	Michael Vernon, Goalie, Cal.	.25	.50

Kraft 1994 Regular Issue
Standup No. 64, Felix Potvin

Kraft 1994 Regular Issue
Disk No. 52, Steve Yzerman

Kraft 1994 Regular Issue
Disk No. 52, Scott Stevens

PANINI

— 1987 - 88 STICKERS —

1987-88 Panini Stickers
Sticker No. 96, Bryan Trottier

Sticker Size: 2 1/8" X 2 11/6"
Face: Four colour; name, Team, Logo
Back: Black and white; Name, Number, Resume
Imprint: MADE IN ITALY BY PANINI SA MODENA 1987
Complete Set No.: 396

	EX	NRMT
Complete Set Price:	10.00	20.00
Common Player:	.03	.05
Album:	2.50	5.00

STANLEY CUP

No.	Player	EX	NRMT
1	Stanley Cup	.03	.05

BOSTON BRUINS

No.	Player	EX	NRMT
2	Boston Bruins "Action Player"	.03	.05
3	Boston Bruins Team Logo	.03	.05
4	Doug Keans, Goalie	.03	.05
5	Bill Ranford, Goalie	.05	.10
6	Raymond Bourque	.25	.50
7	Reed Larson	.03	.05
8	Mike Milbury	.03	.05
9	Michael Thelven	.03	.05
10	Cam Neely	.25	.50
11	Charlie Simmer	.03	.05
12	Rick Middleton	.03	.05
13	Tom McCarthy	.03	.05
14	Keith Crowder	.03	.05
15	Stephen Kasper	.03	.05
16	Ken Linseman	.03	.05
17	Dwight Foster	.03	.05
18	Jay Miller	.03	.05

BUFFALO SABRES

No.	Player	EX	NRMT
19	Buffalo Sabres "Action Player"	.03	.05
20	Buffalo Sabres Team Logo	.03	.05
21	Jacques Cloutier, Goalie	.03	.05
22	Tom Barrasso, Goalie	.10	.20
23	Daren Puppa, Goalie	.05	.10
24	Phil Housley	.03	.05
25	Michael Ramsey	.03	.05
26	Bill Hajt	.03	.05
27	David Andreychuk	.15	.30
28	Christian Ruuttu	.03	.05
29	Mike Foligno	.03	.05
30	John Tucker	.03	.05
31	Adam Creighton	.03	.05
32	Wilf Paiement	.03	.05
33	Paul Cyr	.03	.05
34	Clark Gillies	.03	.05
35	Lindy Ruff	.03	.05

HARTFORD WHALERS

No.	Player	EX	NRMT
36	Hartford Whalers "Action Player"	.03	.05
37	Hartford Whalers Team Logo	.03	.05
38	Mike Liut, Goalie	.03	.05
39	Stephen Weeks, Goalie	.03	.05
40	David Babych	.03	.05
41	Ulf Samuelsson	.03	.05
42	Dana Murzyn	.03	.05
43	Ronald Francis	.12	.25
44	Kevin Dineen	.05	.10
45	John Anderson	.03	.05
46	Ray Ferraro	.03	.05
47	Dean Evason	.03	.05
48	Paul Lawless	.03	.05
49	Robert (Stewart) Gavin	.03	.05
50	Sylvain Turgeon	.03	.05
51	Dave Tippett	.03	.05
52	Doug Jarvis	.03	.05

MONTREAL CANADIENS

No.	Player	EX	NRMT
53	Montreal Canadiens "Action Player"	.03	.05
54	Montreal Canadiens Team Logo	.03	.05
55	Brian Hayward, Goalie	.03	.05
56	Patrick Roy, Goalie	1.50	3.00
57	Larry Robinson	.07	.15
58	Chris Chelios	.05	.10
59	Craig Ludwig	.03	.05
60	Ricchard Green	.03	.05
61	Mats Naslund	.03	.05
62	Robert Smith	.03	.05
63	Claude Lemieux	.05	.10
64	Guy Carbonneau	.05	.10
65	Stephane J.J. Richer	.05	.10
66	Michael McPhee	.03	.05
67	Brian Skrudland	.03	.05
68	Christopher Nilan	.03	.05
69	Bob Gainey	.03	.05

NEW JERSEY DEVILS

No.	Player	EX	NRMT
70	New Jersey Devils "Action Player"	.03	.05
71	New Jersey Devils Team Logo	.03	.05
72	Craig Billington, Goalie	.03	.05
73	Alain Chevrier, Goalie	.03	.05
74	Bruce Driver	.03	.05
75	Joe Cirella	.03	.05
76	Ken Daneyko	.03	.05
77	Craig Wolanin	.03	.05
78	Aaron Broten	.03	.05
79	Kirk Muller	.12	.25
80	John MacLean	.07	.15
81	Patrick Verbeek	.05	.10
82	Douglas Sulliman	.03	.05
83	Mark Johnson	.03	.05
84	Greg Adams	.03	.05
85	Claude Loiselle	.03	.05
86	Andy Brickley	.03	.05

NEW YORK ISLANDERS

No.	Player	EX	NRMT
87	New York Islanders "Action Player"	.03	.05
88	New York Islanders Team Logo	.03	.05
89	Billy Smith, Goalie	.03	.05
90	Kelly Hrudey, Goalie	.05	.10
91	Denis Potvin	.07	.15
92	Tomas Jonsson	.03	.05
93	Ken Leiter	.03	.05
94	Ken Morrow	.03	.05
95	Brian Curran	.03	.05
96	Bryan Trottier	.07	.15
97	Mike Bossy	.10	.20
98	Pat LaFontaine	.50	1.00
99	Brent Sutter	.03	.05
100	Mikko Makela	.03	.05
101	Patrick Flatley	.03	.05
102	Duane Sutter	.03	.05
103	Richard Kromm	.03	.05

NEW YORK RANGERS

No.	Player	EX	NRMT
104	New York Rangers "Action Player"	.03	.05
105	New York Rangers Team Logo	.03	.05
106	John Vanbiesbrouck, Goalie	.25	.50
107	James Patrick	.03	.05
108	Ronald Greschner	.03	.05
109	Willie Huber	.03	.05
110	Curt Giles	.03	.05
111	Larry Melnyk	.03	.05
112	Walter Poddubny	.03	.05
113	Marcel Dionne	.05	.10
114	Tomas Sandstrom	.03	.05
115	Kelly Kisio	.03	.05
116	Pierre Larouche	.03	.05
117	Donald Maloney	.03	.05
118	Anthony McKegney	.03	.05
119	Ron Duguay	.03	.05
120	Jan Erixon	.03	.05

PHILADELPHIA FLYERS

No.	Player	EX	NRMT
121	Philadelphia Flyers "Action Player"	.03	.05
122	Philadelphia Flyers Team Logo	.03	.05
123	Ron Hextall, Goalie	.13	.25
124	Mark Howe	.03	.05
125	Doug Crossman	.03	.05
126	Byron (Brad) McCrimmon	.03	.05
127	Bradley Marsh	.03	.05
128	Tim Kerr	.03	.05
129	Peter Zezel	.03	.05
130	David Poulin	.03	.05
131	Brian Propp	.03	.05
132	Per-Erik Eklund	.03	.05
133	Murray Craven	.03	.05
134	Rick Tocchet	.15	.30
135	Derrick Smith	.03	.05
136	Ilkka Sinisalo	.03	.05
137	Ronald Sutter	.03	.05

PITTSBURGH PENGUINS

No.	Player	EX	NRMT
138	Pittsburgh Penguins "Action Player"	.03	.05
139	Pittsburgh Penguins Team Logo	.03	.05
140	Gilles Meloche, Goalie	.03	.05
141	Doug Bodger	.03	.05
142	Maurice Mantha	.03	.05
143	Jim Johnson	.03	.05
144	Rod Buskas	.03	.05
145	Randy Hillier	.03	.05
146	Mario Lemieux	.75	1.50
147	Dan Quinn	.03	.05
148	Randy Cunneyworth	.03	.05
149	Craig Simpson	.15	.30
150	Terry Ruskowski	.03	.05
151	John Chabot	.03	.05
152	Bob Errey	.05	.10
153	Dan Frawley	.03	.05
154	David Hannan	.03	.05

QUEBEC NORDIQUES

No.	Player	EX	NRMT
155	Quebec Nordiques "Action Player"	.03	.05
156	Quebec Nordiques Team Logo	.03	.05
157	Mario Gosselin, Goalie	.03	.05
158	Clint Malarchuk, Goalie	.03	.05
159	Risto Siltanen	.03	.05
160	Robert Picard	.03	.05
161	Normand Rochefort	.03	.05
162	Randy Moller	.03	.05
163	Michel Goulet	.12	.25
164	Peter Stastny	.12	.25
165	John Ogrodnick	.03	.05
166	Anton Stastny	.03	.05
167	Paul Gillis	.03	.05
168	Dale Hunter	.03	.05
169	Alain Cote	.03	.05
170	Mike Eagles	.03	.05
171	Jason Lafreniere	.03	.05

WASHINGTON CAPITALS

No.	Player	EX	NRMT
172	Washington Capitals "Action Player"	.03	.05
173	Washington Capitals Team Logo	.03	.05
174	Peter Peeters, Goalie	.03	.05
175	Bob Mason, Goalie	.03	.05
176	Lawrence Murphy	.10	.20
177	Scott Stevens	.12	.25
178	Rod Langway	.03	.05
179	Kevin Hatcher	.10	.20

No.	Player	EX	NRMT
180	Michael Gartner	.25	.50
181	Mike Ridley	.03	.05
182	Craig Laughlin	.03	.05
183	Gaetan Duchesne	.03	.05
184	Dave Christian	.03	.05
185	Greg Adams	.03	.05
186	Kelly Miller	.03	.05
187	Alan Haworth	.03	.05
188	Lou Franceschetti	.03	.05

1987 STANLEY CUP

No.	Player	EX	NRMT
189	Stanley Cup	.03	.05
190	Stanley Cup	.03	.05
191	Ron Hextall, Goalie, Phi.	.05	.10
192	Wayne Gretzky, Edm.	2.00	4.00
193	Brian Propp, Phi.	.03	.05
194	Mark Messier, Edm.	.10	.20
195	Mark Messier Skates Through Oilers Defence During Stanley Cup	.05	.10
196	Mark Messier Skates Through Oilers Defence During Stanley Cup	.05	.10
197	Gretzky Hoists The Stanley Cup for the Third Time in Four Years	1.00	2.00
198	Gretzky Hoists The Stanley Cup for the Third Time in Four Years	1.00	2.00
199	Gretzky Hoists The Stanley Cup for the Third Time in Four Years	1.00	2.00
200	Gretzky Hoists The Stanley Cup for the Third Time in Four Years	1.00	2.00

CALGARY FLAMES

No.	Player	EX	NRMT
201	Calgary Flames "Action Player"	.03	.05
202	Calgary Flames Team Logo	.03	.05
203	Mike Vernon, Goalie	.05	.10
204	Rejean Lemelin, Goalie	.03	.05
205	Allan MacInnis	.05	.10
206	Paul Reinhart	.03	.05
207	Gary Suter	.03	.05
208	Jamie Macoun	.03	.05
209	Neil Sheehy	.03	.05
210	Joe Mullen	.05	.10
211	Carey Wilson	.03	.05
212	Joel Otto	.03	.05
213	James Peplinski	.03	.05
214	Hakan Loob	.03	.05
215	Lanny McDonald	.10	.20
216	Timothy Hunter	.03	.05
217	Gary Roberts	.25	.50

CHICAGO BLACK HAWKS

No.	Player	EX	NRMT
218	Chicago Black Hawks "Action Player"	.03	.05
219	Chicago Black Hawks Team Logo	.03	.05
220	Bob Sauve, Goalie	.03	.05
221	Murray Bannerman, Goalie	.03	.05
222	Douglas Wilson	.05	.10
223	Rob Murray	.03	.05
224	Gary Nylund	.03	.05
225	Denis Savard	.10	.20
226	Steve Larmer	.10	.20
227	Troy Murray	.03	.05
228	Wayne Presley	.03	.05
229	Alan Secord	.03	.05
230	Ed Olczyk	.03	.05
231	Curt Fraser	.03	.05
232	Bill Watson	.03	.05
233	Keith Brown	.03	.05
234	Darryl Sutter	.03	.05

DETROIT RED WINGS

No.	Player	EX	NRMT
235	Detroit Red Wings "Action Player"	.03	.05
236	Detroit Red Wings Team Logo	.03	.05
237	Gregory Stefan, Goalie	.03	.05
238	Glen Hanlon, Goalie	.03	.05
239	Darren Veitch	.03	.05
240	Mike O'Connell	.03	.05
241	Harold Snepsts	.03	.05
242	Dave Lewis	.03	.05
243	Steve Yzerman	.50	1.00
244	Brent Ashton	.03	.05

No.	Player	EX	NRMT
245	Gerard Gallant	.05	.10
246	Petr Klima	.05	.10
247	Shawn Burr	.10	.20
248	Adam Oates	.50	1.00
249	Mel Bridgman	.03	.05
250	Tim Higgins	.03	.05
251	Joey Kocur	.03	.05

EDMONTON OILERS

No.	Player	EX	NRMT
252	Edmonton Oilers "Action Player"	.03	.05
253	Edmonton Oilers Team Logo	.03	.05
254	Grant Fuhr, Goalie	.07	.15
255	Andrew Moog, Goalie	.03	.05
256	Paul Coffey	.25	.50
257	Kevin Lowe	.03	.05
258	Craig Muni	.03	.05
259	James (Steve) Smith	.05	.10
260	Charles Huddy	.03	.05
261	Wayne Gretzky	3.00	6.00
262	Jari Kurri	.07	.15
263	Mark Messier	1.00	2.00
264	Esa Tikkanen	.12	.25
265	Glenn Anderson	.10	.20
266	Michael Krushelnyski	.03	.05
267	Craig MacTavish	.03	.05
268	Dave Hunter	.03	.05

LOS ANGELES KINGS

No.	Player	EX	NRMT
269	Los Angeles Kings "Action Player"	.03	.05
270	Los Angeles Kings Team Logo	.03	.05
271	Roland Melanson, Goalie	.03	.05
272	Darren Eliot, Goalie	.03	.05
273	Grant Ledyard	.03	.05
274	Gordon (Jay) Wells	.03	.05
275	Mark Hardy	.03	.05
276	Edward (Dean) Kennedy	.03	.05
277	Luc Robitaille	.50	1.00
278	Bernie Nicholls	.05	.10
279	Jimmy Carson	.10	.20
280	David Taylor	.03	.05
281	Jim Fox	.03	.05
282	Bryan Erickson	.03	.05
283	David Williams	.03	.05
284	Sean McKenna	.03	.05
285	Phil Sykes	.03	.05

MINNESOTA NORTH STARS

No.	Player	EX	NRMT
286	Minnesota North Stars "Action Player"	.03	.05
287	Minnesota North Stars Team Logo	.03	.05
288	Kari Takko, Goalie	.03	.05
289	Donald Beaupre, Goalie	.05	.10
290	Craig Hartsburg	.03	.05
291	Ronald Wilson	.03	.05
292	Frantisek Musil	.03	.05
293	Dino Ciccarelli	.13	.25
294	Brian MacLellan	.03	.05
295	Dirk Graham	.03	.05
296	Brian Bellows	.13	.25
297	Neal Broten	.03	.05
298	Dennis Maruk	.03	.05
299	Keith Acton	.03	.05
300	Brian Lawton	.03	.05
301	Bob Brooke	.03	.05
302	Willi Plett	.03	.05

ST. LOUIS BLUES

No.	Player	EX	NRMT
303	St. Louis Blues "Action Player"	.03	.05
304	St. Louis Blues Team Logo	.03	.05
305	Richard Wamsley, Goalie	.03	.05
306	George (Rob) Ramage	.03	.05
307	Eric Nattress	.03	.05
308	Bruce Bell	.03	.05
309	Charlie Bourgeois	.03	.05
310	Jim Pavese	.03	.05
311	Douglas Gilmour	.50	1.00
312	Bernie Federko	.12	.25
313	Mark Hunter	.03	.05

No.	Player	EX	NRMT
314	Gregory Paslawski	.03	.05
315	Gino Cavallini	.03	.05
316	Richard Meagher	.03	.05
317	Ron Flockhart	.03	.05
318	Douglas Wickenheiser	.03	.05
319	Jocelyn Lemieux	.03	.05

TORONTO MAPLE LEAFS

No.	Player	EX	NRMT
320	Toronto Maple Leafs "Action Player"	.03	.05
321	Toronto Maple Leafs Team Logo	.03	.05
322	Ken Wregget, Goalie	.03	.05
323	Allan Bester, Goalie	.03	.05
324	Todd Gill	.03	.05
325	Al Iafrate	.10	.20
326	Borje Salming	.10	.20
327	Russell Courtnall	.10	.20
328	Richard Vaive	.03	.05
329	Steve Thomas	.03	.05
330	Wendel Clark	.18	.35
331	Gary Leeman	.03	.05
332	Tom Fergus	.03	.05
333	Vincent Damphousse	.10	.20
334	Peter Ihnacak	.03	.05
335	Brad Smith	.03	.05
336	Miroslav Ihnacak	.03	.05

VANCOUVER CANUCKS

No.	Player	EX	NRMT
337	Vancouver Canucks "Action Player"	.03	.05
338	Vancouver Canucks Team Logo	.03	.05
339	Frank Caprice, Goalie	.03	.05
340	Richard Brodeur, Goalie	.03	.05
341	Doug Lidster	.03	.05
342	Michel Petit	.03	.05
343	Garth Butcher	.03	.05
344	Dave Richter	.03	.05
345	Tony Tanti	.03	.05
346	Barry Pederson	.03	.05
347	Petri Skriko	.03	.05
348	Patrik Sundstrom	.03	.05
349	Stanley Smyl	.03	.05
350	Richard Sutter	.03	.05
351	Steve Tambellini	.03	.05
352	Jim Sandlak	.03	.05
353	Dave Lowry	.03	.05

WINNIPEG JETS

No.	Player	EX	NRMT
354	Winnipeg Jets "Action Player"	.03	.05
355	Winnipeg Jets Team Logo	.03	.05
356	Daniel Berthiaume, Goalie	.03	.05
357	Eldon Reddick, Goalie	.03	.05
358	Dave Ellett	.03	.05
359	Mario Marois	.03	.05
360	Randy Carlyle	.05	.10
361	Fredrick Olausson	.05	.10
362	James Kyte	.03	.05
363	Dale Hawerchuk	.13	.25
364	Paul MacLean	.03	.05
365	Thomas Steen	.03	.05
366	Gilles Hamel	.03	.05
367	Douglas Smail	.03	.05
368	Laurie Boschman	.03	.05
369	Ray Neufeld	.03	.05
370	Andrew McBain	.03	.05

1986-87 LEAGUE LEADERS

No.	Player	EX	NRMT
371	Wayne Gretzky, Edm.	1.00	2.00
372	Hart Memorial Trophy	.03	.05
373	Wayne Gretzky, Edm.	1.00	2.00
374	Art Ross Trophy	.03	.05
375	William M. Jennings Trophy	.03	.05
376A	Brian Hayward, Goalie, Mon.	.03	.05
376B	Patrick Roy, Goalie, Mon.	.75	1.50
377	Vezina Trophy	.03	.05
378	Ron Hextall, Goalie, Phi.	.10	.20
379	Luc Robitaille, LA	.35	.75
380	Calder Memorial Trophy	.03	.05
381	Raymond Bourque, Bos.	.03	.05

326 • PANINI — 1988-89 STICKERS —

No.	Player	EX	NRMT
382	James Norris Memorial Trophy	.03	.05
383	lady Byng Memorial Trophy	.03	.05
384	Joe Mullen, Cal.	.03	.05
385	Frank J. Selke Trophy	.03	.05
386	David Poulin, Phi.	.03	.05
387	Doug Jarvis, Har.	.03	.05
388	Bill Masterton Memorial Trophy	.03	.05
389	Wayne Gretzky, Edm.	1.00	2.00
390	Emery Edge Award	.03	.05

1987 STANLEY CUP PLAYOFFS

No.	Player	EX	NRMT
391	Philadelphia Flyers Team Photo	.03	.05
392	Philadelphia Flyers Team Photo	.03	.05
393	Prince of Wales Trophy	.03	.05
394	Clarence S. Campbell Bowl	.03	.05
395	Edmonton Oilers Team Photo	.03	.05
396	Edmonton Oilers Team Photo	.03	.05

— 1988-89 STICKERS —

1988-89 Panini Stickers
Sticker No. 60, Craig McTavish

Sticker Size: 2 1/8" X 2 15/16"
Face: Four colour, white border; Name, Team
Back: Black on white card stock
Imprint: PANINI
Complete Set No.: 408
Complete Set Price: 10.00 20.00
Common Player: .03 .05
Album: 2.50 5.00

No.	Player	EX	NRMT
1	Road to the Cup Stanley Cup Draw	.03	.05

CALGARY FLAMES

No.	Player	EX	NRMT
2	Calgary Flames Team Logo	.03	.05
3	Calgary Flames Uniform	.03	.05
4	Mike Vernon, Goalie	.05	.10
5	Al MacInnis	.05	.10
6	Byron (Brad) McCrimmon	.03	.05
7	Gary Suter	.03	.05
8	Mike Bullard	.03	.05
9	Hakan Loob	.03	.05
10	Lanny McDonald	.05	.10
11	Joe Mullen	.05	.10
12	Joe Nieuwendyk	.25	.50
13	Joel Otto	.03	.05
14	James Peplinski	.03	.05
15	Gary Roberts	.07	.15
16	Calgary Flames Team Photo	.03	.05
17	Calgary Flames Team Photo	.03	.05

CHICAGO BLACK HAWKS

No.	Player	EX	NRMT
18	Chicago Black Hawks Team Logo	.03	.05
19	Chicago Black Hawks Uniform	.03	.05
20	Bob Mason, Goalie	.03	.05
21	Darren Pang, Goalie	.03	.05
22	Rob Murray	.03	.05
23	Gary Nylund	.03	.05
24	Douglas Wilson	.05	.10
25	Dirk Graham	.03	.05
26	Steve Larmer	.03	.05
27	Troy Murray	.03	.05
28	Brian Noonan	.03	.05

No.	Player	EX	NRMT
29	Denis Savard	.10	.20
30	Steve Thomas	.03	.05
31	Richard Vaive	.03	.05
32	Chicago Black Hawks Team	.03	.05
33	Chicago Black Hawks Team	.03	.05

DETROIT RED WINGS

No.	Player	EX	NRMT
34	Detroit Red Wings Team Logo	.03	.05
35	Detroit Red Wings Uniform	.03	.05
36	Glen Hanlon, Goalie	.03	.05
37	Gregory Stefan, Goalie	.03	.05
38	Jeff Sharples	.03	.05
39	Darren Veitch	.03	.05
40	Brent Ashton	.03	.05
41	Shawn Burr	.03	.05
42	John Chabot	.03	.05
43	Gerard Gallant	.03	.05
44	Petr Klima	.03	.05
45	Adam Oates	.25	.50
46	Bob Probert	.15	.30
47	Steve Yzerman	.15	.30
48	Detroit Red Wings Team Photo	.03	.05
49	Detroit Red Wings Team Photo	.03	.05

EDMONTON OILERS

No.	Player	EX	NRMT
50	Edmonton Oilers Team Logo	.03	.05
51	Edmonton Oilers Uniform	.03	.05
52	Grant Fuhr, Goalie	.05	.10
53	Charles Huddy	.03	.05
54	Kevin Lowe	.03	.05
55	James (Steve) Smith	.03	.05
56	Jeff Beukeboom	.03	.05
57	Glenn Anderson	.03	.05
58	Wayne Gretzky	2.50	5.00
59	Jari Kurri	.05	.10
60	Craig MacTavish	.03	.05
61	Mark Messier	.75	1.50
62	Craig Simpson	.05	.10
63	Esa Tikkanen	.05	.10
64	Edmonton Oilers Team Photo	.03	.05
65	Edmonton Oilers Team Photo	.03	.05

LOS ANGELES KINGS

No.	Player	EX	NRMT
66	Los Angeles Kings Team Logo	.03	.05
67	Los Angeles Kings Uniform	.03	.05
68	Glenn Healy, Goalie	.03	.05
69	Roland Melanson, Goalie	.03	.05
70	Steve Duchesne	.05	.10
71	Thomas Laidlaw	.03	.05
72	Gordon (Jay) Wells	.03	.05
73	Mike Allison	.03	.05
74	Robert Carpenter	.03	.05
75	Jimmy Carson	.05	.10
76	Jim Fox	.03	.05
77	Bernie Nicholls	.03	.05
78	Luc Robitaille	.15	.30
79	David Taylor	.03	.05
80	Los Angeles Kings Team Photo	.03	.05
81	Los Angeles Kings Team Photo	.03	.05

MINNESOTA NORTH STARS

No.	Player	EX	NRMT
82	Minnesota North Stars Team Logo	.03	.05
83	Minnesota North Stars Uniform	.03	.05
84	Donald Beaupre, Goalie	.05	.10
85	Kari Takko, Goalie	.03	.05
86	Craig Hartsburg	.03	.05
87	Frantisek Musil	.03	.05
88	Dave Archibald	.03	.05
89	Brian Bellows	.10	.20
90	Scott Bjugstad	.03	.05
91	Bob Brooke	.03	.05
92	Neal Broten	.03	.05
93	Dino Ciccarelli	.10	.20
94	Brian Lawton	.03	.05
95	Brian MacLellan	.03	.05
96	Minnesota North Stars Team Photo	.03	.05
97	Minnesota North Stars Team Photo	.03	.05

ST. LOUIS BLUES

No.	Player	EX	NRMT
98	St. Louis Blues Team Logo	.03	.05
99	St. Louis Blues Uniform	.03	.05
100	Greg Millen, Goalie	.03	.05
101	Brian Benning	.03	.05
102	Gordon Roberts	.03	.05
103	Gino Cavallini	.03	.05
104	Bernie Federko	.03	.05
105	Douglas Gilmour	.35	.75
106	Anthony Hrkac	.03	.05
107	Brett Hull	.75	1.50
108	Mark Hunter	.03	.05
109	Anthony McKegney	.03	.05
110	Richard Meagher	.03	.05
111	Brian Sutter	.03	.05
112	St. Louis Blues Team Photo	.03	.05
113	St. Louis Blues Team Photo	.03	.05

TORONTO MAPLE LEAFS

No.	Player	EX	NRMT
114	Toronto Maple Leafs Team Logo	.03	.05
115	Toronto Maple Leafs Uniform	.03	.05
116	Allan Bester, Goalie	.03	.05
117	Ken Wregget, Goalie	.03	.05
118	Al Iafrate	.10	.20
119	Luke Richardson	.03	.05
120	Borje Salming	.10	.20
121	Wendel Clark	.18	.35
122	Russell Courtnall	.05	.10
123	Vincent Damphousse	.08	.15
124	Dan Daoust	.03	.05
125	Gary Leeman	.03	.05
126	Ed Olczyk	.03	.05
127	Mark Osborne	.03	.05
128	Toronto Maple Leafs Team Photo	.03	.05
129	Toronto Maple Leafs Team Photo	.03	.05

VANCOUVER CANUCKS

No.	Player	EX	NRMT
130	Vancouver Canucks Team Logo	.03	.05
131	Vancouver Canucks Uniform	.03	.05
132	Kirk McLean, Goalie	.50	1.00
133	Jim Benning	.03	.05
134	Garth Butcher	.03	.05
135	Doug Lidster	.03	.05
136	Greg Adams	.03	.05
137	David Bruce	.03	.05
138	Barry Pederson	.03	.05
139	Jim Sandlak	.03	.05
140	Petri Skriko	.03	.05
141	Stanley Smyl	.03	.05
142	Richard Sutter	.03	.05
143	Tony Tanti	.03	.05
144	Vancouver Canucks Team Photo	.03	.05
145	Vancouver Canucks Team Photo	.03	.05

WINNIPEG JETS

No.	Player	EX	NRMT
146	Winnipeg Jets Team Logo	.03	.05
147	Winnipeg Jets Uniform	.03	.05
148	Daniel Berthiaume, Goalie	.03	.05
149	Randy Carlyle	.05	.10
150	Dave Ellett	.03	.05
151	Mario Marois	.03	.05
152	Peter Taglianetti	.03	.05
153	Laurie Boschman	.03	.05
154	Iain Duncan	.03	.05
155	Dale Hawerchuk	.10	.20
156	Paul MacLean	.03	.05
157	Andrew McBain	.03	.05
158	Douglas Smail	.03	.05
159	Thomas Steen	.03	.05
160	Winnipeg Jets Team Photo	.03	.05
161	Winnipeg Jets Team Photo	.03	.05

1988 STANLEY CUP PLAYOFFS

No.	Player	EX	NRMT
162	Prince of Wales Trophy	.03	.05
163	Washington Defeats Flyers	.03	.05
164	Boston Beat Montreal	.03	.05
165	Devils Skate Past the Capitals	.03	.05

1988-89 STICKERS — PANINI • 327

No.	Player	EX	NRMT
166	Bruins Were Victories Over New Jersey	.03	.05
167	Bruins Were Victories Over New Jersey	.03	.05
168	Calgary Too Much For Kings	.03	.05
169	Clarence S. Campbell Bowl	.03	.05
170	Edmonton Put Out Flames	.03	.05
171	Detroit Defeat St. Louis	.03	.05
172	Oilers Overpowered Detroit	.03	.05
173	Oilers Overpowered Detroit	.03	.05
174	Edmonton Celebrate a Victory in Game 1	.03	.05
175	Game 2, Oilers Eyed Another Victory	.03	.05
176	Stanley Cup	.03	.05
177	Stanley Cup	.03	.05
178	Gretzky & Teammates Take a Commanding 3-0 Lead in Boston	.15	.30
179	Gretzky & Teammates Take a Commanding 3-0 Lead in Boston	.15	.30
180	Gretzky & Teammates Take a Commanding 3-0 Lead in Boston	.15	.30
181	Wayne Gretzky, Edm., M.V.Pl.	1.00	2.00
182	Conn Smythe Trophy	.03	.05
183	Edmonton Oilers Celebrate Winning Their Fourth Stanley Cup in Five Years	.03	.05
184	Edmonton Oilers Celebrate Winning Their Fourth Stanley Cup in Five Years	.03	.05
185	Edmonton Oilers Celebrate Winning Their Fourth Stanley Cup in Five Years	.03	.05
186	Edmonton Oilers Celebrate Winning Their Fourth Stanley Cup in Five Years	.03	.05

ACTION STICKERS

No.	Player	EX	NRMT
187	Calgary Flames Action	.03	.05
188	Grant Fuhr, Goalie, Edm.	.08	.15
189	New Jersey Devils Action	.03	.05
190	Marcel Dionne	.05	.10
191	Bruins Action	.03	.05
192	Washington Capitals Action	.03	.05
193	Wayne Gretzky	2.50	5.00
194	Winnipeg Jets	.03	.05
195	Boston Bruins	.03	.05
196	St. Louis Blues	.03	.05
197	Philadelphia Flyers vs Washington Capitals	.03	.05
198	New York Islanders	.03	.05
199	Calgary Flames	.03	.05
200	Pittsburgh Penguins	.03	.05

BOSTON BRUINS

No.	Player	EX	NRMT
201	Boston Bruins Team Logo	.03	.05
202	Boston Bruins Uniform	.03	.05
203	Rejean Lemelin, Goalie	.05	.10
204	Raymond Bourque	.12	.25
205	Gordon Kluzak	.03	.05
206	Michael Thelven	.03	.05
207	Glen Wesley	.03	.05
208	Randy Burridge	.03	.05
209	Keith Crowder	.03	.05
210	Stephen Kasper	.03	.05
211	Ken Linseman	.03	.05
212	Jay Miller	.03	.05
213	Cam Neely	.12	.25
214	Robert Sweeney	.03	.05
215	Boston Bruins Team Photo	.03	.05
216	Boston Bruins Team Photo	.03	.05

BUFFALO SABRES

No.	Player	EX	NRMT
217	Buffalo Sabres Team Logo	.03	.05
218	Buffalo Sabres Uniform	.03	.05
219	Tom Barrasso, Goalie	.10	.20
220	Phil Housley	.03	.05
221	Calle Johansson	.03	.05
222	Michael Ramsey	.03	.05
223	David Andreychuk	.10	.20
224	Scott Arniel	.03	.05
225	Adam Creighton	.03	.05
226	Mike Foligno	.03	.05
227	Christian Ruuttu	.03	.05
228	Ray Sheppard	.15	.30

No.	Player	EX	NRMT
229	John Tucker	.03	.05
230	Pierre Turgeon	.25	.50
231	Buffalo Sabres Team Photo	.03	.05
232	Buffalo Sabres Team Photo	.03	.05

HARTFORD WHALERS

No.	Player	EX	NRMT
233	Hartford Whalers Team Logo	.03	.05
234	Hartford Whalers Uniform	.03	.05
235	Mike Liut, Goalie	.03	.05
236	David Babych	.03	.05
237	Sylvain Cote	.03	.05
238	Ulf Samuelsson	.03	.05
239	John Anderson	.03	.05
240	Kevin Dineen	.05	.10
241	Ray Ferraro	.05	.10
242	Ronald Francis	.07	.15
243	Paul MacDermid	.03	.05
244	Dave Tippett	.03	.05
245	Sylvain Turgeon	.03	.05
246	Carey Wilson	.03	.05
247	Hartford Whalers Team Photo	.03	.05
248	Hartford Whalers Team Photo	.03	.05

MONTREAL CANADIENS

No.	Player	EX	NRMT
249	Montreal Canadiens Team Logo	.03	.05
250	Montreal Canadiens Uniform	.03	.05
251	Brian Hayward, Goalie	.03	.05
252	Patrick Roy, Goalie	1.00	2.00
253	Chris Chelios	.25	.50
254	Craig Ludwig	.03	.05
255	Petr Svoboda	.03	.05
256	Guy Carbonneau	.07	.15
257	Claude Lemieux	.03	.05
258	Michael McPhee	.03	.05
259	Mats Naslund	.03	.05
260	Stephane J.J. Richer	.03	.05
261	Robert Smith	.05	.10
262	Ryan Walter	.03	.05
263	Montreal Canadiens Team Photo	.03	.05
264	Montreal Canadiens Team Photo	.03	.05

NEW JERSEY DEVILS

No.	Player	EX	NRMT
265	New Jersey Devils Team Logo	.03	.05
266	New Jersey Devils Uniform	.03	.05
267	Sean Burke, Goalie	.03	.05
268	Joe Cirella	.03	.05
269	Bruce Driver	.03	.05
270	Craig Wolanin	.03	.05
271	Aaron Broten	.03	.05
272	Doug Brown	.03	.05
273	Claude Loiselle	.03	.05
274	John MacLean	.03	.05
275	Kirk Muller	.10	.20
276	Brendan Shanahan	.18	.35
277	Patrik Sundstrom	.03	.05
278	Patrick Verbeek	.05	.10
279	New Jersey Devils Team Photo	.03	.05
280	New Jersey Devils Team Photo	.03	.05

NEW YORK ISLANDERS

No.	Player	EX	NRMT
281	New York Islanders Team Logo	.03	.05
282	New York Islanders Uniform	.03	.05
283	Kelly Hrudey, Goalie	.03	.05
284	Stephen Konroyd	.03	.05
285	Ken Morrow	.03	.05
286	Patrick Flatley	.03	.05
287	Gregory Gilbert	.03	.05
288	Alan Kerr	.03	.05
289	Derek King	.15	.30
290	Pat LaFontaine	.50	1.00
291	Mikko Makela	.03	.05
292	Brent Sutter	.03	.05
293	Bryan Trottier	.08	.15
294	Randy Wood	.03	.05
295	New York Islanders Team	.03	.05
296	New York Islanders Team	.03	.05

NEW YORK RANGERS

No.	Player	EX	NRMT
297	New York Rangers Team Logo	.03	.05
298	New York Rangers Uniform	.03	.05
299	Robert Froese, Goalie	.03	.05
300	John Vanbiesbrouck, Goalie	.03	.05
301	Brian Leetch	.75	1.50
302	Norm Maciver	.03	.05
303	James Patrick	.03	.05
304	Michel Petit	.03	.05
305	Ulf Dahlen	.03	.05
306	Jan Erixon	.03	.05
307	Kelly Kisio	.03	.05
308	Donald Maloney	.03	.05
309	Walter Poddubny	.03	.05
310	Tomas Sandstrom	.05	.10
311	New York Rangers Team Photo	.03	.05
312	New York Rangers Team Photo	.03	.05

PHILADELPHIA FLYERS

No.	Player	EX	NRMT
313	Philadelphia Flyers Team Logo	.03	.05
314	Philadelphia Flyers Uniform	.03	.05
315	Ron Hextall, Goalie	.05	.10
316	Mark Howe	.03	.05
317	Kerry Huffman	.03	.05
318	Kjell Samuelsson	.03	.05
319	David Brown	.03	.05
320	Murray Craven	.03	.05
321	Tim Kerr	.03	.05
322	Scott Mellanby	.03	.05
323	David Poulin	.03	.05
324	Brian Propp	.03	.05
325	Ilkka Sinisalo	.03	.05
326	Rick Tocchet	1.00	2.00
327	Philadelphia Flyers Team Photo	.03	.05
328	Philadelphia Flyers Team Photo	.03	.05

PITTSBURGH PENGUINS

No.	Player	EX	NRMT
329	Pittsburgh Penguins Team Logo	.03	.05
330	Pittsburgh Penguins Uniform	.03	.05
331	Frank Pietrangelo, Goalie	.08	.15
332	Doug Bodger	.03	.05
333	Paul Coffey	.15	.30
334	Jim Johnson	.03	.05
335	Ville Siren	.03	.05
336	Rob Brown	.15	.30
337	Randy Cunneyworth	.03	.05
338	Dan Frawley	.03	.05
339	Dave Hunter	.03	.05
340	Mario Lemieux	1.50	3.00
341	Troy Loney	.03	.05
342	Dan Quinn	.03	.05
343	Pittsburgh Penguins Team Photo	.03	.05
344	Pittsburgh Penguins Team Photo	.03	.05

QUEBEC NORDIQUES

No.	Player	EX	NRMT
345	Quebec Nordiques Team Logo	.03	.05
346	Quebec Nordiques Uniform	.03	.05
347	Mario Gosselin, Goalie	.03	.05
348	Tommy Albelin	.03	.05
349	Jeff Brown	.08	.15
350	Steven Finn	.03	.05
351	Randy Moller	.03	.05
352	Alain Cote	.03	.05
353	Gaetan Duchesne	.03	.05
354	Mike Eagles	.03	.05
355	Michel Goulet	.07	.15
356	Lane Lambert	.03	.05
357	Anton Stastny	.03	.05
358	Peter Stastny	.07	.15
359	Quebec Nordiques Team Photo	.03	.05
360	Quebec Nordiques Team Photo	.03	.05

WASHINGTON CAPITALS

No.	Player	EX	NRMT
361	Washington Capitals Team Logo	.03	.05
362	Washington Capitals Uniform	.03	.05
363	Clint Malarchuk, Goalie	.03	.05
364	Peter Peeters, Goalie	.03	.05

1989-90 STICKERS

No.	Player	EX	NRMT
365	Kevin Hatcher	.08	.15
366	Rod Langway	.03	.05
367	Lawrence Murphy	.10	.20
368	Scott Stevens	.15	.30
369	Dave Christian	.03	.05
370	Michael Gartner	.20	.40
371	Bengt-ake Gustafsson	.03	.05
372	Dale Hunter	.03	.05
373	Kelly Miller	.03	.05
374	Mike Ridley	.03	.05
375	Washington Capitals Team Photo	.03	.05
376	Washington Capitals Team Photo	.03	.05

SIGNALS AND RULES

No.	Player	EX	NRMT
377	Hockey Rink	.03	.05
378	Hockey Rink	.03	.05
379	Cross-checking	.03	.05
380	Elbowing	.03	.05
381	High-sticking	.03	.05
382	Holding	.03	.05
383	Hooking	.03	.05
384	Interference	.03	.05
385	Spearing	.03	.05
386	Tripping	.03	.05
387	Boarding	.03	.05
388	Charging	.03	.05
389	Delayed Calling of Penalty	.03	.05
390	Kneeing	.03	.05
391	Misconduct	.03	.05
392	Roughing	.03	.05
393	Slashing	.03	.05
394	Unsportsmanlike Conduct	.03	.05
395	Wash-out	.03	.05
396	Icing	.03	.05
397	Off-side	.03	.05
398	Wash-out	.03	.05

1987-88 LEAGUE LEADERS

No.	Player	EX	NRMT
399	**Bill Masterson Memorial Cup:** Bob Borne, Pit.	.03	.05
400	**Hart Memorial Trophy:** Mario Lemieux, Pit.	.50	1.00
401	**Art Ross Trophy:** Mario Lemieux, Pit.	.50	1.00
402	**William M. Jennings Trophy:** Brian Hayward, Mon.; Patrick Roy, Mon.	.35	.75
403	**Vezina Trophy:** Grant Fuhr, Edm.	.05	.10
404	**Calder Memorial Trophy:** Joe Nieuwendyk, Cal.	.05	.10
405	**James Norris Memorial Trophy:** Raymond Bourque, Bos.	.12	.25
406	**Lady Byng Memorial Trophy:** Mats Naslund, Mon.	.05	.10
407	**Frank J. Selke Trophy:** Guy Carbonneau, Mon.	.03	.05
408	**Emery Edge Award:** Byron (Brad) McCrimmon, Cal.	.03	.05

— 1989 - 90 STICKERS —

1989-90 Panini Stickers
Sticker No. 117, Brett Hull

Sticker Size: 1 7/8" X 3"
Face: Four colour; Name, Team
Back: Black and white on card stock; Number
Imprint: PRINTED IN MODENA, ITALY
Complete Set No.: 384
Complete Set Price: 10.00 / 20.00
Common Player: .03 / .05
Album: 2.50 / 5.00

NHL ACTION

No.	Player	EX	NRMT
1	NHL Logo	.03	.05
2	Playoff schedule	.03	.05
3	Calgary Flames vs Chicago Black Hawks	.03	.05
4	Calgary Flames vs Vancouver Canucks	.03	.05
5	Los Angeles Kings vs Edmonton Oilers	.03	.05
6	Mike Vernon, Goalie	.03	.05
7	Mike Vernon, Goalie	.03	.05
8	Boston Bruins vs Buffalo Sabres	.03	.05
9	Montreal Canadiens vs Boston Bruins	.03	.05
10	Philadelphia Flyers score	.03	.05
11	Montreal Canadiens vs Philadelphia Flyers	.03	.05
12	Montreal Canadiens vs Philadelphia Flyers	.03	.05
13	Montreal Canadiens vs Calgary Flames	.03	.05
14	**Celebration:** Montreal Canadiens	.03	.05
15	Montreal Canadiens vs Calgary Flames	.03	.05
16	Montreal Canadiens vs Calgary Flames	.03	.05
17	**Celebration:** Calgary Flames	.03	.05
18	Calgary Flames vs Montreal Canadiens	.03	.05
19	Calgary Flames vs Montreal Canadiens	.03	.05
20	**Conn Smythe Trophy:** Al MacInnis	.05	.10

STANLEY CUP

No.	Player	EX	NRMT
21	Calgary Flames	.03	.05
22	Calgary Flames	.03	.05
23	Calgary Flames	.03	.05
24	Calgary Flames	.03	.05
25	Stanley Cup	.03	.05

CALGARY FLAMES

No.	Player	EX	NRMT
26	Calgary Flames logo	.03	.05
27	Joe Mullen	.10	.20
28	Douglas Gilmour	.20	.40
29	Joe Nieuwendyk	.05	.10
30	Gary Suter	.03	.05
31	Calgary Flames Team Photo	.03	.05
32	Allan MacInnis	.12	.25
33	Byron (Brad) McCrimmon	.03	.05
34	Mike Vernon, Goalie	.03	.05
35	Gary Roberts	.05	.10
36	Colin Patterson	.03	.05
37	James Peplinski	.03	.05
38	Jamie Macoun	.03	.05
39	Lanny McDonald	.05	.10
40	Saddledome	.03	.05

CHICAGO BLACK HAWKS

No.	Player	EX	NRMT
41	Chicago Black Hawks logo	.03	.05
42	Darren Pang, Goalie	.03	.05
43	Steve Larmer	.05	.10
44	Dirk Graham	.03	.05
45	Douglas Wilson	.03	.05
46	Chicago Black Hawks vs Edmonton Oiliers	.03	.05
47	Dave Manson	.05	.10
48	Troy Murray	.03	.05
49	Denis Savard	.08	.15
50	Steve Thomas	.03	.05
51	Adam Creighton	.03	.05
52	Wayne Presley	.03	.05
53	Trent Yawney	.03	.05
54	Alain Chevrier, Goalie	.03	.05
55	Chicago Stadium	.03	.05

DETROIT RED WINGS

No.	Player	EX	NRMT
56	Detroit Red Wings logo	.03	.05
57	Steve Yzerman	.25	.50
58	Gerard Gallant	.03	.05
59	Gregory Stefan	.03	.05
60	David Barr	.03	.05
61	Detroit Red Wings Team Photo	.03	.05
62	Steve Chiasson	.03	.05
63	Shawn Burr	.03	.05
64	Richard Zombo	.03	.05
65	Glen Hanlon, Goalie	.03	.05
66	Jeff Sharples	.03	.05
67	Joey Kocur	.03	.05
68	Lee Norwood	.03	.05
69	Mike O'Connell	.03	.05
70	Joe Louis Arena	.03	.05

EDMONTON OILERS

No.	Player	EX	NRMT
71	Edmonton Oilers logo	.03	.05
72	Jimmy Carson	.05	.10
73	Jari Kurri	.05	.10
74	Mark Messier	.25	.50
75	Craig Simpson	.03	.05
76	Edmonton Oilers vs Philadelphia Flyers	.03	.05
77	Glenn Anderson	.07	.15
78	Craig MacTavish	.03	.05
79	Kevin Lowe	.03	.05
80	Craig Muni	.03	.05
81	Bill Ranford, Goalie	.10	.20
82	Charles Huddy	.03	.05
83	James (Steve) Smith	.03	.05
84	Normand Lacombe	.03	.05
85	Northlands Coliseum	.03	.05

LOS ANGELES KINGS

No.	Player	EX	NRMT
86	Los Angeles Kings Logo	.03	.05
87	Wayne Gretzky	1.50	3.00
88	Bernie Nicholls	.05	.10
89	Kelly Hrudey, Goalie	.05	.10
90	John Tonelli	.03	.05
91	Edmonton Oilers vs Los Angeles Kings	.03	.05
92	Stephen Kasper	.03	.05
93	Steve Duchesne	.03	.05
94	Michael Krushelnyski	.03	.05
95	Luc Robitaille	.15	.30
96	Ron Duguay	.03	.05
97	Glenn Healy, Goalie	.03	.05
98	David Taylor	.03	.05
99	Martin McSorley	.05	.10
100	The Great Western Forum	.03	.05

MINNESOTA NORTH STARS

No.	Player	EX	NRMT
101	Minnesota North Stars logo	.03	.05
102	Kari Takko, Goalie	.03	.05
103	Dave Gagner	.05	.10
104	Michael Gartner	.20	.40
105	Brian Bellows	.03	.05
106	Minnesota North Stars Team Photo	.03	.05
107	Neal Broten	.03	.05
108	Lawrence Murphy	.07	.15
109	Basil McRae	.03	.05
110	Perry Berezan	.03	.05
111	Shawn Chambers	.03	.05
112	Curt Giles	.03	.05
113	Robert (Stewart) Gavin	.03	.05
114	Jon Casey, Goalie	.05	.10
115	Metropolitan Sports Center	.03	.05

ST. LOUIS BLUES

No.	Player	EX	NRMT
116	St. Louis Blues logo	.03	.05
117	Brett Hull	.25	.50
118	Peter Zezel	.03	.05
119	Anthony Hrkac	.03	.05
120	Vincent Riendeau, Goalie	.05	.10
121	St. Louis Blues vs New York Islanders	.03	.05
122	Cliff Ronning	.05	.10
123	Gino Cavallini	.03	.05

1989-90 STICKERS — PANINI

No.	Player	EX	NRMT
124	Brian Benning	.03	.05
125	Richard Meagher	.03	.05
126	Steve Tuttle	.03	.05
127	Paul Cavallini	.03	.05
128	Tom Tilley	.03	.05
129	Greg Millen, Goalie	.03	.05
130	St. Louis Arena	.03	.05

TORONTO MAPLE LEAFS

No.	Player	EX	NRMT
131	Toronto Maple Leafs logo	.03	.05
132	Ed Olczyk	.03	.05
133	Gary Leeman	.03	.05
134	Vincent Damphousse	.08	.15
135	Tom Fergus	.03	.05
136	Toronto Maple Leafs Team Photo	.03	.05
137	Daniel Marois	.05	.10
138	Mark Osborne	.03	.05
139	Allan Bester, Goalie	.03	.05
140	Al Iafrate	.05	.10
141	Bradley Marsh	.03	.05
142	Luke Richardson	.03	.05
143	Todd Gill	.03	.05
144	Wendel Clark	.12	.25
145	Maple Leaf Gardens	.03	.05

VANCOUVER CANUCKS

No.	Player	EX	NRMT
146	Vancouver Canucks logo	.03	.05
147	Petri Skriko	.03	.05
148	Trevor Linden	.15	.30
149	Tony Tanti	.03	.05
150	Stephen Weeks, Goalie	.03	.05
151	Vancouver Canucks vs New York Islanders	.03	.05
152	Brian Bradley	.03	.05
153	Barry Pederson	.03	.05
154	Greg Adams	.03	.05
155	Kirk McLean, Goalie	.12	.25
156	Jim Sandlak	.03	.05
157	Richard Sutter	.03	.05
158	Garth Butcher	.03	.05
159	Stanley Smyl	.03	.05
160	Pacific Coliseum	.03	.05

WINNIPEG JETS

No.	Player	EX	NRMT
161	Winnipeg Jets logo	.03	.05
162	Dale Hawerchuk	.13	.25
163	Thomas Steen	.03	.05
164	Brent Ashton	.03	.05
165	Pat Elynuik	.08	.15
166	Winnipeg Jets vs New York Islanders	.03	.05
167	Dave Ellett	.03	.05
168	Randy Carlyle	.05	.10
169	Laurie Boschman	.03	.05
170	Iain Duncan	.03	.05
171	Douglas Smail	.03	.05
172	Teppo Numminen	.03	.05
173	Bob Essensa, Goalie	.05	.10
174	Peter Taglianetti	.03	.05
175	Winnipeg Arena	.03	.05

ALL STARS

No.	Player	EX	NRMT
176	Steve Duchesne	.05	.10
177	Luc Robitaille	.10	.20
178	Mike Vernon, Goalie	.03	.05
179	Wayne Gretzky	.75	1.50
180	Kevin Lowe	.03	.05
181	Jari Kurri	.05	.10
182	Cam Neely	.07	.15
183	Paul Coffey	.05	.10
184	Mario Lemieux	.50	1.00
185	Sean Burke, Goalie	.03	.05
186	Rob Brown	.05	.10
187	Raymond Bourque	.10	.20

BOSTON BRUINS

No.	Player	EX	NRMT
188	Boston Bruins logo	.03	.05
189	Greg Hawgood	.03	.05
190	Ken Linseman	.03	.05
191	Andrew Moog, Goalie	.05	.10
192	Cam Neely	.15	.30
193	Boston Bruins vs Philadelphia Flyers	.03	.05
194	Andy Brickley	.03	.05
195	Rejean Lemelin, Goalie	.03	.05
196	Robert Carpenter	.03	.05
197	Randy Burridge	.03	.05
198	Craig Janney	.10	.20
199	Bob Joyce	.03	.05
200	Glen Wesley	.03	.05
201	Raymond Bourque	.15	.30
202	Boston Garden	.03	.05

BUFFALO SABRES

No.	Player	EX	NRMT
203	Buffalo Sabres logo	.03	.05
204	Pierre Turgeon	.13	.25
205	Phil Housley	.03	.05
206	Richard Vaive	.03	.05
207	Christian Ruuttu	.03	.05
208	Philadelphia Flyers vs Buffalo Sabres	.03	.05
209	Doug Bodger	.03	.05
210	Mike Foligno	.03	.05
211	Ray Sheppard	.03	.05
212	John Tucker	.03	.05
213	Scott Arniel	.03	.05
214	Daren Puppa, Goalie	.03	.05
215	David Andreychuk	.07	.15
216	Uwe Krupp	.03	.05
217	Memorial Auditorium	.03	.05

HARTFORD WHALERS

No.	Player	EX	NRMT
218	Hartford Whalers logo	.03	.05
219	Kevin Dineen	.03	.05
220	Peter Sidorkiewicz, Goalie	.03	.05
221	Ron Francis	.05	.10
222	Ray Ferraro	.05	.10
223	New York Islanders vs Hartford Whalers	.03	.05
224	Scott Young	.03	.05
225	David Babych	.03	.05
226	Dave Tippett	.03	.05
227	Paul MacDermid	.03	.05
228	Ulf Samuelsson	.03	.05
229	Sylvain Cote	.03	.05
230	Jody Hull	.03	.05
231	Donald Maloney	.03	.05
232	Hartford Civic Center	.03	.05

MONTREAL CANADIENS

No.	Player	EX	NRMT
233	Montreal Canadiens logo	.03	.05
234	Mats Naslund	.03	.05
235	Patrick Roy, Goalie	.50	1.00
236	Robert Smith	.03	.05
237	Chris Chelios	.10	.20
238	Calgary Flames vs Montreal Canadiens	.03	.05
239	Stephane J.J. Richer	.05	.10
240	Claude Lemieux	.03	.05
241	Guy Carbonneau	.05	.10
242	Shayne Corson	.03	.05
243	Michael McPhee	.03	.05
244	Petr Svoboda	.03	.05
245	Larry Robinson	.05	.10
246	Brian Hayward, Goalie	.03	.05
247	Montreal Forum	.03	.05

NEW JERSEY DEVILS

No.	Player	EX	NRMT
248	New Jersey Devils logo	.03	.05
249	John MacLean	.03	.05
250	Patrik Sundstrom	.03	.05
251	Kirk Muller	.05	.10
252	Tom Kurvers	.03	.05
253	Boston Bruins vs New Jersey Devils Action	.03	.05
254	Aaron Broten	.03	.05
255	Brendan Shanahan	.07	.15
256	Sean Burke, Goalie	.03	.05
257	Tommy Albelin	.03	.05
258	Ken Daneyko	.03	.05
259	Randy Velischek	.03	.05
260	Mark Johnson	.03	.05
261	James Korn	.03	.05
262	Brendan Byrne Arena	.03	.05

NEW YORK ISLANDERS

No.	Player	EX	NRMT
263	New York Islanders logo	.03	.05
264	Pat LaFontaine	.25	.50
265	Mark Fitzpatrick	.03	.05
266	Brent Sutter	.03	.05
267	David Volek	.03	.05
268	New York Islanders vs New York Rangers	.03	.05
269	Bryan Trottier	.05	.10
270	Mikko Makela	.03	.05
271	Derek King	.10	.20
272	Patrick Flatley	.03	.05
273	Jeff Norton	.03	.05
274	Gerald Diduck	.03	.05
275	Alan Kerr	.03	.05
276	Jeff Hackett, Goalie	.03	.05
277	Nassau Veterans Memorial Coliseum	.03	.05

NEW YORK RANGERS

No.	Player	EX	NRMT
278	New York Rangers logo	.03	.05
279	Brian Leetch	.35	.75
280	Carey Wilson	.03	.05
281	Tomas Sandstrom	.05	.10
282	John Vanbiesbrouck, Goalie	.07	.15
283	Edmonton Oilers vs New York Rangers	.03	.05
284	Robert Froese, Goalie	.03	.05
285	Tony Granato	.08	.15
286	Brian Mullen	.03	.05
287	Kelly Kisio	.03	.05
288	Ulf Dahlen	.03	.05
289	James Patrick	.03	.05
290	John Ogrodnick	.03	.05
291	Michel Petit	.03	.05
292	Madison Square Garden	.03	.05

PHILADELPHIA FLYERS

No.	Player	EX	NRMT
293	Philadelphia Flyers logo	.03	.05
294	Tim Kerr	.03	.05
295	Rick Tocchet	.05	.10
296	Per-Erik Eklund	.03	.05
297	Terry Carkner	.03	.05
298	Philadelphia Flyers vs Montreal Canadiens	.03	.05
299	Ronald Sutter	.03	.05
300	Mark Howe	.05	.10
301	Keith Acton	.03	.05
302	Ron Hextall, Goalie	.05	.10
303	Gordon Murphy	.03	.05
304	Derrick Smith	.03	.05
305	David Poulin	.03	.05
306	Brian Propp	.03	.05
307	The Spectrum	.03	.05

PITTSBURGH PENGUINS

No.	Player	EX	NRMT
308	Pittsburgh Penguins logo	.03	.05
309	Mario Lemieux	.50	1.00
310	Rob Brown	.05	.10
311	Paul Coffey	.08	.15
312	Tom Barrasso, Goalie	.08	.15
313	Pittsburgh Penguins vs Philadelphia Flyers	.03	.05
314	Dan Quinn	.03	.05
315	Bob Errey	.03	.05
316	John Cullen	.03	.05
317	Phil Bourque	.03	.05
318	Zarley Zalapski	.03	.05
319	Troy Loney	.03	.05
320	Jim Johnson	.03	.05
321	Kevin Stevens	.13	.25
322	Civic Arena	.03	.05

PANINI — 1990-91 STICKERS —

1990-91 STICKERS

1990-91 Panini Stickers
Sticker No. 9, Cam Neely

Sticker Size: 2 1/6" X 2 15/16"
Face: Four colour, white border; Name, Team
Back: Black and white on card stock; Number
Imprint: PANINI
Complete Set No.: 351

	EX	NRMT
Complete Set Price:	10.00	20.00
Common Player:	.03	.05
Album:	2.50	5.00

QUEBEC NORDIQUES

No.	Player	EX	NRMT
323	Quebec Nordiques logo	.03	.05
324	Peter Stastny	.08	.15
325	Jeff Brown	.03	.05
326	Michel Goulet	.03	.05
327	Joe Sakic	.20	.40
328	Philadelphia Flyers vs Quebec Nordiques	.03	.05
329	Iiro Jarvi	.03	.05
330	Paul Gillis	.03	.05
331	Randy Moller	.03	.05
332	Ron Tugnutt, Goalie	.05	.10
333	Robert Picard	.03	.05
334	Curtis Leschyshyn	.03	.05
335	Marc Fortier	.03	.05
336	Mario Marois	.03	.05
337	Le Colisee	.03	.05

WASHINGTON CAPITALS

No.	Player	EX	NRMT
338	Washington Capitals logo	.03	.05
339	Mike Ridley	.03	.05
340	Geoff Courtnall	.05	.10
341	Scott Stevens	.10	.20
342	Dino Ciccarelli	.10	.20
343	Washington Capitals vs Calgary Flames	.03	.05
344	Bob Mason, Goalie	.03	.05
345	Dave Christian	.03	.05
346	Dale Hunter	.03	.05
347	Kevin Hatcher	.05	.10
348	Kelly Miller	.03	.05
349	Stephen Leach	.05	.10
350	Rod Langway	.03	.05
351	Robert Rouse	.03	.05
352	Capital Centre	.03	.05

TEAM LOGOS

No.	Player	EX	NRMT
353	Calgary Flames	.03	.05
354	Edmonton Oilers	.03	.05
355	Winnipeg Jets	.03	.05
356	Toronto Maple Leafs	.03	.05
357	Buffalo Sabres	.03	.05
358	Montreal Canadiens	.03	.05
359	Quebec Nordiques	.03	.05
360	New Jersey Devils	.03	.05
361	Boston Bruins	.03	.05
362	Hartford Whalers	.03	.05
363	Vancouver Canucks	.03	.05
364	Minnesota North Stars	.03	.05
365	Los Angeles Kings	.03	.05
366	St. Louis Blues	.03	.05
367	Chicago Black Hawks	.03	.05
368	Detroit Red Wings	.03	.05
369	Pittsburgh Penguins	.03	.05
370	Washington Capitals	.03	.05
371	Philadelphia Flyers	.03	.05
372	New York Rangers	.03	.05
373	New York Islanders	.03	.05

LEAGUE LEADERS

No.	Player	EX	NRMT
374	Wayne Gretzky	.35	.75
375	Mario Lemieux	.25	.50
376	Patrick Roy, Goalie; Brian Hayward, Goalie	.25	.50
377	Tim Kerr	.03	.05
378	Brian Leetch	.15	.30
379	Chris Chelios	.08	.15
380	Joe Mullen	.03	.05
381	Guy Carbonneau	.03	.05
382	Bryan Trottier	.05	.10
383	Patrick Roy, Goalie	.25	.50
384	Joe Mullen	.03	.05

STANLEY CUP

No.	Player	EX	NRMT
1	Prince of Wales Conference	.03	.05
2	Clarence Campbell Conference	.03	.05
3	Stanley Cup	.03	.05

BOSTON BRUINS

No.	Player	EX	NRMT
4	David Poulin	.03	.05
5	Brian Propp	.03	.05
6	Glen Wesley	.03	.05
7	Robert Carpenter	.03	.05
8	John Carter	.03	.05
9	Cam Neely	.10	.20
10	Greg Hawgood	.03	.05
11	Andrew Moog, Goalie	.03	.05
12	Boston Bruins logo	.03	.05
13	Rejean Lemelin, Goalie	.03	.05
14	Craig Janney	.10	.20
15	Robert Sweeney	.03	.05
16	Andy Brickley	.03	.05
17	Raymond Bourque	.12	.25
18	Dave Christian	.03	.05

BUFFALO SABRES

No.	Player	EX	NRMT
19	Dave Snuggerud	.03	.05
20	Christian Ruuttu	.03	.05
21	Phil Housley	.03	.05
22	Uwe Krupp	.03	.05
23	Richard Vaive	.03	.05
24	Michael Ramsey	.03	.05
25	Mike Foligno	.03	.05
26	Clint Malarchuk, Goalie	.03	.05
27	Buffalo Sabres logo	.03	.05
28	Pierre Turgeon	.13	.25
29	David Andreychuk	.07	.15
30	Scott Arniel	.03	.05
31	Daren Puppa, Goalie	.03	.05
32	Mike Hartman	.03	.05
33	Doug Bodger	.03	.05

HARTFORD WHALERS

No.	Player	EX	NRMT
34	Scott Young	.03	.05
35	Todd Krygier	.03	.05
36	Patrick Verbeek	.03	.05
37	Dave Tippett	.03	.05
38	Peter Sidorkiewicz, Goalie	.03	.05
39	Ron Francis	.05	.10
40	David Babych	.03	.05
41	Randy Ladouceur	.03	.05
42	Hartford Whalers logo	.03	.05
43	Kevin Dineen	.05	.10
44	Dean Evason	.03	.05
45	Ray Ferraro	.05	.10
46	Mike Tomlak	.03	.05
47	Bo-Mikael Andersson	.03	.05
48	Brad Shaw	.03	.05

MONTREAL CANADIENS

No.	Player	EX	NRMT
49	Chris Chelios	.08	.15
50	Petr Svoboda	.03	.05
51	Patrick Roy, Goalie	.50	1.00
52	Robert Smith	.03	.05
53	Stephane J.J. Richer	.03	.05
54	Shayne Corson	.03	.05
55	Brian Skrudland	.03	.05
56	Russell Courtnall	.05	.10
57	Montreal Canadiens logo	.03	.05
58	Guy Carbonneau	.05	.10
59	Sylvain Lefebvre	.05	.10
60	Mathieu Schneider	.05	.10
61	Brian Hayward, Goalie	.03	.05
62	Mats Naslund	.03	.05
63	Michael McPhee	.03	.05

NEW JERSEY DEVILS

No.	Player	EX	NRMT
64	Brendan Shanahan	.03	.05
65	Patrik Sundstrom	.03	.05
66	Mark Johnson	.03	.05
67	Doug Brown	.03	.05
68	Chris Terreri, Goalie	.03	.05
69	Bruce Driver	.03	.05
70	Peter Stastny	.05	.10
71	Sylvain Turgeon	.03	.05
72	New Jersey Devils logo	.03	.05
73	Kirk Muller	.08	.15
74	John MacLean	.05	.10
75	Viacheslav Fetisov	.05	.10
76	Tommy Albelin	.03	.05
77	Sean Burke, Goalie	.03	.05
78	Janne Ojanen	.03	.05

NEW YORK ISLANDERS

No.	Player	EX	NRMT
79	Randy Wood	.03	.05
80	Gary Nylund	.03	.05
81	Pat LaFontaine	.25	.50
82	Patrick Flatley	.03	.05
83	Bryan Trottier	.05	.10
84	Donald Maloney	.03	.05
85	Gerald Diduck	.03	.05
86	Mark Fitzpatrick, Goalie	.03	.05
87			
88	Glenn Healy, Goalie	.03	.05
89	Alan Kerr	.03	.05
90	Brent Sutter	.03	.05
91	Doug Crossman	.03	.05
92	Hubie McDonough	.03	.05
93	Jeff Norton	.03	.05

NEW YORK RANGERS

No.	Player	EX	NRMT
94	Kelly Kisio	.03	.05
95	Brian Leetch	.15	.30
96	Brian Mullen	.03	.05
97	James Patrick	.03	.05
98	Mike Richter, Goalie	.10	.20
99	John Ogrodnick	.03	.05
100	Troy Mallette	.03	.05
101	Mark Janssens	.03	.05
102	New York Rangers logo	.03	.05
103	Michael Gartner	.07	.15
104	Jan Erixon	.03	.05
105	Carey Wilson	.03	.05
106	Bernie Nicholls	.03	.05
107	Darren Turcotte	.05	.10
108	John Vanbiesbrouck, Goalie	.07	.15

PHILADELPHIA FLYERS

No.	Player	EX	NRMT
109	Ronald Sutter	.03	.05
110	Kjell Samuelsson	.03	.05
111	Ken Linseman	.03	.05

1990-91 STICKERS — PANINI • 331

No.	Player	EX	NRMT
112	Ken Wregget, Goalie	.03	.05
113	Per-Erik Eklund	.03	.05
114	Terry Carkner	.03	.05
115	Gordon Murphy	.03	.05
116	Murray Craven	.03	.05
117	Philadelphia Flyers logo	.03	.05
118	Ron Hextall, Goalie	.05	.10
119	Mike Bullard	.03	.05
120	Tim Kerr	.03	.05
121	Rick Tocchet	.05	.10
122	Mark Howe	.05	.10
123	Ilkka Sinisalo	.03	.05

PITTSBURGH PENGUINS

No.	Player	EX	NRMT
124	Tony Tanti	.03	.05
125	John Cullen	.03	.05
126	Zarley Zalapski	.03	.05
127	Wendell Young, Goalie	.03	.05
128	Rob Brown	.03	.05
129	Phil Bourque	.03	.05
130	Mark Recchi	.25	.50
131	Kevin Stevens	.25	.50
132	Pittsburgh Penguins logo	.03	.05
133	Bob Errey	.03	.05
134	Tom Barrasso, Goalie	.07	.15
135	Paul Coffey	.07	.15
136	Mario Lemieux	.50	1.00
137	Randy Hillier	.03	.05
138	Troy Loney	.03	.05

QUEBEC NORDIQUES

No.	Player	EX	NRMT
139	Joe Sakic	.15	.30
140	Lucien DeBlois	.03	.05
141	Joe Cirella	.03	.05
142	Ron Tugnutt, Goalie	.03	.05
143	Paul Gillis	.03	.05
144	Bryan Fogarty	.03	.05
145	Guy Lafleur	.05	.10
146	Anthony Hrkac	.03	.05
147	Quebec Nordiques logo	.03	.05
148	Michel Petit	.03	.05
149	Anthony McKegney	.03	.05
150	Curtis Leschyshyn	.03	.05
151	Claude Loiselle	.03	.05
152	Mario Brunetta, Goalie	.03	.05
153	Marc Fortier	.03	.05

WASHINGTON CAPITALS

No.	Player	EX	NRMT
154	Michal Pivonka	.03	.05
155	Scott Stevens	.10	.20
156	Kelly Miller	.03	.05
157	John Tucker	.03	.05
158	Donald Beaupre, Goalie	.03	.05
159	Geoff Courtnall	.07	.15
160	Alan May	.03	.05
161	Dino Ciccarelli	.07	.15
162	Washington Capitals logo	.03	.05
163	Mike Ridley	.03	.05
164	Robert Rouse	.03	.05
165	Mike Liut, Goalie	.03	.05
166	Stephen Leach	.05	.10
167	Kevin Hatcher	.05	.10
168	Dale Hunter	.03	.05

CALGARY FLAMES

No.	Player	EX	NRMT
169	Prince of Wales Trophy	.03	.05
170	Clarence Campbell Trophy	.03	.05
171	Stanley Cup Championship	.03	.05
172	Douglas Gilmour	.15	.30
173	Byron (Brad) McCrimmon	.03	.05
174	Joe Nieuwendyk	.05	.10
175	Mike Vernon, Goalie	.03	.05
176	Theoren Fleury	.05	.10
177	Gary Suter	.03	.05
178	Jamie Macoun	.03	.05
179	Gary Roberts	.07	.15
180	Calgary Flames logo	.03	.05

No.	Player	EX	NRMT
181	Paul Ranheim	.03	.05
182	Jiri Hrdina	.03	.05
183	Joe Mullen	.05	.10
184	Sergei Makarov	.05	.10
185	Allan MacInnis	.13	.25
186	Richard Wamsley, Goalie	.03	.05

CHICAGO BLACK HAWKS

No.	Player	EX	NRMT
187	Trent Yawney	.03	.05
188	Greg Millen, Goalie	.03	.05
189	Douglas Wilson	.03	.05
190	Jocelyn Lemieux	.03	.05
191	Dirk Graham	.03	.05
192	Keith Brown	.03	.05
193	Adam Creighton	.03	.05
194	Steve Larmer	.03	.05
195	Chicago Black Hawks logo	.03	.05
196	Gregory Gilbert	.03	.05
197	Jacques Cloutier, Goalie	.03	.05
198	Denis Savard	.05	.10
199	Dave Manson	.03	.05
200	Troy Murray	.03	.05
201	Jeremy Roenick	.35	.75

DETROIT RED WINGS

No.	Player	EX	NRMT
202	Lee Norwood	.03	.05
203	Glen Hanlon, Goalie	.03	.05
204	Marc Habscheid	.03	.05
205	Gerard Gallant	.03	.05
206	Richard Zombo	.03	.05
207	Steve Chiasson	.03	.05
208	Steve Yzerman	.13	.25
209	Bernie Federko	.03	.05
210	Detroit Red Wings logo	.03	.05
211	Joey Kocur	.03	.05
212	Tim Cheveldae, Goalie	.10	.20
213	Shawn Burr	.03	.05
214	Jimmy Carson	.03	.05
215	Mike O'Connell	.03	.05
216	John Chabot	.03	.05

EDMONTON OILERS

No.	Player	EX	NRMT
217	Craig Muni	.03	.05
218	Bill Ranford, Goalie	.03	.05
219	Mark Messier	.15	.30
220	Craig MacTavish	.03	.05
221	Charles Huddy	.03	.05
222	Jari Kurri	.05	.10
223	Esa Tikkanen	.03	.05
224	Kevin Lowe	.03	.05
225	Edmonton Oilers logo	.03	.05
226	James (Steve) Smith	.03	.05
227	Glenn Anderson	.05	.10
228	Petr Klima	.03	.05
229	Craig Simpson	.03	.05
230	Grant Fuhr, Goalie	.05	.10
231	Randall Gregg	.03	.05

LOS ANGELES KINGS

No.	Player	EX	NRMT
232	Bob Kudelski	.03	.05
233	Luc Robitaille	.10	.20
234	Martin McSorley	.03	.05
235	John Tonelli	.03	.05
236	David Taylor	.03	.05
237	Mikko Makela	.03	.05
238	Stephen Kasper	.03	.05
239	Tony Granato	.05	.10
240	Los Angeles Kings logo	.03	.05
241	Steve Duchesne	.07	.15
242	Wayne Gretzky	.75	1.50
243	Tomas Sandstrom	.05	.10
244	Larry Robinson	.03	.05
245	Michael Krushelnyski	.03	.05
246	Kelly Hrudey, Goalie	.03	.05

MINNESOTA NORTH STARS

No.	Player	EX	NRMT
247	Aaron Broten	.03	.05
248	Dave Gagner	.03	.05
249	Basil McRae	.03	.05
250	Curt Giles	.03	.05
251	Lawrence Murphy	.05	.10
252	Shawn Chambers	.03	.05
253	Michael Modano	.25	.50
254	Jon Casey, Goalie	.10	.20
255	Minnesota North Stars logo	.03	.05
256	Gaetan Duchesne	.03	.05
257	Brian Bellows	.05	.10
258	Frantisek Musil	.03	.05
259	Don Barber	.03	.05
260	Robert (Stewart) Gavin	.03	.05
261	Neal Broten	.03	.05

ST. LOUIS BLUES

No.	Player	EX	NRMT
262	Brett Hull	.35	.75
263	Sergio Momesso	.03	.05
264	Peter Zezel	.03	.05
265	Gino Cavallini	.03	.05
266	Rod Brind'Amour	.10	.20
267	Mike Lalor	.03	.05
268	Vincent Riendeau, Goalie	.05	.10
269	Gordon Roberts	.03	.05
270	St. Louis Blues logo	.03	.05
271	Paul MacLean	.03	.05
272	Curtis Joseph, Goalie	.10	.20
273	Richard Meagher	.03	.05
274	Jeff Brown	.03	.05
275	Adam Oates	.12	.25
276	Paul Cavallini	.03	.05

TORONTO MAPLE LEAFS

No.	Player	EX	NRMT
277	Bradley Marsh	.03	.05
278	Mark Osborne	.03	.05
279	Gary Leeman	.03	.05
280	George (Rob) Ramage	.03	.05
281	Jeff Reese, Goalie	.03	.05
282	Tom Fergus	.03	.05
283	Ed Olczyk	.03	.05
284	Daniel Marois	.03	.05
285	Toronto Maple Leafs logo	.03	.05
286	Wendel Clark	.12	.25
287	Tom Kurvers	.03	.05
288	Gilles Thibaudeau	.03	.05
289	Lou Franceschetti	.03	.05
290	Al Iafrate	.05	.10
291	Vincent Damphousse	.05	.10

VANCOUVER CANUCKS

No.	Player	EX	NRMT
292	Stanley Smyl	.03	.05
293	Paul Reinhart	.03	.05
294	Igor Larionov	.05	.10
295	Doug Lidster	.03	.05
296	Kirk McLean, Goalie	.10	.20
297	Andrew McBain	.03	.05
298	Petri Skriko	.03	.05
299	Trevor Linden	.08	.15
300	Vancouver Canucks logo	.03	.05
301	Steve Bozek	.03	.05
302	Brian Bradley	.03	.05
303	Greg Adams	.03	.05
304	Vladimir Krutov	.03	.05
305	Dan Quinn	.03	.05
306	Jim Sandlak	.03	.05

WINNIPEG JETS

No.	Player	EX	NRMT
307	Teppo Numminen	.03	.05
308	Douglas Smail	.03	.05
309	Gregory Paslawski	.03	.05
310	Dave Ellett	.03	.05
311	Bob Essensa, Goalie	.03	.05
312	Pat Elynuik	.03	.05
313	Paul Fenton	.03	.05
314	Randy Carlyle	.05	.10

332 • PANINI — 1991-92 STICKERS —

No.	Player	EX	NRMT
315	Winnipeg Jets logo	.03	.05
316	Thomas Steen	.03	.05
317	Dale Hawerchuk	.08	.15
318	Fredrick Olausson	.05	.10
319	Dave McLlwain	.03	.05
320	Laurie Boschman	.03	.05
321	Brent Ashton	.03	.05

REGULAR ISSUE

No.	Player	EX	NRMT
322	Raymond Bourque, Bos.	.12	.25
323	Patrick Roy, Goalie, Mon.	.50	1.00
324	Paul Coffey, Pit.	.05	.10
325	Brian Propp, Phi.	.05	.10
326	Mario Lemieux, Pit.	.50	1.00
327	Cam Neely, Bos.	.25	.50
328	Al MacInnis, Cal.	.07	.15
329	Mike Vernon, Goalie, Cal.	.05	.10
330	Kevin Lowe, Edm.	.03	.05
331	Luc Robitaille, LA	.10	.20
332	Wayne Gretzky, LA	.75	1.50
333	Brett Hull, St.L.	.25	.50
334	Sergei Makarov, Cal.	.03	.05
335	Alexei Kasatonov, Bos.	.03	.05
336	Igor Larionov, Van.	.03	.05
337	Vladamir Krutov, Van.	.03	.05
338	Alexander Mogilny, Bos.	.25	.50
339	Viacheslav Fetisov, NJ	.05	.10
340	Michael Modano, Min.	.20	.40
341	Mark Recchi, Pit.	.20	.40
342	Paul Ranheim, Cal.	.05	.10
343	Rod Brind'Amour, St.L.	.10	.20
344	Brad Shaw, Har.	.03	.05
345	Mike Richter, Goalie, NYR	.10	.20

TROPHIES

No.	Player	EX	NRMT
346	Hart Memorial Trophy	.03	.05
347	Art Ross Trophy	.03	.05
348	Calder Memorial Trophy	.03	.05
349	Lady Byng Memorial Trophy	.03	.05
350	James Norris Memorial Trophy	.03	.05
351	Vezina Trophy	.03	.05

— 1991 - 92 STICKERS —

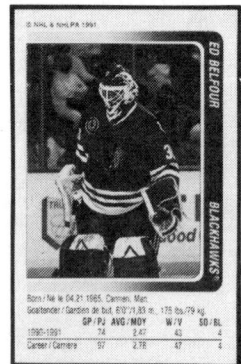

1991-92 Panini Stickers
Sticker No. 9, Ed Belfour

Sticker Size: 1 13/16" X 27/8"
Face: Four colour, white border; Name, Team
Back: Black and white on card stock; Number, Resume
Imprint: PANINI
Complete Set No.: 344
Complete Set Price: 10.00   20.00
Common Player: .03   .05
Album: 2.50   5.00

No.	Player	EX	NRMT
1	NHL Logo	.03	.05
2	NHLPA Logo	.03	.05
3	NHL 75th Anniversary Logo	.03	.05
4	NHL 75th Anniversary Logo	.03	.05
5	Clarence Campbell Conference Logo	.03	.05
6	Prince of Wales Converence Logo	.03	.05
7	Stanley Cup Championship Logo	.03	.05

CHICAGO BLACK HAWKS

No.	Player	EX	NRMT
8	Steve Larmer	.03	.05
9	Ed Belfour, Goalie	.15	.30
10	Chris Chelios	.05	.10
11	Michel Goulet	.05	.10
12	Jeremy Roenick	.20	.40
13	Adam Creighton	.03	.05
14	Steve Thomas	.03	.05
15	Dave Manson	.03	.05
16	Dirk Graham	.03	.05
17	Troy Murray	.03	.05
18	Douglas Wilson	.03	.05
19	Wayne Presley	.03	.05
20	Jocelyn Lemieux	.03	.05
21	Keith Brown	.03	.05

ST. LOUIS BLUES

No.	Player	EX	NRMT
22	Curtis Joseph, Goalie	.12	.25
23	Jeff Brown	.03	.05
24	Gino Cavallini	.03	.05
25	Brett Hull	.15	.30
26	Scott Stevens	.10	.20
27	Dan Quinn	.03	.05
28	Garth Butcher	.03	.05
29	Bob Bassen	.03	.05
30	Rod Brind'Amour	.07	.15
31	Adam Oates	.10	.20
32	Dave Lowry	.03	.05
33	Richard Sutter	.03	.05
34	Ronald Wilson	.03	.05
35	Paul Cavallini	.03	.05

VANCOUVER CANUCKS

No.	Player	EX	NRMT
36	Trevor Linden	.08	.15
37	Troy Gamble, Goalie	.03	.05
38	Geoff Courtnall	.05	.10
39	Greg Adams	.03	.05
40	Doug Lidster	.03	.05
41	Dave Capuano	.03	.05
42	Igor Larionov	.05	.10
43	Tom Kurvers	.03	.05
44	Sergio Momesso	.03	.05
45	Kirk McLean, Goalie	.07	.15
46	Cliff Ronning	.03	.05
47	Robert Kron	.03	.05
48	Steve Bozek	.03	.05
49	Petr Nedved	.10	.20

CALGARY FLAMES

No.	Player	EX	NRMT
50	Al MacInnis	.05	.10
51	Theoren Fleury	.10	.15
52	Gary Roberts	.10	.15
53	Joe Nieuwendyk	.10	.15
54	Paul Ranheim	.03	.05
55	Mike Vernon, Goalie	.05	.10
56	Carey Wilson	.03	.05
57	Gary Suter	.03	.05
58	Sergei Makarov	.03	.05
59	Douglas Gilmour	.13	.25
60	Joel Otto	.03	.05
61	Jamie Macoun	.03	.05
62	Stephane Matteau	.03	.05
63	Robert Reichel	.03	.05

WINNIPEG JETS

No.	Player	EX	NRMT
64	Ed Olczyk	.03	.05
65	Phil Housley	.03	.05
66	Pat Elynuik	.03	.05
67	Fredrik Olausson	.03	.05
68	Thomas Steen	.03	.05
69	Paul MacDermid	.03	.05
70	Brent Ashton	.03	.05
71	Teppo Numminen	.03	.05
72	Danton Cole	.03	.05
73	Dave McLlwain	.03	.05
74	Scott Arniel	.03	.05
75	Bob Essensa, Goalie	.05	.10
76	Randy Carlyle	.03	.05
77	Mark Osborne	.03	.05

LOS ANGELES KINGS

No.	Player	EX	NRMT
78	Wayne Gretzky	.75	1.50
79	Tomas Sandstrom	.05	.10
80	Steve Duchesne	.05	.10
81	Kelly Hrudey, Goalie	.05	.05
82	Larry Robinson	.05	.10
83	Tony Granato	.05	.10
84	Martin McSorley	.03	.05
85	Todd Elik	.03	.05
86	Rob Blake	.05	.10
87	Bob Kudelski	.03	.05
88	Stephen Kasper	.03	.05
89	David Taylor	.03	.05
90	John Tonelli	.03	.05
91	Luc Robitaille	.10	.20

TORONTO MAPLE LEAFS

No.	Player	EX	NRMT
92	Vincent Damphousse	.05	.10
93	Brian Bradley	.03	.05
94	Dave Ellett	.03	.05
95	Daniel Marois	.03	.05
96	George (Rob) Ramage	.03	.05
97	Michael Krushelnyski	.03	.05
98	Michel Petit	.03	.05
99	Peter Ing, Goalie	.03	.05
100	Lucien DeBlois	.03	.05
101	Robert Rouse	.03	.05
102	Wendel Clark	.10	.20
103	Peter Zezel	.03	.05
104	David Reid	.03	.05
105	Aaron Broten	.03	.05

MINNESOTA NORTH STARS

No.	Player	EX	NRMT
106	Brian Hayward, Goalie	.03	.05
107	Neal Broten	.03	.05
108	Brian Bellows	.08	.15
109	Mark Timordi	.03	.05
110	Ulf Dahlen	.03	.05
111	Douglas Smail	.03	.05
112	Dave Gagner	.03	.05
113	Robert Smith	.03	.05
114	Brian Glynn	.03	.05
115	Brian Propp	.03	.05
116	Michael Modano	.12	.25
117	Gaetan Duchesne	.03	.05
118	Jon Casey, Goalie	.05	.10
119	Basil McRae	.03	.05

EDMONTON OILERS

No.	Player	EX	NRMT
120	Glenn Anderson	.05	.10
121	James (Steve) Smith	.03	.05
122	Adam Graves	.03	.05
123	Esa Tikkanen	.03	.05
124	Mark Messier	.10	.20
125	Bill Ranford, Goalie	.05	.10
126	Petr Klima	.03	.05
127	Anatoli Semenov	.03	.05
128	Martin Gelinas	.03	.05
129	Charles Huddy	.03	.05
130	Craig Simpson	.03	.05
131	Kevin Lowe	.03	.05
132	Craig MacTavish	.03	.05
133	Craig Muni	.03	.05

DETROIT RED WINGS

No.	Player	EX	NRMT
134	Steve Yzerman	.13	.25
135	Shawn Burr	.03	.05
136	Tim Cheveldae, Goalie	.05	.10
137	Richard Zombo	.03	.05

1991-92 STICKERS — PANINI • 333

No.	Player	EX	NRMT
138	Marc Habscheid	.03	.05
139	Jimmy Carson	.03	.05
140	Brent Fedyk	.03	.05
141	Yves Racine	.03	.05
142	Gerard Gallant	.03	.05
143	Steve Chiasson	.03	.05
144	Johan Garpenlov	.03	.05
145	Sergei Fedorov	.20	.40
146	Bob Probert	.03	.05
147	Richard Green	.03	.05

CLARENCE CAMPBELL CONFERENCE

No.	Player	EX	NRMT
148	Chicago Black Hawks	.03	.05
149	Detroit Red Wings	.03	.05
150	Minnesota North Stars	.03	.05
151	St. Louis Blues	.03	.05
152	Toronto Maple Leafs	.03	.05
153	Calgary Flames	.03	.05
154	Edmonton Oilers	.03	.05
155	Los Angeles Kings	.03	.05
156	San Jose Sharks	.03	.05
157	Vancouver Canucks	.03	.05
158	Winnipeg Jets	.03	.05

PRINCE OF WALES CONFERENCE

No.	Player	EX	NRMT
159	Boston Bruins	.03	.05
160	Buffalo Sabres	.03	.05
161	Hartford Whalers	.03	.05
162	Montreal Canadiens	.03	.05
163	Quebec Nordiques	.03	.05
164	New Jersey Devils	.03	.05
165	New York Islanders	.03	.05
166	New York Rangers	.03	.05
167	Philadelphia Flyers	.03	.05
168	Pittsburgh Penguins	.03	.05
169	Washington Capitals	.03	.05

BOSTON BRUINS

No.	Player	EX	NRMT
170	Craig Janney	.05	.10
171	Raymond Bourque	.10	.20
172	Rejean Lemelin, Goalie	.03	.05
173	Dave Christian	.03	.05
174	Randy Burridge	.03	.05
175	Garry Galley	.03	.05
176	Cam Neely	.10	.20
177	Robert Sweeney	.03	.05
178	Kenneth Hodge, Jr.	.03	.05
179	Andrew Moog, Goalie	.03	.05
180	Don Sweeney	.03	.05
181	Robert Carpenter	.03	.05
182	Glen Wesley	.03	.05
183	Christopher Nilan	.03	.05

MONTREAL CANADIENS

No.	Player	EX	NRMT
184	Patrick Roy, Goalie	.35	.75
185	Petr Svoboda	.03	.05
186	Russ Courtnall	.03	.05
187	Denis Savard	.05	.10
188	Michael McPhee	.03	.05
189	Eric Desjardins	.03	.05
190	Mike Keane	.03	.05
191	Stephan Lebeau	.05	.10
192	Jean-Jacques Daigneault	.03	.05
193	Stephane J.J. Richer	.03	.05
194	Brian Skrudland	.03	.05
195	Mathieu Schneider	.03	.05
196	Shayne Corson	.03	.05
197	Guy Carbonneau	.05	.10

WASHINGTON CAPITALS

No.	Player	EX	NRMT
198	Kevin Hatcher	.05	.10
199	Mike Ridley	.03	.05
200	John Druce	.03	.05
201	Donald Beaupre, Goalie	.03	.05
202	Kelly Miller	.03	.05
203	Dale Hunter	.03	.05
204	Nicholas Kypreos	.03	.05
205	Calle Johansson	.03	.05
206	Michal Pivonka	.03	.05
207	Dino Ciccarelli	.05	.10
208	Al Iafrate	.05	.10
209	Rod Langway	.03	.05
210	Mikhail Tatarinov	.03	.05
211	Stephen Leach	.05	.10

NEW JERSEY DEVILS

No.	Player	EX	NRMT
212	Sean Burke, Goalie	.03	.05
213	John MacLean	.05	.10
214	Lee Norwood	.03	.05
215	Laurie Boschman	.03	.05
216	Alexei Kasatonov	.03	.05
217	Patrik Sundstrom	.03	.05
218	Ken Daneyko	.03	.05
219	Kirk Muller	.08	.15
220	Peter Stastny	.05	.10
221	Chris Terreri, Goalie	.03	.05
222	Brendan Shanahan	.05	.10
223	Eric Weinrich	.03	.05
224	Claude Lemieux	.03	.05
225	Bruce Driver	.03	.05

PHILADELPHIA FLYERS

No.	Player	EX	NRMT
226	Tim Kerr	.03	.05
227	Ron Hextall, Goalie	.03	.05
228	Per-Erik Eklund	.03	.05
229	Rick Tocchet	.05	.10
230	Gordon Murphy	.03	.05
231	Mike Ricci	.10	.20
232	Derrick Smith	.03	.05
233	Ronald Sutter	.03	.05
234	Murray Craven	.03	.05
235	Terry Carkner	.03	.05
236	Ken Wregget, Goalie	.03	.05
237	Keith Acton	.03	.05
238	Scott Mellanby	.03	.05
239	Kjell Samuelsson	.03	.05

NEW YORK ISLANDERS

No.	Player	EX	NRMT
240	Jeff Hackett, Goalie	.03	.05
241	David Volek	.03	.05
242	Craig Ludwig	.03	.05
243	Pat LaFontaine	.13	.25
244	Randy Wood	.03	.05
245	Patrick Flatley	.03	.05
246	Brent Sutter	.03	.05
247	Derek King	.05	.10
248	Jeff Norton	.03	.05
249	Glenn Healy, Goalie	.03	.05
250	Ray Ferraro	.03	.05
251	Gary Nylund	.03	.05
252	Joe Reekie	.03	.05
253	David Chyzowski	.03	.05

QUEBEC NORDIQUES

No.	Player	EX	NRMT
254	Mike Hough	.03	.05
255	Mats Sundin	.08	.15
256	Curtis Leschyshyn	.03	.05
257	Joe Sakic	.10	.20
258	Stephane Fiset, Goalie	.03	.05
259	Bryan Fogarty	.03	.05
260	Alexei Gusarov	.03	.05
261	Steven Finn	.03	.05
262	Everett Sanipass	.03	.05
263	Stephane Morin	.03	.05
264	Craig Wolanin	.03	.05
265	Randy Velischek	.03	.05
266	Owen Nolan	.05	.10
267	Ron Tugnutt, Goalie	.03	.05

PITTSBURGH PENGUINS

No.	Player	EX	NRMT
268	Mario Lemieux	.35	.75
269	Kevin Stevens	.10	.20
270	Lawrence Murphy	.05	.10
271	Tom Barrasso, Goalie	.05	.10
272	Phil Bourque	.03	.05
273	Scott Young	.03	.05
274	Paul Stanton	.03	.05
275	Jaromir Jagr	.10	.20
276	Paul Coffey	.05	.10
277	Ulf Samuelsson	.03	.05
278	Joe Mullen	.05	.10
279	Bob Errey	.03	.05
280	Mark Recchi	.10	.20
281	Ron Francis	.05	.10

NEW YORK RANGERS

No.	Player	EX	NRMT
282	John Vanbiesbrouck, Goalie	.07	.15
283	Jan Erixon	.03	.05
284	Brian Leetch	.10	.20
285	Darren Turcotte	.03	.05
286	Ray Sheppard	.05	.10
287	James Patrick	.03	.05
288	Bernie Nicholls	.03	.05
289	Brian Mullen	.03	.05
290	Mike Richter, Goalie	.03	.05
291	Kelly Kisio	.03	.05
292	Michael Gartner	.07	.15
293	John Ogrodnick	.03	.05
294	David Shaw	.03	.05
295	Troy Mallette	.03	.05

BUFFALO SABRES

No.	Player	EX	NRMT
296	Dale Hawerchuk	.05	.10
297	Richard Vaive	.03	.05
298	Daren Puppa, Goalie	.03	.05
299	Michael Ramsey	.03	.05
300	Benoit Hogue	.03	.05
301	Clint Malarchuk, Goalie	.03	.05
302	Mikko Makela	.03	.05
303	Pierre Turgeon	.08	.15
304	Alexander Mogilny	.10	.20
305	Uwe Krupp	.03	.05
306	Christian Ruuttu	.03	.05
307	Doug Bodger	.03	.05
308	Dave Snuggerud	.03	.05
309	David Andreychuk	.07	.15

HARTFORD WHALERS

No.	Player	EX	NRMT
310	Peter Sidorkiewicz, Goalie	.03	.05
311	Brad Shaw	.03	.05
312	Dean Evason	.03	.05
313	Patrick Verbeek	.03	.05
314	John Cullen	.05	.10
315	Rob Brown	.03	.05
316	Robert Holik	.03	.05
317	Todd Krygier	.03	.05
318	Adam Burt	.03	.05
319	Mike Tomlak	.03	.05
320	Randy Cunneyworth	.03	.05
321	Paul Cyr	.03	.05
322	Zarley Zalapski	.05	.10
323	Kevin Dineen	.03	.05

1991 NHL ALL-STAR GAME

CLARENCE CAMPBELL CONFERENCE

No.	Player	EX	NRMT
324	Luc Robitaille	.08	.15
325	Brett Hull	.10	.20
326	All-Star Game Logo	.03	.05
327	Wayne Gretzky	.35	.75
328	Mike Vernon, Goalie	.05	.10
329	Chris Chelios	.08	.15
330	Al MacInnis	.03	.05

PRINCE OF WALES CONFERENCE

No.	Player	EX	NRMT
331	Rick Tocchet	.05	.10
332	Cam Neely	.05	.10
333	Patrick Roy, Goalie	.25	.50

334 • PANINI — 1992-93 STICKERS —

No.	Player	EX	NRMT
334	Joe Sakic	.10	.20
335	Raymond Bourque	.10	.20
336	Paul Coffey	.05	.10

TOP NHL ROOKIES

No.	Player	EX	NRMT
337	Ed Belfour, Goalie	.15	.30
338	Mike Ricci	.10	.20
339	Rob Blake	.05	.10
340	Sergei Fedorov	.20	.40
341	Kenneth Hodge, Jr.	.03	.05
342	Robert Holik	.03	.05
343	Robert Reichel	.03	.05
344	Jaromir Jagr	.15	.30

— 1992-93 STICKERS —

This 308-sticker set is the same quality as previous years, but Panini added a unique subset that has since caught the eye of the collector. The subset has the better rookies and second-year cards of the most popular players.

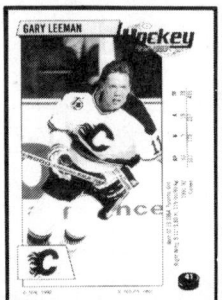 

1992-93 Panini Stickers
Sticker No. 41, Gary Leeman

Sticker Size: 2 1/2" x 3 1/2"
Face: Four colour, white border; Name, Number, Resume
Back: Four colour, Name, Logos, Slap-Shot Game question and answer
Imprint: Printed in Italy by Panini S.r.l. © Panini Canada Ltd
© NHL 1992 © NHLPA 1992
Complete Set No.: 308
Complete Set Price: 20.00 20.00
Common Card: .05 .05
Album: 5.00

1992 STANLEY CUP CHAMPIONS

No.	Player	English NRMT	Frencg NRMT
1	Stanley Cup	.50	.50

CHICAGO BLACKHAWKS

No.	Player	English NRMT	French NRMT
2	Chicago Blackhawks Logo	.10	.10
3	Ed Belfour, Goalie	.20	.20
4	Jeremy Roenick	.25	.25
5	Steve Larmer	.05	.05
6	Michel Goulet	.05	.05
7	Dirk Graham	.05	.05
8	Jocelyn Lemieux	.05	.05
9	Brian Noonan	.05	.05
10	Rob Brown	.05	.05
11	Chris Chelios	.05	.05
12	James (Steve) Smith	.05	.05
13	Keith Brown	.05	.05

ST. LOUIS BLUES

No.	Player	English NRMT	French NRMT
14	St. Louis Blues Logo	.10	.10
15	Curtis Joseph, Goalie	.20	.20
16	Brett Hull	.30	.30
17	Brendan Shanahan	.20	.20
18	Ronald Wilson	.05	.05
19	Richard Sutter	.05	.05
20	Ronald Sutter	.05	.05
21	Dave Lowry	.05	.05
22	Craig Janney	.10	.10
23	Paul Cavallini	.05	.05
24	Garth Butcher	.05	.05
25	Jeff Brown	.05	.05

VANCOUVER CANUCKS

No.	Player	English NRMT	French NRMT
26	Vancouver Canucks Logo	.10	.10
27	Kirk McLean, Goalie	.15	.15
28	Trevor Linden	.15	.15
29	Geoff Courtnall	.10	.10
30	Cliff Ronning	.05	.05
31	Petr Nedved	.10	.10
32	Igor Larionov	.05	.05
33	Robert Kron	.05	.05
34	Jim Sandlak	.05	.05
35	David Babych	.05	.05
36	Jyrki Lumme	.05	.05
37	Doug Lidster	.05	.05

CALGARY FLAMES

No.	Player	English NRMT	French NRMT
38	Calgary Flames Logo	.10	.10
39	Michael Vernon, Goalie	.05	.05
40	Joe Nieuwendyk	.15	.15
41	Gary Leeman	.05	.05
42	Robert Reichel	.15	.15
43	Joel Otto	.05	.05
44	Paul Ranheim	.05	.05
45	Gary Roberts	.05	.05
46	Theoren Fleury	.15	.15
47	Sergei Makarov	.10	.10
48	Gary Suter	.05	.05
49	Allan MacInnis	.05	.05

WINNIPEG JETS

No.	Player	English NRMT	French NRMT
50	Winnipeg Jets Logo	.10	.10
51	Bob Essensa, Goalie	.05	.05
52	Teppo Numminen	.05	.05
53	Thomas Steen	.05	.05
54	Pat Elynuik	.05	.05
55	Ed Olczyk	.05	.05
56	Danton Cole	.05	.05
57	Troy Murray	.05	.05
58	Darrin Shannon	.05	.05
59	Russell Romaniuk	.05	.05
60	Fredrik Olausson	.05	.05
61	Phil Housley	.05	.05

LOS ANGELES KINGS

No.	Player	English NRMT	French NRMT
62	Los Angeles Kings Logo	.10	.10
63	Kelly Hrudey, Goalie	.05	.05
64	Wayne Gretzky	1.00	1.00
65	Luc Robitaille	.25	.25
66	Jari Kurri	.15	.15
67	Tomas Sandstrom	.10	.10
68	Tony Granato	.05	.05
69	Bob Kudelski	.10	.10
70	Corey Millen	.10	.10
71	Robert Blake	.10	.10
72	Paul Coffey	.10	.10
73	Martin McSorley	.05	.05

TORONTO MAPLE LEAFS

No.	Player	English NRMT	French NRMT
74	Toronto Maple Leafs Logo	.10	.10
75	Grant Fuhr, Goalie	.10	.10
76	Glenn Anderson	.10	.10
77	Douglas Gilmour	.25	.25
78	Michael Krushelnyski	.05	.05
79	Wendel Clark	.20	.20
80	Rob Pearson	.05	.05
81	Peter Zezel	.05	.05
82	Todd Gill	.05	.05
83	David Ellett	.05	.05
84	Mike Foligno	.05	.05
85	Ken Baumgartner	.05	.05

MINNESOTA NORTH STARS

No.	Player	English NRMT	French NRMT
86	Minnesota North Stars Logo	.10	.10
87	Jon Casey, Goalie	.10	.10
88	Brian Bellows	.10	.10
89	Neal Broten	.10	.05
90	Dave Gagner	.10	.05
91	Michael Modano	.15	.15
92	Ulf Dahlen	.05	.05
93	Brian Propp	.05	.05
94	Jim Johnson	.05	.05
95	Mike Craig	.05	.05
96	Robert (Bobby) Smith	.05	.05
97	Mark Tinordi	.05	.05

EDMONTON OILERS

No.	Player	English NRMT	French NRMT
98	Edmonton Oilers Logo	.10	.10
99	Bill Ranford, Goalie	.10	.10
100	Joe Murphy	.05	.05
101	Craig MacTavish	.05	.05
102	Craig Simpson	.05	.05
103	Esa Tikkanen	.05	.05
104	Vincent Damphousse	.10	.10
105	Petr Klima	.05	.05
106	Martin Gelinas	.10	.10
107	Kevin Lowe	.05	.05
108	Dave Manson	.05	.05
109	Bernie Nicholls	.10	.10

DETROIT RED WINGS

No.	Player	English NRMT	French NRMT
110	Detroit Red Wings Logo	.10	.10
111	Tim Cheveldae, Goalie	.10	.10
112	Steve Yzerman	.25	.25
113	Sergei Fedorov	.30	.30
114	Jimmy Carson	.05	.05
115	Kevin Miller	.05	.05
116	Gerard Gallant	.05	.05
117	Keith Primeau	.05	.05
118	Paul Ysebaert	.05	.05
119	Yves Racine	.05	.05
120	Steve Chiasson	.05	.05
121	Ray Sheppard	.10	.10

SAN JOSE SHARKS

No.	Player	English NRMT	French NRMT
122	San Jose Sharks Logo	.25	.25
123	Jeff Hackett, Goalie	.05	.05
124	Kelly Kisio	.05	.05
125	Brian Mullen	.05	.05
126	David Bruce	.05	.05
127	Rob Zettler	.05	.05
128	Neil Wilkinson	.05	.05
129	Douglas Wilson	.05	.05
130	Jeff Odgers	.05	.05
131	Dean Evason	.05	.05
132	Brian Lawton	.05	.05
133	Dale Craigwell	.05	.05

BOSTON BRUINS

No.	Player	English NRMT	French NRMT
134	Boston Bruins Logo	.10	.10
135	Andrew Moog, Goalie	.10	.10
136	Adam Oates	.20	.20
137	David Poulin	.05	.05
138	Vladimir Ruzicka	.05	.05
139	Jeff Lazaro	.05	.05
140	Robert Carpenter	.05	.05
141	Peter Douris	.05	.05

1992-93 STICKERS — PANINI • 335

No.	Player	English NRMT	French NRMT
142	Glen Murray	.05	.05
143	Cam Neely	.20	.20
144	Raymond Bourque	.25	.25
145	Glen Wesley	.05	.05

MONTREAL CANADIENS

No.	Player	English NRMT	French NRMT
146	Montreal Canadiens Logo	.10	.10
147	Patrick Roy, Goalie	.75	.75
148	Kirk Muller	.20	.20
149	Guy Carbonneau	.05	.05
150	Shayne Corson	.05	.05
151	Stephan Lebeau	.05	.05
152	Dennis Savard	.10	.10
153	Brent Gilchrist	.05	.05
154	Russell Courtnall	.05	.05
155	Patrice Brisebois	.05	.05
156	Eric Desjardins	.05	.05
157	Mathieu Schneider	.05	.05

WASHINGTON CAPITALS

No.	Player	English NRMT	French NRMT
158	Washington Capitals Logo	.10	.10
159	Donald Beaupre, Goalie	.05	.05
160	Dino Ciccarelli	.10	.10
161	Michal Pivonka	.05	.05
162	Mike Ridley	.05	.05
163	Randy Burridge	.05	.05
164	Peter Bondra	.05	.05
165	Dale Hunter	.05	.05
166	Kelly Miller	.05	.05
167	Kevin Hatcher	.05	.05
168	Al Iafrate	.10	.10
169	Rod Langway	.05	.05

NEW JERSEY DEVILS

No.	Player	English NRMT	French NRMT
170	New Jersey Devils Logo	.10	.10
171	Chris Terreri, Goalie	.05	.05
172	Claude Lemieux	.05	.05
173	Stephane J. J. Richer	.05	.05
174	Peter Stastny	.05	.05
175	Zdeno Ciger	.05	.05
176	Alexander Semak	.05	.05
177	Valeri Zelepukin	.05	.05
178	Bruce Driver	.05	.05
179	Scott Niedermayer	.10	.10
180	Alexei Kasatonov	.05	.05
181	Scott Stevens	.10	.10

PHILADELPHIA FLYERS

No.	Player	English NRMT	French NRMT
182	Philadelphia Flyers Logo	.10	.10
183	Dominic Roussel, Goalie	.05	.05
184	Mike Ricci	.10	.10
185	Mark Recchi	.10	.10
186	Kevin Dineen	.10	.05
187	Rod Brind'Amour	.10	.10
188	Mark Pederson	.05	.05
189	Per-Erik (Pelle) Eklund	.05	.05
190	Terry Carkner	.05	.05
191	Mark Howe	.10	.10
192	Steve Duchesne	.05	.05
193	Andrei Lomakin	.05	.05

NEW YORK ISLANDERS

No.	Player	English NRMT	French NRMT
194	New York Islanders Logo	.10	.10
195	Mark Fitzpatrick, Goalie	.05	.05
196	Pierre Turgeon	.15	.15
197	Benoit Hogue	.05	.05
198	Ray Ferraro	.05	.05
199	Derek King	.10	.10
200	David Volek	.05	.05
201	Patrick Flatley	.05	.05
202	Uwe Krupp	.05	.05
203	Steve Thomas	.05	.05
204	Adam Creighton	.05	.05
205	Jeff Norton	.05	.05

QUEBEC NORDIQUES

No.	Player	English NRMT	French NRMT
206	Quebec Nordiques Logo	.10	.10
207	Stephane Fiset, Goalie	.05	.05
208	Mikhail Tatarinov	.05	.05
209	Joe Sakic	.20	.20
210	Owen Nolan	.15	.15
211	Mike Hough	.05	.05
212	Mats Sundin	.15	.15
213	Claude Lapointe	.05	.05
214	Stephane Morin	.05	.05
215	Alexei Gusarov	.05	.05
216	Steven Finn	.05	.05
217	Curtis Leschyshyn	.05	.05

PITTSBURGH PENGUINS

No.	Player	English NRMT	French NRMT
218	Pittsburgh Penguins Logo	.10	.10
219	Tom Barrasso, Goalie	.05	.05
220	Mario Lemieux	.75	.75
221	Kevin Stevens	.20	.20
222	Shawn McEachern	.50	.50
223	Joe Mullen	.05	.05
224	Ronald Francis	.05	.05
225	Phillippe Bourque	.05	.05
226	Rick Tocchet	.15	.15
227	Bryan Trottier	.05	.05
228	Lawrence (Larry) Murphy	.10	.10
229	Ulf Samuelsson	.05	.05

NEW YORK RANGERS

No.	Player	English NRMT	French NRMT
230	New York Rangers Logo	.10	.10
231	Mike Richter, Goalie	.15	.15
232	John Vanbiesbrouck, Goalie	.15	.15
233	Mark Messier	.50	.50
234	Sergei Nemchinov	.15	.15
235	Darren Turcotte	.05	.05
236	Doug Weight	.10	.10
237	Michael Gartner	.15	.15
238	Adam Graves	.15	.15
239	Brian Leetch	.25	.25
240	James Patrick	.05	.05
241	Jan Erixon	.05	.05

BUFFALO SABRES

No.	Player	English NRMT	French NRMT
242	Buffalo Sabres Logo	.10	.10
243	Tom Draper, Goalie	.05	.05
244	Grant Ledyard	.05	.05
245	Doug Bodger	.05	.05
246	Pat LaFontaine	.30	.30
247	Dale Hawerchuk	.05	.05
248	Alexander Mogilny	.30	.30
249	David Andreychuk	.15	.15
250	Christian Ruuttu	.05	.05
251	Randy Wood	.05	.05
252	Brad May	.05	.05
253	Michael Ramsey	.05	.05

HARTFORD WHALERS

No.	Player	English NRMT	French NRMT
254	Hartford Whalers Logo	.10	.10
255	Kay Whitmore, Goalie	.05	.05
256	Patrick Verbeek	.05	.05
257	John Cullen	.05	.05
258	Bo Mikael Andersson	.05	.05
259	Yvon Corriveau	.10	.10
260	Randy Cunneyworth	.05	.05
261	Robert Holik	.10	.10
262	Murray Craven	.05	.05
263	Zarley Zalapski	.05	.05
264	Adam Burt	.05	.05
265	Brad Shaw	.05	.05

THE 1992 NEWCOMERS
TAMPA BAY LIGHTNING

No.	Player	English NRMT	French NRMT
266	Tampa Bay Lightning Logo	.50	.50
267	Tampa Bay Lighning Jersey	.50	.50

OTTAWA SENATORS

No.	Player	English NRMT	French NRMT
268	Ottawa Senators Logo	.50	.50
269	Ottawa Senators Jersey	.50	.50

1992 NHL'S TOP ROOKIES

No.	Player	English NRMT	French NRMT
270	Anthony Amonte, NYR	.15	.15
271	Pavel Bure, Van.	1.00	1.00
272	Gilbert Dionne, Mon.	.15	.15
273	Pat Falloon, SJ	.25	.25
274	Nicklas Lidstrom, Det.	.15	.15
275	Kevin Todd, NJ	.15	.15

1992 ALL-STAR GAME

No.	Player	English NRMT	French NRMT
276	Prince of Wales Conference Logo	.10	.10
277	Patrick Roy, Goalie, Mon.	.75	.75
278	Paul Coffey, LA	.25	.25
279	Raymond Bourque, Bos.	.25	.25
280	Mario Lemieux, Pit.	.75	.75
281	Kevin Stevens, Pit.	.20	.20
282	Jaromir Jagr, Pit.	.30	.30
283	Clarence Campbell Conference Logo	.10	.10
284	Ed Belfour, Goalie, Chi.	.20	.20
285	Allan MacInnis, Cal.	.10	.10
286	Chris Chelios, Chi.	.10	.10
287	Wayne Gretzky, LA	1.00	1.00
288	Luc Robitaille, LA	.20	.20
289	Brett Hull, St.L	.40	.40

EUROPEAN INVASION

No.	Player	English NRMT	French NRMT
290	Pavel Bure, Van.	.50	.50
291	Sergei Fedorov, Det.	.25	.25
292	Dominik Hasek, Goalie	.10	.10
293	Robert Holik, Har.	.10	.10
294	Jaromir Jagr, Pit.	.50	.50
295	Valeri Kamensky	.20	.20
296	Alexander Semak, NJ	.10	.10
297	Igor Kravchuk, Chi.	.10	.10
298	Nicklas Lidstrom, Det.	.10	.10
299	Alexander Mogilny, Buf.	.50	.50
300	Petr Nedved, Van.	.25	.25
301	Robert Reichel, Cal.	.15	.15
302	Mats Sundin, Que.	.20	.20

THE TROPHIES

No.	Player	English NRMT	French NRMT
303	Calder Trophy	.10	.10
304	Hart Trophy	.10	.10
305	Lady Byng Trophy	.10	.10
306	Norris Trophy	.10	.10
307	Frank J. Selke Trophy	.10	.10
308	Vezina Trophy	.10	.10

336 • PANINI — 1992-93 INSERT SET —

— 1992-93 INSERT SET —

Randomly inserted one card per pack.

1992-93 Panini Insert Set Stickers
Sticker No. E, Luciano Borsato

Sticker Size: 2 1/2" X 3 1/2"
Face: Four colour, glitter border; Name, Resume
Back: Black on white card stock
Imprint: PANINI Printed in Italy
Complete Set No.: 22
Complete Set Price: 20.00 40.00

No.	Player	English NRMT	French NRMT
A	Igor Kravchuk, Chi.	1.00	1.00
B	Nelson Emerson, St.L	1.00	1.00
C	Pavel Bure, Van.	7.00	7.00
D	Tomas Forslund, Cal.	1.00	1.00
E	Luciano Borsato, Win.	1.00	1.00
F	Darryl Sydor, LA	1.00	1.00
G	Felix Potvin, Goalie, Tor.	7.00	7.00
H	Derian Hatcher, Min.	1.00	1.00
I	Josef Beranek, Edm.	3.00	3.00
J	Nicklas Lidstrom, Det.	2.00	2.00
K	Pat Falloon, SJ	3.50	3.50
L	Joseph Juneau, Bos.	5.00	5.00
M	Gilbert Dionne, Mon.	1.00	1.00
N	Dimitri Khristich, Wash.	1.00	1.00
O	Kevin Todd, NJ	1.00	1.00
P	Eric Lindros, Phi.	9.00	10.00
Q	Scott Lachance, NYI	1.00	1.00
R	Valeri Kamensky, Que.	1.00	1.00
S	Jarimir Jagr, Pit.	4.00	4.00
T	Anthony Amonte, NYR	2.00	2.00
U	Donald Audette, Buf.	1.00	1.00
V	Geoff Sanderson, Har.	2.00	2.00

— ACTION FREAKS 1992 - 1993 —

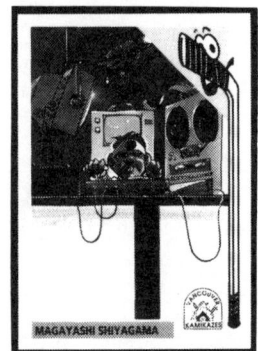

Action Freaks 1992-93
Sticker No. 83, Magayashi Shiyagama

Card Size: 2 1/2" X 3 1/2"
Face: Four colour, white border; Name
Back: Black and white
Imprint: Printed in Italy. Impreme en Italie
Complete Set No.: 100
Complete Set Price: 5.00 10.00
Common Card: .05 .10

CHECKLIST

No.	Player	EX	NRMT
1	Checklist (1-46)	.05	.10

BOSTON STRANGLERS

No.	Player	EX	NRMT
2	Glenn Harvey	.05	.10
3	Chuck "Aaaaarrrggghhh" Manson	.05	.10
4	Drakk Kula	.05	.10
5	Tex Leetch	.05	.10
6	The Stuntson Brothers	.05	.10
7	Jack the Strapper	.05	.10
8	Evil Zattan	.05	.10
9	Ted Knives	.05	.10
10	Levy Waite	.05	.10

CHICAGO GANGSTERS

No.	Player	EX	NRMT
11	Wolfee Bag	.05	.10
12	Real Capote	.05	.10
13	Shirley "High Scream" Vanilla	.05	.10
14	Charlie Horse	.05	.10
15	XXXX	.05	.10
16	Doug Hunter	.05	.10
17	Andy Glover	.05	.10
18	Samantha Puck	.05	.10
19	Pete Soup	.05	.10

DETROIT UNEMPLOYED

No.	Player	EX	NRMT
20	HV-151001	.05	.10
21	Hercule "Pumping Iron" Samson	.05	.10
22	Victor Laforce	.05	.10
23	Brad Luck	.05	.10
24	Pierrot Rinfrette	.05	.10
25	Bernie 40% Turcotte	.05	.10
26	Redd Neck	.05	.10
27	Johnny Bolling	.05	.10
28	Ted Gumbee	.05	.10

LOS ANGELES POLLUTION

No.	Player	EX	NRMT
29	Neil Moony	.05	.10
30	Typhonse Allaire	.05	.10
31	Wayne Grizzly	.05	.10
32	Nico "IQ" Brainstein	.05	.10
33	Everett "Smokey" Garrett	.05	.10
34	Frank Geiger	.05	.10
35	Ernest Murphy	.05	.10
36	Theo Beausoleil	.05	.10
37	Power-22	.05	.10

MONTREAL FLYING HASBEENS

No.	Player	EX	NRMT
38	Jack Dummy	.05	.10
39	Chris "Preacher" Window	.05	.10
40	Mach Five	.05	.10
41	Great Sesame	.05	.10
42	Phil Boulet	.05	.10
43	Darn Yarn	.05	.10
44	Jim Fish	.05	.10
45	Walter Walker	.05	.10
46	Yvan Trilock	.05	.10

NEW YORK SCUMS

No.	Player	EX	NRMT
47	M.D. Grichman	.05	.10
48	Greg Proctor	.05	.10
49	Max "Arson" Burn	.05	.10
50	Bud "Raw" Butcher	.05	.10
51	Dry Klean	.05	.10
52	Herbert Picks	.05	.10
53	Rod Heint	.05	.10
54	Jack Hill	.05	.10
55	Dave Save	.05	.10

OTTAWA MOUNTEES

No.	Player	EX	NRMT
56	Boulhouboulhou Boulhou	.05	.10
57	Pete Puzzle	.05	.10
58	Michael Dundee	.05	.10
59	Robert Rubber	.05	.10
60	Kurt Spider	.05	.10
61	Joe Cooker	.05	.10
62	Mgwo Khull	.05	.10
63	Satan Claus	.05	.10
64	Benny Hull	.05	.10

QUEBEC FROGS

No.	Player	EX	NRMT
65	Jacques Baloune	.05	.10
66	Gino Azzaro	.05	.10
67	Don Nutts	.05	.10
68	Rikki Lindrock	.05	.10
69	Jim Treck	.05	.10
70	Mark Max	.05	.10
71	Charly Moffet	.05	.10
72	Ben Crepeault	.05	.10
73	Billy Bilodeau Jr.	.05	.10

TORONTO GOLD PLATED

No.	Player	EX	NRMT
74	Raven Spitberg	.05	.10
75	Goofy Mandell	.05	.10
76	Rick Shark	.05	.10
77	Buddy Selleck	.05	.10
78	Oscar F. Fecks	.05	.10
79	Jack Flash	.05	.10
80	Alphonse Cadorette	.05	.10
81	Jeff McFly	.05	.10
82	Cammy Lyon	.05	.10

VANCOUVER KAMIKAZES

No.	Player	EX	NRMT
83	Magayashi Shiyagama	.05	.10
84	Martin Chauze	.05	.10
85	Colonel Snaps	.05	.10
86	Tommy Mito	.05	.10
87	Will Van Hish	.05	.10
88	Redd "Alert" Cannon	.05	.10
89	Hiro Gotakaka	.05	.10
90	Mami Blohead	.05	.10
91	Steve Koop	.05	.10

All STARS

No.	Player	EX	NRMT
92	Atomic Hockey League: Mister Ron Royce	.05	.10
93	New York Scums: N.Y. - Studebaker Cup	.05	.10
94	Toronto Cold Plated: Rich Cash, All Star Player	.05	.10
95	New York Scums: Terence Hell, All Star Player	.05	.10
96	Chicago Gangsters: Kelly Nails, All Star Player	.05	.10
97	Ottawa Mounties: Kandy Striker, All Star Player	.05	.10
98	Montreal Flying Hasbeens: Ray Padds, All Star Player	.05	.10
99	Chicago Gangsters: Rodolph Richter, All Star Player	.05	.10

CHECKLIST

No.	Player	EX	NRMT
100	Checklist B (47/100)	.05	.10

— 1992 - 93 INSERT SET —

1992-93 Insert Set
Sticker No. 1, Detroit Unemployed

Sticker Size: 2 1/2" x 3 1/2"
Face: Four colour, silver foil
Back: Black and white; Number
Imprint: © Printed in Italy Imprimé en Italie
Complete Set No.: 10

	English NRMT	French NRMT
Complete Set Price:	.50	1.00
Common Team:	.05	.10

TEAM LOGOS

No.	Player	EX	NRMT
SP 1	Detroit Unemployed	.05	.10
SP 2	Boston Stranglers	.05	.10
SP 3	Chicago Gangsters	.05	.10
SP 4	Quebec Frogs	.05	.10
SP 5	Vancouver Kamikazes	.05	.10
SP 6	Toronto Gold Plated	.05	.10
SP 7	Montreal Flying Hasbeens	.05	.10
SP 8	Ottawa Mounties	.05	.10
SP 9	Los Angeles Pollution	.05	.10
SP 10	New York Scums	.05	.10

— 1993 - 94 STICKERS —

1993-94 Stickers
Sticker No. 177, Kirk McLean

Sticker Size: 2 1/2" x 3 1/2"
Face: Four colour, white border; Name
Back: Black on white card stock
Imprint: Printed in Italy. Imprime en Italie
Complete Set No.: 276

	English NRMT	French NRMT
Complete Set Price:	10.00	20.00
Common Player:	.05	.05

BOSTON BRIUNS

No.	Players	English NRMT	French NRMT
1	Boston Bruin Team Logo	.05	.05
2	Adam Oates	.10	.20
3	Cam Neely	.10	.20
4	David Poulin	.05	.05
5	Stephen Leach	.05	.05
6	Glen Wesley	.05	.05
7	Dmitri Kvartalnov	.05	.05
8	Ted Donato	.05	.05
9	Andrew Moog, Goalie	.05	.05
10	Raymond Bourque	.25	.25
11	Don Sweeney	.05	.05

MONTREAL CANADIENS

No.	Players	English NRMT	French NRMT
12	Montreal Canadiens Team Logo	.05	.05
13	Vincent Damphousse	.20	.20
14	Kirk Muller	.15	.15
15	Brian Bellows	.05	.05
16	Stephan Lebeau	.05	.05
17	Denis Savard	.05	.05
18	Gilbert Dionne	.05	.05
19	Guy Carbonneau	.05	.05
20	Benoit Brunet	.05	.05
21	Eric Desjardins	.05	.05
22	Mathieu Schneider	.05	.05

WASHINGTON CAPITALS

No.	Players	English NRMT	French NRMT
23	Washington Capitals Team Logo	.05	.05
24	Peter Bondra	.05	.05
25	Mike Ridley	.05	.05
26	Dale Hunter	.05	.05
27	Michal Pivonka	.05	.05
28	Dimitri Khristich	.05	.05
29	Pat Elynuik	.05	.05
30	Kelly Miller	.05	.05
31	Calle Johansson	.05	.05
32	Al Iafrate	.05	.05
33	Donald Beaupre, Goalie	.05	.05

NEW JERSEY DEVILS

No.	Players	English NRMT	French NRMT
34	New Jersey Devils Team Logo	.05	.05
35	Claude Lemieux	.05	.05
36	Alexander Semak	.05	.05
37	Stephane J. J. Richer	.07	.15
38	Valeri Zelepukin	.05	.05
39	Bernie Nicholls	.05	.05
40	John MacLean	.05	.05
41	Peter Stastny	.07	.15
42	Scott Niedermayer	.35	.75
43	Scott Stevens	.10	.20
44	Bruce Driver	.05	.05

PHILADELPHIA FLYERS

No.	Players	English NRMT	French NRMT
45	Philadelphia Flyers Team Logo	.05	.05
46	Mark Recchi	.20	.40
47	Rod Brind'Amour	.12	.25
48	Brent Fedyk	.05	.05
49	Kevin Dineen	.05	.05
50	Keith Acton	.05	.05
51	Per-Erik Eklund	.05	.05
52	Andrei Lomakin	.05	.05
53	Garry Galley	.05	.05
54	Terry Carkner	.05	.05
55	Tommy Soderstrom, Goalie	.10	.20

NEW YORK ISLANDERS

No.	Players	English NRMT	French NRMT
56	New York Islanders Team Logo	.05	.05
57	Steve Thomas	.05	.05
58	Derek King	.05	.05
59	Benoit Hogue	.05	.05
60	Patrick Flatley	.05	.05
61	Brian Mullen	.05	.05
62	Marty McInnis	.05	.05
63	Scott Lachance	.10	.20
64	Jeff Norton	.05	.05
65	Glenn Healy, Goalie	.05	.05
66	Mark Fitzpatrick, Goalie	.05	.05

QUEBEC NORDIQUES

No.	Players	English NRMT	French NRMT
67	Quebec Nordiques Team Logo	.05	.05
68	Mats Sundin	.15	.30
69	Mike Ricci	.05	.05
70	Owen Nolan	.10	.20
71	Andrei Kovalenko	.10	.20
72	Valeri Kamensky	.10	.20
73	Scott Young	.05	.05
74	Martin Rucinsky	.05	.05
75	Steven Finn	.05	.05
76	Steve Duchesne	.05	.05
77	Ron Hextall, Goalie	.05	.05

PITTSBURGH PENGUINS

No.	Players	English NRMT	French NRMT
78	Pittsburgh Penguins Team Logo	.05	.05
79	Kevin Stevens	.12	.25
80	Rick Tocchet	.05	.05
81	Ronald Francis	.05	.05
82	Jaromir Jagr	.25	.50
83	Joe Mullen	.05	.05
84	Shawn McEachern	.15	.30
85	Dave Tippett	.05	.05
86	Lawrence Murphy	.05	.05
87	Ulf Samuelsson	.05	.05
88	Tom Barrasso, Goalie	.10	.20

NEW YORK RANGERS

No.	Players	English NRMT	French NRMT
89	New York Rangers Team Logo	.05	.05
90	Anthony Amonte	.12	.25
91	Michael Gartner	.05	.05
92	Adam Graves	.25	.50
93	Sergei Nemchinov	.10	.20
94	Darren Turcotte	.05	.05
95	Esa Tikkanen	.05	.05
96	Brian Leetch	.20	.40
97	Kevin Lowe	.05	.05
98	John Vanbiesbrouck, Goalie	.12	.25
99	Mike Richter, Goalie	.12	.25

BUFFALO SABRES

No.	Players	English NRMT	French NRMT
100	Buffalo Sabres Team Logo	.05	.05
101	Pat LaFontaine	.15	.30
102	Dale Hawerchuk	.05	.05
103	Donald Audette	.05	.05
104	Robert Sweeney	.05	.05
105	Randy Wood	.05	.05
106	Yuri Khmylev	.05	.05
107	Wayne Presley	.05	.05
108	Grant Fuhr, Goalie	.05	.05
109	Doug Bodger	.05	.05
110	Richard Smehlik	.05	.05

OTTAWA SENATORS

No.	Players	English NRMT	French NRMT
111	Ottawa Senators Team Logo	.05	.05
112	Norm Maciver	.05	.05
113	Jamie Baker	.05	.05
114	Bob Kudelski	.05	.05
115	Jody Hull	.05	.05
116	Mike Peluso	.05	.05
117	Mark Lamb	.05	.05
118	Mark Freer	.05	.05
119	Neil Brady	.05	.05
120	Brad Shaw	.05	.05
121	Peter Sidorkiewicz, Goalie	.05	.05

HARTFORD WHALERS

No.	Player	English NRMT	French NRMT
122	Hartford Whalers Team Logo	.05	.05
123	Andrew Cassels	.10	.20
124	Patrick Verbeek	.05	.05
125	Terry Yake	.05	.05

338 • PANINI — 1993-94 INSERT SET

No.	Player	English NRMT	French NRMT
126	Patrick Poulin	.10	.20
127	Mark Janssens	.05	.05
128	Mikael Nylander	.15	.30
129	Zarley Zalapski	.05	.05
130	Eric Weinrich	.05	.05
131	Sean Burke, Goalie	.05	.05
132	Frank Pietrangelo, Goalie	.05	.05

SCORING LEADERS - DEFENSEMEN

No.	Players	English NRMT	French NRMT
133	Phil Housley, Win.	.05	.05
134	Paul Coffey, Det.	.10	.20
135	Lawrence Murphy, Pit.	.05	.05

SCORING LEADERS - FORWARDS

No.	Players	English NRMT	French NRMT
136	Mario Lemieux, Pit.	.75	1.50
137	Pat LaFontaine, Buf.	.15	.30
138	Adam Oates, Bos.	.15	.30

BEST GOALS AGAINST AVERAGE

No.	Players	English NRMT	French NRMT
139	Felix Potvin, Tor.	.50	1.00
140	Ed Belfour, Chi.	.20	.40
141	Tom Barasso, Pit.	.10	.20

SCORING LEADERS - ROOKIES

No.	Players	English NRMT	French NRMT
142	Teemu Selanne, Win.	.75	1.50
143	Joseph Juneau, Bos.	.35	.75
144	Eric Lindros, Phi.	1.50	3.00

CHICAGO BLACK HAWKS

No.	Players	English NRMT	French NRMT
145	Chicago Blackhawks Team Logo	.05	.05
146	Steve Larmer	.05	.05
147	Dirk Graham	.05	.05
148	Michel Goulet	.05	.05
149	Brian Noonan	.05	.05
150	Stephane Matteau	.05	.05
151	Brent Sutter	.05	.05
152	Jocelyn Lemieux	.05	.05
153	Chris Chelios	.05	.05
154	James (Steve) Smith	.05	.05
155	Ed Belfour, Goalie	.20	.40

ST. LOUIS BLUES

No.	Players	English NRMT	French NRMT
156	St. Louis Blues Team Logo	.05	.05
157	Craig Janney	.10	.20
158	Brendan Shanahan	.10	.20
159	Nelson Emerson	.05	.05
160	Richard Sutter	.05	.05
161	Ronald Sutter	.05	.05
162	Ronald Wilson	.05	.05
163	Bob Bassen	.05	.05
164	Garth Butcher	.05	.05
165	Jeff Brown	.05	.05
166	Curtis Joseph, Goalie	.20	.40

VANCOUVER CANUCKS

No.	Players	English NRMT	French NRMT
167	Vancouver Canucks Team Logo	.05	.05
168	Cliff Ronning	.07	.15
169	Murray Craven	.05	.05
170	Geoff Courtnall	.07	.15
171	Petr Nedved	.05	.05
172	Trevor Linden	.20	.40
173	Greg Adams	.05	.05
174	Anatoli Semenov	.05	.05
175	Jyrki Lumme	.05	.05
176	Doug Lidster	.05	.05
177	Kirk McLean, Goalie	.20	.40

CALGARY FLAMES

No.	Players	English NRMT	French NRMT
178	Calgary Flames Team Logo	.05	.05
179	Theoren Fleury	.05	.05
180	Robert Reichel	.05	.05
181	Gary Roberts	.05	.05
182	Joe Nieuwendyk	.05	.05
183	Sergei Makarov	.05	.05
184	Paul Ranheim	.05	.05
185	Joel Otto	.05	.05
186	Gary Suter	.05	.05
187	Jeff Reese, Goalie	.05	.05
188	Michael Vernon, Goalie	.05	.05

WINNIPEG JETS

No.	Players	English NRMT	French NRMT
189	Winnipeg Jets Team Logo	.05	.05
190	Alexei Zhamnov	.15	.30
191	Thomas Steen	.05	.05
192	Darrin Shannon	.05	.05
193	Keith Tkachuk	.35	.75
194	Eugeny Davydov	.05	.05
195	Luciano Borsato	.05	.05
196	Phil Housley	.05	.05
197	Teppo Numminen	.05	.05
198	Fredrick Olausson	.05	.05
199	Bob Essensa, Goalie	.05	.05

LOS ANGELES KINGS

No.	Players	English NRMT	French NRMT
200	Los Angeles Kings Team Logo	.05	.05
201	Luc Robitaille	.05	.05
202	Jari Kurri	.05	.05
203	Tony Granato	.05	.05
204	Jimmy Carson	.05	.05
205	Tomas Sandstrom	.05	.05
206	David Taylor	.05	.05
207	Corey Millen	.05	.05
208	Martin McSorley	.05	.05
209	Robert Blake	.10	.20
210	Kelly Hrudey, Goalie	.05	.05

TAMPA BAY LIGHTNING

No.	Players	English NRMT	French NRMT
211	Tampa Bay Lightning Team Logo	.05	.05
212	John Tucker	.05	.05
213	Chris Kontos	.05	.05
214	Rob Zamuner	.10	.20
215	Adam Creighton	.05	.05
216	Bo Mikael Andersson	.05	.05
217	Bob Beers	.05	.05
218	Robert DiMaio	.05	.05
219	Shawn Chambers	.05	.05
220	Jean-Claude Bergeron, Goalie	.05	.05
221	Wendell Young, Goalie	.05	.05

TORONTO MAPLE LEAFS

No.	Player	English NRMT	French NRMT
222	Toronto Maple Leafs Team Logo	.05	.05
223	David Andreychuk	.10	.20
224	Nikolai Borschevsky	.05	.05
225	Glenn Anderson	.05	.05
226	John Cullen	.05	.05
227	Wendel Clark	.10	.20
228	Mike Foligno	.05	.05
229	Michael Krushelnyski	.05	.05
230	Jamie Macoun	.05	.05
231	David Ellett	.05	.05
232	Felix Potvin, Goalie	.75	1.50

EDMONTON OILERS

No.	Player	English NRMT	French NRMT
233	Edmonton Oilers Team Logo	.05	.05
234	Petr Klima	.05	.05
235	Doug Weight	.05	.05
236	Shayne Corson	.05	.05

No.	Player	English NRMT	French NRMT
237	Craig Simpson	.05	.05
238	Todd Elik	.05	.05
239	Zdeno Ciger	.05	.05
240	Craig MacTavish	.05	.05
241	Kelly Buchberger	.05	.05
242	Dave Manson	.05	.05
243	Scott Mellanby	.05	.05

DETROIT RED WINGS

No.	Player	English NRMT	French NRMT
244	Detroit Red Wings Team Logo	.05	.05
245	Dino Ciccarelli	.05	.05
246	Sergei Fedorov	.50	1.00
247	Ray Sheppard	.10	.20
248	Paul Ysebaert	.05	.05
249	Bob Probert	.05	.05
250	Keith Primeau	.05	.05
251	Steve Chiasson	.05	.05
252	Paul Coffey	.07	.15
253	Nicklas Lidstrom	.05	.05
254	Tim Cheveldae, Goalie	.05	.05

SAN JOSE SHARKS

No.	Player	English NRMT	French NRMT
255	San Jose Sharks Team Logo	.05	.05
256	Kelly Kisio	.05	.05
257	Johan Garpenlov	.05	.05
258	Robert Gaudreau	.20	.40
259	Dean Evason	.05	.05
260	Jeff Odgers	.05	.05
261	Ed Courtenay	.05	.05
262	Mike Sullivan	.05	.05
263	Doug Zmolek	.05	.05
264	Douglas Wilson	.05	.05
265	Brian Hayward, Goalie	.05	.05

DALLAS STARS

No.	Players	English NRMT	French NRMT
266	Dallas Stars Team Logo	.05	.05
267	Brian Propp	.05	.05
268	Russell Courtnall	.05	.05
269	Dave Gagner	.05	.05
270	Ulf Dahlen	.05	.05
271	Mike Craig	.05	.05
272	Neal Broten	.05	.05
273	Gaetan Duchesne	.05	.05
274	Derian Hatcher	.05	.05
275	Mark Tinordi	.05	.05
276	Jon Casey, Goalie	.07	.15

— 1993 - 94 INSERT SET —

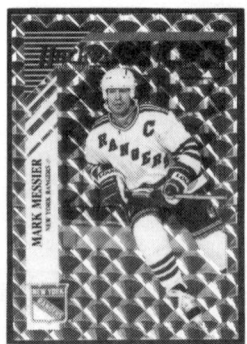

1993-94 Insert Set
Sticker No. 1, Mark Messier

Sticker Size: 2 1/2" x 3 1/2"
Face: Four colour, glitter border; Name
Back: Black on white card stock
Imprint: Printed in Italy. Imprime en Italie
Complete Set No.: 23
Complete Set Price: 75.00

CELEBRITY WATCH INC.

— 1988 PRO-SPORT AUTOGRAPH COLLECTION —

No.	Player	English NRMT	French NRMT
A	Joseph Juneau, Bos.	2.50	5.00
B	Patrick Roy, Goalie, Mon.	2.50	5.00
C	Kevin Hatcher, Wash.	1.50	3.00
D	Chris Terreri, Goalie, NJ	1.50	3.00
E	Eric Lindros, Phi.	4.00	8.00
F	Pierre Turgeon, NYI	1.50	3.00
G	Joe Sakic, Que.	3.00	6.00
H	Mario Lemieux, Pit.	3.50	7.00
I	Mark Messier, NYR	2.00	4.00
J	Alexander Mogilny, Buf.	2.50	5.00
K	Sylvain Turgeon, Ott.	1.50	3.00
L	Geoff Sanderson, Har.	1.50	3.00
M	Jeremy Roenick, Chi.	2.50	5.00
N	Brett Hull, St.L	2.50	5.00
O	Pavel Bure, Van.	3.50	7.00
P	Allan MacInnis, Cal.	1.50	3.00
Q	Teemu Selanne, Win.	3.50	7.00
R	Wayne Gretzky, LA	5.00	10.00
T	Brian Bradley, TB	1.50	3.00
U	Bill Ranford, Goalie, Edm.	1.50	3.00
V	Steve Yzerman, Det.	2.50	5.00
W	Pat Falloon, SJ	1.50	3.00
X	Michael Modano, Dal.	2.50	5.00

CELEBRITY WATCH INC.

— 1988 PRO-SPORT AUTOGRAPH COLLECTION —

This 17-card set is very unique. The cards themselves were part of a folder package for quartz watches. As such they are printed on heavy card stock. The card face is one piece of the actual packaging and the card back is another.

Celebrity Watch Inc.
1988 Pro-Sport Autograph Collection
Card No. CW5, Mario Lemieux

Folder Size: 3 3/8" x 6 3/4
Card Size: 3 11/16" x 6 13/16"
Face: Card face: Four colour, borderless with facimile autograph
Card back: blank
Back: Card back: Four colour, black and white; Name, Jersey number, Resume, Bilingual, Team, NHL and NHLPA logos
Imprint: © Celebrity Watch Inc. Montre Celebrite Inc.
Complete Set No.: 17
Complete Set Price: 40.00 80.00
Common Card: 2.50 5.00

No.	Player	NRMT	Mint
CW1	Larry Robinson, Mon.	2.50	5.00
CW2	Guy Carbonneau, Mon.	2.50	5.00
CW3	Chris Chelios, Mon.	2.50	5.00
CW4	Not issued		
CW5	Mario Lemieux, Pit.	5.00	10.00
CW6	Mike Bossy, NYI	2.50	5.00
CW7	Dale Hawerchuk, Win.	2.50	5.00
CW8	Joe Mullen, Cal.	2.50	5.00
CW9	Richard Vaive, Tor.	2.50	5.00
CW10	Wendel Clark, Tor.	3.00	6.00
CW11	Michel Goulet, Que.	2.50	5.00

No.	Player	EX	NRMT
CW12	Peter Stastny, Que.	2.50	5.00
CW13	Mark Messier, Edm.	3.00	6.00
CW14	Paul Coffey, Edm.	3.00	6.00
CW15	Tony Tanti, Van.	2.50	5.00
CW16	Borje Salming, Tor.	2.50	5.00
CW17	Christopher Nilan, Mon.	2.50	5.00
CW17	Mats Naslund, Mon.	2.50	5.00

FRITO-LAY

— 1988 - 89 STICKERS —

These stickers feature action photographs along with the player's name and uniform number. The stickers are packaged individually in small cello bags. The stickers could be placed on a poster supplied by Hostess/Frito-Lay Canada.

 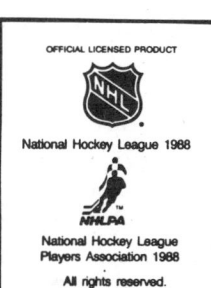

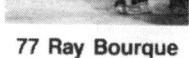

Frito-Lay 1988-89 Stickers
Sticker No. 4, Raymond Bourque

Sticker Size: 1 3/8" X 1 3/4"
Face: Four colour; Name, Jersey number
Back: Black on white; NHL crest
Imprint: All Rights Reserved
Complete Set No.: 42
Complete Set Price: 5.00 10.00
Common Card: .05 .10
Poster: 5.00

No.	Player	EX	NRMT
1	Glenn Anderson, Edm.	.10	.20
2	Tom Barrasso, Goalie, Buf.	.10	.20
3	Brian Bellows, Min.	.10	.20
4	Raymond Bourque, Bos.	.20	.40
5	Neal Broten, Min.	.05	.10
6	Sean Burke, Goalie, NJD	.05	.10
7	Wendel Clark, Tor.	.12	.25
8	Paul Coffey, Pit.	.20	.40
9	Kevin Dineen, Har.	.05	.10
10	Marcel Dionne, NYR	.10	.20
11	Bernie Federko, St. L.	.05	.10
12	Michael Foligno, Buf.	.05	.10
13	Ron Francis, Har.	.10	.20
14	Mike Gartner, Wash.	.20	.40
15	Douglas Gilmour, St. L.	.25	.50
16	Michel Goulet, Que.	.10	.20
17	Dale Hawerchuk, Win.	.08	.15
18	Ron Hextall, Goalie, Phi.	.10	.20
19	Pat LaFontaine, NYI	.20	.40
20	Mario Lemieux, Pit.	.50	1.00
21	Al MacInnis, Cal.	.10	.20
22	Andrew McBain, win.	.05	.10
23	Mark Messier, Edm.	.10	.20
24	Kirk Muller, NJD	.10	.20
25	Troy Murray, Chi.	.05	.10
26	Mats Naslund, Mon.	.05	.10
27	Cam Neely, Bos.	.20	.40
28	Bernie Nicholls, LA	.05	.10
29	Joe Nieuwendyk, Cal.	.05	.10
30	Ed Olczyk, Tor.	.05	.10
31	James Patrick, NYR	.05	.10
32	Barry Pederson, Van.	.05	.10
33	David Poulin, Phi.	.05	.10
34	Bob Probert, Det.	.10	.20
35	Stephane J.J. Richer, Mon.	.08	.15
36	Luc Robitaille, LA	.15	.30
37	Denis Savard, Chi.	.10	.20
38	Peter Stastny, Que.	.10	.20
39	Scott Stevens, Wash.	.10	.20
40	Tony Tanti, Van.	.05	.10
41	Bryan Trottier, NYI	.10	.20
42	Steve Yzerman, Det.	.25	.50

ACTION PACKED

1989 - 90 - PROMOTIONAL SET

 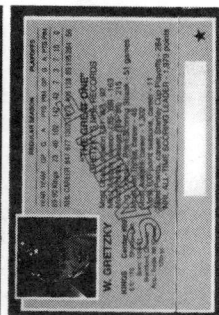

Action Packed 1993 Promotional Set
Card No. 1, Wayne Gretzky

Card Size: 2 1/2" X 3 1/2"
Face: Four colour, gold border Name, Team
Back: Four colour, gold border; Name, Number, Resume
Imprint: HI-PRO MKTG., INC. Copyright 1990
Complete Set No.: 2
Complete Set Price: 7 (Hockey 3) 1,300.00
Complete Set Price: (Hockey) 750.00

No.	Player	EX	NRMT
1	Wayne Gretzky, LA	125.00	250.00
2	Mario Lemieux, Pit.	100.00	200.00
3	Steve Yzerman, Det., SP	135.00	375.00

1993 PROMOTIONAL SET

Action Packed 1993 Promotional Set
Card No. BH1, Bobby Hull

Card Size: 2 1/2" X 3 1/2"
Face: Four colour, embossed
Back: Four colour; Name, Number, Resume
Imprint: Action Packed, Inc. Copyright 1993 Pat. #315,364
Printed in U.S.A.
Complete Set No.: 7 (Hockey: 2)
Complete Set Price: 5.00 10.00

No.	Player	EX	NRMT
BH1	Bobby Hull	2.50	5.00
BH2	Bobby Hull, Gold	2.50	5.00

BOWMAN

— 1990 - 91 ISSUE —

Bowman issued a high quality limited edition set in 1990. The set, with 264 cards plus 22 special glossy insert cards, came in a special serial numbered collectors box. Three thousand sets were issued.

 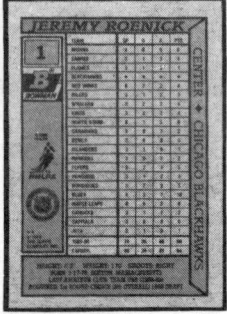

1990-1991 Issue
Card No. 1, Jeremy Roenick

Card Size: 2 1/2" X 3 1/2"
Face: Four colour, white border, Team name
Back: Blue and black on card stock, Number, Resume
Imprint: ** © 1990 THE TOPPS COMPANY, INC.
© 1990 NHLPA
Complete Set No.: 264
Complete Set Price:

Regular:	7.50	15.00
Tiffany:	30.00	60.00
Common Card:	.03	.05
Wax Pack: (15 Cards)		.50
Wax Box: (36 Packs)		10.00
Wax Case: (20 Boxes)		175.00
Factory Set:		20.00

CHICAGO BLACK HAWKS

No.	Player	EX	NRMT
1	Jeremy Roenick, RC	1.00	2.00
2	Douglas Wilson	.03	.05
3	Greg Millen, Goalie	.03	.05
4	Steve Thomas	.03	.05
5	Steve Larmer	.05	.10
6	Denis Savard	.03	.05
7	Ed Belfour, Goalie, RC	.75	1.50
8	Dirk Graham	.03	.05
9	Adam Creighton	.03	.05
10	Keith Brown, RC	.03	.05
11	Jacques Cloutier, Goalie, RC	.03	.05
12	Al Secord, Error	.03	.05
13	Troy Murray	.03	.05

ST. LOUIS BLUES

No.	Player	EX	NRMT
14	Kelly Chase, RC	.12	.25
15	Dave Lowry, RC	.03	.05
16	Adam Oates	.10	.20
17	Sergio Momesso, RC	.07	.15
18	Paul MacLean	.03	.05
19	Peter Zezel	.03	.05
20	Vincent Riendeau, Goalie, RC	.10	.20
21	Dave Thomlinson, RC	.03	.05
22	Paul Cavallini	.03	.05
23	Rod Brind'Amour, RC	.30	.60
24	Brett Hull	.30	.60
25	Jeff Brown	.05	.10
26	Dominic Lavoie, RC	.05	.10

BOSTON BRUINS

No.	Player	EX	NRMT
27	Andy Brickley	.03	.05
28	Robert Sweeney	.03	.05
29	Cam Neely	.12	.25
30	Robert Carpenter	.03	.05
31	Ray Bourque	.13	.25
32	Rejean Lemelin, Goalie	.03	.05
33	Craig Janney	.10	.20
34	Bob Beers, RC	.05	.10
35	Andrew Moog, Goalie	.05	.10
36	David Poulin	.03	.05
37	Brian Propp	.03	.05
38	John Byce, RC	.03	.05
39	John Carter, RC	.03	.05
40	Dave Christian	.03	.05

MONTREAL CANADIENS

No.	Player	EX	NRMT
41	Shayne Corson	.03	.05
42	Chris Chelios	.05	.10
43	Michael McPhee	.03	.05
44	Guy Carbonneau	.03	.05
45	Stephane Richer	.05	.10
46	Petr Svoboda, Error	.03	.05
47	Russ Courtnall	.03	.05
48	Sylvain Lefebvre, RC	.08	.15
49	Brian Skrudland	.03	.05
50	Patrick Roy, Goalie	.35	.75
51	Robert Smith	.03	.05
52	Mathieu Schneider, RC	.15	.30
53	Stephan Lebeau, RC	.20	.40

VANCOUVER CANUCKS

No.	Player	EX	NRMT
54	Petri Skriko	.03	.05
55	Jim Sandlak	.03	.05
56	Doug Lidster	.03	.05
57	Kirk McLean, Goalie	.10	.20
58	Brian Bradley	.03	.05
59	Greg Adams	.03	.05
60	Paul Reinhart	.03	.05
61	Trevor Linden	.10	.20
62	Adrien Plavsic, RC	.03	.05
63	Igor Larionov, RC	.12	.25
64	Steve Bozek	.03	.05
65	Dan Quinn	.03	.05

WASHINGTON CAPITALS

No.	Player	EX	NRMT
66	Michael Liut, Goalie	.03	.05
67	Nicholas Kypreos, RC	.03	.05
68	Michal Pivonka, RC	.13	.25
69	Dino Ciccarelli	.05	.10
70	Kevin Hatcher	.05	.10
71	Dale Hunter	.03	.05
72	Don Beaupre, Goalie	.03	.05
73	Geoff Courtnall	.03	.05
74	Rob Murray, RC	.03	.05
75	Calle Johansson	.03	.05
76	Kelly Miller	.03	.05
77	Mike Ridley	.03	.05
78	Alan May, RC	.05	.10

NEW JERSEY DEVILS

No.	Player	EX	NRMT
79	Bob Brooke	.03	.05
80	Vlacheslav Fetisov, RC	.10	.20
81	Sylvain Turgeon	.03	.05
82	Kirk Muller	.05	.10
83	John MacLean	.03	.05
84	Jon Morris, RC	.06	.12
85	Brendan Shanahan	.10	.20
86	Peter Stastny	.05	.10
87	Bruce Driver	.03	.05
88	Neil Brady, RC	.03	.05
89	Patrik Sundstrom	.03	.05
90	Eric Weinrich, RC	.08	.15

CALGARY FLAMES

No.	Player	EX	NRMT
91	Joe Nieuwendyk	.08	.15
92	Sergei Makarov, RC	.20	.40
93	Allan MacInnis	.05	.10
94	Michael Vernon, Goalie	.03	.05
95	Gary Roberts	.08	.15
96	Douglas Gilmour	.20	.40
97	Joe Mullen	.03	.05
98	Richard Wamsley, Goalie	.03	.05
99	Joel Otto	.03	.05
100	Paul Ranheim, RC	.05	.10
101	Gary Suter	.03	.05
102	Theoren Fleury	.13	.25
103	Sergei Priakin, RC	.05	.10

PHILADELPHIA FLYERS

No.	Player	EX	NRMT
104	Tony Horacek, RC	.03	.05
105	Ron Hextall, Goalie	.05	.10
106	Gordon Murphy, RC	.05	.10
107	Per-Erik Eklund	.03	.05
108	Rick Tocchet	.05	.10
109	Murray Craven	.03	.05
110	Douglas Sulliman	.03	.05
111	Kjell Samuelsson	.03	.05
112	Ilkka Sinisalo	.03	.05
113	Keith Acton	.03	.05
114	Mike Bullard	.03	.05

NEW YORK ISLANDERS

No.	Player	EX	NRMT
115	Doug Crossman	.03	.05
116	Tom Fitzgerald, RC	.03	.05
117	Donald Maloney	.03	.05
118	Alan Kerr	.03	.05
119	Mark Fitzpatrick, RC, Goalie	.07	.15
120	Hubie McDonough, RC	.03	.05
121	Randy Wood	.03	.05
122	Jeff Norton	.03	.05
123	Pat LaFontaine	.18	.35
124	Patrick Flatley	.03	.05
125	Joe Reekie, RC	.05	.10
126	Brent Sutter	.03	.05
127	David Volek	.03	.05

WINNIPEG JETS

No.	Player	EX	NRMT
128	Shawn Cronin, RC	.05	.10
129	Dale Hawerchuk	.05	.10
130	Brent Ashton	.03	.05
131	Bob Essensa, RC, Goalie	.15	.30
132	Dave Ellett	.03	.05
133	Thomas Steen	.03	05
134	Douglas Smail	.03	.05
135	Fredrik Olausson	.03	.05
136	Dave McLlwain, Error	.03	.05
137	Pat Elynuik	.03	.05
138	Teppo Numminen, RC	.10	.20
139	Paul Fenton	.03	.05

LOS ANGELES KINGS

No.	Player	EX	NRMT
140	Tony Granato	.05	.10
141	Tomas Sandstrom	.03	.05
142	Rob Blake, RC	.25	.50
143	Wayne Gretzky	.50	1.00
144	Kelly Hrudey, Goalie	.03	.05
145	Michael Krushelnyski	.03	.05
146	Steve Duchesne	.03	.05
147	Stephen Kasper	.03	.05
148	John Tonelli	.03	.05
149	David Taylor	.03	.05
150	Larry Robinson	.05	.10
151	Todd Elik, RC	.10	.20
152	Luc Robitaille	.13	.25

TORONTO MAPLE LEAFS

No.	Player	EX	NRMT
153	Al Iafrate	.05	.10
154	Allan Bester, Goalie	.03	.05
155	Gary Leeman	.03	.05
156	Mark Osborne	.03	.05
157	Tom Fergus	.03	.05
158	Brad Marsh	.03	.05
159	Wendel Clark	.10	.20
160	Daniel Marois	.03	.05
161	Ed Olczyk	.03	.05
162	George (Rob) Ramage	.03	.05
163	Vincent Damphousse	.05	.10
164	Lou Franceschetti, RC	.03	.05

QUEBEC NORDIQUES

No.	Player	EX	NRMT
165	Paul Gillis	.03	.05
166	Craig Wolanin, RC	.03	.05
167	Marc Fortier	.03	.05
168	Anthony McKegney	.03	.05

1990-91 INSERT SET — BOWMAN

No.	Player	EX	NRMT
169	Joe Sakic	.25	.50
170	Michel Petit	.03	.05
171	Scott Gordon, RC, Goalie	.03	.05
172	Anthony Hrkac	.03	.05
173	Bryan Fogarty, RC	.03	.05
174	Mike Hough	.03	.05
175	Claude Loiselle, RC	.03	.05

MINNESOTA NORTH STARS

No.	Player	EX	NRMT
176	Ulf Dahlen	.03	.05
177	Lawrence Murphy	.03	.05
178	Neal Broten	.03	.05
179	Don Barber, RC	.03	.05
180	Shawn Chambers	.03	.05
181	Clark Donatelli, RC, Error	.03	.05
182	Brian Bellows	.05	.10
183	Jon Casey, Goalie	.05	.10
184	Neil Wilkinson, RC	.10	.20
185	Aaron Broten	.03	.05
186	Dave Gagner	.03	.05
187	Basil McRae	.03	.05
188	Michael Modano, RC	.50	1.00

EDMONTON OILERS

No.	Player	EX	NRMT
189	Grant Fuhr, Goalie	.05	.10
190	Martin Gelinas, RC	.07	.15
191	Jari Kurri	.05	.10
192	Geoff Smith, RC	.03	.05
193	Craig MacTavish	.03	.05
194	Esa Tikkanen	.03	.05
195	Glenn Anderson	.05	.10
196	Joe Murphy, RC	.13	.25
197	Petr Klima	.03	.05
198	Kevin Lowe	.03	.05
199	Mark Messier	.18	.35
200	Steve Smith	.03	.05
201	Craig Simpson	.03	.05

PITTSBURGH PENGUINS

No.	Player	EX	NRMT
202	Rob Brown	.03	.05
203	Wendell Young, Goalie, RC	.06	.12
204	Mario Lemieux	.50	1.00
205	Phil Bourque	.03	.05
206	Mark Recchi, RC	.50	1.00
207	Zarley Zalapski	.03	.05
208	Kevin Stevens, RC	.50	1.00
209	Tom Barrasso, Goalie	.03	.05
210	John Cullen	.03	.05
211	Paul Coffey	.05	.10
212	Bob Errey	.03	.05
213	Tony Tanti	.03	.05

NEW YORK RANGERS

No.	Player	EX	NRMT
214	Carey Wilson	.03	.05
215A	Brian Leetch, Error	.50	1.00
215B	Brian Leetch, Corrected	.30	.60
216	Darren Turcotte, RC	.10	.20
217	Brian Mullen	.03	.05
218	Mike Richter, RC, Goalie	.50	1.00
219	Troy Mallette, RC	.03	.05
220	Michael Gartner	.03	.05
221	Bernie Nicholls	.03	.05
222	John Vanbiesbrouck, Goalie	.10	.20
223	John Ogrodnick	.03	.05
224	Paul Broten, RC	.05	.10
225	James Patrick	.03	.05
226	Mark Janssens, RC	.03	.05

DETROIT RED WINGS

No.	Player	EX	NRMT
227	Randy McKay, RC	.03	.05
228	Marc Habscheid	.03	.05
229	Jimmy Carson	.05	.10
230	Yves Racine, RC	.05	.10
231	Dave Barr	.03	.05
232	Shawn Burr	.03	.05
233	Steve Yzerman	.18	.35

No.	Player	EX	NRMT
234	Steve Chiasson	.03	.05
235	Daniel Shank, RC	.03	.05
236	John Chabot	.03	.05
237	Gerard Gallant	.03	.05
238	Bernie Federko	.03	.05

BUFFALO SABRES

No.	Player	EX	NRMT
239	Phil Housley	.05	.10
240	Alexander Mogilny, RC	.50	1.00
241	Pierre Turgeon	.20	.40
242	Daren Puppa, Goalie	.05	.10
243	Scott Arniel	.03	.05
244	Christian Ruuttu	.03	.05
245	Doug Bodger	.03	.05
246	David Andreychuk	.08	.15
247	Mike Foligno	.03	.05
248	Edward (Dean) Kennedy, RC	.03	.05
249	Dave Snuggerud, RC	.06	.12
250	Richard Vaive	.03	.05

HARTFORD WHALERS

No.	Player	EX	NRMT
251	Todd Krygier, RC	.05	.10
252	Adam Burt, RC	.03	.05
253	Scott Young	.03	.05
254	Ron Francis	.03	.05
255	Peter Sidorkiewicz, Goalie	.03	.05
256	Dave Babych	.03	.05
257	Patrick Verbeek	.03	.05
258	Ray Ferraro	.03	.05
259	Chris Govedaris, RC	.03	.05
260	Brad Shaw, RC	.05	.10
261	Kevin Dineen	.03	.05
262	Dean Evason	.03	.05

CHECKLIST

No.	Checklist	EX	NRMT
263	Checklist 1 (1 - 132)	.08	.15
264	Checklist 2 (133 - 264)	.08	.15

— 1990-91 INSERT SET —

HAT TRICKS

This Hat Trick subset was available only from wax packs and was not included in regular factory sets. There is no checklist with the set and cards are numbered _ of 22. One card was issued in each of the standard wax packs.

1990-91 Insert set
Card No. HT21, Tomas Sandstrom

Card Size: 2 1/2" X 3 1/2"
Front: Four colour, white border
Back: Orange and blue on white card, Number, Date of Hat Trick(s)
Imprint: ** © 1990 THE TOPPS COMPANY, INC.
© 1990 NHLPA
Complete Set No.: 22
Complete Set Price: 2.50 5.00
Common Card: .05 .10

No.	Player	EX	NRMT
HT1	Brett Hull, St. L.	.50	1.00
HT2	Mario Lemieux, Pit.	.50	1.00
HT3	Rob Brown, Pit.	.05	.10
HT4	Mark Messier, Edm.	.25	.50
HT5	Steve Yzerman, Det.	.25	.50
HT6	Vincent Damphousse, Tor.	.13	.25
HT7	Kevin Dineen, Har.	.05	.10
HT8	Michael Gartner, Tor., Error	.13	.25
HT9	Pat LaFontaine, NYI	.25	.50
HT10	Gary Leeman, Tor.	.05	.10
HT11	Stephane Richer, Mon.	.08	.15
HT12	Luc Robitaille, LA	.20	.40
HT13	Steve Thomas, Chi.	.05	.10
HT14	Rick Tocchet, Phi.	.10	.20
HT15	Dino Ciccarelli, Wash.	.10	.20
HT16	John Druce, Wash.	.10	.20
HT17	Michael Gartner, NYR	.13	.25
HT18	Tony Granato, LA	.05	.10
HT19	Jari Kurri, Edm.	.12	.25
HT20	Bernie Nicholls, NYR	.05	.10
HT21	Tomas Sandstrom, LA	.05	.10
HT22	David Taylor, LA	.05	.10

Note: Gretzky also scored a hat trick during the same time frame but was inadvertently overlooked by Bowman when they produced this subset.

— 1991 PROMOTIONAL CARDS —

Promotional cards were issued in a nine-card mini-sheet comprising five Topps and four Bowman cards. The cards are unnumbered and are listed in alphabetical order. (See the 1991 Topps listing for their promotional cards.)

1991 Promotional Cards
Raymond Bourque   Mark Messier

Card Size: 2 1/2" X 3 1/2"
Face: Four colour, white border
Back: White and blue on card stock
Imprint: © 1991 THE TOPPS COMPANY, INC.

No.	Player	EX	NRMT
---	Raymond Bourque, Bos.	1.00	2.00
---	Wayne Gretzky, LA	1.00	2.00
---	Mark Messier, Edm.	1.00	2.00
---	Steve Yzerman, Det.	1.00	2.00

— 1991 - 92 REGULAR ISSUE —

This is the second year of issue for Bowman. This 429-card set is different in design and photography from the Topps 1991-92 set.

1991-92 Issue
Card No. 41, Steve Yzerman

Card Size: 2 1/2" X 3 1/2"
Face: Four colour, white border
Back: Four colour, green and brown on card stock; Number, Resume
Imprint: A, B, C or D * © 1991 THE TOPPS COMPANY, INC.
Complete Set No.: 429

Complete Set Price:	15.00
Common Card: .03	.05
Wax Pack: (15 Cards)	.50
Wax Box: (36 Packs)	10.00
Wax Case: (20 Boxes)	175.00
Factory Set:	15.00

HARTFORD WHALERS

No.	Player	EX	NRMT
1	John Cullen	.03	.05
2	Todd Krygier	.03	.05
3	Kay Whitmore, Goalie	.03	.05
4	Terry Yake	.03	.05
5	Randy Ladouceur	.03	.05
6	Kevin Dineen	.03	.05
7	Jim McKenzie	.03	.05
8	Brad Shaw	.03	.05
9	Mark Hunter	.03	.05
10	Dean Evason	.03	.05
11	Bo Mikael Andersson	.05	.10
12	Patrick Verbeek	.05	.10
13	Peter Sidorkiewicz, Goalie	.03	.05
14	Mike Tomlak	.03	.05
15	Zarley Zalapski	.03	.05
16	Rob Brown	.03	.05
17	Sylvain Coté	.03	.05
18	Robert Holik	.05	.10
19	Daryl Reaugh, Goalie	.03	.05
20	Paul Cyr	.03	.05

BUFFALO SABRES

No.	Player	EX	NRMT
21	Doug Bodger	.03	.05
22	David Andreychuk	.08	.15
23	Clint Malarchuk, Goalie	.03	.05
24	Darrin Shannon	.03	.05
25	Christian Ruuttu	.03	.05
26	Uwe Krupp	.03	.05
27	Pierre Turgeon	.12	.25
28	**Kevin Haller, RC**	**.08**	**.15**
29	Dave Snuggerud	.03	.05
30	Alexander Mogilny	.25	.50
31	Dale Hawerchuk	.03	.05
32	Michael Ramsey	.03	.05
33	**Darcy Wakaluk, Goalie**	**.15**	**.30**
34	Tony Tanti	.03	.05
35	Gordon (Jay) Wells	.03	.05
36	Mikko Makela	.03	.05
37	Daren Puppa, Goalie	.03	.05
38	Benoit Hogue	.03	.05
39	Richard Vaive	.03	.05
40	Grant Ledyard	.03	.05

DETROIT RED WINGS

No.	Player	EX	NRMT
41	**Hat Trick:** Steve Yzerman, Det.	.05	.10
42	Steve Yzerman	.13	.25
43	Shawn Burr	.03	.05
44	Yves Racine	.03	.05
45	Johan Garpenlov	.05	.10
46	Keith Primeau	.08	.15
47	Tim Cheveldae, Goalie	.10	.20
48	Byron (Brad) McCrimmon	.03	.05
49	David Barr	.03	.05
50	Sergei Fedorov, Error	.35	.75
51	Brent Fedyk	.03	.05
52	Jimmy Carson	.03	.05
53	Paul Ysebaert	.03	.05
54	Rick Zombo	.03	.05
55	Bob Probert	.03	.10
56	Gerard Gallant	.03	.05
57	Kevin Miller	.03	.05

NEW YORK RANGERS

No.	Player	EX	NRMT
58	Randy Moller	.03	.05
59	Kris King	.03	.05
60	**Corey Millen, RC**	**.15**	**.30**
61	Brian Mullen, (Now With Sharks 5-30-91)	.03	.05
62	Darren Turcotte	.03	.05
63	Ray Sheppard, (Now With Red Wings 8-6-91)	.05	.10
64	David Shaw	.03	.05
65	Troy Mallette	.03	.05
66	James Patrick	.03	.05
67	Mark Janssens	.03	.05
68	John Vanbiesbrouck, Goalie	.08	.15
69	Joey Kocur	.03	.05
70	Mike Richter, Goalie	.10	.20
71	John Ogrodnick	.03	.05
72	Kelly Kisio, (Now With Sharks 6-4-91)	.03	.05
73	Normand Rochefort	.03	.05
74	Michael Gartner	.08	.15
75	Brian Leetch	.20	.40
76	Bernie Nicholls	.03	.05
77	Jan Erixon	.03	.05

PITTSBURGH PENGUINS

No.	Player	EX	NRMT
78	Lawrence Murphy	.03	.05
79	Joe Mullen	.03	.05
80	Tom Barrasso, Goalie	.05	.10
81	Paul Coffey	.08	.15
82	Jiri Hrdina	.03	.05
83	Mark Recchi	.15	.30
84	Randy Gilhen, (Now With Kings 6-22-91)	.03	.05
85	Bob Errey	.03	.05
86	Scott Young	.03	.05
87	Mario Lemieux	.40	.80
88	Ulf Samuelsson	.03	.05
89	Frank Pietrangelo, Goalie	.03	.05
90	Ronald Francis	.03	.05
91	Paul Stanton	.03	.05
92	Kevin Stevens	.15	.30
93	Bryan Trottier	.03	.05
94	Phillippe Bourque	.03	.05
95	Jaromir Jagr	.30	.60

EDMONTON OILERS

No.	Player	EX	NRMT
96	**Hat Trick:** Petr Klima	.03	.05
97	Adam Graves	.15	.30
98	Esa Tikkanen	.03	.05
99	**Norm MacIver, RC**	**.10**	**.20**
100	Craig MacTavish	.03	.05
101	Bill Ranford, Goalie	.03	.05
102	Martin Gelinas	.03	.05
103	Charles Huddy, (Now With Kings 6-22-91)	.03	.05
104	Petr Klima	.03	.05
105	Ken Linseman	.03	.05
106	James (Steve) Smith	.03	.05
107	Craig Simpson	.03	.05
108	Chris Joseph	.03	.05

No.	Player	EX	NRMT
109	Joe Murphy	.03	.05
110	Jeff Beukeboom	.03	.05
111	Grant Fuhr, Goalie	.05	.10
112	Geoff Smith	.03	.05
113	Anatoli Semenov	.03	.05
114	Mark Messier	.15	.30
115	Kevin Lowe	.03	.05
116	Glenn Anderson	.05	.10

MINNESOTA NORTH STARS

No.	Player	EX	NRMT
117	Robert Smith	.05	.10
118	Douglas Smail	.03	.05
119	Jon Casey, Goalie	.03	.05
120	Gaetan Duchesne	.03	.05
121	Neal Broten	.03	.05
122	Brian Hayward, Goalie (Now With Sharks 5-30-91)	.03	.05
123	Brian Propp	.03	.05
124	Mark Tinordi	.03	.05
125	Michael Modano	.15	.30
126	Marc Bureau	.03	.05
127	Ulf Dahlen	.03	.05
128	Chris Dahlquist	.03	.05
129	Brian Bellows	.05	.10
130	Mike Craig	.03	.05
131	Dave Gagner	.03	.05
132	Brian Glynn	.03	.05

QUEBEC NORDIQUES

No.	Player	EX	NRMT
133	Joe Sakic	.15	.30
134	Owen Nolan	.10	.20
135	Everett Sanipass	.03	.05
136	**Jamie Baker, RC**	**.10**	**.20**
137	Mats Sundin	.13	.25
138	Craig Wolanin	.03	.05
139	Kip Miller	.03	.05
140	Steven Finn	.03	.05
141	Anthony Hrkac, (Now With Sharks 5-30-91)	.03	.05
142	Curtis Leschyshyn	.03	.05
143	Michael McNeill	.03	.05
144	Mike Hough	.03	.05
145	**Alexei Gusarov, RC**	**.05**	**.10**
146	Jacques Cloutier, Goalie	.03	.05
147	Shawn Anderson	.03	.05
148	Stephane Morin	.03	.05
149	Bryan Fogarty	.03	.05
150	Scott Pearson	.03	.05
151	Ron Tugnutt, Goalie	.03	.05
152	Randy Velischek	.03	.05

TORONTO MAPLE LEAFS

No.	Player	NRMT	Mint
153	Dave Reid	.03	.05
154	George (Rob) Ramage, (Now With North Stars 5-30-91)	.03	.05
155	David Hannan	.03	.05
156	Wendel Clark	.10	.20
157	Peter Ing, Goalie	.03	.05
158	Michel Petit	.03	.05
159	Brian Bradley	.03	.05
160	Robert Cimetta	.03	.05
161	Gary Leeman	.03	.05
162	Aaron Broten	.03	.05
163	Dave Ellett	.03	.05
164	Peter Zezel	.03	.05
165	Daniel Marois	.03	.05
166	Michael Krushelnyski	.03	.05
167	Luke Richardson	.03	.05
168	Scott Thornton	.03	.05
169	Mike Foligno	.03	.05
170	Vincent Damphousse	.05	.10
171	Todd Gill	.03	.05
172	Kevin Maguire	.03	.05

LOS ANGELES KINGS

No.	Player	EX	NRMT
173	**Hat Trick:** Wayne Gretzky	.25	.50
174	**Hat Trick:** Tomas Sandstrom	.03	.05

1991-92 REGULAR ISSUE — BOWMAN • 343

No.	Player	EX	NRMT
175	John Tonelli, (Now With Black Hawks 7-1-91)	.03	.05
176	Wayne Gretzky	.50	1.00
177	Larry Robinson	.03	.05
178	Jay Miller	.03	.05
179	Tomas Sandstrom	.03	.05
180	John McIntyre	.03	.05
181	**Brad Jones, RC**	**.03**	**.05**
182	Robert Blake	.10	.20
183	Kelly Hrudey, Goalie	.03	.05
184	Martin McSorley, Error	.03	.05
185	Todd Elik, (Now With North Stars 6-22-91)	.03	.05
186	David Taylor	.03	.05
187	Stephen Kasper, (Now With Flyers 5-30-91)	.03	.05
188	Luc Robitaille	.08	.15
189	Bob Kudelski	.03	.05
190	Daniel Berthiaume, Goalie	.03	.05
191	Steve Duchesne, (Now With Flyers 5-30-91)	.03	.05
192	Tony Granato	.03	.05

WINNIPEG JETS

No.	Player	EX	NRMT
193	Bob Essensa, Goalie	.05	.10
194	Phil Sykes	.03	.05
195	Paul MacDermid	.03	.05
196	Dave McLlwain	.03	.05
197	Phil Housley	.03	.05
198	Pat Elynuik	.03	.05
199	Randy Carlyle	.03	.05
200	Thomas Steen	.03	.05
201	Teppo Numminen	.03	.05
202	Danton Cole	.03	.05
203	Doug Evans	.03	.05
204	Ed Olczyk	.03	.05
205	Maurice Mantha	.03	.05
206	Scott Arniel	.03	.05
207	Richard Tabaracci, Goalie	.03	.05
208	**Bryan Marchment, RC** (Now With Black Hawks 7-22-91)	**.05**	**.10**
209	Mark Osborne	.03	.05
210	Fredrik Olausson	.03	.05
211	Brent Ashton	.03	.05

NEW YORK ISLANDERS

No.	Player	EX	NRMT
212	Ray Ferraro	.03	.05
213	Mark Fitzpatrick, Goalie	.03	.05
214	Hubie McDonough	.03	.05
215	Joe Reekie	.03	.05
216	**Bill Berg, RC**	**.03**	**.05**
217	Wayne McBean	.03	.05
218	Patrick Flatley	.03	.05
219	Jeff Hackett, Goalie, (Now With Sharks 5-30-91)	.05	.10
220	Derek King	.03	.05
221	Craig Ludwig, (Now With North Stars 6-22-91)	.03	.05
222	Pat LaFontaine	.13	.25
223	David Volek	.03	.05
224	Glenn Healy, Goalie	.03	.05
225	Jeff Norton	.03	.05
226	Brent Sutter	.03	.05
227	Randy Wood	.03	.05
228	Gary Nylund	.03	.05
229	David Chyzowski	.03	.05

PHILADELPHIA FLYERS

No.	Player	EX	NRMT
230	Rick Tocchet	.05	.10
231	Ken Wregget, Goalie	.03	.05
232	Terry Carkner	.03	.05
233	Martin Hostak	.03	.05
234	Ron Hextall, Goalie	.03	.05
235	Gordon Murphy	.03	.05
236	Scott Mellanby, (Now With Oilers 5-30-91)	.03	.05
237	Peter Peeters, Goalie	.03	.05
238	Ronald Sutter	.03	.05
239	Murray Craven	.03	.05
240	Kjell Samuelsson	.03	.05

No.	Player	EX	NRMT
241	Per-erik Eklund	.03	.05
242	Mark Pederson	.03	.05
243	Murray Baron	.03	.05
244	Keith Acton	.03	.05
245	Derrick Smith	.03	.05
246	Mike Ricci	.10	.20
247	Dale Kushner	.03	.05
248	Normand Lacombe, Error	.03	.05

CALGARY FLAMES

No.	Player	EX	NRMT
249	**Hat Trick:** Theoren Fleury	.05	.10
250	**Hat Trick:** Sergei Makarov	.03	.05
251	Paul Ranheim	.03	.05
252	Joe Nieuwendyk	.05	.10
253	Michael Vernon, Goalie	.03	.05
254	Gary Suter	.03	.05
255	Douglas Gilmour	.13	.25
256	Paul Fenton	.03	.05
257	Roger Johansson	.03	.05
258	Stephane Matteau	.03	.05
259	Frantisek Musil	.03	.05
260	Joel Otto	.03	.05
261	Tim Sweeney	.03	.05
262	Allan MacInnis	.03	.05
263	Gary Roberts	.05	.10
264	Sergei Makarov	.03	.05
265	Carey Wilson	.03	.05
266	Eric Nattress	.03	.05
267	Robert Reichel	.10	.20
268	Richard Wamsley, Goalie	.03	.05
269	Brian MacLellan, (Now With Red Wings 6-11-91)	.05	.10
270	Theoren Fleury	.10	.20

NEW JERSEY DEVILS

No.	Player	EX	NRMT
271	**Hat Trick:** Claude Lemieux	.03	.05
272	**Hat Trick:** John MacLean	.03	.05
273	Viacheslav Fetisov	.03	.05
274	Kirk Muller	.03	.05
275	Sean Burke, Goalie	.03	.05
276	Alexei Kasatonov	.03	.05
277	Claude Lemieux	.03	.05
278	Eric Weinrich	.03	.05
279	Patrik Sundstrom	.03	.05
280	Zdeno Ciger	.03	.05
281	Bruce Driver	.03	.05
282	Laurie Boschman	.03	.05
283	Chris Terreri, Goalie	.05	.10
284	Kenneth Daneyko	.03	.05
285	Doug Brown	.03	.05
286	Jon Morris	.03	.05
287	Peter Stastny	.03	.05
288	Brendan Shanahan, (Now With Blues 7-24-91)	.12	.25
289	John MacLean	.03	.05

WASHINGTON CAPITALS

No.	Player	EX	NRMT
290	Michael Liut, Goalie	.03	.05
291	Michal Pivonka	.03	.05
292	Kelly Miller	.03	.05
293	John Druce	.03	.05
294	Calle Johansson	.03	.05
295	Alan May	.03	.05
296	Kevin Hatcher	.03	.05
297	Tim Bergland	.03	.05
298	Mikhail Tatarinov, (Now With Nordiques 6-22-91)	.03	.05
299	Peter Bondra	.05	.10
300	Al Iafrate	.03	.05
301	Nicholas Kypreos	.03	.05
302	Dino Ciccarelli	.03	.05
303	Dale Hunter	.03	.05
304	Donald Beaupre, Goalie	.03	.05
305	Jim Hrivnak, Goalie	.03	.05
306	Stephen Leach, (Now With Bruins 6-21-91)	.03	.05
307	Dimitri Khristich, Error	.05	.10
308	Mike Ridley	.03	.05

VANCOUVER CANUCKS

No.	Player	EX	NRMT
309	Sergio Momesso	.03	.05
310	Kirk McLean, Goalie	.12	.25
311	Greg Adams	.03	.05
312	Adrien Plavsic	.03	.05
313	Cliff Ronning	.05	.10
314	Garry Valk	.03	.05
315	Troy Gamble, Goalie	.03	.05
316	Gino Odjick	.03	.05
317	Doug Lidster	.03	.05
318	Geoff Courtnall	.03	.05
319	Tom Kurvers, (Now With Islanders 6-22-91)	.03	.05
320	Robert Kron	.03	.05
321	Jyrki Lumme	.03	.05
322	**Jay Mazur, RC**	**.03**	**.05**
323	Dave Capuano	.03	.05
324	Petr Nedved	.13	.25
325	Steven Bozek	.03	.05
326	Igor Larionov	.03	.05
327	Trevor Linden	.15	.30

MONTREAL CANADIENS

No.	Player	EX	NRMT
328	Shayne Corson	.03	.05
329	Eric Desjardins	.03	.05
330	Stephane Richer	.03	.05
331	Brian Skrudland	.03	.05
332	Sylvain Lefebvre	.03	.05
333	Stephan Lebeau	.10	.20
334	Mike Keane	.03	.05
335	Patrick Roy, Goalie	.25	.50
336	Brent Gilchrist	.03	.05
337	**Andre Racicot, Goalie, RC**	**.08**	**.15**
338	Guy Carbonneau	.03	.05
339	Michael McPhee	.03	.05
340	Andrew Cassels	.03	.05
341	Petr Svoboda	.03	.05
342	Denis Savard	.05	.10
343	Mathieu Schneider	.03	.05
344	**John LeClair, RC**	**.15**	**.30**
345	Tom Chorske	.03	.05
346	Russell Courtnall	.03	.05

BOSTON BRUINS

No.	Player	EX	NRMT
347	**Hat Trick:** Kenneth Hodge, Jr.	.03	.05
348	**Hat Trick:** Cam Neely	.05	.10
349	Randy Burridge, (Now With Capitals 6-21-91)	.03	.05
350	Glen Wesley, Error	.03	.05
351	Christopher Nilan	.03	.05
352	**Jeff Lazaro, RC**	**.03**	**.05**
353	Wes Walz	.03	.05
354	Rejean Lemelin, Goalie	.03	.05
355	Craig Janney	.08	.15
356	Raymond Bourque	.08	.15
357	Robert Sweeney	.03	.05
358	David Christian	.03	.05
359	David Poulin	.03	.05
360	Garry Galley	.03	.05
361	Andrew Moog, Goalie	.05	.10
362	Kenneth Hodge, Jr.	.03	.05
363	James Wiemer	.03	.05
364	Petri Skriko	.03	.05
365	Don Sweeney	.03	.05
366	Cam Neely	.08	.15

ST. LOUIS BLUES

No.	Player	EX	NRMT
367	**Hat Trick:** Brett Hull	.10	.20
368	Gino Cavallini	.03	.05
369	Scott Stevens	.05	.10
370	Richard Sutter	.03	.05
371	Glen Featherstone, (Now With Bruins 7-25-91)	.03	.05
372	Vincent Riendeau, Goalie	.03	.05
373	Dave Lowry	.03	.05
374	Rod Brind'Amour	.10	.20
375	Brett Hull	.25	.50
376	Dan Quinn	.03	.05
377	Tom Tilley	.03	.05

— 1992-93 REGULAR ISSUE —

This 442-card set features the popular gold foil cards that have dramatically increased the price of this set. The 18 short printed gold foiled stamped cards have made this set both collectable and desirable. Very high quality from Bowman in this set has also added to its popularity. Beware of the Eric Lindros counterfeit cards. The gloss on this fake is very slight.

 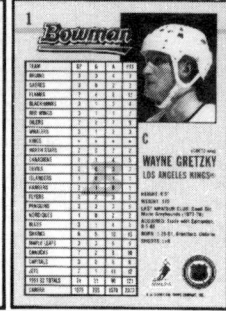

1992-93 Issue
Card No. 1, Wayne Gretzky

Card Size: 2 1/2" x 3 1/2"
Face: Regular: Four colour, white border; Name
Foil: Four colour, gold foil border; Name
Back: Four colour on card stock; Name, Team, Position, Resume
Imprint: © 1992 THE TOPPS COMPANY, INC.
Complete Set No.: 442
Complete Set Price: 200.00   400.00
Common Player: .15   .30
Wax Pack: (16 Cards)   16.00
Wax Box: (36 Packs)   525.00

No.	Player	EX	NRMT
1	Wayne Gretzky, LA	5.00	10.00
2	Michael Krusheinyski, Tor.	.15	.30
3	Raymond Bourque, Bos.	.30	.60
4	Keith Brown, Chi.	.15	.30
5	Robert Sweeney, Bos.	.15	.30
6	Dave Christian, St.L	.15	.30
7	Frantisek Kucera, Chi.	.15	.30
8	John LeClair, Mon.	.15	.30
9	Jamie Macoun, Tor.	.15	.30
10	Robert Carpenter, Bos.	.15	.30
11	Garry Galley, Phi.	.15	.30
12	Bob Kudelski, LA	.15	.30
13	Doug Bodger, Buf.	.15	.30
14	Craig Janney, St.L	.30	.60
15	Glen Wesley, Bos.	.15	.30
16	Daren Puppa, Goalie Buf.	.15	.30
17	Andy Brickley, Bos.	.15	.30
18	Stephen Konroyd, Har.	.15	.30
19	David Poulin, Bos.	.15	.30
20	Phil Housley, Win.	.15	.30
21	Kevin Todd, NJ	.15	.30
22	Tomas Sandstrom, LA	.15	.30
23	Pierre Turgeon, NYI	1.00	2.00
24	James (Steve) Smith, Chi.	.15	.30
25	Ray Sheppard, Det.	.25	.50
26	Stu Barnes, Win.	.15	.30
27	Grant Ledyard, Buf.	.15	.30
28	Benoit Hogue, NYI	.15	.30
29	Randy Burridge, Wash.	.15	.30
30	Clint Malarchuk, Goalie, Buf.	.15	.30
31	Steve Duchesne, Phi.	.15	.30
32	Guy Hebert, Goalie, St.L, RC	.75	1.50
33	Stephen Kasper, Phi.	.15	.30
34	Alexander Mogilny, Buf.	1.75	3.50
35	Martin McSorley, LA	.15	.30
36	Doug Weight, NYR	.15	.30
37	David Taylor, LA	.15	.30
38	Guy Carbonneau, Mon	.15	.30
39	Brian Benning, Phi.	.15	.30
40	Nelson Emerson, St.L	.25	.50
41	Craig Wolanin, Que.	.15	.30
42	Kelly Hrudey, Goalie, LA	.15	.30
43	Chris Chelios, Chi.	.25	.50
44	David Andreychuk, Buf.	.35	.75
45	Russell Courtnall, Mon.	.15	.30
46	Stephane J. J. Richer, NJ	.15	.30
47	Petr Svoboda, Buf.	.15	.30
48	Barry Pederson, Bos.	.15	.30
49	Claude Lemieux, NJ	.15	.30
50	Tony Granato, LA	.15	.30
51	Allan MacInnis, Cal.	.15	.30
52	Luciano Borsato, Win.	.15	.30
53	Sergei Makarov, Cal.	.15	.30
54	Bobby Smith, Min.	.15	.30
55	Gary Suter, Cal.	.15	.30
56	Tom Draper, Goalie, Buf.	.15	.30
57	Corey Millen, LA	.15	.30
58	Joe Mullen, Pit.	.15	.30
59	Joe Nieuwendyk, Cal.	.25	.50
60	Brian Hayward, Goalie, SJ	.15	.30
61	Steve Larmer, Chi.	.15	.30
62	Cam Neely, Bos.	.35	.75
63	Eric Nattress, Tor.	.15	.30
64	Denis Savard, Mon.	.15	.30
65	Gerald Diduck, Van.	.15	.30
66	Pat Jablonski, Goalie, St.L	.15	.30
67	Byron (Brad) McCrimmon, Det.	.15	.30
68	Dirk Graham, Chi.	.15	.30
69	Joel Otto, Cal.	.15	.30
70	Luc Robitaille, LA	.50	1.00
71	Dana Murzyn, Van.	.15	.30
72	Jocelyn Lemieux, Chi.	.15	.30
73	Mike Hudson, Chi.	.15	.30
74	Patrick Roy, Goalie, Mon.	2.00	4.00
75	Douglas Wilson, SJ	.15	.30
76	Wayne Presley, Buf.	.15	.30
77	Felix Potvin, Goalie, Tor.	6.00	12.00
78	Jeremy Roenick Chi.	2.50	5.00
79	Andrew Moog, Goalie, Bos.	.15	.30
80	Joey Kocur, NYR	.15	.30
81	Neal Broten, Min.	.15	.30
82	Shayne Corson, Mon.	.15	.30
83	Douglas Gilmour, Tor.	1.50	3.00
84	Rob Zettler, SJ	.15	.30
85	Bob Probert, Det.	.15	.30
86	Michael Vernon, Goalie, Cal.	.15	.30
87	Richard Zombo, St.L	.15	.30
88	Adam Creighton, NYI	.15	.30
89	Michael McPhee, Mon.	.15	.30
90	Ed Belfour, Goalie, Chi.	.50	1.00
91	Steve Chiasson, Det.	.15	.30
92	Dominic Roussel, Goalie, Phi.	.30	.60
93	Troy Murray, Win.	.15	.30
94	Jari Kurri, LA	.15	.30
95	Geoff Smith, Edm.	.15	.30
96	Paul Ranheim, Det.	.15	.30
97	Richard Wamsley, Goalie, Tor.	.15	.30
98	Brian Noonan, Chi.	.15	.30
99	Kevin Lowe, Edm.	.15	.30
100	Josef Beranek, Edm.	.15	.30
101	Michel Petit, Cal.	.15	.30
102	Craig Billington, Goalie, NJ	.15	.30
103	Steve Yzerman, Det.	1.00	2.00
104	Glenn Anderson, Tor.	.15	.30
105	Perry Berezan, SJ	.15	.30
106	Bill Ranford, Goalie, Edm.	.15	.30
107	Randy Ladouceur, Har.	.15	.30
108	Jimmy Carson, Det.	.15	.30
109	Gary Roberts, Cal.	.15	.30
110	Checklist #1 (1-110)	.15	.30
111	Brad Shaw, Ott.	.15	.30
112	Patrick Verbeek, Har.	.15	.30
113	Mark Messier, NYR	.50	1.00
114	Grant Fuhr, Goalie, Tor.	.15	.30
115	Sylvain Cote, Wash.	.15	.30
116	Mike Sullivan, SJ	.15	.30
117	Steve Thomas, NYI	.15	.30
118	Craig MacTavish, Edm.	.15	.30
119	David Babych Van.	.15	.30
120	Jim Waite. Goalie, Chi.	.15	.30
121	Kevin Dineen, Phi.	.15	.30
122	Shawn Burr, Det.	.15	.30
123	Ronald Francis, Pit.	.15	.30
124	Garth Butcher, St.L	.15	.30
125	Jarmo Myllys, Goalie, Tor.	.15	.30
126	Doug Brown, NJ	.15	.30
127	James Patrick, NYR	.15	.30
128	Ray Ferraro, NYI	.15	.30
129	Terry Carkner, Phi.	.15	.30
130	John MacLean, NJ	.15	.30
131	Randy Velischek, Que.	.15	.30

No.	Player	EX	NRMT
378	Paul Cavallini	.03	.05
379	Bob Bassen	.03	.05
380	Mario Marois	.03	.05
381	Darin Kimble	.03	.05
382	Ronald Wilson	.03	.05
383	Garth Butcher	.03	.05
384	Adam Oates	.12	.25
385	Jeff Brown	.03	.05

CHICAGO BLACK HAWKS

No.	Player	EX	NRMT
386	Hat Trick: Jeremy Roenick	.15	.30
387	Anthony McKegney	.03	.05
388	Troy Murray, (Now With Jets 7-22-91)	.03	.05
389	Dave Manson	.03	.05
390	Ed Belfour, Goalie	.15	.30
391	Steve Thomas	.03	.05
392	Michel Goulet	.03	.05
393	Trent Yawney	.03	.05
394	Adam Creighton	.03	.05
395	Steve Larmer	.03	.05
396	Jimmy Waite, Goalie	.05	.10
397	Dirk Graham	.03	.05
398	Chris Chelios	.05	.10
399	Mike Hudson	.03	.05
400	Douglas Wilson	.03	.05
401	Gregory Gilbert	.03	.05
402	Wayne Presley	.03	.05
403	Jeremy Roenick	.30	.60
404	Frantisek Kucera	.03	.05

STANLEY CUP PLAYOFFS

No.	Teams	EX	NRMT
405	Black Hawks vs North Stars	.03	.05
406	Blues vs Red Wings	.03	.05
407	Flames vs Oilers	.03	.05
408	Penguins vs Devils	.03	.05
409	Rangers vs Capitals	.03	.05
410	Bruins vs Whalers	.03	.05
411	Canadiens vs Sabres	.03	.05
412	Kings vs Canucks	.03	.05
413	Penguins vs Capitals	.03	.05
414	Bruins vs Canadiens	.03	.05
415	North Stars vs Blues	.03	.05
416	Kings vs Oilers	.03	.05
417	North Stars vs Oilers	.03	.05
418	Bruins vs. Penguins	.03	.05

STANLEY CUP FINALS

No.	Game	EX	NRMT
419	Game 1 - May 15th	.03	.05
420	Game 2 - May 17th	.03	.05
421	Game 3 - May 19th	.03	.05
422	Game 4 - May 21st	.03	.05
423	Game 5 - May 23rd	.03	.05
424	Game 6 - May 25th	.03	.05

1991 PLAYOFF M.V.P.

No.	Player	EX	NRMT
425	Mario Lemieux, Pit.	.25	.50

CHECKLISTS

No.	Checklist	EX	NRMT
426	Checklist I (1-108)	.05	.10
427	Checklist II (109-216)	.05	.10
428	Checklist III (217-324)	.05	.10
429	Checklist IV (325-429)	.05	.10

— 1992 - 93 REGULAR ISSUE — BOWMAN • 345

No.	Player	EX	NRMT
132	John Vanbiesbrouck, Goalie, NYR	.35	.75
133	Dean Evason, SJ	.15	.30
134	Patrick Flatley, NYI	.15	.30
135	Petr Klima, Edm.	.15	.30
136	Geoff Sanderson, Har.	1.75	3.50
137	Joe Reekie, TB	.15	.30
138	Kirk Muller, Mon.	.15	.30
139	Brian Mullen, SJ	.15	.30
140	Daniel Berthiaume, Goalie, Bos.	.15	.30
141	David Shaw, Min.	.15	.30
142	Pat LaFontaine, Buf.	.75	1.50
143	Ulf Dahlen, Mln.	.15	.30
144	Esa Tikkanen, Edm.	.15	.30
145	Viacheslav Fetisov, NJ	.15	.30
146	Michael Gartner, NYR	.15	.30
147	Brent Sutter, Chi.	.15	.30
148	Darcy Wakaluk, Goalie, Min.	.15	.30
149	Brian Leetch, NYR	.75	1.50
150	Craig Simpson, Edm.	.15	.30
151	Michael Modano, Min.	.75	1.50
152	Bryan Trottier, Pit.	.15	.30
153	Lawrence Murphy, Pit.	.15	.30
154	Pavel Bure, Van.	6.00	12.00
155	Kay Whitmore, Goalie, Har.	.15	.30
156	Darren Turcotte, NYR	.15	.30
157	Frantisek Musil, Cal.	.15	.30
158	Bo Mikael Andersson, TB	.15	.30
159	Rick Tocchet, Pit.	.15	.30
160	Scott Stevens, NJ	.15	.30
161	Bernie Nicholls, Edm.	.15	.30
162	Peter Sidorkiewicz, Goalie, Ott.	.15	.30
163	Scott Mellanby, Edm.	.15	.30
164	Alexander Semak, NJ	.15	.30
165	Kjell Samuelsson, Pit.	.15	.30
166	Kelly Kisio, SJ	.15	.30
167	Sylvain Turgeon, Ott.	.15	.30
168	Rob Brown, Chi.	.15	.30
169	Gerard Gallant, Det.	.15	.30
170	Jyrki Lumme, Van.	.15	.30
171	Dave Gagner, Min.	.15	.30
172	Tony Tanti, Buf.	.15	.30
173	Zarley Zalapski, Har.	.15	.30
174	Joe Murphy, Edm.	.15	.30
175	Ronald Sutter, St.L	.15	.30
176	Dino Ciccarelli, Det.	.15	.30
177	Jim Johnson, Min.	.15	.30
178	Mike Hough, Que.	.15	.30
179	Per-Erik Eklund, Phi.	.15	.30
180	John Druce, Wash.	.15	.30
181	Paul Coffey, LA	.30	.60
182	Ken Wregget, Goalie, Pit.	.15	.30
183	Brendan Shanahan, St.L	.75	1.50
184	Keith Acton, Phi.	.15	.30
185	Steven Finn, Que.	.15	.30
186	Brett Hull, St.L	2.00	4.00
187	Ronald Melanson, Goalie, Mon.	.15	.30
188	Derek King, NYI	.15	.30
189	Mario Lemieux, Pit.	4.00	8.00
190	Mathieu Schneider, Mon.	.15	.30
191	Claude Vilgrain, NJ	.15	.30
192	Gary Leeman, Cal.	.15	.30
193	Paul Cavallini, St.L	.15	.30
194	John Cullen, Har.	.15	.30
195	Ron Hextall, Goalie, Que.	.15	.30
196	David Volek, NYI	.15	.30
197	Gordon Roberts, Bos.	.15	.30
198	Dale Craigwell, SJ	.15	.30

**43rd NHL ALL STAR GAME
CAMPBELL CONFERENCE ALL STAR**

No.	PLayer	EX	NRMT
199	Ed Belfour, Goalie, Chi.	2.50	5.00
200	Brian Bellows, Min., SP	14.00	28.00
201	Chris Chelios, Chi.	1.25	2.50
202	Tim Cheveldae, Goalie, Det., SP	15.00	30.00
203A	Vincent Damphousse, Error	1.50	3.00
203B	Vincent Damphousse, Corrected	1.50	3.00
204	David Ellett, Tor.	1.00	2.00
205	Sergei Fedorov, Det., SP	30.00	60.00
206	Theoren Fleury, Cal.	1.00	2.00
207	Wayne Gretzky, LA	10.00	20.00
208	Phil Housley, Win.	1.00	2.00
209	Brett Hull, St.L	5.00	10.00

No.	Player	EX	NRMT
210	Trevor Linden, Van., SP	8.00	16.00
211	Allan MacInnis, Cal., SP	5.00	10.00
212	Kirk McLean, Goalie, Van., SP	16.00	32.00
213	Adam Oates, St.L	1.50	3.00
214	Gary Roberts, Cal., SP	7.50	15.00
215	Larry Robinson, LA	1.00	2.00
216	Luc Robitaille, LA	2.00	4.00
217	Jeremy Roenick, Chi., SP	25.00	50.00
218	Mark Tinordi, Min.	1.00	2.00
219	Douglas Wilson, SJ	1.00	2.00
220	Steve Yzerman, Det.	3.50	7.00
221	Checklist #2 (111 - 220)	.15	.30
222	Donald Beaupre, Goalie, Wash., SP	7.50	15.00

WALES CONFERENCE ALL STAR

No.	Player	EX	NRMT
223	Raymond Bourque, Bos.	1.50	3.00
224	Rod Brind'amour Phi., SP	10.00	20.00
225	Randy Burridge, Wash., SP	10.00	20.00
226	Paul Coffey, Pit., SP	10.00	20.00
227	John Cullen, Har., SP	5.00	10.00
228	Eric Desjardins, Mon., SP	10.00	20.00
229	Ray Ferraro, NYI, SP	5.00	10.00
230	Kevin Hatcher, Wash.	1.00	2.00
231	Jaromir Jagr, Pit.	4.50	9.00
232	Brian Leetch, NYR, SP	11.00	22.00
233	Mario Lemieux, Pit.	7.50	15.00
234	Mark Messier, NYR	2.50	5.00
235	Alexander Mogilny, Buf.	3.50	7.00
236	Kirk Muller, Mon.	1.50	3.00
237	Owen Nolan, Que.	1.00	2.00
238	Mike Richter, Goalie, NYR	3.00	6.00
239	Patrick Roy, Goalie, Mon	5.00	10.00
240	Joe Sakic, Que., SP	9.00	18.00
241	Kevin Stevens, Pit.	1.50	3.00
242	Scott Stevens, NJ	1.00	2.00
243	Bryan Trottier, Pit., SP	5.00	10.00

REGULAR ISSUE

No.	Player	EX	NRMT
244	Joe Sakic, Que.	.50	1.00
245	Daniel Marois, NYI	.15	.30
246	Randy Wood, Buf.	.15	.30
247	Jeff Brown, St.L	.15	.30
248	Peter Bondra, Wash.	.15	.30
249	Peter Stastny, NJ	.15	.30
250	Tom Barrasso, Goalie, Pit.	.15	.30
251	Al Iafrate, Wash.	.15	.30
252	James Black, Har.	.15	.30
253	Jan Erixon, NYR	.15	.30
254	Brian Lawton, SJ	.15	.30
255	Luke Richardson, Edm.	.15	.30
256	Richard Sutter, St.L	.15	.30
257	Jeff Chychrun, Pit. Error	.15	.30
258	Adam Oates, Bos.	.35	.75
259	Tom Kurvers. NYI	.15	.30
260	Brian Bellows, Min.	.15	.30
261	Trevor Linden, Van.	.35	.75
262	Vincent Riendeau, Goalie, Det.	.15	.30
263	Peter Zezel, Tor.	.15	.30
264	Rich Pilon, NYI	.15	.30
265	Paul Broten, NYR	.15	.30
266	Gaetan Duchesne, Min.	.15	.30
267	Doug Lidster, Van.	.15	.30
268	Rod Brind'Amour, Phi.	.35	.75
269	Jon Casey, Goalie, Min.	.15	.30
270	Pat Elynuik, Win.	.15	.30
271	Kevin Hatcher, Wash.	.15	.30
272	Brian Propp, Min.	.15	.30
273	Thomas Fergus, Van.	.15	.30
274	Stephen Weeks, Goalie, Ott.	.15	.30
275	Calle Johansson, Wash.	.15	.30
276	Russell Romaniuk, Win.	.15	.30
277	Gregory Paslawski, Que.	.15	.30
278	Ed Olczyk, Win.	.15	.30
279	Rod Langway, Wash.	.15	.30
280	Murray Craven, Har.	.15	.30
281	Guy Larose, Tor.	.15	.30
282	Paul MacDermid, Wash.	.15	.30
283	Brian Bradley, TB	.15	.30
284	Paul Stanton, Pit.	.15	.30
285	Kirk McLean, Goalie, Van.	.35	.75

No.	Player	EX	NRMT
286	Andrei Lomakin, Phi.	.15	.30
287	Randy Carlyle, Win.	.15	.30
288	Donald Audette, Buf.	.15	.30
289	Dan Quinn, Phi.	.15	.30
290	Mike Keane, Mon.	.15	.30
291	David Ellett. Tor.	.15	.30
292	Joseph Juneau, Bos.	2.50	5.00
293	Phillippe Bourque, Pit.	.15	.30
294	Michal Pivonka, Wash.	.15	.30
295	Fredrik Olausson, Win.	.15	.30
296	Randy McKay, NJ	.15	.30
297	Donald Beaupre, Goalie, Wash.	.15	.30
298	Stephen Leach, Bos.	.15	.30
299	Teppo Numminen, Win.	.15	.30
300	Viacheslav Kozlov, Det.	1.75	3.50
301	Kevin Haller, Buf.	.15	.30
302	Jaromir Jagr, Pit.	2.50	5.00
303	Dale Hunter, Wash.	.15	.30
304	Bob Errey, Pit.	.15	.30
305	Nicklas Lidstrom, Det.	.15	.30
306	Bob Essensa, Goalie, Win.	.15	.30
307	Sylvain Lefebvre, Mon.	.15	.30
308	Dale Hawerchuk, Buf.	.15	.30
309	Dave Snuggerud, SJ	.15	.30
310	Michel Goulet, Chi.	.15	.30
311	Eric Desjardins, Mon.	.15	.30
312	Thomas Steen, Win.	.15	.30
313	Scott Niedermayer, NJ	.50	1.00
314	Mark Recchi, Phi.	.85	1.75
315	Gordon Murphy, Bos.	.15	.30
316	Sergio Momesso, Van.	.15	.30
317	Todd Elik, Min.	.15	.30
318	Louie DeBrusk, Edm.	.15	.30
319	Mike Lalor, Win.	.15	.30
320	Jamie Leach, Pit.	.15	.30
321	Darryl Sydor, LA	.15	.30
322	Brent Gilchrist, Mon.	.15	.30
323	Alexei Kasatonov, NJ	.15	.30
324	Richard Tabaracci, Goalie, Win.	.15	.30
325	Wendel Clark, Tor.	.35	.75
326	Vladimir Konstantinov, Det.	.15	.30
327	Randy Gilhen, NYR	.15	.30
328	Owen Nolan, Que.	.15	.30
329	Vincent Damphousse, Edm.	.15	.30
330	Checklist ## (221-331)	.15	.30
331	Yves Racine, Det.	.15	.30
332	Jacques Cloutier, Goalie, Que.	.15	.30
333	Greg Adams, Van.	.15	.30
334	Mike Craig, Min.	.15	.30
335	Curtis Leschyshyn, Que.	.15	.30
336	John McIntyre, LA	.15	.30
337	Stephane Quintal, St.L	.15	.30
338	Kelly Miller, Wash.	.15	.30
339	Dave Manson. Edm.	.15	.30
340	Stephane Matteau, Chi.	.15	.30
341	Christian Ruuttu, Win.	.15	.30
342	Mike Donnelly, LA	.15	.30
343	Eric Weinrich, NJ	.15	.30
344	Mats Sundin, Que.	.50	1.00
345	Geoff Courtnall, Van.	.15	.30
346	Stephan Lebeau, Mon.	.15	.30
347	Jeff Beukeboom, NYR	.15	.30
348	Jeff Hackett, Goalie, SJ	.15	.30
349	Uwe Krupp, NYI	.15	.30
350	Igor Larionov, Van.	.15	.30
351	Ulf Samuelsson, Pit.	.15	.30
352	Marty McInnis, NYI	.15	.30
353	Peter Ahola, LA	.15	.30
354	Mike Richter, Goalie, NYR	1.00	2.00
355	Theoren Fleury, Cal.	.30	.60
356	Dan Lambert, Que.	.15	.30
357	Brent Ashton, Bos.	.15	.30
358	David Bruce, SJ	.15	.30
359	Chris Dahlquist, Min.	.15	.30
360	Mike Ridley, Wash.	.15	.30
361	Pat Falloon, SJ	.30	.60
362	Douglas Smail, Que.	.15	.30
363	Adrien Plavsic, Van.	.15	.30
364	Ronald Wilson, St.L	.15	.30
365	Derian Hatcher, Min.	.15	.30
366	Kevin Stevens, Pit.	.85	1.75
367	Robert Blake, LA	.15	.30
368	Curtis Joseph, Goalie, St.L	1.00	2.00

346 • PRO SET — 1990 PROMOTIONAL CARD —

No.	Player	EX	NRMT
369	Tom Fitzgerald, NYI	.15	.30
370	Dave Lowry, St.L	.15	.30
371	Jean-Jacques Daigneault, Mon	.15	.30
372	Jim Hrivnak, Goalie, Wash.	.15	.30
373	Adam Graves, NYR	1.00	2.00
374	Brad May, Buf.	.15	.30
375	Todd Gill, Tor.	.15	.30
376	Paul Ysebaert, Det.	.15	.30
377	**David Williams, SJ, RC**	.15	.30
378	Bob Bassen, St.L	.15	.30
379	Brian Glynn, Edm.	.15	.30
380	Kris King, NYR	.15	.30
381	Rob Pearson, Tor.	.15	.30
382	Marc Bureau, Min.	.15	.30
383	Jim Paek, Pit	.15	.30
384	Tomas Forslund, Cal.	.15	.30
385	Darrin Shannon, Win.	.15	.30
386	Chris Terreri, Goalie, NJ	.15	.30
387	Andrew Cassels, Har.	.15	.30
388	Jayson More, SJ	.15	.30
389	Anthony Amonte, NYR	.15	.30
390	Mark Pederson, Phi.	.15	.30
391	Kevin Miller, Wash.	.15	.30
392	Igor Ulanov, Win.	.15	.30
393	Kelly Buchberger, Edm.	.15	.30
394	Mark Fitzpatrick, Goalie, NYI	.15	.30
395	Mikhail Tatarinov, Que.	.15	.30
396	Petr Nedved, Van.	.35	.75
397	Jeff Odgers, SJ	.15	.30
398	Stephane Fiset, Goalie, Que.	.25	.50
399	Mark Tinordi, Min.	.15	.30
400	Johan Garpenlov, SJ	.15	.30
401	Robert Reichel, Cal.	.25	.50
402	Don Sweeney, Bos.	.15	.30
403	Robert DiMaio, TB	.15	.30
404	**Bill Lindsay, Que. RC**	.15	.30
405	Stephane Beauregard, Goalie, Win.	.15	.30
406	Mike Ricci, Que.	.35	.75
407	Robert Holik, Har.	.15	.30
408	Igor Kravchuk, Chi.	.15	.30
409	Murray Baron, St.L	.15	.30
410	Troy Gamble, Goalie, Van.	.15	.30
411	Cliff Ronning, Van.	.15	.30
412	Jeff Reese, Goalie, Cal.	.15	.30
413	Robert Kron, Van.	.15	.30
414	Benoit Brunet, Mon.	.30	.60
415	Shawn McEachern, Pit.	.25	.50
416	Sergei Fedorov, Det.	3.50	7.00
417	Joseph Sacco, Tor.	.15	.30
418	Bryan Marchment, Chi.	.15	.30
419	**John LeBlanc, Win. RC**	.15	.30
420	Tim Cheveldae, Goalie, Det.	.15	.30
421	Claude LaPointe, Que.	.15	.30
422	Kenneth Sutton, Buf.	.15	.30
423	Anatoli Semenov, TB	.15	.30
424	Michael McNeill, Que.	.15	.30
425	Norm Maciver, Edm.	.15	.30
426	Sergei Nemchinov, NYR	.15	.30
427	Dimitri Khristich, Wash.	.15	.30
428	Dominik Hasek, Goalie, Chi.	2.50	5.00
429	Robert McGill, TB	.15	.30
430	Valeri Zelepukin, NJ	.30	.60
431	Vladimir Ruzicka, Bos.	.15	.30
432	Valeri Kamensky, Que.	.35	.75
433	**Pat MacLeod, SJ, RC**	.15	.30
434	Glenn Healy, Goalie, NYI	.15	.30
435	Patrice Brisebois, Mon.	.15	.30
436	Jamie Baker, Que.	.15	.30
437	Michel Picard, Har.	.15	.30
438	Scott Lachance, NYI	.15	.30
439	Gilbert Dionne, Mon.	.15	.30

STANLEY CUP CHAMPIONSHIP CONN SMYTHE TROPHY WINNER

No.	Player	EX	NRMT
440	Mario Lemieux, Pit. (Gold Foil)	8.75	17.50
441	Checklist #4 (332-441)	.30	.60
442	Eric Lindros, Phi.	15.00	30.00

PRO SET

— 1990 PROMOTIONAL CARD —

 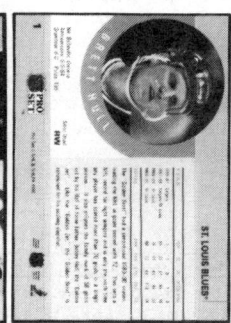

1990 Promotional Card
Brett Hull

Card Size: 2 1/2" X 3 1/2"
Face: Four colour, border as regular issue
Back: Four colour, Number, Resume
Imprint: Pro Set © NHL & NHLPA 1990

No.	Player	EX	NRMT
1	Brett Hull, St.L.	2.00	4.00

— 1990 - 1991 SERIES ONE —

This is the first year of issue for Pro Set hockey cards. Two series were issued. Series One had 405 cards and Series Two had 300 cards. The complete 1990 - 91 set contains 705 cards.

 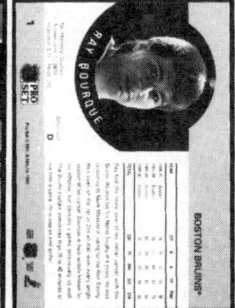

1990-91 Series One
Card No. 1A, Error, Raymond Bourque

Card Size: 2 1/2" X 3 1/2"
Face: Four colour, borders are team colours, Team logo, Position
Back: Four colour, Number, Resume
Imprint: Pro Set © NHL & NHLPA 1990
Complete Set No.: 405
Complete Set Price: 4.00 / 8.00
Common Card: .03 / .05
Wax Pack: (15 Cards) .25
Wax Box: (36 Packs) 6.00
Wax Case (20 Boxes): 100.00

HOLOGRAM

The Stanley Cup hologram is a limited edition card of 5000, issued only in foil packs.

No.	Player	EX	NRMT
—	Stanley Cup Hologram	75.00	150.00

BOSTON BRUINS

No.	Player	EX	NRMT
1A	Raymond Bourque, Error	.15	.30
1B	Raymond Bourque, Corrected	.10	.20
2	Randy Burridge	.03	.05
3	Lyndon Byers, RC	.03	.05
4	Robert Carpenter, Error	.03	.05
5	**John Carter, RC**	.03	.05
6	Dave Christian, Error	.03	.05
7A	**Garry Galley RC, Error**	.05	.10
7B	**Garry Galley RC, Corrected**	.05	.10
8	Craig Janney	.05	.10
9	Rejean Lemelin, Goalie, Error	.03	.05
10	Andrew Moog, Goalie, Error	.05	.10
11	Cam Neely, Error	.08	.15
12	Allen Pedersen	.03	.05
13	David Poulin, Error	.03	.05
14	Brian Propp, Error	.03	.05
15	Robert Sweeney	.03	.05
16	Glen Wesley	.03	.05

BRUINS' ERROR AND VARIATION CARDS

No.	Player	Description
1A	Bourque	Name misspelled on front Borque
4	Carpenter	Front reads "LW", should be "C"
6	Christian	Played 50 games with Boston, not 78
7A	Galley	Name misspelled on back Gary
9	Lemelin	Stats heading wrong, 1989-90 are Andy Moog's
10	Moog	1989-90 stats are Reggie Lemelins'
11	Neely	On back, "The bruins", should be capitalized
13	Poulin	Stats do not include the Flyers numbers
14	Propp	No Philadelphia stats listed

BUFFALO SABRES

No.	Player	EX	NRMT
17A	David Andreychuk, Error, Buffalo	.08	.15
17B	David Andreychuk, Error, Traded	.08	.15
17C	David Andreychuk, Corrected	.08	.15
18A	Scott Arniel, Error (Traded to Jets 6/6/90)	.03	.05
18B	Scott Arniel, Corrected	.03	.05
19	Doug Bodger	.03	.05
20	Mike Foligno	.03	.05
21A	Phil Housley, Error, Buffalo	.03	.05
21B	Phil Housley, Error (Traded to Jets 6/6/90)	.03	.05
22	Edward (Dean) Kennedy, RC, Error	.03	.05
23	Uwe Krupp	.03	.05
24	**Grant Ledyard, RC**	.03	.05
25	Clint Malarchuk, Goalie, Error	.03	.05
26	**Alexander Mogilny, RC**	.35	.75
27	Daren Puppa, Goalie, Error	.03	.05
28	Michael Ramsey	.03	.05
29	Christian Ruuttu, Error	.03	.05
30	**Dave Snuggerud, RC**	.05	.10
31	Pierre Turgeon	.13	.25
32	Richard Vaive, Error	.03	.05

SABRES' ERROR AND VARIATION CARDS

No.	Player	Description
17A	Andreychuk	Photo on back is Scott Arniel
17B	Andreychuk	Traded to Jets, Variety, Photo on back is S. Arniel
18A	Arniel	Photo on back is D. Andreychuk
21	Housley	Variation: Traded to Jets, Name misspelled on back "Frederick" in copy
22	Kennedy	"Redvers" misspelled "Redver" on back
25	Malarchuk	Back in action in 11 days not 2
27	Puppa	Birthdate wrong should be "3/23/65"
29	Ruuttu	Name misspelled on back "Ruutu"
32	Vaive	Jersey No. 12 but listed as 22

CALGARY FLAMES

No.	Player	EX	NRMT
33	Theoren Fleury	.08	.15
34	Douglas Gilmour	.03	.05
35	Al MacInnis, Error	.03	.05
36	Brian MacLellan	.03	.05
37	Jamie Macoun, Error	.03	.05
38	**Sergei Makarov, RC**	.15	.30
39A	Byron (Brad) McCrimmon, Calgary, Error	.03	.05
39B	Byron (Brad) McCrimmon, Corrected, Traded	.03	.05

PRO SET • 347

No.	Player	EX	NRMT
40A	Joe Mullen	.03	.05
40B	Joe Mullen, (Traded to Penguins 6/6/90)	.03	.05
41	Dana Murzyn	.03	.05
42A	Joe Nieuwendyk, Error	1.00	2.00
42B	Joe Nieuwendyk, Corrected	.08	.15
43	Joel Otto	.03	.05
44	Paul Ranheim, RC, Error	.05	.10
45	Gary Roberts	.08	.15
46	Gary Suter	.03	.05
47	Michael Vernon, Goalie	.03	.05
48	Richard Wamsley, Goalie, Error	.03	.05

FLAMES' ERROR AND VARIATION CARDS

No.	Player	Description
35	MacInnes	Name misspelled on back Allan
37	Macoun	Wrong number of games played and birthdate should read "8/17/61"
39A	McCrimmon	Wrong jersey number on face
40B	Mullen	Variation: "Traded to Penguins"
42	Nieuwendyk	Name misspelled on back Niewendyk
44	Ranheim	Position on back reads "C" should be "LW"
48	Wamsley	Name misspelled in text Rich

CHICAGO BLACK HAWKS

No.	Player	EX	NRMT
49	Keith Brown	.03	.05
50	Adam Creighton	.03	.05
51	Dirk Graham, Error	.03	.05
52	Stephen Konroyd, Error	.03	.05
53A	Steve Larmer, Error	.03	.05
53B	Steve Larmer, Corrected	.03	.05
54A	Dave Manson, Error	.03	.05
54B	Dave Manson, Corrected	.03	.05
55	Robert McGill	.03	.05
56	Greg Millen, Goalie	.03	.05
57A	Troy Murray, Error	.03	.05
57B	Troy Murray, Corrected	.25	.50
58	Jeremy Roenick, RC	.50	1.00
59A	Denis Savard, Chicago	.05	.10
59B	Denis Savard, (Traded to Canadiens 6/29/90)	.05	.10
60A	Allan Secord, Error	.03	.05
60B	Allan Secord, Corrected	.03	.05
61A	Duane Sutter, Error	.03	.05
61B	Duane Sutter, Retired	.03	.05
62	Steve Thomas	.03	.05
63A	Douglas Wilson, Error	.03	.05
63B	Douglas Wilson, Corrected	.03	.05
64	Trent Yawney	.05	.10

BLACK HAWK'S ERROR AND VARIATION CARDS

No.	Player	Description
51	Graham	Text on back, season should be "1988-89"
52	Konroyd	Back reads "LW" should be "D"
53A	Larmer	Players position & number should be black on red
54A	Manson	Photos on face and back show Stephen Konroyd
57A	Murray	Players position & number should be black on red
60A	Secord	"Al" on face, "Alan" on back photo
61A	Sutter	Face reads "RW", should be "C"
61B	Sutter	Face is "Retired June 1990" variety
63A	Wilson	Players position & number should be black on red

DETROIT RED WINGS

No.	Player	EX	NRMT
65	David Barr	.03	.05
66A	Shawn Burr, Error	.03	.05
66B	Shawn Burr, Corrected	.03	.05
67	Jimmy Carson	.03	.05
68	John Chabot	.03	.05
69	Steve Chiasson	.03	.05
70	Bernie Federko, Error	.03	.05
71	Gerard Gallant	.03	.05
72	Glen Hanlon, Goalie	.03	.05
73	Joey Kocur, RC	.03	.05
74	Lee Norwood	.03	.05
75	Michael O'Connell, Error	.03	.05
76	Bob Probert	.03	.05
77	Torrie Robertson	.03	.05

No.	Player	EX	NRMT
78	Daniel Shank, RC	.03	.05
79	Steve Yzerman	.13	.25
80	Rick Zombo, RC	.03	.05

WINGS' ERROR AND VARIATION CARDS

No.	Player	Description
66A	Burr	Without resume on back
66B	Burr	With resume on back
70	Federko	Two players come from Foam Lake.
75	O'Connell	Missed the "Retired" band.

EDMONTON OILERS

No.	Player	EX	NRMT
81	Glenn Anderson	.03	.05
82	Grant Fuhr, Goalie	.03	.05
83	Martin Gelinas, RC, Error	.08	.15
84	Adam Graves, RC, Error	.25	.50
85	Charles Huddy, Error	.03	.05
86	Petr Klima, Error	.03	.05
87A	Jari Kurri, Edmonton	.03	.05
87B	Jari Kurri, Milan	.03	.05
88	Mark Lamb, RC	.03	.05
89	Kevin Lowe, Error	.03	.05
90	Craig MacTavish	.03	.05
91	Mark Messier	.13	.25
92	Craig Muni	.03	.05
93	Joe Murphy, RC	.08	.15
94	Bill Ranford, Goalie	.03	.05
95	Craig Simpson, Error	.03	.05
96	Steve Smith, Error	.03	.05
97	Esa Tikkanen	.03	.05

OILERS' ERROR AND VARIATION CARDS

No.	Player	Description
83	Gelinas	Card shows Joe Murphy on back
84	Graves	No stats on 1989/90 Season
85	Huddy	Accent aigu missing from "Défenseur"
86	Klima	Birthplace and stats incorrect
87B	Kurri	Variation: "Signed with Milan, Italy Devils August 1990"
89	Lowe	Accent aigu missing from "Défenseur"
95	Simpson	Position should be "LW"
96	Smith	Accent aigu missing from "Défenseur"

HARTFORD WHALERS

No.	Player	EX	NRMT
98	Bo Mikael Andersson, RC	.03	.05
99	Dave Babych, Error	.03	.05
100	Yvon Corriveau, RC, Error	.03	.05
101	Randy Cunneyworth, Error	.03	.05
102	Kevin Dineen	.03	.05
103	Dean Evason	.03	.05
104	Ray Ferraro	.03	.05
105	Ron Francis	.03	.05
106	Grant Jennings, RC	.03	.05
107	Todd Krygler, RC	.03	.05
108	Randy Ladouceur	.03	.05
109	Ulf Samuelsson	.03	.05
110	Brad Shaw, RC	.03	.05
111	Dave Tippett, Error	.03	.05
112	Patrick Verbeek	.03	.05
113	Scott Young	.03	.05

WHALERS' ERROR AND VARIATION CARDS

No.	Player	Description
99	Babych	Spacing after "Forum" on back
100	Corriveau	Stats grouping for 1989-90 incorrect
101	Cunneyworth	Position on back should be "LW"; stats incorrect
111	Tippett	Postion on back should be "LW"

LOS ANGELES KINGS

No.	Player	EX	NRMT
114	Brian Benning, Error	.03	.05
115	Steve Duchesne, Error	.03	.05
116	Todd Elik, RC	.08	.15
117	Tony Granato, Error	.03	.05
118	Wayne Gretzky	.50	1.00
119	Kelly Hrudey, Goalie	.03	.05
120	Stephen Kasper	.03	.05
121A	Michael Krushelnyski, Error	.03	.05
121B	Michael Krushelnyski, Corrected	.03	.05
122	Bob Kudelski, RC, Error	.10	.20

No.	Player	EX	NRMT
123	Thomas Laidlaw	.03	.05
124	Martin McSorley	.03	.05
125	Larry Robinson	.03	.05
126	Luc Robitaille, Error	.10	.20
127	Tomas Sandstrom, Error	.03	.05
128	David Taylor	.03	.05
129A	John Tonelli, Error	.03	.05
129B	John Tonelli, Corrected	.03	.05

KINGS' ERROR AND VARIATION CARDS

No.	Player	Description
114	Benning	Stats not separated for 1989-90
115	Duchesne	In the text "King's" should be " Kings' "
117	Granato	Position wrong & stats not separated for 89/90
121	Krushelnyski	Missing position & player number on face
122	Kudelski	Birthplace incorrect, should be "Springfield"
126	Robitaille	In the text "King's" should be " Kings' "
127	Sandstrom	Ranger stats not listed.
129A	Tonelli	Name misspelled on front Tonnelli

MINNESOTA NORTH STARS

No.	Player	EX	NRMT
130A	Brian Bellows, Error	.03	.05
130B	Brian Bellows, Corrected	.03	.05
131	Aaron Broten, Error	.03	.05
132	Neal Broten	.03	.05
133	Jon Casey, Goalie, Error	.03	.05
134	Shawn Chambers, Error	.03	.05
135	Shane Churla, RC	.08	.15
136	Ulf Dahlen, Error	.03	.05
137	Gaetan Duchesne	.03	.05
138	Dave Gagner	.03	.05
139	Robert (Stewart) Gavin	.03	.05
140	Curt Giles	.03	.05
141	Basil McRae	.03	.05
142	Michael Modano, RC	.35	.75
143	Lawrence Murphy	.03	.05
144	Ville Siren, RC	.03	.05
145	Mark Tinordi, RC	.05	.10

NORTH STARS' ERROR AND VARIATION CARDS

No.	Player	Description
130A	Bellows	Card shows Dave Gagner on back and wrong position
131	Broten	Stats not separated for 1989-90 season.
133	Casey	GAA for 1989-90 incorrect.
134	Chambers	Back photo reversed.
136	Dahlen	Stats not separated for 1989-90.

MONTREAL CANADIENS

No.	Player	EX	NRMT
146	Guy Carbonneau, Error	.03	.05
147A	Chris Chelios, (Montreal)	.03	.05
147B	Chris Chelios (Traded to Blackhawks 6/29/90)	.03	.05
148	Shayne Corson	.03	.05
149	Russ Courtnall, Error	.03	.05
150	Brian Hayward, Goalie	.03	.05
151	Michael Keane, RC	.08	.15
152	Stephan Lebeau, RC	.15	.30
153	Claude Lemieux, Error	.03	.05
154	Craig Ludwig	.03	.05
155	Mike McPhee	.03	.05
156	Stephane Richer	.03	.05
157	Patrick Roy, Goalie	.25	.50
158	Mathieu Schneider, RC	.10	.20
159	Brian Skrudland	.03	.05
160	Robert Smith, Error	.03	.05
161	Petr Svoboda	.03	.05

CANADIENS' ERROR AND VARIATION CARDS

No.	Player	Description
146	Carbonneau	Birthplace misspelled, should read "Sept-Iles".
147	Chelios	Variation: Traded strip added
149	Courtnall	"C" on back incorrect, should read "RW".
153	Lemieux	In text, misspelled "reason".
160	Smith	Stats not correct, does not list trade.

NEW JERSEY DEVILS

No.	Player	EX	NRMT
162	Tommy Albelin	.03	.05

348 • PRO SET

No.	Player	EX	NRMT
163	Doug Brown, Error	.03	.05
164	Sean Burke, Goalie	.03	.05
165	Ken Daneyko	.03	.05
166	Bruce Driver	.03	.05
167A	Vlacheslav Fetisov RC, Error	.08	.15
167B	Vlacheslav Fetisov RC, Error	.08	.15
167C	Vlacheslav Fetisov RC, Corrected	.05	.10
168	Mark Johnson	.03	.05
169	Alexel Kasatonov, RC, Error	.08	.15
170	John MacLean, Error	.03	.05
171A	David Maley, RC, Error	.03	.05
171B	David Maley, RC, Corrected	.03	.05
172	Kirk Muller	.05	.10
173	Janne Ojanen, RC	.03	.05
174	Brendan Shanahan	.08	.15
175A	Peter Stastny, Error	.03	.05
175B	Peter Stastny, Corrected	.03	.05
176A	Patrik Sundstrom, Error	.03	.05
176B	Patrik Sundstrom, Corrected	.03	.05
177	Sylvain Turgeon	.03	.05

DEVILS' ERROR AND VARIATION CARDS

No.	Player	Description
163	Brown	Birthdate should read "6/12/64"
167A	Fetisov	Name misspelled on front Vlacheslav
167B	Fetisov	"L" airbrushed to appear as an "I"
169	Kasatonov	Stats mixed between NHL and Soviet
170	MacLean	"The Devil's" should read "The Devils'"
171A	Maley	Photo reversed, position on back should be "LW"
175A	Stastny	Photo reversed with card No. 176
176A	Sundstrom	Photo reversed with card No. 175

NEW YORK ISLANDERS

No.	Player	EX	NRMT
178	Ken Baumgartner, RC	.03	.05
179	Doug Crossman, Error	.03	.05
180	Gerald Diduck	.03	.05
181	Mark Fitzpatrick, RC, Goalie	.05	.10
182	Patrick Flatley, Error	.03	.05
183	Glen Healy, RC, Goalie, Error	.08	.15
184	Alan Kerr	.03	.05
185	Derek King	.03	.05
186	Pat LaFontaine	.12	.25
187	Donald Maloney	.03	.05
188	Huble McDonough, RC, Error	.03	.05
189	Jeff Norton, Error	.03	.05
190	Gary Nylund	.03	.05
191	Brent Sutter	.03	.05
192	Bryan Trottier, Error	.03	.05
193	David Volek, Error	.03	.05
194	Randy Wood	.03	.05

ISLANDERS' ERROR AND VARIATION LISTING

No.	Player	Description
179	Crossman	Birthdate should read "6/30/60"
182	Flatley	Position should be "RW" on face
183	Healey	Name misspelled on back Glenn
188	McDonough	1989-90 Stats not separated
189	Norton	Birthplace should read "Cambridge"
192	Trottier	In text, "finish" should read "finished"
193	Volek	Back position should be "LW"

NEW YORK RANGERS

No.	Player	EX	NRMT
195	Jan Erixon	.03	.05
196	Michael Gartner, Error	.03	.05
197	Ronald Greschner	.03	.05

No.	Player	EX	NRMT
198A	Miloslav Horava, RC, Error	.03	.05
198B	Miloslav Horava, RC, Corrected	.03	.05
199	Mark Janssens, RC	.03	.05
200	Kelly Kisio	.03	.05
201	Brian Leetch	.15	.30
202	Randy Moller	.03	.05
203	Brian Mullen	.03	.05
204	Bernie Nicholls, Error	.03	.05
205A	Christopher Nilan, (Rangers)	.03	.05
205B	Christopher Nilan (Traded to Bruins 6/29/90)	.03	.05
206	John Ogrodnick	.03	.05
207	James Patrick	.03	.05
208	Darren Turcotte, RC, Error	.05	.10
209	John Vanbiesbrouck, Goalie, Error	.03	.05
210	Carey Wilson	.03	.05

RANGERS' ERROR AND VARIATION CARDS

No.	Player	Description
196	Gartner	1989-90 stats not separated.
198A	Horava	Name misspelled on face Miroslav, Soviet and NHL stats not separated
204	Nicholls	1989-90 stats not separated.
205B	Nilan	Variation: Traded strip added
208	Turcotte	Career games is "96"
209	Vanbiesbrouck	Should read "G" on face

PHILADELPHIA FLYERS

No.	Player	EX	NRMT
211	Mike Bullard	.03	.05
212	Terry Carkner	.03	.05
213	Jeff Chychrun, RC	.03	.05
214	Murray Craven	.03	.05
215	Per-Erik Eklund, Error	.03	.05
216	Ron Hextall, Goalie, Error	.03	.05
217	Mark Howe	.03	.05
218	Tim Kerr	.03	.05
219	Ken Linseman, Error	.03	.05
220	Scott Mellanby	.03	.05
221	Gordon Murphy, RC	.03	.05
222	Kjell Samuelsson, Error	.03	.05
223	Ilkka Sinisalo	.03	.05
224	Ronald Sutter	.03	.05
225	Rick Tocchet	.03	.05
226	Ken Wregget, Goalie	.03	.05

FLYERS' ERROR AND VARIATION CARDDS

No.	Player	Description
215	Eklund	Spelling errors in "Center" and "Previously"
216	Hextall	Birthdate should read "5/3/64"
219	Linesman	1989-90 stats not separated
222	Samuelsson	Birthdate should read "10/18/58"

PITTSBURGH PENGUINS

No.	Player	EX	NRMT
227	Tom Barrasso, Goalie	.03	.05
228A	Phil Bourque, Error	.03	.05
228B	Phil Bourque, Corrected	.03	.05
229	Rob Brown, Error	.03	.05
230	Alain Chevrier, Goalie, Error	.03	.05
231	Paul Coffey, Error	.05	.10
232	John Cullen	.03	.05
233	Gord Dineen, Error	.03	.05
234	Bob Errey	.03	.05
235	Jim Johnson, Error	.03	.05
236	Mario Lemieux, Error	.38	.75
237	Troy Loney, RC	.03	.05
238	Barry Pederson, Error	.03	.05
239	Mark Recchi, RC	.30	.60
240	Kevin Stevens, RC, Error	.30	.60
241	Tony Tanti, Error	.03	.05
242	Zarley Zalapski, Error	.03	.05

PENGUINS' ERROR AND VARIATION CARDS

No.	Player	Description
228A	Bourque	Name misspelled on face and back Borque
229	Brown	Position should read "RW" on back, 1989-90 stats read Penguins, other years are Pittsburgh
230	Chevrier	1989-90 stats not separated
233	Dineen	Birthplace should read "Toronto, Ontario"
235	Johnson	Birthplace should be "New Hope, Minn."
236	Lemieux	In 1989-90 season, missed 21 games not 11
238	Pederson	Stats not complete
240	Stevens	Back should be "LW"
241	Tanti	1989-90 stats not separated
242	Zalapski	Trade bar missing

QUEBEC NORDIQUES

No.	Player	EX	NRMT
243	Joe Cirella	.03	.05
244	Lucien DeBlois, Error	.03	.05
245A	Marc Fortier, Error	.03	.05
245B	Marc Fortier, Corrected	.03	.05
246	Paul Gillis	.03	.05
247	Mike Hough	.03	.05
248	Anthony Hrkac, Error	.03	.05
249	Jeff Jackson	.03	.05
250	Guy Lafleur	.03	.05
251	Curtis Leschyshyn, RC	.03	.05

No.	Player	EX	NRMT
252	Claude Loiselle, RC	.03	.05
253	Mario Marois	.03	.05
254	Anthony McKegney, Error	.03	.05
255	Ken McRae, RC	.03	.05
256A	Michel Petit, Error	.03	.05
256B	Michel Petit, Corrected	.03	.05
257	Joe Sakic, Error	.13	.25
258	Ron Tugnutt, Goalie	.03	.05

NORDIQUES' ERROR AND VARIATION CARDS

No.	Player	Description
244	DeBlois	Back should be "C"
245A	Fortier	Name misspelled on face and back Mark
248	Hrkac	Stats not separated
254	McKegney	Stats not separated
256	Petit	Wrong player number on face
257	Sakic	Jersey number is "19"

ST. LOUIS BLUES

No.	Player	EX	NRMT
259	Rod Brind'Amour, RC, Error	.18	.35
260	Jeff Brown, Error	.03	.05
261	Gino Cavallini, Error	.03	.05
262	Paul Cavallini	.03	.05
263	Brett Hull	.25	.50
264	Mike Lalor, RC, Error	.03	.05
265	Dave Lowry, RC	.03	.05
266	Paul MacLean	.03	.05
267	Richard Meagher	.03	.05
268	Sergio Momesso, RC, Error	.05	.10
269	Adam Oates	.05	.10
270	Vincent Riendeau, Goalie, RC	.05	.10
271	Gordon Roberts	.03	.05
272	Rich Sutter, Error	.03	.05
273	Steve Tuttle	.03	.05
274	Peter Zezel, Error	.03	.05

BLUES' ERROR AND VARIATION CARDS

No.	Player	Description
259	Brind'Amour	Name misspelled in text Rob
260	Brown	Stats are not separated
261	Cavallini	Name misspelled in text Meagher
264	Lalor	Traded to Washington during off season
268	Momesso	Has "56" points
272	Sutter	Stats not separated
274	Zezel	Traded to Washington during off season

TORONTO MAPLE LEAFS

No.	Player	EX	NRMT
275A	Allan Bester, Goalie, Error	.03	.05
275B	Allan Bester, Goalie, Corrected	.03	.05
276	Wendel Clark	.08	.15
277	Brian Curran, Error	.03	.05
278	Vincent Damphousse	.05	.10
279	Tom Fergus	.03	.05
280	Lou Franceschetti, RC	.03	.05
281	Al Iafrate	.03	.05
282	Tom Kurvers, Error	.03	.05
283	Gary Leeman	.03	.05
284	Daniel Marois	.03	.05
285	Bradley Marsh	.03	.05
286	Ed Olczyk, Error	.03	.05
287	Mark Osborne	.03	.05
288	George (Rob) Ramage	.03	.05
289	Luke Richardson	.03	.05
290	Gilles Thibaudeau, RC, Error	.03	.05

LEAFS' ERROR AND VARIATION CARDS

No.	Player	Description
275	Bester	Name misspelled on face Alan
277	Curran	Text has "plays" should read "played"
282	Kurvers	Played in "71" Toronto games
286	Olczyk	Position should be "C" on back
290	Thibaudeau	Traded to Toronto, stats not separated

VANCOUVER CANUCKS

No.	Player	EX	NRMT
291	Greg Adams, Error	.03	.05
292	Jim Benning	.03	.05
293	Steve Bozek	.03	.05
294	Brian Bradley	.03	.05
295	Garth Butcher	.03	.05
296	Vladimir Krutov, RC	.03	.05

PRO SET • 349

No.	Player	EX	NRMT
297	Igor Larionov, RC, Error	.08	.15
298	Doug Lidster	.03	.05
299	Trevor Linden	.10	.20
300	Jyrki Lumme, RC, Error	.05	.10
301A	Andrew McBain, Error	.13	.25
301B	Andrew McBain, Corrected	.03	.05
302	Kirk McLean, Goalie, Error	.10	.20
303	Dan Quinn, Error	.03	.05
304	Paul Reinhart, Error	.03	.05
305	Jim Sandlak	.03	.05
306	Petri Skriko	.03	.05

CANUCKS' ERROR AND VARIATION CARDS

No.	Player	Description
291	Adams	Position on face should be "C"
297	Larionov	Soviet and NHL stats should not be combined
300	Lumme	Stats are not separated
301	McBain	Wrong photo on back, correction shows player with stick
302	McLean	GAA is "3.46" not "6.50"
303	Quinn	1989-90 stats are not separated
304	Reinhart	Birthdate should be "1/8/60"

WASHINGTON CAPITALS

No.	Player	EX	NRMT
307	Don Beaupre, Goalie	.03	.05
308	Dino Ciccarelli	.03	.05
309	Geoff Courtnall, Error	.03	.05
310	John Druce, RC	.03	.05
311	Kevin Hatcher	.03	.05
312	Dale Hunter, Error	.03	.05
313	Calle Johansson, Error	.03	.05
314	Rod Langway	.03	.05
315	Stephen Leach	.03	.05
316	Michael Liut, Goalie, Error	.03	.05
317	Alan May, RC	.03	.05
318	Kelly Miller, Error	.03	.05
319	Michal Pivonka, RC, Error	.05	.10
320A	Mike Ridley, Error	.03	.05
320B	Mike Ridley, Corrected	.03	.05
321	Scott Stevens, Error	.05	.10
322	John Tucker, Error	.03	.05

CAPITALS' ERROR AND VARIATION CARDS

No.	Player	Description
309	Courtnall	Traded to St. Louis in off season
312	Hunter	Spelling in text should be "Roguish"
313	Johansson	Accent aigu missing in Défenseur
316	Liut	1989-90 stats are combined
318	Miller	Position on back should be "LW"
319	Pivonka	1988-89 stats should show "8" not "88"
320	Ridley	On back: "point.s." should read "points."
321	Stevens	Traded to St. Louis in off season; accent missing; stats has "1987-88b"
322	Tucker	"Ottawa" misspelled; stats are total for 1989-90

WINNIPEG JETS

No.	Player	EX	NRMT
323	Brent Ashton	.03	.05
324	Laurie Boschman	.03	.05
325	Randy Carlyle	.03	.05
326	David Ellett	.03	.05
327	Pat Elynuik	.03	.05
328	Bob Essensa, Goalie, RC	.10	.20
329	Paul Fenton, Error	.03	.05
330A	Dale Hawerchuk, (Winnipeg)	.03	.05
330B	Dale Hawerchuk (Traded to Sabres 6/6/90)	.03	.05
331	Paul MacDermid	.03	.05
332	Maurice Mantha	.03	.05
333	Dave McLlwain, Error	.03	.05
334	Teppo Numminen, RC	.05	.10
335	Fredrik Olausson	.03	.05
336	Greg Paslawski, Error	.03	.05

JETS' ERROR AND VARIATION CARDS

No.	Player	Description
329	Fenton	Position on back should be "LW"
330	Hawerchuk	Year is listed as "1989-90", "Center" should read "Centre", Traded strip added
333	McLlwain	Birthdate should be "1/9/67"
335A	Olausson	Name on face Fred
335B	Olausson	Name on face Fredrik
336	Paslawski	Oversized "TM" after Jets

ALL STAR CAMPBELL CONFERENCE

No.	Player	EX	NRMT
337	Al MacInnis, Cal.	.03	.05
338	Michael Vernon, Goalie, Cal., Error	.03	.05
339	Kevin Lowe, Edm.	.03	.05
340	Wayne Gretzky, LA	.13	.25
341	Luc Robitaille, LA, Error	.05	.10
342	Brett Hull, St. L.	.10	.20
343	Joe Mullen, Cal.	.03	.05
344	Joe Nieuwendyk, Cal., Error	.03	.05
345	Steve Larmer, Chi.	.03	.05
346	Douglas Wilson, Chi., Error	.03	.05
347	Steve Yzerman, Det.	.03	.05
348A	Jari Kurri, Edm., (All Star)	.03	.05
348B	Jari Kurri, Edm., (Signed with Milan)	.03	.05
349	Mark Messier, Edm.	.03	.05
350	Steve Duchesne, LA, Error	.03	.05
351	Michael Gartner, Min., Error	.03	.05
352	Bernie Nicholls, LA	.03	.05
353	Paul Cavallini, St. L.	.03	.05
354	Al Iafrate, Tor.	.03	.05
355	Kirk McLean, Goalie, Van.	.03	.05
356	Thomas Steen, Win., Error	.03	.05

ALL STAR CAMPBELL ERROR AND VARIATION CARDS

No.	Player	Description
341	Robitaille	The record for fewest shots belong to East All Star.
344	Nieuwendyk	Face lists number as "25" should be "26".
346	Wilson	"Premier" is misspelled.
348B	Kurri	Variation: Signed strip added
350	Duchesne	The record for shots is 44 held by Detroit
351	Gartner	Face has number as "11" should be "12".
356	Steen	Photo of Doug Smail, not Steen.

ALL STAR WALES CONFERENCE

No.	Player	EX	NRMT
357	Raymond Bourque, Bos.	.03	.05
358	Cam Neely, Bos.	.03	.05
359	Patrick Roy, Goalie, Mon.	.13	.25
360	Brian Propp, Phi., Error	.03	.05
361	Paul Coffey, Pit., Error	.03	.05
362	Mario Lemieux, Pit.	.13	.25
363	David Andreychuk, Buf.	.03	.05
364	Phil Housley, Buf.	.03	.05
365	Daren Puppa, Goalie, Buf.	.03	.05
366	Pierre Turgeon, Buf.	.03	.05
367	Ron Francis, Har.	.03	.05
368	Chris Chelios, Mon.	.03	.05
369A	Shayne Corson, Mon., Error	.03	.05
369B	Shayne Corson, Mon., Corrected	.03	.05
370	Stephane J. J. Richer, Mon.	.03	.05
371	Kirk Muller, NJ	.03	.05
372	Pat LaFontaine, NYI	.03	.05
373	Brian Leetch, NYR	.03	.05
374	Rick Tocchet, Phi.	.03	.05
375	Joe Sakic, Que.	.03	.05
376	Kevin Hatcher, Wash.	.03	.05

ALL STAR WALES ERROR AND VARIATION CARDS

No.	Player	Description
360	Propp	In the text "games" misspelled
361	Coffey	Lists number as "77" should be "7"
369	Corson	Name misspelled on face Shane

TROPHY WINNERS

No.	Player	EX	NRMT
377	Jack Adams Award: Bob Murdoch, Coach, Error	.03	.05
378	Lady Byng Memorial Trophy: Brett Hull, St. L., Error	.08	.15
379	Calder Memorial Trophy: Sergei Makarov, Cal., RC	.03	.05
380	King Clancy Memorial Trophy: Kevin Lowe, Edm.	.03	.05
381	Hart Memorial Trophy: Mark Messier, Edm.	.05	.10
382	William M. Jennings Trophy: Andy Moog/Rejean Lemelin, Bos.	.03	.05
383	Bill Masterton Memorial Trophy: Gordon Kluzak, Bos., Error	.03	.05
384	James Norris Memorial Trophy: Raymond Bourque, Bos., Error	.03	.05
385A	Lester Patrick Trophy: Len Ceglarski, Error	.03	.05
385B	Lester Patrick Trophy: Len Ceglarski, Corrected	.03	.05
386	Lester B. Pearson Award: Mark Messier, Edm.	.05	.10
387	Presidents' Trophy: Boston Bruins	.03	.05
388	Art Ross Trophy: Wayne Gretzky, LA, Error	.13	.25
389	Frank J. Selke Trophy: Richard Meagher, St. L.	.03	.05
390	Conn Smythe Trophy: Bill Ranford, Goalie, Edm.	.03	.05
391	Vezina Trophy: Patrick Roy, Goalie, Mon.	.13	.25
392	Clarence S. Campbell Bowl: Edmonton Oilers, Error	.03	.05
393	Prince of Wales Trophy: Boston Bruins	.03	.05

TROPHY ERROR AND VARIATION CARDS

No.	Trophy	Description
377	Adams	Jets 1989-90 record is "37-32-11", not "37-32-1"
378	Byng	Should be "Memorial" trophy
383	Masterton	Should be "Memorial" trophy
384	Norris	On the back "Raymond" should be "Ray"
385A	Patrick	Missing card number on back
388	Ross	Gretzky won "8" times, not "7"
392	Campbell	Should be "Bowl", not "Trophy"

LEAGUE LEADERS

No.	Player	EX	NRMT
394	Points: Wayne Gretzky, LA, Error	.13	.25
395	Goals: Brett Hull, St. L., Error	.08	.15
396	Rookie of the Year: Sergei Makarov, Cal.	.05	.10
397	Most Valuable Player: Mark Messier, Edm.	.05	.10
398	Rookie Goals Against Average: Mike Richter, NYR, Error	.03	.05
399	Goals Against Average: Patrick Roy, Mon.	.13	.25
400	Rookie Goal Leader: Darren Turcotte, NYR, Error	.03	.05

LEAGUE LEADER ERROR AND VARIATION CARDS

No.	Player	Description
394	Gretzky	Only Dionne tied
395	Hull	Birthdate is "8/9/64"
398	Richter	Text has "Lays" should be "Plays"
400	Turcotte	Position on face should be "C"

TOP DRAFT CHOICE

No.	Player	EX	NRMT
401	Number One Draft Pick: Owen Nolan, Que., RC	.30	.60
402	Number Two Draft Pick: Petr Nedved, Van., RC	.30	.60

HALL OF FAMER

No.	Player	EX	NRMT
403	Phil Esposito, Chi., Bos., NYR	.05	.10
404	Darryl Sittler, Tor., Error	.05	.10
405	Stan Mikita, Det.	.05	.10

HOF ERROR AND VARIATION CARDS

No.	Player	Description
404	Sittler	Stats heading should be "career: 15 seasons" to match other HOF cards

ADDITIONAL VARIATIONS

Variations of these cards exist with the backs printed upside down, the sheet probably being fed through the press inverted 180 degrees from the normal feed. Listings and prices will show in future editions, when more data becomes available.

Card Nos. 227, 229, 231, 233, 235, 236, 238, 240, 241, 242, 338, 341, 350, 357, 360, 361, 366, 373, 374, 375

1990 - 91 SERIES TWO

There are variations in border colour possibly due to long press runs.

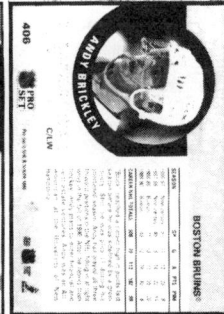

1990-91 Series Two
Card No. 406, Error, Andy Brickley

Card Size: 2 1/2" X 3 1/2"
Face: Four colour, borders are team colours, Team logo, Position
Back: Four colour, Number, Resume
Imprint: Pro Set © NHL & NHLPA 1990
Complete Set No.: 300
Complete Set Price: 5.00   10.00
Common Card: .03   .05
Wax Pack: (15 Cards)   .50
Wax Box: (36 Packs)   7.00
Wax Case: (20 Boxes)   125.00

BOSTON BRUINS

No.	Player	EX	NRMT
406	Andy Brickley, Error	.03	.05
407	Peter Douris, RC	.03	.05
408	Nevin Markwart	.03	.05
409	Christopher Nilan	.03	.05
410	Stephane Quintal, RC	.05	.10
411	Bruce Shoebottom, RC	.03	.05
412	Don Sweeney, RC	.03	.05
413	James Wiemer, RC	.03	.05

BUFFALO SABRES

No.	Player	EX	NRMT
414	Mike Hartman, RC	.03	.05
415	Dale Hawerchuk	.03	.05
416	Benoit Hogue	.03	.05
417	Bill Houlder, RC (Traded to Buffalo Sept. 1990)	.03	.05
418	Mikko Makela	.03	.05
419	Robert Ray, RC	.03	.05
420	John Tucker	.03	.05

CALGARY FLAMES

No.	Player	EX	NRMT
421	Jiri Hrdina, RC (Traded to Pittsburgh Dec. 1990)	.03	.05
422	Mark Hunter	.03	.05
423	Tim Hunter, RC	.05	.10
424	Roger Johansson, RC	.03	.05
425	Frantisek Musil (Traded to Calgary Oct. 1990)	.03	.05
426	Eric Nattress	.03	.05

CHICAGO BLACK HAWKS

No.	Player	EX	NRMT
427	Chris Chelios	.03	.05
428	Jacques Cloutier, Goalie, RC, Error	.03	.05
429	Gregory Gilbert	.03	.05
430	Michel Goulet, Error	.03	.05
431	Mike Hudson, RC	.03	.05
432	Jocelyn Lemieux, RC	.03	.05
433	Brian Noonan	.03	.05
434	Wayne Presley	.03	.05

DETROIT RED WINGS

No.	Player	EX	NRMT
435	Brent Fedyk, RC	.08	.15
436	Richard Green	.03	.05
437	Marc Habscheid	.03	.05
438	Byron (Brad) McCrimmon	.03	.05

EDMONTON OILERS

No.	Player	EX	NRMT
439	Jeff Beukeboom, RC	.08	.15
440	David Brown, RC	.05	.10
441	Kelly Buchberger, RC	.03	.05
442	Greg Hawgood	.03	.05
443	Chris Joseph, RC	.03	.05
444	Ken Linseman	.03	.05
445	Eldon Reddick, Goalie, RC	.03	.05
446	Geoff Smith, RC	.03	.05

HARTFORD WHALERS

No.	Player	EX	NRMT
447	Adam Burt, RC	.03	.05
448	Sylvain Coté	.03	.05
449	Paul Cyr, RC	.03	.05
450	Edward Kastelic, RC	.03	.05
451	Peter Sidorkiewicz, Goalie	.03	.05
452	Mike Tomlak, RC	.03	.05
453	Carey Wilson	.03	.05

LOS ANGELES KINGS

No.	Player	EX	NRMT
454	Daniel Berthiaume, Goalie	.03	.05
455	Scott Bjugstad	.03	.05
456	Rod Buskas, RC	.03	.05
457	John McIntyre, RC (Traded to Los Angeles Nov. 1990)	.03	.05
458	Timothy Watters	.03	.05

MINNESOTA NORTH STARS

No.	Player	EX	NRMT
459	Perry Berezan, RC	.03	.05
460	Brian Propp	.03	.05
461	Ilkka Sinisalo	.03	.05
462	Douglas Smail (Traded to Minnesota Nov. 1990)	.03	.05
463	Robert Smith	.03	.05
464	Chris Dahlquist	.03	.05
465	Neil Wilkinson, RC	.03	.05

MONTREAL CANADIENS

No.	Player	EX	NRMT
466	Jean-Jacques Daigneault, RC	.03	.05
467	Eric Desjardins, RC	.10	.20
468	Gerald Diduck	.03	.05
469	Donald Dufresne, RC	.03	.05
470A	Todd Ewen, RC, Error	.03	.05
470B	Todd Ewen, RC, Corrected	.03	.05
471	Brent Gilchrist, RC	.05	.10
472	Sylvain Lefebvre, RC	.03	.05
473	Denis Savard	.05	.10
474	Sylvain Turgeon (Traded to Montreal Sept. 1990)	.03	.05
475	Ryan Walter, Error	.03	.05

NEW JERSEY DEVILS

No.	Player	EX	NRMT
476	Laurie Boschman	.03	.05
477	Pat Conacher, RC	.05	.10
478	Claude Lemieux	.03	.05
479	Walter Poddubny	.03	.05
480	Allan Stewart, RC, Error	.03	.05
481	Chris Terreri, Goalie, RC	.07	.15

NEW YORK ISLANDERS

No.	Player	EX	NRMT
482	Brad Dalgarno	.03	.05
483	Dave Chyzowski, RC	.03	.05
484	Craig Ludwig	.03	.05
485	Wayne McBean, RC	.03	.05
486	Richard Pilon, RC	.03	.05
487	Joe Reekie, RC	.03	.05
488	Mick Vukota, RC	.03	.05

NEW YORK RANGERS

No.	Player	EX	NRMT
489	Mark Hardy	.03	.05
490	Jody Hull, RC	.03	.05
491	Kris King, RC	.03	.05
492	Troy Mallette, RC	.03	.05
493	Kevin Miller, RC	.08	.15
494	Normand Rochefort	.03	.05
495	David Shaw	.03	.05
496	Ray Sheppard	.03	.05

PHILADELPHIA FLYERS

No.	Player	EX	NRMT
497	Keith Acton	.03	.05
498	Craig Berube, RC	.03	.05
499	Tony Horacek, RC	.03	.05
500	Normand Lacombe, RC	.03	.05
501	Jiri Latal, RC	.03	.05
502	Peter Peeters, Goalie	.03	.05
503	Derrick Smith, RC	.03	.05

PITTSBURGH PENGUINS

No.	Player	EX	NRMT
504	Jay Caufield, RC	.03	.05
505	Peter Taglianetti (Traded to Pittsburgh Dec. 1990)	.03	.05
506	Randy Gilhen, RC	.03	.05
507	Randy Hillier	.03	.05
508	Joe Mullen	.03	.05
509	Frank Pietrangelo, Goalie, RC	.03	.05
510	Gordon Roberts	.03	.05
511	Bryan Trottier	.03	.05
512	Wendell Young, Goalie, RC	.03	.05

QUEBEC NORDIQUES

No.	Player	EX	NRMT
513	Shawn Anderson, RC	.03	.05
514	Steven Finn, RC	.03	.05
515	Bryan Fogarty, RC	.03	.05
516	Mike Hough, Error	.03	.05
517	Darin Kimble, RC	.03	.05
518	Randy Velischek	.03	.05
519	Craig Wolanin, RC	.03	.05

ST. LOUIS BLUES

No.	Player	EX	NRMT
520	Bob Bassen, RC	.03	.05
521	Geoff Courtnall	.03	.05
522	Robert Dirk, RC	.03	.05
523	Glen Featherstone, RC	.05	.10
524	Mario Marois	.03	.05
525	Herb Raglan, RC	.03	.05
526	Cliff Ronning	.03	.05
527	Harold Snepsts	.03	.05
528	Scott Stevens	.03	.05
529	Ronald Wilson	.03	.05

TORONTO MAPLE LEAFS

No.	Player	EX	NRMT
530	Aaron Broten (Traded to Toronto Nov. 1990)	.03	.05
531	Lucien DeBlois	.03	.05
532	Dave Ellett	.03	.05
533A	Paul Fenton, Error	.03	.05
533B	Paul Fenton, Corrected	.03	.05
534	Todd Gill, RC	.08	.15
535	Dave Hannan	.03	.05
536	John Kordic, RC	.03	.05
537	Michael Krushelnyski	.03	.05
538	Kevin Maguire, RC	.03	.05
539	Michel Petit	.03	.05
540	Jeff Reese, Goalie, RC	.03	.05
541	David Reid, RC	.03	.05
542	Douglas Shedden	.03	.05

VANCOUVER CANUCKS

No.	Player	EX	NRMT
543	Dave Capuano, RC	.03	.05
544	Craig Coxe, RC	.03	.05
545	Kevan Guy, RC	.03	.05
546	Rob Murphy, RC	.03	.05
547	Robert Nordmark, RC	.03	.05
548	Stanley Smyl	.03	.05
549	Ronald Stern, RC	.03	.05

1990-91 SERIES TWO — PRO SET • 351

WASHINGTON CAPITALS

No.	Player	EX	NRMT
550	Tim Bergland, RC	.03	.05
551	Nicholas Kypreos, RC	.03	.05
552	Mike Lalor, RC	.03	.05
553	Rob Murray, RC	.03	.05
554	Robert Rouse	.03	.05
555	Dave Tippett	.03	.05
556	Peter Zezel, Error (Traded to Washington July 1990)	.03	.05

WINNIPEG JETS

No.	Player	EX	NRMT
557	Scott Arniel	.03	.05
558	Don Barber, RC	.03	.05
559	Shawn Cronin, RC	.03	.05
560	Gord Donnelly, RC	.03	.05
561	Doug Evans, RC	.03	.05
562	Phil Housley	.03	.05
563	Ed Olczyk	.03	.05
564	Mark Osborne	.03	.05
565	Thomas Steen	.03	.05

TEAM LOGO CARDS

No.	Team	EX	NRMT
566	Boston Bruins	.03	.05
567	Buffalo Sabres	.03	.05
568	Calgary Flames	.03	.05
569	Chicago Black Hawks	.03	.05
570	Detroit Red Wings	.03	.05
571	Edmonton Oilers	.03	.05
572	Hartford Whalers	.03	.05
573A	Los Angeles Kings, Error	.03	.05
573B	Los Angeles Kings, Corrected	.03	.05
574	Minnesota North Stars	.03	.05
575	Montreal Canadiens	.03	.05
576	New Jersey Devils	.03	.05
577	New York Islanders	.03	.05
578	New York Rangers	.03	.05
579	Philadelphia Flyers	.03	.05
580	Pittsburgh Penguins	.03	.05
581	Quebec Nordiques	.03	.05
582	St. Louis Blues	.03	.05
583	Toronto Maple Leafs	.03	.05
584	Vancouver Canucks	.03	.05
585	Washington Capitals	.03	.05
586	Winnipeg Jets	.03	.05

1990-1991 ROOKIE SEASON

BOSTON BRUINS

No.	Player	EX	NRMT
587	Kenneth Hodge Jr., RC	.03	.05
588	Vladimir Ruzicka, RC	.05	.10
589	Wes Walz, RC	.05	.10

BUFFALO SABRES

No.	Player	EX	NRMT
590	Greg Brown, RC	.03	.05
591	Brad Miller, RC	.03	.05
592	Darrin Shannon, RC	.05	.10

CALGARY FLAMES

No.	Player	EX	NRMT
593	Stephane Matteau, RC, Error	.10	.20
594	Sergei Priakin, RC	.03	.05
595	Robert Reichel, RC	.20	.40
596	Ken Sabourin, RC, Error	.03	.05
597	Tim Sweeney, RC, Error	.03	.05

CHICAGO BLACK HAWKS

No.	Player	EX	NRMT
598	Ed Belfour, Goalie, RC, Error	.30	.60
599	Frantisek Kucera, RC	.03	.05
600	Michael McNeill, RC, Error	.03	.05
601	Mike Peluso, RC	.03	.05

DETROIT RED WINGS

No.	Player	EX	NRMT
602	Tim Cheveldae, Goalie, RC	.12	.25
603	Per Olav Djoos, RC	.03	.05
604	Sergei Fedorov, RC	.50	1.00
605	Johan Garpenlov, RC	.10	.20
606	Keith Primeau, RC	.10	.20
607	Paul Ysebaert, RC	.05	.10

EDMONTON OILERS

No.	Player	EX	NRMT
608	Anatoli Semenov, RC	.05	.10

HARTFORD WHALERS

No.	Player	EX	NRMT
609	Robert Holik, RC	.18	.35
610	Kay Whitmore, Goalie, RC	.05	.10

LOS ANGELES KINGS

No.	Player	EX	NRMT
611	Robert Blake, RC	.12	.25
612	Francois Breault, RC	.05	.10

MINNESOTA NORTH STARS

No.	Player	EX	NRMT
613	Mike Craig, RC, Error	.05	.10

MONTREAL CANADIENS

No.	Player	EX	NRMT
614	Jean-Claude Bergeron, Goalie, RC	.03	.05
615	Andrew Cassels, RC	.03	.05
616	Tom Chorske, RC	.03	.05
617	Lyle Odelein, RC	.12	.25
618	Mark Pederson, RC	.03	.05

NEW JERSEY DEVILS

No.	Player	EX	NRMT
619	Zdeno Ciger, RC	.03	.05
620	Troy Crowder, RC	.03	.05
621	Jon Morris, RC	.03	.05
622	Eric Weinrich, RC	.03	.05
623	David Marcinyshyn, RC, Error	.03	.05

NEW YORK ISLANDERS

No.	Player	EX	NRMT
624	Jeff Hackett, Goalie, RC	.05	.10
625	Rob DiMaio, RC	.03	.05

NEW YORK RANGERS

No.	Player	EX	NRMT
626	Steven Rice, RC	.05	.10
627	Mike Richter, Goalie, RC	.30	.60
628	Dennis Vial, RC	.03	.05

PHILDAELPHIA FLYERS

No.	Player	EX	NRMT
629	Martin Hostak, RC	.03	.05
630	Pat Murray, RC	.03	.05
631	Mike Ricci, RC	.12	.25

PITTSBURGH PENGUINS

No.	Player	EX	NRMT
632	Jaromir Jagr, RC, Error	.50	1.00
633	Paul Stanton, RC	.05	.10

QUEBEC NORDIQUES

No.	Player	EX	NRMT
634	Scott Gordon, Goalie, RC, Error	.03	.05
635	Owen Nolan, RC	.20	.40
636	Mats Sundin, RC	.30	.60
637	John Tanner, Goalie, RC	.03	.05

ST. LOUIS BLUES

No.	Player	EX	NRMT
638	Curtis Joseph, Goalie, RC	.20	.40

TORONTO MAPLE LEAFS

No.	Player	EX	NRMT
639	Peter Ing, Goalie, RC	.03	.05
640	Scott Thornton, RC	.03	.05

VANCOUVER CANUCKS

No.	Player	EX	NRMT
641	Troy Gamble, Goalie, RC	.03	.05
642	Robert Kron, RC	.03	.05
643	Petr Nedved, RC	.15	.30
644	Adrien Plavsic, RC	.03	.05

WASHINGTON CAPITALS

No.	Player	EX	NRMT
645	Peter Bondra, RC	.13	.25
646	Jim Hrivnak, Goalie, RC	.08	.15
647	Mikhail Tatarinov, RC	.05	.10

WINNIPEG JETS

No.	Player	EX	NRMT
648	Stephane Beauregard, Goalie, RC, Error	.05	.10
649	Richard Tabaracci, Goalie, RC	.05	.10

CAREER POINT LEADERS

No.	Player	EX	NRMT
650	Mike Bossy, NYI	.03	.05
651	Bobby Clarke, Phi.	.03	.05
652	Alex Delvecchio, Det.	.03	.05
653	Marcel Dionne, Det., LA, NYR	.03	.05
654	Gordie Howe, Det., Har., Hou., NEW	.05	.10
655	Stan Mikita, Chicago Blackhawks	.03	.05
656	Denis Potvin, NYI	.03	.05

HALL OF FAME PLAYER

No.	Player	EX	NRMT
657	Bobby Clarke, Ph.	.03	.05
658	Alex Delvecchio, Det.	.03	.05
659	Tony Esposito, Goalie, Mon., Chi.,	.03	.05
660	Gordie Howe, Det., Har., Hou., NEW	.05	.10

NATIONAL HOCKEY LEAGUE COACHES

No.	Coach	EX	NRMT
661	Mike Milbury, Bos.	.03	.05
662	Rick Dudley, Buf.	.03	.05
663	Doug Risebrough, Cal.	.03	.05
664	Bryan Murray, Det.	.03	.05
665	John Muckler, Edm.	.03	.05
666	Rick Ley, Har.	.03	.05
667	Tom Webster, LA	.03	.05
668	Bob Gainey, Min.	.03	.05
669	Pat Burns, Mon.	.03	.05
670	John Cunniff, NJD	.03	.05
671	Al Arbour, NYI	.03	.05
672	Roger Neilson, NYR	.03	.05
673	Paul Holmgren, Phi.	.03	.05
674	Bob Johnson, Pit.	.10	.20
675	Dave Chambers, Que.	.03	.05
676	Brian Sutter, St.L, Error	.03	.05
677	Tom Watt, Tor.	.03	.05
678	Bob McCammon, Van.	.03	.05
679	Terry Murray, Wash.	.03	.05
680	Bob J. Murdoch, Win.	.03	.05

NATIONAL HOCKEY LEAGUE OFFICIALS

No.	Official	EX	NRMT
681	Ron Asselstine, Linesman	.03	.05
682	Wayne Bonney, Linesman	.03	.05
683	Kevin Collins, Linesman	.03	.05
684	Pat Dapuzzo, Linesman	.03	.05
685	Ron Finn, Linesman	.03	.05
686	Kerry Fraser, Referee	.03	.05
687	Gerard Gauthier, Linesman	.03	.05
688	Terry Gregson, Referee	.03	.05
689	Bob Hodges, Linesman	.03	.05
690	Ron Hoggarth, Referee	.03	.05
691	Don Koharski, Referee	.03	.05
692	Dan Marouelli, Referee	.03	.05
693	Dan McCourt, Linesman	.03	.05
694	Bill Mccreary, Referee	.03	.05
695	Denis Morel, Referee	.03	.05
696	Jerry Pateman, Linesman	.03	.05
697	Ray Scapinello, Linesman	.03	.05
698	Rob Shick, Referee	.03	.05
699	Paul Stewart, Referee	.03	.05
700	Leon Stickle, Linesman	.03	.05

352 • PRO SET — 1990 - 91 PLAYER OF THE MONTH —

No.	Player	EX	NRMT
701	Andy van Hellemond, Referee	.03	.05
702	Mark Vines, Linesman	.03	.05

WAYNE GRETZKY THE 2000TH POINT

No.	Player	EX	NRMT
703	Wayne Gretzky	.35	.75

STANLEY CUP CHAMPIONS

No.	Player	EX	NRMT
704	Edmonton Oilers	.05	.10

THE PUCK

No.	Player	EX	NRMT
705	The Puck	.03	.05

— 1990 - 91 PLAYER OF THE MONTH —

Issued each month to honour the player selected Pro Set "Player of the Month". October 1990 and March 1991 player cards were not issued.

1990-91 Player of the Month
Card No. P2, Wayne Gretzky - January

Card Size: 2 1/2" X 3 1/2"
Face: Four colour, border as regular issue
Back: Four colour, Number, Resume
Imprint: Pro Set © NHL & NHLPA 1990
Complete Set No.: 4
Complete Set Price: 32.50 65.00

No.	Player	EX	NRMT
—	November 1990: Peter Peeters, Goalie, Phi.	6.00	12.00
P1	December 1990: Tom Barrasso, Goalie, Pit.	6.00	12.00
P2	January 1991: Wayne Gretzky, LA	18.00	35.00
P3	February 1991: Brett Hull, St. L.	10.00	20.00

— 1991 - NHL AWARDS SPECIAL —

This set was produced for and given to attendees at the Awards Night Banquet held in Toronto, June 5th, 1991.
The card backs numbered AC1 to AC16 are titled "A Celebration of Excellence" and have a thumbnail sketch of the award nominees and award winners.

1991 NHL Awards Special
Card No. AC1, Ed Belfour

Card Size: 2 1/2" X 3 1/2"
Face: Four colour, Team Logo
Back: Four colour, Number
Imprint: Title Card: © Pro Set Inc.
AC1 to AC 16: Pro Set © NHL & NHLPA 1991
Complete Set No.: 17
Complete Set Price: 175.00 350.00

No.	Player	EX	NRMT
—	**Title Card:** 1990-91 NHL Awards Special	2.50	5.00
AC1	Ed Belfour, Goalie, Chi.,	5.00	10.00
	Winner: William M. Jennings Trophy		
	Nominee: Vezina Trophy, Calder Memorial Trophy and Hart Memorial Trophy		
AC2	Mike Richter, Goalie, NYR,	5.00	10.00
	Nominee: Vezina Trophy		
AC3	Patrick Roy, Mon.,	35.00	75.00
	Nominee: Vezina Trophy		
AC4	Wayne Gretzky, LA	50.00	100.00
	Winner: Art Ross Trophy;		
	Nominee: Lady Byng Trophy Hart Memorial Trophy		
AC5	Joe Sakic, Que,	5.00	10.00
	Nominee: Lady Byng Trophy		
AC6	Brett Hull, St. L.,	18.00	35.00
	Nominee: Lady Byng Trophy Hart Memorial Trophy		
AC7	Raymond Bourque, Bos.,	10.00	20.00
	Nominee: James Norris Trophy		
AC8	Allan MacInnis, Cal.,	2.50	5.00
	Nominee: James Norris Trophy		
AC9	Luc Robitaille, LA	5.00	10.00
	1990/91 First Team All Star		
AC10	Sergei Fedorov, Det.,	12.50	25.00
	Nominee: Calder Memorial Trophy		
AC11	Kenneth Hodge, Jr., Bos.,	2.50	5.00
	Nominee: Calder Memorial Trophy		
AC12	Dirk Graham, Chi.,	2.50	5.00
	Nominee: Frank J. Selke Trophy		
AC13	Steve Larmer, Chi.,	2.50	5.00
	Nominee: Frank J. Selke Trophy		
AC14	Esa Tikkanen, Edm.,	2.50	5.00
	Nominee: Frank J. Selke Trophy		
AC15	Chris Chelios, , Chi.,	5.00	10.00
	Nominee: James Norris Trophy		
AC16	Dave Taylor, LA	2.50	5.00
	Winner: King Clancy Award and Bill Masterton Memorial Trophy		

— 1991 - NHL SPONSOR AWARDS —

These cards were produced for the Hockey News Sponsor Awards Luncheon held in Toronto June 6th, 1991. This limited edition set is a continuation of the "NHL Award Ceremonies" set with numbers AC 17 to AC 23 having the award sponsor's logo on the back of the card.

1991 NHL Sponsor Awards
Card No. AC 17, Kevin Dineen

Card Size: 2 1/2" X 3 1/2"
Face: Four colour, Team Logo
Back: Four colour, Sponsor's Name, Award, Number
Imprint: Title Card: © Pro Set Inc.
AC17 to AC23: Pro Set © NHL & NHLPA 1991
Complete Set No.: 8
Complete Set Price: 50.00 100.00

No.	Player	EX	NRMT
—	**Title Card:** 1990-91 NHL Sponsor Awards	3.50	7.00
AC17	Kevin Dineen, Har., Bud Light/ NHL Man of the Year Award	3.50	7.00
AC18	Brett Hull, St. L., NHL Pro Set Player of the Year Award	25.00	50.00
AC19	Ed Belfour, Chi., Trico Goaltender Award	10.00	20.00
AC20	Theoren Fleury, Cal. Alka-Seltzer Plus Award	3.50	7.00
AC21	Martin McSorley, LA Alka-Seltzer Plus Award	3.50	7.00
AC22	Mike Ilitch, Owner, Detroit Red Wings, Lester Patrick Award	3.50	7.00
AC23	Rod Gilbert, MCR, New York Rangers, Lester Patrick Award	3.50	7.00

— 1991 - 12TH ANNUAL NATIONAL —

At the 12th Annual National Sports Collectors Convention in 1991 Pro Set released a five-card promo set illustrating their full line of cards. The hockey promo card in this set was the Patrick Roy card.

Card Size: 2 1/2" X 3 1/2"
Face: Four colour, borderless, Team Logo
Back: Four colour, Number, Resume
Imprint: Pro Set © NHL & NHLPA 1991

No.	Player	EX	NRMT
125	Patrick Roy, Goalie, Mon.	2.50	5.00

— THE 1991 HOCKEY HALL OF FAME — INDUCTION DINNER & CEREMONIES

These cards were issued for the 1991 Hockey Hall of Fame Dinner and Ceremonies held in Toronto on September 23rd, 1991. The set, printed in sepia, honours the 1991 Hall of Fame inductees.

 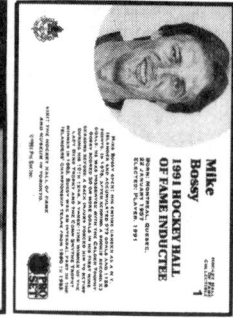

1991 Hockey Hall of Fame
Induction Dinner and Ceremon
Card No. 1, Mike Bossy

Card Size: 2 1/2" X 3 1/2"
Face: Sepia, Emblem: Hockey Hall of Fame and Museum, High gloss card stock
Back: Four colour, Number, Resume
Imprint: © 1991Pro Set Inc.
Complete Set No.: 14
Complete Set Price: 45.00 90.00

No.	Player	EX	NRMT
—	**Title Card:** The 1991 Hockey Hall of Fame Induction Dinner & Ceremonies	4.00	8.00
1	Mike Bossy, 1991 Hockey Hall of Fame Inductee	8.00	16.00
2	Denis Potvin, 1991 Hockey Hall of Fame Inductee	8.00	16.00
3	Bob Pulford, 1991 Hockey Hall of Fame Inductee	6.00	12.00
4	William Scott Bowman, 1991 Hockey Hall of Fame Inductee	6.00	12.00
5	Neil P. Armstrong, 1991 Hockey Hall of Fame Inductee	4.00	8.00
6	Clint Smith, 1991 Hockey Hall of Fame Inductee	6.00	12.00
7	1903-4 Ottawa Silver Seven	4.00	8.00
8	1905 Ottawa Silver Seven	4.00	8.00
9	1909 Ottawa Senators	4.00	8.00

1991 - 92 REGULAR ISSUE — PRO SET • 353

No.	Player	EX	NRMT
10	1911 Ottawa Senators	4.00	8.00
11	1920-21 Ottawa Senators	4.00	8.00
12	1923 Ottawa Senators	4.00	8.00
13	1927 Ottawa Senators	4.00	8.00

— 1991 - HOCKEY HALL OF FAME — NHL 75TH ANNIVERSARY TRIBUTE

Issued in a polyethylene pack of eight cards for the Hockey Hall of Fame's 75th Anniversary Tribute to the NHL. An open house was held in the Hall of Fame allowing collectors the opportunity to have their cards autographed by NHL Greats. These sets were available for authographing. Only the "Title Card" and the "HHOF 1" card were specially issued for this set. The remaining six cards, Nos. 145 to 150 inclusive, are from the Pro Set Platinum Series One set. The specifications below are for the HHF1 card only.

1991 Hockey Hall of Fame
NHL 75th Anniversary Tribute
Card No. 147, Detroit Red Wings

Card Size: 2 1/2" X 3/12"
Face: Sepia, Pro Set logo
Back: Four colour, Number, Resume
Imprint: ©1991 Pro Set Inc.
Complete Set No.: 8
Complete Set Price: 7.50 15.00

No.	Player	EX	NRMT
—	Title Card: Hockey Hall of Fame NHL 75th Anniversary Tribute	5.00	10.00
HHF1	Hockey Hall of Fame Collectible Excellence Education Entertainment	5.00	10.00
145	Boston Bruins	.05	.10
146	Chicago Black Hawks	.05	.10
147	Detroit Red Wings	.05	.10
148	Montreal Canadiens	.05	.10
149	New York Rangers	.05	.10
150	Toronto Maple Leafs	.05	.10

— 1991 - PROMOTIONAL CARDS —

Issued for the 1991-92 season as "Prototype for Review Only" cards. The set contains five player cards and one title card. The cards are not numbered. The missing numbers and the "Review Notice" are the only differences between the promo and the regular issue cards.

1991 Promotional Cards
Bob Essensa

Card Size: 2 1/2" X 3/12"
Face: Four colour, borderless, Pro Set and team logo
Back: Four colour, Resume
Imprint: ©1991 Pro Set Inc.
Complete Set No.: 6
Complete Set Price: 5.00 10.00

PROTOTYPE REVIEW SET

No.	Player	EX	NRMT
—	Title Card:	1.00	2.00
—	Bob Essensa, Goalie, Win.	1.00	2.00
—	Gord Murphy, Phi.	1.00	2.00
—	Dave Reid, Tor.	1.00	2.00
—	Craig Wolanin, Que.	1.00	2.00
—	Randy Wood, NYI	1.00	2.00

— 1991 ST. LOUIS BLUES — MID WEST COLLECTOR SHOW

Issued for the Mid West Collector Show held at St. Louis during October 1991, these cards are identical to the regular issue except for a blue stripe at the right side of the card. The cards are numbered in gold within the strip.

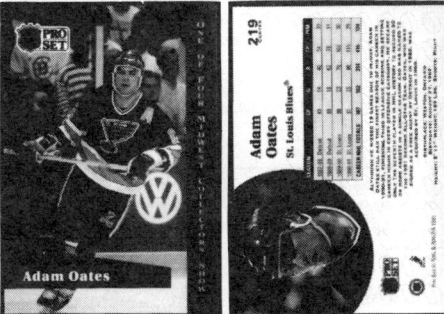

1991 St. Louis Blues
Mid West Collector Show
Card No. 1 of 4, Adam Oates

Card Size: 2 1/2" X 3/12"
Face: Four colour, blue border on right side, Pro Set and team logo
Back: Four colour, Resume
Imprint: Pro Set © NHL & NHLPA 1991
Complete Set No.: 4
Complete Set Price: 15.00 30.00

No.	Player	EX	NRMT
1 of 4	Adam Oates	5.00	10.00
2 of 4	Paul Cavallini	2.00	4.00
3 of 4	Rick Meagher	2.00	4.00
4 of 4	Brett Hull	7.50	15.00

— 1991 - 1992 NATIONAL HOCKEY TOUR — TOUR PROMO CARD

During the 1991-92 season Pro Set sponsored a Hockey Card Collectibles and Memorabilia Show which toured several NHL cities. A limited number of cards were given out at each city the tour visited. The card was not numbered.

1991-92 National Hockey Tour
Tour Promo Card

Card Size: 2 1/2" X 3/12"
Face: Four colour, grey and black, Pro Set and NHL logo
Back: Four colour, orange and black, Pro Set and NHL logo
Imprint: NHL Pro Set © 1991

No.	Player	EX	NRMT
—	National Hockey Tour	5.00	10.00

— 1991 - 92 REGULAR ISSUE —

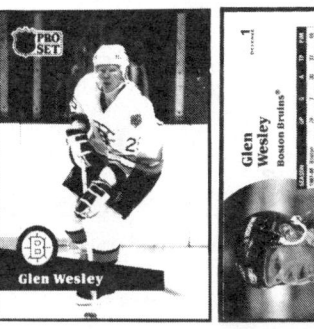

1991-92 Series One
Card No. 1, Glen Wesley

Card Size: 2 1/2" X 3 1/2"
Face: Four colour, borderless, Pro Set and team logo
Back: Four colour, Number, Resume
Imprint:
  Series One: Pro Set © NHL 1991 and Pro Set © NHL & NHLPA 1991
  Series Two: Pro set @ NHL 1992 and Pro Set @ NHL and NHLPA 1992

Complete Set No.: 615
Complete Set Price: 5.00 10.00
Series One: 345 4.00 8.00
Series Two: 270 4.00 8.00
Common Card: .03 .05

Series One:
Regular:	Foil Pack: (15 Cards)	.50
	Foil Box: (36 Packs)	10.00
	Foil Case: (20 Boxes)	150.00
Jumbos:	Foil Pack: (30 Cards)	1.00
	Foil Box: (20 Packs)	15.00
	Foil Cases: (20 Boxes)	200.00
Vending:	Case: (12,000 Cards)	175.00

Series Two:
Regular:	Foil Pack: (15 Cards)	.50
	Foil Box: (36 Packs)	10.00
	Foil Case: (20 Boxes)	125.00

— SERIES ONE —

BOSTON BRUINS

No.	Player	English NRMT	French NRMT
1	Glen Wesley	.05	.05
2	Craig Janney	.10	.10
3	Kenneth Hodge, Jr.	.05	.05
4	Randy Burridge, (Traded to Washington)	.05	.05
5	Cam Neely	.15	.15
6	Robert Sweeney	.05	.05
7	Garry Galley	.05	.05
8	Petri Skriko	.05	.05
9	Raymond Bourque	.15	.15
10	Andrew Moog, Goalie	.05	.05
11	David Christian	.05	.05
12	David Poulin	.05	.05
13	Jeff Lazaro, RC	.05	.05

BUFFALO SABRES

No.	Player	English NRMT	French NRMT
14	Darrin Shannon	.05	.05
15	Pierre Turgeon, Error	.20	.20
16	Alexander Mogilny	.40	.40
17	Benoit Hogue, Error	.05	.05
18	Dave Snuggerud	.05	.05
19	Doug Bodger, Error	.05	.05
20	Uwe Krupp	.05	.05
21	Daren Puppa, Goalie	.05	.05

354 • PRO SET — 1991-92 REGULAR ISSUE —

No.	Player	English NRMT	French NRMT
22	Christian Ruuttu	.05	.05
23	David Andreychuk	.15	.15
24	Dale Hawerchuk	.05	.05
25	Michael Ramsey	.05	.05
26	Richard Vaive	.05	.05

CALGARY FLAMES

No.	Player	English NRMT	French NRMT
27	Stephane Matteau	.05	.05
28	Theoren Fleury	.10	.10
29	Joe Nieuwendyk	.05	.05
30	Gary Roberts	.05	.05
31	Paul Ranheim	.05	.05
32	Gary Suter	.05	.05
33	Allan MacInnis	.05	.05
34	Douglas Gilmour	.25	.25
35	Michael Vernon, Goalie	.05	.05
36	Carey Wilson	.05	.05
37	Joel Otto	.05	.05
38	Jamie Macoun	.05	.05
39	Sergei Makarov	.05	.05

CHICAGO BLACK HAWKS

No.	Player	English NRMT	French NRMT
40	Jeremy Roenick	.50	.50
41	Dave Manson	.05	.05
42	Adam Creighton	.05	.05
43	Ed Belfour, Goalie	.25	.25
44	Wayne Presley	.05	.05
45	Steve Thomas	.05	.05
46	Troy Murray	.05	.05
47	Robert McGill, Drafted By San Jose	.05	.05
48	Chris Chelios	.05	.05
49	Steve Larmer	.05	.05
50	Michel Goulet	.05	.05
51	Dirk Graham	.05	.05
52	Douglas Wilson	.05	.05

DETROIT RED WINGS

No.	Player	English NRMT	French NRMT
53	Sergei Fedorov	.60	.60
54	Yves Racine	.10	.10
55	Jimmy Carson	.05	.05
56	Johan Garpenlov	.05	.05
57	Tim Cheveldae, Goalie	.05	.05
58	Shawn Burr	.05	.05
59	Paul Ysebaert	.05	.05
60	Kevin Miller	.05	.05
61	Bob Probert	.05	.05
62	Steve Yzerman	.20	.20
63	Gerard Gallant	.05	.05
64	Rick Zombo	.05	.05
65	David Barr	.05	.05

EDMONTON OILERS

No.	Player	English NRMT	French NRMT
66	Martin Gelinas	.05	.05
67	Adam Graves	.20	.20
68	Joe Murphy	.05	.05
69	Craig Simpson	.05	.05
70	Bill Ranford, Goalie	.05	.05
71	Esa Tikkanen	.05	.05
72	Petr Klima	.05	.05
73	James (Steve) Smith	.05	.05
74	Mark Messier	.30	.30
75	Glenn Anderson	.05	.05
76	Kevin Lowe	.05	.05
77	Craig MacTavish	.05	.05
78	Grant Fuhr, Goalie	.05	.05

HARTFORD WHALERS

No.	Player	English NRMT	French NRMT
79	Robert Holik	.05	.05
80	Rob Brown	.05	.05
81	Doug Houda	.05	.05
82	Sylvain Coté	.05	.05
83	Todd Krygier	.05	.05
84	Dean Evason	.05	.05
85	John Cullen	.05	.05
86	Patrick Verbeek	.05	.05
87	Brad Shaw	.05	.05
88	Paul Cyr	.05	.05
89	Kevin Dineen	.05	.05
90	Peter Sidorkiewicz, Goalie	.05	.05
91	Zarley Zalapski	.05	.05

LOS ANGELES KINGS

No.	Player	English NRMT	French NRMT
92	Robert Blake	.20	.20
93	Jari Kurri	.10	.10
94	Todd Elik, (Traded to Minnesota)	.05	.05
95	Luc Robitaille	.20	.20
96	Steve Duchesne (Traded to Philadelphia)	.05	.05
97	Tomas Sandstrom	.05	.05
98	Tony Granato	.05	.05
99	Bob Kudelski	.05	.05
100	Martin McSorley	.05	.05
101	Wayne Gretzky	1.00	1.00
102	Kelly Hrudey, Goalie	.05	.05
103	David Taylor	.05	.05
104	Larry Robinson	.05	.05

MINNESOTA NORTH STARS

No.	Player	English NRMT	French NRMT
105	Michael Modano	.12	.25
106	Ulf Dahlen	.05	.05
107	Mark Tinordi	.05	.05
108	Dave Gagner	.05	.05
109	Brian Bellows	.05	.05
110	Gaetan Duchesne	.05	.05
111	Jon Casey, Goalie	.05	.05
112	Neal Broten	.05	.05
113	Brian Propp	.05	.05
114	Curt Giles	.05	.05
115	Robert Smith	.05	.05
116	Jim Johnson	.05	.05
117	Douglas Smail	.05	.05

MONTREAL CANADIENS

No.	Player	English NRMT	French NRMT
118	Eric Desjardins	.05	.05
119	Mathieu Schneider	.05	.05
120	Stephan Lebeau	.10	.10
121	Mike Keane	.05	.05
122	Stephane J. J. Richer	.05	.05
123	Petr Svoboda	.05	.05
124	Jean-Jacques Daigneault	.05	.05
125	Patrick Roy, Goalie	.50	.50
126	Russell Courtnall	.05	.05
127	Brian Skrudland	.05	.05
128	Denis Savard	.05	.05
129	Michael McPhee	.05	.05
130A	Guy Carbonneau	.05	.05
130B	Guy Carbonneau, Error	.05	.05

NEW JERSEY DEVILS

No.	Player	English NRMT	French NRMT
131	Brendan Shanahan	.12	.25
132	Sean Burke, Goalie	.05	.05
133	Eric Weinrich	.05	.05
134	Kirk Muller	.05	.05
135	Claude Lemieux	.05	.05
136	John MacLean	.05	.05
137	Chris Terreri, Goalie	.05	.05
138	Doug Brown	.05	.05
139	Kenneth Daneyko	.05	.05
140	Bruce Driver	.05	.05
141	Patrik Sundstrom	.05	.05
142	Viacheslav Fetisov	.05	.05
143	Peter Stastny	.05	.05

NEW YORK ISLANDERS

No.	Player	English NRMT	French NRMT
144	Wayne McBean	.05	.05
145	**Bill Berg, RC**	**.10**	**.10**
146	Derek King	.05	.05
147	David Volek	.05	.05
148	Jeff Norton	.05	.05
149	Pat LaFontaine	.30	.30
150	Gary Nylund	.05	.05
151	Randy Wood	.05	.05
152	Patrick Flatley	.05	.05
153	Glenn Healy, Goalie	.05	.05
154	Brent Sutter	.05	.05
155	Craig Ludwig, (Traded to Minnesota)	.05	.05
156	Ray Ferraro	.05	.05

NEW YORK RANGERS

No.	Player	English NRMT	French NRMT
157	Troy Mallette	.05	.05
158	Mark Janssens	.05	.05
159	Brian Leetch	.25	.25
160	Darren Turcotte	.05	.05
161	Mike Richter, Goalie	.25	.25
162	Ray Sheppard	.05	.05
163	Randy Moller	.05	.05
164	James Patrick	.05	.05
165	Brian Mullen, (Drafted By San Jose)	.05	.05
166	Bernie Nicholls	.05	.05
167	Michael Gartner	.05	.05
168	Kelly Kisio, (Drafted By Minnesota)	.05	.05
169	John Ogrodnick	.05	.05

PHILADELPHIA FLYERS

No.	Player	English NRMT	French NRMT
170	Mike Ricci	.10	.10
171	Gordon Murphy	.05	.05
172	Scott Mellanby, (Traded to Edmonton)	.05	.05
173	Terry Carkner	.05	.05
174	Derrick Smith	.05	.05
175	Murray Craven	.05	.05
176	Ron Hextall, Goalie	.05	.05
177	Rick Tocchet	.10	.10
178	Ronald Sutter	.05	.05
179	Per-erik Eklund	.05	.05
180	Tim Kerr, (Traded to Rangers, May 1991)	.05	.05
181	Kjell Samuelsson	.05	.05
182	Mark Howe	.05	.05

PITTSBURGH PENGUINS

No.	Player	English NRMT	French NRMT
183	Jaromir Jagr	.20	.40
184	Mark Recchi	.20	.40
185	Kevin Stevens	.20	.40
186	Tom Barrasso, Goalie	.05	.05
187	Bob Errey	.05	.05
188	Ronald Francis	.05	.05
189	Phil Bourque	.05	.05
190	Paul Coffey	.10	.10
191	Joe Mullen	.05	.05
192	Bryan Trottier	.05	.05
193	Lawrence Murphy	.05	.05
194	Mario Lemieux	1.00	1.00
195	Scott Young	.05	.05

QUEBEC NORDIQUES

No.	Player	English NRMT	French NRMT
196	Owen Nolan	.15	.15
197	Mats Sundin	.25	.25
198	Curtis Leschyshyn	.05	.05
199	Joe Sakic	.30	.30
200	Bryan Fogarty	.05	.05
201	Stephane Morin	.05	.05
202	Ron Tugnutt, Goalie	.05	.05
203	Craig Wolanin	.05	.05
204	Steven Finn	.05	.05
205	Anthony Hrkac, (Traded to San Jose)	.05	.05
206	Randy Velischek	.05	.05
207	**Alexei Gusarov, RC**	**.10**	**.10**
208	Scott Pearson	.10	.10

— 1991 - 92 REGULAR ISSUE — PRO SET • 355

ST LOUIS BLUES

No.	Player	English NRMT	French NRMT
209	Dan Quinn	.05	.05
210	Garth Butcher	.05	.05
211	Rod Brind'Amour	.15	.15
212	Jeff Brown	.05	.05
213	Vincent Riendeau, Goalie	.10	.10
214	Paul Cavallini	.05	.05
215	Brett Hull	.40	.40
216	Scott Stevens	.05	.05
217	Richard Sutter	.05	.05
218	Gino Cavallini	.05	.05
219	Adam Oates	.20	.20
220	Ronald Wilson	.05	.05
221	Bob Bassen	.05	.05

TORONTO MAPLE LEAFS

No.	Player	English NRMT	French NRMT
222	Peter Ing, Goalie	.05	.05
223	Daniel Marois	.05	.05
224	Vincent Damphousse	.10	.10
225	Wendel Clark	.20	.20
226	Todd Gill	.05	.05
227	Peter Zezel	.05	.05
228	Robert Rouse	.05	.05
229	David Reid	.05	.05
230	David Ellett	.05	.05
231	Gary Leeman	.05	.05
232	Gordon (Rob) Ramage, (Drafted by Minnesota)	.05	.05
233	Michael Krushelnyski	.05	.05
234	Thomas Fergus	.05	.05

VANCOUVER CANUCKS

No.	Player	English NRMT	French NRMT
235	Petr Nedved	.15	.15
236	Trevor Linden	.30	.30
237	Dave Capuano	.05	.05
238	Troy Gamble, Goalie	.05	.05
239	Robert Kron	.05	.05
240	Jyrki Lumme	.05	.05
241	Cliff Ronning	.05	.05
242	Sergio Momesso	.05	.05
243	Greg Adams	.05	.05
244	Tom Kurvers, (Traded to New York)	.05	.05
245	Geoff Courtnall	.05	.05
246	Igor Larionov	.05	.05
247	Doug Lidster	.05	.05

WASHINGTON CAPITALS

No.	Player	English NRMT	French NRMT
248	Calle Johansson	.05	.05
249	Kevin Hatcher	.05	.05
250	Al Iafrate	.05	.05
251	John Druce	.05	.05
252	Michal Pivonka	.05	.05
253	Stephen Leach, (Traded to Boston)	.05	.05
254	Mike Ridley	.05	.05
255	Mike Lalor	.05	.05
256	Kelly Miller	.05	.05
257	Don Beaupre, Goalie	.05	.05
258	Dino Ciccarelli	.05	.05
259	Rod Langway	.05	.05
260	Dimitri Khristich	.05	.05

WINNIPEG JETS

No.	Player	English NRMT	French NRMT
261	Teppo Numminen	.05	.05
262	Pat Elynuik	.05	.05
263	Danton Cole	.05	.05
264	Fredrik Olausson	.05	.05
265	Ed Olczyk	.05	.05
266	Bob Essensa, Goalie	.05	.05
267	Phil Housley	.05	.05
268	Shawn Cronin	.05	.05
269	Paul MacDermid	.05	.05
270	Mark Osborne	.05	.05
271	Thomas Steen	.05	.05
272	Brent Ashton	.05	.05
273	Randy Carlyle	.05	.05

ALL STAR CAMPBELL CONFERENCE

No.	Player	English NRMT	French NRMT
274	Theoren Fleury, Cal.	.05	.05
275	Allan MacInnis, Cal.	.05	.05
276	Gary Suter, Cal.	.05	.05
277	Michael Vernon, Cal., Goalie	.05	.05
278	Chris Chelios, Chi.	.05	.05
279	Steve Larmer, Chi.	.10	.10
280	Jeremy Roenick, Chi.	.25	.25
281	Steve Yzerman, Det.	.15	.15
282	Mark Messier, Edm.	.15	.15
283	Bill Ranford, Edm., Goalie	.05	.05
284	James (Steve) Smith, Edm.	.05	.05
285	Wayne Gretzky, LA	.35	.35
286	Luc Robitaille, LA	.15	.15
287	Tomas Sandstrom, LA	.05	.05
288	Dave Gagner, Min.	.05	.05
289	Robert Smith, Min.	.05	.05
290	Brett Hull, St. L.	.20	.20
291	Adam Oates, St. L.	.10	.10
292	Scott Stevens, St. L.	.05	.05
293	Vincent Damphousse, Tor.	.05	.05
294	Trevor Linden, Van.	.15	.15
295	Phil Housley, Win.	.05	.05

ALL STAR WALES CONFERENCE

No.	Player	English NRMT	French NRMT
296	Raymond Bourque, Bos.	.10	.10
297	David Christian, Bos.	.05	.05
298	Garry Galley, Bos.	.05	.05
299	Andrew Moog, Bos., Goalie	.05	.05
300	Cam Neely, Bos.	.10	.10
301	Uwe Krupp, Buf.	.05	.05
302	John Cullen, Har.	.05	.05
303	Patrick Verbeek, Har.	.05	.05
304	Patrick Roy, Mon., Goalie	.35	.35
305	Denis Savard, Mon.	.05	.05
306	Brian Skrudland, Mon.	.05	.05
307	John MacLean, NJD	.05	.05
308	Pat LaFontaine, NYI	.15	.15
309	Brian Leetch, NYR	.20	.20
310	Darren Turcotte, NYR	.05	.05
311	Rick Tocchet, Phi.	.05	.05
312	Paul Coffey, Pit.	.05	.05
313	Mark Recchi, Pit.	.10	.10
314	Kevin Stevens, Pit.	.10	.10
315	Joe Sakic, Que.	.10	.10
316	Kevin Hatcher, Wash.	.05	.05
317	Guy Lafleur, Que.	.05	.05

TROPHY WINNERS

No.	Player	English NRMT	French NRMT
318	Conn Smythe Trophy: Mario Lemieux, Pit.	.30	.30
319	1991 Stanley Cup Champions: Pittsburgh Penguins	.15	.15
320	Hart Memorial Trophy: Brett Hull, St. L.	.20	.20
321	Calder Memorial Trophy, Vezina Trophy, William M. Jennings Trophy: Ed Belfour, Goalie, Chi.	.10	.10
322	James Norris Memorial Trophy: Raymond Bourque, Bos.	.10	.10
323	Frank J. Selke Trophy: Dirk Graham, Chi.	.05	.05
324	Art Ross Trophy, Lady Byng Memorial Trophy: Wayne Gretzky, LA	.35	.35
325	King Clancy Memorial Trophy, Bill Masterton Memorial Trophy: David Taylor, LA	.05	.05
326	NHL Pro Set Player of the Year Award: Brett Hull, St. L.	.20	.20

SAN JOSE SHARKS

No.	Player	English NRMT	French NRMT
327	Brian Hayward, Goalie	.05	.05
328	Neil Wilkinson, Error	.05	.05
329	Craig Coxe	.05	.05
330	Rob Zettler	.05	.05
331	Jeff Hackett, Goalie	.05	.05

GREATS OF THE GAME

No.	Player	English NRMT	French NRMT
332	"Phantom" Joe Malone The NHL's First Scoring Leader	.10	.10
333	Georges Vezina, The First Ironman	.10	.10
334	The Modern Arena	.05	.05
335	Ace Bailey Benefit Game First All-Star Game	.10	.10
336	Howie Morenz, The "Stratford Streak"	.15	.15
337	The Punch Line, Knockout Artists	.10	.10
338	The Kid Line, Toronto's Terrific Trio	.10	.10
339	Before the Zamboni	.05	.05
340	Bill Barilko, The End of the Innocence	.10	.10
341	Jacques Plante, The Innovator	.15	.15
342	Arena Designs, Separate and Not Equal	.05	.05
343	Terry Sawchuk, The True Mr. Zero	.15	.15
344	Gordie Howe, "Mr. Hockey"	.15	.15

PLAY SMART

No.	Player	English NRMT	French NRMT
345	Guy Carbonneau	.05	.05

SERIES TWO

BOSTON BRUINS

No.	Player	English NRMT	French NRMT
346	Stephen Leach	.05	.05
347	Peter Douris	.05	.05
348	David Reid	.05	.05
349	Robert Carpenter	.05	.05
350	Stephane Quintal	.05	.05
351	Barry Pederson	.05	.05
352	Brent Ashton	.05	.05
353	Vladimir Ruzicka	.10	.10

BUFFALO SABRES

No.	Player	English NRMT	French NRMT
354	Brad Miller	.05	.05
355	Robert Ray	.05	.05
356	Colin Patterson	.05	.05
357	Gordon Donnelly	.05	.05
358	Pat LaFontaine	.30	.30
359	Randy Wood	.05	.05
360	Randy Hillier	.05	.05

CALGARY FLAMES

No.	Player	English NRMT	French NRMT
361	Robert Reichel	.20	.20
362	Ronald Stern	.05	.05
363	Eric Nattress, (Traded To Toronto)	.05	.05
364	Tim Sweeney	.05	.05
365	Marc Habscheid	.05	.05
366	Timothy Hunter	.05	.05
367	Richard Wamsley, Goalie, (Traded to Toronto)	.05	.05
368	Frankisek Musil	.05	.05

CHICAGO BLACK HAWKS

No.	Player	English NRMT	French NRMT
369	Mike Hudson	.05	.05
370	Steve Smith	.05	.05
371	Keith Brown	.05	.05
372	Gregory Gilbert	.05	.05
373	John Tonelli	.05	.05
374	Brent Sutter	.05	.05
375	Brad Lauer	.05	.05

356 • PRO SET — 1991-92 REGULAR ISSUE —

DETROIT RED WINGS

No.	Player	English NRMT	French NRMT
376	Alan Kerr	.05	.05
377	Bradley McCrimmon	.05	.05
378	Charles (Brad) Marsh	.05	.05
379	Brent Fedyk	.05	.05
380	Ray Sheppard	.05	.05

EDMONTON OILERS

No.	Player	English NRMT	French NRMT
381	Vincent Damphousse	.05	.05
382	Craig Muni	.05	.05
383	Scott Mellanby	.05	.05
384	Geoff Smith	.05	.05
385	Kelly Buchberger	.05	.05
286	Bernie Nicholls	.05	.05
387	Luke Richardson	.05	.05
388	Peter Ing, Goalie	.05	.05
389	Dave Manson	.05	.05

HARTFORD WHALERS

No.	Player	English NRMT	French NRMT
390	Mark Hunter	.05	.05
391	Jim McKenzie, RC	.05	.05
392	Randy Cunneyworth	.05	.05
393	Murray Craven	.05	.05
394	Bo Mikael Andersson	.05	.05
395	Andrew Cassels	.05	.05
396	Randy Ladouceur	.05	.05
397	Marc Bergevin	.05	.05
398	Brian Benning	.05	.05

LOS ANGELES KINGS

No.	Player	English NRMT	French NRMT
399	Mike Donnelly, RC	.15	.15
400	Charles Huddy	.05	.05
401	John McIntyre	.05	.05
402	Jay Miller	.05	.05
403	Randy Gilhen	.05	.05

MINNESOTA NORTH STARS

No.	Player	English NRMT	French NRMT
404	Stewart Gavin	.05	.05
405	Mike Craig	.05	.05
406	Brian Glynn	.05	.05
407	Gordon (Rob) Ramage	.05	.05
408	Chris Dahlquist	.05	.05
409	Basil McRae	.05	.05
410	Todd Elik	.05	.05
411	Craig Ludwig	.05	.05

MONTREAL CANADIENS

No.	Player	English NRMT	French NRMT
412	Kirk Muller	.05	.05
413	Shayne Corson	.05	.05
414	Brent Gilchrist	.05	.05
415	Mario Roberge, RC	.05	.05
416	Sylvain Turgeon	.05	.05
417	Alain Cote	.05	.05
418	Donald Dufresne	.05	.05
419	Todd Ewen	.05	.05

NEW JERSEY DEVILS

No.	Player	English NRMT	French NRMT
420	Stephane J.J. Richer	.05	.05
421	David Maley	.05	.05
422	Randy McKay	.05	.05
423	Scott Stevens	.05	.05
424	Jon Morris	.05	.05
425	Claude Vilgrain	.05	.05
426	Laurie Boschman	.05	.05
427	Patrick Conacher	.05	.05

NEW YORK ISLANDERS

No.	Player	English NRMT	French NRMT
428	Tom Kurvers	.05	.05
429	Joe Reekie	.05	.05
430	Robert DiMaio	.05	.05
431	Tom Fitzgerald	.05	.05
432	Ken Baumgartner	.05	.05
433	Pierre Turgeon	.25	.25
434	Dave McLlwain	.05	.05
435	Benoit Hogue	.05	.05
436	Uwe Krupp	.05	.05
437	Adam Creighton	.05	.05
438	Steve Thomas	.05	.05

NEW YORK RANGERS

No.	Player	English NRMT	French NRMT
439	Mark Messier	.25	.25
440	Tahir (Tie) Domi	.05	.05
441	Sergei Nemchinov	.05	.05
442	Mark Hardy	.05	.05
443	Adam Graves	.25	.25
444	Jeff Beukeboom	.05	.05
445	Kris King	.05	.05
446	Tim Kerr	.05	.05
447	John Vanbiesbrouck, Goalie	.05	.05
448	Steve Duchesne	.05	.05
449	Stephen Kasper	.05	.05
450	Ken Wregget, Goalie	.05	.05
451	Kevin Dineen	.05	.05

PHILADELPHIA FLYERS

No.	Player	English NRMT	French NRMT
452	David Brown	.05	.05
453	Rod Brind'Amour	.15	.15
454	Jiri Latal	.05	.05
455	Tony Horacek	.05	.05
456	Brad Jones, RC	.05	.05

PITTSBURGH PENGUINS

No.	Player	English NRMT	French NRMT
457	Paul Stanton	.05	.05
458	Gordon Roberts	.05	.05
459	Ulf Samuelsson	.05	.05
460	Ken Priestlay, RC	.05	.05
461	Jiri Hrdina	.05	.05

QUEBEC NORDIQUES

No.	Player	English NRMT	French NRMT
462	Mikhail Tatarinov	.05	.05
463	Mike Hough	.05	.05
464	Don Barber	.05	.05
465	Greg Smyth, RC	.05	.05
466	Douglas Smail	.05	.05
467	Michael McNeill	.05	.05
468	John Kordic	.05	.05
469	Gregory Paslawski	.05	.05
470	Herb Raglan	.05	.05

ST. LOUIS BLUES

No.	Player	English NRMT	French NRMT
471	David Christian	.05	.05
472	Murray Baron	.05	.05
473	Curtis Joseph, Goalie	.25	.25
474	Rick Zombo	.05	.05
475	Brendan Shanahan	.25	.25
476	Ronald Sutter	.05	.05
477	Mario Marois, (Traded To Winnipeg)	.05	.05

SAN JOSE SHARKS

No.	Player	English NRMT	French NRMT
478	Douglas Wilson	.05	.05
479	Kelly Kisio	.05	.05
480	Robert McGill	.05	.05
481	Perry Anderson, RC	.05	.05
482	Brian Lawton	.05	.05

No.	Player	English NRMT	French NRMT
483	Neil Wilkinson	.05	.05
484	Ken Hammond	.05	.05
485	David Bruce, RC	.05	.05
486	Steven Bozek	.05	.05
487	Perry Berezan	.05	.05
488	Wayne Presley	.05	.05

TORONTO MAPLE LEAFS

No.	Player	English NRMT	French NRMT
489	Brian Bradley	.05	.05
490	Darryl Shannon, RC	.05	.05
491	Lucien DeBlois	.05	.05
492	Michel Petit, (Traded To Calgary)	.05	.05
493	Claude Loiselle	.05	.05
494	Grant Fuhr, Goalie	.05	.05
495	Craig Berube	.05	.05
496	Michael Bullard	.05	.05

VANCOUVER CANUCKS

No.	Player	English NRMT	French NRMT
497	Jim Sandlak	.05	.05
498	Dana Murzyn	.05	.05
499	Garry Valk	.05	.05
500	Andrew McBain	.05	.05
501	Kirk McLean, Goalie	.20	.20
502	Gerald Diduck	.05	.05
503	David Babych	.05	.05
504	Ryan Walter	.05	.05
505	Gino Odjick	.05	.05

WASHINGTON CAPITALS

No.	Player	English NRMT	French NRMT
506	Dale Hunter	.05	.05
507	Tim Bergland	.05	.05
508	Alan May	.05	.05
509	Jim Hrivnak, Goalie	.05	.05
510	Randy Burridge	.05	.05
511	Peter Bondra	.10	.10
512	Sylvain Coté	.05	.05
513	Nicholas Kypreos	.05	.05

WINNIPEG JETS

No.	Player	English NRMT	French NRMT
514	Troy Murray	.05	.05
515	Darrin Shannon	.05	.05
516	Bryan Erickson	.05	.05
517	Petri Skriko	.05	.05
518	Michael Eagles	.05	.05
519	Mike Hartman	.05	.05

ROOKIES

No.	Player	Englis NRMT	French NRMT
520	Bob Beers, Bos., RC	.05	.05
521	Matt DelGuidice, Goalie, Bos., RC	.05	.05
522	Chris Winnes, Bos., RC	.05	.05
523	Brad May, Buf.	.10	.10
524	Donald Audette, Buf.	.10	.10
525	Kevin Haller, Buf., RC	.20	.20
526	Martin Simard, Cal., RC	.05	.05
527	Tomas Forslund, Cal., RC, Error	.05	.05
528	Mark Osiecki, Cal., RC	.05	.05
529	Dominik Hasek, Goalie, Chi., RC	1.00	1.00
530	Jimmy Waite, Goalie, Chi.	.10	.10
531	Nicklas Lidstrom, Det., RC, Error	.30	.30
532	Martin Lapointe, Det., RC	.05	.05
533	Vladimir Konstantinov, Det., RC	.15	.15
534	Josef Beranek, Edm., RC	.40	.40
535	Louie DeBrusk, Edm., RC	.10	.10
536	Geoff Sanderson, Har., RC	.80	.80
537	Mark Greig, Har., RC	.10	.10
538	Michel Picard, Har., RC	.05	.05
539	Chris Tancill, Det., RC, (Traded To Detroit)	.05	.05
540	Peter Ahola, LA, RC	.10	.10
541	Francois Breault, LA, RC	.05	.05
542	Darryl Sydor, LA	.05	.05

1991 - 92 INSERT SET — PRO SET • 357

No.	Player	English NRMT	French NRMT
543	Derian Hatcher, Min.	.05	.05
544	Marc Bureau, Min., RC	.05	.05
545	John LeClair, Mon., RC	.20	.20
546	Paul Di Pietro, Mon., RC	.15	.15
547	Scott Niedermayer, NJD, Error	.25	.25
548	Kevin Todd, NJD, RC	.20	.20
549	Doug Weight, NYR, RC	.25	.25
550	Anthony Amonte, NYR, RC	.30	.30
551	Corey Foster, Phi., RC	.10	.10
552	Dominic Roussel, Goalie, Phi., RC	.25	.25
553	Dan Kordic, Phi., RC	.10	.10
554	Jim Paek, Pit., RC	.15	.15
555	Kip Miller, Que.	.10	.10
556	Claude Lapointe, Que., RC	.15	.15
557	Nelson Emerson, St. L.	.30	.30
558	Pat Falloon, SJ	.50	.50
559	Pat MacLeod, SJ, RC	.15	.15
560	Rick Lessard, SJ, RC	.10	.10
561	Link Gaetz, SJ, RC	.10	.10
562	Rob Pearson, Tor., RC	.25	.25
563	Alexander Godynyuk, Tor., RC (Traded To Calgary)	.10	.10
564	Pavel Bure, Van.	2.50	2.50
565	Russell Romaniuk, Win., RC	.15	.15
566	Stu Barnes, Win.	.10	.10

CAPTAINS

No.	Player	English NRMT	French NRMT
567	Raymond Bourque, Bos.	.10	.10
568	Michael Ramsey, Buf.	.05	.05
569	Joe Nieuwendyk, Cal.	.05	.05
570	Dirk Graham, Chi.	.05	.05
571	Steve Yzerman, Det.	.10	.10
572	Kevin Lowe, Edm.	.05	.05
573	Randy Ladouceur, Har.	.05	.05
574	Wayne Gretzky, LA	.25	.25
575	Mark Tinordi, Min.	.05	.05
576	Guy Carbonneau, Mon.	.05	.05
577	Bruce Driver, NJD	.05	.05
578	Patrick Flatley, NYI	.05	.05
579	Mark Messier, NYR	.15	.15
580	Rick Tocchet, Phi.	.05	.05
581	Mario Lemieux, Pit.	.25	.25
582	Mike Hough, Que.	.05	.05
583	Garth Butcher, St. L.	.05	.05
584	Douglas Wilson, SJ	.05	.05
585	Wendel Clark, Tor.	.15	.15
586	Trevor Linden, Van.	.10	.10
587	Rod Langway, Was.	.05	.05
588	Troy Murray, Win.	.05	.05

HOCKEY HALL OF FAME AND MUSEUM

No.	Player	English NRMT	French NRMT
589	Montreal Canadiens Practice Outdoors	.05	.05
590	Shape Up or Ship Out	.05	.05
591	Boston Bruins Cartoon	.05	.05
592	Opening Night at Maple Leaf Gardens	.05	.05
593	Rod Gilbert	.05	.05
594	Phil Esposito	.05	.05
595	Dale Tallon	.05	.05
596	Gilbert Perreault	.05	.05
597	Bernie Federko	.05	.05
598	History of the HNL All-Star Game	.05	.05

GOALIE LEADERS

No.	Player	English NRMT	French NRMT
599	Patrick Roy, Goalie, Mon.	.25	.25
600	Ed Belfour, Goalie, Chi.	.10	.10
601	Don Beaupre, Goalie, Wash.	.05	.05
602	Bob Essensa, Goalie, Win.	.05	.05
603	Kirk McLean, Goalie, Van., Error	.05	.05

POWER-PLAY GOAL LEADERS

No.	Player	English NRMT	French NRMT
604	Michael Gartner, NYR	.05	.05
605	Jeremy Roenick, Chi.	.25	.25
606	Rob Brown, Har.	.05	.05
607	Ulf Dahlen, Min.	.05	.05

PLUS/MINUS LEADERS

No.	Player	English NRMT	French NRMT
608	Paul Ysebaert, Det.	.05	.05
609	Byron (Brad) McCrimmon, Det.	.05	.05
610	Nicklas Lidstrom, Det.	.10	.10
611	Kelly Miller, Was.	.05	.05

PLAY SMART

No.	Player	English NRMT	French NRMT
612	James Kyte, Cal., Hockey is For Everyone	.05	.05
613	Patrick Roy, Goalie, Mon., Study Hard	.35	.35
614	Alan May, Was., Stay in School	.05	.05
615	Kelly Miller, Was., Get Involved	.05	.05

— 1991 - 92 INSERT SET —
COLLECTOR CARDS

The four collector cards CC1 to CC4 were randomly inserted into foil packs of Series One. Approximately halfway through the release of this series copyright problems arose with cards CC3 and CC4 and they were withdrawn from the foil packs. No French CC3 and CC4 cards exist.

Cards CC5 to CC9 are a continuation of the Collector Cards begun in Series One. These cards were randomly inserted into Series Two foil packs.

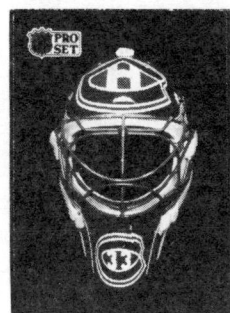 

1991-92 Insert Set
Card No. CC2,   Card No. CC5,
The Mask   Wayne Gretzky

Card Size: 2 1/2" X 3 1/2"
Face: Four colour, borderless; Pro Set and team logo, Name
Back: Four colour on white card stock; Name, Number, Position, Team, Resume
Imprint: Pro Set © NHL 1991
Complete Set No.: 9
Complete Set Price: 60.00   20.00

No.	Player	English NRMT	French NRMT
CC1	1991 Draft Entry	4.00	4.00
CC2	The Mask	7.00	7.00
CC3	Pat Falloon	20.00	—
CC4	Scott Niedermayer	20.00	—
CC5	Wayne Gretzky, LA	5.00	5.00
CC6	Brett Hull, St. L.	4.00	4.00
CC7	Adam Oates, St. L.	3.00	3.00
CC8	Mark Recchi, Pit.	3.00	3.00
CC9	John Cullen, Har.	2.00	2.00

> # THE CHARLTON STANDARD CATALOGUE OF CANADIAN BASEBALL AND FOOTBALL CARDS
> - Fourth Edition -
> *Coming in April!*

— 1991-92 PRO SET —
75TH ANNIVERSARY HOLOGRAM

Card Size: 2 1/2" X 3 1/2"
Face: Four colour
Back: Four colour
Imprint: Pro Set © NHL 1991
Complete Set No.: 1
Complete Set Price: 125.00   125.00

No.	Player	English NRMT	French NRMT
—	Holographic 75th Anniversary Logo	125.00	125.00

— 1991 - 92 AUTOGRAPHED CARD —
PATRICK ROY

In this Canadian Issue an additional collector card was randomly inserted into the packs. This card, No. 125, Patrick Roy, was signed on the face and numbered on the back (1 to 1,000) with silver ink by Roy in a limited edition of 1,000. The foil boxes possibly containing this card are gold stamped and display the Roy mask, differentiating the Canadian boxes from the American.

Card Size: 2 1/2" X 3 1/2"
Face: Four colour, borderless; Pro Set and team logos, Name
Back: Four colour on white card stock; Name, Number, Position, Team, Resume
Imprint: Pro Set © NHL and NHLPA 1991

No.	Player	EX	NRMT
125	Patrick Roy, Signed, Numbered	75.00	150.00

— 1991 - 92 PLATINUM —

This is Pro Set's first issue of Premium Hockey Cards. The 1991-92 season saw the introduction of high-quality action photographs on both the face and back of their cards. The colour process, finish and card designs are far superior to the standard issue.

1991-92 Platinum
Card No. 1, Cam Neely

Card Size: 2 1/2" X 3 1/2"
Face: Four colour, borderless, Pro Set Platinum Logo
Back: Four colour, Number, Resume, Position, Player's signature
Imprint:
   Series One: Pro Set © NHL & NHLPA 1991
   Series Two: PRO SET © NHL AND NHLPA 1992
Complete Set No.: 300
   Series One: 150
   Series Two: 150
Complete Set Price: 8.00   16.00
Series One: 4.00   8.00
Series Two: 4.00   8.00
Common Player: .03   .05
Foil Pack: (15 Cards)   .25
Foil Box: (36 Packs)   7.00
Foil Case: (20 Boxes)   100.00

PRO SET — 1991-92 PLATINUM

— SERIES ONE —

BOSTON BRUINS

No.	Player	EX	NRMT
1	Cam Neely	.05	.10
2	Raymond Bourque	.08	.15
3	Craig Janney	.05	.10
4	Andrew Moog, Goalie	.03	.05
5	David Poulin	.03	.05
6	Kenneth Hodge, Jr.	.03	.05
7	Glen Wesley	.03	.05

BUFFALO SABRES

No.	Player	EX	NRMT
8	David Andreychuk	.08	.15
9	Daren Puppa, Goalie	.03	.05
10	Pierre Turgeon	.13	.25
11	Dale Hawerchuk	.03	.05
12	Doug Bodger	.03	.05
13	Michael Ramsey	.03	.05
14	Alexander Mogilny	.25	.50

CALGARY FLAMES

No.	Player	EX	NRMT
15	Sergei Makarov	.03	.05
16	Theoren Fleury	.08	.15
17	Joel Otto	.03	.05
18	Joe Nieuwendyk	.05	.10
19	Allan MacInnis	.05	.10
20	Gary Suter	.03	.05
21	Michael Vernon, Goalie	.03	.05

CHICAGO BLACK HAWKS

No.	Player	EX	NRMT
22	John Tonelli	.03	.05
23	Dirk Graham	.03	.05
24	Jeremy Roenick	.35	.75
25	Chris Chelios	.03	.05
26	Ed Belfour, Goalie	.12	.25
27	Steve Smith	.03	.05
28	Steve Larmer	.03	.05

DETROIT RED WINGS

No.	Player	EX	NRMT
29	Johan Garpenlov	.03	.05
30	Sergei Fedorov	.35	.75
31	Tim Cheveldae, Goalie	.03	.05
32	Steve Yzerman	.13	.25
33	Jimmy Carson	.03	.05
34	Bob Probert	.03	.05

EDMONTON OILERS

No.	Player	EX	NRMT
35	Vincent Damphousse	.05	.10
36	Bill Ranford, Goalie	.04	.08
37	Petr Klima	.03	.05
38	Kevin Lowe	.03	.05
39	Esa Tikkanen	.03	.05
40	Craig Simpson	.03	.05
41	Peter Ing, Goalie	.03	.05

HARTFORD WHALERS

No.	Player	EX	NRMT
42	Rob Brown	.03	.05
43	Robert Holik	.03	.05
44	Patrick Verbeek	.03	.05
45	Brad Shaw	.03	.05
46	Kevin Dineen	.03	.05
47	Zarley Zalapski	.03	.05

LOS ANGELES KINGS

No.	Player	EX	NRMT
48	Jari Kurri	.03	.05
49	Tony Granato	.03	.05
50	Luc Robitaille	.08	.15
51	Robert Blake	.10	.20
52	Wayne Gretzky	.50	1.00
53	Tomas Sandstrom	.03	.05
54	Kelly Hrudey, Goalie	.03	.05

MINNESOTA NORTH STARS

No.	Player	EX	NRMT
55	Michael Modano	.12	.25
56	Jon Casey	.03	.05
57	Todd Elik	.03	.05
58	Mark Tinordi	.03	.05
59	Brian Bellows	.03	.05
60	Dave Gagner	.03	.05

MONTREAL CANADIENS

No.	Player	EX	NRMT
61	Patrick Roy, Goalie	.25	.50
62	Russell Courtnall	.03	.05
63	Guy Carbonneau	.03	.05
64	Denis Savard	.03	.05
65	Petr Svoboda	.03	.05
66	Kirk Muller	.03	.05

NEW JERSEY DEVILS

No.	Player	EX	NRMT
67	Stephane Richer	.03	.05
68	Chris Terreri, Goalie	.03	.05
69	Bruce Driver	.03	.05
70	John MacLean	.03	.05
71	Patrik Sundstrom	.03	.05
72	Scott Stevens	.05	.10

NEW YORK ISLANDERS

No.	Player	EX	NRMT
73	Glenn Healy, Goalie	.03	.05
74	Brent Sutter	.03	.05
75	David Volek	.03	.05
76	Ray Ferraro	.03	.05
77	Patrick Flatley	.03	.05
78	Jeff Norton	.03	.05

NEW YORK RANGERS

No.	Player	EX	NRMT
79	Brian Leetch	.18	.35
80	Tim Kerr	.03	.05
81	Mark Messier	.15	.30
82	James Patrick	.03	.05
83	Mike Richter, Goalie	.15	.30
84	Michael Gartner	.05	.10

PHILADELPHIA FLYERS

No.	Player	EX	NRMT
85	Mike Ricci	.10	.20
86	Steve Duchesne	.03	.05
87	Ron Hextall, Goalie	.03	.05
88	Rick Tocchet	.05	.10
89	Per-erik Eklund	.03	.05
90	Rod Brind'Amour	.10	.20

PITTSBURGH PENGUINS

No.	Player	EX	NRMT
91	Mario Lemieux	.35	.75
92	Jaromir Jagr	.25	.50
93	Kevin Stevens	.25	.50
94	Paul Coffey	.05	.10
95	Ulf Samuelsson	.03	.05
96	Tom Barrasso, Goalie	.05	.10
97	Mark Recchi	.25	.50

QUEBEC NORDIQUES

No.	Player	EX	NRMT
98	Ron Tugnutt, Goalie	.03	.05
99	Mats Sundin	.18	.35
100	Stephane Morin	.05	.10
101	Owen Nolan	.08	.15
102	Joe Sakic	.18	.35
103	Bryan Fogarty	.03	.05

SAN JOSE SHARKS

No.	Player	EX	NRMT
104	Kelly Kisio	.03	.05
105	Anthony Hrkac	.03	.05
106	Brian Mullen	.03	.05
107	Douglas Wilson	.03	.05

ST. LOUIS BLUES

No.	Player	EX	NRMT
108	Richard Sutter	.03	.05
109	Brett Hull	.25	.50
110	David Christian	.03	.05
111	Brendan Shanahan	.12	.25
112	Vincent Riendeau, Goalie	.05	.10
113	Adam Oates	.12	.25
114	Jeff Brown	.03	.05

TORONTO MAPLE LEAFS

No.	Player	EX	NRMT
115	Gary Leeman	.03	.05
116	David Ellett	.03	.05
117	Grant Fuhr, Goalie	.05	.10
118	Daniel Marois	.03	.05
119	Michael Krushelnyski	.03	.05
120	Wendel Clark	.08	.15

VANCOUVER CANUCKS

No.	Player	EX	NRMT
121	Troy Gamble, Goalie	.03	.05
122	Robert Kron	.03	.05
123	Geoff Courtnall	.03	.05
124	Trevor Linden	.13	.25
125	Greg Adams	.03	.05
126	Igor Larionov	.03	.05

WASHINGTON CAPITALS

No.	Player	EX	NRMT
127	Kevin Hatcher	.03	.05
128	Mike Ridley	.03	.05
129	John Druce	.03	.05
130	Al Iafrate	.03	.05
131	Dino Ciccarelli	.03	.05
132	Michal Pivonka	.03	.05

WINNIPEG JETS

No.	Player	EX	NRMT
133	Fredrik Olausson	.03	.05
134	Ed Olczyk	.03	.05
135	Bob Essensa, Goalie	.03	.05
136	Pat Elynuik	.03	.05
137	Phil Housley	.03	.05
138	Thomas Steen	.03	.05

WASHINGTON CAPITALS

No.	Player	EX	NRMT
139	Don Beaupre, Goalie	.03	.05

CHAMPIONS

No.	Player	EX	NRMT
140	Adams Division Champions: Boston Bruins	.03	.05
141	Norris Division Champions: Chicago Black Hawks	.03	.05
142	Smythe Division Champions: Los Angeles Kings	.03	.05
143	Campbell Conference Champions: Minnesota North Stars	.03	.05
144	Stanley Cup Champions: Pittsburgh Penguins	.03	.05

TEAM COLOURS

No.	Player	EX	NRMT
145	Boston Bruins	.03	.05
146	Chicago Black Hawks	.03	.05
147	Detroit Red Wings	.03	.05
148	Montreal Canadiens	.03	.05
149	New York Rangers	.03	.05
150	Toronto Maple Leafs	.03	.05

1991-92 PLATINUM — PRO SET • 359

— SERIES TWO —

BOSTON BRUINS

No.	Player	EX	NRMT
151	Stephen Leach	.03	.05
152	Vladimir Ruzicka	.03	.05
153	Don Sweeney	.03	.05
154	Bob Carpenter	.03	.05
155	Brent Ashton	.03	.05
156	Gord Murphy	.03	.05

BUFFALO SABRES

No.	Player	EX	NRMT
157	Pat LaFontaine	.15	.30
158	Randy Hillier	.03	.05
159	Clint Malarchuk	.03	.05
160	Randy Wood	.03	.05

CALGARY FLAMES

No.	Player	EX	NRMT
161	Gary Roberts	.03	.05
162	Gary Leeman	.03	.05
163	Robert Reichel	.10	.20

CHICAGO BLACK HAWKS

No.	Player	EX	NRMT
164	Brent Sutter	.03	.05
165	Brian Noonan	.03	.05
166	Michel Goulet	.03	.05

DETROIT RED WINGS

No.	Player	EX	NRMT
167	Paul Ysebaert	.03	.05
168	Kevin Miller	.03	.05
169	Ray Sheppard	.03	.05
170	Brad McCrimmon	.03	.05

EDMONTON OILERS

No.	Player	EX	NRMT
171	Joe Murphy	.03	.05
172	Dave Manson	.03	.05
173	Scott Mellanby	.03	.05
174	Bernie Nicholls	.03	.05

HARTFORD WHALERS

No.	Player	EX	NRMT
175	John Cullen	.03	.05
176	Marc Bergevin	.03	.05
177	Steve Konroyd	.03	.05
178	Kay Whitmore, Goalie	.03	.05
179	Murray Craven	.03	.05
180	Mikael Andersson	.03	.05

LOS ANGELES KINGS

No.	Player	EX	NRMT
181	Bob Kudelski	.03	.05
182	Brian Benning	.03	.05
183	Mike Donnelly	.04	.08
184	Marty McSorley	.03	.05
185	Corey Millen, RC	.13	.25

MINNESOTA NORTH STARS

No.	Player	EX	NRMT
186	Ulf Dahlen	.03	.05
187	Brian Propp	.03	.05
188	Neal Broten	.03	.05
189	Mike Craig	.03	.05

MONTREAL CANADIENS

No.	Player	EX	NRMT
190	Stephan Lebeau	.08	.15
191	Mike Keane	.03	.05
192	Brent Gilchrist	.03	.05
193	Eric Desjardins	.03	.05

NEW JERSEY DEVILS

No.	Player	EX	NRMT
194	Peter Stastny	.03	.05
195	Claude Vilgrain	.03	.05
196	Claude Lemieux	.03	.05
197	Craig Billington, Goalie, RC	.08	.15
198	Alexei Kasatonov	.03	.05
199	Viacheslav Fetisov	.03	.05

NEW YORK ISLANDERS

No.	Player	EX	NRMT
200	Benoit Hogue	.03	.05
201	Derek King	.03	.05
202	Uwe Krupp	.03	.05
203	Steve Thomas	.03	.05

NEW YORK RANGERS

No.	Player	EX	NRMT
204	John Ogrodnick	.03	.05
205	Sergei Nemchinov	.08	.15
206	Jeff Beukeboom	.03	.05
207	Adam Graves	.10	.20

PHILADELPHIA FLYERS

No.	Player	EX	NRMT
208	Andrei Lomakin	.03	.05
209	Dan Quinn	.03	.05
210	Ken Wreggett, Goalie	.03	.05
211	Garry Galley	.03	.05
212	Terry Carkner	.03	.05

PITTSBURGH PENGUINS

No.	Player	EX	NRMT
213	Lawrence Murphy	.03	.05
214	Ron Francis	.03	.05
215	Bob Errey	.03	.05
216	Bryan Trottier	.03	.05

QUEBEC NORDIQUES

No.	Player	EX	NRMT
217	Mike Hough	.03	.05
218	Mikhail Tatarinov	.03	.05
219	Jacques Cloutier	.03	.05
220	Greg Paslawski	.03	.05
221	Alexei Gusarov, RC	.05	.10

ST. LOUIS BLUES

No.	Player	EX	NRMT
222	Ron Sutter	.03	.05
223	Garth Butcher	.03	.05
224	Paul Cavallini	.03	.05
225	Curtis Joseph, Goalie	.10	.20

SAN JOSE SHARKS

No.	Player	EX	NRMT
226	Jeff Hackett, Goalie	.03	.05
227	David Bruce, RC	.05	.10
228	Wayne Presley	.03	.05
229	Neil Wilkinson	.03	.05
230	Dean Evason	.03	.05

TORONTO MAPLE LEAFS

No.	Player	EX	NRMT
231	Brian Bradley	.03	.05
232	Peter Zezel	.03	.05
233	Mike Bullard	.03	.05
234	Doug Gilmour	.13	.25
235	Jamie Macoun	.03	.05

VANCOUVER CANUCKS

No.	Player	EX	NRMT
236	Cliff Ronning	.03	.05
237	Jyrki Lumme	.03	.05
238	Tom Fergus	.03	.05
239	Kirk McLean, Goalie	.05	.10
240	Sergio Momesso	.03	.05

WASHINGTON CAPITALS

No.	Player	EX	NRMT
241	Randy Burridge	.03	.05
242	Dimitri Khristich	.03	.05
243	Calle Johansson	.03	.05
244	Peter Bondra	.03	.05
245	Dale Hunter	.03	.05

WINNIPEG JETS

No.	Player	EX	NRMT
246	Darrin Shannon	.03	.05
247	Troy Murray	.03	.05
248	Teppo Numminen	.03	.05

PLATINUM PROSPECT - ROOKIES

No.	Player	EX	NRMT
249	Donald Audette, Buf.	.05	.10
250	Kevin Haller, Buf., RC	.08	.15
251	Alexander Godynyuk, Cal., RC	.03	.05
252	Dominik Hasek, Goalie, Chi., RC	.50	1.00
253	Nicklas Lidstrom, Det., RC	.25	.50
254	Vladimir Konstantinov, Det., RC	.13	.25
255	Josef Beranek, Edm., RC	.20	.40
256	Geoff Sanderson, Har., RC	.50	1.00
257	Peter Ahola, LA, RC	.03	.05
258	Derian Hatcher, Min.	.03	.05
259	John LeClair, Mon., RC	.10	.20
260	Kevin Todd, NJD, RC	.10	.20
261	Valeri Zelepukin, NJD, RC	.25	.50
262	Anthony Amonte, NYR, RC	.15	.30
263	Doug Weight, NYR, RC	.12	.25
264	Claude Boivin, Phi., RC	.05	.10
265	Corey Foster, Phi., RC	.03	.05
266	Jim Paek, Pit., RC	.08	.15
267	Claude Lapointe, Que., RC	.05	.10
268	Adam Foote, Que., RC	.03	.05
269	Nelson Emerson, St. L.	.15	.30
270	Arturs Irbe, Goalie, SJ	.25	.50
271	Pat Falloon, SJ	.25	.50
272	Pavel Bure, Van.	1.25	2.50
273	Stu Barnes, Win.	.03	.05
274	Russ Romaniuk, Win, RC	.05	.10
275	Luciano Borsato, Win., RC	.08	.15

PLATINUM ALL STAR

No.	Player	EX	NRMT
276	Allan MacInnis, Cal.	.03	.05
277	Sergei Fedorov, Det.	.13	.25
278	Raymond Bourque, Bos.	.03	.05
279	Mike Richter, Goalie, NYR	.03	.05
280	Campbell Conference	.03	.05
281	Wales Conference	.03	.05

PLATINUM PERFORMANCE

No.	Player	EX	NRMT
282	Brett Hull, St. L.	.08	.15
283	Alexander Mogilny, Buf.	.12	.25
284	Brian Leetch, NYR	.10	.20
285	Bob Essensa, Goalie, Win.	.03	.05
286	Derek King, NYI	.03	.05
287	Steve Larmer, Chi.	.03	.05
288	Chris Terreri, Goalie, NJD	.03	.05

CELEBRITY CAPTAINS

No.	Celebrity Captain	EX	NRMT
289	Terry O'Reilly, Bos.	.05	.10
290	Burton Cummins, Win.	.05	.10
291	Marv Albert, NYR	.15	.30
292	Larry King, Wash.	.15	.30
293	Jim Kelly, Buf.	.15	.30
294	David Wheaton, Min.	.05	.10
295	Ralph Macchio, NYI	.05	.10
296	Rick Hansen, Van.	.05	.10
297	Fred Rogers, Pit.	.10	.20
298	Gaetan Boucher, Que.	.05	.10
299	Susan Saint James, Har.	.08	.15
300	James Belushi, Chi.	.15	.30

— 1991 - 92 INSERT SET —

PLATINUM COLLECTIBLES

This insert set was included in packs of Pro Set Platinum Series One and Two. Series One included cards PC1 to PC10 and Series Two PC11 to PC20.

The cards PC1 to PC6 are a re-issue of 1990-91 "Player of the Month" cards, however this time the set is complete.

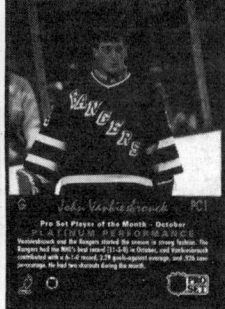

1991-92 Platinum Collectibles
Card No. PC1, John Vanbiesbrouck

Card Size: 2 1/2" X 3 1/2"
Face: Four colour, borderless, Pro Set Platinum Logo
Back: Four colour, Number, Resume
Imprint: Pro Set © NHL & NHLPA 1991
Complete Set No.: 20
Complete Set Price: 15.00 30.00

PLAYER OF THE MONTH

No.	Player	EX	NRMT
PC1	October: John Vanbiesbrouck, Goalie, NYR	1.25	2.50
PC2	November: Pete Peeters, Goalie, Phi.	.75	1.50
PC3	December: Tom Barrasso, Goalie, Pit.	.75	1.50
PC4	January: Wayne Gretzky, LA	3.00	6.00
PC5	February: Brett Hull, St. L.	2.00	4.00
PC6	March: Kelly Hrudey, Goalie, LA	.75	1.50

SENSATIONAL SOPHOMORE

No.	Player	EX	NRMT
PC7	Sergei Fedorov, Det.	2.50	5.00
PC8	Rob Blake, LA	.75	1.50
PC9	Kenneth Hodge, Jr., Bos.	.75	1.50
PC10	Eric Weinrich, NJD	.75	1.50

PLATINUM MILESTONE

No.	Player	EX	NRMT
PC11	Mike Gartner, NYR	1.25	2.50
PC12	Paul Coffey, Pit.	1.00	2.00
PC13	Bobby Smith, Min.	.75	1.50
PC14	Wayne Gretzy, LA	3.00	6.00
PC15	Michel Goulet, Chi.	.75	1.50
PC16	Mike Liut, Goalie, Wash.	.75	1.50
PC17	Brian Propp, Min.	.75	1.50
PC18	Denis Savard, Mon.	.75	1.50
PC19	Bryan Trottier, Pit.	.75	1.50
PC20	Mark Messier, NYR	1.75	3.50

— 1991 - 92 PLAYER OF THE MONTH —

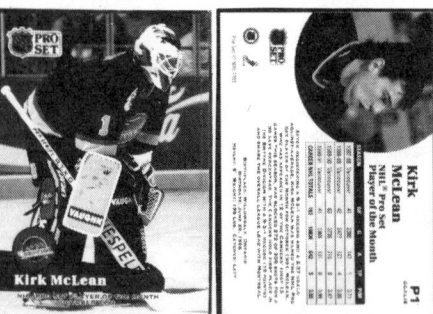

1991-92 Player of the Month
Card No. P1, Kirk McLean

For the 1991-92 season Pro Set again selected a "Player of the Month" and issued a card in recognition of this honour. The design is identical to the regular issue.

Card Size: 2 1/2" X 3 /12"
Face: Four colour, borderless; Pro Set and team logo
Back: Four colour, Number, Resume
Imprint: Pro Set © NHL 1991
Complete Set No.: 7
Complete Set Price: 60.00

No.	Player	EX	NRMT
P1	October: Kirk McLean, Goalie, Van.	5.00	10.00
P2	November: Kevin Stevens, Pit.	5.00	10.00
P3	December: Mario Lemieux, Pit.	10.00	20.00
P4	January: Pat LaFontaine, NYI	7.50	15.00
P5	January: Andrew Moog, Goalie, Bos.	5.00	10.00
P6	February: Luc Robitaille, LA	6.00	12.00

— 1992 PRO SET GAZETTE COLLECTIBLES —

The Gazette is published by Pro Set as a product information magazine. Initially the Gazette was produced twice a year but starting in 1992 the magazine became available three or four times a year.

Sample packs are inserted into the Gazette with each mailing. These packs can contain two types of cards: (1) "Promotional" which are regular issue cards from the various Pro Set products and (2) "Pro Set Gazette" cards. Produced specially for the Gazette only the Pro Set Gazette cards are listed here.

1992 Pro Set Gazette Collectibles
Card No. 2, Patrick Roy

Card Size: 2 1/2" X 3 /12"
Face: Four colour, borderless; Pro Set Gazette logo
Back: Four colour, Number, Resume
Imprint: Pro Set Inc. © NHL 1992 © NHLPA 1992
or © 1991 Pro Set In. © 1991 National Football League

No.	Player	EX	NRMT
2	Patrick Roy, Goalie, Mon.	5.00	10.00

— 1992 THE PUCK —
PROMOTIONAL CARDS

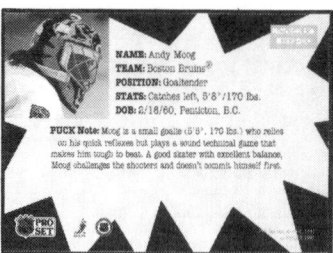

1991 The Puck, Promotional Cards
Andrew Moog (back)

Pro Set issued three "Puck" promotional cards with "Prototype for Review Only" printed on the back in place of numbering. These cards were issued in polyethylene packs to candy wholesalers as sample cards packaged with "Puck" candy bars.

Card Size: 2 1/2" X 3 1/2"
Face: Four colour, borderless, black stripe along bottom; Pro Set and Puck Logo
Back: Four colour, black on yellow, "PFRO", Resume
Imprint: Pro Set Inc. © NHL 1992 © NHLPA 1992

No.	Player	EX	NRMT
—	Andy Moog, Goalie, Bos.	2.50	5.00
—	Kirk McLean, Goalie, Van.	2.50	5.00
—	Patrick Verbeek, Har.	2.50	5.00

— SERIES ONE —

In 1992 Pro Set entered the candy business with the introduction of the "Puck", a chocolate, peanut and caramel candy shaped like a hockey puck. Packaged along with the "Puck" are three cards in a polyethylene pack designed specially as a premium for the candy product.

1992 The Puck
Card No. 1, Raymond Bourque

Card Size: 2 1/2" X 3 1/2"
Face: Four colour, borderless, Black Stripe along bottom; Pro Set and Puck Logo
Back: Four colour; Black on yellow; Number, Resume
Imprint: Pro Set Inc. © NHL 1992 © NHLPA 1992
Complete Set No.: 30
Complete Set Price: 12.50 25.00

No.	Player	EX	NRMT
1	Raymond Bourque, Bos.	.50	1.00
2	Andrew Moog, Goalie, Bos.	.13	.25
3	Doug Bodger, Buf.	.13	.25
4	Theoren Fleury, Cal.	.20	.40
5	Allan MacInnis, Cal.	.13	.25
6	Jeremy Roenick, Chi.	.60	1.25
7	Tim Cheveldae, Goalie, Det.	.13	.25
8	Steve Yzerman, Det.	.25	.50
9	Craig Simpson, Edm.	.13	.25
10	Patrick Verbeek, Har.	.13	.25
11	Wayne Gretzky, LA	2.50	5.00
12	Luc Robitaille, LA	.35	.75
13	Brian Bellows, Min.	.13	.25
14	Patrick Roy, Goalie, Mon.	2.00	4.00
15	Guy Carbonneau, Mon.	.13	.25
16	Peter Stastny, NJD	.13	.25
17	Adam Creighton, NYI	.13	.25
18	Glenn Healy, Goalie, NYI	.13	.25
19	Mark Messier, NYR	.35	.75
20	Rod Brind'Amour, Phi.	.13	.25
21	Paul Coffey, Pit., SP	1.75	3.50
22	Tom Barrasso, Goalie, Pit.	.20	.40
23	Joe Sakic, Que.	.25	.50
24	Brett Hull, St. L.	.75	1.50
25	Adam Oates, St. L.	.25	.50
26	Kelly Kisio, SJ	.13	.25
27	Grant Fuhr, Tor.	.20	.40
28	Kirk McLean, Goalie, Van.	.35	.75
29	Kevin Hatcher, Goalie, Wash.	.13	.25
30	Phil Housley, Win.	.13	.25

— 1992 - 93 REGULAR ISSUE —

This 270-card set includes all the major stars of the game. A relatively limited print run compared to previous years has enabled this set to maintain high price level.

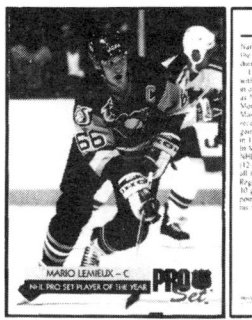

1992-93 Issue
Card No. 1, Mario Lemieux

Card Size: 2 1/2" x 3 1/2"
Face: Four Colour; Grey-white left border; Name, Team
Back: Four colour; Name, Number, Team, Resume
Imprint: PRINTED IN THE U.S.A. © 1992 PRO SET INC.
Complete Set No.: 270

	EX	NRMT
Complete Set Price:	18.00	35.00
Common Card:	.05	.10
Foil Pack:(15 Cards)	.50	1.00
Foil Box: (36 Packs)	17.50	35.00
Jumbo Pack: (31 Cards)	.75	1.50
Jumbo Box: (20 Packs)	17.50	35.00

NHL PRO SET PLAYER OF THE YEAR

No.	Player	EX	NRMT
1	Mario Lemieux, Pit.	.35	.75

GOALIE OF THE YEAR

No.	Player	EX	NRMT
2	Patrick Roy, Goalie, Mon.	.25	.50

BOSTON BRUINS

No.	Player	EX	NRMT
3	Adam Oates	.10	.20
4	Raymond Bourque	.10	.20
5	Vladimir Ruzicka	.05	.10
6	Stephen Leach	.05	.10
7	Andrew Moog, Goalie	.05	.10
8	Cam Neely	.10	.20
9	David Poulin	.05	.10
10	Glen Wesley	.05	.10
11	Gordon Murphy	.05	.10

BUFFALO SABRES

No.	Player	EX	NRMT
12	Dale Hawerchuk	.05	.10
13	Pat LaFontaine	.12	.25
14	Tom Draper, Goalie	.05	.10
15	David Andreychuk	.10	.25
16	Petr Svoboda	.05	.10
17	Doug Bodger	.05	.10
18	Donald Audette	.05	.10
19	Alexander Mogilny	.25	.50
20	Randy Wood	.05	.10

CALGARY FLAMES

No.	Player	EX	NRMT
21	Gary Roberts	.05	.10
22	Allan MacInnes	.05	.10
23	Theoren Fleury	.05	.10
24	Sergei Makarov	.05	.10
25	Michael Vernon, Goalie	.05	.10
26	Joe Nieuwendyke	.05	.10
27	Gary Suter	.05	.10
28	Joel Otto	.05	.10
29	Paul Ranheim	.05	.10

CHICAGO BLACK HAWKS

No.	Player	EX	NRMT
30	Jeremy Roenick	.35	.75
31	Steve Larmer	.05	.10
32	Michel Goulet	.05	.10
33	Ed Belfour, Goalie	.15	.30
34	Chris Chelios	.05	.10
35	Igor Kravchuk	.05	.10
36	Brent Sutter	.05	.10
37	James (Steve) Smith	.05	.10
38	Dirk Graham	.05	.10

DETROIT RED WINGS

No.	Player	EX	NRMT
39	Steve Yzerman	.15	.30
40	Sergei Fedorov	.35	.75
41	Paul Ysebaert	.05	.10
42	Nicklas Lidstrom	.07	.15
43	Tim Cheveldae, Goalie	.05	.10
44	Vladimir Konstantinov	.05	.10
45	Shawn Burr	.05	.10
46	Bob Probert	.05	.10
47	Ray Sheppard	.05	.10

EDMONTON OILERS

No.	Player	EX	NRMT
48	Kelly Buchberger	.05	.10
49	Joe Murphy	.05	.10
50	Norm Maciver	.05	.10
51	Bill Ranford, Goalie	.05	.10
52	Bernie Nicholls	.05	.10
53	Esa Tikkanen	.05	.10
54	Scott Mellanby	.05	.10
55	Dave Manson	.05	.10
56	Craig Simpson	.05	.10

HARTFORD WHALERS

No.	Player	EX	NRMT
57	John Cullen	.05	.10
58	Patrick Verbeek	.05	.10
59	Zarley Zalapski	.05	.10
60	Murray Craven	.05	.10
61	Robert Holik, (Traded to New Jersey)	.05	.10
62	Stephen Konroy	.05	.10
63	Geoff Sanderson	.25	.50
64	Frank Pietrangelo, Goalie	.05	.10
65	Bo Mikael Andersson, (Traded to Tampa Bay)	.05	.10

LOS ANGELES KINGS

No.	Player	EX	NRMT
66	Wayne Gretzky	1.00	2.00
67	Robert Blake	.05	.10
68	Jari Kurri	.05	.10
69	Martin McSorley	.05	.10
70	Kelly Hrudey, Goalie	.05	.10
71	Paul Coffey	.08	.15
72	Luc Robitaille	.12	.25
73	Peter Ahola	.05	.10
74	Tony Granato	.05	.10

MINNESOTA NORTH STARS

No.	Player	EX	NRMT
75	Derian Hatcher	.05	.10
76	Michael Modano	.20	.40
77	Dave Gagner	.05	.10
78	Mark Tinordi	.05	.10
79	Craig Ludwig	.05	.10
80	Ulf Dahlen	.05	.10
81	Bobby Smith	.05	.10
82	Jon Casey, Goalie	.05	.10
83	Jim Johnson	.05	.10

MONTREAL CANADIENS

No.	Player	EX	NRMT
84	Denis Savard	.05	.10
85	Patrick Roy, Goalie	.35	.75
86	Eric Desjardins	.05	.10
87	Kirk Muller	.05	.10
88	Guy Carbonneau	.05	.10
89	Shayne Corson, (Traded to Edmonton)	.05	.10
90	Brent Gilchrist, (Traded to Edmonton)	.05	.10
91	Mathieu Schneider	.05	.10
92	Gilbert Dionne	.05	.10

NEW JERSEY DEVILS

No.	Players	EX	NRMT
93	Stephane J. J. Richer	.05	.10
94	Kevin Todd	.05	.10
95	Scott Stevens	.08	.15
96	Viacheslav Fetisov	.05	.10
97	Chris Terreri, Goalie	.05	.10
98	Claude Lemieux	.05	.10
99	Bruce Driver	.05	.10
100	Peter Stastny	.05	.10
101	Alexei Kasatonov	.05	.10

NEW YORK ISLANDERS

No.	Players	EX	NRMT
102	Patrick Flatley	.05	.10
103	Adam Creighton, (Traded to Tampa Bay)	.05	.10
104	Pierre Turgeon	.12	.25
105	Ray Ferraro	.05	.10
106	Steve Thomas	.05	.10
107	Mark Fitzpatrick, Goalie	.05	.10
108	Benoit Hogue	.05	.10
109	Uwe Krupp	.05	.10
110	Derek King	.05	.10

NEW YORK RANGERS

No.	Player	EX	NRMT
111	Mark Messier	.12	.25
112	Brian Leetch	.20	.40
113	Michael Gartner	.10	.20
114	Darren Turcotte	.05	.10
115	Adam Graves	.15	.30
116	Mike Richter, Goalie	.10	.20
117	Sergei Nemchinov	.07	.15
118	Anthony Amonte	.10	.20
119	James Patrick	.05	.10

OTTAWA SENATORS

No.	Player	EX	NRMT
120	Andrew McBain	.05	.10
121	Rob Murphy	.05	.10
122	Mike Peluso	.05	.10
123	Sylvain Turgeon	.05	.10
124	Brad Shaw	.05	.10
125	Peter Sidorkiewicz, Goalie	.05	.10
126	Bradley Marsh	.05	.10
127	Mark Freer	.05	.10
128	Marc Fortier	.05	.10

PHILADELPHIA FLYERS

No.	Player	EX	NRMT
129	Ron Hextall, Goalie, (Traded to Quebec)	.05	.10
130	Claude Boivin	.05	.10
131	Mark Recchi	.20	.40
132	Rod Brind'Amour	.10	.20
133	Mike Ricci, (Traded to Quebec)	.07	.15
134	Kevin Dineen	.05	.10
135	Brian Benning	.05	.10
136	Kerry Huffman, (Traded to Quebec)	.05	.10
137	Steve Duchesne, (Traded to Quebec)	.05	.10

PITTSBURGH PENGUINS

No.	Player	EX	NRMT
138	Rick Tocchet	.05	.10
139	Mario Lemieux	.85	1.75
140	Kevin Stevens	.05	.10
141	Jaromir Jagr	.30	.60
142	Joe Mullen	.05	.10
143	Ulf Samuelsson	.05	.10
144	Ronald Francis	.05	.10
145	Tom Barrasso, Goalie	.05	.10
146	Lawrence Murphy	.05	.10

QUEBEC NORDIQUES

No.	Player	EX	NRMT
147	Alexei Gusarov	.05	.10
148	Valeri Kamensky	.15	.30
149	Mats Sundin	.18	.35
150	Joe Sakic	.18	.35
151	Claude LaPointe	.05	.10
152	Stephane Fiset, Goalie	.05	.10

362 • PRO SET — 1992 - 93 INSERT SETS —

No.	Player	EX	NRMT
153	Owen Nolan	.05	.10
154	Mike Hough	.05	.10
155	Gregory Paslawski	.05	.10

ST. LOUIS BLUES

No.	Player	EX	NRMT
156	Brett Hull	.30	.60
157	Craig Janney	.08	.15
158	Jeff Brown	.05	.10
159	Paul Cavallini	.05	.10
160	Garth Butcher	.05	.10
161	Nelson Emerson	.10	.20
162	Ronald Sutter	.05	.10
163	Brendan Shanahan	.12	.25
164	Curtis Joseph, Goalie	.12	.25

SAN JOSE SHARKS

No.	Player	EX	NRMT
165	Douglas Wilson	.05	.10
166	Pat Falloon	.17	.35
167	Kelly Kisio	.05	.10
168	Neil Wilkinson	.05	.10
169	Jay More	.05	.10
170	David Bruce	.05	.10
171	Jeff Hackett, Goalie	.05	.10
172	David Williams, RC	.05	.10
173	Brian Lawton	.05	.10

TAMPA BAY LIGHTNING

No.	Player	EX	NRMT
174	Brian Bradley	.05	.10
175	Jock Callander, RC	.05	.10
176	Basil McRae	.05	.10
177	George (Rob) Ramage	.05	.10
178	Pat Jablonski, Goalie	.05	.10
179	Joe Reekie	.05	.10
180	Douglas Crossman	.05	.10
181	Jim Benning	.05	.10
182	Kenneth Hodge Jr.	.05	.10

TORONTO MAPLE LEAFS

No.	Player	EX	NRMT
183	Grant Fuhr, Goalie	.07	.15
184	Douglas Gilmour	.18	.35
185	Glenn Anderson	.05	.10
186	David Ellett	.05	.10
187	Peter Zezel	.05	.10
188	Jamie Macoun	.05	.10
189	Wendel Clark	.10	.20
190	Bob Halkidis, RC	.05	.10
191	Rob Pearson	.07	.15

VANCOUVER CANUCKS

No.	Player	EX	NRMT
192	Pavel Bure	.75	1.50
193	Kirk McLean, Goalie	.12	.25
194	Sergio Momesso	.05	.10
195	Cliff Ronning	.05	.10
196	Jyrki Lumme	.05	.10
197	Trevor Linden	.10	.20
198	Geoff Courtnall	.05	.10
199	Doug Lidster	.05	.10
200	David Babych	.05	.10

WASHINGTON CAPITALS

No.	Player	EX	NRMT
201	Michal Pivonka	.05	.10
202	Dale Hunter	.05	.10
203	Calle Johansson	.05	.10
204	Kevin Hatcher	.05	.10
205	Al Iafrate	.05	.10
206	Donald Beaupre, Goalie	.05	.10
207	Randy Burridge	.05	.10
208	Dimitri Khristich	.05	.10
209	Peter Bondra	.05	.10

WINNIPEG JETS

No.	Player	EX	NRMT
210	Teppo Numminen	.05	.10
211	Bob Essensa, Goalie	.05	.10

No.	Player	EX	NRMT
212	Phil Housley	.05	.10
213	Ed Olczyk	.05	.10
214	Pat Elynuik, (Traded to Washington)	.05	.10
215	Troy Murray	.05	.10
216	Igor Ulanov	.05	.10
217	Thomas Steen	.05	.10
218	Darrin Shannon	.05	.10

1992 - 93 ROOKIES

No.	Player	EX	NRMT
219	Joseph Juneau, Bos.	.85	1.75
220	Steve Heinze, Bos.	.05	.10
221	Ted Donato, Bos.	.05	.10
222	Glen Murray, Bos.	.05	.10
223	Keith Carney, Buf., RC	.07	.15
224	Dean McAmmond, Chi., RC	.12	.25
225	Viacheslav Kozlov, Det.	.08	.15
226	Martin LaPointe, Det.	.05	.10
227	Patrick Poulin, Har.	.05	.10
228	Darryl Sydor, LA	.05	.10
229	Trent Klatt, Min., RC	.12	.25
230	Bill Guerin, NJ, RC	.12	.25
231	Jerrod Skalde, NJ	.05	.10
232	Scott Niedermayer, NJ	.18	.35
233	Marty McInnis, NYI	.05	.10
234	Scott Lachance, NYI	.08	.15
235	Dominic Roussel, Goalie, Phi.	.12	.25
236	Eric Lindros, Phi.	3.25	6.50
237	Shawn McEachern, Pit.	.12	.25
238	Martin Rucinsky, Que.	.08	.15
239	Bill Lindsay, Que., RC	.05	.10
240	Bret Hedican, St.L, RC	.10	.20
241	Ray Whitney, SJ, RC	.12	.25
242	Felix Potvin, Goalie, Tor.	1.00	2.00
243	Keith Tkachuk, Win.	.25	.50
244	Eugeny Davydov, Win. Error	.10	.20

STATISTICAL LEADERS

No.	Player	EX	NRMT
245	Goals Leader: Brett Hull, St.L	.12	.25
246	Assists Leader: Wayne Gretzky, LA	.35	.75
247	Short Handed Goals Leader: Steve Yzerman, Det.	.08	.15
248	Plus/Minus Leader: Paul Ysebaert, Det.	.05	.10
249	PP Goals Leader: David Andreychuk, Buf.	.05	.10
250	Goalie Wins Leader: Kirk McLean, Van.	.10	.20
251	Goalie Wins Leader: Tim Cheveldae, Det.	.05	.10
252	GW Goals Leader: Jeremy Roenick, Chi.	.10	.20

1991-92 NEWSREEL

No.	Player	EX	NRMT
253	NHL Pro Set Youth Clinic	.05	.10
254	NHL Pro Set Hockey Clinic	.05	.10
255	NHL All-Time Team	.05	.10

1991 - 92 MILESTONE

No.	Player	EX	NRMT
256	1,000th Pt/1000th Game: Michael Gartner, NYR	.05	.10
257	400th Goal: Brian Propp, Min.	.05	.10
258	1,000th Game: Dave Taylor, LA	.05	.10
259	1,000th Pt/1000th Game: Bobby Smith, Min.	.05	.10
260	400th Goal: Denis Savard, Mon.	.05	.10
261	1,000th Point: Raymond Bourque, Bos.	.05	.10
262	400th Goal: Joe Mullen, Pit.	.05	.10
263	1,000th Game: John Tonelli, Que.	.05	.10
264	1,000th Game: Bradley Marsh, Det.	.05	.10
265	1,000th Game: Randy Carlyle, Win.	.05	.10

PLAY SMART

No.	Player	EX	NRMT
266	Power: Mike Hough, Que.	.05	.10
267	Achieve: Bob Essensa, Goalie, Win.	.05	.10
268	Motivate: Mike Lalor, Win.	.05	.10
269	Attitude: Terry Carkner, Phi.	.05	.10
270	Responsibility: Todd Krygier, Wash.	.05	.10

— 1992 - 93 INSERT SETS —

AWARD WINNERS

This 5-card set numbered CC1-CC5 is a select group of the 91-92 NHL award winners. The cards were randomly inserted in the Pro Set foil packs. Each card is gold embossed with a "AWARD WINNER" logo.

1992-93 Insert Set, Award Winners
Card No. CC1, Mark Messier

Card Size: 2 1/2" x 3 1/2"
Face: Four colour, borderless
Back: Four colour with white border on card stock; Name, Resume
Imprint: © 1992 PRO SET INC. PRINTED IN THE U.S.A.
Common Set No.: 5
Complete Set Price: 15.00 30.00
Common Card: 1.50 3.00

No.	Player	EX	NRMT
CC1	Hart/Pearson Trophies: Mark Messier, NYR	2.00	4.00
CC2	Vezina/Jennings Trophies: Partick Roy, Goalie, Mon.	6.00	12.00
CC3	Calder Trophy: Pavel Bure, Van.	7.50	15.00
CC4	Norris Trophy: Brian Leetch, NYR	2.50	5.00
CC5	Selke Trophy: Guy Carbonneau, Mon.	1.50	3.00

1991 - 92 ROOKIE GOAL LEADERS

This 12-card set is the most desirable of the Pro-Set insert sets. The cards are numbered _ of 12 and were randomly inserted in the foil packs. Each card is gold embossed "1991-92 Rookie Goal Leader".

1991 Rookie Goal Leaders
Card No. 1, Anthony Amonte

Card Size: 2 1/2" x 3 1/2"
Face: Four colour, purple border
Back: Four colour on card stock
Imprint: © 1992 PRO SET INC. PRINTED IN THE U.S.A.
Common Set No.: 12
Complete Set Price: 22.50 45.00
Common Card: 1.75 3.50

No.	Player	EX	NRMT
1	Anthony Amonte, NYR	2.50	5.00
2	Pavel Bure, Van.	7.50	15.00
3	Donald Audette, Buf.	1.75	3.50
4	Pat Falloon, SJ	2.50	5.00
5	Nelson Emerson, St.L	2.50	5.00

No.	Player	EX	NRMT
6	Gilbert Dionne, Mon.	2.00	4.00
7	Kevin Todd, NJ.	1.75	3.50
8	Luciano Borsato, Win.	1.75	3.50
9	Rob Pearson, Tor.	2.00	4.00
10	Valeri Zelepukin, NJ	2.00	4.00
11	Geoff Sanderson, Har.	3.00	6.00
12	Claude LaPoint, Que.	1.75	3.50

1991 - 92 TEAM LEADERS

This 15-card set was another insert set in the Pro-Set series. The cards are numbered _ of 15. They were randomly inserted into the jumbo packs. Each card is gold embossed "1991-92 Team Leader".

1991-92 Team Leaders
Card No. 6, Wayne Gretzky

Card Size: 2-1/2" x 3-1/2"
Face: Four colour, borderless
Back: Four colour, black border; Campbell Conference logo
Imprint: © 1992 Pro Set Inc. Printed in the U.S.A.
Common Set No.: 15
Complete Set Price: 22.50 45.00
Common Card: .75 1.50

No.	Player	EX	NRMT
1	Gary Roberts, Cal.	.75	1.50
2	Jeremy Roenick, Chi.	2.50	5.00
3	Steve Yzerman, Det.	2.50	5.00
4	Nicklas Lidstrom, Det.	.75	1.50
5	Vincent Damphousse, Edm.	.75	1.50
6	Wayne Gretzky, LA	6.50	13.00
7	Michael Modano, Min.	2.00	4.00
8	Brett Hull, St.L	2.00	4.00
9	Nelson Emerson, St.L	.75	1.50
10	Pat Falloon, SJ	1.00	2.00
11	Douglas Gilmour, Tor.	3.00	6.00
12	Trevor Linden, Van.	1.00	2.00
13	Pavel Bure, Van.	6.00	12.00
14	Phil Housley, Win.	.75	1.50
15	Luciano Borsato, Win.	.75	1.50

1992 - 93 PARKHURST PREVIEWS

This 5-card set was randomly inserted in the Pro-Set foil packs, a marketing strategy to promote their 1992-93 Parkhurst cards.

1992-93 Parkhurst Previews
Card No. PV1, Paul Ysebaert

Card Size: 2 1/2" x 3 1/2"
Face: Four colour, turquoise marble left border; Name
Back: Four colour; Name, Number, Team, Resume, Bilingual
Imprint: © 1992 Pro Set Inc. Printed in the U.S.A.
Complete Set No. 5
Complete Set Price: 4.00 8.00
Common Card: .50 1.00

No.	Player	EX	NRMT
PV1	Paul Ysebaert, Det.	.50	1.00
PV2	Sean Burke, Goalie, Har.	.50	1.00
PV3	Gilbert Dionne, Mon.	1.00	2.00
PV4	Ken Hammond, Ott.	.50	1.00
PV5	Grant Fuhr, Goalie, Tor.	1.50	3.00

Pro Set 1991 Hockey Hall of Fame - Induction
Dinner and Ceremonies
Card No. 13, 1927 Ottawa Senators

SCORE

— 1990 AMERICAN PROMOTIONAL CARDS —

Card Size: 2 1/2" X 3 1/2"
Face: Four colour, White with red and blue striped border; Team logo
Back: Four colour on white card stock; Number, Resume, Canadian and U.S.A. flags
Imprint: © 1990 SCORE, PRINTED IN U.S.A.

No.	Player	EX	NRMT
1A	Wayne Gretzky, LA, Error "Catches"	75.00	100.00
1B	Wayne Gretzky, LA, Corrected "Shoots"	20.00	40.00
179	Jeremy Roenick, Chi.	15.00	30.00
200	Ray Bourque, Bos.	15.00	30.00

— 1990 CANADIAN PROMOTIONAL CARDS —

Promotional or prototype cards differ from the regular issue in various ways, however, identification is made easy by the NHL logo located on the back, bottom right. The logo is 6mm high on the regular issue and 8mm on the promotional cards.

Card Size: 2 1/2" X 3 1/2"
Face: Four colour, white with red and blue striped border, Team logo
Back: Four colour on white card stock, Number, Resume
Imprint: © 1990 SCORE, PRINTED IN U.S.A.

No.	Player	USA NRMT	Can. NRMT
10	Patrick Roy, Goalie, Mon.	25.00	50.00
40	Gary Leeman, Tor.	12.50	25.00
100A	Mark Messier, Edm.	15.00	30.00
100B	Mark Messier, Edm.	15.00	30.00

— 1990-91 REGULAR ISSUE —

Score issued two versions of their regular set for 1990/91. The Canadian set has English and French backs while the American set has only English. The two versions are not identical. Cards 301 to 310 vary between the sets. Only the factory sets (both Canadian and American) contain the Lindros subset. The Canadian set was produced in smaller quantities. The Score logo on top right is red, the American is blue.

 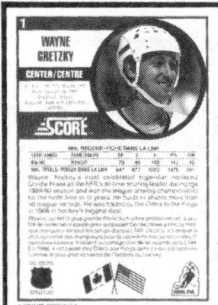

1990-91 Issue
Card No. 1, Wayne Gretzky

Card Size: 2 1/2" X 3 1/2"
Face: Four colour, white with red and blue striped border, Score logo, Team logo
Back: Four colour on white card stock, Number, Resume, Position, Canadian and U.S.A. flags
Imprint: © 1990 SCORE, PRINTED IN U.S.A.

		USA	CAN.
Complete Set No.:	440		
Complete Set Price:		20.00	25.00
Factory Set No.:	445		
Factory Set Price:		35.00	50.00
Common Player:		.05	.05
Foil Pack: (15 Cards)		1.00	1.50
Foil Box: (36 Packs)		35.00	50.00
Foil Case: (20 Boxes)		600.00	900.00

No.	Player	USA NRMT	Can. NRMT
1	Wayne Gretzky, LA	1.00	1.25
2	Mario Lemieux, Pit.	1.00	1.25
3	Steve Yzerman, Det.	.30	.40
4	Cam Neely, Bos.	.20	.25
5	Allan MacInnis, Cal.	.05	.05
6	Paul Coffey, Pit.	.10	.10
7	Brian Bellows, Min.	.05	.05
8	Joe Sakic, Que.	.60	.50
9	Bernie Nicholls, NYR	.05	.05
10	Patrick Roy, Goalie, Mon.	.50	.60
11	Doug Houda, Det., RC	.05	.05
12	David Volek, NYI	.05	.05
13	Esa Tikkanen, Edm.	.05	.05
14	Thomas Steen, Win.	.05	.05
15	Chris Chelios, Mon.	.05	.05
16	Robert Carpenter, Bos.	.05	.05
17	Dirk Graham, Chi.	.05	.05
18	Garth Butcher, Van.	.05	.05
19	Patrik Sundstrom, NJ	.05	.05
20	Rod Langway, Wash.	.05	.05
21	Scott Young, Har.	.05	.05
22	Ulf Dahlen, Min.	.05	.05
23	Michael Ramsey, Buf.	.05	.05
24	Peter Zezel, St. L.	.05	.05
25	Ron Hextall, Goalie, Phi.	.05	.05
26	Stephen Duchesne, LA	.05	.05
27	Allan Bester, Goalie, Tor.	.05	.05
28	Everett Sanipass, Que., RC	.05	.05
29	Steve Konroyd, Chi.	.05	.05
30	Joe Nieuwendyk, Cal.	.15	.15
31	Brent Ashton, Win.	.05	.05
32	Trevor Linden, Van.	.25	.30
33	Mike Ridley, Wash.	.05	.05
34	Sean Burke, Goalie, NJ	.05	.05
35	Patrick Verbeek, Har.	.05	.05
36	George (Rob) Ramage, Tor.	.05	.05
37	Kelly Kisio, NYR	.05	.05
38A	Craig Muni, Edm., "Without helmet"	.05	.05
38B	Craig Muni, Edm., "With helmet"	.05	.05
39	Brent Sutter, NYI	.05	.05
40	Gary Leeman, Tor.	.05	.05
41	Jeff Brown, St. L.	.05	.05
42	Greg Millen, Goalie, Chi.	.05	.05
43	Alexander Mogilny, Buf., RC	1.00	1.25
44	Dale Hunter, Wash.	.05	.05
45	Randy Moller, NYI	.05	.05
46	Peter Sidorkiewicz, Goalie, Har.	.05	.05
47	Terry Carkner, Phi.	.05	.05
48	Tony Granato, LA	.05	.10
49	Shawn Burr, Det.	.05	.05
50	Dale Hawerchuk, Win.	.05	.05
51	Don Sweeney, Bos., RC	.05	.05
52	Michael Vernon, Goalie, Cal., Error	.05	.05
53	Kevin Stevens, Pit., RC	.75	.90
54	Bryan Fogarty, Que., RC	.05	.05
55	Dan Quinn, Van.	.05	.05
56	Murray Craven, Phi.	.05	.05
57	Shawn Chambers, Min.	.05	.05
58	Craig Simpson, Edm	.05	.05
59	Douglas Crossman, NYI	.05	.05
60	Daren Puppa, Goalie, Buf.	.05	.05
61	Robert Smith, Mon.	.05	.05
62	Viacheslav Fetisov, NJ, RC	.10	.10
63	Gino Cavallini, St. L.	.05	.05
64	Jimmy Carson, Det.	.05	.05
65	David Ellett, Win.	.05	.05
66	Steve Thomas, Chi.	.05	.05
67	Mike Lalor, St. L., RC	.05	.05
68	Michael Liut, Goalie, Wash.	.05	.05
69	Thomas Laidlaw, LA	.05	.05
70	Ronald Francis, Har.	.05	.05
71	Sergei Makarov, Cal., RC	.30	.40
72	Randy Burridge, Bos.	.05	.05
73	Doug Lidster, Van.	.05	.05
74	Mike Richter, Goalie, NYR, RC	1.00	1.25
75	Stephane J. J. Richer, Mon.	.05	.05
76	Randy Hillier, Pit.	.05	.05
77	Christian Ruuttu, Buf.	.05	.05
78	Marc Fortier, Que.	.05	.05
79	Bill Ranford, Goalie, Edm.	.05	.05
80	Rick Tocchet, Phi.	.05	.05
81	Fredrik Olausson, Win.	.05	.05

No.	Player	USA NRMT	Can. NRMT
82	Adam Creighton, Chi.	.05	.05
83	Sylvain Cote, Har.	.05	.05
84	Brian Mullen, NYR	.05	.05
85	Adam Oates, St. L.	.15	.15
86	Gary Nylund, NYI	.05	.05
87	Tim Cheveldae, Goalie, Det., RC	.30	.40
88	Gary Suter, Cal.	.05	.05
89	John Tonelli, LA	.05	.05
90	Kevin Hatcher, Wash.	.05	.05
91	Guy Carbonneau, Mon.	.05	.05
92	Curtis Leschyshyn, Que., RC	.05	.05
93	Kirk McLean, Goalie, Van.	.25	.35
94	Curt Giles, Min.	.05	.05
95	Vincent Damphousse, Tor.	.05	.05
96	Peter Stastny, NJ	.05	.05
97	Glen Wesley, Bos.	.05	.05
98	David Shaw, NYR	.05	.05
99	Brad Shaw, Har., RC	.05	.05
100	Mark Messier, Edm.	.25	.35
101	Richard Zombo, Det., RC	.05	.05
102A	Mark Fitzpatrick, Goalie, NYI, RC, Error	.25	30
102B	Mark Fitzpatrick, Goalie, NYI, RC, Corrected	.05	.05
103	Richard Vaive, Buf.	.05	.05
104	Mark Osborne, Tor.	.05	.05
105	Rob Brown, Pit.	.05	.05
106	Gary Roberts, Cal.	.20	.30
107	Vincent Riendeau, Goalie, St. L., RC	.15	.20
108	Dave Gagner, Min.	.05	.05
109	Bruce Driver, NJ	.05	.05
110	Pierre Turgeon, Buf.	.30	.40
111	Claude Lemieux, Mon.	.05	.05
112	Bob Essensa, Goalie, Win., RC	.25	.35
113	John Ogrodnick, NYR	.05	.05
114	Glenn Anderson, Edm.	.05	.05
115	Kelly Hrudey, Goalie, LA	.05	.05
116	Sylvain Turgeon, NJ	.05	.05
117	Gordon Murphy, Phi., RC	.05	.05
118	Craig Janney, Bos.	.20	.25
119	Randy Wood, NYI	.05	.05
120	Michael Modano, Min., RC	.85	1.00
121	Tom Barrasso, Goalie, Pit.	.05	.05
122	Daniel Marois, Tor.	.05	.05
123	Igor Larionov, Van., RC	.25	.35
124	Geoff Courtnall, Wash.	.05	.05
125	Denis Savard, Chi.	.05	.05
126	Ron Tugnutt, Goalie, Que.	.05	.05
127	Mathieu Schneider, Mon., RC	.20	.25
128	Joel Otto, Cal.	.05	.05
129	James (Steve) Smith, Edm.	.05	.05
130	Michael Gartner, NYR	.05	.05
131	Rod Brind'Amour, St. L., RC	.50	.65
132	Jyrki Lumme, Van., RC	.15	.20
133	Mike Foligno, Buf.	.05	.05
134	Ray Ferraro, Har.	.05	.05
135	Steve Larmer, Chi.	.05	.05
136	Randy Carlyle, Win.	.05	.05
137	Tony Tanti, Pit.	.05	.05
138	Jeff Chychrun, Phi., RC	.05	.05
139	Gerald Diduck, NYI	.05	.05
140	Andrew Moog, Goalie, Bos.	.05	.05
141	Paul Gillis, Que.	.05	.05
142	Tom Kurvers, Tor.	.05	.05
143	Bob Probert, Det.	.05	.05
144	Neal Broten, Min.	.05	.05
145	Phil Housley, Buf.	.05	.05
146	Brendan Shanahan, NJ	.25	.35
147	Robert Rouse, Wash.	.05	.05
148	Russell Courtnall, Mon.	.05	.05
149	Normand Rochefort, NYR	.05	.05
150	Luc Robitaille, LA	.55	.05
151	Curtis Joseph, Goalie, St. L., RC	.85	1.00
152	Ulf Samuelsson, Har.	.05	.05
153	Ronald Sutter, Phi.	.05	.05
154	Petri Skriko, Van.	.05	.05
155	Douglas Gilmour, Cal.	.40	.50
156	Paul Fenton, Win.	.05	.05
157	Jeff Norton, NYI	.05	.05
158	Jari Kurri, Edm.	.05	.05
159	Rejean Lemelin, Goalie, Bos.	.05	.05
160	Kirk Muller, NJ	.05	.05

1990 - 91 REGULAR ISSUE — SCORE • 365

No.	Player	USA NRMT	Can. NRMT
161	Keith Brown, Chi.	.05	.05
162	Aaron Broten, Min.	.05	.05
163	**Adam Graves, Edm., RC**	**.85**	**1.00**
164	John Cullen, Pit.	.05	.05
165	Craig Ludwig, Mon.	.05	.05
166	David Taylor, LA	.05	.05
167	**Craig Wolanin, Que., RC**	**.05**	**.05**
168	Kelly Miller, Wash.	.05	.05
169	Uwe Krupp, Buf.	.05	.05
170	Kevin Lowe, Edm.	.05	.05
171	Wendel Clark, Tor.	.15	.20
172	Dave Babych, Har.	.05	.05
173	Paul Reinhart, Van.	.05	.05
174	Patrick Flatley, NYI	.05	.05
175	John Vanbiesbrouck, Goalie, NYR	.05	.05
176	**Teppo Numminen, Win., RC**	**.15**	**.20**
177	Tim Kerr, Phi.	.05	.05
178	Ken Daneyko, NJ	.05	.05
179	**Jeremy Roenick, Chi., RC**	**1.75**	**2.50**
180	Gerard Gallant, Det.	.05	.05
181	Allen Pedersen, Bos.	.05	.05
182	Jon Casey, Goalie, Min.	.05	.05
183	Tomas Sandstrom, LA	.05	.05
184	Byron (Brad) McCrimmon, Cal.	.05	.05
185	Paul Cavallini, St. L.	.05	.05
186	**Mark Recchi, Pit., RC**	**.85**	**1.00**
187	Michel Petit, Que.	.05	.05
188	Scott Stevens, Wash.	.05	.05
189	David Andreychuk, Buf.	.15	.20
190	John MacLean, NJ	.05	.05
191	Petr Svoboda, Mon.	.05	.05
192	Dave Tippett, Har.	.05	.05
193	Dave Manson, Chi.	.05	.05
194	James Patrick, NYR	.05	.05
195	Al Iafrate, Tor.	.05	.05
196	Douglas Smail, Win.	.05	.05
197	Kjell Samuelsson, Phi.	.05	.05
198	Brian Bradley, Van.	.05	.05
199	Charles Huddy, Edm.	.05	.05
200	Raymond Bourque, Bos.	.20	.30
201	**Joey Kocur, Det., RC**	**.05**	**.05**
202	Jim Johnson, Pit., Error	.05	.05
203	Paul MacLean, St. L.	.05	.05
204	Timothy Watters, LA	.05	.05
205	Pat Elynuik, Win.	.05	.05
206	Lawrence Murphy, Min.	.05	.05
207	**Claude Loiselle, Que., RC**	**.05**	**.05**
208	Joe Mullen, Cal.	.05	.05
209	**Alexei Kasatonov, NJ, RC**	**.15**	**.20**
210	Ed Olczyk, Tor.	.05	.05
211	Doug Bodger, Buf.	.05	.05
212	Kevin Dineen, Har.	.05	.05
213	Shayne Corson, Mon.	.05	.05
214	Steve Chiasson, Det.	.05	.05
215	Don Beaupre, Goalie, Wash.	.05	.05
216	Jamie Macoun, Cal.	.05	.05
217	David Poulin, Bos.	.05	.05
218	Zarley Zalapski, Pit.	.05	.05
219	Bradley Marsh, Tor.	.05	.05
220	Mark Howe, Phi.	.05	.05
221	Michel Goulet, Chi.	.05	.05
222	**Hubie McDonough, NYI, RC**	**.05**	**.05**
223	Frantisek Musil, Min.	.05	.05
224	**Sergio Momesso, St. L., RC**	**.10**	**.15**
225	Brian Leetch, NYR	.50	.65
226	Theoren Fleury, Cal.	.25	.35
227	Michael Krushelnyski, LA	.05	.05
228	Glen Hanlon, Goalie, Det.	.05	.05
229	Mario Marois, Que.	.05	.05
230	Dino Ciccarelli, Wash.	.05	.05
231A	Dave McLlwain, Win., Error	.05	.05
231B	Dave McLlwain, Win., Corrected	.05	.05
232	Petr Klima, Edm.	.05	.05
233	**Grant Ledyard, Buf., RC**	**.05**	**.05**
234	Phil Bourque, Pit.	.05	.05
235	Robert Sweeney, Bos.	.05	.05
236	Luke Richardson, Tor.	.05	.05
237	**Todd Krygier, Har., RC**	**.05**	**.05**
238	Brian Skrudland, Mon.	.05	.05
239	**Chris Terreri, Goalie, NJ, RC**	**.25**	**.35**
240	Greg Adams, Van.	.05	.05
241	**Darren Turcotte, NYR, RC**	**.25**	**.35**

No.	Player	USA NRMT	Can. NRMT
242	Scott Mellanby, Phi.	.05	.05
243	Troy Murray, Chi.	.05	.05
244	Robert (Stewart) Gavin, Min.	.05	.05
245	Gordon Roberts, St. L.	.05	.05
246	**John Druce, Wash., RC**	**.05**	**.05**
247	Stephen Kasper, LA	.05	.05
248	**Paul Ranheim, Cal., RC**	**.10**	**.15**
249	Greg Paslawski, Win.	.05	.05
250	Pat LaFontaine, NYI.	.25	.35
251	Scott Arniel, Buf.	.05	.05
252	Bernie Federko, Det.	.05	.05
253	**Garry Galley, Bos., RC**	**.25**	**.35**
254	Carey Wilson, NYR	.05	.05
255	Bob Errey, Pit.	.05	.05
256	Anthony Hrkac, Que.	.05	.05
257	Andrew McBain, Van.	.05	.05
258	Craig MacTavish, Edm.	.05	.05
259A	Dean Evason, Har., Error	.05	.05
259B	Dean Evason, Har., Corrected	.05	.05
260	Larry Robinson, LA	.05	.05
261	Basil McRae, Min.	.05	.05
262	**Stephan Lebeau, Mon., RC**	**.35**	**.45**
263	Ken Wregget, Goalie, Phi.	.05	.05
264	Gregory Gilbert, Chi.	.05	.05
265	**Ken Baumgartner, NYI, RC**	**.10**	**.15**
266	Lou Franceschetti, Tor., RC	.05	.05
267	Richard Meagher, Pit.	.05	.05
268	**Michal Pivonka, Wash., RC**	**.25**	**.35**
269	Brian Propp, Bos.	.05	.05
270	Bryan Trottier, NYI	.05	.05
271	Martin McSorley, LA	.05	.05
272	Jan Erixon, NYR	.05	.05
273	**Vladimir Krutov, Van., RC**	**.05**	**.05**
274	Dana Murzyn, Cal.	.05	.05
275	Grant Fuhr, Goalie, Edm.	.05	.05
276	Randy Cunneyworth, Har.	.05	.05
277	John Chabot, Det.	.05	.05
278	Walter Poddubny, NJ	.05	.05
279	Stephen Leach, Wash.	.05	.05
280	Douglas Wilson, Chi.	.05	.05
281	Richard Sutter, St. L.	.05	.05
282	Stephane Beauregard, Goalie, Win., RC, Error	.10	.15
283	John Carter, Bos., RC	.05	.05
284	Don Barber, Min., RC	.05	.05
285	Tom Fergus, Tor.	.05	.05
286	Ilkka Sinisalo, Phi.	.05	.05
287	Kevin McClelland, Det.	.05	.05
288	**Troy Mallette, NYR, RC**	**.05**	**.05**
289	Clint Malarchuk, Goalie, Buf.	.05	.05
290	Guy Lafleur, Que.	.05	.05
291	Robert Joyce, Wash.	.05	.05
292	Trent Yawney, Chi.	.05	.05
293	**Joe Murphy, Edm., RC**	**.25**	**.35**
294	**Glenn Healy, Goalie, NYI, RC**	**.25**	**.35**
295	Dave Christian, Bos.	.05	.05
296	Paul MacDermid, Win.	.05	.05
297	**Todd Elik, LA, RC**	**.20**	**.25**
298	**Wendell Young, Goalie, Pit., RC**	**.05**	**.05**
299	**Edward (Dean) Kennedy, Buf., RC**	**.05**	**.05**
300	Brett Hull, St. L.	.60	.75

AMERICAN CARDS 301 TO 311

No.	Player	USA NRMT
301	Keith Acton, Phi.	.05
302	Yvon Corriveau	.10
303	Donald Maloney, NYI	.05
304	**Mark Tinordi, Min., RC**	**.15**
305	**Bob Kudelski, LA, RC**	**.10**
306	Brian Benning, LA	.08
307	Alan Kerr, NYI	.05
308	Per-Erik Eklund, Phi.	.15
309	Calle Johansson, Goalie, Wash.	.08
310	David Maley, NJ	.10
311	Christopher Nilan, NYR	.08

CANADIAN CARDS 301 TO 311

No.	Player	Can. NRMT
301	**Martin Gelinas, Edm., RC**	**.35**
302	Eric Nattress, Cal.	.08

No.	Player	Can. NRMT
303	Jim Sandlak, Van.	.08
304	Brian Hayward, Goalie, Mon.	.08
305	Joe Cirella, Que.	.08
306	Randall Gregg, Edm.	.08
307	**Sylvain Lefebvre, Mon., RC**	**.10**
308	**Mark Lamb, Edm., RC**	**.15**
309	Richard Wamsley, Goalie, Cal.	.08
310	Maurice Mantha, Win.	.10
311	Anthony McKegney, Que.	.08

ALL STARS

First Team

No.	Player	USA NRMT	Can. NRMT
312	Patrick Roy, Goalie, Mon.	.25	.35
313	Raymond Bourque, Bos.	.05	.05
314	Allan MacInnis, Cal.	.05	.05
315	Mark Messier, Edm.	.05	.05
316	Luc Robitaille, LA	.05	.05
317	Brett Hull, St. L.	.25	.35

Second Team

No.	Player	USA NRMT	Can. NRMT
318	Daren Puppa, Goalie, Buf.	.05	.05
319	Paul Coffey, Pit.	.05	.05
320	Douglas Wilson, Chi.	.05	.05
321	Wayne Gretzky, LA	.25	.35
322	Brian Bellows, Min.	.05	.05
323	Cam Neely, Bos.	.05	.05

ROOKIE TEAM

No.	Player	USA NRMT	Can. NRMT
324	**Bob Essensa, Goalie, Win., RC**	**.10**	**.15**
325	**Brad Shaw, Har., RC**	**.05**	**.05**
326	**Geoff Smith, Edm., RC**	**.05**	**.05**
327	**Michael Modano, Min., RC**	**.25**	**.35**
328	**Rod Brind'Amour, St. L., RC**	**.15**	**.20**
329	**Sergei Makarov, Cal., RC**	**.05**	**.05**

AMERICAN HOBBEY BAKER

No.	Player	USA NRMT
330	Kip Miller	.30

MEMORIAL CUP CHAMPIONS

No.	Team	Can. NRMT
330	Oshawa Generals	1.00

STANLEY CUP CHAMPIONS

No.	Team	USA NRMT	Can. NRMT
331	Edmonton Oilers	.05	.05
332	Paul Coffey, Pit., Speedster	.05	.05
333	Michael Gartner, NYR, Speedster	.05	.05
334	Al Iafrate, Tor., Blaster	.05	.05
335	Allan MacInnis, Cal., Blaster	.05	.05
336	Wayne Gretzky, LA, Sniper	.25	.35
337	Mario Lemieux, Pit., Sniper	.25	.35
338	Wayne Gretzky, LA, Magician	.25	.35
339	Steve Yzerman, Det., Magician	.05	.05
340	Cam Neely, Bos., Banger	.05	.05
341	Scott Stevens, Wash., Banger	.05	.05
342	Esa Tikkanen, Edm., Shadow	.05	.05
343	Jan Erixon, NYR, Shadow	.05	.05
344	Patrick Roy, Goalie, Mon., Stopper	.20	.20
345	Bill Ranford, Goalie, Edm., Stopper	.05	.05

1990 RECORD SETTERS

No.	Player	USA NRMT	Can. NRMT
346	Brett Hull, St. L.	.25	.35
347	Wayne Gretzky, LA	.25	.35
348	Jari Kurri, Edm.,	.05	.05

1990 SEASON LEADERS

No.	Player	USA NRMT	Can. NRMT
349	Plus - Minus: Paul Cavallini, St. L.	.05	.05
350	Rookie Points: Sergei Makarov, Cal.	.05	.05
351	Goals: Brett Hull, St. L.	.25	.35
352	Assists: Wayne Gretzky, LA	.25	.35
353	Points: Wayne Gretzky, LA	.25	.35
354	Goals Against Average: Patrick Roy/Mike Liut	.20	.30

HALL OF FAMER

No.	Player	USA NRMT	Can. NRMT
355	Gilbert Perreault, Buf.	.05	.05
356	Bill Barber, Phi.	.05	.05
357	Fern Flaman, Bos./Tor.	.05	.05

TROPHY WINNERS

No.	Player	USA NRMT	Can. NRMT
358	The Conn Smythe Trophy: Bill Ranford, Goalie, Edm.	.05	.05
359	The Frank J. Selke Trophy: Richard Meagher, St.L.	.05	.05
360	The Hart Memorial Trophy: Mark Messier, Edm.	.05	.05
361	The Art Ross Trophy: Wayne Gretzky, LA	.25	.35
362	The Calder Memorial Trophy: Sergei Makarov, Cal.	.05	.05
363	The James Norris Memorial Trophy: Ray Bourque, Bos.	.05	.05
364	The Vezina Trophy: Patrick Roy	.20	.30
365	The William M. Jennings Trophy: Rejean Lemelin / Andrew Moog, Bos.	.05	.05
366	The Lady Byng Memorial Trophy: Brett Hull, St.L	.20	.30
367	The Bill Masterton Memorial Trophy: Gordon Kluzak, Bos.	.05	.05

1990 CONFERENCE CHAMPIONS

No.	Team	USA NRMT	Can. NRMT
368	Prince of Wales Conference: Boston Bruins	.05	.05
369	Campbell Conference: Edmonton Oilers	.05	.05

REGULAR ISSUE

No.	Player	USA NRMT	Can. NRMT
370	Adam Burt, Har., RC	.05	.05
371	Troy Loney, Pit., RC	.05	.05
372	Dave Chyzowski, NYI, RC	.05	.05
373	Geoff Smith, Edm., RC	.05	.05
374	Stanley Smyl, Van.	.05	.05
375	Gaetan Duchesne, Min.	.05	.05
376	Bob Murray, Chi., LC	.05	.05
377	Daniel Shank, Det., RC	.05	.10
378	Tommy Albelin, NJ	.05	.05
379	Perry Berezan, Min., RC	.05	.05
380	Ken Linseman, Phi.	.05	.05

NHL PROSPECT '90

No.	Player	USA NRMT	Can. NRMT
381	Stephane Matteau, Cal., RC	.20	.30
382	Mario Thyer, Min., RC	.05	.05
383	Nelson Emerson, St. L., RC	.75	.90
384	Kory Kocur, Det., RC	.05	.05
385	Bob Beers, Bos., RC	.10	.15
386	Jim Hrivnak, Goalie, Wash., RC	.15	.20
387	Mark Pederson, Mon., RC	.05	.05
388	Jeff Hackett, Goalie, NYI, RC	.15	.20
389	Eric Weinrich, NJ, RC	.15	.20
390	Steven Rice, NYR, RC	.15	.20
391	Stu Barnes, Win., RC	.15	.20
392	Olaf Kolzig, Goalie, Wash., RC	.15	.20
393	Francois Leroux, Edm., RC	.05	.05
394	Adrien Plavsic, Van., RC	.05	.05
395	Michel Mongeau, St. L., RC	.05	.05
396	Rick Corriveau, St. L., RC	.05	.05
397	Wayne Doucet, NYI, RC	.05	.05

No.	Player	USA NRMT	Can. NRMT
398	Mats Sundin, Que., RC	1.00	1.25
399	Murray Baron, Phi., RC	.05	.05
400	Rick Bennett, NYR, RC	.05	.05
401	Jon Morris, NJ, RC	.05	.05
402	Kay Whitmore, Goalie, Har., RC	.15	.20
403	Peter Lappin, Min., RC	.05	.05
404	Kris Draper, Win. RC	.05	.05
405	Shayne Stevenson, Bos., RC	.05	.05
406	Paul Ysebaert, NJ, RC	.10	.15
407A	Jimmy Waite, Goalie, Chl., RC, Error	.40	.50
407B	Jimmy Waite, Goalie, Chi., RC, Corrected	.10	.15
408	Cam Russell, Chi., RC	.05	.05
409	Kim Issel, Edm., RC	.05	.05
410	Darrin Shannon, Buf., RC	.15	.20
411	Link Gaetz, Min., RC	.05	.05
412	Craig Fisher, Phi., RC	.05	.05
413	Bruce Hoffort, Goalie, Phi., RC	.05	.05
414	Peter Ing, Goalie, Tor., RC	.05	.05
415	Stephane Fiset, Goalie, Que., RC	.25	.35
416	Dominic Lavoie, St. L., RC	.05	.05
417	Steve Maltais, Wash., RC	.05	.05
418	Wes Walz, Bos., RC	.20	.25
419	Terry Yake, Har., RC	.25	.35
420	Jamie Leach, Pit., RC	.05	.05
421	Rob Blake, LA, RC	.50	.60
422	Andrew Cassels, Mon., RC	.25	.35
423	Marc Bureau, Cal., RC	.05	.05

FIRST ROUND DRAFT CHOICE 1990

No.	Player	USA NRMT	Can. NRMT
424	Scott Allison, Edm., RC	.05	.10
425	Darryl Sydor, LA, RC	.25	.35
426	Turner Stevenson, Mon., RC	.15	.20
427	Brad May, Buf., RC	.25	.35
428	Jaromir Jagr, Pit., RC	1.00	1.25
429	Shawn Antoski, Van., RC	.10	.15
430	Derian Hatcher, Min., RC	.20	.25
431	Mark Greig, Har., RC	.10	.15
432	Scott Scissons, NYI, RC	.05	.05
433	Mike Ricci, Phi., RC	.50	.60
434	Drake Berehowsky, Tor., RC	.30	.40
435	Owen Nolan, Que., RC	.50	.60
436	Keith Primeau, Det., RC	.30	.40
437	Karl Dykhuis, Chi., RC	.05	.05
438	Trevor Kidd, Goalie, Cal., RC	.30	.40
439	Martin Brodeur, Goalie, NJ, RC	1.75	2.50

FUTURE SUPERSTAR

No.	Player	USA NRMT	Can. NRMT
440	Eric Lindros, Osh. Gen.	12.00	20.00

ERIC LINDROS

The Eric Lindros cards B1 to B5 were not available in wax packs, only in factory sets. They were the same in both the American and Canadian sets.

No.	Player	USA NRMT	Can. NRMT
B1	Eric Lindros, Osh. Gen.	3.00	3.00
B2	Eric Lindros, Osh. Gen.	3.00	3.00
B3	Eric Lindros, Osh. Gen.	3.00	3.00
B4	Eric Lindros, Osh. Gen.	3.00	3.00
B5	Eric Lindros, Osh. Gen.	3.00	3.00

— 1990 ROOKIE AND TRADED —

The dating on this set by Score is a little confusing. The set is meant for the 1990-91 season and was issued after the regular set.

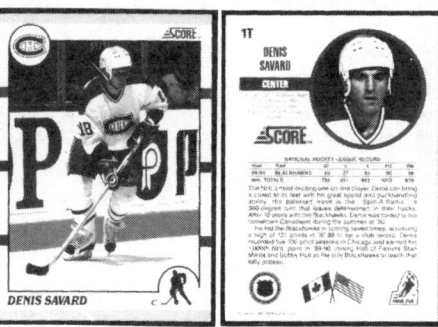

1990 Rookie and Traded
Card No. 1T, Denis Savard

Card Size: 2 1/2" X 3 1/2"
Face: Four colour, white with yellow striped borders, Team Logo
Back: Four colour on white card stock, Number, Resume, Position, Canadian and U.S.A. Flags
Imprint: © 1990 SCORE, PRINTED IN U.S.A.
Complete Set No.: 110
Common Set Price: 10.00 20.00
Common Player: .04 .08

No.	Player	EX	NRMT
1T	Denis Savard, Mon.	.04	.08
2T	Dale Hawerchuk, Buf.	.04	.08
3T	Phil Housley, Win.	.04	.08
4T	Chris Chelios, Chi.	.04	.08
5T	Geoff Courtnall, St. L.	.04	.08
6T	Peter Zezel, Wash.	.04	.08
7T	Joe Mullen, Pit.	.04	.08
8T	Craig Ludwig, NYI	.04	.08
9T	Claude Lemieux, NJ	.05	.10
10T	Robert Holik, Har.	.18	.35
11T	Peter Ing, Goalie, Tor.	.04	.08
12T	Rod Buskas, LA	.04	.08
13T	Tim Sweeney, Cal.	.04	.08
14T	Don Barber, Win.	.04	.08
15T	Ray Ferraro, NYI	.04	.08
16T	Peter Taglianetti, Min.	.04	.08
17T	Johan Garpenlov, Det.	.10	.20
18T	Kevin Miller, NYR	.20	.40
19T	Frantisek Musil, Cal.	.04	.08
20T	Sergei Fedorov, Det.	2.00	4.00
21T	Aaron Broten, Tor.	.04	.08
22T	Christopher Nilan, Bos.	.04	.08
23T	Gerald Diduck, Mon.	.04	.08
24T	Marc Habscheid, Det.	.04	.08
25T	Glen Featherstone, St. L.	.04	.08
26T	Mikko Makela, Buf.	.04	.08
27T	Paul Stanton, Pit.	.04	.08
28T	Mark Osborne, Win.	.04	.08
29T	Dave Tippett, Wash.	.04	.08
30T	Robert Reichel, Cal.	.50	1.00
31T	Grant Jennings, Har.	.04	.08
32T	Troy Gamble, Goalie, Van.	.04	.08
33T	Mark Janssens, NYR	.04	.08
34T	Brian Propp, Min.	.04	.08
35T	Donald Dufresne, Mon.	.04	.08
36T	Martin Hostak, Phi.	.04	.08
37T	Byron (Brad) McCrimmon, Det.	.04	.08
38T	Dave Lowry, St. L.	.04	.08
39T	Anatoli Semenov, Edm.	.15	.30
40T	Scott Stevens, St. L.	.04	.08
41T	Paul Broten, NYR	.04	.08
42T	Carey Wilson, Har.	.04	.08
43T	Troy Crowder, NJ	.04	.08
44T	Vladimir Ruzicka, Bos.	.05	.10
45T	Richard Pilon, NYI	.04	.08
46T	John McIntyre, LA	.04	.08
47T	Michael Krushelnyski, Tor.	.04	.08
48T	Dave Snuggerud, Buf.	.04	.08
49T	Robert McGill, Chi.	.04	.08
50T	Petr Nedved, Van.	.35	.75
51T	Ed Olczyk, Win.	.04	.08
52T	Doug Crossman, Har.	.04	.08
53T	Mikhail Tatarinov, Wash.	.05	.10

No.	Player	EX	NRMT
54T	Michel Petit, Tor.	.04	.08
55T	Frank Pietrangelo, Goalie, Pit.	.04	.08
56T	Brian MacLellan, Cal.	.04	.08
57T	Paul Fenton, Tor.	.04	.08
58T	Eric Desjardins, Mon.	.15	.30
59T	Mike Craig, Min.	.10	.20
60T	Mike Ricci, Phi.	.35	.75
61T	Harold Snepsts, St. L.	.04	.08
62T	John Byce, Bos.	.04	.08
63T	Laurie Boschman, NJ	.04	.08
64T	Randy Velischek, Que.	.04	.08
65T	Robert Kron, Van.	.04	.08
66T	Jocelyn Lemieux, Chi.	.04	.08
67T	David Ellett, Tor.	.04	.08
68T	Scott Arniel, Win.	.04	.08
69T	Douglas Smail, Min.	.04	.08
70T	Jaromir Jagr, Pit.	1.35	2.75
71T	Peter Bondra, Wash.	.25	.50
72T	Paul Cyr, Har.	.04	.08
73T	Daniel Berthiaume, Goalie, LA	.04	.08
74T	Lee Norwood, NJ	.04	.08
75T	Robert Smith, Min.	.04	.08
76T	Kris King, NYR	.04	.08
77T	Mark Hunter, Cal.	.04	.08
78T	Brian Hayward, Goalie, Min.	.04	.08
79T	Greg Hawgood, Edm.	.04	.08
80T	Owen Nolan, Que.	.25	.50
81T	Cliff Ronning, St. L.	.04	.08
82T	Zdeno Ciger, NJ	.13	.25
83T	Gordon Roberts, Pit.	.04	.08
84T	Richard Green, Det.	.04	.08
85T	Kenneth Hodge, Jr., Bos.	.04	.08
86T	Derek King, NYI	.04	.08
87T	Brent Gilchrist, Mon.	.04	.08
88T	Eric Lindros, Can.	6.00	12.00
89T	Steve Bozek, Van.	.04	.08
90T	Keith Primeau, Det.	.25	.50
91T	Roger Johansson, Cal.	.04	.08
92T	Wayne Presley, Chi.	.04	.08
93T	Ilkka Sinisalo, Min.	.04	.08
94T	Mario Marois, St. L.	.04	.08
95T	Ken Linseman, Edm.	.04	.08
96T	Greg Brown, Buf.	.04	.08
97T	Ray Sheppard, NYR	.04	.08
98T	Mike Lalor, Wash.	.04	.08
99T	Norman Lacombe, Phi.	.04	.08
100T	Mats Sundin, Que.	1.00	2.00
101T	Jergus Baca, Har.	.04	.08
102T	Mike Keane, Mon.	1.00	2.00
103T	Ed Belfour, Goalie, Chi.	1.50	3.00
104T	Mark Hardy, NYR	.04	.08
105T	Dave Capuano, Van.	.04	.08
106T	Bryan Trottier, Pit.	.04	.08
107T	Per Olav Djoos, Det.	.04	.08
108T	Sylvain Turgeon, Mon	.04	.08
109T	David Reid, Tor.	.04	.08

WAYNE GRETZKY THE 2000TH POINT

No.	Player	EX	NRMT
110T	Wayne Gretzky, LA	.50	1.00

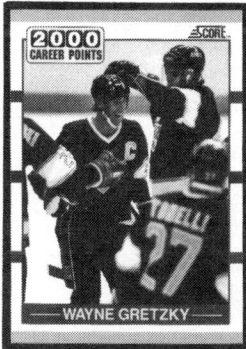

Score
1990 Rookie and traded
Card No. 110T, Wayne Gretzky

— 1990 - 91 YOUNG SUPERSTARS —

1990-91 Young Superstars
Card No. 1, Pierre Turgeon

Card Size: 2 1/2" X 3 1/2"
Face: Four colour, Light blue border with dark blue stripe
Back: Four colour on white card stock, Number, Resume, Position,
Imprint: © 1990 SCORE, PRINTED IN U.S.A.
Complete Set No.: 40
Common Set Price: 7.50 15.00
Common Card: .05 .10

No.	Player	EX	NRMT
1	Pierre Turgeon, Buf.	.15	.30
2	Brian Leetch, NYR	.25	.50
3	Daniel Marois, Tor.	.05	.10
4	Peter Sidorkiewicz, Goalie, Har.	.05	.10
5	Rob Brown, Pit.	.05	.10
6	Theoren Fleury, Cal.	.15	.30
7	Mats Sundin, Que.	.35	.75
8	Glen Wesley, Bos.	.05	.10
9	Sergei Fedorov, Det.	2.00	4.00
10	Joe Sakic, Que.	.15	.30
11	Sean Burke, Goalie, NJ	.05	.10
12	Dave Chyzowski, NYI	.05	.10
13	Gordon Murphy, Phi.	.05	.10
14	Scott Young, Har.	.05	.10
15	Curtis Joseph, Goalie, St. L.	.25	.50
16	Darren Turcotte, NYR	.05	.10
17	Kevin Stevens, Pit.	.35	.75
18	Mathieu Schneider, Mon.	.05	.10
19	Trevor Linden, Van.	.15	.30
20	Michael Modano, Min.	.35	.75
21	Martin Gelinas, Edm.	.10	.20
22	Stephane Fiset, Goalie, Que.	.05	.10
23	Brendan Shanahan, NJ	.08	.15
24	Jeremy Roenick, Chi.	.50	1.00
25	John Druce, Wash.	.18	.35
26	Alexander Mogilny, Buf.	.50	1.00
27	Mike Richter, Goalie, NYR	.35	.75
28	Pat Elynuik, Win.	.05	.10
29	Robert Reichel, Cal.	.05	.10
30	Craig Janney, Bos.	.12	.25
31	Rod Brind'Amour, St. L..	.15	.30
32	Mark Fitzpatrick, Goalie, NYI	.05	.10
33	Tony Granato, LA	.05	.10
34	Robert Holik, Har.	.25	.50
35	Mark Recchi, Pit.	.35	.75
36	Owen Nolan, Que.	.38	.75
37	Petr Nedved, Van.	.15	.30
38	Keith Primeau, Det.	.10	.20
39	Mike Ricci, Phi.	.30	.60
40	Eric Lindros, Osh. Gen.	3.50	7.00

— 1990 - 91 HOCKEY'S 100 HOTTEST AND RISING STARS —

Score renumbered 100 cards from the 1990 - 91 regular issue set for Publications International, Ltd. They included these cards in "Value Pack" which also contained a "Hottest and Rising Star" book.

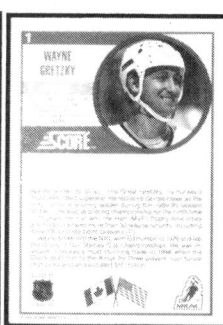

1990-91 Hottest and Rising Stars
Card No. 1, Wayne Gretzky

Card Size: 2 1/2" X 3 1/2"
Face: Four colour, white with red striped border at top and bottom, Team logo
Back: Four colour on white card stock, Number, Resume, Position, Canadian and U.S.A. flags
Imprint: © 1990 SCORE, PRINTED IN U.S.A.
Complete Set No.: 100
Complete Set Price: 7.50 15.00
Common Card: .03 .05

No.	Player	EX	NRMT
1	Wayne Gretzky, LA	.60	1.25
2	Craig Simpson, Edm.	.03	.05
3	Brian Bellows, Min.	.05	.10
4	Steve Yzerman, Det	.13	.25
5	Bernie Nicholls, NYR	.03	.05
6	Esa Tikkanen, Edm.	.03	.05
7	Joe Sakic, Que.	.13	.25
8	Thomas Steen, Win.	.03	.05
9	Chris Chelios, Mon.	.05	.10
10	Patrik Sundstrom, NJD	.03	.05
11	Rod Langway, Wash.	.03	.05
12	Scott Young, Har.	.03	.05
13	Mike Ramsey, Buf.	.03	.05
14	Ron Hextall, Goalie, Phi.	.03	.05
15	Steve Duchesne, LA	.03	.05
16	Trevor Linden, Van.	.10	.20
17	Sean Burke, Goalie, NJD	.03	.05
18	Patrick Verbeek, Har.	.03	.05
19	Brent Sutter, NYI	.03	.05
20	Gary Leeman, Tor.	.03	.05
21	Shawn Burr, Det.	.03	.05
22	Dale Hawerchuk, Win.	.10	.20
23	Mike Vernon, Goalie, Cal.	.03	.05
24	Dan Quinn, Van.	.03	.05
25	Patrick Roy, Goalie, Mon.	.25	.50
26	Daren Puppa, Goalie, Buf.	.03	.05
27	Gino Cavallini, St. L.	.03	.05
28	Jimmy Carson, Det.	.03	.05
29	David Ellett, Win.	.03	.05
30	Steve Thomas, Chi.	.03	.05
31	Jeremy Roenick, Chi.	.60	1.25
32	Mike Liut, Goalie, Wash.	.03	.05
33	Mark Messier, Edm.	.15	.30
34	Mario Lemieux, Pit.	.50	1.00
35	Raymond Bourque, Bos.	.10	.20
36	Allan MacInnis, Cal.	.03	.05
37	Ronald Francis, Har.	.03	.05
38	Stephane J. J. Richer, Mon.	.03	.05
39	Bill Ranford, Goalie, Edm.	.03	.05
40	Rick Tocchet, Phi.	.03	.05
41	Adam Oates, St. L.	.10	.20
42	Kevin Hatcher, Wash.	.03	.05
43	Guy Carbonneau, Mon.	.03	.05
44	Curtis Leschyshyn, Que.	.03	.05
45	Joe Nieuwendyk, Cal.	.03	.05
46	Kirk McLean, Goalie, Van.	.03	.05
47	Vincent Damphousse, Tor.	.08	.15
48	Peter Stastny, NJD	.03	.05
49	Richard Zombo, Det.	.03	.05

SCORE — 1991 PROMOTIONAL CARDS

No.	Player	EX	NRMT
50	Mark Fitzpatrick, Goalie, NYI	.03	.05
51	Rob Brown, Pit.	.03	.05
52	Dave Gagner, Min.	.03	.05
53	Pierre Turgeon, Buf.	.13	.25
54	Glenn Anderson, Edm.	.03	.05
55	Kelly Hrudey, Goalie, LA	.03	.05
56	Gordon Murphy, Phi.	.03	.05
57	Glen Wesley, Bos.	.03	.05
58	Craig Janney, Bos.	.13	.25
59	Denis Savard, Chi.	.03	.05
60	Michael Gartner, NYR	.05	.10
61	Steve Larmer, Chi.	.03	.05
62	Andrew Moog, Goalie, Bos.	.03	.05
63	Phil Housley, Buf.	.03	.05
64	Ulf Samuelsson, Har.	.03	.05
65	Paul Coffey, Pit.	.08	.15
66	Luc Robitaille, LA	.13	.25
67	Cam Neely, Bos.	.10	.20
68	Douglas Wilson, Chi.	.03	.05
69	Douglas Gilmour, Cal.	.13	.25
70	Jeff Norton, NYI	.03	.05
71	Kirk Muller, NJD	.03	.05
72	Aaron Broten, Min.	.03	.05
73	John Cullen, Pit.	.03	.05
74	Craig Ludwig, Mon.	.03	.05
75	Kevin Lowe, Edm.	.03	.05
76	John Vanbiesbrouck, Goalie, NYR	.03	.05
77	Tim Kerr, Phi.	.03	.05
78	Gerard Gallant, Det.	.03	.05
79	Tomas Sandstrom, LA	.03	.05
80	Jon Casey, Goalie, Min.	.03	.05
81	Mark Recchi, Pit.	.25	.50
82	Scott Stevens, Wash.	.05	.10
83	John MacLean, NJD	.03	.05
84	James Patrick, NYR	.03	.05
85	Al Iafrate, Tor.	.08	.15
86	Pat Elynuik, Win.	.03	.05
87	David Andreychuk, Buf.	.08	.15
88	Joe Mullen, Cal.	.03	.05
89	Ed Olczyk, Tor.	.03	.05
90	Kevin Dineen, Har.	.03	.05
91	Shayne Corson, Mon.	.03	.05
92	Marke Howe, Phi.	.03	.05
93	Brian Leetch, NYR	.25	.50
94	Dino Ciccarelli, Wash.	.03	.05
95	Pat LaFontaine, NYI	.12	.25
96	Guy Lafleur, Que.	.03	.05
97	Michael Modano, Min.	.35	.75
98	Rod Brind'Amour, St. L.	.25	.50
99	Sergei Makarov, Cal.	.05	.10
100	Brett Hull, St. L.	.25	.50

— 1991 PROMOTIONAL CARDS —

The 1991 Promotional Cards were distributed at the 12th National Sports Collectors Convention and the National Candy Wholesalers Association Convention.

The sets were also available at Toronto during Fanfest, the location of the 1991 All Star baseball game. The event is printed on the lower green stripe on the back of the cards. Plain cards not domiciled, do not have the green stripe printed and were used for promotional purposes and also given out at 1991 Fanfest.

1991 Promotional Cards
"12th National Sports Collectors Convention"
Card No. 1, Wayne Gretzky

Card Size: 2 1/2" X 3 1/2"
Face: Four colour, printed to edge
Back: Four colour, white design border, Resume, Number
Back Variations: A. Plain (Toronto Fanfest)
B. "12th National Sports Collectors Convention" (60,000 sets)
C. "N.C.W.A. Summer Convention 1991" (National Candy Wholesalers Association)
Imprint: © 1991 SCORE, PRINTED IN U.S.A.
Complete Set No.: 10
Complete Set Price:
A: Plain 75.00
B: 12th Annual 50.00
C: "N.W.C.A. Summer Convention 1991" 40.00

No.	Player	Plain NRMT	12th NRMT	NCWA NRMT
1	Wayne Gretzky, LA	30.00	20.00	15.00
2	Brett Hull, St. L.	10.00	7.00	5.00
3	Raymond Bourque, Bos.	10.00	7.00	5.00
4	Allan MacInnis, Cal.	10.00	7.00	5.00
5	Luc Robitaille, LA	15.00	7.00	5.00
6	Ed Belfour, Goalie, Chi.	10.00	7.00	5.00
7	Steve Yzerman, Det.	15.00	7.00	5.00
8	Cam Neely, Bos.	10.00	7.00	5.00
9	Paul Coffey, Pit.	10.00	7.00	5.00
10	Patrick Roy, Goalie, Mon.	25.00	15.00	12.00

— 1991-92 PROMOTIONAL CARDS —
AMERICAN ISSUE

The card face is identical to the regular card. The back contains two variations. First, the stats table is printed completely in red, while on the regular card the table is red and blue. Second, the Score logo is followed by the letters TM. instead of R on the regular cards.

Card Size: 2 1/2" x 3 1/2"
Face: Four colour, purple border; Score logo
Back: Four colour on white card stock; Number; Resume; Position; American flag
Imprint: ©1991 SCORE, PRINTED IN U.S.A.
Complete Set No.: 6
Complete Set Price: 25.00 50.00

No.	Player	EX	NRMT
1	Brett Hull, St. L	4.00	8.00
2	Allan MacInnis, Cal.	2.50	5.00
3	Luc Robitaille, LA	2.50	5.00
50	Raymond Bourque, Bos.	2.50	5.00
75	Patrick Roy, Goalie, Mon.	12.50	25.00
100	Wayne Gretzky, LA	12.50	25.00

— 1991-92 AMERICAN ISSUE —

The Score American issue differs from the Canadian and Bilingual issues in photographs and border colours. Card nos. 1 to 230 are the same player for all issues, but cards 231 to 440 feature different players.

 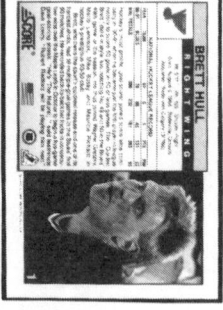

1991-92 American Issue
Card No. 1, Bret Hull

Card Size: 2 1/2" X 3 1/2"
Face: Four colour, purple border, Score logo
Back: Four colour on white card stock, Number, Resume, Position, U.S.A. Flag
Imprint: © 1991 SCORE, PRINTED IN U.S.A.

Complete Set No.: 440
Complete Set Price: 6.00 12.00
Complete Factory Set: 6.00 12.00
Common Card: .03 .05
Foil Pack: (15 Cards) .60
Foil Box: (36 Packs) 8.00
Foil Case: (20 Boxes) 125.00

No.	Player	EX	NRMT
1	Brett Hull, St. L.	.25	.50
2	Allan MacInnis, Cal.	.03	.05
3	Luc Robitaille, LA	.08	.15
4	Pierre Turgeon, Buf.	.13	.25
5	Brian Leetch, NYR	.18	.35
6	Cam Neely, Bos.	.05	.10
7	John Cullen, Har.	.03	.05
8	Trevor Linden, Van.	.15	.30
9	Rick Tocchet, Phi.	.03	.05
10	John Vanbiesbrouck, Goalie, NYR	.03	.05
11	Steve Smith, Edm.	.03	.05
12	Douglas Smail, Min.	.03	.05
13	Craig Ludwig, NYI	.03	.05
14	Paul Fenton, Cal.	.03	.05
15	Dirk Graham, Chi.	.03	.05
16	Byron (Brad) McCrimmon, Det.	.03	.05
17	Dean Evason, Har.	.03	.05
18	Fredrik Olausson, Win.	.03	.05
19	Guy Carbonneau, Mon.	.03	.05
20	Kevin Hatcher, Wash.	.03	.05
21	Paul Ranheim, Cal.	.03	.05
22	Claude Lemieux, NJD	.03	.05
23	Vincent Riendeau, Goalie, St. L.	.03	.05
24	Garth Butcher, St. L.	.03	.05
25	Joe Sakic, Que.	.15	.30
26	Richard Vaive, Buf.	.03	.05
27	Robert Blake, LA	.08	.15
28	Mike Ricci, Phi.	.08	.15
29	Patrick Flatley, NYI	.03	.05
30	Bill Ranford, Goalie, Edm.	.03	.05
31	Lawrence Murphy, Pit.	.03	.05
32	Robert Smith, Min.	.03	.05
33	Michael Krushelnyski, Tor.	.03	.05
34	Gerard Gallant, Det.	.03	.05
35	Douglas Wilson, Chi.	.03	.05
36	John Ogrodnick, NYR	.03	.05
37	Mikhail Tatarinov, Wash.	.03	.05
38	Douglas Crossman, Det.	.03	.05
39	Mark Osborne, Win.	.03	.05
40	Scott Stevens, St. L.	.03	.05
41	Ron Tugnutt, Goalie, Que.	.03	.05
42	Russell Courtnall, Mon.	.03	.05
43	Gordon Murphy, Phi.	.03	.05
44	Greg Adams, Van.	.03	.05
45	Christian Ruuttu, St. L.	.03	.05
46	Kenneth Daneyko, NJD	.03	.05
47	Glenn Anderson, Edm.	.03	.05
48	Ray Ferraro, NYI	.03	.05
49	Tony Tanti, Buf.	.03	.05
50	Raymond Bourque, Bos.	.08	.15
51	Sergei Makarov, Cal.	.03	.05
52	Jim Johnson, Min.	.03	.05
53	Troy Murray, Chi.	.03	.05
54	Shawn Burr, Det.	.03	.05
55	Peter Ing, Goalie, Tor.	.03	.05
56	Dale Hunter, Was.	.03	.05
57	Tony Granato, LA	.03	.05
58	Curtis Leschyshyn, Que.	.03	.05
59	Brian Mullen, NYR	.03	.05
60	Ed Olczyk, Win.	.03	.05
61	Michael Ramsey, Buf.	.03	.05
62	Dan Quinn, St. L.	.03	.05
63	Richard Sutter, St. L.	.03	.05
64	Terry Carkner, Phi.	.03	.05
65	Shayne Corson, Mon.	.03	.05
66	Peter Stastny, NJD	.03	.05
67	Craig Muni, Edm.	.03	.05
68	Glenn Healy, Goalie, NYI	.03	.05
69	Phillippe Bourque, Pit.	.03	.05
70	Patrick Verbeek, Har.	.03	.05
71	Garry Galley, Bos.	.03	.05
72	Dave Gagner, Min.	.03	.05
73	Bob Probert, Det.	.03	.05
74	Craig Wolanin, Que.	.03	.05
75	Patrick Roy, Goalie, Mon.	.25	.50
76	Keith Brown, Chi.	.03	.05
77	Gary Leeman, Tor.	.03	.05

No.	Player	EX	NRMT
78	Brent Ashton, Win.	.03	.05
79	Randy Moller, NYR	.03	.05
80	Michael Vernon, Goalie, Cal.	.03	.05
81	Kelly Miller, Wash.	.03	.05
82	Ulf Samuelsson, Pit.	.03	.05
83	Todd Elik, LA	.03	.05
84	Uwe Krupp, Buf.	.03	.05
85	Rod Brind'Amour, St. L.	.08	.15
86	Dave Capuano, Van.	.03	.05
87	Geoff Smith, Edm.	.03	.05
88	David Volek, NYI	.03	.05
89	Bruce Driver, NJD	.03	.05
90	Andrew Moog, Goalie, Bos.	.03	.05
91	Per-erik Eklund, Phi.	.03	.05
92	Joey Kocur, NYR	.03	.05
93	Mark Tinordi, Min.	.03	.05
94	Steve Thomas, Chi.	.03	.05
95	Petr Svoboda, Mon.	.03	.05
96	Joel Otto, Cal.	.03	.05
97	Todd Krygier, Har.	.03	.05
98	Jaromir Jagr, Pit.	.20	.40
99	Michael Liut, Goalie, Wash.	.03	.05
100	Wayne Gretzky, LA	.50	1.00
101	Teppo Numminen, Win.	.03	.05
102	Randy Burridge, Bos.	.03	.05
103	Michel Petit, Tor.	.03	.05
104	Anthony McKegney, Chi.	.03	.05
105	Mathieu Schneider, Mon.	.03	.05
106	Daren Puppa, Goalie, St. L.	.03	.05
107	Paul Cavallini, St. L.	.03	.05
108	Tim Kerr, Phi.	.03	.05
109	Kevin Lowe, Edm.	.03	.05
110	Kirk Muller, NJD	.03	.05
111	Zarley Zalapski, Har.	.03	.05
112	Mike Hough, Que.	.03	.05
113	Kenneth Hodge, Jr., Bos.	.03	.05
114	Grant Fuhr, Goalie, Edm.	.03	.05
115	Paul Coffey, Pit.	.08	.15
116	Wendel Clark, Tor.	.08	.15
117	Patrik Sundstrom, NJD	.03	.05
118	Kevin Dineen, Har.	.03	.05
119	Eric Desjardins, Mon.	.03	.05
120	Mike Richter, Goalie, NYR	.15	.30
121	Sergio Momesso, Van.	.03	.05
122	Anthony Hrkac, Que.	.03	.05
123	Joe Reekie, NYI	.03	.05
124	Petr Nedved, Van.	.10	.20
125	Randy Carlyle, Win.	.03	.05
126	Kevin Miller, Det.	.03	.05
127	Rejean Lemelin, Goalie, Bos.	.03	.05
128	Dino Ciccarelli, Wash.	.03	.05
129	Sylvain Coté, Har.	.03	.05
130	Mats Sundin, Que.	.12	.25
131	Eric Weinrich, NJD	.03	.05
132	Daniel Berthiaume, Goalie, LA	.03	.05
133	Keith Acton, Phi.	.03	.05
134	Benoit Hogue, Buf.	.03	.05
135	Michael Gartner, NYR	.03	.05
136	Petr Klima, Edm.	.03	.05
137	Curt Giles, Min.	.03	.05
138	Scott Pearson, Que.	.03	.05
139	Luke Richardson, Tor.	.03	.05
140	Steve Larmer, Chi.	.03	.05
141	Ken Wregget, Goalie, Phi.	.03	.05
142	Frantisek Musil, Cal.	.03	.05
143	Owen Nolan, Que.	.08	.15
144	Keith Primeau, Det.	.03	.05
145	Mark Recchi, Pit.	.12	.25
146	Don Sweeney, Bos.	.03	.05
147	Michael McPhee, Mon.	.03	.05
148	Ken Baumgartner, NYI	.03	.05
149	Dave Lowry, St. L.	.03	.05
150	Geoff Courtnall, Van.	.03	.05
151	Chris Terreri, Goalie, NJD	.03	.05
152	Dave Manson, Chi.	.03	.05
153	Robert Holik, Har.	.03	.05
154	Bob Kudelski, LA	.03	.05
155	Calle Johansson, Wash.	.03	.05
156	Mark Hunter, Har.	.03	.05
157	Randy Gilhen, Pit.	.03	.05
158	Yves Racine, Det.	.03	.05
159	Martin Gelinas, Edm.	.03	.05
160	Brian Bellows, Min.	.03	.05

No.	Player	EX	NRMT
161	David Shaw, NYR	.03	.05
162	Robert Carpenter, Bos.	.03	.05
163	Doug Brown, NJD	.03	.05
164	Ulf Dahlen, Min.	.03	.05
165	Denis Savard, Mon.	.03	.05
166	Paul Ysebaert, Det.	.03	.05
167	Derek King, NYI	.03	.05
168	Igor Larionov, Van.	.03	.05
169	Bob Errey, Pit.	.03	.05
170	Joe Nieuwendyk, Cal.	.03	.05
171	Normand Rochefort, NYR	.03	.05
172	John Tonelli, LA	.03	.05
173	David Reid, Tor.	.03	.05
174	Tom Kurvers, Van.	.03	.05
175	Dimitri Khristich, Wash.	.03	.05
176	Robert Sweeney, Bos.	.03	.05
177	Rick Zombo, Det.	.03	.05
178	Troy Mallette, NYR	.03	.05
179	Bob Bassen, St. L.	.03	.05
180	John Druce, Wash.	.03	.05
181	Mike Craig, Min.	.03	.05
182	John McIntyre, LA	.03	.05
183	Murray Baron, Phi.	.03	.05
184	Viacheslav Fetisov, NJD	.03	.05
185	Donald Beaupre, Goalie, Wash.	.03	.05
186	Brian Benning, LA	.03	.05
187	David Barr, Det.	.03	.05
188	Petri Skriko, Bos.	.03	.05
189	Stephen Konroyd, Chi.	.03	.05
190	Steve Yzerman, Det.	.15	.30
191	Jon Casey, Goalie, Min.	.03	.05
192	Gary Nylund, NYI	.03	.05
193	Michal Pivonka, Wash.	.03	.05
194	Alexei Kasatonov, NJD	.03	.05
195	Garry Valk, Van.	.03	.05
196	Darren Turcotte, NYR	.03	.05
197	Christopher Nilan, Bos.	.03	.05
198	Thomas Steen, Win.	.03	.05
199	Gary Roberts, Cal.	.03	.05
200	Mario Lemieux, Pit.	.35	.75
201	Michel Goulet, Chi.	.03	.05
202	Craig MacTavish, Edm.	.03	.05
203	Peter Sidorkiewicz, Goalie, Har.	.03	.05
204	Johan Garpenlov, Det.	.03	.05
205	Steve Duchesne, LA	.03	.05
206	Dave Snuggerud, Buf.	.03	.05
207	Kjell Samuelsson, Phi.	.03	.05
208	Sylvain Turgeon, Mon.	.03	.05
209	Al Iafrate, Wash.	.03	.05
210	John MacLean, NJD	.03	.05
211	Brian Hayward, Goalie, Min.	.03	.05
212	Cliff Ronning, Van.	.03	.05
213	Ray Sheppard, NYR	.03	.05
214	David Taylor, LA	.03	.05
215	Doug Lidster, Van.	.03	.05
216	Peter Bondra, Wash.	.03	.05
217	Martin McSorley, LA	.03	.05
218	Douglas Gilmour, Cal.	.15	.30
219	Paul MacDermid, Win.	.03	.05
220	Jeremy Roenick, Chi.	.25	.50
221	Wayne Presley, Chi.	.03	.05
222	Jeff Norton, NYI	.03	.05
223	Brian Propp, Min.	.03	.05
224	Jimmy Carson, Det.	.03	.05
225	Tom Barrasso, Goalie, Pit.	.03	.05
226	Theoren Fleury, Cal.	.05	.10
227	Carey Wilson, Cal.	.03	.05
228	Rod Langway, Wash.	.03	.05
229	Bryan Trottier, Pit.	.03	.05
230	James Patrick, NYR	.03	.05
231	Kelly Hrudey, Goalie, LA	.03	.05
232	David Poulin, Bos.	.03	.05
233	Gordon (Rob) Ramage, Tor.	.03	.05
234	Stephane Richer, Mon.	.03	.05
235	Chris Chelios, Chi.	.03	.05
236	Alexander Mogilny, Buf.	.20	.40
237	Bryan Fogarty, Que.	.03	.05
238	Adam Oates, St. L.	.08	.15
239	Ron Hextall, Goalie, Phi.	.03	.05
240	Bernie Nicholls, NYR	.03	.05
241	Esa Tikkanen, Edm.	.03	.05
242	Jyrki Lumme, Van.	.03	.05
243	Brent Sutter, NYI	.03	.05

No.	Player	EX	NRMT
244	Gary Suter, Cal.	.03	.05
245	Sean Burke, Goalie, NJD	.03	.05
246	Rob Brown, Har.	.03	.05
247	Michael Modano, Min.	.15	.30
248	Kevin Stevens, Pit.	.15	.30
249	Mike Lalor, Wash.	.03	.05
250	Sergei Fedorov, Det.	.25	.50
251	Bob Essensa, Goalie, Win.	.03	.05
252	Mark Howe, Phi.	.03	.05
253	Craig Janney, Bos.	.05	.10
254	Daniel Marois, Tor.	.03	.05
255	Craig Simpson, Edm.	.03	.05
256	Stephen Kasper, LA	.03	.05
257	Randy Velischek, Que.	.03	.05
258	Gino Cavallini, St. L.	.03	.05
259	Dale Hawerchuk, Buf.	.03	.05
260	Pat LaFontaine, NYI	.10	.20
261	Kirk McLean, Goalie, Van.	.12	.25
262	Murray Craven, Phi.	.03	.05
263	Robert Reichel, Cal.	.08	.15
264	Jan Erixon, NYR	.03	.05
265	Adam Creighton, Chi.	.03	.05
266	Mark Fitzpatrick, Goalie, NYI	.03	.05
267	Ronald Francis, Pit.	.03	.05
268	Joe Mullen, Pit.	.03	.05
269	Peter Zezel, Tor.	.03	.05
270	Tomas Sandstrom, LA	.03	.05
271	Phil Housley, Win.	.03	.05
272	Tim Cheveldae, Goalie, Det.	.03	.05
273	Glen Wesley, Bos.	.03	.05
274	Stephan Lebeau, Mon.	.08	.15
275	David Ellett, Tor.	.03	.05
276	Jeff Brown, St. L.	.03	.05
277	David Andreychuk, Buf.	.08	.15
278	Steven Finn, Que.	.03	.05
279	Scott Mellanby, Phi.	.03	.05
280	Neal Broten, Min.	.03	.05
281	Randy Wood, NYI	.03	.05
282	Troy Gamble, Goalie, Van.	.03	.05
283	Mike Ridley, Wash.	.03	.05
284	Jamie Macoun, Cal.	.03	.05
285	Mark Messier, Edm.	.12	.25
286	Brendan Shanahan, NJD	.12	.25
287	Scott Young, Pit.	.03	.05
288	Kelly Kisio, NYR	.03	.05
289	Brad Shaw, Har.	.03	.05
290	Ed Belfour, Goalie, Chi.	.12	.25
291	Larry Robinson, LA	.03	.05
292	David Christian, Bos.	.03	.05
293	Steve Chiasson, Det.	.03	.05
294	Brian Skrudland, Mon.	.03	.05
295	Pat Elynuik, Win.	.12	.25
296	Curtis Joseph, Goalie, St. L.	.10	.20
297	Doug Bodger, Buf.	.03	.05
298	Ronald Sutter, Phi.	.03	.05
299	Joe Murphy, Edm.	.03	.05
300	Vincent Damphousse, Tor.	.03	.05

CRUNCH CREW

No.	Player	EX	NRMT
301	Cam Neely, Bos.	.05	.10
302	Rick Tocchet, Phi.	.03	.05
303	Scott Stevens, St. L.	.03	.05
304	Ulf Samuelsson, Pit.	.03	.05
305	Jeremy Roenick, Chi.	.10	.20

NHL BROTHERS

No.	Player	EX	NRMT
306	Dale and Mark Hunter	.03	.05
307	Aaron and Neal Broten	.03	.05
308	Gino and Paul Cavallini	.03	.05
309	Kelly and Kevin Miller	.03	.05

TOP PROSPECT

No.	Player	EX	NRMT
310	Dennis Vaske, NYI, RC	.03	.05
311	Rob Pearson, Tor., RC	.10	.20
312	Jason Miller, NJD, RC	.03	.05
313	John LeClair, Mon., RC	.10	.20
314	Bryan Marchment, Win., RC	.05	.10
315	Gary Shuchuk, Det., RC	.03	.05

SCORE — 1991-92 PROMOTIONAL CARDS

No.	Player	EX	NRMT
316	Dominik Hasek, Goalie, Chi., RC, Error	.60	1.25
317	Michel Picard, Har., RC	.05	.10
318	Corey Millen, NYR, RC	.13	.25
319	Joe Sacco, Tor., RC	.05	.10
320	Rejean Savage, Wash., RC	.03	.05
321	Pat Murray, Phi.	.03	.05
322	Myles O'Connor, NJD, RC	.05	.10
323	Shawn Antoski, Van.	.03	.05
324	Geoff Sanderson, Har., RC	.35	.75
325	Chris Govedaris, Har.	.03	.05
326	Alexei Gusarov, Que., RC	.03	.05
327	Mike Sillinger, Det.	.03	.05
328	Bob Wilkie, Det., RC	.03	.05
329	Pat Jablonski, Goalie, St. L., RC	.08	.15

HOBEY BAKER WINNER

No.	Player	EX	NRMT
330	David Emma	.08	.15

FRANCHISE

No.	Player	EX	NRMT
331	Kirk Muller, NJD	.03	.05
332	Pat LaFontaine, NYI	.05	.10
333	Brian Leetch, NYR	.10	.20
334	Rick Tocchet, Phi.	.03	.05
335	Mario Lemieux, Pit.	.12	.25
336	Joe Sakic, Que.	.08	.15
337	Brett Hull, St. L.	.10	.20
338	Vincent Damphousse, Tor.	.03	.05
339	Trevor Linden, Van.	.05	.10
340	Kevin Hatcher, Wash.	.03	.05
341	Pat Elynuik, Win.	.03	.05

DREAM TEAM

No.	Player	EX	NRMT
342	Patrick Roy, Goalie, Mon.	.15	.30
343	Brian Leetch, NYR	.05	.10
344	Raymond Bourque, Bos.	.05	.10
345	Luc Robitaille, LA	.05	.10
346	Wayne Gretzky, LA	.15	.30
347	Brett Hull, St. L.	.10	.20

ALL-ROOKIE TEAM

No.	Player	EX	NRMT
348	Ed Belfour, Goalie, Chi.	.05	.10
349	Robert Blake, LA	.05	.10
350	Eric Weinrich, NJD	.03	.05
351	Jaromir Jagr, Pit.	.10	.20
352	Sergei Fedorov, Det.	.10	.20
353	Kenneth Hodge, Jr. Bos.	.03	.05

ERIC LINDROS

No.	Player	EX	NRMT
354	Eric Lindros 88	.60	1.25
355	Awards and Honors	.60	1.25
356	1991 First Round Draft Choice	.60	1.25

REGULAR ISSUE

No.	Player	EX	NRMT
357	Dana Murzyn, Van.	.03	.05
358	Adam Graves, Edm.	.15	.30
359	Ken Linseman, Edm.	.03	.05
360	Mike Keane, Mon.	.03	.05
361	Stephane Morin, Que.	.03	.05
362	Grant Ledyard, Buf.	.03	.05
363	Kris King, NYR	.03	.05
364	Paul Gillis, Chi.	.03	.05
365	Chris Dahlquist, Min.	.03	.05
366	Paul Stanton, Pit.	.03	.05

SAN JOSE SHARKS

No.	Player	EX	NRMT
367	Jeff Hackett, Goalie	.03	.05
368	Robert McGill	.03	.05
369	Neil Wilkinson	.03	.05
370	Rob Zettler	.03	.05

MAN OF THE YEAR

No.	Player	EX	NRMT
371	Brett Hull, St. L.	.10	.20

1,000 POINT CLUB

No.	Player	EX	NRMT
372	Paul Coffey, Pit.	.05	.10
373	Mark Messier, Edm.	.08	.15
374	David Taylor, LA	.03	.05
375	Michel Goulet, Chi.	.03	.05
376	Dale Hawerchuk, Buf.	.03	.05

NHL BROTHERS

No.	Player	EX	NRMT
377	Pierre and Sylvain Turgeon	.03	.05
378	Rich, Ron and Brian Sutter	.03	.05
379	Brian and Joe Mullen	.03	.05
380	Geoff and Russ Courtnall	.03	.05

TOP PROSPECT

No.	Player	EX	NRMT
381	Trevor Kidd, Goalie, Cal.	.03	.05
382	Patrice Brisebois, Mon.	.08	.15
383	Mark Greig, Har.	.03	.05
384	Kip Miller, Que.	.03	.05
385	Drake Berehowsky, Tor.	.03	.05
386	Kevin Haller, Buf., RC	.08	.15
387	David Gagnon, Goalie, Det.	.03	.05
388	Jason Marshall, St. L.	.03	.05
389	Donald Audette, Buf., RC	.05	.10
390	Patrick Lebeau, Mon., RC	.08	.15
391	Alexander Godynyuk, Tor., RC	.05	.10
392	Jarrod Skalde, NJD, RC	.10	.20
393	Kenneth Sutton, Buf., RC	.05	.10
394	Sergei Kharin, Win., RC	.03	.05
395	Andre Racicot, Goalie, Mon., RC	.05	.10
396	Doug Weight, NYR., RC	.10	.20
397	Kevin Todd, NJD, RC	.10	.20
398	Anthony Amonte, NYR, RC	.18	.35
399	Kimbi Daniels, Phi., RC	.05	.10
400	Jeff Daniels, Pit., RC	.05	.10

TRIBUTE TO GUY LAFLEUR

No.	Player	EX	NRMT
401	"Speed and Grace"	.05	.10
402	"Awards and Achievements"	.05	.10
403	"A Hall of Famer"	.05	.10

SEASON LEADERS

No.	Player	EX	NRMT
404	Goals: Brett Hull, St. L.	.10	.20
405	Assists: Wayne Gretzky, LA	.13	.25
406	Points: Wayne Gretzky, LA	.13	.25
407	Plus/Minus: Theoren Fleury, Cal. Marty McSorley, LA	.03	.05
408	Points/Leading Rookie: Sergei Fedorov, Det	.12	.25
409	Points/Leading Defenseman: Allan McInnes, Cal.	.03	.05
410	Wins: Ed Belfour, Goalie, Chi.	.05	.10
411	Goals Against Average: Ed Belfour, Chi.	.05	.10

1990-91 HIGHLIGHT

No.	Player	EX	NRMT
412	Brett Hull 50 Goals/50 Games	.10	.20
413	Wayne Gretzky's 700th Career Goal	.13	.25

SAN JOSE SHARKS CHECKLIST

No.	Checklist	EX	NRMT
414	San Jose Sharks Checklist	.15	.30

THE FRANCHISE

No.	Player	EX	NRMT
415	Raymond Bourque, Bos.	.05	.10
416	Pierre Turgeon, Buf.	.05	.10
417	Allan MacInnis, Cal.	.03	.05
418	Jeremy Roenick, Chi.	.10	.20
419	Steve Yzerman, Det.	.05	.10
420	Mark Messier, Edm.	.05	.10
421	John Cullen, Har.	.03	.05

No.	Player	EX	NRMT
422	Wayne Gretzky, LA	.13	.25
423	Michael Modano, Min.	.05	.10
424	Patrick Roy, Goalie, Mon.	.12	.25

1991 STANLEY CUP CHAMPIONS

No.	Team	EX	NRMT
425	Pittsburgh Penguins	.12	.25

TROPHY WINNERS

No.	Player	EX	NRMT
426	Conn Smythe Trophy: Mario Lemieux	.13	.25
427	Art Ross Trophy: Wayne Gretzky	.13	.25
428	Hart Memorial Trophy: Brett Hull	.10	.20
429	Norris Trophy: Raymond Bourque	.03	.05
430	Calder Trophy: Ed Belfour, Goalie, Chi.	.05	.10
431	Vezina Trophy: Ed Belfour, Goalie, Chi.	.05	.10
432	Frank J. Selke Trophy: Dirk Graham	.03	.05
433	Jennings Trophy: Ed Belfour, Goalie, Chi.	.05	.10
434	Lady Byng Trophy: Wayne Gretzky	.13	.25
435	Bill Masterton Trophy: David Taylor	.03	.05

REGULAR ISSUE

No.	Player	EX	NRMT
436	Randy Ladouceur, Har.	.03	.05
437	Dave Tippett, Was.	.03	.05
438	Clint Malarchuk, Goalie, Buf.	.03	.05
439	Gordon Roberts, Pit.	.03	.05
440	Frank Pietrangelo, Goalie, Pit.	.03	.05

NOTE: See page no. 374 for American insert "Bobby Orr" Cards

— 1991-92 PROMOTIONAL CARDS —
CANADIAN AND BILINGUAL ISSUE

The fronts of these cards are identical to the regular cards. The back contains two variations. First, the stats table is printed completely in blue while on the regular cards, the table is blue and red. Second, the Score logo is followed by the letters TM. instead of R on the regular cards.

1991-92 Promotional Cards
Card No. 3, Luc Robitaille

Card Size: 2 1/2" x 3 1/2"
Face: Four colour, red border: Name, Score logo
Back: Four colour on white card stock; Name, Number; Resume; Position; Bilingual; Canadian flag
Imprint: ©1991 SCORE, PRINTED IN U.S.A.
Complete Set No.: 6
Complete Set Price: 65.00 65.00

No.	Player	English NRMT	Bilingual NRMT
1	Brett Hull, St. L	8.00	8.00
2	Allan MacInnis, Cal	5.00	5.00
3	Luc Robitaille, LA	5.00	5.00
50	Raymond Bourque, Bos.	5.00	5.00
75	Patrick Roy, Goalie, Mon.	25.00	25.00
100	Wayne Gretzky, LA	50.00	50.00

— 1991 - 92 REGULAR ISSUE —

CANADIAN AND BILINGUAL

The Score Canadian and Bilingual sets are divided into two series of three hundred and thirty cards each. The first two hundred and thirty cards of each set, American, Canadian and Bilingual are identical as to player but the American set shows different photographs. The English and Bilingual sets differ only in the bilingual copy.

 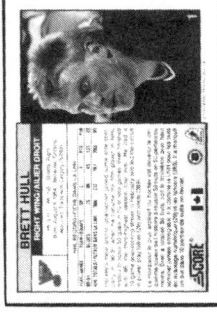

1991-92 Bilingual Issue
Card No. 1, Brett Hull

Card Size: 2 1/2" X 3 1/2"
Face: Four colour, red border, Score logo
Back: Four colour on white card stock, Number, Resume, Position, Canadian Flag
Imprint: © 1991 SCORE, PRINTED IN U.S.A

Complete Set No.: 660	ENG.	BIL.
Complete Set Price:	16.00	16.00
Series One:	8.00	8.00
Series Two:	8.00	8.00
Complete Factory Set:	16.00	16.00
Common Player:	.05	.05
Foil Pack: (15 Cards)		.50
Foil Box: (36 Packs)		8.00
Foil Case: (20 Boxes)		150.00

SERIES ONE

No.	Player	English NRMT	Bilingual NRMT
1	Brett Hull, St. L.	.50	.50
2	Allan MacInnis, Cal.	.05	.05
3	Luc Robitaille, LA	.15	.15
4	Pierre Turgeon, Buf.	.25	.25
5	Brian Leetch, NYR	.35	.35
6	Cam Neely, Bos.	.10	.10
7	John Cullen, Har.	.05	.05
8	Trevor Linden, Van.	.30	.30
9	Rick Tocchet, Phi.	.05	.05
10	John Vanbiesbrouck, Goalie, NYR	.05	.05
11	Steve Smith, Edm.	.05	.05
12	Douglas Smail, Min.	.05	.05
13	Craig Ludwig, NYI	.05	.05
14	Paul Fenton, Cal.	.05	.05
15	Dirk Graham, Chi.	.05	.05
16	Byron (Brad) McCrimmon, Det.	.05	.05
17	Dean Evason, Har.	.05	.05
18	Fredrik Olausson, Win.	.05	.05
19	Guy Carbonneau, Mon.	.05	.05
20	Kevin Hatcher, Wash.	.05	.05
21	Paul Ranheim, Cal.	.05	.05
22	Claude Lemieux, NJD	.05	.05
23	Vincent Riendeau, Goalie, St. L.	.05	.05
24	Garth Butcher, St. L.	.05	.05
25	Joe Sakic, Que.	.30	.30
26	Richard Vaive, Buf.	.05	.05
27	Robert Blake, LA	.15	.15
28	Mike Ricci, Phi.	.15	.15
29	Patrick Flatley, NYI	.05	.05
30	Bill Ranford, Goalie, Edm.	.05	.05
31	Lawrence Murphy, Pit.	.05	.05
32	Robert Smith, Min.	.05	.05
33	Michael Krusheinyski, Tor.	.05	.05
34	Gerard Gallant, Det.	.05	.05
35	Douglas Wilson, Chi.	.05	.05
36	John Ogrodnick, NYR	.05	.05
37	Mikhail Tatarinov, Wash.	.05	.05
38	Douglas Crossman, Det.	.05	.05
39	Mark Osborne, Win.	.05	.05
40	Scott Stevens, St. L.	.05	.05
41	Ron Tugnutt, Goalie, Que.	.05	.05
42	Russell Courtnall, Mon.	.05	.05
43	Gordon Murphy, Phi.	.05	.05
44	Greg Adams, Van.	.05	.05
45	Christian Ruuttu, Buf.	.05	.05
46	Kenneth Daneyko, NJD	.05	.05
47	Glenn Anderson, Edm.	.05	.05
48	Ray Ferraro, NYI	.05	.05
49	Tony Tanti, Buf.	.05	.05
50	Raymond Bourque, Bos.	.15	.15
51	Sergei Makarov, Cal.	.05	.05
52	Jim Johnson, Min.	.05	.05
53	Troy Murray, Chi.	.05	.05
54	Shawn Burr, Det.	.05	.05
55	Peter Ing, Goalie, Tor.	.05	.05
56	Dale Hunter, Wash.	.05	.05
57	Tony Granato, LA	.05	.05
58	Curtis Leschyshyn, Que.	.05	.05
59	Brian Mullen, NYR	.05	.05
60	Ed Olczyk, Win.	.05	.05
61	Michael Ramsey, Buf.	.05	.05
62	Dan Quinn, St. L.	.05	.05
63	Richard Sutter, St. L.	.05	.05
64	Terry Carkner, Phi.	.05	.05
65	Shayne Corson, Mon.	.05	.05
66	Peter Stastny, NJD	.05	.05
67	Craig Muni, Edm.	.05	.05
68	Glenn Healy, Goalie, NYI	.05	.05
69	Phillippe Bourque, Pit.	.05	.05
70	Patrick Verbeek, Har.	.05	.05
71	Garry Galley, Bos.	.05	.05
72	Dave Gagner, Min.	.05	.05
73	Bob Probert, Det.	.05	.10
74	Craig Wolanin, Que.	.05	.05
75	Patrick Roy, Goalie, Mon.	.50	.50
76	Keith Brown, Chi.	.05	.05
77	Gary Leeman, Tor.	.05	.05
78	Brent Ashton, Win.	.05	.05
79	Randy Moller, NYR	.05	.05
80	Michael Vernon, Goalie, Cal.	.05	.05
81	Kelly Miller, Wash.	.05	.05
82	Ulf Samuelsson, Pit.	.05	.05
83	Todd Elik, LA	.05	.05
84	Uwe Krupp, Buf.	.05	.05
85	Rod Brind'Amour, St. L.	.15	.15
86	Dave Capuano, Van.	.05	.05
87	Geoff Smith, Edm.	.05	.05
88	David Volek, NYI	.05	.05
89	Bruce Driver, NJD	.05	.05
90	Andrew Moog, Goalie, Bos.	.05	.05
91	Per-erik Eklund, Phi.	.05	.05
92	Joey Kocur, NYR	.05	.05
93	Mark Tinordi, Min.	.05	.05
94	Steve Thomas, Chi.	.05	.05
95	Petr Svoboda, Mon.	.05	.05
96	Joel Otto, Cal.	.05	.05
97	Todd Krygier, Har.	.05	.05
98	Jaromir Jagr, Pit.	.20	.40
99	Michael Liut, Goalie, Wash.	.05	.05
100	Wayne Gretzky, LA	1.00	1.00
101	Teppo Numminen, Win.	.05	.05
102	Randy Burridge, Bos.	.05	.05
103	Michel Petit, Tor.	.05	.05
104	Anthony McKegney, Chi.	.05	.05
105	Mathieu Schneider, Mon.	.05	.05
106	Daren Puppa, Goalie, Buf	.05	.05
107	Paul Cavallini, St. L.	.05	.05
108	Tim Kerr, Phi.	.05	.05
109	Kevin Lowe, Edm.	.05	.05
110	Kirk Muller, NJD	.05	.05
111	Zarley Zalapski, Har.	.05	.05
112	Mike Hough, Que.	.05	.05
113	Kenneth Hodge, Jr., Bos.	.05	.05
114	Grant Fuhr, Goalie, Edm.	.05	.05
115	Paul Coffey, Pit.	.15	.15
116	Wendel Clark, Tor.	.15	.15
117	Patrik Sundstrom, NJD	.05	.05
118	Kevin Dineen, Har.	.05	.05
119	Eric Desjardins, Mon.	.05	.05
120	Mike Richter, Goalie, NYR	.30	.30
121	Sergio Momesso, Van.	.05	.05
122	Anthony Hrkac, Que.	.05	.05
123	Joe Reekie, NYI	.05	.05
124	Petr Nedved, Van.	.20	.20
125	Randy Carlyle, Win.	.05	.05
126	Kevin Miller, Det.	.10	.10
127	Rejean Lemelin, Goalie, Bos.	.05	.05
128	Dino Ciccarelli, Wash.	.05	.05
129	Sylvain Coté, Har.	.05	.05
130	Mats Sundin, Que.	.25	.25
131	Eric Weinrich, NJD	.05	.05
132	Daniel Berthiaume, Goalie, LA	.05	.05
133	Keith Acton, Phi.	.05	.05
134	Benoit Hogue, Buf.	.05	.05
135	Michael Gartner, NYR	.05	.05
136	Petr Klima, Edm.	.05	.05
137	Curt Giles, Min.	.05	.05
138	Scott Pearson, Que.	.05	.05
139	Luke Richardson, Tor.	.05	.05
140	Steve Larmer, Chi.	.05	.05
141	Ken Wregget, Goalie, Phi.	.05	.05
142	Frantisek Musil, Cal.	.05	.05
143	Owen Nolan, Que.	.15	.15
144	Keith Primeau, Det.	.05	.05
145	Mark Recchi, Pit.	.25	.25
146	Don Sweeney, Bos.	.05	.05
147	Michael McPhee, Mon.	.05	.05
148	Ken Baumgartner, NYI	.05	.05
149	Dave Lowry, St. L.	.05	.05
150	Geoff Courtnall, Van.	.05	.05
151	Chris Terreri, Goalie, NJD	.05	.05
152	Dave Manson, Chi.	.05	.05
153	Robert Holik, Har.	.05	.05
154	Bob Kudelski, LA	.05	.05
155	Calle Johansson, Wash.	.05	.05
156	Mark Hunter, Har.	.05	.05
157	Randy Gilhen, Pit.	.05	.05
158	Yves Racine, Det.	.05	.05
159	Martin Gelinas, Edm.	.05	.05
160	Brian Bellows, Min.	.05	.05
161	David Shaw, NYR	.05	.05
162	Robert Carpenter, Bos.	.05	.05
163	Doug Brown, NJD	.05	.05
164	Ulf Dahlen, Min.	.05	.05
165	Denis Savard, Mon.	.05	.05
166	Paul Ysebaert, Det.	.05	.05
167	Derek King, NYI	.05	.05
168	Igor Larionov, Van.	.05	.05
169	Bob Errey, Pit.	.05	.05
170	Joe Nieuwendyk, Cal.	.05	.05
171	Normand Rochefort, NYR	.05	.05
172	John Tonelli, LA	.05	.05
173	David Reid, Tor.	.05	.05
174	Tom Kurvers, Van.	.05	.05
175	Dimitri Khristich, Wash.	.05	.05
176	Robert Sweeney, Bos.	.05	.05
177	Rick Zombo, Det.	.05	.05
178	Troy Mallette, NYR	.05	.05
179	Bob Bassen, St. L.	.05	.05
180	John Druce, Wash.	.05	.05
181	Mike Craig, Min.	.05	.05
182	John McIntyre, LA	.05	.05
183	Murray Baron, Phi.	.05	.05
184	Viacheslav Fetisov, NJD	.05	.05
185	Donald Beaupre, Goalie, Wash.	.05	.05
186	Brian Benning, LA	.05	.05
187	David Barr, Det.	.05	.05
188	Petri Skriko, Bos.	.05	.05
189	Stephen Konroyd, Chi.	.05	.05
190	Steve Yzerman, Det.	.30	.30
191	Jon Casey, Goalie, Min.	.05	.05
192	Gary Nylund, NYI	.05	.05
193	Michal Pivonka, Wash.	.05	.05
194	Alexei Kasatonov, NJD	.05	.05
195	Garry Valk, Van.	.05	.05
196	Darren Turcotte, NYR	.05	.05
197	Christopher Nilan, Bos.	.05	.05
198	Thomas Steen, Win.	.05	.05
199	Gary Roberts, Cal.	.05	.05
200	Mario Lemieux, Pit.	.75	.75
201	Michel Goulet, Chi.	.05	.05
202	Craig MacTavish, Edm.	.05	.05
203	Peter Sidorkiewicz, Goalie, Har.	.05	.05

SCORE — 1991-92 REGULAR ISSUE

No.	Player	English NRMT	Bilingual NRMT
204	Johan Garpenlov, Det.	.05	.05
205	Steve Duchesne, LA	.05	.05
206	Dave Snuggerud, Buf.	.05	.05
207	Kjell Samuelsson, Phi.	.05	.05
208	Sylvain Turgeon, Mon.	.05	.05
209	Al Iafrate, Wash.	.05	.05
210	John MacLean, NJD	.05	.05
211	Brian Hayward, Goalie, Min.	.05	.05
212	Cliff Ronning, Van.	.05	.05
213	Ray Sheppard, NYR	.05	.05
214	David Taylor, LA	.05	.05
215	Doug Lidster, Van.	.05	.05
216	Peter Bondra, Wash.	.05	.05
217	Martin McSorley, LA	.05	.05
218	Douglas Gilmour, Cal.	.30	.30
219	Paul MacDermid, Win.	.05	.05
220	Jeremy Roenick, Chi.	.50	.50
221	Wayne Presley, Chi.	.05	.05
222	Jeff Norton, NYI	.05	.05
223	Brian Propp, Min.	.05	.05
224	Jimmy Carson, Det.	.05	.05
225	Tom Barrasso, Goalie, Pit.	.05	.05
226	Theoren Fleury, Cal.	.10	.10
227	Carey Wilson, Cal.	.05	.05
228	Rod Langway, Wash.	.05	.05
229	Bryan Trottier, Pit.	.05	.05
230	James Patrick, NYR	.05	.05
231	Dana Murzyn, Van.	.05	.05
232	Richard Wamsley, Goalie, Cal.	.05	.05
233	Dave McLlwain, Win.	.05	.05
234	Thomas Fergus, Tor.	.05	.05
235	Adam Graves, Edm.	.30	.30
236	Jacques Cloutier, Goalie, Que.	.05	.05
237	Gino Odjick, Van.	.05	.05
238	Andrew Cassels, Mon.	.05	.05
239	Ken Linseman, Edm.	.05	.05
240	Danton Cole, Win.	.05	.05
241	David Hannan, Tor.	.05	.05
242	Stephane Matteau, Cal.	.05	.05
243	Gerald Diduck, Van.	.05	.05
244	Richard Tabaracci, Goalie, Win.	.05	.05
245	Sylvain Lefebvre, Mon.	.05	.05
246	Robert Rouse, Tor.	.05	.05
247	Charles Huddy, Edm.	.05	.05
248	Mike Foligno, Tor.	.05	.05
249	Eric Nattress, Cal.	.05	.05
250	Aaron Broten, Tor.	.05	.05
251	Mike Keane, Mon.	.05	.05
252	Steven Bozek, Van.	.05	.05
253	Jeff Beukeboom, Edm.	.05	.05
254	Stephane Morin, Que.	.05	.05
255	Brian Bradley, Tor.	.05	.05
256	Scott Arniel, Win.	.05	.05
257	Robert Kron, Van.	.05	.05
258	Anatoli Semenov, Edm.	.05	.05
259	Brent Gilchrist, Mon.	.05	.05
260	Jim Sandlak, Van.	.05	.05

MAN OF THE YEAR

No.	Player	English NRMT	Bilingual NRMT
261	Brett Hull, St. L.	.15	.15

1000 POINT CLUB

No.	Player	English NRMT	Bilingual NRMT
262	Paul Coffey, Pit.	.10	.10
263	Mark Messier, Edm.	.10	.10
264	David Taylor, LA	.05	.05
265	Michel Goulet, Chi.	.05	.05
266	Dale Hawerchuk, Buf.	.10	.10

NHL BROTHERS

No.	Player	English NRMT	Bilingual NRMT
267	Pierre & Sylvain Turgeon	.10	.10
268	Rich, Brian & Ron Sutter	.05	.05
269	Brian & Joe Mullen	.05	.05
270	Geoff & Russ Courtnall	.05	.05

TOP PROSPECT

No.	Player	English NRMT	Bilingual NRMT
271	Trevor Kidd, Goalie, Cal.	.05	.05
272	Patrice Brisebois, Mon.	.15	.15
273	Mark Greig, Har.	.05	.05
274	Kip Miller, Que.	.08	.05
275	Drake Berehowsky, Tor.	.05	.05
276	Kevin Haller, Buf., RC	.15	.15
277	David Gagnon, Goalie, Det.	.05	.05
278	Jason Marshall, St. L.	.05	.05
279	Donald Audette, Buf., RC	.10	.10
280	Patrick Lebeau, Mon., RC	.15	.15
281	Alexander Godynyuk, Tor., RC	.10	.10
282	Jarrod Skalde, NJD, RC	.20	.20
283	Kenneth Sutton, Buf., RC	.10	.10
284	Sergei Kharin, Win., RC	.05	.05
285	Andre Racicot, Goalie, Mon., RC	.10	.10
286	Doug Weight, NYR, RC	.20	.20
287	Kevin Todd, NJD, RC	.20	.20
288	Anthony Amonte, NYR, RC	.35	.35
289	Kimbi Daniels, Phi., RC	.10	.10
290	Jeff Daniels, Pits., RC	.10	.10

GUY LAFLEUR

No.	Player	English NRMT	Bilingual NRMT
291	"Speed and Grace"	.10	.10
292	"Awards and Achievements"	.10	.10
293	"A Hall of Famer"	.10	.10

SEASON LEADERS

No.	Player	English NRMT	Bilingual NRMT
294	Goals: Brett Hull, St. L.	.20	.20
295	Assists: Wayne Gretzky, LA	.25	.25
296	Points: Wayne Gretzky, LA	.25	.25
297	Plus/Minus: Theoren Fleury, Cal. Marty McSorley, LA	.05	.05
298	Points/Leading Rookie: Sergei Fedorov, Det.	.25	.25
299	Points/Leading Defenseman: Allan MacInnis, Cal.	.05	.05
300	Wins: Ed Belfour, Goalie, Chi.	.10	.10
301	Goals Against Average: Ed Belfour, Goalie, Chi.	.10	.10

1990 - 91 HIGHLIGHT

No.	Player	English NRMT	Bilingual NRMT
302	Brett Hull 50 Goals/50 Games	.20	.20
303	Wayne Gretzky's 700th Career Goal	.25	.25

SAN JOSE SHARKS CHECKLIST

No.	Team	English NRMT	Bilingual NRMT
304	San Jose Sharks Checklist	.30	.30

CRUNCH CREW

No.	Player	English NRMT	Bilingual NRMT
305	Cam Neely, Bos.	.10	.10
306	Rick Tocchet, Phi.	.10	.10
307	Scott Stevens, St. L.	.05	.05
308	Ulf Samuelsson, Pit.	.05	.05
309	Jeremy Roenick, Chi.	.15	.15

THE FRANCHISE

No.	Player	English NRMT	Bilingual NRMT
310	Mark Messier, Edm.	.10	.10
311	John Cullen, Har.	.10	.10
312	Wayne Gretzky, LA	.25	.25
313	Michael Modano, Min.	.10	.10
314	Patrick Roy, Goalie, Mon.	.25	.25

1991 STANLEY CUP CHAMPIONS

No.	Team	English NRMT	Bilingual NRMT
315	Pittsburgh Penguins	.25	.25

TROPHY WINNERS

No.	Player	English NRMT	Bilingual NRMT
316	Conn Smythe Trophy: Mario Lemieux, Pit.	.25	.25
317	Art Ross Trophy: Wayne Gretzky, LA	.25	.25
318	Hart Memorial Trophy: Brett Hull, St. L.	.10	.20
319	Norris Trophy: Raymond Bourque, Bos.	.05	.05
320	Calder Trophy: Ed Belfour, Goalie, Chi.	.10	.10
321	Vezina Trophy: Ed Belfour, Goalie, Chi.	.10	.10
322	Frank J. Selke Trophy: Dirk Graham	.05	.05
323	Jennings Trophy: Ed Belfour, Goalie, Chi.	.10	.10
324	Lady Byng Trophy: Wayne Gretzky, LA David Taylor, LA	.25	.25
325	Bill Masterton Trophy: David Taylor, LA	.05	.05

SAN JOSE SHARKS

No.	Player	English NRMT	Bilingual NRMT
326	Jeff Hackett, Goalie	.05	.05
327	Robert McGill	.05	.05
328	Neil Wilkinson	.05	.05

ERIC LINDROS

No.	Player	English NRMT	Bilingual NRMT
329	1991 First Round Draft Choice	1.25	1.25
330	Awards And Honors	1.25	1.25

SERIES TWO

THE FRANCHISE

No.	Player	English NRMT	Bilingual NRMT
331	Raymond Bourque, Bos.	.10	.10
332	Pierre Turgeon, Buf.	.15	.15
333	Allan MacInnis, Cal.	.10	.10
334	Jeremy Roenick, Chi.	.25	.25
335	Steve Yzerman, Det.	.15	.15

NHL BROTHERS

No.	Player	English NRMT	Bilingual NRMT
336	Dale and Mark Hunter	.05	.05
337	Aaron and Neal Broten	.05	.05
338	Gino and Paul Cavallini	.05	.05
339	Kelly and Kevin Miller	.05	.05

TOP PROSPECT

No.	Player	English NRMT	Bilingual NRMT
340	Dennis Vaske, NYI, RC	.05	.05
341	Rob Pearson, Tor., RC	.20	.20
342	Jason Miller, NJD, RC	.05	.05
343	John LeClair, Mon., RC	.20	.20
344	Bryan Marchment, Win., RC	.10	.10
345	Gary Shuchuk, Det., RC	.05	.05

No.	Player	English NRMT	Bilingual NRMT
346	Dominik Hasek, Goalie, Chi., RC, Error	1.25	1.25
347	Michel Picard, Har., RC	.05	.05
348	Corey Millen, NYR, RC	.25	.25
349	Joe Sacco, Tor., RC	.10	.10
350	Rejean Savage, Wash., RC	.05	.05
351	Pat Murray, Phi.	.05	.05
352	Myles O'Connor, NJD, RC	.05	.05
353	Shawn Antoski, Van.	.05	.05
354	Geoff Sanderson, Har., RC	.75	.75
355	Chris Govedaris, Har.	.05	.05
356	Alexei Gusarov, Que., RC	.05	.05
357	Mike Sillinger, Det.	.05	.05
358	Bob Wilkie, Det., RC	.05	.05

— 1991 - 92 REGULAR ISSUE — SCORE • 373

No.	Team	English NRMT	Bilingual NRMT
359	Pat Jablonski, Goalie, St. L., RC	.15	.15

1991 MEMORIAL CUP CHAMPIONS

No.	Team	English NRMT	Bilingual NRMT
360	1991 Memorial Cup Champions - Spokane Chiefs	.20	.20

THE FRANCHISE

No.	Player	English NRMT	Bilingual NRMT
361	Kirk Muller, NJD	.10	.10
362	Pat LaFontaine, NYI	.15	.15
363	Brian Leetch, NYR	.20	.20
364	Rick Tocchet, Phi.	.05	.05
365	Mario Lemieux, Pit.	.25	.25
366	Joe Sakic, Que.	.10	.10
367	Brett Hull, St. L.	.15	.15
368	Vincent Damphousse, Tor.	.05	.05
369	Trevor Linden, Van.	.10	.10
370	Kevin Hatcher, Wash.	.05	.05
371	Pat Elynuik, Win.	.05	.05

DREAM TEAM

No.	Player	English NRMT	Bilingual NRMT
372	Patrick Roy, Goalie, Mon.	.35	.35
373	Brian Leetch, NYR	.20	.20
374	Raymond Bourque, Bos.	.10	.10
375	Luc Robitaille, LA	.10	.10
376	Wayne Gretzky, LA	.35	.35
377	Brett Hull, St. L.	.20	.20

ALL-ROOKIE TEAM

No.	Player	English NRMT	Bilingual NRMT
378	Ed Belfour, Goalie, Chi.	.10	.10
379	Robert Blake, LA	.05	.05
380	Eric Weinrich, NJD	.05	.05
381	Jaromir Jagr	.20	.20
382	Sergei Fedorov, Det.	.25	.25
383	Kenneth Hodge, Jr., Bos.	.05	.05

REGULAR ISSUE

No.	Player	English NRMT	Bilingual NRMT
384	Eric Lindros	1.25	1.25
385	Eric Lindros and Rob Pearson	1.25	1.25
386	A Look Into the Future Ottawa Senators, Tampa Bay Lightning	.30	.30
387	Mick Vukota, NYI	.05	.05
388	Lou Franceschetti, Buf.	.05	.05
389	Mike Hudson, Chi.	.05	.05
390	Frantisek Kucera, Chi.	.05	.05
391	Basil McRae, Min.	.05	.05
392	Donald Dufresne, Mon.	.05	.05
393	Tommy Albelin, NJD	.05	.05
394	Normand Lacombe, Phi., Error	.05	.05
395	Lucien DeBlois, Tor.	.05	.05
396	Anthony Twist, Que., RC	.10	.10
397	Rob Murphy, Van.	.05	.05
398	Ken Sabourin, Wash.	.05	.05
399	Doug Evans, Win.	.05	.05
400	Walter Poddubny, NJD	.05	.05
401	Grant Ledyard, Buf.	.05	.05
402	Kris King, NYR	.05	.05
403	Paul Gillis, Chi.	.05	.05
404	Chris Dahlquist, Min.	.05	.05
405	Zdeno Ciger, NJD	.05	.05
406	Paul Stanton, Pit.	.05	.05
407	Randy Ladouceur, Har.	.05	.05
408	Ronald Stern, Cal.	.05	.05
409	Dave Tippett, Was.	.05	.05
410	Jeff Reese, Goalie, Tor.	.05	.05
411	Vladimir Ruzicka, Bos.	.05	.05
412	Brent Fedyk, Det.	.05	.05
413	Paul Cyr, Har.	.05	.05
414	Michael Eagles, Win.	.05	.05
415	Chris Joseph, Edm.	.05	.05
416	Bradley Marsh, Cal.	.05	.05
417	Richard Pilon, NYI	.05	.05
418	Jiri Hrdina, Pit.	.05	.05
419	Clint Malarchuk, Goalie, Buf.	.05	.05
420	Steven Rice, NYR	.05	.05
421	Mark Janssens, NYR	.05	.05
422	Gordon Roberts, Pit.	.05	.05
423	Shawn Cronin, Win.	.05	.05
424	Randy Cunneyworth, Har.	.05	.05
425	Frank Pietrangelo, Goalie, Pit.	.05	.05
426	David Maley, NJD	.05	.05
427	Rod Buskas, LA	.05	.05
428	Dennis Vial, Det.	.05	.05
429	Kelly Buchberger, Edm.	.05	.05
430	Wes Walz, Bos.	.05	.05
431	Edward (Dean) Kennedy, Buf.	.05	.05
432	Nicholas Kypreos, Wash.	.05	.05
433	Robert (Stewart) Gavin, Min.	.05	.05
434	Norm MacIver, Edm., RC	.20	.20
435	Mark Pederson, Phi.	.05	.05
436	Laurie Boschman, NJD	.05	.05
437	Stephane Quintal, Bos.	.05	.05
438	Darrin Shannon, Buf.	.05	.05
439	Trent Yawney, Chi.	.05	.05
440	Gaetan Duchesne, Min.	.05	.05
441	Joe Cirella, NYR	.05	.05
442	Doug Houda, Har.	.05	.05
443	Dave Chyzowski, NYI	.05	.05
444	Derrick Smith, Phi.	.05	.05
445	Jeff Lazaro, Bos.	.05	.05
446	Brian Glynn, Min.	.05	.05
447	Jocelyn Lemieux, Chi.	.05	.05
448	Peter Taglianetti, Pit.	.05	.05
449	Adam Burt, Har.	.05	.05
450	Hubie McDonough, NYI	.05	.05
451	Kelly Hrudey, Goalie, LA	.05	.05
452	David Poulin, Bos.	.05	.05
453	Mark Hardy, NYR	.05	.05
454	Mike Hartman, Buf.	.05	.05
455	Chris Chelios, Chi.	.05	.05
456	Alexander Mogilny, Buf.	.40	.40
457	Bryan Fogarty, Que.	.05	.05
458	Adam Oates, St. L.	.15	.15
459	Ron Hextall, Goalie, Phi.	.05	.05
460	Bernie Nicholls, NYR	.05	.05
461	Esa Tikkanen, Edm.	.05	.05
462	Jyrki Lumme, Van.	.05	.05
463	Brent Sutter, NYI	.05	.05
464	Gary Suter, Cal.	.05	.05
465	Sean Burke, Goalie, NJD	.05	.05
466	Rob Brown, Har.	.05	.05
467	Michael Modano, Min.	.30	.30
468	Kevin Stevens, Pit.	.30	.30
469	Mike Lalor, Was.	.05	.05
470	Sergei Fedorov, Det.	.60	.60
471	Bob Essensa, Goalie, Win.	.05	.05
472	Mark Howe, Phi.	.05	.05
473	Craig Janney, Bos.	.10	.10
474	Daniel Marois, Tor.	.05	.05
475	Craig Simpson, Edm.	.05	.05
476	Marc Bureau, Min.	.05	.05
477	Randy Velischek, Que.	.05	.05
478	Gino Cavallini, St. L.	.05	.05
479	Dale Hawerchuk, Buf.	.05	.05
480	Pat LaFontaine, NYI	.20	.20
481	Kirk McLean, Goalie, Van.	.25	.25
482	Murray Craven, Phi.	.05	.05
483	Robert Reichel, Cal.	.20	.20
484	Jan Erixon, NYR	.05	.05
485	Adam Creighton, Chi.	.05	.05
486	Mark Fitzpatrick, Goalie, NYI	.05	.05
487	Ronald Francis, Pit.	.05	.05
488	Joe Mullen, Pit.	.05	.05
489	Peter Zezel, Tor.	.05	.05
490	Tomas Sandstrom, LA	.05	.05
491	Phil Housley, Win.	.05	.05
492	Tim Cheveldae, Goalie, Det.	.05	.05
493	Glen Wesley, Bos.	.05	.05
494	Stephan Lebeau, Mon.	.15	.15
495	David Ellett, Tor.	.05	.05
496	Jeff Brown, St. L.	.05	.05
497	David Andreychuk, Buf.	.15	.15
498	Steven Finn, Que.	.05	.05
499	Mike Donnelly, LA, RC	.20	.20
500	Neal Broten, Min.	.05	.05
501	Randy Wood, NYI	.05	.05
502	Troy Gamble, Goalie, Van.	.05	.05
503	Mike Ridley, Was.	.05	.05
504	Jamie Macoun, Cal.	.05	.05
505	Mark Messier, Edm.	.25	.25
506	Maurice Mantha, Win.	.05	.05
507	Scott Young, Pit.	.05	.05
508	Robert Dirk, Van.	.05	.05
509	Brad Shaw, Har.	.05	.05
510	Ed Belfour, Goalie, Chi.	.25	.25
511	Larry Robinson, LA	.05	.05
512	Dale Kushner, Phi.	.05	.05
513	Steve Chiasson, Det.	.05	.05
514	Brian Skrudland, Mon.	.05	.05
515	Pat Elynuik, Win.	.05	.05
516	Curtis Joseph, Goalie, St. L.	.30	.30
517	Doug Bodger, Buf.	.05	.05
518	Greg Brown, Buf.	.05	.05
519	Joe Murphy, Edm.	.05	.05
520	Jean-Jacques Daigneault, Mon.	.05	.05
521	Todd Gill, Tor.	.05	.05
522	Troy Loney, Pit.	.05	.05
523	Tim Watters, LA	.05	.05
524	Jody Hull, NYR	.05	.05
525	Colin Patterson, Cal.	.05	.05
526	Darin Kimble, St. L.	.05	.05
527	Perry Berezan, Min.	.05	.05
528	Lee Norwood, NJD	.05	.05
529	Mike Peluso, Chi.	.05	.05
530	Wayne McBean, NYI	.05	.05
531	Grant Jennings, Pit.	.05	.05
532	Claude Loiselle, Tor.	.05	.05
533	Ronald Wilson, St. L.	.05	.05
534	Phil Sykes, Win.	.05	.05
535	James Wiemer, Bos.	.05	.05
536	Herb Raglan, Que.	.05	.05
537	Timothy Hunter, Cal.	.05	.05
538	Mike Tomlak, Har.	.05	.05
539	Gregory Gilbert, Chi.	.05	.05
540	Jiri Latal, Phi.	.05	.05
541	Bill Berg, NYI, RC	.10	.10
542	Shane Churla, Min.	.05	.05
543	Jay Miller, LA	.05	.05
544	Peter Peeters, Goalie, Phi.	.05	.05
545	Alan May, Was.	.05	.05
546	Mario Marois, St. L.	.05	.05
547	Jim Kyte, Cal.	.05	.05
548	Jon Morris, NJD	.05	.05
549	Mikko Makela, Buf.	.05	.05
550	Nelson Emerson, St. L.	.25	.25

SAN JOSE SHARKS

No.	Player	English NRMT	Bilingual NRMT
551	Douglas Wilson	.05	.05
552	Brian Mullen	.05	.05
553	Kelly Kisio	.05	.05
554	Brian Hayward, Goalie	.05	.05
555	Anthony Hrkac	.05	.05
556	Steven Bozek	.05	.05
557	John Carter	.05	.05
558	Neil Wilkinson	.05	.05
559	Wayne Presley	.05	.05
560	Robert McGill	.05	.05

REGULAR ISSUE

No.	Player	English NRMT	Bilingual NRMT
561	Craig Ludwig, Min.	.05	.05
562	Mikhail Tatarinov, Que.	.05	.05
563	Todd Elik, Min.	.05	.05
564	Randy Burridge, Wash.	.05	.05
565	Tim Kerr, NYR	.05	.05
566	Randy Gilhen, LA	.05	.05
567	John Tonelli, Chi.	.05	.05
568	Tom Kurvers, NYI	.05	.05
569	Steve Duchesne, Phi.	.05	.05
570	Charles Huddy, LA	.05	.05
571	Alan Kerr, Det.	.05	.05
572	Shawn Chambers	.05	.05
573	George (Rob) Ramage, Min.	.05	.05

374 • SCORE — 1991-92 Insert Sets

No.	Player	English NRMT	Bilingual NRMT
574	Stephen Kasper, Phi.	.05	.05
575	Scott Mellanby, Edm.	.05	.05
576	Stephen Leach, Bos.	.05	.05
577	**Scott Niedermayer, NJD, RC**	.30	.30
578	Craig Berube, Tor.	.05	.05
579	Gregory Paslawski, Que.	.05	.05
580	Randy Hillier, NYI	.05	.05
581	Stephane Richer, NJD	.05	.05
582	Brian MacLellan, Det.	.05	.05
583	Marc Habscheid, Cal.	.05	.05
584	David Babych, Van.	.05	.05
585	Troy Murray, Win.	.05	.05
586	Ray Sheppard, Det.	.05	.05
587	Glen Featherstone, Bos.	.05	.05
588	Brendan Shanahan, St. L.	.20	.20
589	David Christian, St. L.	.05	.05
590	Michael Bullard, Tor.	.05	.05
591	Ryan Walter, Van.	.05	.05
592	Douglas Smail, Que.	.05	.05
593	Paul Fenton, Har.	.05	.05
594	Adam Graves, NYR	.05	.05
595	Scott Stevens, NJD	.05	.05
596	Sylvain Coté, Wash.	.05	.05
597	David Barr, NJD	.05	.05
598	Randall Gregg, Van.	.05	.05
599	Allen Pedersen, Min.	.05	.05
600	Jari Kurri, LA	.05	.05
601	Troy Mallette, Edm.	.05	.05
602	Troy Crowder, Det.	.05	.05
603	Brad Jones, Phi.	.05	.05
604	Randy McKay, NJD	.05	.05
605	Scott Thornton, Edm.	.05	.05
606	**Bryan Marchment, Chi., RC**	.10	.10
607	Andrew Cassels, Har.	.05	.05
608	Grant Fuhr, Goalie, Tor.	.05	.05
609	Vincent Damphousse, Edm.	.05	.05
610	Robert Ray, Buf.	.05	.05
611	Glenn Anderson, Tor.	.05	.05
612	Peter Ing, Goalie, Edm.	.05	.05
613	Tom Chorske, NJD	.05	.05
614	Kirk Muller, Mon.	.05	.05
615	Dan Quinn, Phi.	.05	.05
616	Murray Baron, St. L.	.05	.05
617	Sergei Nemchinov, NYR	.20	.20
618	Rod Brind'Amour, Phi.	.05	.05
619	Ronald Sutter, St. L.	.05	.05
620	Luke Richardson, Edm.	.05	.05
621	**Nicklas Lidstrom, Det., RC**	.35	.35
622	Ken Linseman, Tor.	.05	.05
623	Steve Smith, Chi.	.05	.05
624	Dave Manson, Edm.	.05	.05
625	Kay Whitmore, Goalie, Har.	.05	.05
626	Jeff Chychrun, LA	.05	.05
627	**Russell Romaniuk, Win., RC**	.15	.15
628	Brad May, Buf.	.05	.05
629	**Tomas Forslund, Cal., RC**	.05	.05
630	Stu Barnes, Win.	.05	.10
631	Darryl Sydor, LA	.05	.05
632	Jimmy Waite, Goalie, Chi.	.05	.05
633	Peter Douris, Bos.	.05	.05
634	David Brown, Phi.	.05	.05
635	Mark Messier, NYR	.30	.30
636	Neil Sheehy, Cal.	.05	.05
637	Todd Krygier, Was.	.05	.05
638	Stephane Beauregard, Goalie, Win.	.05	.05
639	Barry Pederson, Har.	.05	.05

SAN JOSE SHARKS

No.	Player	English NRMT	Bilingual NRMT
640	Pat Falloon	.40	.40
641	Dean Evason	.05	.05
642	Jeff Hackett, Goalie	.05	.05
643	Rob Zettler	.05	.05
644	**David Bruce, RC**	.05	.05
645	**Pat MacLeod, RC**	.05	.05
646	Craig Coxe	.05	.05
647	**Ken Hammond, RC**	.05	.05
648	Brian Lawton	.05	.05
649	**Perry Anderson, RC**	.05	.05
650	**Kevin Evans, RC**	.05	.05
651	**Michael McHugh, RC**	.05	.05

REGULAR ISSUE

No.	Player	English NRMT	Bilingual NRMT
652	Mark Lamb, Edm.	.05	.05
653	**Darcy Wakaluk, Goalie, Min., RC**	.30	.30
654	Pat Conacher, NJD	.05	.05
655	Martin Lapointe, Det.	.05	.05
656	Derian Hatcher, Min.	.05	.05
657	Bryan Erickson, Win.	.05	.05
658	**Ken Priestlay, Pit., RC**	.05	.05
659	**Vladimir Konstantinov, Det., RC**	.15	.15
660	Andrei Lomakin, Phi.	.05	.05

— 1991-92 INSERT SETS —

BOBBY ORR COLLECTOR CARDS AUTOGRAPHED

The "Bobby Orr" collector cards were randomly inserted into the regular foil packs of all three issues, Canadian, Bilingual and American. A total of 270,000 cards were inserted, 45,000 of each. In addition 15,000 autographed cards were inserted, 2500 of each.

The "Junior Star" and "The Scoring Leader" cards were inserted in all three packs.

The "Stanley Cup Hero" and the "Hall of America" cards were inserted in the Canadian and bilingual packs.

The "Rookie" and "The Award Winner" cards were inserted in the American packs.

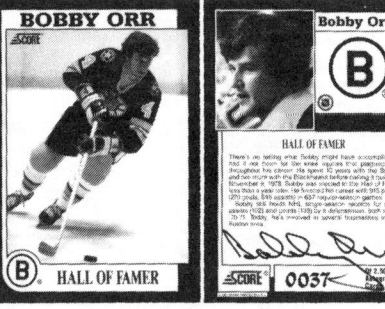

1991-92 Collector Cards
Autographed Bobby Orr, "Hall of Fame"

Card Size: 2 1/2" X 3 1/2"
Face: Four colour, black border, Score logo
Back: Four colour on card stock, Resume
Imprint: © 1991 SCORE, PRINTED IN U.S.A
Complete Set No.: 12

Complete Set Price:	60.00	120.00
Complete Autographed Set Price:	1,000.00	2,000.00

CANADIAN AND AMERICAN ISSUE

No.	Player	USA NRMT	Can. NRMT
—	Bobby Orr, Junior Star	15.00	15.00
—	Bobby Orr, Junior Star, Autographed	400.00	400.00
—	Bobby Orr, Scoring Leader	15.00	15.00
—	Bobby Orr, Scoring Leader, Autographed	400.00	400.00

CANADIAN ISSUE

No.	Player	EX	NRMT
—	Bobby Orr, Stanley Cup Hero	7.50	15.00
—	Bobby Orr, Stanley Cup Hero, Autographed	200.00	400.00
—	Bobby Orr, Hall of Famer	7.50	15.00
—	Bobby Orr, Hall of Famer, Autographed	200.00	400.00

AMERICAN ISSUE

No.	Player	EX	NRMT
—	Bobby Orr, Rookie	7.50	15.00
—	Bobby Orr, Rookie Autographed	200.00	400.00
—	Bobby Orr, Award Winner	7.50	15.00
—	Bobby Orr, Award Winner, Autographed	200.00	400.00

— HOT CARDS —

The Score Canadian set was also available in blister packs, a see-through plastic package which contained one hundred regular issue cards plus a "Hot Card".

1991-92 Insert Set, Hot Cards
Card No. 1, Eric Lindros

Card Size: 2 1/2" X 3 1/2"
Face: Four colour, red border; Score logo
Back: Four colour on white card stock, Number, Resume
Imprint: © 1991 SCORE, PRINTED IN U.S.A.
Complete Set No.: 10

Complete Set Price:	12.50	25.00

No.	Player	EX	NRMT
1	Eric Lindros	7.50	15.00
2	Wayne Gretzky, LA	3.50	7.00
3	Brett Hull, St. L.	1.50	3.00
4	Sergei Fedorov, Det.	2.50	5.00
5	Mario Lemieux, Pit.	2.50	5.00
6	Adam Oates, St. L.	1.00	2.00
7	Theoren Fleury, Cal.	.50	1.00
8	Jaromir Jagr, Pit.	1.50	3.00
9	Ed Belfour, Goalie, Chi.	1.50	3.00
10	Jeremy Roenick, Chi.	2.00	4.00

— 1991 ROOKIE AND TRADED —

 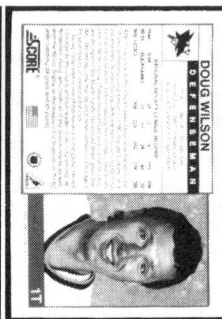

1991 Rookie and Traded
Card No. 1T, Douglas Wilson

Card Size: 2 1/2" X 3 1/2"
Face: Four colour, green border
Back: Four colour on white card stock, Number, Resume, Position
Imprint: © 1991 SCORE, PRINTED IN U.S.A.
Complete Set No.: 110

Complete Set Price:	4.00	8.00
Common Player:	.03	.05

SAN JOSE SHARKS

No.	Player	EX	NRMT
1T	Douglas Wilson	.03	.05
2T	Brian Mullen	.03	.05
3T	Kelly Kisio	.03	.05
4T	Brian Hayward, Goalie	.03	.05
5T	Anthony Hrkac	.03	.05
6T	Steven Bozek	.03	.05
7T	John Carter	.03	.05
8T	Neil Wilkinson	.03	.05
9T	Wayne Presley	.03	.05
10T	Robert McGill	.03	.05

1991 YOUNG SUPERSTARS — SCORE • 375

REGULAR ISSUE

No.	Player	EX	NRMT
11T	Craig Ludwig, Min.	.03	.05
12T	Mikhail Tatarinov, Que.	.03	.05
13T	Todd Elik, Min.	.03	.05
14T	Randy Burridge, Wash.	.03	.05
15T	Tim Kerr, NYR	.03	.05
16T	Randy Gilhen, LA	.03	.05
17T	John Tonelli, Chi.	.03	.05
18T	Tom Kurvers, NYI	.03	.05
19T	Steve Duchesne, Phi.	.03	.05
20T	Charles Huddy, LA	.03	.05
21T	Adam Creighton, NYI	.03	.05
22T	Brent Ashton, Bos.	.03	.05
23T	George (Rob) Ramage, Min.	.03	.05
24T	Steve Kasper, Phi.	.03	.05
25T	Scott Mellanby, Edm.	.03	.05
26T	Steve Leach, Bos.	.03	.05
27T	Scott Niedermayer, NJD	.15	.30
28T	Craig Berube, Tor.	.03	.05
29T	Gregory Paslawski, Que.	.03	.05
30T	Randy Hillier, Buf.	.03	.05
31T	Stephane J.J. Richer, NJD	.05	.10
32T	Brian MacLellan, Det.	.03	.05
33T	Marc Habscheid, Cal.	.03	.05
34T	Dave Babych, Van.	.03	.05
35T	Troy Murray, Win.	.03	.05
36T	Ray Sheppard, Det.	.03	.05
37T	Glen Featherstone, Bos.	.03	.05
38T	Brendan Shanahan, St. L.	.03	.05
39T	Dave Christian, St. L.	.03	.05
40T	Michael Bullard, Tor.	.03	.05
41T	Ryan Walter, Van.	.03	.05
42T	Randy Wood, Buf.	.03	.05
43T	Vincent Riendeau, Goalie, Det.	.03	.05
44T	Adam Graves, NYR	.15	.30
45T	Scott Stevens, NJD	.03	.05
46T	Sylvain Coté, Wash.	.03	.05
47T	David Barr, NJD	.03	.05
48T	Randall Gregg, Van.	.03	.05
49T	Pavel Bure, Van.	1.50	3.00
50T	Jari Kurri, LA	.03	.05
51T	Steve Thomas, NYI	.03	.05
52T	Troy Crowder, Det.	.03	.05
53T	Brad Jones, Phi.	.03	.05
54T	Randy McKay, NJD	.03	.05
55T	Scott Thornton, Edm.	.03	.05
56T	Bryan Marchment, Chi.	.03	.05
57T	Andrew Cassels, Har.	.03	.05
58T	Grant Fuhr, Goalie, Tor.	.03	.05
59T	Vincent Damphousse, Edm.	.03	.05
60T	Richard Zombo, St. L.	.03	.05
61T	Glenn Anderson, Tor.	.03	.05
62T	Peter Ing, Goalie, Edm.	.03	.05
63T	Tom Chorske, NJD	.03	.05
64T	Kirk Muller, Mon.	.03	.05
65T	Dan Quinn, Phi.	.03	.05
66T	Murray Baron, St. L.	.03	.05
67T	Sergei Nemchinov, NYR	.10	.20
68T	Rod Brind'Amour, Phi.	.08	.15
69T	Ronald Sutter, St. L.	.03	.05
70T	Luke Richardson, Edm.	.03	.05
71T	Nicklas Lidstrom, Det., Error	.20	.40
72T	Petri Skriko, Win.	.03	.05
73T	Steve Smith, Chi.	.03	.05
74T	Dave Manson, Edm.	.03	.05
75T	Kay Whitmore, Goalie, Har.	.03	.05
76T	Valeri Kamensky, Que.	.20	.40
77T	Russ Romaniuk, Win.	.08	.15
78T	Brad May, Buf.	.03	.05
79T	Tomas Forslund, Cal.	.03	.05
80T	Stu Barnes, Win.	.03	.05
81T	Darryl Sydor, LA	.03	.05
82T	Jimmy Waite, Goalie, Chi.	.03	.05
83T	Vladimir Ruzicka, Bos.	.03	.05
84T	David Brown, Phi.	.03	.05
85T	Mark Messier, NYR	.13	.25
86T	Neil Sheehy, Cal.	.03	.05
87T	Todd Krygier, Wash.	.03	.05
88T	Eric Lindros, Team Canada	2.00	4.00
89T	Nelson, Emerson, St. L.	.12	.25

SAN JOSE SHARKS

No.	Player	EX	NRMT
90T	Pat Falloon	.20	.40
91T	Dean Evason	.03	.05
92T	Jeff Hackett, Goalie	.05	.10
93T	Rob Zettler	.03	.05
94T	Perry Berezan	.03	.05
95T	Pat MacLeod	.05	.10
96T	Craig Coxe	.03	.05
97T	Ken Hammond	.05	.10
98T	Brian Lawton	.03	.05
99T	Perry Anderson	.05	.10

REGULAR ISSUE

No.	Player	EX	NRMT
100T	Pat LaFontaine	.13	.25
101T	Pierre Turgeon, NYI	.13	.25
102T	Dave McLlwain, NYI	.03	.05
103T	Brent Sutter, Chi.	.03	.05
104T	Uwe Krupp, NYI	.03	.05
105T	Martin Lapointe, Det.	.03	.05
106T	Derian Hatcher, Min.	.03	.05
107T	Darrin Shannon, Win.	.03	.05
108T	Benoit Hogue, NYI	.03	.05
109T	Vladimir Konstantinov, Det.	.08	.15
110T	Andrei Lomakin, Phi.	.03	.05

— 1991 YOUNG SUPERSTARS —

Like the issue from the previous year the Young Superstars set was available only as a factory set.

 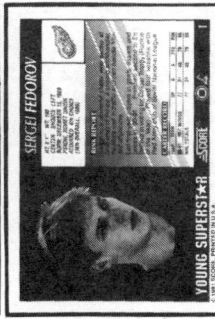

1991 Young Superstars
Card No. 1, Sergei Fedorov

Card Size: 2 1/2" X 3 1/2"
Face: Four colour, brown border, Score logo
Back: Four colour, Number, Resume, Team logo
Imprint: © 1991 SCORE, PRINTED IN U.S.A.
Complete Set No.: 40
Set Price: 3.00 6.00
Common Goalie: .03 .05
Common Player: .03 .05

No.	Player	EX	NRMT
1	Sergei Fedorov, Det.	.20	.40
2	Mike Richter, Goalie, NYR	.15	.30
3	Mats Sundin, Que.	.12	.25
4	Theoren Fleury, Cal.	.05	.10
5	John Cullen, Har.	.03	.05
6	Dimitri Khristich, Wash.	.03	.05
7	Stephan Lebeau, Mon.	.08	.15
8	Robert Blake, LA	.05	.10
9	Kenneth Hodge, Jr., Bos.	.05	.10
10	Mike Ricci, Phi.	.08	.15
11	Trevor Linden, Van.	.10	.20
12	Peter Ing, Goalie, Edm.	.03	.05
13	Alexander Mogilny, Buf.	.20	.40
14	Martin Gelinas, Edm.	.03	.05
15	Chris Terreri, Goalie, NJD	.03	.05
16	Jeff Norton, NYI	.03	.05
17	Bob Essensa, Goalie, Win.	.03	.05
18	Mark Tinordi, Min.	.03	.05
19	Curtis Joseph, Goalie, St. L.	.03	.05
20	Joe Sakic, Que.	.10	.20
21	Jeremy Roenick, Chi.	.13	.25
22	Mark Recchi, Pit.	.10	.20

No.	Player	EX	NRMT
23	Eric Desjardins, Mon.	.03	.05
24	Robert Reichel, Cal.	.03	.05
25	Tim Cheveldae, Goalie, Det.	.05	.10
26	Eric Weinrich, NJD	.03	.05
27	Murray Barron, St. L.	.03	.05
28	Darren Turcotte, NYR	.03	.05
29	Troy Gamble, Goalie, Van.	.05	.10
30	Eric Lindros, Osh.	1.50	3.00
31	Benoit Hogue, Buf.	.03	.05
32	Ed Belfour, Goalie, Chi.	.10	.20
33	Ron Tugnutt, Goalie, Que.	.05	.10
34	Pat Elynuik, Win.	.03	.05
35	Michael Modano, Min.	.05	.10
36	Robert Holik, Har.	.03	.05
37	Yves Racine, Det.	.03	.05
38	Jaromir Jagr, Pit.	.13	.25
39	Stephane Morin, Que.	.03	.05
40	Kevin Miller, Det.	.03	.05

— 1991 - 92 PINNACLE ISSUE —

ENGLISH and FRENCH

With the introduction of this new premium series Score counterfeit-proofed their cards by adding a greyish box on the lower middle back, which, when viewed through a decoder will confirm authenticity.

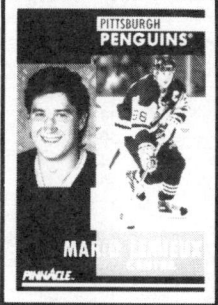 

1991-92 Pinnacle English Issue
Card No. 1, Mario Lemieux

Card Size: 2 1/2" X 3 1/2"
Face: Four colour
Back: Four colour on white card stock, Number, Resume
Imprint: © 1992 SCORE, PRINTED IN U.S.A.
Complete Set No.: 420

	English	French
Complete Set Price:	45.00	45.00
Common Goalie:	.10	.10
Common Player:	.10	.10
Foil Pack: (12 Cards)	1.75	1.75
Foil Box: (36 Packs)	55.00	55.00
Foil Case: (16 Boxes)	750.00	750.00

No.	Player	English NRMT	French NRMT
1	Mario Lemieux, Pit.	2.00	2.00
2	Trevor Linden, Van.	.40	.40
3	Kirk Muller, Mon.	.15	.15
4	Phil Housley, Win.	.10	.10
5	Michael Modano, Min.	.75	.75
6	Adam Oates, St. L.	.40	.40
7	Tom Kurvers, NYI	.10	.10
8	Douglas Bodger, Buf.	.10	.10
9	Rod Brind'Amour, Phi.	.45	.45
10	Mats Sundin, Que.	.75	.75
11	Gary Suter, Cal.	.10	.10
12	Glenn Anderson, Tor.	.10	.10
13	Douglas Wilson, SJ	.10	.10
14	Stephane J.J. Richer, NJD	.10	.10
15	Raymond Bourque, Bos.	.30	.30
16	Adam Graves, NYR	.75	.75
17	Luc Robitaille, LA	.45	.45
18	Steve Smith, Chi.	.10	.10
19	Uwe Krupp, NYI	.10	.10
20	Rick Tocchet, Phi.	.10	.10
21	Tim Cheveldae, Goalie, Det.	.10	.10
22	Kay Whitmore, Goalie, Har.	.10	.10

SCORE — 1991-92 PINNACLE ISSUE

No.	Player	English NRMT	French NRMT
23	Kelly Miller, Wash.	.10	.10
24	Esa Tikkanen, Edm.	.10	.10
25	Pat LaFontaine, Buf.	.50	.50
26	James Patrick, NYR	.10	.10
27	Daniel Marois, Tor.	.10	.10
28	Denis Savard, Mon.	.10	.10
29	Steve Larmer, Chi.	.10	.10
30	Pierre Turgeon, NYI	.50	.50
31	Gary Leeman, Tor.	.10	.10
32	Mike Ricci, Phi.	.30	.30
33	Troy Murray, Win.	.10	.10
34	Sergio Momesso, Van.	.10	.10
35	Martin McSorley, LA	.20	.20
36	Paul Ysebaert, Det.	.10	.10
37	Gary Roberts, Cal.	.10	.10
38	Mike Hudson, Chi.	.10	.10
39	Kelly Hrudey, Goalie, LA	.10	.10
40	Dale Hunter, Wash.	.10	.10
41	Brendan Shanahan, St. L.	.50	.50
42	Steve Duchesne, Phi.	.10	.10
43	Patrick Verbeek, Har.	.10	.10
44	Tom Barrasso, Goalie, Pit.	.10	.10
45	Scott Mellanby, Edm.	.10	.10
46	Stephen Leach, Bos.	.10	.10
47	Darren Turcotte, NYR	.10	.10
48	Jari Kurri, LA	.10	.10
49	Michel Petit, Tor.	.10	.10
50	Mark Messier, NYR	.50	.50
51	Terry Carkner, Phi.	.10	.10
52	Tim Kerr, NYR	.10	.10
53	Jaromir Jagr, Pit.	1.25	1.25
54	Joe Nieuwendyk, Cal.	.10	.10
55	Randy Burridge, Wash.	.10	.10
56	Robert Reichel, Cal.	.30	.30
57	Craig Janney, Bos.	.25	.25
58	Chris Chelios, Chi.	.10	.10
59	Bryan Fogarty, Que.	.10	.10
60	Christian Ruuttu, Buf.	.10	.10
61	Steven Bozek, SJ	.10	.10
62	Dave Manson, Edm.	.10	.10
63	Bruce Driver, NJD	.10	.10
64	Michael Ramsey, Buf.	.10	.10
65	Robert Holik, Har.	.10	.10
66	Bob Essensa, Goalie, Win.	.10	.10
67	Patrick Flatley, NYI	.10	.10
68	Wayne Presley, SJ	.10	.10
69	Michael Bullard, Tor.	.10	.10
70	Claude Lemieux, NJD	.10	.10
71	Dave Gagner, Min.	.10	.10
72	Jeff Brown, St. L.	.10	.10
73	Eric Desjardins, Mon.	.15	.15
74	Fredrik Olausson, Win.	.10	.10
75	Steve Yzerman, Det.	.75	.75
76	Tony Granato, LA	.10	.10
77	Adam Burt, Har.	.10	.10
78	Cam Neely, Bos.	.25	.25
79	Brent Sutter, Chi.	.10	.10
80	Dale Hawerchuk, Buf.	.10	.10
81	Scott Stevens, NJD	.10	.10
82	Adam Creighton, NYI	.10	.10
83	Brian Hayward, Goalie, SJ	.10	.10
84	Dan Quinn, Phi.	.10	.10
85	Garth Butcher, St. L.	.10	.10
86	Shawn Burr, Det.	.10	.10
87	Peter Bondra, Wash.	.10	.10
88	Brad Shaw, Har.	.10	.10
89	Eric Weinrich, NJD	.10	.10
90	Brian Bradley, Tor.	.10	.10
91	Vincent Damphousse, Edm.	.10	.10
92	Douglas Gilmour, Cal.	.75	.75
93	Martin Gelinas, Edm.	.10	.10
94	Michael Ridley, Wash.	.10	.10
95	Ron Sutter, St. L.	.10	.10
96	Mark Osborne, Win.	.10	.10
97	Mikhail Tatarinov, Que.	.15	.15
98	Robert McGill, SJ	.10	.10
99	Robert Carpenter, Bos.	.10	.10
100	Wayne Gretzky, LA	2.50	2.50
101	Viacheslav Fetisov, NJD	.10	.10
102	Shayne Corson, Mon.	.10	.10
103	Clint Malarchuk, Goalie, Buf.	.10	.10
104	Randy Wood, Buf.	.10	.10
105	Curtis Joseph, Goalie, St. L.	.50	.50
106	Cliff Ronning, Van.	.10	.10
107	Derek King, NYI	.10	.10
108	Neil Wilkinson, SJ	.10	.10
109	Michel Goulet, Chi.	.10	.10
110	Zarley Zalapski, Har.	.10	.10
111	David Ellett, Tor.	.10	.10
112	Glen Wesley, Bos.	.10	.10
113	Bob Kudelski, LA	.25	.25
114	Jamie Macoun, Cal.	.10	.10
115	John MacLean, NJD	.10	.10
116	Steve Thomas, NYI	.10	.10
117	Pat Elynuik, Win.	.10	.10
118	Ron Hextall, Goalie, Phi.	.10	.10
119	Jeff Hackett, Goalie, SJ	.10	.10
120	Jeremy Roenick, Chi.	2.00	2.00
121	John Vanbiesbrouck, Goalie, NYR	.30	.30
122	David Andreychuk, Buf.	.30	.30
123	Ray Ferraro, NYI	.10	.10
124	Ronald Tugnutt, Goalie, Que.	.10	.10
125	John Cullen, Har.	.10	.10
126	Andrew Moog, Goalie, Bos.	.10	.10
127	Ed Belfour, Goalie, Chi.	.75	.75
128	Dino Ciccarelli, Wash.	.10	.10
129	Brian Bellows, Min.	.10	.10
130	Guy Carbonneau, Mon.	.10	.10
131	Kevin Hatcher, Wash.	.10	.10
132	Michael Vernon, Goalie, Cal.	.10	.10
133	Kevin Miller, Det.	.10	.10
134	Per-Erik Eklund, Phi.	.10	.10
135	Brian Mullen, SJ	.10	.10
136	Brian Leetch, NYR	.80	.80
137	Daren Puppa, Goalie, Buf.	.10	.10
138	Steven Finn, Que.	.10	.10
139	Stephan Lebeau, Mon.	.30	.30
140	Gordon Murphy, Phi.	.10	.10
141	Robert Brown, Har.	.10	.10
142	Kenneth Daneyko, NJD	.10	.10
143	Lawrence Murphy, Pit.	.10	.10
144	Jon Casey, Goalie, Min.	.10	.10
145	John Ogrodnick, NYR	.10	.10
146	Benoit Hogue, NYI	.10	.10
147	Michael McPhee, Mon.	.10	.10
148	Donald Beaupre, Goalie, Wash.	.10	.10
149	Kjell Samuelsson, Phi.	.10	.10
150	Joe Sakic, Que.	.75	.75
151	Mark Recchi, Pit.	1.00	1.00
152	Ulf Dahlen, Min.	.10	.10
153	Dean Evason, SJ	.10	.10
154	Keith Brown, Chi.	.10	.10
155	Ray Sheppard, Det.	.25	.25
156	Owen Nolan, Que.	.30	.30
157	Sergei Fedorov, Det.	2.00	2.00
158	Kirk McLean, Goalie, Van.	.10	.10
159	Petr Klima, Edm.	.10	.10
160	Brian Skrudland, Mon.	.10	.10
161	Neal Broten, Min.	.10	.10
162	Dimitri Khristich, Wash.	.10	.10
163	Alexander Mogilny, Buf.	1.00	1.00
164	Mike Richter, Goalie, NYR	.65	.65
165	Daniel Berthiaume, Goalie, LA	.10	.10
166	Teppo Numminen, Win.	.10	.10
167	Ronald Francis, Pit.	.10	.10
168	Grant Fuhr, Goalie, Tor.	.10	.10
169	Mike Liut, Goalie, Wash.	.10	.10
170	Bill Ranford, Goalie, Edm.	.10	.10
171	Garry Galley, Bos.	.10	.10
172	Jeff Norton, NYI	.10	.10
173	Jimmy Carson, Det.	.10	.10
174	Peter Zezel, Tor.	.10	.10
175	Patrick Roy, Goalie, Mon.	1.50	1.50
176	Joe Mullen, Pit.	.10	.10
177	Murray Craven, Har.	.10	.10
178	Tomas Sandstrom, LA	.10	.10
179	Joel Otto, Cal.	.10	.10
180	Stephen Konroyd, Chi.	.10	.10
181	Vladimir Ruzicka, Bos.	.10	.10
182	Paul Cavallini, St. L.	.10	.10
183	Bob Probert, Det.	.10	.10
184	Brian Propp, Min.	.10	.10
185	Glenn Healy, Goalie, NYI	.10	.10
186	Paul Coffey, Pit.	.20	.20
187	Jan Erixon, NYR	.10	.10
188	Kevin Lowe, Edm.	.10	.10
189	Doug Lidster, Van.	.10	.10
190	Theoren Fleury, Cal.	.45	.45
191	Kevin Stevens, Pit.	.75	.75
192	Petr Nedved, Van.	.40	.40
193	Ed Olczyk, Win.	.10	.10
194	Mike Hough, Que.	.10	.10
195	Rod Langway, Wash.	.10	.10
196	Craig Simpson, Edm.	.10	.10
197	Petr Svoboda, Mon.	.10	.10
198	David Volek, NYI	.10	.10
199	Mark Tinordi, Min.	.10	.10
200	Brett Hull, St. L.	1.50	1.50
201	Robert Blake, LA	.40	.40
202	Michael Gartner, NYR	.10	.10
203	Kenneth Hodge, Jr., Bos.	.10	.10
204	Murray Baron, St. L.	.10	.10
205	Gerard Gallant, Det.	.10	.10
206	Joe Murphy, Edm.	.10	.10
207	Al Iafrate, Wash.	.10	.10
208	Larry Robinson, LA	.10	.10
209	Mathieu Schneider, Mon.	.10	.10
210	Robert Smith, Min.	.10	.10
211	Gerald Diduck, Van.	.10	.10
212	Luke Richardson, Edm.	.10	.10
213	Rob Zettler, SJ	.10	.10
214	Brad McCrimmon, Det.	.10	.10
215	Craig MacTavish, Edm.	.10	.10
216	Gino Cavallini, St. L.	.10	.10
217	Craig Wolanin, Que.	.10	.10
218	Greg Adams, Van.	.10	.10
219	Mike Craig, Min.	.10	.10
220	Allan MacInnis, Cal.	.20	.20
221	Sylvain Cote, Wash.	.10	.10
222	Robert Sweeney, Bos.	.10	.10
223	Dave Snuggerud, Buf.	.10	.10
224	Randy Ladouceur, Har.	.10	.10
225	Charles Huddy, LA	.10	.10
226	Sylvain Turgeon, Mon.	.10	.10
227	Phillippe Bourque, Pit.	.10	.10
228	George (Rob) Ramage, Min.	.10	.10
229	Jeff Beukeboom, NYR	.10	.10
230	Alexei Gusarov, Que., RC	.20	.20
231	Kelly Kisio, SJ	.10	.10
232	Calle Johansson, Wash.	.10	.10
233	Yves Racine, Det.	.10	.10
234	Peter Sidorkiewicz, Goalie, Har.	.10	.10
235	Jim Johnson, Min.	.10	.10
236	Brent Gilchrist, Mon.	.10	.10
237	Jyrki Lumme, Van.	.10	.10
238	Randy Gilhen, LA	.10	.10
239	Ken Baumgartner, NYI	.10	.10
240	Joe Kocur, NYR	.10	.10
241	Bryan Trottier, Pit.	.10	.10
242	Todd Krygier, Wash.	.10	.10
243	Darrin Shannon, Win.	.10	.10
244	David Christian, St. L.	.10	.10
245	Stephane Morin, Que.	.15	.15
246	Kevin Dineen, Phi.	.10	.10
247	Chris Terreri, Goalie, NJD	.20	.20
248	Craig Ludwig, Min.	.10	.10
249	David Taylor, LA	.10	.10
250	Wendel Clark, Tor.	.25	.25
251	David Shaw, Edm.	.10	.10
252	Paul Ranheim, Cal.	.10	.10
253	Mark Hunter, Har.	.10	.10
254	Russell Courtnall, Mon.	.10	.10
255	Alexei Kasatonov, NJD	.10	.10
256	Randy Moller, NYR	.10	.10
257	Bob Errey, Pit.	.10	.10
258	Curtis Leschyshyn, Que.	.10	.10
259	Richard Zombo, St. L.	.10	.10
260	Dana Murzyn, Van.	.10	.10
261	Dirk Graham, Chi.	.10	.10
262	Craig Muni, Edm.	.10	.10
263	Geoff Courtnall, Van.	.10	.10
264	Todd Elik, Min.	.10	.10
265	Mike Keane, Mon.	.10	.10
266	Peter Stastny, NJD	.10	.10
267	Ulf Samuelsson, Pit.	.10	.10
268	Richard Sutter, St. L.	.10	.10

1991-92 TEAM PINNACLE INSERT SET — SCORE • 377

No.	Player	English NRMT	French NRMT
269	Michael Krushelnyski, Tor.	.10	.10
270	David Babych, Van.	.10	.10
271	Sergei Makarov, Cal.	.10	.10
272	David Maley, NJD	.10	.10
273	Normand Rochefort, NYR	.10	.10
274	Gordon Roberts, Pit.	.10	.10
275	Thomas Steen, Win.	.10	.10
276	Dave Lowry, St. L.	.10	.10
277	Michal Pivonka, Wash.	.10	.10
278	Todd Gill, Tor.	.10	.10
279	Paul MacDermid, Win.	.10	.10
280	Brent Ashton, Bos.	.10	.10
281	Randy Hillier, Buf.	.10	.10
282	Frantisek Musil, Cal.	.10	.10
283	Geoff Smith, Edm.	.10	.10
284	John Tonelli, Chi.	.10	.10
285	Joe Reekie, NYI	.10	.10
286	Gregory Paslawski, Que.	.10	.10
287	Perry Berezan, SJ	.10	.10
288	Randy Carlyle, Win.	.10	.10
289	Christopher Nilan, Bos.	.10	.10
290	Patrik Sundstrom, NJD	.10	.10
291	Garry Valk, Van.	.10	.10
292	Mike Foligno, Tor.	.10	.10
293	Igor Larionov, Van.	.10	.10
294	Jim Sandlak, Van.	.10	.10
295	Tom Chorske, NJD	.10	.10
296	Claude Loiselle, Tor.	.10	.10
297	Mark Howe, Phi.	.10	.10
298	Steve Chiasson, Det.	.10	.10
299	**Mike Donnelly, LA, RC**	.30	.30
300	Bernie Nicholls, Edm.	.10	.10

ROOKIE

No.	Player	English NRMT	French NRMT
301	**Anthony Amonte, NYR, RC**	.75	.75
302	Brad May, Buf.	.10	.10
303	**Josef Beranek, Edm., RC**	.85	.85
304	**Rob Pearson, Tor., RC**	.35	.35
305	Andrei Lomakin, Phi.	.10	.10
306	Kip Miller, Que.	.10	.10
307	**Kevin Haller, Buf., RC**	.20	.20
308	**Kevin Todd, NJD, RC**	.20	.20
309	**Geoff Sanderson, Har., RC**	3.50	3.50
310	**Doug Weight, NYR, RC**	.60	.60
311	**Vladimir Konstantinov, Det., RC**	.40	.40
312	**Peter Ahola, LA, RC**	.10	.10
313	**Claude Lapointe, Que., RC**	.10	.10
314	Nelson Emerson, St. L.	.50	.50
315	Pavel Bure, Van.	4.50	4.50
316	Jimmy Waite, Chi.	.10	.10
317	Sergei Nemchinov, NYR	.25	.25
318	Alexander Godynyuk, Tor.	.20	.20
319	Stu Barnes, Win.	.10	.10
320	**Nicklas Lidstrom, Det., RC**	.75	.75
321	Darryl Sydor, LA	.10	.10
322	**John LeClair, Mon., RC**	.30	.30
323	**Arturs Irbe, Goalie, SJ**	1.25	1.25
324	**Russ Romaniuk, Win., RC**	.20	.20
325	**Kenneth Sutton, Buf., RC**	.20	.20
326	Bob Beers, Bos.	.10	.10
327	**Michel Picard, Har., RC**	.10	.10
328	Derian Hatcher, Min.	.20	.20
329	Pat Falloon, SJ	.75	.75
330	Donald Audette, Buf.	.20	.20
331	**Pat Jablonski, St. L., RC**	.20	.20
332	**Corey Foster, Phi., RC**	.10	.10
333	**Tomas Forslund, Cal., RC**	.20	.20
334	Steven Rice, Edm.	.10	.10
335	Marc Bureau, Min.	.10	.10
336	Kimbi Daniels, Phi.	.10	.10
337	Adam Foote, Que.	.10	.10
338	**Dan Kordic, Phi., RC**	.10	.10
339	Link Gaetz, SJ	.10	.10
340	**Valeri Kamensky, Que., RC**	.75	.75
341	**Tom Draper, Buf., RC**	.10	.10
342	**Jayson More, SJ, RC**	.20	.20
343	**Dominic Roussel, Goalie, Phi., RC**	.80	.80
344	**Jim Paek, Pit., RC**	.20	.20
345	**Felix Potvin, Goalie, Tor.**	4.00	4.00
346	**Dan Lambert, Que., RC**	.20	.20

No.	Player	English NRMT	French NRMT
347	Louis DeBrusk, Edm.	.20	.20
348	**Jamie Baker, Que., RC**	.15	.15
349	**Scott Niedermayer, NJD, RC**	.75	.75
350	**Paul Di Pietro, Mon., RC**	.40	.40
351	**Chris Winnes, Bos., RC**	.20	.20
352	Mark Greig, Har.	.20	.20
353	**Luciano Borsato, Win., RC**	.75	.75
354	**Valeri Zelepukin, NJD, RC**	.75	.75
355	Martin Lapointe, Det.	.25	.25

GAME WINNERS

No.	Player	English NRMT	French NRMT
356	Brett Hull, St. L.	.40	.40
357	Steve Larmer, Chi.	.10	.10
358	Theoren Fleury, Cal.	.10	.10
359	Jeremy Roenick, Chi.	.40	.40
360	Mark Recchi, Pit.	.30	.30

REGULAR ISSUE

No.	Player	English NRMT	French NRMT
361	Brad Marsh, Det.	.10	.10
362	Kris King, NYR	.10	.10
363	Doug Brown, NJD	.10	.10
364	Carey Wilson, Cal.	.10	.10
365	Eric Lindros, Can. Nat. Team	11.00	11.00

GOOD GUYS

No.	Player	English NRMT	French NRMT
366	Kevin Dineen, Phi.	.10	.10
367	John Vanbiesbrouck, Goalie, NYR	.15	.15
368	Raymond Bourque, Bos.	.15	.15
369	Douglas Wilson, SJ	.10	.10
370	Keith Brown, Chi.	.10	.10
371	Kevin Lowe, Edm.	.10	.10
372	Kelly Miller, Wash.	.10	.10
373	David Taylor, LA	.10	.10
374	Guy Carbonneau, Mon.	.10	.10
375	Tim Hunter, Cal.	.10	.10

TECHNICIANS

No.	Player	English NRMT	French NRMT
376	Brett Hull, St. L.	.40	.40
377	Paul Coffey, Pit.	.10	.10
378	Adam Oates, St. L.	.20	.20
379	Andrew Moog, Goalie, Bos.	.15	.15
380	Mario Lemieux, Pit.	.50	.50

IDOLS

No.	Player	English NRMT	French NRMT
381	Joe Sakic, Que., Wayne Gretzky, LA	.60	.60
382	Robert Blake, LA, Larry Robinson, Mon.	.15	.15
383	Doug Weight, NYR, Steve Yzerman, Det.	.35	.35
384	Michael Richter, Goalie, NYR, Bernie Parent, Goalie, Phi.	.35	.35
385	Luc Robitaille, LA, Marcel Dionne, LA	.25	.25
386	Ed Olczyk, Win., Bobby Clarke, Phi.	.15	.15
387	Patrick Roy, Goalie, Mon., Rogatien Vachon, Goalie, Mon.	.50	.50
388	Ed Belfour, Goalie, Chi., Tony Esposito, Goalie, Chi.	.35	.35
389	Mats Sundin, Que., Mats Naslund, Mon.	.20	.20
390	Anthony Amonte, NYR, Mark Messier, NYR	.40	.40
391	John Cullen, Har., Barry Cullen	.15	.15
392	Gary Suter, Cal., Bobby Orr, Bos.	.50	.50
393	Richard Zombo, St. L., Glen Resch, NYI	.15	.15
394	Todd Krygier, Wash.	.10	.10
395	John Druce, Wash.	.10	.10

SIDELINES

No.	Player	English NRMT	French NRMT
396	Robert Carpenter, Bos.	.10	.10
397	Clint Malarchuk, Goalie Buf.	.10	.10
398	Jim Kyte, Cal.	.10	.10
399	Allan MacInnis, Cal.	.10	.10

No.	Player	English NRMT	French NRMT
400	Ed Belfour, Goalie, Chi.	.35	.35
401	Brad Marsh, Det.	.10	.10
402	Brian Benning, LA	.10	.10
403	Larry Robinson, LA	.10	.10
404	Craig Ludwig, Min.	.10	.10
405	Patrick Flatley, NYI	.10	.10
406	Gary Nylund, NYI	.10	.10
407	Kjell Samuelsson, Phi.	.10	.10
408	Dan Quinn, Phi.	.10	.10
409	Garth Butcher, St. L.	.10	.10
410	Richard Zombo, St. L.	.10	.10
411	Paul Cavallini, St. L.	.10	.10

No.	Player	English NRMT	French NRMT
412	Link Gaetz, SJ	.10	.10
413	David Hannan, Tor.	.10	.10
414	Peter Zezel, Tor.	.10	.10
415	Randy Gregg, Van.	.10	.10
416	Pat Elynuik, Win.	.10	.10
417	Rod Buskas, Chi.	.10	.10
418	Mark Howe, Phi.	.10	.10

REGULAR ISSUE

No.	Player	English NRMT	French NRMT
419	Don Sweeney, Bos.	.10	.10
420	Mark Hardy, NYR	.10	.10

— 1991-92 TEAM PINNACLE INSERT SET —

ENGLISH AND FRENCH

Team Pinnacle was randomly inserted in the foil packs of Score Pinnacle. These cards are scarce and numbered B-1 to B-12.

1991-92 Team Pinnacle Insert Set, French Card No. B-8, Allan MacInnis

Card Size: 2 1/2" X 3 1/2"
Face: Black and white, blue or red name plate; Name, Team
Back: Black, white and blue or red on white card stock; Name, Position, Resume, Number
Imprint: © 1991 SCORE, PRINTED IN U.S.A.

	English	French
Complete Set No.: 12		
Complete Set Price:	550.00	550.00
Common Player:	30.00	30.00

WALES CONFERENCE

No.	Player	English NRMT	French NRMT
B-1	Patrick Roy, Goalie, Mon.	100.00	120.00
B-2	Raymond Bourque, Bos.	40.00	40.00
B-3	Brian Leetch, NYR	55.00	55.00
B-4	Kevin Stevens, Pit.	40.00	40.00
B-5	Mario Lemieux, Pit.	100.00	120.00
B-6	Cam Neely, Bos.	35.00	35.00

CAMPBELL CONFERENCE

No.	Player	English NRMT	French NRMT
B-7	Bill Ranford, Goalie, Edm.	30.00	30.00
B-8	Allam MacInnis, Cal.	30.00	30.00
B-9	Chris Chelios, Chi.	40.00	40.00
B-10	Luc Robitaille, LA	50.00	55.00
B-11	Wayne Gretzky, LA	100.00	125.00
B-12	Brett Hull, St.L.	60.00	70.00

1991 FIRE ON ICE

ERIC LINDROS

These 3 cards were given out by Score as a premium when purchasing the book "Fire On Ice" by Eric Lindros.

PHOTOGRAPH
NOT AVAILABLE
AT PRESS TIME

Card Size: 2 1/2" x 3 1/2"
Face: Four colour, Light blue border
Back: Four colour, Light blue border, card stock; Name, Biography
Imprint: © 1991 SCORE. PRINTED
Complete Set No.: 3
Complete Set Price: 7.50   15.00
Common Player: 2.50   5.00

No.	Player	EX	NRMT
1	A Real Corker	2.50	5.00
2	A Little Bit of Heaven	2.50	5.00
3	Graduation Day	2.50	5.00

1992 LINDROS JOINING THE FLYERS

ERIC LINDROS PRESS CONFERENCE CARD

This card was issued at a press conference in Philadelphia, announcing Lindros acceptance of the Flyers offer to join the

PHOTOGRAPH
NOT AVAILABLE
AT PRESS TIME

Philadelphia team.

Card Size: 2 1/2" x 3 1/2"
Face: Four colour, White border
Back: Four colour, white border; Name; Resume on card stock
Imprint: © 1992 SCORE, PRINTED IN U.S.A.

No.	Player	EX	NRMT
--	Eric Lindros	37.50	75.00

1992 - 93 PROMOTIONAL CARDS

CANADIAN ISSUE

This 6-card set was available as a handout at larger shows, usually through a 4-card sheet format that reads "PROMOTIONAL PURPOSES ONLY NOT FOR RESALE" in large red letters on the back. The cards are no different than the regular cards except for the following. The word "SAMPLE" across the Biography in white, and part of the red letters from the words for "PROMOTIONAL PURPOSES ONLY NOT FOR RESALE"

1992-93 Promotional Cards
Card No. 25, Kevin Stevens

Card Size: 2-1/2" x 3-1/2"
Face: Four colour with blue border
Back: Four colour, white border; Name, Resume, Number, Bilingual logo. Resume on card stock
Imprint: © 1992 SCORE, PRINTED IN THE U.S.A.
Complete Set No.: 6
Complete Set Price: 3.00   6.00
Common Player: .50   1.00

SINGLE CARDS

No.	Player	EX	NRMT
2	Chris Chelios, Chi.	.50	1.00
6	Pat LaFontaine, Buf.	1.00	2.00
8	Claude Lemieux, NJ	.50	1.00
16	Esa Tikkanen, Edm.	.50	1.00
23	Eric Desjardins, Mon.	.50	1.00
25	Kevin Stevens, Pit.	1.00	2.00

FOUR CARD SHEETS

No.	Player	EX	NRMT
--	Sheet	2.50	5.00
25	Kevin Stevens, Pit.		
8	Claude Lemieux, NJ		
16	Esa Tikkanen, Edm.		
23	Eric Desjardin, Mon.		
--	Sheet	3.00	6.00
6	Pat LaFontaine, Buf.		
25	Kevins Stevens, Pit.		
2	Chris Chelios, Chi.		
16	Esa Tikkanen, Edm.		

1992 - 93 REGULAR ISSUE

AMERICAN and CANADIAN

 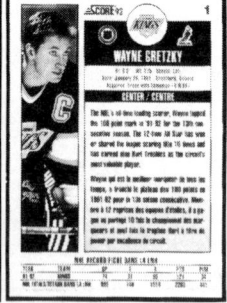

1992-93 Canadian Issue
Card No. 1, Wayne Gretzky

The 550-card Canadian set is numbered identically by player to the American set but the design and pictures used on the cards are different than the American. The set could be obtained either through regular foil or jumbo packs.

Card Size: 2 1/2" x 3 1/2"
Face: Four colour, blue border; Name, Team, Position, Bilingual
Back: Four colour, white border, card stock; Name, Number, Position, Resume, Bilingual
Imprint: © 1992 SCORE, PRINTED IN THE U.S.A.

	USA	Can.
Complete Set No.: 550		
Complete Set Price:	23.00	23.00
Common Player:	.05	.05
Foil Pack: (16 Cards)	1.00	1.00
Foil Box: (36 Packs)	30.00	30.00

No.	Player	USA NRMT	Can. NRMT
1	Wayne Gretzky, LA	1.00	1.00
2	Chris Chelios, Chi.	.10	.10
3	Joe Mullen, Pit.	.10	.10
4	Russell Courtnall, Mon.	.10	.10
5	Mike Richter, Goalie, NYR	.25	.25
6	Pat LaFontaine, Buf.	.20	.20
7	Mark Tinordi, Min.	.10	.10
8	Claude Lemieux, NJ	.10	.10
9	Jimmy Carson, Det.	.10	.10
10	Cam Neely, Bos.	.10	.10
11	Al Iafrate, Wash.	.10	.10
12	Steve Thomas, NYI	.10	.10
13	Fredrick Olausson, Win.	.10	.10
14	Paval Bure, Van.	1.00	1.00
15	Douglas Wilson, SJ	.10	.10
16	Esa Tikkanen, Edm.	.10	.10
17	Gary Suter, Cal.	.10	.10
18	Murray Craven, Har.	.10	.10
19	Garry Galley, Phi.	.10	.10
20	Grant Fuhr, Goalie, Tor.	.10	.10
21	Craig Wolanin, Que.	.10	.10
22	Paul Cavallini, St.L	.10	.10
23	Eric Desjardins, Mon.	.10	.10
24	Joey Kocur, NYR	.10	.10
25	Kevin Stevens, Pit.	.20	.20
26	Martin McSorley, LA	.10	.10
27	Dirk Graham, Chi.	.10	.10
28	Michael Ramsey, Buf.	.10	.10
29	Gordon Murphy, Bos.	.10	.10
30	John MacLean, NJ	.10	.10
31	Vladimir Konstantinov, Det.	.10	.10
32	Neal Broten, Min.	.10	.10
33	Dimitri Khristich, Wash.	.10	.10
34	Gerald Diduck, Van.	.10	.10
35	Ken Baumgartner, Tor.	.10	.10
36	Darrin Shannon, Win.	.10	.10
37	Steven Bozek, SJ	.10	.10
38	Michel Petit, Cal.	.10	.10
39	Kevin Lowe, Edm.	.10	.10
40	Douglas Gilmour, Tor.	.30	.30
41	Peter Sidorkiewicz, Goalie, Har.	.10	.10
42	Gino Cavallini, Que.	.10	.10
43	Dan Quinn, Phi.	.10	.10
44	Steven Finn, Que.	.10	.10
45	Lawrence Murphy, Pit.	.10	.10
46	Brent Gilchrist, Mon.	.10	.10
47	Darren Puppa, Goalie, Buf.	.10	.10
48	James (Steve) Smith, Chi.	.10	.10
49	David Taylor, LA	.10	.10
50	Michael Gartner, NYR	.10	.10
51	Derian Hatcher, Min.	.10	.10
52	Bob Probert, Det.	.10	.10
53	Kenneth Daneyko, NJ	.10	.10
54	Stephen Leach, Bos.	.10	.10
55	Kelly Miller, Wash.	.10	.10
56	Jeff Norton, NYI	.10	.10
57	Kelly Kisio, SJ	.10	.10
58	Igor Larionov, Van.	.10	.10
59	Paul MacDermid, Wash.	.10	.10
60	Michael Vernon, Goalie, Cal.	.10	.10
61	Randy Ladouceur, Har.	.10	.10
62	Luke Richardson, Edm.	.10	.10
63	Daniel Marois, NYI	.10	.10
64	Mike Hough, Que.	.10	.10
65	Garth Butcher, St.L	.10	.10
66	Terry Carkner, Phi.	.10	.10
67	Mike Donnelly, LA	.10	.10
68	Keith Brown, Chi.	.10	.10
69	Mathieu Schneider, Mon.	.10	.10

1992-93 REGULAR ISSUE — SCORE • 379

No.	Player	USA NRMT	Can. NRMT
70	Tom Barrasso, Goalie, Pit.	.10	.10
71	Adam Graves, NYR	.25	.25
72	Brian Propp, Min.	.10	.10
73	Randy Wood, Buf.	.10	.10
74	Yves Racine, Det.	.10	.10
75	Scott Stevens, NJ	.10	.10
76	Christopher Nilan, Mon	.10	.10
77	Uwe Krupp, NYI	.10	.10
78	Sylvain Cote, Wash.	.10	.10
79	Sergio Momesso, Van.	.10	.10
80	Thomas Steen, Win.	.10	.10
81	Craig Muni, Edm.	.10	.10
82	Jeff Hackett, Goalie, SJ	.10	.10
83	Frantisek Musil, Cal.	.10	.10
84	Mike Ricci, Phi.	.15	.15
85	Brad Shaw, Har.	.10	.10
86	Ronald Sutter, St.L	.10	.10
87	Curtis Leschyshyn, Que.	.10	.10
88	Jamie Macoun, Tor.	.10	.10
89	Brian Noonan, Chi.	.10	.10
90	Ulf Samuelsson, Pit.	.10	.10
91	Michael McPhee, Mon.	.10	.10
92	Charles Huddy, LA	.10	.10
93	Tim Kerr, NYR	.10	.10
94	Craig Ludwig, Min.	.10	.10
95	Paul Ysebaert, Det.	.10	.10
96	Brad May, Buf.	.10	.10
97	Viacheslav Fetisov, NJ	.10	.10
98	Todd Krygier, Wash.	.10	.10
99	Patrick Flatley, NYI	.10	.10
100	Raymond Bourque, Bos.	.10	.10
101	Petr Nedved, Van.	.10	.10
102	Teppo Numminen, Win.	.10	.10
103	Dean Evason, SJ	.10	.10
104	Ron Hextall, Goalie, Phi.	.10	.10
105	Josef Beranek, Edm.	.15	.15
106	Robert Reichel, Cal.	.10	.10
107	Mikhail Tatarinov, Que.	.10	.10
108	Geoff Sanderson, Har.	.25	.25
109	Dave Lowry, St.L	.10	.10
110	Wendel Clark, Tor.	.10	.10
111	Corey Millen, LA	.10	.10
112	Brent Sutter, Chi.	.10	.10
113	Jaromir Jagr, Pit.	.40	.40
114	Petr Svoboda, Buf.	.10	.10
115	Sergei Nemchinov, NYR	.10	.10
116	Tony Tanti, Buf.	.10	.10
117	Robert (Stewart) Gavin, Min	.10	.10
118	Doug Brown, NJ	.10	.10
119	Gerard Gallant, Det.	.10	.10
120	Andrew Moog, Goalie, Bos.	.10	.10
121	John Druce, Wash.	.10	.10
122	Dave McLlwain, Tor.	.10	.10
123	Bob Essensa, Win.	.10	.10
124	Doug Lidster, Van.	.10	.10
125	Pat Falloon, SJ	.20	.20
126	Kelly Buchberger, Edm.	.10	.10
127	Carey Wilson, Cal.	.10	.10
128	Robert Holik, Har.	.10	.10
129	Andrei Lomakin, Phi.	.10	.10
130	Robert Rouse, Tor.	.10	.10
131	Adam Foote, Que.	.10	.10
132	Bob Bassen, St.L	.10	.10
133	Brian Benning, Phi.	.10	.10
134	Gregory Gilbert, Chi.	.10	.10
135	Paul Stanton, Pit.	.10	.10
136	Brian Skrudland, Mon.	.10	.10
137	Jeff Beukeboom, NYR	.10	.10
138	Clint Malarchuk, Goalie, Buf.	.10	.10
139	Michael Modano, Min.	.25	.25
140	Stephane J.J. Richer, NJ	.10	.10
141	Byron (Brad) McCrimmon, Det.	.10	.10
142	Robert Carpenter, Bos.	.10	.10
143	Rod Langway, Wash.	.10	.10
144	Adam Creighton, NYI	.10	.10
145	Ed Olczyk, Win.	.10	.10
146	Greg Adams, Van.	.10	.10
147	Jayson More, SJ	.10	.10
148	Scott Mellanby, Edm.	.10	.10
149	Paul Ranheim, Cal.	.10	.10
150	John Cullen, Har.	.10	.10
151	Steve Duchesne, Phi.	.10	.10
152	David Ellett, Tor.	.10	.10
153	Mats Sundin, Que.	.25	.25
154	Richard Zombo, St.L	.10	.10
155	Kelly Hrudey, Goalie, LA	.10	.10
156	Mike Hudson, Chi.	.10	.10
157	Bryan Trottier, Pit.	.10	.10
158	Shayne Corson, Mon.	.10	.10
159	Kevin Haller, Mon.	.10	.10
160	John Vanbiesbrouck, Goalie, NYR	.15	.15
161	Jim Johnson, Min.	.10	.10
162	Kevin Todd, NJ	.10	.10
163	Ray Sheppard, Det.	.10	.10
164	Brent Ashton, Bos.	.10	.10
165	Peter Bondra, Wash.	.10	.10
166	David Volek, NYI	.10	.10
167	Randy Carlyle, Win.	.10	.10
168	Dana Murzyn, Van.	.10	.10
169	Perry Berezan, SJ	.10	.10
170	Vincent Damphousse, Edm.	.10	.10
171	Gary Leeman, Cal.	.10	.10
172	Stephen Konroyd, Har.	.10	.10
173	Per-Erik Eklund, Phi.	.10	.10
174	Peter Zezel, Tor.	.10	.10
175	Gregory Paslawski, Que	.10	.10
176	Murray Baron, St.L	.10	.10
177	Robert Blake, LA	.10	.10
178	Ed Belfour, Goalie, Chi.	.25	.25
179	Mike Keane, Mon.	.10	.10
180	Mark Recchi, Phi.	.25	.25
181	Kris King, NYR	.10	.10
182	Dave Snuggerud, SJ	.10	.10
183	David Shaw, Min.	.10	.10
184	Tom Chorske, NJ	.10	.10
185	Steve Chiasson, Det.	.10	.10
186	Don Sweeney, Bos.	.10	.10
187	Mike Ridley, Wash.	.10	.10
188	Glenn Healy, Goalie, NYI	.10	.10
189	Troy Murray, Win.	.10	.10
190	Thomas Fergus, Van.	.10	.10
191	Rob Zettler, SJ	.10	.10
192	Geoff Smith, Edm.	.10	.10
193	Joe Nieuwendyk, Cal.	.10	.10
194	Mark Hunter, Har.	.10	.10
195	Kjell Samuelsson, Pit.	.10	.10
196	Todd Gill, Tor.	.10	.10
197	Douglas Smail, Que.	.10	.10
198	Dave Christian, St.L	.10	.10
199	Tomas Sandstrom, LA	.10	.10
200	Jeremy Roenick, Chi.	.50	.50
201	Gordon Roberts, Pit.	.10	.10
202	Denis Savard, Mon.	.10	.10
203	James Patrick, NYR	.10	.10
204	David Andreychuk, Buf.	.10	.10
205	Bobby Smith, Min.	.10	.10
206	Valeri Zelepukin, NJ	.20	.20
207	Shawn Burr, Det.	.10	.10
208	Vladimir Ruzicka, Bos.	.10	.10
209	Calle Johansson, Wash.	.10	.10
210	Mark Fitzpatrick, Goalie, NYI	.10	.10
211	Edward (Dean) Kennedy, Win.	.10	.10
212	David Babych, Van.	.10	.10
213	Wayne Presley, Buf.	.10	.10
214	Dave Manson, Edm.	.10	.10
215	Bo Mikael Andersson, Har.	.10	.10
216	Trent Yawney, Cal.	.10	.10
217	Mark Howe, Phi.	.10	.10
218	Michael Bullard, Tor.	.10	.10
219	Claude Lapointe, Que.	.10	.10
220	Jeff Brown, St.L	.10	.10
221	Bob Kudelski, LA	.10	.10
222	Michel Goulet, Chi.	.10	.10
223	Phillippe Bourque, Pit.	.10	.10
224	Darren Turcotte, NYR	.10	.10
225	Kirk Muller, Mon.	.10	.10
226	Doug Bodger, Buf.	.10	.10
227	Dave Gagner, Min.	.10	.10
228	Craig Billington, Goalie, NJ	.10	.10
229	Kevin Miller, Det.	.10	.10
230	Glen Wesley, Bos.	.10	.10
231	Dale Hunter, Wash.	.10	.10
232	Tom Kurvers, NYI	.10	.10
233	Pat Elynuik, Win.	.10	.10
234	Geoff Courtnall, Van.	.10	.10
235	Neil Wilkinson, SJ	.10	.10
236	Bill Ranford, Goalie, Edm.	.10	.10
237	Ronald Stern, Cal.	.10	.10
238	Zarley Zalapski, Har.	.10	.10
239	Kerry Huffman, Phi.	.10	.10
240	Joe Sakic, Que.	.25	.25
241	Glenn Anderson, Tor.	.10	.10
242	Stephane Quintal, St.L	.10	.10
243	Tony Granato, LA	.10	.10
244	Rob Brown, Chi.	.10	.10
245	Rick Tocchet, Pit.	.10	.10
246	Stephan Lebeau, Mon.	.10	.10
247	Mark Hardy, NYR	.10	.10
248	Alexander Mogilny, Buf.	.40	.40
249	Jon Casey, Goalie, Min.	.10	.10
250	Adam Oates, Bos.	.15	.15
251	Bruce Driver, NJ	.10	.10
252	Sergei Fedorov, Det.	.50	.50
253	Michal Pivonka, Wash.	.10	.10
254	Cliff Ronning, Van.	.10	.10
255	Derek King, NYI	.10	.10
256	Luciano Borsato, Win.	.10	.10
257	Paul Fenton, SJ	.10	.10
258	Craig Berube, Cal.	.10	.10
259	Brian Bradley, Tor.	.10	.10
260	Craig Simpson, Edm.	.10	.10
261	Adam Burt, Har.	.10	.10
262	Curtis Joseph, Goalie, St.L, Error	.25	.25
263	Mark Pederson, Phi.	.10	.10
264	Alexei Gusarov, Que.	.10	.10
265	Paul Coffey, LA	.10	.10
266	Steve Larmer, Chi.	.10	.10
267	Ronald Francis, Pit.	.10	.10
268	Randy Gilhen, NYR	.10	.10
269	Guy Carbonneau, Mon.	.10	.10
270	Chris Terreri, Goalie, NJ	.10	.10
271	Mike Craig, Min.	.10	.10
272	Dale Hawerchuk, Buf.	.10	.10
273	Kevin Hatcher, Wash.	.10	.10
274	Kenneth Hodge Jr., Bos.	.10	.10
275	Tim Cheveldae, Goalie, Det.	.10	.10
276	Benoit Hogue, NYI	.10	.10
277	Mark Osborne, Tor.	.10	.10
278	Brian Mullen, SJ	.10	.10
279	Robert Dirk, Van.	.10	.10
280	Theoren Fleury, Cal.	.10	.10
281	Martin Gelinas, Edm.	.10	.10
282	Patrick Verbeek, Har.	.10	.10
283	Michael Krushelnyski, Tor.	.10	.10
284	Kevin Dineen, Phi.	.10	.10
285	Craig Janney, St.L	.10	.10
286	Owen Nolan, Que.	.05	.05
287	Bob Errey, Pit.	.10	.10
288	Bryan Marchment, Chi.	.10	.10
289	Randy Moller, Buf.	.10	.10
290	Luc Robitaille, LA	.20	.20
291	Peter Stastny, NJ	.10	.10
292	Ken Sutton, Buf.	.10	.10
293	Bradley Marsh, Det.	.10	.10
294	Chris Dahlquist, Min.	.10	.10
295	Patrick Roy, Goalie, Mon	.50	.50
296	Andy Brickley, Bos.	.10	.10
297	Randy Burridge, Wash.	.10	.10
298	Ray Ferraro, NYI	.10	.10
299	Phil Housley, Win.	.10	.10
300	Mark Messier, NYR	.25	.25
301	David Bruce, SJ	.10	.10
302	Allan MacInnis, Cal.	.10	.10
303	Craig MacTavish, Edm.	.10	.10
304	Kay Whitmore, Goalie, Har.	.10	.10
305	Trevor Linden, Van.	.20	.20
306	Stephen Kasper, Phi.	.10	.10
307	Todd Elik, Min.	.10	.10
308	Eric Weinrich, NJ	.10	.10
309	Jocelyn Lemieux, Chi.	.10	.10
310	Peter Ahola, LA	.10	.10
311	J.J. Daigneault, Mon.	.10	.10
312	Colin Patterson, Buf.	.10	.10
313	Darcy Wakaluk, Goalie, Min.	.10	.10
314	Doug Weight, NYR	.10	.10
315	David Barr, NJ	.10	.10

SCORE — 1992-93 REGULAR ISSUE

No.	Player	USA NRMT	Can. NRMT
316	Keith Primeau, Det.	.10	.10
317	Robert Sweeney, Bos.	.10	.10
318	Jyrki Lumme, Van.	.10	.10
319	Stu Barnes, Win.	.10	.10
320	Donald Beaupre, Goalie, Wash.	.10	.10
321	Joe Murphy, Edm.	.10	.10
322	Gary Roberts, Cal.	.10	.10
323	Andrew Cassels, Har.	.10	.10
324	Rod Brind'amour Phi.	.15	.15
325	Pierre Turgeon, NYI	.20	.20
326	Claude Vilgrain, NJ	.10	.10
327	Richard Sutter, St.L	.10	.10
328	Claude Loiselle, NYI	.10	.10
329	John Ogrodnick, NYR	.10	.10
330	Ulf Dahlen, Min.	.10	.10
331	Gilbert Dionne, Mon.	.20	.20
332	Joel Otto, Cal.	.10	.10
333	Rob Pearson, Tor.	.20	.20
334	Christian Ruuttu, Buf.	.10	.10
335	Brian Bellows, Min.	.10	.10
336	Anatoli Semenov, Edm.	.10	.10
337	Brent Fedyk, Det.	.10	.10
338	Gaetan Duchesne, Min.	.10	.10
339	Randy McKay, NJ	.10	.10
340	Bernie Nicholls, Edm.	.10	.10
341	Keith Acton, Phi.	.10	.10
342	John Tonelli, Que.	.10	.10
343	Brian Lawton, SJ	.10	.10
344	Eric Nattress, Tor.	.10	.10
345	Mike Eagles, Win.	.10	.10
346	Frantisek Kucera, Chi.	.10	.10
347	John McIntyre, LA	.10	.10
348	Troy Loney, Pit.	.10	.10
349	Norm Maciver, Edm.	.10	.10
350	Brett Hull, St.L	.50	.50
351	George (Rob) Ramage, Min.	.10	.10
352	Claude Boivin, Phi.	.10	.10
353	Paul Broten, NYR	.10	.10
354	Stephane Fiset, Goalie, Que.	.10	.10
355	Garry Valk, Van.	.10	.10
356	Basil McRae, Min.	.10	.10
357	Alan May, Wash.	.10	.10
358	Grant Ledyard, Buf.	.10	.10
359	David Poulin, Bos.	.10	.10
360	Valeri Kamensky, Que.	.15	.15
361	Brian Glynn, Edm.	.10	.10
362	Jan Erixon, NYR	.10	.10
363	Mike Lalor, Win.	.10	.10
364	Jeff Chychrun, Pit.	.10	.10
365	Ronald Wilson, St.L	.10	.10
366	Shawn Cronin, Win.	.10	.10
367	Sylvain Turgeon, Mon.	.10	.10
368	Michael Liut, Goalie, Wash.	.10	.10
369	Joe Cirella, NYR	.10	.10
370	David Maley, Edm.	.10	.10
371	Lucien DeBlois, Win.	.10	.10
372	Per Olav Djoos, NYR	.10	.10
373	Dominik Hasek, Goalie, Chi.	.35	.35
374	Laurie Boschman, NJ	.10	.10
375	Brian Leetch, NYR	.35	.35
376	Nelson Emerson, St.L	.10	.10
377	Normand Rochefort, NYR	.10	.10
378	Jacques Cloutier, Goalie, Que.	.10	.10
379	Jim Sandlak, Van.	.10	.10
380	David Reid, Bos.	.10	.10
381	Gary Nylund, NYI	.10	.10
382	Sergei Makarov, Cal.	.10	.10
383	Petr Klima, Edm.	.10	.10
384	Peter Douris, Bos.	.10	.10
385	Kirk McLean, Goalie, Van.	.20	.20
386	Robert McGill, Det.	.10	.10
387	Ron Tugnutt, Goalie, Edm.	.10	.10
388	Patrice Brisebois, Mon.	.10	.10
389	Anthony Amonte, NYR	.15	.15
390	Mario Lemieux, Pit.	.75	.75
391	Nicklas Lidstrom, Det.	.10	.10
392	Brendan Shanahan, St.L	.20	.20
393	Donald Audette, Buf.	.10	.10
394	Alexei Kasatonov, NJ	.10	.10
395	Dino Ciccarelli, Wash.	.10	.10
396	Vincent Riendeau, Goalie, Det.	.10	.10
397	Joe Reekie, NYI	.10	.10
398	Jari Kurri, LA	.10	.10
399	Ken Wregget, Goalie, Pit.	.10	.10
400	Steve Yzerman, Det.	.25	.25
401	Scott Niedermayer, NJ	.20	.20
402	Stephane Beauregard, Goalie, Win.	.10	.10
403	Timothy Hunter, Cal.	.10	.10
404	Marc Bergevin, Har.	.10	.10
405	Sylvain Lefebvre, Mon.	.10	.10
406	Johan Garpenlov, SJ	.10	.10
407	Anthony Hrkac, Chi.	.10	.10
408	**Tahir Domi, NYR, RC**	.10	.10
409	Martin LaPointe, Det.	.10	.10
410	Darryl Sydor, LA	.10	.10

1992-93 SEASON LEADERS

No.	Player	USA NRMT	Can. NRMT
411	**Goals:** Brett Hull, St.L	.20	.20
412	**Assists:** Wayne Gretzky, LA	.30	.30
413	**Points:** Mario Lemieux, Pit.	.30	.30
414	**Plus/Minus:** Paul Ysabaert, Det.	.05	.05
415	**Points Leading Rookie:** Anthony Amonte, NYR	.05	.05
416	**Points Leading Defenseman:** Brian Leetch, NYR	.15	.15
417	**Goalie Wins:** Kirk McLean, Van.; Tim Cheveldae, Goalie, Det.	.05	.05
418	**Goals Against Average:** Patrick Roy, Goalie, Mon.	.25	.25

FRANCHISE

No.	Player	USA NRMT	Can. NRMT
419	Raymond Bourque, Bos.	.10	.10
420	Pat Lafontaine, Buf.	.10	.10
421	Allan MacInnis, Cal.	.10	.10
422	Jeremy Roenick, Chi.	.20	.20
423	Steve Yzerman, Det.	.10	.10
424	Bill Ranford, Goalie, Edm.	.10	.10
425	John Cullen, Har.	.10	.10
426	Wayne Gretzky, LA	.30	.30
427	Michael Modano, Min.	.10	.10
428	Patrick Roy, Goalie, Mon.	.30	.30
429	Scott Stevens, NJ	.10	.10
430	Pierre Turgeon, NYI	.10	.10
431	Mark Messier, NYR	.10	.10
432	Eric Lindros, Phi.	1.00	2.00
433	Mario Lemieux, Pit.	.30	.30
434	Joe Sakic, Que.	.10	.10
435	Brett Hull, St.L	.20	.20
436	Pat Falloon, SJ	.20	.20
437	Grant Fuhr, Goalie, Tor.	.10	.10
438	Trevor Linden, Van.	.10	.10
439	Kevin Hatcher, Wash.	.10	.10
440	Phil Housley, Win.	.10	.10

1992-1993 HIGHLIGHTS

No.	Player	USA NRMT	Can. NRMT
441	**Highest Scoring Defenseman:** Paul Coffey, Pit.	.10	.10
442	**50 Goals/50 Games:** Brett Hull, St.L	.20	.20
443	**500th Goal:** Michael Gartner, NYR	.10	.10
444	**500th Goal:** Michel Goulet, Chi.	.05	.05
445	**1,000th Point:** Michael Gartner, NYR	.05	.05
446	**1,000th Point:** Robert Smith, Min.	.05	.05
447	**1,000th Point:** Raymond Bourque, Bos.	.10	.10
448	**1,000th Point:** Mario Lemieux, Pit.	.25	.25

NHL TOP PROSPECT '92

No.	Player	USA NRMT	Can. NRMT
449	Scott LaChance, NYI	.05	.05
450	**Keith Tkachuk, Win.**	**.25**	**.25**
451	Alexander Semak, NJ	.05	.05
452	John Tanner, Goalie, Que.	.05	.05
453	Joseph Juneau, Bos.	.75	.75
454	Igor Kravchuk, Chi.	.05	.05
455	Brent Thompson, LA	.05	.05
456	Evgeny Davydov, Win.	.05	.05
457	Arturs Irbe, Goalie, SJ	.40	.40
458	Kent Manderville, Tor.	.05	.05
459	Shawn McEachern, Pit.	.20	.20
460	**Guy Hebert, Goalie, St.L, RC**	**.50**	**.50**
461	**Keith Carney, Buf., RC**	**.10**	**.10**
462	Karl Dykhuis, Chi.	.05	.05
463	**Bill Lindsay, Que., RC**	**.10**	**.10**
464	Dominic Roussel, Goalie, Phi.	.25	.25
465	Marty McInnis, NYI	.05	.05
466	Dale Craigwell, SJ	.05	.05
467	Igor Ulanov, Win.	.05	.05
468	Dimitri Mironov, Tor.	.05	.05
469	**Dean McAmmond, Chi., RC**	**.10**	**.10**
470	**Bill Guerin, NJ, RC**	**.15**	**.15**
471	**Bret Hedican, St.L, RC**	**.25**	**.25**
472	Felix Potvin, Goalie, Tor.	1.00	1.00
473	Viacheslav Kozlov, Det.	.40	.40
474	Martin Rucinsky, Que.	.05	.05
475	**Ray Whitney, SJ, RC**	**.20**	**.20**
476	Stephen Heinze, Bos.	.05	.05
477	Brad Schlegel, Wash.	.05	.05
478	Patrick Poulin, Har.	.05	.05
479	Ted Donato, Bos.	.05	.05
480	Martin Brodeur, Goalie, NJ	.40	.40
481	**Denny Felsner, St.L, RC**	**.10**	**.10**
482	**Trent Klatt, Min., RC**	**.05**	**.05**
483	Gord Hynes, Bos.	.05	.05
484	Glen Murray, Bos.	.05	.05
485	Chris Lindberg, Cal.	.05	.05
486	Raymond LeBlanc, Goalie, Chi.	.05	.05
487	**Yanic Perreault, Tor., RC**	**.20**	**.20**
488	**Jean Francois Quintin, SJ, RC**	**.05**	**.05**

DREAM TEAM

No.	Player	USA NRMT	Can. NRMT
489	Patrick Roy, Goalie, Mon.	.30	.30
490	Raymond Bourque, Bos.	.10	.10
491	Brian Leetch, NYR	.15	.15
492	Kevin Stevens, Pit.	.10	.10
493	Mark Messier, NYR	.15	.15
494	Jaromir Jagr, Pit.	.15	.15
495	Bill Ranford, Goalie, Edm.	.05	.05
496	Allan MacInnis, Cal.	.05	.05
497	Chris Chelios, Chi.	.05	.05
498	Luc Robitaille, LA	.10	.10
499	Jeremy Roenick, Chi.	.20	.20
500	Brett Hull, St.L	.15	.15

ROOKIE DREAM TEAM

No.	Player	USA NRMT	Can. NRMT
501	Felix Potvin, Gaolie, Tor.	.75	.75
502	Nicklas Lidstrom, Det.	.10	.10
503	Vladimir Konstantinov, Det.	.05	.05
504	Pavel Bure, Van.	.75	.75
505	Nelson Emerson, St.L	.05	.05
506	Anthony Amonte, NYR	.05	.05

TAMPA BAY LIGHTNING

No.	Player	USA NRMT	Can. NRMT
507	Tampa Bay Lightning Checklist	.05	.05
508	Shawn Chambers	.05	.05
509	Basil McRae	.05	.05
510	Joe Reekie	.05	.05
511	Wendell Young, Goalie	.05	.05

OTTAWA SENATORS

No.	Player	USA NRMT	Can. NRMT
512	Ottawa Senators Checklist	.05	.05
513	Laurie Boschman	.05	.05
514	Mark Lamb	.05	.05
515	Peter Sidorkiewicz, Goalie	.05	.05
516	Sylvain Turgeon	.05	.05

REGULAR ISSUE

No.	Player	USA NRMT	Can. NRMT
517	Kevin and Bill Dineen, Phi.	.05	.05

1992 - 93 CANADIAN INSERT SETS — SCORE • 381

AWARD WINNERS

No.	Player	USA NRMT	Can. NRMT
518	1992 Stanley Cup Champs, Pit.	.10	.10
519	**Conn Smythe Trophy:** Mario Lemieux, Pit.	.25	.25
520	**King Clancy Trophy:** Raymond Bourque, Bos.	.10	.10
521	**Hart Memorial Trophy:** Mark Messier, NYR	.10	.10
522	**Norris Trophy:** Brian Leetch, NYR	.15	.15
523	**Calder Trophy:** Pavel Bure, Van.	.75	.75
524	**Selke Trophy:** Guy Carbonneau, Mon.	.10	.10
525	**Lady Byng Trophy:** Wayne Gretzky, LA	.30	.30
526	**Bill Masterton Trophy:** Mark Fitzpatrick, NYI	.10	.10
527	**Vezina and Jennings Trophies:** Patrick Roy, Goalie, Mon.	.30	.30

MEMORIAL CUP CHAMPIONS

No.	Player	USA NRMT	Can. NRMT
528	Kamloops Blazers	.10	.10

REGULAR ISSUE

No.	Player	USA NRMT	Can. NRMT
529	Richard Tabaracci, Goalie, Win.	.05	.05
530	Tom Draper, Goalie, Buf.	.05	.05
531	Adrien Plavsic, Van.	.05	.05
532	Joseph Sacco, Tor.	.05	.05
533	Mike Sullivan, SJ	.05	.05
534	Zdeno Ciger, NJ	.05	.05
535	Frank Pietrangelo, Goalie, Har.	.05	.05
536	Mike Peluso, Chi.	.05	.05
537	Jim Paek, Pit.	.05	.05
538	David Hannan, Buf.	.05	.05
539	**David Williams, SJ, RC**	.10	.10
540	Gino Odjick, Van.	.05	.05
541	Yvon Corriveau, Har.	.05	.05
542	Grant Jennings, Pit.	.05	.05
543	Stephane Matteau, Chi.	.05	.05
544	Patrick Conacher, NJ	.05	.05
545	Steven Rice, Edm.	.05	.05
546	Marc Habscheid, Cal.	.05	.05
547	Stephen Weeks, Goalie, LA	.05	.05
548	**50 Goal Scorer:** Maurice Richard, Mon.	.25	.25
549	**The Legend:** Maurice Richard, Mon.	.25	.25
550	Eric Lindros, Phi.	5.00	5.00

— 1992 - 93 CANADIAN INSERT SETS —

CANADIAN OLYMPIC HEROES '92

This 13-card subset was randomly inserted into the Canadian wax packs and is among the most desirable subsets of 1992-93. This subset includes only the Canadian players that participated in the '92 Winter Olympic Games. These cards are numbered _ of 13

Canadian Olympic Heroes '92
Card No. 1, Eric Lindros

Card Size: 2 1/2" x 3 1/2"
Face: Four colour, red border; Name, Position
Back: Four colour, card stock; Name, Number, Biography over Canadian flag, Bilingual
Imprint: © 1992 SCORE, PRINTED IN THE U.S.A.
Complete Set No.: 13
Complete Set Price: 55.00 115.00
Common Card: 2.00 4.00

No.	Player	EX	NRMT
1	Eric Lindros	25.00	50.00
2	Joseph Juneau	17.50	35.00
3	Dave Archibald	2.00	4.00
4	Randy Smith	2.00	4.00
5	Gord Hynes	2.00	4.00
6	Chris Lindberg	2.00	4.00
7	Jason Woolley	2.00	4.00
8	Fabian Joseph	2.00	4.00
9	Brad Schlegel	2.00	4.00
10	Kent Manderville	2.00	4.00
11	Adrien Plavsic	2.00	4.00
12	Trevor Kidd, Goalie	2.00	4.00
13	Sean Burke, Goalie	2.00	4.00

MAURICE RICHARD COLLECTORS SET

This 2-card set was randomly inserted into the Canadian regular foil. The autographed cards are signed with a black Sharpie marker and numbered - of 1,250.

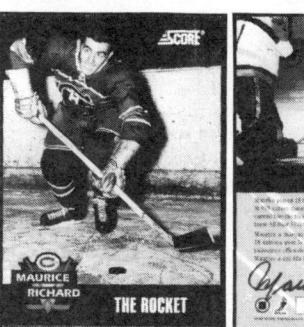

Maurice Richard Collectors Set
"The Rocket" Autographed Card

Card Size: 2 1/2" x 3 1/2"
Face: Three colour, black and white photograph; Name
Back: Three colour, black and white photograph, card stock; Resume, Bilingual
Imprint: © 1992 SCORE, PRINTED IN THE U.S.A.
Complete Set No.: 2
Complete Set Price
Regular 18.00 36.00
Autographed 175.00 350.00

No.	Player	EX	NRMT
--	**The Rocket:**	9.00	18.00
--	**The Rocket:** Autographed	87.50	175.00
--	**Stanley Cup Hero:**	9.00	18.00
--	**Stanley Cup Hero:** Autographed	87.50	175.00

SHARP SHOOTERS

Sharp Shooters
Card No. 30, Craig Simpson

This 30-card subset was inserted in Canadian Jumbo foil, two cards per pack. The set is numbered - of 30. The number on the card is the rank in percentage terms of goals per shots based on the 1991 - 92 season. The Canadian set varies from the American set by different borders and portraits.

Card Size: 2 1/2" x 3 1/2"
Face: Four colour, black border at bottom, gold embossed "SHARP SHOOTERS", Name
Back: Four colour, card stock; Name, Number, Resume, Bilingual
Imprint: © 1992 SCORE, PRINTED IN THE U.S.A.
Complete Set No.: 30 USA Can.
Complete Set Price: 15.00 15.00
Common Card: .40 .40

No.	Player	USA NRMT	Can. NRMT
1	Gary Roberts, Cal.	.40	.40
2	Sergei Makarov, Cal.	.40	.40
3	Ray Ferraro, NYI	.40	.40
4	Dale Hunter, Wash.	.40	.40
5	Sergei Nemchinov, NYR	.40	.40
6	Mike Ridley, Wash.	.40	.40
7	Gilbert Dionne, Mon.	.40	.40
8	Pat LaFontaine, Buf.	1.50	1.50
9	Jimmy Carson, Det.	.40	.40
10	Jeremy Roenick, Chi.	2.00	2.00
11	Kelly Buchberger, Edm.	.40	.40
12	Owen Nolan, Que.	.40	.40
13	Igor Larionov, Van.	.40	.40
14	Claude Vilgrain, NJ	.40	.40
15	Derek King, NYI	.40	.40
16	Gregory Paslawski, Que.	.40	.40
17	Bob Probert, Det.	.40	.40
18	Mark Recchi, Phi.	1.00	1.00
19	Donald Audette, Buf.	.40	.40
20	Ray Sheppard, Det.	.40	.40
21	Benoit Hogue, NYI	.40	.40
22	Rob Brown, Chi.	.40	.40
23	Pat Elynuik, Win.	.40	.40
24	Petr Klima, Edm.	.40	.40
25	Pierre Turgeon, NYI	1.50	1.50
26	Corey Millen, LA	.40	.40
27	Dimitri Khristich, Wash.	.40	.40
28	Anatoli Semenov, Edm.	.40	.40
29	Kirk Muller, Mon.	.40	.40
30	Craig Simpson, Edm.	.40	.40

— 1992 - 93 AMERICAN INSERT SETS —

USA GREATS

This 15-card subset was issued in American foil packs. The player selection was made to represent the NHLs' top American-born players. The cards are numbered - of 15

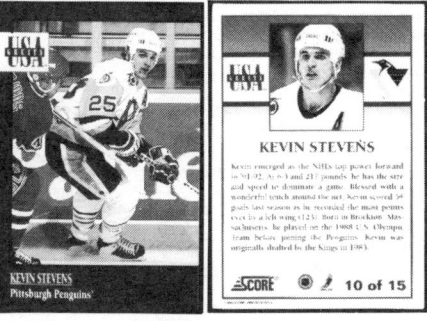

USA Greats
Card No. 10, Kevin Stevens

Card Size: 2 1/2" x 3 1/2"
Face: Four colour with royal blue three sided border; Name Red embossed Score logo
Back: Four colour, white border; Name, Number, Team, Resume, Team logo
Imprint: © 1992 SCORE, PRINTED IN THE U.S.A.
Complete Set No.: 15
Complete Set Price: 32.50 65.00
Common Card: 2.00 4.00

— 1992 - 93 PINNACLE ISSUE —

No.	Player	EX	NRMT
1	Pat LaFontaine, Buf.	3.50	7.00
2	Chris Chelios, Chi.	2.50	5.00
3	Jeremy Roenick, Chi.	4.50	9.00
4	Anthony Granato, LA	2.00	4.00
5	Michael Modano, Min.	3.00	6.00
6	Mike Richter, Goalie, NYR	3.00	6.00
7	John Vanbiesbrouck. Goalie, NYR	3.00	6.00
8	Brian Leetch, NYR	3.50	7.00
9	Joe Mullen, Pit.	2.00	4.00
10	Kevin Stevens, Pit.	2.50	5.00
11	Craig Janney, St.L	3.00	6.00
12	Brian Mullen, SJ	2.00	4.00
13	Kevin Hatcher, Wash.	2.00	4.00
14	Kelly Miller, Wash.	2.00	4.00
15	Ed Olczyk, Win.	2.00	4.00

— 1992 - 93 PINNACLE ISSUE —

FOUR-CARD PROMOTIONAL SHEETS

These 4-card sheets were used to promote the Canadian Pinnacle issue for the 1992 - 93 season. The cards are indentical to the regular issue except they are issued in sheet format. Each sheet is stamped on the back "Not for Resale for Promotional use only".

Card Size: 5" x 7"
Face: Four colour, black border; Name
Back: Four colour, white border on card stock, Name, Number, Resume, Bilingual
Imprint: © 1992 Score, Printed in U.S.A.
Complete Set No.: 3
Complete Set Price: 12.50 25.00

No.	Player	EX	NRMT
--	Sheet 1	2.50	5.00
111	Kirk Muller, Mon		
165	Pierre Turgeon, NYI		
288	Kevin Stevens, Pit.		
387	Brian Bradley, TB		
--	Sheet 2	5.00	10.00
66	Al Iafrate, Wash.		
80	Mark Recchi, Phi.		
110	Pavel Bure, Van.		
280	Scott Stevens, NJ		
--	Sheet 3	5.00	10.00
77	Alaxander Mogilny, Buf.		
175	Luc Robitaille, LA		
279	Douglas Gilmour. Tor.		
406	Teemu Selanne, Win.		

SIX-CARD PROMOTIONAL SHEET

This sheet of 6 cards was used by Score to promote the 1992-93 Pinnacle American issue. The cards are identical to the regular issue. The sheet is printed on the back "Not for Resale for Promotional use only".

Sheet Size: 7 1/2" x 7"
Face: Four colour, black border; Name
Back: Four colour, white border, card stock; Resume
Imprint: © 1992 SCORE, Printed in U.S.A.

No.	Player	EX	NRMT
--	Sheet	15.00	30.00
91	Andrew Moog, Goalie, Bos.		
36	Nelson Emerson, St.L		
61	Denis Savard, Mon.		
6	Owen Nolan, Que.		
22	Michel Goulet, Chi.		
88	Eric Lindros. Phi.		

— 1992 - 93 PINNACLE ISSUE —

AMERICAN and CANADIAN

This 420-card premium set from Score was produced in both Canadian and American editions. The only difference between the two editions are the player's portraits and the bilingual resumes of the Canadian issue.

 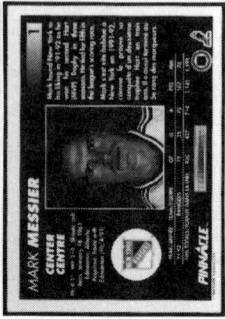

1992-93 Pinnacle Canadian Issue
Card No. 1, Mark Messier

Card Size: 2 1/2" x 3 1/2"
Face: Four colour, black border
Back: Four colour, white border, card stock, Name, Number, Team, Bilingual
Imprint: © 1992 SCORE, PRINTED IN U.S.A.
Complete Set No.: 420
Complete Set Price: USA 35.00 / Can. 35.00
Common Player: .10 / .10
Foil Pack: (16 Cards) 2.50 / 2.50
Foil Box: (36 Packs) 80.00 / 80.00
Jumbo Pack: (27 Cards) 3.50 / 3.50
Jumbo Box: (24 Packs) 70.00 / 70.00

No.	Player	USA NRMT	Can. NRMT
1	Mark Messier, NYR	.30	.30
2	Raymond Bourque, Bos.	.25	.25
3	Gary Roberts, Cal.	.10	.10
4	Bill Ranford, Goalie, Edm.	.10	.10
5	Gilbert Dionne, Mon.	.10	.10
6	Owen Nolan, Que.	.15	.15
7	Pat LaFontaine. Buff.	.35	.35
8	Nicklas Lidstrom, Det.	.20	.20
9	Pat Falloon, SJ.	.25	.25
10	Jeremy Roenick, Chi.	1.25	1.25
11	Kevin Hatcher, Wash.	.10	.10
12	Cliff Ronning, Van.	.10	.10
13	Jeff Brown, St.L	.10	.10
14	Kevin Dineen, Phi.	.10	.10
15	Brian Leetch, NYR	.50	.50
16	Eric Desjardins, Mon.	.10	.10
17	Derek King, NYI	.10	.10
18	Mark Tinordi, Min.	.10	.10
19	Kelly Hrudey, Goalie, LA	.10	.10
20	Sergei Federov, Det.	1.25	1.25
21	Michael Ramsey, Buf.	.10	.10
22	Michel Goulet, Chi.	.10	.10
23	Joe Murphy, Edm.	.10	.10
24	Mark Fitzpatrick, Goalie, NYI	.10	.10
25	Cam Neely, Bos.	.25	.25
26	Rod Brind'Amour, Phi.	.25	.25
27	Neil Wilkinson, SJ	.10	.10
28	Greg Adams, Van.	.10	.10
29	Thomas Steen, Win.	.10	.10
30	Calle Johansson, Wash.	.10	.10
31	Joe Nieuwendyk, Cal.	.10	.10
32	Robert Blake, LA	.10	.10
33	Darren Turcotte, NYR	.10	.10
34	Derian Hatcher, Min.	.10	.10
35	Mikhail Tatarinov, Que.	.10	.10
36	Nelson Emerson, St.L	.25	.25
37	Tim Cheveldae, Goalie, Det.	.10	.10
38	Donald Audette, Buf.	.10	.10
39	Brent Sutter, Chi.	.10	.10
40	Adam Oates, Bos.	.25	.25
41	Luke Richardson, Edm.	.10	.10
42	Jon Casey, Goalie, Min.	.10	.10
43	Guy Carbonneau, Mon.	.10	.10
44	Patrick Flatley, NYI	.10	.10
45	Brian Benning, Phi.	.10	.10

No.	Player	USA NRMT	Can. NRMT
46	Curtis Leschyshyn, Que.	.10	.10
47	Trevor Linden, Van.	.30	.30
48	Donald Beaupre, Goalie, Wash.	.10	.10
49	Troy Murray, Win.	.10	.10
50	Paul Coffey, LA	.20	.20
51	Frantisek Musil, Cal.	.10	.10
52	Douglas Wilson, Goalie, SJ	.10	.10
53	Pat Elynuik, Wash.	.10	.10
54	Curtis Joseph, Goalie, St.L	.30	.30
55	Anthony Amonte, NYR	.25	.25
56	Bob Probert, Det.	.10	.10
57	James (Steve) Smith, Chi.	.10	.10
58	David Andreychuk, Buf.	.20	.20
59	Vladimir Ruzicka, Bos.	.10	.10
60	Jari Kurri, LA	.10	.10
61	Denis Savard, Bos.	.10	.10
62	Benoit Hogue, NYI	.10	.10
63	Terry Carkner, Phi.	.10	.10
64	Valeri Kamensky, Que.	.25	.25
65	Jyrki Lumme, Van.	.10	.10
66	Al Iafrate, Wash.	.10	.10
67	Paul Ranheim, Cal.	.10	.10
68	Ulf Dahlen, Min.	.10	.10
69	Tony Granato, LA	.10	.10
70	Phil Housley, Win.	.10	.10
71	Brian Lawton, SJ	.10	.10
72	Garth Butcher, St.L	.10	.10
73	Stephen Leach, Bos.	.10	.10
74	Steve Larmer, Chi.	.10	.10
75	Mike Richter, Goalie, NYR	.40	.40
76	Vladimir Konstantinov, Det.	.10	.10
77	Alexander Mogilny, Buf.	.75	.75
78	Craig MacTavish, Edm.	.10	.10
79	Mathieu, Schneider, Mon.	.10	.10
80	Mark Recchi, Phi.	.30	.30
81	Gerald Diduck, Van.	.10	.10
82	Peter Bondra, Wash.	.10	.10
83	Allan MacInnis, Cal.	.10	.10
84	Bob Kudelski, LA	.10	.10
85	Dave Gagner, Min.	.10	.10
86	Uwe Krupp, NYI	.10	.10
87	Randy Carlyle, Win.	.10	.10
88	Eric Lindros, Phi.	3.00	6.00
89	Rob Zettler, SJ	.10	.10
90	Mats Sundin, Que.	.35	.35
91	Andrew Moog, Goalie, Bos.	.10	.10
92	Keith Brown, Chi.	.10	.10
93	Paul Ysabaert, Det.	.10	.10
94	Michael Gartner, NYR	.10	.10
95	Kelly Buchberger, Edm.	.10	.10
96	Dominic Roussel, Goalie, Phi.	.30	.30
97	Doug Bodger, Buf.	.10	.10
98	Mike Donnelly, LA	.10	.10
99	Mike Craig, Min.	.10	.10
100	Brett Hull, St.L	1.00	1.00
101	Robert Reichel, Cal.	.10	.10
102	Jeff Norton, NYI	.10	.10
103	Garry Galley, Phi.	.10	.10
104	Dale Hunter, Wash.	.10	.10
105	Jeff Hackett, Goalie, SJ	.10	.10
106	Darrin Shannon, Win.	.10	.10
107	Craig Wolanin, Que.	.10	.10
108	Adam Graves, NYR	.40	.40
109	Chris Chelios, Chi.	.10	.10
110	Pavel Bure, Van.	3.50	3.50
111	Kirk Muller, Mon.	.10	.10
112	Jeff Beukeboom, NYR	.10	.10
113	Mike Hough, Que.	.10	.10
114	Brendan Shanahan, St.L	.30	.30
115	Randy Burridge, Wash.	.10	.10
116	David Poulin, Bos.	.10	.10
117	Petr Svoboda, Buf.	.10	.10
118	Ed Belfour, Goalie, Chi.	.35	.35
119	**Ray Sheppard, Det.**	.10	.10
120	Bernie Nicholls, Edm.	.10	.10
121	Glenn Healy, Goalie, NYI	.10	.10
122	Johan Garpenlov, SJ	.10	.10
123	Mike Lalor, Win.	.10	.10
124	Byron (Brad) McCrimmon, Det.	.10	.10
125	Theoren Fleury, Cal.	.10	.10
126	Randy Gilhen, NYR	.10	.10
127	Petr Nedved, Van.	.25	.25

— 1992 - 93 PINNACLE ISSUE — SCORE • 383

No.	Player	USA NRMT	Can. NRMT
128	Steve Thomas, NYI	.10	.10
129	Richard Zombo, St.L	.10	.10
130	Patrick Roy, Goalie, Mon.	1.25	1.25
131	Rod Langway, Wash.	.10	.10
132	Gordon Murphy, Bos.	.10	.10
133	Randy Wood, Buf.	.10	.10
134	Mike Hudson, Chi.	.10	.10
135	Gerard Gallant, Det.	.10	.10
136	Brian Glynn, Edm.	.10	.10
137	Jim Johnson, Min.	.10	.10
138	Corey Millen, LA	.10	.10
139	Daniel Marois, NYI	.10	.10
140	James Patrick, NYR	.10	.10
141	Claude LaPointe, Que.	.10	.10
142	Bobby Smith, Min.	.10	.10
143	Charles Huddy, LA	.10	.10
144	Murray Baron, St.L	.10	.10
145	Ed Olczyk, Win.	.10	.10
146	Dimitri Khristich, Wash.	.10	.10
147	Doug Lidster, Van.	.10	.10
148	Perry Berezan, SJ.	.10	.10
149	Per-Erik Eklund, Phi.	.10	.10
150	Joe Sakic, Que.	.30	.30
151	Michal Pivonka, Wash.	.10	.10
152	Joey Kocur, NYR	.10	.10
153	Patrice Brisebois, Mon.	.10	.10
154	Ray Ferraro, NYI	.10	.10
155	Michael Modano, Min.	.40	.40
156	Martin McSorley, LA	.10	.10
157	Norm Maciver, Ott.	.10	.10
158	Sergei Nemchinov, NYR	.10	.10
159	David Bruce, SJ	.10	.10
160	Kelly Miller, Wash.	.10	.10
161	Alexei Gusarov, Que.	.10	.10
162	Andrei Lomakin, Phi.	.10	.10
163	Sergio Momesso, Van.	.10	.10
164	Mike Keane, Mon.	.10	.10
165	Pierre Turgeon, NYI	.35	.35
166	Martin Gelinas, Edm.	.10	.10
167	Chris Dahlquist, Cal.	.10	.10
168	Kris King, NYR	.10	.10
169	Dean Evason, SJ	.10	.10
170	Mike Ridley, Wash.	.10	.10
171	Shawn Burr, Det.	.10	.10
172	Dana Murzyn, Van.	.10	.10
173	Dirk Graham, Chi.	.10	.10
174	Trent Yawney, Cal.	.10	.10
175	Luc Robitaille, LA	.25	.25
176	Randy Moller, Buf.	.10	.10
177	Vincent Riendeau, Goalie, Det.	.10	.10
178	Brian Propp, Min.	.10	.10
179	Don Sweeney, Bos.	.10	.10
180	Stephane Matteau, Chi.	.10	.10
181	Garry Valk, Van.	.10	.10
182	Sylvain Cote, Wash.	.10	.10
183	Dave Snuggerud, SJ.	.10	.10
184	Gary Leeman, Cal.	.10	.10
185	John Druce, Win.	.10	.10
186	John Vanbiesbrouck, Goalie, NYR	.10	.10
187	Geoff Courtnall, Van.	.10	.10
188	David Volek, NYI	.10	.10
189	Doug Weight, NYR	.15	.15
190	Bob Essensa, Goalie, Win.	.10	.10
191	Jan Erixon, NYR	.10	.10
192	Geoff Smith, Edm.	.10	.10
193	Dave Christian, Chi.	.10	.10
194	Brian Noonan, Chi.	.10	.10
195	Gary Suter, Cal.	.10	.10
196	Craig Janney, St.L	.20	.20
197	Brad May, Buf.	.10	.10
198	Gaetan Duchesne, Min.	.10	.10
199	Adam Creighton, TB	.10	.10
200	Wayne Gretzky, LA	2.00	2.00
201	David Babych, Van.	.10	.10
202	Fredrik Olausson, Win.	.10	.10
203	Bob Bassen, St.L	.10	.10
204	Todd Krygier, Wash.	.10	.10
205	Grant Ledyard. Buf.	.10	.10
206	Michel Petit, Cal.	.10	.10
207	Todd Elik, Min.	.10	.10
208	Josef Beranek, Edm.	.25	.25
209	Neal Broten, Min.	.10	.10

No.	Player	USA NRMT	Can. NRMT
210	Jim Sandlak, Van.	.10	.10
211	Kevin Haller, Mon.	.10	.10
212	Paul Broten, NYR	.10	.10
213	Mark Pederson, Phi.	.10	.10
214	John McIntyre, LA	.10	.10
215	Teppo Numminen, Win.	.10	.10
216	Kenneth Sutton, Buf.	.10	.10
217	Ronald Stern, Cal.	.10	.10
218	Luciano Borsato, Win.	.10	.10
219	Claude Loiselle, NYI	.10	.10
220	Mark Hardy, NYR	.10	.10

'92 - 93 ROOKIE

No.	Player	USA NRMT	Can. NRMT
221	Joseph Juneau, Bos.	1.75	1.75
222	Keith Tkachuk, Win.	.50	.50
223	Scott Lachance, NYI	.10	.10
224	Glen Murray, Bos.	.10	.10
225	Igor Kravchuk, Chi.	.10	.10
226	Eugeny Davydov, Win.	.10	.10
227	**Ray Whitney, SJ, RC**	**.40**	**.40**
228	**Bret Hedican, St.L, RC**	**.50**	**.50**
229	**Keith Carney, Buf., RC**	**.25**	**.25**
230	Viacheslav Kozlov, Det.	1.25	1.25
231	Drake Berehowsky, Tor.	.10	.10

SIDELINES

No.	Player	USA NRMT	Can. NRMT
232	**Restaurateur:** Cam Neely, Bos.	.10	.10
233	**Actor:** Douglas Gilmour, Tor.	.20	.20
234	**Real Estate Broker:** Randy Wood, Buf.	.10	.10
235	**Rocket Builder:** Luke Rochardson,	.10	.10
236	**Water Skier:** Eric Lindros, Phi.	2.00	2.00
237	**Horse Owner:** Dale Hunter	.10	.10
238	**Farmer:** Pat Falloon, SJ	.20	.20
239	**Rodeo Star:** Dean Kennedy	.10	.10
240	**Sled Dog Trainer:** Uwe Krupp	.10	.10

THE IDOLS

No.	Player	USA NRMT	Can. NRMT
241	Scott Niedermayer, NJ; Steve Yzerman, Det.	.30	.30
242	Gary Roberts, Cal.; Lanny McDonald, Cal.	.10	.10
243	Peter Ahola, LA; Jari Kurri, LA	.10	.10
244	Scott LaChance, NYI; Mark Howe, Det.	.10	.10
245	Rob Pearson, Tor.; Mike Bossy, NYI	.20	.20
246	Kirk McLean, Goalie, Van.; Bernie Parent, Goalie, Phi.	.20	.20
247	Dmitri Mironov, Tor.; Viacheslav Fetisov, NJ	.10	.10
248	Brendan Shanahan, St.L; Darryl Sittler, Tor.	.20	.20
249	Petr Nedved, Van.; Wayne Gretzky, LA	.75	.75
250	Todd Ewen, Mon.; Clark Gilles, NYI	.10	.10

GOOD GUY

No.	Player	USA NRMT	Can. NRMT
251	Luc Robitaille, LA	.10	.10
252	Mark Tinordi, Min.	.10	.10
253	Kris King, NYR	.10	.10
254	Pat LaFontaine, Buf.	.10	.10
255	Ryan Walter, Van.	.10	.10

GAMEWINNERS

No.	Player	USA NRMT	Can. NRMT
256	Jeremy Roenick, Chi.	.25	.25
257	Brett Hull, St.L	.25	.25
258	Steve Yzerman, Det.	.20	.20
259	Claude Lemieux, NJ	.10	.10
260	Michael Modano, Min.	.10	.10
261	Vincent Damphousse, Mon.	.10	.10
262	Tony Granato, LA	.10	.10

MASKS

No.	Player	USA NRMT	Can. NRMT
263	Andrew Moog, Goalie, Bos.	1.00	1.00
264	Curtis Joseph, Goalie, St.L	1.50	1.50
265	Ed Belfour, Goalie, Chi.	1.50	1.50
266	Brian Hayward, Goalie, SJ	1.50	1.50
267	Grant Fuhr, Goalie, Tor.	1.00	1.00
268	Donald Beaupre, Goalie, Wash.	1.00	1.00
269	Tim Cheveldae, Goalie, Det.	1.00	1.00
270	Mike Richter, Goalie, NYR	1.50	1.50

REGULAR ISSUE

No.	Player	USA NRMT	Can. NRMT
271	Zarley Zalapski. Har.	.10	.10
272	Kevin Todd, NJ	.10	.10
273	David Ellett, Tor.	.10	.10
274	Chris Terreri, Goalie, NJ	.10	.10
275	Jaromir Jagr, Pit.	1.00	1.00
276	Wendel Clark, Tor.	.20	.20
277	Robert Holik, NJ	.10	.10
278	Bruce Driver, NJ	.10	.10
279	Douglas Gilmour. Tor.	.40	.40
280	Scott Stevens, NJ	.10	.10
281	Murray Craven, Har.	.10	.10
282	Rick Tocchet, Pit.	.10	.10
283	Peter Zezel, Tor.	.10	.10
284	Claude Lemieux, NJ	.10	.10
285	John Cullen, Har.	.10	.10
286	Valeri Zelepukin, NJ	.30	.30
287	Rob Pearson, Tor.	.10	.10
288	Kevin Stevens, Pit.	.30	.30
289	Alexei Kasatonov, NJ	.10	.10
290	Todd Gill, Tor.	.10	.10
291	Randy Ladouceur, Har.	.10	.10
292	Lawrence Murphy, Pit.	.10	.10
293	Tom Chorske, NJ	.10	.10
294	Jamie Macoun, Tor.	.10	.10
295	Sean Burke, Goalie, Har.	.10	.10
296	Ulf Samuelsson, Pit.	.10	.10
297	Eric Weinrich, Har.	.10	.10
298	Tom Barrasso, Goalie, Pit.	.10	.10
299	Viacheslav Fetisov, NJ	.10	.10
300	Mario Lemieux, Pit.	1.50	1.50
301	Grant Fuhr, Goalie, Tor.	.10	.10
302	Zdeno Ciger, NJ	.10	.10
303	Ronald Francis, Pit.	.10	.10
304	Scott Niedermayer, NJ	.50	.50
305	Mark Osborne, Tor.	.10	.10
306	Kjell Samuelsson, Pit.	.10	.10
307	Geoff Sanderson, Har.	.50	.50
308	Paul Stanton, Pit.	.10	.10
309	Frank Pietrangelo, Goalie, Har.	.10	.10
310	Bob Errey, Pit.	.10	.10
311	Dino Ciccarelli, Det.	.10	.10
312	Gordon Roberts, Bos.	.10	.10
313	Kevin Miller, Wash.	.10	.10
314	Mike Ricci, Que.	.20	.20
315	Robert Carpenter, Wash.	.10	.10
316	Dale Hawerchuk, Buf	.10	.10
317	Christian Ruuttu, Chi.	.10	.10
318	Michael Vernon, Goalie, Cal.	.10	.10
319	Paul Cavallini, St.L	.10	.10
320	Steve Duchesne, Que.	.10	.10
321	Craig Simpson, Edm.	.10	.10
322	Mark Howe, Det.	.10	.10
323	Shayne Corson, Edm.	.10	.10
324	Tom Kurvers, NYI	.10	.10
325	Brian Bellows, Mon.	.10	.10
326	Glen Wesley, Bos.	.10	.10
327	Daren Puppa, Goalie, Buf.	.10	.10
328	Joel Otto, Cal.	.10	.10
329	Jimmy Carson, Det.	.10	.10
330	Kirk McLean, Goalie, Van.	.30	.30
331	Rob Brown, Chi.	.10	.10
332	Yves Racine, Det.	.10	.10
333	Brian Mullen, NYI	.10	.10
334	Dave Manson, Edm.	.10	.10
335	Sergei Makarov, Cal.	.10	.10
336	Esa Tikkanen, Edm.	.10	.10
337	Russell Courtnall, Min.	.10	.10
338	Kevin Lowe, Edm.	.10	.10
339	Steve Chaisson, Det.	.10	.10

384 • SCORE — 1992-93 PINNACLE INSERT SETS

No.	Player	USA NRMT	Can. NRMT
340	Ron Hextall, Goalie, Que.	.10	.10
341	Stephan Lebeau, Mon.	.10	.10
342	Michael McPhee, Min.	.10	.10
343	David Shaw, Bos.	.10	.10
344	Petr Klima, Edm.	.10	.10
345	Tomas Sandstrom, LA	.10	.10
346	Scott Mellanby, Edm.	.10	.10
347	Brian Skrudland, Mon.	.10	.10
348	Patrick Verbeek, Har.	.10	.10
349	Vincent Damphousse, Mon.	.10	.10
350	Steve Yzerman, Det.	.30	.30
351	John MacLean, NJ	.10	.10
352	Stephen Konroyd, Har.	.10	.10
353	Phillippe Bourque, NYR	.10	.10
354	Kenneth Daneyko, NJ	.10	.10
355	Glenn Anderson, Tor.	.10	.10
356	Ken Wregget, Goalie, Pit.	.10	.10
357	Brent Gilchrist, Edm.	.10	.10
358	Robert Rouse, Tor.	.10	.10
359	Peter Stastny, NJ	.10	.10
360	Joe Mullen, Pit.	.10	.10
361	Stephane J.J. Richer, NJ	.10	.10
362	Kelly Kisio, SJ	.10	.10
363	Keith Acton, Phi.	.10	.10
364	Felix Potvin, Goalie, Tor.	3.00	3.00
365	Martin LaPointe, Det.	.20	.20
366	Ron Tugnutt, Goalie, Edm.	.10	.10
367	David Taylor, LA	.10	.10
368	Tim Kerr, Har.	.10	.10
369	Carey Wilson, Cal.	.10	.10
370	Gregory Paslawski, Phi.	.10	.10

OTTAWA SENATORS

No.	Player	USA NRMT	Can. NRMT
371	Peter Sidorkiewicz, Goalie	.10	.10
372	Brad Shaw	.10	.10
373	Sylvain Turgeon	.10	.10
374	Mark Lamb	.10	.10
375	Laurie Boschman	.10	.10
376	Mark Osiecki	.10	.10
377	Douglas Smail	.10	.10
378	Bradley Marsh	.10	.10
379	Mike Peluso	.10	.10
380	Stephen Weeks, Goalie	.10	.10

TAMPA BAY LIGHTNING

No.	Player	USA NRMT	Can. NRMT
381	Wendell Young, Goalie	.10	.10
382	Joe Reekie	.10	.10
383	Peter Taglianetti	.10	.10
384	Bo Mikael Andersson	.10	.10
385	Marc Bergevin	.10	.10
386	Anatoli Semenov	.10	.10
387	Brian Bradley	.10	.10
388	Michel Mongeau	.10	.10
389	George (Rob) Ramage	.10	.10
390	Ken Hodge	.10	.10

1992-93 ROOKIES

No.	Player	USA NRMT	Can. NRMT
391	Richard Matvichuk, Min., RC	.25	.25
392	Alexei Zhitnik, LA	.40	.40
393	Richard Smehlik, Buf., RC	.30	.30
394	Dimitri Yushkevich, Phi., RC	.25	.25
395	Andrei Kovalenko, Que., RC	.50	.50
396	Vladimir Vujtek, Edm., RC	.20	.20
397	Nikolai Borschevsky, Tor., RC	.75	.75
398	Vitali Karamnov, St.L, RC	.30	.30
399	Jim Hiller, LA, RC	.20	.20
400	Michael Nylander, Min., RC	.75	.75
401	Tommy Sjodin, Min., RC	.25	.25
402	Robert Petrovicky, Har., RC	.30	.30
403	Alexei Kovalev, NYR	1.50	1.50
404	Vatali Prokhorov, St.L, RC	.25	.25
405	Dmitri Kvartalnov, Bos., RC	.40	.40
406	Teemu Selanne, Win.	1.50	3.00
407	Darius Kasparaitis, NYI	.20	.20
408	Roman Hamrlik, TB, RC	.50	.50

No.	Player	USA NRMT	Can. NRMT
409	Vladimir Malakhov, NYI	.35	.35
410	Sergei Krivokrasov, Chi.	.25	.25
411	Robert Lang, LA, RC	.30	.30
412	Josef Stumpel, Bos., Error	.10	.10
413	Denny Felsner, St.L, RC	.30	.30
414	Rob Zamuner, TB, RC	.20	.20
415	Jason Woolley, Wash., RC	.20	.20
416	Alexei Zhamnov, Win.	.90	.90
417	Igor Korolev, St.L, RC	.25	.25
418	Patrick Poulin, Har.	.10	.10
419	Dmitri Mironov, Tor.	.25	.25
420	Shawn McEachern, Pit.	.40	.40

— 1992-93 PINNACLE INSERT SETS —

AMERICAN AND CANADIAN TEAM PINNACLE

This 6-card set has two players, one for each side. Six players from each conference are featured. The cards are randomly inserted in foil packs. The Canadian and American versions are different in only one respect; the title bar that reads "TEAM PINNACLE" in the Canadian version is red and in the American version is blue. The set is numbered -- of 6.

1992-93 Team Pinnacle
Card No. 1, Face: Ed Belfour
Card No. 1, Back: Mike Richter

Card Size: 2 1/2" x 3 1/2"
Face: Four colour, black border at bottom; Gold embossed bar
Back: Four colour, black border at bottom, card stock; Gold embossed; Name, Number
Imprint: © 1992 SCORE, PRINTED IN THE U.S.A.

Complete Set No.: 6	USA	Can.
Complete Set Price:	125.00	125.00
Common Card:	15.00	15.00

No.	Player	USA NRMT	Can. NRMT
1	Ed Belfour, Goalie, Chi.	20.00	20.00
	Mike Richter, Goalie, NYR		
2	Chris Chelios, Chi.	15.00	15.00
	Raymond Bourque, Bos.		
3	Paul Coffey, LA	20.00	20.00
	Brian Leetch,		
4	Pavel Bure, Van.	25.00	30.00
	Kevin Stevens, Pit.		
5	Wayne Gretzky, LA	55.00	60.00
	Eric Lindros, Phi.		
6	Brett Hull, St.L	20.00	25.00
	Jaromir Jagr, Pit.		

— TEAM 2000 —

This 30-card insert set was issued two cards per jumbo pack. The difference between the Canadian and American editions are: The Canadian cards have a small gold embossed maple leaf on the face while the American cards have a small gold embossed star. While both editions feature the same player the portraits differ.

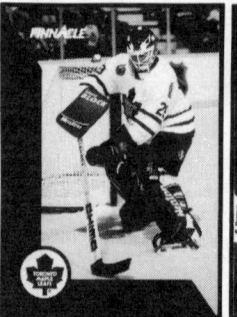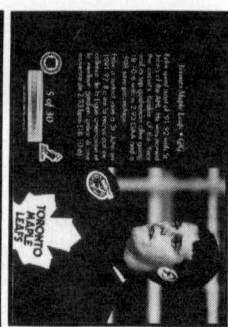

Team 2000
Card No. 5, Felix Potvin

Card Size: 2 1/2" x 3 1/2"
Face: Four colour, black border with gold embossed title bar
Back: Four colour, card stock; Name, Team, Resume
Imprint: © 1992 SCORE, PRINTED IN THE U.S.A.

Complete Set No.: 30	USA	Can.
Complete Set Price:	40.00	40.00
Common Card:	1.25	1.25

No.	Player	USA NRMT	Can. NRMT
1	Eric Lindros, Phi.	8.00	9.00
2	Michael Modano, Min.	2.00	2.00
3	Nicklas Lidstrom, Det.	.40	.50
4	Anthony Amonte, NYR	.60	.60
5	Felix Potvin, Goalie, Tor.	6.00	7.00
6	Scott Lachance, NYI	.40	.40
7	Mats Sundin, Que.	1.00	1.00
8	Pavel Bure, Van.	7.00	8.00
9	Eric Desjardins, Mon.	.40	.40
10	Owen Nolan, Que.	.60	.60
11	Dominic Roussel, Goalie, Phi.	.60	.60
12	Scott Niedermayer, NJ	1.00	1.00
13	Viacheslav Kozlov, Det.	2.50	2.50
14	Patrick Poulin, Har.	.40	.40
15	Jaromir Jagr, Pit.	3.00	3.50
16	Robert Blake, LA	.40	.40
17	Pierre Turgeon, NYI	1.50	1.50
18	Rod Brind'Amour, Phi.	1.50	1.50
19	Joseph Juneau, Bos.	3.00	3.00
20	Tim Cheveldae, Goalie, Det.	.40	.40
21	Joe Sakic, Que.	.40	.40
22	Kevin Todd, NJ	.40	.40
23	Rob Pearson, Tor.	.40	.40
24	Trevor Linden, Van.	1.50	1.50
25	Dimitri Khristich, Wash.	.40	.40
26	Pat Falloon, SJ	2.00	2.00
27	Jeremy Roenick, Chi.	3.50	4.00
28	Alexander Mogilny, Buf.	3.50	4.00
29	Gilbert Dionne, Mon.	.40	.40
30	Sergei Fedorov, Det.	3.50	4.00

— 1993-94 PROMOTIONAL CARDS —

AMERICAN

These six cards were issued singly and in sheet form to promote their 1993-94 Pinnacle issue. The cards are stamped "Sample" on the back to the left of the player's name.

Card Size: 2 1/2" x 3 1/2"
Sheet Size: 7 1/2" x 7"
Face: Four colour, black border; Name, Team
Back: Four colour; Name, Number, Position, Team logo Number, Resume, Logo
Imprint: © 1993 SCORE, PRINTED IN U.S.A.

No.	Player	EX	NRMT
—	Sheet	15.00	30.00
1	Eric Lindros, Phi.	1.50	3.00
2	Mats Sundin, Que.	1.50	3.00
3	Tom Barrasso, Goalie, Pit.	1.50	3.00
4	Teemu Selanne, Win.	1.50	3.00
5	Joseph Juneau, Bos.	1.50	3.00
6	Anthony Amonte, NYR	1.50	3.00

— 1993-94 REGULAR ISSUE — SERIES ONE

AMERICAN AND CANADIAN

The 496th card of this set was only available by sending "Alexandre Daigle" redemption cards to Score. In return they mailed the limited edition 496th card. The only difference between American and Canadian is the bilingual backs on the Canadian cards.

 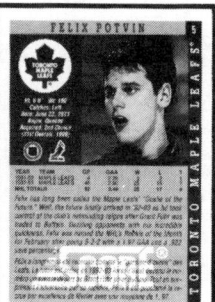

1993-94 Canadian Issue
Card No. 5, Felix Potvin

Card Size: 2 1/2 x 3 1/2
Face: Four colour, White border, Name, Team
Back: Four colour, Name, Team, Resume, Number, Bilingual, Team Logo
Imprint: ©1993 SCORE, PRINTED IN U.S.A.

	USA	Can.
Complete Set No.: 496		
Complete Set Price:	22.00	22.00
Foil Pack: (15 Cards)	1.00	1.00
Foil Box: (36 Packs)	35.00	35.00
Common Card:	.10	.10

No.	Player	USA NRMT	Can. NRMT
1	Eric Lindros, Phil.	2.00	2.00
2	Michael Gartner, NYR	.10	.10
3	Steve Larmer, Chi.	.10	.10
4	Brian Bellows, Mon.	.10	.10
5	Felix Potvin, Goalie, Tor.	.75	.75
6	Pierre Turgeon, NYI	.25	.25
7	Joe Mullen, Pit.	.10	.10
8	Craig MacTavish, Edm.	.10	.10
9	Mats Sundin, Que.	.15	.15
10	Patrick Verbeek, Hart.	.10	.10
11	Andrew Moog, Goalie, Bos.	.10	.10
12	Dirk Graham, Chi.	.10	.10
13	Gary Suter, Cal.	.10	.10
14	Brent Fedyk, Phil.	.10	.10
15	Brad Shaw, Ott.	.10	.10
16	Benoit Hogue, NYI	.10	.10
17	Cliff Ronning, Van.	.10	.10
18	Mathieu Schneider, Mon.	.10	.10
19	Bernie Nicholls, NJ	.10	.10
20	Vladimir Konstantinov, Det.	.25	.25
21	Doug Bodger, Buf.	.10	.10
22	Peter Stastny, NJ	.10	.10
23	Lawrence Murphy, Pit.	.10	.10
24	Darren Turcotte, NYR	.10	.10
25	Doug Crossman, St.L	.10	.10
26	Bob Essensa, Win.	.10	.10
27	Kelly Kisio, SJ	.10	.10
28	Nelson Emerson, St.L	.10	.10
29	Raymond Bourque, Bos.	.15	.15
30	Kelly Miller, Wash.	.10	.10
31	Peter Zezel, Tor.	.10	.10
32	Owen Nolan, Que.	.08	.15
33	Sergei Makarov, Cal.	.10	.10
34	Stephane J.J. Richer, NJ	.10	.10
35	Adam Graves, NYR	.20	.20
36	George (Rob) Ramage, Mon.	.10	.10
37	Ed Olczyk, NYR	.10	.10
38	Jeff Hackett, Goalie, SJ	.10	.10
39	Ronald Sutter, St.L	.10	.10
40	Dale Hunter, Wash.	.10	.10
41	Nikolai Borschevsky, Tor.	.15	.15
42	Curtis Leschyshyn, Que.	.10	.10
43	Mike Vernon, Cal.	.10	.10
44	Brent Sutter,	.10	.10
45	Rod Brind'Amour, Phil.	.15	.15
46	Sylvain Turgeon, Ott.	.10	.10
47	Kirk McLean, Goalie, Van.	.10	.10
48	Derek King, NYI	.10	.10
49	Murray Craven, Van.	.10	.10
50	Jaromir Jagr, Pit.	.40	.40
51	Guy Carbonneau, Mon.	.10	.10
52	Tony Granato, L.A.	.10	.10
53	Mark Tinordi, Dal.	.10	.10
54	Brad McCrimmon, Det.	.10	.10
55	Randy Wood, Buf.	.10	.10
56	Scott Young, Que.	.10	.10
57	Jamie Baker, Ott.	.10	.10
58	Donald Beaupre, Goalie, Wash.	.10	.10
59	Bob Probert, Det.	.10	.10
60	Ray Ferraro, NYI	.10	.10
61	Alexei Kasatonov, NJ	.10	.10
62	Corey Millen, L.A.	.10	.10
63	Scott Mellanby, Edm.	.10	.10
64	Brian Benning, Edm.	.10	.10
65	Doug Lidster, Van.	.10	.10
66	Douglas Gilmour, Tor.	.20	.20
67	Shawn McEachern, Pit.	.10	.10
68	Tim Cheveldae, Goalie, Det.	.10	.10
69	Jeff Norton, NYI	.10	.10
70	Ed Belfour, Goalie, Chi.	.20	.20
71	Thomas Steen, Win.	.10	.10
72	Stephan Lebeau, Mon.	.10	.10
73	James Patrick, NYR	.10	.10
74	Joel Otto, Cal.	.10	.10
75	Grant Fuhr, Goalie, Buf.	.10	.10
76	Calle Johansson, Wash.	.10	.10
77	Donald Audette, Buf.	.10	.10
78	Geoff Courtnall, Van.	.10	.10
79	Fredrik Olausson, Win.	.10	.10
80	Dimitri, Khristich, Wash.	.10	.10
81	John MacLean, Goalie, NJ	.10	.10
82	Dominic Roussel, Phil.	.10	.10
83	Ray Sheppard, Det.	.10	.10
84	Christian Ruuttu, Chi.	.10	.10
85	Mike McPhee, Dal.	.10	.10
86	Adam Creighton, NYI	.10	.10
87	Uwe Krupp, NYI	.10	.10
88	Steve Leach, Bos.	.10	.10
89	Kevin Miller, St.L	.10	.10
90	Charles Huddy, L.A.	.10	.10
91	Mark Howe, Det.	.10	.10
92	Sylvain Cote, Wash.	.10	.10
93	Anatoli Semenov, Van.	.10	.10
94	Jeff Beukeboom, NYR	.10	.10
95	Gord Murphy, Bos.	.10	.10
96	Rob Pearson, Tor.	.10	.10
97	Esa Tikkanen, NYR	.10	.10
98	Dave Gagner, Dal.	.10	.10
99	Mike Richter, Goalie, NYR	.20	.20
100	Jari Kurri, L.A.	.10	.10
101	Chris Chelios, Chi.	.10	.10
102	Peter Sidorkiewicz, Goalie, Ott.	.10	.10
103	Scott Lachance, NYI	.10	.10
104	Zarley Zalapski, Hart.	.10	.10
105	Denis Savard, Mon.	.10	.10
106	Paul Coffey, Det.	.15	.15
107	Ulf Dahlen,	.10	.10
108	Shayne Corson, Edm.	.10	.10
109	Jimmy Carson, L.A.	.10	.10
110	Petr Svoboda, Buf.	.10	.10
111	Scott Stevens, NJ	.10	.10
112	Kevin Lowe, NYR	.10	.10
113	Chris Kontos, TB	.10	.10
114	Eugeny Davydov, Win.	.10	.10
115	Doug Wilson, SJ	.10	.10
116	Curtis Joseph, Goalie, St.L	.15	.15
117	Trevor Linden, Van.	.10	.10
118	Michal Pivonka, Wash.	.10	.10
119	David Ellet, Tor.	.10	.10
120	Mike Ricci, Que.	.10	.10
121	Allan MacInnis, Cal.	.10	.10
122	Kevin Dineen, Phil.	.10	.10
123	Norm Maciver, Ott.	.10	.10
124	Darius Kasparaitis, NYI	.10	.10
125	Adam Oates, Bos.	.15	.15
126	Sean Burke, Hart.	.10	.10
127	Dave Manson, Edm.	.10	.10
128	Eric Desjardins, Mon.	.10	.10
129	Tomas Sandstrom, L.A.	.10	.10
130	Russell Courtnall, Dal.	.10	.10
131	Roman Hamrlik, TB	.15	.15
132	Teppo Numminen, Win.	.10	.10
133	Pat Falloon, SJ	.20	.20
134	Jyrki Lumme, Van.	.10	.10
135	Joe Sakic, Que.	.20	.20
136	Kevin Hatcher, Wash.	.10	.10
137	Wendel Clark, Tor.	.10	.10
138	Neil Wilkinson, SJ	.10	.10
139	Craig Simpson, Edm.	.10	.10
140	Kelly Hrudey, Goalie. L.A.	.10	.10
141	Steve Thomas, NYI	.10	.10
142	Michael Modano, Dal.	.20	.20
143	Garry Galley, Phil.	.10	.10
144	Jim Johnson, Dal.	.10	.10
145	Rod Langway, Wash.	.10	.10
146	Bob Sweeney, Buf.	.10	.10
147	Gary Leeman, Mon.	.10	.10
148	Alexei Zhitnik, L.A.	.10	.10
149	Adam Foote, Que.	.10	.10
150	Mark Recchi, Phil.	.20	.20
151	Ronald Francis, Pit.	.10	.10
152	Ron Hextall, Goalie, Que.	.10	.10
153	Michel Goulet, Chi.	.10	.10
154	Vladimir Ruzicka, Bos.	.10	.10
155	Bill Ranford, Goalie, Edm.	.10	.10
156	Mike Craig, Dal.	.10	.10
157	Vladimir Malakhov, NYI	.10	.10
158	Nicklas Lidstrom, Det.	.15	.15
159	Dale Hawerchuk, Buf.	.10	.10
160	Claude Lemieux, NJ	.10	.10
161	Ulf Samuelsson, Pit.	.10	.10
162	John Vanbiesbrouck, Goalie, NYR	.10	.10
163	Patrice Brisbois, Mon.	.10	.10
164	Andrew Cassels, Hart.	.10	.10
165	Paul Ranheim, Cal.	.10	.10
166	Neal Broten, Dal.	.10	.10
167	Joe Reekie, TB	.10	.10
168	Derian Hatcher, Dal.	.10	.10
169	Don Sweeney, Bos.	.10	.10
170	Mike Keane, Mon.	.10	.10
171	Mark Fitzpatrick, Goalie, NYI	.10	.10
172	Paul Cavallini, Wash.	.10	.10
173	Garth Butcher, St.L	.10	.10
174	Andrei Kovalenko, Que.	.15	.15
175	Shawn Burr, Det.	.10	.10
176	Mike Donnelly, L.A.	.10	.10
177	Glenn Healy, Goalie, NYI	.10	.10
178	Gilbert Dionne, Mon.	.10	.10
179	Mike Ramsey, Pit.	.10	.10
180	Glenn Anderson, Tor.	.10	.10
181	Pelle Eklund, Phil.	.10	.10
182	Kerry Huffman, Que.	.10	.10
183	Johan Garpenlov, SJ	.10	.10
184	Kjell Samuelsson, Pit.	.10	.10

No.	Player	USA NRMT	Can. NRMT
185	Todd Elik, Dal.	.10	.10
186	Craig Janney, St.L	.15	.15
187	Dmitri Kvartalnov, Bos.	.10	.10
188	Al Iafrate, Wash.	.10	.10
189	John Cullen, Tor.	.10	.10
190	Steve Duchesne, Que.	.10	.10
191	Thereon Fleury, Cal.	.10	.10
192	Steve Smith, Chi.	.10	.10
193	Jon Casey, Goalie, Dal.	.10	.10
194	Jeff Brown, St. L	.10	.10
195	Keith Tkachuk, Win.	.20	.20
196	Greg Adams, Van.	.10	.10
197	Mike Ridley, Wash.	.10	.10
198	Bobby Holik, NJ	.15	.15
199	Joe Nieuwendyk, Cal.	.10	.10
200	Mark Messier, NYR	.20	.20
201	Jim Hrivnak, Goalie, Win.	.10	.10
202	Patrick Poulin, Hart.	.10	.10
203	Alexei Kovalev, NYR	.30	.30
204	Robert Reichel, Cal.	.15	.15
205	David Shaw, Bos.	.10	.10
206	Brent Gilchrist, Det.	.10	.10
207	Craig Billington, Goalie, NJ	.10	.10
208	Bob Errey, Buf.	.10	.10
209	Dmitri Mironov, Tor., Error	.15	.15
210	Dixon Ward, Van.	.10	.10
211	Rick Zombo, St. L	.10	.10
212	Marty McSorley, LA	.10	.10
213	Geoff Sanderson, Hart.	.30	.30
214	Dino Ciccarelli, Det.	.10	.10
215	Anthony Amonte, NYR	.10	.10
216	Dimitri Yushkevich, Phi.	.10	.10
217	Scott Niedermayer, NJ	.15	.15
218	Sergei Nemchinov, NYR	.10	.10
219	Steve Konroyd, Det.	.10	.10
220	Patrick Flatley, NYI	.10	.10
221	Steve Chiasson, Det.	.10	.10
222	Alexander Mogilny, Buf.	.30	.30
223	Pat Elynuik, Wash.	.10	.10
224	Jamie Macoun, Tor.	.10	.10
225	Tom Barrasso, Goalie, Pit.	.10	.10
226	Gaetan Duchesne, Det.	.10	.10
227	Eric Weinrich, Hart.	.10	.10
228	Dave Poulin, Bos.	.10	.10
229	Viacheslav Fetisov, NJ	.10	.10
230	Brian Bradley, TB	.10	.10
231	Petr Nedved, Van.	.15	.15
232	Phil Housley, Win.	.10	.10
233	Terry Carkner, Phi.	.10	.10
234	Kirk Muller, Mon.	.10	.10
235	Brian Leetch, NYR	.20	.20
236	Rob Blake, LA	.10	.10
237	Chris Terreri, Goalie, NJ	.10	.10
238	Brendan Shanahan, St. L	.10	.10
239	Paul Ysebaert, Det.	.10	.10
240	Jeremy Roenick, Chi.	.35	.35
241	Gary Roberts, Cal.	.10	.10
242	Petr Klima, Edm.	.10	.10
243	Glen Wesley, Bos.	.10	.10
244	Vincent Damphousse, Mon.	.10	.10
245	Luc Robitaille, LA	.15	.15
246	**Dallas Drake, Det., RC**	.20	.20
247	**Rob Gaudreau, SJ, RC**	.20	.20
248	Tommy Sjodin, Det.	.10	.10
249	Richard Smehlik, SJ	.10	.10
250	Sergei Federov, Det.	.40	.40
251	Stephen Heinze, Bos.	.10	.10
252	Luke Richardson, Edm.	.10	.10
253	Doug Weight, Edm.	.10	.10
254	Martin Rucinsky, Que.	.10	.10
255	Sergio Memesso, Van.	.10	.10
256	Alexei Zhamnov, Win.	.10	.10
257	Bob Kudelski, Ott.	.10	.10
258	Brian Skrudland, Cal.	.10	.10
259	Terry Yake, Hart.	.10	.10
260	Alexei Gusarov, Que.	.10	.10
261	Sandis Ozolinsh, SJ	.15	.15
262	Ted Donato, Bos.	.10	.10
263	Bruce Driver, NJ	.10	.10
264	Yves Racine, Det.	.10	.10
265	Mike Peluso, Ott.	.10	.10
266	Craig Muni, Chi.	.10	.10
267	Bob Carpenter, Wash.	.10	.10
268	Kevin Haller, Mon	.10	.10
269	Brad May, Buf.	.10	.10
270	Joe Kocur, NYR	.10	.10
271	Igor Korolev, St. L	.10	.10
272	Troy Murray, Chi.	.10	.10
273	Daren Puppa, Goalie, Tor.	.10	.10
274	Gordie Roberts, Bos.	.10	.10
275	Michel Petit, Cal.	.10	.10
276	Vincent Riendeau, Det.	.10	.10
277	Robert Petrovicky, Hart.	.10	.10
278	Valeri Zelepukin, NJ	.10	.10
279	Bob Bassen, St. L	.10	.10
280	Darrin Shannon, Win.	.10	.10
281	Dominik Hasek, Goalie, Buf.	.20	.20
282	Craig Ludwig, Cal.	.10	.10
283	Lyle Odelein, Mon.	.10	.10
284	Alexander Semak, NJ	.10	.10
285	Richard Matvichuk, Det.	.10	.10
286	Ken Daneyko, NJ	.10	.10
287	Jan Erixon, NYR	.10	.10
288	Robert Dirk, Van.	.10	.10
289	Laurie Boschman, Ott.	.10	.10
290	Gregory Paslawski, Cal.	.10	.10
291	Rob Zamuner, TB	.10	.10
292	Todd Gill, Tor.	.10	.10
293	Neil Brady, Ott.	.10	.10
294	Murray Baron, St.L	.10	.10
295	Peter Taglianetti, Pit.	.10	.10
296	Wayne Presley, Buf.	.10	.10
297	Paul Broten, NYR	.10	.10
298	Dana Murzyn, Van.	.10	.10
299	Jean-Jacques Daigneault, Mon.	.10	.10
300	Wayne Gretzky, L.A.	1.00	1.00
301	Keith Acton, Phi.	.10	.10
302	Yuri Khmylev, Buf.	.10	.10
303	Frantisek Musil, Cal.	.10	.10
304	Bob Rousse, Tor.	.10	.10
305	Greg Gilbert, Chi.	.10	.10
306	Geoff Smith, Edm.	.10	.10
307	Adam Burt, Hart.	.10	.10
308	Phillippe Bourque, NYR	.10	.10
309	Igor Kravchuk, Edm.	.10	.10
310	Steve Yzerman, Det.	.25	.25
311	Darryl Sydor, LA	.10	.10
312	Tahir Domi, Win.	.10	.10
313	Sergei Zubov, NYR	.10	.10
314	Chris Dahlquist, Cal.	.10	.10
315	Patrick Roy, Goalie, Mon.	.50	.50
316	Mark Osborne, Tor.	.10	.10
317	Kelly Buchberger, Edm.	.10	.10
318	John LeClair, Mon.	.10	.10
319	Randy McKay, NJ	.10	.10
320	Jody Hull, Ott.	.10	.10
321	Paul Stanton, Pit.	.10	.10
322	Steven Finn, Que.	.10	.10
323	Rich Sutter, St. L	.10	.10
324	Ray Whitney, SJ	.10	.10
325	Kevin Stevens, Pit.	.20	.20
326	Valeri Kamensky, Que.	.15	.15
327	Doug Zmolek, SJ	.10	.10
328	Mikhail Tatarinov, Que.	.10	.10
329	Ken Wregget, Goalie, Pit	.10	.10
330	Joseph Juneau, Bos.	.30	.30
331	Teemu Selanne, Win.	.10	.10
332	Trent Yawney, Cal.	.10	.10
333	Pavel Bure, Van.	.80	.80
334	Jim Paek, Pit.	.10	.10
335	Brett Hull, St. L	.30	.30
336	Tommy Soderstrom, Phi.	.10	.10
337	Grigori Panteleyev, Bos.	.10	.10
338	Kevin Todd, Edm.	.10	.10
339	Mark Janssens, Hart.	.10	.10
340	Rick Tocchet, Pit.	.10	.10
341	Wendell Young, Goalie, TB	.10	.10
342	Cam Neely, Bos.	.20	.20
343	David Andreychuk, Tor.	.20	.20
344	Peter Bondra, Wash.	.10	.10
345	Pat LaFontaine, Buf.	.30	.30
346	Robb Stauber, Goalie, LA	.10	.10
347	Brian Muller, NYI	.10	.10
348	Joe Murphy, Chi.	.10	.10
349	Pat Jablonski, Goalie, TB	.10	.10
350	Mario Lemieux, Pit.	.75	.75
351	Sergei Bautin, Win.	.10	.10
352	Claude Lapointe, Que.	.10	.10
353	Dean Evason, St.L	.10	.10
354	John Tucker, TB	.10	.10
355	Drake Berehowsky, Tor.	.10	.10
356	Gerald Diduck, Van.	.10	.10
357	Todd Krygier, Wash.	.10	.10
358	Adrien Plavsic, Van.	.10	.10
359	Sylvain Lefebvre, Tor.	.10	.10
360	Kay Whitmore, Goalie, Van.	.10	.10
361	Sheldon Kennedy, Det.	.10	.10
362	Kris King, Win.	.10	.10
363	Marc Bergevin, TB	.10	.10
364	Keith Primeau, Det.	.10	.10
365	Jimmy Waite, Chi.	.10	.10
366	Dean Kennedy, Win.	.10	.10
367	Michael Krushelnyski, Tor.	.10	.10
368	Ron Tugnutt, Goalie, Edm.	.10	.10
369	Bob Beers, TB	.10	.10
370	Randy Burridge, Wash.	.10	.10
371	Dave Reid, Bos.	.10	.10
372	Frantisek Kucera, Chi.	.10	.10
373	Scott Pellerin, NJ	.10	.10
374	Brad Dalgarno, NYI	.10	.10
375	Martin Straka, Pit.	.10	.10
376	Scott Pearson, Que.	.10	.10
377	Arturs Irbe, Goalie, SJ	.20	.20
378	Jiri Slegr, Van.	.10	.10
379	Stephane Fiset, Goalie, Que.	.10	.10
380	Stu Barnes, Win.	.10	.10
381	Eric Nattress, Phi.	.10	.10
382	Steven King, NYR	.10	.10
383	Michael Nylander, Hart.	.10	.10
384	Keith Brown, Chi.	.10	.10
385	Gino Odjick, Van.	.10	.10
386	Bryan Marchment, Chi.	.10	.10
387	Mike Foligno, Tor.	.10	.10
388	Zdeno Ciger, Edm.	.10	.10
389	Dave Taylor, LA	.10	.10
390	Mike Sullivan, SJ	.10	.10
391	Shawn Chant, TB	.10	.10
392	Brad Marsh, Ott.	.10	.10
393	Mike Hough, Que.	.10	.10
394	Jeff Reese, Cal.	.10	.10
395	Bill Guerin, NJ	.10	.10
396	Greg Hawgood, Phi.	.10	.10
397	Jim Sandlak, Van.	.10	.10
398	Stephane Matteau, Chi.	.10	.10
399	John Blue, Goalie, Bos.	.10	.10
400	Anthony Twist, Que.	.10	.10
401	Luciano Borsato, Win.	.10	.10
402	Gerard Gallant, Det.	.10	.10
403	Rick Tabaracci, Goalie, Wash.	.10	.10
404	Nicholas Kypreos, Hart.	.10	.10
405	Martin McInnis, NYI	.10	.10
406	Craig Wolanin, Que.	.10	.10
407	Mark Lamb, Ott.	.10	.10
408	Martin Gelinas, Edm.	.10	.10
409	Ronnie Stern, Cal.	.10	.10
410	Ken Sutton, Buf.	.10	.10
411	Brian Noonan, Chi.	.10	.10
412	Stephane Quintal, St. L	.10	.10
413	Rob Zettler, SJ	.10	.10
414	Gino Cavallini, Que.	.10	.10
415	Mark Hardy, LA	.10	.10
416	Jay Wells, NYR	.10	.10
417	Keith Jones, Wash.	.10	.10
418	Dave McLlwain, Tor.	.10	.10
419	Frank Pietrangelo, Goalie, Hart.	.10	.10
420	Jocelyn Lemieux, Chi.	.10	.10
421	Vyacheslav Kozlov, Det.	.30	.30
422	Randy Moller, Buf.	.10	.10
423	Kevin Dahl, Cal.	.10	.10
424	**Shjon Podein, Edm., RC**	.10	.10
425	Shane Churla, Dal.	.10	.10
426	Guy Hebert, St. L	.10	.10
427	Bo Mikael Andersson, TB	.10	.10
428	Robert Kron, Hart.	.10	.10
429	Mike Eagles, Win.	.10	.10
430	Alan May, Wash.	.10	.10

No.	Player	USA NRMT	Can. NRMT
431	Ron Wilson, St. L	.10	.10
432	Darcy Wakaluk, Goalie, Dal.	.10	.10
433	Rob Ray, Buf.	.10	.10
434	Brent Ashton, Cal.	.10	.10
435	Jason Woolley, Wash.	.10	.10
436	Basil McRae, St. L	.10	.10
437	Andre Racicot, Goalie, Mon.	.10	.10
438	Brad Werenka, Edm.	.10	.10
439	Josef Beranek, Phi.	.10	.10
440	Dave Christian, Chi.	.10	.10

LITTLE BIG MEN

No.	Player	USA NRMT	Can. NRMT
441	Thereon Fleury, Cal.	.15	.15
442	Mark Recchi, Phi.	.15	.15
443	Cliff Ronning, Van.	.10	.10
444	Tony Granato, LA	.10	.10
445	John Vanbiesbrouck, Goalie, NYR	.15	.15

HIGHLIGHTS

No.	Player	USA NRMT	Can. NRMT
446	Jarri Kurri, LA	.10	.10
447	Michael Gartner, NYR	.15	.15
448	Steve Yzerman, Det.	.15	.15
449	Glenn Anderson, Tor.	.10	.10
450	Teemu Selanne, Win.	.15	.15
451	Luc Robitaille, LA	.10	.10
452	Pittsburgh Penguins	.10	.10

TOP ROOKIE

No.	Player	USA NRMT	Can. NRMT
453	Corey Hirsch, Goalie, NYR	.15	.15
454	Jesse Belanger, Mon., RC	.15	.15
455	Phillippe Boucher, Buf.	.10	.10
456	Robert Lang, LA, RC	.10	.10
457	Doug Barrault, Dal., RC	.10	.10
458	Steve Konowalchuk, Wash., RC	.10	.10
459	Oleg Petrov, Mon., RC	.15	.15
460	Niclas Andersson, Que.	.10	.10
461	Milan Tichy, Chi.	.10	.10
462	Darrin Madeley, Goalie, Ott., RC	.25	.25
463	Tyler Wright, Edm.	.10	.10
464	Sergei Krivokrasov, Chi.	.10	.10
465	Vladimir Vujtek, Edm., RC	.10	.10
466	Rick Knickle, Goalie, LA, RC	.10	.10
467	Gord Kruppke, Det., RC	.10	.10
468	David Emma, NJ, RC	.10	.10
469	Scott Thomas, Buf., RC	.10	.10
470	Shawn Rivers, TB, RC	.10	.10
471	Jason Bowen, Phi., RC	.10	.10
472	Bryan Smolinski, Bos., RC	.25	.25
473	Chris Simon, Que., RC	.15	.15
474	Peter Clavaglia, Buf., RC	.10	.10
475	Sergei Zholtok, Bos.	.10	.10
476	Radek Hamr, Ott., RC	.10	.10

SEASON LEADERS

No.	Player	USA NRMT	Can. NRMT
477	Teemu Selanne, Win. / Alexander Mogilny, Buf.	.25	.25
478	Adam Oates, Bos.	.10	.10
479	Mario Lemieux, Pit.	.20	.20
480	Mario Lemieux, Pit.	.20	.20
481	David Andreychuk, Tor.	.10	.10
482	Phil Housley, Win.	.10	.10
483	Tom Barrasso, Goalie, Pit.	.10	.10
484	Felix Potvin, Goalie, Tor.	.30	.30
485	Shutouts: Ed. Belfour, Goalie, Chi.	.15	.15

EXPANSION DRAFT

No.	Player	USA NRMT	Can. NRMT
486	Sault Ste. Marie Greyhounds, 1993 Memorial Cup Champions	.10	.10
487	Stanley Cup Champions, Montreal	.10	.10
488	Mighty Ducks of Anaheim	.50	.50
489	Guy Hebert, Goalie, Ana.	.10	.10

No.	Players	USA NRMT	Can. NRMT
490	Sean Hill, Ana.	.10	.10
491	Florida Panthers	.50	.50
492	John Vanbiesbrouck, Goalie, Fla.	.10	.10
493	Tom Fitzgerald, Goalie, Fla.	.10	.10
494	Paul DePietro, Mon.	.10	.10
495	David Volek, NYI	.10	.10
496A	Alexandre Daigle Redemption Card	1.00	1.00
496B	Alexandre Daigle, Ott.	8.00	8.00

— 1993 - 94 REGULAR ISSUE — SERIES TWO

AMERICAN AND CANADIAN

The Series Two American and Canadian cards are distinguishable by their different backs, the Canadian back is bilingual. Series Two packs have the "Gold Rush" cards inserted one per pack.

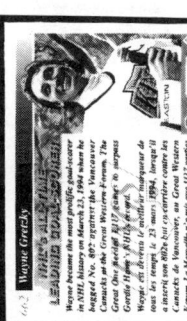

1993-94 American Issue
Card No. 662, Wayne Gretzky

Card Size: 2 1/2 x 3 1/2
Face: Four colour, blue marble border, Name, Team, Logo
Back: Four colour on card stock; Name, Number, Position, Team, Resume
Imprint: ©1994 PINNACLE BRANDS, INC. PRINTED IN U.S.A.

		USA	Can.
Complete Set No.: 166			
Complete Set Price:		12.00	12.00
Common Card:		.10	.10
Foil Pack: (15 Cards)		1.00	1.00
Foil Box: (36 Packs)		35.00	35.00

No.	Players	USA NRMT	Can. NRMT
497	Shawn McEachern, LA	.10	.10
498	Richard Sutter, Chi.	.10	.10
499	Evgeny Davydov, Ott.	.10	.10
500	Sean Hill, MDA	.10	.10
501	John Vanbiesbrouck, Goalie, Fl.	.15	.15
502	Guy Hebert, Goalie, MDA	.20	.20
503	Scott Mellanby, Fl.	.10	.10
504	Ron Tugnutt, Goalie, MDA	.10	.10
505	Brian Skrudland, Fl.	.10	.10
506	Nelson Emerson, Win.	.10	.10
507	Kevin Todd, Chi.	.10	.10
508	Terry Carkner, Det.	.10	.10
509	Stephane Quintal, Win.	.10	.10
510	Paul Stanton, Bos.	.10	.10
511	Terry Yake, MDA	.10	.10
512	Brain Benning, Fl.	.10	.10
513	Brian Propp, Har.	.10	.10
514	Steven King, MDA	.10	.10
515	Joe Cirella, Fl.	.10	.10
516	Andrew Moog, Goalie, Dal.	.10	.10
517	Paul Ysebaert, Win.	.10	.10
518	Petr Klima, TB	.10	.10
519	Corey Millen, NJ	.10	.10
520	Phil Housley, St.L	.10	.10
521	Craig Billington, Goalie, Ott.	.10	.10
522	Jeff Norton, SJ	.10	.10
523	Neil Wilkinson, Chi.	.10	.10
524	Doug Lidster, NYR	.10	.10
525	Steve Larmer, NYR	.10	.10
526	Jon Casey, Goalie, Bos.	.10	.10
527	Byron McCrimmon, Har.	.10	.10
528	Alexei Kasatonov, MDA	.10	.10

No.	Player	USA NRMT	Can. NRMT
529	Andrei Lomakin, Fl.	.10	.10
530	Daren Puppa, Goalie, TB	.10	.10
531	Sergei Makarov, SJ	.15	.15
532	Jim Sandlak, Har.	.10	.10
533	Glenn Healey, Goalie, NYR	.10	.10
534	Martin Gelinas, Van.	.10	.10
535	Igor Larionov, SJ	.10	.10
536	Anatoli Semenov, MDA	.10	.10
537	Mark Fitzpatrick, Goalie, Fl.	.10	.10
538	Paul Cavallini, Dal.	.10	.10
539	Jimmy Waite, Goalie, SJ	.10	.10
540	Yves Racine, Phi.	.10	.10
541	Jeff Hackett, Goalie, Chi.	.10	.10
542	Martin McSorley, Pit.	.10	.10
543	Scott Pearson, Edm.	.10	.10
544	Ron Hextall, Goalie, NYI	.10	.10
545	Gaetan Duchesne, SJ	.10	.10
546	Jamie Baker, SJ	.10	.10
547	Troy Loney, MDA	.10	.10
548	Gordon Murphy, Fl.	.10	.10
549	Bob Kudelski, Fl.	.10	.10
550	Dean Evason, Dal.	.10	.10
551	Mike Peluso, NJ	.10	.10
552	David Poulin, Wash.	.10	.10
553	Randy Ladouceur, MDA	.10	.10
554	Tom Fitzgerald, Fl.	.10	.10
555	Denis Savard, TB	.10	.10
556	Kelly Kisio, Cal.	.10	.10
557	Craig Simpson, Buf.	.10	.10
558	Stu Grimson, MDA	.10	.10
559	Mike Hough, Fl.	.10	.10
560	Gerard Gallant, TB	.10	.10
561	Gregory Gilbert, NYR	.10	.10
562	Vladimir Ruzicka, Ott.	.10	.10
563	Jim Hrivnak, Goalie, St.L	.10	.10
564	Dave Lowry, Fl.	.10	.10
565	Todd Ewen, MDA	.10	.10
566	Bob Errey, SJ	.10	.10
567	Bryan Trottier, Pit.	.10	.10
568	Grant Ledyard, Dal.	.10	.10
569	Keith Brown, Fl.	.10	.10
570	Darren Turcotte, Har.	.10	.10
571	Patrick Poulin, Chi.	.10	.10
572	Jimmy Carson, Van.	.10	.10
573	Eric Weinrich, Chi.	.10	.10
574	James Patrick, Har.	.10	.10
575	Bob Beers, Edm.	.10	.10
576	Chris Joseph, TB	.10	.10
577	Bryan Marchment, Har.	.10	.10
578	Robert Carpenter, NJ	.10	.10
579	Craig Muni, Buf.	.10	.10
580	Pat Elynuik, TB	.10	.10
581	Todd Elik, SJ	.10	.10
582	Doug Brown, Pit.	.10	.10
583	Dave McLlwain, Ott.	.10	.10
584	Dave Tippett, Phi.	.10	.10
585	Jesse Belanger, Fl.	.20	.20

TOP ROOKIE

No.	Player	USA NRMT	Can. NRMT
586	Chris Pronger, RC, Har.	.75	.75
587	Alexandre Daigle, RC, Ott.	.75	.75
588	Cam Stewart, RC, Bos.	.20	.20
589	Derek Plante, RC, Buf.	1.00	1.00
590	Pat Peake, RC, Wash.	.20	.20
591	Alexander Karpovtsev, NYR, RC	.20	.20
592	Rob Niedermayer, Fl., RC	.75	.75
593	Jocelyn Thibault, Goalie, Que., RC	.75	.75
594	Jason Arnott, Edm., RC	2.00	2.00
595	Mike Rathje, SJ, RC	.25	.25
596	Chris Gratton, TB, RC	.75	.75
597	Markus Naslund, Pit., RC	.20	.20
598	Dmitri Filimonov, Ott., RC	.15	.15
599	Andrei Trefilov, Goalie, Cal., RC	.25	.25
600	Michal Sykora, SJ, RC	.15	.15
601	Greg Johnson, Det., RC	.20	.20
602	Mikael Renberg, Phi., RC	.75	.75
603	Alexei Yashin, Ott., RC	1.00	1.00
604	Damian Rhodes, Goalie, Tor., RC	.30	.30
605	Jeff Shantz, Chi., RC	.15	.15
606	Brent Gretzky, TB, RC	.20	.20

388 • SCORE — 1993 - 94 INSERT SETS

No.	Player	USA NRMT	Can. NRMT
607	Boris Mironov, Win., RC	.20	.20
608	Ted Drury, Cal., RC	.20	.20
609	Chris Osgood, Goalie, Det., RC	1.00	1.00
610	Jim Storm, Har., RC	.20	.20
611	Dave Karpa, Que., RC	.20	.20
612	Stewart Malgunas, Phi., RC	.20	.20
613	Jason Smith, NJ, RC	.20	.20
614	German Titov, Cal., RC	.40	.40
615	Patrik Carnback, MDA, RC	.20	.20
616	Jaroslav Modry, NJ, RC	.20.	.20
617	Scott Levins, Ott., RC	.20	.20
618	Fred Brathwaite, Goalie, Edm., RC	.20	.20
619	Ilya Byakin, Edm., RC	.20	.20
620	Jarkko Varvio, Dal., RC	.20	.20
621	Jim Montgomery, St.L, RC	.25	.25
622	Vesa Viitakoski, Cal., RC	.20	.20
623	Alexel Kudashov, Tor., RC	.25	.25
624	Pavol Demitra, Ott., RC	.20	.20
625	Iain Fraser, Que., RC	.20	.20
626	Peter Popovic, Mon., RC	.30	.30
627	Kirk Maltby, Edm., RC	.20	.20
628	Garth Snow, Goalie, Que., RC	.30	.30
629	Peter White, Edm., RC	.20	.20
630	Mike McKee, Edm., RC	.20	.20
631	Darren McCarty, Det., RC	.20	.20
632	Pat Neaton, Pit., RC	.20	.20
633	Sandy McCarthy, Cal., RC	.20	.20
634	Pierre Sevigny, Mon., RC	.20	.20
635	Matt Martin, Tor., RC	.30	.30
636	John Slaney, Wash., RC	.20	.20

REGULAR ISSUE

No.	Player	USA NRMT	Can. NRMT
637	Bob Corkum, MDA	.10	.10
638	Mike Stapleton, Pit.	.10	.10
639	Bill Houlder, MDA	.10	.10
640	Ronald Sutter, Que.	.10	.10
641	Garry Valk, MDA	.10	.10
642	Greg Hawgood, Fl.	.10	.10
643	Bob Bassen, Que.	.10	.10
644	Stu Barnes, Fl.	.10	.10
645	Fredrik Olausson, Edm.	.10	.10
646	Geoff Smith, Fl.	.10	.10
647	Mike Foligno, Fl.	.10	.10
648	Martin Brodeur, Goalie, NJ	.40	.40
649	Ryan McGill, Phi.	.10	.10
650	Jeff Reese, Goalie, Har.	.10	.10
651	Mike Sillinger, Det.	.10	.10
652	Brent Severyn, Fl.	.10	.10
653	George Ramage, Phi.	.10	.10
654	Dixon Ward, LA	.10	.10
655	Danton Cole, TB	.10	.10
656	Vjateslav Butsayev, SJ	.10	.10
657	Garth Butcher, Que.	.10	.10
658	Paul Broten, Dal.	.10	.10
659	Steve Duchesne, St.L	.10	.10
660	Trevor Kidd, Goalie, Cal.	.10	.10
661	Travis Green, NYI	.10	.10
662	**Goal 802:** Wayne Gretzky, LA	1.50	1.50

— 1993 - 94 INSERT SETS —

ERIC LINDROS ALL STAR GAME 1994

Randomly inserted into American and Canadian foil packs.

Size: 2 1/2" x 3 1/2"
Face: Four colour, borderless
Back: Four colour; borderless
Imprint: © 1994 PINNACLE BRANDS INC. PRINTED IN U.S.A

No.	Player	USA NRMT	Can. NRMT
—	Eric Lindros	25.00	50.00

GOLD RUSH SET

This 224-card set comes from one card per American or Canadian Series Two foil pack. Again the Canadian edition of "Gold Rush" is distinguished by the bilingual backs.

1993-94 Gold Rush, Series Two,
Card No. 662, Wayne Gretzky

Size: 2 1/2" x 3 1/2"
Face: Four colour, gold marble border; Name
Back: Four colour; Name, Number, Position, Resume
Imprint: © 1994 PINNACLE BRANDS INC. PRINTED IN U.S.A.
Complete Set No.: 224

	USA	Can.
Complete Set Price:	70.00	70.00
Common Player:	.50	.50

No.	Player	USA NRMT	Can. NRMT
497	Shawn McEachern, LA	.50	.50
498	Richard Sutter, Chi.	.50	.50
499	Evgeny Davydov, Ott.	.50	.50
500	Sean Hill, MDA	.50	.50
501	John Vanbiesbrouck, Goalie, Fl.	.75	.75
502	Guy Hebert, Goalie, MDA	.75	.75
503	Scott Mellanby, Fl.	.50	.50
504	Ron Tugnutt, Goalie, MDA	.50	.50
505	Brian Skrudland, Fl.	.50	.50
506	Nelson Emerson, Win.	.50	.50
507	Kevin Todd, Chi.	.50	.50
508	Terry Carkner, Det.	.50	.50
509	Stephane Quintal, Win.	.50	.50
510	Paul Stanton, Bos.	.50	.50
511	Terry Yake, MDA	.50	.50
512	Brain Benning, Fl.	.50	.50
513	Brian Propp, Har.	.50	.50
514	Steven King, MDA	.50	.50
515	Joe Cirella, Fl.	.50	.50
516	Andrew Moog, Goalie, Dal.	.50	.50
517	Paul Ysebaert, Win.	.50	.50
518	Petr Klima, TB	.50	.50
519	Corey Millen, NJ	.50	.50
520	Phil Housley, St.L	.50	.50
521	Craig Billington, Goalie, Ott.	.50	.50
522	Jeff Norton, SJ	.50	.50
523	Neil Wilkinson, Chi.	.50	.50
524	Doug Lidster, NYR	.50	.50
525	Steve Larmer, NYR	.50	.50
526	Jon Casey, Goalie, Bos.	.50	.50
527	Brad McCrimmon, Har.	.50	.50
528	Alexei Kasatonov, MDA	.50	.50
529	Andrei Lomakin, Fl.	.50	.50
530	Daren Puppa, Goalie, TB	.50	.50
531	Sergei Makarov, SJ	.50	.50
532	Jim Sandlak, Har.	.50	.50
533	Glenn Healy, Goalie, NYR	.50	.50
534	Martin Gelinas, Van.	.50	.50
535	Igor Larionov, SJ	.50	.50
536	Anatoli Semenov, MDA	.50	.50
537	Mark Fitzpatrick, Goalie, Fl.	.50	.50
538	Paul Cavallini, Dal.	.50	.50
539	Jimmy Waite, Goalie, SJ	.50	.50
540	Yves Racine, Phi.	.50	.50
541	Jeff Hackett, Chi.	.50	.50
542	Martin McSorley, Pit.	.50	.50
543	Scott Pearson, Edm.	.50	.50
544	Ron Hextall, Goalie, NYI	.50	.50
545	Gaetan Duchesne, SJ	.50	.50
546	Jamie Baker, SJ	.50	.50
547	Troy Loney, MDA	.50	.50
548	Gordon Murphy, Fl.	.50	.50
549	Bob Kudelski, Fl.	.50	.50

No.	Player	USA NRMT	Can. NRMT
550	Dean Evason, Dal.	.50	.50
551	Mike Peluso, NJ	.50	.50
552	David Poulin, Wash.	.50	.50
553	Randy Ladouceur, MDA	.50	.50
554	Tom Fitzgerald, Fl.	.50	.50
555	Denis Savard, TB	.50	.50
556	Kelly Kisio, Cal.	.50	.50
557	Craig Simpson, Buf.	.50	.50
558	Stu Grimson, MDA	.50	.50
559	Mike Hough, Fl.	.50	.50
560	Gerard Gallant, TB	.50	.50
561	Gregory Gilbert, NYR	.50	.50
562	Vladimir Ruzicka, Ott.	.50	.50
563	Jim Hrivnak, St.L, Goalie	.50	.50
564	Dave Lowry, Fl.	.50	.50
565	Todd Ewen, MDA	.50	.50
566	Bob Errey, SJ	.50	.50
567	Bryan Trottier, Pit.	.50	.50
568	Grant Ledyard, Dal.	.50	.50
569	Keith Brown, Fl.	.50	.50
570	Darren Turcotte, Har.	.50	.50
571	Patrick Poulin, Chi.	.50	.50
572	Jimmy Carson, Van.	.50	.50
573	Eric Weinrich, Chi.	.50	.50
574	James Patrick, Har.	.50	.50
575	Bob Beers, Edm.	.50	.50
576	Chris Joseph, TB	.50	.50
577	Bryan Marchment, Har.	.50	.50
578	Robert Carpenter, NJ	.50	.50
579	Craig Muni, Buf.	.50	.50
580	Pat Elynuik, TB	.50	.50
581	Todd Elik, SJ	.50	.50
582	Doug Brown, Pit.	.50	.50
583	Dave McIlwain, Ott.	.50	.50
584	Dave Tippett, Phi.	.50	.50
585	Jesse Belanger, Fl.	1.00	1.00

TOP ROOKIES

No.	Player	USA NRMT	Can. NRMT
586	Chris Pronger, Har., RC	2.00	2.00
587	Alexandre Daigle, Ott., RC	3.50	3.50
588	Cam Stewart, Bos., RC	.75	.75
589	Derek Plante, Buf., RC	3.50	3.50
590	Pat Peake, Wash., RC	.75	.75
591	Alexander Karpovtsev, NYR, RC	.75	.75
592	Rob Niedermayer, Fl., RC	2.00	2.00
593	Jocelyn Thibault, Goalie, Que., RC	3.50	3.50
594	Jason Arnott, Edm., RC	12.50	12.50
595	Mike Rathje, SJ, RC	.75	.75
596	Chris Gratton, TB, RC	2.00	2.00
597	Markus Naslund, Pit., RC	.75	.75
598	Dmitri Filimonov, Ott., RC	.75	.75
599	Andrei Trefilov, Goalie, Cal., RC	1.50	1.50
600	Michal Sykora, SJ, RC	.75	.75
601	Greg Johnson, Det., RC	.75	.75
602	Mikael Renberg, Phi., RC	3.50	3.50
603	Alexei Yashin, Ott., RC	5.00	5.00
604	Damian Rhodes, Goalie, Tor., RC	1.50	1.50
605	Jeff Shantz, Chi., RC	.75	.75
606	Brent Gretzky, TB, RC	1.50	1.50
607	Boris Mirinov, Win., RC	.50	.50
608	Ted Drury, Cal., RC	.50	.50
609	Chris Osgood, Goalie, Det., RC	5.00	5.00
610	Jim Storm, Har., RC	.75	.75
611	Dave Karpa, Que., RC	.50	.50
612	Stewart Malgunas, Phi., RC	.50	.50
613	Jason Smith, NJ, RC	.50	.50
614	German Titov, Cal., RC	1.50	1.50
615	Patrik Carnback, MDA, RC	.50	.50
616	Jaroslav Modry, NJ, RC	.75	.75
617	Scott Levins, Ott., RC	.75	.75
618	Fred Brathwaite, Goalie, Edm., RC	1.00	1.00
619	Ilya Byakin, Edm., RC	.50	.50
620	Jarkko Varvio, Dal., RC	.50	.50
621	Jim Montgomery, St.L, RC	.75	.75
622	Vesa Viitakoski, Cal., RC	.50	.50
623	Alexei Kudashov, Tor., RC	.50	.50
624	Pavol Demitra, Ott., RC	.50	.50
625	Iain Fraser, Que., RC	.10	.50
626	Peter Popovic, Mon., RC	.10	.50
627	Kirk Maltby, Edm., RC	.10	.50

SCORE • 389

No.	Player	USA NRMT	Can. NRMT
628	Garth Snow, Goalie, Que., RC	.75	.75
629	Peter White, Edm., RC	.50	.50
630	Mike McKee, Que., RC	.50	.50
631	Darren McCarty, Det., RC	.50	.50
632	Pat Neaton, Pit., RC	.50	.50
633	Sandy McCarthy, Cal., RC	.50	.50
634	Pierre Sevigny, Mon., RC	.50	.50
635	Matt Martin, Tor., RC	1.00	1.00
636	John Slaney, Wash., RC	.50	.50
637	Bob Corkum, MDA	.50	.50
638	Mike Stapleton, Pit.	.50	.50
639	Bill Houlder, MDA	.50	.50
640	Ronald Sutter, Que.	.50	.50
641	Garry Valk, MDA	.50	.50
642	Greg Hawgood, Fl.	.50	.50
643	Bob Basson, Que.	.50	.50
644	Stu Barnes, Fl.	.50	.50
645	Fredrik Olausson, Win.	.50	.50
646	Geoff Smith, Fl., RC	.50	.50
647	Mike Folgno, Fl.	.50	.50
648	Martin Brodeur, Goalie, NJ	2.00	2.00
649	Ryan McGill, Phi.	.50	.50
650	Jeff Reese, Goalie, Har.	.50	.50
651	Mike Sillinger, Det.	.50	.50
652	Brent Severyn, Fl., RC	.75	.75
653	Rob Ramage, Phi.	.50	.50
654	Dixon Ward, LA	.50	.50
655	Danton Cole, TB	.50	.50
656	Vjateslav Butsayev, SJ	.50	.50
657	Garth Butcher, Que.	.50	.50
658	Paul Broten, Dal.	.50	.50
659	Steve Duchesne, St.L	.50	.50
660	Trevor Kidd, Goalie, Cal.	.50	.50
661	Travis Green, NYI, RC	.50	.50
662	Goal 802: Wayne Gretzky, LA	15.00	15.00

DREAM TEAM - CANADIAN

Inserted only in Canadian foil packs these cards appear not less than 1 in 24 packs.

1993-94 Canadian Dream Team
Card No. 1, Tom Barrasso

Card Size: 2 1/2" x 3 1/2"
Face: Four colour, borderless; Name, Position
Back: Four colour, borderless, Name, Resume, Number _ of 24, Bilingual, Logo
Imprint: ©1993 SCORE, PRINTED IN U.S.A.
Complete Set No.: 24
Complete Set Price: 110.00 225.00
Common Card: 2.50 5.00

No.	Player	EX	NRMT
1	Tom Barrasso, Goalie, Pit.	4.00	8.00
2	Patrick Roy, Goalie, Mon	12.50	25.00
3	Chris Chelios, Chi.	3.50	7.00
4	Allan MacInnis, Cal.	2.50	5.00
5	Scott Stevens, NJ	2.50	5.00
6	Brian Leetch, NYR	6.00	12.00
7	Raymond Bourque, Bos.	3.50	7.00
8	Paul Coffey, Det.	2.50	5.00
9	Al Iafrate, Wash.	2.50	5.00
10	Mario Lemieux, Pit.	15.00	30.00
11	Wayne Gretzky, L.A.	17.50	35.00
12	Eric Lindros, Phil.	17.50	35.00
13	Pat LaFontaine, Buf.	5.00	10.00

No.	Player	EX	NRMT
14	Joe Sakic, Que.	5.00	10.00
15	Pierre Turgeon, NYI	5.00	10.00
16	Steve Yzerman, Det.	5.00	10.00
17	Adam Oates, Bos.	5.00	10.00
18	Brett Hull, St.L	5.00	10.00
19	Pavel Bure, Van.	10.00	20.00
20	Alexander Mogilny, Buf.	5.00	10.00
21	Teemu Selanne, Win.	7.50	15.00
22	Steve Larmer, Chi.	2.50	5.00
23	Kevin Stevens, Pit.	2.50	5.00
24	Luc Robitaille, L.A.	3.00	6.00

DYNAMIC DUOS - CANADIAN

Randomly inserted in Canadian Series Two foil packs.

1993-94 Dynamic Duos - Canadian
Card No. DD9,
Pierre Turgeon, Derek King

Size: 2 1/2" x 3 1/2"
Face: Four colour; Name, Number, Gold foil logo
Back: Four colour; Name, Number, Gold foil border
Imprint: © 1994 PINNACLE BRANDS INC., PRINTED IN U.S.A.
Complete Set No.: 9
Complete Set Price: 60.00 125.00
Common Card: 4.00 8.00

No.	Player	EX	NRMT
DD1	Douglas Gilmour, Tor. David Andreychuk, Tor.	12.50	25.00
DD2	Teemu Selanne, Win. Alexei Zhamnov, Win.	7.50	15.00
DD3	Alexandre Daigle, Ott. Alexei Yashin, Ott.	7.50	15.00
DD4	Gary Roberts, Cal. Joe Nieuwendyke, Cal.	4.00	8.00
DD5	Joe Sakic, Que. Mats Sundin, Que.	6.00	12.00
DD6	Brian Bellows, Mon. Kirk Muller, Mon.	4.00	8.00
DD7	Shayne Corson, Edm. Jason Arnott, Edm.	12.50	25.00
DD8	Mario Lemieux, Pit. Kevin Stevens, Pit.	15.00	30.00
DD9	Pierre Turgeon, NYI Derek King, NYI	5.00	10.00

DYNAMIC DUOS - AMERICAN

Randomly inserted in American Series Two foil packs.

1993-94 Dynamic Duos - American
Card No. DD1, Mark Recchi, Eric Lindros

Size: 2 1/2" x 3 1/2"
Face: Four colour, white border; Name
Back: Four colour
Imprint: © 1994 PINNACLE BRANDS INC., PRINTED IN U.S.A.
Complete Set No.: 9
Complete Set Price: 60.00 125.00
Common Card: 4.00 8.00

No.	Player	EX	NRMT
DD1	Mark Recchi, Phi. Eric Lindros, Phi.	20.00	40.00
DD2	Pat LaFontaine, Buf. Alexander Mogilny, Buf.	6.00	12.00
DD3	Adams Oates, Bos. Joseph Juneau, Bos.	5.00	10.00
DD4	Brett Hull, St.L Craig Janney, St.L	6.00	12.00
DD5	Mark Messier, NYR Adam Graves, NYR	7.50	15.00
DD6	Jeremy Roenick, Chi. Joe Murphy, Chi.	6.00	12.00
DD7	Jari Kurri, LA Wayne Gretzky, LA	25.00	50.00
DD8	Sergei Makarov, SJ Igor Larionov, SJ	4.00	8.00
DD9	Steve Yzerman, Det. Sergei Fedorov, Det.	12.50	25.00

THE FRANCHISE - AMERICAN

These cards were randomly inserted into American foil packs. The cards are numbered _ of 24. The odds are one in 24 packs.

 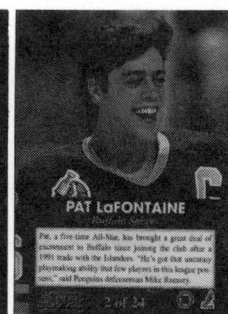

1993-94 The Franchise
Card No. 2, Pat LaFontaine

Card Size: 2 1/2" x 3-1/2"
Face: Four colour, borderless; Name, Logo
Back: Four colour; Name, Team, Resume, Number _ of 24, Logos
Imprint: ©1993 SCORE, PRINTED IN U.S.A.
Complete Set No.: 24
Complete Set Price: 112.50 225.00
Common Card: 2.50 5.00

No.	Player	EX	NRMT
1	Raymond Bourque, Bos.	3.50	7.00
2	Pat LaFontaine, Buf.	5.00	10.00
3	Allan MacInnis, Cal.	2.50	5.00
4	Jeremy Roenick, Chi.	6.00	12.00
5	Michael Modano, Dal.	5.00	10.00
6	Steve Yzerman, Det.	6.00	12.00
7	Bill Ranford, Goalie, Edm.	2.50	5.00
8	Sean Burke, Goalie, Hart.	2.50	5.00
9	Wayne Gretzky, L.A.	17.50	35.00
10	Patrick Roy, Goalie, Mon.	12.50	25.00
11	Scott Stevens, NJ	2.50	5.00
12	Pierre Turgeon, NYI	5.00	10.00
13	Brian Leetch, NYR	5.00	10.00
14	Peter Sidorkiewicz, Goalie, Ott.	2.50	5.00
15	Eric Lindros, Phil.	17.50	35.00
16	Mario Lemieux, Pit.	15.00	30.00
17	Joe Sakic, Que.	5.00	10.00
18	Brett Hull, St.L	5.00	10.00
19	Pat Falloon, SJ	2.50	5.00
20	Brian Bradley, TB	2.50	5.00
21	Douglas Gilmour, Tor.	7.50	15.00
22	Pavel Bure, Van.	12.50	25.00
23	Kevin Hatcher, Wash.	2.50	5.00
24	Teemu Selanne, Win.	12.50	25.00

44TH ALL STAR GAME

Issued in both Canadian and American Series One foils. The differences between the Canadian and American cards are: different player's portraits and the bilingual backs of the Canadian cards. Cards nos. 46 to 50 were not inserted and are available only by mail.

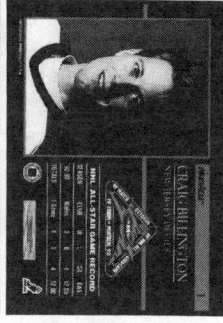

1993-94 44th All Star Game
Card No. 1, Craig Billington

Card Size: 2 1/2" x 3 1/2"
Face: Four colour, borderless; Name, Team, Position, Logo
Back: Four colour, borderless; Name, Team, Number, Resume
Imprint: ©1993 SCORE, PRINTED IN U.S.A.
Complete Set No.: 45
Complete Set Price: 15.00 15.00
Common Card: .25 .25

No.	Player	USA NRMT	Can. NRMT
1	Craig Billington, Goalie, NJ	.25	.25
2	Zarley Zalapski, Ott.	.25	.25
3	Kevin Lowe, NYR	.25	.25
4	Scott Stevens, NJ	.25	.25
5	Pierre Turgeon, NYI	.50	.50
6	Mark Recchi, Phi.	.50	.50
7	Kirk Muller, Mon.	.25	.25
8	Michael Gartner, NYR	.40	.40
9	Adam Oates, Bos.	.50	.50
10	Brad Marsh, Ott.	.25	.25
11	Pat LaFontaine, Buf.	.50	.50
12	Peter Bondra, Wash.	.25	.25
13	Joe Sakic, Que.	.50	.50
14	Rick Tocchet, Phi.	.25	.25
15	Kevin Stevens, Pit.	.25	.25
16	Steve Duchesne, Que.	.25	.25
17	Peter Sidorkiewicz, Goalie, Ott.	.25	.25
18	Patrick Roy, Goalie, Mon.	1.00	1.00
19	Al Iafrate, Wash.	.25	.25
20	Jaromir Jagr, Pit.	.50	.50
21	Raymond Bourque, Bos.	.50	.50
22	Alexander Mogilny, Buf.	.50	.50
23	Steve Chiasson, Det.	.25	.25
24	Garth Butcher, St.L	.25	.25
25	Phil Housley, Win.	.25	.25
26	Chris Chelios, Chi.	.25	.25
27	Randy Carlyle, Win.	.25	.25
28	Michael Modano, Min.	.50	.50
29	Gary Roberts, Cal.	.25	.25
30	Kelly Kisio, SJ	.25	.25
31	Pavel Bure, Van.	1.25	1.25
32	Teemu Selanne, Win.	1.00	1.00
33	Brian Bradley, TB	.25	.25
34	Brett Hull, St.L	.50	.50
35	Jari Kurri, LA	.25	.25
36	Steve Yzerman, Det.	.50	.50
37	Luc Robitaille, L.A.	.40	.40
38	Dave Manson, Edm.	.25	.25
39	Jeremy Roenick, Chi.	.50	.50
40	Mike Vernon, Goalie, Cal.	.25	.25
41	Jon Casey, Goalie, Min.	.25	.25
42	Ed Belfour, Goalie, Chi.	.35	.35
43	Paul Coffey, Det.	.25	.25
44	Douglas Gilmour, Tor.	.50	.50
45	Wayne Gretzky, L.A.	2.00	2.00
46	Michael Gartner, NYR	2.00	2.00
47	Al Iafrate, Wash.	2.00	2.00
48	Raymond Bourque, Bos.	2.00	2.00
49	Jon Casey, Goalie, Bos.	2.00	2.00
50	Campbell Contenders	2.00	2.00

INTERNATIONAL STARS

Inserted in Series One jumbo packs these cards have the standard differences between Canadian and American.

1993-94 International Stars
Card No. 3, Sergei Fedorov

Size: 2 1/2" x 3 1/2"
Face: Four colour, borderless; Name; Country
Back: Four colour, borderless; Name; Resume
Imprint: ©1993 SCORE, PRINTED IN U.S.A.
Complete Set No.: 22
Complete Set Price: 25.00 25.00
Common Card: .75 .75

No.	Player	USA NRMT	Can. NRMT
1	Pavel Bure, Russia	7.00	7.00
2	Teemu Selanne, Finland	3.00	3.00
3	Sergei Fedorov, Russia	3.00	3.00
4	Peter Bondra, Slovak Rep.	.75	.75
5	Tommy Soderstrom, Sweden, Goalie	.75	.75
6	Robert Reichel, Czech Rep.	.75	.75
7	Jari Kurri, Finland	.75	.75
8	Alexander Mogilny, Russia	3.00	3.00
9	Jaromir Jagr, Czech Rep.	3.00	3.00
10	Mats Sundin, Sweden	2.00	2.00
11	Uwe Krupp, Germany	.75	.75
12	Nikolai Borschevsky, Russia	.75	.75
13	Ulf Dahlen, Sweden	.75	.75
14	Alexander Semak, Russia	.75	.75
15	Michal Pivonka, Czech Rep.	.75	.75
16	Sergei Nemchinov, Russia	.75	.75
17	Darius Kasparaitis, Lithuania	.75	.75
18	Sandis Ozolinch, Latvia	1.50	1.50
19	Alexei Kovalev, Russia	1.50	1.50
20	Dimitri Khristich, Ukraine	.75	.75
21	Tomas Sandstrom, Sweden	.75	.75
22	Petr Nedved, Czech Rep.	.75	.75

— 1993 COMMEMORATIVE SHEETS —

Inserted in a case of Score boxes one per case.

Card Size: 10 5/8" X 8 1/8"
Face: Four colour, Coloured border, Numbered
Back: Blank
Imprint: ©1993 SCORE, PRINTED IN U.S.A.
Complete Set No.: 3
Complete Set Price: 20.00 40.00

No.	Player	EX	NRMT
1	Montreal Canadiens Stanley Cup History	7.50	15.00
2	Stanley Cup Champions 1992 - 93	7.50	15.00
3	Montreal Canadiens Player Cards	7.50	15.00

— 1993 - 94 PINNACLE ISSUE —

AMERICAN PROMOTIONAL CARDS

These six cards were issued singly and in sheet format by Score to promote their 1993-94 American issue. These cards are stamped "Sample Card" on the back lower right corner.

Sheet Size: 7 1/2" x 7"
Card Size: 2 1/2" x 3 1/2"
Face: Four colour, white border; Name, Team
Back: Four colour, white border; Name; Numbr, Team, Resume
Imprint: ©1993 SCORE, PRINTED IN U.S.A.

No.	Player	EX	NRMT
—	Sheet	12.50	25.00
1	Eric Lindros, Phi.	7.50	15.00
2	Michael Gartner, NYI	1.50	3.00
3	Steve Larmer, Chi.	1.50	3.00
4	Brian Bellows, Mon.	1.50	3.00
5	Felix Potvin, Goalie, Tor.	1.50	3.00
6	Pierre Turgeon, NYI	1.50	3.00

— 1993 - 94 PINNACLE ISSUE —

This 512-card set is divided into two series with 236 in Series One and 276 cards in Series Two. Series Two contains cards from the World Junior Champions.

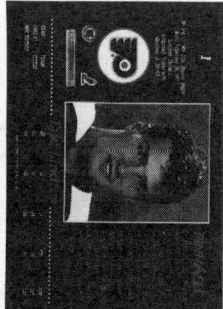

1993-94 Pinnacle Issue
Card No. 1, Eric Lindros

Card Size: 2 1/2" x 3 1/2"
Face: Four colour, black border; Name, Team, Gold foil logo
Back: Four colour; Name, Number, Resume on card stock
Imprint:
  Series One: ©1993 SCORE, PRINTED IN U.S.A.
  Series Two: ©1994 PINNACLE BRANDS, INC.
    PRINTED IN U.S.A.
Complete Set No.: 512
  Series One: 236
  Series Two: 276
Complete Set Price: 25.00 50.00
  Series One: 12.50 25.00
  Series Two: 12.50 25.00
Common Card: .05 .10
Foil Pack: (12 Cards) 2.50
Foil Box: (36 Packs) 80.00

SERIES ONE

No.	Player	EX	NRMT
1	Eric Lindros, Phi.	1.50	3.00
2	Mats Sundin, Que.	.12	.25
3	Tom Barrasso, Goalie, Pit.	.05	.10
4	Teemu Selanne, Win.	.50	1.00
5	Joe Juneau, Bos.	.35	.75
6	Anthony Almonte, NYR	.05	.10
7	Bob Probert, Det.	.05	.10
8	Chris Kontos, TB	.05	.10
9	Geoff Sanderson, Har.	.12	.25
10	Alexander Mogilny, Buf.	.25	.50
11	Kevin Lowe, NYR	.05	.10
12	Nikolai Borschevsky, Tor.	.10	.20
13	Dale Hunter, Wash.	.05	.10
14	Gary Suter, Cal.	.05	.10
15	Curtis Joseph, Goalie, St. L	.12	.25
16	Mark Tinordi, Dal.	.05	.10
17	Doug Weight, Edm.	.05	.10

No.	Player	EX	NRMT
18	Benoit Houge, NYI	.05	.10
19	Tommy Soderstrom, Goalie, Phi.	.10	.20
20	Pat Falloon, SJ	.05	.10
21	Jyrki Lumme, Van.	.05	.10
22	Brian Bellows, Mon.	.05	.10
23	Alexei Zhitnik, LA	.10	.20
24	Dirk Graham, Chi.	.05	.10
25	Scott Stevens, NJ	.07	.15
26	Adam Foote, Que.	.05	.10
27	Michael Gartner, NYR	.07	.15
28	**Dallas Drake, Det., RC**	**.10**	**.20**
29	Ulf Samuelsson, Pit.	.05	.10
30	Cam Neely, Bos.	.10	.20
31	Sean Burke, Goalie, Har.	.05	.10
32	Petr Svoboda, Buf.	.05	.10
33	Keith Tkachuk, Win.	.20	.40
34	Roman Hamrlik, TB	.10	.20
35	Robert Reichel, Cal.	.05	.10
36	Igor Kravchuk, Edm.	.05	.10
37	Mathieu Schneider, Mon.	.05	.10
38	Bob Kudelski, Ott.	.05	.10
39	Jeff Brown, St. L	.05	.10
40	Michael Modano, Dal.	.05	.10
41	**Rob Gaudreau, SJ, RC**	**.20**	**.40**
42	David Andreychuk, Tor.	.10	.20
43	Trevor Linden, Van.	.10	.20
44	Dimitri Khristich, Wash.	.05	.10
45	Joe Murphy, Chi.	.05	.10
46	Robert Blake, LA	.10	.20
47	Alexander Semak, NJ	.05	.10
48	Ray Ferraro, NYI	.05	.10
49	Curtis Leschyshyn, Que.	.05	.10
50	Mark Recchi, Phi.	.12	.25
51	Sergei Nemchinov, NYR	.10	.20
52	Lawrence Murphy, Pit.	.05	.10
53	Stephen Heinze, Bos.	.05	.10
54	Sergei Fedorov, Det.	.50	1.00
55	Gary Roberts, Cal.	.05	.10
56	Alexei Zhamnov, Win.	.20	.40
57	Derian Hatcher, Dal.	.05	.10
58	Kelly Buchberger, Edm.	.05	.10
59	Eric Desjardins, Mon.	.05	.10
60	Brian Bradley, TB	.05	.10
61	Patrick Poulin, Har.	.05	.10
62	Scott Lachance, NYI	.05	.10
63	Johan Garpenlov, SJ	.05	.10
64	Sylvain Turgeon, Ott.	.05	.10
65	Grant Fuhr, Goalie, Buf.	.05	.10
66	Garth Butcher, St. L	.05	.10
67	Michal Pivonka, Wash.	.05	.10
68	Todd Gill, Tor.	.05	.10
69	Cliff Ronning, Van.	.05	.10
70	James (Steve) Smith, Chi.	.05	.10
71	Bobby Holik, NJ	.05	.10
72	Garry Galley, Phi.	.05	.10
73	Stephen Leach, Bos.	.05	.10
74	Ronald Francis, Pit.	.05	.10
75	Jari Kurri, LA	.05	.10
76	Alexei Kovalev, NYR	.30	.60
77	Dave Gagner, Dal.	.05	.10
78	Steve Duchesne, Que.	.05	.10
79	Theoren Fleury, Cal.	.07	.15
80	Paul Coffey, Det.	.07	.15
81	Bill Ranford, Goalie, Edm.	.05	.10
82	Doug Bodger, Buf.	.05	.10
83	Nicholas Kypreos, Har.	.05	.10
84	Darius Kasparaitis, NYI	.07	.15
85	Vincent Damphousse, Mon.	.05	.10
86	Arturs Irbe, Goalie, SJ	.20	.40
87	Shawn Chambers, TB	.05	.10
88	Murray Craven, Van.	.05	.10
89	Rob Pearson, Tor.	.05	.10
90	Kevin Hatcher, Wash.	.05	.10
91	Brent Sutter, Chi.	.05	.10
92	Teppo Numminen, Win.	.05	.10
93	Shawn Burr, Det.	.05	.10
94	Valeri Zelepukin, NJ	.05	.10
95	Ronald Sutter, St. L	.05	.10
96	Craig MacTavish, Edm.	.05	.10
97	Dominic Roussel, Goalie, Phi.	.10	.20
98	Nicklas Lidstrom, Det.	.05	.10
99	Adam Graves, NYR	.15	.30
100	Douglas Gilmour, Tor.	.20	.40

No.	Player	EX	NRMT
101	Frantisek Musil, Cal.	.05	.10
102	Ted Donato, Bos.	.05	.10
103	Andrew Cassels, Har.	.05	.10
104	Vladimir Malakhov, NYI	.10	.20
105	Shawn McEachern, Pit.	.05	.10
106	Petr Nedved, Van.	.05	.10
107	Calle Johansson, Wash.	.05	.10
108	Richard Sutter, St. L	.05	.10
109	Eugeny Davydov, Win.	.05	.10
110	Mike Ricci, Que.	.05	.10
111	Scott Niedermayer, NJ	.12	.25
112	John LeClair, Mon.	.05	.10
113	Darryl Sydor, LA	.05	.10
114	Paul Di Pietro, Mon.	.05	.10
115	Stephane Fiset, Goalie, Que.	.12	.25
116	Christian Ruuttu, Chi.	.05	.10
117	Doug Zmolek, SJ	.05	.10
118	Bob Sweeney, Buf.	.05	.10
119	Brent Fedyk, Phi.	.05	.10
120	Norm Maciver, Ott.	.05	.10
121	Rob Zamuner, TB	.05	.10
122	Joe Mullen, Pit.	.05	.10
123	Trent Yawney, Cal.	.05	.10
124	David Shaw, Bos.	.05	.10
125	Mark Messier, NYR	.10	.20
126	Kevin Miller, St. L	.05	.10
127	Dino Ciccarelli, Det.	.05	.10
128	Derek King, NYI	.05	.10
129	Scott Young, Que.	.05	.10
130	Craig Janney, St. L	.05	.10
131	Jamie Macoun, Tor.	.05	.10
132	Geoff Courtnall, Van.	.05	.10
133	Bob Essensa, Goalie, Win.	.05	.10
134	Kenneth Daneyko, NJ	.05	.10
135	Mike Ridley, Wash.	.05	.10
136	Stephan Lebeau, Mon.	.05	.10
137	Tony Granato, LA	.05	.10
138	Kay Whitmore, Goalie, Van.	.05	.10
139	Luke Richardson, Edm.	.05	.10
140	Jeremy Roenick, Chi.	.35	.75
141	Brad May, Buf.	.05	.10
142	Sandis Ozolinch, SJ	.12	.25
143	Stephane J. J. Richer, NJ	.05	.10
144	John Tucker, TB	.05	.10
145	Luc Robitaille, LA	.10	.20
146	Dimitri Yushkievich, Phi.	.05	.10
147	Sean Hill, MDA	.05	.10
148	John Vanbiesbrouck, Fl.	.05	.10
149	Kevin Stevens, Pit.	.15	.30
150	Patrick Roy, Goalie, Mon.	.35	.75
151	Owen Nolan, Que.	.05	.10
152	Richard Smehlik, Buf.	.05	.10
153	Ray Sheppard, Det.	.10	.20
154	Ed Olczyk, NYR	.05	.10
155	Allan MacInnis, Cal.	.05	.10
156	Sergei Zubov, NYR	.30	.60
157	Wendel Clark, Tor.	.10	.20
158	Kirk McLean, Goalie, Van.	.10	.20
159	Thomas Steen, Win.	.05	.10
160	Pierre Turgeon, NYI	.12	.25
161	Dmitri Kartalnov, Bos.	.05	.10
162	Brian Noonan, Chi.	.05	.10
163	Michael McPhee, Dal.	.05	.10
164	Peter Bondra, Wash.	.05	.10
165	Bernie Nicholls, NJ	.05	.10
166	Michael, Nylander, Har.	.10	.20
167	Guy Hebert, Goalie, MDA	.10	.20
168	Scott Mellanby, Fl.	.05	.10
169	Bob Bassen, St. L	.05	.10
170	Rod Brind'Amour, Phi.	.10	.20
171	Andrei Kovalenko, Que.	.10	.20
172	Mike Donnelley, LA	.05	.10
173	Steve Thomas, NYI	.05	.10
174	Rick Tocchet, Pit.	.05	.10
175	Steve Yzerman, Det.	.20	.40
176	Dixon Ward, Van.	.05	.10
177	Randy Wood, Buf.	.05	.10
178	Dean Kennedy, Win.	.05	.10
179	Joel Otto, Cal.	.05	.10
180	Kirk Muller, Mon.	.07	.15
181	Chris Chelios, Chi.	.07	.15
182	Richard Matvichuk, Dal.	.05	.10
183	John MacLean, NJ	.05	.10

No.	Player	EX	NRMT
184	Joe Kocur, NYR	.05	.10
185	Adam Oates, Bos.	.10	.20
186	Bob Beers, TB	.05	.10
187	Ron Tugnutt, Goalie, MDA	.05	.10
188	Brian Skrudland, Fl.	.05	.10
189	Al Iafrate, Wash.	.05	.10
190	Felix Potvin, Goalie, Tor.	.75	1.50
191	David Reid, Bos.	.05	.10
192	Jim Johnson, Dal.	.05	.10
193	Kevin Haller, Mon.	.05	.10
194	Steve Chiasson, Det.	.05	.10
195	Jaromir Jagr, Pit.	.25	.50
196	Martin Rucinsky, Que.	.05	.10
197	Sergei Bautin, Win.	.05	.10
198	Joe Nieuwendyk, Cal.	.05	.10
199	Gilbert Dionne, Mon.	.05	.10
200	Brett Hull, St. L	.35	.75
201	Yuri Khmylev, Buf.	.05	.10
202	Todd Elik, Edm.	.05	.10
203	Patrick Flatley, NYI	.05	.10
204	Martin Straka, Pit.	.25	.50
205	Brendan Shanahan, St. L	.10	.20
206	Mark Beaufait, SJ	.05	.10
207	**Mike Lenarduzzi, Goalie, Har., RC**	**.10**	**.20**
208	Chris LiPuma, TB	.05	.10
209	Andre Faust, Phi.	.05	.10
210	**Ben Hankinson, NJ, RC**	**.10**	**.20**
211	**Darrin Madeley, Goalie, Ott., RC**	**.15**	**.30**
212	**Oleg Petrov, Mon., RC**	**.12**	**.25**
213	Philippe Boucher, Buf.	.05	.10
214	Tyler Wright, Edm.	.05	.10
215	**Jason Bowen, Phi., RC**	**.12**	**.25**
216	Matthew Barnaby, Buf.	.10	.20
217	Bryan Smolinski, Bos.	.30	.60
218	Dan Keczmer, Har.	.05	.10
219	**Chris Simon, Que., RC**	**.07**	**.15**
220	**Corey Hirsch, Goalie, NYR, RC**	**.12**	**.25**

TROPHY WINNERS

No.	Player	EX	NRMT
221	**Hart Trophy:** Mario Lemieux, Pit.	.20	.40
222	**Calder Trophy:** Teemu Selanne, Win.	.20	.40
223	**Norris Trophy:** Chris Chelios, Chi.	.05	.10
224	**Vezina Trophy:** Ed Belfour, Goalie, Chi.	.10	.20
225	**Lady Byng Trophy:** Pierre Turgeon, NY	.05	.10
226	**Selke Trophy:** Douglas Gilmour, Tor.	.12	.25
227	**Jennings Trophy:** Ed Belfour, Goalie, Chi.	.10	.20
228	**Conn Smythe Trophy:** Patrick Roy, Goalie, Mon.	.20	.40
229	**King Clancy Trophy:** Dave Poulin, Bos.	.05	.10
230	**Art Ross Trophy:** Mario Lemieux, Pit.	.20.	.40

HOMETOWN HEROES

No.	Player	EX	NRMT
231	Mike Vernon, Goalie, Cal.	.05	.10
232	Vincent Damphousse, Mon.	.05	.10
233	Chris Chelios, Chi.	.05	.10
234	Cliff Ronning, Van.	.05	.10
235	Mark Howe, Det.	.05	.10

REGULAR ISSUE

No.	Player	EX	NRMT
236	Alexandre Daigle, Ott.	.50	1.00

SERIES TWO

NOW AND THEN

No.	Player	EX	NRMT
237	Wayne Gretzky, LA	.50	1.00
238	Mark Messier, NYR	.12	.25
239	Dino Ciccarelli, Det.	.05	.10
240	Joe Mullen, Pit.	.05	.10
241	Michael Gartner, NYR	.05	.10

SCORE SERIES TWO

REGULAR ISSUE

No.	Player	EX	NRMT
242	Mike Richter, Goalie, NYR	.12	.25
243	Patrick Verbeek, Har.	.05	.10
244	Valeri Kamensky, Que.	.10	.20
245	Nelson Emerson, Win.	.05	.10
246	James Patrick, Har.	.05	.10
247	Greg Adams, Van.	.05	.10
248	Ulf Dahlen, Dal.	.05	.10
249	Shayne Corson, Edm.	.05	.10
250	Raymond Bourque, Bos.	.10	.20
251	Claude Lemieux, NJ	.05	.10
252	Kelly Hrudey, Goalie, LA	.05	.10
253	Patrice Brisebois, Mon.	.05	.10
254	Mark Howe, Det.	.10	.20
255	Ed Belfour, Goalie, Chi.	.15	.30
256	Per-Erik Eklund, Phi.	.05	.10
257	Zarley Zalapski, Har.	.05	.10
258	Sylvain Cote, Wash.	.05	.10
259	Uwe Krupp, NYI	.05	.10
260	Dale Hawerchuk, Buf.	.05	.10
261	Alexei Gusarov, Que.	.05	.10
262	David Ellett, Tor.	.05	.10
263	Tomas Sandstrom, LA	.05	.10
264	Vladimir Konstantinov, Det.	.05	.10
265	Paul Ranheim, Cal.	.05	.10
266	Darrin Shannon, Win.	.05	.10
267	Chris Terreri, Goalie, NJ	.05	.10
268	Russell Courtnall, Dal.	.05	.10
269	Don Sweeney, Bos.	.05	.10
270	Kevin Todd, Chi.	.05	.10
271	Brad Shaw, Ott.	.05	.10
272	Adam Creighton, TB	.05	.10
273	Dana Murzyn, Van.	.05	.10
274	Donald Audette, Buf.	.05	.10
275	Brian Leetch, NYR	.15	.30
276	Kevin Dineen, Phi.	.05	.10
277	Bruce Driver, NJ	.05	.10
278	Jim Paek, Pit.	.05	.10
279	Esa Tikkanen, NYR	.05	.10
280	Guy Carbonneau, Mon.	.05	.10
281	Eric Weinrich, Chi.	.05	.10
282	Tim Cheveldae, Goalie, Det.	.05	.10
283	Bryan Marchment, Har.	.05	.10
284	Kelly Miller, Wash.	.05	.10
285	Jimmy Carson, LA	.05	.10
286	Terry Carkner, Det.	.05	.10
287	Mike Sullivan, SJ	.05	.10
288	Joe Reekie, TB	.05	.10
289	Robert Rouse, Tor.	.05	.10
290	Joe Sakic, Que.	.15	.39
291	Gerald Diduck, Van.	.05	.10
292	Donald Beaupre, Goalie, Wash.	.05	.10
293	Kjell Samuelsson, Pit.	.05	.10
294	Claude Lapointe, Que.	.05	.10
295	Tahir Domi, Win.	.05	.10
296	Charles Huddy, LA	.05	.10
297	Peter Zezel, Tor.	.05	.10
298	Craig Muni, Buf.	.05	.10
299	Richard Tabaracci, Goalie, Wash.	.05	.10
300	Pat LaFontaine, Buf.	.15	.30
301	Lyle Odelein, Mon.	.05	.10
302	Jocelyn Lemieux, Chi.	.05	.10
303	Craig Ludwig, Dal.	.05	.10
304	Marc Bergevin, TB	.05	.10
305	Bill Guerin, NJ	.05	.10
306	Rick Zombo, St. L	.05	.10
307	Steven Finn, Que.	.05	.10
308	Gino Odjick, Van.	.05	.10
309	Jeff Beukeboom, NYR	.05	.10
310	Mario Lemieux, Pit.	.75	.150
311	Jean Jacques Daigneault, Mon.	.05	.10
312	Vincent Riendeau, Goalie, Det.	.05	.10
313	Adam Burt, Har.	.05	.10
314	Mike Craig, Dal.	.05	.10
315	Bret Hedican, St. L	.05	.10
316	Kris King, Win.	.05	.10
317	Sylvain Lefebvre, Tor.	.05	.10
318	Troy Murray, Chi.	.05	.10
319	Gordie Roberts, Bos.	.05	.10
320	Pavel Bure, Van.	.50	1.00
321	Marc Bureau, TB	.05	.10
322	Randy McKay, NJ	.05	.10
323	Mark Lamb, Ott.	.05	.10
324	Brian Mullen, NYI	.05	.10
325	Ken Wregget, Goalie, Pit.	.05	.10
326	Stephane Quintal, Win.	.05	.10
327	Robert Dirk, Van.	.05	.10
328	Mike Krushelnyski, Tor.	.05	.10
329	Bo Mikael Andersson, TB	.05	.10
330	Paul Stanton, Bos.	.05	.10
331	Phil Bourque, NYR	.05	.10
332	Andre Racicot, Goalie, Mon.	.05	.10
333	Brad Dalgarno, NYI	.05	.10
334	Neal Broten, Dal.	.05	.10
335	John Blue, Goalie, Bos.	.05	.10
336	Ken Sutton, Buf.	.05	.10
337	Gregory Paslawski, Cal.	.05	.10
338	Rob Stauber, Goalie, LA	.05	.10
339	Mike Keane, Mon.	.05	.10
340	Terry Yake, MDA	.05	.10
341	Brian Benning, Fl.	.05	.10
342	Brian Propp, Har.	.05	.10
343	Frank Pietrangelo, Goalie, Har.	.05	.10
344	Stephane Matteau, Chi.	.05	.10
345	Steven King, MDA	.05	.10
346	Joe Cirella, Fl.	.05	.10
347	Andrew Moog, Goalie, Dal.	.05	.10
348	Paul Ysebaert, Win.	.05	.10
349	Petr Klima, TB	.05	.10
350	Corey Millen, NJ	.05	.10
351	Phil Housley, St. L	.05	.10
352	Craig Billington, Goalie, Ott.	.05	.10
353	Jeff Norton, SJ	.05	.10
354	Neil Wilkinson, Chi.	.05	.10
355	Doug Lidster, NYR	.05	.10
356	Steve Larmer, NYR	.05	.10
357	Jon Casey, Goalie, Bos.	.05	.10
358	Brad McCrimmon, Har.	.05	.10
359	Alexei Kasatonov, MDA	.05	.10
360	Andrei Lomakin, Fl.	.05	.10
361	Daren Puppa, Goalie, TB	.05	.10
362	Sergei Makarov, SJ	.07	.15
363	Dave Manson, Edm.	.05	.10
364	Jim Sandlak, Har.	.05	.10
365	Glenn Healy, Goalie, NYR	.05	.10
366	Martin Gelinas, Que.	.05	.10
367	Igor Larionov, SJ	.05	.10
368	Anatoli Semenov, MDA	.05	.10
369	Mark Fitzpatrick, Goalie, Fl.	.05	.10
370	Paul Cavallini, Dal.	.05	.10
371	Jimmy Waite, Goalie, SJ	.05	.10
372	Yves Racine, Phi.	.05	.10
373	Jeff Hackett, Goalie, Chi.	.05	.10
374	Martin McSorley, Pit.	.05	.10
375	Scott Pearson, Edm.	.05	.10
376	Ron Hextall, Goalie, NYI	.05	.10
377	Gaetan Duchesne, SJ	.05	.10
378	Jamie Baker, SJ	.05	.10
379	Troy Loney, MDA	.05	.10
380	Gordon Murphy, Fl.	.05	.10
381	Peter Sidorkiewicz, Goalie, NJ	.05	.10
382	Pat Elynuik, TB	.05	.10
383	Glen Wesley, Bos.	.05	.10
384	Dean Evason, Dal.	.05	.10
385	Mike Peluso, NJ	.05	.10
386	Darren Turcotte, Har.	.05	.10
387	Dave Poulin, Wash.	.05	.10
388	John Cullen, Tor.	.05	.10
389	Randy Ladouceur, MDA	.05	.10
390	Tom Fitzgerald, Fl.	.05	.10
391	Denis Savard, TB	.05	.10
392	Fredrick Olausson, Win.	.05	.10
393	Sergio Momesso, Van.	.05	.10
394	Mike Ramsey, Pit.	.05	.10
395	Kelly Kisio, Cal.	.05	.10
396	Craig Simpson, Buf.	.05	.10
397	Vyacheslav Fetisov, NJ	.05	.10
398	Glenn Anderson, Tor.	.05	.10
399	Michel Goulet, Chi.	.05	.10
400	Wayne Gretzky, LA	.85	.1.75
401	Stu Grimson, MDA	.05	.10
402	Mike Hough, Fl.	.05	.10
403	Dominik Hasek, Goalie, Buf.	.20	.40
404	Gerard Gallant, TB	.05	.10
405	Greg Gilbert, NYR	.05	.10
406	Vladimir Ruzicka, Ott.	.05	.10
407	Jim Hrivnak, Goalie, St. L	.05	.10
408	Dave Lowry, Fl.	.05	.10
409	Todd Ewen, MDA	.05	.10
410	Bob Errey, SJ	.05	.10
411	Bryan Trottier, Pit.	.05	.10
412	David Taylor, LA	.05	.10
413	Grant Ledyard, Dal.	.05	.10
414	Chris Dahlquist, Cal.	.05	.10
415	Brent Gilchrist, Dal.	.05	.10
416	Geoff Smith, Edm.	.05	.10
417	Jiri Slegr, Van.	.07	.15
418	Randy Burridge, Wash.	.05	.10
419	Sergei Krivokrasov, Chi.	.05	.10
420	Keith Primeau, Det.	.05	.10
421	Robert Kron, Har.	.05	.10
422	Keith Brown, Fl.	.05	.10
423	David Volek, NYI	.05	.10
424	Josef Beranek, Phi.	.10	.20
425	Wayne Presley, Buf.	.05	.10
426	Stu Barnes, Win.	.05	.10

1993 - 1994 ROOKIE

No.	Player	EX	NRMT
427	Milos Holan, Phi., RC	.07	.15
428	Jeff Shantz, Chi.	.05	.10
429	Brent Gretzky, TB, RC	.12	.25
430	Jarkko Varvio, Dal.	.10	.20
431	Chris Osgood, Goalie, Det., RC	.35	.75
432	Aaron Ward, Det., RC	.10	.20
433	Jason Smith, NJ, RC	.10	.29
434	Cameron Stewart, Bos., RC	.10	.20
435	Derek Plante, Buf., RC	.50	1.00
436	Pat Peake, Wash.	.05	.10
437	Alexander Karpovtsev, NYR	.05	.10
438	Jim Mongomery, St. L, RC	.10	.20
439	Rob Niedermayer, Fl.	.35	.75
440	Jocelyn Thibault, Goalie, Que., RC	.35	.75
441	Jason Arnott, Edm., RC	1.25	2.50
442	Mike Rathje, SJ, RC	.35	.75
443	Chris Gratton, TB, RC	.35	.75
444	Vesa Vittakoski, Cal., RC	.10	.20
445	Alexei Kudashov, Tor., RC	.12	.25
446	Pavol Demitra, Ott.	.07	.15
447	Ted Drury, Cal.	.05	.10
448	Rene Corbet, Que., RC	.12	.25
449	Markus Naslund, Pit.	.10	.20
450	Dmitri Filimonov, Ott.	.05	.10
451	Roman Oksiuta, Edm., RC	.07	.15
452	Michal Sykora, SJ, RC	.10	.20
453	Greg Johnson, Det.	.05	.10
454	Mikael Renberg, Phi., RC	.50	1.00
455	Alexei Yashin, Ott., RC	.75	.150
456	Chris Pronger, Har., RC	.35	.75

WORLD JUNIOR CHAMPIONSHIP - TEAM CANADA

No.	Player	EX	NRMT
457	Emmanuel Fernandez, Goalie	.35	.75
458	Jamie Storr, Goalie	1.50	3.00
459	Chris Armstrong	.12	.25
460	Drew Bannister	.20	.40
461	Joel Bouchard	.12	.25
462	Bryan McCabe	.18	.35
463	Nick Stajduhar	.25	.50
464	Brent Tully	.12	.25
465	Brendan Witt	.35	.75
466	Jason Allison	.50	1.00
467	Jason Botterill	.50	1.00
468	Curtis Bowen	.25	.50
469	Anson Carter	.12	.25
470	Brandon Convery	.35	.75
471	Yanick Dube	.50	1.00
472	Jeff Friesen	1.00	2.00
473	Aaron Gavey	.50	1.00
474	Martin Gendron	.25	.50
475	Rick Girard	.25	.50
476	Todd Harvey	.50	1.00
477	Marty Murray	.20	.40
478	Mike Peca	.30	.60

WORLD JUNIOR CHAMPIONSHIP TEAM - USA

No.	Player	EX	NRMT
479	Aaron Ellis, Goalie	.15	.30
480	Toby Kvalevog, Goalie	.10	.20
481	Joe Coleman	.12	.25
482	Ashlin Halfnight	.15	.30
483	Jason McBain	.15	.30
484	Chris O'Sullivan	.12	.25
485	Deron Quint	.20	.40
486	Blake Sloan	.12	.25
487	David Wilkie	.15	.30
488	Kevyn Adams	.35	.75
489	Jason Bonsignore	1.00	2.00
490	Andy Brink	.12	.25
491	Adam Deadmarsh	.18	.35
492	John Emmons	.05	.10
493	Kevin Hilton	.15	.30
494	Jason Karmanos	.10	.20
495	Bob Lachance	.10	.20
496	Jamie Langenbrunner	.25	.50
497	Jay Pandolfo	.12	.25
498	Richard Park	.35	.75
499	Ryan Sittler	.12	.25
500	John Varga	.25	.50

WORLD JUNIOR CHAMPIONSHIP TEAM - RUSSIA

No.	Player	EX	NRMT
501	Valeri Bure	.75	1.50
502	Maxim Bets	.50	1.00
503	Vadim Sharifjanov	.20	.40
504	Alexander Kharlamov	.35	.75
505	Pavel Desyatkov	.10	.20
506	Oleg Tverdovsky	1.00	2.00
507	Nikolai Tsulygin	.07	.15
508	Evgeni Ryabchikov, Goalie	.20	.40
509	Sergei Brylin	.15	.30
510	Maxim Sushinski	.10	.20
511	Sergei Kondrashkin	.10	.20

REGULAR ISSUE

No.	Player	EX	NRMT
512	802 Career Goal: Wayne Gretzky, SP	6.00	12.00

Note: Card no. 512 can only be found in Series Two Jumbo packs.

— 1993 - 94 INSERT SETS —

PINNACLE AUTOGRAPHS

The autographed Daigle card was inserted into American and Canadian Series One foils while the autographed Lindros card was obtained by mail through the redemption card process. The redemption cards now have only collector value since they have expired.

Autographed Card, Eric Lindros

Card Size: 2 1/2" x 3 1/2"
Face: Four colour, borderless; Name, Jersey Number
Back: Four colour; Name, Resume on card stock
Imprint: © 1993 SCORE, PRINTED IN U.S.A
Complete Set No.: 2
Complete Set Price: 225.00 450.00

No.	Player	EX	NRMT
—	Alexandre Daigle, Ott.	75.00	150.00
—	Eric Lindros, Phi.	150.00	300.00

PINNACLE TEAM CAPTAINS

Randomly inserted into American and Canadian Series Two Jumbo packs.

 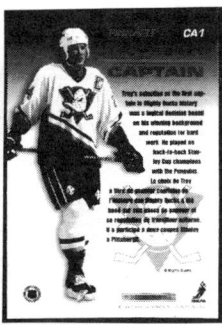

Pinnacle Captains
Card No. 1, Troy Loney

Card Size: 2 1/2" x 3 1/2"
Face: Four colour, borderless; Name
Back: Four colour, borderless; Name, Number, Resume
Imprint: © 1993 SCORE, PRINTED IN U.S.A.
Complete Set No.: 27
Complete Set Price: 80.00 160.00
Common Card: 2.50 5.00

No.	Player	EX	NRMT
1	Troy Loney, MDA	2.50	5.00
2	Raymond Bourque, Bos.	3.00	6.00
3	Pat LaFontaine, Buf.	3.00	6.00
4	Joe Nieuwendyk, Cal.	2.50	5.00
5	Dirk Graham, Chi.	2.50	5.00
6	Mark Tinordi, Dal.	2.50	5.00
7	Steve Yzerman, Det.	6.00	12.00
8	Craig MacTavish, Edm.	2.50	5.00
9	Brian Skrudland, Fl.	2.50	5.00
10	Patrick Verbeek, Har.	2.50	5.00
11	Wayne Gretzky, LA	17.50	35.00
12	Guy Carbonneau, Mon.	2.50	5.00
13	Scott Stevens, NJ	2.50	5.00
14	Pat Flatley, NYI	2.50	5.00
15	Mark Messier, NYR	5.00	10.00
16	Mark Lamb, Ott.	2.50	5.00
17	Kevin Dineen, Phi.	2.50	5.00
18	Mario Lemieux, Pit.	12.50	25.00
19	Joe Sakic, Que.	4.00	8.00
20	Brett Hull, St. L	5.00	10.00
21	Bob Errey, SJ	2.50	5.00
22	Bergevin, Savard, Tucker, TB	2.50	5.00
23	Wendel Clarke, Tor.	5.00	10.00
24	Trevor Linden, Van.	4.00	8.00
25	Kevin Hatcher, Wash.	2.50	5.00
26	Keith Tkachuk, Win.	3.50	7.00
27	Checklist	6.00	12.00

PINNACLE EXPANSION - AMERICAN

Randomly inserted into Series One American Hobby foil. Cards are numbered - of 6.

Pinnacle Expansion
Card No. 1, John Vanbiesbrouck, Guy Hebert

Card Size: 2 1/2" x 3 1/2"
Face: Four colour, borderless; Name, Position
Back: Four colour, borderless; Name, Number, Position
Imprint: © 1993 SCORE, PRINTED IN U.S.A.
Complete Set No.: 6
Complete Set Price: 10.00 20.00
Common Card: 2.00 4.00

No.	Player	EX	NRMT
1	John Vanbiesbrouck, Fl.; Guy Hebert, MDA, Goalies	3.50	7.00
2	Gordon Murphy, Randy Ladouceur	2.00	4.00
3	Joe Cirella; Sean Hill	2.00	4.00
4	Dave Lowry; Troy Loney	2.00	4.00
5	Brian Skrudland; Terry Yake	2.00	4.00
6	Scott Mellanby; Steven King	2.00	4.00

PINNACLE MASKS

Randomly inserted into American and Canadian Series One foils.

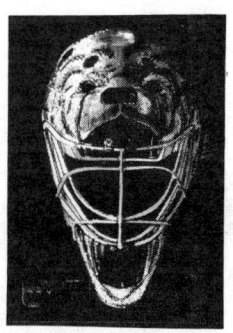

Pinnacle Masks
Card No. 8, Ron Hextall

Card Size: 2 1/2" x 3 1/2"
Face: Four colour; Silver foiled card
Back: Four colour; Name, Silver foil, Resume on card stock
Imprint: © 1993 SCORE, PRINTED IN U.S.A
Complete Set No.: 10
Complete Set Price: 125.00 250.00
Common Card: 12.50 25.00

No.	Player	EX	NRMT
1	Grant Fuhr, Buf.	15.00	30.00
2	Mike Vernon, Van.	15.00	30.00
3	Rob Stauber, LA	12.50	25.00
4	Dominic Roussel,	15.00	30.00
5	Pat Jablonski, TA	12.50	25.00
6	Stephane Fiset, Que.	12.50	25.00
7	Wendell Young, TB	12.50	25.00
8	Ron Hextall, NYI	17.50	35.00
9	John Vanbiesbrouck, Fl.	17.50	35.00
10	Peter Sidorkiewicz, NJ	12.50	25.00

PINNACLE NIFTY FIFTY

Randomly inserted into American and Canadian Series Two foil packs.

Pinnacle Nifty Fifty
Card No. 2, Alexander Mogilny

394 • SCORE — 1993 - 94 INSERT SETS

Card Size: 2 1/2" x 3 1/2"
Face: Four colour; Name, Team, Silver foiled card logo
Back: Four colour; Name, Team, Resume on silver foiled card Stock
Imprint: © 1993 SCORE, PRINTED IN U.K.
Complete Set No.: 15
Complete Set Price: 125.00 250.00
Common Card: 7.50 15.00

No.	Player	EX	NRMT
1	Introductory CL	20.00	40.00
2	Alexander Mogilny, Buf.	9.00	18.00
3	Teemu Selanne, Win.	12.50	25.00
4	Mario Lemieux, Pit.	17.50	35.00
5	Luc Robitaille, LA	7.50	15.00
6	Pavel Bure, Van.	17.50	35.00
7	Pierre Turgeon, NYI	7.50	15.00
8	Steve Yzerman, Det.	12.50	25.00
9	Kevin Stevens, Pit.	7.50	15.00
10	Brett Hull, St.L	10.00	20.00
11	David Andreychuk, Tor.	7.50	15.00
12	Pat LaFontaine, Buf.	10.00	20.00
13	Mark Recchi, Phi.	7.50	15.00
14	Brendan Shanahan, St.L	10.00	20.00
15	Jeremy Roenick, Chi.	12.50	25.00

PINNACLE SUPER ROOKIES - AMERICAN

 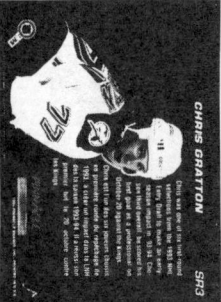

Super Rookies
Card No. SR3, Chris Gratton
Randomly inserted into American Series Two Hobby foils.

Card Size: 2 1/2" x 3 1/2"
Face: Four colour, borderless; Name
Back: Four colour, borderless; Name, Number, Resume
Imprint: © 1994 PINNACLE BRANDS, PRINTED IN U.S.A.
Complete Set No.: 9   USA   Can.
Complete Set Price: 70.00   80.00
Common Card: 5.00   5.00

No.	Player	USA NRMT	Can. NRMT
SR1	Alexandre Daigle, Ott	8.00	10.00
SR2	Chris Pronger, Hart.	8.00	10.00
SR3	Chris Gratton, TB	8.00	10.00
SR4	Rob Niedermayer, Fl.	8.00	10.00
SR5	Alexei Yashin, Ott.	12.00	15.00
SR6	Mikael Renberg, Phi.	12.00	15.00
SR7	Jason Arnott, Edm.	15.00	20.00
SR8	Markus Naslund, Cal.	5.00	5.00
SR9	Pat Peake, Wash.	5.00	5.00

TEAM PINNACLE

These cards were inserted into all American and Canadian Series One and Two foils. The Canadian version has a maple leaf instead of a star between the words TEAM PINNACLE on top of the card. Card numbers 1-6 were randomly inserted into Series One. Numbers 7-12 were randomly inserted into Series Two.

Team Pinnacle
Card No. 8, Paul Coffey, Raymond Bourque

Card Size: 2 1/2" x 3 1/2"
Face: Four colour, black border; Name, Position, Conference
Back: Four colour, black border; Name, Position, Conference
Imprint: © 1993 SCORE, PRINTED IN U.S.A.
Complete Set No.: 12   USA   Can.
Complete Set Price: 450.00   450.00
Common Card: 25.00   25.00

No.	Player	USA NRMT	Can. NRMT
1	Patrick Roy, Goalie, Mon., Ed Belfour, Goalie, Chi.	75.00	80.00
2	Brian Leetch, NYR, Chris Chelios, Chi.	25.00	25.00
3	Allan MacInnis, Cal., Scott Stevens, NJ	25.00	25.00
4	Luc Robitaille, LA, Kevin Stevens, Pit.	25.00	25.00
5	Wayne Gretzky, LA, Mario Lemieux, Pit.	125.00	150.00
6	Brett Hull, St. L, Jaromir Jagr, Pit.	30.00	35.00
7	Tom Barrasso, Goalie, Pit., Kirk McLean, Goalie, Van.	30.00	30.00
8	Paul Coffey, Det., Raymond Bourque, Bos.	25.00	25.00
9	Al Iafrate, Wash., Phil Housley, St. L	25.00	25.00
10	Vincent Damphousse, Mon., Pavel Bure, Van.	40.00	50.00
11	Eric Lindros, Phi., Jeremy Roenick, Chi.	75.00	80.00
12	Teemu Selanne, Win., Alexander Mogilny, Win.	35.00	40.00

PINNACLE TEAM 2001

One card was inserted per American and Canadian Jumbo Series One pack.

 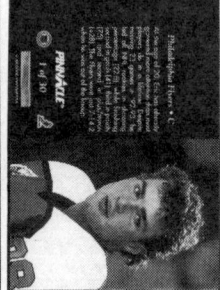

Team 2001
Card No. 1, Eric Lindros

Card Size: 2 1/2" x 3 1/2"
Face: Four colour; Name, Gold foiled logo
Back: Four colour; Name, Gold foiled logo, Resume on card stock
Imprint: © 1993 SCORE, PRINTED IN U.S.A.
Complete Set No.: 30   USA   Can.
Complete Set Price: 35.00   40.00
Common Card: .50   .50

No.	Player	USA NRMT	Can. NRMT
1	Eric Lindros, Phi.	8.00	10.00
2	Alenander Mogilny, Buf.	2.00	2.00
3	Pavel Bure, Van.	5.00	7.00
4	Joseph Juneau, Bos.	2.50	3.00
5	Felix Potvin, Goalie, Tor.	5.00	7.00
6	Niklas Lidstrom, Det.	.50	.50
7	Alexei Kovalev, NYR	2.00	2.00
8	Patrick Poulin, Har.	.50	.50
9	Shawan McEachern, Pit.	.50	.50
10	Teemu Selanne, Win.	2.50	2.50
11	Rod Brind'Amour, Phi.	.50	.50
12	Jaromir Jagr, Pit.	2.00	2.00
13	Pierre Turgeon, NYI	.50	.50
14	Scott Niedermayer, NJ	.50	.50
15	Mats Sundin, Que.	2.00	2.00
16	Trevor Linden, Van.	.50	.50
17	Michael Modano, Dal.	2.00	2.00
18	Roman Hamrlik, TB	.50	.50
19	Anthony Amonte, NYR	.50	.50
20	Jeremy Roenick, Chi.	3.00	3.00
21	Scott Lachance, NYI	.50	.50
22	Mike Ricci, Que.	.50	.50
23	Dmitri Khristich, Wash.	.50	.50
24	Sergei Fedorov, Det.	3.00	3.00
25	Joe Sakic, Que.	1.00	1.00
26	Pat Falloon, SJ	.50	.50
27	Mathiew Schneider, Mon.	.50	.50
28	Owen Nolan, Que.	.50	.50
29	Brendan Shanahan, St.L	2.00	2.00
30	Mark Recchi, Phi.	1.00	1.25

PINNACLE LINDROS BROTHERS

Randomly inserted into all American and Canadian Series Two foil packs.

Lindros Brothers

Card Size: 2 1/2" x 3 1/2"
Face: Four colour
Back: Four colour
Imprint: ©1994 PINNACLE BRANDS, INC., PRINTED IN U.S.A.

No.	Player	USA NRMT	Can. NRMT
—	Eric Lindros, Brett Lindros	30.00	30.00

DRAFT DAY CARD
ALEXANDRE DAIGLE

Given out during the 1994 draft in Quebec City. This card is a double portrait card.

PHOTOGRAPH
NOT AVAILABLE
AT PRESS TIME

1994 Daigle Draft Day

Card Size: 2 1/2" x 3 1/2"
Face: Four colour, white border; Name, Team
Back: Four colour, borderless; Draft day
Imprint: ©1994 PINNACLE BRANDS, INC., PRINTED IN U.S.A.

No.	Player	EX	NRMT
—	Alexandre Daigle	25.00	50.00

— 1994 - 95 PROMOTIONAL CARDS —

 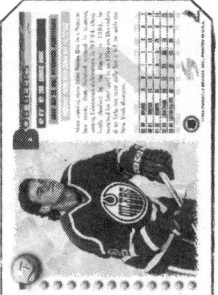

1994-95 Promotional Cards
Card No. 7, Bob Beers

Card Size: 2 1/2" x 3 1/2"
Face: Four colour, white border; Name, Team logo
Back: Four colour, white border, card stock; Name, Number, Resume
Imprint: ©1994 PINNACLE BRANDS, INC., PRINTED IN U.S.A.
Complete Set No.: 10
Complete Set Price: 4.00 8.00

No.	Player	EX	NRMT
—	Title Card: 1994-95 Series 1, Retail Edition	.50	1.00
1	Eric Lindros, Phi.	1.00	2.00
2	Pat LaFontaine, Buf.	.50	1.00
3	Wendel Clark, Tor.	.50	1.00
4	Cam Neely, Bos.	.50	1.00
5	Lawrence Murphy, Pit.	.50	1.00
6	Patrick Poulin, Chi.	.50	1.00
7	Bob Beers, Edm.	.50	1.00
254	Jason Arnott, Edm.	1.00	2.00
—	'94-95 Gold Line Redemption Card	.50	1.00

— 1994 - 95 REGULAR
and GOLD LINE ISSUE —
AMERICAN and CANADIAN

This 275-card set was issued with no variations. The Canadian and American cards are identical. There is however a minimum of five different packs: Canadian Hobby and Retail, American Hobby and Retail, plus the Super packs

1994-95 Regular Issue
Card No. 4, Cam Neely

Card Size: 2 1/2" x 3 1/2"
Face: Four colour, blue border; Name, Team, Position
Back: Four colour, white border, card stock; Name, Number, Position, Resume, Bilingual
Imprint: © 1994 PINNACLE BRANDS INC., PRODUCT OF U.S.A.

	Regular	Gold
Complete Set No.: 275		
Complete Set Price:	20.00	130.00
Common Player:	.10	.50

No.	Player	Regular NRMT	Gold NRMT
1	Eric Lindros, Phi.	2.00	15.00
2	Pat LaFontaine, Buf.	.30	2.00
3	Wendel Clark, Tor.	.20	1.50
4	Cam Neely, Bos.	.20	1.50
5	Lawrence Murphy, Pit.	.10	.50
6	Patrick Poulin, Chi.	.10	.50
7	Bob Beers, Edm.	.10	.50
8	James Patrick, Hart.	.10	.50
9	Gino Odjick, Van.	.10	.50
10	Arturs Irbe, Goalie, SJ.	.25	1.75
11	Darius Kasparaitis, NYI	.10	.50
12	Peter Bondra, Wash.	.10	.50
13	Garth Butcher, Que.	.10	.50
14	Sergei Nemchinov, NYR	.20	1.50
15	Doug Brown, Pit.	.10	.50
16	Anatoli Semenov, NYR	.10	.50
17	Michael McPhee, Dal.	.10	.50
18	Joel Otto, Cal.	.10	.50
19	Dino Ciccarelli, Det.	.10	.50
20	Martin McSorley, LA	.10	.50
21	Ron Tugnutt, Goalie, MDA	.10	.50
22	Scott Niedermayer, NJ	.20	1.50
23	John Tucker, Buf.	.10	.50
24	Norm Maciver, Ott.	.10	.50
25	Kevin Miller, St.L	.10	.50
26	Garry Galley, Phi.	.10	.50
27	Edward Donato, Bos.	.10	.50
28	Bob Kudelski, Ott.	.10	.50
29	Craig Muni, Edm.	.10	.50
30	Nikolai Borschevsky, Tor.	.10	.50
31	Tom Barrasso, Goalie, Pit.	.10	.50
32	Brent Sutter, Chi.	.10	.50
33	Igor Kravchuk, Chi.	.10	.50
34	Andrew Cassels, Hart.	.10	.50
35	Jyrki Lumme, Van.	.10	.50
36	Sandis Ozolinch, SJ	.20	1.50
37	Steve Thomas, NYI	.10	.50
38	David Poulin, Wash.	.10	.50
39	Andrei Kovalenko, Que.	.20	1.50
40	Steve Larmer, NYR	.10	.50
41	Nelson Emerson, Win.	.10	.50
42	Guy Hebert, Goalie, MDA	.20	1.50
43	Russell Courtnall, Dal.	.10	.50
44	Gary Suter, Cal.	.10	.50
45	Steve Chiasson, Det.	.10	.50

No.	Player	Regular NRMT	Gold NRMT
46	Guy Carbonneau, Mon.	.10	.50
47	Robert Blake, LA	.10	.50
48	Roman Hamrlik, TB	.10	.50
49	Valeri Zepelukin, NJ	.10	.50
50	Mark Recchi, Phi.	.10	.50
51	Darrin Madeley, Ott.	.20	1.50
52	Steve Duchesne, St.L	.10	.50
53	Brian Skrudland, Cal.	.10	.50
54	Craig Simpson, Van.	.10	.50
55	Todd Gill, Tor.	.10	.50
56	Dirk Graham, Chi.	.10	.50
57	Joe Mullen, Pit.	.10	.50
58	Doug Weight, Edm.	.10	.50
59	Mikael Nylander, Cal.	.20	1.50
60	Kirk McLean, Goalie, Van.	.25	1.75
61	Igor Larionov, SJ	.10	.50
62	Vladimir Malakhov, NYI	.10	.50
63	Kelly Miller, Wash.	.10	.50
64	Curtis Leschyshyn, Que.	.10	.50
65	Thomas Steen, Win.	.10	.50
66	Jeff Beukeboom, NYR	.10	.50
67	Troy Loney, MDA	.10	.50
68	Mark Tinordi, Dal.	.10	.50
69	Theoren Fleury, Cal.	.10	.50
70	Viacheslav Kozlov, Det.	.25	1.75
71	Tony Granato, LA	.10	.50
72	Daren Puppa, Goalie, TB	.10	.50
73	Brian Bellows, Mon.	.10	.50
74	Bernie Nicholls, NJ	.10	.50
75	Richard Zombo, St.L	.10	.50
76	Brad Shaw, Ott.	.10	.50
77	Josef Beranek, Phi.	.10	.50
78	Dominik Hasek, Goalie, Buf.	.30	2.00
79	Stephen Leach, Bos.	.10	.50
80	David Reid, Bos.	.10	.50
81	Dave Lowry, Fl.	.10	.50
82	Martin Straka, Pit.	.20	1.50
83	David Ellett, Tor.	.10	.50
84	Sean Burke, Goalie, Hart.	.10	.50
85	Craig MacTavish, NYR	.10	.50
86	Cliff Ronning, Van.	.10	.50
87	Bob Errey, SJ	.10	.50
88	Marty McInnis, NYI	.10	.50
89	Mats Sundin, Que.	.20	1.50
90	Randy Burridge, Wash.	.10	.50
91	Teppo Numminen, Win.	.10	.50
92	Anthony Amonte, NYR	.10	.50
93	Terry Yake, MDA	.10	.50
94	Paul Cavallini, Dal.	.10	.50
95	German Titov, Cal.	.25	1.75
96	Vladimir Konstantinov, Det.	.10	.50
97	Darryl Sydor, LA	.10	.50
98	Chris Joseph, TB	.10	.50
99	Corey Millen, LA	.10	.50
100	Brett Hull, St.L	.30	2.00
101	Don Sweeney, Bos.	.10	.50
102	Scott Mellanby, Fl.	.10	.50
103	Mathieu Schneider, Mon.	.10	.50
104	Brad May, Buf.	.10	.50
105	Dominic Roussel, Goalie, Bos.	.10	.50
106	Jamie Macoun, Tor.	.10	.50
107	Bryan Marchment, Hart.	.10	.50
108	Shawn McEachern, Pit.	.10	.50
109	Murray Craven, Van.	.10	.50
110	Eric Desjardins, Mon.	.10	.50
111	Jon Casey, Goalie, Bos.	.10	.50
112	Michael Gartner, Tor.	.15	1.00
113	Neal Broten, Dal.	.10	.50
114	Jari Kurri, La	.10	.50
115	Bruce Driver, NJ	.10	.50
116	Patrick Flatley, NYI	.10	.50
117	Gordon Murphy, Fl.	.10	.50
118	Dimitri Khristich, Wash.	.10	.50
119	Nickias Lidstrom, Det.	.10	.50
120	Allan MacInnis, Cal.	.10	.50
121	James (Steve) Smith, Chi.	.10	.50
122	Zdeno Ciger, Edm.	.10	.50
123	Tahir Domi, Win.	.10	.50
124	Joseph Juneau, Wash.	.30	2.00
125	Todd Elik, SJ	.10	.50
126	Stephane Fiset, Goalie, Que.	.20	1.50
127	Craig Janney, St.L	.10	.50

396 • SCORE — 1994-95 INSERT SETS

No.	Player	Regular NRMT	Gold NRMT
128	Stephan Lebeau, MDA	.10	.50
129	Richard Smehlik, Buf.	.10	.50
130	Mike Richter, Goalie. NYR	.25	1.75
131	Danton Cole, TB	.10	.50
132	Rod Brind'Amour, Phi.	.15	1.00
133	Dave Archibald, Ott.	.10	.50
134	Dana Murzyn, Van.	.10	.50
135	Jaromir Jagr, Pit.	.25	1.75
136	Esa Tikkanen, NYR	.10	.50
137	Rob Pearson, Tor.	.10	.50
138	Stu Barnes, Win.	.10	.50
139	Frantisek Musil, Cal.	.10	.50
140	Ron Hextall, Goalie, NYI	.10	.50
141	Adam Oates, Bos.	.20	1.50
142	Kenneth Daneyko, NJ	.10	.50
143	Dale Hunter, Wash.	.10	.50
144	Geoff Sanderson, Hart.	.20	1.50
145	Kelly Hrudey, Goalie, LA	.10	.50
146	Kirk Muller, Mon.	.10	.50
147	Fredrik Olausson, Win.	.10	.50
148	Derian Hatcher, Dal.	.10	.50
149	Ed Belfour, Goalie, Chi.	.30	2.00
150	Steve Yzerman, Det.	.30	2.00
151	Adam Foote, Que.	.10	.50
152	Pat Falloon, SJ	.10	.50
153	Shawn Chambers, TB	.10	.50
154	Alexei Zhamnov, Win.	.15	1.00
155	Brendan Shanahan, St.L	.15	1.00
156	Ulf Samuelsson, Pit.	.10	.50
157	Donald Audette, Buf.	.10	.50
158	Bob Corkum, MDA	.10	.50
159	Joe Nieuwendyk, Cal.	.10	.50
160	Felix Potvin, Goalie, Tor.	.75	5.00
161	Geoff Courtnall, Van.	.10	.50
162	Yves Racine, Phi.	.10	.50
163	Tom Fitzgerald, Fl.	.10	.50
164	Adam Graves, NYR	.40	3.00
165	Vincent Damphousse, Mon.	.10	.50
166	Pierre Turgeon, NYI	.10	.50
167	Craig Billington, Goalie, Ott.	.10	.50
168	Al Iafrate, Bos.	.10	.50
169	Darren Turcotte, Hart.	.10	.50
170	Joe Murphy, Chi.	.10	.50
171	Alexei Zhitnik, NYI	.10	.50
172	John MacLean, NJ	.10	.50
173	Andrew Moog, Goalie, Dal.	.10	.50
174	Shayne Corson, Edm.	.10	.50
175	Ray Sheppard, Det.	.10	.50
176	Johan Garpenlov, SJ	.10	.50
177	Ronald Sutter, St.L	.10	.50
178	Teemu Selanne, Win.	.50	3.50
179	Brian Bradley, TB	.10	.50
180	Raymond Bourque, Bos.	.20	1.50
181	Curtis Joseph, Goalie, St.L	.20	1.50
182	Kevin Stevens, Pit.	.10	.50
183	Alexei Kasatonov, MDA	.10	.50
184	Brian Leetch, NYR	.30	2.00
185	Douglas Gilmour, Tor.	.30	2.00
186	Gary Roberts, Cal.	.10	.50
187	Mike Keane, Mon.	.10	.50
188	Michael Modano, Dal.	.20	1.50
189	Chris Chelios, Chi.	.10	.50
190	Pavel Bure, Van.	.75	5.00
191	Bob Essensa, Goalie, Det.	.10	.50
192	Dale Hawerchuk, Buf.	.10	.50
193	Scott Stevens, NJ	.15	1.00
194	Claude Lapointe, Que.	.10	.50
195	Scott Lachance, NYI	.10	.50
196	Gaetan Duchesne, Dal.	.10	.50
197	Kevin Dineen, Phi.	.10	.50
198	Doug Bodger, NYR	.10	.50
199	Mike Ridley, Wash.	.10	.50
200	Alexander Mogilny, Buf.	.20	1.50

WORLD JUNIORS

No.	Player	Regular NRMT	Gold NRMT
201	Jamie Storr, Goalie	.50	3.50
202	Jason Botterill	.20	1.50
203	Jeff Friesen	.50	3.50
204	Todd Harvey, Dal.	.10	.50
205	Brendan Witt, Wash.	.10	.50

No.	Player	Regular NRMT	Gold NRMT
206	Jason Allison, Wash	.10	.50
207	Aaron Gavey, TB	.10	.50
208	Deron Quint	.10	.50
209	Jason Bonsignore	.25	1.75
210	Richard Park	.10	.50
211	Kevyn Adams, Bos.	.10	.50
212	Vadim Sharifjanov	.20	1.50
213	Alexander Kharlamov	.25	1.75
214	Oleg Tverdovsky	.30	2.25
215	Valeri Bure, Mon.	.20	1.50
216	Dane Jackson, Van.	.20	1.50
217	Jozef Cierny, Buf.	.20	1.50
218	Yevgeny Namestnikov, Van.	.20	1.50
219	Daniel Laperriere, St.L	.20	1.50
220	Fred Knipscheer	.20	1.50
221	Yan Kaminsky, Win.	.20	1.50
222	David Roberts, St.L	.20	1.50
223	Derek Mayer	.20	1.50
224	Jamie McLennan	.20	1.50
225	Kevin Smyth, Hart.	.20	1.50
226	Todd Marchant	.20	1.50
227	Mariusz Cherkawski	.20	1.50
228	John Lilley, Win.	.20	1.50
229	Aaron Ward, Win.	.20	1.50
230	Brian Savage, Mon.	.20	1.50
231	Jason Allison, Wash.	.20	1.50
232	Maxim Bets, MDA	.20	1.50
233	Edward Crowley, Tor.	.20	1.50
234	Todd Simon, Buf.	.20	1.50
235	Zigmund Palffy, NYI	.20	1.50
236	Rene Corbet, Que.	.20	1.50
237	Michael Peca, Van.	.20	1.50
238	Dwayne Norris, Que.	.20	1.50
239	Andrei Nazarov, St.L	.20	1.50
240	David Sacco, Tor.	.20	1.50

REGULAR ISSUE

No.	Player	Regular NRMT	Gold NRMT
241	Wayne Gretzky, LA	1.50	10.00
242	Michael Gartner, Tor.	.15	3.50
243	Dino Ciccarelli, Det.	.10	.50
244	Ronald Francis, Pit.	.10	.50
245	Bernie Nicholls, NJ	.10	.50
246	Dino Ciccarelli, Det.	.10	.50
247	Brian Propp, Dal.	.10	.50

YOUNG STARS '94

No.	Player	Regular NRMT	Gold NRMT
248	Alexandre Daigle, Ott.	.50	3.50
249	Mikael Renberg, Phi.	.50	3.50
250	Jocelyn Thibault, Goalie, Que.	.40	3.00
251	Derek Plante, Buf.	.50	3.50
252	Chris Pronger, Hart.	.25	1.75
253	Alexei Yashin, Ott.	.50	3.50
254	Jason Arnott, Edm.	1.00	7.50
255	Boris Mironov, Win.	.25	1.75
256	Chris Osgood, Goalie, Det.	.50	3.50
257	Jesse Belanger, Fl.	.30	2.00
258	Darren McCarty, Det.	.10	.50
259	Trevor Kidd, Goalie, Cal.	.20	1.50
260	Oleg Petrov, Mon.	.25	1.75
261	Mike Rathje, Phi.	.10	.50
262	John Slaney, Wash.	.10	.50

CLUB LOGOS

No.	Player	Regular NRMT	Gold NRMT
263	Mighty Ducks of Anaheim, Boston Bruins	.25	1.75
264	Buffalo Sabres, Calgary Flames	.25	1.75
265	Chicago Blackhawks, Dallas Stars	.25	1.75
266	Detroit Red Wings, Edmonton Oilers	.25	1.75
267	Florida Panthers, Hartford Whalers	.25	1.75
268	Los Angeles Kings, Montreal Canadiens	.25	1.75
269	New Jersey Devils, New York Islanders	.25	1.75
270	New York Rangers, Ottawa Senators	.25	1.75
271	Philadelphia Flyers, Pittsburgh Penguins	.25	1.75

No.	Player	Regular NRMT	Gold NRMT
272	Quebec Nordiques, St. Louis Blues	.25	1.75
273	San Jose Sharks, Tampa Bay Lightning	.25	1.75
274	Toronto Maple Leafs, Vancouver Canucks	.25	1.75
275	Washington Capitals, Winnipeg Jets	.25	1.75

— 1994-95 INSERT SETS —

1994 CANADIAN TEAM

Randomly inserted into Canadian Retail and Hobby packs, odds are one in every 36 packs.

1994 Canadian Team
Card No. CT7, Dwayne Norris

Card Size: 2 1/2" x 3 1/2"
Face: Horographic card; Name, Logo
Back: Four colour; Name, Resume on card stock
Imprint: © 1994 PINNACLE BRANDS INC.
PRODUCTS OF U.S.A.
Complete Set No.: 24
Complete Set Price: 65.00 125.00
Common Player: 2.50 5.00

No.	Player	EX	NRMT
CT1	Paul Kariya, MDA	7.50	15.00
CT2	Petr Nedved, St.L	2.50	5.00
CT3	Todd Warriner, Que.	5.00	10.00
CT4	Corey Hirsch, Goalie, NYR	3.50	7.00
CT5	Greg Johnson, Phi.	2.50	5.00
CT6	Chris Kontos, TB	2.50	5.00
CT7	Dwayne Norris, Que.	2.50	5.00
CT8	Brian Savage, Mon.	2.50	5.00
CT9	Todd Hlushko	3.50	7.00
CT10	Fabian Joseph	2.50	5.00
CT11	1Greg Parks, NYI	2.50	5.00
CT12	Jean-Yves Roy, NYR	2.50	5.00
CT13	Mark Astley, Buf.	2.50	5.00
CT14	Adrian Aucoin, Van.	2.50	5.00
CT15	David Harlock, NJ	3.50	7.00
CT16	Ken Lovsin	2.50	5.00
CT17	Derek Mayer	2.50	5.00
CT18	Brad Schlegel, Wash.	2.50	5.00
CT19	Chris Therien, Phi.	2.50	5.00
CT20	Emanuel Legace, Goalie	2.50	5.00
CT21	Brad Werenka, Edm.	2.50	5.00
CT22	Wally Schreiber	2.50	5.00
CT23	Allain Roy	2.50	5.00
CT24	Brett Lindros	10.00	20.00

1994 DREAM TEAM

Randomly inserted into American Series One Hobby and Retail packs. Odds are one in 36 packs.

1994 Dream Team
Card No. DT1, Patrick Roy

Card Size: 2 1/2" x 3 1/2"
Face: Holographic Card; Name, Logo
Back: Four colour; Name, Number, Team, Resume
Imprint: © © 1994PINNACLE BRANDS INC.
PRODUCTS OF U.S.A.
Complete Set No.: 24
Complete Set Price: 125.00 250.00
Common Player: 3.00 6.00

No.	Player	EX	NRMT
DT1	Patrick Roy, Goalie, Mon.	12.50	25.00
DT2	Felix Potvin, Goalie, Tor.	12.50	25.00
DT3	Raymond Bourque, Bos.	5.00	10.00
DT4	Brian Leetch, NYR	7.50	15.00
DT5	Scott Stevens, NJ	3.00	6.00
DT6	Paul Coffey, Det.	3.00	6.00
DT7	Allan MacInnis, Cal.	3.00	6.00
DT8	Chris Chelios, Chi.	3.00	6.00
DT9	Adam Graves, NYR	5.00	10.00
DT10	Luc Robitaille, LA	5.00	10.00
DT11	David Andreychuk, Tor.	3.00	6.00
DT12	Sergei Fedorov, Det.	7.50	15.00
DT13	Douglas Gilmour, Tor.	7.50	15.00
DT14	Wayne Gretzky, LA	15.00	30.00
DT15	Mario Lemieux, Pit.	10.00	20.00
DT16	Mark Messier, NYR	3.00	6.00
DT17	Michael Modano, Dal.	5.00	10.00
DT18	Jeremy Roenick, Chi.	5.00	10.00
DT19	Eric Lindros, Phi.	15.00	30.00
DT20	Steve Yzerman, Det.	5.00	10.00
DT21	Alexandre Daigle, Ott.	5.00	10.00
DT22	Brett Hull, St.L	5.00	10.00
DT23	Cam Neely, Bos.	3.00	6.00
DT24	Pavel Bure, Van.	12.50	25.00

CHECK IT

Randomly inserted into Canadian Hobby packs. The odds are one in 72 packs.

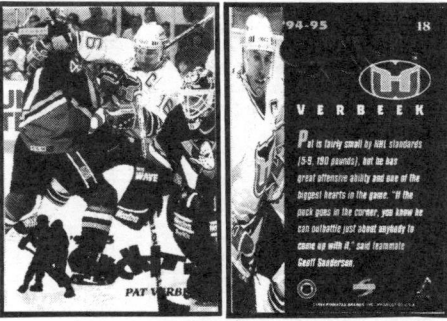

1994-95 Check It
Card No. 18, Patrick Verbeek

Card Size: 2 1/2" x 3 1/2"
Face: Four colour; Name, Red foil logo
Back: Four colour; Name, Team Logo, Resume on card stock
Imprint: © 1994PINNACLE BRANDS INC.
PRODUCTS OF U.S.A.
Complete Set No.: 18
Complete Set Price: 85.00 175.00
Common Player: 4.00 8.00

No.	Player	EX	NRMT
1	Eric Lindros, Phi.	30.00	60.00
2	Scott Stevens, NJ	4.00	8.00
3	Darius Kasparaitis, NYI	4.00	8.00
4	Kevin Stevens, Pit.	6.00	12.00
5	Brendan Shanahan, St.L	6.00	12.00
6	Jeremy Roenick, Chi.	9.00	18.00
7	Ulf Samuelsson, Pit.	4.00	8.00
8	Cam Neely, Bos.	7.50	15.00
9	Adam Graves, NYR	9.00	18.00
10	Owen Nolan, Que	4.00	8.00
11	Rick Tocchet, Pit.	4.00	8.00
12	Gary Roberts, Cal.	4.00	8.00
13	Wendel Clark, Tor.	7.50	15.00
14	Keith Tkachuk, Win.	7.50	15.00
15	Theoren Fleury, Cal.	4.00	8.00
16	Shayne Corson, Edm.	4.00	8.00
17	Chris Chelios, Chi.	4.00	8.00
18	Patrick Verbeek, Hart.	4.00	8.00

FRANCHISE

Randomly inserted into American Hobby packs. The odds are one in 72 packs.

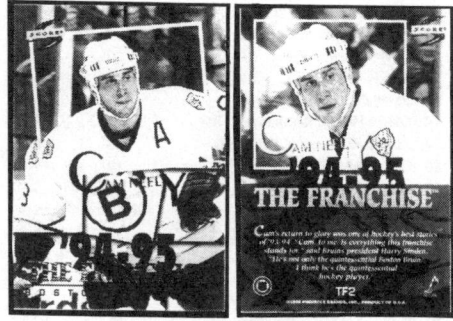

1994-95 Franchise
Card No. TF2, Cam Neely

Card Size: 2 1/2" x 3 1/2"
Face: Four colour; Name, Team, Red foil logo
Back: Four colour; Logo, Resume, Number on card stock
Imprint: © 1994PINNACLE BRANDS INC.
PRODUCTS OF U.S.A.
Complete Set No.: 26
Complete Set Price: 150.00 300.00
Common Player: 4.00 8.00

No.	Player	EX	NRMT
TF1	Guy Hebert, Goalie, MDA	6.00	12.00
TF2	Cam Neely, Bos.	7.50	15.00
TF3	Pat LaFontaine, Buf.	7.50	15.00
TF4	Theoren Fleury, Cal.	4.00	8.00
TF5	Jeremy Roenick, Chi.	7.50	15.00
TF6	Michael Modano, Dal.	7.50	15.00
TF7	Sergei Fedorov, Det.	10.00	20.00
TF8	Jason Arnott, Edm.	12.50	25.00
TF9	John Vanbiesbrouck, Goalie, Fl.	4.00	8.00
TF10	Geoff Sanderson, Hart.	5.00	10.00
TF11	Wayne Gretzky, LA	20.00	40.00
TF12	Patrick Roy, Goalie, Mon.	15.00	30.00
TF13	Scott Stevens, NJ	4.00	8.00
TF14	Pierre Turgeon, NYI	5.00	10.00
TF15	Mark Messier, NYR	6.00	12.00
TF16	Alexandre Daigle, Ott.	6.00	12.00
TF17	Eric Lindros, Phi.	20.00	40.00
TF18	Mario Lemieux, Pit.	15.00	30.00
TF19	Joe Sakic, Que.	5.00	10.00
TF20	Brett Hull, St.L	6.00	12.00
TF21	Arturs Irbe, Goalie, SJ	6.00	12.00
TF22	Brian Bradley, TB	4.00	8.00
TF23	Douglas Gilmour, Tor.	7.50	15.00
TF24	Pavel Bure, Van.	12.50	25.00
TF25	Joseph Juneau, Wash.	5.00	10.00
TF26	Teemu Selanne, Win	7.50	15.00

90 + CLUB

Randomly inserted into Canadian and American super packs, approximately one in every four.

Card Size: 2 1/2" x 3 1/2"
Face: Unknown
Back: Unknown
Imprint: © 1994PINNACLE BRANDS INC.
PRODUCTS OF U.S.A.
Complete Set No.: 18
Complete Set Price: 30.00 60.00
Common Player: 1.50 3.00

No.	Player	EX	NRMT
1	Wayne Gretzky, LA	7.50	15.00
2	Sergei Fedorov, Det.	5.00	10.00
3	Adam Oats, Bos.	1.50	3.00
4	Douglas Gilmour, Tor.	2.50	5.00
5	Pavel Bure, Van.	5.00	10.00
6	Jeremy Roenick, Chi.	2.50	5.00
7	Mark Recchi, Phi.	1.50	3.00
8	Brendan Shanahan, St.L	1.50	3.00
9	Jaromir Jagr, Pit.	1.50	3.00
10	David Andreychuk, Tor.	1.50	3.00
11	Brett Hull, St.L	2.50	5.00
12	Eric Lindros, Phi.	7.50	15.00
13	Rod Brind'Amour, Phi.	1.50	3.00
14	Pierre Turgeon, NYI	2.50	5.00
15	Ray Sheppard, Det.	1.50	3.00
16	Michael Modano, Dal.	2.50	5.00
17	Robert Reichel, Cal.	1.50	3.00
18	Ronald Francis, Pit.	1.50	3.00

PRO DEBUT

Insert redemption cards are in Canadian and American Retail and Hobby packs. They are redeemable for the top ten 1994 draft picks pictured in their NHL team uniforms provided they play an NHL game by December 31, 1994.

These cards were not issed at press time and thus not priced.

UPPER DECK

— 1990 PROMOTIONAL CARDS —

Error: Both promotional cards have feet and inches reversed in their statistical tables.

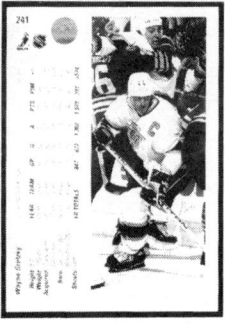

1990 Promotional Cards
Card No. 241, Wayne Gretzky

Card Size: 2 1/2" X 3 1/2"
Face: Four colour, white border, Team logo, Position
Back: Four colour, Hologram, Number, Resume
Imprint: © 1990 The Upper Deck Company Printed in USA

No.	Player	EX	NRMT
241	Wayne Gretzky, LA, Error	12.50	25.00
241	Patrick Roy, Goalie, Mon., Error	12.50	25.00

— 1990 HOCKEY SUPERSTARS — STEREOGRAMS

Upper Deck included six stereogram cards in their set this year. A "Live Action Stereogram" is a hologram that displays pronounced motion as it is turned. They were inserted into all foil packs.

Card Size: 2 1/2" X 3 1/2"
Face: Hologram
Back: Blank
Imprint: UPPER DECK COMPANY © NHL 1990

No.	Player	EX	NRMT
—	Wayne Gretzky, LA, In Action	.50	1.00
—	Wayne Gretzky, LA, In Action	.50	1.00
—	Wayne Gretzky, LA, In Action	.50	1.00
—	Brett Hull, St. L.,	.50	1.00
—	Mark Messier, Edm.	.50	1.00
—	Steven Yzerman, Det.	.50	1.00

— 1990 - 91 ISSUE —

This premier issue of hockey from Upper Deck is divided into low and the high numbered series. The set was available in English and French and the French high number set is very hard to obtain. The low number series set consists of cards 1-400 and the high series set numbers are from 401-550.

1990-91 Issue
Card No. 1, David Volek

Card Size: 2 1/2" X 3 1/2"
Face: Four colour, white border, Team, Logo, Position
Back: Four colour, Hologram, Number, Resume, Position
Imprint: © 1990 The Upper Deck Co. Printed in USA
Complete Set No.: 550
 Low Series No.: 400
 High Series No.: 150

Set Price:	English	French
Low Series:	38.00	65.00
High Series:	38.00	115.00
High Series Factory Set:	38.00	--
Complete Set:	75.00	175.00
Common Card	.10	.15
Foil Packs: No. of Cards		
Low Series: 12	1.50	2.00
High Series: 8 Low + 4 High	1.75	3.50
High Series: 6 Low + 6 High	2.00	5.00
Foil Boxes		
Low Series: 36 Packs	50.00	70.00
High Series: 36 Packs (6 + 6)	60.00	120.00
High Series: 36 Packs (6 + 6)	70.00	150.00
Foil Cases		
Low Series: 24 Boxes	1,000.00	1,500.00
High Series: 24 Boxes (6 + 6)	1,350.00	2,600.00
High Series: 24 Boxes (6 + 6)	1,500.00	3,300.00

No.	Player	English NRMT	French NRMT
1	David Volek, NYI	.10	.15
2	Brian Propp, Bos.	.10	.15
3	Wendel Clark, Tor.	.40	.60
4	Adam Creighton, Chi.	.10	.15
5	Mark Osborne, Tor.	.10	.15
6	Murray Craven, Phi.	.10	.15
7	Doug Crossman, NYI	.10	.15
8	Mario Marois, Que.	.10	.15
9	Curt Giles, Min.	.10	.15
10	Rick Wamsley, Goalie, Cal.	.10	.15
11	Troy Mallette, NYR, RC	.10	.15
12	John Cullen, Pit.	.10	.15
13	Miloslav Horava, NYR, RC	.10	.15
14	Kevin Stevens, Pit., RC	2.50	2.75
15	David Shaw, NYR	.10	.15
16	Randy Wood, NYI	.10	.15
17	Peter Zezel, St. L.	.10	.15
18	Glenn Healy, Goalie, NYI, RC	.50	.75
19	Sergio Momesso, St. L, RC	.35	.50
20	Donald Maloney, NYI	.10	.15
21	Craig Muni, Edm.	.10	.15
22	Phil Housley, Buf.	.10	.15
23	Martin Gelinas, Edm., RC	.30	.50
24	Alexander Mogilny, Buf., RC	4.00	6.00
25	Star-Rookie: John Byce, Bos.	.10	.15
26	Joe Nieuwendyk, Cal.	.30	.50
27	Ron Tugnutt, Goalie, Que.	.10	.15
28	Don Barber, Min., RC	.10	.15
29	Gary Roberts, Cal.	.40	.60
30	Basil McRae, Min.	.10	.15
31	Phil Bourque, Pit.	.10	.15
32	Mike Richter, Goalie, NYR, RC	2.00	3.00
33	Zarley Zalapski, Pit.	.10	.15
34	Bernie Nicholls, NYR	.10	.15
35	Star-Rookie: Bob Corkum, Buf.	.30	.50
36	Rod Brind'Amour, St. L., RC	2.00	3.00
37	Mark Fitzpatrick, Goalie, NYI, RC	.30	.50
38	Gino Cavallini, St. L.	.10	.15
39	Mick Vukota, NYI, RC	.10	.15
40	Mike Lalor, St. L., RC	.10	.15
41	David Andreychuk, Buf.	.30	.50
42	Bill Ranford, Goalie, Edm.	.30	.50
43	Pierre Turgeon, Buf.	.75	1.25
44	Mark Messier, Edm.	.50	.75
45	Star-Rookie: Robert Blake, LA, RC	1.50	2.25
46	Michael Modano, Min., RC	2.50	3.75
47	Theoren Fleury, Cal.	.50	.75
48	Neal Broten, Min.	.10	.15
49	Paul Gillis, Que.	.10	.15
50	Doug Bodger, Buf.	.10	.15
51	Stephan Lebeau, Mon., RC	1.00	1.50
52	Larry Robinson, LA	.10	.15
53	Dale Hawerchuk, Win.	.10	.15
54	Wayne Gretzky, LA	2.50	3.75
55	Ed Belfour, Goalie, Chi., RC	3.00	4.50
56	Steve Yzerman, Det.	.75	1.25
57	Rod Langway, Wash.	.10	.15
58	Bernie Federko, Det.	.10	.15
59	Lemieux's Scoring Streak, Pit.	.50	.75
60	Doug Lidster, Van.	.10	.15
61	Dave Christian, Bos.	.10	.15
62	George (Rob) Ramage, Tor.	.10	.15
63	Jeremy Roenick, Chi., RC	4.00	6.00
64	Raymond Bourque, Bos.	.40	.60
65	Star-Rookie: Jon Morris, NJ	.10	.15
66	Sean Burke, Goalie, NJ	.10	.15
67	Ronald Francis, Har.	.10	.15
68	Ronald Sutter, Phi.	.10	.15
69	Peter Sidorkiewicz, Goalie, Har.	.10	.15
70	Sylvain Turgeon, NJ	.10	.15
71	David Ellett, Win.	.10	.15
72	Robert Smith, Mon.	.10	.15
73	Luc Robitaille, LA	.50	.75
74	Pat Elynuik, Win.	.10	.15
75	Star Rookie: Jason Soules, Edm., RC	.10	.15
76	Dino Ciccarelli, Wash.	.20	.30
77	Vladimir Krutov, Van., RC	.10	.15
78	Lee Norwood, Det.	.10	.15
79	Brian Bradley, Van.	.20	.30
80	Michal Pivonka, Wash., RC	.50	.75
81	Mark LaForest, Goalie, Tor., RC	.10	.15
82	Trent Yawney, Chi.	.10	.15
83	Tom Fergus, Tor.	.10	.15
84	Andy Brickley, Bos.	.10	.15
85	Dave Manson, Chi.	.10	.15
86	Gordon Murphy, Phi., RC	.20	.30
87	Scott Young, Har.,	.10	.15
88	Tommy Albelin, NJ	.10	.15
89	Ken Wregget, Goalie, Phi.	.10	.15
90	Brad Shaw, Har., RC	.10	.15
91	Mario Gosselin, Goalie, LA	.10	.15
92	Paul Fenton, Win.	.10	.15
93	Brian Skrudland, Mon.	.10	.15
94	Thomas Steen, Win.	.10	.15
95	John Tonelli, LA	.10	.15
96	Steve Chiasson, Det.	.10	.15
97	Mike Ridley, Wash.	.10	.15
98	Garth Butcher, Van.	.10	.15
99	Daniel Shank, Det., RC	.10	.15
100	Checklist 1 (1 - 100)	.10	.15
101	Jamie Macoun, Cal.	.10	.15
102	Wendell Young, Goalie, Pit., RC	.10	.15
103	Laurie Boschman, Win.	.10	.15
104	Paul Ranheim, Cal., RC	.20	.30
105	Douglas Small, Win	.10	.15
106	Shawn Chambers, Min.	.10	.15
107	Stephen Weeks, Goalie, Van.	.10	.15
108	Gaetan Duchesne, Min.	.10	.15
109	Kevin Hatcher, Wash.	.10	.15
110	Paul Reinhart, Van.	.10	.15
111	Shawn Burr, Det.	.10	.15
112	Troy Murray, Chi.	.10	.15
113	John Chabot, Det.	.10	.15
114	Jacques Cloutier, Goalie, Chi., RC	.10	.15
115	Richard Zombo, Det., RC	.10	.15
116	Kjell Samuelsson, Phi.	.10	.15
117	Timothy Watters, LA	.10	.15
118	Patrick Flatley, NYI	.10	.15
119	Thomas Laidlaw, LA	.10	.15
120	Ilkka Sinisalo, Phi.	.10	.15
121	Tom Barrasso, Goalie, Pit.	.20	.30
122	Bob Essensa, Goalie, Win., RC	.50	.75
123	Sergei Makarov, Cal., RC	.75	1.25
124	Paul Coffey, Pit.	.20	.30
125	Star-Rookie: Bob Beers, Bos., RC	.20	.30
126	Brian Bellows, Min.	.10	.15
127	Michael Liut, Goalie, Wash.	.10	.15
128	Igor Larionov, Van., RC	.75	1.25
129	Craig Simpson, Edm.	.10	.15
130	Kelly Miller, Wash.	.10	.15
131	Dirk Graham, Chi.	.10	.15
132	Jimmy Carson, Det.	.10	.15
133	Michel Goulet, Chi.	.10	.15
134	Gerard Gallant, Det.	.10	.15
135	Star-Rookie: Bruce Hoffort, Goalie, Phi., RC	.10	.15
136	Steve Duchesne, LA	.10	.15
137	Bryan Trottier, NYI	.10	.15
138	Per-Erik Eklund, Phi	.10	.15
139	Gary Nylund, NYI	.10	.15
140	Stephen Kasper, LA	.10	.15
141	Joel Otto, Cal.	.10	.15

1990 - 91 ISSUE — UPPER DECK • 399

No.	Player	English NRMT	French NRMT
142	Rob Brown, Pit.,	.10	.20
143	Allan MacInnis, Cal.	.20	.30
144	Mario Lemieux, Pit.	2.00	3.00
145	Star-Rookie: Peter Eriksson, Edm., RC	.10	.15
146	Jari Kurri, Edm.	.10	.15
147	Petri Skriko, Van.	.10	.15
148	James (Steve) Smith, Edm.	.10	.15
149	Calle Johansson, Wash.	.10	.15
150	Robert (Stewart) Gavin, Min.	.10	.15
151	Randy Ladouceur, Har.	.10	.15
152	Vincent Riendeau, Goalie, St. L., RC	.25	.35
153	Patrick Roy, Goalie, Mon.	1.00	1.50
154	Brett Hull, St. L.	1.00	1.50
155	Star-Rookie: Craig Fisher, Phi.	.10	.15
156	Cam Neely, Bos.	.35	.50
157	Al Iafrate, Tor.	.10	.15
158	Robert Carpenter, Bos.	.10	.15
159	Doug Brown, NJ	.10	.15
160	Tom Kurvers, Tor.	.10	.15
161	John MacLean, NJ	.10	.15
162	Guy Lafleur, Que.	.10	.20
163	Peter Stastny, NJ	.10	.15
164	Joe Sakic, Que.	1.00	1.50
165	Star Rookie: Robb Stauber, Goalie, LA, RC	.35	.50
166	Daren Puppa, Goalie, Buf.	.10	.15
167	Esa Tikkanen, Edm.	.10	.15
168	Michael Ramsey, Buf.	.10	.15
169	Craig MacTavish, Edm.	.10	.15
170	Christian Ruuttu, Buf.	.10	.15
171	Brian Hayward, Goalie, Mon.	.10	.15
172	Patrick Verbeek, Har.	.10	.15
173	Adam Oates, St. L.	.50	.75
174	Chris Chelios, Mon.	.20	.30
175	Star-Rookie: Curtis Joseph, Goalie, St. L., RC	2.00	3.00
176	Vlacheslav Fetisov, NJ, RC	.35	.50
177	David Poulin, Bos.	.10	.15
178	Mark Recchi, Pit., RC	3.00	4.50
179	Daniel Marois, Tor.	.10	.15
180	Mark Johnson, NJ	.10	.15
181	Michel Petit, Que.	.10	.15
182	Brian Mullen, NYR	.10	.15
183	Chris Terreri, Goalie, NJ, RC	.60	.90
184	Anthony Hrkac, Que.	.10	.15
185	James Patrick, NYR	.10	.15
186	Craig Ludwig, Mon.	.10	.15
187	Uwe Krupp, Buf.	.10	.15
188	Guy Carbonneau, Mon.	.20	.30
189	Dave Snuggerud, Buf., RC	.10	.15
190	Joe Murphy, Edm., RC	.75	1.25
191	Jeff Brown, St. L.	.10	.15
192	Dean Evason, Har.	.10	.15
193	Petr Svoboda, Mon.	.10	.15
194	Dave Babych, Har.	.10	.15
195	Steve Tuttle, St. L.	.10	.15
196	Randy Burridge, Bos.	.10	.15
197	Tony Tanti, Pit.	.10	.15
198	Bob Sweeney, Bos.,	.10	.15
199	Brad Marsh, Tor.	.10	.15
200	Checklist 2 (101 - 200)	.10	.15
201	The Conn Smythe Trophy: Bill Ranford, Goalie, Edm.	.10	.15
202	The Calder Memorial Trophy: Sergei Makarov, Cal.	.20	.30
203	The Lady Byng Memorial Trophy: Brett Hull, St. L	.20	.30
204	The James Norris Memorial Trophy: Raymond Bourque, Bos.	.10	.15
205	The Art Ross Trophy: Wayne Gretzky, LA	.50	.75
206	The Hart Memorial Trophy: Mark Messier, Edm.	.20	.30
207	The Vezina Trophy: Patrick Roy, Goalie, Mon.	.50	.75
208	The Frank J. Selke Trophy: Richard Meagher, St.L	.10	.15
209	The William M. Jennings Trophy: A. Moog; R. Lemelin, Goalies, Bos.	.10	.15

REGULAR ISSUE

No.	Player	English NRMT	French NRMT
210	Aaron Broten, Min.	.10	.15
211	John Carter, Bos., RC	.10	.15
212	Martin McSorley, LA	.25	.40
213	Greg Millen, Goalie, Chi.	.10	.15
214	David Taylor, LA	.10	.15
215	Rejean Lemelin, Goalie, Bos.	.10	.15
216	Dave McLlwain, Win.	.10	.15
217	Donald Beaupre, Goalie, Wash.	.10	.15
218	Paul MacDermid, Win.	.10	.15
219	Dale Hunter, Wash.	.10	.15
220	Brent Ashton, Win.	.10	.15
221	Steve Thomas, Chi.	.10	.15
222	Ed Olczyk, Tor.	.10	.15
223	Douglas Wilson, Chi.	.10	.15
224	Vincent Damphousse, Tor.	.25	.40
225	Star-Rookie: Robert DiMaio, NYI, RC	.10	.15
226	Huble McDonough, NYI, RC	.10	.15
227	Ron Hextall, Goalie, Phi.	.10	.15
228	Dave Chyzowski, NYI, RC, Error	.10	.15
229	Lawrence Murphy, Min.	.10	.15
230	Mike Bullard, Phi.	.10	.15
231	Kelly Hrudey, Goalie, LA	.10	.15
232	Andrew Moog, Goalie, Bos.	.10	.15
233	Todd Elik, LA, RC	.35	.50
234	Craig Janney, Bos.	.50	.75
235	Star-Rookie: Peter Lappin, Min., RC	.10	.15
236	Scott Stevens, Wash.	.10	.15
237	Fredrik Olausson, Win.	.10	.15
238	Geoff Courtnall, Wash.	.10	.15
239	Gregory Paslawski, Win.	.10	.15
240	Alan May, Wash., RC	.10	.15
241	Allan Bester, Goalie, Tor.	.10	.15
242	Steve Larmer, Chi.	.10	.15
243	Gary Leeman, Tor.	.10	.15
244	Denis Savard, Chi.	.10	.15
245	Eric Weinrich, NJ, RC	.25	.40
246	Pat LaFontaine, NYI	.50	.75
247	Tim Kerr, Phi.	.10	.15
248	Dave Gagner, Min.	.10	.15
249	Brent Sutter, NYI	.10	.15
250	Claude Vilgrain, NJ, RC	.13	.25
251	Tomas Sandstrom, LA	.10	.15
252	Joe Mullen, Cal.	.10	.15
253	Brian Leetch, NYR	1.00	1.50
254	Michael Vernon, Goalie, Cal.	.10	.15
255	Star-Rookie: Daniel Doré, Que., RC	.10	.15
256	Trevor Linden, Van.	1.00	1.50
257	David Barr, Det.	.10	.15
258	John Ogrodnick, NYR	.10	.15
259	Russell Courtnall, Mon.	.10	.15
260	Dan Quinn, Van.	.10	.15
261	Mark Howe, Phi.	.10	.15
262	Kevin Lowe, Edm.	.10	.15
263	Rick Tocchet, Phi.	.15	.25
264	Grant Fuhr, Goalie, Edm.	.15	.25
265	Star-Rookie: Andrew Cassels, Mon., RC	.10	.15
266	Kevin Dineen, Har.	.10	.15
267	Kirk Muller, NJ	.10	.15
268	Randy Cunneyworth, Har.	.10	.15
269	Brendan Shanahan, NJ	.50	.75
270	Dave Tippett, Har.	.10	.15
271	Douglas Gilmour, Cal.	.50	.75
272	Tony Granato, LA	.10	.15
273	Gary Suter, Cal.	.10	.15
274	Darren Turcotte, NYR, RC	.40	.60
275	Star-Rookie: Murray Baron, Phi., RC	.10	.15
276	Stephane Richer, Mon.	.10	.15
277	Michael Gartner, NYR	.20	.30
278	Kirk McLean, Goalie, Van.	1.00	1.50
279	John Vanbiesbrouck, Goalie, NYR	.30	.45
280	Shayne Corson, Mon.	.10	.15
281	Paul Cavallini, St. L.	.10	.15
282	Petr Klima, Edm.	.10	.15
283	Ulf Dahlen, Min.	.10	.15
284	Glenn Anderson, Edm.	.10	.15
285	Richard Meagher, St. L.	.10	.15

No.	Player	English NRMT	French NRMT
286	Alexei Kasatonov, NJ, RC	.30	.45
287	Ulf Samuelsson, Har.	.10	.15
288	Patrik Sundstrom, NJ	.10	.15
289	Ray Ferraro, Har.	.10	.15
290	Janne Ojanen, NJ, RC	.10	.15
291	Jeff Jackson, Que.	.10	.15
292	Jiri Hrdina, Cal., RC	.10	.15
293	Joe Cirella, Que.	.10	.15
294	Byron (Brad) McCrimmon, Cal.	.10	.15
295	Curtis Leschyshyn, Que., RC	.10	.15
296	Kelly Kisio, NYR	.10	.15
297	Jyrki Lumme, Van., RC	.30	.45
298	Mark Janssens, NYR, RC	.10	.15
299	Stanley Smyl, Van.	.10	.15
300	Checklist 3 (201 - 300)	.10	.15

THE COLLECTOR'S CHOICE - TEAM CHECKLIST

No.	Team	English NRMT	French NRMT
301	Quebec Nordiques: Joe Sakic	.25	.40
302	Vancouver Canucks: Petri Skriko	.10	.15
303	Detroit Red Wings: Steve Yzerman	.20	.30
304	Philadelphia Flyers: Tim Kerr	.10	.15
305	Pittsburgh Penguins: Mario Lemieux	.50	.75
306	New York Islanders: Pat LaFontaine	.20	.30
307	Los Angeles Kings: Wayne Gretzky	.50	.75
308	Minnesota North Stars: Brian Bellows	.10	.15
309	Washington Capitals: Rod Langway	.10	.15
310	Toronto Maple Leafs: Gary Leeman	.10	.15
311	New Jersey Devils: Kirk Muller	.10	.15
312	St. Louis Blues: Brett Hull	.20	.30
313	Winnipeg Jets: Thomas Steen	.10	.15
314	Hartford Whalers: Ronald Francis	.10	.15
315	New York Rangers: Brian Leetch	.20	.30
316	Chicago Black Hawks: Jeremy Roenick	.40	.60
317	Montreal Canadiens: Patrick Roy, Goalie	.40	.60
318	Buffalo Sabres: Pierre Turgeon	.10	.20
319	Calgary Flames: Allan MacInnis	.10	.15
320	Boston Bruins: Raymond Bourque	.10	.15
321	Edmonton Oilers: Mark Messier	.15	.25

REGULAR ISSUE

No.	Player	English NRMT	French NRMT
322	Jody Hull, Har., RC	.10	.15
323	Chris Joseph, Ed., RC	.10	.15
324	Adam Burt, Har., RC	.10	.15
325	Star-Rookie: Jason Herter, Van., RC	.10	.15
326	All Rookie Team: Geoff Smith, Edm., RC	.10	.15
327	All Rookie Team: Brad Shaw, Har., RC	.10	.15
328	Richard Sutter, St. L.	.10	.15
329	Barry Pederson, Pit.	.10	.15
330	Paul MacLean, St. L.	.10	.15
331	Randy Carlyle, Win.	.10	.15
332	Donald Dufresne, Mon., RC	.10	.15
333	Brent Hughes, Win., RC	.10	.15
334	Mathieu Schneider, Mon., RC	.75	1.25
335	Star-Rookie: Jason Miller, NJ, RC	.10	.15
336	All Rookie Team: Sergei Makarov, Cal., RC	.25	.35
337	All Rookie Team: Bob Essensa, Goalie, Win., RC	.10	.15
338	Claude Loiselle, Que., RC	.10	.15
339	Wayne Presley, Chi.	.10	.15
340	Anthony McKegney, Que.	.10	.15
341	Charles Huddy, Edm.	.10	.15
342	Greg Adams, Van.	.10	.15
343	Mike Tomlak, Har., RC	.10	.15
344	Adam Graves, Edm., RC	4.00	6.00
345	Star-Rookie: Michel Mongeau, St. L., RC	.10	.15
346	All Rookie Team: Michael Modano, Min.	.50	.75
347	All Rookie Team: Rod Brind'Amour, St. L.	.25	.40
348	Dana Murzyn, Cal.	.10	.15
349	Dave Lowry, St. L., RC	.15	.20
350	Star Rookie Checklist	.15	.20

400 • UPPER DECK — 1990-91 ISSUE

NUMBER ONE DRAFT

No.	Player	English NRMT	French NRMT
351	Top Ten Draft Pick Checklist Nolan/Primeau/Nedved/Ricci	1.00	1.50
352	Owen Nolan, Que., RC	2.00	3.00
353	Petr Nedved, Van., RC	1.50	2.25
354	Keith Primeau, Det., RC	1.00	1.50
355	Mike Ricci, Phi., RC	1.00	1.50
356	Jaromir Jagr, Pit., RC	3.00	4.50
357	Scott Scissons, NYI, RC	.10	.15
358	Darryl Sydor, LA, RC	.50	.75
359	Derian Hatcher, Min., RC	.75	1.25
360	John Slaney, Wash., RC	.50	.75
361	Drake Berehowsky, Tor., RC	.75	1.25

REGULAR ISSUE

No.	Player	English NRMT	French NRMT
362	Luke Richardson, Tor.	.10	.15
363	Lucien DeBlois, Que.	.10	.15
364	David Reid, Tor., RC	.10	.15
365	Mats Sundin, Que., RC	3.50	5.25
366	Jan Erixon, NYR	.10	.15
367	Troy Loney, Pit., RC	.15	.20
368	Christopher Nilan, NYR	.10	.15
369	Gord Dineen, Pit.	.10	.15
370	Jeff Bloemberg, NYR, RC	.10	.15
371	John Druce, Wash., RC	.15	.25
372	Brian MacLellan, Cal.	.10	.15
373	Bruce Driver, NJ	.10	.15
374	Marc Habscheid, Det.	.10	.15
375	Paul Ysebaert, NJ, RC	.30	.45
376	Richard Vaive, Buf.	.10	.15
377	Glen Wesley, Bos.	.10	.15
378	Mike Foligno, Buf.	.10	.15
379	Garry Galley, Bos., RC	.30	.45
380	Edward (Dean) Kennedy, Buf., RC	.10	.15
381	Daniel Berthiaume, Goalie, Min.	.10	.15
382	Mike Keane, Mon., RC	.40	.60
383	Frantisek Musil, Min	.10	.15
384	Michael McPhee, Mon.	.10	.15
385	Jon Casey, Goalie, Min.	.10	.15
386	Jeff Norton, NYI	.10	.15
387	John Tucker, Wash.	.10	.15
388	Alan Kerr, NYI	.10	.15
389	Robert Rouse, Wash.	.10	.15
390	Gerald Diduck, NYI	.10	.15
391	Greg Hawgood, Bos.	.10	.15
392	Randy Velischek, NJ	.10	.15
393	Tim Cheveldae, Goalie, Det., RC	.75	1.25
394	Michael Krushelnyski, LA	.10	.15
395	Glen Hanlon, Goalie, Det.	.10	.15
396	Lou Franceschetti, Tor., RC	.10	.15
397	Scott Arniel, Buf.	.10	.15
398	Terry Carkner, Phi.	.10	.15
399	Clint Malarchuk, Goalie, Buf.	.10	.15
400	Checklist 4 (301 - 400)	.10	.15
401	Mikhail Tatarinov, Wash., RC	.20	.40
402	Benoit Hogue, Buf.	.10	.20
403	Frank Pietrangelo, Goalie, Pit., RC	.10	.20
404	Paul Stanton, Pit., RC	.10	.20
405	Anatoli Semenov, Edm., RC	.35	.70
406	Robert Smith, Min.	.10	.20
407	Derek King, NYI	.10	.20
408	Jean-Claude Bergeron, Goalie, Mon., RC	.10	.20
409	Brian Propp, Bos.	.10	.20
410	Jiri Latal, Phi., RC	.10	.20
411	Joey Kocur, Det., RC	.20	.40
412	Daniel Berthiaume, Goalie, LA	.10	.20
413	David Ellett, Win.	.10	.20
414	Jay Miller, LA, RC	.10	.20
415	Stephane Beauregard, Goalie, Win., RC	.10	.15
416	Mark Hardy, NYR	.10	.20
417	Todd Krygier, Har., RC	.10	.20
418	Randy Moller, NYR	.10	.20
419	Douglas Crossman, Har.	.10	.20
420	Ray Sheppard, NYR	.25	.50
421	Sylvain Lefebvre, Mon., RC	.25	.50
422	Chris Chelios, Mon.	.15	.30
423	Joe Mullen, Pit.	.10	.20
424	Peter Peeters, Goalie, Phi.	.10	.20
425	Bryan Trottier, Pit	.10	.20
426	Denis Savard, Mon	.10	.20
427	Ken Daneyko, NJ	.10	.20
428	Eric Desjardins, Mon., RC	.50	1.00
429	Zdeno Ciger, NJ, RC	.25	.50
430	Byron (Brad) McCrimmon, Cal.	.10	.20
431	Ed Olczyk, Win.	.10	.20
432	Peter Ing, Goalie, Tor., RC	.10	.20
433	Bob Kudelski, LA, RC	.75	1.50
434	Troy Gamble, Goalie, Van., RC	.10	.20
435	Phil Housley, Buf.	.10	.20
436	Scott Stevens, St. L.	.10	.20
437	Normand Rochefort, NYR	.10	.20
438	Geoff Courtnall, Wash.	.10	.20
439	Ken Baumgartner, NYI, RC	.10	.20
440	Kris King, NYR, RC	.20	.40
441	Troy Crowder, NJ, RC	.10	.20
442	Christopher Nilan, Bos.	.10	.20
443	Dale Hawerchuk, Buf.	.20	.40
444	Kevin Miller, NYR, RC	.50	1.00
445	Keith Acton, Phi.	.10	.20
446	Jeff Chychrun, Phi., RC	.10	.20
447	Claude Lemieux, Mon.	.10	.20
448	Bob Probert, Det.	.50	1.00
449	Brian Hayward, Goalie, Mon.	.10	.20
450	Craig Berube, Phi, RC	.10	.20

WORLD JUNIOR CHAMPIONS - TEAM CANADA

No.	Player	English NRMT	French NRMT
451	Canadian National Junior Team	1.00	2.00
452	Mike Sillinger	.25	.50
453	Jason Marshall	.30	.60
454	Patrice Brisebois	.50	1.00
455	Brad May	.50	1.00
456	Pierre Sevigny	.25	.50
457	John Slaney	.25	.50
458	Felix Potvin, Goalie	14.00	28.00
459	Scott Thornton	.10	.20
460	Greg Johnson	.50	1.00
461	Scott Niedermayer	3.00	6.00
462	Steven Rice	.20	.40
463	Trevor Kidd, Goalie	1.00	2.00
464	Dale Craigwell	.20	.40
465	Kent Manderville	.25	.50
466	Kris Draper	.25	.50
467	Martin Lapointe	.40	.80
468	Chris Snell	.20	.40
469	Pat Falloon	2.00	4.00
470	David Harlock	.20	.40
471	Karl Dykhuis	.10	.20
472	Mike Craig	.40	.80
473	Canada's Captains: Draper, Rice, Lindros	5.00	10.00

ALL STAR

No.	Player	English NRMT	French NRMT
474	Brett Hull, St. L.	.35	.70
475	Darren Turcotte, NYR	.10	.20
476	Wayne Gretzky, LA	.75	1.50
477	Steve Yzerman, Det.	.25	.50
478	Theoren Fleury, Cal.	.10	.20
479	Pat LaFontaine, NYI	.20	.40
480	Trevor Linden, Van.	.35	.70
481	Jeremy Roenick, Chi.	.50	1.00
482	Scott Stevens, St. L.	.10	.20
483	Adam Oates, St. L.	.10	.20
484	Vincent Damphousse, Tor.	.10	.20
485	Brian Leetch, NYR	.35	.70
486	Kevin Hatcher, Wash.	.10	.20
487	Mark Recchi, Pit.	.30	.60
488	Rick Tocchet, Phi.	.10	.20
489	Raymond Bourque, Bos.	.20	.40
490	Joe Sakic, Que.	.25	.50
491	Chris Chelios, Mon.	.10	.20
492	John Cullen, Pit.	.10	.20
493	Cam Neely, Bos	.15	.30
494	Mark Messier, Edm.	.20	.40
495	Michael Vernon, Goalie, Cal.	.10	.20
496	Patrick Roy, Mon., Goalie	.50	1.00
497	Allan MacInnis, Cal.	.10	.20
498	Paul Coffey, Pit.	.10	.20
499	Steve Larmer, Chi.	.10	.20
500	Checklist 1 (401 - 500)	.10	.20
501	Heroes Checklist	.10	.20

HEROES

No.	Player	English NRMT	French NRMT
502	Red Kelly, Det.	.10	.20
503	Eric Nesterenko, Tor.	.10	.20
504	Darryl Sittler, Tor.	.10	.20
505	Jim Schoenfeld, Buf.	.10	.20
506	Serge Savard, Mon.	.10	.20
507	Glenn Resch, Goalie, NYI	.10	.20
508	Lanny McDonald, Tor.	.10	.20
509	Bobby Clarke, Phi.	.10	.20
510	Phil Esposito, Chi.	.10	.20
511	Harry Howell, NYR	.10	.20
512	Rod Gilbert, NYR	.10	.20
513	Pit Martin, Det.	.10	.20
514	Jimmy Watson, Phi.	.10	.20
515	Denis Potvin, NYI	.10	.20

REGULAR ISSUE

No.	Player	English NRMT	French NRMT
516	Robert Ray, Buf., RC	.10	.20
517	Danton Cole, Win., RC	.20	.40
518	Gino Odjick, Van., RC	.60	1.20
519	Donald Audette, Buf., RC	.50	1.00
520	Richard Tabaracci, Goalie, Pit., RC	.40	.80

YOUNG GUNS

No.	Player	English NRMT	French NRMT
521	Checklist: Fedorov, Garpenlov, Det.	.75	1.50
522	Kip Miller, Que., RC	.10	.20
523	Johan Garpenlov, Det., RC	.40	.80
524	Stephane Morin, Que., RC	.10	.20
525	Sergei Fedorov, Det., RC	12.00	24.00
526	Pavel Bure, Van., RC	18.00	36.00
527	Wes Walz, Bos., RC	.20	.40
528	Robert Kron, Van., RC	.20	.40
529	Kenneth Hodge, Jr., Min., RC	.10	.20
530	Garry Valk, Van., RC	.15	.30
531	Tim Sweeney, Cal., RC	.15	.30
532	Mark Pederson, Mon., RC	.10	.20
533	Robert Reichel, Cal., RC	1.75	3.50
534	Robert Holik, Har., RC	1.00	2.00
535	Stephane Matteau, Cal., RC	.50	1.00
536	Peter Bondra, Wash., RC	.75	1.50

REGULAR ISSUE

No.	Player	English NRMT	French NRMT
537	Dimitri Khristich, Wash., RC	.80	1.60
538	Vladimir Ruzicka, Bos., RC	.25	.50
539	Al Iafrate, Wash.	.10	.20
540	Rick Bennett, NYR, RC	.10	.20
541	Daryl Reaugh, Goalie, Har., RC	.10	.20
542	Martin Hostak, Phi., RC	.10	.20
543	Karl Takko, Goalie, Edm., RC	.10	.20
544	Jocelyn Lemieux, Chi., RC	.10	.20

GRETZKY'S THE 2000TH POINT

No.	Player	English NRMT	French NRMT
545	Wayne Gretzky, LA	1.50	2.50

HULL'S 50 GOALS/50 GAMES

No.	Player	English NRMT	French NRMT
546	Brett Hull, St. L.	.50	1.00

REGULAR ISSUE

No.	Player	English NRMT	French NRMT
547	Neil Wilkinson, Min., RC	.10	.20
548	Bryan Fogarty, Que., RC	.10	.20
549	Frank J. Zamboni / Zamboni Ice Rink Resurfacer	.10	.20
550	Checklist 2 (501 - 550)	.10	.20

— 1991 - 92 REGULAR ISSUE —

Again the Upper Deck set was issued with both a "Low and High" number series. Included in the set are Stereograms, Special Player Cards and the Hockey Heroes Set. The first ninety-nine cards consist of various subsets.

1991-92 Regular Issue, English
Card No. 1, Vladimir Malakhov

Card Size: 2 1/2" X 3 1/2"
Face: Four colour, white border; Name, Position, Logo
Back: Four colour, white border on white card stock; Name, Number, Hologram, Resume, Position
Imprint:
  Low Series: © 1991 The Upper Deck Company. Printed in the U.S.A. All rights reserved
  High Series: © 1992 The Upper Deck Company, Printed in the U.S.A. All rights reserved

		English	French
Complete Set No.:	700		
Low Series:	500		
High Series:	200		
Set Price:			
Low Series:		30.00	30.00
High Series:		15.00	15.00
Factory Set: (High)		16.00	N/I
Complete Set:		45.00	45.00
Common Card:		.05	.05
Foil Pack:			
Low Series: (12 Cards)		1.00	1.00
High Series: (12 Cards)		1.00	1.00
Foil Box:			
Low Series: (36 Packs)		35.00	35.00
High Series: (36 Packs)		35.00	35.00
Foil Case:			
Low Series: (24 Boxes)		600.00	600.00
High Series: (24 Boxes)		600.00	600.00

SOVIET STARS

No.	Player	English NRMT	French NRMT
1	Vladimir Malakhov	.75	.75
2	Alexei Zhamnov	2.50	2.50
3	Dimitri Filimonov, Error	.25	.25
4	Alexander Semak	.40	.40
5	Viacheslav Kozlov, Error	2.00	2.00
6	Sergei Fedorov	.70	.70

1991 CANADA CUP

No.	Player	English NRMT	French NRMT
7	Canada Cup Checklist	1.00	1.00

CANADA

No.	Player	English NRMT	French NRMT
8	Allan MacInnis	.05	.05
9	Eric Lindros	6.00	6.00
10	Bill Ranford, Goalie	.05	.05
11	Paul Coffey	.05	.05
12	Dale Hawerchuk	.05	.05
13	Wayne Gretzky	.50	.50
14	Mark Messier	.20	.20
15	Steve Larmer	.05	.05

CZECHOSLOVAKIA

No.	Player	English NRMT	French NRMT
16	Zigmund Palffy	.50	.50
17	Josef Beranek	.70	.70
18	Jiri Slegr	.40	.40
19	Martin Rucinsky	.30	.30
20	Jaromir Jagr	.50	.50

FINLAND

No.	Player	English NRMT	French NRMT
21	Teemu Selanne	5.00	10.00
22	Janne Laukkanen	.20	.20
23	Markus Ketterer, Goalie	.25	.25
24	Jari Kurri	.05	.05
25	Janne Ojanen	.05	.05

SWEDEN

No.	Player	English NRMT	French NRMT
26	Nicklas Lidstrom, Error	.80	.80
27	Tomas Forslund	.05	.05
28	Johan Garpenlov	.05	.05
29	Niclas Andersson	.15	.15
30	Tomas Sandstrom	.05	.05
31	Mats Sundin	.15	.15

USA

No.	Player	English NRMT	French NRMT
32	Michael Modano	.20	.20
33	Brett Hull	.30	.30
34	Mike Richter, Goalie	.20	.20
35	Brian Leetch	.35	.35
36	Jeremy Roenick	.60	.60
37	Chris Chelios	.05	.05

GRETZKY 99

No.	Player	English NRMT	French NRMT
38	Gretzky 99	.50	.50

ALL ROOKIE TEAM

No.	Player	English NRMT	French NRMT
39	Ed Belfour, Goalie, Chi.	.15	.15
40	Sergei Fedorov, Det.	.35	.35
41	Kenneth Hodge, Jr., Bos.	.05	.05
42	Jaromir Jagr, Pit.	.25	.25
43	Robert Blake, LA	.05	.05
44	Eric Weinrich, NJD	.05	.05

REGULAR ISSUE

No.	Player	English NRMT	French NRMT
45	The "50/50" Club: Lemieux, Gretzky, and Hull	.25	.25
46	Russell Romaniuk, Win., RC	.15	.15
47	White House Welcome: Mario Lemieux/ President G. Bush	.25	.25
48	Michel Picard, Har., RC	.05	.05
49	Dennis Vaske, NYI, RC	.05	.05
50	Eric Murano, Van., RC	.05	.05
51	Enrico Ciccone, Min., RC	.05	.05
52	Shaun Van Allen, Edm., RC	.20	.20
53	Stu Barnes, Win.	.05	.05
54	Pavel Bure, Van.	3.00	3.00

SAN JOSE SHARKS

No.	Player	English NRMT	French NRMT
55	Neil Wilkinson	.05	.05
56	Anthony Hrkac	.05	.05
57	Brian Mullen	.05	.05
58	Jeff Hackett, Goalie	.05	.05
59	Brian Hayward, Goalie	.05	.05
60	Craig Coxe	.05	.05
61	Rob Zettler	.05	.05
62	Robert McGill	.05	.05

1991 DRAFT CHOICE

No.	Player	English NRMT	French NRMT
63	Draft Checklist: M. Lapointe and J. Pushor	.20	.20
64	Peter Forsberg, Phi., RC	5.00	5.00
65	Patrick Poulin, Har., RC	.50	.50
66	Martin Lapointe, Det., RC	.20	.20
67	Tyler Wright, Edm., RC	.20	.20
68	Philippe Boucher, Buf., RC	.20	.20

No.	Team	English NRMT	French NRMT
69	Glen Murray, Bos., RC	.30	.30
70	Martin Rucinsky, Edm., RC	.20	.20
71	Zigmund Palffy, NYI, RC	.50	.50
72	Jassen Cullimore, Van., RC	.15	.15
73	Jamie Pushor, Det., RC	.15	.15
74	Andrew Verner, Goalie, Edm., RC	.15	.15
75	Jason Dawe, Buf., RC	.35	.35
76	Jamie Matthews, Chi., RC	.15	.15
77	Sandy McCarthy, Cal., RC	.30	.30

THE COLLECTOR'S CHOICE TEAM CHECKLIST

No.	Team	English NRMT	French NRMT
78	Boston Bruins: Cam Neely	.10	.10
79	Buffalo Sabres: Dale Hawerchuk	.10	.10
80	Calgary Flames: Theoren Fleury	.05	.05
81	Chicago Black Hawks: Ed Belfour, Goalie	.15	.15
82	Detroit Red Wings: Sergei Fedorov	.20	.20
83	Edmonton Oilers: Esa Tikkanen	.05	.05
84	Hartford Whalers: John Cullen	.05	.05
85	Los Angeles Kings: Tomas Sandstrom	.05	.05
86	Minnesota North Stars: Dave Gagner	.05	.05
87	Montreal Canadiens: Russell Courtnall	.05	.05
88	New Jersey Devils: John MacLean	.05	.05
89	New York Islanders: David Volek	.05	.05
90	New York Rangers: Darren Turcotte	.05	.05
91	Philadelphia Flyers: Rick Tocchet	.05	.05
92	Pittsburgh Penguins: Mark Recchi	.15	.15
93	Quebec Nordiques: Mats Sundin	.15	.15
94	St. Louis Blues: Adam Oates	.05	.05
95	San Jose Sharks: Neil Wilkinson	.05	.05
96	Toronto Maple Leafs: David Ellett	.05	.05
97	Vancouver Canucks: Trevor Linden	.15	.15
98	Washington Capitals: Kevin Hatcher	.05	.05
99	Winnipeg Jets: Ed Olczyk	.05	.05

REGULAR ISSUE

No.	Player	English NRMT	French NRMT
100	Checklist 1 (1 - 100)	.05	.05
101	Bob Essensa, Goalie, Win.	.15	.15
102	Uwe Krupp, Buf.	.05	.05
103	Per-erik Eklund, Phi.	.05	.05
104	Christian Ruuttu, Buf.	.05	.05
105	Kevin Dineen, Har.	.05	.05
106	Phil Housley, Win.	.05	.05
107	Pat Jablonski, Goalie, St. L., RC	.25	.25
108	Jarmo Kekalainen, Bos., RC	.10	.10
109	Pat Elynuik, Win.	.05	.05
110	Corey Millen, NYR, RC	.50	.50
111	Petr Klima, Edm.	.05	.05
112	Mike Ridley, Wash.	.05	.05
113	Peter Stastny, NJD	.05	.05
114	Jyrki Lumme, Van.	.05	.05
115	Chris Terreri, Goalie, NJD	.05	.05
116	Tom Barrasso, Goalie, Pit.	.05	.05
117	Bill Ranford, Goalie, Edm.	.05	.05
118	Peter Ing, Goalie, Tor.	.05	.05
119	John Tanner, Goalie, Que.	.05	.05
120	Troy Gamble, Goalie, Van.	.05	.05
121	Stephane Matteau, Cal.	.05	.05
122	Rick Tocchet, Phi.	.05	.05
123	Wes Walz, Bos.	.05	.05
124	David Andreychuk, Buf.	.20	.20
125	Mike Craig, Min.	.05	.05
126	Dale Hawerchuk, Buf.	.10	.10
127	Dean Evason, Har.	.05	.05
128	Craig Janney, Bos.	.20	.20
129	Tim Cheveldae, Goalie, Det.	.05	.05
130	Richard Wamsley, Goalie, Cal.	.05	.05
131	Peter Bondra, Wash.	.25	.25
132	Scott Stevens, St. L.	.05	.05
133	Kelly Miller, Wash.	.05	.05
134	Mats Sundin, Que.	.50	.50
135	Mick Vukota, NYI	.05	.05
136	Vincent Damphousse, Tor.	.15	.15
137	Patrick Roy, Goalie, Mon.	1.00	1.00

No.	Team	English NRMT	French NRMT
138	Hubie McDonough, NYI	.05	.05
139	Curtis Joseph, Goalie, St. L.	.50	.50
140	Brent Sutter, NYI	.05	.05
141	Tomas Sandstrom, LA	.05	.05
142	Kevin Miller, Det.	.05	.05
143	Mike Ricci, Phi.	.20	.20
144	Sergei Fedorov, Det.	1.25	1.25
145	Luc Robitaille, LA	.30	.30
146	Steve Yzerman, Det.	.50	.50
147	Andrew Moog, Goalie, Bos.	.05	.05
148	Robert Blake, LA	.30	.30
149	Kirk Muller, NJD	.05	.05
150	Daniel Berthiaume, Goalie, LA	.05	.05
151	John Druce, Wash.	.05	.05
152	Garry Valk, Van.	.05	.05
153	Brian Leetch, NYR	.70	.70
154	Kevin Stevens, Pit.	.50	.50
155	Darren Turcotte, NYR	.05	.05
156	Mario Lemieux, Pit.	1.00	1.00
157	Dimitri Khristich, Was.	.25	.25
158	**Brian Glynn, Min., RC**	**.10**	**.10**
159	Benoit Hogue, Buf.	.05	.05
160	Michael Modano, Min.	.50	.50
161	Jimmy Carson, Det.	.05	.05
162	Steve Thomas, Chi.	.05	.05
163	Michael Vernon, Goalie, Cal.	.05	.05
164	Ed Belfour, Goalie, Chi.	.60	.60
165	Joel Otto, Cal.	.05	.05
166	Jeremy Roenick, Chi.	1.00	1.00
167	Johan Garpenlov, Det.	.10	.10
168	Russell Courtnall, Mon.	.05	.05
169	John MacLean, NJD	.05	.05
170	Jean-Jacques Daigneault, Mon.	.05	.05
171	Sylvain Lefebvre, Mon.	.05	.05
172	Tony Granato, LA	.05	.05
173	David Volek, NYI	.05	.05
174	Trevor Linden, Van.	.35	.35
175	Mike Richter, Goalie, NYR	.40	.40
176	Pierre Turgeon, Buf.	.40	.40
177	Paul Coffey, Pit.	.25	.25
178	Jan Erixon, NYR	.05	.05
179	Richard Vaive, Buf.	.05	.05
180	Dave Gagner, Min.	.05	.05
181	Thomas Steen, Win.	.05	.05
182	Esa Tikkanen, Edm.	.05	.05
183	Sean Burke, Goalie, NJD	.05	.05
184	Paul Cavallini, St. L.	.05	.05
185	Alexei Kasatonov, NJD	.05	.05
186	Kevin Lowe, Edm.	.05	.05
187	Gino Cavallini, St. L.	.05	.05
188	Douglas Gilmour, Cal.	.50	.50
189	Rod Brind'Amour, St. L.	.25	.25
190	Gary Roberts, Cal.	.05	.05
191	Kirk McLean, Goalie, Van.	.35	.35
192	**Kevin Haller, Buf., RC**	**.15**	**.15**
193	Patrick Verbeek, Har.	.05	.05
194	Dave Snuggerud, Buf.	.05	.05
195	Gino Odjick, Van.	.05	.05
196	David Ellett, Tor.	.05	.05
197	Donald Beaupre, Goalie, Wash.	.05	.05
198	Rob Brown, Har.	.05	.05
199	Martin McSorley, LA	.05	.05
200	Checklist 2 (101 - 200)	.05	.05
201	Joe Mullen, Pit.	.05	.05
202	Dave Capuano, Van.	.05	.05
203	Paul Stanton, Pit.	.05	.05
204	Terry Carkner, Phi.	.05	.05
205	Jon Casey, Goalie, Min.	.05	.05
206	Ken Wregget, Goalie, Phi.	.05	.05
207	Gaetan Duchesne, Min.	.05	.05
208	Cliff Ronning, Van.	.10	.10
209	Dale Hunter, Wash.	.05	.05
210	Danton Cole, Win.	.05	.05
211	Jeff Brown, St. L.	.05	.05
212	Mike Foligno, Tor.	.05	.05
213	Michel Mongeau, St. L.	.05	.05
214	Doug Brown, NJD	.05	.05
215	Todd Krygier, Har.	.05	.05
216	Jon Morris, NJD	.05	.05
217	David Reid, Tor.	.05	.05
218	John McIntyre, LA	.05	.05
219	Lafleur's Farewell	.05	.05

No.	Player	English NRMT	French NRMT
220	Vincent Riendeau, Goalie, St. L.	.10	.10
221	Timothy Hunter, Cal.	.05	.05
222	Dave McLlwain, Win.	.05	.05
223	Robert Reichel, Cal.	.25	.25
224	Glenn Healy, Goalie, NYI	.05	.05
225	Robert Kron, Van.	.05	.05
226	Patrick Flatley, NYI	.05	.05
227	Petr Nedved, Van.	.30	.30
228	Mark Janssens, NYR	.05	.05
229	Michal Pivonka, Wash.	.05	.05
230	Ulf Samuelsson, Pit.	.05	.05
231	Zarley Zalapski, Har.	.05	.05
232	Neal Broten, Min.	.05	.05
233	Robert Holik, Har.	.10	.10
234	Cam Neely, Bos.	.10	.10
235	John Cullen, Har.	.05	.05
236	Brian Bellows, Min.	.10	.10
237	Christopher Nilan, Bos.	.05	.05
238	Bo Mikael Andersson, Har.	.05	.05
239	Bob Probert, Det.	.10	.10
240	Teppo Numminen, Win.	.05	.05
241	Peter Zezel, Tor.	.05	.05
242	Denis Savard, Mon.	.10	.10
243	Allan MacInnis, Cal.	.10	.10
244	Stephane J. J. Richer, Mon.	.05	.05
245	Theoren Fleury, Cal.	.25	.25
246	Mark Messier, Edm.	.40	.40
247	Michael Gartner, NYR	.10	.10
248	Daren Puppa, Goalie, Buf.	.05	.05
249	Louie DeBrusk, NYR	.10	.10
250	Glenn Anderson, Edm.	.10	.10
251	Kenneth Hodge, Jr., Bos.	.05	.05
252	Adam Oates, St. L.	.25	.25
253	Pat LaFontaine, NYI	.50	.50
254	Adam Creighton, Chi.	.05	.05
255	Raymond Bourque, Bos.	.25	.25
256	Jaromir Jagr, Pit.	1.00	1.00
257	Steve Larmer, Chi.	.05	.05
258	Keith Primeau, Det.	.25	.25
259	Michael Liut, Goalie, Wash.	.05	.05
260	Brian Propp, Min.	.05	.05
261	Stephan Lebeau, Mon.	.25	.25
262	Kelly Hrudey, Goalie, LA	.05	.05
263	Joe Nieuwendyk, Cal.	.10	.10
264	Grant Fuhr, Goalie, Edm.	.05	.05
265	Guy Carbonneau, Mon.	.05	.05
266	Martin Gelinas, Edm.	.10	.10
267	Alexander Mogilny, Buf.	1.00	1.00
268	Adam Graves, Edm.	.40	.40
269	Anatoli Semenov, Edm.	.05	.05
270	David Taylor, LA	.05	.05
271	Dirk Graham, Chi.	.05	.05
272	Gary Leeman, Tor.	.05	.05
273	**Valeri Kamensky, Que., RC**	**.75**	**.75**
274	Marc Bureau, Min.	.05	.05
275	James Patrick, NYR	.05	.05
276	Dino Ciccarelli, Wash.	.05	.05
277	Ron Tugnutt, Goalie, Que.	.05	.05
278	Paul Ysebaert, Det.	.05	.05
279	Laurie Boschman, NJD	.05	.05
280	Dave Manson, Chi.	.05	.05
281	David Chyzowski, NYI	.05	.05
282	Shayne Corson, Mon.	.05	.05
283	Steve Chiasson, Det.	.05	.05
284	Craig MacTavish, Edm.	.05	.05
285	Petr Svoboda, Mon.	.05	.05
286	Craig Simpson, Edm.	.05	.05
287	**Ron Hoover, Bos., RC**	**.05**	**.05**
288	Vladimir Ruzicka, Bos.	.05	.05
289	Randy Wood, NYI	.05	.05
290	Doug Lidster, Van.	.05	.05
291	Kay Whitmore, Goalie, Har.	.05	.05
292	Bruce Driver, NJD	.05	.05
293	Robert Smith, Min.	.05	.05
294	Claude Lemieux, NJD	.05	.05
295	Mark Tinordi, Min.	.05	.05
296	Mark Osborne, Win.	.05	.05
297	Brad Shaw, Har.	.05	.05
298	Igor Larionov, Van.	.05	.05
299	Ronald Francis, Pit.	.10	.10
300	Checklist 3 (201 - 300)	.05	.05
301	Bob Kudelski, LA	.05	.05

No.	Player	English NRMT	French NRMT
302	Lawrence Murphy, Pit.	.05	.05
303	Brent Ashton, Win.	.05	.05
304	**Brad Jones, LA, RC**	**.10**	**.10**
305	Gordon Donnelly, Win.	.05	.05
306	Murray Craven, Phi.	.05	.05
307	Chris Dahlquist, Min.	.05	.05
308	**Jim Paek, Pit., RC**	**.20**	**.20**
309	Ronald Sutter, Phi.	.05	.05
310	Mike Tomlak, Har.	.05	.05
311	Ray Ferraro, NYI	.05	.05
312	David Hannan, Tor.	.05	.05
313	Randy McKay, Det.	.05	.05
314	Rod Langway, Wash.	.05	.05
315	Shawn Burr, Det.	.05	.05
316	Calle Johansson, Wash.	.05	.05
317	Richard Sutter, St. L.	.05	.05
318	Al Iafrate, Was.	.05	.05
319	Bob Bassen, St. L.	.05	.05
320	Michael Krushelnyski, Tor.	.05	.05
321	Sergei Makarov, Cal.	.25	.25
322	Darrin Shannon, Buf.	.05	.05
323	Terry Yake, Har.	.05	.05
324	John Vanbiesbrouck, Goalie, NYR	.25	.25
325	Peter Sidorkiewicz, Goalie, Har.	.05	.05
326	Troy Mallette, NYR	.05	.05
327	Ron Hextall, Goalie, Phi.	.05	.05
328	Mathieu Schneider, Mon.	.10	.10
329	Bryan Trottier, Pit.	.05	.05
330	Kris King, NYR	.05	.05
331	Daniel Marois, Tor.	.05	.05
332	Shayne Stevenson, Bos.	.05	.05
333	Joe Sakic, Que.	.50	.50
334	Petri Skriko, Bos.	.05	.05
335	**Dominik Hasek, Goalie, Chi., RC**	**3.00**	**3.00**
336	Scott Pearson, Que.	.05	.05
337	Bryan Fogarty, Que.	.05	.05
338	Don Sweeney, Bos.	.05	.05
339	Richard Tabaracci, Goalie, Win.	.05	.05
340	Steven Finn, Que.	.05	.05
341	Gary Suter, Cal.	.05	.05
342	Troy Crowder, NJD	.05	.05
343	Jim Hrivnak, Goalie, Wash.	.10	.10
344	Eric Weinrich, NJD	.05	.05
345	**John LeClair, Mon., RC**	**.30**	**.30**
346	Mark Recchi, Pit.	.90	.90
347	**Dan Currie, Edm., RC**	**.20**	**.20**
348	Ulf Dahlen, Min.	.05	.05
349	Robert Ray, Buf.	.05	.05
350	James (Steve) Smith, Edm.	.05	.05
351	Shawn Antoski, Van.	.05	.05
352	Cam Russell, Chi.	.05	.05
353	Scott Thornton, Tor.	.05	.05
354	Chris Chelios, Chi.	.05	.05
355	Sergei Nemchinov, NYR	.25	.25
356	Bernie Nicholls, NYR	.05	.05
357	Jeff Norton, NYI	.05	.05
358	Dan Quinn, St. L.	.05	.05
359	Michel Petit, Tor.	.05	.05
360	Eric Desjardins, Mon.	.10	.10
361	Kevin Hatcher, Wash.	.05	.05
362	**Jiri Sejba, Buf., RC**	**.05**	**.05**
363	Mark Pederson, Phi.	.05	.05
364	**Jeff Lazaro, Bos., RC**	**.10**	**.10**
365	**Alexei Gusarov, Que., RC**	**.15**	**.15**
366	Jari Kurri, LA	.10	.10
367	Owen Nolan, Que.	.25	.25
368	Clint Malarchuk, Goalie, Buf.	.05	.05
369	Patrik Sundstrom, NJD	.05	.05
370	Glen Wesley, Bos.	.05	.05
371	Wayne Presley, Chi.	.05	.05
372	Craig Muni, Edm.	.05	.05
373	Brent Fedyk, Det.	.05	.05
374	Michel Goulet, Chi.	.05	.05
375	Tim Sweeney, Cal.	.05	.05
376	**Gary Shuchuk, Det., RC**	**.10**	**.10**
377	**Andre Racicot, Goalie, Mon., RC**	**.25**	**.25**
378	**Jay Mazur, Van., RC**	**.05**	**.05**
379	Andrew Cassels, Mon.	.05	.05
380	Brian Noonan, Chi.	.05	.05
381	**Sergei Kharin, Win., RC**	**.05**	**.05**
382	Derek King, NYI	.05	.05
383	Fredrik Olausson, Win.	.05	.05

1991-92 REGULAR ISSUE — UPPER DECK

No.	Player	English NRMT	French NRMT
384	Thomas Fergus, Tor.	.05	.05
385	Zdeno Ciger, NJD	.05	.05
386	Wendel Clark, Tor.	.20	.20
387	Ed Olczyk, Win.	.05	.05
388	Basil McRae, Min.	.05	.05
389	Tom Fitzgerald, NYI	.05	.05
390	Ray Sheppard, NYR	.10	.10
391	Robert Sweeney, Bos.	.05	.05
392	Gordon Murphy, Phi.	.05	.05
393	John Chabot, Det.	.05	.05
394	Jeff Beukeboom, Edm.	.05	.05
395	Rick Zombo, Det.	.05	.05
396	Kjell Samuelsson, Phi.	.05	.05
397	Garth Butcher, St. L.	.05	.05
398	Phillippe Bourque, Pit.	.05	.05
399	Lou Franceschetti, Buf.	.05	.05
400	Checklist 4 (301 - 400)	.05	.05
401	**Kevin Todd, NJD, RC**	**.25**	**.25**
402	Ken Baumgartner, NYI	.05	.05
403	Peter Douris, Bos.	.05	.05
404	Jiri Latal, Phi.	.05	.05
405	**Marc Potvin, Det., RC**	**.10**	**.10**
406	Gary Nylund, NYI	.05	.05
407	Yvon Corriveau, Har.	.05	.05
408	Sheldon Kennedy, Det.	.05	.05
409	David Shaw, NYR	.05	.05
410	Viacheslav Fetisov, NJD	.05	.05
411	**Mario Doyon, Que., RC**	**.05**	**.05**
412	Jamie Macoun, Cal.	.05	.05
413	Curtis Leschyshyn, Que.	.05	.05
414	Mike Peluso, Chi.	.05	.05
415	Brian Benning, LA	.05	.05
416	**Stu Grimson, Chi., RC**	**.25**	**.25**
417	Ken Sabourin, Was.	.05	.05
418	Luke Richardson, Tor.	.05	.05
419	**Ken Quinney, Que., RC**	**.10**	**.10**
420	**Mike Donnelly, LA, RC**	**.20**	**.20**
421	**Darcy Loewen, Buf., RC**	**.05**	**.05**
422	Brian Skrudland, Mon.	.05	.05
423	Joel Savage, Buf.	.05	.05
424	Adrien Plavsic, Van.	.05	.05
425	Jergus Baca, Har.	.05	.05
426	Greg Adams, Van.	.05	.05
427	Tom Chorske, Mon.	.05	.05
428	Scott Scissons, NYI	.05	.05
429	Dale Kushner, Phi.	.05	.05
430	**Todd Richards, Har., RC**	**.05**	**.05**
431	Kip Miller, Que.	.05	.05
432	**Jason Prosofsky, NYR, RC**	**.05**	**.05**
433	Stephane Morin, Que.	.05	.05
434	**Brian McReynolds, NYR, RC**	**.05**	**.05**
435	Kenneth Daneyko, NJD	.05	.05
436	Chris Joseph, Edm.	.10	.10
437	Wayne Gretzky, LA	1.00	1.00
438	Jocelyn Lemieux, Chi.	.05	.05
439	Garry Galley, Bos.	.05	.05

STAR ROOKIE

No.	Player	English NRMT	French NRMT
440	**Star Rookie Checklist:** D. Weight, S. Rice, A. Amonte	.30	.30
441	Steven Rice, NYR	.10	.10
442	**Canadiens:** Patrice Brisebois	.20	.20
443	**Black Hawks:** Jim Waite, Goalie	.20	.20
444	**Rangers: Doug Weight, RC**	.50	.50
445	**Blues:** Nelson Emerson	.50	.50
446	**Devils: Jarrod Skalde, RC**	.25	.25
447	**Penguins:** Jamie Leach	.05	.05
448	**Canadiens: Gilbert Dionne, RC**	.50	.50
449	**Flames:** Trevor Kidd, Goalie	.20	.20
450	**Rangers: Anthony Amonte, RC**	.50	.50
451	**Flyers:** Pat Murray	.05	.05
452	**Nordiques:** Stephane Fiset, Goalie	.40	.40
453	**Canadiens: Patrick Lebeau, RC**	.20	.20
454	**Islanders: Chris Taylor, RC**	.05	.05
455	**Whalers: Chris Tancill, RC**	.05	.05
456	**Whalers:** Mark Greig	.10	.10
457	**Red Wings:** Mike Sillinger	.10	.10
458	**Sabres: Kenneth Sutton, RC**	.10	.10
459	**Flyers: Len Barrie, RC**	.10	.10
460	**Maple Leafs:** Felix Potvin, Goalie	2.50	2.50
461	**Capitals: Brian Sakic, RC**	.50	.50
462	**Red Wings: Viacheslav Kozlov, RC**	4.00	4.00

REGULAR ISSUE

No.	Player	English NRMT	French NRMT
463	**Matt DelGuidice, Goalie, Bos., RC**	.10	.10
464	Brett Hull, St. L.	1.00	1.00
465	**Norm Foster, Goalie, Bos., RC**	.05	.05
466	**Alexander Godynyuk, Tor., RC**	.05	.05
467	Geoff Courtnall, Van.	.05	.05
468	Frantisek Kucera, Chi.	.05	.05
469	**Benoit Brunet, Mon., RC**	.25	.25
470	**Mark Vermette, Que., RC**	.05	.05
471	Timothy Watters, LA	.05	.05
472	Paul Ranheim, Cal.	.05	.05
473	Martin Hostak, Phi.	.05	.05
474	Joe Murphy, Edm.	.10	.10
475	**Claude Bolvin, Phi., RC**	.15	.15
476	John Ogrodnick, NYR	.05	.05
477	Doug Bodger, Buf.	.05	.05
478	Shawn Cronin, Win.	.05	.05
479	Mark Hunter, Har.	.05	.05
480	Dave Tippett, Was.	.05	.05
481	Robert DiMaio, NYI	.05	.05
482	Lyle Odelein, Mon.	.05	.05
483	Joe Reekie, NYI	.05	.05
484	Randy Velischek, Que.	.05	.05
485	Myles O'Connor, NJD, RC	.10	.10
486	Craig Wolanin, Que.	.05	.05
487	Michael McPhee, Mon.	.05	.05
488	**Claude Lapointe, Que., RC**	.15	.15
489	Troy Loney, Pit.	.05	.05
490	Bob Beers, Bos.	.05	.05
491	**Sylvain Couturier, LA, RC**	.10	.10
492	**Kimbi Daniels, Phi., RC**	.10	.10
493	**Darryl Shannon, Tor., RC**	.10	.10
494	**Jim McKenzie, Har., RC**	.10	.10
495	**Don Gibson, Van., RC**	.10	.10
496	**Ralph Barahona, Bos., RC**	.10	.10
497	Murray Baron, Phi.	.05	.05
498	Yves Racine, Det.	.05	.05
499	Larry Robinson, LA	.05	.05

CHECKLISTS

No.	Player	English NRMT	French NRMT
500	Checklist 5 (401 to 500)	.05	.05
501	Canada Cup Checklist Paul Coffey, Wayne Gretzky	.25	.25

CANADA

No.	Player	English NRMT	French NRMT
502	Dirk Graham	.05	.05
503	Rick Tocchet	.05	.05
504	Eric Desjardins	.05	.05
505	Shayne Corson	.05	.05
506	Theoren Fleury	.10	.10
507	Luc Robitaille	.15	.15

U.S.A.

No.	Player	English NRMT	French NRMT
508	Tony Granato	.05	.05
509	Eric Weinrich	.05	.05
510	Gary Suter	.05	.05
511	Kevin Hatcher	.05	.05
512	Craig Janney	.05	.05
513	Darren Turcotte	.05	.05

REGULAR ISSUE

No.	Player	Englsih NRMT	French NRMT
514	**Christopher Winnes, Bos., RC**	.10	.10
515	Kelly Kisio, SJ	.05	.05
516	**Joe Day, Har., RC**	.05	.05
517	Ed Courtenay, SJ, RC	.05	.05
518	Andrei Lomakin, Phi.	.05	.05
519	Kirk Muller, Mon.	.05	.05
520	Rick Lessard, SJ	.10	.10
521	Scott Thornton, Edm.	.05	.05
522	Luke Richardson, Edm.	.05	.05
523	Mike Eagles, Win.	.05	.05
524	Michael McNeill, Que.	.05	.05
525	Ken Priestlay, Pit.	.10	.10
526	Louie DeBrusk, Edm.	.10	.10
527	Dave McLlwain, NYI	.05	.05
528	Gary Leeman, Cal.	.05	.05
529	**Adam Foote, Que., RC**	.10	.10
530	Kevin Dineen, Phi.	.05	.05
531	David Reid, Bos.	.05	.05
532	**Arturs Irbe, Goalie, SJ, RC**	1.00	1.00
533	**Mark Osiecki, Cal., RC**	.15	.15
534	Steve Thomas, NYI	.05	.05
535	Vincent Damphousse, Edm.	.10	.10
536	Stephane J.J. Richer, NJD	.05	.05
537	**Jarmo Myllys, Goalie, SJ, RC**	.10	.10
538	Carey Wilson, Cal.	.05	.05
539	Scott Stevens, NJD	.10	.10
540	Uwe Krupp, NYI	.05	.05
541	Dave Christian, St. L.	.05	.05
542	Scott Mellanby, Edm.	.05	.05
543	**Peter Ahola, LA, RC**	.10	.10
544	Todd Elik, Min.	.05	.05
545	Mark Messier, NYR	.40	.40
546	Derian Hatcher, Min.	.15	.15
547	Rod Brind'Amour, Phi.	.25	.25
548	David Manson, Edm.	.05	.05
549	Darryl Sydor, LA	.10	.10
550	Paul Broten, NYR	.05	.05
551	Andrew Cassels, Har.	.05	.05
552	**Tom Draper, Goalie, Buf., RC**	.15	.15
553	Grant Fuhr, Goalie, Tor.	.10	.10
554	Pierre Turgeon, NYI	.40	.40
555	Pavel Bure, Van.	3.00	3.00
556	Pat LaFontaine, Buf.	.40	.40
557	Dave Thomlinson, Bos.	.05	.05
558	Douglas Gilmour, Tor.	.50	.50
559	**Craig Billington, Goalie, NJD, RC**	.30	.30
560	Dean Evason, SJ	.05	.05
561	Brendan Shanahan, St. L.	.30	.30
562	Mike Hough, Que.	.05	.05
563	Dan Quinn, Phi.	.05	.05
564	Jeff Daniels, Pit.	.05	.05
565	Troy Murray, Win.	.05	.05
566	Bernie Nicholls, Edm.	.05	.05
567	Randy Burridge, Wash.	.05	.05
568	**Todd Hartje, Win., RC**	.10	.10
569	Charles Huddy, LA	.05	.05
570	Steve Duchesne, Phi.	.05	.05
571	Sergio Momesso, Van.	.05	.05
572	Brian Lawton, SJ	.05	.05
573	Ray Sheppard, Det.	.05	.05
574	Adam Graves, NYR	.60	.60
575	Roland Melanson, Goalie, Mon.	.05	.05
576	Steve Kasper, Phi.	.05	.05
577	Jim Sandlak, Van.	.05	.05
578	**Pat MacLeod, SJ, RC**	.10	.10
579	Sylvain Turgeon, Mon.	.05	.05
580	**James Black, Har., RC**	.05	.05
581	Darrin Shannon, Win.	.05	.05
582	Todd Krygier, Wash.	.05	.05
583	**Dominic Roussel, Goalie, Phi., RC**	.60	.60

YOUNG GUNS

No.	Player	English NRMT	French NRMT
584	Young Gun Checklist	.15	.15
585	Donald Audette, Buf.	.10	.10
586	Tomas Forslund, Cal.	.05	.05
587	Nicklas Lidstrom, Det., Error	.50	.50
588	**Geoff Sanderson, Har., RC**	2.50	2.50
589	**Valeri Zelepukin, NJD, RC**	.75	.75
590	Igor Ulanov, Win., RC	.20	.20
591	**Corey Foster, Phi., RC**	.15	.15
592	**Dan Lambert, Que., RC**	.15	.15
593	Pat Falloon, SJ	.50	.50
594	**Vladimir Konstantinov, Det., RC**	.25	.25
595	Josef Beranek, Edm.	.60	.60
596	Brad May, Buf.	.10	.10
597	**Jeff Odgers, SJ, RC**	.20	.20
598	**Rob Pearson, Tor., RC**	.25	.25
599	**Luciano Borsato, Win., RC**	.20	.20

404 • UPPER DECK — 1991 - 92 INSERT SETS

REGULAR ISSUE

No.	Player	English NRMT	French NRMT
600	Checklist 1 (501-600)	.05	.05
601	Peter Douris, Bos.	.05	.05
602	Mark Fitzpatrick, Goalie, NYI	.05	.05
603	Randy Gilhen, NYR	.05	.05
604	Corey Millen, LA	.25	.25
605	Jason Cirone, Win., RC	.10	.10
606	Kyosti Karjalainen, LA, RC	.10	.10
607	Garry Galley, Phi.	.05	.05
608	Brent Thompson, LA, RC	.15	.15
609	Alexander Godynyuk, Cal., RC	.10	.10

43RD NHL ALL-STAR GAME

No.	Player	English NRMT	French NRMT
610	All-Star Checklist	.40	.40
611	Mario Lemieux, Pit.	.40	.40
612	Brian Leetch, NYR	.20	.20
613	Kevin Stevens, Pit.	.10	.10
614	Patrick Roy, Goalie, Mon.	.40	.40
615	Paul Coffey, Pit.	.05	.05
616	Joe Sakic, Que.	.20	.20
617	Jaromir Jagr, Pit.	.25	.25
618	Alexander Mogilny, Buf.	.25	.25
619	Owen Nolan, Que.	.10	.10
620	Mark Messier, NYR	.20	.20
621	Wayne Gretzky, LA	.50	.50
622	Brett Hull, St. L.	.20	.20
623	Luc Robitaille, LA	.15	.15
624	Phil Housley, Win.	.05	.05
625	Ed Belfour, Goalie, Chi.	.15	.15
626	Steve Yzerman, Det.	.15	.15
627	Adam Oates, St. L.	.15	.15
628	Trevor Linden, Van.	.15	.15
629	Jeremy Roenick, Chi.	.25	.25
630	Theoren Fleury, Cal.	.10	.10
631	**Fastest Skater:** Sergei Fedorov, Det.	.30	.30
632	**Hardest Shot:** Allan MacInnis, Cal.	.10	.10
633	**Shooting Accuracy:** Raymond Bourque, Bos.	.10	.10
634	**Rapid Fire Goaltending:** Michael Richter, Goalie, NYR	.10	.10

HEROES

No.	Player	English NRMT	French NRMT
635	Alan Secord	.05	.05
636	Marcel Dionne, LA	.10	.10
637	Ken Morrow, NYI	.05	.05
638	Guy Lafleur, Mon.	.10	.10
639	Ed Mio, Goalie, NYR	.05	.05
640	Clark Gillies, NYI	.05	.05
641	Bob Nystrom, NYI	.05	.05
642	Peter Peeters, Goalie, Wash.	.05	.05
643	Ulf Nilsson, NYR	.05	.05

BLOODLINE

No.	Player	English NRMT	French NRMT
644	Stephan and Patrick Lebeau	.30	.30
645	The Sutter Brothers	.05	.05
646	Gino and Paul Cavallini	.05	.05
647	Valeri and Pavel Bure	1.50	1.50
648	Chris and Peter Ferraro	.50	.50

WORLD JUNIOR TOURNAMENT

No.	Player	English NRMT	French NRMT
649	World Junior Checklist	.30	.30

CIS

No.	Player	English NRMT	French NRMT
650	Darius Kasparaitis	.50	.50
651	Alexei Yashin	6.00	6.00
652	Nicolai Khabibulin, Goalie	.30	.30
653	Denis Metlyuk	.10	.10
654	Konstantin Korotkov	.30	.30
655	Alexei Kovalev	5.00	5.00
656	Alexander Kuzminsky	.25	.25
657	Alexander Cherbayev	.60	.60
658	Sergei Krivokrasov	.75	.75
659	Sergei Zholtok	.25	.25
660	Alexei Zhitnik	1.00	1.00
661	Sandis Ozolinch	2.00	2.00
662	Boris Mironov	.75	.75

SWITZERLAND

No.	Player	English NRMT	French NRMT
663	Pauli Jaks, Goalie	.20	.20
664	Gaetan Voisard	.10	.10
665	Nicola Celio	.10	.10
666	Marc Weber	.10	.10
667	Bernhard Schümperli	.10	.10
668	Laurent Bucher	.10	.10
669	Michael Blaha	.10	.10
670	Tiziano Gianini	.10	.10

FINLAND

No.	Player	English NRMT	French NRMT
671	Marko Kiprusoff	.10	.10
672	Janne Gronvall	.20	.20
673	Juha Ylönen	.20	.20
674	Sami Kapanen	.10	.10
675	Marko Tuomainen	.25	.25
676	Jarkko Varvio	.50	.50
677	Tuomas Grönman	.30	.30

GERMANY

No.	Player	English NRMT	French NRMT
678	Andreas Naumann	.10	.10
679	Steffan Ziesche	.10	.10
680	Jens Schwabe	.10	.10
681	Thomas Schubert	.10	.10
682	Hans-Jörg Mayer	.10	.10
683	Marc Seliger, Goalie	.20	.20

CANADA

No.	Player	English NRMT	French NRMT
684	Trevor Kidd, Goalie	.10	.10
685	Martin Lapointe	.10	.10
686	Tyler Wright	.10	.10
687	Kimbi Daniels	.10	.10
688	Karl Dykhuis	.10	.10
689	Jeff Nelson	.30	.30
690	Jassen Cullimore	.15	.15
691	Turner Stevenson	.20	.20

U.S.A.

No.	Player	English NRMT	French NRMT
692	Scott Lachance	.40	.40
693	Mike Dunham, Goalie	.85	.85
694	Brent Bilodeau	.25	.25
695	Ryan Sittler	1.00	1.00
696	Peter Ferraro	1.00	1.00
697	Pat Peake	1.75	1.75
698	Keith Tkachuk	3.50	3.50
699	Brian Rolston	1.00	1.00

CHECKLIST

No.	Player	English NRMT	French NRMT
700	Checklist 2 (601-700)	.05	.05

— 1991 COLLECTOR CARD — HOCKEY SUPERSTARS

Issued as an insert card in the regular low number foil packs.

1991 Collector Card
Card No. SP1, Glasnost on Ice

Card Size: 2 1/2" X 3 1/2"
Face: Four colour, white border
Back: Four colour; Upper Deck hologram, Number
Imprint: © 1991 The Upper Deck Co. Printed in the U.S.A. All Rights Reserved.

No.	Player	English NRMT	French NRMT
SP1	Glasnost on Ice	5.00	7.00

— 1991 - 92 INSERT SETS —

HOCKEY HEROES

The Brett Hull insert set was randomly inserted into low number foil packs. Card No. 9 was also signed and numbered with 2,500 of these cards being randomly inserted into both English and French foil packs. The Title card was a short print.

1991-92 Hockey Heroes
Title Card: "Hockey Heroes"

Card Size: 2 1/2" X 3 1/2"
Face: Four colour, white border
Back: Four colour, Hologram, Number, Resume
Imprint: © 1991 The Upper Deck Co. Printed in the U. S. A. All rights reserved.
Complete Set No.: 9
Complete Set Price:

	English	French
	25.00	25.00

BRETT HULL

No.	Player	English NRMT	French NRMT
—	Title Card: "Hockey Heroes" Brett Hull, SP	7.50	7.50
1	'83-84 Penticton's 105-Goal Man	3.00	3.00
2	1984 Feeling The Draft	3.00	3.00
3	'85-86 NCAA's Goal-Scoring Leader	3.00	3.00
4	'86-87 AHL's Rookie-of-the-Year	3.00	3.00
5	1987 A Full-Time Flame	3.00	3.00
6	'88-89 40-Goal Plateau	3.00	3.00
7	'89-90 NHL's New 70-Goal Scorer	3.00	3.00
8	'90-91 A Season With Hart	3.00	3.00
9	Hockey Heroes Checklist	3.00	3.00

— 1992 - 93 REGULAR ISSUE — UPPER DECK • 405

AUTOGRAPHED CARD
BRETT HULL

These randomly inserted autographed cards are different from the regular issue, first by the autograph, but more importantly by the diamond shape of the hologram.

1991-92 Autographed Card
Brett Hull

Card Size: 2 1/2" X 3 1/2"
Face: Four colour, white border; Name, number - / 2500
Back: Four colour, white border; Number
Imprint: © 1991 The Upper Deck Co. Printed in the U. S. A. All rights reserved.

No.	Player	English NRMT	French NRMT
—	Brett Hull, Autographed	200.00	400.00

— 1991 - 92 AWARD WINNERS —
HOLOGRAMS

Issued as inserts into the "Low" and "High" number foil packs. Card Nos. AW1 to 3 were issued in the Canadian low numbers, AW5 to 7 were issued in the American low numbers, AW 4, 8 and 9 were issued in the high numbers.

Card Size: 2 1/2" X 3 1/2"
Face: Hologram; Trophy, Name, Position
Back: Four colour; Number, Name, Resume
Imprint: © 1991 The Upper Deck Co. Printed in the U.S.A. All rights reserved.
Complete Set No.: 9
Complete Set Price: 5.00 10.00

No.	Player	EX	NRMT
AW1	Wayne Gretzky, LA, Art Ross Trophy Winner	1.00	2.00
AW2	Ed Belfour, Goalie, Chi., William M. Jennings Trophy Winner	.50	1.00
AW3	Brett Hull, St. L., Hart Trophy Winner	.75	1.50
AW4	Ed Belfour, Goalie, Chi., Calder Trophy Winner	.50	1.00
AW5	Raymond Bourque, Bos., Norris Trophy Winner	.50	1.00
AW6	Wayne Gretzy, LA, Lady Byng Trophy Winner	1.00	2.00
AW7	Ed Belfour, Goalie, Chi., Vezina Trophy Winner	.50	1.00
AW8	Dirk Graham, Frank J. Selke Trophy	.50	1.00
AW9	Mario Lemieux, Error Conn Smythe Trophy Winner	1.00	2.00
AW9	Mario Lemieux, Corrected Conn Smythe Trophy Winner	1.00	2.00

EURO STARS

This set was only available from jumbo foil packs, one card per jumbo pack, in both the low and high series.

 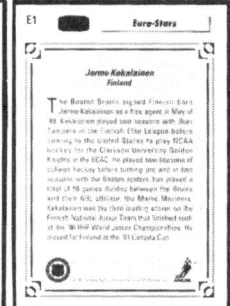

1991-92 Euro Stars, English,
Card No. E1, Jarmo Kekalainen

Card Size: 2 1/2" X 3 1/2"
Face: Four colour, white border
Back: Four colour, Hologram, Number, Resume
Imprint: © 1991 The Upper Deck Co. Printed in the U.S.A. All rights reserved.
Complete Set No.: 18
Complete Set Price: English 12.00 French 15.00

No.	Player	English NRMT	French NRMT
E1	Jarmo Kekalainen, Finland	.50	.70
E2	Alexander Mogilny, Soviet Union	2.00	2.75
E3	Robert Holik, Czechoslovakia	.50	.70
E4	Anatoli Semenov, Soviet Union	.50	.70
E5	Petr Nedved, Czechoslovakia	1.50	2.00
E6	Jaromir Jagr, Czechoslovakia	2.50	3.00
E7	Tomas Sandstrom, Sweden	.50	.70
E8	Robert Kron, Czechoslovakia	.50	.70
E9	Sergei Fedorov, Soviet Union	3.00	4.00
E10	Esa Tikkanen, Finland	.50	.70
E11	Christian Ruuttu, Finland	.50	.70
E12	Peter Bondra, Czechoslovakia	.50	.70
E13	Mats Sundin, Sweden	2.00	2.75
E14	Dominik Hasek, Czech., Goalie	3.00	4.00
E15	Johan Garpenlov, Sweden	1.00	1.25
E16	Alexander Godynyuk, Soviet Union	.50	.70
E17	Ulf Samuelsson, Sweden	.50	.70
E18	Igor Larionov, Soviet Union	1.00	1.25

— 1992 - 93 REGULAR ISSUE —

In 1992 Upper Deck divided their American foil packs into Hobby and Retail, now having five different packs. This 640-card set contains 440 cards in the Low Series and 200 cards in the High Series. The new packaging allowed for many different chase card sets. No French version was produced.

 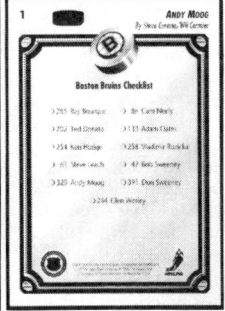

1992-93 Regular Issue
Card No. 1, Andrew Moog, Team Checklist

Card Size: 2 1/2" x 3 1/2"
Face: Four colour, white border; Name, Team logo
Back: Four colour, white border, card stock; Name, Number, Team, Position, Resume, Hologram
Imprint: Upper Deck and the card/hologram combination are trademarks of The Upper Deck Company. © The 1992 Upper Deck Company All Rights Reserved. Printed in the U.S.A.
Complete Set No.: 640
Low Series: 440
High Series: 200

Set Price:	EX	NRMT
Low Series:	12.50	25.00
High Series:	17.50	35.00
Complete Set:	30.00	60.00
Common Player:	.03	.05
Foil Pack		
Low Series: (12 Cards)		1.00
High Series: (12 Cards)		2.25
Foil Box:		
Low Series: (36 Packs)		35.00
High Series: (36 Packs)		70.00
Foil Case:		
Low Series: (20 Boxes)		600.00
High Series: (20 Boxes)		1,200.00

THE COLLECTOR'S CHOICE
TEAM CHECKLISTS

No.	Player	EX	NRMT
1	Andrew Moog, Goalie, Bos.	.03	.05
2	Donald Audette, Buf.	.03	.05
3	Tomas Forslund, Cal.	.03	.05
4	Steve Larmer, Chi.	.03	.05
5	Tim Cheveldae, Goalie, Det.	.03	.05
6	Vincent Damphousse, Edm.	.03	.05
7	Patrick Verbeek, Har.	.03	.05
8	Luc Robitaille, LA	.03	.05
9	Michael Modano, Min.	.03	.05
10	Denis Savard, Mon.	.03	.05
11	Kevin Todd, NJ	.03	.05
12	Ray Ferraro, NYI	.03	.05
13	Anthony Amonte, NYR	.03	.05
14	Peter Sidorkiewicz, Goalie, Ott.	.03	.05
15	Rod Brind'Amour, Phi.	.03	.05
16	Jaromir Jagr, Pit.	.12	.25
17	Owen Nolan, Que.	.05	.10
18	Nelson Emerson, St.L	.07	.15
19	Pat Falloon, SJ	.07	.15
20	Anatoli Semenov, TB	.05	.10
21	Douglas Gilmour, Tor.	.07	.15
22	Kirk McLean, Goalie, Van.	.05	.10
23	Donald Beaupre, Goalie, Was.	.05	.10
24	Phil Housley, Win.	.05	.10

REGULAR ISSUE

No.	Player	EX	NRMT
25	Wayne Gretzky, LA	.50	1.00
26	Mario Lemieux, Pit.	.50	1.00
27	Valeri Kamensky, Que.	.12	.25
28	Jaromir Jagr, Pit.	.35	.75
29	Brett Hull, St.L	.35	.75
30	Neil Wilkinson, SJ	.03	.05
31	Dominic Roussel, Goalie, Phi.	.12	.25
32	Kent Manderville, Tor.	.03	.05
33	1500th Assist: Wayne Gretzky, LA	.25	.50
34	Presidents' Trophy: New York Rangers	.12	.25

BLOODLINES

No.	Player	EX	NRMT
35	Kevin, Kelly, Kip Miller, Was.	.03	.05
36	Joe Sakic, Que., Brian Sakic, NYR	.12	.25
37	Keith Gretzky; Wayne Gretzky, LA Brent Gretzky, TB	.30	.60
38	Trevor Linden, Van.; Jamie Linden	.10	.20
39	Russell Courtnall, Mon.; Geoff Courtnall, Van.	.03	.05

REGULAR ISSUE

No.	Player	EX	NRMT
40	Dale Craigwell, SJ	.03	.05
41	Peter Ahola, LA	.03	.05
42	Robert Reichel, Cal.	.03	.05
43	Chris Terreri, Goalie, NJ	.03	.05
44	John Vanbiesbrouck, Goalie, NYR	.05	.10
45	Alexander Semak, NJ	.03	.05
46	Mike Sullivan, SJ	.03	.05
47	Robert Sweeney, Bos.	.03	.05

UPPER DECK — 1992-93 REGULAR ISSUE

No.	Player	EX	NRMT
48	Corey Millen, LA	.03	.05
49	Murray Craven, Har.	.03	.05
50	Dennis Vaske, NYI	.03	.05
51	**David Williams, SJ, RC**	**.03**	**.05**
52	Tom Fitzgerald, NYI	.03	.05
53	Corey Foster, Phi.	.03	.05
54	Al Iafrate, Was.	.03	.05
55	John LeClair, Mon.	.03	.05
56	Stephane J. J. Richer, NJ	.03	.05
57	Claude Boivin, Phi.	.03	.05
58	Richard Tabaracci, Goalie, Win.	.03	.05
59	Johan Garpenlov, SJ	.03	.05
60	Checklist (1-110)	.03	.05
61	Stephen Leach, Bos.	.03	.05
62	**Trent Klatt, Min., RC**	**.10**	**.20**
63	Darryl Sydor, LA	.03	.05
64	Brian Glynn, Edm.	.03	.05
65	Mike Craig, Min.	.03	.05
66	Gary Leeman, Cal.	.03	.05
67	Jimmy Waite, Goalie, Chi.	.03	.05
68	Jason Marshall, St.L	.03	.05
69	Robert Kron, Van.	.03	.05
70	**Yanic Perreault, Tor., RC**	**.25**	**.50**
71	Daniel Marois, NYI	.03	.05
72	Mark Osborne, Tor.	.03	.05
73	Mark Tinordi, Min.	.03	.05
74	Brad May, Buf.	.03	.05
75	Kimbi Daniels, Phi.	.03	.05
76	Kay Whitmore, Goalie, Har.	.03	.05
77	Luciano Borsato, Win.	.03	.05
78	Kris King, NYR	.03	.05
79	Felix Potvin, Goalie, Tor.	.75	1.50
80	Benoit Brunet, Mon.	.03	.05
81	Shawn Antoski, Van.	.03	.05
82	Randy Gilhen, NYR	.03	.05
83	Dmitri Mironov, Tor., Error	.03	.05
84	Dave Manson, Edm.	.03	.05
85	Sergio Momesso, Van.	.03	.05
86	Cam Neely, Bos.	.07	.15
87	Michael Krushelnyski, Tor.	.03	.05
88	Eric Lindros, Phi., SP	4.00	8.00
89	Wendel Clark, Tor.	.07	.15
90	Enrico Ciccone, Min.	.03	.05
91	Jarrod Skalde, NJ	.03	.05
92	Dominik Hasek, Goalie, Chi.	.25	.50
93	Dave McLlwain, Tor.	.03	.05
94	Russell Courtnall, Mon.	.03	.05
95	Tim Sweeney, Cal.	.03	.05
96	Alexei Kasatonov, NJ	.03	.05
97	Chris Lindberg, Cal.	.03	.05
98	Steven Rice, Edm.	.03	.05
99	Tahir (Tie) Domi, NYR	.03	.05
100	Paul Stanton, Pit.	.03	.05
101	Brad Schlegel, Was.	.03	.05
102	David Bruce, SJ	.03	.05

TAMPA BAY LIGHTNING

No.	Player	EX	NRMT
103	Bo Mikael Andersson	.03	.05
104	Shawn Chambers	.03	.05
105	George (Rob) Ramage	.03	.05
106	Joe Reekie	.03	.05

OTTAWA SENATORS

No.	Player	EX	NRMT
107	Sylvain Turgeon	.03	.05
108	Rob Murphy	.03	.05
109	Brad Shaw	.03	.05
110	**Darren Rumble, RC**	**.05**	**.10**

REGULAR ISSUE

No.	Player	EX	NRMT
111	**Kyosti Karjalainen, LA, RC**	**.03**	**.05**
112	Michael Vernon, Goalie, Cal.	.03	.05
113	Michel Goulet, Chi.	.03	.05
114	Garry Valk, Van.	.03	.05
115	Peter Bondra, Was.	.03	.05
116	Paul Coffey, LA	.07	.15
117	Brian Noonan, Chi.	.03	.05
118	John McIntyre, LA	.03	.05
119	Scott Mellanby, Edm.	.03	.05
120	Jim Sandlak, Van.	.03	.05
121	Mats Sundin, Que.	.12	.25
122	Brendan Shanahan, St.L	.12	.25
123	Kelly Buchberger, Edm.	.03	.05
124	Douglas Smail, Que.	.03	.05
125	Craig Janney, St.L	.05	.10
126	Michael Gartner, NYR	.03	.05
127	Alexei Gusarov, Que.	.03	.05
128	Joe Nieuwendyk, Cal.	.03	.05
129	Troy Murray, Win.	.03	.05
130	Jamie Baker, Que.	.03	.05
131	Dale Hunter, Was.	.03	.05
132	Darrin Shannon, Win.	.03	.05
133	Adam Oates, Bos.	.12	.25
134	Trevor Kidd, Goalie, Cal.	.03	.05
135	Steve Larmer, Chi.	.03	.05
136	Fredrik Olausson, Win.	.03	.05
137	Jyrki Lumme, Van.	.03	.05
138	Anthony Amonte, NYR	.10	.20
139	Calle Johansson, Was.	.03	.05
140	Robert Blake, LA	.03	.05
141	Phillippe Bourque, Pit.	.03	.05
142	Yves Racine, Det.	.03	.05
143	Richard Sutter, St.L	.03	.05
144	Joe Mullen, Pit.	.03	.05
145	Mike Richter, Goalie, NYR	.20	.40
146	Pat MacLeod, SJ	.03	.05
147	Claude LaPointe, Que.	.03	.05
148	Paul Broten, NYR	.03	.05
149	Patrick Roy, Goalie, Mon.	.25	.50
150	Douglas Wilson, SJ	.03	.05
151	Jim Hrivnak, Goalie, Was.	.03	.05
152	Joe Murphy, Edm.	.03	.05
153	Randy Burridge, Was.	.03	.05
154	Thomas Steen, Win.	.03	.05
155	Steve Yzerman, Det.	.15	.30
156	Pavel Bure, Van.	.75	1.50
157	Sergei Fedorov, Det.	.35	.75
158	Trevor Linden, Van.	.10	.20
159	Chris Chelios, Chi.	.03	.05
160	Cliff Ronning, Van.	.03	.05
161	Jeff Beukeboom, NYR	.03	.05
162	Denis Savard, Mon.	.03	.05
163	Claude Lemieux, NJ	.03	.05
164	Mike Keane, Mon.	.03	.05
165	Pat LaFontaine, Buf.	.12	.25
166	Nelson Emerson, St.L	.10	.20
167	Alexander Mogilny, Buf.	.35	.70
168	Jamie Leach, Pit.	.03	.05
169	Darren Turcotte, NYR	.03	.05
170	Checklist (111 - 220)	.03	.05
171	Steve Thomas, NYI	.03	.05
172	Brian Bellows, Min.	.03	.05
173	Mike Ridley, Was.	.03	.05
174	Dave Gagner, Min.	.03	.05
175	Pierre Turgeon, NYI	.15	.30
176	Paul Ysabaert, Det.	.03	.05
177	Brian Propp, Min.	.03	.05
178	Nicklas Lidstrom, Det.	.05	.10
179	Kelly Miller, Was.	.03	.05
180	Kirk Muller, Mon.	.03	.05
181	Bob Bassen, St.L	.03	.05
182	Tony Tanti, Buf.	.03	.05
183	Mikhail Tatarinov, Que.	.03	.05
184	Ronald Sutter, St.L	.03	.05
185	Tony Granato, LA	.03	.05
186	Curtis Joseph, Goalie, St.L	.15	.30
187	Uwe Krupp, NYI	.03	.05
188	Esa Tikkanen, Edm.	.03	.05
189	Ulf Samuelsson, Pit.	.03	.05
190	Jon Casey, Goalie, Min.	.03	.05
191	Derek King, NYI	.03	.05
192	Greg Adams, Van.	.03	.05
193	Ray Ferraro, NYI	.03	.05
194	Dave Christian, St.L	.03	.05
195	Eric Weinrich, NJ	.03	.05
196	Josef Beranek, Edm.	.12	.25
197	Tim Cheveldae, Goalie, Det.	.03	.05
198	Kevin Hatcher, Was.	.03	.05
199	Brent Sutter, Chi.	.03	.05
200	Bruce Driver, NJ	.03	.05
201	Tom Draper, Goalie, Buf.	.03	.05
202	Ted Donato, Bos.	.03	.05
203	Ed Belfour, Goalie, Chi.	.15	.30
204	Patrick Verbeek, Har.	.03	.05
205	John Druce, Was.	.03	.05
206	Neal Broten, Min.	.03	.05
207	Doug Bodger, Buf.	.03	.05
208	Troy Loney, Pit.	.03	.05
209	Mark Pederson, Phi.	.03	.05
210	Todd Elik, Min.	.03	.05
211	Ed Olczyk, Win.	.03	.05
212	Paul Cavallini, St.L	.03	.05
213	Stephan Lebeau, Mon.	.03	.05
214	David Ellett, Tor.	.03	.05
215	Douglas Gilmour, Tor.	.15	.30
216	Luc Robitaille, LA	.15	.30
217	Bob Essensa, Goalie, Win.	.03	.05
218	Jari Kurri, LA	.03	.05
219	Dimitri Khristich, Was.	.03	.05
220	Joel Otto, Cal.	.03	.05
221	Checklist (222-236)	.03	.05

WORLD JUNIOR TOURNAMENT

SWEDEN

No.	Player	EX	NRMT
222	Jonas Hoglund	.03	.05
223	Rolf Wanhainen, Goalie	.03	.05
224	Stefan Klockare	.03	.05
225	Johan Norgren	.03	.05
226	Roger Kyro	.03	.05
227	Niklas Sundblad	.03	.05
228	Calle Carlsson	.15	.30
229	Jakob Karlsson	.03	.05
230	Fredrik Jax	.10	.20
231	Bjorn Nord	.03	.05
232	Kristian Gahn	.03	.05
233	Mikael Renberg	1.50	3.00
234	Markus Näslund	.35	.75
235	Peter Forsberg	.25	.50
236	Mikael Nylander	.25	.50

REGULAR ISSUE

No.	Player	EX	NRMT
237	Stanley Cup Centennial 1893-1993	.03	.05
238	Rick Tocchet, Pit.	.03	.05
239	Igor Kravchuk, Chi.	.03	.05
240	Geoff Courtnall, Van.	.03	.05
241	Lawrence Murphy, Pit.	.03	.05
242	Mark Messier, NYR	.12	.25
243	Tom Barrasso, Goalie, Pit.	.03	.05
244	Glen Wesley, Bos.	.03	.05
245	Randy Wood, Buf.	.03	.05
246	Gerard Gallant, Det.	.03	.05
247	Kip Miller, Min.	.03	.05
248	Bob Probert, Det.	.03	.05
249	Gary Suter, Cal.	.03	.05
250	Ulf Dahlen, Min.	.03	.05
251	Dan Lambert, Que.	.03	.05
252	Robert Holik, Har.	.03	.05
253	Jimmy Carson, Det.	.03	.05
254	Kenneth Hodge Jr., Bos.	.03	.05
255	Joe Sakic, Que.	.15	.30
256	Kevin Dineen, Phi.	.03	.05
257	Allan MacInnis, Cal.	.03	.05
258	Vladimir Ruzicka, Bos.	.03	.05
259	Kenneth Daneyko, NJ	.03	.05
260	Guy Carbonneau, Mon.	.03	.05
261	Michal Pivonka, Was.	.03	.05
262	Bill Ranford, Goalie, Edm.	.03	.05
263	Petr Nedved, Van.	.10	.20
264	Rod Brind'Amour, Phi.	.10	.20
265	Raymond Bourque, Bos.	.10	.20
266	Joe Sacco, Tor.	.03	.05
267	Vladimir Konstantinov, Det.	.03	.05
268	Eric Desjardins, Mon.	.03	.05
269	David Andreychuk, Buf.	.03	.05
270	Kelly Hrudey, Goalie, LA	.03	.05
271	Grant Fuhr, Goalie, Tor.	.03	.05
272	Dirk Graham, Chi.	.03	.05
273	Frank Pietrangelo, Goalie, Har.	.03	.05
274	Jeremy Roenick, Chi.	.35	.75
275	Kevin Stevens, Pit.	.10	.20
276	Phil Housley, Win.	.03	.05
277	Patrice Brisebois, Mon	.03	.05

1992-93 REGULAR ISSUE — UPPER DECK

No.	Player	EX	NRMT
278	Viacheslav Fetisov, NJ	.03	.05
279	Doug Weight, NYR	.03	.05
280	Checklist (221-330)	.03	.05
281	Dean Evason, SJ	.03	.05
282	Martin Gelinas, Edm.	.03	.05
283	Philippe Bozon, St.L	.03	.05
284	Brian Leetch, NYR	.18	.35
285	Theoren Fleury, Cal.	.03	.05
286	Pat Falloon, SJ	.10	.20
287	Derian Hatcher, Min.	.03	.05
288	Andrew Cassels, Har.	.03	.05
289	Gary Roberts, Cal.	.03	.05
290	Bernie Nicholls, Edm.	.03	.05
291	Ronald Francis, Pit.	.03	.05
292	Tom Kurvers, NYI	.03	.05
293	Geoff Sanderson, Har.	.20	.40
294	Vyacheslav Kozlov, Det.	.35	.75
295	Valeri Zelepukin, NJ	.10	.20
296	Ray Sheppard, Det.	.03	.05
297	Scott Stevens, NJ	.03	.05
298	Sergei Nemchinov, NYR	.03	.05
299	Kirk McLean, Goalie, Van.	.10	.20
300	Igor Ulanov, Win.	.03	.05
301	Brian Benning, Phi.	.03	.05
302	Dale Hawerchuk, Buf.	.03	.05
303	Kevin Todd, NJ	.03	.05
304	John Cullen, Har.	.03	.05
305	Michael Modano, Min.	.15	.30
306	Donald Audette, Buf.	.03	.05
307	Vincent Damphousse, Edm.	.03	.05
308	Jeff Hackett, Goalie, SJ	.03	.05
309	Craig Simpson, Edm.	.03	.05
310	Donald Beaupre, Goalie, Was.	.03	.05
311	Adam Creighton, NYI	.03	.05
312	Pat Elynuik, Win.	.03	.05
313	David Volek, NYI	.03	.05
314	Sergei Makarov, Cal.	.03	.05
315	Craig Billington, Goalie, NJ	.03	.05
316	Zarley Zalapski, Har.	.03	.05
317	Brian Mullen, SJ	.03	.05
318	Rob Pearson, Tor.	.03	.05
319	Garry Galley, Phi.	.03	.05
320	James Patrick, NYR	.03	.05
321	Owen Nolan, Que.	.03	.05
322	Martin McSorley, LA	.03	.05
323	James Black, Har.	.03	.05
324	Jacques Cloutier, Goalie, Que.	.03	.05
325	Benoit Hogue, NYI	.03	.05
326	Teppo Numminen, Win.	.03	.05
327	Mark Recchi, Phi.	.18	.35
328	Paul Ranheim, Cal.	.03	.05
329	Andrew Moog, Goalie, Bos.	.03	.05
330	Shayne Corson, Mon.	.03	.05
331	Jean-Jacques Daigneault, Mon.	.03	.05
332	Mark Fitzpatrick, Goalie, NYI	.03	.05

RUSSIAN STARS

No.	Player	EX	NRMT
333	Russian Stars Checklist (342-350)	.12	.25
334	Alexei Yashin	.60	1.25
335	Darius Kasparaitis	.07	.15
336	Alexander Yudin	.10	.20
337	Sergei Bautin	.10	.20
338	Igor Korolyou	.10	.20
339	Sergei Klimovich	.10	.20
340	Andrei Nikolishin	.10	.20
341	Vitali Karamnov	.10	.20
342	Alexander Andriyevski	.10	.20
343	Sergei Sorokin	.10	.20
344	Yan Kaminsky	.20	.40
345	Andrei Trefilov	.30	.60
346	Sergei Petrenko	.12	.25
347	Ravil Khaidarov	.10	.20
348	Dmitri Frolov	.03	.05
349	Ravil Yakubov	.10	.20
350	Dmitri Yushkevich	.12	.25
351	Alexander Karpovtsev	.20	.40
352	Igor Dorofeyev	.07	.15
353	Alexander Galchenyuk	.12	.25

ROOKIE REPORT

No.	Player	EX	NRMT
354	Joseph Juneau, Bos	.35	.75
355	Pat Falloon, SJ	.12	.25
356	Gilbert Dionne, Mon.	.03	.05
357	Vladimir Konstantinov, Det.	.03	.05
358	Richard Tabaracci, Goalie, Win	.03	.05
359	Anthony Amonte, NYR	.10	.20
360	Scott Lachance, NYI	.03	.05
361	Tom Draper, Goalie, Buf.	.03	.05
362	Pavel Bure, Van.	.50	1.00
363	Nicklas Lidstrom, Det.	.03	.05
364	Keith Tkachuk, Win.	.15	.30
365	Kevin Todd, NJ	.03	.05
366	Dominik Hasek, Goalie, Chi.	.18	.35
367	Igor Kravchuk, Chi.	.03	.05
368	Shawn McEachern, Pit.	.12	.25

ICE HOCKEY WORLD CHAMPIONSHIP POOL A SENIORS

No.	Player	EX	NRMT
369	Checklist	.05	.10

GERMANY

No.	Player	EX	NRMT
370	Dieter Hegen	.05	.10
371	Stefan Ustorf	.10	.20
372	Ernst Kopf	.05	.10
373	Raimond Hilger	.05	.10

SWEDEN

No.	Player	EX	NRMT
374	Mats Sundin	.12	.25
375	Peter Forsberg	.25	.50
376	Arto Blomsten	.07	.15
377	Tommy Soderstrom, Goalie	.25	.50
378	Mikael Nylander	.25	.50

UNITED STATES

No.	Player	EX	NRMT
379	David Jensen	.03	.05
380	Christopher Winnes	.03	.05
381	Raymond LeBlanc, Goalie	.03	.05
382	Joe Sacco	.03	.05
383	Dennis Vaske	.03	.05

SWITZERLAND

No.	Player	EX	NRMT
384	Jorg Eberle	.03	.05

CANADA

No.	Player	EX	NRMT
385	Trevor Kidd, Goalie	.03	.05
386	Pat Falloon	.10	.20

REGULAR ISSUE

No.	Player	EX	NRMT
387	Rob Brown, Chi.	.03	.05
388	Adam Graves, NYR	.15	.30
389	Peter Zezel, Tor.	.03	.05
390	Checklist (331-440)	.03	.05
391	Don Sweeney, Bos.	.03	.05

TEAM U.S.A.

No.	Player	EX	NRMT
392	Sean Hill	.12	.25
393	Ted Donato	.03	.05
394	Marty McInnis	.03	.05
395	C.J. Young	.12	.25
396	Ted Drury	.12	.25
397	Scott Young	.03	.05

STAR ROOKIES

No.	Player	EX	NRMT
398	Checklist: S. Lachance; K. Tkachuk	.12	.25
399	Joseph Juneau, Bos.	.50	1.00
400	Stephen Heinze, Bos.	.03	.05
401	Glen Murray, Bos.	.03	.05
402	Keith Carney, Buf., RC	.10	.20
403	Dean McAmmond, Chi., RC	.12	.25

No.	Player	EX	NRMT
404	Karl Dykhuis, Chi.	.03	.05
405	Martin LaPointe, Det.	.03	.05
406	Scott Niedermayer, NJ	.20	.40
407	Ray Whitney, SJ, RC	.15	.30
408	Martin Brodeur, Goalie, NJ	.35	.75
409	Scott Lachance, NYI	.03	.05
410	Marty McInnis, NYI	.03	.05
411	Bill Guerin, NJ, RC	.15	.30
412	Shawn McEachern, Pit.	.12	.25
413	Denny Felsner, St.L, RC	.12	.25
414	Bret Hedican, St.L, RC	.12	.25
415	Drake Berehowsky, Tor.	.03	.05
416	Patrick Poulin, Har.	.03	.05
417	Vladimir Vujtek, Mon., RC	.07	.15
418	Steve Konowalchuk, Was., RC	.12	.25
419	Keith Tkachuk, Win.	.18	.35
420	Eugeny Davydov, Win., Error	.03	.05
421	Yanick Dupre, Phi.	.03	.05
422	Jason Woolley, Was., RC	.05	.10

BACK TO BACK

No.	Player	EX	NRMT
423	Brett Hull, St.L; Wayne Gretzky, LA	.25	.50

REGULAR ISSUE

No.	Player	EX	NRMT
424	Tomas Sandstrom, LA	.03	.05
425	Craig MacTavish, Edm.	.03	.05
426	Stu Barnes, Win.	.03	.05
427	Gilbert Dionne, Mon.	.03	.05
428	Andrei Lomakin, Phi.	.03	.05
429	Tomas Forslund, Cal.	.03	.05
430	Andre Racicot, Goalie, Mon.	.03	.05
431	Calder Memorial Trophy Winner: Pavel Bure, Van.	.50	1.00
432	Lester B. Pearson Award Winner: Mark Messier, NYR	.10	.20
433	Art Ross Trophy Winner: Mario Lemieux, Pit.	.12	.25
434	James Norris Memorial Trophy Winner: Brian Leetch, NYR	.10	.20
435	Lady Byng Memorial Trophy Winner: Wayne Gretzky, LA	.25	.50
436	Conn Smythe Trophy Winner: Mario Lemieux, Pit.	.12	.25
437	Hart Memorial Trophy Winner: Mark Messier, NYR	.07	.15
438	Vezina Trophy Winner: Patrick Roy, Goalie, Mon.	.25	.50
439	Frank J. Selke Trophy Winner: Guy Carbonneau, Mon.	.05	.10
440	William M. Jennings Trophy Winner: Patrick Roy, Goalie, Mon.	.25	.50

REGULAR ISSUE - HIGH SERIES

No.	Player	EX	NRMT
441	Russell Courtnall, Min.	.03	.05
442	Jeff Reese, Goalie, Cal.	.03	.05
443	Brent Fedyk, Phi.	.03	.05
444	Kerry Huffman, Que.	.03	.05
445	Mark Freer, Ott.	.03	.05
446	Christian Ruuttu, Chi.	.03	.05
447	Nicholas Kypreos, Har.	.03	.05
448	Mike Hurlbut, NYR, RC	.03	.05
449	Robert Sweeney, Buf.	.03	.05
450	Checklist (441 - 540)	.03	.05
451	Perry Berezan, SJ	.03	.05
452	Phillippe Bourque, NYR	.03	.05

LETHAL LINES

No.	Player	EX	NRMT
453	Mark Messier; Anthony Amonte; Adam Graves, NYR	.20	.40
454	Mario Lemieux; Kevin Stevens; Rick Tocchet, Pit.	.15	.30
455	Adam Oates; Joseph Juneau; Dmitri Kvartalnov, Bos.	.12	.25
456	Pat LaFontaine; David Andreychuk; Alexander Mogilny, Buf.	.12	.25

REGULAR ISSUE

No	Player	EX	NRMT
457	Zdeno Ciger, NJ	.03	.05
458	Pat Jablonski, Goalie TB	.03	.05

UPPER DECK — 1992-93 INSERT SETS —

No.	Player	EX	NRMT
459	Brent Gilchrist, Edm.	.03	.05
460	Yvon Corriveau, SJ	.03	.05
461	Dino Ciccarelli, Det.	.03	.05
462	David Emma, NJ	.03	.05
463	**Corey Hirsch, Goalie, NYR, RC**	**.35**	**.75**
464	Jamie Baker, Ott.	.03	.05
465	John Cullen, Tor.	.03	.05
466	**Lonnie Loach, LA, RC**	.03	.05
467	Louie DeBrusk, Edm.	.03	.05
468	Brian Mullen, NYI	.03	.05
469	Gaetan Duchesne, Min.	.03	.05
470	Eric Lindros, Phi.	2.50	5.00
471	Brian Bellows, Mon.	.03	.05
472	**Bill Lindsay, Que., RC**	**.05**	**.10**
473	Dave Archibald, Ott.	.03	.05
474	Reggie Savage, Was.	.03	.05
475	**Tommy Soderstrom, Goalie, Phi., RC**	**.15**	**.30**
476	Vincent Damphousse, Mon.	.03	.05
477	Mike Ricci, Que.	.03	.05
478	Robert Carpenter, Was.	.03	.05
479	Kevin Haller, Mon.	.03	.05
480	Peter Sidorkiewicz, Goalie, Ott.	.03	.05
481	**Peter Andersson, NYR, RC**	.07	.15
482	Kevin Miller, St.L	.03	.05
483	**Jean-Francois Quintin, SJ, RC**	.03	.05
484	Philippe Boucher, Buf.	.03	.05
485	Jozef Stumpel, Bos.	.03	.05
486	**Vitali Prokhorov, St.L, RC**	.15	.30
487	**Stan Drulia, TB, RC**	.03	.05
488	Jayson More, SJ	.03	.05
489	**Mike Needham, Pit., RC**	.07	.15
490	**Glenn Mulvenna, Phi., RC**	.03	.05
491	**Ed Ronan, Mon., RC**	.05	.10
492	**Grigori Panteleyev, Bos., RC**	.07	.15
493	**Kevin Dahl, Cal., RC**	.03	.05
494	**Ryan McGill, Phi., RC**	.05	.10
495	Robb Stauber, Goalie, LA	.03	.05
496	**Vladimir Vujtek, Edm., RC**	.05	.10
497	**Tomas Jelinek, Ott., RC**	.03	.05
498	**Patrik Kjellberg, Mon., RC**	.03	.05
499	Sergei Bautin, Win.	.03	.05
500	Robert Holik, NJ	.03	.05
501	**Guy Hebert, Goalie, St.L, RC**	.25	.50
502	**Chris Kontos, TB, RC**	.07	.15
503	**Vjateslav Butsayev, Phi., RC**	.10	.20
504	**Yuri Khmylev, Buf., RC**	.12	.35
505	**Richard Matvichuk, Min., RC**	.10	.20
506	Dominik Hasek, Goalie, Buf.	.25	.50
507	Ed Courtenay, SJ	.03	.05
508	Jeff Daniels, Pit.	.03	.05
509	**Doug Zmolek, SJ, RC**	.07	.15
510	**Vitali Karamnov, St.L, RC**	.07	.15
511	Norm Maciver, Ott.	.03	.05
512	Terry Yake, Har.	.03	.05
513	Steve Duchesne, Que.	.03	.05
514	Andrei Trefilov, Goalie, Cal.	.18	.35
515	**Jiri Slegr, Van., RC**	.03	.05
516	**Sergei Zubov, NYR, RC**	1.50	3.00
517	**Dave Karpa, Que., RC**	.05	.10
518	Sean Burke, Goalie, Har.	.03	.05
519	Adrien Plavsic, Van.	.03	.05
520	**Mikael Nylander, Har., RC**	.15	.30
521	John MacLean, NJ	.03	.05
522	**Jason Ruff, St.L, RC**	.05	.10
523	**Sean Hill, Mon., RC**	.03	.05
524	Mike Sillinger, Det.	.03	.05
525	**Daniel Laperriere, St.L, RC**	.07	.15
526	Peter Ahola, Pit.	.03	.05
527	Guy Larose, Tor.	.03	.05
528	**Tommy Sjodin, Min., RC**	.12	.25
529	Robert DiMaio, TB	.03	.05
530	Mark Howe, Det.	.03	.05
531	Gregory Paslawski, Phi.	.03	.05
532	Ron Hextall, Goalie, Que.	.03	.05
533	**Keith Jones, Was., RC**	**.07**	**.15**
534	**Chris Luongo, Ott., RC**	.07	.15
535	Anatoli Semenov, Van.	.03	.05
536	Stephane Beauregard, Goalie, Phi.	.03	.05
537	Pat Elynuik, Was.	.03	.05
538	Michael McPhee, Min.	.03	.05
539	Jody Hull, Ott.	.03	.05
540	Stephane Matteau, Chi.	.03	.05
541	Shayne Corson, Edm.	.03	.05

No.	Player	EX	NRMT
542	**Mikhail Kravets, SJ, RC**	.07	.15
543	**Kevin Miehm, St.L, RC**	.03	.05
544	Brian Bradley, TB	.03	.05
545	Mathieu Schneider, Mon.	.03	.05
546	Steve Chiasson, Det.	.03	.05
547	**Warren Rychel, LA, RC**	.12	.25
548	John Tucker, TB	.03	.05
549	Todd Ewen, Mon.	.03	.05
550	Checklist (541-640)	.03	.05
551	Petr Klima, Edm.	.03	.05
552	**Robert Lang, LA, RC**	.12	.25
553	Eric Weinrich, Har.	.03	.05

YOUNG GUNS

No.	Player	EX	NRMT
554	Checklist (555-582); Darius Kasparaitis, NYI; Vladimir Malakhov, NYI	.10	.20
555	**Roman Hamrlik, TB, RC**	.25	.50
556	Martin Rucinsky, Que.	.10	.20
557	Patrick Poulin, Har.	.03	.05
558	Tyler Wright, Edm.	.03	.05
559	**Martin Straka, Pit., RC**	.60	1.25
560	Jim Hiller, LA, RC	.05	.10
561	**Dmitri Kvartalnov, Bos., RC**	.15	.30
562	Scott Niedermayer, NJ	.15	.30
563	Darius Kasparaitis, NYI	.07	.15
564	**Richard Smehlik, Buf., RC**	.12	.25
565	Shawn McEachern, Pit.	.03	.05
566	Alexei Zhitnik, LA	.12	.25
567	**Andrei Kovalenko, Que., RC**	.18	.35
568	**Sandis Ozlinch, SJ, RC**	.25	.50
569	**Robert Petrovicky, Har., RC**	.12	.25
570	**Dimitri Yushkevich, Phi., RC**	.12	.25
571	Scott Lachance, NYI	.03	.05
572	**Nikolai Borschevsky, Tor., RC**	.25	.50
573	Alexei Kovalev, NYR	.35	.75
574	Teemu Selanne, Win.	1.00	2.00
575	**Steven King, NYR, RC**	.10	.20
576	**Guy Leveque, LA, RC**	.03	.15
577	Vladimir Malakhov, NYI	.12	.25
578	Alexei Zhamnov, Win.	.30	.65
579	**Viktor Gordijuk, Buf., RC**	.10	.20
580	**Dixon Ward, Van., RC**	.10	.20
581	**Igor Korolev, St.L, RC**	.03	.05
582	Sergei Krivokrasov, Chi.	.12	.25
583	**Rob Zamuner, TB, RC**	.07	.15

WORLD JUNIOR CHAMPIONSHIPS SWEDEN '93

No.	Player	EX	NRMT
584	**Team's Checklist:** Adrian Aucoi; Martin Lapointe; Tyler Wright	.10	.20

CANADA

No.	Player	EX	NRMT
585	Manny Legace, Goalie	.35	.75
586	Paul Kariya	3.00	6.00
587	Alexandre Daigle	3.00	6.00
588	Nathan Lafayette	.35	.75
589	Mike Rathje	.35	.75
590	Chris Gratton	1.25	2.50
591	Chris Pronger	1.25	2.50
592	Brent Tully	.25	.50
593	Rob Niedermayer	1.25	2.50
594	Darcy Werenka	.18	.35

SWEDEN

No.	Player	EX	NRMT
595	Peter Forsberg	.25	.50
596	Kenny Jonsson	.50	1.00
597	Niklas Sundstrom	.50	1.00
598	Reine Rauhala	.12	.25
599	Daniel Johansson	.12	.25

CZECHOSLOVAKIA

No.	Player	EX	NRMT
600	David Vyborny	.25	.50
601	Jan Vopat	.25	.50
602	Pavol Demitra	.25	.50
603	Michal Cerny	.17	.35
604	Ondrej Steiner	.15	.30

U.S.A.

No.	Player	EX	NRMT
605	Jim Campbell	.20	.45
606	Todd Marchant	.20	.40
607	Mike Pomichter	.15	.30
608	John Emmons	.12	.25
609	Adam Deadmarsh	.25	.50

RUSSIA

No.	Player	EX	NRMT
610	Nikolai Semin	.15	.30
611	Igor Alexandrov	.15	.30
612	Vadim Sharifjanov	.35	.75
613	Viktor Kozlov	1.00	2.00
614	Nikolai Tsulygin	.20	.40

FINLAND

No.	Player	EX	NRMT
615	Jere Lehtinen	.15	.30
616	Ville Peltonen	.15	.30
617	Saku Koivu	.50	1.00
618	Kimmo Rintanen	.15	.30
619	Jonni Vauhkonen	.15	.30

PROFILES

No.	Player	EX	NRMT
620	Brett Hull, St.L	.12	.25
621	Wayne Gretzky, LA	.25	.50
622	Jaromir Jagr, Pit.	.12	.25
623	Darius Kasparaitis, NYI	.03	.05
624	Bernie Nicholls, Edm.	.03	.05
625	Gilbert Dionne, Mon	.03	.05
626	Raymond Bourque, Bos.	.05	.10
627	Mike Ricci, Que.	.03	.05
628	Phil Housley, Win.	.03	.05
629	Chris Chelios, Chi.	.03	.05
630	Kevin Stevens, Pit.	.03	.05
631	**Roman Hamrlik, TB, RC**	.12	.25
632	Sergei Fedorov, Det.	.15	.30
633	Alexei Kovalev, NYR	.12	.25
634	Shawn McEachern, Pit.	.03	.05
635	Anthony Amonte, NYR	.03	.05
636	Brian Bellows, Mon.	.03	.05
637	Adam Oates, Bos.	.05	.10
638	Denis Savard, Mon.	.03	.05
639	Douglas Gilmour, Tor.	.12	.25
640	Brian Leetch, NYR	.10	.20

— 1992-93 INSERT SETS —

HOCKEY HEROES — WAYNE GRETZKY

This is a continuing series from the '91-92 Upper Deck with card numbers starting at 10 this season. This 10-card set consists of 9 numbered cards plus a title card. All low series regular foil packs contain the Wayne Gretzky cards (10-18). The title card is a short print card.

1992-93 Hockey Heroes, Wayne Gretzky
Wrapped in the Maple Leaf

1992-93 INSERT SETS — UPPER DECK

Card Size: 2 1/2" x 3 1/2"
Face: Four colour, white border; Name
Back: Four colour, white border, card stock; Name, Number, Resume
Imprint: Upper Deck and the card/hologram combination are trademarks of The Upper Deck Company. © 1992 The Upper Deck Company. All Rights Reserved. Printed in the U.S.A.
Complete Set No.: 10
Complete Set Price: 25.00   50.00 ☐

INSERTED IN LOW NUMBER FOIL

No.	Player	EX	NRMT
—	Title Card: "Hockey Heroes" Wayne Gretzky	6.00	12.00 ☐
10	The Untouchable Greyhound	2.50	5.00 ☐
11	17 Year Old Pro	2.50	5.00 ☐
12	Hart Trophy In NHL Debut	2.50	5.00 ☐
13	Four Cups In Five Seasons	2.50	5.00 ☐
14	Wrapped In The Maple Leaf	2.50	5.00 ☐
15	The Trade that Rocked Sports	2.50	5.00 ☐
16	Athlete of the Decade	2.50	5.00 ☐
17	New Goals	2.50	5.00 ☐
18	Checklist	2.50	5.00 ☐

HOCKEY HEROES — GORDIE HOWE

This is a continuing series from the previous set with card numbers starting at 19. Each 10-card set consists of 9 numbered cards plus a title card. All high number series regular foil packs contain the Gordie Howe cards (19-27). The title card is a short print card.

1992-93 Hockey Heroes
Card No. 19, The Early Years

Card Size: 2 1/2" x 3 1/2"
Face: Four colour, borderless; Name
Back: Four colour, borderless, card stock; Name, Number, Resume
Imprint: Upper Deck and the card/hologram combination are trademarks of The Upper Deck Company. © 1992 The Upper Deck Company. All Rights Reserved. Printed in the U.S.A.
Complete Set No.: 10
Complete Set Price: 12.50   25.00 ☐

INSERTED IN HIGH NUMBER FOIL

No.	Player	EX	NRMT
—	Title Card: "Hockey Heroes" Gordie Howe	3.50	7.00 ☐
19	The Early Years	1.00	2.00 ☐
20	Dynasty in Detroit	1.00	2.00 ☐
21	The First Production Line	1.00	2.00 ☐
22	'50s Scoring Champion	1.00	2.00 ☐
23	Six-Time Hart Trophy Winner	1.00	2.00 ☐
24	Hall of Fame	1.00	2.00 ☐
25	The Comeback	1.00	2.00 ☐
26	"Mr Hockey" and "The Great One"	1.00	2.00 ☐
27	"Hockey Heroes" Checklist	1.00	2.00 ☐

COLLECTORS CARD

The SP1 "Glasnost on Ice" card was issued in 1991-92 (see page no. 404) and it forms part of this set. The SP2 "Pavel Bure" card was inserted in all low number foil pack. The SP3 "Junior Champions" card was inserted in all high number packs.

1992-93 Collectors Card
Card No. SP2, Pavel Bure

Card Size: 2 1/2" x 3 1/2"
Face: Four colour, borderless; Title
Back: Four colour, white border; Title, Number, Stats
Imprint: © The Upper Deck Company

No.	Player	EX	NRMT
SP2	Pavel Bure, Top Vote-Getter	5.00	10.00 ☐
SP3	1993 World Junior Champions	3.00	6.00 ☐

1992 - 93 EURO ROOKIES

This 20-card insert set was obtained from all high series jumbo foil packs, one card per pack. The set is numbered ER1 to ER20. The set features the younger European stars of the NHL.

 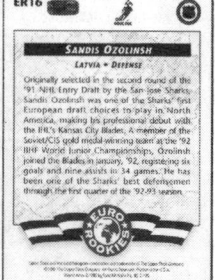

1992-93 Euro Rookies
Card No. ER16, Sandis Ozlinch

Card Size: 2 1/2" x 3 1/2"
Face: Four colour, grey border, Name, Team logo
Back: Four colour, grey border, card stock; Name, Number, Position, Resume
Imprint: Upper Deck and the card/hologram combination are trademarks of The Upper Deck Company. © 1992 The Upper Deck Company. All Rights Reserved. Printed in the U.S.A.
Complete Set No.: 20
Complete Set Price: 15.00   30.00 ☐
Common Card: .50   1.00

INSERTED IN HIGH NUMBER JUMBO FOIL

No.	Player	EX	NRMT
ER1	Richard Smehlik, Buf.	.50	1.00 ☐
ER2	Mikael Nylander, Har.	1.25	2.50 ☐
ER3	Igor Korolev, St.L	.50	1.00 ☐
ER4	Robert Lang, LA	.60	1.25 ☐
ER5	Sergei Krivokrasov, Chi.	.85	1.75 ☐
ER6	Teemu Selanne, Win.	4.00	8.00 ☐
ER7	Darius Kasparaitis, NYI	1.00	2.00 ☐
ER8	Alexei Zhamnov, Win.	2.00	4.00 ☐
ER9	Jiri Slegr, Van.	.75	1.50 ☐
ER10	Alexei Kovalev, NYR	2.50	5.00 ☐
ER11	Roman Hamrlik, TB	1.00	2.00 ☐
ER12	Dimitri Yushkevich, Phi.	.75	1.50 ☐
ER13	Alexei Zhitnik, LA	1.25	2.50 ☐
ER14	Andrei Kovalenko, Que.	1.00	2.00 ☐
ER15	Vladimir Malakhov, NYI	1.00	2.00 ☐
ER16	Sandis Ozlinch, SJ	1.50	3.00 ☐
ER17	Eugeny Davydov, Win., Error	.85	1.75 ☐
ER18	Viktor Gordijuk, Buf.	.50	1.00 ☐
ER19	Martin Straka, Bos.	1.50	5.00 ☐
ER20	Robert Petrovicky, Har.	.50	1.00 ☐

CALDER CANDIDATES

This 20-card insert set was randomly inserted into high number American Retail foil packs. The set consists of all the possible winners for the 1992-93 Calder Memorial Trophy (rookie of the year). The cards are numbered CC1 to CC20.

1992-93 Calder Candidates
Card No. CC10, Teemu Selanne

Card Size: 2 1/2" x 3 1/2"
Face: Four colour, Gold top border; Name
Back: Four colour, white top border, card stock; Name, Number, Resume
Imprint: Upper Deck and the card/hologram combination are trademarks of The Upper Deck Company. © 1992 The Upper Deck Company. All Rights Reserved. Printed in the U.S.A.
Complete Set No.: 20
Complete Set Price: 47.50   95.00 ☐
Common Card: 1.85   3.75

INSERTED IN HIGH NUMBER FOIL

No.	Player	EX	NRMT
CC1	Dixon Ward, Van.	1.85	3.75 ☐
CC2	Igor Korolev, St.L	1.85	3.75 ☐
CC3	Felix Potvin, Goalie, Tor.	6.00	12.00 ☐
CC4	Rob Zamuner, TB	1.85	3.75 ☐
CC5	Scott Niedermayer, NJ	2.50	5.00 ☐
CC6	Eric Lindros, Phi.	10.00	20.00 ☐
CC7	Alexei Zhitnik, LA	3.00	6.00 ☐
CC8	Roman Hamrlik, TB	1.85	3.75 ☐
CC9	Joseph Juneau, Bos.	5.00	10.00 ☐
CC10	Teemu Selanne, Win.	5.00	10.00 ☐
CC11	Alexei Kovalev, NYR	4.00	8.00 ☐
CC12	Vladimir Malakhov, NYI	2.50	5.00 ☐
CC13	Darius Kasparaitis, NYI	2.50	5.00 ☐
CC14	Shawn McEachern, Pit.	1.85	3.75 ☐
CC15	Keith Tkachuk, Win.	3.00	6.00 ☐
CC16	Scott Lachance, NYI	1.85	3.75 ☐
CC17	Andrei Kovalenko, Que.	1.85	3.75 ☐
CC18	Patrick Poulin, Har.	1.85	3.75 ☐
CC19	Eugeny Davydov, Win., Error	1.85	3.75 ☐
CC20	Dimitri Yushkevich, Phi.	1.85	3.75 ☐

1992 - 93 EURO STARS

992-93 Euro Stars
Card No. E1, Sergei Fedorov

UPPER DECK — 1992-93 INSERT SETS

This 20-card insert set was found in all low number jumbo foil packs, one card per pack. The set is numbered E1 to E20 and features the better stars of the game that were born in Europe.

Card Size: 2 1/2" x 3 1/2"
Face: Four colour, silver border; Name
Back: Four colour, white borderless; Name, Number
Imprint: Upper Deck and the card/hologram combination are trademarks of The Upper Deck Company. © 1992 The Upper Deck Company. All Rights Reserved. Printed in the U.S.A.
Complete Set No.: 20
Complete Set Price: 20.00 40.00
Common Card: 1.00 2.00

INSERTED IN LOW NUMBER JUMBO FOIL PACKS

No.	Player	EX	NRMT
E1	Sergei Fedorov, Det.	3.00	6.00
E2	Pavel Bure, Van.	6.25	12.50
E3	Dominik Hasek, Goalie, Chi.	2.50	5.00
E4	Vladimir Ruzicka, Bos.	1.00	2.00
E5	Peter Ahola, LA	1.00	2.00
E6	Kyosti Karjalainen, LA	1.00	2.00
E7	Igor Kravchuk, Chi.	1.00	2.00
E8	Eugeny Davydov, Win., Error	1.00	2.00
E9	Nicklas Lidstrom, Det.	1.25	2.50
E10	Vladimir Konstantinov, Det.	1.00	2.00
E11	Josef Beranek, Edm.	1.00	2.00
E12	Valeri Zelepukin, NJ	1.25	2.50
E13	Sergei Nemchinov, NYR	1.12	2.25
E14	Jaromir Jagr, Pit.	3.00	6.00
E15	Igor Ulanov, Win.	1.00	2.00
E16	Sergei Makarov, Cal.	1.00	2.00
E17	Andrei Lomakin, Phi.	1.00	2.00
E18	Mats Sundin, Que.	2.00	4.00
E19	Jarmo Myllys, SJ	1.00	2.00
E20	Valeri Kamensky, Que.	1.25	2.50

AMERI / CAN ROOKIE TEAM HOLOGRAMS

This 6-card insert set, numbered AC1 to AC6 was randomly inserted into all the high number foil packs. The hologram type cards are very popular.

1992-93 Ameri / Can Rookie Team Holograms
Card No. AC1, Joseph Juneau

Card Size: 2 1/2" X 3 1/2"
Face: Four colour, borderless; Name, Hologram
Back: Four colour, borderless, card stock; Name, Number, Position, Resume
Imprint: Upper Deck and the card/hologram combination are trademarks of The Upper Deck Company. © 1992 The Upper Deck Company. All Rights Reserved. Printed in the U.S.A.
Complete Set No.: 6
Complete Set Price: 7.50 15.00
Common Card: 1.25 2.50

INSERTED IN HIGH NUMBER FOIL PACKS

No.	Player	EX	NRMT
AC1	Joseph Juneau, Bos.	2.50	5.00
AC2	Keith Tkachuk, Win.	2.00	4.00
AC3	Steve Heinze, Bos.	1.25	2.50
AC4	Scott Lachance, NYI	1.25	2.50
AC5	Scott Niedermayer, NJ	1.50	3.00
AC6	Dominic Roussel, Goalie, Phi.	1.25	2.50

1992 - 93 ALL ROOKIE TEAM

This 7-card insert set is Upper Deck's version of their best rookies at the six positions, plus a team photograph of the six players which is used as a checklist. The cards are numbered AR1 to AR7 and can be found randomly inserted in all American low number foil packs.

1992-93 All Rookie Team
Card No. AR7, Checklist

Card Size: 2 1/2" x 3 1/2"
Face: Four colour, borderless; Name
Back: Four colour, white border; Name, Number, Team, Position, Resume
Imprint: Upper Deck and the card/hologram combination are trademarks of The Upper Deck Company. © 1992 The Upper Deck Company. All Rights Reserved. Printed in the U.S.A.
Complete Set No.: 7
Complete Set Price: 25.00 50.00
Common Card: 2.25 4.50

INSERTED IN U.S. LOW NUMBER FOIL PACKS

No.	Player	EX	NRMT
AR1	Anthony Amonte	3.25	6.50
AR2	Gilbert Dionne	2.25	4.50
AR3	Kevin Todd	2.25	4.50
AR4	Nicklas Lidstrom	3.00	6.00
AR5	Vladimir Konstantinov	2.25	4.50
AR6	Dominik Hasek, Goalie	5.00	10.00
AR7	Checklist	10.00	20.00

1992 - 93 EURO - ROOKIE TEAM

This 6-card insert set was randomly inserted in all low number foil packs. These cards are numbered ERT1 to ERT6 and are part picture and part hologram. These six selected players are Upper Deck's most promising European stars at each position.

1992-93 Euro-Rookie Team
Card No. ERT1, Pavel Bure

Card Size: 2 1/2" x 3 1/2"
Face: Four colour, blue-grey border; Hologram, Name, Team logo
Back: Two colour, blue-grey border, card stock; Name, Position, Resume
Imprint: Upper Deck and the card/hologram combination are trademarks of The Upper Deck Company. © 1992 The Upper Deck Company. All Rights Reserved. Printed in the U.S.A.
Complete Set No.: 6
Complete Set Price: 10.00 20.00
Common Player: 1.00 2.00

INSERTED IN LOW NUMBER FOIL PACKS

No.	Player	EX	NRMT
ERT1	Pavel Bure, Van.	6.25	12.50
ERT2	Nicklas Lidstrom, Det.	1.00	2.00
ERT3	Dominik Hasek, Goalie, Chi.	3.50	7.00
ERT4	Peter Ahola, LA	1.00	2.00
ERT5	Alexander Semak, NJ	1.00	2.00
ERT6	Tomas Forslund, Cal.	1.00	2.00

1992 - 93 ALL WORLD TEAM

This 6-card insert set could only be found in the low number Canadian foil packs. This is one of the hardest insert sets to put together as well as one of the more expensive. Upper Deck's quality on these cards is at the highest level. The cards are numbered W1 to W6.

1992-93 All World Team
Card No. W6, Patrick Roy

Card Size: 2-1/2' X 3-1/2"
Face: Four colour, borderless; Name
Back: Four colour, white border; Name, Number, Position, Resume
Imprint: Upper Deck and card/hologram combination are trademarks of The Upper Deck Company. © 1992 The Upper Deck Company. All Rights Reserved. Printed in the U.S.A.
Complete Set No.: 6
Complete Set Price: 20.00 40.00
Common Card: 2.00 4.00

INSERTED IN CANADIAN LOW NUMBER FOIL PACKS

No.	Player	EX	NRMT
W1	Wayne Gretzky, LA	6.00	12.00
W2	Brett Hull, St.L	3.00	6.00
W3	Jaromir Jagr, Pit.	3.00	6.00
W4	Nicklas Lidstrom, Det.	2.00	4.00
W5	Vladimir Konstantinov, Det.	2.00	4.00
W6	Patrick Roy, Goalie, Mon.	6.00	12.00

WORLD JUNIOR GRADS CLASS OF '92

This 20-card set was randomly inserted only in the Canadian high number foil packs. The cards are numbered WG1 to WG20. This insert set not only features the younger stars of the game and also the best superstars of the game.

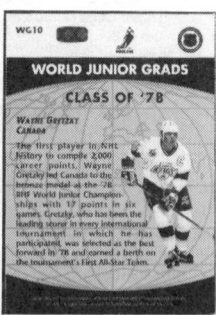

1992-93 World Junior Grads Class of '92
Card No. WG10, Wayne Gretzky

Card Size: 2 1/2" x 3 1/2"
Face: Four colour, borderless; Name, Position
Back: Four colour, borderless, card stock; Name, Number, Team, Resume
Imprint: Upper Deck and the card/hologram combination are trademarks of The Upper Deck Company. © 1992 The Upper Deck Company. All Rights Reserved. Printed in the U.S.A.
Complete Set No.: 20
Complete Set Price: 50.00 100.00
Common Card: 1.75 3.50

1992 - 1993 COMMEMORATIVE SHEETS — UPPER DECK

INSERTED IN CANADIAN HIGH NUMBER FOIL PACKS

No.	Player	EX	NRMT
WG1	Scott Niedermayer, Canada	2.50	5.00
WG2	Viacheslav Kozlov, USSR, Error	4.00	8.00
WG3	Chris Chelios, U.S.A.	1.85	3.50
WG4	Jari Kurri, Finland	1.85	3.50
WG5	Pavel Bure, USSR	9.00	18.00
WG6	Jaromir Jagr, Czechoslovakia	5.00	10.00
WG7	Steve Yzerman, Canada	4.00	8.00
WG8	Joe Sakic, Canada	3.50	7.00
WG9	Alexei Kovalev, USSR/CIS	4.00	8.00
WG10	Wayne Gretzky, Canada	11.00	22.00
WG11	Mario Lemieux, Canada	7.50	15.00
WG12	Eric Lindros, Canada	10.00	20.00
WG13	Pat Falloon, Canada	2.75	5.50
WG14	Trevor Linden, Canada	4.00	8.00
WG15	Brian Leetch, U.S.A.	4.00	8.00
WG16	Sergei Fedorov, USSR	5.00	10.00
WG17	Mats Sundin, Sweden	3.00	6.00
WG18	Alexander Mogilny, USSR	4.00	8.00
WG19	Jeremy Roenick, U.S.A.	4.50	9.00
WG20	Luc Robitaille, Canada	2.00	4.00

GORDIE HOWE SELECTS

This 20-card set was randomly inserted in American Hobby high number foil packs. The set, numbered G1 to G20, features Gordie Howe's favourite players of this year and his biography on that player is on the back of each card.

1992-93 Gordie Howe Selects
Card No. G2, Luc Robitaille

Card Size: 2 1/2" x 3 1/2"
Face: Four colour, borderless
Back: Four colour; Name, Number, Team, Resume
Imprint: Upper Deck and the card/hologram combination are trademarks of The Upper Deck Co. © 1992 The Upper Deck Company. All Rights Reserved. Printed in the U.S.A.
Complete Set No.: 20
Complete Set Price: 50.00 100.00
Common Card: 1.75 3.50

INSERTED IN HIGH NUMBER HOBBY FOIL PACKS

No.	Player	EX	NRMT
G1	Brian Bellows, Mon.	1.75	3.50
G2	Luc Robitaille, LA	2.50	5.00
G3	Pat LaFontaine, Buf.	3.00	6.00
G4	Kevins Stevens, Pit.	2.00	4.00
G5	Wayne Gretzky, LA	11.00	22.00
G6	Steve Larmer, Chi.	1.75	3.50
G7	Brett Hull, St. L	4.00	8.00
G8	Jeremy Roenick, Chi.	4.50	9.00
G9	Mario Lemieux, Pit.	7.50	15.00
G10	Steve Yzerman, Det.	4.00	8.00
G11	Joseph Juneau, Bos.	5.00	10.00
G12	Vladimir Malakhov, NYI	1.75	3.50
G13	Alexei Kovalev, NYR	4.00	8.00
G14	Eric Lindros, Phi.	10.00	20.00
G15	Teemu Selanne, Win.	6.00	12.00
G16	David Poulin, Bos.	1.75	3.50
G17	Shawn McEachern, Pit.	1.75	3.50
G18	Keith Tkachuk, Win.	3.00	6.00
G19	Andrei Kovalenko, Que.	1.75	3.50
G20	Ted Donato, Bos.	1.75	3.50

— 1992 - 1993 NHL ALL STAR LOCKER SERIES —

44TH NHL ALL STAR GAME

This 60-card set was produced after the 1992-93 NHL All Star game in Montreal. It features the Campbell and Wales Conference teams with future and past all stars. There was also a chance to win special autographed cards of Gordie Howe that were randomly inserted in these locker boxed sets.

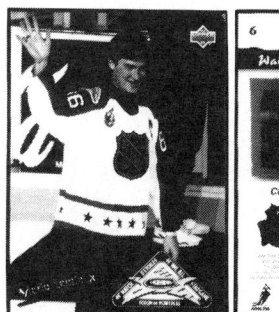

1992-93 NHL All Star Locker Series
Card No. 6, Mario Lemieux

Card Size: 2 1/2" x 3 1/2"
Face: Four colour, borderless; Name
Back: Four colour, white border, card stock; Name, Resume
Imprint: Upper Deck and the card/hologram combination are trademarks of The Upper Deck Company. © 1992 The Upper Deck Company. All Rights Reserved. Printed in the U.S.A.
Complete Set No.: 60
Complete Set Price: 12.50 25.00
Common Card: .12 .25
Locker Box: 1.00

WALES CONFERENCE ALL-STARS

No.	Player	EX	NRMT
1	Peter Bondra, Was.	.12	.25
2	Steve Duchesne, Que.	.12	.25
3	Jaromir Jagr, Pit.	.50	1.00
4	Pat LaFontaine, Buff.	.50	1.00
5	Brian Leetch, NYR	1.00	2.00
6	Mario Lemieux, Pit.	2.50	5.00
7	Mark Messier, NYR	.75	1.50
8	Alexander Mogilny, Buf.	1.50	3.00
9	Kirk Muller, Mon.	.35	.75
10	Adam Oates, Bos.	.50	1.00
11	Mark Recchi, Phi.	.50	1.00
12	Patrick Roy, Goalie, Mon.	2.50	5.00
13	Joe Sakic, Que.	.50	1.00
14	Kevin Stevens,	.35	.75
15	Scott Stevens, NJ	.12	.25
16	Rick Tocchet, Pit.	.12	.25
17	Pierre Turgeon, NJ	.50	1.00
18	Zarley Zalapski, Har.	.12	.25

CAMPBELL CONFERENCE ALL-STARS

No.	Player	EX	NRMT
19	Ed Belfour, Goalie, Chi.	1.00	2.00
20	Brian Bradley, TB	.12	.25
21	Pavel Bure, Van.	2.50	5.00
22	Chris Chelios, Chi.	.25	.50
23	Paul Coffey, Det.	.25	.50
24	Douglas Gilmour, Tor.	1.00	2.00
25	Wayne Gretzky, LA	2.50	5.00
26	Phil Housley, Win.	.12	.25
27	Brett Hull, St.L	.12	.25
28	Kelly Kisio, SJ	.12	.25
29	Jari Kurri, LA	.12	.25
30	Dave Manson, Edm.	.12	.25
31	Michael Modano, Min.	.12	.25
32	Gary Roberts, Cal.	.12	.25
33	Luc Robitaille, LA	.35	.75
34	Jeremy Roenick, Chi.	1.00	2.00
35	Teemu Selanne, Win.	2.00	4.00
36	Steve Yzerman, Det.	.35	.75

ALL STAR SKILLS

No.	Player	EX	NRMT
37	Hardest Shot: Al Iafrate, Was.	.12	.25
38	Fastest Skater: Michael Gartner, NYR	.12	.25

No.	Sheet	EX	NRTM
39	Shooting Accuracy: Raymond Bourque, Bos.	.25	.50
40	Rapid Fire: Jon Casey, Goalie, Min.	.12	.25

ALL-STAR HEROES

No.	Player	EX	NRMT
41	Bob Gainey, Mon.	.12	.25
42	Gordie Howe, Det.	.50	1.00
43	Bobby Hull, Chi.	.50	1.00
44	Frank Mahovlich, Mon.	.35	.75
45	Lanny McDonald, Cal.	.12	.25
46	Stan Mikita, Chi.	.12	.25
47	Henri Richard, Mon.	.50	1.00
48	Larry Robinson, Mon.	.12	.25
49	Glen Sather, NYR	.12	.25
50	Bryan Trottier, NYI	.12	.25

FUTURE ALL-STARS

No.	Player	EX	NRMT
51	Anthony Amonte, NYR	.35	.75
52	Pat Falloon, SJ	.25	.50
53	Joseph Juneau, Bos.	1.00	2.00
54	Alexei Kovalev, NYR	.50	1.00
55	Dmitri Kvartalnov, Bos.	.35	.75
56	Eric Lindros, Phi.	2.50	5.00
57	Vladimir Malakhov, NYI	.12	.25
58	Felix Potvin, Goalie, Tor.	1.50	3.00
59	Mats Sundin, Que.	.50	1.00
60	Alexei Zhamnov, Win.	.50	1.00

AUTOGRAPHED GORDIE HOWE

Card Size: 2 1/2" x 3 1/2"
Face: Four colour, borderless; Name
Back: Four colour, white border, card stock; Name, Resume, Hologram;
Imprint: Upper Deck and the card/hologram combination are trademarks of The Upper Deck Company. © 1992 The Upper Deck Company. All Rights Reserved. Printed in the U.S.A.
Complete Set No.: 1
Complete Set Price: 125.00 250.00

No.	Player	EX	NRMT
—	Gordie Howe	125.00	250.00

— 1992 - 1993 COMMEMORATIVE SHEETS —

These sheets were issued at home team arenas on the dates printed on the sheet. The sheets commemorate a home team game on that date. Complete sets are difficult to obtain and may command a premium.

Card Size: 8 1/2" x 11"
Face: Four colour, white border; Numbered
Back: Blank
Imprint: © 1992 The Upper Deck Company. All Rights Reserved.
Complete Set No.: 18
Complete Set Price: 112.50 225.00

No.	Sheet	EX	NRMT
1	New York Rangers '92-93	3.50	7.00
2	Quebec Nordiques vs New York Rangers, October 29, 1992	3.50	7.00
3	Vancouver Canucks vs. Los Angeles Kings, November 12, 1992	3.50	7.00
4	Pittsburgh Penguins vs. New York Rangers, October 29, 1992	3.50	7.00
5	San Jose vs. Minnesota North North Stars, November 28, 1992	3.50	7.00
6	Calgary Flames vs. Edmonton Oilers, December 8th, 1992	3.50	7.00
7	Pittsburgh Penguins vs. Philadelphia Flyers, December 17th, 1992	3.50	7.00
8	Vancouver Canucks vs New York Rangers, January 11th, 1993	3.50	7.00
9	Tampa Bay Lightning vs. Minnesota North Stars, January 30, 1993	3.50	7.00
10	Philadelphia Flyers vs. New York Rangers, February 3rd, 1993	3.50	7.00

1993 NHL ALL STAR GAME - MONTREAL FORUM

No.	Sheet	EX	NRMT
11	Campbell Conference, February 6th, 1993	5.00	10.00
12	Wales Conference, February 6th, 1993	5.00	10.00
13	St. Louis Blues vs. Washington Capitals, February 21, 1993	3.50	7.00
14	Chicago Blackhawks vs. Detroit Red Wings, February 27th, 1993	3.50	7.00
15	Ottawa Senators vs. Los Angeles Kings, March 4, 1993	3.50	7.00
16	Hartford Whalers vs. Quebec Nordiques, March 8, 1993	3.50	7.00
17	St. Louis Blues vs. Los Angeles Kings, March 20th, 1993	3.50	7.00
18	Vancouver Canucks vs. St. Louis Blues, March 30th, 1993	3.50	7.00

1992 - 93 UPPER DECK FLYERS TEAM SET

Upper Deck issued a set of 45 commemorative sheets for the Philadelphia Flyers. See page no. 622 for a listing of this team set.

— 1993 - 94 REGULAR ISSUE —

This 575-card set is divided into two series with 310 cards in the first and 265 in the second. The second series has many more rookie and world junior cards. The packaging divides the issue into American Hobby and Retail, and Canadian Issues. The Canadian foils and boxes are bilingual.

1993-94 Regular Issue Series Two
Card No. 311, Terry Yake

Size: 2 1/2" x 3 1/2"
Face: Four colour, white border; Name, Team
Back: Four colour, white border; Name, Number, Hologram, Resume
Imprint: © 1993 The Upper Deck Company. All Rights Reserved. Printed in the U.S.A.
Complete Set No.: 575
  Series One: 310
  Series Two: 265
Set Price:
  Series One: 2.50   5.00
  Series Two: 10.00   20.00
Complete Set Price: 22.50   45.00
Common Card: .03   .07
Foil Packs
  American Hobby
    Series 1 (12 Cards)   1.00
    Series 2 (12 Cards)   1.00
  American Retail
    Series 1 (12 Cards)   1.00
    Series 2 (12 Cards)   1.00
  Canadian Bilingual
    Series 1 (12 Cards)   1.00
    Series 2 (12 Cards)   1.00
Foil Boxes
  American Hobby
    Series 1 (36 Packs)   30.00
    Series 2 (36 Packs)   30.00
  American Retail
    Series 1 (36 Packs)   30.00
    Series 2 (36 Packs)   30.00
  Canadian Bilingual
    Series 1 (36 Packs)   30.00
    Series 2 (36 Packs)   30.00

SERIES ONE

No.	Players	EX	NRMT
1	Guy Hebert, Goalie, MDA	.07	.15
2	Bob Bassen, St.L	.03	.07
3	Theoren Fleury, Cal.	.03	.07
4	Ray Whitney, SJ	.03	.07
5	Donald Audette, Buf.	.03	.07
6	Martin Rucinsky, Que.	.03	.07
7	Lyle Odelein, Mon.	.03	.07
8	John Vanbiesbrouck, Goalie, Fl.	.03	.07
9	Tim Cheveldae, Goalie, Det.	.03	.07
10	Jock Callander, TB	.03	.07
11	Nicolas Kypreos, Har.	.03	.07
12	Jarrold Skalde, MDA	.03	.07
13	Gary Shuchuk, LA	.03	.07
14	Kris King, WIN	.03	.07
15	Josef Beranek, Phi.	.07	.15
16	Sean Hill, MDA	.03	.07
17	Bob Kudelski, Ott.	.03	.07
18	Jiri Slegr, Van.	.03	.07
19	Dmitri Kvartalnov, Bos.	.03	.07
20	Drake Berehowsky, Tor.	.03	.07
21	Jean-Francois Quintin, SJ	.03	.07
22	Randy Wood, Buf.	.03	.07
23	Jim McKenzie, Har.	.03	.07
24	Steven King, MDA	.03	.07
25	Scott Niedermayer, NJ	.07	.15
26	Alexander Andrijevski, Chi.	.03	.07
27	Alexei Kovalev, NYR	.20	.40
28	Steve Konowalchuk, Wash.	.03	.07
29	Vladimir Malakhov, NYI	.10	.20
30	Eric Lindros, Phi.	1.00	2.00
31	Mathieu Schneider, Mon.	.03	.07
32	Russell Courtnall, Dal.	.03	.07
33	Ronald Sutter, St. L	.03	.07
34	Radek Hamr, Ott., RC	.07	.15
35	Pavel Bure, Van.	.50	1.00
36	Joseph Sacco, MDA	.03	.07
37	Robert Petrovicky, Har.	.03	.07
38	Anatoli Fedotov, MDA, RC	.07	.15
39	Pat Falloon, SJ	.03	.07
40	Martin Straka, Pit.	.25	.50
41	Brad Werenka, Edm.	.03	.07
42	Mike Richter, Goalie, NYR	.10	.20
43	Mike McPhee, Dal.	.03	.07
44	Sylvain Turgeon, Ott.	.03	.07
45	Tom Barrasso, Goalie, Pit.	.03	.07
46	Anatoli Semenov, MDA	.03	.07
47	Joe Murphy, Chi.	.03	.07
48	Rob Pearson, Tor.	.03	.07
49	Patrick Roy, Goalie, Mon.	.25	.50
50	Dallas Drake, Det., RC	.12	.25
51	Mark Messier, NYR	.10	.20
52	Scott Pellerin, NJ, RC	.10	.20
53	Teppo Numminen, Win.	.03	.07
54	Chris Kontos, TB	.03	.07
55	Richard Matvichuk, Dal.	.03	.07
56	Dale Craigwell, SJ	.03	.07
57	Michael Eastwood, Tor.	.03	.07
58	Bernie Nicholls, NJ	.03	.07
59	Travis Green, NYI	.03	.07
60	Shjon Podein, Edm., RC	.07	.15
61	Darrin Madeley, Goalie, Ott., RC	.10	.20
62	Dixon Ward, Van.	.03	.07
63	Andre Faust, Phi.	.03	.07
64	Anthony Amonte, NYR	.03	.07
65	Joe Cirella, Fl.	.03	.07
66	Michel Petit, Cal.	.03	.07
67	Dave Lowry, Fl.	.03	.07
68	Shawn Chambers, TB	.03	.07
69	Joe Sakic, Que.	.10	.20
70	Mikael Nylander, Har.	.10	.20
71	Peter Andersson, NYR	.03	.07
72	Sandis Ozolinch, SJ	.10	.20
73	Joby Messier, NYR, RC	.07	.15
74	John Blue, Goalie, Bos.	.03	.07
75	Pat Elynuik, Wash.	.03	.07
76	Keith Osborne, TB, RC	.07	.15
77	Greg Adams, Van.	.03	.07
78	Chris Gratton, TB, RC	.25	.50
79	Louie DeBrusk, Edm.	.03	.07
80	Todd Harkins, Cal., RC	.05	.10
81	Neil Brady, Ott.	.03	.07

No.	Players	EX	NRMT
82	Philippe Boucher, Buf.	.03	.07
83	Darryl Sydor, LA	.03	.07
84	Oleg Petrov, Mon., RC	.10	.20
85	Andrei Kovalenko, Que.	.07	.15
86	David Andreychuk, Tor.	.07	.15
87	Jeff Daniels, Pit.	.03	.07
88	Kevin Todd, Edm.	.03	.07
89	Mark Tinordi, Dal.	.03	.07
90	Garry Galley, Phi.	.03	.07
91	Shawn Burr, Det.	.03	.07
92	Tom Pederson, SJ	.03	.07
93	Warren Rychel, LA	.03	.07
94	Stu Barnes, Win.	.03	.07
95	Peter Bondra, Wash.	.03	.07
96	Brian Skrudland, Fl.	.03	.07
97	Doug MacDonald, Buf.	.03	.07
98	Rob Niedermayer, Fl.	.25	.50
99	Wayne Gretzky, LA	.50	1.00
100	Peter Taglianetti, Pit.	.03	.07
101	Don Sweeney, Bos.	.03	.07
102	Andrei Lomakin, Fl.	.03	.07
103	Checklist 1 (1 - 103)	.03	.07
104	Sergio Momesso, Van.	.03	.07
105	Dave Archibald, Ott.	.03	.07
106	Karl Dykhuis, Chi.	.03	.07
107	Scott Mellanby, Fl.	.03	.07
108	Paul Di Pietro, Mon.	.03	.07
109	Neal Broten, Dal.	.03	.07
110	Chris Terreri, Goalie, NJ	.03	.07
111	Craig MacTavish, Edm.	.03	.07
112	Jody Hull, Ott.	.03	.07
113	Philippe Bozon, St. L	.03	.07
114	Geoff Courtnall, Van.	.03	.07
115	Ed Olczyk, NYR	.03	.07
116	Raymond Bourque, Bos.	.07	.15
117	Gilbert Dionne, Mon.	.03	.07
118	Valeri Kamensky, Que.	.07	.15
119	Scott Stevens, NJ	.03	.07
120	Per Erik Eklund, Phi.	.03	.07
121	Brian Bradley, TB	.03	.07
122	Steve Thomas, NYI	.03	.07
123	Donald Beaupre, Goalie, Wash.	.03	.07
124	Joel Otto, Cal.	.03	.07
125	Arturs Irbe, Goalie, SJ	.20	.40
126	Kevin Stevens, Pit.	.10	.20
127	Dimitri Yushkevich, Phi.	.03	.07
128	Adam Graves, NYR	.12	.25
129	Chris Chelios, Chi.	.03	.07
130	Jeff Brown, St. L	.03	.07
131	Paul Ranheim, Cal.	.03	.07
132	Shayne Corson, Edm.	.03	.07
133	Curtis Leschyshyn, Que.	.03	.07
134	John MacLean, NJ	.03	.07
135	Dimitri Khristich, Wash.	.03	.07
136	Dino Ciccarelli, Det.	.03	.07
137	Pat LaFontaine, Buf.	.10	.20
138	Patrick Poulin, Har.	.03	.07
139	Jaromir Jagr, Pit.	.12	.25
140	Kevin Hatcher, Wash.	.03	.07
141	Christian Ruuttu, Chi.	.03	.07
142	Ulf Samuelsson, Pit.	.03	.07
143	Ted Donato, Bos.	.03	.07
144	Bob Essensa, Goalie, Win.	.03	.07
145	Dave Gagner, Dal.	.03	.07
146	Tony Granato, LA	.03	.07
147	Ed Belfour, Goalie, Chi.	.12	.25
148	Kirk Muller, Mon	.03	.07
149	Rob Gaudreau, SJ, RC	.12	.25
150	Nicklas Lidstrom, Det.	.03	.07
151	Gary Roberts, Cal.	.03	.07
152	Trent Klatt, Dal.	.03	.07
153	Ray Ferraro, NYI	.03	.07
154	Michal Pivonka, Wash.	.03	.07
155	Mike Foligno, Tor.	.03	.07
156	Kirk McLean, Goalie, Van.	.07	.15
157	Curtis Joseph, Goalie, St.L	.10	.20
158	Roman Hamrlik, TB	.07	.15
159	Felix Potvin, Goalie, Tor.	.50	1.00
160	Brett Hull, St.L	.25	.50
161	Alexei Zhitnik, LA	.07	.15
162	Alexei Zhamnov, Win.	.20	.40
163	Grant Fuhr, Goalie, Buf.	.03	.07
164	Nikolai Borschevsky, Tor.	.07	.15

— 1993 - 94 REGULAR ISSUE — UPPER DECK • 413

No.	Players	EX	NRMT
165	Tomas Jelinek, Ott.	.03	.07
166	Thomas Steen, Win.	.03	.07
167	John LeClair, Mon.	.03	.07
168	Vladimir Vujtek, Edm.	.03	.07
169	Richard Smehlik, Buf.	.03	.07
170	**Alexandre Daigle, Ott., RC**	**.35**	**.75**
171	Sergei Fedorov, Det.	.35	.75
172	Steve Larmer, Chi.	.03	.07
173	Darius Kasparaitis, NYI	.03	.07
174	Igor Kravchuk, Edm.	.03	.07
175	Owen Nolan, Que.	.07	.15
176	Robert DiMaio, TB	.03	.07
177	Michael Vernon, Goalie, Cal.	.03	.07
178	Alexander Semak, NJ	.03	.07
179	Rick Tocchet, Pit.	.03	.07
180	Bill Ranford, Goalie, Edm.	.03	.07
181	Sergei Zubov, NYR	.25	.50
182	Tommy Soderstrom, Goalie, Phi.	.10	.20
183	Al Iafrate, Wash.	.03	.07
184	Eric Desjardins, Mon.	.03	.07
185	Bret Hedican, St. L	.03	.07
186	Joe Mullen, Pit.	.03	.07
187	Doug Bodger, Buf.	.03	.07
188	Tomas Sandstrom, LA	.03	.07
189	Glen Murray, Bos.	.03	.07
190	**Chris Pronger, Har., RC**	**.25**	**.50**
191	Mike Craig, Dal.	.03	.07
192	Jim Paek, Pit.	.03	.07
193	Doug Zmolek, SJ	.03	.07
194	Yves Racine, Det.	.03	.07
195	Keith Tkachuk, Win	.10	.20
196	Chris Lindberg, Cal.	.03	.07
197	Kelly Buchberger, Edm.	.03	.07
198	Mark Janssens, Har.	.03	.07
199	Peter Zezel, Tor.	.03	.07
200	Bob Probert, Det.	.03	.07
201	Brad May, Buf.	.03	.07
202	Rob Zamuner, TB	.03	.07
203	Stephane Fiset, Goalie, Que.	.07	.15
204	Derian Hatcher, Dal.	.03	.07
205	Michael Gartner, NYR	.07	.15
206	Checklist 2 (104 - 206)	.03	.07
207	Todd Krygier, Wash.	.03	.07
208	Glen Wesley, Bos.	.03	.07
209	Fredrik Olausson, Win.	.03	.07
210	Patrick Flatley, NYI	.03	.07
211	Cliff Ronning, Van.	.03	.07
212	Kevin Dineen, Phi.	.03	.07
213	Zarley Zalapski, Har.	.03	.07
214	Stephane Matteau, Chi.	.03	.07
215	David Ellett, Tor.	.03	.07
216	Kelly Hrudey, Goalie, LA	.03	.07
217	Steve Duchesne, Que.	.03	.07
218	Bobby Holik, NJ	.03	.07
219	Brad Dalgarno, NYI	.03	.07

POINT 100 CLUB

No.	Player	EX	NRMT
220	Checklist No. 3 (221/235)	.03	.07
221	Pat LaFontaine, Buf.	.05	.10
222	Mark Recchi, Phi.	.05	.10
223	Joe Sakic, Que.	.05	.10
224	Pierre Turgeon, NYI	.05	.10
225	Craig Janney, St. L	.05	.10
226	Adam Oates, Bos.	.05	.10
227	Steve Yzerman, Det.	.07	.15
228	Mats Sundin, Que.	.07	.15
229	Theoren Fleury, Cal.	.05	.10
230	Kevin Stevens, Pit.	.07	.15
231	Luc Robitaille, LA	.07	.15
232	Brett Hull, St. L	.07	.15
233	Rick Tocchet, Pit.	.05	.10
234	Alexander Mogilny, Buf.	.07	.15
235	Jeremy Roenick, Chi.	.07	.15

NHL STAR ROOKIE

No.	Player	EX	NRMT
236	Checklist 4 (237 - 249) G. Leveque, LA; T. Stevenson, Mon.	.03	.07
237	**Adam Bennett, Chi., RC**	**.05**	**.10**
238	**Dody Wood, SJ, RC**	**.05**	**.10**
239	**Niclas Andersson, Que., RC**	**.05**	**.10**

No.	Players	EX	NRMT
240	**Jason Bowen, Phi., RC**	**.07**	**.15**
241	**Steve Junker, NYI, RC**	**.05**	**.10**
242	**Bryan Smolinski, Bos., RC**	**.25**	**.50**
243	Chris Simon, Que., RC	.07	.15
244	Sergei Zholtok, Bos., RC	.07	.15
245	Dan Ratushny, Van., RC	.05	.10
246	Guy Leveque, LA	.03	.07
247	Scott Thomas, Buf., RC	.05	.10
248	Turner Stevenson, Mon.	.03	.07
249	Dan Keczmer, Har.	.03	.07

WORLD JUNIOR CHAMPIONSHIPS, SWEDEN '93

No.	Player	EX	NRMT
250	Checklist 5 (251 - 277) Alexandre Daigle, Ott.	.25	.50

CANADA

No.	Player	EX	NRMT
251	Adrian Aucoin	.10	.20
252	Jason Smith	.03	.07
253	Ralph Intranuovo	.12	.25
254	Jason Dawe	.07	.15
255	Jeff Bes	.25	.50
256	Tyler Wright	.03	.07
257	Martin LaPointe	.03	.07
258	Jeff Shantz	.10	.20
259	Martin Gendron	.25	.50
260	Philippe DeRouville, Goalie	.25	.50

CZECHOSLOVAKIA

No.	Player	EX	NRMT
261	Frantisek Kaberle	.07	.15
262	Radim Bicanek	.07	.15
263	Tomas Klimt	.07	.15
264	Tomas Nemcicky	.07	.15
265	Richard Kapus	.07	.15
266	Patrik Krisak	.07	.15
267	Roman Kadera	.07	.15

FINLAND

No.	Player	EX	NRMT
268	Kimmo Timonen	.07	.15
269	Jukka Ollila	.07	.15
270	Tuomas Gronman	.07	.15
271	Mikko Luovi	.07	.15

RUSSIA

No.	Player	EX	NRMT
272	Sergei Gonchar	.07	.15
273	Maxim Golanov	.07	.15
274	Oleg Belov	.07	.15
275	Sergei Klimovich	.07	.15
276	Sergei Brylin	.07	.15
277	Alexei Yashin	.50	1.00
278	Vitali Tomilin	.07	.15
279	Alexander Cherbayev	.07	.15

ALL ROOKIE TEAM

No.	Player	EX	NRMT
280	Eric Lindros, Phi.	.50	1.00
281	Teemu Selanne, Win.	.35	.75
282	Joseph Juneau, Bos.	.15	.30
283	Vladimir Malakhov	.07	.15
284	Scott Niedermayer, NJ	.10	.20
285	Felix Potvin, Goalie, Tor.	.25	.50

TEAM POINT LEADERS

No.	Player	EX	NRMT
286	Adam Oates, Bos.	.05	.10
287	Pat LaFontaine, Buf.	.05	.10
288	Theoren Fleury, Cal.	.05	.10
289	Jeremy Roenick, Chi.	.12	.25
290	Steve Yzerman, Det.	.12	.25
291	Petr Klima, Doug. Weight, Edm.	.05	.10
292	Geoff Sanderson, Har.	.07	.15
293	Luc Robitaille, LA	.07	.15
294	Michael Modano, Dal.	.07	.15
295	Vincent Damphousse, Mon.	.05	.10
296	Claude Lemieux, NJ	.05	.10
297	Pierre Turgeon, NYI	.05	.10

No.	Players	EX	NRMT
298	Mark Messier, NYR	.07	.15
299	Norm Maciver, Ott.	.05	.10
300	Mark Recchi, Phi.	.07	.15
301	Mario Lemieux, Pit.	.15	.30
302	Mats Sundin, Que.	.07	.15
303	Craig Janney, St.L	.05	.10
304	Kelly Kisio, SJ	.05	.10
305	Brian Bradley, TB	.05	.10
306	Douglas Gilmour, Tor.	.07	.15
307	Pavel Bure, Van.	.12	.25
308	Peter Bondra, Wash.	.05	.10
309	Teemu Selanne, Win.	.12	.25
310	Checklist 3 (207 - 310)	.03	.07

SERIES TWO

REGULAR ISSUE

No.	Players	EX	NRMT
311	Terry Yake, MDA	.03	.07
312	Robert Sweeney, Buf.	.03	.07
313	Robert Reichel, Cal.	.03	.07
314	Jeremy Roenick, Chi.	.20	.40
315	Paul Coffey, Det.	.03	.07
316	Geoff Sanderson, Har.	.10	.20
317	Robert Blake, LA	.07	.15
318	Patrice Brisebois, Mon.	.03	.07
319	**Jaroslav Modry, NJ, RC**	**.10**	**.20**
320	**Scott Lachance, NYI, RC**	**.07**	**.15**
321	Glenn Healy, Goalie, NYR	.03	.07
322	Martin Gelinas, Que.	.03	.07
323	Craig Janney, St. L	.03	.07
324	**Bill McDougall, TB, RC**	**.05**	**.10**
325	Shawn Antoski, Van.	.03	.07
326	Olaf Kolzig, Goalie, Wash.	.03	.07
327	Adam Oates, Bos.	.07	.15
328	Dirk Graham, Chi.	.03	.07
329	Brent Gilchrist, Dal.	.03	.07
330	Zdeno Ciger, Edm.	.03	.07
331	Patrick Verbeek, Har.	.03	.07
332	Jari Kurri, LA	.03	.07
333	Kevin Haller, Mon.	.03	.07
334	Martin Brodeur, Goalie, NJ	.20	.40
335	Norm Maciver, Ott.	.03	.07
336	Dominic Roussel, Goalie, Phi.	.10	.20
337	**Iain Fraser, Que., RC**	**.10**	**.20**
338	Vitali Karamnov, St. L	.03	.07
339	**Rene Corbet, Que., RC**	**.07**	**.15**
340	Wendel Clark, Tor.	.07	.15
341	Mike Ridley, Wash.	.03	.07
342	Nelson Emerson, Win.	.03	.07
343	Joseph Juneau, Bos.	.20	.40
344	**Vesa Viitakoski, Cal., RC**	**.07**	**.15**
345	Steve Chiasson, Det.	.03	.07
346	Andrew Cassels, Har.	.03	.07
347	Pierre Turgeon, NYI	.10	.20
348	Brian Leetch, NYR	.12	.25
349	Alexei Yashin, Ott.	.35	.75
350	Mark Recchi, Phi.	.10	.20
351	Ronald Francis, Pit.	.03	.07
352	Mike Ricci, Que.	.03	.07
353	Igor Korolev, St.L	.03	.07
354	**Brent Gretzky, TB, RC**	**.07**	**.15**
355	David Poulin, Wash.	.03	.07
356	Cam Neely, Bos.	.07	.15
357	Gary Suter, Cal.	.03	.07
358	Dave Manson, Edm.	.03	.07
359	Robert Kron, Har.	.03	.07
360	Ulf Dahlen, Dal.	.03	.07
361	Rod Brind'amour, Phi.	.10	.20
362	Alexei Gusarov, Que.	.03	.07
363	Vitali Prokhorov, St. L	.03	.07
364	**Damian Rhodes, Goalie, Tor., RC**	**.15**	**.30**
365	Paul Ysebaert, Win.	.03	.07
366	Vladimir Konstantinov, Det.	.03	.07
367	Steve Rice, Edm.	.03	.07
368	Brian Propp, Har.	.03	.07
369	Valeri Zelepukin, NJ	.03	.07
370	David Violek, NYI	.03	.07
371	Sergei Nemchinov, NYR	.03	.07
372	**Pavol Demitra, Ott., RC**	**.07**	**.15**
373	Brent Fedyk, Phi.	.03	.07

UPPER DECK — 1993-94 INSERTS SETS

No.	Players	EX	NRMT
374	Lawrence Murphy, Pit.	.03	.07
375	Dave Karpa, Que.	.03	.07
376	Dave Babych, Van.	.03	.07
377	Keith Jones, Wash.	.03	.07
378	Neil Wilkinson, Chi.	.03	.07
379	Jozef Stumpel, Bos.	.03	.07
380	Vincent Damphousse, Mon.	.03	.07
381	Tom Kurvers, NYI	.03	.07
382	Douglas Gilmour, Tor.	.15	.30
383	Trevor Linden, Van.	.10	.20
384	Kelly Miller, Wash.	.03	.07
385	Tim Sweeney, MDA	.03	.07
386	Mikhail Tatarinov, Bos.	.03	.07
387	Dominik Hasek, Goalie, Buf.	.10	.20
388	Steve Yzerman, Det.	.15	.30
389	Scott Pearson, Edm.	.03	.07
390	Brian Bellows, Mon.	.03	.07
391	Claude Lemieux, NJ	.03	.07
392	Marty McInnis, NYI	.03	.07
393	Jim Sandlak, Har.	.03	.07
394	**Jocelyn Thibault, Goalie, Que., RC**	.30	.60
395	John Cullen, Tor.	.03	.07
396	Joe Nieuwendyk, Cal.	.03	.07
397	Michael Modano, Dal.	.12	.25
398	Ray Sheppard, Det.	.03	.07
399	Trevor Kidd, Goalie, Cal.	.03	.07
400	Checklist 1 (311 - 400)	.03	.07
401	Frank Pietrangelo, Goalie, Har.	.03	.07
402	Stephan Lebeau, Mon.	.03	.07
403	Stephane J. J. Richer, NJ	.03	.07
404	Gregory Gilbert, NYR	.03	.07
405	**Dmitri Filimonov, Ott., RC**	.07	.15
406	Vjateslav Butsayev, Phi.	.03	.07
407	Mario Lemieux, Pit.	.25	.50
408	Kevin Miller, St. L	.03	.07
409	John Tucker, TB	.03	.07
410	Murray Craven, Van.	.03	.07
411	Dale Hawerchuk, Buf.	.03	.07
412	Allan MacInnis, Cal.	.03	.07
413	Keith Primeau, Det.	.03	.07
414	Luc Robitaille, LA	.10	.20
415	Benoit Brunet, Mon.	.03	.07
416	Tom Chorske, NJ	.03	.07
417	Derek King, NYI	.03	.07
418	Troy Mallette, Ott.	.03	.07
419	Mats Sundin, Que.	.10	.20
420	Kent Manderville, Tor.	.03	.07
421	Kip Miller, SJ	.03	.07
422	Jarkko Varvio, Dal.	.03	.07
423	**Jason Arnott, Edm., RC**	1.00	2.00
424	Craig Billington, Goalie, Ott.	.03	.07
425	**Stewart Malgunas, Phi., RC**	.07	.15
426	Ron Tugnutt, Goalie, MDA	.03	.07
427	**Alexei Kudashov, Tor., RC**	.07	.15
428	**Harijs Vitolinsh, Win., RC**	.07	.15
429	Bill Houlder, MDA	.03	.07
430	Craig Simpson, Buf.	.03	.07
431	Wes Walz, Cal.	.03	.07
432	**Micah Alvazoff, Det., RC**	.07	.15
433	**Scott Levins, Fl., RC**	.07	.15
434	Ron Hextall, Goalie, NYI	.03	.07
435	**Fred Brathwaite, Goalie, Edm., RC**	.10	.20
436	**Chad Penney, Ott., RC**	.12	.25
437	**Vlastimil Kroupa, SJ, RC**	.12	.25
438	Troy Loney, MDA	.03	.07
439	Matthew Barnaby, Buf.	.03	.07
440	Kevin Todd, Chi.	.03	.07
441	Paul Cavallini, Dal.	.03	.07
442	Doug Weight, Edm.	.03	.07
443	Eugeny Davydov, Fl.	.03	.07
444	Dominic Lavoie, LA	.03	.07
445	**Peter Popovic, Mon., RC**	.07	.15
446	Sergei Makarov, SJ	.03	.07
447	**Matt Martin, Tor., RC**	.07	.15
448	Teemu Selanne, Win.	.35	.75
449	Todd Ewen, MDA	.03	.07
450	**Sergei Petrenko, Buf., RC**	.07	.15
451	**Jeff Shantz, Chi., RC**	.07	.15
452	**Greg Johnson, Det., RC**	.07	.15
453	**Brent Severyn, Fl., RC**	.07	.15
454	Shawn McEachern, LA	.07	.15
455	Pierre Sevigny, Mon.	.03	.07
456	Benoit Hogue, NYI	.03	.07
457	Esa Tikkanen, NYR	.03	.07
458	Brian Glynn, Ott.	.03	.07
459	Doug Brown, Pit.	.03	.07
460	**Mike Rathje, SJ, RC**	.07	.15
461	**Rudy Poeschek, TB, RC**	.07	.15
462	Jason Woolley, Wash.	.03	.07
463	**Patrik Carnback, MDA, RC**	.07	.15
464	**Cam Stewart, Bos., RC**	.07	.15
465	Petr Svoboda, Buf.	.03	.07
466	**Ted Drury, Cal., RC**	.07	.15
467	**Ladislav Karabin, Pit., RC**	.10	.20
468	Paul Broten, Dal.	.03	.07
469	Alexander Godynyuk, Fl.	.03	.07
470	**Bob Jay, LA, RC**	.07	.15
471	Steve Larmer, NYR	.03	.07
472	**Jim Montgomery, St.L, RC**	.10	.20
473	Daren Puppa, Goalie, TB	.03	.07
474	Alexei Kasatonov, MDA	.03	.07
475	**Derek Plante, Buf., RC**	.35	.75
476	German Titov, Cal., RC	.12	.25
477	Steve Dubinsky, Chi.	.03	.07
478	Andrew Moog, Dal.	.03	.07
479	**Aaron Ward, Det., RC**	.07	.15
480	Dean McAmmond, Edm.	.03	.07
481	Randy Gilhen, Fl.	.03	.07
482	**Jason Muzzatti, Goalie, Cal., RC**	.07	.15
483	Corey Millen, NJ	.03	.07
484	Alexander Karpovtsev, NYR	.07	.15
485	**Bill Huard, Ott., RC**	.05	.10
486	Mikael Renberg, Phi.	.35	.75
487	Martin McSorley, Pit.	.03	.07
488	Alexander Mogilny, Buf.	.20	.40
489	**Michal Sykora, SJ, RC**	.12	.25
490	Checklist 2 (401 - 490)	.03	.07
491	Tom Tilley, St. L	.03	.07
492	**Boris Mironov, Win., RC**	.10	.20
493	**Sandy McCarthy, Cal., RC**	.07	.15
494	**Mark Astley, Buf., RC**	.07	.15
495	Vyacheslav Kozlov, Det.	.20	.40
496	Brian Benning, Fl.	.03	.07
497	Eric Weinrich, Chi.	.03	.07
498	**Robert Burakovsky, Ott., RC**	.07	.15
499	Patrick Lebeau, Fl.	.03	.07
500	Markus Naslund, Pit.	.07	.15
501	Jimmy Waite, Goalie, SJ	.03	.07
502	Denis Savard, TB	.03	.07
503	Jose Charbonneau, Van.	.03	.07
504	Randy Burridge, Wash.	.03	.07
505	Arto Blomsten, Win.	.03	.07
506	Shaun Van Allen, MDA	.03	.07
507	Jon Casey, Goalie, Bos.	.03	.07
508	**Darren McCarty, Det., RC**	.07	.15
509	**Roman Oksyuta, Edm., RC**	.07	.15
510	Jody Hull, Fl.	.03	.07
511	Scott Scissons NYI	.03	.07
512	Jeff Norton, NJ	.03	.07
513	Dmitri Mironov, Tor.	.03	.07
514	Sergei Bautin, Win.	.03	.07
515	Garry Valk, MDA	.03	.07
516	Keith Carney, Chi.	.03	.07
517	James Black, Dal.	.03	.07
518	Pat Peake, Wash.	.03	.07
519	**Chris Osgood, Goalie, Det., RC**	.25	.50
520	Kirk Maltby, Edm.	.07	.15
521	Gordon Murphy, Fl.	.03	.07
522	**Mattias Norstrom, NYR, RC**	.05	.10
523	**Milos Holan, Phi., RC**	.05	.10
524	Dave McLlwain, Ott.	.03	.07
525	Phil Housley, St. L	.03	.07
526	Petr Klima, TB	.03	.07
527	John McIntyre, Van.	.03	.07
528	Enrico Ciccone, Wash.	.03	.07
529	Stephane Quintal, Win.	.03	.07

WORLD JUNIOR CHAMPIONSHIPS

No.	Players	EX	NRMT
530	Checklist 3 (531 - 568) Brent Tully, Captain	.07	.15

TEAM CANADA

No.	Player	EX	NRMT
531	Anson Carter	.15	.30
532	Jeff Friesen	.75	1.50
533	Yanick Dube	.35	.75
534	Jason Botterill	.35	.75
535	Todd Harvey	.35	.75
536	Emanuel Fernandez, Goalie	.25	.50
537	Jason Allison	.35	.75
538	Jamie Storr, Goalie	1.25	2.50
539	Rick Girard	.20	.40
540	Martin Gendron	.15	.30
541	Joel Bouchard	.07	.15
542	Mike Peca	.07	.15
543	Nick Stajduhar	.25	.50
544	Brendan Witt	.25	.50
545	Aaron Gavey	.35	.75
546	Chris Armstrong	.07	.15
547	Curtis Bowen	.15	.30
548	Brandon Convery	.20	.40
549	Bryan McCabe	.12	.25
550	Marty Murray	.20	.40

TEAM U.S.A.

No.	Players	EX	NRMT
551	Ryan Sittler	.10	.20
552	Jason McBain	.07	.15
553	Richard Park	.35	.75
554	Aaron Ellis, Goalie	.07	.15
555	Toby Kvalevog, Goalie	.07	.15
556	Jay Pandolfo	.10	.20
557	John Emmons	.03	.07
558	David Wilkie	.12	.25
559	John Varga	.15	.30
560	Jason Bonsignore	.50	1.00
561	Deron Quint	.12	.25
562	Adam Deadmarsh	.12	.25
563	Joe Coleman	.10	.20
564	Bob Lachance	.07	.15
565	Chris O'Sullivan	.10	.20
566	Jamie Langenbrunner	.12	.25
567	Kevin Hilton	.12	.25
568	Kevin Adams	.25	.50

ALL WORLD JUNIORS

No.	Players	EX	NRMT
569	Saku Koivu, Finland	.25	.50
570	Mats Lindgren, Sweden	.25	.50
571	Valeri Bure, Russia	.50	1.00
572	Edvin Frylen, Sweden	.10	.20
573	Jaroslav Miklenda, Czech Republic	.12	.25
574	Vadim Sharif Janov, Russia	.15	.30
575	Checklist 3 (491 - 575)	.03	.07

— 1993 - 94 INSERTS SETS —

AWARD WINNERS

Randomly inserted into Canadian Series One packs.

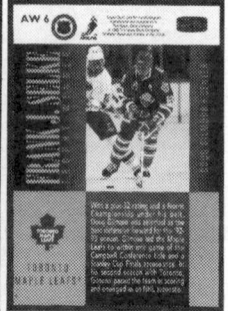

1993-94 Award Winners
Card No. AW6, Douglas Gilmour

Size: 2 1/2" x 3 1/2"
Face: Four colour, borderless; Name in silver foil, Logo
Back: Four colour; Name, Number, Team, Trophy, Resume, Hologram
Imprint: © 1993 The Upper Deck Company.
All Rights Reserved. Printed in the U.S.A.
Complete Set No.: 8
Complete Set Price: 22.50 45.00
Common Card: 1.50 3.00

No.	Players	EX	NRMT
AW1	Mario Lemieux, Pit.	6.00	12.00
AW2	Teemu Selanne, Win.	3.50	7.00
AW3	Ed. Belfour, Goalie, Chi.	2.50	5.00
AW4	Patrick Roy, Goalie, Mon	7.50	15.00
AW5	Chris Chelios, Chi.	1.50	3.00
AW6	Douglas Gilmour, Tor.	2.50	5.00
AW7	Pierre Turgeon, NYI	1.50	.300
AW8	David Poulin, Bos.	1.50	3.00

COLLECTORS CARD

The Collectors Card is another continuation set which first began in the 1991-92 season. SP1 was issued in 1991-92 and SP 2 and 3 in 1992-93. These cards were randomly inserted into all Series One packs.

PHOTOGRAPH NOT AVAILABLE AT PRESS TIME

Size: 2 1/2" x 3 1/2"
Face: Four colour, borderless; Name
Back: Four colour; Name, Number, Resume, Hologram
Imprint: © 1993 The Upper Deck Company.
All Rights Reserved. Printed in the U.S.A.

No.	Players	EX	NRMT
SP4	Teemu Selanne	2.50	5.00

FUTURE HEROES

The Future Heroes insert set is a continuation of a set first begun in the 1991-92 season. Cards nos. 1 to 9 were issued in 1991-92 and cards nos. 10 to 27 were issued in 1992-93. They were randomly inserted into Series One American Hobby packs.

1993-94 Future Heroes
Card No. 35, Joseph Juneau

Size: 2 1/2" x 3 1/2"
Face: Four colour, bronze side borders; Name, Logo
Back: Four colour; Name, Number, Position, Resume, Hologram
Imprint: © 1993 The Upper Deck Company.
All Rights Reserved. Printed in the U.S.A
Complete Set No.: 10
Complete Set Price: 95.00 190.00
Common Card: 2.50 5.00

No.	Players	EX	NRMT
—	Title Card	12.50	25.00
28	Felix Potvin, Goalie, Tor.	12.50	25.00
29	Pat Falloon, SJ	2.50	5.00
30	Pavel Bure, Van.	20.00	40.00
31	Eric Lindros, Phi.	22.50	45.00
32	Teemu Selanne, Win.	8.00	16.00
33	Jaromir Jagr, Pit.	7.50	15.00
34	Alexander Mogilny, Buf.	7.00	14.00
35	Joseph Juneau, Bos.	6.00	12.00
36	Checklist	15.00	30.00

GRETZKY'S GREAT ONES

Randomly inserted into all Series One packs.

 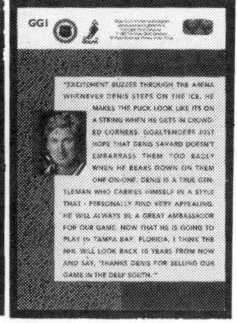

1993-94 Gretzky's Great Ones
Card No. GG1, Denis Savard

Size: 2 1/2" x 3 1/2"
Face: Four colour, borderless; Name, Logo
Back: Four colour, borderless; Number, Resume, Hologram
Imprint: © 1993 The Upper Deck Company.
All Rights Reserved. Printed in the U.S.A.
Complete Set No.: 10
Complete Set Price: 10.00 20.00
Common Card: .25 .50

No.	Players	EX	NRMT
GG1	Denis Savard, Mon.	.25	.50
GG2	Chris Chelios, Chi.	.25	.50
GG3	Brett Hull, St.L	1.50	3.00
GG4	Mario Lemieux, Pit.	4.00	8.00
GG5	Mark Messier, NYR	1.50	3.00
GG6	Paul Coffey, Pit.	.25	.50
GG7	Theoren Fleury, Cal.	.25	.50
GG8	Luc Robitaille, LA	1.00	2.00
GG9	Martin McSorley, LA	.25	.50
GG10	Grant Fuhr, Goalie, Edm.	.25	.50

HAT TRICKS

Inserted in all Series One Jumbo one per pack.

 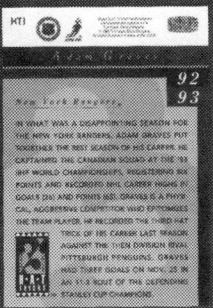

1993-94 Hat Tricks
Card No. HT1, Adam Graves

Size: 2 1/2" x 3 1/2"
Face: Four colour, Name, Logo
Back: Four colour; Name, Number, Team, Resume, Hologram
Imprint: © 1993 The Upper Deck Company.
All Rights Reserved. Printed in the U.S.A.
Complete Set No.: 20
Complete Set Price: 7.50 15.00
Common Card: .25 .50

No.	Players	EX	NRMT
HT1	Adam Graves, NYR	.50	1.00
HT2	Geoff Sanderson, Har.	.50	1.00
HT3	Gary Roberts, Cal.	.25	.50
HT4	Robert Reichel, Cal.	.25	.50
HT5	Adam Oates, Bos.	.50	1.00
HT6	Steve Yzerman, Det.	1.00	2.00
HT7	Alexei Kovalev, NYR	.75	1.50
HT8	Vincent Damphousse, Mon.	.25	.50
HT9	Rob Gaudreau, SJ	.25	.50
HT10	Pat LaFontaine, Buf.	.50	1.00
HT11	Pierre Turgeon, NYI	.50	1.00
HT12	Rick Tocchet, Pit.	.25	.50
HT13	Mikael Nylander, Har.	.25	.50
HT14	Steve Larmer, Det.	.25	.50
HT15	Alexander Mogilny, Buf.	.75	1.50
HT16	Owen Nolan, Que.	.25	.50
HT17	Luc Robitaille, LA	.35	.75
HT18	Jeremy Roenick, Chi.	1.25	2.50
HT19	Kevin Stevens, Pit.	.50	1.00
HT20	Mats Sundin, Que.	.35	.75

NEXT IN LINE

Randomly inserted into all Series One packs.

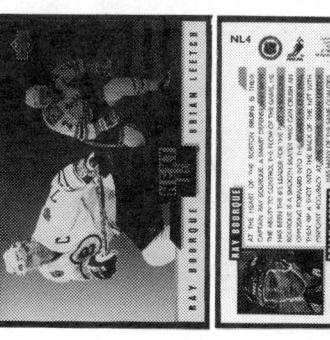

1993-94 Next in Line
Card No. NL4, R. Bourque, B. Leetch

Size: 2 1/2" x 3 1/2"
Face: Four colour, borderless; Names, Holographic picture, Logo
Back: Four colour; Names, Number, Resume, Hologram
Imprint: © 1993 The Upper Deck Company.
All Rights Reserved. Printed in the U.S.A.
Complete Set No.: 6
Complete Set Price: 20.00 40.00
Common Card: 2.00 4.00

No.	Players	EX	NRMT
NL1	Wayne Gretzky/Mats Nylander	6.00	12.00
NL2	Brett Hull/ Patrick Poulin	2.50	5.00
NL3	Steve Yzerman/Joe Sakic	3.00	6.00
NL4	Raymond Bourque/Brian Leetch	2.00	4.00
NL5	Douglas Gilmour/Keith Tkachuk	3.00	6.00
NL6	Patrick Roy/Felix Potvin, Goalies	6.00	12.00

UPPER DECK — 1993-94 INSERTS SETS

NHL'S BEST

Randomly inserted into Series One American retail packs.

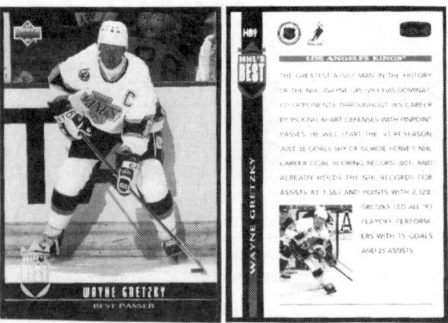

1993-94 NHL's Best
Card No. HB9, Wayne Gretzky

Size: 2 1/2" x 3 1/2"
Face: Four colour, black border at bottom; Name, Logo
Back: Four colour; Name, Number, Team, Hologram
Imprint: 1993 The Upper Deck Company.
All Rights Reserved. Printed in the U.S.A.
Complete Set No.: 10
Complete Set Price: 95.00 190.00
Common Card: 2.50 5.00

No.	Players	EX	NRMT
HB1	Alexander Mogilny, Buf.	7.00	14.00
HB2	Rob Gaudreau, SJ	2.50	5.00
HB3	Brett Hull, St.L	7.50	15.00
HB4	Dallas Drake, Det.	2.50	5.00
HB5	Pavel Bure, Van.	20.00	40.00
HB6	Alexei Kovalev, NYR	5.00	10.00
HB7	Mario Lemieux, Pit.	15.00	30.00
HB8	Eric Lindros, Phi.	22.50	45.00
HB9	Wayne Gretzky, LA	25.00	50.00
HB10	Joseph Juneau, Bos.	5.00	10.00

PROGRAM OF EXCELLENCE

Randomly inserted into Canadian Series Two packs.

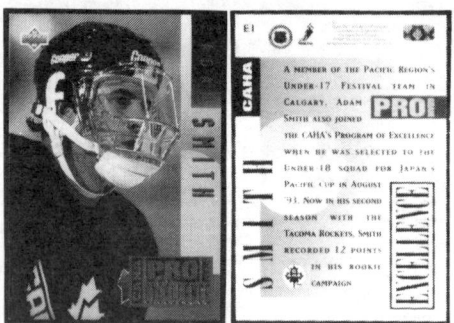

1993-94 Program of Excellence
Card No. E1, Adam Smith

Size: 2 1/2" x 3 1/2"
Face: Four colour, borderless; Name in silver foil, Logo
Back: Four colour; Name, Number, Resume, Hologram
Imprint: © 1993 The Upper Deck Company.
All Rights Reserved. Printed in the U.S.A.
Complete Set No.: 15
Complete Set Price: 110.00 220.00
Common Card: 4.00 8.00

No.	Players	EX	NRMT
E1	Adam Smith	4.00	8.00
E2	Jason Podollan	5.00	10.00
E3	Jason Wiemer	5.00	10.00
E4	Jeff O'Neill	9.00	18.00
E5	Daniel Goneau	4.00	8.00
E6	Christian Laflamme	4.00	8.00
E7	Daymond Langkow	7.00	14.00
E8	Jeff Friesen	9.00	18.00
E9	Wayne Primeau	7.50	15.00
E10	Paul Kariya	12.50	25.00
E11	Rob Niedermayer	5.00	10.00
E12	Eric Lindros	25.00	50.00
E13	Mario Lemieux	15.00	30.00
E14	Steve Yzerman	9.00	18.00
E15	Alexandre Daigle	6.00	12.00

SILVER SKATES

Randomly inserted into Series Two American Hobby packs.

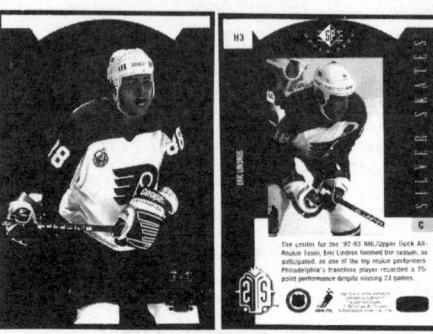

1993-94 Silver Skates American Hobby
Card No. H3, Eric Lindros

Size: 2 1/2" x 3 1/2"
Face: Four colour; Silver foil heading, Name, Logo
Back: Four colour; Name, Number, Resume, Hologram
Imprint: © 1993 The Upper Deck Company.
All Rights Reserved. Printed in the U.S.A.
Complete Set No.: 10
Complete Set Price: 80.00 160.00
Common Card: 6.00 12.00

No.	Players	EX	NRMT
H1	Mario Lemieux, Pit	15.00	30.00
H2	Pavel Bure, Van.	16.00	32.00
H3	Eric Lindros, Phi.	20.00	40.00
H4	Rob Niedermayer, Fl.	6.00	12.00
H5	Chris Pronger, Edm.	6.00	12.00
H6	Adam Oates, Bos.	6.00	12.00
H7	Pierre Turgeon, NYI	6.00	12.00
H8	Alexei Yashin, Ott.	7.50	15.00
H9	Joe Sakic, Que.	6.00	12.00
H10	Alexander Mogilny, Buf.	6.00	12.00
—	Gold Trade Card/Gretzky	30.00	60.00
—	Silver Trade Card/Gretzky	22.50	45.00

GOLD AND SILVER SKATES

These cards were randomly inserted into Series Two American Retail packs. Inserted into American Series Two Hobby foil packs are redemption cards that may be redeemed for either a Silver Skates American Retail or a Gold Silver Skates American Retail set.

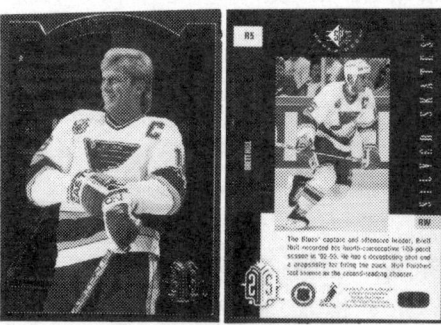

1993-94 Silver Skates American Retail
Card No. R5, Brett Hull

Size: 2 1/2" x 3 1/2"
Face: Four colour, silver or gold heading; Name, Logo
Back: Four colour; Name, Number, Resume, Hologram
Imprint: © 1993 The Upper Deck Company.
All Rights Reserved. Printed in the U.S.A.
Complete Set No.: 10
Complete Set Price: Silver 150.00 Gold 250.00
Common Card: 12.00 16.00

No.	Players	Silver NRMT	Gold NRMT
R1	Wayne Gretzky, LA	45.00	75.00
R2	Teemu Selanne, Win	15.00	20.00
R3	Alexandre Daigle, Ott.	15.00	20.00
R4	Chris Gratton, TB	12.00	16.00
R5	Brett Hull, St.L	15.00	20.00
R6	Steve Yzerman, Det.	18.00	25.00
R7	Douglas Gilmour, Tor.	18.00	25.00
R8	Jaromir Jagr, Pit.	18.00	25.00
R9	Jason Arnott, Edm.	25.00	35.00
R10	Jeremy Roenick, Chi.	18.00	25.00

SPECIAL PRINT

One card was randomly inserted into all Series Two foil packs

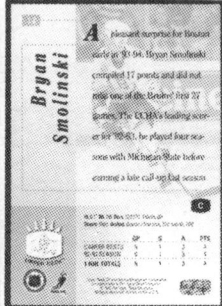

1993-94 Special Print
Card No. 12, Bryan Smolinski

Card Size: 2 1/2" x 3 1/2"
Face: Four colour, borderless; Name, Position, Silver foil logo
Back: Four colour; Number, Resume, logo on card stock
Imprint: ©1993 The Upper Deck Company.
All rights reserved. Printed in the U.S.A.
Complete Set No.: 180
Complete Set Price: 70.00 140.00
Common Card: .15 .30

MIGHTY DUCKS OF ANAHEIM

No.	Players	EX	NRMT
1	Sean Hill	.15	.30
2	Troy Loney	.15	.30
3	Joseph Sacco	.15	.30
4	Anatoli Semenov	.15	.30
5	Ron Tugnutt, Goalie	.15	.30
6	Terry Yake	.15	.30

BOSTON BRUINS

No.	Players	EX	NRMT
7	Raymond Bourque	.50	1.00
8	Jon Casey, Goalie	.15	.30
9	Joseph Juneau	1.00	2.00
10	Cam Neely	.25	.50
11	Adam Oates	.35	.75
12	Bryan Smolinski	.75	1.50

BUFFALO

No.	Player	EX	NRMT
13	Matthew Barnaby	.15	.30
14	Philippe Boucher	.15	.30
15	Grant Fuhr, Goalie	.15	.30
16	Dale Hawerchuk	.15	.30
17	Pat LaFontaine	.35	.75
18	Alexander Mogilny	.75	1.50
19	Craig Simpson	.15	.30

CALGARY FLAMES

No.	Player	EX	NRMT
20	Ted Drury	.15	.30
21	Theoren Fleury	.15	.30
22	Allan MacInnis	.15	.30
23	Joe Nieuwendyk	.15	.30
24	Joel Otto	.15	.30
25	Gary Roberts	.15	.30
26	Vesa Viitakoski	.15	.30

CHICAGO BLACK HAWKS

No.	Player	EX	NRMT
27	Ed. Belfour, Goalie	.35	.75
28	Chris Chelios	.15	.30
29	Joe Murphy	.15	.30
30	Patrick Poulin	.15	.30
31	Jeremy Roenick	1.00	2.00
32	Jeff Shantz	.15	.30
33	Kevin Todd	.15	.30

DALLAS STARS

No.	Player	EX	NRMT
34	Neal Broten	.15	.30
35	Paul Cavallini	.15	.30
36	Russell Courtnall	.15	.30
37	Derian Hatcher	.15	.30
38	Michael Modano	.50	1.00
39	Andrew Moog, Goalie	.15	.30
40	Jurkko Varvio	.15	.30

DETROIT RED WINGS

No.	Player	EX	NRMT
41	Dino Ciccarelli	.15	.30
42	Paul Coffey	.25	.50
43	Dallas Drake	.25	.50
44	Sergei Fedorov	1.50	3.00
45	Keith Primeau	.25	.50
46	Bob Probert	.15	.30
47	Steve Yzerman	.75	1.50

EDMONTON OILERS

No.	Player	EX	NRMT
48	Jason Arnott	4.50	9.00
49	Shayne Corson	.15	.30
50	Dave Manson	.15	.30
51	Dean McAmmond	.15	.30
52	Bill Ranford, Goalie	.15	.30
53	Doug Weight	.15	.30
54	Brad Werenka	.15	.30

FLORIDA PANTHERS

No.	Player	EX	NRMT
55	Eugeny Davydov	.15	.30
56	Scott Levins	.15	.30
57	Scott Mellanby	.15	.30
58	Rob Niedermayer	1.00	2.00
59	Brian Skrudland	.15	.30
60	John Vanbiesbrouck, Goalie	.50	1.00

HARTFORD WHALERS

No.	Player	EX	NRMT
61	Robert Kron	.15	.30
62	Michael Nylander	.35	.75
63	Robert Petrovicky	.15	.30
64	Chris Pronger	.15	.30
65	Geoff Sanderson	.35	.75
66	Darren Turcotte	.15	.30
67	Patrick Verbeek	.15	.30

LOS ANGELES KINGS

No.	Player	EX	NRMT
68	Robert Blake	.15	.30
69	Tony Granato	.15	.30
70	Wayne Gretzky	6.00	12.00
71	Kelly Hrudey, Goalie	.15	.30
72	Shawn McEachern	.25	.50
73	Luc Robitaille	.35	.75
74	Darryl Sydor	.15	.30
75	Alexei Zhitnik	.25	.50

MONTREAL CANADIENS

No.	Player	EX	NRMT
76	Brian Bellows	.15	.30
77	Vincent Damphousse	.15	.30
78	Stephan Lebeau	.15	.30
79	John Leclair	.15	.30
80	Kirk Muller	.15	.30
81	Patrick Roy, Goalie	4.00	8.00
82	Pierre Seveigny	.15	.30

NEW JERSEY DEVILS

No.	Player	EX	NRMT
83	Claude Lemieux	.15	.30
84	Corey Millen	.15	.30
85	Bernie Nicholls	.15	.30
86	Scott Niedermayer	1.00	2.00
87	Stephane J. J. Richer	.15	.30
88	Alexander Semak	.15	.30
89	Scott Stevens	.15	.30

NEW YORK ISLANDERS

No.	Player	EX	NRMT
90	Ray Ferraro	.15	.30
91	Darius Kasparaitis	.15	.30
92	Scott Lachance	.15	.30
93	Vladimir Malakhov	.25	.50
94	Marty McInnis	.15	.30
95	Steve Thomas	.15	.30
96	Pierre Turgeon	.35	.75

NEW YORK RANGERS

No.	Player	EX	NRMT
97	Anthony Amonte	.15	.30
98	Michael Gartner	.15	.30
99	Adam Graves	.35	.75
100	Alexander Karpovtsev	.25	.50
101	Alexei Kovalev	.75	1.50
102	Brian Leetch	.75	1.50
103	Mark Messier	.50	1.00
104	Essa Tikkanen	.15	.30

OTTAWA SENATORS

No.	Player	EX	NRMT
105	Craig Billington, Goalie	.15	.30
106	Robert Burakovsky	.15	.30
107	Alexandre Daigle	1.25	2.50
108	Pavel Demitra	.15	.30
109	Alexei Kovalev	.15	.30
110	Bob Kudelski	.15	.30
111	Norm Maciver	.15	.30
112	Alexei Yashin	1.75	3.50

PHILADELPHIA FLYERS

No.	Player	EX	NRMT
113	Josef Beranek	.15	.30
114	Rod Brind'Amour	.25	.50
115	Milos Holan	.15	.30
116	Eric Lindros	6.00	12.00
117	Mark Recchi	.50	1.00
118	Mikael Renberg	2.00	4.00
119	Dimitri Yushkevich	.15	.30

PITTSBURGH PENGUINS

No.	Player	EX	NRMT
120	Tom Barrasso, Goalie	.15	.30
121	Jaromir Jagr	1.00	2.00
122	Mario Lemieux	4.00	8.00
123	Markus Naslund	.25	.50
124	Kevin Stevens	.35	.75
125	Martin Straka	.35	.75
126	Rick Tocchet	.15	.30

QUEBEC NORDIQUES

No.	Player	EX	NRMT
127	Martin Gelinas	.15	.30
128	Owen Nolan	.15	.30
129	Mike Ricci	.15	.30
130	Joe Sakic	.35	.75
131	Chris Simon	.15	.30
132	Mats Sundin	.35	.75
133	Jocelyn Thibault, Goalie	1.50	3.00

ST. LOUIS BLUES

No.	Player	EX	NRMT
134	Philippe Bozon	.15	.30
135	Jeff Brown	.15	.30
136	Phil Housley	.15	.30
137	Brett Hull	1.50	3.00
138	Craig Janney	.15	.30
139	Curtis Joseph, Goalie	.50	1.00
140	Brendan Shanahan	.35	.75

SAN JOSE SHARKS

No.	Player	EX	NRMT
141	Pat Falloon	.15	.30
142	Johan Garpenlov	.15	.30
143	Rob Gaudreau	.15	.30
144	Vlastimal Kroupa	.15	.30
145	Sergei Makarov	.15	.30
146	Sandis Ozolinch	.75	1.50
147	Mike Rathje	.15	.30

TAMPA BAT LIGHTNING

No.	Player	EX	NRMT
148	Brian Brqadley	.15	.30
149	Chris Gratton	.75	1.50
150	Brent Gretzky	.50	1.00
151	Roman Hamrlik	.25	.50
152	Petr Klima	.15	.30
153	Denis Savard	.15	.30
154	Rob Zamuner	.15	.30

TORONTO MAPLE LEAFS

No.	Player	EX	NRMT
155	David Andreychuk	.25	.50
156	Nickolai Borschevsky	.35	.75
157	David Ellett	.15	.30
158	Douglas Gilmour	1.50	3.00
159	Alexei Kudashov	.15	.30
160	Felix Potvin, Goalie	2.50	5.00

VANCOUVER CANUCKS

No.	Player	EX	NRMT
161	Greg Adams	.15	.30
162	Pavel Bure	3.50	7.00
163	Geoff Courtnall	.15	.30
164	Trevor Linden	.50	1.00
165	Kirk McLean, Goalie	.50	1.00
166	Jiri Slegr	.15	.30
167	Dixon Ward	.15	.30

WASHINGTON CAPITALS

No.	Player	EX	NRMT
168	Peter Bondra	.15	.30
169	Kevin Hatcher	.15	.30
170	Al Iafrate	.15	.30
171	Dimitri Khristich	.15	.30
172	Pat Peake	.25	.50
173	Mike Ridley	.15	.30

WINNIPEG JETS

No.	Player	EX	NRMT
174	Arto Blomsten	.15	.30
175	Nelson Emerson	.15	.30
176	Boris Mironov	.15	.30
177	Teemu Selanne	1.50	3.00
178	Keith Tkachuk	.50	1.00
179	Paul Yserbaert	.15	.30
180	Alexei Zhamnov	.35	.75

— 1994 UPPER DECK WORLD CUP SOCCER —

Issued in the World Cup Soccer set as a chase card. The 'A' card was randomly inserted into foil packs and the 'B' card randomly inserted in cases.

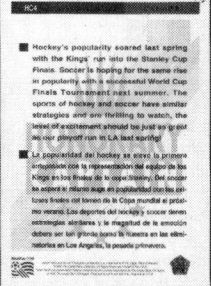

1994 Upper Deck World Cup Soccer
Card No. HC4A, Wayne Gretzky

UPPER DECK — 1993-94 ROOTS "BE A PLAYER" NHLPA

Card Size: 2 1/2" x 3 1/2"
Face: A: Four colour, borderless, Name
B: Four colour, white border, Name
Back: A: Black on white card stock, Name, Number, Resume
B: Black on white card stock, Name, Number, Resume
Imprint: © 1993 The Upper Deck Company. All Rights Reserved.

No.	Player	EX	NRMT
HC4A	Wayne Gretzky, Honorary Captain	25.00	50.00
HC4B	Wayne Gretzky, Honorary Captain	25.00	50.00

— 1993-94 ROOTS "BE A PLAYER" NHLPA —

This two series, 20-card set was issued by Upper Deck / Roots as a promotional premium for the Roots clothing line.

1993-94 Roots "Be A Player" NHLPA
Card No. 3, Felix Potvin

Card Size: 2 1/2" x 3 1/2"
Face: Four colour, borderless
Back: Four colour, borderless; Name, Number, Team, Resume
Imprint: © 1993 The Upper Deck Company. All Rights Reserved. Printed in the U.S.A.

Complete Set No.:	10	
Complete Set Price:	10.00	20.00
Common Card:	.12	.25

SERIES ONE

No.	Player	EX	NRMT
1	Trevor Linden, Van.	.35	.75
2	Guy Carbonneau, Mon.	.12	.25
3	Felix Potvin, Goalie, Tor.	2.00	4.00
4	Steve Yzerman, Det.	.50	1.00
5	Douglas Gilmour, Tor.	.75	1.50
6	Wendel Clark, Tor.	.35	.75
7	Kirk McLean, Goalie, Van.	.35	.75
8	Lawrence Murphy, Pit.	.12	.25
9	Patrick Roy, Goalie, Mon.	2.00	4.00
10	Mike Ricci, Que.	.25	.50

SERIES TWO

No.	Players	EX	NRMT
11	Douglas Gilmour, Tor.	.75	1.50
12	Sergei Fedorov, Det.	1.50	3.00
13	Shayne Corson, Edm.	.25	.50
14	Alexei Yashin, Ott.	.75	1.50
15	Pavel Bure, Van.	1.50	3.00
16	Joe Sakic, Que.	.50	1.00
17	Teemu Selanne, Win.	1.00	2.00
18	David Andreychuk, Tor.	.25	.50
19	Allan McInnis, Cal.	.12	.25
20	Robert Blake, LA	.12	.25

— 1993-94 "BE A PLAYER" NHLPA —

This 45-card boxed set was issued through hobby dealers by Upper Deck as promotional cards for "Roots" products.

 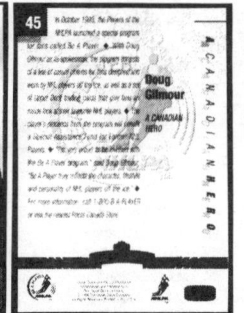

1993-94 "Be A Player" NHLPA
Card No. 45, Douglas Gilmour

Card Size: 3 1/2" X 2 1/2"
Face: Four colour, Borderless
Back: Four colour, Name, Number, Team, Position
Imprint: © 1994 The Upper Deck Company. All Rights Reserved. Printed in the U.S.A.

Complete Set No.:	45	
Complete Set Price:	12.50	25.00
Common Card:	.12	.25

No.	Players	EX	NRMT
1	Anthony Amonte, NYR	.12	.25
2	Chris Chelios, Chi.	.12	.25
3	Alexandre Daigle, Ott.	.50	1.00
4	David Ellett, Tor.	.12	.25
5	Sergei Fedorov, Det.	.75	.150
6	Chris Gratton, TB	.12	.25
7	Wayne Gretzky, LA	2.00	4.00
8	Brett Hull, St.L	.75	1.50
9	Brian Leetch, NYR	.50	1.00
10	Rob Niedermayer, Fl.	.25	.50
11	Felix Potvin, Goalie, Tor.	1.00	2.00
12	Luc Robitaille, LA	.50	1.00
13	Jeremy Roenick, Chi.	.50	1.00
14	Joe Sakic, Que.	.50	1.00
15	Teemu Selanne, Win.	1.00	2.00
16	Brendan Shanahan, St.L	.12	.25
17	Alexei Yashin, Ott.	.50	1.00
18	Steve Yzerman, Det.	.50	1.00
19	Jason Arnott, Edm.	1.00	2.00
20	Pavel Bure, Van.	1.50	3.00
21	Theoren Fleury, Cal.	.12	.25
22	Michael Gartner, NYR	.12	.25
23	Kevin Haller, Mon.	.12	.25
24	Derian Hatcher, Dal.	.12	.25
25	Mark and Gordie Howe, Det.	.50	1.00
26	Al Iafrate, Wash.	.12	.25
27	Joseph Juneau, Bos.	.35	.75
28	Pat LaFontaine, Buf.	.35	.75
29	Eric Lindros, Phi.	1.50	3.00
30	Dave Manson, Win.	.12	.25
31	Michael Modano, Dal.	.35	.75
32	Scott Niedermayer, NJ	.35	.75
33	Owen Nolan, Que.	.12	.25
34	Joel Otto, Cal.	.12	.25
35	Chris Pronger, Har.	.35	.75
36	Scott Stevens, NJ	.12	.25
37	Pierre Turgeon, NYI	.50	1.00
38	Patrick Verbeek, Har.	.12	.25
39	Doug Weight, Edm.	.12	.25
40	Terry Yake, MDA	.12	.25
41	Douglas Gilmour, Tor.	.75	1.50
42	Douglas Gilmour, Tor.	.75	1.50
43	Douglas Gilmour, Tor.	.75	1.50
44	Douglas Gilmour, Tor.	.75	1.50
45	Douglas Gilmour, Tor.	.75	1.50

Available in April!

THE CHARLTON STANDARD CATALOGUE OF CANADIAN BASEBALL & FOOTBALL CARDS

- Fourth Edition -

BASEBALL CARDS FROM 1912
FOOTBALL CARDS FROM 1949

For Canadian Baseball and Football Card Collectors this Catalogue has it all!

IMPERIAL TOBACCO * MAPLE CRISPETTE
BAZOOKA * PARKHURST * O-PEE-CHEE
CANADA STARCH * STUART * POST
TOPPS * WORLD WIDE GUM * NALLEYS
DONRUSS - LEAF * EDDIE SARGENT
WILLARD * TORONTO BLUE JAYS
STANDARD OIL * NABISCO * VACHON
BLUE RIBBON TEA * PANINI * PROVIGO
GENERAL MILLS * SCORE * EXHIBITS
HOSTESS * PURITAN MEATS * JOGO
GULF CANADA * ROYAL STUDIOS
BEN'S AULT FOODS * COCA-COLA * KFC
And All Other Major Manufacturers...

Complete price listings for all Major League Baseball and Canadian Football League cards!
Comprehensive baseball and football minor league card listings!
Regular issues, stickers, inserts, subsets, transfers and much, much more!
All major manufacturers!
Current Pricing for all cards in up to three grades of condition - VG, EX, and NRMT!
All rookie, last, pitcher, quarterback, error and variation cards identified and priced!
Plus Charlton's Fabulous Alphabetical Index!

OVER 300 PAGES * 60,000 PRICES
NEW, LARGER 8 1/2 x 11" FORMAT
RESERVE YOUR COPY TODAY
DIRECTLY FROM THE PUBLISHER...

The Charlton Press

**2010 YONGE STREET,
TORONTO, ONTARIO M4S 1Z9**
FOR TOLL FREE ORDERING PHONE
1-800-442-6042 FAX 1-800-442-1542
from anywhere in Canada or the U.S.

GILLETTE

— 1991 - 92 ISSUE —

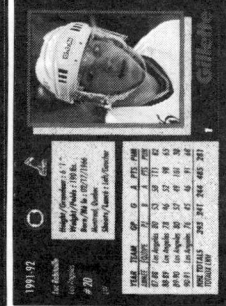

1991-92 Issue
Card No. 1, Luc Robitaille

Card Size: 2 1/2" X 3 1/2"
Face: Six colour, black border; Name, Team logo
Back: Five colour on card stock; Name, Team, Jersey number, Position, Number, Resume, Bilingual
Imprint: Gillette
Complete Set No.: 48
Complete Set Price: 12.50 25.00
Common Player: .13 .25

SMYTHE DIVISION

No.	Player	EX	NRMT
—	Title Card: Smythe Division	.13	.25
1	Luc Robitaille, LA	.35	.75
2	Esa Tikkanen, Edm.	.13	.25
3	Rookie Card: Pat Falloon, SJ	1.00	2.00
4	Theoren Fleury, Cal.	.25	.50
5	Trevor Linden, Van.	.35	.75
6	Robert Blake, LA	.25	.50
7	Al MacInnis, Cal.q	.13	.25
8	Bob Essensa, Goalie, Win.	.25	.50
9	Bill Ranford, Goalie, Edm.	.38	.75
10	Rookie Card: Pavel Bure, Van.	4.00	8.00

NORRIS DIVISION

No.	Player	EX	NRMT
—	Title Card: Norris Division	.13	.25
11	Wendel Clark, Tor.	.50	1.00
12	Sergei Fedorov, Det.	2.00	4.00
13	Jeremy Roenick, Chi.	1.50	3.00
14	Brett Hull, St. L.	1.00	2.00
15	Michael Modano, Min.	1.00	2.00
16	Chris Chelios, Chi.	.25	.50
17	Dave Ellett, Tor.	.13	.25
18	Ed Belfour, Goalie, Chi.	1.50	3.00
19	Grant Fuhr, Goalie, Tor.	.25	.50
20	Rookie Card: Martin Lapointe, Det.	.50	1.00

ADAMS DIVISION

No.	Player	EX	NRMT
—	Title Card: Adams Division	.13	.25
21	Kirk Muller, Mon.	.25	.50
22	Joe Sakic, Que.	.50	1.00
23	Pat LaFontaine, Buf.	.35	.75
24	Patrick Verbeek, Har.	.13	.25
25	Owen Nolan, Que.	.50	1.00
26	Raymond Bourque, Bos.	.25	.50
27	Eric Desjardins, Mon.	.13	.25
28	Patrick Roy, Goalie, Mon.	2.50	5.00
29	Andrew Moog, Goalie, Bos.	.13	.25
30	Rookie Card: Valeri Kamensky, Que.	1.00	2.00

PATRICK DIVISION

No.	Player	EX	NRMT
—	Title Card: Patrick Division	.13	.25
31	Mark Messier, NYR	.75	1.50
32	Mike Ricci, Phi.	.13	.25
33	Mario Lemieux, Pit.	2.00	4.00
34	Jaromir Jagr, Pit.	2.00	4.00
35	Pierre Turgeon, Buf.	.50	1.00
36	Kevin Hatcher, Wash.	.13	.25
37	Paul Coffey, Pit.	.25	.50
38	Chris Terreri, Goalie, NJD	.25	.50
39	Mike Richter, Goalie, NYR	.25	.50
40	Rookie Card: Kevin Todd	.50	1.00

TRIVIA

No.	Trivia	EX	NRMT
—	Trivia	.13	.25
—	Trivia	.13	.25
—	Trivia	.13	.25
—	Trivia	.13	.25

ABALENE SALES AND PROMOTIONS LTD

— 1992 - 93 ARTCARD ISSUE —

Card Size: 5 3/8" x 7 3/8"
Face: Black and white, white border
Back: Black on white postcard stock
Imprint: ©1992 Abalene Sales and Promotions Ltd.
Complete Set No.: 4
Complete Set Price: 10.00 20.00

No.	Player	EX	NRMT
1	Beat Them In The Alley, Calgary	2.50	5.00
2	The Big Steal, Vancouver	2.50	5.00
3	Getting It Going, Toronto	2.50	5.00
4	Road Trip, Vancouer	2.50	5.00

— 1992 - 93 GREETING CARD ISSUE —

Card Size: 5 3/8" x 7 3/8"
Face: Black and white, white border
Back: Black on white postcard stock
Imprint: ©1992 Abalene Sales and Promotions Ltd.
Complete Set No.: 7
Complete Set Price:

No.	Player	EX	NRMT
1	Beat Them In The Alley, Calgary	2.50	5.00
2	The Big Steal, Vancouver	2.50	5.00
3	Getting It Going, Toronto	2.50	5.00
4	Road Trip, Vancouver	2.50	5.00
5	On Trial, Vancouver	2.50	5.00
6	Going For More, Toronto	2.50	5.00
7	Fire on Ice, Calgary Flames	2.50	5.00

Abalene Sales And Promotions Ltd.
1992-93 Artcard Issue, Card No. 3, Getting it Going, Toronto

Abalene Sales And Promotions Ltd.
1992-93 Greeting Card Issue, Card No. 4, Road Trip, Vancouver

DURIVAGE

1992 - 93 LES GRANDS HOCKEYEURS QUEBECOIS

This 50-sticker set was randomly inserted in Durivage Bread during the regular season. It is not uncommon to find creases or bread stains on these cards as they were inserted into bread while still hot, and the cards were often damaged by heat and moisture. There is also a very rare autographed Patrick Roy card limited to 1,000. All of these are individually numbered. A 20-page album was available to hold the 50-sticker collection. The cards are numbered _ de/of 50.

1992-93 Les Grands Hockeyeurs Quebecois
Card No. 3, Benoit Hogue

Card Size: 2 1/2" x 3 1/2"
Face: Four colour, white border; Name, Position, Team and Sponsor logo
Back: Black on white card stock; Name, Number, Resume, Team and sponsor logos, Bilingual
Imprint: IMPRIMÉ EN ITALIE, PANINI PRINTED IN ITALY
Complete Set No.: 50
Complete Set Price: 12.50 / 25.00
Common Card: .12 / .25
Album: 3.00

No.	Player	EX	NRMT
1	Guy Carbonneau, Mon.	.35	.75
2	Lucien DeBlois, Win.	.12	.25
3	Benoit Hogue, NYI	.25	.50
4	Stephen Kasper, Phi.	.12	.25
5	Michael Krushelnyski, Tor.	.12	.25
6	Claude Lapointe, Que.	.12	.25
7	Stephan LeBeau, Mon.	.25	.50
8	Mario Lemieux, Pit.	1.25	2.50
9	Stephane Morin, Que.	.12	.25
10	Denis Savard, Mon.	.25	.50
11	Pierre Turgeon, NYI	.75	1.50
12	Kevin Dineen, Phi.	.12	.25
13	Gordon Donnelly, Buf.	.12	.25
14	Claude Lemieux, NJ	.25	.50
15	Jocelyn Lemieux, Chi.	.12	.25
16	Daniel Marois, NYI	.12	.25
17	Scott Mellanby, Edm.	.12	.25
18	Stephane J. J. Richer, NJ	.25	.50
19	Benoit Brunet, Mon.	.12	.25
20	Vincent Damphousse, Mon.	.35	.75
21	Gilbert Dionne, Mon.	.25	.50
22	Gaetan Duchesne, Min.	.12	.25
23	Bob Errey, Pit.	.12	.25
24	Michel Goulet, Chi.	.12	.25
25	Mike Hough, Que.	.12	.25
26	Sergio Momesso, Van.	.12	.25
27	Mario Roberge, Mon.	.12	.25
28	Luc Robitaille, LA	.75	1.50
29	Sylvain Turgeon, Ott.	.12	.25
30	Marc Bergevin, TB	.12	.25
31	Raymond Bourque, Bos.	.50	1.00
32	Patrice Brisebois, Mon.	.12	.25
33	Jeff Chychrun, Pit.	.12	.25
34	Sylvain Cote, Wash.	.12	.25
35	Jean-Jacques Daigneault, Mon.	.12	.25
36	Eric Desjardins, Mon.	.25	.50
37	Gord Dineen, Ott.	.12	.25
38	Steve Duchesne, Que.	.25	.50
39	Donald Dufresne, Mon.	.12	.25
40	Steven Finn, Que.	.12	.25
41	Garry Galley, Phi.	.12	.25
42	Kevin Lowe, Edm.	.25	.50
43	Michel Petit, Cal.	.12	.25
44	Normand Rochefort, NYR	.12	.25
45	Randy Velischek, Que.	.12	.25
46	Jacques Cloutier, Goalie Que.	.12	.25
47	Stephane Fiset, Goalie, Que.	.25	.50
48	Rejean Lemelin, Goalie, Bos.	.25	.50
49	Andre Racicot, Goalie, Mon.	.35	.75
50	Patrick Roy, Goalie, Mon.	2.50	5.00

PATRICK ROY AUTOGRAPH

Card Size: 2 1/2" x 3 1/2"
Face: Four colour, white border; Name, Position, Team and Sponsor logo
Back: Black on white card stock; Name, Number, Resume, Team and sponsor logos, Bilingual
Imprint: IMPRIMÉ EN ITALIE, PANINI PRINTED IN ITALY

No.	Player	EX	NRMT
—	Patrick Roy, Goalie, Mon. Autographed	87.50	175.00

1993 - 94 DES GRANDS HOCKEYEURS QUEBECOIS

This 51-card set was inserted one per loaf of Durivage Bread. The cards were produced by Score.

 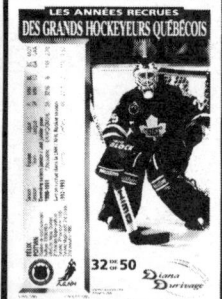

1993-94 Des Grands Hockeyeurs Quebecois
Card No. 41, Luc Robitaille (face)
Card No. 32, Felix Potvin (back)

Card Size: 2 1/2" x 3 1/2"
Face: Four colour, white border; Name, Team, Logo
Back: Four colour; Name, Number, Resume
Imprint: Imprimé én États-Unis Printed in USA
Complete Set No.: 51
Complete Set Price: 12.50 / 25.00
Common Player: .12 / .25

No.	Player	EX	NRMT
1	Alexandre Daigle, Ott.	1.50	3.00
2	Pierre Sevigny, Mon.	.12	.25
3	Jocelyn Thibault, Goalie, Que.	.75	1.50
4	Philippe Boucher, Buf.	.12	.25
5	Martin Brodeur, Goalie, NJ	.50	1.00
6	Martin Lapointe, Det.	.12	.25
7	Patrice Brisebois, Mon.	.25	.50
8	Benoit Brunet, Mon.	.25	.50
9	Guy Carbonneau, Mon.	.25	.50
10	Jean-Jacques Daigneault, Mon.	.12	.25
11	Vincent Damphousse, Mon.	.50	1.00
12	Eric Desjardins, Mon.	.12	.25
13	Gilbert Dionne, Mon.	.12	.25
14	Stephan Lebeau, Mon.	.12	.25
15	Andre Racicot, Goalie, Mon.	.12	.25
16	Mario Roberge, Mon.	.12	.25
17	Patrick Roy, Goalie, Mon.	2.00	4.00
18	Jacques Cloutier, Goalie, Que.	.12	.25
19	Alain Cote, Que.	.12	.25
20	Steve Finn, Que.	.12	.25
21	Stephane Fiset, Goalie, Que.	.75	1.50
22	Martin Gelinas, Que.	.25	.50
23	Reginald Savage, Que.	.12	.25
24	Claude Lapointe, Que.	.12	.25
25	Denis Savard, TB	.50	1.00
26	Raymond Bourque, Bos.	.50	1.00
27	Joseph Juneau, Bos.	1.25	2.50
28	Ronald Stern, Cal.	.12	.25
29	Benoit Hogue, NYI	.12	.25
30	Pierre Turgeon, NYI	1.00	2.00
31	Michael Krushelnyski, Tor.	.12	.25
32	Felix Potvin, Goalie, Tor.	2.00	4.00
33	Sergio Momesso, Van.	.12	.25
34	Yves Racine, Phi.	.12	.25
35	Sylvain Cote, Wash.	.12	.25
36	Sylvain Turgeon, Ott.	.12	.25
37	Kevin Dineen, Phi.	.12	.25
38	Garry Galley, Phi.	.12	.25
39	Dominic Roussel, Goalie, Phi.	.25	.50
40	Gaetan Duchesne, Dal.	.12	.25
41	Luc Robitaille, LA	.75	1.50
42	Michel Goulet, Chi.	.12	.25
43	Jocelyn Lemieux, Chi.	.12	.25
44	Stephane Matteau, Chi.	.12	.25
45	Mike Hough, Fl.	.12	.25
46	Scott Mellanby, Fl.	.25	.50
47	Claude Lemieux, NJ	.25	.50
48	Stephane Richer, NJ	.25	.50
49	Jimmy Waite, Goalie, SJ	.25	.50
50	Patrick Poulin, Hart.	.25	.50
—	Checklist 1 (1 - 50)	.25	.50

AUTOGRAPH CARDS

Card Size: 2 1/2" x 3 1/2"
Face: Four colour, white border; Name, Position, Team and Sponsor logo
Back: Black on white card stock; Name, Number, Resume, Team and sponsor logos, Bilingual
Imprint: IMPRIMÉ EN ITALIE, PANINI PRINTED IN ITALY

No.	Player	EX	NRMT
—	Patrick Roy, Goalie, Mon. Autographed	65.00	125.00
—	Jocelyn Thibault, Goalie, Que. Autographed	37.50	75.00

FLEER ULTRA

1992 - 93 REGULAR ISSUE

This 450-card set is Fleer's first entry into hockey cards. The cards are premium quality. The set is divided into Series One and Series Two.

1992-93 Regular Issue
Card No. 4, Joseph Juneau

Card Size: 2 1/2" x 3 1/2"
Face: Four colour, borderless; Name, Team, Position
Back: Four colour, card stock; Name, Number, Resume, Team logo
Imprint: © 1992 FLEER CORP. PRINTED IN U.S.A.

— 1992 - 93 REGULAR ISSUE — FLEER ULTRA • 421

Complete Set No.:	450		
Series One:	250		
Series Two:	200		
Set Price:			
Series One Price:		9.00	18.00
Series Two Price:		9.00	18.00
Complete Set:		17.50	35.00
Common Player:		.05	.10
Foil Pack:			
Series One: (14 Cards)			1.50
Series Two: (14 Cards)			1.50
Foil Box:			
Series One: (36 Packs)			50.00
Series Two: (36 Packs)			50.00

SERIES ONE

BOSTON BRUINS

No.	Player	EX	NRMT
1	Brent Ashton	.05	.10
2	Raymond Bourque	.15	.30
3	1992 Rookie: Steve Heinze	.05	.10
4	1992 Rookie: Joseph Juneau	1.25	2.50
5	Stephen Leach	.05	.10
6	Andrew Moog, Goalie	.05	.10
7	Cam Neely	.15	.30
8	Adams Oates	.15	.30
9	David Poulin	.05	.10
10	Vladimir Ruzicka	.05	.10
11	Glen Wesley	.05	.10

BUFFALO SABRES

No.	Player	EX	NRMT
12	David Andreychuk	.15	.30
13	1992 Rookie: Keith Carney, RC	.05	.10
14	Tom Draper, Goalie	.05	.10
15	Dale Hawerchuk	.05	.10
16	Pat LaFontaine	.15	.30
17	Brad May	.05	.10
18	Alexander Mogilny	.35	.75
19	Michael Ramsay	.05	.10
20	Kenneth Sutton	.05	.10

CALGARY FLAMES

No.	Player	EX	NRMT
21	Theoren Fleury	.07	.15
22	Gary Leeman	.05	.10
23	Allan MacInnis	.05	.10
24	Sergei Makarov	.05	.10
25	Joe Nieuwendyk	.05	.10
26	Joel Otto	.05	.10
27	Paul Ranheim	.05	.10
28	Robert Reichel	.05	.10
29	Gary Roberts	.05	.10
30	Gary Suter	.05	.10
31	Michael Vernon, Goalie	.05	.10

CHICAGO BLACK HAWKS

No.	Player	EX	NRMT
32	Ed Belfour, Goalie	.20	.40
33	Rob Brown	.05	.10
34	Chris Chelios	.05	.10
35	Michel Goulet	.05	.10
36	Dirk Graham	.05	.10
37	Mike Hudson	.05	.10
38	Igor Kravchuk	.05	.10
39	Steve Larmer	.05	.10
40	1992 Rookie: Dean McAmmond, RC	.12	.25
41	Jeremy Roenick	.50	1.00
42	James (Steve) Smith	.05	.10
43	Brent Sutter	.05	.10

DETROIT RED WINGS

No.	Player	EX	NRMT
44	Shawn Burr	.05	.10
45	Jimmy Carson	.05	.10
46	Tim Cheveldae, Goalie	.05	.10
47	Dino Ciccarelli	.05	.10
48	Sergei Fedorov	.75	1.50
49	Vladimir Konstantinov	.05	.10
50	1992 Rookie: Vyacheslav Kozlov	.60	1.25
51	Nicklas Lidstrom	.12	.25
52	Byron (Brad) McCrimmon	.05	.10
53	Bob Probert	.05	.10
54	Paul Ysebaert	.05	.10
55	Steve Yzerman	.25	.50

EDMONTON OILERS

No.	Player	EX	NRMT
56	Josef Beranek	.15	.30
57	Shayne Corson	.05	.10
58	Brian Glynn	.05	.10
59	Petr Klima	.05	.10
60	Kevin Lowe	.05	.10
61	Norm Maciver	.05	.10
62	Dave Manson	.05	.10
63	Joe Murphy	.05	.10
64	Bernie Nicholls	.05	.10
65	Bill Ranford, Goalie	.05	.10
66	Craig Simpson	.05	.10
67	Esa Tikkanen	.05	.10

HARTFORD WHALERS

No.	Player	EX	NRMT
68	Sean Burke, Goalie	.05	.10
69	Adam Burt	.05	.10
70	Andrew Cassels	.05	.10
71	Murray Craven	.05	.10
72	John Cullen	.05	.10
73	Randy Cunneyworth	.05	.10
74	Tim Kerr	.05	.10
75	Geoff Sanderson	.25	.50
76	Eric Weinrich	.05	.10
77	Zaeley Zalapski	.05	.10

LOS ANGELES KINGS

No.	Player	EX	NRMT
78	Peter Ahola	.05	.10
79	Robert Blake	.05	.10
80	Paul Coffey	.10	.20
81	Mike Donnelly	.05	.10
82	Tony Granato	.05	.10
83	Wayne Gretzky	.75	1.50
84	Kelly Hrudey, Goalie	.05	.10
85	Jari Kurri	.05	.10
86	Corey Millen	.05	.10
87	Luc Robitaille	.15	.30
88	Tomas Sandstrom	.05	.10

MINNESOTA NORTH STARS

No.	Player	EX	NRMT
89	Neal Broten	.05	.10
90	Jon Casey, Goalie	.05	.10
91	Russell Courtnall	.05	.10
92	Ulf Dahlen	.05	.10
93	Todd Elik	.05	.10
94	Dave Gagner	.05	.10
95	Jim Johnson	.05	.10
96	Michael Modano	.20	.40
97	Bobby Smith	.05	.10
98	Mark Tinordi	.05	.10
99	Darcy Wakaluk, Goalie	.05	.10

MONTREAL CANADIENS

No.	Player	EX	NRMT
100	Brian Bellows	.05	.10
101	Benoit Brunet	.05	.10
102	Guy Carbonneau	.05	.10
103	Vincent Damphousse	.05	.10
104	Eric Desjardins	.05	.10
105	Gilbert Dionne	.05	.10
106	Mike Keane	.05	.10
107	Kirk Muller	.05	.10
108	Patrick Roy, Goalie	.50	1.00
109	Denis Savard	.05	.10
110	Mathieu Schneider	.05	.10
111	Brian Skrudland	.05	.10

NEW JERSEY DEVILS

No.	Player	EX	NRMT
112	Tom Chorske	.05	.10
113	Zdeno Ciger	.05	.10
114	Claude Lemieux	.05	.10
115	John MacLean	.05	.10
116	1992 Rookie: Scott Niedermayer	.30	.60
117	Stephane J. J. Richer	.05	.10
118	Peter Stastny	.05	.10
119	Scott Stevens	.05	.10
120	Chris Terreri, Goalie	.05	.10
121	Kevin Todd	.05	.10
122	Valeri Zelepukin	.12	.25

NEW YORK ISLANDERS

No.	Player	EX	NRMT
123	Ray Ferraro	.05	.10
124	Mark Fitzpatrick, Goalie	.05	.10
125	Patrick Flatley	.05	.10
126	Glenn Healy, Goalie	.05	.10
127	Benoit Hogue	.05	.10
128	Derek King	.05	.10
129	Uwe Krupp	.05	.10
130	1992 Rookie: Scott Lachance	.05	.10
131	Steve Thomas	.05	.10
132	Pierre Turgeon	.17	.35

NEW YORK RANGERS

No.	Player	EX	NRMT
133	Anthony Amonte	.12	.25
134	Paul Broten	.05	.10
135	Michael Gartner	.05	.10
136	Adam Graves	.20	.40
137	1992 Rookie: Alexei Kovalev	.60	1.25
138	Brian Leetch	.20	.40
139	Mark Messier	.15	.30
140	Sergei Nemchinov	.05	.10
141	James Patrick	.05	.10
142	Mike Richter, Goalie	.20	.40
143	Darren Turcotte	.05	.10
144	John Vanbiesbrouck, Goalie	.05	.10

OTTAWA SENATORS

No.	Player	EX	NRMT
145	Dominic Lavoie	.05	.10
146	1992 Rookie: Lonnie Loach, RC	.05	.10
147	Andrew McBain	.05	.10
148	1992 Rookie: Darren Rumble, RC	.05	.10
149	Sylvain Turgeon	.05	.10
150	Peter Sidorkiewicz, Goalie	.05	.10

PHILADELPHIA FLYERS

No.	Player	EX	NRMT
151	Brian Benning	.05	.10
152	Rod Brind'Amour	.12	.25
153	1992 Rookie: Vjateslav Butsayev, RC	.12	.25
154	Kevin Dineen	.05	.10
155	Per-Erik Eklund	.05	.10
156	Garry Galley	.05	.10
157	1992 Rookie: Eric Lindros	2.50	5.00
158	Mark Recchi	.17	.35
159	1992 Rookie: Dominic Roussel, Goalie	.17	.35
160	1992 Rookie: Tommy Soderstrom, Goalie, RC	.25	.50
161	1992 Rookie: Dimitri Yushkevich, RC	.12	.25

PITTSBURGH PENGUINS

No.	Player	EX	NRMT
162	Tom Barrasso, Goalie	.05	.10
163	Ronald Francis	.05	.10
164	Jaromir Jagr	.50	1.00
165	Mario Lemieux	.75	1.50
166	Joe Mullen	.05	.10
167	Lawrence Murphy	.05	.10
168	Jim Paek	.05	.10
169	Kjell Samuelsson	.05	.10
170	Ulf Samuelsson	.05	.10
171	Kevin Stevens	.15	.30
172	Rick Tocchet	.05	.10

QUEBEC NORDIQUES

No.	Player	EX	NRMT
173	Alexei Gusarov	.05	.10
174	Ron Hextall, Goalie	.05	.10
175	Mike Hough	.05	.10
176	Claude LaPointe	.05	.10
177	Owen Nolan	.10	.20
178	Mike Ricci	.10	.20
179	Joe Sakic	.17	.35
180	Mats Sundin	.17	.35
181	Mikhail Tatarinov	.05	.10

422 • FLEER ULTRA — 1992-93 REGULAR ISSUE

ST. LOUIS BLUES

No.	Player	EX	NRMT
182	Bob Bassen	.05	.10
183	Jeff Brown	.05	.10
184	Garth Butcher	.05	.10
185	Paul Cavallini	.05	.10
186	Brett Hull	.35	.75
187	Craig Janney	.07	.15
188	Curtis Joseph, Goalie	.15	.30
189	Brendan Shanahan	.12	.25
190	Ronald Sutter	.05	.10

SAN JOSE SHARKS

No.	Player	EX	NRMT
191	David Bruce	.05	.10
192	Dale Craigwell	.05	.10
193	Dean Evason	.05	.10
194	Pat Falloon	.12	.25
195	Jeff Hackett, Goalie	.05	.10
196	Kelly Kisio	.05	.10
197	Brian Lawton	.05	.10
198	Neil Wilkinson	.05	.10
199	Douglas Wilson	.05	.10

TAMPA BAY LIGHTNING

No.	Player	EX	NRMT
200	Marc Bergevin	.05	.10
201	1992 Rookie: Roman Hamrlik, RC	.50	1.00
202	Pat Jablonski, Goalie	.05	.10
203	Michel Mongeau	.05	.10
204	Peter Taglianetti	.05	.10
205	Steve Tuttle	.05	.10
206	Wendell Young, Goalie	.05	.10

TORONTO MAPLE LEAFS

No.	Player	EX	NRMT
207	Glenn Anderson	.05	.10
208	Wendel Clark	.05	.10
209	David Ellett	.05	.10
210	Grant Fuhr, Goalie	.05	.10
211	Douglas Gilmour	.20	.40
212	Jamie Macoun	.05	.10
213	Felix Potvin, Goalie	1.25	2.50
214	Robert Rouse	.05	.10
215	Joseph Sacco	.05	.10
216	Peter Zezel	.05	.10

VANCOUVER CANUCKS

No.	Player	EX	NRMT
217	Greg Adams	.05	.10
218	David Babych	.05	.10
219	Pavel Bure	1.50	3.00
220	Geoff Courtnall	.05	.10
221	Doug Lidster	.05	.10
222	Trevor Linden	.15	.30
223	Jyrki Lumme	.05	.10
224	Kirk McLean, Goalie	.05	.10
225	Sergio Momesso	.05	.10
226	Peter Nedved	.12	.25
227	Cliff Ronning	.05	.10
228	Jim Sandlak	.05	.10

WASHINGTON CAPITALS

No.	Player	EX	NRMT
229	Donald Beaupre, Goalie	.05	.10
230	Peter Bondra	.05	.10
231	Kevin Hatcher	.05	.10
232	Dale Hunter	.05	.10
233	Al Iafrate	.05	.10
234	Calle Johansson	.05	.10
235	Dimitri Khristich	.05	.10
236	Kelly Miller	.05	.10
237	Michal Pivonka	.05	.10
238	Mike Ridley	.05	.10

WINNIPEG JETS

No.	Player	EX	NRMT
239	Luciano Borsato	.05	.10
240	Bob Essensa, Goalie	.05	.10
241	Phil Housley	.05	.10
242	Troy Murray	.05	.10
243	Teppo Numminen	.05	.10
244	Fredrik Olausson	.05	.10
245	Ed Olczyk	.05	.10
246	Darrin Shannon	.05	.10
247	Thomas Steen	.05	.10
248	Checklist 1 (1 - 88)	.05	.10
249	Checklist 2 (89 - 172)	.05	.10
250	Checklist 3 (173 - 250)	.05	.10

SERIES TWO

BOSTON BRUINS

No.	Player	EX	NRMT
251	1992 Rookie: Ted Donato	.05	.10
252	1992 Rookie: Dmitri Kvartalnov, RC	.20	.40
253	Gordon Murphy	.05	.10
254	1992 Rookie: Gregori Panteleyev, RC	.10	.20
255	Gordon Roberts	.05	.10
256	David Shaw	.05	.10
257	Don Sweeney	.05	.10

BUFFALO SABRES

No.	Player	EX	NRMT
258	Doug Bodger	.05	.10
259	Gordon Donnelly	.05	.10
260	1992 Rookie: Yuri Khmylev, RC	.25	.50
261	Daren Puppa, Goalie	.05	.10
262	1992 Rookie: Richard Smehlik, RC	.15	.30
263	Petr Svoboda	.05	.10
264	Robert Sweeney	.05	.10
265	Randy Wood	.05	.10

CALGARY FLAMES

No.	Player	EX	NRMT
266	1992 Rookie: Kevin Dahl, RC	.05	.10
267	Chris Dahlquist	.05	.10
268	Roger Johansson	.05	.10
269	1992 Rookie: Chris Lindberg	.05	.10
270	Frantisek Musil	.05	.10
271	Ronald Stern	.05	.10
272	Carey Wilson	.05	.10

CHICAGO BLACK HAWKS

No.	Player	EX	NRMT
273	Dave Christian	.05	.10
274	1992 Rookie: Karl Dykhuis	.05	.10
275	Gregory Gilbert	.05	.10
276	1992 Rookie: Sergei Krivokrasov, RC	.15	.30
277	Frantisek Kucera	.05	.10
278	Bryan Marchment	.05	.10
279	Stephane Matteau	.05	.10
280	Brian Noonan	.05	.10
281	Christian Ruuttu	.05	.10

DETROIT REDWINGS

No.	Player	EX	NRMT
282	Steve Chiasson	.05	.10
283	Dino Ciccarelli	.05	.10
284	Gerard Gallant	.05	.10
285	Mark Howe	.05	.10
286	Keith Primeau	.05	.10
287	Yves Racine	.05	.10
288	Vincent Riendeau, Goalie	.05	.10
289	Ray Sheppard	.05	.10
290	Mike Sillinger	.05	.10

EDMONTON OILERS

No.	Player	EX	NRMT
291	Kelly Buchberger	.05	.10
292	Shayne Corson	.05	.10
293	Brent Gilchrist	.05	.10
294	Craig MacTavish	.05	.10
295	Scott Mellanby	.05	.10
296	Craig Muni	.05	.10
297	Luke Richardson	.05	.10
298	Ron Tugnutt, Goalie	.05	.10
299	1992 Rookie: Shaun Van Allen	.05	.10

HARTFORD WHALERS

No.	Player	EX	NRMT
300	Stephen Konroyd	.05	.10
301	Nicholas Kypreos	.05	.10
302	1992 Rookie: Robert Petrovicky, RC	.12	.25
303	Frank Pietrangelo, Goalie	.05	.10
304	1992 Rookie: Patrick Poulin	.05	.10
305	Patrick Verbeek	.05	.10
306	Eric Weinrich	.05	.10

LOS ANGELES KINGS

No.	Player	EX	NRMT
307	1992 Rookie: Jim Hiller, RC	.07	.15
308	Charles Huddy	.05	.10
309	1992 Rookie: Lonnie Loach	.05	.10
310	Martin McSorley	.05	.10
311	1992 Rookie: Robb Stauber, Goalie	.05	.10
312	1992 Rookie: Darryl Sydor	.05	.10
313	David Taylor	.05	.10
314	1992 Rookie: Alexei Zhitnik, RC	.17	.35

MINNESOTA NORTH STARS

No.	Player	EX	NRMT
315	Shane Churla	.05	.10
316	Russell Courtnall	.05	.10
317	Mike Craig	.05	.10
318	Gaetan Duchesne	.05	.10
319	Derian Hatcher	.05	.10
320	Craig Ludwig	.05	.10
321	Richard Matvichuk, RC	.12	.25
322	Michael McPhee	.05	.10
323	Tommy Sjodin, RC	.10	.20

MONTREAL CANADIENS

No.	Player	EX	NRMT
324	Brian Bellows	.05	.10
325	Patrice Brisebois	.05	.10
326	Jean-Jacques Daigneault	.05	.10
327	Kevin Haller	.05	.10
328	1992 Rookie: Sean Hill, RC	.12	.25
329	Stephan Lebeau	.05	.10
330	John LeClair	.05	.10
331	Lyle Odelein	.05	.10
332	Andre Racicot, Goalie	.05	.10
333	1992 Rookie: Ed Ronan, RC	.10	.20

NEW JERSEY DEVILS

No.	Player	EX	NRMT
334	Craig Billington, Goalie	.05	.10
335	Kenneth Daneyko	.05	.10
336	Bruce Driver	.05	.10
337	Viacheslav Fetisov	.05	.10
338	1992 Rookie: Bill Guerin	.20	.40
339	Robert Holik	.05	.10
340	Alexei Kasatonov	.05	.10
341	Alexander Semak	.05	.10

NEW YORK ISLANDERS

No.	Player	EX	NRMT
342	Tom Fitzgerald	.05	.10
343	1992 Rookie: Travis Green, RC	.12	.25
344	1992 Rookie: Darius Kasparaitis, RC	.12	.25
345	1992 Rookie: Danny Lorenz, Goalie, RC	.05	.10
346	1992 Rookie: Vladimir Malakhov, RC	.17	.35
347	1992 Rookie: Marty McInnis	.05	.10
348	Brian Mullen	.05	.10
349	Jeff Norton	.05	.10
350	David Volek	.05	.10

NEW YORK RANGERS

No.	Player	EX	NRMT
351	Jeff Beukeboom	.05	.10
352	Phillippe Bourque	.05	.10
353	Paul Broten	.05	.10
354	Mark Hardy	.05	.10
355	1992 Rookie: Steven King, RC	.15	.30
356	Kevin Lowe	.05	.10
357	Ed Olczyk	.05	.10
358	Doug Weight	.05	.10
359	1992 Rookie: Sergei Zubov, RC	1.50	3.00

OTTAWA SENATORS

No.	Player	EX	NRMT
360	Jamie Baker	.05	.10
361	Daniel Berthiaume, Goalie	.05	.10
362	1992 Rookie: Chris Luongo, RC	.05	.10
363	Norm Maciver	.05	.10
364	Bradley Marsh	.05	.10
365	Mike Peluso	.05	.10
366	Brad Shaw	.05	.10
367	Peter Sidorkiewicz, Goalie	.05	.10

PHILADELPHIA FLYERS

No.	Player	EX	NRMT
368	Keith Acton	.05	.10
369	Stephane Beauregard, Goalie	.05	.10
370	Terry Carkner	.05	.10
371	Brent Fedyk	.05	.10
372	Andrei Lomakin	.05	.10
373	1992 Rookie: Ryan McGill, RC	.07	.15
374	Erik Nattress	.05	.10
375	Gregory Paslawski	.05	.10

PITTSBURGH PENGUINS

No.	Player	EX	NRMT
376	Peter Ahola	.05	.10
377	1992 Rookie: Jeff Daniels	.05	.10
378	Troy Loney	.05	.10
379	1992 Rookie: Shawn McEachern	.15	.30
380	1992 Rookie: Mike Needham, RC	.10	.20
381	Paul Stanton	.05	.10
382	1992 Rookie: Martin Straka, RC	.85	1.75
383	Ken Wregget, Goalie	.05	.10

QUEBEC NORDIQUES

No.	Player	EX	NRMT
384	Steve Duchesne	.05	.10
385	Ron Hextall, Goalie	.05	.10
386	Kerry Huffman	.05	.10
387	1992 Rookie: Andrei Kovalenko, RC	.50	1.00
388	1992 Rookie: Bill Lindsay, RC	.07	.15
389	Mike Ricci	.05	.10
390	1992 Rookie: Martin Rucinsky	.12	.25
391	Scott Young	.05	.10

ST. LOUIS BLUES

No.	Player	EX	NRMT
392	1992 Rookie: Philippe Bozon	.05	.10
393	Nelson Emerson	.15	.30
394	1992 Rookie: Guy Hebert, Goalie, RC	.35	.75
395	1992 Rookie: Igor Korolev, RC	.10	.20
396	Kevin Miller	.05	.10
397	1992 Rookie: Vitali Prokhorov, RC	.15	.30
398	Richard Sutter	.05	.10

SAN JOSE SHARKS

No.	Player	EX	NRMT
399	John Carter	.05	.10
400	Johan Garpenlov	.05	.10
401	1992 Rookie: Arturs Irbe, Goalie	.35	.75
402	1992 Rookie: Sandis Ozolinch, RC, Error	.35	.75
403	1992 Rookie: Tom Pederson, RC	.10	.20
404	Michel Picard	.05	.10
405	1992 Rookie: Doug Zmolek, RC	.10	.20

TAMPER BAY LIGHTNING

No.	Player	EX	NRMT
406	Bo Mikael Andersson	.05	.10
407	Bob Beers	.05	.10
408	Brian Bradley	.05	.10
409	Adam Creighton	.05	.10
410	Douglas Crossman	.05	.10
411	Kenneth Hodge Jr.	.05	.10
412	Chris Kontos, RC	.15	.30
413	George (Rob) Ramage	.05	.10
414	John Tucker	.05	.10
415	1992 Rookie: Rob Zamuner, RC	.10	.20

TORONTO MAPLE LEAFS

No.	Player	EX	NRMT
416	Ken Baumgartner	.05	.10
417	1992 Rookie: Drake Berehowsky	.05	.10
418	1992 Rookie: Nikolai Borschevsky, RC	.35	.75
419	John Cullen	.05	.10
420	Mike Foligno	.05	.10
421	Michael Krushelnyski	.05	.10
422	1992 Rookie: Dmitri Mironov, RC	.05	.10
423	Rob Pearson	.05	.10

VANCOUVER CANUCKS

No.	Player	EX	NRMT
424	Gerald Diduck	.05	.10
425	Robert Dirk	.05	.10
426	Thomas Fergus	.05	.10
427	Gino Odjick	.05	.10
428	Adrien Plavsic	.05	.10
429	Anatoli Semenov	.05	.10
430	1992 Rookie: Jiri Slegr, RC	.05	.10
431	1992 Rookie: Dixon Ward, RC	.12	.25

WASHINGTON CAPITALS

No.	Player	EX	NRMT
432	Paul Cavallini	.05	.10
433	Sylvain Cote	.05	.10
434	Pat Elynuik	.05	.10
435	Jim Hrivnak, Goalie	.05	.10
436	1992 Rookie: Keith Jones, RC	.10	.20
437	1992 Rookie: Steve Konowalchuk, RC	.15	.30
438	Todd Krygier	.05	.10
439	Paul MacDermid	.05	.10

WINNIPEG JETS

No.	Player	EX	NRMT
440	1992 Rookie: Sergei Bautin, RC	.15	.30
441	1992 Rookie: Eugeny Davydov, Error	.17	.35
442	John Druce	.05	.10
443	Troy Murray	.05	.10
444	1992 Rookie: Teemu Selanne, RC	2.50	5.00
445	Richard Tabaracci, Goalie	.05	.10
446	1992 Rookie: Keith Tkachuk	.12	.25
447	1992 Rookie: Alexei Zhamnov, RC	.50	1.00
448	Series 2 Checklist (251 - 314)	.07	.15
449	Series 2 Checklist (315 - 383)	.07	.15
450	Series 2 Checklist (384 - 450)	.07	.15

— 1992 - 93 INSERT SETS —

JEREMY ROENICK PERFORMANCE HIGHLIGHTS

Of this 12-card set, 10 cards were randomly inserted into Series One foil packs, cards nos. 11 and 12 were available only through a mail order offer.

 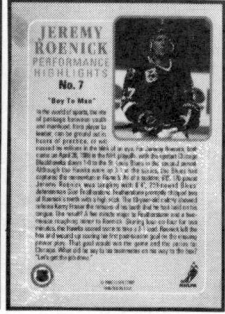

1992-93 Jeremy Roenick Performance Highlights Card No. 7, Boy to Man

Card Size: 2 1/2" x 3 1/2"
Face: Four colour, blue marble border, Name
Back: Four colour, mauve border; Name, Number, Resume
Imprint: © 1992 FLEER CORP. PRINTED IN U.S.A.
Complete Set No.: 12
Complete Set Price: 25.00   50.00

No.	Player	EX	NRMT
1	Blast from the Past	2.50	5.00
2	Early Days on the Road	2.50	5.00
3	Prep School Phenom	2.50	5.00
4	Blackhawk Bound	2.50	5.00
5	Breakfast with a Champion	2.50	5.00
6	The Fast Track	2.50	5.00
7	Boy to Man	2.50	5.00
8	Great Expectations	2.50	5.00
9	Changing of the Guard	2.50	5.00
10	Superstar	2.50	5.00
11	Mail in Card	2.50	5.00
12	Mail in Card	2.50	5.00

JEREMY ROENICK AUTOGRAPH

Card Size: 2 1/2" x 3 1/2"
Face: Four colour, blue marble border, Name
Back: Four colour, mauve border, card stock, Name
Imprint: © 1992 FLEER CORP. PRINTED IN U.S.A.

No.	Player	EX	NRMT
—	Jeremy Roenick Autographed Card	125.00	250.00

ROOKIES

This 8-card set was randomly inserted into Series One foil packs.

1992-93 Rookies
Card No. 4, Family Ties, Gilbert Dionne

Card Size: 2 1/2" x 3 1/2"
Face: Four colour, purple lower border; Name
Back: Four colour, borderless; Name, Number, Resume
Imprint: © 1992 FLEER CORP. PRINTED IN U.S.A.
Complete Set No.: 8
Complete Set Price: 13.50   27.00

No.	Player	EX	NRMT
1	The Blue Flash: Anthony Amonte, NYR	2.00	4.00
2	Sabre Tooth Sniper: Donald Audette, Buf.	1.00	2.00
3	Rapid Fire Road Runner: Pavel Bure, Van.	5.00	10.00
4	Family Ties: Gilbert Dionne, Mon.	1.00	2.00
5	High Note: Nelson Emerson, St.L	2.00	4.00
6	Coming of Age: Pat Falloon, SJ	2.50	5.00
7	Perfect Fit: Nicklas Lidstrom, Det.	1.00	2.00
8	Third Time's a Charm: Kevin Todd, NJ	1.00	2.00

NHL ALL STAR

This 12-card set was randomly inserted in the Series One foil packs as chase cards. The cards are numbered _ of 12.

1992-93 NHL All Star
Card No. 9, Ed Belfour

Card Size: 2 1/2" x 3 1/2"
Face: Four colour, borderless; Name
Back: Four colour, borderless; Name, Number, Resume
Imprint: © 1992 FLEER CORP. PRINTED IN U.S.A.
Complete Set No.: 12

Complete Set Price:		40.00	80.00
Common Card:		1.50	3.00

No.	Player	EX	NRMT
1	**King of Swing:** Paul Coffey, LA	1.50	3.00
2	**Beantown Blueliner:** Raymond Bourque, Bos.	1.50	3.00
3	**Simply the Best:** Patrick Roy, Goalie, Mon.	4.00	8.00
4	**Le Magnifique:** Mario Lemieux, Pit.	4.00	8.00
5	**Super Slot Sniper:** Kevin Stevens, Pit.	1.50	3.00
6	**Jags:** Jaromir Jagr, Pit.	2.50	5.00
7	**Bruising Backliner:** Chris Chelios, Chi.	1.50	3.00
8	**Big-Bang-Boom:** Al McInnis, Cal.	1.50	3.00
9	**Eddie The Eagle:** Ed Belfour, Goalie, Chi.	2.00	4.00
10	**The Great One:** Wayne Gretzky, LA	5.00	10.00
11	**Silent Superstar:** Luc Robitaille, LA	1.50	3.00
12	**Stealth Bomber:** Brett Hull, St.L	2.00	4.00

AWARD WINNERS

This 10-card set was inserted into Series One foil packs as chase cards. The cards are numbered _ of 10.

1992-93 Award Winners
Card No. 1, Mark Messier   Card No. 6, Wayne Gretzky

Card Size: 2 1/2" x 3 1/2"
Face: Four colour, borderless; Name
Back: Four colour, borderless; Name
Imprint: © 1992 FLEER CORP. PRINTED IN U.S.A.
Complete Set No.: 10

Complete Set Price:		16.50	33.00
Common Card:		1.25	2.50

No.	Player	EX	NRMT
1	**Hart Memorial Trophy:** Mark Messier, NYR	1.75	3.50
2	**James Norris Memorial Trophy:** Brian Leetch, NYR	2.25	4.50
3	**Frank J. Selke Trophy:** Guy Carbonneau, Mon.	1.25	2.50
4	**Vezina Trophy:** Patrick Roy, Goalie, Mon	4.00	8.00
5	**Art Ross Trophy:** Mario Lemieux, Pit.	4.00	8.00
6	**Lady Byng Memorial Trophy:** Wayne Gretzky, LA	5.00	10.00
7	**Bill Masterton Memorial Trophy:** Mark Fitzpatrick, NYI	1.25	2.50
8	**King Clancy Memorial Trophy:** Raymond Bourque, Bos.	1.25	2.50
9	**Calder Memorial Trophy:** Pavel Bure, Van.	5.00	10.00
10	**Lester B. Pearson Award:** Mark Messier, NYR	1.75	3.50

IMPORTS

This 25-card set was randomly inserted into Series Two foil packs as chase cards. The cards are numbered _ of 25.

1992-93 Imports
Card No. 17, Petr Nedved

Card Size: 2 1/2" x 3 1/2"
Face: Four colour, borderless; Name
Back: Four colour, borderless; Name, Number, Resume
Imprint: © 1993 FLEER CORP. PRINTED IN U.S.A.
Complete Set No.: 25

Complete Set Price:		35.00	75.00
Common Card:		1.25	2.50

No.	Player	EX	NRMT
1	Nikolai Borschevsky, Tor.	2.00	4.00
2	Pavel Bure, Van.	7.50	15.00
3	Sergei Fedorov, Det.	5.00	10.00
4	Roman Hamrlik, TB	1.50	3.00
5	Arturs Irbe, Goalie, SJ	4.00	8.00
6	Jaromir Jagr, Pit.	3.50	7.00
7	Dimitri Khristich, Wash.	1.25	2.50
8	Petr Klima, Edm.	1.25	2.50
9	Andrei Kovalenko, Que.	1.25	2.50
10	Alexei Kovalev, NYR	2.50	5.00
11	Jari Kurri, LA	1.25	2.50
12	Dmitri Kvartalnov, Bos.	1.25	2.50
13	Nicklas Lidstrom, Det.	1.25	2.50
14	Vladimir Malakhov, NYI	2.00	4.00
15	Dmitri Mironov, Tor.	2.00	4.00
16	Alexander Mogilny, Buf.	3.50	7.00
17	Petr Nedved, Van.	2.00	4.00
18	Fredrick Olausson, Win.	1.25	2.50
19	Sandis Ozolinch, SJ, Error	3.00	6.00
20	Ulf Samuelsson, Pit.	1.25	2.50
21	Teemu Selanne, Win.	5.00	10.00
22	Richard Smehlik, Buf.	1.25	2.50
23	Tommy Soderstrom, Goalie, Phi.	1.50	3.00
24	Peter Stastny, NJ	1.25	2.50
25	Mats Sundin, Que.	2.50	5.00

— 1993 - 94 PROMOTIONAL SHEET —

This 9-card mini sheet profiles the new look for Fleer's '93-'94 hockey cards.

Sheet Size: 7 3/4" x 10 3/4"
Face: Four colour, borderless; Name, Team, Position
Back: Four colour; Name, Number, Resume, Team logo
Imprint: © 1993 FLEER CORP. PRINTED IN U.S.A.
Complete Set No.: 9

No.	Player	EX	NRMT
—	Sheet	7.50	15.00
—	Title Card: '93-94 Fleer Ultra		
30	Felix Potvin, Goalie, Tor.		
49	Joe Juneau, Bos.		
110	Douglas Gilmour, Tor.		
115	Alexei Kovalev, NYR		
121	Sergei Fedorov, Det.		
137	Mats Sundin, Que.		
186	Jeremy Roenick, Chi.		
236	Mark Recchi, Phi.		

— 1993 - 94 REGULAR ISSUE —

This 500-card set was issued in two parts Series One (1 - 250) and Series Two (251 - 500). The set has ten insert sets.

1993-94 Issue
Card No. 350, Guy Carbonneau

Card Size: 2 1/2" x 3 1/2"
Face: Four colour, borderless; Name, Team, Position
Back: Four colour; Name, Number, Resume, Team logo
Imprint: © 1993 FLEER CORP. PRINTED IN U.S.A.
Complete Set No.: 500
  Series One: 250
  Series Two: 250
Set Price:

Series One:	10.00	20.00
Series Two:	12.50	25.00
Complete Set:	22.50	45.00
Common Player:	.05	.10

Foil Pack:
  Series One: (14 Cards) 1.75
  Series Two: (14 Cards) 1.75
Foil Box:
  Series One (36 Packs) 50.00
  Series Two (36 Packs) 50.00

SERIES ONE

No.	Player	EX	NRMT
1	Raymond Bourque, Bos.	.10	.20
2	**Post Season Trade:** Andrew Moog, Goalie, Dal.	.05	.10
3	Brian Benning, Edm.	.05	.10
4	Brian Bellows, Mon.	.05	.10
5	Claude Lemieux, NJ	.05	.10
6	Jamie Baker, Ott.	.05	.10
7	Steve Duchesne, Que.	.05	.10
8	Ed Courtenay, SJ, RC	.05	.10
9	Glenn Anderson, Tor.	.05	.10
10	Sergei Bautin, Win.	.05	.10
11	Al Iafrate, Wash.	.05	.10
12	Gary Shuchuk, LA RC	.07	.15
13	Matthew Barnaby, Buf. RC	.10	.20
14	Tim Cheveldae, Goalie, Det.	.05	.10
15	Sean Burke, Goalie, Hart.	.05	.10
16	Ray Ferraro, NYI	.05	.10
17	Josef Beranek, Phi.	.05	.10
18	Bob Beers, TB	.05	.10

424 • Fleer Ultra — 1993 - 94 Promotional Sheet —

— 1993 - 94 REGULAR ISSUE — FLEER ULTRA • 425

No.	Player	EX	NRMT
19	Greg Adams, Van.	.05	.10
20	John Cullen, Tor.	.05	.10
21	Kirk Muller, Mon.	.05	.10
22	Ed Belfour, Goalie, Chi.	.12	.25
23	Kevin Dahl, Cal.	.05	.10
24	Robert Blake, LA	.05	.10
25	Michael Gartner, NYR	.05	.10
26	Tom Barrasso, Goalie, Pit.	.05	.10
27	Garth Butcher, St.L	.05	.10
28	Donald Beaupre, Goalie, Wash.	.05	.10
29	Kirk McLean, Goalie, Van.	.0	.20
30	Felix Potvin, Goalie, Tor.	.75	1.50
31	Doug Bodger, Buf.	.05	.10
32	Dino Ciccarelli, Det.	.05	.10
33	Andrew Cassels, Har.	.05	.10
34	Patrick Flatley, NYI	.05	.10
35	**Jason Bowen, Phl., RC**	.07	.15
36	Brian Bradley, TB	.05	.10
37	Pavel Bure, Van.	.75	1.50
38	David Ellett, Tor.	.05	.10
39	Patrick Roy, Goalie, Mon.	.35	.75
40	Chris Chelios, Chi.	.05	.10
41	Theoren Fleury, Cal.	.05	.10
42	Jimmy Carson, LA	.05	.10
43	Adam Graves, NYR	.15	.30
44	Ronald Francis, Pit.	.05	.10
45	Nelson Emerson, St.L	.05	.10
46	Peter Bondra, Wash.	.05	.10
47	Sergio Momesso, Van.	.05	.10
48	Teemu Selanne, Win.	.75	1.50
49	Joseph Juneau, Bos.	.25	.50
50	Russell Courtnall, Dal.	.05	.10
51	Shayne Corson, Edm.	.05	.10
52	Patrice Brisebois, Mon.	.05	.10
53	John MacLean, NJ	.05	.10
54	Daniel Berthiaume, Goalie, Ott.	.05	.10
55	Stephane Fiset, Goalie, Que.	.10	.20
56	Pat Falloon, SJ	.05	.10
57	David Andreychuk, Tor.	.07	.15
58	Eugeny Davydov, Win.	.05	.10
59	Dimitri Khristich, Wash.	.05	.10
60	Darryl Sydor, LA	.05	.10
61	Dirk Graham, Chi.	.05	.10
62	Chris Lindberg, Cal.	.05	.10
63	Tony Granato, LA	.05	.10
64	**Corey Hirsch, Goalie, NYR, RC**	.12	.25
65	Jaromir Jagr, Pit.	.25	.50
66	Bret Hedican, St.L	.05	.10
67	Pat Elynuik, Wash.	.05	.10
68	Petr Nedved, Van.	.05	.10
69	Thomas Steen, Win.	.05	.10
70	**Philippe Boucher, Buf., RC**	.07	.15
71	Paul Coffey, Det.	.10	.20
72	**Mike Lenarduzzi, Goalie, Hart., RC**	.07	.15
73	**Iain Fraser, Que., RC**	.10	.20
74	Rod Brind'Amour, Phi.	.10	.20
75	Shawn Chambers, TB	.05	.10
76	Geoff Courtnall, Van.	.05	.10
77	Todd Gill, Tor.	.05	.10
78	Mathieu Schneider, Mon.	.05	.10
79	Vincent Damphousse, Mon.	.05	.10
80	Igor Kravchuk, Edm.	.05	.10
81	Ulf Dahlen, Dal.	.05	.10
82	Dmitri Kvartalnov, Bos.	.05	.10
83	Johan Garpenlov, SJ	.05	.10
84	Valeri Kamensky, Que.	.10	.20
85	Bob Kudelski, Ott.	.05	.10
86	Bernie Nicholls, NJ	.05	.10
87	Alexei Zhitnik, LA	.10	.20
88	Kelly Miller, Wash.	.05	.10
89	Bob Essensa, Goalie, Win.	.05	.10
90	Drake Berehowsky, Tor.	.07	.15
91	**Post Season Trade:** Jon Casey, Goalie, Bos.	.05	.10
92	Dave Gagner, Dal.	.05	.10
93	Dave Manson, Edm.	.05	.10
94	Eric Desjardins, Mon.	.05	.10
95	Scott Niedermayer, NJ	.12	.25
96	**Post Season Trade:** Chris Luongo, NYI	.05	.10
97	**Dave Karpa, Que., RC**	.07	.15
98	**Rob Gaudreau, SJ, RC**	.12	.25
99	Nikolai Borschevsky, Tor.	.10	.20

No.	Player	EX	NRMT
100	Phil Housley, Win.	.05	.10
101	Michal Pivonka, Wash.	.05	.10
102	Dixon Ward, Van.	.05	.10
103	Grant Fuhr, Goalie, Buf.	.05	.10
104	**Dallas Drake, Det., RC**	.12	.25
105	Michael Nylander, Hart.	.10	.20
106	**Post Season Trade:** Glenn Healy, Goalie, NYR	.05	.10
107	Kevin Dineen, Phi.	.05	.10
108	Roman Hamrlik, TB	.10	.20
109	Trevor Linden, Van.	.10	.20
110	Douglas Gilmour, Tor.	.25	.50
111	Keith Tkachuk, Win.	.15	.30
112	Sergei Krivokrasov, Chi.	.05	.10
113	Allan MacInnis, Cal.	.05	.10
114	Wayne Gretzky, LA	.75	1.50
115	Alexei Kovalev, NYR	.30	.60
116	Mario Lemieux, Pit.	.75	1.05
117	Brett Hull, St.L	.25	.50
118	Kevin Hatcher, Wash.	.05	.10
119	Cliff Ronning, Van.	.05	.10
120	**Viktor Gordiouk, Buf. RC**	.07	.15
121	Sergei Fedorov, Det.	.50	1.00
122	Patrick Poulin, Hart.	.05	.10
123	Benoit Hogue, NYI	.05	.10
124	Garry Galley, Phi.	.05	.10
125	Pat Jablonski, Goalie, TB	.05	.10
126	Jyrki Lumme, Van.	.05	.10
127	Dimitri Mironov, Tor.	.05	.10
128	Alexei Zhamnov, Win.	.25	.50
129	Steve Larmer, Chi.	.05	.10
130	Joe Nieuwendyk, Cal.	.05	.10
131	Kelly Hrudey, Goalie, LA	.05	.10
132	Brian Leetch, NYR	.20	.40
133	Shawn McEachern, Pit.	.10	.20
134	Craig Janney, St.L	.05	.10
135	Dale Hunter, Wash.	.05	.10
136	Jiri Slegr, Van.	.05	.10
137	Mats Sundin, Que.	.02	.20
138	Cam Neely, Bos.	.07	.15
139	Derian Hatcher, Dal.	.05	.10
140	**Shjon Podein, Edm., RC**	.10	.20
141	Gilbert Dionne, Mon.	.05	.10
142	**Scott Pellerin, NJ RC**	.10	.20
143	Norm MacIver, Ott.	.05	.10
144	Andrei Kovalenko, Que.	.10	.20
145	Artus Irbe, Goalie, SJ	.17	.35
146	Wendel Clark, Tor.	.07	.15
147	Fredrik Olausson, Win.	.05	.10
148	Mike Ridley, Wash.	.05	.10
149	Dale Hawerchuk, Buf.	.05	.10
150	Vladimir Konstantinov, Det.	.05	.10
151	Geoff Sanderson, Hart.	.15	.30
152	Stephane J. J. Richer, NJ	.07	.15
153	Darren Rumble, Ott.	.05	.10
154	Owen Nolan, Que.	.05	.10
155	Kelly Kisio, SJ	.05	.10
156	Adam Oates, Bos.	.07	.15
157	Trent Klatt, Dal.	.05	.10
158	Bill Ranford, Goalie, Edm.	.05	.10
159	Paul Di Pietro, Mon.	.05	.10
160	Darius Kasparaitis, NYI	.05	.10
161	Eric Lindros, Phi.	1.50	3.00
162	Chris Kontos, TB	.05	.10
163	Joe Murphy, Chi.	.05	.10
164	Robert Reichel, Cal.	.05	.10
165	Jari Kurri, LA	.05	.10
166	Alexander Semak, NJ	.05	.10
167	Brad Shaw, Ott.	.05	.10
168	Mike Ricci, Que.	.05	.10
169	Sandis Ozolinch, SJ	.12	.25
170	**Joby Messier, NYR, RC**	.07	.15
171	Joe Mullen, Pitt.	.05	.10
172	Curtis Joseph, Goalie, St.L	.07	.15
173	Yuri Khmylev, Buf.	.05	.10
174	Vyacheslav Kozlov, Det.	.35	.75
175	Patrick Verbeek, Hart.	.05	.10
176	Derek King, NYI	.05	.10
177	Ryan McGill, Phi.	.05	.10
178	**Chris LiPuma, TB, RC**	.07	.15
179	Gregori Pantaleyev, Bos.	.05	.10
180	Richard Matvichuk, Dal.	.05	.10
181	Steven Rice, Edm.	.05	.10

No.	Player	EX	NRMT
182	**Expansion Draft:** Sean Hill, MDA	.05	.10
183	Mark Messier, NYR	.10	.20
184	Lawrence Murphy, Pitt.	.05	.10
185	Igor Korolev, St.L	.05	.10
186	Jeremy Roenick, Chi.	.35	.75
187	Gary Roberts, Cal.	.05	.10
188	**Robert Lang, LA, RC**	.07	.15
189	Scott Stevens, NJ	.05	.10
190	Sylvain Turgeon, Ott.	.05	.10
191	Martin Rucinsky, Que.	.05	.10
192	**Jean-Francois Quintin, SJ, RC**	.07	.15
193	David Poulin, Bos.	.05	.10
194	Michael Modano, Dal.	.15	.30
195	Doug Weight, Edm.	.05	.10
196	Mike Keane, Mon.	.05	.10
197	Pierre Turgeon, NYI	.10	.20
198	Dimitri Yushkevich, Phi.	.05	.10
199	Rob Zamuner, TB	.05	.10
200	Richard Smehlik, Buf.	.05	.10
201	Steve Yzerman, Det.	.17	.35
202	Anthony Amonte, NYR	.05	.10
203	Sergei Nemchinov, NYR	.05	.10
204	Ulf Samuelsson, Pit.	.05	.10
205	**Kevin Miehm, St.L, RC**	.07	.15
206	Brent Sutter, Chi.	.05	.10
207	Michael Vernon, Goalie, Cal.	.05	.10
208	Luc Robitaille, LA	.10	.20
209	Chris Terreri, Goalie, NJ	.05	.10
210	Philippe Bozon, St.L	.05	.10
211	John Tucker, TB	.05	.10
212	Jozef Stumpel, Bos.	.05	.10
213	Mark Tinordi, Dal.	.05	.10
214	Bruce Driver, NJ	.05	.10
215	John LeClair, Mon.	.05	.10
216	Steve Thomas, NYI	.05	.10
217	Tommy Soderstrom, Goalie, Phi.	.10	.20
218	Kevin Miller, St.L	.05	.10
219	Pat LaFontaine, Buf.	.10	.20
220	Niklas Lidstrom, Det.	.05	.10
221	**Expansion Draft:** Terry Yake, MDA	.05	.10
222	Valeri Zelepukin, NJ	.07	.15
223	Jeff Brown, St.L	.05	.10
224	**Chris Simon, Que., RC**	.10	.20
225	Rick Tocchet, Pit.	.05	.10
226	Gary Suter, Cal.	.05	.10
227	Martin McSorley, LA	.05	.10
228	Mike Richter, Goalie, NYR	.12	.25
229	Kevin Stevens, Pit.	.12	.25
230	Douglas Jr. Wilson, SJ	.05	.10
231	James Stephen (Steve) Smith, Chi.	.05	.10
232	**Bryan Smolinski, Bos. RC**	.30	.60
233	Tommy Sjodin, Dal.	.05	.10
234	Zarley Zalapski, Hart.	.05	.10
235	Vladimir Malakhov, NYI	.10	.20
236	Mark Recchi, Phi.	.15	.30
237	**David Littman, TB RC**	.07	.15
238	Alexander Mogilny, Buf.	.25	.50
239	Keith Primeau, Det.	.05	.10
240	**Tyler Wright, Edm. RC**	.07	.17
241	Stephan Lebeau, Mon.	.05	.10
242	Joe Sakic, Que.	.12	.25
243	Sergei Zubov, NYR	.30	.60
244	Martin Straka, Pit.	.25	.50
245	Brendan Shanahan, St.L	.10	.20
246	Tomas Sandstrom, LA	.05	.10
247	**Expansion Draft:** Milan Tichy, Fl. RC	.10	.20
248	**C.J. Young, Bos. RC**	.07	.15
249	Checklist 1	.05	.10
250	Checklist 2	.05	.10

SERIES TWO

MIGHTY DUCKS OF ANAHEIM

No.	Player	EX	NRMT
251	Rookie: Patrik Carnback, RC	.10	.20
252	Todd Ewen	.05	.10
253	Stu Grimson	.05	.10
254	Guy Hebert, Goalie	.10	.20
255	Sean Hill	.05	.10

FLEER ULTRA — 1993-94 REGULAR ISSUE

No.	Player	EX	NRMT
256	Bill Houlder	.05	.10
257	Alexei Kasatonov	.05	.10
258	Steven King	.05	.10
259	Troy Loney	.05	.10
260	Joseph Sacco	.05	.10
261	Anatoli Semenov	.05	.10
262	Tim Sweeney	.05	.10
263	Ron Tugnutt, Goalie	.05	.10
264	Shaun Van Allen	.05	.10
265	Terry Yake	.05	.10

BOSTON BRUINS

No.	Player	EX	NRMT
266	Jon Casey, Goalie	.05	.10
267	Ted Donato	.05	.10
268	Steven Leach	.05	.10
269	David Reid	.05	.10
270	Rookie: Cameron Stewart, RC	.10	.20
271	Don Sweeney	.05	.10
272	Glen Wesley	.05	.10

BUFFALO SABRES

No.	Player	EX	NRMT
273	Donald Audette	.05	.10
274	Dominik Hasek, Goalie	.15	.30
275	Rookie: Sergei Petrenko, RC	.10	.20
276	Rookie: Derek Plante, RC	.50	1.00
277	Craig Simpson	.05	.10
278	Robert Sweeney	.05	.10
279	Randy Wood	.05	.10

CALGARY FLAMES

No.	Player	EX	NRMT
280	Rookie: Ted Drury, RC	.10	.20
281	Rookie: Trevor Kidd, Goalie	.07	.15
282	Kelly Kisio	.05	.10
283	Frantisek Musil	.05	.10
284	Rookie: Jason Muzzatti, Goalie, RC	.10	.20
285	Joel Otto	.05	.10
286	Paul Ranheim	.05	.10
287	Wes Walz	.05	.10

CHICAGO BLACK HAWKS

No.	Player	EX	NRMT
288	Rookie: Ivan Droppa, RC	.10	.20
289	Michel Goulet	.05	.10
290	Stephane Matteau	.05	.10
291	Brian Noonan	.05	.10
292	Patrick Poulin	.05	.10
293	Richard Sutter	.05	.10
294	Kevin Todd	.05	.10
295	Eric Weinrich	.05	.10

DALLAS STARS

No.	Player	EX	NRMT
296	Neal Broten	.05	.10
297	Mike Craig	.05	.10
298	Dean Evason	.05	.10
299	Grant Ledyard	.05	.10
300	Michael McPhee	.05	.10
301	Andrew Moog, Goalie	.05	.10
302	Rookie: Jarkko Varvio, RC	.10	.20

DETROIT RED WINGS

No.	Players	EX	NRMT
303	Rookie: Micah Alzavoff, RC	.12	.25
304	Terry Carkner	.05	.10
305	Steve Chiasson	.05	.10
306	Rookie: Greg Johnson, RC	.10	.20
307	Rookie: Darren McCarty, RC	.12	.25
308	Rookie: Chris Osgood, Goalie, RC	.50	1.00
309	Bob Probert	.05	.10
310	Ray Ssheppard	.05	.10
311	Mike Sillinger	.05	.10

EDMONTON OILERS

No.	Players	EX	NRMT
312	Rookie: Jason Arnott, RC	1.00	2.00
313	Rookie: Fred Brathwaite, Goalie, RC	.10	.20
314	Kelly Buchberger	.05	.10

No.	Player	EX	NRMT
315	Zdeno Ciger	.05	.10
316	Craig MacTavish	.05	.10
317	Deam McAmmond	.05	.10
318	Luke Richardson	.05	.10
319	Vladimir Vujtek, RC	.10	.20

FLORIDA PANTHERS

No.	Player	EX	NRMT
320	Jesse Belanger	.05	.10
321	Brian Benning	.05	.10
322	Keith Brown	.05	.10
323	Eugeny Davydov	.05	.10
324	Tom Fitzgerald	.05	.10
325	Alexander Godynyuk	.05	.10
326	Rookie: Scott Levins, RC	.10	.20
327	Andrei Lomakin	.05	.10
328	Scott Mallanby	.05	.10
329	Gordon Murphy	.05	.10
330	Rookie: Rob Neidermayer, RC	.30	.60
331	Brent Severyn, RC	.10	.20
332	Brian Skrudland	.05	.10
333	John Vanbiesbrouck, Goalie	.07	.15

HARTFORD WHALERS

No.	Player	EX	NRMT
334	Mark Greig	.05	.10
335	Bryan Marchment	.05	.10
336	James Patrick	.05	.10
337	Robert Petrovicky	.05	.10
338	Frank Pietrangelo, Goalie	.05	.10
339	Rookie: Chris Pronger, RC	.30	.60
340	Brian Propp	.05	.10
341	Darren Turcotte	.05	.10

LOS ANGLES KINGS

No.	Player	EX	NRMT
342	Patrick Conacher	.05	.10
343	Mark Hardy	.05	.10
344	Charles Huddy	.05	.10
345	Shawn McEachern	.05	.10
346	Warren Rychel	.05	.10
347	Robb Stauber, Goalie	.05	.10
348	Dave Tayler	.05	.10

MONTREAL CANADIENS

No.	Player	EX	NRMT
349	Benoit Brunet	.05	.10
350	Guy Carbonneau	.05	.10
351	Jean-Jacques Daigneault	.05	.10
352	Kevin Haller	.05	.10
353	Gary Leeman	.05	.10
354	Lyle Odelein	.05	.10
355	Andre Racicot, Goalie	.05	.10
356	Ron Wilson, RC	.07	.15

NEW JERSEY DEVILS

No.	Player	EX	NRMT
357	Rookie: Martin Brodeur, Goalie, RC	.20	.40
358	Kenneth Daneyko	.05	.10
359	Bill Guerin	.05	.10
360	Robert Holik	.05	.10
361	Corey Millen	.05	.10
362	Rookie: Jaroslav Modry, RC	.12	.25
363	Rookie: Jason Smith, RC	.10	.20

NEW YORK ISLANDERS

No.	Player	EX	NRMT
364	Brad Dalgarno, RC	.07	.15
365	Travis Green, RC	.10	.20
366	Ron Hextall, Goalie	.05	.10
367	Rookie: Steve Junker, RC	.10	.20
368	Tom Kurvers	.05	.10
369	Scott Lachance	.05	.10
370	Marty McInnis	.05	.10

NEW YORK RANGERS

No.	Player	EX	NRMT
371	Glenn Healy, Goalie	.05	.10
372	Rookie: Alexander Karpovtsev, RC	.15	.30
373	Steve Larmer	.05	.10

No.	Player	EX	NRMT
374	Doug Lidster	.05	.10
375	Kevin Lowe	.05	.10
376	Rookie: Mattias Norstrom, RC	.10	.20
377	Esa Tikkanen	.05	.10

OTTAWA SENATORS

No.	Player	EX	NRMT
378	Craig Billington, Goalie	.05	.10
379	Rookie: Robert Burakovsky, RC	.10	.20
380	Rookie: Alexandre Daigle, RC	.50	1.00
381	Rookie: Dmitri Filimonov, RC	.12	.25
382	Rookie: Darrin Madeley, RC	.15	.30
383	Vladimir Ruzicka	.05	.10
384	Rookie: Alexei Yashin, RC	.75	1.50

PHILADELPHIA FLYERS

No.	Player	EX	NRMT
385	Viacheslav Butsayev	.05	.10
386	Pelle Eklund	.05	.10
387	Brent Fedyk	.05	.10
388	Greg Hawgood	.05	.10
389	Rookie: Milos Holan, RC	.10	.20
390	Rookie: Stewart Malgunas, RC	.10	.20
391	Rookie: Mikael Renberg, RC	.30	.60
392	Dominic Roussel, Goalie	.10	.20

PITTSBURGH PENGUINS

No.	Player	EX	NRMT
393	Doug Brown	.05	.10
394	Martin McSorley	.05	.10
395	Rookie: Markus Naslund, RC	.12	.25
396	Mike Ramsey	.05	.10
397	Peter Taglianetti	.05	.10
398	Bryan Trottier	.05	.10
399	Ken Wregget, Goalie	.05	.10

QUEBEC NORDIQUES

No.	Player	EX	NRMT
400	Iain Fraser, RC	.12	.25
401	Martin Gelinas	.05	.10
402	Kerry Huffman	.05	.10
403	Claude Lapointe	.05	.10
404	Curtis Leschyshyn	.05	.10
405	Chris Lindberg, RC	.10	.20
406	Rookie: Jocelyn Thibault, Goalie, RC	.25	.50

ST. LOUIS BLUES

No.	Player	EX	NRMT
407	Murray Baron	.05	.10
408	Bob Bassen	.05	.10
409	Phil Housley	.05	.10
410	Jim Hrivnak	.05	.10
411	Tony Hrkac	.05	.10
412	Rookie: Vitali Karamnov, RC	.12	.25
413	Rookie: Jim Montgomery, RC	.10	.20

SAN JOSE SHARKS

No.	Player	EX	NRMT
414	Rookie: Vlastimil Kroupa, RC	.15	.30
415	Igor Larionov	.05	.10
416	Sergei Makarov	.05	.10
417	Jeff Norton	.05	.10
418	Rookie: Mike Rathje, RC	.10	.20
419	Jim Waite, Goalie	.05	.10
420	Ray Whitney	.05	.10

TAMPA BAY LIGHTNING

No.	Player	EX	NRMT
421	Bo Mikael Andersson	.05	.10
422	Donald Dufresne	.05	.10
423	Rookie: Chris Gratton, RC	.30	.60
424	Rookie: Brent Gretzky, RC	.12	.25
425	Petr Klima	.05	.10
426	Rookie: Bill McDougall, RC	.15	.30
427	Daren Puppa, Goalie	.05	.10
428	Denis Savard	.05	.10

TORONTO MAPLE LEAFS

No.	Player	EX	NRMT
429	Ken Baumgartner	.05	.10
430	Sylvain Lefebvre	.05	.10
431	Jamie Macoun	.05	.10
432	Rookie: Matt Martin, RC	.15	.30
433	Mark Osborne	.05	.10
434	Rob Pearson	.05	.10
435	Rookie: Damian Rhodes, Goalie, RC	.15	.30
436	Peter Zezel	.05	.10

VANCOUVER CANUCKS

No.	Player	EX	NRMT
437	Rookie: Shawn Antoski, RC	.05	.10
438	Jose Charbonneau	.05	.10
439	Murray Craven	.05	.10
440	Gerald Diduck	.05	.10
441	Dana Murzyn	.05	.10
442	Gino Odjick	.05	.10
443	Kay Whitmore, Goalie	.05	.10

WASHINGTON CAPITALS

No.	Player	EX	NRMT
444	Randy Burridge	.05	.10
445	Sylvain Cote	.05	.10
446	Keith Jones	.05	.10
447	Rookie: Olaf Kolzig, Goalie, RC	.12	.25
448	Todd Krygier	.05	.10
449	Rookie: Pat Peake, RC	.05	.10
450	Dave Poulin	.05	.10

WINNIPEG JETS

No.	Player	EX	NRMT
451	Stephane Beauregard, Goalie	.05	.10
452	Luciano Borsata	.05	.10
453	Nelson Emerson	.05	.10
454	Rookie: Boris Mironov, RC	.05	.10
455	Teppo Numminen	.05	.10
456	Stephane Quintal	.05	.10
457	Paul Ysebaert	.05	.10

TEAM CANADA

No.	Player	EX	NRMT
458	Adrian Aucoin	.10	.20
459	Todd Brost	.12	.25
460	Martin Gendron	.12	.25
461	David Harlock	.15	.30
462	Corey Hirsch, Goalie	.10	.20
463	Todd Hlushko	.10	.20
464	Fabian Joseph	.10	.20
465	Paul Kariya	.50	1.00
466	Brett Lindros	2.00	4.00
467	Ken Lovsin	.10	.20
468	Jason Marshall	.05	.10
469	Derek Mayer	.05	.10
470	Dwayne Norris	.10	.20
471	Russ Romaniuk	.10	.20
472	Brian Savage	.10	.20
473	Trevor Sim	.10	.20
474	Chris Therien	.10	.20
475	Brad Turner	.10	.20
476	Todd Warriner	.20	.40
477	Craig Woodcroft	.10	.20

TEAM USA

No.	Player	EX	NRMT
478	Mark Beaufait	.10	.20
479	Jim Campbell	.10	.20
480	Ted Crowley	.10	.20
481	Mike Dunham, Goalie	.10	.20
482	Chris Ferraro	.20	.40
483	Peter Ferraro	.20	.40
484	Brett Hauer	.10	.20
485	Darby Hendrickson	.12	.25
486	Chris Imes	.10	.20
487	Craig Johnson	.10	.20
488	Peter Laviolette	.10	.20
489	Jeff Lazaro	.12	.25
490	John Lilley	.10	.20
491	Todd Marchant	.12	.25
492	Ian Moran	.10	.20
493	Travis Richards	.10	.20

No.	Player	EX	NRMT
494	Barry Richter	.10	.20
495	David Roberts	.10	.20
496	Brian Rolston	.50	1.00
497	David Sacco	.12	.25

CHECKLISTS

No.	Player	EX	NRMT
498	Checklist	.05	.10
499	Checklist	.05	.10
500	Checklist	.05	.10

— 1993 - 94 INSERT SETS —

ADAM OATES CAREER HIGHLIGHTS

Cards nos. 1 - 5 were randomly inserted in Series One foil packs, and cards nos. 6 - 10 were randomly inserted into Series Two foil packs. Cards nos. 11 - 12 were available only by mail.

1993-94 Adam Oates Career Highlights
Card No. 12, Giving till it Hurts

Card Size: 2 1/2" x 3 1/2"
Face: Four Colour, borderless; Name, Silver foil
Back: Four Colour; Name, Number, Resume on card stock
Imprint: ©1993 FLEER CORP. PRINTED IN U.S.A.
Complete Set No.: 12
Complete Set Price: 7.50 15.00
Common Card: .75 1.50

No.	Player	EX	NRMT
1	A Challenge Met	.75	1.50
2	Sowing His Oates, Boston Bruins	.75	1.50
3	Wanted Man, Detroit Red Wings	.75	1.50
4	Making The Grade, Detroit Red Wings	.75	1.50
5	Motor City Motion	.75	1.50
6	Hello and Goodbye, St. Louis Blues 1989-1992	.75	1.50
7	Blues' Brother, St. Louis Blues 1989-1992	.75	1.50
8	Hit the Ignition, St. Louis Blues 1989-1992	.75	1.50
9	The Break-up	.75	1.50
10	The Spotlight Shines	.75	1.50
11	North American Dream	.75	1.50
12	Giving till it Hurts	.75	1.50

ADAM OATES AUTOGRAPHED CARD

The card was randomly inserted into all foil packs.

Card Size: 2 1/2" x 3 1/2"
Face: Four Colour, borderless; Name, Silver foil, Silver sharpie autograph
Back: Four Colour; Name, Number, Resume on card stock
Imprint: ©1993 FLEER CORP. PRINTED IN U.S.A.

No.	Player	EX	NRMT
1	Adam Oates, Bos. Autographed	60.00	125.00

ALL ROOKIE

This 10-card set was randomly inserted into Series One jumbo foil packs only.

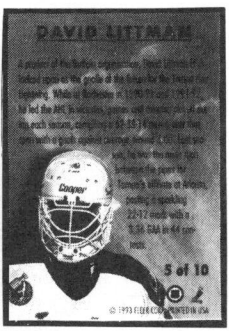

1993-94 All Rookie
Card No. 5, David Littman

Card Size: 2 1/2" x 3 1/2"
Face: Four Colour, borderless; Name, Gold foil
Back: Four Colour; Name, Number, Resume
Imprint: ©1993 FLEER CORP. PRINTED IN U.S.A.
Complete Set. No.: 10
Complete Set Price: 35.00 75.00
Common Card: 3.50 7.00

No.	Player	EX	NRMT
1	Philippe Boucher, Buf.	3.50	7.00
2	Viktor Gordiouk, Buf.	3.50	7.00
3	Corey Hirsch, Goalie, NYR	5.00	10.00
4	Chris LiPuma, TB	3.50	7.00
5	David Littman, TB	3.50	7.00
6	Joby Messier, NYR	3.50	7.00
7	Chris Simon, Que.	3.50	7.00
8	Bryab Smolinski, Bos.	7.50	15.00
9	Jozef Stumpel, Bos.	3.50	7.00
10	Milan Tichy, Chi.	3.50	7.00

ALL STARS

This 18-card set was randomly inserted into Series One foil packs.

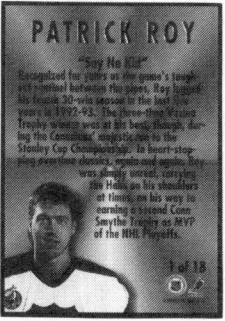

1993-94 All Stars
Card No. 1, Patrick Roy

Card Size: 2 1/2" x 3 1/2"
Face: Four Colour, borderless; Name, Gold foil
Back: Four Colour; Name, Number, Resume, Gold foil
Imprint: ©1993 FLEER CORP. PRINTED IN U.S.A.
Complete Set No.: 18
Complete Set Price: 40.00 85.00
Common Card: 2.00 4.00

No.	Player	EX	NRMT
1	Patrick Roy, Goalie, Mon.	5.00	10.00
2	Raymond Bourque, Bos.	2.50	5.00
3	Pierre Turgeon, NYI	2.50	5.00
4	Pat LaFontaine, Buf.	2.50	5.00
5	Alexander Mogilny, Buf.	2.50	5.00
6	Kevin Stevens, Pit.	2.00	4.00
7	Adam Oates, Bos.	2.50	5.00
8	Al Iafrate, Wash.	2.00	4.00
9	Kirk Muller, Mon.	2.00	4.00

428 • FLEER ULTRA — 1993 - 94 INSERT SETS

No.	Player	EX	NRMT
10	Ed Belfour, Goalie, Chi.	2.50	5.00
11	Temmu Selanne, Win.	3.50	7.00
12	Steve Yzerman, Det.	2.50	5.00
13	Luc Robitaille, LA	2.00	4.00
14	Chris Chelios, Chi.	2.00	4.00
15	Wayne Gretzky, LA	6.00	12.00
16	Douglas Gilmour, Tor.	3.00	6.00
17	Pavel Bure, Van.	5.00	10.00
18	Phil Housley, Win.	2.00	4.00

AWARD WINNERS 93-94

This 6-card set was randomly inserted into Series One foil packs. The set depicts the major trophy winners from the 92-93 season.

 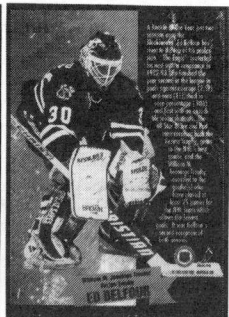

Award Winners 93-94
Card No. 1, Ed Belfour

Card Size: 2 1/2" x 3 1/2"
Face: Four Colour, borderless; Name, Gold foil
Back: Four Colour; Name, Number, Resume on card stock
Imprint: © 1993 FLEER CORP. PRINTED IN U.S.A.
Complete Set No.: 6
Complete Set Price: 17.50 35.00
Common Card: 2.00 4.00

No.	Player	EX	NRMT
1	William M. Jennings Trophy / Vezina Trophy: Ed Belfour, Chi.	2.00	4.00
2	James Norris Memorial Trophy: Chris Chelios, Chi.	2.00	4.00
3	Frank Selke Memorial Trophy: Douglas Gilmour, Tor.	2.50	5.00
4	Masterton Memorial Trophy, Art RossTrophy, Hart Trophy: Mario Lemieux, Pit.	5.00	10.00
5	King Clency Trophy: David Poulin, Bos.	2.00	4.00
6	Calder Trophy: Teemu Selanne, Win.	3.50	7.00

PREMIER PIVOTS

This 10-card set was randomly inserted into Series Two foil packs.

1993-94 Premier Pivots
Card No. 6, Mark Messier

Card Size: 2 1/2" x 3 1/2"
Face: Four Colour, borderless; Name, Gold foil
Back: Four Colour; Name, Number, Resume
Imprint: ©1993 FLEER CORP. PRINTED IN U.S.A.
Complete Set No.: 10
Complete Set Price: 15.00 30.00
Common Card: .50 1.00

No.	Player	EX	NRMT
1	Douglas Gilmour, Tor.	2.50	5.00
2	Wayne Gretzky, LA	5.00	10.00
3	Pat LaFontaine, Buf.	1.50	3.00
4	Mario Lemieux, Pit.	3.00	6.00
5	Eric Lindros, Phi.	5.00	10.00
6	Mark Messier, NYR	1.00	2.00
7	Adam Oates, Bos.	.50	1.00
8	Jeremy Roenick, Chi.	1.50	3.00
9	Pierre Turgeon, NYI	.75	1.50
10	Steve Yzerman, Det.	1.00	2.00

PROSPECTS 93-94

This 10-card set was randomly inserted into Series One foil packs.

 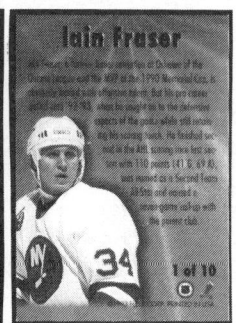

Prospects 93-94
Card No. 1, Iain Fraser

Card Size: 2 1/2" x 3 1/2"
Face: Four Colour, borderless; Name, Gold foil
Back: Four Colour; Name, Number, Resume, Gold foil
Imprint: ©1993 FLEER CORP. PRINTED IN U.S.A.
Complete Set No : 10
Complete Set Price: 12.50 25.00
Common Card: 1.00 2.00

No.	Player	EX	NRMT
1	Iain Fraser, NYI	.50	1.00
2	Rob Gaudreau, SJ	1.50	3.00
3	Dave Karpa, Que.	1.00	2.00
4	Trent Klatt, Min.	1.00	2.00
5	Mike Lenarduzzi, Goalie, Har.	1.00	2.00
6	Kevin Miehm, St.L	1.00	2.00
7	Michael Nylander, Har.	1.50	3.00
8	J.F. Quintin, SJ	1.00	2.00
9	Gary Shuchuk, LA	1.00	2.00
10	Tyler Wright, Edm.	1.00	2.00

RED LIGHT SPECIALS

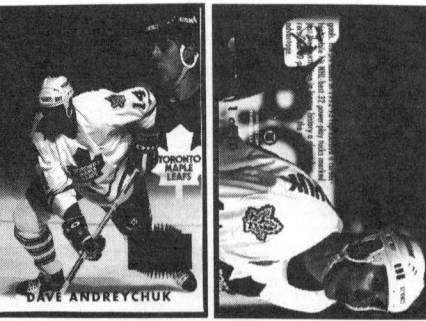

1993-94 Red Light Specials
Card No. 1, David Andreychuk

This 10-card set was randomly inserted into Series Two foil packs.

Card Size: 2 1/2" x 3 1/2"
Face: Four Colour, borderless; Name, Red foil
Back: Four Colour; Name, Number, Team, Resume
Imprint: ©1993 FLEER CORP. PRINTED IN U.S.A.
Complete Set No.: 10
Complete Set Price: 13.50 27.00
Common Card: .50 1.00

No.	Player	EX	NRMT
1	David Andreychuk, Tor.	.75	1.50
2	Pavel Bure, Van.	4.00	8.00
3	Michael Gartner, NYR	.75	1.50
4	Brett Hull, St.L	1.00	2.00
5	Jaromir Jagr, Pit.	1.25	2.50
6	Mario Lemieux, Pit.	3.00	6.00
7	Alexander Mogilny, Buf.	1.25	2.50
8	Mark Recchi, Phi.	.50	1.00
9	Luc Robitaille, LA	.50	1.00
10	Teemu Selanne. Win.	2.00	4.00

SCORING KINGS

This 6-card set was randomly inserted into Series One foil packs.

 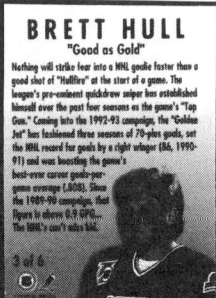

1993-94 Scoring Kings
Card No. 3, Brett Hull

Card Size: 2 1/2" x 3 1/2"
Face: Four Colour, borderless; Name, Gold foil
Back: Four Colour; Name, Number, Resume
Imprint: ©1993 FLEER CORP. PRINTED IN U.S.A.
Complete Set No.: 6
Complete Set Price: 25.00 50.00
Common Card: 3.00 6.00

No.	Player	EX	NRMT
1	Pat LaFontaine, Buf.	3.00	6.00
2	Wayne Gretzky, LA	7.50	15.00
3	Brett Hull, St.L	3.50	7.00
4	Mario Lemieux, Pit.	6.00	12.00
5	Pierre Turgeon, NYI	3.00	6.00
6	Steve Yzerman, Det.	3.75	7.50

SPEED MERCHANTS

This 10-card set was randomly inserted into Series Two jumbo packs.
Card Size: 2 1/2" x 3 1/2"

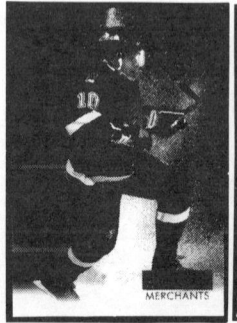 

1993-94 Speed Merchants
Card No. 1, Pavel Bure

Face: Four Colour, borderless; Name, Silver foil
Back: Four Colour; Name, Number, Resume on card stock
Imprint: ©1993 FLEER CORP. PRINTED IN U.S.A.
Complete Set No.: 10
Complete Set Price: 50.00 100.00
Common Card: 2.50 5.00

No.	Player	EX	NRMT
1	Pavel Bure, Van.	12.50	25.00
2	Russell Courtnall, Dal.	2.50	5.00
3	Sergei Fedorov, Det.	7.50	15.00
4	Michael Gartner, NYR	3.00	6.00
5	Al Iafrate, Wash.	3.00	6.00
6	Pat LaFontaine, Buf.	3.50	7.00
7	Alexander Mogilny, Buf.	5.00	10.00
8	Rob Niedermayer, Fl.	5.00	10.00
9	Geoff Sanderson, Hart.	3.50	7.00
10	Teemu Selanne, Win.	7.00	14.00

WAVE OF THE FUTURE

This 20-card set was randomly inserted into Series Two foil packs.

1993-94 Wave of the Future
Card No. 6, Milos Holan

Card Size: 2 1/2" x 3 1/2"
Face: Four Colour, borderless; Name, Gold foil
Back: Four Colour; Name, Number, Resume on card stock
Imprint: ©1993 FLEER CORP. PRINTED IN U.S.A.
Complete Set No.: 20
Complete Set Price: 20.00 40.00
Common Card: .50 1.00

No.	Player	EX	NRMT
1	Jason Arnott, Edm.	5.00	10.00
2	Martin Brodeur, Goalie, NJ.	3.50	7.00
3	Alexandre Daigle, Ott.	2.50	5.00
4	Ted Drury, Cal.	.50	1.00
5	Chris Gratton, TB	1.50	3.00
6	Milos Holan, Phi.	.50	1.00
7	Greg Johnson, Det.	.50	1.00
8	Boris Mironov, Win.	.50	1.00
9	Jaroslav Modry, NJ	.50	1.00
10	Markus Naslund, Cal.	.50	1.00
11	Rob Niedermayer, Fl.	1.50	3.00
12	Chris Osgood, Goalie, Det.	1.50	3.00
13	Derek Plante, Buf.	1.50	3.00
14	Chris Pronger, Har.	1.50	3.00
15	Mike Rathje, SJ	.75	1.50
16	Mikael Renberg, Phi.	2.50	5.00
17	Jason Smith, Cal.	.50	1.00
18	Jocelyn Thibault, Goalie, Que.	2.00	4.00
19	Jarkko Varvio, Dal.	.50	1.00
20	Alexei Yashin, Ott.	2.50	5.00

— 1993 - 94 POWER PLAY —

This 520-card set was divided into two series. Series One contains cards numbered 1 - 280 and Series Two cards numbered 281 to 520. The increased size of these cards allows for clear pictures with a bright overall appearance. The set has eight insert sets.

 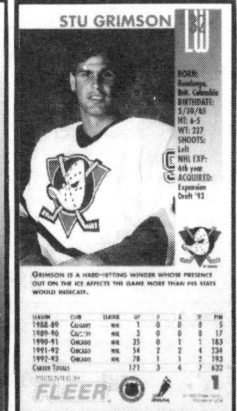

1993-94 Power Play
Card No. 1, Stu Grimson

Card Size: 2 1/2" x 5"
Face: Four colour, team coloured border; Name, Logo
Back: Four colour; Name, Number, Position, Player's number, Resume, Team Logo
Imprint: © 1993 FLEER CORP. PRINTED IN U.S.A.
Complete Set No.: 520
  Series One: 280
  Series Two: 240
Set Price:
  Series One: 15.00 30.00
  Series Two: 15.00 30.00
  Complete Set: 30.00 60.00
Common Card: .05 .10
Foil Pack:
  Series One: (14 Cards) 1.75
  Series Two: (14 Cards) 1.75
Foil Box:
  Series One: (36 Packs) 60.00
  Series Two: (36 Packs) 60.00

SERIES ONE

MIGHTY DUCKS OF ANAHEIM

No.	Player	EX	NRMT
1	Stu Grimson	.05	.10
2	Guy Hebert, Goalie	.10	.20
3	Sean Hill	.05	.10
4	Bill Houlder	.05	.10
5	Alexei Kasatonov	.05	.10
6	Steven King	.05	.10
7	Lonnie Loach	.05	.10
8	Troy Loney	.05	.10
9	Joseph Sacco	.05	.10
10	Anatoli Semenov	.05	.10
11	Jarrod Skalde	.05	.10
12	Tim Sweeney	.05	.10
13	Ron Tugnutt, Goalie	.05	.10
14	Terry Yake	.05	.10
15	Shaun Van Allen	.05	.10

BOSTON BRUINS

No.	Player	EX	NRMT
16	Raymond Bourque	.12	.25
17	Jon Casey, Goalie	.05	.10
18	Ted Donato	.05	.10
19	Joseph Juneau	.30	.60
20	Dmitri Kvartalnov	.05	.10
21	Stephen Leach	.05	.10
22	Cam Neely	.07	.15
23	Adam Oates	.10	.20
24	Don Sweeney	.05	.10
25	Glen Wesley	.05	.10

BUFFALO SABRES

No.	Player	EX	NRMT
26	Doug Bodger	.05	.10
27	Grant Fuhr, Goalie	.07	.15
28	Viktor Gordijuk	.05	.10
29	Dale Hawerchuk	.07	.15
30	Yuri Khmylev	.05	.10
31	Pat LaFontaine	.15	.30
32	Alexander Mogilny	.25	.50
33	Richard Smehlik	.05	.10
34	Robert Sweeney	.05	.10
35	Randy Wood	.05	.10

CALGARY FLAMES

No.	Player	EX	NRMT
36	Theoren Fleury	.07	.15
37	Kelly Kisio	.05	.10
38	Allan MacInnis	.07	.15
39	Joe Nieuwendyk	.07	.15
40	Joel Otto	.05	.10
41	Robert Reichel	.10	.20
42	Gary Roberts	.05	.10
43	Ronald Stern	.05	.10
44	Gary Suter	.05	.10
45	Michael Vernon, Goalie	.07	.15

CHICAGO BLACKHAWKS

No.	Player	EX	NRMT
46	Ed Belfour, Goalie	.12	.25
47	Chris Chelios	.07	.15
48	Karl Dykhuis	.05	.10
49	Michel Goulet	.05	.10
50	Dirk Graham	.05	.10
51	Sergei Krivokrasov	.05	.10
52	Steve Larmer	.05	.10
53	Joe Murphy	.05	.10
54	Jeremy Roenick	.35	.75
55	James (Steve) Smith	.05	.10
56	Brent Sutter	.05	.10

DALLAS STARS

No.	Player	EX	NRMT
57	Neal Broten	.05	.10
58	Russell Courtnall	.07	.15
59	Ulf Dahlen	.05	.10
60	Dave Gagner	.05	.10
61	Derian Hatcher	.05	.10
62	Trent Klatt	.05	.10
63	Michael Modano	.25	.50
64	Andrew Moog, Goalie	.05	.10
65	Tommy Sjodin	.05	.10
66	Mark Tinordi	.05	.10

DETROIT RED WINGS

No.	Player	EX	NRMT
67	Tim Cheveldae, Goalie	.05	.10
68	Steve Chiasson	.05	.10
69	Dino Ciccarelli	.05	.10
70	Paul Coffey	.07	.15
71	Dallas Drake, RC	.07	.15
72	Sergei Fedorov	.50	1.00
73	Vladimir Konstantinov	.05	.10
74	Niklas Lidstrom	.05	.10
75	Keith Primeau	.05	.10
76	Ray Sheppard	.10	.20
77	Steve Yzerman	.15	.30

EDMONTON OILERS

No.	Player	EX	NRMT
78	Zdeno Ciger	.05	.10
79	Shayne Corson	.05	.10
80	Todd Elik	.05	.10
81	Igor Kravchuk	.05	.10
82	Craig MacTavish	.05	.10
83	Dave Manson	.05	.10
84	Shjon Podein, RC	.05	.10
85	Bill Ranford, Goalie	.07	.15
86	Steven Rice	.05	.10
87	Doug Weight	.05	.10

430 • FLEER ULTRA — 1993-94 Power Play

FLORIDA PANTHERS

No.	Player	EX	NRMT
88	**Doug Barrault, RC**	.07	.15
89	Jesse Belanger	.12	.25
90	Brian Benning	.05	.10
91	Joe Cirella	.05	.10
92	Mark Fitzpatrick, Goalie	.05	.10
93	Randy Gilhen	.05	.10
94	Mike Hough	.05	.10
95	Bill Lindsay	.05	.10
96	Andrei Lomakin	.05	.10
97	Dave Lowry	.05	.10
98	Scott Mellanby	.05	.10
99	Gordon Murphy	.05	.10
100	Brian Skrudland	.05	.10
101	**Milan Tichy, RC**	.10	.20
102	John Vanbiesbrouck, Goalie	.05	.10

HARTFORD WHALERS

No.	Player	EX	NRMT
103	Sean Burke, Goalie	.05	.10
104	Andrew Cassels	.07	.15
105	Nickolas Kypreos	.05	.10
106	Mikael Nylander	.10	.20
107	Robert Petrovicky	.05	.10
108	Patrick Poulin	.05	.10
109	Geoff Sanderson	.18	.35
110	Patrick Verbeek	.05	.10
111	Eric Weinrich	.05	.10
112	Zarley Zalapski	.05	.10

LOS ANGELES KINGS

No.	Player	EX	NRMT
113	Robert Blake	.07	.15
114	Jimmy Carson	.05	.10
115	Tony Granato	.05	.10
116	Wayne Gretzky	.75	1.50
117	Kelly Hrudey, Goalie	.05	.10
118	Jari Kurri	.05	.10
119	Shawn McEachern	.05	.10
120	Luc Robitaille	.10	.20
121	Tomas Sandstrom	.05	.10
122	Darryl Sydor	.05	.10
123	Alexei Zhitnik	.10	.20

MONTREAL CANADIENS

No.	Player	EX	NRMT
124	Brian Bellows	.05	.10
125	Patrice Brisebois	.05	.10
126	Guy Carbonneau	.07	.15
127	Vincent Damphousse	.07	.15
128	Eric Desjardins	.05	.10
129	Mike Keane	.05	.10
130	Stephan LeBeau	.05	.10
131	Kirk Muller	.05	.10
132	Lyle Odelein	.05	.10
133	Patrick Roy, Goalie	.50	1.00
134	Mathieu Schneider	.05	.10

NEW JERSEY DEVILS

No.	Player	EX	NRMT
135	Bruce Driver	.05	.10
136	Viacheslav Fetisov	.07	.15
137	Claude Lemieux	.07	.15
138	John MacLean	.05	.10
139	Bernie Nicholls	.05	.10
140	Scott Niedermayer	.12	.25
141	Stephane J. J. Richer	.05	.10
142	Alexander Semak	.05	.10
143	Scott Stevens	.07	.15
144	Chris Terreri, Goalie	.05	.10
145	Valeri Zelepukin	.05	.10

NEW YORK ISLANDERS

No.	Player	EX	NRMT
146	Patrick Flatley	.05	.10
147	Ron Hextall, Goalie	.05	.10
148	Benoit Hogue	.05	.10
149	Darius Kasparaitis	.07	.15
150	Derek King	.05	.10
151	Uwe Krupp	.05	.10
152	Scott Lachance	.07	.15
153	Vladimir Malakhov	.10	.20
154	Steve Thomas	.05	.10
155	Pierre Turgeon	.12	.25

NEW YORK RANGERS

No.	Player	EX	NRMT
156	Anthony Amonte	.05	.10
157	Michael Gartner	.07	.15
158	Adam Graves	.15	.30
159	Alexei Kovalev	.25	.50
160	Brian Leetch	.15	.30
161	**Joby Messier, RC**	.07	.15
162	Sergei Nemchinov	.05	.10
163	James Patrick	.05	.10
164	Mike Richter, Goalie	.12	.25
166	Darren Turcotte	.05	.10
167	Sergei Zubov	.35	.70

OTTAWA SENATORS

No.	Player	EX	NRMT
168	Dave Archibald	.05	.10
169	Craig Billington, Goalie	.05	.10
170	Bob Kudelski	.05	.10
171	Mark Lamb	.05	.10
172	Norm Maciver	.05	.10
173	Darren Rumble	.05	.10
174	Vladimir Ruzicka	.05	.10
175	Brad Shaw	.05	.10
176	Sylvain Turgeon	.05	.10

PHILADELPHIA FLYERS

No.	Player	EX	NRMT
177	Josef Beranek	.07	.15
178	Rod Brind'Amour	.10	.20
179	Kevin Dineen	.05	.10
180	Per-Erik Eklund	.05	.10
181	Brent Fedyk	.05	.10
182	Garry Galley	.05	.10
183	Eric Lindros	1.50	3.00
184	Mark Recchi	.12	.25
185	Tommy Soderstrom, Goalie	.07	.15
186	Dimitri Yushkevich	.05	.10

PITTSBURGH PENGUINS

No.	Player	EX	NRMT
187	Tom Barrasso, Goalie	.07	.15
188	Ronald Francis	.07	.15
189	Jaromir Jagr	.25	.50
190	Mario Lemieux	.75	1.50
191	Martin McSorley	.05	.10
192	Joe Mullen	.05	.10
193	Lawrence Murphy	.05	.10
194	Ulf Samuelsson	.05	.10
195	Kevin Stevens	.12	.25
196	Rick Tocchet	.07	.15

QUEBEC NORDIQUES

No.	Player	EX	NRMT
197	Steve Duchesne	.07	.15
198	Stephane Fiset, Goalie	.10	.20
199	Valeri Kamensky	.10	.20
200	Andrei Kovalenko	.10	.20
201	Owen Nolan	.07	.15
202	Mike Ricci	.07	.15
203	Martin Rucinsky	.05	.10
204	Joe Sakic	.12	.25
205	Mats Sundin	.12	.25
206	Scott Young	.05	.10

ST. LOUIS BLUES

No.	Player	EX	NRMT
207	Jeff Brown	.05	.10
208	Garth Butcher	.05	.10
209	Nelson Emerson	.07	.15
210	Bret Hedican	.05	.10
211	Brett Hull	.25	.50
212	Craig Janney	.07	.15
213	Curtis Joseph, Goalie	.12	.25
214	Igor Korolev	.05	.10
215	Kevin Miller	.05	.10
216	Brendan Shanahan	.10	.20

SAN JOSE SHARKS

No.	Player	EX	NRMT
217	Ed Courtnay	.05	.10
218	Pat Falloon	.10	.20
219	Johan Garpenlov	.05	.10
220	**Rob Gaudreau, RC**	.10	.25
221	Arturs Irbe, Goalie	.18	.35
222	Sergei Makarov (Traded from Whalers)	.07	.15
223	Jeff Norton	.05	.10
224	Jeff Odgers	.05	.10
225	Sandis Ozolinch	.12	.25
226	Tom Pederson	.05	.10

TAMPA BAY LIGHTNING

No.	Player	EX	NRMT
227	Bob Beers	.05	.10
228	Brian Bradley	.05	.10
229	Shawn Chambers	.05	.10
230	Gerard Gallant (Traded from Detroit)	.05	.10
231	Roman Hamrlik	.10	.20
232	Petr Klima (Traded from Oilers)	.05	.10
233	Chris Kontos	.07	.15
234	Daren Puppa, Goalie, (Traded from Toronto)	.05	.10
235	John Tucker	.05	.10
236	Rob Zamuner	.05	.10

TORONTO MAPLE LEAFS

No.	Player	EX	NRMT
237	Glenn Anderson	.07	.15
238	David Andreychuk	.10	.20
239	Drake Berehowsky	.07	.15
240	Nikolai Borschevsky	.07	.15
241	Wendel Clark	.07	.15
242	John Cullen	.05	.10
243	David Ellett	.05	.10
244	Douglas Gilmour	.25	.50
245	Dimitri Mironov	.05	.10
246	Felix Potvin, Goalie	.50	1.00

VANCOUVER CANUCKS

No.	Player	EX	NRMT
247	Greg Adams	.05	.10
248	Pavel Bure	.50	1.00
249	Geoff Courtnall	.07	.15
250	Gerald Diduck	.05	.10
251	Trevor Linden	.10	.20
252	Jyrki Lumme	.05	.10
253	Kirk McLean, Goalie	.10	.20
254	Petr Nedved	.07	.15
255	Cliff Ronning	.07	.15
256	Jiri Slegr	.07	.15
257	Dixon Ward	.05	.10

WASHINGTON CAPITALS

No.	Player	EX	NRMT
258	Peter Bondra	.05	.10
259	Sylvain Cote	.05	.10
260	Pat Elynuik	.05	.10
261	Kevin Hatcher	.07	.15
262	Dale Hunter	.05	.10
263	Al Iafrate	.07	.15
264	Dimitri Khristich	.05	.10
265	Michal Pivonka	.05	.10
266	Mike Ridley	.05	.10
267	Richard Tabaracci, Goalie	.05	.10

WINNIPEG JETS

No.	Player	EX	NRMT
268	Sergei Bautin	.07	.15
269	Eugeny Davydov	.05	.10
270	Bob Essensa, Goalie	.05	.10
271	Phil Housley	.05	.10
272	Teppo Numminen	.05	.10
273	Fredrick Olausson	.05	.10
274	Teemu Selanne	.50	.100
275	Thomas Steen	.05	.10
276	Keith Tkachuk	.12	.25
277	Paul Ysebaert (Traded from Red Wings)	.07	.15
278	Alexei Zhamnov	..20	.40

1993-94 POWER PLAY — FLEER ULTRA • 431

CHECKLISTS

No.	Player	EX	NRMT
279	Checklist 1 (1 - 164)	.05	.10
280	Checklist 2 (165 - 280, Insert Sets)	.05	.10

SERIES TWO

MIGHTY DUCKS OF ANAHEIM

No.	Player	EX	NRMT
281	Patrick Carnback, RC	.07	.15
282	Bob Corkum	.05	.10
283	Bobby Dollas	.05	.10
284	Peter Douris	.05	.10
285	Todd Ewen	.05	.10
286	Garry Valk	.05	.10

BOSTON BRUINS

No.	Player	EX	NRMT
287	John Blue, Goalie	.07	.15
288	Glen Featherstone	.05	.10
289	Stephen Heinze	.05	.10
290	David Reid	.05	.10
291	Bryan Smolinski	.30	.60
292	Cam Stewart, RC	.07	.15
293	Jozef Stumpel	.05	.10
294	Sergei Zholtok	.07	.15

BUFFALO SABRES

No.	Player	EX	NRMT
295	Donald Audette	.05	.10
296	Philippe Boucher	.05	.10
297	Dominik Hasek, Goalie	.12	.25
298	Brad May	.05	.10
299	Craig Muni	.05	.10
300	Derek Plante, RC	.50	1.00
301	Craig Simpson	.05	.10
302	Scott Thomas, RC	.07	.15

CALGARY FLAMES

No.	Player	EX	NRMT
303	Ted Drury	.05	.10
304	Dan Keczmer, RC	.07	.15
305	Trevor Kidd, Goalie	.07	.15
306	Sandy McCarthy	.05	.10
307	Frantisek Musil	.05	.10
308	Michel Petit	.05	.10
309	Paul Ranheim	.05	.10
310	German Titov, RC	.25	.50
311	Andrei Trefilov, Goalie	.15	.30

CHICAGO BLACK HAWKS

No.	Player	EX	NRMT
312	Jeff Hackett, Goalie	.05	.10
313	Stephane Matteau	.05	.10
314	Brian Noonan	.05	.10
315	Patrick Poulin	.05	.10
316	Jeff Shantz, RC	.07	.15
317	Richard Sutter	.05	.10
318	Kevin Todd	.05	.10
319	Eric Weinrich	.05	.10

DALLAS STARS

No.	Player	EX	NRMT
320	David Barr	.05	.10
321	Paul Cavallini	.05	.10
322	Mike Craig	.05	.10
323	Dean Evason	.05	.10
324	Brent Gilchrist	.05	.10
325	Grant Ledyard	.05	.10
326	Michael McPhee	.05	.10
327	Darcy Wakaluk, Goalie	.05	.10

DETROIT RED WINGS

No.	Player	EX	NRMT
328	Terry Carkner	.05	.10
329	Mark Howe	.07	.15
330	Greg Johnson	.10	.20
331	Viacheslav Kozlov	.30	.60
332	Martin Lapointe	.05	.10
333	Darren McCarty, RC	.10	.20
334	Chris Osgood, Goalie, RC	.35	.75
335	Bob Probert	.05	.10
336	Mike Sillinger	.05	.10

EDMONTON OILERS

No.	Player	EX	NRMT
337	Jason Arnott, RC	1.50	3.00
338	Bob Beers	.05	.10
339	Fred Brathwaite, Goalie, RC	.07	.15
340	Kelly Buchberger	.05	.10
341	Ilya Byakin, RC	.07	.15
342	Fredrick Olausson	.05	.10
343	Vladimir Vujtek	.05	.10
344	Peter White, RC	.07	.15

FLORIDA PANTHERS

No.	Player	EX	NRMT
345	Stu Barnes	.05	.10
346	Mike Foligno	.05	.10
347	Greg Hawgood	.05	.10
348	Bob Kudelski	.05	.10
349	Rob Niedermayer	.35	.75

HARTFORD WHALERS

No.	Player	EX	NRMT
350	Igor Chibirev, RC	.10	.20
351	Robert Kron	.05	.10
352	Bryan Marchment	.05	.10
353	James Patrick	.05	.10
354	Chris Pronger	.25	.50
355	Jeff Reese, Goalie	.05	.10
356	Jim Storm	.10	.20
357	Darren Turcotte	.05	.10

LOS ANGELES KINGS

No.	Player	EX	NRMT
358	Patrick Conacher	.05	.10
359	Mike Donnelly	.05	.10
360	John Druce	.05	.10
361	Charles Huddy	.05	.10
352	Warren Rychel	.07	.15
363	Robb Stauber, Goalie	.07	.15
364	David Taylor	.05	.10
365	Dixon Ward	.05	.10

MONTREAL CANADIENS

No.	Player	EX	NRMT
366	Benoit Brunet	.05	.10
367	Jean-Jacques Daigneault	.07	.15
368	Gilbert Dionne	.05	.10
369	Paul Di Pietro	.05	.10
370	Kevin Haller	.05	.10
371	Oleg Petrov	.12	.25
372	Peter Popovic, RC	.12	.25
373	Ronald Wilson	.05	.10

NEW JERSEY DEVILS

No.	Player	EX	NRMT
374	Martin Brodeur, Goalie	.25	.50
375	Tom Chorske	.05	.10
376	Jim Dowd, RC	.18	.35
377	David Emma	.05	.10
378	Robert Holik	.07.	15
379	Corey Millen	.05	.10
380	Jaroslav Modry, RC	.10	.20
381	Jason Smith, RC	.07	.15

NEW YORK ISLANDER

No.	Player	EX	NRMT
382	Ray Ferraro	.05	.10
383	Travis Green, RC	.07	.15
384	Tom Kurvers	.05	.10
385	Martin McInnes	.05	.10
386	Jamie McLennan, Goalie, RC	.07	.15
387	Dennis Vaske	.05	.10
388	David Volek	.05	.10

NEW YORK RANGERS

No.	Player	EX	NRMT
389	Jeff Beukeboom	.05	.10
390	Glenn Healy, Goalie	.05	.10
391	Alexander Karpovtsev	.05	.10
392	Steve Larmer	.07	.15
393	Kevin Lowe	.05	.10
394	Ed Olczyk	.05	.10
395	Esa Tikkanen	.05	.10

OTTAWA SENATORS

No.	Player	EX	NRMT
396	Alexandre Daigle, RC	.50	1.00
397	Eugeny Davydov	.05	.10
398	Dimitri Filimonov	.05	.10
399	Brian Glynn	.05	.10
400	Darrin Madeley, Goalie, RC	.12	.25
401	Troy Mallette	.05	.10
402	Dave McLlwain	.05	.10
403	Alexei Yashin, RC	.85	1.75

PHILADELPHIA FLYERS

No.	Player	EX	NRMT
404	Jason Bowen, RC	.07	.15
405	Jeff Finley	.05	.10
406	Yves Racine	.05	.10
407	George (Rob) Ramage	.05	.10
408	Mikael Renberg	.35	.75
409	Dominic Roussel, Goalie	.10	.20
410	Dave Tippett	.05	.10

PITTSBURG PENGUINS

No.	Player	EX	NRMT
411	Doug Brown	.05	.10
412	Markus Naslund	.07	.15
413	Pat Neaton, RC	.10	.20
414	Kjell Samuelsson	.05	.10
415	Martin Straka	.25	.50
416	Bryan Trottier	.05	.10
417	Ken Wregget, Goalie	.05	.10

QUEBEC NORDIQUES

No.	Player	EX	NRMT
418	Adam Foote	.05	.10
419	Iain Fraser, RC	.07	.15
420	Alexei Gusarov	.05	.10
421	Dave Karpa	.05	.10
422	Claude Lapointe	.05	.10
423	Curtis Leschyshyn	.05	.10
424	Michael McKee	.05	.10
425	Garth Snow, Goalie, RC	.12	.25
426	Jocelyn Thibault, Goalie, RC	.35.	.75

ST. LOUIS BLUES

No.	Player	EX	NRMT
427	Phil Housley	.05	.10
428	Jim Hrivnak, Goalie	.05	.10
429	Vitali Karamnov	.07	.15
430	Basil McRae	.05	.10
431	Jim Montgomery, RC	.10	.20
432	Vitali Prokhorov	.07	.15

SAN JOSE SHARKS

No.	Player	EX	NRMT
433	Gaetan Duchesne	.05	.10
434	Todd Elik	.05	.10
435	Bob Errey	.05	.10
436	Igor Larionov	.07	.15
437	Mike Rathje	.07	.15
438	Jimmy Waite, Goalie	.05	.10
439	Ray Whitney	.07	.15

TAMPA BAY LIGHTNING

No.	Player	EX	NRMT
440	Bo Mikael Andersson	.05	.10
441	Danton Cole	.05	.10
442	Pat Elynuik	.05	.10
443	Chris Gratton	.35	.75
444	Pat Jablonski, Goalie	.05	.10
445	Chris Joseph	.05	.10
446	Chris LiPuma, RC	.07	.15
447	Denis Savard	.07	.15

FLEER ULTRA — 1993 - 94 POWER PLAY INSERT SETS

TORONTO MAPLE LEAFS

No.	Player	EX	NRMT
448	Ken Baumgartner	.05	.10
449	Todd Gill	.05	.10
450	Sylvain Lefebvre	.07	.15
451	Jamie Macoun	.05	.10
452	Mark Osborne	.05	.10
453	Rob Pearson	.05	.10
454	Damian Rhodes, Goalie, RC	.20	.40
455	Peter Zezel	.05	.10

VANCOUVER CANUCKS

No.	Player	EX	NRMT
456	David Babych	.05	.10
457	Jose Charbonneau, RC	.07	.15
458	Murray Craven	.05	.10
459	Neil Eisenhut, RC	.07	.15
460	Dan Kesa, RC	.07	.15
461	Gino Odjick	.05	.10
462	Kay Whitmore, Goalie	.05	.10

WASHINGTON CAPITALS

No.	Player	EX	NRMT
463	Donald Beaupre, Goalie	.05	.10
464	Randy Burridge	.05	.10
465	Calle Johansson	.05	.10
466	Keith Jones	.05	.10
467	Todd Krygier	.05	.10
468	Kelly Miller	.05	.10
469	Pat Peake	.07	.15
470	David Poulin	.05	.10

WINNIPEG JETS

No.	Player	EX	NRMT
471	Luciano Borsato	.05	.10
472	Nelson Emerson	.07	.15
473	Randy Gilhen	.05	.10
474	Boris Mironov	.05	.10
475	Stephane Quintal	.05	.10
476	Thomas Steen	.05	.10
477	Igor Ulanov	.07	.15

HOCKEY CANADA

No.	Player	EX	NRMT
478	Adrian Aucoin	.10	.20
479	Todd Brost	.7	.15
480	Martin Gendron	.20	.40
481	David Harlock	.07	.15
482	Corey Hirsch, Goalie	.12	.25
483	Todd Hlushko	.10	.20
484	Fabian Joseph	.10	.20
485	Paul Kariya	2.00	4.00
486	Brett Lindros	2.50	5.00
487	Ken Lovsin	.07	.15
488	Jason Marshall	.07	.15
489	Derek Mayer	.12	.25
490	Petr Nedved	.05	.10
491	Dwayne Norris	.12	.25
492	Russell Romaniuk	.05	.10
493	Brian Savage	.12	.25
494	Trevor Sim	.07	.15
495	Chris Terien	.07	.15
496	Todd Warriner	.35	.75
497	Craig Woodcroft	.07	.15

U.S.A. HOCKEY

No.	Player	EX	NRMT
498	Mark Beaufait	.07	.15
499	Jim Campbell	.07	.15
500	Ted Crowley	.07	.15
501	Mike Dunham, Goalie	.10	.20
502	Chris Ferraro	.12	.25
503	Peter Ferraro	.12	.25
504	Brett Hauer	.07	.15
505	Darby Hendrickson	.12	.25
506	Chris Imes	.10	.20
507	Craig Johnson	.07	.15
508	Peter Laviolette	.07	.15
509	Jeff Lazaro	.07	.15
510	John Lilley	.12	.25
511	Todd Marchmant	.10	.20
512	Ian Moran	.07	.15
513	Travis Richards	.07	.15
514	Barry Richter	.07	.15
515	David Roberts	.07	.15
516	Brian Rolston	.25	.50
517	David Sacco	.12	.25

CHECKLISTS

No.	Player	EX	NRMT
518	Checklist (281 - 373)	.05	.10
519	Checklist (374 - 462)	.05	.10
520	Checklist (463 - 520, Insert Sets)	.05	.10

— 1993 - 94 POWER PLAY INSERT SETS —

GAMEBREAKERS

This 20-card set was randomly inserted in Series Two foil packs.

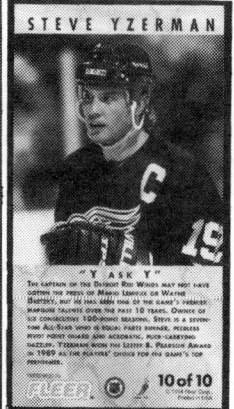

1993-94 Gamebreakers
Card No. 10, Steve Yzerman

Card Size: 2 1/2" x 4 11/16"
Face: Four Colour, borderless; Name, Gold foil
Back: Four Colour; Name, Number, Resume
Imprint: © 1993 FLEER CORP. PRINTED IN U.S.A.
Complete Set No.: 10
Complete Set Price: 15.00 / 30.00
Common Card: 1.00 / 2.00

No.	Player	EX	NRMT
1	Sergei Fedorov, Det.	1.50	3.00
2	Douglas Gilmour, Tor.	1.50	3.00
3	Wayne Gretzky, LA	2.50	5.00
4	Curtis Joseph, Goalie, St.L	1.00	2.00
5	Mario Lemieux, Pit.	2.00	4.00
6	Eric Lindros, Phi.	2.50	5.00
7	Felix Potvin, Goalie, Tor.	2.00	4.00
8	Jeremy Roenick, Det.	1.50	3.00
9	Patrick Roy, Goalie, Mon.	2.50	5.00
10	Steve Yzerman, Det.	1.50	3.00

GLOBAL GREATS

This 10-card set was randomly inserted in Series Two foil packs.

Card Size: 2 1/2" x 4 11/16"
Face: Four Colour; borderless; Name, Gold foil
Back: Four Colour; Name, Number, Resume on card stock
Imprint: ©1993 FLEER CORP. PRINTED IN U.S.A.
Complete Set No.: 10
Complete Set Price: 12.50 / 25.00
Common Card: .35 / .75

1993-94 Global Greats
Card No. 7, Teemu Selanne

No.	Player	EX	NRMT
1	Pavel Bure, Van.	3.00	6.00
2	Sergei Fedorov, Det.	1.50	3.00
3	Jaromir Jagr, Pit.	1.00	2.00
4	Jarri Kurri, LA	.35	.75
5	Alexander Mogilny, Buf.	1.00	2.00
6	Mikael Renberg, Phi.	1.75	3.50
7	Teemu Selanne, Win.	2.00	4.00
8	Mats Sundin, Que.	.75	1.50
9	Esa Tikkanen, NYR	.35	.75
10	Alexei Yashin, Ott.	2.00	4.00

NETMINDERS

This 8-card set was randomly inserted into Series One foil packs.

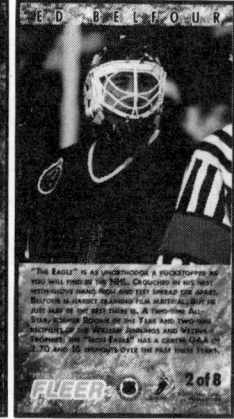

1993-94 Netminders
Card No. 2, Ed Belfour

Card Size: 2 1/2" x 4 11/16"
Face: Four Colour, blue marble border; Name, Blue foil
Back: Four Colour; Name, Number, Resume
Imprint: © 1993 FLEER CORP. PRINTED IN U.S.A.
Complete Set No.: 8
Complete Set Price: 20.00 / 40.00
Common Card: 1.50 / 3.00

GOALIES

No.	Player	EX	NRMT
1	Tom Barrasso, Pit.	1.50	3.00
2	Ed Belfour, Chi.	3.50	7.00
3	Grant Fuhr, Buf.	1.50	3.00
4	Curtis Joseph, St. L	2.50	5.00
5	Felix Potvin, Tor.	7.50	15.00
6	Bill Ranford, Edm.	2.00	4.00
7	Patrick Roy, Mon.	7.50	15.00
8	Tommy Soderstrom, Phi.	1.50	3.00

POINT LEADERS

This 20-card set was randomly inserted in Series One foil packs.

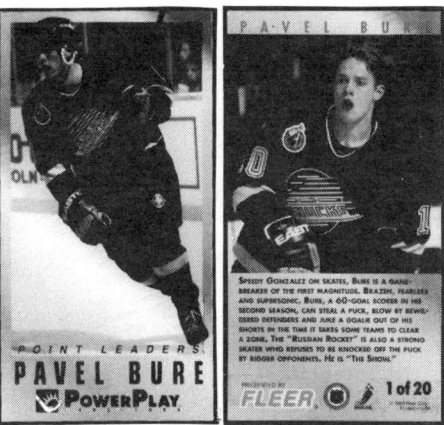

1993-94 Poimt Leaders
Card No. 1, Pavel Bure

Card Size: 2 1/2" x 4 11/16"
Face: Four Colour, gold border; Name, Silver foil
Back: Four Colour, Name, Number, Resume on card stock
Imprint: © 1993 FLEER CORP. PRINTED IN U.S.A.
Complete Set No.: 20
Complete Set Price: 15.00 30.00
Common Card: .35 .75

No.	Player	EX	NRMT
1	Pavel Bure, Van.	2.50	5.00
2	Douglas Gilmour, Tor.	1.50	3.00
3	Wayne Gretzky, LA	2.50	5.00
4	Brett Hull, St. L	.75	1.50
5	Jaromir Jagr, Pit.	.75	1.50
6	Joseph Juneau, Bos	.75	1.50
7	Pat LaFontaine, Buf.	.50	1.00
8	Mario Lemieux, Pit.	2.00	4.00
9	Mark Messier, NYR	.50	1.00
10	Alexander Mogilny, Buf.	.75	1.50
11	Adam Oates, Bos.	.35	.75
12	Mark Recchi, Phi.	.35	.75
13	Luc Robitaille, LA	.35	.75
14	Jeremy Roenick, Chi.	.75	1.50
15	Joe Sakic, Que.	.35	.75
16	Teemu Selanne. Win.	1.50	3.00
17	Kevin Stevens, Pit.	.35	.75
18	Mats Sundin, Que.	.50	1.00
19	Pierre Turgeon, NYI	.50	1.00
20	Steve Yzerman, Det.	.75	1.50

RISING STARS

This 10-card set was randomly inserted in Series Two foil packs.

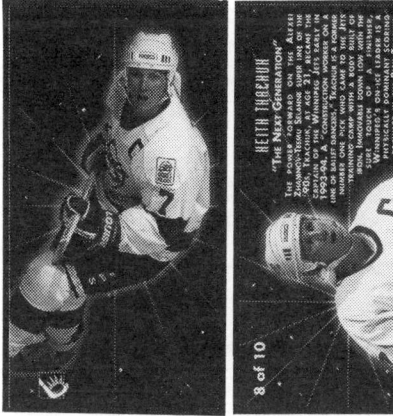

1993-94 Rising Stars
Card No. 8, Keith Tkachuk

Card Size: 2 1/2" x 4 11/16"
Face: Four Colour, borderless; Name, Gold foil
Back: Four Colour; Name, Number, Resume on card stock
Imprint: © 1993 FLEER CORP. PRINTED IN U.S.A.
Complete Set No.: 10
Complete Set Price: 14.00 28.00
Common Card: 1.00 2.00

No.	Player	EX	NRMT
1	Arturs Irbe, Goalie, SJ	2.50	5.00
2	Vyacheslav Kozlov, Det.	1.50	3.00
3	Felix Potvin, Goalie, Tor.	1.50	3.00
4	Keith Primeau, Det.	.50	1.00
5	Robert Reichel, Cal.	.50	1.00
6	Geoff Sanderson, Hart.	1.00	2.00
7	Martin Straka, Pit.	1.00	2.00
8	Keith Tkachuk, Win.	1.00	2.00
9	Alexei Zhamnov, Win.	1.00	2.00
10	Sergei Zubov, NYR	2.00	4.00

ROOKIE STANDOUTS

This 16-card set was randomly inserted in Series Two packs.

1993-94 Rookie Standouts
Card No. 1, Jason Arnott

Card Size: 2 1/2" x 4 11/16"
Face: Four Colour, borderless; Name, Gold foil
Back: Four Colour; Name, Number, Resume on card stock
Imprint: © 1993 FLEER CORP. PRINTED IN U.S.A.
Complete Set No.: 16
Complete Set Price: 17.50 35.00
Common Card: .35 .75

No.	Player	EX	NRMT
1	Jason Arnott, Edm.	3.50	7.00
2	Jesse Belanger, Fl.	.50	1.00
3	Alexandre Daigle, Ott.	2.00	4.00
4	Iain Fraser, Que.	.35	.75
5	Chris Gratton, TB	1.00	2.00
6	Boris Mironov, Win.	.35	.75
7	Jaroslav Modry, NJ	.35	.75
8	Rob Niedermayer, Fl.	1.00	2.00
9	Chris Osgood, Goalie, Det.	1.00	2.00
10	Pat Peake, Wash.	.35	.75
11	Derek Plante, Buf.	1.00	2.00
12	Chris Pronger, Hart.	1.00	2.00
13	Mikael Renberg, Phi.	2.00	4.00
14	Bryan Smolinski, Bos.	1.25	2.50
15	Jocelyn Thibault, Goalie, Que.	1.25	2.50
16	Alexei Yashin, Ott.	2.00	4.00

SECOND YEAR STARS

This 12-card set was randomly inserted into Series One foil packs.

1993-94 Second Year Stars
Card No. 2, Joseph Juneau

Card Size: 2 1/2" x 4 11/16"
Face: Four Colour, blue-grey border, Name, Gold foil
Back: Four Colour; Name, Number, Resume on card stock
Imprint: © 1993 FLEER CORP. PRINTED IN U.S.A.
Complete Set No.: 12
Complete Set Price: 9.00 18.00
Common Card: .35 .75

No.	Player	EX	NRMT
1	Rob Gaudreau, SJ	.35	.75
2	Joseph Juneau, Bos.	.75	1.50
3	Darius Kasparaitis. NYI	.35	.75
4	Dmitri Kvartalnov, Bos.	.35	.75
5	Eric Lindros, Phi.	2.50	5.00
6	Vladimir Malakhov,	.35	.75
7	Shawn McEachern	.35	.75
8	Felix Potvin, Goalie, Tor.	2.00	4.00
9	Patrick Poulin. Hart.	.35	.75
10	Teemu Selanne, Win.	1.50	3.00
11	Tommy Soderstrom, Goalie, Phi.	.35	.75
12	Alexei Zhamnov, Win.	1.00	2.00

SLAPSHOT ARTISTS

This 10-card set was randomly inserted into Series Two packs.

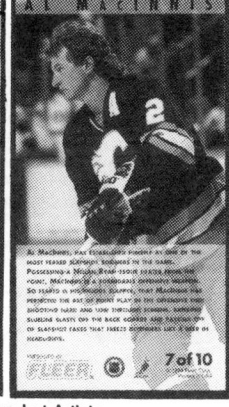

1993-94 Slapshot Artists
Card No. 7, Allan McInnis

Card Size: 2 1/2" x 4 11/16"
Face: Four Colour, borderless; Name, Gold foil
Back: Four Colour; Name, Number, Resume on card stock
Imprint: © 1993 FLEER CORP. PRINTED IN U.S.A.
Complete Set No.: 10
Complete Set Price: 10.00 20.00
Common Card: .35 .75

434 • FLEER ULTRA — 1994-95 ISSUE

No.	Player	EX	NRMT
1	David Andreychuk, Tor.	.50	1.00
2	Raymond Bourque, Bos.	.50	1.00
3	Sergei Fedorov, Det.	2.00	4.00
4	Brett Hull, St.L	1.50	3.00
5	Al Iafrate, Wash.	.35	.75
6	Brian Leetch, NYR	.75	1.50
7	Allan MacInnis, Cal.	.35	.75
8	Michael Modano, Dal.	1.00	2.00
9	Teemu Selanne, Win.	1.50	3.00
10	Brendan Shanahan, St.L	.75	1.50

— 1994-95 ISSUE —

The 1994-95 Fleer set is comprised of two series, Series One contains 250 cards.

1994-95 Issue
Card No. 60, Sergei Fedorov

Card Size: 2 1/2" x 3 1/2"
Face: Four colour; borderless; Name, Team Logo
Back: Four colour, three pictures; Name, Number, Resume
Imprint: © FLEER CORP. Printed in USA
Complete Set No.: 250

Complete Price Set:	10.00	20.00
Common Card:	.05	.10
Foil Pack: (14 Cards)		2.50
Foil Box: (36 Packs)		80.00

SERIES ONE

MIGHTY DUCKS OF ANAHEIM

No.	Player	EX	NRMT
1	Bob Corkum	.05	.10
2	Todd Ewen	.05	.10
3	Guy Hebert, Goalie	.10	.20
4	Bill Houlder	.05	.10
5	Stephan Lebeau	.05	.10
6	Joseph Sacco	.05	.10
7	Anatoli Semenov	.05	.10
8	Tim Sweeney	.05	.10
9	Terry Yake	.05	.10

BOSTON BRUINS

No.	Player	EX	NRMT
10	Raymond Bourque	.10	.20
11	Mariusz Czerkawski, RC	.10	.20
12	Ted Donato	.05	.10
13	Cam Neely	.07	.15
14	Adam Oates	.07	.15
15	Vincent Riendeau, Goalie	.05	.10
16	Bryan Smolinski	.25	.50
17	Don Sweeney	.05	.10
18	Glen Wesley	.05	.10

BUFFALO SABRES

No.	Player	EX	NRMT
19	Donald Audette	.05	.10
20	Doug Bodger	.05	.10
21	Jason Dawe	.05	.10
22	Dominik Hasek, Goalie	.12	.25
23	Dale Hawerchuk	.05	.10
24	Pat LaFontaine	.15	.30
25	Brad May	.05	.10
26	Alexander Mogilny	.15	.30

No.	Player	EX	NRMT
27	Derek Plante	.30	.60
28	Richard Smehlik	.05	.10

CALGARY FLAMES

No.	Player	EX	NRMT
29	Theoren Fleury	.05	.10
30	Trevor Kidd, Goalie	.10	.20
31	Frantisek Musil	.05	.10
32	Mikael Nylander	.05	.10
33	James Patrick	.05	.10
34	Robert Reichel	.05	.10
35	Gary Roberts	.05	.10
36	German Titov	.10	.20
37	Wes Walz	.05	.10
38	Zarley Zalapski	.05	.10

CHICAGO BLACK HAWKS

No.	Player	EX	NRMT
39	Ed Belfour, Goalie	.12	.25
40	Chris Chelios	.05	.10
41	Dirk Graham	.05	.10
42	Bernie Nicholls	.05	.10
43	Patrick Poulin	.05	.10
44	Jeremy Roenick	.15	.30
45	James (Steve) Smith	.05	.10
46	Gary Suter	.05	.10
47	Brent Sutter	.05	.10

DALLAS STARS

No.	Player	EX	NRMT
48	Neal Broten	.05	.10
49	Paul Cavallini	.05	.10
50	Dean Evason	.05	.10
51	Dave Gagner	.05	.10
52	Derian Hatcher	.05	.10
53	Trent Klatt	.05	.10
54	Grant Ledyard	.05	.10
55	Michael Modano	.10	.20
56	Andrew Moog, Goalie	.05	.10
57	Mark Tinordi	.05	.10

DETROIT RED WINGS

No.	Player	EX	NRMT
58	Dino Ciccarelli	.05	.10
59	Paul Coffey	.05	.10
60	Sergei Fedorov	.35	.75
61	Vladimir Konstantinov	.05	.10
62	Nicklas Lidstrom	.05	.10
63	Darren McCarty	.05	.10
64	Chris Osgood, Goalie	.25	.50
65	Keith Primeau	.05	.10
66	Ray Sheppard	.05	.10
67	Steve Yzerman	.15	.30

EDMONTON OILERS

No.	Player	EX	NRMT
68	Jason Arnott	.60	1.25
69	Bob Beers	.05	.10
70	Ilya Byakin	.05	.10
71	Zdeno Ciger	.05	.10
72	Igor Kravchuk	.05	.10
73	Boris Mironov	.05	.10
74	Fredrik Olausson	.05	.10
75	Scott Pearson	.05	.10
76	Bill Ranford, Goalie	.05	.10
77	Doug Weight	.05	.10

FLORIDA PANTHERS

No.	Player	EX	NRMT
78	Stu Barnes	.05	.10
79	Jesse Belanger	.05	.10
80	Bob Kudelski	.05	.10
81	Andrei Lomakin	.05	.10
82	Dave Lowry	.05	.10
83	Gordon Murphy	.05	.10
84	Rob Niedermayer	.15	.30
85	Brian Skrudland	.05	.10
86	John Vanbiesbrouck, Goalie	.10	.20

HARTFORD WHALER

No.	Player	EX	NRMT
87	Sean Burke, Goalie	.05	.10
88	Ted Drury	.05	.10
89	Alexander Godynyuk	.05	.10
90	Robert Kron	.05	.10
91	Chris Pronger	.15	.30
92	Brian Propp	.05	.10
93	Geoff Sanderson	.12	.25
94	Darren Turcotte	.05	.10
95	Patrick Verbeek	.05	.10

LOS ANGELES KINGS

No.	Player	EX	NRMT
96	Robert Blake	.07	.15
97	Mike Donnelly	.05	.10
98	John Druce	.05	.10
99	Kelly Hrudey, Goalie	.05	.10
100	Jari Kurri	.05	.10
101	Robert Lang	.05	.10
102	Martin McSorley	.05	.10
103	Luc Robitaille	.12	.25
104	Alexei Zhitnik	.10	.20

MONTREAL CANADIENS

No.	Player	EX	NRMT
105	Brian Bellows	.05	.10
106	Patrice Brisebois	.05	.10
107	Vincent Damphousse	.05	.10
108	Eric Desjardins	.05	.10
109	Gilbert Dionne	.05	.10
110	Mike Keane	.05	.10
111	John LeClair	.05	.10
112	Lyle Odelein	.05	.10
113	Patrick Roy, Goalie	.25	.50
114	Mathieu Schneider	.05	.10

NEW JERSEY DEVILS

No.	Player	EX	NRMT
115	Martin Brodeur, Goalie	.12	.25
116	Jim Dowd	.07	.15
117	Bill Guerin	.07	.15
118	Claude Lemieux	.05	.10
119	John MacLean	.05	.10
120	Corey Millen	.05	.10
121	Scott Niedermayer	.10	.20
122	Stephane J. J. Richer	.05	.10
123	Scott Stevens	.10	.20
124	Valeri Zelepukin	.05	.10

NEW YORK ISLANDERS

No.	Player	EX	NRMT
125	Patrick Flatley	.05	.10
126	Travis Green	.05	.10
127	Ron Hextall, Goalie	.05	.10
128	Benoit Hogue	.05	.10
129	Darius Kasparaitis	.05	.10
130	Vladimir Malakhov	.10	.20
131	Marty McInnis	.05	.10
132	Steve Thomas	.05	.10
133	Pierre Turgeon	.10	.20
134	Dennis Vaske	.05	.10

NEW YORK RANGERS

No.	Player	EX	NRMT
135	Glenn Anderson	.05	.10
136	Jeff Beukeboom	.05	.10
137	Adam Graves	.15	.30
138	Steve Larmer	.05	.10
139	Brian Leetch	.15	.30
140	Mark Messier	.10	.20
141	Petr Nedved	.05	.10
142	Sergei Nemchinov	.10	.20
143	Mike Richter, Goalie	.10	.20
144	Sergei Zubov	.12	.25

OTTAWA SENATORS

No.	Player	EX	NRMT
145	Craig Billington, Goalie	.05	.10
146	Alexandre Daigle	.20	.40
147	Eugeny Davydov	.05	.10

1994 - 95 INSERT SETS — FLEER ULTRA

No.	Player	EX	NRMT
148	Scott Levins	.07	.15
149	Norm Maciver	.05	.10
150	Troy Mallette	.05	.10
151	Brad Shaw	.05	.10
152	Alexei Yashin	.25	.50

PHILADELPHIA FLYERS

No.	Player	EX	NRMT
153	Josef Beranek	.05	.10
154	Jason Bowen	.05	.10
155	Rod Brind'Amour	.10	.20
156	Kevin Dineen	.05	.10
157	Garry Galley	.05	.10
158	Mark Recchi	.10	.20
159	Mikael Renberg	.12	.25
160	Tommy Soderstrom, Goalie	.05	.10
161	Dimitri Yushkevich	.05	.10

PITTSBURGH PENGUINS

No.	Player	EX	NRMT
162	Tom Barrasso, Goalie	.05	.10
163	Ronald Francis	.05	.10
164	Jaromir Jagr	.15	.30
165	Mario Lemieux	.50	1.00
166	Shawn McEachern	.05	.10
167	Joe Mullen	.05	.10
168	Lawrence Murphy	.05	.10
169	Ulf Samuelsson	.05	.10
170	Kevin Stevens	.12	.25
171	Martin Straka	.12	.25

QUEBEC NORDIQUES

No.	Player	EX	NRMT
172	Wendel Clark	.10	.20
173	Stephane Fiset, Goalie	.10	.20
174	Iain Fraser	.05	.10
175	Andrei Kovalenko	.10	.20
176	Sylvain Lefebvre	.05	.10
177	Owen Nolan	.05	.10
178	Mike Ricci	.05	.10
179	Martin Rucinsky	.05	.10
180	Joe Sakic	.15	.30
181	Scott Young	.05	.10

ST. LOUIS BLUES

No.	Player	EX	NRMT
182	Steve Duchesne	.05	.10
183	Brett Hull	.05	.10
184	Curtis Joseph, Goalie	.15	.30
185	Allan MacInnis	.12	.25
186	Kevin Miller	.05	.10
187	Jim Montgomery	.05	.10
188	Vitali Prokhorov	.05	.10
189	Brendan Shanahan	.07	.15
190	Peter Stastny	.05	.10
191	Esa Tikkanen	.05	.10

SAN JOSE SHARKS

No.	Player	EX	NRMT
192	Ulf Dahlen	.05	.10
193	Todd Elik	.05	.10
194	Johan Garpenlov	.05	.10
195	Arturs Irbe, Goalie	.15	.30
196	Vlastimil Kroupa	.05	.10
197	Igor Larionov	.05	.10
198	Sergei Makarov	.05	.10
199	Jeff Norton	.05	.10
200	Sandis Ozolinch	.12	.25
201	Mike Rathje	.10	.20

TAMPA BAY LIGHTNING

No.	Player	EX	NRMT
202	Brian Bradley	.05	.10
203	Shawn Chambers	.05	.10
204	Danton Cole	.05	.10
205	Chris Gratton	.20	.40
206	Roman Hamrlik	.05	.10
207	Chris Joseph	.05	.10
208	Petr Klima	.05	.10
209	Daren Puppa, Goalie	.05	.10
210	John Tucker	.05	.10

TORONTO MAPLE LEAFS

No.	Player	EX	NRMT
211	David Andreychuk	.07	.15
212	Ken Baumgartner	.05	.10
213	David Ellett	.05	.10
214	Michael Gartner	.07	.15
215	Todd Gill	.05	.10
216	Douglas Gilmour	.15	.30
217	Jamie Macoun	.05	.10
218	Dmitri Mironov	.05	.10
219	Felix Potvin, Goalie	.35	.75
220	Mats Sundin	.10	.20

VANCOUVER CANUCKS

No.	Player	EX	NRMT
221	Jeff Brown	.05	.10
222	Pavel Bure	.35	.75
223	Murray Craven	.05	.10
224	Bret Hedican	.05	.10
225	Nathan Lafayette	.10	.20
226	Trevor Linden	.10	.20
227	Jyrki Lumme	.05	.10
228	Kirk McLean, Goalie	.10	.20
229	Gino Odjick	.05	.10
230	Cliff Ronning	.05	.10

WASHINGTON CAPITALS

No.	Player	EX	NRMT
231	Peter Bondra	.05	.10
232	Sylvain Cote	.05	.10
233	Kevin Hatcher	.05	.10
234	Dale Hunter	.05	.10
235	Calle Johansson	.05	.10
236	Dimitri Khristich	.05	.10
237	Pat Peake	.05	.10
238	Michal Pivonka	.05	.10
239	Rick Tabaracci, Goalie	.05	.10

WINNIPEG JETS

No.	Player	EX	NRMT
240	Tim Cheveldae, Goalie	.05	.10
241	Dallas Drake	.05	.10
242	Nelson Emerson	.05	.10
243	Dave Manson	.05	.10
244	Teppo Numminen	.05	.10
245	Stephane Quintal	.05	.10
246	Teemu Selanne	.20	.40
247	Keith Tkachuk	.15	.30

CHECKLISTS

No.	Player	EX	NRMT
248	Checklist	.05	.10
249	Checklist	.05	.10
250	Checklist	.05	.10

— 1994 - 95 INSERT SETS —

NHL ALL-STARS

Randomly inserted into Series One foil packs. Cards are numbered _ of 12.

1994-95 NHL All-Stars
Card No. 12, Felix Potvin

Card Size: 2 1/2" x 3 1/2"
Face: Four Colour; borderless; Name
Back: Four Colour; Name, Number, Position
Imprint: ©1994 Fleer. Printed in USA
Complete Set No.: 12
Complete Price Set: 22.50 45.00
Common Card: 1.00 2.00

EASTERN CONFERENCE

No.	Player	EX	NRMT
1	Raymond Bourque, Bos.	1.00	2.00
2	Brian Leetch, NYR	1.50	3.00
3	Eric Lindros, Phi.	3.50	7.00
4	Mark Messier, NYR	1.25	2.50
5	Alexander Mogilny, Buf.	1.25	2.50
6	Patrick Roy, Goalie, Mon.	2.50	5.00

WESTERN CONFERENCE

No.	Player	EX	NRMT
7	Pavel Bure, Van.	3.50	7.00
8	Chris Chelios, Chi.	1.00	2.00
9	Paul Coffey, Det.	1.00	2.00
10	Wayne Gretzky, LA	3.50	7.00
11	Brett Hull, St.L	2.00	4.00
12	Felix Potvin, Goalie, Tor.	2.50	5.00

NHL AWARD WINNERS

Randomly inseted into Series One foil packs. Cards are numbered _ of 8.

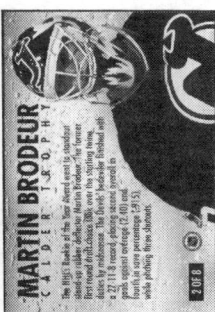

1994-95 NHL Award Winners
Card No. 2, Martin Brodeur

Card Size: 2 1/2" x 3 1/2"
Face: Four Colour; borderless; Name
Back: Four Colour; Name, Number, Trophy
Imprint: ©1994 Fleer
Complete Set No.: 8
Complete Price Set: 11.00 22.00
Common Card: 1.25 2.50

No.	Player	EX	NRMT
1	James Norris Trophy; Raymond Bourque, Bis.	1.25	2.50
2	Calder Trophy; Martin Brodeur, Goalie, NJ	1.75	3.50
3	Hart Trophy; Sergei Fedorov, Det.	2.50	5.00
4	King Clancy Trophy; Adam Graves, NYR	1.75	3.50
5	Art Ross Trophy; Wayne Gretzky, LA	3.75	7.50
6	Vezina Trophy; Dominik Hasek, Goalie, Buf.	1.75	3.50
7	Conn Smythe Trophy; Brian Leetch, NYR	1.75	3.50
8	Bill Masterton Trophy; Cam Neely, Bos.	1.25	2.50

PERFORMANCE HIGHLIGHTS
SERGEI FEDOROV

Cards randomly inserted in Series One foil packs. The set describes the career to date of Sergei Fedorov.

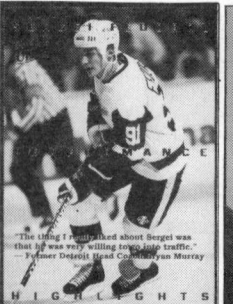

1994-95 Performance Highlights
Card No. 9, Sergei Fedorov

Card Size: 2 1/2" x 3 1/2"
Face: Four colour, borderless, silver foiled; Name, Title
Back: Four colour; Name, Number, Resume
Imprint: ©1994 FLEER CORP. PRINTED IN USA
Complete Set No.: 10
Complete Price Set: 17.50 35.00

No.	Player	EX	NRMT
1	Sergei Fedorov	1.75	3.50
2	Sergei Fedorov	1.75	3.50
3	Sergei Fedorov	1.75	3.50
4	Sergei Fedorov	1.75	3.50
5	Sergei Fedorov	1.75	3.50
6	Sergei Fedorov	1.75	3.50
7	Sergei Fedorov	1.75	3.50
8	Sergei Fedorov	1.75	3.50
9	Sergei Fedorov	1.75	3.50
10	Sergei Fedorov	1.75	3.50

PREMIER PAD MEN

Randomly inserted into Series One foil packs. Cards are numbered _ of 6.

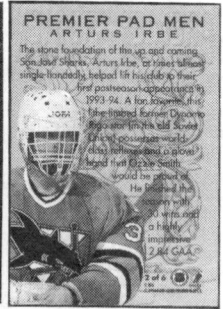

1994-95 Premier Pad Men
Card No. 2, Arturs Irbe

Card Size: 2 1/2" x 3 1/2"
Face: Four Colour; borderless; Name, Team Logo
Back: Four Colour; Name, Number, Resume
Imprint: Printed in USA
Complete Set No.: 6
Complete Price Set: 30.00 60.00
Common Card: 5.00 10.00

GOALIES

No.	Player	EX	NRMT
1	Dominik Hasek, Buf.	5.00	10.00
2	Arturs Irbe, SJ	5.00	10.00
3	Curtis Joseph, St.L	5.00	10.00
4	Felix Potvin, Tor.	7.50	15.00
5	Mike Richter, NYR	6.00	12.00
6	Patrick Roy, Mon.	9.00	18.00

ULTRA POWER

Randomly inserted into Series One foil packs. Cards are numbered _ of 10.

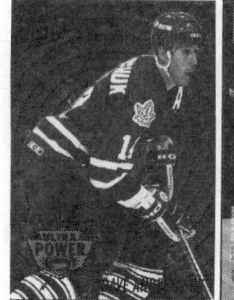

1994-95 Ultra Power
Card No. 1, David Andreychuk

Card Size: 2 1/2" x 3 1/2"
Face: Four colour; borderless; Name, Logo
Back: Four colour; Name, Team, Resume
Imprint: ©1994 Fleer. Printed in USA
Complete Set No.: 10
Complete Price Set: 65.00 125.00
Common Card: 3.50 7.00

No.	Player	EX	NRMT
1	David Andreychuk, Tor.	3.50	7.00
2	Jason Arnott, Edm.	7.00	14.00
3	Chris Gratton, TB	3.50	7.00
4	Adam Graves, NYR	6.00	12.00
5	Eric Lindros, Phi.	12.50	25.00
6	Cam Neely, Bos.	5.00	10.00
7	Mikael Renberg, Phi.	5.00	10.00
8	Jeremy Roenick, Chi.	7.50	15.00
9	Brendan Shanahan, St.L	3.50	7.00
10	Keith Tkachuk, Win.	6.00	12.00

SCORING KINGS

Cards randomly inserted in Series One foil packs. The cards are numbered _ of 7.

1994-95 Scoring Kings
Card No. 7, Steve Yzerman

Card Size: 2 1/2" x 3 1/2"
Face: Four colour, borderless; Name, Team Logo
Back: Four colour;
Imprint: ©1994 Fleer. Printed in USA
Complete Set No.: 7
Complete Price Set: 20.00 40.00
Common Card: 2.00 4.00

No.	Player	EX	NRMT
1	Pavel Bure, Van.	3.50	7.00
2	Sergei Fedorov, Det.	3.50	7.00
3	Douglas Gilmour, Tor.	2.50	5.00
4	Wayne Gretzky, LA	3.50	7.00
5	Mario Lemieux, Pit.	2.50	7.00
6	Eric Lindros, Phi.	3.50	7.00
7	Steve Yzerman, Det.	2.00	4.00

HIGHLINER

— 1992-93 CENTENNIAL COLLECTOR SERIES —

This 28-card set was a sales premium for Highliner Fish Sticks. The cards are numbered _ of /de 28

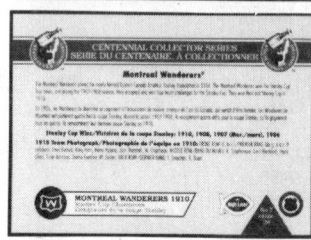

1992-93 Centennial Collector Series
Card No. 7, Montreal Wanderers

Card Size: 2 1/2" x 3 1/2"
Face: Type 1: Black and white borderless
　　　　Type 2: Four colour, borderless
Back: Four colour, borderless, card stock; Team, Team logo, Bilingual
Imprint: Made and printed in USA. Fait et imprime aux Etsts-Unis
Complete Set No.: 28
Complete Set Price: 35.00 75.00
Common Card: 1.00 2.00

TEAM PHOTOGRAPHS

No.	Player	EX	NRMT
1	Montreal AAA, 1893	1.50	3.00
2	Winnipeg Victorias, 1896	1.00	2.00
3	Montreal Victorias, 1896	1.00	2.00
4	Montreal Shamrocks, 1899	1.00	2.00
5	Ottawa Silver Seven, 1903	1.00	2.00
6	Kenora Thistles, 1907	1.00	2.00
7	Montreal Wanderers, 1910	1.00	2.00
8	Quebec Bulldogs, 1913	1.00	2.00
9	Toronto Blueshirts, 1914	1.00	2.00
10	Vancouver Millionaires, 1915	1.00	2.00
11	Seattle Metropolitans, 1917	1.00	2.00
12	Toronto Arenas, 1918	1.00	2.00
13	Toronto St. Patricks, 1922	1.00	2.00
14	Victoria Cougars, 1925	1.00	2.00
15	Ottawa Senators, 1927	1.00	2.00
16	Montreal Maroons, 1935	1.00	2.00
17	New York Rangers, 1940	1.00	2.00
18	Detroit Red Wings, 1955	1.00	2.00
19	Montreal Canadiens, 1956	1.00	2.00
20	Chicago Black Hawks, 1961	1.00	2.00
21	Toronto Maple Leafs, 1967	2.50	5.00
22	Boston Bruins, 1970	1.00	2.00
23	Philadelphia Flyers, 1974	2.50	5.00
24	New York Islanders, 1980	1.00	2.00
25	Edmonton Oilers, 1984	1.00	2.00
26	Calgary Flames, 1989	1.00	2.00
27	Pittsburgh Penguins, 1991	2.50	5.00
28	Checklist	1.00	2.00

— 1993 - 94 GREATEST GOALIES —

This 15-card set was a premium that could be collected by purchasing Highliner Fish Sticks during the 93-94 hockey season. The cards are numbered 7 of/de 15.

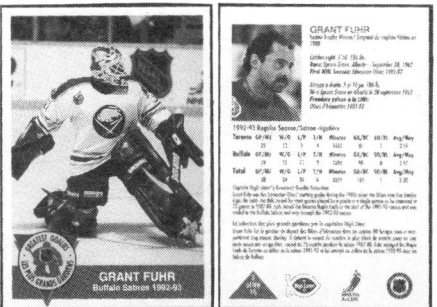

1993-94 Greatest Goalies
Card No. 3, Grant Fuhr

Card Size: 2-1/2" x 3-1/2"
Face: Type 1: Four colour, white border, Name, Team
Type 2: Four colour, white border, black and white picture; Name, Team
Back: Four colour, white border, card stock; Name, Number, Resume
Imprint: None
Complete Set No.: 15
Complete Set Price: 12.50   25.00

GOALIES

No.	Player	EX	NRMT
1	Patrick Roy, Mon.	.75	1.50
2	Ed. Belfour, Chi.	.75	1.50
3	Grant Fuhr, Buf.	.75	1.50
4	Ron Hextall, Que.	.75	1.50
5	John Vanbiesbrouck, NYR	.75	1.50
6	Tom Barrasso, Pit.	.75	1.50
7	Bernie Parent, Phi.	.75	1.50
8	Tony Esposito, Chi.	.75	1.50
9	Johnny Bower, Tor.	.75	1.50
10	Jacques Plante, Mon.	.75	1.50
11	Terry Sawchuk, Det.	.75	1.50
12	Bill Durnan, Mon.	.75	1.50
13	Felix Potvin, Tor.	.75	1.50
14	The Evolution of the Goalie Mask	.75	1.50
15	The Vezina Trophy	.75	1.50

HOCKEY HALL OF FAME & MUSEUM

— 1992 LEGENDS OF HOCKEY —

This 18-card set was produced from original artist Doug West's illustrations and converted to a limited card set.

Card Size: 3 1/2" x 5 1/2"
Face: Four colour, white border
Back: Four colour, dark blue border, card stock; Name, Number, Resume
Imprint: © 1992
Complete Set No.: 18
Complete Set Price: 50.00   100.00
Common Card: 2.50   5.00

SERIES ONE

No.	Player	EX	NRMT
1	Harry Lumley, Goalie, Tor.	2.50	5.00
2	Conn Smythe, M.C.	2.50	5.00
3	Maurice (Rocket) Richard, Mon.	5.00	10.00
4	Bobby Orr, Bos.	5.00	10.00
5	Bernie (Boom Boom) Geoffrion, Mon.	3.75	7.50
6	Hobey Baker	2.50	5.00
7	Tony Esposito, Bos.	3.75	7.50
8	Francis (King) Clancy, Tor.	3.75	7.50
9	Gordon Howe, Det.	5.00	10.00
10	Emile Francis, Goalie	2.50	5.00
11	Jacques Plante, Goalie, Mon.	5.00	10.00
12	Sid Abel, Det.	3.75	7.50
13	Foster Hewitt, Broadcaster	2.50	5.00
14	Charlie Conacher, Sr., Tor.	3.00	6.00
15	Stan Mikita, Chi.	3.25	6.50
16	Bobby Clarke, Phi.	3.00	6.00
17	Norm Ullman, Det.	2.50	5.00
18	Lord Stanley of Preston	2.50	5.00

1992 Legends of Hockey
Card No. 12, Sid Abel

SERIES TWO

No.	Player	EX	NRMT
19	Ted Lindsay	3.00	6.00
20	Duke Keats	2.50	5.00
21	Jack Adams	2.50	5.00
22	Bill Mosienko	3.50	7.00
23	Johnny Bower, Goalie	3.50	7.00
24	Tim Horton	9.00	18.00
25	Punch Imlach	2.50	5.00
26	Georges Vezina	3.50	7.00
27	Earl Seibert	2.50	5.00
28	Bryan Hextall	2.50	5.00
29	Babe Pratt	2.50	5.00
30	Lorne "Gump" Worsley, Goalie	3.50	7.00
31	Ed Giacomin, Goalie	3.50	7.00
32	Ace Bailey	3.00	6.00
33	Harry Sinden	2.50	5.00
34	Lanny McDonald	3.00	6.00
35	Tommy Ivan	2.50	5.00
36	Frank Calder	2.50	5.00

HUMPTY DUMPTY

— 1992 - 93 ISSUE —

1992-93 Issue, Series Two
Card No. 7, Douglas Gilmour

This 52-card set was used as a premium randomly inserted into specially marked bags of Humpty Dumpty potato chips and snacks. The cards, issued in two series, are unnumbered and are listed here in alphabetical order.

Card Size: 1 1/2" x 2"
Face: Four colour borderless; Team logo
Back: Four colour, grey border, card stock; Name, Jersey Number, Resume
Imprint: © NHL & NHLPA 1992
Complete Set No.: 52
Set Price:
  Series One: 7.50   15.00
  Series Two: 7.50   15.00
  Complete Set: 15.00   30.00
Common Card: .25   .50
Album: 5.00

SERIES ONE

No.	Player	EX	NRMT
1	Raymond Bourque, Bos.	.50	1.00
2	Rod Brind'Amour, Phi.	.35	.75
3	Chris Chelios, Chi.	.25	.50
4	Wendel Clark, Tor.	.25	.50
5	Gilbert Dionne, Mon.	.25	.50
6	Pat Falloon, SJ	.25	.50
7	Ray Ferraro, NYI	.25	.50
8	Theoren Fleury, Cal.	.25	.50
9	Grant Fuhr, Goalie, Tor.	.35	.75
10	Wayne Gretzky, LA	3.50	7.00
11	Kevin Hatcher, Wash.	.25	.50
12	Valeri Kamensky, Que.	.25	.50
13	Mike Keane, Mon.	.25	.50
14	Brian Leetch, NYR	.50	1.00
15	Kirk McLean, Goalie, Van.	.35	.75
16	Alexander Mogilny, Buf.	.50	1.00
17	Troy Murray, Win.	.25	.50
18	Patrick Roy, Goalie, Mon.	2.50	5.00
19	Joe Sakic, Que.	.35	.75
20	Brendan Shanahan, St.L	.50	1.00
21	Kevin Stevens, Pit.	.25	.50
22	Scott Stevens, NJ	.25	.50
23	Mark Tinordi, Min.	.25	.50
24	Steve Yzerman, Det.	.50	1.00
25	Zarley Zalapski, Har.	.25	.50
26	Checklist: Series I	.25	.50

SERIES TWO

No.	Player	EX	NRMT
1	Drake Berehowsky, Tor.	.25	.50
2	Shayne Corson, Mon.	.25	.50
3	Russell Courtnall, Mon.	.25	.50
4	David Ellett, Tor.	.25	.50
5	Sergei Fedorov, Det.	1.00	2.00
6	Dave Gagner, Min.	.25	.50
7	Douglas Gilmour, Tor.	1.50	3.00
8	Phil Housley, Win.	.25	.50
9	Brett Hull, St.L	.50	1.00
10	Jaromir Jagr, Pit.	1.00	2.00
11	Pat LaFontaine, Buf.	.50	1.00
12	Mario Lemieux, Pit.	2.50	5.00
13	Trevor Linden, Van.	.50	1.00
14	Allan MacInnis, Cal.	.25	.50
15	Mark Messier, NYR	.50	1.00
16	Cam Neely, Bos.	.35	.75
17	Owen Nolan, Que.	.25	.50
18	Bill Ranford, Goalie, Edm.	.25	.50
19	Jeremy Roenick, Chi.	.75	1.50
20	Luc Robitaille, LA	.35	.75
21	Mats Sundin, Que.	.50	1.00
22	Patrick Verbeek, Har.	.25	.50
23	Chris Terreri, Goalie, NJ	.25	.50
24	Steve Thomas, NYI	.25	.50
25	Neil Wilkinson, SJ	.25	.50
26	Checklist: Series II	.25	.50

SEASON'S

— 1992 - 93 ACTION PLAYER PATCHES —

This 71-patch set was available individually and came wrapped in clear cello. You could pick the player you wanted. These patches were intended to patching clothing. The patches are made of soft cloth.

1992-93 Action Player Patches
Patch No. 54, Grant Fuhr

Patch Size: 3 1/8" x 4 3/8"
Face: Four colour, black border; Player's name and jersey number, Team, Logos
Back: Blank
Imprint: (on packaging) SEASONS TM/MC
Complete Set No.: 71
Complete Set Price: 75.00 / 150.00
Common Card: 1.00 / 2.00

No.	Player	EX	NRMT
1	Jeremy Roenick, Chi.	1.50	3.00
2	Steve Larmer, Chi.	1.00	2.00
3	Ed. Belfour, Goalie, Chi.	1.50	3.00
4	Chris Chelios, Chi.	1.00	2.00
5	Sergei Fedorov, Det.	1.25	2.50
6	Steve Yzerman, Det.	1.25	2.50
7	Tim Cheveldae, Goalie, Det.	1.00	2.00
8	Bob Probert, Det.	1.00	2.00
9	Wayne Gretzky, LA	1.50	3.00
10	Luc Robitaille, LA	1.00	2.00
11	Tony Granato, LA	1.00	2.00
12	Kelly Hrudey, Goalie, LA	1.00	2.00
13	Brett Hull, St.L	1.25	2.50
14	Curtis Joseph, Goalie, St.L	1.00	2.00
15	Brendan Shanahan, St.L	1.00	2.00
16	Nelson Emerson, Bos.	1.00	2.00
17	Raymond Bourque, Bos.	1.00	2.00
18	Joseph Juneau, Bos.	1.50	3.00
19	Andrew Moog, Goalie, Bos.	1.00	2.00
20	Adam Oates, Bos.	1.00	2.00
21	Patrick Roy, Goalie, Mon.	1.75	3.50
22	Prototype	1.50	3.00
23	Denis Savard, Mon.	1.00	2.00
24	Gilbert Dionne, Mon.	1.00	2.00
25	Kirk Muller, Mon.	1.00	2.00
26	Mark Messier, NYR	1.50	3.00
27	Anthony Amonte, NYR	1.00	2.00
28	Brian Leetch, NYR	1.00	2.00
29	Mike Richter, Goalie, NYR	1.00	2.00
30	Trevor Linden, Van.	1.00	2.00
31	Pavel Bure, Van.	1.75	3.50
32	Cliff Ronning, Van.	1.00	2.00
33	Geoff Courtnall, Van.	1.00	2.00
34	Mario Lemieux, Pit.	1.50	3.00
35	Jaromir Jagr, Pit.	1.50	3.00
36	Tom Barrasso, Goalie, Pit.	1.00	2.00
37	Rick Tocchet, Phi.	1.00	2.00
38	Eric Lindros, Phi.	2.00	4.00
39	Rod Brind'Amour, Phi.	1.00	2.00
40	Dominic Roussel, Goalie Phi.	1.00	2.00
41	Mark Recchi, Phi.	1.00	2.00
42	Pat LaFontaine, Buf.	1.50	3.00
43	Donald Audette, Buf.	1.00	2.00
44	Patrick Verbeek, Har.	1.00	2.00
45	John Cullen, Har.	1.00	2.00
46	Owen Nolan, Que.	1.00	2.00
47	Joe Sakic, Que.	1.25	2.50
48	Kevin Hatcher Wash.	1.00	2.00
49	Donald Beaupre, Goalie, Wash.	1.00	2.00
50	Scott Stevens, NJ	1.00	2.00
51	Chris Terreri, Goalie, NJ	1.00	2.00
52	Scott Lachance, NJ	1.00	2.00
53	Pierre Turgeon, NYI	1.00	2.00
54	Grant Fuhr, Goalie, Tor.	1.00	2.00
55	Douglas Gilmour, Tor.	1.50	3.00
56	Dave Manson, Edm.	1.00	2.00
57	Bill Ranford, Goalie, Edm.	1.00	2.00
58	Troy Murray, Chi.	1.00	2.00
59	Phil Housley, Win.	1.00	2.00
60	Allan MacInnis, Cal.	1.00	2.00
61	Michael Vernon, Goalie	1.00	2.00
62	Pat Falloon, SJ	1.00	2.00
63	Douglas Wilson, SJ	1.00	2.00
64	Jon Casey, Goalie, Min.	1.00	2.00
65	Michael Modano, Min.	1.00	2.00
66	Kevin Stevens, Pit.	1.00	2.00
67	Al Iafrate, Wash.	1.00	2.00
68	Dale Hawerchuk,	1.00	2.00
69	Igor Kravchuk, Chi.	1.00	2.00
70	Wendel Clark, Tor.	1.00	2.00
71	Kirk McLean Goalie, Van.	1.00	2.00

— 1993 - 94 ACTION PLAYER PATCHES —

Patch Size: 3 1/8" x 4 3/8"
Face: Four colour, black border; Player's name and jersey number, Team, Logos
Back: Blank
Imprint: (on packaging) SEASONS TM/MC
Complete Set No.: 20
Complete Set Price: 35.00 / 70.00
Common Card: 1.50 / 3.00

No.	Player	EX	NRMT
1	Ed Belfour, Goalie, Chi.	1.50	3.00
2	Pavel Bure, Van.	2.50	5.00
3	Paul Coffey, Det.	1.50	3.00
4	Douglas Gilmour, Tor.	2.50	5.00
5	Wayne Gretzky, LA	5.00	10.00
6	Brett Hull, St.L	2.50	5.00
7	Jaromir Jagr, Pit.	2.50	5.00
8	Joseph Juneau, Bos.	2.50	5.00
9	Mario Lemieux, Pit.	3.50	7.00
10	Eric Lindros, Phi.	5.00	10.00
11	Shawn McEachern, Pit.	1.50	3.00
12	Alexander Mogilny, Buf.	2.50	5.00
13	Adam Oates, Bos.	2.00	4.00
14	Felix Potvin, Goalie, Tor.	3.50	7.00
15	Jeremy Roenick, Chi.	2.50	5.00
16	Patrick Roy, Goalie, Mon.	3.50	7.00
17	Joe Sakic, Que.	1.40	3.00
18	Temmu Selanne, Win.	2.50	5.00
19	Kevin Stevens, Pit.	1.50	3.00
20	Steve Yzerman, Det.	2.50	5.00

ULTIMATE TRADING CARD COMPANY

— 1992 PROMTIONAL CARDS —

The 1992 promotional cards are marked with "SAMPLE" on the back.

 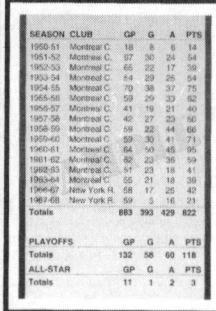

1992 Promotional Card
Bernie Geoffrion

Card Size: 2 1/2" X 3 1/2"
Face: Four colour, white border; Name, Position, Team or
Four colour, white border; Name, Facsimile autograph
Back: Black and grey on white card stock; Facsimile autograph or
Four colour, black and grey on white card stock; Resume
Imprint: None

No.	Player	EX	NRMT
—	Bernie Geoffrion, Mon.	5.00	10.00
—	Bobby Hull, Chi.	7.50	15.00

— 1992 ORIGINAL SIX —

Available only in foil packs the Original six hockey set was produced in both English and French. Game used sticks and lithographs were available through an instant win sweepstakes.

 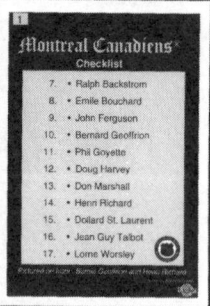

1992 Original Six
Card No. 1, Montreal Canadiens

Card Size: 2 1/2" X 3 1/2"
Face: Four colour, white border; Position, Team
Back: Four colour; Name, Statistics
Imprint: None

		English	French
Complete Set No.:	100		
Complete Set Price:		5.00	5.00
Common Player:		.03	.05
Foil Pack:		.25	.25
Foil Box:		8.00	8.00

BOBBY HULL HOLOGRAM
Limited to 250 signed and numbered hologram cards.

No.	Player	EX	NRMT
—	Bobby Hull, Autographed Hologram	250.00	500.00
—	Bobby Hull, Hologram	35.00	75.00

CHECKLISTS

No.	Player	English NRMT	French NRMT
1	Montreal Canadiens	.05	.10
2	New York Rangers	.05	.10
3	Toronto Maple Leafs	.05	.10

1992 - 93 MASTERS OF HOCKEY — ZELLERS

No.	Player	English NRMT	French NRMT
4	Boston Bruins	.05	.10
5	Chicago Black Hawks	.05	.10
6	Detroit Redwings	.05	.10

MONTREAL CANADIENS

No.	Player	English NRMT	French NRMT
7	Ralph Backstrom	.13	.25
8	Emile (Butch) Bouchard	.13	.25
9	John Ferguson	.08	.15
10	Bernie Geoffrion	.25	.50
11	Phil Goyette	.05	.10
12	Doug Harvey	.13	.25
13	Don Marshall	.03	.05
14	Henri Richard	.10	.20
15	Dollard St. Laurent	.03	.05
16	Jean-Guy Talbot	.03	.05
17	Gump Worsley, Goalie	.13	.25

NEW YORK RANGERS

No.	Player	English NRMT	French NRMT
18	Andy Bathgate	.08	.15
19	Louie Fontinato	.03	.05
20	Ed Giacomin, Goalie	.10	.20
21	Vic Hadfield	.08	.15
22	Camille Henry	.03	.05
23	Harry Howell	.05	.10
24	Orland Kurtenbach	.03	.05
25	Jim Neilson	.03	.05
26	Bob Nevin	.03	.05
27	Dean Prentice	.03	.05
28	Leo Reise, Jr.	.03	.05
29	Red Sullivan	.03	.05

TORONTO MAPLE LEAFS

No.	Player	English NRMT	French NRMT
30	Bob Baun	.08	.15
31	Gus Bodnar	.03	.05
32	Johnny Bower, Goalie	.10	.20
33	Bob Davidson	.03	.05
34	Ron Ellis	.08	.15
35	Billy Harris	.03	.05
36	Larry Hillman	.03	.05
37	Tim Horton	.20	.40
38	Red Kelly	.10	.20
39	Dave Keon	.18	.35
40	Frank Mahovlich	.20	.40
41	Eddie Shack	.10	.20
42	Tod Sloan	.03	.05
43	Sid Smith	.03	.05
44	Allan Stanley	.05	.10
45	Gaye Stewart	.03	.05
46	Harry Watson	.03	.05

BOSTON BRUINS

No.	Player	English NRMT	French NRMT
47	Wayne Carleton	.03	.05
48	Fern Flaman	.08	.15
49	Ken Hodge, Sr.	.10	.20
50	Leo Labine	.03	.05
51	Harry Lumley, Goalie	.35	.75
52	John McKenzie	.05	.10
53	Doug Mohns	.03	.05
54	Fred Stanfield	.03	.05
55	Jerry Toppazzini	.05	.10
56	Ed Westfall	.08	.15

CHICAGO BLACK HAWKS

No.	Player	English NRMT	French NRMT
57	Bobby Hull	.35	.75
58	Ed Litzenberger	.03	.05
59	Gilles Marotte	.03	.05
60	Ab McDonald	.03	.05
61	Bill Mosienko	.03	.05
62	Jim Pappin	.08	.15

No.	Player	English NRMT	French NRMT
63	Pierre Pilote	.08	.15
64	Elmer Vasko	.08	.15
65	Johnny Wilson	.03	.05

DETROIT RED WINGS

No.	Player	English NRMT	French NRMT
66	Sid Abel	.20	.40
67	Gary Bergman	.03	.05
68	Alex Delvecchio	.13	.25
69	Bill Gadsby	.03	.05
70	Ted Lindsay	.13	.25
71	Marcel Pronovost	.03	.05
72	Norm Ullman	.08	.15

HALL OF FAME CHECKLIST

No.	Checklist	English NRMT	French NRMT
73	Montreal Canadiens: Bernie Geoffrion	.05	.10
74	New York Rangers: Andy Bathgate	.05	.10
75	Toronto Maple Leafs: Allan Stanley	.05	.10
76	Boston Bruins: Fern Flaman	.05	.10
77	Chicago Black Hawks: Bobby Hull	.05	.10
78	Detroit Red Wings: Norm Ullman	.05	.10

ALL ULTIMATE TEAM

No.	Player	English NRMT	French NRMT
79	Red Kelly, Tor.	.08	.15
80	Johnny Bower, Goalie, Tor.	.08	.15
81	Henri Richard, Mon.	.08	.15
82	Bobby Hull, Chi.	.15	.30
83	Bernie Geoffrion, Mon.	.10	.20
84	Tim Horton, Tor.	.10	.20

REFEREES

No.	Player	English NRMT	French NRMT
85	Bill Friday	.03	.05
86	Bruce Hood	.03	.05
87	Ron Wicks	.03	.05

THE GOLDEN JET

No.	Player	English NRMT	French NRMT
88	The Electric Slap Shot	.10	.20
89	The Point Race	.10	.20
90	60/61 Stanley Cup Victory	.10	.20
91	The Curse of Muldoon is Lifted	.10	.20
92	Million Dollar Man	.10	.20

RECORDS

No.	Player	English NRMT	French NRMT
93	Bobby Baun's Heroism	.08	.15
94	Terrible Tempered Ted is Back	.08	.15
95	The Pocket Rocket's 99 Year Record Remains	.10	.20
96	The Golden Jet Breaks the 50-Goal Barrier	.10	.20
97	A Tribute to Miles Gordon Horton	.10	.20

REGULAR ISSUE

No.	Player	English NRMT	French NRMT
98	Keith McCreary, Mon.	.03	.05
99	75th Anniversary Checklist 1	.03	.05
100	75th Anniversary Checklist 2	.03	.05

ZELLERS

— 1992 - 93 MASTERS OF HOCKEY —

This 7-card set is unnumbered and listed here alphabetically. The sets were obtained by redeeming Club-Z points.

1992-93 Masters of Hockey
Card No. 7, Maurice (Rocket) Richard

Card Size: 2 1/2" x 3 /15"
Face: Four colour, white border; Name
Back: Four colour, black on white card stock; Name, Jersey number, Resume
Imprint: ZELLERS
Complete Set No. 7
Complete Set Price:

Regular	15.00	30.00
Autographed	300.00	600.00

Production: Regular Sets: 10,000
Autographed Sets: 1,000

REGULAR ISSUE

No.	Player	EX	NRMT
1	Certificate of Authenticity	.50	1.00
2	Johnny Bower, Goalie, Tor.	2.50	5.00
3	Rod Gilbert, NYR	1.50	3.00
4	Ted Lindsay, Det.	2.50	5.00
5	Frank Mahovlich, Tor.	3.50	7.00
6	Stan Mikita, Chi.	2.50	5.00
7	Maurice (Rocket) Richard, Mon.	3.50	7.00

AUTOGRAPHED ISSUE

No.	Player	EX	NRMT
1	Certificate of Authenticity	.50	1.00
2	Johnny Bower, Goalie, Tor.	50.00	100.00
3	Rod Gilbert, NYR	37.50	75.00
4	Ted Lindsay, Det.	50.00	100.00
5	Frank Mahovlich, Tor.	75.00	150.00
6	Stan Mikita, Chi.	50.00	100.00
7	Maurice (Rocket) Richard, Mon.	75.00	150.00

— 1993 - 94 MASTERS OF HOCKEY —

This 8-card set is unnumbered and listed here alphabetically.

1993-94 Masters of Hockey
Card No. 2, John Bucyk

440 • DONRUSS — 1993-94 REGULAR ISSUE

Card Size: 2 1/2" x 3 1/2"
Face: Four colour, white border; Name
Back: Four colour, black on white card stock; Name, Jersey number, Resume
Imprint: ZELLERS
Complete Set No. 8
Complete Set Price: (Regular) 20.00 40.00
Complete Set Price: (Autographed) 400.00 800.00
Production: Regular Sets 10,000
Production: Autographed Sets 2,100

REGULAR ISSUE

No.	Players	EX	NRMT
1	Andy Bathgate	2.50	5.00
2	Johnny Bucyk	2.50	5.00
3	Yvan Cournoyer	2.50	5.00
4	Marcel Dionne	2.50	5.00
5	Bobby Hull	3.50	7.00
6	Brad Park	2.50	5.00
7	Jean Ratelle	2.50	5.00
8	Lorne (Gump) Worsley, Goalie	2.50	5.00

AUTOGRAPHED ISSUE

No.	Players	EX	NRMT
1	Andy Bathgate	50.00	100.00
2	Johnny Bucyk	50.00	100.00
3	Yvan Cournoyer	50.00	100.00
4	Marcel Dionne	50.00	100.00
5	Bobby Hull	75.00	150.00
6	Brad Park	50.00	100.00
7	Jean Ratelle	35.00	75.00
8	Lorne (Gump) Worsley, Goalie	50.00	100.00

— 1994-95 MASTERS OF HOCKEY —

This 8-card set is unnumbered and listed here alphabetically.

Card Size: 2 1/2" x 3 /15"
Face: Four colour, white border; Name
Back: Four colour, black on white card stock; Name, Jersey number, Resume
Imprint: ZELLERS
Complete Set No.
Complete Set Price:
  Regular 20.00 40.00
  Autographed 400.00 800.00
Production: Regular Sets: 10,850
  Autographed Sets: 1,100

REGULAR ISSUE

No.	Player	EX	NRMT
1	Jean Beliveau	2.50	5.00
2	Gerry Cheevers, Goalie	2.50	5.00
3	Red Kelly	2.50	5.00
4	Dave Keon	2.50	5.00
5	Lanny McDonald	2.50	5.00
6	Pierre Pilote	2.50	5.00
7	Henri Richard	2.50	5.00
8	Norm Ullman	2.50	5.00

AUTOGRAPHED ISSUE

No.	Player	EX	NRMT
1	Jean Beliveau	65.00	125.00
2	Gerry Cheevers, Goalie	50.00	100.00
3	Red Kelly	50.00	100.00
4	Dave Keon	50.00	100.00
5	Lanny McDonald	50.00	100.00
6	Pierre Pilote	50.00	100.00
7	Henri Richard	50.00	100.00
8	Norm Ullman	50.00	100.00

DONRUSS

— 1993-94 REGULAR ISSUE —

This 400-card set was Donruss' first entry into hockey cards. The quality of the cards and insert sets made this a premium issue.

1993-94 Issue
Card No. 1, Steven King

Card Size: 2 1/2" x 3 1/2"
Face: Four colour, borderless: Name, Team, Logo
Back: Four colour, borderless: Name, Number, Resume
Imprint: 1993 LEAF INC. PRINTED IN U.S.A.
Complete Set No.: 400
Complete Set Price: 19.00 38.00
Common Card: .05 .10
Foil Pack: (12 Cards) 4.00
Foil Box: (36 Packs) 125.00

MIGHTY DUCKS OF ANAHEIM

No.	Player	EX	NRMT
1	Steven King	.05	.10
2	Joseph Sacco	.05	.10
3	Anatoli Semenov	.05	.10
4	Terry Yake	.05	.10
5	Alexei Kasatonov	.05	.10
6	**Patrik Carnback, RC**	**.10**	**.20**
7	Sean Hill	.05	.10
8	Bill Houlder	.05	.10
9	Todd Ewen	.05	.10
10	Bob Corkum	.05	.10
11	Tim Sweeney	.05	.10
12	Ron Tugnutt, Goalie	.05	.10
13	Guy Hebert, Goalie	.12	.25
14	Shaun Van Allen	.05	.10
15	Stu Grimson	.05	.10

BOSTON BRUINS

No.	Player	EX	NRMT
16	Jon Casey, Goalie	.05	.10
17	Daniel Marois	.05	.10
18	Adam Oates	.10	.20
19	Glen Wesley	.05	.10
20	**Cameron Stewart, RC**	**.10**	**.20**
21	Don Sweeney	.05	.10
22	Glen Murray	.05	.10
23	Jozef Stumpel	.05	.10
24	Raymond Bourque	.10	.20
25	Ted Donato	.05	.10
26	Joseph Juneau	.35	.75
27	Dmitri Kvartalnov	.05	.10
28	Steve Leach	.05	.10
29	Cam Neely	.10	.20
30	Bryan Smolinski	.35	.75

BUFFALO SABRES

No.	Player	EX	NRMT
31	Craig Simpson	.05	.10
32	Donald Audette	.05	.10
33	Doug Bodger	.05	.10
34	Grant Fuhr, Goalie	.05	.10
35	Dale Hawerchuk	.05	.10
36	Yuri Khmylev	.05	.10
37	Pat LaFontaine	.15	.30
38	Brad May	.05	.10
39	Alexander Mogilny	.25	.50
40	Richard Smehlik	.05	.10
41	Petr Svoboda	.05	.10

No.	Player	EX	NRMT
42	**Matthew Barnaby, RC**	**.10**	**.20**
43	**Sergei Petrenko, RC**	**.10**	**.20**
44	Mark Astley	.05	.10
45	**Derek Plante, RC**	**.85**	**1.75**

CALGARY FLAMES

No.	Player	EX	NRMT
46	Theoren Fleury	.05	.10
47	Allan MacInnis	.05	.10
48	Joe Nieuwendyk	.05	.10
49	Joel Otto	.05	.10
50	Paul Ranheim	.05	.10
51	Robert Reichel	.05	.10
52	Gary Roberts	.05	.10
53	Gary Suter	.05	.10
54	Michael Vernon, Goalie	.05	.10
55	Kelly Kisio	.05	.10
56	**German Titov, RC**	**.35**	**.75**
57	Wes Walz	.05	.10
58	**Ted Drury, RC**	**.12**	**.25**
59	**Sandy McCarthy, RC**	**.12**	**.25**
60	**Vesa Viitakoski, RC**	**.12**	**.25**

CHICAGO BLACK HAWKS

No.	Player	EX	NRMT
61	Jeff Hackett, Goalie	.05	.10
62	Neil Wilkinson	.05	.10
63	Dirk Graham	.05	.10
64	Ed Belfour, Goalie	.20	.40
65	Chris Chelios	.05	.10
66	Joe Murphy	.05	.10
67	Jeremy Roenick	.35	.75
68	James (Steve) Smith	.05	.10
69	Brent Sutter	.05	.10
70	**Steve Dubinsky, RC**	**.10**	**.20**
71	Michel Goulet	.05	.10
72	Christian Ruuttu	.05	.10
73	Bryan Marchment	.05	.10
74	Sergei Krivokrasov	.05	.10
75	**Jeff Shantz, RC**	**.10**	**.20**

DALLAS STARS

No.	Player	EX	NRMT
76	Michael Modano	.25	.50
77	Derian Hatcher	.05	.10
78	Ulf Dahlen	.05	.10
79	Mark Tinordi	.05	.10
80	Russell Courtnall	.05	.10
81	Mike Craig	.05	.10
82	Trent Klatt	.05	.10
83	Dave Gagner	.05	.10
84	**Chris Tancill, RC**	**.10**	**.20**
85	James Black	.05	.10
86	Dean Evason	.05	.10
87	Andrew Moog, Goalie	.05	.10
88	Paul Cavallini	.05	.10
89	Grant Ledyard	.05	.10
90	**Jarkko Varvio, RC**	**.10**	**.20**

DETROIT RED WINGS

No.	Player	EX	NRMT
91	Vyacheslav Kozlov	.35	.75
92	Mike Sillinger	.05	.10
93	**Aaron Ward, RC**	**.12**	**.25**
94	**Greg Johnson, RC**	**.12**	**.25**
95	Steve Yzerman	.20	.40
96	Tim Cheveldae, Goalie	.05	.10
97	Steve Chiasson	.05	.10
98	Dino Ciccarelli	.05	.10
99	Paul Coffey	.07	.15
100	**Dallas Drake, RC**	**.20**	**.40**
101	Sergei Fedorov	.50	1.00
102	Nicklas Lidstrom	.05	.10
103	**Darren McCarty, RC**	**.10**	**.20**
104	Bob Probert	.05	.10
105	Ray Sheppard	.10	.20

EDMONTON OILERS

No.	Player	EX	NRMT
106	Scott Pearson	.05	.10
107	Steven Rice	.05	.10

No.	Player	EX	NRMT
108	Louie DeBrusk	.05	.10
109	Dave Manson	.05	.10
110	Dean McAmmond	.05	.10
111	**Roman Oksyuta, RC, Error**	.12	.25
112	Geoff Smith	.05	.10
113	Zdeno Ciger	.05	.10
114	Shayne Corson	.05	.10
115	Luke Richardson	.05	.10
116	Igor Kravchuk	.05	.10
117	Bill Ranford, Goalie	.05	.10
118	Doug Weight	.05	.10
119	**Fred Brathwaite, Goalie, RC**	.12	.25
120	**Jason Arnott, RC**	1.50	3.00

FLORIDA PANTHERS

No.	Player	EX	NRMT
121	Tom Fitzgerald	.05	.10
122	Mike Hough	.05	.10
123	**Jesse Belanger, RC**	.20	.40
124	Brian Skrudland	.05	.10
125	Dave Lowry	.05	.10
126	Scott Mellanby	.05	.10
127	Eugeny Davydov	.05	.10
128	Andrei Lomakin	.05	.10
129	Brian Benning	.05	.10
130	**Scott Levins, RC**	.12	.25
131	Gordon Murphy	.05	.10
132	John Vanbiesbrouck, Goalie	.05	.10
133	Mark Fitzpatrick, Goalie	.05	.10
134	**Rob Niedermayer, RC**	.50	1.00
135	Alexander Godynyuk	.05	.10

HARTFORD WHALERS

No.	Player	EX	NRMT
136	Eric Weinrich	.05	.10
137	Mark Greig	.05	.10
138	Jim Sandlak	.05	.10
139	Adam Burt	.05	.10
140	Nicholas Kypreos	.05	.10
141	Sean Burke, Goalie	.05	.10
142	Andrew Cassels	.05	.10
143	Robert Kron	.05	.10
144	Mikael Nylander	.12	.25
145	Robert Petrovicky	.10	.20
146	Patrick Poulin	.05	.10
147	Geoff Sanderson	.20	.40
148	Patrick Verbeek	.05	.10
149	Zarley Zalapski	.05	.10
150	**Chris Pronger, RC**	.50	1.00

LOS ANGELES KINGS

No.	Player	EX	NRMT
151	Jari Kurri	.05	.10
152	Wayne Gretzky	1.25	2.50
153	Patrick Conacher	.05	.10
154	Shawn McEachern	.10	.20
155	Mike Donnelly	.05	.10
156	Warren Rychel	.05	.10
157	Gary Shuchuk	.05	.10
158	Robert Blake	.05	.10
159	Jimmy Carson	.05	.10
160	Tony Granato	.05	.10
161	Kelly Hrudey, Goalie	.05	.10
162	Luc Robitaille	.15	.30
163	Tomas Sandstrom	.05	.10
164	Darryl Sydor	.05	.10
165	Alexei Zhitnik	.15	.30

MONTREAL CANADIENS

No.	Player	EX	NRMT
166	Benoit Brunet	.05	.10
167	Lyle Odelein	.05	.10
168	Kevin Haller	.05	.10
169	**Pierre Sevigny, RC**	.12	.25
170	Brian Bellows	.05	.10
171	Patrice Brisebois	.05	.10
172	Vincent Damphousse	.10	.20
173	Eric Desjardins	.05	.10
174	Gilbert Dionne	.05	.10
175	Stephan Lebeau	.05	.10
176	John LeClair	.05	.10

No.	Player	EX	NRMT
177	Kirk Muller	.10	.20
178	Patrick Roy, Goalie	.35	.75
179	Mattieu Schneider	.05	.10
180	Peter Popovic	.20	.40

NEW JERSEY DEVILS

No.	Player	EX	NRMT
181	Corey Millen	.05	.10
182	**Jason Smith, RC**	.12	.25
183	Robert Holik	.05	.10
184	John MacLean	.05	.10
185	Bruce Driver	.05	.10
186	Bill Guerin	.05	.10
187	Claude Lemieux	.05	.10
188	Bernie Nicholls	.05	.10
189	Scott Niedermayer	.25	.50
190	Stephane J. J. Richer	.05	.10
191	Alexander Semak	.05	.10
192	Scott Stevens	.05	.10
193	Valeri Zelepukin	.05	.10
194	Chris Terreri, Goalie	.05	.10
195	Martin Brodeur, Goalie	.35	.70

NEW YORK ISLANDERS

No.	Player	EX	NRMT
196	Ron Hextall, Goalie	.05	.10
197	Brad Dalgarno	.05	.10
198	Ray Ferraro	.05	.10
199	Patrick Flatley	.05	.10
200	Travis Green	.05	.10
201	Benoit Hogue	.05	.10
202	**Steve Junker, RC**	.12	.25
203	Darius Kasparaitis	.05	.10
204	Derek King	.05	.10
205	Uwe Krupp	.05	.10
206	Scott Lachance	.07	.15
207	Vladimir Malakhov	.15	.30
208	Steve Thomas	.05	.10
209	Pierre Turgeon	.20	.40
210	Scott Scissons	.05	.10

NEW YORK RANGERS

No.	Player	EX	NRMT
211	Glenn Healy, Goalie	.05	.10
212	**Alexander Karpovtsev, RC**	.20	.40
213	James Patrick	.05	.10
214	Sergei Nemchinov	.05	.10
215	Esa Tikkanen	.05	.10
216	**Corey Hirsch, Goalie, RC**	.20	.40
217	Anthony Amonte	.20	.40
218	Michael Gartner	.10	.20
219	Adam Graves	.25	.50
220	Alexei Kovalev	.50	1.00
221	Brian Leetch	.25	.50
222	Mark Messier	.10	.20
223	Mike Richter, Goalie	.20	.40
224	Darren Turcotte	.05	.10
225	Sergei Zubov	.25	.50

OTTAWA SENATORS

No.	Player	EX	NRMT
226	Craig Billington, Goalie	.05	.10
227	Troy Mallette	.05	.10
228	Vladimir Ruzicka	.05	.10
229	**Darrin Madeley, Goalie, RC**	.20	.40
230	Mark Lamb	.05	.10
231	Dave Archibald	.05	.10
232	Bob Kudelski	.05	.10
233	Norm Maciver	.05	.10
234	Brad Shaw	.05	.10
235	Sylvain Turgeon	.05	.10
236	Brian Glynn	.05	.10
237	**Alexandre Daigle, RC**	.75	1.50
238	**Alexei Yashin, RC**	.85	1.75
239	**Dimitri Filimonov, RC**	.12	.25
240	**Pavol Demitra, RC**	.12	.25

PHILADELPHIA FLYERS

No.	Player	EX	NRMT
241	**Jason Bowen, RC**	.10	.20
242	Eric Lindros	2.00	4.00

No.	Player	EX	NRMT
243	Dominic Roussel, Goalie	.12	.25
244	**Milos Holan, RC**	.10	.20
245	Greg Hawgood	.05	.10
246	Yves Racine	.05	.10
247	Josef Beranek	.05	.10
248	Rod Brind'Amour	.12	.25
249	Kevin Dineen	.05	.10
250	Per-Erik Eklund	.05	.10
251	Garry Galley	.05	.10
252	Mark Recchi	.15	.30
253	Tommy Soderstrom, Goalie	.10	.20
254	Dimitri Yushkevich	.05	.10
255	Mikael Renberg	.75	1.50

PITTSBURGH PENGUINS

No.	Player	EX	NRMT
256	Martin McSorley	.05	.10
257	Joe Mullen	.05	.10
258	Doug Brown	.05	.10
259	Kjell Samuelsson	.05	.10
260	Tom Barrasso, Goalie	.10	.20
261	Ronald Francis	.05	.10
262	Mario Lemieux	1.00	2.00
263	Lawrence Murphy	.05	.10
264	Ulf Samuelsson	.05	.10
265	Kevin Stevens	.15	.30
266	Martin Straka	.35	.75
267	Rick Tocchet	.05	.10
268	Bryan Trottier	.05	.10
269	**Markus Naslund, RC**	.12	.25
270	Jaromir Jagr	.35	.75

QUEBEC NORDIQUES

No.	Player	EX	NRMT
271	Martin Gelinas	.05	.10
272	Adam Foote	.05	.10
273	Curtis Leschyshyn	.05	.10
274	**Stephane Fiset, Goalie, RC**	.20	.40
275	**Jocelyn Thibault, Goalie, RC**	.75	1.50
276	Steve Duchesne	.05	.10
277	Valeri Kamensky	.20	.40
278	Andrei Kovalenko	.20	.40
279	Owen Nolan	.10	.20
280	Mike Ricci	.05	.10
281	Martin Rucinsky	.05	.10
282	Joe Sakic	.12	.25
283	Mats Sundin	.12	.25
284	Scott Young	.05	.10
285	Claude Lapointe	.05	.10

ST. LOUIS BLUES

No.	Player	EX	NRMT
286	Brett Hull	.50	1.00
287	**Vitali Karamnov, RC**	.12	.25
288	Ronald Sutter	.05	.10
289	Garth Butcher	.05	.10
290	**Vitali Prokhorov, RC**	.20	.40
291	Bret Hedican	.05	.10
292	Anthony Hrkac	.05	.10
293	Jeff Brown	.05	.10
294	Phil Housley	.05	.10
295	Craig Janney	.05	.10
296	Curtis Joseph, Goalie	.20	.40
297	**Igor Korolev, RC**	.12	.25
298	Kevin Miller	.05	.10
299	Brendan Shanahan	.10	.20
300	**Jim Montgomery, RC**	.12	.25

SAN JOSE SHARKS

No.	Player	EX	NRMT
301	Gaetan Duchesne	.05	.10
302	Jimmy Waite, Goalie	.05	.10
303	Jeff Norton	.05	.10
304	Sergei Makarov	.05	.10
305	Igor Larionov	.05	.10
306	Mike Lalor	.05	.10
307	Michal Sykora	.05	.10
308	Pat Falloon	.05	.10
309	Johan Garpenlov	.05	.10
310	Rob Gaudreau	.05	.10
311	Arthurs Irbe, Goalie	.05	.10

442 • DONRUSS — 1993-94 UPDATE SET —

No.	Player	EX	NRMT
312	Sandis Ozolinch, Error	.05	.10
313	Doug Zmolek	.05	.10
314	Mike Rathje	.05	.10
315	Vlastimil Kroupa	.05	.10

TAMPA BAY LIGHTNING

No.	Player	EX	NRMT
316	Daren Puppa, Goalie	.05	.10
317	Petr Klima	.05	.10
318	Brent Gretzky	.05	.10
319	Denis Savard	.05	.10
320	Gerard Gallant	.05	.10
321	Joe Reekie	.05	.10
322	Bo Mikael Andersson	.05	.10
323	Bill McDougall	.05	.10
324	Brian Bradley	.05	.10
325	Shawn Chambers	.05	.10
326	Adam Creighton	.05	.10
327	Roman Hamrlik	.05	.10
328	John Tucker	.05	.10
329	Rob Zamuner	.05	.10
330	Chris Gratton	.05	.10

TORONTO MAPLE LEAFS

No.	Player	EX	NRMT
331	Sylvain Lefebvre	.05	.10
332	Nikolai Borschevsky	.05	.10
333	Robert Rouse	.05	.10
334	John Cullen	.05	.10
335	Todd Gill	.05	.10
336	Drake Berehowsky	.05	.10
337	Wendel Clark	.05	.10
338	Peter Zezel	.05	.10
339	Rob Pearson	.05	.10
340	Glenn Anderson	.05	.10
341	Douglas Gilmour	.05	.10
342	David Andreychuk	.05	.10
343	Felix Potvin, Goalie	.05	.10
344	David Ellett	.05	.10
345	Alexei Kudashov	.05	.10

VANCOUVER CANUCKS

No.	Player	EX	NRMT
346	Gino Odjick	.05	.10
347	Jyrki Lumme	.05	.10
348	Dana Murzyn	.05	.10
349	Sergio Momesso	.05	.10
350	Greg Adams	.05	.10
351	Pavel Bure	.05	.10
352	Geoff Courtnall	.05	.10
353	Murray Craven	.05	.10
354	Trevor Linden	.05	.10
355	Kirk McLean, Goalie	.05	.10
356	Petr Nedved	.05	.10
357	Cliff Ronning	.05	.10
358	Jiri Slegr	.05	.10
359	Kay Whitmore, Goalie	.05	.10
360	Gerald Diduck	.05	.10

WASHINGTON CAPITALS

No.	Player	EX	NRMT
361	Pat Peake, RC	.20	.40
362	David Poulin	.05	.10
363	Rick Tabaracci, Goalie	.05	.10
364	Jason Woolley	.05	.10
365	Kelly Miller	.05	.10
366	Peter Bondra	.05	.10
367	Sylvain Cote	.05	.10
368	Pat Elynuik	.05	.10
369	Kevin Hatcher	.05	.10
370	Dale Hunter	.05	.10
371	Al Iafrate	.10	.20
372	Calle Johansson	.05	.10
373	Dimitri Khristich	.05	.10
374	Michal Pivonka	.05	.10
375	Mike Ridley	.05	.10

WINNIPEG JETS

No.	Player	EX	NRMT
376	Paul Ysebaert	.05	.10
377	Stu Barnes	.05	.10
378	Sergei Bautin, RC	.20	.40
379	Kris King	.05	.10
380	Alexei Zhamnov	.35	.75
381	Tahir Domi	.05	.10
382	Bob Essensa, Goalie	.05	.10
383	Nelson Emerson	.05	.10
384	Boris Mironov, RC	.20	.40
385	Teppo Numminen	.05	.10
386	Fredrik Olausson	.05	.10
387	Teemu Selanne	1.00	2.00
388	Darrin Shannon	.05	.10
389	Thomas Steen	.05	.10
390	Keith Tkachuk	.50	1.00

REGULAR ISSUE

No.	Player	EX	NRMT
391	Opening Night: Florida Panthers	.50	1.00
392	Opening Night: Mighty Ducks of Anaheim	.50	1.00
393	1993 NHL Top Draft Picks: Alexandre Daigle, Ott. Chris Pronger, Hart. Chris Gratton, TB	.50	1.00
394	Rookie Record Breakers: Joseoh Juneau, Bos. Teemu Selanne, Win.	.25	.50
395	Record Breaking Kings: Luc Robitaille; Wayne Gretzky	.50	1.00
396	Subset Checklist	.05	.10
397	Checklist: Atlantic Division (1 - 100)	.05	.10
398	Checklist: North East Division (101 - 200)	.05	.10
399	Checklist: Central Division (201 - 300)	.05	.10
400	Checklist: Pacific Division (301 - 400)	.05	.10

— 1993 - 94 UPDATE SET —

Issued late in the season to update the 1993-94 regular issue set. The numbering was carried forward from 401 to 540.

1993-94 Update Set
Card No. 401, Garry Valk

Card Size: 2 1/2" x 3 1/2"
Face: Four colour: Name, Team, Gold foil logo
Back: Four colour: Name, Number, Resume
Imprint: 1993 LEAF INC. PRINTED IN U.S.A.
Complete Set No.: 140
Complete Set Price: 6.00 12.00
Common Card: .05 .10
Foil Pack: (12 Cards) 1.50
Foil Box: (36 Packs) 45.00

No.	Player	EX	NRMT
401	Garry Valk, MDA	.05	.10
402	Al Iafrate, Bos	.05	.10
403	David Reid, Bos.	.05	.10
404	Jason Dawe, Buf.	.10	.20
405	Craig Muni, Buf.	.05	.10

CALGARY FLAMES

No.	Player	EX	NRMT
406	Dan Keczmer, RC	.10	.20
407	Mikael Nylander	.12	.25
408	James Patrick	.05	.10
409	Andrei Trefilov, Goalie, RC	.20	.40
410	Zarley Zalapski	.05	.10

CHICAGO BLACK HAWKS

No.	Player	EX	NRMT
411	Anthony Amonte	.10	.20
412	Keith Carney, RC	.10	.20
413	Randy Cunneyworth	.05	.10
414	Ivan Droppa	.05	.10
415	Gary Suter	.05	.10
416	Eric Weinrich	.05	.10
417	Paul Ysebaert	.05	.10

DALLAS STARS

No.	Player	EX	NRMT
418	Richard Matvichuk	.05	.10
419	Alan May	.05	.10
420	Darcy Wakaluk, Goalie	.05	.10

DETROIT RED WINGS

No.	Player	EX	NRMT
421	Micah Alvazoff, RC	.10	.20
422	Terry Carkner	.05	.10
423	Kris Draper	.05	.10
424	Chris Osgood, Goalie, RC	.50	1.00
425	Keith Primeau	.05	.10

EDMONTON OILERS

No.	Player	EX	NRMT
426	Bob Beers	.05	.10
427	Ilya Byakin, RC	.10	.20
428	Kirk Maltby, RC	.10	.20
429	Boris Mironov, RC	.10	.20
430	Fredrik Olausson	.05	.10
431	Peter White, RC	.10	.20

FLORIDA PANTHERS

No.	Player	EX	NRMT
432	Stu Barnes	.05	.10
433	Mike Foligno	.05	.10
434	Bob Kudelski	.05	.10
435	Geoff Smith	.05	.10

HARTFORD WHALERS

No.	Player	EX	NRMT
436	Igor Chibirev, RC	.15	.30
437	Ted Drury, RC	.10	.20
438	Alexander Godynyuk	.05	.10
439	Frank Kucera	.05	.10
440	Jocelyn Lemieux	.05	.10
441	Brian Propp	.05	.10
442	Paul Ranheim	.05	.10
443	Jeff Reese, Goalie	.05	.10
444	Kevin Smyth, RC	.10	.20
445	Jim Storm, RC	.12	.25

LOS ANGELES KINGS

No.	Player	EX	NRMT
446	Phil Crowe, RC	.12	.25
447	Martin McSorley	.05	.10
448	Keith Redmond, RC	.12	.25
449	Dixon Ward	.05	.10

MONTREAL CANADIENS

No.	Player	EX	NRMT
450	Guy Carbonneau	.05	.10
451	Mike Keane	.05	.10
452	Oleg Petrov, RC	.12	.25
453	Ron Tugnutt, Goalie	.05	.10

NEW JERSEY DEVILS

No.	Player	EX	NRMT
454	Randy McKay, RC	.10	.20
455	Jaroslav Modry, RC	.15	.30

NEW YORK ISLANDERS

No.	Player	EX	NRMT
456	Yan Kaminsky	.05	.10
457	Marty McInnis	.05	.10
458	Jamie McLennan, Goalie, RC	.10	.20
459	Zigmund Palffy	.05	.10

NEW YORK RANGERS

No.	Player	EX	NRMT
460	Glenn Anderson	.05	.10
461	Steve Larmer	.05	.10
462	Craig MacTavish	.05	.10
463	Stephane Matteau	.05	.10
464	Brian Noonan	.05	.10
465	Mattias Norstrom, RC	.10	.20

OTTAWA SENATORS

No.	Player	EX	NRMT
466	Scott Levins, RC	.10	.20
467	Derek Mayer, RC	.12	.25
468	Andy Schneider, RC	.10	.20

PHILADELPHIA FLYERS

No.	Player	EX	NRMT
469	Todd Hlushka, RC	.12	.25
470	Stewart Malgunas, RC	.12	.25

PITTSBURGH PENGUINS

No.	Player	EX	NRMT
471	Justin Duberman, RC	.10	.20
472	Ladislav Karabin, RC	.10	.20
473	Shawn McEachern	.10	.20
474	Ed Patterson	.05	.10
475	Tomas Sandstrom	.05	.10

QUEBEC NORDIQUES

No.	Player	EX	NRMT
476	Bob Bassen	.05	.10
477	Garth Butcher	.05	.10
478	Iain Fraser, RC	.18	.35
479	Mike McKee, RC	.10	.20
480	Dwayne Norris, RC	.15	.30
481	Garth Snow, Goalie, RC	.12	.25
482	Ronald Sutter	.05	.10

ST. LOUIS BLUES

No.	Player	EX	NRMT
483	Kelly Chase	.05	.10
484	Steve Duchesne	.05	.10
485	Daniel Laperriere, RC	.12	.25
486	Petr Nedved	.05	.10
487	Peter Stastny	.05	.10

SAN JOSE SHARKS

No.	Player	EX	NRMT
488	Ulf Dahlen	.05	.10
489	Todd Elik	.05	.10
490	Andrei Nazarov, RC	.15	.30

TAMPA BAY LIGHTNING

No.	Player	EX	NRMT
491	Danton Cole, RC	.10	.20
492	Chris Joseph, RC	.10	.20
493	Chris LiPuma, RC	.10	.20

TORONTO MAPLE LEAFS

No.	Player	EX	NRMT
494	Michael Gartner	.05	.10
495	Mark Greig	.05	.10
496	David Harlock, RC	.10	.20
497	Matt Martin, RC	.10	.20

VANCOUVER CANUCKS

No.	Player	EX	NRMT
498	Shawn Antoski	.05	.10
499	Jeff Brown	.05	.10
500	Jimmy Carson	.05	.10
501	Martin Gelinas	.05	.10
502	Yevgeny Namestnikov, RC	.15	.30

WASHINGTON CAPITALS

No.	Player	EX	NRMT
503	Randy Burridge	.05	.10
504	Joseph Juneau	.35	.75
505	Kevin Kaminski, RC	.12	.25

WINNIPEG JETS

No.	Player	EX	NRMT
506	Arto Blomsten, RC	.12	.25
507	Tim Cheveldae, Goalie	.05	.10
508	Dallas Drake, RC	.20	.40
509	Dave Manson	.05	.10

REGULAR ISSUE

No.	Player	EX	NRMT
510	Checklist (401 - 510)	.05	.10

— 1993 - 94 INSERT SETS —

CONFERENCE INSERTS

Randomly inserted into regular foil packs.

Card Size: 2 1/2" x 3 1/2"
Face: Four colour, Logo
Back: Four colour, Name, Number, Logo
Imprint: © 1993 © LEAF INC. PRINTED IN USA

No.	Player	EX	NRMT
—	Luc Robitaille	15.00	30.00
—	Mario Lemieux	37.50	75.00

ELITE SERIES

Cards 1-10 were randomly inserted into regular foil packs. Cards U1 - U5 were randomly inserted into Update foil packs. There were 10,000 individually numbered cards.

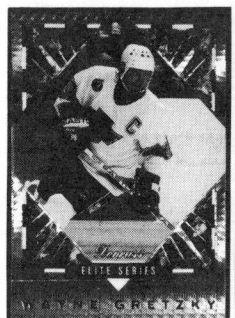 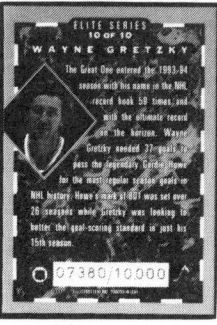

1993-94 Elite Series
Card No. 10, Wayne Gretzky

Card Size: 2 1/2" x 3 1/2"
Face: Four colour, silver foiled border; Name, Logo
Back: Black on card stock; Name, Number, Resume
Imprint: 1993 LEAF INC. PRINTED IN U.S.A.
Complete Set No.: 15
Complete Set Price: 375.00   750.00
Common Card: 20.00   40.00

SERIES ONE

No.	Player	EX	NRMT
1	Mario Lemieux, Pit.	50.00	100.00
2	Alexandre Daigle, Ott.	20.00	40.00
3	Teemu Selanne, Win.	25.00	50.00
4	Eric Lindros, Phi.	55.00	110.00
5	Brett Hull, St.L	30.00	60.00
6	Jeremy Roenick, Chi.	25.00	50.00
7	Douglas Gilmour, Tor.	30.00	60.00
8	Alexander Mogilny, Buf.	20.00	40.00
9	Patrick Roy, Goalie, Mon.	37.50	75.00
10	Wayne Gretzky, LA	60.00	125.00

SERIES TWO UPDATE

No.	Player	EX	NRMT
U1	Mikael Renberg, Phi.	20.00	40.00
U2	Sergei Fedorov, Det.	30.00	60.00
U3	Felix Potvin, Goalie, Tor.	30.00	60.00
U4	Cam Neely, Bos.	20.00	40.00
U5	Alexei Yashin, Ott.	22.50	45.00

ICE KINGS

Randomly inserted into regular foil packs

1993-94 Ice Kings
Card No. 8, Pavel Bure

Card Size: 2 1/3" x 3 1/2"
Face: Four colour, borderless; Name, Logo
Back: Four colour; Name, Resume
Imprint: 1993 LEAF INC. PRINTED IN U.S.A.
Complete Set No.: 10
Complete Set Price: 22.50   45.00
Common Card: 1.50   3.00

No.	Player	EX	NRMT
1	Patrick Roy, Goalie, Mon.	5.00	10.00
2	Pat LaFontaine, Buf.	2.00	4.00
3	Jaromir Jagr, Pit.	2.00	4.00
4	Wayne Gretzky, LA	5.00	10.00
5	Chris Chelios, Chi.	1.50	3.00
6	Felix Potvin, Goalie, Tor.	4.00	8.00
7	Mario Lemieux, Pit.	4.00	8.00
8	Pavel Bure, Van.	4.00	8.00
9	Eric Lindros, Phi.	4.00	8.00
10	Teemu Selanne, Win.	2.50	5.00

RATED ROOKIES

Randomly inserted into regular foil packs.

1993-94 Rated Rookies
Card No. 1, Alexandre Daigle

Card Size: 2 1/2" x 3 1/2"
Face: Four colour, gold foil; Name, Logo
Back: Four colour; Name, Number, Resume on card stock
Imprint: 1993 LEAF INC. PRINTED IN U.S.A.
Complete Set No.: 15
Complete Set Price: 25.00   50.00
Common Card: 1.50   3.00

No.	Player	EX	NRMT
1	Alexandre Daigle, Ott.	3.00	6.00
2	Chris Gratton, TB	2.00	4.00
3	Chris Pronger, Hart.	2.00	4.00
4	Rob Niedermayer, Fl.	2.00	4.00
5	Mikael Renberg, Phi.	3.50	7.00
6	Jarkko Varvio, Dal.	1.50	3.00
7	Alexei Yashin, Ott.	3.50	7.00
8	Markus Naslund, Pit.	1.50	3.00
9	Boris Mironov, Win.	1.50	3.00
10	Martin Brodeur, Goalie, NJ	5.00	10.00
11	Jocelyn Thibault, Goalie, Que.	3.50	7.00
12	Jason Arnott, Edm.	6.00	12.00
13	Jim Montgomery, St.L	1.50	3.00
14	Ted Drury, Cal.	1.50	3.00
15	Roman Oksyuta, Edm., Error	1.50	3.00

444 • KENNER — 1993-94 STARTING LINE UP

SPECIAL PRINT - PREMIER EDITION

Randomly inserted into regular foil packs. The cards are lettered rather than numbered.

1993-94 Special Print - Premier Edition
Card No. A, Ron Tugnutt

Card Size: 2 1/2" x 3 1/2"
Face: Four colour, border;ess; Name, Gold foil, Logo
Back: Four colour; Name, Number, Resume
Imprint: © 1993 LEAF INC., PRINTED IN U.S.A.
Complete Set No.: 26
Complete Set Price: 90.00   180.00
Common Card: 1.50   3.00

No.	Player	EX	NRMT
A	Ron Tugnutt, Goalie, MDA	1.50	3.00
B	Adam Oates, Bos.	2.50	5.00
C	Alexander Mogilny, Buf.	3.50	7.00
D	Theoren Fleury, Cal.	1.50	3.00
E	Jeremy Roenick, Chi.	4.00	8.00
F	Michael Modano, Dal.	2.50	5.00
G	Steve Yzerman, Det.	4.00	8.00
H	Jason Arnott, Edm.	9.00	18.00
I	Rob Niedermayer, Fl.	3.00	6.00
J	Chris Pronger, Hart.	3.00	6.00
K	Wayne Gretzky, LA	12.50	25.00
L	Patrick Roy, Goalie, Mon.	7.50	15.00
M	Scott Niedermayer, NJ	1.50	3.00
N	Pierre Turgeon, NYI	2.50	5.00
O	Mark Messier, NYR	3.00	6.00
P	Alexandre Daigle, Ott.	4.00	8.00
Q	Eric Lindros, Phi.	12.50	25.00
R	Mario Lemieux, Pit.	10.00	20.00
S	Mats Sundin, Que.	2.50	5.00
T	Pat Falloon, SJ	1.50	3.00
U	Brett Hull, St.L	3.50	7.00
V	Chris Gratton, TB	3.00	6.00
W	Felix Potvin, Goalie, Tor.	7.50	15.00
X	Pavel Bure, Van.	9.00	18.00
Y	Al Iafrate, Wash.	1.50	3.00
Z	Teemu Selanne, Win.	5.00	10.00

1994 WORLD JUNIOR CHAMPIONSHIPS

Either Team Canada or Team U.S.A. cards were inserted one per pack into Update foil packs.

1994 World Junior Championships
Card No. 1, Jason Allison

Card Size: 2 1/2" x 3 1/2"
Face: Four colour, borderless, foil; Name, Logo
Back: Four colour; Name, Number, Resume
Imprint: © 1994 LEAF INC., PRINTED IN U.S.A.
Complete Set No.: 46
Complete Set Price: 15.00   45.00
Common Card: .35   .75

TEAM CANADA

No.	Player	EX	NRMT
1	Jason Allison	1.50	3.00
2	Chris Armstrong	.35	.75
3	Drew Bannister	.35	.75
4	Jason Botterill	1.00	2.00
5	Joel Bouchard	.35	.75
6	Curtis Bowen	.35	.75
7	Anson Carter	.50	1.00
8	Brandon Convery	.75	1.50
9	Yannick Dube	.75	1.50
10	Emanuel Fernandez, Goalie	.50	1.00
11	Jeff Friesen	2.50	5.00
12	Aaron Gavey	1.00	2.00
13	Martin Gendron	.50	1.00
14	Rick Girard	.50	1.00
15	Todd Harvey	1.25	2.50
16	Bryan McCabe	.35	.75
17	Marty Murray	.35	.75
18	Mike Peca	.85	1.75
19	Nick Stajduhar	.50	1.00
20	Jamie Storr, Goalie	2.50	5.00
21	Brent Tully	.35	.75
22	Brendan Witt	1.00	2.00
23	Canadian Checklist (1/22)	1.00	2.00

TEAM U.S.A.

No.	Player	EX	NRMT
1	Kevin Adams	.60	1.25
2	Jason Bonsignore	1.50	3.00
3	Andy Brink	.35	.75
4	Joe Coleman	.35	.75
5	Adam Deadmarsh	.35	.75
6	Aaron Ellis, Goalie	.35	.75
7	John Emmons	.35	.75
8	Ashlin Halfnight	.35	.75
9	Kevin Hilton	.35	.75
10	Jason Karmanos	.35	.75
11	Toby Kvalevog, Goalie	.35	.75
12	Bob Lachance	.35	.75
13	Jamie Langenbrunner	.35	.75
14	Jason McBain	.35	.75
15	Chris O'Sullivan	.35	.75
16	Jay Pandolfo	.35	.75
17	Richard Park	.85	1.75
18	Deron Quint	.35	.75
19	Ryan Sittler	.35	.75
20	Blake Sloan	.35	.75
21	John Varga	.35	.75
22	David Wilkie	.35	.75
23	USA Checklist (1 - 22)	1.00	2.00

KENNER

— 1993 - 94 STARTING LINE UP —

1993-94 Staring Line Up
Figure No. 6, Brett Hull

This 12-figure set was available in both the U.S.A. and Canada with the only difference being the Canadian cards are bilingual. Each statue comes packaged with two cards of that player. If removed from the blister pack the value of the statue and cards are decreased dramatically.

Card Size: 2 1/2" x 3 1/2"
Face: Four colour; Name, Logo
Back: Blue on cardstock; Name, Logo
Statue Size: 3 1/2" to 5 1/2"
Statue Colour: Four colour
Imprint: © 1993 NHLPA
Complete Set
  Cards: 12
  Statue: 12
Complete Set Price: 425.00

No.	Player	NRMT
1	Grant Fuhr, Goalie, Buf.	200.00
2	Steve Yzerman, Det.	12.00
3	Mark Messier, NYR	12.00
4	Raymond Bourque, Bos.	12.00
5	Patrick Roy, Goalie, Mon.	50.00
6	Brett Hull, St.L.	12.00
7	Jeremy Roenick, Chi.	12.00
8	Ed. Belfour, Goalie, Chi.	65.00
9	Jarmir Jagr, Pit.	25.00
10	Mario Lemieux, Pit.	12.00
11	Eric Lindros, Phi.	30.00
12	Pat LaFontaine, Buf.	85.00

HOCKEY WIT

— 1993 - 94 ISSUE —

This 108-card set is a game of Trivia with each card having at least three hockey questions on the back.

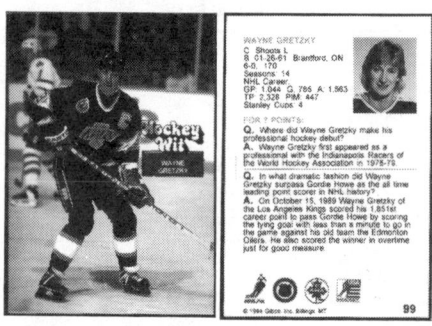

1993-94 Issue
Card No. 99, Wayne Gretzkky

Card Size: 2 1/2" x 3 1/2"
Face: Four colour; Name, Gold foil logo
Back: Four colour; Name, Number, Resume, Trivia
Imprint: © Gibco Inc., Billings, Mt.
Complete Set No.: 108
Complete Price Set: 12.50   25.00
Common Card: .07   .15

No.	Player	EX	NRMT
1	Mike Richter, Goalie, NYR	.25	.50
2	Anthony Amonte, NYR	.07	.15
3	Patrick Roy, Goalie, Mon.	1.25	2.50
4	Craig Janney, St.L	.07	.15
5	Adam Oates, Bos.	.25.	.50
6	Geoff Sanderson, Har.	.07	.15
7	Pavel Bure, Van.	1.25	2.50
8	Steve Duchesne, St.L	.07	.15
9	Gordie Howe, Det.	1.00	2.00
10	Brad Park, NYR	.07	.15
11	Brian Bellows, Mon.	.07	.15
12	Chris Chelios, Chi.	.07	.15
13	Bill Barber, Phi.	.07	.15
14	Lorne (Gump) Worsley, Goalie, NYR	.35	.75
15	Stanley Cup	.50	1.00
16	Maurice Richard, Mon.	.75	1.50
17	Kevin Hatcher, Wash.	.07	.15
18	Ed Belfour, Goalie, Chi.	.50	1.00
19	Kirk Muller, Mon.	.07	.15

— 1993 - 94 ISSUE — SEGA - E M SPORTS • 445

No.	Player	EX	NRMT
20	Kevin Stevens, Pit.	.25	.50
21	David Taylor, LA	.07	.15
22	Dale Hawerchuk, Buf.	.07	.15
23	Jean Beliveau, Mon.	.75	1.50
24	Rogatien Vachon, Goalie, LA	.07	.15
25	Tom Barrasso, Goalie, Pit.	.07	.15
26	Rod Langway, Wash.	.07	.15
27	Pierre Turgeon, NYI	.25	.50
28	Derek King, NYI	.07	.15
29	Brendan Shanahan, St.L	.07	.15
30	Darren Turcotte, NYR	.07	.15
31	Chris Terreri, Goalie, NJ	.07	.15
32	Tony Granato, LA	.07	.15
33	Michel Goulet, Que.	.07	.15
34	Felix Potvin, Goalie, Tor.	1.00	2.00
35	Curtis Joseph, Goalie, St.L	.50	1.00
36	Cam Neely, Bos.	.25	.50
37	Anders Borje Salming, Tor.	.25	.50
38	Denis Savard, Mon.	.07	.15
39	Stan Mikita, Chi.	.75	1.50
40	Grant Fuhr, Goalie, Buf.	.07	.15
41	Gary Suter, Cal.	.07	.15
42	Serge Savard, Mon.	.07	.15
43	Steve Larmer, NYR	.07	.15
44	Bryan Trottier, Pit.	.07	.15
45	Michael Vernon, Goalie, Cal.	.07	.15
46	Paul Coffey, Det.	.25	.50
47	Bernie Federko	.07	.15
48	Lawrence Murphy, Pit.	.07	.15
49	William (Scotty) Bowman, Det.	.07	.15
50	Glenn Anderson, NYR	.07	.15
51	Mats Sundin, Que.	.25	.50
52	Henri Richard, Mon.	.50	1.00
53	Ronald Francis, Pit.	.07	.15
54	Scott Niedermayer, NJ	.25	.50
55	Teemu Selanne, Win.	.75	1.50
56	Frank Mahovlich, Tor.	.75	1.50
57	Owen Nolan, Que.	.25	.50
58	Rick Tocchet, Pit.	.07	.15
59	Rod Brind'Amour, Phi.	.07	.15
60	Michael Modano, Dal.	.25	.50
61	Douglas Gilmour, Tor.	.75	1.50
62	Jimmy Carson, Van.	.07	.15
63	Mike Keane, Mon.	.07	.15
64	Bernie Nicholls, NJ	.07	.15
65	Scott Stevens, NJ	.07	.15
66	Mario Lemieux, Pit.	1.00	2.00
67	Keith Primeau, Det.	.07	.15
68	Robert Carpenter, NJ	.07	.15
69	Sergei Fedorov, Det.	1.00	2.00
70	Peter Stastny, St.L	.07	.15
71	Brian Leetch, NYR	.35	.75
72	Vincent Damphousse, Mon.	.07	.15
73	Darryl Sittler, Tor.	.50	1.00
74	Al Iafrate, Bos.	.07	.15
75	Alexander Mogilny, Buf.	.50	1.00
76	Bill Ranford, Goalie, Edm.	.07	.15
77	Raymond Bourque, Bos.	.50	1.00
78	Joey Mullen, Pit.	.07	.15
79	Mike Ricci, Que.	.25	.50
80	Bobby Clarke, Phi.	.50	1.00
81	Gerry Cheevers, Goalie, Bos.	.25	.50
82	Joe Nieuwendyk, Cal.	.07	.15
83	Terry Sawchuk, Goalie, Det.	.75	1.50
84	Ray Ferraro, Har.	.07	.15
85	Lanny McDonald, Cal.	.07	.15
86	Adam Graves, NYR	.25	.50
87	Tomas Sandstrom	.07	.15
88	Eric Lindros, Phi.	1.00	2.00
89	Jari Kurri, LA	.07	.15
90	Allan MacInnis, Cal.	.07	.15
91	Alexandre Daigle, Ott.	.50	1.00
92	Larry Robinson, Mon.	.07	.15
93	Kelly Hrudey, Goalie, LA	.07	.15
94	Theoren Fleury, LA	.07	.15
95	Billy Smith, Goalie, NYI	.07	.15
96	Luc Robitaille, LA	.25	.50
97	Brett Hull, St.L	.50	1.00
98	Pat Falloon, SJ	.07	.15
99	Wayne Gretzky, LA	1.50	3.00
100	Joe Sakic	.07	.15
101	Phil Housley, St.L	.07	.15
102	Mark Messier, NYR	.25	.50
103	Jeremy Roenick, Chi.	.25	.50
104	Mark Recchi, Phi.	.25	.50
105	Pat LaFontaine, Buf.	.25	.50
106	Trevor Linden, Van.	.25	.50
107	Jaromir Jagr, Pit.	.25	.50
108	Steve Yzerman, Det.	.25	.50

SEGA - E M SPORTS
— 1993 - 94 ISSUE —

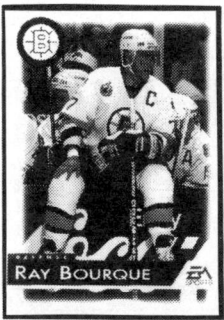

1993-94 Issue
Card No. 7, Raymond Bourque

Card Size: 2 1/2" x 3 1/2"
Face: Four colour, white border; Name, Position, Team logo
Back: Four colour; Name Jersey number, Resume, Team Name, Sponsors logos
Imprint: None
Complete Set No.: 225
Complete Set Price: 37.50 75.00
Common Card: .12 .25

MIGHTY DUCKS OF ANAHEIM

No.	Player	EX	NRMT
1	Alexei Kasatonov	.12	.25
2	Randy Ladouceur	.12	.25
3	Terry Yake	.12	.25
4	Troy Loney	.12	.25
5	Anatoli Semenov	.12	.25
6	Guy Hebert, Goalie	.12	.25

BOSTON BRUINS

No.	Player	EX	NRMT
7	Raymond Bourque	1.50	3.00
8	Don Sweeney	.12	.25
9	Adam Oates	1.00	2.00
19	Joseph Juneau	1.00	2.00
11	Cam Neely	1.00	2.00
12	Andrew Moog, Goalie	.12	.25

BUFFALO SABRES

No.	Players	EX	NRMT
13	Doug Bodger	.12	.25
14	Petr Svoboda	.12	.25
15	Pat LaFontaine	1.50	3.00
16	Dale Hawerchuk	.12	.25
17	Alexander Mogilny	1.50	3.00
18	Grant Fuhr, Goalie	.35	.75

CALGARY FLAMES

No.	Player	EX	NRMT
19	Gary Suter	.12	.25
20	Allan MacInnis	1.00	2.00
21	Joe Nieuwendyk	1.00	2.00
22	Gary Roberts	.50	1.00
23	Theoren Fleury	.50	1.00
24	Mike Vernon, Goalie	.12	.25

CHICAGO BLACK HAWKS

No.	Player	EX	NRMT
25	Chris Chelios	.35	.75
26	James (Steve) Smith	.12	.25
27	Jeremy Roenick	2.00	4.00
28	Michel Goulet	.12	.25
29	Steve Larmer	.12	.25
30	Ed Belfour, Goalie	2.00	4.00

DALLAS STARS

No.	Player	EX	NRMT
31	Mark Tinordi	.12	.25
32	Tommy Sjodin	.12	.25
33	Michael Modano	1.50	3.00
34	Dave Gagner	.12	.25
35	Russell Courtnall	.12	.25
36	Jon Casey, Goalie	.12	.25

DETROIT RED WINGS

No.	Player	EX	NRMT
37	Paul Coffey	.35	.75
38	Steve Chiasson	.12	.25
39	Steve Yzerman	2.50	5.00
40	Sergei Fedorov	2.50	5.00
41	Dino Ciccarelli	.12	.25
42	Tim Cheveldae, Goalie	.12	.25

EDMONTON OILERS

No.	Player	EX	NRMT
43	Dave Manson	.12	.25
44	Igor Kravchuk	.12	.25
45	Doug Weight	.12	.25
46	Shayne Corson	.12	.25
47	Petr Klima	.12	.25
48	Bill Ranford, Goalie	.12	.25

FLORIDA PANTHERS

No.	Player	EX	NRMT
49	Joe Cirella	.12	.25
50	Gordon Murphy	.12	.25
51	Brian Skrudland	.12	.25
52	Andrei Lomakin	.12	.25
53	Scott Mellanby	.12	.25
54	John Vanbiesbrouck, Goalie	.50	1.00

HARTFORD WHALERS

No.	Player	EX	NRMT
55	Zarley Zalapski	.12	.25
56	Eric Weinrich	.12	.25
57	Andrew Cassels	.35	.75
58	Geoff Sanderson	1.00	2.00
59	Patrick Verbeek	.12	.25
60	Sean Burke, Goalie	.12	.25

LOS ANGELES KINGS

No.	Player	EX	NRMT
61	Robert Blake	.12	.25
62	Martin McSorley	.12	.25
63	Wayne Gretzky	7.50	15.00
64	Luc Robitaille	1.00	2.00
65	Tomas Sandstrom	.12	.25
66	Kelly Hrudey, Goalie	.35	.75

MONTREAL CANADIENS

No.	Player	EX	NRMT
67	Eric Desjardins	.12	.25
68	Mathieu Schneider	.12	.25
69	Kirk Muller	.12	.25
70	Vincent Damphousse	.12	.25
71	Brian Bellows	.12	.25
72	Patrick Roy, Goalie	6.00	12.00

NEW JERSEY DEVILS

No.	Player	EX	NRMT
73	Scott Stevens	1.00	2.00
74	Viacheslav Fetisov	.12	.25
75	Alexander Semak	.12	.25
76	Stephane J. J. Richer	.12	.25
77	Claude Lemieux	.12	.25
78	Chris Terreri, Goalie	.12	.25

NEW YORK ISLANDERS

No.	Player	EX	NRMT
79	Vladimir Malakhov	.35	.75
80	Darius Kasparaitis	.35	.75
81	Pierre Turgeon	.75	1.50
82	Steve Thomas	.12	.25
83	Benoit Hogue	.12	.25
84	Glenn Healy, Goalie	.12	.25

NEW YORK RANGERS

No.	Player	EX	NRMT
85	Brian Leetch	1.50	3.00
86	James Patrick	.12	.25
87	Mark Messier	1.50	3.00
88	THE WONG	.12	.25
89	Michael Gartner	.12	.25
90	Mike Richter, Goalie	1.00	2.00

OTTAWA SENATORS

No.	Player	EX	NRMT
91	Norm Maciver	.12	.25
92	Brad Shaw	.12	.25
93	Jamie Baker	.12	.25
94	Sylvain Turgeon	.12	.25
95	Bob Kudelski	.12	.25
96	Peter Sidorkiewicz, Goalie	.12	.25

PHILADELPHIA FLYERS

No.	Player	EX	NRMT
97	Garry Galley	.12	.25
98	Dimitri Yushkevitch	.12	.25
99	Eric Lindros	6.00	12.00
100	Rod Brind'Amour	.35	.75
101	Mark Recchi	.35	.75
102	Tommy Soderstrom, Goalie	.12	.25

PITTSBURGH PENGUINS

No.	Player	EX	NRMT
103	Lawrence Murphy	.12	.25
104	Ulf Samuelsson	.12	.25
105	Mario Lemieux	5.00	10.00
106	Kevin Stevens	1.00	2.00
107	Jaromir Jagr	2.00	4.00
108	Tom Barrasso, Goalie	.12	.25

QUEBEC NORDIQUES

No.	Player	EX	NRMT
109	Steve Duchesne	.12	.25
110	Curtis Leschyshyn	.12	.25
111	Mats Sundin	1.00	2.00
112	Joe Sakic	1.00	2.00
113	Owen Nolan	.12	.25
114	Ron Hextall, Goalie	.12	.25

SAN JOSE SHARKS

No.	Player	EX	NRMT
115	Douglas Wilson	.12	.25
116	Neil Wilkinson	.12	.25
117	Kelly Kisio	.12	.25
118	Johan Garpenlov	.12	.25
119	Pat Falloon	.35	.75
120	Arturs Irbe, Goalie	1.00	2.00

ST. LOUIS BLUES

No.	Player	EX	NRMT
121	Jeff Brown	.12	.25
122	Garth Butcher	.12	.25
123	Craig Janney	.12	.25
124	Brendan Shanahan	1.50	3.00
125	Brett Hull	2.50	5.00
126	Curtis Joseph, Goalie	2.00	4.00

TAMPA BAY LIGHTNING

No.	Player	EX	NRMT
127	Bob Beers	.12	.25
128	Roman Hamrlik	.35	.75
129	Brian Bradley	.12	.25
130	Bo Mikael Andersson	.12	.25
131	Chris Kontos	.12	.25
132	Wendell Young, Goalie	.12	.25

TORONTO MAPLE LEAFS

No.	Player	EX	NRMT
133	Todd Gill	.12	.25
134	David Ellett	.12	.25
135	Douglas Gilmour, Error Pavel Bure photo on back	1.50	3.00
136	David Andreychuk	.35	.75
137	Nikolai Borschevsky	.12	.25
138	Felix Potvin, Goalie	4.00	8.00

VANCOUVER CANUCKS

No.	Player	EX	NRMT
139	Jyrki Lumme	.12	.25
140	Doug Lidster	.12	.25
141	Cliff Ronning	.35	.75
142	Geoff Courtnall	.12	.25
143	Pavel Bure	6.00	12.00
144	Kirk McLean, Goalie	1.00	2.00

WINNIPEG JETS

No.	Player	EX	NRMT
145	Phil Housley	.12	.25
146	Teppo Numminen	.12	.25
147	Alexei Zhamnov	.35	.75
148	Thomas Steen	.12	.25
149	Teemu Selanne	2.00	4.00
150	Bob Essensa, Goalie	.12	.25

WASHINGTON CAPITALS

No.	Player	EX	NRMT
151	Kevin Hatcher	.12	.25
152	Al Iafrate	.50	1.00
153	Mike Ridley	.12	.25
154	Dimitri Khristich	.12	.25
155	Peter Bondra	.12	.25
156	Donald Beaupre, Goalie	.12	.25

ALL STAR EAST

No.	Player	EX	NRMT
157	All Star Standings Statistics	.12	.25

ALL STAR WEST

No.	Player	EX	NRMT
158	All Star Standings Statistics	.12	.25

TEAM STATISICS

No.	Player	EX	NRMT
159	Mighty Ducks of Anaheim	.12	.25
160	Boston Bruins	.12	.25
161	Buffalo Sabres	.12	.25
162	Calgary Flames	.12	.25
163	Chicago Blackhawks	.12	.25
164	Detroit Red Wings	.12	.25
165	Edmonton Oilers	.12	.25
166	Florida Panthers	.12	.25
167	Hartford Whalers	.12	.25
168	Los Angeles Kings	.12	.25
169	Dallas Stars	.12	.25
170	Montreal Canadiens	.12	.25
171	New Jersey Devils	.12	.25
172	New York Islanders	.12	.25
173	New York Rangers	.12	.25
174	Ottawa Senators	.12	.25
175	Philadelphia Flyers	.12	.25
176	Pittsburgh Penguins	.12	.25
177	Quebec Nordiques	.12	.25
178	San Jose Sharks	.12	.25
179	St. Louis Blues	.12	.25
180	Tampa Bay Lightning	.12	.25
181	Toronto Maple Leafs	.12	.25
182	Vancouver Canucks	.12	.25
183	Washington Capitals	.12	.25
184	Winnipeg Jets	.12	.25

SKILL LEADERS

No.	Player	EX	NRMT
185	**Checking:** Raymond Bourque, Bos.	1.00	2.00
186	**Defense:** Chris Chelios, Chi.	.25	.50
187	**Goaltending:** Ed. Belfour, Chi.	1.25	2.50
188	**Passing:** Adam Oates, Bos.	.50	1.00
189	**Shot Accuracy:** Mario Lemieux, Pit.	3.00	6.00
190	**Shot Power:** Al Iafrate, Wash.	.25	.50
191	**Skating:** Alexander Mogilny, Buf.	1.00	2.00
192	**Stickhandling:** Wayne Gretzky, LA	5.00	10.00

NEW FEATURE

No.	Player	EX	NRMT
193	4 Way Play	.12	.25
194	Auto Line Changes	.12	.25
195	Bench Checks	.12	.25
196	Board Checks	.12	.25
197	Clear Zone	.12	.25
198	Crowd Records	.12	.25
199	Expansion Teams	.12	.25
200	Goalie Control: Arturs Irbe, SJ	.50	1.00
201	Hot/Cold Streaks:	.12	.25
202	Local Organ Music:	.12	.25
203	More Stats:	.12	.25
204	NHL Logos	.12	.25
205	One Timers	.12	.25
206	Penalty Shots	.12	.25
207	Player Cards	.12	.25
208	Player Profiles	.12	.25
209	Player Records	.12	.25
210	Reverse Angle	.12	.25
211	Shootout Game	.12	.25
212	User Records	.12	.25

DESIGNER TIPS

No.	Player	EX	NRMT
213	**The Brook:** Delayed Slap Shot	.12	.25
214	**The Costa:** Skate Away From Goal	.12	.25
215	**The Hogan:** Slide Into Goal	.12	.25
216	**The Lange:** Use Goalie To Take Out Shooter	.12	.25
217	**The Lesser:** Screen To Take Out Goalie	.12	.25
218	**The Matulac:** Fake oUtside Shoot I Nside	.12	.25
219	**The Scott:** Fake Inside Shoot Outside	.12	.25
220	**The Probin:** One Timer In The Slot	.12	.25
221	**The Rogers:** One Timer Across The Rease	.12	.25
222	**The Rubinelli:** Fake Outside Fake Inside Shoot	.12	.25
223	**The Shin:** Wrap Around Goal Shoot Wide	.12	.25
224	**The White:** Deflection At The Goal Mouth	.12	.25
225	**The Wike:** One Timer From Behind The Goal	.12	.25

LEAF

— 1993 PROMOTIONAL SHEET —
MARIO LEMIEUX

This sheet was handed out at the National in Chicago, July 1993, to promote Leaf's first hockey card set. The sheet was also issued autographed. The series was issued in American Regular and Canadian Regular Jumbo foil packs. The Canadian issue is bilingual.

Card Size: 8 1/4" x 11 3/8"
Face: Four colour, borderless; Name, Team, Team and Leaf logo
Back: Four colour, borderless; Name, Position, Resume, Team, NHL and NHLPA logos
Imprint: ©1993 Leaf, Inc. Printed in USA

No.	Player	EX	NRMT
—	Mario Lemieux	50.00	100.00
—	Mario Lemieux, Autographed	75.00	150.00

— 1993 - 94 REGULAR ISSUE —

This is Donruss Leaf's premier hockey set. This 440-card set has 220 cards in Series One and 220 cards in Series Two.

1993-94 Issue
Card No. 93, Douglas Gilmour

Card Size: 2 1/2" x 3 1/2"
Face: Four colour, borderless; Name, Team, Team logo
Back: Four colour, borderless; Name, Number, Position, Resume
Imprint: ©1993 Leaf, Inc., Printed in USA
Complete Set. No.: 440
  Series One: 220
  Series Two: 220
Set Price:
  Series One: 12.50 25.00
  Series Two: 12.50 25.00
  Complete Set: 25.00 50.00
Common Card: .05 .10
Foil Pack:
  Series One: (14 Cards) 1.25 2.50
  Series Two: (14 Cards) 1.25 2.50
Foil Box:
  Series One: (36 Packs) 35.00 75.00
  Series Two: (36 Packs) 35.00 75.00

SERIES ONE

No.	Player	EX	NRMT
1	Mario Lemieux, Pit.	.75	1.50
2	Curtis Joseph, Goalie, St.L	.08	.15
3	Stephen Leach, Bos.	.05	.10
4	Vincent Damphousse, Mon.	.08	.15
5	Murray Craven, Van.	.05	.10
6	Pat Elynuik, Wash.	.05	.10
7	Bill Guerin, NJ	.05	.10
8	Zarley Zalapski, Har.	.05	.10
9	Rob Gaudreau, SJ, RC	.12	.25
10	Pavel Bure, Van.	.50	1.00
11	Brad Shaw, Ott.	.05	.10
12	Pat LaFontaine, Buf.	.15	.30
13	Teemu Selanne, Win.	.75	1.50
14	Trent Klatt, Dal.	.05	.10
15	Kevin Todd, Edm.	.05	.10
16	Larry Murphy, Pit.	.05	.10
17	Anthony Amonte, NYR	.05	.10
18	Dino Ciccarelli, Det.	.05	.10
19	Douglas Bodger, Buf.	.05	.10
20	Luc Robitaille, LA	.13	.25
21	John Tucker, TB	.05	.10
22	Todd Gill, Tor.	.05	.10
23	Mike Ricci, Que.	.08	.15
24	Eugeny Davydov, Win.	.05	.10
25	Pierre Turgeon, NYI	.15	.30
26	Rod Brind'Amour, Phi.	.10	.20
27	Jeremy Roenick, Chi.	.35	.75
28	Joel Otto, Cal.	.05	.10
29	Jeff Brown, St.L	.05	.10
30	Brendan Shanahan, St.L	.08	.15
31	Jiri Slegr, Van.	.05	.10
32	Vladimir Malakhov, NYI	.08	.15
33	Patrick Roy, Goalie, Mon.	.35	.75
34	Kevin Hatcher, Wash.	.05	.10
35	Alexander Semak, NJ	.05	.10
36	Gary Roberts, Cal.	.05	.10
37	Tommy Soderstrom, Goalie, Phi.	.10	.20
38	Bob Essensa, Goalie, Win.	.05	.10
39	Kelly Hrudey, Goalie, LA	.05	.10
40	Shawn Chambers, TB	.05	.10
41	Glenn Anderson, Tor.	.05	.10
42	Owen Nolan, Que.	.08	.15
43	Patrick Flatley, NYI	.05	.10
44	Raymond Sheppard, Det.	.05	.10
45	Darren Turcotte, NYR	.05	.10
46	Shayne Corson, Edm.	.05	.10
47	Brad May, Buf.	.05	.10
48	Robert Kudelski, Ott.	.05	.10
49	Pat Falloon, SJ	.08	.15
50	Andrew Cassels, Har.	.05	.10
51	Chris Chelios, Chi.	.08	.15
52	Sylvain Cote, Wash.	.05	.10
53	Matt Schneider, Mon.	.05	.10
54	Ted Donato, Bos.	.05	.10
55	Kirk McLean, Goalie, Van.	.08	.15
56	Bruce Driver, NJ	.05	.10
57	Uwe Krupp, NYI	.05	.10
58	Brent Fedyk, Phi.	.05	.10
59	Robert Reichel, Cal.	.08	.15
60	Scott Stevens, NJ	.08	.15
61	Phil Housley, Win.	.05	.10
62	Ed Belfour, Goalie, Chi.	.13	.25
63	David Andreychuk, Tor.	.08	.15
64	Claude Lapointe, Que.	.05	.10
65	Russell Courtnall, Min.	.05	.10
66	Grant Fuhr, Goalie, Buf.	.05	.10
67	Paul Coffey, Det.	.08	.15
68	Bill Ranford, Goalie, Edm.	.08	.15
69	Kevin Stevens, Pit.	.12	.25
70	Brian Leetch, NYR	.18	.35
71	Dale Hawerchuk, Buf.	.05	.10
72	Geoff Courtnall, Van.	.05	.10
73	Sandis Ozolnich, SJ	.12	.25
74	Sylvain Turgeon, Ott.	.05	.10
75	Nelson Emerson, St.L	.05	.10
76	Brian Bellows, Mon.	.05	.10
77	Geoff Sanderson, Hart.	.20	.40
78	Petr Nedved, Van.	.08	.15
79	Peter Bondra, Wash.	.05	.10
80	Scott Niedermayer, NJ	.15	.30
81	Steve Thomas, NYI	.05	.10
82	Dimitri Yushkevitch, Phi.	.05	.10
83	Mike Vernon, Goalie, Cal.	.05	.10
84	Alexei Zhamnov, Win.	.15	.30
85	Adam Creighton, TB	.05	.10
86	David Ellett, Tor.	.05	.10
87	Joe Sakic, Que.	.15	.30
88	Mike Craig, Min.	.05	.10
89	Nicklas Lidstrom, Det.	.05	.10
90	Ed Olczyk, NYR	.05	.10
91	Alexander Mogilny, Buf.	.25	.50
92	Ulf Samuelsson, Pit.	.05	.10
93	Douglas Gilmour, Tor.	.25	.50
94	Mikael Nylander, Hart.	.10	.20
95	Steve Smith, Chi.	.05	.10
96	Igor Korolev, St.L	.05	.10
97	Dixon Ward, Van.	.05	.10
98	John LeClair, Mon.	.05	.10
99	Cam Neely, Bos.	.10	.20
100	Stanley Cup Champions	.50	1.00
101	Darius Kasparaitis, NYI	.05	.10
102	Mike Ridley, Wash.	.05	.10
103	Josef Beranek, Edm.	.08	.15
104	Valeri Zelepukin, NJ	.05	.10
105	Keith Tkachuk, Win.	.12	.25
106	Tomas Sandstrom, LA	.05	.10
107	Peter Zezel, Tor.	.05	.10
108	Scott Young, Que.	.05	.10
109	Rick Tocchet, Pit.	.08	.15
110	Checklist	.05	.10
111	Steve Chiasson, Det.	.05	.10
112	Doug Zmolek, SJ	.05	.10
113	Patrick Poulin, Hart.	.05	.10
114	Stephane Matteau, Chi.	.05	.10
115	Yves Racine, Det.	.05	.10
116	Steve Heinze, Bos.	.05	.10
117	Gilbert Dionne, Mon.	.05	.10
118	Dale Hunter, Wash.	.05	.10
119	Derek King, NYI	.05	.10
120	Garry Galley, Phi.	.05	.10
121	Ray Ferraro, NYI	.05	.10
122	Andrei Kovalenko, Que.	.10	.20
123	Alexei Zhitnik, LA	.10	.20
124	Fredrik Olausson, Win.	.05	.10
125	Claude Lemieux, NJ	.05	.10
126	Joe Nieuwendyk, Cal.	.08	.15
127	Travis Green, NYI	.05	.10
128	Dave Gagner, Min.	.05	.10
129	Sergei Fedorov, Det.	.50	1.00
130	Adam Graves, NYR	.20	.40
131	Petr Svoboda, Buf.	.05	.10
132	Sean Burke, Goalie, Hart.	.05	.10
133	Johan Garpenlov, SJ	.05	.10
134	Jamie Baker, Ott.	.05	.10
135	Teppo Numminen, Win.	.05	.10
136	Mats Sundin, Que.	.13	.25
137	Nikolai Borschevsky, Tor.	.08	.15
138	Stephane J. J. Richer, NJ	.08	.15
139	Scott Lachance, NYI	.05	.10
140	Gary Suter, Cal.	.05	.10
141	Al Iafrate, Wash.	.05	.10
142	Brent Sutter, Chi.	.05	.10
143	Dmitri Kvartalnov, Bos.	.05	.10
144	Pat Verbeek, Hart.	.05	.10
145	Ed Courtenay, SJ	.05	.10
146	Mark Tinordi, Min.	.05	.10
147	Alexei Kovalev, NYR	.25	.50
148	Dallas Drake, Det., RC	.12	.25
149	Jimmy Carson, LA	.08	.15
150	Florida Panthers	.50	1.00
151	Roman Hamrlik, TB	.05	.10
152	Martin Rucinsky, Que.	.05	.10
153	Calle Johansson, Wash.	.05	.10
154	Theoren Fleury, Cal.	.05	.10
155	Benoit Hogue, NYI	.05	.10
156	Kevin Dineen, Phi.	.05	.10
157	Jody Hull, Ott.	.05	.10
158	Mark Messier, NYR	.13	.25
159	Dave Manson, Edm.	.05	.10
160	Chris Kontos, TB	.05	.10
161	Ronald Francis, Pit.	.05	.10
162	Steve Yzerman, Det.	.20	.40
163	Igor Kravchuk, Edm.	.05	.10
164	Sergei Zubov, NYR	.25	.50
165	Thomas Steen, Win.	.05	.10
166	Wendel Clark, Tor.	.08	.15
167	Scott Pellerin, NJ, RC	.05	.10
168	Dimitri Khristich, Wash.	.05	.10
169	Bernie Nicholls, NJ	.05	.10
170	Paul Ranheim, Cal.	.05	.10
171	Robert Kron, Har.	.05	.10
172	Robert Blake, LA	.05	.10
173	Rob Zamuner, TB	.05	.10
174	Rob Pearson, Tor.	.05	.10
175	Checklist	.05	.10
176	Steve Duchesne, Que.	.05	.10
177	Pelle Eklund, Phi.	.05	.10
178	Michal Pivonka, Wash.	.05	.10
179	Joe Murphy, Chi.	.05	.10
180	Allan MacInnis, Cal.	.05	.10
181	Craig Janney, St.L	.08	.15
182	Kirk Muller, Mon.	.08	.15
183	Cliff Ronning, Van.	.05	.10
184	Doug Weight, Edm.	.05	.10

LEAF SERIES ONE

No.	Player	EX	NRMT
185	Mike Richter, Goalie, NYR	.15	.30
186	Bob Probert, Det.	.05	.10
187	Robert Petrovicky, Hart.	.05	.10
188	Richard Smehlik, Buf.	.05	.10
189	Norm Maciver, Ott.	.05	.10
190	Stephane Lebeau, Mon.	.05	.10
191	Patrice Brisebois, Mon.	.05	.10
192	Kevin Miller, St. L.	.05	.10
193	Trevor Linden, Van.	.10	.20
194	Darrin Shannon, Win.	.05	.10
195	Tim Cheveldae, Goalie, Det.	.05	.10
196	Tom Barrasso, Goalie, Pit.	.05	.10
197	Zdeno Ciger, Edm.	.05	.10
198	Ulf Dahlen, Min.	.05	.10
199	Arturs Irbe, Goalie, SJ	.20	.40
200	Anaheim Mighty Ducks	.50	1.00
201	Tony Granato, LA	.05	.10
202	Michael Modano, Min.	.18	.35
203	Eric Desjardins, Mon.	.05	.10
204	Bryan Smolinski, Bos.	.35	.70
205	Mark Recchi, Phi.	.15	.30
206	Darryl Sydor, LA	.05	.10
207	Valeri Kamensky, Que.	.08	.15
208	Kelly Kisio, SJ	.05	.10
209	Brian Bradley, TB	.05	.10
210	Checklist	.05	.10
211	Yuri Khmylev, Buf.	.05	.10
212	Derian Hatcher, Min.	.05	.10
213	Michael Gartner, NYR	.08	.15
214	Mike Needham, Pit	.05	.10
215	Raymond Bourque, Bos.	.12	.25
216	Tahir Domi, Win.	.05	.10
217	Shawn McEachern, Pit.	.08	.15
218	Joseph Juneau, Bos.	.30	.60
219	Greg Adams, Van.	.05	.10
220	Martin Straka, Pit.	.25	.50

SERIES TWO

No.	Player	EX	NRMT
221	Tom Fitzgerald, Fl.	.05	.10
222	Gary Shuchuk, LA	.05	.10
223	Kevin Haller, Mon.	.05	.10
224	Bryan Marchment, Chi.	.05	.10
225	Louie DeBrusk, Edm.	.05	.10
226	Randy Wood, Buf.	.05	.10
227	Robert Holik, NJ	.05	.10
228	Troy Mallette, Ott.	.05	.10
229	Adam Foote, Que.	.05	.10
230	Robert (Bob) Rouse, Tor.	.05	.10
231	Jyrki Lumme, Van.	.05	.10
232	James Patrick, NYR	.05	.10
233	Eric Lindros, Phi.	1.50	3.00
234	Joe Reekie, TB	.05	.10
235	Adam Oates, Bos.	.10	.20
236	Frantasik Musil, Cal.	.05	.10
237	Vladimir Konstantinov, Det.	.05	.10
238	Dave Lowry, Fl.	.05	.10
239	Garth Butcher, St.L.	.05	.10
240	Jari Kurri, LA	.05	.10
241	Rick Tabaracci, Goalie, Wash.	.05	.10
242	Sergei Bautin, Win.	.05	.10
243	Scott Scissons, NYI	.05	.10
244	Dominic Roussel, Goalie, Phi.	.10	.20
245	John Cullen, Tor.	.05	.10
246	Sheldon Kennedy, Det.	.05	.10
247	Mike Hough, Fl.	.05	.10
248	Paul Di Pietro, Mon.	.05	.10
249	David Shaw, Bos.	.05	.10
250	Sergio Momesso, Van.	.05	.10
251	Jeff Daniels, Pit.	.05	.10
252	Sergei Nemchinov, NYR	.05	.10
253	Kris King, Win.	.05	.10
254	Kelly Miller, Wash.	.05	.10
255	Brett Hull, St.L.	.35	.75
256	Dominik Hasek, Goalie, Buf.	.12	.25
257	Chris Pronger, Hart., RC	.36	.75
258	Derek Plante, Buf., RC	.50	1.00
259	Mark Howe, Det.	.05	.10
260	Oleg Petrov, Mon., RC	.10	.20
261	Ronnie Stern, Cal.	.05	.10

No.	Player	EX	NRMT
262	Scott Mellanby, Fl.	.05	.10
263	Warren Rychel, LA	.05	.10
264	John MacLean, NJ	.05	.10
265	Radek Hamr, Ott., RC	.10	.20
266	Greg Hawgood, Phi.	.05	.10
267	Sylvain Lefebvre, Tor.	.05	.10
268	Glen Wesley, Bos.	.05	.10
269	Joe Cirella, Fl.	.05	.10
270	Dirk Graham, Chi.	.05	.10
271	Eric Weinrich, Hart.	.05	.10
272	Donald Audette, Buf.	.05	.10
273	Jason Woolley, Wash.	.05	.10
274	Kjell Samuelsson, Pit.	.05	.10
275	Ronald Sutter, St.L.	.05	.10
276	Keith Primeau, Det.	.05	.10
277	Ron Tugnutt, Goalie, MDA	.05	.10
278	Jesse Balanger, Fl., RC	.12	.25
279	Mike Keane, Mon.	.05	.10
280	Adam Burt, Hart.	.05	.10
281	Don Sweeney, Bos.	.05	.10
282	Mike Donnelly, LA	.05	.10
283	Lyle Odelein, Mon.	.05	.10
284	Gordon Murphy, Fl.	.05	.10
285	Bo Mikael Andersson, TB	.05	.10
286	Bret Hedican, St.L.	.05	.10
287	Bill Berg, Tor.	.05	.10
288	Esa Tikkanen, NYR	.05	.10
289	Markus Naslund, Pit., RC	.10	.20
290	Checklist 2 (221 - 293), Chris Chelios, Norris Memorial Trophy	.05	.10
291	Kerry Huffman, Que.	.05	.10
292	Dana Murzyn, Van.	.05	.10
293	Rob Niedermayer, Fl., RC	.35	.75
294	Andre Racicot, Goalie, Mon.	.05	.10
295	Ken Sutton, Buf.	.05	.10
296	Shawn Burr, Det.	.05	.10
297	Scott Pearson, Edm.	.05	.10
298	Joby Messier, NYR, RC	.07	.15
299	Darren Madeley, Goalie, Ott., RC	.15	.30
300	Joe Mullen, Pit.	.05	.10
301	Stephane Fiset, Goalie, Que., RC	.10	.20
302	Geoff Smith, Edm.	.10	.20
303	Vyacheslav Kozlov, Det.	.35	.75
304	Wayne Gretzky, LA	.75	1.50
305	Curtis Leschyshyn, Que.	.05	.10
306	Mike Sillinger, Det.	.05	.10
307	Vyacheslav Butsayev, Phi.	.05	.10
308	Mark Lamb, Ott.	.05	.10
309	German Titov, Cal., RC	.25	.50
310	Gerard Gallant, TB	.05	.10
311	Alexandre Daigle, Ott., RC	.50	1.00
312	Jim Hrivnak, Goalie, St.L.	.05	.10
313	Corey Hirsch, Goalie, NYR	.12	.25
314	Craig Berube, Wash.	.05	.10
315	Bill Houlder, MDA	.05	.10
316	Ron Wilson, Mon.	.05	.10
317	Glen Murray, Bos.	.05	.10
318	Bryan Trottier, Pit.	.05	.10
319	Jeff Hackett, Goalie, Chi.	.05	.10
320	Brad Dalgarno, NYI	.05	.10
321	Petr Klima, TB	.05	.10
322	Jon Casey, Goalie, Bos.	.05	.10
323	Mikael Renberg, Phi., RC	.50	1.00
324	Jimmy Waite, Goalie, SJ	.05	.10
325	Brian Skrudland, Fl.	.05	.10
326	Vitali Prokhorov, St.L., RC	.10	.20
327	Glenn Healy, Goalie, NYR	.05	.10
328	Brian Benning, Fl.	.05	.10
329	Tony Hrkac, St.L.	.05	.10
330	Stu Grimson, MDA	.05	.10
331	Chris Gratton, TB, RC	.35	.75
332	David (Dave) Poulin, Wash.	.05	.10
333	Jarrod Skalde, MDA, RC	.12	.25
334	Christian Ruuttu, Chi.	.05	.10
335	Mark Fitzpatrick, Goalie, Fl.	.05	.10
336	Martin Lapointe, Det.	.05	.10
337	Cameron Stewart, Bos., RC	.10	.20
338	Anatoli Semenov, MDA	.05	.10
339	Gaetan Duchesne, SJ	.05	.10
340	Checklist 3 (294 - 366) Pierre Turgeon, Lady Byng Memorial Trophy	.05	.10
341	Ron Hextall, Goalie, NYI	.05	.10
342	Mikhail Tatarinov, Bos.	.05	.10
343	Danny Lorenz, Goalie, NYI	.05	.10

No.	Player	EX	NRMT
344	Craig Simpson, Buf.	.05	.10
345	Martin Brodeur, Goalie, NJ	.15	.30
346	Jaromir Jagr, Pit.	.35	.75
347	Tyler Wright, Edm.	.05	.10
348	Greg Gilbert, NYR	.05	.10
349	Dave Tippett, Phi.	.05	.10
350	Stu Barnes, Win.	.05	.10
351	Daniel Lacroix, NYR	.05	.10
352	Martin McSorley, Pit.	.05	.10
353	Sean Hill, MDA	.05	.10
354	Craig Billington, Goalie, Ott.	.05	.10
355	Donald Dufresne, TB	.05	.10
356	Guy Hebert, Goalie, MDA	.12	.25
357	Neil Wilkinson, Chi.	.05	.10
358	Sandy McCarthy, Cal.	.05	.10
359	Aaron Ward, Det., RC	.10	.20
360	Scott Thomas, Buf., RC	.10	.20
361	Corey Millen, NJ	.05	.10
362	Matthew Barnaby, Buf.	.10	.20
363	Benoit Brunet, Mon.	.05	.10
364	Boris Mironov, Win.	.05	.10
365	Doug Lidster, NYR	.05	.10
366	Pavol Demitra, Ott., RC	.12	.25
367	Damian Rhodes, Goalie, Tor., RC	.15	.30
368	Shawn Antoski, Van.	.05	.10
369	Andrew Moog, Goalie, Dal.	.05	.10
370	Greg Johnson, Det., RC	.10	.20
371	John Vanbiesbrouk, Goalie, Fl.	.07	.15
372	Denis Savard, TB	.05	.10
373	Michel Goulet, Chi.	.05	.10
374	David Taylor, LA	.05	.10
375	Enrico Ciccone, Wash.	.05	.10
376	Sergei Zholtok, Bos.	.07	.15
377	Bob Errey, SJ	.05	.10
378	Doug Brown, Pit.	.05	.10
379	Bill McDougall, TB, RC	.07	.15
380	Pat Conacher, LA	.05	.10
381	Alexei Kasatonov, MDA	.05	.10
382	Jason Arnott, Edm., RC	1.50	3.00
383	Jarkko Varvio, Dal.	.05	.10
384	Sergei Makarov, SJ	.05	.10
385	Trevor Kidd, Goalie, Cal.	.05	.10
386	Alexei Yashin, Ott., RC	.75	1.50
387	Gerald Diduck, Van.	.05	.10
388	Paul Ysabaert, Win.	.05	.10
389	Jason Smith, NJ, RC	.10	.20
390	Jeff Norton, SJ	.05	.10
391	Igor Larionov, SJ	.05	.10
392	Pierre Sevigny, Mon.	.05	.10
393	Wes Walz, Cal.	.05	.10
394	Grant Ledyard, Dal.	.05	.10
395	Brad McCrimmon, Hart.	.05	.10
396	Martin Gelinas, Que.	.05	.10
397	Paul Cavallini, Dal.	.05	.10
398	Brian Noonan, Chi.	.05	.10
399	Mike Lalor, SJ	.05	.10
400	Dimitri Fillmonov, Ott., RC	.10	.20
401	Andrei Lomakin, Fl.	.05	.10
402	Steve Junker, NYI, RC	.10	.20
403	Daren Puppa, Goalie, TB	.05	.10
404	Jozef Stumpel, Bos.	.05	.10
405	Jeff Shantz, Chi., RC	.12	.25
406	Terry Yake, MDA	.05	.10
407	Mike Peluso, NJ	.05	.10
408	Vitali Karamnov, St.L.	.07	.15
409	Felix Potvin, Goalie, Tor.	.50	1.00
410	Steven King, MDA	.05	.10
411	Roman Oksyuta, Edm., RC	.07	.15
412	Mark Greig, Hart.	.05	.10
413	Wayne McBean, NYI	.05	.10
414	Nicholas Kypreos, Hart.	.05	.10
415	Dominic Lavoie, LA	.05	.10
416	Chris Simon, Que., RC	.10	.20
417	Peter Popovic, Mon., RC	.15	.30
418	Gino Odjick, Van.	.05	.10
419	Mike Rathje, SJ, RC	.07	.15
420	Keith Acton, Wash.	.05	.10
421	Robert Carpenter, NJ	.05	.10
422	Steven Finn, Que.	.05	.10
423	Ian Herbers, Edm., RC	.10	.20
424	Ted Drury, Cal., RC	.10	.20
425	Sergei Petrenko, Buf., RC	.12	.25
426	Mattias Norstrom, NYR, RC	.12	.25

— 1993 - 94 INSERT SETS — LEAF • 449

No.	Player	EX	NRMT
427	Todd Ewen, MDA	.05	.10
428	Jocelyn Thibault, Goalie, Que., RC	.35	.75
429	Robert Burakovsky, Ott.	.05	.10
430	Chris Terreri, Goalie, NJ	.05	.10
431	Michal Sykora, SJ, RC	.10	.20
432	Craig Ludwig, Dal.	.05	.10
433	Vesa Viitakoski, Cal., RC	.10	.20
434	Sergei Krivokrasov, Chi.	.05	.10
435	Darren McCarty, Det., RC	.12	.25
436	Dean McAmmond, Edm.	.05	.10
437	Jean-Jacques Daigneault, Mon.	.05	.10
438	Vladimir Ruzicka, Ott.	.05	.10
439	Vlastimil Kroupa, SJ	.12	.25
440	Checklist 4 (367 - 440), Douglas Gilmour, Frank Selke Trophy	.05	.10

— 1993 - 94 INSERT SETS —

FRESHMAN PHENOMS

Randomly inserted into Series Two foil packs.

1993-94 Freshman Phenoms
Card No. 1, Alexandre Daigle

Card Size: 2 1/2" x 3 1/2"
Face: Four colour; borderless; Name, Team Logo
Back: Four colour; Name, Number, Resume
Imprint: Printed in USA, Inc.
Complete Set No.: 10
Complete Price Set: 30.00 60.00
Common Card: 1.50 3.00

No.	Player	EX	NRMT
1	Alexandre Daigle, Ott.	4.00	8.00
2	Chris Pronger, Har.	3.00	6.00
3	Chris Gratton, TB	3.00	6.00
4	Markus Naslund	1.50	3.00
5	Mikael Renberg, Phi.	5.00	10.00
6	Rob Niedermayer, Fl.	3.00	6.00
7	Jason Arnott, Edm.	7.50	15.00
8	Jarkko Varvio	1.50	3.00
9	Alexei Yashin, Ott.	5.00	10.00
10	Jocelyn Thibault, Goalie, Que.	5.00	10.00

GOLD ALL-STARS

This 10-card set was randomly inserted intp all Series One and Series Two foil packs with cards numbered 1 to 5 in Series One and cards 6 to 10 in Series Two.

1993-94 Gold All-Stars
Card No. 2, Chris Chelios, Lawrence Murphy

Card Size: 2 1/2" x 3 1/2"
Face: Four colour, borderless: Name, Team
Back: Four colour, borderless; Name, Number, Team
Imprint: © 1993 Leaf, Inc. Printed in USA
Complete Set No.: 10
 Series One: 5
 Series Two: 5
Set Price:
 Series One: 30.00 60.00
 Series Two: 30.00 60.00
 Complete Set: 55.00 115.00

SERIES ONE

No.	Player	EX	NRMT
1	M. Lemieux, Pit., P. LaFontaine, Buf.	12.50	25.00
2	C. Chelios, Chi., L. Murphy, Pit.	3.00	6.00
3	B. Hull, St.L, T. Selanne, Win.	7.50	15.00
4	K. Stevens, Pit., D. Andreychuk, Tor.	5.00	10.00
5	P. Roy, Mon., T. Barrasso, Goalies	9.00	18.00

SERIES TWO

No.	Player	EX	NRMT
6	W. Gretzky, LA, D. Gilmour, Tor.	20.00	40.00
7	R. Bourque, Bos., P. Coffey, Det.	3.50	7.00
8	A. Mogilny, Buf., P. Bure, Van.	9.00	18.00
9	L. Robitaille, LA, B. Shanahan, St.L	3.50	7.00
10	E. Belfour, Chi., F. Potvin, Tor., Goalies	8.00	16.00

1992 - 93 GOLD LEAF ROOKIES

This 15-card insert set is found in all Series One foil packs. The set features the top rookies for the '92-93 season. The cards bear unique red foil rookies logos and are numbered _ of 15.

1993-94 Gold Leaf Rookies
Card No. 1, Teemu Selanne

Card Size: 2 1/2" x 3 1/2"
Face: Four colour, white border, Name, Team
Back: Four colour, Red and black border; Name, Number, Team
Imprint: © 1993 Leaf, Inc. Printed in U.S.A.
Complete Set. No.: 15
Complete Set Price: 35.00 70.00
Common Card: 1.00 2.00

No.	Player	EX	NRMT
1	Teemu Selanne, Win.	5.00	10.00
2	Joseph Juneau, Bos.	3.00	6.00
3	Eric Lindros, Phi.	15.00	30.00
4	Felix Potvin, Goalie, Tor.	8.00	16.00
5	Alexei Zhamnov, Win.	1.50	3.00
6	Andrei Kovalenko, Que.	1.00	2.00
7	Shawn McEachern, Pit.	1.00	2.00
8	Alexei Zhitnik, LA	1.00	2.00
9	Vladimir Malakhov, NYI	1.00	2.00
10	Patrick Poulin, Hart.	1.00	2.00
11	Keith Tkachuk, Win.	1.50	3.00
12	Tommy Soderstrom, Goalie, Phi.	1.50	3.00
13	Darius Kasparaitis, NYI	1.00	2.00
14	Scott Niedermayer, NJ	1.50	3.00
15	Darryl Sydor, LA	1.00	2.00

HAT TRICK ARTISTS

This 10-card set is randomly inserted into all American regular foil packs and all Jumbo packs. The cards are numbered _ of 10 and represent the players who scored three or more hat tricks during the '92-93 season.

1993-94 Hat Trick Artists
Card No. 7, Eric Lindros

Card Size: 2 1/2" x 3 1/2"
Face: Four colour, borderless; Name
Back: Four colour, grey border; Name, Number, Team, Resume
Imprint: © 1993 Leaf, Inc., Printed in U.S.A.
Complete Set. No.: 10
 Series One: 5
 Series Two: 5
Set Price:
 Series One: 10.00 20.00
 Series Two: 10.00 20.00
 Complete Set: 20.00 40.00
Common Card: 1.50 3.00

SERIES ONE

No.	Player	EX	NRMT
1	Title Card, Mario Lemieux	2.50	5.00
2	Alexander Mogilny, Buf.	2.00	4.00
3	Teemu Selanne, Win.	3.00	6.00
4	Mario Lemieux, Pit.	4.00	8.00
5	Pierre Turgeon, NYI	1.50	3.00

SERIES TWO

No.	Player	EX	NRMT
6	Kevin Dineen, Phi.	1.50	3.00
7	Eric Lindros, Phi.	7.50	15.00
8	Adam Oates, Bos.	2.00	4.00
9	Kevin Stevens, Pit.	2.00	4.00
10	Steve Yzerman, Det.	3.00	6.00

MARIO LEMIEUX COLLECTION

This 10-card insert set was randomly inserted in all Series One and Series Two foil packs. Numbers 1 to 5 in Series One and 6 to 10 in Series Two.

 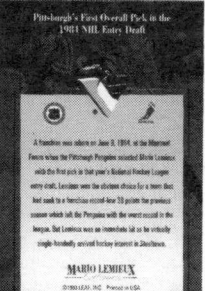

1993-94 Mario Lemieux Collection
Card No. 2, 1st Pick 1984 NHL Draft

Card Size: 2 1/2" x 3 1/2"
Face: Four colour, borderless; Name
Back: Four colour; Name, Number, Resume
Imprint: © 1993 Leaf, Inc. Printed in USA
Complete Set. No.: 10
 Series One: 5
 Series Two: 5

450 • LEAF — 1994-95 REGULAR ISSUE —

		EX	NRMT
Complete Set Price:		25.00	50.00
Series One:		12.50	25.00
Series Two:		12.50	25.00

SERIES ONE

No.	Player	EX	NRMT
1	Title Card	2.00	4.00
2	1st Pick in 1984 NHL Draft	2.00	4.00
3	1984 QMJHL Player of the Year	2.00	4.00
4	1984/85 Calder Trophy Winner	2.00	4.00
5	1987/88 Hart Trophy & Art Ross Trophy Winner	2.00	4.00

SERIES TWO

No.	Player	EX	NRMT
6	Two Time Conn Smythe Trophy Winner	2.00	4.00
7	Six-Time NHL All Star	2.00	4.00
8	Penguins Capture First Stanley Cup	2.00	4.00
9	1992-93: Mario Lemieux Best Season Ever	2.00	4.00
10	Mario's Magnificent Career	2.00	4.00

MARIO LEMIEUX AUTOGRAPH CARD

Randomly inserted into all foil packs.

Card Size: 2 1/2" x 3 1/2"
Face: Four colour; borderless; Name, Team Logo
Back: Four colour; Black autograph
Imprint: Printed in USA

No.	Player	EX	NRMT
—	Mario Lemieux, Pit., Autograph	200.00	400.00

PAINTED WARRIORS

This 10-card set was randomly inserted into all Series One and Series Two foil packs. Cards are numbered _ of 10. Numbers 1 to 5 were in Series One foil packs and 6 to 10 in Series Two.

1993-94 Painted Warriors
Card No. 1, Felix Potvin

Card Size: 2 1/2" x 3 1/2"
Face: Four colour, blue top border; Name, Team
Back: Four colour, borderless; Name, Number, Resume
Imprint: © 1993 Leaf, Inc. Printed in U.S.A.
Complete Set No.: 10
  Series One: 5
  Series Two: 5

		EX	NRMT
Complete Set Price:		22.50	45.00
Series One:		12.50	25.00
Series Two:		10.00	20.00

GOALIES - SERIES ONE

No.	Player	EX	NRMT
1	Felix Potvin, Tor.	5.00	10.00
2	Curtis Joseph, St.L	3.00	6.00
3	Kirk McLean, Van.	3.00	6.00
4	Patrick Roy, Mon.	5.00	10.00
5	Grant Fuhr, Buf.	1.50	3.00

GOALIES - SERIES TWO

No.	Player	EX	NRMT
6	Ed Belfour, Chi.	3.00	6.00
7	Michael Vernon, Cal.	1.50	3.00
8	John Vanbiesbrouk, Fl.	3.00	6.00
9	Tom Barrasso, Pit.	1.50	3.00
10	Bill Ranford, Edm.	2.00	4.00

STUDIO SIGNATURE

This 10-card insert set was randomly inserted into Canadian Series One and Series Two foil and all Jumbo packs. This insert set depicts a facsimile gold stamped autograph of the game's ten premier players. The cards are numered _ of 10. Numbers 1-5 were found in Series One packs and 6-10 were found in Series Two.

 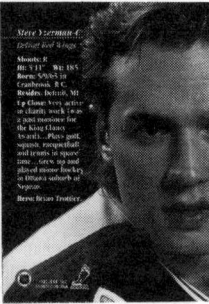

1993-94 Studio Signature
Card No. 5, Steve Yzerman

Card Size: 2 1/2" x 3 1/2"
Face: Four colour, borderless, Name, Facsimile autograph, Team logo
Back: Four colour, borderless
Imprint: © 1993 Leaf, Inc., Printed in U.S.A.
Complete Set. No.: 10
  Series One: 5
  Series Two: 5

	EX	NRMT
Set Price:	37.50	75.00
Series One:	17.50	35.00
Series Two:	22.50	45.00
Complete Set:		
Common Card:	2.50	5.00

SERIES ONE

No.	Player	EX	NRMT
1	Douglas Gilmour, Tor.	5.00	10.00
2	Pat Falloon, SJ	2.50	5.00
3	Pat LaFontaine, Buf.	3.00	6.00
4	Wayne Gretzky, LA	7.50	15.00
5	Steve Yzerman, Det.	3.50	7.00

SERIES TWO

No.	Player	EX	NRMT
6	Patrick Roy, Goalie, Mon.	5.00	10.00
7	Jeremy Roenick, Chi.	4.00	8.00
8	Brett Hull, St.L	4.00	8.00
9	Alexandre Daigle, Ott.	4.00	8.00
10	Eric Lindros, Phi.	10.00	20.00

— 1994-95 REGULAR ISSUE —

This 330-card set has a good player selection and a wide variety of quality insert sets.

1994-95 Issue
Card No. 1, Mario Lemieux

Size: 2 1/2" x 3 1/2"
Face: Four colour; borderless; Name on gold foil, Team Logo
Back: Four colour; Name, Numner, Resume, Logo
Imprint: © DONRUSS INC. PRINTED IN U.S.A.
Complete Set No.: 330

	EX	NRMT
Complete Price Set:	12.50	25.00
Common Card	.05	.10
Foil Pack: (12 Cards)		2.50
Foil Box: (36 Packs)		80.00

SERIES ONE

No.	Player	EX	NRMT
1	Mario Lemieux, Pit.	.50	1.00
2	Anthony Amonte, Chi.	.05	.10
3	Steve Duchesne, St.L	.05	.10
4	Glen Murray, Bos.	.05	.10
5	John LeClair, Mon.	.05	.10
6	Glen Wesley, Bos.	.05	.10
7	Chris Chelios, Chi.	.05	.10
8	Alexei Zhitnik, LA	.05	.10
9	Michael Modano, Dal.	.12	.25
10	Pavel Bure, Van.	.35	.75
11	Mark Messier, NYR	.10	.20
12	Robert Blake, LA	.10	.20
13	Anthony Twist, Que.	.05	.10
14	Glenn Anderson, NYR	.10	.20
15	Keith Redmond, LA	.05	.10
16	Brett Hull, St.L	.15	.30
17	Valeri Zelepukin, NJ	.07	.15
18	Mike Richter, Goalie, NYR	.10	.20
19	Alexei Yashin, Ott.	.25	.50
20	Luc Robitaille, LA	.10	.20
21	Tim Sweeney, Bos.	.05	.10
22	Ted Drury, Cal.	.05	.10
23	Guy Carbonneau, Mon	.05	.10
24	Stephane J. J. Richer, NJ	.05	.10
25	Ulf Dahlen, Dal.	.05	.10
26	Fred Brathwaite, Goalie, Edm.	.05	.10
27	Darius Kasparaitis, NYI	.05	.10
28	Kris Draper, Win	.05	.10
29	Alexander Godynyuk, Cal.	.05	.10
30	Brent Sutter, Chi.	.05	.10
31	Josef Beranek, Phi.	.10	.20
32	Stephane Matteau, NYR	.05	.10
33	Derek Plante, Buf.	.25	.50
34	Vesa Viitakoski, Cal.	.05	.10
35	David Ellett, Tor.	.05	.10
36	Martin Straka, Pit.	.10	.20
37	Dimitri Yushkevich, Phi.	.05	.10
38	John Tucker, TB	.05	.10
39	Robert Gaudreau, SJ	.05	.10
40	Doug Weight, Edm.	.05	.10
41	Patrick Roy, Goalie, Mon.	.05	.10
42	Brian Bradley, TB	.05	.10
43	Bob Beers, TB	.05	.10
44	Dino Ciccarelli, Det.	.05	.10
45	Dean Evason, SJ	.05	.10
46	Ron Tugnutt, Goalie, Mon.	.05	.10
47	Andrew Moog, Goalie, Dal.	.05	.10
48	Jason Dawe, Buf.	.05	.10
49	Ted Donato, Bos.	.05	.10
50	Ron Hextall, Goalie, NYI	.05	.10

1994-95 REGULAR ISSUE — LEAF • 451

No.	Player	EX	NRMT
51	Derek Armstrong, NYI, RC	.10	.20
52	Craig Janney, St.L	.05	.10
53	Geoff Courtnall, Van.	.05	.10
54	Mikael Renberg, Phi.	.15	.30
55	Theoren Fleury, Cal.	.05	.10
56	Martin Brodeur, Goalie, NJ	.10	.20
57	Mattias Norstrom, NYR	.05	.10
58	David Sacco, Tor., RC	.10	.20
59	Jeff Reese, Goalie, Har.	.05	.10
60	Bill Ranford, Goalie, Edm.	.05	.10
61	Dan Quinn, Dal.	.05	.10
62	Joseph Juneau, Wash.	.15	.30
63	Jeremy Roenick, Chi.	.12	.25
64	Donald Audette, Buf.	.05	.10
65	Zdeno Ciger, Edm.	.05	.10
66	Cliff Ronning, Van.	.05	.10
67	Steve Thomas, NYI	.05	.10
68	Norm Maciver, Ott.	.05	.10
69	Vincent Damphousse, Mon.	.05	.10
70	John Vanbiesbrouck, Goalie, Fl.	.07	.15
71	Andrei Kovalenko, Que.	.07	.15
72	David Andreychuk, Tor.	.07	.15
73	Stu Barnes, Win.	.05	.10
74	Jamie McLennan, Goalie, NYI	.05	.10
75	Rudy Poeschek, Tor.	.05	.10
76	Ken Wregger, Goalie, Pit.	.05	.10
77	Raymond Bourque, Bos.	.07	.15
78	Grant Fuhr, Goalie, Buf.	.05	.10
79	Paul Cavallini, Dal.	.05	.10
80	Nelson Emerson, Win.	.05	.10
81	Tim Cheveldae, Goalie, Win.	.05	.10
82	Mariusz Czerkawski, Bos., RC	.15	.30
83	Pat Peake, Wash.	.05	.10
84	Craig Billington, Goalie, Ott.	.05	.10
85	Sean Burke, Goalie, Har.	.05	.10
86	Chris Gratton, TB	.15	.30
87	Andrei Trefilov, Goalie, Cal.	.10	.20
88	Terry Yake, MDA	.05	.10
89	Mark Recchi, Phi.	.10	.20
90	Igor Korolev, St.L	.05	.10
91	Mark Tinordi, Dal.	.05	.10
92	Alexei Kovalev, NYR	.15	.30
93	Bob Essensa, Goalie, Det.	.05	.10
94	Keith Tkachuk, Win.	.10	.20
95	Pat Falloon, SJ	.05	.10
96	John Slaney, Wash.	.05	.10
97	Alexei Zhamnov, Win.	.10	.20
98	Jeff Norton, SJ	.05	.10
99	Douglas Gilmour, Tor.	.15	.30
100	Rick Tocchet, Pit.	.05	.10
101	Robert Kron, Har.	.05	.10
102	Patrik Carnback. MDA	.05	.10
103	Tom Barrasso, Goalie, Pit.	.05	.10
104	Jari Kurri, LA	.05	.10
105	Iain Fraser, Que.	.05	.10
106	Mike Donnelly, LA	.05	.10
107	Ray Sheppard, Det.	.05	.10
108	Scott Young, Que.	.05	.10
109	Kirk McLean, Goalie, Van.	.10	.20
110	Checklist	.05	.10
111	Sergei Zubov, NYR	.15	.30
112	Ivan Droppa, Chi.	.05	.10
113	Brendan Shanahan, St.L	.10	.20
114	Michal Pivonka, Wash.	.05	.10
115	Pavol Demitra, Ott.	.05	.10
116	Doug Brown, NJ	.05	.10
117	Valeri Kamensky, Que.	.05	.10
118	Alexander Karpovtsev, Que.	.05	.10
119	Alexander Daigle, Ott.	.18	.35
120	Dominik Hasek, Goalie, Buf.	.12	.25
121	Murray Craven, Van.	.05	.10
122	Michal Sykora. SJ	.05	.10
123	Aris Brimanis, Phi., RC	.10	.20
124	Benoit Hogue, NYI	.05	.10
125	Arto Blumsten, Win.	.05	.10
126	Russell Courtnall, Dal.	.05	.10
127	Bryan Marchment, Chi.	.05	.10
128	Jeff Hackett, Goalie, Chi.	.05	.10
129	Kevin Miller, St.L	.05	.10
130	Bryan Smolinski, Bos.	.18	.35
131	John Druce, Cal.	.05	.10
132	Roman Hamrlik, TB	.05	.10
133	Jason Arnott, Edm.	.50	1.00
134	Chris Terreri, Goalie, NJ	.05	.10
135	Michael Gartner, Tor.	.05	.10
136	Darryl Sydor, LA	.05	.10
137	Lyle Odelein, Mon.	.05	.10
138	Martin Gelinas, Van.	.05	.10
139	Mike Rathje, SJ	.10	.20
140	Sylvain Cote, Wash.	.05	.10
141	Nicklas Lidstrom, Det.	.05	.10
142	Guy Hebert, Goalie, MDA	.10	.20
143	Jozef Stumpel, Bos.	.12	.25
144	Owen Nolan, Que.	.07	.15
145	Jesse Belanger, Fl.	.07	.15
146	Bill Guerin, NJ	.05	.10
147	Mike Stapleton, Pit.	.05	.10
148	Steve Yzerman, Det.	.05	.10
149	Mikael Nylander, Edm.	.05	.10
150	Rod Brind'Amour, Phi.	.05	.10
151	Jaromir Jagr, Pit.	.18	.35
152	Darcy Wakaluk, Goalie, Dal.	.05	.10
153	Sergei Nemchinov, NYR	.05	.10
154	Wes Walz, Cal.	.05	.10
155	Sergei Fedorov, Det.	.35	.75
156	Daniel Laperriere, St.L	.10	.20
157	Marty McInnis, NYI	.05	.10
158	Chris Joseph, Edm.	.05	.10
159	Matt Martin, Tor.	.10	.20
160	Checklist	.05	.10
161	Denis Tsygurov, Buf., RC	.12	.25
162	Stephan Lebeau, Mon.	.05	.10
163	Kirk Muller, Mon.	.05	.10
164	Shayne Corson, Edm.	.05	.10
165	Joe Sakic, Que.	.10	.20
166	Denis Savard, TB	.05	.10
167	Kevin Dineen, Phi.	.05	.10
168	Paul Coffey, Det.	.07	.15
169	Sandis Ozolinch, SJ	.10	.20
170	Stewart Malgunas, Phi.	.05	.10
171	Petr Klima, TB	.05	.10
172	Patrick Verbeek, Har.	.05	.10
173	Yan Kaminsky, Win.	.05	.10
174	Martin McSorley, LA	.05	.10
175	Arturs Irbe, Goalie, SJ	.10	.20
176	Peter Popovic, Mon.	.10	.20
177	Brian Skrudland, Fl.	.05	.10
178	John Lilley, Win.	.05	.10
179	Boris Mironov, Win.	.05	.10
180	Garth Snow, Goalie, Que.	.05	.10
181	Alexei Kudashov, Tor.	.05	.10
182	Scott Mellanby, Fl.	.05	.10
183	Dale Hunter, Wash.	.05	.10
184	Tommy Soderstrom, Goalie, Phi.	.05	.10
185	Claude Lemieux, NJ	.05	.10
186	Felix Potvin, Goalie, Tor.	.35	.75
187	Corey Millen, NJ	.05	.10
188	Derek King, NYI	.05	.10
189	Kelly Hrudey, Goalie, LA	.05	.10
190	Dimitri Khristich, Wash.	.05	.10
191	Sylvain Turgeon, Ott.	.05	.10
192	John Gruden, Bos., RC	.10	.20
193	Michael Peca, Van.	.05	.10
194	Vladimir Malakhov, NYI	.10	.20
195	Mathieu Schneider, Mon.	.05	.10
196	Jeff Shantz, Chi.	.05	.10
197	Darren McCarty, Det.	.05	.10
198	Craig Simpson, Edm.	.05	.10
199	Jarkko Varvio, Dal.	.05	.10
200	Gino Odjick, Van.	.05	.10
201	Martin Lapointe, Det.	.05	.10
202	Paul Ysebaert, Win.	.05	.10
203	Michael McPhee, Dal.	.05	.10
204	John MacLean, NJ	.05	.10
205	Ulf Samuelsson, Pit.	.05	.10
206	Garry Valk, Van.	.05	.10
207	Tomas Sandstrom, Pit.	.05	.10
208	Curtis Joseph, Goalie, St.L	.10	.20
209	Mikhail Shtalenkov, Goalie, MDA	.05	.10
210	Darren Turcotte, NYR	.05	.10
211	Markus Naslund, Pit.	.10	.20
212	Al Iafrate, Bos.	.05	.10
213	Jim Storm, Har.	.05	.10
214	Dan Plante, NYI	.05	.10
215	Brad May, Buf.	.05	.10
216	Nathan Lafayette, Van.	.10	.20
217	Brian Noonan, Chi.	.05	.10
218	Brent Hughes, Bos.	.05	.10
219	Geoff Sanderson, Har.	.10	.20
220	Checklist	.05	.10
221	Eric Weinrich, Har.	.05	.10
222	Greg Adams, Van.	.05	.10
223	Dominic Roussel, Goalie, Phi.	.07	.15
224	Daren Puppa, Goalie, TB	.05	.10
225	Rob Niedermayer, Fl.	.20	.40
226	Todd Elik, SJ	.05	.10
227	Donald Brashear, Mon., RC	.07	.15
228	Joe Nieuwendyk, Cal.	.05	.10
229	Tony Granatom LA	.05	.10
230	Kirk Maltby, Edm.	.05	.10
231	Jocelyn Thibault, Goalie, Que.	.12	.25
232	Shawn McEachern, LA	.05	.10
233	Teppo Numminen, Win.	.05	.10
234	Johan Garpenlov, SJ	.05	.10
235	Ronald Francis, Pit.	.05	.10
236	Viacheslav Kozlov, Det.	.12	.25
237	Scott Niedermayer, NJ	.20	.40
238	Sergei Krivokrasov, Chi.	.05	.10
239	Dave Manson, Win.	.05	.10
240	Mike Ricci, Que.	.05	.10
241	Chad Penney, Ott., RC	.10	.20
242	Calle Johansson, Wash.	.05	.10
243	Robert Reichel, Cal.	.05	.10
244	Igor Kravchuk, Edm.	.05	.10
245	Jason Smith, NJ	.05	.10
246	Neal Broten, Dal.	.05	.10
247	Jeff Brown, Van.	.05	.10
248	Jason Bowen, Phi.	.05	.10
249	Lawrence Murphy, Pit.	.05	.10
250	Gordon Murphy, Bos.	.05	.10
251	Darrin Shannon, Win.	.05	.10
252	Robert Holik, NJ	.05	.10
253	Zigmund Palffy, NYI	.05	.10
254	Dmitri Mironov, Tor.	.05	.10
255	Adam Graves, NYR	.12	.25
256	Alexander Mogilny, Buf.	.12	.25
257	James (Steve) Smith	.05	.10
258	Jim Montgomery, St.L	.05	.10
259	Danton Cole, TB	.05	.10
260	Dave McLlwain, Ott.	.05	.10
261	German Titov, Cal.	.10	.20
262	Tom Chorske, NJ	.05	.10
263	Grant Ledyard, Buf.	.05	.10
264	Garry Galley, Phi.	.05	.10
265	Vlastimil Kroupa, Sj	.05	.10
266	Keith Primeau, Det.	.05	.10
267	Cam Neely, Bos.	.07	.15
268	Chris Pronger, Har.	.20	.40
269	Richard Matvichuk, Dal.	.05	.10
270	Steve Larmer, NYR	.05	.10
271	James Patrick, Cal.	.05	.10
272	Joel Otto, Cal.	.05	.10
273	Todd Nelson, Pit.	.05	.10
274	Joseph Sacco, MDA	.05	.10
275	Jason York, Det., RC	.10	.20
276	Andrew Cassels, Har.	.05	.10
277	Peter Bondra, Wash.	.05	.10
278	Pat LaFontaine, Buf.	.12	.25
279	Nikolai Borschevsky, Tor.	.07	.15
280	David Mackey, St.L, RC	.10	.20
281	Cameron Stewart, Bos.	.05	.10
282	Sergei Makarov, SJ	.05	.10
283	Byron Dafoe, Goalie	.05	.10
284	Joe Murphy, Chi.	.05	.10
285	Matthew Barnaby. Buf.	.05	.10
286	Derian Hatcher, Dal.	.05	.10
287	Jyrki Lumme, Van.	.05	.10
288	Travis Green, NYI	.05	.10
289	Milos Holan, Phi.	.05	.10
290	Ed Patterson, Pit.	.05	.10
291	Randy Burridge, Wash.	.05	.10
292	Brian Savage, Mon.	.05	.10
293	Stephane Quintal, St.L	.05	.10
294	Zarley Zalapski, Har.	.05	.10
295	Vitali Prokhorov, St.L	.05	.10
296	Ed Belfour, Goalie, Chi.	.12	.25
297	Yuri Khmylev, Buf.	.05	.10
298	Dean McAmmond, Edm.	.05	.10
299	Bob Corkum, MDA	.05	.10

No.	Player	EX	NRMT
300	Darrin Madeley, Goalie, Ott.	.10	.20
301	Brian Bellows, Mon.	.05	.10
302	Andrei Lomakin, Fl.	.05	.10
303	Anatoli Semenov, MDA	.05	.10
304	Claude Lapointe, Que.	.05	.10
305	Adam Oates, Bos.	.05	.10
306	Richard Smehlik, Buf.	.05	.10
307	James Dowd, NJ	.10	.20
308	Mark Fitzpatrick, Goalie, Fl.	.05	.10
309	Pierre Sevigny, Mon.	.05	.10
310	Glenn Healy, Goalie, NYR	.05	.10
311	Igor Larionov, SJ	.05	.10
312	Aaron Ward, Det.	.05	.10
313	Dale Hawerchuk, Buf.	.05	.10
314	Bob Kudelski, Ott.	.05	.10
315	Chris Osgood, Goalie, Det.	.25	.50
316	Trent Klatt, Dal.	.05	.10
317	Gary Suter, Cal.	.05	.10
318	Tahir Domi, Win.	.05	.10
319	Dave Gagner, Dal.	.05	.10
320	Kevin Smyth, Har.	.05	.10
321	Philippe Bozon, St.L	.05	.10
322	Trevor Kidd, Goalie, Cal.	.05	.10
323	Warren Rychel, LA	.05	.10
324	Steven Rice, Edm.	.05	.10
325	Patrice Brisebois, Mon.	.05	.10
326	Gary Roberts, Cal.	.05	.10
327	Fredrik Olausson, Win.	.05	.10
328	Andrei Nazarov, SJ	.05	.10
329	Stephane Fiset, Goalie, Que.	.10	.20
330	Checklist	.05	.10

— 1994-95 INSERT CARDS —

The pictures on the following insert cards are pre-production samples. Actual photographs and numbers may differ with the sets designed to accommodate the series..

GOLD LEAF STARS

This 10-card set was randomly inserted into all Series One American and Canadian foil packs. The chances of finding a Gold Leaf Star is not less that one in 72 packs. All cards are numbered - of 5000. These cards have two different players front and back giving them the appearance of no backs. The cards are numbered - of 10 with a circulation 5000.

1994-95 Gold Leaf Stars
Card No. 1, Mark Messier, Alexei Yashin

Card Size: 2 1/2" X 3 1/2"
Face: Four colour, gold border; Name, Team
Back: Four colour, gold border; Name, Number, Team, Logo
Imprint: ©1994 DONRUSS INC. PRINTED IN U.S.A.
Complete Set No.: 10
Complete Set Price: 250.00 500.00
Common Card 20.00 40.00

No.	Player	EX	NRMT
1	S. Fedorov, Det., W. Gretzky, LA	50.00	100.00
2	D. Gilmour, Tor., J. Roenick, Chi.	25.00	50.00
3	P. Roy, Mon., M. Richter, NYR, Goalies	37.50	75.00
4	B. Hull, St.L, P. Bure, Van.	37.50	75.00
5	M. Messier, NYR, A. Yashin, Ott.	20.00	40.00
6	R. Bourque, Bos., B. Leetch, NYR	20.00	40.00
7	C. Joseph, St.L, E. Belfour, Chi., Goalies	20.00	40.00

No.	Player	EX	NRMT
8	M. Brodeur, NJ, D. Hasek, Buf. Goalies	25.00	50.00
9	C. Neely, Bos., M. Renberg, Phi.	25.00	50.00
10	M. Modano, Dal., J. Arnott, Edm.	37.50	65.00

FIRE ON ICE

This 12-card set was randomly inserted into all Series One American and Canadian foil packs. The chances of finding a card from this set are not less than one in 18 foil packs.

1994-95 Fire on Ice
Card No. 1, Paul Coffey

Card Size: 2 1/2" X 3 1/2"
Face: Four colour, borderless; Name, Logo
Back: Four colour; Name, Number, Resume, Team Logo
Imprint: ©1994 DONRUSS INC. PRINTED IN U.S.A.
Complete Set No.: 12
Complete Set Price: 37.50 75.00
Common Card 2.00 4.00

No.	Player	EX	NRMT
1	Sergei Fedorov, Det.	5.00	10.00
2	Jeremy Roenick, Chi.	4.00	8.00
3	Pavel Bure, VAn.	6.00	12.00
4	Wayne Gretzky, LA	7.50	15.00
5	Douglas Gilmour, Tor.	5.00	10.00
6	Eric Lindros, Phi.	7.50	15.00
7	Joseph Juneau, Bos.	4.00	8.00
8	Paul Coffey, Det.	2.00	4.00
9	Mario Lemieux, Pit.	8.00	16.00
10	Alexander Mogilny, Buf.	4.00	8.00
11	Michael Gartner, Tor.	2.00	4.00
12	Teemu Selanne, Win.	4.00	8.00

LEAF LIMITED

This 18-card set was randomly inserted into all Series One American and Canadian foil packs.

 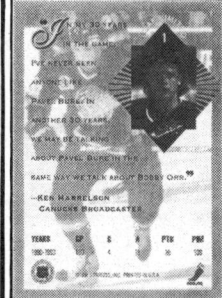

1994-95 Leaf Limited
Card No. 1, Pavel Bure

Card Size: 2 1/2" x 3 1/2"
Face: Four colour, siler foil, borderless; Name, Team logo
Back: Four colour; Name, Number, Position, Resume
Imprint: ©1994 DONRUSS INC. PRINTED IN U.S.A.
Complete Set No.: 18
Complete Set Price: 60.00 120.00
Common Card 2.00 4.00

No.	Player	EX	NRMT
1	Guy Hebert, Goalie, MDA	2.00	4.00
2	Adam Oates, Bos.	2.50	5.00
3	Dominik Hasek, Goalie, Buf.	3.50	7.00
4	Robert Reichel, Cal.	2.00	4.00
5	Jeremy Roenick, Chi.	3.50	7.00
6	Michael Modano, Dal.	3.00	6.00
7	Sergei Fedorov, Det.	6.00	12.00
8	Jason Arnott, Edm.	5.00	10.00
9	John Vanbiesbrouck, Goalie, Fl.	2.50	5.00
10	Chris Pronger, Har.	2.50	5.00
11	Wayne Gretzky, LA	7.50	15.00
12	Patrick Roy, Goalie, Mon.	5.00	10.00
13	Martin Brodeur, Goalie, NJ	3.50	7.00
14	Pierre Turgeon, NYI	2.50	5.00
15	Mark Messier, NYR	3.00	6.00
16	Alexei Yashin, Ott.	3.00	6.00
17	Eric Lindros, Phi.	7.50	15.00
18	Mario Lemieux, Pit.	5.00	10.00

GOLD LEAF ROOKIES

This 15-card set was randomly inserted into all Series One American and Canadian foil packs. Chances of finding these cards are not less than one in 18 packs.

1994-95 Gold Leaf Rookies
Card No. 19, Martin Brodeur

Card Size: 2 1/2" x 3 1/2"
Face: Four colour, borderless; Name, Team, Team logo
Back: Four colour; Name, Number, Resume
Imprint: ©1994 DONRUSS INC. PRINTED IN U.S.A.
Complete Set No.: 15
Complete Set Price: 37.50 75.00
Common Card 2.50 5.00

No.	Player	EX	NRMT
1	Martin Brodeur, Goalie, NJ	2.50	5.00
2	Jason Arnott, Edm.	4.00	8.00
3	Alexei Yashin, Ott.	4.00	8.00
4	Chris Gratton, TB	2.50	5.00
5	Alexandre Daigle, Ott.	3.00	6.00
6	Mikael Renberg, Phi.	3.00	6.00
7	Rob Niedermayer, Fl.	2.50	5.00
8	Boris Mironov, Win.	2.50	5.00
9	Chris Pronger, Har.	2.50	5.00
10	Chris Osgood, Goalie, Det.	3.50	7.00
11	Derek Plante, Buf.	3.50	7.00
12	Pat Peake, Wash.	2.50	5.00
13	Jason Allison, Wash.	2.50	5.00
14	Bryan Smolinski, Bos.	3.00	6.00
15	Jocelyn Thibault, Goalie, Que.	3.00	6.00

**ALPHABETICAL INDEX
NATIONAL HOCKEY ASSOCIATION
NATIONAL HOCKEY LEAGUE**

NHA / NHL ALPHABETICAL INDEX

All players that appear on cards from Imperial Tobacco 1910 - 11 to the modern era 1994 - 95 cards are listed alphabetically by the last name.

COMPANY ABBREVIATIONS

Can. Chew. Gum	Canadian Chewing Gum	Dom. Choc.	Dominion Chocolate
Cel. Watch	Celebrity Watch Co.	Amal. Press	Amalgamated Press
Champ's	Champ's Cigarettes		

SET TYPE ABBREVIATIONS

A	American / Autograph		P/C	Promotional Cards (unnumbered)
AN	Anniversary		PK	Puck
AS	All Star		PO	Photos
AW	Award Winner		PP	Power Play
B	Bilingual		PS	Puck Stickers
BB	Box Bottoms		PT	Platinum / Posters
BK	Booklets		PTC	Platinum Collection
C	Canadian		PM	Premier / Premium
CS	Crest Stickers		PN	Pinnacle
DE	Deckle Edge		PNA	Pinnacle American
E	English		PNE	Pinnacle English
EI	Emerald Ice		QS	Mini-Quad Stickers
EN	Eastern		R	Red Army
ES	Euro Stars		RL	Red Light Special
F	French		RR	Rated Rookies
FS	Future Stars		RS	Rising Stars
G	Gamebreakers		SA	Slapshot Artists
GG	Global Greats		SC	Stadium Club / Scoring Kings
GP	Glossy Photos		SCM	Stadium Club Member
GS	Gold Set		S/G	Sterogram Cards
HB	Hockey Bucks		SK	Stickers
HF	Hall of Fame		SL	Scoring Leaders
HL	Hockey Leader		SM	Speed Merchants
HR	Hottest and Rising		SP	Special Print
HT	Hat Trick		SS	Sticker Stamps / Studio Signature
IK	Ice Kings		ST	Stamps
JCA	Junior Championships American		SY	Second Year Stars
JCC	Junior Championships Canadian		T	Rookie and Traded
N	Netmindersa		TP	Top Prospects
NS	NHL Star		UR	Ultra Rookie
OS	Original Six		W	Wave of the Future
OSF	Original Six French		WN	Western
OSHE	Original Six Holograms English		YS	Young Superstars
OSHF	Original Six Holograms French		(I)'	Series One
P	Promotional Cards (numbered)		(II)	Series Two
PL	Point Leaders			

Abel, Clarence (Taffy)
Can. Chew. Gum: 33/34 - 1
Diamond: 33/35 - 1

Abel, Sid
Beehive: 34/44 - 86; 45/63 - 149
Hall of Fame: 83 - 2, A1P, 87 - 2
HHFM: 92 - 12
O-Pee-Chee: 39/40 - 68
Parkhurst: 51/52 - 64; 60/61 - 23; 62/63 - 34
Royal Desserts: 1952 - 4
Shirriff: 60/61 - 60; 61/62 - 61
Topps: 64/65 - 93; 65/66 - 41; 66/67 - 42
Ultimate: 92 - 66(OSE), 66(OSF)

Acton, Keith
Bowman: 90/91 - 113; 91/92 - 244; 92/93 - 184
Derniere: 72/84 - 136
Fleer: 92/93 - 368
Leaf: 93/94 - 420
O-Pee-Chee: 81/82 - 181; 82/83 - 179, 180, 42SK, 43SK; 83/84 - 184; 84/85 - 93; 85/86 - 82, 38SK; 86/87 - 172; 89/90 - 254; 90/91 - 355; 91/92 - 77; 92/93 - 368; 93/94 - 407, 205SC, 205FD
Panini: 87/88 - 299; 89/90 - 301; 91/92 - 237; 93/94 - 50E, 50F
PepsiCo: 80/81 - 41
Post: 82/83 - 145
Pro Set: 90/91 - 497
Score: 90/91 - 301A; 91/92 - 133A, 133B, 133C; 92/93 - 341C, 341A, 363PNC, 363PNA; 93/94 - 301C, 301A
Topps: 82/83 - 42SK, 43SK; 85/86 - 82; 86/87 - 172; 90/91 - 355; 91/92 - 77, 247SC; 92/93 - 199, 199GS, 223SC; 93/94 - 407, 205SC, 205FD
Upper Deck: 90/91 - 445E, 445F

Adams, Charles
Hall of Fame: 83P - D1, 47; 87 - 47

Adams, Greg
Bowman: 90/91 - 59; 91/92 - 311; 92/93 - 333
Donruss: 93/94 - 350
Fleer: 92/93 - 217; 93/94 - 19, 247PP
Leaf: 93/94 - 219
O-Pee-Chee: 86/87 - 10, A/BB, 196SK; 87/88 - 135; 88/89 - 162, 66SK; 89/90 - 178; 90/91 - 106; 91/92 - 340; 92/93 - 365
Panini: 87/88 - 84; 88/89 - 136; 89/90 - 154; 90/91 - 303; 91/92 - 39; 93/94 - 173E, 173IS
Parkhurst: 91/92 - 183E, 183F; 93/94 - 480, 480EI
Pro Set: 90/91 - 291; 91/92 - 243E, 243F, 125PT
Score: 90/91 - 240A, 240C; 91/92 - 44A; 44B; 44C; 92/93 - 146C, 146A, 218PNE, 218PNF; 92/93 - 28PNC, 28PNA
Topps: 86/87 - 10; 87/88 - 135; 88/89 - 162 89/90 - 178; 90/91 - 106; 91/92 - 340, 52SC; 92/93 - 507, 507GS, 232SC
Upper Deck: 90/91 - 342E, 342F; 91/92 - 426E, 426F; 92/93 - 192; 93/94 - 77

Adams, Greg C.
O-Pee-Chee: 86/87 - 253; 87/88 - 139; 88/89 - 199; 90/91 - 518
Panini: 87/88 - 185
Score: 93/94 - 196C, 196A
Topps: 86/87 - A/BB; 87/88 - 139

Adams, Jack E.
O-Pee-Chee: 40/41 - 104

Adams, Jack J.
Beehive: 34/44 - 133
Champ's: 24/25 - 48
Hall of Fame: 83, 182, J1P; 87 - 182
Wm. Paterson: 23/24 - 24; 24/25 - 53
World Wide Gum: 36/37 - 99

Adams, Kevin
Donruss: 93/94 - 1JCA
Upper Deck: 93/94 - 568

Adams, Sr., Weston W.
Hall of Fame: 83 - 11, 122; 87 - 122

Affleck, Bruce
Loblaws: 74/75 - 55
O-Pee-Chee: 76/77 - 305; 77/78 - 376; 78/79 - 279

Aggatt, J.P.
Dom. Choc.: 1925 - 68

Ahearn, T. Franklin
Hall of Fame: 83 - E1P, 62; 87 - 62

Ahearn, J. Frank
Hall of Fame: 83 - 183, J2P; 87 - 183

Ahern, Fred
O-Pee-Chee: 76/77 - 298; 77/78 - 280; 78/79 - 386

Ahrens, Chris
Loblaws: 74/75 - 145
O-Pee-Chee: 74/75 - 346; 75/76 - 371

Ahola, Peter
Bowman: 92/93 - 353
Fleer: 92/93 - 78, 376
O-Pee-Chee: 92/93 - 268
Parkhurst: 91/92 - 65E, 65F
Pro Set: 91/92 - 540E, 540F, 257PT; 92/93 - 73
Score: 91/92 - 312PNE, 312PNF; 92/93 - 310C, 310A
Topps: 92/93 - 73, 73GS, 192SC
Upper Deck: 91/92 - 543E, 543F; 92/93 - 41, 526, E5, ERT4

Aikenhead, Andy (Goalie)
Diamond: 36/39 - 1 (I)

Aivazoff, Micah
Donruss: 93/94 - 421
O-Pee-Chee: 93/94 - 345
Parkhurst: 93/94 - 253, 253EI
Topps: 93/94 - 345, 263SC, 263FD
Upper Deck: 93/94 - 432

Akulinin, Igor
O-Pee-Chee: 90/91 - 491

Albelin, Tommy
O-Pee-Chee: 88/89 - 210, 184SK; 89/90 - 241; 90/91 - 323
Panini: 88/89 - 348; 89/90 - 257; 90/91 - 76
Pro Set: 90/91 - 162
Score: 90/91 - 378A, 378C; 91/92 - 393B, 393C
Topps: 90/91 - 323
Upper Deck: 90/91 - 88E, 88F

Albert, Marv
Pro-Set: 91/92 - 291PT

Albright, Clint
Beehive: 45/63 - 296

Aldcorn, Gary
Beehive: 45/63 - 371
Parkhurst: 57/58 TOR - 24; 58/59 - 18; 60/61 - 33; 93/94 - 122ML
Shirriff: 60/61 - 53

Alexander, Arthur
La Presse: 27/32 - 70

Alexander, Claire
O-Pee-Chee: 76/77 321

Alexandrov, Igor
Upper Deck 92/93 - 611

Allan, Montagu
Hall of Fame: 83 - 12, I23P; 87 - 123

Allen, George
Beehive: 34/44 - 38
CKAC Radio: 43/47 - 30
O-Pee-Chee: 39/40 - 79
Quaker Oats: 45/54 - 1

Allen, Keith
Parkhurst: 54/55 - 47

Allen, V. (Squee)
Beehive: 34/44 - 211

Allison, Jason
Donruss: 93/94 - 1JCC
Upper Deck: 93/94 - 537

Allison, Mike
O-Pee-Chee: 81/82 - 221; 89/90 - 141; 90/91 - 417
Panini: 88/89 - 73
Post: 82/83 - 193
Topps: 81/82 EN - 94; 89/90 - 141

Allison, Ray
O-Pee-Chee: 80/81 - 126; 83/84 - 259
Topps: 80/81 - 126

Allison Scott
Score: 90/91 - 424A, 424C

Amadio, Dave
O-Pee-Chee: 68/69 - 157; 70/71 - 33
Shirriff: 68/69 - D10
Topps: 70/71 - 33

Amodeo, Mike
O-Pee-Chee: 72/73 - 291; 79/80 - 268

Amonte, Anthony
Bowman: 92/93 - 389
Donruss: 93/94 - 217, 411
Fleer: 92/93 - 133, 1UR; 93/94 - 202, 156PP
Hockey Wit: 93/94 - 2
Leaf: 93/94 - 17
O-Pee-Chee: 91/92 - 26, 11PM; 92/93 - 155, 255, 24AN; 93/94 - 70, 226SC, 226FD
Parkhurst: 91/92 - 114E, 443E, 114F, 443F; 92/93 - 107, 235, 107EI, 235EI; 93/94 - 132, 132EI; 94/95 - V56
Panini: 92/93 - 270E, 270F, T(E), T(F); 93/94 - 90E, 90F
Pro Set: 91/92 - 550E, 550F, 262PT; 92/93 - 118, 1RGL
Score: 91/92 - 398A, 288B, 288C, 301PNE, 390PNE, 301PNF, 390PNF; 92/93 - 389C, 389A, 415C, 415A, 506C, 506A, 55PNC, 55PNA, 4CT, 4AT; 93/94 - 215C, 215A, 6PCE
Season's: 92/93 - 27
Topps: 91/92 - 26; 92/93 6GS, 229GS, 32SC, 250SC; 92/93 - 6, 6GS, 229SC; 93/94 - 70, 226SC, 458SC, 226FD, 458FD
Upper Deck: 92/93 - 13, 138, 359, 635, AR1, 51AS; 93/94 - 64

Anderson, Earl
O-Pee-Chee: 77/78 - 114
Topps: 77/78 - 114

Anderson, Glenn
Bowman: 90/91 - 195; 91/92 - 116; 92/93 - 104
Donruss: 93/94 - 340, 460
Esso: 83/84 - 1E, 1F
Fleer: 92/93 - 207; 93/94 - 9, 237PP
Frito-Lay: 88/89 - 1
Funmate: 83/84 - 37
Hockey Wit: 93/94 - 50
Kraft: 86/87 - 11, 11P; 1990 - 10
Leaf: 93/94 - 41
O-Pee-Chee: 81/82 - 108, 217SK; 82/83 - 100, 99SK, 100SK; 83/84 - 24; 92SK, 93SK, 158SK; 84/85 - 238, 247SK, 248SK; 85/86 - 168, 227SK; 86/87 - 80, 78SK; 87/88 - 199, 95SK, 1HL; 88/89 - 189, 229SK; 89/90 - 226, 218SK; 90/91 - 145; 91/92 - 124, 10PM; 92/93 - 134; 93/94 - 104, 168SC, 168FD
Panini: 87/88 - 265; 88/89 - 57; 89/90 - 77; 90/91 - 227; 91/92 - 120; 92/93 - 76E, 76F; 93/94 - 225E, 225F
Parkhurst: 91/92 - 177E, 177F; 92/93 - 178, 178EI; 93/94 - 201, 201EI
PepsiCo 80/81 - 21
Post: 82/83 - 81
Pro Set: 90/91 - 81; 91/92 - 75E, 75F; 92/93 - 185
Score: 90/91 - 114A, 114C, 54HR; 1991 - 61T; 91/92 - 47A, 47B, 47C, 611B, 611C, 12PNE, 12PNF; 92/93 - 241C, 241A, 355PNC, 355PNA; 93/94 - 449C, 449A

Anderson, Glenn (cont.)
- 7-Eleven: 84/85 - 13
- Topps: 82/83 - 99SK, 100SK; 83/84 - 92SK, 93SK, 158SK; 248SK; 86/87 - 80; 88/89 - 189; 90/91 - 145; 91/92 - 124, 116SC; 92/93 - 162, 162GS, 124SC; 93/94 - 104, 168SC, 168FD
- Upper Deck: 90/91 - 284E, 284F; 91/92 - 250E, 250F
- Vachon Foods: 83/84 - 21

Anderson, Jim
- O-Pee-Chee: 74/75 - 118
- Topps: 74/75 - 118

Anderson, John
- Esso: 83/84 - 2E, 2F
- Funmate: 83/84 - 121
- Kelloggs: 84 - 3
- O-Pee-Chee: 80/81 - 79; 81/82 - 313, 107SK; 82/83 - 315, 73SK, 74SK; 83/84 - 325, 30SK, 31SK; 84/85 - 295, 18SK; 85/86 - 20, 10SK; 86/87 - 13, 54SK; 87/88 - 45, 204SK; 88/89 - 190, 270SK; 89/90 - 124
- Panini: 87/88 - 45; 88/89 - 239
- PepsiCo: 80/81 - 81
- Post: 82/83 - 273
- 7-Eleven: 84/85 - 44
- Topps: 80/81 - 79; 82/83 - 73SK, 74SK; 83/84 - 30SK, 31SK; 84/85 - 136; 85/86 - 20; 86/87 - 13; 87/88 - 45; 88/89 - 190, 89/90 - 124
- Vachon Foods: 83/84 - 81

Anderson, Perry
- O-Pee-Chee: 91/92 - 501; 92/93 - 38
- Parkhurst: 91/92 - 164E, 164F
- Topps: 91/92 - 501
- Pro Set: 91/92 - 481E, 481F
- Score: 91 - 99T; 91/92 - 649B, 649C
- Topps: 92/93 - 286, 286GS, 89SC

Anderson, Ron C.
- Colgate: 70/71 - 48
- Eddie Sargent: 70/71 - 18; 71/72 - 18
- Esso: 70/71 - 20
- O-Pee-Chee: 69/70 - 14; 71/72 - 163; 72/73 - 298

Anderson, Ron H.
- Loblaws: 74/75 - 307
- O-Pee-Chee: 74/75 - 314

Anderson, Russ
- O-Pee-Chee: 78/79 - 156; 79/80 - 264
- Topps: 78/79 - 156; 79/80 - 264

Anderson, Shawn
- Bowman: 91/92 - 147
- Pro Set: 90/91 - 513
- Topps: 91/92 - 358SC

Anderson, Tom
- Beehive: 34/44 - 212
- Diamond: 36/39 - 1(II), 1(III)
- O-Pee-Chee: 39/40 - 61

Andersson, Bo Mikael
- Bowman: 91/92 - 11; 92/93 - 158
- Donruss: 93/94 - 322
- Fleer: 92/93 - 406; 93/94 - 440PP
- Leaf: 93/94 - 285
- O-Pee-Chee: 90/91 - 35; 91/92 - 197; 92/93 - 214, 55PM; 93/94 - 150, 97SC, 97FD
- Panini: 90/91 - 47; 92/93 - 258E, 258F; 93/94 - 216E, 216F
- Parkhurst: 91/92 - 63E, 63F; 92/93 - 169, 169EI; 93/94 - 198, 198EI; 94/95 - 226, 226EI
- Pro Set: 90/91 - 98; 91/92 - 394F, 180PT; 92/93 - 65
- Score: 92/93 - 215C, 215A, 384PNC, 384PNA; 93/94 - 427C, 427A
- Sega: 93/94 - 130
- Topps: 90/91 - 35; 91/92 - 197, 39SC; 92/93 - 151, 151GS, 348SC; 93/94 - 150, 97SC, 97FD, 427FD
- Upper Deck: 91/92 - 238E, 238F; 92/93 -103

Andersson, Kent-Erik
- O-Pee-Chee: 78/79 - 17; 80/81 - 383; 81/82 - 158; 82/83 - 218
- Post: 82/83 - 129
- Topps: 78/79 - 17; 81/82 WN - 102

Andersson, Niclas
- Score: 93/94 - 460C, 460A
- Upper Deck: 91/92 - 29E, 29F; 93/94 - 239

Andersson, Peter
- Parkhurst: 94/95 - 88, 88EI
- Upper Deck: 92/93 - 481; 93/94 - 71

Andrea, Paul
- Esso: 70/71 - 19
- O-Pee-Chee: 70/71 - 77
- Shirriff: 68/69 - K8
- Topps: 70/71 - 77

Andrijevsky, Alexander
- O-Pee-Chee: 91/92 - 31R
- Upper Deck: 92/93 - 342; 93/94 - 26

Andrews, Lloyd
- Champ's: 24/25 - 49
- Wm. Paterson: 23/24 - 21; 24/25 - 59

Andreychuk, David (Dave)
- Bowman: 90/91 - 246; 91/92 - 22; 92/93 - 44
- Donruss: 93/94 - 342
- Fleer: 92/93 - 12; 93/94 - 57, 1SA, 238PP, 1RL
- Leaf: 93/94 - 63
- O-Pee-Chee: 84/85 - 17, 353, 209SK, 210SK; 85/86 - 143, 187SK; 86/87 - 16, 49SK; 87/88 - 3, 147SK; 88/89 - 163, M/BB, 261SK; 89/90 - 106, 258SK; 90/91 - 169; 91/92 - 38; 92/93 - 141; 93/94 - 235, 23SC, 23FD
- Panini: 87/88 - 27; 88/89 - 223; 89/90 - 215; 90/91 - 29; 91/92 - 309; 92/93 - 249E, 249F; 93/94 - 223E, 223F
- Parkhurst: 91/92 - 17E, 437E, 17F, 437F; 92/93 - 10, 409, 10EI, 409EI; 93/94 - 200, 200EI; 94/95 - 303, 303EI, V89
- Pro Set: 90/91 - 17A, 17C, 363; 91/92 - 23E, 23F, 8PT; 92/93 - 15, 249
- Score: 90/91 - 189A, 189C, 87HR; 91/92 - 277A, 497B, 497C, 122PNE, 122PNF; 92/93 - 204C, 204A, 58PNC, 58PNA; 93/94 - 343C, 343A, 481C, 481A
- Sega: 93/94 - 136
- Topps: 84/85 - 13; 85/86 - 143; 86/87 - 16; 87/88 - 3; 88/89 - 163, M/BB; 89/90 - 106; 90/91 - 169; 91/92 - 38, 93SC; 92/93 - 164, 164GS, 132SC; 93/94 - 235, 23SC, 23FD
- Upper Deck: 90/91 - 41E, 41F; 91/92 - 124E; 92/93 - 269; 93/94 - 86

Andruff, Ron
- O-Pee-Chee: 77/78 - 288; 78/79 - 315

Angotti, Lou
- Beehive: 64/67 - 30, 120
- Coca Cola: 64/65 - 73
- Colgate: 70/71 - 8
- Dad's Cookies: 70/71 - 34
- Eddie Sargent: 70/71 - 40; 71/72 - 38; 72/73 - 65
- Esso: 70/71 - 55
- O-Pee-Chee: 68/69 - 103, 11PS; 69/70 - 134; 70/71 - 12; 71/72 - 212; 72/73 - 243; 73/74 - 224; 74/75 - 63
- Shirriff: 68/69 - K11
- Topps: 64/65 - 66; 66/67 - 116; 68/69 - 103; 70/71 - 12; 74/75 - 63
- Toronto Sun: 71/72 - 63

Antoski, Shawn
- Donruss: 93/94 - 498
- Leaf: 93/94 - 368
- O-Pee-Chee: 91/92 - 98, 10PM; 93/94 - 31
- Parkhurst: 93/94 - 479, 479EI; 94/95 - 248, 248EI
- Score: 90/91 - 429A, 429C; 91/92 - 323A, 353B, 353C
- Topps: 91/92 - 98; 93/94 - 288SC, 288FD

Antoski, Shawn (cont)
- Upper Deck: 91/92 - 351E, 351F; 92/93 - 81; 93/94 - 325

Antonovich, Mike
- O-Pee-Chee: 79/80 - 349

Apps, Sr., Syl
- Beehive: 34/44 - 298; 45/63 - 372
- Eddie Sargent: 70/71 - 113
- Hall of Fame: 83 - 212, O1P; 87 - 212
- Loblaws: 74/75 - 235
- O-Pee-Chee: 36/37 - 101; 37/38 - 141; 39/40 - 6; 40/41 - 118, 146
- Parkhurst: 55/56 - 28
- Quaker Oats: 38/39 - 15; 45/54 - 55A, 55B, 55C; 55/56 - 28
- Toronto Sun: 71/72 - 210
- World Wide Gum: 36/37 - 23

Apps, Jr., Syl
- Coca Cola: 77/78 - 1
- Colgate: 70/71 - 26
- Eddie Sargent: 72/73 - 169
- Lipton Soup: 74/75 - 49
- O-Pee-Chee: 71/72 - 77; 72/73 - 115; 73/74 - 76; 74/75 - 13; 75/76 - 130; 76/77 - 50; 77/78 - 248; 78/79 - 56; 79/80 - 366; 80/81 - 362
- Topps: 71/72 - 77; 72/73 - 11; 73/74 - 160; 74/75 - 13; 75/76 - 130; 76/77 - 50; 13PO; 77/78 - 248; 78/79 - 56

Arbour, Al
- Beehive: 45/63 - 75, 150, 373; 64/67 - 150
- Kraft: 93/94 - 30
- O-Pee-Chee: 68/69 - 128; 69/70 - 178, 13QS; 74/75 - 91
- Parkhurst: 53/54 - 37; 93/94 - 61ML
- Pro Set: 90/91 - 671
- Shirriff: 60/61 - 67; 61/62 - 60; 62/63 - 20; 68/69 - L3
- Topps: 57/58 - 38; 58/59 - 64; 59/60 - 35; 60/61 - 64; 74/75 - 91
- Toronto Sun: 71/72 - 232
- York: 61/62 - 33

Arbour, Amos
- Wm. Paterson: 23/24 - 20

Arbour, John
- O-Pee-Chee: 68/69 - 189
- Toronto Sun: 71/72 - 233

Archambault, Michel
- O-Pee-Chee: 72/73 - 320

Archibald, Dave
- Donruss: 93/94 - 231
- Fleer: 93/94 - 168PP
- O-Pee-Chee: 88/89 - 112, 1FS; 89/90 - 10, 201SK; 93/94 - 458
- Panini: 88/89 - 88
- Score: 92/93 - 3COH
- Topps: 88/89 - 112; 89/90 - 10; 93/94 - 458C, 399SC, 399FD
- Upper Deck: 92/93 - 473; 93/94 - 105

Armstrong, Bob
- Beehive: 45/63 - 1
- Parkhurst: 52/53 - 84; 54/55 - 55; 93/94 - 7ML
- Shirriff: 60/61 - 118; 61/62 - 12
- Topps: 54/55 - 7; 57/58 - 3; 58/59 - 1; 59/60 - 39; 60/61 - 56; 61/62 - 13
- Toronto Star: 57/67 - 49

Armstrong, Chris
- Donruss: 93/94 - 2JCC
- Upper Deck: 93/94 - 546

Armstrong, George
- Beehive: 45/63 - 410, 411, 412; 64/67 - 168
- Chex: 63/65 - 40
- Coca Cola: 65/66 - 91
- Hall of Fame: 83 - D1P, 197; 87 - 197
- O-Pee-Chee: 70/71 - 113
- Parkhurst: 52/53 - 51; 53/54 - 11; 54/55 - 24; 55/56 - 4; 57/58 TOR - 1; 58/59 - 48; 59/60 - 7; 60/61 - 17; 61/62 - 17; 62/63 - 13; 63/64 - 13, 73; 92/93 - PR17; 93/94 - PR48, 125ML

Armstrong, George (cont.)
Quaker Oats: 45/54 - 56; 55/56 - 4
Shirriff: 60/61 - 9; 61/62 - 51; 62/63 - 10; 68/69 - M1
Topps: 64/65 - 69; 65/66 - 19; 66/67 - 84; 66/67 US - 17; 67/68 - 83; 70/71 - 113
Toronto Star: 57/67 - 111; 58/67 - 44; 63/64 - 29
York: 60/61 - 20; 61/62 - 37; 62/63 - 17; 63/64 - 16

Armstrong, Murray
Beehive: 34/44 - 213, 299
O-Pee-Chee: 37/38 - 146; 39/40 - 19

Armstrong, Neil (Official)
Pro Set: 5HF

Armstrong, William (Bill)
O-Pee-Chee: 91/92 - 36
Topps: 91/92 - 36

Arnason, Chuck
Deniere: 72/84 - 18
Loblaws: 74/75 - 236
O-Pee-Chee: 74/75 - 385; 75/76 - 57; 76/77 - 92; 77/78 - 379; 78/79 - 389
Topps: 75/76 - 57; 76/77 - 92

Arniel, Scott
Bowman: 90/91 - 243; 91/92 - 206
Funmate: 83/84 - 128
O-Pee-Chee: 83/84 - 379; 84/85 - 333, 286SK; 86/87 - 194; 87/88 - 137; 88/89 - 90, 258SK; 89/90 - 187; 90/91 - 324; 90/91 - 1PM; 91/92 - 137
Panini: 88/89 - 224; 89/90 - 213; 90/91 - 30; 91/92 - 74
Post: 82/83 - 321
Pro Set: 90/91 - 18, 557
Score: 90/91 - 251A, 251C, 68T; 91/92 - 256B, 256C
7-Eleven: 84/85 - 55
Topps: 86/87 - 194; 87/88 - 137; 88/89 - 90; 89/90 - 187; 90/91 - 324; 91/92 - 137, 30SC
Upper Deck: 90/91 - 397 E, 397F
Vachon Foods: 83/84 - 121

Arnott, Jason
Donruss: 93/94 - 120, 12RR, H/PM, H/SP
Fleer: 93/94 - 1RS, 337PP
Kraft: 93/94 - 24
Leaf: 93/94 - 382, 7FP, 345SC, 345FD
Parkhurst: 93/94 - 261, 261EI, W8, CC6; 94/95 - 271, 271EI, H8, R8, C8, V84
Upper Deck: 93/94 - 423

Arthur, Fred
O-Pee-Chee: 82/83 - 245
Post: 82/83 - 209

Ashbee, Barry
Coca Cola: 65/66 - 1
Esso: 70/71 - 163
O-Pee-Chee: 71/72 - 104; 72/73 - 206
Toronto Sun: 71/72 - 188

Ashby, Don
O-Pee-Chee: 77/78 - 365; 78/79 - 351

Ashley, John (Official)
Hall of Fame: 83 - 213, O2P; 87 - 213

Ashton, Brent
Bowman: 90/91 - 130; 91/92 - 211; 92/93 - 357
Fleer: 92/93 - 1
Kraft: 86/87 - 42, 42P; 1990 - 46
O-Pee-Chee: 82/83 - 135, 227SK; 83/84 - 225; 85/86 - 170, 153SK; 86/87 - 181, 25SK; 87/88 - 100, 108SK; 88/89 - 128, 250SK; 89/90 - 181, 138SK; 90/91 - 24; 91/92 - 240; 93/94 - 51SC, 51FD
Panini: 87/88 - 244; 88/89 - 40; 89/90 - 164; 90/91 - 321; 91/92 - 70
Parkhurst: 92/93 - 258, 258EI
PepsiCo: 80/81 - 101
Post: 82/83 - 161
Pro Set: 90/91 - 323; 91/92 - 272E, 352E, 272F, 352F, 155PT

Ashton, Brent (cont.)
Score: 90/91 - 31A, 31C; 91 - 22T; 91/92 - 78A, 78B, 78C, 280PNE, 280PNF; 92/93 - 164C, 164A, 93/94 - 434C, 434A
Topps: 82/83 - 227SK; 86/87 - 181; 87/88 - 100; 88/89 - 128; 89/90 - 181; 90/91 - 24; 91/92 - 240, 90SC; 92/93 - 191, 191GS, 146SC, 51SC, 51FD
Upper Deck: 90/91 - 220E, 220F; 91/92 - 303E, 303F

Asselstine, Ron (Official)
Pro Set: 90/91 - 681

Astley, Mark (Goalie)
Donruss: 93/94 - 44
O-Pee-Chee: 93/94 - 324
Parkhurst: 93/94 -295, 295EI
Topps: 93/94 - 342, 311SC, 311FD
Upper Deck: 93/94 - 494

Astrom, Hardy
O-Pee-Chee: 80/81 - 269

Atchinson, A.
Imperial Tobacco: 12/13 - 4

Atkinson, Steve
Eddie Sargent: 72/73 - 40
Esso: 70/71 - 21
Loblaws: 74/75 - 308
O-Pee-Chee: 71/72 - 162; 72/73 - 40; 73/74 - 245; 74/75 - 192
Topps: 72/73 - 47; 74/75 - 192

Aubin, Normand
O-Pee-Chee: 82/83 - 316
Post: 82/83 - 274

Aubry, Pierre
Deniere: 72/84 - 154
O-Pee-Chee: 82/83 - 277; 83/84 - 289

Aucoin, Adrian
Fleer: 93/94 - 478PP
O-Pee-Chee: 93/94 - 3TC
Upper Deck: 93/94 - 251

Audette, Donald
Bowman: 92/93 - 288
Donruss: 93/94 - 32
Fleer: 92/93 - 2UR; 93/94 - 295PP
Leaf: 93/94 - 272
O-Pee-Chee: 91/92 - 273; 92/93 - 117; 93/94 - 61, 213SC, 213FD
Panini: 92/93 - U(E), U(F); 93/94 - 103E, 103IS
Parkhurst: 91/92 - 11E, 11F; 92/93 - 18, 18EI, 231, 231EI; 93/94 - 26, 26EI
Pro Set: 91/92 - 524E, 524F, 249PT; 92/93 - 18, 3RGL
Score: 91/92 - 389A, 279B, 279C, 330PNE, 330PNF; 92/93 - 393C, 393A, 38PNC, 38PNA, 19CSS, 19ASS; 93/94 - 77C, 77A
Season's: 92/93 - 43
Topps: 91/92 - 273; 92/93 - 12GS, 206GS, 112SC; 92/93 - 12, 12GS, 206, 206GS; 93/94 - 61, 213SC, 213FD
Upper Deck: 90/91 - 519E, 519F; 91/92 - 585E, 585F; 93/94 - 5; 92/93 - 2, 306

Aurie, Larry
Anonymous: 33/34 - 19
Beehive: 34/44 - 87
Can. Chew. Gum: 33/34 - 2
Hamilton Gum: 33/34 - 44
O-Pee-Chee: 34/35 - 51; 36/37 - 131
Sweet Caporal: 34/35 - 8
World Wide Gum: 33/34 - 59

Awrey, Don
Coca Cola: 65/66 - 2
Dad's Cookies: 70/71 - 1
Eddie Sargent: 70/71 - 2; 72/73 - 23
Esso: 70/71 - 1
Loblaws: 74/75 - 253
Shirriff: 68/69 - A3

Awrey, Don (cont.)
O-Pee-Chee: 68/69 - 3; 69/70 - 203; 70/71 - 4; 71/72 - 3; 72/73 - 170; 73/74 - 240; 74/75 80; 75/76 344; 76/77 311; 77/78 137; 78/79 - 383
Topps: 65/66 - 99; 67/68 - 37; 68/69 - 3; 70/71 - 4; 74/75 - 80; 77/78 - 137
Toronto Sun: 71/72 - 2

Ayers, Vern
Diamond: 36/39 - 2/ (I), 2/ (II), 2/ (III)
O-Pee-Chee: 34/35 - 65
World Wide Gum: 33/34 - 51

Babando, Pete
Beehive: 45/63 - 2, 76, 151
Parkhurst: 51/52 - 51; 52/53 - 16

Babcock, Bob
O-Pee-Chee: 92/93 - 56PM
Topps: 92/93 - 56PM

Baby, John
O-Pee-Chee: 78/79 - 366; 79/80 - 357

Babych, David (Dave)
Bowman: 90/91 - 256; 92/93 - 119
Esso: 83/84 - 3E, 3F
Fleer: 92/93 - 218; 93/94 - 456PP
Funmate: 83/84 - 143
Kellogg's: 84 - 11
Kraft: 90/91 - 1
O-Pee-Chee: 81/82 - 358, 137SK; 82/83 - 375, 376, 207SK; 83/84 - 380, 163SK, 285SK, 286SK; 84/85 - 334, 287SK; 85/86 - 10, 249SK; 86/87 - 73, 50SK; 87/88 - 5, 208SK; 88/89 - 164, 267SK; 89/90 - 46, 265SK; 90/91 - 328; 92/93 - 213; 93/94 - 428
Panini: 87/88 - 40; 88/89 - 236; 89/90 - 225; 90/91 - 40; 92/93 - 35E, 35F
Parkhurst: 91/92 - 187E, 187F; 92/93 - 424, 424EI; 93/94 - 481, 481EI
PepsiCo: 80/81 - 121
Post: 81/82 - 26; 82/83 - 322
Pro Set: 90/91 - 99; 91/92 - 503E, 503F; 92/93 - 200
Score: 90/91 - 172A, 172C, 91 - 34T; 91/92 - 584B, 584C, 270PNE, 270PF; 92/93 - 212C, 212A, 201PNC, 201PNA
7-Eleven: 84/85 - 56
Topps: 81/82 - 1; 82/83 - 207SK; 83/84 - 163SK, 285SK, 286SK; 84/85 - 150; 85/86 - 10; 86/87 - 73; 87/88 - 5; 88/89 - 164; 89/90 - 46; 90/91 - 328; 92/93 - 138, 138GS, 120SC; 93/94 - 428C
Upper Deck: 90/91 - 194E, 194F; 93/94 - 376
Vachon Foods: 83/84 - 122

Babych, Wayne
O-Pee-Chee: 79/80 - 142; 80/81 - 281; 81/82 - 290, 130SK; 82/83 - 299, 201SK; 83/84 - 310; 84/85 - 181; 85/86 - 108, 103SK; 86/87 - 213
Post: 82/83 - 257
Topps: 79/80 - 142; 81/82 WN - 114; 82/83 - 201SK; 85/86 - 108

Baca, Jergus
O-Pee-Chee: 90/91 - 2PM; 91/92 - 131
Score: 90/91 - 101T
Topps: 91/92 - 131; 92/93 - 64, 64GS
Upper Deck: 91/92 - 425E, 425F

Backstrom, Ralph
Bazooka: 71/72 - 22
Beehive: 45/63 - 221; 64/67 - 97
Chex: 63/65 - 20
Coca Cola: 64/65 - 55; 65/66 - 55
Colgate: 70/71 - 21
Eddie Sargent: 72/73 - 88
O-Pee-Chee: 68/69 - 60; 69/70 166; 70/71 54; 71/72 - 108; 72/73 - 131
Parkhurst: 58/59 - 16; 59/60 - 29; 60/61 - 41; 61/62 - 39; 62/63 - 44; 63/64 - 24, 83; 92/93 - PR18; 93/94 - 77ML

Backstrom, Ralph (cont.)
- Post: 68/69 - 1
- Shirriff: 60/61 - 31; 61/62 - 114; 62/63 - 26; 68/69 - F8
- Topps: 64/65 - 78; 65/66 - 73; 66/67 - 75; 66/67 US - 6; 67/68 - 67; 68/69 - 60; 70/71 - 54; 71/72 - 108; 72/73 - 133
- Toronto Star: 57/67 - 59; 58/67 - 39
- Toronto Sun: 71/72 - 105
- Ultimate: 92 - 7(OSE), 7(OSF)
- York: 60/61 - 1; 61/62 - 24; 62/63 - 16; 63/64 - 27

Bailey, Ace (Irvine)
- Anonymous: 33/34 - 3
- Canada Starch: 35/40 - 66
- Can. Chew. Gum: 33/34 - 3
- Goudy Gum: 33 - 29
- Hall of Fame: 83 - 198, N2P; 87 - 198
- Hamilton Gum: 33/34 - 11
- Loblaws: 74/75 - 254
- O-Pee-Chee: 33/34 - 13
- Parkhurst: 55/56 - 30
- Quaker Oats: 55/56 - 30
- World Wide Gum: 33/34 - 22

Bailey, Bob
- Beehive: 45/63 - 375
- Parkhurst: 54/55 - 28
- Topps: 57/58 19

Bailey, Garnet
- Eddie Sargent: 70/71 - 13; 72/73 - 28
- Esso: 70/71 - 2
- O-Pee-Chee: 70/71 - 10; 72/73 - 191; 74/75 - 332; 75/76 - 284; 76/77 - 304; 77/78 - 196; 78/79 - 276
- Toronto Sun: 71/72 - 3
- Topps: 70/71 - 10; 75/76 - 284; 77/78 - 196

Bailey, Reid
- Post: 82/83 - 210

Bain, Donald
- Hall of Fame: 83 - 227, B1P; 87 - 227

Baker, Bill
- O-Pee-Chee: 83/84 - 240
- Post: 82/83 - 258

Baker, Hobey
- Hall of Fame: 83 - 17, B2P; 87 - 17
- HHFM: 92 - 6

Baker, Jamie
- Bowman: 91/92 - 136; 92/93 - 436
- Fleer: 92/93 - 360; 93/94 - 6
- Leaf: 93/94 - 134
- O-Pee-Chee: 92/93 - 41; 93/94 - 22
- Panini: 93/94 - 113E, 113IS
- Parkhurst: 92/93 - 353, 353EI; 93/94 - 459, 459EI
- Score: 91/92 - 348PNE, 348PNF; 93/94 - 57C, 57A
- Sega: 93/94 - 93
- Topps: 92/93 - 506, 506GS, 136SC; 93/94 - 22, 461SC, 461FD
- Upper Deck: 92/93 - 130, 464

Baker, Steve (Goalie)
- O-Pee-Chee: 80/81 - 346; 81/82 - 231

Balanger, Jesse
- Leaf: 93/94 - 278

Baldwin, Doug
- Quaker Oats: 45/54 - 57

Balfour, Earl
- Beehive: 45/63 - 77, 376
- Parkhurst: 54/55 - 25
- Shirriff: 60/61 - 68
- Topps: 58/59 - 37; 59/60 - 50; 61/62 - 3

Balfour, Murray
- Beehive: 45/63 - 78; 64/67 - 1
- Coca Cola: 64/65 - 1
- Shirriff: 60/61 - 65; 61/62 - 30
- Topps: 59/60 - 33; 60/61 - 12, 17ST; 61/62 - 33; 62/63 - 36; 63/64 - 35; 64/65 - 90

Ballard, Harold
- Hall of Fame: 83 - 63, E2P; 87 - 63

Balon, Dave
- Beehive: 45/63 - 223, 297A, 297B; 64/67 - 98
- Chex: 63/65 - 21
- Coca Cola: 64/65 - 56
- Colgate: 70/71 - 33
- Eddie Sargent: 70/71 - 119; 72/73 - 220
- Esso: 70/71 - 145
- O-Pee-Chee: 68/69 - 169; 69/70 - 191; 70/71 - 61; 71/72 - 229; 72/73 - 162
- Parkhurst: 63/64 - 38; 63/64 - 97
- Shirriff: 60/61 - 94; 68/69 - G15
- Topps: 62/63 - 56, 17HB; 64/65 - 37; 65/66 - 72; 66/67 - 74; 70/71 - 61; 72/73; - 117
- Toronto Star: 58/67 - 86; 64/65 - 25
- Toronto Sun: 71/72 - 168
- York: 63/64 - 33

Banks, Darren
- O-Pee-Chee: 92/93 - 118PM
- Parkhurst: 93/94 - 286, 286EI

Bannerman, Murray (Goalie)
- O-Pee-Chee: 81/82 - 68; 82/83; - 61; 83/84 - 97, 113SK, 164SK; 84/85 - 32, 135SK; 85/86 - 27, 27SK; 86/87 - 180
- Panini: 87/88 - 221
- Topps: 83/84 - 113SK, 164SK; 84/85 - 27; 85/86 - 27; 86/87 - 180

Bannister, Drew
- Donruss: 93/94 - 3JCC

Barahona, Ralph
- Upper Deck: 91/92 - 496E, 496F

Barber, Bill
- Funmate: 83/84 - 79
- Hockey Wit: 93/94 - 13
- Lipton Soup: 74/75 - 31
- Loblaws: 74/75 - 217
- McDonald's: 82/83 - 11
- O-Pee-Chee: 73/74 - 81; 74/75 - 8; 75/76 - 226; 76/77 - 178; 77/78 - 227; 78/79 - 176; 79/80 - 140; 80/81 - 200; 81/82 - 238, 247, 253, 155SK, 174SK; 82/83 - 244, 246, 247, 110SK, 170SK; 83/84 - 260, 5SK, 194SK; 84/85 - 156
- Panini: 90/91 - 259
- Parkhurst: 92/93 - 469, 469EI
- Post: 82/83 - 211
- Score: 90/91 - 356A, 356C
- Topps: 73/74 - 81; 74/75 - 8; 75/76 - 226; 76/77 - 178, 12PO; 77/78 - 227; 78/79 - 176; 79/80 - 140; 80/81 - 200; 81/82 - 2, 59, EN - 123; 82/83 - 110SK, 170SK; 83/84 - 5SK

Barber, Don
- Bowman: 90/91 - 179
- O-Pee-Chee: 90/91 - 53
- Pro Set: 90/91 - 558; 91/92 - 464E, 464F
- Score: 90/91 - 284A, 284C, 14T
- Topps: 90/91 - 53
- Upper Deck: 90/91 - 28E, 28F

Barilko, Bill
- Beehive: 45/63 - 415
- Quaker Oats: 45/54 - 58A, 58B
- Parkhurst: 51/52 - 52; 93/94 - PR35
- Pro Set: 91/92 - 340E, 340F

Barkley, Doug
- Beehive: 45/63 - 168, 169; 64/67 - 68
- Coca Cola: 64/65 - 37; 65/66 - 39
- Parkhurst: 63/64 - 60
- Topps: 64/65 - 9; 65/66 - 43
- York: 62/63 - 24; 63/64 - 46

Barlow, Bob
- Eddie Sargent: 70/71 - 93
- O-Pee-Chee: 69/70 - 196; 70/71 - 45
- Topps: 70/71 - 45

Barnaby, Matthew
- Donruss: 93/94 - 42
- Fleer: 93/94 - 13

Barnaby, Matthew (cont.)
- Leaf: 93/94 - 362
- O-Pee-Chee: 93/94 - 346
- Parkhurst: 92/93 - 483, 483EI; 93/94 - 296, 296EI
- Topps: 93/94 - 346, 321SC, 321FD
- Upper Deck: 93/94 - 439

Barnes, Norm
- O-Pee-Chee: 80/81 - 308; 81/82 - 67SK;

Barnes, Stu
- Bowman: 92/93 - 26
- Donruss: 93/94 - 377, 432
- Fleer: 93/94 - 345PP
- Leaf: 93/94 = 350
- O-Pee-Chee: 91/92 - 109PM; 92/93 - 39; 93/94 - 351
- Parkhurst: 91/92 - 419E, 419F; 93/94 - 226, 226EI
- Pro Set: 91/92 - 566E, 566F, 273PT
- Score: 90/91 - 391A, 391C; 91 - 80T; 91/92 - 630B, 630C, 319PNE, 319PNF; 92/93 - 319C, 319A; 93/94 - 380C, 380A
- Topps: 92/93 - 210, 210GS, 285SC; 93/94 - 351
- Upper Deck: 91/92 - 53E, 53F; 92/93 - 426; 93/94 - 94

Baron, Murray
- Bowman: 91/92 - 243; 92/93 - 409
- O-Pee-Chee: 91/92 - 373
- Pro Set: 91/92 - 472E, 472F
- Score: 90/91 - 399A, 399C; 91 - 27YS, 66T; 91/92 - 183A, 183B, 183C, 616B, 616C, 204PNE, 204PNF; 92/93 - 176C, 176A, 144PNC, 144PNA; 93/94 - 294C, 294A
- Topps: 91/92 - 373, 334SC; 92/93 - 354, 354GS, 194SC
- Upper Deck: 90/91 - 275E, 275F; 91/92 - 497E, 497F

Barr, David (Dave)
- Bowman: 90/91 - 231; 91/92 - 49
- Fleer: 93/94 - 320PP
- O-Pee-Chee: 86/87 - 237; 89/90 - 13, 250SK; 90/91 - 308; 91/92 - 147, 54PM
- Panini: 89/90 - 60
- Pro Set: 90/91 - 65; 91/92 - 65E, 65F
- Score: 91 - 47T; 91/92 - 187A, 187B, 187C, 597B, 597C; 92/93 - 315C, 315A
- Topps: 89/90 - 13; 90/91 - 308; 91/92 - 147, 141SC; 92/93 - 197, 197GS, 291SC
- Upper Deck: 90/91 - 257E, 257F

Barrasso, Tom (Goalie)
- Bowman: 90/91 - 209; 91/92 - 80; 92/93 - 250
- Donruss: 93/94 - 260
- Fleer: 92/93 - 162; 93/94 - 26, 187PP, 1N
- Frito-Lay: 88/89 - 2
- Highliner: 93/94 - 6
- Hockey Wit: 93/94 - 25
- Kraft: 93/94 - 53
- Leaf: 93/94 - 196, 9PW
- O-Pee-Chee: 84/85 - 18, 212, 375, 379, 205SK, 206SK, 227SK, 228SK; 85/86 - 105, 263, 55SK, 114SK, 179SK, 189SK; 86/87 - 91, 45SK; 87/88 - 78, 148SK; 88/89 - 107, 1NS, 259SK; 89/90 - 36, 235SK; 90/91 - 65; 91/92 - 402, 103PM; 92/93 - 340; 93/94 - 175, 204, 446, 501, 79SC, 79FD
- Panini: 87/88 - 22; 88/89 - 219; 89/90 - 312; 90/91 - 134; 91/92 - 271; 92/93 - 219E, 219F; 93/94 - 88E, 141E, 141IS
- Parkhurst: 91/92 - 139E, 139F; 92/93 - 134, 134EI; 93/94 - 157, 157EI; 94/95 - 182,182EI
- Pro Set: 90/91 - 227, P1; 91/92 - 186E, 186F, 96PT, PC3PL, 22PK; 92/93 - 145
- Score: 90/91 - 121A, 121C; 91/92 - 225A, 225B, 225C, 44PNE, 44PNF; 92/93 - 70C, 70A, 298PNC,

Barrasso, Tom (Goalie) (cont.)
Score: 298PNA; 93/94 - 225C, 225A, 483C, 483A, 1DT, 3PCE
Season's: 92/93 - 36
Sega: 93/94 - 108
7-Eleven: 84/85 - 3
Topps: 84/85 - 14, 158; 85/86 - 105, 12SK; 86/87 - 91; 87/88 - 78; 88/89 - 107; 89/90 - 36; 90/91 - 65; 91/92 - 402, 155SC; 92/93 - 503, 503GS, 416SC; 93/94 - 175, 204, 446, 501, 11BG, 79SC, 79FD, 12MP
Upper Deck: 90/91 - 121E, 121F; 91/92 - 116E, 116F; 92/93 - 243; 93/94 - 45

Barrett, Fred
Esso: 70/71 - 109
Loblaws: 74/75 - 146
O-Pee-Chee: 71/72 - 128; 73/74 - 264; 74/75 - 234; 75/76 - 124; 76/77 - 249; 77/78 - 291; 78/79 - 185; 80/81 - 253
Post: 82/83 - 130
Topps: 74/75 - 234; 75/76 - 124; 76/77 - 249; 78/79 - 185; 80/81 - 253
Toronto Sun: 71/72 - 126

Barrett, John
O-Pee-Chee: 82/83 - 80; 83/84 - 117; 84/85 - 49
Post: 82/83 - 65

Barrie, Doug
Esso: 70/71 - 22
O-Pee-Chee: 71/72 - 22
Topps: 71/72 - 22
Toronto Sun: 71/72 - 23

Barry, Len
Parkhurst: 93/94 - 451, 451EI

Barry, Marty
Anonymous: 33/34 - 38
Amal. Press: 35/36 - 1
Beehive: 34/44 - 88, 134
Canada Starch: 35/40 - 62; 195
Diamond: 33/35 - 2
Hall of Fame: 83 - O3, 214; 87 - 214
O-Pee-Chee: 35/36 - 81; 39/40 - 57; 39/40 - 57
World Wide Gum: 33/34 - 27; 36/37 - 4

Barry, Ray
Beehive: 45/63 - 3
Parkhurst: 51/52 - 32

Bartlett, Jim
Shirriff: 60/61 - 113
Topps: 58/59 - 26; 59/60 - 51

Basalgin, Andrei
O-Pee-Chee: 91/92 - 49R

Bassen, Bob
Bowman: 91/92 - 379; 92/93 - 378
Donruss: 93/94 - 476
Fleer: 92/93 - 182
O-Pee-Chee: 91/92 - 51; 92/93 - 139
Panini: 91/92 - 29; 93/94 - 163E, 163IS
Parkhurst: 91/92 - 379E, 379F; 93/94 - 445, 445EI; 94/95 - 184, 184EI
Pro Set: 90/91 - 520; 91/92 - 221E, 221F
Score: 91/92 - 179A, 179B, 179C; 92/93 - 132C, 132A, 203PNC, 203PNA; 93/94 - 279C, 279A
Topps: 91/92 - 51, 367SC; 92/93 - 454, 454GS, 176SC
Upper Deck: 91/92 - 319E, 319F; 92/93 - 181; 93/94 - 2

Bassen, Hank (Goalie)
Beehive: 45/63 - 153; 64/67 - 62
Coca Cola: 65/66 - 38
Parkhurst: 62/63 - 19
Shirriff: 61/62 - 80
Topps: 65/66 - 106; 66/67 - 107

Bastien, Baz (Aldridge) (Goalie)
CKAC Radio: 43/47 - 14
Quaker Oats: 45/54 - 59

Bastien, Morris
World Wide Gum: 36/37 - 131

Bathe, Frank
O-Pee-Chee: 80/81 - 389

Bathgate, Andy
Bauer: 68/69 - 1
Beehive: 45/63 - 298A, 298B, 378; 64/67 - 63; 152
Coca Cola: 64/65 - 92A, 92B, 96; 65/66 - 91
Eddie Sargent: 70/71 - 173
Esso: 70/71 - 181
Hall of Fame: 83 - O4, 215; 87 - 215
O-Pee-Chee: 68/69 - 104; 70/71 - 207
Parkhurst: 53/54 - 56; 92/93 - PR22; 93/94 - 90ML, 173ML
Shirriff: 60/61 - 89; 61/62 - 88; 62/63 - 48; 68/69 - K5
TCMA: 1981 - 8
Topps: 54/55 - 11; 57/58 - 60; 58/59 - 21; 59/60 - 34; 60/61 - 45, 9ST; 61/62 - 53; 62/63 - 52, 18HB; 63/64 - 52; 64/65 - 86; 65/66 - 48; 66/67 - 44; 68/69 - 104
Toronto Star: 57/67 - 58, 102; 58/67 - 23, 78; 63/64 - 26; 64/65 - 37
Ultimate: 92 - 18(OSE), 74(OSE), 18(OSF), 74(OSF)
Zellers: 93/94 - 1, 1A

Barrault, Doug
Fleer: 93/94 - 88PP
Score: 93/94 - 457C, 457A

Bauer, Bobby
Beehive: 33/44 - 1
O-Pee-Chee: 39/49 - 99

Bauman, Gary (Goalie)
O-Pee-Chee: 68/69 - 145

Baumgartner, Ken
Fleer: 92/93 - 416; 93/94 - 448PP
O-Pee-Chee: 90/91 - 414; 91/92 - 316
Panini: 92/93 - 85E, 85F
Parkhurst: 92/93 - 413, 413EI; 93/94 - 207, 207EI
Pro Set: 90/91 - 178; 91/92 - 432E, 432F
Score: 90/91 - 265A, 265C; 91/92 - 148A, 148B, 148C, 239PNE, 239PNF; 92/93 - 35C, 35A
Topps: 91/92 - 316; 92/93 - 217, 217GS, 103SC
Upper Deck: 90/91 - 439E, 439F; 91/92 - 402E, 402F

Baun, Bob
Beehive: 45/63 - 379; 64/67 - 153A, 153B
Chex: 63/65 - 41
Coca Cola: 64/65 - 93; 65/66 - 92
Colgate: 70/71 - 66
Dad's Cookies: 70/71 - 124
Eddie Sargent: 70/71 - 64; 72/73 - 199
Esso: 70/71 - 217
O-Pee-Chee: 68/69 - 24; 69/70 - 57; 69/70 - 1QS; 70/71 - 223; 71/72 - 196; 72/73 - 66
Parkhurst: 57/58 TOR - 20; 58/59 - 15; 59/60 - 21; 60/61 - 11; 61/62 - 11; 62/63 - 3; 63/64 - 18, 78; 92/93 - PR12; 93/94 - 123ML
Shirriff: 60/61 - 7; 61/62 - 50; 62/63 - 19 68/69 - C13
Topps: 64/65 - 57; 65/66 - 13; 66/67 - 83; 68/69 - 24; 69/70 - 57; 70/71 - 24; 72/73 - 134
Toronto Star: 57/67 - 103, 145; 63/64 - 30; 64/65 - 38
Toronto Sun: 71/72 - 254
Ultimate: 92 - 30(OSE), 93(OSE), 30(OSF), 93(OSF)
York: 60/61 - 21; 61/62 - 1; 63/64 - 7

Bautin, Sergei
Donruss: 93/94 - 378
Fleer: 92/93 - 440; 93/94 - 10, 268PP
Leaf: 93/94 - 242
O-Pee-Chee: 92/93 - 84PM; 93/94 - 332
Parkhurst: 92/93 - 435, 435EI
Score: 93/94 - 351C, 351A
Topps: 93/94 - 332
Upper Deck: 92/93 - 337, 499; 93/94 - 514

Bawa, Robin
Topps: 93/94 - 445SC, 445FD

Baxter, Paul
Derniere: 72/84 - 76, 93
O-Pee-Chee: 79/80 - 372; 82/83 - 238
Post: 82/83 - 225
Vachon Foods: 83/84 - 1

Bawlf, Nick
Imperial Tobacco: 10/11 - 18

Beattie, Red (John)
Anonymous: 33/34 - 35
Beehive: 34/44 - 2, 214
Diamond: 33/35 - 3
World Wide Gum: 33/34 - 29

Beaudin, Norm
O-Pee-Chee: 70/71 - 48; 72/73 - 290
Topps: 70/71 - 48

Beaufait, Mark
Fleer: 93/94 - 498PP
Topps: 93/94 - 6US

Beaupre, Donald (Don) (Goalie)
Bowman: 90/91 - 72; 91/92 - 304; 92/93 - 222, 297
Fleer: 92/93 - 229; 93/94 - 28, 463PP
O-Pee-Chee: 81/82 - 159, 89SK, 149SK; 82/83 - 163, 193SK; 83/84 - 166, 122SK; 84/85 - 94; 85/86 - 142; 86/87 - 89; 87/88 - 132, 51SK; 88/89 - 42, 196SK; 90/91 - 253, O/BB; 91/92 - 505; 92/93 - 28; 93/94 - 304, 71SC, 71FD
Panini: 87/88 - 289; 88/89 - 84; 90/91 - 158; 91/92 - 201; 92/93 - 159E, 159F; 93/94 - 33E, 33F
Parkhurst: 91/92 - 416E, 416F; 92/93 - 197, 197EI; 93/94 - 225, 225EI
Pro Set: 90/91 - 307; 91/92 - 257E, 601E, 257F, 139PT, 601F; 92/93 - 206
Score: 90/91 - 215A, 215C; 91/92 - 185A, 185B, 185C, 148PNE, 148PNF; 92/93 - 320C, 320A, 48PNC, 48PNA, 268PNC, 268PNA; 93/94 - 58C, 58A
Season's: 92/93 - 49
Sega: 93/94 - 156
Topps: 81/82 WN - 103; 82/83 - 193SK; 83/84 - 122SK; 84/85 - 70; 85/86 - 142; 86/87 - 89; 87/88 - 132; 88/89 - 42; 90/91 - 253; 90/91 - O/BB; 91/92 - 505, 246SC; 92/93 - 195, 195GS, 270SC; 93/94 - 304, 71SC, 71FD
Upper Deck: 90/91 - 217E, 217F; 91/92 - 197E, 197F; 92/93 - 23, 310; 93/94 - 123

Beauregard, Stephane (Goalie)
Bowman: 92/93 - 405
Fleer: 92/93 - 369
O-Pee-Chee: 90/91 - 223; 92/93 - 88PM
Parkhurst: 91/92 - 426E, 426F
Pro Set: 90/91 - 648
Score: 90/91 - 282A, 282C; 91/92 - 638B, 638C; 92/93 - 402C, 402A
Topps: 90/91 - 223; 92/93 - 62, 62GS, 304SC
Upper Deck: 90/91 - 415E, 415F; 92/93 - 536

Beck, Barry
Funmate: 83/84 - 86
Kellogg's: 84 - 6
McDonald's: 82/83 - 27
O-Pee-Chee: 78/79 - 121; 79/80 - 35; 80/81 - 90, 170; 81/82 - 220, 230, 168SK; 82/83 - 219, 220, 135SK; 83/84 - 241, 210SK; 84/85 - 140, 100SK; 85/86 - 138, 82SK
Post: 81/82 - 14/ 82/83 - 194
7-Eleven: 84/85 - 34
Topps: 78/79 - 121; 79/80 - 35; 80/81 - 90, 170; 81/82 - 3, EN 124; 82/83 - 135SK; 83/84 210SK; 84/85 - 105; 85/86 - 138

Beckett, Bob
Parkhurst: 93/94 - 13ML

Bedard, Jim (Goalie)
- Beehive: 45/63 - 79
- O-Pee-Chee: 78/79 - 243; 79/80 - 62
- Topps: 78/79 - 243; 79/80 - 62

Bednarski, John
- O-Pee-Chee: 76/77 - 231
- Topps: 76/77 - 231

Beers, Bob
- Bowman: 90/91 - 34
- Donruss: 93/94 - 425
- Fleer: 92/93 - 407; 93/94 - 18, 227PP, 338PP
- O-Pee-Chee: 90/91 - 113; 93/94 - 44
- Panini: 93/94 - 217E, 217F
- Parkhurst: 92/93 - 401, 401EI
- Pro Set: 91/92 - 520E, 520F
- Score: 90/91 - 385A, 385C; 91/92 - 326PNE, 326PNF; 93/94 - 369C, 369A
- Sega: 93/94 - 127
- Topps: 90/91 - 113; 93/94 - 44
- Upper Deck: 90/91 - 125E, 125F; 91/92 - 490E, 490F

Beers, Eddy
- O-Pee-Chee: 83/84 - 76, 141SK; 84/85 - 219, 354, 243SK; 85/86 - 144, 214SK; 86/87 - 238
- Topps: 83/84 - 141SK; 84/85 - 24; 85/86 - 144
- Vachon Foods: 83/84 - 2

Belanger, Jesse
- Donruss: 93/94 - 123
- Fleer: 93/94 - 2RS, 89PP
- O-Pee-Chee: 93/94 - 451
- Parkhurst: 92/93 - 488, 488EI; 93/94 - 346, 346EI, CC15; 94/95 - 86, 284, 86EI, 284EI, V31
- Score: 93/94 - 454C, 454A
- Topps: 93/94 - 451C

Belanger, Raymond
- La Presse: 27/32 - 40

Belanger, Yves (Goalie)
- O-Pee-Chee: 76/77 - 168; 77/78 - 367; 78/79 - 44
- Topps: 76/77 - 168; 78/79 - 44

Belfour, Ed (Goalie)
- Bowman: 90/91 - 7; 91/92 - 390; 92/93 - 90, 199
- Donruss: 93/94 - 64
- Fleer: 92/93 - 32, 9AS; 93/94 - 22, 1AW, 10AS, 46PP, 2N
- Gillete: 91/92 - 18
- Highliner: 93/94 - 2
- Hockey Wit: 93/94 - 18
- Kraft: 93/94 - 1
- Leaf: 1993/94 - 62, 10AS, 6PW
- O-Pee-Chee: 91/92 - 4, 20, 263, 271, 288, 425, 518, 519, 19PM; 92/93 - 81; 93/94 - 60, 95, 16BG, 99SC, 144SC, 150SC, 99FD, 144FD, 150F
- Panini: 91/92 - 9, 337; 92/93 - 3E, 284E, 3F, 284F; 93/94 - 140E, 155E, 140IS, 155IS
- Parkhurst: 91/92 - 30E, 218E, 30F, 218F; 92/93 - 28, 461, 28EI, 461EI; 93/94 - 44, 44EI; 94/95 -41, 41EI
- Pro Set: 90/91 - 598; 91/92 - AC1, AC19, 43E, 321E, 600E, 43F, 321F, 26PT, 600F; 92/93 - 33
- Score: 90/91 - 103T; 91 - 6P, 32YS; 91/92 - 290A, 348A, 410A, 411A, 430A, 431A, 433A, 300B, 301B, 320B, 321B, 323B, 378B, 510B, 300C, 301C, 320C, 321C, 323C, 378C, 510C, 9HC, 127PNE, 388PNE, 400PNE, 127PNF, 388PNF, 400PNF; 92/93 - 178C, 178A, 118PNC, 118PNA, 265PNC, 265PNA, 1CTP, 1ATP; 93/94 - 70C, 70A, 485C, 485A, 42PNC, 42PNA, 42CAS, 42AAS
- Season's: 92/93 - 3
- Sega: 93/94 - 30, 187

Belfour, Ed (Goalie) (cont.)
- Topps: 91/92 - P/C, 4, 20, 263, 271, 288, 425, 518, 519, 333SC, 1SCM, 2SCM; 92/93 - 22GS, 243SC, 333SC; 92/93 - 22, 22GS; 93/94 - 60, 95, 14BG, 99SC, 144SC, 150SC, 99FD, 144FD, 150FD, 1AS
- Upper Deck: 90/91 - 55E, 55F; 91/92 - AW2E, 39E, 164E, 625E, 39F, 164F, 625F, AW2F; 92/93 - 203, 19AS; 93/94 - 147

Belhumeur, Michel (Goalie)
- O-Pee-Chee: 72/73 - 273; 74/75 - 153; 75/76 - 232; 76/77 - 296
- Topps: 74/75 - 153; 75/76 - 232

Beliveau, Jean
- Beehive: 45/63 - 223; 64/67 - 99
- Chex: 63/65 - 22A, 22B
- Coca Cola: 64/65 - 57; 65/66 - 56
- Dad's Cookies: 70/71 - 73
- Derniere: 72/84 - 26, 63
- Eddie Sargent: 70/71 - 108
- El Producto: 62/63 - 1LS, 1
- Esso: 70/71 - 127; 88/89 - 1
- Hall of Fame: 83 - C1P, 31; 87 - 31
- Hockey Wit: 93/94 - 23
- La Patrie: 51/54 - 7
- O-Pee-Chee: 68/69 - 166, 7PS; 69/70 - 10, 220, 1ST, 5QS; 70/71 - 55, 21DE, 1SS; 71/72 - 263
- Parkhurst: 53/54 - 27; 54/55 - 3; 55/56 - 44; 57/58 MON - 3; 58/59 - 34; 59/60 - 6; 60/61 - 49; 61/62 - 45; 62/63 - 39; 63/64 - 30, 89; 92/93 - PR30; 93/94 - 64ML, 138ML, 149ML, 150ML, 156ML, 157ML, 172ML
- Post: 67/68 1L, 1S; 68/69 - 2
- Quaker Oats: 45/54 - 2; 55/56 - 44
- Shirriff: 60/61 - 30; 61/62 - 102; 62/63 - 32; 68/69 - F6
- TCMA: 1981 - 11
- Topps: 64/65 - 33; 65/66 - 6; 66/67 - 73, 127; 66/67 US - 31; 67/68 - 74; 68/69 - 61; 69/70 - 10; 70/71 - 55, 1SK;
- Toronto Star: 57/67 - 110, 112, 116, 135; 58/67 - 43, 104; 63/64 - 18; 64/65 - 26
- York: 60/61 - 2; 61/62 - 10; 62/63 - 8; 63/64 - 26

Bell, Bruce
- O-Pee-Chee: 85/86 - 231, 142SK
- Panini: 87/88 - 308

Bell, Gordie (Goalie)
- Quaker Oats: 45/54 - 60

Bellefeuille, Pete
- Anonymous: 26/27 - 61

Bellows, Brian
- Bowman: 90/91 - 182; 91/92 - 129; 92/93 - 200, 260
- Donruss: 93/94 - 170
- Fleer: 92/93 - 100, 324; 93/94 - 4, 124PP
- Frito-Lay: 88/89 - 3
- Funmate: 83/84- 58
- Hockey Wit: 93/94 - 11
- Kraft: 90/91 - 38
- Leaf: 93/94 - 76
- O-Pee-Chee: 83/84 - 165, 167, 142SK; 84/85 - 95, 359, 44SK, 45SK; 85/86 - 50, A/BB, 41SK; 86/87 - 75, 167SK; 87/88 - 94, 53SK; 88/89 - 95, 203SK; 89/90 - 177, 200SK; 90/91 - 70, 200; 90/91 - 3PM; 91/92 - 110; 92/93 - 384, 75PM; 93/94 - 202, 156SC, 156FD
- Panini: 87/88 - 296; 88/89 - 89; 89/90 - 105; 90/91 - 257; 91/ 92 - 108; 92/93 - 88E, 88F; 93/94 - 15E, 15F
- Parkhurst: 91/92 - 79E, 79F; 92/93 - 87, 87EI; 93/94 - 371, 371EI; 94/95 - 112, 112EI

Bellows, Brian (cont.)
- Pro Set: 90/91 - 130A, 130B; 91/92 - 109E, 109F, 59PT, 13PK
- Score: 90/91 - 7A, 7C, 322A, 322C, 3HR; 91/92 - 160A, 160B, 16JC, 129PNE, 129PNF; 92/93 - 335C, 335A, 325PNC, 325PNA; 93/94 - 4C, 4A, 4PCA
- Sega: 93/94 - 71
- 7-Eleven: 84/85 - 27
- Topps: 83/84 - 142SK; 84/85 - 71; 85/86 - 50, A/BB; 86/87 - 75; 87/88 - 94; 88/89 - 95; 89/90 - 177; 90/91 - 70, 200, 15SL; 91/92 - 110, 87SC, 293SC; 92/93 - 240, 240GS, 293SC; 93/94 - 202, 156SC, 156FD
- Upper Deck: 90/91 - 126E, 126F; 91/92 - 236E, 236F; 92/93 - 172, 471, 636, G1; 93/94 - 390

Belov, Oleg
- Upper Deck: 93/94 - 274

Belushi, James
- Pro-Set: 91/92 - 300PT

Benedict, Clint (Goalie)
- Anonymous: 26/27 - 95
- Champ's: 24/25 - 28
- Hall of Fame: 83 - H1P, 107; 87 - 107
- Imperial Tobacco: 12/13 - 3
- La Presse: 27/32 - 23
- Maple Crispette: 24/25 - 2
- Wm. Paterson: 23/24 - 7; 24/25 - 32

Bennett, Adam
- Parkhurst: 93/94 - 334, 334EI
- Upper Deck: 93/94 - 237

Bennett, Curt
- Loblaws: 74/75 - 1
- O-Pee-Chee: 75/76 - 8; 73/74 - 149; 74/75 - 33; 76/77 - 202; 77/78 - 97; 78/79 - 31; 79/80 - 344
- Topps: 73/74 - 152; 74/75 - 33; 75/76 - 8; 76/77 - 202; 77/78 - 97; 78/79 - 31

Bennett, Harvey
- O-Pee-Chee: 77/78 - 282; 78/79 - 163
- Topps: 78/79 - 163

Bennett, Eric (Ric)
- O-Pee-Chee: 90/91 - 252
- Score: 90/91 - 400A, 400C
- Topps: 90/91 - 252
- Upper Deck: 90/91 - 540E, 540F

Benning, Brian
- Bowman: 92/93 - 39
- Donruss: 93/94 - 129
- Fleer: 92/93 - 151; 93/94 - 3, 90PP
- Leaf: 93/94 - 328
- O-Pee-Chee: 87/88 - 122, 2HL, 124SK; 88/89 - 174, 18SK; 89/90 - 86, 24SK; 90/91 - 365; 91/92 - 359; 92/93 - 68
- Panini: 88/89 - 101; 89/90 - 124
- Parkhurst: 92/93 - 125, 284, 125EI; 284EI; 93/94 - 343, 343EI
- Pro Set: 90/91 - 114; 91/92 - 398E, 398F, 182PT; 92/93 - 135
- Score: 90/91 - 306A; 91/92 - 186A, 186B, 186C, 402PNE, 402PNF; 92/93 - 133C, 133A, 45PNC, 45PNA; 93/94 - 64C, 64A
- Topps: 87/88 - 122; 88/89 - 174; 89/90 - 86; 90/91 - 365; 91/92 - 359; 92/93 - 250, 250GS, 91SC
- Upper Deck: 91/92 - 415E, 415F; 92/93 - 301; 93/94 - 496

Benning, Jim
- O-Pee-Chee: 82/83 - 317, 64SK; 83/84 - 326; 84/85 - 296, 21SK; 85/86 - 250, 16SK; 87/88 - 260, 197SK; 88/89 - 58SK; 90/91 - 455
- Panini: 88/89 - 133
- Post: 82/83 - 275
- Pro Set: 90/91 - 292; 92/93 - 181
- Topps: 82/83 - 64SK

Benning, Jim (cont.)
Vachon Foods: 83/84 - 82

Benoit, Joe
Beehive: 34/44 - 135
CKAC Radio: 43/47 - 30
O-Pee-Chee: 40/41 - 121
Quaker Oats: 45/54 - 3

Benson, Bill
Beehive: 33/44 - 215; 45/63 - 90
O-Pee-Chee: 40/41 - 135

Bentley, Doug
Beehive: 34/44 - 39; 45/63 - 80
Hall of Fame: 83 - 77, F1P; 87 - 77
Parkhurst: 51/52 - 48

Bentley, Max
Beehive: 34/44 - 40; 45/63 - 299, 380
Hall of Fame: 83 - 32, C2P; 87 - 32
O-Pee-Chee: 40/41 - 131
Parkhurst: 51/52 - 81; 52/53 - 95; 53/54 - 55
Quaker Oats: 45/54 - 61A, 61B, 61C

Beranek, Josef
Bowman: 92/93 - 100
Donruss: 93/94 - 247
Fleer: 92/93 - 56; 93/94 - 17, 177PP
Leaf: 93/94 - 103
O-Pee-Chee: 91/92 - 149PM; 92/93 - 178; 93/94 - 467, 69SC, 69FD
Panini: 92/93 - I(E), I(F)
Parkhurst: 91/92 - 47E, 47F; 92/93 - 360, 360EI; 93/94 - 153, 153EI; 94/95 - 166, 166EI
Pro Set: 91/92 - 534E, 534F, 255PT
Score: 91/92 - 303PNE, 303PNF; 92/93 - 105C, 105A, 208PNC, 208PNA; 93/94 - 439C, 439A
Topps: 92/93 - 177, 177GS, 214SC; 93/94 - 467C, 69SC, 69FD
Upper Deck: 91/92 - 17E, 17F, 595E, 595F; 92/93 - 196, E11; 93/94 - 15

Berdichevsky, Lev
O-Pee-Chee: 91/92 - 50R

Berehowsky, Drake
Donruss: 93/94 - 336
Fleer: 92/93 - 417; 93/94 - 90, 239PP
Humpty Dumpty: 92/93 - 1(II)
O-Pee-Chee: 91/92 - 70; 92/93 - 131PM; 93/94 - 69
Parkhurst: 93/94 - 199, 199EI
Score: 90/91 - 434A, 434C; 91/92 - 385A, 275B, 275C, 231PNC, 231PNA; 93/94 - 355C, 355A
Topps: 91/92 - 70; 93/94 - 69,331SC, 331FD
Upper Deck: 90/91 - 361E, 361F; 92/93 - 415; 93/94 - 20

Berenson, Gordon (Red)
Beehive: 45/63 - 224A, 224B, 248; 64/67 - 100
Chex: 63/65 - 23
Colgate: 70/71 - 24
Dad's Cookies: 70/71 - 114
Eddie Sargent: 70/71 - 177; 71/72 - 51; 72/73 - 73
Esso: 70/71 - 199
Lipton Soup: 74/75 - 25
Loblaws: 74/75 - 91
O-Pee-Chee: 68/69 - 114; 69/70 - 20, 2ST, 16QS; 70/71 - 103, 25DE, 2SS; 71/72 - 91, 10PT; 72/73 - 123, 7CS; 73/74 - 10; 74/75 - 19; 75/76 - 22; 76/77 - 236; 77/78 - 107; 78/79 - 218
Parkhurst: 63/64 - 26, 85
Shirriff: 62/63 - 42; 68/69 - L4
Topps: 64/65 - 61; 65/66 - 9; 66/67 - 92; 66/67 US - 10; 67/68 - 24; 68/69 - 114; 69/70 - 20; 70/71 - 103, 2SK; 71/72 - 91; 72/73 - 95; 73/74 - 174; 74/75 - 19; 75/76 - 22; 76/77 - 236; 77/78 - 107; 78/79 - 218
Toronto Star: 64/65 - 27
Toronto Sun: 71/72 - 84
York: 63/64 - 36

Berezan, Perry
Bowman: 92/93 - 105
O-Pee-Chee: 90/91 - 357; 91/92 - 485; 92/93 - 182
Panini: 89/90 - 110
Parkhurst: 91/92 - 381E, 381F
Pro Set: 90/91 - 459; 91/92 - 487E, 487F
Score: 90/91 - 379A, 379C; 91 - 94T; 91/92 - 527B, 527C, 287PNE, 287PNF; 92/93 - 169C, 169A, 148PNC, 148PNA
Topps: 90/91 - 357; 91/92 - 485, 227SC; 92/93 - 342, 342GS, 441SC
Upper Deck: 92/93 - 451

Berg, Bill
Bowman: 91/92 - 216
Leaf: 93/94 - 287
O-Pee-Chee: 91/92 - 122
Parkhurst: 93/94 - 472, 472EI
Pro Set: 91/92 - 145E, 145F
Score: 91/92 - 541B, 541C
Topps: 91/92 - 122, 385SC

Bergeron, Jean-Claude
O-Pee-Chee: 90/91 - 4PM
Panini: 93/94 - 220E, 220F
Pro Set: 90/91 - 614
Upper Deck: 90/91 - 408E, 408F

Bergeron, Michel
Derniere: 72/84 - 139
O-Pee-Chee: 76/77 - 71; 77/78 - 159; 78/79 - 273
Topps: 76/77 - 71; 77/78 - 159

Bergevin, Marc
Durivage: 92/93 - 30
Fleer: 92/93 - 200
O-Pee-Chee: 89/90 - 249; 93/94 - 373, 154SC, 154FD
Pro Set: 91/92 - 397E, 397F, 176PT
Score: 92/93 - 404C, 404A, 385PNC, 385PNA; 93/94 - 363C. 363A
Topps: 92/93 - 61, 61GS, 174SC; 93/94 - 373, 154SC, 154FD

Bergland, Tim
Bowman: 91/92 - 297
O-Pee-Chee: 90/91 - 507; 91/92 - 34
Parkhurst: 91/92 - 409E, 409F
Pro Set: 90/91 - 550; 91/92 - 507E, 507F
Topps: 91/92 - 34, 351SC; 92/93 - 244, 244GS, 127SC

Berglund, Bo
O-Pee-Chee: 84/85 - 276
Vachon Foods: 83/84 - 61

Bergman, Gary
Bauer: 68/69 - 2
Beehive: 64/67 - 64
Coca Cola: 64/65 - 38; 65/66 - 40
Colgate: 70/71 - 73
Dad's Cookies: 70/71 - 45
Eddie Sargent: 70/71 - 49; 71/72 - 54; 72/73 - 79
Esso: 70/71 - 73
Loblaws: 74/75 - 147
Mac's Milk: 73/74 - 1
O-Pee-Chee: 68/69 - 25; 69/70 - 58; 70/71 - 154; 71/72 - 119; 72/73 - 164, 8CS; 73/74 - 65; 75/76 - 236
Shirriff: 68/69 - C1
Topps: 64/65 - 8; 65/66 - 107; 66/67 - 47; 66/67 US - 47; 67/68 - 47; 68/69 - 25; 69/70 - 58; 71/72 - 119; 72/73 - 49; 73/74 - 65; 75/76 - 236; 76/77 - 159
Toronto Sun: 71/72 - 85
Ultimate: 92 - 67(OSE), 67(OSF)

Bergman, Thommie
Loblaws: 74/75 - 92
O-Pee-Chee: 73/74 - 204; 74/75 - 365; 79/80 - 148
Topps: 79/80 - 148

Berlinquette, Louis
Anonymous: 1926/27 - 47
Champ's: 24/25 - 29
Maple Crispette: 24/25 - 30
Wm. Paterson: 24/25 - 41

Bernhardt, Timothy (Tim) (Goalie)
O-Pee-Chee: 85/86 - 166, 9SK

Bernier, Art
Imperial Tobacco: 10/11 - 25, 37L; 11/12 - 37; 12/13 - 6

Bernier, Serge
Bazooka: 71/72 - 24
Deniere: 72/84 - 53, 91
Eddie Sargent: 72/73 - 97
Esso: 70/71 - 164
O-Pee-Chee: 71/72 - 19; 72/73 - 153; 79/80 - 47; 80/81 - 309
PepsiCo: 80/81 - 61
Topps: 71/72 - 19; 72/73 - 36; 79/80 - 47
Toronto Sun: 71/72 - 189

Berry, Bob
Eddie Sargent: 72/73 - 98
Esso: 70/71 - 91
Kraft: 93/94 - 31
Loblaws: 74/75 - 127
O-Pee-Chee: 71/72 - 76; 72/73 - 9; 73/74 - 175; 74/75 - 18; 75/76 - 196; 76/77 - 300; 77/78 - 268
Topps: 71/72 - 76; 72/73 - 21; 73/74 - 172; 74/75 - 18; 75/76 - 196

Berry, Brad
Parkhurst: 92/93 - 312, 312EI

Berthiaume, Daniel (Goalie)
Bowman: 91/92 - 190; 92/93 - 140
Fleer: 92/93 - 361; 93/94 - 54
O-Pee-Chee: 87/88 - 217, 3HL, 249SK; 88/89 - 142, 149SK; 89/90 - 296; 90/91 - 247; 90/91 - 5PM; 91/92 - 313
Panini: 87/88 - 356; 88/89 - 148
Parkhurst: 92/93 - 359, 359EI
Pro Set: 90/91 - 454
Score: 90/91 - 73T; 91/92 - 132A, 132B, 132C, 165PNE, 165PNF
Topps: 88/89 - 142; 90/91 - 247; 91/92 - 313, 290SC; 92/93 - 505, 505GS, 101SC
Upper Deck: 90/91 - 381E, 381F, 412E, 412F; 91/92 - 150E, 150F

Berube, Craig
Leaf: 93/94 - 314
O-Pee-Chee: 90/91 - 448; 91/92 - 47PM; 92/93 - 147
Parkhurst: 91/92 - 246E, 246F
Pro Set: 90/91 - 498; 91/92 - 495E, 495F
Score: 91 - 28T; 91/92 - 578B, 578C; 92/93 - 258C, 258A
Topps: 92/93 - 208, 208GS, 458SC
Upper Deck: 90/91 - 450E, 450F

Bes, Jeff
Upper Deck: 93/94 - 255

Bester, Allan (Goalie)
Bowman: 90/91 - 154
O-Pee-Chee: 84/85 - 297, 20SK; 87/88 - 236, 162SK; 89/90 - 271, 169SK; 90/91 - 32
Panini: 87/88 - 323; 88/89 - 116; 89/90 - 139
Pro Set: 90/91 - 275
Score: 90/91 - 27A, 27C
Topps: 90/91 - 32
Upper Deck: 90/91 - 241E, 241F

Bets, Maxim
Parkhurst: 94/95 - 10, 10EI, V37

Beukeboom, Jeff
Bowman: 91/92 - 110; 92/93 - 347
Fleer: 92/93 - 351; 93/94 - 389PP
O-Pee-Chee: 90/91 - 471; 91/92 - 284; 92/93 - 237; 93/94 - 54, 7SC, 7FD
Panini: 88/89 - 56
Parkhurst: 91/92 - 341E, 341F
Pro Set: 90/91 - 439; 91/92 - 444E, 444F, 206PT
Score: 91/92 - 253B, 253C, 229PNE, 229PNF; 92/93 - 137C, 137A, 112PNC, 112PNA; 93/94 - 94C, 94A
Topps: 91/92 - 284, 350SC; 92/93 - 57GS,

Beukeboom, Jeff (cont.)
Topps: 129SC; 92/93 - 57, 57GS; 93/94 - 54, 7SC, 7FD
Upper Deck: 91/92 - 394E, 394F; 92/93 - 161

Beveridge, Bill (Goalie)
Anonymous: 33/34 - 25
Beehive: 34/44 - 189
Canada Starch: 35/40 - 122
Diamond: 36/39 - 3(I)
O-Pee-Chee: 34/35 - 54; 37/38 - 161
World Wide Gum: 33/34 - 60; 36/37 - 82

Beverley, Nick
O-Pee-Chee: 72/73 - 281; 73/74 - 239; 75/76 - 279; 76/77 - 41; 77/78 - 198; 78/79 - 111
Topps: 75/76 - 279; 76/77 - 41; 77/78 - 198; 78/79 - 111

Bialowas, Dwight
O-Pee-Chee: 74/75 - 372; 75/76 - 106; 76/77 - 198; 77/78 - 271
Topps: 75/76 - 106; 76/77 - 198

Bialowas, Frank
parkhurst: 94/95 - 237, 237EI

Bianchin, Wayne
Loblaws: 74/75 - 237
O-Pee-Chee: 77/78 - 188; 78/79 - 103; 79/80 - 290
Topps: 77/78 - 188; 78/79 - 103

Bibeault, Paul (Goalie)
Beehive: 34/44 - 136
CKAC Radio: 43/47 - 32

Bicanek, Radim
Upper Deck: 93/94 - 262

Bickell, J. P.
Hall of Fame: 83 - 184, J3P; 87 - 184

Billington, Craig (Goalie)
Bowman: 92/93 - 102
Donruss: 93/94 - 226
Fleer: 92/93 - 334; 93/94 - 169PP
Leaf: 93/94 - 354
O-Pee-Chee: 92/93 - 372; 93/94 - 374
Panini: 87/88 - 72
Parkhurst: 91/92 - 320E, 320F; 92/93 - 330, 330EI; 93/94 - 138, 138EI; 94/95 - 158, 158EI
Pro-Set: 91/92 - 197PT
Score: 92/93 - 228C, 228A; 93/94 - 207C, 207A, 1PNC, 1PNA, 1CAS, 1AAS
Topps: 92/93 - 48, 48GS, 343SC; 93/94 - 374, 2AS
Upper Deck: 91/92 - 559E, 559F; 92/93 - 315; 93/94 - 424

Bilodeau, Brent
Upper Deck: 91/92 - 694E, 694F

Binkley, Les (Goalie)
Colgate: 70/71 - 75
Dad's Cookies: 70/71 - 104
Eddie Sargent: 70/71 - 175; 71/72 - 166
Esso: 70/71 - 182
O-Pee-Chee: 68/69 - 100; 69/70 - 110, 3ST, 2QS; 70/71 - 200, 10DE; 71/72 - 192; 72/73 - 300
Shirriff: 68/69 - K6
Topps: 68/69 - 100; 69/70 - 110
Toronto Sun: 71/72 - 211

Bionda, Jack
Beehive: 45/63 - 381
Parkhurst: 93/94 - 13ML
Topps: 57/58 - 2

Bjugstad, Scott
O-Pee-Chee: 86/87 - 23, 168SK
Panini: 88/89 - 90
Pro Set: 90/91 - 455
Topps: 86/87 - 23

Black, James
Bowman: 92/93 - 252
Donruss: 93/94 - 85
O-Pee-Chee: 92/93 - 388
Topps: 92/93 - 232, 232GS, 303SC

Black, James (cont.)
Upper Deck: 91/92 - 580E, 580F; 92/93 - 323; 93/94 - 517

Black, Stephen
Beehive: 45/63 - 154

Blackburn, Bob
Esso: 70/71 - 183
O-Pee-Chee: 69/70 - 113

Blackburn, Don
Shirriff: 68/69 - J8

Bladon, Tom
Loblaws: 74/75 - 218
O-Pee-Chee: 74/75 - 396; 75/76 - 74; 76/77 - 164; 77/78 - 131; 78/79 - 152; 79/80 - 204; 80/81 - 135
Topps: 75/76 - 74; 76/77 - 164; 77/78 - 131; 78/79 - 152; 79/80 - 204; 80/81 - 135

Blaha, Michael
Upper Deck: 91/92 - 669E, 669F

Blair, Andy
Anonymous: 33/34 - 11
Beehive: 34/44 - 300
Diamond: 36/39 - 1(IV)
Hamilton Gum: 33/34 - 9
La Presse: 27/32 - 36
O-Pee-Chee: 34/35 - 70
World Wide Gum: 33/34 - 4; 36/37 - 56

Blaisdell, Michael (Mike)
O-Pee-Chee: 82/83 - 81; 83/84 - 242
Post: 82/83 - 66

Blake, Robert (Rob)
Bowman: 90/91 - 142; 91/92 - 182; 92/93 - 367
Donruss: 93/94 - 158
Fleer: 92/93 - 79; 93/94 - 24, 113PP
Gillette: 91/92 - 6
Kellogg's: 92 - 22
Leaf: 93/94 - 172
O-Pee-Chee: 90/91 - 6PM; 91/92 - 6, 112, 44PM; 92/93 - 243; 93/94 - 56, 246SC, 246FD
Panini: 91/92 - 86, 339; 92/93 - 71E, 71F; 93/94 - 209E, 209F
Parkhurst: 91/92 - 293E, 293F; 92/93 - 302, 302EI; 93/94 - 94, 94EI; 94/95 - 105, 105EI, V85
Pro Set: 90/91 - 611; 91/92 - 92E, 92F, 51PT, PC8PT; 92/93 - 67
Score: 90/91 - 421A, 421C; 91 - 8YS; 91/92 - 27A, 349A, 27B, 379B, 27C, 379C, 201PNE, 382PNE, 201PNF, 382PNF; 92/93 - 177C, 177A, 32PNF, 32PNA, 16CT, 16AT; 93/94 - 236C, 236A
Topps: 91/92 - 6, 112, 348SC; 92/93 - 211, 211GS, 23SC; 93/94 - 56, 246SC, 246FD
Sega: 93/94 - 61
Upper Deck: 90/91 - 45E, 45F; 91/92 - 43E, 148E, 43F, 148F; 92/93 - 140; 93/94 - 317

Blake, Toe (Hector)
Beehive: 34/44 - 137
Canada Starch: 35/40 - 108
Chex: 63/65 - 24
CKAC Radio: 43/47 - 33
Deniere: 72/84 - 61
Hall of Fame: 83 - 92, G1P; 87 - 92
O-Pee-Chee: 37/38 - 160; 40/41 - 101
Parkhurst: 55/56 - 67; 57/58 MON - 16; 58/59 - 9;59/60 - 27; 63/64 - 34, 93; 93/94 - 84ML
Quaker Oats: 38/39 - 1; 45/54 - 4A, 4B, 4C; 55/56 - 67
Shirriff: 60/61 - 40; 61/62 - 101; 62/63 - 31
York: 61/62 - 22
Topps: 64/65 - 43; 65/66 - 1; 66/67 - 1

Blazek, Tomas
Parkhurst: 93/94 - 517, 517EI

Blight, Rick
O-Pee-Chee: 76/77 - 238; 77/78; - 259; 78/79 - 7; 79/80 - 395; 80/81 - 372
Topps: 76/77 - 238; 77/78 - 259; 78/79 - 7

Blinco, Russ
Beehive: 34/44 - 41, 190
Canada Starch: 35/40 - 53
O-Pee-Chee: 35/36 - 75; 36/37 - 127; 37/38 - 169
Sweet Caporal: 34/45 - 26
World Wide Gum: 36/37 - 30

Bloemberg, Jeff
O-Pee-Chee: 90/91 - 483
Upper Deck: 90/91 - 370E, 370F

Blomsten, Arto
Donruss: 93/94 - 506
O-Pee-Chee: 93/94 - 453
Parkhurst: 93/94 - 232, 232EI
Topps: 93/94 - 453C
Upper Deck: 92/93 - 376; 93/94 - 505

Bloom, Mike
Loblaws: 74/75 - 309
O-Pee-Chee: 74/75 - 369; 75/76 - 376; 76/77 - 56; 77/78 - 375
Topps: 76/77 - 56

Blue, John (Goalie)
Fleer: 93/94 - 287PP
O-Pee-Chee: 93/94 - 209
Parkhurst: 92/93 - 245, 245EI, CP19
Score: 93/94 - 399C, 399A
Topps: 93/94 - 209, 334SC, 334FD
Upper Deck: 93/94 - 74

Boddy, Gregg
Esso: 72/73 - 223
Loblaws: 74/75 - 289
O-Pee-Chee: 73/74 - 235; 74/75 - 349; 75/76 - 285
Topps: 75/76 - 285

Bodger, Doug
Bowman: 90/91 - 245; 91/92 - 21; 92/93 - 13
Donruss: 93/94 - 33
Fleer: 92/93 - 258; 93/94 - 31, 26PP
Leaf: 93/94 - 19
O-Pee-Chee: 85/86 - 38, 99SK; 86/87 - 24, 232SK; 87/88 - 125; 88/89 - 96, 234SK; 89/90 - 154, 257SK; 90/91 - 282; 91/92 - 207; 92/93 - 146; 93/94 - 29
Panini: 87/88 - 141; 88/89 - 332; 89/90 - 209; 90/91 - 33; 91/92 - 307; 92/93 - 245E, 245F; 93/94 - 109E, 109IS
Parkhurst: 91/92 - 15E, 15F; 92/93 - 253, 253EI
Pro Set: 90/91 - 19; 91/92 - 19E, 19F, 12PT, 3PK; 92/93 - 17
Score: 90/91 - 211A, 211C; 91/92 - 297A, 517B, 517C, 8PNE, 8PNF; 92/93 - 226C, 226A, 97PNC, 97PNA; 93/94 - 21C, 21A
Sega: 93/94 - 13
Topps: 85/86 - 38; 86/87 - 24; 87/88 - 125; 88/89 - 96; 89/90 - 154; 90/91 - 282; 91/92 - 207, 114SC; 92/93 - 247, 247GS, 147SC; 93/94 - 29, 354SC, 354FD
Upper Deck: 90/91 - 50E, 50F; 91/92 - 477E, 477F; 92/93 - 207; 93/94 - 187

Bodnar, Gus
Beehive: 45/63 - 4, 81
Parkhurst: 51/52 - 40; 52/53 - 37; 53/54 - 75; 54/55 - 62
Quaker Oats: 45/54 - 62
Ultimate: 92 - 31(OSE), 31(OSF)

Boesch, Garth
Beehive: 45/63 - 382
Quaker Oats: 45/54 - 63A, 63B, 63C

Boileau, Marc
O-Pee-Chee: 74/75 - 49
Parkhurst: 62/63 - 29
Topps: 74/75 - 49

Boimistruck, Fred
O-Pee-Chee: 82/83 - 318
Post: 82/83 - 276

Boivin, Claude
Parkhurst: 93/94 - 146, 146EI; 94/95 - 159, 159EI
Pro-Set: 91/92 - 264PT; 92/93 - 130
Score: 92/93 - 352C, 352A
Topps: 92/93 - 427, 427GS, 16SC
Upper Deck: 91/92 - 475E, 475F; 92/93 - 57

Boivin, Leo
Beehive: 45/63 - 5, 383; 64/67 - 2, 65
Coca Cola: 64/65 - 2; 65/66 - 3
Hall of Fame: 87 - 252
O-Pee-Chee: 68/69 - 101; 69/70 - 122, 5QS; 70/71 - 42, 15DE
Parkhurst: 52/53 - 34; 53/54 - 6; 54/55 - 26; 93/94 - 11ML
Quaker Oats: 45/54 - 64
Shirriff: 60/61 - 107; 61/62 - 5; 68/69 - K7
Topps: 57/58 - 18; 58/59 - 20; 59/60 - 26; 60/61 - 62, 1ST; 61/62 - 7; 62/63 - 5, 1HB; 63/64 - 5; 64/65 - 50; 65/66 - 32; 66/67 - 50; 68/69 - 101; 69/70 - 122; 70/71 - 42
Toronto Star: 57/67 - 90; 58/67 - 35; 63/64 - 1; 64/65 - 1

Boldirev, Ivan
Eddie Sargent: 72/73 - 51
Loblaws: 74/75 - 73
O-Pee-Chee: 72/73 - 41; 73/74 - 68; 74/75 - 16; 75/76 - 12; 76/77 - 251; 77/78 - 61; 78/79 - 135; 79/80 - 127; 80/81 - 52; 81/82 - 329; 82/83 - 338, 241SK; 83/84 - 118, 132SK; 84/85 - 50, 39SK; 85/86 - 92, 34SK
PepsiCo: 80/81 - 102
Post: 82/83 - 289
Toronto Sun: 71/72 - 4
Topps: 72/73 - 146; 73/74 - 68; 74/75 - 16; 75/76 - 12; 76/77 - 251; 77/78 - 61; 78/79 - 135; 79/80 - 127; 80/81 - 52; 82/83 - 241SK; 83/84 - 132SK; 84/85 - 38; 85/86 - 92

Bolduc, Alex
World Wide Gum: 36/37 - 119

Bolduc, Danny
O-Pee-Chee: 79/80 - 173
Topps: 79/80 - 173

Boll, Buzz
Anonymous: 33/34 - 4
Beehive: 34/44 - 3, 216, 301
O-Pee-Chee: 35/36 - 90; 36/37 - 119; 37/38 - 140; 39/40 - 21
Quaker Oats: 28/39 - 16
World Wide Gum: 36/37 - 40

Bolonchuk, Larry
O-Pee-Chee: 76/77 - 322; 78/79 - 387

Bolton, Hugh
Beehive: 45/63 - 384
Parkhurst: 51/52 - 79; 55/56 - 14; 57/58 TOR - 13; 93/94 - 124ML
Quaker Oats: 45/54 - 65; 55/56 - 14

Bonar, Dan
O-Pee-Chee: 82/83 - 150

Bondra, Peter
Bowman: 91/92 - 299; 92/93 - 248
Donruss: 93/94 - 366
Fleer: 92/93 - 230; 93/94 - 46, 258PP
Leaf: 93/94 - 79
O-Pee-Chee: 90/91 - 7PM; 91/92 - 362; 92/93 - 106; 93/94 - 12, 82SC, 82FD
Panini: 92/93 - 164E, 164F; 93/94 - 24E, 24F
Parkhurst: 91/92 - 188E, 188F; 92/93 - 204, 204EI; 93/94 - 222, 222EI; 94/95 - 251, 251EI
Pro Set: 90/91 - 645; 91/92 - 511E, 511F, 244PT; 92/93 - 209
Score: 90/91 - 71T; 91/92 - 216A, 216B, 216C, 87PNE, 87PNF;

Bondra, Peter (cont.)
Score: 92/93 - 165C, 165A; 92/93 - 82PNC 82PNA; 93/94 - 344C, 344A, 12PNC, 12PNA, 12CAS, 12AAS
Sega: 93/94 - 155
Topps: 91/92 - 362, 37SC; 92/93 - 294, 294GS, 286SC; 93/94 - 12, 82SC, 83FD, 3AS
Upper Deck: 90/91 - 536E, 536F; 91/92 - 131E, E12(E), 131F, E12(F); 92/93 - 115, 1AS; 93/94 - 95, 308

Bonin, Marcel
Beehive: 45/63 - 155, 225
Parkhurst: 57/58 MON - 18; 58/59 - 32; 59/60 - 12; 60/61 - 51; 61/62 - 47; 62/63 - 45; 93/94 - 19ML
Shirriff: 61/62 - 115; 62/63 - 27
Topps: 54/55 - 59
Toronto Star: 58/67 - 61
York: 60/61 - 3; 61/62 - 29

Bonney, Wayne (Official)
Pro Set: 90/91 - 682

Bonsignore, Jason
Donruss: 93/94 - 2JCA
Parkhurst: 93/94 - 510, 510EI
Upper Deck: 93/94 - 560

Boon, Richard (Dickie)
Hall of Fame: 83 - 108, H2P; 87 - 108
Topps: 60/61 - 17, 27ST

Boothman, George
Beehive: 34/44 - 302

Bordeleau, Christian
Derniere: 72/84 - 204
Eddie Sargent: 70/71 - 185
Esso: 70/71 - 200
O-Pee-Chee: 71/72 - 51; 72/73 - 299
Topps: 71/72 - 51
Toronto Sun: 71/72 - 234

Bordeleau, J. P.
Derniere: 72/84 - 107
Loblaws: 74/75 - 74
O-Pee-Chee: 73/74 - 258; 74/75 - 309; 75/76 - 369; 76/77 - 208; 77/78 - 156; 78/79 - 101; 79/80 - 212; 80/81 - 339
Topps: 76/77 - 208; 77/78 - 156; 78/79 - 101; 79/80 - 212

Bordeleau, Paulin
Loblaws: 74/75 - 290
O-Pee-Chee: 74/75 - 340; 75/76 - 151;
Topps: 75/76 - 151

Borsato, Luciano
Bowman: 92/93 - 52
Fleer: 92/93 - 239; 93/94 - 471PP
O-Pee-Chee: 92/93 - 149; 93/94 - 234
Panini: 92/93 - E(E), E(F); 93/94 - 195E, 195IS
Parkhurst: 91/92 - 425E, 425F; 92/93 - 439, 439EI; 93/94 - 501, 501EI
Pro-Set: 91/92 - 275PT, 8RGL, 15TL
Score: 91/92 - 353PNE, 353PNF; 92/93 - 256C, 256A, 218PNC, 218PNA; 93/94 - 401C, 401A
Topps: 92/93 - 239, 239GS, 81SC; 93/94 - 234, 317SC, 317FD
Upper Deck: 91/92 - 599E, 599F; 92/93 - 77

Borschevsky, Nikolai
Donruss: 93/94 - 332
Fleer: 92/93 - 418, 1UI; 93/94 - 99, 240PP
Leaf: 93/94 - 137
O-Pee-Chee: 92/93 - 100PM; 93/94 - 107
Panini: 93/94 - 224E, 224F
Parkhurst: 92/93 - 186, 216, 186EI, 216EI; 93/94 - 203, 203EI; 94/95 - 231, 231EI
Sega: 93/94 - 137
Score: 92/93 - 397PNC, 397PNA; 93/94 - 41C, 41A
Topps: 93/94 - 107, 375SC, 375FD
Upper Deck: 92/93 - 572; 93/94 - 164

Boschman, Laurie
Bowman: 91/92 - 282
Kraft: 86/87 - 72, 72P
O-Pee-Chee: 80/81 - 179; 81/82 - 314, 103SK; 83/84 - 381; 84/85 - 335, 288SK; 85/86 - 251, 254SK; 86/87 - 184, 111SK; 87/88 - 222; 88/89 - 200, 139SK; 89/90 - 147SK; 90/91 - 39, 8PM; 91/92 - 202; 93/94 - 3SC, 3FD
Panini: 87/88 - 368; 88/89 - 153; 89/90 - 169; 90/91 - 320; 91/92 - 215
Parkhurst: 91/92 - 316E, 316F; 92/93 - 122, 122EI
PepsiCo: 80/81 - 82
Pro Set: 90/91 - 324, 476; 91/92 - 426E, 426F
Score: 90/91 - 63T; 91/92 - 436B, 436C; 92/93 - 374C, 374A, 513C, 513A, 375PNC, 375PNA; 93/94 - 289C, 289A
Topps: 92/93 - 246, 246GS, 310SC
7-Eleven: 84/85 - 57
Topps: 80/81 - 179; 84/85 - 151; 86/87 - 184, 90/91 - 39; 91/92 - 202, 292SC; 93/94 - 3SC, 3FD
Upper Deck: 90/91 - 103E, 103F; 91/92 - 279E, 279F
Vachon Foods: 83/84 - 123

Bossy, Mike
Cel.Watch: 1988 - CW6
Deniere: 72/84 - 57, 166
Esso: 88/89 - 2
Funmate: 83/84 - 79
Kellogg's: 84 - 17
McDonald's: 82/83 - 6, 21
O-Pee-Chee: 78/79 - 1, 115; 79/80 - 161, 230; 80/81 - 25, 204, 12PO; 81/82 - 198, 208, 219, 382, 386, 388, 390, 150SK, 158SK, 253SK; 82/83 - 2, 197, 199, 1SK, 50SK, 51SK, 165SK; 83/84 - 1, 3, 205, 210, 10SK, 78SK, 79SK, 176SK, 306SK, 321SK, 322SK; 84/85 - 122, 209, 362, 376, 82SK, 83SK, 235SK; 85/86 - 130, 66SK, 118SK; 86/87 - 90, B/BB, 117SK, 194SK, 217SK; 87/88 - 105, 244SK; 92/93 - 391, 11AN
Panini: 87/88 - 97
Post: 81/82 - 6; 82/83 - 177
Pro Set: 90/91 - 650; 91 - 1HF
7-Eleven: 84/85 - 36
Topps: 78/79 - 1, 115; 79/80 - 161, 230; 80/81 - 25, 204; 81/82 - 4, 57, EN - 125; 82/83 - 1SK, 51SK, 50SK, 165SK; 83/84 - 10SK, 78SK, 79SK, 176SK, 306SK, 321SK, 322SK; 84/85 - 91, 155; 85/86 - 130, 9SK; 86/87 - 90, B/BB, 4SK; 87/88 - 105
Topps: 165SK; 83/84 - 10SK, 78SK, 79SK, 176SK, 306SK, 321SK, 322SK; 84/85 - 91, 155; 85/86 - 130, 9SK; 86/87 - 90, B/BB, 4SK; 87/88 - 105

Bostrom, Helge
Can. Chew. Gum: 33/34 - 4

Bothwell, Tim
O-Pee-Chee: 84/85 - 182; 85/86 - 161, 49SK; 87/88 - 29, 26SK
Topps: 85/86 - 161; 87/88 - 29

Botterill, Jason
Donruss: 93/94 - 4JCC
Upper Deck: 93/94 - 534

Boucha, Henry
Esso: 72/73 - 84
Lipton Soup: 74/75 - 32
Loblaws: 74/75 - 148
O-Pee-Chee: 73/74 - 33; 74/75 - 38; 76/77 - 209
Topps: 73/74 - 33; 74/75 - 38; 76/77 - 209

Bouchard, Dan (Goalie)
Derniere: 72/84 - 113, 140, 203
Eddie Sargent: 72/73 14
Funmate: 83/84 - 107
Lipton Soup: 74/75 - 44
Loblaws: 74/75 - 2
McDonald's: 82/83 - 1
O-Pee-Chee: 72/73 - 203; 73/74 - 45; 74/75 - 15; 75/76 - 268; 76/77 - 111; 77/78 - 37;

Bouchard, Dan (Goalie) (cont.)
O-Pee-Chee: 78/79 - 169; 79/80 - 28; 80/81 - 68; 81/82 - 270, 73SK, 84SK; 82/83 - 278, 27SK; 83/84 - 290, 245SK; 84/85 - 277, 172SK, 173SK; 85/86 - 246, 143SK
PepsiCo: 80/81 - 1
Topps: 73/74 - 45; 74/75 - 15; 75/76 - 268; 76/77 - 111; 77/78 - 37; 78/79 - 169; 79/80 - 28; 80/81 - 68; 84SK; 82/83 - 27SK; 83/84 - 245SK; 84/85 - 128
Vachon Foods: 83/84 - 62

Bouchard, Edmond
Champ's: 24/25 - 9
Wm. Paterson: 23/24 - 37; 24/25 - 19

Bouchard, Emile (Butch)
Beehive: 34/44 - 138; 45/63 - 226
CKAC Radio: 43/47 - 34, 35
Derniere: 72/84 - 65
Hall of Fame: 83 - M1P, 228; 87 - 228
La Patrie: 51/54 - 2
Parkhurst: 51/52 - 3; 52/53 - 13; 53/54 - 32; 54/55 - 6; 55/56 - 46
Quaker Oats: 45/54 - 5A, 5B, 5C; 55/56 - 46
Ultimate: 92 - 8(OSE), 8(OSF)

Bouchard, Joel
Donruss: 93/94 - 5JCC
Upper Deck: 93/94 - 541

Bouchard, Pierre
Bazooka: 71/72 - 20
Derniere: 72/84 - 6, 32,110
Eddie Sargent: 72/73 - 116
Loblaws: 75/75 - 163
O-Pee-Chee: 71/72 - 2; 72/73 - 165; 73/74 - 261; 74/75 - 254; 75/76 - 304; 76/77 - 177; 77/78 - 20; 78/79 - 116; 79/80 - 289; 80/81 - 373
Topps: 74/75 - 178; 74/75 - 254; 75/76 - 304; 76/77 - 177; 77/78 - 20; 78/79 - 116
Toronto Sun: 71/72 - 147

Boucher, Billy
Anonymous: 1926-27 - 1
Champ's: 24/25 - 20
Maple Crispette: 24/25 - 11
Wm. Paterson: 23/24 - 16; 24/25 - 46

Boucher, Buck
Hall of Fame: 83 - L1P

Boucher, Frank
Beehive: 34/44 - 261
C.C.M.: 33/36 - 3
Canada Starch: 35/40 - 68
Diamond: 33/35 - 4; 36/39 - 3 (II), 4 (II), 3 (III)
Hall of Fame: 83 - G2P, 93; 87 - 93
Topps: 60/61 - 29, 28ST
World Wide Gum: 36/37 - 16

Boucher, Gaetan
Pro-Set: 91/92 - 298PT

Boucher, George
Hall of Fame: 83 - 229; 87 - 229
La Presse: 27/32 - 29
Wm. Paterson: 23/24 - 6; 24/25 - 2

Boucher, Philippe
Durivage: 93/94 - 4
Fleer: 93/94 - 70, 1UR, 296PP
O-Pee-Chee: 92/93 - 72PM
Parkhurst: 92/93 - 16, 16EI; 93/94 - 24, 24EI, CC11
Score: 93/94 - 455C, 455A
Upper Deck: 91/92 - 68E, 68F; 92/93 - 484; 93/94 - 82

Boucher, Robert
Champ's: 24/25 - 39

Boudreau, Bruce
O-Pee-Chee: 78/79 - 280; 79/80 - 354

Boudreau, Rene
World Wide Gum: 36/37 - 117

Boudrias, Andre
Bazooka: 71/72 - 16
Dad's Cookies: 70/71 - 135
Eddie Sargent: 70/71 - 219; 72/73 - 214
Esso: 70/71 - 235
Lipton Soup: 74/75 - 14
Loblaws: 74/75 - 291
O-Pee-Chee: 68/69 - 53; 69/70 - 16; 70/71 - 121; 71/72 - 12; 72/73 - 93; 73/74 - 19; 74/75 - 191; 75/76 - 60
Shirriff: 68/69 - E3
Topps: 68/69 - 53; 69/70 - 16; 70/71 - 121; 71/72 - 12; 72/73 - 158; 73/74 - 19; 74/75 - 191; 75/76 - 60
Toronto Sun: 71/72 - 276

Bourbonnais, Rick
O-Pee-Chee: 77/78 - 312

Bourgeault, Leo
La Presse: 27/32 - 39
O-Pee-Chee: 33/34 - 28

Bourgeois, Charlie
O-Pee-Chee: 86/87 - 239, 178SK
Panini: 87/88 - 309

Bourne, Bob
O-Pee-Chee: 75/76 - 163; 77/78 - 93; 78/79 - 126; 79/80 - 56; 80/81 - 276; 81/82 - 201, 163SK; 82/83 - 198, 53SK; 83/84 - 4, 80SK, 174SK; 84/85 - 123, 89SK; 85/86 - 97, 67SK; 86/87 - 14, 208SK; 87/88 - 167; 88/89 - 101, 2NS, 213SK
Panini: 88/89 - 399
Post: 82/83 - 178
Topps: 75/76 - 163; 77/78 - 93; 78/79 - 126; 79/80 - 56; 81/82 EN - 87; 82/83 - 53SK; 83/84 - 80SK, 174SK; 84/85 - 92; 85/86 - 97; 86/87 - 14; 87/88 - 167; 88/89 - 101

Bourque, Claude (Goalie)
Beehive: 34/44 - 139
Canada Starch: 35/40 - 199
O-Pee-Chee: 39/40 - 28

Bourque, Phillippe (Phil)
Bowman: 90/91 - 205; 91/92 - 94; 92/93 - 293
Fleer: 92/93 - 352
Kraft: 1993 - 19
O-Pee-Chee: 89/90 - 19; 90/91 - 41; 91/92 - 33, 73PM
Panini: 89/90 - 317; 90/91 - 129; 91/92 - 272; 92/93 - 225E, 279E, 225F, 279F
Parkhurst: 91/92 - 136E, 136F
Pro Set: 90/91 - 228; 91/92 - 189E, 189F
Score: 90/91 - 234A, 234C; 91/92 - 69A, 69B, 69C, 227PNE, 227PNF; 92/93 - 223C, 223A, 353PNC, 353PNA
Topps: 89/90 - 19; 90/91 - 41, 282SC; 91/92 - 33, 168SC; 92/93 - 442, 442GS
Upper Deck: 90/91 - 31E, 31F; 91/92 - 398E, 398F; 92/93 - 141, 452

Bourque, Raymond (Ray)
Bowman: 90/91 - 31; 91/92 - P/C, 356; 92/93 - 3, 223
Donruss: 93/94 - 24
Derniere: 72/84 - 96, 161
Durivage: 92/93 - 31; 93/94 - 26
Esso: 88/89 - 3
Fleer: 92/93 - 2, 2AS, 8AW; 93/94 - 1, 2SA, 2AS, 16PP
Frito-Lay: 88/89 - 4
Funmate: 83/84 - 2
Gillette: 91/92 - 26
Hockey Wit: 93/94 - 77
Humpty Dumpty: 92/93 - 1(I)
Kraft: 1990 - 52; 90/91 - 3, 80; 91/92 - 57; 93/94 - 32
Leaf: 93/94 - 215, 7AS
McDonald's: 82/83 - 28; 91/92 - McH3, Mc10

Bourque, Raymond (Ray) (cont.)
O-Pee-Chee: 80/81 - 2, 140; 81/82 - 1, 17, 49SK; 82/83 - 7, 24, 86SK, 87SK, 166SK; 83/84 - 45, 46SK, 47SK, 173SK; 84/85 - 1, 211, 143SK, 183SK; 85/86 - 40, B/BB, 115SK, 157SK; 86/87 - 1, 34SK, 119SK; 87/88 - 87, 4HL, F/BB, 116SK, 140SK, 178SK; 88/89 - 73, 3NS, I/BB, 23SK, 117SK, 208SK; 89/90 - 110, 32SK, 162SK, 33FS, ; 90/91 - 43, 196, 475, I/BB; 90/91 - 9PM; 91/92 - 66, 261, 517, 119PM, 192PM; 92/93 - 126, 348; 93/94 - 93, 350, 383, 160SC, 160FD
Panini: 87/88 - 6, 381; 88/89 - 204, 405; 89/90 - 187, 201; 90/91 - 17, 322; 91/92 - 171, 335; 92/93 - 144E, 279E, 144F, 279F; 93/94 - 10E, 10F
Parkhurst: 91/92 - 9, 221E, 9F, 221F, 469, 472; 92/93 - 1, 464, 1EI, 464EI; 93/94 - 14, 14EI; 94/95 - 13, 304, 13EI, 304EI, H2, R2, C2
Post: 81/82 - 1; 82/83 - 1
Pro Set: 90/91 - 1, 357, 384; 91/92 - AC7, 9E, 296E, 322E, 567E, 9F, 296F, 322F, 2PT, 1PK, 567F, 278PT; 92/93 - 4, 261
Score: 90/91 - 200PC, 200A, 200C, 313A, 313C, 363A, 363C, 35HR; 91/92 - 50A, 344A, 415A, 429A, 50B, 319B, 331B, 374B, 50C, 319C, 331C, 374C, 15PNE, 15PNF, 368PNE, 368PNF, 50PC, B-2E, B-2F; 92/93 - 100C, 419C, 447C, 490C, 520C, 100A, 419A, 447A, 490A, 520A, 2PNC, 2PNA, 2CTP, 2ATP; 93/94 - 29C, 308C, 29A, 308A, 21PNC, 21PNA, 7DT, 21CAS, 21AAS, 1FR
Season's: 92/93 - 17
Sega: 93/94 - 7, 185
7-Eleven: 84/85 - 1
Topps: 80/81 - 2, 140; 81/82 - 5; 81/82 EN - 126; 82/83 - 86SK, 87SK, 166SK; 83/84 - 46SK, 47SK, 173SK; 84/85 - 1, 157; 85/86 - 40, B/BB, 5SK; 86/87 - 1, 11SK; 87/88 - 87, F/BB, 1SK; 88/89 - 73, I/BB, 5SK; 89/90 - 110, 7SK; 90/91 - 43, 196, I/BB; 91/92 - 19SL, 66, 261, 517, 233SC, 3SCM; 92/93 - 221, 262, 221GS, 262GS, 249SC, 267SC; 93/94 - 93, 350, 383, 15BG, 160SC, 160FD, 3MP, 4AS, 12SCSF
Upper Deck: 90/91 - 64E, 64F, 204E, 204F, 489E, 489F; 91/92 - 255E, 255F, 633E, 633F; 92/93 - 265, 626, 39AS; 93/94 - 116

Boutette, Pat
O-Pee-Chee: 76/77 - 367; 77/78 - 284; 78/79 - 374; 79/80 - 319; 80/81 - 14; 81/82 - 255; 82/83 - 263, 148SK; 83/84 - 276, 233SK; 84/85 - 171
Post: 82/83 - 226
Topps: 80/81 - 14; 81/82 EN - 81; 82/83 - 148SK; 83/84 - 233SK

Bouvrette, Lionel (Goalie)
CKAC Radio: 43/47 - 17

Bowen, Curtis
Donruss: 93/94 - 6JCC
Upper Deck: 93/94 - 547

Bowen, Jason
Donruss: 93/94 - 241
Fleer: 93/94 - 35, 404PP
Parkhurst: 93/94 - 418, 418EI
Score: 93/94 - 471C, 471A
Upper Deck: 93/94 - 240

Bower, Johnny (Goalie)
Beehive: 45/63 - 300, 385; 64/67 - 154A, 154B
Chex: 63/65 - 42
Coca Cola: 64/65 94; 65/66 - 93

Bower, Johnny (cont.)
Esso: 88/89 - 4
Hall of Fame: 83 - O5P, 211; 87 - 211
Highliner: 93/94 - 9
O-Pee-Chee: 68/69 - 122, 210, 17PS; 69/70 - 187
Parkhurst: 54/55 - 65; 58/59 - 46; 59/60 - 25, 32; 60/61 - 3; 61/62 - 3; 62/63 - 16; 63/64 - 5, 65; 92/93 - PR3; 93/94 - 103ML
Post: 68/69 - 16
Shirriff: 60/61 - 1; 61/62 - 41; 62/63 - 1; 68/69 - M6
Topps: 64/65 - 40; 65/66 - 77; 66/67 - 12; 66/67 US - 12; 67/68 - 76; 68/69 - 122;
Toronto Star: 57/67 - 46; 58/67 - 63; 63/64 - 31
Ultimate: 92 - 32(OSE), 80(OSE), 32(OSF), 80(OSF)
York: 60/61 - 22; 61/62 - 8; 62/63 - 1; 63/64 - 2
Zellers: 92/93 - 2, 2A

Bowie, Russell
Hall of Fame: 83 - 48, D2P; 87 - 48

Bowman, Kirk
Topps: 78/79 - 61
O-Pee-Chee: 77/78 - 309; 78/79 - 61

Bowman, Ralph
Beehive: 34/44 - 89
Diamond: 36/39 - 4 (I)

Bowman, William (Scotty)
Bowman: 91/92 - 4HF
Deniere: 72/84 - 11
Hockey Wit: 93/94 - 49
Kraft: 93/94 - 33
O-Pee-Chee: 74/75 - 261
Topps: 74/75 - 261

Bowness, Rick
O-Pee-Chee: 77/78 - 265; 78/79 - 173; 81/82 - 361
Topps: 78/79 - 173

Boyce, Arthur (Goalie)
Imperial Tobacco: 12/13 - 40

Boyd, Randy
O-Pee-Chee: 83/84 - 283

Boyd, Yank
Beehive: 34/44 - 4

Boyer, Wally
Beehive: 64/67 - 31, 155
Dad's Cookies: 70/71 - 105
Eddie Sargent: 70/71 - 171
Esso: 70/71 - 184
O-Pee-Chee: 68/69 - 105; 69/70 - 118; 70/71 - 203; 72/73 - 308
Shirriff: 68/69 - K12
Topps: 66/67 - 55; 68/69 - 105; 69/70 - 118
Toronto Sun: 71/72 - 212

Bozek, Steven (Steve)
Bowman: 90/91 - 64; 91/92 - 325
O-Pee-Chee: 82/83 - 151, 233SK; 83/84 - 77; 84/85 - 220; 87/88 - 216; 89/90 - 67SK; 90/91 - 76; 91/92 - 397
Panini: 90/91 - 301; 91/92 - 48
Post: 82/83 - 113
Pro Set: 90/91 - 293; 91/92 - 486E, 486F
Score: 90 - 89T; 91 - 6T; 91/92 - 252B, 252C, 556B, 556C, 61PNE, 61PNF; 92/93 - 37C, 37A
Topps: 82/83 - 233SK; 90/91 - 76; 91/92 - 397, 28SC
Vachon Foods: 83/84 - 3

Bozon, Philippe
Fleer: 92/93 - 392; 93/94 - 210
O-Pee-Chee: 92/93 - 257, 25PM; 93/94 - 68, 214SC, 214FD
Parkhurst: 91/92 - 375E, 375F; 92/93 - 159, 452, 159EI, 452EI; 93/94 - 179, 179EI

Bozon, Philippe (cont.)
Topps: 92/93 - 433, 433GS, 8SC; 93/94 - 68, 214SC, 214FD
Upper Deck: 92/93 - 283; 93/94 - 113

Brackenbury, Curt
Derniere: 72/84 - 87
O-Pee-Chee: 79/80 - 308; 81/82 - 109
PepsiCo: 80/81 - 22
Upper Deck: 92/93 - 283

Bradley, Brian
Bowman: 90/91 - 58; 91/92 - 159; 92/93 - 283
Donruss: 93/94 - 324
Fleer: 92/93 - 408; 93/94 - 36, 228PP
Kraft: 93/94 - 2
Leaf: 93/94 - 209
O-Pee-Chee: 89/90 - 287, 63SK; 90/91 - 115; 91/92 - 234, 185PM; 92/93 - 27; 190PM; 93/94 - 117, 212SC, 212FD
Panini: 89/90 - 152; 90/91 - 302; 91/92 - 93; 93/94 - T(E), T(F)
Parkhurst: 91/92 - 171E, 171F; 92/93 - 174, 174EI; 93/94 - 465, 465EI; 94/95 - 221, 221EI, V71
Pro Set: 90/91 - 294; 91/92 - 489E, 489F, 231PT; 92/93 - 174
Score: 90/91 - 198A, 198C; 91/92 - 255B, 255C, 90PNE, 90PNF; 92/93 - 259C, 259A, 387PNC, 387PNA; 93/94 - 230C,230A, 33PNC, 33PNA, 33CAS, 33AAS, 20FR
Sega: 93/94 - 129
Topps: 90/91 - 115; 91/92 - 234, 257SC; 92/93 - 291, 291GS, 163SC; 93/94 - 117, 212SC, 212FD, 5AS
Upper Deck: 90/91 - 79E, 79F; 92/93 - 544, 20AS; 94/95 - 121, 305

Brady, Neil
Bowman: 90/91 - 88
O-Pee-Chee: 92/93 - 82PM; 93/94 - 17, 199SC, 199FD
Panini: 93/94 - 119E, 119IS
Parkhurst: 92/93 - 124, 124EI
Score: 93/94 - 293C, 293A
Topps: 92/93 - 1SCM; 93/94 - 17, 199SC, 199FD
Upper Deck: 93/94 - 81

Bragnalo, Rick
O-Pee-Chee: 77/78 - 296; 78/79 - 308

Brannigan, Andy
Beehive: 34/44 - 217

Brasar, Per-Olov
O-Pee-Chee: 78/79 - 99; 79/80 - 192; 80/81 - 291; 81/82 - 330, 244SK
PepsiCo: 80/81 - 103
Topps: 78/79 - 99; 79/80 - 192

Brashear, Donald
Parkhurst: 94/95 - 119, 119EI

Bratash, Oleg
O-Pee-Chee: 90/91 - 525

Brathwaite, Fred (Goalie)
Donruss: 93/94 - 119
Fleer: 93/94 - 339PP
Upper Deck: 93/94 - 435

Breault, Francois
O-Pee-Chee: 91/92 - 496
Pro Set: 90/91 - 612; 91/92 - 541E, 541F
Topps: 91/92 - 496

Breitenbach, Ken
O-Pee-Chee: 77/78 - 279

Brennan, Doug
Beehive: 34/44 - 262
Diamond: 33/35 - 5
World Wide Gum: 33/34 - 45

Brennan, Lester
World Wide Gum: 36/37 - 106

Brenneman, John
Beehive: 64/67 - 156
Coca Cola: 64/65 - 27

Brenneman, John (cont.)
O-Pee-Chee: 68/69 - 83
Shirriff: 68/69 - H2
Topps: 68/69 - 83

Brewer, Carl
Beehive: 45/63 - 386; 64/67 - 157
Coca Cola: 64/65 - 95
O-Pee-Chee: 69/70 - 59, 7QS; 70/71 - 243; 71/72 - 222
Parkhurst: 59/60 - 3; 60/61 - 18; 61/62 - 18; 62/63 - 8; 63/64 - 8, 68; 92/93 - PR13
Shirriff: 60/61 - 3; 61/62 - 45; 62/63 - 5, 51
Topps: 64/65 - 75; 65/66 - 78; 69/70 - 59
Toronto Star: 57/67 - 75; 58/67 - 41, 88; 63/64 - 32; 64/65 - 39
Toronto Sun: 71/72 - 235
York: 60/61 - 23; 61/62 - 13; 62/63 - 5; 63/64 - 17

Brezgunov, Vadim
O-Pee-Chee: 91/92 - 11R

Brickley, Andy
Bowman: 90/91 - 27; 92/93 - 17
O-Pee-Chee: 89/90 - 29; 90/91 - 88
Panini: 87/88 - 86; 89/90 - 194; 90/91 - 16
Pro Set: 90/91 - 406
Score: 92/93 - 296C, 296A
Topps: 89/90 - 29; 90/91 - 88; 92/93 - 109, 109GS, 208SC
Upper Deck: 90/91 - 84E, 84F

Bridgman, Mel
O-Pee-Chee: 76/77 - 26; 77/78 - 121; 78/79 - 26; 79/80 - 201; 80/81 - 189; 81/82 - 248; 82/83 - 39, 40, 213SK; 83/84 - 226, 265SK; 84/85 - 109, 361, 71SK; 85/86 - 42, 57SK; 86/87 - 136, 203SK; 87/88 - 17
Panini: 87/88 - 249
Post: 82/83 - 33
7-Eleven: 84/85 - 30
Topps: 76/77 - 26; 77/78 - 121; 78/79 - 26; 79/80 - 201; 80/81 - 189; 82/83 - 213SK; 83/84 - 265SK; 84/85 - 84; 85/86 - 42; 86/87 - 136; 87/88 - 17

Brimsek, Frank (Goalie)
Beehive: 34/44 - 5A, 5B; 45/63 - 6, 82
CKAC Radio: 43/47 - 2
Hall of Fame: 83 - 13, I24P; 87 - 124
O-Pee-Chee: 39/40 - 97

Brind'Amour, Rod
Bowman: 90/91 - 23; 91/92 - 374; 92/93 - 224, 268
Donruss: 93/94 - 248
Fleer: 92/93 - 152; 93/94 - 74, 178PP
Hockey Wit: 93/94 - 59
Humpty Dumpty: 92/93 - 2(I)
Leaf: 93/94 - 26
O-Pee-Chee: 90/91 - 332; 91/92 - 490, 94PM; 92/93 - 49, 9SP; 93/94 - 115, 78SC, 78FD
Panini: 90/91 - 266, 343; 91/92 - 30; 92/93 - 187E, 187F; 93/94 - 47E, 47F
Parkhurst: 91/92 - 124E, 124F; 92/93 - 126, 126EI; 93/94 - 152, 152EI; 94/95 - 167, 167EI
Pro Set: 90/91 - 259; 91/92 - 211E, 453E, 211F, 90PT, 20PK, 453F; 92/93 - 132
Score: 90 - 31YS; 90/91 - 131C, 328C, 131A, 328A, 98HR; 91 - 68T; 91/92 - 85A, 85B, 85C, 618B, 618C; 9PNE, 9PNF; 92/93 - 324C, 324A; 26PNC, 26PNA, 18CT, 18AT; 93/94 - 45C, 45A
Season's: 92/93 - 39
Sega: 93/94 - 100
Topps: 90/91 - 332; 91/92 - 490, 184SC; 92/93 - 90, 90GS, 202SC; 93/94 - 115, 78SC, 78FD
Upper Deck: 90/91 - 36E, 36F, 347E, 347F; 91/92 - 189E, 189F, 547E, 547F; 92/93 - 15, 264; 93/94 - 361

Brink, Andy
    Donruss: 93/94 - 3JCA

Brisebois, Patrice
    Bowman: 92/93 - 435
    Donruss: 93/94 - 171
    Durivage: 92/93 - 32; 93/94 - 7
    Fleer: 92/93 - 325; 93/94 - 52, 125PP
    Leaf: 93/94 - 191
    O-Pee-Chee: 92/93 - 239; 93/94 - 59, 27SC, 27FD
    Panini: 92/93 - 155E, 155F
    Parkhurst: 91/92 - 309E, 309F; 92/93 - 320, 320EI; 93/94 - 105, 105EI; 94/95 - 116, 116EI
    Score: 91/92 - 382A, 272B, 272C; 92/93 - 388C, 388A, 153PNC, 153PN; 93/94 - 163C, 163A
    Topps: 92/93 - 189, 189GS, 238SC; 93/94 - 59, 27SC, 27FD
    Upper Deck: 90/91 - 454E, 454F; 92/93 - 277; 93/94 - 318

Broadbent, Harry (Punch)
    Champ's: 24/25 - 30
    Hall of Fame: 83 - A2P, 3; 87 - 3
    Imperial Tobacco: 12/13 - 2
    Maple Crispette: 24/25 - 18
    Wm. Paterson: 23/24 - 9; 24/25 - 39

Broda, Turk (Walter) (Goalie)
    Beehive: 34/44 - 303; 45/63 - 387; 64/67 - 158
    CKAC Radio: 43/47 - 15
    Hall of Fame: 83 - G3P, 94; 87 - 94
    O-Pee-Chee: 36/37 - 97; 37/38 - 133; 39/40 - 2; 40/41 - 108, 130
    Parkhurst: 51/52 - 75; 55/56 - 23; 92/93 - PR6
    Quaker Oats: 38/39 - 17; 45/54 - 66A, 66B, 66C; 55/56 - 23

Broden, Connie
    Parkhurst: 93/94 - 83ML

Broderick, Ken
    O-Pee-Chee: 69/70 - 197; 75/76 - 340;

Broderick, Len
    Parkhurst: 57/58 - 21

Brodeur, Martin (Goalie)
    Donruss: 93/94 - 195, 10RR
    Durivage: 93/94 - 5
    Fleer: 93/94 - 374PP
    Leaf: 93/94 - 345
    O-Pee-Chee: 92/93 - 59; 93/94 - 401
    Parkhurst: 93/94 - 380, 380EI; 94/95 - 126, 278, 126EI, 278EI
    Score: 90/91 - 439A, 439C; 92/93 - 480C, 480A
    Topps: 92/93 - 513, 513GS, 233SC; 93/94 - 401C, 352SC, 352FD
    Upper deck 92/93 - 408; 93/94 - 334

Brodeur, Richard (Goalie)
    Derniere: 72/84 - 88, 177
    Esso: 83/84 - 4E, 4F
    Funmate: 83/84 - 128
    Kellogg's: 84 - 16
    Kraft: 86/87 - 62, 62P
    McDonald's: 82/83 - 2
    O-Pee-Chee: 79/80 - 176; 81/82 - 331; 82/83 - 339, 340, 7SK, 247SK; 83/84 - 346, 276SK, 277SK; 84/85 - 314, 277SK; 85/86 - 180; 86/87 - 246, 98SK; 87/88 - 257, 189SK
    Panini: 87/88 - 340
    PepsiCo: 80/81 - 105
    Post: 82/83 - 290
    7-Eleven: 84/85 - 48
    Topps: 79/80 - 176; 82/83 - 7SK, 247SK; 83/84 - 276SK, 277SK
    Vachon Foods: 83/84 - 101

Bromley, Gary (Goalie)
    Loblaws: 74/75 - 37
    O-Pee-Chee: 74/75 - 7; 75/76 - 368; 79/80 - 167; 80/81 - 330
    Topps: 74/75 - 7; 79/80 - 167

Brooke, Bob
    Bowman: 90/91 - 79
    O-Pee-Chee: 85/86 - 202; 86/87 - 48, 219SK; 87/88 - 64; 88/89 - 61; 89/90 - 215; 90/91 - 105
    Panini: 87/88 - 301; 88/89 - 91
    Topps: 86/87 - 48; 87/88 - 64; 88/89 - 61; 90/91 - 105

Brooks, Gord
    Loblaws: 74/75 - 310

Brooks, Ross (Goalie)
    Loblaws: 74/75 - 19
    O-Pee-Chee: 74/75 - 376

Brossart, Willie
    Loblaws: 74/75 - 271

Brost, Todd
    Fleer: 93/94 - 479PP
    O-Pee-Chee: 93/94 - 8TC

Broten, Aaron
    Bowman: 90/91 - 185; 91/92 - 162
    O-Pee-Chee: 82/83 - 136; 83/84 - 227, 226SK; 85/86 - 249, 62SK; 87/88 - 46, 62SK; 88/89 - 138, 76SK; 89/90 - 180, 88SK; 90/91 - 118; 90/91 - 10PM
    Panini: 87/88 - 78; 88/89 - 271; 89/90 - 254; 90/91 - 247; 91/92 - 105
    Pro Set: 90/91 - 131, 530
    Score: 90/91 - 162A, 162C, 21T, 72HR; 91/92 - 250B, 337B, 250C, 337C
    Topps: 83/84 - 226SK; 87/88 - 46; 88/89 - 138; 89/90 - 180; 90/91 - 118
    Upper Deck: 90/91 - 210E, 210F

Broten, Neal
    Bowman: 90/91 - 178; 91/92 - 121; 92/93 - 81
    Fleer: 92/93 - 89; 93/94 - 57PP
    Frito-Lay: 88/89 - 5
    Funmate: 83/84 - 59
    O-Pee-Chee: 82/83 - 164, 190SK; 83/84 - 168, 120SK; 84/85 - 96, 46SK; 85/86 - 124, 40SK; 86/87 - 99, 166SK; 87/88 - 11, 52SK; 88/89 - 144, 201SK; 89/90 - 87, 202SK; 90/91 - 90; 91/92 - 420; 92/93 - 62; 93/94 - 131, 28SC, 28FD
    Panini: 87/88 - 297; 88/89 - 92; 89/90 - 107; 90/91 - 261; 91/92 - 107; 92/93 - 89E, 89F; 93/94 - 272E, 272F
    Parkhurst: 91/92 - 80E, 80F; 92/93 - 313, 313EI; 93/94 - 54, 54EI; 94/95 - 53, 53EI
    Pro Set: 90/91 - 132, 91/92 - 112E, 112F, 188PT
    Score: 90/91 - 144A, 144C; 91/92 - 280A, 338B, 500B, 338C, 500C, 161PNE, 161PNF; 92/93 - 32C, 32A, 209PNC, 209PNA; 93/94 - 166C, 166A
    Topps: 82/83 - 190SK; 83/84 - 120SK; 84/85 - 72; 85/86 - 124; 86/87 - 99; 87/88 - 11; 88/89 - 144; 89/90 - 87; 90/91 - 90; 91/92 - 420, 99SC; 92/93 - 309, 309GS, 90SC; 93/94 - 131, 28SC, 28FD
    Upper Deck: 90/91 - 48E, 48F; 91/92 - 232E, 323F, 550E; 92/93 - 206; 93/94 - 109

Broten, Paul
    Bowman: 90/91 - 22; 92/93 - 265
    Fleer: 92/93 - 134, 353
    Parkhurst: 91/92 - 336E, 336F; 92/93 - 364, 364EI; 93/94 - 324, 324EI; 94/95 - 60, 60EI
    Score: 90/91 - 41T; 92/93 - 353C, 353A, 212PNC, 212PNA; 93/94 - 297, 297A
    Topps: 91/92 - 376SC; 92/93 - 355, 355GS, 109SC
    Upper Deck: 91/92 - 550E, 550F; 92/93 - 148; 93/94 - 468

Broughton, George (Goalie)
    Imperial Tobacco: 12/13 - 39

Broune, Cecil
    Dom. Choc.: 1925 - 103

Brown, Adam
    Beehive: 34/44 - 90; 45/63 - 7, 83
    Parkhurst: 51/52 - 30
    Topps: 92/93 - 52

Brown, Andy (Goalie)
    Eddie Sargent: 72/73 - 83

Brown, Arnie
    Beehive: 64/67 - 121
    Coca Cola: 64/65 - 74; 65/66 - 75
    Colgate: 70/71 - 76
    Dad's Cookies: 70/71 - 84
    Eddie Sargent: 70/71 - 116; 72/73 - 72
    Esso: 70/71 - 146
    Loblaws: 74/75 - 3
    O-Pee-Chee: 68/69 - 68; 69/70 - 34; 70/71 - 66; 71/72 - 14; 72/73 - 144; 73/74 - 225
    Shirriff: 68/69 - G6
    Topps: 64/65 - 74; 65/66 - 90; 66/67 - 90; 66/67 US - 48; 67/68 - 89; 68/69 - 68; 69/70 - 34; 70/71 - 66; 71/72 - 14; 72/73 - 111
    Toronto Sun: 71/72 - 86

Brown, Connie
    Beehive: 34/44 - 91

Brown, David (Dave)
    Panini: 88/89 - 272, 319; 90/91 - 67
    Pro Set: 90/91 - 440; 91/92 - 452E, 452F
    Score: 91 - 84T; 91/92 - 634B, 634C

Brown, Doug
    Bowman: 91/92 - 285; 92/93 - 126
    Donruss: 93/94 - 258
    Fleer: 93/94 - 411PP
    Leaf: 93/94 - 378
    O-Pee-Chee: 88/89 - 115, 80SK, 2FS; 89/90 - 242; 90/91 - 117; 91/92 - 42; 92/93 - 333
    Parkhurst: 93/94 - 424, 424EI
    Pro Set: 90/91 - 163; 91/92 - 138E, 138F
    Score: 91/92 - 163A, 163B, 163C, 363PNE, 363PNF; 92/93 - 118C, 118A
    Topps: 88/89 - 115; 90/91 - 117; 91/92 - 42, 47SC; 92/93 - 139, 139GS, 331SC
    Upper Deck: 90/91 - 159E, 159F; 91/92 - 214E, 214F; 93/94 - 459

Brown, George Allan
    Beehive: 34/44 - 140
    O-Pee-Chee: 37/38 - 157

Brown, George V.
    Hall of Fame: 83 - L2P, 152; 87 - 152

Brown, Greg
    O-Pee-Chee: 90/91 - 11PM
    Pro Set: 90/91 - 590
    Score: 90/91 - 96T; 91/92 - 518B, 518C

Brown, Jeff
    Bowman: 90/91 - 25; 91/92 - 385; 92/93 - 247
    Donruss: 93/94 - 293, 499
    Fleer: 92/93 - 183; 93/94 - 223, 207PP
    Leaf: 93/94 - 29
    Kraft: 1990 - 28
    O-Pee-Chee: 88/89 - 201, 192SK; 89/90 - 28, 193SK; 90/91 - 295; 91/92 - 222; 93/94 - 363, 381, 188SC, 188FD
    Panini: 88/89 - 349; 89/90 - 325; 90/91 - 274; 91/92 - 23; 92/93 - 25E, 25F; 93/94 - 165E, 165IS
    Parkhurst: 91/92 - 156E, 156F; 93/94 - 173, 173EI; 94/95 - 244, 244EI, V45
    Pro Set: 90/91 - 260; 91/92 - 212E, 212F, 114PT; 92/93 - 158
    Score: 90/91 - 41A, 41C; 91/92 - 276A, 496B, 496C, 72PNE, 72PNF; 92/93 - 220C, 220A, 13PNC, 13PNA; 93/94 - 194C, 194A
    Sega: 93/94 - 121
    Topps: 89/90 - 28; 90/91 - 295; 91/92 - 222, 148SC; 92/93 - 174, 174GS,263SC; 93/94 - 363, 381C, 188SC, 188FD, 2SCF
    Upper Deck: 90/91 - 191E, 191F; 91/92 - 211E, 211F; 93/94 - 130

Brown, Jerry
    Beehive: 34/44 - 92

Brown, Keith
Bowman: 90/91 - 10; 92/93 - 4
O-Pee-Chee: 80/81 - 98; 81/82 - 55, 115SK; 82/83 - 62; 83/84 - 98; 84/85 - 33, 28SK; 85/86 - 59; 86/87 - 206; 87/88 - 47; 90/91 - 276, 92/93 - 48; 93/94 - 58SC, 58FD
Panini: 87/88 - 233; 90/91 - 192; 91/92 - 21; 92/93 - 13E, 13F
Parkhurst: 91/92 - 261E, 261F; 92/93 - 274, 274EI
Pro Set: 90/91 - 49; 91/92 - 371E, 371F
Score: 90/91 - 161A, 161C; 91/92 - 76A, 76B, 76C, 154PNE, 370PNE, 154PNF, 370PNF; 92/93 - 68C, 68A, 92PNC, 92PNA; 93/94 - 384C, 384A
Topps: 80/81 - 98; 81/82 WN - 67; 84/85 - 28; 85/86 - 59; 87/88 - 47; 90/91 - 276; 92/93 - 52, 52GS, 274SC; 93/94 - 58SC, 58FD, 281SC, 281FD

Brown, Larry
Eddie Sargent: 72/73 - 95
Esso: 70/71 - 74
O-Pee-Chee: 74/75 - 271; 75/76 - 377; 76/77 - 355; 77/78 - 289; 78/79 - 361; 79/80 - 323
Toronto Sun: 71/72 - 190

Brown, Rob
Bowman: 90/91 - 202, HT3; 91/92 - 16; 92/93 - 168
Fleer: 92/93 - 33
O-Pee-Chee: 88/89 - 109, 131SK, 237SK, 3FS; 89/90 - 193, 163SK, 236SK, 31FS; 90/91 - 19; 91/92 - 83; 92/93 - 170
Panini: 88/89 - 336; 89/90 - 186, 310; 90/91 - 128; 91/92 - 315; 92/93 - 10E, 10F
Parkhurst: 91/92 - 60E, 258E, 60F, 258F
Pro Set: 90/91 - 229; 91/92 - 80E, 606E, 80F, 42PT, 606F
Score: 90 - 5YS; 90/91 - 105A, 105C, 51HR; 91/92 - 246A, 466B, 466C, 141PNE, 141PNF; 92/93 - 244C, 244A, 331PNC, 331PNA, 22CSS, 22ASS
Topps: 88/89 - 109; 89/90 - 193, 8SK; 90/91 - 19; 91/92 - 83, 200SC; 92/93 - 72, 72GS, 295SC
Upper Deck: 90/91 - 142E, 142F; 91/92 - 198E, 198F; 92/93 - 387

Brown, Walter
Hall of Fame: 83 - 78, F2P; 87 - 78

Brownschidle, Jack
O-Pee-Chee: 78/79 - 379; 79/80 - 278; 80/81 - 101; 81/82 - 302; 82/83 - 300; 83/84 - 311
Post: 82/83 - 259
Topps: 80/81 - 101

Bruce, David
Bowman: 92/93 - 358
Fleer: 92/93 - 191
O-Pee-Chee: 92/93 - 246
Panini: 88/89 - 137; 92/93 - 126E, 126F
Parkhurst: 91/92 - 384E, 384F
Pro Set: 91/92 - 485E, 485F, 227PT; 92/93 - 170
Score: 91/92 - 644B, 644C; 92/93 - 301C, 301A, 159PNC, 159PNA
Topps: 92/93 - 448, 448GS, 284SC
Upper Deck: 92/93 - 102

Brumwell, James (Murray)
O-Pee-Chee: 83/84 - 228, 179SK
Topps: 83/84 - 179SK

Brunet, Benoit
Bowman: 92/93 - 414
Donruss: 93/94 - 166
Durivage: 92/93 - 19; 93/94 - 8
Fleer: 92/93 - 101; 93/94 - 366PP
Leaf: 93/94 - 363
O-Pee-Chee: 92/93 - 352; 93/94 - 84
Panini: 93/94 - 20E, 20F
Parkhurst: 93/94 - 375, 375EI

Brunet, Benoit (cont.)
Topps: 92/93 - 137, 137GS, 134SC; 93/94 - 84, 422SC, 422FD
Upper Deck: 91/92 - 469E, 469F; 92/93 - 80; 93/94 - 415

Brunet, Lucien
La Presse: 27/32 - 28

Bruneteau, Eddie
CKAC Radio: 43/47 - 9, 10

Bruneteau, Modere (Mud)
Beehive: 34/44 - 93
CKAC Radio: 43/47 - 10
O-Pee-Chee: 39/40 - 43; 40/41 - 138
World Wide Gum: 36/37 - 47

Brunetta, Mario (Goalie)
Panini: 90/91 - 152

Brydge, Bill
Anonymous: 33/34 - 22
Can. Chew. Gum: 33/34 - 5
Diamond: 33/35 - 6; 36/39 - 5 (I), 5 (II), 4 (III)
Dom. Choc.: 1925 - 101
World Wide Gum: 33/34 - 2

Brydson, Glenn
Beehive: 34/44 - 42
Can. Chew. Gum: 33/34 - 6
Diamond: 36/39 - 6 (I), 2 (IV), 1 (V), 1 (VI)
O-Pee-Chee: 34/35 - 64
World Wide Gum: 33/34 - 39

Brylin, Sergei
Upper Deck: 93/94 - 276

Bubla, Jiri
O-Pee-Chee: 83/84 - 347, 143SK; 84/85 - 315
Topps: 83/84 - 143SK
Vachon Foods: 83/84 - 102

Buchberger, Kelly
Bowman: 92/93 - 393
Fleer: 92/93 - 291; 93/94 - 340PP
O-Pee-Chee: 92/93 - 125
Panini: 93/94 - 241E, 241F
Parkhurst: 91/92 - 275E, 275F
Pro Set: 90/91 - 441; 91/92 - 385E, 385F; 92/93 - 48
Score: 91/92 - 429B, 429C; 92/93 - 126C, 126A, 95PNC, 95PNA, 11CSS, 11ASS; 93/94 - 317C, 317A
Topps: 92/93 - 455, 455GS, 235SC
Upper Deck: 92/93 - 123; 93/94 - 197

Bucher, Laurent
Upper Deck: 91/92 - 668E, 668F

Buckland, Frank
Hall of Fame: 83 - 216, O6P; 87 - 216

Bucyk, John
Beehive: 45/63 - 8, 156; 64/67 - 3
Coca Cola: 64/65 - 3; 65/66 - 4
Colgate: 70/71 - 46
Dad's Cookies: 70/71 - 2
Eddie Sargent: 70/71 - 8; 72/73 - 16
Esso: 70/71 - 3
Hall of Fame: 83 - J4P, 181; 87 - 181
Loblaws: 74/75 - 20
Mac's Milk: 73/74 - 2
O-Pee-Chee: 68/69 - 5; 69/70 - 26; 70/71 - 2; 71/72 - 35, 249, 255; 72/73 - 1; 73/74 - 147; 74/75 - 239, 245; 75/76 - 9; 76/77 - 95; 77/78 - 155
Parkhurst: 93/94 - 56ML
Shirriff: 60/61 - 104; 61/62 - 7; 68/69 - A6
TCMA: 1981 - 5
Topps: 57/58 - 10; 58/59 - 40; 59/60 - 23; 60/61 - 11, 2ST; 61/62 - 8; 62/63 - 11, 2HB; 63/64 - 11; 64/65 - 100; 65/66 - 101; 66/67 - 39; 66/67 US - 39; 67/68 - 42; 68/69 - 5; 69/70 - 26; 70/71 - 2; 71/72 - 35; 72/73 - 60; 73/74 - 26; 74/75 - 239, 245; 75/76 - 9; 76/77 - 95, 14PO; 77/78 - 155
Toronto Star: 57/67 - 95; 58/67 - 50; 63/64 - 2
Toronto Sun: 71/72 - 5
Zellers: 93/94 - 2, 2A

Bullard, Michael (Mike)
Bowman: 90/91 - 114
Funmate: 83/84 - 100
O-Pee-Chee: 82/83 - 262, 264, 149SK; 83/84 - 277, 235SK; 84/05 - 172, 365, 118SK; 85/86 - 67, 104SK; 86/87 - 83, 228SK; 87/88 - 210, 37SK; 88/89 - 152, 93SK, 119SK; 89/90 - 21, 104SK; 90/91 - 274
Panini: 88/89 - 8; 90/91 - 119
Parkhurst: 91/92 - 397E, 397F
Post: 82/83 - 227
Pro Set: 90/91 - 211; 91/92 - 496E, 496F, 233PT
Score: 91 - 40T; 91/92 - 590B, 590C, 69PNE, 69PNF; 92/93 - 218C, 218A
7-Eleven: 84/85 - 40
Topps: 82/83 - 149SK; 83/84 - 235SK; 84/85 - 123; 85/86 - 67; 86/87 - 83; 88/89 - 152; 89/90 - 21; 90/91 - 274; 92/93 - 146, 146GS, 494SC
Upper Deck: 90/91 - 230E, 230F

Buller, Hyman (Hy)
Beehive: 45/63 - 301
Parkhurst: 51/52 - 91; 52/53 - 98; 53/54 - 58

Bulley, Ted
O-Pee-Chee: 78/79 - 217; 79/80 - 128; 80/81 - 229; 81/82 - 56; 82/83 - 360
Post: 82/83 - 49
Topps: 78/79 - 217; 79/80 - 128; 80/81 - 229; 81/82 WN - 68

Burakovsky, Robert
Leaf: 93/94 - 429
Parkhurst: 93/94 - 144, 144EI
Upper Deck: 93/94 - 498

Burch, Billy
Anonymous: 26/227 - 79
Champ's: 24/25 - 10
Hall of Fame: 83 - E3P, 64; 87 - 64
Maple Crispette: 24/25 - 21
Wm. Paterson: 23/24 - 35; 24/25 - 13

Burchell, Skippy
La Patrie: 51/54 - 27

Bure, Pavel
Bowman: 92/93 - 154
Donruss: 93/94 - 351, 8IK, X/PM, X/SP
Fleer: 92/93 - 219, 3UR, 9AW, 2UI; 93/94 - 37, 1GG, 17AS, 248PP, 1PL, 1SM, 2RL
Gillette: 91/92 - 10
Hockey Wit: 93/94 - 7
Kraft: 93/94 - 3, 54
Leaf: 93/94 - 10, 8AS
O-Pee-Chee: 91/92 - 67PM; 92/93 - 25, 324, 25AN, 10SP, 1BB
Panini: 92/93 - 271E, 290E, C(E), 271F, 290F, C(F); 93/94 - O(E), O(F), 260, 440
Parkhurst: 91/92 - 404E, 446E, 462E, 404F, 446F; 92/93 - 188, 234, 460, 506, 188EI, 234EI, 460EI, 506EI; 93/94 - 211, 509, 211EI, 509EI, G7, W2; 94/95 - 297, 297EI, H24, R24, C24, V18
Pro-Set: 91/92 - 564F, 272PT; 92/93 - 192, CC3, 2RGL, 13TL
Score: 91 - 49T; 91/92 - 315PNE, 315PNF; 92/93 - 14C, 14A, 504C, 504A, 523C, 523A, 110PMC, 110PNA, 4CTP, 8CT, 4ATP, 8AT; 93/94 - 333C, 333A, 31PNC, 31PNA, 19DT, 31CAS, 31AAS, 22FR
Season's: 92/93 - 31
Sega: 93/94 - 143
Topps: 92/93 - 8, 8GS, 353, 353GS, 246SC, 489SC; 93/94 - 260, 440C, 480SC, 480FD, 6AS
Upper Deck: 90/91 - 526E, 526F; 91/92 - 54E, 54F, 555E, 555F; 92/93 - 156, 362, 431, SP2, E2, ERT1; WJG5, 21AS; 93/94 - 35, 307

Bure, Valeri
- Parkhurst: 93/94 - 528, 528EI
- Upper Deck: 93/94 - 571

Bureau, Marc
- Bowman: 91/92 - 126; 92/93 - 382
- O-Pee-Chee: 91/92 - 93; 92/93 - 78; 93/94 - 344, 134SC, 134FD
- Parkhurst: 91/92 - 302E, 302F; 92/93 - 400, 400EI; 93/94 - 461, 461EI
- Pro Set: 91/92 - 544E, 544F
- Score: 90/91 - 423A, 423C; 91/92 - 476B, 476C, 335PNE, 335PNF
- Topps: 91/92 - 93, 322SC; 92/93 - 179, 179GS, 30SC; 93/94 - 344,134SC, 134FD
- Upper Deck: 91/92 - 274E, 274F

Burke, Claude
- World Wide Gum: 36/37 - 112

Burke, Eddie
- Diamond: 33/35 - 7; 36/39 - 7 (I)

Burke, Marty
- Beehive: 34/44 - 43
- Canada Starch: 35/40 - 69
- Can. Chew. Gum: 33/34 - 7
- Diamond: 33/35 - 8; 36/39 - 8 (I) 6 (II), 5 (III) 3 (IV), 3 (V), 2 (VI)
- Hamilton Gum: 33/34 - 3
- La Presse: 27/32 - 19
- World Wide Gum: 33/34 - 14; 36/37 - 72

Burke, Sean (Goalie)
- Bowman: 91/92 - 275
- Donruss: 93/94 - 141
- Fleer: 92/93 - 68; 93/94 - 15, 103PP
- Frito-Lay: 88/89 - 6
- Kraft: 1990 - 53; 90/91 - 4
- Leaf: 1993/94 - 132
- O-Pee-Chee: 87/88 - 72SK; 88/89 - 94, 82SK, 4FS; 89/90 - 92, 34SK, 86SK, 8FS; 90/91 - 140; 91/92 - 67; 92/93 - 92PM; 93/94 - 241, 207SC, 207FD
- Panini: 88/89 - 267; 89/90 - 185, 256; 90/91 - 77; 91/92 - 212; 93/94 - 131E, 131IS
- Parkhurst: 92/93 - 57, 57EI
- Pro Set: 90/91 - 164; 91/92 - 132E, 132F; 92/93 - PV2
- Score: 90 - 11YS; 90/91 - 34A, 34C, 17HR; 91/92 - 245A, 465B, 465C; 92/93 - 13COH, 295PNC, 295PNA; 93/94 - 126C, 126A, 8FR
- Sega: 93/94 - 60
- Topps: 88/89 - 94; 89/90 - 92; 90/91 - 140; 91/92 - 67, 76SC; 93/94 - 241, 207SC, 207FD
- Upper Deck: 90/91 - 66E, 66F; 91/92 - 183E, 183F; 92/93 - 518

Burns, Charlie
- Bauer: 68/69 - 4
- Beehive: 45/63 - 9
- Colgate: 70/71 - 19
- Dad's Cookies: 70/71 - 63
- Eddie Sargent: 70/71 - 87; 72/73 - 106
- Esso: 70/71 - 110
- O-Pee-Chee: 68/69 - 108; 69/70 - 129; 70/71 - 44, 13DE; 71/72 - 238; 72/73 - 178
- Shirriff: 61/62 - 4
- Topps: 58/59 - 43; 59/60 - 40; 60/61 - 24, 3ST; 61/62 - 11; 62/63 - 15; 63/64 - 9; 68/69 - 108; 69/70 - 129; 70/71 - 44; 71/72 - 21
- Toronto Star: 57/67 - 86
- Toronto Sun: 71/72 - 127

Burns, Norm
- Beehive: 34/44 - 263

Burns, Pat
- Kraft: 93/94 - 34
- Pro Set: 90/91 - 669

Burns, Robin
- Loblaws: 74/75 - 109
- O-Pee-Chee: 75/76 - 104
- Topps: 75/76 - 104

Burr, Shawn
- Bowman: 90/91 - 232; 91/92 - 43; 92/93 - 122
- Fleer: 92/93 - 44
- Leaf: 93/94 - 296
- O-Pee-Chee: 87/88 - 164, 5HL, 125SK; 88/89 - 78; 89/90 - 101, 252SK; 90/91 - 74; 91/92 - 184; 92/93 - 24; 93/94 - 83
- Panini: 87/88 - 247; 88/89 - 41; 89/90 - 63; 90/91 - 213; 91/92 - 135
- Parkhurst: 91/92 - 45E, 45F;93/94 - 328, 328EI; 94/95 - 62, 62EI
- Pro Set: 90/91 - 66; 91/92 - 58E, 58F; 92/93 - 45
- Score: 90/91 - 49A, 49C, 21HR; 91/92 - 54A, 54B, 54C, 86PNE, 86PNF; 92/93 - 207C, 207A, 171PNC, 171PNA; 93/94 - 175C, 175A
- Topps: 87/88 - 164; 88/89 - 78; 89/90 - 101; 90/91 - 74; 91/92 - 184, 101SC; 92/93 - 178, 178GS, 126SC; 93/94 - 83, 313SC, 313FD
- Upper Deck: 90/91 - 111E, 111F; 91/92 - 315E, 315F; 93/94 - 91

Burridge, Randy
- Bowman: 91/92 - 349; 92/93 - 29, 225
- Donruss: 93/94 - 503
- Fleer: 93/94 - 464PP
- O-Pee-Chee: 86/87 - 70; 88/89 - 33, 29SK; 89/90 - 121, 28SK; 90/91 - 190; 91/92 - 358, 43PM, 92/93 - 370
- Panini: 88/89 - 208; 89/90 - 197; 91/92 - 174; 92/93 - 163E, 163F
- Parkhurst: 91/92 - 190E, 190F; 93/94 - 492, 492EI
- Pro Set: 90/91 - 2; 91/92 - 4E, 510E, 4F, 510F, 241PT; 92/93 - 207
- Score: 90/91 - 72A, 72C; 91 - 14T; 91/92 - 102A, 102B, 102C, 564B, 564C, 55PNE, 55PNF; 92/93 - 297C, 297A; 93/94 - 370C, 370A, 297A, 115PNC, 115PNA
- Topps: 86/87 - 70; 88/89 - 33; 89/90 - 121 90/91 - 190; 91/92 - 358, 119SC; 92/93 - 83, 83GS, 61SC; 93/94 - 416SC, 416FD
- Upper Deck: 90/91 - 196E, 196F; 91/92 - 567E; 567F; 92/93 - 153; 93/94 - 504

Burrows, Dave
- Coca Cola: 77/78 - 2
- Eddie Sargent: 72/73 - 182
- Loblaws: 74/75 - 238
- O-Pee-Chee: 72/73 - 133; 73/74 - 140; 74/75 - 137, 241; 75/76 - 186; 76/77 - 83; 77/78 - 66; 78/79 - 254; 80/81 - 147
- Topps: 72/73 - 82; 73/74 - 27; 74/75 - 137, 241; 75/76 - 186; 76/77 - 83; 77/78 - 66; 78/79 - 254; 80/81 - 147

Burt, Adam
- Bowman: 90/91 - 252
- Donruss: 93/94 - 139
- Fleer: 92/93 - 69
- Leaf: 93/94 - 280
- O-Pee-Chee: 90/91 - 431
- Panini: 91/92 - 318; 92/93 - 264E, 264F
- Parkhurst: 91/92 - 291E, 291F
- Pro Set: 90/91 - 447
- Score: 90/91 - 370A, 370C; 91/92 - 449B, 449C, 77PNE, 77PNF; 92/93 - 261C, 261A; 93/94 - 307C, 307A
- Topps: 92/93 - 283, 283GS, 139SC
- Upper Deck: 90/91 - 324E, 324F

Bush, Eddie
- Beehive: 34/44 - 94

Buskas, Rod
- O-Pee-Chee: 90/91 - 509
- Panini: 87/88 - 144
- Pro Set: 90/91 - 456
- Score: 90/91 - 12T; 91/92 - 427B, 427C, 417PNE, 417PNF

Busniuk, Mike
- O-Pee-Chee: 80/81 - 326; 81/82 - 249

Buswell, Walt
- Beehive: 34/44 - 141
- Canada Starch: 35/40 - 113
- Diamond: 36/39 - 6 (III)
- O-Pee-Chee: 37/38 - 174; 39/40 - 32
- Quaker Oats: 38/39 - 2
- World Wide Gum: 36/37 - 32

Butcher, Garth
- Bowman: 91/92 - 383; 92/93 - 124
- Donruss: 93/94 - 289, 477
- Fleer: 92/93 - 184; 93/94 - 27, 208PP
- Leaf: 93/94 - 239
- O-Pee-Chee: 87/88 - 200SK; 88/89 - 202, 54SK; 89/90 - 72SK; 90/91 - 150; 91/92 - 204; 92/93 - 280; 93/94 - 316, 21SC, 21FD
- Panini: 87/88 - 343; 88/89 - 134; 89/90 - 158; 91/92 - 28; 92/93 - 24E, 24F; 93/94 - 164E, 164IS
- Parkhurst: 91/92 - 374E, 374F; 92/93 - 390, 390EI; 93/94 - 449, 449EI; 94/95 - 188, 188EI
- Pro Set: 90/91 - 295; 91/92 - 210E, 583E, 210F. 583F, 223PT; 92/93 - 160
- Score: 90/91 - 18A, 18C; 91/92 - 24A, 24B, 24C, 85PNE, 409PNE, 85PNF, 409PNF; 92/93 - 65C, 65A, 72PNC, 72PNA; 93/94 - 173C, 173A, 24PNC, 24PNA, 24CAS, 21AAS
- Sega: 93/94 - 122
- Topps: 90/91 - 150; 91/92 - 204, 223SC; 92/93 - 281, 281GS, 287SC; 93/94 - 316, 21SC, 21FD, 7AS
- Upper Deck: 90/91 - 98E, 98F; 91/92 - 397E, 397F
- Vachon Foods: 83/84 - 103

Butler, Jerry
- Loblaws: 74/75 - 199
- O-Pee-Chee: 74/75 - 393; 75/76 - 167; 76/77 - 336; 77/78 - 349; 78/79 - 304; 79/80 - 393; 80/81 - 351; 81/82 - 332
- PepsiCo: 80/81 - 106
- Topps: 75/76 - 167

Butsayev, Vjateslav
- Fleer: 92/93 - 153
- Leaf: 93/94 - 307
- O-Pee-Chee: 91/92 - 12R; 92/93 - 31PM; 93/94 - 79, 94SC, 94FD
- Parkhurst: 92/93 - 363, 363EI; 93/94 - 151, 151EI; 94/95 - 213, 213EI
- Topps: 93/94 - 79, 94SC, 94FD
- Upper Deck: 92/93 - 503; 93/94 - 406

Jack Butterfield
- Hall of Fame: 83 - M2P, 167; 87 - 167

Byakin, Ilya
- Donruss:. 93/94 - 427
- Fleer: 93/94 - 341PP
- O-Pee-Chee: 91/92 - 13R
- Parkhurst: 93/94 - 341, 341EI; 94/95 - 73, 73EI

Byalsin, Ilya
- O-Pee-Chee: 90/91 - 1R

Byce, John
- Bowman: 90/91 - 38
- Score: 90/91 - 62T
- Upper Deck: 90/91 - 25E, 25F

Byers, Jerry
- Loblaws: 74/75 - 4
- O-Pee-Chee: 74/75 - 273

Byers, Lyndon
- O-Pee-Chee: 90/91 - 464
- Pro Set: 90/91 - 3

Byers Mike
- Colgate: 70/71 - 55
- Esso: 70/71 - 92
- O-Pee-Chee: 70/71 - 160; 71/72 - 34
- Shirriff: 68/69 - M17
- Topps: 71/72 - 34;
- Toronto Sun: 71/72 - 107

Bykov, Viacheslav
- O-Pee-Chee: 90/91 - 10R

Caffery, Jack
- Beehive: 45/63 - 10
- Parkhurst: 55/56 - 19; 93/94 - 12ML
- Quaker Oats: 55/56 - 19
- Topps: 57/58 - 8

Caffery, Terry
- O-Pee-Chee: 69/70 - 135

Cahan, Larry
- Beehive: 45/63 - 302A, 302B, 302C, 388; 64/67 - 122
- Dad's Cookies: 70/71 - 55
- Eddie Sargent: 70/71 - 79
- Esso: 70/71 - 93
- O-Pee-Chee: 68/69 - 35; 70/71 - 164; 72/73 - 307
- Parkhurst: 55/56 - 16; 93/94 - 87ML
- Quaker Oats: 55/56 - 16
- Shirriff: 61/62 - 95
- Topps: 57/58 - 59; 58/59 - 23; 61/62 - 52; 62/63 - 48; 63/64 - 51; 68/69 - 35
- Toronto Sun: 71/72 - 108

Cain, Herbert
- Beehive: 34/44 - 6, 142, 191
- Canada Starch: 35/40 - 78, 152
- O-Pee-Chee: 35/36 - 77; 36/37 - 110; 37/38 - 172; 39/40 - 42
- Quaker Oats: 38/39 - 3
- Sweet Caporal: 34/35 - 27
- World Wide Gum: 36/37 - 46

Cain, Jim (Dutch)
- Anonymous: 26/27 - 91
- Champ's: 24/25 - 31
- Maple Crispette: 24/25 - 16
- Wm. Paterson: 24/25 - 35

Calder, Frank
- Hall of Fame: 83 - B5P, 18; 87 - 18

Callander, Jock
- Pro-Set: 92/93 - 175
- Upper Deck: 93/94 - 10

Callighen, Brett
- O-Pee-Chee: 79/80 - 315; 80/81 - 114; 81/82 - 110, 212SK; 82/83 - 103
- PepsiCo: 80/81 - 23
- Post: 82/83 - 82
- Topps: 80/81 - 114

Camback, Patrik
- Donruss: 93/94 - 6
- Topps: 93/94 - 379

Cameron, Angus
- Beehive: 34/44 - 264

Cameron, Al
- O-Pee-Chee: 77/78 - 48; 78/79 - 396
- PepsiCo: 80/81 - 122
- Topps: 77/78 - 48

Cameron, Craig
- Loblaws: 74/75 - 181
- O-Pee-Chee: 72/73 - 13; 73/74 - 42; 74/75 - 263; 75/76 - 239; 76/77 - 327
- Topps: 72/73 - 22; 73/74 - 147; 74/75 - 263; 75/76 - 239

Cameron, Dave
- Post: 82/83 - 162

Cameron, Harry
- Hall of Fame: 83 - 95, G4P; 87 - 95

Cameron, J. (Goalie)
- Dom. Choc.: 1925 - 70

Campbell, Angus
- Hall of Fame: 83 - 14, I25P; 87 - 125
- Imperial Tobacco: 10/11 - 9

Campbell, Bryan
- Esso: 70/71 - 56
- O-Pee-Chee: 69/70 - 106; 71/72 - 214
- Toronto Sun: 71/72 - 64

Campbell, Clarence
- Hall of Fame: 83 - A3, 4; 87 - 4

Campbell, Colin
- O-Pee-Chee: 75/76 - 346; 76/77 - 372; 78/79 - 269; 79/80 - 339;

Campbell, Colin (cont.)
- O-Pee-Chee: 80/81 - 380; 81/82 - 333; 82/83 - 82; 83/84 - 119; 84/85 - 51
- PepsiCo: 80/81 - 107
- Topps: 84/85 - 39

Campbell, Jim
- Fleer: 93/94 - 499PP
- Topps: 93/94 - 17US
- Upper Deck: 92/93 - 605

Campbell, Scott
- PepsiCo: 80/81 - 123

Campbell, Spiff (Earl)
- Wm. Paterson: 24/25 - 8
- Champ's: 24/25 - 40

Campbell, Wade
- O-Pee-Chee: 83/84 - 382; 84/85 - 336
- Vachon Foods: 83/84 - 124

Campeau, Jean-Claude
- CKAC: 43/47 - 36

Campeau, J.P.
- CKAC: 43/47 - 37

Campeau, Tod
- Beehive: 45/63 - 227
- La Patrie: 51/54 - 32
- Quaker Oats: 45/54 - 6

Caprice, Frank (Goalie)
- Panini: 87/88 - 339

Capuano, Dave
- Bowman: 91/92 - 323
- O-Pee-Chee: 90/91 - 170; 91/92 - 318
- Panini: 91/92 - 41
- Pro Set: 90/91 - 543; 91/92 - 237E, 237F
- Score: 90/91 - 105T; 91/92 - 86A, 86B, 86C
- Topps: 90/91 - 170; 91/92 - 318, 53SC
- Upper Deck: 91/92 - 202E, 202F

Carbonneau, Guy
- Bowman: 90/91 - 44; 91/92 - 338; 92/93 - 38
- Cel.Watch: 1988 - CW2
- Donruss: 93/94 - 450
- Durivage: 92/93 - 1; 93/94 - 9
- Fleer: 92/93 - 102, 3AW; 93/94 - 126PP
- Kraft: 86/87 - 21, 21P; 1990 - 19; 93/94 - 35
- O-Pee-Chee: 83/84 - 185, 180SK; 84/85 - 257, 160SK; 85/86 - 233, 135SK; 86/87 - 176, 7SK; 87/88 - 232, 7SK; 88/89 - 203, 4NS, 41SK, 209SK; 89/90 - 53, 48SK, 213SK; 90/91 - 93; 91/92 - 54, 152PM; 92/93 - 206; 93/94 - 250, 1SC, 1FD
- Panini: 87/88 - 64; 88/89 - 256, 407; 89/90 - 241, 381; 90/91 - 58; 91/92 - 197; 92/93 - 149E, 149F; 93/94 - 19E, 19F
- Parkhurst: 91/92 - 92E, 466E, 92F; 92/93 - 485, 508, 485EI, 508EI; 93/94 - 372, 372EI
- Pro Set: 90/91 - 146; 91/92 - 130E, 345E, 576E, 130F, 345F, 63PT, 15PK, 576F; 92/93 - 88, CC5
- Roots: 93/94 - 2
- Score: 90/91 - 91A, 91C, 43HR; 91/92 - 19A, 19B, 19C, 130E, 130PNE, 130PNF, 374PNE, 374PNF; 92/93 - 269C, 269A, 524C, 524A, 43PNC, 43PNA; 93/94 - 51C, 51A
- Topps: 83/84 - 180SK; 86/87 - 176; 89/90 - 53; 90/91 - 93; 91/92 - 54, 41SC; 92/93 - 125, 125GS, 260SC, 289SC; 93/94 - 250, 1SC, 1FD
- Upper Deck: 90/91 - 188E, 188F; 91/92 - 265E, 265F; 92/93 - 260, 439; 92/93 - 439
- Vachon Foods: 83/84 - 41

Carkner, Terry
- Bowman: 91/92 - 232; 92/93 - 129
- Donruss: 93/94 - 422
- Fleer: 92/93 - 370; 93/94 - 328PP
- O-Pee-Chee: 89/90 - 3; 90/91 - 381; 91/92 - 291; 92/93 - 180; 93/94 - 152

Carkner, Terry (cont.)
- Panini: 89/90 - 297; 90/91 - 114; 91/92 - 235; 92/93 - 190E, 190F; 93/94 - 54E, 54F
- Parkhurst: 91/92 - 342E, 342F; 92/93 - 362, 362EI; 93/94 - 332, 332EI; 94/95 - 69, 69EI
- Pro Set: 90/91 - 212; 91/92 - 173E, 173F, 212PT; 92/93 - 269
- Score: 90/91 - 47A, 47C; 91/92 - 64A, 64B, 64C, 51PNE, 51PNF; 92/93 - 66C, 66A, 63PNC, 63PNA; 93/94 - 233C, 233A
- Topps: 89/90 - 3; 90/91 - 381; 91/92 - 291, 219SC; 92/93 - 465, 465GS, 463SC; 93/94 - 152, 252SC, 252FD
- Upper Deck: 90/91 - 398E, 398F; 91/92 - 204E, 204F

Carleton, Wayne
- Eddie Sargent: 70/71 - 6; 71/72 - 131
- Esso: 70/71 - 4
- O-Pee-Chee: 69/70 - 184; 70/71 - 9, 3SS; 71/72 - 178; 72/73 - 337
- Post: 68/69 - 17
- Shirriff: 68/69 - M2
- Topps: 67/68 - 77; 70/71 - 9, 3SK
- Toronto Sun: 71/72 - 43
- Ultimate: 92 - 47(OSE), 47(OSF)

Carlson, Kent
- Vachon Foods: 83/84 - 42

Carlsson, Calle
- UpperDeck: 92/93 - 228

Carlyle, Randy
- Bowman: 91/92 - 199; 92/93 - 287
- Funmate: 83/84 - 101
- Kraft: 86/87 - 73, 73P; 1990 - 47
- O-Pee-Chee: 78/79 - 312; 79/80 - 124; 80/81 - 367; 81/82 - 256; 183SK, 255SK; 82/83 - 265, 266, 144SK; 83/84 - 278, 227SK; 84/85 - 337, 291SK; 85/86 - 57, 251SK; 86/87 - 144, 107SK; 87/88 - 9, 248SK; 88/89 - 204, 148SK; 89/90 - 291, 143SK; 90/91 - 51; 91/92 - 72; 92/93 - 12; 93/94 - 86
- Panini: 87/88 - 360; 88/89 - 149; 89/90 - 168; 90/91 - 314; 91/92 - 76
- Parkhurst: 91/92 - 418E, 418F
- Post: 81/82 - 8; 82/83 - 228
- Pro Set: 90/91 - 325; 91/92 - 273E, 273F; 92/93 - 265
- Score: 90/91 - 136A, 136C; 91/92 - 125A, 125B, 125C, 288PNE, 288PNF; 92/93 - 167C, 167A; 93/94 - 27PNC, 27PNA
- Topps: 79/80 - 124; 81/82 EN - 112; 82/83 - 144SK; 83/84 - 227SK; 85/86 - 57; 86/87 - 144; 87/88 - 9; 90/91 - 51; 91/92 - 72, 94SC; 92/93 - 147, 147GS, 332SC; 93/94 - 86, 27CAS, 27AAS, 8AS
- Upper Deck: 90/91 - 331E, 331F

Carnback, Patrik
- Fleer: 93/94 - 281PP
- O-Pee-Chee: 93/94 - 379
- Parkhurst: 93/94 - 8, 8EI; 94/95 - 7, 7EI, V28
- Topps: 93/94 - 434SC, 434FD
- Upper Deck: 93/94 - 463

Carnegie, Herbie
- La Patrie: 51/54 - 28

Carney, Keith
- Donruss: 93/94 - 412
- Fleer: 92/93 - 13
- O-Pee-Chee: 92/93 - 81PM
- Pro Set: 92/93 - 223
- Score: 92/93 - 229PNC, 229PNA
- Upper Deck: 92/93 - 402; 93/94 - 516

Caron, Alain
- O-Pee-Chee: 72/73 - 324

Caron, Jacques (Goalie)
Eddie Sargent: 72/73 - 193
O-Pee-Chee: 72/73 - 140, 18CS
Topps: 72/73 - 86

Carpenter, Robert (Bob)
Bowman: 90/91 - 30; 92/93 - 10
Funmate: 83/84 - 135
Hockey Wit: 93/94 - 68
Leaf: 93/94 - 421
O-Pee-Chee: 82/83 - 361, 154SK; 83/84 - 366, 206SK; 84/85 - 194, 132SK; 85/86 - 26, C/BB, 112SK; 86/87 - 150, 250SK; 87/88 - 30; 88/89 - 72, 153SK; 89/90 - 167; 90/91 - 139; 91/92 - 404, 148PM; 92/93 - 131, 78PM; 93/94 - 413, 175SC, 175FD
Panini: 88/89 - 74; 89/90 - 196; 90/91 - 7; 91/92 - 181, 226; 92/93 - 140E, 140F
Parkhurst: 91/92 - 226E, 226F
Post: 82/83 - 305
Pro Set: 90/91 - 4; 91/92 - 349E, 349F, 154PT
Score: 90/91 - 16A, 16C; 91/92 - 162A, 162B, 162C, 99PNE, 396PNE, 99PNF, 396PNF; 92/93 - 142C, 142A, 315PNC, 315PNA; 93/94 - 267C, 267A
Topps: 82/83 - 154SK; 83/84 - 206SK; 85/86 - 26, C/BB; 86/87 - 150; 87/88 - 30; 88/89 - 72; 89/90 - 167; 90/91 - 139; 91/92 - 404, 161SC; 92/93 - 378, 378GS, 122SC; 93/94 - 413C, 175SC, 175FD
Upper Deck: 90/91 - 158E, 158F; 92/93 - 478

Carr, Gene
Loblaws: 74/75 - 128
O-Pee-Chee: 74/75 - 320; 75/76 - 343; 76/77 - 290; 77/78 - 298; 78/79 - 14
Topps: 78/79 - 14
Toronto Sun: 71/72 - 236

Carr, Lorne
Beehive: 34/441 - 218, 304
Diamond: 36/39 - 9(I), 7(II), 7(III)
O-Pee-Chee: 39/40 - 62
Quaker Oats: 45/54 - 67
World Wide Gum: 36/37 - 26

Carriere, Larry
Loblaws: 74/75 - 38
O-Pee-Chee: 72/73 - 282; 73/74 - 260; 74/75 - 43; 75/76 - 154; 76/77 - 297; 77/78 - 304; 78/79 - 272
Topps: 74/75 - 43; 75/76 - 154

Carroll, Billy
O-Pee-Chee: 83/84 - 5; 85/86 - 203, 224SK

Carroll, George
Champ's: 24/25 - 32
Maple Crispette: 24/25 - 20
Wm. Paterson: 24/25 - 42

Carroll, Greg
O-Pee-Chee: 79/80 - 184
Topps: 79/80 - 184

Carse, Bill
Beehive: 34/44 - 44, 45
CKAC Radio: 43/47 - 37
O-Pee-Chee: 39/40 - 80
Quaker Oats: 45/54 - 13

Carse, Bob
Beehive: 34/44 - 45, 45/54 - 7
CKAR Radio: 43/47 - 38

Carson, Gerry
Beehive: 34/44 - 192
Can. Chew. Gum: 33/34 - 8
Diamond: 33/35 - 9; 36/39 - 10(I)
Sweet Caporal: 34/35 - 12
World Wide Gum: 33/34 - 24

Carson, Jimmy
Bowman: 90/91 - 229; 91/92 - 52; 92/93 - 108
Donruss: 93/94 - 159, 500

Carson, Jimmy (cont.)
Fleer: 92/93 - 45; 93/94 - 42, 114PP
Hockey Wit: 93/94 - 62
Kraft: 90/91 - 5
Leaf: 93/94 - 149
O-Pee-Chee: 87/88 - 92, 6HL, 126SK, 210SK; 88/89 - 9, 5NS, 158SK; 89/90 - 127, 222SK; 90/91 - 231, 12PM; 91/92 - 104, 167PM; 92/93 - 152; 93/94 - 376, 118SC, 118FD
Panini: 87/88 - 279; 88/89 - 75; 89/90 - 72; 90/91 - 214; 91/92 - 139; 92/93 - 114E, 114F; 93/94 - 204E, 204F
Parkhurst: 91/92 - 43E, 43F; 92/93 - 308, 308EI; 93/94 - 368, 368EI; 94/95 - 239, 239EI
Pro Set: 90/91 - 67; 91/92 - 55E, 55F, 33PT
Score: 90/91 - 64A, 64C, 28HR; 91/92 - 224B, 224C, 173PNE, 173PNF; 92/93 - 9C, 9A, 329PNC, 329PNA, 9CSS, 9ASS; 93/94 - 109C, 109A
Topps: 87/88 - 92; 88/89 - 9; 89/90 - 127; 90/91 - 231; 91/92 - 104, 121SC; 92/93 - 398, 398GS, 277SC; 93/94 - 376, 118SC, 118FD
Upper Deck: 90/91 - 132E, 132F; 91/92 - 161E, 161F; 92/93 - 253

Carson, Lindsay
O-Pee-Chee: 83/84 - 261, 181SK
Topps: 83/84 - 181SK

Carter, Anson
Donruss: 93/94 - 7JCC
Upper Deck: 93/94 - 531

Carter, Billy
Shirriff: 60/61 - 115

Carter, John
Bowman: 90/91 - 39
Fleer: 92/93 - 399
O-Pee-Chee: 91/92 - 300
Panini: 90/91 - 8
Pro Set: 90/91 - 5
Score: 90/91 - 283A, 283C; 91 - 7T; 91/92 - 557B, 557C
Topps: 91/92 - 300
Upper Deck: 90/91 - 211E, 211F

Carter, Lyle (Goalie)
Toronto Sun: 71/72 - 44

Carveth, Joe
Beehive: 34/44 - 95; 45/63 - 228
CKAC Radio: 43/47 - 39
O-Pee-Chee: 40/41 - 123
Quaker Oats: 45/54 - 8

Casavant, Denys
CKAC Radio: 43/47 - 18

Casey, Jon (Goalie)
Bowman: 90/91 - 183; 91/92 - 119; 92/93 - 269
Donruss: 93/94 - 16
Fleer: 92/93 - 90; 93/94 - 91, 17PP
Leaf: 93/94 - 322
O-Pee-Chee: 89/90 - 48, 197SK; 90/91 - 269, B/BB; 91/92 - 237, 112PM; 92/93 - 16, 7SP; 93/94 - 437
Panini: 89/90 - 114; 90/91 - 254; 91/92 - 118; 92/93 - 87E, 87F; 93/94 - 276E, 276F
Parkhurst: 91/92 - 77E, 77F; 92/93 - 73, 73EI; 93/94 - 12, 12EI; 94/95 - V55
Pro Set: 90/91 - 133; 91/92 - 111E, 111F, 56PT; 92/93 - 82
Score: 90/91 - 182A, 182C, 80HR; 91/92 - 191A, 191B, 191C, 144PNE, 144PNF; 92/93 - 249C, 249A, 42PNC, 42PNA; 93/94 - 193C, 193A, 41CAS, 41AAS
Season's: 92/93 - 64
Sega: 93/94 - 36
Topps: 89/90 - 48; 90/91 - 269, B/BB; 91/92 - 237, 138SC; 92/93 - 379, 379GS, 198SC; 93/94 - 437C, 303SC, 456SC, 303FD, 456FD, 2AS

Casey, Jon (Goalie) (cont.)
Upper Deck: 90/91 - 385E, 385F; 91/92 - 205E, 205F; 92/93 - 190, 40AS; 93/94 - 507

Cashman, Wayne
Eddie Sargent: 72/73 - 18
Esso: 70/71 - 5
Lipton Soup: 74/75 - 9
Loblaws: 74/75 - 21
Mac's Milk: 73/74 - 3
O-Pee-Chee: 70/71 - 7; 71/72 - 129; 72/73 - 68; 73/74 - 85; 74/75 - 206; 75/76 - 63; 76/77 - 165; 77/78 - 234, 1GP; 78/79 - 124; 79/80 - 79; 80/81 - 318; 81/82 - 11; 82/83 - 8
Post: 82/83 - 2
Topps: 70/71 - 7; 71/72 - 129; 72/73 - 29; 73/74 - 166; 74/75 - 206; 75/76 - 63; 76/77 - 165; 77/78 - 234; 77/78 - 1/PO; 78/79 - 124; 79/80 - 79
Toronto Sun: 71/72 - 6

Cassels, Andrew
Bowman: 91/92 - 340; 92/93 - 387
Donruss: 93/94 - 142
Fleer: 92/93 - 70; 93/94 - 33, 104PP
Leaf: 93/94 - 50
O-Pee-Chee: 91/92 - 176, 72PM; 92/93 - 222; 93/94 - 65, 74SC, 74FD
Panini: 93/94 - 123E
Parkhurst: 91/92 - 285E, 285F; 92/93 - 298, 298EI; 93/94 - 359, 359EI; 94/95 - 97, 97EI, V58
Pro Set: 90/91 - 615; 91/92 - 395E, 395F
Score: 90/91 - 422A, 422C; 91 - 57T; 91/92 - 323C, 323A, 238B, 238C, 607B, 607C; 93/94 - 164C, 164A
Sega: 93/94 - 57
Topps: 91/92 - 176, 329SC; 92/93 - 23, 23GS, 39SC; 93/94 - 65, 74SC, 74FD
Upper Deck: 90/91 - 265E, 265F; 91/92 - 379E, 551E, 379F, 551F; 92/93 - 288; 93/94 - 346

Cattarinich, Joseph (Goalie)
Hall of Fame: 83 - 168, M3P; 87 - 168
Imperial Tobacco: 10/11 - 16

Caufield, Jay
Pro Set: 90/91 - 504

Cavallini, Gino
Bowman: 91/92 - 368
Donruss: 93/94 - 88
O-Pee-Chee: 87/88 - 146; 88/89 - 149; 89/90 - 176; 90/91 - 36; 91/92 - 218; 93/94 - 232, 152SC, 152FD
Panini: 87/88 - 315; 88/89 - 103; 89/90 - 123; 90/91 - 265; 91/92 - 24
Parkhurst: 93/94 - 50, 50EI
Pro Set: 90/91 - 261; 91/92 - 218E, 218F, 224PT
Score: 90/91 - 63A, 63C, 27HR; 91/92 - 258A, 338B, 478B, 338C, 478C, 216PNE, 216PNF; 92/93 - 42C, 42A; 93/94 - 414C, 414A
Topps: 87/88 - 146; 88/89 - 149; 89/90 - 176; 90/91 - 36; 91/92 - 281, 34SC; 92/93 - 234, 234GS, 480SC; 93/94 - 232, 152SC, 152FD
Upper Deck: 90/91 - 38E, 38F; 91/92 - 187E, 646E, 187F, 646F

Cavallini, Paul
Bowman: 90/91 - 22; 91/92 - 378; 92/93 - 193
Fleer: 92/93 - 185, 432; 93/94 - 321PP
Leaf: 93/94 - 397
O-Pee-Chee: 89/90 - 269, 19SK; 90/91 - 57; 91/92 - 328; 92/93 - 379
Panini: 89/90 - 127; 90/91 - 276; 91/92 - 35; 92/93 - 23E, 23F
Parkhurst: 91/92 - 154E, 154F; 94/95 - V12
Pro Set: 90/91 - 262, 353; 91/92 - 214E, 214F, MWCS2; 92/93 - 159
Score: 90/91 - 185A, 185C, 349A, 349C; 91/92 - 107A, 107B, 338B, 107C, 338C, 182PNE, 182PNF, 411PNE,

Cavallini, Paul (cont.)
Score: 411PNF; 92/93 - 22C, 22A, 319PNC, 319PNA; 93/94 - 172C, 172A
Topps: 90/91 - 57; 91/92 - 328, 48SC; 92/93 - 233, 233GS, 447SC
Upper Deck: 90/91 - 281E, 281F; 91/92 - 184E, 646E, 184F, 646F; 92/93 - 212; 93/94 - 441

Ceglarski, Len
Pro Set: 90/91 - 385

Celio, Nicola
Upper Deck: 91/92 - 665E, 665F

Ceresino, Ray
Beehive: 45/63 - 389

Cerny, Michal
Upper Deck: 92/93 - 603

Chabot, John
Bowman: 90/91 - 236
O-Pee-Chee: 84/85 - 258; 85/86 - 244, 101SK; 86/87 - 230SK87/88 - 32, 169SK; 88/89 - 39; 89/90 - 225; 90/91 - 163
Panini: 87/88 - 151; 88/89 - 42; 90/91 - 216
Pro Set: 90/91 - 68
Score: 90/91 - 277A, 277C
Topps: 87/88 - 32; 88/89 - 39; 90/91 - 163
Upper Deck: 90/91 - 113E, 113F; 91/92 - 393E, 393F

Chabot, Frederic
Parkhurst: 94/95 - 169, 169EI

Chabot, Lorne (Chiseler) (Goalie)
Annonymous: 33/34 - 45
Beehive: 34/44 - 46
C.C.M.: 33/36 - 4
Can. Chew. Gum: 33/34 - 9
Diamond: 33/35 - 10; 36/39 - 11(I), 7(II), 8(III)
Hamilton Gum: 33/34 - 30
O-Pee-Chee: 33/34 - 18
Parkhurst: 55/56 - 21
Quaker Oats: 55/56 - 21
Sweet Caporal: 34/35 - 5
World Wide Gum: 33/34 - 71

Chad, John
Beehive: 34/44 - 47

Chadwick, Bill (Official)
Hall of Fame: 83 - 65, E4P; 87 - 65

Chadwick, Ed (Goalie)
Beehive: 45/63 - 428
Parkhurst: 57/58 TOR - 2; 58/59 - 12; 59/60 - 5; 93/94 - 128ML
Shirriff: 61/62 - 20

Chamberlain, Murph
Beehive: 34/44 - 7, 143, 305; 45/63 - 229
CKAC Radio: 43/47 - 40
O-Pee-Chee: 37/38 - 147; 39/40 - 12
Quaker Oats: 38/39 - 18; 45/54 - 9A, 9B, 9C

Chambers, Dave
Pro Set: 90/91 - 675

Chambers, Shawn
Bowman: 90/91 - 180
Donruss: 93/94 - 325
Fleer: 93/94 - 75, 229PP
Leaf: 93/94 - 40
O-Pee-Chee: 89/90 - 142; 90/91 - 192; 93/94 - 101
Panini: 89/90 - 111; 90/91 - 252; 93/94 - 219E, 219F
Parkhurst: 92/93 - 406, 406EI
Pro Set: 90/91 - 134
Score: 90/91 - 57A, 57C; 91/92 - 572B, 572C; 92/93 - 508C, 508A
Topps: 89/90 - 142; 90/91 - 192; 93/94 - 101, 412SC, 412FD
Upper Deck: 90/91 - 106E, 106F; 92/93 - 104; 93/94 - 68

Chant, Shawn
Score: 93/94 - 391C, 391A

Chapman, Art
Beehive: 34/44 - 219

Chapman, Art (cont.)
Diamond: 33/35 - 11; 36/39 - 12(I), 9(II), 9(III)
O-Pee-Chee: 35/36 - 94; 39/40 - 18
World Wide Gum: 33/34 - 32; 36/37 - 42

Chapman, Blair
O-Pee-Chee: 77/78 - 174; 78/79 - 33; 79/80 - 21; 80/81 - 48; 81/82 - 291
Topps: 77/78 - 174; 78/79 - 33; 79/80 - 21; 80/81 - 48; 81/82 WN - 115

Charbonneau, Jose
Fleer: 93/94 - 457PP
Parkhurst: 93/94 - 484, 484EI
Upper Deck: 93/94 - 503

Charlebois, Bob
O-Pee-Chee: 72/73 - 309

Charron, Eric
Parkhurst: 94/95 - 223, 223EI

Charron Guy
Derniere: 72/84 - 103
Eddie Sargent: 72/73 - 80
Loblaws: 74/75 - 93
O-Pee-Chee: 72/73 - 223; 73/74 - 220; 74/75 - 57; 75/76 - 32; 76/77 - 186; 77/78 - 145; 78/79 - 22; 79/80 - 152; 80/81 - 352
Topps: 74/75 - 57; 75/76 - 32; 76/77 - 186; 77/78 - 145; 78/79 - 22; 79/80 - 152
Toronto Sun: 71/72 - 87

Chartraw, Rick
O-Pee-Chee: 75/76 - 388; 76/77 - 244; 77/78 - 363; 78/79 - 238; 79/80 - 243; 80/81 - 364
Post: 82/83 - 114
Topps: 76/77 - 244; 78/79 - 238; 79/80 - 243

Chase, Kelly
Bowman: 90/91 - 14
Donruss: 93/94 -483
O-Pee-Chee: 90/91 - 432; 91/92 - 23
Topps: 91/92 - 23

Cheevers, Gerry (Goalie)
Coca Cola: 65/66 - 5
Colgate: 70/71 - 71
Dad's Cookies: 70/71 - 3
Eddie Sargent: 70/71 - 15
Esso: 70/71 - 6
Hall of Fame: 87 - 250
Hockey Wit: 93/94 - 81
O-Pee-Chee: 68/69 - 140; 69/70 - 22, 12QS; 70/71 - 1; 71/72 - 54; 72/73 - 340; 76/77 - 120; 77/78 - 260, 2GP; 78/79 - 140; 79/80 - 85; 92/93 - 343, 5AN
Shirriff: 68/69 - A4
Topps: 65/66 - 31; 67/68 - 99; 68/69 - 1; 69/70 - 22; 70/71 - 1; 71/72 - 54; 76/77 - 120; 77/78 - 260; 77/78 - 2PO78/79 - 140; 79/80 - 85
Toronto Sun: 71/72 - 7

Chelios, Chris
Bowman: 90/91 - 42; 91/92 - 398; 92/93 - 43, 201
Donruss: 93/94 - 65, 5IK
Cel.Watch: 1988 - CW3
Fleer: 92/93 - 34, 7AS; 93/94 - 40, 2AW, 14AS, 47PP
Gillette: 91/92 - 16
Hockey Wit: 93/94 - 12
Humpty Dumpty: 92/93 - 3(I)
Kraft: 86/87 - 22, 22P; 1990 - 20; 90/91 - 6, 81; 91/92 - 18; 1993 - 13; 93/94 - 25
Leaf: 93/94 - 51, 290, 2AS
McDonald's: 91/92 - Mc22, McH2
O-Pee-Chee: 84/85 - 259; 85/86 - 51, D/BB, 125SK; 86/87 - 171, 6SK; 87/88 - 106, 9SK; 88/89 - 49, 51SK; 89/90 - 174, 323, 156SK, 212SK, 26FS; 90/91 - 29, 90/91 - 13PM; 92/93 - 13 91/92 - 13, 233, 268, 17PM; 93/94 - 94, 237, 147SC, 147FD

Chelios, Chris (cont.)
Panini: 87/88 - 58; 88/89 - 253; 89/90 - 237, 379; 90/91 - 49; 91/92 - 10, 329; 92/93 - 11E, 286E, 11F, 286F; 93/94 - 153E
Parkhurst: 91/92 - 32E, 32F; 92/93 - 29, 457, 29EI, 457EI, CP16; 93/94 - 45, 45EI; 94/95 - 45, 45EI
Pro Set: 90/91 - 147, 368, 427; 91/92 - AC15, 48E, 278E, 48F, 278F, 25PT; 92/93 - 34
Score: 90 - 4T; 90/91 - 15A, 15C, 9HR; 91/92 - 235A, 455B, 455C, 58PNE, 58PNF,B-9E, B-9F; 92/93 - 2C, 496C, 2A, 496A, 109PNC, 109PNA, 2PC(S); 2PC(F), 2USG,2CTP, 2ATP; 93/94 - 101C, 101A, 3DT, 26CAS. 26AAS
Season's: 92/93 - 4
Sega: 93/94 - 25, 186
Topps: 85/86 - 51, D/BB; 86/87 - 171; 87/88 - 106; 88/89 - 49; 89/90 - 174, 1SK; 90/91 - 29; 91/92 - 233, 268, 6SC; 92/93 - 98, 98GS, 87SC; 93/94 - 237, 147SC, 420SC, 459SC, 147FD, 420FD, 459FD, 9AS
Upper Deck: 90/91 - 174E, 174F, 422E, 422F, 491E, 491F; 91/92 - 37E, 354E, 37F, 354F; 92/93 - 159, 629, WJG3, 22AS; 93/94 - 129

Cherbayev, Alexander
Upper Deck: 91/92 - 657E, 657F; 93/94 - 279

Cherry, Dick
O-Pee-Chee: 69/70 - 173

Cherry, Don
O-Pee-Chee: 74/75 - 161
Topps: 74/75 - 161

Cheveldae, Tim (Goalie)
Bowman: 91/92 - 47; 92/93 - 202, 420
Donruss: 93/94 - 96, 507
Fleer: 92/93 - 46; 93/94 - 14, 67PP
Leaf: 93/93 - 195
O-Pee-Chee: 90/91 - 430; 91/92 - 35, 175PM; 92/93 - 128; 93/94 - 66, 166SC, 166FD
Panini: 90/91 - 212; 91/92 - 136; 92/93 - 111E, 111F; 93/94 - 254E, 245F
Parkhurst: 91/92 - 39E, 39F, 441E, 441F; 92/93 - 37, 37EI; 93/94 - 59, 59EI
Pro Set: 90/91 - 602; 91/92 - 57E, 57F, 31PT, 7PK; 92/93 - 43, 251
Score: 90/91 - 87A, 87C; 91 - 25YS; 91/92 - 272A, 492B, 492C, 21PNE, 21PNF; 92/93 - 275C, 417A, 275A, 417A, 37PNC, 269PNC, 37PNA, 269PNA, 20CT, 20AT; 93/94 - 68C, 68A
Season's: 92/93 - 7
Sega: 93/94 - 42
Topps: 91/92 - 35, 92/93 - 225, 310, 225GS, 310GS, 199SC; 93/94 - 66, 166SC, 166FD
Upper Deck: 90/91 - 393E, 393F; 91/92 - 129E, 129F; 92/93 - 5, 197; 93/94 - 9

Chevrefils, Real
Beehive: 45/63 - 11
Parkhurst: 52/53 - 80; 53/54 - 89; 54/55 - 63; 93/94 - 9ML
Topps: 54/55 - 6; 57/58 - 1

Chevrier, Alain (Goalie)
O-Pee-Chee: 86/87 - 225; 87/88 - 58, 63SK; 89/90 - 132; 90/91 - 436
Panini: 87/88 - 73; 89/90 - 54
Pro Set: 90/91 - 230
Topps: 87/88 - 58; 89/90 - 132

Chiasson, Steve
Bowman: 90/91 - 234; 92/93 - 91
Donruss: 93/94 - 97
Fleer: 92/93 - 282; 93/94 - 68PP
Leaf: 93/94 - 111

Chiasson, Steve (cont.)
O-Pee-Chee: 89/90 - 164; 90/91 - 94; 91/92 - 508; 92/93 - 160; 93/94 - 196, 247SC. 247FD
Panini: 89/90 - 62; 90/91 - 207; 91/92 - 143; 92/93 - 120E, 120F; 93/94 - 251E, 251F
Parkhurst: 91/92 - 268E, 268F; 92/93 - 282, 282EI; 93/94 - 55, 55EI; 94/95 - 68, 68EI
Pro Set: 90/91 - 69
Score: 90/91 - 214A, 214C; 91/92 - 293A, 513B, 513C, 298PNE, 298PNF; 92/93 - 339PNC, 339PNA; 93/94 - 221C, 221A, 23CAS, 23AAS
Sega: 93/94 - 38
Topps: 89/90 - 164; 90/91 - 94; 91/92 - 508; 92/93 - 37, 37GS, 105SC; 93/94 - 196(I), 247SC, 247FD, 10AS
Upper Deck: 90/91 - 96E, 96F; 91/92 - 283E, 283F; 92/93 - 546; 93/94 - 345

Chibirev, Igor
Donruss: 93/94 - 436
Fleer: 93/94 - 350PP
O-Pee-Chee: 90/91 - 8R; 91/92 - 14R
Parkhurst: 94/95 - 98, 98EI

Chipperfield, Ron
O-Pee-Chee: 80/81 - 280

Chisholm, Lex (Alexander)
Beehive: 34/44 - 306
O-Pee-Chee: 40/41 - 148

Cholette, Jules
World Wide Gum: 36/37 - 127

Chorney, Marc
Post: 82/83 - 229

Chorske, Tom
Bowman: 91/92 - 345
Fleer: 92/93 - 112; 93/94 - 375PP
O-Pee-Chee: 90/91 - 490; 91/92 - 287, 91PM; 93/94 - 524
Parkhurst: 91/92 - 95E, 95F; 93/94 - 384, 384EI
Pro Set: 90/91 - 616
Score: 91 - 63T; 91/92 - 613B, 613C, 295PNE, 295PNF; 92/93 - 184C, 184A, 293PNC, 293PNA
Topps: 91/92 - 287, 276SC; 92/93 - 313, 313GS, 351SC; 93/94 - 524A
Upper Deck: 91/92 - 427E, 427F; 93/94 - 416

Chouinard, Guy
Derniere: 72/84 - 95
O-Pee-Chee: 76/77 - 316; 77/78 - 237; 78/79 - 340; 79/80 - 60; 80/81 - 45; 81/82 - 33, 219SK; 82/83 - 41, 215SK; 83/84 - 78
PepsiCo: 80/81 - 2; 82/83 - 34
Topps: 77/78 - 237; 79/80 - 60; 80/81 - 45; 81/82 - 6; 82/83 - 215SK

Christian, Dave
Bowman: 90/91 - 40; 91/92 - 358; 92/93 - 6
Fleer: 92/93 - 273
O-Pee-Chee: 80/81 - 176; 81/82 - 359, 360, 378; 82/83 - 377; 83/84 - 367; 84/85 - 195; 85/86 - 99; 86/87 - 21; 87/88 - 88; 88/89 - 14; 89/90 - 159; 90/91 - 263; 91/92 - 276, 53PM; 92/93 - 289, 1PM; 93/94 - 118
Panini: 87/88 - 184; 88/89 - 369; 89/90 - 345; 90/91 - 18; 91/92 - 173
Parkhurst: 91/92 - 159E, 159F
PepsiCo: 80/81 - 124
Post: 82/83 - 323
Pro Set: 90/91 - 6; 91/92 - 11E, 297E, 471E, 11F, 297F, 110PT, 471F
Score: 90/91 - 295A, 295C; 91 - 39T; 91/92 - 292A, 589B, 589C, 244PNE, 244PNF; 92/93 - 198C, 198A, 193PNC, 193PNA; 93/94 - 440C, 440A
Topps: 80/81 - 176; 81/82 - 7, 66; 82/83 - 206SK; 84/85 - 142; 85/86 - 99, 110SK; 86/87 - 21, C/BB, 248SK; 87/88 - 88, 235SK; 88/89 - 14, 70SK; 89/90 - 159, 78SK; 90/91 - 263; 91/92 - 276, 95SC; 92/93 - 21, 21GS, 216SC; 93/94 - 118
Upper Deck: 90/91 - 61E, 61F; 91/92 - 541E, 541F; 92/93 - 194

Christie, Mike
Loblaws: 74/75 - 56
O-Pee-Chee: 74/75 - 278; 75/76 - 366; 76/77 - 333; 77/78 - 357; 78/79 - 291; 79/80 - 345; 80/81 - 358

Christoff, Steve
O-Pee-Chee: 80/81 - 103; 81/82 - 160; 82/83 - 42, 194SK; 83/84 - 169; 84/85 - 81
Post: 82/83 - 131
Topps: 80/81 - 103; 81/82 WN - 104; 82/83 - 194SK

Chrystal, Bob
Parkhurst: 54/55 - 69
Topps: 54/55 - 2

Church, Jack
Beehive: 34/44 - 307
O-Pee-Chee: 39/40 - 52

Churla, Shane
Fleer: 92/93 - 315
O-Pee-Chee: 93/94 - 368
Parkhurst: 92/93 - 316, 316EI
Pro Set: 90/91 - 135
Score: 91/92 - 542B, 542C; 93/94 - 425C, 425A
Topps: 93/94 - 368

Chychrun, Jeff
Bowman: 92/93 - 257
Durivage: 92/93 - 33
O-Pee-Chee: 90/91 - 465
Pro Set: 90/91 - 213
Score: 90/91 - 138A, 138C; 91/92 - 626B, 626C; 92/93 - 364C, 364A
Topps: 92/93 - 196, 196GS, 298SC
Upper Deck: 90/91 - 446E, 446F

Chyzowski, David
Bowman: 91/92 - 229
O-Pee-Chee: 90/91 - 146; 91/92 - 435
Panini: 91/92 - 253
Pro Set: 90/91 - 483
Score: 90/91 - 372A, 372C; 90 - 12YS; 91/92 - 43B, 443C
Topps: 90/91 - 146; 91/92 - 435, 250SC
Upper Deck: 90/91 - 228E, 228F; 91/92 - 281E, 281F

Ciavaglia, Peter
Score: 93/94 - 474C, 474A

Ciccarelli, Dino
Bowman: 90/91 69, HT15; 91/92 - 302; 92/93 - 176
Donruss: 93/94 - 98
Fleer: 92/93 - 47, 283; 93/94 - 32, 69PP
Funmate: 83/84 - 60
Kellogg's: 84 - 18
Kraft: 90/91 - 7; 91/92 - 14
Leaf: 93/94 - 18
McDonald's: 82/83 - 7
O-Pee-Chee: 81/82 - 161; 82/83 - 162, 165, 189SK; 83/84 - 164, 170, 118SK, 119SK; 84/85 - 97, 47SK; 85/86 - 13, 39SK; 86/87 - 138, 86/87 - 169SK; 87/88 - 81, 7HL, 57SK, 118SK; 88/89 - 175, 202SK; 89/90 - 41, 75SK; 90/91 - 100, 14PM; 91/92 - 429; 92/93 - 249, 44PM; 93/94 - 49
Panini: 87/88 - 293; 88/89 - 93; 89/90 - 342; 90/91 - 161;

Ciccarelli, Dino (cont.)
Panini: 91/92 - 207; 92/93 - 160E, 160F; 93/94 - 245E, 245F
Parkhurst: 91/92 - 193E, 193F; 92/93 - 45, 45EI; 93/94 - 60, 60EI, D5; 93/94 - 65, 65EI
Post: 82/83 - 132
Pro Set: 90/91 - 308; 91/92 - 258E, 258F, 131PT
Score: 90/91 - 230A, 230C, 94HR; 91/92 - 128A, 128B, 128C, 128PNE, 128PNF; 92/93 - 395C, 395A, 311PNC, 311PNA; 93/94 - 214C, 214A
Sega: 93/94 - 41
7-Eleven: 84/85 - 28
Topps: 81/82 WN - 105; 82/83 - 189SK, 194SK; 83/84 - 118SK, 119SK; 84/85 - 73; 85/86 - 13, 47SK; 86/87 - 138; 87/88 - 81; 88/89 - 175; 89/90 - 41; 90/91 - 100, 6SL; 91/92 - 429, 118SC; 92/93 - 318, 318GS, 399SC; 93/94 - 49, 294SC, 294FD
Upper Deck: 90/91 - 76E, 76F; 91/92 - 276E, 276F; 92/93 - 461; 93/94 - 136

Ciccone, Enrico
Leaf: 93/94 - 375
O-Pee-Chee: 92/93 - 122PM
Parkhurst: 93/94 - 219, 219EI
Upper Deck: 91/92 - 51E, 51F; 92/93 - 90; 93/94 - 528

Cichocki, Chris
O-Pee-Chee: 86/87 - 41; 124SK
Topps: 86/87 - 41

Ciesla, Hank
Beehive: 45/63 - 84
Parkhurst: 63/64 - 51; 93/94 - 29ML
Topps: 58/59 - 49

Ciger, Zdeno
Bowman: 91/92 - 280
Donruss: 93/94 - 113
Fleer: 92/93 - 113; 93/94 - 78PP
Leaf: 93/94 - 197
O-Pee-Chee: 90/91 - 15PM; 91/92 - 352; 92/93 - 88; 93/94 - 4546, 73SC, 73FD
Panini: 92/93 - 175E, 175F; 93/94 - 239E, 239F
Parkhurst: 92/93 - 286, 286EI; 93/94 - 336, 336EI; 94/95 - 76, 76EI
Pro Set: 90/91 - 619
Score: 90/91 - 82T; 91/92 - 405B, 405C; 92/93 - 534C, 534A, 302PNC, 302PNA; 93/94 - 388C, 388A
Topps: 91/92 - 352, 379SC; 92/93 - 496, 496GS, 228SC; 93/94 - 456C, 73SC, 73FD
Upper Deck: 90/91 - 429E, 429F; 91/92 - 385E, 385F; 92/93 - 457; 93/94 - 330

Cimetta, Robert
Bowman: 91/92 - 160
O-Pee-Chee: 90/91 - 288; 91/92 - 256, 160PM
Topps: 90/91 - 288; 91/92 - 256, 9SC; 92/93 - 181, 181GS, 83SC

Cirella, Joe
Fleer: 93/94 - 91PP
Leaf: 93/94 - 269
O-Pee-Chee: 82/83 - 137; 84/85 - 110, 74SK; 85/86 - 98; 86/87 - 163, 198SK; 87/88 - 170, 61SK; 88/89 - 188, 79SK; 89/90 - 130; 90/91 - 107; 91/92 - 502; 93/94 - 41, 414, 2SC, 2FD
Panini: 87/88 - 75; 88/89 - 268; 90/91 - 141
Parkhurst: 91/92 - 340E, 340F; 93/94 - 347, 347EI
Post: 82/83 - 163
Pro Set: 90/91 - 243
Score: 90/91 - 305C; 91/92 - 441B, 441C; 92/93 - 369C, 369A
Sega: 93/94 - 49

Cirella, Joe (cont.)
　　Topps: 84/85 - 85; 85/86 - 98; 86/87 - 163; 87/88 - 170; 88/89 - 188; 89/90 - 130; 90/91 - 107; 91/92 - 502; 92/93 - 163SC, 479SC; 93/94 - 41, 414C, 2SC, 2FD
　　Upper Deck: 90/91 - 293E, 293F; 93/94 - 65

Cirone, Jason
　　Upper Deck: 91/92 - 605E, 605F

Clackson, Kim
　　O-Pee-Chee: 81/82 - 271
　　PepsiCo: 80/81 - 62

Clancy, Francis (King)
　　Amal. Press: 35/36 - 2
　　Anonymous: 25/26 - 18; 26/27 - 17; 33/34 - 8
　　Beehive: 34/44 - 193, 308
　　Canada Starch: 35/40 - 111
　　Can. Chew. Gum: 33/34 - 10
　　Champ's: 24/25 - 41
　　Hall of Fame: 83 - 33, C3P; 87 - 33
　　Hamilton Gum: 33/34 - 17
　　HHFM: 92 - 8
　　La Presse: 27/32 - 37
　　O-Pee-Chee: 33/34 - 31; 36/37 - 125
　　Parkhurst: 55/56 - 33; 59/60 - 50; 63/64 - 20
　　Quaker Oats: 55/56 - 33
　　Sweet Caporal: 34/35 - 44
　　Topps: 61/62 - 47, 29ST
　　Wm. Paterson: 23/24 - 3; 24/25 - 3
　　World Wide Gum: 33/34 - 1P, 13; 36/37 - 29
　　York: 61/62 - 39

Clapper, Dit (Aubrey Victor)
　　Anonymous: 33/34 - 36
　　Beehive: 34/44 - 8
　　Can. Chew. Gum: 33/34 - 8, 11; 39/40 - 95
　　Diamond: 33/35 - 12
　　Hall of Fame: 83 - 79, F3P; 87 - 79
　　Topps: 60/61 - 26, 30ST
　　World Wide Gum: 33/34 - 1; 36/37 - 36

Clark, Wendel
　　Bowman: 90/91 - 159; 91/92 - 156; 92/93 - 325
　　Cel.Watch: 1988 - CW10
　　Donruss: 93/94 - 337
　　Fleer: 92/93 - 208; 93/94 - 146, 241PP
　　Frito-Lay: 88/89 - 7
　　Gillette: 91/92 - 11
　　Humpty Dumpty: 92/93 - 4(I)
　　Kellogg's: 92 - 3
　　Kraft: 86/87 - 52, 52P; 1990 - 34; 91/92 - 42; 93/94 - 38
　　Leaf: 93/94 - 166
　　O-Pee-Chee: 86/87 - 149, 125SK, 141SK; 87/88 - 12, 152SK; 88/89 - 172SK 90/91 - 79; 91/92 - 464, 116PM, 177PM; 92/93 - 96; 93/94 - 359, 9HR, 192SC, 192FD
　　Panini: 87/88 - 330; 88/89 - 121; 89/90 - 144; 90/91 - 286; 91/92 - 102; 92/93 - 79E, 79F; 93/94 - 227E, 227F
　　Parkhurst: 91/92 - 170E, 170F; 92/93 - 179, 179EI, CP11; 93/94 - 475, 475EI, F9
　　Pro Set: 90/91 - 276; 91/92 - 225E, 585E, 225F, 120PT, 585F; 92/93 - 189
　　Roots: 93/94 - 6
　　Score: 90/91 - 171A, 171C; 91/92 - 116A, 116B, 116C, 250PNE, 250PNF; 92/93 - 110C, 110A, 276PNC, 276PNA; 93/94 - 137C, 137A
　　Season's: 92/93 - 70
　　Topps: 86/87 - 149; 87/88 - 12; 90/91 - 79; 91/92 - 464, 124SC; 92/93 - 325, 325GS, 204SC; 93/94 - 359, 9PF, 192SC, 192FD
　　Upper Deck: 90/91 - 3E, 3F; 91/92 - 386E, 386F; 92/93 - 89; 93/94 - 340

Clarke, Herb
　　Imperial Tobacco: 10/11 - 11

Clarke, Bobby
　　Coca Cola: 77/78 - 3
　　Dad's Cookies: 70/71 - 94
　　Derniere: 72/84 - 106, 168

Clarke, Bobby (cont.)
　　Eddie Sargent: 70/71 - 148; 72/73 - 162
　　Esso: 70/71 - 165; 88/89 - 5
　　Funmate: 83/84 - 94
　　Hall of Fame: 87 - 258
　　HHFM: 92 - 16
　　Hockey Wit: 93/94 - 80
　　Lipton Soup: 74/75 - 21
　　Loblaws: 74/75 - 219
　　Mac's Milk: 73/74 - 4
　　O-Pee-Chee: 70/71 - 195;71/72 - 114, 10BK; 72/73 - 14; 73/74 - 50;74/75 - 135, 260; 75/76 - 250, 286; 76/77 - 70; 77/78 - 115, 3GP; 78/79 - 215; 79/80 - 125; 80/81 - 55, 16PO; 81/82 - 240, 178SK; 82/83 -248, 115SK; 83/84 - 262, 12SK, 198SK, 302SK; 92/93 - 43, 3AN
　　Parkhurst: 92/93 - 468, 468EI
　　Post: 81/82 - 7; 82/83 - 212
　　Pro Set: 90/91 - 651, 657
　　Topps: 71/72 - 114, 10BK; 72/73 - 90; 73/74 - 50; 74/75 - 135, 260; 75/76 - 250, 286; 76/77 - 70, 1PO; 77/78 - 115, 3PO; 78/79 - 215; 79/80 - 125; 80/81 - 55; 81/82 EN - 103; 82/83 - 115SK; 83/84 - 12SK, 198SK, 302SK
　　Toronto Sun: 71/72 - 191
　　Upper Deck: 90/91 - 509E, 509F

Clarke, George
　　Dom. Choc.: 1926 - 26

Cleghorn, Odie (Ogilvie)
　　Anonymous: 1925/26 - 46; 26/27 - 46
　　Champ's: 24/25 - 21
　　Dom. Choc.: 1925 - 117
　　Imperial Tobacco: 10/11 - 25L; 11/12 - 25; 12/13 - 50
　　Wm. Paterson: 23/24 - 18; 24/25 - 45

Cleghorn, Sprague
　　Anonymous: 1925/26 - 41; 26/27 - 31
　　Champ's: 24/25 - 22
　　Hall of Fame: 83 - 66, E5P; 87 - 66
　　Imperial Tobacco: 10/11 - 24L; 11/12 - 24; 12/13 - 15
　　Maple Crispette: 24/25 - 15
　　Topps: 60/61 - 31ST
　　Wm. Paterson: 23/24 - 11; 24/25 - 49

Clement, Bill
　　Eddie Sargent: 72/73 - 168
　　Loblaws: 74/75 - 220
　　O-Pee-Chee: 74/75 - 357; 75/76 - 189; 76/77 - 82; 77/78 - 292; 78/79 - 364; 79/80 - 295; 80/81 - 376; 81/82 - 39; 82/83 - 44
　　Parkhurst: 92/93 - 478, 478EI
　　PepsiCo: 80/81 - 3
　　Topps: 75/76 - 189; 76/77 - 82

Climie, Ron
　　O-Pee-Chee: 72/73 - 318

Cline, Bruce
　　Parkhurst: 93/94 - 106ML

Cloutier, Jacques (Goalie)
　　Bowman: 90/91 - 11; 91/92 - 146; 92/93 - 332
　　Durivage: 92/93 - 46; 93/94 - 18
　　O-Pee-Chee: 90/91 - 378; 91/92 - 286; 92/93 - 113
　　Panini: 87/88 - 21; 90/91 - 197
　　Parkhurst: 91/92 - 368E, 368F
　　Pro Set: 90/91 - 428; 91/92 - 219PT
　　Score: 91/92 - 236B, 236C; 92/93 - 378C, 378A
　　Topps: 90/91 - 378; 91/92 - 286, 166SC; 92/93 - 66, 66GS, 118SC
　　Upper Deck: 90/91 - 114E, 114F; 92/93 - 324

Cloutier, Real
　　Derniere: 72/84 - 48, 51, 86, 155, 198
　　Funmate: 83/84 - 9
　　O-Pee-Chee: 79/80 - 239; 80/81 - 178, 238; 81/82 - 74SK; 82/83 - 279, 280, 23SK; 83/84 - 62, 246SK; 84/85 - 19
　　Post: 81/82 - 17; 82/83 - 241

Cloutier, Real (cont.)
　　Topps: 79/80 - 239; 80/81 - 178, 238; 82/83 - 23SK; 83/84 - 2456SK; 84/85 - 15

Coalter, Gary
　　Loblaws: 74/75 - 110
　　O-Pee-Chee: 74/75 - 17; 75/76 - 334
　　Topps: 74/75 - 17

Cochrane, Glen
　　Kraft: 86/87 - 63, 63P
　　Post: 82/83 - 213

Cockburn, William
　　La Presse: 27/32 - 69

Coffey, Paul
　　Bowman: 90/91 - 211; 91/92 - 81; 92/93 - 181, 226
　　Cel.Watch: 1988 - CW14
　　Donruss: 93/94 - 99
　　Esso: 83/84 - 5E, 5F; 88/89 - 6
　　Fleer: 92/93 - 80, 1AS; 93/94 - 71, 70PP
　　Frito-Lay: 88/89 - 8
　　Funmate: 83/84 - 38
　　Gillette: 91/92 - 37
　　Hockey Wit: 93/94 - 46
　　Kellogg's: 84 - 1
　　Kraft: 86/87 - 12, 12P; 1990 - 54; 90/91 - 8, 82, 92/93 - 20, 4SP; 93/94 - 4
　　Leaf: 93/94 - 67, 7AS
　　McDonald's: 91/92 - Mc11
　　O-Pee-Chee: 81/82 - 111; 82/83 - 101, 102, 104SK, 105SK, 160SK; 83/84 - 25, 94SK, 95SK; 84/85 - 217, 239, 134SK,251SK, 252SK; 85/86 - 85, 56SK, 124SK, 191SK, 217SK; 86/87 - 137, 68SK, 112SK, 188SK; 87/88 - 99, 8HL, 89SK; 88/89 - 179, 6NS, 233SK;89/90 - 95, 237SK; 90/91 - 116, 202, C/BB, 16PM; 91/92 - 183, 504, 79PM; 92/93 - 5, 187, 318, 14AN; 93/94 - 145
　　Panini: 87/88 - 256; 88/89 - 333; 89/90 - 183, 311; 90/91 - 135, 324; 91/92 - 276, 336; 92/93 - 72E, 278E, 72F, 278F ; 93/94 - 252E, 134E, 252F
　　Parkhurst: 91/92 - 140E, 212E, 225E, 297E140F, 212F, 225F, 297F; 92/93 - 63, 276, 458, 63EI, 276EI, 458EI; 93/94 - 56, 56EI, D8; 94/95 - 63, 63EI
　　PepsiCo: 80/81 - 24
　　Post: 82/83 - 83
　　Pro Set: 90/91 - 231, 361; 91/92 - 190E, 312E, 190F, 312F, 94PT, 21PK; 92/93 - 71
　　Score: 90/91 - 6A, 6C, 319A, 319C, 332A, 332C, 65HR; 91 - 6P; 91/92 - 115A, 372A, 115B, 262B, 115C, 262C, 186PNE, 377PNE, 186PNF, 377PNF; 92/93 - 265C, 441C, 441A, 265A, 50PNC, 50PNA, 3CTP, 3ATP; 93/94 - 106C, 106A, 8DT, 43CAS, 43AAS
　　Sega: 93/94 - 37
　　7-Eleven: 84/85 - 14
　　Topps: 82/83 - 104SK, 105SK, 160SK; 83/84 - 94SK, 95SK; 84/85 - 50, 163; 85/86 - 85, 4SK; 86/87 - 137, 5SK; 87/88 - 99; 88/89 - 179; 89/90 - 95; 90/91 - 116, 202, C/BB; 91/92 - 183, 504, 212SC, 4SCM; 92/93 - 5, 182, 5GS, 182GS, 169SC; 93/94 - 145, 6BG, 450SC, 450FD, 4AS, 4SCF
　　Upper Deck: 90/91 - 124E, 124F, 498E, 498F; 91/92 - 11E, 177E, 615E, 11F, 177F, 615F; 92/93 - 116, 23AS; 93/94 - 315
　　Vachon Foods: 83/84 - 22

Cole, Danton
　　Bowman: 91/92 - 202
　　Donruss: 93/94 - 491

Cole, Danton (cont.)
- Fleer: 93/94 - 441PP
- O-Pee-Chee: 90/91 - 17PM; 91/92 - 27; 93/94 - 239SC, 239FD
- Panini: 91/92 - 72; 92/93 - 56E, 56F
- Parkhurst: 92/93 - 408, 408EI; 93/94 - 464, 464EI
- Pro Set: 91/92 - 263E, 263F
- Score: 91/92 - 240B, 240C
- Topps: 91/92 - 27, 342SC; 93/94 - 239SC, 239FD
- Upper Deck: 90/91 - 517E, 517F; 91/92 - 210E 210F

Coleman, Joe
- Donruss: 93/94 - 4JCA
- Upper Deck: 93/94 - 563

Collett, E.J.
- Dom. Choc.: 1925 - 55
- Willards: 1925 - 45

Collins, Bill
- Eddie Sargent: 70/71 - 104; 72/73 - 71
- Esso: 70/71 - 128
- Loblaws: 74/75 - 255
- O-Pee-Chee: 69/70 - 126; 71/72 - 139; 72/73 - 265; 73/74 - 163; 74/75 - 364
- Shirriff: 68/69 - E7A
- Topps: 73/74 - 158
- Toronto Sun: 71/72 - 88

Collins, Gary
- Parkhurst: 57/58 TOR - 23

Collins, Kevin
- Pro Set: 90/91 - 683

Collyard, Bob
- Loblaws: 74/75 - 311

Colville, Mac (Matthew)
- Beehive: 34/44 - 265
- World Wide Gum: 36/37 - 89
- O-Pee-Chee: 39/40 - 90

Colville, Neil
- Beehive: 34/44 - 266
- Hall of Fame: 83 - 5, A4P; 87 - 5
- O-Pee-Chee: 36/37 - 105; 39/40 - 39
- World Wide Gum: 36/37 - 91

Colwill, Les
- Topps: 58/59 - 19

Comeau, Rey
- Loblaws: 74/75 - 5
- O-Pee-Chee: 72/73 - 239; 73/74 - 29; 74/75 - 296; 75/76 - 248; 76/77 - 343; 77/78 - 346; 78/79 - 293; 79/80 - 385
- Topps: 73/74 - 29; 75/76 - 248

Conacher, Brian
- Beehive: 64/67 - 159
- O-Pee-Chee: 71/72 - 138; 92/93 - 49PM
- Shirriff: 68/69 - C14
- Topps: 67/68 - 17
- Toronto Sun: 71/72 - 89

Conacher, Charlie
- Amal. Press: 35/36 - 3
- Anonymous: 33/34 - 5
- Beehive: 34/44 - 96, 220, 309
- C.C.M.: 33/36 - 5
- Can. Chew. Gum: 33/34 - 12
- Hall of Fame: 83 - 6, A5P; 87 - 6
- Hamilton Gum: 33/34 - 49
- HHFM: 92 - 14
- La Presse: 27/32 - 60
- O-Pee-Chee: 33/34 - 34; 36/37 - 123; 37/38 - 138; 39/40 - 59
- Parkhurst: 55/56 - 26
- Quaker Oats: 55/56 - 26
- Sweet Caporal: 34/35 - 45
- World Wide Gum: 36/37 - 1

Conacher, Jim
- Beehive: 45/63 - 85, 304
- Parkhurst: 51/52 - 105; 52/53 - 103

Conacher, John
- Beehive: 45/63 - 157

Conacher, Lionel
- Can. Chew. Gum: 33/34 - 13
- Diamond: 33/35 - 13
- Dom. Choc.: 1925 - 118
- La Presse: 27/32 - 16
- O-Pee-Chee: 36/37 - 102
- Sweet Caporal: 34/35 - 28
- World Wide Gum: 36/37 - 10

Conacher, Patrick (Pat)
- Donruss: 93/94 - 1
- Fleer: 93/94 - 358PP
- Leaf: 93/94 - 380
- O-Pee-Chee: 93/94 - 252, 179SC, 179FD
- Parkhurst: 93/94 - 363, 363EI; 94/95 - 107, 107EI
- Pro Set: 90/91 - 477; 91/92 - 427E, 427F
- Score: 91/92 - 654B, 654C; 92/93 - 544C, 544A
- Topps: 91/92 - 387SC; 93/94 - 252, 179SC, 179FD

Conacher, Pete
- Beehive: 45/63 - 86, 391
- Parkhurst: 52/53 - 33; 53/54 - 70; 54/55 - 86; 57/58 TOR - 14
- Topps: 54/55 - 33

Conacher, Roy
- Beehive: 34/44 - 9; 45/63 - 87
- Parkhurst: 51/52 - 50

Conn, Joe
- Beehive: 45/63 - 88

Conn, Red
- Diamond: 33/35 - 14; 36/39 - 13(I)

Connell, Alex (Goalie)
- Anonymous: 1926/27 - 16
- Beehive: 34/44 - 194
- Can. Chew. Gum: 33/34 - 14
- Champ's: 24/25 - 42
- Hall of Fame: 83 - 169, M4P; 87 - 169
- Sweet Caporal: 34/35 - 29
- Wm. Paterson: 24/25 - 10

Connelly, Bert
- Diamond: 36/39 - 14(I), 10(II), 10(III)

Connelly, Wayne
- Beehive: 45/63 - 12A, 12B; 64/67 - 4
- Dad's Cookies: 70/71 - 46
- Eddie Sargent: 70/71 - 54
- Esso: 70/71 - 75
- O-Pee-Chee: 68/69 - 50; 69/70 - 60; 70/71 - 159; 71/72 - 237; 72/73 - 296
- Shirriff: 68/69 - E1
- Parkhurst: 61/62 - 44
- Topps: 62/63 - 18; 66/67 - 40; 68/69 - 50; 69/70 - 60; 71/72 - 127
- Toronto Sun: 71/72 - 237

Connor, Cam
- O-Pee-Chee: 79/80 - 138; 80/81 - 387
- Topps: 79/80 - 138

Conroy, Allan
- O-Pee-Chee: 93/94 - 352
- Topps: 92/93 - 525GS; 93/94 - 352

Convery, Brandon
- Donruss: 93/94 - 8JCC
- Upper Deck: 93/94 - 548

Cook, Bill
- Amal. Paper: 35/36 - 5
- Beehive: 34/44 - 257
- Diamond: 33/35 - 15; 36/39 - 15(I), 11(II), 12(II), 11(III)
- Hall of Fame: 83 - 126, I5P; 87 - 126
- O-Pee-Chee: 33/34 - 38
- Sweet Caporal: 34/35 - 40
- Topps: 60/61 - 10, 33ST
- Wm. Paterson: 24/25 - 24
- World Wide Gum: 33/34 - 30

Cook, Bun (Fred)
- Anonymous: 26/27 - 41; 33/34 - 46

Cook, Bunn (Fred) (cont.)
- Beehive: 34/44 - 10
- Can. Chew. Gum: 33/34 - 15
- Diamond: 33/35 - 16; 36/39 - 15(I), 13(II), 12(III)
- La Presse: 27/32 - 31
- O-Pee-Chee: 34/35 - 72
- Sweet Caporal: 34/35 - 41
- World Wide Gum: 33/34 - 66

Cook, Lloyd
- Maple Crispette: 24/25 - 6

Cook, Tom
- Beehive: 34/44 - 195
- Diamond: 33/35 - 17; 36/39 - 16(I), 14(II), 13(III) 4(IV), 3(V(, 3(VI)
- La Presse: 27/32 - 67
- O-Pee-Chee: 37/38 - 180

Cooper, Carson
- Anonymous: 26/27 - 32
- Champ's: 24/25 - 1
- Maple Crispette: 24/25 - 9
- Wm. Paterson: 24/25 - 21

Cooper, Joe
- Beehive: 34/44 - 48, 268

Copp, Bob
- Beehive: 34/44 - 310

Corbeau, Bert
- Champ's: 24/25 - 50
- Wm. Paterson: 23/24 - 25; 24/25 - 58

Corbet, Rene
- Parkhurst: 93/94 - 433, 433EI; 94/95 - 193, 193EI
- Upper Deck: 93/94 - 339

Corkum, Bob
- Donruss: 93/94 - 10
- Fleer: 93/94 - 282PP
- Parkhurst: 91/91 - 238E, 238F; 93/94 - 6, 6EI
- Topps: 92/93 - 74, 74GS, 179SC; 93/94 - 284SC, 284FD
- Upper Deck: 90/91 - 35E, 35F

Corrigan Mike
- Eddie Sargent: 72/73 - 94
- Esso: 70/71 - 236
- Loblaws: 74/75 - 129
- O-Pee-Chee: 70/71 - 227; 71/72 - 157; 72/73 - 74; 73/74 - 48; 74/75 - 37; 75/76 - 361; 76/77 - 268; 77/78 - 236
- Topps: 72/73 - 89; 73/74 - 48; 74/75 - 37; 77/78 - 236

Corriveau, Andre
- La Patrie: 51/54 - 17

Corriveau, Rick
- Score: 90/91 - 396A, 396C

Corriveau, Yvon
- O-Pee-Chee: 90/91 - 364; 92/93 - 74PM; 93/94 - 208, 9SC, 9FD
- Panini: 92/93 - 259E, 259F
- Parkhurst: 92/93 - 295, 295EI
- Pro Set: 90/91 - 100
- Score: 90/91 - 302A; 92/93 - 541C, 541A
- Topps: 90/91 - 364; 92/93 - 474, 474GS, 476SC; 93/94 - 208, 9SC, 9FD
- Upper Deck: 91/92 - 407E, 407F; 92/93 - 460

Corsi, Jim (Goalie)
- Derniere: 72/84 - 78

Corson, Jimmy
- Score: 91/92 - 224A

Corson, Shayne
- Bowman: 90/91 - 41; 91/92 - 328; 92/93 - 82
- Donruss: 93/94 - 114
- Fleer: 92/93 - 57, 292; 93/94 - 51, 79PP
- Humpty Dumpty: 92/93 - 2(II)
- Kraft: 89/90 - 21; 1990 -21
- Leaf: 93/94 - 46
- O-Pee-Chee: 87/88 - 127SK; 89/90 - 248, 49SK; 90/91 - 58; 92/93 - 231; 91/92 - 157, 161PM; 93/94 - 38, 40SC, 40FD

Corson, Shayne (cont.)
Panini: 89/90 - 242; 90/91 - 54; 91/92 - 196; 92/93 - 150E, 150F; 93/94 - 236E, 236F
Parkhurst: 91/92 - 86E, 86F; 92/93 - 53, 53EI; 93/94 - 338, 338EI; 94/95 - 75, 75EI, V3
Pro Set: 90/91 - 148, 369; 91/92 - 413E, 413F; 92/93 - 89
Score: 90/91 - 213A, 213C, 91HR; 91/92 - 65A, 65B, 65C, 102PNE, 102PNF; 92/93 - 158C, 158A, 323PNC, 323PNA; 93/94 - 108C, 108A
Sega: 93/94 - 46
Topps: 90/91 - 58; 91/92 - 157, 5SC; 92/93 - 201, 201GS, 221SC; 93/94 - 38, 40SC, 40FD
Upper Deck: 90/91 - 280E, 280F; 91/92 - 282E, 282F, 505E, 505F; 92/93 - 330, 541; 93/94 - 132

Costello, Les
Beehive: 45/63 - 392
Quaker Oats: 45/54 - 68

Costello, Murray
Beehive: 45/63 - 13, 89
Parkhurst: 93/94 - 60ML

Costello, Rich
O-Pee-Chee: 84/85 - 298

Coté, Alain
Derniere: 72/84 - 82, 156
Durivage: 93/94 - 19
Kraft: 86/87 - 43, 43P
O-Pee-Chee: 79/80 - 324; 81/82 - 272; 82/83 - 281; 83/84 - 291; 84/85 - 278; 85/86 - 205, 149SK; 86/87 - 233, 20SK; 87/88 - 254; 88/89 - 205, 186SK; 91/92 - 188PM
Panini: 87/88 - 169; 88/89 - 352
Post: 82/83 - 242
Pro Set: 91/92 - 417E, 417F
Vachon Foods: 83/84 - 63

Coté, Sylvain
Bowman: 91/92 - 17; 92/93 - 115
Donruss: 93/94 - 367
Durivage: 92/93 - 34; 93/94 - 35
Fleer: 92/93 - 433; 93/94 - 259PP
Leaf: 93/94 - 52
O-Pee-Chee: 89/90 - 162; 91/92 - 249; 92/93 - 277; 93/94 - 138, 66SC, 66FD
Panini: 88/89 - 237; 89/90 - 229
Parkhurst: 92/93 - 431, 431EI; 93/94 - 489, 489EI
Pro Set: 90/91 - 448; 91/92 - 82E, 512E, 82F, 512F
Score: 90/91 - 83A, 83C; 91 - 46T; 91/92 - 129A, 129B, 129C, 596B, 596C, 221PNE, 221PNF; 92/93 - 78, 78A, 182PNC, 182PNA; 93/94 - 92C, 92A
Topps: 89/90 - 162; 91/92 - 249, 183SC; 92/93 - 428, 428GS, 145SC; 93/94 - 138, 66SC, 66FD
Upper Deck: 91/92 - 221E

Cotton, Baldy (Harold)
Anonymous: 33/34 - 12
Beehive: 34/44 - 311
Hamilton Gum: 33/34 - 39
O-Pee-Chee: 33/34 - 35
Parkhurst: 55/56 - 32
Quaker Oats: 55/56 - 32
World Wide Gum: 33/34 - 33; 36/37 - 35

Coulter, Art
Beehive: 34/44 - 269
Diamond: 36/39 - 17(I), 15(II), 14(III)
Hall of Fame: 83 - 185, J5P; 87 - 185
O-Pee-Chee: 35/36 - 93; 39/40 - 34

Cournoyer, Yvan
Bazooka: 71/72 - 15
Beehive: 64/67 - 101
Coca-Cola: 64/65 - 58; 65/66 - 57; 77/78 - 4
Colgate: 70/71 - 60; 71/72 - 1

Cournoyer, Yvan (cont.)
Derniere: 72/84 - 25, 30
Dom. Choc.: 70/71 - 74
Eddie Sargent: 70/71 - 109; 71/72 - 102; 72/73 - 117
Esso: 70/71 - 129; 88/89 - 7
Hall of Fame: 83 - 138, K1P; 87 - 136
Letraset: 74/75 - 13
Loblaws: 74/75 - 164
Mac's Milk: 73/74 - 5
O-Pee-Chee: 68/69 - 62; 69/70 - 6, 221, 4ST, 3QS; 70/71 - 50, 23DE; 71/72 - 15, 260, 4PT; 72/73 - 29, 44; 73/74 - 157; 74/75 - 140; 75/76 - 70; 76/77 - 30; 77/78 - 230; 78/79 - 60
Post: 68/69 - 3
Shirriff: 68/69 - F13
Topps: 65/66 - 76; 66/67 - 72; 66/67 US - 13; 67/68 - 70; 68/69 - 62; 69/70 - 6; 70/71 - 50; 71/72 - 15; 72/73 - 10, 131; 73/74 - 115; 74/75 - 140; 75/76 - 70; 76/77 - 30; 77/78 - 230; 78/79 - 60
Toronto Sun: 71/72 - 148
Zellers: 93/94 - 3, 3A

Courtenay, Ed
Fleer: 93/94 - 8
Leaf: 93/94 - 145
O-Pee-Chee: 92/93 - 8PM; 93/94 - 72SC, 72FD
Panini: 93/94 - 261E, 261F
Topps: 93/94 - 72SC, 72FD
Upper Deck: 91/92 - 517E, 517F

Courtnall, Geoff
Bowman: 90/91 - 73; 91/92 - 318; 92/93 - 345
Donruss: 93/94 - 352
Fleer: 92/93 - 220; 93/94 - 76, 249PP
Kraft: 90/91 - 9; 91/92 - 15
Leaf: 93/94 - 72
O-Pee-Chee: 88/89 - 222SK; 89/90 - 111, 80SK, 164SK, 29FS; 90/91 - 273; 90/91 - 18PM; 91/92 - 305, 101PM; 92/93 - 176; 93/94 - 337, 55SC, 55FD
Panini: 89/90 - 340; 90/91 - 159; 91/92 - 38; 92/93 - 29E, 29F; 93/94 - 170E
Parkhurst: 91/92 - 186E, 186F; 92/93 - 189, 189EI; 93/94 - 216, 216EI; 94/95 - 240, 240EI
Pro Set: 90/91 - 309, 521; 91/92 - 245E, 245F, 123PT; 92/93 - 198
Score: 90/91 - 124A, 124C, 5T; 91/92 - 150A, 150B, 150C, 263PNE, 263PNF; 92/93 - 234C, 234A, 187PNC, 187PNA; 93/94 - 78C, 78A
Season's: 92/93 - 33
Sega: 93/94 - 142
Topps: 89/90 - 111, 9SK; 90/91 - 273; 91/92 - 305, 149SC; 92/93 - 472, 472GS, 265SC; 93/94 - 337, 413SC, 413FD
Upper Deck: 90/91 - 238E, 238F, 438E, 438F; 91/92 - 467E, 467F; 92/93 - 240; 93/94 - 114

Courtnall, Russell (Russ)
Bowman: 90/91 - 47; 91/92 - 346; 92/93 - 45
Donruss: 93/94 - 80
Fleer: 92/93 - 91, 316; 93/94 - 50, 58PP, 2SM
Humpty Dumpty: 92/93 - 3(II)
Kraft: 86/87 - 53, 53P; 1990 - 22; 91/92 - 49
Leaf: 93/94 - 65
O-Pee-Chee: 85/86 - 20SK; 86/87 - 174, 149SK; 87/88 - 62, P/BB, 156SK; 88/89 - 183, 175SK; 89/90 - 239, 53SK; 90/91 - 124; 91/92 - 119, 58PM, 194PM; 92/93 - 284, 20PM; 93/94 - 153
Panini: 87/88 - 32788/89 - 122; 90/91 - 56; 91/92 - 186; 92/93 - 154E, 154F; 93/94 - 268E, 268F
Parkhurst: 91/92 - 308E, 308F; 92/93 - 78, 78EI; 93/94 - 53, 53EI; 94/95 - 52, 52EI
Pro Set: 90/91 - 149; 91/92 - 126E, 126F, 62PT

Courtnall, Russell (Russ) (cont.)
Score: 90/91 - 148A, 148C; 91/92 - 42A, 42B, 42C, 254PNE, 254PNF; 92/93 - 4C, 4A, 337PNC, 337PNA; 93/94 - 130C, 130A
Sega: 93/94 - 35
Topps: 86/87 - 174; 87/88 - 62, P/BB; 88/89 - 183; 90/91 - 124; 91/92 - 119, 18SL, 43SC; 92/93 - 276, 276GS, 152SC; 93/94 - 153, 55SC, 55FD
Upper Deck: 90/91 - 259E, 259F; 91/92 - 168E, 168F; 92/93 - 94, 441; 93/94 - 32

Courtnay, Ed
Fleer: 93/94 - 217PP

Couture, Billy
Anonymous: 1926/27 - 2
Champ's: 24/25 - 23
Dom. Choc.: 1925 - 89
Wm. Paterson: 23/24 - 17; 24/25 - 44

Couture, Gerald (Gerry)
Beehive: 45/63 - 90, 158
Parkhurst: 51/52 - 17; 52/53 - 41; 53/54 - 84
Quaker Oats: 45/54 - 10

Couture, Nick (Doc)
Beehive: 45/63 - 254

Couture, Rosario (Lolo)
Diamond: 33/35 - 18; 36/39 - 18(I), 16(II), 15(III)
La Presse: 27/32 - 64

Couturier, Sylvain
Upper Deck: 91/92 - 491E, 491F

Cowick, Bruce
O-Pee-Chee: 74/75 - 386

Cowley, Bill (Cowboy)
Beehive: 34/44 - 11
CKAC Radio: 43/47 - 3
Diamond: 36/39 - 19(II)
Hall of Fame: 83 - 170, M5P, 87 - 170
O-Pee-Chee: 39/40 - 98

Cox, Danny
Anonymous: 33/34 - 48
Can. Chew. Gum: 33/34 - 16
O-Pee-Chee: 33/34 - 1
World Wide Gum: 33/34 - 69

Coxe, Craig
O-Pee-Chee: 90/91 - 339; 91/92 - 447
Pro Set: 90/91 - 544; 91/92 - 329E, 329F
Score: 91 - 96T; 91/92 - 646B, 646C
Topps: 90/91 - 339; 91/92 - 447
Upper Deck: 91/92 - 60E, 60F

Craig, Jim (Goalie)
O-Pee-Chee: 80/81 - 22
Topps: 80/81 - 22

Craig, Mike
Bowman: 91/92 - 130; 92/93 - 334
Donruss: 93/94 - 81
Fleer: 92/93 - 317; 93/94 - 322PP
Leaf: 93/94 - 88
O-Pee-Chee: 90/91 - 19PM; 91/92 - 187; 92/93 - 103; 93/94 - 309
Panini: 92/93 - 95E, 95F; 93/94 - 271E, 271F
Parkhurst: 91/92 - 301E, 301F; 92/93 - 314, 314EI; 93/94 - 323, 323EI; 94/95 - 54, 54EI
Pro Set: 90/91 - 613; 91/92 - 405E, 405F, 189PT
Score: 90 - 59T; 91/92 - 181A, 181B, 181C, 219PNE, 219PNF; 92/93 - 271C, 271A, 99PNC, 99PNA; 93/94 - 156C, 156A
Topps: 91/92 - 187, 344SC; 92/93 - 238, 238GS, 268SC; 93/94 - 309, 355SC, 355FD
Upper Deck: 90/91 - 472E, 472F; 91/92 - 125E, 125F; 92/93 - 65; 93/94 - 191

Craigwell, Dale
Bowman: 92/93 - 198
Fleer: 92/93 - 192
O-Pee-Chee: 92/93 - 271; 93/94 - 348

Craigwell, Dale (cont.)
Panini: 92/93 - 133E, 133F
Parkhurst: 91/92 - 389E, 389F;
92/93 - 168, 168EI
Score: 92/93 - 466C, 466A
Topps: 92/93 - 60, 60GS, 464SC; 93/94 - 348
Upper Deck: 90/91 - 464E, 464F; 92/93 - 40;
93/94 - 56

Crashley, Bart
O-Pee-Chee: 72/73 - 295
Topps: 67/68 - 105

Craven, Murray
Bowman: 90/91 - 109; 91/92 - 239; 92/93 - 280
Donruss: 93/94 - 353
Fleer: 92/93 - 71; 93/94 - 458PP
Leaf: 93/94 - 5
O-Pee-Chee: 83/84 - 120; 85/86 - 53, 95SK;
86/87 - 167, 244SK; 87/88 - 22,
69SK; 88/89 - 79, 98SK; 89/90 - 44;
90/91 - 318; 91/92 - 254; 92/93 - 127,
3S; 93/94 - 400
Panini: 87/88 - 133; 88/89 - 320; 90/91 - 116;
91/92 - 234; 92/93 - 262E, 262F;
93/94 - 169E
Parkhurst: 91/92 - 288E, 288F; 92/93 - 55, 495,
55EI, 495EI; 93/94 - 208, 208EI;
94/95 - 242, 242EI
Pro Set: 90/91 - 214; 91/92 - 175E, 393E,
175F, 393F, 179PT; 92/93 - 60
Score: 90/91 - 56A, 56C; 91/92 - 262A,
482B, 482C, 177PNE, 177PNF;
92/93 - 18C, 18A, 281PNC, 281PNA;
93/94 - 49C, 49A
Topps: 85/86 - 53; 86/87 - 167; 87/88 - 22;
88/89 - 79; 89/90 - 44; 90/91 - 318;
91/92 - 254, 176SC; 92/93 - 248,
248GS, 442SC; 93/94 - 400C,
264SC, 264FD
Upper Deck: 90/91 - 6E, 6F; 91/92 - 306E, 306F;
92/93 - 49; 93/94 - 410

Crawford, Bob
O-Pee-Chee: 84/85 - 68, 197SK;
85/86 - 162, 167SK
Topps: 83/84 - 126SK; 84/85 - 53;
85/86 - 162

Crawford, John (Jack)
Beehive: 34/44 - 14; 45/63 - 15
O-Pee-Chee: 40/41 - 134

Crawford, Marc
O-Pee-Chee: 82/83 - 342
Post: 82/83 - 291

Crawford, Rusty
Hall of Fame: 83 - 67, E6P; 87 - 67

Creighton, Adam
Bowman: 90/91 - 9; 91/92 - 394; 92/93 - 88
Donruss: 93/94 - 326
Fleer: 92/93 - 409
Kraft: 91/92 - 47
Leaf: 93/94 - 85
O-Pee-Chee: 89/90 - 218; 90/91 - 83; 91/92 - 314,
171PM; 92/93 - 85, 61PM;
93/94 - 2SC, 5FD
Panini: 87/88 - 31; 88/89 - 225; 89/90 - 51
90/91 - 193; 91/92 - 13; 92/93 - 204E,
204F; 93/94 - 215E, 215F
Parkhurst: 91/92 - 113E, 113F; 92/93 - 172,
172EI; 94/95 - 222, 222EI
Pro Set: 90/91 - 50; 91/92 - 42E, 437E,
42F, 17PK, 437F; 92/93 - 103
Score: 90/91 - 82A, 82C; 91 - 21T;
91/92 - 265A, 485B, 485C, 82PNE,
82PNF; 92/93 - 144C, 144A,
199PNC, 199PNA; 93/94 - 86C, 86A
Topps: 90/91 - 83; 91/92 - 314, 89SC;
92/93 - 451, 451GS, 45SC;
93/94 - 5SC, 5FD
Upper Deck: 90/91 - 4E, 4F; 91/92 - 254E, 254F;
92/93 - 311

Creighton, Dave
Beehive: 45/63 - 15A, 15B, 393
Parkhurst: 52/53 - 76; 53/54 - 85; 54/55 - 58;
60/61 - 10; 93/94 - 99ML

Creighton, Dave (cont.)
Topps: 57/58 - 66

Crha, Jiri (Goalie)
O-Pee-Chee: 81/82 - 315, 106SK
PepsiCo: 80/81 - 83

Crisp, Terry
Eddie Sargent: 70/71 - 182; 71/72 - 179; 72/73 - 128
Esso: 70/71 - 201
Loblaws: 74/75 - 221
O-Pee-Chee: 71/72 - 127; 72/73 - 88;
74/75 - 352; 75/76 - 337
Shirriff: 68/69 - L10
Topps: 72/73 - 103
Toronto Sun: 71/72 - 238

Crogan, Maurice
World Wide Gum: 36/37 - 103

Crombeen, Mike
O-Pee-Chee: 83/84 - 312, 126SK
Post: 82/83 - 260

Cronin, Shawn
Bowman: 90/91 - 128
O-Pee-Chee: 92/93 - 42PM
Parkhurst: 91/92 - 423E, 423F
Pro Set: 90/91 - 559; 91/92 - 268E, 268F
Score: 91/92 - 423B, 423C;
92/93 - 366C, 366A
Topps: 92/93 - 489, 489GS, 471SC
Upper Deck: 91/92 - 478E, 478F

Crossman, Douglas (Doug)
Bowman: 90/91 - 115
Fleer: 92/93 - 410
Kraft: 90/91 - 10
O-Pee-Chee: 82/83 - 63; 83/84 - 263;
84/85 - 157; 86/87 - 237SK;
87/88 - 182; 88/89 - 197, 100SK;
90/91 - 72; 91/92 - 341;
92/93 - 59PM; 93/94 - 159
Panini: 87/88 - 125; 90/91 - 91
Parkhurst: 92/93 - 388, 388EI
Post: 82/83 - 50
Pro Set: 90/91 - 179; 92/93 - 180
Score: 90/91 - 59A, 59C, 52T; 91/92 - 38A,
38B, 38C; 93/94 - 25C, 25A
Topps: 87/88 - 182; 88/89 - 197; 90/91 - 72;
91/92 - 341; 93/94 - 159
Upper Deck: 90/91 - 7E, 7F, 419E, 419F

Croteau, Gary
Eddie Sargent: 70/71 - 141 72/73 - 48
Esso: 70/71 - 37
Loblaws: 74/75 - 111
O-Pee-Chee: 70/71 - 189; 71/72 - 17; 72/73 - 3;
73/74 - 228; 74/75 - 36; 76/77 - 283;
77/78 - 52; 78/79 - 362; 79/80 - 158
Topps: 71/72 - 17; 72/73 - 83; 74/75 - 36;
77/78 - 52; 79/80 - 158
Toronto Sun: 71/72 - 45

Crowder, Bruce
O-Pee-Chee: 82/83 - 9; 83/84 - 46
Post: 82/83 - 3

Crowder, Keith
O-Pee-Chee: 82/83 - 10, 80SK; 83/84 - 47, 56SK;
84/85 - 2; 85/86 - 159, 163SK;
86/87 - 130, 37SK; 87/88 - 194,
136SK; 88/89 - 206; 89/90 - 199;
90/91 - 476
Panini: 87/88 - 14; 88/89 - 209
Topps: 82/83 - 80SK; 83/84 - 56SK;
84/85 - 2; 85/86 - 159; 86/87 - 130;
87/88 - 194

Crowder, Troy
O-Pee-Chee: 91/92 - 374, 169PM
Pro Set: 90/91 - 620
Score: 90 - 43T; 91 - 52T;
91/92 - 602B, 602C
Topps: 91/92 - 374
Upper Deck: 90/91 - 441E, 441F;
91/92 - 342E, 342F

Crowe, Phil
Donruss: 93/94 - 446

Crowley, Ted
Fleer: 93/94 - 500PP
Parkhurst: 94/95 - 93, 93EI
Topps: 93/94 - 12US

Crozier, Roger (Goalie)
Bazooka: 71/72 - 32
Beehive: 64/67 - 66
Coca-Cola: 64/65 - 39; 65/66 - 41
Colgate: 70/71 - 83
Dom. Choc.: 70/71 - 12
Eddie Sargent: 70/71 - 26; 72/73 - 32
Esso: 70/71 - 23
Loblaws: 74/75 - 39
O-Pee-Chee: 68/69 - 23, 10PS; 69/70 - 55, 10QS;
70/71 - 145, 11DE; 71/72 - 36, 5BK
72/73 - 50; 73/74 - 153; 75/76 - 350
Shirriff: 68/69 - C2
Topps: 64/65 - 47; 65/66 - 42; 66/67 - 43;
66/67 US - 43; 67/68 - 48;
68/69 - 23; 69/70 - 55; 71/72 - 36,
5BK; 72/73 - 31; 73/74 - 108
Toronto Star: 57/67 - 101; 58/67 - 88
Toronto Sun: 71/72 - 24

Crutchfield, Nels
Sweet Caporal: 34/35 - 12

Crystal, Bob
Beehive: 45/63 - 303

Cude, Wilf (Goalie)
Beehive: 34/44 - 144
Canada Starch: 35/40 - 59
Diamond: 36/39 - 20(I), 17(II), 16(III)
O-Pee-Chee: 35/36 - 73; 36/37 - 120; 37/38 - 149
Quaker Oats: 38/39 - 4
Sweet Caporal: 34/35 - 14
World Wide Gum: 36/37 - 9

Cullen, Barry
Beehive: 45/63 - 394A, 394B
Leaf: 93/94 - 245
Parkhurst: 57/58 MON - 22; 57/58 TOR - 21;
58/59 - 31, 36; 60/61 - 32;
93/94 - 120ML
Shirriff: 60/61 - 47
Topps: 59/60 - 25

Cullen, Brian
Beehive: 45/63 - 305, 395
Parkhurst: 55/56 - 13; 57/58 TOR - 9;
58/59 - 50; 93/94 - 118ML
Quaker Oats: 55/56 - 13
Shirriff: 60/61 - 99
Topps: 59/60 - 55

Cullen, John
Bowman: 90/91 - 210; 91/92 - 1;
92/93 - 194, 227
Donruss: 93/94 - 334
Fleer: 92/93 - 72, 419; 93/94 - 20, 242PP
Kraft: 91/92 - 24
O-Pee-Chee: 89/90 - 145, 231SK, 13FS;
90/91 - 208, 20PM; 91/92 - 226,
127PM; 92/93 - 104; 93/94 - 479,
209SC, 209FD
Panini: 89/90 - 316; 90/91 - 125;
91/92 - 314; 92/93 - 257E, 257F;
93/94 - 226E, 226F
Parkhurst: 91/92 - 59E, 59F; 92/93 - 180, 180EI;
93/94 - 473, 473EI; 94/95 - 232,
232EI
Pro Set: 90/91 - 232; 91/92 - 85E, 302E,
CC9, 85F, 302F, 175PT; 92/93 - 57
Score: 90/91 - 164A, 164C, 73HR;
91 - 5YS; 91/92 - 7A, 421A, 7B,
311B, 7C, 311C, 125PNE, 391PNE,
125PNF, 391PNF; 92/93 - 150C,
425C, 150A, 425A, 285PNC,
285PNA; 93/94 - 189C, 189A
Season's: 92/93 - 45
Topps: 89/90 - 145; 90/91 - 208;
91/92 - 226, 289SC; 92/93 - 132,
132GS, 160SC; 93/94 - 479C,
209SC, 209FD
Upper Deck: 90/91 - 12E, 12F, 492E, 492F;
91/92 - 235E, 235F; 92/93 - 304,
465; 93/94 - 395

Cullen, Ray
  Bauer: 68/69 - 4
  Colgate: 70/71 - 15
  Dom. Choc.: 70/71 - 136
  Eddie Sargent: 70/71 - 216
  Esso: 70/71 - 237
  O-Pee-Chee: 68/69 - 54; 69/70 - 130, 5ST, 15QS; 70/71 - 228, 31DE
  Shirriff: 68/69 - E9
  Topps: 68/69 - 54; 69/70 - 130

Cullimore, Jason
  Upper Deck: 91/92 - 72E, 690E, 72F, 690F

Cummins, Burton
  Pro-Set: 91/92 - 290PT

Cummins, Jim
  Topps: 93/94 - 448SC, 448FD

Cunneyworth, Randy
  Donruss: 93/94 - 413
  Fleer: 92/93 - 73
  Kraft: 1990 - 48
  O-Pee-Chee: 87/88 - 150; 88/89 - 19, 231SK; 89/90 - 63; 90/91 - 67; 93/94 - 423
  Panini: 87/88 - 148; 88/89 - 337; 91/92 - 320; 92/93 - 260E, 260F
  Parkhurst: 91/92 - 284E, 284F
  Pro Set: 90/91 - 101; 91/92 - 392E, 392F
  Score: 90/91 - 276A, 276C; 91/92 - 424B, 424C
  Topps: 87/88 - 150; 88/89 - 19; 89/90 - 63; 91/92 - 67; 93/94 - 423C, 341SC, 341FD
  Upper Deck: 90/91 - 268E, 268F

Cunniff, John
  Pro Set: 90/91 - 670

Cunningham, Bob
  Shirriff: 61/62 - 96

Cunningham, Les
  Beehive: 34/44 - 49
  O-Pee-Chee: 39/40 - 78

Curran, Brian
  O-Pee-Chee: 87/88 - 90
  Panini: 87/88 - 95
  Pro Set: 90/91 - 277
  Topps: 87/88 - 90

Currie, Alex
  Imperial Tobacco: 10/11 - 13L; 11/12 - 13; 12/13 - 32

Currie, Dan
  Upper Deck: 91/92 - 347E, 347F

Currie, Glen
  Post: 82/83 - 306

Currie, Tony
  O-Pee-Chee: 80/81 - 384; 81/82 - 292; 82/83 - 341
  Topps: 81/82 WN - 116

Curry, Floyd
  Beehive: 45/63 - 255
  CKAC Radio: 43/47 - 41
  Derniere: 72/84 - 64
  La Patrie: 51/54 - 12
  Parkhurst: 51/52 - 12; 52/53 - 7; 53/54 - 35; 54/55 - 15, 89; 55/56 - 40; 57/58 MON - 20; 93/94 - 78ML
  Quaker Oats: 45/54 - 11A, 11B; 55/56 - 40

Curtis, Paul
  Eddie Sargent: 72/73 - 85
  Esso: 70/71 - 94
  O-Pee-Chee: 71/72 - 4; 72/73 - 266
  Toronto Sun: 71/72 - 109

Cushenan, Ian
  Beehive: 45/63 - 232, 306
  Parkhurst: 58/59 - 24; 63/64 - 49

Cyr, Denis
  O-Pee-Chee: 82/83 - 43
  Post: 82/83 - 35

Cyr, Paul
  Bowman: 91/92 - 20
  O-Pee-Chee: 85/86 - 183SK; 86/87 - 200; 91/92 - 73

Cyr, Paul (cont.)
  Panini: 87/88 - 33; 91/92 - 321
  Pro Set: 90/91 - 449; 91/92 - 88E, 88F
  Score: 90/91 - 72T; 91/92 - 413B, 413C
  Topps: 91/92 - 73, 279SC

Czerkaeski, Mariusz
  Parkhurst: 94/95 - 20, 20EI

Dafoe, Byron Goalie
  Parkhurst: 94/95 - 255, 255EI

Dahl, Kevin
  Fleer: 92/93 - 266; 93/94 - 23
  O-Pee-Chee: 92/93 - 22PM; 93/94 - 362
  Parkhurst: 92/93 - 261, 261EI; 93/94 - 298, 298EI
  Score: 93/94 - 423C, 423A
  Topps: 93/94 - 362, 432SC, 432FD
  Upper Deck: 92/93 - 493

Dahlen, Ulf
  Bowman: 90/91 - 176; 91/92 - 127; 92/93 - 143
  Donruss: 93/94 - 78, 488
  Fleer: 92/93 - 92; 93/94 - 81, 59PP
  Leaf: 93/94 - 198
  O-Pee-Chee: 88/89 - 47, 7NS, 128SK, 5FS; 89/90 - 2; 90/91 - 12; 91/92 - 177; 92/93 - 129; 93/94 - 75, 238SC, 238FD
  Panini: 88/89 - 305; 89/90 - 288; 91/92 - 23; 92/93 - 92E, 92F; 93/94 - 270E, 270F
  Parkhurst: 91/92 - 76E, 76F; 92/93 - 310, 310EI; 93/94 - 322, 322EI; 94/95 - 215, 215EI
  Pro Set: 90/91 - 136; 91/92 - 106E, 607E, 106F, 607F, 186PT; 92/93 - 80
  Score: 90/91 - 22A, 22C; 91/92 - 164A, 164B, 164C, 152PNE, 152PNF, 92/93 - 330C, 330A, 68PNC, 68PNA; 93/94 - 107C, 107A
  Topps: 88/89 - 47; 89/90 - 2; 90/91 - 12; 91/92 - 177, 55SC; 92/93 - 28, 28GS, 207SC; 93/94 - 75, 238SC, 428SC, 238FD, 428FD
  Upper Deck: 90/91 - 283E, 283F; 91/92 - 348E, 348F; 92/93 - 250; 93/94 - 360

Dahlin, Kjell
  Kraft: 86/87 - 23, 23P
  O-Pee-Chee: 86/87 - 15, 262, 18SK, 126SK; Topps: 86/87 - 15; 87/88 - 14SK

Dahlquist, Chris
  Bowman: 91/92 - 128; 92/93 - 359
  Fleer: 92/93 - 267
  O-Pee-Chee: 90/91 - 528; 91/92 - 142; 92/93 - 22, 38PM
  Pro Set: 90/91 - 464; 91/92 - 408E, 408F
  Score: 91/92 - 365A, 404B, 404C; 92/93 - 294C, 294A, 167PNC, 167PNA; 93/94 - 314C, 314A
  Topps: 91/92 - 142, 314SC; 92/93 - 231, 231GS, 57SC; 93/94 - 266SC, 266FD
  Upper Deck: 91/92 - 307E, 307F

Dahlstrom, Cully
  Beehive: 34/44 - 50
  Diamond: 36/39 - 4(V), 4(VI)
  O-Pee-Chee: 39/40 - 46; 40/41 - 137

Daigle, Alain
  O-Pee-Chee: 75/76 - 394; 76/77 - 156; 77/78 - 208; 78/79 - 117; 79/80 - 227
  Topps: 76/77 - 156; 77/78 - 208; 78/79 - 117; 79/80 - 227

Daigle, Alexandre
  Donruss: 93/94 - 237, 393, 2ES, 1RR, P/PM, P/SP
  Durivage: 93/94 - 1
  Fleer: 93/94 - 3RS, 396PP
  Hockey Wit: 93/94 - 91
  Kraft: 93/94 - 5
  Leaf: 93/94 - 311, 1FP, 9SS
  O-Pee-Chee: 93/94 - 405, 1HR
  Parkhurst: 93/94 - 244, 244EI, F1, G6, E3, CC1, D11; 94/95 - 285, 285EI, V42

Daigle, Alexandre (cont.)
  Score: 93/94 - 496C, 496A
  Topps: 93/94 - 405C, 1PF, 300SC, 300FD
  Upper Deck: 92/93 - 587; 93/94 - 170, 250; E15

Daigneault, Jean-Jacques
  Bowman: 92/93 - 371
  Durivage: 92/93 - 35; 93/94 - 10
  Fleer: 92/93 - 326; 93/94 - 367PP
  Leaf: 93/94 - 437
  O-Pee-Chee: 91/92 - 456; 92/93 - 304; 93/94 - 372
  Panini: 91/92 - 192
  Parkhurst: 91/92 - 312E, 312F; 92/93 - 324, 324EI; 93/94 - 377, 377EI
  Pro Set: 90/91 - 466; 91/92 - 124E, 124F
  Score: 91/92 - 520B, 520C; 92/93 - 311C, 311A, 93/94 - 299C, 299A
  Topps: 91/92 - 456; 92/93 - 334, 334GS, 308SC; 93/94 - 372, 475SC, 475FD
  Upper Deck: 91/92 - 170E, 170F; 92/93 - 331

Dailey, Bob
  Loblaws: 74/75 - 292
  O-Pee-Chee: 74/75 - 240; 75/76 - 231; 76/77 - 350; 77/78 - 98; 78/79 - 131; 79/80 - 226; 80/81 - 131; 81/82 - 241
  Topps: 74/75 - 240; 75/76 - 231; 77/78 - 98; 78/79 - 131; 79/80 - 226; 80/81 - 131; 81/82 EN - 104

Daley, Joe (Goalie)
  Eddie Sargent: 70/71 - 17
  O-Pee-Chee: 68/69 - 188; 69/70 - 152; 71/72 - 137
  Toronto Sun: 71/72 - 90

Dalgarno, Brad
  Donruss: 93/94 - 197
  Leaf: 93/94 - 320
  O-Pee-Chee: 89/90 - 246; 93/94 - 223, 167SC, 167FD
  Upper Deck: 93/94 - 219
  Parkhurst: 92/93 - 336, 336EI; 93/94 - 393, 393EI
  Pro Set: 90/91 - 482
  Score: 93/94 - 374C, 374A
  Topps: 91/92 - 371SC; 93/94 - 223, 167SC, 167FD

Dame, Bunny
  Beehive: 34/44 - 145

Damphousse, Vincent
  Bowman: 90/91 - 163, HT6; 91/92 - 170; 92/93 - 203A, 203B, 329
  Donruss: 93/94 - 172
  Durivage: 92/93 - 20; 93/94 - 11
  Fleer: 92/93 - 103; 93/94 - 79, 127PP
  Hockey Wit: 93/94 - 72
  Kraft: 1990 - 35
  Leaf: 93/94 - 4
  McDonald's: 91/92 - Mc16
  O-Pee-Chee: 87/88 - 243, 128SK; 88/89 - 207, 171SK; 89/90 - 272, 179SK; 90/91 - 121, 21PM; 91/92 - 299, 104PM; 92/93 - 192, 3PM; 93/94 - 233, 240SC, 240FD
  Panini: 87/88 - 333; 88/89 - 123; 89/90 - 134; 90/91 - 291; 91/92 - 92; 92/93 - 104E, 104F; 93/94 - 13E, 13F
  Parkhurst: 91/92 - 48E, 48F; 92/93 - 86, 496, 86EI, 496EI; 93/94 - 104, 104EI; 94/95 - 115, 115EI, V23
  Pro Set: 90/91 - 278; 91/92 - 224E, 293E, 381E, 224F, 293F, 35PT, 381F, 5TL
  Score: 90/91 - 95A, 95C, 47HR; 91 - 59T; 91/92 - 300A, 338A, 368B, 609B, 368C, 609C, 91PNE, 91PNF; 92/93 - 170C, 170A, 261PNC, 261PNA, 349PNC, 349PNA; 93/94 - 244C, 244A
  Sega: 93/94 - 70
  Topps: 90/91 - 121; 91/92 - 299, 9SL, 146SC; 92/93 - 55, 55GS, 191SC; 93/94 - 233, 240SC, 240FD
  Upper Deck: 90/91 - 224E, 224F, 484E, 484F; 91/92 - 136E, 136F,

Damphousse, Vincent (cont.)
Upper Deck: 535E, 535F; 92/93 - 6, 307, 476; 93/94 - 295, 380

Dandurand, Leo
Anonymous: 1926/27 - 15
Hall of Fame: 83 - 96, G5P, 87 - 96

Daneyko, Kenneth (Ken)
Bowman: 91/92 - 284
Fleer: 92/93 - 335
O-Pee-Chee: 89/90 - 243; 91/92 - 118; 93/94 - 236, 206SC, 206FD
Panini: 87/88 - 76; 89/90 - 258; 91/92 - 218
Parkhurst: 91/92 - 317E, 317F; 92/93 - 332, 332EI; 93/94 - 387, 387EI; 94/95 - 131, 131EI
Pro Set: 90/91 - 165; 91/92 - 139E, 139F
Score: 90/91 - 178A, 178C; 91/92 - 46A, 46B, 46C, 142PNE, 142PNF; 92/93 - 53C, 53A, 354PNC, 354PNA; 93/94 - 286C, 286A
Topps: 91/92 - 118, 103SC; 92/93 - 357, 357GS; 93/94 - 236, 206SC, 206FD
Upper Deck: 90/91 - 427E, 427F; 91/92 - 435E, 435F; 92/93 - 259

Daniels, Jeff
Fleer: 92/93 - 377
Leaf: 93/94 - 251
O-Pee-Chee: 92/93 - 58PM; 93/94 - 343
Parkhurst: 92/93 - 492, 492EI; 93/94 - 429, 429EI
Score: 91/92 - 400A, 290B, 290C
Topps: 93/94 - 343, 483SC, 483FD
Upper Deck: 91/92 - 564E, 564F; 92/93 - 508; 93/94 - 87

Daniels, Kimbi
Parkhurst: 91/92 - 346E, 346F
Score: 91/92 - 399A, 289B, 289C, 336PNE, 336PNF
Topps: 92/93 - 453SC
Upper Deck: 91/92 - 492E, 687E, 492F, 687F; 92/93 - 75

Daoust, Dan
Derniere: 72/84 - 181
Kraft: 86/87 - 54, 54P
O-Pee-Chee: 83/84 - 328, 28SK, 29SK; 84/85 - 299, 9SK, 10SK; 85/86 - 164, 11SK; 86/87 - 241, 146SK; 88/89 - 169SK 89/90 - 277, 177SK
Panini: 88/89 - 124
Topps: 83/84 - 28SK, 29SK; 84/85 - 137; 85/86 - 164
Vachon Foods: 83/84 - 83

Dapuzzo, Pat (Official)
Pro Set: 90/91 - 684

Darragh, Jack
Hall of Fame: 83 - 199, N3P, 87 - 199
Imperial Tobacco: 10/11 - 17(L); 11/12 - 17; 12/13 - 29
Wm. Paterson: 23/24 - 4

David, Richard
Derniere: 72/84 - 83

Davidson, Bob
Beehive: 34/44 - 312
O-Pee-Chee: 36/37 - 100; 37/38 - 136; 39/40 - 5
Quaker Oats: 38/39 - 19; 45/54 - 69
Ultimate: 92 - 33(OSE), 33(OSF)
World Wide Gum: 36/37 - 48

Davidson, Gord
Beehive: 34/44 - 270

Davidson, John (Goalie)
Coca-Cola: 77/78 - 5
Loblaws: 74/75 - 256
O-Pee-Chee: 74/75 - 11; 75/76 - 183; 76/77 - 204; 77/78 - 28; 78/79 - 211; 79/80 - 110; 80/81 - 190; 81/82 - 222
Topps: 74/75 - 11; 75/76 - 183; 76/77 - 204; 77/78 - 28; 78/79 - 211; 79/80 - 110; 80/81 - 190; 81/82 EN - 95

Davidson, Scotty
Hall of Fame: 83 - 137, K2P; 87 - 137

Davidson, Robert
Ultimate: 92 - 33OS

Davidsson, Johan
Parkhurst: 93/94 - 538, 538EI

Davie, Bob
Diamond: 33/35 - 19

Davis, Lorne
Beehive: 45/63 - 233

Davis Mal
O-Pee-Chee: 85/86 - 186SK

Davydov, Eugeny
Donruss: 93/94 - 127
Fleer: 92/93 - 441; 93/94 - 58, 269PP, 397PP
Leaf: 93/94 - 24
O-Pee-Chee: 90/91 - 18R; 92/93 - 66PM; 93/94 - 200, 444, 34SC, 34FD
Panini: 93/94 - 194E
Parkhurst: 91/92 - 422E, 422F; 92/93 - 211, 226, 211EI, 226EI; 93/94 - 78, 78EI; 94/95 - 161, 161EI
Pro-Set: 92/93 - 244
Score: 92/93 - 456C, 456A, 226PNC, 226PNA; 93/94 - 114C, 114A
Topps: 92/93 - 115, 115GS; 93/94 - 200, 444C, 34SC, 487SC, 34FD, 487FD
Upper Deck: 92/93 - 420, ER17, CC19, E8; 93/94 - 443

Dawe, Jason
Donruss: 93/94 - 404
Upper Deck: 91/92 - 75E, 75F; 93/94 - 254

Dawes, Robert
Beehive: 45/63 - 396

Day, Hap (Clarence)
Anonymous: 33/34 - 2
Beehive: 34/44 - 221, 313
Can. Chew. Gum: 33/34 - 17
Champ's: 24/25 - 51
Hall of Fame: 83 - 80, F4P; 87 - 80
Hamilton Gum: 33/34 - 33
La Presse: 27/32 - 22
O-Pee-Chee: 33/34 - 32
Parkhurst: 55/56 - 34; 93/94 - 134ML
Quaker Oates: 55/56 - 34
World Wide Gum: 33/34 - 2PM, 10; 36/37 - 52

Day, Joseph
Parkhurst: 94/95 - 138, 138EI
Upper Deck: 91/92 - 516E, 516F

Dea, Billy
Beehive: 45/63 - 159, 307
Eddie Sargent: 70/71 - 53
Esso: 70/71 - 76
O-Pee-Chee: 68/69 - 190; 70/71 - 30
Parkhurst: 93/94 - 47ML
Topps: 57/58 - 39; 70/71 - 30

Deacon, Doug
Beehive: 34/44 - 97

Deacon, Ed
Imperial Tobacco: 10/11 - 13

Deadmarsh, Adam
Donruss: 93/94 - 5JCA
Upper Deck: 92/93 - 609; 93/94 - 562

Deadmarsh, Butch
O-Pee-Chee: 74/75 - 73
Topps: 74/75 - 73

Dean, Barry
O-Pee-Chee: 77/78 - 183; 78/79 - 142; 79/80 - 318
Topps: 77/78 - 183; 78/79 - 142

Debenedet, Nelson
Loblaws: 74/75 - 239
O-Pee-Chee: 74/75 - 293

DeBlois, Lucien
Derniere: 72/84 - 56
Durivage: 92/93 - 2
O-Pee-Chee: 78/79 - 136; 80/81 - 146; 81/82 - 74, 232SK; 82/83 - 379, 212SK; 83/84 - 370, 383, 284SK;

DeBlois, Lucien (cont.)
O-Pee-Chee: 84/85 - 260, 290SK; 90/91 - 441; 91/92 - 102
Panini: 90/91 - 140; 91/92 - 100
Post: 82/83 - 324
Pro Set: 90/91 - 244, 531; 91/92 - 491E, 491F
Score: 91/92 - 395B, 395C; 92/93 - 371C, 371A
Topps: 78/79 - 136; 80/81 - 146; 81/82 WN - 79; 82/83 - 212SK; 83/84 - 284SK; 91/92 - 102
Upper Deck: 90/91 - 363E, 363F
Vachon Foods: 83/84 - 125

Debol, Dave
O-Pee-Chee: 79/80 - 363; 80/81 - 381

DeBrusk, Louie
Bowman: 92/93 - 318
Donruss: 93/94 - 108
Leaf: 93/94 - 225
O-Pee-Chee: 93/94 - 319
Parkhurst: 91/92 - 281E, 281F; 93/94 - 337, 337EI
Pro Set: 91/92 - 535E, 535F
Score: 91/92 - 347PNE, 347PNF
Topps: 92/93 - 392, 392GS, 290SC; 93/94 - 319
Upper Deck: 91/92 - 249E, 526E, 249F, 526F; 92/93 - 467; 93/94 - 79

Decarie, Ed
Imperial Tobacco: 1910/11 - 13

DeGray, Dale
Topps: 89/90 - 18
O-Pee-Chee: 89/90 - 18

DeJordy, Denis (Goalie)
Bazooka: 71/72 - 8
Beehive: 64/67 - 32
Coca-Cola: 64/65 - 20
Colgate: 70/71 - 84
Dom. Choc.: 70/71 - 56
Eddie Sargent: 70/71 - 73; 72/73 - 130
Esso: 70/71 - 95
O-Pee-Chee: 68/69 - 12; 69/70 - 66, 7QS; 70/71 - 31; 71/72 - 63; 72/73 - 184
Shirriff: 68/69 - B4
Topps: 61/62 - 37; 62/63 - 25; 63/64 - 24; 64/65 - 22; 65/66 - 113; 66/67 - 115; 66/67 US - 50; 67/68 - 115; 68/69 - 12; 69/70 - 66; 70/71 - 31; 71/72 - 63; 72/73 - 144
Toronto Sun: 71/72 - 110
Vachon Foods: 83/84 - 43

DelGuidice, Matt (Goalie)
Parkhurst: 91/92 - 1E, 1F
O-Pee-Chee: 91/92 - 96PM
Pro Set: 91/92 - 521E, 521F
Upper Deck: 91/92 - 463E

Dellaire, Henri
Imperial Tobacco: 10/11 - 39; 11/12 - 39; 12/13 - 7

Delorme, Gilbert
O-Pee-Chee: 83/84 - 186, 70SK; 86/87 - 234, 28SK; 90/91 - 517
Topps: 83/84 - 70SK

Delorme, Ron
O-Pee-Chee: 78/79 - 323; 79/80 - 284; 80/81 - 321; 81/82 - 82, 231SK; 82/83 - 347; 83/84 - 348; 84/85 - 316
Post: 82/83 - 292
Vachon Foods: 83/84 - 104

Delvecchio, Alex
Bazooka: 71/72 - 7
Beehive: 45/63 - 160; 64/67 - 67A, 67B
Chex: 63/65 - 11
Coca-Cola: 64/65 - 40; 65/66 - 42
Colgate: 70/71 - 4
Dom. Choc.: 70/71 - 47
Eddie Sargent: 70/71 - 59; 72/73 - 76
Esso: 70/71 - 77
Hall of Fame: 83 - 230, E7P; 87 - 230

Delvecchio, Alex (cont.)
O-Pee-Chee: 68/69 - 28; 69/70 - 157, 206, 18QS; 70/71 - 157; 71/72 - 37, 12BK; 72/73 - 26; 73/74 - 1; 74/75 - 222
Parkhurst: 51/52 - 63; 52/53 - 53; 53/54 - 47; 54/55 - 36; 60/61 - 36; 61/62 - 25; 62/63 - 32; 63/64 - 50; 91/92 - PHC2E, PHC2F; 92/93 - PR19; 93/94 - 59ML
Pro Set: 90/91 - 652, 658
Shirriff: 60/61 - 44; 61/62 - 70; 68/69 - C4
Topps: 54/55 - 39; 57/58 - 34; 58/59 - 52; 59/60 - 8; 64/65 - 95; 65/66 - 47; 66/67 - 102; 66/67 US - 63; 67/68 - 51; 68/69 - 28; 69/70 - 64;
Topps: 71/72 - 37, 12BK; 72/73 - 141; 73/74 - 141; 74/75 - 222
Toronto Star: 58/67 - 27, 71; 63/64 - 11; 64/65 - 17
Toronto Sun: 71/72 - 91
Ultimate: 92 - 68(OSE), 68(OSF)
York: 62/63 - 21; 63/64 - 50

Delvecchio, Bill
Beehive: 45/63 - 161

DeMarco, Ab (Albert)
Loblaws: 74/75 - 240
O-Pee-Chee: 39/40 - 82; 71/72 - 90; 73/74 - 118; 74/75 - 89; 75/76 - 78; 76/77 - 374; 77/78 - 283
Topps: 73/74 - 118; 74/75 - 89; 75/76 - 78
Toronto Sun: 71/72 - 169

Demers, Jacques
Derniere: 72/84 - 84
Kraft: 93/94 - 36

DeMeres, Tony
Beehive: 34/44 - 146
CKAC Radio: 43/47 - 42
O-Pee-Chee: 40/41 - 144

Demitra, Pavol
Donruss: 93/94 - 240
Leaf: 93/94 - 366
Parkhurst: 93/94 - 140, 140EI
Upper Deck: 92/93 - 602; 93/94 - 372

Denis, Lulu (Louis)
World Wide Gum: 36/37 - 125

Denneny, Corbett
Wm. Paterson: 23/24 - 40

Denneny, Cy
Champ's: 24/25 - 43
Hall of Fame: 83 - 138, K3P; 87 - 138
Topps: 60/61 - 8, 34ST
Wm. Paterson: 23/24 - 10; 24/25 - 7

Dennison, Joe
Imperial Tobacco: 12/13 - 42

Derlago, Bill
Esso: 83/84 - 6E, 6F
Funmate: 83/84 - 122
Kraft: 86/87 - 74, 74P
O-Pee-Chee: 80/81 - 11; 81/82 - 305, 99SK; 108SK; 82/83 - 319, 320, 67SK, 68SK; 83/84 - 327, 35SK; 84/85 - 300, 14SK; 85/86 - 71, 7SK; 86/87 - 254, 105SK; 87/88 - 224SK
PepsiCo: 80/81 - 84
Post: 82/83 - 277
7-Eleven: 84/85 - 45
Topps: 80/81 - 11; 82/83 - 67SK, 68SK; 83/84 - 35SK, 85/86 - 71
Vachon Foods: 83/84 - 84

DeRouville, Phillippe, Goalie
Upper Deck: 93/94 - 260

Desilets, Joffre
Beehive: 34/44 - 51, 147
Canada Starch: 35/40, 109
O-Pee-Chee: 36/37 - 114; 37/38 - 156; 39/40 - 44

Desjardins, Eric
Bowman: 91/92 - 329; 92/93 - 228; 92/93 - 311
Donruss: 93/94 - 173
Durivage: 92/93 - 36; 93/94 - 12
Fleer: 92/93 - 104; 93/94 - 94, 128PP

Desjardins, Eric (cont.)
Gillette: 91/92 - 27
Leaf: 93/94 - 203
O-Pee-Chee: 90/91 - 425; 91/92 - 14, 157PM; 92/93 - 360; 93/94 - 32, 170SC, 170FD
Panini: 91/92 - 189; 92/93 - 156E, 156F; 93/94 - 21E, 21F
Parkhurst: 91/92 - 85E, 85F; 92/93 - 80, 80EI; 93/94 - 102, 102EI; 94/95 - 118, 118EI
Pro Set: 90/91 - 467; 91/92 - 118E, 118F, 193PT; 92/93 - 86
Score: 90/91 - 58T; 91 - 23YS; 91/92 - 119A, 119B, 119C, 73PNE, 73PNF; 92/93 - 23C, 23A, 16PNC, 16PNA, 23PC(S), 23PC(F), 9CT, 9AT; 93/94 - 128C, 128A
Sega: 93/94 - 67
Topps: 91/92 - 14, 214SC; 92/93 - 192, 192GS, 326SC; 93/94 - 32, 170SC, 170FD
Upper Deck: 90/91 - 428E, 428F; 91/92 - 360E, 360F, 504E, 504F; 92/93 - 268; 93/94 - 184

Desjardins, Gerry (Goalie)
Colgate: 70/71 - 67
Eddie Sargent: 70/71 - 45; 72/73 - 129
Esso: 70/71 - 57
O-Pee-Chee: 69/70 - 99, 6ST, 14QS; 70/71 - 152; 72/73 - 119; 73/74 - 178; 75/76 - 125; 76/77 - 230; 77/78 - 150
Topps: 69/70 - 99; 72/73 - 38; 73/74 - 114; 75/76 - 125; 76/77 - 230; 77/78 - 150

Dessureault, Gaetan
La Patrie: 51/54 - 36

Dewsbury, Al
Beehive: 45/63 - 91, 162
Parkhurst: 51/52 - 38; 52/53 - 17; 53/54 - 78; 54/55 - 78; 93/94 - 22ML

Dey, Edgar
Imperial Tobacco: 10/11 - 6

Dickens, Ernie
Beehive: 34/44 - 314; 45/63 - 92

Dickenson, Herb
Parkhurst: 52/53 - 57

Diduck, Gerald
Bowman: 92/93 - 65
Donruss: 93/94 - 360
Fleer: 92/93 - 424; 93/94 - 250PP
Leaf: 93/94 - 387
O-Pee-Chee: 89/90 - 182, 117SK; 90/91 - 421, 22PM; 91/92 - 280; 92/93 - 309
Panini: 89/90 - 274; 90/91 - 85
Parkhurst: 91/92 - 407E, 407F; 92/93 - 419, 419EI
Pro Set: 90/91 - 180, 468; 91/92 - 502E, 502F
Score: 90 - 23T; 90/91 - 139A, 139C; 91/92 - 243B, 243C, 211PNE, 211PNF; 92/93 - 34C, 34A, 81PNC, 81PNA; 93/94 - 356C, 356A
Topps: 89/90 - 182; 91/92 - 280; 92/93 - 44, 44GS, 97SC
Upper Deck: 90/91 - 390E, 390F

Dilio, Frank
Hall of Fame: 83 - 81, F5P; 87 - 81

Dillabough, Bob
Beehive: 64/67 - 5
Coca-Cola: 65/66 - 6
Dad's Cookies: 70/71 - 137
Eddie Sargent: 70/71 - 217
O-Pee-Chee: 68/69 - 191; 69/70 - 150
Parkhurst: 63/64 - 47
Topps: 65/66 - 39; 66/67 - 98

Dillon, Cecil
Anonymous: 33/34 - 32
Beehive: 34/44 - 98, 271
Can. Chew. Gum: 33/34 - 18; 34/35 - 71
Diamond: 33/35 - 20; 36/39 - 18(II), 19(II), 17(III)

Dillon, Cecil (cont.)
World Wide Gum: 33/34 - 15

Dillon, Wayne
O-Pee-Chee: 75/76 - 363; 76/77 - 9; 77/78 - 166; 78/79 - 73; 79/80 - 359
Topps: 76/77 - 9; 77/78 - 166; 78/79 - 73

DiMaio, Robert (Rob)
Bowman: 92/93 - 403
O-Pee-Chee: 90/91 - 27PM; 92/93 - 62PM; 93/94 - 242, 182SC, 182FD
Panini: 93/94 - 218E, 218F
Parkhurst: 91/92 - 325E, 325F; 92/93 - 402, 402EI; 93/94 - 196, 196EI
Pro Set: 90/91 - 625; 91/92 - 430E, 430F
Topps: 92/93 - 488, 488GS, 33SC; 93/94 - 242, 182SC, 182FD
Upper Deck: 90/91 - 225E, 225F; 91/92 - 481E, 481F; 92/93 - 529; 93/94 - 176

Dineen, Bill
Beehive: 45/63 - 163
Parkhurst: 53/54 - 38; 54/55 - 48; 93/94 - 50ML
Topps: 54/55 - 57; 57/58 - 49

Dineen, Gord
Durivage: 92/93 - 37
O-Pee-Chee: 89/90 - 256; 90/91 - 470
Pro Set: 90/91 - 233
Upper Deck: 90/91 - 369E, 369F

Dineen, Kevin
Bowman: 90/91 - 261, HT7; 91/92 - 6; 92/93 - 121
Donruss: 93/94 - 249
Durivage: 92/93 - 12; 93/94 - 37
Fleer: 92/93 - 154; 93/94 - 107, 179PP
Fritolay: 88/89 - 9
Kellogg's: 92 - 11
Kraft: 90/91 - 11; 93/94 - 37
Leaf: 93/94 - 156, 6HT
O-Pee-Chee: 85/86 - 34, 168SK; 86/87 - 88, 56SK; 87/88 - 124, 202SK; 88/89 - 36, 269SK; 89/90 - 20, M/BB, 270; 90/91 - 213, 23PM; 91/92 - 285; 92/93 - 200; 93/94 - 167, 43SC, 43FD
Panini: 87/88 - 44; 88/89 - 240; 89/90 - 219; 90/91 - 43; 91/92 - 323; 92/93 - 186E, 186F; 93/94 - 49E, 49F
Parkhurst: 91/92 - 348E, 348F; 92/93 - 127, 127EI; 93/94 - 421, 421EI; 94/95 - 172, 172EI
Pro Set: 90/91 - 102; 91/92 - AC17, 89E, 451E, 89F, 46PT, 451F; 92/93 - 134
Score: 90/91 - 212A, 212C, 90HR; 91/92 - 118A, 118B, 118C, 246PNE, 366PNE, 246PNF, 366PNF; 92/93 - 284C, 284A, 14PNC, 14PNA; 93/94 - 122C, 122A
Topps: 85/86 - 34; 86/87 - 88; 87/88 - 124; 88/89 - 36; 89/90 - 20, M/BB; 90/91 - 213; 91/92 - 285, 162SC; 92/93 - 131, 131GS, 365SC; 93/94 - 167, 43SC, 43FD
Upper Deck: 90/91 - 266E, 266F; 91/92 - 105E, 530E, 105F, 530F; 92/93 - 256; 93/94 - 212

Dinsmore, Chuck
Champ's: 24/25 - 33
Maple Crispette: 24/25 - 17
Wm. Paterson: 24/25 - 40

Dion, Connie (Goalie)
CKAC Radio: 43/47 - 19

Dion, Michel (Goalie)
Funmate: 83/84 - 102
O-Pee-Chee: 79/80 - 316; 80/81 - 223; 82/83 - 267, 146SK, 168SK; 83/84 - 279, 234SK; 84/85 - 173
Post: 82/83 - 230
Topps: 80/81 - 223; 82/83 - 146SK, 168SK; 83/84 - 234SK

Dionne, Gilbert
Bowman: 92/93 - 439

Dionne, Gilbert (cont.)
- Derniere: 72/84 - 193
- Donruss: 93/94 - 174
- Durivage: 92/93 - 21; 93/94 - 13
- Fleer: 92/93 - 105, 4UR; 93/94 - 141, 368PP
- Humpty Dumpty: 92/93 - 5(I)
- Leaf: 93/94 - 117
- O-Pee-Chee: 92/93 - 307; 93/94 - 480, 115SC, 115FD
- Panini: 92/93 - 272E, M(E), 272F, M(F); 93/94 - 18E, 18F
- Parkhurst: 91/92 - 313E, 447E, 313F, 447F; 92/93 - 81, 237, 81EI, 237EI; 93/94 - 101, 101EI; 94/95 - V14
- Pro-Set: 91/92 - 6RGL; 92/93 - 92, PV3
- Score: 92/93 - 331C, 331A, 7CSS, 7ASS, 29CT, 29AT; 93/94 - 178C, 178A
- Topps: 92/93 - 13, 19, 13GS, 19GS, 403SC; 93/94 - 480C, 115SC, 115FD
- Upper Deck: 92/93 - 356, 427, 625, AR1; 93/94 - 117

Dionne, Marcel
- Coca-Cola: 77/78 - 6
- Colgate: 71/72 - 2
- Derniere: 72/84 - 99, 197
- Esso: 88/89 - 8
- Frito-Lay: 88/89 - 10
- Funmate: 83/84 - 51
- Kellogg's: 84 - 23
- Loblaws: 74/75 - 94
- O-Pee-Chee: 71/72 - 133; 72/73 - 8; 73/74 - 17; 74/75 - 72; 75/76 - 140; 76/77 - 91; 77/78 - 240, 4GP; 78/79 - 120; 79/80 - 160; 80/81 - 20, 81, 8PO; 81/82 - 141, 150, 156, 147SK, 235SK, 267SK; 82/83 - 149, 152, 153, 230SK; 83/84 - 150, 151, 152, 211, 1SK, 294SK, 295SK, 323SK, 324SK; 84/85 - 82, 264SK, 265SK; 85/86 - 90, E/BB, 235SK; 86/87 - 30, 88SK; 87/88 - 129, 34SK; 88/89 - 13, 8NS, 244SK; 92/93 - 294, 4AN
- Panini: 87/88 - 113; 88/89 - 190
- Post: 81/82 - 12; 82/83 - 115
- Pro Set: 90/91 653
- 7-Eleven: 84/85 - 23
- Score: 92/93 - 5PNC, 5PNA
- Season's: 92/93 - 24
- Topps: 72/73 - 18; 73/74 - 17; 74/75 - 72; 75/76 - 140; 76/77 - 91, 4PO; 77/78 - 240, 4PO; 78/79 - 120; 79/80 - 160; 80/81 - 20, 81; 81/82 - WN 125, 9, 54; 82/83 - 230SK; 83/84 - 1SK, 294SK, 295SK, 323SL, 324SK; 84/85 - 64; 85/86 - 90, E/BB; 86/87 - 30; 87/88 - 129; 88/89 - 13
- Toronto Sun: 71/72 - 92
- Upper Deck: 91/92 - 636E, 636F
- Zellers: 93/94 - 4, 4A

Di Pietro, Paul
- Fleer: 93/94 - 159, 369PP
- Leaf: 93/94 - 248
- O-Pee-Chee: 93/94 - 288, 194SC, 194FD
- Parkhurst: 92/93 - 489, 489EI; 93/94 - 108, 108EI
- Pro Set: 91/92 - 546E, 546F
- Score: 91/92 - 350PNE, 350PNF; 93/94 - 494C, 494A
- Topps: 92/93 - 361, 361GS; 93/94 - 288, 194SC, 194FD
- Upper Deck: 93/94 - 108

Dirk, Robert
- Fleer: 92/93 - 425
- O-Pee-Chee: 91/92 - 493; 93/94 - 284
- Parkhurst: 91/92 - 403; 92/93 - 425, 425EI
- Pro Set: 90/91 - 522
- Score: 91/92 - 508B, 508C; 92/93 - 279C, 279A; 93/94 - 288C, 288A
- Topps: 91/92 - 493; 92/93 - 437, 437GS, 98SC; 93/94 - 284

Djoos, Per Olav
- O-Pee-Chee: 90/91 - 24PM

Djoos, Per Olav (cont.)
- Pro Set: 90/91 - 603
- Score: 90/91 - 107T; 92/93 - 372C, 372A
- Topps: 92/93 - 93, 93GS, 492SC

Doak, Gary
- Dad's Cookies: 70/71 - 138
- Eddie Sargent: 70/71 - 218; 71/72 - 214
- Esso: 70/71 - 238
- O-Pee-Chee: 68/69 - 138; 69/70 - 202; 70/71 - 114; 71/72 - 87; 72/73 - 73; 74/75 - 361; 75/76 - 358; 76/77 - 7; 77/78 - 181; 78/79 - 305; 80/81 - 374
- Shirriff: 68/69 - A14
- Topps: 67/68 - 97; 70/71 - 114; 71/72 - 87; 72/73 - 81; 76/77 - 7; 77/78 - 181

Dollas, Bobby
- Fleer: 93/94 - 283PP
- O-Pee-Chee: 93/94 - 491
- Topps: 93/94 - 491C, 463SC, 463FD

Domi, Tahir (Tie)
- Donruss: 93/94 - 381
- Leaf: 93/94 - 216
- O-Pee-Chee: 90/91 - 25PM; 93/94 - 513
- Parkhurst: 91/92 - 333E, 333F; 92/93 - 434, 434EI; 93/94 - 230, 230EI
- Pro Set: 91/92 - 440E, 440F
- Score: 92/93 - 408C, 408A; 93/94 - 312C, 312A
- Topps: 92/93 - 395, 395GS; 93/94 - 513A
- Upper Deck: 92/93 - 99

Donatelli, Clark
- Bowman: 90/91 - 181
- O-Pee-Chee: 90/91 - 458

Donato, Ted
- Donruss: 93/94 - 25
- Fleer: 92/93 - 251; 93/94 - 18PP
- Leaf: 93/94 - 54
- O-Pee-Chee: 92/93 - 30PM; 93/94 - 146, 83SC, 83FD
- Panini: 93/94 - 8E, 8F
- Parkhurst: 91/92 - 230E, 230F; 92/93 - 8, 8EI; 93/94 - 283, 283EI
- Pro-Set: 92/93 - 221
- Score: 92/93 - 479C, 479A; 93/94 - 262C, 262A
- Topps: 92/93 - 271; 93/94 - 146, 83SC, 83FD
- Upper Deck: 92/93 - 202, 393, G20; 93/94 - 143

Donnelly, Gordon (Gord)
- Durivage: 92/93 - 13
- Fleer: 92/93 - 259
- Pro Set: 90/91 - 560; 91/92 - 357E, 357F
- Topps: 93/94 - 396SC, 396FD
- Upper Deck: 91/92 - 305E, 305F

Donnelly, Mike
- Bowman: 92/93 - 342
- Donruss: 93/94 - 155
- Fleer: 92/93 - 81; 93/94 - 359PP
- Leaf: 93/94 - 282
- O-Pee-Chee: 92/93 - 151; 93/94 - 33
- Parkhurst: 91/92 - 294E, 294F; 93/94 - 369, 369EI
- Pro Set: 91/92 - 399E, 399F, 183PT
- Score: 91/92 - 499B, 499C, 299PNE, 299PNF; 92/93 - 67C, 67A, 98PNC, 98PNA
- Topps: 92/93 - 121, 121GS, 411SC; 93/94 - 33, 374SC, 374FD
- Upper Deck: 91/92 - 420E, 420F

Donnelly, Truman
- World Wide Gum: 36/37 - 134

Doraty, Ken
- Anonymous: 33/34 - 14
- O-Pee-Chee: 33/34 - 4
- World Wide Gum: 33/34 - 49

Doré, Andre
- O-Pee-Chee: 83/84 - 313; 84/85 - 279
- Post: 82/83 - 195

Doré, Daniel
- Upper Deck: 90/91 - 255E, 255F

Dorey, Jim
- Colgate: 70/71 - 79
- Derniere: 72/84 - 79
- Eddie Sargent: 70/71 - 197
- Esso: 70/71 - 218
- O-Pee-Chee: 69/70 - 45; 70/71 - 106; 71/72 - 57; 72/73 - 339
- Topps: 70/71 - 106; 71/72 - 57
- Toronto Sun: 71/72 - 255

Dornhoefer, Gary
- Bauer: 68/69 - 5
- Beehive: 64/67 - 6
- Coca-Cola: 64/65 - 4
- Colgate: 70/71 - 40
- Dad's Cookies: 70/71 - 95
- Eddie Sargent: 70/71 - 149; 72/73 - 161
- Esso: 70/71 - 166
- Loblaws: 74/75 - 222
- O-Pee-Chee: 68/69 - 94; 69/70 - 94; 70/71 - 85, 33DE; 71/72 - 202; 72/73 - 146; 73/74 - 182; 74/75 - 44; 75/76 - 129; 76/77 - 256; 77/78 - 202
- Shirriff: 68/69 - J4
- Topps: 64/65 - 72; 65/66 - 38; 68/69 - 94; 69/70 - 94; 70/71 - 85; 71/72 - 89; 72/73 - 41; 73/74 - 167; 74/75 - 44; 75/76 - 129; 76/77 - 256; 77/78 - 202
- Toronto Sun: 71/72 - 192

Dorofeyev, Igor
- O-Pee-Chee: 91/92 - 32R
- Upper Deck: 92/93 - 352

Dorohoy, Eddie
- Beehive: 45/63 - 234
- Quaker Oats: 45/54 - 12

Doucet, Wayne
- Score: 90/91 - 397A, 397C

Douglas, Jordy
- O-Pee-Chee: 79/80 - 335; 80/81 - 97; 81/82 - 65SK; 84/85 - 338
- Post: 82/83 - 97
- Topps: 80/81 - 97

Douglas, Kent
- Bauer: 68/69 - 6
- Beehive: 45/63 - 397; 64/67 - 160
- Coca-Cola: 64/65 - 96; 65/66 - 94
- Chex: 63/65 - 43
- O-Pee-Chee: 68/69 - 26
- Parkhurst: 63/64 - 7, 67
- Shirriff: 68/69 - C6
- Topps: 65/66 - 14; 66/67 - 82; 68/69 - 26
- Toronto Star: 57/67 - 94; 63/64 - 33
- York: 62/63 - 13; 63/64 - 13

Douglas, Les
- Beehive: 34/44 - 99
- O-Pee-Chee: 40/41 - 129

Douris, Peter
- Fleer: 93/94 - 284PP
- O-Pee-Chee: 90/91 - 26PM; 91/92 - 141PM; 93/94 - 265
- Panini: 92/93 - 141E, 141F
- Pro Set: 90/91 - 407; 91/92 - 347E, 347F
- Score: 91/92 - 633B, 633C; 92/93 - 384C, 384A
- Topps: 92/93 - 190, 190GS, 402SC; 93/94 - 265
- Upper Deck: 91/92 - 403E, 601E, 403F, 601F

Dowd, Jim
- Fleer: 93/94 - 376PP

Doyon, Mario
- Upper Deck: 91/92 - 411E, 411F

Drake, Dallas
- Donruss: 93/94 - 100, 508
- Fleer: 93/94 - 104, 71PP
- Leaf: 93/94 - 148
- O-Pee-Chee: 93/94 - 365
- Parkhurst: 93/94 - 61, 61EI; 94/95 - 261, 261EI, V90
- Score: 93/94 - 246C, 246A
- Topps: 93/94 - 365, 484SC, 484FD
- Upper Deck: 93/94 - 50

Draper, Kris
  Donruss: 93/94 - 423
  O-Pee-Chee: 92/93 - 374, 27PM
  Score: 90/91 - 404A, 404C
  Topps: 92/93 - 249, 249GS
  Upper Deck: 90/91 - 466E, 466F

Draper, Tom (Goalie)
  Bowman: 92/93 - 56
  Fleer: 92/93 - 14
  O-Pee-Chee: 92/93 - 376
  Panini: 92/93 - 243E, 243F
  Parkhurst: 91/92 - 240E, 448E, 240F, 448F
  Pro-Set: 92/93 - 14
  Score: 91/92 - 341PNE, 341PNF; 92/93 - 530C, 530A
  Topps: 92/93 - 278, 278GS, 395SC
  Upper Deck: 91/92 - 552E, 552F; 92/93 - 201, 361

Drillon, Gordie
  Beehive: 34/44 - 148, 315
  Hall of Fame: 83 - 109, H3P, 87 - 109
  O-Pee-Chee: 37/38 - 142; 39/40 - 4; 40/41 - 110
  Parkhurst: 55/56 - 25
  Quaker Oats: 38/39 - 20; 55/56 - 25

Drinkwater, Graham
  Hall of Fame: 83 - 186, J6P, 87 - 186

Driver, Bruce
  Bowman: 90/91 - 87; 91/92 - 281
  Donruss: 93/94 - 185
  Fleer: 92/93 - 336; 93/94 - 214, 135PP
  Leaf: 93/94 - 56
  O-Pee-Chee: 85/86 - 127; 86/87 - 19; 87/88 - 79, 60SK; 88/89 - 157, 77SK; 90/91 - 172; 91/92 - 294; 93/94 - 377, 126SC, 126FD
  Panini: 87/88 - 74; 88/89 - 269; 90/91 - 69; 91/92 - 225; 92/93 - 178E, 178F; 93/94 - 44E, 44F
  Parkhurst: 91/92 - 322E, 322F; 92/93 - 333, 333EI
  Pro Set: 90/91 - 166; 91/92 - 140E, 577E, 140F, 69PT, 577F; 92/93 - 99
  Score: 90/91 - 109A, 109C; 91/92 - 89A, 89B, 89C, 63PNE, 63PNF; 92/93 - 251C, 251A, 278PNC, 278PNA; 93/94 - 263C, 263A
  Topps: 85/86 - 127; 86/87 - 19; 87/88 - 79; 88/89 - 157; 90/91 - 172; 91/92 - 294; 122SC; 92/93 - 384, 384GS, 376SC; 93/94 - 377, 126SC, 126FD
  Upper Deck: 90/91 - 373E, 373F; 91/92 - 294E, 294F; 92/93 - 200

Droppa, Ivan
  Donruss: 93/94 - 414
  Parkhurst: 93/94 - 42, 42EI; 94/95 - 49, 49EI

Drouin, Jude
  Colgate: 70/71 - 18
  Eddie Sargent: 70/71 - 88; 71/72 - 82
  Esso: 72/73 - 100
  Loblaws: 74/75 - 149
  O-Pee-Chee: 70/71 - 171; 71/72 - 68, 21BK; 72/73 - 47; 73/74 - 125; 74/75 - 255; 75/76 - 224; 76/77 - 106; 77/78 - 182; 78/79 - 93; 79/80 - 329; 80/81 - 285
  PepsiCo: 80/81 - 125
  Topps: 71/72 - 68, 21BK; 72/73 - 153; 73/74 - 125; 74/75 - 255; 75/76 - 224; 76/77 - 106; 77/78 - 182; 78/79 - 93
  Toronto Sun: 71/72 - 128

Drouin, Polly (Emile Paul)
  Beehive: 34/44 - 149
  Canada Starch: 35/40 - 118
  O-Pee-Chee: 37/38 - 158; 39/40 - 24
  Quaker Oats: 38/39 - 5
  World Wide Gum: 36/37 - 50

Druce, John
  Bowman: 90/91 - HT16; 91/92 - 293; 92/93 - 180
  Fleer: 92/93 - 442; 93/94 - 360PP

Druce, John (cont.)
  O-Pee-Chee: 90/91 - 298; 91/92 - 203; 92/93 - 105, 80PM
  Panini: 91/92 - 200
  Parkhurst: 91/92 - 415E, 415F; 92/93 - 437, 437EI
  Pro Set: 90/91 - 310; 91/92 - 251E, 251F, 129PT
  Score: 90 - 25YS; 90/91 - 246A, 246C; 91/92 - 180A, 180B, 180C, 395PNE, 395PNF; 92/93 - 121C, 121A, 185PNC, 185PNA
  Topps: 90/91 - 298; 91/92 - 206, 331SC; 92/93 - 188, 188GS, 405SC
  Upper Deck: 90/91 - 371E, 371F; 91/92 - 151E, 151F; 92/93 - 205

Drulia, Stan
  O-Pee-Chee: 92/93 - 105PM
  Parkhurst: 92/93 - 177, 177EI; 93/94 - 191, 191EI
  Upper Deck: 92/93 - 487

Drury, Ted
  Donruss: 93/94 - 58, 437, 14RR
  Fleer: 93/94 - 303PP
  Leaf: 93/94 - 424
  Parkhurst: 93/94 - 35, 35EI
  Topps: 93/94 - 443SC, 443FD
  Upper Deck: 92/93 - 396; 93/94 - 466

Dryden, Dave (Goalie)
  Beehive: 64/67 - 33
  Coca-Cola: 65/66 - 19
  Colgate: 70/71 - 80
  Esso: 72/73 - 34
  O-Pee-Chee: 68/69 - 150; 71/72 - 159; 72/73 - 241; 73/74 - 63; 79/80 - 71
  Shirriff: 68/69 - B13
  Topps: 67/68 - 57; 73/74 - 187; 79/80 - 71
  Toronto Sun: 71/72 - 25

Dryden, Ken (Goalie)
  Colgate: 71/72 - 3
  Derniere: 72/84 - 1
  Eddie Sargent: 72/73 - 124
  Esso: 88/89 - 9
  Hall of Fame: 83 - 196, N4P; 87 - 196
  Letraset: 74/75 - 19
  Loblaws: 74/75 - 165
  O-Pee-Chee: 71/72 - 45, 17BK, 22PT; 72/73 - 134, 145, 247, 12CS; 74/75 - 155; 75/76 - 35; 76/77 - 200; 77/78 - 100, 5GP; 78/79 - 50, 330; 79/80 - 150
  Topps: 71/72 - 45, 17BK; 72/73 - 127, 160; 73/74 - 10; 74/75 - 155; 75/76 - 35; 76/77 - 200, 5PO; 77/78 - 100, 5PO; 78/79 - 50; 79/80 - 150
  Toronto Sun: 71/72 - 149

Dube, Gilles
  Beehive: 45/63 - 235

Dube, Normand
  Derniere: 72/84 - 77

Dube, Yannick
  Donruss: 93/94 - 9JCC
  Parkhurst: 93/94 - 512, 512EI
  Upper Deck: 93/94 - 533

Duberman, Justin
  Donruss: 93/94 - 471
  Parkhurst: 94/95 - 181, 181EI

Dubinsky, Steve
  Donruss: 93/94 - 70
  Parkhurst: 93/94 - 40, 40EI
  Upper Deck: 93/94 - 477

Duchesne, Gaetan
  Bowman: 91/92 - 120; 92/93 - 266
  Donruss: 93/94 - 301
  Durivage: 92/93 - 22
  Fleer: 92/93 - 318; 93/94 - 433PP
  Leaf: 93/94 - 339
  O-Pee-Chee: 88/89 - 208, 187SK; 89/90 - 194SK; 90/91 - 319; 91/92 - 433; 92/93 - 143
  Panini: 87/88 - 183; 88/89 - 353; 90/91 - 256; 91/92 - 117;

Duchesne, Gaetan (cont.)
  Panini: 93/94 - 273E, 273F
  Parkhurst: 91/92 - 305E, 305F; 93/94 - 456, 456EI
  Post: 82/83 - 307
  Pro Set: 90/91 - 137; 91/92 - 110E, 110F
  Score: 90/91 - 375A, 375C; 91/92 - 440B, 440C; 92/93 - 338C, 338B, 198PNC, 198PNA; 93/94 - 226C, 226A
  Topps: 90/91 - 319; 91/92 - 433, 153SC; 92/93 - 406, 406GS, 307SC
  Upper Deck: 90/91 - 108E, 108F; 91/92 - 207E, 207F; 92/93 - 469

Duchesne, Steve
  Bowman: 90/91 - 146; 91/92 - 191; 92/93 - 31
  Donruss: 93/94 - 276, 484
  Durivage: 92/93 - 38; 93/94 - 40
  Fleer: 92/93 - 384; 93/94 - 7, 197PP
  Hockey Wit: 93/94 - 8
  Kraft: 1990 - 58; 90/91 - 65
  Leaf: 93/94 - 176
  O-Pee-Chee: 88/89 - 182, 152SK; 89/90 - 123, 150SK, 165SK, 32FS; 90/91 - 86; 91/92 - 31, 13PM; 92/93 - 296, 130PM; 93/94 - 151
  Panini: 88/89 - 70, 89/90 - 93, 176; 90/91 - 241; 91/92 - 80; 92/93 - 192E, 192F; 93/94 - 76E, 76F
  Parkhurst: 91/92 - 125E, 125F; 92/93 - 143, 143EI; 93/94 - 168, 168EI; 94/95 - 205, 205EI, V26
  Pro Set: 90/91 - 115, 350; 91/92 - 96E, 448E, 96F, 86PT, 448F; 92/93 - 137
  Score: 90/91 - 26A, 26C, 15HR; 91 - 19T; 91/92 - 205A, 205B, 205C, 569B, 569C, 42PNE, 42PNF; 92/93 - 151C, 151A, 320PNC, 320PNA; 93/94 - 190C, 190A, 16CAS, 16AAS
  Sega: 93/94 - 109
  Topps: 88/89 - 182, 10SK; 89/90 - 123; 90/91 - 86; 91/92 - 31, 58SC; 92/93 - 271, 271GS, 313SC; 93/94 - 151, 2BG, 10AS
  Upper Deck: 90/91 - 136E, 136F; 91/92 - 570E, 570F; 92/93 - 513, 2AS; 93/94 - 217

Dudley, George
  Hall of Fame: 83 - 68, E8P; 87 -68

Dudley, Rick
  Loblaws: 74/75 - 40
  O-Pee-Chee: 74/75 - 268; 79/80 - 37; 80/81 - 355; 81/82 - 362
  Pro Set: 90/91 - 662
  Topps: 79/80 - 37

Duff, Dick
  Beehive: 45/63 - 398; 64/67 - 102, 123
  Chex: 63/65 - 44
  Coca-Cola: 64/65 - 75
  Dad's Cookies: 70/71 - 13
  Eddie Sargent: 70/71 - 65
  O-Pee-Chee: 68/69 - 161; 69/70 - 11; 71/72 - 164
  Parkhurst: 55/56 - 18; 57/58 TOR - 3; 58/59 - 29; 59/60 - 38; 60/61 - 12; 61/62 - 12; 62/63 - 2; 63/64 - 4, 64; 1992/93 - PR24; 93/94 - 126ML
  Quaker Oats: 55/56 - 18
  Shirriff: 60/61 - 2; 61/62 - 53; 62/63 - 12; 68/69 - F11
  Topps: 64/65 - 46; 65/66 - 7; 66/67 - 71; 67/68 - 2
  Toronto Star: 58/67 - 29; 63/64 - 34
  Toronto Sun: 71/72 - 26
  York: 60/61 - 24; 61/62 - 2; 62/63 - 7; 63/64 - 9

Dufour, Claude
  La Patrie: 51/54 - 42

Dufour, Guy
  O-Pee-Chee: 72/73 - 328

Dufour, Luc
  O-Pee-Chee: 83/84 - 48, 172SK, 182SK; 84/85 - 3
  Topps: 83/84 - 172SK, 182SK

Dufresne, Donald
    Durivage: 92/93 - 39
    Leaf: 93/94 - 355
    Parkhurst: 93/94 - 467, 467EI
    Pro Set: 90/91 - 469; 91/92 - 418E, 418F
    Score: 90/91 - 35T; 91/92 - 392B, 392C
    Upper Deck: 90/91 - 332E, 332F

Duguay, Ron
    Derniere: 72/84 - 167
    Funmate: 83/84 - 30
    O-Pee-Chee: 78/79 - 177; 79/80 - 208; 80/81 - 37; 81/82 - 223, 171SK; 82/83 - 217, 221, 134SK; 83/84 - 121; 84/85 - 52, 42SK; 85/86 - 116, 32SK; 87/88 - 110
    Panini: 87/88 - 119; 89/90 - 96
    Post: 82/83 - 196
    Topps: 78/79 - 177; 79/80 - 208; 80/81 - 37; 81/82 EN - 96; 82/83 - 134SK 84/85 - 40; 85/86 - 116; 87/88 - 110

Duguid, Lorne
    Can. Chew. Gum: 33/34 - 19
    O-Pee-Chee: 34/35 - 58
    World Wide Gum: 33/34 - 52

Dumart, Woody
    Beehive: 34/44 - 13; 44/63 - 16
    O-Pee-Chee: 39/40 - 94
    Parkhurst: 51/52 - 28; 52/53 - 72; 53/54 - 96

Duncan, Iain
    O-Pee-Chee: 88/89 - 209, 132SK, 140SK, 6FS; 89/90 - 293, 136SK
    Panini: 88/89 - 154; 89/90 - 170

Dunderdale, Tom
    Hall of Fame: 83 - 126, I6P; 87 - 127
    Imperial Tobacco: 10/11 - 6L, 14; 11/12 - 6; 12/13 - 5

Dunham, Mike
    Fleer: 93/94 - 501PP
    Topps: 93/94 - 1US
    Upper Deck: 91/92 - 693E, 693F

Dunlop, Blake
    Funmate: 83/84 - 114
    Loblaws: 74/75 - 150
    O-Pee-Chee: 74/75 - 308; 75/76 - 16; 76/77 - 263; 79/80 - 174 80/81 - 370; 81/82 - 293, 131SK; 82/83 - 301, 199SK; 83/84 - 314, 131SK
    Post: 82/83 - 261
    Topps: 75/76 - 16; 76/77 - 263; 79/80 - 174; 81/82 WN - 117; 82/83 - 199SK; 83/84 - 131SK

Dunn, Dave
    Loblaws: 74/75 - 293
    O-Pee-Chee: 74/75 - 152; 75/76 - 187
    Topps: 74/75 - 152; 75/76 - 187

Dunn, James
    Hall of Fame: 83 - 217, O7P; 87 - 217

Dunn, Richard (Richie)
    O-Pee-Chee: 80/81 - 109; 81/82 - 29; 82/83 - 45; 83/84 - 137; 84/85 - 69
    Post: 82/83 - 17
    Topps: 80/81 - 109

Dupere, Denis
    Esso: 72/73 - 210
    O-Pee-Chee: 71/72 - 200; 72/73 - 167; 73/74 - 210; 74/75 - 105; 75/76 - 159; 76/77 - 334; 77/78 - 388; 78/79 -283
    Topps: 74/75 - 105; 75/76 - 159
    Toronto Sun: 71/72 - 256

Dupont, Andre
    Derniere: 72/84 - 108, 144
    Esso: 72/73 - 194
    Loblaws: 74/75 - 223
    O-Pee-Chee: 72/73 - 16; 73/74 - 113; 74/75 - 67; 75/76 - 56; 76/77 - 131; 77/78 - 164; 78/79 - 98; 79/80 - 178; 81/82 - 273; 82/83 - 282
    PepsiCo: 80/81 - 65
    Post: 82/83 - 243

Dupont, Andre (cont.)
    Topps: 72/73 - 19; 73/74 - 183; 74/75 - 67; 75/76 - 56; 76/77 - 131; 77/78 - 164; 78/79 - 98; 79/80 - 178

Dupont, Norm
    O-Pee-Chee: 81/82 - 363, 139SK; 82/83 - 378
    PepsiCo: 80/81 - 126
    Post: 82/83 - 325

Dupre, Yanic
    O-Pee-Chee: 91/92 - 16PM
    Topps: 92/93 - 515, 515GS, 137SC
    Upper Deck: 92/93 - 421

Durbano, Steve
    Loblaws: 74/75 - 241
    O-Pee-Chee: 73/74 - 124; 74/75 - 106; 76/77 - 19
    Topps: 73/74 - 168; 74/75 - 106; 76/77 - 19

Duris, Vitezslav
    O-Pee-Chee: 81/82 - 316
    PepsiCo: 80/81 -85

Durnan, Bill (Goalie)
    Beehive: 45/63 - 236
    Berk Ross: 1951 - 1-17
    CKAC Radio: 43/47 - 43, 44
    Hall of Fame: 83, 139, K4P, 87 - 139
    Highliner: 93/94 - 12
    Parkhurst: 55/56 - 63
    Quaker Oats: 45/54 - 13A, 13B; 55/56 - 63

Dussault, Norm
    Beehive: 45/63 - 237
    CKAC Radio: 43/47 - 45
    Quaker Oats: 45/54 - 14A, 14B

Dutkowski, Duke (Joseph)
    Can. Chew. Gum: 33/34 - 20
    Diamond: 33/35 - 21
    World Wide Gum: 33/34 - 56

Dutton, Red (Mervyn)
    Anonymous: 33/34 - 23
    Beehive: 34/44 - 222
    Can. Chew. Gum: 33/34 - 21
    Diamond: 33/35 - 22; 36/39 - 21(I), 20(II), 18(III)
    Hall of Fame: 83 - 7, A6P; 87 - 7
    La Presse: 27/32 - 24
    Topps: 60/61 - 16
    World Wide Gum: 33/34 - 25; 36/37 - 14

Dye, Babe (Cecil)
    Champ's: 24/25 - 52
    Hall of Fame: 83 - 34, C4P; 87 - 34
    Wm. Paterson: 23/24 - 23; 24/25 - 54

Dykhuis, Karl
    Fleer: 92/93 - 274; 93/94 - 48PP
    O-Pee-Chee: 91/92 - 172
    Parkhurst: 91/92 - 262E, 262F
    Score: 90/91 - 437A, 437C; 92/93 - 462C, 462A
    Topps: 91/92 - 172
    Upper Deck: 90/91 - 471E, 471F; 91/92 - 688E, 688F; 92/93 - 404; 93/94 - 106

Dykstra, Steve
    O-Pee-Chee: 87/88 - 146SK

Eagan, Pat
    Beehive: 45/63 - 17

Eagles, Mike
    O-Pee-Chee: 87/88 - 253; 88/89 - 191SK; 93/94 - 116, 14SC, 14FD
    Panini: 87/88 - 170; 88/89 - 354
    Parkhurst: 91/92 - 420E, 420F; 93/94 - 229, 229EI
    Pro Set: 91/92 - 518E, 518F
    Score: 91/92 - 414B, 414C; 92/93 - 345C, 345A, 93/94 - 429C, 429A
    Topps: 93/94 - 116, 14SC, 14FD
    Upper Deck: 91/92 - 523E, 523F

Eastwood, Michael
    Parkhurst: 92/93 - 494, 494EI
    Upper Deck: 93/94 - 57

Eaves, Mike
    O-Pee-Chee: 80/81 - 206; 1/82 - 171; 83/84 - 79; 84/85 - 221, 244SK; 85/86 - 213

Eaves, Mike (cont.)
    Topps: 80/81 - 206
    Vachon Foods: 83/84 - 4

Eaves, Murray
    O-Pee-Chee: 83/84 - 384

Eberle, Jorg
    Upper Deck: 92/93 - 384

Ecclestone, Tim
    Bauer: 68/69 - 7
    Bazooka: 71/72 - 27
    Colgate: 70/71 - 58
    Dad's Cookies: 70/71 - 115
    Eddie Sargent: 70/71 - 188; 72/73 - 78
    Esso: 70/71 - 202
    Loblaws: 74/75 - 272
    O-Pee-Chee: 68/69 - 178; 69/70 - 179; 70/71 - 102, 4SS; 71/72 - 52; 72/73 - 55; 73/74 - 144; 74/75 - 323; 76/77 - 351; 77/78 - 364
    Topps: 70/71 - 102, 4SK; 71/72 - 52; 72/73 - 33; 73/74 - 124
    Toronto Sun: 71/72 - 93

Edberg, Rolf
    Topps: 80/81 - 65
    O-Pee-Chee: 80/81 - 65

Eddolls, Frank
    Beehive: 45/63 - 308
    CKAC Radio: 43/47 - 46
    Parkhurst: 51/52 - 89
    Quaker Oats: 45/54 - 15

Edestrand, Darryl
    Esso: 72/73 - 181
    Loblaws: 74/75 - 22
    O-Pee-Chee: 71/72 - 187; 72/73 - 195; 73/74 - 216; 74/75 - 313; 75/76 - 11; 76/77 - 179; 77/78 - 321; 78/79 - 377; 79/80 - 280
    Topps: 75/76 - 11; 76/77 - 179
    Toronto Sun: 71/72 - 213

Edmundson, Garry
    Beehive: 45/63 - 399
    Parkhurst: 59/60 - 48; 60/61 - 5
    Shirriff: 60/61 - 14

Edur, Tom
    O-Pee-Chee: 77/78 - 169; 78/79 - 119
    Topps: 77/78 - 169; 78/79 - 119

Edwards, Don (Goalie)
    Funmate: 83/84 - 16
    O-Pee-Chee: 77/78 - 201; 78/79 - 150, 336; 79/80 - 105; 80/81 - 92, 215; 81/82 - 21, 389, 55SK; 82/83 - 46, 124SK; 83/84 - 80; 84/85 - 222; 85/86 - 183; 86/87 - 139SK
    Post: 82/83 - 18
    Topps: 77/78 - 201; 78/79 - 150; 79/80 - 105; 80/81 - 92, 215; 81/82 EN - 75; 82/83 - 124SK
    Vachon Foods: 83/84 - 5

Edwards, Gary (Goalie)
    Loblaws: 74/75 - 130
    O-Pee-Chee: 71/72 - 155; 72/73 - 113, 9CS; 73/74 - 199; 75/76 - 105; 76/77 - 365; 77/78 - 345; 78/79 - 6; 80/81 - 335
    Topps: 72/73 - 151; 75/76 - 105; 78/79 - 6
    Toronto Sun: 71/72 - 111

Edwards, Marv (Goalie)
    Esso: 72/73 - 49
    O-Pee-Chee: 69/70 - 185

Edwards, Roy (Goalie)
    Bazooka: 71/72 - 21
    Dad's Cookies: 70/71 - 48
    Eddie Sargent: 71/72 - 62; 72/73 - 174
    Esso: 70/71 - 78
    O-Pee-Chee: 68/69 - 144; 69/70 - 56; 70/71 - 21; 71/72 - 99; 73/74 - 82
    Shirriff: 68/69 - C7
    Topps: 67/68 - 106; 69/70 - 56; 70/71 - 21; 71/72 - 99; 73/74 - 82
    Toronto Sun: 71/72 - 214

Egan, Pat
  Beehive: 34/44 - 223; 45/63 - 309
Egers, Jack
  Eddie Sargent: 72/73 - 196
  Esso: 70/71 - 147
  Loblaws: 74/75 - 312
  O-Pee-Chee: 72/73 - 107; 73/74 - 79; 74/75 - 93; 75/76 - 134;
  Topps: 72/73 - 147; 73/74 - 79; 74/75 - 93; 75/76 - 134
  Toronto Sun: 71/72 - 170
Ehman, Gerry
  Beehive: 45/63 - 400
  Dad's Cookies: 70/71 - 24
  Eddie Sargent: 70/71 - 144
  Esso: 70/71 - 38
  O-Pee-Chee: 68/69 - 84; 69/70 - 83; 70/71 - 187
  Parkhurst: 59/60 - 19; 60/61 - 8
  Shirriff: 60/61 - 19; 68/69 - H1
  Topps: 68/69 - 84; 69/70 - 83
Eisenhut, Neil
  Fleer: 93/94 - 459PP
Eklund, Per-Erik (Pelle)
  Bowman: 90/91 - 107; 91/92 - 241; 92/93 - 179
  Donruss: 93/94 - 250
  Fleer: 92/93 - 155; 93/94 - 180PP
  Leaf: 93/94 - 177
  O-Pee-Chee: 86/87 - 127SK; 87/88 - 98, 9HL; 88/89 - 211; 89/90 - 105SK 90/91 - 254; 91/92 - 111; 92/93 - 242; 93/94 - 449
  Panini: 87/88 - 132; 89/90 - 296; 90/91 - 113; 91/92 - 228; 92/93 - 189E, 189F; 93/94 - 51E
  Parkhurst: 91/92 - 128E, 128F; 93/94 - 147, 147EI; 94/95 - 56, 56EI
  Pro Set: 90/91 - 215; 91/92 - 179E, 179F, 89PT
  Score: 90/91 - 308A; 91/92 - 91A, 91B, 91C, 134PNE, 134PNF; 92/93 - 173C, 173A, 149PNC, 149PNA; 93/94 - 181C, 181A
  Topps: 87/88 - 98; 90/91 - 254; 91/92 - 111, 182SC; 92/93 - 117, 117GS, 154SC; 93/94 - 449C, 289SC, 289FD
  Upper Deck: 90/91 - 138E, 138F; 91/92 - 103E, 103F; 93/94 - 120
Elik, Todd
  Bowman: 90/91 - 151; 91/92 - 185; 92/93 - 317
  Donruss: 93/94 - 489
  Fleer: 92/93 - 93; 93/94 - 80PP, 434PP
  O-Pee-Chee: 90/91 - 352; 91/92 - 251, 74PM; 92/93 - 20
  Panini: 91/92 - 85; 93/94 - 238E, 238F
  Parkhurst: 91/92 - 300E, 300F; 92/93 - 77, 292, 77EI. 292EI; 93/94 - 71, 71EI; 94/95 - 210, 210EI
  Pro Set: 90/91 - 116; 91/92 - 94E, 410E, 94F, 57PT, 410F
  Score: 90/91 - 297A, 297C; 91 - 13T; 91/92 - 83A, 83B, 83C, 563B, 563C, 264PNE, 264PNF; 92/93 - 307C, 307A, 207PNC, 207PNA; 93/94 - 185C, 185A
  Topps: 90/91 - 352; 91/92 - 251, 310SC; 92/93 - 97, 97GS, 226SC, 363SC, 363FD
  Upper Deck: 90/91 - 233E, 233F; 91/92 - 544E, 544F; 92/93 - 210
Eliot, Darren (Goalie)
  Panini: 87/88 - 272
Ellett, David (Dave)
  Bowman: 90/91 - 132; 91/92 - 163; 92/93 - 204, 291
  Donruss: 93/94 - 344
  Fleer: 92/93 - 209; 93/94 - 38, 243PP
  Gillette: 91/92 - 17
  Humpty Dumpty: 92/93 - 4(II)
  Kellogg's: 89 - 23

Ellett, David (cont.)
  Kraft: 1990 - 49
  Leaf: 93/94 - 86
  O-Pee-Chee: 85/86 - 185; 87/88 - 35, 251SK; 88/89 - 167, 150SK; 89/90 - 69, 139SK; 90/91 - 104; 91/92 - 381, 180PM; 92/93 - 9; 93/94 - 297
  Panini: 87-88 - 358; 88/89 - 150; 89-90 - 167; 90/91 - 310; 91/92 - 94; 92/93 - 83E, 83F; 93/94 - 231E, 231F
  Parkhurst: 91/92 - 172E, 172F; 92/93 - 181, 181EI; 93/94 - 205, 205EI; 94/95 - 227, 227EI, V8
  Pro Set: 90/91 - 326, 532; 91/92 - 230E, 230F, 116PT; 92/93 - 186
  Score: 90 - 67T; 90/91 - 65A, 65C, 29HR; 91/92 - 275A, 495B, 495C, 111PNE, 111PNF; 92/93 - 152C, 152A, 273PNC, 273PNA; 93/94 - 119C, 119A
  Topps: 87/88 - 35; 88/89 - 167; 89/90 - 69; 90/91 - 104; 91/92 - 381, 274SC; 92/93 - 30, 30GS, 283SC; 93/94 - 297, 469SC, 469FD
  Upper Deck: 90/91 - 71E, 71F, 413E, 413F; 91/92 - 196E, 196F; 92/93 - 214; 93/94 - 215
Elliott, Chaucer
  Hall of Fame: 83 - 171, M6P; 87 - 171
Ellis, Aaron (Goalie)
  Donruss: 93/94 - 6JCA
  Upper Deck: 93/94 - 554
Ellis, Ron
  Bazooka: 71/72 - 34
  Beehive: 64/67 - 161
  Coca-Cola: 64/65 - 97; 65/66 - 95
  Colgate: 70/71 - 54
  Dad's Cookies: 70/71 - 125
  Eddie Sargent: 70/71 - 200; 72/73 - 201
  Esso: 70/71 - 219
  Kellogg's: 70 - 1
  Letraset: 74/75 - 6
  Loblaws: 74/75 - 273
  Mac's Milk: 73/74 - 6
  O-Pee-Chee: 68/69 - 126; 69/70 - 46; 70/71 - 221, 46DE, 5SS; 71/72 - 113; 72/73 - 36; 73/74 - 55; 74/75 - 12; 75/76 - 59; 77/78 - 311; 78/79 - 92; 79/80 - 373; 80/81 - 329
  PepsiCo: 80/81 - 86
  Shirriff: 68/69 - M7
  Topps: 65/66 - 82; 66/67 - 81; 67/68 - 14; 68/69 - 126; 69/70 - 46; 70/71 - 5SK; 71/72 - 113; 72/73 - 152; 73/74 - 55; 74/75 - 12; 75/76 - 59; 78/79 - 92
  Toronto Star: 57/67 - 119
  Toronto Sun: 71/72 - 257
  Ultimate: 92 - 34(OSE), 34(OSF)
Eloranta, Kari
  O-Pee-Chee: 83/84 - 81, 270SK; 84/85 - 223
  Topps: 83/84 - 270SK
  Vachon Foods: 83/84 -6
Elynuik, Pat
  Bowman: 90/91 - 137; 91/92 - 198; 92/93 - 270
  Donruss: 93/94 - 368
  Fleer: 92/93 - 434; 93/94 - 67, 260PP, 442PP
  Kraft: 91/92 - 12
  Leaf: 93/94 - 6
  O-Pee-Chee: 89/90 - 94, 35SK, 142SK, 20FS; 90/91 - 71, 28PM; 91/92 - 326; 92/93 - 201, 119PM; 93/94 - 51, 49SC, 49FD
  Panini: 89/90 - 165; 90/91 - 312; 91/92 - 66; 92/93 - 54E, 54F; 93/94 - 29E, 29F, 51F
  Parkhurst: 91/92 - 202E, 202F; 92/93 - 205, 205EI; 93/94 - 224, 224EI;
  Pro Set: 90/91 - 327; 91/92 - 262E, 262F, 136PT; 92/93 - 214
  Score: 90 - 28YS; 90/91 - 205A, 205C, 86HR; 91 - 34YS; 91/92 - 295A, 341A, 371B, 371C, 515B, 515C,

Elynuik, Pat (cont.)
  Score: 117PNE, 416PNE, 117PNF, 416PNF; 92/93 - 233C, 233A, 53PNC, 53PNA, 23CSS, 23ASS; 93/94 - 223C, 223A
  Topps: 89/90 - 94; 90/91 - 71; 91/92 - 326, 132SC; 92/93 - 56, 56GS, 410SC; 93/94 - 51, 49SC, 447SC, 49FD, 447FD
  Upper Deck: 90/91 - 74E, 74F; 91/92 - 109E, 109F; 92/93 - 312, 537; 93/94 - 75
Emerson, Nelson
  Bowman: 92/93 - 40
  Donruss: 93/94 - 383
  Fleer: 92/93 - 393, 5UR; 93/94 - 45, 209PP, 472PP
  Leaf: 93/94 - 75
  O-Pee-Chee: 91/92 - 138PM; 92/93 - 181; 93/94 - 35, 223SC, 223FD
  Panini: 92/93 - B(E), B(F); 93/94 - 159E, 159F
  Parkhurst: 91/92 - 151E, 151F; 92/93 - 152, 232, 152EI, 232EI; 93/94 - 497, 497EI; 94/95 - 267, 267EI
  Pro Set: 91/92 - 557E, 557F, 269PT, 5RGL; 92/93 - 161, 9TL
  Score: 90/91 - 383A, 383C; 91 - 89T; 91/92 - 550B, 550C, 314PNE, 314PNF; 92/93 - 376C, 505C, 376A, 505A, 36PNC, 36PNA; 93/94 - 28C, 28A
  Season's: 92/93 - 16
  Topps: 92/93 - 11, 480, 11GS, 480GS, 306SC; 93/94 - 223SC, 223FD
  Upper Deck: 92/93 - 18, 166; 93/94 - 342
Emma, David
  Fleer: 93/94 - 377PP
  O-Pee-Chee: 93/94 - 448
  Score: 91/92 - 330A; 93/94 - 468C, 468A
  Topps: 93/94 - 35, 448C
  Upper Deck: 92/93 - 462
Emmons, John
  Donruss: 93/94 - 7JCA
  Upper Deck: 92/93 - 608; 93/94 - 557
Emms, Hap (Leighton)
  Beehive: 34/44 - 224
  Can. Chew. Gum: 33/34 - 22
  Diamond: 36/39 - 21(II), 19(III)
  O-Pee-Chee: 33/34 - 40
  World Wide Gum: 33/34 - 55; 36/37 - 59
Engblom, Brian
  Derniere: 72/84 - 127, 180
  Funmate: 83/84 - 136
  McDonald's: 82/83 - 29
  O-Pee-Chee: 79/80 - 361; 80/81 - 304; 81/82 - 175, 33SK; 82/83 - 362; 83/84 - 368, 203SK; 84/85 - 83, 271SK; 85/86 - 5, 233SK; 86/87 - 40, 46SK
  PepsiCo: 80/81 - 42
  Post: 82/83 - 146
  Topps: 81/82 - 10; 83/84 - 203SK; 84/85 - 65; 85/86 - 5; 86/87 - 40
Enio, Jim
  Beehive: 45/63 - 164
Erickson, Aut
  Shirriff: 60/61 - 112; 61/62 - 18
Erickson, Bryan
  O-Pee-Chee: 85/86 - 80; 86/87 - 101, 93SK; 87/88 - 130; 93/94 - 294
  Panini: 87/88 - 282
  Pro Set: 91/92 - 516E, 516F
  Score: 91/92 - 657B, 657C
  Topps: 85/86 - 80; 86/87 - 101; 87/88 - 130; 93/94 - 294
Eriksson, Anders
  Parkhurst: 93/94 - 540, 540EI
Eriksson, Peter
  Upper Deck: 90/91 - 145E, 145F

Eriksson, Rolie
O-Pee-Chee: 77/78 - 123; 78/79 - 241; 79/80 - 350
Topps: 77/78 - 123; 78/79 - 241

Eriksson, Thomas
O-Pee-Chee: 84/85 - 158

Erixon, Jan
Bowman: 91/92 - 77; 92/93 - 253
O-Pee-Chee: 88/89 - 212; 89/90 - 96; 90/91 - 187; 91/92 - 152; 92/93 -207
Panini: 87/88 - 120; 88/89 - 306; 90/91 - 104; 91/92 - 283; 92/93 - 241E, 241F
Pro Set: 90/91 - 195;
Score: 90/91 - 272A, 272C, 343A, 343C; 91/92 - 264A, 484B, 484C, 187PNE, 187PNF; 92/93 - 362C, 362A, 191PNC, 191PNA; 93/94 - 287C, 287A
Topps: 89/90 - 96; 90/91 - 187; 91/92 - 152, 151SC; 92/93 - 153, 153GS, 161SC
Upper Deck: 90/91 - 366E, 366F; 91/92 - 178E, 178F

Errey, Bob
Bowman: 90/91 - 212; 91/92 - 85; 92/93 - 304
Durivage: 92/93 - 23
Fleer: 93/94 - 435PP
Leaf: 93/94 - 377
O-Pee-Chee: 89/90 - 50, 233SK; 90/91 - 230; 92/93 - 323
Panini: 87/88 - 152; 89/90 - 315; 90/91 - 133; 91/92 - 279
Parkhurst: 91/92 - 138E, 138F; 92/93 - 374, 374EI; 93/94 - 453, 453EI
Pro Set: 90/91 - 234; 91/92 - 187E, 187F, 215PT
Score: 90/91 - 255A, 255C; 91/92 - 169A, 169B, 169C, 257PNE, 257PNF; 92/93 - 287C, 287A, 310PNC, 310PNA; 93/94 - 208C, 208A
Topps: 89/90 - 50; 90/91 - 230; 91/92 - 94, 191SC; 92/93 - 95, 95GS, 170SC; 93/94 - 404SC, 404FD

Esau, Leonard
Parkhurst: 94/95 - 37, 37EI

Esmantovich, Igor
O-Pee-Chee: 90/91 - 479

Esposito, Phil
Bazooka: 71/72 - 1
Beehive: 64/67 - 34A, 34B
Chex: 63/65 - 1
Coca-Cola: 64/65 - 21; 65/66 - 20
Dad's Cookies: 70/71 - 4
Eddie Sargent: 70/71 - 14; 72/73 - 21
Esso: 70/71 - 7; 88/89 - 10
Hal of Fame: 87 - 244
Kellogg's: 70 - 2
Loblaws: 74/75 - 23
O-Pee-Chee: 68/69 - 7, 208, 5PS; 69/70 - 30, 205, 214, 7ST, 18QS; 70/71 - 11, 237, 6DE, 6SS;71/72 - 20, 247, 253, 2BK, 21PT; 72/73 - 76, 111, 148, 230, 2CS; 73/74 - 120; 74/75 - 129, 200, 244, 246; 75/76 - 200, 292; 76/77 - 245; 77/78 - 55; 78/79 - 2, 100; 79/80 - 220; 80/81 - 100, 149, 14PO; 92/93 - 283, 10AN
Pro Set: 90/91 - 403; 91/92 - 594E, 594F
Shirriff: 68/69 - A8
Topps: 65/66 - 116; 66/67 - 63; 67/68 - 32; 68/69 - 7; 69/70 - 30; 70/71 - 11, 6SK; 71/72 - 20, 2BK; 72/73 - 124,
Topps: 150; 73/74 - 120; 74/75 - 129, 200, 244, 246; 75/76 - 200, 292; 76/77 - 245, 7PO; 77/78 - 55; 78/79 - 2, 100; 79/80 - 220; 80/81 - 100, 149
Toronto Sun: 71/72 - 8
Upper Deck: 90/91 - 510E, 510F

Esposito, Tony (Goalie)
Bazooka: 71/72 - 29
Dad's Cookies: 70/71 - 35
Eddie Sargent: 70/71 - 33; 72/73 - 66
Esso: 70/71 - 58; 88/89 - 11
Funmate: 83/84 - 23
HHFM: 92 - 7
Highliner: 93/94 - 8
Letraset: 74/75 - 45
Loblaws: 74/75 - 75
O-Pee-Chee: 69/70 - 138; 70/71 - 153, 234, 247, 250, 32DE, 7SS; 71/72 - 110, 13BK; O-Pee-Chee: 8PT; 72/73 - 137, 155, 196, 226; 73/74 - 90; 74/75 - 170; 75/76 - 240; 76/77 - 100; 77/78 - 170; 78/79 - 250; 79/80 - 80; 80/81 - 86, 150, 4PO; 81/82 - 54, 67, 113SK; 82/83 - 64; 83/84 - 99; 92/93 - 194, 2AN
Post: 82/83 - 51
Pro Set: 90/91 - 659
Topps: 70/71 - 7SK; 71/72 - 110, 13BK; 72/73 - 20, 121; 73/74 - 90; 74/75 - 170; 75/76 - 240; 76/77 - 100, 3PO; 77/78 - 170; 78/79 - 250; 79/80 - 80; 80/81 - 86, 150; 81/82 - WN 126
Toronto Sun: 71/72 - 65

Essensa, Bob (Goalie)
Bowman: 90/91 - 131; 91/92 - 193; 92/93 - 306
Donruss: 93/94 - 382
Fleer: 92/93 - 240; 93/94 - 89, 270PP
Gillette: 91/92 - 8
Leaf: 93/94 - 38
O-Pee-Chee: 89/90 - 21FS; 90/91 - 119, 29PM; 91/92 - 307; 92/93 - 226; 93/94 - 161
Panini: 89/90 - 173; 90/91 - 311; 91/92 - 75; 92/93 - 51E, 51F; 93/94 - 199E
Parkhurst: 91/92 - 199E, 199F; 92/93 - 207, 207EI; 93/94 - 234, 234EI; 94/95 - 64, 64EI
Pro Set: 90/91 - 328; 91/92 - P/C, 266E, 602E, 266F, 135PT, 602F, 285PT; 92/93 - 211, 267
Score: 90/91 - 112A, 112C, 324A, 324C; 91 - 17YS; 91/92 - 251A, 471B, 471C, 66PNE, 66PNF; 92/93 - 123C, 123A, 190PNC, 190PNA; 93/94 - 26C. 26A
Sega: 93/94 - 150
Topps: 90/91 - 119; 91/92 - 307, 152SC; 92/93 - 183, 183GS, 210SC; 93/94 - 161, 254SC, 254FD
Upper Deck: 90/91 - 122E, 337E, 122F, 337F; 91/92 - 101E; 92/93 - 217; 93/94 - 144

Evans, Chris
Eddie Sargent: 72/73 - 192
Loblaws: 74/75 - 112
O-Pee-Chee: 72/73 - 236; 73/74 - 208; 74/75 - 59
Topps: 74/75 - 59

Evans, Daryl
O-Pee-Chee: 83/84 - 153; 92/93 - 381
Topps: 83/84 - 144SK

Evans, Doug
Bowman: 91/92 - 203
O-Pee-Chee: 90/91 - 413; 91/92 - 438; 92/93 - 45PM; 93/94 - 203
Pro Set: 90/91 - 561
Score: 91/92 - 399B, 399C
Topps: 91/92 - 438, 321SC; 93/94 - 203

Evans, Jack
Beehive: 45/63 - 93, 310A, 310B
Parkhurst: 51/52 - 90; 53/54 - 54; 54/55 - 72; 93/94 - 101ML
Shirriff: 60/61 - 76; 61/62 - 39
Topps: 54/55 - 14; 57/58 - 55; 58/59 - 31; 59/60 - 30; 60/61 - 30, 18ST; 62/63 - 26

Evans, Kevin
Score: 91/92 - 650B, 650C

Evans, Stewart
Beehive: 34/44 - 150, 196
Canada Starch: 35/40 - 77. 155
O-Pee-Chee: 37/38 - 164
Quaker Oats: 38/39 - 6
Sweet Caporal: 34/35 - 30
World Wide Gum: 36/37 - 67

Evason, Dean
Bowman: 90/91 - 262; 91/92 - 10; 92/93 - 133
Donruss: 93/94 - 86
Fleer: 92/93 - 193; 93/94 - 323PP
O-Pee-Chee: 87/88 - 166; 90/91 - 376; 91/92 - 325, 36PM; 92/93 - 381
Panini: 87/88 - 47; 90/91 - 44; 91/92 - 312; 92/93 - 131E, 131F; 93/94 - 259E, 259F
Parkhurst: 91/92 - 388E, 388F; 92/93 - 392, 392EI; 93/94 - 319, 319EI
Pro Set: 90/91 - 103; 91/92 - 84E, 84F, 230PT
Score: 90/91 - 259A, 259C; 91 - 91T; 91/92 - 17A, 17B, 17C, 641B, 641C, 153PNE, 153PNF; 92/93 - 103C, 103A, 169PNC, 169PNA; 93/94 - 353C, 353A
Topps: 87/88 - 166; 90/91 - 376; 91/92 - 325, 145SC; 92/93 - 304, 304GS, 11SC
Upper Deck: 90/91 - 192E, 192F; 91/92 - 127E, 560E, 127F, 560F; 92/93 - 281

Ewen, Todd
Donruss: 93/94 - 9
Fleer: 93/94 - 285PP
O-Pee-Chee: 93/94 - 369
Parkhurst: 93/94 - 5, 5EI
Pro Set: 90/91 - 470; 91/92 - 419E, 419F
Topps: 91/92 - 340SC; 93/94 - 369, 309SC, 309FD
Upper Deck: 92/93 - 549; 93/94 - 449

Ezinicki, Bill
Beehive: 45/63 - 18, 401
Quaker Oats: 45/54 - 70A, 70B, 70C, 70D

Fairbairn, Bill
Eddie Sargent: 70/71 - 123; 72/73 - 150
Esso: 70/71 - 148
Loblaws: 74/75 - 200
O-Pee-Chee: 71/72 - 215; 72/73 - 87; 73/74 - 41; 74/75 - 231; 75/76 - 109; 76/77 - 57; 77/78 - 303; 78/79 - 267
Topps: 73/74 - 41; 74/75 - 231; 75/76 - 109; 76/77 - 57; 77/78 - 255
Toronto Sun: 71/72 - 171

Falkenberg, Bob
O-Pee-Chee: 68/69 - 141; 72/73 - 310

Falloon, Pat
Bowman: 92/93 - 361
Donruss: 93/94 - 308, T/PM, T/SP
Fleer: 92/93 - 194, 6UR; 93/94 - 56, 218PP
Gillette: 91/92 - 3
Hockey Wit: 93/94 - 98
Humpty Dumpty: 92/93 - 6(I)
Kraft: 91/92 - 8; 93/94 - 6
Leaf: 93/94 - 49, 2SS
O-Pee-Chee: 91/92 - 56PM; 92/93 - 227, 12SP; 93/94 - 259, 224SC, 224FD
Panini: 92/93 - 273E, K(E), 273F, K(F); 93/94 - W(E), W(F)
Parkhurst: 91/92 - 160E, 160F; 92/93 - 161, 233, 161EI, 233EI; 93/94 - 183, 183EI, V70
Pro Set: 91/92 - CC3, 558E, 558F, 271PT, 4RGL; 92/93 - 166, 10TL
Score: 91 - 90T; 91/92 - 640B, 640C, 329PNE, 329PNF, 9PNC, 9PNA; 92/93 - 125C, 436C, 125A, 436A,
Score: 238PNC, 238PNA, 26CT, 26AT; 93/94 - 133C, 133A, 19FR
Season's: 92/93 - 62
Sega: 93/94 - 119
Topps: 92/93 - 7, 418, 7GS, 418GS, 56SC, 259SC; 93/94 - 259, 224SC, 224FD
Upper Deck: 90/91 - 469E, 469F; 91/92 - 593E, 593F; 92/93 - 19, 286, 355, 386, WJG13, 52AS; 93/94 - 39

Farrell, Arthur
  Hall of Fame: 83 - 153, L3P; 87 - 153
Farrish, Dave
  O-Pee-Chee: 77/78 - 179; 78/79 - 41; 79/80 - 299;
    80/81 - 311; 81/82 - 317;
    83/84 - 329; 84/85 - 301
  PepsiCo: 80/81 - 87
  Topps: 77/78 - 179; 78/79 - 41
  Vachon Foods: 83/84 - 85
Faubert, Mario
  O-Pee-Chee: 78/79 - 296; 81/82 - 261, 189SK
Faulkner, Alex
  Beehive: 45/63 - 165; 64/67 - 68
  Parkhurst: 63/64 - 42
  York: 63/64 - 49
Faust, Andre
  Parkhurst: 92/93 - 365, 365EI;
    93/94 - 419, 419EI
  Topps: 93/94 - 462SC, 462FD
  Upper Deck: 93/94 - 63
Favell, Doug (Goalie)
  Coca-Cola: 77/78 - 7
  Colgate: 70/71 - 91
  Dad's Cookies: 70/71 - 96
  Eddie Sargent: 70/71 - 152; 72/73 - 157
  Esso: 70/71 - 167
  Loblaws: 74/75 - 274
  O-Pee-Chee: 69/70 - 88; 70/71 - 199; 71/72 - 72;
    72/73 - 89, 16CS; 73/74 - 158;
    74/75 - 46; 75/76 - 381; 76/77 - 292;
    77/78 - 370; 78/79 - 54; 79/80 - 274
  Shirriff: 68/69 - J5
  Topps: 69/70 - 88; 71/72 - 72; 72/73 - 74;
    73/74 - 119; 74/75 - 46; 78/79 - 54
  Toronto Sun: 71/72 - 193
Feamster, Dave
  O-Pee-Chee: 83/84 - 100
Featherstone, Glen
  Bowman: 91/92 - 371
  Fleer: 93/94 - 288PP
  O-Pee-Chee: 90/91 - 387; 91/92 - 436, 66PM;
    93/94 - 14
  Pro Set: 90/91 - 523
  Score: 90 - 25T; 91 - 37T; 91/92 - 587B, 587C
  Topps: 90/91 - 387; 91/92 - 436, 319SC;
    93/94 - 14, 372SC, 372FD
Featherstone, Tony
  Esso: 70/71 - 39
  Topps: 71/72 - 106
Federko, Bernie
  Bowman: 90/91 - 238
  Frito-Lay: 88/89 - 11
  Funmate: 83/84 - 115
  Hockey Wit: 93/94 - 47
  Kellogg's: 84 - 11
  O-Pee-Chee: 78/79 - 143; 79/80 - 215;
    80/81 - 71, 136, 18PO; 81/82 - 288;
    81/82 - 300, 304, 128SK;
    82/83 - 302, 303, 197SK;
    83/84 - 315, 125SK; 84/85 - 184,
    54SK, 55SK; 85/86 - 104, 53SK;
    86/87 - 105, 174SK; 87/88 - 83,
    24SK; 88/89 - 81, E/BB, 21SK;
    89/90 - 107, 247SK; 90/91 - 191
  Panini: 87/88 - 312; 88/89 - 104;
    90/91 - 209
  Post: 82/83 - 262
  Pro Set: 90/91 - 70; 91/92 - 597E, 597F
  Score: 90/91 - 252A, 252C
  7-Eleven: 84/85 - 42
  Topps: 78/79 - 143; 79/80 - 215; 80/81 - 71,
    136; 81/82 - WN 127, 12, 62;
    82/83 - 197SK; 83/84 - 125SK;
    84/85 - 131; 85/86 - 104; 86/87 - 105;
    87/88 - 83; 88/89 - 81, E/BB;
    89/90 - 107; 90/91 - 191
  Upper Deck: 90/91 - 58E, 58F
Fedorov, Sergei
  Bowman: 91/92 - 50; 92/93 - 205, 416
  Donruss: 93/94 - 101, U5

Fedorov, Sergei (cont.)
  Fleer: 92/93 - 48, 3UI; 93/94 - 121, 3SA,
    1G, 2GG, 72PP, 3SM
  Gillette: 91/92 - 12
  Hockey Wit: 93/94 - 69
  Humpty Dumpty: 92/93 - 5
  Kraft: 91/92 - 51
  Leaf: 93/94 - 129
  O-Pee-Chee: 90/91 - 19R, 30PM; 91/92 - 8, 401,
    68PM, 173PM; 92/93 - 195, 20SP;
    93/94 - 318, 441, 45SC, 45FD
  Panini: 91/92 - 145, 340; 92/93 - 113E, 291E,
    113F, 291F; 93/94 - 246E, 246F
  Parkhurst: 91/92 - 38E, PHC5E, 38F, PHC5F;
    92/93 - 39, 219, 39EI, 219EI;
    93/94 - 58, 58EI, W10; 94/95 - 305,
    305EI, H7, R7, C7, V39
  Pro Set: 90/91 - 604; 91/92 - AC10, 53E,
    53F, PC7PT, 30PT, 277PT;
    92/93 - 40
  Score: 90 - 9YS, 20T; 91 - 1YS;
    91/92 - 250A, 352A, 408A, 298B,
    382B, 470B, 298C, 382C, 470C,
    157PNE, 157PNF, 4HC, 30CT, 30AT;
    92/93 - 252C, 252A, 20PNC, 20PNA
  Season's: 92/93 - 5
  Sega: 93/94 - 40
  Topps: 91/92 - 8, 401, 316SC; 92/93 - 252,
    252GS, 244SC, 300SC; 93/94 - 318,
    441C, 45SC, 45FD
  Upper Deck: 90/91 - 525E, 525F; 91/92 - 6E, 40E,
    144E, 631E, E9(E), 6F, 40F, 144F,
    E9(F), 631F; 92/93 - 157, 632, E1,
    WG16; 93/94 - 171
Fedotov, Anatoli
  Upper Deck: 93/94 - 38
Fedyk, Brent
  Bowman: 91/92 - 51
  Fleer: 92/93 - 371; 93/94 - 181PP
  Leaf: 93/94 - 58
  O-Pee-Chee: 90/91 - 31PM; 91/92 - 376;
    92/93 - 26PM; 93/94 - 211, 181SC,
    181FD
  Panini: 91/92 - 140; 93/94 - 48E, 48F
  Parkhurst: 91/92 - 270E, 270F; 92/93 - 131,
    131EI; 93/94 - 148, 148EI;
    94/95 - 170, 170EI
  Pro Set: 90/91 - 435; 91/92 - 379E, 379F
  Score: 91/92 - 412B 412C; 92/93 - 337C,
    337A, 93/94 - 14C, 14A
  Topps: 91/92 - 376, 238SC; 92/93 - 401,
    401GS, 390SC; 93/94 - 211,181SC,
    181FD
  Upper Deck: 91/92 - 373E; 92/93 - 443; 93/94 - 373
Felsner, Denny
  Parkhurst: 92/93 - 493, 493EI;
    93/94 - 267, 267EI
  Score: 92/93 - 481C, 481A, 413PNC,
    413PNA
  Topps: 92/93 - 514, 514GS
  Upper Deck: 92/93 - 413
Fenton, Paul
  Bowman: 90/91 - 139; 91/92 - 256
  O-Pee-Chee: 88/89 - 213; 90/91 - 313;
    91/92 - 331, 187PM; 92/93 - 380
  Panini: 90/91 - 313
  Pro Set: 90/91 - 329, 533
  Score: 90/91 - 156A, 156C, 57T;
    91/92 - 14A, 14B, 14C, 593B, 593C
    92/93 - 257C, 257A
  Topps: 90/91 - 313; 91/92 - 331, 327SC;
    92/93 - 173. 173GS, 224SC
  Upper Deck: 91/92 - 92E, 92F
Fergus, Thomas (Tom)
  Bowman: 91/92 - 157; 92/93 - 273
  Fleer: 92/93 - 426
  Kraft: 86/87 - 55; 55P
  O-Pee-Chee: 82/83 - 11, 88SK; 83/84 - 49, 55SK;
    84/85 - 4, 189SK; 85/86 - 113,
    164SK; 86/87 - 84, 143SK;
    87/88 - 120, 159SK; 88/89 - 214,
    170SK; 89/90 - 103, 173SK;
    90/91 - 63; 92/93 - 356

Fergus, Thomas (Tom) (cont.)
  Panini: 87/88 - 332; 89/90 - 135;
    90/91 - 282
  Parkhurst: 91/92 - 400E, 400F
  Post: 82/83 - 4
  Pro Set: 90/91 - 279; 91/92 - 234E, 234F, 238PT
  Score: 90/91 - 285A, 285C; 91/92 - 190C,
    190A, 234B, 234C
  Topps: 82/83 - 88SK; 83/84 - 55SK;
    84/85 - 3; 85/86 - 113; 86/87 - 84;
    87/88 - 120; 89/90 - 103; 90/91 - 63;
    92/93 - 311, 311GS, 278SC
  Upper Deck: 90/91 - 83E, 83F; 91/92 - 384E, 384F
Ferguson, George
  O-Pee-Chee: 74/75 - 302; 75/76 - 77; 76/77 - 286;
    77/78 - 266; 78/79 - 395;
    79/80 - 139; 80/81 - 44; 81/82 - 262,
    184SK; 82/83 - 268, 150SK;
    83/84 - 171
  Post: 82/83 - 231
  Topps: 75/76 - 77; 79/80 - 139; 80/81 - 44;
    82/83 - 150SK
Ferguson, John
  Beehive: 45/63 - 238; 64/67 - 103
  Chex: 63/65 - 25
  Coca-Cola: 64/65 - 59; 65/66 - 59
  Dad's Cookies: 70/71 - 75
  Esso: 70/71 - 130
  O-Pee-Chee: 68/69 - 20; 69/70 - 7; 70/71 - 264
  Parkhurst: 63/64 - 33, 92
  Post: 68/69 - 4
  Shirriff: 68/69 - F10
  Topps: 64/65 - 4; 65/66 - 10; 66/67 - 70;
    66/67 US - 65; 67/68 - 69; 69/70 - 7
  Toronto Star: 58/67 - 91
  Ultimate: 92 - 9(OSE), 9(OSF)
  York: 63/64
Ferguson, Lorne
  Beehive: 45/63 - 19
  Parkhurst: 51/52 - 35; 93/94 - 54ML
  Topps: 54/55 - 31; 57/58 - 40; 58/59 - 55
Ferguson, Norm
  Colgate: 70/71 - 56
  Dad's Cookies: 70/71 - 25
  Eddie Sargent: 70/71 - 142
  O-Pee-Chee: 69/70 - 146; 71/72 - 179
  Toronto Sun: 71/72 - 46
Fernandez, Emanuel (Goalie)
  Donruss: 93/94 - 10JCC
  Upper Deck: 93/94 - 536
Ferner, Mark
  O-Pee-Chee: 93/94 - 478
  Parkhurst: 93/94 - 275, 275EI
  Topps: 93/94 - 478C, 342SC, 342FD
Ferraro, Chris
  Fleer: 93/94 - 648E, 648F, 502PP
  Topps: 93/94 - 9US
Ferraro, Peter
  Fleer: 93/94 - 503PP
  Topps: 93/94 - 15US
  Upper Deck: 91/92 - 648E, 696E, 648F, 696F
Ferraro, Ray
  Bowman: 90/91 - 258; 91/92 - 212;
    92/93 - 128, 229
  Donruss: 93/94 - 198
  Fleer: 92/93 - 123; 93/94 - 16, 382PP
  Hockey Wit: 93/94 - 84
  Humpty Dumpty: 92/93 - 7(I)
  Leaf: 93/94 - 121
  O-Pee-Chee: 86/87 - 160, 57SK; 87/88 - 109;
    88/89 - 114, 268SK; 89/90 - 70,
    263SK; 90/91 - 336; 91/92 - 304;
  O-Pee-Chee: 92/93 - 42, 1SP; 93/94 - 349,
    50SC, 50FD
  Panini: 87/88 - 46; 88/89 - 241; 89/90 - 222
    90/91 - 45; 91/92 - 250;
    92/93 - 198E, 198F
  Parkhurst: 91/92 - 110E, 110F; 92/93 - 98, 499,
    98EI, 499EI; 93/94 - 123, 123EI;
    94/95 - 134, 134EI, V86

Ferraro, Ray (cont.)
  Pro Set: 90/91 - 104; 91/92 - 156E, 156F, 76PT; 92/93 - 105
  Score: 90/91 - 134A, 134C, 15T; 91/92 - 48A, 48B, 48C, 123PNE, 123PNF; 92/93 - 298C, 298A, 154PNC, 154PNA, 3CSS, 3ASS; 93/94 - 60C, 60A
  Topps: 86/87 - 160; 87/88 - 109; 88/89 - 114; 89/90 - 70; 90/91 - 336; 91/92 - 304, 3SC; 92/93 - 324, 324GS, 123SC; 93/94 - 349, 50SC, 50FD, 6MP
  Upper Deck: 90/91 - 289E, 289F; 91/92 - 311E, 311F; 92/93 - 12; 92/93 - 193; 93/94 - 153

Fetisov, Viacheslav
  Bowman: 90/91 - 80; 91/92 - 273; 92/93 - 145
  Fleer: 92/93 - 337; 93/94 - 136PP
  O-Pee-Chee: 90/91 - 27; 91/92 - 175; 92/93 - 162
  Panini: 90/91 - 75, 339
  Parkhurst: 91/92 - 96E, 96F; 92/93 - 334, 334EI
  Pro Set: 90/91 - 167; 91/92 - 142E, 142F, 199PT; 92/93 - 96
  Score: 90/91 - 62A, 62C; 91/92 - 184A, 184B, 184C, 101PNE, 101PNF; 92/93 - 97C, 97A, 299PNC, 299PNA; 93/94 - 229C, 229A
  Sega: 93/94 - 74
  Topps: 90/91 - 27; 91/92 - 175, 24SC; 92/93 - 458, 458GS, 392SC; 93/94 - 265SC, 265FD
  Upper Deck: 90/91 - 176E, 176F; 91/92 - 410E, 410F; 92/93 - 278

Fidler, Mike
  O-Pee-Chee: 77/78 - 290; 78/79 - 84; 79/80 - 219; 81/82 - 136
  Topps: 78/79 - 84; 79/80 - 219

Field, Wilf
  Beehive: 34/44 - 225
  O-Pee-Chee: 39/40 - 64

Fielder, Guyle
  Topps: 57/58 - 36

Filimonov, Dimitri
  Donruss: 93/94 - 239
  Fleer: 93/94 - 398PP
  Leaf: 93/94 - 400
  O-Pee-Chee: 93/94 - 496
  Parkhurst: 93/94 - 139, 139EI; 94/95 - 162, 162EI
  Topps: 93/94 - 496C, 468SC, 468FD
  Upper Deck: 91/92 - 3E, 3F; 93/94 - 405

Fillion, Bob
  Beehive: 45/63 - 239
  CKAC Radio: 43/47 - 47, 48
  Quaker Oats: 45/54 - 16A, 16B, 16C, 16D; 45/63 - 263

Finley, Jeff
  Fleer: 93/94 - 405PP
  Topps: 92/93 - 426SC

Finn, Ron (Official)
  Pro Set: 90/91 - 685

Finn, Steven
  Bowman: 91/92 - 140; 92/93 - 185
  Durivage: 92/93 - 40; 93/94 - 20
  Leaf: 93/94 - 422
  O-Pee-Chee: 89/90 - 191; 91/92 - 139; 92/93 - 7; 93/94 - 326
  Panini: 88/89 - 350; 91/92 - 261; 92/93 - 216E, 216F; 93/94 - 75E, 75F
  Parkhurst: 92/93 - 379, 379EI
  Pro Set: 90/91 - 514; 91/92 - 204E, 204F
  Score: 91/92 - 278A, 498B, 498C, 138PNE, 138PNF; 92/93 - 44C, 44A; 93/94 - 322C, 322A
  Topps: 91/92 - 139, 56SC; 92/93 - 449, 449GS, 384SC; 93/94 - 326, 464SC, 464FD, 21MP
  Upper Deck: 91/92 - 340E, 340F

Finnigan, Frank
  Anonymous: 33/34 - 26
  Beehive: 34/44 - 316

Finnigan, Frank (cont.)
  Can. Chew. Gum: 33/34 - 23
  Champ's: 24/25 - 44
  Diamond: 36/39 - 22(I)
  La Presse: 27/32 - 68
  O-Pee-Chee: 33/34 - 25
  Wm. Paterson: 24/25 - 9

Fiset, Stephane (Goalie)
  Bowman: 92/93 - 398
  Donruss: 93/94 - 274
  Durivage: 92/93 - 47; 93/94 - 21
  Fleer: 93/94 - 55, 198PP
  Kraft: 93/94 - 55
  Leaf: 93/94 - 301
  O-Pee-Chee: 90/91 - 312; 92/93 - 75; 93/94 - 165
  Panini: 91/92 - 258; 92/93 - 207E, 207F
  Parkhurst: 91/92 - 363E, 363F; 92/93 - 378, 378EI; 93/94 - 164, 164EI
  Pro-Set: 92/93 - 152
  Score: 90 - 22YS; 90/91 - 415A, 415C; 92/93 - 354C, 354A; 93/94 - 379C, 379A
  Topps: 90/91 - 312; 92/93 - 285, 285GS, 196SC; 93/94 - 165, 315SC, 315FD
  Upper Deck: 93/94 - 203

Fisher, Bud (Goalie)
  Dom. Choc.: 1926 - 29

Fisher, Dunc
  Beehive: 45/63 - 311

Fisher, Craig
  O-Pee-Chee: 90/91 - 126
  Score: 90/91 - 412A, 412C
  parkhurst: 94/95 - 265, 265EI
  Topps: 90/91 - 126
  Upper Deck: 90/91 - 155E, 155F

Fisher, Robert
  Parkhurst: 51/52 - 24

Fitchner, Bob
  Derniere: 72/84 - 81

Fitzgerald, Tom
  Bowman: 90/91 - 116; 92/93 - 369
  Donruss: 93/94 - 121
  Fleer: 92/93 - 342
  Leaf: 93/94 - 221
  O-Pee-Chee: 91/92 - 279; 92/93 - 394; 93/94 - 338
  Parkhurst: 93/94 - 348, 348EI
  Pro Set: 91/92 - 431E, 431F
  Topps: 91/92 - 279; 92/93 - 31, 31GS, 102SC; 93/94 - 338, 392SC, 392FD
  Upper Deck: 90/91 - 389E, 389F; 92/93 - 52

Fitzpatrick, Mark (Goalie)
  Bowman: 90/91 - 119; 91/92 - 213; 92/93 - 394
  Donruss: 93/94 - 133
  Fleer: 92/93 - 124, 7AW; 93/94 - 92PP
  Leaf: 93/94 - 335
  O-Pee-Chee: 90/91 - 395; 91/92 - 47; 92/93 - 204
  Panini: 89/90 - 265; 90/91 - 87; 92/93 - 195E, 195F; 93/94 - 66E, 66F
  Parkhurst: 92/93 - 99, 99EI; 93/94 - 344, 344EI; 94/95 - 87, 87EI
  Pro Set: 90/91 - 181; 92/93 - 107
  Score: 90 - 32YS; 90/91 - 102A, 102C, 50HR; 91/92 - 266A, 486B, 486C; 92/93 - 210C, 210A, 24PNC, 24PNA
  Topps: 90/91 - 395; 91/92 - 47, 345SC; 92/93 - 216, 216GS, 12SC; 93/94 - 307SC, 307FD
  Upper Deck: 90/91 - 37E, 37F; 91/92 - 602E, 602F; 92/93 - 332

Flaman, Fern
  Beehive: 45/63 - 20A, 20B, 402
  Parkhurst: 51/52 - 80; 52/53 - 47; 53/54 - 14; 93/94 - PR49, 2ML
  Quaker Oats: 45/54 - 71
  Score: 90/91 - 357A, 357C
  Shirriff: 60/61 - 102
  Topps: 54/55 - 20, 25; 57/58 - 4; 58/59 - 56; 59/60 - 29; 60/61 - 57
  Toronto Star: 57/67 - 60; 58/67 - 24
  Ultimate: 92 - 48(OSE), 76(OSE), 48(OSF), 76(OSF)

Flatley, Patrick (Pat)
  Bowman: 90/91 - 124; 91/92 - 218; 92/93 - 134
  Donruss: 93/94 - 199
  Fleer: 92/93 - 125; 93/94 - 34, 146PP
  Kraft: 93/94 - 32
  Leaf: 93/94 - 43
  O-Pee-Chee: 84/85 - 124; 85/86 - 83, 73SK; 86/87 - 162, 207SK; 87/88 - 136, 245SK; 88/89 - 191; 89/90 - 250; 90/91 - 350; 91/92 - 343; 92/93 - 342; 93/94 - 28, 24SC, 24FD
  Panini: 87/88 - 101; 88/89 - 286; 89/90 - 272; 90/91 - 82; 91/92 - 245; 92/93 - 201E, 201F; 93/94 - 60E, 60F
  Parkhurst: 91/92 - 111E, 111F; 92/93 - 342, 342EI; 93/94 - 391, 391EI
  Pro Set: 90/91 - 182; 91/92 - 152E, 578E, 152F, 77PT, 578F; 92/93 - 102
  Score: 90/91 - 174A, 174C; 91/92 - 29A, 29B, 29C, 67PNE, 405PNE, 67PNF, 405PNF; 92/93 - 99C, 99A, 44PNC, 44PNA; 93/94 - 220C, 220A
  Topps: 85/86 - 83; 86/87 - 162; 87/88 - 136; 88/89 - 191; 90/91 - 350; 91/92 - 343, 20SC; 92/93 - 135, 135GS, 477SC; 93/94 - 28, 24SC, 24FD
  Upper Deck: 90/91 - 118E, 118F; 91/92 - 226E, 226F; 93/94 - 210

Fleming, Gerry
  Parkhurst: 94/95 - 117, 117EI

Fleming, Reggie
  Beehive: 45/63 - 94; 64/67 - 7, 124
  Coca-Cola: 64/65 - 5; 65/66 - 7
  Dad's Cookies: 70/71 - 14
  Eddie Sargent: 70/71 - 21
  Esso: 70/71 - 24
  O-Pee-Chee: 68/69 - 167; 69/70 - 95, 2QS; 70/71 - 128, 12DE; 72/73 - 316
  Shirriff: 60/61 - 78; 61/62 - 24; 68/69 - G4
  Topps: 61/62 - 26; 62/63 - 42, 9HB; 63/64 - 31; 64/65 - 35; 65/66 - 104; 66/67 - 93; 66/67 US - 54; 67/68 - 30; 69/70 - 95; 70/71 - 128

Flesch, John
  O-Pee-Chee: 75/76 - 353

Flett, Bill
  Bauer: 68/69 - 8
  Dad's Cookies: 70/71 - 57
  Eddie Sargent: 70/71 - 75; 71/72 - 67; 72/73 - 164
  Esso: 70/71 - 96
  Loblaws: 74/75 - 275
  O-Pee-Chee: 68/69 - 159; 69/70 - 102; 70/71 - 161, 8SS; 71/72 - 47; 72/73 - 187; 73/74 - 20; 74/75 - 64; 75/76 - 349; 76/77 - 332; 79/80 - 266
  Shirriff: 68/69 - D8
  Topps: 69/70 - 102; 70/71 - 8SK; 71/72 - 47; 72/73 - 139; 73/74 - 20; 74/75 - 64
  Toronto Sun: 71/72 - 112

Fleury, Theoren (Theo)
  Bowman: 90/91 - 102; 91/92 - 249, 270; 92/93 - 206, 355
  Donruss: 93/94 - 46, D/PM, D/SP
  Fleer: 92/93 - 21; 93/94 - 41, 36PP
  Gillette: 91/92 - 4
  Hockey Wit: 93/94 - 94
  Humpty Dumpty: 92/93 - 8(I)
  Kraft: 1990 - 2; 91/92 - 13; 93/94 - 7
  Leaf: 93/94 - 154
  McDonald's: 91/92 - Mc18
  O-Pee-Chee: 89/90 - 232; 90/91 - 386; 91/92 - 282, 92PM; 92/93 - 99; 93/94 - 100, 13BG
  Panini: 90/91 - 176; 91/92 - 51; 92/93 - 46E, 46F; 93/94 - 179F
  Parkhurst: 91/92 - 22E, 22F; 92/93 - 19, 19EI; 93/94 - 28, 28EI; 94/95 - V20
  Pro Set: 90/91 - 33; 91/92 - AC20, 28E, 274E, 28F, 274F, 16PT, 4PK; 92/93 - 23
  Score: 90 - 6YS; 90/91 - 226A, 226C; 91 - 4YS; 91/92 - 226A, 226B,

Fleury, Theoren (Theo) (cont.)
Score: 226C, 7HC, 190PNE, 358PNE, 190PNF, 358PNF; 92/93 - 280C, 280A, 125PNC, 125PNA; 93/94 - 191C, 191A, 441C, 441A
Sega: 93/94 - 23
Topps: 90/91 - 386; 91/92 - 282, 14SL, 355SC; 92/93 - 220, 220GS, 2SC; 93/94 - 100, 17MP
Upper Deck: 90/91 - 47E, 47F, 478E, 478F; 91/92 - 245E, 245F, 506E, 630E, 506F, 630F; 92/93 - 285, 390SC, 390FD; 93/94 - 3, 229, 288

Flockhart, Ron
O-Pee-Chee: 82/83 - 249, 113SK; 83/84 - 264, 192SK; 84/85 - 174, 115SK, 116SK; 85/86 - 171, 128SK; 86/87 - 146, 176SK; 87/88 - 103, 25SK
Panini: 87/88 - 317
Topps: 82/83 - 113SK; 83/84 - 192SK; 84/85 - 124; 86/87 - 146; 87/88 - 103

Fogarty, Bryan
Bowman: 90/91 - 173; 91/92 - 149
O-Pee-Chee: 91/92 - 500
Panini: 90/91 - 144; 91/92 - 259
Parkhurst: 91/92 - 146E, 146F
Pro Set: 90/91 515; 91/92 - 200E, 200F, 103PT
Score: 90/91 - 54A, 54C; 91/92 - 237A, 457B, 457C, 59PNE, 59PNF
Topps: 91/92 - 500
Upper Deck: 90/91 - 548E, 548F; 91/92 - 337E, 337F

Fogolin, Lidio (John Lee)
Beehive: 45/63 - 95, 166
Parkhurst: 51/52 - 46; 52/53 - 55; 53/54 - 72; 54/55 - 84

Fogolin, Lee
Loblaws: 74/75 - 41
O-Pee-Chee: 75/76 - 306; 76/77 - 253; 77/78 - 94; 78/79 - 27; 79/80 - 183; 80/81 - 63; 81/82 - 112, 215SK; 82/83 - 104, 106SK; 83/84 - 26, 17SK, 100SK; 84/85 - 240, 254SK; 85/86 - 235, 218SK; 86/87 - 210, 71SK
PepsiCo: 80/81 - 25
Post: 82/83 - 84
Topps: 75/76 - 306; 76/77 - 253; 77/78 - 94; 78/79 - 27; 79/80 - 183; 80/81 - 63; 82/83 - 106SK; 83/84 - 17SK, 100SK
Vachon Foods: 83/84 - 23

Foley, Gerry
Parkhurst: 93/94 - 94ML
Topps: 57/58 - 57

Foley, Rick
Esso: 72/73 - 165
O-Pee-Chee: 72/73 - 80
Topps: 72/73 - 98

Foligno, Mike
Bowman: 90/91 - 247; 91/92 - 169
Donruss: 93/94 - 433
Fleer: 92/93 - 420; 93/94 - 346PP
Frito-Lay: 88/89 - 12
Funmate: 83/84 - 10
O-Pee-Chee: 80/81 - 16, 187; 81/82 - 87, 122SK; 82/83 - 26, 120SK; 83/84 - 63, 234SK; 84/85 - 20, 212SK; 85/86 - 17, 174SK; 86/87 - 127, 42SK; 87/88 - 40, 150SK; 88/89 - 184, 257SK; 89/90 - 78, 260SK; 90/91 - 123; 91/92 - 18; 93/94 - 262
Panini: 87/88 - 29; 88/89 - 226; 89/90 - 210; 90/91 - 25; 92/93 - 84E, 84F; 93/94 - 228E, 228F
Parkhurst: 92/93 - 415, 415EI
Post: 82/83 - 19
Pro Set: 90/91 - 20

Foligno, Mike (cont.)
Score: 90/91 - 133A, 133C; 91/92 - 248B, 248C, 292PNE, 292PNF; 93/94 - 387C, 387A
Topps: 80/81 - 16, 187; 81/82 WN - 87; 82/83 - 120SK; 83/84 - 237SK; 84/85 - 16; 85/86 - 17; 86/87 - 127, D/BB; 87/88 - 40; 88/89 - 184; 89/90 - 78; 90/91 - 123; 91/92 - 18, 29SC; 93/94 - 262
Upper Deck: 90/91 - 378E, 378F; 91/92 - 212E, 212F; 93/94 - 155

Fontaine, Len
O-Pee-Chee: 72/73 - 244

Fonteyne, Val
Beehive: 45/63 - 167; 64/67 - 69
Coca-Cola: 64/65 - 76; 65/66 - 43
Eddie Sargent: 70/71 - 176; 71/72 - 163
O-Pee-Chee: 68/69 - 109; 69/70 - 119; 70/71 - 208; 71/72 - 189; 72/73 - 319
Parkhurst: 60/61 - 21; 61/62 - 21; 62/63 - 27
Shirriff: 60/61 - 48; 61/62 - 67; 68/69 - K3
Topps: 63/64 - 61; 66/67 - 108; 68/69 - 109; 69/70 - 119

Fontinato, Louie
Beehive: 45/63 - 240, 312
Parkhurst: 62/63 - 52; 93/94 - 93ML
Shirriff: 60/61 - 97; 61/62 - 111; 62/63 - 23
Topps: 57/58 - 64; 58/59 - 41; 59/60 - 5; 60/61 - 61
Toronto Star: 57/67 - 83; 58/67 - 46
Ultimate: 92 - 19(OSE). 19(OSF)
York: 61/62 - 40

Foote, Adam
Donruss: 93/94 - 272
Fleer: 93/94 - 418PP
Leaf: 93/94 - 229
Parkhurst: 91/92 - 371E, 371F
Pro-Set: 91/92 - 268PT
Score: 91/92 - 337PNE, 337PNF; 92/93 - 131C, 131A; 93/94 - 149C, 149A
TCMA: 1981 - 4
Topps: 92/93 - 528GS, 496SC, 468SC, 496FD
Upper Deck: 91/92 - 529E, 529F

Forbes, Dave
Loblaws: 74/75 - 24
O-Pee-Chee: 74/75 - 266; 75/76 - 173; 76/77 - 246; 77/78 - 143; 78/79 - 167
Topps: 75/76 - 173; 76/77 - 246; 77/78 - 143; 78/79 - 167

Forbes, Vernon (Goalie)
Anonymous: 26/27 - 77
Champ's: 24/25 - 11
Dom. Choc.: 1925 - 82
Maple Crispette: 24/25 - 25
Wm. Paterson: 23/24 - 29; 24/25 - 11

Ford, Brian (Goalie)
Vachon Foods: 83/84 - 64

Forsberg, Peter
Upper Deck: 91/92 - 64E, 64F; 92/93 - 235, 375, 595

Forsey, Jack
Beehive: 34/44 - 317

Forslund, Tomas
Bowman: 92/93 - 384
O-Pee-Chee: 91/92 - 31PM; 92/93 - 70, D(E), D(F)
Parkhurst: 91/92 - 20E, 20F
Pro Set: 91/92 - 527E, 527F
Score: 91 - 79T; 91/92 - 629B, 629C, 333PNE, 333PNF
Topps: 92/93 - 186. 186GS, 280SC
Upper Deck: 91/92 - 27E, 586E, 27F, 586F; 92/93 - 3, 429, ERT6

Fortier, Dave
O-Pee-Chee: 74/75 - 382; 75/76 - 336; 76/77 - 328

Fortier, Marc
Bowman: 90/91 - 167
O-Pee-Chee: 89/90 - 262, 189SK; 90/91 - 176
Panini: 89/90 - 335; 90/91 - 153
Pro Set: 90/91 - 245; 92/93 - 128
Score: 90/91 - 78A, 78C
Topps: 90/91 - 176; 92/93 - 226, 226GS, 173SC

Fortin, Emile
World Wide Gum: 36/37 - 122

Foster, Corey
Parkhurst: 91/92 - 344E, 344F
Pro Set: 91/92 - 551E, 551F, 265PT
Score: 91/92 - 332PNE, 332PNF
Upper Deck: 91/92 - 591E, 591F; 92/93 - 53

Foster, Dwight
O-Pee-Chee: 78/79 - 271; 81/82 - 3, 52SK; 82/83 - 138; 83/84 - 122, 153SK; 84/85 - 53; 85/86 - 14
Panini: 87/88 - 17
Post: 82/83 - 164
Topps: 81/82 EN - 67; 83/84 - 133SK 84/85 - 41; 85/86 - 14

Foster, Norm
Upper Deck: 91/92 - 465E, 465F

Fotiu, Nick
O-Pee-Chee: 77/78 - 11; 78/79 - 367; 79/80 - 286; 80/81 - 184; 82/83 - 222; 83/84 - 243; 85/86 - 22
Post: 82/83 - 197
Topps: 77/78 - 11; 80/81 - 184; 85/86 - 22

Fournier, Jack
Imperial Tobacco: 12/13 - 36

Fowler, Hec (Norman) (Goalie)
Champ's: 24/25 - 2
Maple Crispette: 24/25 - 3
Wm. Paterson: 24/25 - 30

Fowler, Jimmy
Beehive: 34/44 - 318
O-Pee-Chee: 36/37 - 103; 37/38 - 135; 39/40 - 55
Quaker Oats: 38/39 - 21

Fox, Greg
O-Pee-Chee: 79/80 - 116; 80/81 - 268; 81/92 - 69 82/83 - 65; 83/84 - 101; 84/85 - 175
Post: 82/83 - 52
Topps: 79/80 - 116

Fox, Hughie J.
Dom. Choc.: 1925 - 56

Fox, Jim
Funmate: 83/84 - 52
O-Pee-Chee: 81/82 - 153; 82/83 - 154, 235SK; 83/84 - 154, 293SK; 84/85 - 84, 268SK; 85/86 - 61, 236SK; 86/87 - 215, 89SK; 87/88 - 75; 216SK; 88/89 - 139, 154SK
Panini: 87/88 - 281; 88/89 - 76
Post: 82/83 - 116
Topps: 82/83 - 235SK; 83/84 - 293SK; 84/85 - 66; 85/86 - 61; 87/88 - 75; 88/89 - 139

Foyston, Frank
Hall of Fame: 83 - 20, B4P; 87 - 20

Franceschetti, Lou
Bowman: 90/91 - 164
O-Pee-Chee: 90/91 - 303; 91/92 - 354
Panini: 87/88 - 188; 90/91 - 289
Pro Set: 90/91 - 280
Score: 90/91 - 266A, 266C; 91/92 - 388B, 388C
Topps: 90/91 - 303; 91/92 - 354
Upper Deck: 90/91 - 396E, 396F; 91/92 - 399

Francis, Emile
Hall of Fame: 83 - 231, I7P; 87 - 231
HHFM: 92 - 10
O-Pee-Chee: 74/75 - 9
Topps: 66/67 - 21; 74/75 - 9

Francis, Ronald (Ron)
- Bowman: 90/91 - 254; 91/92 - 90; 92/93 - 123
- Donruss: 93/94 - 261
- Fleer: 92/93 - 163; 93/94 - 44, 188PP
- Frito-Lay: 88/89 - 13
- Funmate: 83/84 - 44
- Hockey Wit: 93/94 - 53
- Kellogg's: 84 - 8
- Kraft: 90/91 - 13, 83
- Leaf: 93/94 - 161
- O-Pee-Chee: 82/83 - 123, 129SK; 83/84 - 138, 255SK; 84/85 - 70, 196SK; 85/86 - 140, F/BB, 172SK; 86/87 - 43, 51SK; 87/88 - 187, 10HL, J/BB, 206SK; 88/89 - 52, A/BB, 264SK; 89/90 - 175, 269SK; 90/91 - 311, 32PM; 91/92 - 130, 120PM; 92/93 - 188; 93/94 - 424
- Panini: 87/88 - 43; 88/89 - 242; 89/90 - 221 90/91 - 39; 91/92 - 281; 92/93 - 224E, 224F; 93/94 - 81E, 81F
- Parkhurst: 91/92 - 353E, 353F; 92/93 - 141, 141EI; 93/94 - 160, 160EI; 94/95 - 176, 176EI
- Post: 82/83 - 98
- Pro Set: 90/91 - 105, 367; 91/92 - 188E, 188F, 214PT; 92/93 - 144
- Score: 90/91 - 70A, 70C, 37HR; 91/92 - 267A, 487B, 487C, 167PNE, 167PNF; 92/93 - 267C, 267A, 303PNC, 303PNA; 93/94 - 151C, 151A
- 7-Eleven: 84/85 - 21
- Topps: 82/83 - 129SK; 83/84 - 255SK; 84/85 - 54; 85/86 - 140F/BB; 86/87 - 43; 87/88 - 187, J/BB, 88/89 - 52, A/BB; 89/90 - 175; 90/91 - 311, 21SL; 91/92 - 130, 73SC; 92/93 - 322, 322GS, 352SC; 93/94 - 424C, 385SC, 385FD
- Upper Deck: 90/91 - 67E, 67F; 91/92 - 299E, 299F; 92/93 - 291; 93/94 - 351

Franks, Jim (Goalie)
- Beehive: 34/44 - 272

Fraser, Charles
- Wm. Paterson: 23/24 - 39

Fraser Curt
- O-Pee-Chee: 79/80 - 117; 80/81 - 287; 81/82 - 334; 82/83 - 343, 244SK; 83/84 - 102; 84/85 - 34; 85/86 - 3, 24SK; 86/87 - 31
- Panini: 87/88 - 231
- PepsiCo: 80/81 - 108
- Post: 82/83 - 293
- Topps: 79/80 - 117; 82/83 - 244SK; 84/85 - 29; 85/86 - 3; 86/87 - 31

Fraser, Gord
- Anonymous: 26/27 - 136;
- La Presse: 27/32 - 33

Fraser, Iain
- Donruss: 93/94 - 478
- Fleer: 93/94 - 73, 4RS, 1TP, 419PP
- O-Pee-Chee: 93/94 - 525
- Parkhurst: 93/94 - 434, 434EI, CC19; 94/95 - 187, 280, 187EI, 280EI
- Topps: 93/94 - 525A, 485SC, 485FD
- Upper Deck: 93/94 - 337

Fraser, Kerry (Official)
- Pro Set: 90/91 - 686

Fraser, William
- Dom. Choc.: 1925 - 81

Frawley, Dan
- Panini: 87/88 - 153; 88/89 - 338

Frederickson, Frank
- Hall of Fame: 83 - 49, D3P; 87 - 49
- Topps: 60/61 - 34, 35ST

Freer, Mark
- O-Pee-Chee: 93/94 - 142, 29SC, 29FD
- Panini: 93/94 - 118E
- Parkhurst: 91/92 - 343E, 343F; 92/93 - 354, 354EI

Freer, Mark (cont.)
- Pro-Set: 92/93 - 127
- Topps: 93/94 - 142, 29SC, 29FD
- Upper Deck: 92/93 - 445

Frews, Irvine
- Diamond: 36/39 - 23(I), 22(II), 20(III)

Friday, Bill (Official)
- Ultimate: 92 - 85(OSE), 85)OSF

Friesen, Jeff
- Donruss: 93/94 - 11JCC
- Parkhurst: 93/94 - 505, 505EI
- Upper Deck: 93/94 - 532, e8

Frig, Len
- Loblaws: 74/75 - 57
- O-Pee-Chee: 74/75 - 242; 75/76 - 174; 76/77 - 352; 77/78 - 384
- Topps: 74/75 - 242; 75/76 - 174

Froese, Robert (Bob) (Goalie)
- O-Pee-Chee: 83/84 - 265, 183SK; 84/85 - 159, 113SK; 86/87 - 55, 263, 264, 182SK, 186SK, 193SK, 236SK; 87/88 - 195
- Panini: 88/89 - 299; 89/90 - 284
- Topps: 83/84 - 183SK; 84/85 - 117; 86/87 - 55, 7SK; 87/88 - 195

Frolikov, Alexei
- O-Pee-Chee: 90/91 - 502

Frolov, Dmitri
- O-Pee-Chee: 90/91 - 523
- Upper Deck: 92/93 - 348

Frycer, Miroslav
- Derniere: 72/84 - 159
- O-Pee-Chee: 82/83 - 321, 65SK; 83/84 - 330, 38SK; 85/86 - 198, 21SK; 86/87 - 68, 142SK; 87/88 - 158SK
- Post: 82/83 - 278
- Topps: 82/83 - 65SK; 83/84 - 38SK; 86/87 - 68
- Vachon Foods: 83/84 - 86

Frylen, Edvin
- Parkhurst: 93/94 - 536, 536EI
- Upper Deck: 93/94 - 572

Ftorek, Robbie
- Derniere: 72/84 - 145
- O-Pee-Chee: 79/80 - 267; 80/81 - 35; 81/82 - 274, 72SK; 82/83 - 223; 83/84 - 244
- Pepsi-Cola: 80/81 - 66
- Post: 81/82 - 24; 82/83 - 85, 198
- Season's: 92/93 - 54
- Topps: 80/81 - 35;

Fuhr, Grant (Goalie)
- Bowman: 90/91 - 189; 91/92 - 111; 92/93 - 114
- Donruss: 93/94 - 34
- Esso: 88/89 - 12
- Fleer: 92/93 - 210; 93/94 - 103, 27PP, 3N
- Gillette: 91/92 - 19
- Highliner: 93/94 - 3
- Hockey Wit: 93/94 - 40
- Humpty Dumpty: 92/93 - 9(I)
- Kraft: 86/87 - 13, 13P; 1990 - 11; 91/92 - 9
- Leaf: 93/94 - 66, 5PW
- O-Pee-Chee: 82/83 - 105, 95SK, 161SK; 83/84 - 27; 84/85 - 241, 259SK; 85/86 - 207, 221SK; 86/87 - 56, 67SK, 121SK; 87/88 - 178, 85SK; 88/89 - 59, 9NS, 122SK, 212SK, 223SK; 89/90 - 192, 228SK; 90/91 - 321; 91/92 - 84, 100PM, 191PM; 92/93 - 31, 119, 15AN; 93/94 - 218
- Panini: 87/88 - 254; 88/89 - 52, 493; 90/91 - 230; 92/93 - 75E, 75F; 93/94 - 108E
- Parkhurst: 91/92 - 175E, 175F; 92/93 - 250, 497, 250EI, 497EI; 93/94 - 22, 22EI, D7
- Pro Set: 90/91 - 82; 91/92 - 78E, 494E, 78F, 117PT, 27PK, 494F; 92/93 - 182, 182EI, PV5

Fuhr, Grant (Goalie) (cont.)
- Score: 90/91 - 275A, 275C; 90 - 58T; 91/92 - 114A, 114B, 114C, 608B, 608C, 168PNE, 168PNF; 92/93 - 20C, 437C, 20A, 437A, 267PNC, 267PNA, 301PNC, 301PNA; 93/94 - 75C, 75A
- Sega: 93/94 - 18
- Topps: 82/83 - 95SK, 161SK; 86/87 - 56; 87/88 - 178; 88/89 - 59, 6SK; 89/90 - 192; 90/91 - 321; 91/92 - 84, 258SC; 92/93 - 350, 350GS, 412SC; 93/94 - 218, 260SC, 260FD, 15MP
- Upper Deck: 90/91 - 264E, 264F; 91/92 - 264E, 553E, 264F, 553F; 92/93 - 271; 93/94 - 163
- Vachon Foods: 83/84 - 24

Fullan, Lawrence
- Loblaws: 74/75 - 313

Fusco, Mark
- O-Pee-Chee: 85/86 - 74
- Topps: 85/86 - 74

Gadsby, Bill
- Bee Hive: 45/63 - 96, 168A, 168B, 313; 64/67 - 70
- Chex: 63/65 - 12
- Coca Cola: 64/65 - 41; 65/66 - 44
- Hall Of Fame: 1983 - 110, H4P, 110
- Parkhurst: 51/52 - 37; 52/53 - 56; 53/54 - 76; 54/55 - 87; 61/62 - 27; 62/63 - 25; 63/64 - 59; 92/93 - PR9; 93/94 - 89ML, 137ML
- Shirriff: 60/61 - 90; 61/62 - 79
- Topps: 54/55 - 20; 57/58 - 65; 58/59 - 34; 59/60 - 62; 60/61 - 22; 64/65 - 96; 65/66 - 44
- Toronto Star: 57/67 - 53, 77; 58/67 - 13; 63/64 - 12
- Ultimate: 92 - 69(OSE), 69(OSF)
- York: 62/63 - 31; 63/64 - 39

Gaetz, Link
- O-Pee-Chee: 90/91 - 33PM; 91/92 - 1S
- Pro Set: 91/92 - 561E, 561F
- Score: 90/91 - 411A, 411C, 339PNE, 412PNE, 339PNF, 412PNF

Gagne, Art
- Anonymous: 1926/27 - 12
- La Presse: 27/32 - 6

Gagne, Paul
- O-Pee-Chee: 81/82 - 75, 233SK; 82/83 - 139; 85/86 - 163, 60SK
- Topps: 81/82 WN - 80; 85/86 - 163

Gagner, Dave
- Bowman: 90/91 - 186; 91/92 - 131; 92/93 - 171
- Donruss: 93/94 - 83
- Fleer: 92/93 - 94; 93/94 - 92, 60PP
- Humpty Dumpty: 92/93 - 6(II)
- Leaf: 93/94 - 128
- O-Pee-Chee: 88/89 - 215; 89/90 - 109, N/BB, 203SK; 90/91 - 168; 91/92 - 74, 128PM; 92/93 - 80; 93/94 - 183
- Panini: 89/90 - 103; 90/91 - 248; 91/92 - 112; 92/93 - 90E, 90F; 93/94 - 269E, 269F
- Parkhurst: 91/92 - 78E, 78F; 92/93 - 311, 311EI; 93/94 - 317, 317EI; 94/95 - 58, 58EI
- Pro Set: 90/91 - 138; 91/92 - 108E, 288E, 108F, 288F, 60PT; 92/93 - 77
- Score: 90/91 - 108A, 108C, 52HR; 91/92 - 72A, 72B, 72C, 71PNE, 71PNF; 92/93 - 227C, 227A, 85PNC, 85PNA; 93/94 - 98C, 98A
- Sega: 93/94 - 34
- Topps: 89/90 - 109, N/BB; 90/91 - 168; 91/92 - 74, 7SL, 117SC; 92/93 - 254, 254GS, 121SC; 93/94 - 183, 436SC, 436FD
- Upper Deck: 90/91 - 248E, 248F; 91/92 - 180E, 180F; 93/94 - 145

Gagnon, David (Dave) (Goalie)
- Score: 91/92 - 387A, 277B, 277C

Gagnon, Germain
- Eddie Sargent: 72/73 - 133

Gagnon, Germain (cont.)
  Loblaws: 74/75 - 76
  O-Pee-Chee: 72/73 - 200; 73/74 - 161; 74/75 - 344; 75/76 - 101
  Topps: 73/74 - 178; 75/76 - 101

Gagnon, Johnny
  Anonymous: 33/34 - 43
  Bee Hive: 34/44 - 151
  CKAC Radio: 43/47 - 49
  Canada Starch: 35/40 - 58
  Diamond: 33/35 - 23, 36/39 - 23(II), 21(III)
  La Presse: 27/32 - 50
  O-Pee-Chee: 33/34 - 19; 37/38 - 154; 39/40 - 25
  Parkhurst: 55/56 - 65
  Quaker Oats: 38/39 - 7; 55/56 - 65
  World Wide Gum: 33/34 - 21; 36/37 - 83

Gahn, Kristian
  Upper Deck: 92/93 - 232

Gainey, Bob
  Derniere: 72/84 - 43, 116
  Esso: 83/84 - 7E, 7F
  Kraft: 86/87 - 24, 24P
  McDonald's: 82/83 - 12
  O-Pee-Chee: 74/75 - 388; 75/76 - 278; 76/77 - 44; 77/78 - 129; 78/79 - 76; 79/80 - 170; 80/81 - 58, 9PO; 81/82 - 176, 194, 30SK, 43SK, 269SK; 82/83 - 181, 36SK; 83/84 - 187, 66SK; 84/85 - 261, 153SK; 85/86 - 169, 138SK; 86/87 - 96, 12SK; 87/88 - 228, 12SK; 88/89 - 216, 42SK; 89/90 - 58SK
  Panini: 87/88 - 69
  PepsiCo: 80/81 - 43
  Post: 82/83 - 14
  Pro Set: 90/91 - 668
  7-Eleven: 84/85 - 28
  Vachon Foods: 83/84 - 44
  Topps: 75/76 - 278; 76/77 - 44; 77/78 - 129; 78/79 - 76; 79/80 - 170; 80/81 - 58; 81/82 - 13, 82/83 - 36SK; 83/84 - 66SK; 86/87 - 96
  Upper Deck: 92/93 - 41AS

Gainor, Dutch (Norman)
  La Presse: 27/32 - 43
  Sweet Caporal: 34/35 - 31
  World Wide Gum: 36/37 - 98

Galbraith, Walter
  O-Pee-Chee: 33/34 - 7

Galchenyuk, Alexander
  O-Pee-Chee: 91/92 - 33R
  Upper Deck: 92/93 - 353

Gallagher, John
  Beehive: 34/44 - 226
  La Presse: 27/32 - 53
  O-Pee-Chee: 36/37 - 108
  World Wide Gum: 36/37 - 41

Gallant, Gerard
  Bowman: 90/91 - 237; 91/92 - 56; 92/93 - 169
  Donruss: 93/94 - 320
  Fleer: 92/93 - 284; 93/94 - 230PP
  Kraft: 90/91 - 14; 91/92 - 58; 91/92 - 58
  Leaf: 93/94 - 310
  O-Pee-Chee: 87/88 - 67, 106SK; 88/89 - 12, 254SK; 89/90 - 172, 157SK, 253SK, 25FS; 90/91 - 322; 91/92 - 443; 92/93 - 163; 93/94 - 511, 16SC, 16FD
  Panini: 87/88 - 245; 88/89 - 43; 89/90 - 58; 90/91 - 205; 91/92 - 142; 92/93 - 116E, 116F
  Parkhurst: 91/92 - 269E, 269F
  Pro Set: 90/91 - 71; 91/92 - 63E, 63F
  Score: 90/91 - 180A, 180C, 78HR; 91/92 - 34A, 34B, 34C, 205PNE, 205PNF; 92/93 - 119C, 119A, 135PNC, 135PNA; 93/94 - 402C, 402A
  Topps: 87/88 - 67; 88/89 - 12; 89/90 - 172, 2SK; 90/91 - 322; 91/92 - 443, 165SC; 92/93 - 92, 92GS, 218SC; 93/94 - 511A, 346SC, 346FD, 16SC, 16FD
  Upper Deck: 90/91 - 134E, 134F; 92/93 - 246

Galley, Garry
  Bowman: 91/92 - 360; 92/93 - 11
  Donruss: 93/94 - 251
  Durivage: 92/93 - 41; 93/94 - 38
  Fleer: 92/93 - 156; 93/94 - 124, 182PP
  Leaf: 93/94 - 120
  O-Pee-Chee: 90/91 - 331; 91/92 - 86; 92/93 - 317; 93/94 - 255
  Panini: 91/92 - 175; 93/94 - 53E, 53F
  Parkhurst: 91/92 - 7E, 350E, 7F, 350F; 92/93 - 364, 364EI; 93/94 - 423, 423EI, V87
  Pro Set: 90/91 - 7; 91/92 - 7E, 298E, 7F, 298F, 211PT
  Score: 90/91 - 253A, 253C; 91/92 - 71A, 71B, 71C, 171PNE, 171PNF; 92/93 - 19C, 19A, 103PNC, 103PNA; 93/94 - 143C, 143A
  Sega: 93/94 - 97
  Topps: 90/91 - 331; 91/92 - 86, 175SC; 92/93 - 360, 360GS, 424SC; 93/94 - 255, 381SC, 381FD
  Upper Deck: 90/91 - 379E, 379F; 91/92 - 439E, 607E, 439F, 607F; 92/93 - 319; 93/94 - 90

Gallinger, Don
  Beehive: 34/44 - 14

Gamble, Bruce (Goalie)
  Beehive: 45/63 - 21; 64/67 - 162)
  Colgate: 70/71 - 82
  Dom. Choc.: 70/71 - 126
  Eddie Sargent: 70/71 - 193
  Esso: 70/71 - 220
  O-Pee-Chee: 68/69 - 197; 69/70 - 44, 4QS; 70/71 - 105, 44DE; 71/72 - 201, 16PT
  Post: 68/69 - 19
  Shirriff: 60/61 - 119; 68/69 - 15
  Topps: 62/63 - 3; 67/68 - 18; 69/70 - 44; 70/71 - 105; 71/72 - 104
  Toronto Sun: 71/72 - 194

Gamble, DickS
  Beehive: 45/63 - 241
  La Patrie: 51/54 - 9
  Parkhurst: 51/52 - 16; 52/53 - 5; 53/54 - 18
  Quaker Oats: 45/54 - 17
  Topps: 54/55 - 1

Gamble, Troy (Goalie)
  Bowman: 91/92 - 315; 92/93 - 410
  O-Pee-Chee: 90/91 - 34PM; 91/92 - 446
  Panini: 91/92 - 37
  Parkhurst: 91/92 - 402E, 402F
  Pro Set: 90/91 - 641; 91/92 - 238E, 238F, 121PT
  Score: 90/91 - 32T; 91 - 29YS; 91/92 - 282A, 502B, 502C
  Topps: 91/92 - 446, 218SC; 92/93 - 412, 412GS
  Upper Deck: 90/91 - 434E, 434F; 91/92 - 120E, 120F

Gardiner, Bert (Goalie)
  Beehive: 34/44 - 52, 152

Gardiner Chuck (Goalie)
  Can. Chew. Gum: 33/34 - 24
  Diamond: 33/34 - 24
  Hall of Fame: 83 - 128, I8P; 87 - 128
  La Presse: 27/32 - 66
  Topps: 60/61 - 32, 36ST

Gardiner Herb
  Hall of Fame: 83 - 154, L4P; 87 - 154
  La Presse: 27/32 - 7
  Topps: 60/61 - 44, 37ST

Gardiner, James
  Imperial Tobacco: 10/11 - 36; 11/12 - 36; 12/13 - 24

Gardner, Bill
  O-Pee-Chee: 83/84 - 103; 84/85 - 35
  Post: 82/83 - 53

Gardner, Cal
  Beehive: 45/63 - 22, 403
  Parkhurst: 51/52 - 85; 52/53 - 30; 53/54 - 99; 54/55 - 53; 93/94 - 10ML
  Quaker Oats: 45/54 - 72A, 73B
  Topps: 54/55 - 47

Gardner, Dave
  Loblaws: 74/75 - 257
  O-Pee-Chee: 74/75 - 47; 75/76 - 119; 76/77 - 274; 77/78 - 258; 78/79 - 278
  Topps: 74/75 - 47; 75/76 - 119; 77/78 - 258

Gardner, George, (Goalie)
  Eddie Sargent: 70/71 - 222
  O-Pee-Chee: 70/71 - 224; 71/72 - 235
  Toronto Sun: 71/72 - 277

Gardner, Jimmy
  Hall of Fame: 83 - 172, M7P; 87 - 172

Gardner, Paul
  Funmate: 83/84 - 103
  O-Pee-Chee: 77/78 - 24; 78/79 - 88; 81/82 - 257, 187SK; 82/83 - 236, 269, 145SK; 83/84 - 275, 280, 230SK
  Post: 82/83 - 232
  Topps: 77/78 - 24; 78/79 - 88; 81/82 EN - 113; 82/83 - 145SK; 83/84 - 230SK

Gare, Danny
  Funmate: 83/84 - 31
  O-Pee-Chee: 75/76 - 64; 76/77 - 222; 77/78 - 42; 78/79 - 209; 79/80 - 61; 80/81 - 38, 88, 260; 81/82 - 20, 27, 28, 53SK; 82/83 - 83, 184SK; 83/84 - 123, 135SK; 84/85 - 54; 85/86 - 37, 35SK; 86/87 - 69, 159SK
  Post: 82/83 - 67
  Topps: 75/76 - 64; 76/77 - 222; 77/78 - 42; 78/79 - 209; 79/80 - 61; 80/81 - 38, 88, 260; 81/82 - EN 127, 14, 47; 82/83 - 184SK; 83/84 - 135SK; 84/85 - 42; 85/86 - 37; 86/87 - 69

Gariepy, Ray
  Beehive: 45/63 - 23

Garland, Scott
  O-Pee-Chee: 76/77 - 243; 77/78 - 302; 78/79 - 274

Garpenlov, Johan
  Bowman: 91/92 - 45; 92/93 - 400
  Donruss: 93/94 - 309
  Fleer: 92/93 - 400; 93/94 - 83, 219PP
  Leaf: 93/94 - 133
  O-Pee-Chee: 90/91 - 35PM; 91/92 - 278; 93/94 - 53, 44SC, 44FD
  Panini: 91/92 - 144; 93/94 - 257E, 257F
  Parkhurst: 91/92 - 385E, 385F; 92/93 - 397, 397EI; 94/95 - 209, 209EI
  Pro Set: 90/91 - 605; 91/92 - 56E, 56F, 29PT
  Score: 90/91 - 17T; 91/92 - 204A, 204B, 204C; 92/93 - 406C, 406A 93/94 - 183C, 183A
  Sega: 93/94 - 118
  Topps: 91/92 - 268SC; 91/92 - 278; 92/93 - 359, 359GS, 212SC; 93/94 - 53, 44SC, 44FD
  Upper Deck: 90/91 - 523E, 523F; 91/92 - 28E, 167E, E15(E), 28F, 167F, E15(F); 92/93 - 59

Garrett, John (Goalie)
  O-Pee-Chee: 79/80 - 293; 80/81 - 77; 81/82 - 137, 68SK; 82/83 -283; 83/84 - 349, 275SK; 84/85 - 317; 85/86 - 220
  Post: 82/83 - 244
  Topps: 80/81 - 77; 83/84 - 275SK
  Vachon Foods: 83/84 - 105

Garrett, Red (Dudley)
  Beehive: 34/44 - 273

Gartner, Michael (Mike)
  Bowman: 90/91 220, HT8, HT17; 91/92 - 74; 92/93 - 146
  Donruss: 93/94 - 218, 494
  Fleer: 92/93 - 135; 93/94 - 25, 157PP, 4SM, 3RL
  Frito-Lay: 88/89 - 14
  Funmate: 83/84 - 137
  Kellogg's: 84 - 10
  Kraft: 90/91 - 69; 91/92 - 27
  Leaf: 93/94 - 213

Gartner, Michael (Mike) (cont.)
O-Pee-Chee: 80/81 - 49, 195; 81/82 - 347, 190SK; 82/83 - 363, 153SK; 83/84 - 364, 369, 207SK; 84/85 - 197, 370, 131SK; 85/86 - 46, 111SK; 86/87 - 59, 251SK; 87/88 - 168, 239SK; 88/89 - 50, 67SK; 89/90 - 30, 196SK; 90/91 - 373, 36PM; 91/92 - 46, 147PM, 164PM; 92/93 - 245, 300; 93/94 - 375, 384, 110SC, 110FD
Panini: 87/88 - 180; 88/89 - 370; 89/90 - 104; 90/91 - 103; 91/92 - 292; 92/93 - 237E, 237F; 93/94 - 91E, 91F
Parkhurst: 91/92 - 122E, 430E, 122F, 430F; 92/93 - 108, 108EI; 93/94 - 400, 400EI; 94/95 - 228, 228EI
Post: 82/83 - 308
Pro Set: 90/91 - 196, 351; 91/92 - 167E, 604E, 167F, 84PT, 604F; 92/93 - 113, 256
Score: 90/91 - 130A, 130C, 333A, 333C, 60HR; 91/92 - 135A, 135B, 135C, 202PNE, 202PNF; 92/93 - 50C, 443C, 445C, 50A, 443A, 445A, 94PNC, 94PNA; 93/94 - 2C, 2A, 447C, 447A, 8PNC, 8PNA, 8CAS, 8AAS, 2PCA
Sega: 93/94 - 89
7-Eleven: 84/85 - 53
Topps: 80/81 - 49, 195; 81/82 EN - 117; 82/83 - 153SK; 83/84 - 207SK; 84/85 - 143; 85/86 - 46; 86/87 - 59; 87/88 - 168; 88/89 - 50, N/BB; 89/90 - 30; 90/91 - 373; 91/92 - 46, 51SC; 92/93 - 264, 404, 264GS, 404GS, 311SK; 93/94 - 375, 384SC, 110SC, 110FD, 11AS, 6SCF
Upper Deck: 90/91 - 277E, 277F; 91/92 - 247E, 247F; 92/93 - 126, 38AS; 93/94 - 205

Gassoff, Bob
Loblaws: 74/75 - 258
O-Pee-Chee: 75/76 - 58; 76/77 - 301
Topps: 75/76 - 58

Gassoff, Brad
O-Pee-Chee: 78/79 - 388; 79/80 - 353

Gaudreau, Rob
Donruss: 93/94 - 310
Fleer: 93/94 - 98, 2TP, 220PP, 1SY
Leaf: 93/94 - 9
O-Pee-Chee: 93/94 - 199, 174SC, 174FD
Panini: 93/94 - 258E, 258F
Parkhurst: 93/94 - 189, 189EI; 94/95 - 207, 207EI
Score: 93/94 - 247C, 247A
Topps: 93/94 - 199, 174SC, 174FD
Upper Deck: 93/94 - 149

Gaudreault, Armand
CKAC Radio: 43/47 - 4

Gaudreault, Leonard
La Presse: 27/32 - 10

Gaul, Horace
Imperial Tobacco: 10/11 - 31

Gauthier, Fern
Beehive: 45/63 - 169A, 169B
CKAC Radio: 43/47 - 51

Gauthier, Gerard (Official)
Pro Set: 90/91 - 687

Gauthier, Jean
Chex: 63/65 - 26
Parkhurst: 63/64 - 28, 87
Shirriff: 61/62 - 120
York: 61/62 - 42; 63/64 - 29

Gavey, Aaron
Donruss: 93/94 - 12JCC
Upper Deck: 93/94 - 545

Gavin, Robert (Stewart)
O-Pee-Chee: 83/84 - 331; 84/85 - 302; 85/86 - 17SK; 87/88 - 61; 88/89 - 217; 89/90 - 214; 90/91 - 402

Gavin, Robert (Stewart) (cont.)
Panini: 87/88 - 49; 89/90 - 113; 90/91 - 260
PepsiCo: 80/81 - 88
Post: 82/83 - 279
Pro Set: 90/91 - 139; 91/92 - 404E, 404F
Score: 90/91 - 244A, 244C; 91/92 - 433B, 433C; 92/93 - 117C, 117A
Topps: 87/88 - 61
Upper Deck: 90/91 - 150E, 150F
Vachon Foods: 83/84 - 87

Gee, George
Beehive: 45/63 - 97, 170
Parkhurst: 51/52 - 43; 52/53 - 36; 53/54 - 83; 54/55 - 80

Gelinas, Martin
Bowman: 90/91 - 190; 91/92 - 102
Donruss: 93/94 - 271, 501
Durivage: 93/94 - 22
Leaf: 93/94 - 396
O-Pee-Chee: 90/91 - 64; 91/92 - 244; 92/93 - 19
Panini: 91/92 - 128; 92/93 - 106, 106F
Parkhurst: 91/92 - 283E, 283F; 93/94 - 166, 166EI; 94/95 - V36
Pro Set: 90/91 - 83; 91/92 - 66E, 66F
Score: 90 - 21YS; 90/91 - 301C; 91 - 14YS; 91/92 - 159A, 159B, 159C, 93PNE, 93PNF; 92/93 - 281C, 281A, 166PNC, 166PNA; 93/94 - 408C, 408A
Topps: 90/91 - 64; 91/92 - 244, 11SC; 92/93 - 292, 292GS, 314SC
Upper Deck: 90/91 - 23E, 23F; 91/92 - 266E, 266F; 92/93 - 282; 93/94 - 322

Gelineau, Jack (Goalie)
Beehive: 45/63 - 24

Gendron, Jean-Guy
Beehive: 45/63 - 25, 314; 64/67 - 8
Dom. Choc.: 70/71 - 97
Eddie Sargent: 70/71 - 157
Esso: 70/71 - 168
La Patrie: 51/54 - 41
O-Pee-Chee: 68/69 - 185; 69/70 - 169, 11QS; 70/71 - 86; 71/72 - 204; 72/73 - 302
Parkhurst: 93/94 - 88ML
Shirriff: 60/61 - 109; 61/62 - 93
Toronto Sun: 71/72 - 195
Toronto Star: 63/64 - 3
Topps: 57/58 - 52; 58/59 - 51; 59/60 - 24; 60/61 - 31; 61/62 - 57; 62/63 - 16; 63/64 - 16; 69/70 - 96; 70/71 - 86
York: 60/61 - 4

Gendron, Martin
Donruss: 93/94 - 13JCC
Fleer: 93/94 - 480PP
Upper Deck: 93/94 - 259, 540

Geoffrion, Bernie (Boom Boom)
Beehive: 45/63 - 242; 64/67 - 125, 214
Chex: 63/65 - 27
Derniere: 72/84 - 67
Hall of Fame: 83 - 166, M8P; 87 - 166
HHFM: 92/93 - 5
La Patrie: 51/54 - 5
O-Pee-Chee: 74/75 - 147
Parkhurst: 51/52 - 14; 52/53 - 3; 53/54 - 29; 54/55 - 8; 55/56 - 43; 57/58 MON - 2; 58/59 - 28; 59/60 - 33; 60/61 - 46; 61/62 - 35; 62/63 - 48, 53; 63/64 - 29, 88; 92/93 - PR32, 93/94 - PR44, 68ML
Quaker Oats: 45/54 - 18; 55/56 - 43
Shirriff: 60/61 - 28; 61/62 - 104; 62/63 - 34
Topps: 66/67 - 85; 66/67 US - 36; 67/68 - 29; 74/75 - 147
Toronto Star: 58/67 - 48; 63/64 - 19
Ultimate: 92 - 10(OSE), 73(OSE), 83(OSE), 10(OSF), 73(OSF), 83(OSF), PC
York: 60/61 - 5; 61/62 - 28; 62/63 - 12; 63/64 - 20

Geoffrion, Danny
Derniere: 72/84 - 75
O-Pee-Chee: 81/82 - 364, 141SK
PepsiCo: 80/81 - 127
Topps: 81/82 - 141SK

Gerard, Eddie
Wm. Patterson: 23/24 - 1
Hall of Fame: 83 - 200, N5P; 87 - 200
Imperial Tobacco: 12/13 - 34
Topps: 61/62 - 38ST

Getliffe, Ray
Beehive: 34/44 - 15, 153
Canada Starch: 35/40 - 197
O-Pee-Chee: 39/40 - 29; 40/41 - 147

Giacomin, Ed (Goalie)
Bauer: 68/69 - 9
Beehive: 64/67 - 126
Coca-Cola: 65/66 - 76
Colgate: 70/71 - 70
Dom. Choc.: 70/71 - 85
Eddie Sargent: 70/71 - 115; 72/73 - 147
Esso: 70/71 - 149
Hall of Fame: 87 - 259
Lipton Soup: 74/75 - 26
Loblaws: 74/75 - 201
O-Pee-Chee: 68/69 - 67, 205; 69/70 - 33, 217, 8ST5QS; 70/71 - 68, 244, 42DE, 9SS; 71/72 - 220, 250, 7BK; 72/73 - 173; 73/74 - 160; 74/75 - 160; 75/76 - 55; 76/77 - 160; 77/78 - 70
Shirriff: 68/69 - G3
Topps: 65/66 - 21; 66/67 - 23; 67/68 - 85, 123; 68/69 - 67; 69/70 - 33; 70/71 - 68, 9SK; 71/72 - 90, 7BK; 72/73 - 165; 73/74 - 140; 74/75 - 160; 75/76 - 55; 76/77 - 160; 77/78 - 70
Toronto Star: 57/67 - 134
Toronto Sun: 71/72 - 172
Ultimate: 92 - 20(OSE), 20(OSF)

Gianini, Tiziano
Upper Deck: 91/92 - 670E, 670F

Gibbs, Barry
Eddie Sargent: 70/71 - 91; 72/73 - 108
Esso: 70/71 - 111
Loblaws: 74/75 - 151
O-Pee-Chee: 72/73 - 101; 73/74 - 174; 74/75 - 203; 75/76 - 214; 76/77 - 341; 77/78 - 319; 78/79 - 390; 79/80 - 304; 80/81 - 334
Topps: 72/73 - 169; 73/74 - 30; 74/75 - 203; 75/76 - 214
Toronto Sun: 71/72 - 129

Gibson, Don
Upper Deck: 91/92 - 495E, 495F

Gibson, Doug
O-Pee-Chee: 75/76 - 375

Gibson, Jack
Hall of Fame: 83 - 201, N6P; 87 - 201

Giesebrecht, Gus (Roy)
Beehive: 34/44 - 100
O-Pee-Chee: 39/40 - 69

Gilbert, Ed
Loblaws: 74/75 - 113
O-Pee-Chee: 75/76 - 370; 76/77 - 329

Gilbert, Gilles (Goalie)
Loblaws: 74/75 - 25
O-Pee-Chee: 73/74 - 74; 74/75 - 10, 132; 75/76 - 45; 76/77 - 255; 77/78 - 125; 78/79 - 95; 79/80 - 209; 80/81 - 175; 81/82 - 88, 123SK; 82/83 - 84
Topps: 73/74 - 74; 74/75 - 10, 132; 75/76 - 45; 76/77 - 255; 77/78 - 125; 78/79 - 95; 79/80 - 209; 80/81 - 175; 81/82 WN - 88
Toronto Sun: 71/72 - 130

Gilbert, Gregory (Greg)
Bowman: 91/92 - 401
Fleer: 92/93 - 275
Leaf: 93/94 - 348
O-Pee-Chee: 84/85 - 125, 90SK; 85/86 - 126, 75SK; 88/89 - 83; 90/91 - 255; 91/92 - 149; 93/94 - 216, 37SC, 37FD
Panini: 88/89 - 287; 90/91 - 196
Parkhurst: 93/94 - 404A, 494A(EI)
Pro Set: 90/91 - 429; 91/92 - 372E, 372F

Gilbert, Gregory (Greg) (cont.)
- Score: 90/91 - 264A, 264C; 91/92 - 539B, 539C; 92/93 - 134C, 134A; 93/94 - 305C, 305A
- Topps: 84/85 - 93; 85/86 - 126; 88/89 - 83; 90/91 - 255; 91/92 - 149, 242SC; 92/93 - 218, 218GS, 323SC; 93/94 - 216, 37SC, 37FD
- Upper Deck: 93/94 - 404

Gilbert, Rod
- Bazooka: 71/72 - 30
- Beehive: 45/63 - 315; 64/67 - 127
- Coca-Cola: 64/65 - 77; 65/66 - 77; 77/78 - 8
- Colgate: 70/71 - 53
- Dom. Choc.: 70/71 - 86
- Eddie Sargent: 70/71 - 122; 72/73 - 141
- Esso: 70/71 - 150
- Hall of Fame: 83 - 111, H5P; 87 - 111
- Kellogg's: 70 - 3
- Lipton Soup: 74/75 - 40
- Loblaws: 74/75 - 202
- Mac's Milk: 73/74 - 7
- O-Pee-Chee: 68/69 - 72, 209, 9PS; 69/70 - 37, 9ST, 12QS; 70/71 - 63, 39DE, 10SS; 71/72 - 123, 18BK, 7PT; 72/73 - 152, 229; 73/74 - 156; 74/75 - 201; 75/76 - 225; 76/77 - 90; 77/78 - 25
- Pro Set: 91/92 - AC23, 593E, 593F
- Shirriff: 68/69 - G10
- Topps: 61/62 - 62; 62/63 - 59; 63/64 - 57; 64/65 - 24; 65/66 - 91; 66/67 - 26; 66/67 US - 26; 67/68 - 90; 68/69 - 72; 69/70 - 37; 70/71 - 63, 10SK; 71/72 - 123, 18BK; 72/73 - 80, 125; 73/74 - 88; 76/77 - 18PO 74/75 - 201; 75/76 - 225; 76/77 - 90; 77/78 - 25
- Toronto Star: 57/67 - 87, 120; 64/65 - 33
- Toronto Sun: 71/72 - 173
- Upper Deck: 90/91 - 512E, 512F
- Zellers: 92/93 - 3, 3A

Gilbertson, Stan
- Eddie Sargent: 72/73 - 52
- Loblaws: 74/75 - 58
- O-Pee-Chee: 71/72 - 183; 72/73 - 70; 73/74 - 212; 74/75 - 223; 75/76 - 382; 76/77 - 187
- Topps: 72/73 - 101; 74/75 - 223; 76/77 - 187; 77/78 - 203
- Toronto Sun: 71/72 - 47

Gilchrist, Brent
- Bowman: 91/92 - 336; 92/93 - 322
- Fleer: 92/93 - 293; 93/94 - 324PP
- O-Pee-Chee: 90/91 - 422; 91/92 - 90; 92/93 - 221, 129PM
- Panini: 92/93 - 153E, 153F
- Parkhurst: 91/92 - 315E, 315F; 93/94 - 52, 52EI; 94/95 - 55, 55EI, V21
- Pro Set: 90/91 - 471; 91/92 - 414E, 414F, 192PT; 92/93 - 90
- Score: 90/91 - 87T; 91/92 - 259B, 259C, 236PNE, 236PNF; 92/93 - 46C, 46A, 357PNC, 357PNA; 93/94 - 206C, 206A
- Topps: 91/92 - 90; 92/93 - 386, 386GS, 449SC
- Upper Deck: 92/93 - 459; 93/94 - 329

Giles, Curt
- O-Pee-Chee: 82/83 - 166; 85/86 - 96; 86/87 - 119, 172SK; 89/90 - 213; 90/91 - 228; 91/92 - 17
- Panini: 87/88 - 110; 89/90 - 112; 90/91 - 250
- Post: 82/83 - 133
- Pro Set: 90/91 - 140; 91/92 - 114E, 114F
- Score: 90/91 - 94A, 94C; 91/92 - 137A, 137B, 137C
- Topps: 85/86 - 96; 86/87 - 119; 90/91 - 228; 91/92 - 17; 92/93 - 202, 202GS, 64SC
- Upper Deck: 90/91 - 9E, 9F

Gilhen, Randy
- Bowman: 91/92 - 84; 92/93 - 327
- Fleer: 93/94 - 93PP, 473PP
- O-Pee-Chee: 90/91 - 250; 91/92 - 418, 123PM; 92/93 - 26

Gilhen, Randy (cont.)
- Parkhurst: 91/92 - 335E, 335F
- Pro Set: 90/91 - 506; 91/92 - 403E, 403F
- Score: 91 - 16T; 91/92 - 157A, 157B, 157C, 566B, 566C, 238PNE, 238PNF; 92/93 - 238C, 268A, 126PNC, 126PNA
- Topps: 90/91 - 250; 91/92 - 418, 275SC; 92/93 - 27, 27GS, 318SC
- Upper Deck: 91/92 - 603E, 603F; 92/93 - 82; 93/94 - 481

Gill, Todd
- Bowman: 91/92 - 171; 92/93 - 375
- Donruss: 93/94 - 335
- Fleer: 93/94 - 77, 449PP
- Leaf: 93/94 - 22
- O-Pee-Chee: 87/88 - 163SK; 91/92 - 361; 93/94 - 4, 62SC, 62FD
- Panini: 87/88 - 324; 89/90 - 143; 92/93 - 82E, 82F
- Parkhurst: 91/92 - 393E, 393F
- Pro Set: 90/91 - 534; 91/92 - 226E, 226F
- Score: 91/92 - 521B, 521C, 278PNE, 278PNF; 92/93 - 196C, 196A, 290PNC, 290PNA; 93/94 - 292C, 292A
- Sega: 93/94 - 133
- Topps: 91/92 - 361, 336SC; 92/93 - 374, 374GS, 261SC; 93/94 - 4, 62SC, 62FD

Gillies, Clark
- Esso: 88/89 - 13
- Funmate: 83/84 - 80
- Loblaws: 74/75 - 182
- McDonald's: 82/83 - 13
- O-Pee-Chee: 75/76 - 199; 76/77 - 126; 77/78 - 250, 6GP; 78/79 - 220, 327; 79/80 - 130; 80/81 - 75; 81/82 - 202, 164SK; 82/83 - 201, 54SK, 55SK; 83/84 - 6, 84SK; 84/85 - 126; 85/86 - 81, 68SK; 86/87 - 141, 205SK; 87/88 - 96; 88/89 - 80
- Panini: 87/88 - 34
- Post: 82/83 - 179
- Topps: 75/76 - 199; 76/77 - 126; 77/78 - 250, 6PO; 78/79 - 220, 327; 79/80 - 130; 80/81 - 75; 81/82 EN - 88; 82/83 - 54SK, 55SK; 83/84 - 84SK; 84/85 - 94; 85/86 - 81; 86/87 - 141; 87/88 - 96; 88/89 - 80
- Upper Deck: 91/92 - 640E, 640F

Gillis, Jere
- Derniere: 72/84 - 59
- O-Pee-Chee: 78/79 - 109; 79/80 - 322; 80/81 - 283; 81/82 - 232; 84/85 - 318
- Post: 82/83 - 245
- Topps: 78/79 - 109
- Vachon Foods: 83/84 - 106

Gillis, Mike
- O-Pee-Chee: 81/82 - 12
- Post: 82/83 - 5

Gillis, Paul
- Bowman: 90/91 - 165
- Kraft: 1990 - 29
- O-Pee-Chee: 85/86 - 150SK; 86/87 - 168, 24SK; 87/88 - 247, 221SK; 89/90 - 265, 183SK; 90/91 - 22; 91/92 - 469
- Panini: 87/88 - 167; 89/90 - 330; 90/91 - 143
- Pro Set: 90/91 - 246
- Score: 90/91 - 141A, 141C; 91/92 - 364A, 403B, 403C
- Topps: 86/87 - 168; 90/91 - 22; 91/92 - 469
- Upper Deck: 90/91 - 49E, 49F

Gilmour, Billy
- Hall of Fame: 83 - 50, D4P; 87 - 50

Gilmour, Douglas (Doug)
- Bowman: 90/91 - 96; 91/92 - 255; 92/93 - 83
- Donruss: 93/94 - 341, 7ES
- Fleer: 92/93 - 211; 93/94 - 110, 2G, 3AW, 16AS, 244PP, 2PL, 1PM
- Frito-Lay: 88/89 - 15

Gilmour, Douglas (Doug) (cont.)
- Hockey Wit: 93/94 - 61
- Humpty Dumpty: 92/93 - 7(II)
- Kraft: 1990 - 1; 93/94 - 8, 56
- Leaf: 93/94 - 93, 440, 6AS, 1SS
- O-Pee-Chee: 84/85 - 185, 60SK; 85/86 - 76, 48SK; 86/87 - 93, 177SK; 87/88 - 175, 11HL, E/BB, 27SK; 88/89 - 56, 20SK; 89/90 - 74, 103SK; 90/91 - 136; 91/92 - 208; 92/93 - 177, 8SP; 93/94 - 390, 140SC, 149SC, 140FD, 149FD
- Panini: 87/88 - 311; 88/89 - 105; 89/90 - 28; 90/91 - 172; 91/92 - 59; 92/93 - 77E, 77F
- Parkhurst: 91/92 - 26E, 396E, 26F, 396F; 92/93 - 183, 502, 183EI, 502EI; -CP; 93/94 - 469, 469EI, G10, W4, D9; 94/95 - 313, 313EI, H23, R23, C23, V80
- Pro Set: 90/91 - 34; 91/92 - 34E, 34F, 234PT; 92/93 - 184; CP1, 11TL
- Roots: 93/94 - 5
- Score: 90/91 - 155A, 155C, 69HR; 91/92 - 218A, 218B, 218C, 92PNE, 92PNF; 92/93 - 40C, 40A, 233PNC, 233PNA, 279PNC, 279PNA, -PC; 93/94 - 66C, 66A, 44PNC, 44PNA, 44CAS, 44AAS, 21FR
- Season's: 92/93 - 55
- Sega: 93/94 - 135
- Topps: 85/86 - 76; 86/87 - 93; 87/88 - 175, E/BB; 88/89 - 56; 89/90 - 74; 90/91 - 136; 91/92 - 208, 96SC; 92/93 - 122, 122GS, 359SC; 93/94 - 390PM, 140SC, 149SC, 140FD, 149FD
- Upper Deck: 90/91 - 271E, 271F; 91/92 - 188E, 558E, 188F, 558F; 92/93 - 21, 215, 639, 24AS; 93/94 - 306, 382

Gilmour, Larry
- Imperial Tobacco: 10/11 - 22L; 11/12 - 22

Gingras, Gaston
- Derniere: 72/84 - 125, 176
- Kraft: 86/87 - 25; 86/87 - 25
- O-Pee-Chee: 80/81 - 322; 81/82 - 182; 82/83 - 182; 83/84 - 332, 40SK; 84/85 - 303; 87/88 - 229, 8SK; 88/89 - 35; 89/90 - 270, 21SK
- PepsiCo: 80/81 - 44
- Topps: 83/84 - 40SK; 88/89 - 35
- Vachon Foods: 83/84 - 88

Girard Bob
- O-Pee-Chee: 76/77 - 362; 77/78 - 255; 78/79 - 339

Girard, Kenny
- Parkhurst: 57/58 TOR - 18, 93/94 - 132ML

Girard, Rick
- Donruss: 93/94 - 14JCC
- Upper Deck: 93/94 - 539

Giroux, Larry
- Loblaws: 74/75 - 259
- O-Pee-Chee: 75/76 - 273
- Topps: 75/76 - 273

Gladu, Jean
- CKAC Radio: 43/47 - 5

Glass, Frank
- Imperial Tobacco: 10/11 - 5, 34L; 11/12 - 34; 12/13 - 21

Glennie, Brian
- Coca-Cola: 77/78 - 9
- Eddie Sargent: 70/71 - 196; 72/73 - 205
- Esso: 70/71 - 221
- Loblaws: 74/75 - 276
- Mac's Milk: 73/74 - 8
- O-Pee-Chee: 70/71 - 216; 71/72 - 197; 72/73 - 216; 73/74 - 170; 74/75 - 310; 75/76 - 365; 76/77 - 99; 77/78 - 275; 78/79 - 345; 79/80 - 341
- Topps: 72/73 - 37; 73/74 - 163; 76/77 - 99
- Toronto Sun: 71/72 - 258

Glover, Fred
- Beehive: 45/63 - 171
- Parkhurst: 51/52 - 60; 52/53 - 40

Glover, Howie
- Beehive: 45/63 - 172, 316
- Parkhurst: 61/62 - 19; 62/63 - 28
- Shirriff: 60/61 - 57; 61/62 - 65

Glynn, Brian
- Bowman: 91/92 - 132; 92/93 - 379
- Donruss: 93/94 - 236
- Fleer: 92/93 - 58; 93/94 - 399PP
- O-Pee-Chee: 91/92 - 506
- Panini: 91/92 - 114
- Parkhurst: 92/93 - 287, 287EI; 93/94 - 141, 141EI
- Pro Set: 91/92 - 406E, 406F
- Score: 91/92 - 446B, 446C; 92/93 - 361C, 361A, 136PNC, 136PNA
- Topps: 91/92 - 506, 388SC; 92/93 - 198, 198GS, 472SC
- Upper Deck: 91/92 - 158E, 158F; 92/93 - 64; 93/94 - 458

Godfrey, Warren
- Beehive: 45/63 - 26A, 26B, 26C, 173; 64/67 - 9, 71
- Coca-Cola: 65/66 - 45
- Parkhurst: 52/53 - 85; 53/54 - 95; 54/55 - 56; 60/61 - 30; 61/62 - 30; 62/63 - 36, 3HB; 93/94 - 51ML
- Shirriff: 60/61 - 49; 61/62 - 62
- Topps: 54/55 - 50; 57/58 - 41; 58/59 - 58; 59/60 - 27; 62/63 - 4
- Toronto Star: 58/67 - 58

Godynyuk, Alexander
- Donruss: 93/94 - 135, 438
- O-Pee-Chee: 91/92 - 471; 92/93 - 10; 93/94 - 289
- Parkhurst: 91/92 - 248E, 248F; 93/94 - 74, 74EI
- Pro Set: 91/92 - 563E, 563F, 251PT
- Score: 91/92 - 391A, 281B, 281C, 318PNE, 318PNF
- Topps: 91/92 - 471; 92/93 - 256, 256GS, 88SC; 93/94 - 289, 268SC, 268FD
- Upper Deck: 91/92 - 466E, 609E, E16(E), 466F, 609F, E16(F); 93/94 - 469

Goegan, Peter
- Beehive: 45/63 - 174; 64/67 - 72
- Parkhurst: 60/61 - 34; 61/62 - 23; 63/64 - 43
- Shirriff: 60/61 - 50; 61/62 - 75
- Topps: 58/59 - 47; 59/60 - 4
- York: 63/64 - 53

Goheen, Francis (Moose)
- Hall of Fame: 83 - 112, H6P; 87 - 112
- Topps: 60/61 - 63, 39ST

Golsnov, Maxim
- Upper Deck: 93/94 - 273

Goldham, Bob
- Beehive: 34/44 - 319; 45/63 - 98, 175
- Parkhurst: 51/52 - 67; 52/53 - 64; 53/54 - 49; 54/55 - 39
- Quaker Oats: 45/54 - 73A, 73B
- Topps: 54/55 - 46

Goldsworthy, Bill
- Colgate: 70/71 - 52
- Dom. Choc.: 70/71 - 64
- Eddie Sargent: 70/71 - 95; 71/72 - 86; 72/73 - 104
- Esso: 70/71 - 112
- Loblaws: 74/75 - 152
- O-Pee-Chee: 68/69 - 148; 69/70 - 195; 70/71 - 46; 71/72 - 55, 10CS; 72/73 - 159; 73/74 - 62; 74/75 - 134, 220; 75/76 - 180; 76/77 - 169; 77/78 - 99
- Shirriff: 68/69 - E4
- Topps: 70/71 - 46; 71/72 - 55; 72/73 - 115; 73/74 - 62; 74/75 - 134, 220; 75/76 - 180; 76/77 - 169; 77/78 - 99
- Toronto Sun: 71/72 - 131

Goldsworthy, Leroy
- Beehive: 34/44 - 16, 53, 227
- Diamond: 36/39 - 24(I), 24(II), 22(III)
- O-Pee-Chee: 35/36 - 96
- World Wide Gum: 36/37 - 73

Goldup, Glenn
- O-Pee-Chee: 74/75 - 275; 75/76 - 391; 78/79 - 337; 79/80 - 376; 80/81 - 382

Goldup, Hank
- Beehive: 34/44 - 274, 320
- O-Pee-Chee: 39/40 - 54

Gonchar, Sergei
- Upper Deck: 93/94 - 272

Goodenough, Larry
- Topps: 76/77 - 96
- O-Pee-Chee: 75/76 - 373; 76/77 - 96; 77/78 - 359; 79/80 - 383

Goodfellow, Ebbie (Ebenezer)
- Anonymous: 33/34 - 20
- Beehive: 34/44 - 101
- Can. Chew. Gum: 33/34 - 25
- Hall of Fame: 83 - 35, C5P; 87 - 35
- Hamilton Gum: 33/34 - 42
- La Presse: 27/32/ - 62
- O-Pee-Chee: 34/35 - 52; 36/37 - 117; 39/40 - 66
- Sweet Caporal: 34/35 - 37
- World Wide Gum: 36/37 - 11

Goodman, Paul (Goalie)
- Beehive: 34/44 - 54
- O-Pee-Chee: 40/41 - 150

Gordijuk, Viktor
- Fleer: 93/94 - 120, 28PP
- O-Pee-Chee: 91/92 - 15R; 92/93 - 60PM
- Parkhurst: 92/93 - 17, 17EI
- Upper Deck: 92/93 - 579, ER18

Gordon, Jackie
- Beehive: 45/63 - 317
- O-Pee-Chee: 74/75 - 238
- Topps: 74/75 - 238

Gordon, Scott (Goalie)
- Bowman: 90/91 - 171
- Pro Set: 90/91 - 634

Gorence, Tom
- O-Pee-Chee: 79/80 - 51; 80/81 - 368; 81/82 - 250; 82/83 - 250
- Topps: 79/80 - 51

Goring, Butch
- Coca-Cola: 77/78 - 10
- Eddie Sargent: 72/73 - 92
- Loblaws: 74/75 - 131
- O-Pee-Chee: 71/72 - 152; 72/73 - 56; 73/74 - 155; 74/75 - 74; 75/76 - 221; 76/77 - 239; 77/78 - 67; 78/79 - 151; 79/80 - 98; 80/81 - 254; 81/82 - 203, 20SK; 82/83 - 200; 83/84 - 7, 13SK, 177SK; 84/85 - 127, 84SK
- Post: 82/83 - 180
- Toronto Sun: 71/72 - 113
- Topps: 72/73 - 72; 73/74 - 138; 74/75 - 74; 75/76 - 221; 76/77 - 239; 77/78 - 67; 78/79 - 151; 79/80 - 98; 80/81 - 254; 81/82 EN - 89; 83/84 - 13SK, 177SK 84/85 - 95

Gorman, Tommy
- Hall of Fame: 83 - 113, H7P; 87 - 113
- World Wide Gum: 36/37 - 17

Gosselin, Mario (Goalie)
- Kraft: 86/87 - 44, 44P
- O-Pee-Chee: 85/86 - 18, 146SK; 86/87 - 235, 21SK; 87/88 - 250, 231SK; 88/89 - 173, 193SK; 89/90 - 258; 90/91 - 442
- Panini: 87/88 - 157; 88/89 - 347
- Topps: 85/86 - 18; 88/89 - 173
- Upper Deck: 90/91 - 91E, 91F

Gottselig, Johnny
- Beehive: 34/44 - 55
- Can. Chew. Gum: 33/34 - 26; 35/36 - 80; 39/40 - 50
- Diamond: 33/35 - 25, 36/39 - 25(I), 25(II), 23(III) 5(IV), 5(V), 5(VI)
- La Presse: 27/32 - 52
- World Wide Gum: 36/37 - 55

Gould, John
- Loblaws: 74/75 - 294

Gould, John (cont.)
- O-Pee-Chee: 74/75 - 381; 75/76 - 266; 76/77 - 85; 77/78 - 382; 78/79 - 309; 79/80 - 282
- Topps: 75/76 - 266; 76/77 - 85

Gould, Robert (Bobby)
- O-Pee-Chee: 84/85 - 196; 87/88 - 55, 237SK; 89/90 - 289; 90/91 - 398
- Post: 82/83 - 309
- Topps: 87/88 - 55

Goulet, Michel
- Bowman: 91/92 - 392; 92/93 - 310
- Cel.Watch: 1988 - CW11
- Derniere: 72/84 - 143
- Donruss: 93/94 - 71
- Durivage: 92/93 - 24, 93/94 - 42
- Esso: 83/84 - 8E, 8F; 88/89 - 14
- Fleer: 92/93 - 35; 93/94 - 49PP
- Frito-Lay: 88/89 - 16
- Funmate: 83/84 - 108
- Hockey Wit: 93/94 - 33
- Kellogg's: 84 - 15
- Kraft: 86/87 - 45, 45P; 1990 - 30
- Leaf: 93/94 - 373
- McDonald's: 82/83 - 14, 19
- O-Pee-Chee: 80/81 - 67; 81/82 - 275, 75SK; 82/83 - 284, 25SK; 83/84 - 287, 288, 292, 166SK, 249SK, 250SK; 84/85 - 207, 280, 366, 384, 391, 64SK, 140SK, 168SK, 169SK; 85/86 - 150; 86/87 - 92, E/BB, 141SK; 86/87 - 22SK, 113SK; 87/88 - 77, 12HL, M/BB, 113SK, 225SK; 88/89 - 54, 10NS, 188SK; 89/90 - 57, 186SK; 90/91 - 329; 91/92 - 336; 92/93 - 358; 93/94 - 386, 12SC, 12FD
- Panini: 87/88 - 163; 88/89 - 355; 89/90 - 326; 91/92 - 11; 92/93 - 6E, 6F; 93/94 - 148E, 148F
- Parkhurst: 91/92 - 36E, 215E, 428E, 36F, 215F, 428F; 92/93 - 272, 272EI; 93/94 - 313, 313EI
- PepsiCo: 80/81 - 67
- Post: 82/83 - 246
- Pro Set: 90/91 - 430; 91/92 - 50E, 50F, 166PT; 92/93 - 32
- Score: 90/91 - 221A, 221C; 91/92 - 201A, 375A, 201B, 265B, 201B, 265C, 109PNE, 109PNF; 92/93 - 222C, 444C, 222A, 444A, 22PNC, 22PNA; 93/94 - 153C, 153A
- Sega: 93/94 - 28
- 7-Eleven: 84/85 - 40
- Topps: 80/81 - 67; 82/83 - 25SK; 83/84 - 166SK, 249SK, 250SK; 84/85 - 129, 153; 85/86 - 150; 86/87 - 92, E/BB, 2SK; 87/88 - 77, M/BB, 6SK; 88/89 - 54, 7SK; 89/90 - 57; 90/91 - 329; 91/92 - 336, 66SC; 92/93 - 255, 347, 255GS, 347GS, 69SC; 93/94 - 386C, 12SC, 12FD
- Upper Deck: 90/91 - 133E, 133F; 91/92 - 374E, 374F; 92/93 - 113
- Vachon Foods: 83/84 - 65

Goupille, Red (Clifford)
- Beehive: 34/44 - 154
- Canada Starch: 35/40 - 116
- O-Pee-Chee: 37/38 - 178; 39/40 - 22; 40/41 - 120

Govedaris, Chris
- Bowman: 90/91 - 259
- Score: 91/92 - 325A, 355B, 355C

Goyer, Gerry
- Topps: 67/68 - 54

Goyette, Phil
- Beehive: 45/63 - 243, 318; 64/67 - 128
- Coca-Cola: 64/65 - 78; 65/66 - 78
- Colgate: 70/71 - 10
- Dom. Choc.: 70/71 - 15
- Esso: 70/71 - 25
- O-Pee-Chee: 68/69 - 73; 69/70 - 21, 6QS; 70/71 - 127, 251; 71/72 - 88

Goyette, Phil (cont.)
Parkhurst:	57/58 MON - 11; 58/59 - 47; 59/60 - 4; 60/61 - 50; 61/62 - 46; 62/63 - 37; 93/94 - 74ML
Shirriff:	60/61 - 27; 61/62 - 116; 62/63 - 28; 68/69 - G5
Topps:	63/64 - 58; 64/65 - 87; 65/66 - 92; 66/67 - 28; 66/67 US - 28; 67/68 - 25; 68/69 - 73; 69/70 - 21; 70/71 - 127; 71/72 - 88
Toronto Star:	58/67 - 87
Toronto Sun:	71/72 - 27
Ultimate:	92 - 11(OSE), 11(OSF)
York:	60/61 - 6; 61/62 - 30

Graboski, Tony
Beehive:	34/44 - 155

Gracie, Bob
Anonymous:	33/34 - 40
Beehive:	34/44 - 156, 197
Canada Starch:	35/40 - 55, 153
Can. Chew. Gum:	33/34 - 27
Diamond:	33/35 - 36, 36/39 - 26(I)
O-Pee-Chee:	34/35 - 66; 37/38 - 171
Quaker Oats:	38/39 - 8
World Wide Gum:	33/34 - 63; 36/37 - 38

Gradin, Thomas
Funmate:	83/84 - 129
Kellogg's:	84 - 36
O-Pee-Chee:	79/80 - 53; 80/81 - 241; 81/82 - 327, 346, 243SK; 82/83 - 337, 344, 345, 240SK; 83/84 - 350, 273SK; 84/85 - 319, 282SK; 85/86 - 16, 240SK
PepsiCo:	80/81 - 109
Post:	82/83 - 294
Topps:	79/80 - 53; 80/81 - 241; 81/82 - 15, 64; 82/83 - 240SK; 83/84 - 273SK; 85/86 - 16
Vachon Foods:	83/84 - 107

Graham, Dirk
Bowman:	90/91 - 8; 91/92 - 397; 92/93 - 68
Donruss:	93/94 - 63
Fleer:	92/93 - 36; 93/94 - 61, 50PP
Leaf:	93/94 - 270
O-Pee-Chee:	86/87 - 143, 171SK; 87/88 - 184; 88/89 - 135, 7SK; 89/90 - 52, 12SK; 90/91 - 179; 91/92 - 217, 521, 131PM; 92/93 - 210; 93/94 - 88, 90SC, 90FD
Panini:	87/88 - 295; 88/89 - 25; 89/90 - 44; 90/91 - 191; 91/92 - 16; 92/93 - 7E, 7F; 93/94 - 147E, 147F
Parkhurst:	91/92 - 33E, 33F; 92/93 - 271, 271EI
Pro Set:	90/91 - 51; 91/92 - AC12, 51E, 323E, 570E, 51F, 323F, 23PT, 570F; 92/93 - 38
Score:	90/91 - 17A, 17C; 91/92 - 15A, 432A, 15B, 322B, 15C, 322C, 261PNE, 261PNF; 92/93 - 27C, 27A, 173PNC, 173PNA; 93/94 - 12C, 12A
Topps:	86/87 - 143; 87/88 - 184; 88/89 - 135; 89/90 - 52; 90/91 - 179; 91/92 - 217, 521, 181SC; 92/93 - 376, 376GS, 342SC; 93/94 - 88, 90SC, 90FD
Upper Deck:	90/91 - 131E, 131F; 91/92 - 271E, 271F, 502E, 502F; 92/93 - 272; 93/94 - 328

Graham, Pat
Post:	82/83 - 233

Grahame, Ron (Goalie)
O-Pee-Chee:	78/79 - 219
Topps:	78/79 - 219

Granato, Tony
Bowman:	90/91 - 140, HT18; 91/92 - 192; 92/93 - 50
Donruss:	93/94 - 160
Fleer:	92/93 - 82; 93/94 - 63, 115PP
Hockey Wit:	93/94 - 32
Kraft:	91/92 - 35
Leaf:	93/94 - 201

Granato, Tony (cont.)
O-Pee-Chee:	89/90 - 161, 36SK, 241SK, 10FS; 90/91 - 62; 91/92 - 88; 92/93 - 65; 93/94 - 144, 504
Panini:	89/90 - 285; 90/91 - 239; 91/92 - 83; 92/93 - 68E, 68F; 93/94 - 203E, 203F
Parkhurst:	91/92 - 66E, 66F; 92/93 - 301, 301EI; 93/94 - 93, 93EI; 94/95 - V76
Pro Set:	90/91 - 117; 91/92 - 98E, 98F, 49PT; 92/93 - 74
Score:	90 - 33YS; 90/91 - 48A, 48C; 91/92 - 57A, 57B, 57C, 76PNE, 76PNF; 92/93 - 243C, 243A, 69PMC, 69PNA, 262PNC, 262PNA, 4USG; 93/94 - 52C, 52A, 444C, 444A
Season's:	92/93 - 11
Topps:	89/90 - 161; 90/91 - 62; 91/92 - 88, 97SC; 92/93 - 242, 242GS, 281SC; 93/94 - 146(I), 504A, 285SC, 285FD
Upper Deck:	90/91 - 272E, 272F; 91/92 - 172E, 508E, 172F, 508F; 92/93 - 185; 93/94 - 146

Grant, Danny
Colgate:	70/71 - 36
Dom. Choc.:	70/71 - 65
Eddie Sargent:	70/71 - 92; 72/73 - 103
Esso:	70/71 - 113
Loblaws:	74/75 - 95
O-Pee-Chee:	68/69 - 52; 69/70 - 125, 208, 10ST, 17QS; 70/71 - 47, 11SS; 71/72 - 79, 11BK;72/73 - 57; 73/74 - 214; 74/75 - 174; 75/76 - 49; 76/77 - 16; 77/78 - 147; 78/79 - 306
Topps:	68/69 - 52; 69/70 - 125; 70/71 - 47, 11SK; 71/72 - 79, 11BK; 72/73 - 39; 73/74 - 161; 74/75 - 174; 75/76 - 49; 76/77 - 16; 77/78 - 147
Toronto Sun:	71/72 - 132

Grant, Doug (Goalie)
Loblaws:	74/75 - 96
O-Pee-Chee:	74/75 - 347; 77/78 - 294; 78/79 - 373

Grant, Mike
Hall of Fame:	83 - 218, O8P; 87 - 218

Gratton, Chris
Donruss:	93/94 - 330, 393, 2RR, V/PM, V/SP
Fleer:	93/94 - 5RS, 443PP
Leaf:	93/94 - 331, 3FP
O-Pee-Chee:	93/94 - 410
Parkhurst:	93/94 - 250, 250EI, E6, CC3, D12 94/95 - 220, 282, 220EI, 282EI, H22, R22, C22
Topps:	93/94 - 410C, 320SC, 320FD
Upper Deck:	92/93 - 590; 93/94 - 78

Gratton, Gilles (Goalie)
O-Pee-Chee:	76/77 - 28; 77/78 - 207
Topps:	76/77 - 28; 77/78 - 207

Gratton, Norm
Loblaws:	74/75 - 42
O-Pee-Chee:	74/75 - 288; 75/76 - 34
Topps:	75/76 - 34

Gravelle, Leo
Beehive:	45/63 - 244
CKAC Radio:	43/47 - 52
Quaker Oats:	45/54 - 38

Graves, Adam
Bowman:	91/92 - 97; 92/93 - 373
Donruss:	93/94 - 219
Fleer:	92/93 - 136; 93/94 - 43, 158PP
Hockey Wit:	93/94 - 86
Kraft:	93/94 - 9
Leaf:	93/94 - 130
O-Pee-Chee:	90/91 - 480; 91/92 - 167, 28PM; 92/93 - 158; 93/94 - 106
Panini:	91/92 - 122; 92/93 - 238E, 238F; 93/94 - 92E, 92F
Parkhurst:	91/92 - 339E, 399F; 92/93 - 346, 346EI; 93/94 - 134, 134EI; 94/95 - 147, 307, 147EI, 307EI, H15, R15, C15
Pro Set:	90/91 - 84; 91/92 - 67E, 443E, 67F, 443F, 207PT; 92/93 - 115

Graves, Adam (cont.)
Score:	90/91 - 163A, 163C; 91 - 44T; 91/92 - 358A, 235B, 235C, 594B, 594C, 16PNE, 16PNF; 92/93 - 71C, 71A, 108PNC, 108PNA; 93/94 - 35C, 35A
Topps:	91/92 - 167, 332SC; 92/93 - 329, 329GS, 150SC; 93/94 - 106, 270SC, 270FD, 18MP
Upper Deck:	90/91 - 344E, 344F; 91/92 - 268E, 574E, 268F, 574F; 92/93 - 388; 93/94 - 128

Graves, Hilliard
O-Pee-Chee:	73/74 - 110; 74/75 - 306; 75/76 - 62; 76/77 - 273; 77/78 - 286; 78/79 - 357; 79/80 - 294
Topps:	73/74 - 110; 75/76 - 62

Gray, Terry
O-Pee-Chee:	68/69 - 44
Topps:	61/62 - 16; 62/63 - 20; 68/69 - 44

Green, Red (Redvers)
Wm. Paterson:	23/24 - 31; 24/25 - 15
Champ's:	24/25 - 12
Dom. Choc.:	1925 - 84
Maple Crispette:	24/25 - 10

Green, Richard (Rick)
Kraft:	86/87 - 26, 26P
O-Pee-Chee:	77/78 - 245; 78/79 - 363; 79/80 - 309; 80/81 - 33; 81/82 - 348, 193SK; 82/83 - 183, 156SK; 83/84 - 188; 84/85 - 262; 87/88 - 234, 11SK; 90/91 - 37PM
Panini:	87/88 - 60; 91/92 - 147
Post:	82/83 - 310
Pro Set:	90/91 - 436
Score:	90/91 - 84T
Topps:	77/78 - 245; 80/81 - 33; 81/82 EN - 118; 82/83 - 156SK

Green, Wilf (Shorty)
Wm. Paterson:	23/24 - 30; 24/25 - 14
Champ's:	24/25 - 13
Dom. Choc.:	1925 - 83
Hall of Fame:	83 - 140, K5P; 87 - 140
Maple Crispette:	24/25 - 22

Green, Ted
Beehive:	64/67 - 10
Coca-Cola:	64/65 - 6; 65/66 - 8
Dom. Choc.:	70/71 - 5
Eddie Sargent:	70/71 - 4; 71/72 - 5
Esso:	70/71 - 8
O-Pee-Chee:	68/69 - 4; 69/70 - 23, 218, 6QS; 70/71 - 134; 71/72 - 173
Shirriff:	61/62 - 16; 68/69 - A12
Topps:	61/62 - 2; 62/63 - 7, 4HB; 63/64 - 7; 64/65 - 32; 65/66 - 98; 66/67 - 37; 66/67 US - 37; 67/68 - 94; 68/69 - 4; 69/70 - 23
Toronto Star:	57/67 - 139; 64/65 - 2
Toronto Sun:	71/72 - 9

Green, Travis
Donruss:	93/94 - 200
Fleer:	92/93 - 343; 93/94 - 383PP
Leaf:	93/94 - 127
O-Pee-Chee:	93/94 - 489
Parkhurst:	92/93 - 343, 343EI; 93/94 - 126, 126EI
Topps:	93/94 - 489C, 394SC, 394FD
Upper Deck:	93/94 - 59

Gregg, Randall (Randy)
O-Pee-Chee:	83/84 - 28, 145SK; 84/85 - 242, 257SK; 85/86 - 199, 225SK; 87/88 - 94SK; 89/90 - 229; 90/91 - 275
Panini:	90/91 - 231
Score:	90/91 - 306C; 91 - 48T; 91/92 - 598B, 598C, 415PNE, 415PNF
Topps:	83/84 - 145SK; 90/91 - 275
Vachon Foods:	83/84 - 25

Gregson, Terry (Official)
Pro Set:	90/91 - 688

Greig, Mark
- Donruss: 93/94 - 137, 495
- Leaf: 93/94 - 412
- O-Pee-Chee: 92/93 - 186, 99PM; 93/94 - 301
- Pro Set: 91/92 - 537E, 537F
- Score: 90/91 - 431A, 431C; 91/92 - 383A, 273B, 273C, 352PNE, 352PNF
- Topps: 92/93 - 175, 175GS, 421SC; 93/94 - 301, 386SC, 386FD

Grenier, Lucien
- Eddie Sargent: 72/73 - 1
- Toronto Sun: 71/72 - 114

Greschner, Ronald (Ron)
- O-Pee-Chee: 75/76 - 146; 76/77 - 154; 77/78 - 256; 78/79 - 154; 79/80 - 78; 80/81 - 248; 81/82 - 224, 167SK; 82/83 - 224; 84/85 - 141; 85/86 - 182; 86/87 - 18, 222SK; 87/88 - 159; 90/91 - 447
- Panini: 87/88 - 108
- Post: 82/83 - 199
- Pro Set: 90/91 - 197
- Topps: 75/76 - 146; 76/77 - 154; 77/78 - 256; 78/79 - 154; 79/80 - 78; 80/81 - 248; 81/82 EN - 97; 86/87 - 18; 87/88 - 159

Gretzky, Brent
- Donruss: 93/94 - 318
- Parkhurst: 93/94 - 248, 248EI, CC14; 94/95 - 218, 295, 218EI, 295EI
- Upper Deck: 93/94 - 354

Gretzky, Wayne
- Action Packed: 89/90 - 1
- Bowman: 90/91 - 143; 91/92 - P/C, 173, 176 92/93 - 1, 207
- Donruss: 93/94 - 152, 395, 10ES, 4IK, K/PM, K/SP
- Derniere: 72/84 - 160
- Esso: 88/89 - 15
- Fleer: 92/93 - 83, 10AS, 6AW; 93/94 - 114, 3G, 15AS, 116PP, 3PL, 2PM, 2SC
- Funmate: 83/84 - 39
- Hockey Wit: 93/94 - 99
- Humpty Dumpty: 92/93 - 10(l)
- Kraft: 86/87 - 14, 14P; 1990 - 59; 90/91 - 15, 67; 1993 - 14; 93/94 - 38, 57
- Leaf: 93/94 - 304, 6AS, 4SS
- McDonald's: 82/83 - 20, 22; 91/92 - McH1, Mc17
- O-Pee-Chee: 79/80 - 18; 80/81 - 3, 87, 182, 250, 7PO; 81/82 - 106, 125, 126, 383, 384, 392, 209SK, 252SK, 264SK; 82/83 - 1, 99, 106, 107, 235, 237, 240, 242, 243, 97SK, 98SK, 162SK, 256SK, 257SK, 258SK, 259SK; 83/84 - 22, 29, 203, 204, 212, 215, 216, 217, 7SK, 89SK, 90SK, 161SK, 301SK, 307SK, 325SK, 326SK; 84/85 - 208, 243, 357, 373, 374, 380, 381, 382, 383, 388, 63SK, 138SK, 226SK, 229SK, 255SK, 256SK; 85/86 - 120, 257, 258, 259, G/BB, 5SK, 54SK, 120SK, 198SK, 202SK, 222SK; 86/87 - 3, 259, 260, F/BB, 72SK, 115SK, 183SK, 191SK, 195SK; 87/88 - 53, 13HL, A/BB, 86SK, 115SK, 174SK, 180SK, 181SK; 88/89 - 120, 11NS, B/BB, 1SK, 121SK, 224SK; 89/90 - 156, 320, 325, E/BB, 154SK, 166SK, 209SK, 30FS; 90/91 - 1, 2, 3, 120, 199, 522, D/BB, 38PM; 91/92 - 201, 224, 257, 258, 321, 520, 522, 524, 3PM; 92/93 - 15, 220, 12AN; 93/94 - 330, 380, 1BG, 200SC, 200FD
- Panini: 87/88 - 192, 261, 371, 373, 389; 88/89 - 58, 181, 193; 89/90 - 87, 179, 374; 90/91 - 242, 332; 91/92 - 78, 327; 92/93 - 64E, 287E, 64F, 287F; 93/94 - R(E), R(F)
- Parkhurst: 91/92 - 73E, 207E, 222E, 429E, 465, 73F, 207F, 222F, 429F, 433; 92/93 - 65, 509, 65EI, 509EI; 93/94 - 99, 99EI, G1, W1, D1;

Gretzky, Wayne (cont.)
- Parkhurst: 94/95 - 103, 306, 103EI, 306EI, H11, R11, C11, V62
- Post: 82/83 - 86
- Pro Set: 90/91 - 118, 340, 388, 394, 703, P2; 91/92 - AC4, 101E, 285E, 324E, CC5E, 574E, 101F, 285F, 324F, PC4PT, 52PT, 11PK, 574F; 92/93 - 66, 246, 6TL
- 7-Eleven: 84/85 - 15
- Score: 90/91 - 1A/PC, 1B/PC, 1A, 1C, 321A, 321C, 336A, 336C, 338A, 338C, 347A, 347C, 352A, 352C, 353A, 353C, 361A, 361C, 110T, 1HR; 91 - 1PC; 91/92 - 100A, 346A, 405A, 406A, 413A, 422A, 427A, 434A, 100B, 295B, 296B, 303B, 312B, 317B, 324B, 376B, 100C, 295C, 296C, 303C, 312C, 317C, 324C, 376C, 100PC, B-11E, B-11F; 92/93 - 296C, 303C, 312C, 317C, 324C, 376C, 2HC, 100PNE, 100PNF, 200PNC, 200PNA; 92/93 - 1C, 412C, 426C, 525C, 1A, 412A, 426A, 525A, 5CTP, 5ATP; 93/94 - 300C, 300A, 45PNC, 45PNA, 11DT, 45CAS, 45AAS, 9FR
- Season's: 92/93 - 9
- Sega: 92/93 - 63
- Topps: 79/80 - 18; 80/81 - 3, 87, 182, 250; 81/82 - 16, 52; 82/83 - 97SK, 98SK, 162SK, 256SK, 257SK, 258SK, 259SK; 83/84 - 7SK, 89SK, 90SK, 161SK, 301SK, 307SK, 325SK, 326SK; 84/85 - 51, 154; 85/86 - 120, G/BB, 2SK; 86/87 - 3, F/BB, 3SK; 87/88 - 53, A/BB, 5SK; 88/89 - 120, B/BB, 8SK; 89/90 - 156, E/BB, 11SK; 90/91 - 1, 2, 3, 120, 199, 12SL, D/BB; 91/92 - 224, 257, 258, 321, 520, 522, 524, 10SL, 1SC, 5SCM, 91/92 - 6SCM; 92/93 - 1, 123, 1GS, 123GS, 18SC, 256SC; 93/94 - 330(II), 380C, 7BG, 200SC, 200FD, 8MP, 17AS, 1SCF
- Upper Deck: 90/91 - P/C, S/G (3), 54E, 54F, 205E, 205F, 476E, 476F, 545E, 545F, 241PC; 91/92 - 13E, 38E, 437E, 621E, AW1E, BBE, 13F, 38F, 437F, 621F, AW1F, BBF; 92/93 - 25, 33, 435, 621, 10-18HH, W1, WJG10, G5, 25AS; 93/94 - 99

- Vachon Foods: 83/84 - 26

Grieve, Brent
- Parkhurst: 94/95 - 79, 79EI

Griffis, Si
- Hall of Fame: 83 - 155, L5P; 87 - 155

Griffiths, Tuffy
- World Wide Gum: 36/37 - 132

Grimson, Stu
- Donruss: 93/94 - 15
- Fleer: 93/94 - 1PP
- Kraft: 93/94 - 10
- Leaf: 93/94 - 330
- O-Pee-Chee: 93/94 - 357
- Parkhurst: 93/94 - 277, 277EI; 94/95 - 3, 3EI
- Topps: 93/94 - 357
- Upper Deck: 91/92 - 416E, 416F

Grisdale, John
- O-Pee-Chee: 75/76 - 339; 77/78 - 277; 78/79 - 318

Gronman, Tuomas
- Parkhurst: 93/94 - 523, 523EI
- Upper Deck: 91/92 - 677E, 677F; 93/94 - 270

Gronvall, Janne
- Upper Deck: 91/92 - 672E, 672F

Grosso, Don
- Beehive: 34/44 - 102
- O-Pee-Chee: 40/41 - 128

Gryp, Bob
- Loblaws: 74/75 - 314
- O-Pee-Chee: 75/76 - 348

Guay, Paul
- O-Pee-Chee: 84/85 - 160

Guerin, Bill
- Donruss: 93/94 - 186
- Fleer: 92/93 - 338
- Leaf: 93/94 - 7
- O-Pee-Chee: 92/93 - 308, 120PM; 93/94 - 421
- Parkhurst: 91/92 - 453E; 92/93 - 97, 97EI; 93/94 - 382, 382EI; 94/95 - 127, 127EI
- Pro-Set: 92/93 - 230
- Score: 92/93 - 470C, 470A; 93/94 - 395C, 395A
- Topps: 92/93 - 516, 516GS, 17SC; 93/94 - 421SC, 467SC, 467FD
- Upper Deck: 92/93 - 411

Guevremont, Jocelyn
- Eddie Sargent: 72/73 - 222
- Lipton Soup: 74/75 - 48
- Loblaws: 74/75 - 294
- O-Pee-Chee: 71/72 - 232; 72/73 - 37; 73/74 - 143; 74/75 - 122; 75/76 - 216; 76/77 - 108; 77/78 - 242; 78/79 - 94; 79/80 - 381
- Topps: 72/73 - 75; 73/74 - 142; 74/75 - 122; 75/76 - 216; 76/77 - 108; 77/78 - 242; 78/79 - 94
- Toronto Sun: 71/72 - 2

Guidolin, Aldo
- Beehive: 34/44 - 17, 45/63 - 99, 319
- Parkhurst: 51/52 - 42, 53/54 - 66
- Topps: 74/75 - 34
- O-Pee-Chee: 74/75 - 34

Gusarov, Alexei
- Bowman: 91/92 - 145
- Fleer: 92/93 - 173; 93/94 - 420PP
- O-Pee-Chee: 91/92 - 355; 92/93 - 389; 93/94 - 293
- Panini: 91/92 - 260; 92/93 - 215E, 215F
- Parkhurst: 91/92 - 364E, 364F; 93/94 - 441, 441EI
- Pro Set: 91/92 - 207E, 207F, 221PT; 92/93 - 147
- Score: 91/92 - 230PNE, 230PNF, 326A; 91/92 - 356B, 356C; 92/93 - 264C, 264A, 161PNC, 161PNA; 93/94 - 260C, 260A
- Topps: 91/92 - 355, 330SC; 92/93 - 451SC; 93/94 - 293, 424SC, 424FD
- Upper Deck: 91/92 - 365E, 365F; 92/93 - 127; 93/94 - 362

Gustafsson, Bengt-ake
- O-Pee-Chee: 80/81 - 222; 81/82 - 353; 82/83 - 364, 157SK; 83/84 - 370; 84/85 - 198, 130SK; 88/89 - 151; 91/92 - 2S
- Panini: 88/89 - 371
- Post: 82/83 - 311
- Topps: 80/81 - 222; 82/83 - 157SK; 84/85 - 144; 88/89 - 151

Guy, Kevan
- Pro Set: 90/91 - 545

Habscheid, Marc
- Bowman: 90/91 - 228
- O-Pee-Chee: 89/90 - 151, 198SK; 90/91 - 342; 91/92 - 250
- Panini: 90/91 - 204; 91/92 - 138
- Pro Set: 90/91 - 437; 91/92 - 365E, 365F
- Score: 90 - 24T; 91 - 33T; 91/92 - 583B, 583C; 92/93 - 546C, 546A
- Topps: 89/90 - 151; 90/91 - 342; 91/92 - 250
- Upper Deck: 90/91 - 374E, 374F

Hackett, Jeff (Goalie)
- Bowman: 91/92 - 219; 92/93 - 348
- Donruss: 93/94 - 61
- Fleer: 92/93 - 195; 93/94 - 312PP
- Leaf: 93/94 - 319
- O-Pee-Chee: 90/91 - 39PM; 91/92 - 382, 108PM; 92/93 - 218
- Panini: 89/90 - 276; 91/92 - 240; 92/93 - 123E, 123F

Hackett, Jeff (Goalie) (cont.)
Parkhurst: 92/93 - 162, 162EI; 93/94 - 312, 312EI
Pro Set: 90/91 - 624; 91/92 - 331E, 331F, 226PT; 92/93 - 171
Score: 90/91 - 388A, 388C; 91 - 92T; 91/92 - 367A, 326B, 326C, 642B, 642C, 119PNE, 119PNF; 92/93 - 82C, 82A, 105PNC, 105PNA; 93/94 - 38C, 38A
Topps: 91/92 - 382; 92/93 - 185, 185GS, 108SC; 93/94 - 326SC, 326FD
Upper Deck: 91/92 - 58E, 58F; 92/93 - 308

Hadfield, Vic
Beehive: 45/63 - 320; 64/67 - 129
Coca-Cola: 64/65 - 79; 65/66 - 79
Colgate: 70/71 - 45
Dom. Choc.: 70/71 - 87
Esso: 70/71 - 151
Eddie Sargent: 70/71 - 126; 72/73 - 151
Loblaws: 74/75 - 243
O-Pee-Chee: 68/69 - 171; 69/70 - 38; 70/71 - 62; 71/72 - 9; 72/73 - 31; 73/74 - 108; 74/75 - 65; 75/76 - 165; 76/77 - 226
Shirriff: 61/62 - 97; 68/69 - G13
Topps: 62/63 - 60; 63/64 - 54; 64/65 - 62; 65/66 - 27; 66/67 - 86; 66/67 US - 19; 67/68 - 88; 68/69 - 74; 69/70 - 38; 70/71 - 62; 71/72 - 9; 72/73 - 110, 132; 73/74 - 181; 74/75 - 65; 75/76 - 165; 76/77 - 226
Toronto Star: 57/67 - 106, 125
Toronto Sun: 71/72 - 174
Ultimate: 92 - 21(OSE), 21(OSF)

Hagman, Matti
O-Pee-Chee: 81/82 - 113, 213SK; 82/83 - 108, 103SK
PepsiCo: 80/81 - 26
Post: 82/83 - 87
Topps: 82/83 - 103SK

Hainsworth, George (Goalie)
Anonymous: 33/34 - 13
Beehive: 34/44 - 321
Can. Chew. Gum: 33/34 - 15, 28
Hall of Fame: 83 - 187, J7P; 87 - 187
La Presse: 27/32 - 5
Parkhurst: 55/56 - 59
Quaker Oats: 55/56 - 59

Hajt, Bill
O-Pee-Chee: 75/76 - 233; 76/77 - 128; 77/78 - 27; 78/79 - 108; 79/80 - 221; 80/81 - 337; 83/84 - 64; 84/85 - 21, 214SK; 85/86 - 119, 176SK; 86/87 - 52
Panini: 87/88 - 26
Post: 82/83 - 20
Topps: 75/76 - 233; 76/77 - 128; 77/78 - 27; 78/79 - 108; 79/80 - 221; 84/85 - 17; 85/86 - 119; 86/87 - 52

Hakansson, Anders
O-Pee-Chee: 84/85 - 85

Hakansson, Mikael
Parkhurst: 93/94 - 539, 539EI

Hale, Larry
Eddie Sargent: 70/71 - 155
Esso: 70/71 - 169
Topps: 72/73 - 44
Toronto Sun: 71/72 - 196
O-Pee-Chee: 72/73 - 53

Halfnight, Ashlin
Donruss: 93/94 - 8JCA

Halkidis, Bob
Pro-Set: 92/93 - 190

Hall, Glenn (Goalie)
Beehive: 45/63 - 100, 176; 64/67 - 35
Chex: 63/65 - 2
Coca-Cola: 64/65 -22; 65/66 - 21
El Producto: 62/63 - 2LS
Esso: 70/71 - 203
Eddie Sargent: 62/63 - 4
Hall of Fame: 83 - 114, H8P; 87 - 114

Hall, Glenn (Goalie) (cont.)
O-Pee-Chee: 68/69 - 111, 215, 13PS; 69/70 - 12, 211, 11ST; 70/71 - 210, 27DE
Parkhurst: 93/94 - 46ML, 141ML, 152ML,159ML
Post: 66/67 - 1L, 1S
Shirriff: 60/61 - 61; 61/62 - 29; 62/63 - 49; 68/69 - L5
Topps: 57/58 - 20; 58/59 - 13; 59/60 - 32; 60/61 - 25, 19ST; 61/62 - 32; 62/63 - 24, 10HB; 63/64 - 23; 64/65 - 12, 110;65/66 - 55; 66/67 - 54, 126;67/68 - 129; 68/69 - 111; 69/70 - 12
Toronto Star: 57/67 - 52, 72, 104, 127; 58/67 - 16, 74, 92; 63/64 - 4; 64/65 - 7

Hall, Joe
Hall of Fame: 83 - 97, , G6P; ; 87 - 97
Imperial Tobacco: 10/11 - 2L; 11/12 - 2; 12/13 - 16

Hall, Murray
Beehive: 45/63 - 101; 64/67 - 36, 73
Eddie Sargent: 70/71 - 224; 71/72 - 211; 72/73 - 212
Esso: 70/71 - 239
O-Pee-Chee: 70/71 - 118; 71/72 - 109; 72/73 - 294
Topps: 62/63 - 43; 66/67 - 105; 70/71 - 118; 71/72 - 109
Toronto Sun: 71/72 - 279

Haller, Kevin
Bowman: 91/92 - 28; 92/93 - 301
Donruss: 93/94 - 168
Fleer: 92/93 - 327; 93/94 - 370PP
Leaf: 93/94 - 223
O-Pee-Chee: 91/92 - 473; 92/93 - 290; 93/94 - 339, 53SC, 53FD
Parkhurst: 93/94 - 376, 376EI; 94/95 - 120, 120EI
Pro Set: 91/92 - 525E, 525F, 250PT
Score: 91/92 - 386A, 276B, 276C, 307PNE, 307PNF; 92/93 - 159C, 159A, 211PNC, 211PNA; 93/94 - 268C, 268A
Topps: 91/92 - 473, 382SC; 92/93 - 445, 445GS, 38SC; 93/94 - 339, 53SC, 53FD
Upper Deck: 91/92 - 192E, 192F; 92/93 - 479; 93/94 - 333

Hallin, Mats
O-Pee-Chee: 83/84 - 8, 184SK
Topps: 83/84 - 184SK

Halward, Doug
Kraft: 86/87 - 64, 64P
O-Pee-Chee: 76/77 - 306; 78/79 - 392; 80/81 - 207; 81/82 - 335; 83/84 - 351, 278SK; 84/85 - 320, 278SK; 85/86 - 189, 243SK; 86/87 - 248, 97SK; 88/89 - 113
Post: 82/83 - 295
Topps: 80/81 - 207; 83/84 - 278SK; 88/89 - 113
Vachon Foods: 83/84 - 108

Hamel, Gilles
O-Pee-Chee: 84/85 - 22; 85/86 - 185SK; 87/88 - 218, 253SK
Panini: 87/88 - 366

Hamel, Jean
Loblaws: 74/75 - 97
O-Pee-Chee: 74/75 - 383; 75/76 - 257; 76/77 - 340; 77/78 - 348; 78/79 - 281; 79/80 - 262; 81/82 - 97; 84/85 - 263, 158SK
Topps: 75/76 - 257; 79/80 - 262
Vachon Foods: 83/84 - 45

Hamel, Pierre (Goalie)
O-Pee-Chee: 80/81 - 205; 81/82 - 365, 143SK
PepsiCo: 80/81 - 128
Topps: 80/81 - 205; 81/82 - 143SK

Hamill, Red
Beehive: 34/44 - 18; 45/63 - 102

Hamilton, Al (Allan)
Eddie Sargent: 70/71 - 22
Esso: 70/71 - 26
Dom. Choc.: 70/71 - 16

Hamilton, Al (Allan) (cont.)
O-Pee-Chee: 68/69 - 70; 69/70 - 192; 71/72 - 49; 79/80 - 355
Topps: 71/72 - 49
Toronto Sun: 71/72 - 28

Hamilton, Reg
Beehive: 34/44 - 322
O-Pee-Chee: 37/38 - 137; 39/40 - 1; 40/41 - 119
Quaker Oats: 38/39 - 22

Hammarstrom, Inge
Loblaws: 74/75 - 277
O-Pee-Chee: 74/75 - 88; 75/76 - 168; 76/77 - 358; 77/78 - 320; 78/79 - 53
Topps: 74/75 - 88; 75/76 - 168; 78/79 - 53

Hammond, Ken
Parkhurst: 92/93 - 358, 358EI
Pro Set: 91/92 - 484E, 484F; 92/93 - PV4
Score: 91 - 97T; 91/92 - 647B, 647C

Hampson, Ted
Beehive: 45/63 - 321, 404; 64/67 - 74
Colgate: 70/71 - 9
Dom. Choc.: 70/71 - 26
Eddie Sargent: 70/71 - 137
Esso: 70/71 - 40
O-Pee-Chee: 68/69 - 85; 69/70 - 86, 12ST, 7QS; 70/71 - 190; 71/72 - 101
Parkhurst: 59/60 - 34
Shirriff: 60/61 - 98; 61/62 - 92; 68/69 - H3
Topps: 61/62 - 59; 62/63 - 55; 67/68 - 108; 68/69 - 85; 69/70 - 86; 71/72 - 101
Toronto Sun: 71/72 - 133
York: 63/64 - 52

Hampton, Rick
Loblaws: 74/75 - 59
O-Pee-Chee: 74/75 - 329; 75/76 - 65; 76/77 - 113; 77/78 - 63; 78/79 - 174; 79/80 - 330
Panini: 79 - 54
Topps: 75/76 - 65; 76/77 - 113; 77/78 - 63; 78/79 - 174

Hamr, Radek
Leaf: 93/94 - 265
Parkhurst: 93/94 - 143, 143EI
Score: 93/94 - 476C, 476A
Upper Deck: 93/94 - 34

Hamrlik, Roman
Donruss: 93/94 - 327
Fleer: 92/93 - 201, 4UI; 93/94 - 108, 231PP
Leaf: 93/94 - 151
O-Pee-Chee: 92/93 - 46PM; 93/94 - 281, 323, 2HR, 75SC, 57FD
Parkhurst: 92/93 - 173, 443, 173EI, 443EI; 93/94 - 190, 190EI, F2; 94/95 - V53
Score: 92/93 - 408PNC, 408PNA, 2TR; 93/94 - 131C, 131A
Sega: 93/94 - 128
Topps: 93/94 - 281, 323, 2PF, 75SC, 75FD
Upper Deck: 92/93 - 555, 631, ER11, CC8; 93/94 - 158

Hangsleben, Al (Alan)
O-Pee-Chee: 79/80 - 307; 81/82 - 354, 197SK

Hanley, Rick
Hall of Fame: 87 - 251

Hanlon, Glen (Goalie)
O-Pee-Chee: 79/80 - 337; 80/81 - 141, 22PO; 81/82 - 336, 245SK; 84/85 - 142, 98SK; 85/86 - 149, 87SK; 87/88 - 89, 14HL, 109SK; 88/89 - 150; 89/90 - 144; 90/91 - 266
Panini: 87/88 - 238; 88/89 - 36; 89/90 - 65; 90/91 - 203
Pro Set: 90/91 - 72
Score: 90/91 - 228A, 288C
Topps: 80/81 - 141; 84/85 - 106; 85/86 - 149; 87/88 - 89; 88/89 - 150; 89/90 - 144; 90/91 - 266
Upper Deck: 90/91 - 395E, 395F

Hanna, John
Beehive: 45/63 - 245; 64/67 - 104
Topps: 58/59 - 7; 59/60 - 31
Shirriff: 60/61 - 85

Hannan, David (Dave)
- Bowman: 91/92 - 155
- O-Pee-Chee: 83/84 - 281; 89/90 - 257; 90/91 - 449; 91/92 - 360; 93/94 - 47SC, 47FD
- Panini: 87/88 - 154
- Pro Set: 90/91 - 535
- Score: 91/92 - 241B, 241C, 413PNE, 413PNF; 92/93 - 538C, 538A
- Topps: 91/92 - 360, 220SC; 93/94 - 47SC, 47FD
- Upper Deck: 91/92 - 312E, 312F

Hannigan, Gord
- Beehive: 45/63 - 405
- Parkhurst: 52/53 - 54; 53/54 - 3; 54/55 - 27
- Quaker Oats: 45/54 - 74

Hannigan, Pat
- Shirriff: 61/62 - 83; 68/69 - J12
- Topps: 61/62 - 58; 62/63 - 64

Hansen, Rick
- Pro-Set: 91/92 - 296PT

Harbaruk, Nick
- Eddie Sargent: 70/71 - 172; 72/73 - 171
- Esso: 70/71 - 185
- O-Pee-Chee: 71/72 - 191; 72/73 - 106
- Toronto Sun: 71/72 - 215

Hardy, Joe
- Esso: 70/71 - 41

Hardy, Mark
- Fleer: 92/93 - 354
- O-Pee-Chee: 82/83 - 155; 83/84 - 155; 84/85 - 86, 272SK; 85/86 - 234SK; 89/90 - 252; 91/92 - 406
- Panini: 87/88 - 275
- Post: 82/83 - 117
- Pro Set: 90/91 - 489; 91/92 - 442E, 442F
- Score: 90 - 104T; 91/92 - 453B, 453C, 420PNE, 420PNF; 92/93 - 247C, 247A, 220PNC, 220PNA; 93/94 - 415C, 415A
- Topps: 91/92 - 406, 414SC, 414FD
- Upper Deck: 90/91 - 416E, 416F

Harlock, David
- Donruss: 93/94 - 496
- Fleer: 93/94 - 481PP
- Parkhurst: 94/95 - 233, 233EI
- Upper Deck: 90/91 - 470E, 470F

Harkins, Todd
- Upper Deck: 93/94 - 80

Harmon, Glen
- Beehive: 45/63 - 246
- CKAC Radio: 43/47 - 54, 55
- Quaker Oats: 45/54 - 20A, 20B, 20C

Harper, Terry
- Beehive: 45/63 - 247; 64/67 - 105A, 105B
- Chex: 63/65 - 28
- Coca-Cola: 64/65 - 60; 65/66 - 60
- Dom. Choc.: 70/71 - 76
- Eddie Sargent: 70/71 - 111; 72/73 - 96
- Esso: 70/71 - 131
- Loblaws: 74/75 - 132
- O-Pee-Chee: 68/69 - 57; 69/70 - 164; 70/71 - 53; 71/72 - 59; 72/73 - 172; 73/74 - 80; 74/75 - 55; 75/76 - 255; 76/77 - 262; 77/78 - 16; 78/79 - 214
- Parkhurst: 63/64 - 32, 91
- Post: 68/69 - 5
- Shirriff: 68/69 - F12
- Topps: 64/65 - 3; 65/66 - 68; 66/67 - 68; 67/68 - 6; 68/69 - 57; 70/71 - 53; 71/72 - 59; 72/73 - 119; 73/74 - 80; 74/75 - 55; 75/76 - 255; 76/77 - 262; 77/78 - 16; 78/79 - 214
- Toronto Sun: 71/72 - 150
- York: 63/64 - 31

Harris, Billy
- Coca Cola: 65/66 - 46
- Eddie Sargent: 72/73 - 131
- Lipton Soup: 74/75 - 35
- Loblaws: 74/75 - 183

Harris, Billy (cont.)
- O-Pee-Chee: 73/74 - 130; 74/75 - 228; 75/76 - 242; 76/77 - 252; 77/78 - 126; 78/79 - 182; 79/80 - 115; 80/81 - 46; 81/82 - 144, 242SK; 82/83 - 322; 83/84 - 333, 27SK
- Parkhurst: 93/94 - PR46, 129ML
- Topps: 73/74 - 130; 74/75 - 228; 75/76 - 242; 76/77 - 252; 77/78 - 126; 78/79 - 182; 79/80 - 115; 80/81 - 46; 81/82 WN - 96
- Toronto Star: 58/67 - 37
- Ultimate: 92 - 35(OSE), 35(OSF)
- Vachon Foods: 83/84 - 89

Harris, Ron
- Eddie Sargent: 70/71 - 52
- Esso: 70/71 - 79
- Loblaws: 74/75 - 203
- O-Pee-Chee: 68/69 - 27; 69/70 - 64; 70/71 - 23; 71/72 - 70; 72/73 - 5; 74/75 - 276
- Topps: 68/69 - 27; 70/71 - 23; 72/73 - 138
- Toronto Sun: 71/72 - 94

Harris, Smokey
- Maple Crispette: 24/25 - 7
- Wm. Paterson: 24/25 - 22

Harris, Ted
- Bauer: 68/69 - 10
- Bazooka: 71/72 - 9
- Beehive: 64/67 - 106
- Coca-Cola: 64/65 - 61; 65/66 - 61
- Dom. Choc.: 70/71 - 66
- Eddie Sargent: 70/71 - 82; 72/73 - 109
- Esso: 70/71 - 114
- O-Pee-Chee: 68/69 - 162; 69/70 - 2, 219; 70/71 - 166; 71/72 - 32; 72/73 - 118; 73/74 - 154
- Post: 68/69 - 6
- Shirriff: 68/69 - F3
- Topps: 65/66 - 5; 66/67 - 69; 66/67 US - 41; 67/68 - 10; 69/70 - 2; 71/72 - 32; 72/73 - 23; 73/74 - 14
- Toronto Sun: 71/72 - 134

Harris, William (Billy)
- Beehive: 45/63 - 406; 64/67 - 75, 163A, 163B
- Chex: 63/65 - 45
- Coca-Cola: 65/66 - 46
- O-Pee-Chee: 68/69 - 80
- Parkhurst: 55/56 - 20; 57/58 TOR - 15; 58/59 - 4; 59/60 - 9; 60/61 - 15; 61/62 - 15; 62/63 - 1; 63/64 - 11, 71
- Quaker Oats: 55/56 - 20
- Shirriff: 60/61 - 8; 61/62 - 54; 62/63 - 13; 68/69 H4
- Topps: 64/65 - 27; 65/66 - 53; 68/69 - 80
- Toronto Star: 58/67 - 24; 64/65 - 40
- Ultimate: 92 - 35OS
- York: 60/61 - 25; 61/62 - 15; 62/63 - 26; 63/64 - 10

Harrison, Ed
- Beehive: 45/63 - 27

Harrison, Jim
- Eddie Sargent: 70/71 - 194
- Esso: 70/71 - 223
- O-Pee-Chee: 70/71 - 220; 71/72 - 10; 72/73 - 292, 20CS; 76/77 - 183; 77/78 - 243
- Topps: 77/78 - 243
- Toronto Sun: 71/72 - 259

Harrison, Paul (Goalie)
- O-Pee-Chee: 78/79 - 123; 80/81 - 391
- Topps: 78/79 - 123

Hart, Cecil
- World Wide Gum: 36/37 - 97

Hart, Gerry
- Eddie Sargent: 72/73 - 138
- Loblaws: 74/75 - 184
- O-Pee-Chee: 72/73 - 139; 73/74 - 34; 74/75 - 199; 75/76 - 18; 76/77 - 77; 77/78 - 162; 78/79 - 77; 79/80 - 365; 80/81 - 349

Hart, Gerry (cont.)
- Topps: 72/73 - 92; 73/74 - 34; 74/75 - 199; 75/76 - 18; 76/77 - 77; 77/78 - 162; 78/79 - 77
- Toronto Sun: 71/72 - 95

Hart, Gizzy
- La Presse: 27/32 - 11

Hartje, Todd
- Upper Deck: 91/92 - 568E, 568F

Hartman, Mike
- Panini: 90/91 - 32
- Parkhurst: 92/93 - 407, 407EI
- O-Pee-Chee: 90/91 - 16; 91/92 - 363
- Pro Set: 90/91 - 414; 91/92 - 519E, 519F
- Score: 91/92 - 454B, 454C
- Topps: 90/91 - 16; 91/92 - 363, 341SC; 92/93 - 518, 518GS, 497SC

Hartsburg, Craig
- Funmate: 83/84 - 61
- McDonald's: 82/83 - 30
- O-Pee-Chee: 80/81 - 317; 81/82 - 162, 91SK; 82/83 - 167, 192SK; 83/84 - 172, 117SK; 84/85 - 98; 85/86 - 242; 86/87 - 12, 173SK; 87/88 - 165, 54SK; 88/89 - 159, 199SK
- Panini: 87/88 - 290; 88/89 - 86
- Topps: 81/82 WN - 106; 82/83 - 192SK; 83/84 - 117SK; 86/87 - 12; 87/88 - 165; 88/89 - 159

Harvey, Doug
- Beehive: 45/63 - 248, 322; 64/67 - 130
- CKAC Radio: 43/47 - 56
- Hall of Fame: 83 - 219, O9P; 87 - 219
- La Patrie: 51/54 - 6
- O-Pee-Chee: 68/69 - 1, 14PS
- Parkhurst: 51/52 - 10; 52/53 - 14; 53/54 - 26; 54/55 - 14; 55/56 - 45; 57/58 MON - 1; 58/59 - 49; 59/60 - 8; 60/61 - 48; 92/93 - PR14; 93/94 - PR39, 67ML, 136ML, 148ML
- Quaker Oats: 45/65 - 21A, 21B; 55/56 - 45
- Shirriff: 60/61 - 26; 61/62 - 81; 62/63 - 60; 62/63 - 45
- Topps: 60/61 - 10ST; 61/62 - 45; 63/64 - 47
- Toronto Star: 57/67 - 73; 58/67 - 25, 66; 63/64 - 27
- Ultimate: 92 - 12(OSE), 12(OSF)
- York: 60/61 - 7

Harvey, Fred (Buster)
- Esso: 70/71 - 115
- Loblaws: 74/75 - 6
- O-Pee-Chee: 72/73 - 246; 73/74 - 190; 74/75 - 319; 75/76 - 298; 76/77 - 212; 77/78 - 122
- Topps: 73/74 - 78; 75/76 - 298; 76/77 - 212; 77/78 - 122
- Toronto Sun: 71/72 - 135

Harvey, Todd
- Donruss: 93/94 - 15JCC
- Parkhurst: 93/94 - 513, 513EI
- Upper Deck: 93/94 - 535

Hasek, Dominik (Goalie)
- Fleer: 93/94 - 297PP
- Leaf: 93/94 - 256
- O-Pee-Chee: 92/93 - 301, 50PM; 93/94 - 320, 463, 178SC, 178FD
- Panini: 92/93 - 292E, 292F
- Parkhurst: 91/92 - 263E, 449E, 263F, 449F; 94/95 - 24, 24EI, V1
- Pro Set: 91/92 - 529E, 529F, 252PT
- Score: 91/92 - 316A, 346B, 346C; 92/93 - 373C, 373A, 93/94 - 281C, 281A
- Topps: 92/93 - 136, 136GS, 107SC; 93/94 - 320(II), 463C, 178SC, 178FD
- Upper Deck: 91/92 - 335E, E14(E), 335F, E14(F); 92/93 - 92, 366, 506, E3, AR6, ERT3; 93/94 - 387

Hassard, Bob
- Beehive: 45/63 - 407
- Parkhurst: 52/53 - 105; 53/54 - 4
- Quaker Oats: 45/54 - 75

Hatcher, Derian
  Bowman: 92/93 - 365
  Donruss: 93/94 - 77
  Fleer: 92/93 - 319; 93/94 - 139, 61PP
  Leaf: 93/94 - 212
  O-Pee-Chee: 91/92 - 143PM; 92/93 - 123; 93/94 - 520
  Panini: 92/93 - H(E), H(F)93/94 - 274E, 274F
  Parkhurst: 91/92 - 75E, 75F; 92/93 - 72, 72EI; 93/94 - 46, 46EI, V30
  Pro Set: 91/92 - 543E, 543F, 258PT; 92/93 - 75; 92/93 - 204
  Score: 90/91 - 430A, 430C; 91 - 106T; 91/92 - 656E, 656C, 328PNE, 328PNF; 92/93 - 51C, 51A, 34PNC, 34PNA; 93/94 - 168C, 168A
  Topps: 92/93 - 405, 405GS, 414SC; 93/94 - 520, 494SC, 494FD
  Upper Deck: 90/91 - 359E, 546E, 359F, 546F; 92/93 - 287; 93/94 - 204

Hatcher, Kevin
  Bowman: 90/91 - 70; 91/92 - 296; 92/93 - 230, 271
  Donruss: 93/94 - 369
  Fleer: 92/93 - 231; 93/94 - 118, 261PP
  Hockey Wit: 93/94 - 17
  Humpty Dumpty: 92/93 - 11(I)
  Gillette: 91/92 - 36
  Kellogg's: 92 - 7
  Kraft: 91/92 - 20; 93/94 - 37
  Leaf: 93/94 - 34
  O-Pee-Chee: 87/88 - 68; 88/89 - 86; 89/90 - 146; 90/91 - 147; 91/92 - 310, 88PM; 92/93 - 145; 93/94 - 435, 153SC, 153FD
  Panini: 87/88 - 179; 88/89 - 365; 89/90 - 347; 90/91 - 167; 91/92 - 198; 92/93 - 167E, 167F; 93/94 - C(E), C(F)
  Parkhurst: 91/92 - 191E, 191F; 92/93 - 198, 198EI; 93/94 - 221, 221EI; 94/95 - V54
  Pro Set: 90/91 - 311, 376; 91/92 - 249E, 316E, 249F, 316F, 127PT, 29PK
  Score: 90/91 - 90A, 90C, 42HR; 91/92 - 20A, 340A, 20B, 20C, 370B, 370C, 131PNE, 131PNF; 92/93 - 273C, 439C, 273A, 439A, 11PNC, 11PNA, 13USG; 93/94 - 136C, 136A, 23FR
  Season's: 92/93 - 48
  Sega: 93/94 - 151
  Topps: 87/88 - 68; 88/89 - 86; 89/90 - 146; 90/91 - 147; 91/92 - 310, 16SL, 140SC; 92/93 - 149, 149GS, 301SC; 93/94 - 435PM, 153SC, 153FD
  Upper Deck: 90/91 - 109E, 486E, 511E, 109F, 486F, 511F; 91/92 - 361E, 361F, 511E; 92/93 - 198; 93/94 - 140

Hauer, Brett
  Fleer: 93/94 - 504PP
  Topps: 93/94 - 20US

Hawerchuk, Dale
  Bowman: 90/91 - 129; 91/92 - 31; 92/93 - 308
  Cel.Watch: 1988 - CW7
  Donruss: 93/94 - 35
  Derniere: 72/84 - 178
  Esso: 83/84 - 9E, 9F; 88/89 - 16
  Fleer: 92/93 - 15; 93/94 - 149, 29PP
  Frito-Lay: 88/89 - 17
  Funmate: 83/84 - 144
  Hockey Wit: 93/94 - 22
  Kellogg's: 84 - 4
  Kraft: 86/87 - 75, 75P; 1990 - 50; 90/91 - 16; 91/92 - 36
  Leaf: 93/94 - 71
  O-Pee-Chee: 82/83 - 3, 374, 380, 381, 204SK, 249SK; 83/84 - 377, 385, 282SK; 84/85 - 339, 393, 284SK, 285SK; 85/86 - 109, 248SK; 86/87 - 74, 104SK; 87/88 - 149, I/BB, 255SK; 88/89 - 65, 12NS, K/BB, 143SK; 89/90 - 122, 134SK; 90/91 - 141, 40PM; 91/92 - 65, 1PM; 92/93 - 212; 93/94 - 7, 11HR, 220SC, 220FD

Hawerchuk, Dale (cont.)
  Panini: 87/88 - 363; 88/89 - 155; 89/90 - 162; 90/91 - 317; 91/92 - 296; 92/93 - 247E, 247F; 93/94 - 102E, 102F
  Parkhurst: 91/92 - 18E, 216E, 18F, 216F; 92/93 - 11, 11EI; 93/94 - 23, 23EI; 94/95 - 29, 29EI
  Post: 82/83 - 326
  Pro Set: 90/91 - 330, 415; 91/92 - 24E, 24F, 11PT; 92/93 - 12
  Score: 90 - 2T; 90/91 - 50A, 50C, 22HR; 91/92 - 259A, 376A, 266B, 266C, 479B, 479C, 80PNE, 80PNF; 92/93 - 272C, 272A, 316PNC, 316PNA; 93/94 - 159C, 159A
  Season's: 92/93 - 68; 93/94 - 16
  7-Eleven: 84/85 - 58
  Topps: 82/83 - 204SK; 83/84 - 282; 84/85 - 152; 85/86 - 109, 8SK; 86/87 - 74; 87/88 - 149, I/BB; 88/89 - 65, K/BB; 89/90 - 122; 90/91 - 141, 11SL; 91/92 - 65, 2SL, 312SC; 92/93 - 296, 296GS, 419SC; 93/94 - 7, 11PF, 220SC, 220FD
  Upper Deck: 90/91 - 53E, 53F, 443E, 443F; 91/92 - 12E, 126E, 12F, 126F; 92/93 - 302; 93/94 - 411
  Vachon Foods: 83/84 - 126

Hawgood, Greg
  Donruss: 93/94 - 245
  Fleer: 93/94 - 347PP
  Leaf: 93/94 - 266
  O-Pee-Chee: 89/90 - 81, 1FS; 90/91 - 236; 93/94 - 422
  Panini: 89/90 - 189; 90/91 - 10
  Parkhurst: 92/93 - 361, 361EI
  Pro Set: 90/91 - 442
  Score: 90/91 - 79T; 93/94 - 396C, 396A
  Topps: 89/90 - 81; 90/91 - 236; 92/93 - 358, 358GS, 495SC; 93/94 - 422C
  Upper Deck: 90/91 - 391E, 391F

Hawk, Henry
  Loblaws: 74/75 - 98

Haworth, Alan
  O-Pee-Chee: 84/85 - 199; 85/86 - 117, 108SK; 86/87 - 107, 255SK; 88/89 - 131, 195SK
  Panini: 87/88 - 187
  Topps: 85/86 - 117; 86/87 - 107; 88/89 - 131

Hay, Billy (Red)
  Beehive: 45/63 - 103; 64/67 - 37
  Chex: 63/65 - 3
  Coca-Cola: 64/65 - 23; 65/66 - 22
  Shirriff: 60/61 - 77; 61/62 - 34
  Topps: 60/61 - 6, 20ST; 61/62 - 35; 62/63 - 35, 11HB; 63/64 - 34; 64/65 - 7; 65/66 - 62
  Toronto Star: 57/67 - 85, 142; 58/67 - 45; 63/64 - 5; 64/65 - 8

Hay, Charles
  Hall of Fame: 83 - 36, C6P; 87 - 36

Hay, George
  Hall of Fame: 83 - 98, G7P; 87 - 98
  Topps: 60/61 - 15, 40ST

Haynes, Paul
  Beehive: 34/44 - 157
  Canada Starch: 35/40 - 61
  Diamond: 36/39 - 26(II), 24(III)
  O-Pee-Chee: 35/36 - 95; 37/38 - 155; 39/40 - 31; 40/41 - 112
  Quaker Oats: 38/39 - 9
  Sweet Caporal: 34/35 - 32
  World Wide Gum: 33/34 - 6; 36/37 - 33

Hayward, Brian (Goalie)
  Bowman: 91/92 - 122; 92/93 - 60
  Kraft: 86/87 - 27, 27P
  O-Pee-Chee: 85/86 - 226; 86/87 - 255; 87/88 - 230, 15HL, 175SK, 184SK; 88/89 - 195, 13NS, 52SK; 89/90 - 237, 50SK; 90/91 - 23; 91/92 - 178

Hayward, Brian (Goalie) (cont.)
  Panini: 87/88 - 55, 376A; 88/89 - 251; 89/90 - 246; 90/91 - 61; 91/92 - 106; 93/94 - 265E, 265F
  Pro Set: 90/91 - 150; 91/92 - 327E, 327F
  Score: 90 - 78T; 90/91 - 304C; 91 - 4T; 91/92 - 211A, 211B, 211C, 554B, 554C, 83PNE, 83PNF; 92/93 - 266PNC, 266PNA
  Topps: 88/89 - 195; 90/91 - 23; 91/92 - 178, 19SC; 92/93 - 436, 436GS, 364SC
  Upper Deck: 90/91 - 171E, 449E, 171F, 449F; 91/92 - 59E, 59F
  Vachon Foods: 83/84 - 127

Head, Don (Goalie)
  Beehive: 45/63 - 28
  Shirriff: 61/62 - 11
  Topps: 61/62 - 17

Headley, Fern (Curley)
  Champ's: 24/25 - 3
  Maple Crispette: 24/25 - 4
  Wm. Paterson: 24/25 - 23

Healy, Glenn (Goalie)
  Bowman: 91/92 - 224; 92/93 - 434
  Donruss: 93/94 - 211
  Fleer: 92/93 - 126; 93/94 - 106, 390PP
  Leaf: 93/94 - 327
  O-Pee-Chee: 88/89 - 7FS; 90/91 - 400; 91/92 - 368; 92/93 - 262; 93/94 - 486
  Panini: 88/89 - 68; 89/90 - 97; 90/91 - 88; 91/92 - 249; 93/94 - 65E, 65F
  Parkhurst: 91/92 - 107E, 107F; 92/93 - 341, 505, 341EI, 505EI; 93/94 - 405. 405EI
  Pro Set: 90/91 - 183; 91/92 - 1535E, 153F, 73PT, 18PK
  Score: 90/91 - 294A, 294C; 91/92 - 68A, 68B, 68C, 185PNE, 185PNF; 92/93 - 188C, 188A, 121PNC, 121PNA; 93/94 - 177C, 177A
  Sega: 93/94 - 84
  Topps: 91/92 - 368, 369SC; 92/93 - 305, 305GS, 356SC; 93/94 - 486PM, 93/94 - 453SC, 453FD
  Upper Deck: 90/91 - 18E, 18F; 91/92 - 224E, 224F; 93/94 - 321

Heaslip, Mark
  O-Pee-Chee: 76/77 - 376; 79/80 - 320

Hebenton, Andy
  Beehive: 45/63 - 29, 323; 64/67 - 11
  Parkhurst: 93/94 - 97ML
  Shirriff: 60/61 - 91; 61/62 - 90
  Topps: 57/58 - 58; 58/59 - 46; 59/60 - 16; 60/61 - 42, 11ST; 61/62 - 55; 62/63 - 54, 19HB; 63/64 - 15
  Toronto Star: 58/67 - 34

Hebert, Guy (Goalie)
  Bowman: 92/93 - 32
  Donruss: 93/94 - 13
  Fleer: 92/93 - 394; 93/94 - 2PP
  Leaf: 93/94 - 356
  O-Pee-Chee: 92/93 - 116, 40PM; 93/94 - 519
  Parkhurst: 92/93 - 386, 386EI; 93/94 - 279, 279EI
  Score: 92/93 - 4460C, 460A; 93/94 - 426C, 426A, 489C, 489A
  Sega: 93/94 - 6
  Topps: 92/93 - 112, 112GS, 401SC; 93/94 - 519A, 295SC, 295FD
  Upper Deck: 92/93 - 501; 93/94 - 1

Hedberg, Anders
  Derniere: 72/84 - 100
  Funmate: 83/84 - 87
  O-Pee-Chee: 78/79 - 25; 79/80 - 240; 80/81 - 73, 15PO; 81/82 - 225, 237, 166SK; 82/83 - 225; 83/84 - 245, 215SK; 84/85 - 143, 102SK; 85/86 - 200SK
  Topps: 78/79 - 25; 79/80 - 240; 80/81 - 73; 81/82 - EN 98, 58; 83/84 - 215SK; 84/85 - 107

Hedican, Bret
  Donruss: 93/94 - 291
  Fleer: 93/94 - 66, 210PP

Hedican, Brett (cont.)
Leaf: 93/94 - 286
O-Pee-Chee: 93/94 - 224, 81SC, 81FD
Parkhurst: 92/93 - 385, 385EI; 93/94 - 177, 177EI; 94/95 - 243, 243EI
Pro-Set: 92/93 - 240
Score: 92/93 - 471C, 471A, 228PNC, 228PNA
Topps: 92/93 - 517, 517GS, 203SC; 93/94 - 224, 81SC, 81FD
Upper Deck: 92/93 - 414; 93/94 - 185

Heffernan, Gerry
Beehive: 34/44 - 158

Heffernan, Jimmy
World Wide Gum: 36/37 - 130

Hegen, Dieter
Upper Deck: 92/93 - 370

Heinze, Stephen
Fleer: 92/93 - 3; 93/94 - 289PP
Leaf: 93/94 - 116
O-Pee-Chee: 92/93 - 92, 24PM; 93/94 - 378,15SC, 15FD
Parkhurst: 91/92 - 232E, 232F; 92/93 - 247, 247EI
Pro-Set: 92/93 - 220
Score: 92/93 - 476C, 476A; 93/94 - 251C, 251A
Topps: 92/93 - 519, 519GS, 166SC; 93/94 - 378, 15SC, 15FD
Upper Deck: 92/93 - 400, AC3

Heiskala, Earl
Esso: 70/71 - 170
O-Pee-Chee: 69/70 - 170; 70/71 - 193

Heller, Ott (Ehrhardt)
Anonymous: 33/34 - 34
Beehive: 34/44 - 275
Can. Chew. Gum: 33/34 - 29
Diamond: 33/35 - 28; 36/39 - 27(I), 27(II), 25(III)
O-Pee-Chee: 33/34 - 16; 39/40 - 33; 40/41 - 142
World Wide Gum: 36/37 - 87

Helman, Harry
Wm. Paterson: 23/24 - 5

Henderson, John (Goalie)
Parkhurst: 51/52 - 23

Henderson, Murray
Beehive: 45/63 - 30

Henderson, Paul
Bauer: 68/69 - 11
Beehive: 64/67 - 76
Chex: 63/65 - 13
Coca-Cola: 64/65 - 42; 65/66 - 47
Colgate: 71/72 - 4
Dom. Choc.: 70/71 - 127
Eddie Sargent: 70/71 - 195; 72/73 - 203
Esso: 70/71; 222
Mac's Milk: 73/74 - 9
O-Pee-Chee: 68/69 - 127; 69/70 - 47; 70/71 - 217; 71/72 - 67; 72/73 - 126, 19CS; 73/74 - 7
Post: 68/69 - 2O
Shirriff: 68/69 - M3
Topps: 65/66 - 51; 66/67 - 46; 66/67 US - 46; 67/68 - 103; 68/69 - 127, 69/70 - 47; 71/72 - 67; 72/73 - 73; 73/74 - 7
Toronto Star: 64/65 - 18
Toronto Sun: 71/72 - 260

Hendrickson, Darby
Fleer: 93/94 - 505PP
Topps: 93/94 - 4US

Hendy, Jim
Hall of Fame: 83 - 19, B5P; 87 - 19

Henning, Lorne
Coca-Cola: 77/78 - 11
Eddie Sargent: 72/73 - 135
Loblaws: 74/75 - 185
O-Pee-Chee: 73/74 - 218; 74/75 - 367; 75/76 - 354; 76/77 - 193; 77/78 - 219; 78/79 - 313; 79/80 - 193

Henning, Lorne (cont.)
Topps: 76/77 - 193; 77/78 - 219; 79/80 - 193

Henry, Camille
Beehive: 45/63 - 324; 64/67 - 38, 131
Coca-Cola: 64/65 - 80
La Patrie: 51/54 - 24
O-Pee-Chee: 68/69 - 116; 69/70 - 17
Parkhurst: 54/55 - 73; 93/94 - PR38, 100ML
Shirriff: 60/61 - 83; 61/62 - 87
Topps: 54/55 - 32; 57/58 - 63; 58/59 - 54; 59/60 - 46; 60/61 - 53, 12ST; 61/62 - 56; 62/63 - 62; 63/64 - 56; 64/65 - 14; 65/66 - 58; 67/68 - 26; 68/69 - 116; 69/70 - 17
Toronto Star: 57/67 - 89; 58/67 - 19; 63/64 - 28
Ultimate: 92 - 22(OSE), 22(OSF)

Henry, Jim (Goalie)
Beehive: 34/44 - 276A, 276B; 45/63 - 31, 104
CKAC Radio: 43/47 - 19
Chex: 43/47 - 19
Parkhurst: 51/52 - 19; 52/53 - 74; 53/54 - 86; 54/55 - 49
Topps: 54/55 - 37

Herbers, Ian
Leaf: 93/94 - 423
Parkhurst: 93/94 - 70, 70EI

Herberts, James
Champ's: 24/25 - 4
Maple Crispette: 24/25 - 8
Wm. Paterson: 24/25 - 25

Hergesheimer, Philip
Beehive: 34/44 - 56
O-Pee-Chee: 40/41 - 143

Hergesheimer, Wally
Beehive: 45/63 - 325
La Patrie: 51/54 - 31
Parkhurst: 51/52 - 100; 52/53 - 20; 53/54 - 67; 54/55 - 71; 93/94 - 26ML
Topps: 54/55 - 22; 57/58 - 33
Toronto Star: 58/67 - 7

Hern, Riley (Goalie)
Hall of Fame: 83 - 232, K6P; 87 - 232
Imperial Tobacco: 10/11 - 22, 32L; 11/12 - 32

Heron, Red (Bob)
Beehive: 34/44 - 228, 323
O-Pee-Chee: 39/40 - 53; 40/41 - 140

Herron, Denis (Goalie)
Derniere: 72/84 - 137
Loblaws: 74/75 - 242
O-Pee-Chee: 74/75 - 45; 75/76 - 68; 76/77 - 55; 77/78 - 119; 78/79 - 172; 79/80 - 94; 80/81 - 130; 81/82 - 258SK; 82/83 - 239, 241, 270, 41SK; 84/85 - 176, 122SK; 85/86 - 186
Panini: 79 - 52
PepsiCo: 80/81 - 45
Topps: 74/75 - 45; 75/76 - 68; 76/77 - 55; 77/78 - 119; 78/79 - 172; 79/80 - 94; 80/81 - 130; 82/83 - 41SK

Herter, Jason
Upper Deck: 90/91 - 325E, 325F

Hess, Bob
O-Pee-Chee: 75/76 - 264; 76/77 - 277; 77/78 - 394; 78/79 - 358
Topps: 75/76 - 264

Hewitson, Bobby
Hall of Fame: 83 - 82, F6P; 87 - 82

Hewitt, Foster
Beehive: 34/44 - 356
C.C.M.: 33/36 - 7
Hall of Fame: 83 - 8, A7P; 87 - 8
Quaker Oats: 38/39 - 30

Hewitt, William A.
Hall of Fame: 83 - 99, G8P; 87 - 99

Hextall, Bryan Sr.
Beehive: 34/44 - 277
Hall of Fame: 83 - 141, K7P; 87 - 141

Hextall, Bryan Jr.
Dom. Choc.: 70/71 - 106
Eddie Sargent: 72/73 - 173
Esso: 70/71 - 186
O-Pee-Chee: 69/70 - 154; 70/71 - 94; 71/72 - 16; 72/73 - 174; 73/74 - 43; 75/76 - 26; 76/77 - 13
Topps: 70/71 - 94; 71/72 - 16; 72/73 - 116, 157; 73/74 - 43; 75/76 - 26; 76/77 - 13
Toronto Sun: 71/72 - 216

Hextall, Dennis
Eddie Sargent: 70/71 - 133
Esso: 70/71 - 42
Loblaws: 74/75 - 153
O-Pee-Chee: 69/70 - 107; 70/71 - 186; 71/72 - 244; 72/73 - 225; 73/74 - 115; 74/75 - 115; 75/76 - 310; 76/77 - 32; 77/78 - 197; 78/79 - 48; 79/80 - 392
Topps: 69/70 - 107; 71/72 - 128; 73/74 - 136; 74/75 - 115; 75/76 - 310; 76/77 - 32; 77/78 - 197; 78/79 - 48

Hextall, Ron (Goalie)
Bowman: 90/91 - 105; 91/92 - 234; 92/93 - 195
Donruss: 93/94 - 196
Esso: 88/89 - 17
Fleer: 92/93 - 174, 385; 93/94 - 148PP
Frito-Lay: 88/89 - 18
Highliner: 93/94 - 4
Kraft: 90/91 - 17
Leaf: 93/94 - 341
O-Pee-Chee: 87/88 - 169, 16HL, 1SK, 101SK, 114SK, 129SK, 182SK; 88/89 - 34, 14NS, 103SK; 89/90 - 155, 111SK; 90/91 - 243, 41PM; 91/92 - 470, 38PM; 92/93 - 84, 57PM; 93/94 - 468
Panini: 87/88 - 123, 191, 378; 88/89 - 315; 89/90 - 302; 90/91 - 118; 91/92 - 227; 93/94 - 77E, 77F
Parkhurst: 91/92 - 126E, 126F; 92/93 - 144, 144EI; CP20; 93/94 - 118, 118EI; 94/95 - 136, 136EI
Pro Set: 90/91 - 216; 91/92 - 176E, 176F, 87PT; 92/93 - 129
Score: 90/91 - 25A, 25C, 14HR; 91/92 - 239A, 459B, 459C, 118PNE, 118PNF; 92/93 - 104C, 104A, 340PNC, 340PNA; 93/94 - 152C, 152A
Sega: 93/94 - 114
Topps: 87/88 - 169, 2SK; 88/89 - 34; 89/90 - 155; 90/91 - 243; 91/92 - 470, 173SC; 92/93 - 40, 40GS, 288SC; 93/94 - 468C, 433SC, 433FD
Upper Deck: 90/91 - 227E, 227F; 91/92 - 327E, 327F; 92/93 - 532; 93/94 - 434

Heyliger, Vic
Diamond: 36/39 - 6(V), 6(VI)

Hicke, Bill
Beehive: 45/63 - 249; 64/67 - 107, 132
Chex: 63/65 - 29
Coca-Cola: 64/65 - 62; 65/66 - 80
Dom. Choc.: 70/71 - 27
Eddie Sargent: 70/71 - 143
Esso: 70/71 - 43
O-Pee-Chee: 68/69 - 86; 69/70 - 145, 6QS; 70/71 - 76, 38DE, 12SS; 71/72 - 142; 72/73 - 327
Parkhurst: 59/60 - 31; 60/61 - 40; 61/62 - 38; 62/63 - 40; 63/64 - 25, 84; 70/71 - 12SK
Shirriff: 60/61 - 38; 61/62 - 108; 62/63 - 38; 68/69 - H9
Topps: 64/65 - 98; 65/66 - 30; 68/69 - 86; 69/70 - 76; 70/71 - 76
Toronto Sun: 71/72 - 217
York: 60/61 - 8; 61/62 - 16; 63/64 - 30

Hicke, Ernie
Eddie Sargent: 72/73 - 3
Esso: 70/71 - 44
Loblaws: 74/75 - 186

Hicke, Ernie (cont.)
    O-Pee-Chee: 71/72 - 61; 72/73 - 72; 73/74 - 18; 74/75 - 387; 75/76 - 71; 76/77 - 87; 77/78 - 132
    Topps: 71/72 - 61; 72/73 - 154; 73/74 - 18; 75/76 - 71; 76/77 - 87; 77/78 - 132
    Toronto Sun: 71/72 - 48

Hickey, Pat
    O-Pee-Chee: 75/76 - 345; 76/77 - 107; 77/78 - 221; 78/79 - 112; 79/80 - 86; 80/81 - 28; 81/82 - 318, 104SK; 82/83 - 304
    Panini: 79 - 68
    PepsiCo: 80/81 - 89
    Topps: 76/77 - 107; 77/78 - 221; 78/79 - 112; 79/80 - 86; 80/81 - 28; 81/82 - 104SK

Hicks, Doug
    Post: 82/83 - 312
    O-Pee-Chee: 77/78 - 361; 78/79 - 228; 79/80 - 379; 80/81 - 221; 81/82 - 114; 82/83 - 365
    Topps: 78/79 - 228; 80/81 - 221

Hicks, Glenn
    O-Pee-Chee: 81/82 - 98

Hicks, Wayne
    O-Pee-Chee: 70/71 - 95
    Topps: 70/71 - 95

Hiemer, Ullie
    O-Pee-Chee: 86/87 - 226

Higgins, Tim
    O-Pee-Chee: 81/82 - 57; 82/83 - 66, 177SK; 83/84 - 104; 84/85 - 111; 86/87 - 227
    Panini: 87/88 - 250
    Post: 82/83 - 54
    Topps: 81/82 WN - 69; 82/83 - 177SK

Hildebrand, Ike
    Beehive: 45/63 - 250, 326
    Parkhurst: 54/55 - 83

Hilger, Raimond
    Upper Deck: 92/93 - 373

Hill, Al
    O-Pee-Chee: 79/80 - 166; 80/81 - 348
    Topps: 79/80 - 166;

Hill, Mel
    Beehive: 34/44 - 19, 229, 324
    O-Pee-Chee: 39/40 - 96
    Quaker Oats: 45/54 - 76

Hill, Sean
    Donruss: 93/94 - 7
    Fleer: 92/93 - 328; 93/94 - 182, 3PP
    Leaf: 93/94 - 353
    O-Pee-Chee: 93/94 - 312
    Parkhurst: 92/93 - 487, 487EI; 93/94 - 2, 2EI; 94/95 - 6, 6EI
    Score: 93/94 - 490C, 490A
    Topps: 93/94 - 312, 387SC, 387FD
    Upper Deck: 92/93 - 392, 523; 93/94 - 16

Hillebrandt, Jon (Goalie)
    Topps: 93/94 - 10US

Hiller, Dutch (Wilbur)
    Beehive: 34/44 - 103, 159, 278
    CKAC Radio: 43/47 - 58
    O-Pee-Chee: 39/40 - 89
    Quaker Oats: 45/54 - 22

Hiller, Jim
    Fleer: 92/93 - 307
    O-Pee-Chee: 92/93 - 34PM
    Parkhurst: 92/92 - 70, 281, 70EI, 281EI
    Score: 92/93 - 399PNC, 399PNA
    Upper Deck: 92/93 - 560

Hillier, Randy
    O-Pee-Chee: 85/86 - 212; 88/89 - 158; 89/90 - 126; 90/91 - 408; 91/92 - 122PM
    Panini: 87/88 - 145; 90/91 - 137
    Pro Set: 90/91 - 507; 91/92 - 360E, 360F, 158PT

Hiller, Randy (cont.)
    Score: 90/91 - 76A, 76C; 91 - 30T; 91/92 - 580B, 580C, 281PNE, 281PNF
    Topps: 88/89 - 158; 89/90 - 126

Hillman, Larry
    Beehive: 45/63 - 32, 177, 408; 64/67 - 164
    Dom. Choc.: 70/71 - 98
    Eddie Sargent: 70/71 - 158; 72/73 - 39
    Esso: 70/71 - 171
    O-Pee-Chee: 68/69 - 48; 69/70 - 90, 4QS; 70/71 - 81; 71/72 - 168; 72/73 - 176
    Parkhurst: 61/62 - 14; 62/63 - 17; 93/94 - 55ML
    Shirriff: 61/62 - 59; 62/63 - 17; 68/69 - E12
    Topps: 57/58 - 17; 58/59 - 25; 67/68 - 80; 68/69 - 48; 69/70 - 90; 70/71 - 81
    Toronto Sun: 71/72 - 115
    Ultimate: 92 - 36(OSE), 36(OSF)
    York: 60/61 - 26; 61/62 - 31; 63/64 - 11

Hillman, Wayne
    Bazooka: 71/72 - 26
    Beehive: 45/63 - 105; 64/67 - 39, 133
    Chex: 63/65 - 4
    Coca-Cola: 64/65 - 34; 65/66 - 81
    Dom. Choc.: 70/71 - 99
    Eddie Sargent: 70/71 - 160; 71/72 - 146; 72/73 - 156
    Esso: 70/71 - 172
    O-Pee-Chee: 68/69 - 47; 69/70 - 91; 70/71 - 198; 71/72 - 62; 72/73 - 255
    Shirriff: 61/62 - 21
    Topps: 61/62 - 31; 62/63 - 31; 63/64 - 27; 64/65 - 41; 66/67 - 87; 66/67 US - 34; 67/68 - 22; 68/69 - 47; 69/70 - 91; 71/72 - 62
    Toronto Star: 64/65 - 9
    Toronto Sun: 71/72 - 197

Hilton, Kevin
    Donruss: 93/94 - 9JCA
    Upper Deck: 93/94 - 567

Himes, Normie
    Anonymous: 33/34 - 21
    Can. Chew. Gum: 33/34 - 30
    Diamond: 33/35 - 29; 36/39 - 28(I)
    La Presse: 27/32 - 63
    O-Pee-Chee: 33/34 - 29
    World Wide Gum: 33/34 - 44; 36/37 - 92

Hindmarch, Dave
    O-Pee-Chee: 83/84 - 82; 84/85 - 224
    Vachon Foods: 83/84 - 7

Hirsch, Corey (Goalie)
    Donruss: 93/94 - 216
    Fleer: 93/94 - 64, 3UR, 482PP
    Leaf: 93/94 - 313
    Parkhurst: 92/93 - 344, 344EI; 94/95 - 149, 149EI
    Score: 93/94 - 453C. 453A
    Upper Deck: 92/93 - 463

Hirsch, Tom
    O-Pee-Chee: 84/85 - 99

Hirschfeld, Bert
    Beehive: 45/63 - 251
    Quaker Oats: 45/54 - 23

Hislop, Jamie
    O-Pee-Chee: 79/80 - 380; 80/81 - 327; 81/82 - 40; 82/83 - 47; 83/84 - 83
    Post: 82/83 - 36
    Vachon Foods: 83/84 - 8

Hitchman, Lionel (Fred)
    Wm. Paterson: 23/24 - 8; 24/25 - 4
    Champ's: 24/25 - 45
    Diamond: 33/35 - 30
    La Presse: 27/32 - 41
    O-Pee-Chee: 33/34 - 5
    World Wide Gum: 33/34 - 34

Hlinka, Ivan
    O-Pee-Chee: 82/83 - 346
    Panini: 79 - 83
    Post: 82/83 - 296

Hlushka, Todd
    Donruss: 93/94 - 469

Hlushka, Todd (cont.)
    Fleer: 93/94 - 483PP
    O-Pee-Chee: 93/94 - 12TC
    Parkhurst: 94/95 - 164, 164EI

Hocking, Justin
    Parkhurst: 94/95 - 102, 102EI

Hodge, Charlie (Goalie)
    Beehive: 45/63 - 252A, 252B; 64/67 - 108
    Chex: 63/65 - 30
    Coca-Cola: 64/65 - 63; 65/66 - 62
    Colgate: 70/71 - 68
    Dom. Choc.: 70/71 - 139
    Eddie Sargent: 70/71 - 211
    Esso: 70/71 - 240
    O-Pee-Chee: 68/69 - 78, 12PS; 69/70 - 77, 8QS; 70/71 - 229
    Parkhurst: 57/58 MON - 17; 58/59 - 17; 59/60 - 16
    Shirriff: 60/61 - 39; 68/69 - H7
    Topps: 64/65 - 17; 65/66 - 67; 68/69 - 78; 69/70 - 77
    Toronto Star: 57/67 - 109, 124, 64/65 - 28
    York: 60/61 - 9

Hodge, Ken Sr.
    Bauer: 68/69 - 12
    Beehive: 64/67 - 40
    Coca-Cola: 65/66 - 23
    Colgate: 70/71 - 62
    Dom. Choc.: 70/71 - 6
    Eddie Sargent: 70/71 - 10; 72/73 - 22
    Esso: 70/71 - 9
    Kraft: 91/92 - 17
    Lipton Soup: 74/75 - 28
    Loblaws: 74/75 - 26
    O-Pee-Chee: 68/69 - 8; 69/70 - 27, 13ST, 2QS; 70/71 - 8; 71/72 - 115, 254; 72/73 - 49, 169; 73/74 - 26; 74/75 - 128, 230; 75/76 - 215; 76/77 - 25; 77/78 - 192
    Shirriff: 68/69 - A10
    Topps: 65/66 - 65; 66/67 - 114; 67/68 - 98; 68/69 - 8; 69/70 - 27; 70/71 - 8; 71/72 - 115; 72/73 - 166; 73/74 - 133; 74/75 - 128, 230; 75/76 - 215; 76/77 - 25; 77/78 - 192
    Toronto Sun: 71/72 - 10
    Ultimate: 92 - 49(OSE), 49(OSF)

Hodge, Kenneth (Ken) Jr.
    Fleer: 92/93 - 411
    Bowman: 91/92 - 347, 362
    O-Pee-Chee: 91/92 - 5, 440, 41PM, 154PM
    Panini: 91/92 - 178, 341
    Parkhurst: 91/92 - 2E, PHC3E, 2F, PHC3F
    Pro Set: 90/91 - 587; 91/92 - AC11, 3E, 3F, PC9PT, 6PT; 92/93 - 182
    Score: 90/91 - 85T; 91 - 9YS; 91/92 - 113A, 353A, 113B, 383B, 113C, 383C, 203PNE, 203PNF; 92/93 - 274C, 274A, 390PNC, 390PNA
    Topps: 91/92 - 5, 440, 357SC; 92/93 - 306, 306GS
    Upper Deck: 90/91 - 529E, 529F; 91/92 - 41E, 251E, 41F, 251F; 92/93 - 254

Hodges, Bob (Official)
    Pro Set: 90/91 - 689

Hoekstra, Cecil
    Shirriff: 60/61 - 79

Hoekstra, Ed
    O-Pee-Chee: 68/69 - 98
    Shirriff: 68/69 - J3A
    Topps: 68/69 - 98

Hoffort, Bruce (Goalie)
    O-Pee-Chee: 90/91 PREM - 42
    Score: 90/91 - 413A, 413C
    Upper Deck: 90/91 - 135E, 135F

Hollinger, Terry
    Parkhurst: 94/95 - 204, 204EI

Hogaboam, Bill
    Loblaws: 74/75 - 98
    O-Pee-Chee: 74/75 - 116; 75/76 - 67; 76/77 - 73; 77/78 - 148; 79/80 - 362

Hogaboam, Bill (cont.)
Topps: 74/75 - 116; 75/76 - 67; 76/77 - 73; 77/78 - 148

Hoganson, Dale
Derniere: 72/84 - 21, 89, 148
Eddie Sargent: 70/71 - 68
Esso: 70/71 - 97
O-Pee-Chee: 71/72 - 149; 80/81 - 155; 81/82 - 276
PepsiCo: 80/81 - 68
Topps: 80/81 - 155
Toronto Sun: 71/72 - 116

Hoggarth, Ron (Official)
Pro Set: 90/91 - 690

Hoglund, Jonas
Upper Deck: 92/93 - 222

Hogue, Benoit
Bowman: 91/92 - 38; 92/93 - 28
Donruss: 93/94 - 201
Durivage: 92/93 - 3; 93/94 - 29
Fleer: 92/93 - 127; 93/94 - 123, 148PP
Leaf: 93/94 - 155
O-Pee-Chee: 89/90 - 201, 37SK, 4FS; 90/91 - 215; 91/92 - 292, 179PM; 92/93 - 132, 425SC; 93/94 - 140, 76SC, 76FD
Panini: 91/92 - 300; 92/93 - 197E, 197F; 93/94 - 59E, 59F
Parkhurst: 91/92 - 332E, 332F; 92/93 - 104, 104EI; 93/94 - 396, 396EI
Pro Set: 90/91 - 416; 91/92 - 17E, 435E, 17F, 435F, 200PT; 92/93 - 108
Score: 91 - 31YS, 108T; 91/92 - 134A, 134B, 134C, 146PNE, 146PNF; 92/93 - 276C, 276A, 62PNC, 62PNA, 21CSS, 21ASS; 93/94 - 16C, 16A
Sega: 93/94 - 83
Topps: 90/91 - 215; 91/92 - 292, 157SC; 92/93 - 103, 103GS; 93/94 - 140, 76SC, 76FD
Upper Deck: 90/91 - 402E, 402F; 91/92 - 159E, 159F; 92/93 - 325; 93/94 - 456

Holden, Barney
Imperial Tobacco: 10/11 - 3L, 4; 11/12 - 3

Holan, Milos
Donruss: 93/94 - 244
Parkhurst: 93/94 - 268, 268EI
Upper Deck: 93/94 - 523

Holik, Robert (Bobby)
Bowman: 91/92 - 18; 92/93 - 407
Donruss: 93/94 - 183
Fleer: 92/93 - 339; 93/94 - 378PP
Leaf: 93/94 - 227
O-Pee-Chee: 90/91 - 43PM; 91/92 - 7, 56; 92/93 - 254, 77PM; 93/94 - 52, 322, 159SC, 159FD
Panini: 91/92 - 316, 342; 92/93 - 261E, 293E, 261F, 293F
Parkhurst: 91/92 - 290E, 290F; 92/93 - 96, 96EI; 93/94 - 385, 385EI; 94/95 - 128, 128EI
Pro Set: 90/91 - 609; 91/92 - 79E, 79F, 43PT; 92/93 - 61
Score: 90 - 34YS, 10T; 91 - 36YS; 91/92 - 153A, 153B, 153C, 65PNE, 65PNF; 92/93 - 128C, 128A, 277PNC, 277PNA; 93/94 - 198C, 198A
Topps: 91/92 - 7, 56, 299SC; 92/93 - 330, 330GS, 106SC; 93/94 - 52, 322, 159SC, 159FD
Upper Deck: 90/91 - 534E, 534F; 91/92 - 233E, E3(E), 233F, E3(F); 92/93 - 252, 500; 93/94 - 218

Holland, Jerry
O-Pee-Chee: 75/76 - 392; 76/77 - 315

Hollett, Bill (Flash)
Beehive: 34/44 - 20, 325
O-Pee-Chee: 35/36 - 83; 39/40 - 41
World Wide Gum: 36/37 - 62

Hollingworth, Bucky
Parkhurst: 93/94 - 62ML
Topps: 54/55 - 12

Holmes, Bill
Anonymous: 1926/27 - 14

Holmes, Harry (Goalie)
Anonymous: 1926/27 - 121
Hall of Fame: 83 - 156, L6P; 87 - 156

Holmgren, Paul
O-Pee-Chee: 77/78 - 307; 78/79 - 234; 79/80 - 156; 80/81 - 172; 81/82 - 242, 179SK; 82/83 - 251, 116SK; 83/84 - 266; 84/85 - 100
Post: 82/83 - 214
Pro Set: 90/91 - 673
Topps: 78/79 - 234; 79/80 - 156; 80/81 - 172; 81/82 EN - 105; 82/83 - 116SK; 84/85 - 74

Holt, Randy
O-Pee-Chee: 77/78 - 34; 78/79 - 341; 81/82 - 41; 83/84 - 220
PepsiCo: 80/81 - 4
Post: 82/83 - 313
Topps: 77/78 - 34

Holway, Albert
Wm. Paterson: 24/25 - 56
Champ's: 24/25 - 53

Hood, Bruce (Official)
Ultimate: 92 - 86(OSE), 86(OSF)

Hooper, Tom
Hall of Fame: 173, M9P; 87 - 173

Hoover, Ron
Upper Deck: 91/92 - 287E, 287F

Hopkins, Dean
Post: 82/83 - 118

Horacek, Tony
Bowman: 90/91 - 104
Pro Set: 90/91 - 499; 91/92 - 455E, 455F

Horava, Miloslav
O-Pee-Chee: 90/91 - 337
Pro Set: 90/91 - 198
Topps: 90/91 - 337
Upper Deck: 90/91 - 13E, 13F

Horbul, Doug
Loblaws: 74/75 - 114
O-Pee-Chee: 74/75 - 317

Horeck, Pete
Beehive: 45/63 - 33, 106, 178

Horner, Red (Reginald)
Anonymous: 33/34 - 1
Beehive: 34/44 - 326
Can. Chew. Gum: 33/34 - 31
Hall of Fame: 83 - 115, H9P; 87 - 115
Hamilton Gum: 33/34 - 21
O-Pee-Chee: 33/34 - 10; 36/37 - 122; 37/38 - 134; 39/40 - 10
Quaker Oats: 38/39 - 23
Sweet Caporal: 34/35 - 46
World Wide Gum: 33/34 - 16; 36/37 - 8

Hornung, Larry
O-Pee-Chee: 72/73 - 317

Horton, Tim
Beehive: 45/63 - 409; 64/67 - 165A, 165B
Chex: 63/65 - 46
Coca-Cola: 64/65 - 98; 65/66 - 96
Eddie Sargent: 70/71 - 125; 72/73 - 37
Esso: 70/71 - 152
Hall of Fame: 83 - 188, J8P; 87 - 188
O-Pee-Chee: 68/69 - 123, 201, 18PS; 69/70 - 182, 213, 1QS; 70/71 - 59; 71/72 - 186, 18PT; 72/73 - 197; 73/74 - 189
Parkhurst: 52/53 - 58; 53/54 - 13; 54/55 - 31; 55/56 - 3; 57/58 TOR - 22; 58/59 - 42; 59/60 - 23; 60/61 - 1; 61/62 - 1; 62/63 - 7; 63/64 - 16, 76; 92/93 - PR16; 93/94 - PR34, 127ML
Post: 66/67 - 2; 68/69 - 21
Quaker Oats: 45/54 - 77; 55/56 - 3
Shirriff: 60/61 - 5; 61/62 - 44; 62/63 - 4; 68/69 - M14

Horton, Tim (cont.)
Topps: 64/65 - 102, 105; 65/66 - 79; 66/67 - 80; 67/68 - 16, 127; 68/69 - 123; 69/70 - 45; 70/71 - 59
Toronto Star: 57/67 - 101, 115, 140; 58/67 - 73; 63/64 - 35; 64/65 - 41
Toronto Sun: 71/72 - 218
Ultimate: 92 - 37(OSE), 84(OSE), 97(OSE), 37(OSF), 84(OSF), 97(OSF)
York: 60/61 - 27; 61/62 - 7; 62/63 - 3; 63/64 - 1

Horvath, Bronco (Rudy)
Beehive: 45/63 - 34, 107, 327, 410; 64/67 - 166
parkhurst: 93/94 - 105ML
Shirriff: 60/61 - 105; 61/62 - 31
Topps: 57/58 - 7; 58/59 - 35; 59/60 - 56; 60/61 - 54, 21ST; 61/62 - 40; 62/63 - 63
Toronto Star: 58/67 - 33

Hospodar, Ed
O-Pee-Chee: 80/81 - 366; 81/82 - 233

Hostak, Martin
Bowman: 91/92 - 233
O-Pee-Chee: 90/91 - 44PM
Pro Set: 90/91 - 629
Score: 90/91 - 36T
Topps: 91/92 - 337sc
Upper Deck: 90/91 - 542E, 542F; 91/92 - 473E, 473F

Houda, Doug
O-Pee-Chee: 90/91 - 410; 91/92 - 512
Pro Set: 91/92 - 81E, 81F
Score: 90/91 - 11A, 11C; 91/92 - 442B, 442C
Topps: 91/92 - 512

Hough, Mike
Bowman: 92/93 - 178
Donruss: 93/94 - 122
Durivage: 92/93 - 25; 93/94 - 45
Fleer: 92/93 - 175; 93/94 - 94PP
Leaf: 93/94 - 247
Panini: 91/92 - 254; 92/93 - 211E, 211F
Bowman: 90/91 - 174; 91/92 - 144
O-Pee-Chee: 87/88 - 220SK; 89/90 - 266; 90/91 - 427; 91/92 - 113; 92/93 - 392; 93/94 - 482
Parkhurst: 91/92 - 150E, 150F; 92/93 - 380, 380EI
Pro Set: 90/91 - 247, 516; 91/92 - 463E, 582E, 463F, 582F, 217PT; 92/93 - 154, 266
Score: 91/92 - 112A, 112B, 112C, 194PNE, 194PNF; 92/93 - 64C, 64A, 113PNC, 113PNA; 93/94 - 393C, 393A
Topps: 91/92 - 113, 80SC; 92/93 - 297, 297GS, 434SC; 93/94 - 482C, 466SC, 466FD
Upper Deck: 91/92 - 562E, 562F

Houlder, Bill
Donruss: 93/94 - 8
Fleer: 93/94 - 4PP
Leaf: 93/94 - 315
O-Pee-Chee: 90/91 399; 93/94 - 403
Parkhurst: 93/94 - 272, 272EI
Pro Set: 90/91 - 417
Topps: 93/94 - 403C, 419SC, 419FD
Upper Deck: 93/94 - 429

Houle, Rejean
Derniere: 72/84 - 23, 117
Eddie Sargent: 72/73 - 125
O-Pee-Chee: 70/71 - 174; 71/72 - 147; 72/73 - 210; 76/77 - 360; 77/78 - 241; 78/79 - 227; 79/80 - 34; 80/81 - 261; 81/82 - 183, 37SK; 82/83 - 184
PepsiCo: 80/81 - 46
Topps: 77/78 - 241; 78/79 - 227; 79/80 - 34; 80/81 - 261
Toronto Sun: 71/72 - 151

Housley, Phil
Bowman: 90/91 - 239; 91/92 - 197; 92/93 - 20, 208
Donruss: 93/94 - 294

Housley, Phil (cont.)
- Fleer: 92/93 - 241; 93/94 - 100, 18AS, 271PP, 427PP
- Funmate: 83/84 - 11
- Hockey Wit: 93/94 - 101
- Humpty Dumpty: 92/93 - 8(II)
- Kraft: 90/91 - 18, 33, 85
- Leaf: 93/94 - 61
- O-Pee-Chee: 83/84 - 65, 238SK; 84/85 - 23, 203SK, 204SK; 85/86 - 63, 173SK; 86/87 - 154, 47SK; 87/88 - 33, 17HL, 151SK; 88/89 - 119, 255SK; 89/90 - 59, 261SK; 90/91 - 89, 45PM; 91/92 - 395, 50PM; 92/93 - 298, 16SP; 93/94 - 36, 503, 104SC, 104FD
- Panini: 87/88 - 24; 88/89 - 220; 89/90 - 205; 90/91 - 21; 91/92 - 65; 92/93 - 61E, 61F; 93/94 - 133E, 196E, 133F, 196F
- Parkhurst: 91/92 - 205E, 205F; 92/93 - 208; 93/94 - 174, 174EI; 94/95 - 197, 197EI
- Pro Set: 90/91 - 21, 364, 562; 91/92 - 267E, 295E, 267F, 295F, 137PT, 30PK; 92/93 - 208, 208EI, 14TL
- Score: 90 - 3T; 90/91 - 145A, 145C, 63HR; 91/92 - 271A, 491B, 491C, 4PNE, 4PNF; 92/93 - 299C, 440C, 299A, 440A, 70PNC, 70PNA; 93/94 - 232C, 482C, 232A, 482A, 25PNC, 25PNA, 25CAS, 25AAS
- Season's: 92/93 - 59
- Sega: 93/94 - 145
- Topps: 83/84 - 238SK; 84/85 - 18; 85/86 - 63; 86/87 - 154; 87/88 - 33; 88/89 - 119; 89/90 - 59; 90/91 - 89; 91/92 - 395, 11SL, 65SC; 92/93 - 268, 456, 268GS, 456GS, 14SC; 93/94 - 36(I), 503A, 19BG, 104SC, 104FD, 13AS
- Upper Deck: 90/91 - 22E, 22F, 435E, 435F; 91/92 - 106E, 624E, 106F, 624F; 92/93 - 24, 276, 628, 26AS; 93/94 - 525

Houston, Ken
- O-Pee-Chee: 77/78 - 274; 78/79 - 348; 79/80 - 310; 80/81 - 303; 82/83 - 366, 221SK; 83/84 - 371, 200SK
- PepsiCo: 80/81 - 5
- Post: 82/83 - 37
- Topps: 82/83 - 221SK; 83/84 - 200SK

Howatt, Garry
- Loblaws: 74/75 - 187
- O-Pee-Chee: 74/75 - 375; 75/76 - 54; 76/77 - 206; 77/78 - 194; 78/79 - 29; 79/80 - 205; 80/81 - 386; 82/83 - 140, 133SK; 83/84 - 229
- Post: 82/83 - 99
- Topps: 75/76 - 54; 76/77 - 206; 77/78 - 194; 78/79 - 29; 79/80 - 205; 82/83 - 133SK

Howe, Gordie
- Beehive: 45/63 - 179A, 179B; 64/67 - 77A, 77B
- Chex: 63/65 - 14
- Coca-Cola: 64/65 - 43A, 43B; 65/66 - 48
- Colgate: 70/71 - 47
- Dom. Choc.: 70/71 - 49
- Eaton's: 64/67 - 1, 2, 3
- Eddie Sartgent: 70/71 - 56
- El Producto: 62/63 - 1SS, 2
- Esso: 70/71 - 80; 88/89 - 18
- Hall of Fame: 83 - 16, B6P; 87 - 16
- HHFM: 92 - 9
- Hockey Wit: 93/94 - 9
- O-Pee-Chee: 68/69 - 29, 203, 22PS; 69/70 - 61, 193, 215, 14ST, 14QS; 70/71 - 29, 238, 18DE, 13SS; 71/72 - 262, 23BK; 79/80 - 175
- Parkhurst: 51/52 - 66; 52/53 - 88; 53/54 - 50; 54/55 - 41; 60/61 - 20; 61/62 - 20; 62/63 - 30, 31; 63/64 - 55; 70/71 - 13SK; 71/72 - 23BK; 91/92 - PHC1E, PHC1F;

Howe, Gordie (cont.)
- Parkhurst: 93/94 - PR33, PR42, 43ML, 145ML, 160ML, 162ML, 171ML, D17
- Post: 66/67 - 2S, ; 67/68 - 2L, 2S3L
- Pro Set: 90/91 - 654, 660; 91/92 - 344E, 344F
- Royal Desserts: 1952 - 8
- Shirriff: 60/61 - 42; 61/62 - 66; 62/63 - 54; 68/69 - C11
- Topps: 54/55 - 8; 57/58 - 42; 58/59 - 8; 59/60 - 63; 64/65 - 89; 65/66 - 108, 122; 66/67 - 109, 121; 66/67 US - 23; 67/68 - 43, 131; 68/69 - 29; 69/70 - 61; 70/71 - 29; 71/72 - 70; 79/80 - 175
- Toronto Star: 57/67 - 45, 71, 108; 58/67 - 42, 85, 95; 63/64 - 13; 64/65 - 19
- Toronto Sun: 71/72 - 96
- Upper Deck: 92/93 - 19-27HH, 42AS
- Wonder Bread: 1960 - 1W, 1PM
- York: 62/63 - 19; 63/64 - 45

Howe, Mark
- Derniere: 72/84 - 172
- Esso: 88/89 - 19
- Fleer: 92/93 - 285; 93/94 - 329PP
- Funmate: 83/84 - 95
- Kraft: 90/91 - 19
- Leaf: 93/94 - 259
- McDonald's: 82/83 - 31
- O-Pee-Chee: 80/81 - 91, 160; 81/82 - 128, 62SK, 145SK; 82/83 - 252, 131SK; 83/84 - 267, 171SK, 195SK, 196SK; 84/85 - 161, 109SK; 85/86 - 35, 93SK; 86/87 - 123, 116SK, 184SK, 246SK; 87/88 - 54, 18HL, 100SK, 112SK, 176SK; 88/89 - 6, 104SK, 124SK; 89/90 - 191, 109SK; 90/91 - 185; 91/92 - 466; 93/94 - 157, 112SC, 112FD
- Panini: 87/88 - 124; 88/89 - 316; 89/90 - 300; 90/91 - 122; 92/93 - 191E, 191F
- Parkhurst: 91/92 - 130E, 130F; 92/93 - 279, 279EI
- Post: 81/82 - 11; 82/83 - 100
- Pro Set: 90/91 - 217; 91/92 - 182E, 182F
- Score: 90/91 - 220A, 220C, 90HR; 91/92 - 252A, 472B, 472C, 297PNE, 418PNE, 297PNF, 418PNF; 92/93 - 217C, 217A, 322PNC, 322PNA; 93/94 - 91C, 91A
- Topps: 79/80 - 216; 80/81 - 91, 160; 81/82 EN - 82; 82/83 - 131SK; 83/84 - 171SK, 195SK, 196SK; 84/85 - 118; 85/86 - 35; 86/87 - 123, 6SK; 87/88 - 54, 3SK; 88/89 - 6; 89/90 - 191; 90/91 - 185; 91/92 - 466; 93/94 - 157, 112SC, 112FD
- Upper Deck: 90/91 - 261E, 261F; 92/93 - 530

Howe, Marty
- O-Pee-Chee: 79/80 - 46; 83/84 - 139, 54SK; 84/85 - 71
- Topps: 79/80 - 46; 83/84 - 54SK; 84/85 - 55

Howe, Syd
- Beehive: 34/44 - 104
- Diamond: 36/39 - 29(I)
- Hall of Fame: 83 - 174, M10P; 87 - 174
- O-Pee-Chee: 33/34 - 24; 39/40 - 72
- World Wide Gum: 33/34 - 72; 36/37 - 75

Howell, Harry
- Bauer: 68/69 - 13
- Beehive: 45/63 - 328; 64/67 - 134
- Coca-Cola: 64/65 - 81; 65/66 - 82
- Dom. Choc.: 70/71 - 28
- Eddie Sargent: 70/71 - 134; 72/73 - 90
- Esso: 70/71 - 45
- Hall of Fame: 83 - 83, F7P; 87 - 83
- O-Pee-Chee: 68/69 - 69; 69/70 - 79; 70/71 - 72, 37DE; 71/72 - 153; 72/73 - 193
- Parkhurst: 53/54 - 57; 54/55 - 70; 92/93 - PR15; 93/94 - 96ML
- Post: 66/67 - 4L; 67/68 - 3L, 3S, 4L
- Shirriff: 60/61 - 86; 61/62 - 89; 68/69 - G11
- TCMA: 1981 - 6

Howell, Harry (cont.)
- Topps: 54/55 - 3; 57/58 - 51; 58/59 - 60; 59/60 - 20; 60/61 - 49, 13ST; 61/62 - 51; 62/63 - 46, 20HB; 63/64 - 89; 64/65 - 83; 65/66 - 22; 66/67 - 91; 66/67 US - 18; 67/68 - 84, 119, 121; 68/69 - 69; 69/70 - 79; 70/71 - 72
- Toronto Star: 58/67 - 109; 64/65 - 34
- Toronto Sun: 71/72 - 117
- Upper Deck: 90/91 - 511E, 511F
- Ultimate: 92 - 23(OSE), 23(OSF)

Hoyda, Dave
- O-Pee-Chee: 79/80 - 338; 80/81 - 332; 81/82 - 366

Hrdina, Jiri
- Bowman: 91/92 - 82
- O-Pee-Chee: 89/90 - 97SK, 5FS; 90/91 - 234; 91/92 - 213
- Panini: 90/91 - 182
- Pro Set: 90/91 - 421; 91/92 - 461E, 461F
- Score: 91/92 - 418B, 418C
- Topps: 89/90 - 234; 91/92 - 213, 36SC; 92/93 - 272, 272GS, 158SC
- Upper Deck: 90/91 - 292E, 292F

Hrechkosy, Dave
- Loblaws: 74/75 - 60
- O-Pee-Chee: 75/76 - 156; 76/77 - 364
- Topps: 75/76 - 156

Hrivnak, Jim (Goalie)
- Bowman: 91/92 - 305; 92/93 - 372
- Fleer: 92/93 - 435; 93/94 - 428PP
- Leaf: 93/94 - 312
- O-Pee-Chee: 90/91 - 9; 91/92 - 487
- Parkhurst: 92/93 - 430, 430EI
- Pro Set: 90/91 - 646; 91/92 - 509E, 509F
- Score: 90/91 - 386A, 386C; 93/94 - 201C, 201A
- Topps: 90/91 - 9; 91/92 - 487, 264SC; 92/93 - 18, 18GS, 325SC; 93/94 - 421SC, 421FD
- Upper Deck: 91/92 - 343E; 92/93 - 151

Hrkac, Anthony (Tony)
- Bowman: 90/91 - 172; 91/92 - 141
- Donruss: 93/94 - 292
- Leaf: 93/94 - 329
- O-Pee-Chee: 88/89 - 129, 15NS, 19SK, 129SK, 8FS; 89/90 - 64, 25SK; 91/92 - 241, 40PM
- Panini: 88/89 - 106; 89/90 - 119; 90/91 - 146
- Parkhurst: 93/94 - 448, 448EI
- Pro Set: 90/91 - 248; 91/92 - 205E, 205F, 105PT
- Score: 90/91 - 256A, 256C; 91 - 5T; 91/92 - 122A, 122B, 122C, 555B, 555C
- Topps: 88/89 - 129; 89/90 - 64; 91/92 - 241, 136SC; 92/93 - 524, 524GS
- Upper Deck: 90/91 - 184E, 184F; 91/92 - 56E, 56F

Hrudey, Kelly (Goalie)
- Bowman: 90/91 - 144; 91/92 - 183; 92/93 - 42
- Donruss: 93/94 - 161
- Fleer: 92/93 - 84; 93/94 - 131, 117PP
- Hockey Wit: 93/94 - 93
- Kraft: 93/94 - 58
- Leaf: 93/94 - 39
- O-Pee-Chee: 85/86 - 122, 79SK; 86/87 - 27, 212SK; 87/88 - 119, 242SK; 88/89 - 155, 109SK; 89/90 - 166, 149SK; 90/91 - 103; 91/92 - 195; 92/93 - 44; 93/94 - 471, 54SC, 54FD
- Panini: 87/88 - 90; 88/89 - 283; 89/90 - 89; 90/91 - 246; 91/92 - 81; 92/93 - 63E, 63F; 93/94 - 210E, 210F
- Parkhurst: 91/92 - 71E, 71F; 92/93 - 66, 66EI; 93/94 - 97, 97EI
- Pro Set: 90/91 - 119; 91/92 - 102E, 102F, PC6PT, 54PT; 92/93 - 70
- Score: 90/91 - 115A, 115C, 55HR; 91/92 - 231A, 451B, 451C, 39PNE, 39PNF; 92/93 - 155C, 155A, 19PNC, 19PNA; 93/94 - 140C, 140A

Hrudey, Kelly (Goalie) (cont.)
Season's: 92/93 - 12
Sega: 93/94 - 66
Topps: 85/86 - 122; 86/87 - 27; 87/88 - 119; 88/89 - 155; 89/90 - 166; 90/91 - 103; 91/92 - 195, 120SC; 92/93 - 29, 29GS, 391SC; 93/94 - 471C, 54SC, 54FD
Upper Deck: 90/91 - 231E, 231F; 91/92 - 262E, 262F; 92/93 - 270; 93/94 - 216

Hrychuik, Jim
Loblaws: 74/75 - 315

Huard, Bill
Parkhurst: 93/94 - 414, 414EI
Upper Deck: 93/94 - 485

Huber, Willie
Funmate: 83/84 - 88
O-Pee-Chee: 79/80 - 17; 80/81 - 173; 81/82 - 89, 126SK; 82/83 - 85, 185SK; 83/84 - 246, 139SK; 87/88 - 93, 31
Panini: 87/88 - 109
Post: 82/83 - 68
Topps: 79/80 - 17; 80/81 - 173; 81/82 WN - 89; 82/83 - 185SK; 83/84 - 139SK; 87/88 - 93

Huck, Fran
Esso: 70/71 - 132
Topps: 73/74 - 63

Hucul, Fred
Beehive: 45/63 - 108
Parkhurst: 51/52 - 45; 52/53 - 26; 53/54 - 71

Huddy, Charles (Charlie)
Bowman: 91/92 - 103
Fleer: 92/93 - 308; 93/94 - 361PP
Kraft: 1990 - 12
O-Pee-Chee: 83/84 - 30, 96; 84/85 - 244, 258; 85/86 - 187, 216SK; 86/87 - 211, 69SK; 87/88 - 207, 87SK; 88/89 - 218, 221SK; 89/90 - 158, 220SK; 90/91 - 344; 91/92 - 125PM; 93/94 - 219
Panini: 87/88 - 260; 88/89 - 53; 89/90 - 82; 90/91 - 221; 91/92 - 129
Parkhurst: 91/92 - 298E, 298F
Pro Set: 90/91 - 85; 91/92 - 400E, 400F
7-Eleven: 84/85 - 16
Score: 90/91 - 199A, 199C; 91 - 20T; 91/92 - 247B, 247C, 570B, 570C, 225PNE, 225PNF; 92/93 - 92C, 92A, 143PNC, 143PNA; 93/94 - 90C, 90A
Topps: 83/84 - 96SK; 89/90 - 158; 90/91 - 344; 91/92 - 203SC; 92/93 - 279, 279GS, 372SC; 93/94 - 219, 308SC, 308FD
Upper Deck: 90/91 - 341E, 341F; 91/92 - 569E, 569F
Vachon Foods: 83/84 - 27

Hudson, Dave
Eddie Sargent: 72/73 - 134
Loblaws: 74/75 - 115
O-Pee-Chee: 72/73 - 211; 73/74 - 234; 74/75 - 335; 75/76 - 122; 76/77 - 299; 77/78 - 343; 78/79 - 299
Topps: 75/76 - 122

Hudson, Mike
Bowman: 91/92 - 399; 92/93 - 73
Fleer: 92/93 - 37
O-Pee-Chee: 90/91 - 424; 91/92 - 495; 92/93 - 331
Parkhurst: 91/92 - 260E, 260F
Pro Set: 90/91 - 431; 91/92 - 369E, 369F
Score: 91/92 - 389B, 389C, 38PNE, 38PNF; 92/93 - 156C, 156A, 134PNC, 134PNA
Topps: 91/92 - 495, 22SC; 92/93 - 172, 172GS, 182SC

Huffman, Kerry
Fleer: 92/93 - 386
Leaf: 93/94 - 291

Huffman, Kerry (cont.)
O-Pee-Chee: 90/91 - 516; 92/93 - 48PM, 127PM; 93/94 - 43, 33SC, 33FD
Panini: 88/89 - 317
Parkhurst: 91/92 - 349E, 349F; 92/93 - 382, 382EI
Pro-Set: 92/93 - 136
Score: 92/93 - 239C, 239A; 93/94 - 182C, 182A
Topps: 92/93 - 387, 387GS, 381SC; 93/94 - 43, 33SC, 33FD
Upper Deck: 92/93 - 444

Huggins, Al
La Presse: 27/32 - 58

Hughes, Brent
Eddie Sargent: 70/71 - 147; 71-72 - 147
Esso: 72/73 - 155
Loblaws: 74/75 - 116
O-Pee-Chee: 69/70 - 144; 71/72 - 205; 72/73 - 234; 73/74 - 184
Toronto Sun: 71/72 - 198

Hughes, Brent Allen
Upper Deck: 90/91 - 333E, 333F

Hughes, Howie
Eddie Sargent: 70/71 - 80
O-Pee-Chee: 68/69 - 158; 69/70 - 142

Hughes, J.
Dom. Choc.: 1925 - 92

Hughes, John
PepsiCo: 80/81 - 27

Hughes, Pat
O-Pee-Chee: 79/80 - 65; 80/81 - 347; 82/83 - 109; 83/84 - 31, 213, 327SK, 328SK; 84/85 - 245; 85/86 - 229SK
Post: 82/83 - 88
7-Eleven: 84/85 - 17
Topps: 79/80 - 65; 83/84 - 327SK, 328SK
Vachon Foods: 83/84 - 28

Hull, Bobby
Bazooka: 71/72 - 4
Beehive: 45/63 - 109A, 109B; 64/67 - 41, 42, 43, 44
Chex: 63/65 - 5
Coca-Cola: 64/65 - 25; 65/66 - 24
Derniere: 72/84 - 101
Dom. Choc.: 70/71 - 36
Eddie Sargent: 70/71 - 43; 71/72 - 34
Esso: 70/71 - 59; 88/89 - 20
Hall of Fame: 87 - 242
Kellogg's: 70 - 4
Kraft: 1993 - 15
O-Pee-Chee: 68/69 - 16, 204, 3PS; 69/70 - 70, 216, 15ST, 9QS; 70/71 - 15, 235, 30DE, 14SS; 71/72 - 50, 261, 1BK, 9PT; 72/73 - 228, 336; 79/80 - 185
Shirriff: 60/61 - 63; 61/62 - 25; 62/63 - 47, 57; 68/69 - B1; 71/72 - 66
Topps: 58/59 - 66; 59/60 - 47; 60/61 - 58, 22ST; 61/62 - 29; 62/63 - 33, 12HB; 63/64 - 33; 64/65 - 20, 107; 65/66 - 59; 66/67 - 64, 125, 112; 66/67 US - 40; 67/68 - 113, 124; 68/69 - 16; 69/70 - 70; 70/71 - 15, 14SK; 71/72 - 50, 1BK; 72/73 - 126; 79/80 - 185
Toronto Star: 57/67 - 54, 82, 99, 114; 58/67 - 32, 90, 97; 63/64 - 6; 64/65 - 10
Ultimate: 92 - 57(OSE), 77(OSE), 82(OSE), 88(OSE), 89(OSE), 90(OSE), 91(OSE), 92(OSE), 96(OSE); 57(OSF), 77(OSF), 82(OSF), 88(OSF), 89(OSF), 90(OSF), 91(OSF), 92(OSF), 96(OSF), PC, OSHE, OSHF
Upper Deck: 92/93 - 43AS
Wonder Bread: 1960 - 2W, 2PM
Upper Deck: 93/94 - 539
Zellers: 93/94 - 5, 5A

Hull, Brett
Bowman: 90/91 - 24, HT1; 91/92 - 367, 375; 92/93 - 186, 209

Hull, Brett (cont.)
Donruss: 93/94 - 286, 5ES, U/PM, U/SP
Fleer: 92/93 - 186, 12AS; 93/94 - 117, 4SA, 211PP, 4PL, 4RL, 3SC
Gillette: 91/92 - 14
Hockey Wit: 93/94 - 97
Humpty Dumpty: 92/93 - 9(II)
Kellogg's: 92 - 21
Kraft: 90/91 - 20, 66; 93/94 - 39
Leaf: 93/94 - 255, 3AS, 8SS
McDonald's: 91/92 - McH4, Mc13
O-Pee-Chee: 88/89 - 66, 16NS, 16SK, 127SK, 9FS; 89/90 - 186, F/BB, 22SK; 90/91 - 4, 77, 195, 513, 47PM; 91/92 - 190, 259, 303, 403, 516, 49PM; 92/93 - 87, 124, 21AN; 93/94 - 425, 65SC, 65FD
Panini: 88/89 - 107; 89/90 - 117; 90/91 - 262, 333; 91/92 - 25, 325; 92/93 - 16E, 289E, 16F, 289F; 93/94 - N(E), N(F)
Parkhurst: 91/92 - 157E, 219E, 432E, PHC6E, 157F, 219F, 432F, PHC6F; 92/93 - 153, 459, 153EI, 459EI; 93/94 - 180, 180EI, G4, W7; 94/95 - 309, 309EI, H20, R20, C20, V35
Pro Set: 90/91 - 1PC, 263, 342, 378, 395, P3; 91/92 - AC6, AC18, 215E, 290E, 320E, 326E, 215F, 290F, 320F, 326F, PC5PT, 109PT, 24PK, 282PT; 92/93 - 156, 245, 8TL
Score: 90/91 - 300A, 300C, 317A, 317C, 346A, 346C, 351A, 351C, 366A, 366C, 100HR; 91 - 2PC; 91/92 - 1A, 337A, 347A, 371A, 404A, 412A, 428A, 1B, 261B, 294B, 302B, 318B, 367B, 377B, 1C, 261C, 294C, 302C, 318C, 367C, 377C, 3HC, 200PNE, 356PNE, 376PNE, 200PNF, 356PNF, 376PNF, 1PC, B-12E, B-12F; 92/93 - 350C, 411C, 435C, 443C, 500C, 350A, 411A, 435A, 443A, 500A, 100PNC, 100PNA, 257PNC, 257PNA, 6CTP, 6ATP; 93/94 - 335C, 335A, 34PNC, 34PNA, 18DT, 34CAS, 34AAS, 18FR
Season's: 92/93 - 13
Sega: 93/94 - 125
Topps: 88/89 - 66; 89/90 - 186, F/BB; 90/91 - 4, 77, 195, 2SL; 91/92 - P/C, 190, 259, 303, 403, 516, 20SL, 67SC, 7SCM, 8SCM; 92/93 - 2, 260, 340, 2GS, 260GS, 340GS, 1SC, 259SC; 93/94 - 425C, 21BG, 65SC, 65FD, 9MP, 14AS, 3SCF
Upper Deck: 90/91 - S/G, 154E, 154F, 203E, 203F, 474E, 474F, 546E, 546F; 91/92 - 33E, 464E, 622E, AW3E, BBE, TCHH, 1 to 9HHE, 33F, 464F, 622F, BBF, TCHH, 1 to 9HHF; 92/93 - 29, 620. W2, G7, 27AS; 93/94 - 160, 232

Hull, Dennis
Beehive: 64/67 - 42
Coca-Cola: 65/66 - 25
Colgate: 70/71 - 32
Dom. Choc.: 70/71 - 37
Eddie Sargent: 70/71 - 36; 72/73 - 67
Esso: 70/71 - 60
Lipton Soup: 74/75 - 17
Loblaws: 74/75 - 77
O-Pee-Chee: 68/69 - 153; 69/70 - 71; 70/71 - 14; 71/72 - 85; 72/73 - 52; 73/74 - 171; 74/75 - 150; 75/76 - 254; 76/77 - 195; 77/78 - 225
Shirriff: 68/69 - B11A, B11B
Topps: 65/66 - 64; 66/67 - 113; 66/67 US - 1; 67/68 - 56; 69/70 - 71; 70/71 - 14; 71/72 - 85; 72/73 - 164; 73/74 - 60; 74/75 - 150; 75/76 - 254; 76/77 - 195, 16PO; 77/78 - 225
Toronto Sun: 71/72 - 67

Hull, Jody
    Leaf: 93/94 - 157
    O-Pee-Chee: 90/91 - 46PM; 93/94 - 212
    Panini: 93/94 - 115E, 115F
    Parkhurst: 92/93 - 119, 119EI; 93/94 - 76, 76EI; 94/95 - 89, 89EI
    Pro Set: 90/91 - 490
    Score: 91/92 - 524B, 524C; 93/94 - 320C, 320A
    Topps: 91/92 - 100SC; 93/94 - 212, 344SC, 344FD; 93/94 - 112
    Upper Deck: 90/91 - 322E, 322F; 92/93 - 539; 93/94 - 510

Hume, Fred
    Hall of Fame: 83 - 233, A8P; 87 - 233

Hunter, Dale
    Bowman: 90/91 - 71; 91/92 - 303; 92/93 - 303
    Derniere: 72/84 - 152
    Donruss: 93/94 - 370
    Esso: 83/84 - 10E, 10F
    Fleer: 92/93 - 232; 93/94 - 135, 262PP
    Kellogg's: 84 - 35
    Kraft: 86/87 - 46, 46P
    Leaf: 93/94 - 118
    O-Pee-Chee: 81/82 - 277; 82/83 - 285, 26SWK; 83/84 - 293; 84/85 - 281, 179SK; 85/86 - 179, 151SK; 86/87 - 192, 32SK; 87/88 - 245; 88/89 - 70, 73SK; 89/90 - 76; 90/91 - 129; 91/92 - 229; 92/93 - 18, 2SP
    Panini: 87/88 - 168; 88/89 - 372; 89/90 - 346; 90/91 - 168; 91/92 - 203; 92/93 - 165E, 165F; 93/94 - 26E, 26F
    Parkhurst: 91/92 - 195E, 195F; 92/93 - CP7; 93/94 - D6; 94/95 - 254, 254EI
    PepsiCo: 80/81 - 69
    Post: 82/83 - 247
    Pro Set: 90/91 - 312; 91/92 - 506E, 506F, 245PT; 92/93 - 202
    Score: 90/91 - 44A, 44C; 91/92 - 56A, 56B, 336B, 56C, 336C, 40PNE, 40PNF; 92/93 - 231C, 231A, 104PNC, 104PNA, 237PNC, 237PNA, 4CSS, 4ASS; 93/93 - 40C, 40A
    Topps: 82/83 - 26SK; 86/87 - 192; 88/89 - 70; 89/90 - 76; 90/91 - 129; 91/92 - 229, 164SC; 92/93 - 464, 464GS, 40SC
    Upper Deck: 90/91 - 219E, 219F; 91/92 - 209E, 209F; 92/93 - 131
    Vachon Foods: 83/84 - 66

Hunter, Dave
    O-Pee-Chee: 79/80 - 387; 80/81 - 293; 81/82 - 115; 82/83 - 110, 102SK; 83/84 - 32, 154SK; 84/85 - 246; 88/89 - 62, 235SK
    Panini: 87/88 - 268; 88/89 - 339
    PepsiCo: 80/81 - 28
    Post: 82/83 - 89
    Topps: 82/83 - 102SK; 83/84 - 154; 88/89 - 62
    Vachon Foods: 83/84 - 29

Hunter, Mark
    Bowman: 91/92 - 9
    O-Pee-Chee: 82/83 - 185; 85/86 - 137SK; 86/87 - 57, 181; 87/88 - 50, 21; 88/89 - 187, 14SK; 91/92 - 109
    Panini: 87/88 - 313; 88/89 - 108
    Post: 82/83 - 148
    Pro Set: 90/91 - 422; 91/92 - 390E, 390F
    Score: 90 - 77T; 91/92 - 156A, 156B, 156C, 253PNE, 253PNF; 92/93 - 194C, 194A
    Topps: 86/87 - 57; 87/88 - 50; 88/89 - 187; 91/92 - 109, 15SC; 92/93 - 36, 36GS, 396SC
    Upper Deck: 91/92 - 479E, 479F
    Vachon Foods: 83/84 - 46

Hunter, Timothy (Tim)
    O-Pee-Chee: 90/91 - 434
    Panini: 87/88 - 216

Hunter, Timothy (Tim) (cont.)
    Pro Set: 90/91 - 423; 91/92 - 366E, 366F
    Score: 91/92 - 537B, 537C, 375PNE, 375PNF; 92/93 - 403C, 403A
    Upper Deck: 91/92 - 221E, 221F

Hurlbut, Mike
    Upper Deck: 92/93 - 448

Hurst, Ron
    Beehive: 45/63 - 441

Huston, Ron
    Loblaws: 74/75 - 61

Hutchison, Dave
    Loblaws: 74/75 - 133
    O-Pee-Chee: 75/76 - 390; 76/77 - 346; 77/78 - 380; 78/79 - 289; 79/80 - 302; 80/81 - 78
    Post: 82/83 - 55
    Topps: 80/81 - 78

Hutton, J.B. (Goalie)
    Hall of Fame: 83 - 100, G9P; 87 - 100

Hyland, Harry
    Hall of Fame: 83 - 157, L7P; 87 - 157
    Imperial Tobacco: 10/11 - 10, 30L; 11/12 - 30; 12/13 - 19

Hynes, Gord
    O-Pee-Chee: 92/93 - 8
    Parkhurst: 91/92 - 235E, 235F
    Score: 92/93 - 483C, 483A, 5COH
    Topps: 92/93 - 49SC

Iafrate, Al
    Bowman: 90/91 - 153; 91/92 - 300; 92/93 - 251
    Donruss: 93/94 - 371, 402, Y/PM, Y/SP
    Fleer: 92/93 - 233; 93/94 - 11, 5SA, 8AS, 263PP, 5SM
    Hockey Wit: 93/94 - 74
    Kraft: 90/91 - 21; 93/94 - 11
    Leaf: 93/94 - 141
    O-Pee-Chee: 85/86 - 210, 13SK; 86/87 - 26, 148SK; 87/88 - 238, 160SK; 88/89 - 71, 180SK; 89/90 - 79, 178; 90/91 - 91, 48PM; 91/92 - 148; 92/93 - 341; 93/94 - 45, 174, 80SC, 80FD
    Panini: 87/88 - 325; 88/89 - 118; 89/90 - 140; 90/91 - 290; 91/92 - 208; 92/93 - 168E, 168F; 93/94 - 32E, 32F
    Parkhurst: 91/92 - 194E, 194F; 92/93 - 203, 203EI; 93/94 - 217, 217EI; 94/95 - 15, 15EI
    Pro Set: 90/91 - 281, 354; 91/92 - 250E, 250F, 130PT; 92/93 - 205
    Season's: 92/93 - 67
    Score: 90/91 - 195A, 195C, 334A, 334C, 85HR; 91/92 - 209A, 209B, 209C, 207PNE, 207PNF; 92/93 - 11C, 11A, 66PNC, 66PNA; 93/94 - 188C, 188A, 19PNC, 19PNA, 9DT, 19CAS, 19AAS
    Sega: 93/94 - 152, 190
    Topps: 86/87 - 26; 88/89 - 71; 89/90 - 79; 90/91 - 91; 91/92 - 148, 372SC; 92/93 - 133, 133GS, 301SC; 93/94 - 45(I), 174, 80SC, 455SC, 80FD, 455FD, 9AS
    Upper Deck: 90/91 - 157E, 157F, 539E, 539F; 91/92 - 318E, 318F; 92/93 - 54, 37AS; 93/94 - 183

Ihnacak, Miroslav
    Panini: 87/88 - 336

Ihnacak, Peter
    Funmate: 83/84 - 123
    O-Pee-Chee: 83/84 - 334, 32SK; 85/86 - 19SK;
    Panini: 87/88 - 334
    Topps: 83/84 - 32SK
    Vachon Foods: 83/84 - 90

Ilitch, Mike
    Pro Set: 91/92 - AC22

Ilyin, Roman
    O-Pee-Chee: 91/92 - 34R

Imes, Chris
    Fleer: 93/94 - 506PP
    Topps: 93/94 - 11US

Imlach, Punch
    Chex: 63/65 - 47
    Hall of Fame: 87 - 243
    Parkhurst: 59/60 - 15; 63/64 - 19, 79
    Shirriff: 60/61 - 20; 61/62 - 57; 62/63 - 15
    Topps: 64/65 - 45; 65/66 - 11; 66/67 - 11; 66/67 US - 11
    York: 61/62 - 38

Ing, Peter (Goalie)
    Bowman: 91/92 - 157
    O-Pee-Chee: 90/91 - 49PM; 91/92 - 145, 33PM
    Panini: 91/92 - 99
    Pro Set: 90/91 - 639; 91/92 - 222E, 388E, 222F, 41PT, 388F
    Score: 90 - 11T; 90/91 - 414A, 414C; 91 - 12YS, 62T; 91/92 - 55A, 55B, 55C. 612B, 612C
    Topps: 91/92 - 145, 352SC; 92/93 - 423, 423GS, 347SC
    Upper Deck: 90/91 - 432E, 432F; 91/92 - 118E, 118F

Ingarfield, Earl
    Bauer: 68/69 - 14
    Beehive: 45/63 - 329A, 329B; 64/67 - 135
    Coca-Cola: 64/65 - 82; 65/66 - 83
    Dom. Choc.: 70/71 - 29
    Eddie Sargent: 70/71 - 132
    Esso: 70/71 - 46
    O-Pee-Chee: 68/69 - 102; 69/70 - 87, 9QS; 70/71 - 191; 15SK
    Shirriff: 60/61 - 92; 61/62 - 8268/69 - K2
    Topps: 58/59 - 18; 59/60 - 10; 61/62 - 49; 62/63 - 51, 21HB; 63/64 - 55; 64/65 - 65; 66/67 - 30; 68/69 - 102; 69/70 - 87; 70/71 - 15SK
    Toronto Star: 58/67 - 72

Inglis, Bill
    Eddie Sargent: 70/71 - 27
    O-Pee-Chee: 70/71 - 130
    Topps: 70/71 - 130

Ingram, Ron
    Beehive: 45/63 - 180; 64/67 - 78
    Parkhurst: 63/64 - 54; 93/94 - 33ML
    York: 63/64 - 54

Inkpen, Dave
    O-Pee-Chee: 79/80 - 321

Inness, Gary
    O-Pee-Chee: 75/76 - 227; 76/77 - 331; 79/80 - 358
    Topps: 75/76 - 227

Intranuovo, Ralph
    Upper Deck: 93/94 - 253

Ion, Mickey (Official)
    Hall of Fame: 83 - 9, A9P; 87 - 9

Irbe, Arturs, Goalie
    Donruss: 93/94 - 311
    Fleer: 92/93 - 401, 5UI; 93/94 - 145, 1RS, 221PP
    Leaf: 93/94 - 199
    O-Pee-Chee: 90/91 - 501, 7R; 93/94 - 110, 442, 4SC, 4FD
    Parkhurst: 92/93 - 396, 396EI; 93/94 - 451, 451EI; 94/95 - V79
    Pro-Set: 91/92 - 270PT
    Score: 91/92 - 323PNE, 323PNF; 92/93 - 457C, 457A; 93/94 - 377C, 377A
    Sega: 93/94 - 120
    Topps: 92/93 - 25, 25GS, 131SC; 93/94 - 110(I), 442C, 4SC, 4FD
    Upper Deck: 91/92 - 532E, 532F; 93/94 - 125

Ironstone, Joe (Goalie)
    Wm. Paterson: 24/25 - 1

Irvin, Dick
    Anonymous: 26/27 - 138
    Hall of Fame: 83 - 101, G10P; 87 - 101
    Topps: 60/61 - 60, 41ST

Irvine, Ted
- Eddie Sargent: 70/71 - 114; 72/73 - 152
- Esso: 70/71 - 153
- Loblaws: 74/75 - 204
- O-Pee-Chee: 68/69 - 39; 69/70 - 103; 70/71 - 65; 71/72 - 74; 72/73 - 212; 73/74 - 248; 74/75 - 264; 75/76 - 244; 76/77 - 347
- Shirriff: 68/69 - D2
- Topps: 68/69 - 39; 69/70 - 103; 70/71 - 65; 74/75 - 264; 75/76 - 244
- Toronto Sun: 71/72 - 175

Irwin, Ivan
- Parkhurst: 93/94 - 197ML
- Topps: 54/55 - 44

Issel, Kim
- Score: 90/91 - 409A, 409C

Ivan, Tommy
- Hall of Fame: 83 - 158, L8P; 87 - 158
- Parkhurst: 93/94 - 42ML
- Shirriff: 60/61 - 80

Jablonski, Pat (Goalie)
- Bowman: 92/93 - 66
- Fleer: 92/93 - 202; 93/94 - 125, 444PP
- O-Pee-Chee: 91/92 - 246, 29PM; 92/93 - 311, 95PM; 93/94 - 186
- Parkhurst: 92/93 - 404, 404EI; 93/94 - 192, 192EI
- Pro-Set: 92/93 - 178
- Score: 91/92 - 329A, 359B, 359C, 331PNE, 331PNF; 93/94 - 349C, 349A
- Topps: 91/92 - 246; 92/93 - 396, 396GS, 231SC; 93/94 - 186
- Upper Deck: 91/92 - 107E, 107F; 92/93 - 458

Jackson, Art
- Beehive: 34/44 - 21, 230, 327
- O-Pee-Chee: 35/36 - 88; 39/40 - 93

Jackson, Don
- O-Pee-Chee: 83/84 - 33; 84/85 - 247
- Vachon Foods: 83/84 - 30

Jackson, Hal
- Diamond: 1936/39 - 6(IV)
- O-Pee-Chee: 36/37 - 112

Jackson, Harvey (Busher)
- Amal. Press: 35/36 - 2
- Anonymous: 33/34 - 6
- Beehive: 34/44 - 22, 231, 328
- Can. Chew. Gum: 33/34 - 32
- Hall of Fame: 83 - 175, M11P; 87 - 175
- Hamilton Gum: 33/34 - 29
- La Presse: 27/32 - 59
- O-Pee-Chee: 33/34 - 33; 36/37 - 124; 37/38 - 139; 39/40 - 20
- Parkhurst: 55/56 - 22
- Quaker Oats: 38/39 - 24; 55/56 - 22
- Sweet Caporal: 34/35 - 47
- World Wide Gum: 36/37 - 51

Jackson, James (Jim)
- O-Pee-Chee: 83/84 - 84, 146SK; 84/85 - 225
- Topps: 83/84 - 146SK

Jackson, Jeff
- O-Pee-Chee: 88/89 - 219, 190SK; 89/90 - 180SK; 90/91 - 249
- Pro Set: 90/91 - 249
- Topps: 90/91 - 249
- Upper Deck: 90/91 - 291E, 291F

Jackson, Stan
- Champ's: 24/25 - 54
- Wm. Paterson: 23/24 - 27; 24/25 - 60

Jackson, Walter (Red)
- Can. Chew. Gum: 33/34 - 33
- Diamond: 33/35 - 31

Jacobs, Tim
- O-Pee-Chee: 76/77 - 370

Jaffres, Irving
- Diamond: 36/39 - 28(II)

Jagr, Jaromir
- Bowman: 91/92 - 95; 92/93 - 231, 301

Jagr, Jaromir (cont.)
- Donruss: 93/94 - 270, 3IK
- Fleer: 92/93 - 164, 6AS, 6UI; 93/94 - 65, 3GG, 189PP, 5PL, 5RL
- Gillette: 91/92 - 34
- Hockey Wit: 93/94 - 107
- Humpty Dumpty: 92/93 - 10(II)
- Kraft: 91/92 - 3; 1993 - 21; 93/94 - 12
- Leaf: 93/94 - 346
- O-Pee-Chee: 90/91 - 50PM; 91/92 - 9, 40, 24PM; 92/93 - 102; 93/94 - 105, 325, 19BG, 98SC, 98FD
- Panini: 91/92 - 275, 344; 92/93 - 282E, 294E, S(E), 282F, 294F, S(F); 93/94 - 82E, 82F
- Parkhurst: 91/92 - 132E, 132F; 92/93 - 135, 220, 465, 135EI, 220EI, 465EI; 93/94 - 154, 154EI; 94/95 - 174, 174EI; 94/95 - 314, 314EI
- Pro Set: 90/91 - 632; 91/92 - 183E, 183F, 92PT; 92/93 - 141
- Score: 90 - 70T; 90/91 - 428A, 428C; 91 - 38YS; 91/92 - 98A, 351A, 98B, 381B, 98C, 381C, 53PNE, 53PNF, 8HC; 92/93 - 113C, 494C, 113A, 494A, 275PNC, 275PNA, 6CTP, 15CT, 6ATP, 15AT; 93/94 - 50C, 50A, 20PNC, 20PNA, 20CAS, 29AAS
- Season's: 92/93 - 35
- Sega: 93/94 - 107
- Topps: 91/92 - 9, 40, 343SC; 92/93 - 24, 24GS, 498SC; 93/94 - 105, 325, 98SC, 98FD, 14AS
- Upper Deck: 90/91 - 356E, 356F; 91/92 - 20E, 42E, 256E, 617E, E(E), 20F, 42F, 256F, 617F, E6(F); 92/93 - 16, 28, 622, E14, W3, WJG6, 2AS; 93/94 - 139

Jaks, Pauli
- Upper Deck: 91/92 - 663E, 663F

James, Gerry
- Beehive: 45/63 - 412
- Parkhurst: 57/58 TOR - 8; 60/61 - 7; 93/94 - 117ML
- Shirriff: 60/61 - 17

Janecyk, Bob (Goalie)
- O-Pee-Chee: 85/86 - 223, 239SK; 86/87 - 131, 91SK
- Topps: 86/87 - 131

Jankowski, Lou
- Beehive: 45/63 - 110
- Parkhurst: 54/55 - 79
- Topps: 54/55 - 28

Janney, Craig
- Bowman: 90/91 - 33; 91/92 - 355; 92/93 - 14
- Donruss: 93/94 - 295
- Fleer: 92/93 - 187; 93/94 - 134, 212PP
- Hockey Wit: 93/94 - 4
- Kraft: 91/92 - 31
- Leaf: 93/94 - 181
- O-Pee-Chee: 88/89 - 10FS; 89/90 - 190, 29SK, 38SK, 2FS; 90/91 - 212; 91/92 - 41, 93PM; 92/93 - 325; 93/94 - 120
- Panini: 89/90 - 198; 90/91 - 14; 91/92 - 170; 92/93 - 22E, 22F; 93/94 - 157E, 157F
- Parkhurst: 91/92 - 4E, 378E, 4F, 378F; 92/93 - 154, 154EI; 93/94 - 443, 443EI; 94/95 - 200, 200EI
- Pro Set: 90/91 - 8; 91/92 - 2E, 2F, 3PT; 92/93 - 157
- Score: 90 - 30YS; 90/91 - 118A, 118C, 58HR; 91/92 - 253A, 473B, 473C, 57PNE, 57PNF; 92/93 - 285C, 285A, 196PNC, 196PNA, 11USG; 93/94 - 186C, 186A
- Sega: 93/94 - 123
- Topps: 89/90 - 190; 90/91 - 212; 91/92 - 41, 147SC; 92/93 - 134, 134GS, 41SC; 93/94 - 120, 335SC, 335FD, 22MP
- Upper Deck: 90/91 - 234E, 234F; 91/92 - 128E, 512E, 128F, 512F; 92/93 - 125; 93/94 - 225, 303, 323

Janssens, Mark
- Bowman: 90/91 - 226; 91/92 - 67
- O-Pee-Chee: 90/91 - 391; 91/92 - 186; 92/93 - 117PM; 93/94 - 133, 180SC, 180FD
- Panini: 90/91 - 101; 93/94 - 127E, 127F
- Parkhurst: 93/94 - 355, 355EI
- Pro Set: 90/91 - 199; 91/92 - 158E, 158F
- Score: 90/91 - 337; 91/92 - 421B, 421C; 93/94 - 339C, 339A
- Topps: 90/91 - 391; 91/92 - 186, 113SC; 93/94 - 133, 180SC, 180FD
- Upper Deck: 90/91 - 298E, 298F; 91/92 - 228E, 228F; 93/94 - 198

Jarrett, Doug
- Beehive: 64/67 - 43
- Coca-Cola: 65/66 - 26
- Dom. Choc.: 70/71 - 38
- Eddie Sargent: 70/71 - 34; 72/73 - 58
- Esso: 70/71 - 61
- Loblaws: 74/75 - 78
- O-Pee-Chee: 68/69 - 13; 69/70 - 67, 6QS; 70/71 - 150; 71/72 - 208; 72/73 - 97; 73/74 - 187; 74/75 - 351; 75/76 - 333
- Shirriff: 68/69 - B10
- Topps: 66/67 - 111; 67/68 - 112; 68/69 - 13; 69/70 - 67; 73/74 - 76
- Toronto Sun: 71/72 - 68

Jarrett, Gary
- Colgate: 70/71 - 49
- Dom. Choc.: 70/71 - 30
- Eddie Sargent: 70/71 - 140
- Esso: 70/71 - 47
- O-Pee-Chee: 68/69 - 87; 69/70 - 85; 70/71 - 75; 71/72 - 93
- Shirriff: 68/69 - H11
- Topps: 67/68 - 44; 68/69 - 87; 69/70 - 85; 70/71 - 75; 71/72 - 93
- Toronto Sun: 71/72 - 49

Jarry, Pierre
- Eddie Sargent: 72/73 - 208
- Loblaws: 74/75 - 99
- O-Pee-Chee: 72/73 - 237; 73/74 - 186; 74/75 - 171; 75/76 - 359; 76/77 - 49; 77/78 - 106
- Topps: 74/75 - 171; 76/77 - 49; 77/78 - 106

Jarvenpaa, Hannu
- O-Pee-Chee: 89/90 - 292, 145SK

Jarvi, Iiro
- O-Pee-Chee: 89/90 - 264, 192SK, 15FS; 90/91 - 52
- Panini: 89/90 - 329
- Topps: 90/91 - 52

Jarvis, Doug
- Derniere: 72/84 - 119, 184
- O-Pee-Chee: 76/77 - 313; 77/78 - 139; 78/79 - 13; 79/80 - 112; 80/81 - 76; 81/82 - 184, 34SK; 82/83 - 367, 40SK; 83/84 - 372, 208SK; 84/85 - 200, 129SK, 234SK; 85/86 - 151, 109SK; 86/87 - 28; 87/88 - 95, 19HL, 183SK, 207SK
- Panini: 87/88 - 52, 387
- PepsiCo: 80/81 - 47
- Post: 82/83 - 149
- Topps: 77/78 - 139; 78/79 - 13; 79/80 - 112; 80/81 - 76; 82/83 - 40SK; 83/84 - 208SK; 84/85 - 145; 85/86 - 151; 86/87 - 28; 87/88 - 95

Jax, Fredrik
- Upper Deck: 92/93 - 230

Jay, Bob
- Parkhurst: 93/94 - 361, 361EI
- Upper Deck: 93/94 - 470

Jeffrey, Larry
- Beehive: 45/63 - 181; 64/67 - 79A, 79B, 167
- Coca-Cola: 64/65 - 44
- O-Pee-Chee: 68/69 - 74; 70/71 - 28
- Parkhurst: 63/64 - 48

Jeffrey, Larry (cont.)
- Shirriff: 68/69 - G14
- Topps: 64/65 - 49; 65/66 - 83; 67/68 - 21; 70/71 - 28
- Toronto Star: 64/65 - 20
- York: 63/64 - 41

Jelinek, Tomas
- Upper Deck: 92/93 - 497; 93/94 - 165

Jenkins, Roger
- Beehive: 34/44 - 57, 160
- Canada Starch: 35/40 - 80
- Diamond: 33/35 - 32; 36/39 - 30(I)
- O-Pee-Chee: 35/36 - 92
- Sweet Caporal: 34/35 - 15

Jennings, Bill
- Beehive: 34/44 - 23, 105
- Hall of Fame: 83 - 142, K8P; 87 - 142

Jennings, Grant
- O-Pee-Chee: 90/91 - 510; 91/92 - 468
- Parkhurst: 93/94 - 427, 427EI
- Pro Set: 90/91 - 106
- Score: 90/91 - 31T; 91/92 - 531B, 531C; 92/93 - 542C, 542A
- Topps: 91/92 - 468

Jensen, Al (Goalie)
- O-Pee-Chee: 83/84 - 373, 202SK; 84/85 - 201, 128SK, 232SK; 86/87 - 135, 252SK
- Post: 82/83 - 314
- Topps: 83/84 - 202SK; 84/85 - 146; 86/87 - 135

Jensen, Darren (Goalie)
- O-Pee-Chee: 86/87 - 187SK

Jensen, David
- Upper Deck: 92/93 - 379

Jensen, Steve
- O-Pee-Chee: 77/78 - 238; 78/79 - 45; 79/80 - 292; 80/81 - 294; 81/82 - 154
- Panini: 79 - 220
- Post: 82/83 - 119
- Topps: 77/78 - 238; 78/79 - 45

Jerwa, Joe
- Beehive: 34/44 - 232
- Diamond: 36/39 - 29(II), 26(III)

Joanette, Rosaro
- CKAC Radio: 43/47 - 59

Johansen, Trevor
- O-Pee-Chee: 78/79 - 320

Johansson, Calle
- Bowman: 90/91 - 75; 91/92 - 294; 92/93 - 275
- Donruss: 93/94 - 372
- Fleer: 92/93 - 234; 93/94 - 465PP
- Leaf: 93/94 - 153
- O-Pee-Chee: 88/89 - 134SK, 11FS; 89/90 - 16; 90/91 - 164; 91/92 - 126; 92/93 - 223; 93/94 - 253, 93/94 - 278
- Panini: 88/89 - 221; 91/92 - 205; 93/94 - 31E, 31F
- Parkhurst: 91/92 - 410E, 410F; 92/93 - 201, 201EI
- Pro Set: 90/91 - 313; 91/92 - 248E, 248F, 243PT; 92/93 - 203
- Score: 90/91 - 309A; 91/92 - 155A, 155B, 155C, 232PNE, 232PNF; 92/93 - 209C, 209A, 30PNC, 30PNA; 93/94 - 76C, 76A
- Topps: 89/90 - 16; 90/91 - 164; 91/92 - 126, 188SC; 92/92 - 498, 498GS, 341SC; 93/94 - 278, 451SC, 451FD
- Upper Deck: 90/91 - 149E, 149F; 91/92 - 316E, 316F; 92/93 - 139

Johansson, Daniel
- Upper Deck: 92/93 - 599

Johansson, Roger
- Bowman: 91/92 - 257
- Fleer: 92/93 - 268
- O-Pee-Chee: 90/91 - 96; 91/92 - 53; 93/94 - 133SC, 133FD
- Parkhurst: 92/93 - 263, 263EI

Johansson, Roger (cont.)
- Pro Set: 90/91 - 424
- Score: 90/91 - 91T
- Topps: 90/91 - 96; 91/92 - 53, 375SC; 93/94 - 253, 133SC, 133FD

Johansson, Mathias
- Parkhurst: 93/94 - 537, 537EI

Johns, Don
- Beehive: 64/67 - 136
- Coca-Cola: 64/65 - 83
- Shirriff: 60/61 - 93
- Topps: 63/64 - 64

Johnson, Al
- Beehive: 45/63 - 182
- Parkhurst: 61/62 - 22
- Shirriff: 61/62 - 72

Johnson, Bob (Goalie)
- Loblaws: 74/75 - 244
- Pro Set: 90/91 - 674

Johnson, Craig
- Fleer: 93/94 - 507PP
- Topps: 93/94 - 19US

Johnson, Danny
- Eddie Sargent: 70/71 - 214; 71/72 - 210
- Esso: 70/71 - 241
- O-Pee-Chee: 71/72 - 95
- Toronto Sun: 71/72 - 280

Johnson, Ernest (Moose)
- Hall of Fame: 83 - 10, A10P; 87 - 10
- Imperial Tobacco: 10/11 - 28L, 30; 11/12 - 28; 12/13 - 25
- Topps: 60/61 - 4, 42ST

Johnson, Greg
- Donruss: 93/94 - 94
- Fleer: 93/94 - 330PP
- Leaf: 93/94 - 370
- O-Pee-Chee: 93/94 - 457
- Parkhurst: 93/94 - 270, 270EI
- Topps: 92/93 - 413, 413GS; 93/94 - 457C, 367SC, 367F
- Upper Deck: 90/91 - 460E, 460F; 93/94 - 452

Johnson, Ivan (Ching)
- Amal. Press: 35/36 - 3
- Anonymous: 33/34 - 33
- Beehive: 34/44 - 279
- Diamond: 36/39 - 31(I), 30(II), 27(III)
- Goudy Gum: 1933 - 30
- Hall of Fame: 83 - 51, D5P; 87 - 51
- O-Pee-Chee: 33/34 - 39
- Sweet Caporal: 34/35 - 42
- World Wide Gum: 36/37 - 21

Johnson, Jim
- Eddie Sargent: 70/71 - 153
- Esso: 70/71 - 173
- O-Pee-Chee: 68/69 - 186; 69/70 - 97; 71/72 - 48
- Topps: 69/70 - 97; 71/72 - 48
- Toronto Sun: 71/72 - 199

Johnson, Jim
- Bowman: 92/93 - 177
- Fleer: 92/93 - 95
- O-Pee-Chee: 86/87 - 231, 128SK; 87/88 - 196, 172SK; 88/89 - 148; 89/90 - 77; 90/91 - 98; 91/92 - 426; 93/94 - 98
- Panini: 87/88 - 143; 88/89 - 334; 89/90 - 320; 92/93 - 94E, 94F
- Parkhurst: 91/92 - 303E, 303F
- Pro Set: 90/91 - 235; 91/92 - 116E, 116F; 92/93 - 83
- Score: 90/91 - 202A, 202C; 91/92 - 52A, 52B, 52C, 235PNE, 235PNF; 92/93 - 161C, 161A, 137PNC, 137PNA; 93/94 - 144C, 144A
- Topps: 87/88 - 196; 88/89 - 148; 89/90 - 77; 90/91 - 98; 91/92 - 426; 92/93 - 54, 54GS, 75SC; 93/94 - 98, 298SC, 298FD

Johnson, Mark
- Funmate: 83/84 - 45
- O-Pee-Chee: 80/81 - 69; 83/84 - 140, 254SK; 84/85 - 72, 193SK; 85/86 - 44,

Johnson, Mark (cont.)
- O-Pee-Chee: 50SK; 86/87 - 112, 200SK; 87/88 - 101, 64SK; 88/89 - 45; 89/90 - 244; 90/91 - 178
- Panini: 79 - 213; 87/88 - 83; 89/90 - 260; 90/91 - 66
- Pro Set: 90/91 - 168
- Topps: 80/81 - 69; 83/84 - 254SK; 84/85 - 56; 85/86 - 44; 86/87 - 112; 87/88 - 101; 88/89 - 45; 90/91 - 178
- Upper Deck: 90/91 - 180E, 180F

Johnson, Norm
- Topps: 58/59 - 17

Johnson, Terry
- O-Pee-Chee: 84/85 - 186

Johnson, Tom
- Beehive: 45/63 - 35, 253; 64/67 - 13
- Coca-Cola: 64/65 - 7
- Derniere: 72/84 - 66
- Hall of Fame: 83 - 52, D6P; 87 - 52
- La Patrie: 51/54 - 19
- Parkhurst: 51/52 - 7; 52/53 - 9; 54/55 - 10; 55/56 - 49; 57/58 MON - 6; 58/59 - 10; 59/60 - 10; 60/61 - 44; 61/62 - 42; 62/63 - 50; 93/94 - 79ML, 143ML
- Quaker Oats: 45/54 - 24; 55/56 - 49
- Shirriff: 60/61 - 25; 61/62 - 106; 62/63 - 36
- Topps: 63/64 - 4; 64/65 - 101
- Toronto Star: 57/67 - 51; 58/67 - 28; 64/65 - 3
- York: 60/61 - 10; 61/62 - 11

Johnston, Eddie (Goalie)
- Beehive: 45/63 - 41; 64/67 - 12
- Coca-Cola: 64/65 - 8
- Dom. Choc.: 70/71 - 7
- Eddie Sargent: 70/71 - 5; 72/73 - 20
- Esso: 70/71 - 20
- Kraft: 93/94 - 40
- Loblaws: 74/75 - 260
- Mac's Milk: 73/74 - 10
- O-Pee-Chee: 68/69 - 133; 69/70 - 200; 70/71 - 133; 71/72 - 172; 72/73 - 261; 73/74 - 23; 74/75 - 265; 75/76 - 185; 76/77 - 285; 77/78 - 276
- Topps: 63/64 - 2; 64/65 - 21; 65/66 - 97; 66/67 - 99; 66/67 US - 64; 67/68 - 96; 72/73 - 13; 73/74 - 23; 75/76 - 185
- Toronto Sun: 71/72 - 11

Johnston, Greg
- O-Pee-Chee: 87/88 - 102
- Topps: 87/88 - 102

Johnston, Joey
- Eddie Sargent: 72/73 - 45
- Loblaws: 74/75 - 62
- O-Pee-Chee: 71/72 - 182; 72/73 - 96; 73/74 - 172; 74/75 - 185; 75/76 - 193; 76/77 - 325
- Topps: 72/73 - 48; 73/74 - 143; 74/75 - 185; 75/76 - 193
- Toronto Sun: 71/72 - 50

Johnston, Larry
- Eddie Sargent: 72/73 - 82
- O-Pee-Chee: 73/74 - 251; 75/76 - 352

Johnston, Marshall
- Eddie Sargent: 72/73 - 44
- O-Pee-Chee: 72/73 - 171; 73/74 - 21; 74/75 - 189
- Topps: 73/74 - 21; 74/75 - 189
- Toronto Sun: 71/72 - 51

Johnston, George (Wingy)
- Beehive: 34/44 - 58

Johnstone, Eddie
- O-Pee-Chee: 79/80 - 179; 80/81 - 277; 81/82 - 226, 169SK; 82/83 - 226, 139SK; 83/84 - 124; 84/85 - 55
- Post: 82/83 - 200
- Topps: 79/80 - 179; 81/82 EN - 99; 82/83 - 139SK; 84/85 - 43

Joliat, Aurel (Quetto)
- Amal. Press: 35/36 - 5
- Anonymous: 23/24 - 14; 24/25 - 48, 26/27 - 8
- Beehive: 34/44 - 161
- Canada Starch: 35/40 - 112
- Can. Chew. Gum: 33/34 - 34
- Champ's: 24/25 - 24
- Diamond: 33/35 - 33; 36/39 - 32(I), 31(II), 28(III)
- Dom. Chocs.: 1925 - 119
- Hall of Fame: 83 - 53, D7P; 87 - 53
- Hamilton Gum: 33/34 - 27
- La Presse: 27/32 - 2
- Maple Crispette: 24/25 - 14
- O-Pee-Chee: 33/34 - 50; 36/37 - 129; 37/38 - 152
- Parkhurst: 55/56 - 58
- Quaker Oats: 55/56 - 58
- Sweet Caporal: 34/35 - 16
- World Wide Gum: 33/34 - 3, 3P; 36/37 - 65

Joly, Greg
- Loblaws: 74/75 - 316
- O-Pee-Chee: 74/75 - 294; 75/76 - 170; 76/77 - 52; 77/78 - 273; 78/79 - 148; 79/80 - 311; 80/81 - 270; 82/83 - 86
- Post: 82/83 - 69
- Topps: 75/76 - 170; 76/77 - 52; 78/79 - 148

Jonathan, Stan
- O-Pee-Chee: 77/78 - 270; 78/79 - 181; 79/80 - 263; 80/81 - 113; 81/82 - 13
- Post: 82/83 - 6
- Topps: 78/79 - 181; 79/80 - 263; 80/81 - 113

Jones, Brad
- Bowman: 91/92 - 181
- O-Pee-Chee: 91/92 - 478, 115PM
- Parkhurst: 91/92 - 127E, 127F
- Pro Set: 91/92 - 456E, 456F
- Score: 91 - 53T; 91/92 - 603B, 603C
- Topps: 91/92 - 478, 368SC; 92/92 - 299, 299GS, 141SC
- Upper Deck: 91/92 - 304E, 304F

Jones, J. ("Chief") (Goalie)
- Imperial Tobacco: 10/11 - 19

Jones, Jimmy
- O-Pee-Chee: 78/79 - 288; 79/80 - 288

Jones, Keith
- Fleer: 92/93 - 436; 93/94 - 466PP
- O-Pee-Chee: 92/93 - 14PM; 93/94 - 96, 234SC, 234FD
- Parkhurst: 92/93 - 427, 427EI; 93/94 - 495, 495EI
- Score: 93/94 - 417C, 417A
- Topps: 93/94 - 96, 234SC, 234FD
- Upper Deck: 92/93 - 533; 93/94 - 377

Jones, Ron
- O-Pee-Chee: 75/76 - 247
- Topps: 75/76 - 247

Jonsson, Kenny
- Parkhurst: 93/94 - 535, 535EI
- Upper Deck: 92/93 - 596

Jonsson, Tomas
- O-Pee-Chee: 82/83 - 202; 83/84 - 9, 87SK; 84/85 - 128; 85/86 - 154, 78SK; 86/87 - 78, 214SK; 87/88 - 190; 88/89 - 108
- Panini: 87/88 - 92
- Post: 82/83 - 182
- Topps: 83/84 - 87SK; 85/86 - 154; 86/87 - 78; 87/88 - 190; 88/89 - 108

Joseph, Chris
- Bowman: 91/92 - 108
- Donruss: 93/94 - 492
- Fleer: 93/94 - 445PP
- O-Pee-Chee: 88/89 - 218SK; 89/90 - 225SK; 91/92 - 432; 92/93 - 203, 222
- Pro Set: 90/91 - 443
- Score: 91/92 - 415B, 415C
- Topps: 91/92 - 432, 362SC
- Upper Deck: 90/91 - 323E, 323F; 91/92 - 436E, 436F

Joseph, Curtis (Goalie)
- Bowman: 92/93 - 368
- Donruss: 93/94 - 296
- Fleer: 92/93 - 188; 93/94 - 172, 4G, 213PP, 4N
- Hockey Wit: 93/94 - 35
- Leaf: 1993/394 - 2, 2PW
- O-Pee-Chee: 90/91 - 171, 51PM; 91/92 - 417, 165PM; 92/93 - 339; 93/94 - 87, 272, 162SC, 162FD
- Panini: 90/91 - 272; 91/92 - 22; 92/93 - 15E, 15F; 93/94 - 166E, 166F
- Parkhurst: 91/92 - 152E, 152F; 92/93 - 155, 503, 155EI, 503EI; 93/94 - 175, 175EI; 94/95 - 199, 199EI, V17
- Pro Set: 90/91 - 638; 91/92 - 473E, 473F, 225PT; 92/93 - 164
- Score: 90 - 15YS; 90/91 - 151A, 151C; 91 - 19YS; 91/92 - 296A, 516B, 516C, 105PNE, 105PNF; 92/93 - 262C, 262A, 54PNC, 54PNA, 264PNC, 264PNA; 93/94 - 116C, 116A
- Season's: 92/93 - 14
- Sega: 93/94 - 126
- Topps: 90/91 - 171; 91/92 - 417; 92/93 - 237, 237GS, 327SC; 93/94 - 87(I), 222(I), 272, 18BG, 162SC, 162FD
- Upper Deck: 90/91 - 175E, 175F; 91/92 - 139E, 139F; 92/93 - 186; 93/94 - 157

Joseph, Fabian
- Fleer: 93/94 - 484PP
- O-Pee-Chee: 93/94 - 7TC
- Score: 92/93 - 8COH

Jotkus, Pete
- World Wide Gum: 36/37 - 104

Joyal, Eddie
- Beehive: 64/67 - 80A, 80B, 168
- Coca-Cola: 64/65 - 45
- Eddie Sargent: 70/71 - 67
- Esso: 70/71 - 98
- O-Pee-Chee: 68/69 - 40; 69/70 - 108, 16ST5QS; 70/71 - 39, 3DE, 16SS; 71/72 - 23
- Shirriff: 68/69 - D6
- Topps: 65/66 - 85; 68/69 - 40; 69/70 - 108; 70/71 - 39, 16SK; 71/72 - 23
- Toronto Sun: 71/72 - 118
- York: 63/64 - 48

Joyce, Robert (Bob)
- O-Pee-Chee: 88/89 - 2; 89/90 - 73, 31SK, 3FS
- Panini: 89/90 - 199
- Score: 90/91 - 291A, 291C
- Topps: 88/89 - 2; 89/90 - 73

Juckes, Bing (Winston Bryan)
- Beehive: 45/63 - 330
- Hall of Fame: 83 - 143, K9P; 87 - 143

Juneau, Joseph (Joe)
- Bowman: 92/93 - 292
- Donruss: 93/94 - 26, 394, 504
- Durivage: 93/94 - 27
- Fleer: 92/93 - 4; 93/94 - 49, 19PP, 2SY, 6PL
- Kraft: 9 3/94 - 13
- Leaf: 93/94 - 218, 1R
- O-Pee-Chee: 92/93 - 189, 101PM; 93/94 - 125, 299, 202SC, 202FD
- Panini: 92/93 - L(E), L(F); 93/94 - 143E, 143F, A(E), A(F)
- Parkhurst: 91/92 - 234E, 234F; 92/93 - 2, 2EI; 93/94 - 241, 280, 241EI, 280EI; 94/95 - 253, 253EI, H25, R25, C25
- Pro-Set: 92/93 - 219
- Score: 92/93 - 453C, 453A, 2COH, 221PNC, 221PNA, 19CT, 19AT; 93/94 - 330C, 330A, 5PCE
- Season's: 92/93 - 18
- Sega: 93/94 - 19
- Topps: 92/93 - 365, 365GS, 297SC; 93/94 - 299(II), 125, 12BG, 202SC, 202FD
- Upper Deck: 92/93 - 354, 399, CC9, AC1, G11, 53AS; 93/94 - 282, 343

Junker, Steve
- Donruss: 93/94 - 202
- Leaf: 93/94 - 402
- Parkhurst: 93/94 - 394, 394EI
- Upper Deck: 93/94 - 241

Juzda, Bill
- Beehive: 34/44 - 280; 45/63 - 413
- Parkhurst: 51/52 - 77
- Quaker Oats: 45/54 - 78A, 78B

Kaberle, Frantisek
- Upper Deck: 93/94 - 261

Kachur, Eddie
- Parkhurst: 93/94 - 37ML

Kadera, Roman
- Upper Deck: 93/94 - 267

Kaiser, Vern
- Beehive: 45/63 - 254
- Quaker Oats: 45/54 - 25

Kaleta, Alex
- Beehive: 34/44 - 59; 45/63 - 331

Kallur, Anders
- O-Pee-Chee: 80/81 - 156; 81/82 - 204, 162SK; 82/83 - 203, 57SK
- Post: 82/83 - 181
- Topps: 80/81 - 156; 81/82 EN - 90; 82/83 - 57SK

Kamensky, Valeri
- Bowman: 92/93 - 432
- Donruss: 93/94 - 277
- Fleer: 93/94 - 84, 199PP
- Gillette: 91/92 - 30
- Humpty Dumpty: 92/93 - 12(I)
- Leaf: 93/94 - 207
- O-Pee-Chee: 90/91 - 4R; 91/92 - 513; 92/93 - 266; 93/94 - 85, 237SC, 237FD
- Panini: 92/93 - 295E, R(E), 295F, R(F); 93/94 - 72E, 72F
- Parkhurst: 91/92 - 362E, 362F; 92/93 - 230, 377, 230EI, 377EI; 93/94 - 438, 438EI; 94/95 - 190, 190EI
- Pro-Set: 92/93 - 148
- Score: 91 - 76T; 91/92 - 340PNE, 340PNF; 92/93 - 360C, 360A, 64PNC, 64PNA; 93/94 - 326C, 326A
- Topps: 91/92 - 513; 92/93 - 53, 53GS, 344SC; 93/94 - 85, 237SC, 237FD
- Upper Deck: 91/92 - 273E, 273F; 92/93 - 27, E20; 93/94 - 118

Kaminski, Kevin
- Donruss: 93/94 - 505
- Parkhurst: 93/94 - 493, 493EI

Kaminsky, Max
- Beehive: 34/44 - 198

Kaminsky, Yan
- Donruss: 93/94 - 456
- Upper Deck: 92/93 - 344

Kampman, Bingo (Rudolph)
- Beehive: 34/44 - 329
- O-Pee-Chee: 39/40 - 3; 40/41 - 109
- Quaker Oats: 38/39 - 25

Kannegiesser, Sheldon
- Loblaws: 74/75 - 134
- Topps: 75/76 - 69
- O-Pee-Chee: 71/72 - 190; 74/75 - 338; 75/76 - 69; 76/77 - 335; 78/79 - 310
- Toronto Sun: 71/72 - 219

Kapanen, Sami
- Upper Deck: 91/92 - 674E, 674F

Kapkaikin, Konstantin
- O-Pee-Chee: 91/92 - 51R

Kapus, Richard
- Upper Deck: 93/94 - 265

Karabin, Ladislav
- Donruss: 93/94 - 472
- Parkhurst: 93/94 - 426, 426EI
- Upper Deck: 93/94 - 467

Karakas, Mike (Goalie)
Beehive: 34/44 - 60
CKAC Radio: 43/47 - 7
Diamond: 36/39 - 29(III), 7(IV), 7(V), 7(VI)
O-Pee-Chee: 36/37 - 107; 39/40 - 47
World Wide Gum: 36/37 - 123

Karamnov, Vitali
Donruss: 93/94 - 287
Fleer: 93/94 - 429PP
Leaf: 93/94 - 408
O-Pee-Chee: 93/94 - 292
Score: 92/93 - 398
Parkhurst: 92/93 - 387, 387EI; 93/94 - 444, 444EI
Topps: 93/94 - 292, 478SC, 478FD
Upper Deck: 92/93 - 341, 510; 93/94 - 338

Kariya, Paul
Fleer: 93/94 - 485PP
Upper Deck: 92/93 - 586

Karjalainen, Kyosti
Parkhurst: 91/92 - 295E, 295F
Upper Deck: 91/92 - 606E, 606F; 92/93 - 111, E6

Karlander, Al
Eddie Sargent: 70/71 - 58
Esso: 70/71 - 81
Toronto Sun: 71/72 - 97

Karlsson, Jakob
Upper Deck: 92/93 - 229

Karmanos, Jason
Donruss: 93/94 - 10JCA

Karpa, Dave
Fleer: 93/94 - 97, 3TP, 421PP
O-Pee-Chee: 93/94 - 408
Parkhurst: 92/93 - 151, 151EI; 93/94 - 165, 165EI
Topps: 93/94 - 408C, 296SC, 296FD
Upper Deck: 92/93 - 517; 93/94 - 375

Karpovtsev, Alexander
Donruss: 93/94 - 212
Fleer: 93/94 - 391PP
O-Pee-Chee: 91/92 - 35R; 93/94 - 358
Parkhurst: 93/94 - 269, 259EI
Topps: 93/94 - 358, 291SC, 291FD
Upper Deck: 92/93 - 351; 93/94 - 484

Kasatonov, Alexei
Bowman: 91/92 - 276; 92/93 - 323
Donruss: 93/94 - 5
Fleer: 92/93 - 340, 5PP
Leaf: 93/94 - 381
O-Pee-Chee: 90/91 - 358; 91/92 - 439; 92/93 - 353; 93/94 - 492
Parkhurst: 91/92 - 319E, 319F; 93/94 - 276, 276EI; 94/95 - 195, 195EI
Panini: 90/91 - 335; 91/92 - 216, 319; 92/93 - 180E, 180F
Pro Set: 90/91 - 169; 91/92 - 198PT; 92/93 - 101
Score: 90/91 - 209A, 209C; 91/92 - 194A, 194B, 194C, 255PNE, 255PNF; 92/93 - 394C, 394A, 289PNC, 289A 93/94 - 61C, 61A
Sega: 93/94 - 1
Topps: 90/91 - 358; 91/92 - 439, 282SC; 92/93 - 152, 152GS, 406SC; 93/94 - 492C, 332SC, 332FD
Upper Deck: 90/91 - 286E, 286F; 91/92 - 185E, 185F; 92/93 - 96; 93/94 - 474

Kasparaitis, Darius
Donruss: 93/94 - 203
Fleer: 92/93 - 344; 93/94 - 160, 149PP, 3SY
Leaf: 93/94 - 101, 13R
O-Pee-Chee: 92/93 - 103PM; 93/94 - 112, 443, 101SC, 101FD
Parkhurst: 92/93 - 102, 215, 102EI, 215EI; 93/94 - 122, 122EI; 94/95 - 133, 133EI
Score: 92/93 - 407PNC, 407PNA; 93/94 - 124C, 124A
Sega: 93/94 - 80
Topps: 93/94 - 112(I), 443C, 101SC, 101FD
Upper Deck: 91/92 - 650E, 650F; 92/93 - 335, 563, 623, ER7, CC13; 93/94 - 173

Kasper, Stephen (Steve)
Bowman: 90/91 - 147; 91/92 - 187; 92/93 - 33
Durivage: 92/93 - 4
O-Pee-Chee: 81/82 - 4 51SK; 82/83 - 12, 81SK, 253SK; 83/84 - 50, 53SK; 85/86 - 79; 86/87 - 97, 40SK; 87/88 - 162, 66BSK; 88/89 - 176, 27SK; 89/90 - 194, 152SK; 90/91 - 153; 91/92 - 302, 85PM; 93/94 - 73, 122SC, 122FD
Panini: 87/88 - 15; 88/89 - 210; 89/90 - 92; 90/91 - 238; 91/92 - 88
Parkhurst: 92/93 - 403, 403EI
Post: 82/83 - 7
Pro Set: 90/91 - 120; 91/92 - 449E, 449F
Score: 90/91 - 247A, 247C; 91 - 24T; 91/92 - 256A, 574B, 574C; 92/93 - 306C, 306A
Topps: 81/82 EN - 68; 82/83 - 81SK, 253SK; 83/84 - 53SK; 85/86 - 79; 86/87 - 97; 87/88 - 162; 88/89 - 176; 89/90 - 194; 90/91 - 153; 91/92 - 302, 139SC; 92/93 - 150, 150GS, 71SC; 93/94 - 73, 122SC, 122FD
Upper Deck: 90/91 - 140E, 140F; 91/92 - 576E, 576F

Kastelic, Edward (Ed)
O-Pee-Chee: 90/91 - 404
Pro Set: 90/91 - 450

Kaszycki, Mike
O-Pee-Chee: 78/79 - 171; 79/80 - 87; 80/81 - 371
Topps: 78/79 - 171; 79/80 - 87

Kea, Ed
O-Pee-Chee: 75/76 - 383; 76/77 - 361; 77/78 - 301; 78/79 - 277; 79/80 - 390; 81/82 - 294
Post: 82/83 - 263
Topps: 81/82 WN - 118

Keane, Mike
Bowman: 91/92 - 34
Donruss: 93/94 - 451
Fleer: 92/93 - 106; 93/94 - 196, 129PP
Hockey Wit: 93/94 - 63
Humpty Dumpty: 92/93 - 13(I)
Leaf: 93/94 - 279
O-Pee-Chee: 90/91 - 325; 91/92 - 434; 92/93 - 274; 93/94 - 139, 92SC, 92FD
Panini: 91/92 - 190
Parkhurst: 91/92 - 311E, 311F; 92/93 - 318, 318EI
Pro Set: 90/91 - 151; 91/92 - 121E, 121F, 191PT
Score: 90/91 - 102T; 91/92 - 360A, 251B, 251C, 265PNE, 265PNF; 92/93 - 179C, 179A, 164PNC, 164PNA; 93/94 - 170C, 170A
Topps: 90/91 - 325; 91/92 - 434, 236SC; 92/93 - 478, 478GS, 349SC; 93/94 - 139, 92SC, 92FD
Upper Deck: 90/91 - 382E, 382F; 92/93 - 164

Keans, Doug (Goalie)
O-Pee-Chee: 84/85 - 5; 85/86 - 133; 86/87 - 22; 87/88 - 147, 139SK
Panini: 87/88 - 4
Topps: 84/85 - 4; 85/86 - 133; 86/87 - 22; 87/88 - 147

Kearns, Dennis
Eddie Sargent: 72/73 - 224
Loblaws: 74/75 - 296
O-Pee-Chee: 71/72 - 231; 73/74 - 162; 74/75 - 366; 75/76 - 188; 76/77 - 338; 77/78 - 175; 78/79 - 191; 79/80 - 76; 80/81 - 392; 81/82 - 337, 249SK
Panini: 79 - 58
PepsiCo: 80/81 - 110
Topps: 73/74 - 173; 75/76 - 188; 77/78 - 175; 78/79 - 191; 79/80 - 76
Toronto Sun: 71/72 - 281

Keating, Jack
Beehive: 34/44 - 106
O-Pee-Chee: 39/40 - 67

Keats, Duke
Hall of Fame: 83 - 54, D8P; 87 - 54

Keczmer, Dan
Donruss: 93/94 - 406
Fleer: 93/94 - 304PP
O-Pee-Chee: 91/92 - 3S; 93/94 - 461
Parkhurst: 93/94 - 82, 82EI
Topps: 93/94 - 461C
Upper Deck: 93/94 - 249

Keeling, Butch (Melville)
Anonymous: 33/34 - 30
Beehive: 34/44 - 281
Diamond: 33/35 - 34; 36/39 - 34(I), 32(II), 30(III)
O-Pee-Chee: 33/34 - 36
World Wide Gum: 33/34 - 203; 36/37 - 15

Keenan, Larry
Esso: 70/71 - 27
O-Pee-Chee: 68/69 - 115; 70/71 - 104
Parkhurst: 61/62 - 13
Shirriff: 61/62 - 55; 68/69 - L9
Topps: 68/69 - 115; 70/71 - 104
Toronto Sun: 71/72 - 29
York: 61/62 - 32

Kehoe, Rick
Eddie Sargent: 72/73 - 209
Funmate: 83/84 - 104
Kellogg's: 84 - 5
Loblaws: 74/75 - 245
Mac's Milk: 73/74 - 11
O-Pee-Chee: 72/73 - 277; 73/74 - 60; 74/75 - 81; 75/76 - 39; 76/77 - 124; 77/78 - 33; 78/79 - 213; 79/80 - 109; 80/81 - 18, 117; 81/82 - 254, 260, 267, 182SK, 261SK; 82/83 - 271, 143SK; 83/84 - 274, 282, 11SK, 231SK, 232SK; 84/85 - 177, 117SK
Post: 82/83 - 234
7-Eleven: 84/85 - 39
Topps: 73/74 - 179; 74/75 - 81; 75/76 - 39; 76/77 - 124; 77/78 - 33; 78/79 - 213; 79/80 - 109; 80/81 - 18, 117; 81/82 - EN 128, 17, 60; 82/83 - 143SK; 83/84 - 11SK, 231SK, 232SK; 84/85 - 125

Keiller, Jimmy
World Wide Gum: 36/37 - 120

Kekalainen, Jarmo
Upper Deck: 91/92 - 108E, E1(E), 108F, E1(F)
Parkhurst: 93/94 - 410, 410EI

Kelly Bob
Eddie Sargent: 72/73 - 163
Esso: 70/71 - 174
Loblaws: 74/75 - 224
O-Pee-Chee: 71/72 - 203; 73/74 - 253; 74/75 - 380; 75/76 - 184; 76/77 - 219; 77/78 - 178; 78/79 - 71; 79/80 - 14; 81/82 - 349, 195SK
Parkhurst: 92/93 - 477, 477EI
Topps: 75/76 - 184; 76/77 - 219; 77/78 - 178; 78/79 - 71; 79/80 - 14; 81/82 EN - 119
Toronto Sun: 71/72 - 200

Kelly, Jim
Pro-Set: 91/92 - 293PT

Kelly, J. Bob
Loblaws: 74/75 - 246
O-Pee-Chee: 74/75 - 143; 75/76 - 263; 76/77 - 261; 77/78 - 14; 78/79 - 189; 79/80 - 306
Topps: 74/75 - 143; 75/76 - 263; 76/77 - 261; 77/78 - 14; 78/79 - 189

Kelly, John Paul
Post: 82/83 - 120

Kelly, Pete
Beehive: 34/44 - 107, 233
Canada Starch: 35/740 - 63

Kelly, Red
- Beehive: 45/63 - 183, 414A, 414B; 64/67 - 169
- Chex: 63/65 - 48
- Coca-Cola: 64/65 - 99; 65/66 - 97
- Hall of Fame: 83 - 55, D9P; 87 - 55
- O-Pee-Chee: 74/75 - 76
- Parkhurst: 51/52 - 55; 52/53 - 67; 53/54 - 40; 54/55 - 42; 60/61 - 9; 61/62 - 9; 62/63 - 5; 63/64 - 3, 63; 92/93 - PR10; 93/94 - 52ML, 142ML
- Royal Desserts: 1952 - 7
- Shirriff: 60/61 - 4; 61/62 - 49; 62/63 - 9
- Topps: 54/55 - 5; 57/58 - 48; 58/59 - 61; 59/60 - 65; 64/65 - 44; 65/66 - 15; 66/67 - 79; 66/67 US - 42; 74/75 - 76
- Toronto Star: 58/67 - 49; 63/64 - 36
- Ultimate: 92 - 38(OSE), 79(OSE), 38(OSF), 79(OSF)
- Upper Deck: 90/91 - 502E, 502F
- York: 60/61 - 28; 61/62 - 21; 62/63 - 20; 63/64 - 12

Kelly, Reg (Pep)
- Amal. Press: 35/36 - 7
- Beehive: 34/44 - 61, 330
- O-Pee-Chee: 35/36 - 87; 37/38 - 145; 39/40 - 9
- Quaker Oats: 38/39 - 26
- World Wide Gum: 36/37 - 86

Kendall, Carl
- Imperial Tobacco: 12/13 - 35

Kendall, William
- Beehive: 34/44 - 62, 331
- Diamond: 33/35 - 35; 36/39 - 35(I), 33(II)

Kennedy, Edward (Dean)
- Bowman: 90/91 - 248
- Kraft: 93/94 - 41
- O-Pee-Chee: 91/92 - 388
- Panini: 87/88 - 276
- Pro Set: 90/91 - 22
- Score: 90/91 - 299A, 299C; 91/92 - 431B, 431C; 92/93 - 211C, 211A, 239PNC, 239PNA; 93/94 - 366C, 366A
- Topps: 91/92 - 388
- Upper Deck: 90/91 - 380E, 380F

Kennedy, Forbes
- Beehive: 45/63 - 37, 111, 184; 64/67 - 14
- Coca-Cola: 64/65 - 9; 65/66 - 9
- O-Pee-Chee: 68/69 - 97
- Parkhurst: 93/94 - 35ML
- Shirriff: 68/69 - J10
- Topps: 57/58 - 50; 58/59 - 11; 59/60 - 52; 63/64 - 19; 68/69 - 97
- Toronto Star: 64/65 - 4

Kennedy, Sheldon
- Leaf: 93/94 - 246
- O-Pee-Chee: 90/91 - 520; 91/92 - 317; 93/94 - 221
- Score: 93/94 - 361C, 361A
- Topps: 91/92 - 317; 92/93 - 368, 368GS; 93/94 - 221
- Upper Deck: 91/92 - 408E, 408F

Kennedy, Ted
- Beehive: 45/63 - 415; 64/67 - 170
- Hall of Fame: 83 - 69, E9P; 87 - 69
- Parkhurst: 51/52 - 86; 52/53 - 44; 53/54 - 7; 54/55 - 29; 55/56 - 29; 93/94 - PR41, 116ML
- Quaker Oats: 45/54 - 79A, 79B, 79C, 79D, 79E; 55/56 - 29
- Toronto Star: 58/57 - 1

Keon, Dave
- Bazooka: 71/72 - 11
- Beehive: 45/63 - 416; 64/67 - 171A, 171B
- Chex: 63/65 - 49
- Coca-Cola: 64/65 - 100; 65/66 - 98
- Dom. Choc.: 70/71 - 128
- Eddie Sargent: 62/63 - 3; 70/71 - 208; 72/73 - 206
- Esso: 70/71 - 224
- Hall of Fame: 87 - 255
- Lipton Soup: 74/75 - 50
- Loblaws: 74/75 - 278

Keon, Dave (cont.)
- O-Pee-Chee: 68/69 - 198, 19PS; 69/70 - 51, 17ST, 11QS; 70/71 - 219, 47DE, 17SS; 71/72 - 80, 259, 16BK, 3PT; 72/73 - 108, 209; 73/74 - 150; 74/75 - 151; 79/80 - 279; 80/81 - 272; 81/82 - 129
- Parkhurst: 61/62 - 5; 62/63 - 15; 63/64 - 75; 92/93 - PR21
- Post: 66/67 - 3S, 5L; 68/69 - 22; 82/83 - 101
- Shirriff: 61/62 - 58; 62/63 - 16, 52, 55; 68/69 - M11
- Topps: 64/65 - 94; 65/66 - 17; 66/67 - 78; 66/67 US - 30; 67/68 - 11; 68/69 - 128; 69/70 - 51; 70/71 - 17SK; 71/72 - 80, 16BK; 72/73 - 88; 73/74 - 85; 74/75 - 151; 81/82 EN - 83
- Toronto Star: 57/67 - 76, 143; 58/67 - 57; 63/64 - 37; 64/65 - 42
- Toronto Sun: 71/72 - 261
- Ultimate: 92 - 39(OSE), 39(OSF)
- Wonder Bread: 1960 - 3W, 3PM
- York: 60/61 - 29; 61/62 - 27; 62/63 - 9; 63/64 - 6

Kerch, Alexander
- O-Pee-Chee: 90/91 - 474
- Parkhurst: 94/95 - 80, 80EI

Kerr, Alan
- Bowman: 90/91 - 118
- O-Pee-Chee: 88/89 - 63, 106SK; 90/91 - 50
- Panini: 88/89 - 288; 89/90 - 275; 90/91 - 89
- Parkhurst: 91/92 - 273E, 273F
- Pro Set: 90/91 - 184; 91/92 - 376E, 376F
- Score: 90/91 - 307A; 91/92 - 571B, 571C
- Topps: 88/89 - 63; 90/91 - 50
- Upper Deck: 90/91 - 388E, 388F

Kerr, Albert
- Imperial Tobacco: 10/11 - 10L; 11/12 - 10; 12/13 - 33

Kerr, Dave (Goalie)
- Beehive: 34/44 - 282
- Canada Starch: 35/40 - 64
- Can. Chew. Gum: 33/34 - 35
- Diamond: 36/39 - 34(II), 31(III)
- La Presse: 27/32 - 56
- O-Pee-Chee: 34/35 - 59; 39/40 - 37; 40/41 - 139
- Sweet Caporal: 34/35 - 43
- World Wide Gum: 33/34 - 19; 36/37 - 53

Kerr, Reg
- O-Pee-Chee: 79/80 - 67; 80/81 - 377; 81/82 - 58, 118SK; 82/83 - 67, 176SK
- Post: 82/83 - 56
- Topps: 79/80 - 67; 81/82 WN - 70; 82/83 - 176SK

Kerr, Tim
- Esso: 88/89 - 21
- Fleer: 92/93 - 74
- O-Pee-Chee: 81/82 - 251; 82/83 - 253; 84/85 - 162, 364, 105SK, 106SK; 85/86 - 91, 260, H/BB, 96SK; 86/87 - 134, 261, G/BB, 240SK; 87/88 - 144, 20HL, B/BB, 103SK; 89/90 - 72, G/BB, 110SK, 216SK; 90/91 - 210; 91/92 - 164, 83PM
- Panini: 87/88 - 128; 88/89 - 321; 89/90 - 294, 377; 90/91 - 120; 91/92 - 226
- Post: 82/83 - 215
- Pro Set: 90/91 - 218; 91/92 - 180E, 446E, 180F, 80PT, 446F
- Score: 90/91 - 177A, 177C, 77HR; 91 - 15T; 91/92 - 108A, 108B, 108C, 565B, 565C, 52PNE, 52PNF; 92/93 - 93C, 93A, 368PNC, 368PNA
- 7-Eleven: 84/85 - 36
- Topps: 84/85 - 119; 85/86 - 91, H/BB; 86/87 - 134, G/BB; 87/88 - 144, B/BB, 10SK; 89/90 - 72, G/BB; 90/91 - 210; 91/92 - 164, 130SC; 92/93 - 351, 351GS
- Upper Deck: 90/91 - 247E, 247F

Kesa, Dan
- Fleer: 93/94 - 460PP

Kessell, Rick
- Eddie Sargent: 72/73 - 177

Ketterer, Markus
- Upper Deck: 91/92 - 23E, 23F

Khabibulin, Nicolai
- Upper Deck: 91/92 - 652E, 652F

Khaidarov, Ravil
- O-Pee-Chee: 91/92 - 36R
- Upper Deck: 92/93 - 347

Kharin, Sergei
- Score: 91/92 - 394A, 284B, 284C
- Upper Deck: 91/92 - 381E, 381F

kharlamov, Alexander
- Parkhurst: 93/94 - 529, 529EI

Khmylev, Yuri
- Donruss: 93/94 - 36
- Fleer: 92/93 - 260; 93/94 - 173, 30PP
- Leaf: 93/94 - 211
- O-Pee-Chee: 91/92 - 16R; 93/94 - 389, 241SC, 241FD
- Panini: 93/94 - 106E, 106F
- Parkhurst: 92/93 - 255, 255EI; 94/95 - 22, 22EI
- Score: 93/94 - 302C, 302A
- Topps: 93/94 - 389C, 241SC, 241FD
- Upper Deck: 92/93 - 504

Khomutov, Andrei
- O-Pee-Chee: 90/91 - 3R
- Bowman: 91/92 - 307
- Fleer: 92/93 - 235, 7UI; 93/94 - 59
- Leaf: 93/94 - 168
- O-Pee-Chee: 90/91 - 16R; 91/92 - 78, 176PM; 92/93 - 286
- Panini: 93/94 - 28E, 28F
- Parkhurst: 91/92 - 189E, 189F
- Pro Set: 91/92 - 260E, 260F
- Score: 91 - 6YS; 91/92 - 175A, 175B, 175C, 162PNE, 162PNF; 92/93 - 146PNC, 146PNA; 93/93 - 80C, 80A
- Topps: 91/92 - 78, 359SC
- Upper Deck: 90/91 - 537E, 537F; 91/92 - 157E, 157F

Khristich, Dimitri
- Bowman: 92/93 - 427
- Donruss: 93/94 - 373
- Fleer: 93/94 - 59, 264PP
- O-Pee-Chee: 93/94 - 210
- Panini: 92/93 - N(E), N(F)
- Parkhurst: 92/93 - 428, 428EI; 93/94 - 220, 220EI; 94/95 - 252, 252EI
- Pro-Set: 91/92 - 242PT; 92/93 - 208
- Score: 92/93 - 33C, 33A, 27CSS, 27ASS, 25CT, 25AT
- Sega: 93/94 - 154
- Topps: 92/93 - 470, 470GS, 86SC; 93/94 - 210, 277SC, 277F
- Upper Deck: 92/93 - 219; 93/94 - 135

Kidd, Trevor (Goalie)
- Fleer: 93/94 - 305PP
- Leaf: 93/94 - 385
- O-Pee-Chee: 91/92 - 312
- Parkhurst: 94/95 - 288, 288EI
- Score: 90/91 - 438A, 438C; 91/92 - 381A, 271B, 271C; 92/93 - 12COH
- Topps: 91/92 - 312; 92/93 - 280, 280GS
- Upper Deck: 90/91 - 463E, 463F; 91/92 - 684E, 684F; 92/93 - 134, 385; 93/94 - 399

Kilpatrick, John
- Hall of Fame: 83 - 116, HF83P; 87 - 116

Kilrea, Hec
- Anonymous: 26/27 - 19; 33/34 - 17
- Beehive: 34/44 - 108, 332
- La Presse: 27/32 - 35
- O-Pee-Chee: 35/36 - 86; 39/40 - 71
- World Wide Gum: 33/34 - 64; 36/37 - 24

Kilrea, Ken
- Beehive: 34/44 - 109

Kilrea, Wally
Beehive: 34/44 - 110
O-Pee-Chee: 34/35 - 63
World Wide Gum: 33/34 - 53

Kimble, Darin
Bowman: 91/92 - 381
O-Pee-Chee: 90/91 - 437; 91/92 - 156
Parkhurst: 91/92 - 377E, 377F
Pro Set: 90/91 - 517
Score: 91/92 - 526B, 526C
Topps: 91/92 - 156, 278SC; 92/93 - 511, 511GS, 486SC

Kindrachuk, Orest
Loblaws: 74/75 - 225
O-Pee-Chee: 74/75 - 334; 75/76 - 389; 76/77 - 233; 77/78 - 26; 78/79 - 114; 79/80 - 218; 80/81 - 292
Parkhurst: 92/93 - 476, 476EI
Topps: 76/77 - 233; 77/78 - 26; 78/79 - 114; 79/80 - 218

King, Dave
Kraft: 93/94 - 42

King, Derek
Bowman: 91/92 - 220; 92/93 - 188
Donruss: 93/94 - 204
Fleer: 92/93 - 128; 93/94 - 176, 150PP
Hockey Wit: 93/94 - 28
Leaf: 93/94 - 119
O-Pee-Chee: 89/90 - 6, 116SK; 90/91 - 128; 91/92 - 455; 92/93 - 79; 93/94 - 176, 215SC, 215FD
Panini: 88/89 - 289; 89/90 - 271; 91/92 - 247; 92/93 - 199E, 199F; 93/94 - 58E, 58F
Parkhurst: 91/92 - 108E, 108F; 92/93 - 100, 100EI; 93/94 - 119, 119EI; 94/95 - 132, 132EI
Pro Set: 90/91 - 185; 91/92 - 146E, 146F, 201PT, 286PT; 92/93 - 110
Score: 90 - 86T; 91/92 - 167A, 167B, 167C, 91/92 - 255C, 255A, 107PNE, 107PNF; 92/93 - 17PNC, 17PNA, 15CSS, 15ASS; 93/94 - 48C, 48A
Topps: 89/90 - 6; 90/91 - 128; 91/92 - 455, 82SC; 92/93 - 431, 431GS, 82SC; 93/94 - 176, 215SC, 215FD
Upper Deck: 90/91 - 407E, 407F; 91/92 - 382E, 382F; 92/93 - 191; 93/94 - 417

King, Frank
Beehive: 45/63 - 255

King, Kris
Bowman: 91/92 - 59; 92/93 - 380
Donruss: 93/94 - 379
Leaf: 93/94 - 253
O-Pee-Chee: 90/91 - 526; 91/92 - 498; 92/93 - 86
Parkhurst: 91/92 - 337E, 337F; 92/93 - 442, 442EI; 93/94 - 478B, 478B(EI); 94/95 - 269, 269EI
Pro Set: 90/91 - 491; 91/92 - 445E, 445F
Score: 90 - 76T; 91/92 - 363A, 402B, 402C, 362PNE, 362PNF; 92/93 - 181C, 181A, 168PNC, 168PNA, 253PNC, 253PNA; 93/94 - 362C, 362A
Topps: 91/92 - 498, 26SC; 92/93 - 509, 509GS, 187SC
Upper Deck: 90/91 - 440E, 440F; 91/92 - 330E, 330F; 92/93 - 78; 93/94 - 14

King, Larry
Pro-Set: 91/92 - 292PT

King, Scott (Goalie)
Topps: 92/93 - 269SC

King, Steven
Donruss: 93/94 - 1
Fleer: 92/93 - 355; 93/94 - 6PP
Leaf: 93/94 - 410
O-Pee-Chee: 93/94 - 303
Parkhurst: 92/93 - 347, 347EI; 93/94 - 1, 1EI
Score: 93/94 - 382C, 382A
Topps: 93/94 - 303, 377SC, 377FD
Upper Deck: 92/93 - 575; 93/94 - 24

King, Wayne
Loblaws: 74/75 - 63

Kiprusoff, Marko
Upper Deck: 91/92 - 671E, 671F

Kirk, Bobby
Beehive: 34/44 - 283

Kirkpatrick, Bob
Beehive: 34/44 - 284

Kirton, Mark
O-Pee-Chee: 81/82 - 90; 82/83 - 87; 83/84 - 352
Post: 82/83 - 70
Topps: 81/82 WN - 90
Vachon Foods: 83/84 - 109

Kisio, Kelly
Bowman: 91/92 - 72; 92/93 - 166
Donruss: 93/94 - 55
Fleer: 92/93 - 196; 93/94 - 155, 37PP
Leaf: 93/94 - 208
O-Pee-Chee: 84/85 - 56, 40; 85/86 - 101; 86/87 - 116, 163SK; 87/88 - 76, 28SK; 88/89 - 143, 239SK; 89/90 - 171; 90/91 - 239; 91/92 - 335, 69PM; 92/93 - 232; 93/94 - 455, 30SC, 30FD
Panini: 87/88 - 115; 88/89 - 307; 89/90 - 287; 90/91 - 94; 91/92 - 291; 92/93 - 124E, 124F; 93/94 - 256E, 256F
Parkhurst: 91/92 - 165E, 165F; 92/93 - 166, 166EI; 93/94 - 33, 33EI
Pro Set: 90/91 - 200; 91/92 - 168E, 479E, 168F, 104PT, 26PK, 479F; 92/93 - 167
Score: 90/91 - 37A, 37C; 91 - 3T; 91/92 - 288A, 553B, 553C, 231PNE, 231PNF; 92/93 - 57C, 57A, 362PNC, 362PNA; 93/94 - 27C, 27A, 30PNC, 30PNA, 30CAS, 30AAS
Sega: 93/94 - 117
Topps: 85/86 - 101; 86/87 - 116; 87/88 - 76; 88/89 - 143; 89/90 - 171; 90/91 - 239; 91/92 - 335, 186SC; 92/93 - 331, 331GS, 454SC; 93/94 - 455C, 30SC, 30FD, 3AS
Upper Deck: 90/91 - 296E, 296F; 91/92 - 515E, 515F, 28AS; 93/94 - 304

Kitchen, Mike
O-Pee-Chee: 77/78 - 267; 78/79 - 338; 81/82 - 83
Post: 82/83 - 165

Kjellberg, Patric
O-Pee-Chee: 92/93 - 29PM
Upper Deck: 92/93 - 498

Klassen, Ralph
O-Pee-Chee: 76/77 - 282; 77/78 - 372; 78/79 - 346

Klatt, Trent
Donruss: 93/94 - 82
Fleer: 93/94 - 157, 4TP, 62PP
Leaf: 93/94 - 14
O-Pee-Chee: 93/94 - 523
Parkhurst: 91/92 - 452E; 92/93 - 317, 317EI; 93/94 - 48, 48EI
Pro-Set: 92/93 - 229
Topps: 93/94 - 523A
Upper Deck: 92/93 - 62; 93/94 - 152

Klein, Jim
Beehive: 34/44 - 234

Klein, Lloyd
Diamond: 33/35 - 36; 36/39 - 36(I), 35(II), 32(III)

Klemm, Jon
Parkhurst: 94/95 - 194, 194EI

Klima, Petr
Bowman: 90/91 - 197; 91/92 - 96, 104; 92/93 - 135
Donruss: 93/94 - 317
Fleer: 92/93 - 59, 8UI; 93/94 - 232PP
Kellogg's: 92 - 17
Leaf: 93/94 - 321

Klima, Petr (cont.)
O-Pee-Chee: 86/87 - 98, 129SK, 162SK; 87/88 - 26, 104SK; 88/89 - 28, 251SK; 90/91 - 85; 91/92 - 193, 61PM
Panini: 87/88 - 246; 88/89 - 44; 90/91 - 228; 91/92 - 126; 92/93 - 105E, 105F; 93/94 - 234E, 234F
Parkhurst: 91/92 - 280E, 280F; 92/93 - 54, 54EI; 93/94 - 195, 195EI; 94/95 - 219, 219EI
Pro Set: 90/91 - 91/92 - 72E, 72F, 37PT
Score: 90/91 - 232A, 232C; 91/92 - 136A, 136B, 136C, 159PNE, 159PNF; 92/93 - 383C, 383A, 344PNC, 344PNA, 24CSS, 24ASS; 93/94 - 242C, 242A
Sega: 93/94 - 47
Topps: 86/87 - 98; 87/88 - 26; 88/89 - 28; 90/91 - 85; 91/92 - 193, 61SC; 92/93 - 26, 26GS, 368SC
Upper Deck: 90/91 - 282E, 282F; 91/92 - 111E, 111F; 92/93 - 551; 93/94 - 526

Klimovich, Sergei
Upper Deck: 92/93 - 339; 93/94 - 275

Klima, Tomas
Upper Deck: 93/94 - 263

Klockare, Stefan
Upper Deck: 92/93 - 224

Klukay, Joe
Beehive: 45/63 - 38, 417
Parkhurst: 51/52 - 74; 52/53 - 75; 53/54 - 94; 54/55 - 54; 55/56 - 6
Quaker Oats: 45/54 - 80A, 80B; 55/56 - 6

Kluzak, Gordon (Gord)
O-Pee-Chee: 83/84 - 51, 185SK; 84/85 - 6, 186SK; 85/86 - 167; 86/87 - 54; 88/89 - 23, 25SK; 90/91 - 495
Panini: 88/89 - 205
Pro Set: 90/91 - 383
Score: 90/91 - 367A, 367C
Topps: 83/84 - 185SK; 84/85 - 5; 86/87 - 54; 88/89 - 23

Knickle, Rick (Goalie)
Score: 93/94 - 466C, 466A

Knipscheer, Fred
Parkhurst: 93/94 - 18, 18EI

Knott, Nick
Beehive: 34/44 - 235

Kocur, Joey
Bowman: 91/92 - 69; 92/93 - 80
O-Pee-Chee: 90/91 - 55; 91/92 - 427; 92/93 - 169; 93/94 - 512
Panini: 87/88 - 25189/90 - 67; 90/91 - 211
Parkhurst: 93/94 - 401, 401EI
Pro Set: 90/91 - 73
Score: 90/91 - 201A, 201C; 91/92 - 92A, 92B, 92C, 240PNE, 240PNF; 92/93 - 24C, 24A, 152PNC, 152PNA; 93/94 - 270C, 270A
Topps: 90/91 - 55; 91/92 - 427, 365SC; 92/93 - 128, 128GS, 417SC; 93/94 - 512A
Upper Deck: 90/91 - 411E, 411F

Kocur, Kory
Score: 90/91 - 384A, 384C

Koharski, Don (Official)
Pro Set: 90/91 - 691

Koivu, Saku
Upper Deck: 92/93 - 617; 93/94 - 569

Kolstad, Dean
O-Pee-Chee: 91/92 - 4S

Kolvu, Saku
Parkhurst: 93/94 - 521, 521EI

Kolzig, Olaf (Goalie)
O-Pee-Chee: 91/92 - 290; 93/94 - 291
Score: 90/91 - 392A, 392C
Topps: 91/92 - 290; 93/94 - 291,

Kolzig, Olaf (Goalie) (cont.)
   Topps: 438SC, 438FD
   Upper Deck: 93/94 - 326

Komadoski, Neil
   Loblaws: 74/75 - 135
   O-Pee-Chee: 73/74 - 16; 74/75 - 358; 75/76 - 238; 76/77 - 284; 77/78 - 344; 78/79 - 382
   Topps: 73/74 - 16; 75/76 - 238

Kondrashkin, Sergei
   Parkhurst: 93/94 - 532, 532EI

Konowalchuk, Steve
   Fleer: 92/93 - 437
   O-Pee-Chee: 92/93 - 15PM
   Parkhurst: 92/93 - 202, 202EI; 93/94 - 223, 223EI
   Score: 93/94 - 458C, 458A
   Topps: 93/94 - 481SC, 481FD
   Upper Deck: 92/93 - 418; 93/94 - 28

Konroyd, Stephen (Steve)
   Bowman: 92/93 - 18
   Fleer: 92/93 - 300
   O-Pee-Chee: 82/83 - 48; 83/84 - 85; 84/85 - 226; 87/88 - 153; 88/89 - 171, 110SK; 89/90 - 220; 91/92 - 366; 92/93 - 238
   Panini: 88/89 - 284
   Parkhurst: 91/92 - 287E, 287F; 92/93 - 299, 299EI
   Pro Set: 90/91 - 52, 177PT; 92/93 - 62
   Score: 90/91 - 29A, 29C; 91/92 - 189A, 189B, 189C, 180PNE, 180PNF; 92/93 - 172C, 172A, 352PNC, 352PNA; 93/94 - 219C, 219A
   Topps: 87/88 - 153; 88/89 - 171; 91/92 - 366; 92/93 - 411, 411GS, 236SC
   Vachon Foods: 83/84 - 9

Konstantinov, Vladimir
   Bowman: 92/93 - 326
   Fleer: 92/93 - 49; 93/94 - 150, 73PP
   Leaf: 93/94 - 237
   O-Pee-Chee: 90/91 - 21R; 91/92 - 118PM, 155PM; 92/93 - 267; 93/94 - 108
   Parkhurst: 91/92 - 46E, 46F; 92/93 - 283, 283EI; 93/94 - 325, 325EI
   Pro Set: 91/92 - 533E, 533F, 254PT; 92/93 - 44
   Score: 91 - 109T; 91/92 - 659B, 659C, 311PNE, 311PNF; 92/93 - 31C, 503C, 31A, 503A, 76PNC, 76PNA; 93/94 - 20C, 20A
   Topps: 92/93 - 14, 165, 14GS, 165GS, 418SC; 93/94 - 108, 333SC, 333FD
   Upper Deck: 91/92 - 594E, 594F; 92/93 - 267, 357, E10, AR5, W5; 93/94 - 366

Kontos, Chris
   Fleer: 92/93 - 412; 93/94 - 162, 233PP
   Leaf: 93/94 - 160
   O-Pee-Chee: 92/93 - 123PM; 93/94 - 215, 14TC
   Panini: 93/94 - 213E, 213F
   Parkhurst: 92/93 - 176, 176EI; 93/94 - 197, 197EI
   Score: 93/94 - 113C, 113A
   Sega: 93/94 - 131
   Topps: 92/93 - 2SCM; 93/94 - 215
   Upper Deck: 92/93 - 502; 93/94 - 54

Kopf, Ernst
   Upper Deck: 92/93 - 372

Korab, Jerry
   Loblaws: 74/75 - 43
   O-Pee-Chee: 72/73 - 285; 73/74 - 203; 74/75 - 354; 75/76 - 192; 76/77 - 27; 77/78 - 128; 78/79 - 231; 79/80 - 74; 80/81 - 300; 81/82 - 145, 240SK; 83/84 - 297SK
   Post: 82/83 - 121
   Topps: 75/76 - 192; 76/77 - 27; 77/78 - 128; 78/79 - 231; 79/80 - 74; 81/82 WN - 97; 83/84 - 297SK
   Toronto Sun: 71/72 - 69

Kordic, Dan
   Pro Set: 91/92 - 553E, 553F
   Score: 91/92 - 338PNE, 338PNF

Kordic, John
   O-Pee-Chee: 90/91 - 401
   Pro Set: 90/91 - 536; 91/92 - 468E, 468F

Korn, James (Jim)
   O-Pee-Chee: 81/82 - 91, 127SK; 82/83 - 323; 83/84 - 335; 84/85 - 304, 17SK; 90/91 - 450
   Panini: 89/90 - 261
   Topps: 81/82 WN - 9
   Vachon Foods: 83/84 - 91

Korney, Mike
   O-Pee-Chee: 75/76 - 342

Koroll, Cliff
   Coca-Cola: 77/78 - 12
   Eddie Sargent: 70/71 - 37; 71/72 - 35; 72/73 - 59
   Esso: 70/71 - 62
   Loblaws: 74/75 - 79
   O-Pee-Chee: 70/71 - 147; 71/72 - 209; 72/73 - 222; 73/74 - 28; 74/75 - 35; 75/76 - 139; 76/77 - 242; 77/78 - 146; 78/79 - 239; 79/80 - 102
   Topps: 73/74 - 28; 74/75 - 35; 75/76 - 139; 76/77 - 242; 77/78 - 146; 78/79 - 239; 79/80 - 102
   Toronto Sun: 71/72 - 70

Korolev, Igor
   Donruss: 93/94 - 297
   Fleer: 92/93 - 395, 93/94 - 185, 214PP
   Leaf: 93/94 - 185
   O-Pee-Chee: 92/93 - 53PM, 37R; 93/94 - 409, 119SC, 119FD
   Parkhurst: 92/93 - 158, 158EI; 93/94 - 446, 446EI
   Score: 93/94 - 271C, 271A, 417PNC, 417PNA
   Topps: 93/94 - 409C, 119SC, 119FD
   Upper Deck: 92/93 - 581, ER3, CC2; 93/94 - 353

Korolyou, Igor
   Upper Deck: 92/93 - 338

Korotkov, Konstantin
   Upper Deck: 91/92 - 654E, 654F

Kostichkin, Pavel
   O-Pee-Chee: 90/91 - 20R; 91/92 - 17R

Kotsopoulos, Christopher (Chris)
   O-Pee-Chee: 82/83 - 124, 132; 84/85 - 73; 87/88 - 244; 89/90 - 279, 180SK
   Post: 82/83 - 102
   Topps: 82/83 - 132SK

Kovalenko, Andrei
   Donruss: 93/94 - 278
   Fleer: 92/93 - 387, 9UI; 93/94 - 144, 200PP
   Leaf: 93/94 - 122, 6R
   O-Pee-Chee: 91/92 - 18R; 92/93 - 93PM; 93/94 - 124, 198, 77SC, 77FD
   Panini: 93/94 - 71E, 71F
   Parkhurst: 92/93 - 150, 223, 150EI, 223EI; 93/94 - 167, 167EI
   Score: 92/93 - 395PNC, 395PNA; 93/94 - 174C, 174A
   Topps: 93/94 - 198(I), 124, 17BG, 77SC, 77FD
   Upper Deck: 92/93 - 567, ER14, CC17, G19; 93/94 - 85

Kovalev, Alexei
   Donruss: 93/94 - 220
   Fleer: 92/93 - 137, 10UI; 93/94 - 115, 159PP
   Leaf: 93/94 - 147
   O-Pee-Chee: 92/93 - 126PM; 93/94 - 187, 129SC, 129FD
   Parkhurst: 92/93 - 109, 225, 109EI, 225EI; 93/94 - 130, 130EI; 93/94 - 238, 238EI; 94/95 - 142, 142EI, V24
   Score: 92/93 - 403PNC, 403PNA; 93/94 - 203C, 203A
   Topps: 93/94 - 187, 129SC, 129FD

Kovalev, Alexei (cont.)
   Upper Deck: 91/92 - 655E, 655F; 92/93 - 573, 633, ER10, CC11, WJG9, G13, 54AS; 93/94 - 27

Kovalyov, Andrei
   O-Pee-Chee: 91/92 - 38R

Kozak, Don
   Loblaws: 74/75 - 136
   O-Pee-Chee: 74/75 - 111; 75/76 - 276; 76/77 - 185; 77/78 - 316; 79/80 - 342
   Topps: 74/75 - 111; 75/76 - 276; 76/77 - 185

Kozlov, Viacheslav
   Bowman: 92/93 - 300
   Donruss: 93/94 - 91
   Fleer: 92/93 - 50; 93/94 - 174, 2RS, 331PP
   Leaf: 93/94 - 303
   O-Pee-Chee: 92/93 - 235, 71PM; 93/94 - 494
   Parkhurst: 91/92 - 266E, 266F; 92/93 - 40, 40EI; 93/94 - 57, 57EI; 94/95 - 66, 66EI, V49
   Pro-Set: 92/93 - 225
   Score: 92/93 - 473C, 473A, 230PNC, 230PNA, 13CT, 13AT; 93/94 - 421C, 421A
   Topps: 92/93 - 35, 35GS, 62SC; 93/94 - 494C, 388SC, 388FD
   Upper Deck: 91/92 - 5E, 5F; 92/93 - 294, WJG2; 93/94 - 495

Kozlov, Viktor
   Upper Deck: 92/93 - 613

Kraftcheck, Stephen
   Beehive: 45/63 - 332, 418
   Parkhurst: 51/52 - 92; 52/53 - 23; 58/59 - 37

Krake, Skip
   Eddie Sargent: 70/71 - 24
   Esso: 70/71 - 28
   Dom. Choc.: 70/71 - 17
   O-Pee-Chee: 68/69 - 43; 69/70 - 141; 70/71 - 126
   Shirriff: 68/69 - D11
   Topps: 67/68 - 93; 68/69 - 43; 70/71 - 126

Kravchuk, Igor
   Bowman: 92/93 - 408
   Donruss: 93/94 - 116
   Fleer: 92/93 - 38; 93/94 - 80, 81PP
   Leaf: 93/94 - 163
   O-Pee-Chee: 91/92 - 19R; 92/93 - 161; 93/94 - 495, 204SC, 204FD
   Parkhurst: 91/92 - 257E, 257F; 92/93 - 35, 291, 35EI, 291EI; 93/94 - 65, 65EI
   Panini: 92/93 - 297E, A (E), 297F, A(F)
   Pro-Set: 92/93 - 35
   Score: 92/93 - 454C, 454A, 225PNC, 225PNA; 93/94 - 309C, 309A
   Season's: 92/93 - 69
   Sega: 93/94 - 44
   Topps: 92/93 - 200, 200GS, 7SC; 93/94 - 495C, 204SC, 204FD
   Upper Deck: 92/93 - 239, 367, E7; 93/94 - 174

Kravets, Mikhail
   Upper Deck: 92/93 - 542

Krisak, Patrik
   Upper Deck: 93/94 - 266

Krivokrasov, Sergei
   Donruss: 93/94 - 74
   Fleer: 92/93 - 276; 93/94 - 112, 51PP
   Leaf: 93/94 - 434
   O-Pee-Chee: 92/93 - 9PM
   Parkhurst: 92/93 - 36, 36EI; 94/95 - 50, 50EI
   Score: 92/93 - 410PNC, 410PNA; 93/94 - 464C, 464A
   Upper Deck: 91/92 - 658E, 658F; 92/93 - 582, ER5

Krol, Joe
   Beehive: 34/44 - 236

Kromm, Richard (Rich)
O-Pee-Chee: 84/85 - 227; 85/86 - 222; 86/87 - 229
Panini: 87/88 - 103

Kron, Robert
Bowman: 91/92 - 320; 92/93 - 413
Donruss: 93/94 - 143
Fleer: 93/94 - 351PP
Leaf: 93/94 - 171
O-Pee-Chee: 90/91 - 52PM; 91/92 - 52; 92/93 - 2
Panini: 91/92 - 47; 92/93 - 33E, 33F
Parkhurst: 91/92 - PHC4E, PHC4F; 93/94 - 90, 90EI
Pro Set: 90/91 - 642; 91/92 - 239E, 239F, 122PT
Score: 90/91 - 65T; 91/92 - 257B, 257C; 93/94 - 428C, 428A
Topps: 91/92 - 52, 240SC; 92/93 - 80, 80GS, 155SC
Upper Deck: 90/91 - 528E, 528F; 91/92 - 225E, E8(E), 225F, E8(F); 92/93 - 69; 93/94 - 359

Kroupa, Vlastimil
Donruss: 93/94 - 315
Leaf: 93/94 - 439
Parkhurst: 93/94 - 266, 266EI
Upper Deck: 93/94 - 437

Krupp, Uwe
Bowman: 91/92 - 26; 92/93 - 349
Donruss: 93/94 - 205
Fleer: 92/93 - 129; 93/94 - 151PP
Leaf: 93/94 - 57
O-Pee-Chee: 88/89 - 220; 90/91 - 390; 91/92 - 155, 140PM; 92/93 - 173; 93/94 - 3, 138SC, 138FD
Panini: 89/90 - 216; 90/91 - 22; 91/92 - 305; 92/93 - 202E, 202F
Parkhurst: 91/92 - 109E, 109F; 92/93 - 101, 453, 101EI, 453EI; 93/94 - 388, 388EI
Pro Set: 90/91 - 23; 91/92 - 20E, 301E, 436E, 20F, 301F, 436F, 202PT; 92/93 - 109
Score: 90/91 - 169A, 169C; 91 - 104T; 91/92 - 84A, 84B, 84C, 19PNE, 19PNF; 92/93 - 77C, 77A, 86PNC, 86PNA, 240PNC, 240PNA; 93/94 - 87C, 87A
Topps: 90/91 - 390; 91/92 - 155, 62SC; 92/93 - 158, 158GS, 177SC; 93/94 - 3, 138SC, 138FD
Upper Deck: 90/91 - 187E, 187F; 91/92 - 102E, 540E, 102F, 540F; 92/93 - 187

Kruppke, Gord
Score: 93/94 - 467C, 467A

Krushelnyski, Michael (Mike)
Bowman: 90/91 - 145; 91/92 - 166; 92/93 - 2
Durivage: 92/93 - 5; 93/94 - 31
Fleer: 92/93 - 421
Kraft: 86/87 - 15, 15P
O-Pee-Chee: 83/84 - 52, 43SK; 84/85 - 248, 188SK; 85/86 - 49, 223SK; 86/87 - 193, 74SK; 87/88 - 202, 90SK; 88/89 - 221, 226SK; 89/90 - 104, 153SK; 90/91 - 167; 91/92 - 324, 189PM; 92/93 - 335; 93/94 - 169
Panini: 87/88 - 266; 89/90 - 94; 90/91 - 245; 91/92 - 97; 92/93 - 78E, 78F; 93/94 - 229E, 229F
Parkhurst: 92/93 - 411, 411EI
Pro Set: 90/91 - 121, 537; 91/92 - 233E, 233F, 119PT
Score: 90/91 - 227A, 227C, 47T; 91/92 - 33A, 33B, 33C, 269PNE, 269PNF; 92/93 - 283C, 283A, 93/94 - 367C, 367A
Topps: 83/84 - 43SK; 84/85 - 6; 85/86 - 49; 86/87 - 193; 89/90 - 104; 90/91 - 167; 91/92 - 324, 54SC; 92/93 - 450, 450GS, 487SC; 93/94 - 306SC, 306FD
Upper Deck: 90/91 - 394E, 394F; 91/92 - 320E, 320F; 92/93 - 87

Krutov, Vladimir
Kraft: 1990 - 40
O-Pee-Chee: 90/91 - 380
Panini: 90/91 - 304, 337
Pro Set: 90/91 - 296
Score: 90/91 - 273A, 273C
Upper Deck: 90/91 - 77E, 77F
Topps: 90/91 - 380

Krygier, Todd
Bowman: 90/91 - 251; 91/92 - 2
Fleer: 92/93 - 438; 93/94 - 467PP
O-Pee-Chee: 90/91 - 260; 91/92 - 449; 93/94 - 188
Panini: 90/91 - 35; 91/92 - 317
Parkhurst: 91/92 - 408E, 408F; 94/95 - 258, 258EI
Pro Set: 90/91 - 107; 91/92 - 83E, 83F; 92/93 - 270
Score: 90/91 - 237A, 237C; 91 - 87T; 91/92 - 97A, 97B, 97C, 637B, 637C, 242PNE, 394PNE, 242PNF, 394PNF; 92/93 - 98C, 98A, 204PNC, 204PNA; 93/94 - 357C, 357A
Topps: 90/91 - 260; 91/92 - 449, 45SC; 92/93 - 502, 502GS, 474SC; 93/94 - 188, 337SC, 337FD
Upper Deck: 90/91 - 417E, 417F; 91/92 - 215E, 582E, 215F, 582F; 93/94 - 207

Kryskow, Dave
Loblaws: 74/75 - 317
O-Pee-Chee: 74/75 - 62; 75/76 - 158
Topps: 74/75 - 62; 75/76 - 158

Kryznowski, Edward (Ted)
Beehive: 45/63 - 39
Parkhurst: 51/52 - 33; 52/53 - 29

Kucera, Frantisek (Frank)
Bowman: 91/92 - 404; 92/93 - 7
Donruss: 93/94 - 439
Fleer: 92/93 - 277
O-Pee-Chee: 90/91 - 53PM
Parkhurst: 92/93 - 269, 269EI
Pro Set: 90/91 - 599
Score: 91/92 - 390B, 390C; 92/93 - 346C, 346A; 93/94 - 372C, 372A
Topps: 92/93 - 520, 520GS, 438SC; 93/94 - 442SC, 442FD
Upper Deck: 91/92 - 468E, 468F

Kudashov, Alexei
Donruss: 93/94 - 345
Parkhurst: 93/94 - 260, 260EI
Upper Deck: 93/94 - 427

Kudelski, Bob
Bowman: 91/92 - 189; 92/93 - 12
Donruss: 93/94 - 232, 434
Fleer: 93/94 - 85, 170PP, 348PP
Leaf: 93/94 - 48
O-Pee-Chee: 90/91 - 46; 91/92 - 61, 129PM; 92/93 - 326; 93/94 - 40, 120SC, 120FD
Panini: 90/91 - 232; 91/92 - 87; 92/93 - 69E, 69F; 93/94 - 114E, 114F
Parkhurst: 91/92 - 299E, 299F; 92/93 - 357, 357EI; 93/94 - 408, 408EI; 94/95 - 83, 83EI
Pro Set: 90/91 - 122; 91/92 - 99E, 99F, 181PT
Score: 90/91 - 305A; 91/92 - 154A, 154B, 154C, 113PNE, 113PNF; 92/93 - 221C, 221A, 84PNC, 84PNA; 93/94 - 257C, 257A
Sega: 93/94 - 95
Topps: 90/91 - 46; 91/92 - 61, 40SC; 92/93 - 145, 145GS, 149SC; 93/94 - 40, 120SC, 120FD
Upper Deck: 90/91 - 433E, 433F; 91/92 - 301E, 301F; 93/94 - 17

Kullman, Eddie
Beehive: 45/63 - 333
Parkhurst: 51/52 - 101; 52/53 - 18; 53/54 - 61

Kuminsky, Max
Diamond: 36/39 - 33(I)

Kumpel, Mark
O-Pee-Chee: 90/91 - 444

Kurashov, Konstanin
O-Pee-Chee: 90/91 - 469; 91/92 - 52R

Kurri, Jari
Bowman: 90/91 - 191, HT19; 92/93 - 94
Donruss: 93/94 - 151
Esso: 88/89 - 22
Fleer: 92/93 - 85, 11UI; 93/94 - 165, 4GG, 118PP
Funmate: 83/84 - 40
Hockey Wit: 93/94 - 89
Kellogg's: 84 - 14
Kraft: 86/87 - 16, 16P; 1990 - 13; 90/91 - 68
Leaf: 93/94 - 240
O-Pee-Chee: 81/82 - 107, 11SK, 211SK; 82/83 - 111, 108SK, 109SK; 83/84 - 34, 104SK; 84/85 - 215, 249, 250SK, 249SK; 85/86 - 155, 261, 121SK, 201SK, 231SK; 86/87 - 108, 258, H/BB, 73SK, 118SK, 185SK; 87/88 - 148, 21HL, 82SK, 117SK; 88/89 - 147, 221SK, 227SK; 89/90 - 43, I/BB; 90/91 - 5, 108; 91/92 - 295, 111PM; 92/93 - 205; 93/94 - 206
Panini: 87/88 - 262; 88/89 - 59; 89/90 - 181; 89/90 - 73; 90/91 - 222; 92/93 - 66E, 66F; 93/94 - 202E, 202F
Parkhurst: 91/92 - 72E, 210E, 223E, 72F, 210F, 223F; 92/93 - 67, 445, 67EI, 445EI; 93/94 - 365, 365EI; 94/95 - 104, 104EI
PepsiCo: 80/81 - 29
Post: 82/83 - 90
Pro Set: 90/91 - 87, 348; 91/92 - 93E, 93F, 48PT; 92/93 - 68
Score: 90/91 - 158A, 158C, 348A, 348C; 91 - 50T; 91/92 - 600B, 600C, 48PNE, 48PNF; 92/93 - 398C, 398A, 60PNC, 60PNA; 93/94 - 100C, 100A; 446C, 446A, 35PNC, 35PNA, 35CAS, 35AAS
7-Eleven: 84/85 - 18
Topps: 81/82 - 18; 82/83 - 108SK, 109SK; 83/84 - 104SK; 84/85 - 52, 161; 85/86 - 155, 3SK; 86/87 - 108, H/BB, 10SK; 87/88 - 148, 4SK; 88/89 - 147; 89/90 - 43, I/BB; 90/91 - 5, 108; 91/92 - 295; 92/93 - 51, 51GS, 138SC, 3SCM; 93/94 - 206, 400SC, 400FD, 13MP,15AS
Upper Deck: 90/91 - 146E, 146F; 91/92 - 24E, 366E, 24F, 366F; 92/93 - 218, WJG4, 29AS; 93/94 - 332
Vachon Foods: 83/84 - 31

Kurt, Gary (Goalie)
O-Pee-Chee: 71/72 - 181; 72/73 - 306

Kurtenbach, Orland
Bazooka: 71/72 - 13
Beehive: 45/63 - 40; 64/67 - 15, 137, 172
Coca-Cola: 64/65 - 10; 65/66 - 99
Colgate: 70/71 - 23
Dom. Choc.: 70/71 - 140
Eddie Sargent: 70/71 - 212; 72/73 - 215
Esso: 70/71 - 242
Mac's Milk: 73/74 - 12
O-Pee-Chee: 68/69 - 170; 69/70 - 188; 70/71 - 117, 45DE; 71/72 - 42, 20BK, 12PT; 72/73 - 141, 149, 22CS; 73/74 - 4
Shirriff: 61/62 - 14; 68/69 - G8
Topps: 61/62 - 15; 63/64 - 20; 64/65 - 18; 65/66 - 20; 66/67 - 25; 66/67 US - 25; 67/68 - 87; 70/71 - 117; 71/72 - 42, BK/20; 72/73 - 46; 73/74 - 157
Toronto Star: 64/65 - 5
Toronto Sun: 71/72 - 282
Ultimate: 92 - 24(OSE), 24(OSF)

Kurvers, Tom
Bowman: 91/92 - 319; 92/93 - 259
Fleer: 93/94 - 384PP
O-Pee-Chee: 85/86 - 219, 129SK; 86/87 - 10SK; 88/89 - 222; 89/90 - 9, 84SK;

Kurvers, Tom (cont.)
O-Pee-Chee: 90/91 - 11; 91/92 - 98PM; 92/93 - 202; 93/94 - 279
Panini: 89/90 - 252; 90/91 - 287; 91/92 - 43
Parkhurst: 91/92 - 112E, 112F; 93/94 - 392, 392EI
Pro Set: 90/91 - 282; 91/92 - 244E, 428E, 244F, 428F
Score: 90/91 - 142A, 142C; 91 - 18T; 91/92 - 174A, 174B, 174C, 568B, 568C, 7PNE, 7PNF; 92/93 - 232C, 232A, 324PNC, 324PNA
Topps: 89/90 - 9; 90/91 - 11; 92/93 - 118, 118GS, 409SC; 93/94 - 279, 279SC, 279FD
Upper Deck: 90/91 - 160E, 160F; 92/93 - 292; 93/94 - 381

Kushner, Dale
Bowman: 91/92 - 247
O-Pee-Chee: 90/91 - 54PM; 91/92 - 415
Score: 91/92 - 512B, 512C
Topps: 91/92 - 415, 349SC
Upper Deck: 91/92 - 429E, 429F

Kusnetsov, Yuri
O-Pee-Chee: 90/91 - 489

Kuzminsky, Alexander
Upper Deck: 91/92 - 656E, 656F

Kvalevog, Toby (Goalie
Donruss: 93/94 - 11JCA
Upper Deck: 93/94 - 555

Kvartalnov, Andrei
O-Pee-Chee: 91/92 - 53R; 93/94 - 197
Score: 92/93 - 405PNC, 405PNA

Kvartalnov, Dmitri
Donruss: 93/94 - 27
Leaf: 93/94 - 143
Fleer: 92/93 - 252, 12UI; 93/94 - 82, 20PP, 4SY
O-Pee-Chee: 92/93 - 6PM
Panini: 93/94 - 7E, 7F
Parkhurst: 92/93 - 7, 222, 7EI, 222EI; 93/94 - 287, 287EI
Score: 93/94 - 187C, 187A
Topps: 93/94 - 197
Upper Deck: 92/93 - 561, 55AS; 93/94 - 19

Kyle, Gus
Beehive: 45/63 - 334

Kyle, Walter
Parkhurst: 51/52 - 21

Kypreos, Nicholas (Nick)
Bowman: 90/91 - 67; 91/92 - 301
Donruss: 93/94 - 140
Fleer: 92/93 - 301
Leaf: 93/94 - 414
O-Pee-Chee: 90/91 - 440; 91/92 - 511
Panini: 91/92 - 204
Parkhurst: 91/92 - 411E, 411F; 92/93 - 297, 297EI
Pro Set: 90/91 - 551; 91/92 - 513E, 513F
Score: 91/92 - 432B, 432C; 93/94 - 404C, 404A
Topps: 91/92 - 511, 307SC; 92/93 - 193, 193GS
Upper Deck: 92/93 - 447; 93/94 - 11

Kyro, Roger
Upper Deck: 92/93 - 226

Kyte, James (Jim)
O-Pee-Chee: 87/88 - 226; 88/89 - 145SK; 89/90 - 295, 140SK
Panini: 87/88 - 362
Pro Set: 91/92 - 612E, 612F
Score: 91/92 - 547B, 547C, 398PNE, 398PNF
Vachon Foods: 83/84 - 128

Labine, Leo
Beehive: 45/63 - 41, 185
Parkhurst: 52/53 - 81; 53/54 - 93; 54/55 - 61; 61/62 - 33; 62/63 - 26; 93/94 - 4ML
Shirriff: 60/61 - 117; 61/62 - 64
Topps: 54/55 - 19; 57/58 - 9; 58/59 - 4;

Labine, Leo (cont.)
Topps: 59/60 - 7; 60/61 - 13
Ultimate: 92 - 50(OSE), 50(OSF)

Labossiere, Gord
Beehive: 45/63 - 335; 64/67 - 138
Esso: 70/71 - 99
O-Pee-Chee: 68/69 - 38; 69/70 - 109; 70/71 - 38; 72/73 - 303
Shirriff: 68/69 - D5
Topps: 68/69 - 38; 69/70 - 109; 70/71 - 38

Labraaten, Dan
O-Pee-Chee: 79/80 - 92; 80/81 - 217; 81/82 - 42
Topps: 79/80 - 92; 80/81 - 217

Labre, Yvon
O-Pee-Chee: 73/74 - 247; 74/75 - 345; 75/76 - 61; 76/77 - 161; 77/78 - 31; 78/79 - 324; 79/80 - 343
Topps: 75/76 - 61; 76/77 - 161; 77/78 - 31

Lach, Elmer
Beehive: 34/44 - 162; 45/63 - 256
Chex: 43/47 - 60
Derniere: 72/84 - 62
Hall of Fame: 83 - 129, I9P; 87 - 129
La Patrie: 51/54 - 3
O-Pee-Chee: 40/41 - 125
Parkhurst: 51/52 - 1; 52/53 - 6; 53/54 - 31; 93/94 - PR36
Quaker Oats: 45/54 - 26A, 26B, 26C, 26D
Toronto Star: 58/67 - 2

Lachance, Bob
Donruss: 93/94 - 12JCA
Upper Deck: 93/94 - 564

Lachance, Scott
Bowman: 92/93 - 438
Donruss: 93/94 - 206
Fleer: 92/93 - 130,; 93/94 - 152PP
Leaf: 93/94 - 139
O-Pee-Chee: 92/93 - 390, 79PM; 93/94 - 257
Panini: 92/93 - Q(E), Q(F); 93/94 - 63E, 63F
Parkhurst: 91/92 - 326E, 326F; 92/93 - 105, 105EI; 93/94 - 120, 120EI; 94/95 - 140, 140EI
Pro-Set: 92/93 - 234
Score: 92/93 - 449C, 449A, 223PNC, 223PNA, 6CT, 6AT; 93/94 - 103C, 103A
Season's: 92/93 - 52
Topps: 92/93 - 366, 366GS, 201SC; 93/94 - 257, 465SC, 465FD, 16MP
Upper Deck: 91/92 - 692E, 692F; 92/93 - 360, 409, 571, CC16, AC4; 93/94 - 320

Lacombe, Francois
Derniere: 72/84 - 85

Lacombe, Normand
Bowman: 91/92 - 248
O-Pee-Chee: 91/92 - 357; 92/93 - 390
Panini: 89/90 - 84
Pro Set: 90/91 - 500
Score: 90/91 - 99T; 91/92 - 394B, 394C
Topps: 91/92 - 357, 363SC

Lacroix, L (Alphonse) (Goalie
Anonymous: 1926/27 - 11

Lacroix, Andre
Colgate: 70/71 - 29
Dom. Choc.: 70/71 - 100
Eddie Sargent: 70/71 - 154
Esso: 70/71 - 175
O-Pee-Chee: 68/69 - 184; 69/70 - 98, 18ST, 10QS; 70/71 - 84, 18SS; 71/72 - 33; 79/80 - 107
Shirriff: 68/69 - J6
Topps: 69/70 - 98; 70/71 - 84, 18SK; 71/72 - 33; 79/80 - 107
Toronto Sun: 71/72 - 201

Lacroix, Daniel
Leaf: 93/94 - 351
Parkhurst: 94/95 - 148, 148EI

Lacroix, Eric
Parkhurst: 94/95 - 234, 234EI

Lacroix, Pierre
Derniere: 72/84 - 147
O-Pee-Chee: 81/82 - 278; 82/83 - 286; 83/84 - 261SK
PepsiCo: 80/81 - 70
Topps: 83/84 - 261SK

Ladouceur, Randy
Bowman: 91/92 - 5; 92/93 - 107
O-Pee-Chee: 84/85 - 60; 85/86 - 216; 90/91 - 162; 92/93 - 299; 93/94 - 469
Panini: 90/91 - 41
Parkhurst: 91/92 - 289E, 289F
Pro Set: 90/91 - 108; 91/92 - 396E, 573E, 396F, 573F
Score: 91/92 - 436A, 407B, 407C, 224PNE, 224PNF; 92/93 - 61C, 61A, 291PNC, 291PNA;
Topps: 90/91 - 162; 92/93 - 344, 344GS, 156SC; 93/94 - 469C, 271SC, 271FD
Sega: 93/94 - 2
Upper Deck: 90/91 - 151E, 151F

Lafayette, Nathan
Parkhurst: 94/95 - 247, 247EI
Upper Deck: 92/93 - 588

Lafleur, Guy
Colgate: 71/72 - 5
Derniere: 72/84 - 8, 31, 130, 188
Esso: 88/89 - 23
Funmate: 83/84 - 65
Kellogg's: 84 - 27
Kraft: 1990 - 31; 90/91 - 22
Loblaws: 74/75 - 166
McDonald's: 82/83 - 8
O-Pee-Chee: 71/72 - 148, 13PT; 72/73 - 59; 73/74 - 72; 74/75 - 232; 75/76 - 126, 290; 76/77 - 163; 77/78 - 200, 214, 216, 218, 7GP;78/79 - 3, 90, 326; 79/80 - 200; 80/81 - 10, 82, 10PO; 81/82 - 177, 195, 29SK, 41SK; 82/83 - 186, 187, 28SK, 29SK; 83/84 - 183, 189, 2SK, 58SK, 59SK; 84/85 - 264, 360, 149SK, 150SK; 89/90 - 189, 245SK; 90/91 - 142, 55PM; 91/92 - 1, 2, 3
Panini: 90/91 - 145
Post: 82/83 - 150
Pro Set: 90/91 - 250; 91/92 - 317E, 317F
Score: 90/91 - 290A, 290C, 96HR; 91/92 - 401A, 402A, 403A, 291B, 292B, 293B, 291C, 292C, 293C
Topps: 72/73 - 79; 73/74 - 72; 74/75 - 232; 75/76 - 126, 290; 76/77 - 163, 11PO; 77/78 - 200, 214, 216, 218, 7PO; 78/79 - 3, 90; 79/80 - 200; 80/81 - 10, 82; 81/82 - 19; 82/83 - 28SK, 29SK; 83/84 - 2SK, 58SK, 59SK; 84/85 - 81; 89/90 - 189, 90/91 - 142; 91/92 - 1, 2, 3
Toronto Sun: 71/72 - 152
Upper Deck: 90/91 - 162E, 162F; 91/92 - 219E, 638E, 219F, 638F
Vachon Foods: 83/84 - 47

LaFontaine, Pat
Bowman: 90/91 - 123, HT9; 91/92 - 222; 92/93 - 142
Derniere: 72/84 - 179
Donruss: 93/94 - 37, 2IK
Fleer: 92/93 - 16; 93/94 - 219, 4AS, 31PP, 7PL, 1SC, 3PM, 6SM
Frito-Lay: 88/89 - 19
Gillette: 91/92 - 23
Hockey Wit: 93/94 - 105
Humpty Dumpty: 92/93 - 11(II)
Kellogg's: 92 - 15
Kraft: 90/91 - 23, 86; 91/92 - 25; 93/94 - 43
Leaf: 93/94 - 12, 3SS
McDonald's: 91/92 - Mc6
O-Pee-Chee: 84/85 - 129, 392; 85/86 - 137, 74SK; 86/87 - 2, 206SK; 87/88 - 173, 22HL, 243SK; 88/89 - 123, C/BB, 111SK; 89/90 - 60, 119SK; 90/91 - 184, 56PM; 91/92 - 80, 64PM; 93/94 - 171, 490, 14BG, 20SC, 20FD

LaFontaine, Pat (cont.)
O-Pee-Chee: 92/93 - 285, 17SP
Panini: 87/88 - 98; 88/89 - 290; 89/90 - 264; 90/91 - 81; 91/92 - 243; 92/93 - 246E,246F; 93/94 - 101E, 137E, 101F, 137F
Parkhurst: 91/92 - 16E, 16F; 92/93 - 12; 93/94 - 289, 289EI, E8; 94/95 - 310, 310EI, H3, R3, C3, V73
Pro Set: 90/91 - 186, 372, 95HR; 91/92 - 149E, 308E, 358E, 149F, 308F, 25PNE, 25PNF, 358F, 157PT; 92/93 - 12, 12EI
Score: 90/91 - 250A, 250C; 91/92 - 260A, 332A, 362B, 480B, 362C, 480C; 92/93 - 6C, 420C, 6A, 420A, 7PNC, 7PNA, 254PNC, 254PNA, 6PC(S), 6PC(F), 8CSS, 8ASS, 1USG; 93/94 - 345C, 345A, 11PNC, 11PNA, 13DT, 11CAS, 11AAS, 2FR
Season's: 92/93 - 42
Sega: 93/94 - 15
Topps: 84/85 - 96; 85/86 - 137; 86/87 - 2; 87/88 - 173; 88/89 - 123, C/BB; 89/90 - 60; 90/91 - 184, 10SL; 91/92 - P/C, 80, 12SL, 123SC; 92/93 - 345, 345GS, 95SC; 93/94 - 490, 171, 20SC, 460SC, 20FD, 460FD, 1MP, 16AS
Upper Deck: 90/91 - 246E, 479E, 246F, 479F; 91/92 - 253E, 556E, 253F, 556F, Mc6; 92/93 - 165M, G3, 4AS; 93/94 - 137, 221, 287

Laforce, Ernie
Chex: 43/47 - 21

LaForest, Mark (Goalie)
Upper Deck: 90/91 - 81E, 81F

Laforge, Claude
Parkhurst: 62/63 - 24
Topps: 58/59 - 33; 59/60 - 64

Laframboise, Pete
Eddie Sargent: 72/73 - 53
Loblaws: 74/75 - 318
O-Pee-Chee: 72/73 - 263; 73/74 - 244; 74/75 - 166; 75/76 - 364
Topps: 74/75 - 166

Lafreniere, Jason
O-Pee-Chee: 87/88 - 130SK, 219SK; 88/89 - 223, 185SK
Panini: 87/88 - 171
Parkhurst: 93/94 - 466, 466EI

Lagace, Jean-Guy
O-Pee-Chee: 74/75 - 299; 75/76 - 141
Topps: 75/76 - 141

Laidlaw, Thomas (Tom)
O-Pee-Chee: 81/82 - 234; 82/83 - 227; 83/84 - 247; 84/85 - 144; 86/87 - 147, 223SK; 88/89 - 37; 89/90 - 34; 90/91 - 524
Panini: 88/89 - 71
Post: 82/83 - 201
Pro Set: 90/91 - 123
Score: 90/91 - 69A, 69C
Topps: 86/87 - 147; 88/89 - 37; 89/90 - 34
Upper Deck: 90/91 - 119E, 119F

Lajeunesse, Serge
Esso: 70/71 - 82
O-Pee-Chee: 71/72 - 136

Lake, Fred
Imperial Tobacco: 10/11 - 9L, 27; 11/12 - 9; 12/13 - 31

Lalande, Hec
Parkhurst: 93/94 - 38ML
Topps: 57/58 - 31

Lalonde, Bobby
Eddie Sargent: 72/73 - 221
Loblaws: 74/75 - 247
O-Pee-Chee: 72/73 - 217; 73/74 - 179; 74/75 - 392; 75/76 - 246; 76/77 - 278; 77/78 - 313; 78/79 - 285; 79/80 - 326;

Lalonde, Bobby (cont.)
O-Pee-Chee: 80/81 - 265
Topps: 73/74 - 189; 75/76 - 246
Toronto Sun: 71/72 - 283

Lalonde, Edouard (Newsy)
Dom. Choc.: 1925 - 95
Hall of Fame: 83 - 70, E10P; 87 - 70
Imperial Tobacco: 10/11 - 36, 42L; 11/12 - 42; 12/13 - 44
Maple Crispette: 24/25 - 27
Parkhurst: 55/56 - 55
Quaker Oats: 55/56 - 55
Topps: 60/61 - 48, 43ST

Lalonde, Herve
La Patrie: 51/54 - 39

Lalonde, Ron
O-Pee-Chee: 75/76 - 152; 76/77 - 339; 77/78 - 378; 78/79 - 371
Topps: 75/76 - 152

Lalor, Mike
Bowman: 92/93 - 319
Donruss: 93/94 - 306
Kraft: 86/87 - 28, 28P; 93/94 - 44
Leaf: 93/94 - 399
O-Pee-Chee: 90/91 - 341, 57PM; 91/92 - 483
Panini: 90/91 - 267
Parkhurst: 91/92 - 427E, 427F
Pro Set: 90/91 - 264, 552; 91/92 - 255E, 255F; 92/93 - 268
Score: 90/91 - 67A, 67C, 98T; 91/92 - 249A, 469B, 469C; 92/93 - 363C, 363A, 123PNC, 123PNA
Topps: 90/91 - 341; 91/92 - 483; 92/93 - 140, 140GS, 190SC
Upper Deck: 90/91 - 40E, 40F

Lamb, Joe
Beehive: 34/44 - 237
Diamond: 33/35 - 37; 36/39 - 37(l)
O-Pee-Chee: 33/34 - 2
Sweet Caporal: 34/35 - 17
World Wide Gum: 33/34 - 41; 36/37 - 37

Lamb, Mark
Donruss: 93/94 - 230
Fleer: 93/94 - 171PP
Leaf: 93/94 - 308
O-Pee-Chee: 90/91 - 25; 92/93 - 322; 93/94 - 271, 172SC, 172FD
Panini: 93/94 - 117E, 117F
Parkhurst: 92/93 - 116, 116EI
Pro Set: 90/91 - 88
Score: 90/91 - 308C; 91/92 - 652B, 652C; 92/93 - 514C, 514A, 374PNC, 374PNA; 93/94 - 407C, 407A
Topps: 90/91 - 25; 92/93 - 230, 230GS; 93/94 - 271, 172SC, 172FD

Lambert, Dan
Bowman: 92/93 - 356
O-Pee-Chee: 92/93 - 357
Score: 91/92 - 346PNE, 346PNF
Topps: 92/93 - 364, 364GS
Upper Deck: 91/92 - 592E, 592F; 92/93 - 251

Lambert, Lane
O-Pee-Chee: 84/85 - 57; 88/89 - 224, 183SK
Panini: 88/89 - 356

Lambert, Yvon
Derniere: 72/84 - 46, 115
Loblaws: 74/75 - 167
O-Pee-Chee: 74/75 - 342; 75/76 - 17; 76/77 - 232; 77/78 - 151; 78/79 - 147; 79/80 - 24; 80/81 - 246; 81/82 - 185, 35SK; 82/83 - 27, 125SK
PepsiCo: 80/81 - 48
Post: 82/83 - 21
Topps: 75/76 - 17; 76/77 - 232; 77/78 - 151; 78/79 - 147; 79/80 - 24; 80/81 - 246, 35SK; 82/83 - 125SK

Lamby, Dick
Panini: 79 - 208

Lamirande, Jean Paul
La Patrie: 51/54 - 25

Lammens, Hank
Parkhurst: 93/94 - 409, 409EI

Lamoureaux, Leo
Beehive: 34/44 - 163
Chex: 43/47 - 61
Quaker Oats: 45/54 - 27A, 27b

Lampman, Mike
O-Pee-Chee: 76/77 - 375; 77/78 - 396

Lane, Gord
O-Pee-Chee: 77/78 - 287; 78/79 - 284; 79/80 - 325; 80/81 - 323; 81/82 - 212; 83/84 - 10; 85/86 - 77SK

Lang, Robert
Fleer: 93/94 - 188
O-Pee-Chee: 92/93 - 47PM
Parkhurst: 92/93 - 64, 227, 64EI, 227EI; 94/95 - 286. 286EI
Score: 92/93 - 411PNC, 411PNA; 93/94 - 456C, 456A
Upper Deck: 92/93 - 552, ER4

Langelle, Pete
Beehive: 34/44 - 333
O-Pee-Chee: 39/40 - 7; 40/41 - 117

Langenbrunner, Jamie
Donruss: 93/94 - 13JCA
Upper Deck: 93/94 - 566

Langevin, Dave
O-Pee-Chee: 80/81 - 188; 81/82 - 213; 82/83 - 204, 83SK; 83/84 - 11, 83SK; 86/87 - 218
Post: 82/83 - 183
Topps: 80/81 - 188

Langlois, Al
Beehive: 45/63 - 257, 336; 64/67 - 81
Coca-Cola: 64/65 - 46; 65/66 - 10
Parkhurst: 58/59 - 5; 59/60 - 45; 60/61 - 39; 61/62 - 37; 62/63 - 22HB
Shirriff: 60/61 - 2461/62 - 94
Topps: 60/61 - 14ST; 61/62 - 46; 62/63 - 47; 63/64 - 49; 64/65 - 13; 65/66 - 33
York: 60/61 - 11

Langlois, Charlie (Louis)
Anonymous: 26/27 - 76
Champ's: 24/25 - 14
La Presse: 27/32 - 12
Maple Crispette: 24/25 - 26
Wm. Paterson: 24/25 - 17

Langtry, Jack
Dom. Choc.: 1925 - 86

Langway, Rod
Bowman: 92/93 - 279
Derniere: 72/84 - 129, 183
Esso: 88/89 - 24
Funmate: 83/84 - 138
Hockey Wit: 93/94 - 26
Kraft: 90/91 - 24
McDonald's: 82/83 - 32
O-Pee-Chee: 80/81 - 344; 81/82 - 186, 39SK; 82/83 - 368, 34SK; 83/84 - 207, 365, 374, 201SK, 313SK; 84/85 - 202, 210, 377, 125SK, 126SK, 230SK; 85/86 - 8, 105SK, 113SK; 86/87 - 164, 249SK; 87/88 - 108, 236SK; 88/89 - 192, 69SK; 89/90 - 55, 77SK; 90/91 - 353; 91/92 - 105; 92/93 - 347
Panini: 87/88 - 178; 88/89 - 366; 89/90 - 350; 91/92 - 209; 92/93 - 169E, 169F
PepsiCo: 80/81 - 49
Post: 82/83 - 151
Pro Set: 90/91 - 314; 91/92 - 259E, 587E, 259F, 587F
7-Eleven: 84/85 - 54
Score: 90/91 - 20A, 20C, 11HR; 91/92 - 228A, 228B, 228C, 195PNE, 195PNF;

Langway, Rod (cont.)
Score: 92/93 - 143C, 143A, 131PNC, 131PNA; 93/94 - 145C, 145A
Topps: 82/83 - 34SK; 83/84 - 201SK, 313SK; 84/85 - 147, 156; 85/86 - 8, 10SK; 86/87 - 164; 87/88 - 108; 88/89 - 192; 89/90 - 55; 90/91 - 353; 91/92 - 105, 225SC; 92/93 - 46, 46GS, 215SC
Upper Deck: 90/91 - 57E, 57F; 91/92 - 314E, 314F

Lanz, Rick
O-Pee-Chee: 81/82 - 338; 82/83 - 348; 83/84 - 353, 280SK; 84/85 - 321, 276SK; 85/86 - 197; 86/87 - 179; 87/88 - 239, 157SK; 88/89 - 225, 176SK
PepsiCo: 80/81 - 111
Topps: 83/84 - 280SK; 86/87 - 179
Vachon Foods: 83/84 - 110

Laperriere, Daniel
Donruss: 93/94 - 485
O-Pee-Chee: 92/93 - 39PM; 93/94 - 526
Topps: 93/94 - 526A
Upper Deck: 92/93 - 525

Laperriere, Jacques
Beehive: 45/63 - 258; 64/67 - 109
Chex: 63/65 - 31
Coca-Cola: 64/65 - 64; 65/66 - 63
Derniere: 72/84 - 9, 34
Dom. Choc.: 70/71 - 77
Eddie Sargent: 70/71 - 97; 72/73 - 121
Esso: 70/71 - 134; 88/89 - 25
Hall of Fame: 87 - 260
Loblaws: 74/75 - 168
O-Pee-Chee: 68/69 - 58; 69/70 - 3, 2QS; 70/71 - 52, 245, 20DE, 19SS; 71/72 - 144; 72/73 - 205, 11SK; 73/74 - 40; 74/75 - 202
Parkhurst: 63/64 - 27, 86
Post: 66/67 - 13L; 68/69 - 7
Shirriff: 68/69 - F4
Topps: 64/65 - 53; 65/66 - 3; 66/67 - 67, 122; 67/68 - 7; 68/69 - 58; 69/70 - 3; 70/71 - 52, 19SK; 73/74 - 137; 74/75 - 202
Toronto Star: 57/67 - 121, 141; 58/67 - 93; 64/65 - 29
Toronto Sun: 71/72 - 153

Laperriere, Ian
Parkhurst: 94/95 - 201, 201EI

Lapointe, Claude
Bowman: 92/93 - 421
Donruss: 93/94 - 285
Durivage: 92/93 - 6; 93/94 - 24
Fleer: 92/93 - 176; 93/94 - 422PP
Leaf: 93/94 - 64
O-Pee-Chee: 91/92 - 431; 92/93 - 320; 93/94 - 251
Panini: 92/93 - 213E, 213F
Parkhurst: 91/92 - 370E, 370F; 93/94 - 437, 437EI
Pro Set: 91/92 - 556E, 556F, 267PT; 92/93 - 151, 226, 12RGL
Score: 91/92 - 313PNE, 313PNF; 92/93 - 219C, 219A, 141PNC, 141PNA; 93/94 - 352C, 352A
Topps: 91/92 - 431; 92/93 - 94, 94GS, 93SC; 93/94 - 251
Upper Deck: 91/92 - 488E, 488F; 92/93 - 147

Lapointe, Guy
Coca-Cola: 77/78 - 13
Derniere: 72/84 - 3, 28, 124
Eddie Sargent: 70/71 - 105; 71/72 - 98; 72/73 - 113
Esso: 71/72 - 133; 88/89 - 26
Lipton Soup: 74/75 - 16
Loblaws: 74/75 - 169
Mac's Milk: 73/74 - 13
O-Pee-Chee: 70/71 - 177; 71/72 - 145; 72/73 - 86; 73/74 - 114; 74/75 - 70; 75/76 - 198, 293; 76/77 - 223; 77/78 - 60; 78/79 - 260; 79/80 - 135; 80/81 - 201; 82/83 - 305

Lapointe, Guy (cont.)
PepsiCo: 80/81 - 50
Post: 82/83 - 265
Topps: 72/73 - 57; 73/74 - 170; 74/75 - 70; 75/76 - 198, 293; 76/77 - 223, 17PO; 77/78 - 60; 78/79 - 260; 79/80 - 135; 80/81 - 201
Toronto Sun: 71/72 - 154

Lapointe, Martin
Durivage: 93/94 - 6
Fleer: 93/94 - 332PP
Gillette: 91/92 - 20
Leaf: 93/94 - 336
Parkhurst: 91/92 - 267E, 267F; 93/94 - 63, 63EI; 94/95 - 70, 70EI
Pro Set: 91/92 - 532E, 532F
Score: 91 - 105T; 91/92 - 655B, 655C, 355PNE, 355PNF; 92/93 - 409C, 409A, 365PNC, 365PNA
Upper Deck: 90/91 - 467E, 467F; 91/92 - 66E, 685E, 66F, 685F; 92/93 - 405; 93/94 - 257

Lapointe, Rick
O-Pee-Chee: 76/77 - 48; 77/78 - 152; 78/79 - 322; 79/80 - 121; 81/82 - 295, 134SK; 83/84 - 294
Post: 82/83 - 264
Topps: 76/77 - 48; 77/78 - 152; 79/80 - 121; 81/82 WN - 119

Lappin, Peter
O-Pee-Chee: 91/92 - 5S
Score: 90/91 - 403A, 403C
Upper Deck: 90/91 - 235E, 235F

Laprade, Edgar
Beehive: 45/63 - 337
CKAC Radio: 43/47 - 12
Parkhurst: 51/52 - 96; 52/53 - 100
Royal Desserts: 1952 - 3
Topps: 54/55 - 56

Larionov, Igor
Bowman: 90/91 - 63; 91/92 - 326; 92/93 - 350
Donruss: 93/94 - 305
Fleer: 93/94 - 436PP
Kraft: 1990 - 41; 90/91 - 25
Leaf: 93/94 - 391
O-Pee-Chee: 90/91 - 359; 91/92 - 480; 92/93 - 159
Panini: 90/91 - 294, 336; 91/92 - 42 92/93 - 32E, 32F
Parkhurst: 91/92 - 406E, 406F; 93/94 - 185, 185EI; 94/95 - V88
Pro Set: 90/91 - 297; 91/92 - 246E, 246F, 126PT
Score: 90/91 - 123A, 123C; 91/92 - 168A, 168B, 168C, 293PNE, 293PNF; 92/93 - 58C, 58A, 13CSS, 13ASS
Topps: 90/91 - 359; 91/92 - 480, 150SC; 92/93 - 512, 512GS, 299SC
Upper Deck: 90/91 - 128E, 128F; 91/92 - 298E, E18(E), 298F, E18(F)

Lariviere, Garry
Derniere: 72/84 - 92
O-Pee-Chee: 79/80 - 291; 81/82 - 116; 82/83 - 116
PepsiCo: 80/81 - 71
Post: 82/83 - 91

Larmer, Jeff
O-Pee-Chee: 83/84 - 230, 186SK; 84/85 - 36
Topps: 83/84 - 186SK

Larmer, Steve
Bowman: 90/91 - 5; 91/92 - 398; 92/93 - 61
Donruss: 93/94 - 461
Fleer: 92/93 - 39; 93/94 - 129, 52PP, 392PP
Funmate: 83/84 - 24
Hockey Wit: 93/94 - 43
Kraft: 90/91 - 26
McDonald's: 91/92 - Mc15
O-Pee-Chee: 83/84 - 105, 108SK; 83/84 - 206, 312SK; 84/85 - 37, 29SK; 85/86 - 132, 28SK; 86/87 - 139, 157SK; 87/88 - 59, 81SK; 88/89 - 154, 17NS, 12SK;

Larmer, Steve (cont.)
O-Pee-Chee: 89/90 - 179, J/BB, 17SK; 90/91 - 56, 58PM; 91/92 - 75, 60PM, 135PM; 92/93 - 32; 93/94 - 240, 236SC, 236FD
Panini: 87/88 - 226; 88/89 - 26; 89/90 - 43; 90/91 - 194; 91/92 - 8; 92/93 - 5E, 5F; 93/94 - 146E, 146F
Parkhurst: 91/92 - 34E, 34F; 92/93 - 30, 30EI; 93/94 - 404B, 404B(EI); 94/95 - 1446, 146EI
Pro Set: 90/91 - 53, 345; 91/92 - AC13, 49E, 279E, 49F, 279F, 28PT, 287PT; 92/93 - 31
Score: 90/91 - 135A, 135C, 61HR; 91/92 - 140A, 140B, 140C, 29PNE, 357PNE, 29PNF, 357PNF; 92/93 - 266C, 266A, 74PNC, 74PNA; 93/94 - 3C, 3A, 22DT, 3PCA
Season's: 92/93 - 2
Sega: 93/94 - 29
Topps: 83/84 - 108SK, 312SK; 84/85 - 30; 85/86 - 132; 86/87 - 139; 87/88 - 59; 88/89 - 154; 89/90 - 179, J/BB; 90/91 - 56, 1SL; 91/92 - 75, 21SL, 270SC; 92/93 - 497. 497GS, 54SC; 93/94 - 240, 236SC, 398SC, 236FD, 398FD
Upper Deck: 90/91 - 242E, 242F, 499E, 499F; 91/92 - 15E, 257E, 15F, 257F; 92/93 - 4, 135, G6; 93/94 - 172, 471

Larochelle, Wildor
Anonymous; 26/27 - 7
Diamond: 33/35 - 38; 36/39 - 38(I), 36(II), 33(III), 8(IV)
Hamilton Gum: 33/34 - 14
La Presse: 27/32 - 9
O-Pee-Chee: 33/34 - 21
Sweet Caporal: 34/35 - 7
World Wide Gum: 33/34 - 28; 36/37 - 34

Larocque, Michel (Bunny) (Goalie)
Derniere: 72/84 - 39, 120
Loblaws: 74/75 - 170
O-Pee-Chee: 74/75 - 297; 75/76 - 362; 76/77 - 79; 77/78 - 177; 78/79 - 158; 79/80 - 296; 81/82 - 319, 105SK, 259SK; 82/83 - 324, 77SK
Post: 82/83 - 280
Topps: 76/77 - 79; 77/78 - 177; 78/79 - 158; 82/83 - 77SK

Larose, Claude
Beehive: 64/67 - 110A, 110B
Coca-Cola: 64/65 - 65; 65/66 - 64
Derniere: 72/84 - 15, 37,
Eddie Sargent: 70/71 - 101; 72/73 - 122
Esso: 70/71 - 135
Loblaws: 74/75 - 171
O-Pee-Chee: 68/69 - 51; 69/70 - 194, 12QS; 70/71 - 56; 71/72 - 146; 75/76 - 112; 76/77 - 310; 77/78 - 167
Shirriff: 68/69 - E7B
Topps: 65/66 - 75; 66/67 - 10; 67/68 - 4; 68/69 - 51; 69/70 - 126; 70/71 - 56; 75/76 - 112; 77/78 - 167
Toronto Sun: 71/72 - 155

Larose, Guy
Bowman: 92/93 - 281
O-Pee-Chee: 92/93 - 269, 128PM
Parkhurst: 91/92 - 399E, 399F
Topps: 92/93 - 47, 47GS, 237SC
Upper Deck: 92/93 - 527

Larouche, Pierre
Derniere: 72/84 - 121, 174, 199
Funmate: 83/84 - 46
O-Pee-Chee: 75/76 - 305; 76/77 - 199; 77/78 - 102; 78/79 - 35; 79/80 - 233; 80/81 - 151; 81/82 - 187, 38SK; 82/83 - 125, 127SK; 84/85 - 145, 363, 103SK; 85/86 - 54, 85SK
Panini: 87/88 - 116
PepsiCo: 80/81 - 51
Post: 82/83 - 103

Larouche, Pierre (cont.)
Topps: 75/76 - 305; 76/77 - 199; 77/78 - 102; 78/79 - 35; 79/80 - 233; 80/81 - 151; 82/83 - 127SK; 84/85 - 108; 85/86 - 54

Larson, Norman
Beehive: 34/44 - 238
O-Pee-Chee: 40/41 - 127

Larson, Reed
Funmate: 83/84 - 32
Kellogg's: 84 - 24
O-Pee-Chee: 78/79 - 226; 79/80 - 213; 80/81 - 43; 81/82 - 92, 124SK; 82/83 - 88, 89, 180SK; 83/84 - 125, 134SK; 84/85 - 58, 36SK; 85/86 - 55, 33SK; 86/87 - 110, 39SK; 87/88 - 131, 142SK; 88/89 - 145
Panini: 87/88 - 7
Post: 82/83 - 71
Topps: 78/79 - 226; 79/80 - 213; 80/81 - 43; 81/82 WN - 92; 82/83 - 180SK; 83/84 - 134SK; 84/85 - 44; 85/86 - 55; 86/87 - 110; 87/88 - 131; 88/89 - 145

Larue, Albert
Anonymous: 1926/27 - 6

Laskoski, Gary (Goalie)
O-Pee-Chee: 83/84 - 156, 296
Topps: 83/84 - 296SK

Latal, Jiri
O-Pee-Chee: 90/91 - 59PM; 91/92 - 444
Pro Set: 90/91 - 501; 91/92 - 454E, 454F
Score: 91/92 - 540B, 540C
Topps: 91/92 - 444
Upper Deck: 90/91 - 410E, 410F; 91/92 - 404E, 404F

Lauer, Brad
O-Pee-Chee: 88/89 - 226; 90/91 - 217
Pro Set: 91/92 - 375E, 375F
Topps: 90/91 - 217; 91/92 - 142SC

Laughlin, Craig
O-Pee-Chee: 83/84 - 375; 84/85 - 203; 85/86 - 190; 86/87 - 35, 253; 87/88 - 161; 89/90 - 275, 171
Panini: 87/88 - 182
Post: 82/83 - 152
Topps: 86/87 - 35; 87/88 - 161

Laughton, Mike
Eddie Sargent: 70/71 - 136
O-Pee-Chee: 69/70 - 148; 70/71 - 74
Topps: 70/71 - 74

Laukkanen, Janne
Upper Deck: 91/92 - 22E, 22F

Laurence, Red (Don)
O-Pee-Chee: 79/80 - 369

Laus, Paul
O-Pee-Chee: 93/94 - 402
Topps: 93/94 - 402C, 292SC, 292FD

LaVallee, Kevin
O-Pee-Chee: 81/82 - 43; 82/83 - 49, 220; 83/84 - 157; 84/85 - 183
PepsiCo: 80/81 - 6
Post: 82/83 - 38
Topps: 82/83 - 220SK

Lavender, Brian
O-Pee-Chee: 72/73 - 270

Lavoie, Dominic
Parkhurst: 93/94 - 366, 366EI
Upper Deck: 93/94 - 444

Laviolette, Jack
Hall of Fame: 83 - 159, L9P; 87 - 159
Imperial Tobacco: 10/11 - 21, 45L; 11/12 - 45; 12/13 - 46

Laviolette, Peter
Fleer: 93/94 - 508PP
Topps: 93/94 - 3US

Lavoie, Dominic
Bowman: 90/91 - 26
Fleer: 92/93 - 145
Leaf: 93/94 - 415
Score: 90/91 - 416A, 416C

Lawless, Paul
O-Pee-Chee: 83/84 - 141
Panini: 87/88 - 48

Lawson, Danny
Esso: 70/71 - 116
Toronto Sun: 71/72 - 30

Lawton, Brian
Bowman: 92/93 - 254
Fleer: 92/93 - 197
O-Pee-Chee: 87/88 - 145; 88/89 - 20, 198SK; 89/90 - 91; 92/93 - 276
Panini: 87/88 - 300; 88/89 - 94; 92/93 - 132E, 132F
Parkhurst: 91/92 - 167E, 167F; 92/93 - 163, 163EI
Pro Set: 91/92 - 482E, 482F; 92/93 - 173
Score: 91 - 98T; 91/92 - 648B, 648C; 92/93 - 343C, 343A, 71PNC, 71PNA
Topps: 87/88 - 145; 88/89 - 20; 89/90 - 91; 92/93 - 435, 435GS, 171SC
Upper Deck: 91/92 - 572E, 572F

Laxdal, Derek
O-Pee-Chee: 89/90 - 169; 181SK
Topps: 89/90 - 169

Laycoe, Hal
Beehive: 45/63 - 42, 259
CKAC Radio: 43/47 - 63
Parkhurst: 51/52 - 25; 52/53 - 71; 53/54 - 87; 54/55 - 52
Quaker Oats: 45/54 - 28A, 28B
Topps: 54/55 - 38

Lazaro, Jeff
Bowman: 91/92 - 352
Fleer: 93/94 - 509PP
O-Pee-Chee: 91/92 - 380
Panini: 92/93 - 139E, 139F
Pro Set: 91/92 - 13E, 13F
Score: 91/92 - 445B, 445C
Topps: 91/92 - 380, 397SC; 92/93 - 224, 224GS; 93/94 - 21US
Upper Deck: 91/92 - 364E, 364F

Leach, Jamie
Bowman: 92/93 - 320
O-Pee-Chee: 90/91 - 377, 60PM; 91/92 - 492
Score: 90/91 - 420A, 420C
Topps: 90/91 - 377; 91/92 - 492, 296SC; 92/93 - 362, 362GS, 329SC
Upper Deck: 92/93 - 168

Leach, Reggie (Reg)
Eddie Sargent: 72/73 - 54
Loblaws: 74/75 - 226
O-Pee-Chee: 71/72 - 175; 72/73 - 51; 73/74 - 84; 74/75 - 95; 75/76 - 166; 76/77 - 65, 110; 77/78 - 185, 8GP; 78/79 - 165; 79/80 - 95; 80/81 - 70, 249; 81/82 - 243, 181SK; 82/83 - 90; 83/84 - 9SK
Parkhurst: 92/93 - 471, 471EI; 93/94 - D19
Post: 82/83 - 216
Topps: 72/73 - 17; 73/74 - 84; 74/75 - 95; 75/76 - 166; 76/77 - 65, 110, 21PO; 77/78 - 185, 8PO; 78/79 - 165; 79/80 - 95; 80/81 - 70, 249; 81/82 EN - 106; 83/84 - 9SK
Toronto Sun: 71/72 - 12

Leach, Stephen
Bowman: 91/92 - 306; 92/93 - 298
Donruss: 93/94 = 28
Fleer: 92/93 - 5; 93/94 - 21PP
Leaf: 93/94 - 3
O-Pee-Chee: 89/90 - 67, 79SK; 90/91 - 235; 91/92 - 100, 12PM; 92/93 - 112; 93/94 - 507, 187SC, 187FD
Panini: 89/90 - 349; 90/91 - 166; 91/92 - 211; 93/94 - 5E, 5F
Parkhurst: 91/92 - 6E, 6F; 92/93 - 241, 241EI;

Leach, Stephen (cont.)
Parkhurst: 93/94 - 285, 285EI
Pro Set: 90/91 - 315; 91/92 - 253E, 346E, 253F, 346F, 151PT; 92/93 - 6
Score: 90/91 - 279A, 279C; 91 - 26T; 91/92 - 576B, 576C, 46PNE, 46PNF; 92/93 - 54C, 54A, 73PNC, 73PNA; 93/94 - 88C, 88A
Topps: 89/90 - 67; 90/91 - 235; 91/92 - 100, 226SC; 92/93 - 16, 16GS, 68SC; 93/94 - 507A, 187SC, 187FD
Upper Deck: 92/93 - 61

Leader, Al
Hall of Fame: 83 - 176, M12P; 87 - 176

Lebeau, Patrick
Score: 91/92 - 390A, 280B, 280C
Topps: 91/92 - 373SC
Upper Deck: 91/92 - 644E, 644F; 93/94 - 499

Lebeau, Stephan
Bowman: 90/91 - 53; 91/92 - 333; 92/93 - 346
Donruss: 93/94 - 175
Durivage: 92/93 - 7; 93/94 - 14
Fleer: 92/93 - 329; 93/94 - 241
Kraft: 91/92 - 26
Leaf: 93/94 - 190
O-Pee-Chee: 90/91 - 388; 91/92 - 135; 92/93 - 293; 93/94 - 462
Panini: 91/92 - 191; 92/93 - 151E, 151F; 93/94 - 16E, 16F
Parkhurst: 91/92 - 87E, 87F; 92/93 - 82, 82EI; 93/94 - 374, 374EI; 94/95 - 2, 2EI, H1, R1, C1
Pro Set: 90/91 - 152; 91/92 - 120E, 120F, 190PT
Score: 90/91 - 262A, 262C; 91 - 7YS; 91/92 - 274A, 494B, 494C, 139PNE, 139PNF; 92/93 - 246C, 246A, 341PNC, 341PNA; 93/94 - 72C, 72A
Topps: 90/91 - 388; 91/92 - 135, 283SC; 92/93 - 69, 69GS, 431SC; 93/94 - 462C, 343SC, 343FD
Upper Deck: 90/91 51E, 51F; 91/92 - 261E, 644E, 261F, 644F; 92/93 - 213; 93/94 - 402

Lebedev, Gennady
O-Pee-Chee: 90/91 - 508

LeBel, Robert
Hall of Fame: 83 - 117, H11P; 87 - 117

LeBlanc, J. P.
O-Pee-Chee: 76/77 - 326; 77/78 - 133
Topps: 77/78 - 133

LeBlanc, John
Bowman: 92/93 - 419
O-Pee-Chee: 92/93 - 287
Score: 92/93 - 486C, 486A
Topps: 92/93 - 88, 88GS, 388SC

LeBlanc, Raymond (Goalie)
Parkhurst: 91/92 - 255E, 255F
Score: 92/93 - 486C, 486A
Upper Deck: 92/93 - 381

LeBrun, Al
Topps: 61/62 - 61; 62/63 - 50

Leclair, Jackie
Beehive: 45/63 - 260
Parkhurst: 55/56 - 36; 93/94 - 83ML
Quaker Oats: 55/56 - 36

LeClair, John
Bowman: 91/92 - 344; 92/93 - 8
Donruss: 93/94 -176
Fleer: 92/93 - 330; 93/94 - 215
Leaf: 93/94 - 98
O-Pee-Chee: 91/92 - 209, 105PM, 186PM; 92/93 - 386; 93/94 - 181, 95SC, 95FD
Parkhurst: 91/92 - 84E, 84F; 92/93 - 326, 326EI; 93/94 - 107, 107EI; 94/95 - 111, 111EI
Pro Set: 91/92 - 545E, 545F, 259PT
Score: 91/92 - 313A, 343B, 343C, 322PNE, 322PNF; 93/94 - 318C, 318A

LeClair, John (cont.)
Topps: 91/92 - 209; 92/93 - 500, 500GS, 181SC; 93/94 - 181, 95SC, 95FD
Upper Deck: 91/92 - 345E, 345F; 92/93 - 55; 93/94 - 167

Lecuyer, Doug
O-Pee-Chee: 81/82 - 367

LeDuc, Albert (Battleship)
Anonymous: 33/34 - 27
La Presse: 27/32 - 8
O-Pee-Chee: 33/34 - 46
Parkhurst: 55/56 - 61
Quaker Oats: 55/56 - 61

Leduc, Bob
O-Pee-Chee: 72/73 - 322

LeDuc, Rich
O-Pee-Chee: 79/80 - 283; 80/81 - 122
PepsiCo: 80/81 - 72
Topps: 80/81 - 122

Ledyard, Grant
Bowman: 91/92 - 40; 92/93 - 27
Donruss: 93/94 - 89
Fleer: 93/94 - 325PP
Leaf: 93/94 - 394
O-Pee-Chee: 90/91 - 406; 91/92 - 386; 92/93 - 393
Panini: 87/88 - 273; 92/93 - 244E, 244F
Parkhurst: 91/92 - 241; 93/94 - 321, 321EI
Pro Set: 90/91 - 24
Score: 90/91 - 233A, 233C; 91/92 - 362A, 401B, 401C; 92/93 - 358C, 358A, 205PNC, 205PNA
Topps: 91/92 - 386, 169SC; 92/93 - 321, 321GS, 79SC

Lee, Peter
O-Pee-Chee: 78/79 - 244; 79/80 - 45; 80/81 - 278; 81/82 - 258, 185SK
Post: 82/83 - 235
Topps: 78/79 - 244; 79/80 - 45; 81/82 EN - 114

Leeman, Gary
Bowman: 90/91 - 155, HT10; 91/92 - 161; 92/93 - 192
Fleer: 92/93 - 22
Kraft: 86/87 - 56, 56P; 1990 - 36; 90/91 - 27; 91/92 - 10
O-Pee-Chee: 84/85 - 305; 87/88 - 240, 161SK; 88/89 - 11, 178SK; 89/90 - 22, 168SK; 90/91 - 135; 91/92 - 188, 106PM, 134PM; 92/93 - 33; 93/94 - 397, 244SC, 244FD
Panini: 87/88 - 331; 88/89 - 125; 89/90 - 133; 90/91 - 279; 92/93 - 41E, 41F
Parkhurst: 91/92 - 173E, 173F, 254E, 254F; 92/93 - 323, 323EI
Pro Set: 90/91 - 283; 91/92 - 231E, 231F, 115PT, 162PT
Score: 90/91 - 40A, 40C, 40PC, 20HR; 91/92 - 77A, 77B, 77C, 31PNE, 31PNF; 92/93 - 171C, 171A, 184PNC, 184PNA; 93/94 - 147C, 147A
Topps: 88/89 - 11; 89/90 - 22; 90/91 - 135, 13SL; 91/92 - 188, 158SC; 92/93 - 85, 85GS, 272SC; 93/94 - 397, 244SC, 244FD
Upper Deck: 90/91 - 243E, 243F; 91/92 - 272E, 528E, 272F, 528F; 92/93 - 66

Leetch, Brian
Bowman: 90/91 - 215; 92/93 - 149, 232
Donruss: 93/94 - 221
Fleer: 92/93 - 138, 2AW; 93/94 - 132, 6SA, 160PP
Hockey Wit: 93/94 - 71
Humpty Dumpty: 92/93 - 14(I)
Kellogg's: 92 - 8
Kraft: 90/91 - 28
McDonald's: 91/92 - Mc12
O-Pee-Chee: 88/89 - 12FS; 89/90 - 136, 321, 326, 39SK, 215SK, 240SK, 11FS; 90/91 - 221, 61PM; 91/92 - 108, 269, 57PM, 183PM; 92/93 - 378;

Leetch, Brian (cont.)
O-Pee-Chee: 93/94 - 25, 505, 88SC, 88FD
Panini: 88/89 - 301; 89/90 - 279, 378; 90/91 - 95; 91/92 - 284; 92/93 - 239E, 239F, 2BB; 93/94 - 96E, 96F
Parkhurst: 91/92 - 119E, 438E, 465E, 471E, 119F, 438F; 92/93 - 110, 467, 110EI, 467EI; 93/94 - 131, 131EI; 94/95 - 151, 151EI, V15
Pro Set: 90/91 - 201, 373; 91/92 - 159E, 309E, 159F, 309F, 79PT, 284PT; 92/93 - 112, CC4
Score: 90 - 2YS; 90/91 - 225A, 225C, 93HR; 91/92 - 5A, 333A, 343A, 5B, 5C, 363B, 373B, 363C, 373C, 136PNE, 136PNF, B-3E, B-3F; 92/93 - 375C, 416C, 491C, 522C, 375A, 416A, 491A, 522A, 15PNC, 15PNA, 8USG, 3CTP, 3ATP; 93/94 - 235C, 235A, 6DT, 13FR
Season's: 92/93 - 28
Sega: 93/94 - 85
Topps: 89/90 - 136; 90/91 - 221; 91/92 - 108, 269, 4SL, 201SC; 92/93 - 261, 293, 261GS, 293GS, 73SC, 248SC; 93/94 - 25, 505A, 88SC, 88FD
Upper Deck: 90/91 - 253E, 253F, 485E, 485F; 91/92 - 35E, 153E, 612E, 35F, 153F, 612F; 92/93 - 284, 434, 640, WJG15, 5AS; 93/94 - 348

Lefebvre, Sylvain
Bowman: 90/91 - 48; 91/92 - 332; 92/93 - 307
Donruss: 93/94 - 331
Fleer: 93/94 - 450PP
Leaf: 93/94 - 267
O-Pee-Chee: 90/91 - 159; 91/92 - 489; 92/93 - 303, 108PM; 93/94 - 331, 48SC, 48FD
Panini: 90/91 - 59
Parkhurst: 91/92 - 307E, 307F; 92/93 - 416, 416EI
Pro Set: 90/91 - 472
Score: 90/91 - 307C; 91/92 - 245B, 245C, 359C, 359A; 92/93 - 405C, 405A
Topps: 90/91 - 159; 91/92 - 489, 208SC; 92/93 - 341, 341GS, 367SC; 93/94 - 331, 48SC, 48FD
Upper Deck: 90/91 - 421E, 421F; 91/92 - 171E, 171F

Lefley, Bryan
Eddie Sargent: 72/73 - 139
Loblaws: 74/75 - 117
O-Pee-Chee: 72/73 - 252; 76/77 - 159; 77/78 - 297; 78/79 - 370

Lefley, Chuck
Derniere: 72/84 - 14, 29
Loblaws: 74/75 - 172
O-Pee-Chee: 73/74 - 44; 74/75 - 178; 75/76 - 282; 76/77 - 63; 77/78 - 340; 80/81 - 395
Topps: 73/74 - 154; 75/76 - 282; 76/77 - 63

Legace, Manny
O-Pee-Chee: 93/94 - 2TC
Upper Deck: 92/93 - 585

Leger, Roger
Beehive: 45/63 - 286
CKAC Radio: 43/47 - 64
La Patrie: 51/54 - 22
Quaker Oats: 45/54 - 29A, 29B, 29C

Legge, Barry
PepsiCo: 80/81 - 129

Lehman, Hugh (Goalie)
Hall of Fame: 83 - 202, N7P; 87 - 202
Topps: 60/61 - 38, 44ST

Lehtinen, Jere
Upper Deck: 92/93 - 615

Leinonen, Mikko
O-Pee-Chee: 82/83 - 4; 83/84 - 248

Leiter, Bobby
Beehive: 64/67 - 16

Leiter, Bobby (cont.)
Coca-Cola: 64/65 - 11
Eddie Sargent: 72/73 - 9
Loblaws: 74/75 - 7
O-Pee-Chee: 72/73 - 218; 73/74 - 117; 74/75 - 51; 75/76 - 191
Topps: 63/64 - 14; 64/65 - 63; 73/74 - 117; 74/75 - 51; 75/76 - 191
Toronto Sun: 71/72 - 220

Leiter, Ken
O-Pee-Chee: 87/88 - 131SK
Panini: 87/88 - 93

Lemaire, Jacques
Colgate: 70/71 - 30
Derniere: 72/84 - 5, 47,
Dom. Choc.: 70/71 - 78
Eddie Sargent: 70/71 - 103; 72/73 - 115
Esso: 70/71 - 136
Hall of Fame: 87 - 245
Lipton Soup: 74/75 - 38
Loblaws: 74/75 - 173
Mac's Milk: 73/74 - 14
O-Pee-Chee: 68/69 - 63; 69/70 - 8; 70/71 - 57, 19DE, 20SS; 71/72 - 71; 72/73 - 77; 73/74 - 56; 74/75 - 24; 75/76 - 258; 76/77 - 129; 77/78 - 254; 78/79 - 180
Post: 68/69 - 8
Shirriff: 68/69 - F14
Topps: 67/68 - 3; 68/69 - 63; 69/70 - 8; 70/71 - 57, 20SK; 71/72 - 71; 72/73 - 25; 73/74 - 56; 74/75 - 24; 75/76 - 258; 76/77 - 129; 77/78 - 254; 78/79 - 180
Toronto Sun: 71/72 - 156

Lemay, Moe
O-Pee-Chee: 84/85 - 322; 85/86 - 173, 246SK; 86/87 - 249

Lemelin, Rejean (Reggie) (Goalie)
Bowman: 90/91 - 32; 91/92 - 354
Durivage: 92/93 - 48
Kraft: 86/87 - 1, 1P
O-Pee-Chee: 81/82 - 44; 82/83 - 50; 83/84 - 86, 266SK; 84/85 - 228, 240SK; 85/86 - 95, 210SK; 86/87 - 102, 83SK; 88/89 - 186, 18NS, 24SK; 89/90 - 40; 90/91 - 343; 91/92 - 497
Pro Set: 90/91 - 9
Score: 90/91 - 159A, 159C; 91/92 - 127A, 127B, 127C
7-Eleven: 84/85 - 5
Topps: 83/84 - 266SK; 84/85 - 25; 85/86 - 95; 86/87 - 102; 88/89 - 186; 89/90 - 40; 90/91 - 343; 91/92 - 497, 23SC
Upper Deck: 90/91 - 215E, 215F
Vachon Foods: 83/84 - 10

Lemieux, Claude
Bowman: 91/92 - 271, 277; 92/93 - 49
Donruss: 93/94 - 187
Durivage: 92/93 - 14; 93/94 - 47
Fleer: 92/93 - 114; 93/94 - 5, 137PP
Kraft: 86/87 - 29, 29P
Leaf: 93/94 - 125
O-Pee-Chee: 87/88 - 227, 19SK; 88/89 - 227, 43SK; 89/90 - 234, 52SK; 90/91 - 451, 62PM; 91/92 - 394; 92/93 - 67; 93/94 - 134, 39SC, 39FD
Panini: 87/88 - 63; 88/89 - 257; 89/90 - 240; 91/92 - 224; 92/93 - 172E, 172F; 93/94 - 35E, 35F
Parkhurst: 91/92 - 101E, 101F; 92/93 - 89, 89EI; 93/94 - 110, 110EI; 94/95 - 129, 129EI, V59
Pro Set: 90/91 - 153, 478; 91/92 - 135E, 135, 196PT; 92/93 - 98
Score: 90 - 9T; 90/91 - 111A, 111C; 91/92 - 22A, 22B, 22C, 70PNE, 79PNF; 92/93 - 8C, 8A, 259PNC, 259PNA, 284PNC, 284PNA, 8PC(S), 8PC(F); 93/94 - 160C, 160A
Sega: 93/94 - 77

Lemieux, Claude (cont.)
  Topps: 91/92 - 394, 18SC; 92/93 - 43, 43GS, 50SC; 93/94 - 134, 39SC, 39FD
  Upper Deck: 90/91 - 447E, 447F; 91/92 - 294E, 294F; 92/93 - 163; 93/94 - 296, 391

Lemieux, Jean
  Loblaws: 74/75 - 8
  O-Pee-Chee: 75/76 - 367; 76/77 - 272

Lemieux, Jocelyn
  Bowman: 92/93 - 72
  Donruss: 93/94 - 440
  Durivage: 92/93 - 15; 93/94 - 43
  O-Pee-Chee: 90/91 - 237; 91/92 - 453; 92/93 - 153; 93/94 - 295
  Panini: 87/88 - 319; 90/91 - 190; 91/92 - 20; 92/93 - 8E, 8F; 93/94 - 152E, 152F
  Parkhurst: 91/92 - 256E, 256F; 92/93 - 275, 275EI; 93/94 - 43, 43EI; 94/95 - 91, 91EI
  Pro Set: 90/91 - 432
  Score: 90/91 - 66T; 91/92 - 447B, 447C; 92/93 - 309C, 309A; 93/94 - 420C, 420A
  Topps: 90/91 - 237; 91/92 - 453, 356SC; 92/93 - 300, 300GS, 446SC; 93/94 - 295, 255SC, 255FD
  Upper Deck: 90/91 - 544E, 544F; 91/92 - 438E, 438F

Lemieux, Mario
  Action Packed: 89/90 - 2
  Bowman: 90/91 - 204, HT2; 91/92 - 87; 92/93 - 189, 233, 440
  Cel.Watch: 1988 - CW5
  Donruss: 93/94 -262, 1ES, 7IK, R/PM, R/SP
  Durivage: 92/93 - 8
  Esso: 88/89 - 27
  Fleer: 92/93 - 165, 4AS, 5AW; 93/94 - 116, 5G, 4AW, 190PP, 8PL, 4PM, 6RL, 4SC
  Frito-Lay: 88/89 - 20
  Gillette: 91/92 - 33
  Hockey Wit: 93/94 - 66
  Humpty Dumpty: 92/93 - 12(II)
  Kellogg's: 92/93 - 1P
  Kraft: 1990 - 55; 90/91 - 29, 87; 91/92 - 1; 93 - 22; 93/94 - 26, 45
  Leaf: 93/94 - 1, 1-10C/C, 1AS, 4HT
  O-Pee-Chee: 85/86 - 9, 262, I/BB, 97SK, 199SK; 86/87 - 122, I/BB, 120SK, 233SK; 87/88 - 15, 23HL, 120SK, 170SK; 88/89 - 1, 19NS, 116SK, 204SK, 210SK, 211SK, 232SK; 89/90 - 1, 319, 327, A/BB, 158SK, 208SK, 238SK, 24FS; 90/91 - 175, G/BB, 63PM; 91/92 - 153, 523, 114PM; 92/93 - 138, 240, 292, 18AN, 22SP; 93/94 - 37, 91, 185. 220, 18BG, 10HR, 143SC, 146SC, 148SC, 143FD, 146FD, 148FD
  Panini: 87/88 - 146; 88/89 - 340, 400, 401; 89/90 - 184, 309, 375; 90/91 - 136, 326; 91/92 - 268; 92/93 - 220E, 280E, 220F, 280F
  Parkhurst: 91/92 - 137E, 467E, PHC-7E, 137F, PHC-7F; 92/93 - 136, 462, 498, 136EI, 462EI, 498EI, H(E), H(F); 93/94 - 425, 425EI, F10, G2, E2, D2; 94/94 - 296, 296EI, H18, R18, C18, V6
  Pro Set: 90/91 - 236, 362; 91/92 - P3E, 194E, 318E, 581E, 194F, 318F, 91PT, 581F; 92/93 - 1, 139
  Score: 90/91 - 2A, 2C, 337A, 337C, 34HR; 91/92 - 200A, 335A, 426A, 200B, 316B, 365B, 200C, 316C, 365C, 1PNE, 380PNE, 1PNF, 380PNF, 5HC, B-5E, B-5F; 92/93 - 390C, 413C, 433C, 519C, 390A, 413A, 433A, 519A, 300PNC, 300PNA; 93/94 - 350C, 479C, 480C, 350A, 479A, 480A, 10DT, 16FR
  Season's: 92/93 - 34
  Sega: 93/94 - 105, 189
  Topps: 85/86 - 9, I/BB; 86/87 - 122, I/BB, 9SK;

Lemieux, Mario (cont.)
  Topps: 87/88 - 15, 11SK; 88/89 - 1, 2SK; 89/90 - 1, A/BB, 3SK; 90/91 - 175, 17SL, G/BB; 91/92 - P/C, 153, 523, 174SC, 9SCM; 92/93 - 265, 504, 265GS, 504GS, 94SC, 251SC; 93/94 - 37, 91, 185, 220, 9BG, 10PF,143SC, 146SC, 148SC, 143FD, 146FD, 148FD, 310SC, 310FD, 17AS, 19SCF
  Upper Deck: 90/91 - 59E, 144E, 59F, 144F; 91/92 - 156E, 611E, 156F, 611F; 92/93 - 26, 433, 436, WJG11, G9, 6AS; 93/94 - 301, 407

Lemieux, Real
  Eddie Sargent: 70/71 - 70; 72/73 - 91
  O-Pee-Chee: 68/69 - 36; 69/70 - 190; 71/72 - 154; 73/74 - 122
  Shirriff: 68/69 - D1
  Topps: 68/69 - 36; 73/74 - 122
  Toronto Sun: 71/72 - 119

Lemieux, Richard
  Eddie Sargent: 72/73 - 218
  Loblaws: 74/75 - 118
  O-Pee-Chee: 72/73 - 202; 73/74 - 53; 74/75 - 114; 75/76 - 274
  Topps: 73/74 - 53; 74/75 - 114; 75/76 - 274

Lenarduzzi, Mike
  Fleer: 93/94 - 72, 5TP
  Parkhurst: 93/94 - 87, 87EI

Lepine, Hector
  Anonymous: 1926/27 - 10

Lepine, Pete
  Sweet Caporal: 34/35 - 19

Lepine, Pit (Alfred)
  Anonymous: 33/34 - 42
  Beehive: 34/44 - 164
  Canada Starch: 35/40 - 115
  Can. Chew. Gum: 33/34 - 36
  Diamond: 33/35 - 39; 36/39 - 39(I), 37(II), 34(III)
  Hamilton Gum: 33/34 - 23
  La Presse: 27/32 - 4
  O-Pee-Chee: 33/34 - 20; 37/38 - 159
  World Wide Gum: 33/34 - 46; 36/37 - 78

Leonov, Yuri
  O-Pee-Chee: 91/92 - 39R

Leroux, Francois
  Parkhurst: 93/94 - 412. 412EI
  Score: 90/91 - 393A, 393C

Leschyshyn, Curtis
  Bowman: 91/92 - 142; 92/93 - 335
  Donruss: 93/94 - 273
  Fleer: 93/94 - 423PP
  Leaf: 93/94 - 305
  O-Pee-Chee: 90/91 - 216; 91/92 - 39; 92/93 - 306; 93/94 - 487
  Panini: 89/90 - 334; 90/91 - 150; 91/92 - 256; 92/93 - 217E, 217F
  Parkhurst: 91/92 - 367E, 367F; 93/94 - 436, 436EI
  Pro Set: 90/91 - 251; 91/92 - 198E, 198F
  Score: 90/91 - 92A, 92C, 44HR; 91/92 - 58A, 58B, 58C, 258PNE, 258PNF; 92/93 - 87C, 87A, 46PNC, 46PNA; 93/94 - 42C, 42A
  Sega: 93/94 - 110
  Topps: 90/91 - 216; 91/92 - 39, 156SC; 92/93 - 124, 124GS, 413SC; 93/94 - 487C, 336SC, 336FD
  Upper Deck: 90/91 - 295E, 295F; 91/92 - 413E, 413F; 93/94 - 133

Lesieur, Art
  Diamond: 36/39 - 38(II), 35(III)
  Canada Starch: 35/40 - 67

Lessard, Mario (Goalie)
  O-Pee-Chee: 79/80 - 389; 81/82 - 146, 238SK; 82/83 - 156, 236SK
  Post: 82/83 - 122
  Topps: 81/82 WN - 98; 82/83 - 236SK

Lessard, Rick
  Pro Set: 91/92 - 560E, 560F
  Upper Deck: 91/92 - 520E, 520F

Lesueur, Percy (Goalie)
  Hall of Fame: 83 - 37, C7P; 87 - 37
  Imperial Tobacco: 10/11 - 2, 16L; 11/12 - 16; 12/13 - 27

Lesuk, Bill
  O-Pee-Chee: 72/73 - 245; 73/74 - 205; 79/80 - 312
  Toronto Sun: 71/72 - 202

Leswick, Tony
  Beehive: 45/63 - 186, 338
  Parkhurst: 51/52 - 59; 52/53 - 65; 53/54 - 43; 54/55 - 45
  Royal Desserts: 1952 - 1
  Topps: 54/55 - 45

Leveille, Normand
  O-Pee-Chee: 82/83 - 13

Lever, Don
  Funmate: 83/84 - 72
  Loblaws: 74/75 - 297
  O-Pee-Chee: 72/73 - 259; 73/74 - 111; 74/75 - 94; 75/76 - 206; 76/77 - 53; 77/78 - 111; 78/79 - 86; 79/80 - 203; 80/81 - 124; 81/82 - 45; 82/83 - 141, 224SK; 83/84 - 224, 231, 218SK; 84/85 - 112, 70SK
  Panini: 79 - 65
  PepsiCo: 80/81 - 7
  Post: 82/83 - 166
  Topps: 73/74 - 111; 74/75 - 94; 75/76 - 206; 76/77 - 53; 77/78 - 111; 78/79 - 86; 79/80 - 203; 80/81 - 124; 82/83 - 224SK; 83/84 - 218SK; 84/85 - 86

Leveque, Guy
  Upper Deck: 92/93 - 576; 93/94 - 246

Levie, Craig
  O-Pee-Chee: 82/83 - 382

Levins, Scott
  Donruss: 93/94 - 130, 466
  Parkhurst: 93/94 - 80, 80EI; 94/95 - 155, 292, 155EI, 292EI
  Upper Deck: 93/94 - 433

Levinsky, Alex
  Anonymous: 33/34 - 9
  Beehive: 34/44 - 63
  Canada Starch: 35/40 - 70
  Diamond: 36/39 - 39(I), 40(I), 36(II), 9(IV), 8(V), 8(VI)
  Hamilton Gum: 33/34 - 36
  O-Pee-Chee: 33/34 - 11
  World Wide Gum: 33/34 - 47; 36/37 - 61

Levo, Tapio
  Funmate: 83/84 - 73

Lewicki, Danny
  Beehive: 45/63 - 339, 419
  Parkhurst: 51/52 - 71; 93/94 - 98ML
  Quaker Oats: 45/54 - 81
  Topps: 54/55 - 23; 57/58 - 61; 58/59 - 6

Lewis, Dave
  Loblaws: 74/75 - 188
  O-Pee-Chee: 74/75 - 324; 75/76 - 108; 76/77 - 221; 77/78 - 116; 78/79 - 162; 79/80 - 44; 80/81 - 196; 82/83 - 157; 83/84 - 158; 84/85 - 113; 85/86 - 66, 59SK; 86/87 - 85, 197SK; 87/88 - 37
  Panini: 87/88 - 242
  Post: 82/83 - 123
  Topps: 75/76 - 108; 76/77 - 221; 77/78 - 116; 78/79 - 162; 79/80 - 44; 80/81 - 196; 84/85 - 87; 85/86 - 66; 86/87 - 85; 87/88 - 37

Lewis, Herbbie
  Amal. Press: 35/36 - 4
  Beehive: 34/44 - 111
  Sweet Caporal: 34/35 - 10
  World Wide Gum: 36/37 - 64

Ley, Rick
  Dom. Choc.: 70/71 - 129
  Eddie Sargent: 70/71 - 198; 71/72 - 195
  Esso: 70/71 - 225
  O-Pee-Chee: 69/70 - 183; 70/71 - 108;
    71/72 - 194; 79/80 - 314;
    80/81 - 198; 81/82 - 64SK
  Pro Set: 90/91 - 666
  Topps: 70/71 - 108; 80/81 - 198;
  Toronto Sun: 71/72 - 262

Libett, Nick
  Eddie Sargent: 70/71 - 60; 72/73 - 75
  Esso: 70/71 - 83
  Loblaws: 74/75 - 100
  O-Pee-Chee: 69/70 - 162; 70/71 - 158;
    71/72 - 140; 72/73 - 45; 73/74 - 49;
    74/75 - 193; 75/76 - 13; 76/77 - 171;
    77/78 - 103; 78/79 - 251; 79/80 - 198
  Shirriff: 68/69 - C16
  Topps: 72/73 - 67; 73/74 - 49; 74/75 - 193;
    75/76 - 13; 76/77 - 171; 77/78 - 103;
    78/79 - 251; 79/80 - 198
  Toronto Sun: 71/72 - 98

Lidster, Doug
  Bowman: 90/91 - 56; 91/92 - 317;
    92/93 - 267
  Fleer: 92/93 - 221
  Kraft: 86/87 - 65, 65P
  Leaf: 93/94 - 365
  O-Pee-Chee: 85/86 - 241; 86/87 - 32, 102SK;
    87/88 - 256, 191SK; 88/89 - 228,
    63SK; 89/90 - 284, 69SK;
    90/91 - 207; 91/92 - 179;
    92/93 - 51; 93/94 - 315
  Panini: 87/88 - 341; 88/89 - 135;
    90/91 - 295; 91/92 - 40; 92/93 - 37E,
    37F; 93/94 - 176E, 176F
  Parkhurst: 91/92 - 184E, 184F;
    93/94 - 403, 403EI
  Pro Set: 90/91 - 298; 91/92 - 247E, 247F;
    92/93 - 199
  Score: 90/91 - 73A, 73C; 91/92 - 215A,
    215B, 215C, 189PNE, 189PNF;
    92/93 - 124C, 124A, 147PNC, 147PNA;
    93/94 - 65, 65A
  Sega: 93/94 - 140
  Topps: 86/87 - 32; 90/91 - 207;
    91/92 - 179, 72SC; 92/93 - 403,
    403GS, 404SC; 93/94 - 315, 406SC,
    406FD
  Upper Deck: 90/91 - 60E, 60F; 91/92 - 290E, 290F

Lidstrom, Nicklas
  Bowman: 92/93 - 305
  Donruss: 93/94 - 102
  Fleer: 92/93 - 51, 7UR, 13UI;
    93/94 - 220, 74PP
  Leaf: 93/94 - 89
  O-Pee-Chee: 91/92 - 117PM, 163PM;
    92/93 - 369; 93/94 - 9, 196SC, 196FD
  Panini: 92/93 - 274E, 298E, J(E), 274F,
    298F, J(F); 93/94 - 253E, 253F
  Parkhurst: 91/92 - 37E, 445E, 37F, 445F;
    92/93 - 42, 239, 451, 42EI, 239EI, 452EI;
    93/94 - 62, 62EI; 94/95 - 61, 61EI
  Pro Set: 91/92 - 531E, 610E, 531F, 610F,
    253PT; 92/93 - 42, 4TL
  Score: 91 - 71T; 91/92 - 621B, 621C,
    320PNE, 320PNF; 92/93 - 391C,
    502C, 391A, 502A, 8PNC, 8PNA, 3
    CT, 3AT; 93/94 - 158C, 158A
  Topps: 92/93 - 9, 440, 9GS, 440GS, 43SC,
    253SC; 93/94 - 9, 196SC,
    429SC, 196FD, 429FD
  Upper Deck: 91/92 - 26E, 587E, 26F, 587F;
    93/94 - 178, 363, E9, AR4, ERT2, W4;
    93/94 - 150

Lilley, John
  Fleer: 93/94 - 510PP
  Parkhurst: 94/95 - 8, 8EI
  Topps: 93/94 - 8US

Lindberg, Chris
  Fleer: 92/93 - 269; 93/94 - 62
  O-Pee-Chee: 92/93 - 4PM; 93/94 - 76, 84SC, 84FD

Lindberg, Chris (cont.)
  Parkhurst: 91/92 - 251E, 251F;
    92/93 - 27, 27EI; 93/94 - 440, 440EI
  Score: 92/93 - 485C, 485A, 6COH
  Topps: 92/93 - 320, 320GS, 407SC;
    93/94 - 76, 84SC, 84FD
  Upper Deck: 92/93 - 97; 93/94 - 196

Lindbergh, Pelle (Goalie)
  O-Pee-Chee: 83/84 - 268, 197SK; 85/86 - 110,
    91SK, 193SK
  Topps: 83/84 - 197SK; 85/86 - 110

Linden, Trevor
  Bowman: 90/91 - 61; 91/92 - 327;
    92/93 - 210, 261
  Donruss: 93/94 - 354
  Fleer: 92/93 - 222; 93/94 - 109, 251PP
  Gillette: 91/92 - 5
  Hockey Wit: 93/94 - 106
  Humpty Dumpty: 92/93 - 13(II)
  Kellogg's: 92 - 20
  Kraft: 1990 - 42; 90/91 - 30; 91/92 - 30;
    1993 - 16; 93/94 - 46
  Leaf: 93/94 - 193
  O-Pee-Chee: 89/90 - 89, 40SK, 61SK, 19FS;
    90/91 - 225; 91/92 - 364, 77PM;
    92/93 - 120; 93/94 - 225
  Panini: 89/90 - 148; 90/91 - 299; 91/92 - 36;
    92/93 - 28E, 28F; 93/94 - 172E, 172F
  Parkhurst: 91/92 - 179E, 179F; 92/93 - 190,
    190EI; 93/94 - 215, 215EI;
    94/95 - 241, 241EI
  Pro Set: 90/91 - 299; 91/92 - 236E, 294E,
    586E, 236F, 294F, 124PT, 586F;
    92/93 - 197, 12TL
  Roots: 93/94 - 1
  Score: 90 - 19YS; 90/91 - 32A, 32C, 16HR;
    91 - 11YS; 91/92 - 8A, 8B, 8C,
    369B, 369C, 2PNE, 2PNF;
    92/93 - 305C, 438C, 305A, 438A,
    47PNC, 47PNA, 24CT, 24AT;
    93/94 - 117C, 117A
  Season's: 92/93 - 30
  Topps: 89/90 - 89; 90/91 - 225; 91/92 - 364,
    17SL, 84SC; 92/93 - 499, 499GS,
    80SC; 93/94 - 225, 357SC, 357FD
  Upper Deck: 90/91 - 256E, 256F, 480E, 480F;
    91/92 - 174E, 628E, 174F, 628F;
    92/93 - 158, WJG14; 93/94 - 383

Lindgren, Lars
  O-Pee-Chee: 80/81 - 177; 82/83 - 349;
    83/84 - 354
  PepsiCo: 80/81 - 112
  Post: 82/83 - 297
  Topps: 80/81 - 177

Lindgren, Mats
  Parkhurst: 93/94 - 511, 534, 511EI, 534EI
  Upper Deck: 93/94 - 570

Lindros, Brett
  Fleer: 93/94 - 486PP
  O-Pee-Chee: 93/94 - 1TC

Lindros, Eric
  Bowman: 92/93 - 442
  Donruss: 93/94 - 242, 4ES, 9IK, Q/PM, Q/SP
  Fleer: 92/93 - 157; 93/94 - 161, 6G, 183PP,
    5SY, 5PM
  Hockey Wit: 93/94 - 88
  Kraft: 93/94 - 14
  Leaf: 93/94 - 233, 3R, 10SS, 7HT
  O-Pee-Chee: 92/93 - 102PM; 93/94 - 121, 310,
    3HR, 10SC, 10FD
  Panini: 92/93 - P(E), P(F); 93/94 - 144E,
    144F, E(E), E(F)
  Parkhurst: 92/93 - 128, 128EI; CP6; 93/94 - 236,
    416, 236EI, 416EI, F3, G3, E1, D15;
    94/95 - 301, 301EI, H17, R17, C17,
    V69
  Pro-Set: 92/93 - 236
  Score: 90 - 40YS; 90/91 - 440A, 440C,
    B1A to B5A, B1C to B5C; 91 - 30YS,
    88T; 91/92 - 354A, 355A, 356A,
    329B, 330B, 384B, 385B, 329C,
    330C, 384C, 385C, 1HC, 365PNE,
    365PNF, PC; 92/93 - 432C, 550C,

Lindros, Eric (cont,)
  Score: 432A, 550A, 88PNC, 88PNA,
    236PNC, 236PNA, 1TR, 1COH,
    5CTP, 1CT, 5ATP, 1AT; 93/94 - 1C,
    1A, 12DT, 1PCA, 1PCE15FR
  Season's: 92/93 - 38
  Sega: 93/94 - 99
  Topps: 92/93 - 529, 529GS, 501SC, 4SCM;
    93/94 - 121, 310, 13BG, 3PF, 10SC,
    10FD, 5MP
  Upper Deck: 91/92 - 9E, 9F; 92/93 - 88, 470,
    CC6, WJG12, G14, 56AS;
    93/94 - 30, 280

Lindsay, Bert (Goalie)
  Imperial Tobacco: 10/11 - 21; 11/12 - 21; 12/13 - 13

Lindsay, Bill
  Bowman: 92/93 - 404
  Fleer: 92/93 - 388; 93/94 - 95PP
  O-Pee-Chee: 92/93 - 5PM; 93/94 - 436
  Parkhurst: 92/93 - 376, 376EI;
    93/94 - 350, 350EI
  Pro-Set: 92/93 - 239
  Score: 92/93 - 463C, 463A
  Topps: 92/93 - 373, 373GS; 93/94 - 436C,
    253SC, 254FD
  Upper Deck: 92/93 - 472

Lindsay, Ted
  Beehive: 45/63 - 112, 187; 64/67 - 82
  Coca-Cola: 64/65 - 47
  Hall of Fame: 83 - 151, L10P; 87 - 151
  Parkhurst: 51/52 - 56; 52/53 - 87;
    53/54 - 52; 54/55 - 46; 92/93 - PR31;
    93/94 - PR47, 44ML, 140ML, 155ML
  Royal Desserts: 1952 - 5
  Topps: 54/55 - 51; 57/58 - 21; 58/59 - 63;
    59/60 - 6; 64/65 - 82
  Toronto Star: 58/67 - 4
  Ultimate: 92 - 70(OSE), 94(OSE),
    70(OSF), 94(OSF)
  Zellers: 92/93 - 4, 4A

Lindstrom, Willy
  O-Pee-Chee: 79/80 - 368; 80/81 - 142;
    81/82 - 368; 82/83 - 384, 209SK;
    83/84 - 35, 91SK; 84/85 - 250,
    260SK; 85/86 - 217, 226SK;
    86/87 - 232, 227SK
  PepsiCo: 80/81 - 130
  Post: 82/83 - 327
  Topps: 80/81 - 142; 82/83 - 209;
    83/84 - 91SK
  Vachon Foods: 83/84 - 32

Linseman, Ken
  Bowman: 91/92 - 105
  Funmate: 83/84 - 41
  O-Pee-Chee: 79/80 - 241; 80/81 - 24; 81/82 - 244,
    176SK; 82/83 - 115, 112SK;
    83/84 - 36, 102SK; 84/85 - 7;
    88/89 - 118; 89/90 - 62, 26SK;
    90/91 - 345; 91/92 - 146
  Panini: 87/88 - 16; 88/89 - 211; 89/90 - 190;
    90/91 - 111
  Post: 82/83 - 217
  Pro Set: 90/91 - 219, 444
  Score: 90/91 - 380A, 380C, 95T;
    91/92 - 359A, 239B, 622B, 239C,
    622C, 102SK
  Topps: 79/80 - 241; 80/81 - 24;
    81/82 EN - 107; 82/83 - 112SK;
    83/84 - 102SK; 88/89 - 118;
    88/89 - 118; 89/90 - 62; 622C
    89/90 - 6290/91 - 345;
    91/92 - 146, 295SC
  Vachon Foods: 83/84 - 33

LiPuma, Chris
  Donruss: 93/94 - 493
  Fleer: 93/94 - 178, 4UR, 446PP

Liscombe, Carl
  Beehive: 34/44 - 112
  O-Pee-Chee: 39/40 - 74

Littman, David
  Fleer: 93/94 - 237

Litzenberger, Ed
  Beehive: 45/63 - 113, 188, 262, 420; 64/67 - 173
  Chex: 63/65 - 50
  La Patrie: 51/54 - 26
  Parkhurst: 61/62 - 28; 62/63 - 12; 63/64 - 6, 66; 93/94 - 24ML
  Shirriff: 60/61 - 62; 61/62 - 71; 62/63 - 18
  Topps: 57/58 - 26; 58/59 - 16; 59/60 - 61; 60/61 - 21
  Toronto Star: 58/67 - 21
  Ultimate: 92 - 58)OSE), 58(OSF)

Liut, Michael (Mike) (Goalie)
  Bowman: 90/91 - 66; 91/92 - 290
  Funmate: 83/84 - 116
  Kraft: 90/91 - 31
  O-Pee-Chee: 80/81 - 31; 81/82 - 289, 301, 129SK, 153SK; 82/83 - 306, 196SK; 83/84 - 309, 316, 129SK; 84/85 - 187, 57SK; 85/86 - 88, 169SK; 86/87 - 133, 52SK; 87/88 - 152, 24HL, 121SK, 209SK; 88/89 - 127, 20NS, 263SK; 89/90 - 97, 267SK; 90/91 - 44; 91/92 - 154
  Panini: 87/88 - 38; 88/89 - 235; 90/91 - 165
  Parkhurst: 91/92 - 196E, 196F
  Post: 81/82 - 13; 82/83 - 266
  Pro Set: 90/91 - 316
  Score: 90/91 - 68A, 68C, 32HR; 91/92 - 99A, 99B, 99C, 169PNE, 169PNF; 92/93 - 368C, 368A
  Topps: 80/81 - 31; 81/82 - WN 128, 20; 82/83 - 196SK; 83/84 - 129SK 84/85 - 132; 85/86 - 88; 86/87 - 133; 87/88 - 152, 8SK; 88/89 - 127; 89/90 - 97; 90/91 - 44; 91/92 - 154, 10SC; 92/93 - 307, 307GS
  Upper Deck: 90/91 - 127E, 127F; 91/92 - 259E, 259F

Loach, Lonnie
  Fleer: 92/93 - 146, 309; 93/94 - 7PP
  Parkhurst: 92/93 - 305, 305EI
  Upper Deck: 92/93 - 466

Locas, Jacques
  Chex: 43/47 - 65
  Quaker Oats: 45/54 - 30

Lochead, Bill
  Loblaws: 74/75 - 101
  O-Pee-Chee: 74/75 - 318; 75/76 - 103; 76/77 - 122; 77/78 - 212; 78/79 - 122; 79/80 - 301
  Topps: 75/76 - 103; 76/77 - 122; 77/78 - 212; 78/79 - 122

Lockett, Ken (Goalie)
  Loblaws: 74/75 - 298

Lockhart, Thomas
  Hall of Fame: 83 - 38, C8P; 87 - 38

Locking, Norman
  Diamond: 36/39 - 40(I), 41(II), 37(III)

Loewen, Darcy
  O-Pee-Chee: 92/93 - 7PM; 93/94 - 184
  Parkhurst: 92/93 - 355, 355EI; 93/94 - 407, 407EI
  Topps: 93/94 - 184, 318SC, 318FD
  Upper Deck: 91/92 - 421E, 421F

Lofthouse, Mark
  O-Pee-Chee: 80/81 - 331

Logan, Dave
  O-Pee-Chee: 78/79 - 343
  PepsiCo: 80/81 - 113

Loicq, Paul
  Hall of Fame: 83 - 234, F8P; 87 - 234

Loiselle, Claude
  Bowman: 90/91 - 175
  O-Pee-Chee: 93/94 - 328
  Panini: 87/88 - 85; 88/89 - 273; 90/91 - 151
  Pro Set: 90/91 - 252; 91/92 - 493E, 493F

Loiselle, Claude (cont.)
  Score: 90/91 - 207A, 207C; 91/92 - 532B, 532C, 296PNE, 296PNF; 92/93 - 328C, 328A, 219PNC, 219PNA
  Topps: 92/93 - 338, 338GS; 93/94 - 328
  Upper Deck: 90/91 - 338E, 338F

Lomakin, Andrei
  Bowman: 92/93 - 286
  Donruss: 93/94 - 128
  Fleer: 92/93 - 372; 93/94 - 96PP
  Leaf: 93/94 - 401
  O-Pee-Chee: 90/91 - 472; 91/92 - 40R, 178PM; 92/93 - 37; 93/94 - 82, 57SC, 57FD
  Panini: 92/93 - 193E, 193F; 93/94 - 52E, 52F
  Parkhurst: 91/92 - 131E, 131F; 93/94 - 349, 349EI; 94/95 - 84, 84EI
  Pro-Set: 91/92 - 208PT
  Score: 91 - 110T; 91/92 - 660B, 660C, 305PNE, 305PNF; 92/93 - 129C, 129A, 162PNC, 162PNA
  Sega: 93/94 - 52
  Topps: 92/93 - 380, 380GS; 93/94 - 82, 57SC, 402SC, 57FD, 402FD
  Upper Deck: 91/92 - 518E, 518F; 92/93 - 428, E17; 93/94 - 102

Loney, Troy
  Fleer: 92/93 - 378; 93/94 - 8PP
  Kraft: 93/94 - 46
  O-Pee-Chee: 90/91 - 347; 93/94 - 340
  Panini: 88/89 - 341; 89/90 - 319; 90/91 - 138
  Parkhurst: 91/92 - 352, 352F; 93/94 - 9, 9EI; 94/95 - 5, 5EI
  Pro Set: 90/91 - 237
  Score: 90/91 - 371A, 371C; 91/92 - 522B, 522C; 92/93 - 348C, 348A
  Topps: 90/91 - 347; 92/93 - 397, 397GS, 357SC; 93/94 - 340, 395SC, 395FD
  Sega: 93/94 - 4
  Upper Deck: 90/91 - 367E, 367F; 91/92 - 489E, 489F; 92/93 - 208; 93/94 - 438

Long, Barry
  O-Pee-Chee: 72/73 - 288; 80/81 - 258; 81/82 - 369, 142SK
  PepsiCo: 80/81 - 131
  Topps: 80/81 - 258; 81/82 - 142SK

Lonsberry, Ross
  Eddie Sargent: 70/71 - 66; 72/73 - 166
  Esso: 70/71 - 100
  Loblaws: 74/75 - 227
  O-Pee-Chee: 69/70 - 104; 70/71 - 37; 71/72 - 121; 72/73 - 166; 73/74 - 36; 74/75 - 144; 75/76 - 110; 76/77 - 201; 77/78 - 257; 78/79 - 186; 79/80 - 58; 80/81 - 388; 81/82 - 263
  Topps: 67/68 - 35; 69/70 - 104; 70/71 - 37; 71/72 - 121; 72/73 - 112; 73/74 - 36; 74/75 - 144; 75/76 - 110; 76/77 - 201; 77/78 - 257; 78/79 - 186; 79/80 - 58
  Toronto Sun: 71/72 - 120

Loob, Hakan
  Kraft: 86/87 - 2, 2P
  O-Pee-Chee: 84/85 - 229; 85/86 - 184; 87/88 - 208, 44SK; 88/89 - 110, 21NS, O/BB, 94SK, 118SK
  Panini: 87/88 - 214; 88/89 - 9
  Topps: 84/85 - 242SL; 88/89 - 110, O/BB, 3SK
  Vachon Foods: 83/84 - 11

LoPresti, Pete (Goalie)
  O-Pee-Chee: 76/77 - 184; 77/78 - 13; 78/79 - 230; 79/80 - 364
  Topps: 76/77 - 184; 77/78 - 13; 78/79 - 230

LoPresti, Sam (Goalie)
  Beehive: 34/44 - 64

Loswick, Jack
  Diamond: 33/35 - 40

Lorentz, Jim
  Eddie Sargent: 70/71 - 192; 72/73 - 36
  Esso: 70/71 - 204
  Loblaws: 74/75 - 44

Lorentz, Jim (cont.)
  O-Pee-Chee: 70/71 - 209; 71/72 - 227; 72/73 - 116; 73/74 - 75; 74/75 - 61; 75/76 - 28; 76/77 - 162; 77/78 - 58; 78/79 - 161
  Topps: 71/72 - 13; 72/73 - 68; 73/74 - 171; 74/75 - 61; 75/76 - 28; 76/77 - 162; 77/78 - 58; 78/79 - 161
  Toronto Sun: 71/72 - 239

Lorenz, Danny
  Fleer: 92/93 - 345
  Leaf: 93/94 - 343

Lorimer, Bob
  O-Pee-Chee: 79/80 - 181; 80/81 - 138; 81/82 - 214; 82/83 - 142, 228SK; 83/84 - 232; 84/85 - 114
  Post: 82/83 - 167
  Topps: 79/80 - 181; 80/81 - 138; 82/83 - 228SK

Lorraine, Rod (Rodrigue)
  Beehive: 34/44 - 166
  Canada Starch: 35/40 - 117
  O-Pee-Chee: 37/38 - 176; 39/40 - 23
  Quaker Oats: 38/39 - 10

Loughlin, Glenn
  Anonymous: 26/27 - 127
  Diamond: 36/39 - 10(IV)

Lovsin, Ken
  Fleer: 93/94 - 487PP
  O-Pee-Chee: 93/94 - 4TC

Low, Ron (Goalie)
  Loblaws: 74/75 - 319
  O-Pee-Chee: 72/73 - 258; 74/75 - 39; 75/76 - 25; 76/77 - 69; 77/78 - 305; 78/79 - 237; 79/80 - 348; 80/81 - 333; 82/83 - 112, 107SK; 83/84 - 233; 84/85 - 115
  PepsiCo: 80/81 - 30
  Topps: 74/75 - 39; 75/76 - 25; 76/77 - 69; 78/79 - 237; 82/83 - 107SK

Lowe, Kevin
  Bowman: 90/91 - 198; 91/92 - 115; 92/93 - 99
  Durivage: 92/93 - 42
  Fleer: 92/93 - 60, 356; 93/94 - 393PP
  Kellogg's: 84 - 26
  Kraft: 86/87 - 17, 17P; 1990 - 14
  O-Pee-Chee: 81/82 - 117; 82/83 - 113, 96SK; 83/84 - 37, 101SK; 84/85 - 251, 253SK; 85/86 - 239, 219SK; 86/87 - 197, 70SK; 87/88 - 200, 25HL, 84SK; 88/89 - 229, 219SK; 89/90 - 227, 224SK; 90/91 - 307; 91/92 - 220; 92/93 - 302; 93/94 - 464, 165SC, 165FD
  Panini: 87/88 - 257; 88/89 - 54; 89/90 - 180; 89/90 - 79; 90/91 - 224, 330; 91/92 - 131; 92/93 - 107E, 107F; 93/94 - 97E, 97F
  Parkhurst: 91/92 - 51E, 51F; 92/93 - 348, 348EI
  PepsiCo: 80/81 - 31
  Post: 82/83 - 92
  Pro Set: 90/91 - 89, 339, 380; 91/92 - 76E, 572E, 76F, 38PT, 572F
  Score: 90/91 - 170A, 170C, 75HR; 91/92 - 109A, 109B, 109C, 188PNE, 371PNE, 188PNF, 371PNF; 92/93 - 39C, 39A, 338PNC, 338PNA; 93/94 - 112C, 112A, 3PNC, 3PNA, 3CAS, 3AAS
  7-Eleven: 84/85 - 19
  Topps: 82/83 - 96SK; 83/84 - 101SKL 86/87 - 197, 90/91 - 307; 91/92 - 220, 179SC; 92/93 - 290, 290GS, 385SC; 93/94 - 464C, 165SC, 165FD, 7AS
  Upper Deck: 90/91 - 262E, 262F; 91/92 - 186E, 186F
  Vachon Foods: 83/84 - 34

Lowe, Ross
  Beehive: 45/63 - 263
  Parkhurst: 51/52 - 18
  Quaker Oats: 45/54 - 31

Lowrey, Fred (Frock)
  Champ's: 24/25 - 34
  Maple Crispette: 24/25 - 28
  Wm. Paterson: 24/25 - 36

Lowry, Dave
  Bowman: 90/91 - 15; 91/92 - 373; 92/93 - 370
  Donruss: 93/94 - 125
  Fleer: 93/94 - 97PP
  Leaf: 93/94 - 238
  O-Pee-Chee: 90/91 - 370; 91/92 - 180; 92/93 - 219; 93/94 - 244, 121SC, 121FD
  Panini: 87/88 - 353; 91/92 - 32 92/93 - 21E, 21F
  Parkhurst: 91/92 - 376E, 376F; 93/94 - 79, 79EI
  Pro Set: 90/91 - 265
  Score: 90/91 - 38T; 91/92 - 149A, 149B, 149C, 276PNE, 276PNF; 92/93 - 109C, 109A
  Topps: 90/91 - 370; 91/92 - 180, 303SC; 92/93 - 42, 42GS, 10SC; 93/94 - 244, 121SC, 379SC, 121FD, 379FD
  Upper Deck: 90/91 - 349E, 349F; 93/94 - 67

Lozinski, Larry (Goalie)
  O-Pee-Chee: 81/82 - 99

Luce, Don
  Eddie Sargent: 72/73 - 33
  Esso: 70/71 - 84
  Loblaws: 74/75 - 45
  O-Pee-Chee: 71/72 - 166; 72/73 - 95; 73/74 - 38; 74/75 - 79; 75/76 - 113; 76/77 - 94; 77/78 - 231; 78/79 - 58; 79/80 - 194; 80/81 - 302; 81/82 - 147
  Topps: 72/73 - 106; 73/74 - 38; 74/75 - 79; 75/76 - 113; 76/77 - 94; 77/78 - 231; 78/79 - 58; 79/80 - 194; 81/82 WN - 99
  Toronto Sun: 71/72 - 31

Ludvig, Jan
  O-Pee-Chee: 84/85 - 116, 76SK

Ludwig, Craig
  Bowman: 91/92 - 221
  Fleer: 92/93 - 320
  Kraft: 86/87 - 30, 30P
  Leaf: 93/94 - 432
  O-Pee-Chee: 83/84 - 190; 84/85 - 265, 154SK; 85/86 - 192, 130SK; 86/87 - 220, 14SK; 88/89 - 230, 48SK; 89/90 - 236; 90/91 - 412, 64PM; 91/92 - 150, 80PM; 93/94 - 191, 173SC, 173FD
  Panini: 87/88 - 59; 88/89 - 254; 91/92 - 242
  Pro Set: 90/91 - 154, 484; 91/92 - 155E, 411E, 155F, 411F; 92/93 - 79
  Score: 90 - 8T; 90/91 - 165A, 165C, 74HR; 91 - 11T; 91/92 - 13A, 13B, 13C, 561B, 561C, 248PNE, 404PNE, 248PNF, 404PNF; 92/93 - 94C, 94A, 93/94 - 282C, 282A
  Topps: 91/92 - 150, 38SC; 92/93 - 154, 154GS, 354SC; 93/94 - 191, 173SC, 173FD
  Upper Deck: 90/91 - 186E, 186F
  Vachon Foods: 83/84 - 48

Ludzik, Steve
  O-Pee-Chee: 83/84 - 106; 84/85 - 38

Lukowich, Morris
  Esso: 83/84 - 11E, 11F
  Funmate: 83/84 - 145
  O-Pee-Chee: 79/80 - 202; 80/81 - 107, 227, 24PO; 81/82 - 370, 138SK; 82/83 - 383, 205SK; 83/84 - 386, 281SK; 84/85 - 340; 85/86 - 129
  Post: 81/82 - 19; 82/83 - 329
  Topps: 79/80 - 202; 80/81 - 107, 227; 82/83 - 205SK; 83/84 - 281SK; 85/86 - 129
  Vachon Foods: 83/84 - 129

Luksa, Chuck
  O-Pee-Chee: 79/80 - 370

Lumley, Dave
  O-Pee-Chee: 80/81 - 271; 82/83 - 114, 101SK; 83/84 - 38; 84/85 - 252
  PepsiCo: 80/81 - 32
  Post: 82/83 - 93
  Topps: 82/83 - 101SK
  Vachon Foods: 83/84 - 35

Lumley, Harry (Goalie)
  Beehive: 45/63 - 43, 114, 189, 421
  CKAC: 43/47 - 11
  Hall of Fame: 83 - 21, B7P; 87-21
  HHFM: 92 - 1
  Parkhurst: 51/52 - 47; 52/53 - 59; 53/54 - 1; 54/55 - 16; 55/56 - 1; 92/93 - PR5
  Quaker Oats: 45/54 - 82; 55/56 - 1
  Toronto Star: 57/67 - 42; 58/67 - 8
  Ultimate: 92 - 51(OSE), 51(OSF)

Lumme, Jyrki
  Bowman: 91/92 - 321; 92/93 - 170
  Donruss: 93/94 - 347
  Fleer: 92/93 - 223; 93/94 - 126, 252PP
  Leaf: 93/94 - 231
  O-Pee-Chee: 91/92 - 419; 92/93 - 265; 93/94 - 475, 108SC, 108FD
  Panini: 92/93 - 36E, 36F; 93/94 - 175E, 175F
  Parkhurst: 91/92 - 180E, 180F; 92/93 - 191, 191EI; 93/94 - 483, 483EI
  Pro Set: 90/91 - 300; 91/92 - 240E, 240F, 237PT; 92/93 - 196
  Score: 90/91 - 132A, 132C; 91/92 - 242A, 462B, 462C, 237PNE, 237PNF; 92/93 - 318C, 318A, 65PNC, 65PNA; 93/94 - 134C, 134A
  Sega: 93/94 - 139
  Topps: 91/92 - 419, 154SC; 92/93 - 510, 510GS, 321SC; 93/94 - 475C, 108SC, 108FD
  Upper Deck: 90/91 - 297E, 297F; 91/92 - 114E, 114F; 92/93 - 137

Lund, Pentti
  Beehive: 45/63 - 44, 340
  Parkhurst: 51/52 - 31; 52/53 - 83

Lunde, Len
  Beehive: 45/63 - 115A, 115B, 190; 64/67 - 44
  Esso: 70/71 - 243
  O-Pee-Chee: 70/71 - 230
  Parkhurst: 60/61 - 35; 61/62 - 24; 62/63 - 35
  Shirriff: 60/61 - 54
  Topps: 58/59 - 15; 59/60 - 22

Lundholm, Bengt
  O-Pee-Chee: 82/83 - 385; 83/84 - 387; 84/85 - 341
  Post: 82/83 - 328
  Vachon Foods: 83/84 - 130

Lundrigan, Joe
  Loblaws: 74/75 - 320
  O-Pee-Chee: 74/75 - 277

Lundy, Pat
  Beehive: 45/63 - 116

Luongo, Chris
  Fleer: 92/93 - 362; 93/94 - 96
  O-Pee-Chee: 92/93 - 35PM
  Upper Deck: 92/93 - 534

Luovi, Mikko
  Upper Deck: 93/94 - 271

Lupien, Gilles
  O-Pee-Chee: 80/81 - 298

Lupul, Gary
  O-Pee-Chee: 82/83 - 354; 83/84 - 355; 84/85 - 323
  Post: 82/83 - 298
  7-Eleven: 84/85 - 49
  Vachon Foods: 83/84 - 111

Lyle, George
  O-Pee-Chee: 80/81 - 379; 81/82 - 100
  Post: 82/83 - 104

Lynch, Jack
  Loblaws: 74/75 - 102
  O-Pee-Chee: 72/73 - 160; 73/74 - 232; 74/75 - 331;

Lynch, Jack (cont.)
  O-Pee-Chee: 75/76 - 116; 76/77 - 288; 77/78 - 369
  Topps: 75/76 - 116

Lynn, Vic
  Beehive: 45/63 - 117, 422
  Parkhurst: 51/52 - 20
  Quaker Oats: 45/54 - 83A, 83B

Lysenko, Alexander
  O-Pee-Chee: 90/91 - 500

Lysiak, Tom
  Funmate: 83/84 - 25
  Loblaws: 74/75 - 9
  O-Pee-Chee: 74/75 - 68; 75/76 - 230; 76/77 - 174; 77/78 - 127; 78/79 - 97; 79/80 - 41; 80/81 - 247; 81/82 - 59; 81/82 - 73, 114SK; 82/83 - 68, 14SK, 174SK; 83/84 - 107, 110SK; 84/85 - 39, 31SK; 85/86 - 23
  Post: 82/83 - 57
  Topps: 74/75 - 68; 75/76 - 230; 76/77 - 174; 77/78 - 127; 78/79 - 97; 79/80 - 41; 80/81 - 247; 81/82 - WN 71, 49; 82/83 - 14SK, 174SK; 83/84 - 110SK; 84/85 - 31; 85/86 - 23

MacAdam, Al
  Loblaws: 74/75 - 64
  O-Pee-Chee: 74/75 - 301; 75/76 - 253; 76/77 - 237; 77/78 - 149; 78/79 - 381; 79/80 - 104; 80/81 - 34; 81/82 - 163, 90SK; 82/83 - 171; 83/84 - 173; 84/85 - 324; 85/86 - 209, 242SK
  Post: 82/83 - 136
  Topps: 75/76 - 253; 76/77 - 237; 77/78 - 149; 79/80 - 104; 80/81 - 34; 81/82 WN - 107; 84/85 - 75

McCarty, Darren
  Donruss: 93/94 - 103
  Fleer: 93/94 - 333PP

Macchio, Ralph
  Pro-Set: 91/92 - 295PT

MacDermid, Paul
  Bowman: 91/92 - 195; 92/93 - 282
  Fleer: 92/93 - 439
  O-Pee-Chee: 89/90 - 183, 266SK; 90/91 - 338; 91/92 - 463
  Panini: 88/89 - 243; 89/90 - 227; 91/92 - 69
  Pro Set: 90/91 - 331; 91/92 - 269E, 269F
  Score: 90/91 - 296A, 296C; 91/92 - 219A, 219B, 219C, 279PNE, 279PNF; 92/93 - 59C, 59A
  Topps: 89/90 - 183; 90/91 - 338; 91/92 - 463, 254SC; 92/93 - 391, 391GS, 178SC
  Upper Deck: 90/91 - 218E, 218F

MacDonald, Blair
  O-Pee-Chee: 80/81 - 32; 81/82 - 340; 82/83 - 350
  PepsiCo: 80/81 - 33
  Topps: 80/81 - 32

MacDonald, Doug
  Upper Deck: 93/94 - 97

MacDonald, Jack
  Imperial Tobacco: 10/11 - 8L; 11/12 - 8; 12/13 - 17

MacDonald, Kevin
  Parkhurst: 94/95 - 160, 160EI

MacDonald, Kilby
  Beehive: 34/44 - 285
  O-Pee-Chee: 39/40 - 87

MacDonald, Lowell
  Loblaws: 74/75 - 248
  O-Pee-Chee: 68/69 - 42; 70/71 - 206; 72/73 - 214; 73/74 - 128; 74/75 - 30, 133; 75/76 - 204; 76/77 - 33; 77/78 - 390
  Shirriff: 68/69 - D7
  Topps: 68/69 - 42; 73/74 - 128; 74/75 - 30, 133; 75/76 - 204; 76/77 - 33

MacDonald, Parker
Beehive: 45/63 - 191; 64/67 - 17, 83
Chex: 63/65 - 15
Coca-Cola: 64/65 - 48; 65/66 - 11
O-Pee-Chee: 68/69 - 55
Parkhurst: 55/56 - 9; 63/64 - 44; 93/94 - 104ML
Quaker Oats: 55/56 - 9
Shirriff: 60/61 - 59; 61/62 - 69; 68/69 - E8
Topps: 64/65 - 11; 65/66 - 105; 68/69 - 55
Toronto Star: 57/67 - 92; 58/67 - 68; 63/64 - 14; 64/65 - 21
York: 62/63 - 27; 63/64 - 40

MacGregor, Bruce
Beehive: 45/63 - 192; 64/67 - 84A, 84B
Chex: 63/65 - 16
Coca-Cola: 64/65 - 49; 65/66 - 49
Dom. Choc.: 70/71 - 50
Eddie Sargent: 70/71 - 51; 72/73 - 153
Esso: 70/71 - 85
O-Pee-Chee: 68/69 - 30; 69/70 - 63; 70/71 - 27; 71/72 - 216; 72/73 - 103; 73/74 - 201
Parkhurst: 62/63 - 23; 63/64 - 41
Shirriff: 61/62 - 73; 68/69 - C8
Topps: 64/65 - 76; 65/66 - 110; 66/67 - 104; 66/67 US - 56; 67/68 - 102; 68/69 - 30; 69/70 - 63; 70/71 - 27
Toronto Sun: 71/72 - 176
York: 62/63 - 36; 63/64 - 51

MacInnis, Allan (Al)
Bowman: 90/91 - 93; 91/92 - 262; 92/93 - 51, 211
Donruss: 93/94 - 47
Fleer: 92/93 - 23, 8AS; 93/94 - 113, 7SA, 38PP
Frito-Lay: 88/89 - 21
Gillette: 91/92 - 7
Hockey Wit: 93/94 - 90
Humpty Dumpty: 92/93 - 14(II)
Kellogg's: 92 - 16
Kraft: 1990 - 3; 90/91 - 33; 91/92 - 32
Leaf: 93/94 - 180
McDonald's: 91/92 - Mc23
O-Pee-Chee: 85/86 - 237, 211SK; 86/87 - 173, 86SK; 87/88 - 72, 26HL, 40SK, 123SK; 88/89 - 231, 22NS, 92SK; 89/90 - 49, 5SK, 95SK, 159SK, 27FS; 90/91 - 127, 197, H/BB, 65PM; 91/92 - 262, 491, 81PM; 92/93 - 330; 93/94 - 276, 105SC, 105FD
Panini: 87/88 - 205; 88/89 - 5; 89/90 - 32; 90/91 - 185, 328; 91/92 - 50, 330; 92/93 - 49E, 285E, 49F, 285F; 93/94 - P(E), P(F)
Parkhurst: 91/92 - 28E, 28F; 92/93 - 20; 93/94 - 36, 36EI, D3; 94/95 - 35, 35EI
Pro Set: 90/91 - 35, 337; 91/92 - AC8, 33E, 92/93 - 20, 20EI
Score: 90/91 - 5A, 5C, 314A, 314C, 335A, 335C, 36HR; 91/92 - 4PC, 2A, 417A, 2A, 2B, 299B, 2C, 299C, 333B, 333C, 220PNE, 399PNE, 220PNF, 399PNF, 2PC, B-8E, B-8F; 92/93 - 302C, 421C, 496C, 302A, 421A, 496A 83PNC, 83PNA; 93/94 - 121C, 121A, 4DT, 3FR
Season's: 92/93 - 60
Sega: 93/94 - 20
Topps: 86/87 - 173; 87/88 - 72, 9SK; 89/90 - 49, 4SK; 90/91 - 127, 197, H/BB; 91/92 - 262, 491, 79SC; 92/93 - 452, 452GS, 128SC; 93/94 - 276, 105SC, 105FD
Upper Deck: 90/91 - 143E, 143F, 497E, 497F; 91/92 - 8E, 243E, 632E, 8F, 243F, 632F; 92/93 - 257; 93/94 - 412

Maciver, Norm
Bowman: 91/92 - 99; 92/93 - 425
Donruss: 93/94 - 233
Fleer: 92/93 - 61, 363; 93/94 - 143, 172PP
Leaf: 93/94 - 189
O-Pee-Chee: 92/93 - 344, 107PM; 93/94 - 64

Maciver, Norm (cont.)
Panini: 88/89 - 302; 93/94 - 112E, 112F
Parkhurst: 91/92 - 282E, 282F; 92/93 - 117, 117EI; 93/94 - 137, 137EI; 94/95 - 154, 154EI
Pro-Set: 92/93 - 50
Score: 91/92 - 434B, 434C; 92/93 - 349C, 349A, 157PNC, 157PNA; 93/94 - 123C, 123A
Sega: 93/94 - 91
Topps: 92/93 - 96, 96GS, 46SC; 93/94 - 64, 267SC, 267FD
Upper Deck: 92/93 - 511; 93/94 - 299, 335

MacKay, Calum
La Patrie: 51/54 - 44
Parkhurst: 51/52 - 9; 54/55 - 11; 55/56 - 41
Quaker Oats: 45/54 - 32; 55/56 - 41

Mackay, Dave
Beehive: 34/44 - 65

MacKay, Mickey
Hall of Fame: 83 - 203, N8P; 87 - 203

MacKay, Murdo
Quaker Oats: 45/54 - 33

Mackell, Fleming
Beehive: 45/63 - 45, 423
Parkhurst: 51/52 - 83; 52/53 - 82; 53/54 - 91; 54/55 - 50; 93/94 - 3ML
Quaker Oats: 45/54 - 84A, 84B
Topps: 54/55 - 36; 57/58 - 16; 58/59 - 29; 59/60 - 19
Toronto Star: 58/67 - 9

MacKenzie, Bill
Beehive: 34/44 - 66, 199
Canada Starch: 35/40 - 114
O-Pee-Chee: 36/37 - 111; 37/38 - 151; 39/40 - 81
World Wide Gum: 33/34 - 61; 36/37 - 44

MacKey, Dave
Parkhurst: 94/95 - 202, 202EI

MacLean, John
Bowman: 90/91 - 83; 91/92 - 272, 289; 92/93 - 130
Donruss: 93/94 - 184
Fleer: 92/93 - 115; 93/94 - 53, 138PP
Kellogg's: 92 - 13
Leaf: 93/94 - 264
O-Pee-Chee: 86/87 - 37; 87/88 - 191; 88/89 - 10, 78SK; 89/90 - 102, 87SK; 90/91 - 224; 91/92 - 239, 4PM; 93/94 - 193
Panini: 87/88 - 80; 88/89 - 274; 89/90 - 249; 90/91 - 74; 91/92 - 213; 93/94 - 40E, 40F
Parkhurst: 92/93 - 90, 90EI; 93/94 - 115, 115EI; 94/95 - 125, 125EI
Pro Set: 90/91 - 170; 91/92 - 136E, 307E, 136F, 307F, 70PT
Score: 90/91 - 190A, 190C, 83HR; 91/92 - 210A, 210B, 210C, 115PNE, 115PNF; 92/93 - 30C, 30A, 351PNC, 351PNA; 93/994 - 81C, 81A
Topps: 86/87 - 37; 87/88 - 191; 88/89 - 10; 89/90 - 102; 90/91 - 224; 91/92 - 239, 15SL, 144SC; 92/93 - 273, 273GS, 28SC; 93/94 - 193, 287SC, 287FD
Upper Deck: 90/91 - 161E, 161F; 91/92 - 169E, 169F; 92/93 - 521; 93/94 - 134

MacLean, Paul
Bowman: 90/91 - 18
Funmate: 83/84 - 146
Kellogg's: 84 - 21
Kraft: 86/87 - 76, 76P
O-Pee-Chee: 82/83 - 386, 208SK; 83/84 - 388, 283SK; 84/85 - 342, 371, 289SK; 85/86 - 145, 250SK; 86/87 - 114, 108SK; 87/88 - 91, 252SK; 88/89 - 38, 23SK, 144SK; 89/90 - 129, 18SK; 90/91 - 110
Panini: 87/88 - 364; 88/89 - 156; 90/91 - 271
Post: 82/83 - 330

MacLean, Paul (cont.)
Pro Set: 90/91 - 266
Score: 90/91 - 203A, 203C
7-Eleven: 84/85 - 59
Topps: 82/83 - 208SK; 83/84 - 283SK; 85/86 - 145; 86/87 - 114; 87/88 - 91; 88/89 - 38; 89/90 - 129; 90/91 - 110
Upper Deck: 90/91 - 330E, 330F
Vachon Foods: 83/84 - 131

MacLeish, Rick
Eddie Sargent: 72/73 - 167
Lipton Soup: 74/75 - 20
Loblaws: 74/75 - 228
O-Pee-Chee: 71/72 - 207; 72/73 - 105; 73/74 - 146; 74/75 - 163; 75/76 - 20; 76/77 - 121; 77/78 - 15, 9GP; 78/79 - 125; 79/80 - 75; 80/81 - 115; 81/82 - 133; 82/83 - 273, 147SK
Parkhurst: 92/93 - 472, 472EI
Topps: 73/74 - 135; 74/75 - 163; 75/76 - 20; 76/77 - 121; 77/78 - 15, 9PO; 78/79 - 125; 79/80 - 75; 80/81 - 115; 81/82 EN - 108; 82/83 - 147SK
Toronto Sun: 71/72 - 203

MacLellan, Brian
Bowman: 91/92 - 269
O-Pee-Chee: 84/85 - 87; 85/86 - 204; 86/87 - 33; 87/88 - 31; 88/89 - 193, 197SK; 89/90 - 208; 90/91 - 286; 91/92 - 50
Panini: 87/88 - 294; 88/89 - 95
Pro Set: 90/91 - 36
Score: 90 - 56T; 91 - 32T; 91/92 - 582B, 582C
Topps: 86/87 - 33; 87/88 - 31; 88/89 - 193; 90/91 - 286; 91/92 - 50, 206SC
Upper Deck: 90/91 - 372E, 372F

MacLeod, Pat
Bowman: 92/93 - 433
O-Pee-Chee: 91/92 - 87PM; 92/93 - 273
Parkhurst: 91/92 - 161E, 161F
Pro Set: 91/92 - 559E, 559F
Score: 91 - 95T; 91/92 - 645B, 645C
Topps: 92/93 - 317, 317GS, 336SC
Upper Deck: 91/92 - 578E, 578F; 92/93 - 146

MacMillan, Billy
Eddie Sargent: 70/71 - 205; 71/72 - 198; 72/73 - 5
Esso: 70/71 - 226
Loblaws: 74/75 - 189
O-Pee-Chee: 72/73 - 98; 74/75 - 339; 76/77 - 312
Topps: 72/73 - 77
Toronto Sun: 71/72 - 263

MacMillan, Bob
Funmate: 83/84 - 74
O-Pee-Chee: 76/77 - 38; 77/78 - 141; 78/79 - 82; 79/80 - 210; 80/81 - 267; 81/82 - 46; 82/83 - 143, 225SK; 83/84 - 234, 220SK; 84/85 - 40, 72SK; 85/86 - 193
Panini: 79 - 66
PepsiCo: 80/81 - 8
Post: 82/83 - 169
Topps: 76/77 - 38; 77/78 - 141; 78/79 - 82; 79/80 - 210; 82/83 - 225SK; 83/84 - 220SK

MacMillan, John
Beehive: 45/63 - 424
Chex: 63/65 - 51
Parkhurst: 63/64 - 15
Shirriff: 61/62 - 56; 62/63 - 14

MacNeil, Al
Beehive: 45/63 - 118A, 118B, 264, 425; 64/67 - 45, 139
Coca-Cola: 64/65 - 26; 65/66 - 27
Parkhurst: 57/58 TOR - 19; 93/94 - 121ML
Shirriff: 61/62 - 119; 62/63 - 40
Topps: 62/63 - 32; 63/64 - 28; 64/65 - 26; 65/66 - 57; 66/67 - 89
Toronto Star: 64/65 - 11
York: 61/62 - 36

Macoun, Jamie
- Bowman: 92/93 - 9
- Fleer: 92/93 - 212; 93/94 - 451PP
- O-Pee-Chee: 84/85 - 230; 85/86 - 201, 212SK; 86/87 - 203, 85SK; 87/88 - 214, 48SK; 89/90 - 207; 90/91 - 265; 91/92 - 168; 92/93 - 371; 93/94 - 517
- Panini: 87/88 - 208; 89/90 - 38; 90/91 - 178; 91/92 - 61; 93/94 - 230E, 230F
- Pro Set: 90/91 - 37; 91/92 - 38E, 38F, 235PT; 92/93 - 188
- Score: 90/91 - 216A, 216C; 91/92 - 284A, 504C, 114PNE, 114PNF; 92/93 - 88C, 88A, 294PNC, 294PNA; 93/94 - 224C, 224A
- Topps: 90/91 - 265; 91/92 - 168, 160SC; 92/93 - 348, 348GS, 309SC; 93/94 - 517(II)
- Upper Deck: 90/91 - 101E, 101F; 91/92 - 412E, 412F
- Vachon Foods: 83/84 - 12

MacPherson, Bud
- Beehive: 45/63 - 265
- La Patrie: 51/54 - 20
- Parkhurst: 51/52 - 6; 52/53 - 11; 53/54 - 22; 55/56 - 47
- Quaker Oats: 55/56 - 47

MacQuisten, Doug
- World Wide Gum: 36/37 - 105

MacSweyn, Ralph
- Eddie Sargent: 70/71 - 145
- O-Pee-Chee: 69/70 - 96

MacTavish, Craig
- Bowman: 90/91 - 193; 91/92 - 100; 92/93 - 118
- Donruss: 93/94 - 462
- Fleer: 92/93 - 294; 93/94 - 82PP
- Kraft: 93/94 - 47
- O-Pee-Chee: 86/87 - 178, 76SK; 87/88 - 203, 91SK; 88/89 - 232, 217SK; 89/90 - 230, 26SK; 90/91 - 189; 91/92 - 63; 92/93 - 118; 93/94 - 23
- Panini: 87/88 - 267; 88/89 - 60; 89/90 - 78; 90/91 - 220; 91/92 - 132; 92/93 - 101E, 101F; 93/94 - 240E, 240F
- Parkhurst: 91/92 - 276E, 276F; 92/93 - 48, 48EI; 93/94 - 342, 342EI; 94/95 - 145, 145EI
- Pro Set: 90/91 - 90; 91/92 - 77E, 77F
- Score: 90/91 - 258A, 258C; 91/92 - 202A, 202B, 202C, 215PNE, 215PNF; 92/93 - 303C, 303A, 78PNC, 78PNA; 93/94 - 8C, 8A
- Topps: 86/87 - 178; 90/91 - 189; 91/92 - 63, 133SC; 92/93 - 336, 336GS, 125SC; 93/94 - 23(I), 410SC, 410FD
- Upper Deck: 90/91 - 169E, 169F; 91/92 - 284E, 284F; 92/93 - 425; 93/94 - 111

Madeley, Darrin (Goalie)
- Donruss: 94/93 - 229
- Fleer: 93/94 - 400PP
- Leaf: 93/94 - 299
- O-Pee-Chee: 93/94 - 283
- Parkhurst: 93/94 - 142, 142EI
- Score: 93/94 - 462C, 462A
- Topps: 93/94 - 283, 431SC, 431FD
- Upper Deck: 93/94 - 61

Madill, Jeff
- O-Pee-Chee: 91/92 - 6S

Maggs, Daryl
- Toronto Sun: 71/72 - 71

Magnuson, Keith
- Dom. Choc.: 70/71 - 39
- Eddie Sargent: 70/71 - 35; 72/73 - 57
- Esso: 70/71 - 63
- Loblaws: 74/75 - 80
- O-Pee-Chee: 70/71 - 151; 71/72 - 69; 72/73 - 71; 73/74 - 151; 74/75 - 75; 75/76 - 176; 76/77 - 125; 77/78 - 89; 78/79 - 34
- Topps: 71/72 - 69; 72/73 - 87; 73/74 - 44; 74/75 - 75; 75/76 - 176; 76/77 - 125;

Magnuson, Keith, (cont.)
- Topps: 77/78 - 89; 78/79 - 34
- Toronto Sun: 71/72 - 72

Maguire, Kevin
- Bowman: 91/92 - 172
- Pro Set: 90/91 - 538

Mahaffy, John
- World Wide Gum: 36/37 - 133

Mahovlich, Frank
- Bazooka: 71/72 - 2
- Beehive: 45/63 - 426; 64/67 - 174A, 174B
- Chex: 63/65 - 52
- Coca-Cola: 64/65 - 101; 65/66 - 100
- Colgate: 71/72 - 6
- Derniere: 72/84 - 2, 36
- Dom. Choc.: 70/71 - 51
- Eddie Sargent: 70/71 - 63; 72/73 - 120
- El Producto: 62/63 - 6
- Esso: 70/71 - 86; 88/89 - 28
- Hall of Fame: 83 - 121, I10P; 87 - 121
- Hockey Wit: 93/94 - 56
- Kellogg's: 70 - 5
- Mac's Milk: 73/74 - 15
- O-Pee-Chee: 68/69 - 31, 2PS; 69/70 - 62, 222, 19ST, 4QS; 70/71 - 22, 242, 17DE, 21SS; 71/72 - 105; 72/73 - 102, 128; 73/74 - 145
- Parkhurst: 57/58 TOR - 17; 58/59 - 33; 59/60 - 24; 60/61 - 2; 61/62 - 2; 62/63 - 4, 18; 63/64 - 17, 77; 92/93 - PR29; 93/94 - PR50
- Post: 66/67 - 4S, 6L
- Shirriff: 60/61 - 12; 61/62 - 43; 62/63 - 3, 53; 68/69 - C12
- TCMA: 1981 - 10
- Topps: 64/65 - 85; 65/66 - 81; 66/67 - 77, 131; 66/67 US - 51; 67/68 - 79; 68/69 - 31; 69/70 - 62; 70/71 - 22, 21SK; 71/72 - 105; 72/73 - 140; 73/74 - 40
- Toronto Star: 57/67 - 55, 84, 126, 133; 58/67 - 17, 68, 98; 63/64 - 38; 64/65 - 43
- Toronto Sun: 71/72 - 157
- Ultimate: 92 - 40(OSE), 40(OSF)
- Upper Deck: 92/93 - 44AS
- York: 60/61 - 30; 61/62 - 3; 62/63 - 11; 63/64 - 5
- Zellers: 92/93 - 5, 5A

Mahovlich, Pete
- Beehive: 64/67 - 85
- Derniere: 72/84 - 12, 40
- Eddie Sargent: 70/71 - 102; 71/72 - 99; 72/73 - 114
- Esso: 70/71 - 137
- Lipton Soup: 74/75 - 39
- Loblaws: 74/75 - 174
- Mac's Milk: 73/74 - 16
- O-Pee-Chee: 68/69 - 143; 70/71 - 58; 71/72 - 84; 72/73 - 124; 73/74 - 164; 74/75 - 97; 75/76 - 50; 76/77 - 15; 77/78 - 205; 78/79 - 51; 79/80 - 187; 80/81 - 72, 6PO
- Shirriff: 68/69 - C3
- Topps: 66/67 - 103; 66/67 US - 21; 70/71 - 58; 71/72 - 84; 72/73 - 42; 73/74 - 186; 74/75 - 97; 75/76 - 50; 76/77 - 15; 77/78 - 205; 78/79 - 51; 79/80 - 187; 80/81 - 72
- Toronto Sun: 71/72 - 158

Mair, Jim
- Esso: 72/73 - 140
- O-Pee-Chee: 72/73 - 232

Majeau, Fern
- CKAC Radio: 43/47 - 66

Makarov, Sergei
- Bowman: 90/91 - 92; 91/92 - 250, 264; 92/93 - 53
- Donruss: 93/94 - 304
- Fleer: 92/93 - 24; 93/94 - 222PP
- Kraft: 1990 - 4
- Leaf: 93/94 - 384(II)

Makarov, Sergei (cont.)
- O-Pee-Chee: 90/91 60, 485, 503, P/BB; 91/92 - 482, 45PM; 92/93 - 90
- Panini: 90/91 - 184, 334; 91/92 - 58; 92/93 - 47E, 47F; 93/94 - 183E, 183F
- Parkhurst: 91/92 - 247E, 247F; 92/93 - 25, 25 EI; 93/94 - 188, 188EI; 94/95 - 211, 211EI
- Pro Set: 90/91 - 38, 379, 396; 91/92 - 39E, 39F, 15PT; 92/93 - 24
- Score: 90/91 - 71A, 71C, 329A, 329C, 350A, 350C, 362A, 362C, 99HR; 91/92 - 51A, 51B, 51C, 271PNE, 271PNF; 92/93 - 382C, 382A, 335PNC, 335PNA, 2CSS, 2ASS; 93/94 - 33C, 33A
- Topps: 90/91 - 60, P/BB; 91/92 - 482, 31SC; 92/93 - 467, 467GS, 217SC
- Upper Deck: 90/91 - 123E, 123F, 202E, 202F, 336E, 336F; 91/92 - 321E, 321F; 92/93 - 314, E16; 93/94 - 446

Makela, Mikko
- Bowman: 91/92 - 36
- O-Pee-Chee: 88/89 - 44, 108SK; 89/90 - 247, 112SK; 90/91 - 229, 66PM; 91/92 - 503
- Panini: 87/88 - 100; 88/89 - 291; 89/90 - 270; 90/91 - 237; 91/92 - 302
- Pro Set: 90/91 - 418
- Score: 90/91 - 26T; 91/92 - 549B, 549C
- Topps: 88/89 - 44; 90/91 - 229; 91/92 - 503, 261SC

Maki, Chico
- Beehive: 45/63 - 119A, 119B; 64/67 - 46A, 46B
- Chex: 63/65 - 6
- Coca-Cola: 64/65 - 27; 65/66 - 28
- Dom. Choc.: 70/71 - 40
- Eddie Sargent: 70/71 - 46; 72/73 - 60
- Esso: 70/71 - 64
- Loblaws: 74/75 - 81
- O-Pee-Chee: 68/69 - 17; 69/70 - 137; 70/71 - 149; 71/72 - 210; 72/73 - 198; 73/74 - 227; 74/75 - 395
- Shirriff: 61/62 - 28; 68/69 - B7
- Topps: 62/63 - 37; 63/64 - 41; 64/65 - 73; 65/66 - 117; 66/67 - 110; 66/67 US - 53; 67/68 - 111; 68/69 - 17
- Toronto Star: 64/65 - 12
- Toronto Sun: 71/72 - 73

Maki, Wayne
- Eddie Sargent: 70/71 - 210; 72/73 - 216
- Esso: 70/71 - 244
- O-Pee-Chee: 70/71 - 116; 71/72 - 58; 72/73 - 84
- Shirriff: 68/69 - B3
- Topps: 67/68 - 55; 70/71 - 116; 71/72 - 58; 72/73 - 32
- Toronto Sun: 71/72 - 284

Malakhov, Vladimir
- Donruss: 93/94 - 207
- Fleer: 92/93 - 346, 14UI; 93/94 - 235, 153PP, 6SY
- Leaf: 93/94 - 32, 9R
- O-Pee-Chee: 90/91 - 2R; 92/93 - 89PM; 93/94 - 129, 445, 515, 248SC, 248FD
- Parkhurst: 92/93 - 339, 339EI; 93/94 - 125, 125EI; 93/94 - 239, 239EI, V77
- Score: 92/93 - 409PNC, 409PNA; 93/94 - 157C, 157A
- Sega: 93/94 - 79
- Topps: 93/94 - 129(I), 445(II), 515(II), 248SC, 248FD
- Upper Deck: 91/92 - 1E, 1F; 92/93 - 577, ER15, CC12, G12, 57AS; 93/94 - 29, 283

Malarchuk, Clint (Goalie)
- Bowman: 91/92 - 23; 92/93 - 30
- Kraft: 86/87 - 47, 47P
- O-Pee-Chee: 86/87 - 47, 33SC; 87/88 - 246; 88/89 - 25, 72SK; 89/90 - 170; 90/91 - 371; 91/92 - 97
- Panini: 87/88 - 158; 88/89 - 363; 90/91 - 26; 91/92 - 301

Malarchuk, Clint (Goalie) (cont.)
Parkhurst: 91/92 - 244E, 244F
Pro Set: 90/91 - 25; 91/92 - 159PT
Score: 90/91 - 289A, 289C; 91/92 - 419B, 419C, 438A, 103PNE, 397PNE, 103PNF, 397PNF; 92/93 - 138C, 138A
Topps: 86/87 - 47; 88/89 - 25; 89/90 - 173 90/91 - 371; 91/92 - 97, 251SC; 92/93 - 363, 363GS, 186SC
Upper Deck: 90/91 - 399E, 399F; 91/92 - 368E, 368F

Malenfant, Ray
World Wide Gum: 36/37 - 108

Maley, David
O-Pee-Chee: 90/91 - 438; 91/92 - 476
Parkhurst: 91/92 - 99E, 99F
Pro Set: 90/91 - 171; 91/92 - 421E, 421F
Score: 90/91 - 310A; 91/92 - 426B, 426C, 272PNE, 272PNF; 92/93 - 370C, 370A
Topps: 91/92 - 476; 93/94 - 259SC, 259FD

Malgin, Albert
O-Pee-Chee: 91/92 - 54R

Malgunas, Stewart
Donruss: 93/94 - 470
O-Pee-Chee: 93/94 - 516
Parkhurst: 93/94 - 420, 420EI
Topps: 93/94 - 516(II), 409SC, 409FD
Upper Deck: 93/94 - 425

Malinowski, Merlin
O-Pee-Chee: 81/82 - 76, 228SK; 82/83 - 128, 229SK; 83/84 - 142
Post: 82/83 - 168
Topps: 81/82 WN - 81; 82/83 - 229SK

Mallen, Ken
Imperial Tobacco: 10/11 - 7L; 11/12 - 7

Mallette, Troy
Bowman: 90/91 - 219; 91/92 - 65
Donruss: 93/94 - 227
Fleer: 93/94 - 401PP
Leaf: 93/94 - 228(II)
O-Pee-Chee: 90/91 - 277; 91/92 - 474, 39PM
Panini: 90/91 - 100; 91/92 - 295
Parkhurst: 93/94 - 413, 413EI
Pro Set: 90/91 - 492; 91/92 - 157E, 157F
Score: 90/91 - 288A, 288C; 91/92 - 178A, 178B, 178C, 601B, 601C
Topps: 90/91 - 277; 91/92 - 474, 134SC; 92/93 - 335, 335GS, 432SC; 93/94 - 444SC, 444FD
Upper Deck: 90/91 - 11E, 11F; 91/92 - 326E, 326F; 93/94 - 418

Malone, Greg
Funmate: 83/84 - 105
O-Pee-Chee: 78/79 - 233; 79/80 - 9; 80/81 - 186; 81/82 - 264; 82/83 - 272; 83/84 - 284, 229SK; 84/85 - 74, 194SK; 85/86 - 118, 166SK
Post: 82/83 - 236
Topps: 78/79 - 233; 79/80 - 9; 80/81 - 186; 83/84 - 229SK; 84/85 - 57; 85/86 - 118

Malone, Joe
Anonymous: 23/24 - 13
Hall of Fame: 83 - 204, N9P; 87 - 204
Imperial Tobacco: 10/11 - 4L; 11/12 - 4; 12/13 - 48
Pro Set: 91/92 - 332E, 332F
Topps: 60/61 - 3, 45ST

Maloney, Dan
Eddie Sargent: 72/73 - 70
Loblaws: 74/75 - 137
O-Pee-Chee: 72/73 - 264; 73/74 - 32; 74/75 - 172; 75/76 - 177; 76/77 - 101; 77/78 - 172; 78/79 - 21; 79/80 - 271; 80/81 - 118; 81/82 - 320, 102SK; 82/83 - 326, 72SK
PepsiCo: 80/81 - 90
Topps: 73/74 - 32; 74/75 - 172; 75/76 - 177; 76/77 - 101; 77/78 - 172; 78/79 - 21; 80/81 - 118; 82/83 - 72SK
Toronto Sun: 71/72 - 74

Maloney, Dave
Coca Cola: 77/78 - 14
O-Pee-Chee: 76/77 - 181; 77/78 - 41, 10GP; 78/79 - 221; 79/80 - 159; 80/81 - 7; 81/82 - 227, 173SK; 82/83 - 228, 140SK; 83/84 - 249, 211SK; 84/85 - 146; 85/86 - 89, 177SK
Post: 82/83 - 202
Topps: 76/77 - 181; 77/78 - 41, 10PO; 78/79 - 221; 79/80 - 159; 80/81 - 7; 81/82 EN - 100; 82/83 - 140SK; 83/84 - 211SK; 85/86 - 89

Maloney, Donald (Don)
Bowman: 90/91 - 117
Funmate: 83/84 - 89
O-Pee-Chee: 79/80 - 42, 162; 80/81 - 231; 81/82 - 228, 170SK; 82/83 - 229, 137SK; 83/84 - 250, 212SK; 84/85 - 147, 95SK, 96SK; 85/86 - 94; 86/87 - 81; 87/88 - 49, 29SK; 90/91 - 31
Panini: 87/88 - 117; 88/89 - 308, 89/90 - 231; 90/91 - 84
Post: 82/83 - 203
Pro Set: 90/91 - 187
7-Eleven: 84/85 - 35
Score: 90/91 - 303A
Topps: 79/80 - 42, 162; 80/81 - 231; 81/82 EN - 101; 82/83 - 137SK; 83/84 - 212SK; 84/85 - 109 85/86 - 94; 86/87 - 81; 87/88 - 49; 90/91 - 31
Upper Deck: 90/91 - 20E, 20F

Maloney, Phi.
Beehive: 45/63 - 46, 427
Quaker Oats: 45/54 - 85

Maloney, Phil
O-Pee-Chee: 74/75 - 104
Topps: 74/75 - 104

Maltais, Steve
Score: 90/91 - 417A, 417C

Maltby, Kirk
Donruss: 93/94 - 428
O-Pee-Chee: 93/94 - 290
Topps: 93/94 - 290(II), 299SC, 299FD
Upper Deck: 93/94 - 520

Malykhin, Igor
O-Pee-Chee: 90/91 - 15R; 91/92 - 20R

Manderville, Kent
O-Pee-Chee: 92/93 - 14, 23PM
Parkhurst: 91/92 - 392E, 392F; 92/93 - 184, 184EI; 93/94 - 204, 204EI; 94/95 - 235, 235EI
Score: 92/93 - 458C, 458A; 10COH
Topps: 92/93 - 148, 148GS, 339SC; 93/94 - 417SC, 417FD
Upper Deck: 90/91 - 465E, 465F; 92/93 - 32; 93/94 - 420

Manery, Kris
O-Pee-Chee: 78/79 - 107; 79/80 - 151; 81/82 - 371
PepsiCo: 80/81 - 132
Topps: 78/79 - 107; 79/80 - 151

Manery, Randy
Eddie Sargent: 72/73 - 10
Loblaws: 74/75 - 10
O-Pee-Chee: 72/73 - 260; 73/74 - 131; 74/75 - 86; 75/76 - 44; 76/77 - 24; 77/78 - 389; 78/79 - 266; 79/80 - 317; 80/81 - 342
Topps: 73/74 - 131; 74/75 - 86; 75/76 - 44; 76/77 - 24

Maniago, Cesare (Goalie)
Beehive: 45/63 - 266, 428; 64/67 - 140
Colgate: 70/71 - 63
Eddie Sargent: 70/71 - 81; 72/73 - 110
Esso: 70/71 - 117
Lipton Soup: 74/75 - 27
Loblaws: 74/75 - 154
O-Pee-Chee: 68/69 - 45; 69/70 - 121, 11QS; 70/71 - 173; 71/72 - 117;

Maniago, Cesare (Goalie) (cont.)
O-Pee-Chee: 72/73 - 138; 73/74 - 127; 74/75 - 26; 75/76 - 261; 76/77 - 240; 77/78 - 23
Parkhurst: 63/64 - 40, 99
Shirriff: 68/69 - E5
Topps: 68/69 - 45; 69/70 - 121; 71/72 - 117; 72/73 - 104; 73/74 - 146; 74/75 - 26; 75/76 - 261; 76/77 - 240; 77/78 - 23
Toronto Sun: 71/72 - 136
York: 61/62 - 41

Mann, Jimmy
O-Pee-Chee: 80/81 - 353; 81/82 - 372
PepsiCo: 80/81 - 133

Mann, Norm
Beehive: 34/44 - 335A, 335B

Manno, Bob
O-Pee-Chee: 78/79 - 349; 79/80 - 270; 81/82 - 396; 82/83 - 325, 71SK; 83/84 - 132; 84/85 - 59; 85/86 - 134
Post: 82/83 - 281
Topps: 82/83 - 71SK; 85/86 - 134

Manson, Dave
Bowman: 91/92 - 389; 92/93 - 339
Donruss: 93/94 - 109, 509
Fleer: 92/93 - 62; 93/94 - 93, 83PP
Leaf: 93/94 - 159
O-Pee-Chee: 89/90 - 150, 13SK; 90/91 - 397; 91/92 - 409, 137PM; 92/93 - 56; 93/94 - 71, 183SC, 183FD
Panini: 89/90 - 47; 90/91 - 199; 91/92 - 15; 92/93 - 108E, 108F; 93/94 - 242E, 242F
Parkhurst: 91/92 - 49E, 49F; 92/93 - 47, 47EI, CP15; 93/94 - 335, 335EI; 94/95 - 262, 262EI, V9
Pro Set: 90/91 - 54; 91/92 - 41E, 41F, 389E, 389F, 172PT; 92/93 - 55
Score: 90/91 - 193A, 193C; 91 - 74T; 91/92 - 152A, 152B, 152C, 624B, 624C, 62PNE, 62PNF; 92/93 - 214C, 214A, 334PNC, 34PNA; 93/94 - 127C, 127A, 38PNC, 38PNA, 38CAS, 38AAS
Season's: 92/93 - 56
Sega: 93/94 - 43
Topps: 89/90 - 150; 91/92 - 409, 308SC; 92/93 - 389, 389GS, 436SC; 93/94 - 71(I), 183SC, 183FD, 18AS
Upper Deck: 90/91 - 85E, 85F; 91/92 - 280E, 548E, 208F, 548F; 92/93 - 84, 30AS; 93/94 - 358

Mantha, Billy
Anonymous: 24/25 - 50

Mantha, Georges
Beehive: 34/41 - 166
CKAC Radio: 43/47 - 67, 68
Canada Starch: 35/40 - 60
Can. Chew. Gum.: 33/34 - 37
Diamond: 33/35 - 41; 36/39 - 41(I), 42(II), 38(III)
La Presse: 27/32 - 32
O-Pee-Chee: 33/34 - 22; 37/38 - 153; 39/40 - 26
Quaker Oats: 38/39 - 11
Sweet Caporal: 34/35 - 20
World Wide Gum: 33/34 - 26; 36/37 - 45

Mantha, Maurice (Moe)
Bowman: 91/92 - 205
O-Pee-Chee: 81/82 - 373; 85/86 - 125, 98SK; 86/87 - 45, 231SK; 87/88 - 51, 171SK; 88/89 - 30, 200SK; 90/91 - 354; 91/92 - 477
Panini: 87/88 - 142
PepsiCo: 80/81 - 134
Pro Set: 90/91 - 332
Score: 90/91 - 310C; 91/92 - 506B, 506C
Topps: 85/86 - 125; 86/87 - 45; 87/88 - 51; 88/89 - 30; 90/91 - 354; 91/92 - 477, 287SC
Vachon Foods: 83/84 - 132

Mantha, Sylvio
Amal. Press: 35/36 - 5
Anonymous: 23/24 - 12; 26/27 - 4
Beehive: 34/41 - 167

Mantha, Sylvio (cont.)
  Champ's: 24/25 - 25
  Diamond: 33/35 - 42; 36/39 - 42(I), 43(II), 39(III)
  Hall of Fame: 83 - 84, F9P; 87 - 84
  Hamilton Gum: 33/34 - 18
  La Presse: 27/32 - 3
  O-Pee-Chee: 35/36 - 82
  Parkhurst: 55/56 - 60
  Quaker Oats: 55/56 - 60
  Sweet Caporal: 34/35 - 21
  World Wide Gum: 33/34 - 42

Marcel, Bernard
  Hall of Fame: 87 - 246

Marcetta, Milan
  Shirriff: 68/69 - E6

March, Mush (Harold)
  Amal. Press: 35/36 - 8
  Beehive: 34/41 - 67
  Canada Starch: 35/40 - 82
  Diamond: 33/35 - 43; 36/39 - 43(I), 44(II), 40(III), 11IV), 9(V), 9(VI)
  World Wide Gum: 36/37 - 13
  O-Pee-Chee: 39/40 - 45
  Sweet Caporal: 34/35 - 6

Marchant, Todd
  Parkhurst: 94/95 - 77, 77EI
  Topps: 93/94 - 14US
  Upper Deck: 92/93 - 606

Marchinko, Brian
  Eddie Sargent: 72/73 - 136
  O-Pee-Chee: 72/73 - 179

Marchment, Bryan
  Bowman: 91/92 - 208; 92/93 - 418
  Donruss: 93/94 - 73
  Fleer: 92/93 - 278; 93/94 - 352PP
  Leaf: 93/94 - 224(II)
  O-Pee-Chee: 91/92 - 116, 99PM; 93/94 - 161SC, 161FD
  Parkhurst: 92/93 - 267, 267EI
  Score: 91 - 56T; 91/92 - 314A, 344B, 344C, 606B, 606C; 92/93 - 288C, 288A; 93/94 - 386C, 386A
  Topps: 91/92 - 116, 384SC; 92/93 - 501, 501GS, 148SC; 93/94 - 161SC, 161FD

Marchment, Todd
  Fleer: 93/94 - 511PP

Marcinyshyn, David
  O-Pee-Chee: 90/91 - 67PM
  Pro Set: 90/91 - 623

Marcon, Lou
  Topps: 59/60 - 49

Marcotte, Don
  Eddie Sargent: 72/73 - 27
  Esso: 70/71 - 11
  Loblaws: 74/75 - 27
  O-Pee-Chee: 70/71 - 138; 71/72 - 176; 72/73 - 219; 74/75 - 221; 75/76 - 269; 76/77 - 234; 77/78 - 165; 78/79 - 236; 79/80 - 99; 80/81 - 336; 81/82 - 14; 82/83 - 14, 91SK
  Topps: 73/74 - 89; 74/75 - 221; 75/76 - 269; 76/77 - 234; 77/78 - 165; 78/79 - 236; 79/80 - 99; 82/83 - 91SK
  Toronto Sun: 71/72 - 13

Marcotte, Jacques
  La Patrie: 51/54 - 43

Marha, Josef
  Parkhurst: 93/94 - 516, 516EI

Marini, Hector
  Funmate: 83/84 - 75
  O-Pee-Chee: 83/84 - 235, 221SK
  Topps: 83/84 - 221SK

Mariucci, John
  Beehive: 34/44 - 68
  Hall of Fame: 87 - 254

Marker, Gus (August)
  Beehive: 34/44 - 200, 239, 336
  Canada Starch: 35/40 - 56
  O-Pee-Chee: 35/36 - 78; 37/38 - 173; 39/40 - 16; 40/41 - 113
  Sweet Caporal: 34/35 - 33

Marks, Jack
  Imperial Tobacco: 12/13 - 38

Marks, John
  Loblaws: 74/82
  O-Pee-Chee: 74/75 - 282; 75/76 - 121; 76/77 - 114; 77/78 - 47; 78/79 - 157; 79/80 - 16; 80/81 - 194; 81/82 - 70
  Topps: 75/76 - 121; 76/77 - 114; 77/78 - 47; 78/79 - 157; 79/80 - 16; 80/81 - 194

Markwart, Nevin
  O-Pee-Chee: 84/85 - 8; 91/92 - 238
  Pro Set: 90/91 - 408
  Topps: 84/85 - 7; 91/92 - 238

Marois, Daniel
  Bowman: 90/91 - 160; 91/92 - 165; 92/93 - 245
  Donruss: 93/94 - 17
  Durivage: 92/93 - 16
  Kraft: 1990 - 37
  O-Pee-Chee: 89/90 - 273, 176SK, 18FS; 90/91 - 267; 91/92 - 212; 92/93 - 58
  Panini: 89/90 - 137; 90/91 - 284; 91/92 - 95
  Parkhurst: 91/92 - 329E, 329F; 93/94 - 282, 282EI; 94/95 - 18, 18EI
  Pro Set: 90/91 - 284; 91/92 - 223E, 223F, 118PT
  Score: 90 - 3YS; 90/91 - 122A, 122C; 91/92 - 254A, 474B, 474C, 27PNE, 27PNF; 92/93 - 63C, 63A, 139PNC, 139PNA
  Topps: 90/91 - 267; 91/92 - 212, 197SC; 92/93 - 49, 49GS, 63SC
  Upper Deck: 90/91 - 179E, 179F; 91/92 - 331E, 331F; 92/93 - 71

Marois, Jean (Goalie)
  CKAC Radio: 43/47 - 22
  La Patrie: 51//54 - 29

Marois, Mario
  Bowman: 91/92 - 380
  Derniere: 72/84 - 149
  Kraft: 86/87 - 77P; 86/87 - 77
  O-Pee-Chee: 81/82 - 279; 82/83 - 287; 83/84 - 295; 84/85 - 282, 166SK, 167SK; 85/86 - 194, 144SK; 87/88 - 220, 250SK; 88/89 - 233, 142SK; 89/90 - 260, 185SK; 90/91 - 158; 91/92 - 82
  Panini: 88/89 - 151; 89/90 - 336
  PepsiCo: 80/81 - 114
  Post: 82/83 - 248
  Vachon Foods: 83/84 - 67
  Pro Set: 90/91 - 253, 524; 91/92 - 477E, 477F
  Score: 90/91 - 229A, 229C, 94T; 91/92 - 546B, 546C
  Topps: 90/91 - 158; 91/92 - 82, 12SC
  Upper Deck: 90/91 - 8E, 8F

Marotte, Gilles
  Bauer: 68/69 - 15
  Colgate: 70/71 - 65
  Dad's Cookies: 70/71 - 58
  Esso: 70/71 - 101
  Eddie Sargent: 70/71 - 78; 71/72 - 70; 72/73 - 89
  Loblaws: 74/75 - 205
  Shirriff: 68/69 - B15
  O-Pee-Chee: 68/69 - 14; 69/70 - 68; 70/71 - 34; 71/72 - 151; 72/73 - 27; 73/74 - 5; 74/75 - 373; 75/76 - 164; 76/77 - 192
  Topps: 66/67 - 36; 67/68 - 59; 68/69 - 14; 69/70 - 68; 70/71 - 34; 72/73 - 167; 73/74 - 188; 75/76 - 164; 76/77 - 192
  Ultimate: 92 - 59(OSE), 59(OSF)

Marouelli, Dan (Official)
  Pro Set: 90/91 - 692

Marseille, Frank
  Eddie Sargent: 70/71 - 180

Marsh, Bradley (Brad)
  Bowman: 90/91 - 158
  Fleer: 92/93 - 364
  O-Pee-Chee: 80/81 - 338; 81/82 - 47, 225SK; 82/83 - 254; 83/84 - 269; 84/85 - 163; 85/86 - 72; 86/87 - 175, 235SK; 87/88 - 128; 8 8/89 - 64, 101SK; 89/90 - 276, 175SK; 90/91 - 155; 91/92 - 19
  Panini: 87/88 - 127; 89/90 - 141; 90/91 - 277
  Parkhurst: 92/93 - 123, 123EI
  PepsiCo: 80/81 - 9
  Post: 82/83 - 218
  Pro Set: 90/91 - 285; 91/92 - 378E, 378F; 92/93 - 126, 264
  Score: 90/91 - 219A, 219C; 91/92 - 416B, 416C, 361PNE, 401PNE, 361PNF, 401PNF; 92/93 - 293C, 293A, 378PNC, 378PNA; 93/94 - 392C, 392A, 10PNC, 10PNA, 10CAS, 10AAS
  Topps: 85/86 - 72; 86/87 - 175; 87/88 - 128 88/89 - 64; 90/91 - 155; 91/92 - 19; 92/93 - 215, 215GS, 482SC, 8AS
  Upper Deck: 90/91 - 199E, 199F

Marsh, Peter
  O-Pee-Chee: 79/80 - 147; 80/81 - 314; 81/82 - 71
  Topps: 79/80 - 147

Marshall, Bert
  Bazooka: 71/72 - 25
  Beehive: 64/67 - 86
  Coca Cola: 65/66 - 50
  Dad's Cookies: 70/71 - 31
  Eddie Sargent: 70/71 - 131; 71/72 - 134; 72/73 - 47
  Loblaws: 74/75 - 190
  O-Pee-Chee: 68/69 - 79; 69/70 - 80; 70/71 - 188; 71/72 - 73; 72/73 - 130; 73/74 - 51; 74/75 - 177; 75/76 - 72; 76/77 - 62; 77/78 - 206; 78/79 - 49
  Shirriff: 68/69 - H8
  Topps: 66/67 - 51; 67/68 - 45; 68/69 - 79; 69/70 - 80, 17QS; 71/72 - 73; 72/73 - 162; 73/74 - 51; 74/75 - 177; 75/76 - 72; 76/77 - 62; 77/78 - 206; 78/79 - 49
  Toronto Sun: 71/72 - 52

Marshall, Don
  Beehive: 45/63 - 267, 341; 64/67 - 141
  Coca Cola: 64/65 - 84; 65/66 - 84
  Colgate: 70/71 - 27
  Dad's Cookies: 70/71 - 18
  Esso: 70/71 - 29
  O-Pee-Chee: 68/69 - 75; 69/70 - 39; 70/71 - 129; 71/72 - 199
  Parkhurst: 55/56 - 35; 57/58 MON - 8; 58/59 - 44; 59/60 - 37; 60/61 - 42; 61/62 - 40; 62/63 - 43; 93/94 - 76ML
  Quaker Oats: 55/56 - 35
  Shirriff: 60/61 - 23; 61/62 - 103; 62/63 - 33; 68/89 - G7
  Topps: 63/64 - 59; 64/65 - 97; 65/66 - 29; 66/67 - 24; 66/67 US - 24; 67/68 - 23, 130; 68/69 - 75; 69/70 - 39; 70/71 - 129
  Toronto Star: 57/67 - 65, 58/67 - 54, 102
  Toronto Sun: 71/72 - 264
  Ultimate: 92 - 13(OSE), 13(OSF)
  York: 60/61 - 12; 61/62 - 6; 62/63 - 28

Marshall, Jack
  Hall of Fame: 83 - 39; 83 - C9P; 87 - 39
  Imperial Tobacco: 10/11 - 29L, 33, 35; 11/12 - 29

Marshall, Jason
  Fleer: 93/94 - 488PP
  Score: 91/92 - 388A, 278B, 278C
  Upper Deck: 90/91 - 453E, 453F; 92/93 - 68

Marshall, Willie
  Parkhurst: 55/56 - 17; 58/59 - 19
  Quaker Oats: 55/56 - 17

Marson, Mike
  Loblaws: 74/75 - 321

Marson, Mike (cont.)
O-Pee-Chee: 75/76 - 43
Topps: 75/76 - 43

Martin, Clare
Beehive: 45/63 - 193

Martin, Frank
Beehive: 45/63 - 47
Parkhurst: 53/54 - 97; 93/94 - 34ML
Topps: 54/55 - 30

Martin, George
Parkhurst: 51/52 - 39

Martin, Matt
Donruss: 93/94 - 497
Parkhurst: 93/94 - 471, 471EI
Topps: 93/94 - 23US
Upper Deck: 93/94 - 447

Martin, Pete
World Wide Gum: 36/37 - 31

Martin, Pit
Beehive: 64/67 - 87
Chex: 63/65 - 17
Coca Cola: 64/65 - 50; 77/78 - 15
Colgate: 70/71 - 31
Dad's Cookies: 70/71 - 41
Eddie Sargent: 70/71 - 39; 72/73 - 68
Esso: 70/71 - 65
Lipton Soup: 74/75 - 37
Loblaws: 74/75 - 83
O-Pee-Chee: 68/69 - 18; 69/70 - 75; 70/71 - 18; 70/71 - 253; 71/72 - 39; 72/73 - 24; 73/74 - 73; 74/75 - 58; 75/76 - 48; 76/77 - 76; 77/78 - 135; 78/79 - 286
Shirriff: 68/89 - B6
Topps: 64/65 - 1; 65/66 - 52; 66/67 - 41; 67/68 - 116; 68/69 - 18; 69/70 - 75; 70/71 - 18; 71/72 - 39; 72/73 - 99; 73/74 - 164; 74/75 - 58; 75/76 - 48; 76/77 - 76; 77/78 - 135
Toronto Star: 58/67 - 107
Toronto Sun: 71/72 - 75
Upper Deck: 90/91 - 513E, 513F

Martin, Richard (Rick)
Colgate: 71/72 - 7
Derniere: 72/84 - 200
Eddie Sargent: 72/73 - 35
Lipton Soup: 74/75 - 33
Loblaws: 74/75 - 46
Mac's Milk: 73/74 - 17
O-Pee-Chee: 71/72 - 161, 6PT; 72/73 - 157, 182, 4CS; 73/74 - 173; 74/75 - 127; 74/75 - 190; 75/76 - 175, 289; 76/77 - 210; 77/78 - 180, 11GP; 78/79 - 80; 79/80 - 149; 80/81 - 51
Topps: 72/73 - 145; 73/74 - 155; 74/75 - 127, 190; 75/76 - 175, 289; 76/77 - 210, 19PO; 77/78 - 180, 11PO; 78/79 - 80; 79/80 - 149; 80/81 - 51
Toronto Sun: 71/72 - 32

Martin, Ron
Beehive: 34/44 - 240
Diamond: 33/35 - 44
World Wide Gum: 33/34 - 7

Martin, Terry
O-Pee-Chee: 77/78 - 318; 78/79 - 118; 81/82 - 321; 82/83 - 329, 66SK; 83/84 - 336; 84/85 - 306
PepsiCo: 80/81 - 91
Post: 82/83 - 282
Topps: 78/79 - 118; 82/83 - 66SK
Vachon Foods: 83/84 - 92

Martineau, Don
Loblaws: 74/75 - 155

Maruk, Dennis
Funmate: 83/84 - 62
O-Pee-Chee: 76/77 - 86; 77/78 - 21; 78/79 - 141; 79/80 - 223; 80/81 - 284; 81/82 - 350, 357, 191SK; 82/83 - 359, 369, 370, 151SK; 83/84 - 174, 204SK, 205SK;

Maruk, Dennis (cont.)
O-Pee-Chee: 84/85 - 101, 48SK; 85/86 - 111; 86/87 - 60, 170SK; 87/88 - 117, 50SK
Panini: 87/88 - 298
Post: 82/83 - 315
Topps: 76/77 - 86; 77/78 - 21; 78/79 - 141; 79/80 - 223; 81/82 - 65; 81/82 EN - 120; 82/83 - 151SK; 83/84 - 204SK, 205SK; 84/85 - 76; 85/86 - 111; 86/87 - 60; 87/88 - 117

Maslennikov, Igor
O-Pee-Chee: 90/91 - 14R; 91/92 - 21R

Maslov, Nikolai
O-Pee-Chee: 91/92 - 55R

Masnick, Paul
Beehive: 45/63 - 268
Parkhurst: 51/52 - 8; 54/55 - 13
Quaker Oats: 45/54 - 128

Mason, Bob (Goalie)
O-Pee-Chee: 87/88 - 238SK; 89/90 - 188SK
Panini: 87/88 - 175; 88/89 - 20; 89/90 - 344

Mason, Charley
Beehive: 34/44 - 113
Diamond: 36/39 - 44(I), 45(II), 41(III), 42(III)

Mathers, Frank
Beehive: 45/63 - 429
Quaker Oats: 45/54 - 173

Matte, Joe
Beehive: 34/44 - 69

Matteau, Stephane
Bowman: 91/92 - 258; 92/93 - 340
Donruss: 93/94 - 463
Durivage: 93/94 - 44
Fleer: 92/93 - 279; 93/94 - 313PP
Leaf: 93/94 - 114
O-Pee-Chee: 90/91 - 68PM; 91/92 - 383; 92/93 - 69; 93/94 - 415, 127SC, 127FD
Panini: 91/92 - 62; 93/94 - 150E, 150F
Parkhurst: 91/92 - 259E, 259F; 92/93 - 268, 268EI; 93/94 - 41, 41EI; 94/95 - 150, 150EI
Pro Set: 90/91 - 593; 91/92 - 27E, 27F
Score: 90/91 - 381A, 381C; 91/92 - 242B, 242C; 92/93 - 543C, 543A, 180PNC, 180PNA; 93/94 - 398C, 398A
Topps: 91/92 - 383, 391SC; 92/93 - 463, 463GS, 363SC; 93/94 - 415(II), 127SC, 127FD
Upper Deck: 90/91 - 535E, 535F; 91/92 - 121E, 121F; 92/93 - 540; 93/94 - 214

Matthews, Jamie
Upper Deck: 91/92 - 76E, 76F

Mattiussi, Dick
Eddie Sargent: 70/71 - 139
Esso: 70/71 - 48
O-Pee-Chee: 69/70 - 147; 70/71 - 192

Mattson, Markus (Goalie)
O-Pee-Chee: 80/81 - 394; 81/82 - 374

Matvichuk, Richard
Donruss: 93/94 - 418
Fleer: 92/93 - 321; 93/94 - 180
O-Pee-Chee: 92/93 - 83PM
Parkhurst: 92/93 - 74, 74EI; 94/95 - 57, 57EI
Score: 92/93 - 391PNC, 391PNA; 93/94 - 285C, 285A
Upper Deck: 92/93 - 505; 93/94 - 55

Maxwell, Brad
O-Pee-Chee: 78/79 - 83; 79/80 - 231; 80/81 - 152; 81/82 - 102; 82/83 - 168; 83/84 - 175; 84/85 - 102, 50SK; 85/86 - 224, 154SK; 86/87 - 242, 145SK
Panini: 79 - 56
Post: 82/83 - 135
PepsiCo: 80/81 - 135
Topps: 78/79 - 83; 79/80 - 231; 80/81 - 152; 84/85 - 77

Maxwell, Bryan
O-Pee-Chee: 78/79 - 216; 82/83 - 387
Post: 82/83 - 331
Topps: 78/79 - 216

Maxwell, Fred
Hall of Fame: 83 - 177; 87 - 177

Maxwell, Kevin
Post: 82/83 - 170

Maxwell, F.G. (Steamer)
Hall of Fame: 83 - M13

May, Alan
Bowman: 90/91 - 78; 91/92 - 295
Donruss: 93/94 - 419
O-Pee-Chee: 91/92 - 57; 93/94 - 518
Panini: 90/91 - 160
Parkhurst: 91/92 - 417E, 417F
Pro Set: 90/91 - 317; 91/92 - 508E, 614E, 508F, 614F
Score: 91/92 - 545B, 545C; 92/93 - 357C, 357A; 93/94 - 430C, 430A
Topps: 91/92 - 57, 288SC; 93/94 - 518(II)
Upper Deck: 90/91 - 240E, 240F

May, Brad
Bowman: 92/93 - 374
Donruss: 93/94 - 38
Fleer: 92/93 - 17; 93/94 - 298PP
Leaf: 93/94 - 47
O-Pee-Chee: 92/93 - 256; 93/94 - 192, 203SC, 203FD
Panini: 92/93 - 252E, 252F
Parkhurst: 91/92 - 10E, 10F; 92/93 - 240, 257, 240EI, 257EI; 93/94 - 27, 27EI; 94/95 - 26, 26EI
Pro Set: 91/92 - 523E, 523F
Score: 90/91 - 427A, 427C; 91 - 78T; 91/92 - 628B, 628C, 302PNE, 302PNF; 92/93 - 96C, 96A, 197PNC, 197PNA; 93/94 - 269C, 269A
Topps: 92/93 - 34, 34GS, 51SC; 93/94 - 192(I), 203SC, 203FD
Upper Deck: 90/91 - 455E, 455F; 91/92 - 596E; 92/93 - 74; 93/94 - 201, 596E, 596F;

Mayer, Derek
Donruss: 93/94 - 467
Fleer: 93/94 - 489PP
O-Pee-Chee: 93/94 - 6TC
Parkhurst: 94/95 - 156, 156EI, V60

Mayer, Hans-Jorg
Upper Deck: 91/92 - 682E, 682F

Mazur, Eddie
Beehive: 45/63 - 269
Parkhurst: 53/54 - 20; 54/55 - 4

Mazur, Jay
Bowman: 91/92 - 322
O-Pee-Chee: 91/92 - 28
Topps: 91/92 - 28, 272SC
Upper Deck: 91/92 - 378E, 378F

McAdam, Gary
Post: 82/83 - 39
O-Pee-Chee: 77/78 - 253; 78/79 - 42; 79/80 - 72; 80/81 - 288; 81/82 - 93; 84/85 - 117
Topps: 77/78 - 253; 78/79 - 42; 79/80 - 72; 81/82 WN - 93

McAffrey, Bert
La Presse: 27/32 - 34

McAmmond Dean
Donruss: 93/94 - 110
Fleer: 92/93 - 40
Leaf: 93/94 - 436(II)
O-Pee-Chee: 93/94 - 366
Parkhurst: 93/94 - 64, 64EI, CC9
Pro-Set: 92/93 - 224
Score: 92/93 - 469C, 469A
Topps: 93/94 - 366(II)
Upper Deck: 92/93 - 403; 93/94 - 480

McAndrew, Hazen
Beehive: 34/44 - 241

McAneeley, Ted
Loblaws: 74/75 - 65

McAneeley, Ted (cont.)
O-Pee-Chee: 72/73 - 242; 73/74 - 37; 74/75 - 148
Topps: 73/74 - 37; 74/75 - 148

McBain, Andrew
Fleer: 92/93 - 147
Frito-Lay: 88/89 - 22
O-Pee-Chee: 84/85 - 343; 88/89 - 105, 147SK;
89/90 - 38, 135SK; 90/91 - 248;
93/94 - 238
Panini: 87/88 - 370; 88/89 - 157; 90/91 - 297
Pro Set: 90/91 - 301; 91/92 - 500E, 500F;
92/93 - 120
Score: 90/91 - 257A, 257C
Topps: 88/89 - 105; 89/90 - 38; 90/91 - 248;
93/94 - 238
Vachon Foods: 83/84 - 133

McBain, Jason
Donruss: 93/94 - 14JCA
Upper Deck: 93/94 - 552

McBean, Wayne
Bowman: 91/92 - 217
Leaf: 93/94 - 413(II)
O-Pee-Chee: 91/92 - 62; 92/93 - 50
Parkhurst: 93/94 - 330E, 330F
Pro Set: 90/91 - 485; 91/92 - 144E, 144F
Score: 91/92 - 530B, 530C
Topps: 91/92 - 62, 353SC; 92/93 - 443,
443GS, 397SC; 93/94 - 493SC,
493FD

McCabe, Bryan
Donruss: 93/94 - 16JCC
Upper Deck: 93/94 - 549

McCaig, Douglas
Beehive: 34/44 - 114; 45/63 - 120

McCallum, Dunc
Esso: 70/71 - 187
Shirriff: 68/69 - K9
Topps: 71/72 - 132

McCammon, Bob
Pro Set: 90/91 - 678

McCaffery, Bert
Champ's: 24/25 - 55
Dom. Choc.: 1925 - 60
Wm. Paterson: 24/25 - 57

McCartan, Jack (Goalie)
Beehive: 45/63 - 342
Shirriff: 60/61 - 81
Topps: 60/61 - 39

McCarthy, Kevin
Funmate: 83/84 - 130
O-Pee-Chee: 79/80 - 287; 80/81 - 21; 81/82 - 34,
248SK; 82/83 - 351, 246SK;
83/84 - 356, 279SK;
84/85 - 178, 119SK
PepsiCo: 80/81 - 115
Post: 82/83 - 299
Topps: 80/81 - 21; 82/83 - 246SK;
83/84 - 279SK; 84/85 - 126
Vachon Foods: 83/84 - 112

McCarthy, Sandy
Donruss: 93/94 - 59
Fleer: 93/94 - 306PP
Leaf: 93/94 - 358(II)
Parkhurst: 93/94 - 30, 30EI
Upper Deck: 91/92 - 77E, 77F; 93/94 - 493

McCarthy, Tom
Topps: 57/58 - 37

McCarthy, Tom
O-Pee-Chee: 80/81 - 93; 81/82 - 164, 95SK;
82/83 - 169; 83/84 - 176, 115SK;
84/85 - 103, 52SK;
87/88 - 38, 141SK
Panini: 87/88 - 13
Post: 82/83 - 137
Topps: 80/81 - 93; 81/82 WN - 108;
83/84 - 115SK; 84/85 - 78; 87/88 - 38

McCarty, Darren
Leaf: 93/94 - 435(II)
O-Pee-Chee: 93/94 - 412

McCarty, Darren (cont.)
Parkhurst: 93/94 - 265, 265EI
Topps: 93/94 - 412(II), 441SC, 441FD
Upper Deck: 93/94 - 508

McClanahan, Rob
Funmate: 83/84 - 90
O-Pee-Chee: 80/81 - 232; 83/84 - 251; 84/85 - 325
Topps: 80/81 - 232

McClelland, Kevin
O-Pee-Chee: 84/85 - 253; 85/86 - 230SK;
86/87 - 77SK; 87/88 - 201;
90/91 - 389
Parkhurst: 94/95 - 266, 266EI
Score: 90/91 - 287A, 287C
Topps: 90/91 - 389

McCool, Frank (Goalie)
Quaker Oats: 45/54 - 87

McCord, Bob
Beehive: 64/67 - 18, 88
Coca Cola: 64/65 - 12
Shirriff: 68/69 - E11
O-Pee-Chee: 68/69 - 146; 69/70 - 123; 70/71 - 41
Topps: 63/64 - 6; 64/65 - 10; 65/66 - 46;
69/70 - 123; 70/71 - 41

McCormack, John
Beehive: 45/63 - 270, 430
La Patrie: 51/54 - 21
Parkhurst: 52/53 - 15; 53/54 - 34; 54/55 - 9
Quaker Oats: 45/54 - 35A, 35B, 88

McCourt, Dale
Derniere: 72/84 - 112
Funmate: 83/84 - 12
Post: 81/82 - 4; 82/83 - 22
O-Pee-Chee: 78/79 - 132; 79/80 - 63; 80/81 - 245;
81/82 - 86, 96, 105, 120SK;
82/83 - 28, 119SK; 83/84 - 66,
236SK; 84/85 - 13SK
Topps: 78/79 - 132; 79/80 - 63; 80/81 - 245;
81/82 - WN 129, 21, 51;
82/83 - 119SK; 83/84 - 236SK
Vachon Foods: 83/84 - 93

McCourt, Dan (Official)
Pro Set: 90/91 - 693

McCreary, Bill E.
Esso: 70/71 - 205
O-Pee-Chee: 68/69 - 182; 69/70 - 181

McCreary, Bill (Official)
Pro Set: 90/91 - 694

McCreary, Keith
Colgate: 70/71 - 34
Dad's Cookies: 70/71 - 107
Eddie Sargent: 70/71 - 168; 72/73 - 4
Esso: 70/71 - 188
Loblaws: 74/75 - 11
O-Pee-Chee: 68/69 - 193; 69/70 - 114, 20ST,
12QS; 70/71 - 93, 22SS;
71/72 - 188; 72/73 - 25; 73/74 - 13;
74/75 - 103
Shirriff: 68/69 - K10
Topps: 69/70 - 114; 70/71 - 93, 22SK;
72/73 - 27; 73/74 - 13; 74/75 - 103
Toronto Sun: 71/72 - 221
Ultimate: 92 - 98(OSE), 98(OSF)

McCreedy, Johnny
Beehive: 34/44 - 337

McCrimmon, Byron (Brad)
Bowman: 91/92 - 48; 92/93 - 67
Fleer: 92/93 - 52
Leaf: 93/94 - 395(II)
O-Pee-Chee: 80/81 - 354; 81/82 - 15; 82/83 - 255,
90SK; 83/84 - 270, 193SK;
84/85 - 164; 85/86 - 158, 92SK;
86/87 - 5, 247SK; 87/88 - 85, 27HL,
99SK; 88/89 - 178, 24NS, 96SK,
120SK, 206SK; 89/90 - 203, 91SK;
90/91 - 320, 69PM; 91/92 - 79;
93/94 - 391
Panini: 87/88 - 126; 88/89 - 6, 408;
89/90 - 33; 90/91 - 173
Parkhurst: 91/92 - 271E, 271F;

McCrimmon, Byron (Brad) (cont.)
Parkhurst: 93/94 - 358, 358EI
Post: 82/83 - 8
Pro Set: 90/91 - 39, 438; 91/92 - 377E, 609E,
377F, 609F, 170PT
Score: 90 - 37T; 90/91 - 184A, 184C;
91/92 - 16A, 16B, 16C, 214PNE,
214PNF; 92/93 - 141C, 141A,
124PNC, 124PNA; 93/94 - 54C, 54A
Topps: 82/83 - 90SK; 83/84 - 193SK;
85/86 - 158; 86/87 - 5;
87/88 - 85; 88/89 - 178, 10SK;
90/91 - 320; 91/92 - 79, 14SC;
92/93 - 301, 301GS, 21SC;
93/94 - 391(II)
Upper Deck: 90/91 - 294E, 294F, 430E, 430F

McDonagh, Bill
Beehive: 45/63 - 343

McDonald, Ab
Beehive: 45/63 - 121; 64/67 - 19, 89
Coca Cola: 64/65 - 13; 65/66 - 51
Dad's Cookies: 70/71 - 116
Eddie Sargent: 70/71 - 178
Esso: 70/71 - 206
Shirriff: 60/61 - 72; 61/62 - 33; 68/69 - L12
O-Pee-Chee: 68/69 - 107, 180; 69/70 - 18;
70/71 - 215
Parkhurst: 58/59 - 30; 59/60 - 20; 60/61 - 60
Topps: 60/61 - 33; 61/62 - 27; 62/63 - 38,
13HB; 63/64 - 37; 64/65 - 16;
65/66 - 50; 68/69 - 107; 69/70 - 18;
71/72 - 134; 72/73 - 321
Toronto Star: 58/67 - 70
Toronto Sun: 71/72 - 99
Ultimate: 92 - 60(OSE), 60(OSF)
Upper Deck: 92/93 - 45AS

McDonald, Alvin
Beehive: 45/63 - 271

McDonald, Bucko (Wilfred)
Beehive: 34/44 - 115A, 115B, 334
O-Pee-Chee: 39/40 - 13

McDonald, Lanny
Esso: 83/84E - 12; 83/84F - 12; 88/89 - 29
Funmate: 83/84 - 17
Hockey Wit: 93/94 - 85
Kellogg's: 84 - 12
Kraft: 86/87P - 3; 86/87 - 3
Loblaws: 74/75 - 279
O-Pee-Chee: 74/75 - 168; 75/76 - 23; 76/77 - 348;
77/78 - 110; 78/79 - 78; 79/80 - 153;
80/81 - 62, 5PO; 81/82 - 77, 85,
227SK; 82/83 - 38, 51, 52, 214SK;
83/84 - 74, 75, 87, 208, 8SK,
162SK, 263SK, 303SK; 84/85 - 231,
237SK, 238SK; 85/86 - 1, 215SK;
86/87 - 8, J/BB, 80SK; 87/88 - 20,
43SK; 88/89 - 234, 85SK;
89/90 - 7, 92SK
Panini: 87/88 O 215; 88/89 - 10; 89/90 - 39
Post: 82/83 - 40
7-Eleven: 84/85 - 6
Topps: 74/75 - 168; 75/76 - 23; 77/78 - 110;
78/79 - 78; 79/80 - 153; 80/81 - 62;
81/82 - WN 82, 50; 82/83 - 214SK;
83/84 - 8SK, 162SK, 263SK, 303SK;
84/85 - 26; 85/86 - 1; 86/87 - 8,
J/BB; 87/88 - 20; 89/90 - 7
Upper Deck: 90/91 - 508E, 508F
Vachon Foods: 83/84 - 13

McDonald, Parker
Beehive: 45/63 - 431

McDonough, Al
O-Pee-Chee: 71/72 - 150; 72/73 - 235;
73/74 - 89
Toronto Sun: 71/72 - 121
Topps: 73/74 - 176

McDonough, Hubie
Bowman: 90/91 - 120; 91/92 - 214
O-Pee-Chee: 90/91 - 366; 91/92 - 389
Panini: 90/91 - 92
Pro Set: 90/91 - 188

McDonough, Hubie (cont.)
Score: 90/91 - 222A, 222C; 91/92 - 450B, 450C
Topps: 90/91 - 366; 91/92 - 389, 260SC; 92/93 - 335SC
Upper Deck: 90/91 - 226E, 226F; 91/92 - 138E, 138F

McDougall, Bill
Donruss: 93/94 - 323
Leaf: 93/94 - 379(II)
Parkhurst: 93/94 - 463, 463EI
Upper Deck: 93/94 - 324

McDuffe, Pete (Goalie)
Loblaws: 74/75 - 119
O-Pee-Chee: 71/72 - 225; 74/75 - 173; 75/76 - 256
Topps: 74/75 - 173; 75/76 - 256
Toronto Sun: 71/72 - 240

McEachern, Shawn
Bowman: 92/93 - 415
Donruss: 93/94 - 154, 473
Fleer: 92/93 - 379; 93/94 - 133, 119PP, 7SY
Leaf: 93/94 - 217, 7R
O-Pee-Chee: 92/93 - 359, 94PM; 93/94 - 123, 353, 189SC, 189FD
Panini: 92/93 - 222E, 222F; 93/94 - 84E, 84F
Parkhurst: 91/92 - 355E, 355F; 92/93 - 142, 142EI; 93/94 - 242, 364, 242EI, 364EI; 94/95 - 173, 173EI
Pro-Set: 92/93 - 237
Score: 92/93 - 459C, 459A, 420PNC, 420PNA; 93/94 - 67C, 67A
Topps: 92/93 - 481, 481GS, 205SC; 93/94 - 123, 353, 4BG, 189SC, 189FD
Upper Deck: 92/93 - 368, 412, 565, 634, CC14, G17; 93/94 - 454

McElmury, Jim
O-Pee-Chee: 75/76 - 14, 77/78 - 352
Topps: 75/76 - 14

McEwen, Mike
O-Pee-Chee: 77/78 - 232; 78/79 - 187; 79/80 - 66; 80/81 - 185; 81/82 - 215; 82/83 - 207
Post: 82/83 - 184
Topps: 77/78 - 232; 78/79 - 187; 79/80 - 66; 80/81 - 185

McFadden, Jim
Beehive: 45/63 - 122, 194
Parkhurst: 51/52 - 44; 52/53 - 38; 53/54 - 77

McFayden, Donnie
Diamond: 1936/39 - 45(I), 46(II), 43(III)

McGee, Frank
Hall of Fame: 83 - 56, D10; 87 - 56

McGill, Jack
Canada Starch: 35/40 - 81
Diamond: 1936/39 - 46(I), 47(II), 44(III)
Sweet Caporal: 34/35 - 22
O-Pee-Chee: 35/36 - 74
World Wide Gun: 36/37 - 77

McGill, Robert (Bob)
Bowman: 92/93 - 429
O-Pee-Chee: 82/83 - 327; 85/86 - 15SK; 91/92 - 216, 8PM
Post: 82/83 - 283
Pro Set: 90/91 - 55; 91/92 - 47E, 47F, 480E, 480F
Score: 90 - 49T; 91 - 10T; 91/92 - 327B, 327C, 368A, 560B, 560C, 98PNE, 98PNF; 92/93 - 386C, 386A
Topps: 91/92 - 216; 92/93 - 209, 209GS, 483SC
Upper Deck: 91/92 - 62E, 62F

McGill, Ryan
Fleer: 92/93 - 373; 93/94 - 177
Parkhurst: 92/93 - 366, 366EI; 93/94 - 415, 415EI
Upper Deck: 92/93 - 494

McGimsie, Billy
Hall of Fame: 83 - 71, E11; 87 - 71

McHugh, Michael (Mike)
O-Pee-Chee: 91/92 - 7S
Score: 91/92 - 651B, 651C

McIlhargey, Jack
O-Pee-Chee: 78/79 - 294; 79/80 - 367
Post: 82/83 - 105

McInenly, Bert (Bertram)
O-Pee-Chee: 33/34 - 41

McInnis, Marty
Bowman: 92/93 - 352
Donruss: 93/94 - 457
Fleer: 92/93 - 347; 93/94 - 385PP
O-Pee-Chee: 92/93 - 135, 12PM; 9394 - 57
Panini: 93/94 - 62E, 62F
Parkhurst: 91/92 - 327E, 327F; 92/93 - 106, 106EI; 93/94 - 390, 390EI
Pro-Set: 92/93 - 233
Score: 92/93 - 465C, 465A; 93/94 - 405C, 405A
Topps: 92/93 - 302, 302GS, 213SC; 93/94 - 57, 257SC, 257FD
Upper Deck: 92/93 - 394, 410; 93/94 - 392

McIntyre, Jack
Beehive: 45/63 - 48
Parkhurst: 52/53 - 77; 54/55 - 88; 60/61 - 24; 93/94 - 27ML
Shirriff: 60/61 - 46
Topps: 54/55 - 43; 57/58 - 28, 117SC

McIntyre, John
Bowman: 91/92 - 180; 92/93 - 336
O-Pee-Chee: 90/91 - 382; 91/92 - 37
Parkhurst: 91/92 - 296E, 296F; 93/94 - 482, 482EI
Pro Set: 90/91 - 457; 91/92 - 401E, 401F
Score: 90/91 - 46T; 91/92 - 182A, 182B, 182C; 92/93 - 347C, 347A, 214PNC, 214PNA
Topps: 90/91 - 382; 91/92 - 37, 324SC; 92/93 - 369, 369GS, 117SC
Upper Deck: 91/92 - 218E, 218F; 92/93 - 118; 93/94 - 527

McIntyre, Lloyd
World Wide Gum: 36.37 - 121

McKay, Callum
Beehive: 45/63 - 272

McKay, Randy
Bowman: 90/91 - 227; 92/93 - 296
Donruss: 93/94 - 454
Parkhurst: 92/93 - 331, 331EI
Pro Set: 91/92 - 422E, 422F
Score: 91 - 54T; 91/92 - 604B, 604C; 92/93 - 339C, 339A; 93/94 - 319C, 319A
Topps: 92/93 - 106, 106GS, 450SC
Upper Deck: 91/92 - 313E, 313F

McKay, Ray
Toronto Sun: 71/72 - 33

McKechnie, Walt
Bazooka: 71/72 - 28
Colgate: 70/71 - 1
Esso: 70/71 - 118
Eddie Sargent: 70/71 - 89; 72/73 - 43
Funmate: 83/84 - 33
Loblaws: 74/75 - 28
O-Pee-Chee: 70/71 - 172; 71/72 - 124, 17PT; 72/73 - 192; 73/74 - 152; 75/76 - 194; 76/77 - 196; 77/78 - 32; 78/79 - 344; 79/80 - 68; 80/81 - 378; 82/83 - 91, 186SK
Post: 82/83 - 72
Topps: 73/74 - 127; 75/76 - 194; 76/77 - 196; 77/78 - 32; 79/80 - 68; 82/83 - 186S
Toronto Sun: 71/72 - 53

McKee, Mike
Donruss: 93/94 - 479
Fleer: 93/94 - 424PP

McKegney, Anthony (Tony)
Bowman: 90/91 - 168; 91/92 - 387
Funmate: 83/84 - 109

McKegney, Anthony (Tony) (cont.)
O-Pee-Chee: 80/81 - 144; 81/82 - 22, 57SK; 82/83 - 29, 122SK; 83/84 - 60, 296, 239SK; 84/85 - 283, 171SK; 85/86 - 156, 45SK; 87/88 - 172; 88/89 - 4, 17SK; 89/90 - 4; 90/91 - 333; 91/92 - 484
Panini: 87/88 - 118; 88/89 - 109; 90/91 - 149
Post: 82/83 - 23
Pro Set: 90/91 - 254
Score: 90/91 - 311C; 91/92 - 104A, 104B, 104C
Topps: 80/81 - 144; 81/82 EN - 76; 82/82 - 122SK; 83/84 - 238SK; 85/86 - 156; 87/88 - 172; 88/89 - 4; 89/90 - 4; 90/91 - 333; 91/92 - 484, 281SC
Upper Deck: 90/91 - 340E, 340F
Vachon Foods: 83/84 - 68

McKenna, Sean
Panini: 87/88 - 284

McKenney, Don
Beehive: 45/63 - 49, 344, 432; 64/67 - 175A, 175B
Coca Cola: 64/54 - 102
Parkhurst: 93/94 - 6ML
Shirriff: 60/61 - 108; 61/62 - 6
Topps: 54/55 - 35; 57/58 - 13; 58/59 - 62; 59/60 - 9; 60/61 - 40, 4ST; 61/62 - 12; 62/63 - 10, 5HB; 63/64 - 53; 64/65 - 81; 65/66 - 112
Toronto Star: 57/67 - 68; 58/67 - 65; 64/65 - 44

McKenny, Jim
Dad's Cookies: 70/71 - 130
Eddie Sargent: 70/71 - 201; 71/72 - 195; 72/73 - 198
Esso: 70.71 - 227
Loblaws: 74/75 - 280
Lipton Soup: 74/75 - 23
Mac's Milk: 73/74 - 18
O-Pee-Chee: 71/72 - 43; 72/73 - 83; 73/74 - 39; 74/75 - 198; 75/76 - 311; 76/77 - 302; 77/78 - 374
Shirriff: 68/69 - M16
Topps: 71/72 - 43; 72/73 - 54; 73/74 - 39; 74/75 - 198; 75/76 - 311
Toronto Sun: 71/72 - 265

McKenzie, Bill
Beehive: 34/44 - 168
O-Pee-Chee: 76/77 - 267; 78/79 - 27

McKenzie, Jim
Bowman: 91/92 - 7
O-Pee-Chee: 91/92 - 24
Parkhurst: 93/94 - 357, 357EI
Pro Set: 91/92 - 391E, 391F
Topps: 91/92 - 24, 354SC
Upper Deck: 91/92 - 494E, 494F; 93/94 - 23

McKenzie, John
Beehive: 64/67 - 47
Coca Cola: 64/65 - 28; 65/66 - 29
Colgate: 70/71 - 59
Dad's Cookies: 70/71 - 8
Eddie Sargent: 70/71 - 9; 71/72 - 3;
Esso: 70/71 - 12
Shirriff: 60/61 - 43; 68/69 - A11
O-Pee-Chee: 68/69 - 9; 69/70 - 28; 70/71 - 6, 241; 71/72 - 82; 72/73 - 338
Parkhurst: 60/61 - 37; 61/62 - 34
Topps: 63/64 - 42; 64/65 - 30; 65/66 - 94; 66/67 - 97; 66/67 US - 66; 67/68 - 39; 68/69 - 9; 69/70 - 28; 70/71 - 6; 71/72 - 82
Toronto Sun: 71/72 - 14
Toronto Star: 64/65 - 13
Ultimate: 92 - 52(OSE), 52(OSF)

McKim, Andrew
Parkhurst: 94/95 - 16, 16EI

McKinnon, Kenny (Goalie)
World Wide Gum: 36/37 - 118

McKinnos, Alex (Goalie)
Champ's: 24/25 - 15
Wm. Paterson: 24/25 - 16

McKnight, Wes
Beehive: 34/44 - 357

McLaughlin, Frederic
Hall of Fame: 83 - 189, J9P; 87 - 189

McLean, Jack (Goalie)
Beehive: 34/44 - 338

McLean, Kirk (Goalie)
Bowman: 90/91 - 57; 91/92 - 310; 92/93 - 212, 285
Donruss: 93/94 - 355
Fleer: 92/93 - 224; 93/94 - 29, 253PP
Humpty Dumpty: 92/93 - 15(I)
Kraft: 1990 - 43; 90/91 - 70
Leaf: 93/94 - 55, 3PW
O-Pee-Chee: 88/89 - 55SK, 136SK, 13FS; 89/90 - 61, 64SK; 90/91 - 257, 70PM; 91/92 - 221, 158PM; 92/93 - 349; 93/94 - 113, 163SC, 163FD
Panini: 88/90 - 132; 89/90 - 155; 90/91 - 296; 91/92 - 45; 92/93 - 27E, 27F; 93/94 - 177E, 177F
Parkhurst: 91/92 - 181E, 440E, 181F, 440F; 92/93 - 192, 192EI; 93/94 - 213, 213EI; 94/95 - 238, 238EI
Pro Set: 90/91 - 302, 355; 91/92 - P1E, 501E, 603E, 28PK, 501F, 603F, 239PT, PC; 92/93 - 193, 250
Roots: 93/94 - 7
Season's: 92/93 - 71
Sega: 93/94 - 144
Score: 90/91 - 93A, 93C, 46HR; 91/92 - 261A, 481B, 481C, 158PNE, 158PNF; 92/93 - 385C, 385A, 330PNC, 330PNA; 93/94 - 47C, 47A
Topps: 89/90 - 61; 90/91 - 257; 91/92 - 221, 105SC; 92/93 - 130, 225, 270, 130GS, 225GS, 270GS,193SC; 93/94 - 163SC, 163FD
Upper Deck: 90/91 - 278E, 278F; 91/92 - 191E, 191F; 92/93 - 22, 299; 93/94 - 156

McLennan, Jamie (Goalie)
Donruss: 93/94 - 458
Fleer: 93/94 - 386PP

McLeod, Jackie
Beehive: 45/63 - 378
Parkhurst: 51/52 - 98; 52/53 - 102

McLlwain, Dave
Bowman: 90/91 - 136; 91/92 - 196
Fleer: 93/94 - 402PP
O-Pee-Chee: 88/89 - 132; 90/91 - 299; 91/92 - 95
Panini: 90/91 - 319; 91/92 - 73
Parkhurst: 94/95 - 157, 157EI
Pro Set: 90/91 - 333; 91/92 - 434E, 434F
Score: 90/91 - 231A, 231C; 91 - 102T; 91/92 - 233B, 233C; 92/93 - 122C, 122A; 93/94 - 418C, 418A
Topps: 88/89 - 132; 90/91 - 299; 91/92 - 95, 202SC; 92/93 - 393, 393GS, 491SC
Upper Deck: 90/91 - 216E, 216F; 91/92 - 222E, 527E, 222F, 527F; 92/93 - 93; 93/94 - 524

McMahon, Mike
Bauer: 68/69 - 16
Coca Cola: 65/66 - 85
CKAC Radio: 43/47 - 69
Dad's Cookies: 70/71 - 19
Eddie Sargent: 70/71 - 28
O-Pee-Chee: 68/69 - 46; 70/71 - 143; 72/73 - 305
Quaker Oats: 45/54 - 36
Shirriff: 68/69 - E10
Topps: 65/66 - 24; 68/69 - 46

McManus, Sammy
World Wide Gum: 36/37 - 79

McNab, Max
Beehive: 45/63 - 123, 195

McNab, Peter
O-Pee-Chee: 75/76 - 252; 76/77 - 118; 77/78 - 18; 78/79 - 212; 79/80 - 39; 80/81 - 220; 81/82 - 5, 46SK; 82/83 - 16, 83SK, 84/85; 83/84 - 53, 51SK; 84/85 - 326; 85/86 - 244SK
Post: 82/83 - 9
Topps: 75/76 - 252; 76/77 - 118; 77/78 - 18; 78/79 - 212; 79/80 - 39; 80/81 - 220; 81/82 EN - 69; 82/83 - 83SK, 84SK; 83/84 - 51SK

McNamara, George
Hall of Fame: 83 -220, O10P; 87 - 220

McNamara, Harold
Imperial Tobacco: 10/11 - 32

McNeil, Gerry (Goalie)
Beehive: 45/63 - 273
Chex: 43/47 - 23
La Patrie: 51/54 - 4
Parkhurst: 51/52 - 15; 52/53 - 12; 53/54 - 25; 54/55 - 1; 55/56 - 52
Quaker Oats: 45/54 - 37; 55/56 - 52

McNeill, Billy
Parkhurst: 63/64 - 56; 93/94 - 48ML
Topps: 57/58 - 44; 59/60 - 41

McNeill, Michael
Bowman: 91/92 - 143; 92/93 - 424
O-Pee-Chee: 91/92 - 408
Pro Set: 90/91 - 600; 91/92 - 467E, 467F
Topps: 91/92 - 241SC, 408; 92/93 - 166, 166GS, 294SC
Upper Deck: 91/92 - 524E, 524F

McPhee, George
O-Pee-Chee: 85/86 - 252

McPhee, Michael (Mike)
Bowman: 90/91 - 43; 91/92 - 339; 92/93 - 89
Fleer: 92/93 - 322; 93/94 - 326PP
Kraft: 86/87P - 31; 86/87 - 31
O-Pee-Chee: 85/86 - 225; 86/87 - 221, 15SK; 88/89 - 237, 47SK; 89/90 - 84, 59SK; 90/91 - 137; 91/92 - 252; 91/92 - 252, 210SC; 92/93 - 199; 93/94 - 214, 6SC, 6FD
Panini: 87/88 - 66; 88/89 - 258; 89/90 - 243; 90/91 - 63; 91/92 - 188; 91/92 - 310
Parkhurst: 91/92 - 310E, 310F; 93/94 - 51, 51EI
Pro Set: 90/91 - 155; 91/92 - 129E, 129F
Score: 91/92 - 147A, 147B, 147C, 147PNE, 147PNF; 92/93 - 91C, 91A,342PNC, 342PNA; 93/94 - 85C, 85A
Topps: 89/90 - 84; 90/91 - 137; 92/93 - 45, 45GS, 452SC; 93/94 - 214(I), 6SC, 6FD
Upper Deck: 90/91 - 384E, 384F; 91/92 - 487E, 487F; 92/93 - 538; 93/94 - 43

McPherson, Jim
Quaker Oats: 45/54 - 134

McRae, Basil
Bowman: 90/91 - 187
Fleer: 93/94 - 430PP
O-Pee-Chee: 87/88 - 227SK89/90 - 216; 90/91 - 151
Panini: 89/90 - 109; 90/91 - 249; 91/92 - 119
Parkhurst: 92/93 - 391, 391EI
Pro Set: 90/91 - 141; 91/92 - 409E, 409F; 92/93 - 176
Score: 90/91 - 261A, 261C; 91/92 - 391B, 391C; 92/93 - 356C, 356A, 509C, 509A; 93/94 - 436C, 436A
Topps: 90/91 - 151; 93/94 - 273SC, 273FD
Upper Deck: 90/91 - 30E, 30F; 91/92 - 388E, 388F

McRae, Gord (Goalie)
O-Pee-Chee: 75/76 - 203; 76/77 - 337
Topps: 75/76 - 203

McRae, Ken
O-Pee-Chee: 90/91 - 411
Pro Set: 90/91 - 255

McReavy, Pat
Beehive: 34/44 - 24, 116

McReynolds, Brian
Upper Deck: 91/92 - 434E, 434F

McSheffrey, Bryan
Loblaws: 74/75 - 299
O-Pee-Chee: 73/74 - 219

McSorley, Martin (Marty)
Bowman: 91/92 - 184; 92/93 - 35
Donruss: 93/94 - 256, 447
Fleer: 92/93 - 310; 93/94 - 227, 191PP
Leaf: 93/94 - 352(II)
O-Pee-Chee: 87/88 - 205; 90/91 - 392; 91/92 - 225; 92/93 - 261; 93/94 - 395, 155SC, 155FD
Panini: 89/90 - 99; 90/91 - 234; 91/92 - 84; 92/93 - 73E, 73F, 208E, 208F
Parkhurst: 91/92 - 69E, 69F; 92/93 - 304, 304EI, CP17; 93/94 - 161, 161EI; 94/95 - 106, 106EI
Pro Set: 90/91 - 124; 91/92 - AC21, 100E, 100F, 184PT; 92/93 - 69
Score: 90/91 - 271A, 271C; 91/92 - 217A, 217B, 217C, 35PNE, 35PNF; 92/93 - 26C, 26A, 156PNC, 156PNA; 93/94 - 212C, 212A
Sega: 93/94 - 62
Topps: 90/91 - 392; 91/92 - 225, 267SC; 92/93 - 171, 171GS; 93/94 - 395(II), 155SC, 155FD, 8SCF
Upper Deck: 90/91 - 212E, 212F; 91/92 - 199E, 199F; 92/93 - 322; 93/94 - 487

McVeigh, Charley
Beehive: 34/44 - 242
Diamond: 33/35 - 45; 36/39 - 47(I)
O-Pee-Chee: 33/34 - 44
World Wide Gum: 33/34 - 38; 36/37 - 93

McVicar, Jack
La Presse: 27/32 - 55

Meagher, Richard (Rick)
O-Pee-Chee: 82/83 - 144; 88/89 - 235; 89/90 - 116; 90/91 - 125, 488; 91/92 - 58
Panini: 87/88 - 316; 88/89 - 110; 89/90 - 125; 90/91 - 273
Pro Set: 90/91 - 267, 389; 91/92 - MWCS3
Score: 90/91 - 267A, 267C, 359A, 359C
Topps: 89/90 - 116; 90/91 - 125; 91/92 - 58, 85SC
Upper Deck: 90/91 - 208E, 208F, 285E, 285F

Meehan, Gerry
Colgate: 70/71 - 20
Esso: 70/71 - 30
Eddie Sargent: 70/71 - 20; 72/73 - 29
Loblaws: 74/75 - 47
O-Pee-Chee: 70/71 - 125; 71/72 - 160; 72/73 - 22; 73/74 - 22; 74/75 - 99; 76/77 - 35; 77/78 - 53; 78/79 - 128
Topps: 70/71 - 125; 71/72 - 74; 72/73 - 16; 73/74 - 22; 74/75 - 99; 76/77 - 35; 77/78 - 53; 78/79 - 128
Toronto Sun: 71/72 - 34

Meeker, Howie
Beehive: 45/63 - 433
Parkhurst: 51/52 - 72; 52/53 - 42; 93/94 - 133ML
Quaker Oats: 45/54 - 176

Meger, Paul
Beehive: 45/63 - 274
La Patrie: 51/54 - 10
Parkhurst: 51/52 - 2; 52/53 - 4; 53/54 - 21; 55/56 - 51
Quaker Oats: 45/54 - 135; 55/56 - 51

Meissner, Dick
Beehive: 45/63 - 50
Shirriff: 60/61 - 111; 61/62 - 15
Topps: 61/62 - 6; 63/64 - 60

Melanson, Roland (Rollie) (Goalie)
Bowman: 92/93 - 187
O-Pee-Chee: 83/84 - 12, 88SK, 317SK;

Melanson, Roland (Rollie) (Goalie) (cont.)
O-Pee-Chee: 84/85 - 130, 387, 92SK; 85/86 - 230; 87/88 - 19, 213SK; 88/89 - 160, 151SK; 91/92 - 97PM
Panini: 87/88 - 271; 88/89 - 69
Topps: 83/84 - 88SK, 317SK; 87/88 - 19; 88/89 - 160; 92/93 - 298, 298GS, 184SC
Upper Deck: 91/92 - 575E, 575F

Mellanby, Scott
Bowman: 91/92 - 236I; 92/93 - 163
Donruss: 93/94 - 126
Durivage: 92/93 - 17; 93/94 - 46
Fleer: 92/93 - 295; 93/94 - 98PP
Leaf: 93/94 - 262(II)
O-Pee-Chee: 88/89 - 21; 89/90 - 253; 90/91 - 173; 91/92 - 200, 30PM; 92/93 - 140; 93/94 - 249, 31SC, 31FD
Panini: 88/89 - 322; 91/92 - 238; 93/94 - 243E, 243F
Parkhurst: 91/92 - 50E, 50F; 92/93 - 52, 52EI; 93/94 - 81, 82EI; 94/95 - 85, 85EI
Pro Set: 90/91 - 220; 91/92 - 172E, 383E, 172F, 383F, 173PT; 92/93 - 54
Score: 90/91 - 242A, 242C; 91 - 25T; 91/92 - 279A, 575B, 575C, 45PNE, 45PNF; 92/93 - 148C, 148A, 346PNC, 346PNA; 93/94 - 63C, 63A
Sega: 93/94 - 53
Topps: 88/89 - 21; 90/91 - 173; 91/92 - 200, 110SC; 92/93 - 444, 444GS, 462SC; 93/94 - 249(I), 31SC, 369SC, 31FD, 369FD
Upper Deck: 91/92 - 542E, 542F; 92/93 - 119; 93/94 - 107

Melnyk, Gerry
Beehive: 45/63 - 124, 196; 64/67 - 48
Shirriff: 60/61 - 51; 61/62 - 38
O-Pee-Chee: 68/69 - 120
Parkhurst: 60/61 - 28
Topps: 68/69 - 120

Melnyk, Larry
O-Pee-Chee: 86/87 - 95, 224SK; 88/89 - 53SK; 89/90 - 288, 73SK; 90/91 - 419
Panini: 87/88 - 111
Post: 82/83 - 10
Topps: 86/87 - 95

Meloche, Gilles (Goalie)
Eddie Sargent: 72/73 - 50
Loblaws: 74/75 - 66
McDonald's: 82/83 - 3
O-Pee-Chee: 72/73 - 112; 73/74 - 2; 74/75 - 205; 75/76 - 190; 76/77 - 36; 77/78 - 109; 78/79 - 28; 79/80 - 136; 80/81 - 47; 81/82 - 165, 93SK; 82/83 - 170, 195SK; 83/84 - 177; 84/85 - 104, 51SK; 87/88 - 107, 168SK; 88/89 - 8, 238SK
Panini: 87/88 - 140
Post: 82/83 - 138
Topps: 72/73 - 69; 73/74 - 175; 74/75 - 205; 75/76 - 190; 76/77 - 36; 77/78 - 109; 78/79 - 28; 79/80 - 136; 80/81 - 47; 81/82 WN - 109; 82/83 - 195SK; 84/85 - 79; 87/88 - 107; 88/89 - 8

Melrose, Barry
Kraft: 93/94 - 48
O-Pee-Chee: 79/80 - 386; 82/83 - 328
PepsiCo: 80/81 - 92
Post: 82/83 - 284

Menard, Howie
O-Pee-Chee: 69/70 - 73; 70/71 - 124
Topps: 70/71 - 124

Meredith, Greg
O-Pee-Chee: 83/84 - 88

Merrick, Wayne
Loblaws: 74/75 - 261
O-Pee-Chee: 74/75 - 66; 75/76 - 228; 76/77 - 18; 77/78 - 176; 78/79 - 258; 79/80 - 169; 80/81 - 345; 81/82 - 216; 82/83 - 205

Merrick, Wayne (cont.)
Post: 82/83 - 185
Topps: 74/75 - 66; 75/76 - 228; 76/77 - 18; 77/78 - 176; 78/79 - 258; 79/80 - 169

Messier, Joby
Fleer: 93/94 - 170, 6UR, 161PP
Leaf: 93/94 - 298(II)
O-Pee-Chee: 93/94 - 522
Parkhurst: 93/94 - 399, 399EI
Topps: 93/94 - 522(II), 339SC, 339FD
Upper Deck: 93/94 - 73

Messier, Mark
Bowman: 90/91 - 199, HT4; 91/92 - P/C, 114; 92/93 - 113, 234
Cel.Watch: 1988 - CW13
Donruss: 93/94 - 222, O/PM. O/SP
Esso: 83/84E - 13; 83/84F - 13; 88/89 - 30
Fleer: 92/93 - 139, 1AW, 10AW; 93/94 - 183, 9PL, 6PM
Frito-Lay: 88/89 - 23
Funmate: 83/84 - 42
Gillette: 91/92 - 31
Hockey Wit: 93/94 - 102
Humpty Dumpty: 92/93 - 15(II)
Kellogg's: 92/93 - 2P
Kraft: 86/87P - 18; 86/87 - 18; 1990 - 15; 90/91 - 32, 71; 91/92 - 16; 1993 - 23; 93/94 - 45
Leaf: 93/94 - 158
McDonald's: 80/81 - 289; 81/82 - 118, 210SK; 82/83 - 117, 94SK, 159SK; 83/84 - 39, 97SK, 98SK, 157SK; 84/85 - 213, 254, 5SK, 261SK; 85/86 - 177, 228SK; 86/87 - 186, 79SK; 87/88 - 112, 28HL, 92SK; 88/89 - 93, 25NS, 230SK; 89/90 - 65, 227SK; 90/91 - 130, 193, 519, 71PM; 91/92 - 346, 51PM; 92/93 - 208, 258, 13AN, 3BB, 15SP; 93/94 - 430, 35SC, 35FD
Panini: 87/88 - 263; 87/88 - 194; 88/89 - 61; 89/90 - 74; 90/91 - 219; 91/92 - 124; 92/93 - 233E, 233F; 93/94 - I(E), I(F)
Parkhurst: 91/92 - 121E, 213E, 121F, 213F, 468E, 475E; 92/93 - 111, 111EI, CP4; 93/94 - 127, 127EI, D4; 94/95 - V33
PepsiCo: 80/81 - 34
Post: 81/82 - 15; 82/83 - 94
Pro Set: 90/91 - 91, 349, 381, 386, 397; 91/92 - 74E, 282E, 439E, 579E, 74F, 282F, 81PT, 19PK, 439F, 579F; 92/93 - 111, CC1
Season's: 92/93 - 26
Sega: 93/94 - 87
Score: 90/91 - 10PC(A) 10PC(C),100A, 100C, 315A, 315C, 360A, 360C, 33HR; 91 - 85T; 91/92 - 285A, 373A, 420A, 263B, 310B, 505B, 635B, 263C, 310C, 505C, 635C, 50PNE, 50PNF; 92/93 - 300C, 300A, 431C, 431A, 493C, 493A, 521C, 521A, 1PNC, 1PNA; 93/94 - 200C, 200A
7-Eleven: 84/85 - 20
Topps: 82/83 - 94SK, 159SK; 83/84 - 97SK, 98SK, 157SK; 84/85 - 159; 86/87 - 186; 87/88 - 112; 88/89 - 93; 89/90 - 65; 90/91 - 130, 193, 16SL; 91/92 - 346, 111SC; 92/93 - 258, 274, 258GS, 274GS, 241SC, 443SC; 93/94 - 430(II), 35SC, 35FD
Upper Deck: 90/91 - S/G, 44E, 44F, 206E, 206F, 494E, 494F; 91/92 - BBE, 14E, 246E, 545E, 620E, BBF, 14F, 246F, 545F, 620F; 92/93 - 242, 432, 437, 7AS; 93/94 - 51, 298
Vechon Foods: 83/84 - 36

Metlyuk, Denis
Upper Deck: 91/92 - 653E, 653F

Metz, Don
Beehive: 34/44 - 339; 45/63 - 434
O-Pee-Chee: 39/40 - 8; 40/41 - 111
Quaker Oats: 45/54 - 90A, 90B

Metz, Nick
Amal. Press: 35/36 - 6
Beehive: 34/44 - 340; 45/63 - 435
O-Pee-Chee: 35/36 - 84; 37/38 - 144; 39/40 - 51; 40/41 - 133, 141
Quaker Oats: 38/39 - 27; 45/54 - 91A, 91B
World Wide Gum: 36/37 - 28

Micalef, Corrado (Goalie)
O-Pee-Chee: 83/84 - 116, 147SK; 83/84 - 126; 85/86 - 200
Topps: 83/84 - 147SK

Micheletti, Joe
Post: 82/83 - 171

Mickey, Larry
Dad's Cookies: 70/71 - 59
Eddie Sargent: 70/71 - 74
Esso: 70/71 - 102
Loblaws: 74/75 - 48
O-Pee-Chee: 68/69 - 195; 70/71 - 162; 71/72 - 167
Toronto Sun: 71/72 - 204

Mickoski, Nick
Beehive: 45/63 - 346
Parkhurst: 51/52 - 97; 52/53 - 101; 53/54 - 62; 54/55 - 75; 93/94 - 25ML
Topps: 54/55 - 29; 57/58 - 32; 58/59 - 27; 59/60 - 37

Middleton, Rick
Funmate: 83/84 - 3
Kellogg's: 84 - 28
McDonald's: 82/83 - 9
O-Pee-Chee: 74/75 - 304; 75/76 - 37; 76/77 - 127; 77/78 - 246; 78/79 - 113; 79/80 - 10; 80/81 - 251; 81/82 - 2, 18, 19, 45SK; 82/83 - 6, 15, 78SK, 79SK, 262SK; 83/84 - 43, 54, 214, 14SK, 44SK, 45SK, 329SK, 330SK; 84/85 - 9, 352, 142SK, 181SK, 182SK; 85/86 - 64, 159SK; 86/87 - 157, 35SK; 87/88 - 115, 138SK; 88/89 - 87, 26SK
Panini: 87/88 - 12
Post: 82/83 - 11
7-Eleven: 84/85 - 2
Topps: 75/76 - 37; 76/77 - 127; 77/78 - 246; 78/79 - 113; 79/80 - 10; 80/81 - 251; 81/82 - 22, 46; 81/82 EN - 129; 82/83 - 78SK, 79SK, 262SK; 83/84 - 14SK, 44SK, 45SK, 330SK; 84/85 - 8; 85/86 - 64; 86/87 - 157; 87/88 - 115; 88/89 - 87

Miehm, Kevin
Fleer: 93/94 - 205, 6TP
Parkhurst: 93/94 - 447, 447EI
Upper Deck: 92/93 - 543

Miettinen, Tommi
Parkhurst: 93/94 - 522, 522EI

Migay, Rudy
Beehive: 45/63 - 436
Parkhurst: 52/53 - 96; 53/54 - 17; 54/55 - 21; 55/56 - 12; 57/58 TOR - 6; 93/94 - 111ML
Quaker Oats: 45/54 - 92; 55/56 - 12
Shirriff: 60/61 - 18

Mikhailovsky, Maxim
O-Pee-Chee: 90/91 - 9R; 91/92 - 22R

Mikita, Stan
Beehive: 45/63 - 125; 64/67 - 49
Bazooka: 71/72 - 35
Coca Cola: 64/65 - 29; 65/66 - 30
Chex: 63/65 - 7
Dad's Cookies: 70/71 - 42
Esso: 70/71 - 66; 88/89 - 31
Eddie Sargent: 70/71 - 48; 72/73 - 63
Hall of Fame: 83 - 226; 87 - 226; 83 - O11
HHFM: 92 - 15
Hockey Wit: 93/94 - 39
Kellogg's: 70 - 6
Loblaws: 74/75 - 84
O-Pee-Chee: 68/69 - 155, 202, 211, 1PS; 69/70 - 76, 21ST, 13QS; 70/71 - 20,

Mikita, Stan (cont.)
O-Pee-Chee: 240, 23SS; 71/72 - 125; 72/73 - 156, 177, 5CS; 73/74 - 6; 74/75 - 20; 75/76 - 30; 76/77 - 225; 77/78 - 195; 78/79 - 75; 79/80 - 155
Post: 66/67L - 7; 67.68L - 5; 67/68S - 4
Pro Set: 90/91 - 405, 655
Shirriff: 60/61 - 71; 61/62 - 22; 62/63 - 46; 68/69 - B9
1981 - 13
Topps: 60/61 - 14, 23ST; 61/62 - 36; 62/63 - 34, 14HB; 63/64 - 36; 64/65 - 31 ,106; 65/66 - 60; 66/67 - 62, 124; 66/67 US - 62; 67/68 - 64, 114, 126; 68/69 - 20; 69/70 - 76; 70/71 - 20, 23SK; 71/72 - 125; 72/73 - 56; 73/74 - 145; 74/75 - 20, 75/76 - 30; 76/77 - 225; 77/78 - 195; 78/79 - 75; 79/80 - 155
Toronto Star: 57/67 - 97, 113; 58/67 - 64, 96; 63/64 - 7; 64/65 - 14
Toronto Sun: 71/72 - 76
Upper Deck: 92/93 - 46AS
Zellers: 92/93 - 6, 6A

Mikkelson, Bill
Loblaws: 74/75 - 322
O-Pee-Chee: 72/73 - 79; 74/75 - 23; 75/76 - 207
Topps: 72/73 - 118; 74/75 - 23; 75/76 - 207

Miklenda, Jaroslav
Parkhurst: 93/94 - 519, 519EI
Upper Deck: 93/94 - 573

Mikol, Jim
Beehive: 45/63 - 437; 64/67 - 142
Coca Cola: 64/65 - 85
Topps: 64/65 - 36

Milbury, Mike
O-Pee-Chee: 77/78 - 134; 78/79 - 59; 79/80 - 114; 80/81 - 191; 81/82 - 16; 83/84 - 55; 84/85 - 10
Panini: 87/88 - 8
Post: 82/83 - 12
Topps: 77/78 - 134; 78/79 - 59; 79/80 - 114; 80/81 - 191
Pro Set: 90/91 - 661

Milford, Jake
Hall of Fame: 87 - 253

Milks, Heb (Hibbert)
Anonymous: 1925/26 - 52; 26/27 - 48

Millen, Corey
Bowman: 91/92 - 60; 92/93 - 57
Donruss: 93/94 - 181
Fleer: 92/93 - 86; 93/94 - 379PP
Leaf: 93/94 - 361(II)
O-Pee-Chee: 91/92 - 461; 92/93 - 334; 93/94 - 493
Panini: 92/93 - 70E, 70F; 93/94 - 207E, 207F
Parkhurst: 91/92 - 292E, 292F; 92/93 - 306, 306EI; 93/94 - 381, 381EI; 94/95 - 122, 122EI
Pro-Set: 91/92 - 185PT
Score: 91/92 - 318A, 348B, 348C; 92/93 - 111C, 111A, 138PNC, 138PNA, 26CSS, 26ASS; 93/94 - 62C, 62A
Topps: 91/92 - 461, 71SC; 92/93 - 326, 326GS, 296SC; 93/94 - 493(II), 437SC, 437FD
Upper Deck: 91/92 - 110E, 110F, 604E; 92/93 - 48; 93/94 - 483

Millen, Greg (Goalie)
Bowman: 90/91 - 3
Funmate: 83/84 - 47
O-Pee-Chee: 79/80 - 281; 80/81 - 158; 81/82 - 134; 82/83 - 126, 130SK; 83/84 - 143, 262SK; 84/85 - 75, 198SK; 85/86 - 221, 51SK; 88/89 - 117; 89/90 - 137; 90/91 - 335
Panini: 88/89 - 100; 89/90 - 129; 90/91 - 188
Post: 82/83 - 106
Pro Set: 90/91 - 56
Score: 90/91 - 42A, 42C
Topps: 80/81 - 158; 81/82 EN - 115; 82/83 - 130SK; 83/84 - 262SK;

Millen, Greg (Goalie) (cont.)
Topps: 84/85 - 58; 88/89 - 117; 89/90 - 137; 90/91 - 335
Upper Deck: 90/91 - 213E, 213F

Miller, Bob
O-Pee-Chee: 79/80 - 196; 80/81 - 236
Post: 82/83 - 172
Topps: 79/80 - 196; 80/81 - 236

Miller, Brad
Parkhurst: 91/92 - 243E, 243F; 93/94 - 306, 306EI
Pro Set: 90/91 - 591; 91/92 - 354E, 354F
Topps: 92/93 - 475SC

Miller, Earl
La Presse: 27/32 - 49

Miller, Jason
O-Pee-Chee: 91/92 - 163
Score: 91/92 - 312A, 342B, 342C
Topps: 91/92 - 163
Upper Deck: 90/91 - 335E, 335F

Miller, Jay
Bowman: 91/92 - 178
O-Pee-Chee: 91/92 - 467
Panini: 87/88 - 18; 88/89 - 212
Pro Set: 91/92 - 402E, 402F
Score: 91/92 - 543B, 543C
Topps: 91/92 - 467, 63SC
Upper Deck: 90/91 - 414E, 414F

Miller, Kelly
Bowman: 90/91 - 76; 91/92 - 292; 92/93 - 338
Donruss: 93/94 - 365
Fleer: 92/93 - 236, 396; 93/94 - 88, 468PP
Leaf: 93/94 - 254(II)
O-Pee-Chee: 87/88 - 189; 88/89 - 130; 89/90 - 131, 74SK; 90/91 - 81, 72PM; 91/92 - 342; 92/93 - 142; 93/94 - 474, 17SC, 17FD
Panini: 87/88 - 186; 88/89 - 373; 89/90 - 348; 90/91 - 156; 91/92 - 202; 92/93 - 166E, 166F; 93/94 - 30E, 30F
Parkhurst: 91/92 - 414E, 414F; 93/94 - 491, 491EI; 94/95 - 256, 256EI
Pro Set: 90/91 - 318; 91/92 - 256E, 611E, 615E, 256F, 611F, 615F
Score: 90/91 - 168A, 168C; 91/92 - 81A, 81B, 339B, 81C, 339C, 23PNE, 372PNE, 23PNF, 372PNF, 14USG; 92/93 - 55C, 55A, 160PNC, 160PNA; 93/94 - 30C, 30A
Topps: 87/88 - 189; 88/89 - 130; 89/90 - 131; 90/91 - 81; 91/92 - 342, 106SC; 92/93 - 479, 479GS, 361SC; 93/94 - 474(II), 17SC, 17FD
Upper Deck: 90/91 - 130E, 130F; 91/92 - 133E, 133F; 92/93 - 179; 93/94 - 384

Miller, Kevin
Bowman: 91/92 - 57; 92/93 - 391
Donruss: 93/94 - 298
Fleer: 94/92 - 218, 215PP
Leaf: 93/94 - 192
O-Pee-Chee: 90/91 - 73PM; 91/92 - 125; 92/93 - 291; 93/94 - 8, 193SC, 193FD
Panini: 92/93 - 115E, 115F
Parkhurst: 94/94 - 40E, 40F; 93/94 - 178, 178EI
Pro Set: 90/91 - 493; 91/92 - 60E, 60F; 168PT
Score: 90 - 18T; 91 - 40YS; 91/92 - 126A, 126B, 126C, 133PNE, 133PNF; 92/93 - 229C, 229A, 313PNC, 313PNA; 93/94 - 89C, 89A
Topps: 91/92 - 125, 286SC; 92/93 - 129, 129GS, 229SC; 93/94 - 8(I), 193SC, 193FD
Upper Deck: 90/91 - 444E, 444F; 91/92 - 142E, 142F; 92/93 - 482; 93/94 - 408

Miller, Kip
Bowman: 91/92 - 139
O-Pee-Chee: 91/92 - 387, 42PM
Parkhurst: 91/92 - 142E, 142F
Pro Set: 91/92 - 555E, 555F
Score: 90 - 330A; 91/92 - 384A, 274B, 274C, 306PNE, 306PNF
Topps: 91/92 - 387

Miller, Kip (cont.)
Upper Deck: 90/91 - 522E, 522F; 91/92 - 431E, 431F; 92/93 - 247; 93/94 - 421

Miller, Perry
O-Pee-Chee: 78/79 - 16; 79/80 - 157; 81/82 - 101
Topps: 78/79 - 16; 79/80 - 157

Miller, Tom
Eddie Sargent: 72/73 - 137
O-Pee-Chee: 72/73 - 32; 73/74 - 249
Topps: 72/73 - 76

Miller, Warren
O-Pee-Chee: 81/82 - 130; 82/83 - 127
Post: 82/83 - 107
Topps: 81/82 EN - 84

Minor, Gerry
O-Pee-Chee: 81/82 - 342; 82/83 - 352
PepsiCo: 80/81 - 116

Mio, Ed (Goalie)
O-Pee-Chee: 80/81 - 341; 81/82 - 119, 216SK; 82/83 - 230, 142SK; 83/84 - 127, 209SK; 84/85 - 61
PepsiCo: 80/81 - 35
Topps: 82/83 - 142SK; 83/84 - 209SK; 84/85 - 45
Upper Deck: 91/92 - 639E, 639F

Mironov, Boris
Donruss: 93/94 - 384, 429, 9RR
Fleer: 93/94 - 6RS, 474PP
Leaf: 93/94 - 364
O-Pee-Chee: 93/94 - 394
Parkhurst: 93/94 - 264, 264EI; 94/95 - 279, 279EI
Topps: 93/94 - 394, 338SC, 338FD
Upper Deck: 91/92 - 662E, 662F; 93/94 - 492

Mironov, Dimitri
Fleer: 92/93 - 422, 15UI; 93/94 - 127, 245PP
O-Pee-Chee: 90/91 - 514; 91/92 - 515, 23R; 92/93 - 71; 93/94 - 419
Parkhurst: 91/92 - 391E, 391F; 92/93 - 417, 417EI; 93/94 - 477, 477EI
Score: 92/93 - 468C, 468A, 419PNC, 419PNA; 93/94 - 209C, 209A
Topps: 91/92 - 515; 92/93 - 144, 144GS, 5SC; 93/94 - 419(II)
Upper Deck: 92/93 - 83; 93/94 - 513

Miszuk, John
Shirriff: 68/69 - J2
O-Pee-Chee: 68/69 - 93; 69/70 - 124, 3QS
Topps: 68/69 - 93; 69/70 - 124

Mitchell Red
Beehive: 34/44 - 70

Mitchell, Herb
Anonymous: 26/27 - 38
Champ's: 24/25 - 5
Wm. Paterson: 24/25 - 29

Modano, Michael (Mike)
Bowman: 90/91 - 188; 91/92 - 125; 92/93 - 151
Donruss: 93/94 - 76,F/PM, F/SP
Fleer: 92/93 - 96; 93/94 - 194, 8SA, 63PP
Kellogg's: 92 - 4
Gillette: 91/92 - 15
Hockey Wit: 93/94 - 60
Kraft: 90/91 - 34; 91/92 - 48
Leaf: 93/94 - 202
O-Pee-Chee: 90/91 - 348, F/BB, 74PM; 91/92 - 367; 92/93 - 313; 93/94 - 46, 6HR, 130SC, 130FD
Panini: 90/91 - 340, 253; 91/92 - 116; 92/93 - 91E, 91F; 93/94 - X(E), X(F)
Parkhurst: 91/92 - 81E, 81F; 92/93 - 75, 75EI; 93/94 - 49, 49EI, F6; 94/95 - 308, 308EI, H6, R6, C6, V2
Pro Set: 90/91 - 142; 91/92 - 105E, 105F, 55PT; 92/93 - 76, 7TL
Score: 90 - 20YS; 90/91 - 120A, 120C, 327A, 327C, 97HR; 91 - 35YS; 91/92 - 247A, 423A, 313B, 313C, 467B, 467C, 5PNE, 5PNF; 92/93 - 139C,139A, 427C, 427A, 155PNC, 260PNC, 155PNA,

Modano, Michael (Mike) (cont.)
- Score: 260PNA, 5USG, 2CT, 2AT; 93/94 - 142C,142A, 28PNC, 28PNA, 28CAS, 28AAS, 5FR
- Season's: 92/93 - 65
- Sega: 93/94 - 33
- Topps: 90/91 - 348, F/BB; 91/92 - 367, 187SC; 92/93 - 441, 441GS, 4SC; 93/94 - 46(I), 6PF,130SC, 130FD, 19AS
- Upper Deck: 90/91 - 46E, 46F, 346E, 346F; 91/92 - 32E, 160E, 32F, 160F; 92/93 - 9, 305, 31AS; 93/94 - 294, 397

Modry, Jaroslav
- Donruss: 93/94 - 455
- Fleer: 93/94 - 7RS, 380PP
- O-Pee-Chee: 93/94 - 307
- Parkhurst: 93/94 - 386, 386EI; 94/95 - 123, 290, 123EI, 290EI
- Topps: 93/94 - 307(II), 411SC, 411FD
- Upper Deck: 93/94 - 319

Moe, Billy
- Beehive: 45/63 - 347

Moffat, Lyle
- O-Pee-Chee: 74/75 - 379; 79/80 - 277

Mogilny, Alexander
- Bowman: 90/91 - 240; 91/92 - 30; 92/93 - 34, 235
- Donruss: 93/94 - 39, 8ES, C/PM, C/SP
- Fleer: 93/94 - 18, 16UI; 93/94 - 238, 5GG, 5AS, 32PP, 10PL, 7RL, 7SM
- Hockey Wit: 93/94 - 75
- Humpty Dumpty: 92/93 - 16(I)
- Kraft: 91/92 - 60
- Leaf: 93/94 - 91, 2HT, 8AS
- O-Pee-Chee: 90/91 - 42, A/BB, 75PM; 91/92 - 171; 92/93 - 279; 93/94 - 148, 172, 245, 91SC, 91FD
- Panini: 90/91 - 338; 91/92 - 304; 92/93 - 248E, 299E, 248F, 299F; 93/94 - J(E), J(F), 172
- Parkhurst: 91/92 - 12E, 12F; 92/93 - 13, 13EI, 218, 218EI; 93/94 - 21, 21EI; 94/95 - 21, 21EI
- Pro Set: 90/91 - 26; 91/92 - 16E, 16F, 14PT, 283PT; 92/93 - 19
- Score: 90 - 26YS; 90/91 - 43A, 43C; 91 - 13YS; 91/92 - 236A, 456B, 456C, 163PNE, 163PNF; 92/93 - 248C, 248A, 77PNC, 77PNA, 28CT, 28AT; 93/94 - 222C, 222A, 22PNC, 22PNA, 20DT, 22CAS, 22AAS
- Sega: 93/94 - 17, 191
- Topps: 90/91 - 42, A/BB; 91/92 - 171, 195SC; 92/93 - 382, 382GS, 320SC; 93/94 - 148(I), 172(I), 245(I), 91SC, 91FD, 15AS
- Upper Deck: 90/91 - 24E, 24F; 91/92 - 267E, 618E, E2(E), 267F, 618F, E2(F); 92/93 - 167, WJG18, 8AS; 93/94 - 234, 488

Mohns, Doug
- Bauer: 68/69 - 17
- Beehive: 45/63 - 51; 64/67 - 50
- Coca Cola: 64/65 - 30; 65/66 - 31
- Dad's Cookies: 70/71 - 43
- Esso: 70/71 - 67
- Eddie Sargent: 70/71 - 47; 72/73 - 102
- Loblaws: 74/75 - 323
- Shirriff: 60/61 - 106; 61/62 - 10; 68/69 - B8
- O-Pee-Chee: 68/69 - 19; 69/70 - 72, 14QS; 70/71 - 16, 29DE; 71/72 - 242; 72/73 - 75; 73/74 - 241; 74/75 - 181
- Parkhurst: 54/55 - 57; 93/94 - 18ML
- Topps: 54/55 - 18; 57/58 - 12; 58/59 - 50; 59/60 - 58; 60/61 - 52, 5ST; 61/62 - 10; 62/63 - 6, 6HB; 63/64 - 3; 64/65 - 25; 65/66 - 118; 66/67 - 61; 66/67 US - 61; 67/68 - 63; 68/69 - 19; 69/70 - 72; 70/71 - 16, 72/73 - 78; 74/75 - 181
- Toronto Star: 57/67 - 136; 58/67 - 60, 105

Mohns, Doug (cont.)
- Toronto Sun: 71/72 - 137
- Ultimate: 92 - 53(OSE), 53(OSF)

Molin, Lars
- O-Pee-Chee: 82/83 - 353, 245SK
- Post: 82/83 - 300
- Topps: 82/83 - 245SK
- Vachon Foods: 83/84 - 113

Moller, Randy
- Bowman: 91/92 - 58
- Kraft: 86/87P - 48; 86/87 - 48
- O-Pee-Chee: 83/84 - 297, 248SK; 84/85 - 284, 174SK; 85/86 - 240, 145SK; 87/88 - 251, 229SK;89/90 - 259, 195SK; 90/91 - 515; 91/92 - 371
- Panini: 87/88 - 162; 88/89 - 351; 89/90 - 331
- Pro Set: 90/91 - 202; 91/92 - 163E, 163F
- Score: 90/91 - 45A, 45C; 91/92 - 79A, 79B, 79C, 256PNE, 256PNF; 92/93 - 289C, 289A, 176PNC, 176PNA; 93/94 - 422C, 422A
- Topps: 83/84 - 248SK; 91/92 - 371, 2SC; 92/93 - 407, 407GS, 484SC; 93/94 - 435SC, 435FD
- Upper Deck: 90/91 - 418E, 418F
- Vachon Foods: 83/84 - 69

Momesso, Sergio
- Bowman: 90/91 - 17; 91/92 - 309; 92/93 - 316
- Donruss: 93/94 - 349
- Durivage: 92/93 - 26; 93/94 - 33
- Fleer: 92/93 - 225; 93/94 - 47
- Kraft: 86/87P - 32; 86/87 - 32
- Leaf: 93/94 - 250(II)
- O-Pee-Chee: 90/91 - 244; 91/92 - 462, 55PM; 92/93 - 377; 93/94 - 6
- Panini: 90/91 - 263; 91/92 - 185F, 185F; 92/93 - 421, 421EI; 93/94 - 212, 212EI; 94/95 - 249, 249EI
- Pro Set: 90/91 - 268; 91/92 - 242E, 242F, 240PT; 92/93 - 194
- Score: 90/91 - 224A, 224C; 91/92 - 121A, 121B, 121C, 34PNE, 34PNF; 92/93 - 79C, 79A, 163PNC, 163PNA; 93/94 - 255C. 255A
- Topps: 90/91 - 244; 91/92 - 462, 17SC; 92/93 - 214, 214GS, 42SC; 93/94 - 323SC, 323FD
- Upper Deck: 90/91 - 19E, 19F; 91/92 - 571E, 571F; 92/93 - 85; 93/94 - 104

Molson, Hartland
- Hall of Fame: 83 - 221; 87 - 221

Molson, Sen. H.
- Hall of Fame: 83 - O12P

Molyneau, Larry
- Beehive: 34/44 - 288

Monahan, Garry
- Colgate: 70/71 - 13
- Esso: 70/71 - 228
- Eddie Sargent: 70/71 - 207; 72/73 - 202
- O-Pee-Chee: 69/70 - 160; 70/71 - 112; 72/73 - 207; 73/74 - 226; 75/76 - 357; 76/77 - 295; 77/78 - 341; 78/79 - 268
- Topps: 67/68 - 8; 70/71 - 112
- Toronto Sun: 71/72 - 266

Monahan, Hartland
- O-Pee-Chee: 76/77 - 203; 77/78 - 96; 78/79 - 393
- Topps: 76/77 - 203; 77/78 - 96

Mondou, Armand
- Anonymous: 33/34 - 44
- Beehive: 34/44 - 169
- Canada Starch: 35/40 - 125
- Diamond: 36/39 - 48(I), 48(II), 45(III)
- La Presse: 27/32 - 30
- O-Pee-Chee: 33/34 - 48; 37/38 - 177; 39/40 - 27
- Sweet Caporal: 34/35 - 23
- World Wide Gum: 33/34 - 17

Mondou, Pierre
- Derniere: 72/84 - 135, 194
- O-Pee-Chee: 78/79 - 102; 79/80 - 211; 80/81 - 42; 81/82 - 188; 82/83 - 188, 35SK; 83/84 - 191, 68SK; 84/85 - 266, 162SK; 85/86 - 211, 133SK
- PepsiCo: 80/81 - 52
- Post: 82/83 - 153
- Topps: 78/79 - 102; 79/80 - 211; 80/81 - 42; 82/83 - 35SK; 83/84 - 68SK
- Vachon Foods: 83/84 - 49

Mongeau, Michel
- Fleer: 92/93 - 203
- Score: 90/91 - 395A, 395C; 92/93 - 388PNC, 388PNA
- Topps: 92/93 - 415SC
- Upper Deck: 90/91 - 345E, 345F; 91/92 - 213E, 213F

Montgomery, Jim
- Donruss: 93/94 - 300, 13RR
- Fleer: 93/94 - 431PP
- O-Pee-Chee: 93/94 - 488
- Parkhurst: 93/94 - 176, 176EI; 94/95 - 198, 198EI
- Topps: 93/94 - 488(II)
- Upper Deck: 93/94 - 472

Moog, Andrew (Andy) (Goalie)
- Bowman: 90/91 - 35; 91/92 - 361; 92/93 - 79
- Donruss: 93/94 - 87
- Fleer: 92/93 - 6; 93/94 - 2, 64PP
- Gillette: 91/92 - 29
- Kellogg's: 92 - 10
- Kraft: 86/87 - 19P; 86/76 - 19; 90/91 - 35; 91/92 - 59
- Leaf: 93/94 - 369(II)
- McDonald's: 91/92 - Mc9
- O-Pee-Chee: 81/82 - 120; 83/84 - 40, 99SK, 155SK; 84/85 - 255, 262SK; 85/86 - 12, 123SK, 220SK; 86/87 - 212, 66SK; 87/88 - 204, 93SK; 89/90 - 160, 30SK; 90/91 - 294, 76PM; 91/92 - 338, 133PM; 92/93 - 184; 93/94 - 476
- Panini: 87/88 - 255; 89/90 - 191; 90/91 - 11; 981/92 - 179; 92/93 - 135E, 135F; 93/94 - 9E, 9F
- Parkhurst: 91/92 - 8E, 8F; 92/93 - 3, 3EI; 93/94 - 47, 47EI; 94/95 - 51, 51EI
- Pro Set: 90/91 - 10; 91/92 - 10E, 299E, 10F, 299F, 4PT, 2PK, PC; 92/93 - 7
- Score: 90/91 - 140A, 140C, 62HR; 91/92 - 90A, 90B, 90C, 126PNE, 379PNE, 126PNF, 379PNF; 92/93 - 120C, 120A, 91PNC, 91PNA, 263PNC, 263PNA; 93/94 - 11C, 11A
- Season's: 92/93 - 19
- Sega: 93/94 - 12
- Topps: 83/84 - 99SK, 155SK; 85/86 - 12; 89/90 - 160; 90/91 - 294; 91/92 - 338, 211SC; 92/93 - 394, 394GS, 430SC; 93/94 - 476(II), 470SC, 470FD
- Upper Deck: 90/91 - 209E, 209F, 232E, 232F; 91/92 - 147E, 147F; 92/93 - 1, 329; 93/94 - 478
- Vachon Foods: 83/84 - 37

Moore, Dickie
- Beehive: 45/63 - 275; 64/67 - 176
- Coca Cola: 64/65 - 103
- Derniere: 72/84 - 69
- Hall of Fame: 83 - 190, J10P; 87 - 190
- La Patrie: 51/54 - 15
- Parkhurst: 52/53 - 10; 53/54 - 28; 54/55 - 2; 55/56 - 38; 57/58 MON - 14; 58/59 - 8; 59/60 - 14; 60/61 - 38; 61/62 - 36; 62/63 - 42; 92/93 - PR26, 70ML
- Quaker Oats: 45/54 - 40; 55/56 - 38
- Shirriff: 60/61 0 22; 61/62 - 107; 62/63 - 37
- Toronto Star: 57/67 - 91; 58/67 - 15; 64 - 20
- York: 60/61 - 13; 61/62 - 5; 62/63 - 22

Moran, Ian
- Fleer: 93/94 - 512PP
- Topps: 93/94 - 2US

Moran, Paddy (Goalie)
- Hall of Fame: 83 - 144, K10P; 87 - 144
- Imperial Tobacco: 10/11 - 1L, 28; 11/12 - 1; 12/13 - 18
- Topps: 60/61 - 2, 46ST

More, Jayson
- Bowman: 92/93 - 388
- O-Pee-Chee: 92/93 - 312; 93/94 - 227, 208SC, 208FD
- Parkhurst: 91/92 - 387E, 387F; 92/93 - 394, 394EI; 93/94 - 452, 452EI
- Pro-Set: 92/93 - 169
- Score: 91/92 - 342PNE, 342PNF; 92/93 - 147C, 147A
- Topps: 92/93 - 245, 245GS, 60SC; 93/94 - 227(I), 208SC, 208FD
- Upper Deck: 92/93 - 488

Morel, Denis (Official)
- Pro Set: 90/91 - 695

Morenz Jr., Howie
- World Wide Gum: 36/37 - 100

Morenz Sr., Howie
- Anonymous: 26/27 - 9
- Beehive: 34/44 - 170
- Canada Starch: 35/40 - 57
- Can. Chew. Gum.: 33/34 - 38
- Champ's: 24/25 - 26
- Diamond: 33/35 - 46; 36/39 - 49(I), 49(II), 46(III)
- Goudy Gum: 33 - 24
- Hall of Fame: 83 - 106, H12P; 87 - 106
- Hamilton Gum: 33/34 - 8
- La Presse: 1927/32 - 1
- Maple Crispette: 24/25 - 12
- O-Pee-Chee: 33/34 - 23; 36/37 - 121
- Pro Set: 91/92 - 336E, 336F
- Parkhurst: 55/56 - 57
- Quaker Oats: 55/56 - 57
- Sweet Caporal: 34/35 - 7
- Topps: 60/61 - 59, 47ST
- Wm. Paterson: 23/24 - 15; 24/25 - 47; 33/34 - 41
- World Wide Gum: 33/34P - 4; 33/34 - 36; 36/37 - 18

Morin Pete
- Beehive: 34/44 - 171
- World Wide Gum: 36/67 - 129

Morin, Stephane
- Bowman: 91/92 - 148
- Durivage: 92/93 - 9
- O-Pee-Chee: 91/92 - 159
- Panini: 91/92 - 263; 92/93 - 214E, 214F
- Parkhurst: 91/92 - 147E, 147F
- Pro Set: 91/92 - 201E, 201F, 100PT
- Score: 91 - 39YS; 91/92 - 361A, 254B, 254C, 245PNE, 245PNF
- Topps: 91/92 - 159, 216SC; 92/93 - 316, 316GS, 469SC
- Upper Deck: 90/91 - 524E, 524F; 91/92 - 433E, 433F

Morris, Elwyn
- Beehive: 45/63 - 348
- Quaker Oats: 45/54 - 93

Morris, Jon
- Bowman: 90/91 - 84; 91/92 - 286
- O-Pee-Chee: 90/91 - 457; 91/92 - 332
- Pro Set: 90/91 - 621; 91/92 - 424E, 424F
- Score: 90/91 - 401A, 401C; 91/92 - 548B, 548C
- Topps: 91/92 - 332, 360SC
- Upper Deck: 90/91 - 65E, 65F; 91/92 - 216E, 216F

Morrison, Don
- Beehive: 45/63 - 126, 197

Morrison, George
- Esso: 70/71 - 207
- O-Pee-Chee: 71/72 - 223; 72/73 - 314
- Toronto Sun: 71/72 - 241

Morrison, Jim
- Beehive: 45/63 - 438
- Eddie Sargent: 70/71 - 169
- Esso: 70/71 - 189
- O-Pee-Chee: 69/70 - 156; 70/71 - 90
- Quaker Oats: 45/54 - 94; 55/56 - 8

Morrison, Jim (cont.)
- Parkhurst: 52/53 - 28; 53/54 - 15; 54/55 - 18; 55/56 - 8; 57/58 TOR - 11; 60/61 - 61; 93/94 - 115ML
- Shirriff: 60/61 - 95
- Topps: 59/60 - 36; 60/61 - 9; 70/71 - 90

Morrison, Lew
- Esso: 70/71 - 176
- Eddie Sargent: 72/73 - 13
- Loblaws: 74/75 - 324
- O-Pee-Chee: 70/71 - 197; 71/72 - 89; 72/73 - 143; 74/75 - 125; 76/77 - 307; 77/78 - 300
- Topps: 72/73 - 58; 74/75 - 125

Morrison, Roderick
- Beehive: 45/63 - 198

Morrow, Ken
- O-Pee-Chee: 80/81 - 9; 81/82 - 205, 165SK; 82/83 - 206, 58SK; 83/84 - 13, 73SK; 84/85 - 131, 93SK; 85/86 - 93; 86/87 - 65, 215SK; 87/88 - 66, 246SK; 88/89 - 53
- Panini: 87/88 - 94; 88/89 - 285
- Post: 82/83 - 186
- Topps: 80/81 - 9; 81/82 EN - 91; 82/83 - 58SK; 83/84 - 73SK; 84/85 - 97, 93SK; 85/86 - 93; 86/87 - 65; 87/88 - 66; 88/89 - 53
- Upper Deck: 91/92 - 637E, 637F

Mortson, Gus
- Beehive: 45/63 - 127, 439
- Parkhurst: 51/52 - 73; 52/53 - 39; 53/54 - 81; 54/55 - 81; 93/94 - 30ML
- Quaker Oats: 45/54 - 95A, 95B
- Topps: 54/55 - 17; 57/58 - 25; 58/59 - 38
- Toronto Star: 58/67 - 3

Mosdell, Kenny
- Beehive: 34/44 - 243; 45/63 - 276
- CKAC Radio: 43/47 - 70
- La Patrie: 51/54 - 8
- Parkhurst: 51/52 - 11; 52/53 - 8; 53/54 - 33; 54/55 - 12; 55/56 - 39; 93/94 - 41ML
- Quaker Oats: 45/54 - 41A, 41B, 41C; 55/56 - 39

Mosienko, Bill
- Beehive: 45/63 - 128
- Hall of Fame: 83 - 11, A11P; 87 - 11
- Parkhurst: 51/52 - 49; 52/53 - 27; 53/54 - 80; 92/93 - PR20
- Topps: 54/55 - 54
- Ultimate: 92 - 61(OSE), 61(OSF)

Motkov, Dimitri
- O-Pee-Chee: 90/91 - 5R

Mott, Morris
- O-Pee-Chee: 74/75 - 48
- Topps: 74/75 - 48

Motter, Alex
- Beehive: 34/44 - 25, 117
- O-Pee-Chee: 40/41 - 115

Mowers, Johnny
- Beehive: 34/44 - 119
- O-Pee-Chee: 40/41 - 105

Moxey, Jim
- O-Pee-Chee: 76/77 - 349

Muckler, John
- Kraft: 93/94 - 49
- Pro Set: 90/91 - 665

Muir, Jimmy
- World Wide Gum: 36/37 - 128

Mulhern, Richard
- O-Pee-Chee: 76/77 - 265; 77/78 - 373; 78/79 - 256; 79/80 - 133; 80/81 - 350
- Topps: 78/79 - 256; 79/80 - 133

Mullen, Brian
- Bowman: 90/91 - 217; 91/92 - 61; 92/93 - 139
- Fleer: 92/93 - 348
- Funmate: 83/84 - 147

Mullen, Brian (cont.)
- Kraft: 86/87P - 78; 86/87 - 78
- O-Pee-Chee: 83/84 - 389, 148SK; 84/85 - 344; 85/86 - 195; 86/87 - 38, 109SK; 88/89 - 91; 89/90 - 24, 243SK; 90/91 - 292; 91/92 - 129, 166PM; 92/93 - 260, 111PM; 93/94 - 154, 227SC, 227FD
- Panini: 89/90 - 286; 90/91 - 96; 91/92 - 289; 92/93 - 125E, 125F; 93/94 - 61E, 61F
- Parkhurst: 91/92 - 166E, 166F
- Pro Set: 90/91 - 203; 91/92 - 165E, 165F, 106PT
- 7-Eleven: 84/86 - 60
- Score: 90/91 - 84A, 84C; 91 - 2T; 91/92 - 59A, 59B, 59C, 552B, 552C, 135PNE, 135PNF; 92/93 - 278C, 278A, 333PNC, 333PNA, 12USG; 93/94 - 347C, 347A
- Topps: 83/84 - 148SK; 86/87 - 38; 88/89 - 91; 89/90 - 24; 90/91 - 292; 91/92 - 129, 222SC; 92/93 - 104, 104GS, 420SC; 93/94 - 154, 227SC, 227FD
- Upper Deck: 90/91 - 182E, 182F; 91/92 - 57E, 57F; 92/93 - 317, 468
- Vachon Foods: 83/84 - 134

Mullen, Corey
- O-Pee-Chee: 92/93 - 334

Mullen, Joe
- Bowman: 90/91 - 97; 91/92 - 79; 92/93 - 58
- Cel.Watch: 1988 - CW8
- Donruss: 93/94 - 257
- Fleer: 92/93 - 166; 93/94 - 171, 192PP
- Hockey Wit: 93/94 - 78
- Kraft: 86/87P - 4; 86/87 - 4; 1990 - 60; 90/91 - 36; 90/91 - 72
- Leaf: 93/94 - 300
- O-Pee-Chee: 82/83 - 307, 200SK; 83/84 - 317; 84/85 - 188, 61SK; 85/86 - 7, 47SK; 86/87 - 44, 82SK; 87/88 - 126, 29HL, G/BB, 36SK, 186SK; 88/89 - 76, 95SK; 89/90 - 196, 324, O/BB, 90SK, 160SK, 214SK, 23FS;90/91 - 218, 77PM; 91/92 - 69, 153PM; 92/93 - 23; 93/94 - 498, 19SC, 19FD
- Panini: 87/88 - 210; 87/88 - 384; 88/89 - 11; 89/90 - 27; 89/90 - 380; 89/90 - 384; 90/91 - 183; 91/92 - 278; 92/93 - 223E, 223F; 93/94 - 83E, 83F
- Parkhurst: 91/92 - 141E, 141F; 92/93 - 368, 368E; 93/94 - 159, 159EI; 94/95 - 180, 180EI
- Pro Set: 90/91 - 40, 343, 508; 91/92 - 191E, 191F; 92/93 - 142
- Score: 90 - 7T; 90/91 - 208A, 208C, 88HR; 91/92 - 268A, 488B, 488C, 176PNE, 176PNF; 92/93 - 3C, 3A, 360PNC, 360PNA, 9USG; 93/94 - 7C, 7A
- Topps: 82/83 - 200SK; 84/85 - 133; 85/86 - 7; 86/87 - 44; 87/88 - 126, G/BB; 88/89 - 76; 89/90 - 196, O/BB, 5SK; 90/91 - 218; 91/92 - 69, 7SC; 92/93 - 113, 113GS, 20SC; 93/94 - 498(II), 19SC, 19FD
- Upper Deck: 90/91 - 252E, 252F, 423E, 423F; 91/92 - 201E, 201F; 92/93 - 144; 93/94 - 186

Muller, Kirk
- Bowman: 90/91 - 82; 91/92 - 274; 92/93 - 138, 236
- Donruss: 93/94 - 177
- Fleer: 92/93 - 107; 93/94 - 21, 9AS, 131PP
- Frito-Lay: 88/89 - 24
- Gillette: 91/92 - 21
- Hockey Wit: 93/94 - 19
- Kraft: 90/91 - 37, 88; 91/92 - 12; 93/94 - 15
- Leaf: 93/94 - 182
- O-Pee-Chee: 85/86 - 84, 64SK; 86/87 - 94, 201SK; 87/88 - 157, 65SK; 88/89 - 84, F/BB, 75SK; 89/90 - 117, 83SK; 90/91 - 245, 78PM;

Muller, Kirk (cont.)
    O-pee-Chee: 91/92 - 22, 86PM, 145PM; 92/93 - 327; 93/94 - 509, 67SC, 67FD
    Panini: 87/88 - 79; 88/89 - 275; 89/90 - 251; 90/91 - 73; 91/92 - 219; 92/93 - 148E, 148F; 93/94 - 14E, 14F
    Parkhurst: 91/92 - 89E, 89F; 92/93 - 83, 504, 83EI, 504EI, CP5; 93/94 - 378, 378EI; 94/95 - V4
    Pro Set: 90/91 - 172, 371; 91/92 - 134E, 412E, 134F, 66PT, 412F; 92/93 - 87
    Score: 90/91 - 160A, 160C, 71HR; 91 - 64T; 91/92 - 110A, 331A, 110B, 110C, 361B, 614C, 361C, 614C, 3PNE, 3PNF; 92/93 - 225C, 225A, 111PNC, 111PNA, 29CSS, 29ASS; 93/94 - 234C, 234A, 7PNC, 7PNA, 7CAS, 7AAS
    Season's: 92/93 - 25
    Sega: 93/94 - 69
    Topps: 85/86 - 84; 86/87 - 94; 87/88 - 157; 88/89 - 84, F/BB; 89/90 - 117; 90/91 - 245, 7SL; 91/92 - 22, 193SC; 92/93 - 490, 490GS, 387SC; 93/94 - 509, 67SC, 67FD, 20AS
    Upper Deck: 90/91 - 267E, 267F; 91/92 - 149E, 519E, 149F, 519F; 92/93 - 180, 9AS; 93/94 - 148

Muloin, Wayne
    Dad's Cookies: 70/71 - 32
    Eddie Sargent: 70/71 - 135
    Esso: 70/71 - 49

Mulvenna, Glenn
    O-Pee-Chee: 92/93 - 97PM
    Upper Deck: 92/93 - 490

Mulvey, Grant
    O-Pee-Chee: 75/76 - 272; 76/77 - 167; 77/78 - 101; 78/79 - 261; 79/80 - 88; 80/81 - 27, 212; 81/82 - 60; 82/83 - 69, 173SK
    Post: 82/83 - 58
    Topps: 75/76 - 272; 76/77 - 167; 77/78 - 101; 78/79 - 261; 79/80 - 88; 80/81 - 27, 212; 81/82 WN - 72; 82/83 - 173SK

Mundy, Buster
    World Wide Gum: 36/37 - 101

Muni, Craig
    Donruss: 93/94 - 405
    Fleer: 92/93 - 296; 93/94 - 299PP
    O-Pee-Chee: 87/88 - 206, 30HL; 88/89 - 236; 89/90 - 231, 229SK; 90/91 - 423; 91/92 - 479
    Panini: 87/88 - 258; 89/90 - 80; 90/91 - 217; 91/92 - 133
    Parkhurst: 93/94 - 291, 291EI
    Pro Set: 90/91 - 92; 91/92 - 382E, 382F
    Score: 90/91 - 38A, 38C; 91/92 - 67A, 67B, 67C, 262PNE, 262PNF; 92/93 - 81C, 81A; 93/94 - 266C, 266A
    Topps: 91/92 - 479
    Upper Deck: 90/91 - 21E, 21F; 91/92 - 372E, 372F

Munro, Dunc
    Champ's: 24/25 - 35
    Dom. Choc.: 1925 - 57
    Maple Crispette: 24/25 - 1
    Willards: 1925 - 52
    Wm. Paterson: 24/25 - 34

Munro, Gerry
    Anonymous: 26/27 - 62
    Champ's: 24/25 - 36
    Wm. Paterson: 24/25 - 33

Murano, Eric
    Upper Deck: 91/92 - 50E, 50F

Murdoch, Bob L.
    Loblaws: 74/75 - 138
    Derniere: 72/84 - 17

Murdoch, Bob L (cont.)
    O-Pee-Chee: 76/77 - 54; 77/78 - 39; 79/80 - 351
    Topps: 76/77 - 54; 77/78 - 39

Murdoch, Bob J.
    O-Pee-Chee: 74/75 - 194; 75/76 - 33; 76/77 - 74; 77/78 - 371; 78/79 - 91; 79/80 - 276; 81/82 - 48; 82/83 - 53
    Pro Set: 90/91 - 377, 680
    Topps: 74/75 - 194; 75/76 - 33; 76/77 - 74; 78/79 - 91

Murdoch, Don
    O-Pee-Chee: 77/78 - 244, 12GP; 78/79 - 11; 79/80 - 168; 80/81 - 203
    PepsiCo: 80/81 - 36
    Topps: 77/78 - 244, 12PO; 78/79 - 11; 79/80 - 168; 80/81 - 203

Murdoch, John Murray
    Anonymous: 33/34 - 29
    Beehive: 34/44 - 287
    Can. Chew. Gum: 33/34 - 39
    Diamond: 33/35 - 47; 36/39 - 50(I), 50(II), 47(III)
    O-Pee-Chee: 33/34 - 37
    World Wide Gum: 33/34 - 68; 36.67 - 88

Murphy, Gordon (Gord)
    Bowman: 90/91 - 106; 91/92 - 235; 92/93 - 315
    Donruss: 93/94 - 131
    Fleer: 92/93 - 253; 93/94 - 99PP
    Leaf: 93/94 - 284
    O-Pee-Chee: 89/90 - 12FS; 90/91 - 302; 91/92 - 89; 92/93 - 101; 93/94 - 465
    Panini: 89/90 - 303; 90/91 - 115; 91/92 - 230
    Parkhurst: 91/92 - 227E, 227F; 93/94 - 345, 345EI
    Pro Set: 90/91 - 221; 91/92 - P/C, 171E, 171F, 156PT; 92/93 - 11
    Score: 90 - 13YS; 90/91 - 117A, 117C, 56HR; 91/92 - 43A, 43B, 43C, 140PNF, 140PNF; 92/93 - 29C, 29A, 132PNC, 132PNA; 93/94 - 95C. 95A
    Sega: 93/94 - 50
    Topps: 90/91 - 302; 91/92 - 89, 248SC; 92/93 - 114, 114GS, 445SC; 93/94 - 465, 439SC, 439FD
    Upper Deck: 90/91 - 86E, 86F; 91/92 - 392E, 392F; 93/94 - 521

Murphy, Joe
    Bowman: 90/91 - 196; 91/92 - 109; 92/93 - 174
    Donruss: 93/94 - 66
    Fleer: 92/93 - 63; 93/94 - 163, 53PP
    Leaf: 93/94 - 179
    O-Pee-Chee: 90/91 - 429; 91/92 - 48; 92/93 - 100; 93/94 - 273, 8HR
    Panini: 92/93 - 100E, 100F
    Parkhurst: 91/92 - 52E, 52F; 92/93 - 273, 273EI; 93/94 - 38, 38EI, F8; 94/95 - 44, 44EI
    Pro Set: 90/91 - 93; 91/92 - 68E, 68F, 171PT; 92/93 - 49
    Score: 90/91 - 293A, 293C; 91/92 - 299A, 519B, 519C, 206PNE, 206PNF; 92/93 - 321C, 321A; 92/93 - 23PNC, 23PNA; 93/94 - 348C, 348A
    Topps: 91/92 - 48, 313SC; 92/93 - 38, 38GS, 34SC; 93/94 - 273, 8PF
    Upper Deck: 90/91 - 190E, 190F; 91/92 - 474E, 474F; 92/93 - 152; 93/94 - 47

Murphy, Lawrence (Larry)
    Bowman: 90/91 - 177; 91/92 - 78; 92/93 - 153
    Donruss: 93/94 - 263
    Fleer: 92/93 - 167; 93/94 - 184, 193PP
    Funmate: 83/84 - 53
    Hockey Wit: 93/94 - 48
    Leaf: 93/94 - 16
    O-Pee-Chee: 81/82 - 148, 393, 239SK; 82/83 - 158, 232SK; 83/84 - 159, 298SK; 84/85 - 204, 127SK; 85/86 - 236; 86/87 - 185; 87/88 - 133, 31HL, H/BB, 119SK, 232SK; 88/89 - 141, 71SK;

Murphy, Lawrence (Larry) (cont.)
    O-Pee-Chee: 89/90 - 128, 199SK; 90/91 - 47; 91/92 - 277; 92/93 - 209; 93/94 - 173, 189
    Panini: 87/88 - 176; 88/89 - 367; 89/90 - 108; 90/91 - 251; 91/92 - 270; 92/93 - 228E, 228F; 93/94 - 135E, 86F, 135F, 86E
    Parkhurst: 91/92 - 358E, 358F; 92/93 - 137, 137EI; 93/94 - 162, 162EI; 94/95 - 179, 179EI
    Post: 82/83 - 124
    Pro Set: 90/91 - 143; 91/92 - 193E, 193F, 213PT; 92/93 - 146
    Roots: 93/94 - 8
    Topps: 81/82 WN - 100; 82/83 - 232SK; 83/84 - 298SK; 86/87 - 185; 87/88 - 133, H/BB, 7SK; 88/89 - 141; 89/90 - 128; 90/91 - 47; 91/92 - 277, 112SC; 92/93 - 447, 447GS, 375SC; 93/94 - 173, 189, 283SC, 283FD
    Score: 90/91 - 206A, 206C; 91/92 - 31A, 31B, 31C, 143PNE, 143PNF; 92/93 - 45C, 45A, 292PNC, 292PNA; 93/94 - 23C. 23A
    Sega: 93/94 - 103
    Topps: 93/94 - 23BG
    Upper Deck: 90/91 - 229E, 229F; 91/92 - 302E, 302F; 92/93 - 241; 93/94 - 374

Murphy, Mike
    Eddie Sargent: 72/73 - 195
    Loblaws: 74/75 - 139
    O-Pee-Chee: 72/73 - 215; 74/75 - 224; 75/76 - 52; 76/77 - 21; 77/78 - 22; 78/79 - 229; 79/80 - 31; 80/81 - 286; 81/82 - 149, 241SK
    Topps: 74/75 - 224; 75/76 - 52; 76/77 - 21; 77/78 - 22; 78/79 - 229; 79/80 - 31; 81/82 WN - 101

Murphy, Rob
    O-Pee-Chee: 90/91 - 37
    Pro Set: 90/91 - 546; 92/93 - 121
    Score: 91/92 - 397B, 397C
    Topps: 90/91 - 37
    Upper Deck: 92/93 - 108

Murphy, Ron
    Beehive: 45/63 - 129, 349; 64/67 - 90
    Coca Cola: 64/65 - 51; 65/66 - 52
    O-Pee-Chee: 68/69 - 139; 69/70 - 204
    Parkhurst: 54/55 - 76; 93/94 - 102ML
    Shirriff: 60/61 - 75; 61/62 - 36
    Topps: 57/58 - 29; 58/59 - 59; 59/60 - 66; 60/61 - 41, 24ST; 61/62 - 34; 62/63 - 40; 63/64 - 40; 64/65 -56; 65/66 - 111; 66/67 - 96; 66/67 US - 33; 67/68 - 100

Murray, Allan
    Beehive: 34/44 - 244
    Diamond: 36/39 - 51(I), 51(II), 48(III)
    O-Pee-Chee: 36/37 - 104
    World Wide Gum: 36/37 - 54

Murray, Bob J.
    Loblaws: 74/75 - 12
    O-Pee-Chee: 74/75 - 336; 75/76 - 386; 76/77 - 363

Murray, Bob
    O-Pee-Chee: 76/77 - 309; 77/78 - 12; 78/79 - 89; 79/80 - 55; 80/81 - 181; 81/82 - 61, 119SK; 82/83 - 70; 83/84 - 108, 109SK; 84/85 - 41, 26SK; 85/86 - 114; 86/87 - 64; 87/88 - 156; 90/91 - 138
    Panini: 87/88 - 223; 88/89 - 22
    Topps: 77/78 - 12; 78/79 - 89; 79/80 - 55; 80/81 - 181; 81/82 WN - 73; 83/84 - 109SK; 84/85 - 32; 85/86 - 114; 86/87 - 64; 87/88 - 156; 90/91 - 138
    Score: 90/91 - 376A, 376C

Murray, Bryan
    Pro Set: 90/91 - 664

Murray, Glen
    Donruss: 93/94 - 22

Murray, Glen (cont.)
- Leaf: 93/94 - 317(II)
- O-Pee-Chee: 92/93 - 74, 52PM; 93/94 - 477, 59SC, 59FD
- Panini: 92/93 - 142E, 142F
- Parkhurst: 91/92 - 229E, 229F; 92/93 - 9, 9EI; 93/94 - 16, 16EI
- Pro-Set: 92/93 - 222
- Score: 92/93 - 484C, 484A, 224PNC, 224PNA
- Topps: 92/93 - 370, 370GS, 393SC; 93/94 - 477(II), 59SC, 59FD
- Upper Deck: 91/92 - 69E, 69F; 92/93 - 401; 93/94 - 189

Murray, Herman
- World Wide Gum: 36/37 - 113

Murray, Ken
- World Wide Gum: 36/37 - 109

Murray, Marty
- Donruss: 93/94 - 17JCC
- Upper Deck: 93/94 - 550

Murray, Pat
- O-Pee-Chee: 90/91 - 79PM
- Pro Set: 90/91 - 630
- Score: 91/92 - 321A, 351B, 351C

Murray, Rob
- Bowman: 90/91 - 74
- O-Pee-Chee: 90/91 - 460
- Pro Set: 90/91 - 553

Murray, Terry
- O-Pee-Chee: 73/74 - 259; 74/75 - 126
- Post: 82/83 - 316
- Pro Set: 90/91 - 679
- Topps: 74/75 - 126

Murray, Troy
- Bowman: 90/91 - 13; 91/92 - 388; 92/93 - 93
- Fleer: 92/93 - 242, 443
- Frito-Lay: 88/89 - 25
- Humpty Dumpty: 92/93 - 17(I)
- O-Pee-Chee: 84/85 - 42; 85/86 - 146, 29SK; 86/87 - 25, 154SK, 189SK; 87/88 - 74, 79SK; 88/89 - 106, 10SK; 89/90 - 219, 11SK; 90/91 - 160; 91/92 - 87, 75PM; 92/93 - 64; 93/94 - 182, 230SC, 230FD
- Panini: 87/88 - 227; 88/89 - 27; 89/90 - 48; 90/91 - 200; 91/92 - 17; 92/93 - 57E, 57F
- Parkhurst: 91/92 - 206E, 206F
- Pro Set: 90/91 - 57; 91/92 - 46E, 514E, 588E, 46F, 514F, 588F, 247PT; 92/93 - 215
- Score: 90/91 - 243A, 243C; 91 - 35T; 91/92 - 53A, 53B, 53C, 585B, 585C, 33PNE, 33PNF; 92/93 - 189C, 189A, 49PNC, 49PNA; 93/94 - 272C, 272A
- Season's: 92/93 - 58
- Topps: 85/86 - 146; 86/87 - 25; 87/88 - 74; 88/89 - 106; 90/91 - 160; 91/92 - 87, 167SC; 92/93 - 284, 284GS, 31SC; 93/94 - 182, 230SC, 230FD
- Upper Deck: 90/91 - 112E, 112F; 91/92 - 565E, 565F; 92/93 - 129

Murzyn, Dana
- Bowman: 92/93 - 71
- Donruss: 93/94 - 348
- Leaf: 93/94 - 292(II)
- O-Pee-Chee: 86/87 - 58; 87/88 - 138; 90/91 - 304; 92/93 - 241; 93/94 - 311
- Parkhurst: 93/94 - 486, 486EI
- Pro Set: 90/91 - 41; 91/92 - 498E, 498F
- Score: 90/91 - 274A, 274C; 91/92 - 357A, 231B, 231C, 260PNE, 260PNF; 92/93 - 168C, 168A, 172PNC, 172PNA; 93/94 - 298C, 298A
- Panini: 87/88 - 42
- Topps: 86/87 - 58; 87/88 - 138; 90/91 - 304; 92/93 - 194, 194GS, 353SC; 93/94 - 311(II)
- Upper Deck: 90/91 - 348E, 348F

Musil, Frantisek
- Bowman: 91/92 - 259; 92/93 - 157

Musil, Frantisek (cont.)
- Fleer: 92/93 - 270; 93/94 - 307PP
- Leaf: 93/94 - 236(II)
- O-Pee-Chee: 89/90 - 217; 91/92 - 68; 92/93 - 66; 93/94 - 229, 169SC, 169FD
- Panini: 87/88 - 292; 88/89 - 87; 90/91 - 258
- Pro Set: 90/91 - 425; 91/92 - 368E, 368F
- Score: 90/91 - 223A, 223C, 19T; 91/92 - 142A, 142B, 142C, 282PNE, 282PNF; 92/93 - 83C, 83A, 51PNC, 51PNA; 93/94 - 303C, 303A
- Topps: 91/92 - 68, 235SC; 92/93 - 142, 142GS, 67SC; 93/94 - 229(I), 169SC, 160FD
- Upper Deck: 90/91 - 383E, 383F

Muzzatti, Jason
- Upper Deck: 93/94 - 482

Myles, Vic
- Beehive: 34/44 - 288

Myllys, Jarmo
- Bowman: 92/93 - 125
- O-Pee-Chee: 90/91 - 80PM; 91/92 - 8S, 15PM
- Parkhurst: 91/92 - 162E, 162F
- Topps: 92/93 - 251, 251GS, 113SC
- Upper Deck: 91/92 - 537E, 537; 92/93 - E19

Mylnikov, Sergei
- O-Pee-Chee: 90/91 - 445

Myre, Phil (Goalie)
- Derniere: 72/84 - 104
- Esso: 70/71 - 138
- Eddie Sargent: 70/71 - 112; 72/73 - 2
- Loblaws: 74/75 - 13
- O-Pee-Chee: 72/73 - 43; 73/74 - 77; 74/75 - 270; 75/76 - 308; 76/77 - 17; 77/78 - 193; 78/79 - 87; 79/80 - 189; 80/81 - 8
- Topps: 72/73 - 109; 73/74 - 77; 75/76 - 308; 76/77 - 17; 77/78 - 193; 78/79 - 87; 79/80 - 189; 80/81 - 8
- Toronto Sun: 71/72 - 159

Nachbauer, Donald (Don)
- O-Pee-Chee: 81/82 - 138
- Post: 82/83 - 108

Naida, Anatoli
- O-Pee-Chee: 91/92 - 56R

Namestnikov, Yevgeny
- Donruss: 93/94 - 502
- parkhurst: 94/95 - 246, 246EI

Nanne, Lou
- Coca Cola: 77/78 - 16
- Esso: 70/71 - 119
- Eddie Sargent: 72/73 - 111
- Loblaws: 74/75 - 156
- O-Pee-Chee: 69/70 - 198; 71/72 - 240; 72/73 - 10; 73/74 - 246; 74/75 - 325; 75/76 - 143; 76/77 - 173; 77/78 - 36
- Topps: 72/73 - 93; 75/76 - 143; 76/77 - 173; 77/78 - 36
- Toronto Sun: 71/72 - 138

Nantais, Richard
- O-Pee-Chee: 76/77 - 357

Napier, Mark
- Derniere: 72/84 - 132
- Kraft: 86/87P - 20; 86/87 - 20
- O-Pee-Chee: 79/80 - 222; 80/81 - 111; 81/82 - 178; 82/83 - 178, 189, 38SK, 39SK; 83/84 - 182, 192, 64SK, 65SK; 84/85 - 105; 85/86 - 253; 86/87 - 183, 75SK
- PepsiCo: 82/83 - 154
- Topps: 79/80 - 222; 80/81 - 111; 81/82 - 23; 82/83 - 38SK, 39SK; 83/84 - 64SK, 65SK; 86/87 - 183

Naslund, Markus
- Donruss: 93/94 - 269, 8RR
- Fleer: 93/94 - 412PP
- Leaf: 93/94 - 289, 4FP
- Parkhurst: 93/94 - 245, 245EI, CC5; 94/95 - 287, 287EI
- Topps: 93/94 - 393SC, 393FD
- Upper Deck: 92/93 - 234; 93/94 - 500

Naslund, Mats
- Cel.Watch: 1988 - CW17
- Derniere: 72/84 - 190
- Esso: 88/89 - 32
- Frito-Lay: 88/89 - 26
- Funmate: 83/84 - 66
- Kraft: 86/76P - 33; 86/87 - 33; 1990 - 23
- O-Pee-Chee: 83/84 - 193, 71SK; 84/85 - 267, 155SK, 156SK; 85/86 - 102, 131SK; 86/87 - 161, 11SK, 122SK; 87/88 - 16, L/BB, 6SK; 88/89 - 156, 26NS, 50SK, 215SK; 89/90 - 118, H/BB, 46SK
- Panini: 87/88 - 61; 88/89 - 259; 88/89 - 406; 89/90 - 234; 90/91 - 62
- Topps: 83/84 - 71SK; 85/86 - 102; 86/87 - 161, 8SK; 87/88 - 16, L/BB; 88/89 - 156; 89/90 - 118, H/BB
- Vachon Foods: 83/84 - 50

Nattress, Eric (Ric)
- Bowman: 91/92 - 266; 92/93 - 63
- Fleer: 92/93 - 374
- O-Pee-Chee: 88/89 - 238, 91SK; 90/91 - 459; 92/93 - 98
- Panini: 87/88 - 307
- Pro Set: 90/91 - 426; 91/92 - 363E, 363F
- Score: 90/91 - 302C; 91/92 - 249B, 249C; 92/93 - 344C, 344A; 93/94 - 381C, 381A
- Topps: 91/92 - 217SC; 92/93 - 219, 219GS, 328SC

Nattress, Ralph
- Beehive: 45/63 - 130

Naumann, Andreas
- Upper Deck: 91/92 - 678E, 678F

Nazarov, Andrei
- Donruss: 93/94 - 490
- Parkhurst: 94/95 - 216, 216EI

Neaton, Pat
- Fleer: 93/94 - 413PP

Nedomansky, Vaclav
- O-Pee-Chee: 79/80 - 132; 80/81 - 202; 81/82 - 94, 125SK
- Post: 82/83 - 73
- Topps: 79/80 - 132; 80/81 - 202; 81/82 WN - 94

Nedved, Petr
- Bowman: 91/92 - 324; 92/93 - 396
- Donruss: 93/94 - 356, 486
- Fleer: 92/93 - 226, 17UI; 93/94 - 68, 254PP, 490PP
- Kraft: 90/91 - 38; 91/92 - 11
- Leaf: 93/94 - 78
- O-Pee-Chee: 90/91 - 81PM; 91/92 - 141; 92/93 - 89; 93/94 - 15TC, 17SC, 18FD
- Panini: 91/92 - 49; 92/93 - 31E, 31F, 300E, 300F; 93/94 - 171E, 171F
- Parkhurst: 91/92 - 178E, 178F; 92/93 - 418, 418EI, 449, 449EI; 94/95 - V44
- Pro Set: 90/91 - 402, 643; 91/92 - 235E, 235F
- Score: 90 - 37YS, 50T; 91/92 - 124A, 124B, 124C, 192PNE, 192PNF; 92/93 - 101C, 101A, 127PNC, 127PNA; 93/94 - 231C, 231A
- Topps: 91/92 - 141, 280SC; 92/93 - 422, 422GS, 457SC; 93/94 - 6(I), 18SC, 18FD
- Upper Deck: 90/91 - 353E, 353F; 91/92 - 227E, E5(E), 227F, E5(F); 92/93 - 263

Nedved, Zdenek
- Parkhurst: 93/94 - 518, 518EI

Needham, Mike
- Fleer: 92/93 - 380
- Leaf: 93/94 - 214
- O-Pee-Chee: 92/93 - 106PM; 93/94 - 472
- Parkhurst: 93/94 - 370, 370EI
- Topps: 93/94 - 472(II), 452SC, 452FD
- Upper Deck: 92/93 - 489

Neely, Bob
- Loblaws: 74/75 - 281

Neely, Bob (cont.)
O-Pee-Chee: 74/75 - 272; 75/76 - 245; 76/77 - 194; 77/78 - 347
Topps: 75/76 - 245; 76/77 - 194

Neely, Cam
Bowman: 90/91 - 29; 91/92 - 348, 366; 92/93 - 62
Donruss: 93/94 - 29, U1
Fleer: 92/93 - 7; 93/94 - 138, 22PP
Frito-Lay: 88/89 - 27
Hockey Wit: 93/94 - 36
Humpty Dumpty: 92/93 - 16(II)
Kraft: 1990 - 56; 90/91 - 39, 84
Leaf: 93/94 - 99
McDonald's: 91/92 - Mc1; 91/92 0 McH5
O-Pee-Chee: 84/85 - 327; 85/86 - 228; 86/87 - 250; 87/88 - 69, 143SK; 88/89 - 58, 27NS, 22SK; 89/90 - 15, K/BB, 33SK; 90/91 - 69, 201, 82PM; 91/92 - 192, 266, 107PM; 92/93 - 174; 93/94 - 254, 216SC, 216FD
Panini: 87/88 - 10; 88/89 - 213; 89/90 - 182; 89/90 - 192; 90/91 - 9; 90/91 - 327; 91/92 0 176; 91/92 - 332; 92/93 - 143E, 143F; 93/94 - 3E, 3F
Parkhurst: 92/93 - 248, 248EI, CP14; 93/94 - 10, 10EI; 94/95 - 11, 11EI, V64
Pro Set: 90/91 - 11, 358; 91/92 - 5E, 300E, 5F, 1PT; 92/93 - 8
Score: 90/91 - 4A, 4C, 323A, 323C, 340A, 340C, 67HR; 91 - 8PC; 91/92 - 6A, 301A, 6B, 305B, 6C, 305C, 78PNE, 78PNF, B-6E, B-6F; 92/93 - 10C, 10A, 25PNA, 25PNC, 232PNC, 232PNA; 93/94 - 342C, 342A
Sega: 93/94 - 11
Season's: 92/93 - 33
Topps: 87/88 - 69; 88/89 - 58, 9SK; 89/90 - 15, K/BB; 90/91 - 69, 201, 3SL; 91/92 - 192, 266, 64SC; 92/93 - 32, 32GS, 316SC; 93/94 - 254(I), 216SC, 216FD
Upper Deck: 90/91 - 156E, 156F, 493E, 493F; 91/92 - 234E, 234F, McH5; 92/93 - 86; 93/94 - 356

Neilson, Jim
Beehive: 64/67 - 160
Coca Cola: 64/65 - 86; 65/66 - 86
Dad's Cookies: 70/71 - 88
Esso: 70/71 - 154
Eddie Sargent: 70/71 - 121; 72/73 - 154
Loblaws: 74/75 - 67
Shirriff: 68/69 - G12
O-Pee-Chee: 68/69 - 172, 207; 69/70 - 35, 3QS; 70/71 - 185; 71/72 - 112; 72/73 - 60; 73/74 - 123; 74/75 - 109; 75/76 - 270; 76/77 - 344; 77/78 - 317
Topps: 62/63 - 49; 63/64 - 50; 64/65 - 103; 65/66 - 89; 66/67 - 88; 67/68 - 91; 68/69 - 70; 69/70 - 35; 66/67 US - 55; 71/72 - 112; 72/73 - 66; 73/74 - 123; 74/75 - 109; 75/76 - 270
Toronto Star: 64/65 - 35
Toronto Sun: 71/72 - 177
Ultimate: 92 - 25(OSE), 25(OSF)

Nelson, Francis
Hall of Fame: 83 - 160, L11P; 87 - 160

Nelson, Todd
Topps: 92/93 - 50, 50GS

Neilson, Roger
Pro Set: 90/91 - 672

Nelson, Jeff
Upper Deck: 91/92 - 689E, 689F

Nemchinov, Sergei
Bowman: 92/93 - 426
Donruss: 93/94 - 214
Fleer: 92/93 - 140; 93/94 - 203, 162PP
Leaf: 93/94 - 252
O-Pee-Chee: 90/91 - 493; 91/92 - 514, 24R, 25PM; 92/93 - 316; 93/94 - 42, 245SC, 245FD

Nemchinov, Sergei (cont.)
Panini: 92/93 - 234E, 234F; 93/94 - 93E, 93F
Parkhurst: 91/92 - 334E, 334F; 92/93 - 114, 114EI, 236, 236EI, 447, 447EI; 93/94 - 128, 128EI
Pro Set: 91/92 - 441E, 441F, 205PT; 92/93 - 117
Score: 91 - 67T; 91/92 - 617B, 617C, 317PNE, 317PNF; 92/93 - 115C, 115A, 158PNC, 158PNA, 5CSS, 5ASS; 93/94 - 218C, 218A
Topps: 91/92 - 514; 92/93 - 287, 287GS, 340SC; 93/94 - 42, 245SC, 245FD
Upper Deck: 91/92 - 355E, 355F; 92/93 - 298, E13; 93/94 - 371

Nemcicky, Tomas
Upper Deck: 93/94 - 264

Nesterenko, Eric
Beehive: 45/63 - 131, 440; 64/67 - 51A, 51B
Coca Cola: 64/65 - 31; 65/66 - 32
Eddie Sargetn: 70/71 - 38
Esso: 70/71 - 686
O-Pee-Chee: 68/69 - 154; 69/70 - 136; 70/71 - 19; 71/72 - 213
Parkhurst: 53/54 - 10; 54/55 - 19; 55/56 - 15; 93/94 - 39ML
Quaker Oats: 45/54 - 96; 55/56 - 15
Shirriff: 60/61 - 69; 61/62 - 23; 68/69 - B14
Topps: 57/58 - 24; 58/59 - 53; 59/60 - 1; 61/62 - 28; 62/63 - 41; 63/64 - 39; 64/65 - 91; 65/66 - 119; 66/67 - 60; 66/67 US - 60; 67/68 - 60; 70/71 - 19
Toronto Star: 63/64 - 8
Toronto Sun: 71/72 - 77
Upper Deck: 90/91 - 503E, 503F

Neufeld, Ray
O-Pee-Chee: 83/84 - 144, 260SK; 84/85 - 76, 199SK; 85/86 - 58, 171SK; 86/87 - 177, 106SK; 88/89 - 239, 141SK
Panini: 87/88 - 369
Topps: 83/84 - 260SK; 84/85 - 59; 85/86 - 58; 86/87 - 177

Neville, Dave
World Wide Gum: 36/37 - 111

Nevin, Bob
Beehive: 45/63 - 441; 64/67 - 144
Bazooka: 71/72 - 14
Coca Cola: 64/65 - 87; 65/66 - 87
Colgate: 70/71 0 38
CKAR Radio: 63/65 - 53
Dad's Cookies: 70/71 - 89
Esso: 70/71 - 155
Eddie Sargent: 70/71 - 127; 72/73 - 112
Loblaws: 74/75 - 140
O-Pee-Chee: 68/69 - 76; 69/70 - 40, 15QS; 70/71 - 60; 71/72 - 44; 72/73 - 267; 74/75 - 378; 75/76 - 123
Parkhurst: 58/59 - 13; 61/62 - 10; 62/63 - 10; 63/64 - 10, 70
Post: 66/67L - 8; 66/67S - 5
Shirriff: 61/62 - 47; 62/63 - 7; 68/69 - G9
Topps: 64/65 - 77; 65/66 - 93; 66/67 - 27; 66/67 US - 27; 67/68 - 28; 68/69 - 76; 69/70 - 40; 70/71 - 60; 71/72 - 44; 75/76 - 123
Toronto Star: 58/67 - 106
Toronto Sun: 71/72 - 139
Ultimate: 92 - 26(OSE), 26(OSF)
York: 60/61 - 31; 61/62 - 26; 63/64 - 8

Newman, Dan
O-Pee-Chee: 77/78 - 362; 78/79 - 270

Nicholls, Bernie
Bowman: 90/91 - 221, HT20; 91/92 - 76; 92/93 - 161
Donruss: 93/94 - 188
Fleer: 92/93 - 64; 93/94 - 86, 139PP
Frito-Lay: 88/89 - 28
Funmate: 83/84 - 54
Hockey Wit: 93/94 - 64
Kraft: 90/91 - 73; 90/91 - 40

Nicholls, Bernie (cont.)
Leaf: 93/94 - 169
O-Pee-Chee: 83/84 - 160, 292SK; 84/85 - 88, 269SK; 85/86 - 148, 232SK; 86/87 - 159, K/BB, 95SK; 87/88 - 183, 214SK; 88/89 - 169, 28NS, 156SK; 89/90 - 47, 155SK; 90/91 - 13, 83PM; 91/92 - 174; 92/93 - 52; 93/94 - 274, 111SC, 111FD
Panini: 87/88 - 278; 88/89 - 77; 89/90 - 88; 90/91 - 106; 91/92 - 288; 92/93 - 109E, 109F; 93/94 - 39E, 39F
Parkhurst: 91/92 - 278E, 278F; 92/93 - 49, 328 49EI, 328EI; 93/94 - 117, 117EI
Pro Set: 90/91 - 204, 352; 91/92 - 166E, 286E, 166F, 286F, 174PT; 92/93 - 52
Score: 90/91 - 9A, 9C, 5HR; 91/92 - 240A, 460B, 460C, 300PNE, 300PNF; 92/93 - 340C, 340A, 120PNC, 120PNA; 93/94 - 19C, 19A
Topps: 83/84 - 292SK; 84/85 - 67; 85/86 - 148; 86/87 - 159, K/BB; 87/88 - 183, 88/89 - 169; 89/90 - 47; 90/91 - 13; 91/92 - 174, 245SC; 92/93 - 438, 438GS, 448SC; 93/94 - 274(II), 111SC, 111FD
Upper Deck: 90/91 - 34E, 34F; 91/92 - 356E, 566E, 356F, 566F; 92/93 - 290, 624; 93/94 - 58

Niedermayer, Rob
Donruss: 93/94 - 134, 4RR, I/PM, I/SP
Fleer: 93/94 - 8RS, 349PP, 8SM
Kraft: 93/94 - 27
Leaf: 93/94 - 293(II), 6FP
O-Pee-Chee: 93/94 - 270
Parkhurst: 93/94 - 246, 246EI, G5, E5, CC4; 94/95 - 294, 294EI, V22
Topps: 93/94 - 270(II), 449SC, 449FD
Upper Deck: 92/93 - 593; 93/94 - 98

Niedermayer, Scott
Bowman: 92/93 - 313
Donruss: 93/94 - 189, M/PM, M/SP
Fleer: 92/93 - 116; 93/94 - 95, 140PP
Hockey Wit: 93/94 - 54
Leaf: 93/94 - 80, 14R
O-Pee-Chee: 91/92 - 35PM; 92/93 - 113PM; 93/94 - 470
Panini: 92/93 - 179E, 179F; 93/94 - 42E, 42F
Parkhurst: 91/92 - 94E, 94F; 92/93 - 95, 95EI; 93/94 - 111, 111EI; 93/94 - 240, 240EI
Pro Set: 91/92 - CC4, 547E, 547F; 92/93 - 232
Score: 91 - 27T; 91/92 - 577B, 577C, 349PNE, 349PNF; 92/93 - 401C, 401A, 304PNC, 304PNA, 12CT, 12AT; 93/94 - 217C, 217A
Topps: 92/93 - 223, 223GS, 209SC; 93/94 - 470(II), 403SC, 403FD
Upper Deck: 90/91 - 461E, 461F; 92/93 - 406, 562, CC5, AC5, WJG1; 93/94 - 25, 284

Niekamp, Jim
Toronto Sun: 71/72 - 100

Nieuwendyk, Joe
Bowman: 90/91 - 91; 91/92 - 252; 92/93 - 59
Donruss: 93/94 - 48
Fleer: 92/93 - 25; 93/94 - 130, 39PP
Frito-Lay: 88/89 - 29
Hockey Wit: 93/94 - 82
Kraft: 89/90 - 5; 1990 - 5; 90/91 - 41, 74; 93/94 - 126, 50
O-Pee-Chee: 88/89 - 16, 29NS, 90SK, 125SK, 205SK, 216SK, 14FS; 89/90 - 138, 101SK; 90/91 - 87, 84PM; 91/92 - 223, 48PM; 92/93 - 354; 93/94 - 205, 96SC, 96FD
Panini: 88/89 - 404; 88/89 - 12; 89/90 - 29; 90/91 - 174; 91/92 - 53; 92/93 - 40E, 40F; 93/94 - 182E, 182F
Parkhurst: 91/92 - 23E, 23F; 92/93 - 21, 21EI; 93/94 - 31, 31EI; 94/95 - 33, 33EI, H4, R4, C4
Pro Set: 90/91 - 42, 344; 91/92 - 29E, 569E, 29F, 18PT, 569F; 92/93 - 26
Score: 90/91 - 30A, 30C, 45HR; 91/92 - 170A, 170B, 170C, 54PNE,

Nieuwendyk, Joe (cont.)
- Score: 54PNF; 92/93 - 193C, 193A, 31PNC, 31PNA; 93/94 - 199C. 199A
- Sega: 93/94 - 21
- Topps: 88/89 - 16; 89/90 - 138; 90/91 - 878SL; 91/92 - 223, 60SC; 92/93 - 105, 105GS, 37SC; 93/94 - 205(I), 96SC, 96FD
- Upper Deck: 90/91 - 26E, 26F; 91/92 - 263E, 263F; 92/93 - 128; 93/94 - 396

Nighbor, Frank
- Topps: 60/61 - 35; 61/62 - 48/ST

Nigro, Frank
- Champ's: 24/25 - 46
- Hall of Fame: 83 - E12; 83 - 72; 87 - 72
- O-Pee-Chee: 83/84 - 337, 149SK
- Topps: 83/84 - 149SK
- Wm. Paterson: 23/24 - 2; 24/25 - 6

Niinimaa, Janne
- Parkhurst: 93/94 - 520, 520EI

Nikolshin, Vitali
- Upper Deck: 92/93 - 340

Nikko, Jani
- Parkhurst: 93/94 - 524, 524EI

Nilan, Christopher (Chris)
- Bowman: 91/92 - 351
- Cel.Watch: 1988 - CW17
- Derniere: 72/84 - 134, 191
- Kraft: 86/87P - 34; 86/87 - 34
- O-Pee-Chee: 83/84 - 194; 84/85 - 268; 85/86 - 127SK; 86/87 - 199; 87/88 - 15SK; 88/89 - 31, 245SK; 90/91 - 454, 85PM; 91/92 - 311
- Panini: 87/88 - 68; 91/92 - 183
- PepsiCo: 80/81 - 54
- Pro Set: 90/91 - 205, 409
- Score: 90/91 - 311A, 22T; 91/92 - 197A, 197B, 197C, 289PNE, 289PNF; 92/93 - 76C, 76A
- Topps: 88/89 - 31; 91/92 - 311, 244SC
- Upper Deck: 90/91 - 368E, 368F, 442E, 442F; 91/92 - 237E, 237F
- Vachon Foods: 83/84 - 51

Nill, James (Jim)
- O-Pee-Chee: 83/84 - 357; 84/85 - 11; 89/90 - 224
- Vachon Foods: 83/84 - 114

Nilsson, Kent
- Funmate: 83/84 - 18
- O-Pee-Chee: 80/81 - 106, 197, 3PO; 81/82 - 34, 52, 53, 218SK; 82/83 - 54, 217SK; 83/84 - 89, 267SK, 268SK; 84/85 - 232, 245SK; 85/86 - 208SK; 87/88 - 88SK
- PepsiCo: 80/81 - 11
- Post: 81/82 - 28; 82/83 - 42
- Topps: 80/81 - 106, 197; 81/82 - 24, 48; 82/83 - 217SK; 83/84 - 267SK, 268SK
- Vachon Foods: 83/84 - 14

Nilsson, Ulf
- O-Pee-Chee: 78/79 - 255; 79/80 - 30; 80/81 - 116; 81/82 - 229, 172SK
- Topps: 78/79 - 255; 79/80 - 30, 163; 80/81 - 116; 81/82 EN - 102, 172SK
- Upper Deck: 91/92 - 643E, 643F

Noble, Reg
- Anonymous: 26/27 - 96
- Champ's: 24/25 - 56
- Hall of Fame: 83 - 22; 87 - 22
- Wm. Paterson: 23/24 - 26; 24/25 - 51

Nolan, Owen
- Bowman: 91/92 - 134; 92/93 - 237, 328
- Donruss: 93/94 - 279
- Fleer: 92/93 - 177; 93/94 - 154, 201PP
- Gillette: 91/92 - 25
- Hockey Wit: 93/94 - 57
- Humpty Dumpty: 92/93 - 17(II)
- Kraft: 91/92 - 55
- Leaf: 93/94 - 42

Nolan, Owen (cont.)
- O-Pee-Chee: 90/91 - 86PM; 91/92 - 64, 193PM; 92/93 - 382; 93/94 - 267, 4HR
- Panini: 91/92 - 266; 92/93 - 210E, 210F; 93/94 - 70F, 70F
- Parkhurst: 91/92 - 143E, 143F; 92/93 - 145, 455, 145EI, 455EI, CP13; 93/94 - 163, 163EI, F4; 94/95 - V43
- Pro Set: 90/91 - 401, 635; 91/92 - 196E, 196F, 101PT; 92/93 - 153
- Score: 90 - 36YS; 90/91 - 435A, 435C, 80T; 91/92 - 143A, 143B, 143C, 156PNE, 156PNF; 92/93 - 286C, 286A, 6PNC, 6PNA, 12CSS, 12ASS, 10CT, 10AT; 93/94 - 32C, 32A
- Season's: 92/93 - 46
- Sega: 93/94 - 113
- Topps: 91/92 - 64, 259SC; 92/93 - 349, 349GS, 78SC; 93/94 - 267, 4PF, 397SC, 397FD
- Upper Deck: 90/91 - 352E, 352F; 91/92 - 367E, 619E, 367F, 619F; 92/93 - 17, 321; 93/94 - 175

Nolet, Simon
- Colgate: 70/71 - 51
- Eddie Sargent: 70/71 - 150; 72/73 - 158
- Loblaws: 74/75 - 119
- O-Pee-Chee: 68/69 - 187; 70/71 - 194; 71/72 - 206; 72/73 - 125; 73/74 - 222; 74/75 - 187; 75/76 - 220; 76/77 - 64
- Topps: 72/73 - 26; 74/75 - 187; 75/76 - 220; 76/77 - 64
- Toronto Sun: 71/72 - 205

Noonan, Brian
- Bowman: 92/93 - 98
- Donruss: 93/94 - 464
- Fleer: 92/93 - 280; 93/94 - 314PP
- Leaf: 93/94 - 398(II)
- O-Pee-Chee: 88/89 - 165, 11SK, 15FS; 90/91 - 87PM; 92/93 - 234; 93/94 - 13
- Panini: 88/89 - 28; 92/93 - 9E, 9F; 93/94 - 149E, 149F
- Parkhurst: 91/92 - 264E, 264F; 94/95 - 143, 143EI
- Pro Set: 90/91 - 433; 91/92 - 165PT
- Score: 92/93 - 89C, 89A, 194PNC, 194PNA; 93/94 - 411C, 411A
- Topps: 88/89 - 165; 92/93 - 159, 159GS, 400SC; 93/94 - 13(I)
- Upper Deck: 91/92 - 380E, 380F; 92/93 - 117

Nord, Bjorn
- Upper Deck: 92/93 - 231

Nordmark, Robert
- O-Pee-Chee: 89/90 - 66SK; 90/91 - 433
- Pro Set: 90/91 - 547

Norgren, Johan
- Upper Deck: 92/93 - 225

Noris, Joe
- Toronto Sun: 71/72 - 222

Norris, Bruce
- Hall of Fame: 83 - 205, N10P; 87 - 205

Norris, Dwayne
- Donruss: 93/94 - 480
- Fleer: 93/94 - 491PP
- O-Pee-Chee: 93/94 - 13TC
- Parkhurst: 94/95 - 192, 192EI

Norris, Jack (Goalie)
- Esso: 70/71 - 103
- O-Pee-Chee: 70/71 - 165

Norris, James
- Hall of Fame: 83 - 57, 145, D11P, K11P; 87 - 57, 145

Norstrom, Mattias
- Donruss: 93/94 - 465
- Leaf: 93/94 - 426(II)
- O-Pee-Chee: 93/94 - 418
- Parkhurst: 93/94 - 256, 256EI; 94/95 - 152, 152EI
- Topps: 93/94 - 418(II), 371SC, 371FD
- Upper Deck: 93/94 - 522

Northcott, Baldy (Lawrence)
- Amal. Press: 35/36 - 7
- Anonymous: 33/34 - 49
- Beehive: 34/44 - 71, 201
- Canada Starch: 35/40 - 51
- Sweet Caporal: 34/35 - 34
- Can. Chew. Gum.: 33/34 - 40
- O-Pee-Chee: 34/35 - 60; 36/37 - 130; 37/38 - 166
- World Wide Gum: 33/34 - 48; 36/67 - 22

Northey, William
- Hall of Fame: 83 - 161, L12P; 87 - 161

Norton, Jeff
- Bowman: 90/91 - 122; 91/92 - 225
- Donruss: 93/94 - 303
- Fleer: 92/93 - 349; 93/94 - 223PP
- Leaf: 93/94 - 390
- O-Pee-Chee: 89/90 - 120; 90/91 - 166; 91/92 - 243; 93/94 - 447
- Panini: 89/90 - 273; 90/91 - 93; 91/92 - 248; 92/93 - 205E, 205F; 93/94 - 64E, 65F
- Parkhurst: 91/92 - 331E, 331F; 92/93 - 337, 337EI; 93/94 - 455, 455EI
- Pro Set: 90/91 - 189; 91/92 - 148E, 148F, 78PT
- Score: 90/91 - 157A, 157C, 70HR; 91 - 16YS; 91/92 - 222A, 222B, 222C, 172PNE, 172PNF; 92/93 - 56C, 56A, 102PNC, 102PNA; 93/94 - 69C. 69A
- Topps: 89/90 - 120; 90/91 - 166; 91/92 - 243, 98SC; 92/93 - 324SC, 526GS; 93/94 - 447, 495SC, 495FD
- Upper Deck: 90/91 - 386E, 386F; 91/92 - 357E, 357F; 93/94 - 512

Norwich, Craig
- O-Pee-Chee: 80/81 - 53
- Topps: 80/81 - 53

Norwood, Lee
- O-Pee-Chee: 88/89 - 240; 89/90 - 75; 90/91 - 285
- Panini: 89/90 - 68; 90/91 - 202; 91/92 - 214
- Parkhurst: 91/92 - 373E, 373F
- Pro Set: 90/91 - 74
- Score: 90/91 - 74T; 91/92 - 528B, 528C
- Topps: 89/90 - 75, 251SK; 90/91 - 285; 91/92 - 317SC
- Upper Deck: 90/91 - 78E, 78F

Novy, Milan
- Funmate: 83/84 - 139
- O-Pee-Chee: 83/84 - 187SK
- Topps: 83/84 - 187SK

Nowak, Hank
- Loblaws: 74/75 - 103
- O-Pee-Chee: 76/77 - 224
- Topps: 76/77 - 224

Numminen, Teppo
- Bowman: 90/91 - 138; 91/92 - 201; 92/93 - 299
- Donruss: 93/94 - 385
- Fleer: 92/93 - 243; 93/94 - 272PP
- Leaf: 93/94 - 135
- O-Pee-Chee: 90/91 - 385; 91/92 - 274; 92/93 - 4; 93/94 - 269, 164SC, 164FD
- Panini: 89/90 - 172; 90/91 - 307; 91/92 - 71; 92/93 - 52E, 52F; 93/94 - 197E, 197F
- Parkhurst: 91/92 - 200E, 200F; 92/93 - 438, 438EI; 93/94 - 231, 231EI; 94/95 - 270, 270EI
- Pro Set: 90/91 - 334; 91/92 - 261E, 261F, 248PT; 92/93 - 210
- Score: 90/91 - 176A, 176C; 91/92 - 101A, 101B, 101C, 166PNE, 166PNF; 92/93 - 102C, 102A, 215PNC, 215PNA; 93/94 - 132C. 132A
- Sega: 93/94 - 146
- Topps: 90/91 - 385; 91/92 - 274, 302SC; 92/93 - 339, 339GS, 77SC; 93/94 - 269(II), 164SC, 164FD
- Upper Deck: 91/92 - 240E, 240F; 92/93 - 326; 93/94 - 53

Nykoluk, Mike
- Beehive: 45/63 - 482
- Parkhurst: 57/58 TOR - 16; 93/94 - 130ML

Nylander, Mikael
- Donruss: 93/94 - 144, 407
- Fleer: 93/94 - 105, 7TP, 106PP
- Leaf: 93/94 - 94
- O-Pee-Chee: 92/93 - 19PM; 93/94 - 99, 186SC, 186FD
- Panini: 93/94 - 128E, 128F
- Parkhurst: 92/93 - 294, 294EI; 93/94 - 83, 38EI; 94/95 - 32, 32EI, V38
- Score: 92/93 - 400PNC, 400PNA; 93/94 - 383C, 383A
- Topps: 93/94 - 99(I), 186SC, 186FD
- Upper Deck: 92/93 - 236, 378, 520, ER2; 93/94 - 70

Nylund, Gary
- Bowman: 91/92 - 228
- O-Pee-Chee: 84/85 - 307, 15SK, 16SK; 85/86 - 172, 14SK; 86/87 - 243, 137SK; 87/88 - 82, 80SK; 88/89 - 15; 89/90 - 105, 114SK; 90/91 - 233; 91/92 - 101
- Panini: 87/88 - 224; 88/89 - 23; 90/91 - 80; 91/92 - 251
- Pro Set: 90/91 - 190; 91/92 - 150E, 150F
- 7-Eleven: 84/85 - 46
- Score: 90/91 - 86A, 86C; 91/92 - 192A, 192B, 192C, 406PNE, 406PNF; 92/93 - 381C, 381A
- Topps: 87/88 - 82; 88/89 - 15; 89/90 - 105, 90/91 - 233; 91/92 - 101, 163SC
- Upper Deck: 90/91 - 139E, 139F; 91/92 - 406E, 406F
- Vachon Foods: 83/84 - 94

Nyrop, Bill
- O-Pee-Chee: 76/77 - 188; 77/78 - 91; 78/79 - 134
- Topps: 76/77 - 188; 77/78 - 91; 78/79 - 134

Nystrom, Bob
- Loblaws: 74/75 - 191
- O-Pee-Chee: 73/74 - 202; 74/75 - 123; 75/76 - 259; 76/77 - 153; 77/78 - 62; 78/79 - 153; 79/80 - 217; 80/81 - 102; 81/82 - 217; 82/83 - 208, 59SK; 83/84 - 14, 85SK; 84/85 - 132, 85SK; 85/86 - 11, 69SK; 86/87 - 104, 204SK
- Post: 82/83 - 187
- Topps: 74/75 - 123; 75/76 - 259; 76/77 - 153; 77/78 - 62; 78/79 - 153; 79/80 - 217; 80/81 - 102; 82/83 - 59SK; 83/84 - 85SK; 84/85 - 98; 85/86 - 11; 86/87 - 104
- Upper Deck: 91/92 - 641E, 641F

Oates, Adam
- Bowman: 90/91 - 16; 91/92 - 384; 92/93 - 213, 258
- Donruss: 93/94 - 18, B/PM, B/SP
- Fleer: 92/93 - 8; 93/94 - 156, 7AS, 23PP, 11PL, 7PM
- Hockey Wit: 93/94 - 5
- Kraft: 91/92 - 5
- Leaf: 93/94 - 235(II), 8HT
- O-Pee-Chee: 87/88 - 123, 105SK; 88/89 - 161; 89/90 - 185; 90/91 - 149, 88PM; 91/92 - 265, 448, 7PM; 92/93 - 172, 272, 20AN, 13SP; 93/94 - 50, 74, 93SC, 93FD
- Panini: 87/88 - 248; 88/89 - 45; 90/91 - 275; 91/92 - 31; 92/93 - 136E, 136F; 93/94 - 2E, 138E, 2F, 138F
- Parkhurst: 91/92 - 155E, 233E, 155F, 233F; 92/93 - 4, 4EI; 93/94 - 11, 11EI; 94/95 - 311, 311EI, V46
- Pro Set: 90/91 - 269; 91/92 - CC7, 219E, 291E, 219F, 291F, 113PT, 25PK, MWCS1; 92/93 - 3
- Score: 90/91 - 85A, 85C, 41HR; 91/92 - 238A, 458B, 458C, 6HC, 6PNE, 378PNE, 6PNF, 378PNF; 92/93 - 250C, 250A, 40PNC, 40PNA; 93/94 - 125C, 125A, 478C, 478A, 9PNC, 9PNA, 17DT, 9CAS, 9AAS
- Season's: 92/93 - 20
- Sega: 93/94 - 8, 188
- Topps: 87/88 - 123; 88/89 - 161; 89/90 - 185; 90/91 - 149; 91/92 - 265, 448, 108SC; 92/93 - 475, 475GS, 188SC, 245SC; 93/94 - 50, 74, 5BG, 93SC, 93FD, 11MP, 5AS
- Upper Deck: 90/91 - 173E, 173F, 483E, 483F; 91/92 - 252E, 627E, 252F, 627F; 92/93 - 133, 637, 10AS; 93/94 - 226, 286, 327

Oatman, Ed
- Imperial Tobacco: 10/11 - 5L; 11/12 - 5; 12/13 - 47

O'Brien, Dennis
- Loblaws: 74/75 - 157
- O-Pee-Chee: 73/74 - 88; 74/75 - 96; 75/76 - 53; 76/77 - 34; 77/78 - 173; 78/79 - 104; 79/80 - 375
- Topps: 73/74 - 177; 74/75 - 96; 75/76 - 53; 76/77 - 34; 77/78 - 173; 78/79 - 104
- Toronto Sun: 71/72 - 140

O'Brien, J.A.
- Hall of Fame: 83 - 206, N11P; 87 - 206

O'Callahan, Jack
- O-Pee-Chee: 84/85 - 43; 86/87 - 207
- Topps: 84/85 - 33

O'Connell, Jack
- World Wide Gum: 36/37 - 107

O'Connell, Michael (Mike)
- O-Pee-Chee: 80/81 - 61; 81/82 - 6; 82/83 - 17, 89SK; 83/84 - 56, 52SK; 84/85 - 12, 185SK; 85/86 - 2, 161SK; 86/87 - 140, 160SK; 87/88 - 141, 107SK; 88/89 - 92, 248SK; 89/90 - 223, 249SK; 90/91 - 114
- Panini: 87/88 - 240; 89/90 - 69; 90/91 - 215
- Post: 82/83 - 13
- Pro Set: 90/91 - 75
- Topps: 80/81 - 61; 81/82 EN - 70; 82/83 - 89SK; 83/84 - 52SK; 84/85 - 9; 85/86 - 2; 86/87 - 140; 87/88 - 141; 88/89 - 92; 90/91 - 114

O'Connor, Buddy
- Beehive: 34/44 - 172; 45/63 - 350
- CKAC Radio: 43/47 - 71
- Quaker Oats: 45/54 - 42A, 42B
- World Wide Gum: 36/37 - 114

O'Connor, Myles
- O-Pee-Chee: 91/92 - 509
- Score: 91/92 - 322A, 352B, 352C
- Topps: 91/92 - 509
- Upper Deck: 91/92 - 485E, 485F

Oddleifson, Chris
- Loblaws: 74/75 - 300
- O-Pee-Chee: 74/75 - 108; 75/76 - 169; 76/77 - 112; 77/78 - 209; 78/79 - 183; 79/80 - 305; 80/81 - 295; 81/82 - 246
- Topps: 74/75 - 108; 75/76 - 169; 76/77 - 112; 77/78 - 209; 78/79 - 183, 81/82 - 246SK

Odelein, Lyle
- Donruss: 93/94 - 167
- Fleer: 92/93 - 331; 93/94 - 132PP
- Leaf: 93/94 - 283
- O-Pee-Chee: 91/92 - 350
- Parkhurst: 92/93 - 325, 325EI; 93/94 - 370, 370EI
- Pro Set: 90/91 - 617
- Score: 93/94 - 283C, 283A
- Topps: 91/92 - 350
- Upper Deck: 91/92 - 482E, 482F; 93/94 - 7

Odgers, Jeff
- Bowman: 92/93 - 397
- Fleer: 93/94 - 224PP
- O-Pee-Chee: 93/94 - 497,114SC, 114FD
- Panini: 92/93 - 130E, 130F; 93/94 - 260E, 260F
- Parkhurst: 91/92 - 386E, 386F, 93/93 - 398, 398EI
- Topps: 92/93 - 483, 483GS, 142SC; 93/94 - 497(II), 114SC, 114FD
- Upper Deck: 91/92 - 597E, 597F

Odjick, Gino
- Bowman: 91/92 - 316
- Donruss: 93/94 - 346
- Fleer: 92/93 - 427
- Leaf: 93/94 - 418(II)
- O-Pee-Chee: 91/92 - 260; 92/93 - 190
- Parkhurst: 92/93 - 422, 422EI;Z; 93/94 - 485, 485EI
- Pro Set: 91/92 - 505E, 505F
- Score: 91/92 - 237B, 237C; 92/93 - 540C, 540A; 93/94 - 385C, 385A
- Topps: 91/92 - 203, 338SC
- Upper Deck: 90/91 - 518E, 518F; 91/92 - 195E, 195F

O'Donnell, Fred
- O-Pee-Chee: 73/74 - 223

O'Donoghue, Don
- O-Pee-Chee: 71/72 - 180
- Toronto Sun: 71/72 - 54

Odrowski, Gerry
- Beehive: 45/63 - 219
- O-Pee-Chee: 72/73 - 304
- Parkhurst: 62/63 - 20
- Toronto Sun: 60/61 - 58; 61/62 - 78

O'Flaherty, Gerry
- Loblaws: 74/75 - 301
- O-Pee-Chee: 72/73 - 278; 73/74 - 250; 74/75 - 71; 75/76 - 307; 76/77 - 287; 77/78 - 377; 78/79 - 365
- Topps: 74/75 - 71; 75/76 - 307

O'Flaherty, John
- Beehive: 34/44 - 245

Ogilvie, Brian
- Loblaws: 74/75 - 262

Ogrodnick, John
- Bowman: 90/91 - 223; 91/92 - 71
- Funmate: 83/84 - 34
- O-Pee-Chee: 80/81 - 359; 81/82 - 95, 121SK; 82/83 - 79, 92, 179SK; 83/84 - 115, 128, 137SK, 138SK; 84/85 - 62, 356, 34SK, 35SK, 137SK; 85/86 - 70, J/BB, 37SK, 119SK; 86/87 - 87, 158SK; 87/88 - 134, 218SK; 88/89 - 153; 90/91 - 174; 91/92 - 365; 92/93 - 351
- Panini: 87/88 - 165; 89/90 - 290; 90/91 - 99; 91/92 - 293
- Parkhurst: 91/92 - 115E, 115F
- Post: 82/83 - 74
- Pro Set: 90/91 - 206; 91/92 - 169E, 169F, 204PT
- Score: 90/91 - 113A; 113C; 91/92 - 36A, 36B, 36C, 145PNE, 145PNF; 92/93 - 329C, 329A
- Topps: 81/82 WN - 95; 82/83 - 179SK; 83/84 - 137SK, 138SK; 84/85 - 46; 85/86 - 70, J/BB, 1SK; 86/87 - 87; 87/88 - 134; 88/89 - 153; 90/91 - 174, 18SL; 91/92 - 365, 273SC; 92/93 - 222SC
- Upper Deck: 90/91 - 258E, 258F; 91/92 - 476E, 476F

Ojanen, Janne
- O-Pee-Chee: 90/91 - 30; 92/93 - 17PM; 93/94 - 16, 184SC, 184FD
- Panini: 90/91 - 78
- Pro Set: 90/91 - 173
- Topps: 90/91 - 30; 93/94 - 16(I), 184SC, 184FD
- Upper Deck: 90/91 - 290E, 290F; 91/92 - 25E, 25F

Oksyuta, Roman
- Donruss: 93/94 - 111, 15RR
- Leaf: 93/94 - 411(II)
- O-Pee-Chee: 91/92 - 57R

Oksyuta, Roman (cont.)
Parkhurst: 93/94 - 258, 258EI
Upper Deck: 93/94 - 509

Olausson, Fredrik
Bowman: 90/91 - 135; 91/92 - 210; 92/93 - 295
Donruss: 93/94 - 386, 430
Fleer: 92/93 - 244, 18UI; 93/94 - 147, 273PP, 342PP
Kraft: 89/90 - 51; 90 - 51
Leaf: 93/94 - 124
O-Pee-Chee: 87/88 - 225; 90/91 - 242; 91/92 - 45; 92/93 - 121; 93/94 - 63
Panini: 90/91 - 318; 87/88 - 361; 91/92 - 67; 92/93 - 60E, 60F; 93/94 - 198E, 198F
Parkhurst: 91/92 - 203E, 203F; 92/93 - 212, 212EI; 93/94 - 227, 227EI
Pro Set: 90/91 - 335; 91/92 - 264E, 264F, 133PT
Score: 90/91 - 81A, 81C; 91/92 - 18A, 18B, 18C, 74PNE, 74PNF; 92/93 - 13C, 13A, 202PNC, 202PNA; 93/94 - 79C, 79A
Topps: 90/91 - 242; 91/92 - 45, 185SC; 92/93 - 120, 120GS, 346SC; 93/94 - 63(I)
Upper Deck: 90/91 - 237E, 237F; 91/92 - 383E, 383F; 92/93 - 136; 93/94 - 209

Olczyk, Ed
Bowman: 90/91 - 161; 91/92 - 204; 92/93 - 278
Fleer: 92/93 - 245, 357; 93/94 - 394PP
Frito-Lay: 88/89 - 30
Kellogg's: 92 - 18
Kraft: 1990 - 38; 91/92 - 62
Leaf: 93/94 - 90
O-Pee-Chee: 85/86 - 86, 26SK; 86/87 - 82, 156SK; 87/88 - 104, 76SK; 88/89 - 125, G/BB, 181SK; 89/90 - 133, 172SK; 90/91 - 206; 91/92 - 182, 196PM; 92/93 - 375; 93/94 - 398, 197SC, 197FD
Panini: 87/88 - 230; 88/89 - 126; 89/90 - 132; 90/91 - 283; 91/92 - 64; 92/93 - 55E, 55F
Parkhurst: 91/92 - 204E, 204F; 92/93 - 213, 213EI, 350, 350EI; 93/94 - 402, 402EI
Pro Set: 90/91 - 286, 563; 91/92 - 265E, 265F, 134PT; 92/93 - 213
Score: 90 - 51T; 90/91 - 210A, 210C, 89HR; 91/92 - 60A, 60B, 60C, 193PNE, 386PNE, 193PNF, 386PNF; 92/93 - 145C, 145A, 145PNC, 145PNA, 16USG; 93/94 - 37C, 37A
Topps: 85/86 - 86; 86/87 - 82; 87/88 - 104 88/89 - 125, G/BB; 89/90 - 133; 90/91 - 206; 91/92 - 182, 57SC; 92/93 - 17, 17GS, 157SC; 93/94 - 398(II), 197SC, 197FD
Upper Deck: 90/91 - 222F, 222F, 431E, 431F; 91/92 - 387E, 387F; 92/93 - 21; 93/94 - 115

O'Leary, Mickey
Champ's: 24/25 - 57
Diamond: 33/35 - 48; 36/39 - 52(I), 52(II), 49(III)

Oliver, Harry
Diamond: 33/35 - 48; 36/39 - 52(I), 52(II), 49(III)
Hall of Fame: 83 - 146, K12P; 87 - 146
O-Pee-Chee: 33/34 - 9
World Wide Gum: 33/34 - 23

Oliver, Murray
Beehive: 45/63 - 52, 200; 64/67 - 20
Coca Cola: 64/65 - 14; 65/66 - 12
Dad's Cookies: 70/71 - 67
Esso: 70/71 - 120
Eddie Sargent: 70/71 - 86; 72/73 - 107
Loblaws: 74/75 - 158
O-Pee-Chee: 68/69 - 194; 69/70 - 52; 70/71 - 167; 71/72 - 239; 74/75 - 291; 75/76 - 335
Parkhurst: 60/61 - 22
Post: 66/67 - 9; 68/69 - 23
Shirriff: 60/61 - 55; 61/62 - 8; 68/69 - M9
Topps: 60/61 - 6ST; 61/62 - 14;

Oliver, Murray (cont.)
Topps: 62/63 - 12, 7HB; 63/64 - 10; 64/65 - 79; 65/66 - 34; 66/67 - 95; 67/68 - 82; 69/70 - 52
Toronto Star: 58/67 - 75
Toronto Sun: 71/72 - 141

Ollila, Jukka
Upper Deck: 93/94 - 269

Olmstead, Bert
Beehive: 45/63 - 132; 45/63 - 277,443
Hall of Fame: 87 - 248
La Patrie: 51/54 - 16
Parkhurst: 51/52 - 5; 52/53 - 93; 53/54 - 19; 54/55 - 5; 55/56 - 42; 57/58 MON - 19; 58/59 - 27; 59/60 - 40; 60/61 - 4; 61/62 - 4; 93/94 - 71ML, 146ML
Quaker Oats: 45/54 - 43; 55/56 - 42
Shirriff: 60/61 - 11; 61/62 - 52; 62/63 - 11
Topps: 62/63 - 57
Toronto Star: 57/67 - 43
York: 60/61 - 32; 61/62 - 19

Orban, Bill
Topps: 67/68 - 109

O'Neil, Peggy
Beehive: 34/44 - 26, 173
World Wide Gum: 36/37 - 63

O'Neill, Michael (Goalie)
Parkhurst: 92/93 - 441, 441EI; 94/95 - 268, 268EI

O'Ree, Willie
Beehive: 45/63 - 53

O'Reilly, Terry
Funmate: 83/84 - 4
Loblaws: 74/75 - 29
O-Pee-Chee: 73/74 - 254; 74/75 - 295; 75/76 - 301; 76/77 - 130; 77/78 - 220; 78/79 - 40, 332; 79/80 - 238; 80/81 - 56; 81/82 - 7, 50SK; 82/83 - 18, 85SK; 84/85 - 13; 85/86 - 162SK
Post: 82/83 - 14
Pro-Set: 91/92 - 289PT
Topps: 75/76 - 301; 76/77 - 130; 77/78 - 220; 78/79 - 40; 79/80 - 238; 80/81 - 56; 81/82 EN - 71; 82/83 - 85SK, 84/85 - 10

O'Sullivan, Chris
Donruss: 93/94 - 15JCA
Upper Deck: 93/94 - 565

Orlando, Jimmy
Beehive: 34/44 - 119
O-Pee-Chee: 39/40 - 65

Orr, Bobby
Bauer: 68/69 - 18
Bazooka: 71/72 - 36
Coca Cola: 77/78 - 17
Colgate: 70/71 - 87; 71/72 - 8
Dad's Cookies: 70/71 - 9
Esso: 70/71 - 13; 88/89 - 33
Eddie Sargent: 70/71 - 1; 72/73 - 17
Hall of Fame: 83 - 61, E13P; 87 - 61
HHFM: 92 - 4
Loblaws: 74/75 - 30
Lipton Soup: 74.75 - 8
Mac's Milk: 73/74 - 19
O-Pee-Chee: 68/69 - 2, 200, 214, 4PS; 69/70 - 24, 209, 212, 22ST, 11QS; 70/71 - 3, 236, 246, 248, 249, 252, 4DE, 24SS; 71/72 - 100, 245, 251, 24BK, 1PT; 72/73 - 58, 127, 129, 142, 175, 3CS; 73/74 - 30; 74/75 - 100,.130, 248; 75/76 - 100, 288; 76/77 - 213; 77/78 - 251; 78/79 - 300
Post: 67/68 - 6; 67/68 - 5
Shirriff: 68/69 - A5
Score: 91/92 - CCA (2), CCC (4)
TCMA: 1981 - 9
Topps: 66/67 - 35; 66/67 US - 35; 67/68 - 92, 118, 128; 68/69 - 2;

Orr, Bobby (cont.)
Topps: 69/70 - 24; 70/71 - 3, 24SK; 71/72 - 100, 24BK; 72/73 - 100, 122; 73/74 - 150; 74/75 - 100, 130, 248; 75/76 - 100, 288; 76/77 - 213, 20PO; 77/78 - 251
Toronto Sun: 71/72 - 15

Osborne, Mark
Bowman: 90/91 - 156; 91/92 - 209
Fleer: 93/94 - 452PP
O-Pee-Chee: 82/83 - 93, 182SK; 83/84 - 252; 84/85 - 148; 88/89 - 241, 168SK; 89/90 - 274, 174SK; 90/91 - 227; 91/92 - 345; 93/94 - 268
Panini: 88/89 - 1127; 89/90 - 138; 90/91 - 278; 91/92 - 77
Parkhurst: 93/94 - 476, 476EI
Post: 82/83 - 75
Pro Set: 90/91 - 287, 564; 91/92 - 270E, 270F
Score: 90/91 - 104A, 104C, 28T; 91/92 - 39A, 39B, 39C, 96PNE, 96PNF; 92/93 - 277C, 277A, 305PNC, 305PNA; 93/94 - 316C, 316A
Topps: 82/83 - 182SK; 84/85 - 110; 90/91 - 227; 91/92 - 345, 21SC; 92/93 - 77, 77GS, 379SC; 93/94 - 268(II)
Upper Deck: 90/91 - 5E, 5F; 91/92 - 296E, 296F; 92/93 - 72

Osborne, Keith
Upper Deck: 93/94 - 76

Osgood, Chris (Goalie)
Donruss: 93/94 - 424
Fleer: 93/94 - 9RS, 334PP
Parkhurst: 93/94 - 329, 329EI, CC17; 94/95 - 283, 283EI
Topps: 93/94 - 350SC, 350FD
Upper Deck: 93/94 - 519

O'Shea, Danny
Colgate: 70/71 - 16
Dad's Cookies: 70/71 - 68
Esso: 70/71 - 121
Eddie Sargent: 70/71 - 90; 72/73 - 189
O-Pee-Chee: 69/70 - 131; 71/72 - 211; 72/73 - 201
Topps: 69/70 - 131
Toronto Sun: 71/72 - 78; 71/72 - 35

O'Shea, Kevin
Eddie Sargent: 70/71 - 25; 71/72 - 22; 72/73 - 190
O-Pee-Chee: 72/73 - 257

Osiecki, Mark
Pro Set: 91/92 - 528E, 528F
Score: 92/93 - 376PNC, 376PNA
Upper Deck: 91/92 - 533E, 533F

Otevrel, Jaroslav
Parkhurst: 92/93 - 399, 399EI
Topps: 93/94 - 293SC, 293FD

Otto, Joel
Bowman: 90/91 - 99; 91/92 - 260; 92/93 - 69
Donruss: 93/94 - 49
Fleer: 92/93 - 26; 93/94 - 40PP
Kraft: 1990 - 6
Leaf: 93/94 - 28
O-Pee-Chee: 86/87 - 247, 130SK; 87/88 - 212, 42SK; 88/89 - 242, 83SK; 89/90 - 205, 96SK; 90/91 - 369; 91/92 - 428, 102PM; 92/93 - 82; 93/94 - 48, 128SC, 128FD
Panini: 87/88 - 212; 88/89 - 13; 91/92 - 60; 91/92 - 253; 92/93 - 43E, 43F; 93/94 - 185E, 185F
Parkhurst: 91/92 - 253E, 253F; 92/93 - 259, 259EI; 93/94 - 34, 34EI
Pro Set: 90/91 - 43; 91/92 - 37E, 37F, 17PT; 92/93 - 28
Score: 90/91 - 128A, 128C; 91/92 - 96A, 96B, 96C, 179PNE, 179PNF; 92/93 - 332C, 332A, 328PNC, 328PNA; 93/94 - 74C, 74A
Topps: 90/91 - 369; 91/92 - 428, 170SC; 92/93 - 471, 471GS, 305SC;

Otto, Joel (cont.)
Topps: : 93/94 - 48(I), 128SC, 128FD
Upper Deck: 90/91 - 141E, 141F; 91/92 - 165E, 165F; 92/93 - 220; 93/94 - 124

Ouellette, Adelard
Diamond: 36/39 - 53(II), 50(III)

Owchar, Dennis
O-Pee-Chee: 75/76 - 380; 76/77 - 314; 77/78 - 391; 78/79 - 19
Topps: 78/79 - 19

Owen, George
La Presse: 27/32 - 65

Ozolinch, Sandis
Donruss: 93/94 - 312
Fleer: 92/93 - 402, 19UI; 93/94 - 169, 225PP
Leaf: 93/94 - 73
O-Pee-Chee: 92/93 - 104PM; 93/94 - 168
Parkhurst: 92/93 - 164, 164EI; 93/94 - 187, 187EI; 94/95 - 208, 208EI, H21, R21, C21, V7
Score: 93/94 - 261C, 261A
Topps: 93/94 - 168, 362SC, 362FD
Upper Deck: 91/92 - 661E, 661F; 92/93 - 568, ER16; 93/94 - 72

Paddock, John
PepsiCo: 80/81 - 73

Paek, Jim
Bowman: 92/93 - 383
Fleer: 92/93 - 168
O-Pee-Chee: 91/92 - 437; 92/93 - 328; 93/94 - 243
Parkhurst: 91/92 - 133E, 133F; 92/93 - 375, 375EI
Pro Set: 91/92 - 554E, 554F, 266PT
Score: 91/92 - 344PNE, 344PNF; 92/93 - 537C, 537A; 93/94 - 334C. 334A
Topps: 92/93 - 243, 243GS, 437SC; 93/94 - 401SC, 401FD
Upper Deck: 91/92 - 308E, 308F; 93/94 - 192

Paice, Frank
Topps: 62/63 - 61

Paiement, Rosaire
Colgate: 70/71 - 39
Dad's Cookies: 70/71 0 141
Eddie Sargent: 70/71 - 220
Esso: 70/71 - 245
O-Pee-Chee: 70/71 - 226; 71/72 - 233; 72/73 - 333
Topps: 71/72 - 24
Toronto Sun: 71/72 - 285

Paiement, Wilf
Derniere: 72/84 - 102, 165
O-Pee-Chee: 74/75 - 292; 75/76 - 195; 76/77 - 37; 77/78 - 130; 78/79 - 145; 79/80 - 190; 80/81 - 225; 81/82 - 306, 311, 326, 96SK, 110SK; 82/83 - 288, 22SK; 83/84 - 298; 84/85 - 285, 175SK; 85/86 - 152SK; 87/88 - 180
Panini: 87/88 - 32
PepsiCo: 80/81 - 93
Post: 81/82 - 22; 82/83 - 249
Topps: 75/76 - 195; 76/77 - 37; 77/78 - 130; 78/79 - 145; 79/80 - 190; 80/81 - 225; 81/82 - 25, 63; 82/83 - 22SK; 87/88 - 180
Vachon Foods: 83/84 - 70

Paille, Marcel (Goalie)
Bee Hive: 45/63 - 351; 64/67 - 145
Coca Cola: 64/65 - 88
Topps: 64/65 - 92

Page, Pierre
Kraft: 93/94 - 51

Palangio, Peter
Bee Hive: 34/44 - 72

Palazzari, Doug
O-Pee-Chee: 77/78 - 354

Palffy, Zigmund
Donruss: 93/94 - 459
Parkhurst: 93/94 - 397, 397EI; 94/95 - 137, 137EI
Upper Deck: 91/92 - 16E, 16F, 71E, 71F

Palmateer, Mike (Goalie)
Funmate: 83/84 - 124
O-Pee-Chee: 77/78 - 211; 78/79 - 160; 79/80 - 197; 80/81 - 95, 23PO; 81/82 - 351, 394, 194SK; 83/84 - 338, 39SK; 84/85 - 308, 22SK
Post: 81/82 - 9
Topps: 77/78 - 211; 78/79 - 160; 79/80 - 197; 80/81 - 95; 81/82 EN - 121; 83/84 - 39SK
Vachon Foods: 83/84 - 95

Palmer, Rob
O-Pee-Chee: 78/79 - 298; 79/80 - 352; 80/81 - 104
Topps: 80/81 - 104

Palmer, Brad
O-Pee-Chee: 82/83 - 21
Post: 82/83 - 139

Pandolfo, Jay
Donruss: 93/94 - 16JCA
Upper Deck: 93/94 - 556

Pang, Darren (Goalie)
O-Pee-Chee: 88/89 - 51, 8SK, 135SK, 16FS; 89/90 - 31, 10SK
Panini: 88/89 - 21; 89/90 - 42
Topps: 88/89 - 51; 89/90 - 31

Panin, Mikhail
O-Pee-Chee: 90/91 - 492

Panteleyev, Grigori
Fleer: 92/93 - 254; 93/94 - 179
Parkhurst: 92/93 - 243, 243EI
Score: 93/94 - 337C, 337A
Upper Deck: 92/93 - 492

Papike, Joe
Bee Hive: 34/44 - 73

Pappin, Jim
Bee Hive: 64/67 - 201
Colgate: 70/71 - 43
Esso: 70/71 - 69
Eddie Sargent: 70/71 - 41; 72/73 - 64
Loblaws: 74/75 - 85
Lipton Soup: 74/75 - 36
O-Pee-Chee: 68/69 - 21; 69/70 - 133; 70/71 - 13; 71/72 - 98; 72/73 - 42; 73/74 - 112; 74/75 - 113; 75/76 - 234
Shirriff: 68/69 - B16
Topps: 64/65 - 64; 65/66 - 16; 66/67 - 76; 66/67 US - 49; 67/68 - 78; 68/69 - 21; 69/70 - 73; 70/71 - 13; 71/72 - 98; 72/73 - 148; 73/74 - 112; 74/75 - 113; 75/76 - 234
Toronto Sun: 71/72 - 79
Toronto Star: 64/65 - 45
Ultimate: 92 - 62(OSE). 62(OSF)

Paradise, Bob
Eddie Sargent: 72/273 - 11
Loblaws: 74/75 - 249
O-Pee-Chee: 74/75 - 343; 75/76 - 21; 76/77 - 368; 77/78 - 203; 78/79 - 375
Topps: 75/76 - 21

Parent, Bernie (Goalie)
Bee Hive: 64/67 - 21
Coca Cola: 65/66 - 13
Colgate: 70/71 - 93
Dad's Cookies: 70/71 - 101
Derniere: 72/84 - 50
Eddie Sargent: 70/71 - 146
Esso: 70/71 - 177
Highliner: 93/94 - 7
Lipton Soup: 74/75 - 18

Parent, Bernie (Goalie) (cont.)
Loblaws: 74/75 - 229
O-Pee-Chee: 68/69 - 89; 69/70 - 8923ST, 1QS; 70/71 - 78; 71/72 - 131; 73/74 - 66; 74/75 - 60, 138, 249, 251; 75/76 - 291, 300; 76/77 - 10; 77/78 - 65; 78/79 - 15; 92/93 - 217, 1AN
Parkhurst: 92/93 - 470, 470EI
Shirriff: 68/69 - J1
Topps: 68/69 - 89; 69/70 - 89; 70/71 - 78; 71/72 - 131; 73/74 - 66; 74/75 - 60, 138, 249, 251; 75/76 - 291, 300; 76/77 - 10; 77/78 - 65; 78/79 - 15
Toronto Sun: 71/72 - 267

Parise, Jean Paul
Dad's Cookies: 70/71 - 69
Esso: 70/71 - 122
Eddie Sargent: 70/71 - 94; 71/72 - 83; 72/73 - 101
Loblaws: 74/75 - 159
Lipton Soup: 74/75 - 4
Mac's Milk: 73/74 - 20
O-Pee-Chee: 68/69 - 149; 69/70 - 127; 70/71 - 168, 25SS; 71/72 - 243; 72/73 - 199; 73/74 - 46; 74/75 - 83; 75/76 - 127; 76/77 - 182; 77/78 - 29; 78/79 - 350; 79/80 - 118
Topps: 69/70 - 127; 70/71 - 25SK; 73/74 - 46; 74/75 - 83; 75/76 - 127; 76/77 - 182; 77/78 - 29; 79/80 - 118
Toronto Sun: 71/72 - 142

Parizeau, Michel
O-Pee-Chee: 72/73 - 335
Toronto Sun: 71/72 - 242

Park, Brad
Coca Cola: 77/78 - 18
Colgate: 71/72 - 9
Dad's Cookies: 70/71 - 90
Derniere: 72/84 - 109
Eddie Sargent: 70/71 - 124; 72/73 - 144
Esso: 70/71 - 156; 88/89 - 34
Funmate: 83/84 - 35
Hockey Wit: 93/94 - 10
Loblaws: 74/75 - 206
Lipton Soup: 74/75 - 10
Mac's Milk: 73/74 - 21
O-Pee-Chee: 70/71 - 67, 239, 43DE; 71/72 - 40, 257; 72/73 - 85, 114, 15CS; 73/74 - 165; 74/75 - 50, 131; 75/76 - 260; 76/77 - 60; 77/78 - 190, 13GP; 78/79 - 79; 79/80 - 23, 164; 80/81 - 74, 1PO;81/82 - 8, 48SK; 82/83 - 19, 82SK; 83/84 - 129, 48SK, 178SK; 84/85 - 63, 378, 390, 38SK, 231SK
Post: 82/83 - 15
Topps: 70/71 - 67; 71/72 - 40; 72/73 - 30, 123; 73/74 - 165; 74/75 - 50, 131; 75/76 - 260; 76/77 - 60, 2PO; 77/78 - 190, 13PO; 78/79 - 79; 79/80 - 23, 164; 80/81 - 74; 81/82 EN - 72; 82/83 - 82SK; 83/84 - 48SK, 178SK; 84/85 - 47
Toronto Sun: 71/72 - 178
Zellers: 93/94 - 6, 6A

Park, Richard
Donruss: 93/94 - 17JCA
Upper Deck: 93/94 - 553

Parker, Jeff
O-Pee-Chee: 90/91 - 497

Parks, Greg
O-Pee-Chee: 90/91 - 89PM
Parkhurst: 92/93 - 491, 491EI

Parro, Dave (Goalie)
Topps: 82/83 - 158SK
O-Pee-Chee: 82/83 - 371, 158SK

Parsons, George
Bee Hive: 34/44 - 341
Quaker Oats: 38/39 - 28

Pasin, Dave
O-Pee-Chee: 86/87 - 76
Topps: 86/87 - 76

Paslawski, Gregory (Greg)
Bowman: 92/93 - 277
92/93 - 375
O-Pee-Chee: 87/88 - 10, 23SK; 89/90 - 268; 90/91 - 154; 92/93 - 193
Panini: 87/88 - 314; 90/91 - 309
Parkhurst: 91/92 - 365E., 365F; 92/93 - 132, 132EI
Pro Set: 90/91 - 336; 91/92 - 469E, 469F; 220PT; 92/93 - 155
Score: 90/91 - 249A, 249C; 91 - 29T; 91/92 - 579B, 579C; 286PNE, 286PNF; 92/93 - 175C, 175A, 370PNC, 370PNA, 16CSS, 16ASS; 93/94 - 290C, 290A
Topps: 87/88 - 10; 90/91 - 154; 92/93 - 33, 33GS, 275SC
Upper Deck: 90/91 - 239E, 239F; 92/93 - 531
Vachon Foods: 83/84 - 52

Pateman, Jerry (Official)
Pro Set: 90/91 - 696

Paterson, Rick
O-Pee-Chee: 83/84 - 109; 84/85 - 44
Post: 82/83 - 59

Patey, Doug
O-Pee-Chee: 79/80 - 298

Patey, Larry
Loblaws: 74/75 - 68
O-Pee-Chee: 75/76 - 137; 76/77 - 320; 77/78 - 199; 78/79 - 8; 79/80 - 57; 80/81 - 310; 81/82 - 303; 82/83 - 308; 84/85 - 149
Post: 82/83 - 267
Topps: 75/76 - 137; 77/78 - 199; 78/79 - 8; 79/80 - 57; 84/85 - 111

Patrick, Craig
Eddie Sargent: 72/73 - 55
Loblaws: 74/75 - 69
Lipton Soup: 74/75 - 46
O-Pee-Chee: 71/72 - 184; 72/73 - 221; 73/74 - 52; 74/75 - 262; 75/76 - 178; 77/78 - 278
Topps: 73/74 - 52; 74/75 - 262; 75/76 - 178

Patrick, Frank
Hall of Fame: 83 - 23, B9P; 87 - 23
Imperial Tobacco: 10/11 - 1

Patrick, James
Bowman: 90/91 - 225; 91/92 - 66; 92/93 - 127
Donruss: 93/94 -213, 408
Fleer: 92/93 - 141; 93/94 - 163PP, 353PP
Frito-Lay: 88/89 - 31
Leaf: 93/94 - 232
O-Pee-Chee: 84/85 - 150; 85/86 - 15, 83SK; 86/87 - 113, 220SK; 87/88 - 18, 30SK; 88/89 - 69, 246SK; 89/90 - 90, 242SK; 90/91 - 131; 91/92 - 253, 172PM; 92/93 - 215; 93/94 - 149
Panini: 87/88 - 107; 88/89 - 303; 89/90 - 289; 90/91 - 97; 91/92 - 287; 92/93 - 240E, 240F
Parkhurst: 91/92 - 120E, 120F; 92/93 - 113, 113EI; 93/94 - 360, 360EI; 94/95 - 40, 40EI
Pro Set: 90/91 - 207; 91/92 - 164E, 164F, 82PT; 92/93 - 119
Score: 90/91 - 194A, 194C, 84HR; 91/92 - 230A, 230B, 230C, 26PNE, 26PNF; 92/93 - 203C, 203A, 140PNC, 140PNA; 93/94 - 73C, 73A
Sega: 93/94 - 86
Topps: 84/85 - 112; 85/86 - 15; 86/87 - 113; 92/93 - 71; 87/88 - 18; 88/89 - 69; 89/90 - 90; 90/91 - 131; 91/92 - 253,

Patrick, James (cont.)
Topps: 277SC; 92/93 - 71, 71GS, 394SC; 93/94 - 149, 302SC, 392FD
Upper Deck: 90/91 - 185E, 185F; 91/92 - 275E, 275F; 92/93 - 320

Patrick, Lester
Hall of Fame: 83 - 40, C10P; 87 - 40
Imperial Tobacco: 10/11 - 26; 12/13 - 41
Topps: 60/61 - 1
World Wide Gum: 36/37 - 94

Patrick, Lynn
Beehive: 34/44 - 289
Diamond: 36/39 - 54(II), 55(II), 51(III)
Hall of Fame: 83 - 207, N12P; 87 - 207
O-Pee-Chee: 35/36 - 79; 36/37 - 128; 39/40 - 36; 40/41 - 136
World Wide Gum: 36/37 - 57

Patrick, Murray
Beehive: 34/44 - 290
O-Pee-Chee: 39/40 - 38

Patterson, Colin
Kraft: 1990 - 7
O-Pee-Chee: 89/90 - 71, 102SK; 90/91 - 420
Panini: 89/90 - 36
Pro Set: 91/92 - 356E, 356F
Score: 91/92 - 525B, 525C; 92/93 - 312C, 312A
Topps: 89/90 - 71; 92/93 - 91, 91GS
Vachon Foods: 83/84 - 15

Patterson, Dennis
Loblaws: 74/75 - 121
O-Pee-Chee: 75/76 - 51
Topps: 75/76 - 51

Patterson, Ed
Donruss: 93/94 - 474

Patterson, George
Diamond: 33/35 - 49
La Presse: 27/32 - 18
O-Pee-Chee: 33/34 - 14
World Wide Gum: 33/34 - 35

Paulhus, Ronald
Anonymous: 1926/27 - 5

Pavelich, Mark
O-Pee-Chee: 82/83 - 231, 138SK; 83/84 - 238, 239, 253, 213SK, 214SK; 84/85 -151, 97SK; 85/86 - 69, 84SK
Post: 82/83 - 204
Topps: 82/83 - 138SK; 83/84 - 213SK, 214SK, 84/85 - 113; 85/86 - 69

Pavelich, Matt
Hall of Fame: 87 - 261

Pavelich, Marty
Beehive: 45/63 - 201
Parkhurst: 51/52 - 54; 52/53 - 66; 53/54 - 44; 54/55 - 43; 93/94 - 53ML
Topps: 54/55 - 34

Pavese, Jim
Panini: 87/88 - 310
Post: 82/83 - 268

Payan, Eugene
Imperial Tobacco: 10/11 - 43L; 11/12 - 43; 12/13 - 9

Payette, Jean
O-Pee-Chee: 72/73 - 311

Payne, Steve
O-Pee-Chee: 79/80 - 64; 80/81 - 274; 81/82 - 166, 22SK, 92SK; 82/83 - 172, 191SK; 83/84 - 178, 121SK; 84/85 - 106, 4 9SK; 85/86 - 65, 42SK; 86/87 - 219; 87/88 - 56SK
Post: 82/83 - 140
Topps: 79/80 - 64; 81/82 WN - 110; 82/83 - 191SK; 83/84 - 121SK; 84/85 - 80; 85/86 - 65

Peake, Pat
Donruss: 93/94 - 361
Fleer: 93/94 - 10RS, 469PP
Parkhurst: 93/94 - 490, 490EI;

Peake, Pat (cont.)
Parkhurst: 94/95 - 281, 281EI, V63
Upper Deck: 91/92 - 697E, 697F; 93/94 - 518

Pearson, Rob
Bowman: 92/93 - 381
Donruss: 93/94 - 339
Fleer: 92/93 - 423; 93/94 - 453PP
Leaf: 93/94 - 174,
O-Pee-Chee: 91/92 - 65PM; 92/93 - 136; 93/94 - 137
Panini: 92/93 - 80E, 80F
Parkhurst: 91/92 - 169E, 169F; 92/93 - 414, 414EI; 93/94 - 474, 474EI
Pro Set: 91/92 - 562E, 562F, 9RGL; 92/93 - 191
Score: 91/92 - 311A, 341B, 341C, 304PNE, 304PNF; 92/93 - 333C, 333A, 287PNC, 287PNA, 23CT, 23AT; 93/94 - 96C, 96A
Topps: 92/93 - 168, 168GS, 377SC; 93/94 - 137, 498SC, 498FD
Upper Deck: 91/92 - 598E, 598F; 92/93 - 318; 93/94 - 48

Pearson, Scott
Bowman: 91/92 - 150
Donruss: 93/94 - 106
Leaf: 93/94 - 297
O-Pee-Chee: 90/91 - 356; 91/92 - 297
Parkhurst: 92/93 - 381, 381EI; 94/95 - 78, 78EI
Pro Set: 91/92 - 208E, 208F
Score: 91/92 - 138A, 138B, 138C 93/94 - 376C, 376A
Topps: 90/91 - 356; 91/92 - 297, 178SC
Upper Deck: 91/92 - 336E, 336F; 93/94 - 389

Peca, Mike
Donruss: 93/94 - 18JCC
Parkhurst: 94/95 - 245, 245EI
Upper Deck: 93/94 - 542

Pedersen, Allen
O-Pee-Chee: 87/88 - 174, 132SK; 88/89 - 103; 90/91 - 505; 91/92 - 128; 93/94 - 439
Parkhurst: 92/93 - 300, 300EI
Pro Set: 90/91 - 12
Score: 90/91 - 181A, 181C; 91/92 - 599B, 599C
Topps: 87/88 - 174; 88/89 - 103; 91/92 - 128; 93/94 - 439C, 366SC, 366FD

Pederson, Barry
Bowman: 92/93 - 48
Frito-Lay: 88/89 - 32
Funmate: 83/84 - 5
Kraft: 86/87 - 66; 86/87P - 66
O-Pee-Chee: 82/83 - 20, 92SK, 93SK; 83/84 - 57, 49SK, 50SK; 84/85 - 14, 187SK; 85/86 - 52; 86/87 - 34, 38SK; 87/88 - 177, 188SK; 88/89 - 32, 65SK; 89/90 - 281, 60SK; 90/91 - 134; 91/92 - 124PM; 92/93 - 295
Panini: 87/88 - 346; 88/89 - 138; 89/90 - 153
Pro Set: 90/91 - 238; 91/92 - 351E, 351F
Score: 91/92 - 639B, 639C
Topps: 82/83 - 92SK; 83/84 - 50SK; 83/84 - 49SK; 84/85 - 11; 85/86 - 52; 86/87 - 34; 87/88 - 177; 88/89 - 32; 90/91 - 134; 92/93 - 241, 241GS
Upper Deck: 90/91 - 329E, 329F; 93/94 - 92

Pederson, Mark
Bowman: 91/92 - 242; 92/93 - 390
O-Pee-Chee: 90/91 - 82; 91/92 - 399; 92/93 - 157
Panini: 92/93 - 188E, 188F
Parkhurst: 91/92 - 345E, 345F
Pro Set: 90/91 - 618
Score: 90/91 - 387A, 387C; 91/92 - 263C, 263A, 435B, 435C; 92/93 - 213PNC, 213PNA
Topps: 90/91 - 82; 91/92 - 399, 291SC; 92/93 - 327, 327GS, 168SC
Upper Deck: 90/91 - 532E, 532F; 91/92 - 363E, 363F; 92/93 - 209

Pederson, Tom
  Fleer: 92/93 - 403; 93/94 - 226PP
  O-Pee-Chee: 92/93 - 33PM
  Parkhurst: 93/94 - 184, 184EI

Peeters, Peter (Goalie)
  Bowman: 91/92 - 237
  Funmate: 83/84 - 6
  O-Pee-Chee: 80/81 - 279; 81/82 - 245, 177SK;
    82/83 - 22, 117SK; 83/84 - 44, 58,
    209, 221, 222, 41SK, 42SK, 170SK,
    318SK; 84/85 - 15, 144SK, 184SK;
    85/86 - 75, 160SK; 86/87 - 77;
    87/88 - 44; 88/89 - 180, 90NS,
    207SK; 89/90 - 195; 90/91 - 109;
    91/92 - 29
  Panini: 87/88 - 174; 88/89 - 364
  Post: 82/83 - 219
  Pro Set: 90/91 - 502; 91/92 - PC2PT
  Score: 91/92 - 544B, 544C
  Topps: 81/82 EN - 109; 82/83 - 117SK;
    83/84 - 41SK, 42SK, 170SK, 318SK;
    84/85 - 12; 85/86 - 75; 86/87 - 77;
    87/88 - 44; 88/89 - 180; 89/90 - 195;
    90/91 - 109; 91/92 - 29, 88SC
  Upper Deck: 90/91 - 424E, 424F;
    91/92 - 642E, 642F

Peirson, Johnny
  Beehive: 45/63 - 54A, 54B
  Parkhurst: 51/52 - 34; 52/53 - 78; 53/54 - 88;
    54/55 - 60; 93/94 - 5ML

Pellerin, Scott
  Fleer: 93/94 - 142
  Leaf: 93/94 - 167
  O-Pee-Chee: 93/94 - 13SC, 13FD
  Parkhurst: 93/94 - 116, 116EI
  Score: 93/94 - 373C, 373A
  Topps: 93/94 - 13SC, 13FD
  Upper Deck: 93/94 - 52

Pelletier, Marcel
  La Patrie: 51/54 - 18

Peltonen, Ville
  Upper Deck: 92/93 - 616

Peluso, Mike
  Fleer: 92/93 - 365
  Leaf: 93/94 - 407
  O-Pee-Chee: 91/92 - 293
  Panini: 93/94 - 116E, 116F
  Parkhurst: 92/93 - 118, 118EI
  Pro Set: 90/91 - 601; 92/93 - 122
  Score: 91/92 - 529B, 529C; 92/93 - 536C,
    536A, 379PNC, 379PNA;
    93/94 - 265C, 265A
  Topps: 91/92 - 293; 93/94 - 497SC, 497FD
  Upper Deck: 91/92 - 414E, 414F

Pelyk, Mike
  Dad's Cookies: 70/71 - 131
  Eddie Sargent: 70/71 - 203; 72/73 - 200
  Esso: 70/71 - 229
  O-Pee-Chee: 70/71 - 107; 71/72 - 92; 72/73 - 17;
    73/74 - 71; 76/77 - 342
  Post: 68/69 - 24
  Shirriff: 68/69 - M8
  Topps: 70/71 - 107; 71/72 - 92; 72/73 - 107;
    73/74 - 71; 86/87 - 182
  Toronto Sun: 71/72 - 268

Penney, Chad
  Upper Deck: 93/94 - 436

Penney, Steve (Goalie)
  Kraft: 86/87 - 79; 86/87P - 79
  O-Pee-Chee: 84/85 - 269; 85/86 - 4, 126SK;
    86/87 - 222
  Topps: 85/86 - 4

Pennington, Cliff
  Beehive: 45/63 - 55A, 55B; 64/67 - 22
  Topps: 61/62 - 19; 62/63 - 14
  Toronto Sun: 61/62 - 1

Pepin, Robert
  CKAC Radio: 43/47 - 24

Peplinski, James (Jim)
  Esso: 83/84E - 14; 83/84F - 14

Peplinski, James (Jim) (cont.)
  Kraft: 86/87 - 5; 86/87P - 5
  O-Pee-Chee: 81/82 - 49; 82/83 - 55, 216SK;
    83/84 - 90; 84/85 - 233; 86/87 - 182,
    84SK; 87/88 - 209, 46SK;
    88/89 - 243, 88SK;
    89/90 - 206, 99SK
  Panini: 87/88 - 213; 88/89 - 14; 89/90 - 37
  PepsiCo: 80/81 - 12
  Post: 82/83 - 43
  Topps: 82/83 - 216SK; 86/87 - 182
  Vachon Foods: 83/384 - 16

Perreault, Albert
  World Wide Gum: 36/37 - 115

Perreault, Gilbert
  Bazooka: 71/72 - 6
  Colgate: 70/71 - 28
  Dad's Cookies: 70/71 - 20
  Derniere: 72/84 - 175, 201
  Eddie Sargent: 70/71 - 23; 71/72 - 19;
    72/73 - 31
  Esso: 70/71 - 31; 88/89 - 35
  Funmate: 83/84 - 13
  Kellogg's: 84 - 29
  Lipton Soup: 74/75 - 2
  Loblaws: 74/75 - 49
  O-Pee-Chee: 70/71 - 131; 71/72 - 60, 246, 8BK,
    14PT; 72/73 - 136; 73/74 - 70;
    74/75 - 25; 75/76 - 10; 76/77 - 180;
    77/78 - 210, 14GP; 78/79 - 130;
    79/80 - 180; 80/81 - 80, 2PO;
    81/82 - 30, 60SK; 82/83 - 25, 30,
    118SK; 83/84 - 67, 4SK, 240SK,
    241SK; 84/85 - 24, 201SK, 202SK;
    85/86 - 160, K/BB, 188SK;
    86/87 - 79, 43SK
  Post: 81/82 - 2; 82/83 - 24
  Pro Set: 91/92 - 596E, 596F
  7-Eleven: 84/85 - 4
  Score: 90/91 - 355A, 355C
  Topps: 70/71 - 131; 71/72 - 60, 8BK;
    72/73 - 120; 73/74 - 70; 74/75 - 25;
    75/76 - 10; 76/77 - 180, 9PO;
    77/78 - 210, 14PO; 78/79 - 130;
    79/80 - 180; 80/81 - 80;
    82/83 - 118SK; 83/84 - 4SK, 240SK,
    241SK 85/86 - 160, K/BB; 86/87 - 79
  Toronto Sun: 71/72 - 36

Perreault, Robert (Bob) (Goalie)
  Beehive: 45/63 - 56A 56B; 64/67 - 23
  Topps: 62/63 - 2
  Toronto Star: 57/67 - 79

Perreault, Yanic
  Parkhurst: 94/95 - 230, 230EI
  Score: 92/93 - 487C, 487A
  Upper Deck: 92/93 - 70

Perry, Brian
  O-Pee-Chee: 69/70 - 84

Perry, Robert
  Toronto Sun: 71/72 - 106

Persson, Stefan
  O-Pee-Chee: 78/79 - 144; 79/80 - 32; 80/81 - 219;
    81/82 - 206; 82/83 - 209; 83/84 - 15;
    84/85 - 133
  Post: 82/83 - 188
  Topps: 78/79 - 144; 79/80 - 32; 80/81 - 219;
    81/82 EN - 92; 84/85 - 99

Pesut, George
  O-Pee-Chee: 75/76 - 360

Peters, Garry
  Coca Cola: 65/66 - 65
  Colgate: 65/66 - 65
  Eddie Sargent: 70/71 - 151
  Esso: 70/71 - 178
  O-Pee-Chee: 68/69 - 99; 69/70 - 171;
    70/71 - 196
  Topps: 65/66 - 28; 68/69 - 99

Peters, Jim
  Beehive: 45/63 - 57, 133, 202
  CKAC Radio: 43/47 - 72
  Eddie Sargent: 70/71 - 77

Peters, Jim (cont.)
  Parkhurst: 51/52 - 41; 52/53 - 35; 53/54 - 69
  Quaker Oats: 45/54 - 44A, 44B

Peters, Jimmy
  O-Pee-Chee: 69/70 - 143; 72/73 - 224;
    73/74 - 231

Peters, Peter
  Pro-Set: 90/91 - P

Peterson, Brent
  Kraft: 86/87 - 67; 86/87P - 67
  O-Pee-Chee: 83/84 - 68; 84/85 - 25; 85/86 - 47,
    178SK; 86/87 - 251, 100SK;
    87/88 - 263, 199SK
  Topps: 85/86 - 47

Petit, Michel
  Bowman: 90/91 - 170; 91/92 - 158; 92/93 - 101
  Durivage: 92/93 - 43
  Fleer: 93/94 - 308PP
  O-Pee-Chee: 87/88 - 262, 196SK; 89/90 - 251;
    90/91 - 271; 91/92 - 166; 92/93 - 185;
    93/94 - 141, 232SC, 232FD
  Panini: 87/88 - 342; 88/89 - 304;
    89/90 - 291; 90/91 - 148; 91/92 - 98
  Parkhurst: 91/92 - 252E, 252F; 93/94 - 304,
    304EI; 94/95 - 39, 39EI
  Pro Set: 90/91 - 256, 539; 91/92 - 492E
  Score: 90/91 - 187A, 187C, 54T;
    91/92 - 103A, 103B, 103C,
    49PNE, 49PNF; 92/93 - 38C,
    38A, 206PNC, 206PNA;
    93/94 - 275C, 275A
  Topps: 90/91 - 271; 91/92 - 166, 311SC;
    92/93 - 337, 337GS, 195SC;
    93/94 - 141, 232SC, 232FD
  Upper Deck: 90/91 - 181E, 181F; 91/92 - 359E,
    359F; 93/94 - 66

Petrenko, Sergei
  Donruss: 93/94 - 43
  Leaf: 93/94 - 425
  Parkhurst: 93/94 - 292, 292EI
  Topps: 93/94 - 373SC, 373FD
  Upper Deck: 92/93 - 346; 93/94 - 450

Petrov, Oleg
  Donruss: 93/94 - 452
  Fleer: 93/94 - 371PP
  Leaf: 93/94 - 260
  O-Pee-Chee: 92/93 - 96PM
  Parkhurst: 92/93 - 486, 486EI;
    94/95 - 291, 291EI
  Score: 93/94 - 459C, 459A
  Upper Deck: 93/94 - 84

Petrovicky, Robert
  Donruss: 93/94 - 145
  Fleer: 92/93 - 302; 93/94 - 107PP
  Leaf: 93/94 - 187
  O-Pee-Chee: 92/93 - 36PM
  Parkhurst: 92/93 - 61, 61EI; 93/94 - 89, 89EI
  Score: 92/93 - 402PNC, 402PNA;
    93/94 - 277C, 277A
  Upper Deck: 92/93 - 569, ER20; 93/94 - 37

Pettersson, Jorgen
  Funmate: 83/84 - 117
  O-Pee-Chee: 81/82 - 296, 135SK; 82/83 - 309,
    202SK; 83/84 - 318, 123SK;
    84/85 - 189, 59SK
  Post: 82/83 - 269
  Topps: 81/82 WN - 121; 82/83 - 202SK;
    83/84 - 123SK

Pettinger, Gord
  Beehive: 34/44 - 27, 120
  World Wide Gum: 36/37 - 76

Phillipoff, Harold
  O-Pee-Chee: 79/80 - 27
  Topps: 79/80 - 27

Phillippe, Charles
  Beehive: 34/44 - 174

Phillips, Bill
  La Presse: 27/32 - 26
  O-Pee-Chee: 33/34 - 43

Phillips, Tom
Hall of Fame: 83 - 208, N13P; 87 - 208

Picard, Michel
Bowman: 92/93 - 437
Fleer: 92/93 - 404
O-Pee-Chee: 91/92 - 20PM; 92/93 - 179
Parkhurst: 91/92 - 56E, 56F
Pro Set: 91/92 - 538E, 538F
Score: 91/92 - 317A, 347B, 347C, 327PNE, 327PNF
Topps: 92/93 - 439, 439GS, 119SC
Upper Deck: 91/92 - 48E, 48F

Picard, Noel
Colgate: 70/71 - 88
Dad's Cookies: 70/71 - 117
Eddie Sargent: 70/71 - 190; 72/73 - 185
Esso: 70/71 - 208
O-Pee-Chee: 69/70 - 175, 70/71 - 212; 71/72 - 224; 72/73 - 180
Shirriff: 68/69 - L7
Toronto Sun: 71/72 - 243

Picard, Robert
Derniere: 72/84 - 55, 97
O-Pee-Chee: 78/79 - 39; 79/80 - 91; 80/81 - 255; 81/82 - 189, 82/83 - 190; 84/85 - 345; 85/86 - 215, 252SK; 86/87 - 30SK; 87/88 - 248, 230SK; 89/90 - 261, 190SK
Panini: 79 - 55; 87/88 - 160; 89/90 - 333
PepsiCo: 80/81 - 94
Post: 82/83 - 155
Topps: 78/79 - 39; 79/80 - 91; 80/81 - 255
Vachon Foods: 83/84 - 135

Pichette, Dave
Derniere: 72/84 - 153
O-Pee-Chee: 81/82 - 280; 82/83 - 289; 83/84 - 299; 85/86 - 21, 63SK
Topps: 85/86 - 21

Pickard, Allan
Hall of Fame: 83 - 209, N14P; 87 - 209

Picketts, Hal
Diamond: 33/35 - 50

Pierce, Randy
O-Pee-Chee: 79/80 - 137; 80/81 - 340
Topps: 79/80 - 137

Pietrangelo, Frank (Goalie)
Bowman: 91/92 - 89
Fleer: 92/93 - 303
O-Pee-Chee: 91/92 - 114; 92/93 - 115; 93/94 - 287
Panini: 88/89 - 331; 93/94 - 132E, 132F
Parkhurst: 92/93 - 296, 296EI; 93/94 - 352, 352EI
Pro Set: 90/91 - 509; 92/93 - 64
Score: 90/91 - 55T; 91/92 - 440A, 425B, 425C; 92/93 - 535C, 535A, 309PNC, 309PNA; 93/94 - 419C, 419A
Topps: 91/92 - 114, 364SC; 92/93 - 522, 522GS, 96SC; 93/94 - 287, 272SC, 272FD
Upper Deck: 90/91 - 403E, 403F; 92/93 - 273; 93/94 - 401

Pike, Alf
Beehive: 34/44 - 291
Shirriff: 60/61 - 100
O-Pee-Chee: 39/40 - 84

Pilon, Richard
Bowman: 92/93 - 264
O-Pee-Chee: 91/92 - 379; 93/94 - 417, 113SC, 113FD
Parkhurst: 92/93 - 490, 490EI
Pro Set: 90/91 - 486
Score: 90/91 - 45T; 91/92 - 417B, 417C
Topps: 91/92 - 379; 92/93 - 492, 492GS, 230SC; 93/94 - 417C, 113SC, 113FD

Pilote, Pierre
Beehive: 45/63 - 134; 64/67 - 52A, 52B
CHEX: 63/65 - 8
Coca Cola: 64/65 - 32; 65/66 - 33
Colgate: 64/65 - 21; 65/66 - 33

Pilote, Pierre (cont.)
Hall of Fame: 83 - 191, J11P; 87 - 191
O-Pee-Chee: 68/69 - 124
Parkhurst: 93/94 - 32ML
Post: 66/67 - 10L; 68/69 - 25
Shirriff: 60/61 - 66; 61/62 - 27; 62/63 - 50; 68/69 - M18
Topps: 57/58 - 22; 58/59 - 36; 59/60 - 2, 60; 60/61 - 65, 25ST; 61/62 - 24; 62/63 - 28, 15HB; 63/64 - 25; 64/65 - 59, 109; 65/66 - 56; 66/67 - 59, 123; 66/67 US - 59; 67/68 - 62, 122; 68/69 - 124
Toronto Star: 58/67 - 52, 94; 64/65 - 15
Ultimate: 92 - 63(OSE), 63(OSF)

Pilous, Rudy
Hall of Fame: 87 - 247
Shirriff: 61/62 - 40
Topps: 61/62 - 23; 62/63 - 23

Pinder, Gerry
Eddie Sargent: 70/71 - 42
Esso: 70/71 - 70
O-Pee-Chee: 70/71 - 148; 71/72 - 185; 72/73 - 341
Toronto Sun: 71/72 - 55

Pirus, Alex
O-Pee-Chee: 77/78 - 204
Topps: 77/78 - 204

Pitre, Didier
Hall of Fame: 83 - 130, I11P; 87 - 130
Imperial Tobacco: 10/11 - 23, 41L; 11/12 - 41; 12/13 - 45

Pivonka, Michal
Bowman: 90/91 - 68; 91/92 - 291; 92/93 - 294
Donruss: 93/94 - 374
Fleer: 92/93 - 237; 93/94 - 101, 265PP
Leaf: 93/94 - 178
O-Pee-Chee: 90/91 - 68; 91/92 - 327; 92/93 - 30; 93/94 - 321, 360
Panini: 90/91 - 154; 91/92 - 206; 92/93 - 161E, 161F; 93/94 - 27E, 27F
Parkhurst: 91/92 - 412E, 412F; 92/93 - 432, 432EI; 93/94 - 487, 487EI
Pro Set: 90/91 - 319; 91/92 - 252E, 252F, 132PT; 92/93 - 201
Score: 90/91 - 268A, 268C; 91/92 - 193A, 193B, 193C, 277PNE, 277PNF; 92/93 - 253C, 253A, 151PNC, 151PNA 93/94 - 118C, 118A
Topps: 90/91 - 68; 91/92 - 327, 44SC; 92/93 - 107, 107GS, 382SC; 93/94 - 321, 360, 405SC, 405FD
Upper Deck: 90/91 - 80E, 80F; 91/92 - 229E, 229F; 92/93 - 261; 93/94 - 154

Plager, Barclay
Dad's Cookies: 70/71 - 118
Eddie Sargent: 70/71 - 184; 71/72 - 182; 72/73 - 187
Esso: 70/71 - 210
Loblaws: 74/75 - 263
O-Pee-Chee: 68/69 - 177; 69/70 - 176; 70/71 - 99; 71/72 - 66; 72/73 - 35; 73/74 - 47; 74/75 - 87; 75/76 - 205
Shirriff: 68/69 - L8
Topps: 70/71 - 99; 71/72 - 66; 72/73 - 136; 73/74 - 47; 74/75 - 87; 75/76 - 205
Toronto Sun: 71/72 - 244

Plager, Bob
Eddie Sargent: 70/71 - 183; 72/73 - 186
Esso: 70/71 - 209
Loblaws: 74/75 - 264
O-Pee-Chee: 68/69 - 112; 69/70 - 13; 70/71 - 211; 71/72 - 103; 72/73 - 161; 73/74 - 148; 74/75 - 107; 75/76 - 131; 76/77 - 369; 77/78 - 285
Shirriff: 68/69 - L2
Topps: 68/69 - 112; 69/70 - 13; 71/72 - 103; 72/73 - 96; 73/74 - 134; 74/75 - 107; 75/76 - 131
Toronto Sun: 71/72 - 245

Plager, William
Eddie Sargent: 70/71 - 187; 72/73 - 7

Plager, William (cont.)
O-Pee-Chee: 72/73 - 122
Topps: 72/73 - 12

Plamondon Gerry
Beehive: 45/63 - 278
CKAC Radio: 43/47 - 25
Quaker Oats: 45/54 - 45

Plante, Derek
Donruss: 93/94 - 45
Fleer: 93/94 - 11RS, 300PP
Leaf: 93/94 - 258
O-Pee-Chee: 93/94 - 285
Parkhurst: 93/94 - 293, 293EI, CC18; 94/95 - 25, 277, 25EI, 277EI, V82
Topps: 93/94 - 285, 491SC, 491FD
Upper Deck: 93/94 - 475

Plante, Jacques Goalie)
Beehive: 45/63 - 279, 352; 64/67 - 146
Coca Cola: 64/65 - 89
Colgate: 71/72 - 10
Dad's Cookies: 70/71 - 132
Derniere: 72/84 - 72
Eddie Sargent: 70/71 - 199; 72/73 - 207
Esso: 70/71 - 230
Hall of Fame: 83 - 76, F10P; 87 - 76
Highliner: 93/94 - 10
HHFM: 92 - 11
Mac's Milk: 73/74 - 22
O-Pee-Chee: 68/69 - 181, 15PS; 69/70 - 180, 15QS; 70/71 - 222; 71/72 - 195, 256, 4BK, 15PT; 72/73 - 92
Parkhurst: 55/56 - 50; 57/58 MON - 15; 58/59 - 22, 26; 59/60 - 41; 60/61 - 53; 61/62 - 49; 62/63 - 49; 92/93 - PR1; 93/94 - PR43, 72ML, 135ML, 151ML, 161ML, 163ML
Pro Set: 91/92 - 341E, 341F
Quaker Oats: 55/56 - 50
Shirriff: 60/61 - 21; 61/62 - 113; 62/63 - 25, 43, 58, 59
TCMA: 1981 - 12
Topps: 63/64 - 45; 64/65 - 68; 71/72 - 10, 4BK; 72/73 - 24
Toronto Star: 57/67 - 50, 74; 58/67 - 31, 82; 64/65 - 36
Toronto Sun: 71/72 - 269
York: 60/61 - 14; 61/62 - 23; 62/63 - 2

Plante, Pierre
Loblaws: 74/75 - 265
O-Pee-Chee: 73/74 - 255; 74/75 - 149; 75/76 - 309; 76/77 - 371; 77/78 - 385; 78/79 - 179; 79/80 - 275; 80/81 - 369
Topps: 74/75 - 149; 75/76 - 309; 78/79 - 179
Toronto Sun: 71/72 - 206

Plasse, Michel (Goalie)
Derniere: 72/84 - 13, 38, 146
Loblaws: 74/75 - 122
O-Pee-Chee: 73/74 - 252; 74/75 - 257; 75/76 - 249; 76/77 - 172; 77/78 - 92; 78/79 - 36; 79/80 - 69; 81/82 - 281
PepsiCo: 80/81 - 74
Topps: 74/75 - 257; 75/76 - 249; 76/77 - 172; 77/78 - 92; 78/79 - 36; 79/80 - 69

Plavsic, Adrien
Bowman: 90/91 - 62; 91/92 - 312; 92/93 - 363
Fleer: 92/93 - 428
O-Pee-Chee: 90/91 - 90PM; 91/92 - 162; 92/93 - 156; 93/94 - 201, 201SC, 201FD
Pro Set: 90/91 - 644
Score: 90/91 - 394A, 394C; 92/93 - 531C, 531A, 11COH; 93/94 - 358C, 358A
Topps: 91/92 - 162, 196SC; 92/93 - 323, 323GS, 15SC; 93/94 - 201, 201SC, 201FD
Upper Deck: 91/92 - 424E, 424F; 92/93 - 519

Playfair, Larry
O-Pee-Chee: 80/81 - 296; 84/85 26, 207SK;

Playfair, Larry (cont.)
O-Pee-Chee: 85/86 - 131; 86/87 - 195; 87/88 - 57, 211SK
Post: 82/83 - 25
Topps: 84/85 - 20; 85/86 - 131; 86/87 - 195; 87/88 - 57
Toronto Sun: 71/72 - 160

Pleau, Larry
Eddie Sargent: 70/71 - 107

Plett, Willi
O-Pee-Chee: 77/78 - 17; 78/79 - 317; 79/80 - 382; 80/81 - 320; 81/82 - 35, 222SK; 82/83 - 173; 83/84 - 179
Panini: 87/88 - 302
PepsiCo: 80/81 - 13
Post: 81/82 - 27; 82/83 - 44
Topps: 77/78 - 17; 81/82 - 26

Plumb, Ron
O-Pee-Chee: 79/80 - 328

Poddubny, Walter (Walt)
O-Pee-Chee: 83/84 - 339, 150SK; 84/85 - 309; 87/88 - 142, K/BB, 32SK; 88/89 - 170, 240SK; 89/90 - 184, 85SK; 90/91 - 426
Panini: 87/88 - 112; 88/89 - 309
Post: 82/83 - 285
Pro Set: 90/91 - 479
Score: 90/91 - 278A 278C; 91/92 - 400B, 400C
Topps: 83/84 - 150SK; 87/88 - 142, K/BB; 88/89 - 170; 89/90 - 184; 91/92 - 177SC
Vachon Foods: 83/84 - 96A, 96B

Podein, Shjon
Fleer: 93/94 - 140, 84PP
Parkhurst: 93/94 - 66, 66EI; 94/95 - 81, 81EI
Score: 93/94 - 424C, 424A
Topps: 93/94 - 474SC, 474FD
Upper Deck: 93/94 - 60

Poeschek, Rudy
Upper Deck: 93/94 - 461

Poile, Bud (Norman)
Beehive: 34/44 - 342; 45/63 - 203, 353
Quaker Oats: 45/54 - 97

Polich, Mike
O-Pee-Chee: 79/80 - 333; 80/81 - 363; 81/82 - 172

Polis, Greg
Eddie Sargent: 72/73 - 178
Loblaws: 74/75 - 206
O-Pee-Chee: 71/72 - 41, 9BK; 72/73 - 34; 73/74 - 176; 74/75 - 164; 75/76 - 201; 76/77 - 117; 77/78 - 112; 78/79 - 246; 79/80 - 273
Topps: 71/72 - 41, 9BK; 72/73 - 43; 73/74 - 75; 74/75 - 164; 75/76 - 201; 76/77 - 117; 77/78 - 112; 78/79 - 246
Toronto Sun: 71/72 - 223

Pollock, Sam
Hall of Fame: 83 - 147, K13P; 87 - 147

Polonic, Tom
O-Pee-Chee: 69/70 - 199

Polonich, Dennis
O-Pee-Chee: 77/78 - 228; 78/79 - 106; 79/80 - 224; 80/81 - 54
Topps: 77/78 - 228; 78/79 - 106; 79/80 - 224; 80/81 - 54

Pomichter, Mike
Upper Deck: 92/93 - 607

Popein, Larry
Beehive: 45/63 - 354
Parkhurst: 93/94 - 95ML
Shirriff: 60/61 - 84
Topps: 54/55 - 55; 57/58 - 54; 58/59 - 28; 59/60 - 21

Popiel, Paul
Eddie Sargent: 70/71 - 213
Esso: 70/71 - 246
O-Pee-Chee: 69/70 - 158; 70/71 - 122; 71/72 - 1; 72/73 - 67
Topps: 65/66 - 40; 70/71 - 122; 72/73 - 142
Toronto Sun: 71/72 - 286

Popikhin, Evgeny
O-Pee-Chee: 91/92 - 41R

Popovic, Peter
Donruss: 93/94 - 180
Fleer: 93/94 - 372PP
Leaf: 93/94 - 417
O-Pee-Chee: 93/94 - 361
Parkhurst: 93/94 - 103, 103EI
Topps: 93/94 - 361
Upper Deck: 93/94 - 445

Porter, J.C. (Red)
Dom. Choc.: 1925 - 106
La Presse: 27/32 - 17

Portland, Jack
Beehive: 34/44 - 28, 74, 175
O-Pee-Chee: 39/40 - 40

Potvin, Denis
Derniere: 72/84 - 54
Funmate: 83/84 - 81
Loblaws: 74/75 - 192
McDonald's: 82/83 - 18, 33
O-Pee-Chee: 74/75 - 195, 252; 75/76 - 275, 287; 76/77 - 170; 77/78 - 10, 15GP; 78/79 - 245, 334; 79/80 - 70; 80/81 - 120, 13PO; 81/82 - 199, 209, 151SK, 159SK; 82/83 - 210, 46SK; 83/84 - 2, 16, 81SK, 82SK, 169SK, 175SK; 84/85 - 134, 216, 389, 66SK, 78SK, 79SK, 145SK; 85/86 - 25; 86/87 - 129, 70SK; 209SK; 87/88 - 1, 247SK; 92/93 - 57, 7AN
Panini: 87/88 - 91
Post: 82/83 - 189
Pro Set: 90/91 - 656; 91/92 - 2HF
Topps: 74/75 - 195, 252; 75/76 - 275, 287; 76/77 - 170, 10PO; 77/78 - 10, 15PO; 78/79 - 245; 79/80 - 70; 80/81 - 120; 81/82 - 27; 81/82 EN - 130; 82/83 - 46SK; 83/84 - 81SK, 82SK, 169SK, 175SK; 84/85 - 100, 162; 85/86 - 25; 86/87 - 129; 87/88 - 1; 92/93 - 10
Upper Deck: 90/91 - 515E, 515F

Potvin, Felix (Goalie)
Bowman: 92/93 - 77
Donruss: 93/94 - 343, 6IK, W/PM, W/SP, U2
Durivage: 93/94 - 32
Fleer: 92/93 - 213; 93/94 - 30, 3RS, 7G, 246PP, 5N, 8SY
Highliner: 93/94 - 13
Hockey Wit: 93/94 - 34
Leaf: 93/94 - 409, 1PW, 4R, 10AS
O-Pee-Chee: 92/93 - 73, 114PM, 4TR; 93/94 - 30, 111, 126, 385, 17BG
Panini: 92/93 - G(E), G(F); 93/94 - 139E, 232E, 139F, 232F
Parkhurst: 91/92 - 398E, 398F; 92/93 - 187, 507, 187EI, 507EI; 93/94 - 202, 237, 202EI, 237EI, W9, D14; 94/95 - 229, 229EI
Pro-Set: 92/93 - 242
Roots: 93/94 - 3
Score: 91/92 - 345PNE, 345PNF; 92/93 - 501C, 501A, 364PNC, 364PNA, 5CT, 5AT; 93/94 - 5C, 5A, 484C, 484A, 5PCA
Sega: 93/94 - 138
Topps: 92/93 - 3, 3GS, 338SC; 93/94 - 30, 111, 126, 385, 3BG, 280SC, 280FD, 24MP, 5SCF
Upper Deck: 90/91 - 458E, 458F; 92/93 - 79, CC3, 58AS; 93/94 - 159, 285

Potvin, Jean
Loblaws: 74/75 - 193

Potvin, Jean (cont.)
O-Pee-Chee: 74/75 - 101; 75/76 - 36; 76/77 - 93; 77/78 - 144; 78/79 - 287; 79/80 - 334
Topps: 74/75 - 101; 75/76 - 36; 76/77 - 93; 77/78 - 144
Toronto Sun: 71/72 - 122

Potvin, Marc
Upper Deck: 91/92 - 405E, 405F

Poulin, David (Dave)
Bowman: 90/91 - 36; 91/92 - 359; 92/93 - 19
Donruss: 93/94 - 362
Fleer: 92/93 - 9, 304; 93/94 - 193, 5AW, 470PP
Frito-Lay: 88/89 - 33
Leaf: 93/94 - 332
O-Pee-Chee: 84/85 - 165, 110SK; 85/86 - 128, 89SK; 86/87 - 71, 241SK; 87/88 - 39, 32HL, 98SK, 179SK; 88/89 - 100; 89/90 - 115; 90/91 - 362; 91/92 - 507; 92/93 - 367; 93/94 - 228, 142SC, 142FD
Panini: 87/88 - 386; 87/88 - 130; 88/89 - 323; 89/90 - 305; 90/91 - 4; 92/93 - 137E, 137F
Parkhurst: 92/93 - 242, 242EI; 93/94 - 488, 488EI
Pro Set: 90/91 - 13; 91/92 - 12E, 12F, 5PT; 92/93 - 9
Score: 90/91 - 217A, 217C; 91/92 - 232A, 452B, 452C; 92/93 - 359C, 359A, 116PNC, 116PNA; 93/94 - 228C, 228A
Topps: 84/85 - 120; 85/86 - 128; 86/87 - 71; 87/88 - 39; 88/89 - 100; 89/90 - 115; 90/91 - 362; 91/92 - 507, 253SC; 92/93 - 155, 155GS, 13SC; 93/94 - 228, 142SC, 301SC, 142FD, 301FD
Upper Deck: 90/91 - 177E, 177F; 92/93 - G16; 93/94 - 355

Poulin, George (Skinner)
Imperial Tobacco: 10/11 - 24, 44L; 11/12 - 44; 12/13 - 8

Poulin, Patrick
Donruss: 93/94 - 146
Durivage: 93/94 - 50
Fleer: 93/94 - 122, 108PP, 315PP, 9SY
Leaf: 93/94 - 113, 10R
O-Pee-Chee: 92/93 - 85PM; 93/94 - 157SC, 157FD
Panini: 93/94 - 126E, 126F
Parkhurst: 92/93 - 60, 60EI; 93/94 - 307, 307EI
Pro-Set: 92/93 - 227
Score: 92/93 - 478C, 478A, 418PNC, 418PNA, 14CT, 14AT; 93/94 - 202C, 202A
Topps: 92/93 - 328, 328GS, 211SC; 93/94 - 157SC, 157FD
Upper Deck: 91/92 - 65E, 65F; 92/93 - 416, 557, CC18; 93/94 - 138

Pouzar, Jaroslav
O-Pee-Chee: 83/84 - 41, 151SK, 159SK; 84/85 - 256
Topps: 83/84 - 151SK, 159SK
Vachon Foods: 83/84 - 38

Power, R.
Imperial Tobacco: 10/11 - 40L; 11/12 - 40

Powis, Jeff
Topps: 67/68 - 110

Powis, Lynn
Loblaws: 74/75 - 123
O-Pee-Chee: 73/74 - 209; 74/75 - 227;
Topps: 74/75 - 227

Prajsler, Petr
O-Pee-Chee: 90/91 - 481

Pratt, Babe (Walter)
Beehive: 34/44 - 292, 343
Hall of Fame: 83 -162, L13P; 87 - 162
O-Pee-Chee: 39/40 - 85

Pratt, Babe (Walter)
    Parkhurst: 55/56 - 31
    Quaker Oats: 45/54 - 98; 55/56 - 31

Pratt, Stan
    World Wide Gum: 36/37 - 126

Pratt, Tracy
    Dad's Cookies: 70/71 - 21
    Eddie Sargent: 70/71 - 19; 72/73 - 30
    Esso: 70/71 - 32
    Loblaws: 74/75 - 302
    O-Pee-Chee: 69/70 - 111; 70/71 - 146; 71/72 - 107; 72/73 - 69; 73/74 - 54; 74/75 - 41; 75/76 - 133; 76/77 - 275
    Shirriff: 68/69 - H10
    Topps: 69/70 - 111; 71/72 - 107; 72/73 - 84; 73/74 - 54; 74/75 - 41; 75/76 - 133
    Toronto Sun: 71/72 - 37

Prentice, Dean
    Beehive: 45/63 - 58, 355A, 355B, 355C; 64/67 - 24, 91
    Coca Cola: 64/65 - 12; 65/66 - 15
    Dad's Cookies: 70/71 - 108
    Eddie Sargent: 70/71 - 165
    Esso: 70/71 - 190
    O-Pee-Chee: 68/69 - 32; 69/70 - 115; 70/71 - 201; 72/73 - 289
    Parkhurst: 54/55 - 74; 93/94 - 91ML
    Shirriff: 61/62 - 84; 68/69 - C5
    Topps: 57/58 - 62; 58/59 - 32; 59/60 - 17; 60/61 - 37, 15ST; 61/62 - 54; 62/63 - 53, 23HB; 63/64 - 13; 64/65 - 19; 65/66 - 102; 66/67 - 45; 66/67 US - 45; 67/68 - 46; 68/69 - 32; 69/70 - 115
    Toronto Star: 57/67 - 80, 118; 58/67 - 51
    Toronto Sun: 71/72 - 143
    Ultimate: 92 - 27(OSE), 27(OSF)

Presley, Wayne
    Bowman: 91/92 - 402; 92/93 - 76
    O-Pee-Chee: 87/88 - 179; 88/89 - 185; 89/90 - 98; 90/91 - 456; 91/92 - 385, 89PM; 93/94 - 162, 233SC, 233FD
    Panini: 87/88 - 228; 89/89 - 52; 91/92 - 19; 93/94 - 107E, 107F
    Parkhurst: 91/92 - 163E, 163F; 93/94 - 294, 294EI; 94/95 - 27, 27EI
    Pro Set: 90/91 - 434; 91/92 - 44E, 488E, 44F, 488F, 228PT
    Score: 90 - 92T; 91 - 9T; 91/92 - 221A, 221B, 221C, 559B, 559C, 68PNE, 68PNF; 92/93 - 213C, 213A; 93/94 - 296C, 296A
    Topps: 87/88 - 179; 88/89 - 185; 89/90 - 98; 91/92 - 385, 215SC; 92/93 - 424, 424GS, 24SC; 93/94 - 162, 233SC, 233FD
    Upper Deck: 90/91 - 339E, 339F; 91/92 - 371E, 371F

Preston, Rich
    O-Pee-Chee: 80/81 - 41; 82/83 - 71; 83/84 - 110; 84/85 - 118; 85/86 - 139; 86/87 - 61, 199SK
    Post: 82/83 - 60
    Topps: 80/81 - 41; 84/85 - 34; 85/86 - 139; 86/87 - 61

Priakin, Sergei
    Bowman: 90/91 - 103
    Kraft: 1990 - 8
    Pro Set: 90/91 - 594

Price, Noel
    Esso: 70/71 - 104
    Eddie Sargent: 72/73 - 8
    Loblaws: 74/75 - 14
    O-Pee-Chee: 68/69 - 110; 70/71 - 163; 72/73 - 163; 73/74 - 256; 74/75 - 356; 75/76 - 331
    Parkhurst: 58/59 - 6; 59/60 - 42; 93/94 - 131ML
    Shirriff: 68/69 - K4
    Topps: 68/69 - 110

Price, Pat
    Kraft: 86/87 - 49; 86/87P - 49

Price, Pat (cont.)
    O-Pee-Chee: 76/77 - 318; 77/78 - 308; 78/79 - 368; 79/80 - 347; 80/81 - 299; 81/82 - 265; 82/83 - 274; 84/85 - 286
    PepsiCo: 80/81 - 37; 82/83 - 237
    Vachon Foods: 83/84 - 71

Priestlay, Ken
    Parkhurst: 91/92 - 359E, 359F
    Pro Set: 91/92 - 460E, 460F
    Score: 91/92 - 658B, 658C
    Upper Deck: 91/92 - 525E, 525F

Primeau, Joe
    Anonymous: 33/34 - 7
    Beehive: 34/44 - 344
    Hall of Fame: 83 - 131, I12P; 87 - 131
    Hamilton Gum: 33/34 - 2
    La Presse: 27/32 - 42
    O-Pee-Chee: 33/34 - 12
    Parkhurst: 55/56 - 24
    Quaker Oats: 55/56 - 24
    Sweet Caporal: 34/35 - 48
    World Wide Gum: 33/34 - 40

Primeau, Keith
    Bowman: 91/92 - 46
    Donruss: 93/94 - 425
    Fleer: 92/93 - 286; 93/94 - 239, 4RS
    Hockey Wit: 93/94 - 67
    Leaf: 93/94 - 276
    O-Pee-Chee: 90/91 - 91PM; 91/92 - 309; 93/94 - 256, 217SC, 217FD
    Panini: 92/93 - 117E, 117F; 93/94 - 250E, 250F
    Parkhurst: 92/93 - 277, 277EI; 93/94 - 327, 327EI; 94/95 - 67, 67EI, V66
    Pro Set: 90/91 - 606
    Score: 90 - 38YS; 90/91 - 436A, 436C, 90T; 91/92 - 144A, 144B, 144C; 92/93 - 316C, 316A; 93/94 - 364C, 364A
    Topps: 91/92 - 309, 305SC; 92/93 - 99, 99GS, 485SC; 93/94 - 256, 217SC, 217FD
    Upper Deck: 90/91 - 354E, 354F; 91/92 - 258E, 258F; 93/94 - 413

Probert, Bob
    Bowman: 91/92 - 55; 92/93 - 85
    Donruss: 93/94 - 104
    Fleer: 92/93 - 53; 93/94 - 335PP
    Frito-Lay: 88/89 - 34
    Leaf: 93/94 - 186
    O-Pee-Chee: 88/89 - 181, 247SK; 91/92 - 198; 92/93 - 252; 93/94 - 177, 137SC, 137FD
    Panini: 88/89 - 46; 91/92 - 146; 93/94 - 249E, 249F
    Parkhurst: 91/92 - 272E, 272F; 92/93 - CP9; 93/94 - 333, 333EI; 94/95 - 71, 71EI
    Pro Set: 90/91 - 76; 91/92 - 61E, 61F, 34PT; 92/93 - 46
    Score: 90/91 - 143A, 143C; 91/92 - 73A, 73B, 73C, 183PNE, 183PNF; 92/93 - 52C, 52A, 56PNC, 56PNA, 17CSS, 17ASS; 93/94 - 59C, 59A
    Season's: 92/93 - 8
    Topps: 88/89 - 181; 91/92 - 198, 59SC; 92/93 - 63, 63GS, 355SC; 93/94 - 177, 137SC, 137FD
    Upper Deck: 90/91 - 448E, 448F; 91/92 - 239E; 92/93 - 248; 93/94 - 200

Prodgers, Goldie
    Champ's: 24/25 - 16
    Imperial Tobacco: 12/13 - 37
    Wm. Paterson: 23/24 - 32

Prokhorov, Vitali
    Donruss: 93/94 -290
    Fleer: 92/93 - 397; 93/94 - 432PP
    Leaf: 93/94 - 326
    O-Pee-Chee: 92/93 - 64, 64PM; 93/94 - 452
    Parkhurst: 92/93 - 157, 157EI; 93/94 - 450, 450EI; 94/95 - 206, 206EI
    Score: 92/93 - 404PNC, 404PNA

Prokhorov, Vitali (cont.)
    Topps: 93/94 - 452C
    Upper Deck: 92/93 - 486; 93/94 - 363

Prokopjev, Alexander
    O-Pee-Chee: 91/92 - 25R
    Panini: 87/88 - 181; 88/89 - 374; 89/90 - 339; 90/91 - 163; 91/92 - 199; 92/93 - 162E, 162F; 93/94 - 25E, 25F

Prokupek, Ladislav
    Parkhurst: 93/94 - 514, 514EI

Pronger, Chris
    Donruss: 93/94 - 150, 393, 3RR, J/PM, J/SP
    Fleer: 93/94 - 12RS, 354PP
    Kraft: 93/94 - 28
    Leaf: 93/94 - 257, 2FP
    O-Pee-Chee: 93/94 - 485
    Parkhurst: 93/94 - 249, 249EI, CC2, D13; 94/95 - 274, 274EI, V40
    Topps: 93/94 - 485C, 290SC, 290FD
    Upper Deck: 92/93 - 591; 93/94 - 190

Pronovost, Andre
    Beehive: 45/63 - 59, 204, 280; 64/67 - 92
    Parkhurst: 57/58 MON - 7; 58/59 - 3; 59/60 - 35; 60/61 - 55; 61/62 - 51; 63/64 - 45; 93/94 - 75ML
    Shirriff: 60/61 - 32; 61/62 - 3
    Topps: 60/61 - 7ST; 61/62 - 5; 62/63 - 19

Pronovost, Claude
    La Patrie: 51/54 - 38
    Parkhurst: 93/94 - 15ML

Pronovost, Jean
    Colgate: 70/71 - 50
    Dad's Cookies: 70/71 - 109
    Derniere: 72/84 - 202
    Eddie Sargent: 70/71 - 162; 72/73 - 176
    Esso: 70/71 - 191
    Loblaws: 74/75 - 250
    O-Pee-Chee: 69/70 - 155; 70/71 - 202; 71/72 - 118; 72/73 - 64; 73/74 - 11; 74/75 - 110; 75/76 - 280; 76/77 - 14; 77/78 - 261; 78/79 - 184; 79/80 - 77; 81/82 - 355, 196SK
    Panini: 79 - 64
    Topps: 71/72 - 118; 72/73 - 143; 73/74 - 11; 74/75 - 110; 75/76 - 280; 76/77 - 14; 77/78 - 261; 78/79 - 184; 79/80 - 77
    York: 62/63 - 30A; 63/64 - 43
    Toronto Sun: 71/72 - 224

Pronovost, Marcel
    Beehive: 45/63 - 205; 64/67 - 93, 178A, 179B
    Chex: 63/65 - 18
    Coca Cola: 64/65 - 52; 65/66 - 102
    Hall of Fame: 83 - 14, K14P; 87 - 148
    O-Pee-Chee: 68/69 - 125
    Parkhurst: 51/52 - 68; 52/53 - 61; 53/54 - 41; 54/55 - 34; 60/61 - 29; 61/62 - 29; 62/63 - 33; 63/64 - 46; 93/94 - 58ML
    Post: 68/69 - 26
    Shirriff: 60/61 - 56; 61.62 - 68; 68/69 - M13
    Topps: 54/55 - 27; 57/58 - 43; 58/59 - 24; 59/60 - 44; 64/65 - 39; 65/66 - 80; 66/67 - 20; 66/67 US - 20; 67/68 - 81; 68/69 - 125
    Toronto Star: 57/67 - 64, 110, 130; 58/67 - 20, 76; 63/64 - 15; 64/65 - 30
    Ultimate: 92 - 71(OSE), 71(OSF)
    York: 62/63 - 23; 63/64 - 38

Propp, Brian
    Bowman: 90/91 - 37; 91/92 - 123; 92/93 - 272
    Donruss: 93/94 - 441
    Funmate: 83/84 - 96
    O-Pee-Chee: 80/81 - 39; 81/82 - 246, 180SK; 82/83 - 256, 111SK; 83/84 - 218, 271, 199SK; 84/85 - 166, 112SK; 85/86 - 141, 90SK; 86/87 - 86, 239SK; 87/88 - 158, 33, 97SK; 88/89 - 168, 97SK; 89/90 - 139, 106SK; 90/91 - 8, 92PM; 91/92 - 227; 92/93 - 350;
    Panini: 92/93 - 93E, 93F; 93/94 - 267E, 267F

Propp, Brian (cont.)
Parkhurst: 91/92 - 82E, 82F; 93/94 - 85, 85EI
Post: 82/83 - 222
Pro Set: 90/91 - 14, 360, 460; 91/92 - 113E, 113F, 187PT; 92/93 - 257
Score: 90/91 - 269A, 269C, 34T; 91/92 - 223A, 223B, 223C, 184PNE, 184PNF; 92/93 - 72C, 72A, 178PNC, 178PNA
Topps: 80/81 - 39; 81/82 EN - 110; 82/83 - 111SK; 83/84 - 199SK 85/86 - 141; 86/87 - 86; 87/88 - 158; 88/89 - 168; 89/90 - 139; 90/91 - 8; 91/92 - 227, 237SC; 92/93 - 65, 65GS, 374SC
Upper Deck: 90/91 - 2E, 2F, 409E, 409F; 91/92 - 260E, 260F; 92/93 - 177; 93/94 - 368

Prosofsky, Jason
Upper Deck: 91/92 - 432E, 432F

Provost, Claude
Bauer: 68/69 - 19
Beehive: 45/63 - 281; 64/67 - 111
Chex: 63/65 - 32
Coca Cola: 64/65 - 66; 65/66 - 66
Derniere: 72/84 - 70
La Patrie: 51/54 - 35
Parkhurst: 57/58 MON - 12; 58/59 - 43; 59/60 - 18; 60/61 - 54; 61/62 - 50; 62/63 - 41; 63/64 - 36, 95; 93/94 - 73ML
O-Pee-Chee: 68/69 - 163, 216; 67/68 - 71
Shirriff: 60/61 - 33; 61/62 - 105; 62/63 - 35; 68/69 - F16
Topps: 64/65 - 23; 65/66 - 8; 66/67 - 9; 66/67 US - 9; 69/70 - 167; 72/73 - 231
Toronto Star: 57/67 -70, 138; 58/67 - 55; 63/64 - 21; 64/65 - 30
York: 60/61 - 15; 61/62 - 17; 62/63 - 14; 63/64 - 28

Prystai, Metro
Beehive: 45/63 - 135, 206; 64/67 - 203, 204
Coca Cola: 64/65 - 103; 65/66 - 101
Colgate: 70/71 - 2
Parkhurst: 51/52 - 65; 52/53 - 60; 53/54 - 42; 54/55 - 35 ; 93/94 - 57ML
Topps: 54/55 - 24

Pulford, Bob
Beehive: 45/63 - 444; 64/67 - 180A, 180B
Chex: 63/65 - 54
Coca-Cola: 64/65 - 104; 65/66 - 101
Dad's Cookies: 70/71 - 60
Eddie Sargent: 70/71 - 72; 71/72 - 66
Esso: 70/71 - 105
O-Pee-Chee: 68/69 - 129; 69/70 - 53, 16QS; 70/71 - 36; 71/72 - 94, 2PT; 74/75 - 229
Parkhurst: 57/58 TOR - 4; 58/59 - 1, 45; 59/60 - 28; 60/61 - 19; 61/62 - 8; 62/63 - 11; 63/64 - 12; 63/64 - 72; 93/94 - 113ML
Post: 66/67L - 11; 66/67S - 6; 68/69 - 27
Pro Set: 91/92 - 3HF
Shirriff: 60/71 - 13; 61/62 - 46; 62/63 - 6; 68/69 - M4
Topps: 64/65 - 60; 65/66 - 18; 66/67 - 19; 67/68 - 19; 68/69 - 129; 69/70 - 53; 70/71 - 36; 71/72 - 94; 74/75 - 229
Toronto Star: 57/67 - 96, 117; 58/67 - 22, 80; 63/64 - 39; 64/65 - 46
Toronto Sun: 71/72 - 123
York: 60/61 - 33; 61/62 - 14; 62/63 - 15; 63/64 - 18

Pulford, Harvey
Hall of Fame: 83 - 24, B10P; 87 - 24

Puppa, Daren (Goalie)
Bowman: 90/91 - 242; 91/92 - 37; 92/93 - 16
Donruss: 93/94 -316
Fleer: 92/93 - 261; 93/94 - 234PP

Puppa, Daren (Goalie) (cont.)
Kraft: 90/91 - 43
Leaf: 93/94 - 403
O-Pee-Chee: 89/90 - 200; 90/91 - 204, 238; 91/92 - 333; 92/93 - 53; 93/94 - 364
Panini: 87/88 - 23: 89/90 - 214; 90/91 - 31; 91/92 - 298
Parkhurst: 91/92 - 14E, 14F; 92/93 - 412, 412EI; 93/94 - 468, 468EI; 94/95 - 225, 225EI
Pro Set: 90/91 - 27, 365; 91/92 - 21E, 21F, 9PT
Score: 90/91 - 60A, 60C, 318A, 318C, 26HR; 91/92 - 106A, 106B, 106C, 137PNE, 137PNF; 92/93 - 47C, 47A; 92/93 - 327PNC, 327PNA; 93/94 - 273C, 273A
Topps: 90/91 - 204, 238; 91/92 - 333, 231SC; 92/93 - 457, 457GS, 370SC; 93/94 - 364, 275SC, 275FD
Upper Deck: 90/91 - 166E, 166F; 91/92 - 248E, 248F; 93/94 - 473

Purpur. Cliff (Fido)
Beehive: 34/44 - 75

Pushor, Jamie
Upper Deck: 91/92 - 73E, 73F

Pusie, Jean
Diamond: 36/39 - 53(I)
O-Pee-Chee: 35/36 - 91

Pyatt, Nelson
Loblaws: 74/75 - 104
O-Pee-Chee: 76/77 - 98; 77/78 - 252; 78/79 - 354
Topps: 76/77 - 98; 77/78 - 252

Quackenbush, Bill
Beehive: 45/63 - 60, 207
Berk Ross: 1951 - 1-18
Hall of Fame: 83 - 235, C11P; 87 - 235
Parkhurst: 51/52 - 26; 52/53 - 68; 53/54 - 100; 54/55 - 51
Topps: 54/55 - 49
Toronto Star: 58/67 - 12

Quackenbush, Max
Beehive: 45/63 - 136

Quenneville, Joel
O-Pee-Chee: 79/80 - 336; 80/81 - 19; 81/82 - 78, 234SK; 83/84 - 145, 225SK; 84/85 77; 85/86 - 103, 170SK; 86/87 - 118, 55SK; 88/89 - 3; 89/90 - 211; 90/91 - 418
Topps: 80/81 - 19; 81/82 WN - 83; 83/84 - 225SK; 84/85 - 60; 85/86 - 103; 86/87 - 118; 88/89 - 3

Quilty, John
Beehive: 34/44 - 176
CKAC Radio: 43/47 - 73
O-Pee-Chee: 40/41 - 106
Quaker Oats: 45/54 - 46

Quinn, Dan
Bowman: 90/91 - 65; 91/92 - 376; 92/93 - 289
O-Pee-Chee: 84/85 - 234; 85/86 - 176; 86/87 - 204, 87SK; 87/88 - 171, 173SK; 88/89 - 41, 236SK; 89/90 - 152, 234SK; 90/9 - 272, 93PM; 91/92 - 393, 27PM; 92/93 - 264
Panini: 87/88 - 147; 88/89 - 342; 89/90 - 314; 90/91 - 305; 01/92 - 27
Parkhurst: 91/92 - 351E, 351F
Pro Set: 90/91 - 303; 91/92 - 209E, 209F, 209PT
Score: 90/91 - 55, 55C, 24HR; 91 - 65T; 91/92 - 62A, 62B, 62C, 615B, 615C, 84PNE, 408PNE, 84PNF, 408PNF; 92/93 - 43C, 43A
Topps: 87/88 - 171; 88/89 - 41; 89/90 - 152; 90/91 - 272; 91/92 - 393, 243SC; 92/93 - 143, 143GS, 22SC
Upper Deck: 90/91 - 260E, 260F; 91/92 - 358E, 563E, 358F, 563F

Quinn, Pat
Colgate: 70/71 - 72

Quinn, Pat (cont.)
Dad's Cookies: 70/71 - 142
Eddie Sargent: 70/71 - 209; 72/73 - 6
Esso: 70/71 - 247
Loblaws: 74/75 - 15
O-Pee-Chee: 69/70 - 186, 8QS; 70/71 - 120, 1DE; 71/72 - 122; 72/73 - 183, 1CS; 73/74 - 61; 74/75 - 286; 75/76 - 172; 76/77 - 289
Topps: 70/71 - 120; 71/72 - 122; 73/74 - 61; 75/76 - 172
Toronto Sun: 71/72 - 287

Quinney, Ken
Upper Deck: 91/92 - 419E, 419F

Quint, Deron
Upper Deck: 93/94 - 561

Quintal, Stephane
Bowman: 92/93 - 337
Fleer: 93/94 - 475PP
O-Pee-Chee: 93/94 - 242SC, 242FD
Parkhurst: 92/93 - 384, 384EI; 93/94 - 500, 500EI
Pro Set: 90/91 - 410; 91/92 - 350E, 350F
Score: 91/92 - 437B, 437C; 92/93 - 242, 242A; 93/94 - 412C, 412A
Topps: 92/93 - 484, 484GS, 350SC; 93/94 - 242SC, 242FD
Upper Deck: 93/94 - 529

Quintin, Jean-Francois
Fleer: 93/94 - 192, 8TP
O-Pee-Chee: 92/93 - 37PM
Parkhurst: 94/95 - 212, 212EI
Score: 92/93 - 488C, 488A
Upper Deck: 92/93 - 483; 93/94 - 21

Racicot, Andre (Goalie)
Bowman: 91/92 - 337
Durivage: 92/93 - 49; 93/94 - 15
Fleer: 92/93 - 332
Leaf: 93/94 - 294
O-Pee-Chee: 91/92 - 450; 92/93 - 11PM; 93/94 - 313, 26SC, 26FD
Parkhurst: 92/93 - 321E, 321F
Score: 91/92 - 395A, 285B, 285C 93/94 - 437C, 437A
Topps: 91/92 - 450, 377SC; 93/94 - 313, 26SC, 26FD
Upper Deck: 91/92 - 377E, 377F; 92/93 - 430

Racine, Yves
Bowman: 90/91 - 230; 91/92 - 44; 92/93 - 331
Donruss: 93/94 - 246
Durivage: 93/94 - 34
Fleer: 92/93 - 287; 93/94 - 406PP
Leaf: 93/94 - 115
O-Pee-Chee: 90/91 - 361; 91/92 - 228; 92/93 - 297
Panini: 91/92 - 141; 92/93 - 119E, 119F
Parkhurst: 91/92 - 265E, 265F; 93/94 - 422. 422EI; 94/95 - 168, 168EI
Pro Set: 91/92 - 54E, 54F
Score: 91 - 37YS; 91/92 - 158A, 158B, 158C, 233PNE, 233PNF; 92/93 - 74C, 74A, 332C, 332A; 93/94 - 264C, 264A
Topps: 90/91 - 361; 91/92 - 228, 198SC; 92/93 - 277, 277GS, 6SC; 93/94 - 304SC, 304FD
Upper Deck: 91/92 - 498E, 498F; 92/93 - 142; 93/94 - 194

Raglan, Clare
Beehive: 45/63 - 137
Parkhurst: 51/52 - 36; 53/54 - 79

Raglan, Herb
Pro Set: 90/91 - 525; 91/92 - 470E, 470F
Score: 91/92 - 536B, 536C

Raleigh, Don
Beehive: 45/63 - 356
La Patrie: 51/54 - 30
Parkhurst: 51/52 - 93; 52/53 - 99; 53/54 - 68; 54/55 - 68
Topps: 54/55 - 53

Ramage, George (Rob)
Bowman: 90/91 - 162; 91/92 - 154

Ramage, George (Rob) (cont.)
- Fleer: 92/93 - 413; 93/94 - 407PP
- Funmate: 83/84 - 118
- Kraft: 1990 - 39; 90/91 - 44
- O-Pee-Chee: 80/81 - 213; 81/82 - 79, 154SK, 229SK; 82/83 - 310, 223SK; 83/84 - 319, 130SK; 84/85 - 190, 62SK, 136SK; 85/86 - 196; 86/87 - 17, 180SK; 87/88 - 160, 20SK; 88/89 - 244, 84SK; 90/91 - 317; 91/92 - 55, 76PM; 93/94 - 12HR
- Panini: 87/88 - 306; 90/91 - 280; 91/92 - 96
- Parkhurst: 92/93 - 175, 175EI
- Post: 81/82 - 21; 82/83 - 173
- Pro Set: 90/91 - 288; 91/92 - 232E, 407E, 232F, 407F; 92/93 - 177
- Score: 90/91 - 36A, 36C; 91 - 23T; 91/92 - 233A, 573B, 573C, 228PNE, 228PNF; 92/93 - 351A, 351A, 389PNC, 389PNA; 93/94 - 36C, 36A
- 7-Eleven: 84/85 - 43
- Topps: 80/81 - 213; 81/82 WN - 84; 82/83 - 223SK ;83/84 - 130SK; 84/85 - 134; 86/87 - 17; 87/88 - 160; 90/91 - 317; 91/92 - 55, 239SC; 93/94 - 12PF
- Upper Deck: 90/91 - 62E, 62F; 92/93 - 105

Ramsay, Beattie
- Dom. Choc.: 1925 - 59

Ramsay, Craig
- Coca Cola: 77/78 - 19
- Eddie Sargent: 72/73 - 38
- Loblaws: 74/75 - 50
- O-Pee-Chee: 72/73 - 262; 73/74 - 213; 74/75 - 305, 75/76 - 271; 76/77 - 78; 77/78 - 191; 78/79 - 9; 79/80 - 207; 80/81 - 13; 81/82 - 31; 83/84 - 69; 84/85 - 27, 215SK; 85/86 - 32, 175SK, 192SK
- Post: 82/83 - 26
- Topps: 75/76 - 271; 76/77 - 78; 77/78 - 191; 78/79 - 9; 79/80 - 207; 80/81 - 13; 84/85 - 21; 85/86 - 32

Ramsay, Michael (Mike)
- Bowman: 91/92 - 32
- Fleer: 92/93 - 19
- O-Pee-Chee: 80/81 - 127; 82/83 - 32; 83/84 - 70, 243SK; 84/85 - 28, 211SK; 85/86 - 77, 180SK; 86/87 - 115, 44SK; 87/88 - 63, 149SK; 88/89 - 133, 260SK; 89/90 - 140; 90/91 - 102; 91/92 - 236
- Panini: 87/88 - 25; 88/89 - 222; 90/91 - 24; 91/92 - 299; 92/93 - 253E, 253F
- Post: 82/83 - 27
- Parkhurst: 91/92 - 19E, 19F; 92/93 - 256, 256EI
- Pro Set: 90/91 - 28; 91/92 - 25E, 568E, 25F, 13PT, 568F
- Score: 90/91 - 23A, 23C, 13HR; 91/92 - 61A, 61B, 61C, 64PNE, 64PNF; 92/93 - 28C, 28A, 21PNC, 21PNA; 93/94 - 179C, 179A
- Topps: 80/81 - 127; 83/84 - 243SK; 84/85 - 22; 85/86 - 77; 86/87 - 115; 87/88 - 63; 88/89 - 133; 89/90 - 140; 90/91 - 102; 91/92 - 236, 135SC; 92/93 - 473, 473GS, 386SC
- Upper Deck: 90/91 - 168E, 168F

Randall, Ken
- Champ's: 24/25 - 17
- Maple Crispette: 24/25 - 24
- Wm. Paterson: 23/34 - 34; 24/25 - 12

Ranford, Bill (Goalie)
- Bowman: 91/92 - 101; 92/93 - 106
- Donruss: 93/94 - 117
- Fleer: 92/93 - 65; 93/94 - 158, 85PP, 6N
- Gillette: 91/92 - 9
- Hockey Wit: 93/94 - 76
- Humpty Dumpty: 92/93 - 18(II)
- Kraft: 90/91 - 45; 91/92 - 44; 93/94 - 16
- Leaf: 93/94 - 68, 10PW

Ranford, Bill (Goalie) (cont.)
- McDonald's: 91/92 - Mc21
- O-Pee-Chee: 87/88 - 13; 89/90 - 233, 230SK; 90/91 - 226, 467, 94PM; 91/92 - 356, 18PM; 92/93 - 137, 19SP; 93/94 - 258, 131SC, 131FD
- Panini: 87/88 - 5; 89/90 - 81; 90/91 - 218; 91/92 - 125; 92/93 - 99E, 99F; 93/94 - U(E), U(F)
- Parkhurst: 91/92 - 53E, 53F; 92/93 - 50, 50EI; 93/94 - 67, 67EI; 94/95 - 72, 72EI, V75
- Pro Set: 90/91 - 94, 390; 91/92 - 70E, 283E, 70F, 283F, 36PT; 92/93 - 51
- Score: 90/91 - 79A, 79C, 345A, 345C, 358A, 358C, 39HR; 91/92 - 30A, 30B, 30C, 170PNE, 170PNF, B-7E, B-7F; 92/93 - 236C, 424C, 495C, 236A, 424A, 495A, 4PNC, 4PNA; 93/94 - 155C, 155A, 7FR
- Season's: 92/93 - 57
- Topps: 87/88 - 13; 90/91 - 226; 91/92 - 356, 249SC; 92/93 - 126, 126GS, 66SC; 93/94 - 258, 426, 131SC, 131FD
- Upper Deck: 90/91 - 42E, 42F, 201E, 201F; 91/92 - 10E, 117E, 10F, 117F; 92/93 - 262; 93/94 - 180

Ranheim, Paul
- Bowman: 90/91 - 100; 91/92 - 251; 92/93 - 96
- Donruss: 93/94 - 50, 442
- Fleer: 92/93 - 27; 93/94 - 309PP
- Kraft: 1990 - 9
- Leaf: 93/94 - 170
- O-Pee-Chee: 90/91 - 20; 91/92 - 15; 92/93 - 36; 93/94 - 481, 151SC, 131FD
- Panini: 90/91 - 181, 342; 91/92 - 54 92/93 - 44E, 44F; 93/94 - 184E, 184F
- Parkhurst: 91/92 - 249E, 249F; 92/93 - 260, 260EI; 93/94 - 32, 32EI; 94/95 - 94, 94EI
- Pro Set: 90/91 - 44; 91/92 - 31E, 31F; 92/93 - 29
- Score: 90/91 - 248A, 248C; 91/92 - 21A, 21B, 21C, 252PNE, 252PNF; 92/93 - 149C, 149A; 93/94 - 165C, 165A
- Topps: 90/91 - 20; 91/92 - 15, 50SC; 92/93 - 486, 486GS, 144SC; 93/94 - 481C, 151SC, 151FD
- Upper Deck: 90/91 - 104E, 104F; 91/92 - 472E, 472F; 92/93 - 328; 93/94 - 131

Rankin, Frank
- Hall of Fame: 83 - 132, I13P; 87 - 132

Ratelle, Jean
- Beehive: 45/63 - 357A, 357B; 64/67 - 147
- Coca Cola: 65/66 - 88
- Colgate: 70/71 - 25
- Colgate: 71/72 - 11
- Dad;s Cookies: 70/71 - 91
- Derniere: 72/84 - 94
- Eddie Sargent: 70/71 - 118; 71/72 - 114; 72/73 - 142
- Esso: 70/71 - 157
- Hall of Fame: 87 - 249
- Loblaws: 74/75 - 208
- Mac's Milk: 73/74 - 23
- O-Pee-Chee: 68/69 - 77; 69/70 - 42, 24ST, 17QS; 70 71 - 181, 40DE, 26SS; 71/72 - 97, 19PT; 72/73 - 12, 48, 168; 73/74 - 141;74/75 - 145; 75/76 - 243; 76/77 - 80; 77/78 - 40, 16GP; 78/79 - 155; 79/80 - 225; 80/81 - 6
- Shirriff: 61/62 - 98; 68/69 - G2
- Topps: 61/62 - 60; 62/63 - 58; 63/64 - 63; 65/66 - 25; 66/67 - 29; 66/67 US - 29; 67/68 - 31; 68/69 - 77; 69/70 - 42; 70/71 - 26SK; 71/72 - 97; 72/73 - 50, 130; 73/74 - 73;74/75 - 145; 75/76 - 243; 76/77 - 80, 22PO; 77/78 - 40, 16PO; 78/79 - 155; 79/80 - 225; 80/81 - 6
- Toronto Sun: 71/72 - 179
- Zellers: 93/94 - 7, 7A

Rathje, Mike
- Donruss: 93/94 - 314
- Fleer: 93/94 - 437PP
- Leaf: 93/94 - 419
- O-Pee-Chee: 93/94 - 427
- Parkhurst: 93/94 - 4458, 458EI
- Topps: 93/94 - 427C, 322SC, 322FD
- Upper Deck: 92/93 - 589; 93/94 - 460

Ratushny, Dan
- Upper Deck: 93/94 - 245

Rauhala, Reine
- Upper Deck: 92/93 - 598

Rautakallio, Pekka
- O-Pee-Chee: 80/81 - 356; 81/82 - 50, 223SK; 82/83 - 218SK
- Panini: 79 - 164
- PepsiCo: 14
- Post: 82/83 - 45
- Topps: 82/83 - 218SK

Ravlich, Matt
- Beehive: 64/67 - 53
- Coca Cola: 65/66 - 34
- Colgate: 70/71 - 69
- Dad's Cookies: 70/71 - 61
- Eddie Sargent: 70/71 -71
- Esso: 70/71 - 106
- O-Pee-Chee: 68/69 - 152; 69/70 - 161; 70/71 - 32
- Shirriff: 68/69 - B12
- Topps: 65/66 - 115; 66/67 - 58; 66/67 US - 58; 70/71 - 32

Ray, Robert
- Parkhurst: 92/93 - 252, 252EI; 94/95 - 30, 30EI
- Pro Set: 90/91 - 419; 91/92 - 355E, 355F
- Score: 91/92 - 610B, 610C; 93/94 - 433C, 433A
- Upper Deck: 90/91 - 516E, 516F; 91/92 - 349E, 349F

Raymond, Donat
- Hall of Fame: 83 - 73, E14P; 87 - 73

Raymond, Paul
- CKAC Radio: 43/47 - 74
- Diamond: 36/39 - 54(I)
- Sweet Caporal: 34/35 - 24
- World Wide Gum: 33/34 - 18

Rayner, Chuck (Goalie)
- Beehive: 34/44 - 246; 45/63 - 358
- Hall of Fame: 83 - L14; 83 - 163; 87 - 163
- Parkhurst: 51/52 - 104; 52/53 - 22; 53/54 - 59
- Royal Desserts: 1952 - 2

Reardon, Ken
- Beehive: 34/44 - 177; 45/63 - 282
- CKAR Radio: 43/47 - 75
- Hall of Fame: 83 - B11; 83 - 25; 87 0 25
- O-Pee-Chee: 40/41 - 116
- Parkhurst: 55/56 - 64; 59/60 - 22
- Quaker Oats: 45/54 - 47A, 47B, 47C; 55/56 - 64

Reardon, Terry
- Beehive: 34/44 - 178

Reaugh, Daryl (Goalie)
- Bowman: 91/92 - 19
- O-Pee-Chee: 91/92 - 391
- Topps: 91/92 - 391, 326SC
- Upper Deck: 90/91 - 541E, 541F

Reaume, Marc
- Beehive: 45/63 - 445
- Chex: 63/65 - 33
- Esso: 70/71 - 248
- O-Pee-Chee: 70/71 - 119
- Parkhurst: 55/56 - 7; 57/58 TOR - 12; 58/59 - 20; 59/60 - 11; 60/61 - 25; 63/64 - 37, 96; 93/94 - 114ML
- Quaker Oats: 55/56 - 7
- Shirriff: 60/61 - 52
- Topps: 70/71 - 119
- York: 63/64 - 32

Reay, Billy
- Beehive: 45/63 - 283

Reay, Billy (cont.)
  CKAC Radio: 43/47 - 76
  La Patrie: 51/54 - 11
  O-Pee-Chee: 74/75 - 204
  Parkhurst: 51/52 - 13; 52/53 - 2; 55/56 - 66; 57/58 TOR - 25; 58/59 - 25
  Quaker Oats: 45/54 - 48A, 48B, 48C; 55/56 - 66
  Topps: 63/64 - 22; 64/65 - 38; 65/66 - 54; 66/67 - 53; 74/75 - 204

Recchi, Mark
  Bowman: 90/91 - 206; 91/92 - 83; 92/93 - 314
  Donruss: 93/94 - 252
  Fleer: 92/93 - 158; 93/94 - 236, 184PP, 12PL, 8RL
  Hockey Wit: 93/94 - 104
  Kellogg's: 92 - 9
  Kraft: 91/92 - 2
  Leaf: 93/94 - 205
  McDonald's: 91/92 - Mc4
  O-Pee-Chee: 90/91 - 280; 91/92 - 196; 92/93 - 373; 93/94 - 230, 136SC, 136FD
  Panini: 90/91 - 130, 341; 91/92 - 280; 92/93 - 185E, 185F; 93/94 - 46E, 46F
  Parkhurst: 91/92 - 134E, 347E, 134F, 347F; 92/93 - 130, 130EI; 93/94 - 149, 149EI; 94/95 - 165, 315, 165EI, 315EI
  Pro Set: 90/91 - 239; 91/92 - CC8E, 184E, 313E, 184F, 313F, 97PT; 92/93 - 131
  Score: 90 - 35YS; 90/91 - 186A, 186C, 81HR; 91 - 22YS; 91/92 - 145A, 145B, 145C, 151PNE, 360PNE, 151PNF, 360PNF; 92/93 - 180C, 180A, 80PNC, 80PNA, 18CSS, 18ASS; 93/94 - 150C,150A, 442C, 442A, 6PNC, 6PNA, 6CAS, 6AAS
  Season's: 92/93 - 41
  Sega: 93/94 - 101
  Topps: 90/91 - 280; 91/92 - 196, 5SL, 256SC; 92/93 - 267, 410, 267GS, 410GS, 183SC; 93/94 - 230, 136SC, 136FD, 21AS
  Upper Deck: 90/91 - 178E, 178F, 487E, 487F; 91/92 - 346E, 346F; 92/93 - 327, 11AS; 93/94 - 222, 300, 350

Reddick, Eldon (Goalie)
  O-Pee-Chee: 88/89 - 146SK; 89/90 - 137SK; 90/91 - 452
  Panini: 87/88 - 357
  Pro Set: 90/91 - 445

Redding, George
  Champ's: 24/25 - 6
  Wm. Paterson: 24/25 - 28

Redmond, Craig
  O-Pee-Chee: 85/86 - 121
  Topps: 85/86 - 121

Redmond, Dick
  Eddie Sargent: 72/73 - 46
  Loblaws: 74/75 - 85
  O-Pee-Chee: 71/72 - 106; 72/73 - 151; 73/74 - 12; 74/75 - 186; 75/76 - 218; 76/77 - 12; 77/78 - 213; 78/79 - 23; 79/80 - 129; 80/81 - 36; 81/82 - 9
  Topps: 72/73 - 113; 73/74 - 12; 74/75 - 186; 75/76 - 218; 76/77 - 12; 77/78 - 213; 78/79 - 23; 79/80 - 129; 81/82 EN - 73
  Toronto Sun: 71/72 - 56

Redmond, Keith
  Donruss: 93/94 - 448
  Parkhurst: 94/95 - 110, 110EI

Redmond, Mickey
  Colgate: 70/71 - 44
  Dad's Cookies: 70/71 - 79
  Eddie Sargent: 70/71 - 106; 72/73 - 74
  Esso: 70/71 - 139
  Loblaws: 74/75 - 105
  Mac's Milk: 73/74 - 24
  O-Pee-Chee: 68/69 - 64; 70/71 - 175; 71/72 - 102; 72/73 - 99; 73/74 - 180; 74/75 - 120; 75/76 - 120
  Shirriff: 68/69 - F18
  Topps: 71/72 - 102; 72/73 - 155;

Redmond, Mickey (cont.)
  Topps: 73/74 - 190; 74/75 - 120; 75/76 - 120; 76/77 - 243
  Toronto Sun: 71/72 - 101

Reekie, Joe
  Bowman: 90/91 - 125; 91/92 - 215; 92/93 - 137
  Donruss: 93/94 - 321
  Leaf: 93/94 - 234
  O-Pee-Chee: 91/92 - 144; 92/93 - 224, 70PM; 93/94 - 433
  Panini: 91/92 - 252
  Parkhurst: 91/92 - 328; 93/94 - 460, 460EI
  Pro Set: 90/91 - 487E, 328F; 91/92 - 429E, 429F; 92/93 - 179
  Score: 91/92 - 123A, 123B, 123C, 285PNE, 285PNF, 510C, 510A, 382PNC, 382PNA; 92/93 - 397C, 397A, 93/94 - 167C, 167A
  Topps: 91/92 - 144, 304SC; 92/93 - 184, 184GS, 264SC; 93/94 - 433C, 486SC, 486FD
  Upper Deck: 91/92 - 483E, 483F; 92/93 - 106

Reese, Jeff (Goalie)
  Bowman: 92/93 - 412
  Donruss: 93/94 - 443
  Fleer: 93/94 - 355PP
  O-Pee-Chee: 90/91 - 349; 91/92 - 81; 92/93 - 77; 93/94 - 302, 22SC, 22FD
  Panini: 90/91 - 281; 93/94 - 187E, 187F
  Parkhurst: 91/92 - 250E, 250F; 92/93 - 264, 264EI; 94/95 - 96, 96EI
  Pro Set: 90/91 - 540
  Score: 91/92 - 410B, 410C; 93/94 - 394C, 394A
  Topps: 90/91 - 349; 91/92 - 81; 92/93 - 385, 385GS, 322SC; 93/94 - 302,22SC, 22FD
  Upper Deck: 92/93 - 442

Regan, Larry
  Beehive: 45/63 - 61, 446
  Parkhurst: 59/60 - 17; 60/61 - 13; 93/94 - 16ML
  Shirriff: 60/61 - 16
  Topps: 57/58 - 6; 58/59 - 10
  York: 60/61 - 34

Reibel, Earl
  Beehive: 45/63 - 62, 208
  Parkhurst: 53/54 - 36; 54/55 - 37; 93/94 - 49ML, 147ML
  Topps: 54/55 - 52; 57/58 - 45; 58/59 - 57
  Toronto Star: 58/67 - 11

Reichel, Robert
  Bowman: 91/92 - 267; 92/93 - 401
  Donruss: 93/94 - 51
  Fleer: 92/93 - 28; 93/94 - 164, 5RS, 41PP
  Leaf: 93/94 - 59
  O-Pee-Chee: 90/91 - 95PM; 91/92 - 411; 92/93 - 93; 93/94 - 404, 198SC, 198FD
  Panini: 91/92 - 63, 343; 92/93 - 42E, 42F, 301E, 301F; 93/94 - 180E, 180F
  Parkhurst: 91/92 - 21E, 21F; 92/93 - 26, 26EI, PC; 93/94 - 300, 300EI; 94/95 - 34, 34EI, V47
  Pro Set: 90/91 - 595; 91/92 - 361E, 361F, 163PT
  Score: 90 - 29YS, 30T; 91 - 24YS; 91/92 - 263A, 483B, 483C, 56PNE, 56PNF; 92/93 - 106C, 106A, 101PNC, 101PNA; 93/94 204C, 204A
  Topps: 91/92 - 411, 393SC; 92/93 - 157, 157GS, 180SC; 93/94 - 404C, 198SC, 198FD
  Upper Deck: 90/91 - 533E, 533F; 91/92 - 223E, 223F; 92/93 - 42; 93/94 - 313

Reid, Dave
  Beehive: 45/63 - 447

Reid, David
  Bowman: 91/92 - 153
  Donruss: 93/94 - 403
  Fleer: 93/94 - 290PP
  O-Pee-Chee: 89/90 - 170SK 90/91 - 290; 91/92 - 423; 93/94 - 67, 100SC, 100FD

Reid, David (cont.)
  Panini: 91/92 - 104
  Parkhurst: 92/93 - 249, 249EI
  Pro Set: 90/91 - 541; 91/92 - P/C, 229E, 348E, 229F, 348F
  Score: 90/91 - 109T; 91/92 - 173A, 173B, 173C; 92/93 - 380C, 380A; 93/94 - 371C, 371A
  Topps: 90/91 - 290; 91/92 - 423; 78SC; 92/93 - 521 521GS; 93/94 - 67, 100SC, 100FD
  Upper Deck: 90/91 - 364E, 364F; 91/92 - 217E, 531E, 217F, 531F

Reid, Tom
  Esso: 70/71 - 123
  Eddie Sargent: 70/71 - 85; 72/73 - 99
  Loblaws: 74/75 - 160
  O-Pee-Chee: 70/71 - 43; 71/72 - 21; 73/74 - 109; 74/75 - 52; 75/76 - 277; 76/77 - 123; 77/78 - 306
  Topps: 70/71 - 43; 73/74 - 109; 74/75 - 52; 75/76 - 277; 76/77 - 123
  Toronto Sun: 71/72 - 144

Reid, Reg
  Wm. Paterson: 24/25 - 55

Reinhart, Paul
  Bowman: 90/91 - 60
  Esso: 83/84E - 15; 83/84F - 15
  Funmate: 83/84 - 19
  Kellogg's: 84 - 13
  Kraft: 86/87 - 6; 86/87P - 6; 1990 - 44
  O-Pee-Chee: 80/81 - 157; 81/82 - 36, 224SK; 82/83 - 56, 219SK; 83/84 - 91, 264SK; 84/85 - 235; 85/86 - 48, 209SK; 86/87 - 205; 87/88 - 143, 34HL, 39SK; 89/90 - 148, 65SK; 90/91 - 293
  Panini: 87/88 - 206; 90/91 - 293
  PepsiCo: 80/81 - 15
  Post: 82/83 - 46
  Pro Set: 90/91 - 304
  Score: 90/91 - 173A, 173C
  7-Eleven: 84/85 - 7
  Topps: 80/81 - 157; 81/82 - 28; 82/83 - 219SK; 83/84 - 264SK; 85/86 - 48; 87/88 - 143; 89/90 - 148; 90/91 - 293, 5SL;
  Upper Deck: 90/91 - 110E, 110F
  Vachon Foods: 83/84 - 17

Reise, Leo Jr.
  Beehive: 45/63 - 209, 359
  Parkhurst: 51/52 - 69; 52/53 - 49; 53/54 - 65; 54/55 - 67
  Royal Desserts: 1952 - 6
  Ultimate: 92 - 28(OSE), 28(OSF)

Reise, Leo
  Wm. Paterson: 23/24 - 33

Renberg, Mikael
  Donruss: 93/94 - 255, 5RR, U3
  Fleer: 93/94 - 13RS, 6GG, 408PP
  Leaf: 93/94 - 323, 5FP
  Parkhurst: 93/94 - 251, 251EI, CC12; 94/95 - 272, 272EI, V78
  Topps: 93/94 - 269SC, 269FD
  Upper Deck: 92/93 - 233; 93/94 - 486

Resch, Glenn (Chico) (Goalie)
  Kellogg's: 84 - 32
  Funmate: 83/84 - 76
  Loblaws: 74/75 - 194
  O-Pee-Chee: 74/75 - 353; 75/76 - 145; 76/77 - 250; 77/78 - 50, 17GP; 78/79 - 105; 79/80 -20; 80/81 - 235; 81/82 - 80, 230SK; 82/83 - 145, 146, 222SK; 83/84 - 236, 222SK, 223SK; 84/85 - 119, 69SK; 85/86 - 36, L/BB, 61SK; 86/87 - 158, 234SK
  Post: 82/83 - 174
  7-Eleven: 84/85 - 31
  Topps: 75/76 - 145; 76/77 - 250;

Resch, Glenn (Chico) (Goalie) (cont.)
- Topps: 76/77 - 6PO77/78 - 50; 78/79 - 105; 79/80 - 20; 80/81 - 235; 81/82 WN - 85; 82/83 - 222SK; 83/84 - 222SK, 223SK; 84/85 - 89; 85/86 - 36, L/BB; 86/87 - 158
- Upper Deck: 90/91 - 507E, 507F

Rheaume, Herb (Goalie)
- Anonymous: 1925/26 - 12

Rhodes, Damian
- Fleer: 93/94 - 454PP
- Leaf: 93/94 - 367
- Parkhurst: 93/94 - 470, 470EI
- Upper Deck: 93/94 - 364

Riabchikov, Evgeny
- Parkhurst: 93/94 - 533, 533EI

Ribble, Pat
- O-Pee-Chee: 79/80 - 199; 80/81 - 393; 81/82 - 339
- Topps: 79/80 - 199

Ricci, Mike
- Bowman: 91/92 - 246; 92/93 - 406
- Donruss: 93/94 - 280
- Fleer: 92/93 - 178, 389; 93/94 - 168, 202PP
- Gillette: 91/92 - 32
- Hockey Wit: 93/94 - 79
- Kraft: 91/92 - 52; 93/94 - 17
- Leaf: 93/94 - 23
- O-Pee-Chee: 90/91 - 96PM; 91/92 - 13, 194, 23PM; 92/93 - 329, 91PM; 93/94 - 62, 176SC, 176FD
- Panini: 91/92 - 231, 338; 92/93 - 184E, 184F; 93/94 - 69E, 69F
- Parkhurst: 91/92 - 123E, 123F; 92/93 - 146, 146EI; 93/94 - 439, 439EI; 94/95 - 186, 186EI
- Pro Set: 90/91 - 631; 91/92 - 170E, 170F, 85PT; 92/93 - 133
- Roots: 93/94 - 10
- Score: 90 - 39YS; 90/91 - 433A, 433C, 60T; 91 - 10YS; 91/92 - 28A, 28B, 28C, 32PNE, 32PNF; 92/93 - 84C, 84A, 314PNC, 314PNA; 93/94 - 120C, 120A
- Topps: 91/92 - 13, 194, 386SC; 92/93 - 86, 86SC, 408SC; 93/94 - 62, 176SC, 176FD
- Upper Deck: 90/91 - 355E, 355F; 91/92 - 143E, 143F; 92/93 - 477, 627; 93/94 - 352

Rice, Steven
- Donruss: 93/94 - 107
- Fleer: 93/94 - 181, 93/94 - 86PP
- O-Pee-Chee: 90/91 - 97PM
- Parkhurst: 93/94 - 72, 72EI
- Pro Set: 90/91 - 626
- Score: 90/91 - 390A, 390C; 91/92 - 420B, 420C, 334PNE, 334PNF; 92/93 - 545C, 545A
- Topps: 93/94 - 446SC, 446FD
- Upper Deck: 90/91 462E, 462F; 91/92 - 441E, 441F; 92/93 - 98; 93/94 - 367

Richard, Henri
- Bazooka: 71/72 - 5
- Beehive: 45/63 - 284; 64/67 - 112
- Chex: 63/65 - 34
- Coca Cola: 64/65 - 67; 65/66 - 67
- Colgate: 70/71 - 14
- Dad's Cookies: 70/71 - 80
- Derniere: 72/84 - 7, 27, 68
- Eddie Sragent: 70/71 - 98; 72/73 - 119
- El Producto: 62/63 - 5
- Esso: 70/71 - 140
- Hall of Fame: 83 - G11;83 - 91; 87 - 91
- Hockey Wit: 93/94 - 52
- La Patrie: 51/54 - 23
- Loblaws: 74/75 - 175
- O-Pee-Chee: 68/69 - 165, 21PS; 69/70 - 163, 16QS; 70/71 - 176, 24DE; 71/72 - 120, 6BK; 72/73 - 251; 73/74 - 87; 74/75 - 243, 321
- Parkhurst: 57/58 MON - 4; 58/59 - 2; 59/60 - 39; 60/61 - 47; 61/62 - 43;

Richard, Henri (cont.)
- Parkhurst: 62/63 - 38; 63/64 - 23, 82 ; 92/93 - PR28, 66ML, D18
- Post: 66/67 - 14; 68/69 - 9
- Shirriff: 60/61 - 34; 61/62 - 110; 62/63 - 41; 68/69 - F15
- TCMA: 1981 - 7
- Topps: 64/65 - 48; 65/66 - 71; 66/67 - 8; 66/67 US - 8; 67/68 - 72; 68/69 - 64; 69/70 - 11; 71/72 - 120, 6BK; 73/74 - 87
- Toronto Star: 57/67 - 44, 88, 98, 131; 58/67 - 18, 77; 63/64 - 22; 64/65 - 31
- Toronto Sun: 71/72 - 161
- Ultimate: 92 - 14(OSE), 81(OSE), 14(OSF), 81(OSF)
- Upper Deck: 92/93 - 47
- York: 60/61 - 16; 61/62 - 18; 62/63 - 10; 63/64 - 19

Richard, Jacques
- Derniere: 72/84 - 141
- Loblaws: 74/75 - 16
- O-Pee-Chee: 72/73 - 279; 73/74 - 169; 74/75 - 139; 75/76 - 117; 76/77 - 8; 77/78 - 366; 81/82 - 268, 285, 71SK; 82/83 - 290
- PepsiCo: 80/81 - 75; 82/83 - 250
- Topps: 73/74 - 169; 74/75 - 139; 75/76 - 117; 76/77 - 8; 81/82 - 29

Richard, Maurice (Rocket)
- Beehive: 34/44 - 179; 45/63 - 285; 64/67 - 113
- CKAC Radio: 43/47 - 77A, 77B
- Derniere: 72/84 - 60
- Hall of Fame: 83 - A12; 83 - 1; 87 - 1
- HHFM: 92 - 3
- Hockey Wit: 93/94 - 16
- La Patrie: 51/54 - 1
- Parkhurst: 51/52 - 4; 52/53 - 1; 53/54 - 24; 54/55 - 7; 55/56 - 37; 57/58 MON - 5;58/59 - 38; 59/60 - 2; 60/61 - 45; 93/94 - PR40, 65ML, 139ML, D16
- Quaker Oats: 45/54 - 49A, 49B, 49C, 49D; 5 5/56 - 37
- Score: 92/93 - 548C, 549C
- Ultimate: 92 - 95(OSE), 95(OSF)
- Wonder Bread: 1960 - 4W, 4PM
- Zellers: 92/93 - 7, 7A

Richards, Todd
- Topps: 92/93 - 79, 79GS

Richards, Travis
- Fleer: 93/94 - 513PP
- Topps: 93/94 - 7US
- Upper Deck: 91/92 - 430E, 430F

Richardson, George
- Hall of Fame: 83 - 85, F11P; 87 - 85

Richardson, Luke
- Bowman: 91/92 - 167; 92/93 - 255
- Donruss: 93/94 - 115
- Fleer: 92/93 - 297
- O-Pee-Chee: 88/89 - 245, 173SK; 90/91 - 428; 91/92 - 351, 46PM; 92/93 - 171
- Panini: 88/89 - 119; 89/90 - 142
- Parkhurst: 91/92 - 274E, 274F
- Pro Set: 90/91 - 289; 91/92 - 387E, 378F
- Score: 90/91 - 236A, 236C; 91 - 70T; 91/92 - 139A, 139B, 139C, 620B, 620C, 212PNE, 212PNF; 92/93 - 62C, 62A, 41PNC, 41PNA, 235PNC, 235A; 93/94 - 252C. 252A
- Topps: 91/92 - 351, 172SC; 92/93 - 409, 409GS, 456SC
- Upper Deck: 90/91 - 362E, 362F; 91/92 - 418E, 522E, 418F, 522F

Richardson, Terry (Goalie)
- O-Pee-Chee: 79/80 - 377

Richer, Stephane J.J.
- Bowman: 90/91 - 45; HT11; 91/92 - 330; 92/93 - 46
- Donruss: 93/94 - 190
- Durivage: 92/93 - 18; 93/94 - 48

Richer, Stephane J.J. (cont.)
- Fleer: 92/93 - 117; 93/94 - 152, 141PP
- Frito-Lay: 88/89 - 35
- Kraft: 86/87 - 35; 86/87P - 35; 1990 - 24; 90/91 - 46, 89; 91/92 - 21
- Leaf: 93/94 - 138
- O-Pee-Chee: 87/88 - 233; 88/89 - 5, 31NS, 49SK; 89/90 - 153, 51SK; 90/91 - 186, 98PM; 91/92 - 369, 113PM; 92/93 - 76, 18SP; 93/94 - 158, 327, 61SC, 61FD
- Panini: 87/88 - 65; 88/89 - 260; 89/90 - 239; 90/91 - 53; 91/92 - 193; 92/93 - 173E, 173F; 93/94 - 37E, 37F
- Parkhurst: 91/92 - 100E, 100F; 92/93 - 91, 91EI; 93/94 - 113, 113EI; 94/95 - V50
- Pro Set: 90/91 - 156, 370; 91/92 - 122E, 420E, 122F, 67PT, 420F; 92/93 - 93
- Score: 90/91 - 75A, 75C, 38HR; 91 - 31T; 91/92 - 234A, 581B, 581C, 14PNE, 14PNF; 92/93 - 140C, 140A, 361PNC, 361PNA; 93/94 - 34C, 34A
- Sega: 93/94 - 76
- Topps: 88/89 - 5; 89/90 - 153; 90/91 - 186, 4SL; 91/92 - 369, 86SC; 92/93 - 160, 160GS, 9SC; 93/94 - 158, 327, 61SC, 347SC, 61FD, 347FD
- Upper Deck: 90/91 - 276E, 276F; 91/92 - 244E, 536E, 244F, 536F; 92/93 - 56; 93/94 - 403

Richmond, Steve
- O-Pee-Chee: 86/87 - 208

Richter, Barry
- Fleer: 93/94 - 514PP
- O-Pee-Chee: 93/94 - 135
- Topps: 93/94 - 18US

Richter, Dave
- Panini: 87/88 - 344
- O-Pee-Chee: 87/88 - 261, 190SK

Richter, Mike (Goalie)
- Bowman: 90/91 - 218; 91/92 - 70; 92/93 - 238, 354
- Donruss: 93/94 - 223
- Fleer: 92/93 - 142; 93/94 - 228; 164PP
- Gillette: 91/92 - 39
- Hockey Wit: 93/94 - 1
- Leaf: 93/94 - 185
- O-Pee-Chee: 90/91 - 330; 91/92 - 11, 91, 78PM; 92/93 - 259, 93/94 - 64SC, 64FD
- Panini: 90/91 - 98, 345; 91/92 - 290; 92/93 - 231E, 231F; 93/94 - 99E, 99F
- Parkhurst: 91/92 - 117E, 117F; 92/93 - 112, 112EI; 93/94 - 129, 129EI; 94/95 - V5
- Pro Set: 90/91 - 398, 627; 91/92 - AC2, 161E, 161F, 83PT, 279PT; 92/93 - 116
- Score: 90 - 27YS; 90/91 - 74A, 74C; 91 - 2YS; 91/92 - 120A, 120B, 120C, 164PNE, 384PNE, 164PNF, 384PNF; 92/93 - 5C, 5A, 75PNC, 270PNC, 75PNA, 270PNA, 6USG, 1CTP, 1ATP; 93/94 - 99C, 99A
- Season's: 92/93 - 29
- Sega: 93/94 - 90
- Topps: 90/91 - 330; 91/92 - 11, 91, 92SC; 92/93 - 267, 367GS, 242SC, 266SC; 93/94 - 135, 64SC, 64FD
- Upper Deck: 90/91 - 32E, 32F; 91/92 - 34E, 175E, 634E, 34F, 175F, 634F; 92/93 - 145; 93/94 - 42

Ridley, Curt (Goalie)
- O-Pee-Chee: 76/77 - 197; 77/78 - 395; 78/79 - 302
- Topps: 76/77 - 197

Ridley, Mike
- Bowman: 90/91 - 77; 91/92 - 308; 92/93 - 360
- Donruss: 93/94 - 375
- Fleer: 92/93 - 238; 93/94 - 148, 266PP
- Leaf: 93/94 - 102
- O-Pee-Chee: 86/87 - 66, L/BB, 131SK, 221SK; 87/88 - 8, 234SK; 88/89 - 104, 74SK; 89/90 - 165, B/BB, 81SK; 90/91 - 327; 91/92 - 245; 92/93 - 305;

Ridley, Mike (cont.)
O-Pee-Chee: 93/94 - 78, 123SC, 123FD
Panini: 87/88 - 181; 88/89 - 374;
89/90 - 339; 90/91 - 163;
91/92 - 199; 92/93 - 162E, 162F;
93/94 - 25E, 25F
Parkhurst: 91/92 - 192E, 192F; 92/93 - 200,
200EI; 93/94 - 218, 218EI;
94/95 - 250, 250EI, V72
Pro Set: 90/91 - 320; 91/92 - 254E, 254F,
128PT
Score: 90/91 - 33A, 33C; 91/92 - 283A,
503B, 503C, 94PNE, 94PNF;
92/93 - 187C, 187A; 92/93 - 170PNC,
170PNA, 6CSS, 6ASS;
93/94 - 197C, 197A
Sega: 93/94 - 153
Topps: 86/87 - 66, L/BB; 87/88 - 8;
88/89 - 104; 89/90 - 165, B/BB;
90/91 - 327; 91/92 - 245;
91/92 - 245, 68SC; 91/92 - 245
92/93 - 236, 236GS, 200SC;
93/94 - 78, 123SC. 123FD
Upper Deck: 90/91 - 97E, 97F; 91/92 - 112E, 112F;
92/93 - 173; 93/94 - 341

Ridpath, Bruce
Imperial Tobacco: 10/11 - 14L, 34; 11/12 - 14;
12/13 - 28

Riendeau, Vincent
Bowman: 90/91 - 20; 91/92 - 372; 92/93 - 262
Fleer: 92/93 - 288
O-Pee-Chee: 89/90 - 17FS90/91 - 177;
91/92 - 370; 93/94 - 411
Panini: 89/90 - 120; 90/91 - 268
Parkhurst: 92/93 - 278, 278EI;
94/95 - 14, 14EI
Pro Set: 90/91 - 270; 91/92 - 213E, 213F,
112PT
Score: 90/91 - 107A, 107C; 91 - 43T;
91/92 - 23A, 23B, 23C; 92/93 - 396C,
396A, 177PNC, 177PNA
93/94 - 276C, 276A
Topps: 90/91 - 177; 91/92 - 370, 128SC
92/93 - 466, 466GS, 172SC;
93/94 - 411C
Upper Deck: 90/91 - 152E, 152F;
91/92 - 220E, 220F

Riggin, Pat (Goalie)
Funmate: 83/84 - 140
O-Pee-Chee: 81/82 - 37, 12SK, 221SK;
82/83 - 372; 84/85 - 205, 218,
386, 65SK, 233SK;
85/86 - 136, 106SK; 86/87 - 41SK
PepsiCo: 80/81 - 16
Post: 82/83 - 47
Topps: 81/82 - 30; 84/85 - 148, 164;
85/86 - 136

Riley, Bill
O-Pee-Chee: 77/78 - 360; 78/79 - 292;
79/80 - 303

Riley, Jack
Diamond: 36/39 - 55(I)
Sweet Caporal: 34/35 - 25

Rintanen, Kimmo
Upper Deck: 92/93 - 618

Ripley, Vic
Diamond: 33/35 - 51; 36/39 - 56(I)
O-Pee-Chee: 34/35 - 67
World Wide Gum: 33/34 - 54

Riopelle, Howard (Rip)
Beehive: 45/63 - 286
CKAC Radio: 43/47 - 78
Quaker Oats: 45/54 - 50A, 50B

Risebrough, Doug
Derniere: 72/84 - 128, 182
Funmate: 83/84 - 20
Kellogg's: 84 - 20
Kraft: 86/87 - 7; 86/87P - 7
O-Pee-Chee: 75/76 - 107; 76/77 - 109;
77/78 - 189; 78/79 - 249;
79/80 - 13; 80/81 - 275; 81/82 - 190;

Risebrough, Doug (cont.)
O-Pee-Chee: 82/83 - 57; 83/84 - 92, 269SK;
84/85 - 236, 241SK;
85/86 - 243; 86/87 - 196
PepsiCo: 80/81 - 55
Post: 82/83 - 156
Pro Set: 90/91 - 663
7-Eleven: 84/85 - 8
Topps: 75/76 - 107; 76/77 - 109;
77/78 - 189; 78/79 - 249;
79/80 - 13; 83/84 - 269SK;
86/87 - 196
Vachon Foods: 83/84 - 18

Rivard, Fern (Goalie)
Loblaws: 74/75 - 161

Rivers, Gus
La Presse: 27/32 - 45

Rivers, Wayne
O-Pee-Chee: 72/73 - 315
Topps: 63/64 - 17
Toronto Star: 64/65 - 6

Rivers, Shawn
Score: 93/94 - 470C, 470A

Roach, John (Goalie)
Anonymous: 33/34 - 18
Can. Chew Gum: 33/34 - 41
Champ's: 24/25 - 58
La Presse: 27/32 - 38
O-Pee-Chee: 33/34 - 53

Roach, John (Goalie) (cont.)
Wm. Paterson: 23/24 - 28; 24/25 - 52;
World Wide Gum: 33/34 - 67

Roach, Mickey
Champ's: 24/25 - 18
Maple Crispette: 24/25 - 23
Wm. Paterson: 23/24 - 38; 24/25 - 18

Robazza, Rino
Topps: 61/62 - 39

Roberge, Mario
Durivage: 92/93 - 27; 93/94 - 16
Parkhurst: 92/93 - 322, 322EI
Pro Set: 91/92 - 415E, 415F

Robert, Rene
Derniere: 72/84 - 105
Eddie Sargent: 72/73 - 42
Loblaws: 74/75 - 51
Lipton Soup: 74/75 - 24
O-Pee-Chee: 72/73 - 2; 73/74 - 139; 74/75 - 142;
75/76 - 46, 296; 76/77 - 42;
77/78 - 222; 78/79 - 188; 79/80 - 12;
80/81 - 239, 259; 81/82 - 322;
82/83 - 330
Topps: 72/73 - 161; 73/74 - 139;
74/75 - 142; 75/76 - 46, 296;
76/77 - 42; 77/78 - 222; 78 79 - 188;
79/80 - 12; 80/81 - 239, 259
Toronto Sun: 71/72 - 225

Roberto, Phil
Loblaws: 74/75 - 266
O-Pee-Chee: 71/72 - 228; 72/73 - 82; 73/74 - 3;
74/75 - 208; 75/76 - 80; 76/77 - 345
Topps: 72/73 - 52; 73/74 - 151;
74/75 - 208; 75/76 - 80
Toronto Sun: 71/72 - 162

Roberts, David
Fleer: 93/94 - 515PP
Topps: 93/94 - 16US

Roberts, Doug
Esso: 70/71 - 50
Eddie Sargent: 70/71 - 138; 72/73 - 26
Loblaws: 74/75 - 106
O-Pee-Chee: 68/69 - 88; 69/70 - 81; 70/71 - 71;
73/74 - 207; 74/75 - 312
Topps: 67/68 - 50; 68/69 - 88; 69/70 - 81;
70/71 - 71; 71/72 - 83

Roberts, Gary
Bowman: 90/91 - 95; 91/92 - 263;
92/93 - 109, 214
Donruss: 93/94 - 52

Roberts, Gary (cont.)
Fleer: 92/93 - 29; 93/94 - 187, 42PP
Leaf: 93/94 - 36
O-Pee-Chee: 89/90 - 202, 98SK; 90/91 - 161;
91/92 - 320, 126PM; 92/93 - 72,
14SP; 93/94 - 382, 510, 235SC,
235FD
Panini: 87/88 - 217; 88/89 - 15; 89/90 - 35;
90/91 - 179; 91/92 - 52; 92/93 - 45E,
45F; 93/94 - 181E, 181F
Parkhurst: 91/92 - 24E, 436E, 24F, 436F;
92/93 - 22, 22EI, CP8;
93/94 - 302, 302EI; 94/95 - V29
Pro Set: 90/91 - 45; 91/92 - 30E, 30F, 161PT;
92/93 - 21, 1TL
Score: 90/91 - 106A, 106C; 91/92 - 199A,
199B, 199C, 37PNE, 37PNF;
92/93 - 322C, 322A, 3PNC,
3PNA, 1CSS, 1ASS; 93/94 - 241C,
241A, 29PNC, 29PNA, 29CAS,
29AAS
Sega: 93/94 - 22
Topps: 90/91 - 161; 91/92 - 320, 126SC;
92/93 - 116, 116GS, 48SC;
93/94 - 382C, 510A, 235SC, 235FD,
9SCF, 20AS
Upper Deck: 90/91 - 29E, 29F; 91/92 - 190E, 190F;
92/93 - 289, 32AS; 93/94 - 151

Roberts, Gordon
Hall of Fame: 83 - O13; 83 - 222; 87 - 222
Imperial Tobacco: 10/11 - 3, 33L; 11/12 - 33;
12/13 - 23

Roberts, Gordon (Gordie)
Bowman: 92/93 - 197
Fleer: 92/93 - 255
O-Pee-Chee: 79/80 - 265; 80/81 - 112;
81/82 - 167; 82/83 - 174;
83/84 - 180, 114SK; 84/85 - 107;
85/86 - 28, 43SK; 86/87 - 42;
87/88 - 41, 55SK; 90/91 - 256;
91/92 - 494; 92/93 - 233, 86PM;
93/94 - 275, 41SC, 41FD
Panini: 88/89 - 102; 90/91 - 269
Post: 82/83 - 141
Pro Set: 90/91 - 271, 510; 91/92 - 458E, 458F
Score: 90/91 - 245A, 245C, 83T;
91/92 - 439A, 422B, 422C, 274PNE,
274PNF; 92/93 - 201C, 201A,
312PNC, 312PNA;
93/94 - 274C, 274A
Topps: 80/81 - 112; 81/82 WN - 111;
83/84 - 114SK; 85/86 - 28;
86/87 - 42; 87/88 - 41; 90/91 - 256;
91/92 - 494; 92/93 - 176, 176GS,
185SC; 93/94 - 275, 41SC, 41FD

Roberts, Jim
Beehive: 64/67 - 114
Coca Cola: 64/65 - 68; 65/66 - 68
Dad's Cookies: 70/71 - 119
Derniere: 72/84 - 16, 42
Eddie Sargent: 70/71 - 179, 72/73 - 126
Esso: 70/71 - 211
Loblaws: 74/75 - 176
O-Pee-Chee: 68/69 - 113; 69/70 - 174, 9QS;
70/71 - 213; 71/72 - 116;
72/73 - 269; 73/74 - 181;
74/75 - 78; 75/76 - 378;
76/77 - 119; 77/78 - 281
Shirriff: 68/69 - L6
Topps: 65/66 - 74; 66/67 - 6; 68/69 - 113;
69/70 - 14; 71/72 - 116; 74/75 - 78;
76/77 - 119
Toronto Sun: 71/72 - 246

Roberts, Jimmy
O-Pee-Chee: 77/78 - 392; 78/79 - 342

Robertson, Earl (Cooper) (Goalie)
Beehive: 34/44 - 247

Robertson, Torrie
O-Pee-Chee: 85/86 - 218; 86/87 - 214
Pro Set: 90/91 - 77

Robertson, Fred
Anonymous: 33/34 - 15

Robertson, George
    Beehive: 45/63 - 287
    Quaker Oats: 45/54 - 51

Robertson, John
    Hall of Fame: 83 - 102, G12P; 87 - 102

Robinson, Claude
    Hall of Fame: 83 - 192, J12P; 87-192

Robinson, Doug
    Coca Cola: 64/65 - 33; 65/66 - 89
    Esso: 70/71 - 107
    O-Pee-Chee: 68/69 - 160
    Shirriff: 68/69 - D12
    Topps: 64/65 - 84; 65/66 - 26

Robinson, Earl (Henry)
    Beehive: 34/44 - 76, 180, 202
    Canada Starch: 35/40 - 54, 196
    O-Pee-Chee: 34/35 - 55; 36/37 - 115; 37/38 - 165; 39/40 - 63
    Sweet Caporal: 34/35 - 35
    World Wide Gum: 33/34 - 5; 36/37 - 85

Robinson, Larry
    Bowman: 90/91 - 150; 91/92 - 177; 92/93 - 215
    Cel.Watch: 1988 - CW1
    Coca Cola: 77/78 - 20
    Derniere: 72/84 - 22, 45, 122, 187
    Esso: 83/84E - 16; 83/84F - 16;88/90 - 37
    Funmate: 83/84 - 67
    Hockey Wit: 93/94 - 92
    Kellogg's: 84 - 9
    Kraft: 86/87 - 36; 86/87P - 36; 90/91 - 47
    Loblaws: 74/75 - 177
    McDonald's: 82/83 - 17, 34
    O-Pee-Chee: 73/74 - 237; 74/75 - 280; 75/76 - 241; 76/77 - 151; 77/78 - 30, 18GP; 78/79 - 210, 329; 79/80 - 50; 80/81 - 84, 230, 11PO; 81/82 - 179, 196, 42SK, 148SK; 82/83 - 191, 31SK, 169SK; 83/84 - 195, 60SK, 61SK; 84/85 - 270, 147SK, 148SK; 85/86 - 147, 140SK; 86/87 - 62, M/BB, 8SK, 123SK; 87/88 - 192, 16SK; 88/89 - 246, 39SK; 89/90 - 235, 55SK; 90/91 - 261; 91/92 - 458; 92/93 - 167, 6AN
    Panini: 87/88 - 57; 89/90 - 245; 90/91 - 244; 91/92 - 82
    PepsiCo: 80/81 - 56
    Parkhurst: 91/92 - 74E, 74F
    Post: 81/82 - 16; 82/83 - 157
    Pro Set: 90/91 - 125; 91/92 - 104E, 104F
    7-Eleven: 84/85 - 29
    Score: 90/91 - 260A, 260C; 91/92 - 291A, 511B, 511C, 208PNE, 403PNE, 208PNF, 403PNF
    Topps: 75/76 - 241; 76/77 - 151; 77/78 - 30, 18PO; 78/79 - 210; 79/80 - 50; 80/81 - 84, 230; 81/82 - 31; 82/83 - 31SK, 169SK; 83/84 - 60SK, 61SK; 84/85 - 82; 85/86 - 147; 86/87 - 62, M/BB, 12SK; 87/88 - 192; 90/91 - 261; 91/92 - 458, 252SC
    Upper Deck: 90/91 - 52E, 52F; 91/92 - 499E, 499F; 92/93 - 48
    Vachon Foods: 83/84 - 53

Robinson, Rob
    Topps: 92/93 - 527GS

Robitaille, Luc
    Bowman: 90/91 - 152, HT12; 91/92 - 188; 92/93 - 70, 216
    Donruss: 93/94 - 162, 395
    Durivage: 92/93 - 28; 93/94 - 41
    Esso: 88/89 - 38
    Fleer: 92/93 - 87, 11AS; 93/94 - 208, 13AS, 120PP, 13PL, 9RL
    Frito-Lay: 88/89 - 36
    Gillette: 91/92 - 1
    Hockey Wit: 93/94 - 96
    Humpty Dumpty: 92/93 - 20(II)
    Kellogg's: 92/93 - 3P
    Kraft: 90/91 - 48, 75; 93/94 - 18

Robitaille, Luc (cont.)
    Leaf: 93/94 - 20, 9AS
    McDonald's: 91/92 - Mc14
    O-Pee-Chee: 87/88 - 42, 35HL, D/BB, 122SK, 133SK, 177SK, 187SK, 217SK; 88/89 - 124, 32NS, P/BB, 114SK, 157SK; 89/90 - 88, 148SK; 90/91 - 194, 209, 99PM; 91/92 - 260, 405, 34PM; 92/93 - 6; 93/94 - 90, 180, 87SC, 87FD
    Panini: 87/88 - 277; 87/88 - 379; 88/89 - 78; 89/90 - 95, 177; 90/91 - 233 ,331; 91/92 - 91. 324; 92/93 - 65E, 65F, 288E, 288F; 93/94 - 201E, 201F
    Parkhurst: 91/92 - 68E, 224E, 68F, 224F; 92/93 - 68, 501, 68EI, 501EI; 93/94 - 91, 91EI; 94/95 - V67
    Pro Set: 90/91 - 126, 341; 91/92 - AC9, 95E, 286E, 95F, 286F, 50PT, 12PK; 92/93 - 72
    Score: 90/91 - 150A, 150C, 316A, 316C, 66HR; 91/92 - 5PC, 3A, 345A, 3B, 3C, 375B, 375C, 17PNE, 385PNE, 17PNF, 385PNF, 3PC, B-10E, B-10F; 92/93 - 290C, 498C, 290A, 498A, 175PNC, 175PNA, 251PNC,251PNA; 93/94 - 245C, 245A, 451C, 451A, 37PNC, 37PNA, 24DT, 37CAS, 37AAS
    Season's: 92/93 - 10
    Sega: 93/94 - 64
    Topps: 87/88 - 42, D/BB, 12SK; 88/89 - 124, P/BB, 1SK; 89/90 - 88; 90/91 - 194, 209; 91/92 - 260, 405, 159SC; 92/93 - 101, 266, 101GS, 266GS, 44SC, 247SC; 93/94 - 90, 180, 87SC, 87FD, 21AS, 7SCF
    Upper Deck: 90/91 - 73E, 73F; 91/92 - 145E, 507E, 623E; 145F, 507F, 623F; 92/93 - 8, 216, WJG20, G2, 33AS; 93/94 - 231, 293, 414

Robitaille, Mike
    Loblaws: 74/75 - 52
    O-Pee-Chee: 71/72 - 8; 73/74 - 121; 74/75 - 159; 75/76 - 24; 76/77 - 359
    Topps: 71/72 - 8; 73/74 - 121; 74/75 - 159; 75/76 - 24
    Toronto Sun: 71/72 - 38

Roche, Desse (Desmond)
    Diamond: 36/39 - 57(I)
    La Presse: 27/32 - 57
    World Wide Gum: 33/34 - 70

Roche, Earl
    Diamond: 36/39 - 58(I)
    La Presse: 27/32 - 54
    World Wide Gum: 33/34 - 62

Rochefort, Leon
    Eddie Sargent: 72/73 - 81
    O-Pee-Chee: 68/69 - 95; 69/70 - 105, 7QS; 71/72 - 135; 72/73 - 204; 75/76 - 374
    Shirriff: 68/69 - J9
    Topps: 68/69 - 95; 69/70 - 105
    Toronto Sun: 71/72 - 102

Rochefort, Normand
    Bowman: 91/92 - 73
    Derniere: 72/84 - 150
    Durivage: 92/93 - 44
    O-Pee-Chee: 82/83 - 291; 83/84 - 300; 84/85 - 287, 176SK; 85/86 - 148SK; 88/89 - 182SK
    McDonald's: 82/83 - 35
    Panini: 87/88 - 161
    Post: 82/83 - 251
    Pro Set: 90/91 - 494
    Score: 90/91 - 149A, 149C; 91/92 - 171A, 171B, 171C, 273PNE, 273PNF; 92/93 - 377C, 377A
    Topps: 84/85 - 176SK
    Upper Deck: 90/91 - 437E, 437F
    Vachon Foods: 83/84 - 72

Rodden, Mike
    Hall of Fame: 83 - 164, L15P; 87 - 164

Roenick, Jeremy
    Bowman: 90/91 - 1; 91/92 - 386, 403; 92/93 - 78, 217
    Donruss: 93/94 - 67, 6ES, E/PM, E/SP
    Fleer: 92/93 - 41, 1-12PH; 93/94 - 186, 8G, 54PP, 14PL, 8PM
    Gillette: 91/92 - 13
    Hockey Wit: 93/94 - 103
    Humpty Dumpty: 92/93 - 19(II)
    Kellogg's: 92 - 5
    Kraft: 91/92 - 56: 93 - 17; 93/94 - 35
    Leaf: 93/94 - 27, 7SS
    O-Pee-Chee: 90/91 - 7, 100PM; 91/92 - 106, 52PM, 174PM; 92/93 - 345, 383, 23AN, 5SP; 93/94 - 450, 500, 190SC, 190FD
    Panini: 90/91 - 201; 91/92 - 12; 92/93 - 4E, 4F; 93/94 - M(E), M(F)
    Parkhurst: 91/92 - 29E, 439E, 29F, 439F; 92/93 - 31, 31EI, CP2; 93/94 - 309. 309EI, W6; 94/95 - 302, 302EI, H5, R5, C5, V65
    Pro Set: 90/91 - 58; 91/92 - 40E, 280E, 605E, 40F, 280F, 24PT, 6PK, 605F; 92/93 - 30, 252, 2TL
    Score: 90 - 24YS; 90/91 - 179PC, 179A, 179C, 31HR; 91 - 21YS; 91/92 - 220A, 305A, 418A, 220B, 309B, 334B, 220C, 309C, 334C, 10HC, 120PNE, 359PNE, 120PNF, 359PNF; 92/93 - 200C, 422C, 499C, 200A, 422A, 499A, 10PNC,10PNA, 256PNC, 256PNA, 10CSS, 10ASS, 3USG, 27CT, 27AT; 93/94 - 240C, 240A, 39PNC, 39PNA, 39CAS, 39AAS, 4FR
    Season's: 92/93 - 1
    Sega: 93/94 - 27
    Topps: 90/91 - 7; 91/92 - 106, 46SC; 92/93 - 400, 400GS, 167SC, 255SC; 93/94 - 450C, 500A, 190SC, 190FD, 22AS
    Upper Deck: 90/91 - 63E, 63F, 481E, 481F; 91/92 - 36E, 166E, 629E, 36F, 166, 629F; 92/93 - 274, WJG19, G8, 34AS; 93/94 - 235, 289, 314

Rogers, Fred
    Pro-Set: 91/92 - 297PT

Rogers, Mike
    Derniere: 72/84 - 169
    O-Pee-Chee: 79/80 - 43; 80/81 - 143; 81/82 - 127, 135, 140, 61SK; 82/83 - 232, 136SK; 83/84 - 254, 217SK; 84/85 - 152, 99SK; 85/86 - 39, 86SK
    Post: 82/83 - 205
    Topps: 79/80 - 43; 80/81 - 143; 81/82 - EN 131, 32, 53; 82/83 - 136SK; 83/84 - 217SK; 84/85 - 114; 85/86 - 39

Rolfe, Dale
    Dad's Cookies: 70/71 - 52
    Eddie Sargent: 70/71 - 55; 71/72 - 118; 72/73 - 146
    Esso: 70/71 - 87
    Loblaws: 74/75 - 209
    O-Pee-Chee: 68/69 - 41; 69/70 - 100, 18QS; 70/71 - 156; 71/72 - 219; 72/73 - 271; 73/74 - 177; 74/75 - 341
    Topps: 68/69 - 41; 69/70 - 100
    Toronto Sun: 71/72 - 180

Rollins, Al (Goalie)
    Beehive: 45/63 - 138A, 138B, 448
    Parkhurst: 51/52 - 76; 52/53 - 31; **53/54 - 82; 54/55 - 77**; 92/93 - PR8; 93/94 - 28ML, 166ML
    Topps: 54/55 - 26
    Quaker Oats: 45/54 - 99

Rolston, Brian
    Fleer: 93/94 - 516PP
    Topps: 93/94 - 5us
    Upper Deck: 91/92 - 699E, 699F

Romanchych, Larry
Eddie Sargent: 72/73 - 12
Loblaws: 74/75 - 17
O-Pee-Chee: 73/74 - 185; 74/75 - 157; 75/76 - 153; 76/77 - 281
Topps: 73/74 - 185; 74/75 - 157; 75/76 - 153

Romaniuk, Russell
Bowman: 92/93 - 276
Fleer: 93/94 - 492PP
O-Pee-Chee: 91/92 - 162PM; 92/93 - 263
Panini: 92/93 - 59E, 59F
Parkhurst: 91/92 - 198E, 198F
Pro Set: 91/92 - 565E, 565F, 274PT
Score: 91 - 77T; 91/92 - 627B, 627C, 324PNE, 324PNF
Topps: 92/93 - 390, 390GS, 164SC
Upper Deck: 91/92 - 46E, 46F

Romano, Roberto (Goalie)
O-Pee-Chee: 86/87 - 152, 229
Topps: 86/87 - 152

Rombough, Doug
Loblaws: 74/75 - 195
O-Pee-Chee: 74/75 - 279; 75/76 - 161
Topps: 75/76 - 161

Romnes, Doc (Elwin)
Beehive: 34/44 - 77, 248, 345
Diamond: 33/35 - 52; 36/39 - 59(I)

Ronan, Ed
Fleer: 92/93 - 333
O-Pee-Chee: 92/93 - 41PM
Parkhurst: 92/93 - 88, 88EI
Topps: 93/94 - 262SC, 262FD
Upper Deck: 92/93 - 491

Ronan, Skene (Erskine)
Imperial Tobacco: 10/11 - 26L; 11/12 - 26; 12/13 - 14

Ronning, Cliff
Bowman: 91/92 - 313; 92/93 - 411
Donruss: 93/94 - 357
Fleer: 92/93 - 227; 93/94 - 119, 255PP
Leaf: 93/94 - 183
O-Pee-Chee: 89/90 - 45, 20SK; 91/92 - 59; 92/93 - 94; 93/94 - 81, 125SC, 125FD
Panini: 89/90 - 122; 91/92 - 46; 92/93 - 30F, 30F; 93/94 - 168E, 168F
Parkhurst: 91/92 - 182E, 182F; 92/93 - 193, 193EI; 93/94 - 210, 210EI
Pro Set: 90/91 - 526; 91/92 - 241E, 241F, 236PT; 92/93 - 195
Score: 90/91 - 81T; 91/92 - 212A, 212B, 212C, 106PNE, 106PNF; 92/93 - 254C, 254A, 12PNC, 12PNA; 93/94 - 17C, 17A, 443C, 443A
Season's: 92/93 - 32
Sega: 93/94 - 141
Topps: 89/90 - 45; 91/92 - 59, 298SC; 92/93 - 81, 81GS, 373SC; 93/94 - 81 125SC, 125FD
Upper Deck: 91/92 - 208E, 208F; 92/93 - 160; 93/94 - 211

Ronty, Paul
Beehive: 45/63 - 63, 360
Parkhurst: 51/52 - 95; 52/53 - 24; 53/54 - 63; 54/55 - 66
Topps: 54/55 - 15

Rooney, Steve
O-Pee-Chee: 87/88 - 223

Root, William (Bill)
Derniere: 72/84 - 196
O-Pee-Chee: 83/84 - 196; 84/85 - 271

Ross, Art
Hall of Fame: 83 - 74, E15P; 87 - 74
Imperial Tobacco: 10/11 - 8, 12, 31L; 11/12 - 31; 12/13 - 20
Topps: 60/61 - 27, 49ST
World Wide Gum: 36/37 - 96

Ross, Phillip D.
Hall of Fame: 83 - 58, D12P; 87 - 58

Rota, Darcy
Funmate: 83/83 - 131
Loblaws: 74/75 - 86
O-Pee-Chee: 74/75 - 269; 75/76 - 66; 76/77 - 47; 77/78 - 117; 78/79 - 47; 79/80 - 360; 80/81 - 301; 81/82 - 343; 82/83 - 355; 83/84 - 344, 345, 358, 272SK; 84/85 - 328, 280SK
PepsiCo: 80/81 - 117; 82/83 - 301
7-Eleven: 84/85 - 50
Topps: 75/76 - 66; 76/77 - 47; 77/78 - 117; 78/79 - 47; 83/84 - 272SK; 84/85 - 139
Vachon Foods: 83/84 - 115

Rota, Randy
Loblaws: 74/75 - 124
O-Pee-Chee: 74/75 - 362; 75/76 - 237; 76/77 - 353
Topps: 75/76 - 237

Rothschild, Sam
Anonymous: 26/27 - 100
Champ's: 24/25 - 37
Maple Crispette: 24/25 - 19
Wm. Paterson: 24/25 - 37

Roulston, Tom
O-Pee-Chee: 82/83 - 118; 83/84 - 42, 103SK; 84/85 - 179, 123SK
Topps: 83/84 - 103SK
Vachon Foods: 83/84 - 39

Rouse, Robert (Bob)
Donruss: 93/94 - 333
Fleer: 92/93 - 214
Leaf: 93/94 - 230
O-Pee-Chee: 89/90 - 26; 91/92 - 151PM; 93/94 - 207
Panini: 89/90 - 351; 90/91 - 164; 91/92 - 101
Parkhurst: 91/92 - 176E, 176F
Pro Set: 90/91 - 554; 91/92 - 228E, 228F
Score: 90/91 - 147A, 147C; 91/92 - 246B, 246C; 92/93 - 130C, 130A, 358PNC, 358PNA; 93/94 - 304C, 304A
Topps: 89/90 - 26; 93/94 - 207, 353SC, 353FD
Upper Deck: 90/91 - 389E, 389F

Rousseau, Bobby
Beehive: 45/63 - 288; 64/67 - 115
Chex: 63/65 - 35A, 35B
Coca Cola: 64/65 - 65; 65/66 - 69
Colgate: 70/71 - 35
Dad's Cookies: 70/71 - 70
Eddie Sargent: 70/71 - 96; 72/73 - 145
Esso: 70/71 - 124
Loblaws: 74/75 - 210
O-Pee-Chee: 68/69 - 65; 69/70 - 9; 70/71 - 170, 14DE; 71/72 - 218; 72/73 - 233; 73/74 - 233; 74/75 - 326
Parkhurst: 62/63 - 47; 63/64 - 35, 94
Post: 66/67L - 15; 66/67S - 7; 68/69 - 10
Shirriff: 61/62 - 117; 62/63 - 29; 62/63 - 56; 68/69 - F9
Topps: 64/65 - 80; 65/66 - 70; 66/67 - 7, 132; 66/67 US - 7; 67/68 - 68; 68/69 - 65; 69/70 - 9
Toronto Star: 57/67 - 100; 58/67 - 79, 99
Toronto Sun: 71/72 - 181
York: 61/62 - 35; 62/63 - 18; 63/64 - 25

Rousseau, Guy
La Patrie: 51/54 - 33, 40

Roussel, Dominic (Goalie)
Bowman: 92/93 - 92
Donruss: 93/94 - 243
Durivage: 93/94 - 39
Fleer: 92/93 - 159; 93/94 - 409PP
Leaf: 93/94 - 244
O-Pee-Chee: 92/93 - 198, 51PM, 3TR; 93/94 - 335, 109SC, 109FD
Panini: 92/93 - 183E, 183F
Parkhurst: 91/92 - 450E, 450F; 92/93 - 129, 129EI; 93/94 - 417, 417EI
Pro Set: 91/92 - 552E, 552F; 92/93 - 235
Score: 91/92 - 343PNE, 343PNF; 92/93 - 96PNC, 96PNA, 11CT, 11AT;

Roussel, Dominic (Goalie) (cont.)
Score: 93/94 - 82C, 82A
Season's: 92/93 - 40
Topps: 92/93 - 10, 213, 10GS, 213GS, 315SC; 93/94 - 335, 109SC, 109FD
Upper Deck: 91/92 - 583E, 583F; 92/93 - 31; 93/94 - 336

Rowe, Bobby
Imperial Tobacco: 10/11 - 23L; 11/12 - 23; 12/13 - 11

Rowe, Tom
O-Pee-Chee: 79/80 - 113; 80/81 - 214; 81/82 - 139
Topps: 79/80 - 113; 80/81 - 214

Roy, Patrick (Goalie)
Bowman: 90/91 - 50; 91/92 - 335; 92/93 - 74, 239
Donruss: 93/94 - 178, 9ES, 1IK, L/PM, L/SP
Durivage: 92/93 - 50; 93/94 - 17
Fleer: 92/93 - 3AS, 4AW; 93/94 - 39, 9G, 1AS, 133PP, 7N
Gillette: 91/92 -28
Highliner: 92/93 - 1
Hockey Wit: 93/94 - 3
Humpty Dumpty: 92/93 - 18(I)
Kellogg's: 92 - 1; 92/93 - 4P
Leaf: 92/93 - 5AS, 4PW, 6SS
Kraft: 86/87 - 37; 86/87P - 37; 1990 - 25; 90/91 - 49; 1993 - 24; 93 - 33; 93/94 - 29
McDonald's: 91/92 - Mc6, McH8
O-Pee-Chee: 86/87 - 53, 5SK, 19SK, 132SK; 87/88 - 163, 36HL, 13SK, 73SK, 185SK; 88/89 - 116, 33NS, 45SK, 115SK; 89/90 - 17, 322, 57SK, 161SK, 210SK, 28FS; 90/91 - 198, 219, 512, E/BB, 101PM; 91/92 - 270, 413, 14PM, 170PM; 92/93 - 111, 164, 19AN, 4BB; 93/94 - 231SC, 231FD
Panini: 87/88 - 376B; 87/88 - 56; 88/89 - 252; 89/90 - 235, 383; 90/91 - 51, 323; 91/92 - 184, 333; 92/93 - 147E, 147F, 277E, 277F; 93/94 - B(E), B(F)
Parkhurst: 91/92 - 90E, 220E, 90F, 220F, 442, 463, 470; 92/93 - 84, 463, 510, 84EI, 463EI, 510EI; 93/94 - 100. 100EI, G9, E4, D10; 94/95 - 113, 312, 113EI, 312EI, H12, R12, C12
Pro Set: 90/91 - 157, 359, 391, 399, ; 91/92 - AC3, 125P, 125CC, 125E, 304E, 599E, 613E, 125F, 304F, 61PT, 14PK, 125CCE, 125CCF, 599F, 613F, 599CC, 2CC; 92/93 - 2, 85, CC2
Roots: 93/94 - 9
Score: 90/91 - 10A, 10C, 10PC, 312A, 312C, 344A, 344C, 364A, 364C, 25HR; 91/92 - 10PC, 75A, 342A, 424A, 75B, 314B, 372B, 75C, 314C, 372C, 175PNE, 387PNE, 175PNF, 387PNF, 75PC, B-1E, B-1F; 92/93 - 298C, 418C, 428C, 489C, 527C, 298A, 418A, 428A, 489A, 527A, 130PNC, 130PNA; 93/94 - 315C, 315A, 18PNC, 18PNA, 2DT, 18CAS, 18AAS, 10FR
Season's: 92/93 - 21
Sega: 93/94 - 72
Topps: 86/87 - 53; 87/88 - 163; 88/89 - 116, 12SK; 89/90 - 17, 6SK; 90/91 - 198, 219, E/BB; 91/92 - 270, 413, 107SC; 92/93 - 110, 263, 491, 508, 110GS, 263GS, 491GS, 508GS, 133SC, 252SC; 93/94 - 1, 22BG, 231SC, 231FD, 7MP, 1AS, 11SCF
Upper Deck: 90/91 - P/C, 153E, 153F, 207E, 207F, 496E, 496F; 91/92 - 241PC, 137E, 614E, 137F, 614F; 92/93 - 149, 438, 440, W6, 12AS; 93/94 - 49

Rucinsky, Martin
Donruss: 93/94 - 281

Rucinsky, Martin (cont.)
Fleer: 92/93 - 390; 93/94 - 191, 203PP
Leaf: 93/94 - 152
O-Pee-Chee: 92/93 - 124PM; 93/94 - 367, 11SC, 11FD
Panini: 93/94 - 74E, 74F
Parkhurst: 91/92 - 366E, 366F; 92/93 - 149, 149EI; 93/94 - 170, 170EI
Pro-Set: 92/93 - 238
Score: 92/93 - 474C, 474A; 93/94 - 254C, 254A
Topps: 92/93 - 523, 523GS; 93/94 - 367, 11SC, 11FD
Upper Deck: 91/92 - 19E, 19F, 70E, 70F; 92/93 - 556; 93/94 - 6

Ruel, Claude
Demiere: 72/84 - 118

Ruff, Jason
Upper Deck: 92/93 - 522

Ruff, Lindy
O-Pee-Chee: 80/81 - 319; 82/83 - 31; 84/85 - 29, 213SK; 86/87 - 4; 88/89 - 40; 90/91 - 143
Panini: 87/88 - 35
Post: 82/83 - 28
Topps: 84/85 - 23; 86/87 - 4; 88/89 - 40; 90/91 - 143

Rumble, Darren
Fleer: 92/93 - 148; 93/94 - 153, 173PP
O-Pee-Chee: 93/94 - 356
Parkhurst: 92/93 - 356, 356EI; 93/94 - 411, 411EI
Topps: 93/94 - 356, 418SC, 418FD
Upper Deck: 92/93 - 110

Runge, Paul
Beehive: 34/44 - 204
Diamond: 36/39 - 56(II), 52(III)
O-Pee-Chee: 36/37 - 106; 37/38 - 167
World Wide Gum: 36/37 - 81

Ruotsalainen, Reijo
Funmate: 83/84 - 91
O-Pee-Chee: 82/83 - 233; 83/84 - 255, 216SK; 84/85 - 153, 101SK; 85/86 - 112, 81SK; 86/87 - 128, 225SK
Post: 82/83 - 206
Topps: 83/84 - 216SK; 84/85 - 115; 85/86 - 112, M/BB; 86/87 - 128

Rupp, Duane
Esso: 70/71 - 192
Eddie Sargent: 70/71 - 166; 72/73 - 180
O-Pee-Chee: 69/70 - 153, 8QS; 70/71 - 89; 72/73 - 154
Topps: 67/68 - 20; 70/71 - 89; 72/73 - 28;
Toronto Sun: 71/72 - 226

Ruskowski, Terry
O-Pee-Chee: 79/80 - 141; 80/81 - 119; 81/82 - 62, 117SK; 82/83 - 72, 178SK; 83/84 - 161, 291SK; 84/85 - 89, 270SK; 85/86 - 33, 237SK; 86/87 - 111, 226SK; 87/88 - 73, 167SK
Panini: 87/88 - 150
Post: 82/83 - 61
Topps: 80/81 - 119; 81/82 WN - 74; 82/83 - 178SK; 83/84 - 291SK; 84/85 - 68; 85/86 - 33; 86/87 - 111; 87/88 - 73

Russell, Blair
Hall of Fame: 83 - 178, M14; 87 - 178

Russell, Cam
Upper Deck: 91/92 - 352E, 352F
Score: 90/91 - 408A, 408C
Topps: 93/94 - 286SC, 286FD

Russell, Ernest
Hall of Fame: 83 - 133, I14P; 87 - 133
Imperial Tobacco: 10/11 - 20, 35L; 11/12 - 35; 12/13 - 26

Russell, Phil
Funmate: 83/84 - 77
Loblaws: 74/75 - 87
O-Pee-Chee: 73/74 - 243; 74/75 - 226; 75/76 - 102; 76/77 - 31; 77/78 - 235; 78/79 - 12; 79/80 - 143; 80/81 - 226; 81/82 - 51, 226SK; 82/83 - 58; 83/84 - 237, 271SK; 84/85 - 120, 75SK; 85/86 - 30, 58SK; 86/87 - 142
PepsiCo: 80/81 - 17
Post: 82/83 - 48
Topps: 74/75 - 226; 75/76 - 102; 76/77 - 31; 77/78 - 235; 78/79 - 12; 79/80 - 143; 80/81 - 226; 83/84 - 271SK; 85/86 - 30; 86/87 - 142

Rutherford, Jim (Goalie)
Coca Cola: 77/78 - 21
Esso: 70/71 - 88
Eddie Sargent: 72/73 - 175
Loblaws: 74/75 - 107
O-Pee-Chee: 72/73 - 15; 73/74 - 59; 74/75 - 225; 75/76 - 219; 76/77 - 88; 77/78 - 239; 78/79 - 74; 79/80 - 122; 80/81 - 125
PepsiCo: 80/81 - 95
Topps: 72/73 - 97; 73/74 - 59; 74/75 - 225; 75/76 - 219; 76/77 - 88; 77/78 - 239; 78/79 - 74; 79/80 - 122; 80/81 - 125

Rutherford, N.
Dom. Choc.: 1925 - 58

Rutledge, Wayne (Goalie)
O-Pee-Chee: 72/73 - 329
Shirriff: 68/69 - D9

Ruttan, Jack
Hall of Fame: 83 - 149, K15P; 87 - 149

Ruuttu, Christian
Bowman: 90/91 - 244; 91/92 - 25; 92/93 - 341
Donruss: 93/94 - 72
Fleer: 92/93 - 281
Leaf: 93/94 - 334
O-Pee-Chee: 87/88 - 121, 37HL, 134SK, 144SK; 88/89 - 18, 256SK; 89/90 - 68, 255SK; 90/91 - 182; 91/92 - 115; 92/93 - 2PM; 93/94 - 355, 103SC, 103FD
Panini: 87/88 - 28; 88/89 - 227; 89/90 - 207; 90/91 - 20; 91/92 - 306; 92/93 - 250E, 250F
Parkhurst: 91/92 - 242E, 242F; 92/93 - 34, 34EI; 93/94 - 39, 39EI; 94/95 - 42, 42EI
Pro Set: 90/91 - 29; 91/92 - 22E, 22F
Score: 90/91 - 77A, 77C; 91/92 - 45A, 45B, 45C, 60PNE, 60PNF; 92/93 - 334C, 334A, 317PNC, 317PNA; 93/94 - 84C, 84A
Topps: 87/88 - 121; 88/89 - 18; 89/90 - 68; 90/91 - 182; 91/92 - 115, 33SC; 92/93 - 485, 485GS, 330SC; 93/94 - 355, 103SC, 103FD
Upper Deck: 90/91 - 170E, 170F; 91/92 - 104E, E11(E), 104F, E11(F); 92/93 - 446; 93/94 - 141

Ruzicka, Vladimir
Bowman: 92/93 - 431
Donruss: 93/94 - 228
Fleer: 92/93 - 10; 93/94 - 174PP
Leaf: 93/94 - 438
O-Pee-Chee: 90/91 - 393; 91/92 - 144PM; 92/93 - 228
Panini: 92/93 - 138E, 138F
Parkhurst: 91/92 - 3E, 3F; 92/93 - 5, 5EI
Pro Set: 90/91 - 588; 91/92 - 353E, 353F, 152PT; 92/93 - 5
Score: 90/91 - 44T; 91/92 - 411B, 411C; 181PNE,191PNF; 92/93 - 208C, 208A, 59PNC, 59PNA; 93/94 - 154C, 154A
Topps: 90/91 - 393; 91/92 - 383SC; 92/93 - 333, 333GS, 358SC
Upper Deck: 90/91 - 538E, 538F; 91 - 83T; 91/92 - 288E, 288F; 92/93 - 258, E4

Rychel, Warren
Donruss: 93/94 - 156
Fleer: 93/94 - 352PP
Leaf: 93/94 - 263

Rychel, Warren (cont.)
O-Pee-CHee: 93/94 - 266
Parkhurst: 92/93 - 309, 309EI; 93/94 - 98, 98EI
Topps: 93/94 - 266, 258SC, 258FD
Upper Deck: 92/93 - 547; 93/94 - 93

Sabourin, Gary
Bauer: 68/69 - 20
Colgate: 70/71 - 57
Dad's Cookies: 70/71 - 120
Eddie Sargent: 70/71 - 186; 72/73 - 183
Esso: 70/71 - 212
Loblaws: 74/75 - 282
O-Pee-Chee: 68/69 - 117 69/70 - 19, 3QS; 70/71 - 96, 28DE; 71/72 - 13; 72/73 - 91; 73/74 - 168; 74/75 - 368; 75/76 - 299; 76/77 - 266
Shirriff: 68/69 - L11
Topps: 68/69 - 117; 69/70 - 19; 70/71 - 96; 72/73 - 163; 73/74 - 184; 75/76 - 299
Toronto Sun: 71/72 - 247

Sabourin, Ken
O-Pee-Chee: 91/92 - 43
Pro Set: 90/91 - 596
Score: 91/92 - 398B, 398C
Topps: 91/92 - 43, 396SC
Upper Deck: 91/92 - 417E, 417F

Sacco, David
Fleer: 93/94 - 517PP
Parkhurst: 94/95 - 236, 236EI
Topps: 93/94 - 13US

Sacco, Joseph (Joe)
Bowman: 92/93 - 417
Donruss: 93/94 - 2
Fleer: 92/93 - 21593/94 - 9PP
O-Pee-Chee: 92/93 - 355; 93/94 - 329
Parkhurst: 91/92 - 395E, 395F; 92/93 - 185, 185EI; 93/94 - 273, 273EI
Score: 91/92 - 319A, 349B, 349C; 92/93 - 532C, 532A
Topps: 92/93 - 398SC; 93/94 - 329, 256SC, 256FD
Upper Deck: 92/93 - 266, 382; 93/94 - 36

Sacharuk, Larry
Loblaws: 74/75 - 267
O-Pee-Chee: 75/76 - 76
Topps: 75/76 - 76E

Saganiuk, Rocky
O-Pee-Chee: 80/81 - 64; 81/82 - 323; 82/83 - 331, 69SK
PepsiCo: 80/81 - 96
Post: 82/83 - 286
Topps: 80/81 - 64; 82/83 - 69SK

Saint James, Susan
Pro-Set: 91/92 - 299PT

Sakic, Joe
Bowman: 90/91 - 169; 91/92 - 133; 92/93 - 240, 244
Donruss: 92/93 - 282
Fleer: 92/93 - 179; 93/94 - 242, 204PP, 15PL
Gillette: 91/92 - 22
Hockey Wit: 93/94 - 100
Humpty Dumpty: 92/93 - 19(I)
Kellogg's: 92 - 12
Kraft: 1990 - 32; 90/91 - 50, 79; 91/92 - 41; 93/94 - 50
Leaf: 93/94 - 87
McDonald's: 91/92 - Mc5
O-Pee-Chee: 89/90 - 113, 41SK, 187SK; 16FS; 90/91 - 384, 102PM; 91/92 - 16, 70PM; 92/93 - 54, 55, 22AN, 11SP; 93/94 - 101, 15BG, 32SC, 32FD
Panini: 89/90 - 327; 90/91 - 139; 91/92 - 334, 257; 92/93 - 209E, 209F; 93/94 - G(E), G(F)
Parkhurst: 91/92 - 148E, 148F; 92/93 - 147, 147EI; 93/94 - 169, 169EI, E9; 94/95 - V34
Pro Set: 90/91 - 257, 375; 91/92 - AC5,

Sakic, Joe (cont.)
Pro Set: 199E, 199F, 315E, 315F, 102PT, 23PK; 92/93 - 150
Score: 90 - 10YS; 90/91 - 8A, 8C, 7HR; 91 - 20YS; 91/92 - 25A, 336A, 25B, 25C, 366B, 366C, 105PNE, 381PNE, 105PNF, 381PNF; 92/93 - 240C, 434C, 240A, 434A, 150PNC, 150PNA, 21CT, 21AT; 93/94 - 135C, 135A, 13PNC, 13PNA, 14DT, 13CAS, 13AAS, 17FR
Season's: 92/93 - 47
Sega: 93/94 - 112
Topps: 89/90 - 113; 90/91 - 384, 14SL; 91/92 - P/C, 16, 8SL, 389SC; 92/93 - 495, 495GS, 3SC; 93/94 - 10, 32SC, 32FD, 12AS
Upper Deck: 90/91 - 164E, 164F, 490E, 490F; 91/92 - 333E, 616E, 333F, 616F; 92/93 - 255, WJG8, 13AS; 93/94 - 69, 223

Saleski, Don
Coca-Cola: 77/78 - 22
Loblaws: 74/75 - 230
O-Pee-Chee: 72/73 - 213; 74/75 - 283; 75/76 - 262; 76/77 - 81; 77/78 - 233; 78/79 - 257
Topps: 75/76 - 262; 76/77 - 81; 77/78 - 233; 78/79 - 257

Salming, Borje
Cel.Watch: 1988 - CW16
Derniere: 72/84 - 111
Esso: 88/89 - 39
Funmate: 83/84 - 125
Hockey Wit: 93/94 - 37
Kellogg's: 84 - 25
Kraft: 86/87 - 57, 57P
Lipton Soup: 74/75 - 41A, 41B
Loblaws: 74/75 - 283
O-Pee-Chee: 74/75 - 180; 75/76 - 283, 294; 76/77 - 22; 77/78 - 140; 78/79 - 240, 328; 79/80 - 40; 80/81 - 85, 210, 19PO; 81/82 - 307, 98SK, 111SK; 82/83 - 332, 75SK, 76SK; 83/84 - 341, 33SK, 34SK; 84/85 - 311, 7SK, 8SK; 85/86 - 248, 12SK; 86/87 - 169, 136SK; 87/88 - 237, 165SK; 88/89 - 247, 174SK; 89/90 - 278
Panini: 87/88 - 326; 88/89 - 120
PepsiCo: 80/81 - 97
Post: 81/82 - 18; 82/83 - 287
Topps: 74/75 - 180; 75/76 - 283, 294; 76/77 - 22; 77/78 - 140; 78/79 - 240; 79/80 - 40; 80/81 - 85, 210; 81/82 - 33; 82/83 - 75SK, 76SK; 83/84 - 33SK, 34SK; 86/87 - 169
Vachon Foods: 83/84 - 97

Samuelsson, Kjell
Bowman: 90/91 - 111; 91/92 - 240; 92/93 - 165
Donruss: 93/94 - 259
Fleer: 92/93 - 169; 93/94 - 414PP
Leaf: 93/94 - 274
O-Pee-Chee: 89/90 - 100; 90/91 - 61; 91/92 - 211; 92/93 - 230; 93/94 - 34
Panini: 88/89 - 318; 90/91 - 110; 91/92 - 239
Parkhurst: 91/92 - 356E, 356F; 92/93 - 373, 373EI; 93/94 - 432, 432EI
Pro Set: 90/91 - 222; 91/92 - 181E, 181F
Score: 90/91 - 197A, 197C; 91/92 - 207A, 207B, 207C, 149PNE, 407PNE, 149PNF, 407PNF; 92/93 - 195C, 195A, 306PNC, 306PNA; 93/94 - 184C, 184A
Topps: 89/90 - 100; 90/91 - 61; 91/92 - 211, 70SC; 92/93 - 352, 352GS, 466SC; 93/94 - 34, 251SC, 251FD
Upper Deck: 90/91 - 116E, 116F; 91/92 - 396E, 396F

Samuelsson, Ulf
Bowman: 91/92 - 88; 92/93 - 351
Donruss: 93/94 - 264
Fleer: 92/93 - 170, 20UI; 93/94 - 204, 194PP
Leaf: 93/94 - 92
O-Pee-Chee: 87/88 - 23, 205SK; 88/89 - 136, 265; 89/90 - 210; 90/91 - 511; 91/92 - 323; 92/93 - 270; 93/94 - 132
Panini: 87/88 - 41; 88/89 - 238; 89/90 - 228; 91/92 - 277; 92/93 - 229E, 229F; 93/94 - 87E, 87F
Parkhurst: 91/92 - 361E, 361F; 92/93 - 369, 446, 369EI, 446EI; 93/94 - 155, 155EI; 94/95 - 183, 183EI
Pro Set: 90/91 - 109; 91/92 - 459E, 95PT, 459F; 92/93 - 143
Score: 90/91 - 152A, 152C, 64HR; 91/92 - 82A, 304A, 82B, 308B, 82C, 308C, 267PNE, 267PNF; 92/93 - 90C, 90A, 296PNC, 296PNA; 93/94 - 135C, 135A
Topps: 87/88 - 23; 88/89 - 136; 91/92 - 323, 328SC; 92/93 - 127, 127GS; 93/94 - 132, 356SC, 426SC, 356FD, 426FD
Upper Deck: 90/91 - 287E, 287F; 91/92 - 230E, E17(E), 230F, E17(F); 92/93 - 189; 93/94 - 142

Sanderson, Derek
Bazooka: 71/72 - 12
Colgate: 70/71 - 6; 71/72 - 12
Dad's Cookies: 70/71 - 10
Eddie Sargent: 70/71 - 3
Esso: 70/71 - 14
Loblaws: 74/75 - 211
O-Pee-Chee: 68/69 - 6, 213; 69/70 - 201, 8QS; 70/71 - 136, 5DE, 27SS; 71/72 - 65; 73/74 - 183; 74/75 - 290; 75/76 - 73; 76/77 - 20; 77/78 - 46
Shirriff: 68/69 - A7
Topps: 67/68 - 33; 68/69 - 6; 69/70 - 31; 70/71 - 28SK; 71/72 - 65; 73/74 - 182; 75/76 - 73; 76/77 - 20; 77/78 - 46
Toronto Sun: 71/72 - 16

Sanderson, Geoff
Bowman: 92/93 - 136
Donruss: 93/94 - 147
Fleer: 92/93 - 75; 93/94 - 151, 6RS, 109PP, 9SM
Hockey Wit: 93/94 - 6
Kraft: 93/94 - 19
Leaf: 93/94 - 77
O-Pee-Chee: 92/93 - 122; 93/94 - 156
Panini: 92/93 - V(E), V(F); 93/94 - L(E), L(F)
Parkhurst: 91/92 - 57E, 57F; 92/93 - 62, 62EI; 93/94 - 86, 86EI; 94/95 - 95, 95EI, H10, R10, C10, V49
Pro Set: 91/92 - 536E, 536F, 256PT; 92/93 - 63, 11RGL
Score: 91/92 - 324A, 354B, 354C, 309PNE, 309PNF; 92/93 - 108C, 108A, 307PNC, 307PNA; 93/94 - 213C, 213A
Sega: 93/94 - 58
Topps: 92/93 - 402, 402GS, 111SC; 93/94 - 156, 408SC, 408FD
Upper Deck: 91/92 - 588E, 588F; 92/93 - 293; 93/94 - 292, 316

Sandford, Ed
Beehive: 45/63 - 64
Parkhurst: 51/52 - 22; 52/53 - 69; 53/54 - 90; 54/55 - 64
Topps: 54/55 - 48
Toronto Star: 58/67 - 6

Sandlak, Jim
Bowman: 90/91 - 55
Donruss: 93/94 - 138
Fleer: 92/93 - 228
O-Pee-Chee: 87/88 - 264, 66ASK, 135SK, 194SK; 89/90 - 267; 90/91 - 18; 92/93 - 168
Panini: 87/88 - 352; 88/89 - 139; 89/90 - 156; 90/91 - 306; 92/93 - 34E, 34F
Parkhurst: 91/92 - 405E, 405F;

Sandlak, Jim (cont.)
Parkhurst: 93/94 - 84, 84EI
Pro Set: 90/91 - 305; 91/92 - 497E, 497F
Score: 90/91 - 303C; 91/92 - 260B, 260C, 294PNE, 294PNF; 92/93 - 379C, 379A, 210PNC, 210PNA; 93/94 - 397C, 397A
Topps: 90/91 - 18; 92/93 - 41GS, 175SC
Upper Deck: 91/92 - 577E, 577F; 92/93 - 120; 93/94 - 393

Sands, Charlie
Anonymous: 33/34 - 16
Beehive: 34/44 - 29, 181
Canada Starch: 35/40 - 198
O-Pee-Chee: 39/40 - 56; 40/41 - 102
World Wide Gum: 33/34 - 58; 36/37 - 27

Sandstrom, Tomas
Bowman: 90/91 - 141, HT21; 91/92 - 174, 179; 92/93 - 22
Donruss: 93/94 - 163, 475
Fleer: 92/93 - 88; 93/94 - 246, 121PP
Hockey Wit: 93/94 - 87
Kraft: 91/92 - 63]
Leaf: 93/94 - 106
O-Pee-Chee: 85/86 - 123; 86/86 - 230; 87/88 - 28, 38HL, 35SK; 88/89 - 121, 242SK; 89/90 - 54, C/BB, 244SK; 90/91 - 301; 91/92 - 173, 82PM; 92/93 - 91; 93/94 - 434, 25SC, 25FD
Panini: 87/88 - 114; 88/89 - 310; 89/90 - 281; 90/91 - 243; 91/92 - 79; 92/93 - 67E, 67F; 93/94 - 205E, 205F
Parkhurst: 91/92 - 70E, 70F; 93/94 - 362, 362EI; 94/95 - 175, 175EI
Pro-Set: 90/91 - 127, 91/92 - 97E, 287E, 97F, 287F, 53PT
Score: 90/91 - 183A, 183C, 79HR; 91/92 - 270A, 490B, 490C, 178PNE, 178PNF; 92/93 - 199C, 199A, 345PNC, 345PNA; 93/94 - 129C, 129A
Sega: 93/94 - 65
Topps: 85/86 - 123; 87/88 - 28; 88/89 - 121; 89/90 - 54, C/BB; 90/91 - 301; 91/92 - 173, 209SC; 92/93 - 421, 421GS, 220SC; 93/94 - 434, 25SC, 25FD
Upper Deck: 90/91 - 251E, 251F; 91/92 - 30E, 141E, E7(E), 30F, 141F, E7(F); 92/93 - 424; 93/94 - 188

Sanipass, Everett
Bowman: 91/92 - 135
O-Pee-Chee: 91/92 - 315
Panini: 91/92 - 262
Score: 90/91 - 28A, 28C
Topps: 91/92 - 315, 284SC

Sargent, Gary
O-Pee-Chee: 77/78 - 113; 78/79 - 37; 79/80 - 52; 80/81 - 237
Post: 82/83 - 142
Topps: 77/78 - 113; 78/79 - 37; 79/80 - 52; 80/81 - 237

Sasakamoose, Fred
Parkhurst: 54/55 - 82

Sather, Glen
Dad's Cookies: 70/71 - 110
Eddie Sargent: 70/71 - 167
Esso: 70/71 - 193
O-Pee-Chee: 68/69 - 134; 69/70 - 116; 70/71 - 205; 71/72 - 221; 75/76 - 222
Shirriff: 68/69 - A15
Topps: 67/68 - 38; 69/70 - 116; 75/76 - 222
Toronto Sun: 71/72 - 182
Upper Deck: 92/93 - 49AS

Saunders, David
O-Pee-Chee: 88/89 - 248, 61SK

Sauve, Bob (Goalie)
O-Pee-Chee: 76/77 - 308; 78/79 - 265; 79/80 - 49; 80/81 - 266; 81/82 - 23, 56SK; 82/83 - 34, 181SK; 83/84 - 61, 71, 242SK; 84/85 - 30, 208SK;

Sauve, Bob (Goalie) (cont.)
O-Pee-Chee: 85/86 - 174, 181SK, 190SK; 86/87 - 124, 152SK; 87/88 - 140, 75SK
Panini: 87/88 - 220
Post: 82/83 - 76
Topps: 79/80 - 49; 81/82 EN - 77; 82/83 - 181SK; 83/84 - 242SK; 86/87 - 124; 87/88 - 140

Sauvé, Jenn-Francois
O-Pee-Chee: 82/83 - 33; 85/86 - 155SK; 86/87 - 23SK
Post: 82/83 - 30

Savage, Brian
Fleer: 93/94 - 493PP
O-Pee-Chee: 93/94 - 16TC
Parkhurst: 94/95 - 121, 121EI

Savage, Joel
Upper Deck: 91/92 - 423E, 423F

Savage, Reginald (Reggie)
Durivage: 93/94 - 23
O-Pee-Chee: 92/93 - 121PM
Parkhurst: 92/93 - 426, 426EI
Score: 91/92 - 320A, 350B, 350C
Topps: 92/93 - 5SCM
Upper Deck: 92/93 - 474

Savard, Andre
Loblaws: 74/75 - 31
O-Pee-Chee: 74/75 - 285; 75/76 - 155; 76/77 - 43; 77/78 - 118; 78/79 - 253; 79/80 - 25; 80/81 - 375; 81/82 - 24, 54SK; 84/85 - 288, 170SK
Post: 82/83 - 31
Topps: 75/76 - 155; 76/77 - 43; 77/78 - 118; 78/79 - 253; 79/80 - 25; 81/82 EN - 78
Vachon Foods: 83/84 - 73

Savard, Denis
Bowman: 90/91 - 6; 91/92 - 342; 92/93 - 64
Derniere: 72/84 - 162
Donruss: 93/94 - 319
Durivage: 92/93 - 10; 93/94 - 25
Eddie Sargent: 70/71 - 110
Esso: 88/89 - 40
Fleer: 92/93 - 109; 93/94 - 447PP
Frito-Lay: 88/89 - 37
Funmate: 83/84 -26
Hockey Wit: 93/94 - 38
Kraft: 90/91 - 51; 93/94 - 41
Leaf: 93/94 - 372(II)
McDonald's: 82/83 - 23
O-Pee-Chee: 81/82 - 63, 112SK; 82/83 - 73, 171SK; 83/84 - 96, 111, 106SK, 107SK, 153SK; 84/85 - 45, 355, 24SK, 25SK; 85/86 - 73, 22SK; 86/87 - 7, N/B, B, 150SK; 87/88 - 127, 39HL, N/BB, 78SK; 88/89 - 26, 34NS, H/BB, 13SK; 89/90 - 5, 16SK; 90/91 - 28, 103PM; 91/92 - 330, 71PM; 92/93 - 35, 6SP; 93/94 - 305
Panini: 87/88 - 225; 88/89 - 29; 89/90 - 49; 90/91 - 198; 91/92 - 187; 92/93 - 152E, 152F; 93/94 - 17E, 17F
Parkhurst: 91/92 - 93E, 211E, 93F, 211F; 92/93 - 85, 85EI; 93/94 - 193, 193EI; 94/95 - 217, 217EI
Post: 81/82 - 3; 82/83 - 62
Pro Set: 90/91 - 59, 473; 91/92 - 128E, 305E, 28F, 305F, 64PT; 92/93 - 84, 260
Score: 90 - 1T; 90/91 - 125A, 125C, 59HR; 91/92 - 165A, 165B, 165C, 28PNE, 28PNF; 92/93 - 202C, 202A, 61PNC, 61PNA; 93/94 - 105C, 105A
Season's: 92/93 - 23
7-Eleven: 84/85 - 9
Topps: 81/82 WN - 75; 82/83 - 171SK; 83/84 - 106SK, 107SK, 153SK; 84/85 - 35; 85/86 - 73; 86/87 - 7, N/BB; 87/88 - 127, N/BB; 88/89 - 26, H/BB; 89/90 - 5; 90/91 - 28; 91/92 - 330, 213SC; 92/93 - 414, 414GS, 467SC;

Savard, Denis (cont.)
Topps: 93/94 - 305, 297SC, 297FD
Upper Deck: 90/91 - 244E, 244F, 426E, 426F; 91/92 - 242E, 242F; 92/93 - 10, 162, 638; 93/94 - 502

Savard, Jean
Derniere: 72/84 - 58

Savard, Serge
Colgate: 70/71 - 74
Dad's Cookies: 70/71 - 81
Derniere: 72/84 - 4, 35, 114, 163
Eddie Sargent: 72/73 - 123
Esso: 70/71 - 141; 88-89 - 41
Hall of Fame: 87 - 256C
Hockey Wit: 93/94 - 42
Lipton Soup: 74/75 - 11
Loblaws: 74/75 - 178
Mac's Milk: 73/74 - 25
O-Pee-Chee: 69/70 - 4, 210, 10QS; 70/71 - 51; 71/72 - 143; 72/73 - 185; 73/74 - 24; 74/75 - 53; 75/76 - 144; 76/77 - 205; 77/78 - 45; 78/79 - 190, 335; 79/80 - 101; 80/81 - 26; 82/83 - 390
PepsiCo: 80/81 - 57
Post: 68/69 - 11; 82/83 - 332
Shirriff: 68/69 - F17
Topps: 69/70 - 4; 70/71 - 51; 73/74 - 24; 74/75 - 53; 75/76 - 144; 76/77 - 205; 77/78 - 45; 78/79 - 190; 79/80 - 101; 80/81 - 26
Toronto Sun: 71/72 - 163
Upper Deck: 90/91 - 506E, 506F

Sawchuk, Terry (Goalie)
Bee Hive: 45/63 - 65, 210A, 210B; 64/67 - 181
Coca-Cola: 64/65 - 105; 65/66 - 103
Hall of Fame: 83 - D13, 46C; 87 - 46C
Highliner: 93/94 - 11
Hockey Wit: 93/94 - 83
O-Pee-Chee: 68/69 - 34, 20PS; 69/70 - 189; 70/71 - 231
Parkhurst: 51/52 - 61; 52/53 - 86; 53/54 - 46; 54/55 - 33; 60/61 - 31; 61/62 - 31; 63/64 - 53; 91/92 - PHC9; 92/93 -PR2; 93/94 - PR37, 17ML, 153ML, 167ML, 168ML
Pro Set: 91/92 - 343E, 343F
Shirriff: 60/61 - 41; 61/62 - 77
Topps: 54/55 - 58; 57/58 - 35; 58/59 - 2; 59/60 - 42; 64/65 - 6; 65/66 - 12; 66/67 - 13; 68/69 - 34
Toronto Star: 57/67 - 56, 81, 122; 58/67 - 36, 89, 103; 120; 63/64 - 16
York: 62/63 - 25; 63/64 - 37

Scanlan, Fred
Hall of Fame: 83 - 118, H13p; 87 - 118

Scapinello, Ray (Official)
Pro Set: 90/91 - 697

Schella, John
Toronto Sun: 71/72 - 288

Schewchuk, Jack
O-Pee-Chee: 40/41 - 126

Schinkel, Ken
Bazooka: 71/72 - 33
Bee Hive: 45/63 - 361
Colgate: 70/71 - 61
Dad's Cookies: 70/71 - 111
Eddie Sargent: 70/71 - 174; 71/72 - 162; 72/73 - 170
Esso: 70/71 - 194
O-Pee-Chee: 68/69 - 106; 69/70 - 117, 1QS; 70/71 - 92; 71/72 - 64; 72/73 - 256
Shirriff: 60/61 - 96; 61/62 - 99; 68/69 - K1
Topps: 60/61 - 50; 63/64 - 62; 68/69 - 106; 69/70 - 117; 70/71 - 92; 71/72 - 64
Toronto Sun: 71/72 - 227

Schlegel, Brad
O-Pee-Chee: 92/93 - 28PM
Parkhurst: 91/92 - 413E, 413F; 92/93 - 199, 199EI
Score: 92/93 - 477C, 477A, 9COH
Topps: 92/93 - 377, 377GS, 29SC
Upper Deck: 92/93 - 101

Schliebener, Andy
O-Pee-Chee: 84/85 - 329

Schmautz, Bobby
Eddie Sargent: 72/73 - 219
Loblaws: 74/75 - 32
O-Pee-Chee: 72/73 - 181; 73/74 - 35; 74/75 - 27; 75/76 - 251; 76/77 - 189; 77/78 - 59; 78/79 - 248; 79/80 - 144
Topps: 73/74 - 35; 74/75 - 27; 75/76 - 251; 76/77 - 189; 77/78 - 59; 78/79 - 248; 79/80 - 144
Toronto Sun: 71/72 - 289

Schmautz, Cliff
Eddie Sargent: 70/71 - 29
Esso: 70/71 - 33
O-Pee-Chee: 40/41 - 132; 70/71 - 142

Schmidt, Jackie
Bee Hive: 34/44 - 30

Schmidt, Milt
Bee Hive: 34/44 - 31
Hall of Fame: 83 - L16, 165C; 87 - 165C
O-Pee-Chee: 40/41 - 132
Parkhurst: 51/52 - 29; 52/53 - 70; 53/54 - 92; 54/55 - 59 ; 92/93 - PR23; 93/94 - 21ML
Shirriff: 60/61 - 120
Topps: 54/55 - 60; 63/64 - 1; 64/65 - 70; 65/66 - 96
Toronto Star: 58/67 - 5

Schnarr, Werner
Champ's: 24/25 - 7
Wm. Paterson: 24/25 - 26

Schneider, Andy
Donruss: 93/94 - 468

Schneider, Mathieu
Bowman: 90/91 - 52; 91/92 - 343; 92/93 - 190
Donruss: 93/94 - 179
Fleer: 92/93 - 110; 93/94 - 78, 134PP
Leaf: 93/94 - 53
O-Pee-Chee: 90/91 - 372; 91/92 - 392, 181PM; 92/93 - 166; 93/94 - 163
Panini: 90/91 - 60; 91/92 - 195; 92/93 - 157E, 157F; 93/94 - 22E, 22F
Parkhurst: 91/92 - 88E, 88F; 92/93 - 319, 319EI; 93/94 - 373, 373EI; 94/95 - V32
Pro Set: 90/91 - 158; 91/92 - 119E, 119F; 92/93 - 91
Score: 90 - 18YS; 90/91 - 127A, 127C; 91/92 - 105A, 105B, 105C, 209PNE, 209PNF; 92/93 - 69C, 69A, 79PNC, 79PNA; 93/94 - 18C, 18A
Sega: 93/94 - 68
Topps: 90/91 - 372; 91/92 - 392, 262SC; 92/93 - 253, 253GS, 70SC; 93/94 - 163, 391SC, 391FD, 23MP
Upper Deck: 90/91 - 334E, 334F; 91/92 - 328E, 328F; 92/93 - 545; 93/94 - 31

Schock, Ron
Bee Hive: 64/67 - 25
Coca-Cola: 64/65 - 16
Colgate: 70/71 - 42
Eddie Sargent: 70/71 - 170; 72/73 - 179
Esso: 70/71 - 195
Lipton Soup: 74/75 - 43
Loblaws: 74/75 - 251
O-Pee-Chee: 68/69 - 118; 69/70 - 120, 13QS; 70/71 - 91, 9DE, 29SS; 71/72 - 56; 72/73 - 81; 73/74 - 200; 74/75 - 167; 75/76 - 75; 76/77 - 248; 77/78 - 51; 78/79 - 384
Shirriff: 68/69 - L1
Topps: 65/66 - 36; 66/67 - 100; 68/69 - 118; 69/70 - 120; 70/71 - 91, 29SK; 71/72 - 56; 72/73 - 59; 73/74 - 113; 74/75 - 167; 75/76 - 75; 76/77 - 248; 77/78 - 51
Toronto Sun: 71/72 - 228

Schoenfeld, Jim
Eddie Sargent: 72/73 - 41
Funmate: 83/84 - 7

Schoenfeld, Jim (cont.)
Loblaws: 74/75 - 53
O-Pee-Chee: 72/73 - 220; 73/74 - 86; 74/75 - 121; 75/76 - 138; 76/77 - 241; 77/78 - 108; 78/79 - 178; 79/80 - 171; 80/81 - 96; 82/83 - 94, 183SK; 83/84 - 59, 136SK
Post: 82/83 - 77
Topps: 73/74 - 86; 74/75 - 121; 75/76 - 138; 76/77 - 241; 77/78 - 108; 78/79 - 178; 79/80 - 171; 80/81 - 96; 82/83 - 183SK; 83/84 - 136SK
Upper Deck: 90/91 - 505E, 505F

Schofield, Dwight
O-Pee-Chee: 84/85 - 191

Schriner, Sweeney (David)
Amalg. Press: 35/36 - 9
Bee Hive: 34/44 - 249, 346
Diamond: 36/39 - 60(I), 57(II), 53(III),
Hall of Fame: 83 - J13, 236C; 87 - 236C
O-Pee-Chee: 36/37 - 98; 39/40 - 14; 40/41 - 122
Parkhurst: 55/56 - 27
Quaker Oats: 45/54 - 100; 55/56 - 27
World Wide Gum: 36/37 - 58

Schubert, Thomas
Upper Deck: 91/92 - 681E, 681F

Schultz, Dave
Lipton Soup: 74/75 - 30
Loblaws: 74/75 - 231
O-Pee-Chee: 73/74 - 166; 74/75 - 196; 75/76 - 147; 76/77 - 150; 77/78 - 353; 78/79 - 225; 79/80 - 134
Parkhurst: 92/93 - 473, 473EI
Topps: 73/74 - 149; 74/75 - 196; 75/76 - 147; 76/77 - 150; 78/79 - 225; 79/80 - 134

Schumperli, Bernard
Upper Deck: 91/92 - 667E, 667F

Schutt, Rod
O-Pee-Chee: 79/80 - 234; 80/81 - 307; 81/82 - 259, 186SK
Topps: 79/80 - 234; 81/82 EN - 116

Schwabe, Jens
Upper Deck: 91/92 - 680E, 680F

Scissons, Scott
Donruss: 93/94 - 210
Leaf: 93/94 - 243(II)
Parkhurst: 93/94 - 121, 121EI
Score: 90/91 - 432A, 432C
Upper Deck: 90/91 - 357E, 357F; 91/92 - 428E, 428F; 93/94 - 511

Sclisizzi, Enio
Parkhurst: 52/53 - 32

Scott, Ganton
Champ's: 24/25 - 38
Maple Crispette: 24/25 - 29
Wm. Paterson: 24/25 - 38

Secord, Alan (Al)
Bowman: 90/91 - 12
Funmate: 83/84 - 27
O-Pee-Chee: 80/81 - 129; 81/82 - 72; 82/83 - 60, 74, 175SK; 83/84 - 95, 112, 111SK, 156SK, 160SK; 84/85 - 46; 86/87 - 100, 155SK; 87/88 - 111, 74SK; 88/89 - 249, 179SK
Panini: 87/88 - 229
Post: 82/83 - 63
Pro Set: 90/91 - 60
7-Eleven: 84/85 - 10
Topps: 80/81 - 129; 82/83 - 175SK; 83/84 - 111SK, 156SK, 160SK; 86/87 - 100; 87/88 - 111
Upper Deck: 91/92 - 635E, 635F

Sedlbauer, Ron
O-Pee-Chee: 76/77 - 271; 77/78 - 368; 78/79 - 139; 79/80 - 19; 80/81 - 134; 81/82 - 324
Topps: 78/79 - 139; 79/80 - 19; 80/81 - 134

Seibert, Earl
Bee Hive: 34/44 - 78
Diamond: 36/39 - 61(I), 12(IV), 10(V), 10(VI)
Hall of Fame: 83 - 150, K16P; 150
O-Pee-Chee: 39/40 - 76

Seiling, Ric
O-Pee-Chee: 78/79 - 242 ;79/80 - 119; 80/81 - 159; 81/82 - 32; 82/83 - 35, 123SK; 83/84 - 72; 84/85 - 31, 216SK; 85/86 - 182SK; 86/87 - 201
Post: 82/83 - 29
Topps: 78/79 - 242; 79/80 - 119; 80/81 - 159; 82/83 - 123SK

Seiling, Rod
Bee Hive: 64/67 - 148
Coca-Cola: 64/65 - 90
Dad's Cookies: 70/71 - 92
Eddie Sargent: 70/71 - 128; 72/73 - 148
Esso: 70/71 - 158
Loblaws: 74/75 - 212
O-Pee-Chee: 68/69 - 71; 69/70 - 36, 13QS; 70/71 - 184; 71/72 - 53; 72/73 - 194; 73/74 - 9; 74/75 - 102; 75/76 - 229; 76/77 - 280; 77/78 - 226; 78/79 - 394
Shirriff: 68/69 - G1
Topps: 64/65 - 67; 65/66 - 23; 66/67 - 22; 66/67 US - 22; 67/68 - 27; 68/69 - 71; 69/70 - 36; 71/72 - 53; 72/73 - 149; 73/74 - 9; 74/75 - 102; 75/76 - 229; 77/78 - 226
Toronto Sun: 71/72 - 183

Sejba, Jiri
Upper Deck: 91/92 - 362E, 362F

Selanne, Teemu
Donruss: 93/94 - 387, 394, 3ES, 10IK, Z/PM, Z/SP
Fleer: 92/93 - 444, 21UI; 93/94 - 48, 9SA, 7GG, 6AW, 11AS, 274PP, 10SY, 16PL, 10RL, 10SM
Hockey Wit: 93/94 - 55
Kraft: 93/94 - 20
Leaf: 93/94 - 13, 1R, 3HT
O-Pee-Chee: 92/93 - 68PM; 93/94 - 92, 130, 148, 483, 20BG, 141SC, 210SC, 141FD, 210FD
Panini: 93/94 - 142E, 142F, Q(E), Q(F)
Parkhurst: 92/93 - 209, 217, 500, 209EI, 217EI, 500EI; 93/94 - 233, 235, 233EI, 235EI, G8, W3; 94/95 - 300, 300EI, H26, R26, C26, V81
Score: 92/93 - 406PNC, 406PNA; 93/94 - 331C, 331A, 450C, 450A, 32PNC, 32PNA, 21DT, 32CAS, 32AAS, 24FR, 4PCE
Sega: 93/94 - 149
Topps: 93/94 - 92(I), 130(I), 148(I), 483, 1BG, 141SC, 210SC, 141FD, 210FD, 4MP, 11AS
Upper Deck: 91/92 - 21E, 21F; 92/93 - 574, ER6, CC10, G15, 35AS; 93/94 - 281, 309, 448

Selby, Brit
Bee Hive: 64/67 - 182
Coca-Cola: 65/66 - 104
Colgate: 70/71 - 37
Dad's Cookies: 70/71 - 121
Eddie Sargent: 70/71 - 202
Esso: 70/71 - 213
O-Pee-Chee: 68/69 - 96; 69/70 - 48; 70/71 - 111; 71/72 - 226
Shirriff: 68/69 - J7
Topps: 66/67 - 18; 68/69 - 96; 69/70 - 48; 70/71 - 111

Seliger, Marc
Upper Deck: 91/92 - 683E, 683F

Selke, Frank
Hall of Fame: 83 - 41, C12P; 87 - 41
Parkhurst: 55/56 - 68; 59/60 - 47; 93/94 - 85ML
Quaker Oats: 55/56 - 68

Selwood, Brad
Toronto Sun: 71/72 - 270

Selyanin, Sergei
O-Pee-Chee: 91/92 - 58R

Semak, Alexander
Bowman: 92/93 - 164
Donruss: 93/94 - 191
Fleer: 92/93 - 341; 93/94 - 166, 142PP
Leaf: 93/94 - 35
O-Pee-Chee: 91/92 - 42R; 93/94 - 102
Panini: 92/93 - 176E, 176F, 296E, 296F; 93/94 - 36E, 36F
Parkhurst: 91/92 - 323E, 323F; 92/93 - 329, 329EI; 93/94 - 109, 109EI
Score: 92/93 - 451C, 451A; 93/94 - 284C, 284A
Sega: 93/94 - 75
Topps: 92/93 - 419, 419GS, 444SC; 93/94 - 102(I), 365SC, 365FD
Upper Deck: 91/92 - 4E, 4F; 92/93 - 45, ERT5; 93/94 - 178

Semenko, Dave
O-Pee-Chee: 79/80 - 371; 80/81 - 360; 81/82 - 121; 82/83 - 119
PepsiCo: 80/81 - 38
Post: 82/83 - 95
Vachon Foods: 83/84 - 40

Semenov, Anatoli
Bowman: 91/92 - 113; 92/93 - 423
Donruss: 93/94 - 3
Fleer: 92/93 - 429; 93/94 - 10PP
Leaf: 93/94 - 338
O-Pee-Chee: 90/91 - 468, 104PM; 91/92 - 390; 92/93 - 83; 93/94 - 506
Panini: 91/92 - 127; 93/94 - 174E, 174F
Parkhurst: 91/92 - 279; 92/93 - 420, 420EI; 93/94 - 3, 3EI; 94/95 - 1, 1EI
Pro Set: 90/91 - 608
Score: 90/91 - 39T; 91/92 - 258B, 258C; 92/93 - 336C, 336A, 386PNC, 386PNA, 28CSS, 28ASS; 93/94 - 93C, 93A
Sega: 93/94 - 5
Topps: 91/92 - 390, 366SC; 92/93 - 68, 68GS, 143SC; 93/94 - 506, 368SC, 368FD
Upper Deck: 90/91 - 405E, 405F; 91/92 - 269E, E4(E), 269F, E4(F); 92/93 - 20, 535; 93/94 - 46

Semin, Nikolai
Upper Deck: 92/93 - 610

Severyn, Brent
O-Pee-Chee: 93/94 - 392
Parkhurst: 93/94 - 77, 77EI; 94/95 - 90, 90EI
Topps: 93/94 - 392
Upper Deck: 93/94 - 453

Sevigny, Pierre
Donruss: 93/94 - 169
Durivage: 93/94 - 2
Leaf: 93/94 - 392
Parkhurst: 93/94 - 106, 106EI, CC7
Upper Deck: 90/91 - 456E, 456F; 93/94 - 455

Sevigny, Richard (Goalie)
Derniere: 72/84 - 133
O-Pee-Chee: 80/81 - 385; 81/82 - 191, 387, 40SK, 256SK; 83/84 - 197; 84/85 - 289
Post: 82/83 - 158
Vachon Foods: 83/84 - 54

Shack, Eddie
Bee Hive: 45/63 - 362, 449A, 449B; 64/67 - 207
Chex: 63/65 - 55
Coca-Cola: 64/65 - 106; 65/66 - 105
Colgate: 70/71 - 41
Dad's Cookies: 70/71 - 22
Eddie Sargent: 70/71 - 69
Esso: 70/71 - 34
O-Pee-Chee: 68/69 - 137; 69/70 - 139, 16QS; 70/71 - 35, 2DE; 71/72 - 96;

Shack, Eddie (cont.)
O-Pee-Chee: 72/73 - 186, 274, 17CS; 73/74 - 242
Parkhurst: 61/62 - 7; 62/63 - 14; 63/64 - 9, 69
Shirriff: 60/61 - 87; 61/62 - 48; 62/63 - 8; 68/69 - A1
Topps: 58/59 - 30; 59/60 - 57; 60/61 - 7; 64/65 - 71; 66/67 - 17; 67/68 - 34; 69/70 - 106; 70/71 - 35; 71/72 - 96
Toronto Star: 57/67 - 69, 137; 63/64 - 40
Toronto Sun: 71/72 - 39
Ultimate: 92 - 41(OSE), 41(OSF)
York: 60/61 - 35; 61/62 - 25; 62/63 - 32; 63/64 - 4

Shanahan, Brendan
Bowman: 90/91 - 85; 91/92 - 288; 92/93 - 183
Donruss: 93/94 - 299
Fleer: 92/93 - 189; 93/94 - 245, 10SA, 216PP
Hockey Wit: 93/94 - 29
Humpty Dumpty: 92/93 - 20(I)
Kraft: 91/92 - 7
Leaf: 93/94 - 30, 9AS
O-Pee-Chee: 88/89 - 122; 89/90 - 147; 90/91 - 259, 105PM; 91/92 - 140, 130PM; 92/93 - 244; 93/94 - 247
Panini: 88/89 - 276; 89/90 - 255; 90/91 - 64; 91/92 - 222; 92/93 - 17E, 17F; 93/94 - 158E, 158F
Parkhurst: 91/92 - 153E, 153F; 92/93 - 156, 156EI, CP10; 93/94 - 172, 172EI; 94/95 - 196, 298, 196EI, 298EI
Pro Set: 90/91 - 174; 91/92 - 131E, 475E, 131F, 111PT, 475F; 92/93 - 163
Score: 90 - 23YS; 90/91 - 146A, 146C; 91 - 38T; 91/92 - 286A, 588B, 588C, 41PNE, 41PNF; 92/93 - 114PNC, 114PNA; 93/94 - 238C, 238A
Season's: 92/93 - 15
Sega: 93/94 - 124
Topps: 88/89 - 122; 89/90 - 147, 89SK; 90/91 - 259; 91/92 - 140, 199SC; 92/93 - 295, 295GS, 371SC; 93/94 - 247(I), 389SC, 389FD
Upper Deck: 90/91 - 269E, 561E, 269F, 561F; 92/93 - 12

Shand, Dave
O-Pee-Chee: 77/78 - 355; 78/79 - 356; 79/80 - 394; 80/81 - 282
PepsiCo: 80/81 - 98

Shank, Daniel
Bowman: 90/91 - 235
O-Pee-Chee: 90/91 - 34
Pro Set: 90/91 - 78
Score: 90/91 - 377A, 377C
Topps: 90/91 - 34
Upper Deck: 90/91 - 99E, 99F

Shannon, Darrin
Bowman: 91/92 - 24; 92/93 - 385
Donruss: 93/94 - 388
Fleer: 92/93 - 246
Leaf: 93/94 - 194
O-Pee-Chee: 90/91 - 310; 91/92 - 214, 146PM; 92/93 - 332; 93/94 - 261, 191SC, 191FD
Panini: 92/93 - 58E, 58F; 93/94 - 192E, 192F
Parkhurst: 91/92 - 201E, 201F; 92/93 - 436, 436EI; 93/94 - 499, 499EI
Pro Set: 90/91 - 592; 91/92 - 14E, 515E, 14F, 515F, 246PT; 92/93 - 218
Score: 90/91 - 410A, 410C; 91 - 107T; 91/92 - 438B, 438C, 243PNE, 243PNF; 92/93 - 36C, 36A, 106PNC, 106PNA; 93/94 - 280C, 280A
Topps: 90/91 - 310; 91/92 - 214, 361SC; 92/93 - 167, 167GS, 55SC; 93/94 - 261(I), 191SC, 191FD
Upper Deck: 91/92 - 322E, 322F; 91/92 - 581E, 581F; 92/93 - 132

Shannon, Darryl
Parkhurst: 91/92 - 390E, 390F
Pro Set: 91/92 - 490E, 490F
Upper Deck: 91/92 - 493E, 493F

Shannon, Gerry
Bee Hive: 34/44 - 204
Diamond: 36/39 - 62(I)
Canada Starch: 35/40 - 123
O-Pee-Chee: 37/38 - 179

Shantz, Jeff
Donruss: 93/94 - 75
Fleer: 93/94 - 316PP
Leaf: 93/94 - 405
Parkhurst: 93/94 - 314, 314EI; 94/95 - 46. 289, 46EI, 289EI
Topps: 93/94 - 348SC, 348FD
Upper Deck: 93/94 - 258, 451

Sharifjanov, Vadim
Parkhurst: 93/94 - 527, 527EI
Upper Deck: 92/93 - 612

Sharples, Jeff
O-Pee-Chee: 88/89 - 48, 249SK, 17FS; 89/90 - 42
Panini: 88/89 - 38; 89/90 - 66
Topps: 88/89 - 48; 89/90 - 42

Sharpley, Glen
O-Pee-Chee: 77/78 - 158; 78/79 - 175; 79/80 - 93; 80/81 - 218; 81/82 - 64, 116SK; 82/83 - 75
Panini: 79 - 63
Topps: 77/78 - 158; 78/79 - 175; 79/80 - 93; 80/81 - 218; 81/82 WN - 76

Shashov, Vladimir
O-Pee-Chee: 90/91 - 506

Shastin, Evgeny
O-Pee-Chee: 90/91 - 6R

Shaw, Brad
Bowman: 90/91 - 260; 91/92 - 8; 92/93 - 111
Donruss: 93/94 - 234
Fleer: 92/93 - 366; 93/94 - 167, 175PP
Kraft: 93/94 - 39
Leaf: 93/94 - 11
O-Pee-Chee: 90/91 - 279; 91/92 - 442
Panini: 90/91 - 48, 344; 91/92 - 311; 92/93 - 265GS, 265F; 93/94 - 120E, 120F
Parkhurst: 91/92 - 62E, 62F; 92/93 - 352, 352EI
Pro Set: 90/91 - 110; 91/92 - 87E, 87F, 45PT; 92/93 - 124
Score: 90/91 - 99A, 99C, 325A, 325C; 91/92 - 289A, 509B, 509C, 88PNE, 88PNF; 92/93 - 85A, 85, 372PNC, 372PNA; 93/94 - 15C, 15A
Sega: 93/94 - 92
Topps: 90/91 - 279; 91/92 - 442, 83SC; 92/93 - 89, 89GS, 65SC
Upper Deck: 90/91 - 90E, 90F, 327E, 327F; 91/92 - 297E, 297F; 92/93 - 109

Shaw, David
Bowman: 91/92 - 64; 92/93 - 141
Fleer: 92/93 - 256
Leaf: 93/94 - 249
O-Pee-Chee: 86/87 - 236, 31SK, 133SK; 87/88 - 252, 223SK; 88/89 - 57, 243SK; 89/90 - 39; 90/91 - 403; 91/92 - 306; 93/94 - 179, 229SC, 229FD
Panini: 91/92 - 294
Pro Set: 90/91 - 495
Score: 90/91 - 98A, 98C; 91/92 - 161A, 161B, 161C, 251PNE, 251PNF; 92/93 - 183C, 183A, 343PNC, 343PNA; 93/94 - 205C, 205A
Topps: 88/89 - 57; 89/90 - 39; 91/92 - 306, 306SC; 92/93 - 420, 420GS, 162SC; 93/94 - 179, 229SC, 229FD
Upper Deck: 90/91 - 15E, 15F; 91/92 - 409E, 409F

Shedden, Douglas (Doug)
O-Pee-Chee: 83/84 - 285, 228SK; 84/85 - 120SK; 85/86 - 247, 102SK; 86/87 - 153, 164SK; 87/88 - 249, 226SK
Post: 82/83 - 238
Pro Set: 90/91 - 542
Topps: 83/84 - 228SK; 86/87 - 153

Sheehan, Bobby
O-Pee-Chee: 71/72 - 177; 72/73 - 297; 78/79 - 311

Sheehan, Bobby (cont.)
Topps: 76/77 - 183
Toronto Sun: 71/72 - 57

Sheehy, Neil
O-Pee-Chee: 87/88 - 213, 38SK; 90/91 - 188; 91/92 - 407
Panini: 87/88 - 209
Score: 91 - 86T; 91/92 - 636B, 636C
Topps: 90/91 - 188; 91/92 - 407

Shelton, Doug
Topps: 67/68 - 53

Sheppard, Gregg
Lipton Soup: 74/75 - 29
Loblaws: 74/75 - 33
O-Pee-Chee: 72/73 - 240; 73/74 - 8; 74/75 - 184; 75/76 - 235; 76/77 - 155; 77/78 - 95; 78/79 - 18; 79/80 - 172; 80/81 - 325
Post: 82/83 - 239
Topps: 73/74 - 8; 74/75 - 184; 75/76 - 235; 76/77 - 155; 77/78 - 95; 78/79 - 18; 79/80 - 172

Sheppard, Johnny
Anonymous: 1926/27 - 129
Can. Chew. Gum: 33/34 - 42
Diamond: 33/35 - 53
Topps: 33/34 - 30

Sheppard, Ray
Bowman: 91/92 - 63; 92/93 - 25
Donruss: 93/94 - 105
Fleer: 92/93 - 289; 93/94 - 76PP
Leaf: 93/94 - 44
O-Pee-Chee: 88/89 - 55, 35NS, 126SK, 262SK, 18FS; 89/90 - 119, 259SK; 90/91 - 446, 106PM; 91/92 - 289, 2PM; 92/93 - 154
Panini: 88/89 - 228; 89/90 - 211; 91/92 - 286; 92/93 - 121E, 121F; 93/94 - 247E, 247F
Parkhurst: 91/92 - 41E, 41F; 92/93 - 280, 280EI; 93/94 - 330, 330EI
Pro Set: 90/91 - 496; 91/92 - 162E, 380E, 162F, 380F, 169PT; 92/93 - 47
Score: 90/91 - 97T; 91 - 36T; 91/92 - 213A, 213B, 213C, 586B, 586C, 155PNE, 155PNF, 92/93 - 163C, 163A, 119PNC,119PNA; 20CSS, 20ASS; 93/94 - 83C, 83A
Topps: 88/89 - 55; 89/90 - 119; 91/92 - 289, 381SC; 92/93 - 257, 257GS; 85SC
Upper Deck: 90/91 - 420E, 420F; 91/92 - 390E, 573E. 390F, 573F; 92/93 - 296; 93/94 - 398

Sherf, John
Bee Hive: 34/44 - 121

Shero, Fred
Bee Hive: 45/63 - 363
O-Pee-Chee: 74/75 - 21
Parkhurst: 92/93 - 480, 480EI
Topps: 74/75 - 21

Shewchuk, Jack
Bee Hive: 34/44 - 32

Shibicky, Alex
Bee Hive: 34/44 - 293
O-Pee-Chee: 36/37 - 109; 39/40 - 88
World Wide Gum: 36/37 - 90

Shick, Rob (Official)
Pro Set: 90/91 - 698

Shields, Al (Allan)
Bee Hive: 34/44 - 205, 250
Canada Starch: 35/40 - 120
O-Pee-Chee: 35/36 - 89; 37/38 - 162
World Wide Gum: 33/34 - 5P; 36/37 - 60

Shill, Jack
Bee Hive: 34/44 - 79, 251, 347
O-Pee-Chee: 36/37 - 99
World Wide Gum: 36/37 - 39

Shires, Jim
Toronto Sun: 71/72 - 248

Shiryev, Valeri
O-Pee-Chee: 90/91 - 13R; 91/92 - 59R

Shmyr, Paul
O-Pee-Chee: 71/72 - 6; 80/81 - 66
Post: 82/83 - 109
Topps: 80/81 - 66
Toronto Sun: 71/72 - 58

Shoebottom, Bruce
Pro Set: 90/91 - 411

Shore, Eddie
Amal. Press: 35/36 - 8
Anonymous: 33/34 - 37
Bee Hive: 34/44 - 33
Diamond: 33/35 - 54
Goudy Gum: 33 - 19
Hall of Fame: 83 - 223, O14P; 87 - 223
La Presse: 27/32 - 15
O-Pee-Chee: 33/34 - 3; 36/37 - 118; 39/40 - 100
Sweet Caporal: 34/35 - 1
Topps: 60/61 - 20
World Wide Gum: 36/37 - 5

Shore, Hamby
Imperial Tobacco: 10/11 - 12L; 11/12 - 12; 12/13 - 30

Shtalenkov, Mikhail
O-Pee-Chee: 91/92 - 43R
Parkhurst: 94/95 - 4, 4EI

Shuchuk, Gary
Donruss: 93/94 - 157
Fleer: 93/94 - 12, 9TP
Leaf: 93/94 - 222(II)
O-Pee-Chee: 93/94 - 499
Parkhurst: 92/93 - 484, 484EI;
92/93 - 95, 95EI
Score: 91/92 - 315A, 345B, 345C
Topps: 93/94 - 499(II), 351SC, 351FD
Upper Deck: 91/92 - 376E, 376F; 93/94 - 13

Shutt, Steve
Coca-Cola: 77/78 - 23
Derniere: 72/84 - 24, 41, 131, 195
Esso: 88/89 - 42
Funmate: 83/84 - 68
Loblaws: 74/75 - 179
O-Pee-Chee: 74/75 - 316; 75/76 - 181; 76/77 - 59;
77/78 - 120, 217, 19GP;
78/79 - 170, 333; 79/80 - 90;
80/81 - 89, 180; 81/82 - 180, 197,
32SK, 44SK; 82/83 - 192, 32SK,
33SK; 83/84 - 198, 6SK, 57SK;
84/85 - 272
PepsiCo: 80/81 - 58
Post: 82/83 - 159
Topps: 75/76 - 181; 76/77 - 59; 77/78 - 120,
217, 19PO; 78/79 - 170; 79/80 - 90;
80/81 - 89, 180; 81/82 - 34, 56;
82/83 - 32SK, 33SK;
83/84 - 6SK, 57SK
Vachon Foods: 83/84 - 55

Sidorkiewicz, Peter (Goalie)
Bowman: 90/91 - 255; 91/92 - 13;
92/93 - 162
Fleer: 92/93 - 150, 367
O-Pee-Chee: 89/90 - 11, 42SK, 6FS; 90/91 - 14;
91/92 - 296; 92/93 - 175, 112PM
Panini: 89/90 - 220; 90/91 - 38; 91/92 - 310;
93/94 - 121E, 121F
Parkhurst: 91/92 - 286E, 286F; 92/93 - 120,
450, 120EI, 450EI
Pro Set: 90/91 - 451; 91/92 - 90E, 90F;
92/93 - 125
Score: 90 - 4YS; 90/91 - 46A, 46C;
91/92 - 203A, 203B, 203C,
234PNE, 234PNF; 92/93 - 41C,
41A, 515C, 515A, 371PNC, 371PNA;
93/94 - 102C, 102A, 17PNC,
17PNA, 17CAS, 17AAS, 14FR
Sega: 93/94 - 96
Topps: 89/90 - 11; 90/91 - 14; 91/92 - 296,
25SC; 92/93 - 332, 332GS, 27SC;
93/94 - 23AS
Upper Deck: 90/91 - 69E, 69F; 91/92 - 325E,
325F; 92/93 - 14, 480

Siebert, Babe (Albert)
Anonymous: 33/34 - 28
Bee Hive: 34/44 - 182
Canada Starch: 35/40 - 110
Can. Chew. Gum: 33/34 - 43
Hall of Fame: 83 - D14, 59C; 87 - 59C
La Presse: 27/32 - 21
O-Pee-Chee: 34/35 - 49; 37/38 - 150
Parkhurst: 55/56 - 62
Quaker Oats: 38/39 - 12; 55/56 - 62
Sweet Caporal: 34/35 - 2
World Wide Gum: 33/34 - 8; 36/37 - 3

Silk, Dave
O-Pee-Chee: 84/85 - 16

Sillinger, Mike
Donruss: 93/94 - 92
Fleer: 92/93 - 290; 93/94 - 336PP
Leaf: 93/94 - 306(II)
O-Pee-Chee: 90/91 - 107PM; 91/92 - 337
Parkhurst: 92/93 - 38, 38EI;
93/94 - 331, 331EI
Score: 91/92 - 327A, 357B, 357C
Topps: 91/92 - 337
Upper Deck: 90/91 - 452E, 452F; 92/93 - 524

Siltanen, Risto
Funmate: 83/84 - 48
O-Pee-Chee: 80/81 - 315; 81/82 - 122, 214SK;
82/83 - 129; 83/84 - 146, 257SK;
84/85 - 78; 86/87 - 187, 29SK
Panini: 79 - 166; 87/88 - 159
PepsiCo: 80/81 - 39
Post: 82/83 - 96
Topps: 83/84 - 257SK; 84/85 - 61;
86/87 - 187

Sim, Trevor
Fleer: 93/94 - 494PP
O-Pee-Chee: 93/94 - 11TC

Simard, Martin
Pro Set: 91/92 - 526E, 526F

Simmer, Charlie
Funmate: 83/84 - 83/84 - 55
O-Pee-Chee: 79/80 - 191; 80/81 - 4, 83, 171, 240;
81/82 - 142, 151, 144SK, 236SK,
266SK; 82/83 - 159, 237SK;
83/84 - 162, 290SK; 84/85 - 90, 358,
266SK; 85/86 - 87, 158SK;
86/87 - 145, 36SK; 87/88 - 52,
137SK; 88/89 - 250
Panini: 87/88 - 11
Post: 82/83 - 125
Topps: 79/80 - 191; 80/81 - 4, 83, 171, 240;
81/82 - WN 130, 35; 82/83 - 237SK,
290SK; 84/85 - 69; 85/86 - 87;
86/87 - 145; 87/88 - 52

Simmons, Don (Goalie)
Bee Hive: 45/63 - 66A, 66B, 450; 64/67 - 184
Chex: 63/65 - 56
Coca-Cola: 65/66 - 70
Parkhurst: 63/64 - 2, 62
Shirriff: 60/61 - 101; 62/63 - 22
Topps: 57/58 - 14; 58/59 - 44; 59/60 - 11;
60/61 - 43; 65/66 - 88
York: 63/64 - 15

Simmons, Gary (Goalie)
O-Pee-Chee: 74/75 - 371; 75/76 - 29;
76/77 - 176; 78/79 - 385
Topps: 75/76 - 29; 76/77 - 176

Simon, Chris
Fleer: 93/94 - 224, 7UR
Leaf: 93/94 - 416(II)
Parkhurst: 93/94 - 171, 171EI, CC13
Score: 93/94 - 473C, 473A
Upper Deck: 93/94 - 243

Simon, Cully
Bee Hive: 34/44 - 122

Simpson, Bobby
O-Pee-Chee: 77/78 - 310; 78/79 - 372

Simpson, Craig
Bowman: 90/91 - 201; 91/92 - 107; 92/93 - 150
Donruss: 93/94 - 31

Simpson, Craig (cont.)
Fleer: 92/93 - 66; 93/94 - 301PP
Kraft: 1990 - 16; 90/91 - 52
Leaf: 93/94 - 344(II)
O-Pee-Chee: 87/88 - 80, 166SK; 88/89 - 27,
36NS, 123SK, 228SK; 89/90 - 99;
90/91 - 240; 91/92 - 460;
92/93 - 225; 93/94 - 231, 333
Panini: 87/88 - 149; 88/89 - 62; 89/90 - 75;
90/91 - 229; 91/92 - 130; 92/93 - 102E,
102F; 93/94 - 237E, 237F
Parkhurst: 91/92 - 54E, 54F; 92/93 - 51, 51EI;
93/94 - 19, 19EI; 94/95 - V11
Pro Set: 90/91 - 95; 91/92 - 69E, 69F, 40PT,
9PK; 92/93 - 56
Score: 90/91 - 58A, 58C, 2HR;
91/92 - 255A, 475B, 475C, 196PNE,
196PNF; 92/93 - 260C, 260A,
321PNC, 321PNA, 30CSS, 30ASS;
93/94 - 139C, 139A
Topps: 87/88 - 80; 88/89 - 27; 89/90 - 99;
90/91 - 240; 91/92 - 460, 137SC;
92/93 - 356, 356GS, 473SC;
93/94 - 231, 333, 305SC, 305FD
Upper Deck: 90/91 - 129E, 129F; 91/92 - 286E,
286F; 92/93 - 309; 93/94 - 430

Simpson, Joe (Bullet)
Anonymous: 26/27 - 82
Hall of Fame: 83 - B12, 26C; 87 - 26C

Sims, Al
Loblaws: 74/75 - 34
O-Pee-Chee: 74/75 - 333; 75/76 - 136;
79/80 - 272; 80/81 - 233;
81/82 - 131, 66SK
Topps: 75/76 - 136; 80/81 - 233;
81/82 EN - 85

Sinclair, Reg
Bee Hive: 45/63 - 364
Parkhurst: 51/52 - 103; 52/53 - 104

Sinden, Harry
Hall of Fame: 87 - 241
Topps: 66/67 - 31

Singbush, Alex
Bee Hive: 34/44 - 183
O-Pee-Chee: 40/41 - 114

Sinisalo, Ilkka
Bowman: 90/91 - 112
O-Pee-Chee: 84/85 - 167; 85/86 - 188; 86/87 - 36,
238SK; 88/89 - 111; 90/91 - 152,
108PM; 91/92 - 510
Panini: 87/88 - 136; 88/89 - 325;
90/91 - 123
Post: 82/83 - 220
Pro Set: 90/91 - 223, 461
Score: 90/91 - 286A, 286C, 93T
Topps: 86/87 - 36; 88/89 - 111; 90/91 - 152;
91/92 - 510
Upper Deck: 90/91 - 120E, 120F

Siren, Ville
O-Pee-Chee: 90/91 - 383
Panini: 88/89 - 335
Pro Set: 90/91 - 144
Topps: 90/91 - 383

Sirois, Bob
O-Pee-Chee: 76/77 - 323; 77/78 - 351; 78/79 - 96;
79/80 - 29; 80/81 - 313
Topps: 78/79 - 96; 79/80 - 29

Sittler, Darryl
Coca-Cola: 77/78 - 24
Derniere: 72/84 - 170
Eddie Sargent: 72/73 - 204
Esso: 70/71 - 231; 88/89 - 43
Funmate: 83/84 - 97
Hockey Wit: 93/94 - 73
Kellogg's: 84 - 33
Lipton Soup: 74/75 - 3
Loblaws: 74/75 - 284
Mac's Milk: 73/74 - 26
O-Pee-Chee: 70/71 - 218; 71/72 - 193;
72/73 - 188; 73/74 - 132; 74/75 - 40;
75/76 - 150; 76/77 - 66, 207;

Sittler, Darryl (cont.)
O-Pee-Chee: 77/78 - 38, 20GP; 78/79 - 4, 30, 331; 79/80 - 120; 80/81 - 50, 193, 20PO; 81/82 - 308, 312, 97SK, 109SK; 82/83 - 257, 114SK; 83/84 - 257, 258, 272, 3SK, 191SK; 84/85 - 168, 108SK; 85/86 - 36SK; 92/93 - 191, 8AN
Post: 82/83 - 221
Pro Set: 90/91 - 404
7-Eleven: 84/85 - 37
Topps: 73/74 - 132; 74/75 - 40; 75/76 - 150, 328; 76/77 - 66, 207, 8PO; 77/78 - 38, 28PO; 78/79 - 4, 30; 79/80 - 120; 80/81 - 50, 193; 81/82 - 36; 82/83 - 114SK; 83/84 - 3SK, 191SK; 84/85 - 121
Toronto Sun: 71/72 - 271
Upper Deck: 90/91 - 504E, 504F

Sittler, Ryan
Donruss: 93/94 - 19JCA
Upper Deck: 91/92 - 695E, 695F; 93/94 - 551

Sjoberg, Lars-Erik
O-Pee-Chee: 79/80 - 396

Sjodin, Tommy
Fleer: 92/93 - 323; 93/94 - 233, 65PP
O-Pee-Chee: 92/93 - 109PM; 93/94 - 106SC, 106FD
Parkhurst: 92/93 - 79, 79EI, 224, 224EI
Score: 92/93 - 401PNC, 401PNA; 93/94 - 248C, 248A
Sega: 93/94 - 32
Topps: 93/94 - 106sc, 106fd
Upper Deck: 92/93 - 528

Skalde, Jarrod
Fleer: 93/94 - 11PP
Leaf: 93/94 - 333
Pro-Set: 92/93 - 231
Score: 91/92 - 392A, 282B, 282C
Topps: 92/93 - 84, 84GS, 189SC
Upper Deck: 92/93 - 91; 93/94 - 12

Skinner, Alf
Champ's: 24/25 - 8
Maple Crispette: 24/25 - 5
Wm. Paterson: 24/25 - 27

Skinner, Jim
Parkhurst: 93/94 - 63ML

Skorodenski, Warren
O-Pee-Chee: 85/86 - 255, 264

Skosyrev, Sergei
O-Pee-Chee: 90/91 - 496

Skov, Glen
Bee Hive: 45/63 - 211
Parkhurst: 51/52 - 57; 52/53 - 63; 53/54 - 48; 54/55 - 40; 93/94 - 23ML
Topps: 54/55 - 16; 57/58 - 30; 58/59 - 3; 59/60 - 12

Skriko, Petri
Bowman: 90/91 - 54; 91/92 - 364
Kraft: 86/87 - 68, 68P
O-Pee-Chee: 86/87 - 252, 103SK; 87/88 - 255, 40HL, 192SK; 88/89 - 137, 64SK; 89/90 - 33, D/BB, 70SK; 90/91 - 316; 91/92 - 30
Panini: 87/88 - 347; 88/89 - 140; 89/90 - 147; 90/91 - 298
Pro Set: 90/91 - 306; 91/92 - 8E, 517E, 8F, 517F
Score: 90/91 - 154A, 154C; 91 - 72T; 91/92 - 188A, 188B, 188C
Topps: 88/89 - 137; 89/90 - 33, D/BB; 90/91 - 316; 91/92 - 30, 315SC
Upper Deck: 90/91 - 147E, 147F; 91/92 - 334E, 334F

Skrudland, Brian
Bowman: 90/91 - 49; 91/92 - 331
Donruss: 93/94 - 124
Fleer: 92/93 - 111; 93/94 - 100PP
Kraft: 93/94 - 47

Skrudland, Brian (cont.)
Leaf: 93/94 - 325(II)
O-Pee-Chee: 87/88 - 235; 90/91 - 270; 91/92 - 349; 92/93 - 45; 93/94 - 26, 508, 177SC, 177FD
Panini: 87/88 - 67; 90/91 - 55; 91/92 - 194
Parkhurst: 91/92 - 314E, 314F; 92/93 - 266, 266EI; 93/94 - 75, 75EI
Pro Set: 90/91 - 159; 91/92 - 127E, 306E, 127F, 306F
Score: 90/91 - 238A, 238C; 91/92 - 294A, 514B, 514C, 160PNE, 160PNF; 92/93 - 136C, 136A, 347PNC, 347PNA; 93/94 - 258C, 258A
Sega: 93/94 - 51
Topps: 90/91 - 270; 91/92 - 349, 129SC; 92/93 - 408, 408GS, 114SC; 93/94 - 26(I), 508(II), 177SC, 349SC, 177FD, 349FD
Upper Deck: 90/91 - 93E, 93F; 91/92 - 422E, 422F; 93/94 - 96

Slaney, John
Parkhurst: 93/94 - 494, 494EI; 94/95 - 257, 257EI
Upper Deck: 90/91 - 360E, 360F, 457E, 457F

Slegr, Jiri
Donruss: 93/94 - 358
Fleer: 92/93 - 430; 93/94 - 136, 256PP
Leaf: 93/94 - 31
O-Pee-Chee: 92/93 - 54PM; 93/94 - 164, 42SC, 42FD
Parkhurst: 92/93 - 195, 195EI; 93/94 - 214, 214EI; 94/95 - V27
Score: 93/94 - 378C, 378A
Topps: 93/94 - 164(I), 42SC, 42FD
Upper Deck: 91/92 - 18E, 18F; 92/93 - 515, ER9; 93/94 - 18

Sleigher, Louis
O-Pee-Chee: 83/84 - 301; 84/85 - 290
Vachon Foods: 83/84 - 74

Sloan, Blake
Donruss: 93/94 - 20JCA

Sloan, Tod
Bee Hive: 45/63 - 139, 451
Parkhurst: 51/52 - 87; 52/53 - 48; 53/54 - 5; 54/55 - 30; 55/56 - 10; 57/58 - TOR 5; 93/94 - 112ML, 144ML, 174ML
Quaker Oats: 45/54 - 101A, 101B; 55/56 - 10
Shirriff: 60/61 - 64
Toronto Star: 57/67 - 48; 58/67 - 38
Topps: 58/59 - 42; 59/60 - 13; 60/61 - 51
Ultimate: 92 - 42(OSE), 42(OSF)

Slobodzian, Peter
Bee Hive: 34/44 - 252

Slowinski, Eddie
Bee Hive: 45/63 - 365
Parkhurst: 51/52 - 102; 52/53 - 19

Sly, Darryl
Eddie Sargent: 70/71 - 221
Esso: 70/71 - 249
O-Pee-Chee: 70/71 - 115
Topps: 70/71 - 115

Smail, Douglas (Doug)
Bowman: 90/91 - 134; 91/92 - 118; 92/93 - 362
O-Pee-Chee: 82/83 - 388; 83/84 - 390, 287SK; 84/85 - 346; 85/86 - 175, 255SK; 86/87 - 256; 87/88 - 181, 254SK; 88/89 - 251, 137SK; 89/90 - 294, 141SK; 90/91 - 268; 91/92 - 334; 92/93 - 196
Panini: 87/88 - 367; 88/89 - 158; 89/90 - 171; 90/91 - 308; 91/92 - 111
PepsiCo: 80/81 - 137
Pro Set: 90/91 - 462; 91/92 - 117E, 466E, 117F, 466F
Score: 90/91 - 196A, 196C, 69T; 91/92 - 12A, 12B, 12C, 592B, 592C; 92/93 - 197C, 197A, 377PNC, 377PNA
Topps: 83/84 - 287SK; 87/88 - 181; 90/91 - 268; 91/92 - 334, 255SC; 92/93 - 459, 459GS, 334SC

Smail, Douglas (Doug) (cont.)
Upper Deck: 90/91 - 105E, 105F; 92/93 - 124
Vachon Foods: 83/84 - 136

Smaill, Walter
Imperial Tobacco: 10/11 - 27L; 11/12 - 27; 12/13 - 22

Smeaton, Cooper
Hall of Fame: 83 - 42, 13CP; 87 - 42

Smehlik, Richard
Donruss: 93/94 - 40
Fleer: 92/93 - 262, 22UI; 93/94 - 200, 33PP
Leaf: 93/94 - 188
O-Pee-Chee: 92/93 - 90PM; 93/94 - 521, 107SC, 107FD
Panini: 93/94 - 110E, 110F
Parkhurst: 92/93 - 14, 14EI; 93/94 - 20, 20EI; 94/95 - 28, 28EI
Score: 92/93 - 393PNC, 393PNA; 93/94 - 249C, 249A
Topps: 93/94 - 521(II), 197SC, 107FD
Upper Deck: 92/93 - 564, ER1; 93/94 - 169

Smirnov, Alexander
O-Pee-Chee: 90/91 - 499; 91/92 - 60R

Smith, Al (Goalie)
Eddie Sargent: 70/71 - 161
Esso: 70/71 - 196
O-Pee-Chee: 70/71 - 87; 71/72 - 27; 76/77 - 152; 79/80 - 300; 80/81 - 252
Topps: 70/71 - 87; 71/72 - 27; 76/77 - 152; 80/81 - 252
Toronto Sun: 71/72 - 103

Smith, Alex
Anonymous: 33/34 - 47
Can. Chew. Gum: 33/34 - 44
Diamond: 36/39 - 63(I)

Smith, Alfred
Hall of Fame: 83 - 194; 87 - 194

Smith, Billy (Goalie)
Coca-Cola: 77/78 - 25
Esso: 88/89 - 44
Funmate: 83/84 - 82
Hockey Wit: 93/94 - 95
Loblaws: 74/75 - 196
McDonald's: 82/83 - 4, 16
O-Pee-Chee: 73/74 - 142; 74/75 - 82; 75/76 - 372; 76/77 - 46; 77/78 - 229; 78/79 - 62; 79/80 - 242; 80/81 - 5, 60; 81/82 - 207, 161SK; 82/83 - 211, 60SK, 61SK, 251SK; 83/84 - 17, 86SK, 16SK, 316SK; 84/85 - 135, 91SK; 85/86 - 76SK; 86/87 - 228, 213SK; 88/89 - 17
Panini: 87/88 - 89
Post: 82/83 - 190
Topps: 73/74 - 162; 74/75 - 82; 76/77 - 46; 77/78 - 229; 78/79 - 62; 79/80 - 242; 80/81 - 5, 60; 81/82 EN - 93; 82/83 - 60SK, 61SK, 251SK; 83/84 - 16SK, 86SK, 316SK; 84/85 - 101; 88/89 - 17

Smith, Brad
O-Pee-Chee: 81/82 - 103
Panini: 87/88 - 335
PepsiCo: 80/81 - 18

Smith, Brian
Bauer: 68/69 - 21
Parkhurst: 60/61 - 27

Smith, Clint
Bee Hive: 34/44 - 294
O-Pee-Chee: 39/40 - 35
Pro Set: 91/92 - 6HF

Smith, Dallas
Eddie Sargent: 70/71 - 16; 72/73 - 19
Esso: 70/71 - 15
Loblaws: 74/75 - 35
O-Pee-Chee: 68/69 - 136; 69/70 - 25; 70/71 - 137; 71/72 - 170; 72/73 - 21, 135; 73/74 - 167; 74/75 - 146; 75/76 - 118; 76/77 - 105
Shirriff: 60/61 - 116I; 61/62 - 2; 68/69 - A13
Topps: 60/61 - 8ST; 61/62 - 4; 62/63 - 9;

Smith, Dallas (cont.)
Topps: 66/67 - 101; 66/67 US - 3; 67/68 - 41; 69/70 - 25; 72/73 - 45; 73/74 - 42; 74/75 - 146; 75/76 - 118; 76/77 - 105
Toronto Sun: 71/72 - 17

Smith, Des
Bee Hive: 34/44 - 34, 80, 206
Canada Starch: 35/40 - 124
O-Pee-Chee: 37/38 - 148; 39/40 - 77

Smith, Derek
O-Pee-Chee: 78/79 - 222; 79/80 - 89; 80/81 - 199; 81/82 - 25, 59SK; 82/83 - 95
Post: 82/83 - 78
Topps: 78/79 - 222; 79/80 - 89; 80/81 - 199; 81/82 EN - 79

Smith, Derrick
Bowman: 91/92 - 245
O-Pee-Chee: 90/91 - 463; 91/92 - 486; 92/93 - 363
Panini: 87/88 - 135; 89/90 - 304; 91/92 - 232
Parkhurst: 94/95 - 59, 59EI
Pro Set: 90/91 - 503; 91/92 - 174E, 174F
Score: 91/92 - 444B, 444C
Topps: 91/92 - 486

Smith, Don
Imperial Tobacco: 10/11 - 19L; 11/12 - 19; 12/13 - 12

Smith, Douglas (Doug)
O-Pee-Chee: 82/83 - 160; 84/85 - 91; 86/87 - 202
Post: 82/83 - 126

Smith, Floyd
Bee Hive: 45/63 - 212; 64/67 - 94A, 94B, 94C
Coca-Cola: 64/65 - 53; 65/66 - 53
Dad's Cookies: 70/71 - 23
Eddie Sargent: 70/71 - 30
Esso: 70/71 - 35
O-Pee-Chee: 68/69 - 130; 69/70 - 49; 70/71 - 140; 71/72 - 158; 74/75 - 176
Parkhurst: 63/64 - 57
Post: 68/69 - 28
Shirriff: 68/69 - M12
Topps: 64/65 - 42; 65/66 - 109; 66/67 - 106; 67/68 - 52; 68/69 - 130; 69/70 - 49; 74/75 - 176
Toronto Star: 64/65 - 23
York: 63/64 - 42

Smith, Frank D.
Hall of Fame: 83 - G13, 103C; 87 - 103C

Smith, Gary (Goalie)
Colgate: 70/71 - 90
Eddie Sargent: 70/71 - 129; 72/73 - 61
Esso: 70/71 - 51
Lipton Soup: 74/75 - 15
Loblaws: 74/75 - 303
O-Pee-Chee: 68/69 - 176; 69/70 - 78; 70/71 - 69; 71/72 - 22BK; 72/73 - 117; 73/74 - 126; 74/75 - 22; 75/76 - 115; 76/77 - 317; 77/78 - 184; 79/80 - 103
Shirriff: 68/69 - H6
Topps: 69/70 - 78; 70/71 - 69; 71/72 - 124, 22BK; 72/73 - 114; 73/74 - 126; 74/75 - 22; 75/76 - 115; 77/78 - 184; 79/80 - 103
Toronto Sun: 71/72 - 80

Smith, Geoff
Bowman: 90/91 - 192; 91/92 - 112; 92/93 - 95
Donruss: 93/94 - 112, 435
Leaf: 93/94 - 302(II)
O-Pee-Chee: 90/91 - 33; 91/92 - 301; 92/93 - 338
Parkhurst: 94/95 - 82, 82EI
Pro Set: 90/91 - 446; 91/92 - 384E, 384F
Score: 90/91 - 326A, 326C, 373A, 373C; 91/92 - 87B, 87C, 283PNE, 283PNF; 92/93 - 192C, 192A, 192PNC, 192PNA; 93/94 - 306C, 306A
Topps: 90/91 - 33; 91/92 - 301, 42SC; 92/93 - 275, 275GS, 84SC
Upper Deck: 90/91 - 326E, 326F

Smith, Gord
O-Pee-Chee: 76/77 - 303; 77/78 - 387; 78/79 - 347; 79/80 - 285

Smith, Greg
O-Pee-Chee: 77/78 - 269; 78/79 - 303; 79/80 - 11; 81/82 - 168; 82/83 - 96; 83/84 - 130, 140SK; 84/85 - 64
Post: 82/83 - 79
Topps: 79/80 - 11; 81/82 WN - 112; 83/84 - 140SK

Smith, Hooley (Reginald)
Anonymous: 1925/26 - 22; 26/27 - 21
Amal. Press: 35/36 - 10
Bee Hive: 34/44 - 207, 253
Champ's: 24/25 - 47
Dom. Choc.: 1925 - 69
Hall of Fame: 83 - 43, C14P; 87 - 43
La Presse: 27/32 - 46
O-Pee-Chee: 34/35 - 69; 35/36 - 76; 36/37 - 132; 39/40 - 17
Sweet Caporal: 34/35 - 36
Willards: 1923 - 47
Willards: 1925 - 47
Wm. Paterson: 24/25 - 5
World Wide Gum: 33/34 - 6P, 31; 36/37 - 20

Smith, James (Steve)
Bowman: 90/91 - 200; 91/92 - 106; 92/93 - 24
Donruss: 93/94 - 68
Fleer: 92/93 - 42; 93/94 - 231, 55PP
Kraft: 1990 - 17
Leaf: 93/94 - 95
O-Pee-Chee: 88/89 - 252, 225SK; 89/90 - 228, 223SK; 90/91 - 368; 91/92 - 21, 136PM; 92/93 - 108; 93/94 - 39. 218SC, 218FD
Panini: 87/88 - 259; 88/89 - 55; 89/90 - 83; 90/91 - 226; 91/92 - 121; 92/93 - 12E, 12F; 93/94 - 154E, 154F
Parkhurst: 91/92 - 31E, 31F; 92/93 - 32, 32EI, 444, 444EI; 93/94 - 310, 310EI
Pro Set: 90/91 - 96; 91/92 - 73E, 284E, 370E, 73F, 284F, 27PT, 370F; 92/93 - 37
Score: 90/91 - 129A, 129C; 91 - 73T; 91/92 - 11A, 11B, 11C, 623B, 623C, 18PNE, 18PNF; 92/93 - 48C, 48A, 57PNC, 57PNA; 93/94 - 192C, 192A
Sega: 93/94 - 26
Topps: 90/91 - 368; 91/92 - 21, 230SC; 92/93 - 315, 315GS, 383SC; 93/94 - 39(I), 218SC, 218FD
Upper Deck: 90/91 - 148E, 148F; 91/92 - 350E, 350F

Smith, Jason
Donruss: 93/94 - 182
Fleer: 93/94 - 381PP
Leaf: 93/94 - 389(II)
Parkhurst: 93/94 - 379, 379EI; 94/95 - 130, 130EI
Upper Deck: 93/94 - 252

Smith, Kenny
Bee Hive: 45/63 - 67

Smith, Norman (Goalie)
Bee Hive: 34/44 - 123
World Wide Gum: 36/37 - 74

Smith, Randy
Score: 92/93 - 4COH

Smith, Rick
Eddie Sargent: 70/71 - 11
Esso: 70/71 - 16
O-Pee-Chee: 70/71 - 135; 71/72 - 174; 72/73 - 23, 284; 76/77 - 269; 77/78 - 104; 78/79 - 164; 79/80 - 59
Topps: 72/73 - 34; 77/78 - 104; 78/79 - 164; 79/80 - 59
Toronto Sun: 71/72 - 18

Smith, Robert (Bobby)
Bowman: 90/91 - 51; 91/92 - 117; 92/93 - 54
Fleer: 92/93 - 97
Funmate: 83/84 - 63
Kraft: 86/87 - 39, 39P; 1990 - 26; 90/91 - 53
O-Pee-Chee: 79/80 - 206; 80/81 - 17; 81/82 - 157, 170, 174, 88SK; 82/83 - 175, 176, 188SK; 83/84 - 181, 116SK; 84/85 - 273, 151SK, 152SK; 85/86 - 181, 132SK; 86/87 - 188, 13SK; 87/88 - 48, 10SK; 88/89 - 88, D/BB, 46SK; 89/90 - 188, 47SK; 90/91 - 287, 109PM; 91/92 - 398; 92/93 - 396
Panini: 87/88 - 62; 88/89 - 261; 89/90 - 236; 90/91 - 52; 91/92 - 113; 92/93 - 96F, 96F
Parkhurst: 91/92 - 83E, 217E, 83F, 217F
Post: 81/82 - 5; 82/83 - 143
Pro Set: 90/91 - 160, 463; 91/92 - 115E, 289E, 115F, 289F; 92/93 - 81, 259
Score: 90 - 75T; 90/91 - 61A, 61C; 91/92 - 32A, 32B, 32C, 210PNE, 210PNF; 92/93 - 205C, 446C, 205A, 446A, 142PNC, 142PNA
Topps: 79/80 - 206; 80/81 - 17; 81/82 - WN 131, 37, 55; 82/83 - 188SK; 83/84 - 116SK; 84/85 - 83; 86/87 - 188; 87/88 - 48; 88/89 - 88, D/BB; 89/90 - 188; 90/91 - 287; 91/92 - 398, 25SC; 92/93 - 388, 388GS, 427SC
Upper Deck: 90/91 - 72E, 72F, 406E, 406F; 91/92 - 293E, 293F
Vachon Foods: 83/84 - 56

Smith, Sid
Bee Hive: 45/63 - 452
Parkhurst: 51/52 - 84; 52/53 - 45; 53/54 - 2; 54/55 - 22; 55/56 - 2; 57/58 TOR - 10; 93/94 - 109ML
Quaker Oats: 45/54 - 102A, 102B; 55/56 - 2
Ultimate: 92 - 43(OSE), 43(OSF)

Smith, Tommy
Hall of Fame: 83 - 237, H14P; 87 - 237

Smolinski, Bryan
Donruss: 93/94 - 30
Fleer: 93/94 - 232, 14RS, 291PP
Leaf: 93/94 - 204
O-Pee-Chee: 93/94 - 466
Parkhurst: 92/93 - 481, 481EI; 93/94 - 259, 259EI; 94/95 - 12, 276, 12EI, 276EI
Score: 93/94 - 472C, 472A
Topps: 93/94 - 466(II), 274SC, 274FD
Upper Deck: 93/94 - 242

Smrke, John
O-Pee-Chee: 79/80 - 340

Smyl, Stanley (Stan)
Esso: 83/84 - 17E, 17F
Funmate: 83/84 - 132
Kellogg's: 84 - 9
Kraft: 86/87 - 69, 69P
O-Pee-Chee: 80/81 - 128, 208; 81/82 - 328; 82/83 - 356, 242SK; 83/84 - 359, 274SK; 84/85 - 330, 281SK; 85/86 - 68, 247SK; 86/87 - 50, 96SK; 87/88 - 4, 198SK; 88/89 - 253, 60SK; 89/90 - 283, 68SK
Panini: 87/88 - 349; 88/89 - 141; 89/90 - 159; 90/91 - 292
PepsiCo: 80/81 - 118
Post: 81/82 - 25; 82/83 - 302
Pro Set: 90/91 - 548
Score: 90/91 - 374A, 374C
7-Eleven: 84/85 - 51
Topps: 80/81 - 128, 208; 81/82 - 38; 82/83 - 242SK; 83/84 - 274SK; 84/85 - 140; 85/86 - 68; 86/87 - 50; 87/88 - 4
Upper Deck: 90/91 - 299E, 299F
Vachon Foods: 83/84 - 116

Smyth, Greg
Donruss: 93/94 - 444
O-Pee-Chee: 93/94 - 306
Pro Set: 91/92 - 465E, 465F
Topps: 93/94 - 306(II)

Smyth, Kevin
Parkhurst: 94/95 - 99, 99EI

Smythe, Conn
    Hall of Fame: 83 - 27, B13P; 87 - 27
    HHFM: 92 - 2
  World Wide Gum: 36/37 - 95

Smythe, Stafford
    Parkhurst: 59/60 - 36

Sneddon, Bob (Goalie)
    Esso: 70/71 - 52

Snell, Chris
    Upper Deck: 90/91 - 468E, 468F

Snell, Ted
    Loblaws: 74/75 - 125

Snepsts, Harold
    Esso: 83/84 - 18E, 18F
    O-Pee-Chee: 75/76 - 396; 76/77 - 366; 77/78 - 295; 78/79 - 380; 79/80 - 186; 80/81 - 312; 81/82 - 344, 250SK; 82/83 - 357, 243SK; 83/84 - 360; 84/85 - 108; 85/86 - 232, 44SK; 87/88 - 110SK; 89/90 - 286
    Panini: 87/88 - 241
    PepsiCo: 80/81 - 119
    Post: 82/83 - 303
    Pro Set: 90/91 - 527
    Score: 90/91 - 61T
    7-Eleven: 84/85 - 27
    Topps: 79/80 - 186; 82/83 - 243SK
  Vachon Foods: 83/84 - 117

Snow, Garth
    Donruss: 93/94 - 481
    Fleer: 93/94 - 425PP
    Parkhurst: 94/95 - 191, 191EI

Snuggerud, Dave
    Bowman: 90/91 - 249; 91/92 - 29; 92/93 - 309
    O-Pee-Chee: 90/91 - 340; 91/92 - 441
    Panini: 90/91 - 19; 91/92 - 308
    Pro Set: 90/91 - 30; 91/92 - 18E, 18F
    Score: 90/91 - 48T; 91/92 - 206A, 206B, 206C, 223PNE, 223PNF; 92/93 - 182C, 182A, 183PNC, 183PNA
    Topps: 90/91 - 340; 91/92 - 441, 320SC
    Upper Deck: 90/91 - 189E, 189F; 91/92 - 194E, 194F

Soderstrom, Tommy (Goalie)
    Donruss: 93/94 - 253
    Fleer: 92/93 - 160, 23UI; 93/94 - 217, 185PP, 8N, 11SY
    Leaf: 93/94 - 37, 12R
    O-Pee-Chee: 93/94 - 55, 122
    Panini: 93/94 - 55E, 55F
    Parkhurst: 92/93 - 367, 367EI, 448, 448EI; 93/94 - 150, 150EI
    Score: 93/94 - 336C, 336A
    Sega: 93/94 - 102
    Topps: 93/94 - 55, 122, 340SC, 430SC 340FD, 430FD
    Upper Deck: 92/93 - 377, 475; 93/94 - 182

Soetaert, Doug (Goalie)
    O-Pee-Chee: 80/81 - 324; 82/83 - 389, 211SK; 83/84 - 391, 288SK; 84/85 - 347; 85/86 - 136SK; 86/87 - 16SK
    Topps: 82/83 - 211SK; 83/84 - 288SK
  Vachon Foods: 83/84 - 137

Solheim, Ken
    O-Pee-Chee: 83/84 - 131

Solinger, Bob
    Bee Hive: 45/63 - 453
    Parkhurst: 51/52 - 88; 52/53 - 50;53/54 - 16
    Quaker Oats: 45/54 - 103

Somers, Art
    Diamond: 33/35 - 55; 36/39 - 58(II)
    La Presse: 27/32 - 51
    O-Pee-Chee: 33/34 - 17

Somerville, Ross
    Dom. Choc.: 1925 - 113

Sorokin, Serguei
    O-Pee-Chee: 91/92 - 44R
    Upper Deck: 92/93 - 343

Sorrell, John
    Bee Hive: 34/44 - 124, 254
  Can. Chew. Gum: 33/34 - 45
    O-Pee-Chee: 33/34 - 42; 39/40 - 60
  World Wide Gum: 36/37 - 25

Soules, Jason
    Upper Deck: 90/91 - 75E, 75F

Speck, Fred
    O-Pee-Chee: 72/73 - 331
    Toronto Sun: 71/72 - 290

Spencer, Brian
    Eddie Sargent: 72/73 - 132
    Loblaws: 74/75 - 54
    O-Pee-Chee: 71/72 - 198; 72/73 - 61; 73/74 - 83; 74/75 - 328; 75/76 - 384; 76/77 - 191; 77/78 - 9; 78/79 - 137
    Topps: 72/73 - 53; 73/74 - 83; 76/77 - 191; 77/78 - 9; 78/79 - 137
    Toronto Sun: 71/72 - 272

Spencer, Irv
    Shirriff: 60/61 - 88; 61/62 - 86
    Topps: 61/62 - 47; 62/63 - 17

Speyer, Chris
    Champ's: 24/25 - 59
    Diamond: 33/35 - 56

Spring, Don
    O-Pee-Chee: 81/82 - 375; 82/83 - 392; 83/84 - 392
    PepsiCo: 80/81 - 136
    Post: 82/83 - 333

Spring, Frank
    O-Pee-Chee: 75/76 - 341

Spring, Jesse
    Champ's: 24/25 - 19
  Wm. Paterson: 23/24 - 36; 24/25 - 20

Spruce, Andy
    O-Pee-Chee: 78/79 - 378

Stackhouse, Ron
    Eddie Sargent: 72/73 - 77
    Esso: 70/71 - 53
    Loblaws: 74/75 - 252
    O-Pee-Chee: 71/72 - 83; 72/73 - 287; 73/74 - 236; 74/75 - 188; 75/76 - 111; 76/77 - 72; 77/78 - 157; 78/79 - 72; 79/80 - 154; 80/81 - 228; 81/82 - 266, 188SK; 82/83 - 275
    Post: 82/83 - 240
    Topps: 74/75 - 188; 75/76 - 111; 76/77 - 72; 77/78 - 157; 78/79 - 72; 79/80 - 154; 80/81 - 228
    Toronto Sun: 71/72 - 59

Stajduhar, Nick
    Donruss: 93/94 - 19JCC
    Parkhurst: 93/94 - 507, 507EI
    Upper Deck: 93/94 - 543

Stamler, Lorne
    O-Pee-Chee: 78/79 - 301

Stanfield, Fred
    Bee Hive: 64/67 - 55A, 55B
    Coca-Cola: 64/65 - 34; 65/66 - 35
  Dad's Cookies: 70/71 - 11
    Eddie Sargent: 70/71 - 12 72/73 - 15
    Esso: 70/71 - 17
    Loblaws: 74/75 - 162
    O-Pee-Chee: 68/69 - 10; 69/70 - 32; 70/71 - 5, 7DE; 71/72 - 7; 72/73 - 150; 74/75 - 31; 75/76 - 332; 76/77 - 58; 77/78 - 161; 78/79 - 352
    Shirriff: 68/69 - A9
    Topps: 65/66 - 63; 66/67 - 56; 67/68 - 36; 68/69 - 10; 69/70 - 32; 70/71 - 5; 71/72 - 7; 72/73 - 135; 74/75 - 31; 76/77 - 58; 77/78 - 161
    Toronto Sun: 71/72 - 19
    Ultimate: 92 - 54(OSE), 54(OSF)

Stanfield, Jim
    Eddie Sargent: 72/73 -86

Stangle, Frank
  World Wide Gum: 36/37 - 110

Staniowski, Ed (Goalie)
    O-Pee-Chee: 76/77 - 104; 77/78 - 54; 79/80 - 327; 80/81 - 328; 82/83 - 393, 210SK
    Post: 82/83 - 334
    Topps: 76/77 - 104; 77/78 - 54; 82/83 - 210SK

Stanley, Allan
    Bee Hive: 45/63 - 366, 454A, 454B; 64/67 - 185
    Chex: 63/65 - 57
    Coca-Cola: 64/65 - 107; 65/66 - 106
    Hall of Fame: 83 - 238, G14P; 87 - 238
    O-Pee-Chee: 68/69 - 183, 16PS
    Parkhurst: 51/52 - 94; 52/53 - 21; 53/54 - 64; 58/59 - 23; 59/60 - 44; 60/61 - 16; 61/62 - 16; 62/63 - 9; 63/64 - 1, 61; 92/93 - PR11; 93/94 - 20ML
    Shirriff: 60/61 - 6; 61/62 - 42; 62/63 - 2; 68/69 - J3B, J11
    Topps: 54/55 - 41; 57/58 - 15; 64/65 - 104; 66/67 - 16, 128; 66/67 US - 16; 67/68 - 13
    Toronto Star: 57/67 - 61, 105; 58/67 - 62, 108; 63/64 - 41; 64/65 - 47
    Ultimate: 92 - 44(OSE), 75(OSE), 44(OSF), 75(OSF)
    York: 60/61 - 36; 61/62 - 9; 63/64 - 14

Stanley, Lord
    Hall of Fame: 83 - 13, A14P; 87 - 13

Stanley, Russell (Barney)
    Hall of Fame: 83 - 12, A13P; 87 - 12

Stanowski, Wally
    Bee Hive: 34/44 - 348; 45/63 - 367, 455
    O-Pee-Chee: 39/40 - 11; 40/41 - 103
    Quaker Oats: 45/54 - 104A, 104B

Stanton, Paul
    Bowman: 91/92 - 91; 92/93 - 284
    Fleer: 92/93 - 381
    O-Pee-Chee: 90/91 - 110PM; 91/92 - 339; 92/93 - 361; 93/94 - 5, 52SC, 52FD
    Panini: 91/92 - 274
    Parkhurst: 93/94 - 288
    Pro Set: 90/91 - 633; 91/92 - 457E, 457F
    Score: 90/91 - 27T; 91/92 - 366A, 406B, 406C; 92/93 - 135C, 135A, 308PNC, 208PNA; 93/94 - 321C, 321A
    Topps: 91/92 - 339, 380SC; 92/93 - 460, 460GS, 52SC; 93/94 - 5(I), 52SC, 52FD
    Upper Deck: 90/91 - 404E, 404F; 91/92 - 203E, 203F; 92/93 -100

Stapleton, Pat
    Bee Hive: 45/63 - 68A, 68B; 64/67 - 26, 56
    Colgate: 70/71 - 77
  Dad's Cookies: 70/71 - 44
    Eddie Sargent: 70/71 - 44; 73/73 - 69
    Esso: 70/71 - 71
    Mac's Milk: 73/74 - 27
    O-Pee-Chee: 68/69 - 15; 69/70 - 69; 70/71 - 17; 71/72 - 25; 71/72 - 258; 72/73 - 4, 249
    Shirriff: 61/62 - 13; 68/69 - B2
    Topps: 61/62 - 18; 62/63 - 8; 65/66 - 120; 66/67 - 57, 129; 66/67 US - 57; 67/68 - 61; 68/69 - 15; 69/70 - 69, 17QS; 70/71 - 17; 71/72 - 25; 72/73 - 70, 129
    Toronto Star: 58/67 - 100
    Toronto Sun: 71/72 - 81

Starke, Joe
    Diamond: 36/39 - 64

Starr, Harold
    Diamond: 1936/39 - 59(II), 54(III)

Stasiuk, Vic
    Bee Hive: 45/63 - 69, 213A, 213B, 213C
    Parkhurst: 51/52 - 62; 52/53 - 90; 53/54 - 39; 61/62 - 32; 62/63 - 22; 63/64 - 58; 93/94 - 9ML, 169ML
    Shirriff: 60/61 - 103; 61/62 - 63

Stasiuk, Vic (cont.)
- Topps: 57/58 - 11; 58/59 - 9; 59/60 - 14; 60/61 - 66
- Toronto Star: 58/67 - 26
- York: 62/63 - 30B

Stastny, Anton
- Derniere: 72/84 - 151
- Funmate: 83/84 - 110
- Kraft: 86/87 - 50, 50P
- O-Pee-Chee: 81/82 - 282, 70SK; 82/83 - 294, 24SK; 83/84 - 302, 252SK; 84/85 - 291, 178SK; 85/86 - 78, 147SK; 86/87 - 125, 27SK; 87/88 - 185, 228SK; 88/89 - 98, 194SK
- Panini: 87/88 - 166; 88/89 - 357
- PepsiCo: 80/81 - 76
- Post: 82/83 - 252
- Topps: 82-83 - 24SK; 83/84 - 252SK; 85/86 - 78; 86/87 - 125; 87/88 - 185; 88/89 - 98
- Vachon Foods: 83/84 - 75

Stastny, Marian
- Derniere: 72/84 - 142
- Funmate: 83/84 - 111
- McDonald's: 82/83 - 10
- O-Pee-Chee: 82/83 - 295, 20SK; 83/84 - 303, 168SK, 251SK; 84/85 - 292, 177SK; 86/87 - 144SK
- Panini: 79 - 90
- Post: 82/83 - 253
- Topps: 82/83 - 20SK; 83/84 - 168SK, 251SK
- Vachon Foods: 83/84 - 76

Stastny, Peter
- Bowman: 90/91 - 86; 91/92 - 287; 92/93 - 249
- Cel.Watch: 1988 - CW12
- Donruss: 93/94 - 487
- Derniere: 72/84 - 158
- Fleer: 92/93 - 118, 24UI
- Frito-Lay: 88/89 - 38
- Funmate: 83/84 - 112
- Hockey Wit: 93/94 - 70
- Kellogg's: 84 - 22
- Kraft: 86/87 - 51, 51P; 1990 - 33; 90/91 - 54
- McDonald's: 82/83 - 24
- O-Pee-Chee: 81/82 - 269, 286, 287, 395, 69SK, 263SK; 82/83 - 276, 292, 293, 15SK, 19SK, 167SK; 83/84 - 304, 167SK, 253SK; 84/85 - 293, 141SK, 164SK, 165SK; 85/86 - 31, 156SK; 86/87 - 20, 26SK; 87/88 - 21, 222SK; 88/89 - 22, 37SK, 182SK, 189SK; 89/90 - 143; 90/91 - 334; 91/92 - 275; 92/93 - 216
- Panini: 79 - 84; 87/88 - 164; 88/89 - 358; 89/90 - 324; 9/91 - 70; 91/92 - 220; 92/93 - 174E, 174F; 93/94 - 41E, 41F
- Parkhurst: 91/92 - 103E, 209E, 103F, 209F; 94/95 - 203, 203EI
- PepsiCo: 8/81 - 77
- Post: 82/83 - 254
- Pro Set: 90/91 - 175; 91/92 - 143E, 143F, 16PK, 194PT; 92/93 - 100
- Score: 90/91 - 96A, 96C, 48HR; 91/92 - 66A, 66B, 66C, 266PNE, 266PNF; 92/93 - 291C,291A, 359PNC, 359PNA; 93/94 - 22C, 22A
- 7-Eleven: 84/85 - 41
- Topps: 81/82 - 39, 61; 82/83 - 15SK, 19SK, 167SK; 83/84 - 167SK, 253SK; 84/85 - 130; 85/86 - 31; 86/87 - 20; 87/88 - 21; 88/89 - 22; 89/90 - 143; 90/91 - 334; 91/92 - 275, 263SC; 92/93 - 469, 469GS, 140SC
- Upper Deck: 90/91 - 163E, 163F; 91/92 - 113E, 113F
- Vachon Foods: 83/84 - 77

Stauber, Robb (Goalie)
- Fleer: 92/93 - 311; 93/94 - 363PP
- O-Pee-Chee: 92/93 - 115PM
- Parkhurst: 92/93 - 303, 303EI; 94/95 - 109, 109EI
- O-Pee-Chee: 90/91 - 181; 93/94 - 109

Stauber, Robb (Goalie) (cont.)
- Score: 93/94- 346C, 346A
- Topps: 90/91 - 181; 93/94 - 109(I), 327SC, 327FD
- Upper Deck: 90/91 - 165E, 165F; 92/93 - 495

Steen, Anders
- PepsiCo: 80/81 - 138

Steen, Thomas
- Bowman: 90/91 - 133; 91/92 - 200; 92/93 - 312
- Donruss: 93/94 - 389
- Fleer: 92/93 - 247; 93/94 - 69, 275PP, 476PP
- Kraft: 86/87 - 80, 80P; 9/91 - 55
- Leaf: 93/94 - 165
- O-Pee-Chee: 82/83 - 391; 83/84 - 393, 289SK; 84/85 - 348, 292SK; 85/86 - 206, 253SK; 86/87 - 257, 110SK; 87/88 - 221; 88/89 - 254, 138SK; 89/90 - 290, 144SK; 90/91 - 283; 91/92 - 218; 92/93 - 385; 93/94 - 11
- Panini: 87/88 - 365; 88/89 - 159; 89/9 - 163; 9/91 - 316; 91/92 - 68; 92/93 - 53E, 53F; 93/94 - 191E, 191F
- Parkhurst: 92/93 - 214, 214EI; 93/94 - 502, 502EI; 94/95 - 263, 263EI
- Pro Set: 90/91 - 356, 565; 91/92 - 271E, 271F, 138PT; 92/93 - 217
- Score: 90/91 - 14A, 14C, 8HR; 91/92 - 198A, 198B, 198C, 275PNE, 275PNF; 92/93 - 80C, 80A, 29PNC, 29PNA; 93/94 - 71C, 71A
- Sega: 93/94 - 148
- Topps: 83/84 - 289SK; 90/91 - 283; 91/92 - 218, 207SC; 92/93 - 141, 141GS; 93/94 - 5(I), 195SC, 282SC, 195FD, 282FD
- Upper Deck: 90/91 - 94E, 94F; 91/92 - 181E, 181F; 92/93 - 154; 93/94 - 166
- Vachon Foods: 83/84 - 138

Stefan, Gregory (Greg) (Goalie)
- Bee Hive: 34/44 - 352
- O-Pee-Chee: 84/85 - 65, 41SK; 85/86 - 157, 31SK; 86/87 - 51, 165SK; 87/88 - 186; 88/89 - 68, 38NS, 252SK; 89/90 - 23, 248SK
- Panini: 87/88 - 237; 88/89 - 37; 89/90 - 59
- Topps: 84/85 - 48; 85/86 - 157; 86/87 - 51; 87/88 - 186; 88/89 - 68; 89/90 - 23

Stein, Phil (Goalie)
- Beehive: 34/44 - 349

Steiner, Ondrej
- Upper Deck: 92/93 - 604

Stelnov, Igor
- O-Pee-Chee: 91/92 - 26R

Stemkowski, Pete
- Bee Hive: 64/67 - 186
- Coca-Cola: 65/66 - 107
- Eddie Sargent: 70/71 - 50; 71/72 - 115; 72/73 - 143
- Esso: 7/71 - 159
- Lipton Soup: 74/75 - 42
- Loblaws: 74/75 - 213
- O-Pee-Chee: 68/69 - 33; 69/70 - 65; 70/71 - 26, 182; 71/72 - 217; 72/73 - 78; 73/74 - 217; 74/75 - 77; 75/76 - 303; 76/77 - 166; 77/78 - 272; 78/79 - 290
- Shirriff: 68/69 - C10
- Topps: 65/66 - 84; 66/67 - 15; 66/67 US - 15; 67/68 - 12; 68/69 - 33; 69/70 - 65; 70/71 - 25; 74/75 - 77; 75/76 - 303; 76/77 - 166
- Toronto Sun: 71/72 - 184

Stephenson, Bob
- O-Pee-Chee: 79/80 - 391

Stephenson, Wayne (Goalie)
- Eddie Sargent: 72/73 - 191
- O-Pee-Chee: 72/73 - 275; 73/74 - 31; 74/75 - 218; 75/76 - 355; 76/77 - 190; 77/78 - 142; 78/79 - 223; 79/80 - 38; 80/81 - 121
- Topps: 73/74 - 31; 74/75 - 218; 76/77 - 190;

Stephenson, Wayne (Goalie) (cont.)
- Topps: 77/78 - 142; 78/79 - 223; 79/80 - 38; 80/81 - 121

Stern, Ronald (Ronnie)
- Durivage: 93/94 - 28
- Fleer: 92/93 - 271; 93/94 - 43PP
- Leaf: 93/94 - 261(I)'
- O-Pee-Chee: 93/94 - 341, 68SC, 68FD
- Parkhurst: 92/93 - 265, 265EI; 93/94 - 303. 303EI;z
- Pro Set: 90/91 - 549; 91/92 - 362E, 362F
- Score: 91/92 - 408B, 408C; 92/93 - 237C, 237A, 217PNC, 217PNA; 93/94 - 409C, 409A
- Topps: 93/94 - 341(II), 68SC, 68FD

Stevens, John
- Parkhurst: 94/95 - 100, 100EI

Stevens, Kevin
- Bowman: 90/91 - 208; 91/92 - 92; 92/93 - 241, 366
- Donruss: 93/94 - 265
- Fleer: 92/93 - 171, 5AS; 93/94 - 229, 6AS, 195PP, 17PL
- Hockey Wit: 93/94 - 20
- Humpty Dumpty: 92/93 - 21(I)
- Leaf: 93/94 - 69, 4AS, 9HT
- McDonald's: 91/92 - Mc3
- O-Pee-Chee: 90/91 - 360, 111PM; 91/92 - 267, 421, 26PM; 92/93 - 29; 93/94 - 170, 370, 158SC, 158FD
- Panini: 89/90 - 321; 90/91 - 131; 91/92 - 269; 92/93 - 221E, 221F, 281E, 281F; 93/94 - 79E, 79F
- Parkhurst: 91/92 - 135E, 135F, 473; 92/93 - 138, 138EI, 466, 466EI; 93/94 - 158, 158EI; 94/95 - 177, 177EI
- Pro Set: 90/91 - 240; 91/92 - P2, 185E, 314E, 185F, 314F, 93PT; 92/93 - 140
- Score: 90 - 17YS; 90/91 - 53A, 53C; 91/92 - 248A, 468B, 468C, 191PNE, 191PNF, B-4E, B-4F; 92/93 - 25C, 25A, 492C,492A, 288PNC, 288PNA, 25PC(S), 25PC(F), 10USG, 4CTP, 4ATP; 93/94 - 325C, 325A, 15PNC, 15PNA, 23DT, 15CAS, 15AAS
- Season's: 92/93 - 66
- Sega: 93/94 - 106
- Topps: 90/91 - 360; 91/92 - 267, 421, 234SC; 92/93 - 259, 343, 429, 259GS, 343GS, 429GS, 110SC, 257SC; 93/94 - 170, 370, 158SC, 457SC, 158FD, 457FD, 6AS
- Upper Deck: 90/91 - 14E, 14F; 91/92 - 154E, 613E, 154F, 613F, Mc3; 92/93 - 275, 630, G4, 14AS; 93/94 - 126, 230

Stevens, Scott
- Bowman: 91/92 - 369; 92/93 - 160, 242
- Donruss: 93/94 - 192
- Fleer: 92/93 - 119; 93/94 - 189, 143PP
- Frito-Lay: 88/89 - 39
- Hockey Wit: 93/94 - 65
- Humpty Dumpty: 92/93 - 22(I)
- Kraft: 90/91 - 56; 91/92 - 53; 93/94 - 52
- Leaf: 93/94 - 60
- McDonald's: 91/92 - Mc24
- O-Pee-Chee: 83/84 - 376, 188SK; 84/85 - 206, 85/86 - 62, 107SK; 86/87 - 126, 254SK; 87/88 - 25, 233SK; 88/89 - 60, 39NS, 68SK; 89/90 - 93, 76SK; 90/91 - 211, 112PM; 91/92 - 481, 84PM; 92/93 - 251, 336, 16AN; 93/94 - 80
- Panini: 87/88 - 177; 88/89 - 368; 89/90 - 341; 9/91 - 155; 91/92 - 26; 92/93 - 181E, 181F; 93/94 - 43E, 43F
- Parkhurst: 91/92 - 102E, 102F; 92/93 - 92, 92EI, CP18;93/94 - 114, 114F; 94/95 - H13, R13, C13, V41
- Pro Set: 90/91 - 321, 528; 91/92 - 216E, 292E, 423E, 216F, 292F, 72PT, 423F; 92/93 - 95
- Score: 90 - 40T; 90/91 - 188A, 188C, 341A, 341C, 82HR; 91 - 45T;

Stevens, Scott (cont.)
Score: 91/92 - 40A, 303A, 40B, 40C, 307C, 595B, 595C, 81PNE, 81PNF; 92/93 - 75C, 75A, 429C, 429A, 280PNC, 280PNA; 93/94 - 111C, 111A, 4PNC, 4PNA, 5DT, 4CAS, 4AAS, 11FR
Season's: 92/93 - 50
Sega: 93/94 - 73
Topps: 83/84 - 188SK; 84/85 - 149; 85/86 - 62; 86/87 - 126; 87/88 - 25; 88/89 - 60, 4SK; 89/90 - 93; 90/91 - 211; 91/92 - 481, 265SC; 92/93 - 156, 269, 156GS, 269GS, 151SC; 93/94 - 80(I), 383SC, 383FD, 13AS
Upper Deck: 90/91 - 236E, 236F, 436E, 436F, 482E, 482F; 91/92 - 132E, 539E, 132F, 539F; 92/93 - 297, 15AS; 93/94 - 119

Stevenson, Shayne
O-Pee-Chee: 91/92 - 121
Score: 90/91 - 405A, 405C
Topps: 91/92 - 121
Upper Deck: 91/92 - 332E, 332F

Stevenson, Turner
Score: 90/91 - 426A, 426C
Upper Deck: 91/92 - 691E, 691F; 93/94 - 248

Stewart, Allan
O-Pee-Chee: 90/91 - 113PM
Pro Set: 90/91 - 480

Stewart, Bill
O-Pee-Chee: 79/80 - 313

Stewart, Bill
Diamond: 36/39 - 11(V), 11(VI)
World Wide Gum: 36/37 - 135

Stewart Blair
O-Pee-Chee: 78/79 - 355; 79/80 - 332

Stewart, Bob
Coca-Cola: 77/78 - 26
Eddie Sargent: 72/73 - 56
Loblaws: 74/75 - 70
O-Pee-Chee: 73/74 - 188; 74/75 - 92; 75/76 - 47; 76/77 - 291; 77/78 - 299; 78/79 - 46; 79/80 - 297
Topps: 73/74 - 159; 74/75 - 92; 75/76 - 47; 78/79 - 46

Stewart, Cameron
Donruss: 93/94 - 20
Fleer: 93/94 - 292PP
Leaf: 93/94 - 337
Parkhurst: 93/94 - 284, 284EI
Topps: 93/94 - 440SC. 440FD
Upper Deck: 93/94 - 464

Stewart, Charles (Goalie)
Anonymous: 26/27 - 39

Stewart, Gaye
Bee Hive: 34/44 - 351A, 351B; 45/63 - 141, 214
CKAC Radio: 43/47 - 16
Parkhurst: 51/52 - 99; 52/53 - 25
Quaker Oats: 45/54 - 105
Ultimate: 92 - 45(OSE), 45(OSF)

Stewart, Jack
Bee Hive: 34/44 - 125; 45/63 - 142, 215
Hall of Fame: 83 - 210, N15; 87 - 210
O-Pee-Chee: 40/41 - 124
Parkhurst: 51/52 - 53

Stewart, John
O-Pee-Chee: 74/75 - 175
Topps: 74/75 - 175

Stewart, Nels
Anonymous: 26/27 - 97
Bee Hive: 34/44 - 255
Can. Chew. Gum: 33/34 - 46
Diamond: 33/35 - 57; 36/39 - 65(I), 60(II), 55(III)
Hall of Fame: 83 - F12, 86; 87 - 86C
La Presse: 27/32 - 20
O-Pee-Chee: 33/34 - 6

Stewart, Nels (cont.)
Sweet Caporal: 34/35 - 3
Topps: 60/61 - 5, 50ST
World Wide Gum: 33/34 - 12

Stewart, Paul (Official)
Pro Set: 90/91 - 699

Stewart, Ralph
Loblaws: 74/75 - 197
O-Pee-Chee: 74/75 - 158; 75/76 - 182; 76/77 - 229; 77/78 - 386
Topps: 74/75 - 158; 75/76 - 182; 76/77 - 229

Stewart, Ron
Bee Hive: 45/63 - 456; 64/67 - 27, 187A, 187B
Chex: 63/65 - 58
Coca-Cola: 64/65 - 108; 65/66 - 15
Eddie Sargent: 70/71 - 120
Esso: 7/71 - 160
O-Pee-Chee: 68/69 - 168; 69/70 - 41; 70/71 - 64; 71/72 - 236
Parkhurst: 52/53 - 94; 53/54 - 9; 54/55 - 23; 55/56 - 5; 57/58 TOR - 7; 58/59 - 14; 59/60 - 26; 60/61 - 6; 61/62 - 6; 62/63 - 6; 63/64 - 14, 74; 93/94 - 110ML
Quaker Oats: 45/54 - 106; 55/56 - 5
Shirriff: 60/61 - 10; 62/63 - 21; 68/69 - G16
Topps: 64/65 - 99; 65/66 - 103; 66/67 - 94; 69/70 - 41; 70/71 - 64
Toronto Star: 57/67 - 78; 58/67 - 53; 63/64 - 42; 64/65 - 48
York: 60/61 - 37; 61/62 - 20; 63/64 - 3

Stickle, Leon (Official)
Pro Set: 90/91 - 700

Stoddard, Jack (John)
Parkhurst: 52/53 - 97; 53/54 - 60

Storey, Red (Official)
Hall of Fame: 83 - B14, 28C; 87 - 28C

Storm, Jim
Donruss: 93/94 - 445
Fleer: 93/94 - 356PP
parkhurst: 93/94 - 354, 354EI

Storr, Jamie (Goalie)
Donruss: 93/94 - 20JCC
Parkhurst: 93/94 - 508, 508EI
Upper Deck: 93/94 - 538

Stoughton, Blaine
Funmate: 83/84 - 49
O-Pee-Chee: 74/75 - 348; 75/76 - 265; 79/80 - 356; 80/81 - 30, 59; 81/82 - 132, 63SK; 82/83 - 122, 130, 131, 126SK; 83/84 - 135, 136, 147, 258SK, 259SK; 84/85 - 154
Post: 82/83 - 110
Topps: 75/76 - 265; 80/81 - 30, 59; 81/82 EN- 86; 82/83 - 126SK; 83/84 - 258SK, 259SK

Straka, Martin
Donruss: 93/94 - 266
Fleer: 92/93 - 382; 93/94 - 244, 7RS, 415PP
Leaf: 93/94 - 220
O-Pee-Chee: 92/93 - 21PM; 93/94 - 155
Parkhurst: 92/93 - 140, 140EI; 93/94 - 156, 156EI; 94/95 - V16
Score: 93/94 - 375C, 375A
Topps: 93/94 - 155(I), 415SC, 415FD
Upper Deck: 92/93 - 559, ER19; 93/94 - 40

Strakhov, Yuri
O-Pee-Chee: 90/91 - 484

Stratton, Art
York: 63/64 - 44

Stuart, Billy
Wm. Paterson: 23/24 - 22; 24/25 - 31

Stuart, Bruce
Hall of Fame: 83 - 224, O15P; 87 - 224
Imperial Tobacco: 10/11 - 15L, 17; 11/12 - 15

Stuart, Hod
Hall of Fame: 83 - F13, 87C; 87 - 87C

Stumpel, Jozef
Donruss: 93/94 - 23
Fleer: 93/94 - 212, 293PP
Leaf: 93/94 - 404
O-Pee-Chee: 93/94 - 416
Parkhurst: 91/92 - 231E, 231F; 93/94 - 15, 15EI; 94/95 - 19, 293, 19EI, 293EI
Score: 92/93 - 412PNC, 412PNA
Topps: 93/94 - 416, 488SC, 488FD
Upper Deck: 92/93 - 485; 93/94 - 379

Sturgeon, Peter
O-Pee-Chee: 75/76 - 393

St. Croix, Rick (Goalie)
O-Pee-Chee: 81/82 - 252; 82/83 - 258; 83/84 - 340, 36SK; 84/85 - 310; 85/86 - 8SK
Topps: 83/84 - 36SK
Vachon Foods: 83/84 - 98

St. Laurent, Andre
O-Pee-Chee: 75/76 - 387; 76/77 - 29; 77/78 - 171; 78/79 - 32; 79/80 - 73; 80/81 - 316; 83/84 - 286
Topps: 76/77 - 29; 77/78 - 171; 78/79 - 32; 79/80 - 73

St. Laurent, Dollard
Bee Hive: 45/63 - 140, 289; 64/67 - 54
La Patrie: 51/54 - 13
Parkhurst: 52/53 - 52; 53/54 - 23; 55/56 - 48; 57/58 MON - 10; 93/94 - 69ML
Quaker Oats: 45/54 - 52; 55/56 - 48
Shirriff: 60/61 - 74; 61/62 - 35
Topps: 58/59 - 5; 59/60 - 43; 61/62 - 31, 44; 62/63 - 30
Ultimate: 92 - 15(OSE), 15(OSF)

St. Marseille, Frank
Bazooka: 71/72 - 17
Colgate: 7/71 - 22
Dad's Cookies: 7/71 - 122
Eddie Sargent: 72/73 - 188
Esso: 7/71 - 214
Loblaws: 74/75 - 141
O-Pee-Chee: 69/70 - 177; 70/71 - 214, 26DE, 28SS; 71/72 - 38, 15BK; 72/73 - 65; 73/74 - 262; 74/75 - 374; 75/76 - 15; 76/77 - 276
Topps: 70/71 - 27SK; 71/72 - 38, 15BK; 72/73 - 71; 75/76 - 15
Toronto Sun: 71/72 - 249

Sulliman, Douglas (Doug)
Bowman: 90/91 - 110
O-Pee-Chee: 80/81 - 306; 82/83 - 132, 128SK; 83/84 - 148, 256SK; 85/86 - 234; 86/87 - 121; 87/88 - 116, 59SK; 88/89 - 172; 90/91 - 473
Panini: 87/88 - 82
Post: 82/83 - 111
Topps: 82/83SK - 128; 83/84 - 256SK; 86/87 - 121; 87/88 - 116; 88/89 - 172

Sullivan, Bob
O-Pee-Chee: 83/84 - 149, 189SK
Topps: 83/84 - 152SK

Sullivan, Mike
Bowman: 92/93 - 116
O-Pee-Chee: 92/93 - 144; 93/94 - 21, 139SC, 139FD
Panini: 93/94 - 262E, 262F
Parkhurst: 91/92 - 383E, 383F; 92/93 - 395, 395EI; 93/94 - 454, 454EI
Score: 92/93 - 533C, 533A; 93/94 - 390C, 390A
Topps: 92/93 - 282, 282GS, 262SC; 93/94 - 21, 139SC, 139FD
Upper Deck: 92/93 - 46

Sullivan, Peter
O-Pee-Chee: 79/80 - 378; 80/81 - 29
PepsiCo: 80/81 - 139
Topps: 80/81 - 29

Sullivan, Red (George)
  Bee Hive: 45/63 - 70, 368; 64/67 - 149
  Parkhurst: 51/52 - 27; 52/53 - 79; 93/94 - 86ML, 170ML
  Shirriff: 60/61 - 82; 61/62 - 91
  Topps: 54/55 - 42; 57/58 - 56; 58/59 - 48; 59/60 - 59; 60/61 - 18; 61/62 - 48; 63/64 - 44; 64/65 - 2965/66 - 87
  Toronto Star: 57/67 - 47; 58/67 - 40
  Ultimate: 92 - 29(OSE), 29(OSF)

Summerhill, Bill
  Bee Hive: 34/44 - 184

Sundblad, Niklas
  Upper Deck: 92/93 - 227

Sundin, Mats
  Bowman: 91/92 - 137; 92/93 - 344
  Donruss: 93/94 - 283,S/PM, S/SP
  Fleer: 92/93 - 180, 25UI; 93/94 - 137 8GG, 205PP, 18PL
  Hockey Wit: 93/94 - 51
  Humpty Dumpty: 92/93 - 21(II)
  Kraft: 90/91 - 42; 91/92 - 4
  Leaf: 93/94 - 136
  O-Pee-Chee: 90/91 - 114PM; 91/92 - 12, 219; 92/93 - 110; 93/94 - 460, 5HR
  Panini: 91/92 - 255; 92/93 - 212E, 212F, 302E, 302F; 93/94 - 68E, 68F
  Parkhurst: 91/92 - 144E, 144F; 92/93 - 148, 148EI, 221, 221EI; 93/94 - 435, 435EI, F5; 94/95 - 185, 185EI, H19. R19. C19, V52
  Pro Set: 90/91 - 636; 91/92 - 197E, 197F, 99PT; 92/93 - 149
  Score: 90 - 7YS, 100T; 90/91 - 398A, 398C; 91 - 3YS; 91/92 - 130A, 130B, 130C, 10PNE, 389PNE, 10PNF, 389PNF; 92/93 - 153C, 153A, 90PNC, 90PNA, 7CT, 7AT; 93/94 - 9C, 9A, 2PCE
  Sega: 93/94 - 111
  Topps: 91/92 - 12, 219, 300SC; 92/93 - 415, 415GS, 478SC; 93/94 - 460(II), 5PF, 370SC, 425SC, 370FD, 425FD
  Upper Deck: 90/91 - 365E, 365F; 91/92 - 31E, 134E, E13(E), 31F, 134F, E13(F); 92/93 - 121, 374, E18, WJG17, 59AS; 93/94 - 228, 302, 419

Sundstrom, Niklas
  Parkhurst: 93/94 - 506, 5056EI
  Upper Deck: 92/93 - 597

Sundstrom, Patrik
  Bowman: 90/91 - 89; 91/92 - 279
  Kraft: 86/87 - 70, 70P
  O-Pee-Chee: 83/84 - 361, 152SK; 84/85 - 331, 279SK; 85/86 - 115, 241SK; 86/87 - 156, 101SK; 87/88 - 34, 201SK; 88/89 - 67; 89/90 - 56, 82SK; 90/91 - 306; 91/92 - 451
  Panini: 87/88 - 348; 88/89 - 277; 89/90 - 250; 90/91 - 65; 91/92 - 217
  Pro Set: 90/91 - 176; 91/92 - 141E, 141F, 71PT
  Score: 90/91 - 19A, 19C, 10HR; 91/92 - 117A, 117B, 117C, 290PNE, 290PNF
  Topps: 83/84 - 152SK; 85/86 - 115; 86/87 - 156; 87/88 - 34; 88/89 - 67; 89/90 - 56; 90/91 - 306; 91/92 - 451, 229SC
  Upper Deck: 90/91 - 288E, 288F; 91/92 - 369E, 369F
  Vachon Foods: 83/84 - 118

Sundstrom, Peter
  O-Pee-Chee: 84/85 - 155
  Topps: 84/85 - 116

Suter, Gary
  Bowman: 90/91 - 101; 91/92 - 254; 92/93 - 55
  Donruss: 93/94 - 53, 415
  Fleer: 92/93 - 30; 93/94 - 226, 44PP
  Hockey Wit: 93/94 - 41

Suter, Gary (cont.)
  Kraft: 86/87 - 8, 8P; 1990 - 61
  Leaf: 93/94 - 140
  O-Pee-Chee: 86/87 - 189, 134SK, 192SK; 87/88 - 176, 49SK; 88/89 - 43, 40NS, 89SK, 113SK; 89/90 - 108, 100SK; 90/91 - 205; 91/92 - 151; 92/93 - 278; 93/94 - 178, 228SC, 228FD
  Panini: 87/88 - 207; 88/89 - 7; 89/90 - 30; 90/91 - 177; 91/92 - 57; 92/93 - 48E, 48F; 93/94 - 186E, 186F
  Parkhurst: 91/92 - 25E, 25F; 92/93 - 23, 23EI; 93/94 - 299, 299EI; 94/95 - 47, 47EI, V74
  Pro Set: 90/91 - 46; 91/92 - 32E, 276E, 32F, 276F, 20PT; 92/93 - 27
  Score: 90/91 - 88A, 88C; 91/92 - 244A, 464B, 464C, 11PNE, 392PNE, 11PNF, 392PNF; 92/93 - 17C, 17A, 195PNC, 195PNA; 93/94 - 13C, 13A
  Sega: 93/94 - 19
  Topps: 86/87 - 189; 87/88 - 176; 88/89 - 43, 11SK; 89/90 - 108; 90/91 - 205; 91/92 - 151, 143SC; 92/93 - 308, 308GS, 423SC; 93/94 - 178, 10BG, 228SC, 228FD
  Upper Deck: 90/91 - 273E, 273F; 91/92 - 341E, 510E, 341F, 510F; 92/93 - 249; 93/94 - 357

Sutherland, Bill
  O-Pee-Chee: 68/69 - 196; 69/70 - 172; 70/71 - 83; 71/72 - 141
  Topps: 70/71 - 83
  Toronto Sun: 71/72 - 250

Sutherland, James T.
  Hall of Fame: 83 - 44, C15P; 87 - 44

Sutter, Brent
  Bowman: 90/91 - 126; 91/92 - 226; 92/93 - 147
  Donruss: 93/94 - 69
  Fleer: 92/93 - 43; 93/94 - 206, 56PP
  Kraft: 90/91 - 57; 91/92 - 43
  Leaf: 93/94 - 142
  O-Pee-Chee: 82/83 - 216, 56SK; 83/84 - 18; 84/85 - 136; 85/86 - 107, 71SK, 117SK; 86/87 - 117, 211SK; 87/88 - 27, 241SK; 88/89 - 7, 105SK; 89/90 - 14, 115SK; 90/91 - 258, 115PM; 91/92 - 165, 156PM; 92/93 - 60; 93/94 - 147,211SC, 211FD
  Panini: 87/88 - 99; 88/89 - 292; 89/90 - 266; 90/91 - 90; 91/92 - 246; 93/94 - 151E, 151F
  Parkhurst: 91/92 - 35E, 35F; 92/93 - 33, 33EI, CP3; 93/94 - 308, 308EI
  Pro Set: 90/91 - 191; 91/92 - 154E, 374E, 154F, 74PT, 374F, 164PT; 92/93 - 36
  Score: 90/91 - 39A, 39C, 19HR; 91 - 103T; 91/92 - 243A, 463B, 463C, 79PNE, 79PNF; 92/93 - 112C, 112A, 39PNC, 39PNA; 93/94 - 44C, 44A
  Topps: 82/83 - 56SK; 84/85 - 102; 85/86 - 107; 86/87 - 117; 87/88 - 27; 88/89 - 7; 89/90 - 14; 90/91 - 258; 91/92 - 165, 180SC; 92/93 - 75, 75GS, 428SC; 93/94 - 147(I), 211SC, 211FD
  Upper Deck: 90/91 - 249E, 249F; 91/92 - 140E, 140F; 92/93 - 199

Sutter, Brian
  Funmate: 83/84 - 119
  O-Pee-Chee: 78/79 - 319; 79/80 - 84; 80/81 - 244; 81/82 - 297, 133SK; 82/83 - 298, 311, 198SK; 83/84 - 308, 320, 127SK, 128SK; 84/85 - 192, 56SK; 85/86 - 135, N/BB, 46SK; 86/87 - 72, O/BB, 175SK; 88/89 - 15SK
  Panini: 88/89 - 111
  Post: 82/83 - 270
  Pro Set: 90/91 - 676
  Topps: 79/80 - 84; 80/81 - 244; 81/82 WN - 122; 82/83 - 198SK; 83/84 - 127SK, 128SK; 84/85 - 135;

Sutter, Brian (cont.)
  Topps: 85/86 - 135, N/BB; 86/87 - 72, O/BB

Sutter, Darryl
  O-Pee-Chee: 81/82 - 65; 82/83 - 76; 83/84 - 113, 105SK; 84/85 - 47, 30SK; 85/86 - 100, 23SK; 86/87 - 49, 151SK
  Panini: 87/88 - 234
  Topps: 81/82 WN - 77; 83/84 - 105SK; 84/85 - 36; 85/86 - 100; 86/87 - 49

Sutter, Duane
  O-Pee-Chee: 81/82 - 211; 82/83 - 212, 52SK; 83/84 - 19; 84/85 - 137; 85/86 - 227, 72SK; 86/87 - 39, 210SK; 87/88 - 43; 89/90 - 221; 90/91 - 466
  Panini: 87/88 - 102
  Pro Set: 90/91 - 61
  Topps: 82/83 - 52SK; 86/87 - 39; 87/88 - 43

Sutter, Richard (Rich)
  Bowman: 91/92 - 370; 92/93 - 256
  Fleer: 92/93 - 398; 93/94 - 317PP
  O-Pee-Chee: 84/85 - 169, 111SK; 85/86 - 208; 86/87 - 29, 242SK; 87/88 - 258, 193SK; 88/89 - 255, 57SK; 89/90 - 282, 62SK; 90/91 - 405; 91/92 - 143; 93/94 - 46SC, 46FD
  Panini: 87/88 - 350; 88/89 - 142; 89/90 - 157; 91/92 - 33; 92/93 - 19E, 19F; 93/94 - 160E, 160F
  Parkhurst: 91/92 - 372E, 372F
  Pro Set: 90/91 - 272; 91/92 - 217E, 217F, 108PT
  Score: 90/91 - 281A, 281C; 91/92 - 63A, 63B, 63C, 268PNE, 268PNF; 92/93 - 327C, 327A; 93/94 - 3232C, 323A
  Topps: 86/87 - 29; 91/92 - 143, 192SC; 92/93 - 434, 434GS, 389SC; 93/94 - 46SC, 46FD
  Upper Deck: 90/91 - 328E, 328F; 91/92 - 317E, 317F; 92/93 - 143

Sutter, Ronald (Ron)
  Bowman: 91/92 - 238; 92/93 - 175
  Donruss: 93/94 - 288, 482
  Fleer: 92/93 - 190
  Leaf: 93/94 - 275(II)
  O-Pee-Chee: 84/85 - 170, 107SK; 85/86 - 6; 86/87 - 109, 243SK; 87/88 - 113, 102SK; 88/89 - 126; 89/90 - 173, 107SK; 90/91 - 45; 91/92 - 232, 95PM; 92/93 - 362; 93/94 - 103, 86SC, 86FD
  Panini: 87/88 - 137; 89/9 - 299; 90/91 - 109; 91/92 - 233; 92/93 - 20E, 20F; 93/94 - 161E, 161F
  Parkhurst: 91/92 - 158E, 158F; 92/93 - 389, 389EI
  Pro Set: 90/91 - 224; 91/92 - 178E, 476E, 178F, 476F, 222PT; 92/93 - 162
  Score: 90/91 - 153A, 153C; 91 - 69T; 91/92 - 298A, 619B, 619C, 95PNE, 95PNF; 92/93 - 86C, 86A; 93/94 - 39C, 39A
  Topps: 84/85 - 122; 85/86 - 6; 86/87 - 109; 87/88 - 113; 88/89 - 126; 89/90 - 173; 90/91 - 45; 91/92 - 232, 49SC; 92/93 - 371, 371GS, 36SC; 93/94 - 103(I), 86SC, 86FD
  Upper Deck: 90/91 - 68E, 68F; 91/92 - 309E, 309F; 92/93 - 184; 93/94 - 33

Sutton, Kenneth (Ken)
  Bowman: 92/93 - 422
  Fleer: 92/93 - 20
  Leaf: 93/94 - 295
  O-Pee-Chee: 92/93 - 165; 93/94 - 89, 219SC, 219FD
  Parkhurst: 91/92 - 239E, 239F; 92/93 - 254, 254EI
  Score: 91/92 - 393A, 283B, 283C, 325PNE, 325PNF; 92/93 - 292C, 292A, 216PNC, 216PNA; 93/94 - 410C, 410A
  Topps: 92/93 - 59, 59GS, 292SC; 93/94 - 89, 219SC, 219FD

Suzor, Mark
    O-Pee-Chee: 78/79 - 307

Svensson, Leif
    O-Pee-Chee: 79/80 - 374

Svoboda, Petr
    Bowman: 90/91 - 46; 91/92 - 341; 92/93 - 47
    Donruss: 93/94 - 41
    Fleer: 92/93 - 263
    Kraft: 86/87 - 40, 40P; 1990 - 27
    Leaf: 93/94 - 131
    O-Pee-Chee: 85/86 - 139SK; 86/87 - 17SK; 87/88 - 18aSK; 88/89 - 256, 41NS, 44SK; 89/90 - 238, 54SK; 90/91 - 246; 91/92 - 76, 168PM; 92/93 - 109; 93/94 - 308, 324, 132SC, 132FD
    Panini: 88/89 - 255; 89/90 - 244; 90/91 - 50; 91/92 - 185
    Parkhurst: 91/92 - 237E, 237F
    Pro Set: 90/91 - 161; 91/92 - 123E, 123F, 65PT; 92/93 - 16
    Score: 90/91 - 191A, 191C; 91/92 - 95A, 95B, 95C, 197PNE, 197PNF; 92/93 - 114C, 114A, 117PNC, 117PNA; 93/94 - 110C, 110A
    Topps: 90/91 - 246; 91/92 - 76, 127SC; 92/93 - 312, 312GS, 227SC; 93/94 - 308, 324, 132SC, 132FD
    Upper Deck: 90/91 - 193E, 193F; 91/92 - 285E, 285F; 93/94 - 465

Swarbrick, George
    O-Pee-Chee: 68/69 - 174; 70/71 - 82
    Sherriff: 68/69 - H5A
    Topps: 70/71 - 82

Sweeney, Don
    Bowman: 91/92 - 365; 92/93 - 402
    Donruss: 93/94 - 21
    Fleer: 92/93 - 257; 93/94 - 24PP
    Leaf: 93/94 - 281(II)
    O-Pee-Chee: 91/92 - 319; 92/93 - 40; 93/94 - 334, 117SC, 117FD
    Panini: 91/92 - 180; 93/94 - 11E, 11F
    Parkhurst: 91/92 - 228E, 228F; 92/93 - 244, 244EI; 93/94 - 13, 13EI
    Pro Set: 90/91 - 412; 91/92 - 153PT
    Score: 90/91 - 51A, 51C; 91/92 - 146A, 146B, 146C, 419PNE, 419PNF; 92/93 - 186C, 186A, 179PNC, 179PNA; 93/94 - 169C, 169A
    Sega: 93/94 - 8
    Topps: 91/92 - 319, 370SC; 92/93 - 417, 417GS, 337SC; 93/94 - 334(II), 117SC, 117FD
    Upper Deck: 91/92 - 338E, 338F; 92/93 - 391; 93/94 - 101

Sweeney, Robert (Bob)
    Bowman: 90/91 - 28; 91/92 - 357; 92/93 - 5
    Fleer: 92/93 - 264; 93/94 - 34PP
    O-Pee-Chee: 88/89 - 134, 28SK, 130SK, 19FS; 89/90 - 135; 90/91 - 99; 91/92 - 99; 92/93 - 21, 110PM; 93/94 - 431, 63SC, 63FD
    Panini: 88/89 - 214; 90/91 - 15; 91/92 - 177; 93/94 - 104E, 104F
    Parkhurst: 92/93 - 251, 251EI; 93/94 - 290, 29EI
    Pro Set: 90/91 - 15; 91/92 - 6E, 6F
    Score: 90/91 - 235A, 235C; 91/92 - 176A, 176B, 176C, 222PNE, 222PNF; 92/93 - 317C, 317A; 93/94 - 146C, 146A
    Topps: 88/89 - 134; 89/90 - 135; 90/91 - 99; 91/92 - 99, 75SC; 92/93 - 111, 111GS, 455SC; 93/94 - 431(II), 63SC, 63FD
    Upper Deck: 90/91 - 198E, 198F; 91/92 - 391E, 391F; 92/93 - 47, 449; 93/94 - 312

Sweeney, Tim
    Bowman: 91/92 - 261
    Donruss: 93/94 - 11
    Fleer: 93/94 - 12PP

Sweeney, Tim (cont.)
    O-Pee-Chee: 90/91 - 116PM; 93/94 - 426
    Parkhurst: 93/94 - 7, 7EI; 94/95 - 9, 9EI
    Pro Set: 90/91 - 597; 91/92 - 364E, 364F
    Score: 90/91 - 13T
    Topps: 91/92 - 394SC; 93/94 - 426(II), 473SC, 473FD
    Upper Deck: 90/91 - 531E, 531F; 91/92 - 375E, 375F; 92/93 - 95; 93/94 - 385

Sydor, Darryl
    Bowman: 92/93 - 321
    Donruss: 93/94 - 164
    Fleer: 92/93 - 312; 93/94 - 60, 122PP
    Leaf: 93/94 - 206, 15R
    O-Pee-Chee: 91/92 - 90PM; 92/93 - 11, 16PM; 93/94 - 226, 225SC, 225FD
    Panini: 92/93 - F(E), F(F)
    Parkhurst: 92/93 - 69, 69EI; 93/94 - 96, 96EI
    Pro Set: 91/92 - 542E, 542F; 92/93 - 228
    Score: 90/91 - 425A, 425C; 91 - 81T; 91/92 - 631B, 631C, 321PNE, 321PNF; 92/93 - 410C, 410A; 93/94 - 311C, 311A
    Topps: 92/93 - 39, 39GS, 72SC; 93/94 - 226(I), 225SC, 225FD
    Upper Deck: 90/91 - 358E, 358F; 91/92 - 549E, 549F; 92/93 - 63; 93/94 - 83

Sykes, Phil
    Bowman: 91/92 - 194
    O-Pee-Chee: 86/87 - 216; 91/92 - 189
    Panini: 87/88 - 285
    Score: 91/92 - 534B, 534C
    Topps: 91/92 - 189, 271SC

Sykora, Michal
    Donruss: 93/94 - 307
    Leaf: 93/94 - 431(II)
    Parkhurst: 93/94 - 257, 257EI
    Upper Deck: 93/94 - 489

Szura, Joe
    O-Pee-Chee: 68/69 - 175; 70/71 - 73; 72/73 - 313
    Topps: 70/71 - 73

Tabaracci, Richard (Rick) (Goalie)
    Bowman: 91/92 - 207; 92/93 - 324
    Donruss: 93/94 - 363
    Fleer: 92/93 - 445; 93/94 - 267PP
    Leaf: 93/94 - 241(II)
    O-Pee-Chee: 91/92 - 375; 93/94 - 239
    Pro Set: 90/91 - 649
    Score: 91/92 - 244B, 244C; 92/93 - 529C, 529A; 93/94 - 403C, 403A
    Topps: 91/92 - 375, 395SC; 92/93 - 453, 453GS,135SC; 93/94 - 239(I), 378SC, 378FD, 19MP
    Upper Deck: 90/91 - 520E, 520F; 91/92 - 339E, 339F; 92/93 - 58, 358

Taglianetti, Peter
    Fleer: 92/93 - 204
    O-Pee-Chee: 88/89 - 257, 146SK; 89/90 - 297; 90/91 - 435, 117PM; 93/94 - 248, 243SC, 243FD
    Panini: 88/89 - 152; 89/90 - 174
    Parkhurst: 93/94 - 430, 430EI
    Pro Set: 90/91 - 505
    Score: 90/91 - 16T; 91/92 - 448B, 448C; 92/93 - 383PNC, 383PNA; 93/94 - 295C, 295A
    Topps: 93/94 - 248(I), 243SC, 243FD
    Upper Deck: 93/94 - 100

Takko, Kari (Goalie)
    Panini: 87/88 - 288; 88/89 - 85; 89/90 - 102
    Upper Deck: 90/91 - 543E, 543F

Talafous, Dean
    O-Pee-Chee: 75/76 - 197; 76/77 - 103; 77/78 - 49; 78/79 - 149; 79/80 - 54; 80/81 - 132; 81/82 - 235
    Topps: 75/76 - 197; 76/77 - 103; 77/78 - 49; 78/79 - 149; 79/80 - 54; 80/81 - 132

Talbot, Jean-Guy
    Bee Hive: 45/63 - 290; 64/67 - 116
    Chex: 63/65 - 36
    Coca-Cola: 64/65 - 70; 65/66 - 71

Talbot, Jean-Guy (cont.)
    Derniere: 72/84 - 71
    Eddie Sargent: 70/71 - 189
    La Patrie: 51/54 - 14
    O-Pee-Chee: 68/69 - 179; 69/70 - 15; 70/71 - 100
    Parkhurst: 55/56 - 53; 57/58 MON - 9; 58/59 - 41; 59/60 - 49; 60/61 - 52; 61/62 - 48; 62/63 - 51; 63/64 - 22; 63/64 - 81; 93/94 - 80ML
    Quaker Oats: 55/56 - 53
    Shirriff: 60/61 - 35; 61/62 - 109; 62/63 - 39, 44; 63/64 - 26
    Topps: 64/65 - 52; 65/66 - 4; 66/67 - 3; 67/68 - 104; 69/70 - 15; 70/71 - 100
    Toronto Star: 58/67 - 67; 63/64 - 23
    Ultimate: 92 - 16(OSE), 16(OSF)
    York: 60/61 - 17; 61/62 - 12; 62/63 - 4; 63/64 - 23

Tallon, Dale
    Colgate: 70/71 - 81; 71/72 - 13
    Dad's Cookies: 70/71 - 143
    Eddie Sargent: 70/71 - 215; 72/73 - 211
    Esso: 70/71 - 250
    Lipton Soup: 74/75 - 22
    Loblaws: 74/75 - 88
    Mac's Milk: 73/74 - 28
    O-Pee-Chee: 70/71 - 225; 71/72 - 234, 3BK, 5PT; 72/73 - 121, 21CS; 73/74 - 211; 74/75 - 360; 75/76 - 351; 76/77 - 89; 77/78 - 124; 78/79 - 146
    Pro Set: 91/92 - 595E, 595F
    Topps: 71/72 - 95, 3BK; 72/73 - 15; 73/74 - 129; 76/77 - 89; 77/78 - 124; 78/79 - 146
    Toronto Sun: 71/72 - 291

Tamer, Chris
    Parkhurst: 94/95 - 178, 178EI

Tambellini, Steve
    Funmate: 83/84 - 21
    O-Pee-Chee: 80/81 - 365; 81/82 - 81; 82/83 - 134, 147, 226SK; 83/84 - 93, 223, 219SK; 84/85 - 237, 239SK; 87/88 - 259; 88/89 - 258, 62SK
    Panini: 87/88 - 351
    Post: 82/83 - 175
    Topps: 81/82 WN - 86; 82/83 - 226SK; 83/84 - 219SK
    Vachon Foods: 83/84 - 19

Tancill, Chris
    Donruss: 93/94 - 84
    O-Pee-Chee: 93/94 - 429
    Parkhurst: 93/94 - 318, 318EI
    Pro Set: 91/92 - 539E, 539F
    Topps: 93/94 - 429

Tannahill, Don
    O-Pee-Chee: 72/73 - 238; 73/74 - 69
    Topps: 73/74 - 69

Tanner, John (Goalie)
    O-Pee-Chee: 90/91 - 118PM
    Pro Set: 90/91 - 637
    Score: 92/93 - 452C, 452A
    Upper Deck: 91/92 - 119E, 119F

Tanti, Tony
    Bowman: 90/91 - 213; 91/92 - 34; 92/93 - 172
    Cel.Watch: 1988 - CW15
    Frito-Lay: 88/89 - 400
    Kraft: 86/87 - 71, 71P; 1990 - 45
    O-Pee-Chee: 83/84 - 362; 84/85 - 332, 369, 274SK, 275SK; 85/86 - 153, 245SK; 86/87 - 120, 99SK; 87/88 - 97, 195SK; 88/89 - 82, 59SK; 89/90 - 280, 71SK; 90/91 - 157; 91/92 - 133; 92/93 - 34
    Panini: 87/88 - 345; 88/89 - 143; 89/90 - 149; 9/91 - 124
    Parkhurst: 91/92 - 236E, 236F
    Pro Set: 90/91 - 241
    Score: 90/91 - 137A, 137C; 91/92 - 49A, 49B, 49C; 92/93 - 116C, 116A
    7-Eleven: 84/85 - 52
    Topps: 84/85 - 141; 85/86 - 153;

Tanti, Tony (cont.)
Topps: 86/87 - 120; 87/88 - 97; 88/89 - 82; 90/91 - 157; 91/92 - 133, 285SC; 92/93 - 235, 235GS, 312SC
Upper Deck: 90/91 - 197E, 197F; 92/93 - 182
Vachon Foods: 83/84 - 119

Tarasov, Anatoli
Hall of Fame: 83 - 239, D15P; 87 - 239

Tardif, Marc
Colgate: 70/71 - 17
Derniere: 72/84 - 10, 80, 138
Eddie Sargent: 72/73 - 118
Esso: 70/71 - 142; 83/84 - 19E, 19F
O-Pee-Chee: 70/71 - 179; 71/72 - 29; 72/73 - 11; 79/80 - 108; 80/81 - 256, 17PO; 81/82 - 283, 76SK; 82/83 - 296, 21SK; 83/84 - 305, 247SK
PepsiCo: 80/81 - 78
Post: 82/83 - 255
Topps: 71/72 - 29; 72/73 - 105; 79/80 - 108; 80/81 - 256; 82/83 - 21SK; 83/84 - 247SK
Toronto Sun: 71/72 - 164

Tatarinov, Mikhail
Bowman: 91/92 - 298; 92/93 - 395
Fleer: 92/93 - 181
Leaf: 93/94 - 342(II)
O-Pee-Chee: 91/92 - 465, 62PM; 92/93 - 253
Panini: 91/92 - 210; 92/93 - 208E, 208F
Parkhurst: 91/92 - 145E, 145F
Pro Set: 90/91 - 647; 91/92 - 462E, 462F, 218PT
Score: 90 - 53T; 91 - 12T; 91/92 - 37A, 37B, 37C, 562B, 562C, 97PNE, 97PNF; 92/93 - 107C, 107A, 35PNC, 35PNA; 93/94 - 328C, 328A
Topps: 91/92 - 465, 390SC; 92/93 - 180, 180GS; 47SC
Upper Deck: 90/91 - 401E, 401F; 92/93 - 183GS; 93/94 - 386

Taugher, Johnny
World Wide Gum: 36/37 - 116

Taylor, Billy
Bee Hive: 34/44 - 351
O-Pee-Chee: 39/40 - 15; 40/41 - 107

Taylor, Bobby
O-Pee-Chee: 73/74 - 238
Parkhurst: 92/93 - 475, 475EI

Taylor, David (Dave)
Bowman: 90/91 - 149, HT22; 91/92 - 186; 92/93 - 37
Fleer: 92/93 - 313; 93/94 - 364PP
Funmate: 8/84 - 56
Hockey Wit: 93/94 - 21
Leaf: 93/94 - 374
O-Pee-Chee: 78/79 - 353; 79/80 - 232; 80/81 - 137; 81/82 - 143, 152, 149SK, 237SK, 268SK; 82/83 - 161, 164SK, 231SK; 83/84 - 163; 84/85 - 92, 267SK; 85/86 - 214, 238SK; 86/87 - 63, 90SK; 87/88 - 118, 215SK; 88/89 - 46, 155SK; 89/90 - 58, 151SK; 90/91 - 314; 91/92 - 138
Panini: 87/88 - 280; 88/89 - 79; 89/90 - 98; 90/91 - 236; 91/92 - 89; 93/94 - 206E, 206F
Parkhurst: 91/92 - 67E, 214E, 67F, 214F; 92/93 - 307, 307EI; 93/94 - 367, 367EI
Post: 82/83 - 127
Pro Set: 90/91 - 128; 91/92 - AC16, 103E, 325E, 103F, 325F; 92/93 - 258
Score: 90/91 - 166A, 166C; 91/92 - 214A, 374A, 435A, 214B, 264B, 325B, 214C, 264C, 325C, 249PNE, 249PNF, 373PNE, 373PNF; 92/93 - 49C, 49A, 367PNC, 367PNA; 93/94 - 389C, 389A
7-Eleven: 84/85 - 24
Topps: 79/80 - 232; 80/81 - 137; 81/82 - WN 132, 40; 82/83 - 164SK;

Taylor, David (Dave) Cont.
Topps: 82/83 - 231SK; 86/87 - 63; 87/88 - 118; 88/89 - 46; 89/90 - 58; 90/91 - 314; 91/92 - 138, 232SC; 92/93 - 446, 446GS, 234SC
Upper Deck: 90/91 - 214E, 214F; 91/92 - 270E, 270F

Taylor, Fred Eric (Cyclone)
Hall of Fame: 83 - 14, A15P; 87 - 14
Imperial Tobacco: 10/11 - 15, 20L; 11/12 - 20; 12/13 - 43
Topps: 60/61 - 46, 51ST

Taylor, Harry
Bee Hive: 45/63 - 457
Quaker Oats: 45/54 - 107

Taylor, Mark
O-Pee-Chee: 83/84 - 273, 190SK; 84/85 - 180, 121SK
Topps: 83/84 - 190SK; 84/85 - 127

Taylor, Ted
O-Pee-Chee: 72/73 - 312
Topps: 65/66 - 95

Taylor, W.J.
Quaker Oats: 45/54 - 108

Teno, Harvey (Goalie)
Bee Hive: 34/44 - 126

Terbenche, Paul
O-Pee-Chee: 70/71 - 123; 73/74 - 229
Topps: 67/68 - 58; 70/71 - 123

Terien, Chris
Fleer: 93/94 - 495PP

Terreri, Chris (Goalie)
Bowman: 91/92 - 283; 92/93 - 386
Donruss: 93/94 - 194
Fleer: 92/93 - 120; 93/94 - 209, 144PP
Gillette: 91/92 - 38
Hockey Wit: 93/94 - 31
Humpty Dumpty: 92/93 - 22(II)
Leaf: 93/94 - 430
O-Pee-Chee: 90/91 - 375; 91/92 - 422, 197PM; 92/93 - 282; 93/94 - 213
Panini: 90/91 - 68; 91/92 - 221; 92/93 - 171E, 171F; 93/94 - D(E), D(F)
Parkhurst: 91/92 - 98E, 98F; 92/93 - 93, 93EI; 93/94 - 112, 112EI
Pro Set: 90/91 - 481; 91/92 - 137E, 137F, 68PT, 288PT; 92/93 - 97
Score: 90/91 - 239A, 239C; 91 - 15YS; 91/92 - 151A, 151B, 151C, 247PNE, 247PNF; 92/93 - 270C, 270A, 274PNC, 274PNA; 93/94- 237C, 237A
Season's: 92/93 - 51
Sega: 93/94 - 78
Topps: 90/91 - 375; 91/92 - 422, 297SC; 92/93 - 303, 303GS, 74SC; 93/94 - 213(I), 328SC, 328FD
Upper Deck: 90/91 - 183E, 183F; 91/92 - 115E, 115F; 92/93 - 43; 93/94 - 110

Terrion, Greg
Kraft: 86/87 - 58, 58P
O-Pee-Chee: 81/82 - 155; 82/83 - 333, 234SK; 83/84 - 342, 37SK; 84/85 - 312, 19SK; 85/86 - 18SK; 86/87 - 244, 147SK; 87/88 - 241, 153SK
Topps: 82/83 - 234SK; 83/84 - 37SK; 84/86 - 19SK
Vachon Foods: 83/84 - 99

Tessier, Orval
Shirriff: 60/61 - 114

Theberge, Greg
Post: 82/83 - 317

Thelven, Michael
O-Pee-Chee: 87/88 - 24
Panini: 87/88 - 9; 88/89 - 206
Topps: 87/88 - 24

Therien, Chris
O-Pee-Chee: 93/94 - 9TC

Thibaudeau, Gilles
Panini: 90/91 - 288
Pro Set: 90/91 - 290

Thibault, Jocelyn (Goalie)
Donruss: 93/94 - 275, 11RR
Durivage: 93/94 - 3
Fleer: 93/94 - 15RS, 426PP
Leaf: 93/94 - 428(II), 10FP
O-Pee-Chee: 93/94 - 393
Parkhurst: 93/94 - 247, 247EI, CC16; 94/95 - 189, 275, 189EI, 275EI, V61
Topps: 93/94 - 393(II), 479SC, 479FD
Upper Deck: 93/94 - 395

Thomas, Cy
Quaker Oats: 45/54 - 10

Thomas, Scott
Fleer: 93/94 - 302PP
Leaf: 93/94 - 360(II)
O-Pee-Chee: 93/94 - 336
Parkhurst: 93/94 - 25, 25EI
Score: 93/94 - 469C, 469A
Topps: 93/94 - 336(II), 471SC, 471FD

Thomas, Steve
Bowman: 90/91 - 4, HT13; 91/92 - 391; 92/93 - 117
Donruss: 93/94 - 208
Fleer: 92/93 - 13193/94 - 216, 154PP
Humpty Dumpty: 92/93 - 23(II)
Kraft: 86/87 - 59, 59P
Leaf: 93/94 - 81
O-Pee-Chee: 86/87 - 245, 135SK, 140SK; 87/88 - 188, 154SK; 88/89 - 259; 89/90 - 82, 15SK; 90/91 - 92; 91/92 - 210, 195PM; 92/93 - 395; 93/94 - 300, 195SC, 195FD
Panini: 87/88 - 329; 88/89 - 30; 89/90 - 50; 91/92 - 14; 92/93 - 203E, 203F; 93/94 - 57E, 57F
Parkhurst: 91/92 - 105E, 105F; 92/93 - 338, 338EI, 454, 454EI; 93/94 - 124, 124EI; 94/95 - V68
Pro Set: 90/91 - 62; 91/92 - 45E, 438E, 45F, 438F, 203PT; 92/93 - 106
Score: 90/91 - 66A, 66C, 30HR; 91 - 51T; 91/92 - 94A, 94B, 94C, 116PNE, 116PNF; 92/93 - 12C, 12A, 128PNC, 129PNA; 93/94 - 141C, 141A
Sega: 93/94 - 82
Topps: 87/88 - 188; 89/90 - 82; 90/91 - 92; 91/92 - 210, 109SC; 92/93 - 222, 222GS, 369SC; 93/94 - 300(II)
Upper Deck: 90/91 - 221E, 221F; 91/92 - 162E, 534E, 162F, 534F; 92/93 - 171; 93/94 - 122, 247

Thomas, Wayne
Derniere: 72/84 - 20, 33
O-Pee-Chee: 73/74 - 221; 75/76 - 347; 76/77 - 84; 77/78 - 19; 78/79 - 166; 79/80 - 126
Topps: 76/77 - 84; 77/78 - 19; 78/79 - 166; 79/80 - 126

Thomlinson, Dave
Bowman: 90/91 - 21
Upper Deck: 91/92 - 557E, 557F

Thompson, Brent
O-Pee-Chee: 93/94 - 406
Score: 92/93 - 455C, 455A
Topps: 92/93 - 161, 161GS, 92SC; 93/94 - 406(II), 489SC, 490FD
Upper Deck: 91/92 - 608E, 608F

Thompson, Errol
Loblaws: 74/75 - 285
O-Pee-Chee: 75/76 - 114; 76/77 - 259; 77/78 - 293; 78/79 - 57; 79/80 - 106; 80/81 - 234
Topps: 75/76 - 114; 76/77 - 259; 78/79 - 57; 79/80 - 106; 80/81 - 234

Thompson, Paul
Amal. Press: 35/36 - 9
Anonymous: 33/34 - 50
Bee Hive: 34/44 - 81
Diamond: 1936/39 - 66(I), 61(II), 56(III),

Thompson, Paul (cont.)
    Diamond: 13(IV), 12(V), 12(VI)
    World Wide Gum: 36/37 - 6
Thompson, Rhys
    Bee Hive: 34/44 - 352
Thompson, Tiny (Cecil) (Goalie)
    Bee Hive: 34/44 - 35, 127
    Diamond: 33/35 - 58
    Hall of Fame: 83 - A16, 15C; 87 - 15C
    La Presse: 27/32 - 44
    O-Pee-Chee: 34/35 - 68; 39/40 - 75
    Sweet Caporal: 34/35 - 4
    Topps: 60/61 - 55
    World Wide Gum: 33/34 - 57; 36/37 - 12
Thoms, Bill
    Anonymous: 33/34 - 10; 34/44 - 82, 357
    Beehive: 34/44 - 82, 353
    Hamilton Gum: 33/34 - 7
    O-Pee-Chee: 35/36 - 85; 37/38 - 143; 39/40 - 48
    Quaker Oats: 38/39 - 29
    World Wide Gum: 33/34 - 50
Thomson, Floyd
    Loblaws: 74/75 - 268
    O-Pee-Chee: 75/76 - 149; 74/75 - 298; 76/77 - 356; 77/78 - 358
    Topps: 75/76 - 149
Thomson, Jim
    Bee Hive: 45/63 - 458
    Parkhurst: 51/52 - 82; 52/53 - 43; 53/54 - 8; 54/55 - 32; 55/56 - 11; 93/94 - 119ML
    Quaker Oats: 45/54 - 110A, 110B; 55/56 - 11
    Topps: 57/58 - 23GS
    Toronto Star: 58/67 - 14
Thomson, Jim
    Topps: 92/93 - 67, 67GS
Thornton, Scott
    Bowman: 91/92 - 168
    Pro Set: 90/91 - 640
    Score: 91 - 55T; 91/92 - 605B, 605C
    Topps: 91/92 - 378SC
    Upper Deck: 90/91 - 459E, 459F; 91/92 - 353E, 521E, 353F, 521F
Thurier, Fred (Alfred)
    Bee Hive: 34/44 - 256
Thyer, Mario
    Score: 90/91 - 382A, 382C
Tichy, Milan
    Fleer: 93/94 - 247, 10UR, 101PP
    Score: 93/94 - 461C, 461A
Tikhonov, Viktor
    O-Pee-Chee: 90/91 - 17R
Tikkanen, Esa
    Bowman: 90/91 - 194; 91/92 - 98; 92/93 - 144
    Donruss: 93/94 - 215
    Fleer: 92/93 - 56; 93/94 - 9GG, 395PP
    Gillette: 91/92 - 2
    Kraft: 1990 - 18
    Leaf: 93/94 - 288
    O-Pee-Chee: 87/88 - 7, 83SK; 88/89 - 260, 220SK; 89/90 - 12, 328, 219SK; 90/91 - 156; 91/92 - 378, 121PM; 92/93 - 319; 93/94 - 282
    Panini: 87/88 - 264; 88/89 - 63; 90/91 - 223; 91/92 - 123; 92/93 - 103E, 103F; 93/94 - 95E, 95F
    Parkhurst: 91/92 - 55E, 55F; 92/93 - 46, 46EI; 93/94 - 135, 135EI
    Pro Set: 90/91 - 97; 91/92 - AC14, 71E, 71F 39PT; 92/93 - 53
    Score: 90/91 - 13A, 13C, 342A, 342C, 6HR; 91/92 - 241A, 461B, 461C, 24PNE, 24PNF; 92/93 - 16, 16A, 336PNC, 336PNA, 16PC(S), 16PC(F); 93/94 - 97C, 97A
    Topps: 87/88 - 7; 89/90 - 12; 90/91 - 156; 91/92 - 378, 6SL, 69SC; 92/93 - 476, 476GS, 104SC; 93/94 - 282, 477SC, 447FD, 14MP
    Upper Deck: 90/91 - 167E, 167F; 91/92 - 182E, E10(E), 182F, E10(F); 92/93 - 188;

Tikkanen, Esa (Cont.)
    Upper Deck: 93/94 - 457
Tilley, Tom
    Bowman: 91/92 - 377
    O-Pee-Chee: 90/91 - 498
    Panini: 89/90 - 128
    Parkhurst: 93/94 - 442, 442EI
    Upper Deck: 93/94 - 491
Timgren, Ray
    Bee Hive: 45/63 - 459
    Parkhurst: 51/52 - 78
    Quaker Oats: 45/54 - 111A, 111B
    Topps: 54/55 - 13
Timonen, Kimmo
    Upper Deck: 93/94 - 268
Tinordi, Mark
    Bowman: 91/92 - 124; 92/93 - 218, 399
    Donruss: 93/94 - 79
    Fleer: 92/93 - 98; 93/94 - 213, 66PP
    Humpty Dumpty: 92/93 - 23(I)
    Kraft: 91/92 - 22; 92/93 - 44
    Leaf: 93/94 - 146
    O-Pee-Chee: 91/92 - 308; 92/93 - 17; 93/94 - 24
    Panini: 91/92 - 109; 92/93 - 97E, 97F; 93/94 - 275E, 275F
    Parkhurst: 91/92 - 304E, 304F; 92/93 - 76, 76EI; 93/94 - 320, 320EI
    Pro Set: 90/91 - 145; 91/92 - 107E, 575E, 107F, 58PT, 575F; 92/93 - 78
    Score: 90/91 - 304A; 91 - 18YS; 91/92 - 93A, 93B, 93C, 199PNE, 199PNF; 92/93 - 7C, 7A, 18PNC, 18PNA, 252PNC, 252PNA; 93/94 - 53C, 53A
    Sega: 93/94 - 31
    Topps: 91/92 - 308, 392SC; 92/93 - 4, 4GS, 435SC; 93/94 - 24(I), 384SC, 384FD
    Upper Deck: 91/92 - 295E, 295F; 92/93 - 73; 93/94 - 89
Tippett, Dave
    Fleer: 93/94 - 410PP
    Leaf: 93/94 - 349(II)
    O-Pee-Chee: 86/87 - 148; 87/88 - 86; 88/89 - 85; 89/90 - 134, 268SK; 90/91 - 183, 119PM; 93/94 - 387, 124SC, 124FD
    Panini: 87/88 - 51; 88/89 - 244; 89/90 - 226; 90/91 - 37; 93/94 - 85E, 85F
    Parkhurst: 92/93 - 372, 372EI
    Pro Set: 90/91 - 111, 555
    Score: 90/91 - 192A, 192C, 29T; 91/92 - 437A, 409B, 409C
    Topps: 86/87 - 148; 87/88 - 86; 88/89 - 85; 89/90 - 134; 90/91 - 183; 93/94 - 387, 124SC, 124FD
    Upper Deck: 90/91 - 270E, 270F; 91/92 - 480E, 480F
Titov, German
    Donruss: 93/94 - 56
    Fleer: 93/94 - 310PP
    Leaf: 93/94 - 309(II)
    Parkhurst: 93/94 - 255, 255EI
    Topps: 93/94 - 364SC, 364FD
    Upper Deck: 93/94 - 476
Tkachuk, Keith
    Donruss: 93/94 - 390
    Fleer: 92/93 - 446; 93/94 - 111, 8RS, 276PP
    Leaf: 93/94 - 105, 11R
    O-Pee-Chee: 92/93 - 346, 43PM; 93/94 - 27, 502, 135SC, 135FD
    Panini: 93/94 - 193E, 193F
    Parkhurst: 91/92 - 424E, 424F; 92/93 - 206, 206EI; 93/94 - 228, 228EI; 94/95 - 264, 264EI
    Pro-Set: 92/93 - 243
    Score: 92/93 - 450C, 450A, 222PNC, 222PNA; 93/94 - 195C, 195A
    Topps: 92/93 - 102, 102GS, 116SC; 93/94 - 27(I), 502(II), 135SC, 135FD
    Upper Deck: 91/92 - 698E, 698F; 92/93 - 364, 419, CC15, AC2, G18; 93/94 - 195

Tkaczuk, Walt
    Bazooka: 71/72 - 31
    Colgate: 71/72 - 14
    Dad's Cookies: 70/71 - 93
    Eddie Sargent: 70/71 - 117
    Esso: 70/71 - 161; 72/73 - 149
    Lipton Soup: 74/75 - 12
    Loblaws: 74/75 - 214
    O-Pee-Chee: 69/70 - 43; 70/71 - 180, 41DE; 71/72 - 75; 72/73 - 110, 14CS; 73/74 - 25; 74/75 - 119; 75/76 - 128; 76/77 - 220; 77/78 - 90; 78/79 - 235; 79/80 - 15; 80/81 - 211
    Topps: 69/70 - 43; 71/72 - 75; 72/73 - 14; 73/74 - 25; 74/75 - 119; 75/76 - 128; 76/77 - 220; 77/78 - 90; 78/79 - 235; 79/80 - 15; 80/81 - 211
    Toronto Sun: 71/72 - 185
Tocchet, Rick
    Bowman: 90/91 - 108, HT14; 91/92 - 230; 92/93 - 159
    Donruss: 93/94 - 267
    Fleer: 92/93 - 172; 93/94 - 225, 196PP
    Hockey Wit: 93/94 - 58
    Kellogg's: 92 - 2
    Kraft: 1990 - 57; 90/91 - 58; 91/92 - 45
    Leaf: 93/94 - 109
    McDonald's: 91/92 - Mc2
    O-Pee-Chee: 87/88 - 2; 88/89 - 177, 99SK; 89/90 - 80, 108SK; 90/91 - 26, 120PM; 91/92 - 160, 63PM; 92/93 - 148; 93/94 - 72
    Panini: 87/88 - 134; 88/89 - 326; 89/90 - 295; 90/91 - 121; 91/92 - 229, 331; 92/93 - 226E, 226F; 93/94 - 80E, 80F
    Parkhurst: 91/92 - 129E, 354E 129F, 354F; 92/93 - 139, 139EI, CP12; 93/94 - 428, 428EI; 94/95 - V25
    Pro Set: 90/91 - 225, 374; 91/92 - 177E, 311E, 580E, 177F, 311F, 88PT, 580F; 92/93 - 138
    Score: 90/91 - 80A, 80C, 40HR; 91/92 - 9A, 302A, 334A, 9B, 306B, 364B, 9C, 306C, 364C, 20PNE, 20PNF; 92/93 - 245C, 245A, 282PNC, 282PNA; 93/94 - 340C, 340A, 14PNC, 14PNA, 14CAS, 14AAS
    Season's: 92/93 - 37
    Topps: 87/88 - 2; 88/89 - 177; 89/90 - 80; 90/91 - 26, 9SL; 91/92 - 160, 13SL, 35SC; 92/93 - 70, 70GS, 76SC; 93/94 - 72, 329SC, 329FD, 22AS
    Upper Deck: 90/91 - 263E, 263F, 488E, 488F; 91/92 - 122E, 503E, 122F, 503F, Mc2; 92/93 - 238, 16AS; 93/94 - 179, 233
Todd, Kevin
    Bowman: 92/93 - 21
    Fleer: 92/93 - 121, 8UR; 93/94 - 318PP
    Gillette: 91/92 - 40
    Leaf: 93/94 - 15
    O-Pee-Chee: 91/92 - 400, 22PM; 92/93 - 1; 93/94 - 8SC, 8FD
    Panini: 92/93 - 275E, 275F, O(E), O(F)
    Parkhurst: 91/92 - 97E, 444E, 97F, 444F; 92/93 - 94, 238, 285, 94EI, 238EI, 285EI; 93/94 - 37, 37EI; 94/95 - 108, 108EI
    Pro Set: 91/92 - 548E, 548F, 260PT, 7RGL; 92/93 - 94
    Score: 91/92 - 397A, 287B, 287C, 308PNE, 308PNF; 92/93 - 162C, 162A, 272PNC, 272PNA, 22CT, 22AT; 93/94 - 338C, 338A
    Topps: 91/92 - 400; 92/93 - 15, 228, 15GS, 228GS, 465SC; 93/94 - 8SC, 8FD
    Upper Deck: 91/92 - 401E, 401F; 92/93 - 11, 303, 365; 93/94 - 88, 440
Tomilin, Vitali
    Upper Deck: 93/94 - 278
Tomlak, Mike
    Bowman: 91/92 - 14
    O-Pee-Chee: 90/91 - 95; 91/92 - 410
    Panini: 90/91 - 46; 91/92 - 319

Tomlak, Mike (cont.)
Pro Set: 90/91 - 452
Score: 91/92 - 538B, 538C
Topps: 90/91 - 95; 91/92 - 410, 266SC
Upper Deck: 90/91 - 343E, 343F; 91/92 - 310E, 310F; 92/93 - AR3

Toms, C.
Imperial Tobacco: 10/11 - 29

Tonelli, John
Bowman: 90/91 - 148; 91/92 - 175
Esso: 88/89 - 45
Funmate: 83/84 - 83
O-Pee-Chee: 79/80 - 146; 80/81 - 305; 81/82 - 218; 82/83 - 213, 49SK; 83/84 - 20, 74SK, 75SK; 84/85 - 138, 80SK, 81SK; 85/86 - 41, O/BB, 80SK, 116SK; 86/87 - 132, 81SK; 87/88 - 84, 47SK; 89/90 - 8, 87SK; 90/91 - 281; 91/92 - 161, 37PM, 159PM
Panini: 89/90 - 90; 90/91 - 235; 91/92 - 90
Post: 82/83 - 191
Pro Set: 90/91 - 129; 91/92 - 373E, 22PT, 373F; 92/93 - 263
Score: 90/91 - 89A. 89C; 91 - 17T; 91/92 - 172A, 172B, 172C, 567B, 567C, 284PNE, 284PNF; 92/93 - 342C, 342A
Topps: 79/80 - 146; 82/83 - 49SK; 83/84 - 74SK, 75SK; 84/85 - 103; 85/86 - 41, O/BB, 7SK; 86/87 - 132; 87/88 - 84; 89/90 - 8; 90/91 - 281; 91/92 - 161, 189SC; 92/93 - 119, 119GS, 159SC
Upper Deck: 90/91 - 95E, 95F

Topoll, Del
La Patrie: 51/54 - 37

Toppazzini, Jerry
Bee Hive: 45/63 - 71
Parkhurst: 53/54 - 98; 92/93 - PR27; 93/94 - 1ML
Shirriff: 60/61 - 110; 61/62 - 9
Topps: 54/55 - 21; 57/58 - 5; 58/59 - 45; 59/60 - 38; 60/61 - 28; 61/62 - 9; 62/63 - 13, 8HB; 63/64 - 18
Toronto Star: 58/67 - 47
Ultimate: 92 - 55(OSE), 55(OSF)

Toppazzini, Zellio
Bee Hive: 45/63 - 72, 369
Parkhurst: 52/53 - 73

Touhey, Bill
Can. Chew. Gum: 33/34 - 48
O-Pee-Chee: 33/34 - 26

Trefilov, Andrei (Goalie)
Donruss: 93/94 - 409
Fleer: 93/94 - 311PP
O-Pee-Chee: 91/92 - 45R
Parkhurst: 93/94 - 29, 29EI; 94/95 - 36, 36EI
Upper Deck: 92/93 - 345, 514

Tremblay, Gilles
Bee Hive: 45/63 - 291A, 291B; 64/67 - 117A, 117B
Chex: 63/65 - 37
Coca-Cola: 64/65 - 71; 65/66 - 72
O-Pee-Chee: 68/69 - 66; 69/70 - 168
Parkhurst: 62/63 - 46; 63/64 - 21, 80
Post: 66/67 - L16; 68-69 - 12
Shirriff: 61/62 - 112; 62/63 - 24; 68/69 - F7
Topps: 64/65 - 2; 66/67 - 4; 66/67 US - 4; 67/68 - 5; 68/69 - 66
Toronto Star: 58/67 - 69; 63/64 - 24
York: 60/61 - 18; 61/62 - 4; 63/64 - 21

Tremblay, J. C.
Bee Hive: 45/63 - 392A, 292B; 64/67 - 118
Chex: 63/65 - 38A, 38B
Coca-Cola: 64/65 - 72; 65/66 - 73
Colgate: 70/71 - 64
Dad's Cookies: 70/71 - 82
Derniere: 72/84 - 52, 73
Eddie Sargent: 70/71 - 99
Esso: 70/71 - 143

Tremblay, J. C. (cont.)
O-Pee-Chee: 68/69 - 59, 206; 69/70 - 5; 70/71 - 178; 71/72 - 130, 252; 72/73 - 293
Parkhurst: 62/63 - 54; 63/64 - 31, 90
Post: 66/67 - L17, S8; 68/69 - 13
Shirriff: 60/61 - 36; 61/62 - 118; 62/63 - 30; 68/69 - F5
TCMA: 1981 - 3
Topps: 64/65 - 88; 65/66 - 69; 66/67 - 5; 66/67 US - 5; 67/68 - 73; 68/69 - 59; 69/70 - 5; 71/72 - 130
Toronto Star: 57/67 - 144; 63/64 - 25; 64/65 - 32
Toronto Sun: 71/72 - 165
York: 61/62 - 34; 62/63 - 6; 63/64 - 24

Tremblay, Mario
Derniere: 72/84 - 123, 189
Esso: 73/84 - 20E, 20F
Funmate: 83/84 - 69
Kellogg's: 84 - 2
O-Pee-Chee: 75/76 - 223; 76/77 - 97; 77/78 - 163; 78/79 - 376; 79/80 - 123; 80/81 - 297; 81/82 - 192; 82/83 - 193, 30SK; 83/84 - 199, 69SK; 84/85 - 274, 161SK; 85/86 - 245, 134SK; 86/87 - 223, 9SK
PepsiCo: 80/81 - 59
Post: 81/82 - 23; 82/83 - 160
Topps: 75/76 - 223; 76/77 - 97; 77/78 - 163; 79/80 - 123; 82/83 - 30SK; 83/84 - 69SK
Vachon Foods: 83/84 - 57

Tremblay, Vince (Goalie)
O-Pee-Chee: 82/83 - 334, 70SK
Topps: 82/83 - 70SK

Tretiak, Vladislav (Goalie)
Derniere: 72/84 - 173

Trihey, Harry
Hall of Fame: 83 - 88, F14P; 87 - 88

Trimper, Tim
O-Pee-Chee: 80/81 - 357; 81/82 - 376; 82/83 - 394
Post: 82/83 - 335

Trottier, Bryan
Bowman: 91/92 - 93; 92/93 - 152, 243
Donruss: 93/94 - 268
Derniere: 72/84 - 164
Esso: 88/89 - 46
Fleer: 93/94 - 416PP
Frito-Lay: 88/89 - 41
Funmate: 83/84 - 84
Hockey Wit: 93/94 - 44
Leaf: 93/94 - 318(II)
McDonald's: 82/83 - 25
O-Pee-Chee: 76/77 - 67, 115; 77/78 - 105; 78/79 - 10, 325; 79/80 - 100, 165; 80/81 - 40; 81/82 - 200, 210, 152SK, 160SK; 82/83 - 5, 214, 215, 47SK, 48SK; 83/84 - 21, 76SK, 77SK; 84/85 - 139, 214, 86SK, 87SK; 85/86 - 60, 65SK; 86/87 - 155, P/BB, 216SK; 87/88 - 60, 41HL, O/BB, 240SK; 88/89 - 97, 112SK; 89/90 - 149, 118SK; 90/91 - 6, 291, 121PM; 91/92 - 472; 92/93 - 107, 130, 9AN; 93/94 - 296
Panini: 87/88 - 96; 88/89 - 293; 89/90 - 269, 382; 90/91 - 83; 92/93 - 227E, 227F
Parkhurst: 91/92 - 208E, 360E, 431E, 208F, 360F, 431F; 93/94 - 431, 431EI
Post: 82/83 - 192
Pro Set: 90/91 - 192, 511; 91/92 - 192E, 192F, 216PT
Score: 90/91 - 270A, 270C, 106T; 91/92 - 229A, 229B, 229C, 241PNE, 241PNF; 92/93 - 157C, 157A
7-Eleven: 84/85 - 33
Topps: 76/77 - 67, 115, 15PO; 77/78 - 105; 78/79 - 10; 79/80 - 100, 165, 26SC; 80/81 - 40; 81/82 - EN 132, 41; 82/83 - 47SK, 48SK; 83/84 - 76SK, 77SK; 84/85 - 104, 160; 85/86 - 60;

Trottier, Bryan (cont.)
Topps: 86/87 - 155, P/BB; 87/88 - 60, O/BB; 88/89 - 97; 89/90 - 149; 90/91 - 6, 291; 91/92 - 472, 91SC; 92/93 - 15; 92/93 - 416, 416GS, 26SC; 93/94 - 294(II)
Upper Deck: 90/91 - 137E, 137F, 425E, 425F; 91/92 - 329E, 329F, 50AS

Trottier, Dave
Bee Hive: 34/44 - 208
Canada Starch: 35/40 - 52
Can. Chew. Gum: 33/34 - 47
O-Pee-Chee: 34/35 - 62; 36/37 - 126; 37/38 - 168
Sweet Caporal: 34/35 - 37
World Wide Gum: 36/37 - 70

Trottier, Guy
Bazooka: 71/72 - 23
Esso: 70/71 - 232
O-Pee-Chee: 71/72 - 5; 72/73 - 326
Toronto Sun: 71/72 - 273

Trudel, Louis
Bee Hive: 34/44 - 83, 185
Canada Starch: 35/40 - 156
Diamond: 33/34 - 59; 35/39 - 67(I), 62(II) 57(III), 14(IV), 13(V), 13(VI)
World Wide Gum: 36/37 - 71

Trukhno, Leonid
O-Pee-Chee: 91/92 - 61R

Tsulygin, Nikolai
Parkhurst: 93/94 - 526, 526EI
Upper Deck: 614

Tsygurov, Denis
parkhurst: 94/95 - 23, 23EI

Tucker John
Donruss: 93/94 - 328
Fleer: 92/93 - 414; 93/94 - 211, 235PP
Leaf: 93/94 - 21
O-Pee-Chee: 85/86 - 184SK; 86/87 - 67, 48SK; 87/88 - 154, 145SK; 88/89 - 74; 89/90 - 37; 90/91 - 374, 122PM; 93/94 - 473, 38SC, 38FD
Panini: 87/88 - 30; 88/89 - 229; 89/90 - 212; 90/91 - 157; 93/94 - 212E, 212F
Parkhurst: 92/93 - 405, 405EI; 9394 - 462, 462EI
Pro Set: 90/91 - 322, 420
Score: 93/94 - 354C, 354A
Topps: 86/87 - 67; 87/88 - 154; 88/89 - 74; 89/90 - 37; 90/91 - 374; 91/92 - 335SC; 93/94 - 473(II), 38SC, 38FD
Upper Deck: 90/91 - 387E, 387F; 92/93 - 548; 93/94 - 409

Tugnutt, Ron (Goalie)
Bowman: 91/92 - 151
Donruss: 93/94 - 12, 453, A/PM, A/SP
Fleer: 92/93 - 298; 93/94 - 13PP
Leaf: 93/94 - 277(II)
O-Pee-Chee: 89/90 - 263; 90/91 - 367; 91/92 - 181; 92/93 - 221; 93/94 - 286
Panini: 89/90 - 332; 90/91 - 142; 91/92 - 267
Parkhurst: 91/92 - 149E, 149F, 277E, 277F; 92/93 - 290, 290EI
Pro Set: 90/91 - 258; 91/92 - 202E, 202F, 277, 98PT
Score: 90/91 - 126A, 126C; 91 - 33YS; 91/92 - 41A, 41B, 41C, 124PNE, 124PNF; 92/93 - 387C, 387A, 366PNC, 366PNA; 93/94 - 368C, 368A
Topps: 90/91 - 367; 91/92 - 181, 115SC; 93/94 - 286, 325SC, 325FD
Upper Deck: 90/91 - 27E, 27F; 91/92 - 277E, 277F; 93/94 - 426

Tully, Brent
Donruss: 93/94 - 21JCC
Upper Deck: 92/93 - 592

Tuomainen, Marko
Upper Deck: 91/92 - 675E, 675F

Turcotte, Darren
Bowman: 90/91 - 216; 91/92 - 62; 92/93 - 156

Turcotte, Darren (cont.)
- Donruss: 93/94 - 224
- Fleer: 92/93 - 143; 93/94 - 166PP, 357PP
- Hockey Wit: 93/94 - 30
- Leaf: 93/94 - 45
- McDonald's: 91/92 - Mc7
- O-Pee-Chee: 90/91 - 48, K/BB, 123PM; 91/92 - 71; 92/93 - 387; 93/94 - 246
- Panini: 90/91 - 107; 91/92 - 285; 92/93 - 235E, 235F; 93/94 - 94E, 94F
- Parkhurst: 91/92 - 118E, 118F; 92/93 - 345, 345EI; 93/94 - 356, 356EI
- Pro Set: 90/91 - 208, 400; 91/92 - 160E, 310E, 160F, 310F; 92/93 - 114
- Score: 90 - 16YS; 90/91 - 241A, 241C; 91 - 28YS; 91/92 - 196A, 196B, 196C, 47PNE, 47PNF; 92/93 - 224C, 224A, 33PNC, 33PNA; 93/94 - 24C, 24A
- Topps: 90/91 - 48, K/BB; 91/92 - 71, 346SC; 92/93 - 203, 203GS, 360SC; 93/94 - 246(I), 476SC, 476FD
- Upper Deck: 90/91 - 274E, 274F, 475E, 475F; 91/92 - 155E, 513E, 155F, 513F; 92/93 - 169

Turgeon, Pierre
- Bowman: 90/91 - 241; 91/92 - 27; 92/93 - 23
- Donruss: 93/94 - 209, N/PM. N/SP
- Durivage: 92/93 - 11; 93/94 - 30
- Fleer: 92/93 - 132; 93/94 - 197, 3AS, 155PP, 19PL, 9PM, 5SC
- Gillette: 91/92 - 35
- Hockey Wit: 93/94 - 27
- Kellogg's: 92 - 6
- Kraft: 90/91 - 59, 91; 93/94 - 21
- Leaf: 93/94 - 25, 340(II), 5HT
- O-Pee-Chee: 88/89 - 194, 133SK, 20FS; 89/90 - 25, P/BB, 262SK; 90/91 - 66, M/BB, 124PM; 91/92 - 416, 59PM; 92/93 - 47; 93/94 - 190, 7HR, 145SC, 145FD
- Panini: 88/89 - 230; 89/90 - 204; 90/91 - 28; 91/92 - 303; 92/93 - 196E, 196F; 93/94 - F(E), F(F)
- Parkhurst: 91/92 - 106E, 106F; 92/93 - 103, 103EI; 93/94 - 389, 389EI, F7, E10; 94/95 - 135, 135EI, H14, R14, C14
- Pro Set: 90/91 - 31, 366; 91/92 - 15E, 433E, 15F, 10PT, 433F; 92/93 - 104
- Score: 90 - 1YS; 90/91 - 110A, 110C, 53HR; 91 - 101T; 91/92 - 4A, 416A, 4B, 332B, 4C, 332C, 30PNE, 30PNF; 92/93 - 325C, 430C, 325A, 430A, 165PNC, 165PNA, 25CSS, 25ASS, 17CT, 17AT; 93/94 - 6C, 6A, 5PNC, 5PNA, 15DT, 5CAS, 5AAS, 6PCA, 12FR
- Season's: 92/93 - 53
- Sega: 93/94 - 81
- Topps: 88/89 - 194; 89/90 - 25, P/BB; 90/91 - 66, 20SL, M/BB; 91/92 - 416, 77SC; 92/93 - 289, 289GS, 276SC; 93/94 - 190(I), 20BG, 7PF, 145SC, 380SC, 145FD, 380FD, 20MP, 19AS
- Upper Deck: 90/91 - 43E, 43F; 91/92 - 176E, 554E, 176F, 554F; 92/93 - 175, 17AS; 93/94 - 224, 297, 347

Turgeon, Sylvain
- Bowman: 90/91 - 81; 92/93 - 167
- Donruss: 93/94 - 235
- Durivage: 92/93 - 29; 93/94 - 36
- Fleer: 92/93 - 149; 93/94 - 190, 176PP
- Leaf: 93/94 - 74
- O-Pee-Chee: 84/85 - 79, 372, 191SK, 192SK; 85/86 - 43, 165SK; 86/87 - 103, 53SK; 87/88 - 70, 203SK; 88/89 - 24; 90/91 - 73; 91/92 - 231, 184PM; 92/93 - 315, 116PM; 93/94 - 97
- Panini: 87/88 - 50; 88/89 - 245; 90/91 - 71; 93/94 - K(E), K(F)
- Parkhurst: 91/92 - 91E, 91F; 92/93 - 121, 12EI; 93/94 - 136, 136EI; 94/95 - 153, 153EI, V51

Turgeon, Sylvain (cont.)
- Pro Set: 90/91 - 177, 474; 91/92 - 416E, 416F; 92/93 - 123
- Score: 90/91 - 116A, 116C, 108T; 91/92 - 208A, 208B, 208C, 226PNE, 226PNF; 92/93 - 367C, 367A, 516C, 516A, 373PNC, 373PNA
- Sega: 93/94 - 94
- 7-Eleven: 84/85 - 22
- Topps: 84/85 - 62; 85/86 - 43; 86/87 - 105; 87/88 - 70; 88/89 - 24; 90/91 - 73; 91/92 - 231; 92/93 - 375, 375GS, 59SC; 93/94 - 97(I), 482SC, 482FD
- Upper Deck: 90/91 - 70E, 70F; 91/92 - 579E, 579F; 92/93 - 107; 93/94 - 44

Turnbull, Ian
- Loblaws: 74/75 - 286
- O-Pee-Chee: 74/75 - 289; 75/76 - 41; 76/77 - 39; 77/78 - 186, 77/78 - 215; 78/79 - 127; 79/80 - 228; 80/81 - 133, 21PO; 81/82 - 309, 100SK; 82/83 - 203SK; 83/84 - 124SK
- PepsiCo: 80/81 - 99
- Topps: 75/76 - 41; 76/77 - 39; 77/78 - 186, 215; 78/79 - 127; 79/80 - 228; 80/81 - 133; 81/82 - 42

Turnbull, Perry
- Kraft: 86/87 - 81, 81P
- O-Pee-Chee: 80/81 - 169; 81/82 - 298; 82/83 - 312; 83/84 - 321; 84/85 - 349; 85/86 - 254; 86/87 - 170
- Post: 82/83 - 271
- Topps: 80/81 - 169; 81/82 WN - 123; 82/83 - 203SK; 83/84 - 124SK; 86/87 - 170

Turner, Bob
- Bee Hive: 45/63 - 143A, 143B, 293; 64/67 - 57
- Parkhurst: 55/56 - 54; 57/58 MON - 13; 58/59 - 40; 59/60 - 43; 60/61 - 43; 61/62 - 41; 93/94 - 81ML
- Quaker Oats: 55/56 - 54
- Shirriff: 60/61 - 37; 61/62 - 37
- Topps: 61/62 - 41; 62/63 - 29; 63/64 - 32
- York: 60/61 - 19

Turner, Brad
- O-Pee-Chee: 93/94 - 10TC

Tustin, Norman
- Bee Hive: 34/44 - 295

Tuten, Audley
- Bee Hive: 34/44 - 84

Tuttle, Steve
- Fleer: 92/93 - 205
- O-Pee-Chee: 89/90 - 157; 90/91 - 278
- Panini: 89/90 - 126
- Pro Set: 90/91 - 273
- Topps: 89/90 - 157; 90/91 - 278
- Upper Deck: 90/91 - 195E, 195F

Tverdovski, Oleg
- Parkhurst: 93/94 - 531, 531EI

Twist, Anthony (Tony)
- Score: 91/92 - 396B, 396C; 93/94 - 400C, 400A

Ubriaco, Gene
- O-Pee-Chee: 69/70 - 149

Udvari, Frank
- Hall of Fame: 83 - 240, N16P; 87 - 240

Ulanov, Igor
- Bowman: 92/93 - 392
- Fleer: 93/94 - 477PP
- Leaf: 92/93 - 392
- O-Pee-Chee: 91/92 - 62R; 92/93 - 229
- Parkhurst: 91/92 - 421E, 421F; 92/93 - 440, 440EI
- Pro-Set: 92/93 - 216
- Score: 92/93 - 467C, 467A
- Topps: 92/93 - 468, 468GS, 366SC
- Upper Deck: 91/92 - 590E, 590F; 92/93 - 300, E15

Ullman, Norm
- Bazooka: 71/72 - 18
- Bee Hive: 45/63 - 216; 64/67 - 95
- Chex: 63/65 - 19
- Coca-Cola: 64/65 - 54; 65/66 - 54
- Colgate: 70/71 - 121; 71/72 - 15
- Dad's Cookies: 70/71 - 133
- Eddie Sargent: 70/71 - 204; 72/73 - 197
- Esso: 70/71 - 233; 88/89 - 47
- Hall of Fame: 83 - G15, 104C; 87 - 104C
- HHFM: 92 - 17
- Lipton Soup: 74/75 - 1
- Loblaws: 74/75 - 287
- Mac's Milk: 73/74 - 29
- O-Pee-Chee: 68/69 - 131; 69/70 - 54, 25ST; 70/71 - 110, 48DE; 71/72 - 30, 11PT; 72/73 - 147; 73/74 - 27; 74/75 - 236
- Parkhurst: 60/61 - 26; 61/62 - 26; 62/63 - 21; 63/64 - 52; 92/93 - PR25; 93/94 - 45ML
- Post: 66/67 - L12; 68/69 - 29
- Shirriff: 60/61 - 45; 61/62 - 76; 68/69 - M10
- TCMA: 1981 - 1
- Topps: 57/58 - 46; 58/59 - 65; 59/60 - 45; 64/65 - 15; 65/66 - 49; 66/67 - 52; 66/67 US - 52; 67/68 - 101, 132; 68/69 - 131; 69/70 - 54; 70/71 - 110; 71/72 - 30; 72/73 - 168; 73/74 - 148; 74/75 - 236
- Toronto Star: 57/67 - 129, 132; 58/67 - 30; 63/64 - 17; 64/65 - 24
- Toronto Sun: 71/72 - 274
- Ultimate: 92 - 72(OSE), 78(OSE), 72(OSF), 78(OSF)
- York: 62/63 - 29; 63/64 - 47

Unger, Garry
- Bazooka: 71/72 - 19
- Colgate: 70/71 - 7; 71/72 - 16
- Dad's Cookies: 70/71 - 53
- Eddie Sargent: 70/71 - 61; 71/72 - 178; 72/73 - 184
- Esso: 70/71 - 89
- Lipton Soup: 74/75 - 5
- Loblaws: 74/75 - 269
- O-Pee-Chee: 68/69 - 142; 69 70 - 159; 70 71 - 26, 16DE, 30SS; 71/72 - 26, 14BK, 50PT; 72/73 - 120; 73/74 - 15; 74/75 - 237; 75/76 - 40; 76/77 - 68, 260; 77/78 - 35; 78/79 - 5, 110; 79/80 - 33; 80/81 - 273; 81/82 - 123; 82/83 - 120
- Shirriff: 68/69 - C9
- Topps: 70/71 - 26, 30SK; 71/72 - 26, 14BK; 72/73 - 35; 73/74 - 15; 74/75 - 237; 75/76 - 40; 76/77 - 68, 260; 77/78 - 35; 78/79 - 5, 110; 79/80 - 33
- Toronto Sun: 71/72 - 251

Ustorf, Stefan
- Upper Deck: 92/93 - 371

Vachon, Rogatien (Rogie) (Goalie)
- Coca-Cola: 77/78 - 27
- Colgate: 70/71 - 85
- Dad's Cookies: 70/71 - 83
- Derniere: 72/84 - 49
- Eddie Sargent: 70/71 - 100; 72/73 - 87
- Esso: 70/71 - 144
- Hockey Wit: 93/94 - 24
- Lipton Soup: 74/75 - 7
- Loblaws: 74/75 - 142
- O-Pee-Chee: 68/69 - 164; 69/70 - 165; 70/71 - 49, 22DE; 71/72 - 156; 72/73 - 100; 73/74 - 64; 74/75 - 235; 75/76 - 160, 297; 76/77 - 40; 77/78 - 160, 21GP; 78/79 - 20; 79/80 - 235; 80/81 - 110; 81/82 - 10, 47SK; 82/83 - 23
- Post: 68/69 - 14; 82/83 - 16
- Shirriff: 68/69 - F2
- Topps: 67/68 - 75; 70/71 - 49; 72/73 - 51; 73/74 - 64; 74/75 - 235; 75/76 - 160, 297; 76/77 - 40; 77/78 - 160, 21PO; 78/79 - 20; 79/80 - 235; 80/81 - 110; 81/82 EN - 74
- Toronto Sun: 71/72 - 166

Vadnais, Carol
  Colgate: 70/71 - 86
  Dad's Cookies: 70/71 - 33
  Derniere: 72/84 - 98, 171
  Eddie Sargent: 70/71 - 130; 72/73 - 25
  Esso: 70/71 - 54
  Loblaws: 74/75 - 36
  O-Pee-Chee: 68/69 - 81; 69/70 - 82, 26ST, 4QS; 70/71 - 70, 36DE, 31SS; 71/72 - 46; 72/73 - 39; 73/74 - 58; 74/75 - 165; 75/76 - 27; 76/77 - 257; 77/78 - 154; 78/79 - 85; 79/80 - 145; 80/81 - 57; 81/82 - 236; 82/83 - 148; 83/84 - 224SK
  Shirriff: 68/69 - H5B
  Topps: 67/68 - 9; 68/69 - 81; 69/70 - 82; 70/71 - 70, 31SK; 71/72 - 46; 72/73 - 85; 73/74 - 58; 74/75 - 165; 75/76 - 27; 76/77 -257; 77/78 - 154; 78/79 - 85; 79/80 - 145; 80/81 - 57; 83/84 - 224SK
  Toronto Sun: 71/72 - 60

Vail, Eric
  Loblaws: 74/75 - 18
  O-Pee-Chee: 74/75 - 391; 75/76 - 135; 76/77 - 51; 77/78 - 168; 78/79 - 129; 79/80 - 188; 80/81 - 15; 81/82 - 38, 220SK; 82/83 - 97
  PepsiCo: 80/81 - 19
  Topps: 75/76 - 135; 76/77 - 51; 77/78 - 168; 78/79 - 129; 79/80 - 188; 80/81 - 15; 81/82 - 43

Vair, Steve
  Imperial Tobacco: 10/11 - 18L; 11/12 - 18; 12/13 - 10

Vaive, Richard (Rick)
  Bowman: 90/91 - 250; 91/92 - 39
  Cel.Watch: 1988 - CW9
  Esso: 83/84 - 21E, 21F
  Funmate: 83/84 - 112
  Kellogg's: 84 - 3
  Kraft: 86/87 - 60, 60P
  O-Pee-Chee: 80/81 - 242; 81/82 - 310, 101SK; 82/83 - 314 335, 336, 62SK, 63SK; 83/84 - 323, 324, 343, 25SK, 26SK; 84/85 - 313, 368, 11SK, 12SK, 139SK; 85/86 - 106, 6SK; 86/87 - 191, 138SK; 87/88 - 155, 155SK; 88/89 - 77, 9SK; 89/90 - 125, 256SK; 90/91 - 148; 91/92 - 457
  Panini: 87/88 - 328; 88/89 - 31; 89/90 - 206; 90/91 - 23; 91/92 - 297
  PepsiCo: 80/81 - 100
  Post: 82/83 - 288
  Pro Set: 90/91 - 32; 91/92 - 26E, 26F
  Score: 90/91 - 103A, 103C; 91/92 - 26A, 26B, 26C
  7-Eleven: 84/85 - 47
  Topps: 80/81 - 242; 81/82 - 44; 82/83 - 62SK, 63SK; 83/84 - 25SK, 26SK; 84/85 - 138; 85/86 - 106; 86/87 - 191; 87/88 - 155; 88/89 - 77; 89/90 - 125; 90/91 - 148; 91/92 - 457, 13SC
  Upper Deck: 90/91 - 376E, 376F; 91/92 - 179E, 179F
  Vachon Foods: 83/84 - 100

Valentine, Chris
  O-Pee-Chee: 82/83 - 373, 155SK
  Post: 82/83 - 318
  Topps: 82/83 - 155SK

Valiquette, Jack
  O-Pee-Chee: 76/77 - 294; 77/78 - 64; 78/79 - 391; 79/80 - 229; 80/81 - 108
  Topps: 77/78 - 64; 79/80 - 229; 80/81 - 108

Valk, Garry
  Bowman: 91/92 - 314
  Donruss: 93/94 - 401
  O-Pee-Chee: 91/92 - 117; 93/94 - 354
  Parkhurst: 93/94 - 4, 4EI; 94/95 - V19
  Pro Set: 91/92 - 499E, 499F
  Score: 91/92 - 195A, 195B, 195C, 291PNE, 291PNF; 92/93 - 355C, 355A, 181PNC, 181PNA

Valk, Garry (cont.)
  Topps: 91/92 - 117, 318SC; 92/93 - 383, 383GS, 493SC; 93/94 - 354(II), 407SC, 407FD
  Upper Deck: 90/91 - 530E, 530F; 91/92 - 152E, 152F; 92/93 - 114, 515

Vallis, Lindsay
  Parkhurst: 94/95 - 114, 114EI

Van Allen, Shaun
  Donruss: 93/94 - 14
  Fleer: 92/93 - 299; 93/94 - 15PP
  O-Pee-Chee: 91/92 - 414; 93/94 - 396
  Parkhurst: 92/93 - 288, 288EI; 93/94 - 278, 278EI
  Topps: 91/92 - 414; 93/94 - 396(II), 361SC, 361FD
  Upper Deck: 91/92 - 52E, 52F; 93/94 - 506

Van Boxmeer, John
  Funmate: 83/84 - 14
  O-Pee-Chee: 76/77 - 330; 77/78 - 315; 78/79 - 224; 79/80 - 96; 80/81 - 183; 81/82 - 26, 58SK; 82/83 - 36, 37, 121SK; 83/84 - 73, 244SK
  Post: 82/83 - 32
  Topps: 78/79; - 224; 79/80 - 96; 80/81 - 183; 81/82 EN - 80; 82/83 - 121SK; 83/84 - 244SK
  Vachon Foods: 83/84 - 78

Van Dorp, Wayne
  O-Pee-Chee: 90/91 - 527

Van Hellemond, Andy (Official)
  Pro Set: 90/91 - 701

Van Impe, Ed
  Bazooka: 71/72 - 3
  Bee Hive: 64/67 - 58
  Colgate: 70/71 - 78
  Dad's Cookies: 70/71 - 102
  Eddie Sargent: 70/71 - 159; 71/72 - 150; 72/73 - 160
  Esso: 70/71 - 179
  Loblaws: 74/75 - 232
  O-Pee-Chee: 68/69 - 91; 69/70 - 92, 18QS; 70/71 - 80, 34DE, 32SS; 71/72 - 126; 72/73 - 33; 73/74 - 206; 74/75 - 85; 75/76 - 38; 76/77 - 157
  Parkhurst: 92/93 - 479, 479EI
  Topps: 63/64 - 30; 68/69 - 91; 69/70 - 92; 70/71 - 80, 32SK; 71/72 - 126; 72/73 - 9; 74/75 - 85; 75/76 - 38; 76/77 - 157
  Toronto Sun: 71/72 - 207

Vanbiesbrouck, John (Goalie)
  Bowman: 90/91 - 222; 91/92 - 68; 92/93 - 132
  Donruss: 93/94 - 132
  Fleer: 92/93 - 144; 93/94 - 102PP
  Highliner: 93/94 - 5
  Kraft: 90/91 - 60; 93/94 - 22
  Leaf: 93/94 - 371(II), 8PW
  O-Pee-Chee: 85/86 - 88SK; 86/87 - 9, 114SK, 190SK, 218SK; 87/88 - 36, 33SK; 88/89 - 102, 42NS, 241SK; 89/90 - 114, 246; 90/91 - 75; 91/92 - 353; 92/93 - 275; 93/94 - 314, 85SC, 85FD
  Panini: 87/88 - 106; 88/89 - 300; 89/90 - 282; 90/91 - 108; 91/92 - 282; 92/93 - 232E, 232F; 93/94 - 98E, 98F
  Parkhurst: 91/92 - 338E, 238F; 92/93 - 349, 349EI; 93/94 - 73, 73EI, H9, R9, C9, V13
  Pro Set: 90/91 - 209; 91/92 - 447E, PC1PT, 447F
  Score: 90/91 - 175A, 175C, 76HR; 91/92 - 10A, 10B, 10C, 121PNE, 367PNE, 121PNF, 367PNF; 92/93 - 160C, 160A, 186PNC, 186PNA; 93/94 - 162C, 445C, 492C, 162A, 445A; 492A, 7USG;
  Sega: 93/94 - 54
  Topps: 86/87 - 9, 1SK; 87/88 - 36; 88/89 - 102; 89/90 - 114; 90/91 - 75;

Vanbiesbrouck, John (Goalie) (cont.)
  Topps: 91/92 - 353, 323SC; 92/93 - 169, 169GS, 58SC; 93/94 - 160, 314, 85SC, 330SC, 85FD, 330FD, 10MP
  Upper Deck: 90/91 - 279E, 279F; 91/92 - 324E, 324F; 92/93 - 44; 93/94 - 8

Varga, John
  Donruss: 93/94 - 21JCA
  Upper Deck: 93/94 - 559

Varjanov, Nikolai
  O-Pee-Chee: 90/91 - 504

Varvio, Jarkko
  Donruss: 93/94 - 90, 6RR
  Leaf: 93/94 - 383(II), 8FP
  Parkhurst: 93/94 - 252, 252EI, CC8
  Upper Deck: 91/92 - 676E, 676F; 93/94 - 422

Vaske, Dennis
  Fleer: 93/94 - 387PP
  O-Pee-Chee: 91/92 - 230; 93/94 - 438
  Parkhurst: 92/93 - 335, 335EI; 94/95 - 141, 141EI
  Score: 91/92 - 310A, 340B, 340C
  Topps: 91/92 - 230; 92/93 - 87, 87GS, 362SC; 93/94 - 438(II). 358SC, 358FD
  Upper Deck: 91/92 - 49E, 49F; 92/93 -50, 383

Vasko, Elmer
  Bee Hive: 45/63 - 144; 64/67 - 59
  Chex: 63/65 - 9
  Coca-Cola: 64/65 - 35; 65/66 - 36
  O-Pee-Chee: 68/69 - 147, 8PS
  Parkhurst: 93/94 - 31ML
  Shirriff: 60/61 - 73; 61/62 - 26; 63/64 - 9; 64/65 - 16
  Topps: 57/58 - 27; 58/59 - 12; 59/60 - 3; 60/61 - 23, 26ST; 61/62 - 25; 62/63 - 27, 16HB; 63/64 - 26; 64/65 - 5; 65/66 - 114
  Toronto Star: 57/67 - 57, 66; 58/67 - 56; 63/64 - 9, 64/65 - 16
  Ultimate: 92 - 64(OSE), 64(OSF)

Vauhkonen, Jonni
  Parkhurst: 93/94 - 525, 525EI
  Upper Deck: 92/93 - 619

Vautour, Yvon
  O-Pee-Chee: 81/82 - 84

Velsor, Mike (Goalie)
  O-Pee-Chee: 75/76 - 385; 77/78 - 393; 80/81 - 361

Veitch, Darren
  O-Pee-Chee: 87/88 - 114
  Panini: 87/88 - 239; 88/89 - 39
  Post: 82/83 - 319
  Topps: 87/88 - 114

Velischek, Randy
  Bowman: 91/92 - 152; 92/93 - 131
  Durivage: 92/93 - 45
  O-Pee-Chee: 89/90 - 245; 90/91 453, 125PM; 91/92 - 377, 92/93 - 288
  Panini: 89/90 - 259; 91/92 - 265
  Pro Set: 90/91 - 518; 91/92 - 206E, 206F
  Score: 90/91 - 64T; 91/92 - 257A, 477B, 477C
  Topps: 91/92 - 377, 27SC; 92/93 - 430, 430GS, 460SC
  Upper Deck: 90/91 - 392E, 392F; 91/92 - 484E, 484F

Venasky, Vic
  O-Pee-Chee: 74/75 - 389; 75/76 - 312; 76/77 - 211; 77/78 - 187; 78/79 - 321; 79/80 - 269; 80/81 - 290
  Topps: 75/76 - 312; 76/77 - 211; 77/78 - 187

Veneruzzo, Gary
  O-Pee-Chee: 68/69 - 119; 70/71 - 101; 72/73 - 330
  Topps: 68/69 - 119; 70/71 - 101

Verbeek, Patrick (Pat)
  Bowman: 90/91 - 257; 91/92 - 12; 92/93 - 112
  Donruss: 93/94 - 148

Verbeek, Patrick (Pat) (cont.)
- Fleer: 92/93 - 305; 93/94 - 175, 110PP
- Gillette: 91/92 - 24
- Humpty Dumpty: 92/93 - 24(II)
- Kraft: 91/92 - 23; 93/94 - 43
- Leaf: 93/94 - 144
- O-Pee-Chee: 84/85 - 121, 73SK; 85/86 56; 86/87 - 46, 202SK; 87/88 - 6, 58SK; 88/89 - 29, 43NS, 81SK; 89/90 - 32; 90/91 - 112; 91/92 - 499, 5PM; 92/93 - 197; 93/94 - 47, 36SC, 36FD
- Panini: 87/88 - 81; 88/89 - 278; 90/91 - 36; 91/92 - 313; 92/93 - 256E, 256F; 93/94 - 124E, 124F
- Parkhurst: 91/92 - 64E, 64F; 92/93 - 58, 58EI; 93/94 - 353, 353EI; 94/95 - 92, 93EI
- Pro Set: 90/91 - 112; 91/92 - 86E, 303E, 86F, 303F, 44PT, 10PK, PC; 92/93 - 58
- Score: 90/91 - 35A, 35C, 18HR; 91/92 - 70A, 70B, 70C, 43PNE, 43PNF; 92/93 - 282C, 282A, 348PNC, 348PNA; 93/94 - 10C, 10A
- Season's: 92/93 - 44
- Sega: 93/94 - 59
- Topps: 84/85 - 90; 85/86 - 56; 86/87 - 46; 87/88 - 6; 88/89 - 29; 89/90 - 32; 90/91 - 112; 91/92 - 499, 1SL, 102SC; 92/93 - 493, 493GS, 197SC; 93/94 - 47(I), 36SC, 36FD
- Upper Deck: 90/91 - 172E, 172F; 91/92 - 193E, 193F; 92/93 - 7, 204; 93/94 - 331

Vermette, Mark
- Upper Deck: 91/92 - 470E, 470F

Verner, Andrew
- Upper Deck: 91/92 - 74E, 74F

Vernon, Michael (Mike) (Goalie)
- Bowman: 90/91 - 94; 91/92 - 253; 92/93 - 86
- Donruss: 93/94 - 54
- Fleer: 93/94 - 207, 45PP
- Hockey Wit: 93/94 - 45
- Kraft: 86/87 - 9, 9P; 1990 - 62; 90/91 - 61, 76; 91/92 - 19
- Leaf: 93/94 - 83, 7PW
- McDonald's: 91/92 - Mc20
- O-Pee-Chee: 87/88 - 215, 41SK; 88/89 - 261, 44NS, 86SK; 89/90 - 163, 94SK, 167SK, 34FS; 90/91 - 351, L/BB, 126PM; 91/92 - 107, 9PM; 92/93 - 247; 93/94 - 15
- Panini: 87/88 - 203; 88/89 - 4; 89/90 - 34, 178; 90/91 - 175, 329; 91/92 - 55, 328; 92/93 - 39E, 39F; 93/94 - 188E, 188F
- Parkhurst: 91/92 - 27E, 27F; 92/93 - 24, 24EI; 93/94 - 301, 301EI
- Pro Set: 90/91 - 47, 338; 91/92 - 35E, 277E, 35F, 277F, 21PT; 92/93 - 25
- Score: 90/91 -52A, 52C, 23HR; 91/92 - 80A, 80B, 80C, 132PNE, 132PNF; 92/93 - 60C, 60A, 318PNC, 318PNA; 93/94 - 43C, 43A, 40PNC, 40PNA, 40CAS, 40AAS
- Season's: 92/93 - 61
- Sega: 93/94 - 24
- Topps: 89/90 - 163, 12SK; 90/91 - 351, L/BB; 91/92 - 107, 269SC; 92/93 - 20, 20GS, 345SC; 93/94 - 15(I), 319SC, 319FD, 23AS
- Upper Deck: 90/91 - 254E, 254F, 495E, 495F; 91/92 - 163E, 163F; 92/93 -112; 93/94 - 177

Ververgaert, Dennis
- Loblaws: 74/75 - 304
- O-Pee-Chee: 74/75 - 207; 75/76 - 42; 76/77 - 175; 77/78 - 56; 78/79 - 52; 79/80 - 214; 80/81 - 99; 81/82 - 356
- Topps: 74/75 - 207; 75/76 - 42; 76/77 - 175; 77/78 - 56; 78/79 - 52; 79/80 - 214; 80/81 - 99

Vezina, Georges (Goalie)
- Anonymous: 1926/27 - 3
- Champ's: 24/25 - 27

Vezina, Georges (Goalie) (cont.)
- Dom. Choc.: 1925 - 120
- Hall of Fame: 83 - 30, B16P; 87 - 30
- Imperial Tobacco: 10/11 - 38; 11/12 - 38; 12/13 - 1
- La Presse: 27/32 - 13
- Maple Crispette: 24/25 - 13
- Parkhurst: 55/56 - 56
- Pro Set: 91/92 - 333E, 333F
- Quaker Oats: 55/56 - 56
- Topps: 60/61 - 19, 52ST
- Wm. Paterson: 23/24 - 19; 24/25 - 43

Vial, Dennis
- Parkhurst: 93/94 - 406, 406EI
- Pro Set: 90/91 - 628
- Score: 91/92 - 428B, 428C

Vickers, Steve
- Lipton Soup: 74/75 - 34
- Loblaws: 74/75 - 215
- O-Pee-Chee: 72/73 - 254; 73/74 - 57; 74/75 - 29; 75/76 - 19, 295; 76/77 - 75; 77/78 - 136; 78/79 - 55; 79/80 - 195; 80/81 - 23
- Post: 82/83 - 208
- Topps: 73/74 - 57; 74/75 - 29; 75/76 - 19, 295; 76/77 - 75; 77/78 - 136; 78/79 - 55; 79/80 - 195; 80/81 - 23

Viitakoski, Vesa
- Donruss: 93/94 - 60
- Leaf: 93/94 - 433(II)
- Parkhurst: 93/94 - 263, 263EI, CC20
- Upper Deck: 93/94 - 344

Vilgrain, Claude
- Bowman: 92/93 - 191
- O-Pee-Chee: 92/93 - 133
- Parkhurst: 91/92 - 321E, 321F
- Pro Set: 91/92 - 425E, 425F, 195PT
- Score: 92/93 - 326C, 326A, 14CSS, 14ASS
- Topps: 92/93 - 187, 187GS, 422SC
- Upper Deck: 90/91 - 250E, 250F

Villemure, Gilles (Goalie)
- Bazooka: 71/72 - 10
- Colgate: 70/71 - 89
- Esso: 70/71 - 162
- Loblaws: 74/75 - 216
- O-Pee-Chee: 70/71 - 183; 71/72 - 18; 72/73 - 132; 73/74 - 119; 74/75 - 179; 75/76 - 379; 76/77 - 61
- Topps: 63/64 - 46; 64/65 - 74; 67/68 - 86; 71/72 - 18; 72/73 - 137; 73/74 - 153; 74/75 - 179; 76/77 - 61
- Toronto Sun: 71/72 - 186

Vines, Mark (Official)
- Pro Set: 90/91 - 702

Vitolinsh, Harijs
- O-Pee-Chee: 90/91 - 521
- Parkhurst: 93/94 - 496, 496EI
- Upper Deck: 93/94 - 428

Vlolek, David
- Upper Deck: 93/94 - 370

Vlasak, Tomas
- Parkhurst: 93/94 - 515, 515EI

Voisard, Gaetan
- Upper Deck: 91/92 - 664E, 664F

Volcan, Mickey
- O-Pee-Chee: 83/84 - 94
- Vachon Foods: 83/84 - 20

Volek, David
- Bowman: 90/91 - 127; 91/92 - 223; 92/93 - 196
- Fleer: 92/93 - 350; 93/94 - 388PP
- O-Pee-Chee: 89/90 - 85, 43SK, 113SK, 9FS; 90/91 - 300; 91/92 - 488; 92/93 - 3; 93/94 - 371
- Panini: 89/90 - 267; 91/92 - 241; 92/93 - 200E, 200F
- Parkhurst: 91/92 - 104E, 104F; 92/93 - 340, 340EI; 93/94 - 395, 395EI; 94/95 - 139, 139EI
- Pro Set: 90/91 - 193; 91/92 - 147E, 147F, 75PT
- Score: 90/91 - 12A, 12C; 91/92 - 88A, 88B,

Volek, David (cont.)
- Score: 88C, 198PNE, 198PNF; 92/93 - 166C, 166A, 188PNC, 188PNA; 93/94 - 495C, 495A
- Topps: 89/90 - 85; 90/91 - 300; 91/92 - 488, 204SC; 92/93 - 204, 204GS, 319SC; 93/94 - 371(II), 324SC, 324FD
- Upper Deck: 90/91 - 1E, 1F; 91/92 - 173E; 92/93 - 313

Volmar, Doug
- O-Pee-Chee: 73/74 - 215

Vopat, Jan
- Upper Deck: 92/93 - 601

Voss, Carl
- Bee Hive: 34/44 - 128
- Canada Starch: 35/40 - 79
- Diamond: 36/39 - 68(I), 63(II), 58(III)
- Hall of Fame: 83 - 225, O16P; 87 - 225
- O-Pee-Chee: 37/38 - 175
- World Wide Gum: 36/37 - 66

Vostrikov, Sergei
- O-Pee-Chee: 91/92 - 27R

Vujtek, Vladimir
- Fleer: 93/94 - 343PP
- O-Pee-Chee: 93/94 - 459
- Parkhurst: 93/94 - 339, 339EI
- Score: 92/93 - 396PNC, 396PNA; 93/94 - 465C, 465A
- Topps: 93/94 - 459, 278SC, 278FD
- Upper Deck: 92/93 - 417, 496; 93/94 - 168

Vukota, Mick
- O-Pee-Chee: 90/91 - 10; 91/92 - 25
- Pro Set: 90/91 - 488
- Score: 91/92 - 387B, 387C; 92/93 - 549A
- Topps: 90/91 - 10; 91/92 - 25, 309SC
- Upper Deck: 90/91 - 39E, 39F; 91/92 - 135E, 135F

Vyborny, David
- Upper Deck: 92/93 - 600

Waghorne, Fred C.
- Hall of Fame: 83 - 119, H15P; 87 - 119

Waite, Jimmy (Goalie)
- Bowman: 91/92 - 396; 92/93 - 120
- Donruss: 93/94 - 302
- Fleer: 93/94 - 438PP
- Leaf: 93/94 - 324(II)
- O-Pee-Chee: 90/91 - 214; 91/92 - 127; 93/94 - 388
- Parkhurst: 92/93 - 270, 270EI; 93/94 - 181, 181EI; 94/95 - 214, 214EI
- Pro Set: 91/92 - 530E, 530F
- Score: 90/91 - 407A, 407C; 91 - 82T; 91/92 - 632B, 632C, 316PNE, 316PNF; 93/94 - 365C, 365A
- Topps: 90/91 - 214; 91/92 - 127; 92/93 - 100, 100GS, 35SC; 93/94 - 388
- Upper Deck: 92/93 - 67; 93/94 - 501

Wakaluk, Darcy (Goalie)
- Bowman: 91/92 - 33; 92/93 - 148
- Donruss: 93/94 - 420
- Fleer: 92/93 - 99; 93/94 - 327PP
- O-Pee-Chee: 92/93 - 63; 93/94 - 399
- Parkhurst: 91/92 - 306E, 306F; 92/93 - 315, 315EI
- Score: 91/92 - 653B, 653C; 92/93 - 313C, 313A; 93/94 - 432C, 432A
- Topps: 92/92 - 108, 108GS, 153SC; 93/94 - 399(II), 276SC, 276FD

Wakely, Ernie (Goalie)
- Colgate: 70/71 - 92
- Eddie Sargent: 70/71 - 181
- Esso: 70/71 - 216
- O-Pee-Chee: 70/71 - 97; 71/72 - 81
- Topps: 70/71 - 97; 71/72 - 81
- Toronto Sun: 71/72 - 252

Walanin, Craig
- Topps: 92/93 - 317SC

Walker, Howard
 O-Pee-Chee: 82/83 - 59

Walker, Jack
 Hall of Fame: 83 - 75, E16P; 87 - 75

Walker, Kurt
 O-Pee-Chee: 78/79 - 282

Wall, Bob
 Bee Hive: 64/67 - 96
 Dad's Cookies: 70/71 - 123
 Eddie Sargent: 70/71 - 191; 71/72 - 50
 Esso: 70/71 - 215
 O-Pee-Chee: 68/69 - 156; 69/70 - 140, 10QS; 70/71 - 98; 72/73 - 323
 Shirriff: 68/69 - D3
 Topps: 66/67 - 49; 70/71 - 98

Walsh, James Patrick (Flat)
 La Presse: 27/32 - 47

Walsh, Marty
 Hall of Fame: 83 - 89, F15P; 87 - 89
 Imperial Tobacco: 10/11 - 7, 11L; 11/12 - 11; 12/13 - 49

Walter, Ryan
 Funmate: 83/84 - 70
 Kraft: 86/87 - 41, 41P
 O-Pee-Chee: 79/80 - 236; 80/81 - 154; 81/82 - 352, 192SK; 82/83 - 194, 152SK; 83/84 - 200, 62SK, 63SK; 84/85 - 275, 159SK; 86/87 - 224; 87/88 - 231, 17SK; 88/89 - 262, 40SK; 89/90 - 240; 90/91 - 296; 93/94 - 185SC, 185FD
 Panini: 88/89 - 262
 Parkhurst: 91/92 - 401E, 401F
 Post: 82/83 - 320
 Pro Set: 90/91 - 475; 91/92 - 504E, 504F
 Score: 91 - 41T; 91/92 - 591B, 591C; 92/93 - 255PNC, 255PNA
 Topps: 79/80 - 236; 80/81 - 154; 81/82 EN - 122; 82/83 - 152SK; 83/84 - 62SK, 63SK; 90/91 - 296; 93/94 - 185SC, 185FD
 Vachon Foods: 83/84 - 58

Walters, Ron
 O-Pee-Chee: 72/73 - 301

Walton, Mike
 Bee Hive: 64/67 - 188
 Coca-Cola: 65/66 - 108
 Colgate: 70/71 - 3
 Dad's Cookies: 70/71 - 134
 Eddie Sargent: 70/71 - 206; 72/73 - 24
 Esso: 70/71 - 234
 O-Pee-Chee: 68/69 - 132; 69/70 - 50, 15QS; 70/71 - 109; 71/72 - 171; 72/73 - 94; 76/77 - 23; 77/78 - 350; 78/79 - 38
 Post: 68/69 - 30
 Shirriff: 68/69 - M5
 Topps: 65/66 - 86; 66/67 - 14; 66/67 US - 14; 67/68 - 15; 68/69 - 132; 69/70 - 50; 70/71 - 109; 76/77 - 23; 78/79 - 38; 79/80 - 141
 Toronto Sun: 71/72 - 20

Walz, Wes
 Bowman: 91/92 - 353
 Donruss: 93/94 - 57
 Leaf: 93/94 - 393(II)
 O-Pee-Chee: 90/91 - 127PM; 91/92 - 134
 Parkhurst: 93/94 - 305, 305EI; 94/95 - 38, 38EI
 Pro Set: 90/91 - 589
 Score: 90/91 - 418A, 418C; 91/92 - 430B, 430C
 Topps: 91/92 - 134, 325SC
 Upper Deck: 90/91 - 527E, 527F; 91/92 - 123E, 123F; 93/94 - 431

Wamsley, Richard (Rick) (Goalie)
 Bowman: 90/91 - 98; 91/92 - 268; 92/93 - 97
 Derniere: 72/84 - 186
 McDonald's: 82/83 - 5
 O-Pee-Chee: 82/83 - 195, 37SK; 83/84 - 201, 72SK; 84/85 - 157SK; 86/87 - 240, 179SK; 87/88 - 65, 22SK;

Wamsley, Richard (Rick) (Goalie) (cont.)
 O-Pee-Chee: 89/90 - 204, 93SK; 90/91 - 409; 91/92 - 459; 92/93 - 310
 Panini: 87/88 - 305; 90/91 - 186
 Parkhurst: 91/92 - 394E, 394F
 Pro Set: 90/91 - 48; 91/92 - 367E, 367F
 Score: 90/91 - 309C; 91/92 - 232B, 232C
 Topps: 82/83 - 37SK; 83/84 - 72SK; 87/88 - 65; 91/92 - 459, 294SC; 92/93 - 425, 425GS, 53SC
 Upper Deck: 90/91 - 10E, 10F; 91/92 - 130E, 130F
 Vachon Foods: 83/84 - 59

Wanhainen, Rolf
 Upper Deck: 92/93 - 2

Ward, Aaron
 Donruss: 93/94 - 93
 Leaf: 93/94 - 359(II)
 O-Pee-Chee: 93/94 - 484
 Parkhurst: 93/94 - 262, 262EI
 Topps: 93/94 - 484(II), 423SC, 423FD
 Upper Deck: 93/94 - 479

Ward, Dixon
 Donruss: 93/94 - 449
 Fleer: 92/93 - 431; 93/94 - 102, 257PP, 365PP
 Leaf: 93/94 - 97
 O-Pee-Chee: 92/93 - 67PM; 93/94 - 58, 127
 Parkhurst: 92/93 - 194, 194EI; 93/94 - 209, 209EI
 Score: 93/94 - 210C, 210A
 Topps: 93/94 - 58, 127, 454SC, 454FD
 Upper Deck: 92/93 - 580, CC1; 93/94 - 62

Ward, Jimmy
 Bee Hive: 34/44 - 186, 209
 Canada Starch: 35/40 - 121, 154
 Can. Chew. Gum: 33/34 - 49
 La Presse: 27/32 - 25
 O-Pee-Chee: 34/35 - 56; 37/38 - 170
 Quaker Oats: 38/39 - 13
 Sweet Caporal: 34/35 - 38
 Toronto Sun: 71/72 - 292
 World Wide Gum: 33/34 - 37; 36/37 - 2

Ward, Ron
 O-Pee-Chee: 72/73 - 332

Wares, Eddie
 Bee Hive: 34/44 - 129
 O-Pee-Chee: 39/40 - 73

Warner, Jim
 O-Pee-Chee: 79/80 - 384

Warriner, Todd
 Fleer: 93/94 - 496PP

Warwick, Grant
 Bee Hive: 34/44 - 296; 45/63 - 73, 294
 Quaker Oats: 45/54 - 53

Wasnie, Nick
 Can. Chew. Gum: 33/34 - 50
 Hamilton Gum: 33/34 - 1
 O-Pee-Chee: 33/34 - 47

Watson, Bill
 O-Pee-Chee: 86/87 - 151
 Panini: 87/88 - 232
 Topps: 86/87 - 151

Watson, Bryan
 Dad's Cookies: 70/71 - 112
 Eddie Sargent: 70/71 - 164; 72/73 - 172
 Esso: 70/71 - 197
 Loblaws: 74/75 - 108
 O-Pee-Chee: 68/69 - 173; 69/70 - 112; 70/71 - 204; 71/72 - 132; 72/73 - 90; 73/74 - 14; 74/75 - 259; 75/76 - 31; 76/77 - 228; 77/78 - 342; 78/79 - 316
 Topps: 65/66 - 45; 66/67 - 48; 69/70 - 112; 73/74 - 144; 74/75 - 259; 75/76 - 31; 76/77 - 228
 Toronto Sun: 71/72 - 229

Watson, Harry
 Bee Hive: 34/44 - 130, 257; 45/63 - 460
 Dom. Choc.: 25 - 114

Watson, Harry (cont.)
 Hall of Fame: 83 - 105, G16P; 87 - 105
 Parkhurst: 51/52 - 70; 52/53 - 46; 53/54 - 12; 54/55 - 17; 93/94 - 36ML
 Quaker Oats: 45/54 - 112A, 112B, 112C
 Toronto Star: 58/67 - 10
 Ultimate: 92 - 46(OSE), 46(OSF)
 Willards: 1925 - 43

Watson, Jim (James Arthur)
 Eddie Sargent: 70/71 - 32
 Esso: 70/71 - 36
 O-Pee-Chee: 70/71 - 144; 71/72 - 165
 Shirriff: 68/69 - C15
 Topps: 67/68 - 107
 Toronto Sun: 71/72 - 40

Watson, Jimmy (James Charles)
 Coca-Cola: 77/78 - 28
 Loblaws: 74/75 - 233
 O-Pee-Chee: 74/75 - 303; 75/76 - 202; 76/77 - 247; 77/78 - 43; 78/79 - 247; 79/80 - 26; 80/81 - 224; 82/83 - 259
 Post: 82/83 - 223
 Topps: 75/76 - 202; 76/77 - 247; 77/78 - 43; 78/79 - 247; 79/80 - 26; 80/81 - 224
 Upper Deck: 90/91 - 514E, 514F

Watson, Joe
 Coca-Cola: 77/78 - 29
 Dad's Cookies: 70/71 - 103
 Eddie Sargent: 70/71 - 156; 72/73 - 159
 Esso: 70/71 - 180
 Loblaws: 74/75 - 234
 O-Pee-Chee: 68/69 - 90; 69/70 - 93; 70/71 - 79; 72/73 - 62; 73/74 - 91; 74/75 - 217; 75/76 - 281; 76/77 - 45; 77/78 - 247; 78/79 - 43
 Parkhurst: 92/93 - 474, 474EI
 Topps: 66/67 - 33; 68/69 - 90; 69/70 - 93; 70/71 - 79; 72/73 - 156; 73/74 - 91; 74/75 - 217; 75/76 - 281; 76/77 - 45; 77/78 - 247; 78/79 - 43
 Toronto Sun: 71/72 - 208

Watson, Phil
 Bee Hive: 34/44 - 297
 CKAC Radio: 43/47 - 13
 O-Pee-Chee: 39/40 - 83
 Parkhurst: 93/94 - 108ML
 Shirriff: 61/62 - 19
 Topps: 61/62 - 1; 62/63 - 1
 World Wide Gum: 36/37 - 80

Watt, Tom
 Pro Set: 90/91 - 677

Watters, Timothy (Tim)
 O-Pee-Chee: 82/83 - 395; 83/84 - 394; 84/85 - 350; 87/88 - 219; 89/90 - 212; 90/91 - 461; 93/94 - 298
 Post: 82/83 - 336
 Pro Set: 90/91 - 458
 Score: 90/91 - 204A, 204C; 91/92 - 523B, 523C
 Topps: 93/94 - 298(II)
 Upper Deck: 90/91 - 117E, 117F; 91/92 - 471E, 471F
 Vachon Foods: 83/84 - 139

Weber, Marc
 Upper Deck: 91/92 - 666E, 666F

Webster, Tom
 Dad's Cookies: 70/71 - 54
 Eddie Sargent: 70/71 - 57
 Esso: 70/71 - 90
 O-Pee-Chee: 70/71 - 155; 71/72 - 78
 Pro Set: 90/91 - 667
 Topps: 71/72 - 78

Weeks, Stephen (Steve) (Goalie)
 Bowman: 92/93 - 274
 O-Pee-Chee: 82/83 - 234, 141SK; 89/90 - 285; 90/91 - 407
 Panini: 87/88 - 39; 89/90 - 150
 Post: 82/83 - 207
 Score: 92/93 - 547C, 547A, 380PNC, 380PNA

Weeks, Stephen, (Steve) (Goalie) (cont.)
- Topps: 82/83 - 141SK; 92/93 - 461, 461GS, 273SC
- Upper Deck: 90/91 - 107E, 107F

Weight, Doug
- Bowman: 92/93 - 36
- Donruss: 93/94 - 118
- Fleer: 92/93 - 358; 93/94 - 195, 87PP
- Leaf: 93/94 - 184
- O-Pee-Chee: 91/92 - 32PM, 139PM; 92/93 - 114; 93/94 - 136
- Panini: 92/93 - 236E, 236F; 93/94 - 235E, 235F
- Parkhurst: 91/92 - 116E, 116F; 92/93 - 115, 115EI, 229, 229EI; 93/94 - 69, 69EI; 94/95 - 74, 74EI
- Pro Set: 91/92 - 549E, 549F, 263PT
- Score: 91/92 - 396A, 286B, 286C, 310PNE, 383PNE, 310PNF, 383PNF; 92/93 - 314C, 314A, 189PNE, 189PNA; 93/94 - 253C, 253A
- Sega: 93/94 - 45
- Topps: 92/93 - 477, 477GS, 380SC; 93/94 - 136, 382SC, 382FD
- Upper Deck: 92/93 - 279; 93/94 - 442

Weiland, Cooney (Ralph)
- Anonymous: 33/34 - 24
- Bee Hive: 34/44 - 36
- Hall of Fame: 83 - H16, 120C; 87 - 120C
- O-Pee-Chee: 33/34 - 27; 39/40 - 92
- Sweet Caporal: 34/35 - 11
- World Wide Gum: 33/34 - 65; 36/37 - 69

Weinrich, Eric
- Bowman: 90/91 - 90; 91/92 - 278; 92/93 - 343
- Donruss: 93/94 - 136, 416
- Fleer: 92/93 - 76, 306; 93/94 - 111PP, 319PP
- Leaf: 93/94 - 271(II)
- O-Pee-Chee: 90/91 - 416; 91/92 - 10, 92; 92/93 - 95, 63PM; 93/94 - 195
- Panini: 91/92 - 223; 93/94 - 130E, 130F
- Parkhurst: 91/92 - 318E, 318F; 92/93 - 56, 56EI; 93/94 - 311, 311EI; 94/95 - 43, 43EI, V83
- Pro Set: 90/91 - 622; 91/92 - 133E, 133F, PC10PT
- Score: 90/91 - 389A, 389C; 91 - 26YS; 91/92 - 131A, 350A, 131B, 131C, 380B, 380C, 89PNE, 89PNF; 92/93 - 308C, 308A, 297PNC, 297PNA; 93/94 - 227C, 227A
- Sega: 93/94 - 56
- Topps: 91/92 - 10, 92, 339SC; 92/93 - 399, 399GS, 165SC; 93/94 - 195(I)
- Upper Deck: 90/91 - 245E 245F; 91/92 - 44E, 344E, 509E, 44F, 344F, 509F; 92/93 - 195,553; 93/94 - 497

Weir, Stan
- Loblaws: 74/75 - 71
- O-Pee-Chee: 74/75 - 355; 75/76 - 132; 76/77 - 270; 77/78 - 356; 79/80 - 331; 80/81 - 153; 81/82 - 124
- PepsiCo: 80/81 - 40
- Topps: 75/76 - 132; 80/81 - 153

Weir, Wally
- Derniere: 72/84 - 90, 157
- O-Pee-Chee: 79/80 - 388; 81/82 - 284; 82/83 - 297; 83/84 - 306
- PepsiCo: 80/81 - 79
- Post: 82/83 - 256
- Vachon Foods: 83/84 - 79

Wells, Gordon (Jay)
- Bowman: 91/92 - 25
- O-Pee-Chee: 85/86 - 178; 86/87 - 217, 92SK; 87/88 - 151, 212SK
- Panini: 87/88 - 274; 88/89 - 72
- Post: 82/83 - 128
- Score: 92/93 - 548A; 93/94 - 416C, 416A
- Topps: 87/88 - 151

Wensink, John
- O-Pee-Chee: 78/79 - 133; 79/80 - 182; 80/81 - 390

Wensink, John (cont.)
- PepsiCo: 80/81 - 80
- Post: 82/83 - 176
- Topps: 78/79 - 133; 79/80 - 182

Wentworth, Cy (Marvin)
- Bee Hive: 34/44 - 186, 210
- Canada Starch: 35/40 - 119, 157
- O-Pee-Chee: 34/35 - 61; 36/37 - 116; 37/38 - 163; 39/40 - 30
- Quaker Oats: 38/39 - 14
- Sweet Caporal: 34/35 - 39
- World Wide Gum: 33/34 - 43; 36/37 - 19

Werenka, Brad
- Parkhurst: 92/93 - 289, 289EI; 93/94 - 68, 68EI
- Score: 93/94 - 438C, 438A
- Upper Deck: 93/94 - 41

Werenka, Darcy
- Upper Deck: 92/93 - 594

Wesley, Blake
- O-Pee-Chee: 82/83 - 133; 83/84 - 307; 84/85 - 294
- Post: 82/83 - 112
- Vachon Foods: 83/84 - 80

Wesley, Glen
- Bowman: 91/92 - 350; 92/93 - 15
- Donruss: 93/94 - 19
- Fleer: 92/93 - 11; 93/94 - 25PP
- Leaf: 93/94 - 268(II)
- O-Pee-Chee: 88/89 - 166, 27SK, 21FS; 89/90 - 51; 90/91 - 379; 91/92 - 452; 92/93 - 150; 93/94 - 114, 222SC, 222FD
- Panini: 88/89 - 207; 89/90 - 200; 90/91 - 6; 91/92 - 182; 92/93 - 145E, 145F; 93/94 - 6E, 6F
- Parkhurst: 91/92 - 5E, 5F; 92/93 - 6, 6EI; 93/94 - 17, 17EI; 94/95 - 17, 17EI
- Pro Set: 90/91 - 16; 91/92 - 1E, 1F, 7PT; 92/93 - 10
- Score: 90 - 8YS; 90/91 - 97A, 97C, 57HR; 91/92 - 273A, 493B, 493C, 112PNE, 112PNF; 92/93 - 230C, 230A, 326PNC, 326PNA; 93/94 - 243C, 243A
- Topps: 88/89 - 166; 89/90 - 51; 90/9 - 379 91/92 - 452, 190SC; 92/93 - 346, 346GS, 279SC; 93/94 - 114, 222SC, 222FD
- Upper Deck: 90/91 - 377E, 377F; 91/92 - 370E, 370F; 92/93 - 244; 93/94 - 208

Westfall, Ed
- Bee Hive: 64/67 - 28
- Coca-Cola: 64/65 - 17; 65/66 - 16; 77/78 - 30
- Eddie Sargent: 70/71 - 7; 71/72 - 2; 72/73 - 127
- Esso: 70/71 - 18
- Lipton Soup: 74/75 - 47
- Loblaws: 74/75 - 198
- O-Pee-Chee: 68/69 - 135; 69/70 - 29; 70/71 - 139; 71/72 - 169; 72/73 - 104, 13CS; 73/74 - 67; 74/75 - 32; 75/76 - 302; 76/77 - 11; 77/78 - 153; 78/79 - 232
- Shirriff: 68/69 - A2
- Topps: 63/64 - 8; 64/65 - 51; 65/66 - 37; 66/67 - 32; 66/67 US - 32; 67/68 - 95; 69/70 - 29; 72/73 - 159; 73/74 - 67; 74/75 - 32; 75/76 - 302; 76/77 - 11; 77/78 - 153; 78/79 - 232
- Toronto Sun: 71/72 - 21
- Ultimate: 92 - 56(OSE), 56(OSF)

Westwick, Harry
- Hall of Fame: 83 - 135, I16P; 87 - 135

Wharram, Kenny
- Bee Hive: 45/63 - 145; 64/67 - 60
- Chex: 63/65 - 10
- Coca-Cola: 64/65 - 36; 65/66 - 37
- O-Pee-Chee: 68/69 - 22; 69/70 - 74
- Shirriff: 60/61 - 70; 61/62 - 32; 68/69 - B5
- Topps: 58/59 - 14; 61/62 - 30, 43; 62/63 - 39; 63/64 - 38; 64/65 - 28, 108; 65/66 - 61; 66/67 - 117;

Wharram, Kenny (cont.)
- Topps: 66/67 US - 44; 67/68 - 117, 125; 68/69 - 22; 69/70 - 74
- Toronto Star: 57/67 - 93, 107, 128; 58/67 - 83; 63/64 - 10

Wheaton, David
- Pro-Set: 91/92 - 294PT

Whitcroft, Fred
- Hall of Fame: 83 - 45, C16P; 87 - 45

White, Bill
- Eddie Sargent: 72/73 - 62
- Esso: 70/71 - 72
- Loblaws: 74/75 - 89
- Mac's Milk: 73/74 - 30
- O-Pee-Chee: 68/69 - 37; 69/70 - 101; 71/72 - 11; 72/73 - 158, 6CS; 72/73 - 248; 73/74 - 78; 74/75 - 90, 136; 75/76 - 157; 76/77 - 235
- Shirriff: 68/69 - D4
- Topps: 68/69 - 37; 69/70 - 101; 71/72 - 11; 72/73 - 128; 72/73 - 40; 73/74 - 180; 74/75 - 90, 136; 75/76 - 157; 76/77 - 235
- Toronto Sun: 71/72 - 82

White, Peter
- Donruss: 93/94 - 431
- Fleer: 93/94 - 344PP

White, Sherman
- La Patrie: 51/54 - 34

White, Tony
- O-Pee-Chee: 76/77 - 279; 77/78 - 314

Whitmore, Kay (Goalie)
- Bowman: 91/92 - 3; 92/93 - 155
- Donruss: 93/94 - 359
- Fleer: 93/94 - 462PP
- O-Pee-Chee: 90/91 - 232; 91/92 - 182PM; 92/93 - 87PM; 93/94 - 514, 60SC, 60FD
- Panini: 92/93 - 255E, 255F
- Parkhurst: 91/92 - 58E, 58F; 92/93 - 423, 423EI; 93/94 - 478A, 478A(EI)
- Pro Set: 90/91 - 610; 91/92 - 178PT
- Score: 90/91 - 402A, 402C; 91 - 75T; 91/92 - 625B, 625C, 22PNE, 22PNF; 92/93 - 304C, 304A; 93/94 - 360C, 360A
- Topps: 90/91 - 232; 92/93 - 381, 381GS, 459SC; 93/94 - 514(II), 60SC, 60FD
- Upper Deck: 91/92 - 291E, 291F; 92/93 - 76

Whitney, Ray
- Fleer: 93/94 - 439PP
- Parkhurst: 91/92 - 454; 92/93 - 160, 160EI; 93/94 - 182, 182EI
- Pro-Set: 92/93 - 241
- Score: 92/93 - 475C, 475S, 227PNC, 227PNA; 93/94 - 324C, 324A
- Topps: 92/93 - 205, 205GS, 490SC
- Upper Deck: 92/93 - 407; 93/94 - 4

Wickenheiser, Douglas (Doug)
- McDonald's: 82/83 - 26
- O-Pee-Chee: 81/82 - 193; 82/83 - 196; 83/84 - 202, 67SK; 84/85 - 193, 58SK; 85/86 - 229, 52SK; 87/88 - 193; 88/89 - 263, 56SK
- Panini: 87/88 - 318
- PepsiCo: 80/81 - 60
- Topps: 83/84 - 97SK; 87/88 - 193
- Vachon Foods: 83/84 - 60

Wicks, Ron (Official)
- Ultimate: 92 - 87(OSE), 87(OSF)

Widing, Juha
- Colgate: 70/71 - 11
- Dad's Cookies: 70/71 - 62
- Eddie Sargent: 70/71 - 76; 72/73 - 93
- Esso: 70/71 - 108
- Loblaws: 74/75 - 143
- O-Pee-Chee: 75/76 - 142; 71/72 - 86, 19BK; 72/73 - 46; 73/74 - 159; 74/75 - 258; 76/77 - 354
- Topps: 71/72 - 86, 19BK; 72/73 - 108;

Widing, Juha (cont.)
Topps: 73/74 - 156; 74/75 - 258; 75/76 - 142
Toronto Sun: 71/72 - 124

Wiebe, Art
Bee Hive: 34/44 - 85
Diamond: 36/39 - 69(I), 64(II), 59(III), 15(IV), 14(V), 14(VI)
O-Pee-Chee: 36/37 - 113; 39/40 - 49
World Wide Gum: 36/37 - 124

Wiemer, James (Jim)
Bowman: 91/92 - 363
O-Pee-Chee: 90/91 - 439; 91/92 - 475
Pro Set: 90/91 - 413
Score: 91/92 - 535B, 535C
Topps: 91/92 - 475, 16SC

Wilcox, Archie
O-Pee-Chee: 34/35 - 57
World Wide Gum: 33/34 - 9

Wilder, Arch
Bee Hive: 34/44 - 131
O-Pee-Chee: 40/41 - 145

Wiley, Jim
Loblaws: 74/75 - 305

Wilkie, Bob
Parkhurst: 94/95 - 171, 171EI
Score: 91/92 - 328A, 358B, 358C

Wilkie, David
Upper Deck: 93/94 - 558

Wilkins, Barry
Eddie Sargent: 72/73 - 217
Esso: 70/71 - 251
Loblaws: 74/75 - 306
O-Pee-Chee: 71/72 - 230; 72/73 - 109; 74/75 - 182; 75/76 - 148
Topps: 72/73 - 102; 74/75 - 182; 75/76 - 148; 76/77 - 102
Toronto Sun: 71/72 - 293

Wilkinson, Neil
Bowman: 90/91 - 184
Donruss: 93/94 - 62
Fleer: 92/93 - 198
Humpty Dumpty: 92/93 - 25(II)
Leaf: 93/94 - 357
O-Pee-Chee: 90/91 - 443; 91/92 - 348, 110PM
Panini: 92/93 - 128E, 128F
Parkhurst: 91/92 - 382E, 382F; 92/93 - 165, 165EI; 93/94 - 315, 315EI
Pro Set: 90/91 - 465; 91/92 - 328E, 483E, 328F, 483F, 229PT; 92/93 - 168
Score: 91 - 8T; 91/92 - 369A, 328B, 328C, 558B, 558C, 108PNE, 108PNF; 92/93 - 235C, 235A, 27PNC, 27PNA; 93/94 - 138C, 138A
Sega: 93/94 - 116
Topps: 91/92 - 348, 293SC; 92/93 - 76, 76GS, 219SC
Upper Deck: 90/91 - 547E, 547F; 91/92 - 55E, 55F; 92/93 - 30; 93/94 - 378

Wilkie, David
Donruss: 93/94 - 22jca

Williams, David (Dave)
Bowman: 92/93 - 377
Funmate: 83/84 - 133
O-Pee-Chee: 76/77 - 373; 77/78 - 383; 78/79 - 359; 79/80 - 97; 80/81 - 105; 81/82 - 345, 385, 247SK; 82/83 - 358; 83/84 - 363; 86/87 - 6, 94SK; 92/93 - 250
Panini: 87/88 - 283
PepsiCo: 80/81 - 120
Post: 81/82 - 10; 82/83 - 304
Pro-Set: 92/93 - 172
7-Eleven: 84/85 - 11
Score: 92/93 - 539C, 539A
Topps: 79/80 - 97; 80/81 - 105; 86/87 - 6; 92/93 - 372, 372GS
Upper Deck: 92/93 - 51
Vachon Foods: 83/84 - 120

Williams, Ernie
Dom. Choc.: 1926 - 18

Williams, Tom (Thomas Mark)
Bee Hive: 45/63 - 74; 64/67 - 29
Coca-Cola: 64/65 - 18; 65/66 - 17
Colgate: 70/71 - 5
Dad's Cookies: 70/71 - 71
Eddie Sargent: 70/71 - 83; 71/72 - 130
Esso: 70/71 - 125
Loblaws: 74/75 - 144
O-Pee-Chee: 68/69 - 11; 69/70 - 128; 70/71 - 169; 71/72 - 31; 75/76 - 79
Shirriff: 61/62 - 17; 68/69 - A16
Topps: 62/63 - 21; 63/64 - 12; 64/65 - 58; 65/66 - 35; 66/67 - 38; 66/67 US - 38; 67/68 - 40; 68/69 - 11; 69/70 - 128; 71/72 - 31; 75/76 - 79
Toronto Star: 58/67 - 84
Toronto Sun: 71/72 - 61

Williams, Tommy (Thomas Charles)
O-Pee-Chee: 74/75 - 394; 75/76 - 179; 76/77 - 319; 77/78 - 44; 78/79 - 314
Topps: 75/76 - 179; 77/78 - 44

Williams, Warren
O-Pee-Chee: 75/76 - 217
Topps: 75/76 - 217

Wilson, Behn
Funmate: 83/84 - 98
O-Pee-Chee: 79/80 - 111; 80/81 - 145; 81/82 - 239, 175SK; 82/83 - 260
Post: 82/83 - 224
Topps: 79/80 - 111; 80/81 - 145; 81/82 - 45

Wilson, Bert
O-Pee-Chee: 74/75 - 384; 75/76 - 338; 76/77 - 378; 78/79 - 369
PepsiCo: 80/81 - 20

Wilson, Carey
Bowman: 90/91 - 214; 91/92 - 265
Fleer: 92/93 - 272
Kraft: 86/87 - 10, 10P
O-Pee-Chee: 85/86 - 191, 213SK; 86/87 - 166, 45SK; 87/88 - 211; 88/89 - 75, 45NS, 266SK; 89/90 - 66, 239SK; 90/91 - 54, 128PM; 91/92 - 85
Panini: 87/88 - 211; 88/89 - 246; 89/90 - 280; 90/91 - 105; 91/92 - 56
Pro Set: 90/91 - 210, 453; 91/92 - 36E, 36F
Score: 90/91 - 254A, 254C, 42T; 91/92 - 227A, 227B, 227C, 364PNE, 364PNF; 92/93 - 127C, 127A, 369PNC, 360PNA
Topps: 86/87 - 166; 88/89 - 75; 89/90 - 66; 90/91 - 54; 91/92 - 85, 301SC
Upper Deck: 91/92 - 538E, 538F

Wilson, Douglas (Doug)
Bowman: 90/91 - 2; 91/92 - 400;
Fleer: 92/93 - 199; 93/94 - 230
Funmate: 83/84 - 28
Kellogg's: 84 - 34; 92 - 19
Kraft: 90/91 - 62, 77; 91/92 - 34
McDonald's: 82/83 - 36
O-Pee-Chee: 78/79 - 168; 80/81 - 12; 81/82 - 66; 82/83 - 77, 78, 163SK, 172SK, 254SK; 83/84 - 114, 112SK, 165SK; 84/85 - 48, 27SK; 85/86 - 45, P/BB, 25SK, 122SK; 86/87 - 153SK; 87/88 - 14, 77SK; 88/89 - 89, 6SK; 89/90 - 112, 14SK; 90/91 - 111, 203, N/BB, 129PM; 91/92 - 49, 6PM; 92/93 - 281; 93/94 - 79
Panini: 87/88 - 222; 88/89 - 24; 89/90 - 45; 90/91 - 189; 91/92 - 18; 92/93 - 129E, 129F; 93/94 - 264E, 264F
Parkhurst: 91/92 - 168E, 168F; 92/93 - 167, 167EI
Post: 82/83 - 64
Pro Set: 90/91 - 63, 346; 91/92 - 52E, 478E, 584E, 52F, 107PT, 478F, 584F; 92/93 - 165
Score: 90/91 - 280A, 280C, 320A, 320C,

Wilson, Douglas (Doug) (cont.)
Score: 68HR; 91 - 1T; 91/92 - 35A, 35B, 35C, 551B, 551C, 13PNE, 369PNE, 13PNF, 369PNF; 92/93 - 15C, 15A, 52PNC, 52PNA; 93/94 - 115C, 115A
Season's: 92/93 - 63
Sega: 93/94 - 115
Topps: 78/79 - 168; 80/81 - 12; 81/82 WN - 78; 82/83 - 163SK, 172SK, 254SK; 83/84 - 112SK, 165SK; 84/85 - 37; 85/86 - 45, P/BB, 11SK; 86/87 - 106; 87/88 - 14; 88/89 - 79; 89/90 - 112; 90/91 - 111, 203, N/BB; 91/92 - 49, 131SC; 92/93 - 482, 482GS, 470SC; 93/94 - 77(I)
Upper Deck: 90/91 - 223E, 223F; 92/93 - 150

Wilson, Dunc (Goalie)
Eddie Sargent: 72/73 - 213
Esso: 70/71 - 252
Loblaws: 74/75 - 288
O-Pee-Chee: 71/72 - 24; 72/73 - 18; 73/74 - 257; 74/75 - 327; 76/77 - 102; 77/78 - 224
Topps: 72/73 - 91; 77/78 - 224
Toronto Sun: 71/72 - 294

Wilson, Gord
Hall of Fame: 83 - 195C; 87 - 195C

Wilson, Johnny
Bee Hive: 45/63 - 217, 461
Parkhurst: 52/53 - 89; 53/54 - 51; 54/55 - 44; 59/60 - 13; 60/61 - 14
Shirriff: 60/61 - 15; 61/62 - 100
Topps: 54/55 - 4; 57/58 - 47; 58/59 - 22
Ultimate: 92 - 65(OSE), 65(OSF)

Wilson, Larry
Bee Hive: 45/63 - 146
Parkhurst: 52/53 - 92; 53/54 - 74; 54/55 - 85
Topps: 54/55 - 40

Wilson, Murray
Derniere: 72/84 - 19, 44
Loblaws: 74/75 - 180
O-Pee-Chee: 74/75 - 359; 75/76 - 162; 76/77 - 254; 77/78 - 69
Topps: 75/76 - 162; 76/77 - 254; 77/78 - 69

Wilson, Rick
Loblaws: 74/75 - 270
O-Pee-Chee: 74/75 - 284; 75/76 - 356; 76/77 - 293; 77/78 - 57
Topps: 77/78 - 57

Wilson, Ronald Lee (Ron)
Bowman: 91/92 - 382; 92/93 - 364
Leaf: 93/94 - 316(II)
Panini: 91/92 - 34; 92/93 - 18E, 18F; 93/94 - 162E, 162F
PepsiCo: 80/81 - 140
O-Pee-Chee: 80/81 - 243; 81/82 - 377, 140SK; 87/88 - 224; 91/92 - 120; 93/94 - 194
Pro Set: 90/91 - 529; 91/92 - 220E, 220F
Score: 91/92 - 533B, 533C; 92/93 - 365C, 365A; 93/94 - 431C, 431A
Topps: 80/81 - 243; 91/92 - 120, 347SC; 92/93 - 78, 78GS, 429SC

Wilson, Ron (Ronald Lawrence)
Panini: 87/88 - 291

Wing, Johnny
World Wide Gum: 36/37 - 102

Winnes, Christopher (Chris)
Pro Set: 91/92 - 522E, 522F
Score: 91/92 - 351PNE, 351PNF
Upper Deck: 91/92 - 514E, 514F; 92/93 - 380

Wirtz, Arthur
Hall of Fame: 83 - 90, F16P; 87 - 90

Wirtz, Bill
Hall of Fame: 83 - 179, M15P; 87 - 179

Wiseman, Eddie
Bee Hive: 34/44 - 37, 258

Wiseman, Eddie (cont.)
O-Pee-Chee: 40/41 - 149

Wiste, Jim
Dad's Cookies: 70/71 - 144
Eddie Sargent: 70/71 - 223

Witt, Brendan
Donruss: 93/94 - 22JCC
Upper Deck: 93/94 - 544

Woit, Benny
Bee Hive: 45/63 - 218
Parkhurst: 51/52 - 58; 52/53 - 62; 53/54 - 45; 54/55 - 38; 93/94 - 40ML
Topps: 54/55 - 9

Wolanin, Craig
Bowman: 90/91 - 166; 91/92 - 138; 92/93 - 41
O-Pee-Chee: 90/91 - 40; 91/92 - 199
Panini: 87/88 - 77; 88/89 - 270; 91/92 - 264
Parkhurst: 91/92 - 369E, 369F
Pro Set: 90/91 - 519; 91/92 - P/C, 203E, 203F
Score: 90/91 - 167A, 167C; 91/92 - 74A, 74B, 74C, 217PNE, 217PNF; 92/93 - 21C, 21A, 107PNC, 107PNA; 93/94 - 406C, 406A
Topps: 90/91 - 40; 91/92 - 199, 4SC; 92/93 - 487, 487GS
Upper Deck: 91/92 - 486E, 486F

Wolfe, Bernie
O-Pee-Chee: 76/77 - 227; 77/78 - 138; 78/79 - 81
Topps: 76/77 - 227; 77/78 - 138; 78/79 - 81

Wood, Dody
Parkhurst: 93/94 - 186, 186EI
Upper Deck: 93/94 - 238

Wood, Randy
Bowman: 90/91 - 121; 91/92 - 227; 92/93 - 246
Fleer: 92/93 - 265; 93/94 - 35PP
Leaf: 93/94 - 226(II)
O-Pee-Chee: 88/89 - 140, 107SK, 22FS; 89/90 - 35; 90/91 - 97; 91/92 - 205; 93/94 - 119, 89SC, 89FD
Panini: 88/89 - 294; 90/91 - 79; 91/92 - 244; 92/93 - 251E, 251F; 93/94 - 105E, 105F
Parkhurst: 91/92 - 13E, 13F; 93/94 - 297, 297EI
Pro Set: 90/91 - 194; 91/92 - P/C, 151E, 359E, 151F, 359F, 160PT; 92/93 - 20
Score: 90/91 - 119A, 119C; 91 - 42T; 91/92 - 281A, 501B, 501C, 104PNE, 104PNF; 92/93 - 73C, 73A, 133PNC, 133PNA, 234PNC, 234PNA; 93/94 - 55C, 55A
Topps: 88/89 - 140; 89/90 - 35; 90/91 - 97; 91/92 - 205, 221SC; 92/93 - 170, 170GS, 206SC; 93/94 - 119(I), 89SC, 89FD
Upper Deck: 90/91 - 16E, 16F; 91/92 - 289E, 289F; 92/93 - 245; 93/94 - 22

Woodcroft, Craig
Fleer: 93/94 - 497PP
O-Pee-Chee: 93/94 - 5TC

Woods, Paul
O-Pee-Chee: 78/79 - 159; 79/80 - 48; 80/81 - 148; 81/82 - 104; 82/83 - 98, 187SK; 83/84 - 133; 84/85 - 66
Post: 82/83 - 80
Topps: 78/79 - 159; 79/80 - 48; 80/81 - 148; 82/83 - 187SK

Woolley, Jason
Donruss: 93/94 - 364
Leaf: 93/94 - 273(II)
O-Pee-Chee: 92/93 - 98PM
Parkhurst: 92/93 - 429, 429EI; 94/95 - 259, 259EI
Score: 92/93 - 7COH, 415PNC, 415PNA; 93/94 - 435C, 435A
Upper Deck: 92/93 - 422; 93/94 - 462

Worsley, Lorne (Gump) (Goalie)
Bee Hive: 45/63 - 295, 370; 64/67 - 119
Chex: 63/65 - 39
Coca-Cola: 65/66 - 74
Dad's Cookies: 70/71 - 72
Eddie Sargent: 70/71 - 84; 72/73 - 105
Esso: 70/71 - 126; 88/89 - 48
Hall of Fame: 83 - 180, M16P; 87 - 180
O-Pee-Chee: 68/69 - 56, 199, 6PS; 69/70 - 1, 9QS; 70/71 - 40; 71/72 - 241, 23PT; 72/73 - 28, 189; 73/74 - 230
Hockey Wit: 93/94 - 14
Parkhurst: 53/54 - 53; 63/64 - 39, 98; 92/93 - PR4; 93/94 - PR45, 92ML, 165ML
Post: 66/67 - L18, S9; 68/69 - 15
Shirriff: 61/62 - 85; 68/69 - F1
TCMA: 1981 - 2
Topps: 54/55 - 10; 57/58 - 53; 58/59 - 39; 59/60 - 15; 60/61 - 36, 16ST; 61/62 - 50, 65; 62/63 - 45, 24HB; 65/66 - 2; 66/67 - 2, 130; 66/67 US - 2; 67/68 - 1; 68/69 - 56; 69/70 - 1; 70/71 - 40; 72/73 - 55
Toronto Star: 57/67 - 62, 67; 58/67 - 59
Toronto Sun: 71/72 - 145
Ultimate: 92 - 17(OSE), 17(OSF)
York: 63/64 - 22
Zellers: 93/94 - 8, 8A

Worters, Roy (Goalie)
Amal. Press: 35/36 - 10
Bee Hive: 34/44 - 259
Canada Starch: 35/40 - 65
Diamond: 33/35 - 60; 36/39 - 70(I), 65(II), 60(III)
Hall of Fame: 83 - D16, 60C; 87 - 60C
O-Pee-Chee: 33/34 - 45
World Wide Gum: 33/34 - 11; 36/37 - 7

Woytowich, Bob
Bauer: 68/69 - 22
Coca-Cola: 65/66 - 18
Dad's Cookies: 70/71 - 113
Eddie Sargent: 70/71 - 163
Esso: 70/71 - 198
O-Pee-Chee: 68/69 - 49, 192; 69/70 - 151, 14QS; 70/71 - 88, 8DE, 33SS; 71/72 - 28; 72/73 - 325
Shirriff: 68/69 - E2
Topps: 65/66 - 100; 66/67 - 34; 68/69 - 49; 69/70 - 113; 70/71 - 88, 33SK; 71/72 - 28
Toronto Sun: 71/72 - 230

Wregget, Ken (Goalie)
Bowman: 91/92 - 231; 92/93 - 182
Fleer: 92/93 - 383; 93/94 - 417PP
Kraft: 86/87 - 61, 61P
O-Pee-Chee: 87/88 - 242, 164SK; 88/89 - 264, 177SK; 89/90 - 255; 90/91 - 415; 91/92 - 136; 93/94 - 277
Panini: 87/88 - 322; 88/89 - 117; 90/91 - 112; 91/92 - 236
Parkhurst: 91/92 - 357E, 357F; 92/93 - 371, 371EI
Pro Set: 90/91 - 226; 91/92 - 450E, 450F, 210PT
Score: 90/91 - 263A, 263C; 91/92 - 141A, 141B, 141C; 92/93 - 399C, 399A, 356PNC, 356PNA; 93/94 - 329C, 329A
Topps: 91/92 - 136, 8SC; 92/93 - 494, 494GS, 130SC; 93/94 - 277
Upper Deck: 90/91 - 89E, 89F; 91/92 - 206E, 206F

Wright, John
Loblaws: 74/75 - 126
O-Pee-Chee: 74/75 - 156
Topps: 74/75 - 156

Wright, Larry
Loblaws: 74/75 - 72
O-Pee-Chee: 78/79 - 360

Wright, Tyler
Fleer: 93/94 - 240, 10TP
Leaf: 93/94 - 347
O-Pee-Chee: 92/93 - 32PM
Parkhurst: 93/94 - 340, 340EI

Wright, Tyler (cont.)
Score: 93/94 - 463C, 463A
Upper Deck: 91/92 - 67E, 686E, 67F, 686F; 92/93 - 558; 93/94 - 256

Wycherly, Ralph
Bee Hive: 34/44 - 260

Wyrozub, Randy
Eddie Sargent: 70/71 - 31
O-Pee-Chee: 70/71 - 141

Yake, Terry
Bowman: 91/92 - 4
Donruss: 93/94 - 4
Fleer: 93/94 - 221, 14PP
Leaf: 93/94 - 406(II)
O-Pee-Chee: 91/92 - 169; 93/94 - 432
Panini: 93/94 - 125E, 125F
Parkhurst: 92/93 - 293, 293EI; 93/94 - 271, 271EI; 94/95 - V10
Score: 90/91 - 419A, 419C; 93/94 - 259C, 259A
Sega: 93/94 - 3
Topps: 91/92 - 169, 374SC; 92/93 - 432, 432GS, 496SC; 93/94 - 432(II), 490SC, 490FD
Upper Deck: 91/92 - 323E, 323F; 92/93 - 512; 93/94 - 311

Yakovenko, Andrei
O-Pee-Chee: 91/92 - 63R

Yakubov, Ravil
O-Pee-Chee: 91/92 - 46R
Upper Deck: 92/93 - 349

Yashin, Alexei
Donruss: 93/94 - 238, 7RR, U5
Fleer: 93/94 - 16RS, 10GG, 403PP
Leaf: 93/94 - 386(II), 9FP
O-Pee-Chee: 93/94 - 317
Parkhurst: 93/94 - 254, 254EI, E7, CC10; 94/95 - 273, 273NI, H16, R16, C16
Topps: 93/94 - 317(II), 359SC, 359FD
Upper Deck: 91/92 - 651E, 651F; 92/93 - 334; 93/94 - 277, 349

Yashin, Oleg
O-Pee-Chee: 91/92 - 64R

Yashin, Sergei
O-Pee-Chee: 90/91 - 482

Yawney, Trent
Bowman: 91/92 - 393
O-Pee-Chee: 89/90 - 222; 90/91 - 297; 91/92 - 255
Panini: 89/90 - 53; 90/91 - 187
Parkhurst: 91/92 - 245E, 245F; 92/93 - 262, 262EI
Pro Set: 90/91 64
Score: 90/91 - 292A, 292C; 91/92 - 439B, 439C; 92/93 - 216C, 216A, 174PNC, 174PNA; 93/94 - 332C, 332A
Topps: 90/91 - 297; 91/92 - 255, 205SC; 93/94 - 472SC, 472FD
Upper Deck: 90/91 - 82E, 82F

Ylonen, Juha
Upper Deck: 91/92 - 673E, 673F

Young, C.J.
Fleer: 93/94 - 248
O-Pee-Chee: 93/94 - 347
Parkhurst: 92/93 - 246, 246EI
Topps: 93/94 - 347(II), 316SC, 316FD
Upper Deck: 92/93 - 395

Young, Douglas
Bee Hive: 34/44 - 132, 188
Canada Starch: 35/40 - 200
O-Pee-Chee: 39/40 - 58
World Wide Gum: 36/37 - 49

Young, Howie
Bee Hive: 45/63 - 147, 219
O-Pee-Chee: 68/69 - 82, 151
Shirriff: 61/62 - 74; 68/69 - H12
Topps: 63/64 - 29; 67/68 - 49; 68/69 - 82
York: 62/63 - 35

Young, Scott
Bowman: 90/91 - 253; 91/92 - 86

Young, Scott (cont.)
  Donruss: 93/94 - 284
  Fleer: 92/93 - 391; 93/94 - 206PP
  Leaf: 93/94 - 108
  O-Pee-Chee: 89/90 - 209, 44SK, 264SK, 7FS; 90/91 - 84; 91/92 - 235
  Panini: 89/90 - 224; 90/91 - 34; 91/92 - 273; 93/94 - 73E, 73F
  Parkhurst: 92/93 - 383, 383EI
  Pro Set: 90/91 - 113; 91/92 - 195E, 195F
  Score: 90 - 14YS; 90/91 - 21A, 21C, 12HR; 91/92 - 287A, 507B, 507C; 93/94 - 56C, 56A
  Topps: 90/91 - 84; 91/92 - 235, 74SC; 93/94 - 261SC, 261FD
  Upper Deck: 90/91 - 87E, 87F; 92/93 - 397

Young, Tim
  O-Pee-Chee: 76/77 - 158; 77/78 - 223, 22GP; 78/79 - 138; 79/80 - 36; 80/81 - 174; 81/82 - 169, 94SK; 82/83 - 177; 83/84 - 395; 84/85 - 351
  Post: 82/83 - 144
  Topps: 76/77 - 158; 77/78 - 223, 22PO; 78/79 - 138; 79/80 - 36; 80/81 - 174; 81/82 WN - 113
  Vachon Foods: 83/84 - 140

Young, Warren
  O-Pee-Chee: 85/86 - 152, 100SK; 86/87 - 209
  Topps: 85/86 - 152

Young, Wendell (Goalie)
  Bowman: 90/91 - 203
  Fleer: 92/93 - 206
  O-Pee-Chee: 90/91 - 309; 92/93 - 76PM; 93/94 - 166
  Panini: 90/91 - 127; 93/94 - 221E, 221F
  Pro Set: 90/91 - 512
  Parkhurst: 92/93 - 170, 170EI
  Score: 90/91 - 298A, 298C; 92/93 - 511C, 511A, 381PNC, 381PNA; 93/94 - 341C, 341A
  Sega: 93/94 - 132
  Topps: 90/91 - 309; 93/94 - 166(I)
  Upper Deck: 90/91 - 102E, 102F

Younghans, Tom
  O-Pee-Chee: 78/79 - 295; 79/80 - 177; 80/81 - 343; 81/82 - 173
  Topps: 79/80 - 177

Ysebaert, Paul
  Bowman: 91/92 - 53; 92/93 - 376
  Donruss: 93/94 - 376, 417
  Fleer: 92/93 - 54; 93/94 - 277PP
  Kraft: 91/92 - 46
  Leaf: 93/94 - 388(II)
  O-Pee-Chee: 90/91 - 49; 91/92 - 248; 92/93 - 46
  Panini: 92/93 - 118E, 118F; 93/94 - 248E, 248F
  Parkhurst: 91/92 - 42E, 42F, 435; 92/93 - PV1, 43, 43EI; 93/94 - 504, 504EI; 94/95 - 48, 48EI
  Pro Set: 90/91 - 607; 91/92 - 59E, 608E, 59F, 608F, 167PT; 92/93 - 41, 248
  Score: 90/91 - 406, 406C; 91/92 - 166A, 166B, 166C, 36PNE, 36PNF; 92/93 - 95A, 95A, 414C, 414A, 93PNC, 93PNA; 93/94 - 239C, 239A
  Topps: 90/91 - 49; 91/92 - 248, 171SC; 92/93 - 58, 314, 58GS, 314GS, 378SC; 93/94 - 360SC, 360FD
  Upper Deck: 90/91 - 375E, 375F; 91/92 - 278E, 278F; 92/93 -176; 93/94 - 365

Yudin, Alexander
  O-Pee-Chee: 91/92 - 47R
  Upper Deck: 92/93 - 336

Yurzinov, Vladimir
  O-Pee-Chee: 90/91 - 494

Yushkevich, Dimitri
  Donruss: 93/94 - 254
  Fleer: 92/93 - 161; 93/94 - 198, 186PP
  Leaf: 93/94 - 82
  O-Pee-Chee: 92/93 - 65PM; 93/94 - 18
  Parkhurst: 92/93 - 133, 133EI; 93/94 - 145, 145EI; 94/95 - 163, 163EI

Yushkevich, Dimitri (cont.)
  Score: 92/93 - 394PNC, 394PNA; 93/94 - 216C, 216A
  Sega: 93/94 - 98
  Topps: 93/94 - 18(I), 492SC, 492FD
  Upper Deck: 92/93 - 350, 570, ER12, CC20; 93/94 - 127

Yzerman, Steve
  Action Packed: 89/90 - 3
  Bowman: 90/91 - 233, HT5; 91/92 - P/C, 41, 42; 92/93 - 103, 220
  Donruss: 93/94 - 95, G/PM, G/SP
  Fleer: 92/93 - 55; 93/94 - 201, 10G, 12AS, 77PP, 20PL, 10PM, 6SC
  Frito-Lay: 88/89 - 42
  Hockey Wit: 93/94 - 108
  Humpty Dumpty: 92/93 - 24(I)
  Kellogg's: 92 - 14
  Kraft: 1990 - 63; 90/91 - 63, 78; 93 - 18; 93/94 - 52
  Leaf: 93/94 - 162, 5SS, 10HT
  McDonald's: 91/92 - Mc19
  O-Pee-Chee: 84/85 - 67, 385, 37SK; 85/86 - 29, 30SK; 86/87 - 11, 161SK; 87/88 - 56, C/BB, 111SK; 88/89 - 196, L/BB, 253SK; 89/90 - 83, L/BB, 254SK; 90/91 - 222, J/BB, 130PM; 91/92 - 424, 73PM, 142PM; 92/93 - 61, 321, 17AN; 93/94 - 280, 70SC, 70FD
  Panini: 87/88 - 243; 88/89 - 47; 89/90 - 57; 90/91 - 208; 91/92 - 134; 92/93 - 112E, 112F; 93/94 - V(E), V(F)
  Parkhurst: 91/92 - 44E, 434E, 44F, 434F; 92/93 - 44, 456, 44EI, 456EI; 93/94 - 326, 326EI, W5; 94/95 - 299, 299EI, V57
  Pro Set: 90/91 - 79, 347; 91/92 - 62E, 281E, 571E, 62F, 281F, 32PT, 8PK, 571F; 92/93 - 39, 247, 3TL, PV1
  Roots: 93/94 - 4
  Score: 90/91 - 3A, 3C, 339A, 339C, 4HR; 91 - 7PC; 91/92 - 190A, 419A, 190B, 335B, 190C, 335C, 75PNE, 75PNF; 92/93 - 400C, 400A, 423C, 423A, 258PNC, 258PNA, 350PNC, 350PNA; 93/94- 310C, 310A, 448C, 448A, 36PNC, 36PNA, 16DT, 36CAS, 38AAS, 6FR
  Season's: 92/93 - 6
  Sega: 93/94 - 39
  7-Eleven: 84/85 - 12
  Topps: 84/85 - 49; 85/86 - 29; 86/87 - 11; 87/88 - 56, C/BB; 88/89 - 196, L/BB; 89/90 - 83, L/BB; 90/91 - 222, J/BB, 19SL; 91/92 - 424, 3SL, 81SC; 92/93 - 107, 207GS, 19SC, 254SC; 93/94 - 280, 16BG, 70SC, 70FD, 16AS
  Upper Deck: 90/91 - S/G, 56E, 56F, 477E, 477F; 91/92 - BBE, BBF, 146E, 626E, 146F, 626F; 92/93 - 155. WJG7, G10, 36AS; 93/94 - 227, 290, 388

Zaine, Rod
  Toronto Sun: 71/72 - 41

Zaitsev, Sergei
  O-Pee-Chee: 90/91 - 487

Zalapski, Zarley
  Bowman: 90/91 - 207; 91/92 - 15; 92/93 - 173
  Donruss: 93/94 - 149, 410
  Fleer: 92/93 - 77; 93/94 - 234, 112PP
  Humpty Dumpty: 92/93 - 25(I)
  Leaf: 93/94 - 8
  O-Pee-Chee: 89/90 - 168, 45SK, 232SK, 14FS; 90/91 - 78; 91/92 - 344; 92/93 - 248; 93/94 - 20, 102SC, 102FD
  Panini: 89/90 - 318; 90/91 - 126; 91/92 - 322; 92/93 - 263E, 263F; 93/94 - 129E, 129F
  Parkhurst: 91/92 - 61E, 61F; 92/93 - 59, 59EI; 93/94 - 88, 88EI; 94/95 - 31, 31EI
  Pro Set: 90/91 - 242; 91/92 - 91E, 91F, 47PT; 92/93 - 59

Zalapski, Zarley (cont.)
  Score: 90/91 - 218A, 218C; 91/92 - 111A, 111B, 111C, 110PNE, 110PNF; 92/93 - 238C, 238A, 271PNC, 271PNA; 93/94 - 104C, 104A, 2PNC, 2PNA, 2CAS. 2AAS
  Sega: 93/94 - 55
  Topps: 89/90 - 168; 90/91 - 78; 91/92 - 344, 228SC; 92/93 - 82, 82GS, 25SC; 93/94 - 20(I), 102SC, 102FD, 18AS
  Upper Deck: 90/91 - 33E, 33F; 91/92 - 231E, 231F; 92/93 - 316, 18AS; 93/94 - 213

Zamuner, Rob
  Donruss: 93/94 - 329
  Fleer: 92/93 - 415; 93/94 - 199, 236PP
  Leaf: 93/94 - 173
  O-Pee-Chee: 92/93 - 69PM; 93/94 - 19
  Panini: 93/94 - 214E, 214F
  Parkhurst: 92/93 - 171, 171EI; 93/94 - 194, 194EI; 94/95 - 224, 224EI
  Score: 92/93 - 414PNC, 414PNA; 93/94 - 291C, 291A
  Topps: 92/93 - 426, 426GS, 439SC; 93/94 - 19, 376SC, 376FD
  Upper Deck: 92/93 - 583, CC4; 93/94 - 202

Zanussi, Joe
  O-Pee-Chee: 76/77 - 324

Zanussi, Ron
  O-Pee-Chee: 78/79 - 252; 79/80 - 22; 80/81 - 192; 81/82 - 325
  Topps: 78/79 - 252; 79/80 - 22; 80/81 - 192;

Zavarukhin, Nikolai
  Parkhurst: 93/94 - 530, 530EI

Zeidel, Larry
  Bee Hive: 45/63 - 148, 220
  O-Pee-Chee: 68/69 - 92
  Parkhurst: 52/53 - 91; 53/54 - 73
  Topps: 68/69 - 92

Zelepukin, Valeri
  Bowman: 92/93 - 430
  Donruss: 93/94 - 193
  Fleer: 92/93 - 122; 93/94 - 222, 145PP
  Kraft: 93/94 - 23
  Leaf: 93/94 - 104
  O-Pee-Chee: 91/92 - 65R
  Panini: 92/93 - 177E, 177F; 93/94 - 38E, 38F
  Parkhurst: 91/92 - 324E, 324F; 92/93 - 228, 228EI, 327, 327EI; 93/94 - 383, 383EI; 94/95 - 124, 124EI
  Pro-Set: 91/92 - 261PT; 92/93 - 10RGL
  Score: 91/92 - 354PNE, 354PNF; 92/93 - 206C, 206A, 286PNC, 28PNA; 93/94 - 278C, 278A
  Topps: 92/93 - 462, 462GS, 99SC; 93/94 - 314SC, 314FD
  Upper Deck: 91/92 - 589E, 589F; 92/93 - 295, E12; 93/94 - 369

Zettler, Rob
  Bowman: 92/93 - 84
  O-Pee-Chee: 90/91 - 289; 91/92 - 272, 21PM; 92/93 - 366
  Panini: 92/93 - 127E, 127F
  Pro Set: 91/92 - 330E, 330F
  Score: 91 - 93T; 91/92 - 370A, 643B, 643C, 213PNE, 213PNF; 92/93 - 191C, 191A, 89PNC, 89PNA; 93/94 - 413C, 413A
  Topps: 90/91 - 289; 91/92 - 272, 194SC; 92/93 - 227, 227GS, 225SC
  Upper Deck: 91/92 - 61E, 61F

Zezel, Peter
  Bowman: 90/91 - 19; 91/92 - 164; 92/93 - 263
  Donruss: 93/94 - 338
  Leaf: 92/93 - 216; 93/94 - 107
  O-Pee-Chee: 85/86 - 24, 94SK; 86/87 - 190, 245SK; 87/88 - 71, 96SK; 88/89 - 146, 102SK; 89/90 - 27, 23SK; 90/91 - 15, 131PM; 91/92 - 445; 92/93 - 337; 93/94 - 454, 116SC, 116FD

Zezel, Peter (cont.)
    Panini: 87/88 - 129; 89/90 - 118; 90/91 - 264; 91/92 - 103; 92/93 - 81E, 81F
    Parkhurst: 91/92 - 174E, 174F; 92/93 - 410, 410E; 93/94 - 206, 206EI
    Pro Set: 90/91 - 274, 556; 91/92 - 227E, 227F, 232PT; 92/93 - 187
    Score: 90 - 6T; 90/91 - 24A, 24C; 91/92 - 269A, 489B, 489C, 174PNE, 414PNE, 174PNF, 414PNF; 92/93 - 174C, 174A, 283PNC, 283PNA; 93/94 - 31C, 31A
    Topps: 85/86 - 24; 86/87 - 190; 87/88 - 71 88/89 - 146; 89/90 - 27; 90/91 - 15; 91/92 - 445, 104SC; 92/93 - 319, 319GS, 433SC; 93/94 - 454(II), 116SC, 116FD
    Upper Deck: 90/91 - 17E, 17F; 91/92 - 241E, 241F; 92/93 - 389; 93/94 - 199

Zhamnov, Alexei
    Donruss: 93/94 - 380
    Fleer: 92/93 - 447; 93/94 - 128, 9RS, 278PP, 12SY
    Leaf: 93/94 - 84, 5R
    O-Pee-Chee: 91/92 - 48R; 92/93 - 13PM; 93/94 - 128, 420, 56SC, 56FD
    Panini: 93/94 - 190E, 190F
    Parkhurst: 92/93 - 210, 210EI; 93/94 - 243, 503, 243EI, 503EI; 94/95 - 260, 260EI
    Score: 92/93 - 416PNC, 416PNA; 93/94 - 256C, 256A
    Sega: 93/94 - 147
    Topps: 93/94 - 128(I), 420(II), 8BG, 56SC, 56FD
    Upper Deck: 91/92 - 2E, 2F; 92/93 - 578, ER8, 60AS; 93/94 - 162

Zhitnik, Alexei
    Donruss: 93/94 - 165
    Fleer: 92/93 - 314; 93/94 - 87, 123PP
    Leaf: 93/94 - 123, 8R
    O-Pee-Chee: 92/93 - 125PM; 93/94 - 2, 221SC, 221FD
    Parkhurst: 92/93 - 71, 71EI; 93/94 - 92, 93EI; 94/95 - 101, 101EI
    Score: 92/93 - 392PNC, 392PNA; 93/94 - 148C, 148A
    Topps: 93/94 - 2(I), 221SC, 221FD
    Upper Deck: 91/92 - 660E, 660F; 92/93 - 566, ER13, CC7; 93/94 - 161

Zholtok, Sergei
    Fleer: 93/94 - 294PP
    Leaf: 93/94 - 376(II)
    Parkhurst: 92/93 - 482, 284EI; 93/94 - 281, 281EI
    Score: 93/94 - 475C, 475A
    Upper Deck: 91/92 - 659E, 659F; 93/94 - 244

Ziegler, John
    Hall of Fame: 87 - 257C

Ziesche, Steffan
    Upper Deck: 91/92 - 679E, 679F

Zinovjev, Dimitri
    O-Pee-Chee: 90/91 - 478

Zmolek, Doug
    Donruss: 93/94 - 313
    Fleer: 92/93 - 405
    Leaf: 93/94 - 112
    O-Pee-Chee: 91/92 - 9S; 92/93 - 18PM; 93/94 - 143, 171SC, 171FD
    Panini: 93/94 - 263E, 263F
    Parkhurst: 92/93 - 393, 393EI; 92/93 - 4457, 457EI
    Score: 93/94 - 327C, 327A
    Topps: 93/94 - 143(I), 171SC, 171FD
    Upper Deck: 92/93 - 509; 93/94 - 193

Znarok, Oleg
    O-Pee-Chee: 90/91 - 477

Zombo, Richard (Rick)
    Bowman: 91/92 - 54; 92/93 - 87
    O-Pee-Chee: 90/91 - 21; 91/92 - 454; 92/93 - 97
    Panini: 89/90 - 64; 90/91 - 206; 91/92 - 137

Zombo, Richard (Rick) (cont.)
    Parkhurst: 91/92 - 380E, 380F
    Pro Set: 90/91 - 80; 91/92 - 64E, 474E, 64F, 474F
    Score: 90/91 - 101A, 101C, 49HR; 91 - 60T; 91/92 - 177A, 177B, 177C, 259PNE, 393PNE, 410PNE, 259PNF, 393PNF, 410PNF; 92/93 - 154C, 154A, 129PNC, 129PNA; 93/94 - 211C, 211A
    Topps: 90/91 - 21; 91/92 - 454, 32SC; 92/93 - 288, 288GS, 100SC
    Upper Deck: 90/91 - 115E, 115F; 91/92 - 395E, 395F

Zubov, Sergei
    Donruss: 93/94 - 225
    Fleer: 92/93 - 359; 93/94 - 243, 10RS, 167PP
    Leaf: 93/94 - 164
    O-Pee-Chee: 91/92 - 28R; 93/94 - 217
    Parkhurst: 92/93 - 351, 351EI; 93/94 - 133, 133EI; 94/95 - 144, 144EI
    Score: 93/94 - 313C, 313A
    Topps: 93/94 - 217(I), 312SC, 312FD
    Upper Deck: 92/93 - 516; 93/94 - 181

Zuke, Mike
    O-Pee-Chee: 80/81 - 209; 81/82 - 299, 132SK; 82/83 - 313; 83/84 - 322; 84/85 - 80, 195SK; 85/86 - 19
    Post: 82/83 - 272
    Topps: 80/81 - 209; 81/82 WN - 124; 84/85 - 63, 195SK; 85/86 - 19

CHAPTER FIVE
NATIONAL HOCKEY LEAGUE
TEAM SETS

ALPHABETICAL LISTING OF MANUFACTURERS
NATIONAL HOCKEY LEAGUE TEAM SETS

Action Magazine Edmonton Oilers	597
Anonymous Winnipeg Jets	651
Atlanta Flames Team Sets	579
Baybank Boston Bruins	581
Bells Market Buffalo Sabres	582
Black's Photography Toronto Maple Leafs	640
Blue Shield Buffalo Sabres	583
Boston Bruins Team Sets	580
Buffalo Sabres Team Sets	582
Calgary Flames Team Sets	588
Campbell's Buffalo Sabres	586
Card Night Los Angeles Kings	603
Carretta Trucking New Jersey Devils	617
Chicago Black Hawks Team Sets	590
Clark Buns Pittsburgh Penguins	626
Cloverleaf Dairy Minnesota North Stars	606
Coca-Cola	
Atlanta Flames	579
Chicago Black Hawks	590
Hartford Whalers	602
Los Angeles Kings	604
Pittsburgh Penguins	624
Colorado Rockies Team Sets	592
Courant Hartford Whalers	602
Dairymart Hartford Whalers	602
Detroit Red Wings Team Sets	593
Edmonton Oilers Team Sets	596
Elby's \ Big Boy Pittsburgh Penguins	625
Elby's \ Coca-Cola PittsburghPenguins	625
Esso Hockey Talks Toronto Maple Leafs	639
Foodland Pittsburgh Penguins	625
Generdal Foods Quebec Nordiques	629
Ground Round Junior Whalers	601
Hartford Whalers Team Sets	601
Heinz Pittsburgh Penguins	624
Tim Horton Toronto Maple Leafs	639
I.G.A.	
Calgary Flames	589
Edmonton Oilers	600
Montreal Canadiens	612
Winnipeg Jets	653
Islander News New York Islanders	618
Jubilee Foods Buffalo Sabres	586
Kodak	
Pittsburgh Penguins	624
St. Louis Blues	630
Toronto Maple Leafs	640
Washington Capitals	648
La Patrie Montreal Canadiens	612
Little Caesars Pizza Detroit Red Wings	595
Los Angeles Kings Team Sets	603
Linnett Buffalo Sabres	582
Marathon Detroit Red Wings	595
Marine Midland New York Rangers	620
McDonald's Restaurants	
Detroit Red Wings Hockey Heroes Gordie Howe	595
Edmonton Oilers	599
Pittsburgh Penguins	624
McDonald's \ Upper Deck St. Louis Blues	631
Mohawk Vancouver Canucks	645
Montreal Canadiens Team Sets	608
Mighty Milk Philadelphia Flyers	623
Minnesota North Stars Team Sets	605
Molson	
Montreal Canadiens	612
Vancouver Canucks	645
Nalley's Box Vancouver Canucks	644

Neilson's Edmonton Oilers	599
New Jersey Devils Team Sets	616
New York Islanders Team Set	618
New York Rangers Team Sets	620
Noco Express Shop	587
Northwest Airlines Los Angeles Kings	604
O'Keefe Beverages Toronto Maple Leafs	638
O-Pee-Chee Montreal Canadiens	615
Ottawa Senators Team Sets	621
J. C. Penny Stores Philadelphia Flyers	623
Philadelphia Flyers Team Sets	622
Pittsburgh Penguins Team Set	624
Pizza Hut Washington Capitals	648
Playing Cards	612
Police	
New Jersey Devils	617
Toronto Maple Leafs	639
Vancouver Canucks	644
Washington Capitals	649
Winnipeg Jets	652
Pro Star Promotions Montreal Canadiens	613
Provigo	
Montreal Canadiens	614
Quebec Nordiques	629
Quebec Nordiques Team Sets	627
RC Cola Los Angeles Kings	
Real Milk Hartford Whalers	601
Red Rooster	
Calgary Flames	588
Edmonton Oilers	597
Royal Bank Vancouver Canucks	642
Ruffles Winnipeg Jets	653
Safeway Winnipeg Jets	653
Score Pinnacle Philadelphia Flyers	623
St. Louis Blues Team Sets	630
San Jose Sharks Team Set	632
7-Eleven	
Hartford Whalers	601
Minnesota North Stars	606
Shell Oil Vancouver Canucks	645
Silverwood Dairies	
Vancouver Canucks	644
Winnipeg Jets	653
Smokey	
Los Angeles Kings	603
Washington Capitals	649
Sports Action Boston Bruins	580
Stater Mint Ltd.	
Calgary Flames	588
Edmonton Oilers	600
Winnipeg Jets	651
Steinberg Montreal Canadiens	614
Tampa Bay Lightning Team Sets	634
Target Los Angeles Kings	604
Thomas Hartford Whalers	602
Toronto Maple Leafs Team Sets	635
Upper Deck Los Angeles Kings	604
Vachon Montreal Canadiens	614
Vancouver Canucks Team Sets	641
Vancouver Millionairs Team Sets	646
Washington Capitals Team Sets	647
Wendy's Hartford Whalers	602
Wendz Buffalo Sabres	582
Winnipeg Jets Team Sets	650
Wonder Bread \ Hostess Cakes Buffalo Sabres	585
Yum-Yum Quebec Nordiques	629

A NOTE ON TEAM SET LISTINGS

In this publication there are two types of Team Sets, "Team Issues" and "Miscellaneous Issues". The term "Team Issues" designates items produced specifically for and under the auspices of the NHL team in question. These products can include regular card issues, postcard issues, posters, buttons, pins, as well as various other products.

The term "Miscellaneous Items" designates items produced, printed or manufactured by companies or interests other than the team itself. These products can include all of the items mentioned above issued with the authorization of the team and/or the National Hockey League. "Team Issues" are listed first and are then followed by all "Miscellaneous" items.

ATLANTA FLAMES - TEAM SETS

COCA-COLA

— 1978 - 79 POSTCARD ISSUE —

Postcard Size: 3 1/2" x 5 1/2"
Face: Four colour, borderless; Facsimile autograph
Back: Black on white postcard stock; Name,
Imprint: None
Complete Set No.: 20
Complete Set Price: 15.00 30.00
Common Player: .50 1.00

No.	Player	EX	NRMT
1	Dan Bouchard, Goalie	1.50	3.00
2	Guy Chouinard	.75	1.50
3	Bill Clement	.75	1.50
4	Greg Fox	.75	1.50
5	Ken Houston	.50	1.00
6	Ed Kea	.50	1.00
7	Bobby Lalonde	.50	1.00
8	Red Laurence	.50	1.00
9	Rejean Lemelin, Goalie	1.50	3.00
10	Tom Lysiak	1.50	3.00
11	Bob MacMillan	.50	1.00
12	Brad Marsh	1.00	2.00
13	Bob Murdoch	.50	1.00
14	Harold Phillippof	.50	1.00
15	Willi Plett	.75	1.50
16	Jean Pronovost	.75	1.50
17	Pat Ribble	.50	1.00
18	Rod Seiling	.50	1.00
19	Dave Shand	.50	1.00
20	Eric Vail	1.00	2.00

— 1979 - 80 ISSUE —

Card Size: 3 7/16" X 5 1/2"
Face: Four colour, borderless; Facsimile autograph
Back: Black on white card stock, Name, Jersey number, Position, Resume
Imprint: The Atlanta Coca Cola Bottling Company
Complete Set No.: 20
Complete Set Price: 12.50 25.00
Common Card: .25 .50

No.	Player	EX	NRMT
1	Curt Bennett	.25	.50
2	Dan Bouchard, Goalie	1.00	2.00
3	Guy Chouinard	.50	1.00
4	Bill Clement	.50	1.00
5	Jim Craig, Goalie	.25	.50
6	Ken Houston	.25	.50
7	Don Lever	.25	.50
8	Bob MacMillan	.25	.50
9	Brad Marsh	1.00	2.00
10	Bob Murdoch	.25	.50
11	Kent Nilsson	1.00	2.00
12	Willi Plett	1.00	2.00
13	Jean Pronovost	.50	1.00
14	Pekka Rautakallio	.25	.50
15	Paul Reinhardt	.25	.50
16	Pat Riggin, Goalie	.25	.50
17	Phil Russell	.25	.50
18	David Shand	.25	.50
19	Garry Unger	1.00	2.00
20	Eric Vail	1.00	2.00

BOSTON BRUINS - TEAM SETS

TEAM ISSUES

STANLEY CUP CHAMPIONS - 1970

— 1970 - 71 ISSUE —

Cards are unnumbered and are listed below in alphabetical order by issue. They were issued in two different nine card sets.

Card Size: 6" X 8"
Face: Four colour; Name, Team
Back: Blank
Imprint: None
Complete Set No.: 18
Complete Set Price: 25.00 50.00
Common Card: 1.00 2.00

No.	Player	EX	NRMT
1	Garnet Bailey	1.00	2.00
2	John Bucyk	2.00	4.00
3	Gary Doak	1.00	2.00
4	Phil Esposito	4.00	8.00
5	Ed Johnston, Goalie	1.00	2.00
6	Don Marcotte	1.50	3.00
7	Derek Sanderson	2.50	5.00
8	Dallas Smith	1.50	3.00
9	Ed Westfall	1.50	3.00
10	Don Awrey	1.00	2.00
11	Wayne Carleton	1.00	2.00
12	Wayne Cashman	1.50	3.00
13	Gerry Cheevers, Goalie	1.50	3.00
14	Ken Hodge	1.00	2.00
15	John McKenzie	2.50	5.00
16	Bobby Orr	7.50	15.00
17	Rick Smith	1.00	2.00
18	Fred Stanfield	1.00	2.00

— 1984 - 85 POSTCARD ISSUE —

Card Size: 3 5/8" x 5 5/8"
Face: Four colour; Number
Back: Black on white card stock; Name, Number
Imprint: None
Complete Set No.: 20
Complete Set Price: Unknown
Common Card: .35 .75

No.	Player	EX	NRMT
1	Pete Peeters, Goalie	.75	1.50
2	Louis Sleigher	.35	.75
3	Raymond Bourque	1.50	3.00
4	Mike Milbury	.50	1.00
5	Keith Crowder	.50	1.00
6	Stephen Kasper	.50	1.00
7	Mats Thelin	.35	.75
8	Ken Linseman	.50	1.00
9	Terry O'Reilly	.50	1.00
10	Barry Pederson	.35	.75
11	Nevin Markwart	.35	.75
12	Mike O'Connell	.35	.75
13	Geoff Courtnall	.35	.75
14	Doug Keans	1.00	2.00
15	Charlie Simmers	.35	.75
16	Rick Middleton	.50	1.00
17	Tom Fergus	.35	.75
18	Mike Gillis	.35	.75
19	Gordon Kluzak	.75	1.50
20	Lindon Byers	.50	1.00

— 1988 - 89 SPORTS ACTION ISSUE —

Cards are unnumbered and are listed below in alphabetical order.

1988-89 Regular Issue,
Card No. 4, Keith Crowder

Card Size: 2 1/2" X 3 1/2"
Face: Four colour; Name, Jersey number; Team logo
Back: Black on white card stock; Name, Position, Resume
Imprint: None
Complete Set No.: 24
Complete Set Price: 7.50 15.00
Common Card: .25 .50

No.	Player	EX	NRMT
1	Raymond Bourque	1.50	3.00
2	Randy Burridge	.25	.50
3	Lyndon Byers	.25	.50
4	Keith Crowder	.25	.50
5	Craig Janney	1.00	2.00
6	Robert Joyce	.25	.50
7	Stephen Kasper	.25	.50
8	Gordie Kluzak	.25	.50
9	Reed Larson	.25	.50
10	Rejean Lemelin, Goalie	.35	.75
11	Ken Linseman	.25	.50
12	Tom McCarthy	.25	.50
13	Rick Middleton	.25	.50
14	Jay Miller	.25	.50
15	Andrew Moog, Goalie	.75	1.50
16	Cam Neely	1.00	2.00
17	Terry O'Reilly, Coach	.25	.50
18	Allen Pederson	.25	.50
19	Willi Plett	.25	.50
20	Robert Sweeney	.25	.50
21	Michael Thelven	.25	.50
22	Glen Wesley	.25	.50
23	Robert Joyce; Craig Janney	.50	1.00
24	Dynamic Duo: Raymond Bourque; Cam Neely	1.00	2.00
—	24 Card Team Sheet	10.00	20.00

— 1989 - 90 SPORTS ACTION ISSUE —

1989-90 Regular Issue
Card No. 1, Raymond Bourque

Cards are unnumbered and are listed below in alphabetical order.

Card Size: 2 1/2" X 3 1/2"
Face: Four colour, borderless; Team logo
Back: Black on white card stock; Name, Position, Jersey number, Resume
Imprint: None
Complete Set No.: 26
Complete Set Price: 6.00 12.00
Common Card: .25 .50

No.	Player	EX	NRMT
1	Raymond Bourque	1.00	2.00
2	Andy Brickley	.25	.50
3	Randy Burridge	.25	.50
4	Lyndon Byers	.25	.50
5	Robert Carpenter	.25	.50
6	John Carter	.25	.50
7	David Christian	.25	.50
8	Robert Cimetta	.25	.50
9	Garry Galley	.25	.50
10	Bob Gould	.25	.50
11	Greg Hawgood	.25	.50
12	Craig Janney	.50	1.00
13	Bobby Joyce	.25	.50
14	Rejean Lemelin, Goalie	.25	.50
15	Ken Linseman	.25	.50
16	Andrew Moog, Goalie	.50	1.00
17	Nevin Markwart	.25	.50
18	Cam Neely	1.00	2.00
19	Allen Pedersen	.25	.50
20	David Poulin	.25	.50
21	Stephane Quintal	.35	.75
22	Robert Sweeney	.25	.50
23	Michael Thelven	.25	.50
24	Glen Wesley	.25	.50
25	Bruins All-Time Top 10 Scorers	.50	1.00
26	Stanly Cup Championship Teams	.25	.50

— 1989 - 90 SPORTS ACTION UPDATE —

Cards are unnumbered and are listed below in alphabetical order.

1989-90 Update
Card No. 1, Raymond Bourque

Card Size: 2 1/2" X 3 1/2"
Face: Four colour, borderless; Team logo
Back: Black on white card stock; Name, Position, Jersey number, Resume
Imprint: None
Complete Set No.: 12
Complete Set Price: 4.00 8.00
Common Card: .25 .50

No.	Player	EX	NRMT
1	Raymond Bourque	1.00	2.00
2	David Christian	.25	.50
3	Peter Douris	.25	.50
4	Gordon Kluzak	.25	.50
5	Brian Lawton	.25	.50
6	Mike Millar	.25	.50
7	David Poulin	.50	1.00
8	Brian Propp	.35	.75

BOSTON BRUINS - TEAM SETS • 581

No.	Player	EX	NRMT
9	Don Sweeney	.25	.50
10	Graeme Townshend	.25	.50
11	Jim Weimer	.35	.75
12	Bruins Leaders: R. Bourque; R. Lemelin, Goalie; C. Neely	.75	1.50

— 1990 - 91 SPORTS ACTION ISSUE —

Cards are unnumbered and are listed below in alphabetical order.

1990-91 Regular Issue
Card No. 2, Raymond Bourque

Card Size: 2 1/2" X 3 1/2"
Face: Four colour, borderless
Back: Black and white photo, black on white card stock; Name, Position, Resume
Imprint: ©1990 Sports Action
Complete Set No.: 24
Complete Set Price: 7.50 15.00
Common Card: .25 .50

No.	Player	EX	NRMT
1	Bob Beers	.25	.50
2	Raymond Bourque	1.00	2.00
3	Andy Brickley	.25	.50
4	Randy Burridge	.25	.50
5	John Byce	.25	.50
6	Lyndon Byers	.25	.50
7	Robert Carpenter	.25	.50
8	John Carter	.25	.50
9	David Christian	.25	.50
10	Peter Douris	.25	.50
11	Garry Galley	.25	.50
12	Kenneth Hodge, Jr.	.50	1.00
13	Craig Janney	.50	1.00
14	Rejean Lemelin, Goalie	.25	.50
15	Andrew Moog, Goalie	.35	.75
16	Cam Neely	.50	1.00
17	Christopher Nilan	.25	.50
18	Allen Pedersen	.25	.50
19	David Poulin	.35	.75
20	Robert Sweeney	.25	.50
21	Don Sweeney	.25	.50
22	Wes Walz	.25	.50
23	Glen Wesley	.25	.50
24	William M. Jennings Trophy: R. Lemelin, Goalie; A. Moog, Goalie	.35	.75

— 1991 - 92 SPORTS ACTION ISSUE —

1991-92 Regular Issue
Card No. 24, The Big Three
A. Moog, R. Bourque, C. Neely

The cards in this set are unnumbered and are listed below in alphabetical order.

Card Size: 2 1/2" X 3 1/2"
Face: Four colour, borderless
Back: Black on white card stock; Name, Position, Resume, Jersey number
Imprint: Sports Action © 1992
Complete Set No.: 24
Complete Set Price: 5.00 10.00
Common Card: .12 .25

No.	Player	EX	NRMT
1	Brent Ashton	.12	.25
2	Bob Beers	.12	.25
3	Daniel Berthiaume, Goalie	.12	.25
4	Raymond Bourque	.50	1.00
5	Robert Carpenter	.12	.25
6	Peter Douris	.12	.25
7	Glen Featherstone	.12	.25
8	Kenneth Hodge, Jr.	.25	.50
9	Jeff Lazaro	.12	.25
10	Stephen Leach	.25	.50
11	Andrew Moog, Goalie	.25	.50
12	Gordon Murphy	.12	.25
13	Cam Neely	.50	1.00
14	Adam Oates	.50	1.00
15	David Poulin	.12	.25
16	David Reid	.12	.25
17	Vladimir Ruzicka	.12	.25
18	Robert Sweeney	.12	.25
19	Don Sweeney	.12	.25
20	Glen Wesley	.12	.25
21	James Vesey	.12	.25
22	Jim Wiemer	.12	.25
23	Christopher Winnes	.12	.25
24	The Big Three: Andrew Moog, Goalie; Raymond Bourque; Cam Neely	.50	1.00

— 1991 - 92 BOSTON BRUINS LEGENDS —

This 36-card set was produced by The Boston Bruins commemorating the past greats that played in their organization.

1991-92 Boston Bruins Legends
Card No. 3, Raymond Bourque

Card Size: 2-1/2" x 3-1/2"
Face: Black and white, borderless
Back: Black on white card stock; Name, Position, Resume
Imprint: © 1991 - BOSTON BRUINS
Complete Set No.: 36
Complete Set Price: 10.00 20.00
Common Card: .25 .50

No.	Player	EX	NRMT
1	Bob Armstrong	.25	.50
2	Leo Boivin	.25	.50
3	Raymond Bourque	.50	1.00
4	Frank Brimsek, Goalie	.25	.50
5	Bruins Defence: Bill Quackenbush; Fern Flaman; Terry Sawchuk, Goalie; Bob Armstrong; Leo Boivin	.50	1.00
6	John Bucyk	.50	1.00
7	Wayne Cashman	.25	.50
8	Gerry Cheevers, Goalie	.50	1.00
9	Dit Clapper	.50	1.00
10	Bill Cowley	.25	.50
11	Phil Esposito	1.00	2.00
12	Fern Flaman	.25	.50
13	Mel Hill; Bill Cowley; Roy Conacher	.25	.50
14	Lionel Hitchman	.25	.50
15	"The Kraut Line": Milt Schmidt; Woody Dumart; Bobby Bauer	.50	1.00
16	Fleming Mackell	.25	.50
17	Don Marcotte	.25	.50
18	Don McKenney	.25	.50
19	Rick Middleton	.25	.50
20	Doug Mohns	.25	.50
21	Terry O'Reilly	.25	.50
22	Bobby Orr	1.00	2.00
23	Brad Park	.50	1.00
24	John Pierson	.25	.50
25	Bill Quackenbush	.25	.50
26	Jean Ratelle	.25	.50
27	Art Ross	.25	.50
28	Ed Sandford	.25	.50
29	Terry Sawchuk, Goalie	.75	1.50
30	Milt Schmidt	.25	.50
31	M. Schmidt; R. Weiland; B. Cowley	.25	.50
32	Eddie Shore	.75	1.50
33	Harry Sinden, Coach/GM/Pres.	.25	.50
34	Tiny (Cecil) Thompson, Goalie	.25	.50
35	Cooney Weiland	.25	.50
36	Ed Westfall	.50	1.00

BAYBANK

1992 - 93 BOBBY ORR

The first card was issued in 1992, the second in 1993 and so on. These cards were available at Baybank branches for autographing by Bobby Orr during his visits.

1992-93 Bobby Orr
Card No. 2A

Card Size: 2 1/2" x 3 1/2"
Face: Four colour, White border, Name
Back: Black and green, White border, Name, Position, Team, Resume
Imprint: ® Baybank
Complete Set No. 3
Complete Set Price: 3.00 6.00
Complete Autographed Set: 45.00 90.00

No.	Player	EX	NRMT
1A	Bobby Orr	1.50	3.00
1B	Bobby Orr, Autographed	22.50	45.00
2A	Bobby Orr	1.50	3.00
2B	Bobby Orr, Autographed	22.50	45.00
3A	Bobby Orr	1.50	3.00
3B	Bobby Orr, Autographed	22.50	45.00

BUFFALO SABRES - TEAM SETS

TEAM ISSUES

— 1972 - 73 POSTCARD ISSUE —

Postcard Size: 3 1/2" x 5 1/2"
Face: Black and white; Facsimile autograph
Back: Black on white postcard stock; Name, Position, Team
Imprint: None
Complete Set No.: 19
Complete Set Price: 15.00 30.00
Common Card: .75 1.50

No.	Player	EX	NRMT
1	Steve Atkinson	.75	1.50
2	Larry Carriere	1.00	2.00
3	Roger Crozier, Goalie	2.00	4.00
4	Butch Deadmarsh	.75	1.50
5	Larry Hillman	1.00	2.00
6	Tim Horton	2.00	4.00
7	Jim Lorentz	1.00	2.00
8	Don Luce	1.25	2.50
9	Richard Martin	1.50	3.00
10	Gerry Meehan	.75	1.50
11	Larry Mickey	.75	1.50
12	Gilbert Perreault	1.50	3.00
13	Tracy Pratt	.75	1.50
14	Craig Ramsay	1.25	2.50
15	Rene Robert	1.00	2.00
16	Mike Robitaille	.75	1.50
17	Jim Schoenfeld	1.50	3.00
18	Paul Terbenche	.75	1.50
19	Randy Wyrozub	.75	1.50

— 1973 - 74 POSTCARD ISSUE —

Postcard Size: 3 1/2" x 5 1/2"
Face: Black and white, white border
Back: Black on white postcard stock; Number, Position, Team
Imprint: Unknown
Complete Set No.: 22
Complete Set Price: 15.00 30.00
Common Card: .75 1.50

No.	Player	EX	NRMT
1	Steve Atkinson	.75	1.50
2	Larry Carriere	1.00	2.00
3	Joe Crozier, Coach	.75	1.50
4	Roger Crozier, Goalie	1.75	3.50
5	Dave Dryden, Goalie	1.00	2.00
6	Rick Dudley	1.50	3.00
7	John Gould	.75	1.50
8	Tim Horton	1.50	3.00
9	Jim Lorentz	1.00	2.00
10	Don Luce	1.00	2.00
11	Richard Martin	1.50	3.00
12	Gerry Meehan	.75	1.50
13	Larry Mickey	.75	1.50
14	Joe Noris	.75	1.50
15	Gilbert Perreault	1.50	3.00
16	Tracy Pratt	.75	1.50
17	Craig Ramsay	1.10	2.25
18	Rene Robert	1.10	2.25
19	Mike Robitaille	.75	1.50
20	Doug Rombough	.75	1.50
21	Jim Schoenfeld	1.25	2.50
22	Paul Terbenche	.75	1.50

— 1974 - 75 POSTCARD ISSUE —

Post card Size: 3 1/2" x 5 1/2"
Face: Black and white
Back: Black on white postcard stock; Name, Number, Positon, Team
Imprint: None
Complete Set No.: 21
Complete Set Price: 14.00 28.00
Common Card: .60 1.25

No.	Player	EX	NRMT
1	Gary Bromley	.60	1.25
2	Larry Carriere	.60	1.25
3	Roger Crozier, Goalie	1.50	3.00
4	Rick Dudley	1.00	2.00
5	Rocky Farr	.60	1.25
6	Lee Fogolin	1.25	2.50
7	Danny Gare	1.25	2.50
8	Norm Gratton	.60	1.25
9	Jocelyn Guevremont	.85	1.75
10	Bill Hajt	1.00	2.00
11	Jerry Korab	1.00	2.00
12	Jim Lorentz	.75	1.50
13	Don Luce	1.00	2.00
14	Richard Martin	1.50	3.00
15	Peter McNab	.60	1.25
16	Larry Mickey	.60	1.25
17	Gilbert Perreault	1.50	3.00
18	Craig Ramsay	.60	1.25
19	Rene Robert	1.00	2.00
20	Jim Schoenfeld	1.00	2.00
21	Brian Spencer	.60	1.25

— 1986 - 87 POSTCARD ISSUE —

This set is incomplete. We would appreciate hearing from anyone who could supply further information.

Card Size: 5 1/4" x 7 1/4"
Face: Four colour, Name, Number, Facsimile autograph
Back: Blank
Imprint: None
Complete Set No.: 12
Complete Set Price: 4.00 8.00
Common Card: .25 .50

No.	Player	EX	NRMT
1	Scott Arniel	.50	1.00
2	Jacques Cloutier, Goalie	.35	.75
3	Paul Cyr	.25	.50
4	Clark Gillies	.75	1.50
5	Uwe Krupp	.25	.50
6	Tom Kurvers	.75	1.50
7	Normand Lacombe	.25	.50
8	Wilf Paiement	.35	.75
9	Mike Ramsey	.50	1.00
10	Joe Reekie	.50	1.00
11	Christian Ruuttu	.50	1.00
12	Doug Smith	.25	.50

BELLS MARKETS

— 1973 - 74 POSTCARD ISSUE —

Postcard Size: 3 3/8" x 5 1/2"
Face: Four colour, white border; Name, Team, Position, Resume, Sponsor and Team logos
Back: Blank
Imprint: BELLS
Complete Set No.: 4
Complete Set Price: 12.50 25.00
Common Card: 2.50 5.00

No.	Player	EX	NRMT
1	Roger Crozier, Goalie	3.50	7.00
2	Jim Lorentz	2.50	5.00
3	Richard Martin	4.00	8.00
4	Gilbert Perreault	4.00	8.00

— 1979 - 80 PHOTO ISSUE —

Card Size: 7 1/2" X 10"
Face: Four colour, white border; Name, Team
Back: Blue on white card stock; Team logo, Name, Position, Resume
Imprint: BELLS
Complete Set No.: 9
Complete Set Price: 10.00 20.00
Common Card: 1.25 2.50

No.	Player	EX	NRMT
1	Don Edwards, Goalie	1.25	2.50
2	Danny Gare	1.25	2.50
3	Jerry Korab	1.25	2.50
4	Richard Martin	2.00	4.00
5	Anthony McKegney	1.25	2.50
6	Craig Ramsay	1.25	2.50
7	Bob Sauve, Goalie	1.25	2.50
8	Jim Schoenfeld	1.75	3.50
9	John Van Boxmeer	1.25	2.50

LINNETT

— 1975 - 76 PHOTO ISSUE —

We have little information on this set. We would appreciate hearing from anyone who could supply further information.

Card Size: 8 1/2" x 11"
Face:
Back: Unknown
Imprint: All Rights Reserved by Charles Linnett Studios, Inc., Walpole, Mass. 02081
Complete Set No.: 12
Complete Set Price: Unknown
Common Card: Unknown

No.	Player	EX	NRMT
1	Jim Lorentz	1.50	3.00
2	Don Luce	1.50	3.00
3	Richard Martin	3.00	6.00
4	Gerry Meehan	1.50	3.00
5	Gilbert Perreault	4.00	8.00
6	Rene Robert	1.50	3.00
7	Jim Schoenfeld	1.50	3.00

WENDZ

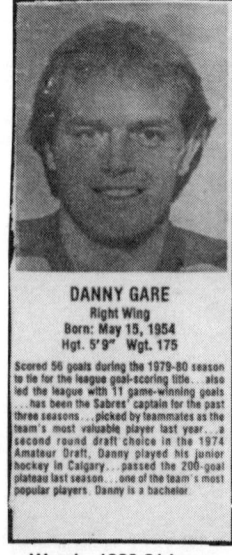

Wendz, 1980-81 Issue
Card No. 2, Danny Gare

BUFFALO SABRES - TEAM SETS • 583

— 1980 - 81 REGULAR ISSUE —

Issued in pairs on the backs of milk cartons this 16-card set had to be cut from the carton along the dotted lines provided. The two cards known are listed alphabetically. As this list is incomplete we would appreciate hearing from anyone who could provide further information.

Card Size: 1 13/16" x 4 3/16"
Face: Blue, white border; Name, Position, Resume
Back: Blank
Imprint: None
Complete Set No. 16 Panels
Complete Set Price: Unknown

No.	Player	EX	NRMT
1	Don Edwards, Goalie	.50	1.00
2	Danny Gare	1.00	2.00

— 1981 - 82 REGULAR ISSUE —

Postcard Size: 2 1/4" x 4 1/2"
Face: Four colour, white border; Name, Position, Resume
Back: Black on white card stock; Information and Ticket Coupon
Imprint: Unknown
Complete Set No.: 16 Panels
Complete Set Price: 60.00 125.00
Common Card: 4.00 8.00

No.	Player	EX	NRMT
1	Richie Dunn	4.00	8.00
2	Don Edwards, Goalie	7.00	14.00
3	Alan Haworth	4.00	8.00
4	Bill Hajt	5.00	10.00
5	Yvon Lambert	5.00	10.00
6	Dale McCourt	5.00	10.00
7	Tony McKegney	5.00	10.00
8	Gil Perreault	10.00	20.00
9	Larry Playfair	4.00	8.00
10	Craig Ramsey	6.00	12.00
11	Mike Ramsey	5.00	10.00
12	Bob Sauve, Goalie	5.00	10.00
13	Andre Savard	4.00	8.00
14	Jim Schoenfeld	6.00	12.00
15	Ric Seiling	4.00	8.00
16	John Van Boxmeer	4.00	8.00

— 1982 - 83 REGULAR ISSUE —

Card Size: 2 1/4" x 3 1/2"
Face: Four colour, white border, Name, Position,
Back: Blank
Imprint: None
Complete Set No.: 16
Complete Set Price: 60.00 125.00
Common Card: 4.00 8.00

No.	Player	EX	NRMT
1	Scott Bowman, General Manager	7.50	15.00
2	Jacques Cloutier, Goalie	2.50	5.00
3	Mike Foligno	5.00	10.00
4	Phil Housley	12.50	25.00
5	Dale McCourt	4.00	8.00
6	Tony McKegney	4.00	8.00
7	Gil Perreault	10.00	20.00
8	Brent Peterson	4.00	8.00
9	Larry Playfair	4.00	8.00
10	Craig Ramsey	4.00	8.00
11	Mike Ramsey	4.00	8.00
12	Lindy Ruff	5.00	10.00
13	Bob Sauve, Goalie	4.00	8.00
14	Ric Seiling	4.00	8.00
15	John Van Boxmeer	4.00	8.00
16	Hannu Virta	4.00	8.00

— 1984 - 85 PHOTO ISSUE —

Card Size: 8" x 10"
Face: Black and white; Team logo
Back: Blank
Imprint: None
Complete Set No.: 32
Complete Set Price: 15.00 30.00
Common Card: .50 1.00

No.	Player	EX	NRMT
1	David Andreychuk	3.00	6.00
2	Tom Barrasso, Goalie	2.50	5.00
3	Scott Bowman, Coach	1.00	2.00
4	Jacques Cloutier, Goalie	.50	1.00
5	Real Cloutier	.75	1.50
6	Adam Creighton	1.00	2.00
7	Joseph Crozier, Coach	.50	1.00
8	Paul Cyr	.50	1.00
9	Malcolm Davis	.50	1.00
10	David Fenyves	.50	1.00
11	Michael Foligno	1.00	2.00
12	Bill Hajt	.50	1.00
13	Gilles Hamel	.50	1.00
14	Phil Housley	1.50	3.00
15	Timo Jutila	.50	1.00
16	Normand Lacombe	.75	1.50
17	Sean McKenna	.60	1.25
18	Gerry Meehan	.50	1.00
19	Mike Moller	.50	1.00
20	Steve Patrick	.50	1.00
21	Gilbert Perreault	1.25	2.50
22	Brent Peterson	.50	1.00
23	Larry Playfair	.75	1.50
24	Craig Ramsey	.75	1.50
25	Mike Ramsey	.75	1.50
26	Lindy Ruff	.50	1.00
27	Bob Sauve, Goalie	.50	1.00
28	Ric Seiling	.60	1.25
29	John Tucker	.60	1.25
30	Claude Verret	.50	1.00
31	Hannu Virta	.50	1.00
32	Jim Wiemer	.50	1.00

BLUE SHIELD

— 1984 - 85 REGULAR ISSUE —

Card Size: 2 1/2" x 3 3/4"
Face: Four colour
Back: Blue on card stock
Imprint: Blue Shield of Western New York, Inc.
Complete Set No.: 21
Complete Set Price: 50.00 100.00
Common Card: 1.75 3.50

No.	Player	EX	NRMT
1	David Andreychuk	7.50	15.00
2	Tom Barrasso, Goalie	7.50	15.00
3	Adam Creighton	2.50	5.00
4	Paul Cyr	2.00	4.00
5	Malcolm Davis	2.00	4.00
6	Mike Foligno	2.50	5.00
7	Bill Hajt	2.00	4.00
8	Gilles Hamel	2.00	4.00
9	Phil Housley	7.50	15.00
10	Sean McKenna	2.00	4.00
11	Mike Moller	2.00	4.00
12	Gilbert Perreault	5.00	10.00
13	Brent Peterson	2.00	4.00
14	Larry Playfair	2.00	4.00
15	Craig Ramsey	2.00	4.00
16	Michael Ramsey	2.00	4.00
17	Lindy Ruff	2.00	4.00
18	Bob Sauve, Goalie	2.00	4.00
19	Ric Seiling	2.00	4.00
20	John Tucker	2.00	4.00
21	Hannu Virta	2.00	4.00

— 1985 - 86 REGULAR ISSUE —

This set was issued in two sizes, regular and postcard.

Card Size: 2 1/2" X 3 1/2"
Face: Four colour
Back: Blue on card stock; Logo
Imprint: Blue Shield of Western New York, Inc.
Complete Set No.: 28
Complete Set Price: 25.00 50.00
Common Card: .75 1.50

No.	Player	EX	NRMT
1	Bo Mikael Andersson	1.00	2.00
2	David Andreychuk	3.50	7.00
3	Tom Barrasso, Goalie	3.50	7.00
4	Adam Creighton	1.00	2.00
5	Paul Cyr	1.00	2.00
6	Malcolm Davis	1.00	2.00
7	Steven Dykstra	1.00	2.00
8	David Fenyves	1.00	2.00
9	Mike Foligno	1.50	3.00
10	Bill Hajt	1.00	2.00
11	Bob Halkidis	1.00	2.00
12	Gilles Hamel	1.00	2.00
13	Phil Housley	3.00	6.00
14	Pat Hughes	1.00	2.00
15	Normand Lacombe	1.00	2.00
16	Chris Langevin	1.00	2.00
17	Sean McKenna	1.00	2.00
18	Gaetano Orlando	1.00	2.00
19	Gilbert Perreault	3.00	6.00
20	Larry Playfair	1.00	2.00
21	Daren Puppa, Goalie	2.00	4.00
22	Craig Ramsey, Assistant Coach	1.00	2.00
23	Michael Ramsey	1.00	2.00
24	Lindy Ruff	1.00	2.00
25	Jim Schoenfeld, Coach, SP	5.00	10.00
26	Ric Seiling	1.00	2.00
27	John Tucker	1.00	2.00
28	Hannu Virta	1.00	2.00

— 1985 - 86 POSTCARD ISSUE —

Postcard Size: 4" X 6"
Face: Four colour; Name, Resume
Back: Blue on card stock; Logo
Imprint: Blue Shield of Western New York, Inc.
Complete Set No.: 28
Complete Set Price: 20.00 40.00
Common Card: .75 1.50

No.	Player	EX	NRMT
1	Bo Mikael Andersson	.75	1.50
2	David Andreychuk	3.50	7.00
3	Tom Barrasso, Goalie	3.50	7.00
4	Adam Creighton	.75	1.50
5	Paul Cyr	.75	1.50
6	Malcolm Davis	.75	1.50
7	Steven Dykstra	.75	1.50
8	David Fenyves	.75	1.50
9	Mike Foligno	.75	1.50
10	Bill Hajt	.75	1.50
11	Bob Halkidis	.75	1.50
12	Gilles Hamel	.75	1.50
13	Phil Housley	3.00	6.00
14	Pat Hughes	.75	1.50
15	Normand Lacombe	.75	1.50
16	Chris Langevin	.75	1.50
17	Sean McKenna	.75	1.50
18	Gaetano Orlando	.75	1.50
19	Gilbert Perreault	3.00	6.00
20	Larry Playfair	.75	1.50
21	Daren Puppa, Goalie	2.00	4.00
22	Craig Ramsey, Assistant Coach	.75	1.50
23	Michael Ramsey	.75	1.50
24	Lindy Ruff	.75	1.50
25	Jim Schoenfeld, Coach	1.50	3.00
26	Ric Seiling	.75	1.50
27	John Tucker	.75	1.50
28	Hannu Virta	.75	1.50

584 • BUFFALO SABRES - TEAM SETS

— 1986 - 87 POSTCARD ISSUE —

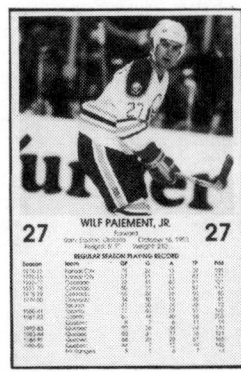

Blue Shield, 1986-87 Postcard Issue
Postcard No. 21, Wil Paiement

Postcard Size: 4" X 6"
Face: Four colour; Name, Jersey number, Resume
Back: Blue on card stock; Logo
Imprint: Blue Shield of Western New York, Inc.
Complete Set No.: 28

Complete Set Price:		15.00	30.00
Common Card:		.50	1.00

No.	Player	EX	NRMT
1	Shawn Anderson	.50	1.00
2	David Andreychuk	2.00	4.00
3	Scott Arniel	.50	1.00
4	Tom Barrasso, Goalie	2.00	4.00
5	Jacques Cloutier, Goalie	1.00	2.00
6	Adam Creighton	1.00	2.00
7	Paul Cyr	.50	1.00
8	Steven Dykstra	.50	1.00
9	David Fenyves	.50	1.00
10	Mike Foligno	.75	1.50
11	Clark Gilles	.75	1.50
12	Bill Hajt	.50	1.00
13	Bob Halkidis	.50	1.00
14	Jim Hofford	.50	1.00
15	Phil Housley	2.00	4.00
16	James Korn	.50	1.00
17	Uwe Krupp	1.00	2.00
18	Tom Kurvers	.50	1.00
19	Normand Lacombe	.50	1.00
20	Gaetano Orlando	.50	1.00
21	Wilf Paiement	1.00	2.00
22	Gilbert Perreault	2.00	4.00
23	Daren Puppa, Goalie	1.00	2.00
24	Michael Ramsey	.50	1.00
25	Lindy Ruff	.50	1.00
26	Christian Ruuttu	1.00	2.00
27	Douglas Smith	.50	1.00
28	John Tucker	.50	1.00

— 1987 - 88 POSTCARD ISSUE —

Postcard Size: 4" X 5"
Face: Four colour; Name, Team, Team logo, Jersey number, Facsimile autograph
Back: Blue on card stock; Logo
Imprint: Blue Shield of Western New York, Inc.
Complete Set No.: 28

Complete Set Price:		14.00	28.00
Common Card:		.25	.50

No.	Player	EX	NRMT
1	Bo Mikael Andersson	.25	.50
2	David Andreychuk	1.50	3.00
3	Scott Arniel	.25	.50
4	Tom Barrasso, Goalie	1.50	3.00
5	Jacques Cloutier, Goalie	.25	.50
6	Adam Creighton	.25	.50
7	Mike Donnelly	.25	.50
8	Mike Foligno	.35	.75
9	Clark Gillies	.25	.50
10	Bob Halkidis	.25	.50
11	Mike Hartman	.25	.50
12	Ed Hospodar	.25	.50
13	Phil Housley	1.50	3.00
14	Calle Johansson	.25	.50
15	Uwe Krupp	.25	.50
16	Jan Ludvig	.25	.50
17	Kevin Maguire	.25	.50
18	Mark Napier	.25	.50
19	Ken Priestlay	.25	.50
20	Daren Puppa, Goalie	.75	1.50
21	Michael Ramsey	.25	.50
22	Joe Reekie	.25	.50
23	Lindy Ruff	.25	.50
24	Christian Ruuttu	.25	.50
25	Ray Sheppard	2.50	5.00
26	Douglas Smith	.25	.50
27	John Tucker	.25	.50
28	Pierre Turgeon	5.00	10.00

— 1988 - 89 POSTCARD ISSUE —

Blue Shield, 1988-89 Postcard Issue
Postcard No. 1, Bo Mikael Andersson

Postcard Size: 4" X 6"
Face: Four colour, yellow top and bottom border; Team logo, Name, Team, Position, Jersey number, Resume
Back: Blue on white card stock; Logo
Imprint: Blue Shield of Western New York, Inc.
Complete Set No.: 28

Complete Set Price:		11.00	22.00
Common Card:		.25	.50

No.	Player	EX	NRMT
1	Bo Mikael Andersson	.25	.50
2	David Andreychuk	1.50	3.00
3	Scott Arniel	.25	.50
4	Doug Bodger	.25	.50
5	Jacques Cloutier, Goalie	.25	.50
6	Mike Donnelly	.50	1.00
7	Mike Foligno	.50	1.00
8	Bob Halkidis	.25	.50
9	Mike Hartman	.25	.50
10	Benoit Hogue, SP	1.25	2.50
11	Phil Housley	1.00	2.00
12	Calle Johansson	.25	.50
13	Uwe Krupp	.25	.50
14	Jan Ludvig	.25	.50
15	Kevin Maguire	.25	.50
16	Mark Napier, SP	1.25	2.50
17	Jeff Parker	.25	.50
18	Larry Playfair	.25	.50
19	Daren Puppa, Goalie	.50	1.00
20	Michael Ramsey	.25	.50
21	Joe Reekie, SP	1.25	2.50
22	Lindy Ruff	.25	.50
23	Christian Ruuttu	.50	1.00
24	Ray Sheppard	.50	1.00
25	John Tucker	.25	.50
26	Pierre Turgeon	3.00	6.00
27	Richard Vaive	.50	1.00
28	Sabretooth, Mascot	.25	.50

— 1989 - 90 POSTCARD ISSUE —

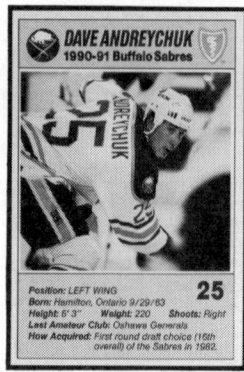

Blue Shield, 1989-90 Postcard Issue,
Postcard No. 1, David Andreychuk

Postcard Size: 4" X 6"
Face: Four colour, yellow top and bottom borders; Team logo, Name, Team, Position, Jersey number, Resume
Back: Blue on white card stock; Logo
Imprint: Blue Shield of Western New York, Inc.
Complete Set No.: 24

Complete Set Price:		9.00	18.00
Common Card:		.13	.25

No.	Player	EX	NRMT
1	David Andreychuk	1.00	2.00
2	Scott Arniel	.13	.25
3	Doug Bodger	.13	.25
4	Mike Foligno	.25	.50
5	Mike Hartman	.13	.25
6	Benoit Hogue	.50	1.00
7	Phil Housley	1.00	2.00
8	Edward (Dean) Kennedy	.13	.25
9	Uwe Krupp	.13	.25
10	Grant Ledyard	.13	.25
11	Kevin Maguire	.13	.25
12	Clint Malarchuk, Goalie	.13	.25
13	Alexander Mogilny	3.50	7.00
14	Jeff Parker	.13	.25
15	Larry Playfair	.13	.25
16	Ken Priestlay	.13	.25
17	Daren Puppa, Goalie	.35	.75
18	Michael Ramsey	.13	.25
19	Christian Ruuttu	.35	.75
20	Ray Sheppard	.35	.75
21	Dave Snuggerud	.13	.25
22	Pierre Turgeon	2.00	4.00
23	Richard Vaive	.50	1.00
24	Sabretooth, Mascot	.13	.25

— 1990 - 91 POSTCARD ISSUE —

Blue Shield, 1990-91 Postcard Issue
Postcard No. 1, David Andreychuk

Postcard Size: 4" X 6"
Face: Four colour, yellow top and bottom borders; Team logo, Name, Blue Shield logo, Position, Jersey number, Resume
Back: Blue on white card stock; Logo
Imprint: Blue Shield of Western New York, Inc.
Complete Set No.: 26

Complete Set Price:		7.50	15.00
Common Card:		.13	.25

BUFFALO SABRES - TEAM SETS • 585

No.	Player	EX	NRMT
1	David Andreychuk	1.00	2.00
2	Donald Audette	.35	.75
3	Doug Bodger	.13	.25
4	Greg Brown	.13	.25
5	Brian Curran	.13	.25
6	Lou Franceschetti	.13	.25
7	Mike Hartman	.13	.25
8	Dale Hawerchuk	.75	1.50
9	Benoit Hogue	.13	.25
10	Edward (Dean) Kennedy	.13	.25
11	Uwe Krupp	.25	.50
12	Grant Ledyard	.13	.25
13	Mikko Makela	.13	.25
14	Clint Malarchuk, Goalie	.13	.25
15	Alexander Mogilny	2.00	4.00
16	Daren Puppa, Goalie	.25	.50
17	Michael Ramsey	.13	.25
18	Robert Ray	.13	.25
19	Christian Ruuttu	.25	.50
20	Jiri Sejba	.13	.25
21	Dave Snuggerud	.13	.25
22	John Tucker	.13	.25
23	Pierre Turgeon	2.00	4.00
24	Richard Vaive	.25	.50
25	Gordon (Jay) Wells	.13	.25
26	Sabretooth, Mascot	.13	.25

— 1991 - 1992 POSTCARD ISSUE —

This 23-postcard set was a promotion in conjunction with Blue Shield of Western New York.

Blue Shield, 1991-92 Postcard Issue
Postcard No. 9, Pat LaFontaine

Postcard Size: 4" x 6"
Face: Four colour, white border; Name, Resume, Team and Sponsor logos
Back: Blue on white card stock; Blue Shield logo
Imprint: Allied Printing Trades Union Lable, Buffalo NY 1991
Complete Set No.: 26
Complete Set Price: 7.50 15.00
Common Card: .35 .75

No.	Player	EX	NRMT
1	David Andreychuk	.75	1.50
2	Donald Audette	.35	.75
3	Doug Bodger	.35	.75
4	Gordon Donnelly	.35	.75
5	Tom Draper, Goalie	.75	1.50
6	Kevin Haller	.50	1.00
7	Dale Hawerchuk	.75	1.50
8	Randy Hillier	.35	.75
9	Pat LaFontaine	2.00	4.00
10	Grant Ledyard	.35	.75
11	Clint Malarchuk, Goalie	.35	.75
12	Brad May	.35	.75
13	Brad Miller	.35	.75
14	Alexander Mogilny	1.50	3.00
15	Colin Patterson	.35	.75
16	Daren Puppa, Goalie	.35	.75
17	Michael Ramsey	.35	.75
18	Robert Ray	.35	.75
19	Christian Ruuttu	.35	.75
20	Dave Snuggerud	.35	.75
21	Kenneth Sutton	.35	.75

No.	Player	EX	NRMT
22	Tony Tanti	.35	.75
23	Richard Vaive	.35	.75
24	Gordon (Jay) Wells	.35	.75
25	Randy Wood	.35	.75
26	Sabretooth, Mascot	.35	.75

— 1992 - 1993 POSTCARD ISSUE —

This 26-postcard set was a promotion in conjunction with Blue Shields of Western New York.

Postcard Size: 4" x 6"
Face: Four colour, white border; Name, Number, Resume, Team and Sponsor logos
Back: Blue on white card stock; Blue Shield logo
Imprint: Allied Printing Trades Union Lable, Buffalo NY 1991
Complete Set No.: 26
Complete Set Price: 7.50 15.00
Common Card: .25 .50

No.	Player	EX	NRMT
1	David Andreychuk	.75	1.50
2	Donald Audette	.35	.75
3	Doug Bodger	.25	.50
4	Bob Corkum	.25	.50
5	Gordon Donnelly	.25	.50
6	Dave Hannan	.25	.50
7	Dominik Hasek, Goalie	2.00	4.00
8	Dale Hawerchuk	.50	1.00
9	Yuri Khmylev	.50	1.00
10	Pat LaFontaine	1.00	2.00
11	Grant Ledyard	.25	.50
12	Brad May	.25	.50
13	Alexander Mogilny	1.25	2.50
14	Randy Moller	.25	.50
15	John Muckler, Coach	.25	.50
16	Colin Paterson	.25	.50
17	Wayne Presley	.25	.50
18	Daren Puppa, Goalie	.25	.50
19	Mike Ramsey	.25	.50
20	Rob Ray	.25	.50
21	Richard Smehlik	.25	.50
22	Ken Sutton	.25	.50
23	Petr Svoboda	.25	.50
24	Bob Sweeney	.25	.50
25	Randy Wood	.25	.50
26	Mascot: Sabretooth	.25	.50

WONDER BREAD / HOSTESS CAKES

— 1987 - 88 REGULAR ISSUE —

This set is comprised of three perforated sheets attached and unnumbered. The cards are listed below in alphabetical order.

1987-88 Issue
Card No. 7, Adam Creighton

Card Size: 2 5/8" X 3 5/16"
Face: Four colour, red, blue and yellow dotted border; Name, Position, Jersey number, Team and sponsor logos
Back: Red, blue and black on white card stock; Name, Position, Resume
Imprint: None

Photo Size: 13 1/2" X 10 11/16"
Face: Four colour; Team and sponsor logos, Player's names
Back: Four colour; Team and sponsor logos
Imprint: None
Complete Set No.: 31
Complete Set Price: 12.50 25.00
Common Card: .25 .50

No.	Player	EX	NRMT
1	Bo Mikael Andersson	.25	.50
2	Shawn Anderson	.25	.50
3	David Andreychuk	1.50	3.00
4	Scott Arniel	.25	.50
5	Tom Barrasso, Goalie	1.50	3.00
6	Jacques Cloutier, Goalie	.50	1.00
7	Adam Creighton	.50	1.00
8	Steven Dykstra	.25	.50
9	Mike Foligno	.35	.75
10	Clark Gillies	.25	.50
11	Ed Hospodar	.25	.50
12	Phil Housley	1.50	3.00
13	Calle Johansson	.25	.50
14	Uwe Krupp	.50	1.00
15	Don Lever, Assistant Coach	.25	.50
16	Robert Logan	.25	.50
17	Jan Ludvig	.25	.50
18	Kevin Maguire	.25	.50
19	Mark Napier	.50	1.00
20	Daren Puppa, Goalie	.50	1.00
21	Michael Ramsey	.25	.50
22	Joe Reekie	.25	.50
23	Lindy Ruff	.25	.50
24	Christian Ruuttu	.50	1.00
25	Ted Sator, Head Coach	.25	.50
26	Ray Sheppard	1.50	3.00
27	Barry Smith, Assistant Coach	.25	.50
28	Douglas Smith	.25	.50
29	John Tucker	.25	.50
30	Pierre Turgeon	5.00	10.00
—	1987 - 1988 Team Photo	1.00	2.00

— 1988 - 89 REGULAR ISSUE —

This set is comprised of three perforated sheets attached and unnumbered. The cards are listed here in alphabetical order.

1988-89 Issue
Card No. 17, Brad Miller

Card Size: 2 5/8" X 3 3/8"
Face: Four colour, blue striped background; Name, Position, Jersey number, Team and sponsor logos
Back: Red, blue and black on white card stock; Name, Position, Resume
Imprint: None
Photo Size: 13 1/2" X 10 3/4"
Face: Four colour; Team logo, Player's names
Back: Four colour, blue striped background; Team and sponsor logos
Imprint: Photography BILL WIPPERT
Complete Set No.: 31
Complete Set Price: 9.00 18.00
Common Card: .25 .50

No.	Player	EX	NRMT
1	Bo Mikael Andersson	.25	.50
2	David Andreychuk	1.00	2.00
3	Scott Arniel	.25	.50
4	Doug Bodger	.25	.50
5	Jacques Cloutier, Goalie	.35	.75
6	Adam Creighton	.25	.50

586 • BUFFALO SABRES - TEAM SETS

No.	Player	EX	NRMT
7	Mike Foligno	.35	.75
8	Bob Halkidis	.25	.50
9	Mike Hartman	.25	.50
10	Benoit Hogue	.50	1.00
11	Phil Housley	.50	1.00
12	Calle Johansson	.25	.50
13	Uwe Krupp	.35	.75
14	Don Lever, Assistant Coach	.25	.50
15	Jan Ludvig	.25	.50
16	Kevin Maguire	.25	.50
17	Brad Miller	.25	.50
18	Mark Napier	.25	.50
19	Jeff Parker	.25	.50
20	Larry Playfair	.25	.50
21	Daren Puppa, Goalie	.50	1.00
22	Michael Ramsey	.25	.50
23	Joe Reekie	.25	.50
24	Lindy Ruff	.25	.50
25	Christian Ruuttu	.50	1.00
26	Ted Sator, Head Coach	.25	.50
27	Ray Sheppard	.25	.50
28	Barry Smith, Assistant Coach	.25	.50
29	John Tucker	.25	.50
30	Pierre Turgeon	3.00	6.00
—	'88-'89 Team Photo	.25	.50

CAMPBELL'S

— 1989 - 90 REGULAR ISSUE —

This set came in three perforated sheets attached and unnumbered. Cards are listed in alphabtical order.

1989-90 Issue
Card No. 9, Phil Housley

Card Size: 2 1/2" X 3 3/8"
Face: Four colour, blue border; Name, Jersey number, Team and sponsor logos
Back: Red and black on card stock; Name, Position, Resume
Imprint: None
Photo Size: 10" X 13 1/2"
Face: Four colour; Team logo
Back: Four colour
Imprint: None
Complete Set No.: 29
Complete Set Price: 9.00 18.00
Common Card: .25 .50

No.	Player	EX	NRMT
—	Title Card: 1970-1990	.25	.50
1	Shawn Anderson	.25	.50
2	David Andreychuk	1.00	2.00
3	Scott Arniel	.25	.50
4	Doug Bodger	.25	.50
5	Rick Dudley, Head Coach	.25	.50
6	Mike Foligno	.25	.50
7	Mike Hartman	.25	.50
8	Benoit Hogue	.35	.75
9	Phil Housley	.50	1.00
10	Edward (Dean) Kennedy	.25	.50
11	Uwe Krupp	.35	.75
12	Grant Ledyard	.25	.50
13	Don Lever, Assistant Coach	.25	.50
14	Kevin Maguire	.25	.50
15	Clint Malarchuk, Goalie	.35	.75

No.	Player	EX	NRMT
16	Alexander Mogilny	3.00	6.00
17	Jeff Parker	.25	.50
18	Larry Playfair	.25	.50
19	Daren Puppa, Goalie	.35	.75
20	Michael Ramsey	.25	.50
21	Robert Ray	.25	.50
22	Christian Ruuttu	.35	.75
23	Ray Sheppard	.25	.50
24	Dave Snuggerud	.25	.50
25	John Tortorella, Assistant Coach	.25	.50
26	Pierre Turgeon	2.00	4.00
27	Richard Vaive	.35	.75
—	'89-90 Team Photo		.50

— 1990 - 91 REGULAR ISSUE —

This set came in three perforated sheets. The cards are unnumbered and are listed here in alphabetical order.

1990-91 Issue
Card No. 18, Alexander Mogilny

Card Size: 2 1/2" X 3 3/8"
Face: Four colour, blue border; Name, Jersey number, Team and sponsor logos
Back: Red and black on white card stock; Name, Jersey number, Position, Resume
Imprint: None
Photo Size: 10" X 13 1/2"
Face: Four colour, white bottom strip; Player's names
Back: Four colour, blue border, Team logo, Campbell's logo
Imprint: None
Complete Set No.: 33
Complete Set Price: 7.50 15.00
Common Card: .25 .50

No.	Player	EX	NRMT
—	Title Card: Team Logo	.25	.50
1	David Andreychuk	1.00	2.00
2	Donald Audette	.60	1.25
3	Doug Bodger	.25	.50
4	Greg Brown	.25	.50
5	Bob Corkum	.25	.50
6	Rick Dudley, Head Coach	.25	.50
7	Mike Foligno	.25	.50
8	Mike Hartman	.25	.50
9	Dale Hawerchuk	.75	1.50
10	Benoit Hogue	.35	.75
11	Edward (Dean) Kennedy	.25	.50
12	Uwe Krupp	.35	.75
13	Grant Ledyard	.25	.50
14	Darcy Loewen	.25	.50
15	Mikko Makela	.25	.50
16	Clint Malarchuk, Goalie	.25	.50
17	Brad Miller	.25	.50
18	Alexander Mogilny	2.00	4.00
19	Daren Puppa, Goalie	.35	.75
20	Michael Ramsey	.25	.50
21	Robert Ray	.25	.50
22	Christian Ruuttu	.35	.75
23	Jiri Sejba	.25	.50
24	Darrin Shannon	.25	.50
25	Dave Snuggerud	.25	.50
26	John Tortorella, Assistant Coach	.25	.50
27	John Tucker	.25	.50
28	Pierre Turgeon	1.50	3.00
29	Richard Vaive	.25	.50
30	John Van Boxmeer, Associate Coach	.25	.50
31	Gordon (Jay) Wells	.25	.50
—	'90-91 Team Photo	.13	.25

— 1991 - 92 REGULAR ISSUE —

1991-92 Issue
Card No. 9, Pat LaFontaine

Card Size: 2 1/2" X 3 1/4"
Face: Four colour, blue vertical strip at side; Jersey number, Team logo, Name
Back: Black on white card stock; Name, Jersey number, Position, Resume.
Imprint: None
Photo Size: 10" X 13"
Face: Four colour; Player's names
Back: Four colour; Team logo, Campbell's logo
Imprint: None
Complete Set No.: 29
Complete Set Price: 7.50 15.00
Common Card: .13 .25

No.	Player	EX	NRMT
—	Title Card: Team logo	.13	.25
—	75th Anniversary NHL	.13	.25
1	David Andreychuk	1.00	2.00
2	Donald Audette	.50	1.00
3	Doug Bodger	.13	.25
4	Gord Donnelly	.25	.50
5	Tom Draper, Goalie	.50	1.00
6	Kevin Haller	.13	.25
7	Dale Hawerchuk	.50	1.00
8	Randy Hillier	.13	.25
9	Pat LaFontaine	2.00	4.00
10	Grant Ledyard	.13	.25
11	Clint Malarchuk, Goalie	.13	.25
12	Brad May	.25	.50
13	Brad Miller	.13	.25
14	Alexander Mogilny	1.50	3.00
15	Colin Patterson	.13	.25
16	Daren Puppa, Goalie	.35	.75
17	Michael Ramsey	.13	.25
18	Robert Ray	.13	.25
19	Christian Ruuttu	.25	.50
20	Dave Snuggerud	.13	.25
21	Ken Sutton	.13	.25
22	Tony Tanti	.13	.25
23	Richard Vaive	.13	.25
24	Gordon (Jay) Wells	.13	.25
25	Randy Wood	.13	.25
26	Sabretooth, Mascot	.13	.25
—	'91-92 Team Photo	.13	.25

JUBILEE FOODS

— 1992 - 93 REGULAR ISSUE —

Card Size: 2 1/2" X 4 1/2"
Face: Four colour, borderless; Name, Sponsor and Team logos
Back: Black on white card stock; Name, Jersey number, Position, Resume.
Imprint: © Copyright - 1992
Complete Set No.: 16
Complete Set Price: 5.00 10.00
Common Card: .25 .50

No.	Player	EX	NRMT
1	David Andreychuk	.75	1.50
2	Doug Bpdger	.25	.50
3	Gordon Donnelly, Rob Ray	.25	.50

No.	Player	EX	NRMT
4	Dominik Hasek, Daren Puppa, Goalies	1.25	2.50
5	Dale Hawerchuk	.35	.75
6	Yuri Khmylev, Viktor Gordijuk	.50	1.00
7	Pat LaFontaine	1.25	2.50
8	Brad May	.25	.50
9	Alexander Mogilny	1.00	2.00
10	Randy Moller, Ken Sutton	.25	.50
11	Wayne Presley, Donald Audette	.25	.50
12	Mike Ramsey	.25	.50
13	Richard Smehlik, Bob Corkum	.25	.50
14	Bob Sweeney	.25	.50
15	Petr Svoboda	.25	.50
16	Randy Wood	.25	.50

NOCO EXPRESS SHOP

— 1993 - 94 REGULAR ISSUE —

This set is unnumbered and listed alphabetically. This set is incomplete and we would appreciate hearing from anyone who could supply further information.

Card Size: 2 1/2" X 3 1/2"
Face: Four colour, borderless; Name
Back: Black on white card stock; Name, Jersey number, Resume, Sponsor logo
Imprint: None
Complete Set No.: Unknown
Complete Set Price: Unknown
Common Card: .50 1.00

No.	Player	EX	NRMT
1	Grant Fuhr, Goalie	.75	1.50
2	Mike Foligno	.50	1.00
3	Danny Gare	.75	1.50
4	Mike Ramsey	.75	1.50
5	Jim Schoenfeld	1.00	2.00

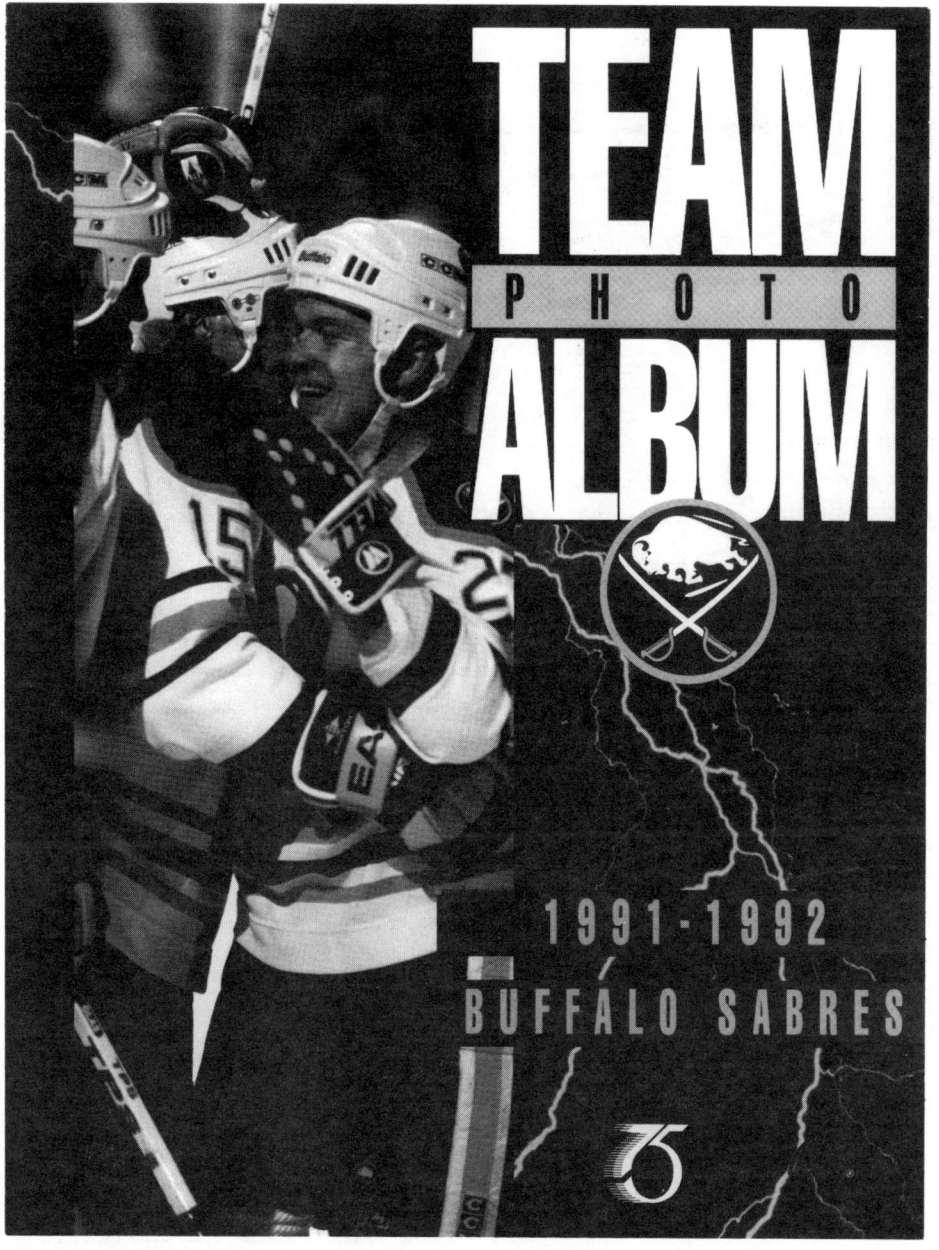

Buffalo Sabres - Team Sets
1991-92 Team Photo Album

CALGARY FLAMES - TEAM SETS

TEAM ISSUES

— 1980 - 81 POSTCARD ISSUE —

Postcard Size: 3 3/4" x 5"
Face: Four colour; Name
Back: Blank
Imprint: None
Complete Set No.: 21

		EX	NRMT
Complete Set Price:		7.50	15.00
Common Card:		.35	.75

No.	Player	EX	NRMT
1	Guy Chouinard	.35	.75
2	Bill Clement	.35	.75
3	Denis Cyr	.35	.75
4	Randy Holt	.35	.75
5	Ken Houston	.35	.75
6	Kevin Lavallee	.35	.75
7	Rejean Lemelin, Goalie	1.00	2.00
8	Don Lever	.35	.75
9	Bob MacMillan	.35	.75
10	Brad Marsh	.75	1.50
11	Bob Murdoch	.35	.75
12	Kent Nilsson	.50	1.00
13	Jim Peplinski	.50	1.00
14	Willi Plett	.35	.75
15	Pekka Rautakallio	.35	.75
16	Paul Reinhart	.35	.75
17	Pat Riggin, Goalie	.35	.75
18	Phil Russell	.35	.75
19	Eric Vail	.35	.75
20	Bert Wilson	.35	.75
21	Unknown	.35	.75

— 1981 - 82 POSTCARD ISSUE —

Postcard Size: 3 3/4" x 5"
Face: Four colour, borderless; Name
Back: Blank
Imprint: None
Complete Set No.: 21

		EX	NRMT
Complete Set Price:		7.50	15.00
Common Card:		.35	.75

No.	Player	EX	NRMT
1	Charles Bourgeois	.35	.75
2	Mel Bridgeman	.50	1.00
3	Guy Chouinard	.35	.75
4	Bill Clement	.35	.75
5	Denis Cyr	.35	.75
6	Jamie Hislop	.35	.75
7	Ken Houston	.35	.75
8	Steve Konroyd	.35	.75
9	Dan Labraaten	.35	.75
10	Kevin Lavallee	.35	.75
11	Rejean Lemelin, Goalie	1.00	2.00
12	Lanny MacDonald	.35	.75
13	Gary McAdam	.35	.75
14	Bob Murdoch	.35	.75
15	Kent Nilsson	.35	.75
16	Jim Peplinski	.50	1.00
17	Willi Plett	.35	.75
18	Pekka Rautakallio	.35	.75
19	Paul Reinhart	.35	.75
20	Pat Riggin, Goalie	.35	.75
21	Phil Russell	.35	.75

— 1982 - 83 POSTCARD ISSUE —

Card Size: 4" x 5 3/4"
Face: Four colour, borderless
Back: Black on white postcard stock; Name, Resume
Imprint: Unknown
Complete Set No.: 24

		EX	NRMT
Complete Set Price:		7.50	15.00
Common Card:		.25	.50

No.	Player	EX	NRMT
1	Charles Bourgeois	.25	.50
2	Mel Bridgeman	.35	.75
3	Guy Chouinard	.25	.50
4	Steve Christoff	.25	.50
5	Richie Dunn	.25	.50
6	Don Edwards, Goalie	.50	1.00
7	Kari Eloranta	.25	.50
8	David Hindmarch	.25	.50
9	Jamie Hislop	.25	.50
10	Tim Hunter	.35	.75
11	Kari Jalonen	.25	.50
12	Bob Johnson, Coach	.75	1.50
13	Steve Konroyd	.25	.50
14	Kevin Lavallee	.25	.50
15	Rejean Lemelin, Goalie	.50	1.00
16	Allan MacInnis	3.00	6.00
17	Lanny MacDonald	1.50	3.00
18	Carl Mokosak	.25	.50
19	Kent Nilsson	.25	.50
20	Jim Peplinski	.35	.75
21	Paul Reinhart	.50	1.00
22	Pat Ribble	.25	.50
23	Doug Risebrough	.50	1.00
24	Phil Russell	.25	.50

STATER MINT LTD

— 1982 - 83 HOCKEY DOLLARS —

Issued in sets of 6 coins, these dollars were available in cupro-nickel, bronze, silver or gold. The prices below are for the cupro-nicke set. They were also available singlely in cupro-nickel. There were 20,000 of each player issued except for Lanny McDonald where there were 110,000 issued.

Stater Mint Ltd/. 1982-83 Hockey Dollars
Lanny McDonald

Coin Size: 1 1/4" Diameter
Face: Player portrait, Name
Back: Team logo
Imprint: None
Complete Set No.: 6

		EX	NRMT
Complete Set Price:		22.50	45.00
Common Card:		4.00	8.00

No.	Player	EX	NRMT
1	Lanny McDonald	5.00	10.00
2	Mel Bridgman	5.00	10.00
3	Kent Nilsson	4.00	8.00
4	Paul Reinhart	5.00	10.00
5	Jim Peplinski	4.00	8.00
6	Don Edwards, Goalie	5.00	10.00

— 1983 - 84 HOCKEY DOLLARS —

This set is not complete. Any information you may have regarding this set would be greatly appreciated. The hockey dollars were available in silver, bronze and cupronickel. The price below is for the bronze dollars.

Coin Size: 1 1/4" Diameter
Face: Player portrait, Name
Back: Team logo
Imprint: None
Complete Set No.: Unknown

			NRMT
Complete Set Price:			Unknown

No.	Player	EX	NRMT
1	Doug Risebrough	5.00	10.00

RED ROOSTER

— 1985 - 86 REGULAR ISSUE —

Sponsored by Red Rooster Food Store, Old Dutch Potato Chips and Post. "Support Crime Stoppers" is printed on the backs and the cards are unnumbered. Cards are listed in alphabetical order.

Card Size: 2 3/4" X 3 9/16"
Face: Four colour, white border; Team logo, Jersey number, Name, Facsimile autograph
Back: Black on card stock; Name, Position, Resume, Sponsor logos
Imprint: None
Complete Set No.: 30

		EX	NRMT
Complete Set Price:		7.50	15.00
Common Card:		.25	.50

No.	Player	EX	NRMT
1	Paul Baxter	.25	.50
2	Eddy Beers	.25	.50
3	Perry Berezan	.25	.50
4	Charlie Bourgeois	.25	.50
5	Steve Bozek	.25	.50
6	Gino Cavallini	.25	.50
7	Mark D'Amour, Goalie	.25	.50
8	Timothy Hunter	.25	.50
9	Bob Johnson, Head Coach	.50	1.00
10	Stephen Konroyd	.25	.50
11	Richard Kromm	.25	.50
12	Rejean Lemelin, Goalie	.35	.75
13	Haken Loob	.25	.50
14	Lanny McDonald	1.00	2.00
15	Lanny McDonald	1.00	2.00
16	Al MacInnis	2.00	4.00
17	Jamie Macoun	.35	.75
18	Bob Murdoch, Asssistant Coach	.25	.50
19	Joel Otto	.35	.75
20	Pierre Page, Assistant Coach	.25	.50
21	Colin Patterson	.25	.50
22	James Peplinski	.35	.75

CALGARY FLAMES - TEAM SETS

No.	Player	EX	NRMT
23	Dan Quinn	.25	.50
24	Paul Reinhart	.35	.75
25	Doug Risebrough	.35	.75
26	Doug Risebrough	.35	.75
27	Neil Sheehy	.25	.50
28	Gary Suter	1.00	2.00
29	Michael Vernon, Goalie	1.00	2.00
30	Carey Wilson	.25	.50

— 1986 - 87 REGULAR ISSUE —

These cards are unnumbered and are listed here in alphabetical order.

Red Rooster, 1986-87 Issue
Card No. 12, Jamie Macoun

Card Size: 2 3/4" X 3 9/16"
Face: Four colour, white border; Facsimile autograph, Team logo, Jersey number, Name, Hockey tip
Back: Black on white card stock; Name, Position, Resume, Sponsor logos
Imprint: None
Complete Set No.: 30
Complete Set Price: 5.50 11.00
Common Card: .13 .25

No.	Player	EX	NRMT
1	Paul Baxter	.13	.25
2	Perry Berezan	.13	.25
3	Steve Bozek	.13	.25
4	Brian Bradley	.25	.50
5	Brian Engblom	.13	.25
6	Nick Fotiu	.13	.25
7	Timothy Hunter	.13	.25
8	Bob Johnson, Head Coach	.50	1.00
9	Rejean Lemelin, Goalie	.35	.75
10	Hakan Loob	.35	.75
11	Allan MacInnis	1.50	3.00
12	Jamie Macoun	.25	.50
13	Lanny McDonald, "When chasing a puck"	.75	1.50
14	Lanny McDonald, "Practice one-timing"	.75	1.50
15	Joe Mullen, "...Checking the opposition"	.50	1.00
16	Joe Mullen, "If you position"	.50	1.00
17	Bob Murdoch, Assistant Coach	.13	.25
18	Joel Otto	.25	.50
19	Pierre Page, Assistant Coach	.13	.25
20	Colin Patterson	.13	.25
21	James Peplinski	.13	.25
22	Paul Reinhart, Autograph Left	.13	.25
23	Paul Reinhart, Autograph, Right	.13	.25
24	Doug Risebrough	.13	.25
25	Gary Roberts	.13	.25
26	Neil Sheehy	.13	.25
27	Gary Suter	.75	1.50
28	John Tonelli	.13	.25
29	Michael Vernon, Goalie	.75	1.50
30	Carey Wilson	.13	.25

— 1987 - 88 REGULAR ISSUE —

These cards are unnumbered and are listed here in alphabetical order. They are not uniform in size.

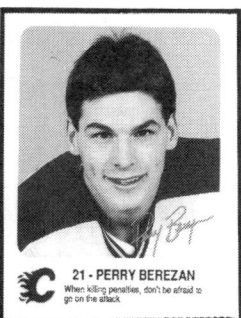

Red Rooster, 1987-88 Issue
Card No. 1, Perry Berezan

Card Size: 2 3/4" X 3 9/16" (approx.)
Face: Four colour, white border; Facsimile autograph, Team logo, Jersey number, Name, Hockey tip
Back: Black on card stock; Name, Position, Resume, Sponsor logos
Imprint: None
Complete Set No.: 30
Complete Set Price: 22.50 45.00
Common Card: .13 .25

No.	Player	EX	NRMT
1	Perry Berezan	.13	.25
2	Steve Bozek	.13	.25
3	Mike Bullard	.13	.25
4	Shane Churla	.13	.25
5	Terry Crisp, Head Coach	.13	.25
6	Doug Dadswell, Goalie	.13	.25
7	Brian Glynn	.13	.25
8	Brett Hull	12.50	25.00
9	Timothy Hunter	.13	.25
10	Hakan Loob, Light grey background	.25	.50
11	Hakan Loob, Dard grey background	.25	.50
12	Al MacInnis	1.00	2.00
13	Byron (Brad) McCrimmon	.13	.25
14	Lanny McDonald, Light grey background	.75	1.50
15	Lanny McDonald, Dark grey background	.75	1.50
16	Joe Mullen	.50	1.00
17	Dana Murzyn	.13	.25
18	Eric Nattress	.13	.25
19	Joe Nieuwendyk, Dark grey background	3.00	6.00
20	Joe Nieuwendyk, Blue background	3.00	6.00
21	Joel Otto	.13	.25
22	Pierre Page, Assistant Coach	.13	.25
23	Colin Patterson	.13	.25
24	James Peplinski	.13	.25
25	Paul Reinhart	.13	.25
26	Doug Risebrough, Assistant Coach	.13	.25
27	Gary Roberts	.75	1.50
28	Gary Suter	.13	.25
29	John Tonelli	.13	.25
30	Mike Vernon, Goalie	1.00	2.00

I.G.A.

— 1990 - 91 REGULAR ISSUE —

The set was issued in card and sheet form. The cards are unnumbered and are listed below in alphabetical order.

Card Size: 2-1/2" x 3-1/2"
Sheet Size: 15" x 18 1/4"
Face: Four colour, orange, red, yellow border; Name
Back: Two colour on card stock; Name, Resume, Team and sponsor's logo
Imprint: © Home and Pitfield Foods Limited 1990-91
Complete Set No.: 30
Complete Set Price: 12.50 25.00
Common Card: .12 .25

No.	Player	EX	NRMT
1	Paul Baxter, Coach	.12	.25
2	Guy Charron, Coach	.12	.25
3	Theoren Fleury	.75	1.50
4	Douglas Gilmour	2.00	4.00
5	Jiri Hrdina	.12	.25
6	Mark Hunter	.12	.25
7	Timothy Hunter	.12	.25
8	Roger Johansson	.12	.25
9	James Macoun	.25	.50
10	Allan MacInnis	.60	1.25
11	Brian MacLellan	.12	.25
12	Sergei Makarov	.50	1.00
13	Allan MacInnis, Sergei Makarov	.50	1.00
14	Stephane Matteau	.25	.50
15	Dana Murzyn	.12	.25
16	Frank Musil	.12	.25
17	Eric Nattress	.12	.25
18	Joe Nieuwendyk	1.00	2.00
19	Joel Otto	.12	.25
20	Colin Patterson	.12	.25
21	Sergei Priakin	.12	.25
22	Paul Ranheim	.12	.25
23	Robert Reichel	1.50	3.00
24	Doug Risebrough, Coach/GM	.12	.25
25	Gary Roberts	.35	.75
26	Gary Suter	.75	1.50
27	Tim Sweeney	.12	.25
28	Michael Vernon, Goalie	.50	1.00
29	Rick Wamsley, Goalie	.12	.25
30	Checklist	.12	.25
—	Uncut sheet of cards	15.00	30.00

— 1991 - 92 REGULAR ISSUE —

These cards are unnumbered and are listed below in alphabetical order.

Card No. 3, Douglas Gilmour

Card Size: 2 1/2" X 3 1/2"
Face: Four colour, red border; Name, Position, Jersey number, Team
Back: Black on white card stock; Name, Team logo, Position, Team, Resume
Imprint: © Home & Pitfield Foods Limited 1991-92
Complete Set No.: 25
Complete Set Price: 7.50 15.00
Common Card: .13 .25

No.	Player	EX	NRMT
1	Theoren Fleury	.75	1.50
2	Tomas Forslund	.25	.50
3	Douglas Gilmour	1.00	2.00
4	Marc Habscheid	.13	.25
5	Timothy Hunter	.13	.25
6	James Kyte	.13	.25
7	Allan MacInnis	.60	1.25
8	Jamie Macoun	.25	.50
9	Sergei Makarov	.35	.75
10	Stephane Matteau	.25	.50
11	Frantisek Musil	.13	.25
12	Eric Nattress	.13	.25
13	Joe Nieuwendyk	.75	1.50
14	Joel Otto	.25	.50
15	Paul Ranheim	.13	.25
16	Robert Reichel	1.00	2.00
17	Gary Roberts	.50	1.00
18	Neil Sheehy	.13	.25
19	Martin Simard	.13	.25
20	Ronnald Stern	.13	.25
21	Gary Suter	.13	.25
22	Tim Sweeney	.13	.25
23	Michael Vernon, Goalie	.50	1.00
24	Richard Wamsley, Goalie	.13	.25
25	Carey Wilson	.13	.25

CHICAGO BLACK HAWKS - TEAM SETS

TEAM ISSUES

— 1979 - 80 POSTCARD ISSUE —

These unnumbered cards are listed below in alphabetical order. Cards numbered 18 and 20 have stats on the back.

Card Size: 4" X 6"
Face: Four colour, borderless
Back: Blank or black on white postcard stock
Imprint: None
Complete Set No.: 22
Complete Set Price: 13.50 / 27.00
Common Card: .50 / 1.00

No.	Player	EX	NRMT
1	Keith Brown	1.50	3.00
2	J.P. Bordeleau	3.75	7.50
3	Ted Bulley	.50	1.00
4	Alain Daigle	.50	1.00
5	Tony Esposito, Goalie	2.00	4.00
6	Greg Fox	1.00	2.00
7	Tim Higgins	.50	1.00
8	Ed. Johnston, Goalie	1.00	2.00
9	Reg Kerr	.50	1.00
10	Cliff Koroll	.75	1.50
11	Tom Lysiak	1.25	2.50
12	Keith Magnuson	1.00	2.00
13	John Marks	.50	1.00
14	Stan Mikita	1.50	3.00
15	Grant Mulvey	.50	1.00
16	Bob Murray	.50	1.00
17	Mike O'Connell	.50	1.00
18	Richard Preston	.50	1.00
19	Bob Pulford, Coach	.50	1.00
20	Terry Ruskowski	.75	1.50
21	Mike Veisor	.75	1.50
22	Douglas Wilson	2.00	4.00

— 1980 - 81 POSTCARD ISSUE —

These unnumbered cards are listed below in alphabetical order. These are studio photos of the players in front of blue or brown backdrops.

Postcard Size: 4" X 6"
Face: Unknown
Back: Blank
Imprint: None
Complete Set No.: 25
Complete Set Price: 12.50 / 25.00
Common Card: .35 / .75

No.	Player	EX	NRMT
1	Murray Bannerman, Goalie		
2	J. P. Bordeleau		
3	Keith Brown		
4	Ted Bulley		
5	Tony Esposito, Goalie		
6	Greg Fox		
7	Tim Higgins		
8	Dave Hutchinson		
9	Reg Kerr		
10	Cliff Koroll		
11	Doug Lecuyer		
12	Tom Lysiak		
13	Keith Magnuson		
14	John Marks		
15	Grant Mulvey		
16	Bob Murray		
17	Mike O'Connell		
18	Rick Paterson		
19	Richard Preston		
20	Terry Ruskowski		
21	Denis Savard		
22	Ron Sedlbauer		
23	Darryl Sutter		
24	Tim Trimper		
25	Douglas Wilson		

— 1981 - 82 POSTCARD ISSUE —

These unnumbered cards are listed below in alphabetical order.

Postcard Size: 3 1/2" X 5 1/2"
Face: Four colour; Facsimile autograph
Back: Black on white postcard stock; Name, Resume
Imprint: Unknown
Complete Set No.: 26
Complete Set Price: 12.50 / 25.00
Common Card: .35 / .75

No.	Player	EX	NRMT
1	Murray Bannerman, Goalie	1.25	2.50
2	Keith Brown	1.00	2.00
3	Ted Bulley	.35	.75
4	Doug Crossman	.75	1.50
5	Jerome Dupont	.35	.75
6	Tony Esposito, Goalie	1.50	3.00
7	Greg Fox	.50	1.00
8	Bill Gardner	.35	.75
9	Tim Higgins	.35	.75
10	Dave Hutchinson	.35	.75
11	Reg Kerr	.35	.75
12	Tom Lysiak	.50	1.00
13	John Marks	.35	.75
14	Peter Marsh	.35	.75
15	Grant Mulvey	.35	.75
16	Bob Murray	.35	.75
17	Rick Paterson	.35	.75
18	Richard Preston	.35	.75
19	Bob Pulford, Coach	.35	.75
20	Terry Ruskowski	.35	.75
21	Denis Savard	2.50	5.00
22	Al Secord	1.50	3.00
23	Glen Sharpley	.35	.75
24	Darryl Sutter	1.50	3.00
25	Toni Tanti	.75	1.50
26	Douglas Wilson	1.50	3.00

— 1982 - 83 POSTCARD ISSUE —

These unnumbered cards are listed below in alphabetical order.

Card Size: 3 1/2" X 5 1/2"
Face: Unknown
Back: Blank
Imprint: Unknown
Complete Set No.: 23
Complete Set Price: .35 / .75
Common Card: .35 / .75

No.	Player	EX	NRMT
1	Murray Bannerman, Goalie	.85	1.75
2	Keith Brown	.75	1.50
3	Doug Crossman	.35	.75
4	Denis Cyr	.35	.75
5	Tony Esposito, Goalie	.75	1.50
6	Dave Feamster	.35	.75
7	Bill Gardner	.35	.75
8	Greg Fox	.35	.75
9	Tim Higgins	.35	.75
10	Steve Larmer	2.00	4.00
11	Steve Ludzik	.75	1.50
12	Tom Lysiak	.50	1.00
13	Peter Marsh	.35	.75
14	Grant Mulvey	.35	.75
15	Bob Murray	.35	.75
16	Troy Murray	.75	1.50
17	Rick Paterson	.35	.75
18	Richard Preston	.35	.75
19	Denis Savard	2.00	4.00
20	Al Secord	.35	.75
21	Darryl Sutter	1.25	2.50
22	Orval Tessier, Coach	.35	.75
23	Douglas Wilson	1.25	2.50

— 1983 - 84 POSTCARD ISSUE —

This set is not complete. We would like to hear from anyone who could supply further information.

Card Size: 3 1/2" X 5 1/2"
Face: Four colour, borderless
Back: Black on white card stock; Name, Position, Resume
Imprint: None
Complete Set No.: Unknown
Complete Set Price: Unknown

No.	Player	EX	NRMT
1	Murray Bannerman, Goalie	.50	1.00
2	Keith Brown	.50	1.00
3	Doug Crossman	.50	1.00
4	Denis Cyr	.50	1.00
5	Tony Esposito, Goalie	1.00	2.00
6	Dave Feamster	.50	1.00
7	Steve Larmer	1.00	2.00
8	Steve Ludzik	.50	1.00
9	Rob Murray	.50	1.00
10	Troy Murray	.50	1.00
11	Rich Preston	.50	1.00
12	Denis Savard	1.50	3.00
13	Alan Secord	.50	1.00
14	Darryl Sutter	.50	1.00
15	Orval Tessier, Coach	.50	1.00

No.	Player	EX	NRMT
1	Greg Fox	.50	1.00

COCA-COLA

— 1986 - 87 POSTCARD ISSUE —

These unnumbered cards are listed below in alphabetical order.

Coca-Cola, 1986-87 Postcard Issue
Postcard No. 1, Murray Bannerman

Card Size: 3 1/2" X 6 1/2"
Face: Four colour, white strip at bottom; Name, Position, Resume
Back: Blank
Imprint: None
Complete Set No.: 24
Complete Set Price: 10.00 / 20.00
Common Card: .35 / .75

No.	Player	EX	NRMT
1	Murray Bannerman, Goalie	.35	.75
2	Marc Bergevin	.35	.75
3	Keith Brown	.35	.75
4	Dave Donnelly	.35	.75
5	Curt Fraser	.35	.75

No.	Player	EX	NRMT
6	Steve Larmer	1.50	3.00
7	Steve Ludzik	.35	.75
8	Dave Manson	.75	1.50
9	Rob Murray	.35	.75
10	Troy Murray	.50	1.00
11	Gary Nylund	.35	.75
12	Jack O'Callahan	.35	.75
13	Ed Olczyk	.35	.75
14	Rick Paterson	.35	.75
15	Wayne Presley	.35	.75
16	Rich Preston	.35	.75
17	Bob Sauve, Goalie	.35	.75
18	Denis Savard	1.00	2.00
19	Alan Secord	.35	.75
20	Mike Stapleton	.35	.75
21	Darryl Sutter	.35	.75
22	Bill Watson	.35	.75
23	Behn Wilson	.35	.75
24	Douglas Wilson	.75	1.50

— 1987 - 88 POSTCARD ISSUE —

These unnumbered cards are listed below in alphabetical order.

Coca-Cola, 1987-88 Postcard Issue,
Postcard No. 14, Troy Murray

Postcard Size: 3 1/2" X 6 1/2"
Face: Four colour, white strip at bottom; Name, Position, Resume, Sponsor's logo
Back: Blank
Imprint: None
Complete Set No.: 30
Complete Set Price: 10.00 20.00
Common Card: .25 .50

No.	Player	EX	NRMT
1	Murray Bannerman, Goalie	.35	.75
2	Marc Bergevin	.25	.50
3	Keith Brown	.35	.75
4	Glen Cochrane	.25	.50
5	Curt Fraser	.25	.50
6	Steve Larmer	1.00	2.00
7	Mark LaVarre	.25	.50
8	Steve Ludzik	.25	.50
9	Dave Manson	.50	1.00
10	Bob Mason, Goalie	.35	.75
11	Robert McGill	.25	.50
12	Bob Murdoch, Head Coach	.25	.50
13	Rob Murray	.25	.50
14	Troy Murray	.35	.75
15	Brian Noonan	.50	1.00
16	Gary Nylund	.25	.50
17	Darren Pang, Goalie	.25	.50
18	Wayne Presley	.25	.50
19	Everett Sanipass	.25	.50
20	Denis Savard	1.00	2.00
21	Mike Stapleton	.25	.50
22	Darryl Sutter, Assistant Coach	.35	.75
23	Duane Sutter	.35	.75
24	Steve Thomas	1.00	2.00
25	Wayne Thomas, Assistant Coach	.25	.50

No.	Player	EX	NRMT
26	Richard Vaive	.35	.75
27	Daniel Vincelette	.25	.50
28	Bill Watson	.25	.50
29	Behn Wilson	.25	.50
30	Douglas Wilson	.75	1.50

— 1988 - 89 POSTCARD ISSUE —

These unnumbered cards are listed below in alphabetical order.

Coca-Cola, 1988-89 Postcard Issue,
Postcard No. 1, Ed Belfour

Postcard Size: 3 1/2" X 6 1/2"
Face: Four colour, white strip at bottom; Name, Position, Resume, Sponsor's logo
Back: Blank
Imprint: None
Complete Set No.: 25
Complete Set Price: 7.50 15.00
Common Card: .13 .25

No.	Player	EX	NRMT
1	Ed Belfour, Goalie	3.00	6.00
2	Keith Brown	.25	.50
3	Bruce Cassidy	.13	.25
4	Mike Eagles	.13	.25
5	Dirk Graham	.13	.25
6	Mike Hudson	.13	.25
7	Mike Keenan, Head Coach	.50	1.00
8	Steve Larmer	.50	1.00
9	Dave Manson	.35	.75
10	Jacques Martin, Assistant Coach	.13	.25
11	Robert McGill	.13	.25
12	E.J. McGuire, Assistant Coach	.13	.25
13	Troy Murray	.25	.50
14	Brian Noonan	.13	.25
15	Darren Pang, Goalie	.13	.25
16	Wayne Presley	.13	.25
17	Everett Sanipass	.13	.25
18	Denis Savard	1.50	3.00
19	Duane Sutter	.25	.50
20	Steve Thomas	.25	.50
21	Richard Vaive	.25	.50
22	Daniel Vincelette	.13	.25
23	Jimmy Waite	.25	.50
24	Douglas Wilson	.50	1.00
25	Trent Yawney	.25	.50

COLORADO ROCKIES - TEAM SETS

TEAM ISSUES

— 1979 - 80 POSTCARD ISSUE —

Card Size: 3 7/8" x 6"
Face: Black and white, white border; Name
Back: Black on white card stock; Team logo
Imprint: None
Complete Set No.: 23
Complete Set Price: 12.50 25.00 ☐
Common Card: .50 1.00

No.	Player	EX	NRMT
1	Hardy Astrom	.50	1.00 ☐
2	Doug Berry	.50	1.00 ☐
3	Nick Beverley	1.00	2.00 ☐
4	Mike Christie	.50	1.00 ☐
5	Gary Croteau	.50	1.00 ☐
6	Lucien Deblois	1.50	3.00 ☐
7	Ron Delorme	.50	1.00 ☐
8	Mike Gillis	.50	1.00 ☐
9	Trevor Johanson	.50	1.00 ☐
10	Lanny MacDonald	2.50	5.00 ☐
11	Mike McEwen	.50	1.00 ☐
12	Bill McKenzie	.50	1.00 ☐
13	Kevin Morrisson	.50	1.00 ☐
14	Bill Oleschuk	.50	1.00 ☐
15	Dennis Owchar	.50	1.00 ☐
16	Randy Pierce	.50	1.00 ☐
17	Michel Plasse, Goalie	.75	1.50 ☐
18	Joel Quenneville	.75	1.50 ☐
19	Rob Ramage	2.00	4.00 ☐
20	Rene Robert	1.00	2.00 ☐
21	Don Saleki	.75	.150 ☐
22	Barry Smith	.50	1.00 ☐
23	Jack Valiquette	1.00	2.00 ☐

— 1981 - 82 POSTCARD ISSUE —

Card Size: 3 1/2" x 5 1/2"
Face: Unknown
Back: Unknown
Imprint: Unknown
Complete Set No.: 30
Complete Set Price: 15.00 30.00 ☐
Common Card: .50 1.00

No.	Player	EX	NRMT
1	Team Crest	1.00	2.00 ☐
2	Brent Ashton	1.00	2.00 ☐
3	Arron Broten	1.75	3.50 ☐
4	Dave Cameron	.50	1.00 ☐
5	Joe Cirella	2.00	4.00 ☐
6	Dwight Foster	.50	1.00 ☐
7	Paul Gagne	1.00	2.00 ☐
8	Marshall Johnson	.50	1.00 ☐
9	Velipekka Ketola	.50	1.00 ☐
10	Mike Kitchen	.50	1.00 ☐
11	Rick Laferriere	.50	1.00 ☐
12	Don Lever	.75	1.50 ☐
13	Tapio Levo	.50	1.00 ☐
14	Bob Lorimer	.50	1.00 ☐
15	Bill MacMillan	.50	1.00 ☐
16	Bob MacMillan	.50	1.00 ☐
17	Merlin Malinovski	.50	1.00 ☐
18	Bert Marshall	.50	1.00 ☐
19	Kevin Maxwell	.50	1.00 ☐
20	Joe Micheletti	.50	1.00 ☐
21	Bobby Miller	.50	1.00 ☐
22	Phil Myre, Goalie	.50	1.00 ☐
23	Graeme Nicolson	.50	1.00 ☐
24	Jukka Porvari	.50	1.00 ☐
25	Joel Quenneville	.50	1.00 ☐
26	Rob Ramage	1.50	3.00 ☐
27	Glenn Resch, Goalie	1.25	2.50 ☐
28	Steve Tambellini	.75	1.50 ☐
29	Yvon Vautour	.50	1.00 ☐
30	John Wensink	.50	1.00 ☐

DETROIT RED WINGS - TEAM SETS

TEAM ISSUES

— 1956 - 57 POSTCARD ISSUE —

1956-57 Postcard Issue
Postcard No. 1, Jerry Toppazzini

Card Size: 3 1/4" x 5 1/2"
Face: Black and white; Facsimile autograph
Back: Black on white card stock
Imprint: J.D. McCarthy
Complete Set No.: Unknown
Complete Set Price: Unknown

No.	Player	EX	NRMT
1	Jerry Toppazzini	.50	1.00

— 1958 - 59 POSTCARD ISSUE —

1958-59 Postcard Issue
Postcard No. 2, Pete Goegan

Card Size: 3 1/4" x 5 1/2"
Face: Black and white; Facsimile autograph
Back: Black on white postcard stock
Imprint: J.D. McCarthy
Complete Set No.: Unknown
Complete Set Price: Unknown

No.	Player	EX	NRMT
1	Charlie Burns	.50	1.00
2	Pete Goegan	.50	1.00

— 1959 - 60 POSTCARD ISSUE —

1959-60 Postcard Issue
Postcard No. 3, Gerry Melnyk

Card Size: 3 1/4" x 5 1/2"
Face: Black and white; Facsimilue autograph
Back: Black on white postcard stock
Imprint: J.D. McCarthy
Complete Set No.: Unknown
Complete Set Price: Unknown

No.	Player	EX	NRMT
1	Barry Cullen	.50	1.00
2	Val Fonteyne	.50	1.00
3	Gerry Melnyk	.50	1.00
4	Vic Stasiuk	.50	1.00

— 1964 - 65 POSTCARD ISSUE —

The Gordie Howe and Sid Abel cards differ from the rest of the set in that they have facsimile autographs.

Card Size: 3 1/4" x 5 1/2"
Face: Black and white, borderless; Name, Facsimile autograph
Back: Black on white postcard stock; Name
Imprint: None
Complete Set No.: 21
Complete Set Price: 30.00   60.00
Common Card: 1.00   2.00

No.	Player	EX	NRMT
1	Sid Abel	2.00	4.00
2	Doug Barkley	1.00	2.00
3	Gary Bergman	1.25	2.50
4	Roger Crozier, Goalie	1.00	2.00
5	Alex Delvecchio	2.00	4.00
6	Bill Gadsby	1.50	3.00
7	Gordie Howe	5.00	10.00
8	Larry Jeffrey	1.00	2.00
9	Ed Joyal	1.00	2.00
10	Al Langlois	1.00	2.00
11	Ted Lindsay	1.75	3.50
12	Parker MacDonald	1.00	2.00
13	Bruce MacGregor	1.00	2.00
14	John MacMillan	1.00	2.00
15	Pit Martin	1.50	3.00
16	Ron Murphy	1.00	2.00
17	Andre Pronovost	1.00	2.00
18	Marcel Pronovost	1.75	3.50
19	Terry Sawchuk, Goalie	3.50	7.00
20	Floyd Smith	1.00	2.00
21	Norm Ullman	1.50	3.00

— 1968 PHOTO ISSUE —

Card Size: 8" x 10"
Face: Black and white, white border; Name, Team name and logo
Back: Blank
Imprint: None
Complete Set No.: Unknown
Complete Set Price: Unknown

No.	Player	EX	NRMT
1	Frank Mahovlich	.50	1.00

— 1972 - 73 PHOTO ISSUE —

The players on these card can be identified by the name shown on the hockey stick.

Card Size: 8 3/8" x 10 5/8"
Face: Four colour
Back: Blank
Imprint: None
Complete Set No.: 18
Complete Set Price: 17.50   35.00
Common Card: .75   1.50

No.	Player	EX	NRMT
1	Garnet Bailey	.75	1.50
2	Red Berenson	1.00	2.00
3	Gary Bergman	1.00	2.00
4	Tommie Bergman	1.00	2.00
5	Guy Charron	.75	1.50
6	Bill Collins	.75	1.50
7	Denis Dejordy, Goalie	1.25	2.50
8	Alex Delvecchio	2.00	4.00
9	Marcel Dionne	2.50	5.00
10	Tim Ecclestone	.75	1.50
11	Roy Edwards, Goalie	.75	1.50
12	Larry Johnston	.75	1.50
13	Al Karlander	.75	1.50
14	Brian Lavender	.75	1.50
15	Nick Libbett	1.00	2.00
16	Ken Murray	.75	1.50
17	Mickey Redman	1.25	2.50
18	Ron Stackhouse	1.00	2.00

— 1974 - 75 POSTCARD ISSUE —

These cards are unnumbered and are listed below alphabetically.

Card Size: 3 1/4" x 5 1/4"
Face: Four colour; Name
Back: Black on white postcard stock
Imprint: J.D. McCarthy
Complete Set No.: 20
Complete Set Price: 22.50   45.00
Common Card: .75   1.50

No.	Player	EX	NRMT
1	Earl Anderson	.75	1.50
2	Red Berenson	1.00	2.00
3	Gary Bergman	1.00	2.00
4	Tommie Bergman	1.00	2.00
5	Guy Charron	.75	1.50
6	Alex Delvecchio	2.00	4.00
7	Marcel Dionne	2.50	5.00
8	Jean Hamel	.75	1.50
9	Bill Hogaboam	.75	1.50
10	Danny Grant	1.00	2.00
11	Doug Grant	.75	1.50
12	Nick Libbett	1.00	2.00
13	Bill Lochead	.75	1.50
14	Jack Lynch	.75	1.50
15	Hank Nowak	.75	1.50
16	Doug Roberts	.75	1.50
17	Jim Rutherford, Goalie	1.00	2.00
18	Barry Salovaara	.75	1.50
19	Blair Stewart	.75	1.50
20	Bryan Watson	1.00	2.00

594 • DETROIT RED WINGS - TEAM SETS

DETROIT RED WINGS TEAM ISSUE
1968 ISSUE, CARD NO. 1, FRANK MAHOVLICH

DETROIT RED WINGS - TEAM SETS • 595

— 1976 REGULAR ISSUE —

1976 Issue
Card No. 2, Sid Abel

Card Size: 2 1/2" x 3 1/2"
Face: Black and white, white border; Name, Team name and logo
Back: Blank
Imprint: None
Complete Set No.: 16
Complete Set Price: 10.00 20.00

Common Card: .50 1.00

No.	Player	EX	NRMT
1	Gerry Abel, Old Timers	1.00	2.00
2	Sid Abel, Old Timers	1.00	2.00
3	Doug Barkley	.50	1.00
4	Joe Carveth	.50	1.00
5	Alex Delvecchio	1.00	2.00
6	Bill Gadsby	.75	1.50
7	Hal Jackson	.50	1.00
8	Joe Klukay	.50	1.00
9	Ted Lindsay	1.00	2.00
10	Jim Orlando	.50	1.00
11	Marty Pavlich	.50	1.00
12	Marcel Pronovost	1.00	2.00
13	Marc Reaume	.50	1.00
14	Leo Reise	.50	1.00
15	Glen Skov	.50	1.00
16	Jack Stewart	1.00	2.00

— 1979 - 80 POSTCARD ISSUE —

Card Size: 4" x 5"
Face: Four colour, borderless; Name
Back: Black on white postcard stock
Imprint: None
Complete Set No.: 19
Complete Set Price: 10.00 20.00
Common Card: .50 1.00

No.	Player	EX	NRMT
1	Tommy Bergman	.50	1.00
2	Dan Bolduc	.50	1.00
3	Michael Foligno	1.50	3.00
4	Jean Hamel	.50	1.00
5	Glen Hicks	.50	1.00
6	Bill Hogaboam	.50	1.00
7	Greg Joly	.75	1.50
8	Willie Huber	.50	1.00
9	Jim Korn	.75	1.50
10	Dan Labraaten	.50	1.00
11	Barry Long	.50	1.00
12	Reed Larson	.50	1.00
13	Dale McCourt	.50	1.00
14	Vaclav Nedomansky	1.00	2.00
15	Jim Rutherford, Goalie	.75	1.50
16	Dennis Polonich	.50	1.00
17	Errol Thompson	.75	1.50
18	Rogatien Vachon, Goalie	1.25	2.50
19	Paul Woods	.50	1.00

— 1980 - 81 PHOTO ISSUE —

Card Size: 8" x 10 1/2"
Face: Black and white, Team, NHL logo
Back: Blank postcard
Imprint: None
Complete Set No.: 32
Complete Set Price: 14.00 28.00
Common Card: .50 1.00

No.	Player	EX	NRMT
1	Mike Blaisdell	.50	1.00
2	Rejean Cloutier	.50	1.00
3	Michael Foligno	1.00	2.00
4	Jody Gage	.50	1.00
5	Gilles Gilbert	.75	1.50
6	Jean Hamel	.50	1.00
7	Glenn Hicks	.50	1.00
8	Bill Hogaboam	.50	1.00
9	Willie Huber	.50	1.00
10	Al Jensen, Goalie	.50	1.00
11	Greg Joly	.50	1.00
12	Jim Korn	.75	1.50
13	Dan Labraaten	.50	1.00
14	Reed Larson	.75	1.50
15	Ted Lindsay, Coach	1.00	2.00
16	George Lyle	.50	1.00
17	Peter Mahovlich	1.25	2.50
18	Dale McCourt	.75	1.50
19	Perry Miller	.50	1.00
20	Vaclav Nedomansky	.75	1.50
21	Dan Olesevich	.50	1.00
22	John Ogrodnick	1.25	2.50
23	Joe Paterson	.50	1.00
24	Brent Peterson	.75	1.50
25	Dennis Polonich	.50	1.00
26	Marcel Pronovost	1.25	2.50
27	Jim Rutherford, Goalie	.75	1.50
28	Jim Skinner	.50	1.00
29	Errol Thompson	.50	1.00
30	Rick Vasko	.50	1.00
31	Russ Wilson	.50	1.00
32	Paul Woods	.50	1.00

— 1988 - 89 POSTCARD ISSUE —

We have no information on this team set. We would appreciate hearing from anyone who could supply further information.

MARATHON

— 1970 - 71 PHOTO ISSUE —

Part of a Pro Star Portraits promotion by Marathon Oil. These cards are unnumbered and are listed below in alphabetical order.

Card Size: 7 1/2" X 14"
Face: Four colour; Facsimile autograph, Name
Back: Promotional offer
Imprint: None
Complete Set No.: 11
Complete Set Price: 30.00 60.00
Common Card: 2.00 4.00

No.	Player	EX	NRMT
1	Gary Bergman	2.00	4.00
2	Wayne Connelly	2.00	4.00
3	Alex Delvecchio	5.00	10.00
4	Roy Edwards, Goalie	2.00	4.00
5	Gordie Howe	15.00	30.00
6	Bruce MacGregor	2.00	4.00
7	Frank Mahovlich	6.00	12.00
8	Dale Rolfe	2.00	4.00
9	Jim Rutherford, Goalie	2.00	4.00
10	Garry Unger	3.00	6.00
11	Tom Webster	2.50	5.00

LITTLE CAESARS PIZZA

— 1987 - 88 POSTCARD ISSUE —

These cards are unnumbered and are listed below in alphabetical order.

Little Caesars Pizza, 1987-88 Postcard Issue
Postcard No. 26, Greg Smith

Postcard Size: 3 3/4" X 6 1/16"
Face: Four colour, white border; Name, Team and sponsor logos
Back: Blank
Imprint: John Hartman
Complete Set No.: 30
Complete Set Price: 12.50 25.00
Common Card:

No.	Player	EX	NRMT
1	Brent Ashton	.25	.50
2	David Barr	.25	.50
3	Mel Bridgman	.25	.50
4	Shawn Burr	.25	.50
5	Steve Chiassen	.25	.50
6	John Chabot	.25	.50
7	Jacques Demers, Coach	.25	.50
8	Ron Dugay	.25	.50
9	Adam Graves	3.00	6.00
10	Joe Kocur	1.50	3.00
11	Dwight Foster	.25	.50
12	Tim Friday	.25	.50
13	Gerard Gallant	.25	.50
14	Glen Hanlon	.25	.50
15	Doug Halward	.25	.50
16	Tim Higgins	.25	.50
17	Petr Klima	.25	.50
18	Lane Lambert	.25	.50
19	Joe Murphy	1.50	3.00
20	Lee Norwood	.25	.50
21	Mike O'Connell	.25	.50
22	Adam Oates	3.00	6.00
23	John Ogrodnick	.25	.50
24	Bob Probert	2.00	4.00
25	Jeff Sharples	.25	.50
26	Greg Smith	.25	.50
27	Greg Stephan, Goalie	.25	.50
28	Darrem Veitch	.25	.50
29	Steve Yzerman	2.50	5.00
30	Rick Zombo	.25	.50

MCDONALDS RESTAURANTS

HOCKEY HEROES - GORDIE HOWE

Sheet Size: 8 1/2" x 11"
Face: Four coloue, white border
Back: Blank
Imprint: ©1993 The Upper Deck Company

No.	Player	EX	NRMT
	65th Birthday Celebration Tour Limited Edition -- of 25,000	7.50	15.00

EDMONTON OILERS - TEAM SETS

TEAM ISSUES

— 1979 - 80 POSTCARD ISSUE —

The cards in this set are unnumbered and are listed below in alphabetical order.

1979-80 Postcard Issue
Postcard No. 18, Ed Mio

Postcard Size: 3 3/8" X 5 1/4"
Face: Four colour, borderless; Facsimile autograph
Back: Black on white card stock; Name, Position, Resume, Team logo, Team
Imprint: None
Complete Set No.: 23
Complete Set Price: 20.00 / 40.00
Common Card: .50 / 1.00

No.	Player	EX	NRMT
1	Brett Callighen	.50	1.00
2	Colin Campbell	.50	1.00
3	Ron Chipperfield	.50	1.00
4	Cam Connor	.50	1.00
5	Peter Driscoll	.50	1.00
6	Dave Dryden, Goalie	.50	1.00
7	Bill Flett	.50	1.00
8	Lee Fogolin	.50	1.00
9	Wayne Gretzky	15.00	30.00
10	Al Hamilton	.50	1.00
11	Doug Hicks	.50	1.00
12	Dave Hunter	.50	1.00
13	Kevin Lowe	1.00	2.00
14	Dave Lumley	.50	1.00
15	Blair MacDonald	.50	1.00
16	Kari Makkonen	.50	1.00
17	Mark Messier	4.00	8.00
18A	Ed Mio, Goalie, Error	.50	1.00
18B	Ed Mio, Goalie, Corrected	.50	1.00
19	Pat Price	.50	1.00
20	Bobby Schmautz	.50	1.00
21	Dave Semenko	.50	1.00
22	Risto Siltanen	.50	1.00
23	Stan Weir	.50	1.00

— 1984 - 85 POSTCARD ISSUE —

The cards in this set are unnumbered and are listed here in alphabetical order.

Postcard Size: 4 1/2" X 6 1/2"
Face: Four colour, on white glossy paper stock; Jersey number, Team logo, Name, Resume
Back: Blank
Imprint: None
Complete Set No.: 23
Complete Set Price: 12.50 / 25.00
Common Card: .25 / .50

No.	Player	EX	NRMT
1	Glenn Anderson	.25	.50
2	Billy Carroll	.25	.50
3	Paul Coffey	1.50	3.00
4	Lee Fogolin	.25	.50
5	Grant Fuhr, Goalie	1.00	2.00
6	Randy Gregg	.25	.50
7	Wayne Gretzky	7.50	15.00
8	Charles Huddy	.25	.50
9	Pat Hughes	.25	.50
10	Dave Hunter	.25	.50
11	Don Jackson	.35	.75
12	Jari Kurri	1.00	2.00
13	Mike Krushelnyski	.25	.50
14	Willy Lindstrom	.25	.50
15	Kevin Lowe	.50	1.00
16	Dave Lumley	.25	.50
17	Kevin McClelland	.25	.50
18	Larry Melnyk	.25	.50
19	Mark Messier	2.50	5.00
20	Andrew Moog, Goalie	.75	1.50
21	Mark Napier	.25	.50
22	Jaroslav Pouzar	.25	.50
23	Dave Semenko	.25	.50

— 1986 - 87 POSTCARD ISSUE —

The cards in this set are unnumbered and are listed here in alphabetical order.

1986-87 Postcard Issue
Postcard No. 7, Wayne Gretzky

Postcard Size: 3 3/4" X 6 7/8"
Face: Four colour, white border; Jersey number, Name, Resume, Team logo
Back: Blank
Imprint: None
Complete Set No.: 24
Complete Set Price: 10.00 / 20.00
Common Card: .13 / .25

No.	Player	EX	NRMT
1	Glenn Anderson	.50	1.00
2	Jeff Beukeboom	.25	.50
3	Paul Coffey	1.00	2.00
4	Lee Fogolin	.13	.25
5	Grant Fuhr, Goalie	.75	1.50
6	Randall Gregg	.13	.25
7	Wayne Gretzky	5.00	10.00
8	Charles Huddy	.13	.25
9	Dave Hunter	.13	.25
10	Michael Krushelnyski	.13	.25
11	Stuart Kulak	.13	.25
12	Jari Kurri	.75	1.50
13	Kevin Lowe	.35	.75
14	Craig MacTavish	.13	.25
15	Kevin McClelland	.13	.25
16	Martin McSorley	.75	1.50
17	Mark Messier	2.00	4.00
18	Andrew Moog, Goalie	.50	1.00
19	Craig Muni	.13	.25
20	Mark Napier	.13	.25
21	Jaroslav Pouzar	.13	.25
22	Steve Smith	.25	.50
23	Raimo Summanen	.13	.25
24	Esa Tikkanen	.50	1.00

— 1987 - 88 POSTCARD ISSUE —

The cards in this set are unnumbered and are listed here in alphabetical order.

1987-88 Postcard Issue
Postcard No. 1, Keith Acton

Postcard Size: 3 11/16" X 6 13/16"
Face: Four colour, white border; Jersey number, Name, Resume, Team logo
Back: Blank
Imprint: None
Complete Set No.: 22
Complete Set Price: 8.00 / 16.00
Common Card: .13 / .25

No.	Player	EX	NRMT
1	Keith Acton	.13	.25
2	Glenn Anderson	.50	1.00
3	Jeff Beukeboom	.25	.50
4	Grant Fuhr, Goalie	.50	1.00
5	Wayne Gretzky	5.00	10.00
6	David Hannah	.13	.25
7	Charles Huddy	.13	.25
8	Michael Krushelnyski	.13	.25
9	Jari Kurri	.50	1.00
10	Normand Lacombe	.13	.25
11	Kevin Lowe	.35	.75
12	Craig MacTavish	.13	.25
13	Kevin McClelland	.13	.25
14	Martin McSorley	.35	.75
15	Mark Messier	2.00	4.00
16	Craig Muni	.13	.25
17	Selmar Odelein	.13	.25
18	Daryl Reaugh, Goalie	.13	.25
19	Craig Simpson	.13	.25
20	Warren Skorodenski, Goalie	.13	.25
21	Steve Smith	.25	.50
22	Esa Tikkanen	.35	.75

EDMONTON OILERS - TEAM SETS • 597

— 1988 - 89 POSTCARD ISSUE —

We have no information on this postcard set. We would appreciate hearing from anyone who could supply further information.

— 1988 - 89 TENTH ANNIVERSARY — ACTION MAGAZINE

Issued in four card panels these cards were inserted in the Action magazine (Oilers game program).

Action Magazine 1988-89 Tenth Anniversary
Card No. 1, Garry Unger

Panel Size: 9 1/4" X 7 1/2"
Card Size: 2 9/16" X 4 5/16"
Face: Four colour, white border; Name, Logos
Back: Name, Position, Resume, Number
Imprint: QUALITY COLOUR PRESS INC.
Complete Set No.: 164
Complete Set Price: 65.00 / 125.00
Common Card: .25 / .50

No.	Player	EX	NRMT
1	Garry Unger	.30	.60
2	Chris Joseph	.30	.60
3	Raimo Summanen	.25	.50
4	Mike Zanier, Goalie	.25	.50
5	Kevin Lowe	.50	1.00
6	Dave Semenko	.25	.50
7	Peter Driscoll	.25	.50
8	Ken Solheim	.25	.50
9	Glenn Anderson	.50	1.00
10	Curt Brackenbury	.25	.50
11	Ron Shudra	.25	.50
12	Gord Sherven	.25	.50
13	Randall Gregg	.35	.75
14	Larry Melnyk	.25	.50
15	Tom Roulston	.25	.50
16	Billy Carroll	.25	.50
17	Jeff Beukeboom	.25	.50
18	Jaroslav Pouzar	.25	.50
19	Jeff Brubaker	.25	.50
20	Danny Gare	.25	.50
21	Craig MacTavish	.25	.50
22	Reijo Ruotsalainen	.25	.50
23	Willy Lindstrom	.25	.50
24	Pat Hughes	.25	.50
25	James Wiemer	.25	.50
26	Selmar Odelein	.25	.50
27	Kent Nilsson	.30	.60
28	Mark Napier	.25	.50
29	Esa Tikkanen	.50	1.00
30	John Miner	.25	.50
31	Tom McMurchy	.25	.50
32	Steve Graves	.25	.50
33	Craig Muni	.25	.50
34	Maurice Mantha	.25	.50
35	Dave Lumley	.25	.50
36	Ron Low, Goalie	.25	.50
37	Martin McSorley	.75	1.50
38	Steven Dykstra	.25	.50
39	Risto Jalo	.25	.50
40	Dave Hunter	.25	.50
41	Jari Kurri	.75	1.50
42	Lee Fogolin	.25	.50
43	Moe Lemay	.25	.50
44	Stuart Kulak	.25	.50
45	Charles Huddy	.25	.50
46	Wayne Gretzky	5.00	10.00
47	Ken Linseman	.25	.50
48	Risto Siltanen	.30	.60
49	Glen Sather	.50	1.00
50	Brett Callighen	.25	.50
51	Ed Mio	.25	.50
52	Ken Hammond	.25	.50
53	Jimmy Carson	.75	1.50
54	Paul Coffey	1.50	3.00
55	Oilers' Milestone: Wayne Gretzky's 1050th	2.50	5.00
56	Reed Larson	.25	.50
57	Ted Green, Assistant Coach	.25	.50
58	Matti Hagman	.25	.50
59	Marc Habscheid	.25	.50
60	Bill Ranford, Goalie	.50	1.00
61	Mark Lamb	.30	.60
62	Daryl Reaugh, Goalie	.25	.50
63	Al Hamilton	.25	.50
64	Oilers' Milestone: Paul Coffey's 47th	.35	.75
65	Grant Fuhr, Goalie	.85	1.75
66	Stan Weir	.25	.50
67	Kenneth Berry	.25	.50
68	John Muckler, Co-Coach	.25	.50
69	Douglas Smith	.25	.50
70	Lance Nethery	.25	.50
71	Bill Flett	.25	.50
72	Mike Forbes	.25	.50
73	Martin Gelinas	.50	1.00
74	Ron Chipperfield	.25	.50
75	Reg Kerr	.25	.50
76	Don Jackson	.25	.50
77	Keith Acton	.25	.50
78	Gary Edwards, Goalie	.25	.50
79	Michael Krushelnyski	.25	.50
80	Oilers' Training Staff: Lyle Kulchisky; Peter Millar; Barrie Stafford	.25	.50
81	Normand Lacombe	.25	.50
82	Pat Price	.25	.50
83	David Hannah	.25	.50
84	Garry Lariviere	.25	.50
85	Gregory Adams	.25	.50
86	Poul Popiel, Error	.25	.50
87	Tom Gorence	.25	.50
88	Geoff Courtnall	.50	1.00
89	Mark Messier	2.50	5.00
90	Dave Dryden, Goalie	.25	.50
91	Andrew Moog, Goalie	.85	1.75
92	Jim Ennis	.25	.50
93	Craig Simpson	.50	1.00
94	Laurie Boschman	.25	.50
95	Doug Hicks	.25	.50
96	Rick Chartraw	.25	.50
97	1984 Stanley Cup Champions	.25	.50
98	Ron Carter	.25	.50
99	Blair MacDonald	.25	.50
100	Dean Clark	.25	.50
101	Glen Cochrane	.25	.50
102	Lindsay Middlebrook, Goalie	.25	.50
103	Ronald Areshenkoff	.25	.50
104	Billy Harris, Assistant Coach	.25	.50
105	Award Winner: Mark Messier, Conn Smythe Trophy	.35	.75
106	John Blum	.25	.50
107	Wayne Bianchin	.25	.50
108	Tom Bladon	.25	.50
109	Kevin McClelland	.25	.50
110	Roy Sommer	.25	.50
111	Mike Toal	.25	.50
112	Don Ashby	.25	.50
113	Donald Nachbaur	.25	.50
114	1985 Stanley Cup Champions	.25	.50
115	Jim Corsi, Goalie	.25	.50
116	John Hughes	.25	.50
117	Award Winner: Glen Sather, Coach of the Year	.25	.50
118	Bob Dupuis, Goalie	.25	.50
119	Jim Harrison	.25	.50
120	Don Murdoch	.25	.50
121	Steve Smith	.35	.75
122	Peter LoPresti, Goalie	.25	.50
123	Colin Campbell	.25	.50
124	Bryan Watson, Coach	.25	.50
125	John Bednarski	.25	.50
126	1987 Stanley Cup Champions	.25	.50
127	Scott Metcalfe	.25	.50
128	Mike Rogers	.25	.50
129	Dan Newman	.25	.50
130	Oilers' Milestone: Grant Fuhr's 75th	.35	.75
131	Warren Skorodenski, Goalie	.25	.50
132	Todd Strueby	.25	.50
133	Kelly Buchberger	.25	.50
134	Cam Connor	.25	.50
135	Dean Hopkins	.25	.50
136	Mike Moller	.25	.50
137	1988 Stanley Cup Champions	.25	.50
138	Byron Baltimore, Error	.25	.50
139	Patrick Conacher	.25	.50
140	Ray Cote	.25	.50
141	Walter Poddubny	.25	.50
142	James Playfair	.25	.50
143	Nick Fotiu	.25	.50
144	Kari Makkonen	.25	.50
145	David Brown	.25	.50
146	Terry Martin	.25	.50
147	Francois Leroux	.25	.50
148	Kari Jalonen	.25	.50
149	Tomas Jonsson	.25	.50
150	Dave Donnelly	.25	.50
151	Michael Ware	.25	.50
152	Don Cutts, Goalie	.25	.50
153	Miroslav Frycer	.25	.50
154	Bruce MacGregor, Asst. General Manager	.25	.50
155	Kim Issel	.25	.50
156	Marco Baron, Goalie	.25	.50
157	Doug Halward	.25	.50
158	Barry Fraser, Director	.25	.50
159	Alan May	.25	.50
160	Bobby Schmautz	.25	.50
161	Craig Redmond	.25	.50
162	Oilers' Milestone: Oilers Host 1989 NHL All-Star Game	.25	.50
163	Alex Tidey	.25	.50
164	Wayne Van Dorp	.25	.50

RED ROOSTER

— 1981 - 82 REGULAR ISSUE —

The cards in this set are unnumbered and are listed in here inalphabetical order. The sponsors are Red Rooster, Sun-Rype, Jell-O, Maxwell House and Post.

Red Rooster, 1981-82 Issue
Card No. 9, Wayne Gretzky

Card Size: 2 3/4" X 3 5/8"
Face: Four colour, white border; Team logo, Facsimile autograph, Name, Jersey number, Hockey tip
Back: Black on white card stock; Name, Position, Resume, Sponsor logos
Imprint: None
Complete Set No.: 30
Complete Set Price: 30.00 / 55.00
Common Card: .25 / .50

598 • EDMONTON OILERS - TEAM SETS

No.	Player	EX	NRMT
—	Title Card: Edmonton Oilers	1.50	3.00
1	Glenn Anderson	1.50	3.00
2	Curt Brackenbury	.25	.50
3	Brett Callighen	.25	.50
4	Paul Coffey	2.50	5.00
5	Lee Fogolin	.25	.50
6	Mike Forbes	.25	.50
7	Grant Fuhr, Goalie	2.00	4.00
8	Ted Green, Assistant Coach	.25	.50
9	Wayne Gretzky: "Headman the Puck ..."	5.00	10.00
10	Wayne Gretzky: "Penalties don't help.."	5.00	10.00
11	Wayne Gretzky: "The positions on a hockey team..."	5.00	10.00
12	Wayne Gretzky: "Q—Where can you run?.."	5.00	10.00
13	Matti Hagman	.25	.50
14	Billy Harris, Assistant Coach	.25	.50
15	Doug Hicks	.25	.50
16	Pat Hughes	.25	.50
17	Dave Hunter	.25	.50
18	Jari Kurri	1.00	2.00
19	Garry Lariviere	.25	.50
20	Ron Low, Goalie	.25	.50
21	Kevin Lowe	1.00	2.00
22	Dave Lumley	.25	.50
23	Mark Messier	2.25	4.50
24	Andrew Moog, Goalie	1.50	3.00
25	Glen Sather, Coach	.25	.50
26	Dave Semenko	.25	.50
27	Risto Siltanen	.25	.50
28	Garry Unger	.25	.50
29	Stan Weir	.25	.50

— 1982 - 83 REGULAR ISSUE —

The cards in this set are unnumbered and are listed below in alphabetcial order.

Red Rooster, 1982-83 Issue
Card No. 1, Glenn Anderson

Card Size: 2 3/4" X 3 11/16"
Face: Four colour, white border; Team logo, Facsimile autograph, Name, Jersey number, Hockey tip
Back: Black on white card stock; Name, Position, Resume
Imprint: None
Complete Set No.: 30
Complete Set Price: 17.50 35.00
Common Card: .25 .50

No.	Player	EX	NRMT
1	Glenn Anderson	.50	1.00
2	Laurie Boschman	.25	.50
3	Paul Coffey	1.00	2.00
4	Lee Fogolin	.25	.50
5	Grant Fuhr, Goalie	.75	1.50
6	Ted Green, Assistant Coach	.25	.50
7	Randall Gregg	.25	.50
8	Wayne Gretzky, "Follow the rules..."	4.00	8.00
9	Wayne Gretzky "Passing makes hockey..."	4.00	8.00
10	Wayne Gretzky, "Physical size is not..."	4.00	8.00
11	Wayne Gretzky, Stickhandling allows a player..."	4.00	8.00
12	Marc Habscheid	.25	.50
13	Charles Huddy	.25	.50
14	Pat Hughes	.25	.50

No.	Player	EX	NRMT
15	Dave Hunter	.25	.50
16	Don Jackson	.25	.50
17	Jari Kurri	1.00	2.00
18	Garry Lariviere	.25	.50
19	Ken Linseman	.25	.50
20	Ron Low, Goalie	.25	.50
21	Kevin Lowe	.50	1.00
22	Dave Lumley	.25	.50
23	Mark Messier	2.00	4.00
24	Andrew Moog, Goalie	.75	1.50
25	John Muckler, Assistant Coach	.25	.50
26	Jaroslav Pouzar	.25	.50
27	Tom Roulston	.25	.50
28	Glen Sather, Coach/General Manager	.50	1.00
29	Dave Semenko	.25	.50
30	Garry Unger	.25	.50

— 1984 - 85 REGULAR ISSUE —

The sponsors of this set are Old Dutch, Post and Red Rooster. The cards are unnumbered and listed below in alphabetical order.

Red Rooster, 1984-85 Issue
Card No. 19, Willy Lindstrom, Error

Card Size: 2 3/4" X 3 11/16"
Face: Four colour, white border; Team logo, Facsimile autograph, Name, Jersey number, Hockey tip
Back: Black on white card stock; Name, Position, Resume, Sponsor logos
Imprint: None
Complete Set No.: 30
Complete Set Price: 10.00 20.00
Common Card: .13 .25

No.	Player	EX	NRMT
1	Glenn Anderson	.35	.75
2	Billy Carroll	.13	.25
3	Paul Coffey	.50	1.00
4	Lee Fogolin	.13	.25
5	Grant Fuhr, Goalie	.50	1.00
6	Ted Green, Assistant Coach	.13	.25
7	Randall Gregg	.25	.50
8	Wayne Gretzky: "An accurate shot is..."	2.00	4.00
9	Wayne Gretzky: Hockey is a team sport, ."	2.00	4.00
10	Wayne Gretzky: "Try to be aware..."	2.00	4.00
11	Wayne Gretzky: "Try to perfect..."	2.00	4.00
12	Marc Habscheid	.13	.25
13	Charles Huddy	.25	.50
14	Pat Hughes	.13	.25
15	Dave Hunter	.13	.25
16	Don Jackson	.13	.25
17	Michael Krushelnyski	.13	.25
18	Jari Kurri	.75	1.50
19	Willy Lindstrom, Error	.13	.25
20	Kevin Lowe	.35	.75
21	Dave Lumley	.13	.25
22	Kevin McClelland	.13	.25
23	Larry Melnyk	.13	.25
24	Mark Messier	1.50	3.00
25	Andrew Moog, Goalie	.50	1.00
26	John Muckler, Assistant Coach	.13	.25
27	Mark Napier	.13	.25
28	Jaroslav Pouzar	.13	.25
29	Glen Sather, Head Coach/GM	.25	.50
30	Dave Semenko	.13	.25

— 1985 - 86 REGULAR ISSUE —

The sponsors of this set are Old Dutch, Post and Red Rooster. The cards are unnumbered and listed below in alphabetical order.

Red Rooster, 1985-86 Issue
Card No. 1, Glenn Anderson

Card Size: 2 3/4" X 3 9/16"
Face: Four colour, white border; Name, Jersey number, Team logo, Facsimile autograph
Back: Black on card stock; Name, Position, Resume, Sponsor logos
Imprint: None
Complete Set No.: 30
Complete Set Price: 10.00 20.00
Common Card: .13 .25

No.	Player	EX	NRMT
1	Glenn Anderson	.35	.75
2	Paul Coffey	.50	1.00
3	Lee Fogolin	.13	.25
4	Grant Fuhr, Goalie	.35	.75
5	Randall Gregg	.13	.25
6	Wayne Gretzky	2.00	4.00
7	Wayne Gretzky	2.00	4.00
8	Wayne Gretzky	2.00	4.00
9	Charles Huddy	.25	.50
10	Dave Hunter	.13	.25
11	Don Jackson	.13	.25
12	Michael Krushelnyski	.13	.25
13	Jari Kurri	.75	1.50
14	Kevin Lowe	.13	.25
15	Dave Lumley	.13	.25
16	Craig McTavish	.13	.25
17	Bob McCammon, Assistant Coach	.13	.25
18	Kevin McClelland	.13	.25
19	Martin McSorley	1.50	3.00
20	Mark Messier	1.25	2.50
21	Andrew Moog, Goalie	.35	.75
22	John Muckler, Assistant Coach	.13	.25
23	Mark Napier	.13	.25
24	Mike Rogers	.13	.25
25	Glen Sather, Head Coach/GM	.25	.50
26	Dave Semenko	.13	.25
27	Gord Sherven	.13	.25
28	Steve Smith	.75	1.50
29	Raimo Summanen	.13	.25
30	Esa Tikkanen	.50	1.00

— 1986 - 87 REGULAR ISSUE —

Red Rooster, 1986-87 Issue
Card No. 1, Glenn Anderson

The sponsors of this set are Old Dutch, Post and Red Rooster. The cards are unnumbered and listed below in alphabetical order.

Card Size: 2 3/4" X 3 9/16"
Face: Four colour, white border; Team logo, Facsimile autograph, Jersey number, Name, Hockey/Safety tip
Back: Blank on white card stock; Name, Position, Resume, Sponsor logos
Imprint: None
Complete Set No.: 30
Complete Set Price: 7.50 / 15.00
Common Card: .13 / .25

No.	Player	EX	NRMT
1	Glenn Anderson	.35	.75
2	Jeff Beukeboom	.25	.50
3	Paul Coffey	.50	1.00
4	Lee Fogolin	.13	.25
5	Grant Fuhr, Goalie	.35	.75
6	Danny Gare	.13	.25
7	Steve Graves	.13	.25
8	Ted Green, Assistant Coach	.13	.25
9	Randall Gregg	.13	.25
10	Wayne Gretzky, "Know Where Your Parents Work" (Eyes looking forward)	2.00	4.00
11	Wayne Gretzky, "Know Where Your Parents Work" (Eyes looking to the side)	2.00	4.00
12	Charles Huddy	.13	.25
13	Dave Hunter	.13	.25
14	Michael Krushelnyski	.13	.25
15	Stuart Kulak	.13	.25
16	Jari Kurri	.75	1.50
17	Kevin Lowe	.13	.25
18	Craig MacTavish	.13	.25
19	Kevin McClelland	.13	.25
20	Martin McSorley	.35	.75
21	Mark Messier	1.00	2.00
22	Andrew Moog, Goalie "Your Police are Friendly"	.50	1.00
23	Andrew Moog, Goalie "Never Walk Coles to..."	.50	1.00
24	John Muckler, Assistant Coach	.13	.25
25	Craig Muni	.13	.25
26	Mark Napier	.13	.25
27	Glen Sather, Coach / GM	.13	.25
28	Steve Smith	.35	.75
29	Raimo Summanen	.13	.25
30	Esa Tikkanen	.25	.50

— 1993 - 94 PHOTO ISSUE —

These 8" x 10" pictures were instered into programmes at each home game duering the 199-93 season at Northlands Colliseum.

1993-94 Program Insert
Program No. 34. Tyler Wright

Size: 8" X 10"
Face: Four colour, white border; Name, Number
Back: Blank
Imprint: None
Complete Set No.: 41
Complete Set Price: 110.00 / 225.00
Common Card: 2.50 / 5.00

No.	Player	EX	NRMT
1	Todd Elik, October 6	2.50	5.00
2	Igor Kravchuk, October 8	2.50	5.00
3	Dave Manson, October 16	2.50	5.00
4	Kelly Buchberger, October 20	2.50	5.00
5	Bill Ranford, Goalie, October 22	3.50	7.00
6	Craig MacTavish, October 24	2.50	5.00
7	Alexander Kerch, October 29	2.50	5.00
8	Chris Joseph, November 3	2.50	5.00
9	Geoff Smith, November 20	2.50	5.00
10	Ian Herbers, November 21	2.50	5.00
11	Fred Brathwaite, Goalie, November 24	2.50	5.00
12	Doug Weight, November 27	2.50	5.00
13	Ilya Byakin, November 29	2.50	5.00
14	Luke Richardson, December 1	2.50	5.00
15	Scott Pearson, December 15	2.50	5.00
16	Adam Bennett, December 17	2.50	5.00
17	Zdeno Ciger, December 19	2.50	5.00
18	Louie DeBrusk, December 22	2.50	5.00
19	Brad Werenka, December 27	2.50	5.00
20	Shayne Corson, December 29	2.50	5.00
21	Steve Rice, January 2	2.50	5.00
22	Kirk Maltby, January 7	2.50	5.00
23	Shjon Podein, January 26	2.50	5.00
24	Peter White, January 28	2.50	5.00
25	Vladimir Vujtek, January 29	2.50	5.00
26	Scott Thornton, February 2	2.50	5.00
27	Roman Oksiuta, February 4	2.50	5.00
28	Bob Beers, February 6	2.50	5.00
29	Fredrik Olausson, February 9	2.50	5.00
30	Wayne Cowley, February 12	2.50	5.00
31	Dean McAmmond, February 13	2.50	5.00
32	Jason Arnott, February 23	5.00	10.00
33	Ron Low, February 25	2.50	5.00
34	Tyler Wright, February 27	2.50	5.00
35	Kevin Primeau, March 9	2.50	5.00
36	Unknown, March 11	2.50	5.00
37	Gord Mark, March 23	2.50	5.00
38	Brent Grieve, March 25	2.50	5.00
39	Brad Zavisha, March 27	2.50	5.00
40	Mike Stapleton, April 8	2.50	5.00
41	Glen Sather, April 10	2.50	5.00

NEILSON'S

— 1982 - 1983 WAYNE GRETZKY —

A card was obtained by purchasing a Neilson's candy bar.

Neilson's 1982-83 Wayne Gretzky
Card No. 1, Discard Broken Stick

Card Size: 2 1/2" X 3 1/2"
Face: Black and white or Four colour photographs, blue border; Number, Facsimile autograph
Back: Blue and black on grey card stock; Facsimile autograph, Hockey tip, Bilingual
Imprint: Neilson
Complete Set No.: 50
Complete Set Price: 90.00 / 175.00
Common Card: 2.50 / 5.00

No.	Player	EX	NRMT
1	Discard Broken Stick	2.50	5.00
2	Handling the Puck	2.50	5.00
3	Offsides	2.50	5.00
4	Penalty Shot	2.50	5.00
5	Icing the Puck	2.50	5.00
6	Taping your Stick	2.50	5.00
7	Skates	2.50	5.00
8	The Helmet	2.50	5.00
9	Selecting Skates	2.50	5.00
10	Choosing a Stick	2.50	5.00
11	General Equipment Care	2.50	5.00
12	The Hook Check	4.00	8.00
13	The Hip Check	2.50	5.00
14	Forward Skating	2.50	5.00
15	Stopping	2.50	5.00
16	Sharp Turning	2.50	5.00
17	Fast Starts	2.50	5.00
18	Backward Skating	2.50	5.00
19	The Grip	2.50	5.00
20	The Wrist Shot	2.50	5.00
21	The Back Hand Shot	2.50	5.00
22	The Slap Shot	2.50	5.00
23	The Flip Shot	2.50	5.00
24	Pass Receiving	2.50	5.00
25	Faking	2.50	5.00
26	Puck Handling	2.50	5.00
27	Deflecting Shots	2.50	5.00
28	One On One	2.50	5.00
29	Keep Your Head Up	2.50	5.00
30	Passing to the Slot	2.50	5.00
31	Winning Face-Offs	2.50	5.00
32	Forechecking	2.50	5.00
33	Body Checking	2.50	5.00
34	Breaking Out	2.50	5.00
35	The Drop Pass	2.50	5.00
36	Backchecking	2.50	5.00
37	Using the Boards	2.50	5.00
38	The Power Play	2.50	5.00
39	Passing the Puck	2.50	5.00
40	Clear the Slot	2.50	5.00
41	Leg Lifts	2.50	5.00
42	Balance Exercise	2.50	5.00
43	Leg Stretches	2.50	5.00
44	Hip and Groin Stretch	2.50	5.00
45	Toe Touches	2.50	5.00
46	Goalie Warm Up Drill	2.50	5.00
47	Leg Exercises	2.50	5.00
48	Arm Exercises	2.50	5.00
49	Wrist Exercises	2.50	5.00
50	Flip Pass	2.50	5.00

McDONALD'S RESTAURANTS

— 1983 - 84 BUTTONS —

We have no information on this button set. We would appreciate hearing from anyone who could supply information on this set.

Button Size: Unknown
Face: Unknown
Back: Unknown
Imprint: Unknown
Complete Set No.: Unknown
Complete Set Price: Unknown

No.	Player	EX	NRMT

— 1984 REGULAR ISSUE —

These cards are unnumbered and are listed here in alphabetical order.

McDonald's Restaurants, 1984 Issue
Card No. 6, Grant Fuhr

Card Size: 1 9/16" X 2 1/2" or 3" X 2 1/2"
Face: Four colour, blue border; Jersey number, Sponsor's logo
Back: Black on card stock; Name, Jersey number, Player trivia
Imprint: None
Complete Set No.: 25

Complete Set Price:		8.00	16.00
Common Card:		.13	.25
Album:		2.50	5.00

No.	Player	EX	NRMT
1	Glenn Anderson	.35	.75
2	Rick Chartraw	.13	.25
3	Paul Coffey	.50	1.00
4	Patrick Conacher	.13	.25
5	Lee Fogolin	.13	.25
6	Grant Fuhr, Goalie	.75	1.50
7	Randall Gregg	.13	.25
8	Wayne Gretzky	4.00	8.00
9	Charles Huddy	.13	.25
10	Pat Hughes	.13	.25
11	Dave Hunter	.13	.25
12	Don Jackson	.13	.25
13	Jari Kurri	.50	1.00
14	Willy Lindstrom	.13	.25
15	Ken Linseman	.13	.25
16	Kevin Lowe	.13	.25
17	Dave Lumley	.13	.25
18	Kevin McClelland	.13	.25
19	Mark Messier	1.00	2.00
20	Andrew Moog, Goalie	.50	1.00
21	Jaroslav Pouzar	.13	.25
22	Dave Semenko	.13	.25
23	Raimo Summanen	.13	.25
24	Ted Green; Glen Sather; John Muckler, Coaches	.13	.25
25	Emery Award	.13	.25

STATER MINT LTD

— 1983 - 84 HOCKEY DOLLARS —

These cupro-nickel coins were sold singlely and packaged with a 8 3/8" X 3" perforated card.

Coin Size: 1 1/4" Diameter
Face: Player portrait, Name
Back: Team logo
Imprint: None
Card Size: 5" X 3"
Face: Grey, black and oranger; Jersey number, Name
Back: Grey and black on white card stock; Jersey number, Name, Resume, Number
Imprint: 1983 — MADE IN CANADA
Complete Set No.: 7

Complete Set Price:	25.00	50.00
Common Card:	3.75	7.50

No.	Player	EX	NRMT
H14	Wayne Gretzky	12.50	25.00
H15	Andrew Moog, Goalie	5.00	10.00
H16	Dave Hunter	3.75	7.50
H17	Ken Linseman	3.75	7.50
H18	Lee Fogolin	3.75	7.50
H19	Dave Semenko	3.75	7.50
H20	Mark Messier	7.50	15.00

I.G.A.

— 1990 - 91 REGULAR ISSUE —

This set is unnumbered and the cards are listed below in alphabetical order.

I.G.A. 1990-91 Issue
Card No. 1, Glenn Anderson

Card Size: 2 1/2" X 3 1/2"
Face: Four colour, blue and oranger border; Jersey number, Team logo
Back: Black and red on white card stock; Team logo, Name, Resume, Sponsor logos
Imprint: © Horne & Pitfield Foods Limied 1990-91
Complete Set No.: 30

Complete Set Price:	10.00	20.00
Common Card:	.13	.25

No.	Player	EX	NRMT
1	Glenn Anderson	1.00	2.00
2	Dave Brown	.13	.25
3	Jeff Beukeboom	.13	.25
4	Kelly Buchberger	.13	.25
5	Martin Gelinas	.35	.75
6	Adam Graves	1.50	3.00
7	Ted Green, Assistant Coach	.13	.25
8	Charles Huddy	.13	.25
9	Chris Joseph	.13	.25
10	Petr Klima	.25	.50
11	Mark Lamb	.13	.25
12	Ken Linseman	.13	.25
13	Ron Low, Assistant Coach	.13	.25
14	Kevin Lowe	.25	.50
15	Craig MacTavish	.13	.25
16	Mark Messier	2.00	4.00
17	Joey Moss, Assistant	.13	.25
18	John Muckler, Coach	.13	.25
19	Craig Muni	.13	.25
20	Joe Murphy	.35	.75
21	Bill Ranford, Goalie	.50	1.00
22	Anatoli Semenov	.35	.75
23	Craig Simpson	.25	.50
24	Geoff Smith	.13	.25
25	Steve Smith	.25	.50
26	Kari Takko, Goalie	.13	.25
27	Esa Tikkanen	.25	.50
28	Training Staff: K. Low; L. Kulchisky; B. Stafford; S. Poirier	.13	.25
29	Five Time Stanley Cup Champions	.25	.50
30	Checklist	.50	1.00

— 1991 - 1992 REGULAR ISSUE —

I.G.A. 1991-92 Issue
Card No. 25, Esa Tikkanen

Card Size: 2 1/2" X 3 1/2"
Face: Four colour, blue border; Name, Position, Jersey number, Team
Back: Black on card stock; Name, Team logo, Position, Resume
Imprint: © Horne & Pitfield Foods Limited 1991-92
Complete Set No.: 30

Complete Set Price:	7.50	15.00
Common Card:	.10	.20

No.	Player	EX	NRMT
1	Josef Beranek	.50	1.00
2	Kelly Buchberger	.10	.20
3	Vincent Damphousse	.50	1.00
4	Louie DeBrusk	.25	.50
5	Martin Gelinas	.25	.50
6	Peter Ing, Goalie	.10	.20
7	Petr Klima	.20	.40
8	Mark Lamb	.10	.20
9	Kevin Lowe	.25	.50
10	Norm Maciver	.25	.50
11	Craig MacTavish	.13	.25
12	Troy Mallette	.10	.20
13	Dave Manson	.25	.50
14	Scott Mellanby	.20	.40
15	Craig Muni	.10	.20
16	Joe Murphy	.25	.50
17	Bill Ranford, Goalie	.50	1.00
18	Steven Rice	.10	.20
19	Luke Richardson	.10	.20
20	Anatoli Semenov	.25	.50
21	David Shaw	.10	.20
22	Craig Simpson	.10	.20
23	Geoff Smith	.10	.20
24	Scott Thornton	.10	.20
25	Esa Tikkanen	.25	.50
26	Training Staff, SP	.50	1.00
27	Ted Green, Coach, SP	.50	1.00
28	Ron Low, Asst. Coach, SP	.50	1.00
29	Kevin Primeau, Asst. Coach, SP	.50	1.00
30	Checklist, SP	.50	1.00

HARTFORD WHALERS - TEAM SETS

TEAM ISSUES

THE JUNIOR WHALERS

— 1983 - 84 JUNIOR ISSUE —

These cards are unnumbered and are listed below alphabetically.

Postcard Size: 3 3/4" x 8 1/4"
Face: Four colour
Back: Black on white card stock; Resume, Facsimile crest
Imprint: None
Complete Set No.: 22
Complete Set Price: 10.00 20.00
Common Card: .35 .75

No.	Player	EX	NRMT
1	Bob Crawford	.35	.75
2	Mike Crombeen	.35	.75
3	Richard Dunn	.35	.75
4	Normand Dupont	.35	.75
5	Ronald Francis	1.75	3.50
6	Ed Hospodar	.35	.75
7	Marty Howe	.50	1.00
8	Mark Johnson	.35	.75
9	Chris Kotsopoulos	.50	1.00
10	Pierre Lacroix	.35	.75
11	Greg Malone	.35	.75
12	Greg Millen, Goalie	.75	1.50
13	Ray Neufeld	.50	1.00
14	Joel Quenneville	.50	1.00
15	Torrie Robertson	.50	1.00
16	Risto Siltanen	.35	.75
17	Blaine Stoughton	.75	1.50
18	Steve Stoyanovich	.35	.75
19	Doug Sulliman	.35	.75
20	Sylvain Turgeon	1.00	2.00
21	Mike Veisor	.35	.75
22	Mike Zuke	.35	.75

— 1988 - 89 GROUND ROUND POSTCARD ISSUE —

These cards are unnumbered and are listed below in alphabetical order.

1988-89 Ground Round Junior Whalers
Postcard No. 1, John Anderson

Postcard Size: 3 11/16" X 8 1/4"
Face: Four colour, borderless; Team logo
Back: Black on card stock; Name, Jersey number, Resume, Drug tip
Imprint: None
Complete Set No.: 18
Complete Set Price: 7.50 15.00
Common Card: .25 .50

No.	Player	EX	NRMT
1	John Anderson	.25	.50
2	David Babych	.50	1.00
3	Sylvain Cote	.25	.50
4	Kevin Dineen	.75	1.50
5	Dean Evason	.25	.50
6	Ray Ferraro	.50	1.00
7	Ron Francis	1.25	2.50
8	Scot Kleinendorst	.25	.50
9	Randy Ladouceur	.25	.50
10	Michael Liut, Goalie	.75	1.50
11	Paul MacDermid	.25	.50
12	Brent Peterson, Error	.25	.50
13	Joel Quenneville	.25	.50
14	Torrie Robertson	.25	.50
15	Ulf Samuelsson	.50	1.00
16	Dave Tippett	.25	.50
17	Sylvain Turgeon	.35	.75
18	Carey Wilson, Error	.25	.50

— 1989 - 90 REAL MILK POSTCARD ISSUE —

The cards in this set are unnumbered are are listed here in alphabetical order.

Postcard Size: 3 11/16" X 8 1/4"
Face: Four colour, borderless; Team logo
Back: Black on card stock; Name, Jersey number, Resume, Drug tip
Imprint: None
Complete Set No.: 23
Complete Set Price: 6.00 12.00
Common Card: .25 .50

No.	Player	EX	NRMT
1	Bo Mikael Andersson	.25	.50
2	David Babych	.35	.75
3	Sylvain Cote	.25	.50
4	Randy Cunneyworth	.25	.50
5	Kevin Dineen	.75	1.50
6	Dean Evason	.35	.75
7	Ray Ferraro	.50	1.00
8	Ron Francis	1.25	2.50
9	Jody Hull	.25	.50
10	Grant Jennings	.25	.50
11	Edward Kastelic	.25	.50
12	Todd Krygier	.50	1.00
13	Randy Ladouceur	.25	.50
14	Michael Liut, Goalie	.60	1.25
15	Paul MacDermid	.25	.50
16	Joel Quenneville	.25	.50
17	Ulf Samuelsson	.35	.75
18	Brad Shaw	.35	.75
19	Peter Sidorkiewicz, Goalie	.60	1.25
20	Dave Tippett	.25	.50
21	Mike Tomlak	.25	.50
22	Patrick Verbeek	.75	1.50
23	Scott Young	.35	.75

— 1990 - 91 7-ELEVEN POSTCARD ISSUE —

Postcard Size: 3 3/4" X 8 1/4"
Face: Four colour, borderless; Team logo
Back: Black on card stock; Name, Jersey number, Resume, Drug tip
Imprint: None
Complete Set No.: 23
Complete Set Price: 7.50 15.00
Common Card: .25 .50

No.	Player	EX	NRMT
1	Bo Mikael Andersson	.25	.50
2	David Babych	.25	.50
3	Yvon Corriveau	.35	.75
4	Sylvain Cote	.25	.50
5	Doug Crossman	.25	.50
6	Randy Cunneyworth	.25	.50
7	Paul Cyr	.25	.50
8	Kevin Dineen	.75	1.50
9	Dean Evason	.25	.50
10	Ron Francis	1.00	2.00
11	Robert Holik	1.50	3.00
12	Gordie Howe	2.00	4.00
13	Grant Jennings	.25	.50
14	Edward Kastelic	.25	.50
15	Todd Krygier	.35	.75
16	Randy Ladouceur	.25	.50
17	Ulf Samuelsson	.25	.50
18	Brad Shaw	.25	.50
19	Peter Sidorkiewicz, Goalie	.50	1.00
20	Mike Tomlak	.25	.50
21	Patrick Verbeek	.60	1.25
22	Carey Wilson	.25	.50
23	Scott Young	.25	.50

Note: There are possibly four Short Printed cards in this set. We would appreciate hearing from anyone with this information.

— 1991 - 92 7-ELEVEN POSTCARD ISSUE —

Postcard Size: 3 3/4" X 8 1/4"
Face: Four colour, borderless; Team logo
Back: Black on card stock; Name, Jersey number, Resume
Imprint: None
Complete Set No.: 22
Complete Set Price: 7.50 15.00
Common Card: .25 .50

No.	Player	EX	NRMT
1	Bo Michael Andersson	.25	.50
2	Adam Burt	.25	.50
3	Marc Bergevin	.25	.50
4	Rob Brown	.75	1.50
5	Murray Craven	.35	.75
6	John Cullen	.35	.75
7	Randy Cunneyworth	.25	.50
8	Joe Day	.25	.50
9	Mark Greig	.30	.60
10	Robert Holik	.75	1.50
11	Doug Houda	.25	.50
12	Mark Hunter	.25	.50
13	Ed Kastelic	.25	.50
14	Randy Ladouceur	.25	.50
15	Kim McKenzie	.25	.50
16	Michel Picard	.25	.50
17	Geoff Sanderson	2.50	5.00
18	Brad Shaw	.25	.50
19	Peter Sidorkiewicz, Goalie	.35	.75
21	Pat Verbeek	.50	1.00
20	Kay Whitmore, Goalie	.35	.75
22	Zarley Zalapski	.35	.75

Note: There are possibly six Short Printed cards in this set. We would appreciate hearing from anyone with this information.

COURANT

— 1982 - 83 POSTCARD ISSUE —

This set is incomplete. We would appreciate hearing from anyone who could supply further information.

THOMAS

— 1982 - 83 JUNIOR ISSUE —

We have no information on the this set. We would appreciate hearing from anyone who could supply information to help complete this set.

WENDY'S

— 1984 - 85 JUNIOR ISSUE —

We have no information on the this set. We would appreciate hearing from anyone who could supply information to help complete this set.

— 1985 - 86 JUNIOR ISSUE —

We have no information on the this set. We would appreciate hearing from anyone who could supply information to help complete this set.

DAIRYMART

— 1992 - 93 REGULAR ISSUE —

Card Size: 2 3/8" X 3 1/2"
Face: Four colour, white border; Name, Team name, Position
Back: Black on white card stock; Name, Number, Position, Resume, Sponsor logo
Imprint: None
Complete Set No.: 25
Complete Set Price: 7.50 / 15.00
Common Card: .25 / .50

No.	Player	EX	NRMT
1	Jim Agnew	.25	.50
2	Sean Burke, Goalie	.25	.50
3	Adam Burt	.25	.50
4	Andrew Cassels	.50	1.00
5	Murray Craven	.25	.50
6	Randy Cunneyworth	.25	.50
7	Paul Gillis	.25	.50
8	Paul Holmgren, Head Coach	.25	.50
9	Doug Houda	.25	.50
10	Mark Janssens	.25	.50
11	Tim Kerr	.35	.75
12	Steve Konroyd	.25	.50
13	Nicolas Kypreos	.25	.50
14	Randy Ladouceur	.25	.50
15	Jim McKenzie	.25	.50
16	Michael Nylander	1.00	2.00
17	Allen Pedersen	.25	.50
18	Robert Petrovicky	.75	1.50
19	Frank Pietrangelo, Goalie	.25	.50
20	Patrick Poulin	.25	.50
21	Geoff Sanderson	1.50	3.00
22	Pat Verbeek	.50	1.00
23	Eric Weinrich	.25	.50
24	Terry Yake	.25	.50
25	Zarley Zalapski	.25	.50

COCA COLA

— 1993 - 94 REGULAR ISSUE —

Card Size: 2 3/8" X 3 1/2"
Face: Four colour, white border; Name, Team name, Position
Back: Black on white card stock; Name, Number, Position, Resume, Sponsor logo
Imprint: None
Complete Set No.: 25
Complete Set Price: 5.00 / 10.00
Common Card: .12 / .25

No.	Player	EX	NRMT
1	Sean Burke, Goalie	.12	.25
2	Adam Burt	.12	.25
3	Andrew Cassels	.50	1.00
4	Randy Cunneyworth	.12	.25
5	Alexander Godynyuk	.12	.25
6	Mark Greig	.12	.25
7	Mark Janssens	.12	.25
8	Robert Kron	.12	.25
9	Bryan Marchment	.12	.25
10	Brad McCrimmon	.12	.25
11	Pierre McGuire, Head Coach	.12	.25
12	Michael Nylander	1.00	2.00
13	James Patrick	.12	.25
14	Frank Pietrangelo, Goalie	.12	.25
15	Marc Potvin	.12	.25
16	Chris Pronger	.12	.25
17	Brian Propp	.12	.25
18	Jeff Reese, Goalie	.12	.25
19	Geoff Sanderson	1.00	2.00
20	Jim Sandlak	.12	.25
21	Jim Storm	.12	.25
22	Darren Turcotte	.35	.75
23	Pat Verbeek	.50	1.00
24	Zarley Zalapski	.12	.25

Hartford Whalers - Team Sets
Dairy Mart 1992-93 Issue, Card No. 21, Geoff Sanderson

Hartford Whalers - Team Sets
Coca-Cola 1993-94 Issue, Card No. 12, Michael Nylander

LOS ANGELES KINGS - TEAM SETS

CARD NIGHT

— 1980 - 81 REGULAR ISSUE —

These cards were given away at the Kings "Card Night".

Card Night, 1980-81 Issue,
Card No. 1, Marcel Dionne

Card Size: 2 1/2 X 3 1/2"
Face: Four colour, blue strip at bottom, white border; Name, Team logo
Back: Black on white card stock; Number, Name, Resume, Position
Imprint: © 1980 All-Star Cards Ltd.
Complete Set No.: 14
Complete Set Price: 7.50   15.00
Common Card: .35   .75

No.	Player	EX	NRMT
1	Marcel Dionne	2.50	5.00
2	Glenn Goldup	.35	.75
3	Doug Halward	.35	.75
4	Billy Harris	.50	1.00
5	Steve Jensen	.35	.75
6	Jerry Korab	.35	.75
7	Mario Lessard, Goalie	.50	1.00
8	Dave Lewis	.35	.75
9	Mike Murphy	.35	.75
10	Rob R. Palmer	.35	.75
11	Charlie Simmer	1.00	2.00
12	David Taylor	1.50	3.00
13	Garry Unger	.35	.75
14	Gordon (Jay) Wells	.35	.75

SMOKEY

— 1984 - 85 ISSUE —

Smokey, 1984-85 Issue,
Card No. 2, Marcel Dionne

Card Size: 2 15/16" X 4 3/8"
Face: Four colour, white border; Name, Team and sponsor logos
Back: Black on white card stock; Number, Name, Position, Resume, Fire Safety tips
Imprint: None
Complete Set No.: 23
Complete Set Price: 7.50   15.00
Common Card: .25   .50

No.	Player	EX	NRMT
1	Russ Anderson	.25	.50
2	Marcel Dionne	2.00	4.00
3	Brian Engblom	.25	.50
4	Daryl Evans	.25	.50
5	Jim Fox	.25	.50
6	Garry Galley	.25	.50
7	Anders Hakansson	.25	.50
8	Mark Hardy	.25	.50
9	Bob Janecyk, Goalie	.25	.50
10	John Paul Kelly	.25	.50
11	Brian MacLellan	.25	.50
12	Bernie Nicholls	.75	1.50
13	Craig Redmond	.25	.50
14	Terry Ruskowski	.25	.50
15	Douglas Smith	.25	.50
16	David Taylor	.75	1.50
17	Gordon (Jay) Wells	.25	.50
18	Darren Eliot, Goalie	.25	.50
19	Rick Lapointe	.25	.50
20	Bob Miller	.25	.50
21	Steve Seguin	.25	.50
22	Phil Sykes	.25	.50
23	Pat Quinn, Coach	.50	1.00

— 1988 - 89 REGULAR ISSUE —

The cards are unnumbered and are listed in alphabetical order.

Smokey, 1988-89 Issue,
Card No. 1, Mike Allison

Card Size: 2 1/2' X 3 1/2"
Face: Four colour, white border; Team, Name, Position, Team and sponsor logos
Back: Black on white card stock; Name, Position, Resume, Fire Safety tip
Imprint: A Public Service in Wildfire Prevention, 1989 Forest Service, USDA - Bureau of Land Management, USDI California Department of Forestry and Fire Protection
Complete Set No.: 25
Complete Set Price: 10.00   20.00
Common Card: .13   .25

No.	Player	EX	NRMT
1	Mike Allison	.13	.25
2	Ken Baumgartner	.13	.25
3	Robert Carpenter	.25	.50
4	Doug Crossman	.13	.25
5	Dale DeGray	.13	.25
6	Steve Duchesne	.75	1.50
7	Ron Duguay	.25	.50
8	Mark Fitzpatrick, Goalie	.25	.50
9	Jim Fox	.13	.25
10	Robbie Ftorek, Head Coach	.25	.50
11	Wayne Gretzky	5.00	10.00
12	Gilles Hamel	.13	.25
13	Glenn Healy, Goalie	.50	1.00
14	Michael Krushelnyski	.25	.50
15	Thomas Laidlaw	.13	.25
16	Bryan Maxwell, Coach	.13	.25
17	Wayne McBean	.35	.75
18	Martin McSorley	.60	1.25
19	Bernie Nicholls	.75	1.50
20	Cap Raeder, Coach	.13	.25
21	Luc Robitaille	1.50	3.00
22	David Taylor	.35	.75
23	John Tonelli	.25	.50
24	Timothy Watters	.13	.25
25	Checklist	.13	.25

— 1989 - 90 REGULAR ISSUE —

Smokey, 1989-90 Issue,
Card No. 1, Wayne Gretzky

Card Size: 2 1/2" X 3 1/2"
Face: Four colour, grey and white border; Team, Team and sponsor logos, Position, Name
Back: Black and white on card stock; Name, Position, Number, Resume, Fire Safety tip
Imprint: A Public Service in Fire Prevention by USDA Forest Service. In Cooperation with California Dept. of Forestry and Fire Protection, and USDI Bureau of Land Management, 1990.
Complete Set No.: 24
Complete Set Price: 10.00   20.00
Common Card: .13   .25

No.	Player	EX	NRMT
1	Wayne Gretzky	5.00	10.00
2	Timothy Watters	.13	.25
3	Mikael Lindholm	.13	.25
4	Mike Allison	.13	.25
5	Stephen Kasper	.25	.50
6	David Taylor	.75	1.50
7	Larry Robinson	.75	1.50
8	Luc Robitaille	1.50	3.00
9	Barry Beck	.25	.50
10	Keith Crowder	.13	.25
11	Petr Prajsler	.13	.25
12	Michael Krushelnyski	.25	.50
13	John Tonelli	.20	.40
14	Steve Duchesne	.50	1.00
15	Jay Miller	.13	.25
16	Kelly Hrudey, Goalie	.50	1.00
17	Martin McSorley	.35	.75
18	Mario Gosselin, Goalie	.25	.50
19	Craig Duncanson	.13	.25
20	Bob Kudelski	.25	.50
21	Brian Benning	.13	.25
22	Mikko Makela	.13	.25
23	Thomas Laidlaw	.13	.25
24	Checklist	.13	.25

LOS ANGELES KINGS - TEAM SETS

— 1989 - 90 GRETZKY —

We have no information regarding this card. We would appreciate hearing from anyone who could supply further information.

— 1990 - 91 REGULAR ISSUE —

This set was sponsored by RC Cola in cooperation with A. S. Forest Services.

Smokey, 1990-91 Issue
Card No. 17, Kelly Hrudey

Card Size: 2 1/2" X 3 1/2"
Face: Four colour, white border; Name, Position, Team and sponsor logos
Back: Black on white card stock; Number, name, Position, Resume, Fire Safety tip
Imprint: A Public Service in Fire Prevention by USDA Forest Service, in cooperation with California Dept of Forestry and Fire Protection, USDI Bureau of Land Management, National Park Service, and the Los Angeles Kings, 1991.
Complete Set No.: 25
Complete Set Price: 6.00 12.00
Common Card: .13 .25
Album: 2.50 5.00

No.	Player	EX	NRMT
—	Title Card: Take the RC Challenge	.13	.25
1	Wayne Gretzky	5.00	10.00
2	Brian Benning	.13	.25
3	Rob Blake	1.00	2.00
4	Timothy Watters	.13	.25
5	Todd Elik	.35	.70
6	Tomas Sandstrom	.60	1.25
7	Stephen Kasper	.13	.25
8	David Taylor	.50	1.00
9	Larry Robinson	.50	1.00
10	Luc Robitaille	1.00	2.00
11	Tony Granato	.13	.25
12	Thomas Laidlaw	.13	.25
13	Francois Breault	.13	.25
14	John Tonelli	.25	.50
15	Steve Duchesne	.50	1.00
16	Jay Miller	.13	.25
17	Kelly Hrudey, Goalie	.35	.75
18	Martin McSorley	.50	1.00
19	Daniel Berthiaume, Goalie	.13	.25
20	Bob Kudelski	.25	.50
21	Brad Jones	.13	.25
22	John McIntyre	.13	.25
23	Rod Buskas	.13	.25
24	Kingston, Mascot	.13	.25

— 1991 - 92 ISSUE —

We have no information regarding this card. We would appreciate hearing from anyone who could supply further information.

NORTHWEST AIRLINES

— 1990 - 91 ISSUE —

We have no information regarding this card. We would appreciate hearing from anyone who could supply further information.

TARGET

— 1991 - 92 ISSUE —

We have no information regarding this card. We would appreciate hearing from anyone who could supply further information.

UPPER DECK

— 1991 - 92 SEASON TICKET HOLDERS —

Sent out to 1992 season ticket holders. Numbered _ of 7,000.

Upper Deck 1991-92 Season Ticket Holders
The Silver Season 25th Anniversary

Card Size: 5" X 3 1/2"
Face: Four colour, borderless; Team logo
Back: Four colour, borderless; Team logo
Imprint: © 1991 The Upper Deck Co.

No.	Player	EX	NRMT
—	The Silver Season 25th Anniversary	75.00	150.00

— 1992 - 93 SEASON TICKET HOLDERS —

Sent out to 1993 season ticket holders. Numbered _ of 7000
A Seasons Greeting from the L. A. Kings

Upper Deck 1992-93 Season Ticket Holders
Season's Greetings from the LA Kings

Card Size: 5 3/8" x 3 5/8"
Face: Four colour, borderless; Upper Deck and Team logos
Back: Four colour, borderless, card stock
Imprint: Upper Deck is a trademark of The Upper Deck Company © 1992 The Upper Deck Company. All Rights Reserved. Printed in the U.S.A

No.	Player	EX	NRMT
1	Season's Greetings from the Los Angeles Kings	75.00	150.00

COCA-COLA

— 1993 - 94 WAYNE GRETZKY POG SET —

This 18-pog set was a premium gift with a purchase of a coca-cola product at Mac's Milk across Canada except Quebec. You receive one pog free with every Coke product purchased.

Card Size: 1 11/16" diameter
Face: Four colour, gold foil border; The Great one, Coke logo
Back: Black print on white card stock
Imprint: © "Coca-Cola", "Coke", "Always" and the Distinctive Bottle are registered trade marks of Coca-Cola Ltd. TM and ©1994 WPF
Complete Set No.: 18
Complete Set Price: 10.00 20.00
Common Card: .75 1.50

THE GREAT ONE

No.	Player	EX	NRMT
1	Most Assists in a Career	.75	1.50
2	Most Points in a Career	.75	1.50
3	Most 100 Point Seasons	.75	1.50
4	Most 3 Goal Games in a Career	.75	1.50
5	Most Goals in a Single Season	.75	1.50
6	Most Points in a Season	.75	1.50
7	Longest Consecutive Point Streak	.75	1.50
8	Most Assists in a Game	.75	1.50
9	Most Goals, One Period	.75	1.50
10	Most Playoff Points (Career)	.75	1.50
11	Most Points One Playoff Year	.75	1.50
12	Most Goals All-Star Game (Career)	.75	1.50
13	Most Goal One Period All-Star Game	.75	1.50
14	Most Valuable Player (Hart Trophy)	.75	1.50
15	NHL Leading Scorer (Art Ross Trophy)	.75	1.50
16	MVP As Voted By Players (Lester B. Pearson Trophy)	.75	1.50
17	Most Game Winning Goals in Playoff (Career)	.75	1.50
18	Most Goals	2.00	4.00

MINNESOTA NORTH STARS - TEAM SETS

TEAM ISSUES

— 1973 - 74 POSTCARD ISSUE —

Postcard Size: 3 5/8" X 5"
Face: Black and white; Name
Back: White postcard stock
Imprint: None
Complete Set No.: 20
Complete Set Price: 16.50 33.00
Common Card: .75 1.50

No.	Player	EX	NRMT
1	Fred Barrett	.75	1.50
2	Gary Bergman	.75	1.50
3	Jude Drouin	.75	1.50
4	Tony Featherstone	.75	1.50
5	Barry Gibbs	.75	1.50
6	Bill Goldsworthy	1.00	2.00
7	Danny Grant	1.25	2.50
8	Buster Harvey	.75	1.50
9	Dennis Hextall	.75	1.50
10	Parker MacDonald	.75	1.50
11	Cesare Maniago, Goalie	1.00	2.00
12	Lou Nanne	1.00	2.00
13	Rod Norrish	.75	1.50
14	Dennis O'Brien	.75	1.50
15	Murray Oliver	1.00	2.00
16	Jean-Paul Parise	1.25	2.50
17	Dean Prentice	.75	1.50
18	Tom Reid	.75	1.50
19	Fred Stanfield	1.00	2.00
20	Lorne "Gump" Worsley, Goalie	2.25	4.50

— 1978 POSTCARD ISSUE —

We have no information on the 1978 postcard issue. We would appreciate hearing from any who could help us complete this set.

1978 Postcard Issue
Card No. 1, Gilles Meloche

Card Size: 3 1/2" X 5 1/2"
Face: Black and white, borderless; Facsimile autograph
Back: Black on white card stock; Name, Position, Resume, Team logo
Imprint: None
Complete Set No.: Unknown
Complete Set Price: Unknown

No.	Player	EX	NRMT
1	Gilles Meloche, Goalie	.50	1.00

— 1979 - 80 POSTCARD ISSUE —

This 25-postcard set was produced as a promotion for the Minnesota North Stars.

1979-80 Postcard Issue
Postcard No. 21, Robert Smith

Postcard Size: 3 1/2" x 5 1/2"
Face: Black and white, borderless
Back: Black print on postcard; Name, Resume, Team logo
Imprint: None
Complete Set No.: 26
Complete Set Price: 10.00 20.00
Common Card: .35 .75

No.	Player	EX	NRMT
1	Kent-Erik Andersson	.35	.75
2	Fred Barrett	.35	.75
3	Per-Olov Brasar	.35	.75
4	Gary Edwards, Goalie	.35	.75
5	Steve Christoff	.35	.75
6	Mike Fidler	.35	.75
7	Craig Hartsburg	1.00	2.00
8	Harry Howell	.75	1.50
9	Al MacAdam	.35	.75
10	Kris Manery	.35	.75
11	Brad Maxwell	.35	.75
12	Tom McCarthy	.35	.75
13	Gilles Meloche, Goalie	.75	1.50
14	Lou Nanne	.50	1.00
15	Murray Oliver Assis. Coach	.35	.75
16	Steve Payne	.35	.75
17	Mike Polich	.35	.75
18	Gary Sargent	.35	.75
19	Glen Sharpley	.35	.75
20	Paul Shmyr	.35	.75
21	Robert Smith	2.50	5.00
22	Greg Smith	.35	.75
23	Glen Sonmor, Coach	.35	.75
24	Tim Young	.35	.75
25	Tom Younghans	.35	.75
26	Ron Zanussi	.35	.75

— 1980 - 81 POSTCARD ISSUE —

This 24-postcard set was produced as a promotion for the Minnesota North Stars.

Postcard Size: 3 1/2" x 5 1/2"
Face: Black and white, borderless
Back: Black print on postcard; Name, Resume, Team logo
Imprint: None
Complete Set No.: 24
Complete Set Price: 9.00 18.00
Common Card: .35 .75

No.	Player	EX	NRMT
1	Kent E. Andersson	.35	.75
2	Fred Barrett	.35	.75
3	Donald Beaupre, Goalie	1.00	2.00
4	Jack Carlson, GM	.35	.75
5	Steve Christoff	1.00	2.00
6	Mike Eaves	.35	.75
7	Gary Edwards	.35	.75
8	Curt Giles	1.00	2.00
9	Craig Hartsburg	1.25	2.50
10	Al McAdam	.50	1.00
11	Brad Maxwell	.50	1.00
12	Tom McCarthy	.35	.75
13	Gilles Meloche, Goalie	.75	1.50
14	Oliver, Sonmor, Parise, Coaches	.50	1.00
15	Steve Payne	.75	1.50
16	Mike Polich	.35	.75
17	Gary Sargent	.35	.75
18	Glen Sharpley	.35	.75
19	Paul Shmyr	.35	.75
20	Robert Smith	2.00	4.00
21	Greg Smith	.35	.75
22	Tim Young	.35	.75
23	Tom Younghans	.35	.75
24	Ron Zanussi	.35	.75

— 1981 - 82 POSTCARD ISSUE —

Card Size: 3 1/2" X 5 1/2"
Face: Four colour, borderless
Back: Green on white card stock; Name, Resume, Position, Team logo
Imprint: Unknown
Complete Set No.: 24
Complete Set Price: 10.00 20.00
Common Card: .35 .75

No.	Player	EX	NRMT
1	Kent-Erik Andersson	.35	.75
2	Fred Barrett	.35	.75
3	Donald Beaupre, Goalie	.75	1.50
4	Neal Broten	1.00	2.00
5	Jack Carlson	.35	.75
6	Steve Christoff	.50	1.00
7	Dino Ciccarelli	2.50	5.00
8	Mike Eaves	.35	.75
9	Curt Giles	.35	.75
10	Anders Hakansson	.35	.75
11	Craig Hartsburg	.50	1.00
12	Al MacAdam	.35	.75
13	Brad Maxwell	.35	.75
14	Kevin Maxwell	.35	.75
15	Tom McCarthy	.35	.75
16	Gilles Meloche, Goalie	.50	1.00
17	Bill Nyrop	.35	.75
18	Murray Oliver, J.P. Parise, Glen Sonmor, Coaches	.50	1.00
19	Brad Palmer	.35	.75
20	Steve Payne	.35	.75
21	Gordon Roberts	.50	1.00
22	Gary Sargent	.35	.75
23	Robert Smith	1.50	3.00
24	Tim Young	.35	.75

— 1982 - 83 POSTCARD ISSUE —

These cards are unnumbered and are listed below alphabetically.

Card Size: 3 1/2" x 5 1/2"
Face: Four colour, borderless
Back: Green on white card stock; Name, Resume, Position, Team logo
Imprint: None
Complete Set No.: 25
Complete Set Price: 10.00 20.00
Common Card: .25 .50

No.	Player	EX	NRMT
1	Neal Broten, Dino Ciccarelli	1.00	2.00
2	Fred Battett	.25	.50
3	Donald Beaupre, Goalie	.50	1.00
4	Brian Bellows	1.00	2.00
5	Neal Broten	1.00	2.00
6	Dino Ciccarelli	1.50	3.00
7	Jordy Douglas	.25	.50
8	Mike Eaves	.25	.50

MINNESOTA NORTH STARS - TEAM SETS

No.	Player	EX	NRMT
9	George Ferguson	.25	.50
10	Ron Friest	.25	.50
11	Curt Giles	.75	1.50
12	Craig Hartsburg	.75	1.50
13	Al MacAdam	.35	.75
14	Dan Mandich	.25	.50
15	Brad Maxwell	.50	1.00
16	Tom McCarthy	.50	1.00
17	Gilles Meloche, Goalie	.75	1.50
18	Steve Payne	.35	.75
19	Willi Plett	.35	.75
20	Gordon Roberts	.25	.50
21	Gary Sargent	.25	.50
22	Bobby Smith	.75	1.50
23	Ken Solheim	.25	.50
24	Tim Young	.25	.50
25	Team Photograph	1.00	2.00

— 1983 - 1984 POSTCARD ISSUE —

This 25-postcard set was produced as a promotion for the Minnesota North Stars.

1983-84 Postcard Issue
Postcard No. 2, Donald Beaupre

Postcard Size: 3 1/2" x 5 7/16"
Face: Four colour, borderless
Back: Green print on card stock; Name, Resume, Team Logo
Imprint: Park Press Inc. Waite Park, Minnesota
Complete Set No.: 25
Complete Set Price: 7.50 / 15.00
Common Card: .25 / .50

No.	Player	EX	NRMT
1	Keith Acton	.25	.50
2	Donald Beaupre, Goalie	.35	.75
3	Brian Bellows	1.00	2.00
4	Scott Bjugstad	.25	.50
5	Neal Broten	.50	1.00
6	Dino Ciccarelli	.75	1.50
7	Curt Giles	.35	.75
8	Craig Hartsburg	.35	.75
9	Tom Hirsch	.25	.50
10	Paul Holmgren	.25	.50
11	Brian Lawton	.25	.50
12	Tom McCarthy	.25	.50
13	Dan Mandich	.25	.50
14	Dennis Maruk	.25	.50
15	Brad Maxwell	.25	.50
16	Roland Melanson, Goalie	.25	.50
17	Gilles Meloche, Goalie	.25	.50
18	Mark Napier	.25	.50
19	Steve Payne	.25	.50
20	Willi Plett	.25	.50
21	Dave Richter	.25	.50
22	Gordon Roberts	.25	.50
23	Robert Rouse	.25	.50
24	Harold Snepsts	.35	.75
25	Ken Solhein	.25	.50

— 1986 - 87 ISSUE —

We have no information on the 1986-87 team set. We would appreciate hearing from anyone who could supply further information.

— 1987 - 88 POSTCARD ISSUE —

Postcard Size: 3 1/2" X 5 3/8"
Face: Four colour, borderless
Back: Green on white card stock; Jersey number, Name, Resume, Team logo
Imprint: None
Complete Set No.: 31
Complete Set Price: 5.00 / 10.00
Common Card: .13 / .25

No.	Player	EX	NRMT
1	Keith Acton	.13	.25
2	Dave Archibald	.13	.25
3	Warren Babe	.13	.25
4	Donald Beaupre, Goalie	.25	.50
5	Brian Bellows	.75	1.50
6	Mike Berger	.13	.25
7	Scott Bjugstad	.13	.25
8	Bob Brooke	.13	.25
9	Herb Brooks, Coach	.25	.50
10	Neal Broten	.25	.50
11	Dino Ciccarelli	.50	1.00
12	Larry DePalma	.13	.25
13	Dave Gagner	1.00	2.00
14	Curt Giles	.13	.25
15	Dirk Graham	.13	.25
16	Craig Hartsburg	.25	.50
17	Tom Hirsch	.13	.25
18	Brian Lawton	.13	.25
19	Brian MacLellan	.13	.25
20	Dennis Maruk	.25	.50
21	Basil McRae	.13	.25
22	Frantisek Musil	.13	.25
23	Steve Payne	.13	.25
24	Pat Price	.13	.25
25	Chris Pryor	.13	.25
26	Gordon Roberts	.13	.25
27	Robert Rouse	.13	.25
28	Terry Ruskowski	.13	.25
29	Kari Takko, Goalie	.13	.25
30	Ronald Wilson	.13	.25
31	Richard Zemlak	.13	.25

CLOVERLEAF DAIRY

— 1978 - 79 ISSUE —

We have no information this set. We would appreciate hearing from anyone would could supply further information.

— 1979 - 80 ISSUE —

We have no information on this set. We would appreciate hearing from anyone would could supply further information.

7 - ELEVEN

— 1984 - 85 REGULAR ISSUE —

7-Eleven, 1984-85 Issue
Card No. 2, Willi Plett

Card Size: 2 5/8" X 4 1/8"
Face: Four colour, white border; Team logo, Jersey number, Name, Position, Team
Back: Black, green and yellow on white card stock; Team logo, Number, Jersey number, Name, Position, Resume, Fire prevention tip
Imprint: Produced in cooperation with the Fire Marshalls Assn. of Minnesota, The Southland Corporation, and the Minnesota North Stars. ©Cueno and Associates 1984.
Complete Set No.: 12
Complete Set Price: 4.00 / 8.00
Common Card: .25 / .50

No.	Player	EX	NRMT
1	Neal Broten	.50	1.00
2	Willi Plett, Error	.25	.50
3	Craig Hartsburg	.25	.50
4	Brian Bellows	.75	1.50
5	Gordon Roberts	.25	.50
6	Keith Acton	.25	.50
7	Paul Holmgren	.35	.75
8	Gilles Meloche, Goalie	.35	.75
9	Dennis Maruk	.50	1.00
10	Tom McCarthy	.25	.50
11	Steve Payne	.25	.50
12	Dino Ciccarelli	.75	1.50

— 1985 - 86 REGULAR ISSUE —

7-Eleven, 1985-86 Issue
Card No. 1, Dino Ciccarelli

Card Size: 2 1/2" X 3 1/2"
Face: Four colour, white border; Team logo, Jersey number, Name, Position, Team
Back: Black, green and yellow on white card stock; Team and sponsor logos, Number, Jersey number, Name, Position, Resume, Fire prevention tip
Imprint: Produced in cooperation with the Fire Marshal's Assn. of Minnesota, The Southland Corporation, and the Minnesota North Stars. ©Cueno and Preston Productions 1986.
Complete Set No.: 12
Complete Set Price: 3.50 / 7.00
Common Card: .25 / .50

MINNESOTA NORTH STARS - TEAM SETS • 607

No.	Player	EX	NRMT
1	Dino Ciccarelli	.75	1.50
2	Scott Bjugstad	.25	.50
3	Curt Giles	.25	.50
4	Donald Beaupre, Goalie	.50	1.00
5	Anthony McKegney	.25	.50
6	Neal Broten	.50	1.00
7	Willi Plett	.25	.50
8	Craig Hartsburg	.35	.75
9	Brian Bellows	.75	1.50
10	Keith Acton	.25	.50
11	Dave Langevin	.25	.50
12	Dirk Graham	.25	.50

— 1986 - 87 REGULAR ISSUE —

7-Eleven, 1986-87 Issue
Card No. 12, Brian Bellows

Card Size: 2 1/2" X 3 1/2"
Face: Four colour, white border; Team logo, Jersey number, Name, Position, Team
Back: Black, green and yellow on white card stock; Team logo, Number, name, jersey number, Position, Resume, Fire prevention tip
Imprint: Produced in cooperation with The Southland Corporation, The Fire Marshal's Assn. of Minnesota, and the Minnesota North Stars. Photo by Frank Howard/Protography. ©Cueno-Preston Productions 1987.

Complete Set No.: 12
Complete Set Price: 3.50 7.00
Common Card: .25 .50

No.	Player	EX	NRMT
1	Neal Broten	.35	.75
2	Brian MacLellan	.25	.50
3	Willi Plett	.25	.50
4	Scott Bjugstad	.25	.50
5	Donald Beaupre, Goalie	.35	.75
6	Dino Ciccarelli	.75	1.50
7	Craig Hartsburg	.25	.50
8	Dennis Maruk	.35	.75
9	Robert Rouse	.25	.50
10	Gordon Roberts	.25	.50
11	Bob Brooke	.25	.50
12	Brian Bellows	.75	1.50

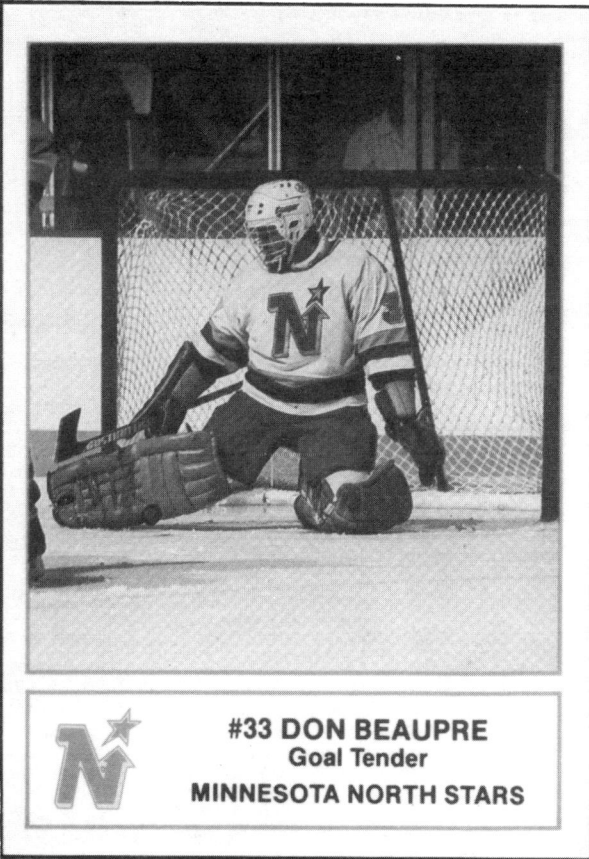

Minnesota North Stars - Team Sets
1986-87 Issue, Card No. 5, Donald Beaupre

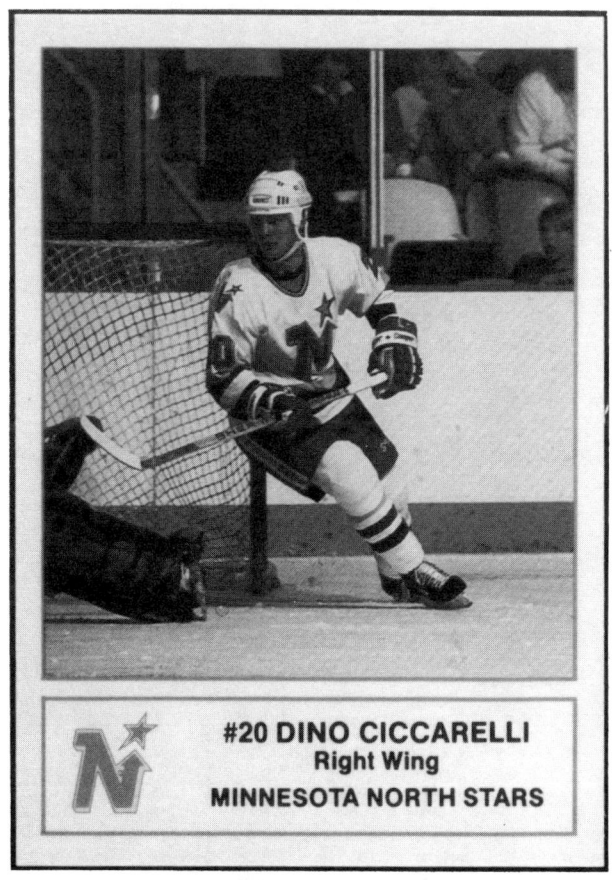

Minnesota North Stars - Team Sets
1986-87 Issue, Card No. 6, Dino Ciccarelli

MONTREAL CANADIENS - TEAMS SETS

TEAMS ISSUES

— 1967 - 68 POSTCARD ISSUE —

This 28-card, black and white set, is unnumbered and is listed below alphabetically.

Card Size: 3 1/2" x 5 3/8"
Face: Black and white, borderless, Facsimile autograph
Back: Blank
Imprint: None
Complete Set No.: 28
Complete Set Price: 25.00 50.00
Common Card: .75 1.50

No.	Player	EX	NRMT
1	Toe Blake, Coach	1.50	3.00
2	Ralph Backstrom	.75	1.50
3	Dave Balon	.75	1.50
4	Jean Beliveau	2.00	4.00
5	Yvan Cournoyer	1.50	3.00
6	Dick Duff	1.00	2.00
7	John Ferguson	.75	1.50
8	Danny Grant	.75	1.50
9	Terry Harper	.75	1.50
10	Ted Harris	.75	1.50
11	Charlie Hodge, Goalie	1.00	2.00
12	Jacques Laperriere	.75	1.50
13	Claude Larose	.75	1.50
14	Jacques Lemaire	1.25	2.50
15	Gary Monahan	.75	1.50
16	Claude Provost	.75	1.50
17	Mickey Redmond	1.00	2.00
18	Henri Richard	1.25	2.50
19	Jim Roberts	.75	1.50
20	Leon Rochefort	.75	1.50
21	Bobby Rousseau	.75	1.50
22	Jean-Guy Talbot	.75	1.50
23	Gilles Tremblay	.75	1.50
24	J. C. Tremblay	.75	1.50
25	Rogatien Vacho, Goalie	1.25	2.50
26	Carol Vadnais	.75	1.50
27	Bryan Watson	.75	1.50
28	Lorne (Gump) Worlsey	1.50	3.00

— 1970 - 71 POSTCARD ISSUE —

This 23-card set is unnumbered and is listed below alphabetically.

Card Size: 3 1/2" x 5 1/2"
Face: Four colour, Facsimile autograph
Back: Blank
Imprint: None
Complete Set No.: 28
Complete Set Price: 15.00 30.00
Common Card: .50 1.00

No.	Player	EX	NRMT
1	Ralph Backstrom	.50	1.00
2	Jean Beliveau	2.00	4.00
3	Pierre Bouchard	.50	1.00
4	Guy Charron	.50	1.00
5	Bill Collins	.50	1.00
6	Yvan Cournoyer	1.50	3.00
7	John Ferguson	1.00	2.00
8	Terry Harper	.50	1.00
9	Rejean Houle	.50	1.00
10	Jacques Laperriere	.75	1.50
11	Guy Lapointe	1.00	2.00
12	Claude Larose	.50	1.00
13	Jacques Lemaire	1.00	2.00
14	Frank Mahovlich	2.00	4.00
15	Peter Mahovlich	.75	1.50
16	Phil Myre, Goalie	.50	1.00
17	Larry Pleau	.50	1.00
18	Mickey Redmond	.75	1.50
19	Henri Richard	1.00	2.00
20	Serge Savard	1.25	2.50
21	Marc Tardiff	.50	1.00
22	J. C. Tremblay	.50	1.00
23	Rogatien Vacho, Goalie	1.50	3.00

— 1971 PINS ISSUE —

The pins are unnumbered and are listed below in alphabetical order.

Pins, 1971 Issue
Pin No. 1, Jean Beliveau

Pin Size: 1 3/4" Diameter
Face: Black and white photo; Name
Back: Blank
Imprint: None
Complete Set No.: 15
Complete Set Price: 7.50 15.00 30.00
Common Player: .25 .50 1.00

No.	Player	VG	EX	NRMT
1	Jean Beliveau	1.75	3.50	7.00
2	Yvan Cournoyer	.65	1.25	2.50
3	John Ferguson	.25	.50	1.00
4	Terry Harper	.25	.50	1.00
5	Guy Lafleur	1.25	2.50	5.00
6	Jacques Laperriere	.50	1.00	2.00
7	Guy Lapointe	.50	1.00	2.00
8	Jacques Lemaire	.25	.50	1.00
9	Frank Mahovlich	1.25	2.50	5.00
10	Pete Mahovlich	.25	.50	1.00
11	Henri Richard	.75	1.50	3.00
12	Claude Ruel, Coach	.25	.50	1.00
13	Serge Savard	.50	1.00	2.00
14	J.C. Tremblay	.25	.50	1.00
15	Rogatien Vachon, Goalie	.85	1.75	3.50

— 1971 - 72 ISSUE —

We have no information on this set. We would appreciate hearing from anyone who can supply any further information.

— 1973 - 74 POSTCARD ISSUE —

Card Size: 3 1/2" x 5 1/2"
Face: Four colour, borderless
Back: Blank
Imprint: None
Complete Set No.: 24
Complete Set Price: 17.50 35.00

No.	Player	EX	NRMT
1	Jean Beliveau, Portrait	1.50	3.00
2	Pierre Bouchard	.50	1.00
3	Scotty Bowman, Coach	.75	1.50
4	Yvan Cournoyer	1.00	2.00
5	Bob Gainey	1.00	2.00
6	Dave Gardner	.50	1.00
7	Guy Lafleur	1.50	3.00
8	Yvon Lambert	.50	1.00
9	Jacques Laperriere	.50	1.00
10	Guy Lapointe	.75	1.50
11	Michel Larocque, Goalie	.50	1.00
12	Claude Larose (Rare)	3.00	6.00
13	Chuck Lefley	.50	1.00
14	Jacques Lemaire	.50	1.00
15	Frank Mahovlich	1.00	2.00
16	Peter Mahovlich	.50	1.00
17	Michel Plasse, Goalie (Rare)	3.00	6.00
18	Henri Richard	1.50	3.00
19	Jim Roberts, (Rare)	3.00	6.00
20	Larry Robinson	1.50	3.00
21	Serge Savard	1.00	2.00
22	Steve Shutt	1.00	2.00
23	Wayne Thomas	.50	1.00
24	Murray Wilson (Rare)	3.00	6.00

— 1974 - 75 POSTCARD ISSUE —

All cards have a facsimile autographed unless otherwise indicated.

Card Size: 3 1/2" x 5 1/2"
Face: Four colour, borderless, facsimile autograph
Back: Blank
Imprint: None
Complete Set No.: 27
Complete Set Price: 15.00 30.00
Common Card: .50 1.00

No.	Player	EX	NRMT
1a	Pierre Bouchard	.50	1.00
1b	Pierre Bouchard, No autograph	.50	1.00
2	Scotty Bowman, Coach	.75	1.50
3	Rick Chartraw	.50	1.00
4	Yvan Cournoyer	1.50	3.00
5	Ken Dryden, Goalie	2.00	4.00
6	Bob Gainey	1.00	2.00
7	Glenn Goldup	.50	1.00
8	Guy Lafleur	1.50	3.00
9a	Yvon Lambert	.50	1.00
9b	Yvon Lambert, No autograph	.50	1.00
10	Jacques Laperrier	.50	1.00
11	Guy Lapointe	.75	1.50
12	Michel Larocque, Goalie	.50	1.00
13	Claude Larose, No autograph	3.00	6.00
14	Chuck Lefley, No autograph	3.00	6.00
15	Jacques Lemaire	.75	1.50
16	Peter Mahovlich	.50	1.00
17	Henri Richard	1.00	2.00
18	Doug Risebrough, No autograph	.50	1.00
19	Jim Roberts	.50	1.00
20	Larry Robinson	1.50	3.00
21	Glen Sather	.50	1.00
22	Serge Savard	1.00	2.00
23	Steve Shutt	.75	1.50
24	Wayne Thomas, Goalie	.50	1.00
25	Mario Tremblay, No autograph	.50	1.00
26	John Van Boxmeer	.50	1.00
27	Murray Wilson	.50	1.00

— 1974 - 75 PHOTO ISSUE —

Card Size: 8" x 10"
Face: Unknown
Back: Unknown
Imprint: Unkown
Complete Set No.: 28
Complete Set Price: 20.00 40.00
Common Card: .60 1.25

No.	Player	EX	NRMT
1	Jean Beliveau	1.75	3.50
2	Scotty Bowman, Coach	.85	1.75

MONTREAL CANADIENS - TEAMS SETS • 609

No.	Player	EX	NRMT
3	Pierre Bouchard	.60	1.25
4	Rick Chartraw	.60	1.25
5	Yvan Cournoyer	1.25	2.50
6	Ken Dryden, Goalie	3.50	7.00
7	Bob Gainey	1.25	2.50
8	Glenn Goldup	.60	1.25
9	Guy Lafleur	2.25	4.50
10	Yvon Lambert	1.00	2.00
11	Jacques Laperriere	.85	1.75
12	Guy Lapointe	.60	1.25
13	Michel Laroque, Goalie	1.00	2.00
14	Claude Larose	.60	1.25
15	Chuck Lefley	.60	1.25
16	Jacques Lemaire	1.25	2.50
17	Peter Mahovlich	.60	1.25
18	Henri Richard	1.00	2.00
19	Doug Risebrough	.60	1.25
20	Jim Roberts	.60	1.25
21	Larry Robinson	3.50	7.00
22	Claude Ruel	.60	1.25
23	Glenn Sather	1.00	2.00
24	Serge Savard	1.00	2.00
25	Steve Shutt	2.00	4.00
26	Wayne Thomas, Goalie	.60	1.25
27	John Vanboxmeer	.60	1.25
28	Murray Wilson	.60	1.25

— 1975 - 76 POSTCARD ISSUE —

Card Size: 3 1/2" x 5 1/2"
Face: Four colour, borderless, Facsimile autograph
Back: Blank
Imprint: None
Complete Set No.: 19
Complete Set Price: 10.00   20.00
Common Card: .50   1.00

No.	Player	EX	NRMT
1	Don Awrey	.50	1.00
2	Pierre Bouchard	.50	1.00
3	Scotty Bowman, Coach	1.00	2.00
4	Yvan Cournoyer, Colour variation	1.00	2.00
5	Ken Dryden, Goalie	2.00	4.00
6	Bob Gainey	.75	1.50
7	Doug Jarvis, White uniform	.50	1.00
8	Guy Lafleur	1.50	3.00
9	Yvon Lambert	.50	1.00
10	Guy Lapointe	.75	1.50
11	Michel Larocque, Goalie	.50	1.00
12	Peter Mahovlich	.50	1.00
13	Doug Risebrough	.50	1.00
14	Jim Roberts	.50	1.00
15	Larry Robinson	1.00	2.00
16	Serge Savard	.75	1.50
17	Steve Shutt	.75	1.50
18	Mario Tremblay	.50	1.00
19	Murray Wilson	.50	1.00

— 1976 - 77 POSTCARD ISSUE —

Card Size: 3 1/2" x 5 1/2"
Face: Four colour, white border, facsimile autograph
Back: Blank
Imprint: None
Complete Set No.: 22
Complete Set Price: 10.00   20.00
Common Card: .35   .75

No.	Player	EX	NRMT
1	Pierre Bouchard	.35	.75
2	Scotty Bowman, Coach	.60	1.25
3	Rick Chartraw	.35	.75
4	Yvan Cournoyer	.75	1.50
5	Ken Dryden, Goalie	1.00	2.00
6	Bob Gainey	.60	1.25
7	Rejean Houle	.35	.75
8	Doug Jarvis	.35	.75
9	Yvon Lambert	.35	.75
10	Guy Lapointe	.60	1.25
11	Michel Larocque, Goalie	.35	.75
12	Jacques Lemaire	.50	1.00
13	Peter Mahovlich	.35	.75
14	Bill Nyrop	.35	.75
15	Doug Risebrough	.50	1.00
16	Jim Roberts	.35	.75
17	Larry Robinson	.75	1.50
18	Claude Ruel	.35	.75
19	Serge Savard	.75	1.50
20	Steve Shutt	.60	1.25
21	Mario Tremblay	.35	.75
22	Murray Wilson	.35	.75

— 1977 - 78 POSTCARD ISSUE —

Card Size: 3 1/2" x 5 1/2"
Face: Four colour, white border, Facsimile autograph
Back: Blank
Imprint: None
Complete Set No.: 25
Complete Set Price: 12.50   25.00
Common Card: .35   .75

No.	Player	EX	NRMT
1	Pierre Bouchard	.35	.75
2	Scotty Bowman, Coach	.60	1.25
3	Rick Chartraw	.35	.75
4	Yvan Cournoyer	.60	1.25
5	Ken Dryden, Goalie	1.50	3.00
6	Brian Engblom	.35	.75
7	Bob Gainey	.60	1.25
8	Rejean Houle	.35	.75
9	Doug Jarvis	.35	.75
10	Guy Lafleur	1.00	2.00
11	Yvon Lambert	.35	.75
12	Guy Lapointe	.60	1.25
13	Michel Larocque, Goalie	.35	.75
14	Pierre Larouche	.35	.75
15	Jacques Lemaire	.60	1.25
16	Gilles Lupien	.35	.75
17	Pierre Mondou	.35	.75
18	Bill Nyrop	.35	.75
19	Doug Risebrough	.50	1.00
20	Larry Robinson	.75	1.50
21	Claude Ruel	.35	.75
22	Serge Savard	.60	1.25
23	Steve Shutt	.60	1.25
24	Mario Tremblay	.35	.75
25	Murray Wilson	.35	.75

— 1978 - 79 POSTCARD ISSUE —

Card Size: 3 1/2" x 5 1/2"
Face: Four colour, white border, Facsimile autograph
Back: Blank
Imprint: None
Complete Set No.: 25
Complete Set Price: 10.00   20.00

No.	Player	EX	NRMT
1	Scotty Bowman, Coach	.50	1.00
2	Rick Chartraw	.35	.75
3	Cam Conner	.35	.75
4	Yvan Cournoyer	.50	1.00
5	Ken Dryden, Goalie	.75	1.50
6	Brian Engblom	.35	.75
7	Bob Gainey	.50	1.00
8	Rejean Houle	.35	.75
9	Pat Hughes	.35	.75
10	Doug Jarvis	.35	.75
11	Guy Lafleur	.75	1.50
12	Yvon Lambert	.35	.75
13	Rod Langway	.50	1.00
14	Guy Lapointe	.50	1.00
15	Michel Larocque, Goalie	.35	.75
16	Pierre Larouche	.35	.75
17	Jacques Lemaire	.50	1.00
18	Gilles Lupien	.35	.75
19	Pierre Mondou	.35	.75
20	Mark Napier	.35	.75
21	Doug Risebrough	.50	1.00
22	Larry Robinson	.60	1.25
23	Claude Ruel	.35	.75
24	Serge Savard	.50	1.00
25	Steve Shutt	.50	1.00

— 1979 - 80 POSTCARD ISSUE —

Card Size: 3 1/2" x 5 1/2"
Face: Four colour, white border, Facsimile autograph
Back: Blank
Imprint: None
Complete Set No.: 25
Complete Set Price: 10.00   20.00

No.	Player	EX	NRMT
1	Rick Chartraw	.30	.60
2	Normand Dupont	.30	.60
3	Brian Engblom	.30	.60
4	Bob Gainey	.50	1.00
5	Bernie Geoffrion	.50	1.00
6	Danny Geoffrion	.30	.60
7	Denis Herron, Goalie	.30	.60
8	Rejean Houle	.30	.60
9	Doug Jarvis	.30	.60
10	Guy Lafleur	.75	1.50
11	Yvon Lambert	.30	.60
12	Rod Langway	.50	1.00
13	Guy Lapointe	.50	1.00
14	Michel Larocque, Goalie	.30	.60
15	Pierre Larouoche	.30	.60
16	Gilles Lupien	.30	.60
17	Pierre Mondou	.30	.60
18	Mark Napier	.30	.60
19	Doug Risebrough	.35	.75
20	Larry Robinson	.50	1.00
21	Claude Ruel	.30	.60
22	Serge Savard	.50	1.00
23	Richard Sevigny, Goalie	.30	.60
24	Steve Shutt	.50	1.00
25	Mario Tremblay	.30	.60

— 1980 - 81 POSTCARD ISSUE —

Card Size: 3 1/2" x 5 1/2"
Face: Four colour, white border
Back: Blank
Imprint: None
Complete Set No.: 26
Complete Set Price: 9.00   18.00

No.	Player	EX	NRMT
1	Keith Acton	.30	.60
2	Bill Baker	.30	.60
3	Rick Chartraw	.30	.60
4	Brian Engblom	.30	.60
5	Bob Gainey	.50	1.00
6	Gaston Gingras	.30	.60
7	Denis Herron, Goalie	.30	.60
8	Rejean Houle	.30	.60
9	Doug Jarvis	.30	.60
10	Guy Lafleur	.75	1.50
11	Yvon Lambert	.30	.60
12	Rod Langway	.50	1.00
13	Guy Lapointe	.35	.75
14	Michel Larocque, Goalie	.30	.60
15	Pierre Larocque	.30	.60
16	Pierre Mondou	.30	.60
17	Mark Napier	.30	.60
18	Chris Nilan	.30	.60
19	Doug Risebrough	.35	.75
20	Larry Robinson	.60	1.25
21	Claude Ruel	.30	.60
22	Serge Savard	.60	1.25
23	Richard Sevigny, Goalie	.30	.60
24	Steve Shutt	.60	1.25
25	Mario Tremblay	.30	.60
26	Doug Wickenheiser	.30	.60

610 • MONTREAL CANADIENS - TEAMS SETS

—1981-82 POSTCARD ISSUE—
SET No. 1

Card Size: 3 1/2" X 5 1/2"
Face: Four colour, white bottom strip; Facsimile autograph
Back: Blank
Imprint: None
Complete Set No.: Unknown
Complete Set Price: Unknown
Common Player: .13 .25

No.	Player	EX	NRMT
1	Keith Acton	.13	.25
2	Bob Barry, Coach	.13	.25
3	Jeff Brubaker	.13	.25
4	Gilbert Delorme	.13	.25
5	Brian Engblom	.13	.25
6	Bob Gainey	.50	1.00
7	Gaston Gingras	.13	.25
8	Denis Herron, Goalie	.13	.25
9	Rejean Houle	.13	.25
10	Mark Hunter	.13	.25
11	Doug Jarvis	.13	.25
12	Guy Lafleur	1.50	3.00
13	Yvon Lambert	.13	.25
14	Rod Langway	.35	.75
15	Jacques Laperriere	.15	.30
16	Guy Lapointe	.50	1.00
17	Pierre Larouche	.25	.50
18	Craig Laughlin	.13	.25
19	Pierre Mondou	.13	.25
20	Mark Napier	.13	.25
21	Christopher Nilan	.13	.25
22	Robert Picard	.13	.25
23	Doug Risebrough	.25	.50
24	Larry Robinson	.50	1.00
25	Serge Savard	.50	1.00
26	Richard Sevigny, Goalie	.13	.25
27	Steve Shutt	.25	.50
28	Mario Tremblay	.25	.50
29	Rick Wamsley, Goalie	.15	.30
30	Douglas Wickenheiser	.13	.25
31	Team Photo	.13	.25

—1981-82 POSTCARD ISSUE—
SET No. 2

Players with an asterisk beside their name had the same postcard photograph issued the previous year.

Card Size: 3 1/2" x 5 1/2"
Face: Four colour, white border, Facsimile autograph
Back: Blank
Imprint: None
Complete Set No.: 28
Complete Set Price: 10.00 20.00

No.	Player	EX	NRMT
1	Team Photograph	.50	1.00
2	Keith Acton	.30	.60
3	Bob Berry	.30	.60
4	Jeff Brubaker	.30	.60
5	Gilbert Delorme	.30	.60
6	Brian Engblom *	.30	.60
7	Bob Gainey *	.50	1.00
8	Gaston Gingras *	.30	.60
9	Denis Herron *, Goalie	.30	.60
10	Rejean Houle	.30	.60
11	Mark Hunter	.30	.60
12	Doug Jarvis *	.30	.60
13	Guy Lafleur *	.75	1.50
14	Rod Langway *	.50	1.00
15	Jacques Laperriere	.30	.60
16	Craig Laughlin	.30	.60
17	Guy Lapointe *	.35	.75
18	Pierre Mondou *	.30	.60
19	Mark Napier *	.30	.60
20	Chris Nilan	.30	.60
21	Robert Picard	.30	.60
22	Doug Risebrough *	.30	.60
23	Larry Robinson	.50	1.00
24	Richard Sevigny *, Goalie	.30	.60
25	Steve Shutt	.50	1.00
26	Mario Tremblay *	.30	.60
27	Rick Walmsley, Goalie	.30	.60
28	Doug Wickenheiser *	.30	.60

—1982-83 POSTCARD ISSUE—

This is the first year that printing appeared on the back of the postcards. The asterisk means that it was the same postcard photograph as the previous year.

Card Size: 3 1/2" x 5 1/2"
Face: Four colour, white border, Facsimile autograph
Back: Blue writing on postcard stock
Imprint: None
Complete Set No.: 28
Complete Set Price: 9.00 18.00

No.	Player	EX	NRMT
1	Keith Acton	.30	.60
2	Bob Berry, *	.30	.60
3	Guy Carbonneau	1.00	2.00
4	Dan Daoust	.30	.60
5	Gilbert Delorme *	.30	.60
6	Bob Gainey	.50	1.00
7	Gaston Gingras *	.30	.60
8	Rick Green	.50	1.00
9	Rejean Houle	.30	.60
10	Mark Hunter *	.30	.60
11	Guy Lafleur *	.75	1.50
12	Jacques Laperriere *	.30	.60
13	Craig Ludwig	.30	.60
14	Pierre Mondou *	.30	.60
15	Mark Napier *	.30	.60
16	Mats Naslund	.30	.60
17	Eric Nattress	.30	.60
18	Chris Nilan *	.30	.60
19	Robert Picard *	.30	.60
20	Henri Richard	.50	1.00
21	Larry Robinson *	.30	.60
22	Bill Root	.30	.60
23	Richard Sevigny, Goalie	.30	.60
24	Steve Shutt	.50	1.00
25	Mario Tremblay *	.30	.60
26	Ryan Walter	.30	.60
27	Rick Walmsley *, Goalie	.30	.60
28	Doug Wickenheiser *	.30	.60

—1983-84 POSTCARD ISSUE—

The players with an asterisk beside their name had the same postcard photograph as the previous year.

Card Size: 3 1/2" x 5 1/2"
Face: Four colour, white border, Facsimile autograph
Back: Blue writing on postcard stock
Imprint: None
Complete Set No.: 32
Complete Set Price: 11.00 22.00

No.	Player	EX	NRMT
1	Jean Beliveau, Action shot	1.00	2.00
2	Bob Berry *	.25	.50
3	Guy Carbonneau	.50	1.00
4	Kent Carlson	.25	.50
5	John Charbot	.25	.50
6	Chris Chelios	1.50	3.00
7	Gilbert Delorme *	.25	.50
8	Bob Gainey	.50	1.00
9	Rick Green	.35	.75
10	Jean Hamel	.25	.50
11	Mark Hunter	.25	.50
12	Guy Lafleur *	.75	1.50
13	Jacques Lemaire	.35	.75
14a	Jacques Laperriere	.25	.50
14b	Jacques Laperriere *	.25	.50
15	Craig Ludwig	.25	.50
16	Pierre Mondou *	.25	.50
17	Mats Naslund	1.00	2.00
18	Eric Nattress	.25	.50
19	Chris Nilan *	.25	.50
20	Steve Penney, Goalie	.25	.50
21	Jacques Plante, Goalie	1.00	2.00
22	Larry Robinson *	.50	1.00
23	Bill Root	.25	.50
24	Richard Sevigny *, Goalie	.25	.50
25	Steve Shutt *	.35	.75
26	Bobby Smith	.35	.75
27	Mario Tremblay	.25	.50
28	Alfie Turcotte	.25	.50
29	Perry Turnbull	.25	.50
30	Ryan Walter	.25	.50
31	Rick Walmsley *, Goalie	.25	.50
32	Doug Wickenheiser *	.25	.50

—1984-85 POSTCARD ISSUE—

The players with an asterisk beside their name had the same postcard photograph as the previous year.

Card Size: 3 1/2" x 5 1/2"
Face: Four colour, borderless,
Back: Two colour, Canadians logo, Name, Player number, Facsimileautograph on postcard stock
Imprint: © Copyright - Tous droits reserves club de Hockey Canadiens Inc.
Complete Set No.: 28
Complete Set Price: 8.00 16.00

No.	Player	EX	NRMT
1a	Guy Carbonneau, *	.35	.75
1b	Guy Carbonneau, No puck	.35	.75
2	Kent Carlson *	.25	.50
3	Chris Chelios, Autographed	.75	1.50
4	Lucien Deblois	.25	.50
5	Ron Flockhart	.25	.50
6	Bob Gainey *	.50	1.00
7	Rick Green *	.35	.75
8	Jean Hamel *	.25	.50
9	Mark Hunter *	.25	.50
10	Tom Kurvers	.25	.50
11	Guy Lafleur *	.75	.150
12	Jacques Laperriere *	.35	.75
13	Jacques Lemaire *	.35	.75
14	Craig Ludwig *	.25	.50
15	Pierre Mondou *	.25	.50
16	Mats Naslund *	.75	1.50
17	Eric Nattress *	.25	.50
18	Chris Nilan *	.25	.50
19	Mike McPhee	.50	1.00
20a	Steve Penney, Goalie (same as 83-84)	.25	.50
20b	Steve Penney, Goalie	.25	.50
21	Jean Perron	.25	.50
22	Larry Robinson	.50	1.00
23	Bobby Smith	.50	1.00
24	Doug Soetaert, Goalie	.35	.75
25	Petr Svoboda	.50	1.00
26	Mario Tremblay *	.35	.75
27a	Alfie Turcotte *	.35	.75
27b	Alfie Turcotte, * Autographed	.35	.75
28	Ryan Walter *	.35	.75

—1985-86 POSTCARD ISSUE—

1985-86 Postcard Issue
Postcard No. 24, Patrick Roy

Card Size: 3 1/2" x 5 1/2"
Face: Four colour, borderless, Facsimile autograph
Back: Two colour, Printing on postcard stock
Imprint: © copyright - Tous droits reserves club de Hockey Canadiens Inc.
Complete Set No.: 30
Complete Set Price: 11.50 23.00

MONTREAL CANADIENS - TEAMS SETS • 611

No.	Player	EX	NRMT
1a	Serge Boisvert, No autograph	.25	.50
1b	Serge Boisvert, Portrait	.25	.50
2	Randy Bucyk, No autograph	.25	.50
3	Guy Carbonneau	.50	1.00
4	Chris Chelios	.75	1.50
5	Kjell Dahlin, Autograph varieties	.25	.50
6	Bob Gainey	.35	.75
7	Gaston Gingras, No autograph	.25	.50
8	Rick Green	.25	.50
9	John Kordic	.25	.50
10	Tom Kurvers	.25	.50
11	Mike Lalor	.25	.50
12	Claude Lemieux	1.00	2.00
13	Craig Ludwig	.25	.50
14	David Maley	.25	.50
15	Mike McPhee	.35	.75
16	Sergio Momesso	.25	.50
17	Mats Naslund	.35	.75
18	Chris Nilan	.25	.50
19	Steve Penney, Goalie	.25	.50
20	Jean Perron, Portrait	.25	.50
21	Stephane J. J. Richer	1.00	2.00
22	Larry Robinson, Autograph varieties	.50	1.00
23	Steve Rooney, Autograph varieties	.25	.50
24	Patrick Roy, Goalie	2.50	5.00
25	Brian Skrudland	.50	1.00
26	Bobby Smith	.35	.75
27	Doug Soetaert, Goalie, autograph varieties	.25	.50
28	Petr Svoboda	.35	.75
29	Mario Tremblay, Autograph varieties	.25	.50
30	Ryan Walter	.25	.50

— 1985 - 86 PLACEMATS —

1985-86 Placemats
Placemat No. 5, M. Naslund, K. Dahlin, P. Svoboda

Card Size: 16" x 10"
Face: Four colour, borderless, Name, Number
Back: Four colour, Team logo
Imprint: Copyright - Tons Droits Reserves - Club De Hockey Canadien Inc.
Complete Set No.: 8
Complete Set Price: Unknown

No.	Player	EX	NRMT
1	Guy Carbonneau, Steve Rooney, Michael McPhee	2.50	5.00
2	Chris Chelios, Patrick Roy, Goalie Sergio Momesso	5.00	10.00
3	Lucien Deblois, Tom Kurvers, Craig Ludwig	2.50	5.00
4	Rick Green, Bobby Smith, Mike Lalar	2.50	5.00
5	Mats Naslund, Kjell Dahlin Petr Svoboda	2.50	5.00
6	Cris Nilan, Doug Soetaert, Larry Robinson	2.50	5.00
7	Stephane J. J.Richer, Ryan Walter, Brian Skrudland	2.50	5.00
8	Mario Tremblay, Steve Penney, Goalie; Bob Gainey	2.50	5.00

— 1986 - 87 POSTCARD ISSUE —
SET No. 1

Card Size: 3 3/8" X 5 1/2"
Face: Four colour, white background; Name
Back: Black on white postcard stock; Name, Resume
Imprint: None
Complete Set No.: 27
Complete Set Price: 12.50 25.00
Common Card: .25 .50

No.	Player	EX	NRMT
1	Guy Carbonneau	1.25	2.50
2	Chris Chelios	2.00	4.00
3	Shane Corson	1.50	3.00
4	Kjell Dahlin	.50	1.00
5	Bob Gainey	.50	1.00
6	Gaston Gingras	.25	.50
7	Rick Green	.50	1.00
8	Brian Hayward, Goalie	.50	1.00
9	John Kordic	.25	.50
10	Mike Lalor	.25	.50
11	Jacques Laperriere, Asst. Coach	.25	.50
12	Claude Lemieux	1.50	3.00
13	Craig Ludwig	.25	.50
14	David Maley	.25	.50
15	Mike McPhee	.60	1.25
16	Sergio Momesso	.25	.50
17	Mats Naslund	1.00	2.00
18	Chris Nilan	.25	.50
19	Jean Perron, Coach	.25	.50
20	Stephane J. J. Richer	1.50	3.00
21	Larry Robinson	.75	.150
22	Steve Rooney	.75	1.50
23	Patrick Roy, Goalie	5.00	10.00
24	Brian Skrudland	.50	1.00
25	Bobby Smith	.75	1.50
26	Petr Svoboda	.25	.50
27	Ryan Walter	.25	.50

— 1986 - 87 POSTCARD ISSUE —
SET No. 2

The asterisk beside the players name indicates the same postcard photograph was used as in the 1985-86 set.

Card Size: 3 1/2" x 5 1/2"
Face: Four colour, borderless, Facsimile autograph
Back: Two colour, printing on postcard stock
Imprint: © Copyright - Tous droits reserves Club de Hockey Canadiens Inc.
Complete Set No.: 27
Complete Set Price: 11.00 22.00

No.	Player	EX	NRMT
1	Guy Carbonneau *	.50	1.00
2	Chris Chelios *	.75	1.50
3	Shayne Coson	.35	.75
4	Kjell Dahlen *	.25	.50
5	Bob Gainey *	.35	.75
6	Gaston Gingras *	.25	.50
7	Rick Green *	.25	.50
8	Brian Hayward, Goalie	.25	.50
9	John Kordic	.25	.50
10	Mike Lalor *	.25	.50
11	Jacques Laperriere, With headphones	.25	.50
12	Claude Lemieux *	1.00	2.00
13	Craig Ludwig *	.25	.50
14	David Maley *	.25	.50
15	Mike McPhee	.25	.50
16	Sergio Momesso	.25	.50
17	Mats Naslund	.35	.75
18	Chris Nilan	.25	.50
19	Jean Perron, In front of team jersey	.25	.50
20	Stephane J. J. Richer	1.00	2.00
21	Larry Robinson	.50	1.00
22	Steve Rooney	.25	.50
23	Patrick Roy, Goalie	2.00	4.00
24	Brian Skrudland	.50	1.00
25	Bobby Smith	.35	.75
26	Petr Svoboda	.25	.50
27	Ryan Walter	.25	.50

— 1987 - 88 POSTCARD ISSUE —

This set is the same as the 1986-87 set but with seven more cards, plus a variation of the Stephane Richer card.

Card Size: 3 1/2" x 5 1/2"
Face: Four colour, borderless, Facsimile autograph
Back: Two colour, printing on postcard stock
Imprint: © Copyright - Tous droits reserves - club de Hockey Canadiens Inc.
Complete Set No.: 33
Complete Set Price: 12.50 25.00

No.	Player	EX	NRMT
1	Francois Allaire	.25	.50
2	Guy Carbonneau	.50	1.00
3	Jose Charbonneau	.25	.50
4	Shayne Corson	.35	.75
5	Kjell Dahlen	.25	.50
6	Bob Gainey	.35	.75
7	Gaston Gingras	.25	.50
8	Rick Green	.25	.50
9	Brian Hayward, Goalie	.25	.50
10	John Kordic	.25	.50
11	Mike Lalor	.25	.50
12	Jacques Laperriere, With headphones	.25	.50
13	Claude Lemieux	1.00	2.00
14	Craig Ludwig	.25	.50
15	David Maley	.25	.50
16	Mike McPhee	.25	.50
17	Sergio Momesso	.25	.50
18	Claude Mouton, Announcer	.50	1.00
19	Mats Naslund	.35	.75
20	Chris Nilan	.25	.50
21	Jean Perron, In front of team jersey	.25	.50
22a	Stephane J. J. Richer	1.00	2.00
22b	Stephane J. J. Richer, No moustache	.50	1.00
23	Larry Robinson	.50	1.00
24	Steve Rooney	.25	.50
25	Patrick Roy, Goalie	2.00	4.00
26	Scott Sandelin	.25	.50
27	Serge Savard	.35	.75
28	Brian Skrudland	.50	1.00
29	Bobby Smith	.35	.75
30	Petr Svoboda	.25	.50
31	Gilles Thibodeau	.25	.50
32	Larry Trader	.25	.50
33	Ryan Walter	.25	.50

— 1988 - 89 POSTARD ISSUE —

The asterisk beside the players names indicate the same photograph was used for the previous year.

Card Size: 3 1/2" x 5 1/2"
Face: Four colour, borderlesss, Facsimile autograph
Back: Two colour, printing on postcard stock
Imprint: © Copyright - Tous droits reserves club de Hockey Canadiens Inc.
Complete Set No.: 31
Complete Set Price: 10.00 20.00

No.	Player	EX	NRMT
1	Francois Allaire	.25	.50
2	Pat Burns, Coach	.50	1.00
3	Guy Carbonneau	.35	.75
4	Jose Carbonneau, *	.25	.50
5	Chris Chelios	.50	1.00
6	Ronald Corey	.25	.50
7	Shayne Corson	.25	.50
8	Russell Courtnall	.50	1.00
9	Eric Desjardins	.50	1.00
10	Bob Gainey, *	.35	.75
11	Brent Gilchrist	.25	.50
12	Rick Green	.25	.50
13	Brian Hayward, Goalie	.25	.50
14	Mike Keene	.25	.50
15	Mike Lalor	.25	.50
16	Jacques Laperriere	.25	.50
17	Claude Lemieux	.35	.75
18	Craig Ludwig	.25	.50
19	Steve Martinson	.25	.50
20	Mike McPhee	.25	.50
21	Mats Naslund *	.35	.75
22	Stephane J. J. Richer *	.35	.75

MONTREAL CANADIENS - TEAMS SETS

No.	Player	EX	NRMT
23	Larry Robinson	.35	.75
24	Patrick Roy, Goalie	1.50	3.00
25	Serge Savard *	.35	.75
26	Brian Skrudland	.25	.50
28	Bobby Smith	.25	.50
29	Petr Svoboda	.25	.50
30	Gilles Thibodeau *	.25	.50
31	Ryan Walter	.25	.50

— 1989 - 90 POSTCARD ISSUE —

Card Size: 3 1/2" x 5 1/2"
Face: Four colour, white background; Facsimile autograph
Back: Black on white ard stock; Facsimile autograph, Resume
Imprint: None
Complete Set No.: 32
Complete Set Price: 7.50 15.00
Common Card: .25 .50

No.	Player	EX	NRMT
1	Francois Allaire	.25	.50
2	Pat Burns, Coach	1.00	2.00
3	Guy Carbonneau	.50	1.00
4	Chris Chelios	1.00	2.00
5	Tom Chorske	.35	.75
6	Ronald Corey, President	.25	.50
7	Shayne Corson	.50	1.00
8	Russell Courtnall	.75	1.50
9	Jean-Jacques Daigneault	.50	1.00
10	Eric Desjardins	.75	1.50
11	Martin Desjardins	.25	.50
12	Donald Dufresne	.25	.50
13	Brent Gilchrist	.50	1.00
14	Brian Hayward, Goalie	.25	.50
15	Mike Keane	.25	.50
16	Jacques Laperriere, Asst. Coach	.25	.50
17	Stephane Lebeau	.50	1.00
18	Sylvain Lefebvre	.50	1.00
19	Claude Lemieux	.75	1.50
20	Jocelyn Lemieux	.25	.50
21	Craig Ludwig	.35	.75
22	Jyrkke Lumme	.50	1.00
23	Steve Martinson	.25	.50
24	Mike McPhee	.25	.50
25	Mats Naslund	.50	1.00
26	Stephane J. J. Richer	.75	1.50
27	Patrick Roy, Goalie	2.00	4.00
28	Serge Savard	.35	.75
29	Brian Skrudland	.35	.75
30	Robert Smith	.50	1.00
31	Petr Svoboda	.35	.75
32	Ryan Walter	.25	.50

— 1989 - 90 POSTCARD ISSUE —

During the 1989-90 season these were inserted into the Canadiens magazine "Magazine Les Canadiens". Same set as Kraft Canadiens.

Card Size: 3 3/4" x 5 1/2"
Face: Four colour; Name
Back: Black on white card stock; Resume
Imprint: None
Complete Set No.: 24
Complete Set Price: 7.50 15.00
Common Card: .25 .50

No.	Player	EX	NRMT
1	Pat Burns, Coach	.50	1.00
2	Guy Carbonneau	.75	1.50
3	Chris Chelios	1.00	2.00
4	Shayne Corson	.50	1.00
5	Russell Courtnall	1.00	2.00
6	Jean-Jacques Daigneault	.50	1.00
7	Eric Desjardins	.75	1.50
8	Todd Ewen	.50	1.00
9	Brent Gilchrist	.50	1.00
10	Brian Hayward, Goalie	.25	.50
11	Mike Keane	.25	.50
12	Stephane Lebeau	.50	1.00
13	Sylvain Lefebvre	.50	1.00
14	Claude Lemieux	.75	1.50
15	Craig Ludwig	.25	.50
16	Mike McPhee	.25	.50
17	Mats Naslund	.50	1.00
18	Stephane J. J. Richer	.25	.50
19	Patrick Roy, Goalie	2.00	4.00
20	Mathew Schneider	.50	1.00
21	Brian Skrudland	.25	.50
22	Robert Smith	.50	1.00
23	Petr Svoboda	.25	.50
24	Ryan Walter	.25	.50

LA PATRIE

— 1927 - 28 PHOTO ISSUE —

La Patrie, 1927-28 Issue
Card No. 13, Leo Gaudreault

Photo Size: 8 1/2" X 11"
Face: Sepia; Name, Number, Year
Back: Blank
Imprint: None
Complete Set No.: 21
Complete Set Price: 325.00 650.00 1,300.00
Common Player: 7.50 15.00 30.00

No.	Player	G	VG	EX
1	Sylvio Mantha	13.00	25.00	50.00
2	Art Gagne	7.50	15.00	30.00
3	Leo Lafrance	7.50	15.00	30.00
4	Aurel Joliat	35.00	75.00	150.00
5	Pit Lepine	7.50	15.00	30.00
6	Gizzy Hart	7.50	15.00	30.00
7	Wildor Larochelle	7.50	15.00	30.00
8	George Hainsworth, Goalie	13.00	25.00	50.00
9	Herb Gardiner	13.00	25.00	50.00
10	Albert Le Duc	5.00	13.00	25.00
11	Marty Burke	13.00	25.00	50.00
12	Charlie Langlois	5.00	13.00	25.00
13	Leo Gaudreault	5.00	13.00	25.00
14	Howie Morenz	85.00	175.00	350.00
15	Cecil M. Hart, Coach	17.50	35.00	75.00
16	Leo Dandurand, Coach	5.00	13.00	25.00
17	Edouard Lalonde	30.00	60.00	125.00
18	Didier Pitre	5.00	13.00	25.00
19	Jack Laviolette	13.00	25.00	50.00
20	George Patterson	5.00	13.00	25.00
21	Georges Vezina, Goalie	60.00	125.00	250.00

PLAYING CARDS

1948 CIRCA

Maurice Richard is illustrated on the face of this playing card deck. The back, beside the card number, has various advertisers listed top and bottom

Card Size: 2 1/4" x 3 3/8"
Face: Four colour, Autographed
Back: Red and black, Card number, Advertising
Imprint: None
Complete Set No. 54
Complete Set Price: Unknown

No.	Player	EX	NRMT
1	Maurice Richard (all 5¢ cards)	30.00	60.00

MOLSON'S

— 1953 - 67 PHOTO ISSUE —

This set was released by the Molson's company as a promotion that continued from 1953 to 1967.

Photograph Size: 8" X 10"
Face: Type 1: (1953-54) Black and white, white border; Team players
Type 2: (1955-67) Four colour, white border Team players
Back: Type 1: (1953-57) Blank; Type 2: (1957-57) Light blue sketch of team to identify the players
Imprint: None
Complete Set No.: 15
Complete Set Price: 87.50 175.00

No.	Player	EX	NRMT
1	1952-53 Champions	12.50	25.00
2	1953-54	12.50	25.00
3	1954-55	10.00	20.00
4	1955-56 Champions	10.00	20.00
5	1956-57 Champions	10.00	20.00
6	1957-58 Champions	7.50	15.00
7	1958-59 Champions	7.50	15.00
8	1959-60 Champions	7.50	15.00
9	1960-61	5.00	10.00
10	1961-62	5.00	10.00
11	1962-63	5.00	10.00
12	1963-64	5.00	10.00
13	1964-65 Champions	5.00	10.00
14	1965-66 Champions	5.00	10.00
15	1966-67	5.00	10.00

IGA

— 1967 - 68 REGULAR ISSUE —

These cards are unnumbered and are listed below in alphabetical order.

IGA, 1967-68 Issue
Card No. 11, Claude Larose

Card Size: 1 5/8" X 1 7/8"
Face: Four colour; Jersey number, Name
Back: Promotional offer, Bilingual
Imprint: None
Complete Set No.: 23
Complete Set Price: 110.00 225.00 450.00
Common Player: 3.75 7.50 15.00

No.	Player	VG	EX	NRMT
1	Ralph Backstrom	3.75	7.50	15.00
2	Jean Beliveau	15.00	30.00	65.00
3	Toe Blake, Coach	6.00	12.00	25.00
4	Yvan Cournoyer	7.50	15.00	30.00
5	Dick Duff	3.75	7.50	15.00
6	John Ferguson	3.75	7.50	15.00
7	Danny Grant	3.75	7.50	15.00
8	Terry Harper	3.75	7.50	15.00
9	Ted Harris	3.75	7.50	15.00
10	Jacques Laperriere	5.00	10.00	20.00
11	Claude Larose	3.75	7.50	15.00
12	Jacques Lemaire	10.00	20.00	40.00
13	Garry Monahan	3.75	7.50	15.00
14	Claude Provost	3.75	7.50	15.00
15	Mickey Redmond	3.75	7.50	15.00
16	Henri Richard	10.00	20.00	40.00
17	Bobby Rousseau	3.75	7.50	15.00
18	Serge Savard	10.00	20.00	40.00
19	Gilles Tremblay	3.75	7.50	15.00

MONTREAL CANADIENS - TEAMS SETS • 613

No.	Player	EX	NRMT
20	J.C. Tremblay	3.75	7.50	15.00
21	Carol Vadnais	3.75	7.50	15.00
22	Rogatien Vachon, Goalie	10.00	20.00	40.00
23	Gump Worsley, Goalie	12.50	25.00	50.00

— 1968 - 69 REGULAR ISSUE —

These cards are unnumbered and are listed below in alphabetical order.

Card Size: 1 1/4" X 2 1/4"
Face: Four colour; Name, Jersey number
Back: Black on white card stock; Promotional offer, Bilingual
Imprint: None
Complete Set No.: 19
Complete Set Price: 90.00 185.00 375.00
Common Player: 3.75 7.50 15.00

No.	Player	VG	EX	NRMT
1	Ralph Backstrom	3.75	7.50	15.00
2	Jean Beliveau	15.00	30.00	60.00
3	Yvan Cournoyer	7.50	15.00	30.00
4	Dick Duff	3.75	7.50	15.00
5	John Ferguson	3.75	7.50	15.00
6	Terry Harper	3.75	7.50	15.00
7	Ted Harris	3.75	7.50	15.00
8	Jacques Laperriere	8.00	10.00	20.00
9	Jacques Lemaire	3.75	7.50	15.00
10	Garry Monahan	3.75	7.50	15.00
11	Claude Provost	3.75	7.50	15.00
12	Mickey Redmond	3.75	7.50	15.00
13	Henri Richard	10.00	20.00	40.00
14	Bobby Rousseau	3.75	7.50	15.00
15	Serge Savard	7.50	15.00	30.00
16	Gilles Tremblay	3.75	7.50	15.00
17	J.C. Tremblay	3.75	7.50	15.00
18	Rogatien Vachon, Goalie	7.50	15.00	30.00
19	Gump Worsley, Goalie	12.50	25.00	50.00

PRO STAR PROMOTIONS

— 1969 - 70 POST CARD ISSUE —

Card Size: 3 1/2" X 5 1/2"
Face: Four colour, borderless, Facsimile Autograph
Back: Blank
Imprint: None
Complete Set No.: 31
Complete Set Price: 25.00 50.00

No.	Player	EX	NRMT
1A	Ralph Backstrom, Large image, autograph at left	1.00	2.00
1B	Ralph Backstrom, Small image, autograph at right	1.00	2.00
2A	Jean Bealiveau,	2.50	5.00
2B	Jean Bealiveau, Autograph slightly lower	2.50	5.00
3	Christian Bordeleau	.75	1.50
4	Pierre Bouchard	.75	1.50
5	Guy Charron	.75	1.50
6	Bill Collins	.75	1.50
7	Yvan Cournoyer (Colour variation exists)	1.50	3.00
8A	John Ferguson, Autograph Touches skate	.75	1.50
8B	John Ferguson, Autograph touches stick	.75	1.50
9A	Terry Harper, Y touches puck	.75	1.50
9B	Terry Harper, Y touches border and away from puck	.75	1.50
10	Ted Harris	.75	1.50
11	Rejean Houle	.75	1.50
12A	Jacques Laperriere, P touches puck	.75	1.50
12B	Jacques Laperriere, P away from puck	.75	1.50
13	Guy Lapointe	1.00	2.00
14	Claude Larose	.75	1.50
15	Jacques Lamaire (Colour variation exists)	1.00	2.00
16	Frank Mahovlich	1.50	3.00
17	Peter Mahovlich (Colour variation exists)	.75	1.50

No.	Player	EX	NRMT
18	Phil Myre	.75	1.50
19	Larry Pleau	.75	1.50
20	Claude Provost	.75	1.50
21	Mickey Redman	.75	1.50
22	Henri Richard	1.50	3.00
23	Phil Roberto	.75	1.50
24	Jim Roberts	.75	1.50
25	Robert Rousseau	.75	1.50
26	Claude Ruel	.75	1.50
27	Serge Savard	1.50	3.00
28	Marc Tardiff	.75	1.50
29	Giles Tremblay	3.00	6.00
30a	J. C. Tremblay, with autograph	.75	1.50
30b	J. C. Tremblay, without autograph	.75	1.50
31	Rogatien Vachon, Goalie (Colour variation exists)	1.50	3.00

— 1970 - 71 POST CARD ISSUE —

Card Size: 3 1/2" X 5 1/2"
Face: Four colour
Back: Blank
Imprint: None
Complete Set No.: 23
Complete Set Price: 20.00 40.00
Common Card: .75 1.50

No.	Player	EX	NRMT
1	Ralph Backstrom	.75	1.50
2	Jean Beliveau	2.50	5.00
3	Pierre Bouchard	.75	1.50
4	Guy Charron	.75	1.50
5	Bill Collins	.75	1.50
6	Yvan Cournover	2.50	5.00
7	John Ferguson	.75	1.50
8	Terry Harper	.75	1.50
9	Rejean Houle	.75	1.50
10	Jacques Laperriere	.75	1.50
11	Guy Lapointe	1.50	3.00
12	Claude Larose	.75	1.50
13	Jacques Lemaire	1.50	3.00
14	Frank Mahovlich	1.50	3.00
15	Pete Mahovlich	.75	1.50
16	Phil Myre	.75	1.50
17	Larry Pleau	.75	1.50
18	Mickey Redmond	.75	1.50
19	Henri Richard	1.50	3.00
20	Serge Savard	2.00	4.00
21	Marc Tardiff	.75	1.50
22	Jean-Claude Tremblay	.75	1.50
23	Rogatien Vachon, Goalie	1.50	3.00

— 1971 - 72 POSTCARD ISSUE —

Pro Star Promotions 1971-72 Issue
Card No. 5, Ken Dryden

Card Size: 3 1/2" x 5 1/2"
Face: Four colour, borderless, Facsimile autograph
Back: Blank
Imprint: Pro Star Promotions Inc. Printed in Canada
Complete Set No.: 25
Complete Set Price: 22.50 45.00

No.	Player	EX	NRMT
1	Pierre Bouchard (Colour variation exists)	.75	1.50
2	Scotty Bowman, Coach	1.00	2.00
3	Yvan Cournoyer	1.50	3.00

No.	Player	EX	NRMT
4	Denis DeJordy, Goalie	.75	1.50
5	Ken Dryden, Goalie	4.00	8.00
6	Terry Harper	.75	1.50
7	Dale Hoganson	.75	1.50
8	Rejean Houle	.75	1.50
9	Guy Lafleur (Colour variation exists)	2.50	'5.00
10	Jacques Laperriere	1.00	2.00
11	Guy Lapointe	1.00	2.00
12	Claude Larose	.75	1.50
13	Jacques Lemaire	1.00	2.00
14	Frank Mahovlich	1.50	3.00
15	Peter Mahovlich	.75	1.50
16	Al MacNeil (Rare)	6.00	12.00
17	Phil Myre, Goalie	.75	1.50
18	Larry Pleau	.75	1.50
19	Henri Richard (Colour variation)	1.50	3.00
20	Phil Roberto	.75	1.50
21a	Jim Roberts, Autograph touches puck	.75	1.50
21b	Jim Roberts, Autograph away from puck	.75	1.50
22	Serge Savard	1.25	2.50
23	Marc Tardiff	.75	1.50
24	Jean-Claude Tremblay	.75	1.50
25	Rogatien Vachon, Goalie	1.50	3.00

— 1971 - 72 POSTCARD UPDATED ISSUE —

All these cards are considered rare, with the Bobby Sheehan card particularly difficult to find.

Card Size: 3 1/2" x 5 1/2"
Face: Four Colour, borderless
Back: Blank
Imprint: PRO STAR PROMOTIONS 1971, PRINTED IN CANADA
Complete Set No.: 8
Complete Set Price: 35.00 75.00

No.	Player	EX	NRMT
1	Jean Beliveau	7.50	15.00
2	Yvan Cournoyer	5.00	10.00
3	Ken Dryden, Goalie	9.00	18.00
4	Frank Mahovlich	5.00	10.00
5	Phil Roberto	1.00	2.00
6	Leon Rochefort	1.00	2.00
7	Bobby Sheehan	10.00	20.00
8	Rogatein Vachon, Goalie (Colour variation exists)	5.00	10.00

— 1972 - 73 POSTCARD ISSUE —

All cards have facsimile autographs.

Card Size: 3 1/2" x 5 1/2"
Face: Four colour, borderless
Back: Blank
Imprint: Pro Star Promotions Inc.
Complete Set No.: 21
Complete Set Price: 14.00 28.00
Common Card: .50 1.00

No.	Player	EX	NRMT
1	Chuck Arnason	.50	1.00
2	Pierre Bouchard	.50	1.00
3	Scotty Bowman, Coach	1.50	3.00
4	Yvan Cournoyer	1.00	2.00
5	Ken Dryden, Goalie	2.50	5.00
6	Rejean Houle	.50	1.00
7	Guy Lafleur	2.50	5.00
8	Jacques Laperriere	.50	1.00
9	Guy Lapointe	1.00	2.00
10	Claude Larose	.50	1.00
11	Chuck Lefley	.50	1.00
12	Jacques Lemaire	.75	1.50
13	Frank Mahovlich	1.00	2.00
14	Peter Mahovlich	.50	1.00
15	Bob Murdoch	.50	1.00
16	Michel Plasse, Goalie	.50	1.00
17	Henri Richard	1.50	3.00
18	Jim Roberts	.50	1.00
19	Serge Savard	1.00	2.00
20	Steve Shutt	1.50	3.00
21	Marc Tardiff	.50	1.00

STEINBERG

— 1982 - 83 POSTCARD ISSUE —

Store coupons were attached to bottom of these cards.

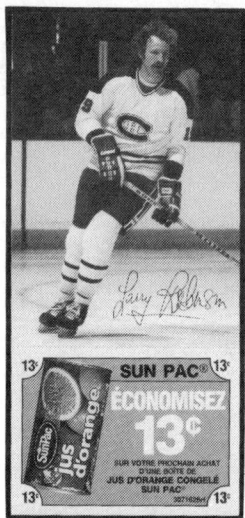

Steinberg, 1982-83 Issue
Card No. 16, Larry Robinson

Card Size: 3 1/2" X 5"; With coupon 3 1/2" X 7 1/2"
Face: Four colour, borderless; Facsimile autograph
Back: Four colour on white card stock; Jersey number, Name, Resume, French
Imprint: ©1982 N.Leroux—M.Fournier
Complete Set No.: 24

Complete Set Price:	9.00	18.00
Common Player:	.25	.50
Album:	2.50	5.00

No.	Player	EX	NRMT
—	Title Card: Montreal Canadiens	.25	.50
1	Keith Acton	.75	1.50
2	Guy Carbonneau	1.00	2.00
3	Gilbert Delorme	.25	.50
4	Bob Gainey	.50	1.00
5	Richard Green	.35	.75
6	Rejean Houle	.25	.50
7	Mark Hunter	.25	.50
8	Guy Lafleur	1.75	3.50
9	Craig Ludwig	.25	.50
10	Pierre Mondou	.25	.50
11	Mark Napier	.25	.50
12	Mats Naslund	.75	1.50
13	Eric Nattress	.25	.50
14	Christopher Nilan	.25	.50
15	Robert Picard	.25	.50
16	Larry Robinson	1.25	2.50
17	Bill Root	.25	.50
18	Richard Sevigny, Goalie	.25	.50
19	Steve Shutt	1.00	2.00
20	Mario Tremblay	.25	.50
21	Ryan Walter	.25	.50
22	Richard Wamsley, Goalie	.25	.50
23	Douglas Wickenheiser	.25	.50

— 1983 - 84 POSTCARD ISSUE —

This 24-postcard set had coupons attached to the base of the postcards. It was used in conjuction with many other food companies to promote their food products with a coupon for Steinbergs. Players are listed here alphabetically.

Steinberg, 1983-84 Postcard Issue
Postcard No. 1, Keith Acton

Postcard Size: 3 1/2" x 5" Plus tear off coupon
Face: Four colour, Borderless; Facsimile Autograph
Back: Four colour, White border; Number; Name; Resume; Steinberg logo on white postcard stock
Imprint: (On Coupon) © 1982 N. Leroux - M. Fournier
Complete Set No.: 24

Complete Set Price:	12.50	25.00
Common Goalie:	.35	.75
Common Player:	.35	.75

No.	Player	EX	NRMT
1	Keith Acton	.35	.75
2	Guy Carbonneau	1.00	2.00
3	Gilbert Delorme	.35	.75
4	Robert (Bob) Gainey	1.00	2.00
5	Richard (Rick) Green	.35	.75
6	Rejean Houle	.35	.75
7	Mark Hunter	.35	.75
8	Guy Lafleur	1.50	3.00
9	Craig Ludwig	.35	.75
10	Pierre Mondou	.35	.75
11	Mark Napier	.35	.75
12	Mats Naslund	1.00	2.00
13	Eric Natress	.35	.75
14	Chris Nilan	.35	.75
15	Robert Picard	.35	.75
16	Larry Robinson	1.25	2.50
17	Bill Root	.35	.75
18	Richard Sevigny, Goalie	.35	.75
19	Stephen (Steve) Shutt	.75	1.50
20	Mario Tremblay	.35	.75
21	Ryan Walter	.35	.75
22	Rick Wamsley, Goalie	.35	.75
23	Douglas Wickenheiser	.35	.75
24	Team Photograph	.35	.75

PROVIGO

— 1985 - 86 REGULAR ISSUE —

Provigo, 1985-86 Issue
Sticker No. 16, Stephane J.J. Richer

These Puffy stickers are unnumbered and are listed below in alphabetical order.

Sticker Size: 1 1/8" X 2 1/4"
Face: Four colour; Jersey number, Name, Team logo
Back: Black type on sticker back
Imprint: Crest-O-Matic
Poster Size: 20 1/16" X 11"
Face: Red, blue and black, white side borders; Jersey number, Names, Team logo
Back: Red and blue on white card stock; Team logo, Checklist
Imprint: PROMOTION BLITZ INC.
Complete Set No.: 25

Complete Set Price:	6.00	12.00
Common Player:	.13	.25

No.	Player	EX	NRMT
1	Guy Carbonneau	.50	1.00
2	Chris Chelios	.50	1.00
3	Kjell Dahlin	.13	.25
4	Lucien Deblois	.13	.25
5	Bob Gainey	.50	1.00
6	Richard Green	.13	.25
7	Tom Kurvers	.13	.25
8	Mike Lalor	.13	.25
9	Craig Ludwig	.13	.25
10	Michael McPhee	.35	.75
11	Sergio Momesso	.25	.50
12	Mats Naslund	.35	.75
13	Christopher Nilan	.13	.25
14	Steve Penney, Goalie	.25	.50
15	Jean Perron, Coach	.13	.25
16	Stephane J.J. Richer	1.00	2.00
17	Larry Robinson	.75	1.50
18	Steve Rooney	.13	.25
19	Patrick Roy, Goalie	2.50	5.00
20	Brian Skrudland	.25	.50
21	Robert Smith	.50	1.00
22	Doug Soetaert, Goalie	.13	.25
23	Petr Svoboda	.13	.25
24	Mario Tremblay	.13	.25
25	Ryan Walter	.13	.25

VACHON

— 1988 REGULAR ISSUE —

Vachon, 1988 Super Collection
Sticker Nos. 1, 38, 41, 67

Panel Size: 2 7/8" X 5 9/16"
Sticker Size: 1 1/2" X 2 9/16" or 1" X 1 13/16"
Face: Four colour; Number
Back: Black on white paper stock; Album offer
Imprint: None
Complete Set No.: 88

Complete Set Price:	7.50	15.00
Common Player:	.03	.05
Album:	2.50	5.00

No.	Player	EX	NRMT
1	Team Photo	.05	.10
2	Team Photo	.05	.10
3	Team Photo	.05	.10

MONTREAL CANADIENS - TEAMS SETS • 615

No.	Player	EX	NRMT
4	Team Photo	.05	.10
5	Team Photo	.05	.10
6	Team Photo	.05	.10
7	Jean Perron, Head Coach	.05	.10
8	Jacques Laperrière, Assistant Coach	.05	.10
9	François Allaire, Goaltending Instructor	.05	.10
10	Jean Perron, Head Coach	.05	.10
11A	Jacques Laperrière, Error	.10	.20
11B	Jacques Laperrière, With number	.10	.20
12	Bob Gainey	.10	.20
13	Bob Gainey	.10	.20
14	Guy Carbonneau	.20	.40
15	Guy Carbonneau	.20	.40
16	Guy Carbonneau	.20	.40
17A	Michael McPhee, Error	.03	.05
17B	Michael McPhee, With number	.03	.05
18	Bob Gainey	.10	.20
19	Christopher Nilan	.03	.05
20	Christopher Nilan	.03	.05
21	Guy Carbonneau	.20	.40
22	Mike Lalor	.03	.05
23	Patrick Roy, Goalie; Guy Carbonneau	.50	1.00
24	Ryan Walter	.03	.05
25	Ryan Walter	.03	.05
26	Robert Smith	.03	.05
27	Mats Naslund	.10	.20
28	Robert Smith	.03	.05
29	Michael McPhee	.03	.05
30	Robert Smith	.03	.05
31	Claude Lemieux	.13	.25
32	Robert Smith	.03	.05
33	Claude Lemieux	.13	.25
34	Brian Skrudland	.03	.05
35	Craig Ludwig	.03	.05
36	Brian Skrudland	.03	.05
37	Michael McPhee	.03	.05
38	Michael McPhee	.03	.05
39	Kjell Dahlin	.03	.05
40	Kjell Dahlin	.03	.05
41	Robert Smith	.03	.05
42	Patrick Roy, Goalie	.50	1.00
43	Patrick Roy, Goalie	.50	1.00
44	Larry Trader	.03	.05
45	Mats Naslund	.13	.25
46	Mats Naslund	.13	.25
47	Mats Naslund	.13	.25
48	Mats Naslund	.13	.25
49	Shayne Corson	.08	.15
50	Shayne Corson	.08	.15
51	Stéphane J.J. Richer	.08	.15
52	Stéphane J.J. Richer	.08	.15
53	Bob Gainey	.05	.10
54	Stéphane J.J. Richer	.08	.15
55	Sergio Momesso	.03	.05
56	Sergio Momesso	.03	.05
57	John Kordic	.03	.05
58	John Kordic	.03	.05
59	Mike Lalor	.03	.05
60A	Mike Lalor, Error	.03	.05
60B	Mike Lalor, With number	.03	.05
61	Brian Hayward, Goalie	.05	.10
62	Guy Carbonneau	.20	.40
63	Guy Carbonneau	.20	.40
64	Brian Hayward, Goalie	.03	.05
65	Richard Green	.03	.05
66	Richard Green	.03	.05
67	Brian Hayward, Goalie	.03	.05
68	Richard Green	.10	.20
69	Patrick Roy, Goalie	.50	1.00
70	Richard Green	.10	.20
71	Patrick Roy, Goalie	.50	1.00
72	Larry Robinson	.10	.20
73	Larry Robinson	.10	.20
74	Patrick Roy, Goalie	.50	1.00
75	Petr Svoboda	.03	.05
76	Patrick Roy, Goalie	.50	1.00
77	Petr Svoboda	.10	.20
78	Chris Chelios	.10	.20
79	Chris Chelios	.10	.20
80	Craig Ludwig	.03	.05
81	Craig Ludwig	.03	.05
82	Chris Chelios	.25	.50
83	Chris Chelios	.25	.50
84	Brian Hayward, Goalie	.03	.05
85	Craig Ludwig	.03	.05
86	Robert Smith	.10	.20
87	Mats Naslund	.10	.20
88	Bob Gainey	.10	.20

O-PEE-CHEE

— 1993 HOCKEYFEST PROMOTIONAL SHEET —

This 4-card mini sheet was handed out by O-Pee-Chee at the Hockeyfest 1993 held at Montreal to promote the special set they produced for the Montreal Canadiens.

Card Size: 5" x 7"
Face: Four colour, white border; Name
Back: Three colour with red border on white card stock; Name, Resume, Bilingual
Imprint: © 1993 O-PEE-CHEE CO. LTD. IMPRIMÉ AU CANADA / PRINTED IN CANADA

No.	Player	EX	NRMT
—	Sheet	3.50	7.00
∑	Henri Richard		
—	Jean Beliveau		
—	Yvan Cournoyer		
—	Maurice Richard		

— 1993 HOCKEYFEST —

This special 66-card set was a promotional set sold at Hockeyfest 1993 commemorating the Montreal Canadiens. The cards were issued as a set in a round black puck-like box.

O-Pee-Chee, 1993 Hockeyfest
Card No. 14, Jean Beliveau

Card Size: 2 1/2" x 3 1/2"
Face: Type 1: Four colour, white border; Name, Team logo
  Type 2: Four colour, blue border; Name, Number, Position, Team logo, Resume, Bilingual
Back: Four colour on a card stock, blue border; Name, Resume
Imprint: © 1993 O-PEE-CHEE CO. LTD. IMPRIMÉ AU CANADA / PRINTED IN CANADA
Complete Set No.: 66
Complete Set Price: 35.00 70.00
Common Goalie: .17 .35
Common Player: .17 .35
Puck: 5.00

No.	Player	EX	NRMT
1	Forum de Montreal	.50	1.00
2	Emilr (Butch) Bouchard	.50	1.00
3	Henri Richard	1.00	2.00
4	Serge Savard	.50	1.00
5	Toe (Hector) Blake	1.00	2.00
6	Maurice (Rocket) Richard	1.50	3.00
7	Stephan Lebeau	.35	.75
8	Kevin Haller	.35	.75
9	Guy Carbonneau	.50	1.00
10	Jacques Demers, Coach	.50	1.00
11	Serge Savard, Managing Director	.50	1.00
12	Forum de Montreal	.50	1.00
13	Howie Morenz	1.25	2.50
14	Jean Beliveau	1.00	2.00
15	Jacques Laperriere	.50	1.00
16	Bob Gainey	.50	1.00
17	Guy "The Flower" Lafleur	1.00	2.00
18	Jacques Raymond	.35	.75
19	Sean Hill	.35	.75
20	Eric Desjardins	.35	.75
21	Aurele Joliate, Error	.75	1.50
22	Doug Harvey	1.00	2.00
23	Yvan Cournoyer	.75	1.50
24	Frank Mahovlich	.75	1.50
25	Jean-Jacques Daigneault	.35	.75
26	Kirk Muller	.75	1.50
27	Jean Beliveau	1.00	2.00
28	Georges Vezina, Goalie	1.00	2.00
29	Maurice (Rocket) Richard	1.50	3.00
30	Patrick Roy, Goalie	2.50	5.00
31	Benoit Brunet	.35	.75
32	Jacques Plante, Goalie	1.50	3.00
33	Ralph Backstrom	.35	.75
34	Elmer Lach	.35	.75
35	Stanley Cup Winners	.50	1.00
36	Jacques Laperriere	.50	1.00
37	Stats	.35	.75
38	Vincent Damphousse	.50	1.00
39	Frank Mahovlich	.75	1.50
40	Jacques Plante, Goalie	1.50	3.00
41	Champions, Coupe Stanley	.50	1.00
42	Ken Reardon	.35	.75
43	Claude Provost	.35	.75
44	Jean Beliveau	1.00	2.00
45	Edward Ronan	.35	.75
46	Stats	.35	.75
47	Bill Durnan, Goalie	.35	.75
48	Coupe Stanley Cup	.50	1.00
49	Patrice Brisebois	.35	.75
50	Denis Savard	.50	1.00
51	Ken Dryden, Goalie	.75	1.50
52	Louie Fontinato	.50	1.00
53	Jean-Guy Talbot	.50	1.00
54	Bernie (Boom Boom) Geoffrion	1.00	2.00
55	Joe Malone	.75	1.50
56	Oleg Petrov	.50	1.00
57	Guy Lafleur	1.00	2.00
58	Bert Olmstead	.35	.75
59	The Dream Team	.50	1.00
60	Brian Bellows	.50	1.00
61	Henri Richard	1.00	2.00
62	Jacques Lemaire	.50	1.00
63	Dickie Moore	.75	1.50
64	Lorne (Gump) Worsley, Goalie	1.00	2.00
65	Toe Blake	1.00	2.00
66	Checklist	.35	.75

THE CHARLTON STANDARD CATALOGUE OF CANADIAN BASEBALL AND FOOTBALL CARDS
- Fourth Edition -

Coming in April!

NEW JERSEY DEVILS - TEAM SETS

TEAM ISSUES

— 1983 - 84 POSTCARD ISSUE —

Card Size: 3 1/4" X 6"
Face: Four colour, borderless
Back: Black and white photo; Name,, Resume Team logo
Imprint: None
Complete Set No.: 25
Complete Set Price: 7.50 15.00
Common Card: .25 .50

No.	Player	EX	NRMT
1	Mike Antonovitch	.25	.50
2	Mel Bridgeman	.35	.75
3	Aaron Broten	.50	1.00
4	Murray Bromwell	.25	.50
5	Dave Cameron	.25	.50
6	Rich Chernomaz	.25	.50
7	Joe Cirella	.75	1.50
8	Kenneth Daneyko	.50	1.00
9	Larry Floyd	.25	.50
10	Paul Gagne	.25	.50
11	Mike Kitchen	.25	.50
12	Jeff Larmer	.25	.50
13	Don Lever	.50	1.00
14	Dave Lewis	.25	.50
15	Bob Lorimer	.25	.50
16	Ron Low, Goalie	.35	.75
17	Jan Ludwig	.25	.50
18	John MacLean	2.00	4.00
19	Bob MacMillan	.25	.50
20	Hector Marini	.25	.50
21	Rick Meagher	.25	.50
22	Grant Mulvey	.25	.50
23	Glenn Resch, Goalie	.50	1.00
24	Phil Russell	.25	.50
25	Pat Verbeek	1.50	3.00

— 1984 - 85 POSTCARD ISSUE —

Card Size: 3 1.4" X 6"
Face: Four colour, borderless
Back: Black and white photograph; Name, Resume, Team logo
Imprint: None
Complete Set No.: 25
Complete Set Price: 7.50 15.00
Common Card: .25 .50

No.	Player	EX	NRMT
1	Doug Carpenter	.35	.75
2	Mel Bridgeman	.35	.75
3	Aaron Broten	.50	1.00
4	Rich Chernoaz	.25	.50
5	Joe Cirella	.75	1.50
6	Bruce Driver	.75	1.50
7	Paul Gagne	.25	.50
8	Uli Hiemer	.25	.50
9	Tim Higgins	.25	.50
10	Bob Hoffmeyer	.25	.50
11	Hanhu Kampurri	.25	.50
12	Don Lever	.35	.75
13	Dave Lewis	.25	.50
14	Bob Lorimer	.25	.50
15	Ron Low, Goalie	.35	.75
16	Jan Ludwig	.25	.50
17	John MacLean	1.00	2.00
18	Rick Meagher	.25	.50
19	Kirk Muller	2.00	4.00
20	Dave Pichette	.25	.50
21	Rich Preston	.25	.50
22	Glen (Chico) Resch, Goalie	.50	1.00
23	Phil Russell	.25	.50
24	Doug Sulliman	.25	.50
25	Pat Verbeek	1.00	2.00

— 1985 - 86 POSTCARD ISSUE —

1985-86 Postcard Issue
Postcard No. 9, Kirk Muller

Postcard Size: 3 5/8" X 5 1/2"
Face: Four colour, borderless
Back: Black and white on card stock; Number, Name, Resume
Imprint: None
Complete Set No.: 10
Complete Set Price: 4.00 8.00
Common Player: .13 .25

No.	Player	EX	NRMT
1	Mark Johnson	.13	.25
2	Craig Billington, Goalie	.50	1.00
3	Alain Chevrier	.13	.25
4	Paul Gagne	.13	.25
5	Chico Resch, Goalie	.25	.50
6	Greg Adams	.35	.75
7	Craig Wolanin	.13	.25
8	Perry Anderson	.13	.25
9	Kirk Muller	3.00	6.00
10	Randy Valischek	.13	.25

— 1989 - 90 REGULAR ISSUE —

Card Size: 2 7/8" X 4 1/4"
Face: Four colour, white border; Team logo, Team, Name, Jersey number, Position
Back: Black on white card stock; Team, Jersey number, Name, Position, Team logo, resume
Imprint: © 1989 NEW JERSEY DEVILS
Complete Set No.: 29
Complete Set Price: 6.00 12.00
Common Player: .13 .25

No.	Player	EX	NRMT
1	Tommy Albelin	.13	.25
2	Bob Bellemore, Coach	.13	.25
3	Neil Brady	.13	.25
4	Aaron Broten	.13	.25
5	Doug Brown	.13	.25
6	Sean Burke, Goalie	.50	1.00
7	Patrick Conacher	.13	.25
8	John Cunniff, Coach	.13	.25
9	Ken Daneyko	.13	.25
10	Bruce Driver	.13	.25
11	Viacheslav Fetisov	.50	1.00
12	Mark Johnson	.13	.25
13	James Korn	.13	.25
14	Lou Lamoriello, President / General Manager	.13	.25
15	John MacLean	.75	1.50
16	David Maley	.13	.25
17	Kirk Muller	1.50	3.00
18	Janne Ojanen	.25	.50
19	Walter Poddubny	.25	.50
20	Reijo Ruotsalainen	.25	.50
21	Brendan Shanahan	.75	1.50
22	Sergei Starikov	.35	.75
23	Patrik Sundstrom	.35	.75
24	Peter Sundstrom	.25	.50
25	Chris Terreri, Goalie	.50	1.00
26	Sylvain Turgeon	.13	.25
27	Randy Velischek	.13	.25
28	Eric Weinrich	.50	1.00
29	Craig Wolanin	.13	.25

— 1990 - 91 REGULAR ISSUE —

Card Size: 2 1/2" X 3 1/2"
Face: Four colour; Name, Logo
Back: Black on white card stock; Resume
Imprint: © 1990 New Jersey Devils
Complete Set No.: 30
Complete Set Price: 5.00
Common Player: .13

No.	Player	EX	NRMT
1	Tommy Albelin	.13	.25
2	Laurie Boschman	.13	.25
3	Doug Brown	.13	.25
4	Sean Burke, Goalie	.25	.50
5	Tim Burke	.13	.25
6	Zdeno Ciger	.25	.50
7	Patrick Conacher	.13	.25
8	Troy Crowder	.25	.50
9	John Cunniff, Coach	.13	.25
10	Ken Daneyko	.13	.25
11	Bruce Driver	.25	.50
12	Viacheslav Fetisov	.35	.75
13	Alexei Kasatonov	.25	.50
14	Lou Lamoriello, President / General Manager	.13	.25
15	Claude Lemieux	.35	.75
16	David Maley	.13	.25
17	John McLean	.35	.75
18	Jon Morris	.13	.25
19	Kirk Muller	.50	1.00
20	Lee Norwood	.13	.25
21	Myles O'Connor	.13	.25
22	Walter Poddubny	.13	.25
23	Brendan Shanahan	.50	1.00
24	Peter Stastny	.50	1.00
25	Allan Stewart	.13	.25
26	Warren Strelow	.13	.25
27	Doug Sulliman	.13	.25
28	Patrik Sundstrom	.25	.50
29	Chris Terreri, Goalie	.50	1.00
30	Eric Weinrich	.25	.50

THE CHARLTON STANDARD CATALOGUE OF CANADIAN BASEBALL AND FOOTBALL CARDS
- Fourth Edition -

Coming in April!

POLICE

— 1986 - 87 REGULAR ISSUE —

This set was sponsored by the New Jersey Devils, S.O.B.E.R. the Howard and the Independent Insurance Agents of Bergen County.

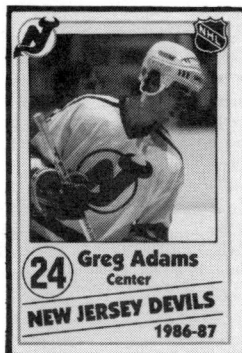

Police, 1986-87 Issue
Card No. 1, Gregory Adams

Card Size: 2 7/8" X 4 1/8"
Face: Four colour, yellow with green and white border; Team logo, Jersey number, Name, Position, Team
Back: Black on white card stock; Jersey number, Name, Resume, Police tip, Sponsor logos; Number
Imprint: None
Complete Set No.: 20
Complete Set Price: 15.00   30.00
Common Player: .50   1.00

No.	Player	EX	NRMT
1	Gregory Adams	1.00	2.00
2	Perry Anderson	.50	1.00
3	Timo Blomqvist	.50	1.00
4	Andy Brickley	.50	1.00
5	Mel Bridgman	.50	1.00
6	Aaron Broten	.50	1.00
7	Alain Chevrier, Goalie	1.00	2.00
8	Joe Cirella	1.00	2.00
9	Ken Daneyko	.50	1.00
10	Bruce Driver	1.00	2.00
11	Uli Hiemer	.50	1.00
12	Mark Johnson	1.00	2.00
13	Jan Ludvig	.50	1.00
14	John MacLean	2.50	5.00
15	Peter McNab	.50	1.00
16	Kirk Muller	3.00	6.00
17	Doug Sulliman	.50	1.00
18	Randy Velischek	.50	1.00
19	Patrick Verbeek	2.00	4.00
20	Craig Wolanin	.50	1.00

CARRETTA TRUCKING

— 1988 - 89 REGULAR ISSUE —

These cards are unnumbered and are listed below in alphabetical order.

Card Size: 2 7/8" X 4 1/4"
Face: Four colour, white border; Team logo, Team, Jersey Number, Name, Position
Back: Black on white card stock; Team, Jersey number, Name, Postion, Team and sponsor logos, Resume
Imprint: None
Complete Set No.: 30
Complete Set Price: 7.50   15.00
Common Player: .13   .25

No.	Player	EX	NRMT
1	Perry Anderson	.13	.25
2	Bob Bellemore	.13	.25
3	Aaron Broten	.13	.25
4	Doug Brown	.13	.25
5	Sean Burke, Goalie	.35	.75
6	Anders Carlsson	.13	.25
7	Joe Cirella	.25	.50
8	Patrick Conacher	.13	.25
9	Ken Daneyko	.13	.25
10	Bruce Driver	.25	.50
11	Bob Hoffmeyer	.13	.25
12	Jamie Huscroft	.13	.25
13	Mark Johnson	.25	.50
14	James Korn	.13	.25
15	Tom Kurvers	.25	.50
16	Lou Lamoriello	.13	.25
17	Claude Loiselle	.25	.50
18	John MacLean	.35	.75
19	David Maley	.25	.50
20	Doug McKay	.13	.25
21	Kirk Muller	1.00	2.00
22	Jack O'Callahan	.13	.25
23	Steve Rooney	.13	.25
24	Bob Sauve, Goalie	.25	.50
25	Jim Schoenfeld, Coach	.25	.50
26	Brendan Shanahan	.50	1.00
27	Patrik Sundstrom	.35	.75
28	Randy Velischek	.13	.25
29	Patrick Verbeek	.50	1.00
30	Craig Wolanin	.13	.25

NEW YORK ISLANDERS - TEAM SETS

TEAM ISSUES

— 1979 - 80 POSTCARD ISSUE —

Card Size: 3" x 5"
Face: Black and white; Name, Facsimile autgraph
Back: Blank
Imprint: None
Complete Set No.: 22
Complete Set Price: 11.00   22.00
Common Card: .50   1.00

No.	Player	EX	NRMT
1	Team Crest	.50	1.00
2	Mike Bossy	1.50	3.00
3	Bob Bourne	.50	1.00
4	Clark Gilles	.75	1.50
5	Billy Harris	.75	1.50
6	Lorne Henning	.50	1.00
7	Garry Howatt	.50	1.00
8	Anders Kallur	.50	1.00
9	Mike Kaszycki	.50	1.00
10	Dave Langevin	.50	1.00
11	Dave Lewis	.50	1.00
12	Bob Lorimer	.50	1.00
13	Wayne Merrick	.50	1.00
14	Bob Nystrom	.75	1.50
15	Stefan Persson	.50	1.00
16	Denis Potvin	1.25	2.50
17	Jean Potvin	.50	1.00
18	Glenn Resch, Goalie	1.25	2.50
19	Billy Smith, Goalie	1.25	2.50
20	Steve Tambellini	.50	1.00
21	John Tonelli	.75	1.50
22	Bryan Trottier	1.50	3.00

ISLANDER NEWS

— 1984 REGULAR ISSUE —

Islander News, 1984 Issue
Card No. 2, Mike Bossy

Card Size: 2 1/2" X 3 1/2"
Face: Four colour, pale blue and white border; Name, Team logo
Back: Black on white card stock; Team logo, Number, Name, Position, Resume, Player trivia
Imprint: None
Complete Set No.: 38
Complete Set Price: 12.50   25.00
Common Player: .25   .50

No.	Player	EX	NRMT
1	Checklist / The Stanley Cup	.25	.50
2	Mike Bossy	1.50	3.00
3	Bob Bourne	.25	.50
4	Billy Carroll	.25	.50
	Bill on face; Billy on back		
5	Gregory Gilbert	.25	.50
6	Clark Gillies	.35	.75

No.	Player	EX	NRMT
7	Butch Goring	.35	.75
8	Mats Hallin	.25	.50
9	Anders Kallur	.25	.50
10	Wayne Merrick	.25	.50
11	Bob Nystrom	.50	1.00
12	Brent Sutter	.50	1.00
13	Duane Sutter	.50	1.00
14	John Tonelli	.50	1.00
15	Bryan Trottier	1.50	3.00
16	Tomas Jonsson	.25	.50
17	Gord Lane	.25	.50
18	Dave Langevin	.25	.50
19	Ken Morrow	.35	.75
20	Stefan Persson	.35	.75
21	Denis Potvin	1.50	3.00
22	Roland Melanson, Goalie	.35	.75
23	Billy Smith, Goalie	1.00	2.00
24	Cup No. 1	.25	.50
25	Cup No. 2	.25	.50
26	Cup No. 4	.25	.50
27	Lorne Henning, Assistant Coach	.25	.50
28	Bill Torrey, General Manager	.25	.50
29	Al Arbour, Coach	.35	.75
30	Ron Waske, Head Trainer; Jim Pickard, Assistant Trainer	.25	.50

TEAM PHOTOS

No.	Player	EX	NRMT
31	1979 - 80	.35	.75
32	1980 - 81	.35	.75
33	1981 - 82	.35	.75
34	1982 - 83	.35	.75

CONN SMYTHE WINNERS

No.	Player	EX	NRMT
35	1982: Mike Bossy	.75	1.50
36	1983: Billy Smith, Goalie	.50	1.00
37	1980: Bryan Trottier	.60	1.25
38	1981: Butch Goring	.35	.75

— 1984 - 85 REGULAR ISSUE —

Islander News, 1984-85 Issue
Card No. 11, Pat LaFontaine

Card Size: 2 1/2" X 3 1/2"
Face: Four colour, white border; Name
Back: Black on white card stock; Name, Number, Resume
Imprint: ISLANDER NEWS (2nd Series)
Complete Set No.: 37
Complete Set Price: 1400   28.00
Common Player: .25   .50

No.	Player	EX	NRMT
1	Checklist 1984-85	.25	.50
2	Mike Bossy	1.25	2.50
3	Bob Bourne	.25	.50
4	Patrick Flatley	.35	.75
5	Gregory Gilbert	.25	.50
6	Clark Gillies	.35	.75

No.	Player	EX	NRMT
7	Mats Hallin	.25	.50
8	Anders Kallur	.25	.50
9	Alan Kerr	.25	.50
10	Roger Kortko	.25	.50
11	Pat LaFontaine	4.50	9.00
12	Bob Nystrom	.25	.50
13	Brent Sutter	.50	1.00
14	Duane Sutter	.50	1.00
15	John Tonelli	.50	1.00
16	Bryan Trottier	1.50	3.00
17	Paul Boutilier	.25	.50
18	Gerald Diduck	.25	.50
19	Gord Dineen	.25	.50
20	Tomas Jonsson	.25	.50
21	Gord Lane	.25	.50
22	Dave Langevin	.25	.50
23	Ken Morrow	.35	.75
24	Stefan Persson	.35	.75
25	Denis Potvin	1.00	2.00
26	Kelly Hrudey, Goalie	1.50	3.00
27	Billy Smith, Goalie	.75	1.50
28	Bill Torrey, General Manager / President	.25	.50
29	Al Arbour, Head Coach	.25	.50
30	Brian Kilrea, Assistant Coach	.25	.50
31	Craig Smith, Athletic Trainer; Jim Packard, Equipment Trainer	.25	.50

MILESTONE

No.	Player	EX	NRMT
32	Mike Bossy, 400 Goals	.50	1.00
33	Denis Potvin, 600 Assists	.50	1.00
34	Billy Smith, Goalie, 500 Games	.50	1.00
35	Bryan Trottier, 1000 Points	.50	1.00

REGULAR ISSUE

No.	Player	EX	NRMT
36	1984 - 85 Team Photo	.35	.75
37	Wales Champs	.35	.75

— 1985 BRYAN TROTTIER — REGULAR ISSUE

Islander News, 1985 Bryan Trottier Issue
Card No. 27, "You Don't Need Drugs"

Card Size: 2 1/2" X 3 1/2"
Face: Four colour or black and white photo, pale blue border; Number, Facsimile autograph
Back: Black on white card stock; Number, Drug and Alcohol prevention tips
Imprint: ISLANDER NEWS
Complete Set No.: 33
Complete Set Price: 10.00   20.00
Common Player: .25   .50

No.	Player	EX	NRMT
1	Using Drugs Puts You In A Permanent Penalty Box	.25	.50
2	Say NO to Drugs!	.25	.50

NEW YORK ISLANDERS - TEAM SETS • 619

No.	Player	EX	NRMT
3	Don't Drink. Don't Smoke. Don't Play With Drugs... The Perfect Hat Trick	.25	.50
4	Don't Let Your Mind Go To Pot	.25	.50
5	Friends Don't Let Friends Drive Drunk	.25	.50
6	Enjoy Alternatives To Drugs & Booze	.25	.50
7	Help Friends Feel Good About Themselves	.25	.50
8	People Who Are Involved Don't Need Drugs	.25	.50
9	Think Before You Drink	.25	.50
10	It's Your Choice. Don't Be A Victim	.25	.50
11	Drugs...Don't Let This Five Letter Word Ruin Your Life	.25	.50
12	Living With Drugs Can Hurt	.25	.50
13	Alcohol Is The Worst Drug Of All	.25	.50
14	Drugs And School Don't Mix	.25	.50
15	Don't Be Embarrassed If You Have A Problem...Get Help	.25	.50
16	Be A Winner... Don't Play With Drugs	.25	.50
17	Develop Good Habits... Not Drug Habits	.25	.50
18	Alcohol is A Drug Think Don't Drink	.25	.50
19	It May Take Five Years To Cure A Drug Addict	.25	.50
20	Grow Up Tall, Use No Drugs At All	.25	.50
21	Don't Play With Drugs... It's A Losing Game	.25	.50
22	Keep Off The Grass	.25	.50
23	Don't Be A Fool Trying To Act Cool..."Be Straight"	.25	.50
24	Even A Kid Can Become An Alcoholic	.25	.50
25	Drugs...Be Smart.. Don't Start	.25	.50
26	You Can't Take Your Best Shot When You're High On Drugs	.25	.50
27	You Don't Need Drugs... You Can Make It On Your Own	.25	.50
28	Drugs Can Cause Genetic Damage	.25	.50
29	Make The Save Of Your Life...Don't Drink	.25	.50
30	Be A Winner... Shut Out Drugs	.25	.50
31	Stopping Is Hard... Don't Start On Drugs	.25	.50
32	Starting With Drugs Can Finish Your Life	.25	.50
33	Real Life Is Fun... Don't Drop Out With Drugs	.25	.50

— 1990 - 91 ISSUE —

We have no information on the 1990-91 team set. We would appreciate hearing from anyone who could supply any further information.

New York Islanders - Team Sets
1984 Issue, Card No. 2, Mike Bossy

New York Islanders - Team Sets
1984 Issue, Card No. 23, Billy Smithh

NEW YORK RANGERS - TEAM SETS

MARINE MIDLAND

— 1989 - 90 REGULAR ISSUE —

These cards are unnumbered and are listed here in alphabetical order.

Marine Midland, 1989-90 Issue
Card No. 12, Brian Leetch

Card Size: 2 5/8" X 3 5/8"
Face: Four colour, white border; Name, Position, Jersey number, Team logo
Back: Black and blue on white card stock; Name, Jersey number, Resume
Imprint: MARINE MIDLAND BANK
Complete Set No.: 30
Complete Set Price: 9.00 18.00
Common Player: .25 .50

No.	Player	EX	NRMT
1	Jeff Bloemberg	.25	.50
2	Paul Broten	.25	.50
3	Ulf Dahlen	.25	.50
4	Jan Erixon	.25	.50
5	Robert Froese, Goalie	.25	.50
6	Ronald Greschner	.25	.50
7	Mark Hardy	.25	.50
8	Miloslav Horava	.25	.50
9	Mark Janssens	.25	.50
10	Kris King	.35	.75
11	Kelly Kisio	.25	.50
12	Brian Leetch	1.50	3.00
13	Troy Mallette	.25	.50
14	Corey Millen	.35	.75
15	Randy Moller	.25	.50
16	Brian Mullen	.25	.50
17	Roger Neilson, Head Coach	.25	.50
18	Bernie Nicholls	.35	.75
19	Christopher Nilan	.25	.50
20	John Ogrodnick	.25	.50
21	James Patrick	.35	.75
22	Rudy Poeschek	.25	.50
23	Mike Richter, Goalie	.60	1.25
24	Normand Rochefort	.25	.50
25	Lindy Ruff	.25	.50
26	David Shaw	.35	.75
27	Darren Turcotte	.50	1.00
28	John Vanbiesbrouck, Goalie	.50	1.00
29	Carey Wilson	.25	.50
30	New York Rangers / Marine Midland Bank MasterCard	.25	.50

HIGH-STICKING

Available in April!

THE CHARLTON STANDARD CATALOGUE OF CANADIAN BASEBALL & FOOTBALL CARDS

- Fourth Edition -

BASEBALL CARDS FROM 1912
FOOTBALL CARDS FROM 1949

For Canadian Baseball and Football Card Collectors this Catalogue has it all!

IMPERIAL TOBACCO * MAPLE CRISPETTE
BAZOOKA *PARKHURST * O-PEE-CHEE
CANADA STARCH * STUART * POST
TOPPS * WORLD WIDE GUM * NALLEYS
DONRUSS - LEAF * EDDIE SARGENT
WILLARD * TORONTO BLUE JAYS
STANDARD OIL * NABISCO * VACHON
BLUE RIBBON TEA * PANINI * PROVIGO
GENERAL MILLS * SCORE * EXHIBITS
HOSTESS * PURITAN MEATS * JOGO
GULF CANADA * ROYAL STUDIOS
BEN'S AULT FOODS * COCA-COLA * KFC
And All Other Major Manufacturers...

Complete price listings for all Major League Baseball and Canadian Football League cards!
Comprehensive baseball and football minor league card listings!
Regular issues, stickers, inserts, subsets, transfers and much, much more!
All major manufacturers!
Current Pricing for all cards in up to three grades of condition - VG, EX, and NRMT!
All rookie, last, pitcher, quarterback, error and variation cards identified and priced!
Plus Charlton's Fabulous Alphabetical Index!

OVER 300 PAGES * 60,000 PRICES
NEW, LARGER 8 1/2 x 11" FORMAT
RESERVE YOUR COPY TODAY
DIRECTLY FROM THE PUBLISHER...

The Charlton Press

**2010 YONGE STREET,
TORONTO, ONTARIO M4S 1Z9**
FOR TOLL FREE ORDERING PHONE
1-800-442-6042 FAX 1-800-442-1542
from anywhere in Canada or the U.S.

OTTAWA SENATORS - TEAM SETS

TEAM ISSUES

1992 - 93 POSTCARD ISSUE

Card Size: 4.0" x 5 7/8"
Face: Four colour, borderless, Advertising
Back: Blank
Imprint: None
Complete Set No.: 23
Complete Set Price: 6.00 12.00

No.	Player	EX	NRMT
1	Dave Archibald	.25	.50
2	Jamie Baker	.35	.75
3	Daniel Berthiaume, Goalie	.25	.50
4	Laurie Boschman	.25	.50
5	Neil Brady	.25	.50
6	Kimbi Daniels	.25	.50
7	Mark Freer	.25	.50
8	Ken Hammond	.25	.50
9	Jody Hull	.25	.50
10	Tomas Jelinek	.25	.50
11	Bob Kudelski	.25	.50
12	Mark Lamb	.35	.75
13	Jeff Lazaro	.25	.50
14	Christopher Luongo	.25	.50
15	Darcy Loewen	.25	.50
16	Norm Maciver	.50	1.00
17	Andrew McBain	.25	.50
18	Mike Peluso	.35	.75
19	Brad Shaw	.25	.50
20	Peter Sidorkiewicz, Goalie	.35	.75
21	Doug Smail	.25	.50
22	Sylvain Turgeon	.25	.50
23	Steve Weeks, Goalie	.25	.50

TEAM ISSUES, 1992-93 POSTCARD SET
POSTCARD No. 20, Peter Sidorkiewiez

PHILADELPHIA FLYERS - TEAM SETS

TEAM ISSUES

— 1981 - 82 TICKET ISSUE —

Issued in the form of ticket stubs these card strips have the Flyers home games as the headline on each card.
This set is incomplete. We would appreciate hearing from anyone with further information.

Card Size: 1 5/8" X 4"
Face: Four colour, Game date and time, Opposing team, Number
Back: Black and white, Advertising message for the Delaware Group
Complete Set No.: 40
Complete Set Price: 37.50 75.00

THE DELAWARE GROUP

No.	Player	EX	NRMT
1	Hartford Whalers, November 12	1.00	2.00
2	New York Islanders, November 15	1.00	2.00
3	Washington Capitals, November 22	1.00	2.00
4	Toronto Maple Leafs, November 24	1.00	2.00
5	Winnipeg Jets, December 1	1.00	2.00
6	Calgary Flames, December 3	1.00	2.00
7	St. Louis Blues, December 6	1.00	2.00
8	New York Rangers, December 12	1.00	2.00

— 1986 - 87 POSTCARD ISSUE —

These cards are unnumbered and are listed below in alphabetical order.

1986-87 Postcard Issue
Postcard No. 9, Ron Hextall

Card Size: 4 1/8" X 6"
Face: Four colour; Team logo, Name, Position, Resume, Jersey number, Facsimile autograph
Back: Black on white card stock; Jersey number, Name, Position, Resume, Team logo
Imprint: None
Complete Set No.: 29
Complete Set Price: 7.50 15.00
Common Player: .25 .50

No.	Player	EX	NRMT
1	Bill Barber, Assistant Coach	.25	.50
2	Dave Brown	.25	.50
3	Lindsay Carson	.25	.50
4	Murray Craven	.25	.50
5	Pat Croce, Assistant Coach	.25	.50
6	Doug Crossman	.25	.50
7	Jean-Jacques Daigneault	.50	1.00
8	Per-Erik (Pelle) Eklund	.35	.75
9	Ron Hextall, Goalie	1.00	2.00
10	Paul Holmgren, Assistant Coach	.25	.50
11	Ed Hospodar	.25	.50
12	Mark Howe	.50	1.00
13	Mike Keenan, Coach	.50	1.00
14	Tim Kerr	.50	1.00
15	Brad Marsh	.25	.50
16	Byron (Brad) McCrimmon	.25	.50
17	E.J. McGuire, Assistant Coach	.25	.50
18	Scott Mellanby	.25	.50
19	Bernie Parent, Assistant Coach	.50	1.00
20	Dave Poulin	.35	.75
21	Brian Propp	.35	.75
22	Glenn Resch, Goalie	.25	.50
23	Ilkka Sinisalo	.25	.50
24	Derrick Smith	.25	.50
25	Daryl Stanley	.25	.50
26	Ron Sutter	.35	.75
27	Rick Tocchet	1.00	2.00
28	Peter Zezel	.25	.50
29	1986-87 Philadelphia Flyers	.50	1.00

— 1992 - 93 PHOTO ISSUE —

A sheet was given out to spectators at the Flyers home game on the date that appears on the sheet.

Card Size: 8 1/2" x 11"
Face: Four colour, white border; Team Name
Back: Two colour, white border; Date; Teams Roster
Imprint: © 1992 UPPER DECK
Complete Set No.: 45
Complete Set Price: 175.00 350.00
Common Card: 5.00 10.00

No.	Player	EX	NRMT
1	Kevin Dineen, September 19, 1992	5.00	10.00
2	Brian Benning, September 24, 1992	5.00	10.00
3	Mark Recchi, October 3, 1992	5.00	10.00
4	Keith Acton, October 9, 1992	5.00	10.00
5	Rod Brind'Amour, October 15, 1992	5.00	10.00
6	Dave Brown, October 18, 1992	5.00	10.00
7	Dominic Roussel, Goalie, October 22, 1992	5.00	10.00
8	Gordon Hynes, October 24, 1992	5.00	10.00
9	Claude Boivin, November 7, 1992	5.00	10.00
10	Dimitri Yushkevich, November 12, 1992	5.00	10.00
11	Eric Lindros, November 15, 1992	5.00	10.00
12	Stephen Kasper, November 19, 1992	5.00	10.00
13	1992-93 Philadelphia Flyers, November 22, 1992	5.00	10.00
14	Gregory Paslawski, November 27, 1992	5.00	10.00
15	Terry Carkner, December 3, 1992	5.00	10.00
16	Shawn Cronin, December 6, 1992	5.00	10.00
17	Brent Fedyk, December 12, 1992	5.00	10.00
18	Garry Galley, December 17, 1992	5.00	10.00
19	Andrei Lomakin, December 19, 1992	5.00	10.00
20	Bill and Kevin Dineen, December 23, 1992	5.00	10.00
21	Stephane Beauregard, Goalie, January 7, 1993	5.00	10.00
22	Mark Recchi, January 9, 1993	5.00	10.00
23	Ryan McGill, January 10, 1993	5.00	10.00
24	Douglas Evans, January 14, 1993	5.00	10.00
25	**The Captains:** K. Dineen, K. Acton, Terry Carkner, January 17, 1993	5.00	10.00
26	Eric Nattress, January 21, 1993	5.00	10.00
27	Rod Brind'Amour, January 24, 1993	5.00	10.00
28	Tommy Soderstrom, Goalie, January 26, 1993	5.00	10.00
29	Per-Erik Eklund, January 28, 1993	5.00	10.00
30	David Brown, February 9, 1993	5.00	10.00
31	**The Rookies:** T. Soderstrom, D. Yushkevitch, D. Roussel, R. McGill E. Lindros, February 11, 1993	5.00	10.00
32	Josef Beranek, February 14, 1993	5.00	10.00
33	Gregory Paslawski, February 25, 1993	5.00	10.00
34	**The Coaches:** C. Hartsburg, B. Dineen, K. Hitchcock, February 27, 1993	5.00	10.00
35	Keith Acton, March 2, 1993	5.00	10.00
36	**NHL All Star:** Mark Recchi, March 11, 1993	5.00	10.00
37	Garry Galley, March 13, 1993	5.00	10.00
38	Terry Carkner, March 16, 1993	5.00	10.00
39	D. Roussel, Goalie, March 21, 1993	5.00	10.00
40	Greg Hawgood, March 25, 1993	5.00	10.00
41	Viacheslav Butsayev, April 3, 1993	5.00	10.00
42	**Crazy 8's:** M. Recchi, E. Lindros, B. Fedyk, April 4, 1993	5.00	10.00
43	**European Style:** Andrei Lomakin, Dimitri Yushkevich, Viacheslav Butsayev, April 8, 1993	5.00	10.00
44	**Hockey Hall of Famers:** B. Clarke, Ed.Snider, B. Barber, B. Parent, Goalie, K. Allen, April 12, 1993	5.00	10.00

PIZZA HUT TEAM PHOTOGRAPH

No.	Player	EX	NRMT
45	Team Photograph	7.50	15.00

— 1993 - 94 PHOTO ISSUE —

Card Size: 8 1/2" x 11"
Face: Four colour, borderles; Name, Team logo
Back: Two colour, borderless; Date, Team Roster
Imprint: None
Complete Set No.: 44
Complete Set Price: 85.00 175.00
Common Card: 2.00 4.00

No.	Player	EX	NRMT
1	Greg Hawgood, Sept. 16, 1993	2.00	4.00
2	Brent Fedyk, Sept. 21, 1993	2.00	4.00
3	Terry Carkner, Sept. 26, 1993	2.00	4.00
4	Mark Recchi, Oct. 5, 1993	3.50	7.00
5	Dave Brown, Oct. 10, 1993	2.00	4.00
6	Jason Bowen, Oct. 12, 1993	2.00	4.00
7	Kevin Dineen, Oct. 16, 1993	2.00	4.00
8	Per-Eric Eklund, Oct. 21, 1993	2.00	4.00
9	Eric Lindros, Oct. 23, 1993	7.50	15.00
10	Mikael Renberg, Nov. 4, 1993	5.00	10.00
11	Ryan McGill, Nov. 7, 1993	2.00	4.00
12	Garry Galley, Nov. 11, 1993	2.00	4.00
13	Yves Racine, Nov. 13, 1993	2.00	4.00
14	Stewart Malgunas, Nov. 18, 1993	2.00	4.00
15	Rod Brind'Amour, Nov. 21, 1993	3.50	7.00
16	The Coaches, Nov. 24, 1993	2.00	4.00
17	Al Conray, Nov. 26, 1993	2.00	4.00
18	Dominic Roussel, Goalie, Dec. 9, 1993	2.50	5.000
19	Dimitri Yushkevich, Dec. 12, 1993	2.00	4.00
20	Team Picture, Dec. 16, 1993	2.00	4.00
21	Mark Recchi, Dec. 18, 1993	3.50	7.00
22	Viacheslav Butsayev, Dec. 21, 1993	2.00	4.00
23	The Rookies, Dec. 23, 1993	2.00	4.00
24	Josef Beranek, Jan. 11, 1994	2.50	5.00
25	The Captains, Jan. 13, 1994	2.00	4.00
26	Dave Tippett, Jan. 16, 1994	2.00	4.00
27	Tommy Soderstrom, Goalie, Jan. 19, 1994	2.50	5.00
28	Eric Lindros, January 29, 1994	7.50	15.00
29	Claude Boivin, February 3, 1994	2.00	4.00
30	Dimitri Yushkevich, Feb. 10, 1994	2.00	4.00
31	Jeff Finley, Feb. 13, 1994	2.00	4.00
32	Rob Ramage, Feb. 21, 1994	2.00	4.00
33	Rob Zettler, Feb. 24, 1994	2.00	4.00
34	Tim Kerr, March 8, 1994	2.00	4.00
35	Kevin Dineen, March 10, 1994	2.00	4.00
36	FLyers' All-Stars, March 13, 1994	2.00	4.00
37	Dominic Roussel, Goalie, March 19, 1994	2.50	5.00
38	Andre Faust, March 24, 1994	2.00	4.00
39	Rod Brind'Amour, March 27, 1994	3.50	7.00
40	Brent Fedyk, March 29, 1994	2.00	4.00
41	Mark Lamb, March 31, 1994	2.00	4.00
42	1973-74 Team Picture, April 7, 1994	2.00	4.00
43	Eric Lindros, April 10, 1994	7.50	15.00
44	Players Thank You, April 12, 1994	2.00	4.00

MIGHTY MILK

— 1972 - 73 ISSUE —

We have no information on the 1972-73 milk set. We would appreciate hearing from anyone who could supply further information.

SCORE PINNACLE

— 1993 ERIC LINDROS —

Score, 1993 Eric Lindros
Card No 22, Regular Season Debut

Card Size: 2 1/2" x 3 1/2"
Face: Four colour, black border; Name
Back: Four colour, black border; Name, Number, Resume
Imprint: © 1992 SCORE, PRINTED IN U.S.A.
Complete Set No.: 30
Complete Set Price: 10.00   20.00

No.	Player	EX	NRMT
1	St. Michael's Buzzers	.50	1.00
2	Detroit Compuware	.50	1.00
3	Oshawa Generals	.50	1.00
4	Oshawa Generals	.50	1.00
5	Oshawa Generals	.50	1.00
6	Oshawa Generals	.50	1.00
7	Memorial Cup	.50	1.00
8	World Junior Championships	.50	1.00
9	World Junior Championships	.50	1.00
10	World Junior Championships	.50	1.00
11	Canada Cup	.50	1.00
12	Canada Cup	.50	1.00
13	Canadian National Team	.50	1.00
14	Canadian National Team	.50	1.00
15	Canadian National Team	.50	1.00
16	Canadian National Team	.50	1.00
17	First-Round Draft Pick	.50	1.00
18	Trade to Philadelphia	.50	1.00
19	Happy Flyer	.50	1.00
20	Preseason Action	.50	1.00
21	Preseason Action	.50	1.00
22	Regular Season Debut	.50	1.00
23	First NHL Goal	.50	1.00
24	Game-Winning Goal Home Debut	.50	1.00
25	First NHL Hat Trick	.50	1.00
26	Playing Golf	.50	1.00
27	Backyard Fun	.50	1.00
28	Fan Favorite	.50	1.00
29	Welcome to Philly	.50	1.00
30	Philly Hero	.50	1.00

J. C. PENNY STORES

— 1993 - 94 POSTCARD ISSUE —

1993-94 Postcard Issue
Postcard No. 13, Eric Lindros

Card Size: 4 1/8" x 6"
Face: Four colour, black border; Name, Position, Jersey number, Team logo
Back: Black on white card stock; Name, Position, Jersey number, Resume, Sponsors logos
Imprint: Compliments of J C PENNY STORES in the Delaware Valley
Complete Set No.: 24
Complete Set Price: 9.00   18.00

No.	Player	EX	NRMT
1	Josef Beranek	1.50	3.00
2	Claude Boivin	.25	.50
3	Jason Bowen	.25	.50
4	Rod Brind'Amour	1.00	2.00
5	Viacheslav Butsayev	.25	.50
6	Dave Brown	.25	.50
7	Al Conroy	.25	.50
8	Kevin Dineen	.25	.50
9	Per-Eric Eklund	.25	.50
10	Brent Fedyk	.25	.50
11	Jeff Finley	.25	.50
12	Garry Galley	.25	.50
13	Eric Lindros	2.50	5.00
14	Stewart Malgunas	.25	.50
15	Ryan McGill	.25	.50
16	George (Rob) Ramage	.50	1.00
17	Mark Recchi	1.25	2.50
18	Mikael Renberg	1.25	2.50
19	Dominic Roussel, Goalie	.50	1.00
20	Yves Racine	.25	.50
21	Tommy Soderstrom, Goalie	.50	1.00
22	Dave Tippett	.25	.50
23	Dimitri Yushkevich	.25	.50
24	1993-94 Team Photo	.25	.50

PITTSBURGH PENGUINS - TEAM SETS

TEAM ISSUES

— 1971 - 72 POSTCARD ISSUE —

These cards are unnumbered and are listed below in alphabetical order.

Card Size: 3 1/2" x 6"
Face: Four colour, Crossed hockey stick, Team logo
Back: Black on white postcrd stock; Name, Resume
Imprint: None
Complete Set No.: 21
Complete Set Price: 22.50 45.00
Common Card: .75 1.50

No.	Player	EX	NRMT
1	Syl Apps	1.25	2.50
2	Les Binkley, Goalie	1.25	2.50
3	Dave Burrows	1.25	2.50
4	Darryl Edestrand	.75	1.50
5	Roy Edwards, Goalie	.75	1.50
6	Val Fonteyne	.75	1.50
7	Nick Harbaruk	.75	1.50
8	Bryan Hextall	1.00	2.00
9	Sheldon Kanne Giesser	.75	1.50
10	Red Kelly, Coach	1.25	2.50
11	Bob Leiter	.75	1.50
12	Keith McCreary	.75	1.50
13	Joe Noris	.75	1.50
14	Greg Polis	.75	1.50
15	Jean Pronovost	1.00	2.00
16	Rene Robert	1.00	2.00
17	Jim Rutherford, Goalie	1.00	2.00
18	Ken Schinkel	.75	1.50
19	Ron Schock	.75	1.50
20	Bryan Watson	1.25	2.50
21	Bob Woytowich	.75	1.50

— 1974 - 75 POSTCARD ISSUE —

We have no information on the set. We would appreciate hearing from anyone who could supply further information.

— 1983 - 84 POSTCARD ISSUE —

Card Size: 5" x 7"
Face: Black and white; Name, Team logo
Back: Blank
Imprint: None
Complete Set No.: 19
Complete Set Price: 8.50 17.00
Common Card: .35 .75

No.	Player	EX	NRMT
1	Pat Boutette	.50	1.00
2	Andy Brickley	.35	.75
3	Mike Bullard	1.00	2.00
4	Ted Bulley	.35	.75
5	Rod Buskas	.35	.75
6	Randy Carlyle	.75	1.50
7	Michael Dion	.35	.75
8	Bob Errey	1.25	2.50
9	Ron Flockhart	.35	.75
10	Steve Gatzos	.35	.75
11	Jim Hamilton	.35	.75
12	Dave Hannan	.75	1.50
13	Denis Herron, Goalie	.50	1.00
14	Troy Loney	.50	1.00
15	Bryan Maxwell	.35	.75
16	Martin McSorley	2.00	4.00
17	Norm Schmidt	.35	.75
18	Mark Taylor	.35	.75
19	Greg Tebbutt	.35	.75

McDONALD'S RESTAURANTS

— 1977 - 78 PUCK BUCKS —

The "Puck Bucks" are unnumbered and are listed below in alphabetical order.

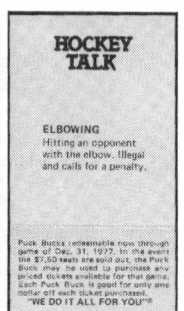

McDonald's Restaurants 1977-78 Puck Bucks
Card No. 15, Jean Pronovost

Card Size: With Coupon: 2" X 3 1/2"; Without Coupon: 2" X 2 7/8"
Face: Four colour, yellow border, orange coupon; Jersey number, Name, Resume, Sponsors logo
Back: Green and black on card stock, Blue coupon; Hockey talk
Imprint: None
Complete Set No.: 18
Complete Set Price: 7.50 15.00
Common Player: .50 1.00

No.	Player	EX	NRMT
1	Russ Anderson	.50	1.00
2	Syl Apps, Jr.	.75	1.50
3	Wayne Bianchin	.50	1.00
4	Dave Burrows	1.00	2.00
5	Colin Campbell	.50	1.00
6	Blair Chapman	.50	1.00
7	Mike Corrigan	.50	1.00
8	Jim Hamilton	.50	1.00
9	Denis Herron, Goalie	.75	1.50
10	Rick Kehoe	.50	1.00
11	Pierre Larouche	1.00	2.00
12	Lowell MacDonald	.50	1.00
13	Greg Malone	.50	1.00
14	Dennis Owchar	.50	1.00
15	Jean Pronovost	1.00	2.00
16	Ron Stackhouse	.75	1.50
17	Dunc Wilson, Goalie	.75	1.50
18	Johnny Wilson, Coach	.50	1.00

COCA-COLA

— 1983 - 84 ISSUE —

We have no information on the 1983-84 Coca-Cola set. We would appreciate hearing from anyone who could supply further information.

HEINZ

— 1983 - 84 ISSUE —

We have no information on the 1983-84 Heinz team set. We would appreciate hearing from anyone who could supply further information.

KODAK

— 1986 - 87 REGULAR ISSUE —

Card Size: 2 3/16" X 2 1/2"
Face: Four colour, yellow border; Jersey number, Name, Position
Back: Jersey number, Name, Position, Resume
Imprint: None
Complete Set No.: 26
Complete Set Price: 19.00 38.00
Common Player: .25 .50

No.	Player	EX	NRMT
1	Bob Berry, Coach	.50	1.00
2	Michael Blaisdell	.25	.50
3	Doug Bodger	.50	1.00
4	Rod Buskas	.25	.50
5	John Chabot	.25	.50
6	Randy Cunneyworth	1.00	2.00
7	Ron Duguay	.50	1.00
8	Bob Errey	.75	1.50
9	Dan Frawley	.25	.50
10	David Hannah	.50	1.00
11	Randy Hillier	.25	.50
12	Jim Johnson	.25	.50
13	Kevin LaVallee	.25	.50
14	Mario Lemieux	12.50	25.00
15	Willy Lindstrom	.25	.50
16	Maurice Mantha	.25	.50
17	Gilles Meloche, Goalie	.35	.75
18	Dan Quinn	.35	.75
19	Jim Roberts, Coach	.25	.50
20	Roberto Romano, Goalie	.25	.50
21	Terry Ruskowski	.35	.75
22	Norm Schmidt	.25	.50
23	Craig Simpson	1.25	2.50
24	Ville Siren	.25	.50
25	Warren Young	.35	.75
—	Team Photo	1.50	3.00

— 1987 - 88 REGULAR ISSUE —

Card Size: 2 3/16' X 2 1/2"
Face: Four colour, yellow background; Team, Name, Jersey number, Position
Back: Resume
Imprint: None
Complete Set No.: 26
Complete Set Price: 14.00 28.00
Common Player: .25 .50

No.	Player	EX	NRMT
1	Doug Bodger	.35	.75
2	Rob Brown	.75	1.50
3	Rod Buskas	.25	.50
4	John (Jock) Callander	.25	.50
5	Paul Coffey	1.00	2.00
6	Randy Cunneyworth	.75	1.50
7	Chris Dahlquist	.25	.50
8	Bob Errey	.75	1.50
9	Dan Frawley	.25	.50
10	Steve Guenette, Goalie	.35	.75
11	Randy Hillier	.35	.75
12	Dave Hunter	.35	.75
13	Jim Johnson	.25	.50
14	Mark Kachowski	.25	.50
15	Christopher Kontos	1.00	2.00
16	Mario Lemieux	7.50	15.00
17	Troy Loney	.35	.75
18	Dwight Mathiasen	.25	.50
19	Dave McLlwain	.35	.75
20	Gilles Meloche, Goalie	.35	.75
21	Dan Quinn	.35	.75
22	Pat Riggin, Goalie	.35	.75
23	Charlie Simmer	.35	.75
24	Ville Siren	.25	.50
25	Wayne Van Dorp	.25	.50
—	Team Photo	1.50	3.00

PITTSBURGH PENGUINS - TEAM SETS • 625

ELBY'S / BIG BOY

— 1989 - 90 POSTCARD ISSUE —

Cards are unnumbered and are listed below in alphabetical order. This set is not complete, any information you may have regarding this issue would be greatly appreciated.

Elby's\Big Boy 1989-90 Issue
Card No. 1, Phil Bourque

Card Size: 4" X 6"
Face: Four colour, white border; Name, Jersey number, Resume, Team and sponsor logos
Back: Black on white card stock; Coupon
Imprint: None
Complete Set No.: 15
Complete Set Price: 9.00 18.00

No.	Player	EX	NRMT
1	Phil Bourque	.25	.50
2	Rob Brown	.35	.75
3	Mario Lemieux	5.00	10.00

ELBY'S / COCA-COLA

— 1991 - 92 POSTCARD ISSUE —

We have no information on the 1991-92 Elby's/Coca-Cola set. We would appreciate hearing from anyone who could supply any further information.

FOODLAND

— 1989 - 90 REGULAR ISSUE —

Foodland, 1989-90 Issue
Card No. 7, Kevin Stevens

Card Size: 2 5/8" X 4 1/8"
Face: Four colour, white border; Team logo, Jersey number, Name, Position
Back: Black on white card stock; Numbered _ of 15, Hockey tip; Safety tip
Imprint: Courtesy of Foodland, the Pittsburgh Penguins, and the Crime Prevention Officers of Western Pennsylvania.
Complete Set No.: 15
Complete Set Price: 10.00 20.00
Common Player: .25 .50

No.	Player	EX	NRMT
1	Rob Brown	.50	1.00
2	Jim Johnson	.25	.50
3	Zarley Zalapski	.50	1.00
4	Paul Coffey	.75	1.50
5	Phil Bourque	.25	.50
6A	Dan Quinn	.25	.50
6B	Gilbert Delorme	.25	.50
7	Kevin Stevens	2.50	5.00
8	Bob Errey	.25	.50
9	John Cullen	.35	.75
10	Mario Lemieux	4.00	8.00
11	Randy Hillier	.25	.50
12	Jay Caufield	.25	.50
13A	Andrew McBain	.25	.50
13B	Troy Loney	.25	.50
14	Wendell Young, Goalie	.25	.50
15	Tom Barrasso, Goalie	1.25	2.50

— 1990 - 91 REGULAR ISSUE —

Foodland, 1990-91 Issue
Card No. 11, Jaromir Jagr

Card Size: 2 3/4" X 4 1/8"
Face: Four colour, yellow border; Jersey number, Name, Team logo, Position
Back: Black on white card stock; Numbered _ of 15, Hockey tip; Safety tip
Imprint: Courtesy of Foodland, the Pittsburgh Penguins, and the Crime Prevention Officers of Western Pennsylvania.
Complete Set No.: 15
Complete Set Price: 9.00 18.00
Common Player: .25 .50

No.	Player	EX	NRMT
1	Phil Bourque	.25	.50
2	Paul Coffey	.75	1.50
3	Randy Hillier	.25	.50
4	Barry Pederson	.25	.50
5	Tom Barrasso, Goalie	.75	1.50
6	Mark Recchi	2.00	4.00
7	Bob Johnson, Coach	.25	.50
8	Joe Mullen	.50	1.00
9	Kevin Stevens	.35	.75
10	John Cullen	.35	.75
11	Jaromir Jagr	2.50	5.00
12	Zarley Zalapski	.25	.50
13	Mario Lemieux	4.00	8.00
14	Tony Tanti	.25	.50
15	Bryan Trottier	.50	1.00

— 1991 - 92 REGULAR ISSUE — 25TH ANNIVERSARY

Card Size: 2 1/2" X 3 1/2"
Face: Four colour, yellow border; Jersey number, Name, Team logo, Position
Back: Black on white card stock; Numbered _ of 15, Hockey tip; Safety tip
Imprint: Courtesy of Foodland, the Pittsburgh Penguins, and the Crime Prevention Officers of Western Pennsylvania.
Complete Set No.: 15
Complete Set Price: 7.50 15.00
Common Player: .25 .50

No.	Player	EX	NRMT
1	Jim Paek	.25	.50
2	Ulf Samuelsson	.35	.75
3	Ronald Francis	.50	1.00
4	Mario Lemieux	3.50	7.00
5	Rick Rocchet	.50	1.00
6	Joe Nullen	.50	1.00
7	Troy Loney	.25	.50
8	Kevin Stevens	1.00	2.00
9	Tom Barrasso, Goalie	.75	1.50
10	Lawrence Murphy	.50	1.00
11	Jaromir Jagr	1.25	2.50
12	Brian Trottier	.50	1.00
13	Paul Stanton	.25	.50
14	Peter Taglianetti	.25	.50
15	Phil Bourque	.25	.50

— 1991 - 92 STICKER ISSUE —

These stickers were issued by Foodland over a four week period in strips of three stickers. Foodland also provided an 18" x 24" poster "Stanley Cup Champs" on which the stickers may be placed. The sticker backing carries discount coupons for various food products.

Card Size: 2 1/2" X 3 1/2"
Face: Four colour, White border, Name, Position
Back: Sticker
Imprint: None
Complete Set No.: 12
Complete Set Price: 5.00 10.00
Poster Price: 1.50 3.00

No.	Player	EX	NRMT
—	Strip No. 1	.50	1.00
1	Bryan Trottier	.25	.50
2	Joe Mullen	.25	.50
3	Larry Murphy	.25	.50
—	Strip No. 2	1.0	2.00
4	Tom Barrasso, Goalie	.35	.75
5	Ran Francis	.35	.75
6	Ulf Samuelsson	.25	.50
—	Strip No. 3	2.00	4.00
7	Jaromir Jagr	1.00	2.00
8	Mario Lemieux	1.00	2.00
9	Keven Stevens	.50	1.00
—	Strip No. 4	1.00	2.00
10	Mark Recchi	.50	1.00
11	Paul Coffey	.50	1.00
12	Frank Pietrangelo, Goalie	.25	.50

PITTSBURGH PENGUINS - TEAM SETS

— 1993 - 94 REGULAR ISSUE —

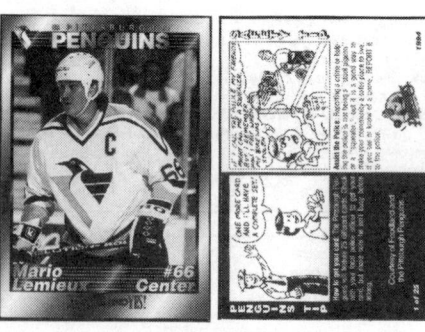

Foodland, 1993-94 Issue
Card No. 1, Mario Lemieux

Card Size: 2 1/2" X 3 1/2"
Face: Four colour, Grey border; Name, Jersey number, Position
Back: Black on white card stock; Numbered _ of 15, Hockey tip, Safety tip
Imprint: Courtesy of Foodland, the Pittsburgh Penguins
Complete Set No.: 25
Complete Set Price: 7.50 15.00
Common Player: .25 .50

No.	Player	EX	NRMT
1	Mario Lemieux	2.50	5.00
2	Grant Jennings	.25	.50
3	Ulf Samuelsson	.25	.50
4	Rock Tocchet	.35	.75
5	Martin McSorley	.50	1.00
6	Rick Kehoe, Assistant Coach	.25	.50
7	Doug Brown	.25	.50
8	Martin Straka	1.00	2.00
9	Jim Paek	.25	.50
10	Ken Wregget, Goalie	.25	.50
11	Jeff Danels	.25	.50
12	Bryan Trottier	.25	.50
13	Lawrence Murphy	.50	1.00
14	Ronald Francis	.50	1.00
15	Mike Needham	.50	1.00
16	Mike Ramsey	.25	.50
17	Kevin Stevens	1.00	2.00
18	Kjell Samuelsson	.25	.50
19	Ed Johnson, Head Coach	.50	1.00
20	Markus Naslund	.25	.50
21	Mike Stapleton	.25	.50
22	Peter Taglianetti	1.25	2.50
23	Jaromir Jagr	.25	.50
24	Tom Barrasso, Goalie	.50	1.00
25	Joe Mullen	.35	.75

CLARK BUNS

— 1993 MARIO LEMIEUX —

This 3-card set was issued along with the Mario Bun by Clark Candy Company. Stains from chocolate are normal.

Clark Buns, 1993 Mario Lemieux
Card No. 3, Facing Action Photo

Card Size: 3" x 3"
Face: Four colour, black border; Name, Facsimile Autograph
Back: Black on white card stock; Name, Position, Resume
Imprint: None
Complete Set No.: 3
Complete Set Price: 2.50 5.00

No.	Player	EX	NRMT
1	Close-up	.85	1.75
2	Side Action Photo	.85	1.75
3	Facing Action Photo	.85	1.75

WEEK #3

Foodland 1991-92 Issue
Strip No. 3, Jagr, Lemieux, Stevens

QUEBEC NORDIQUES - TEAM SETS

TEAM ISSUES

— 1980 - 81 POSTCARD ISSUE —

This set is unnumbered and is listed below in alphabetical order.

Card Size: 3 1/2" x 5 1/2"
Face: Four colour; Facsimile autograph
Back: Black on white postcard stock; Resume
Imprint: None
Complete Set No.: 28
Complete Set Price: 14.00 28.00
Common Card: .35 .75

No.	Player	EX	NRMT
1	Michel Bergeron, Coach, SP	1.25	2.50
2	Serge Bernier	.35	.75
3	Ron Chipperfield	.35	.75
4	Kim Clackson	.35	.75
5	Real Cloutier	.75	1.50
6	Alain Cote	1.00	2.00
7	Michel Dion	.35	.75
8	Andre Dupont	.35	.75
9	Robbie Ftorek	.50	1.00
10	Michel Goulet	2.50	5.00
11	Ron Grahame, SP	1.00	2.00
12	Jamie Hislop	.35	.75
13	Dale Hoganson	.35	.75
14	Dale Hunter	1.25	2.50
15	Pierre Lacroix	.35	.75
16	Gary Lariviere	.35	.75
17	Richard Leduc	.35	.75
18	Lee Norwood	.50	1.00
19	John Paddock	.35	.75
20	Dave Pichette, SP	1.00	2.00
21	Michel Plasse, Goalie	.50	1.00
22	Jacques Richard	.35	.75
23	Normand Rochefort	.75	1.50
24	Anton Stastny	.50	1.00
25	Peter Stastny	2.50	5.00
26	Marc Tardif	.35	.75
27	Wally Weir, SP	1.00	2.00
28	John Wensink	.35	.75

— 1981 - 1982 POSTCARD ISSUE —

This 21-card set features the first postcards of the Stastny brothers in the NHL. Permission was granted by the Nordiques Hockey Club.

1981-82 Postcard Issue
Postcard No. 7, Michel Goulet

Card Size: 3 1/2" x 5 1/2"
Face: Four colour, borderless
Back: Blue, card stock; Name, Resume, Team logo
Imprint:
Complete Set No.: 21
Complete Set Price: 12.50 25.00
Common Card: .35 .75

No.	Player	EX	NRMT
1	Pierre Aubry	.35	.75
2	Michel Bergeron, Coach	.75	1.50
3	Daniel (Dan) Bouchard, Goalie	.50	1.00
4	Real Cloutier	.35	.75
5	Alain Cote	.75	1.50
6	Andre Dupont	.35	.75
7	Michel Goulet	2.00	4.00
8	Dale Hunter	1.00	2.00
9	Pierre Lacroix	.35	.75
10	Mario Marois	.35	.75
11	Miroslav Frycer	.35	.75
12	Dave Pichette	.35	.75
13	Michel Plasse, Goalie	.35	.75
14	Jacques Richard	.35	.75
15	Normand Rochefort	.35	.75
16	Anton Stastny	.50	1.00
17	Marian Stastny	.50	1.00
18	Peter Stastny	2.50	5.00
19	Marc Tardif	.35	.75
20	Charles Thiffault, Ass. Coach	.35	.75
21	Wally Weir	.50	1.00

— 1982 - 83 POSTCARD ISSUE —

This set is unnumbered and is listed below in alphabetical order. The photographs were taken inside the Montreal Forum.

Card Size: 3 1/2" X 5 1/2"
Face: Four colour
Back: Black on white postcard stock; Name, Resume
Imprint: None
Complete Set No.: 26
Complete Set Price: 11.00 22.00
Common Card: .35 .75

No.	Player	EX	NRMT
1	Presentation	.35	.75
2	Michel Bergeron, Coach	.50	1.00
3	Charles Thiffault	.35	.75
4	Pierre Aubry	.35	.75
5	Daniel Bouchard, Goalie	.50	1.00
6	Real Cloutier	.50	1.00
7	Alain Cote	.50	1.00
8	Andre Dupont	.35	.75
9	John Garrett	.35	.75
10	Michel Goulet	2.00	4.00
11	Jean Hamel	.35	.75
12	Dale Hunter	.50	1.00
13	Rick Lapointe	.35	.75
14	Clint Malarchuk, Goalie	1.00	2.00
15	Mario Marois	.50	1.00
16	Randy Moller	.50	1.00
17	Wilfrid Paiement	1.00	2.00
18	Dave Pichette	.35	.75
19	Jacques Richard	.35	.75
20	Normand Rochefort	.35	.75
21	Louis Sleigher	.35	.75
22	Anton Stastny	.50	1.00
23	Marian Stastny	.50	1.00
24	Peter Stastny	2.00	4.00
25	Wally Weir	.35	.75
26	Marc Tardif	.35	.75

— 1983 - 84 POSTCARD ISSUE —

These cards are unnumbered and are listed here in alphabetical order.

Postcard Size: 3 1/2" X 5 1/2"
Face: Four colour, borderless
Back: Team logo, Jersey number, Name
Imprint: None
Complete Set No.: 24
Complete Set Price: 7.50 15.00
Common Card: .25 .50

No.	Player	EX	NRMT
1	Pierre Aubry	.25	.50
2	Michel Bergeron, Coach	.50	1.00
3	Dan Bouchard, Goalie	.50	1.00
4	Real Cloutier	.25	.50
5	Alain Cote	.35	.75
6	Andre Dupont	.25	.50
7	John Garrett	.25	.50
8	Michel Goulet	1.00	2.00
9	Jean Hamel	.25	.50
10	Dale Hunter	.50	1.00
11	Rick Lapointe	.25	.50
12	Clint Malarchuk, Goalie	.75	1.50
13	Mario Marois	.25	.50
14	Randy Moller	.35	.75
15	Wilf Paiement	.35	.75
16	Dave Pichette	.25	.50
17	Jacques Richard	.25	.50
18	Normand Rochefort	.25	.50
19	Louis Sleigher	.25	.50
20	Anton Stastny	.25	.50
21	Marian Stastny	.25	.50
22	Peter Statsny	1.25	2.50
23	Marc Tardif	.25	.50
24	Wally Weir	.25	.50

— 1985 - 1986 POSTCARD ISSUE —

This 28-postcard set was issued as promotion for the Quebec Nordiques Hockey Club.

1985-86 Postcard Issue
Postcard No. 10, Mario Gosselin

Card Size: 3-1/2" x 5-1/2"
Face: Four colour, White bottom; Logo; Players #; Name
Back: Blank
Imprint: Photo: Andre Pichette or Photo: Kedl
Complete Set No.: 28
Complete Set Price: 10.00 20.00
Common Card: .25 .50

No.	Player	EX	NRMT
1	Peter Andersson	.25	.50
2	Brent Ashton	.50	1.00
3	Michel Bergeron, Coach	.35	.75
4	Jeff Brown	.50	1.00
5	Alain Cote	.35	.75
6	Gilbert Delorme	.25	.50
7	Gordon Donnelly	.75	1.50
8	Mike Eagles	.25	.50
9	Paul Gillis	.25	.50
10	Mario Gosselin, Goalie	.50	1.00
11	Michel Goulet	1.25	2.50
12	Ron Harris, Coach	.25	.50
13	Mark Kumpel	.25	.50
14	Clint Malarchuk, Goalie	.50	1.00
15	Greg Malone	.25	.50
16	Jimmy Mann	.25	.50
17	Randy Moller	.35	.75

No.	Player	EX	NRMT
18	Simon Nolet, Coach	.25	.50

628 • QUEBEC NORDIQUES - TEAM SETS

No.	Player	EX	NRMT
19	Steve Patrick	.25	.50
20	Robert Picard	.25	.50
21	Pat Price	.25	.50
22	Normand Rochefort	.25	.50
23	Jenn-Francois Sauve	.25	.50
24	Richard Sevigny, Goalie	.25	.50
25	David Shaw	.25	.50
26	Risto Siltanen	.25	.50
27	Anton Stastny	.25	.50
28	Peter Stastny	1.75	3.50

1986 - 1987 POSTCARD ISSUE

Card Size: 3 1/2" x 5 1/2"

1986-87 Postcard Issue
Postcard No. 10, Michel Goulet

Face: Four colour, borderless; Name, Number
Back: Blank
Imprint: None
Complete Set No.: 29
Complete Set Price: 10.00 20.00
Common Card: .25 .50

No.	Player	EX	NRMT
1	Michel Bergeron, Coach	.35	.75
2	Jeff Brown	.50	1.00
3	Alain Cote	.35	.75
4	Bill Derlago	.25	.50
5	Gord Donnelly	.50	1.00
6	Mike Eagles	.35	.75
7	Steven Finn	.35	.75
8	Paul Gillis	.25	.50
9	Mario Gosselin, Goalie	.50	1.00
10	Michel Goulet	1.00	2.00
11	Mike Hough	.50	1.00
12	Dale Hunter	.50	1.00
13	Jason Lafreniere	.25	.50
14	Clint Malarchuk, Goalie	.50	1.00
15	Randy Moller	.35	.75
16	Simon Nolet, Assistant Coach	.25	.50
17	John Ogrodnick	.35	.75
18	Robert Picard	.25	.50
19	Pat Price	.25	.50
20	Doug Shedden	.35	.75
21	Normand Rochefort	.35	.75
22	Richard Sevigny, Goalie	.50	1.00
23	Risto Siltanen	.25	.50
24	Anton Stastny	.35	.75
25	Peter Stastny	1.00	2.00
26	David Shaw	.25	.50
27	Charles Thiffault, Assistant Coach	.25	.50
28	Richard Zemlack	.35	.75
29	Team Photo	.50	1.00

— 1987 - 88 POSTCARD ISSUE —

These cards are unnumbered and are listed here in alphabetical order.

1987-88 Postcard Issue
Postcard No. 1, Tommy Albelin

Postcard Size: 3 3/4" X 5 5/8"
Face: Four colour; Team logo, Jersey number, Name
Back: Blank
Imprint: None
Complete Set No.: 32
Complete Set Price: 6.50 13.00
Common Card: .25 .50

No.	Player	EX	NRMT
1	Tommy Albelin	.25	.50
2	Jeff Brown	.35	.75
3	Mario Brunetta, Goalie	.25	.50
4	Terry Carkner	.25	.50
5	Alain Cote	.25	.50
6	Gord Donnelly	.25	.50
7	Gaetan Duchesne	.35	.75
8	Mike Eagles	.25	.50
9	Steven Finn	.25	.50
10	Paul Gillis	.25	.50
11	Mario Gosselin, Goalie	.35	.75
12	Michel Goulet	.50	1.00
13	Stephane Guerard	.25	.50
14	Alan Haworth	.25	.50
15	Mike Hough	.35	.75
16	Jeff Jackson	.25	.50
17	Stuart Kulak	.25	.50
18	Jason Lafreniere	.25	.50
19	Lane Lambert	.25	.50
20	David Lotta	.25	.50
21	Max Middendorf	.25	.50
22	Randy Moller	.25	.50
23	Robert Picard	.25	.50
24	Daniel Poudrier	.25	.50
25	Ken Quinney	.25	.50
26	Normand Rochefort	.25	.50
27	Richard Sevigny, Goalie	.35	.75
28	Anton Stastny	.25	.50
29	Peter Stastny	.50	1.00
30	Ron Tugnutt, Goalie	.50	1.00
31	Alain Chainey; Andre Savard; Guy Lapointe	.25	.50
32	Badaboun, Mascot	.25	.50

— 1988 - 89 POSTCARD ISSUE —

1988-89 Postcard Issue
Postcard No. 3, Joel Baillargeon

Card Size: 3 3/4" x 6 5/8"
Face: Four colour; Name, Facsimile autograph
Back: Four colour
Imprint: Unkown
Complete Set No.: 32
Complete Set Price: 9.00 18.00
Common Card: .25 .50

No.	Player	EX	NRMT
1	Tommy Abelin	.25	.50
2	Badaboun, Mascot	.25	.50
3	Joel Baillargeon	.25	.50
4	Jeff Brown	.50	1.00
5	Mario Brunetta	.25	.50
6	Alain Cote	.35	.75
7	Gordon Donnelly	.35	.75
8	Daniel Dore	.25	.50
9	Gaetan Duchesne	.50	1.00
10	Steven Finn	.25	.50
11	Marc Fortier	.25	.50
12	Paul Gillis	.25	.50
13	Michel Goulet	.75	1.50
14	Jari Grondstrand	.25	.50
15	Stephane Guerard	.25	.50
16	Jeff Jackson	.25	.50
17	Iiro Jarvi	.25	.50
18	Lane Lambert	.25	.50
19	David Latta	.25	.50
20	Curtis Leschyshyn	.35	.75
21	Bob Mason	.25	.50
22	Randy Moller	.35	.75
23	Robert Picard	.25	.50
24	Walt Puddubny	.35	.75
25	Joe Sakic	2.50	5.00
26	Greg Smyth	.35	.75
27	Anton Stastny	.35	.75
28	Peter Stastny	.75	1.50
29	Trevor Stienberg	.25	.50
30	Team Coaches	.25	.50
31	Team Photo	.50	1.00
32	Mark Vermetti	.25	.50

QUEBEC NORDIQUES - TEAM SETS • 629

— 1989 - 90 POSTCARD ISSUE —

1989-90 Postcard Issue
Postcard No. 25, Joe Sakic

Card Size: 3 3/4" X 5 5/8"
Face: Four colour, white border; Name, Number, Sponsor logos
Back: Blank
Imprint: None
Complete Set No.: 27
Complete Set Price: 10.00 20.00
Common Card: .25 .50

No.	Player	EX	NRMT
1	Michel Bergeron	.25	.50
2	Jeff Brown	.35	.75
3	Joe Cirella	.25	.50
4	Lucien Deblois	.25	.50
5	Daniel Dore	.25	.50
6	Steven Finn	.25	.50
7	Stephane Fiset, Goalie	1.50	3.00
8	Marc Fortier	.25	.50
9	Michel Goulet	.75	1.50
10	Jari Gronstrand	.25	.50
11	Stephane Guerard	.25	.50
12	Mike Hough	.25	.50
13	Liro Jarvi	.25	.50
14	Kevin Kaminski	.25	.50
15	Darin Kimble	.35	.75
16	Guy Lafleur	.60	1.25
17	David Latta	.25	.50
18	Curtis Leschyshyn	.35	.75
19	Claude Loiselle	.35	.75
20	Mario Marois	.25	.50
21	Ken McRae	.25	.50
22	Sergei Mylnikov	.25	.60
23	Michel Petit	.25	.50
24	Robert Picard	.25	.50
25	Joe Sakic	2.00	4.00
26	Peter Stastny	.75	1.50
27	Ron Tugnutt, Goalie	.50	1.00

YUM-YUM

— 1984 - 85 ISSUE —

We have no information on this 1984-85 set. We would appreciate hearing from anyone who could supply further information.

— 1987 - 88 ISSUE —

These cards are unnumbered and are listed here in alphabetical order.

Yum-Yum, 1987-88 Issue
Card No. 1, Alain Cote

Card Size: 2" X 2 1/2"
Face: Four colour, red and blue border; Team logo, Jersey number, Name
Back: Red and blue on white card stock; Checklist, French
Imprint: None
Complete Set No.: 10
Complete Set Price: 5.00 10.00
Common Player: .50 1.00

No.	Player	EX	NRMT
1	Alain Cote	.75	1.50
2	Paul Gillis	.50	1.00
3	Mario Gosselin, Goalie	.50	1.00
4	Michel Goulet	1.50	3.00
5	Alan Haworth	.50	1.00
6	Jason LeFreniere	.50	1.00
7	Robert Picard	.50	1.00
8	Normand Rochefort	.50	1.00
9	Anton Stastny	.50	1.00
10	Peter Stastny	1.50	3.00

GENERAL FOODS

— 1985 - 86 ISSUE —

— 1986 - 87 ISSUE —

— 1987 - 88 ISSUE —

— 1988 - 89 ISSUE —

— 1989 - 90 ISSUE —

We have no information on these sets. We would appreciate hearing from anyone who could supply further information.

PROVIGO FOODS

— 1985 - 86 STICKER ISSUE —

These stickers are unnumbered and are listed below in alphabetical order.

Sticker Size: 1 1/8" X 2 1/4"
Face: Four colour; Jersey number, Name, Team logo
Back: Black type on sticker back
Imprint: Crest-O-Matic
Poster Size: 20 1/16" x 11"
Face: Red, blue and black, white side borders; Jersey number, Names, Team logo
Back: Red and blue on white card stock; Team logo, Checklist
Imprint: PROMOTION BLITZ INC.
Complete Set No.: 25
Complete Set Price: 6.50 13.00
Common Player: .20 .40
Display Board: 2.50 5.00

No.	Player	EX	NRMT
1	John Anderson	.35	.75
2	Brent Ashton	.20	.40
3	Wayne Babych	.20	.40
4	Michel Bergeron, Coach	.35	.75
5	Alain Cote	.25	.50
6	Gilbert Delorme	.20	.40
7	Mike Eagles	.35	.75
8	Steven Finn	.20	.40
9	Paul Gillis	.20	.40
10	Mario Gosselin, Goalie	.25	.50
11	Michel Goulet	1.00	2.00
12	Dale Hunter	.25	.50
13	Mark Kumpel	.20	.40
14	Clint Malarchuk, Goalie	.50	1.00
15	Jimmy Mann	.20	.40
16	Mario Marois	.20	.40
17	Randy Moller	.20	.40
18	Wilf Paiement	.35	.75
19	Pat Price	.20	.40
20	Normand Rochefort	.20	.40
21	Jenn F. Sauve	.20	.40
22	Richard Sevigny, Goalie	.20	.40
23	David Shaw	.20	.40
24	Anton Stastny	.25	.50
25	Peter Stastny	1.00	2.00

THE CHARLTON STANDARD CATALOGUE OF CANADIAN BASEBALL AND FOOTBALL CARDS
- Fourth Edition -

Coming in April!

ST. LOUIS BLUES - TEAM SETS

TEAM ISSUES

— 1978 - 79 POSTCARD ISSUE —

Card Size: 3 1/2" x 5 1/2"
Face: Four colour, borderless
Back: Black on white postcard stock; Year, Team logo
Imprint: None
Complete Set No.: 21
Complete Set Price: 15.00 30.00
Common Card: .50 1.00

No.	Player	EX	NRMT
1	Barclay Plager	.75	1.50
2	Wayne Babych	.75	1.50
3	Curt Bennett	.50	1.00
4	Harvey Bennett	.50	1.00
5	Jack Brownchidle	.50	1.00
6	Mike Crombeen	.50	1.00
7	Tony Currie	.50	1.00
8	Bernie Federko	2.00	4.00
9	Barry Gibbs	.50	1.00
10	Larry Giroux	.50	1.00
11	Inge Hammarstrom	.75	1.50
12	Phil Myre, Goalie	.75	1.50
13	Larry Patey	.75	1.50
14	Rick Shinske	.50	1.00
15	John Smrke	.50	1.00
16	Ed Stanioski	.50	1.00
17	Bob Stewart	.50	1.00
18	Brian Sutter	1.50	3.00
19	Gary Unger	1.00	2.00
20	Blue Angels	1.00	2.00
21	Fan Van	1.00	2.00

— 1979 - 80 ISSUE —

We have no information on this 1979-80 set. We would appreciate hearing from anyone who could supply further information.

— 1981 - 82 ISSUE —

We have no information on this 1981-82 set. We would appreciate hearing from anyone who could supply further information.

— 1982 - 83 ISSUE —

We have no information on this 1982-83 set. We would appreciate hearing from anyone who could supply further information.

— 1988 - 89 ISSUE —

We have no information on this 1988-89 set. We would appreciate hearing from anyone who could supply further information.

KODAK

— 1987 - 88 REGULAR ISSUE —

Card Size: 2 3/16" X 3"
Face: Four colour; Jersey number, Name, Position
Back: Jersey number, Name, Position, Team logo, Resume
Imprint:
Complete Set No.: 26
Complete Set Price: 12.50 25.00
Common Player: .35 .75

No.	Player	EX	NRMT
1	Brian Benning	.75	1.50
2	Tim Bothwell	.35	.75
3	Charlie Bourgeois	.35	.75
4	Paul Cavallini	1.00	2.00
5	Gino Cavallini	1.00	2.00
6	Michael Dark	.35	.75
7	Doug Evans	.35	.75
8	Todd Ewen	.35	.75
9	Bernie Federko	1.50	3.00
10	Ron Flockhart	.35	.75
11	Douglas Gilmour	3.50	7.00
12	Gaston Gingras	.35	.75
13	Anthony Hrkac	.50	1.00
14	Mark Hunter	.50	1.00
15	Jocelyn Lemieux	.35	.75
16	Anthony McKegney	.35	.75
17	Richard Meagher	.75	1.50
18	Greg Millen, Goalie	.75	1.50
19	Robert Nordmark	.35	.75
20	Gregory Paslawski	.50	1.00
21	Herb Raglan	.35	.75
22	George (Rob) Ramage	.75	1.50
23	Cliff Ronning	1.50	3.00
24	Brian Sutter	1.00	2.00
25	Perry Turnbull	.35	.75
26	Richard Wamsley, Goalie	.75	1.50

— 1988 - 89 REGULAR ISSUE —

Card Size: 2 3/16" X 3"
Face: Four colour, blue and yellow border; Jersey number, Name, Position
Back: Jersey number, Name, Position, Resume
Imprint:
Complete Set No.: 25
Complete Set Price: 12.50 25.00
Common Player: .35 .75

No.	Player	EX	NRMT
1	Brian Benning	.50	1.00
2	Tim Bothwell	.35	.75
3	Gino Cavallini	.35	.75
4	Paul Cavallini	.50	1.00
5	Craig Coxe	.35	.75
6	Doug Evans	.35	.75
7	Todd Ewen	.50	1.00
8	Bernie Federko	.75	1.50
9	Gaston Gingras	.35	.75
10	Anthony Hrkac	.50	1.00
11	Brett Hull	6.00	12.00
12	Mike Lalor	.35	.75
13	Anthony McKegney	.35	.75
14	Richard Meagher	.35	.75
15	Greg Millen, Goalie	.50	1.00
16	Sergio Momesso	.50	1.00
17	Gregory Paslawski	.35	.75
18	Herb Raglan	.35	.75
19	Dave Richter	.35	.75
20	Vincent Riendeau, Goalie	1.00	2.00
21	Gordon Roberts	.50	1.00
22	Cliff Ronning	1.00	2.00
23	Tom Tilley	.35	.75
24	Steve Tuttle	.35	.75
25	Peter Zezel	.50	1.00

— 1989 - 90 REGULAR ISSUE —

Card Size: 2 3/8" X 3 1/2"
Face: Four colour, yellow border; Name, Position
Back: Name, Resume
Imprint: None
Complete Set No.: 25
Complete Set Price: 10.00 20.00
Common Player: .25 .50

No.	Player	EX	NRMT
1	Rod Brind'Amour	1.00	2.00
2	Jeff Brown	.35	.75
3	Gino Cavallini	.35	.75
4	Paul Cavallini	.35	.75
5	Kelly Chase	.35	.75
6	Brett Hull	3.50	7.00
7	Pat Jablonski, Goalie	.50	1.00
8	Curtis Joseph	2.00	4.00
9	Mike Lalor	.25	.50
10	Dominic Lavoie	.25	.50
11	Dave Lowry	.35	.75
12	Richard Meagher	.25	.50
13	Paul MacLean	.25	.50
14	Sergio Momesso	.35	.75
15	Adam Oates	2.50	5.00
16	Adrien Plavsic	.25	.50
17	Herb Raglan	.25	.50
18	Vincent Riendeau, Goalie	.50	1.00
19	Gordon Roberts	.35	.75
20	Brian Sutter, Head Coach	.25	.50
21	Dave Thomlinson	.25	.50
22	Tom Tilley	.25	.50
23	Steve Tuttle	.25	.50
24	Anthony Twist	.35	.75
25	Peter Zezel	.35	.75

— 1990 - 91 REGULAR ISSUE —

Sponsored by Kodak and KMOX Radio, these cards are unnumbered and are listed here in alphabetical order.

Kodak, 1990-91 Issue
Card No. 17, Adam Oates

Card Size: 2 1/2" X 3 1/2"
Face: Four colour, yellow border; Team, Team and sponsor logos, Name, Position
Back: Black on white card stock; Jersey number, Name, Position, Team and sponsor logos, Resume
Imprint: None
Complete Set No.: 25
Complete Set Price: 10.00 20.00
Common Player: .25 .50

No.	Player	EX	NRMT
1	Bob Bassen	.25	.50
2	Rod Brind'Amour	1.00	2.00
3	Jeff Brown	.50	1.00
4	David Bruce	.25	.50
5	Geoff Courtnall	.35	.75

No.	Player	EX	NRMT
6	Paul Cavallini	.25	.50
7	Gino Cavallini	.25	.50
8	Robert Dirk	.25	.50
9	Glen Featherstone	.25	.50
10	Brett Hull	2.50	5.00
11	Curtis Joseph, Goalie	1.50	3.00
12	Dave Lowry	.25	.50
13	Mario Marois	.25	.50
14	Paul MacLean	.25	.50
15	Richard Meagher	.25	.50
16	Sergio Momesso	.25	.50
17	Adam Oates	2.00	4.00
18	Vincent Riendeau, Goalie	.60	1.25
19	Cliff Ronning	.50	1.00
20	Brian Sutter, Head Coach	.25	.50
21	Scott Stevens	1.50	3.00
22	Harold Snepsts	.25	.50
23	Richard Sutter	.25	.50
24	Steve Tuttle	.25	.50
25	Ronald Wilson	.25	.50

McDONALDS / UPPER DECK

— 1967 - 92 THE BEST OF THE BLUES —

This 28-card set was available as a promotion to sell with food products. The set is numbered _ of 28.

Card Size: 2 1/2" x 3 1/2"
Face: Four colour, white border; Name, Position, Sponsor's logos
Back: Four colour, white border, card stock; Name; Resume, Sponsor's logos
Imprint: Upper Deck, The Upper Deck logo and the card/hologram combination are trademarks of The Upper Deck Company © 1992 The Upper Deck Company. All Rights Reserved. Printed in the U.S.A.

Complete Set No.: 28
Complete Set Price:		10.00	20.00
Common Goalie:		.25	.50
Common Player:		.25	.50

No.	Player	EX	NRMT
1	Glenn Hall, Goalie	.75	1.50
2	Douglas Gilmour	1.00	2.00
3	Al Arbour	.25	.50
4	Michael Liut, Goalie	.25	.50
5	Blake Dunlop	.25	.50

No.	Player	EX	NRMT
6	Noel Picard	.25	.50
7	Bob Plager	.25	.50
8	Ab McDonald	.25	.50
9	Curtis Joseph, Goalie	1.00	2.00
10	Wayne Babych	.25	.50
11	Gordon (Red) Berenson	.25	.50
12	Brett Hull	1.25	2.50
13	Bob Gassoff	.25	.50
14	Bernie Federko	.25	.50
15	Gary Sabourin	.25	.50
16	Joe Mullen	.50	1.00
17	Adam Oates	1.00	2.00
18	Jorgen Pettersson	.25	.50
19	Frank St. Marseille	.25	.50
20	Scott Stevens	.50	1.00
21	George (Rob) Ramage	.25	.50
22	Jacques Plante, Goalie	1.00	2.00
23	Richard Meagher	.25	.50
24	Barclay Plager	.25	.50
25	Brian Sutter	.25	.50
26	Perry Turnbull	.25	.50
27	Garry Unger	.35	.75
28	Checklist	.25	.50

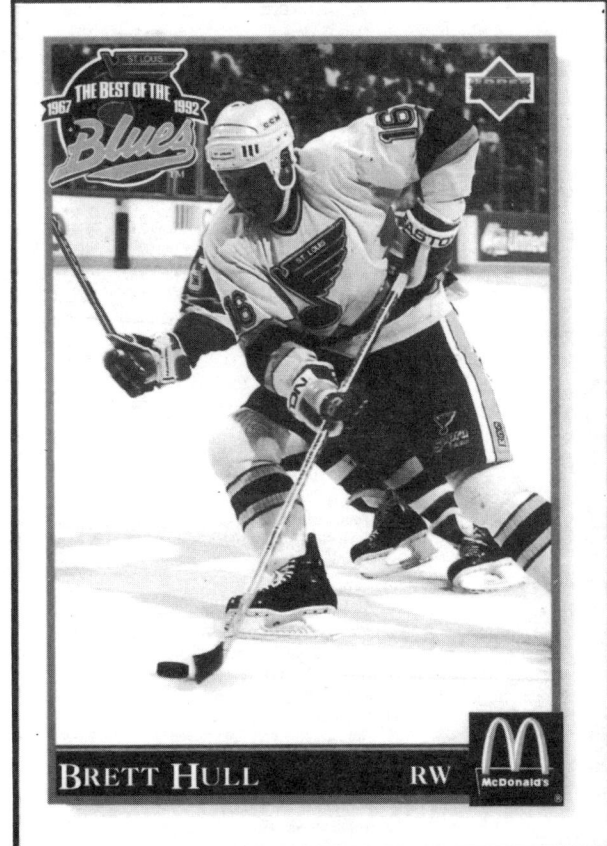

St. Louis Blues - Team Sets
McDonald's / Upper Deck 1967 - 92 The Best of the Blues
Card No. 12, Brett Hull

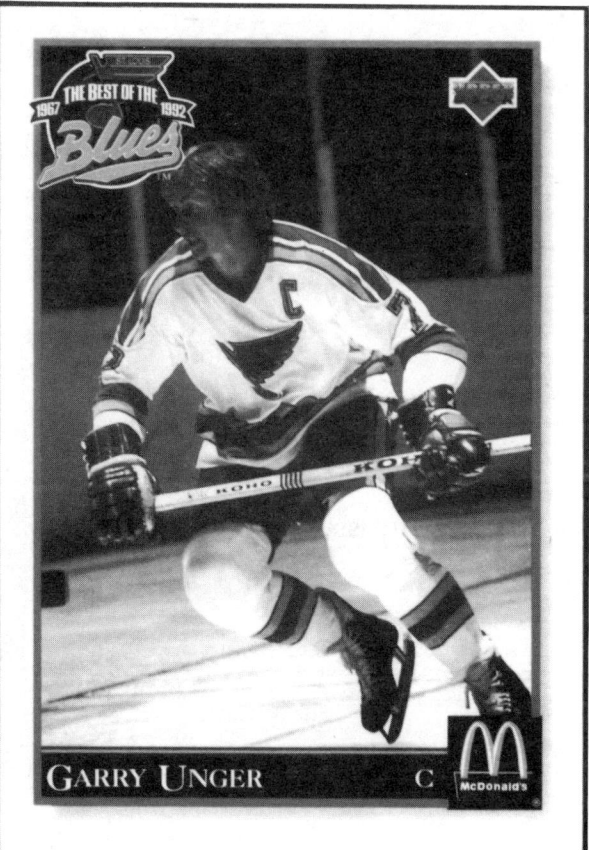

St. Louis Blues - Team Sets
McDonald's / Upper Deck 1967 - 92 The Best of the Blues
Card No. 27, Garry Unger

SAN JOSE SHARKS - TEAM SETS

TEAM ISSUES

— 1991 - 92 REGULAR ISSUE —

These cards are unnumbered are listed here in alphabetical order.

1991-92 Issue
Card No. 5, Pat Falloon

Card Size: 2 1/2" X 3 1/2"
Face: Four colour, borderless
Back: Black on white card stock; Name, Position, Resume, Team logo
Imprint: © 1991 - SAN JOSE SHARKS
Complete Set No.: 22
Complete Set Price: 6.00 12.00
Common Player: .25 .50

No.	Player	EX	NRMT
—	Title Card: San Jose Sharks	.25	.50
1	Perry Anderson	.25	.50
2	Steve Bozek	.25	.50
3	Perry Berezan	.25	.50
4	Dean Evason	.25	.50
5	Pat Falloon	2.50	5.00
6	Paul Fenton	.25	.50
7	Link Gaetz	.25	.50
8	Jeff Hackett, Goalie	.35	.75
9	Ken Hammond	.25	.50
10	Brian Hayward, Goalie	.35	.75
11	Anthony Hrkac	.25	.50
12	Kelly Kisio	.50	1.00
13	Brian Lawton	.25	.50
14	Pat MacLeod	.25	.50
15	Robert McGill	.25	.50
16	Brian Mullen	.35	.75
17	Jarmo Myllys, Goalie	.50	1.00
18	Wayne Presley	.25	.50
19	Neil Wilkinson	.35	.75
20	Douglas Wilson	.50	1.00
21	Rob Zettler	.35	.75

— 1991 - 92 PHOTO ISSUE —

Card Size: 8" x 10"
Face: Four colour, white border; Team Names
Back: Blank
Imprint: San Jose Sharks Photo by Rocky Widner/Don Smith

No.	Player	EX	NRMT
	Team Photograph	2.50	15.00

— 1993 - 94 COMMEMORATIVE SHEETS —

Card Size: 8 1/2" x 11"
Face: Four colour, teal border; Name,
Back: Black on white card stock; Team and Player names, Statistics, Logos
Imprint:
Complete Sheet No.: 3
Complete Sheet Price: 45.00 95.00

No.	Player	EX	NRMT
1	March 20, 1994; Ticket Tying Game - 801st Goal, Wayne Gretzky	25.00	50.00
2	March 20, 1994; Ticket stub Tying Game - 801st Goal, Wayne Gretzky	12.50	25.00
3	March 20, 1994; Penthouse Suite Ticket, Tying game - 801st Goal, Wayne Gretzky	10.00	20.00

— 1993 - 94 COMMEMORATIVE TICKETS — COMING HOME TO A NEW BEGINNING

This is a Limited Edition commemorative set of seven tickets of the first seven games in the new San Jose Arena.
Card Size: 5 1/2" x 13 1/4"
Face: Four colour; Team Names, Game date and time, Black and white historical pictures of San Jose not previously published
Back: Black on white card stock,
Imprint: MERCURY TICKETS/Saskatoon, Canada Lithographed in Canada
Complete Sheet No.: 7
Complete Sheet Price: 10.00 20.00

No.	Player	EX	NRMT
1	Game A, September 30, 1993, New York Islanders	1.50	3.00
2	Game 1, October 14, 1993, Calgary Flames	1.50	3.00
3	Game 2, October 16, 1993, Boston Bruins	1.50	3.00
4	Game 3, October 19, 1993, St. Louis Blues	1.50	3.00
5	Game 4, October 23, 1994, Vancouver Canucks	1.50	3.00
6	Game 5, October 26, 1993, Edmonton Oilers	1.50	3.00
7	Game 7, October 28, 1993, Anaheim Mighty Ducks	1.50	3.00

— 1993 - 94 SINGLE TICKET — COMING HOME TO A NEW BEGINNING

1993-94 Single Ticket
Coming Home to a New Beginning

Card Size: 2 3/4" x 6 1/4"
Face: Four colour; Team Names, Game date and time, Black and white historical pictures of San Jose overlaid with silver hockey player
Back: Black on white card stock
Imprint: MERCURY TICKETS/Saskatoon, Canada Lithographed in Canada

No.	Player	EX	NRMT
1	Game 1, 1993 - Calgary Flames Penthouse Suite Ticket P44 No. 7	12.50	25.00

— SEASON TICKET — COMING HOME TO A NEW BEGINNING 1993 - 1994 LIMITED EDITION COMMEMORATIVE SHEET

Card Size: 2 3/4" x 6 1/4"
Face: Four colour; Black and white historical pictures of San Jose, Coloured picture of Opening of San Jose Arena
Back: Black on white card stock; Home schedule
Imprint: None

No.	Player	EX	NRMT
1	Limited Edition Commemorative 5,000 Set No. _____ of	7.50	15.00

— 1993 - 94 GAMELINE PHOTO INSERTS —

Card Size: 8 1/2" x 11"
Face: Four colour, teal border; Name,
Back: Black on white card stock; Team and Player names, Statistics, Logos
Imprint:
Complete Photo No.: 2
Complete Photo Price: 60.00 125.00
Common Card: 1.50 3.00

No.	Player	EX	NRMT
1	Air Shark, Blimp	1.50	3.00
2	Jamie Baker	2.50	5.00
3	Mark Beaufait	1.50	3.00
4	Viacheslav Butsayev	1.50	3.00
5	Dale Craigwell	1.50	3.00
6	Shawn Cronin	1.50	3.00
7	Gaetan Duchesne	1.50	3.00
8	Todd Elik	2.50	5.00
9	Bob Errey/Rob Zettler	1.50	3.00
10	Pat Falloon	2.50	5.00
11	First Faceof at San Jose Arena	1.50	3.00
12	Wade Flaherty	1.50	3.00
13	John Garpenlov	1.50	3.00
14	Rob Gaudreau	2.00	4.00
15	Arturs Irbe, Goalie	3.00	6.00
16	Arturs Irbe, Goalie, All Star Uniform	2.50	5.00
17	Viktor Kozlov	3.00	6.00
18	Vlastimil Kroupa	1.50	3.00
19	Mike Lalor	1.50	3.00
20	Igor Larionov	2.00	4.00
21	Sergei Makarov	2.00	4.00
22	David Maley	1.50	3.00
23	Jason More	1.50	3.00
24	Jeff Norton	2.00	4.00
25	Jeff Odgers	2.00	4.00
26	Sandis Ozolinch, All Star Uniform	2.50	5.00
27	Tom Pederson	1.50	3.00
28	Mike Rathje/Andrei Nazarov	1.50	3.00
29	San Jose Arena	1.50	3.00
30	Pete Stemkowski	1.50	3.00
31	Mike Sullivan	1.50	3.00
32	Michael Sykora	2.00	4.00
33	The Coaches: Kevin Constantine Duane Thomas, Vasily Tikhonov	1.50	3.00
34	Team Photo	2.50	5.00
35	Ray Whitney	2.00	4.00
36	Ray Whitney and Pat Falloon	2.00	4.00
37	Dody Wood	1.50	3.00
38	Jimmy Waite, Goalie	1.50	3.00
39	Doug Zmolek	1.50	3.00
40	Zamboni with Fin	1.50	3.00

SAN JOSE SHARKS - TEAM SETS • 633

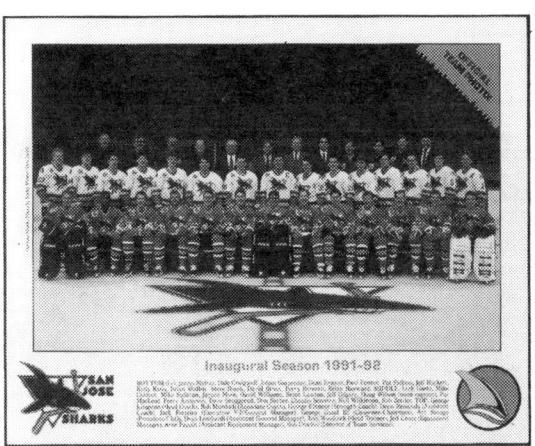

San Jose Sharks
1991-92 Team Photo Inaugural Season

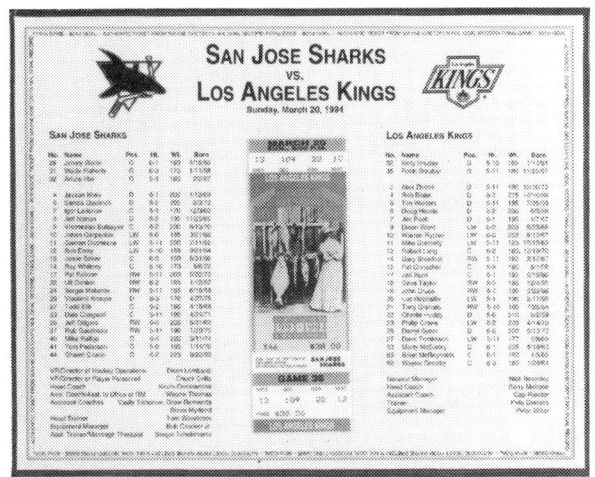

San Jose Sharks 1993-94 Commemmorative Sheet
Suite Ticket, Tying Game, 801st Goal Wayne Gretzky

San Jose Sharks, 1993-94 Commemmorative Season Tickets
Coming Home to a New Beginning 1993-94

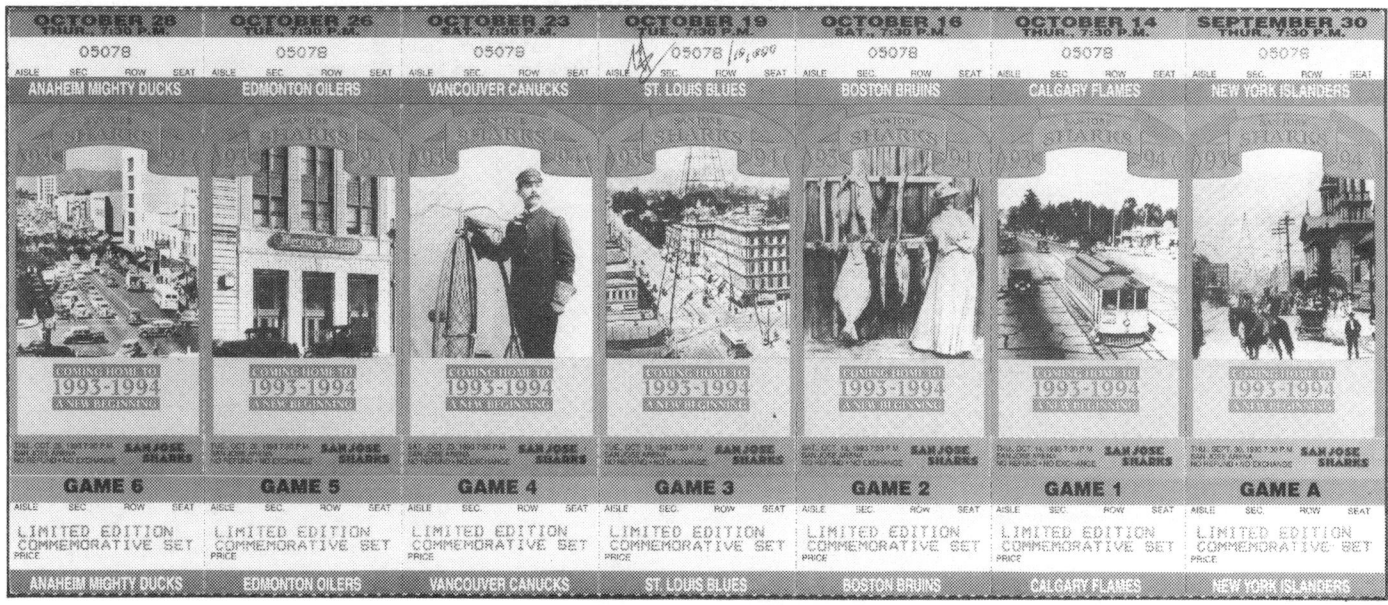

San Jose Sharks, 1993-94 Commemmorative Ticket Set

TAMPA BAY - TEAM SETS

TEAM ISSUES

— 1992 - 93 BLEACHERS MANON RHEAUME —

Issued in a Limited Edition of 10,000 sets these cards reportly have 23 karat gold borders. The cards are numbered _ 0f 10,000. The cards came packaged in a three card lucite holder.

Card Size: 2 1/2" x 3 1/2"
Face: Four colour, Gold borders, Name, Team, Position
Back: Four colour, White border, Number, Name, Resume, Logos
Imprint: © 1993 BLEACHERS
Complete Set No.: 3
Complete Set Price: 20.00 40.00
Complete uncut Strip Price: 22.50 45.00

No.	Player	EX	NRMT
1	Trois Rivieres	7.50	15.00
2	Atlanta Knights	7.50	15.00
3	Tampa Bay	7.50	15.00

Tampa Bay - Team Sets
1992-93 Bleachers Manon Rheaume

TORONTO MAPLE LEAFS - TEAM SETS

TEAM ISSUES

EXHIBIT CARDS

— LATE 1940s TO EARLY 1950s —

This set is incomplete. We would appreciate hearing from anyone who could supply further information.

Card Size: 3 1/4" X 5 1/4"
Face: Black and white, Name
Back: Back on thick grey cardboard stock
Imprint: None
Complete Set No.: Unknown
Complete Set Price: Unknown
Common Card: 2.50   5.00

No.	Player	EX	NRMT
1	Bill Barilko	25.00	50.00
2	Turk Broda, Goalie	3.50	7.00
3	Bill Juzda	2.50	5.00
4	Ted Kennedy	2.50	5.00
5	Gus Mortson	2.50	5.00
6	Ray Timgren	2.50	5.00
7	Jim Thomson	2.50	5.00
8	Joe Klukay	2.50	5.00
9	Sid Smith	2.50	5.00

— SET "A" - Circa 1964-65 — POSTCARD ISSUE

Card Size: 3 1/2" X 5 1/2"
Face: Black and white; Facsimile autograph
Back: Blank
Imprint: None
Complete Set No.: Unknown
Complete Set Price: Unknown
Common Card: 1.50   3.00

No.	Player	EX	NRMT
1	George Armstrong	5.00	10.00
2	Andy Bathgate	3.50	7.50
3	Bobby Baun	1.50	3.00
4	Johnny Bower, Goalie	2.50	5.00
5	Carl Brewer	1.50	3.00
6	Ron Ellis	3.00	6.00
7	Tim Horton	5.00	10.00
8	Punch Imlach, Coach	2.50	5.00
9	Red Kelly	2.50	5.00
10	Dave Keon	3.50	7.00
11	Frank Mahovlich	5.00	10.00
12	Don McKenney	1.50	3.00
13	Dickie Moore	2.50	5.00
14	Bob Pulford	1.50	3.00
15	Terry Sawchuk, Goalie	5.00	10.00
16	Ed Shack	2.50	5.00
17	Ron Stewart	1.50	3.00

— SET "B" - Circa 1965-66 — POSTCARD ISSUE

Card Size: 3 1/2" X 5 1/2"
Face: Black and white; Name, Facsimile autograph, Position
Back: Blank
Imprint: None
Complete Set No.: Unknown
Complete Set Price: Unknown
Common Card: 1.50   3.00

No.	Player	EX	NRMT
1	Billy Harris	2.00	4.00
2	Larry Hillman	1.50	3.00
3	Tim Horton	5.00	10.00
4	Dickie Moore	2.50	5.00
5	Bob Pulford (Home uniform)	2.00	4.00
6	Bob Pulford (Away uniform)	2.00	4.00
7	Ron Stewart	1.50	3.00
8	Carl Brewer	1.50	3.00
9	Kent Douglas	1.50	3.00
10	Dick Duff	2.00	4.00
11	Dave Keon	3.50	7.00
12	Frank Mahovlich	5.00	10.00
13	Bob Pulford, Bust Photo	1.50	3.00
14	Don Simmons	1.50	3.00
15	Bob Baun	2.00	4.00
16	Dick Duff	1.50	3.00
17	George Armstrong	3.50	7.00
18	Carl Brewer	1.50	3.00
19	Bert Olmstead	1.50	3.00

— Set "C" — POSTCARD ISSUE

Card Size: 3 1/2" X 5 1/2"
Face: Black and white; Name
Back: Blank
Imprint: None
Complete Set No.: Unknown
Complete Set Price: Unknown
Common Card: 1.50   3.00

No.	Player	EX	NRMT
1	George Armstrong	3.50	7.00
2	Bob Baun	1.50	3.00
3	Johnny Bower, Goalie	2.50	5.00
4	Kent Douglas	1.50	3.00
5	Ron Ellis	2.50	5.00
6	Tim Horton	3.50	7.00
7	Red Kelly	2.00	4.00
8	Bob Pulford	1.50	3.00
9	Allan Stanley	1.50	3.00

— Set "D" — POSTCARD ISSUE

Card Size: 3 1/2" X 5 1/2"
Face: Black and white; Name, Facsimile autograph
Back: Blank
Imprint: None
Complete Set No.: Unknown
Complete Set Price: Unknown
Common Card: 1.25   2.50

No.	Player	EX	NRMT
1	Johnny Bower, Goalie	2.50	5.00
2	Wally Boyer	1.25	2.50
3	John Brenneman	1.25	2.50
4	Brian Conacher	1.25	2.50
5	Tim Horton	3.50	7.00
6	Larry Jeffrey	1.25	2.50
7	David Keon	2.50	5.00
8	Orland Kurtenbach	1.25	2.50
9	Frank Mahovlich	2.50	5.00
10	Bob Pulford	1.25	2.50
11	Eddie Shack	2.00	2.50

— 1962-63 TO 1967-1968 — POSTCARD ISSUE

Card Size: 5" X 7"
Face: Black and white, glossy photos; Name, Facsimile authograph
Back: Blank
Imprint: None
Complete Set No.: Unknown
Complete Set Price: Unknown
Common Card: 1.00   2.00

No.	Player	EX	NRMT
1	Andy Bathgate	1.50	3.00
2	Johnny Bower, Goalie	1.50	3.00
3	Ron Ellis	1.50	3.00
4	Bruce Gamble, Goalie	1.00	2.00
5	Tim Horton	2.50	5.00
6	Orland Kurtenbach	1.00	2.00
7	Don McKenney	1.00	2.00
8	Dickie Moore	1.25	2.50
9	Marcel Pronovost	1.25	2.50
10	Bob Pulford	1.25	2.50
11	Terry Sawchuk, Goalie	2.50	5.00
12	Brit Selby	1.00	2.00
13	Peter Stemkowski, Jersey No. 16	1.00	2.00
14	Peter Stemkowski, Jersey No. 12	1.00	2.00
15	Norm Ullman	1.50	3.00
16	David Keon	2.00	4.00

— 1964-1965 POSTCARD ISSUE —

Card Size: 3 1/2" x 5 1/2"
Face:
Back: Blank
Imprint: None
Complete Set No.: 23
Complete Set Price: 25.00   50.00
Common Card: 1.00   2.00

No.	Player	EX	NRMT
1	George Armstrong	2.00	4.00
2	Andy Bathgate	1.50	3.00
3	Bob Baun	1.50	3.00
4	Johnny Bower, Goalie	2.00	4.00
5	Carl Brewer	1.00	2.00
6	Kent Douglas	1.00	2.00
7	Dick Duff	1.00	2.00
8	Ron Ellis	2.50	5.00
9	Billy Harris	1.00	2.00
10	Tim Horton	2.50	5.00
11	Punch Imlach, Coach	1.00	2.00
12	Red Kelly	1.50	3.00
13	Dave Keon	2.00	4.00
14	Frank Mahovlich	2.50	5.00
15	Don McKenney	1.00	2.00
16	Dickie Moore	1.50	3.00
17	Jim Pappin	1.00	2.00
18	Bob Pulford	1.00	2.00
19	Terry Sawchuk, Goalie	2.00	4.00
20	Eddie Shack	1.25	2.50
21	Don Simmons, Goalie	1.00	2.00
22	Allan Stanley	1.25	2.50
23	Ron Stewart	1.00	2.00

— 1968-69 TO 1970-71 POSTCARD ISSUE —

Card Size: 3 1/2" X 5 1/2"
Face: Black and white; Name; Some have facsimile autograph
Back: Blank
Imprint: None
Complete Set No.: Unknown
Complete Set Price: Unknown
Common Card: .75   1.50

No.	Player	EX	NRMT
1	George Armstrong	1.50	3.00
2	Johnny Bower, Goalie	1.50	3.00
3	Jim Dorey	.75	1.50
4	Ron Ellis	1.25	2.50
5	Bruce Gamble, facing straight ahead, Goalie	.75	1.50
6	Bruce Gamble, facing to his left, Goalie	.75	1.50
7	Brian Glennie	.75	1.50
8	Jim Harrison	.75	1.50
9	Paul Henderson, facing straight ahead	1.00	2.00
10	Paul Henderson, facing to his right	1.00	2.00
11	Dave Keon "A" on jersey	1.00	2.00
12	Dave Keon "C" on jersey	1.25	2.50
13	Rick Ley	.75	1.50
14	Bob Liddington	.75	1.50
15	Bill MacMillan	.75	1.50
16	Larry McIntyre	.75	1.50
17	Jim McKenny	1.00	2.00

TORONTO MAPLE LEAFS – TEAM SETS

No.	Player	EX	NRMT
18	Garry Monahan	.75	1.50
19	Bernie Parent, Goalie	2.00	4.00
20	Mike Pelyk	.75	1.50
21	Jacques Plante, Goalie	2.00	4.00
22	Brit Selby	.75	1.50
23	Brand Selwood	.75	1.50
24	Darryl Sittler	2.00	4.00
25	Al Smith	.75	1.50
26	Floyd Smith	.75	1.50
27	Brian Spencer	.75	1.50
28	Guy Trottier	.75	1.50
29	Norm Ullman	1.00	2.00
30	Mike Walton, smiling in photo	1.00	2.00
31	Mike Walton, not smiling in photo	1.00	2.00
32	Mike Walton, black tape on stick	1.00	2.00
33	Frank (King) Clancy	1.00	2.00
34	Jim Gregory	.75	1.50
35	John McLellan	.75	1.50

— 1971-72 TO 1972-73 POSTCARD ISSUE —

Card Size: 3 1/2" X 5 1/2"
Face: Colour on black; Facsimile autograph
Back: Blank
Imprint: None
Complete Set No.: Unknown
Complete Set Price: Unknown
Common Card: .60   1.25

No.	Player	EX	NRMT
1	Bob Baun	1.00	2.00
2	Jim Dorey	.60	1.25
3	Denis Dupere	.60	1.25
4	Ron Ellis	1.00	2.00
5	George Ferguson	.60	1.25
6	Brian Glennie	.60	1.25
7	Jim Harrison	.60	1.25
8	Paul Henderson	.85	1.75
9	Pierre Jarry	.60	1.25
10	Rick Kehoe	.60	1.25
11	David Keon	1.25	2.50
12	Rick Ley	.60	1.25
13	Bill MacMillan	.60	1.25
14	Jim McKenny	.60	1.25
15	Bernie Parent, Goalie	2.00	4.00
16	Jacques Plante, leaning on the net, Goalie	2.00	4.00
17	Jacques Plante, crouched in front of the net, Goalie	2.00	4.00
18	Brad Selwood	.60	1.25
19	Darryl Sittler, white tape on stick	2.00	4.00
20	Darryl Sittler, black tape on stick	2.00	4.00
21	Guy Trottier	.60	1.25
22	Norm Ullman, no mustache	.85	1.75
23	Norm Ullman, with mustache	.85	1.75
24	Mike Pelyk	.60	1.25

— 1972-73 POSTCARD ISSUE —

These cards are unnumbered and are listed here in alphabetical order. This set is not complete, any information you may have regarding this issue would be greatly appreciated.

1972-73 Postcard Issue
Postcard No. 6, Darryl Sittler

Card Size: 3 1/2" X 5 1/2"
Face: Four colour, borderless; Facsimile autograph
Back: Blank
Imprint: None
Complete Set No.: 12
Complete Set Price: Unknown

No.	Player	EX	NRMT
1	Denis Dupere	.50	1.00
2	Ron Ellis	.50	1.00
3	Brian Glennie	.50	1.00
4	Paul Henderson	1.00	2.00
5	Brad Selwood	.50	1.00
6	Darryl Sittler	1.00	2.00
7	Norm Ullman	1.00	2.00

— 1973-74 TO 1974-75 POSTCARD ISSUE —

Card Size: 3 1/2" X 5 1/2"
Face: Colour on light blue background; Facsimile autograph
Back: Blank
Imprint: None
Complete Set No.: Unknown
Complete Set Price: 17.50   35.00
Common Card: .60   1.25

No.	Player	EX	NRMT
1	Willy Brossart	.60	1.25
2	Denis Dupere	.60	1.25
3	Ron Ellis, hockey pose	.85	1.75
4	Ron Ellis, standing straight	.85	1.75
5	Doug Favell, Goalie	.75	1.50
6	George Ferguson	.60	1.25
7	Bill Flett	.60	1.25
8	Inge Hammarstrom, number on sleeve visible	.75	1.50
9	Inge Hammarstrom, number on sleeve not visible	.75	1.50
10	Ed Johnston	.60	1.25
11	David Keon	1.25	2.50
12	Gord McRae	.60	1.25
13	Lanny McDonald	1.75	3.50
14	Borje Salming, number on sleeve visible	1.75	3.50
15	Borje Salming, number on sleeve not visible	1.75	3.50
16	Ed Shack, tape on blade of stick	.75	1.50
17	Ed Shack, no tape on blade of stick	.75	1.50
18	Darryl Sittler	1.50	3.00
19	Errol Thompson	.75	1.50
20	Ian Turnbull	1.00	2.00
21	Dunc Wilson, Sherwood hockey stick, Goalie	.60	1.25
22	Dunc Wilson, Louisville hockey stick, Goalie	.60	1.25
23	Jim Gregory	.60	1.25
24	Red Kelly, Coach	1.00	2.00

— 1975-76 POSTCARD ISSUE —

Card Size: 3 1/2" X 5 1/2"
Face: Four colour, Name, Facsimile autograph
Back: Black on white card stock; Name, Resume
Imprint: None
Complete Set No.: Unknown
Complete Set Price: 17.50   35.00
Common Card: .50   1.00

No.	Player	EX	NRMT
1	Claire Alexander	.50	1.00
2	Don Ashby	.50	1.00
3	Pat Boutette	.50	1.00
4	Dave Dunn	.50	1.00
5	Doug Favell, Goalie	.50	1.00
6	George Ferguson	.75	1.50
7	Brian Glennie	.75	1.50
8	Inge Hammarstrom	1.00	2.00
9	Greg Hubick	.50	1.00
10	Lanny McDonald	1.50	3.00
11	Jim McKenny	.75	1.50
12	Gord McRae	.50	1.00
13	Bob Neely	.50	1.00
14	Borje Salming, facing straight ahead	1.50	3.00
15	Borje Salming, facing left	1.50	3.00
16	Rod Selling	.50	1.00
17	Darryl Sittler	1.50	3.00
18	Blaine Stoughton	.50	1.00
19	Wayne Thomas, Goalie	.50	1.00
20	Ian Turnbull	.75	1.50
21	Stan Weir	.50	1.00
22	Dave Williams, hockey pose	.75	1.50
23	Dave Williams, standing straight	.75	1.50
24	Ian Turnbull, hockey pose	.75	1.50
25	Ian Turnbull, standing straight	.75	1.50

— 1976-77 POSTCARD ISSUE 50TH ANNIVERSARY YEAR —

Card Size: 3 1/2" X 5 1/2"
Face: Four colour; Name, Facsimile autograph
Back: Black on white card stock
Imprint: None
Complete Set No.: Unknown
Complete Set Price: Unknown
Common Card: .50   1.00

No.	Player	EX	NRMT
1	Pat Boutette	.50	1.00
2	Inge Hammarstrom	.75	1.50
3	Lanny McDonald	1.25	2.50
4	Gord McRae	.50	1.00
5	Mike Palmateer, Goalie	1.50	3.00
6	Borje Salming	1.50	3.00
7	Darryl Sittler	1.50	3.00
8	Wayne Thomas, Goalie	.50	1.00
9	Ian Turnbull	.75	1.50
10	Dave Williams	.75	1.50
11	Scott Garland	.50	1.00

— 1977-78 POSTCARD ISSUE —

Card Size: 3 1/2" X 5 1/2"
Face: Colour
Back: Blank
Imprint: None
Complete Set No.: Unknown
Complete Set Price: Unknown
Common Card: .50   1.00

No.	Player	EX	NRMT
1	Don Ashby	.50	1.00
2	Pat Boutette	.50	1.00
3	Ron Ellis	.75	1.50
4	George Ferguson	.75	1.50
5	Brian Glennie	.75	1.50
6	Inge Hammarstrom	.75	1.50
7	Trevor Johansen	.50	1.00
8	Jim Jones	.50	1.00
9	Gord McRae	.50	1.00
10	Bob Neely	.50	1.00
11	Borje Salming	1.25	2.50
12	Darryl Sittler	1.25	2.50
13	Errol Thompson	.50	1.00
14	Ian Turnbull	.75	1.50
15	Jack Valiquette	.50	1.00
16	Dave Williams	.75	1.50
17	Kurt Walker	.50	1.00

— 1978-79 POSTCARD ISSUE —

Card Size: 3 1/2" X 5 1/2"
Face: Colour; Name, Facsimile autograph
Back: Black on white card stock
Imprint: None
Complete Set No.: Set of 23
Complete Set Price: Unknown
Common Card: .50   1.00

No.	Player	EX	NRMT
1	John Anderson	.50	1.00
2	Pat Boutette	.50	1.00
3	Jerry Butler	.50	1.00
4	Dave Burrows	.50	1.00

TORONTO MAPLE LEAFS - TEAM SETS • 637

No.	Player	EX	NRMT
5	Bruce Boudreau, black and white	.50	1.00
6	Ron Ellis	.75	1.50
7	Paul Harrison, Goalie	.50	1.00
8	Dave Hutchison	.50	1.00
9	Trevor Johansen	.50	1.00
10	Dan Maloney	1.00	2.00
11	Lanny McDonald	1.25	2.50
12	Walt McKechnie	.50	1.00
13	Garry Monahan	.50	1.00
14	Mike Palmateer, Goalie	1.00	2.00
15	Borje Salming	1.25	2.50
16	Darryl Sittler	1.25	2.50
17	Lorne Stamler	.50	1.00
18	Ian Turnbull	.75	1.50
19	Dave Williams	.75	1.50
20	Ron Wilson	.50	1.00
21	Harold Ballard and King Clancy	.60	1.25
22	Maple Leaf Gardens	.75	1.50
23	Roger Neilson, Coach	.75	1.50

— 1979 - 80 POSTCARD ISSUE —

Card Size: 3 1/2" x 5 1/2"
Face: Colour; Name, Facsimile autograph
Back: Black on white card stock
Imprint: Unkown
Complete Set No.: 31
Complete Set Price: Unknown
Common Card: .35 .75

No.	Player	EX	NRMT
1	John Anderson	.50	1.00
2	Harold Ballard, Pres.	.50	1.00
3	Laurie Boschman	.50	1.00
4	Pat Boutette	.35	.75
5	Carl Brewer, without autograph	.35	.75
6	Dave Burrows	.35	.75
7	Jiri Crha, Goalie	.35	.75
8	Ron Ellis	.75	1.50
9	Paul Gardner	.50	1.00
10	Paul Harrison, Goalie	.35	.75
11	Pat Hickey, without autograph	.35	.75
12	Greg Hotham	.35	.75
13	Dave Hutchison	.35	.75
14	Punch Imlach, Coach	.35	.75
15	Jim Jones	.35	.75
16	Mark Kirton	.35	.75
17	Dan Maloney	.50	1.00
18	Terry Martin	.35	.75
19	Lanny McDonald	1.25	2.50
20	Walt McKechnie	.35	.75
21	Wilf Paiement, without autograph	.35	.75
22	Mike Palmateer, Goalie	1.00	2.00
23	Joel Quenneville	.35	.75
24	Rocky Saganiuk, with autograph	.50	1.00
25	Rocky Saganiuk, without autograph	.50	1.00
26	Borje Salming	1.00	2.00
27	Darryl Sittler	1.25	2.50
28	Floyd Smith	.35	.75
29	Bob Stephenson, without autograph	.35	.75
30	Ian Turnbull	.50	1.00
31	Ron Wilson	.35	.75

— 1980 - 81 POSTCARD ISSUE —

Card Size: 3 1/2" x 5 1/2"
Face: Colour; Name, Position, Facsimile autograph
Back: Blank
Imprint: Unkown
Complete Set No.: 26
Complete Set Price: 9.00 18.00
Common Card: .35 .75

No.	Player	EX	NRMT
1	John Anderson	.35	.75
2	Laurie Boschman	.35	.75
3	Jiri Crha, Goalie	.35	.75
4	Bill Derlago	.35	.75
5	Vitezslav Duris	.35	.75
6	Dave Farrish	.35	.75
7	Stewart Gavin	.50	1.00

No.	Player	EX	NRMT
8	Paul Harrison, Goalie	.35	.75
9	Pat Hickey	.35	.75
10	Mark Kirton	.35	.75
11	Terry Martin	.35	.75
12	Wilf Paiement	.50	1.00
13	Robert Picard	.35	.75
14	Curt Ridley	.35	.75
15	Rocky Saganiuk	.50	1.00
16	Borje Salming	.75	1.50
17	Dave Shand	.35	.75
18	Darryl Sittler	1.00	2.00
19	Ian Turnbull	.50	1.00
20	Rick Vaive	1.25	2.50
21	Harold Ballard, Pres.	.50	1.00
22	Johnny Bower, Goalie	.50	1.00
23	Francis (King) Clancy	.50	1.00
24	Joe Crozier, Goalie	.35	.75
25	Dick Duff	.35	.75
26	Gerry McNamara	.35	.75

— 1981 - 82 POSTCARD ISSUE —

1981-82 Postcard Issue
Postcard No. 1, John Anderson

Card Size: 3 1/2" x 5 1/2"
Face: Four colour; Name and jersey number, Facsimile autograph, Team logo
Back: Blue on card stock
Imprint: None
Complete Set No.: 26
Complete Set Price: 7.50 15.00
Common Player: .25 .50

No.	Player	EX	NRMT
1	John Anderson	.50	1.00
2	Harold Ballard, Pres.	.50	1.00
3	Jim Benning	.25	.50
4	Fred Boimistruck	.25	.50
5	Laurie Boschman	.25	.50
6	Bill Derlago	.25	.50
7	Stewart Gavin	.25	.50
8	Michelle Larocque, Goalie	.25	.50
9	Don Luce	.25	.50
10	Bob McGill	.25	.50
11	Dan Maloney	.25	.50
12	Bob Manno	.25	.50
13	Paul Marshall	.25	.50
14	Terry Martin	.25	.50
15	Barry Melrose	.50	1.00
16	Mike Nykoluk, Coach	.25	.50
17	Wilf Paiement	.25	.50
18	Rene Robert	.25	.50
19	Rocky Saganiuk	.25	.50
20	Borje Salming	1.00	2.00
21	Darryl Sittler	1.00	2.00
22	Vincent Tremblay, Goalie	.25	.50
23	Rick Vaive	.50	1.00
24	Gary Yaremchuk	.25	.50
25	Ron Zanussi	.25	.50
26	Harold Ballard, Frank J. Selke.	.50	1.00

— 1982 - 83 POSTCARD ISSUE —

Card Size: 3 1/2" x 5 1/2"
Face: Four colour; Name, Number, Facsimile autograph
Back: Postcard in blue ink
Imprint: Unkown
Complete Set No.: 29
Complete Set Price: Unknown
Common Card: .35 .75

No.	Player	EX	NRMT
1	Russ Adam	.35	.75
2	John Anderson	.50	1.00
3	Normand Aubin	.35	.75
4	Harold Ballard, Pres.	.50	1.00
5	Jim Benning	.35	.75
6	Serge Boisvert	.35	.75
7	Dan Daoust	.35	.75
8	Bill Derlago	.35	.75
9	Miroslav Frycer	.35	.75
10	Stewart Gavin	.50	1.00
11	Gaston Gingras, action background	.50	1.00
12	Gaston Gingras	.50	1.00
13	Billy Harris	.50	1.00
14	Paul Higgins	.35	.75
15	Peter Ihnacak	.75	1.50
16	Jim Korn	.35	.75
17	Dan Maloney	.50	1.00
18	Terry Martin	.35	.75
19	Frank Nigro	.35	.75
20	Mike Nykoluk, Coach	.35	.75
21	Gary Nylund	.50	1.00
22	Mike Palmateer, Goalie	1.00	2.00
23	Walt Poddubny	.35	.75
24	Borje Salming	1.00	2.00
25	Rick St. Croix, Goalie	.35	.75
26	Greg Terrion, action background	.50	1.00
27	Greg Terrion	.50	1.00
28	Vincent Tremblay, Goalie	.35	.75
29	Rick Vaive	.75	1.50

— 1983 - 84 POSTCARD ISSUE —

Card Size: 3 1/2" x 5 1/2"
Face: Four colour; Name, Facsimile autograph
Back: Black on white card stock
Imprint: Unkown
Complete Set No.: 26
Complete Set Price: 7.50 15.00
Common Card: .25 .50

No.	Player	EX	NRMT
1	John Anderson	.35	.75
2	Jim Benning	.25	.50
3	Dan Daoust	.25	.50
4	Bill Derlago	.25	.50
5	Dave Farrish	.25	.50
6	Miroslav Frycer	.35	.75
7	Stewart Gavin	.25	.50
8	Gaston Gingras	.25	.50
9	Pat Graham	.25	.50
10	Bill Harris	.50	1.00
11	Peter Ihnacak	.50	1.00
12	Jim Korn	.25	.50
13	Gary Leeman	1.50	3.00
14	Dan Maloney	.50	1.00
15	Terry Martin	.25	.50
16	Basil McRae	.25	.50
17	Frank Nigro	.25	.50
18	Mike Nykoluk, Coach	.25	.50
19	Gary Nylund	.25	.50
20	Mike Palmateer, Goalie	.75	1.50
21	Walt Poddubny	.25	.50
22	Borje Salming	.75	1.50
23	Rick St. Croix, Goalie	.25	.50
24	Bill Stewart	.25	.50
25	Greg Terrion	.25	.50
26	Rick Vaive	.50	1.00

TORONTO MAPLE LEAFS - TEAM SETS

— 1984 - 85 POSTCARD ISSUE —

Card Size: 3 1/2" x 5 1/2"
Face: Four colour; Name, Number, Facsimile autograph
Back: Black on white card stocl
Imprint: Unkown
Complete Set No.: 24
Complete Set Price: 7.50 15.00
Common Card: .25 .50

No.	Player	EX	NRMT
1	John Anderson	.25	.50
2	Jim Benning	.25	.50
3	Allan Bester, Goalie	.50	1.00
4	John Brophy, Coach	.25	.50
5	Jeff Brubaker	.25	.50
6	Russell Courtnall	1.50	3.00
7	Dan Daoust	.25	.50
8	Bill Derlago	.25	.50
9	Miroslav Frycer	.25	.50
10	Stewart Gavin	.25	.50
11	Al Iafrate	1.50	3.00
12	Peter Ihnacak	.25	.50
13	Jeff Jackson	.25	.50
14	Jim Korn	.25	.50
15	Gary Leeman	.35	.75
16	Dan Maloney	.50	1.00
17	Bob McGill	.25	.50
18	Gary Nylund	.25	.50
19	Walt Poddubny	.25	.50
20	Bill Root	.25	.50
21	Borje Salming	.50	1.00
22	Greg Terrion	.25	.50
23	Rick Vaive	.25	.50
24	Ken Wregget, Goalie	.50	1.00

— 1985 - 86 POSTCARD ISSUE —

Card Size: 3 1/2" x 5 1/2"
Face: Four colour; Name, Number, Facsimile autograph
Back: Black on wqhite card stock
Imprint: Unkown
Complete Set No.: 29
Complete Set Price: 10.00 20.00
Common Card:

No.	Player	EX	NRMT
1	Harold Ballard, Pres.	.50	1.00
2	Jim Benning	.25	.50
3	Tim Bernhardt, Goalie	.25	.50
4	Johnny Bower, Goalie	.50	1.00
5	Jeff Brubaker	.25	.50
6	Wendel Clark	2.50	5.00
7	Russell Courtnall	1.50	3.00
8	Dan Daoust	.25	.50
9	Don Edwards, Goalie	.50	1.00
10	Tom Fergus	.25	.50
11	Miroslav Frycer	.25	.50
12	Al Iafrate	1.25	2.50
13	Peter Ihnacak	.35	.75
14	Jeff Jackson	.25	.50
15	Jim Korn	.25	.50
16	Chris Kotsopolous	.25	.50
17	Gary Leeman	.50	1.00
18	Brad Maxwell	.25	.50
19	Bob McGill	.25	.50
20	Gary Nylund	.25	.50
21	Walt Poddubny	.25	.50
22	Borje Salming	.75	1.50
23	Marian Stastny	.25	.50
24	Steve Thomas	1.25	2.50
25	Greg Terrion	.25	.50
26	Rick Vaive	.50	1.00
27	Rick Vaive (C) on sweater	.50	1.00
28	Blake Wesley	.25	.50
29	Ken Wregget, Goalie	.50	1.00

— 1986 - 87 POSTCARD ISSUE —

Card Size: 3 1/2" x 5 1/2"
Face: Four colour; Name, Number, Facsimile autograph
Back: Black on white card stock
Imprint: Unkown
Complete Set No.: 24
Complete Set Price: 9.00 18.00
Common Card: .25 .50

No.	Playe	EX	NRMT
1	Mike Allison	.25	.50
2	Wendel Clark	2.00	4.00
3	Russell Courtnall	1.25	2.50
4	Vincent Damphousse	2.50	5.00
5	Dan Daoust	.25	.50
6	Jerome Dupont	.25	.50
7	Tom Fergus	.25	.50
8	Miroslav Frycer	.25	.50
9	Todd Gill	1.00	2.00
10	Dan Hodgson	.25	.50
11	Al Iafrate	1.00	2.00
12	Miroslav Ihnacak	.25	.50
13	Peter Ihnacak	.25	.50
14	Terry Johnson	.25	.50
15	Chris Kotsopoulos	.25	.50
16	Gary Leeman	.50	1.00
17	Bob McGill	.25	.50
18	Bill Root	.25	.50
19	Borje Salming	.75	1.50
20	Brad Smith	.25	.50
21	Steve Thomas	1.00	2.00
22	Greg Terrion	.25	.50
23	Rick Vaive	.35	.75
24	Ken Wregget, Goalie	.35	.75

— 1987 - 88 PHOTO ISSUE —

These cards are unnumbered and are listed here in alphabetical order. This set is not complete, any information you may have regarding this issue would be greatly appreciated.

1987-88 Photo Issue
Photo No. 1, Allan Bester

Photo Size: 5" X 8"
Face: Four colour, white strip at bottom; Jersey number, Name, Team logo
Back: Blank
Imprint: None
Complete Set No.: 24
Complete Set Price: 12.50 25.00
Common Player: .50 1.00

No.	Player	EX	NRMT
1	Allan Bester, Goalie	.50	1.00
2	Wendel Clark	1.50	3.00
3	Russell Courtnall	.50	1.00
4	Vincent Damphousse	1.50	3.00
5	Dan Daoust	.50	1.00
6	Dale DeGray	.50	1.00
7	Tom Fergus	.50	1.00
8	Miroslav Frycer	.50	1.00
9	Todd Gill	.50	1.00
10	Al Iafrate	1.25	2.50
11	Peter Ihnacak	.50	1.00
12	Christopher Kotsopoulos	.50	1.00
13	Rick Lanz	.50	1.00

No.	Player	EX	NRMT
14	Gary Leeman	.50	1.00
15	Ed Olczyk	.50	1.00
16	Mark Osborne	.50	1.00
17	Luke Richardson	.50	1.00
18	Borje Salming	1.00	2.00
19	Alan Secord	.50	1.00
20	Dave Semenko	.50	1.00
21	Brad Smith	.50	1.00
22	Greg Terrion	.50	1.00
23	Ken Wregget, Goalie	.50	1.00
24	Team Photograph	.50	1.00

— 1988 - 89 POSTCARD SET —

Photo Size: 5" X 8"
Face: Colour, Jersey number, Name, Team logo
Back: Postcard back
Imprint: None
Complete Set No.: 21
Complete Set Price:
Common Player:

No.	Player	EX	NRMT
1	Allan Bester, Goalie	.35	.75
2	Wendel Clark	1.50	3.00
3	Brian Curran	.25	.50
4	Vincent Damphousse	1.25	2.50
5	Dan Daoust	.25	.50
6	Tom Fergus	.25	.50
7	Todd Gill	.75	1.50
8	Al Iafrate	.75	1.50
9	Chris Kotsopoulos	.25	.50
10	Rick Lanz	.25	.50
11	Gary Leeman	.50	1.00
12	Daniel Marois	.25	.50
13	Brad Marsh	.35	.75
14	Sean McKenna	.25	.50
15	Ed Olczyk	.25	.50
16	Mark Osborne	.35	.75
17	David Reid	.35	.75
18	Luke Richardson	.25	.50
19	Borje Salming	.75	1.50
20	Al Secord	.25	.50
21	Ken Wregget, Goalie	.35	.75

O'KEEFE BEVERAGES

— 1932 - 33 COASTER ISSUE —

Issued in the Toronto area after Toronto's first Stanley Cup win. Sixteen sided, intended to be used as a coaster.

Card Size: 3" Diameter
Face: Blue, black and white; Name, Team; Number, Trivia
Back: Blank
Imprint: O'KEEFE'S
Complete Set No.: 20
Complete Set Price: 100.00 200.00 400.00
Common Player: 5.00 10.00 20.00

No.	Player	G	VG	EX
1	Lorne Chabot, Goalie	7.50	15.00	30.00
2	Red Horner	5.00	10.00	20.00
3	Alex Levinsky	7.50	15.00	30.00
4	Hap Day	8.75	17.50	35.00
5	Andy Blair	5.00	10.00	20.00
6	Ace Bailey	12.50	25.00	50.00
7	Francis Clancy	12.50	25.00	50.00
8	Baldy Cotton	5.00	10.00	20.00
9	Charlie Conacher	8.75	17.50	35.00
10	Joe Primeau	8.75	17.50	35.00
11	Harvey Jackson	8.75	17.50	35.00
12	Frank Finnigan	5.00	10.00	20.00
13	Unknown	5.00	10.00	20.00
14	Bob Gracie	5.00	10.00	20.00
15	Ken Doraty	5.00	10.00	20.00
16	Harry Darragh	5.00	10.00	20.00
17	Ben Grant, Goalie	5.00	10.00	20.00
18	Fred Robertson	5.00	10.00	20.00
19	Bill Thoms	5.00	10.00	20.00
20	Unknown	5.00	10.00	20.00

TORONTO MAPLE LEAFS - TEAM SETS • 639

ESSO HOCKEY TALKS

— 1966 - 67 COASTER ISSUE —

Issued in the Toronto area after Toronto's Stanley Cup win. Intended to be used as a coaster.

Dick Size: 8" Diameter
Face: Record
Back: Photo
Imprint:
Complete Set No.: 10
Complete Set Price: 60.00 125.00
Common Player: 5.00 10.00

No.	Player	EX	NRMT
1	George Armstrong	7.50	15.00
2	Johnny Bower, Goalie	7.50	15.00
3	Dave Keon	10.00	20.00
4	Frank Mahovlich	10.00	20.00
5	Tim Horton	10.00	20.00
6	Bob Pulford	5.00	10.00
7	Brit Selby	5.00	10.00
8	Eddie Shack	6.00	12.00
9	Ron Ellis	7.50	15.00
10	Punch Imlach, Coach	6.00	12.00

POLICE LAW AND YOUTH

— 1987 - 88 REGULAR ISSUE —

P.L.A.Y. The London City Police and the London and District Detachments of the O.P.P. Sponsored by Kellogg's Salada Canada Inc.

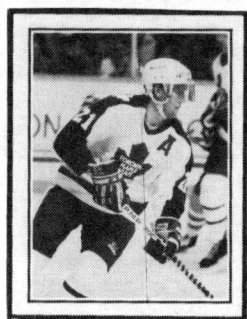

1987-88 P.L.A.Y.
Card No. 8, Borje Salming

Card Size: 2 3/4" X 3 1/2"
Face: Four colour, white border
Back: Black on white card stock; Number, Name, Jersey number, Team, Safety tips
Imprint: Kellogg Salada Canada Inc.
Complete Set No.: 30
Complete Set Price: 7.50 15.00
Common Player: .25 .50

No.	Player	EX	NRMT
1	N. LaVerne Shipley, Chief of Police	.25	.50
2	Tom Gosnell, Mayor	.25	.50
3	1987-88 Checklist	.25	.50
4	Harold Ballard, President	.25	.50
5	Superintendent D. Almond	.25	.50
6	Wendel Clark	1.25	2.50
7	Tom Fergus	.25	.50
8	Borje Salming	.50	1.00
9	Ed Olczyk	.25	.50
10	Gary Leeman	.25	.50
11	Rick Lanz	.25	.50
12	Allan Bester, Goalie	.25	.50
13	Todd Gill	.25	.50
14	Alan Secord	.25	.50
15	Miroslav Frycer	.25	.50
16	Christopher Kotsopoulos	.25	.50
17	Vincent Damphousse	1.50	3.00
18	Mike Allison	.25	.50
19	Al Iafrate	.75	1.50
20	Dan Daoust	.25	.50
21	Greg Terrion	.25	.50
22	Brad Smith	.25	.50
23	Mark Osborne	.25	.50
24	Peter Ihnacak	.25	.50
25	Dale DeGray	.25	.50
26	Dave Semenko	.25	.50
27	Luke Richardson	.25	.50
28	John Brophy, Coach	.25	.50
29	Ken Wregget, Goalie	.25	.50
30	Russell Courtnall	.50	1.00

— 1988 - 89 REGULAR ISSUE —

1988-89 P.L.A.Y.
Card No. 8, Gary Leeman

Card Size: 2 3/4" X 3 1/2"
Face: Four colour, white border
Back: Black on white card stock; Number, Name, Jersey number, Team, Tips
Imprint: Kellogg's Canada Inc.
Complete Set No.: 30
Complete Set Price: 6.00 12.00
Common Player: .13 .25
Album: 1.50 3.00

No.	Player	EX	NRMT
1	Police, Law & Youth	.13	.25
2	Wendel Clark	.75	1.50
3	Tom Fergus	.13	.25
4	Superintendent D. Almond	.13	.25
5	Borje Salming	.35	.75
6	Ed Olczyk	.35	.75
7	1988-89 Checklist	.13	.25
8	Gary Leeman	.25	.50
9	Rick Lanz	.13	.25
10	N. LaVerne Shipley, Chief of Police	.13	.25
11	Allan Bester, Goalie	.25	.50
12	Todd Gill	.13	.25
13	Harold Ballard, President	.13	.25
14	Alan Secord	.25	.50
15	Daniel Marois	.25	.50
16	Christopher Kotsopoulos	.13	.25
17	Vincent Damphousse	.85	1.75
18	Craig Laughlin	.13	.25
19	Al Iafrate	.25	.50
20	Dan Daost	.13	.25
21	Derek Laxdal	.13	.25
22	Darren Veitch	.13	.25
23	Mark Osborne	.13	.25
24	David Reid	.13	.25
25	Bradley Marsh	.25	.50
26	Brian Curran	.13	.25
27	Sean McKenna	.13	.25
28	John Brophy, Coach	.13	.25
29	Ken Wregget, Goalie	.25	.50
30	Russell Courtnall	.25	.50

— 1990 - 91 REGULAR ISSUE —

1990-91 P.L.A.Y.
Card No. 28, Brian Bradley

Card Size: 2 3/4" X 3 1/2"
Face: Four colour, white border; Name, Jersey number, Position, Team logo
Back: Black on white card stock; Name, Jersey number, Position, Drug warning
Imprint: Consumers Gas
Complete Set No.: 30
Complete Set Price: 5.00 10.00
Common Card: .13 .25

No.	Player	EX	NRMT
1	Chief Donald Hillock	.13	.25
2	Deputy Cheif Bryan Cousineau	.13	.25
3	Lanny the Police Dog	.13	.25
4	Cliff Fletcher, General Manager	.50	1.00
5	Tom Watt, Coach	.13	.25
6	Robert Rouse	.35	.75
7	David Ellett	.35	.75
8	David Hannan	.25	.50
9	Glenn Anderson	.50	1.00
10	Gary Leeman	.35	.75
11	Rob Pearson	.50	1.00
12	Claude Loiselle	.13	.25
13	Craig Berube	.25	.50
14	Wendel Clark	1.50	3.00
15	Tom Fergus	.13	.25
16	Michael Bullard	.13	.25
17	Todd Gill	.50	1.00
18	Michel Petit	.13	.25
19	Peter Zezel	.25	.50
20	Michael Krushelnyski	.13	.25
21	Lucien Deblois	.13	.25
22	Darryl Shannon	.13	.25
23	Grant Fuhr, Goalie	.50	1.00
24	Daniel Marois	.50	1.00
25	Robert Cimetta	.13	.25
26	Jeff Reese, Goalie	.25	.50
27	Bob Halkidis	.13	.25
28	Brian Bradley	.50	1.00
29	Michael Foligno	.25	.50
30	Alexander Godynyuk	.13	.25

TIM HORTON

— 1991 REGULAR ISSUE —

Issued to advertise the Sports Collectible Show in Oakville, Ontario during May 1991.

Card Size: 2 1/2" X 3 1/2"
Face: Black and white, White border
Back: Red, black and blue
Imprint: None

No.	Player	EX	NRMT
1	Tim Horton	1.50	3.00

KODAK

— 1992 - 93 PHOTO ISSUE —

Kodak, 1992-93 Photo Issue
Card No. 2, David Andreychuck

Card Size: 4" X 6 1/8"
Face: Four colour, Borderless; Name, Team logo
Back: Blank
Imprint: None
Complete Set No.: 22
Complete Set Price: 10.00 20.00
Common Card: .25 .50

No.	Player	EX	NRMT
1	Glenn Anderson	.35	.75
2	David Andreychuk	.50	1.00
3	David Andreychuk	.50	1.00
4	Ken Baumgartner	.25	.50
5	Drake Berehowsky	.50	1.00
6	Bill Berg	.25	.50
7	Nikolai Borschevsky	.75	1.50
8	Wendel Clark	1.00	2.00
9	John Cullen	.25	.50
10	Mike Eastwood	.25	.50
11	David Ellett	.35	.75
12	Douglas Gilmour	1.25	2.50
13	Sylvain Lefebvre	.25	.50
14	Jamie Macoun	.25	.50
15	Kent Manderville	.35	.75
16	Dave McLlwain	.25	.50
17	Dmitri Mironov	.35	.75
18	Mark Osborne	.25	.50
19	Rob Pearson	.25	.50
20	Felix Potvin, Goalie	1.25	2.50
21	Robert Rouse	.25	.50
22	Peter Zezel	.35	.75

BLACK'S PHOTOGRAPHY

— 1993 - 94 POP-UP ISSUE —

This 24-cad set was a die-cut image of the hocker palyer.

Card Size: 2 1/2" x 3 1/2"
Face: Four colour, purple border; Name, Position, Logo
Back: Four colour; Name, Resume, Logo
Imprint: © Player Portraits by Silvia
Complete Set No.: 24
Complete Set Price: 12.50 25.00
Common Player: .25 .50
Album: 2.50 5.00

No.	Player	EX	NRMT
1	Wendel Clark	1.00	2.00
2	Douglas Gilmour	1.50	3.00
3	Glenn Anderson	.35	.75
4	Peter Zezel	.35	.75
5	Robert Rouse	.25	.50
6	Rob Pearson	.25	.50
7	Mark Osborne	.25	.50
8	Dmitri Mironov	.35	.75
9	Dave McLlwain	.25	.50
10	Kent Manderville	.35	.75
11	Jamie Macoun	.35	.75
12	Sylvain Lefebvre	.35	.75
13	David Andreychuk	.60	1.25
14	Drake Berehowsky	.50	1.00
15	Bill Berg	.25	.50
16	John Cullen	.25	.50
17	Ken Baumgartner	.25	.50
18	Nikolai Borschevsky	.35	.75
19	Michael Eastwood	.25	.50
20	David Ellett	.25	.50
21	Michael Foligno	.35	.75
22	Todd Gill	.35	.75
23	Michael Krushelnyski	.25	.50
24	Felix Potvin, Goalie	1.50	3.00

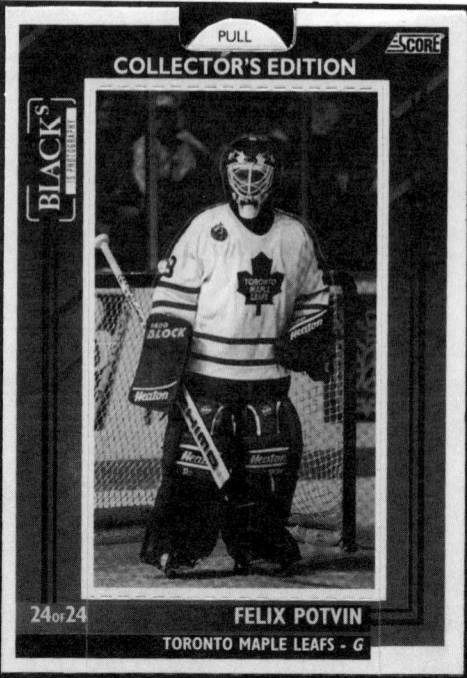

Toronto Maple Leafs - Team Sets
Black's Photography 1993-94 Pop-Up Issue
Card No. 24, Felix Potvin

Toronto Maple Leafs - Team Sets
Black's Photography 1993-94 Pop-Up Issue
Card No. 24, Felix Potvin

THE CHARLTON STANDARD CATALOGUE OF CANADIAN BASEBALL AND FOOTBALL CARDS
- Fourth Edition -
Coming in April!

VANCOUVER CANUCKS - TEAM SETS

TEAM ISSUES

— 1979 - 80 POSTCARD ISSUE —

These cards are unnumbered and are listed here in alphabetical order.

1979-80 Postcard Issue
Postcard No. 1, Brent Ashton

Card Size: 4 1/4" X 5 1/2"
Face: Four colour, white border; Team, Team logo, Name, Jersey number
Back: Blank
Imprint: None
Complete Set No.: 21
Complete Set Price: 12.50 25.00
Common Card: .25 .50

No.	Player	EX	NRMT
1	Brent Ashton	.25	.50
2	Rick Blight	.25	.50
3	Gary Bromley	.25	.50
4	Drew Callander	.25	.50
5	Bill Derlago	.25	.50
6	Curt Fraser	.25	.50
7	Jere Gillis	.25	.50
8	Thomas Gradin	.75	1.50
9	Glen Hanlon, Goalie	.75	1.50
10	John Hughes	.25	.50
11	Dennis Kearns	.25	.50
12	Don Lever	.50	1.00
13	Lars Lindgren	.25	.50
14	Bob Manno	.25	.50
15	Jack McIlhargey	.25	.50
16	Kevin McCarthy	.35	.75
17	Chris Oddleifson	.25	.50
18	Curt Ridley	.25	.50
19	Stan Smyl	.50	1.00
20	Harold Snepsts	.75	1.50
21	Rick Vaive	.75	1.50

— 1980 POSTCARD ISSUE —

These cards are unnumbered and are listed here in alphabetical order. This set is not complete. Any information collectors may have regarding this issue would be greatly appreciated.

Card Size: 3 3/4" X 4 7/8"
Face: Four colour, white border; Name, Position, Jersey number, Team logo
Back: Blank
Imprint: None
Complete Set No.: 22
Complete Set Price: 12.50 25.00

No.	Player	EX	NRMT
1	Brent Ashton	.75	1.50

— 1981 - 82 POSTCARD ISSUE —

This set was obtained by writing to the Vancouver Cannucks Team.

Team Card Size: 3 3/4" x 4 7/8"
Card Size: 3 11/16" X 4 13/16"
Face: Four colour, white border; Name, Position, Jersey number, Facsimile autograph, Team logo
Back: Blank
Imprint: None
Complete Set No.: 19
Complete Set Price: 12.50 25.00
Common Card: .50 1.00

No.	Player	EX	NRMT
1	Ivan Boldirev	.50	1.00
2	Per-Olav Brasar	.50	1.00
3	Richard Brodeur, Goalie	1.50	3.00
4	Gary Bromley	.50	1.00
5	Jerry Butler	.50	1.00
6	Colin Campbell	.50	1.00
7	Curt Fraser	.50	1.00
8	Thomas Gradin	.85	1.75
9	Glen Hanlon	.50	1.00
10	Rick Lanz	.75	1.50
11	Lars Lindgren	.50	1.00
12	Gary Lupul	.50	1.00
13	Kevin McCarthy	.50	1.00
14	Gerry Minor	.50	1.00
15	Darcy Rota	.50	1.00
16	Bobby Schmautz	.50	1.00
17	Stan Smyl	1.00	2.00
18	Harold Snepsts	1.50	3.00
19	Dave Williams	1.50	3.00

— 1982 - 83 POSTCARD ISSUE —

These cards are unnumbered and are listed here in alphabetical order. The cards were issued in four and six panels.

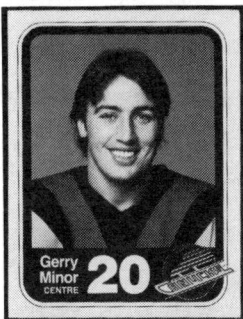

1982-83 Postcard Issue
Postcard No. 2, Gerry Minor

Team Card Size: 7 1/2" X 4 13/16"
Card Size: 3 11/16" X 4 13/16"
Face: Four colour, white border; Name, Position, Jersey number, Team
Back: Black on white card stock; Name, Position, Jersey number, Resume
Imprint: None
Complete Set No.: 23
Complete Set Price: 10.00 20.00
Common Card: .50 1.00

No.	Player	EX	NRMT
1	Yvan Boldirev	.35	.75
2	Richard Brodeur, Goalie	1.00	2.00
3	Jiri Bubla	.35	.75
4	Garth Butcher	.50	1.00
5	Ron Delorme	.35	.75
6	Ken Ellacott	.35	.75
7	Curt Fraser	.35	.75
8	Thomas Gradin	.50	1.00
9	Doug Halward	.35	.75
10	Ivan Hlinka	.35	.75
11	Moe Lemay	.35	.75
12	Rick Lanz	.35	.75
13	Lars Lindgren	.35	.75
14	Kevin McCarthy	.50	1.00
15	Gerry Minor	.35	.75
16	Lars Molin	.35	.75
17	Jim Nill	.35	.75
18	Darcy Rota	.50	1.00
19	Stan Smyl	.50	1.00
20	Harold Snepsts	.75	1.50
21	Patrick Sundstrom	.35	.75
22	Team Photo	.50	1.00
23	Dave Williams	.75	1.50

— 1983 - 84 POSTCARD ISSUE —

1983-84 Postcard Issue
Postcard No. 2, Jiri Bubla

Panel Size: 11 1/16" X 9 3/8"
Card Size: 3 11/16" X 4 3/4"
Face: Four colour, white border; Name, Position, Jersey number, Team logo
Back: Black on white card stock; Jersey number, Name, Position, Resume
Imprint: None
Complete Set No.: 4 Panels / 23 Cards
Complete Set Price: 9.00 18.00
Common Player: .35 .75

No.	Player	EX	NRMT
1	Richard Brodeur, Goalie	1.00	2.00
2	Jiri Bubla	.35	.75
3	Garth Butcher	1.00	2.00
4	Marc Crawford	.35	.75
5	Ron Delorme	.35	.75
6	John Garrett	.35	.75
7	Jere Gillis	.35	.75
8	Thomas Gradin	.75	1.50
9	Doug Halward	.35	.75
10	Mark Kirton	.35	.75
11	Rick Lanz	.50	1.00
12	Gary Lupul	.35	.75
13	Kevin McCarthy	.35	.75
14	Lars Molin	.35	.75
15	James Nill	.35	.75
16	Michel Petit	.75	1.50
17	Darcy Rota	.35	.75
18	Stan Smyl	.75	1.50
19	Harold Snepsts	1.00	2.00
20	Patrik Sundstrom	.85	1.75
21	Tony Tanti	.50	1.00
22	David Williams	.35	.75
23	1983-84 Vancouver Canucks	.50	1.00

VANCOUVER CANUCKS - TEAM SETS

— 1984 - 85 POSTCARD ISSUE —

Card Size: 3 1/4" x 4 1/4"
Face: Four colour; Name, Number
Back: Name, Number, Position, Resume
Imprint: None
Complete Set No.: 26
Complete Set Price: 10.00 20.00
Common Card: .35 .75

No.	Player	EX	NRMT
1	Air Canuck	.35	.75
2	Neil Belland	.35	.75
3	Richard Brodeur, Goalie	1.00	2.00
4	Jiri Bubla	.35	.75
5	Garth Butcher	1.00	2.00
6	Frank Caprice	.35	.75
7	Jean-Jacques Daigneault	1.00	2.00
8	Ron Delorme	.35	.75
9	John Garrett, Goalie	.35	.75
10	Thomas Gradin	.85	1.75
11	Taylor Hall	.35	.75
12	Doug Halward	.35	.75
13	Rick Lanz	.35	.75
14	Moe Lemay	.35	.75
15	Doug Lidster	1.00	2.00
16	Al MaAdam	.50	1.00
17	Peter McNab	.35	.75
18	Gary Lupul	.35	.75
19	Cam Neely	2.50	5.00
20	Michel Petit	.50	1.00
21	Darcy Rota	.35	.75
22	Petri Skriko	.35	.75
23	Stan Smyl	.50	1.00
24	Patrick Sundstrom	.50	1.00
25	Tony Tanti	.50	1.00
26	Team Photo	.50	1.00

— 1985 - 86 REGULAR ISSUE —

We have no information on this set. We would appreciate hearing from anyone who could supply further information.

— 1986 - 87 REGULAR ISSUE —

There were six cards per panel and four panels per set.

Card Size: 2 1/2" x 3 1/3"
Face: Four colour; Name, Number
Back: Name, Number, Position, Resume
Imprint: None
Complete Set No.: 24
Complete Set Price: 9.00 18.00
Common Card: .25 .50

No.	Player	EX	NRMT
1	Richard Brodeur, Goalie	.50	1.00
2	Garth Butcher	.50	1.00
3	Frank Caprice	.25	.50
4	Glen Cochrane	.25	.50
5	Craig Coxe	.35	.75
6	Taylor Hall	.25	.50
7	Stu Kulak	.25	.50
8	Rick Lanz	.25	.50
9	Moe Lemay	.25	.50
10	Doug Lidster	.35	.75
11	Dave Lowrey	.50	1.00
12	Brad Maxwell	.25	.50
13	Barry Pederson	.35	.75
14	Brent Peterson	.25	.50
15	Michel Petit	.25	.50
16	Dave Richter	.25	.50
17	Jim Sandlak	.35	.75
18	Petri Skriko	.25	.50
19	Stan Smyl	.35	.75
20	Patrick Sundstrom	.35	.75
21	Richard Sutter	.50	1.00
22	Steve Tambellini	.25	.50
23	Toni Tanti	.35	.75
24	Wendell Young, Goalie	.25	.50

— 1987 - 88 ISSUE —

Card Size: Unknown
Face: Four colour
Back: Unknown
Imprint: Unkown
Complete Set No.: 24
Complete Set Price: 7.50 15.00
Common Card: .25 .50

No.	Player	EX	NRMT
1	Greg Adams	.50	1.00
2	Jim Benning	.25	.50
3	Randy Boyd	.25	.50
4	Richard Brodeur, Goalie	.50	1.00
5	David Bruce	.25	.50
6	Garth Butcher	.35	.75
7	Frank Caprice	.25	.50
8	Craig Coxe	.35	.75
9	Willie Huber	.25	.50
10	Doug Lidster	.25	.50
11	Dave Lowrey	.50	1.00
12	Kirk McLean, Goalie	2.00	4.00
13	Larry Melnyk	.25	.50
14	Barry Pederson	.25	.50
15	Dave Richter	.25	.50
16	Jim Sanklak	.25	.50
17	David Saunders	.25	.50
18	Petri Skriko	.25	.50
19	Stan Smyl	.25	.50
20	Daryl Stanley	.25	.50
21	Richard Sutter	.50	1.00
22	Steve Tambellini	.25	.50
23	Tony Tanti	.35	.75
24	Doug Wickenheiser	.25	.50

— 1991 - 92 ISSUE —

We have no information on this set. We would appreciate hearing from anyone who could supply further information.

— 1991 - 92 AUTOGRAPHED CARDS —

We have no information on this 1991-92 autographed card set. We would appreciate hearing from anyone who could supply any further information.

— 1992 - 93 POSTCARD ISSUE —

This 25-postcard set was issued by Albalene Sales and Promotions. A very unique series that is the second of five. We have listed these postcards alphabetically.

1992-93 Road Trip
Card No. 4, Pavel Bure

Card Size: 4 3/4" x 7.0"
Face: Black and white, borderless; Number, Gold facsimile autograph
Back: Three colour card stock; Red border at top, yellow border at bottom; Name
Imprint: © 1993 Albalene Sales and Promotions Ltd.,
Complete Set No.: 25
Complete Set Price: 10.00 20.00
Common Card: .25 .50

No.	Player	EX	NRMT
1	Greg Adams	.25	.50
2	Shawn Antoski	.25	.50
3	David Babych	.25	.50
4	Pavel Bure	2.50	5.00
5	Geoff Courtnall	.75	1.50
6	Robert Dirk	.25	.50
7	Gerald Diduck	.25	.50
8	Thomas Fergus	.25	.50
9	Robert Kron	.25	.50
10	Doug Lidster	.25	.50
11	Trevor Linden	1.50	3.00
12	Jyrki Lumme	.25	.50
13	Kirk McLean, Goalie	1.50	3.00
14	Sergio Momesso	.25	.50
15	Dana Murzyn	.25	.50
16	Petr Nedved	1.00	2.00
17	Gino Odjick	.25	.50
18	Adrien Plavsic	.25	.50
19	Cliff Ronning	.75	1.50
20	Jim Sandlak	.25	.50
21	Jiri Slegr	.50	1.00
22	Garry Valk	.25	.50
23	Ryan Walter	.25	.50
24	Dixon Ward	.75	1.50
25	Kay Whitmore, Goalie	.25	.50

ROYAL BANK

— 1970 - 71 POSTCARD ISSUE —

This set features the Canuck's Player of the Week. The posters are unnumbered and are listed in here in alphabetical order. This set is not complete. Any information collectors may have regarding this issue would be greatly appreciated.

Royal Bank 1970-71 Leo's Leaders
Card No. 12, Dunc Wilson

Poster Size: 5" X 7"
Face: Black and white photo; Facsimile autograph, Team logo
Back: Blank
Imprint: None
Complete Set No.: 20
Complete Set Price: 20.00 40.00
Common Player: 1.50 3.00

No.	Player	EX	NRMT
1	Ray Allen	1.50	3.00
2	Mike Corrigan	1.50	3.00
3	Gary Doak	1.50	3.00
4	Murray Hall, Goalie	1.50	3.00
5	Orland Kurtenbach	1.50	3.00
6	Wayne Maki	1.50	3.00
7	Rosaire Paiement	1.50	3.00
8	Poul Popiel	1.50	3.00
9	Marc Reaume	1.50	3.00
10	Darryl Sly	1.50	3.00
11	Ted Taylor	1.50	3.00
12	Dunc Wilson, Goalie	1.50	3.00

— 1971 - 72 POSTCARD ISSUE —

These posters are unnumbered and are listed here in alphabetical order. This set is not be complete. Any information collectors may have regarding this issue would be greatly appreciated.

Royal Bank, 1971-72 Leo's Leaders
Card No. 1, Bobby Lalonde

Poster Size: 5" X 7"
Face: Black and white photo; Number, Facsimile autograph, Team and sponsor logos
Back: Blank
Imprint: None
Complete Set No.: 20
Complete Set Price: 20.00 40.00
Common Player: 1.25 2.50

No.	Player	EX	NRMT
1	Bobby Lalonde	1.25	2.50
2	Murray Hall, Goalie	1.25	2.50
3	Jocelyn Guevremont	1.25	2.50
4	Pat Quinn	1.75	3.50
5	Orland Kurtenbach	1.25	2.50
6	Poul Popiel	1.25	2.50
7	Ron Ward	1.25	2.50
8	Rosaire Paiement	1.25	2.50
9	Dale Tallon	1.25	2.50
10	Bobby Schmautz	1.25	2.50
11	Dennis Kearns	1.25	2.50
12	Barry Wilkins	1.25	2.50
13	Dunc Wilson, Goalie	1.75	3.50
14	Andre Boudrias	1.25	2.50
15	Ted Taylor	1.25	2.50
16	George Gardner, Goalie	1.25	2.50
17	John Schella	1.25	2.50
18	Wayne Maki	1.25	2.50
19	Unknown	1.25	2.50
20	Unknown	1.25	2.50

— 1972 - 73 POSTCARD ISSUE —

These posters are unnumbered and are listed here in alphabetical order. This set is not be complete. Any information collectors may have regarding this issue would be greatly appreciated.

Royal Bank, 1972-73 Leo's Leaders
Card No. 2, Gary Smith

Poster Size: 5" X 7"
Face: Four colour, white border; Facsimile autograph, Team logo
Back: Blank
Imprint: None
Complete Set No.: 21
Complete Set Price: 17.50 35.00
Common Player: 1.00 2.00

No.	Player	EX	NRMT
1	Dennis Kearns	1.00	2.00
2	Gary Smith, Goalie	1.25	2.50

— 1973 - 74 POSTCARD ISSUE —

This set features the Canuck's Player of the Week. The posters are unnumbered and are listed here in alphabetical order. This set is not be complete. Any information collectors may have regarding this issue would be greatly appreciated.

Royal Bank, 1973-74 Leo's Leaders
Card No. 1, Andre Boudrias

Poster Size: 5" X 7"
Face: Four colour, white border; Facsimile autograph, Team logo
Back: Blank
Imprint: None
Complete Set No.: 21
Complete Set Price: 15.00 30.00
Common Player: 1.00 2.00

No.	Player	EX	NRMT
1	Andre Boudrias	1.00	2.00
2	James Hargreaves	1.00	2.00
3	Bryan McSheffrey	1.00	2.00
4	Gerry O'Flaherty	1.00	2.00
5	Dave Tallon	1.00	2.00
6	Dunc Wilson, Goalie	1.50	3.00
7	John Wright	1.00	2.00

— 1974 - 75 POSTCARD ISSUE —

This set features the Royal Leaders Player of the Week. The posters are unnumbered are are listed here in alphabetical order.

Poster Size: 5" X 7"
Face: Four colour, white border; Facsimile autograph, Team and sponsor logos
Back: Blank
Imprint: None
Complete Set No.: 20
Complete Set Price: 15.00 30.00
Common Player: 1.00 2.00

No.	Player	EX	NRMT
1	Paulin Bordeleau	1.00	2.00
2	Andre Boudrias	1.00	2.00
3	Bob Dailey	1.00	2.00
4	Ab DeMarco	1.00	2.00
5	John Gould	1.00	2.00
6	John Grisdale	1.00	2.00
7	Dennis Kearns	1.00	2.00
8	Don Lever	1.00	2.00
9	Ken Lockett	1.00	2.00
10	Garry Monahan	1.00	2.00
11	Gerry O'Flaherty	1.00	2.00
12	Chris Oddleifson	1.00	2.00
13	Tracy Pratt	1.25	2.50
14	Mike Robitaille	1.00	2.00
15	Leon Rochefort	1.00	2.00
16	Gary Smith, Goalie	1.25	2.50
17	Dennis Ververgaert	1.00	2.00

— 1975 - 76 POSTCARD ISSUE —

These posters are unnumbered and are listed here in alphabetical order. This set is not be complete. Any information collectors may have regarding this issue would be greatly appreciated.

Royal Bank, 1975-76 Royal Leaders
Card No. 20, Dennis Ververgaert

Poster Size: 4 3/4" X 7 1/4"
Face: Four colour, white border; Facsimile autograph, Team and sponsor logos
Back: Blank
Imprint: None
Complete Set No.: 22
Complete Set Price: 12.50 25.00
Common Player: .75 1.50

No.	Player	EX	NRMT
1	Rick Blight	.75	1.50
2	Gregg Boddy	.75	1.50
3	Paulin Bordeleau	.75	1.50
4	Andre Boudrias	.75	1.50
5	Bob Dailey	.75	1.50
6	Ab DeMarco	.75	1.50
7	John Gould	.75	1.50
8	John Grisdale	.75	1.50
9	Bobby Lalonde	.75	1.50
10	Don Lever	1.00	2.00
11	Garry Monahan	.75	1.50
12	Bob J. Murray	.75	1.50
13	Chris Oddleifson	.75	1.50
14	Gerry O'Flaherty	.75	1.50
15	Tracy Platt	.75	1.50
16	Mike Robitaille	.75	1.50
17	Ron Sedlbauer	.75	1.50
18	Gary Smith, Goalie	.75	1.50
19	Harold Snepsts	2.50	5.00
20	Dennis Ververgaert	1.00	2.00
21	Unknown		
22	Unknown		

— 1976 - 77 POSTCARD ISSUE —

These posters are unnumbered and are listed here in alphabetical order.

Royal Bank, 1976-77 Royal Leaders
Card No. 11, Garry Monahan

644 • VANCOUVER CANUCKS - TEAM SETS

Poster Size: 4 3/4" X 7 1/4"
Face: Four colour, white border; Facsimile autograph, Team and sponsor logos
Back: Blank
Imprint: None
Complete Set No.: 23
Complete Set Price: 12.50 25.00
Common Card: .75 1.50

No.	Player	EX	NRMT
1	Rick Blight	.75	1.50
2	Bob Dailey	.75	1.50
3	Dave Fortier	.75	1.50
4	Brad Gassoff	.75	1.50
5	John Gould	.75	1.50
6	John Grisdale	.75	1.50
7	Dennis Kearns	.75	1.50
8	Bobby Lalonde	.75	1.50
9	Don Lever	.75	1.50
10	Cesare Maniago, Goalie	1.50	3.00
11	Garry Monahan	.75	1.50
12	Bob J. Murray	.75	1.50
13	Chris Oddleifson	.75	1.50
14	Gerry O'Flaherty	.75	1.50
15	Curt Ridley, Goalie	.75	1.50
16	Mike Robitaille	.75	1.50
17	Ron Sedlbauer	.75	1.50
18	Harold Snepsts	2.00	4.00
19	Andy Spruce	.75	1.50
20	Ralph Stewart	.75	1.50
21	Dennis Ververgaert	.75	1.50
22	Mike Walton	.75	1.50
23	Jim Wiley	.75	1.50

— 1977 - 78 POSTCARD ISSUE —

These posters are unnumbered and are listed here in alphabetical order. This set is not complete. Any information collectors may have regarding this issue would be greatly appreciated.

Poster Size: 4 1/4" X 5 1/2"
Face: Four colour, white border; Facsimile autograph, Team and sponsor logos
Back: Blank
Imprint: None
Complete Set No.: 21
Complete Set Price: 12.50 25.00
Common Card: .75 1.50

No.	Player	EX	NRMT
1	Rick Blight	.75	1.50
2	Rob Flockhart	.75	1.50
3	Brad Gassoff	.75	1.50
4	Jere Gillis	.75	1.50
5	John Grisdale	.75	1.50
6	Dennis Kearns	.75	1.50
7	Don Lever	.75	1.50
8	Cesare Maniago, Goalie	1.25	2.50
9	Jack McIlhargey	.75	1.50
10	Garry Monahan	.75	1.50
11	Chris Oddleifson	.75	1.50
12	Curt Ridley, Goalie	.75	1.50
13	Harold Snepsts	1.50	3.00
14	Mike Walton	.75	1.50

— 1978 - 79 POSTCARD ISSUE —

Royal Bank, 1978-79 Royal Leaders,
Card No. 1, Rick Blight

These posters are unnumbered and are listed here in alphabetical order. This set is not complete. Any information you may have regarding this issue would be greatly appreciated.

Card Size: 4 1/4" X 5 1/2"
Face: Four colour, white border; Facsimile autograph, Team and sponsor logos
Back: Black on white card stock; Name, Resume, Team logo
Imprint: None
Complete Set No.: 22
Complete Set Price: 12.50 25.00
Common Card: .65 1.25

No.	Player	EX	NRMT
1	Rick Blight	.65	1.25
2	Gary Bromley	.65	1.25
3	Bill Derlago	.85	1.75
4	Rolie Eriksson	.65	1.25
5	Curt Fraser	.65	1.25
6	Jere Gillis	.65	1.25
7	Thomas Gradin	1.00	2.00
8	Hilliard Graves	.65	1.25
9	John Grisdale	.65	1.25
10	Glen Hanlon, Goalie	1.25	2.50
11	Randy Holt	.65	1.25
12	Dennis Kearns	.65	1.25
13	Don Lever	.65	1.25
14	Lars Lindgren	.65	1.25
15	Bob Manno	.65	1.25
16	Pit Martin	.65	1.25
17	Jack McIlhargey	.65	1.25
18	Chris Oddleifson	.65	1.25
19	Ron Sedlbauer	.75	1.50
20	Stan Smyl	.65	1.25
21	Harold Snepsts	1.25	2.50
22	Dennis Ververgaert	.65	1.25

NALLEY'S BOX

— 1972 - 73 ISSUE —

We have no information on this set. We would appreciate hearing from anyone who could supply further information.

POLICE SET

— 1979 - 80 ISSUE —

We have no information on this set. We would appreciate hearing from anyone who could supply further information.

SILVERWOOD DAIRIES

— 1980 - 81 REGULAR ISSUE —

This set has three unnumbered cards per panel. The cards are listed here in alphabetical order.

Silverwood Dairies, 1980-81 Issue
Panel No. 1, T. Gradin, D. Kearns, B. Ashton

Panel Size: 7 3/8" X 4 1/8"
Card Size: 2 7/16" X 4 1/8"
Face: Four colour, white border; Jersey number, Name, Team logo
Back: Black on white card stock; Name, Resume, Facsimile autograph
Imprint: None
Complete Set No.: 8 Panels / 24 Cards
Complete Set Price: 16.00 32.00
Common Card: .75 1.50

No.	Player	EX	NRMT
1	Brent Ashton	1.00	2.00
2	Ivan Boldirev	1.10	2.25
3	Per-Olov Brasar	.75	1.50
4	Richard Brodeur, Goalie	1.75	3.50
5	Gary Bromley	.75	1.50
6	Jerry Butler	.75	1.50
7	Colin Campbell	.75	1.50
8	Curt Fraser	.75	1.50
9	Thomas Gradin	1.25	2.50
10	Glen Hanlon, Goalie	.75	1.50
11	Dennis Kearns	.75	1.50
12	Rick Lanz	.75	1.50
13	Lars Lindgren	.75	1.50
14	Dave Logan	.75	1.50
15	Gary Lupul	.75	1.50
16	Bob Manno	.75	1.50
17	Kevin McCarthy	.75	1.50
18	Gerry Minor	.75	1.50
19	Kevin Primeau	.75	1.50
20	Darcy Rota	1.00	2.00
21	Bobby Schmautz	.75	1.50
22	Stan Smyl	1.00	2.00
23	Harold Snepsts	1.00	2.00
24	David Williams	.75	1.50

PANELS

No.	Player	EX	NRMT
1	Thomas Gradin; Dennis Kearns; Brent Ashton	3.00	6.00
2	Glen Hanlon, Goalie; Per-Olov Brasar; Colin Campbell	2.25	4.50
3	Rick Lanz; Darcy Rota; Gerry Minor	2.75	5.50
4	Kevin McCarthy; Richard Brodeur, Goalie; Gary Lupul	3.50	7.00
5	Bobby Schmautz; Curt Fraser; Dave Logan	2.25	4.50
6	Stan Smyl; Jerry Butler; Bob Manno	2.25	4.50
7	Harold Snepsts; Ivan Boldirev; Gary Bromley	3.00	6.00
8	David Williams; Lars Lingren; Kevin Primeau	2.25	4.50

— 1981 - 82 REGULAR ISSUE —

This set has three unnumbered cards per panel. The cards are listed here alphabetical order.

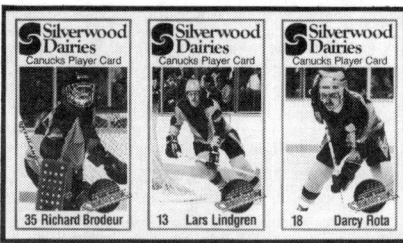

Silverwood Dairies, 1981-82 Issue
Panel No. 1, R. Brodeur, L. Lindgren, D. Rota

Panel Size: 7 3/8" X 4 1/8"
Card Size: 2 7/16" X 4 1/8"
Face: Four colour, white border; Jersy number, Name, Team logo
Back: Blank on white card stock; Name, Resume, Facsimile autograph
Imprint: None
Complete Set No.: 8 Panels / 24 Cards
Complete Set Price: 12.50 25.00
Common Card: .50 1.00

No.	Player	EX	NRMT
1	Ivan Boldirev	.50	1.00
2	Per-Olov Brasar	.50	1.00
3	Richard Brodeur, Goalie	1.50	3.00
4	Jiri Bubla	.50	1.00
5	Jerry Butler	.50	1.00
6	Colin Campbell	.50	1.00
7	Marc Crawford	.50	1.00
8	Anders Eldebrink	.50	1.00
9	Curt Fraser	.50	1.00
10	Thomas Gradin	1.00	2.00
11	Doug Halward	.50	1.00

VANCOUVER CANUCKS - TEAM SETS • 645

No.	Player	EX	NRMT
12	Glen Hanlon, Goalie	.85	1.75
13	Ivan Hlinka	.50	1.00
14	Rick Lanz	.75	1.50
15	Lars Lindgren	.50	1.00
16	Gary Lupul	.50	1.00
17	Blair MacDonald	.50	1.00
18	Kevin McCarthy	.50	1.00
19	Gerry Minor	.50	1.00
20	Lars Molin	.50	1.00
21	Darcy Rota	.50	1.00
22	Stan Smyl	.50	1.00
23	Harold Snepsts	1.00	2.00
24	David Williams	.75	1.50

PANELS

No.	Player	EX	NRMT
1	Richard Brodeur, Goalie; Lars Lindgren, Darcy Rota	3.00	6.00
2	Thomas Gradin; Jiri Bubla; Blair MacDonald	2.00	4.00
3	Glen Hanlon, Goalie; Harold Snepsts; Gerry Minor	2.00	4.00
4	Ivan Hlinka; Jerry Butler; Doug Halward	1.75	3.50
5	Rick Lanz; Curt Fraser; Marc Crawford	1.75	3.50
6	Kevin McCarthy; Ivan Boldirev; Lars Molin	2.00	4.00
7	Stan Smyl; Colin Campbell; Per-Olov Braser	2.00	4.00
8	David Williams; Anders Eldebrink; Gary Lupul	2.00	4.00

SHELL OIL

— 1986 - 1987 ISSUE —

We have no information on this set. We would appreciate hearing from anyone who could supply further information.

— 1987 - 88 REGULAR ISSUE —

This issue features three player cards and one $5 coupon per panel.

Shell Oil, 1987-88 Issue
Card No. 1, Gregory Adams

Card Size: 2 1/2" X 3 1/2"
Face: Four colour, white border; Team and sponsor logos, Name, Position
Back: Black on white card stock; Name, Position, Resume
Imprint: None
Complete Set No.: 8 Panels / 24 cards
Complete Set Price: 5.00 10.00
Common Player: .13 .25

No.	Player	EX	NRMT
1	Gregory Adams	.50	1.00
2	Jim Benning	.13	.25
3	Randy Boyd	.13	.25
4	Richard Brodeur, Goalie	.25	.50
5	David Bruce	.13	.25
6	Garth Butcher	.25	.50
7	Frank Caprice, Goalie	.13	.25
8	Craig Coxe	.13	.25
9	Willie Huber	.13	.25
10	Doug Lidster	.13	.25
11	Dave Lowry	.13	.25
12	Kirk McLean, Goalie	1.50	3.00
13	Larry Melnyk	.13	.25
14	Barry Pederson	.25	.50
15	Dave Richter	.13	.25
16	Jim Sandlak	.13	.25
17	David Saunders	.13	.25
18	Petri Skriko	.25	.50
19	Stan Smyl	.50	1.00
20	Daryl Stanley	.13	.25
21	Richard Sutter	.25	.50
22	Steve Tambellini	.13	.25
23	Tony Tanti	.25	.50
24	Douglas Wickenheiser	.13	.25

PANELS

No.	Player	EX	NRMT
1	Randy Boyd; Jim Benning; Greg Adams	.75	1.50
2	Garth Butcher; David Bruce, Richard Brodeur, Goalie	.75	1.50
3	Willie Huber; Craig Coxe; Frank Caprice	.75	1.50
4	Dave Lowry; Doug Lidster; Kirk McLean, Goalie	2.00	4.00
5	Dave Richter; Barry Pederson; Larry Melnyk	.75	1.50
6	Petri Skriko; Dave Saunders; Jim Sandlak	.75	1.50
7	Rich Sutter; Daryl Stanley; Stan Smyl	.75	1.50
8	Douglas Wickenheiser; Tony Tanti; Steve Tambellini	.75	1.50

MOHAWK

— 1988 - 89 REGULAR ISSUE —

These cards are unnumbered and are listed here in alphabetical order.

Card Size: 2 1/2" X 3 1/2"
Face: Four colour, white border; Jersey number, Name, Position, Team and sponsor logos
Back: Blank
Imprint: None
Complete Set No.: 6 Panels / 24 Cards
Complete Set Price: 6.00 12.00
Common Player: .25 .50

No.	Player	EX	NRMT
1	Gregory Adams	.35	.75
2	Jim Benning	.25	.50
3	Kenneth Berry	.25	.50
4	Randy Boyd	.25	.50
5	Steve Bozek	.25	.50
6	Brian Bradley	.25	.50
7	David Bruce	.25	.50
8	Garth Butcher	.35	.75
9	Kevan Guy	.25	.50
10	Doug Lidster	.25	.50
11	Trevor Linden	1.00	2.00
12	Kirk McLean, Goalie	1.25	2.50
13	Larry Melnyk	.25	.50
14	Robert Nordmark	.25	.50
15	Barry Pederson	.25	.50
16	Paul Reinhart	.35	.75
17	Jim Sandlak	.25	.50
18	Petri Skriko	.35	.75
19	Stan Smyl	.35	.75
20	Harold Snepsts	.35	.75
21	Ronald Stern	.25	.50
22	Richard Sutter	.35	.75
23	Tony Tanti	.35	.75
24	Stephen Weeks, Goalie	.35	.75

— 1989 - 90 REGULAR ISSUE —

This issue commemorates the Canucks' 20th Anniversary in the NHL. The cards are unnumbered and are listed here in alphabetical order.

Card Size: 2 1/2" X 3 1/2"
Face: Four colour, white border; Jersey number, Name, Position, Team and sponsor logos
Back: Blank
Imprint: None
Complete Set No.: 6 Panels / 24 Cards
Complete Set Price: 10.00 20.00
Common Player: .25 .50

No.	Player	EX	NRMT
1	Gregory Adams	.50	1.00
2	Jim Benning	.25	.50
3	Steve Bozek	.25	.50
4	Brian Bradley	.50	1.00
5	Garth Butcher	.50	1.00
6	Craig Coxe	.25	.50
7	Vladimir Krutov	.25	.50
8	Igor Larionov	.75	1.50
9	Doug Lidster	.50	1.00
10	Trevor Linden	1.25	2.50
11	Kirk McLean, Goalie	1.00	2.00
12	Larry Melnyk	.25	.50
13	Robert Nordmark	.25	.50
14	Barry Pederson	.25	.50
15	Paul Reinhart	.35	.75
16	Jim Sandlak	.25	.50
17	Petri Skriko	.35	.75
18	Douglas Smith	.25	.50
19	Stan Smyl	.50	1.00
20	Harold Snepsts	.50	1.00
21	Daryl Stanley	.25	.50
22	Richard Sutter	.35	.75
23	Tony Tanti	.35	.75
24	Stephen Weeks, Goalie	.35	.75

— 1990 - 91 REGULAR ISSUE —

Card Size: 2 1/2" x 3 1/2"
Face: Name, Position, Team logo
Back: Name, Jersey number, Resume
Imprint: None
Complete Set No.: 27
Complete Set Price: 8.00 16.00
Common Card: .25 .50

No.	Player	EX	NRMT
1	Jim Agnew	.25	.50
2	Steve Bozek	.35	.75
3	Garth Butcher	.35	.75
4	Dave Capuano	.35	.75
5	Craig Coxe	.35	.75
6	Gerald Diduck	.25	.50
7	Don Gibson	.25	.50
8	Kevin Guy	.25	.50
9	Ronald Kron	.25	.50
10	Tom Kurvers	.35	.75
11	Igor Larionov	1.00	2.00
12	Doug Lidster	.50	1.00
13	Trevor Linden	1.50	3.00
14	Jyrki Lumme	.50	1.00
15	Jay Mazur	.25	.50
16	Andrew McBain	.25	.50
17	Kirk McLean, Goalie	1.50	3.00
18	Rob Murphy	.25	.50
19	Petr Nedved	1.00	2.00
20	Robert Nordmark	.25	.50
21	Gino Odjick	.50	1.00
22	Adrien Plavsic	.25	.50
23	Dan Quinn	.25	.50
24	Jim Sandlak	.25	.50
25	Stan Smyl	.35	.75
26	Ronald Stern	.25	.50
27	Garry Valk	.25	.50

MOLSON

— 1990 - 91 ISSUE —

— 1991 - 92 ISSUE —

We have no information on these sets. We would appreciate hearing from anyone who could supply further information.

VANCOUVER MILLIONAIRS - TEAM SETS

— 1919 POSTCARD ISSUE —

These postcards are unnumbered and are listed below in alphabetical order.

Card Size: 3 1/3" X 5 1/2"
Face: Black and white
Back: Black on card stock; Postcard notation
Imprint: None
Complete Set No.: 18
Complete Set Price: 265.00   525.00
Common Card: 15.00   30.00

REGULAR ISSUE

No.	Player	EX	NRMT
1	Lloyd Cook	15.00	30.00
2	Art Duncan	15.00	30.00
3	F. (Smokey) Harris	15.00	30.00
4	Alex Irvin	15.00	30.00
5	Hughie Lehman, Goalie	15.00	30.00
6	Duncan (Mickey) MacKay	15.00	30.00
7	Barney Stanley	20.00	40.00
8	Fred (Cyclone) Taylor	30.00	60.00
9	C. Uksila	15.00	30.00

CARICATURES

No.	Player	EX	NRMT
10	Lloyd Cook	15.00	30.00
11	Art Duncan	15.00	30.00
12	F. (Smokey) Harris	15.00	30.00
13	Alex Irvin	15.00	30.00
14	Hughie Lehman, Goalie	15.00	30.00
15	Duncan (Mickey) MacKay	15.00	30.00
16	Barney Stanley	20.00	40.00
16	Fred (Cyclone) Taylor	30.00	60.00
18	C. Uksila	15.00	30.00

Vancouver Millionairs
1919 Postcard Issue
Postcard No. 5, Hughie Lehman

Vancouver Millionairs
1919 Postcard Issue
Postcard No. 5, Hughie Lehman

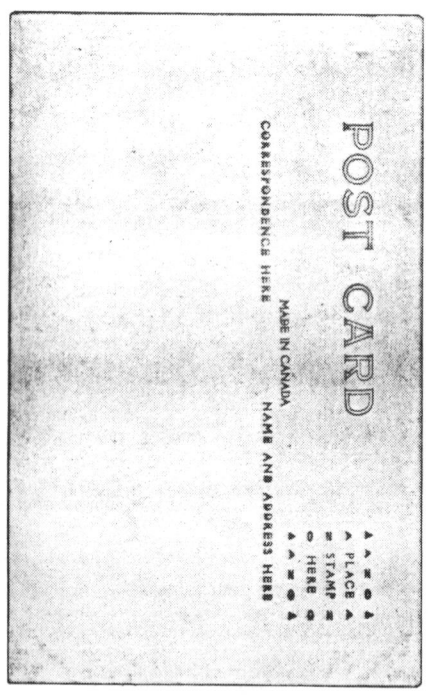

Vancouver Millionairs
1919 Postcard Issue
Postcard Back

Vancouver Millionairs
1919 Postcard Issue
Postcard No. 17, Fred (Cyclone) Taylor

Vancouver Millionairs
1919 Postcard Issue
Postcard No. 17, Fred (Cyclone) Taylor

WASHINGTON CAPITALS - TEAM SETS

TEAM ISSUES

POSTCARD ISSUE

We have no information on this set. We would appreciate hearing from anyone who could supply further information.

Card Size: 5" x 7"
Face: Black and white, white border; Name; Position; Number; Team logo
Back: Blank
Imprint: None
Complete Set No.: Unknown
Complete Set Price: Unknown

No.	Player	EX	NRMT
1	Michael Gartner	2.50	5.00

— 1978 - 79 POSTCARD ISSUE —

We have no information on this set. We would appreciate hearing from anyone who could supply further information.

— 1979 - 80 POSTCARD ISSUE —

The cards are unnumbered and are listed below in alphabetical order. This set is not complete. Any information collectors may have regarding this set would be greatly appreciated.

1979-80 Postcard Issue
Postcard No. 1, Pierre Bouchard

Card Size: 5 1/4" X 7 7/8"
Face: Black and white photos; Team logo, Name, Position, Jersey number
Back: Blank
Imprint: None
Complete Set No.: 23
Complete Set Price: 10.00 20.00
Common Player Price: .50 1.00

No.	Player	EX	NRMT
1	Pierre Bouchard	.50	1.00
2	Guy Charron	.50	1.00
3	Rolf Edberg	.50	1.00
4	Michael Gartner	2.00	4.00
5	Rick Green	.50	1.00
6	Bengt Gustafsson	.50	1.00
7	Dennis Hextall	.50	1.00
8	Gary Inness	.50	1.00
9	Yvon Labre	.50	1.00
10	Antero Lehtonen	.50	1.00
11	Mark Lofthouse	.50	1.00
12	Paul MacKinnon	.50	1.00
13	Dennis Maruk	.50	1.00
14	Paul Mulvey	.50	1.00
15	Robert Picard	.50	1.00
16	Greg Polis	.50	1.00
17	Errol Rausse	.50	1.00
18	Tom Rowe	.50	1.00
19	Peter Scamurra	.50	1.00
20	Bob Sirois	.50	1.00
21	Wayne Syephenson	.50	1.00
22	Leif Svensson	.50	1.00
23	Ryan Walter	.50	1.00

— 1979 - 80 ISSUE —

We have no information on this 1979-80 set. We would appreciate hearing from anyone who could supply any further information.

— 1980 - 81 POSTCARD ISSUE —

Card Size: 5" x 7"
Face: Black and white; Name, Number, Position
Back: Blank
Imprint: None
Complete Set No.: 24
Complete Set Price: 9.00 18.00
Common Card: .35 .75

No.	Player	EX	NRMT
1	Pierre Bouchard	.35	.75
2	Guy Charron	.35	.75
3	Rolf Edberg	.35	.75
4	Michael Gartner	2.50	5.00
5	Gary Green	.35	.75
6	Rick Green	1.00	2.00
7	Bengt Gustafsson	.75	.150
8	Alan Hangsleben	.35	.75
9	Nes Jarvis	.35	.75
10	Bob Kelly	.35	.75
11	Yvon Labre	.35	.75
12	Bill Mahoney	.35	.75
13	Dennis Maruk	.75	1.50
14	Paul McKinnon	.35	.75
15	Paul Mulvey	.35	.75
16	Mike Palmateer, Goalie	.50	1.00
17	Jean Pronovost	.35	.75
18	Pat Ribble	.35	.75
19	Rick Smith	.35	.75
20	Wayne Stephenson, Goalie	.50	1.00
21	Darren Veitch	.75	1.50
22	Dennis Ververgaer	.35	.75
23	Howard Walker	.35	.75
24	Ryan Walter	1.25	2.50

— 1981 - 82 POSTCARD ISSUE —

Card Size: 5" x 7"
Face: Black and white; Name, Number, Position
Back: Blank
Imprint: None
Complete Set No.: 20
Complete Set Price: 9.00 18.00
Common Card: .35 .75

No.	Player	EX	NRMT
1	Timo Blomavist	.35	.75
2	Robert Carpenter	1.00	2.00
3	Glenn Currie	.35	.75
4	Gaetan Duchesne	1.00	2.00
5	Michael Gartner	2.00	4.00
6	Bob Gould	.35	.75
7	Rick Green	.50	1.00
8	Randy Holt	.35	.75
9	Al Jensen, Goalie	.35	.75
10	Dennis Maruk	.50	1.00
11	Terry Murray	.35	.75
12	Lee Norwood	.60	1.25
13	Mike Palmateer, Goalie	.60	1.25
14	Dave Parro	.35	.75
15	Torrie Robertson	.35	.75
16	Greg Theberge	.35	.75
17	Chris Valentine	.35	.75
18	Darren Veitch	.50	1.00
19	Ryan Walter	.50	1.00
20	Doug Hicks	.35	.75

— 1982 - 83 POSTCARD ISSUE —

Card Size: 5" x 7"
Face: Black and white; Name, Number, Position
Back: Blank
Imprint: None
Complete Set No.: 25
Complete Set Price: 7.50 15.00
Common Card: .35 .75

No.	Player	EX	NRMT
1	Timo Blomqvist	.35	.75
2	Ted Bulley	.35	.75
3	Robert Carpenter	.75	1.50
4	Glen Currie	.35	.75
5	Brian Engblom	.35	.75
6	Michael Gartner	1.75	3.50
7	Bob Gould	.35	.75
8	Bengt Gustafsson	.50	1.00
9	Alan Haworth	.35	.75
10	Randy Holt	.35	.75
11	Ken Houston	.35	.75
12	Doug Jarvis	.60	1.25
13	Rod Langway	1.50	3.00
14	Craig Laughlin	.35	.75
15	Dennis Maruk	.50	1.00
16	Bryan Murray	.35	.75
17	Terry Murray	.35	.75
18	Lee Norwood	.35	.75
19	Milan Novi	.35	.75
20	Dave Parro	.35	.75
21	David Poile	.35	.75
22	Pat Riggin, Goalie	.35	.75
23	Scott Stevens	2.00	4.00
24	Chris Valentine	.35	.75
25	Daren Veitch	.35	.75

— 1990 - 91 POSTCARD ISSUE —

Card Size: Unknown
Face: Four colour
Back: Four colour
Imprint: None
Complete Set No.: 23
Complete Set Price: 8.00 16.00
Common Player: .25 .50

No.	Player	EX	NRMT
1	Donald Beaupre, Goalie	.50	1.00
2	David Christian	.35	.75
3	Dino Ciccarelli	.50	1.00
4	Yvon Corriveau	.50	1.00
5	Geoff Courtnall	.35	.75
6	Kevin Hatcher	.75	1.50
7	Bill Houlder	.25	.50
8	Dale Hunter	.50	1.00
9	Calle Johansson	.35	.75
10	Doug Wickenheiser	.25	.50
11	Nickolas (Nick) Kypreos	.25	.50
12	Scott Kleinendorst	.25	.50
13	Rod Langway	.50	1.00
14	Stephen Leach	.50	1.00
15	Bob Mason, Goalie	.25	.50
16	Kelly Miller	.35	.75
17	Michal Pivonka	.50	1.00
18	Mike Ridley	.25	.50

648 • WASHINGTON CAPITALS - TEAM SETS

No.	Player	EX	NRMT
19	Robert (Bob) Rouse	.25	.50
20	Neil Sheehy	.25	.50
21	Scott Stevens	1.00	2.00
22	Unknown	.25	.50
23	Unknown	.25	.50

PIZZA HUT

— 1984 - 85 ISSUE —

We have no information on this set. We would appreciate hearing from anyone who could supply further information.

— 1985 - 86 ISSUE —

We have no information on this set. We would appreciate hearing from anyone who could supply further information.

KODAK

— 1986 - 87 REGULAR ISSUE —

These cards are unnumbered and are listed here in alphabetical order.

Kodak, 1986-87 Issue
Card No. 1, Gregorary Adams
Card No. 2, John Barrett

Card Size: 2" X 2 5/8"
Face: Four colour; Name, Resume
Back: Black on white card stock
Imprint: None
Photo Size: 10" X 8"
Face: Four colour, Team photo, Team
Back: Black on white card stock
Imprint: None
Complete Set No.: 26
Complete Set Price: 15.00 30.00
Common Card: .35 .75

No.	Player	EX	NRMT
1	Gregory Adams	.50	1.00
2	John Barrett	.35	.75
3	John Blum	.35	.75

No.	Player	EX	NRMT
4	David Christian	.50	1.00
5	Bob Crawford	.35	.75
6	Gaetan Duchesne	.35	.75
7	Lou Franceschetti	.35	.75
8	Michael Gartner	2.00	4.00
9	Robert Gould	.35	.75
10	Jeff Greenlaw	.35	.75
11	Kevin Hatcher	1.00	2.00
12	Alan Haworth	.35	.75
13	David Jensen	.35	.75
14	Rod Langway	1.00	2.00
15	Craig Laughlin	.35	.75
16	Bob Mason, Goalie	.50	1.00
17	Kelly Miller	.50	1.00
18	Lawrence Murphy	.75	1.50
19	Bryan Murray, Coach	.50	1.00
20	Peter Peeters, Goalie	.50	1.00
21	Michal Pivonka	1.00	2.00
22	Mike Ridley	.50	1.00
23	Gary Sampson	.35	.75
24	Greg Smith	.35	.75
25	Scott Stevens	1.50	3.00
26	Team Photo	2.50	5.00

— 1987 - 88 REGULAR ISSUE —

Card Size: 2 3/16" X 2 15/16"
Face: Four colour; Jersey number, Name, Position, Team logo
Back: Jersey number, Name, Position, Resume
Imprint: None
Complete Set No.: 25
Complete Set Price: 12.50 25.00
Common Card: .25 .50

No.	Player	EX	NRMT
1	Gregory Adams	.50	1.00
2	John Barrett	.35	.75
3	David Christian	.35	.75
4	Lou Franceschetti	.25	.50
5	Garry Galley	.25	.50
6	Michael Gartner	1.50	3.00
7	Robert Gould	.25	.50
8	Bengt-ake Gustafsson	.25	.50
9	Kevin Hatcher	1.00	2.00
10	Bill Houlder	.25	.50
11	Dale Hunter	.25	.50
12	Edward Kastelic	.25	.50
13	Rod Langway	.50	1.00
14	Craig Laughlin	.25	.50
15	Clint Malarchuk, Goalie	.35	.75
16	Kelly Miller	.25	.50
17	Lawrence Murphy	.50	1.00
18	Bryan Murray, Coach	.35	.75
19	Peter Peeters, Goalie	.60	1.25
20	Michal Pivonka	.50	1.00
21	David Poile, Vice-President / General Manager	.25	.50
22	Mike Ridley	.35	.75
23	Greg Smith	.25	.50
24	Scott Stevens	1.00	2.00
25	Peter Sundstrom	.35	.75

— 1989 - 90 REGULAR ISSUE —

This set was issued in three sheets 11" x 8 1/4". It was sponsored by Kodak and W. Bell and Co. The cards are unnumbered are listed here in alphabetical order.

Card Size: 2 3/16" X 2 1/2"
Face: Four colour; Jersey number, Name, Position, Team logo
Back: Jersey number, Name, Position, Resume
Imprint: None
Complete Set No.: 25
Complete Set Price: 10.00 20.00
Common Card: .25 .50

No.	Player	EX	NRMT
1	Donald Beaupre, Goalie	.50	1.00
2	Tim Bergland	.25	.50
3	Dino Ciccarelli	.60	1.25
4	Geoff Courtnall	.60	1.25
5	John Druce	.50	1.00

No.	Player	EX	NRMT
6	Kevin Hatcher	.65	1.25
7	Dale Hunter	.25	.50
8	Calle Johansson	.25	.50
9	Robert Joyce	.35	.75
10	Scot Kleinendorst	.25	.50
11	Rob Laird, Assistant Coach	.25	.50
12	Rod Langway	.50	1.00
13	Stephen Leach	.35	.75
14	Michael Liut, Goalie	.50	1.00
15	Steve Maltais	.25	.50
16	Alan May	.25	.50
17	Kelly Miller	.35	.75
18	Terry Murray, Coach	.35	.75
19	Michal Pivonka	.35	.75
20	David Poile, Vice-President / General Manger	.25	.50
21	Mike Ridley	.35	.75
22	Robert Rouse	.25	.50
23	Neil Sheehy	.25	.50
24	Scott Stevens	.60	1.25
25	John Tucker	.25	.50

— 1990 - 91 REGULAR ISSUE —

This set was issued in three unnumbered sheets. . The cards are listed here in alphabetical order.

Card Size: 2" X 2 5/8"
Face: Four colour; Jersey number, Name, Position, Team logo
Back: Jersey number, Name, Position, Resume
Imprint: None
Photo Size: 10" X 8"
Face: Four colour
Back: Black on white card stock
Imprint: None
Complete Set No.: 26
Complete Set Price: 7.50 15.00
Common Card: .13 .25

No.	Player	EX	NRMT
1	Donald Beaupre, Goalie	.35	.75
2	Tim Bergland	.13	.25
3	Peter Bondra	.50	1.00
4	Dino Ciccarelli	.50	1.00
5	John Druce	.35	.75
6	Kevin Hatcher	.75	1.50
7	Dale Hunter	.13	.25
8	Al Iafrate	.50	1.00
9	Calle Johansson	.35	.75
10	Dimitri Khristich	.35	.75
11	Nicholas Kypreos	.13	.25
12	Mike Lalor	.13	.25
13	Rod Langway	.35	.75
14	Stephen Leach	.25	.50
15	Michael Liut, Goalie	.35	.75
16	Alan May	.13	.25
17	Kelly Miller	.25	.50
18	Terry Murray, Coach	.25	.50
19	John Perpich	.13	.25
20	Michal Pivonka	.25	.50
21	David Poile, Vice-President/General Manager	.13	.25
22	Mike Ridley	.25	.50
23	Ken Sabourin	.25	.50
24	Mikhail Tatarinov	.25	.50
25	Dave Tippett	.25	.50
26	Team Photo	1.00	2.00

— 1991 - 92 REGULAR ISSUE —

Card Size: 2 3/16" x 2 13/16"
Face: Four colour, white border; Name, Jersey number, Team logo
Back: Black on white card stock; Name, Jersey number, Position, Resume
Imprint: None
Complete Set No.: 25
Complete Set Price: 9.00 18.00
Common Card: .25 .50

No.	Player	EX	NRMT
1	Donald Beapre, Goalie	.35	.75
2	Tim Bergand	.25	.50

WASHINGTON CAPITALS - TEAM SETS • 649

No.	Player	EX	NRMT
3	Peter Bondra	.50	1.00
4	Randy Burridge	.25	.50
5	Shawn Chambers	.25	.50
6	Dino Ciccarelli	.50	1.00
7	Sylvain Cote	.25	.50
8	John Druce	.35	.75
9	Kevin Hatcher	.35	.75
10	Jim Hrivnak, Goalie	.35	.75
11	Dale Hunter	.35	.75
12	Al Iafrate	1.00	2.00
13	Calle Johansson	.35	.75
14	Dimitri Khristich	.35	.75
15	Todd Krygier	.25	.50
16	Nicholas Kypreos	.25	.50
17	Rod Langway	.25	.50
18	Mike Liut, Goalie	.25	.50
19	Alan May	.25	.50
20	Paul MacDermid	.25	.50
21	Kelly Miller	.35	.75
22	Michal Pivonka	.35	.75
23	Mike Ridley	.35	.75
24	Brad Schlegel	.25	.50
25	Dave Tippet	.25	.50

— 1992 - 93 REGULAR ISSUE —

Card Size: 2 3/4" x 2 1/4"
Face: Four colour, white border; Name, Jersey number, Position, Team logo
Back: Black on white card stock; Name, Jersey number, Position, Resume
Imprint: None
Complete Set No.: 25
Complete Set Price: 9.00 18.00
Common Card: .25 .50

No.	Player	EX	NRMT
1	Shawn Anderson	.25	.50
2	Donald Beaupre, Goalie	.35	.75
3	Peter Bondra	.50	1.00
4	Randy Burridge	.25	.50
5	Robert Carpenter	.25	.50
6	Paul Cavallini	.25	.50
7	Sylvain Cote	.25	.50
8	Pat Elynuik	.35	.75
9	Kevin Hatcher	.50	1.00
10	Jim Hrivnak, Goalie	.35	.75
11	Dale Hunter	.35	.75
12	Al Iafrate	.75	1.50
13	Calle Johansson	.35	.75
14	Keith Jones	.25	.50
15	Dimitri Khristich	.35	.75
16	Steve Konowalchuk	.25	.50
17	Todd Krygier	.25	.50
18	Rod Langway	.25	.50
19	Paul MacDermid	.25	.50
20	Alan May	.25	.50
21	Kelly Miller	.25	.50
22	Michal Pivonka	.25	.50
23	Mike Ridley	.35	.75
24	Reggie Savage	.25	.50
25	Jason Woolley	.25	.50

POLICE

— 1986 - 87 REGULAR ISSUE —

Endorsed by Virginia State Police, Metropolitan Police, Washington, D.C., and the Maryland State Police. These cards are unnumbered and are listed below in alphabetical order.

Panel Size: 2 5/8" X 7 1/2"
Card Size: 2 5/8" X 3 3/4"
Face: Four colour, white border; Team logo, Jersey number, Name, Position
Back: Black on white card stock; Team logo, Hockey and safety tips
Imprint: Litho'd In Canada
Complete Set No.: 12 Panels / 24 Cards
Complete Set Price: 6.00 12.00
Common Card: .13 .25

No.	Player	EX	NRMT
1	Gregory Adams	.25	.50
2	John Barrett	.13	.25
3	Robert Carpenter	.25	.50
4	David Christian	.25	.50
5	Yvon Corriveau	.13	.25
6	Gaetan Duchesne	.13	.25
7	Lou Franceschetti	.13	.25
8	Michael Gartner	1.00	2.00
9	Robert Gould	.13	.25
10	Kevin Hatcher	1.00	2.00
11	Alan Haworth	.13	.25
12	Al Jensen	.13	.25
13	David Jensen	.13	.25
14	Rod Langway	.35	.75
15	Craig Laughlin	.13	.25
16	Stephen Leach	.25	.50
17	Lawrence Murphy	.35	.75
18	Bryan Murray, Head Coach	.25	.50
19	Peter Peeters, Goalie	.35	.75
20	Jorgen Pettersson	.13	.25
21	Michal Pivonka	.25	.50
22	David Poile, Vice-President/General Manager	.13	.25
23	Greg Smith	.13	.25
24	Scott Stevens	.50	1.00

SMOKEY

— 1988 - 89 REGULAR ISSUE —

Issued by the Maryland Department of Natural Resources Forest, Park & Wildlife Service. These cards are unnumbered and are listed here in alphabetical order.

Card Size: 2 5/8" X 3 3/4"
Face: Four colour, white border; Name, Position, Jersey number, Team logo
Back: Black on white card stock; Hockey and fire prevention tips
Imprint: None
Complete Set No.: 24
Complete Set Price: 6.00 12.00
Common Player: .12 .25

No.	Player	EX	NRMT
1	Title Card: Smokey the Bear	.13	.25
2	David Christian	.25	.50
3	Geoff Courtnall	.75	1.50
4	Yvon Corriveau	.13	.25
5	Lou Franceschetti	.13	.25
6	Michael Gartner	.75	1.50
7	Robert Gould	.13	.25
8	Bengt-ake Gustafsson	.13	.25
9	Kevin Hatcher	.50	1.00
10	Dale Hunter	.13	.25
11	Rod Langway	.50	1.00
12	Stephen Leach	.25	.50
13	Grant Ledyard	.25	.50
14	Clint Malarchuk, Goalie	.13	.25
15	Kelly Miller	.25	.50
16	Lawrence Murphy	.25	.50
17	Bryan Murray, Coach	.25	.50
18	Peter Peeters, Goalie	.35	.75
19	Michal Pivonka	.25	.50
20	David Poile, Vice-President/General Manager	.13	.25
21	Mike Ridley	.25	.50
22	Neil Sheehy	.13	.25
23	Scott Stevens	.50	1.00
24	Peter Sundstrom	.25	.50

— 1990 - 91 REGULAR ISSUE —

Issued by the Maryland Department of Natural Resources Forest, Park & Wildlife Service. These cards are unnumbered and are listed here in alphabetical order.

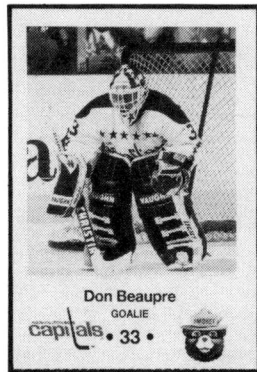

Smokey, 1990-91 Issue
Card No. 1, Donald Beaupre

Card Size: 2 5/8" X 3 3/4"
Face: Four colour, white border; Name, Position, Jersey number, Team logo
Back: Black on white card stock; Hockey and fire prevention tips
Imprint: Lith'd in Canada or None
Complete Set No.: 22
Complete Set Price: 5.00 10.00
Common Player: .13 .25

No.	Player	EX	NRMT
1	Donald Beaupre, Goalie	.35	.75
2	Tim Bergland	.13	.25
3	Peter Bondra, Error	.50	1.00
4	Dino Ciccarelli	.75	1.50
5	John Druce	.25	.50
6	Kevin Hatcher	.50	1.00
7	Jim Hrivnak, Goalie	.25	.50
8	Dale Hunter	.13	.25
9	Calle Johansson	.25	.50
10	Nicholas Kypreos	.13	.25
11	Mike Lalor	.13	.25
12	Rod Langway	.35	.75
13	Stephen Leach	.25	.50
14	Michael Liut, Goalie	.35	.75
15	Alan May	.13	.25
16	Kelly Miller	.25	.50
17	Rob Murray	.13	.25
18	Michal Pivonka	.25	.50
19	Mike Ridley	.25	.50
20	Neil Sheehy	.13	.25
21	Mikhail Tatarinov	.25	.50
22	Dave Tippett	.13	.25

WINNIPEG JETS - TEAM SETS

— 1979 - 80 POSTCARD ISSUE —

Card Size: 3 1/2" x 5 1/2"
Face: Four colour; Name, Facsimile autograph
Back: Resume
Imprint: Unkown
Complete Set No.: 28
Complete Set Price: 8.50 17.00
Common Card: .35 .75

No.	Player	EX	NRMT
1	Team Crest	.75	1.50
2	John Ferguson	.50	1.00
3	Tom McVie	.50	1.00
4	Bill Sutherland	.35	.75
5	Michael Amodeo	.35	.75
6	Al Cameron	.35	.75
7	Scott Campbell	.35	.75
8	Wayne Dillon	.35	.75
9	Jude Drouin	.50	1.00
10	Hilliard Graves	.35	.75
11	Pierre Hamel, Goalie	.35	.75
12	Dave Hoyda	.35	.75
13	Bobby Hull	1.50	3.00
14	Bill Lesuk	.35	.75
15	Willy Lindstrom	.50	1.00
16	Moris Lukovich	.75	1.50
17	Jimmy Mann	.35	.75
18	Peter Marsh	.35	.75
19	Gordon McTavish	.35	.75
20	Barry Melrose	1.00	2.00
21	Lyle Moffat	.35	.75
22	Craig Norwich	.35	.75
23	Lare-s Sjoberg	.35	.75
24	Gary Smith, Goalie	.35	.75
25	Gordon Smith	.35	.75
26	Lorne Stamler	.35	.75
27	Peter Sullivan	.35	.75
28	Ron Wilson	.50	1.00

— 1980 - 81 POSTCARD ISSUE —

These cards are unnumbered and are listed here in alphabetical order.

1980-81 Postcard Issue
Postcard No. 1, David Babych

Card Size: 3 1/2" X 5 5 1/2"
Face: Black and white photo, borderless; Facsimile autograph
Back: Blank
Imprint: None
Complete Set No.: 21
Complete Set Price: 10.00 20.00
Common Player: .50 1.00

No.	Player	EX	NRMT
1	David Babych	.50	1.00
2	Al Cameron	.50	1.00
3	Scott Campbell	.50	1.00
4	Dave Christian	.50	1.00
5	Jude Drouin	.50	1.00
6	Norm Dupont	.50	1.00
7	Danny Geoffrion	.50	1.00
8	Pierre Hamel, Goalie	.50	1.00
9	Barry Legge	.50	1.00
10	Willy Lindstrom	.50	1.00
11	Barry Long	.50	1.00
12	Morris Lukowich	.50	1.00
13	Kris Manery	.50	1.00
14	Jimmy Mann	.50	1.00
15	Maurice Mantha	.50	1.00
16	Markus Mattsson, Goalie	.50	1.00
17	Richard Mulhern	.50	1.00
18	Douglas Smail	.75	1.50
19	Don Spring	.50	1.00
20	Anders Steen	.75	1.50
21	Peter Sullivan	.50	1.00
22	Tim Trimper	.50	1.00
23	Ronald Wilson	.50	1.00

— 1981 - 82 POSTCARD ISSUE —

This 24-postcard set is the first Jets set since entering the NHL.

Postcard Size: 3 1/2" x 5 1/2"
Face: Black and white, white border; Fascimile autograph
Back: Black on card stock
Imprint: None
Complete Set No.: 24
Complete Set Price: 12.50 25.00
Common Goalie: .50 1.00
Common Player: .50 1.00

No.	Player	EX	NRMT
1	Scott Arniel	.75	1.50
2	David Babych	1.00	2.00
3	Dave Christian	.50	1.00
4	Lucien DeBlois	.75	1.50
5	Norm Dupont	.50	1.00
6	Larry Hopkins	.50	1.00
7	Dale Hawerchuk	3.50	7.00
8	Craig Levie	.50	1.00
9	Willy Lindstrom	.50	1.00
10	Morris Lukowich	.50	1.00
11	Bengt Lundholm	.50	1.00
12	Paul MacLean	.75	1.50
13	Jimmy Mann	.50	1.00
14	Bryan Maxwell	.50	1.00
15	Serge Savard	1.00	2.00
16	Douglas Smail	.75	1.50
17	Doug Soetaert, Goalie	.75	1.50
18	Don Spring	.50	1.00
19	Ed Staniowski, Goalie	.50	1.00
20	Thomas Steen	1.00	2.00
21	Bill Sutherland	.50	1.00
22	Tim Trimper	.50	1.00
23	Timothy Watters	.50	1.00
24	Tom Watt	.75	1.50

— 1982 - 83 POSTCARD ISSUE —

Postcard Size: 3 1/2" x 5 1/2"
Face:
Back: Blank
Imprint: None
Complete Set No.: 22
Complete Set Price: 9.00 18.00
Common Card: .35 .75

No.	Player	EX	NRMT
1	Scott Arniel	.50	1.00
2	David Babych	.50	1.00
3	Dave Christian	.75	1.50
4	Lucien Deblois	.35	.75
5	Dale Hawerchuk	2.50	5.00
6	Larry Hopkins	.35	.75
7	Craig Levie	.35	.75
8	Willi Lindstrom	.35	.75
9	Morris Lukowich	.35	.75
10	Paul MacLean	.50	1.00
11	Bryan Maxwell	.35	.75
12	Serge Savard	.50	1.00
13	Doug Smail	.35	.75
14	Douglas Soetaert, Goalie	.35	.75
15	Don Spring	.35	.75
16	Ed Staniowski, Goalie	.35	.75
17	Thomas Steen	.50	1.00
18	Bill Sutherland, Asst. Coach	.25	.75
19	Tim Trimper	.35	.75
20	Tom Watt, Coach	.50	1.00
21	Timothy Watters	.35	.75
22	Unknown	.35	.75

— 1983 - 84 POSTCARD ISSUE —

Card Size: 3 1/4" X 5 1/4"
Face: Four colour, borderless; Name, Jersey number
Back: Blank
Imprint: None
Complete Set No.: 25
Complete Set Price: 10.00 20.00
Common Card: .35 .75

No.	Player	EX	NRMT
1	Scott Arniel	.50	1.00
2	Dave Babych	.50	1.00
3	Laurie Boschman	.50	1.00
4	Wade Campbell	.35	.75
5	Lucien DeBlois	.35	.75
6	John B. Ferguson, VP and GM	.35	.75
7	John Gibson	.35	.75
8	Dale Hawerchuk	2.00	4.00
9	Brian Hayward, Goalie	.50	1.00
10	Jim Kyte	.35	.75
11	Barry Long, Coach	.35	.75
12	Morris Lukowich	.35	.75
13	Bengt Lundholm	.35	.75
14	Paul MacLean	.35	.75
15	Jimmy Mann	.35	.75
16	Moe Mantha	.35	.75
17	Andrew McBain	.35	.75
18	Brian Mullen	.35	.75
19	Robert Picard	.35	.75
20	Doug Smail	.35	.75
21	Doug Soetaert, Goalie	.35	.75
22	Thomas Steen	.50	1.00
23	Tim Watters	.35	.75
24	Ron Wilson	.35	.75
25	Tim Young	.35	.75

— 1985 - 86 POSTCARD ISSUE —

1985-86 Postcard Issue
Postcard No. 8, Dave Ellett

Postcard Size: 3 1/4" x 5 1/4"
Face: Four colour, borderless; Name
Back: Blank
Imprint: None
Complete Set No.: 22
Complete Set Price: 10.00 20.00
Common Card: .35 .75

No.	Player	EX	NRMT
1	Team Photograph	.35	.75
2	Team Coaches: Bill Sutherland, Barry Long, Rick Bowness	.35	.75
3	John B. Ferguson, General Manager	.35	.75
4	Scott Arniel	.35	.75
5	Laurie Boschman	.35	.75
6	Dan Bouchard, Goalie	.75	1.50
7	Randy Carlyle	.35	.75
8	David Ellett	1.50	3.00
9	Dale Hawerchuk	2.50	5.00
10	Brian Hayward, Goalie	1.00	2.00
11	James Kyte	.35	.75
12	Paul MacLean	.35	.75
13	Andrew McBain	.75	1.50
14	Anssi Melametsa	.35	.75
15	Brian Mullen	.35	.75
16	Jim Nill	.35	.75
17	Dave Silk	.35	.75
18	Douglas Smail	.75	1.50
19	Thomas Steen	.75	1.50
20	Perry Turnbull	.35	.75
21	Timothy Watters	.35	.75
22	Ronald Wilson	.35	.75

1986 - 87 POSTCARD ISSUE

1986-87 Postcard Issue
Postcard No. 20, Steve Penney

Postcard Size: 3 1/4" x 5 1/4"
Face: Four colour, Borderless; Name on card stock
Back: Blank
Imprint: None
Complete Set No.: 26
Complete Set Price: 9.00 18.00
Common Card: .35 .75

No.	Player	EX	NRMT
1	Winnipeg Jets Hockey Club	.35	.75
2	Team Coaches: Bill Sutherland, Dan Maloney, Rick Bowness	.35	.75
3	John B. Ferguson GM	.35	.75
4	Brad Berry	.35	.75
5	Laurie Boschman	1.00	2.00
6	Randy Carlyle	1.25	2.50
7	Bill Derlago	.35	.75
8	David Ellett	1.00	2.00
9	Gilles Hamel	.35	.75
10	Dale Hawerchuk	1.50	3.00
11	Hannu Jarvenpaa	.35	.75
12	James Kyte	.35	.75
13	Paul MacLean	.35	.75
14	Andrew McBain	.35	.75
15	Mario Marois	.75	1.50
16	Brian Mullen	.35	.75
17	Ray Neufeld	.50	1.00
18	James Nill	.35	.75
19	Fredrick Olausson, Error	1.00	2.00
20	Steve Penney, Goalie	.50	1.00
21	Eldon Reddick, Goalie	.35	.75
22	Douglas Smail	.50	1.00
23	Thomas Steen	.75	1.50
24	Perry Turnbull	.35	.75
25	Timothy Watters	.35	.75
26	Ronald Wilson	.35	.75

— 1987 - 88 POSTCARD ISSUE —

Postcard Size: 3 1/4" x 5 1/4"
Face: Four colour, Borderless; Name, Jersey number,
Back: Blank
Imprint: None
Complete Set No.: 24
Complete Set Price: 6.00 12.00
Common Card: .25 .50

No.	Player	EX	NRMT
1	Brad Berry	.25	.50
2	Daniel Berthaume, Goalie	.50	1.00
3	Laurie Boschman	.25	.50
4	Randy Carlyle	.50	1.00
5	Iain Duncan	.25	.50
6	David Ellett	.35	.75
7	Pat Elynuik	.50	1.00
8	Gilles Hamel	.25	.50
9	Dale Hawerchuk	1.50	3.00
10	Hanno Jarvenpaa	.25	.50
11	Jim Kyte	.25	.50
12	Paul MacLean	.25	.50
13	Marios Marois	.25	.50
14	Andrew McBain	.25	.50
15	Ray Neufeld	.25	.50
16	Fredrik Olausson	1.00	2.00
17	Eldon Reddick, Goalie	.25	.50
18	Steve Rooney	.25	.50
19	Doug Smail	.25	.50
20	Thomas Steen	.75	1.50
21	Peter Taglianetti	.25	.50
22	Timothy Watters	.25	.50
23	Ronald Wilson	.50	1.00
24	Team Picture	.50	1.00

— 1988 - 89 POSTCARD ISSUE —

We have no information on this set. We would appreciate hearing from anyone who could supply further information.

ANONYMOUS

— 1982 - 83 POSTCARD ISSUE —

This 28-card set is unnumbered and is listed below in alphabetical order.

Card Size: 3 1/2" x 5 1/2"
Face: Four colour; Name
Back: Blank
Imprint: None
Complete Set No.: 28
Complete Set Price: 10.00 20.00
Common Card: .25 .50

No.	Player	EX	NRMT
1	Scott Arniel	.50	1.00
2	Dave Babych	1.00	2.00
3	Jerry Butler	.50	1.00
4	Wade Campbell	.25	.50
5	Dave Christian	.25	.50
6	Lucien Deblois	.75	1.50
7	Norm Dupont	.25	.50
8	Dale Hawerchuk	2.00	4.00
9	Jim Kyte	.25	.50
10	Craig Levie	.25	.50
11	Morris Lukowich	.25	.50
12	Bengt Lundholm	.25	.50
13	Paul MacLean	.50	1.00
14	Jimmy Mann	.25	.50
15	Bryan Maxwell	.25	.50
16	Brian Mullen	.25	.50
17	Serge Savard	.25	.50
18	Doug Smail	.25	.50
19	Doug Soetaert, Goalie	.25	.50
20	Don Spring	.25	.50
21	Ed Staniowski	.25	.50
22	Thomas Steen	1.00	2.00
23	Bill Sutherland, Coach	.25	.50
24	Tom Watt, Coach	.25	.50
26	Tim Watters	.25	.50

STATER MINT LTD

— 1983 - 84 HOCKEY DOLLARS —

These cupro-nickel coins were sold singly and packaged with a 8 3/8" X 3" perforated card.

Coin Size: 1 1/4" Diameter
Face: Player portrait, Name
Back: Team logo
Imprint: None

Card Size: 3" X 5"
Face: Blue and red; Team logo, Jersey number, Name
Back: Blue on white card stock; Jersey number, Name, Position, Resume, Number
Imprint: 1983 — MADE IN CANADA
Complete Set No.: 7
Complete Set Price: 25.00 50.00
Common Player: 3.75 7.50

No.	Player	EX	NRMT
H7	Dale Hawerchuk	5.00	10.00
H8	David Babych	3.75	7.50
H9	Morris Lukowich	3.75	7.50
H10	Brian Mullen	3.75	7.50
H11	Lucien Deblois	3.75	7.50
H12	Brian Hayward, Goalie	3.75	7.50
H13	Tim Watters	3.75	7.50

WINNIPEG JETS - TEAM SETS

POLICE

— 1984 - 85 REGULAR ISSUE —

Endorsed by The Kinsemen Club of Winnipeg and all Police Forces in Manitoba. Cards are unnumbered and are listed below in alphabetical order.

Police, 1984-85 Issue
Card No. 4, Laurie Boschman

Card Size: 2 5/8" X 3 11/16"
Panel Size: 2 5/8" X 7 1/2"
Face: Four colour, white border; Name, Jersey number, Position, Team, Team and sponsor logos
Back: Black on white card stock; Hockey and Safety tips, Team and sponsor logos
Imprint: None
Complete Set No.: 12 Panels / 24 Cards
Complete Set Price: 5.00 10.00
Common Card: .13 .25

No.	Player	EX	NRMT
1	Scott Arniel	.13	.25
2	David Babych	.25	.50
3	Marc Behrend, Goalie	.13	.25
4	Laurie Boschman	.25	.50
5	Randy Carlyle	.35	.75
6	Dave Ellett	.35	.75
7	John B. Ferguson, Vice-President/General Manager	.13	.25
8	Dale Hawerchuk	.75	1.50
9	Brian Hayward, Goalie	.13	.25
10	James Kyte	.13	.25
11	Morris Lukowich	.13	.25
12	Bengt Lundholm	.13	.25
13	Paul MacLean	.25	.50
14	Andrew McBain	.13	.25
15	Brian Mullen	.35	.75
16	Robert Picard	.13	.25
17	Poul Pooley, Error	.13	.25
18	Douglas Smail	.25	.50
19	Thomas Steen	.25	.50
20	Perry Turnbull	.13	.25
21	Timothy Watters	.13	.25
22	Ronald Wilson	.13	.25
23	Bill Sutherland, Assistant Coach; Barry Long, Head Coach; Rick Bowness, Assistant Coach	.13	.25
24	Team Photo	.35	.75

— 1985 - 86 REGULAR ISSUE —

This set was endorsed by The Kinsemen Club of Winnipeg and all Police Forces in Manitoba

Police, 1985-86 Issue
Card No. 1, Scott Arniel

Card Size: 2 5/8" X 3 3/4"
Panel Size: 2 5/8" X 7 1/2"
Face: Four colour, white border; Name, Jersey number, Position, Team, Team and sponsor logos
Back: Black on white card stock; Hockey and Safety tips, Team logo, Sponsor logos
Imprint: None
Complete Set No.: 12 Panels / 24 Cards
Complete Set Price: 4.00 8.00
Common Card: .13 .25

No.	Player	EX	NRMT
1	Scott Arniel	.13	.25
2	Laurie Boschman	.13	.25
3	Dan Bouchard, Goalie	.13	.25
4	Randy Carlyle	.25	.50
5	Dave Ellett	.20	.40
6	John B. Ferguson, Vice-President / General Manager	.13	.25
7	Dale Hawerchuk	.50	1.00
8	Brian Hayward, Goalie	.13	.25
9	James Kyte	.13	.25
10	Paul MacLean	.18	.35
11	Mario Marois	.13	.25
12	Andrew McBain	.13	.25
13	Anssi Melametsa	.13	.25
14	Brian Mullen	.13	.25
15	Ray Neufeld	.13	.25
16	James Nill	.13	.25
17	Dave Silk	.13	.25
18	Douglas Smail	.18	.35
19	Thomas Steen	.18	.35
20	Perry Turnbull	.13	.25
21	Timothy Watters	.13	.25
22	Ronald Wilson	.13	.25
23	Bill Sutherland, Assistant Coach; Barry Long, Head Coach; Rick Bowness, Assistant Coach	.13	.25
24	Team Photo	.25	.50

— 1988 - 89 REGULAR ISSUE —

This set was endorsed by The Kinsemen Club of Winnipeg and all Police Forces in Manitoba

Police, 1988-89 Issue
Card No. 6, Dave Ellett

Card Size: 2 5/8" X 3 3/4"
Panel Size: 2 5/8" X 7 1/2"
Face: Four colour, white border; Name, Jersey number, Position, Team, Team and sponsor logos
Back: Black on white card stock; Hockey and Safety tips, Team logo, Sponsor logos
Imprint: None
Complete Set No.: 12 Panels / 24 Cards
Complete Set Price: 4.00 8.00
Common Player: .13 .25

No.	Player	EX	NRMT
1	Brent Ashton	.13	.25
2	Laurie Boschman	.13	.25
3	Randy Carlyle	.25	.50
4	Alain Chevrier, Goalie	.18	.35
5	Iain Duncan	.13	.25
6	Dave Ellett	.13	.25
7	Pat Elynuik	.35	.75
8	Randy Gilhen	.25	.50
9	Dale Hawerchuk	.35	.75
10	Dave Hunter	.13	.25
11	Hannu Jarvenpaa	.13	.25
12	James Kyte	.13	.25
13	Dan Maloney, Head Coach	.13	.25
14	Mario Marois	.13	.25
15	Andrew McBain	.13	.25
16	Ray Neufeld	.13	.25
17	Teppo Numminen	.13	.25
18	Frederik Olausson	.13	.25
19	Eldon Reddick, Goalie	.18	.35
20	Douglas Smail	.18	.35
21	Thomas Steen	.18	.35
22	Peter Taglianetti	.13	.25
23	Assistant Coaches: Bill Sutherland; Bruce Southern; Rick St. Croix	.13	.25
24	Team Picture	.25	.50

SILVERWOOD DAIRY

— 1985 - 86 ISSUE —

We have no information on the following three sets. We would appreciate hearing from anyone who could supply further information.

SAFEWAY

— 1989 - 90 ISSUE —

We have no information on the following three sets. We would appreciate hearing from anyone who could supply further information.

I.G.A.

— 1990 - 91 ISSUE —

We have no information on the following three sets. We would appreciate hearing from anyone who could supply further information.

RUFFLES

— 1993 - 94 POSTCARD ISSUE —

Card Size: 3 1/2" x 6 1/2"
Face: Four colour, white border; Name, Jersey number
Back: Black on white card stock; Name, Jersey number, Position, Resume, Sponsor and Team logo
Imprint: None
Complete Set No.: 29

Complete Set Price:		7.50	15.00
Common Card:		.25	.50

No.	Players	EX	NRMT
1	Stu Barnes	.25	.50
2	Sergei Bautin	.35	.75
3	Stephane Beauregard, Goalie	.25	.50
4	Zinetula Bilyaletdinov, Asst. Coach	.25	.50
5	Arto Blomsten	.25	.50
6	Luciano Borsato	.25	.50
7	Tahir Domi	.50	1.00
8	Mike Eagles	.25	.50
9	Nelson Emerson	.50	1.00
10	Bryan Erickson	.25	.50
11	Bob Essensa, Goalie	.50	1.00
12	Yan Kaminsky	.35	.75
13	Dean Kennedy	.25	.50
14	Kris King	.25	.50
15	Boris Mironov	.35	.75
16	Andy Murray, Asst. Coach	.25	.50
17	Teppo Numminen	.25	.50
18	Stephane Quintal	.25	.50
19	Fredrik Olausson	.50	1.00
20	John Paddock, Head Coach	.25	.50
21	Teemu Selanne	2.00	4.00
22	Darrin Shannon	.25	.50
23	Thomas Steen	.25	.50
24	Keith Tkachuk	1.00	2.00
25	Igor Ulanov	.25	.50
26	Paul Ysebaert	.50	1.00
27	Alexei Zhamnov	.75	1.50
28	1993-94 Team Picture	.50	1.00
29	Mascot: Benny	.25	.50

Ruffles, 1993 - 94 Postcard Issue
Postcard No. 21, Teemu Selanne

WINNIPEG JETS TEAM SETS, 1986-87 Postcard Issue
Postcard No. 1, Winnipeg Jets Hockey Club

CANADIENS
CHAMPIONS 1953

Hector Dubois, Doug Harvey, Johnny McCormack, Eddie Mazur, Bud Macpherson, Emile Bouchard, Tom Johnson, Dollard St. Laurent, Gaston Bettez, Camil Desroches, Calum Mackay, Dickie Moore, Dick Gamble, Ken Mosdell, Floyd Curry, Lorne Davis, Paul Masnick, Frank D. Selke. Jacques Plante, Maurice Richard, Elmer Lach, Bert Olmstead, Dick Irvin, Frank J. Selke, Bernard Geoffrion, Billy Reay, Paul Meger, Gerry McNeil.

COMPLIMENTS *Molson's*

David Bier Photo

CHAPTER SIX
WORLD HOCKEY ASSOCIATION
1973 - 1978

ALPHABETICAL LISTING OF MANUFACTURERS
WORLD HOCKEY ASSOCIATION

O-Pee-Chee	657	Team Sets		664
Quaker Oats	661			

O-PEE-CHEE WHA Wax Pack Wrapper

O-PEE-CHEE

— 1972 - 73 TEAM LOGO STICKERS —

Poster Size: 2 1/2" X 3 1/2"
Face: Four colour; Team logo or WHA logo
Back: Blank
Imprint: © O.P.C. PRINTED IN CANADA
Complete Set No.: 12

Complete Set Price:		100.00	200.00	400.00 ☐
Common Team:		6.25	12.50	25.00

No.	Player	VG	EX	NRMT
—	Title Card: World Hockey Association - WHA	8.75	17.50	35.00 ☐
1	Chicago Cougars	6.25	12.50	25.00 ☐
2	Cleveland Crusaders	8.75	17.50	35.00 ☐
3	Edmonton Oilers	7.50	15.00	30.00 ☐
4	Houston Aeros	6.25	12.50	25.00 ☐
5	Los Angeles Sharks	7.50	15.00	30.00 ☐
6	Minnesota Fighting Saints	6.25	12.50	25.00 ☐
7	New England Whalers	6.25	12.50	25.00 ☐
8	New York Raiders	6.25	12.50	25.00 ☐
9	Ottawa Nationals	6.25	12.50	25.00 ☐
10	Philadelphia Blazers	6.25	12.50	25.00 ☐
11	Winnipeg Jets	6.25	12.50	25.00 ☐

— 1972 - 73 WORLD HOCKEY ASSOCIATION —

For a listing of the World Hockey Association section of the 1972-73 O-Pee-Chee set, card nos. 290 to 341, see page no. 52.

— 1973 - 74 POSTERS —

Poster Size: 7 1/2" x 12 1/2"
Face: Four colour, white border; Team logo or WHA logo, Name, Position, Numbered _ of 20, Bilingual
Back: Blank
Imprint: © O.P.C. PRINTED IN CANADA
Complete Set No.: 20

Complete Set Price:		12.50	25.00	50.00 ☐
Common Player:		.25	.50	1.00

No.	Player	VG	EX	NRMT
1	Al Smith, Goalie, NEW	.35	.75	1.50 ☐
2	J.C. Tremblay, QuN	.35	.75	1.50 ☐
3	Guy Dufour, QuN	.25	.50	1.00 ☐
4	Pat Stapleton, ChC	.35	.75	1.50 ☐
5	Rosaire Paiement, ChC	.25	.50	1.00 ☐
6	Gerry Cheevers, Goalie, CIC	1.50	3.00	6.00 ☐
7	Gerry Pinder, CIC	.35	.75	1.50 ☐
8	Wayne Carleton, ToT	.25	.50	1.00 ☐
9	Bob LeDuc, ToT	.25	.50	1.00 ☐
10	Andre Lacroix, NJR	.25	.50	1.00 ☐
11	Jim Harrison, EdO	.25	.50	1.00 ☐
12	Ron Climie, EdO	.25	.50	1.00 ☐
13	Gordie Howe, HoA	6.75	13.50	27.00 ☐
14	The Howe Family: Marty; Gordie; Mark	2.50	5.00	10.00 ☐
15	Mike Walton, MFS	.35	.75	1.50 ☐
16	Bobby Hull, WiN	3.00	6.00	12.00 ☐
17	Chris Bordeleau, WiN	.25	.50	1.00 ☐
18	Claude St. Sauveur, VaB	.25	.50	1.00 ☐
19	Bryan Campbell, VaB, Error	.25	.50	1.00 ☐
20	Marc Tardif, LAS	.35	.75	1.50 ☐

O-Pee-Chee
1974-75 Issue
Card No. 1,
The Howes

O-Pee-Chee
1974-75 Issue
Card No. 4,
Ulf Nilsson

O-Pee-Chee
1974-75 Issue
Card No. 30,
Gerry Cheevers

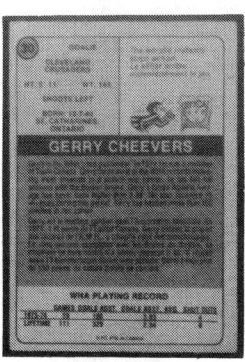

O-Pee-Chee
1974-75 Issue
Card No. 30,
Gerry Cheevers

— 1974 - 75 REGULAR ISSUE —

Mint cards command a premium of 50% over NRMT prices.

PRICE MOVEMENT OF NRMT SETS

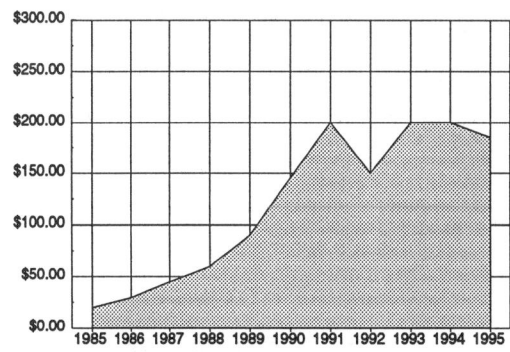

Card Size: 2 1/2" X 3 1/2"
Face: Four colour, white border, Position
Back: Two colour, brown and blue on card stock, Number, Resume, Hockey trivia, Bilingual
Imprint: O.P.C. PTD. IN CANADA
Complete Set No.: 66

Complete Set Price:		45.00	95.00	185.00 ☐
Common Card:		.50	1.00	2.00

No.	Player	VG	EX	NRMT
1	The Howes; Gordie, Mark, Marty, HoA.	20.00	40.00	80.00 ☐
2	Bruce MacGregor, EdO.	.50	1.00	2.00 ☐
3	Wayne Dillon, ToT., RC	.50	1.00	2.00 ☐
4	Ulf Nilsson, WiN., RC	2.25	4.50	9.00 ☐
5	Serge Bernier, QuN.	.50	1.00	2.00 ☐
6	Bryan Campbell, VaB.	.50	1.00	2.00 ☐
7	Rosaire Paiement, ChC.	.50	1.00	2.00 ☐
8	Tom Webster, NEW	.60	1.25	2.50 ☐
9	Gerry Pinder, CIC	.50	1.00	2.00 ☐
10	Mike Walton, MFS	.50	1.00	2.00 ☐
11	Norm Beaudin, WiJ., LC	.50	1.00	2.00 ☐
12	Bob Whitlock, InR., RC	.60	1.25	2.50 ☐
13	Wayne Rivers, SDM	.50	1.00	2.00 ☐
14	Gerry Odrowski, PhR., LC	.50	1.00	2.00 ☐
15	Ron Climie, EdO.	.50	1.00	2.00 ☐
16	Tom Simpson, ToT., RC	.50	1.00	2.00 ☐
17	Anders Hedberg, WiJ., RC	2.25	4.50	9.00 ☐
18	J. C. Tremblay, QuN.,	.50	1.00	2.00 ☐
19	Mike Pelyk, VaB.	.50	1.00	2.00 ☐
20	Dave Dryden, Goalie, ChC.	.50	1.00	2.00 ☐
21	Ron Ward, CIC.	.50	1.00	2.00 ☐
22	Larry Lund, HoA., RC	.50	1.00	2.00 ☐
23	Ron Buchanan, EdO., RC	.50	1.00	2.00 ☐
24	Pat Hickey, ToT., RC	1.25	2.50	5.00 ☐
25	Danny Lawson, VaB., RC	.75	1.50	3.00 ☐
26	Bobby Guindon, QuN., RC, LC	.50	1.00	2.00 ☐
27	Gene Peacosh, SDM, RC	.50	1.00	2.00 ☐
28	Fran Huck, MFS	.50	1.00	2.00 ☐
29	Al Hamilton, EdO.	.50	1.00	2.00 ☐
30	Gerry Cheevers, Goalie, CIC	3.00	6.00	12.00 ☐
31	Heikki Riihiranta, WiN., RC	.50	1.00	2.00 ☐
32	Don Burgess, VaB., RC	.50	1.00	2.00 ☐
33	John French, NEW, RC	.50	1.00	2.00 ☐
34	Jim Wiste, InR., RC	.50	1.00	2.00 ☐
35	Pat Stapleton, ChC., LC	.50	1.00	2.00 ☐
36	J. P. LeBlanc, MiS., RC	.50	1.00	2.00 ☐
37	Mike Antonovich, MFS, RC	.50	1.00	2.00 ☐
38	Joe Daley, Goalie, WiN.	.50	1.00	2.00 ☐
39	Ross Perkins, EdO., RC, LC	.50	1.00	2.00 ☐
40	Frank Mahovlich, ToT.	3.00	6.00	12.00 ☐
41	Réjean Houle, QuN.	.50	1.00	2.00 ☐
42	Ron Chipperfield, VaB., RC	.50	1.00	2.00 ☐
43	Marc Tardif, MiS.	.50	1.00	2.00 ☐
44	Murray Keogan, PhR., RC, LC	.50	1.00	2.00 ☐
45	Wayne Carleton, NEW	.50	1.00	2.00 ☐
46	André Gaudette, QuN., RC, LC	.50	1.00	2.00 ☐
47	Ralph Backstrom, ChC.	.50	1.00	2.00 ☐
48	Don McLeod, Goalie, VaB.	.50	1.00	2.00 ☐
49	Vaclav Nedomansky, ToT., RC	1.25	2.50	5.00 ☐

O-PEE-CHEE — 1975 - 76 REGULAR ISSUE

No.	Player	VG	EX	NRMT
50	Bobby Hull, WiN.	8.75	17.50	35.00
51	Rusty Patenaude, EdO., RC	.50	1.00	2.00
52	Michel Parizeau, QuN., LC	.50	1.00	2.00
53	Checklist (1- 66), Error	5.00	10.00	20.00
54	Wayne Connelly, MFS	.50	1.00	2.00
55	Gary Veneruzzo, MiS	.50	1.00	2.00
56	Dennis Sobchuk, PhR., RC	.50	1.00	2.00
57	Paul Henderson, ToT.	.50	1.00	2.00
58	Andy Brown, Goalie, InR., RC, LC	.50	1.00	2.00
59	Poul Popiel, HoA.	.50	1.00	2.00
60	André Lacroix, SDM	.75	1.50	3.00
61	Gary Jarrett, CIC	.50	1.00	2.00
62	Claude St. Sauveur, VaB., RC	.50	1.00	2.00
63	Réal Cloutier, QuN., RC	.75	1.50	3.00
64	Jacques Plante, Goalie, EdO.	8.00	16.00	32.00
65	Gilles Gratton, Goalie, ToT., RC	1.25	2.50	5.00
66	Lars-Erik Sjoberg, WIN., RC	1.50	3.00	6.00

— 1975 - 76 REGULAR ISSUE —

Mint cards command a 50% premium over NRMT prices.

PRICE MOVEMENT OF NRMT SETS

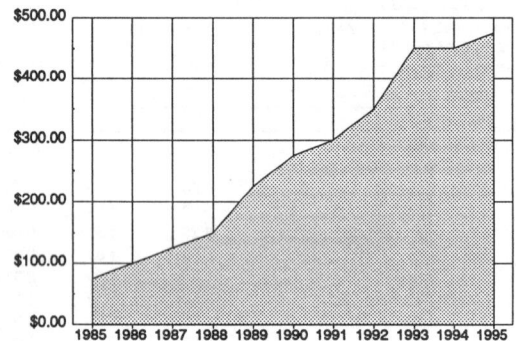

Card Size: 2 1/2" X 3 1/2"
Front: Four colour, white border, position
Back: Black and brown on card stock, Number, Resume, Bilingual
Imprint: O.P.C. PTD. IN CANADA
Complete Set No.: 132

		VG	EX	NRMT
Complete Set Price:		120.00	240.00	475.00
Common Card:		.60	1.25	2.50

No.	Player	VG	EX	NRMT
1	Bobby Hull, WiN	16.00	35.00	65.00
2	Dale Hoganson, Goalie, QuN	.60	1.25	2.50
3	Serge Aubry, CiS, RC, LC, Error	.60	1.25	2.50
4	Ron Chipperfield, CaC	.60	1.25	2.50
5	Paul Shmyr, CIC	.60	1.25	2.50
6	Perry Miller, WIN, RC	.60	1.25	2.50
7	Mark Howe, HoA, RC	8.75	17.50	35.00
8	Mike Rogers, EdO, RC	1.10	2.25	4.50
9	Byron Baltimore, OtC, RC, LC, Error	.60	1.25	2.50
10	Andre Lacroix, SDM	.85	1.75	3.50
11	Nick Harbaruk, InR, LC	.60	1.25	2.50
12	John Garrett, Goalie, MFS, RC	1.25	2.50	5.00
13	Lou Nistico, ToT, RC, LC	.60	1.25	2.50
14	Rick Ley, NEW	.60	1.25	2.50
15	Veli-Pekka Ketola, WIN, RC, Error	.60	1.25	2.50
16	Real Cloutier, QuN	.75	1.50	3.00
17	Pierre Guite, CiS, RC	.60	1.25	2.50
18	Duane Rupp, CaC, LC	.60	1.25	2.50
19	Robbie Ftorek, PhR, RC	1.50	3.00	6.00
20	Gerry Cheevers, Goalie, CIC	4.25	8.50	17.00
21	John Schella, HoA, RC	.60	1.25	2.50
22	Bruce MacGregor, EdO, LC	.60	1.25	2.50
23	Ralph Backstrom, OtC	.60	1.25	2.50
24	Gene Peacosh, SDM	.60	1.25	2.50
25	Pierre Roy, QuN, RC, LC	.50	1.25	2.50
26	Mike Walton, MFS	.60	1.25	2.50
27	Vaclav Nedomansky, ToT	.60	1.25	2.50
28	Christer Abrahamsson, Goalie, NEW, RC	.75	1.50	3.00

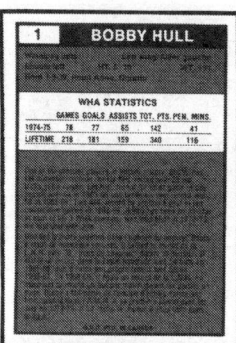

O-Pee-Chee 1975-76 Issue Card No. 1, Bobby Hull

O-Pee-Chee 1975-76 Issue Card No. 7, Mark Howe

O-Pee-Chee 1975-76 Issue Card No. 66, Gordie Howe

No.	Player	VG	EX	NRMT
29	Thommie Bergman, WiN	.60	1.25	2.50
30	Marc Tardif, QuN	.60	1.25	2.50
31	Bryan Campbell, CiS	.60	1.25	2.50
32	Don McLeod, Goalie, CaC	.75	1.50	3.00
33	Al McDonough, CIC	.60	1.25	2.50
34	Jacques Plante, Goalie, EdO LC	8.75	17.50	35.00
35	Andre Hinse, HoA, RC	.60	1.25	2.50
36	Eddie Joyal, EdO, LC	.60	1.25	2.50
37	Ken Baird, EdO, RC	.60	1.25	2.50
38	Wayne Rivers, SDM, LC	.60	1.25	2.50
39	Ron Buchanan, InR, LC	.60	1.25	2.50
40	Anders Hedberg, WiN	1.10	2.25	4.50
41	Rick Smith, MFS	.60	1.25	2.50
42	Paul Henderson, ToT	.60	1.25	2.50
43	Wayne Carleton, NEW, LC	.60	1.25	2.50
44	Richard Brodeur, Goalie, QuN, RC	3.25	6.50	13.00
45	John Hughes, CIS, RC	.60	1.25	2.50
46	Larry Israelson, CaC, RC, LC	.60	1.25	2.50
47	Jim Harrison, CIC.	.60	1.25	2.50
48	Cam Connor, PhR, RC	.75	1.50	3.00
49	Al Hamilton, EdO	.60	1.25	2.50
50	Ron Grahame, Goalie, HoA, RC	.85	1.75	3.50
51	Frank Rochon, OtC, RC, LC	.60	1.25	2.50
52	Ron Climie, NEW, LC	.60	1.25	2.50
53	Murray Heatley, InR, RC, LC	.60	1.25	2.50
54	John Arbour, OtC, LC	.60	1.25	2.50
55	Jim Shaw, ToT, Goalie, RC, LC	.60	1.25	2.50
56	Larry Pleau, NEW, RC	.85	1.75	3.50
57	Ted Green, WiN	1.10	2.25	4.50
58	Rick Dudley, CiS	.60	1.25	2.50
59	Butch Deadmarsh, CaC	.60	1.25	2.50
60	Serge Bernier, QuN	.60	1.25	2.50

ALL STARS

First Team

No.	Player	VG	EX	NRMT
61	Ron Grahame, Goalie, HoA	.50	1.25	2.50
62	J. C. Tremblay, QuN	.50	1.25	2.50
63	Kevin Morrison, SDM	.50	1.25	2.50
64	Andre Lacroix, SDM	.50	1.25	2.50
65	Bobby Hull, WiN	7.50	15.00	30.00
66	Gordie Howe, HoA	9.00	18.00	36.00

Second Team

No.	Player	VG	EX	NRMT
67	Gerry Cheevers, Goalie, CIC	1.85	3.75	7.50
68	Poul Popiel, HoA	.60	1.25	2.50
69	Barry Long, EdO	.60	1.25	2.50
70	Serge Bernier, QuN	.60	1.25	2.50
71	Marc Tardif, QuN	.60	1.25	2.50
72	Anders Hedberg, WiN	.60	1.25	2.50

REGULAR ISSUE

No.	Player	VG	EX	NRMT
73	Ron Ward, CIC	.60	1.25	2.50
74	Michel Cormier, PhR, RC, LC	.60	1.25	2.50
75	Marty Howe, HoA, RC	1.50	3.00	6.00
76	Rusty Patenaude, EdO	.60	1.25	2.50
77	John McKenzie, MFS	.60	1.25	2.50
78	Mark Napier, ToT, RC	1.25	2.50	5.00
79	Henry Boucha, MFS	.60	1.25	2.50
80	Kevin Morrison, SDM, RC	.60	1.25	2.50
81	Tom Simpson, ToT, LC	.60	1.25	2.50
82	Brad Selwood, NEW, RC, LC	.60	1.25	2.50
83	Ulf Nilsson, WiN	1.50	3.00	6.00
84	Rejean Houle, Que.	.60	1.25	2.50
85	Normand Lapointe, Cle., RC, LC, Error	.60	1.25	2.50
86	Danny Lawson, Cal.	.75	1.50	3.00
87	Gary Jarrett, Cle., LC, Error	.60	1.25	2.50
88	Al McLeod, PhR, RC	.60	1.25	2.50
89	Gord Labossierre, HoA, LC, Error	.60	1.25	2.50
90	Barry Long, EdO	.60	1.25	2.50
91	Rick Morris, OtC, RC, LC	.60	1.25	2.50
92	Norm Ferguson, SDM	.60	1.25	2.50
93	Bob Whitlock, InR, LC	.60	1.25	2.50
94	Jim Dorey, ToT	.60	1.25	2.50
95	Tom Webster, NEW	.85	1.75	3.50
96	Gordie Gallant, QuN, RC, LC	.60	1.25	2.50
97	Dave Keon, MFS	1.50	3.00	6.00
98	Ron Plumb, CiS, RC	.75	1.50	3.00

— 1976 - 77 REGULAR ISSUE — O-PEE-CHEE • 659

No.	Player	VG	EX	NRMT
99	Rick Jodzio, CaC, RC	.60	1.25	2.50
100	Gordie Howe, HoA	13.75	27.50	55.00
101	Joe Daley, Goalie, WIN	.75	1.50	3.00
102	Wayne Muloin, CIC, RC, LC	.60	1.25	2.50
103	Gavin Kirk, ToT, RC	.60	1.25	2.50
104	Dave Dryden, Goalie, EdO	.75	1.50	3.00
105	Bob Liddington, OtC, RC, LC	.60	1.25	2.50
106	Rosaire Palement, NEW	.60	1.25	2.50
107	John Sheridan, InR, RC, LC	.60	1.25	2.50
108	Nick Fotiu, NEW, RC	.85	1.75	3.50
109	Lars-Erik Sjoberg, Win., Error	.60	1.25	2.50
110	Frank Mahovlich, Tot	3.50	7.00	14.00
111	Mike Antonovich, Mfs	.60	1.25	2.50
112	Paul Terbenche, CaC, LC	.60	1.25	2.50
113	Rich LeDuc, CIC, RC	.60	1.25	2.50
114	Jack Norris, Goalie, PhR, LC	.50	1.25	2.50
115	Dennis Sobchuk, CiS	.60	1.25	2.50
116	Chris Bordeleau, QuN	.60	1.25	2.50
117	Doug Barrie, EdO	.60	1.25	2.50
118	Hugh Harris, CaC, RC	.60	1.25	2.50
119	Cam Newton, Goalie, OtC, RC, LC	.50	1.25	2.50
120	Poul Popiel, HoA	.60	1.25	2.50
121	Fran Huck, MFS, LC	.60	1.25	2.50
122	Tony Featherstone, ToT, LC	.60	1.25	2.50
123	Bob Woytowich, InR, LC	.60	1.25	2.50
124	Claude St. Sauveur, CaC (Now with Atlanta of the NHL)	.60	1.25	2.50
125	Heikki Riihiranta, WiN	.60	1.25	2.50
126	Gary Kurt, PhR	.60	1.25	2.50
127	Thommy Abrahamsson, NEW, RC	.60	1.25	2.50
128	Danny Gruen, CIC, RC, LC	.60	1.25	2.50
129	Jacques Locas, CiS, RC, LC	.60	1.25	2.50
130	J.C. Tremblay, QuN	.60	1.25	2.50
131	Checklist (1 - 132), Error	10.00	20.00	40.00
132	Ernie Wakely, Goalie, SDM	1.50	3.00	6.00

— 1976 - 77 REGULAR ISSUE —

Mint cards command a 50% premium over NRMT cards.

PRICE MOVEMENT OF NRMT SETS

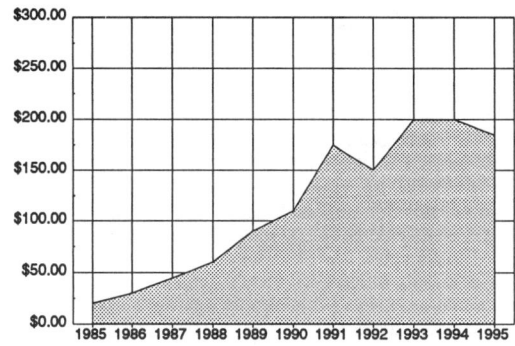

Card Size: 2 1/2" X 3 1/2"
Face: Four colour, white border, Team logo, Position
Back: Blue and brown on card stock; Number, Resume, Bilingual
Imprint: © O-PEE-CHEE PRINTED IN CANADA
Complete Set No.: 132
Complete Set Price: 45.00 95.00 185.00
Common Card: .35 .75 1.50

1975 - 76 LEAGUE LEADERS

No.	Player	VG	EX	NRMT
1	Goal Leaders: M. Tardif, QuN.; R. Cloutier, QuN,; V. Nedomansky, ToT	1.00	2.00	4.00
2	Assist Leaders: J.C. Tremblay, QuN, M. Tardif,QuN; U. Nilsson, WiN	.35	.75	1.50
3	Scoring Leaders: M. Tardif, QuN; B. Hull, WinN; R. Cloutier, QuN; U. Nilsson,WiN	1.50	3.00	6.00
4	Penalty Minute Leaders: C. Brackenbury, QuN, G. Gallant; QuN	.35	.75	1.50

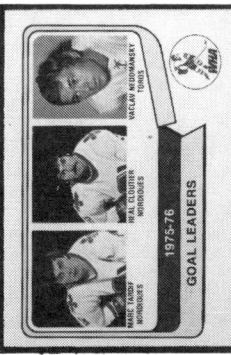

O-Pee-Chee
1976-77 Issue
Card No. 1,
Goal Leaders

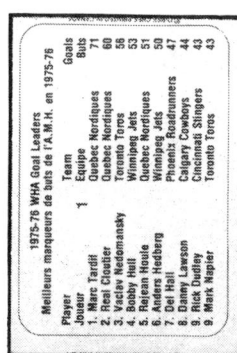

O-Pee-Chee
1976-77 Issue
Card No. 1
Goal Leaders

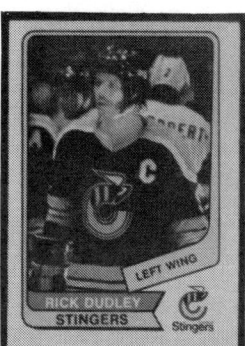

O-Pee-Chee
1976-77 Issue
Card No. 17,
Rick Dudley

O-Pee-Chee
1976-77 Issue
Card No. 51,
Thommie Bergman

No.	Player	VG	EX	NRMT
5	Important Point Leaders: M. Tardif, QuN, B. Hull, WIN, U. Nilsson, WiN	1.50	3.00	6.00
6	Goals Against Avg Leaders: M. Dion, InR, J. Daley, WiN, W. Rutledge, HuA	.35	.75	1.50

REGULAR ISSUE

No.	Player	VG	EX	NRMT
7	Barry Long, WiN	.35	.75	1.50
8	Danny Lawson, CaC, LC	.35	.75	1.50
9	Ulf Nilsson, WiN	.75	1.50	3.00
10	Kevin Morrison, SDM, LC	.35	.75	1.50
11	Gerry Pinder, MFS, LC	.35	.75	1.50
12	Richard Brodeur, Goalie, QuN	1.50	3.00	6.00
13	Robbie Ftorek, PhR	.50	1.00	2.00
14	Tom Webster, NEW	.50	1.00	2.00
15	Marty Howe, HoA	.60	1.25	2.50
16	Bryan Campbell, EdO	.35	.75	1.50
17	Rick Dudley, CiS	.35	.75	1.50
18	Jim Turkiewicz, BIB, RC, LC	.35	.75	1.50
19	Rusty Patenaude, EdO	.35	.75	1.50
20	Joe Daley, Goalie, WiN	.35	.75	1.50
21	Gary Veneruzzo, SDM, LC	.35	.75	1.50
22	Chris Evans, CaC, LC	.35	.75	1.50
23	Mike Antonovich, MFS	.35	.75	1.50
24	Jim Dorey, QuN, LC	.35	.75	1.50
25	John Gray, HoA, RC, LC	.35	.75	1.50
26	Larry Pleau, NEW, LC	.35	.75	1.50
27	Poul Popiel, HoA	.35	.75	1.50
28	Rene Leclerc, InR, RC, LC	.35	.75	1.50
29	Dennis Sobchuk, CiS	.35	.75	1.50
30	Lars-Erik Sjoberg, WiN	.35	.75	1.50
31	Wayne Wood, Goalie, BIB, RC	.55	1.10	2.25
32	Ron Chipperfield, CaC	.35	.75	1.50
33	Tim Sheehy, EdO, RC, LC	.35	.75	1.50
34	Brent Hughes, SDM, LC	.35	.75	1.50
35	Ron Ward, MFS, LC	.35	.75	1.50
36	Ron Huston, PhR, RC, LC	.35	.75	1.50
37	Rosaire Paiement, InR	.35	.75	1.50
38	Terry Ruskowski, HuA, RC	1.25	2.50	5.00
39	Hugh Harris, InR, LC	.35	.75	1.50
40	J.C.Tremblay, QuN	.35	.75	1.50
41	Rich LeDuc, CiS	.35	.75	1.50
42	Peter Sullivan, WiN, RC	.35	.75	1.50
43	Jerry Rollins, PhR, RC, LC	.35	.75	1.50
44	Ken Broderick, Goalie, EdO	.35	.75	1.50
45	Pete Driscoll, CaC, RC, LC	.35	.75	1.50
46	Joe Noris, SDM, RC	.50	1.00	2.00
47	Al McLeod, HoA, LC	.35	.75	1.50
48	Bruce Landon, Goalie, NEW, RC, LC	.35	.75	1.50
49	Chris Bordeleau, QuN, LC	.60	1.25	2.50
50	Gordie Howe, HoA	10.00	20.00	40.00
51	Thommie Bergman, WiN	.35	.75	1.50
52	Dave Keon, MFS	1.50	3.00	6.00
53	Butch Deadmarsh, MFS, LC	.35	.75	1.50
54	Bryan Maxwell, CIS, RC	.35	.75	1.50
55	John Garrett, Goalie, BiB	.40	.85	1.75
56	Glen Sather, EdO, LC	.85	1.75	3.50
57	John Miszuk, CaC, LC	.35	.75	1.50
58	Heikki Riihiranta, WiN, LC	.35	.75	1.50
59	Richard Grenier, QuN, RC, LC	.35	.75	1.50
60	Gene Peacosh, InR, LC	.35	.75	1.50

CANADIAN ALL STAR

No.	Player	VG	EX	NRMT
61	Joe Daley, Goalie, WiN	.35	.75	1.50
62	J. C. Tremblay, QuN	.35	.75	1.50
63	Lars-Erik Sjoberg, WiN	.35	.75	1.50
64	Vaclav Nedomansky, ToT	.35	.75	1.50
65	Bobby Hull, WiN	5.50	11.00	22.00
66	Anders Hedberg, WiN	.35	.75	1.50

AMERICAN ALL STAR

No.	Player	VG	EX	NRMT
67	Christer Abrahamsson, NEW, Goalie	.35	.75	1.50.
68	Kevin Morrison, SDM, LC	.35	.75	1.50
69	Paul Shmyr, CIC	.35	.75	1.50
70	Andre Lacroix, SDM	.50	1.00	2.00
71	Gene Peacosh, SDM	.35	.75	1.50
72	Gordie Howe, HoA	6.00	12.50	25.00

660 • O-PEE-CHEE — 1977-78 REGULAR ISSUE —

REGULAR ISSUE

No.	Player	VG	EX	NRMT
73	Bob Nevin, EdO, LC	.35	.75	1.50
74	Richard Lemieux, CaC, LC	.35	.75	1.50
75	**Mike Ford, CaC, RC, LC**	**.35**	**.75**	**1.50**
76	Real Cloutier, QuN	.35	.75	1.50
77	Al McDonough, MFS, LC	.35	.75	1.50
78	**Del Hall, PhR, RC, LC**	**.35**	**.75**	**1.50**
79	Thommy Abrahamsson, NEW, LC	.35	.75	1.50
80	Andre Lacroix, SDM	.35	.75	1.50
81	**Frank Hughes, PhR, RC, LC**	**.35**	**.75**	**1.50**
82	Reg Thomas, InR, RC	.35	.75	1.50
83	**Dave Inkpen, CiS, RC**	**.35**	**.75**	**1.50**
84	Paul Henderson, BiB	.35	.75	1.50
85	Dave Dryden, Goalie, EdO	.35	.75	1.50
86	Lynn Powis, CaC, LC	.35	.75	1.50
87	Andre Boudrias, QuN, LC	.35	.75	1.50
88	Veli-Pekka Ketola, WiN, LC	.35	.75	1.50
89	Cam Connor, HoA	.35	.75	1.50
90	Claude St. Sauver, CaC	.35	.75	1.50
91	**Garry Swain, NEW, RC, LC**	**.35**	**.75**	**1.50**
92	Ernie Wakely, SDM, Goalie, LC	.35	.75	1.50
93	**Blair MacDonald, InR, RC**	**.35**	**.75**	**1.50**
94	Ron Plumb, CiS	.35	.75	1.50
95	Mark Howe, HoA	3.00	6.00	12.00
96	**Peter Marrin, BiB, RC**	**.35**	**.75**	**1.50**
97	Al Hamilton, EdO	.35	.75	1.50
98	Paulin Bordeleau, QuN	.35	.75	1.50
99	Gavin Kirk, LC	.35	.75	1.50
100	Bobby Hull, WiN	8.25	16.50	33.00
101	Rick Ley, NEW	.35	.75	1.50
102	Gary Kurt, Goalie, PhR, LC	.35	.75	1.50
103	John McKenzie, MFS	.35	.75	1.50
104	**Al Karlander, InR, RC, LC**	**.35**	**.75**	**1.50**
105	John French, SDM, LC	.35	.75	1.50
106	John Hughes, CiS, LC	.35	.75	1.50
107	Ron Grahame, Goalie, HoA	.35	.75	1.50
108	Mark Napier, BiB	.50	1.00	2.00
109	Serge Bernier, QuN	.35	.75	1.50
110	Christer Abrahamsson, Goalie, , NE, LC	.35	.75	1.50
111	Frank Mahovlich, BiB	1.60	3.25	6.50
112	Ted Green, WiN, LC	.35	.75	1.50
113	Rick Jodzio, CaC, LC	.35	.75	1.50
114	**Michel Dion, Goalie, InR, RC**	**.75**	**1.50**	**3.00**
115	Rich Preston, HoA, RC	.35	.75	1.50
116	Pekka Rautakallio, PhR, RC	.50	1.00	2.00
117	Checklist (1 - 132)	3.75	7.50	15.00
118	Marc Tardif, QuN	.35	.75	1.50
119	Doug Barrie, EdO, LC	.35	.75	1.50
120	Vaclav Nedomansky, BiB	.35	.75	1.50
121	Bill Lesuk, WiN	.35	.75	1.50
122	Wayne Connelly, CaC, LC	.35	.75	1.50
123	Pierre Guite, CiS, LC	.35	.75	1.50
124	Ralph Backstrom, NEW, LC	.35	.75	1.50
125	Anders Hedberg, WiN	.75	1.50	3.00
126	Norm Ullman, EdO, LC	.85	1.75	3.50
127	**Steve Sutherland, QuN, RC, LC**	**.35**	**.75**	**1.50**
128	John Schella, HoA, LC	.35	.75	1.50
129	Don McLeod, Goalie, CaC	.35	.75	1.50

1976 PLAYOFFS

No.	Team	VG	EX	NRMT
130	**Canadian O'Keefe Finals:** Winnipeg Wins 4 - 1	**.35**	**.75**	**1.50**
131	U.S. Finals: Houston wins 4 - 3	.35	.75	1.50
132	**World Trophy Finals:** Winnipeg wins Trophy 4 - 0	**1.75**	**3.50**	**7.00**

O-Pee-Chee
1976-77 Issue
Card No. 95,
Mark Howe

O-Pee-Chee
1976-77 Issue
Card No. 119,
Doug Barrie

O-Pee-Chee
1977-78 Issue
Card No. 1,
Gordie Howe

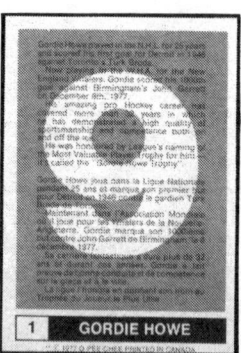

O-Pee-Chee
1977-78 Issue
Card No. 1,
Gordie Howe

— 1977 - 78 REGULAR ISSUE —

This was the final set produced by O-Pee-Chee for the World Hockey Association. Card number 1 recognizes Gordie Howe's 1,000th career goal. Mint cards command a premium of 50% over NRMT cards.

PRICE MOVEMENT OF NRMT SETS

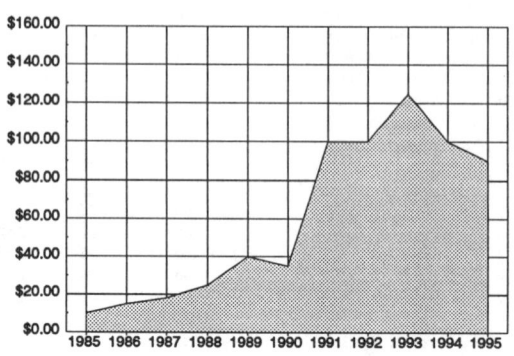

Card Size: 2 1/2" X 3 1/2"
Face: Four colour, white border; Team logo, Position
Back: Blue and brown on card stock, Number, Resume, Bilingual
Imprint: ** © 1977 O-PEE-CHEE PRINTED IN CANADA
Complete Set No.: 66

Complete Set Price:	22.50	45.00	90.00
Common Card:	.18	.35	.75

HOWE'S 1000TH GOAL

No.	Player	VG	EX	NRMT
1	Gordie Howe, NEW (Now with New England Whalers)	11.25	22.50	45.00

REGULAR ISSUE

No.	Player	VG	EX	NRMT
2	Jean Bernier, QuN, RC, LC	.18	.35	.75
3	Anders Hedberg, WiN	.50	1.00	2.00
4	Ken Broderick, Goalie, QuN, LC (Now with Quebec Nordiques)	.18	.35	.75
5	Joe Noris, BiB, LC	.18	.35	.75
6	Blaine Stoughton, CiC	.18	.35	.75
7	Claude St. Sauveur, InR, LC	.18	.35	.75
8	Real Cloutier, QuN	.18	.35	.75
9	Joe Daley, Goalie, WiN, LC	.30	.60	1.25
10	Ron Chipperfield, EdO, (Now with Edmonton Oilers)	.18	.35	.75
11	Wayne Rutledge, Goalie, HoA, LC	.18		.75
12	Mark Napier, BiB	.18	.35	.75
13	Rich LeDuc, CiS	.18	.35	.75
14	Don McLeod, Goalie, QuN, LC (Now with Quebec Nordiques)	.18	.35	.75
15	Ulf Nilsson, WiN	.50	1.00	2.00
16	Blair MacDonald, EdO	.18	.35	.75
17	Mike Rogers, NEW	.18	.35	.75
18	Gary Inness, Goalie, InR	.18	.35	.75
19	Larry Lund, HoA, LC	.18	.35	.75
20	Marc Tardif, QuN, (Now with Quebec Nordiques)	.18	.35	.75
21	Lars-Erik Sjoberg, WiN	.18	.35	.75
22	Bryan Campbell, EdO, LC	.18	.35	.75
23	John Garrett, Goalie, BiB., (Now with Birmingham Bulls)	.30	.60	1.25
24	Ron Plumb, CiS	.18	.35	.75
25	Mark Howe, NEW (Now with New England Whalers)	2.00	4.00	8.00
26	**Garry Lariviere, QuN, RC**	**.18**	**.35**	**.75**
27	Peter Sullivan, WiN	.18	.35	.75
28	Dave Dryden, Goalie, EdN	.18	.35	.75
29	Reg Thomas, InR, LC	.18	.35	.75
30	Andre Lacroix, HoA, (Now with Houston Aeros)	.60	1.25	2.50
31	Paul Henderson, BiB, LC	.35	.75	1.50
32	Paulin Bordeleau, QuN, LC (Now with Quebec Nordiques)	.18	.35	.75
33	Juha Widing, EdO, LC (Now with Edmonton Oilers)	.18	.35	.75
34	Mike Antonovich, NEW	.18	.35	.75
35	Robbie Ftorek, CiS, (Now with Cincinnati Stingers)	.40	.85	1.75

— 1973 - 74 ISSUE — QUAKER OATS • 661

No.	Player	VG	EX	NRMT
36	Rosaire Paiement, InR, LC, (Now with Indianapolis Racers)	.18	.35	.75
37	Terry Ruskowski, HoA	.18	.35	.75
38	Richard Brodeur, Goalie, QuN	.75	1.50	3.00
39	**Willy Lindstrom, WiN, RC**	.40	.85	1.75
40	Al Hamilton, EdO	.18	.35	.75
41	John McKenzie, NEW, LC	.18	.35	.75
42	Wayne Wood, Goalie, BiB, LC (Now with Birmingham Bulls)	.18	.35	.75
43	Claude Larose, CiS, LC	.18	.35	.75
44	J. C. Tremblay, QuN, LC	.18	.35	.75
45	Gary Bromley, Goalie, WiN	.30	.60	1.25
46	Ken Baird, EdO, LC	.18	.35	.75
47	Bobby Sheehan, InR	.18	.35	.75
48	**Don Larway, HoA, RC, LC**	.18	.35	.75
49	Al Smith, Goalie, NEW	.18	.35	.75
50	Bobby Hull, WiN.	6.25	12.50	25.00
51	Peter Marrin, BiB, LC	.18	.35	.75
52	Norm Ferguson, EdO, LC (Now with Edmonton Oilers)	.18	.35	.75
53	Dennis Sobchuk, CiS, LC	.18	.35	.75
54	**Norm Dube, QuN, RC, LC,** (Now with Quebec Nordiques)	.18	.35	.75
55	Tom Webster, NEW, LC	.35	.75	1.50
56	**Jim Park, Goalie, InR, RC, LC**	.18	.35	.75
57	**Dan Labraaten, WiN, RC**	.30	.60	1.25
58	Checklist (1 - 66), Error	2.50	5.00	10.00
59	Paul Shmyr, EdO	.18	.35	.75
60	Serge Bernier, QuN	.18	.35	.75
61	Frank Mahovlich, BiB, LC	1.25	2.50	5.00
62	Michel Dion, Goalie, CiS, (Now with Cincinnati Stingers)	.18	.35	.75
63	Poul Popiel, HoA, LC	.18	.35	.75
64	Lyle Moffat, WiN	.18	.35	.75
65	Marty Howe, NEW (Now with New England Whalers)	.35	.75	1.50
66	Don Burgess, InR, LC	.60	1.25	2.50

QUAKER OATS

— 1973 - 74 ISSUE —

There cards were issued as panels of five cards in Quaker Oats products.

Card Size: 2 1/4" X 3 1/4"
Face: Four colour, white border; Name, Team
Back: Black and blue on white card stock; Name, Team, Position, Team logo, Number, Resume, Bilingual
Imprint: None
Complete Set No.: 10 Panels / 50 Cards

Complete Set Price:	60.00	125.00	250.00
Common Player:	1.00	2.00	4.00

No.	Player	VG	EX	NRMT
—	Panel 1	5.00	10.00	20.00
1	Jim Wiste, CiC	1.00	2.00	4.00
2	Al Smith, Goalie, NEW	1.00	2.00	4.00

O-Pee-Chee
1977-78 Issue
Card No. 54,
Norm Dube

Quaker Oats
1973-74 Issue
Panel No. 1

No.	Player	VG	EX	NRMT
3	Rosaire Paiement, ChC	1.00	2.00	4.00
4	Ted Hampson, MFS	1.00	2.00	4.00
5	Gavin Kirk, ToT	1.00	2.00	4.00
—	Panel 2	8.00	16.00	32.00
6	Andre Lacroix, NeR	1.00	2.00	4.00
7	John Schella, HoA	1.00	2.00	4.00
8	Gerry Cheevers, Goalie, CiC	4.50	9.00	18.00
9	Norm Beaudin, WiN	1.00	2.00	4.00
10	Jim Harrison, AlO	1.00	2.00	4.00
—	Panel 3	5.00	10.00	20.00
11	Gerry Pinder, CiC	1.00	2.00	4.00
12	Bob Sicinski, ChC	1.00	2.00	4.00
13	Bryan Campbell, VaB	1.00	2.00	4.00
14	Murray Hall, HoA	1.00	2.00	4.00
15	Chris Bordeleau, WiN	1.00	2.00	4.00
—	Panel 4	5.00	10.00	20.00
16	Al Hamilton, AlO	1.00	2.00	4.00
17	Jim McLeod, Goalie, NeR	1.00	2.00	4.00
18	Larry Pleau, NEW	1.00	2.00	4.00
19	Larry Lund, HoA	1.00	2.00	4.00
20	Bobby Sheehan, NeR	1.00	2.00	4.00
—	Panel 5	5.00	10.00	20.00
21	Jan Popiel, ChC	1.00	2.00	4.00
22	Andre Gaudette, QuN	1.00	2.00	4.00
23	Bob Charlebois, NEW	1.00	2.00	4.00
24	Gene Peacosh, NeR	1.00	2.00	4.00
25	Rick Ley, NEW	1.00	2.00	4.00
—	Panel 6	5.00	10.00	20.00
26	Larry Hornung, WiN	1.00	2.00	4.00
27	Gary Jarrett, CiC	1.00	2.00	4.00
28	Ted Taylor, HoA	1.00	2.00	4.00
29	Pete Donnelly, Goalie, VaB	1.00	2.00	4.00
30	J.C. Tremblay, QuN	1.00	2.00	4.00
—	Panel 7	5.00	10.00	20.00
31	Jim Cardiff, VaB	1.00	2.00	4.00
32	Gary Veneruzzo, LAS	1.00	2.00	4.00
33	John French, NEW	1.00	2.00	4.00
34	Ron Ward, VaB	1.00	2.00	4.00
35	Wayne Connelly, MFS	1.00	2.00	4.00
—	Panel 8	5.00	10.00	20.00
36	Ron Buchanan, CiC	1.00	2.00	4.00
37	Ken Block, NeR	1.00	2.00	4.00
38	Alain Caron, QuN	1.00	2.00	4.00
39	Brit Selby, ToT	1.00	2.00	4.00
40	Guy Trottier, ToT	1.00	2.00	4.00
—	Panel 9	5.00	10.00	20.00
41	Ernie Wakely, Goalie, WiN	1.00	2.00	4.00
42	J.P. LeBlanc, LAS	1.00	2.00	4.00
43	Michel Parizeau, QuN	1.00	2.00	4.00
44	Wayne Rivers, NeR	1.00	2.00	4.00
45	Reggie Fleming, ChC	1.00	2.00	4.00
—	Panel 10	20.00	40.00	75.00
46	Don Herriman, NeR	1.00	2.00	4.00
47	Jim Dorey, NEW	1.00	2.00	4.00
48	Danny Lawson, VaB	1.00	2.00	4.00
49	Dick Paradise, MFS	1.00	2.00	4.00
50	Bobby Hull, WiN	15.00	30.00	60.00

WORLD HOCKEY ASSOCIATION - TEAM SETS

CLEVELAND CRUSADERS

— 1972 - 73 POSTCARD ISSUE —

Card Size: 3 1/2" X 5 1/2"
Face: Four colour; Name, Jersey number, Team logo
Back: Black on white postcard stock, Name, Resume
Imprint: None
Complete Set No.: 19
Complete Set Price: 22.50 45.00
Common Card: 1.00 2.00

No.	Player	EX	NRMT
1	Paul Andrea	1.75	3.50
2	Doug Brindley	1.00	2.00
3	Ron Buchanan	1.25	2.50
4	Gerry Cheevers, Goalie	7.50	15.00
5	Ray Clearwater	1.00	2.00
6	Bob Dillabough	1.00	2.00
7	John Hanna	1.00	2.00
8	Joe Hardy	1.00	2.00
9	Ted Hodgson	1.00	2.00
10	Ralph Hopiavuori	1.00	2.00
11	Bill Horton	1.00	2.00
12	Gary Jarrett	1.00	2.00
13	Skip Krake	1.00	2.00
14	Jim McMasters	1.00	2.00
15	Wayne Muloin	1.00	2.00
16	Gerry Pinder	1.00	2.00
17	Richard Pumple	1.00	2.00
18	Paul Shmyr	1.00	2.00
19	Bob Whidden	1.00	2.00

LA Sharks
1972-73 Issue
Card No. 3,
George Gardner

LOS ANGELES SHARKS

— 1972 - 73 ISSUE —

Card Size: 2 5/8" X 3 9/16"
Face: Black and white, white border; Name
Back: Black on white card stock; Team logo
Imprint: None
Complete Set No.: 19
Complete Set Price: 12.00 25.00
Common Player: .75 1.50

No.	Player	EX	NRMT
1	Mike Byers	.75	1.50
2	Bart Crashley	.75	1.50
3	George Gardner, Goalie	.75	1.50
4	Russ Gillow, Goalie	.75	1.50
5	Tom Gilmore	.75	1.50
6	Earl Heiskala	.75	1.50
7	J.P. LeBlanc	.75	1.50
8	Ralph MacSweyn	.75	1.50
9	Ted McCaskill	.75	1.50
10	Jim Niekamp	.75	1.50
11	Gerry Odrowski	.75	1.50
12	Tom Serviss	.75	1.50
13	Peter Slater	.75	1.50
14	Steve Sutherland	.75	1.50
15	Joe Szura	.75	1.50
16	Gary Veneruzzo	.75	1.50
17	Jim Watson	1.00	2.00
18	Alton White	.75	1.50
19	Bill Young	.75	1.50

HOUSTON AEROS

— 1975 - 76 POSTCARD ISSUE —

Card Size: 3 1/2" x 5 1/2"
Face: Four colour: Name
Back: Black on white postcard stock; Name, Resume
Imprint: None
Complete Set No.: 19
Complete Set Price: 20.00 40.00
Common Player: .75 1.50

No.	Player	EX	NRMT
1	Ron Grahame, Goalie	.75	1.50
2	Larry Hale	.75	1.50
3	Murray Hall	.75	1.50
4	Gordie Howe	7.50	15.00
5	Mark Howe	4.00	8.00
6	Marty Howe	1.25	2.50
7	Andre Hinse	.75	1.50
8	Frank Hughes	.75	1.50
9	Glen Irwin	.75	1.50
10	Gordon Labossiere	.75	1.50
11	Don Larway	.75	1.50
12	Larry Lund	.75	1.50
13	Paul Popiel	.75	1.50
14	Richard Preston	.75	1.50
15	Terry Ruskowski	1.75	3.50
16	Wayne Rutledge	.75	1.50
17	John Schella	.75	1.50
18	Ted Taylor	.75	1.50
19	John Tonelli	4.00	8.00

ICING

NEW ENGLAND WHALERS

— 1972 - 73 ISSUE —

Card Size: 4 7/8" X 4 5/8"
Face: Black and white: Name
Back: Blank
Imprint: None
Complete Set No.: 17
Complete Set Price: 11.00 22.00
Common Player: .75 1.50

No.	Player	EX	NRMT
1	Mike Byers	.75	1.50
2	Terry Caffery	.75	1.50
3	John Cunniff	.75	1.50
4	John Danby	.75	1.50
5	Jim Dorey	1.00	2.00
6	Tom Earl	.75	1.50
7	John French	.75	1.50
8	Ted Green	1.50	3.00
9	Ric Jordan	.75	1.50
10	Bruce Landon	.75	1.50
11	Rick Ley	1.25	2.50
12	Larry Pleau	.75	1.50
13	Brad Selwood	.75	1.50
14	Tim Sheehy	.75	1.50
15	Al Smith	.75	1.50
16	Tom Webster	1.00	2.00
17	Tom Williams	.75	1.50

Note: Cards are listed in this catalogue chronologically by manufacturer's first date of issue. For all manufacturers, subsequent cards appear in issue date order following that manufacturer's first listing. See the last page of this catalogue for an alphabetical index of issuers.

Note: Cards are listed in this catalogue chronologically by manufacturer's first date of issue. For all manufacturers, subsequent cards appear in issue date order following that manufacturer's first listing. See the last page of this catalogue for an alphabetical index of issuers.

OTTAWA NATIONALS

— 1972 - 73 ISSUE —

Card Size: 4 1/8" X 4 3/4"
Face: Black and white, white border; Name, Team logo
Back: Blank
Imprint: None
Complete Set No.: 23
Complete Set Price: 20.00 40.00
Common Player: 1.00 2.00

No.	Player	EX	NRMT
1	Mike Amodeo	1.00	2.00
2	Les Binkley, Goalie	1.50	3.00
3	Mike Boland	1.00	2.00
4	Wayne Carleton	1.50	3.00
5	Bob Charlebois	1.00	2.00
6	Ron Climie	1.00	2.00
7	Brian Conacher	1.00	2.00
8	Rick Cunningham	1.00	2.00
0	John Donnelly	1.00	2.00
10	Brian Gibbons	1.00	2.00
11	Jack Gibson	1.00	2.00
12	Gilles Gratton, Goalie	1.50	3.00
13	Steve King	1.00	2.00
14	Gavin Kirk	1.00	2.00
15	Bob Leduc	1.00	2.00
16	Tom Martin	1.00	2.00
17	Chris Meloff	1.00	2.00
18	Ron Riley	1.00	2.00
19	Rick Sentes	1.00	2.00
20	Tom Simpson	1.00	2.00
21	Ken Stephenson	1.00	2.00
22	Guy Trottier	1.00	2.00
23	Steve Warr	1.00	2.00

PHOENIX ROADRUNNERS

— 1975 - 76 ISSUE —

Card Size: 3" x 4"
Face: Black and white, white border; Name, Number, Position
Back: Blank
Imprint: None
Complete Set No.: 22
Complete Set Price: 9.00 18.00
Common Player: .50 1.00

No.	Player	EX	NRMT
1	Serge Beaudoin	.50	1.00
2	Jim Boyd	.50	1.00
3	Jim Clarke	.50	1.00
4	Cam Connors	.50	1.00
5	Michel Cormier	.50	1.00
6	Barry Dean	.50	1.00
7	Robbie Ftorek	1.25	2.50
8	Dave Gorman	.50	1.00
9	John Gray	.50	1.00
10	Del Hall	.50	1.00
11	Ron Huston	.50	1.00
12	Murray Keogan	.50	1.00
13	Gary Kurt, Goalie	.50	1.00
14	Garry Lariviere	.50	1.00
15	Al McLeod	.50	1.00
16	Peter McNamee	.50	1.00
17	John Migneault	.50	1.00
18	Lauri Mononen	.50	1.00
19	Jim Niekamp	.50	1.00
20	Jack Norris, Goalie	.50	1.00
21	Pekka Rautakallio	.50	1.00
22	Ron Serafini	.50	1.00

Note: *The Charlton Standard Catalogue of Hockey Cards* arranges cards in their issue date order. This means the first date a manufacturer issues a card set determines the sequence of the manufacturer in the Standard Catalogue. In this manner the historical importance of early cards is maintained. See the last page of this catalogue for an alphabetical index of issuers.

Quebec Nordiques
1972 - 73 Issue
Card No. 1,
Maurice Filion

— 1976 - 77 ISSUE —

Card Size: 3 7/16" x 4 3/8"
Face: Black and white photograph, white border; Name, Resume
Back: Blank
Imprint: None
Complete Set No.: 18
Complete Set Price: 9.00 18.00
Common Card: .50 1.00

No.	Player	EX	NRMT
1	Serge Beaudoin	.50	1.00
2	Michael Cormier	.50	1.00
3	Robbie Ftorek	1.25	2.50
4	Del Hall	.50	1.00
5	Clay Hebenton, Goalie	.50	1.00
6	Andre Hinse	.50	1.00
7	Mike Hobin	.50	1.00
8	Frank Hughes	.50	1.00
9	Ron Huston	.50	1.00
10	Gary Kurt, Goalie	.50	1.00
11	Garry Lariviere	.50	1.00
12	Bob Liddington	.50	1.00
13	Lauri Mononen	.50	1.00
14	Jim Niekamp	.50	1.00
15	Pekka Rautakallio	.50	1.00
16	Seppo Repo	.50	1.00
17	Jerry Rollins	.50	1.00
18	Juhani Tamminen	.50	1.00

QUEBEC NORDIQUES

— 1972 - 73 ISSUE —

These cards are unnumbered. This set is not complete. Any information collectors may have regarding this issue would be greatly appreciated.

Card Size: 3 1/2" X 5 1/2"
Face: Four colour, white border; Facsimile autograph, WHA and team logos
Back: Blank
Imprint: COPY RIGHTS PRO STAR PROMOTIONS INC. Printed in Canada © W.H.A. PROPERTIES CO.
Complete Set No.: 21
Complete Set Price: 35.00

No.	Player	EX	NRMT
1	Maurice Filion, Coach	.50	1.00	2.00

— 1973 - 74 POSTCARD ISSUE —

Card Size: 3 1/2" X 5 1/2"
Face: Four colour; Name, Number, Jersey Number, Team logo
Back: Blank
Imprint: None
Complete Set No.: 19
Complete Set Price: 15.00 30.00
Common Card: .75 1.50

No.	Player	EX	NRMT
1	Serge Aubry	.75	1.50
2	Alain Beaule	.75	1.50
3	Serge Bernier	.75	1.50
4	Richard Brodeau, Goalie	2.00	4.00
5	Alain Caron	.75	1.50
6	Michel Deguise	.75	1.50
7	Ken Desjardins	1.00	2.00
8	Guy Dufour	1.25	2.50
9	Andre Gaudette	.75	1.50
10	Jean-Guy Gendron	1.00	2.00
11	Jeannot Gilbert	.75	1.50
12	Robert Guindon	.75	1.50
13	Pierre Guite	.75	1.50
14	Dale Hoganson	.75	1.50
15	Rejean Houle	1.00	2.00
16	Francois Lacombe	.75	1.50
17	Renald Leclerc	1.00	2.00
18	Michel Parizeau	.75	1.50
19	Jean-Claude Tremblay	1.00	2.00

664 • VANCOUVER BLAZERS — 1973-74 POSTCARD ISSUE —

— 1976 - 77 MARIE ANTOINETTE —

We have no information on this set. We would appreciate hearing from anyone who could supply further information.

— 1976 - 1977 POSTCARD ISSUE —

This 20-card set was used with permission granted from the Quebec Nordiques Hockey Club.

Card Size: 3 1/2" x 5 1/2"
Face: Four colour, borderless; Facsimile autograph
Back: Black on white card stock; Name, Position, Team logo
Imprint: PHBLIE Par La Societe Kent Inc. 105 St. Oliver, QUEBEC
Complete Set No.: 20
Complete Set Price: 12.50 25.00
Common Card: .50 1.00

No.	Player	EX	NRMT
1	Serge Aubry, Goalie	.50	1.00
2	Paul Baxter	.50	1.00
3	Jean Bernier	.50	1.00
4	Serge Bernier	.50	1.00
5	Chris Bordeleau	.50	1.00
6	Paulin Bordeleau	.50	1.00
7	Andre Boudrias	.50	1.00
8	Curt Brackenbury	.50	1.00
9	Richard Brodeur, Goalie	2.50	5.00
10	Real Cloutier	.50	1.00
11	Charles Constantin	.50	1.00
12	Jim Dorey	1.50	3.00
13	Bob Fitchner	.50	1.00
14	Richard Grenier	.50	1.00
15	Francois Lacombe	.50	1.00
16	Pierre Roy	.50	1.00
17	Steve Sutherland	.50	1.00
18	Marc Tardif	1.50	3.00
19	Jean-Claude Tremblay	.50	1.00
20	Wally Weir	1.00	2.00

VANCOUVER BLAZERS

— 1973 - 74 POSTCARD ISSUE —

Card Size: 3 1/2" x 5"
Face: Four colour; Name, Team logo
Back: Blank
Imprint: None
Complete Set No.: 19
Complete Set Price: 15.00 30.00
Common Card: .75 1.50

No.	Player	EX	NRMT
1	Jim Adair	.75	1.50
2	Don Burgess	.75	1.50
3	Bryan Campbell	.75	1.50
4	Colin Campbell	.75	1.50
5	Mike Chernoff	.75	1.50
6	Peter Donnelly	.75	1.50
7	George Gardner, Goalie	1.50	3.00
8	Sam Gellard	.75	1.50
9	Ed Hatoum	.75	1.50
10	Dave Hutchinson	2.00	4.00
11	Danny Lawson	.75	1.50
12	Ralph Macsweyn	.75	1.50
13	Denis Meloche	.75	1.50
14	John Micneault	.75	1.50
15	Murray Myers	.75	1.50
16	Michel Plante	.75	1.50
17	Irvin Spencer	.75	1.50
18	Claude St. Sauveur	.75	1.50
19	Ron Plumb	.75	1.50

Winnipeg Jets
1977-78 Postcard Issue
Card No. 1,
Mike Amodeao

Winnipeg Jets
1977-78 Postcard Issue
Card No. 20,
Lars-Erik Sjoberg

WINNIPEG JETS

— 1978 - 79 POSTCARD ISSUE —

This 23-postcard set is the only known WHA Winnipeg postcard set.

Card Size: 3 1/2" x 5 1/2"
Face: Four colour, borderless; Facsimile autograph
Back: Black on card stock; Name, Resume
Imprint: Printed by Baker & Sons Ltd., Winnipeg
Complete Set No.: 23
Complete Set Price: 10.00 20.00
Common Player: .50 1.00

No.	Player	EX	NRMT
1	Mike Amodeo	.50	1.00
2	Scott Campbell	.50	1.00
3	Kim Clackson	.50	1.00
4	Joe Daley, Goalie	1.00	2.00
5	John Gray	.50	1.00
6	Ted Green	.50	1.00
7	Robert Guindon	.50	1.00
8	Glen Hicks	.50	1.00
9	Larry Hillman, Coach	1.00	2.00
10	Bill Lesuk	.50	1.00
11	Willy Lindstrom	.50	1.00
12	Barry Long	.50	1.00
13	Morris Lukowich	1.50	3.00
14	Paul MacKinnon	.50	1.00
15	Markus Mattsson, Goalie	.50	1.00
16	Lyle Moffatt	.50	1.00
17	Kent Nilsosn	1.00	2.00
18	Rich Preston	.50	1.00
19	Terry Ruskowski	1.25	2.50
20	Lars-Erik Sjoberg	1.50	3.00
21	Peter Sullivan	.50	1.00
22	Paul Terbenche	.50	1.00
23	Steve West	.50	1.00

Note: Your cards must be accurately graded before they can be priced.

Quebec Nordiques, 1976-77 Issue
Card No. 9, Richard Brodeur

**WORLD HOCKEY ASSOCIATION
ALPHABETICAL INDEX**

Abrahamsson, Christer
O-Pee-Chee: 75/76 - 28; 76/77 - 110; 76/77 - 67

Abrahamsson, Thommy
O-Pee-Chee: 75/76 - 127; 76/77 - 79

Amodeo, Mike
Winnipeg Jets: 77/78 - 1

Antonovich, Mike
O-Pee-Chee: 74/75 - 37; 75/76 - 111; 76/77 - 23; 77/78 - 34

Arbour, John
O-Pee-Chee: 75/76 - 54

Aubry, Serge (Goalie)
O-Pee-Chee: 75/76 - 3
Quebec Nord.: 76/77 - 1

Backstrom, Ralph
O-Pee-Chee: 74/75 - 47; 75/76 - 23; 76/77 - 124

Baird, Ken
O-Pee-Chee: 75/76 - 37; 77/78 - 46

Baltimore, Byron
O-Pee-Chee: 75/76 - 9

Barrie, Doug
O-Pee-Chee: 75/76 - 117; 76/77 - 119

Baxter, Paul
Quebec Nord.: 76/77 - 2

Beaudin, Norm
O-Pee-Chee: 74/75 - 11
Quaker Oats: 73/74 - 9

Beaudoin, Serge
Phoenix RR: 75/76 - 1; 76/77 - 1

Bergman, Thommie
O-Pee-Chee: 75/76 - 29; 76/77 - 51

Bernier, Jean
O-Pee-Chee: 77/78 - 2
Quebec Nord.: 76/77 - 3

Bernier, Serge
O-Pee-Chee: 74/75 - 5; 75/76 - 60, 70; 76/77 - 109; 77/78 - 60
Quebec Nord.: 76/77 - 4

Block, Ken
Quaker Oats: 73/74 - 37

Bordeleau, Chris
O-Pee-Chee: 73/74 - 17P; 75/76 - 116; 76/77 - 49
Quaker Oats: 73/74 - 15
Quebec Nord.: 76/77 - 5

Bordeleau, Paulin
O-Pee-Chee: 76/77 - 98; 77/78 - 32
Quebec Nord.: 76/77 - 6

Boucha, Henry
O-Pee-Chee: 75/76 - 79

Boudrias, Andre
O-Pee-Chee: 76/77 - 87
Quebec Nord.: 76/77 - 7

Boyd, Jim
Phoenix RR: 75/76 - 2

Brackenbury, Curt
Quebec Nord.: 76/77 - 8

Broderick, Ken
O-Pee-Chee: 76/77 - 44; 77/78 - 4

Brodeur, Richard
O-Pee-Chee: 75/76 - 44; 76/77 - 12; 77/78 - 38
Quebec Nord.: 76/77 - 9

Bromley, Gary
O-Pee-Chee: 77/78 - 45

Brown, Andy
O-Pee-Chee: 74/75 - 58

Buchanan, Ron
O-Pee-Chee: 74/75 - 23; 75/76 - 39
Quaker Oats: 73/74 - 36

Burgess, Don
O-Pee-Chee: 74/75 - 32; 77/78 - 66

Byers, Mike
LA Sharks: 72/73 - 1

Campbell, Bryan
O-Pee-Chee: 73/74 - 19P; 74/75 - 6; 75/76 - 31; 76/77 - 16; 77/78 - 22
Quaker Oats: 73/74 - 13

Campbell, Scott
Winnipeg Jets: 77/78 - 2

Cardiff, Jim
Quaker Oats: 73/74 - 31

Carleton, Wayne
O-Pee-Chee: 73/74 - 8P; 74/75 - 45; 75/76 - 43

Caron, Alain
Quaker Oats: 73/74 - 38

Charlebois, Bob
Quaker Oats: 73/74 - 23

Cheevers, Gerry
O-Pee-Chee: 73/74 - 6P; 74/75 - 30; 75/76 - 20, 67
Quaker Oats: 73/74 - 8

Chipperfield, Ron
O-Pee-Chee: 74/75 - 42; 75/76 - 4; 76/77 - 32; 77/78 - 10
Quebec Nord.: 76/77 - 10

Clackson, Kim
Winnipeg Jets: 77/78 - 3

Clarke, Jim
Phoenix RR: 75/76 - 3

Climie, Ron
O-Pee-Chee: 73/74 - 12P; 74/75 - 15; 75/76 - 52

Cloutier, Real
O-Pee-Chee: 74/75 - 63; 75/76 - 16; 76/77 - 76; 77/78 - 8

Connelly, Wayne
O-Pee-Chee: 74/75 - 54; 76/77 - 122
Quaker Oats: 73/74 - 35

Connor, Cam
O-Pee-Chee: 75/76 - 48; 76/77 - 89
Phoenix RR: 75/76 - 4

Cormier, Michel
O-Pee-Chee: 75/76 - 74
PHoenix RR: 75/76 - 5; 76/77 - 2

Constantin, Charles
Quebec Nord.: 76/77 - 11

Crashley, Bart
LA Sharks: 72/73 - 2

Daley, Joe
O-Pee-Chee: 74/75 - 38; 75/76 - 101; 76/77 - 20, 61; 77/78 - 9
Winnipeg Jets: 77/78 - 4

Deadmarsh, Butch
O-Pee-Chee: 75/76 - 59; 76/77 - 53

Dean, Barry
Phoenix RR: 75/76 - 6

Dillon, Wayne
O-Pee-Chee: 74/75 - 3

Dion, Michel
O-Pee-Chee: 76/77 - 114; 77/78 - 62

Donnelly, Pete
Quaker Oats: 73/74 - 29

Dorey, Jim
O-Pee-Chee: 75/76 - 94; 76/77 - 24
Quaker Oats: 73/74 - 47
Quebec Nord.: 76/77 - 12

Driscoll, Pete
O-Pee-Chee: 76/77 - 45

Dryden, Dave
O-Pee-Chee: 74/75 - 20; 75/76 - 104; 76/77 - 85; 77/78 - 28

Dube, Norm
O-Pee-Chee: 77/78 - 54

Dudley, Rick
O-Pee-Chee: 75/76 - 58; 76/77 - 17

Dufour, Guy
O-Pee-Chee: 73/74 - 3P

Evans, Chris
O-Pee-Chee: 76/77 - 22

Featherstone, Tony
O-Pee-Chee: 75/76 - 122

Ferguson, Norm
O-Pee-Chee: 75/76 - 92; 77/78 - 52

Filion, Maurice
Quebec Nord.: 72/73 - 1

Fitchner, Bob
Quebec Nord.: 76/77 - 13

Fleming, Reggie
Quaker Oats: 73/74 - 45

Ford, Mike
O-Pee-Chee: 76/77 - 75

Fotiu, Nick
O-Pee-Chee: 75/76 - 108

French, John
O-Pee-Chee: 74/75 - 33; 76/77 - 105
Quaker Oats: 73/74 - 33

Ftorek, Robbie
O-Pee-Chee: 75/76 - 19; 76/77 - 13; 77/78 - 35
Phoenix RR: 75/76 - 7; 76/77 - 3

Gallant, Gordie
O-Pee-Chee: 75/76 - 96

Gardner, George
LA Sharks: 72/73 - 3

Garrett, John
O-Pee-Chee: 75/76 - 12; 76/77 - 55; 77/78 - 23

Gaudette, André
O-Pee-Chee: 74/75 - 46
Quaker Oats: 73/74 - 22

Gillow, Russ
LA Sharks: 72/73 - 4

Gilmore, Tom
LA Sharks: 72/73 - 5

Gorman, Dave
Phoenix RR: 75/76 - 8

Grahame, Ron
O-Pee-Chee: 75/76 - 50, 61; 76/77 - 107

Gratton, Gilles
O-Pee-Chee: 74/75 - 65

Gray, John
O-Pee-Chee: 76/77 - 25
Phoenix RR: 75/76 - 9
Winnipeg Jets: 77/78 - 5

Green, Ted
O-Pee-Chee: 75/76 - 57; 76/77 - 112
Winnipeg Jets: 77/78 - 6

Grenier, Richard
O-Pee-Chee: 76/77 - 59
Quebec Nord.: 76/77 - 14

Gruen, Danny
O-Pee-Chee: 75/76 - 128

Guindon, Bobby
O-Pee-Chee: 74/75 - 26
Winnipeg Jets: 77/78 - 7

Guite, Pierre
O-Pee-Chee: 75/76 - 17; 76/77 - 123

Hall, Del
O-Pee-Chee: 76/77 - 78
Phoenix RR: 75/77 - 10; 76/77 - 4

Hall, Murray
Quaker Oats: 73/74 - 14

Hamilton, Al
O-Pee-Chee: 74/75 - 29; 75/76 - 49; 76/77 - 97; 77/78 - 40
Quaker Oats: 73/74 - 16

Hampson, Ted
Quaker Oats: 73/74 - 4

Harbaruk, Nick
O-Pee-Chee: 75/76 - 11

Harris, Hugh
O-Pee-Chee: 75/76 - 118; 76/77 - 39

Harrison, Jim
O-Pee-Chee: 73/74 - 11P; 75/76 - 47
Quaker Oats: 73/74 - 10

Heatley, Murray
O-Pee-Chee: 75/76 - 53

Hebenton, Clay (Goalie)
Phoenix RR: 76/77 - 5

Hedberg, Anders
O-Pee-Chee: 74/75 - 17; 75/76 - 40, 72; 76/77 - 66, 125; 77/78 - 3

Heiskala, Earl
LA Sharks: 72/73 - 6

Henderson, Paul
O-Pee-Chee: 74/75 - 57; 75/76 - 42; 76/77 - 84; 77/78 - 31

Herriman, Don
Quaker Oats: 73/74 - 46

Hicks, Glen
Winnipeg Jets: 77/78 - 8

Hickey, Pat
O-Pee-Chee: 74/75 - 24

HillMan, Larry
Winnipeg Jets: 77/78 - 9

Hinse, Andre
O-Pee-Chee: 75/76 - 35
Phoenix RR: 76/77 - 6

Hobin, Mike
Phoenix RR: 76/77 - 7

Hoganson, Dale
O-Pee-Chee: 75/76 - 2

Hornung, Larry
Quaker Oats: 73/74 - 26

Houle, Rejean
O-Pee-Chee: 74/75 - 41; 75/76 - 84

Howe, Gordie
O-Pee-Chee: 73/74 - 13P; 75/76 - 66, 100; 76/77 - 50, 72; 77/78 - 1

Howe, Mark
O-Pee-Chee: 75/76 - 7; 76/77 - 95; 77/78 - 25

Howe, Marty
O-Pee-Chee: 75/76 - 75; 76/77 - 15; 77/78 - 65

Huck, Fran
O-Pee-Chee: 74/75 - 28; 75/76 - 121

Hughes, Brent
O-Pee-Chee: 76/77 - 34

Hughes, Frank
O-Pee-Chee: 76/77 - 81
Phoenix RR: 76/77 - 8

Hughes, John
O-Pee-Chee: 75/76 - 45; 76/77 - 106

Hull, Bobby
O-Pee-Chee: 73/74 -P 16; 74/75 - 50; 75/76 - 1, 65; 76/77 - 65, 100; 77/78 - 50
Quaker Oats: 73/74 - 50

Huston, Ron
O-Pee-Chee: 76/77 - 36
Phoenix RR: 75/76 - 11; 76/77 - 9

Inkpen, Dave
O-Pee-Chee: 76/77 - 83

Inness, Gary
O-Pee-Chee: 77/78 - 18

Israelson, Larry
O-Pee-Chee: 75/76 - 46

Jarrett, Gary
O-Pee-Chee: 74/75 - 61; 75/76 - 87
Quaker Oats: 73/74 - 27

Jodzio, Rick
O-Pee-Chee: 75/76 - 99; 76/77 - 113

Joyal, Eddie
O-Pee-Chee: 75/76 - 36

Karlander, Al
O-Pee-Chee: 76/77 - 104

Keogan, Murray
O-Pee-Chee: 74/75 - 44
Phoenix RR: 75/76 - 12

Keon, Dave
O-Pee-Chee: 75/76 - 97; 76/77 - 52

Ketola, Veli-Pekka
O-Pee-Chee: 75/76 - 15; 76/77 - 88

Kirk, Gavin
O-Pee-Chee: 75/76 - 103; 76/77 - 99
Quaker Oats: 73/74 - 5

Kurt, Gary (Goalie)
O-Pee-Chee: 75/76 - 126; 76/77 - 102
Phoenix RR: 75/76 - 13; 76/77 - 10

Labossierre, Gord
O-Pee-Chee: 75/76 - 89

Labraaten, Dan
O-Pee-Chee: 77/78 - 57

Lacombe, Francois
Quebec Nord.: 76/77 - 15

Lacroix, Andre
O-Pee-Chee: 73/74 - 10P; 74/75 - 60; 75/76 - 10, 64; 76/77 - 70, 80; 77/78 - 30
Quaker Oats: 73/74 - 6

Landon, Bruce
O-Pee-Chee: 76/77 - 48

Lapointe, Normand
O-Pee-Chee: 75/76 - 85

Lariviere, Garry
O-Pee-Chee: 77/78 - 26
Phoenix RR: 75/76 - 14; 76/77 - 11

Larose, Claude
O-Pee-Chee: 77/78 - 43

Larway, Don
O-Pee-Chee: 77/78 - 48

Lawson, Danny
O-Pee-Chee: 74/75 - 25; 75/76 - 86; 76/77 - 8
Quaker Oats: 73/74 - 48

LeBlanc, J. P.
O-Pee-Chee: 74/75 - 36
LA Sharks: 72/73 - 7
Quaker Oats: 73/74 - 42

Leclerc, Rene
O-Pee-Chee: 76/77 - 28

LeDuc, Bob
O-Pee-Chee: 73/74 -P 9

LeDuc, Rich
O-Pee-Chee: 75/76 - 113; 76/77 - 41; 77/78 - 13

Lemieux, Richard
O-Pee-Chee: 76/77 - 74

Lesuk, Bill
O-Pee-Chee: 76/77 - 121
Winnipeg Jets: 77/78 - 10

Ley, Rick
O-Pee-Chee: 75/76 - 14; 76/77 - 101
Quaker Oats: 73/74 - 25

Liddington, Bob
O-Pee-Chee: 75/76 - 105
Phoenix RR: 76/77 - 12

Lindstrom, Willy
O-Pee-Chee: 77/78 - 39
Winnipeg Jets: 77/78 - 11

Locas, Jacques
O-Pee-Chee: 75/76 - 129

Long, Barry
O-Pee-Chee: 75/76 - 69, 90; 76/77 - 7
Winnipeg Jets: 77/78 - 12

Lukowich, Morris
Winnipeg Jets: 77/78 - 13

Lund, Larry
O-Pee-Chee: 74/75 - 22; 77/78 - 19
Quaker Oats: 73/74 - 19

MacDonald, Blair
O-Pee-Chee: 76/77 - 93; 77/78 - 16

MacGregor, Bruce
O-Pee-Chee: 75/76 - 22

MacKinnon, Paul
Winnipeg Jets: 77/78 - 14

MacSweyn, Ralph
LA Sharks: 72/73 - 8

Mahovlich, Frank
O-Pee-Chee: 74/75 - 40; 75/76 - 110; 76/77 - 111; 77/78 - 61

Marrin, Peter
O-Pee-Chee: 76/77 - 96; 77/78 - 51

Mattsson, Markus (Goalie)
Winnipeg Jets: 77/78 - 15

Maxwell, Bryan
O-Pee-Chee: 76/77 - 54

McCaskill, Ted
LA Sharks: 72/73 - 9

McDonough, Al
O-Pee-Chee: 75/76 - 33; 76/77 - 77

McKenzie, John
O-Pee-Chee: 75/76 - 77; 76/77 - 103; 77/78 - 41

McLeod, Al
O-Pee-Chee: 75/76 - 88; 76/77 - 47
Phoenix RR: 75/76 - 15

McLeod, Don
O-Pee-Chee: 74/75 - 48; 75/76 - 32; 76/77 - 129; 77/78 - 14

McLeod, Jim
Quaker Oats: 73/74 - 17

McNamee, Peter
Phoenix RR: 75/76 - 16

Migneault, John
Phoenix RR: 75/76 - 17

Miller, Perry
O-Pee-Chee: 75/76 - 6

Miszuk, John
O-Pee-Chee: 76/77 - 57

Moffat, Lyle
O-Pee-Chee: 77/78 - 64
Winnipeg Jets: 77/78 - 16

Mononen, Larry
Phoenix RR: 75/76 - 18; 76/77 - 13

Morris, Rick
O-Pee-Chee: 75/76 - 91

Morrison, Kevin
O-Pee-Chee: 75/76 - 63, 80; 76/77 - 10, 68

Muloin, Wayne
O-Pee-Chee: 75/76 - 102

Napier, Mark
O-Pee-Chee: 75/76 - 78; 76/77 - 108; 77/78 - 12

Nedomansky, Vaclav
O-Pee-Chee: 74/75 - 49; 75/76 - 27; 76/77 - 64, 120

Nevin, Bob
O-Pee-Chee: 76/77 - 73

Newton, Cam
O-Pee-Chee: 75/76 - 119

Niekamp, Jim
LA Sharks: 72/73 - 10
Phoenix RR: 75/76 - 19; 76/77 - 14

Nilsson, Kent
Winnipeg Jets: 77/78 - 17

Nilsson, Ulf
O-Pee-Chee: 74/75 - 4; 75/76 - 83; 76/77 - 9; 77/78 - 15

Nistico, Lou
O-Pee-Chee: 75/76 - 13

Noris, Joe
O-Pee-Chee: 76/77 - 46; 77/78 - 5

Norris, Jack
O-Pee-Chee: 75/76 - 114
Phoenix RR: 75/76 - 20

Odrowski, Gerry
LA Sharks: 72/73 - 11
O-Pee-Chee: 74/75 - 14

Paiement, Rosaire
O-Pee-Chee: 73/74 - 5P; 74/75 - 7; 75/76 - 106; 76/77 - 37; 77/78 - 36
Quaker Oats: 73/74 - 3

Paradise, Dick
Quaker Oats: 73/74 - 49

Parizeau, Michel
O-Pee-Chee: 74/75 - 52
Quaker Oats: 73/74 - 43

Park, Jim
O-Pee-Chee: 77/78 - 56

Patenaude, Rusty
O-Pee-Chee: 74/75 - 51; 75/76 - 76; 76/77 - 19

Peacosh, Gene
O-Pee-Chee: 74/75 - 27; 75/76 - 24; 76/77 - 60, 71
Quaker Oats: 73/74 - 24

Pelyk, Mike
O-Pee-Chee: 74/75 - 19

Perkins, Ross
O-Pee-Chee: 74/75 - 39

Pinder, Gerry
O-Pee-Chee: 73/74 - 7P; 74/75 - 9; 76/77 - 11
Quaker Oats: 73/74 - 11

Plante, Jacques
O-Pee-Chee: 74/75 - 64; 75/76 - 34

Pleau, Larry
O-Pee-Chee: 75/76 - 56; 76/77 - 26
Quaker Oats: 73/74 - 18

Plumb, Ron
O-Pee-Chee: 75/76 - 98; 76/77 - 94; 77/78 - 24

Popiel, Jan
Quaker Oats: 73/74 - 21

Popiel, Poul
O-Pee-Chee: 74/75 - 59; 75/76 - 68, 120; 76/77 - 27; 77/78 - 63

Powis, Lynn
O-Pee-Chee: 76/77 - 86

Preston, Rich
O-Pee-Chee: 76/77 - 115
Winnipeg Jets: 77/78 - 18

Rautakallio, Pekka
O-Pee-Chee: 76/77 - 116
Phoenix RR: 75/76 - 21; 76/77 - 15

Repo, Seppo
Phoenix RR: 76/77 - 16

Riihiranta, Heikki
O-Pee-Chee: 74/75 - 31; 75/76 - 125; 76/77 - 58

Rivers, Wayne
O-Pee-Chee: 74/75 - 13; 75/76 - 38
Quaker Oats: 73/74 - 44

Rochon, Frank
O-Pee-Chee: 75/76 - 51

Rogers, Mike
O-Pee-Chee: 75/76 - 8; 77/78 - 17

Rollins, Jerry
O-Pee-Chee: 76/77 - 43
Phoenix RR: 76/77 - 17

Roy, Pierre
O-Pee-Chee: 75/76 - 25
Quebec Nord.: 76/77 - 16

Rupp, Duane
O-Pee-Chee: 75/76 - 18

Ruskowski, Terry
O-Pee-Chee: 76/77 - 38; 77/78 - 37
Winnipeg Jets: 77/78 - 19

Rutledge, Wayne
O-Pee-Chee: 77/78 - 11

Sather, Glen
O-Pee-Chee: 76/77 - 56

Schella, John
O-Pee-Chee: 75/76 - 21; 76/77 - 128
Quaker Oats: 73/74 - 7

Selby, Brit
Quaker Oats: 73/74 - 39

Selwood, Brad
O-Pee-Chee: 75/76 - 82

Serafini, Ron
Phoenix RR: 75/76 - 22

Serviss, Tom
LA Sharks: 72/73 - 12

Shaw, Jim
O-Pee-Chee: 75/76 - 55

Sheehan, Bobby
O-Pee-Chee: 77/78 - 47
Quaker Oats: 73/74 - 20

Sheehy, Tim
O-Pee-Chee: 76/77 - 33

Sheridan, John
O-Pee-Chee: 75/76 - 107

Shmyr, Paul
O-Pee-Chee: 75/76 - 5; 76/77 - 69; 77/78 - 59

Sicinski, Bob
Quaker Oats: 73/74 - 12

Simpson, Tom
O-Pee-Chee: 74/75 - 16; 75/76 - 81

Sjoberg, Lars-Erik
O-Pee-Chee: 74/75 - 66; 75/76 - 109; 76/77 - 30, 63; 77/78 - 21
Winnipeg Jets: 77/78 - 20

Slater, Peter
LA Sharks: 72/73 - 13

Smith, Al
O-Pee-Chee: 73/74 - 1P; 77/78 - 49
Quaker Oats: 73/74 - 2

Smith, Rick
O-Pee-Chee: 75/76 - 41

Sobchuk, Dennis
O-Pee-Chee: 74/75 - 56; 75/76 - 115; 76/77 - 29; 77/78 - 53

Stapleton, Pat
O-Pee-Chee: 73/74 - 4P; 74/75 - 35

Stoughton, Blaine
O-Pee-Chee: 77/78 - 6

St. Sauveur, Claude
O-Pee-Chee: 73/74 - 18P; 74/75 - 62; 75/76 - 124; 76/77 - 90; 77/78 - 7

Sullivan, Peter
O-Pee-Chee: 76/77 - 42; 77/78 - 27
Winnipeg Jets: 77/78 - 21

Sutherland, Steve
LA Sharks: 72/73 - 14
O-Pee-Chee: 76/77 - 127
Quebec Nord.: 76/77 - 17

Swain, Garry
O-Pee-Chee: 76/77 - 91

Szura, Joe
LA Sharks: 72/73 - 15

Tamminen, Juhani
Phoenix RR: 76/77 - 18

Tardif, Marc
O-Pee-Chee: 73/74 - 20P; 74/75 - 43; 75/76 - 30, 71; 76/77 - 118; 77/78 - 20
Quebec Nord.: 76/77 - 18

Taylor, Ted
Quaker Oats: 73/74 - 28

Terbenche, Paul
O-Pee-Chee: 75/76 - 112
Winnipeg Jets: 77/78 - 22

Thomas, Reg
O-Pee-Chee: 76/77 - 82; 77/78 - 29

Tremblay, J. C.
O-Pee-Chee: 73/74 - 2P; 74/75 - 18; 75/76 - 62, 130; 76/77 - 40, 62; 77/78 - 44
Quaker Oats: 73/74 - 30
Quebec Nord.: 76/77 - 19

Trottier, Guy
Quaker Oats: 73/74 - 40

Turkiewicz, Jim
O-Pee-Chee: 76/77 - 18

Ullman, Norm
O-Pee-Chee: 76/77 - 126

Veneruzzo, Gary
LA Sharks: 72/73 - 16
O-Pee-Chee: 74/75 - 55; 76/77 - 21
Quaker Oats: 73/74 - 32

Wakely, Ernie
O-Pee-Chee: 75/76 - 132; 76/77 - 92
Quaker Oats: 73/74 - 41

Walton, Mike
O-Pee-Chee: 73/74 - 15P; 74/75 - 10; 75/76 - 26

Ward, Ron
O-Pee-Chee: 74/75 - 21; 75/76 - 73; 76/77 - 35
Quaker Oats: 73/74 - 34

Watson, Jim
LA Sharks: 72/73 - 17

Webster, Tom
O-Pee-Chee: 74/75 - 8; 75/76 - 95; 76/77 - 14; 77/78 - 55

Weir, Wally
Quebec Nord.: 76/77 - 20

West, Steve
Winnipeg Jets: 77/78 - 23

White, Alton
LA Sharks: 72/73 - 18

Whitlock, Bob
O-Pee-Chee: 74/75 - 12; 75/76 - 93

Widing, Juha
O-Pee-Chee: 77/78 - 33

Wiste, Jim
O-Pee-Chee: 74/75 - 34
Quaker Oats: 73/74 - 1

Wood, Wayne
O-Pee-Chee: 76/77 - 31; 77/78 - 42

Woytowich, Bob
O-Pee-Chee: 75/76 - 123

Young, Bill
LA Sharks: 72/73 - 19

**CHAPTER SEVEN
TEAM CANADA**

ALPHABETICAL LISTING OF MANUFACTURERS
TEAM CANADA

Alberta Lotteries	673	O-Pee-Chee	671
Future Trends	671	Scotia Bank	671

O-PEE-CHEE

— 1972 - 73 TEAM CANADA —

This unnumbered set features the 28 Team Canada members who played an eight game series against the Russian team in the fall of 1972. This set was an insert issued with the regular O-Pee-Chee second series issue of the same year. Players are listed alphabetically.

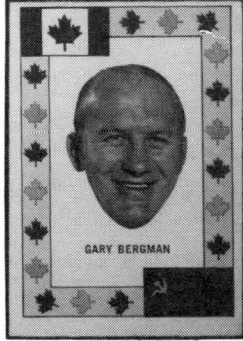

O-Pee-Chee, 1972-73 Issue
Card No. 3, Gary Bergman

Card Size: 2 1/2" X 3 1/2"
Face: Four colour, white border; Name
Back: Orange and black on buff card stock; Name, Resume, Bilingual
Imprint: © O.P.C. PRINTED IN CANADA
Complete Set No.: 28
Complete Set Price: 45.00 90.00 175.00
Common Player: 1.00 2.00 4.00

No.	Player	VG	EX	NRMT
1	Don Awrey	1.00	2.00	4.00
2	Red Berenson	1.00	2.00	4.00
3	Gary Bergman	1.00	2.00	4.00
4	Wayne Cashman	1.25	2.50	5.00
5	Bobby Clarke	3.00	6.00	12.00
6	Yvan Cournoyer	2.50	5.00	10.00
7	Ken Dryden, Goalie	7.00	14.00	28.00
8	Ron Ellis	1.25	2.50	5.00
9	Phil Esposito	6.25	12.50	25.00
10	Tony Esposito, Goalie	2.50	5.00	10.00
11	Rod Gilbert	2.25	4.50	9.00
12	Bill Goldsworthy	1.25	2.50	5.00
13	Vic Hadfield	1.25	2.50	5.00
14	Paul Henderson	1.25	2.50	5.00
15	Dennis Hull	1.25	2.50	5.00
16	Guy Lapointe	1.25	2.50	5.00
17	Frank Mahovlich	3.75	7.50	15.00
18	Pete Mahovlich	1.25	2.50	5.00
19	Stan Mikita	3.00	6.00	12.00
20	Jean Paul Parise	1.00	2.00	4.00
21	Brad Park	2.25	4.50	9.00
22	Gilbert Perreault	2.25	4.50	9.00
23	Jean Ratelle	2.25	4.50	9.00
24	Mickey Redmond	1.00	2.00	4.00
25	Serge Savard	2.25	4.50	9.00
26	Rod Seiling	1.00	2.00	4.00
27	Pat Stapleton	1.00	2.00	4.00
28	Bill White	1.00	2.00	4.00

SCOTIA BANK

— 1972 POSTCARD ISSUE —

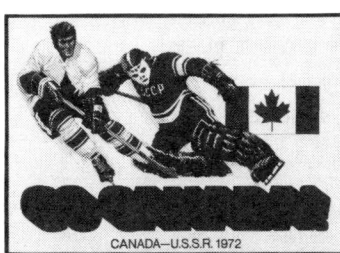

Scotia Bank, 1972 Postcard Issue
Team Canada

Postcard Size: 5 13/16" X 3 15/16"
Face: Four colour
Back: Red and blue on white card stock
Imprint: Scotia Bank

No.	Player	EX	NRMT
—	Team Canada	5.00	10.00

— 1974 POSTCARD ISSUE —

Scotia Bank, 1974 Postcard Issue
Team Canada

Postcard Size: 3 1/2" X 5 3/4"
Face: Four colour, white border
Back: Red and black on card stock
Imprint: Scotia Bank

No.	Player	EX	NRMT
—	Team Canada	5.00	10.00

FUTURE TRENDS

'72 HOCKEY CANADA

— 1991 PROMOTIONAL CARDS —

Three promotional cards were issued to introduce the "Team Canada '72" set. 7,200 of each English promotional card were available through the Hudson Bay Stores in Canada.

Card Size: 2 1/2" x 3 1/2"
Face: Black and white, borderless, red stripe at bottom of photograph, Logo
Back: Black and white, red stripe at bottom of photograph, Logo
Imprint: ©1991 Future Trends Experience Ltd. Printed in Canada

No.	Player	English NRMT	French NRMT
—	The Goal/The Scoreboard	5.00	25.00
—	The Leader/Phil Esposito	5.00	25.00
—	The Legend/The Kid	2.50	25.00

— 1991 ISSUE —

The 20th anniversary of the Canada/Russia series was honoured in 1992 by Future Trends who issued a 101-card set of the 1972 NHL/National Team series. This set was issued in foil cases with an autographed Canadian player card randomly inserted into each case. Each inserted card had a special clear, wavy varnish applied to the face before the player signed it in gold ink. This will distinguish officially issued signed cards from others.

Future Trends, 1991 Issue, Card No. 30
Face: Mahovlich Brothers
Back: Esposito Brothers

Card Size: 2 1/2" x 3 1/2"
Face: Black and white, borderless, red stripe at bottom of photograph, Number, Logo
Back: Three colour, black and white photograph, red stripe at bottom of photograph, Number, Resume, Quote
Imprint: ©1991 Future Trends Experience Ltd. Printed in Canada
Complete Set No.: 101
Complete Set Price: 3.75 7.50
Common Card: .13 .25
Wax Pack: (10 Cards) English or French 1.25
Wax Box: (24 Packs) English or French 30.00
Wax Case: (12 Boxes) English or French 300.00
Production: 9,000 Cases

No.	Player	English NRMT	French NRMT
1	In the Beginning	.13	.25
2	The Backyard Rink/More Months a Year	.13	.25
3	It Didn't Take Long/7-2	.13	.25
4	The Patriarch/Anatoli Tarasov	.13	.25
5	...More Hours a Day	.13	.25
6	Coming Out Party	.13	.25
7	Never in Doubt	.13	.25
8	Team Canada	.13	.25
9	Pat Stapleton	.15	.30
10	Vsevolod Bobrov, Coach	.13	.25
11	Vladislav Tretiak, Goalie	1.50	3.00
12	Faceoff	.13	.25
13	30 Seconds	.13	.25
14	Yevgeny Zimin	.13	.25
15	Bill White	.13	.25
16	7-3/Game 1 Statistics	.13	.25
17	Don Awrey	.13	.25
18	Mickey Redmond	.13	.25
19	Alexander Gusev	.13	.25
20	Alexander Maltsev	.13	.25
21	Rod Seiling	.13	.25
22	Dale Tallon	.13	.25
23	Coming Back	.13	.25
24	Unforgettable/Game 2 Statistics	.13	.25
25	Wayne Cashman	.13	.25
26	Frank Mahovlich	.35	.75
27	Peter Mahovlich	.20	.40
28	Alexander Sidelnikov/Vyacheslav Solodukhin	.13	.25
29	Yuri Shatalov	.13	.25
30	**Brothers:** Phil and Tony Esposito Frank and Peter Mahovlich	.35	.75
31	**The Goalies:** Ken Dryden, Tony Esposito, V. Tretiak	.35	.75
32	Alexander Bodunov	.13	.25

FUTURE TRENDS — CANADA CUP 76

No.	Player	English NRMT	French NRMT
33	All Even/Game 3 Statistics	.13	.25
34	Yuri Blinov	.13	.25
35	Jocelyn Guevremont	.13	.25
36	Vic Hadfield	.13	.25
37	Yuri Lebedev	.13	.25
38	Vyacheslav Starshinov, Yevgeny Poladiev	.13	.25
39	Disaster/Game 4 Statistics	.13	.25
40	Address to the Nation	.13	.25
41	Victor Kuzkin	.13	.25
42	Vladimir Lutchenko	.13	.25
43	Boris Mikhailov	.35	.75
44	Grace Under Pressure	.13	.25
45	Afraid to Lose...	.13	.25
46	...Ready to Win/Game 5 Statistics	.13	.25
47	Vladimir Vikulov	.13	.25
48	Red Berenson	.13	.25
49	Richard Martin	.35	.75
50	Alexander Martynyuk	.13	.25
51	Gilbert Perreault	.35	.75
52	Vladimir Petrov	.35	.75
53	Serge Savard	.25	.50
54	Vladimir Shadrin	.35	.75
55	Da Da Ka-na-da/Nyet Nyet Sov-j-et	.13	.25
56	One Step Back/Game 6 Statistics	.13	.25
57	Bobby Clarke	.75	1.50
58	Valeri Kharlamov	.75	1.50
59	Alexander Volchkov	.13	.25
60	Standing Guard	.13	.25
61	Stan Mikita	.35	.75
62	One More to Go/Game 7 Statistics	.13	.25
63	The Winner	.13	.25
64	The Fans Go Wild	.13	.25
65	Alexander Ragulin	.13	.25
66	Jean Ratelle	.13	.25
67	Gennady Tsygankov	.13	.25
68	Valeri Vasiliev	.13	.25
69	International Dialogue	.13	.25
70	Series Stars: P. Esposito/Yakushev	.35	.75
71	Series Stars: Henderson/Tretiak	.35	.75
72	No Solitudes/The Telegrams	.13	.25
73	2 - 2/3 - 3	.13	.25
74	Rod Gilbert	.13	.25
75	Yevgeny Mishakov	.13	.25
76	Ron Ellis	.50	1.00
77	5 - 4/5 - 5	.13	.25
78	Different Games/Interlude	.13	.25
79	Bill Goldsworthy	.13	.25
80	The Huddle.../...1:30 To Go	.13	.25
81	The Moment	.13	.25
82	Yvan Cournoyer	.50	1.00
83	Yuri Liapkin	.13	.25
84	Phil Esposito	.75	1.50
85	Ken Dryden, Goalie	.75	1.50
86	Peace/Game 8 Statistics	.25	.50
87	Gary Bergman	.13	.25
88	Brian Glennie	.13	.25
89	Dennis Hull	.13	.25
90	Vyacheslav Anisin	.13	.25
91	Marcel Dionne	.25	.50
92	Guy Lapointe	.13	.25
93	Ed Johnston, Goalie	.13	.25
94	Harry Sinden, Coach	.13	.25
95	Brad Park	.13	.25
96	Tony Esposito, Goalie	.35	.75
97	Alexander Yakushev	.35	.75
98	Paul Henderson	.75	1.50
99	J. P. Parise	.13	.25
100	V. Kharlamov 1948-1981	.50	1.00
101	Checklist	.13	.25

— '72 HOCKEY CANADA — 1991 AUTOGRAPHED CARDS

This 36-card autographed set was randomly inserted into foil packs. They are fairly scarce and sets are hard to come by.

Card Size: 2 1/2" X 3 1/2"
Face: Black and white, borderless, red stripe at bottom of photograph, Number, Logo
Back: Three colour, black and white photograph, red stripe at bottom of photograph, Number, Resume, Quote
Imprint: © 1991 Future Trends Experience Ltd. Printed in Canada
Complete Set No.: 36
Complete Set Price: 850.00 / 850.00
Common Card: 20.00 / 20.00

No.	Player	English NRMT	French NRMT
9	Pat Stapleton	20.00	20.00
11	Vladislav Tretiak, Goalie	125.00	125.00
15	Bill White	20.00	20.00
17	Don Awrey	20.00	20.00
18	Mickey Redmond	20.00	20.00
21	Rod Seiling	20.00	20.00
22	Dale Tallon	20.00	20.00
25	Wayne Cashman	20.00	20.00
26	Frank Mahovlich	45.00	45.00
27	Peter Mahovlich	20.00	20.00
35	Jocelyn Guevremont	20.00	20.00
36	Vic Hatfield	20.00	20.00
48	Red Berenson	20.00	20.00
49	Richard Martin	20.00	20.00
51	Gilbert Perreault	20.00	20.00
53	Serge Savard	20.00	20.00
57	Bobby Clarke	50.00	50.00
61	Stan Mikita	40.00	40.00
66	Jean Ratelle	20.00	20.00
74	Rod Gilbert	20.00	20.00
76	Ron Ellis	20.00	20.00
79	Bill Goldsworthy	20.00	20.00
82	Yvan Cournoyer	20.00	20.00
84	Phil Esposito	65.00	65.00
85	Ken Dryden, Goalie	150.00	150.00
87	Gary Bergman	20.00	20.00
88	Brian Glennie	20.00	20.00
89	Dennis Hull	20.00	20.00
91	Marcel Dionne	50.00	50.00
92	Guy Lapointe	20.00	20.00
93	Ed Johnston, Goalie	20.00	20.00
94	Harry Sinden, Coach	20.00	20.00
95	Brad Park	35.00	35.00
96	Tony Esposito, Goalie	50.00	50.00
98	Paul Henderson	50.00	50.00
99	J.P. Parise	20.00	20.00

— CANADA CUP 76 — COMMEMORATIVE SHEETS

These three sheets were handed out to promote the 76 Future Trends Canada Cup sets.

Sheet Size: 8 1/2" x 11"
Face: Four colour
Back: Type 1: Blank
Type 2: Checklist for set, printed on cardboard stock
Complete Set No.: 3
Complete Set Price: 15.00 / 30.00

No.	Player	EX	NRMT
1	Bauer presents Canada Cup '76	5.00	10.00
2	Canada Cup	5.00	10.00
3	Team U.S.A.	5.00	10.00

— CANADA CUP 76 —

This 100-card set is a continuation of the previous year's set. The '76 Canada Cup also includes other countries.

Canada Cup 76 Card No. 102, Sergeant Pepper, Phil Esposito

Card Size: 2 1/2" x 3 1/2"
Face: Four colour, white border, Name
Back: Four colour, white border; Name, Number, Resume
Imprint: © 1992 Future Trends Experience Ltd.
Complete Set No.: 100
Complete Set Price: 7.50 / 15.00
Common Player: .05 / .10

No.	Player	EX	NRMT
—	Vladislav Tretiak, Goalie, Promo	2.50	5.00
102	Sergeant Pepper, Phil Esposito	.13	.25
103	Soviet Ambassador, Vladislav Tretiak	.13	.25
104	Impossible, Bobby Orr	.50	1.00
105	The Goal	.05	.10
106	IF, Alexander Yakishov	.10	.20
107	The Golden Jet, Bobby Hull	.13	.25
108	Soviet Superstar, Vladislav Tretiak	.25	.50
109	Great Goalies	.05	.10
110	What If Series?	.05	.10
111	A Soviet Suprise	.05	.10
112	World Champs	.05	.10
113	Tournament Underdogs	.05	.10
114	Sweden's Best Ever	.05	.10
115	Team U.S.A. Trains	.05	.10
116	Canada Cup Camp	.05	.10
117	Serge Savard	.05	.10
118	Team Finland	.05	.10
119	Team Sweden	.05	.10
120	Team Czechoslovakia	.05	.10
121	Soviets	.05	.10
122	Team U.S.A.	.05	.10
123	Team Canada	.05	.10
124	The Opening Barrage	.05	.10
125	Richard Martin	.05	.10
126	Bobby Orr	.50	1.00
127	Power Play	.05	.10
128	Ivan Hlinka	.05	.10
129	CSSR 5 - CCCP 3	.05	.10
130	Helmut Balderis	.05	.10
131	Peter Stastny	.05	.10
132	Valeri Vasiliev	.05	.10
133	Out Of Contention	.05	.10
134	Standing Alone	.05	.10
135	"The Miracle on Ice" ...Almost	.05	.10
136	Josef Augusta	.05	.10
137	A Soviet Rout	.05	.10
138	Viktor Zhluktov	.05	.10
139	Hull's A Hit	.05	.10
140	Bob Gainey	.05	.10
141	Anders Hedberg	.05	.10
142	Bobby Hull	.05	.10
143	Ulf Nilsson	.05	.10
144	Sergei Kapustin	.05	.10
145	Borje Salming	.10	.20
146	Well Enough to Win	.05	.10
147	Biggest Upset	.05	.10
148	Matti Hagman	.05	.10
149	Unbeatable	.05	.10
150	Boris Alexandrov	.05	.10
151	A Goaltending Duel	.05	.10
152	Vladimir Dzurilla, Goalie	.05	.10
153	Phil Esposito	.10	.20

No.	Player	EX	NRMT
154	Rogatien Vachon, Goalie	.13	.25
155	Milan Novy	.05	.10
156	Vladimir Martinec	.05	.10
157	Good For Hockey	.05	.10
158	Bill Nyrop	.05	.10
159	Pride	.05	.10
160	Another Summit	.05	.10
161	Alexander Maltsev	.05	.10
162	Gilbert Perreault	.05	.10
163	Vladislav Tretiak, Goalie	.25	.50
164	Vladimir Vikulov	.05	.10
165	Canada Cup Final, Game 1	.05	.10
166	Not There Yet	.05	.10
167	Fast & Furious, Game 2	.05	.10
168	4 - 3(Front) 4 - 4 (Back)	.05	.10
169	Bill Barber	.05	.10
170	The Grapevine	.05	.10
171	Guy Lapointe	.05	.10
172	Reggie Leach	.05	.10
173	Sittler's Goal	.08	.15
174	Lanny McDonald	.08	.15
175	Darryl Sittler	.08	.15
176	The Canada Cup	.05	.10
177	Bobby Clarke	.13	.25
178	Last Time For #9	.05	.10
179	Marcel Dionne	.05	.10
180	Peter Mahovlich	.05	.10
181	Denis Potvin	.05	.10
182	Larry Robinson	.10	.20
183	Steve Shutt	.05	.10
184	Tournament MVP: Bobby Orr	.05	.10
185	M.V.P. Canada: Rogatien Vachon, Goalie	.05	.10
186	M.V.P. CSSR: Milan Novy	.05	.10
187	M.V.P. Finland: Matti Hagman	.05	.10
188	M.V.P. Sweden: Borje Salming	.05	.10
189	M.V.P. USA: Robbie Ftorek	.05	.10
190	M.V.P. USSR: Alexander Maltsev	.05	.10
191	Canada Final Series Totals	.05	.10
192	Canada Series Totals	.05	.10
193	CSSR Final Series Totals	.05	.10
194	CSSR Series Totals	.05	.10
195	All Star Team: Rogatien Vachon, Goalie	.05	.10
196	All Star Team: Bobby Orr	.05	.10
197	All Star Team: Borje Salming	.05	.10
198	All Star Team: Milan Novy	.05	.10
199	All Star Team: Darryl Sittler	.05	.10
200	All STar Team: Alexander Maltsev	.05	.10
201	Checklist	.05	.10

— CANADA CUP 76 AUTOGRAPHED CARDS —

Card Size: 2 1/2" x 3 1/2"
Face: Four colour, white border, Autographed in permanent marker.
Back: Four colour, white border, card stock; Name, Resume
Imprint: © 1992 Future Trends Experience Ltd.
Complete Set No.: 5
Complete Set Price: 250.00 500.00

No.	Player	EX	NRMT
—	Bobby Clarke, Phi.	65.00	125.00
—	Bobby Hull, Chi.	75.00	150.00
—	Bobby Orr, Bos.	90.00	175.00
—	Darryl Sittler, Tor.	50.00	100.00
—	Rogatien Vachon, Goalie, Mon.	50.00	100.00

ALBERTA LOTTERIES

— ALBERTA INTERNATIONAL HOCKEY — TOUR '91

This 23-card set represents the players on the Canadian Olympic team in 1992.

Alberta Int'l Hockey Tour '91
Card No. 1, Craig Billington

Card Size: 2 1/2" x 3 1/2"
Face: Four colour, black border at top; grey border at bottom; Name; Number, Position
Back: Four colour on card stock, black border at top; grey border at bottom; Name, Resume, Team Canada logo
Imprint: None
Complete Set No.: 23
Complete Set Price: 7.50 15.00
Common Player: .25 .50

No.	Player	EX	NRMT
1	Craig Billington, Goalie	1.50	3.00
2	Doug Dadswell, Goalie	.25	.50
3	Greg Andrusak	.25	.50
4	Karl Dykhuis	1.00	2.00
5	Gord Hynes	.25	.50
6	Ken MacArthur	.25	.50
7	Jim Paek	.75	1.50
8	Brad Schlegel	.75	1.50
9	Dave Archibald	.25	.50
10	Stu Barnes	1.00	2.00
11	Brad Bennett	.25	.50
12	Todd Brost	.25	.50
13	Jose Charbonneau	.25	.50
14	Jason Lafreniere	.25	.50
15	Chris Lindberg	.25	.50
16	Ken Priestlay	.25	.50
17	Stephane Roy	.25	.50
18	Randy Smith	.25	.50
19	Todd Strueby	.25	.50
20	Vladislav Tretiak, CCCP	1.00	2.00
21	David King, GM/Head Coach	.75	1.50
22	Wayne Fleming, Asst.GM/Asst.Coach	.25	.50
23	Checklist	.25	.50

— ALBERTA INTERNATIONAL TOUR '93 —

CANADA'S NATIONAL TEAM COLLECTOR'S EDITION

This set may be incomplete and we would appreciate hearing from anyone who could supply further information.

Card Size: Unknown
Face: Four colour
Back: Yellow on white card stock; Statistics
Imprint: Unknown
Complete Set No.: 31
Complete Set Price: Unknown
Common Card: .25 .50

No.	Player	EX	NRMT
—	Title Card	.25	.50
—	Canadian Captain: Mike Myres	.35	.75
—	Russian Captain: Vladislav Tretiak, Goalie	.35	.75
—	Coach: Danny Dube	.25	.50
1	Mike Fountain, Goalie	.35	.75
3	Adrian Aucoin	.25	.50
4	Derek Mayer	.25	.50
5	Garth Premak	.25	.50
6	Mike Brewer	.25	.50
7	Hank Lammens	.25	.50
9	Keith Morris	.25	.50
14	Jackson Penney	.25	.50
16	Stephane Roy	.25	.50
17	Trevor Sim	.25	.50
19	Dominic Amodeo	.25	.50
20	Mark Astley	.25	.50
21	Todd Hlushko	.50	1.00
22	Eric Bellerose	.25	.50
27	Mark Bassen	.25	.50
29	Derek Laxdal	.25	.50
31	Allain Roy, Goalie	.25	.50

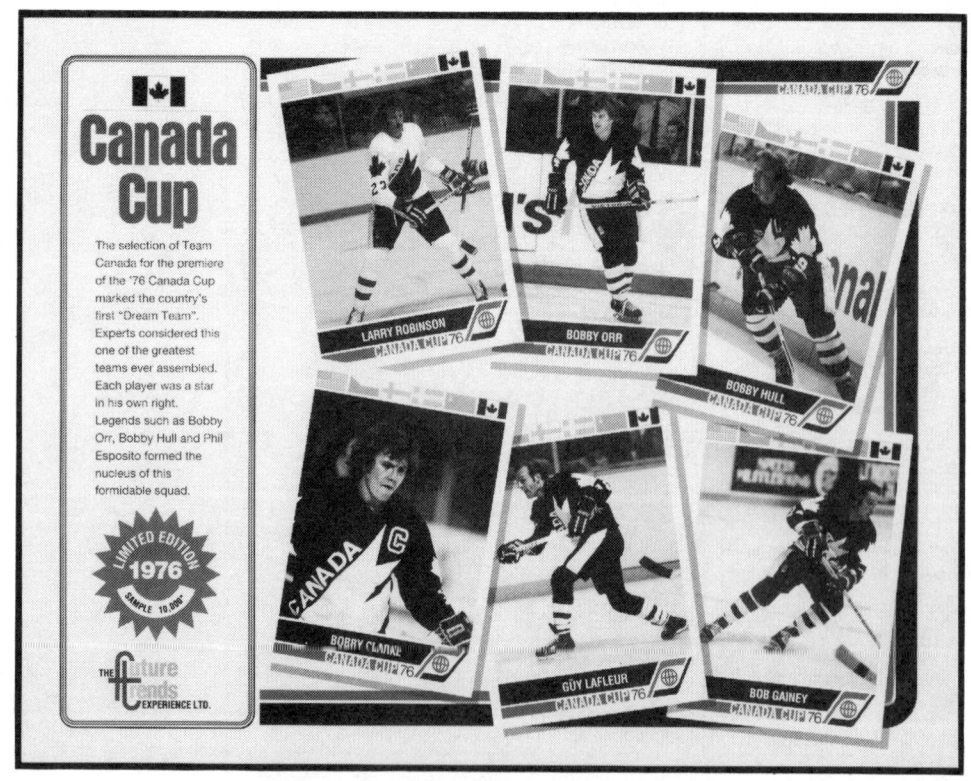

CANADA CUP 1976, COMMEMMORATIVE SHEET

**CHAPTER EIGHT
WORLD HOCKEY**

ALPHABETICAL LISTING OF MANUFACTURERS
WORLD HOCKEY

Ivan Fiodorov Press	677	Russian Team Sets	677
Panini	679	Tri-Globe International	678
Red Ace International	677	U.S.A. Olympic Team Set	681

RUSSIAN TEAM SETS

— 1978 SOVIET NATIONAL TEAM —

WORLD CHAMPIONSHIPS PRAGUE

This 24-postcard set has two well known Russian hockey figures in it. Vladislav Tretiak, goalie and Viktor Tikanov, coach.

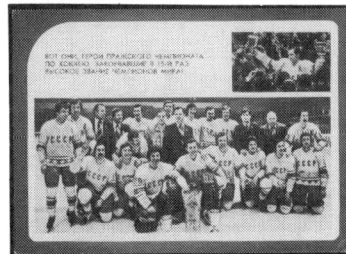

1978 Soviet National Team
World Championships Prague
Card No. 1, Team Photograph

Card Size: 8 1/4" x 5 7/8"
Face: Four colour; Name, Resume
Back: Black and white; Stats, Resume
Imprint: © N3Aarenbctbo Nnafat Mockba 1979
Complete Set No.: 24 plus Checklist Envelope
Complete Set Price: 20.00 — 40.00
Common Goalie: .85 — 1.75
Common Player: .85 — 1.75

No.	Player	EX	NRMT
1	Title Card: Team Photograph	.85	1.75
2	Victor Tikhonov, Coach	1.50	3.00
3	Vladimir Urzinov, Coach	.85	1.75
4	Vladislav Tretjak, Goalie	3.00	6.00
5	Alexander Pashkov, Goalie	.85	1.75
6	Vladimir Lutchenko	.85	1.75
7	Valeri Vasiliev	.85	1.75
8	Gennady Tsygankov	.85	1.75
9	Uri Fedorov	.85	1.75
10	Viacheslav Fetisov	.85	1.75
11	Zinatula Beleletdinov	.85	1.75
12	Vasiliy Pervukhin	.85	1.75
13	Boris Mikhailov	.85	1.75
14	Vladimir Petrov	.85	1.75
15	Valesy Kharlamov	.85	1.75
16	Alexander Maltsev	.85	1.75
17	Sergei Kapustin	.85	1.75
18	Uriy Lebedev	.85	1.75
19	Viktor Zluktov	.85	1.75
20	Helmut Balderis	.85	1.75
21	Alexander Golikov	.85	1.75
22	Sergei Makarov	.85	1.75
23	Vladimir Golikov	.85	1.75
24	Closing Ceremonies	.85	1.75
25	Envelope with checklist	.85	1.75

— 1979 SOVIET NATIONAL TEAM — WORLD CHAMPIONSHIPS MOSCOW

1979 Soviet National Team
World Championships Moscow
Team Photograph

Card Size: 8 1/4" x 5 7/8"
Face: Four colour; Moscow 1979
Back: Black and white; Sketch of Championship
Imprint: © N3Aatembctbo Anakat Mockba 1980

No.	Player	EX	NRMT
1	Team Photograph	.85	1.75

— 1988 HISTORY OF THE SOVIET NATIONAL TEAM IN THE OLYMPIC GAMES —

Card Size: 3 5/8" x 5 5/8"
Face: Black and white photo card
Back: Black and white; Number, Title, Resume
Imprint: © Moscow 1985-1988
Complete Set No.: 14
Complete Set Price: 17.50 — 35.00

No.	Player	EX	NRMT
1	Sweden vs USR, Corinta 1956	1.25	2.50
2	Tregubov, Alexaudsov, Puchkov, Squaw Valley 1960	1.25	2.50
3	Statshinov, Konovaleuko, Ivanov, Jakushev, Innsbruck 1964	1.25	2.50
4	Three Times Olympic Champions Grenoble 1968	1.25	2.50
5	A. Firsov, Sapporo 1972	1.25	2.50
6	Soviets vs Finland, Innsbruck 1976	1.25	2.50
7	Silver Medalist, Lake Placid 1980	1.25	2.50
8	Olympic Champions, Sarajevo 1984	1.25	2.50
9	Soviet Coaches of Olympic Teams	1.25	2.50
10	Captains of Olympic Gold Teams	1.25	2.50
11	Three Time Winners of Olympic Gold Medals	1.25	2.50
12	Vsevolod Bobrov, Coach, Gold Medalist	1.25	2.50
13	Valeri Kharlamov, Twice Gold Medalist	1.25	2.50
14	Makarov, Larionov, Krutov, Fetisov, Kasatomov, Calgary 1988	2.50	5.00

— 1989 - 90 STARS OF SOVIET HOCKEY —

This is the first set to illustrate Soviet players that played in the NHL. The cards are not numbered and are listed here in alphabetical order.

Card Size: 4 1/8" x 5 5/8"
Face: Four colour, borderless; Facsimile autograph
Back: Black and white; Name, Team, Position, Resume
Imprint: None
Complete Set No.: 24
Complete Set Price: 7.50 — 13.00
Common Card: .25 — .50
Folder: .50 — 1.00

No.	Player	EX	NRMT
1	Ilya Biakin	.25	.50
2	Viacheslav Bikov	.25	.50
3	Igor Dmitriev, Assistant Coach	.25	.50
4	Sergei Fedorov	2.50	5.00
5	Viatcheslav Fetisov	.50	1.00
6	Aleksei Gusarov	.75	1.50
7	Artur Irbe, Goalie	1.50	3.00
8	Valeri Kamenski	.50	1.00
9	Aleksei Kasatonov	.25	.50
10	Sviatoslav Khalizov	.25	.50
11	Juri Khmilev	.25	.50
12	Andrei Khomlitov	.25	.50
13	Vladimir Konstantinov	.25	.50
14	Vladimir Krutov	.25	.50
15	Dmitri Kvartalnov	.50	1.00
16	Igor Larionov	.50	1.00
17	Sergei Makarov	.25	.50
18	Sergei Milnikov, Goalie	.25	.50
19	Vladimir Mishkin, Goalie	.25	.50
20	Sergei Nemchinov	.25	.50
21	Valeri Shiriaev	.25	.50
22	Victor Tikhonov, Head Coach	.25	.50
23	Aleksander Tchernikh	.25	.50
24	Sergei Yashin	.25	.50

IVAN FIODOROV PRESS

— 1991 SPORT UNITES HEARTS —

This 11-card set was printed in Leningrad. This special limited edition set was supposedly produced in a quantity of 50,000.

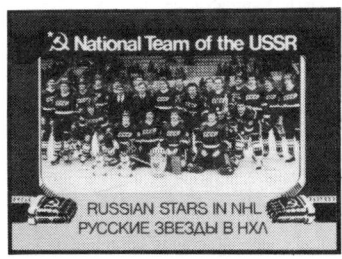

Ivan Fiodorov Press, 1991 Sport Unites Hearts
Card No. 1, USSR National Team

Card Size: 2 1/2" x 3 1/2"
Face: Four colour, blue border; Name, Bilingual
Back: Four colour, white border, card stock; Name, Resume, Bilingual
Imprint: Ivan Fiodorov Leningrad, Printed in USSR
Complete Set No.: 11
Complete Set Price: 5.00 — 10.00
Common Card: .75 — 1.50

No.	Player	EX	NRMT
1	USSR National Team	1.00	2.00
2	Sergei Fedorov	2.50	5.00
3	Viacheslav Fetisov	.75	1.50
4	Alexei Gusarov	.75	1.50
5	Alexei Kasatonov	.75	1.50
6	Vladimir Konstantinov	.75	1.50
7	Igor Larionov	.75	1.50
8	Sergei Makarov	.75	1.50
9	Alexander Mogilny	.75	4.00
10	Mikhail Tatarinov	.75	1.50
11	Vladislav Tretiak, Goalie	.75	1.50

RED ACE INTERNATIONAL

— 1991 RUSSIAN NHL STARS —

This is the first Red Ace set. It shows seventeen of the Russian players in their former team uniforms. They all played for NHL teams in the 1991-92 season. The cards are not numbered and are listed below in alphabetical order. The set was issued in a limited edition of 50,000.

Red Ace International, 1991 Russian NHL Stars
Card No. 1, Pavel Bure

Card Size: 2 1/2" x 3 2/2"
Face: Four colour, borderless; Name
Back: Four colour, card stock; Name, Resume, Bilingual
Imprint: © 1991 Moscow
Complete Set No.: 17
Complete Set Price: 7.50 — 15.00
Common Card: .50 — 1.00

No.	Player	EX	NRMT
1	Pavel Bure, Van.	2.50	5.00
2	Evgeny Davydov, Win.	.50	1.00

TRI-GLOBE INTERNATIONAL — 1992 SERGEI FEDOROV —

No.	Player	EX	NRMT
3	Sergei Fedorov, Det.	2.50	5.00
4	Viacheslav Fetisov, NJ	.50	1.00
5	Alexei Gusarov, Que.	.50	1.00
6	Valeri Kamensky, Que.	1.00	2.00
7	Alexei Kasatonov, NJ	.50	1.00
8	Ravil Khaidarov	.50	1.00
9	Vladimir Konstantinov, Que.	.50	1.00
10	Igor Kravchuk, Chi.	.50	1.00
11	Alexander Mogilny, Buf.	1.50	3.00
12	Igor Larionov, Cal.	.50	1.00
13	Andrei Lomakin, Cal.	.50	1.00
14	Sergei Makarov, Cal.	.50	1.00
15	Sergei Nemchinov, NYR	.50	1.00
16	Anatoli Semenov, Edm.	.50	1.00
17	Mikhail Tatarinov, Que.	.50	1.00
31	Dmitri Starostenko	.50	1.00
32	Ravil Yakubov	.50	1.00
33	Alexei Yashin	2.00	4.00
34	Dmitri Yushkevich	.75	1.50
35	Alexei Zhamnov	1.00	2.00
36	Alexei Zhitnik	1.00	2.00
37	Checklist	.50	1.00

— 1992 RUSSIAN NHL STARS —

This 37-card set was the second year Red Ace produced cards. Again, the Russians who are playing in the NHL are shown playing in their former team uniforms. The set is limited to 25,000.

Red Ace International, 1992 Russian NHL Stars
Card No. 9, Sergei Gonchar

Card Size: 2-1/2" x 3 1/2"
Face: Four colour, white border; Name; Red Ace logo
Back: Four colour, white border, card stock; Name, Numbner, Resume, Bilingual
Imprint: © 1992 Moscow
Complete Set No.: 37
Complete Set Price: 9.00 18.00
Common Card: .50 1.00

No.	Player	EX	NRMT
1	Alexander Barkov	.50	1.00
2	Sergei Bautin	.75	1.50
3	Igor Boldin	.50	1.00
4	Nikolai Bortchevski, Error	1.50	3.00
5	Sergei Brylin	.50	1.00
6	Vyacheslav Butsayev, Error	1.00	2.00
7	Alexander Cherbayev, Error	.75	1.50
8	Evgeny Garanin	.50	1.00
9	Sergei Gonchar	.50	1.00
10	Alexander Karpovtsev	.50	1.00
11	Darius Kasparaitis	1.25	2.50
12	Alexander Kharlamov	.75	1.50
13	Yuri Khmylev	.75	1.50
14	Sergei Klimovich	.50	1.00
15	Igor Korolev	.50	1.00
16	Andrei Kovalenko	.75	1.50
17	Alexei Kovalev	2.00	4.00
18	Dmitri Kvartalnov	.50	1.00
19	Vladimir Malakhov	1.00	2.00
20	Maxim Mikhailovsky, Goalie	.50	1.00
21	Boris Mironov	.75	1.50
22	Dmitri Mironov	.75	1.50
23	Andrei Nazarov	.50	1.00
24	Roman Oksyuta	.50	1.00
25	Arthur Oktyabrev	.50	1.00
26	Sergei Petrenko	.50	1.00
27	Oleg Petrov	.50	1.00
28	Andrei Potaichuk	.50	1.00
29	Vitali Prokhorov	.75	1.50
30	Alexander Semak	.50	1.00

— 1992 RUSSIAN STARS —

This 35-card set was co-sponsored by the World of Hockey Magazine and World Sport. It features Russian stars who played on championship teams in Russia during various tournaments.

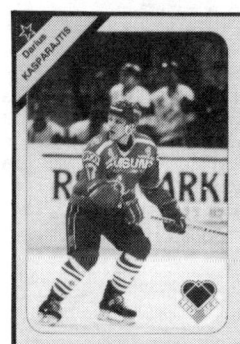

Red Ace International, 1992 Russian Stars
Card No. 1, Darius Kasparaitis

Card Size: 2 1/2" x 3 1/2"
Face: Four colour, blue border; Name, Red Ace logo
Back: Four colour, white border, card stock; Name, Numbner, Resume, Bilingual
Imprint: © 1992 Moscow
Complete Set No.: 35
Complete Set Price: 10.00 20.00
Common Card: .50 1.00

No.	Player	EX	NRMT
--	Title card/Checklist	.50	1.00
1	Darius Kasparaitis, Error	1.25	2.50
2	Alexei Zhamnov	1.25	2.50
3	Dmitri Khristich	1.00	2.00
4	Andrei Trefilov, Goalie	.75	1.50
5	Vitali Prokhorov	.75	1.50
6	Dmitri Filimonov	.75	1.50
7	Valeri Zelepukin	1.25	2.50
8	Alexei Kovalev	1.25	2.50
9	Dmitri Kvartalnov	.75	1.50
10	Igor Korolev	.50	1.00
11	Nikolai Borschevski	1.00	2.00
12	Igor Boldin	.50	1.00
13	Arturs Irbe, Goalie, Error	1.25	2.50
14	Viacheslav Butsayev	.50	1.00
15	Boris Mironov	.50	1.00
16	Sergei Bautin	.50	1.00
17	Alexander Kharlamov	.75	1.50
18	Viacheslav Kozlov	1.50	3.00
19	Mikhail Shtalenkov	.50	1.00
20	Roman Oksyuta	.50	1.00
21	Sandis Ozolnich, Error	.75	1.50
22	Dmitri Mironov	.75	1.50
23	Sergei Brylin	.50	1.00
24	Vladimir Grachev	.50	1.00
25	Dmitri Starostenko	.50	1.00
26	Andrei Nazarov	.50	1.00
27	Alexei Yashin	1.50	3.00
28	Vladimir Malakhov	1.00	2.00
29	Ravil Jakubov	.50	1.00
30	Sergei Klimovich	.50	1.00
31	Artur Oktjabrev	.50	1.00
32	Lev Berdichevsky, Error	.50	1.00
33	Yan Kaminski	.50	1.00
34	Andrei Kovalenko	.50	1.00
35	Dmitri Yushkevich	.75	1.50

TRI-GLOBE INTERNATIONAL

— 1992 SERGEI FEDOROV —

Tr-Globe International
1992 Sergei Fedorov, Card No. 1

Card Size: 2 1/2" X 3 1/2"
Face: Four colour, green side border; Name
Four colour, yellow bottom border; Name
Back: Four colour, yellow and black on textured stock; Number, Resume, English, Russian
Imprint: © TRI-GLOBE INTERNATIONAL IVAN FIODOROV PRESS LENINGRAD PRINTED IN USSR
Complete Set No.: 5
Complete Set Price: 5.00 10.00
Common CarD: 1.00 2.00
Case: (25 Sets) 200.00

No.	Player	EX	NRMT
1	Sergei Fedorov	1.50	3.00
2	Some Men Are Faster	1.50	3.00
3	Some Men Are Tougher	1.50	3.00
4	Some Men Are Stronger	1.50	3.00
5	Some Men Are Better	1.50	3.00
6	Poster	1.50	3.00

— 1992 MAGNIFICENT FIVE —

 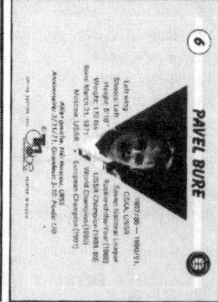

Tri-Globe International, 1992 Magnificent Five
Card No. 6, Pavel Bure, One of the Worlds Best

Card Size: 2 1/2" X 3 1/2"
Face: Four colour; Name;
Border Colours: Valeri Kamensky - Purple;
Pavel Bure - Green; Anatolie Semenov - Blue;
Arturs Irbe - Orange
Back: Four colour, border colour and black on textured stock; Name, Number, Resume, Bilingual
Imprint: LIMITED EDITION, 1992 PRINTED IN RUSSIA © TRI-GLOBE INTERNATIONAL, INC.
Complete Set No.: 21
Complete Set Price: 15.00 30.00
Common Card: .50 1.00

VALERI KAMENSKY

No.	Player	EX	NRMT
1	One Of The Worlds Best	1.00	2.00
2	A World Champion	1.00	2.00
3	A World Class Forward	1.00	2.00
4	Champion Of The USSR	1.00	2.00
5	There Are Only Few Of Them	1.00	2.00

PAVEL BURE

No.	Player	EX	NRMT
6	One Of The Worlds Best	1.50	3.00
7	A World Champion	1.50	3.00
8	A World Class Forward	1.50	3.00
9	Champion Of The USSR	1.50	3.00
10	A European Champion	1.50	3.00

ANATOLI SEMENOV

No.	Player	EX	NRMT
11	One Of The Worlds Best	.50	1.00
12	An Olympic Champion	.50	1.00
13	A World Class Forward	.50	1.00
14	Champion Of The USSR	.50	1.00
15	There Are Only Few Of Them	.50	1.00

ARTURS IRBE

No.	Player	EX	NRMT
16	One Of The Worlds Best	1.00	2.00
17	A European Champion	1.00	2.00
18	A World Class Goaltender	1.00	2.00
19	A World Champion	1.00	2.00
20	There Are Only Few Of Them	1.00	2.00

SERGEI FEDOROV

No.	Checklist	EX	NRMT
—	Checklist	1.50	3.00

— 1992 FROM RUSSIA WITH PUCK —

This 24-card set features the Russians playing in the NHL. The issue is limited to 50,000 sets.

Tri Globe International
1992 From Russia with Puck
Card No. 1, Igor Laionov

Card Size: 2 1/2" x 3 1/2"
Face: Four colour, white border; Name, Position
Back: Four colour, white border; Name, Resume
Imprint: © Tri Globe International, Inc. Limited Edition 50,000
Printed in Russia, 1992
Complete Set No.: 24
Complete Set Price: 7.50 15.00
Common Player: .35 .75

No.	Player	EX	NRMT
1	Igor Larionov	.35	.75
2	Igor Larionov	.35	.75
3	Andrei Lomakin	.35	.75
4	Andrei Lomakin	.35	.75
5	Pavel Bure	1.50	3.00
6	Pavel Bure	1.50	3.00
7	Alexei Zhamnov	.75	1.50
8	Alexei Zhamnov	.75	1.50
9	Sergei Krivokrasov	.35	.75
10	Sergei Krivokrasov	.35	.75
11	Valeri Kamensky	.75	1.50
12	Valeri Kamensky	.75	1.50
13	Viacheslav Kozlov	.75	1.50
14	Viacheslav Kozlov	.75	1.50
15	Valeri Zelepukhin	.75	1.00
16	Valeri Zelepukhin	.75	1.00
17	Igor Kravchuk	.50	1.00
18	Igor Kravchuk	.50	1.00
19	Vladimir Malakhov	.50	1.00
20	Vladimir Malakhov	.50	1.00
21	Boris Mironov	.50	1.00
22	Boris Mironov	.50	1.00
23	Arturs Irbe, Goalie	.50	1.00
24	Arturs Irbe, Goalie	.50	1.00

PANINI
— 1979 STICKERS —

Panini, 1979 Stickers
Sticker No. 61, Marcel Dionne

Sticker Size: 15/16" X 2 11/16"
Face: Four colour, white border; Name, Team
Back: Blue on white stock; Number, English, German, French
Imprint: © PRINTED IN ITALY BY EDIZIONI PANINI S.p.a.-MODENA
Complete Set No.: 400
Complete Set Price: 35.00 75.00
Common Player: .06 .12
Album: 5.00 10.00

REFEREE SIGNALS

No.	Player	EX	NRMT
1	Wash-Out	.06	.12
2	Butt-Ending	.06	.12
3	Delayed Calling of Penalty	.06	.12
4	Hooking	.06	.12
5	Charging	.06	.12
6	Misconduct	.06	.12
7	Holding	.06	.12
8	High-Sticking	.06	.12
9	Tripping	.06	.12
10	Cross-Checking	.06	.12
11	Elbowing	.06	.12
12	Off-Side	.06	.12
13	Icing	.06	.12
14	Boarding	.06	.12
15	Kneeing	.06	.12
16	Slashing	.06	.12
17	Roughness	.06	.12
18	Spearing	.06	.12
19	Interference	.06	.12

FINALS

No.	Player	EX	NRMT
20	MA 78 PRAHA, Ceskoslovensko	.08	.15
21	Ceskoslovensko - SSSR 6-4	.08	.15
22	Ceskoslovensko - SSSR 6-4	.08	.15
23	SSSR - Ceskoslovensko 3-1	.08	.15
24	SSSR - Ceskoslovensko 3-1	.08	.15
25	SSSR - Ceskoslovensko 3-1	.08	.15
26	SSSR - Ceskoslovensko 3-1	.08	.15
27	Canada - Sverige 3-2	.10	.20
28	Canada - Sverige 3-2	.10	.20
29	SSSR - Canada 5-1	.15	.30
30	SSSR - Canada 5-1	.15	.30
31	Ceskoslovensko - Canada 3-2	.08	.15
32	Ceskoslovensko - Canada 3-2	.08	.15
33	SSSR - Sverige 7-1	.08	.15
34	SSSR - Sverige 7-1	.08	.15
35	USA - Suomi-Finland 4-3	.10	.20
36	USA - Suomi-Finland 4-3	.10	.20
37	Suomi-Finland - DDR 7-2	.06	.12
38	DDR - BRD 0-0	.06	.12
39	DDR - BRD 0-0	.06	.12

TEAM LOGOS

No.	Player	EX	NRMT
40	Ceskoslovensko	.06	.12
41	Polska	.06	.12
42	SSSR	.10	.20
43	USA	.10	.20
44	Canada	.10	.20
45	Deutschland - BRD	.06	.12
46	Suomi-Finland	.06	.12
47	Sverige	.06	.12

CANADA

No.	Player	EX	NRMT
48	Canada, Team Photo	.10	.20
49	Canada, Team Photo	.10	.20
50	Canada, Team Photo	.10	.20
51	Canada, Team Photo	.10	.20
52	Denis Herron, Goalie	.15	.30
53	Daniel Bouchard, Goalie	.15	.30
54	Rick Hampton	.10	.20
55	Robert Picard	.10	.20
56	Brad Maxwell	.10	.20
57	David Shand	.10	.20
58	Dennis Kearns	.10	.20
59	Thomas Lysiak	.15	.30
60	Dennis Maruk	.15	.30
61	Marcel Dionne	1.10	2.25
62	Guy Charron	.10	.20
63	Glen Sharpley	.10	.20
64	Jean Pronovost	.15	.30
65	Don Lever	.10	.20
66	Robert MacMillan	.15	.30
67	Wilfred Paiement	.25	.50
68	Pat Hickey	.10	.20
69	Michael Murphy	.10	.20

CESKOSLOVENSKO

No.	Player	EX	NRMT
70	Ceskoslovensko, Team Photo.08	.15	
71	Ceskoslovensko, Team Photo	.08	.15
72	Ceskoslovensko, Team Photo	.08	.15
73	Ceskoslovensko, Team Photo	.08	.15
74	Jiri Holecek, Goalie	.10	.20
75	Jiri Crha, Goalie	.15	.35
76	Jiri Bubla	.15	.35
77	Milan Kajkl	.06	.12
78	Miroslav Dvorak	.06	.12
79	Milan Chalupa	.06	.12
80	Frantisek Kaberle	.06	.12
81	Jan Zajicek	.06	.12
82	Jiri Novak	.06	.12
83	Ivan Hlinka	.10	.20
84	Peter Stastny	2.00	4.00
85	Milan Novy	.06	.12
86	Vladimir Martinec	.06	.12
87	Jaroslav Pouzar	.06	.12
88	Pavel Richter	.06	.12
89	Bohuslav Ebermann	.06	.12
90	Marian Stastny	.15	.35
91	Frantisek Cernick	.06	.12

DEUTSCHLAND - BRD

No.	Player	EX	NRMT
92	Deutschland - BRD Team Photo	.08	.15
93	Deutschland - BRD Team Photo	.08	.15
94	Deutschland - BRD Team Photo	.08	.15
95	Deutschland - BRD Team Photo	.08	.15
96	Erich Weishaupt, Goalie	.06	.12
97	Bernhard Engelbrecht, Goalie	.06	.12
98	Ignaz Berndaner	.06	.12
99	Robert Murray	.06	.12
100	Udo Kiessling	.06	.12
101	Klaus Auhuber	.06	.12
102	Horst Kretschmer	.06	.12
103	Erich Kuhnhackl	.06	.12
104	Martin Wild	.06	.12
105	Lorenz Funk	.06	.12

680 • PANINI — 1979 STICKERS

No.	Player	EX	NRMT
106	Martin Hinterstocker	.06	.12
107	Alois Schloder	.06	.12
108	Rainer Philipp	.06	.12
109	Hermann Hinterstocker	.06	.12
110	Franz Reindl	.06	.12
111	Walter Koberle	.06	.12
112	Johann Zach	.06	.12
113	Marcus Kuhl	.06	.12

POLSKA

No.	Player	EX	NRMT
114	Polska Team Photo	.08	.15
115	Polska Team Photo	.08	.15
116	Polska Team Photo	.08	.15
117	Polska Team Photo	.08	.15
118	Henryk Wojtynek, Goalie	.06	.12
119	Tadeusz Slowakiewicz, Goalie	.06	.12
120	Henryk Janiszewski	.06	.12
121	Henryk Gruth	.06	.12
122	Andrzej Slowakiewicz	.06	.12
123	Andrzej Iskrzycki	.06	.12
124	Jerzy Potz	.06	.12
125	Marek Marcinczak	.06	.12
126	Jozef Batkiewicz	.06	.12
127	Stefan Chowaniec	.06	.12
128	Andrzej Malysiak	.06	.12
129	Walenty Zietara	.06	.12
130	Henryk Pytel	.06	.12
131	Mieczyslaw Jaskierski	.06	.12
132	Andrzej Zabawa	.06	.12
133	Tadeusz Obloj	.06	.12
134	Jan Piecko	.06	.12
135	Leszek Tokarz	.06	.12

SSSR

No.	Player	EX	NRMT
136	SSSR Team Photo	.10	.20
137	SSSR Team Photo	.10	.20
138	SSSR Team Photo	.10	.20
139	SSSR Team Photo	.10	.20
140	Vladislav Tretiak, Goalie, Error	2.00	4.00
141	Vjacheslav Fetisov	1.50	3.00
142	Vladimir Lutchenko	.35	.75
143	Vasilij Pervukhin	.15	.35
144	Valerij Vasiljev	.50	1.00
145	Gennadij Tsygankov	.25	.50
146	Juri Fedorov	.35	.75
147	Vladimir Petrov	.35	.75
148	Vladimir Golikov	.25	.50
149	Victor Zhluktov	.15	.35
150	Boris Mikhajlov	.25	.50
151	Valerij Kharlamov	1.00	2.00
152	Helmut Balderis	.25	.50
153	Sergej Kapustin	.15	.35
154	Alexander Golikov	.15	.35
155	Alexander Maltsev	.50	1.00
156	Juri Lebedev	.15	.35
157	Sergej Makarov	1.50	3.00

SUOMI

No.	Player	EX	NRMT
158	Suomi-Finland Team Photo	.08	.15
159	Suomi-Finland Team Photo	.08	.15
160	Suomi-Finland Team Photo	.08	.15
161	Suomi-Finland Team Photo	.08	.15
162	Urpo Ylonen	.06	.12
163	Antero Kivela, Goalie	.06	.12
164	Pekka Rautakallio	.15	.35
165	Timo Nummelin	.06	.12
166	Risto Siltanen	.25	.50
167	Pekka Marjamaki	.06	.12
168	Tapio Levo	.06	.12
169	Lasse Litma	.06	.12
170	Esa Peltonen	.06	.12
171	Martti Jarkko	.06	.12
172	Matti Hagman	.10	.20
173	Seppo Repo	.06	.12
174	Pertti Koivulahti	.06	.12
175	Seppo Ahokainen	.06	.12
176	Juhani Tamminen	.06	.12
177	Jukko Provari	.06	.12
178	Mikko Leinonen	.15	.30
179	Matti Rautiainen	.06	.12

SVERIGE

No.	Player	EX	NRMT
180	Sverige Team Photo	.06	.12
181	Sverige Team Photo	.06	.12
182	Sverige Team Photo	.06	.12
183	Sverige Team Photo	.06	.12
184	Goran Hogosta	.06	.12
185	Hardy Astrom	.10	.20
186	Stig Ostling	.06	.12
187	Ulf Weinstock	.06	.12
188	Mats Waltin	.06	.12
189	Stig Salming	.08	.15
190	Lars Zetterstrom	.06	.12
191	Lars Lindgren	.08	.15
192	Leif Holmgren	.06	.12
193	Roland Eriksson	.06	.12
194	Rolf Edberg	.06	.12
195	Per Olov Brasar	.10	.20
196	Mats Ahlberg	.06	.12
197	Bengt Lundholm	.06	.12
198	Lars Gunnar Lundberg	.06	.12
199	Nils Olov Olsson	.06	.12
200	Kent Erik Andersson	.15	.35
201	Thomas Gradin	.15	.35

USA

No.	Player	EX	NRMT
202	USA Team Photo	.10	.20
203	USA Team Photo	.10	.20
204	USA Team Photo	.10	.20
205	USA Team Photo	.10	.20
206	Peter LoPresti, Goalie	.10	.20
207	Jim Warden	.10	.20
208	Dick Lamby	.10	.20
209	Craig Norwich	.10	.20
210	Glen Patrick	.10	.20
211	Patrick Westrum	.10	.20
212	Don Jackson	.10	.20
213	Mark Johnson	.15	.30
214	Curt Bennett	.10	.20
215	Dave Debol	.10	.20
216	Robert Collyard	.10	.20
217	Mike Fidler	.10	.20
218	Tom Younghans	.10	.20
219	Harvey Bennett	.10	.20
220	Steve Jensen	.10	.20
221	Jim Warner	.10	.20
222	Mike Eaves	.10	.20
223	William Gilligan	.10	.20

JUGOSLAVIJA

No.	Player	EX	NRMT
224	HOCKEY 76, Jugoslavija	.06	.12
225	Polska - Romania 8-6	.06	.12
226	Polska - Romania 8-6	.06	.12
227	Polska - Romania 8-6	.06	.12
228	Polska - Romania 8-6	.06	.12
229	Polska - Magyarorszag 7-2	.06	.12
230	Polska - Magyarorszag 7-2	.06	.12
231	Nippon - Jugoslavija 6-1	.06	.12
232	Nippon - Jugoslavija 6-1	.06	.12
233	Italia - Jugoslavija 12-3	.06	.12
234	Italia - Jugoslavija 12-3	.06	.12
235	Romania - Italia 5-5	.06	.12
236	Romania - Italia 5-5	.06	.12
237	Polska	.06	.12
238	Polska	.06	.12

TEAM LOGS

No.	Player	EX	NRMT
239	Deutschland - DDR	.06	.12
240	Magyarorszag	.06	.12
241	Nederland	.06	.12
242	Romania	.06	.12
243	Helvetia	.06	.12
244	Nippon	.06	.12
245	Norge	.06	.12
246	Osterreich	.06	.12

DEUTSCHLAND - DDR

No.	Player	EX	NRMT
247	Deutschland - DDR	.06	.12
248	Deutschland - DDR	.06	.12
249	Roland Herzig; Wolfgang Kraske	.06	.12
250	Dieter Simon; Dietmar Peters	.06	.12
251	Dieter Frenzel; Joachim Lempio	.06	.12
252	Reinhard Frengler; Peter Slapke	.06	.12
253	Rainer Patschinski; Rolf Bielas	.06	.12
254	Roland Peters; Eckhard Scholz	.06	.12
255	Friedhelm Bogelsack; Joachim Stasche	.06	.12

HELVETIA

No.	Player	EX	NRMT
256	Helvetia	.06	.12
257	Helvetia	.06	.12
258	Edgar Grubauer; Olivier Anken	.06	.12
259	Aldo Zenhausern; Andreas Meyer	.06	.12
260	Jakob Kolliker; Jean-Claude Locher	.06	.12
261	Georg Mattli; Giovanni Conte	.06	.12
262	Renzo Holzer; Roland Dellsperger	.06	.12
263	Michael Horisberger; Luca Rossetti	.06	.12
264	Jurg Berger; Lorenz Schmid	.06	.12

MAGYARORSZAG

No.	Player	EX	NRMT
265	Magyarorszag	.06	.12
266	Magyarorszag	.06	.12
267	Janos Balogh; Andras Farkas	.06	.12
268	Csaba Kovacs; Janos Hajzer	.06	.12
269	Peter Flora; Adam Kereszty	.06	.12
270	Antal Palla; Andras Meszoly	.06	.12
271	Gaspar Menyhart; Peter Havran	.06	.12
272	Janos Poth; Albert Muhr	.06	.12
273	Gyorgy Buzas; Gyorgy Pek	.06	.12

NEDERLAND

No.	Player	EX	NRMT
274	Nederland	.06	.12
275	Nederland	.06	.12
276	Harry Van Bilsen; Henk Krikke	.06	.12
277	Frank Van Soldt; George Peternousek	.06	.12
278	Patrick Kolijn; Klaas Van Den Broek	.06	.12
279	Larry Van Wieren; Johan Toren	.06	.12
280	Robert Van Onlangs; Jerry Schaffer	.06	.12
281	Jan Janssen; John Van Der Griendt	.06	.12
282	Jack De Heer; Leo Koopmans	.06	.12

NIPPON

No.	Player	EX	NRMT
283	Nippon	.06	.12
284	Nippon	.06	.12
285	Takeshi Iwamoto; Minoru Misawa	.06	.12
286	Norio Ito; Kazuma Tonozaki	.06	.12
287	Hiroshi Hori; Iwao Nakayama	.06	.12
288	Yasushin Tanaka; Yoshiaki Kyoya	.06	.12
289	Katsutoshi Kawamura; Yoshio Hoshino	.06	.12
290	Satoru Misawa; Teruo Sakurai	.06	.12
291	Sadaki Honma; Tsutomu Hanzawa	.06	.12

NORGE

No.	Player	EX	NRMT
292	Norge	.06	.12
293	Norge	.06	.12
294	Tore Walberg; Jorn Goldstein	.06	.12
295	Thor Martisen; Rune Molberg	.06	.12
296	Nils Nilsen; Jone Erevik	.06	.12
297	Sven Lien; Tom Roymark	.06	.12
298	Per Erik Eriksen; Roar Ovstedal	.06	.12
299	Vidar Johansen; Harry Haraldsen	.06	.12
300	Morten Sethereng; Kjell Thorkildsen	.06	.12

OSTERREICH

No.	Player	EX	NRMT
301	Osterreich	.06	.12
302	Osterreich	.06	.12
303	Schilcheri; Prohaska	.06	.12

No.	Player	EX	NRMT
304	Pentti Hyytiainen; Othmar Russ	.06	.12
305	Silvester Staribacher; Walter Schneider	.06	.12
306	Franz Kotnauer; Herbert Pok	.06	.12
307	Alexander Sadjina; Rudolf Konig	.06	.12
308	Herbert Mortl; Gerhard Pepeunig	.06	.12
309	Werner Schilcher; Herbert Haiszan	.06	.12

ROMANIA

No.	Player	EX	NRMT
310	Romania	.06	.12
311	Romania	.06	.12
312	Gheorghe Hutan; Valerian Netedu	.06	.12
313	Elod Antal; Sandor Gall	.06	.12
314	Gheorghe Iustinian; Ion Ionita	.06	.12
315	Vasile Hutanu; Alexandru Halauca	.06	.12
316	Doru Tureanu; Dimitru Axinte	.06	.12
317	Zoltan Nagy; Marian Costea	.06	.12
318	Constantin Nistor; Adrian Olenici	.06	.12
319	World Championship Ice Hockey 1978	.06	.12
320	Danmark - Nederland 3-3	.06	.12
321	Danmark - Nederland 3-3	.06	.12
322	Nederland - Espana 19-0	.06	.12
323	Nederland - Espana 19-0	.06	.12
324	Osterreich - Danmark 7-4	.06	.12
325	Osterreich - Danmark 7-4	.06	.12
326	Nederland - Bulgaria 8-0	.06	.12
327	China - Danmark 3-2	.06	.12
328	China - France 8-4	.06	.12

TEAM LOGOS

No.	Player	EX	NRMT
329	Bulgaria	.06	.12
330	France	.06	.12
331	Italia	.06	.12
332	Jugoslavija	.06	.12
333	Belgique	.06	.12
334	China	.06	.12
335	Danmark	.06	.12
336	Espana	.06	.12

BELGIQUE

No.	Player	EX	NRMT
337	Belgique	.06	.12
338	Belgique	.06	.12
339	Pierre Smeets; Guy Lauwers	.06	.12
340	Georges Andriaensen; Alain Zwikel	.06	.12
341	Christian Cuvelier; Pierre Sarazin	.06	.12
342	Philippe Vermeulen; Christian Voskertian	.06	.12
343	Bob Verschraegen; Patrick Arnould	.06	.12
344	Jozef Lejeune; Pierre Langh	.06	.12

BULGARIA

No.	Player	EX	NRMT
345	Bulgaria	.06	.12
346	Bulgaria	.06	.12
347	Atanas Iliev; Dimitar Lazarov	.06	.12
348	Gueorgui Iliev; Dimo Krastinov	.06	.12
349	Kroum Hristov; Nikolay Petrov	.06	.12
350	Ivan Atanasov; Milcho Nenov	.06	.12
351	Atanas Todorov; Lubomir Stoilov	.06	.12
352	Kiril Guerasimov; Marin Batchvarov	.06	.12

CHINA

No.	Player	EX	NRMT
353	China	.06	.12
354	China	.06	.12
355	Tsui Ting Wen; Yang Yung Ke	.06	.12
356	Cheng Ke; Pien Shao Tang	.06	.12
357	Wan Ta Chun; Chang Yung Sheng	.06	.12
358	Chen Hsi Kiang; Wei Chang Shun	.06	.12
359	Li Cheng Hsin; Liu Te Hsi	.06	.12
360	Hsiang Shu Ching; Chen Sheng Wen	.06	.12

DANMARK

No.	Player	EX	NRMT
361	Danmark	.06	.12
362	Danmark	.06	.12
363	Bent Hansen; Per Holten Moller	.06	.12
364	Richard Andersen; Tommy Pedersen	.06	.12
365	Kenneth Henriksen; Jesper Hviid	.06	.12
366	Frits Nielsen; Steen Thomsen	.06	.12
367	Carsten Nielsen; Egon Kahl	.06	.12
368	Jens Jensen; Soren Gjerding	.06	.12

ESPANA

No.	Player	EX	NRMT
369	Espana	.06	.12
370	Espana	.06	.12
371	Sergio Estrada; Josian Lizarraga	.06	.12
372	Francisco Gonzalez; Ramon Munitiz	.06	.12
373	Alberto Marin; Bievenido Aguado	.06	.12
374	Toni Raventos; Ezequiel Encinas	.06	.12
375	Antonio Capillas; Jose Sarazibar	.06	.12
376	Perico Labayen; Antonio Plaza	.06	.12

FRANCE

No.	Player	EX	NRMT
377	France	.06	.12
378	France	.06	.12
379	Daniel Maric; Pascal Del Monaco	.06	.12
380	Robert Oprandi; Bernard Combe	.06	.12
381	Allard; Le Blond	.06	.12
382	Jean Vassieux; Philippe Rey	.06	.12
383	Guy Galiay; Jean Le Blond	.06	.12
384	Alain Vinard; Louis Smaniotto	.06	.12

ITALIA

No.	Player	EX	NRMT
385	Italia	.06	.12
386	Italia	.06	.12
387	Giorgio Tigliani; Norbert Gasser	.06	.12
388	Kostner; Pasqualotto	.06	.12
389	Renato Lacedelli; Fabio Polloni	.06	.12
390	Adolf Insam; Renato De Toni	.06	.12
391	Herbert Strohmaier; Fabrizio Kasslatter	.06	.12
392	pat De Marchi; Mario Pugliese	.06	.12

JUGOSLAVIJA

No.	Player	EX	NRMT
393	Jugoslavija	.06	.12
394	Jugoslavija	.06	.12
395	Marjan Zbontar; Ivan Scap	.06	.12
396	Bojan Kumar; Tomaz Kosir	.06	.12
397	Ignac Kavec; Roman Smolej	.06	.12
398	Edvard Hafner; Tomaz Lepsa	.06	.12
399	Silvo Poljansek; Saso Kosir	.06	.12
400	Petar-Igor Klemenc; Milan Jan	.06	.12

U.S.A. OLYMPIC TEAM

— 1979 - 80 ISSUE —

Card Size: 1 3/4" x 2 3/4"
Front: Black and white; Name, Position
Back: Black and white; Gold medal winners
Imprint: None
Complete Set No.: 15
Complete Set Price: 10.00 20.00
Common Card: .35 .75

No.	Player	EX	NRMT
1	Jim Craig, Goalie	.75	1.50
2	Mike Eruzione	.75	1.50
3	John Harrington	.35	.75
4	Mark Johnson	.35	.75
5	Rob McClanahan	.35	.75
6	Jack O'Callahan	.35	.75
7	Phil Verchota	.35	.75
8	Bob Suter	.35	.75
9	Eric Strobel	.35	.75
10	Dave Silk	.35	.75
11	Mike Ramsey	.35	.75
12	Mark Pavelich	.35	.75
13	Steve Christoff	.75	1.50
14	Dave Christian	.75	1.50
15	Herb Brooks, Coach	.75	1.50

682 • U.S.A. OLYMPIC TEAM — 1979-80 ISSUE

Upper Deck 1991-92 World Junior Championships
Card No. 22, Sandis Ozolinch

Upper Deck 1991-92 World Junior Championships
Card No. 50, Paul Kariya

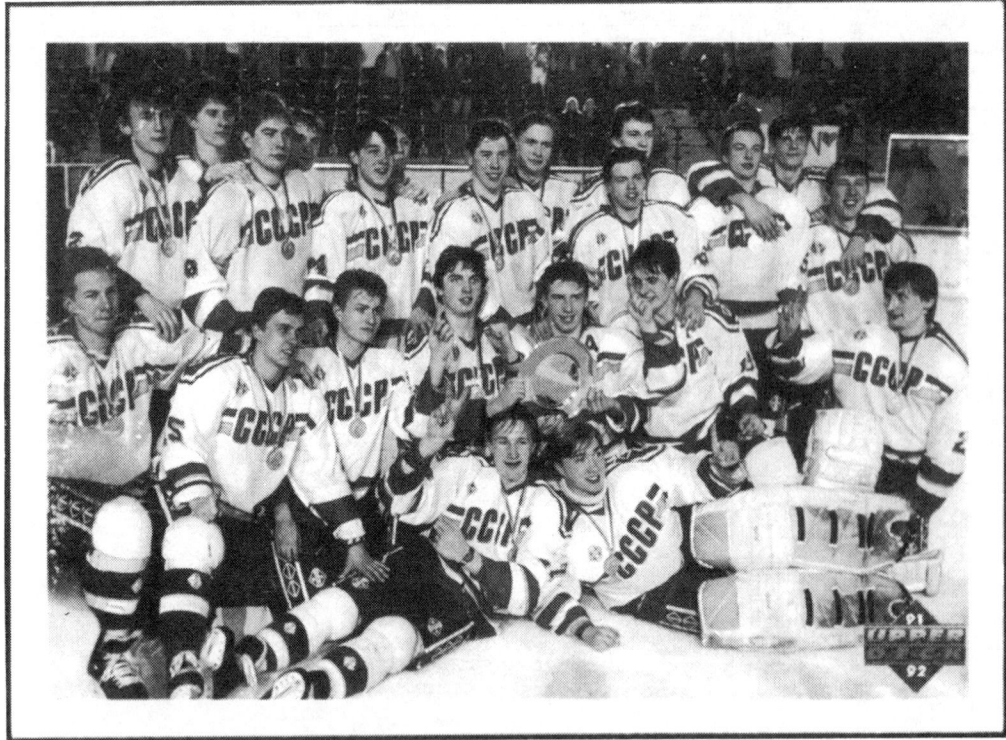

The Gold Medal-Winning Commonwealth of Independent States Team

**CHAPTER NINE
WORLD JUNIOR HOCKEY**

ALPHABETICAL LISTING OF MANUFACTURERS
WORLD JUNIOR HOCKEY

Canada Junior Team   685
Leaf   686

Upper Deck   685

CANADA JUNIOR TEAM

— 1982 CELEBRATION —

Card Size: 7 3/16" X 5"
Face: Black and white photo, red border
Back: Blank
Imprint: None

No.	Player	EX	NRMT
—	Celebration	5.00	10.00

— 1982 WORLD CHAMPIONS —

Card Size: 9 3/4" X 7 3/16"
Face: Four colour, red border; Player's names
Back: Blank
Imprint: None

No.	Player	EX	NRMT
—	Champions	5.00	10.00

— 1983 POSTCARD ISSUE —

These cards are unnumbered and are listed here in alphabetical order.

Canada Junior Team
1983 Postcard Issue
Card No. 10,
Mario Lemieux

Card Size: 3 9/16" X 5"
Face: Four colour, red border; Name
Back: Blank
Imprint: None
Complete Set No.: 21
Complete Set Price: 75.00 150.00
Common Player: .25 .50

No.	Player	EX	NRMT
1	Title Card	.25	.50
2	David Andreychuk	7.00	14.00
3	Joe Cirella	.50	1.00
4	Paul Cyr	.35	.75
5	Dale Derkatch	.25	.50
6	Mike Eagles	.50	1.00
7	Pat Flately	2.00	4.00
8	Mario Gosselin, Goalie	.50	1.00
9	Gary Leeman	1.00	2.00
10	Mario Lemieux	50.00	100.00
11	Mark Morrison	.25	.50
12	James Patrick	1.50	3.00
13	Mike Sands, Goalie	.25	.50
14	Gord Sherven	.25	.50
15	Tony Tanti	1.50	3.00
16	Larry Trader	.25	.50
17	Sylvain Turgeon	1.00	2.00
18	Patrick Verbeek	2.50	5.00
19	Mike Vernon, Goalie	1.75	3.50
20	Steve Yzerman	20.00	40.00
21	Canada's National Junior Team	1.00	2.00

— 1983 TEAM PHOTO —

Canada Junior Team
1983 Team Photo

Card Size: 3 9/16" X 5"
Face: Four colour, red border; Player's names
Back: Blank
Imprint: None

No.	Player	EX	NRMT
—	Team Photo	5.00	10.00

UPPER DECK

— 1991 - 92 WORLD JUNIOR CHAMPIONSHIPS —

Card Size: 2 1/2" X 3 1/2"
Face: Four colour; Name, Position
Back: Four colour; Number
Imprint: © 1992 The Upper Deck Company Printed in the U.S.A.
Complete Set No.: 100
Complete Set Price: 30.00 65.00
Common Card: .25 .50
Foil Pack (12 Cards): 6.00
Foil Box (34 Packs): 175.00
Foil Case (24 Boxes): 3,500.00

No.	Player	EX	NRMT
1	Description Card	.75	1.50
2	Vladislav Buljin	.25	.50
3	Ravil Gusmanov	.25	.50
4	Denis Vinokurov	.25	.50
5	Mikhail Volkov	.25	.50
6	Alexei Troschinsky	.25	.50
7	Andrei Nikolishin	.25	.50
8	Alexander Sverztov	.25	.50
9	Artim Kopot	.25	.50
10	Ildar Mukhometov	.25	.50
11	Darius Kasparaitis	3.00	6.00
12	Alexei Yashin	5.00	10.00
13	Nicolai Khabibulin, Goalie	.75	1.50
14	Denis Metlyuk	.25	.50
15	Konstantin Korotkov	.25	.50
16	Alexei Kovalev	5.00	10.00
17	Alexander Kuzminsky	.25	.50
18	Slexander Cherbayev	1.50	3.00
19	Sergei Krivokrasov	1.50	3.00
20	Sergei Zholtok	.25	.50
21	Alexei Zhitnik	2.50	5.00
22	Sandis Ozolinch	2.50	5.00
23	Boris Mironov	.50	1.00
24	Pauli Jaks	1.00	2.00
25	Gaetan Voisard	.25	.50
26	Nicola Celio	.25	.50
27	Marc Weber	.25	.50
28	Bernhard Schumperli	.25	.50
29	Laurent Bucher	.25	.50
30	Michael Blaha	.25	.50
31	Tiziano Gianini	.25	.50
32	Tero Lehtera	.25	.50
33	Mikko Luovi	.25	.50
34	Marko Kiprusoff	.25	.50
35	Janne Gronvall	.25	.50
36	Juha Ylonen	.25	.50
37	Sami Kapanen	.25	.50
38	Marko Tuomainen	.25	.50
39	Jarkko Varvio	1.50	3.00
40	Tuomas Gronman	.25	.50
41	Andreas Naumann	.25	.50
42	Steffen Ziesche	.25	.50
43	Jens Schwabe	.25	.50
44	Thomas Schubert	.25	.50
45	Hans-Jorg Mayer	.25	.50
46	Marc Seliger	.25	.50
47	Ryan Hughes	.25	.50
48	Richard Matvichuk	.25	.50
49	David St. Pierre	.25	.50
50	Paul Kariya	7.50	15.00
51	Patrick Poulin	.75	1.50
52	Mike Fountain	.25	.50
53	Scott Niedermayer	1.50	3.00
54	John Slaney	.25	.50
55	Brad Bombardir	.25	.50
56	Andy Schneider	.25	.50
57	Steve Junker	.25	.50
58	Trevor Kidd, Goalie	.25	.50
59	Martin Lapointe	2.00	4.00
60	Tyler Wright	.25	.50
61	Kimbi Daniels	.25	.50
62	Karl Dykhuis	.25	.50
63	Jeff Nelson	.25	.50
64	Jassen Cullimore	.25	.50
65	Turner Stevenson	.25	.50
66	Brian Mueller	.25	.50
67	Chris Tucker	.25	.50
68	Marty Schriner	.25	.50
69	Mike Pendergast	.25	.50
70	John Lilley	.25	.50
71	Jim Campbell	.25	.50
72	Brian Holzinger	.50	1.00
73	Steve Konowalchuk	.25	.50
74	Chris Ferraro	1.50	3.00
75	Chris Imes	.25	.50
76	Rich Brennan	.25	.50
77	Todd Hall	.25	.50
78	Brian Rafalski	.25	.50
79	Scott Lachance	1.50	3.00
80	Mike Dunham	.25	.50
81	Brent Bilodeau	.25	.50
82	Ryan Sittler	2.00	4.00
83	Peter Ferraro	1.50	3.00
84	Pat Peake	1.00	2.00
85	Keith Tkachuk	3.00	6.00
86	Brian Rolston	.75	1.50
87	Milan Hnilicka	.25	.50
88	Roman Hamrlik	3.00	6.00
89	Milan Nedoma	.25	.50
90	Patrik Luza	.25	.50
91	Jan Caloun	2.00	4.00
92	Viktor Ujcik	.25	.50
93	Robert Petrovicky	1.50	3.00
94	Roman Meluzin	.25	.50
95	Jan Vopat	.75	1.50
96	Martin Prochazka	.25	.50
97	Zigmund Palffy	1.75	3.00
98	Ivan Droppa	3.00	6.00
99	Martin Straka	5.00	10.00
100	Checklist (1-100)	.50	1.00
—	Hologram: Wayne Gretzky, Art Ross	2.50	5.00
—	Hologram: Wayne Gretzky, Lady Byng	2.50	5.00

LEAF

— 1993 - 94 FINLAND —

Available in Finland from Leaf Confections.

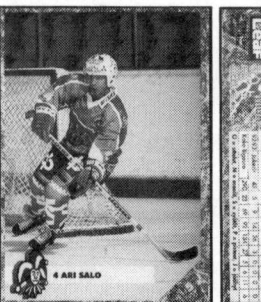 

Leaf, 1993-94 Finland
Card No. 5, Ari Salo

Card Size: 2 1/2" x 3 1/2"
Face: Four colour, orange marble border; Name, Team
Back: Four colour; Name, Number, Team, Resume
Imprint: © 1993 Leaf Turko/Abo Finland
Complete Set No.: 396
Complete Set Price: 20.00 40.00
Common Card: .10 .20

No.	Player	EX	NRMT
1	Jokerit	.10	.20
2	Alpo Suhonen	.10	.20
3	Ari Sulander, Goalie	.10	.20
4	Marko Rantanen	.10	.20
5	Ari Salo	.10	.20
6	Kalle Koskinen	.10	.20
7	Sebastian Sulku	.10	.20
8	Waltteri Immonen	.10	.20
9	Mika Strömberg	.10	.20
10	Heikki Riihijärvi	.10	.20
11	Kari Martikainen	.10	.20
12	Erik Hämäläinen	.10	.20
13	Juha Jokiharju	.10	.20
14	Timo Norppa	.10	.20
15	Rami Koivisto	.10	.20
16	Antti Törmänen	.10	.20
17	Keijo Säilynoja	.10	.20
18	Jere Keskinen	.10	.20
19	Jali Wahlsten	.10	.20
20	Mikko Konttila	.10	.20
21	Juha Ylönen	.10	.20
22	Jussi Vielonen	.10	.20
23	Petri Varis	.10	.20
24	Juha Lind	.10	.20
25	Timo Saarikoski	.10	.20
26	Otakar Janecky	.10	.20

TPS

No.	Player	EX	NRMT
27	TPS	.10	.20
28	Vladimir Jursinov	.10	.20
29	Juoni Rokama, Goalie	.12	.25
30	Kimmo Lecklin	.10	.20
31	Jouko Narvanmaa	.10	.20
32	Petteri Nummelin	.10	.20
33	Erik Kakko	.10	.20
34	Tom Koivisto	.10	.20
35	Marko Kiprusoff	.10	.20
36	Kari Harila	.10	.20
37	Hannu Virta	.25	.50
38	Aki-Petteri Berg	.10	.20
39	Aleksander Smirnov	.20	.40
40	Esa Keskinen	.10	.20
41	Saku Koivu	.50	1.00
42	Jukka Vilander	.10	.20
43	Antti Aalto	.10	.20
44	Mika Karapuu	.10	.20
45	Toni Sihvonen	.10	.20
46	Pavel Torgajev	.10	.20
47	Jere Lehtinen	.10	.20
48	Kai Nurminen	.10	.20
49	Harri Sillgren	.10	.20
50	Niko Mikkola	.10	.20
51	Ari Vuori	.10	.20
52	Lasse Pirjetä	.10	.20
53	Reijo Mikkolainen	.10	.20
54	Marko Jantunen	.10	.20
55	Mikko Virolainen	.10	.20

TAPPARA

No.	Player	EX	NRMT
56	Tappara	.10	.20
57	Boris Majorov	.10	.20
58	Jaromir Sindel, Goalie	.10	.20
59	Timo Hankela, Goalie	.10	.20
60	Teemu Kivinen	.10	.20
61	Petri Kalteva	.10	.20
62	Jari Harjumäki	.10	.20
63	Timo Jutila	.10	.20
64	Janne Grönvall	.20	.40
65	Jari Grönstand	.12	.25
66	Pekka Laksola	.10	.20
67	Tommi Haapsaari	.10	.20
68	Veli-Pekka Kautonen	.10	.20
69	Mikko Peltola	.20	.40
70	Kari Heikkinen	.10	.20
71	Teemu Numminen	.35	.75
72	Jiri Kucera	.10	.20
73	Pauli Järvinen	.10	.20
74	Pasi Forsberg	.25	.50
75	Tero Toivola	.10	.20
76	Ari Haanpää	.10	.20
77	Tommi Pohja	.10	.20
78	Samuli Rautio	.10	.20
79	Markus Oijennus	.10	.20
80	Petri Aaltonen	.10	.20

HIFK

No.	Player	EX	NRMT
81	HIFK	.10	.20
82	Harri Rindell	.10	.20
83	Sakari Lindfors, Goalie	.10	.20
84	Mikael Granlund, Goalie	.10	.20
85	Kimmo Hyttinen	.10	.20
86	Jere Karalahti	.10	.20
87	Dan Lambert	.10	.20
88	Simo Saarinen	.10	.20
89	Pasi Sormunen	.10	.20
90	Tommi Hämäläinen	.10	.20
91	Pertti Lehtonen	.10	.20
92	Jari Munck	.10	.20
93	Kai Tervonen	.10	.20
94	Kim Ahlroos	.10	.20
95	Teppo Kivelä	.10	.20
96	Darren Boyko	.10	.20
97	Pekka Peltola	.10	.20
98	Marco Poulsen	.10	.20
99	Valeri Krykov	.10	.20
100	Jari Laukkanen	.10	.20
101	Ville Peltonen	.10	.20
102	Pekka Tuomisto	.10	.20
103	Miro Haapaniemi	.10	.20
104	Mika Kortelainen	.10	.20
105	Marko Ojanen	.20	.40
106	Iiro Järvi	.35	.75

ILVES TAMPERE

No.	Player	EX	NRMT
107	Ilves Tampere	.10	.20
108	Jukka Jalonen	.10	.20
109	Jukka Tammi, Goalie	.10	.20
110	Mika Manninen, Goalie	.10	.20
111	Jani Nikko	.10	.20
112	Jukka Ollila	.10	.20
113	Juha Lampinen	.10	.20
114	Hannu Henriksson	.10	.20
115	Sami Lehtonen	.10	.20
116	Mikko Niemi	.10	.20
117	Juha-Matti Märijärvi	.10	.20
118	Jarkko Glad	.10	.20
119	Allan Measures	.10	.20
120	Mikko Luovi	.10	.20
121	Risto Jalo	.10	.20
122	Juha Järvenpää	.10	.20
123	Jarno Peltonen	.10	.20
124	Matti Kaipainen	.10	.20
125	Timo Peltomaa	.10	.20
126	Esa Tommila	.10	.20
127	Hannu Mattila	.10	.20
128	Jari Neuvonen	.10	.20
129	Pasi Määttänen	.10	.20
130	Juha Hautamaa	.10	.20
131	Janne Seva	.10	.20
132	Sami Ahlberg	.10	.20
133	Jari Virtanen	.25	.50

JyP HT

No.	Player	EX	NRMT
134	JyP HT	.10	.20
135	Kari Savolainen	.10	.20
136	Ari-Pekka Siekkinen, Goalie	.10	.20
137	Marko Leinonen, Goalie	.10	.20
138	Jan Latvala	.10	.20
139	Markku Heikkinen	.10	.20
140	Jarmo Jokilahti	.10	.20
141	Veli-Pekka Hård	.10	.20
142	Kalle Koskinen	.10	.20
143	Vesa Ponto	.10	.20
144	Petri Kujala	.10	.20
145	Jarmo Rantanen	.20	.40
146	Harri Laurila	.10	.20
147	Lasse Nieminen	.10	.20
148	Mika Paananen	.10	.20
149	Mika Arvaja	.10	.20
150	Marko Virtanen	.10	.20
151	Marko Ek	.10	.20
152	Joni Lius	.10	.20
153	Teemu Kohvakka	.10	.20
154	Jari Lindroos	.10	.20
155	Marko Kupari	.10	.20
156	Markku Ikonen	.10	.20
157	Jyrki Jokinen	.10	.20
158	Risto Kurkinen	.10	.20

KalPa

No.	Player	EX	NRMT
159	KalPa	.10	.20
160	Hannu Kapanen	.10	.20
161	Pasi Kuivalainen, Goalie	.10	.20
162	Kimmo Kapanen	.10	.20
163	Kimmo Timonen	.10	.20
164	Jari Järvinen	.10	.20
165	Mikko Tavi	.10	.20
166	Jermu Pisto	.10	.20
167	Antti Tuomenoksa	.10	.20
168	Vesa Ruotsalainen	.25	.50
169	Vesa Salo	.10	.20
170	Veli-Pekka Pekkarinen	.10	.20
171	Tuomas Kalliomäki	.10	.20
172	Dimitri Zinine	.10	.20
173	Jani Rautio	.10	.20
174	Janne Kekäläinen	.10	.20
175	Arto Sirviö	.10	.20
176	Sami Mettovaara	.10	.20
177	Sami Simonen	.10	.20
178	Pekka Tirkkonen	.10	.20
179	Sami Kapanen	.10	.20
180	Jussi Tarvainen	.10	.20

LUKKO

No.	Player	EX	NRMT
181	Lukko	.10	.20
182	Vaclav Sykora	.25	.50
183	Jarmo Myllys, Goalie	.50	1.00
184	Kimmo Vesa, Goalie	.10	.20
185	Mika Yli-Mäenpää	.10	.20
186	Jarmo Kuusisto	.10	.20
187	Marko Tuulola	.10	.20
188	Tuomas Grönman	.75	1.50
189	Timo Kulonen	.10	.20
190	Kari-Pekka Friman	.10	.20
191	Pasi Huura	.10	.20
192	Harri Suvanto	.10	.20
193	Kamil Kastak	.10	.20

1993 - 94 FINLAND — LEAF

No.	Player	EX	NRMT
194	Jari Torkki	.10	.20
195	Kalle Sahlstedt	.10	.20
196	Tommi Pullola	.10	.20
197	Mika Välilä	.10	.20
198	Tero Arkiomaa	.10	.20
199	Pasi Saarela	.10	.20
200	Matti Forss	.10	.20
201	Jussi Kiuru	.10	.20
202	Mika Alatalo	.10	.20
203	Kimmo Rintanen	.10	.20
204	Petri Lätti	.35	.75
205	Petr Korinek	.10	.20

ÄSSÄT

No.	Player	EX	NRMT
206	Ässät	.10	.20
207	Veli-Pekka Ketola	.10	.20
208	Kari Takko, Goalie	.50	1.00
209	Timo Järvinen, Goalie	.35	.75
210	Marko Sten	.10	.20
211	Pasi Peltonen	.10	.20
212	Olli Kaski	.10	.20
213	Jarno Miikkulainen	.10	.20
214	Juoni Vento	.10	.20
215	Karri Kivi	.10	.20
216	Stanislav Meciar	.10	.20
217	Nemo Nokkosmäki	.10	.20
218	Arto Javanainen	.10	.20
219	Janne Virtanen	.10	.20
220	Vjatseslav Fandul	.10	.20
221	Jari Levonen	.10	.20
222	Jarno Levonen	.10	.20
223	Jari Korpisalo	.10	.20
224	Jokke Heinänen	.10	.20
225	Harri Lönnberg	.10	.20
226	Ari Saarinen	.10	.20
227	Kari Syväsalmi	.10	.20
228	Jarno Mäkelä	.10	.20
229	Rauli Raitanen	.10	.20
230	Arto Heiskanen	.10	.20
231	Mikael Kotkaniemi	.10	.20

HPK

No.	Player	EX	NRMT
232	HPK	.10	.20
233	Pentti Matikainen	.10	.20
234	Kari Rosenberg, Goalie	.10	.20
235	Petri Vilen, Goalie	.10	.20
236	Marko Allen	.10	.20
237	Mikko Myllykoski	.10	.20
238	Kim Vähänen	.10	.20
239	Janne Laukkanen	.10	.20
240	Jari Haapamäki	.10	.20
241	Niko Marttila	.10	.20
242	Esa Sateri	.10	.20
243	Toni Virta	.10	.20
244	Marko Palo	.10	.20
245	Markku Piikkilä	.10	.20
246	Jani Hassinen	.10	.20
247	Jarkko Nikander	.10	.20
248	Pasi Kivilä	.10	.20
249	Mika Lartama	.10	.20
250	Tomas Kapusta	.10	.20
251	Tommi Varjonen	.10	.20
252	Teemu Tamminen	.10	.20
253	Jukka Seppo	.10	.20

KIEKKO-ESPOO

No.	Player	EX	NRMT
254	Kiekko-Espoo	.10	.20
255	Martti Merra	.10	.20
256	Scott Brower, Goalie	.10	.20
257	Timo Mäki, Goalie	.10	.20
258	Petri Pulkkinen	.10	.20
259	Robert Salo	.10	.20
260	Sami Nuutinen	.10	.20
261	Teemu Sillanpää	.10	.20
262	Marko Halonen	.10	.20
263	Jimi Helin	.10	.20
264	Kari Haakana	.10	.20
265	Jukka Tiilikainen	.10	.20
266	Jan Långbacka	.10	.20

No.	Player	EX	NRMT
267	Jarmo Muukkonen	.10	.20
268	Timo Hirvonen	.10	.20
269	Pasi Heinistö	.10	.20
270	Kimmo Maki-Kokkila	.10	.20
271	Mikko Lempiäinen	.10	.20
272	Tero Lehterä	.20	.40
273	Hannu Järvenpää	.35	.75
274	Riku Kuusisto	.10	.20
275	Mikko Halonen	.10	.20
276	Markku Takala	.10	.20
277	Petro Koivunen	.10	.20

REIPAS LAHTI

No.	Player	EX	NRMT
278	Reipas Lahti	.25	.50
279	Kari Mäkinen	.10	.20
280	Oldrich Svoboda, Goalie	.10	.20
281	Pekka Ilmivalta, Goalie	.10	.20
282	Matti Vuorio	.10	.20
283	Jari Parviainen	.10	.20
284	Timo Kahelin	.10	.20
285	Ville Skinnari	.10	.20
286	Petri Koski	.10	.20
287	Jarkko Hämäläinen	.10	.20
288	Pasi Ruponen	.10	.20
289	Oldrich Valek	.10	.20
290	Juha Nurminen	.10	.20
291	Erkki Laine	.10	.20
292	Sami Lekkerimaki	.10	.20
293	Tommy Kiviaho	.10	.20
294	Jyrki Poikolainen	.10	.20
295	Sami Wikström	.10	.20
296	Jonni Vauhkonen	.10	.20
297	Erkki Mäkelä	.10	.20
298	Jani Uski	.10	.20
299	Jari Multanen	.10	.20
300	Toni Koivunen	.10	.20

RUNKOSARJAN KIERROS

No.	Player	EX	NRMT
301	Runkosarjan 1. Kierros	.12	.25
302	Runkosarjan 2. Kierros	.12	.25
303	Runkosarjan 3. Kierros	.12	.25
304	Runkosarjan 4. Kierros	.12	.25
305	Runkosarjan 5. Kierros	.12	.25
306	Runkosarjan 6. Kierros	.12	.25
307	Runkosarjan 7. Kierros	.12	.25
308	Runkosarjan 8. Kierros	.12	.25
309	Runkosarjan 9. Kierros	.12	.25
310	Runkosarjan 10. Kierros	.12	.25
311	Runkosarjan 11. Kierros	.12	.25
312	Runkosarjan 12. Kierros	.12	.25
313	Runkosarjan 13. Kierros	.12	.25
314	Runkosarjan 14. Kierros	.12	.25
315	Runkosarjan 15. Kierros	.12	.25
316	Runkosarjan 16. Kierros	.12	.25
317	Runkosarjan 17. Kierros	.12	.25
318	Runkosarjan 18. Kierros	.12	.25
319	Runkosarjan 19. Kierros	.12	.25
320	Runkosarjan 20. Kierros	.12	.25
321	Runkosarjan 21. Kierros	.12	.25
322	Runkosarjan 22. Kierros	.12	.25
323	Runkosarjan 23. Kierros	.12	.25
324	Runkosarjan 24. Kierros	.12	.25
325	Runkosarjan 25. Kierros	.12	.25
326	Runkosarjan 26. Kierros	.12	.25
327	Runkosarjan 27. Kierros	.12	.25
328	Runkosarjan 28. Kierros	.12	.25
329	Runkosarjan 29. Kierros	.12	.25
330	Runkosarjan 30. Kierros	.12	.25
331	Runkosarjan 31. Kierros	.12	.25
332	Runkosarjan 32. Kierros	.12	.25
333	Runkosarjan 33. Kierros	.12	.25
334	Runkosarjan 34. Kierros	.12	.25
335	Runkosarjan 35. Kierros	.12	.25
336	Runkosarjan 36. Kierros	.12	.25
337	Runkosarjan 37. Kierros	.12	.25
338	Runkosarjan 38. Kierros	.12	.25
339	Runkosarjan 39. Kierros	.12	.25
340	Runkosarjan 40. Kierros	.12	.25
341	Runkosarjan 41. Kierros	.12	.25
342	Runkosarjan 42. Kierros	.12	.25

No.	Player	EX	NRMT
343	Runkosarjan 43. Kierros	.12	.25
344	Runkosarjan 44. Kierros	.12	.25
345	Paikallisottelut 1.	.12	.25
346	Paikallisottelut 2.	.12	.25
347	Paikallisottelut 3.	.12	.25
348	Paikallisottelut 4.	.12	.25
349	Puolivälieria HPK - Lukko	.12	.25
350	Puolivälieria Jokerit - Ässät	.12	.25
351	Puolivälieria Jokerit - Ässät	.12	.25
352	Puolivälieria TPS - Ilves	.12	.25
353	Välieriä HPK - JyP HT	.12	.25
354	Välieriä TPS - Ässät	.12	.25
355	Pronssiottelu	.12	.25
356	Finaali	.10	.20
357	Finaali	.10	.20
358	Finaali	.10	.20
359	Finaali	.10	.20

SISU SPECIAL KRTIT

No.	Player	EX	NRMT
360	Most Points - Esa Keskinen	.20	.40
361	Most goals - Tomas Kapusta	.20	.40
362	(+/-) Leader - Erik Hamalainen	.10	.20
363	Penalty minutes - Brian Tutt	.10	.20
364	Otakar Janecky	.10	.20
365	Ville Peltonen	.10	.20

ALL STARS

No.	Player	EX	NRMT
366	Petr Briza, Goalie	.25	.50
367	Janne Laukkanen	.25	.50
368	Timo Jutila	.20	.40
369	Juha Riihijarvi	.15	.30
370	Esa Keskinen	.15	.30
371	Jarkko Varvio	.35	.75

FAIR PLAY

No.	Player	EX	NRMT
372	Esa Keskinen	.10	.20

COACH OF THE YEAR

No.	Player	EX	NRMT
373	Vladirmir Jursinov	.10	.20

REGULAR ISSUE

No.	Player	EX	NRMT
374	Erik Hämäläinen	.10	.20
375	Timo Lehkonen, Goalie	.10	.20

PLAY OFFS

No.	Player	EX	NRMT
376	German Titov	.35	.75
377	Raimo Summanen	.10	.20
378	Mikko Haapakoski	.10	.20
379	Marko Palo	.10	.20
380	Seppo Mäkelä, (Referee)	.10	.20
381	TPS, Turku Team Card	.10	.20
382	HPK Hämeenlinna	.10	.20
383	JyP HT Jyväskylä	.10	.20
384	Juha Riihijärvi	.10	.20
385	Jukka Virtanen	.10	.20
386	Kari Jalonen	.10	.20
387	Matti Forss	.10	.20
388	Arto Javanainen	.10	.20

NHL DRAFT

No.	Player	EX	NRMT
389	Saku Koivu, Mon.	.50	1.00
390	Janne Niinimaa, Phi.	.20	.40
391	Ville Peltonen, SJ	.15	.30
392	Jonni Vauhkonen, Chi.	.15	.30
393	Petri Varis, SJ	.15	.30
394	Antti Aalto, MDA	.15	.30
395	Jere Karalahti, LA	.15	.30
396	Kimmo Timonen, LA	.15	.30

1994 - 95 FINLAND

Leaf, 1994-95 Finland
Card No. 97, Fredrik Norrena

Card Size: 2 1/2" x 3 1/2"
Face: Four colour; Name, Team
Back: Four colour; Name, Number, Team, Resume
Imprint: © 1994 Leaf Turko/Abo Finland
Complete Set No.: 200
Complete Set Price: 12.50 25.00
Common Card: .10 .20

No.	Player	EX	NRMT
1	Pasi Kuivalainen	.10	.20
2	Jere Karalahti	.10	.20
3	Markku Heikkinen	.10	.20
4	Marko Allen	.10	.20
5	Jarmo Kuusisto	.10	.20
6	Marko Tuulola	.10	.20
7	Marko Kiprusoff	.10	.20
8	Vesa Ponto	.10	.20
9	Tero Lehtera	.50	1.00
10	Darren Boyko	.10	.20
11	Kari Heikkinen	.10	.20
12	Niko Marttila	.10	.20
13	Jari Torkki	.10	.20
14	Jiri Kucera	.25	.50
15	Jari Levonen	.10	.20
16	Juha Ikonen	.10	.20
17	Joni Lius	.10	.20
18	Pekka Tuomisto	.10	.20
19	Petri Kokko	.10	.20
20	Jere Lehtinen	.10	.20
21	Janne Kekalainen	.10	.20
22	Ari Haanpaa	.20	.40
23	Hannu Jarvenpaa	.30	.60
24	Waltteri Immonen	.10	.20
25	Jari Lindroos	.10	.20
26	Jan Langbacka	.10	.20
27	Kari Takko, Goalie	.20	.40
28	Pasi Maattanen	.10	.20
29	Jan Latvala	.10	.20
30	Arto Heiskanen	.10	.20
31	Iiro Jarvi	.10	.20
32	Igor Boldin	.10	.20
33	Sami Simonen	.10	.20
34	Kari Rosenberg, Goalie	.10	.20
35	Sakari Lindfors, Goalie	.10	.20
36	Veli-Pekka Hard	.10	.20
37	Jari Halme	.10	.20
38	Jukka Tammi	.10	.20
39	Kalle Koskinen	.10	.20
40	Pekka Tirkkonen	.10	.20
41	Ari Sulander, Goalie	.10	.20
42	Jani Hassinen	.10	.20
43	Timo Peltomaa	.10	.20
44	Sami Mettovaara	.10	.20
45	Mika Yli-Maenpaa	.10	.20
46	Toni Virta	.10	.20
47	Kimmo Lecklin	.10	.20
48	Rauli Raitanen	.10	.20
49	Juha Lind	.10	.20
50	Ari-Pekka Siekkinen, Goalie	.10	.20
51	Kim Ahlroos	.10	.20
52	Jarkko Nikander	.10	.20
53	Jouni Vento	.10	.20
54	Juha Lampinen	.10	.20
55	Kalle Sahlstedt	.10	.20
56	Teemu Sillanpaa	.10	.20
57	Lasse Nieminen	.10	.20
58	Janne Niinimaa	.10	.20
59	Timo Jutila	.10	.20
60	Tommi Haapsaari	.10	.20
61	Allan Measures	.10	.20
62	Petteri Nummelin	.10	.20
63	Antti Tormanen	.10	.20
64	Pekka Laksola	.10	.20
65	Esa Sateri	.10	.20
66	Petro Koivunen	.10	.20
67	Janne Virtanen	.10	.20
68	Pekka Peltola	.10	.20
69	Matti Kaipainen	.10	.20
70	Sami Pekki	.10	.20
71	Jussi Tarvainen	.10	.20
72	Jari Virtanen	.10	.20
73	Kimmo Salminen	.10	.20
74	Tommi Varjonen	.10	.20
75	Pauli Jarvinen	.10	.20
76	Hannu Mattila	.10	.20
77	Aleksander Smirnov	.15	.30
78	Arto Kulmala	.10	.20
79	Roland Karlsson	.10	.20
80	Jarno Miikkulainen	.10	.20
81	Jarmo Muukkonen	.10	.20
82	Mika Paananen	.10	.20
83	Pasi Kivila	.10	.20
84	Jari Laukkanen	.10	.20
85	Tero Arkiomaa	.10	.20
86	Tommi Miettinen	.10	.20
87	Juha Jarvenpaa	.10	.20
88	Niko Mikkola	.10	.20
89	Antti Tuomenoksa	.10	.20
90	Ilkka Sinisalo	.25	.50
91	Otakar Janecky	.10	.20
92	Arto Sirvio	.10	.20
93	Robert Salo	.10	.20
94	Ari Saarinen	.10	.20
95	Kari Martikainen	.10	.20
96	Miro Haapaniemi	.10	.20
97	Fredrik Norrena, Goalie	.10	.20
98	Erik Hamalainen	.10	.20
99	Simo Saarinen	.10	.20
100	Harri Suvanto	.10	.20
101	Kai Nurminen	.10	.20
102	Rami Koivisto	.10	.20
103	Pasi Peltonen	.10	.20
104	Kari-Pekka Friman	.10	.20
105	Mika Kortelainen	.10	.20
106	Timo Hirvonen	.10	.20
107	Jari Haapamaki	.10	.20
108	Mika Manninen	.10	.20
109	Ari Vuori	.10	.20
110	Markku Ikonen	.10	.20
111	Mikko Konttila	.10	.20
112	Harri Siligren	.10	.20
113	Mikko Tavi	.10	.20
114	Markus Oijennus	.10	.20
115	Kimmo Hyttinen	.10	.20
116	Jokke Heinanen	.10	.20
117	Sami Ahlberg	.10	.20
118	Mika Rautio	.10	.20
119	Ari Salo	.10	.20
120	Juha Hautamaa	.10	.20
121	Kari Haakana	.10	.20
122	Sami Nuutinen	.10	.20
123	Lasse Pirjeta	.10	.20
124	Keijo Sailynoja	.10	.20
125	Mikael Kotkaniemi	.10	.20
126	Samuli Rautio	.10	.20
127	Veli-Pekka Pekkarinen	.10	.20
128	Hannu Henriksson	.10	.20
129	Antti Aalto	.10	.20
130	Jyrki Jokinen	.10	.20
131	Marko Ek	.10	.20
132	Marko Ojanen	.25	.50
133	Mika Arvaja	.10	.20
134	Karri Kivi	.10	.20
135	Timo Saarikoski	.10	.20
136	Toni Sihvonen	.10	.20
137	Mika Laaksonen	.10	.20
138	HIFK, Helsinki	.10	.20
139	HPK, Hameenlinna	.10	.20
140	Ilves, Tampere	.10	.20
141	Jokerit, Helsinki	.10	.20
142	JyP HT, Jyvaskyla	.10	.20
143	KalPa, Kuopio	.10	.20
144	Kiekko-Espoo, Espoo	.10	.20
145	Lukko, Rauma	.10	.20
146	Tappara, Tampere	.10	.20
147	TPS, Turku	.10	.20
148	TuTo, Turku	.10	.20
149	Assat, Pori	.10	.20
150	Checklist 1, Juha Lind, Goalie	.10	.20
151	Checklist 2, Kari Takko	.10	.20
152	Checklist 3, V. Jursinov	.10	.20
153	Checklist 4, P. Nummelin	.10	.20
154	Maalit/runkosarja	.10	.20
155	Maalit/playoffs	.10	.20
156	Pisteet/runkosarja	.10	.20
157	Pisteet/Playoffs	.10	.20
158	Jaahyt/runkosarja	.10	.20
159	Jaahyt/playoffs	.10	.20
160	All Stars MV	.20	.40
161	All Stars VP	.20	.40
162	All Stars OP	.20	.40
163	All Stars VH	.20	.40
164	All Stars KH	.20	.40
165	All Stars OH	.20	.40
166	HIFK/tilastot	.10	.20
167	HPK/tilastot	.10	.20
168	Ilves/tilastot	.10	.20
169	Jokerit/tilastot	.10	.20
170	JyP HT/tilastot	.10	.20
171	KalPa/tilastot	.10	.20
172	Kiekko-Espoo/tilastot	.10	.20
173	Lukko/tilastot	.10	.20
174	Reipas/tilastot	.10	.20
175	Tappara/tilastot	.10	.20
176	TPS/tilastot	.10	.20
177	Assat/tilastot	.10	.20
178	HIFK/ottelut	.10	.20
179	HPK/ottelut	.10	.20
180	Ilves/ottelut	.10	.20
181	Jokerit/ottelut	.10	.20
182	JyP HT/ottelut	.10	.20
183	KalPa/ottelut	.10	.20
184	Kiekko-Espoo/ottelut	.10	.20
185	Lukko/ottelut	.10	.20
186	Reipas/ottelut	.10	.20
187	Tappara/ottelut	.10	.20
188	TPS/ottelut	.10	.20
189	Assat/ottelut	.10	.20
190	SM-kulta/Jokerit	.10	.20
191	SM-hopea/TPS	.10	.20
192	SM-pronssi/Lukko	.10	.20
193	EM-kulta/TPS	.10	.20
194	Puolivalierat	.10	.20
195	Valierat	.10	.20
196	Pronssiottelu	.10	.20
197	1. finaali	.10	.20
198	2. finaali	.10	.20
199	3. finaali	.10	.20
200	4. finaali	.10	.20

ERIKOISKORTIT

SISU SPECIALS

No.	Player	EX	NRMT
1	Mika Alatalo	.25	.50
2	Jari Korpisalo	.25	.50
3	Petteri Nummelin	.25	.50
4	Janne Ojanen	.75	1.50
5	Sami Kapanen	.25	.50
6	Kari Takko, Goalie	.50	1.00
7	Esa Keskinen	.25	.50
8	Ari Sulander, Goalie	.25	.50
9	Jarmo Myllys, Goalie	.75	1.50
10	Saku Koivu	1.25	2.50

NOLLAKORTIT

No.	Player	EX	NRMT
1	Mika Manninen, Goalie	.25	.50
2	Kari Takko, Goalie	.35	.75
3	Ari Sulander, Goalie	.25	.50

1994-95 FINLAND — LEAF

No.	Player	EX	NRMT
4	Jouni Rokama, Goalie	.25	.50
5	Kari Rosenberg, Goalie	.25	.50
6	Ari-Pekka Siekkinen, Goalie	.25	.50
7	Allain Roy, Goalie	.25	.50
8	Pasi Kuivalainen, Goalie	.25	.50
9	Sakari Lindfors, Goalie	.25	.50
10	Mika Rautio, Goalie	.25	.50

FIRE ON ICE

No.	Player	EX	NRMT
1	Saku Koivu	.75	1.50
2	Esa Keskinen	.35	.75
3	Igor Boldin	.25	.50
4	Juha Nurminen	.25	.50

No.	Player	EX	NRMT
5	Marko Jantunen	.25	.50
6	Janne Ojanen	.25	.50
7	Sami Kapanen	.25	.50
8	Kai Nurminen	.25	.50
9	Jari Korpisalo	.25	.50
10	Tero Lehtera	.25	.50
11	Timo Jutila	.25	.50
12	Vjatseslav Fandul	.25	.50
13	Otakar Janecky	.25	.50
14	Tero Arkiomaa	.25	.50
15	Jari Torkki	.25	.50
16	Risto Kurkinen	.25	.50
17	Petr Korinek	.25	.50
18	Petro Koivunen	.25	.50
19	Tomas Kapusta	.25	.50
20	Pauli Jarvinen	.25	.50

JUNIOR

No.	Player	EX	NRMT
1	Saku Koivu	.75	1.50
2	Jokke Heinanen	.25	.50
3	Tommi Miettinen	.25	.50
4	Jere Karalahti	.25	.50
5	Kalle Koskinen	.25	.50
6	Kari Rosenberg, Goalie	.35	.75
7	Mika Manninen, Goalie	.35	.75
8	Jussi Tarvainen	.25	.50
9	Mika Stromberg	.25	.50
10	Kalle Sahlstedt	.25	.50

SUPER CHASE

No.	Player	EX	NRMT
	The Canada Bowl	12.50	25.00

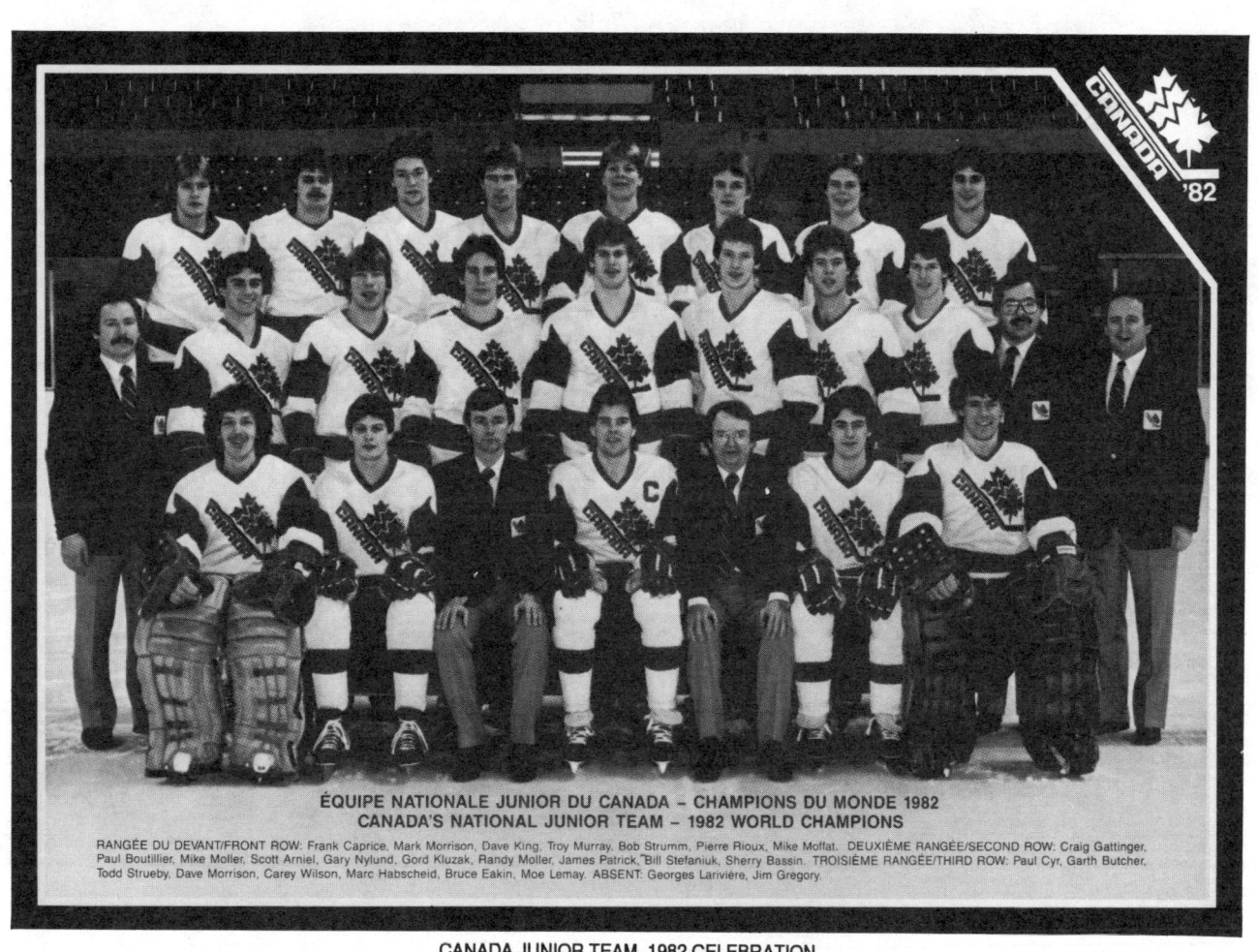

CANADA JUNIOR TEAM, 1982 CELEBRATION

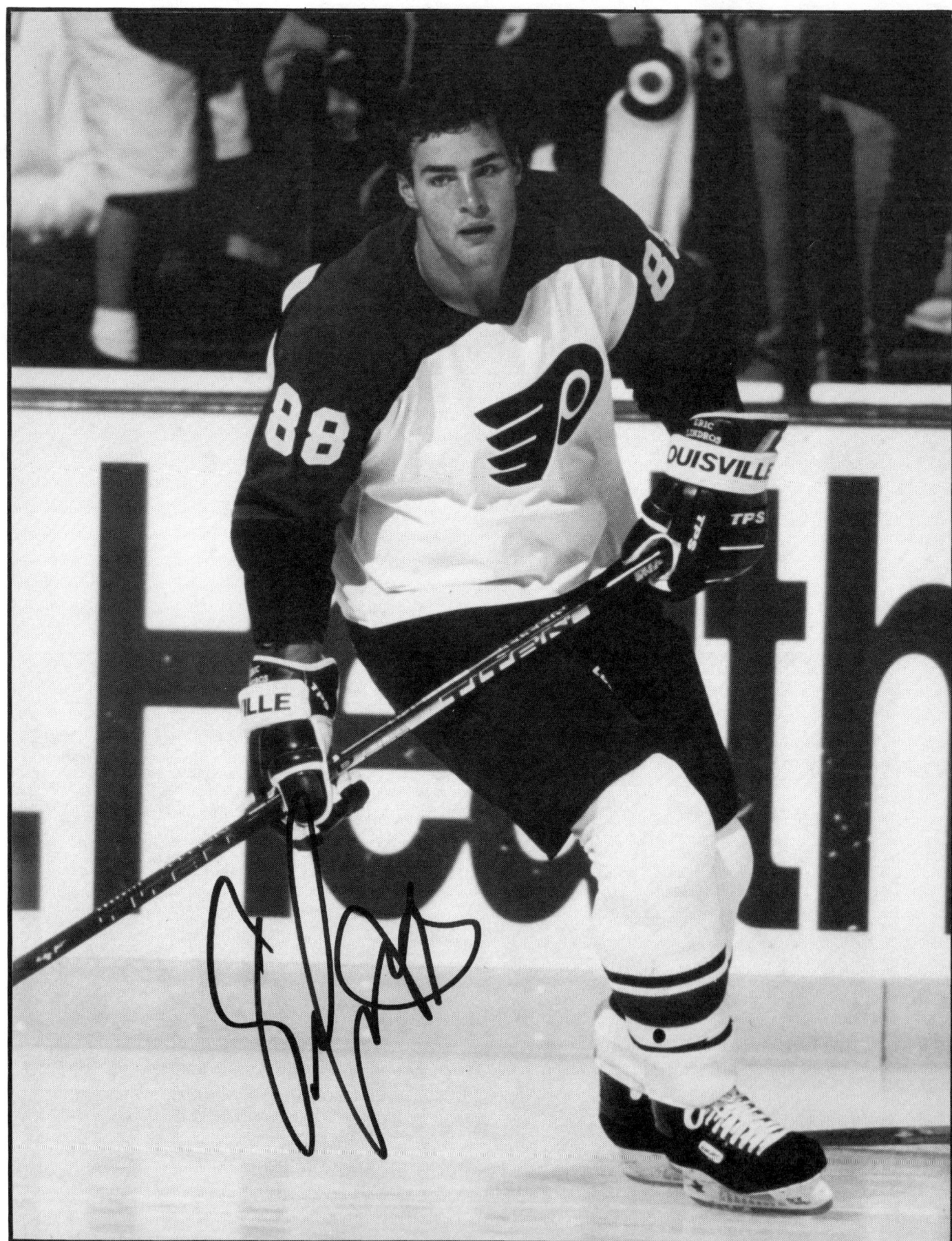

Eric Lindros

**CHAPTER TEN
MINOR LEAGUES**

ALPHABETICAL LISTING OF MANUFACTURERS
MINOR LEAGUES

Air Canada (SJHL)	748
Anonymous (OHL/QHL)	719
Arena Holograms	707
Classic Games	707
Crescent Ice Cream (WCHL)	741
Holland Creameries (WCHL)	741
Laval Dairy (QHL)	731
MPS Photographics	749
Paulin's Candy (WCHL)	741
ProCards (AHL/IHL)	693

7th Inning Sketch	
Memorial Cup	717
Ontario Hockey League	720
Quebec Minor Junior Hockey League	731
Western Hockey League	741
Safeway Phoenix Roadrunners	705
Saskatchewan Junior Hockey League	748
Slapshot Images Ltd.	750
St. Lawrence Sales	733
Star Pics Pro Prospects Hockey Card Art	715
Ultimate Trading Card Company	716

AMERICAN AND INTERNATIONAL HOCKEY LEAGUES

PROCARDS

— 1988 - 89 AMERICAN HOCKEY LEAGUE —

This set of cards is not numbered. The teams are first listed alphabetically and then the players are listed alphabetically within their respective teams.

1988-89 American Hockey League
Card No. 1, John Blum

Card Size: 2 1/2" X 3 1/2"
Face: Four colour, red border, League logo, Position
Back: Black on white card stock, Resume, Team Logo
Imprint: © 1988 ProCards, Inc.
Complete Set No.: 346
Complete Set Price: 75.00   150.00
Common Card: .15   .30

ADIRONDACK RED WINGS
(Detroit Red Wings)

No.	Player	EX	NRMT
1	John Blum	.15	.30
2	Jeff Brubaker	.15	.30
3	Dave Casey, Head Trainer	.15	.30
4	Tim Cheveldae, Goalie	2.50	5.00
5	Lou Crawford	.15	.30
6	Bill Dineen, Coach	.15	.30
7	Peter Dineen	.15	.30
8	Rob Doyle	.15	.30
9	Murray Eaves	.25	.50
10	Brent Fedyk	1.50	3.00
11	Joe Ferras	.15	.30
12	Mike Gober	.15	.30
13	Miroslav Ihnacak	.25	.50
14	Dave Korol	.15	.30
15	Dale Krentz	.15	.30
16	Randy McKay	.35	.75
17	Glenn Merkosky	.25	.50
18	John Mokosak	.15	.30
19	Dean Morton	.15	.30
20	Rob Nichols	.15	.30
21	Tim Paris, Assistant Trainer	.15	.30
22	Mark Reimer, Goalie	.20	.40
23	Sam St. Laurent, Goalie	.20	.40
24	Daniel Shank	.50	1.00
25	Dennis Smith	.15	.30
	Team Set (25 cards)	7.50	15.00

BALTIMORE SKIPJACKS
(Washington Capitals)

No.	Player	EX	NRMT
26	Robin Bawa	.15	.30
27	Tim Bergland	.25	.50
28	Shawn Cronin	.25	.50
29	Frank Dimuzio	.25	.50
30	Dallas Eakins	.15	.30
31	David Farrish	.25	.50
32	Chris Felix	.15	.30
33	Lou Franceschetti	.25	.50
34	Jeff Greenlaw	.15	.30
35	Mark Hatcher	.15	.30
36	Bill Houlder	.25	.50
37	Doug Keans, Goalie	.25	.50
38	Tyler Larter	.15	.30
39	J. P. Mattingly, Trainer	.15	.30
40	Scott McCrory	.15	.30
41	Mike Millar	.15	.30
42	Rob Murray	.50	1.00
43	Terry Murray, General Manager/Coach	.15	.30
44	Mike Richard	.15	.30
45	Steve Seftel	.15	.30
46	Dave Sherrid, Head Trainer	.15	.30
47	Shawn Simpson, Goalie	.20	.40
48	Rob Whistle	.15	.30
	Team Set (23 cards)	5.00	10.00

BINGHAMTON WHALERS
(Hartford Whalers)

No.	Player	EX	NRMT
49	Charles Bourgeois	.25	.50
50	Chris Brant	.15	.30
51	Richard Brodeur, Goalie	.50	1.00
52	Lindsay Carson, Error	.25	.50
53	Gary Callaghan	.15	.30
54	Brian Chapman	.15	.30
55	Jim Culhane	.15	.30
56	Mark Dumas, Equip. Manager	.15	.30
57	Dallas Gaume	.15	.30
58	Roger Kortko	.15	.30
59	Todd Krygier	1.00	2.00
60	Marc Laforge	.15	.30
61	Claude Larose, Coach	.15	.30
62	Mark Lavarre	.15	.30
63	Tom Mitchell, General Manager	.15	.30
64	David O'Brien	.15	.30
65	Mark Reeds	.15	.30
66	Dave Rowbotham	.15	.30
67	Jon Smith, Trainer	.15	.30
68	Larry Trader	.15	.30
69	Allan Tuer	.25	.50
70	Mike Vellucci	.15	.30
71	Kay Whitmore, Goalie	1.00	2.00
72	Terry Yake	.75	1.50
	Team Set (24 cards)	7.00	14.00

CAPE BRETON OILERS
(Edmonton Oilers)

No.	Player	EX	NRMT
73	Mario Barbe	.15	.30
74	Darren Beals, Goalie	.20	.40
75	Nicholas Beaulieu	.15	.30
76	Dan Currie	.15	.30
77	Jim Ennis	.15	.30
78	Larry Floyd	.15	.30
79	Mike Glover	.15	.30
80	David Haas	.15	.30
81	John B. Hanna	.15	.30
82	Kim Issel	.25	.50
83	Fabian Joseph	.25	.50
84	Mark Lamb	1.25	2.50
85	Brad MacGregor	.15	.30
86	Rob MacInnes	.15	.30
87	Don Martin	.15	.30
88	Alan May	.50	1.00
89	Jamie Nicolls	.15	.30
90	Selmar Odelein	.15	.30
91	Daryl Reaugh, Goalie	.25	.50
92	Dave Roach, Goalie	.20	.40
93	Ron Shudra	.15	.30
94	Shaun Van Allen	.75	1.50
95	Mike Ware	.15	.30
96	Jim Wiemer	.75	1.50
	Team Set (24 cards)	5.00	10.00

HALIFAX CITADELS
(Quebec Nordiques)

No.	Player	EX	NRMT
97	Joel Baillargeon	.15	.30
98	Gerald Bzdel	.15	.30
99	Doug Carpenter, Head Coach/ General Manager	.15	.30
100	Bobby Dollas	.15	.30
101	Marc Fortier	.50	1.00
102	Scott Gordon, Goalie	.50	1.00
103	Dean Hopkins	.15	.30
104	Mike Hough	1.50	3.00
105	Claude Julien	.15	.30
106	Darin Kimble	.75	1.50
107	Jacques Mailhot	.15	.30
108	Ken McRae	.15	.30
109	Max Middendorf	.15	.30
110	Keith Miller	.15	.30
111	Mike Natyshak	.15	.30
112	Ken Quinney	.15	.30
113	Jean-Marc Richard	.15	.30
114	Jean-Marc Routhier	.15	.30
115	Jaroslav Sevcik	.15	.30
116	Brent Severyn	.15	.30
117	Scott Shaunessy	.15	.30
118	Ladislav Tresl	.15	.30
119	Ron Tugnutt, Goalie	1.50	3.00
	Team Set (23 cards)	7.50	15.00

HERSHEY BEARS
(Philadelphia Flyers)

No.	Player	EX	NRMT
120	Don Biggs	.15	.30
121	Brian Bucciarelli, Assistant Trainer	.15	.30
122	Jean-Jacques Daigneault	1.50	3.00
123	Marc D'Amour, Goalie	.15	.30
124	David Fenyves	.25	.50
125	Mark Freer	.15	.30
126	Darryl Gilmour, Goalie	.15	.30
127	Jeff Harding	.15	.30
128	Warren Harper	.15	.30
129	Kent Hawley	.15	.30
130	Al Hill	.15	.30
131	Tony Horacek	.50	1.00
132	Chris Jensen	.15	.30
133	Craig Kitteringham	.15	.30
134	Mark Lofthouse	.15	.30
135	Frank Mathers, President/ General Manager	.15	.30
136	Kevin McCarthy, Assistant Coach	.15	.30
137	Don Nachbaur	.25	.50
138	Gordon Paddock	.15	.30
139	John Paddock, Coach	.15	.30
140	Jocelyn Perrault, Goalie	.15	.30
141	Bruce Randall	.15	.30
142	Shawn Sabol	.15	.30
143	Glen Seabrooke	.25	.50
144	John Stevens	.15	.30
145	Mike Stothers	.25	.50
146	Dan Stuck, Head Trainer	.15	.30
147	Doug Yingst, Assist.General Manager	.15	.30
	Team Set (28 cards)	5.00	10.00

MAINE MARINERS
(Boston Bruins)

No.	Player	EX	NRMT
148	Paul Beraldo	.15	.30
149	John Carter	.50	1.00
150	Phil Degaetano	.15	.30
151	Scott Drevitch	.15	.30
152	Joe Flaherty	.15	.30
153	Doug Foerster, Public Relations/Tickets	.15	.30
154	Norm Foster, Goalie	.35	.75
155	Paul Guay	.15	.30
156	Greg Hawgood	1.25	2.50
157	Mike Jeffrey, Goalie	.20	.40
158	Jeff Lamb	.15	.30
159	Jean-Marc Lanthier	.15	.30
160	Darren Lowe	.15	.30
161	Carl Mokosak	.15	.30
162	Mitch Molloy	.25	.50
163	Mike Neill	.15	.30

PROCARDS — 1988 - 1989 INTERNATIONAL HOCKEY LEAGUE

No.	Player	EX	NRMT
164	Ray Podloski	.15	.30
165	Stephane Quintal	1.25	2.50
166	Bruce Shoebottom	.35	.75
167	Terry Taillefer, Goalie	.20	.40
168	Steve Tsujiura	.15	.30
169	Scott Wykoff, Broadcaster/ PR	.15	.30
	Team Set (22 cards)	6.00	12.00

MONCTON HAWKS
(Winnipeg Jets)

No.	Player	EX	NRMT
170	Stephane Beauregard, Goalie	1.00	2.00
171	Rick Bowness, Coach	.50	1.00
172	Sean Clement	.15	.30
173	Tom Draper, Goalie	.75	1.50
174	Wayne Flemming, Equipment Manager	.15	.30
175	Steven Fletcher	.15	.30
176	Todd Flichel	.15	.30
177	Guy Gosselin	.15	.30
178	Gilles Hamel	.25	.50
179	Matt Hervey	.15	.30
180	Brent Hughes	.60	1.25
181	Jamie Husgen	.15	.30
182	Stuart Kulak	.25	.50
183	Guy Larose	.50	1.00
184	Neil Meadmore	.15	.30
185	Len Nielson	.15	.30
186	Chris Norton	.15	.30
187	Scott Schneider	.15	.30
188	Rob Snitzer, Athletic Therapist	.15	.30
189	Mike Warus	.15	.30
190	Ron Wilson	.25	.50
	Team Set (21 cards)	4.00	8.00

NEW HAVEN NIGHTHAWKS
(Independent)

No.	Player	EX	NRMT
191	Ken Baumgartner	.50	1.00
192	Francois Breault	.35	.75
193	Mario Chitaroni	.25	.50
194	Sylvain Couturier	.25	.50
195	Rick Dudley, Head Coach	.25	.50
196	John English	.15	.30
197	Mark Fitzpatrick, Goalie	1.00	2.00
198	Eric Germain	.15	.30
199	Dan Gratton	.15	.30
200	Scott Green, Medical Trainer	.15	.30
201	Pat Hickey, Director of Operations	.15	.30
202	Brad Hyatt	.15	.30
203	Paul Kelly	.15	.30
204	Bob Kudelski	.60	1.25
205	Denis Larocque	.15	.30
206	Bob Logan	.15	.30
207	Sal Lombardi, Athletic Trainer	.15	.30
208	Al Loring, Goalie	.20	.40
209	Hubie McDonough	.50	1.00
210	Chris Panek	.15	.30
211	Dave Pasin	.20	.40
212	Joe Paterson	.25	.50
213	Lyle Phair	.15	.30
214	Petr Prajsler	.35	.75
215	Tom Pratt	.15	.30
216	Steve Richmond	.25	.50
217	Phil Sykes	.25	.50
218	Tim Tookey	.25	.50
219	John Tortorella, Assistant Coach	.15	.30
220	Gordie Walker	.15	.30
221	Brian Wilks	.35	.75
222	Darryl Williams	.15	.30
	Team Set (32 cards)	7.50	15.00

NEWMARKET SAINTS
(Toronto Maple Leafs)

No.	Player	EX	NRMT
223	Tim Armstrong	.15	.30
224	Tim Bernhardt, Goalie	.35	.75
225	Brian Blad	.15	.30
226	Mike Blaisdell	.25	.50
227	Jack Capuano	.35	.75
228	Marty Dallman	.25	.50
229	Daryl Evans	.15	.30
230	Paul Gagne	.30	.60

No.	Player	EX	NRMT
231	Alan Hepple	.15	.30
232	Brian Hoard	.15	.30
233	Greg Hotham	.15	.30
234	Wes Jarvis	.15	.30
235	Trevor Jobe	.15	.30
236	Mark Kirton	.35	.75
237	Sean McKenna	.25	.50
238	Jim Ralph, Goalie, Error	.50	1.00
239	Jeff Reese, Goalie	.75	1.50
240	Bill Root	.25	.50
241	Darryl Shannon	.75	1.50
242	Doug Shedden	.25	.50
243	Greg Terrion	.25	.50
244	Ken Yaremchuk	.25	.50
	Team Set (22 cards)	5.00	10.00

ROCHESTER AMERICANS
(Buffalo Sabres)

No.	Player	EX	NRMT
245	Shawn Anderson	.25	.50
246	Mikael Andersson	.75	1.50
247	John Van Boxmeer, Coach	.15	.30
248	Paul Brydges	.15	.30
249	Jeff Capello	.15	.30
250	Jacques Cloutier, Goalie	.50	1.00
251	Mike Donnelly	1.50	3.00
252	Richie Dunn	.25	.50
253	Mark Ferner	.15	.30
254	Jody Gage	.35	.75
255	Francois Guay	.25	.50
256	Jim Hofford	.15	.30
257	Jim Jackson	.15	.30
258	Kevin Kerr	.15	.30
259	Don McSween	.15	.30
260	Scott Metcalfe	.15	.30
261	The Moose, Mascot	.15	.30
262	Jeff Parker	.35	.75
263	Ken Priestlay	.35	.75
264	Robert Ray	1.25	2.50
265	Steve Smith	.15	.30
266	Grant Tkachuk	.15	.30
267	Wayne Van Dorp	.25	.50
268	Darcy Wakaluk, Goalie	1.50	3.00
	Team Set (24 cards)	5.00	10.00

SHERBROOKE CANADIENS
(Montreal Canadiens)

No	Player	EX	NRMT
269	Steve Bisson	.15	.30
270	Bobby Boulanger, Equip. Manager	.15	.30
271	Benoit Brunet	1.00	2.00
272	Rob Bryden	.15	.30
273	Jose Charbonneau	.25	.50
274	Ron Chyzowski	.20	.40
275	Jean-Jacques Daigneault	1.25	2.50
276	Martin Desjardins	.35	.75
277	Donald Dufresne	.50	1.00
278	Rocky Dundas	.15	.30
279	Randy Exelby, Goalie	.25	.05
280	Luc Gauthier	.15	.30
281	Francois Gravel, Goalie	.25	.50
282	Jean Hamel, Head Coach	.15	.30
283	Claude Larose, Assistant Coach	.15	.30
284	Stephan Lebeau	1.50	3.00
285	Sylvain Lefebvre	1.00	2.00
286	Jocelyn Lemieux	.75	1.50
287	Jyrki Lumme	1.00	2.00
288	Steven Martinson	.25	.50
289	Jim Nesich	.15	.30
290	Martin Nicoletti	.15	.30
291	Jacques Parent, Athletic Therapist	.15	.30
292	Mark Pederson	.35	.75
293	Stephane J. J. Richer	1.00	2.00
294	Mario Roberge	.15	.30
295	Serge Roberge	.15	.30
296	Scott Sandelin	.15	.30
297	Marc Saumier	.15	.30
	Team Set (29 cards)	9.00	18.00

SPRINGFIELD INDIANS
(Hartford Whalers)

No.	Player	EX	NRMT
298	Bill Berg	.75	1.50
299	Bruce Boudreau	.35	.75
300	Stu Burnie	.15	.30
301	Shawn Byram	.15	.30
302	Ralph Calvanese, Equipment Manager	.15	.30
303	Kerry Clark	.25	.50
304	Rod Dallman	.25	.50
305	Rob Dimaio	.75	1.50
306	Shawn Evans	.25	.50
307	Jeff Finley	.25	.50
308	Tom Fitzgerald	.50	1.00
309	Jeff Hackett, Goalie	1.00	2.00
310	Dale Henry	.25	.50
311	Richard Kromm	.50	1.00
312	Hank Lammens	.15	.30
313	Duncan MacPherson	.15	.30
314	George Maneluk, Goalie	.25	.50
315	Todd McLellan	.25	.50
316	Chris Prior	.15	.30
317	Jim Roberts, Coach	.15	.30
318	Vern Smith	.25	.50
319	Mike Stevens	.25	.50
320	Ed Tyburski, Head Trainer	.15	.30
321	Mike Walsh	.15	.30
322	Doug Weiss	.15	.30
	Team Set (25 cards)	7.50	15.00

UTICA DEVILS
(New Jersey Devils)

No.	Player	EX	NRMT
323	Robert Bill, Athletic Trainer	.15	.30
324	Craig Billington, Goalie	1.50	3.00
325	John Blessman	.15	.30
326	Neil Brady	.35	.75
327	Murray Brumwell	.25	.50
328	Anders Carlsson	.25	.50
329	Chris Cichocki	.25	.50
330	Jeff Croop, Head Trainer	.15	.30
331	Dan Delianedis, Goalie	.25	.50
332	Dan Dorion	.25	.50
333	Jamie Huscroft	.25.	.50
334	Marc Laniel	.15	.30
335	Tim Lenardon	.15	.30
336	Jeff Madill	.50	1.00
337	David Marcinyshyn	.35	.75
338	Tom McVie, Coach	.15	.30
339	Scott Moon, Trainer's Assistant	.15	.30
338	Janne Ojanen	.75	1.50
339	Alan Stewart	.25	.50
340	Chris Terreri, Goalie	2.00	4.00
341	Kevin Todd	1.00	2.00
342	John Walker	.15	.30
343	Eric Weinrich	2.00	4.00
344	Paul Ysebaert	1.50	3.00
	Team Set (24 cards)	7.50	15.00

— 1988 - 1989 INTERNATIONAL HOCKEY LEAGUE —

This set of cards was not numbered. The teams are first listed alphabetically and then the players are listed alphabetically within their respective teams.

1988-89 International Hockey League
Card No. 1, Dave Allison

1989-90 AMERICAN HOCKEY LEAGUE — PROCARDS

Card Size: 2 1/2" X 3 1/2"
Face: Four colour, red border, League logo, Position
Back: Black on white card stock, Resume, Team logo
Imprint: © 1988 ProCards, Inc.
Complete Set No.: 119
Complete Set Price: 35.00 75.00
Common Card: .15 .30

INDIANAPOLIS ICE
(Chicago Black Hawks)

No.	Player	EX	NRMT
1	Dave Allison	.15	.30
2	Rick Barkovich	.15	.30
3	Brad Beck	.15	.30
4	Geoff Benic	.15	.30
5	Graham Bonar	.15	.30
6	Rick Boyd	.15	.30
7	Scott Clements	.15	.30
8	Shane Doyle	.15	.30
9	Ron Handy	.25	.50
10	Archie Henderson	.15	.30
11	Paul Houck	.15	.30
12	Glen Johannesen	.15	.30
13	Bob Lakso	.15	.30
14	Jimmy Mann	.15	.30
15	Darwin McCutcheon	.15	.30
16	Chris McSorley	.15	.30
17	Rich Oberlin, Trainer	.15	.30
18	Alan Perry, Goalie	.15	.30
19	Brent Sapergia	.15	.30
20	Gary Stewart	.25	.50
21	Randy Taylor	.15	.30
22	Mark Teevens	.15	.30
	Team Set (22 cards)	2.50	5.00

KALAMAZOO WINGS
(Minnesota North Stars)

No.	Player	EX	NRMT
23	Andy Akervik	.15	.30
24	Warren Babe	.25	.50
25	Darin Baker, Goalie	.20	.40
26	Mike Berger	.15	.30
27	Scott Bjugstad	.50	1.00
28	Larry Dyck, Goalie	.15	.30
29	Ken Hodge	2.50	5.00
30	Joe Lockwood	.15	.30
31	Gary McColgan	.15	.30
32	Scott McCrady	.15	.30
33	Michael McHugh	.25	.50
34	Mitch Messier	.25	.50
35	Jarmo Myllys, Goalie	.50	1.00
36	D'Arcy Norton	.15	.30
37	Stephane Roy	.25	.50
38	Dave Schofield	.15	.30
39	Randy Smith	.25	.50
40	Kirk Tomlinson	.15	.30
41	Emanuel Viveiros	.25	.50
42	Neil Wilkinson	.50	1.00
43	Rob Zettler	1.00	2.00
	Team Set (21 cards)	6.00	12.00

MUSKEGON LUMBERJACKS
(Pittsburgh Penguins)

No.	Player	EX	NRMT
44	Brad Aitken	.15	.30
45	Jock Callander	.25	.50
46	Todd Charlesworth	.25	.50
47	Jeff Cooper, Goalie	.20	.40
48	Jeff Daniels	.15	.30
49	Greg Davies	.15	.30
50	Lee Giffin	.25	.50
51	Dave Goertz	.25	.50
52	Steve Gotaas	.25	.50
53	Scott Gruhl	.25	.50
54	Doug Hobson	.15	.30
55	Kevin MacDonald	.15	.30
56	Pat Mayer	.15	.30
57	Dave McIlwain	.75	1.50
58	Dave Michayluk	.25	.50
59	Glenn Mulvenna	.15	.30
60	Jim Paek	.75	1.50
61	Frank Pietrangelo, Goalie	1.00	2.00
62	Bruce Racine, Goalie	.15	.30
63	Mark Recchi	30.00	60.00
64	Troy Vollhoffer	.15	.30

No.	Player	EX	NRMT
65	Jeff Waver	.15	.30
66	Mitch Wilson	.25	.50
	Team Set (23 cards)	37.50	75.00

PEORIA RIVERMEN
(St. Louis Blues)

No.	Player	EX	NRMT
67	Timothy Bothwell	.35	.75
68	Kelly Chase	.20	.40
69	Peter Douris	.20	.40
70	Toby Ducolon	.15	.30
71	Greg Eberle, Head Trainer	.15	.30
72	Glen Featherstone	.50	1.00
73	Wayne Gagne	.15	.30
74	Scott Harlow	.20	.40
75	Pat Jablonski, Goalie	.30	.60
76	Dominic Lavoie	.50	1.00
77	Dave Lowry	.50	1.00
78	Shane MacEachern	.15	.30
79	Terry MacLean	.15	.30
80	Darrell May, Goalie	.20	.40
81	Brad McCaughey	.15	.30
82	Ed McMurray, Assistant General Manager	.15	.30
83	Lyle Odelein	.50	1.00
84	Scott Paluch	.15	.30
85	Peoria Rivermen 1988-1989	.15	.30
86	Skip Probst, General Manager	.15	.30
87	Sheryl Reeves, Administration	.15	.30
88	Cliff Ronning	1.25	2.50
89	Darin Smith	.15	.30
90	Wayne Thomas, Coach	.15	.30
91	Dave Thomlinson	.75	1.50
92	Charlie Thompson, Sales Manager	.15	.30
93	Tony Twist	.85	1.75
94	Jim Vesey	.25	.50
	Team Set (28 cards)	6.00	12.00

SAGINAW HAWKS
(Chicago Black Hawks)

No.	Player	EX	NRMT
95	Ed Belfour, Goalie	15.00	30.00
96	Bruce Cassidy	.20	.40
97	Chris Clifford, Goalie	.15	.30
98	Mario Doyon	.25	.50
99	Bill Gardner	.20	.40
100	Mark Kurzawski	.15	.30
101	Lonnie Loach	.50	1.00
102	Steve Ludzik	.50	1.00
103	David Mackey	.20	.40
104	Dale Marquette	.20	.40
105	Gary Moscaluk	.15	.30
106	Marty Nanne	.15	.30
107	Brian Noonan	.75	1.50
108	Mark Paterson	.20	.40
109	Kent Paynter	.20	.40
110	Guy Phillips	.20	.40
111	John Reid, Goalie	.20	.40
112	Mike Rucinski	.20	.40
113	Warren Rychel	1.00	2.00
114	Everett Sanipass	.50	1.00
115	Mike Stapleton	.20	.40
116	Darryl Sutter, Coach	.35	.75
117	Jari Torkki, Error	.15	.30
118	Bill Watson	.25	.50
119	Sean Williams	.50	1.00
	Team Set (25 cards)	19.00	38.00

— 1989 - 90 AMERICAN HOCKEY LEAGUE —

1989-90 American Hockey League
Card No. 1, New Haven Nighthawks Checklist

Card Size: 2 1/2" X 3 1/2"
Face: Four colour, yellow border, League logo, Position
Back: Black on white card stock, Number, Resume, Team logo
Imprint: © 1989 ProCards, Inc.
Complete Set No.: 360
Complete Set Price: 60.00 120.00
Common Card: .10 .20

NEW HAVEN NIGHTHAWKS
(Los Angeles Kings)

No.	Player	EX	NRMT
1	New Haven Nighthawks, Checklist	.10	.20
2	Francois Breault	.25	.50
3	Paul Kelly	.10	.20
4	Phil Skyes	.20	.40
5	Ron Scott, Goalie	.15	.30
6	Micah Aivazoff	.10	.20
7	Sylvain Couturier	.10	.20
8	Carl Repp, Goalie	.15	.30
9	Murray Brumwell	.35	.75
10	Todd Elik	1.00	2.00
11	Darwin Bozek	.10	.20
12	Eric Germain	.25	.50
13	Scott Young	.20	.40
14	Chris Kontos	1.00	2.00
15	Scot Bjugstad	.50	1.00
16	Eric Ricard	.10	.20
17	Ross Wilson	.10	.20
18	Graham Stanley	.10	.20
19	Chris Panek	.10	.20
20	Nick Fotiu	.10	.20
21	Rene Chapdelaine	.10	.20
22	Gordie Walker	.10	.20
23	Tim Bothwell	.20	.40
24	Kevin MacDonald	.10	.20
25	Darryl Williams	.10	.20
26	John Van Kessel	.10	.20
27	Paul Brydges	.10	.20
	Team Set (27 cards)	3.75	7.50

MONCTON HAWKS
(Winnipeg Jets)

No.	Player	EX	NRMT
28	Moncton Hawks, Checklist	.10	.20
29	Guy Larose	.35	.75
30	Danton Cole	.35	.75
31	Brent Hughes	.25	.50
32	Larry Bernard	.10	.20
33	Stu Kulak	.10	.20
34	Bob Essensa, Goalie	2.50	5.00
35	Luciano Borsato	.50	1.00
36	Guy Gosselin	.10	.20
37	Todd Flichel	.10	.20
38	Brian Hunt	.10	.20
39	Neil Meadmore	.10	.20
40	Matt Hervey	.10	.20
41	Dallas Eakins	.10	.20
42	Brad Jones	.10	.20
43	Chris Norton	.10	.20
44	Bryan Marchment	.50	1.00
45	Rick Tabaracci, Goalie	.75	1.50
46	Grant Richison	.10	.20
47	Brian McReynolds	.10	.20
48	Tony Joseph	.10	.20
49	Dave Farish, Head Coach/G.M.	.10	.20

696 • PROCARDS — 1989-90 AMERICAN HOCKEY LEAGUE

No.	Player	EX	NRMT
50	Rob Snitzer, Trainer	.10	.20
51	Ron Wilson	.10	.20
52	Scot Schneider	.10	.20
	Team Set (25 cards)	4.25	8.50

MAINE MARINERS
(Boston Bruins)

No.	Player	EX	NRMT
53	Maine Mariners, Checklist	.10	.20
54	Dave Buda	.10	.20
55	Paul Beraldo	.10	.20
56	Lou Crawford	.10	.20
57	Mark Montanari	.10	.20
58	Don Sweeney	.75	1.50
59	Jeff Sirkka	.10	.20
60	Norm Foster, Goalie	.30	.60
61	Greg Poss	.10	.20
62	Gord Cruickshank	.10	.20
63	Bruce Shoebottom	.25	.50
64	Mark Ziliotto	.10	.20
65	Ron Hoover	.10	.20
66	Scott Harlow	.10	.20
67	Mike Millar	.20	.40
68	Bob Beers	.75	1.50
69	Ray Neufeld	.35	.75
70	Greame Townshend	.10	.20
71	Billy O'Dwyer	.10	.20
72	Frank Caprice, Goalie	.15	.30
73	John Blum	.10	.20
74	Jerry Foster, Trainer	.10	.20
75	Bill Sutherland, Assistant Coach/ Rick Bowness, Coach	.35	.75
76	Scott Drevitch	.10	.20
	Team Set (24 cards)	3.75	7.50

BALTIMORE SKIPJACKS
(Washington Capitals)

No.	Player	EX	NRMT
77	Baltimore Skipjacks, Checklist	.10	.20
78	John Purves	.10	.20
79	Jeff Greenlaw	.15	.30
80	Tim Taylor	.10	.20
81	Alfie Turcotte	.15	.30
82	Dan Redmond, Trainer	.10	.20
83	Chris Felix	.15	.30
84	Bobby Babcock	.10	.20
85	Steve Maltais	.35	.75
86	Mike Richard	.10	.20
87	Baltimore Skipjacks, Team Photo	.10	.20
88	Bob Mason, Goalie	.25	.50
89	Mark Ferner	.10	.20
90	Steve Seftel	.10	.20
91	Brain Tutt	.10	.20
92	Terry Murray, Coach	.25	.50
93	Jim Hrivnak, Goalie	.75	1.50
94	Tyler Larter	.10	.20
95	Tim Bergland	.10	.20
96	Dennis Smith	.10	.20
97	Steve Hollett	.10	.20
98	Shawn Simpson, Goalie	.15	.30
99	Robin Bawa	.10	.20
100	John Druce	.50	1.00
101	Kent Paynter	.10	.20
102	Alain Cote	.60	1.25
103	J.P. Mattingly, Trainer	.10	.20
	Team Set (27 cards)	3.75	7.50

NEWMARKET SAINTS
(Toronto Maple Leafs)

No.	Player	EX	NRMT
104	Newmarket Saints, Checklist	.10	.20
105	Dean Anderson, Goalie	.15	.30
106	Wes Jarvis	.10	.20
107	Brian Blad	.10	.20
108	Derek Laxdal	.35	.75
109	Kent Hulst	.10	.20
110	Tim Berhardt, Goalie	.15	.30
111	Brian Hoard	.10	.20
112	Bill Root	.10	.20
113	Paul Gardner, Coach	.10	.20
114	Tim Armstrong	.10	.20
115	Sean McKenna	.15	.30
116	Tim Bean	.10	.20

No.	Player	EX	NRMT
117	Alan Hepple	.10	.20
118	Greg Hotham	.10	.20
119	Scott Pearson	.35	.75
120	Peter Ihnacak	.10	.20
121	John McIntyre	.30	.60
122	Paul Gagne	.10	.20
123	Darren Veitch	.15	.30
124	Mark LaForest, Goalie	.15	.30
125	Doug Shedden	.15	.30
126	Bobby Reynolds	.10	.20
127	Tahir Domi	1.50	3.00
128	Ken Hammond	.15	.30
	Team Set (25 cards)	3.75	7.50

CAPE BRETON OILERS
(Edmonton Oilers)

No.	Player	EX	NRMT
129	Cape Breton Oilers, Checklist	.10	.20
130	Wade Campbell	.10	.20
131	Chris Joseph	.35	.75
132	Mario Barbe	.10	.20
133	Mike Greenlay, Goalie	.15	.30
134	Peter Soberlak	.10	.20
135	Bruce Bell	.15	.30
136	Dan Currie	.15	.30
137	Fabian Joseph	.25	.50
138	Stan Drulia	.10	.20
139	Todd Charlesworth	.10	.20
140	Norm MacIver	1.10	2.25
141	David Haas	.10	.20
142	Tim Tisdale	.10	.20
143	Eldon Reddick, Goalie, (Pokey)	.50	1.00
144	Alexander Tyjnych, Goalie	.15	.30
145	Kim Issel	.30	.60
146	Corey Foster	.10	.20
147	Tomas Kapusta	.10	.20
148	Brian Wilks	.25	.50
149	John LeBlanc	.10	.20
150	Ivan Matulik	.10	.20
151	Shaun Van Allen	.15	.30
	Team Set (23 cards)	4.25	8.50

HALIFAX CITADELS
(Quebec Nordiques)

No.	Player	EX	NRMT
152	Halifax Citadels, Checklist	.10	.20
153	Scott Gordon, Goalie	.20	.40
154	Trevor Steinburg	.10	.20
155	Miroslav Ihnacak	.20	.40
156	Jamie Baker	.10	.20
157	Robbie Ftorek, Coach	.10	.20
158	Chris McQuaid, Equipment Manager/ Brent Smith, Trainer	.10	.20
159	Mario Burnetta, Goalie	.15	.30
160	Jean-Marc Routhier	.10	.20
161	David Espe	.10	.20
162	Ken Quinney	.10	.20
163	Mark Vermette	.10	.20
164	Dean Hopkins	.20	.40
165	Claude Julien	.10	.20
166	Claude Lapointe	.20	.40
167	Stephane Morin	.15	.30
168	Bryan Fogarty	.25	.50
169	Dave Pichette	.10	.20
170	Kevin Kaminski	.10	.20
171	Brent Severyn	.10	.20
172	Max Middendorf	.10	.20
173	Jean-Marc Richard	.15	.30
174	Gerald Bzdel	.10	.20
175	Ladislav Tresl	.10	.20
176	Jaroslav Sevcik	.10	.20
177	Greg Smyth	.10	.20
178	Joel Baillargeon	.15	.30
	Team Set (27 cards)	5.00	10.00

SHERBROOKE CANADIENS
(Montreal Canadiens)

No.	Player	EX	NRMT
179	Sherbrook Canadiens, Checklist	.10	.20
180	Andre Racicot, Goalie	.50	1.00
181	Jean-Claude Bergeron, Goalie	.25	.50
182	Jim Nesich	.10	.20
183	Todd Richards	.10	.20

No.	Player	EX	NRMT
184	Francois Gravel, Goalie	.15	.30
185	Lyle Odelein	1.00	2.00
186	Benoit Brunet	.75	1.50
187	Mario Roberge	.50	1.00
188	Marc Saumier	.10	.20
189	Normand Desjardins	.15	.30
190	Dan Woodley	.10	.20
191	Andrew Cassels	1.50	3.00
192	Roy Mitchell	.10	.20
193	Guy Darveau	.10	.20
194	Ed Cristofoli	.10	.20
195	Stephane J. J. Richer	1.50	3.00
196	Jacques Parent, Athletic Therapist	.10	.20
197	Luc Gauthier	.10	.20
198	John Ferguson	.15	.30
199	Mathieu Schneider	.75	1.50
200	Serge Roberge	.10	.20
201	Jean Hamel, Coach	.10	.20
	Team Set (23 cards)	7.00	14.00

UTICA DEVILS
(New Jersey Devils)

No.	Player	EX	NRMT
202	Utica Devils, Checklist	.10	.20
203	Jason Simon	.10	.20
204	Jeff Madill	.25	.50
205	Kevin Todd	.35	.75
206	Myles O'Connor	.15	.30
207	Jon Morris	.20	.40
208	Bob Hoffmeyer, Associate Coach	.10	.20
209	Paul Ysebaert	.75	1.50
210	Steve Rooney	.20	.40
211	Claude Vilgrain	.75	1.50
212	Paul Guay	.10	.20
213	Roland Melanson, Goalie	.20	.40
214	Tom McVie	.50	1.00
215	Dave Marcinyshyn	.20	.40
216	Perry Anderson	.20	.40
217	Jamie Huscroft	.10	.20
218	Bob Woods	.10	.20
219	Pat Conacher	.50	1.00
220	Jean-Marc Lanthier	.10	.20
221	Chris Kiene	.10	.20
222	Eric Weinrich	.50	1.00
223	Brian Fitzgerald, Assistant Trainer	.10	.20
224	Craig Billington, Goalie	.75	1.50
225	Jim Thomson	.10	.20
226	Tim Budy	.10	.20
227	Marc Laniel	.10	.20
228	Robert Bill, Trainer	.10	.20
	Team Set (27 cards)	5.00	10.00

SPRINGFIELD INDIANS
(Hartford Whalers)

No.	Player	EX	NRMT
229	Springfield Indians, Checklist	.10	.20
230	Mike Walsh	.10	.20
231	Dale Henry	.10	.20
232	Bill Berg	.50	1.00
233	Hank Lammens	.10	.20
234	Rob Dimaio	.50	1.00
235	Shawn Byram	.10	.20
236	Jeff Hackett, Goalie	.60	1.25
237	Wayne McBean	.25	.50
238	Tim Hanley	.10	.20
239	Tom Fitzgerald	.25	.50
240	Mike Stevens	.10	.20
241	George Maneluk, Goalie	.15	.30
242	Dean Ewen	.10	.20
243	Dale Kushner	.10	.20
244	Shawn Evans	.10	.20
245	Rod Dallman	.10	.20
246	Mike Kelfer	.10	.20
247	Sean Lebrun	.10	.20
248	Kerry Clark	.10	.20
249	Ed Tyburski, Trainer	.10	.20
250	Derek King	1.25	2.50
251	Marc Bergevin	.10	.20
252	Jeff Finley	.10	.20
253	Jim Roberts, Coach	.10	.20
254	Chris Pryor	.10	.20
	Team Set (26 cards)	4.50	9.00

1989 - 1990 INTERNATIONAL HOCKEY LEAGUE — PROCARDS

ROCHESTER AMERICANS
(Buffalo Sabres)

No.	Player	EX	NRMT
255	Rochester Americans, Checklist	.10	.20
256	Robert Ray	.50	1.00
257	Ken Priestlay	.50	1.00
258	Darcey Wakaluk, Goalie	.75	1.50
259	Richie Dunn	.10	.20
260	Ken Sutton	.50	1.00
261	Terry Martin, Assistant Coach	.10	.20
262	Scott Metcalfe	.10	.20
263	Joel Savage	.10	.20
264	Brad Miller	.10	.20
265	Donald Audette	.50	1.00
266	John Van Boxmeer, Coach	.10	.20
267	The Moose, Mascot	.10	.20
268	Brian Ford, Goalie	.15	.30
269	Darcy Loewen	.10	.20
270	Bob Halkidis	.25	.50
271	Steve Ludzik	.10	.20
272	Steve Smith	.10	.20
273	Francois Guay	.10	.20
274	Mike Donnelly	.75	1.50
275	Darrin Shannon	.50	1.00
276	Jody Gage	.10	.20
277	Dave Baseggio	.10	.20
278	Bob Corkum	.50	1.00
279	Jim Jackson	.10	.20
280	Don McSween	.10	.20
281	Jim Hofford	.10	.20
282	Scott McCrory	.10	.20
	Team Set (28 cards)	5.00	10.00

BINGHAMTON WHALERS
(Hartford Whalers)

No.	Player	EX	NRMT
283	Binghamton Whalers, Checklist	.10	.20
284	Raymond Saumier	.10	.20
285	Mike Berger	.10	.20
286	Corey Beaulieu	.10	.20
287	Doug McKay, Coach	.10	.20
288	Blair Atcheynum	.10	.20
289	Al Tuer	.10	.20
290	Chris Lindberg	.20	.40
291	Daryl Reaugh, Goalie	.15	.30
292	James Black	.10	.20
293	Vern Smith	.10	.20
294	Todd Krygier	.50	1.00
295	Bob Bodak	.10	.20
296	Jon Smith, Trainer	.10	.20
297	Michel Picard	.10	.20
298	Jim Culhane	.10	.20
299	Brian Chapman	.15	.30
300	Jim Ennis	.10	.20
301	Jacques Caron, Goaltend Coach	.10	.20
302	Jim McKenzie	.10	.20
303	Kay Whitmore, Goalie	.75	1.50
304	Terry Yake	.50	1.00
305	Mike Moller	.20	.40
	Team Set (23 cards)	3.25	6.50

ADIRONDACK RED WINGS
(Detroit Red Wings)

No.	Player	EX	NRMT
306	Adirondack Red Wings, Checklist	.10	.20
307	Bob Wilkie	.10	.20
308	Chris McRae	.10	.20
309	Chris Kotsopoulos	.25	.50
310	Steve Sumner, Assistant Trainer	.10	.20
311	Timothy Abbott, Assistant Trainer	.10	.20
312	Gordon Kruppke	.10	.20
313	Mike Gober	.10	.20
314	Al Conroy	.10	.20
315	Sam St. Laurent, Goalie	.25	.50
316	Dave Casey, Trainer	.10	.20
317	Yves Racine	.50	1.00
318	Randy McKay	.10	.20
319	Dale Krentz	.20	.40
320	Sheldon Kennedy	.50	1.00
321	Barry Melrose, Coach	.50	1.00
322	Dennis Holland	.10	.20
323	Glenn Merkosky	.10	.20
324	Murray Eaves	.10	.20
325	Mark Reimer, Goalie	.15	.30
326	Tim Cheveldae, Goalie	1.25	2.50
327	Peter Dineen	.10	.20
328	Dean Morton	.10	.20
329	Derek Mayer	.10	.20
	Team Set (24 cards)	4.50	9.00

HERSHEY BEARS
(Philadelphia Flyers)

No.	Player	EX	NRMT
330	Hershey Bears, Checklist	.10	.20
331	Don Biggs	.10	.20
332	Scott Sandelin	.15	.30
333	Shaun Sabol	.10	.20
334	Murray Baron	.30	.60
335	David Fenyves	.20	.40
336	Glen Seabrooke	.10	.20
337	Mark Freer	.25	.50
338	Ray Allison	.10	.20
339	Chris Jensen	.10	.20
340	Ross Fitzpatrick	.10	.20
341	Brian Dobbin	.10	.20
342	Darren Rumble	.50	1.00
343	Mike Stothers	.10	.20
344	Jiri Latal	.50	1.00
345	Don Nachbaur	.10	.20
346	John Stevens	.10	.20
347	Steven Fletcher	.10	.20
348	Kent Hawley	.10	.20
349	Bill Armstrong	.10	.20
350	Bruce Hoffort, Goalie	.30	.60
351	Gordon Paddock	.10	.20
352	Marc D'Amour, Goalie	.15	.30
353	Tim Tookey	.10	.20
354	Reid Simpson	.10	.20
355	Mark Bassen	.10	.20
356	Rockey Trottier	.20	.40
357	Harry Bricker, Assistant Trainer	.10	.20
358	Dan Stuck, Head Trainer	.10	.20
359	Al Hill, Assistant Coach	.10	.20
360	Kevin McCarthy, Coach	.10	.20
	Team Set (31 cards)	5.00	10.00

— 1989 - 1990 INTERNATIONAL HOCKEY LEAGUE —

1989-90 International Hockey League
Card No. 1, Peoria Rivermen, Checklist

Card Size: 2 1/2" X 3 1/2"
Face: Four colour, yellow border, League logo, Position
Back: Black on white card stock, Number, Resume, Team logo
Imprint: © 1989 ProCards, Inc.
Complete Set No.: 208
Complete Set Price: 30.00   60.00
Common Card: .10   .20

PEORIA RIVERMAN
(St. Louis Blues)

No.	Player	EX	NRMT
1	Peoria Rivermen, Checklist	.10	.20
2	Darwin McPherson	.10	.20
3	Pat Jablonski, Goalie	.60	1.25
4	Scott Paluch	.10	.20
5	Guy Hebert, Goalie, Error	1.50	3.00
6	Richard Pion	.35	.75
7	Curtis Joseph, Goalie	5.00	10.00
8	Robert Dirk	.35	.75
9	Darin Smith	.10	.20
10	Terry MacLean	.10	.20
11	Kevin Miehm	.10	.20
12	Toby Ducolon	.10	.20
13	Mike Wolak	.10	.20
14	Adrien Plavsic	.50	1.00
15	Dave Thomlinson	.50	1.00
16	Jim Vesey	.30	.60
17	Michel Mongeau	.50	1.00
18	Tom Nash, Trainer	.10	.20
19	David O'Brien	.10	.20
20	Dominic Lavoie	.30	.60
21	Keith Osborne	.10	.20
22	Rob Robinson	.10	.20
23	Wayne Thomas, Coach	.10	.20
	Team Set (23 cards)	7.50	15.00

FLINT SPIRITS
(New York Rangers)

No.	Player	EX	NRMT
24	Flint Spirits, Checklist	.10	.20
25	Jason Lafreniere	.30	.60
26	Rick Knickle, Goalie	.75	1.50
27	Jerry Tarrant	.10	.20
28	Paul Broten	.50	1.00
29	Kevin Miller	.50	1.00
30	James Latos	.10	.20
31	Daniel Lacroix	.10	.20
32	Dennis Vial	.20	.40
33	Denis Larocque	.10	.20
34	Mike Golden	.10	.20
35	Mike Hurlbut	.10	.20
36	Scott Brower, Goalie	.10	.20
37	Lee Giffin	.10	.20
38	Jeff Bloemberg	.30	.60
39	Simon Wheeldon	.10	.20
40	Rob Zamuner	.50	1.00
41	Joe Paterson	.10	.20
42	Barry Chyzowski	.10	.20
43	Peter Laviolette	.10	.20
44	Corey Millen	.30	.60
45	Darren Lowe	.30	.60
46	Peter Fiorentino	.10	.20
47	Soren True	.10	.20
48	Mike Richter, Goalie	3.00	6.00
	Team Set (25 cards)	6.50	13.00

INDIANAPOLIS ICE
(Chicago Black Hawks)

No.	Player	EX	NRMT
49	Indianapolis Ice, Checklist	.10	.20
50	Sean Williams	.25	.50
51	Bruce Cassidy	.10	.20
52	Mark Kurzawski	.10	.20
53	Bob Bassen	.50	1.00
54	Marty Nanne	.10	.20
55	Jari Torkki	.10	.20
56	Ryan McGill	.10	.20
57	Mike Peluso	.60	1.25
58	Darryl Sutter, Coach	.10	.20
59	Dan Vincelette	.10	.20
60	Lonnie Loach	.50	1.00
61	Mike Rucinski	.10	.20
62	Jim Playfiar	.10	.20
63	Everett Sanipass	.35	.75
64	Dale Marquette	.10	.20
65	Gary Moscaluk	.10	.20
66	Mario Doyon	.10	.20
67	Ray Leblanc, Goalie	.10	.20
68	Mike Eagles	.10	.20
69	Warren Rychel	.75	1.50
70	Jim Johannson	.10	.20
71	Cam Russell	.25	.50
72	Michael McNeill	.10	.20
73	Jim Waite, Goalie	.50	1.00
	Team Set (25 cards)	4.50	9.00

KALAMAZOO WINGS
(Minnesota North Stars)

No.	Player	EX	NRMT
74	Kalamazoo Wings, Checklist	.10	.20
75	Kevin Schamehorn	.10	.20
76	Kevin Evans	.10	.20
77	D'Arcy Norton	.10	.20
78	Scott Robinson	.10	.20
79	Larry PePalma	.10	.20
80	Ed Courtenay	.25	.50
81	Rob Zettler	.50	1.00
82	Dusan Pasek	.10	.20
83	Gary Emmons	.10	.20
84	Peter Lappin	.30	.60
85	Mario Thyer	.15	.30
86	Mike McHugh	.30	.60
87	Randy Smith	.30	.60
88	Link Gaetz	.30	.60
89	Ken Hodge, Jr.	1.50	3.00
90	Pat MacLeod	.10	.20
91	Neil Wilkinson	.50	1.00
92	Brett Barnett	.10	.20
93	Larry Dyck, Goalie	.10	.20
94	Dean Kolstad	.10	.20
95	Jarmo Myllys, Goalie	.75	1.50
96	Paul Jerrard	.10	.20
97	Jean-Francois Quintin	.35	.75
98	Mitch Messier	.20	.40
	Team Set (25 cards)	4.00	8.00

PHOENIX ROADRUNNERS
(Los Angeles Kings)

No.	Player	EX	NRMT
99	Phoenix Roadrunners, Checklist	.10	.20
100	Bryant Perrier	.10	.20
101	Keith Gretzky	.50	1.00
102	Don Martin	.10	.20
103	David Littman, Goalie	.35	.75
104	Mike Decarle	.10	.20
105	Grant Tkachuk	.10	.20
106	Richard Novak	.10	.20
107	Chris Luongo	.15	.30
108	Bruce Boudreau	.10	.20
109	Nick Beaulieu	.15	.30
110	Jeff Lamb	.10	.20
111	Rob Nichols	.10	.20
112	Gary Unger, Coach	.10	.20
113	Larry Floyd	.10	.20
114	Brent Sapergia	.10	.20
115	Randy Exelby, Goalie	.10	.20
116	Jim McGeough	.10	.20
117	Tom Karalis	.10	.20
118	Ken Spangler	.10	.20
119	Jacques Mailhot	.10	.20
120	Shawn Dineen, Assistant Coach	.10	.20
121	Dave Korol	.10	.20
	Team Set (23 cards)	3.00	6.00

FORT WAYNE KOMETS
(Independent)

No.	Player	EX	NRMT
122	Fort Wayne Komets, Checklist	.10	.20
123	Colin Chin	.10	.20
124	Scott Shaunessy	.10	.20
125	Bob Lakso	.10	.20
126	Duane Joyce	.10	.20
127	Joe Stephan	.10	.20
128	Ron Shudra	.20	.40
129	Bob Fowler	.10	.20
130	Steve Bisson	.10	.20
131	Craig Endean	.10	.20
132	Carl Mokosak	.10	.20
133	Carey Lucyk	.10	.20
134	Craig Channell	.10	.20
135	Frederic Chabot, Goalie	.10	.20
136	Brian Hannon	.10	.20
137	Keith Miller	.35	.75
138	Al Sims, Coach	.10	.20
139	Stephane Beauregard, Goalie	.30	.60
140	Ron Handy	.10	.20
141	Byron Lomow	.10	.20
	Team Set (20 cards)	3.00	6.00

MUSKEGON LUMBERJACKS
(Pittsburgh Penguins)

No.	Player	EX	NRMT
142	Muskegon Lumberjacks, Checklist	.10	.20
143	Jamie Leach	.35	.75
144	Chris Clifford, Goalie	.10	.20
145	Dave Capuano	.25	.50
146	Jeff Daniels	.10	.20
147	Dave Goertz	.20	.40
148	Perry Ganchar	.10	.20
149	Mitch Wilson	.20	.40
150	Scott Gruhl	.20	.40
151	Randy Taylor	.10	.20
152	Bruce Racine, Goalie	.10	.20
153	Dave Michayluk	.10	.20
154	Richard Zemlak	.50	1.00
155	Brad Aitken	.10	.20
156	Paul Stanton	.20	.40
157	Darren Stolk	.10	.20
158	Jim Paek	.60	1.25
159	Mark Kachowski	.10	.20
160	Dan Frawley	.10	.20
161	Mike Mersch	.10	.20
162	Glenn Mulvenna	.10	.20
163	Phil Russell, Assistant Coach	.10	.20
164	Blair MacDonald, Coach	.10	.20
	Team Set (23 cards)	3.00	6.00

MILWAUKEE ADMIRALS
(Vancouver Canucks)

No.	Player	EX	NRMT
165	Milwaukee Admirals, Checklist	.10	.20
166	Shaun Clouston	.10	.20
167	Steve Veilleux	.10	.20
168	Peter George Bakovic	.10	.20
169	Peter Deboer	.10	.20
170	Ernie Vargas	.10	.20
171	Keith Street	.10	.20
172	Rob Murphy	.20	.40
173	David Bruce	.20	.40
174	Shannon Travis	.10	.20
175	Jeff Rohlicek	.10	.20
176	Jay Mazur	.25	.50
177	Kevan Guy	.20	.40
178	Troy Gamble, Goalie	.75	1.50
179	Ronnie Stern	.35	.75
180	Jime Revenberg	.10	.20
181	Jose Charbonneau	.20	.40
182	Ian Kidd	.10	.20
183	Todd Hawkins	.10	.20
184	Carl Valimont	.10	.20
185	Jim Agnew	.10	.20
186	Curtis Hunt	.10	.20
187	Dean Cook, Goalie	.10	.20
188	Ron Wilson, Assistant Coach	.10	.20
189	Ron Lapointe, Coach	.10	.20
	Team Set (25 Cards)	3.00	6.00

SALT LAKE GOLDEN EAGLES
(Calgary Flames)

No.	Player	EX	NRMT
190	Salt Lake Golden Eagles, Checklist	.20	.40
191	Brian Glynn	.35	.75
192	Stephane Matteau	.60	1.25
193	Rick Barkovich	.10	.20
194	Jeff Wenaas	.10	.20
195	Darryl Olsen	.10	.20
196	Rick Lessard	.10	.20
197	Kevin Grant	.20	.40
198	Rich Chernomaz	.20	.40
199	Stu Grimson	.75	1.50
200	Jamie Hislop, Assistant Coach/ Bob Francis, Coach	.10	.20
201	Doug Pickell	.10	.20
202	Chris Biotti	.10	.20
203	Tim Sweeney	.50	1.00
204	Ken Sabourin	.35	.75
205	Randy Bucyk	.10	.20
206	Wayne Cowley, Goalie	.35	.75
207	Rick Hayward	.10	.20
208	Marc Bureau	.35	.75
	Team Set (19 cards)	3.00	6.00

— 1990 - 1991 —
AMERICAN HOCKEY LEAGUE
INTERNATIONAL HOCKEY LEAGUE

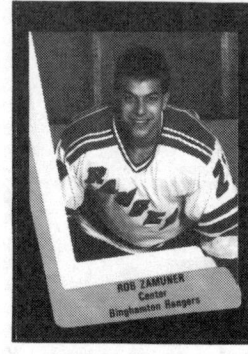

1990-91 AHL \ IHL
Card No. 1, Rob Zamuner

Card Size: 2 1/2" X 3 1/2"
Face: Four colour, red border, Position
Back: Black and buff on white card stock, Number, Resume, Team Logo
Imprint: © 1990 ProCards, Inc. Made in USA
Complete Set No.: 628

Complete Set Price:	50.00	100.00
Common Goalie:	.10	.20
Common Player:	.07	.15

BINGHAMTON RANGERS - AHL
(New York Rangers)

No.	Player	EX	NRMT
1	Rob Zamuner	.50	1.00
2	Todd Charlesworth	.07	.15
3	Bob Bodak	.07	.15
4	Len Hachborn	.07	.15
5	Peter Fiorentino	.07	.15
6	Kord Cernich	.07	.15
7	Daniel Lacroix	.07	.15
8	Joe Paterson	.25	.50
9	Sam St. Laurent, Goalie	.10	.20
10	Jeff Bloemberg	.25	.50
11	Mike Golden	.07	.15
12	Mike Hurlbut	.07	.15
13	Mark Laforest, Goalie	.10	.20
14	Chris Cichocki	.25	.50
15	John Paddock, Coach	.07	.15
16	Peter Laviolette	.07	.15
17	Martin Bergeron	.07	.15
18	Rudy Poeschek	.25	.50
19	Eric Germain	.07	.15
20	Al Hill, Assistant Coach	.07	.15
21	Ric Bennett, Error	.25	.50
22	Tahir Domi	.60	1.25
23	Ross Fitzpatrick	.15	.30
24	Brian McReynolds	.25	.50
25	Binghamton Rangers Checklist	.07	.15
	Team Set (25 cards)	3.00	6.00

HERSHEY BEARS - AHL
(Philadelphia Flyers)

No.	Player	EX	NRMT
26	Mike Eaves, Coach	.07	.15
27	Lance Pitlick	.07	.15
28	Dale Kushner	.07	.15
29	Reid Simpson	.07	.15
30	Craig Fisher	.35	.75
31	Dominic Roussel, Goalie	.75	1.50
32	David Fenyves	.07	.15
33	Brian Dobbin	.35	.75
34	Darren Rumble	.35	.75
35	Murray Baron	.07	.15
36	Bruce Hoffort, Goalie	.10	.20
37	Steve Beadle	.07	.15
38	Chris Jensen	.20	.40
39	Mike Stothers	.07	.15
40	Kent Hawley	.07	.15
41	Scott Sandelin	.07	.15
42	Guy Phillips	.07	.15
43	Mark Bassen	.07	.15
44	Steve Scheifele	.07	.15
45	Bill Armstrong	.25	.50

No.	Player	EX	NRMT
46	Shaun Sabol	.07	.15
47	Mark Freer	.25	.50
48	Claude Boivin	.20	.40
49	Len Barrie	.25	.50
50	Bill Armstrong	.25	.50
51	Tim Tookey	.25	.50
52	Harry Bricker, Assistant Coach	.07	.15
53	Hershey Bears Checklist	.07	.15
	Team Set (28 cards)	3.00	6.00

FREDERICTON CANADIENS - AHL
(Montreal Canadiens)

No.	Player	EX	NRMT
54	Alain Cote	.50	1.00
55	Luc Gauthier	.07	.15
56	Eric Charron	.07	.15
57	Mario Roberge	.25	.50
58	Tom Sagissor	.07	.15
59	Brent Bobyck	.07	.15
60	John Ferguson	.07	.15
61	Jim Nesich	.20	.40
62	Gilbert Dionne	1.00	2.00
63	Herbert Hohenberger	.07	.15
64	Dan Woodley	.07	.15
65	Roy Mitchell	.07	.15
66	Frederic Chabot, Goalie	.10	.20
67	Andre Racicot, Goalie	1.00	2.00
68	Paul Dipietro	.25	.50
69	Norman Desjardins	.07	.15
70	Martin St. Amour	.07	.15
71	Jessie Belanger	.35	.75
72	Ed Cristofoli	.07	.15
73	Patrick Lebeau	1.50	3.00
74	Paulin Bordeleau, Coach	.07	.15
75	Fredericton Canadiens Checklist	.07	.15
	Team Set (22 cards)	4.50	9.00

PEORIA RIVERMEN - IHL
(St. Louis Blues)

No.	Player	EX	NRMT
76	Keith Osborne	.07	.15
77	Richard Pion	.35	.75
78	Alain Raymond, Goalie	.10	.20
79	Rob Robinson	.07	.15
80	Andy Rymsha	.07	.15
81	Randy Skarda	.20	.40
82	Dave Thomlinson	.50	1.00
83	Tom Tilley	.20	.40
84	Steve Tuttle	.25	.50
85	Tony Twist	.35	.75
86	David Bruce	.50	1.00
87	Kelly Chase	.07	.15
88	Nelson Emerson	.50	1.00
89	Guy Hebert, Goalie	.35	.75
90	Tony Hejna	.07	.15
91	Michel Mongeau	.50	1.00
92	David O'Brien	.07	.15
93	Kevin Miehm	.25	.50
94	Darwin McPherson	.07	.15
95	Dominic Lavoie	.07	.15
96	Yves Heroux	.07	.15
97	Pat Jablonski, Goalie	.35	.75
98	Bob Plager, Coach	.07	.15
99	Peoria Rivermen Checklist	.07	.15
	Team Set (24 cards)	3.00	6.00

KALAMAZOO WINGS - IHL
(Minnesota North Stars)

No.	Player	EX	NRMT
99	Jayson More	.35	.75
100	Kevin Evans	.07	.15
101	Warren Babe	.07	.15
102	Mitch Messier	.10	.20
103	John Blue, Goalie	.35	.75
104	Larry Dyck, Goalie	.10	.20
105	Duane Joyce	.20	.40
106	Kari Takko, Goalie	.25	.50
107	Brett Barnett	.07	.15
108	Pat MacLeod	.20	.40
109	Peter Lappin	.25	.50
110	Link Gaetz	.07	.15
111	Larry DePalma	.25	.50

No.	Player	EX	NRMT
112	Steve Gotaas	.35	.75
113	Mike McHugh	.25	.50
114	Dan Keczmer	.07	.15
115	Jackson Penney	.07	.15
116	Ed Courtenay	.25	.50
117	Jean-Francois Quintin	.25	.50
118	Scott Robinson	.07	.15
119	Mario Thyer	.25	.50
120	Enrico Ciccone	.25	.50
121	Kevin Constantine, Assistant Coach; John Marks, Coach	.07	.15
122	Kalamazoo Wings Checklist	.07	.15
	Team Set (24 cards)	3.00	6.00

MAINE MARINERS - AHL
(Boston Bruins)

No.	Player	EX	NRMT
123	Shayne Stevenson	.25	.50
124	Jeff Lazaro	.25	.50
125	Matt Delguidice, Goalie	.35	.75
126	Ron Hoover	.20	.40
127	John Mokosak	.07	.15
128	John Blum	.07	.15
129	Mike Parson, Goalie	.10	.20
130	Bruce Shoebottom	.07	.15
131	Dave Donnelly	.25	.50
132	Ralph Barahona	.25	.50
133	Graeme Townshend	.07	.15
134	Ken Hodge	.25	.50
135	Norm Foster, Goalie	.25	.50
136	Greg Poss	.07	.15
137	Brad James	.07	.15
138	Lou Crawford	.07	.15
139	Rick Allain	.07	.15
140	Bob Beers	.35	.75
141	Ken Hammond	.25	.50
142	Mark Montanari	.07	.15
143	Rick Bowness, Coach	.07	.15
144	Bob Gould, Player/Coach	.07	.15
145	Maine Mariners Checklist	.07	.15
	Team Set (23 cards)	3.00	6.00

NEWMARKET SAINTS - AHL
(Toronto Maple Leafs)

No.	Player	EX	NRMT
146	Mike Stevens	.20	.40
147	Greg Walters	.07	.15
148	Mike Moes	.07	.15
149	Kent Hulst	.25	.50
150	Len Esau	.07	.15
151	Darryl Shannon	.25	.50
152	Bobby Reynolds	.07	.15
153	Derek Langille	.07	.15
154	Jeff Serowik	.07	.15
155	Darren Veitch	.07	.15
156	Joe Sacco	.25	.50
157	Alan Hepple	.07	.15
158	Doug Shedden	.20	.40
159	Steve Bancroft	.07	.15
160	Greg Johnston	.35	.75
161	Trevor Jobe	.07	.15
162	Bill Root	.07	.15
163	Tim Bean	.07	.15
164	Brian Blad	.07	.15
165	Robert Horyna, Goalie	.10	.20
166	Dean Anderson, Goalie	.10	.20
167	Damian Rhodes, Goalie	.50	1.00
168	Mike Millar	.25	.50
169	Mike Jackson	.07	.15
170	Newmarket Saints Checklist	.07	.15
	Team Set (25 cards)	3.00	6.00

SPRINGFIELD INDIANS - AHL
(Hartford Whalers)

No.	Player	EX	NRMT
171	Cal Brown	.13	.25
172	Michel Picard	.13	.25
173	Cam Brauer	.13	.25
174	Jim Burke	.13	.25
175	Jim McKenzie	.13	.25
176	Mike Tomlak	.13	.25
177	Ross McKay, Goalie	.10	.20
178	Blair Atcheynum	.25	.50

No.	Player	EX	NRMT
179	Chris Tancill	.25	.50
180	Mark Greig	.25	.50
181	Joe Day	.25	.50
182	Jim Roberts, Coach	.13	.25
183	Emanuel Viveiros	.13	.25
184	Daryl Reaugh, Goalie	.10	.20
185	Tommie Eriksen	.13	.25
186	Terry Yake	.60	1.25
187	Chris Govedaris	.25	.50
188	Chris Bright	.13	.25
189	John Stevens	.13	.25
190	Brian Chapman	.13	.25
191	James Black	.35	.75
192	Scott Daniels	.13	.25
193	Kelly Ens	.13	.25
194	Springfield Indians Checklist	.13	.25
	Team Set (24 cards)	3.00	6.00

BALTIMORE SKIPJACKS - AHL
(Washington Capitals)

No.	Player	EX	NRMT
195	Ken Lovsin	.07	.15
196	Kent Paynter	.07	.15
197	Jim Mathieson	.07	.15
198	Bob Mendel	.07	.15
199	Reggie Savage	.25	.50
200	Alfie Turcotte	.35	.75
201	Victor Gervais	.07	.15
202	Todd Hlushko	.20	.40
203	Steve Seftel	.20	.40
204	Thomas Sjogren	.25	.50
205	Steve Maltais	.35	.75
206	Bob Joyce	.35	.75
207	Tyler Larter	.07	.15
208	Mark Ferner	.25	.50
209	Bobby Babcock	.07	.15
210	Jeff Greenlaw	.07	.15
211	Tim Taylor	.25	.50
212	John Purves	.25	.50
213	Chris Felix	.07	.15
214	Jiri Vykoukal	.07	.15
215	Shawn Simpson, Goalie	.10	.20
216	Jim Hrivnak, Goalie	.60	1.25
217	Rob Laird, Coach/General Manager	.07	.15
218	Barry Trotz, Assistant Coach	.07	.15
219	Baltimore Skipjacks Checklist	.07	.15
	Team Set (25 cards)	3.00	6.00

CAPE BRETON OILERS - AHL
(Edmonton Oilers)

No.	Player	EX	NRMT
220	David Haas	.20	.40
221	Wade Campbell	.07	.15
222	Dan Currie	.35	.75
223	Shaun Van Allen	.35	.75
224	Norm MacIver	.75	1.50
225	Mike Greenlay, Goalie	.10	.20
226	Peter Soberlak	.07	.15
227	Tim Tisdale	.07	.15
228	Mario Barbe	.07	.15
229	Shjon Podein	.35	.75
230	Trevor Sim	.07	.15
231	Corey Foster	.07	.15
232	Mike Ware	.07	.15
233	Marc LaForge	.07	.15
234	Bruce Bell	.07	.15
235	Tomas Kapusta	.25	.50
236	Alexander Tyjnych, Goalie	.10	.20
237	Tomas Srsen	.07	.15
238	Collin Bauer	.07	.15
239	Francois Leroux	.13	.25
240	Don MacAdam, Coach	.07	.15
241	Norm Ferguson, Assistant Coach	.07	.15
242	Cape Breton Oilers Checklist	.07	.15
	Team Set (23 cards)	3.00	6.00

MONCTON HAWKS - AHL
(Winnipeg Jets)

No.	Player	EX	NRMT
243	Tony Joseph	.07	.15
244	Brent Hughes	.35	.75
245	Larry Bernard	.07	.15
246	Simon Wheeldon	.25	.50

No.	Player	EX	NRMT
247	Todd Flichel	.07	.15
248	Craig Duncanson	.25	.50
249	Iain Duncan	.25	.50
250	Bryan Marchment	.50	1.00
251	Matt Hervey	.07	.15
252	Chris Norton	.07	.15
253	Dallas Eakins	.07	.15
254	Peter Hankinson	.07	.15
255	Grant Richison	.07	.15
256	Lee Davidson	.07	.15
257	Denis Larocque	.07	.15
258	Scott Levins	.35	.75
259	Guy Larose	.35	.75
260	Scott Schneider	.20	.40
261	Sergei Kharin	.25	.50
262	Hawk, Mascot	.07	.15
263	Dave Farrish, Coach/General Manager	.07	.15
264	Moncton Hawks Checklist	.07	.15
	Team Set (24 cards)	3.00	6.00
	(See also card nos. 343-344)		

ROCHESTER AMERICANS - AHL
(Buffalo Sabres)

No.	Player	EX	NRMT
265	Kevin Haller	.35	.75
266	Joel Savage	.20	.40
267	Scott Metcalfe	.07	.15
268	Ian Boyce	.07	.15
269	David Littman, Goalie	.25	.50
270	Dave Baseggio	.07	.15
271	Ken Sutton	.25	.50
272	Brad Miller	.07	.15
273	Bill Houlder	.35	.75
274	Dan Frawley	.20	.40
275	Scott McCrory	.25	.50
276	Steve Ludzik	.25	.50
277	Robert Ray	.50	1.00
278	Darrin Shannon	.50	1.00
279	Dale Degray	.07	.15
280	Bob Corkum	.35	.75
281	Grant Tkachuk	.07	.15
282	Kevin Kerr	.07	.15
283	Mitch Molloy	.07	.15
284	Darcy Loewen	.35	.75
285	Jody Gage	.20	.40
286	Jiri Sejba	.07	.15
287	Steve Smith	.50	1.00
288	Darcy Wakaluk, Goalie	.50	1.00
289	Donald Audette	.35	.75
290	Don McSween	.25	.50
291	Francois Guay	.25	.50
292	Terry Martin, Assistant Coach	.07	.15
293	Don Lever, Coach	.07	.15
294	The Moose, Mascot	.07	.15
295	Rochester Americans Checklist	.07	.15
	Team Set (31 cards)	3.00	6.00

SAN DIEGO GULLS - IHL
(Independent)

No.	Player	EX	NRMT
296	Mike O'Connell, Head Coach	.07	.15
297	Paul Marshall	.07	.15
298	Darin Bannister	.07	.15
299	Rob Nichols	.07	.15
300	Charlie Simmer, Player/Asst. Coach	.20	.40
301	Bob Jones	.07	.15
302	Scott Brower, Goalie	.10	.20
303	Taylor Hall	.07	.15
304	Carl Mokosak	.07	.15
305	Glen Hanlon, Goalie	.20	.40
306	Peter Dineen	.07	.15
307	Mike Sullivan	.07	.15
308	Steven Martinson	.07	.15
309	Dave Korol	.07	.15
310	Darren Lowe	.25	.50
311	Mark Reimer, Goalie	.10	.20
312	Mike Gober	.07	.15
313	Al Tuer	.07	.15
314	Dean Morton	.07	.15
315	Jim McGeough	.07	.15
316	Clark Donatelli	.07	.15
317	Steven Dykstra	.07	.15
318	Brent Sapergia	.07	.15
319	Larry Floyd	.35	.75
320	D'Arcy Norton	.20	.40
321	San Diego Gulls Checklist	.07	.15
	Team Set (26 cards)	3.00	6.00

MILWAUKEE ADMIRALS
(Vancouver Canucks)

No.	Player	EX	NRMT
322	Garry Valk	.07	.15
323	Ian Kidd	.07	.15
324	Todd Hawkins	.07	.15
325	Carl Valimont	.07	.15
326	Peter DeBoer	.07	.15
327	Curt Fraser, Assistant Coach	.07	.15
328	David Mackey	.25	.50
329	Jim Benning	.07	.15
330	Peter George Bakovic	.25	.50
331	Steve Weeks, Goalie	.35	.75
332	Steve Veilleux	.07	.15
333	Shaun Clouston	.20	.40
334	Gino Odjick	.50	1.00
335	Mike Murphy, Coach	.25	.50
336	Cam Brown	.07	.15
337	Patrice Lefebvre	.07	.15
338	Eric Murano	.25	.50
339	Jim Revenberg	.07	.15
340	Don Gibson	.07	.15
341	Steve McKichan, Goalie	.20	.40
342	Milwaukee Admirals Checklist	.07	.15
	Team Set (21 cards)	3.00	6.00

MONCTON HAWKS - AHL
(Winnipeg Jets)

No.	Player	EX	NRMT
343	Rick Tabaracci, Goalie	.60	1.25
344	Mike O'Neill, Goalie	.20	.40

PHOENIX ROADRUNNERS - IHL
(Los Angeles Kings)

No.	Player	EX	NRMT
345	Rick Hayward	.07	.15
346	Sean Whyte	.07	.15
347	Petr Prajsler	.20	.40
348	John Van Kessel	.07	.15
349	Mario Gosselin, Goalie	.20	.40
350	Kyosti Karjalainen	.20	.40
351	Mikael Lindholm	.25	.50
352	David Goverde, Goalie	.10	.20
353	Graham Stanley	.07	.15
354	Stephane Richer	.20	.40
355	Brian Lawton	.35	.75
356	Jerome Bechard	.07	.15
357	Jeff Rohlicek	.07	.15
358	Steve Jaques	.07	.15
359	Chris Kontos	.60	1.25
360	Sylvain Couturier	.35	.75
361	Peter Sentner	.07	.15
362	Steve Graves	.07	.15
363	Daryn McBride	.20	.40
364	Steve Rooney	.07	.15
365	Mickey Volcan	.20	.40
366	Kevin MacDonald	.07	.15
367	Ralph Backstrom, Coach	.07	.15
368	Gary Unger, Assistant Coach	.07	.15
369	Phoenix Roadrunners, Checklist	.07	.15
	Team Set (25 cards)	3.00	6.00

MUSKEGON LUMBERJACKS - IHL
(Pittsburgh Penguins)

No.	Player	EX	NRMT
370	Rob Dopson, Goalie	.10	.20
371	John Callander	.07	.15
372	Chris Olifford, Goalie	.10	.20
373	Sandy Smith	.25	.50
374	Jim Kyte	.07	.15
375	Mike Needham	.75	1.50
376	Mitch Wilson	.07	.15
377	Dave Goertz	.07	.15
378	Mark Kachowski	.07	.15
379	Perry Ganchar	.35	.75
380	Mark Major	.07	.15
381	Joel Gardner	.07	.15
382	Scott Gruhl	.07	.15
383	Todd Nelson	.07	.15
384	Darren Stolk	.07	.15
385	Scott Shaunessy	.07	.15
386	Mike Mersch	.07	.15
387	Glenn Mulvenna	.07	.15
388	Brad Aitken	.07	.15
389	Dave Michayluk	.50	1.00
390	Blair MacDonald, Coach	.07	.15
391	Phil Russell, Assistant Coach	.07	.15
392	Muskegon Lumberjacks Checklist	.07	.15
	Team Seat (23 cards)	3.00	6.00

INDIANAPOLIS ICE - IHL
(Chicago Black Hawks)

No.	Player	EX	NRMT
393	Sean Williams	.25	.50
394	Ryan McGill	.35	.75
395	Mike Eagles	.35	.75
396	Jim Johannson	.25	.50
397	Marty Nanne	.07	.15
398	Jim Playfair	.07	.15
399	Warren Rychel	.50	1.00
400	Cam Russell	.07	.15
401	Jim Waite, Goalie	.60	1.25
402	Mike Stapleton	.35	.75
403	Trevor Dam	.07	.15
404	Tracey Egeland	.07	.15
405	Owen Lessard	.07	.15
406	Jeff Sirkka	.07	.15
407	Mike Dagenais	.07	.15
408	Alex Roberts	.07	.15
409	Dominik Hasek, Goalie	2.50	5.00
410	Martin Desjardins	.25	.50
411	Frantisek Kucera	.50	1.00
412	Carl Mokosak	.07	.15
413	Dave McDowall, Coach	.07	.15
414	Indianapolis Ice Checklist	.07	.15
	Team Set (22 cards)	3.50	7.00

NEW HAVEN NIGHTHAWKS - AHL
(Independent)

No.	Player	EX	NRMT
415	Paul Saundercook	.07	.15
416	Darryl Williams	.07	.15
417	Micah Aivazoff	.20	.40
418	Robb Stauber, Goalie	.50	1.00
419	Tom Martin	.07	.15
420	Billy O'Dwyer	.07	.15
421	Scott Harlow	.07	.15
422	Jim Thomson	.07	.15
423	Jim Pavese	.07	.15
424	Ron Scott, Goalie	.10	.20
425	Dave Pasin	.07	.15
426	Serge Roy	.07	.15
427	Darryl Gilmour, Goalie	.10	.20
428	Mike Donnelly	.60	1.25
429	Rene Chapdelaine	.07	.15
430	Brandy Semchuk	.07	.15
431	Paul Holden	.07	.15
432	Bob Berg	.07	.15
433	Ladislav Tresl	.25	.50
434	Eric Ricard	.07	.15
435	Murray Brumwell, Player/Assist. Coach	.07	.15
436	Shawn McCosh	.07	.15
437	Ross Wilson	.07	.15
438	Scott Young	.07	.15
439	David Moylan	.07	.15
440	Marcel Comeau, Coach	.07	.15
441	New Haven Nighthawks, Checklist	.07	.15
	Team Set (27 cards)	3.00	6.00

HALIFAX CITADELS - AHL
(Quebec Nordiques)

No.	Player	EX	NRMT
442	David Espe	.07	.15
443	Mario Doyon	.07	.15
444	Gerald Bzdel	.07	.15
445	Claude LaPointe	.07	.15
446	Dean Hopkins, Assistant Coach	.07	.15
447	Clement Jodoin, General Manager/Coach	.07	.15
448	Kevin Kaminski	.07	.15

No.	Player	EX	NRMT
449	Jamie Baker	.35	.75
450	Mark Vermette	.20	.40
451	Iiro Jarvi	.35	.75
452	Kip Miller	.35	.75
453	Greg Smyth	.07	.15
454	Serge Roberge	.07	.15
455	Stephane Morin	.25	.50
456	Brent Severyn	.35	.75
457	Jean-Marc Richard	.20	.40
458	Ken Quinney	.20	.40
459	Jeff Jackson	.25	.50
460	Jaroslav Sevcik	.20	.40
461	Dave Latta	.07	.15
462	Trevor Stienburg	.07	.15
463	Miroslav Ihnacak	.35	.75
464	Jim Sprott	.07	.15
465	Mike Bishop, Goalie	.10	.20
466	Stephane Fiset, Goalie	1.10	2.25
467	Scott Gordon, Goalie	.10	.20
468	Halifax Citadels, Checklist	.07	.15
	Team Set (27 cards)	3.50	7.00

ADIRONDACK RED WINGS - AHL
(Detroit Red Wings)

No.	Player	EX	NRMT
469	Gord Kruppke	.07	.15
470	Glenn Merkosky	.25	.50
471	Dennis Holland	.07	.15
472	Chris McRae	.25	.50
473	Al Conroy	.25	.50
474	Yves Racine	.50	1.00
475	Jim Nill, Player/Assistant Coach	.07	.15
476	Barry Melrose, Coach	.25	.50
477	Bob Wilkie	.07	.15
478	Guy Dupuis	.07	.15
479	Doug Houda	.07	.15
480	Tom Bissett	.13	.25
481	Bill McDougall	.13	.25
482	Glen Goodall	.20	.40
483	Kory Kocur	.25	.50
484	Chris Luongo	.07	.15
485	Serge Anglehart	.07	.15
486	Marc Potvin	.35	.75
487	Stewart Malgunas	.25	.50
488	John Chabot	.35	.75
489	Daniel Shank	.25	.50
490	Randy Hansch, Goalie	.10	.20
491	Dave Gagnon, Goalie	.10	.20
492	Scott King, Goalie	.10	.20
493	Adirondack Red Wings, Checklist	.07	.15
	Team Set (25 cards)	3.00	6.00

CAPITAL DISTRICT ISLANDERS - AHL
(New York Islanders)

No.	Player	EX	NRMT
494	Derek Laxdal	.35	.75
495	Sean Lebrun	.07	.15
496	Shawn Byram	.07	.15
497	Wayne Doucet	.07	.15
498	Rich Kromm	.35	.75
499	Chris Pryor, Player/Assistant Coach	.07	.15
500	George Maneluk, Goalie	.10	.20
501	Brad Lauer	.25	.50
502	Wayne McBean	.25	.50
503	Jeff Finley	.07	.15
504	Jim Culhane	.07	.15
505	Paul Cohen, Goalie	.07	.15
506	Brent Grieve	.07	.15
507	Kevin Cheveldayoff	.07	.15
508	Dennis Vaske	.25	.50
509	Dave Chyzowski	.20	.40
510	Travis Green	.13	.25
511	Dean Chynoweth	.07	.15
512	Rob Dimaio	.35	.75
513	Paul Guay	.25	.50
514	Capital District Islanders, Checklist	.07	.15
	Team Set (21 cards)	3.00	6.00

ALBANY CHOPPERS - IHL
(Independent)

No.	Player	EX	NRMT
515	Rick Knickle, Goalie	.35	.75

No.	Player	EX	NRMT
516	Curtis Hunt	.07	.15
517	Bruce Racine, Goalie	.10	.20
518	Yves Heroux	.10	.20
519	Joe Stefan	.07	.15
520	Torrie Robertson	.35	.50
521	Nicholas Beaulieu	.07	.15
522	Dave Richter	.07	.15
523	Jeff Waver	.07	.15
524	Gordon Paddock	.07	.15
525	Darryl Noren	.07	.15
526	Byron Lomow	.07	.15
527	Ivan Matulik	.07	.15
528	Dan Woodley	.07	.15
529	Dale Henry	.07	.15
530	Soren True	.07	.15
531	Stuart Burnie	.07	.15
532	Rob MacInnis	.07	.15
533	Vern Smith	.07	.15
534	Paul Laus	.07	.15
535	Albany Choppers, Checklist	.07	.15
	Team Set (21 cards)	3.00	6.00

FORT WAYNE KOMETS - IHL
(Independent)

No.	Player	EX	NRMT
536	Robin Bawa	.10	.20
537	Steven Fletcher	.10	.20
538	Lonnie Loach	.60	1.25
539	Al Sims, Coach	.07	.15
540	Colin Chin	.25	.50
541	Bruce Boudreau, Player/Assistant Coach	.07	.15
542	Bob Lasko	.25	.50
543	John Anderson	.35	.75
544	Kevin Kaminski	.07	.15
545	Bruce Major	.07	.15
546	Stephane Brochu	.20	.40
547	Peter Hankinson	.07	.15
548	Carey Lucyk	.07	.15
549	Tom Karalis	.07	.15
550	Bob Jay	.07	.15
551	Mike Butters	.07	.15
552	Brian McKee	.25	.50
553	Ray LeBlanc, Goalie	.25	.50
554	Tom Draper, Goalie	.25	.50
555	Steve Laurin, Goalie	.10	.20
556	Fort Wayne Komets, Checklist	.07	.15
	Team Set (21 cards)	3.00	6.00

UTICA DEVILS - AHL
(New Jersey Devils)

No.	Player	EX	NRMT
557	Sergel Starikov	.25	.50
558	Claude Vilgrain	.35	.75
559	Jeff Sharples	.35	.75
560	Bob Woods	.07	.15
561	Perry Anderson	.07	.15
562	Brennan Maley	.07	.15
563	Mike Posma	.07	.15
564	Tom McVie, General Manager/Coach	.07	.15
565	Chris Palmer	.07	.15
566	Bill Huard	.07	.15
567	Marc Laniel	.07	.15
568	Neil Brady	.35	.75
569	Jason Simon	.07	.15
570	Kevin Todd	.75	1.50
571	Jeff Madill	.35	.75
572	Jeff Christian	.25	.50
573	Todd Copeland	.07	.15
574	Mike Bodnarchuk	.25	.50
575	Chris Kiene	.07	.15
576	Myles O'Connor	.07	.15
577	Jamie Huscroft	.25	.50
578	Mark Romaine, Goalie	.25	.50
579	Rollie Melanson, Goalie	.10	.20
580	Team Picture	.07	.15
581	Utica Devils, Checklist	.07	.15
	Team Set (25 cards)	3.00	6.00

KANSAS CITY BLADES - IHL
(Independent)

No.	Player	EX	NRMT
582	Ron Handy	.25	.50

No.	Player	EX	NRMT
583	Cam Plante	.07	.15
584	Lee Giffin	.25	.50
585	Jim Latos	.07	.15
586	Stu Kulak	.15	.30
587	Claude Julien	.07	.15
588	Rick Barkovich	.07	.15
589	Randy Exelby, Goalie	.15	.30
590	Mark Vichorek	.07	.15
591	Darin Smith	.25	.50
592	Mike Kelfer	.07	.15
593	Andy Akervik	.07	.15
594	Mike Hiltner	.07	.15
595	Kevin Sullivan	.07	.15
596	Troy Frederick	.07	.15
597	Claudio Scremin	.07	.15
598	Kurt Semandel	.07	.15
599	Mike Colman	.07	.15
600	Jeff Odgers	.50	1.00
601	Wade Flaherty, Goalie	.10	.20
602	Kansas City Blades, Checklist	.07	.15
	Team Set (21 cards)	3.00	6.00

SALT LAKE GOLDEN EAGLES - IHL
(Calgary Flames)

No.	Player	EX	NRMT
603	Marc Bureau	.50	1.00
604	Darryl Olsen	.25	.50
605	Rick Lessard	.07	.15
606	Kevin Grant	.07	.15
607	Rich Chernomaz	.35	.75
608	Randy Bucyk	.07	.15
609	Wayne Cowley, Goalie	.10	.20
610	Ken Sabourin	.35	.75
611	Bob Francis, Head Coach	.07	.15
612	Jamie Hislop, Coach	.07	.15
613	Kevan Melrose	.07	.15
614	Scott McCrady	.25	.50
615	Corey Lyons	.07	.15
616	Martin Simard	.07	.15
617	C. J. Young	.50	1.00
618	Mark Osiecki	.35	.75
619	Bryan Deasley	.07	.15
620	Kerry Clark	.15	.30
621	Paul Kruse	.07	.15
622	Darren Banks	.07	.15
623	Richard Zemlak	.35	.75
624	Todd Harkins	.07	.15
625	Warren Sharples, Goalie	.25	.50
626	Andrew McKim	.35	.75
627	Steve Guenette, Goalie	.25	.50
628	Salt Lake Golden Eagles Checklist	.07	.15
	Team Set (26 cards)	3.00	6.00

— 1991 - 1992 —
AMERICAN HOCKEY LEAGUE
INTERNATIONAL LEAGUE

Twenty-six team sets are required to complete a set of AHL and IHL cards.

1991-92 AHL\IHL
Card No. 1, Bill Houlder

702 • PROCARDS — 1991 - 92 AHL \ IHL

Card Size: 2 1/2" X 3 1/2"
Face: Four colour, white border, League logo
Back: Yellow, blue and black on white card stock, Number, Resume, Position
Imprint: © 1991 ProCards, Inc. ® Made in USA
Complete Set No.: 620
Complete Set Price: 35.00 75.00
Common Card: .05 .10

ROCHESTER AMERICANS - AHL
(Buffalo Sabres)

No.	Player	EX	NRMT
1	Bill Houlder	.25	.50
2	Brian Curran	.05	.10
3	Dan Frawley	.05	.10
4	Darcy Loewen	.05	.10
5	Jiri Sejba	.05	.10
6	Lindy Ruff	.35	.75
7	Chris Snell	.18	.35
8	Bob Corkum	.35	.75
9	Dave Baseggio	.05	.10
10	Sean O'Donnell	.05	.10
11	Brad Rubachuk	.05	.10
12	Peter Ciavaglia	.25	.50
13	Joel Savage	.05	.10
14	Jason Winch	.05	.10
15	Steve Ludzik	.20	.40
16	Don McSween	.20	.40
17	David DiVita	.05	.10
18	Greg Brown	.05	.10
19	David Littman, Goalie	.20	.40
20	Tom Draper, Goalie	.35	.75
21	Jody Gage	.05	.10
22	Terry Martin, Asst. Coach	.05	.10
23	Don Lever, Coach	.05	.10
24	Rochester Americans, Checklist, Error	.05	.10
	Team Set (24 cards)	2.75	5.50

PEORIA RIVERMEN - IHL
(St. Louis Blues)

No.	Player	EX	NRMT
25	Jason Marshall	.05	.10
26	Michel Mongeau	.25	.50
27	Derek Frenette	.05	.10
28	Kevin Miehm	.20	.40
29	Guy Hebert, Goalie	.50	1.00
30	Greg Poss	.05	.10
31	Dave Mackey	.05	.10
32	Dan Fowler	.05	.10
33	Mark Bassen	.05	.10
34	Yves Heroux	.25	.50
35	Harold Snepsts, Coach	.05	.10
36	Bruce Shoebottom	.05	.10
37	Jaan Luik	.05	.10
38	Alain Raymond, Goalie	.07	.15
39	Kyle Reeves	.05	.10
40	Brian McKee	.05	.10
41	Steve Tuttle	.25	.50
42	Rob Tustian	.05	.10
43	Richard Pion	.20	.40
44	Joe Hawley	.05	.10
45	Brian Pellerin	.05	.10
46	Jason Ruff	.05	.10
47	Peoria Rivermen, Checklist	.05	.10
	Team Set (23 cards)	2.75	5.50

MAINE MARINERS - AHL
(Boston Bruins)

No.	Player	EX	NRMT
48	Wes Walz	.50	1.00
49	Steve Bancroft	.05	.10
50	John Blue, Goalie	.50	1.00
51	Rick Allain	.05	.10
52	Mike Walsh	.05	.10
53	Dave Thomlinson	.35	.75
54	Dennis Smith	.05	.10
55	Jack Capuano	.15	.30
56	Mike Rossetti	.05	.10
57	Petr Prajsler	.05	.10
58	Matt Glennon	.05	.10
59	John Byce	.35	.75
60	Howie Rosenblatt	.05	.10
61	Brad Tiley	.05	.10
62	Lou Crawford	.05	.10
63	Matt Hervey	.05	.10
64	Peter Douris	.30	.60
65	Jeff Lazaro	.35	.75
66	Dave Reid	.35	.75
67	E. J. McGuire, Coach	.05	.10
68	Frank Bathe, Asst. Coach	.05	.10
69	Maine Mariners, Checklist	.05	.10
	Team Set (22 cards)	2.75	5.50

FREDERICTON CANADIENS - AHL
(Montreal Canadiens)

No.	Player	EX	NRMT
70	Paul DiPietro	.60	1.25
71	Darcy Simon	.05	.10
72	Patrick Lebeau	.25	.50
73	Gilbert Dionne	.35	.75
74	John Ferguson	.05	.10
75	Norman Desjardins	.05	.10
76	Luc Gauthier	.05	.10
77	Jean-Claude Bergeron, Goalie	.13	.25
78	Andre Racicot, Goalie	.35	.75
79	Steve Veilleux	.05	.10
80	Patrice Brisebois	.50	1.00
81	Tom Sagissor	.05	.10
82	Lindsay Vallis	.05	.10
83	Steve Larouche	.05	.10
84	Sean Hill	.50	1.00
85	Jesse Belanger	.75	1.50
86	Stephane Richer	.05	.10
87	Marc Labelle	.05	.10
88	Pierre Sevigny	.05	.10
89	Eric Charron	.05	.10
90	Ed Ronan	.35	.75
91	Paulin Bordeleau, Coach	.05	.10
92	Fredericton Canadiens, Checklist, Error	.05	.10
	Team Set (23 cards)	3.50	7.00

SPRINGFIELD INDIANS - AHL
(Hartford Whalers)

No.	Player	EX	NRMT
93	Daryl Reaugh, Goalie	.13	.25
94	Jergus Baca	.25	.50
95	Karl Johnston	.13	.25
96	Shawn Evans	.13	.25
97	Scott Humeniuk	.13	.25
98	Cam Brauer	.13	.25
99	Scott Eichstadt	.13	.25
100	Paul Cyr	.13	.25
101	James Black	.25	.50
102	Chris Govedaris	.20	.40
103	Joe Day	.20	.40
104	Chris Tancill	.20	.40
105	Kerry Russell	.13	.25
106	Denis Chalifoux	.13	.25
107	Blair Atcheynum	.20	.40
108	John Stevens	.13	.25
109	Brian Chapman	.13	.25
110	Chris Bright	.13	.25
111	Jim Burke	.13	.25
112	Scott Daniels	.13	.25
113	Kelly Ens	.13	.25
114	Mike Tomlak	.13	.25
115	Mario Gosselin, Goalie	.07	.15
116	Jay Leach, Coach	.13	.25
117	Springfield Indians, Checklist	.13	.25
	Team Set (25 cards)	3.00	6.00

ADIRONDACK RED WINGS - AHL
(Detroit Red Wings)

No.	Player	EX	NRMT
118	Allan Bester, Goalie	.25	.50
119	Daniel Shank	.25	.50
120	Lonnie Loach	.50	1.00
121	Mark Reimer, Goalie	.07	.15
122	Kirk Tomlinson	.05	.10
123	Stewart Malgunas	.25	.50
124	Serge Anglehart	.05	.10
125	Chris Luongo	.25	.50
126	Keith Primeau	.50	1.00
127	Ken Quinney	.05	.10
128	Dave Flanagan	.05	.10
129	Pete Stauber	.05	.10
130	Mike Sillinger	.35	.75
131	Micah Aivazoff	.05	.10
132	Gary Shuchuk	.35	.75
133	Bill McDougall	.25	.50
134	Sheldon Kennedy	.25	.50
135	Derek Mayer	.05	.10
136	Darin Bannister	.05	.10
137	Guy Dupuis	.05	.10
138	Gord Kruppke	.05	.10
139	Jason York	.05	.10
140	Barry Melrose, Coach	.25	.50
141	Glenn Merkosky, Asst. Coach	.20	.40
142	Adirondack Red Wings, Checklist	.05	.10
	Team Set (25 cards)	3.00	6.00

KALAMAZOO WINGS - IHL
(Minnesota North Stars)

No.	Player	EX	NRMT
143	Larry Dyck, Goalie	.05	.10
144	Roy Mitchell	.05	.10
145	Greg Spenrath	.05	.10
146	Steve Herniman	.05	.10
144	Brad Berry	.05	.10
145	Jim Nesich	.05	.10
146	Tim Lenardon	.05	.10
147	Steve Guenette, Goalie	.07	.15
148	Paul Jerrard	.05	.10
149	Cal McGowan	.05	.10
150	Scott Robinson	.05	.10
151	Mitch Messier	.25	.50
152	Tony Joseph	.05	.10
153	Steve Maltais	.35	.75
154	Steve Gotaas	.25	.50
155	Doug Barrault	.05	.10
156	Dave Moylan	.05	.10
157	Mario Thyer	.25	.50
158	Bob Hoffmeyer, Coach	.05	.10
159	Wade Dawson, Asst. Coach	.05	.10
160	Kalamazoo Wings, Checklist	.05	.10
	Team Set (21 cards)	3.00	6.00

MONCTON HAWKS - AHL
(Winnipeg Jets)

No.	Player	EX	NRMT
164	Rob Murray	.05	.10
165	Chris Kiene	.05	.10
166	Lee Davidson	.05	.10
167	Rudy Poeschek	.25	.50
168	Kent Paynter	.05	.10
169	John LeBlanc	.05	.10
170	Dallas Eakins	.05	.10
171	Claude Julien	.05	.10
172	Bob Joyce	.25	.50
173	Derek Langille	.05	.10
174	Rob Cowie	.05	.10
175	Warren Rychel	.60	1.25
176	Tom Karalis	.05	.10
177	Kris Draper	.20	.40
178	Ken Gernander	.05	.10
179	Tod Hartje	.05	.10
180	Sean Gauthier, Goalie	.07	.15
181	Tyler Larter	.05	.10
182	Scott Levins	.05	.10
183	Jason Cirone	.05	.10
184	Mark Kumpel	.05	.10
185	Rick Tabaracci, Goalie	.60	1.25
186	Luciano Borsato	.35	.75
187	Dave Farrish, Head Coach/GM	.05	.10
188	Dave Prior, Goaltender Coach	.05	.10
189	Moncton Hawks, Checklist	.05	.10
	Team Set (26 cards)	3.00	6.00

BINGHAMTON RANGERS - AHL
(New York Rangers)

No.	Player	EX	NRMT
190	Peter Fiorentino	.05	.10
191	Glen Goodall	.05	.10
192	John Mokosak	.05	.10
193	Sam St. Laurent, Goalie	.07	.15
194	Daniel Lacroix	.05	.10
195	Guy LaRose	.25	.50
196	Mike Hurlbut	.05	.10
197	Peter Laviolette	.05	.10

1991-92 AHL \ IHL — PROCARDS • 703

No.	Player	EX	NRMT
198	Rick Bennett	.20	.40
199	Steven King	.50	1.00
200	Boris Rousson, Goalie	.25	.50
201	Jody Hull	.20	.40
202	Shaun Sabol	.05	.10
203	Joe Paterson	.05	.10
204	Rob Zamuner	.50	1.00
205	Don Biggs	.05	.10
206	Chris Cichocki	.20	.40
207	Ross Fitzpatrick	.05	.10
208	Mark LaForest	.05	.10
209	Brian McReynolds	.05	.10
210	Jeff Bloemberg	.20	.40
211	Kord Cernich	.05	.10
212	Ron Smith, Coach	.05	.10
213	Al Hill, Asst. Coach	.05	.10
214	Binghamton Rangers, Checklist	.05	.10
	Team Set (25 cards)	3.00	6.00

CAPE BRETON OILERS - AHL
(Edmonton Oilers)

No.	Player	EX	NRMT
215	Francois Leroux	.05	.10
216	Marc Laforge	.05	.10
217	Max Middendorf	.05	.10
218	Shjon Podein	.05	.10
219	Jason Soules	.20	.40
220	Collin Bauer	.05	.10
221	Shaun Van Allen	.25	.50
222	Eldon Reddick	.05	.10
223	Eugeny Belosheikin, Goalie	.05	.10
224	David Haas	.15	.30
225	Norm Foster, Goalie	.05	.10
226	Greg Hawgood	.35	.75
227	Steven Rice	.13	.25
228	Dan Currie	.13	.25
229	Peter Soberlak	.05	.10
230	Martin Rucinsky	.35	.75
231	Tomas Kapusta	.20	.40
232	Dean Antos	.05	.10
233	Craig Fisher	.05	.10
234	Tomas Srsen	.20	.40
235	Don MacAdam, Coach	.05	.10
236	Norm Ferguson, Asst. Coach	.05	.10
237	Coaching Staff,	.05	.10
238	Cape Breton Oilers, Checklist, Error	.05	.10
	Team Set (24 cards)	3.00	6.00

FORT WAYNE KOMETS - IHL
(Independent)

No.	Player	EX	NRMT
239	Peter Hankinson	.05	.10
240	Chris McRae	.05	.10
241	Craig Martin	.05	.10
242	Carey Lucyk	.05	.10
243	Jean-Marc Richard	.25	.50
244	Grant Richison	.05	.10
245	Mark Turner	.05	.10
246	Todd Flichel	.05	.10
247	Scott Shaunessy	.05	.10
248	Darin Smith	.05	.10
249	Ian Boyce	.05	.10
250	Colin Chin	.25	.50
251	Bob Jones	.05	.10
252	Bob Jay	.05	.10
253	Kelly Hurd	.05	.10
254	Scott Gruhl	.35	.75
255	Kory Kocur	.05	.10
256	Steven Fletcher	.05	.10
257	Bob Lakso	.20	.40
258	Dusty Imoo, Goalie	.07	.15
259	Mike O'Neill, Goalie	.20	.40
260	Bruce Boudreau, Asst. Coach	.25	.50
261	Al Sims, Coach	.05	.10
262	Fort Wayne Komets, Checklist, Error	.05	.10
	Team Set (24 cards)	3.00	6.00

HERSHEY BEARS - AHL
(Philadelphia Flyers)

No.	Player	EX	NRMT
263	Ray Letourneau, Goalie	.05	.10
264	Marc D'Amour, Goalie	.05	.10
265	Dominic Roussel, Goalie	1.00	2.00
266	Bill Armstrong	.05	.10
267	Al Conroy	.05	.10
268	Dale Kushner	.05	.10
269	Toni Porkka	.05	.10
270	Mike Stothers	.05	.10
271	Darren Rumble	.35	.75
272	Reid Simpson	.05	.10
273	Claude Bolvin	.05	.10
274	Len Barrie	.05	.10
275	Chris Jensen	.15	.30
276	Pat Murray	.20	.40
277	Eric Dandenault	.05	.10
278	Rod Dallman	.05	.10
279	Mark Freer	.35	.75
280	Bill Armstrong	.20	.40
281	Tim Tookey	.35	.75
282	Jamie Cooke	.05	.10
283	David Fenyves	.05	.10
284	Steve Morrow	.05	.10
285	Martin Hostak	.35	.75
286	Mike Eaves, Coach	.05	.10
287	Hershey Bears, Checklist	.05	.10
	Team Set (25 cards)	3.00	6.00

MUSKEGON LUMBERJACKS - IHL
(Pittsburgh Penguins)

No.	Player	EX	NRMT
288	Dave Michayluk	.35	.75
289	Glenn Mulvenna	.05	.10
290	Jean Blouin	.05	.10
291	Jock Callander	.35	.75
292	Perry Ganchar	.25	.50
293	Paul Laus	.05	.10
294	Mark Major	.05	.10
295	Bruce Racine, Goalie	.07	.15
296	Daniel Gauthier	.05	.10
297	Mike Needham	.50	1.00
298	Jeff Daniels	.20	.40
299	Sandy Smith	.20	.40
300	Gilbert Delorme	.05	.10
301	Rob Dopson, Goalie	.07	.15
302	Eric Brule	.05	.10
303	Alain Morissette, Goalie	.07	.15
304	Paul Dyck	.05	.10
305	Jason Smart	.15	.30
306	Gord Dineen	.05	.10
307	Todd Nelson	.05	.10
308	Jamie Heward	.05	.10
309	Phil Russell, Coach	.05	.10
310	Muskegon Lumberjacks, Checklist	.05	.10
	Team Set (23 cards)	3.00	6.00

SAN DIEGO GULLS - IHL
(Independent)

No.	Player	EX	NRMT
311	Soren True	.05	.10
312	Murray Duval	.05	.10
313	Dmitri Kvartalnov	2.50	5.00
314	Larry Floyd	.25	.50
315	Alan Leggett	.05	.10
316	Alan Hepple	.05	.10
317	Ron Duguay	.05	.10
318	Len Hachborn	.13	.25
319	Steve Martinson	.15	.30
320	Rick Knickle, Goalie	.50	1.00
321	Darcy Norton	.15	.30
322	Keith Gretzky	.20	.40
323	Brian Straub	.05	.10
324	Denny Lambert	.05	.10
325	Jason Prosofsky	.05	.10
326	Bruce Hoffort, Goalie	.07	.15
327	Sergei Starikov	.05	.10
328	Dave Korol	.05	.10
329	Robbie Nichols	.05	.10
330	Kord Cernich	.05	.10
331	Brent Sapergia	.05	.10
332	Don Waddell, Coach	.05	.10
333	Charlie Simmer, Asst. Coach	.05	.10
334	San Diego Gulls, Checklist	.05	.10
	Team Set (24 cards)	3.00	6.00

ST. JOHN'S MAPLE LEAFS - AHL
(Toronto Maple Leafs)

No.	Player	EX	NRMT
335	Rob Mendel	.05	.10
336	Curtis Hunt	.05	.10
337	Jeff Serowik	.05	.10
338	Bruce Bell	.05	.10
339	Yanic Perreault	.25	.50
340	Brad Aitken	.05	.10
341	Keith Osborne	.05	.10
342	Todd Hawkins	.05	.10
343	Andrew McKim	.25	.50
344	Kevin McClelland	.05	.10
345	Mike Stevens	.05	.10
346	Dave Tomlinson	1.00	2.00
347	Kevin Maguire	.05	.10
348	Mike MacWilliam	.05	.10
349	Greg Walters	.05	.10
350	Guy Lehoux	.05	.10
351	Todd Gillingham	.05	.10
352	Len Esau	.05	.10
353	Greg Johnston	.05	.10
354	Felix Potvin, Goalie	5.00	10.00
355	Damian Rhodes, Goalie	2.50	5.00
356	Joel Quenneville, Asst. Coach	.05	.10
357	Marc Crawford, Coach	.05	.10
358	Mike Eastwood	2.00	4.00
359	St. John's Maple Leafs, Checklist	.05	.10
	Team Set (25 cards)	10.00	20.00

NEW HAVEN NIGHTHAWKS - AHL
(Los Angeles Kings)

No.	Player	EX	NRMT
360	Lou Franceschetti	.20	.40
361	John Murray Anderson	.05	.10
362	Scott Schneider	.05	.10
363	Jerome Bechard	.05	.10
364	Mario Doyon	.05	.10
365	Jeff Jackson	.25	.50
366	John Tanner, Goalie	.07	.15
367	Al Tuer	.25	.50
368	Paul Willett	.05	.10
369	Darryl Williams	.05	.10
370	George Maneluk, Goalie	.07	.15
371	Eric Ricard	.05	.10
372	Trevor Stienburg	.05	.10
373	Jerry Tarrant	.05	.10
374	Michael McEwen	.05	.10
375	Brian Dobbin	.05	.10
376	David Latta	.05	.10
377	Jim Sprott	.05	.10
378	Trevor Pochipinski	.05	.10
379	Stan Drulia	.25	.50
380	Kent Hulst	.05	.10
381	Brad Turner	.05	.10
382	Doug Carpenter, Coach	.05	.10
383	New Haven Nighthawks, Checklist	.05	.10
	Team Set (24 cards)	3.00	6.00

PHOENIX ROADRUNNERS - IHL
(Los Angeles Kings)

No.	Player	EX	NRMT
384	Bob Berg	.13	.25
385	Steve Jaques	.13	.25
386	Chris Norton	.13	.25
387	Vern Smith	.13	.25
388	Kevin MacDonald	.13	.25
389	Ross Wilson	.13	.25
390	Shawn McCosh	.13	.25
391	Mike Vukonich	.13	.25
392	Marc Saumier	.20	.40
393	Mike Ruark	.13	.25
394	Kris Miller	.13	.25
395	Tim Breslin	.13	.25
396	Paul Holden	.13	.25
397	Jeff Rohlicek	.13	.25
398	Kyosti Karjalainen	.13	.25
399	David Goverde, Goalie	.13	.25
400	John Van Kessel	.13	.25
401	Sean Whyte	.13	.25
402	Brent Thompson	.13	.25
403	Darryl Gilmour, Goalie	.13	.25
404	Scott Bjugstad	.25	.50
405	Ralph Backstrom, Coach, Error	.13	.25

No.	Player	EX	NRMT
406	Rick Kozuback, Asst. Coach, Error	.13	.25
407	Phoenix Roadrunners, Checklist, Error	.13	.25
	Team Set (24 cards)	3.00	6.00

UTICA DEVILS - AHL
(New Jersey Devils)

No.	Player	EX	NRMT
408	Brent Severyn	.13	.25
409	Dean Malkoc	.13	.25
410	Matt Ruchty	.13	.25
411	Jarrod Skalde	.60	1.25
412	Brian Sullivan	.25	.50
413	Ben Hankinson, Error	.13	.25
414	Bill Huard	.13	.25
415	Jeff Christian	.13	.25
416	Corey Schwab, Goalie	.13	.25
417	Kevin Dean	.13	.25
418	Todd Copeland	.13	.25
419	Mike Bodnarchuk	.20	.40
420	Jason Miller	.25	.50
421	Chad Erickson, Goalie	.13	.25
422	David Craievich	.13	.25
423	Jim Dowd	.13	.25
424	Jamie Huscroft	.13	.25
425	Myles O'Connor	.13	.25
426	Jon Morris	.13	.25
427	Valeri Zelepukin	.60	1.25
428	Utica Devils, Checklist, Error	.13	.25
	Team Set (20 cards)	1.50	3.00

FLINT BULLDOGS - CHL
(Independent)

No.	Player	EX	NRMT
429	Brad Beck	.13	.25
430	Brett MacDonald	.13	.25
431	Jacques Mailhot	.13	.25
432	Francis Ouellette	.13	.25
433	Ron Kinghorn, Goalie	.13	.25
434	Dennis Miller	.13	.25
435	Darren Miciak	.13	.25
436	Tom Sasso	.50	1.00
437	Peter Corbett	.13	.25
438	Brian Horan	.13	.25
439	John Messuri	.13	.25
440	E. J. Sauer	.13	.25
441	Tom Mutch	.13	.25
442	Jason Simon	.13	.25
443	Steve Sullivan	.13	.25
444	Scott Allen	.13	.25
445	Stephane Brochu	.13	.25
446	Ken Spangler	.13	.25
447	Lee Odelein	.13	.25
448	Antti Autere	.13	.25
449	John Reid	.13	.25
450	Skip Probst, Coach/G.M.	.13	.25
451	Flint Bulldogs, Checklist	.13	.25
	Team Set (23 cards)	3.00	6.00

CAPITAL DISTRICT ISLANDERS - AHL
(New York Islanders)

No.	Player	EX	NRMT
452	Dean Ewen	.13	.25
453	Brent Grieve	.13	.25
454	Jim Culhane	.13	.25
455	Joni Lehto	.13	.25
456	Graeme Townshend	.13	.25
457	Danny Lorenz, Goalie	.13	.25
458	Phil Huber	.13	.25
459	Kevin Cheveldayoff	.13	.25
460	Dennis Vaske	.35	.75
461	Wayne Doucet	.13	.25
462	Greg Parks	.35	.75
463	Dean Chynoweth	.13	.25
464	Lee Giffin	.13	.25
465	Richard Kromm	.20	.40
466	Derek Laxdal	.15	.30
467	Travis Green	.20	.40
468	Iain Fraser	.35	.75
469	Rick Hayward	.13	.25
470	Jeff Finley	.15	.30
471	Dave Chyzowski	.13	.25
472	Mark Fitzpatrick, Goalie	.50	1.00
473	Hubie McDonough	.35	.75
474	Sean LeBrun	.15	.30
475	Chris Pryor	.13	.25
476	Capital District Islanders, Checklist	.13	.25
	Team Set (25 cards)	3.00	6.00

INDIANAPOLIS ICE - IHL
(Chicago Black Hawks)

No.	Player	EX	NRMT
477	Jeff Sirkka	.05	.10
478	Owen Lessard	.05	.10
479	Jim Playfair	.05	.10
480	Dan Vincelette	.05	.10
481	Tracey Egeland	.15	.30
482	Shawn Byram	.05	.10
483	Trevor Dam	.05	.10
484	Martin Desjardins	.05	.10
485	Milan Tichy	.20	.40
486	Cam Russell	.05	.10
487	Mike Speer	.05	.10
488	Sean Williams	.25	.50
489	Paul Gillis	.05	.10
490	Brad Laurer	.20	.40
491	Trent Yawney	.35	.75
492	Craig Woodcroft	.05	.10
493	Justin Lafayette	.05	.10
494	Robb Conn	.05	.10
495	Frantisek Kucera	.35	.75
496	Mike Peluso	.50	1.00
497	Roch Belley, Goalie	.05	.10
498	Ryan McGill	.35	.75
499	Kerry Toporowski	.05	.10
500	Dominik Hasek, Goalie	1.50	3.00
501	Adam Bennett	.05	.10
502	Ray LeBlanc, Goalie	.35	.75
503	John Marks, Coach	.05	.10
504	Indianapolis Ice, Checklist	.05	.10
	Team Set (28 cards)	3.00	6.00

KANSAS CITY BLADES - IHL
(Independent)

No.	Player	EX	NRMT
505	Mikhail Kravets	.05	.10
506	Gary Emmons	.05	.10
507	Ed Courtenay	.35	.75
508	Claudio Scremin	.05	.10
509	Jarmo Myllys, Goalie	.35	.75
510	Mike Colman	.05	.10
511	Kevin Evans	.05	.10
512	Troy Frederick	.05	.10
513	Ron Handy	.05	.10
514	Murray Garbutt	.05	.10
515	Gord Frantti	.05	.10
516	Dale Craigwell	.25	.50
517	Wade Flaherty, Goalie	.07	.15
518	Dean Kolstad	.05	.10
519	Rick Lessard	.05	.10
520	Craig Coxe	.25	.50
521	Jeff Madill	.05	.10
522	Peter Lappin	.05	.10
523	Duane Joyce	.05	.10
524	Larry DePalma	.05	.10
525	Pat MacLeod	.25	.50
526	Andy Akervik	.05	.10
527	Kansas City Blades, Checklist	.05	.10
	Team Set (23 cards)	3.00	6.00

HALIFAX CITADELS - AHL
(Quebec Nordiques)

No.	Player	EX	NRMT
528	Mike Dagenais	.05	.10
529	Gerald Bzdel	.05	.10
530	Stephane Fiset, Goalie	.50	1.00
531	David Espe	.05	.10
532	Patrick Lebrecque, Goalie	.07	.15
533	Niclas Andersson	.05	.10
534	Jon Klemm	.05	.10
535	Denis Chasse	.05	.10
536	Stephane Charbonneau	.05	.10
537	Ivan Matulik	.05	.10
538	Serge Roberge	.05	.10
539	Daniel Dore	.05	.10
540	Sergei Kharin	.25	.50
541	Jamie Baker	.05	.10
542	Ken McRae	.15	.35
543	Dave Marcinyshyn	.05	.10
544	Clement Jodoin, Coach	.05	.10
545	Dean Hopkins, Asst. Coach	.05	.10
546	Halifax Citadels, Checklist	.05	.10
	Team Set (19 cards)	3.00	6.00

BALTIMORE SKIPJACKS - AHL
(Washington Capitals)

No.	Player	EX	NRMT
547	Jeff Greenlaw	.05	.10
548	Byron Dafoe, Goalie	.07	.15
549	Jim Hrivnak, Goalie	.50	1.00
550	Olaf Kolzig, Goalie	.35	.75
551	John Purves	.20	.40
552	Bobby Reynolds	.20	.40
553	Simon Wheeldon	.35	.75
554	Jim Mathieson	.05	.10
555	Trevor Halverson	.05	.10
556	Steve Seftel	.15	.30
557	Ken Lovsin	.05	.10
558	Victor Gervais	.05	.10
559	Steve Martell	.05	.10
560	Chris Clarke	.05	.10
561	Brent Hughes	.35	.75
562	Jiri Vykoukal	.05	.10
563	Tim Taylor	.20	.40
564	Richie Walcott	.05	.10
565	Harry Mews	.05	.10
566	Craig Duncanson	.05	.10
567	Todd Hlushko	.25	.50
568	Mark Ferner	.20	.40
569	Bob Babcock	.05	.10
570	Reggie Savage	.05	.10
571	Rob Laird, Coach	.05	.10
572	Barry Trotz, Asst. Coach	.05	.10
573	Baltimore Skipjacks, Checklist	.05	.10
	Team Set (27 cards)	3.00	6.00

SALT LAKE GOLDEN EAGLES
(Calgary Flames)

No.	Player	EX	NRMT
574	Kevan Melrose	.13	.25
575	Kevin Grant	.13	.25
576	Kevan Guy	.13	.25
577	Darryl Olsen	.20	.40
578	Kevin Wortman	.13	.25
579	Darren Stolk	.13	.25
580	Bryan Deasley	.15	.30
581	Paul Kruse	.15	.30
582	Darren Banks	.13	.25
583	Corey Lyons	.13	.25
584	Kerry Clark	.13	.25
585	Todd Strueby	.13	.25
586	Rich Chernomaz	.25	.50
587	Tim Harris	.13	.25
588	Shawn Heaphy	.25	.50
589	Todd Harkins	.13	.25
590	Richard Zemlak	.35	.75
591	Warren Sharples, Goalie	.13	.25
592	Jason Muzzatti, Goalie	.20	.40
593	Dennis Holland	.13	.25
594	Salt Lake Golden Eagles, Checklist	.13	.25
	Team Set (21 cards)	3.00	6.00

MILWAUKEE ADMIRALS - IHL
(Vancouver Canucks)

No.	Player	EX	NRMT
595	Shawn Antoski	.25	.50
596	Peter Bakovic	.20	.40
597	Robin Bawa	.13	.25
598	Cam Brown	.13	.25
599	Neil Eisenhut	.13	.25
600	Jason Herter	.35	.75
601	Ian Kidd	.13	.25
602	Troy Neumeier	.13	.25
603	Carl Valimont	.13	.25
604	Phil Von Stefenelli	.13	.25
605	Andrew McBain	.35	.75
606	Eric Murano	.25	.50

SAFEWAY

— 1992 - 93 PHOENIX ROADRUNNERS —

This 28-card set was produced in association with Safeway and was distributed through their chain of food stores.

Card Size: 2 1/2" x 3 1/2"
Face: Four colour; Name, Number, IHL and Team logo
Back: Two colour, card stock; Name, Resume, Sponsor's logo
Imprint: Photo by: Jessen Associates
Complete Set No.: 28
Complete Set Price: 6.00 12.00
Common Card: .25 .50

No.	Player	EX	NRMT
607	Rob Murphy	.25	.50
608	Brian Blad	.13	.25
609	Randy Boyd	.13	.25
610	Don Gibson	.13	.25
611	Paul Guay	.20	.40
612	Jay Mazur	.13	.25
613	Jeff Larmer	.20	.40
614	Ladislav Tresl	.13	.25
615	Dennis Snedden	.13	.25
616	Corrie D'Alessio, Goalie	.13	.25
617	Bob Mason, Goalie	.13	.25
618	Jack McIlhargey, Coach	.13	.25
619	Curt Fraser, Asst. Coach, Error	.13	.25
620	Milwaukee Admirals, Checklist	.13	.25
	Team Set (26 cards)	3.00	6.00

No.	Player	EX	NRMT
1	Tim Bothwell, Head Coach	.25	.50
2	Frank Breault	.25	.50
3	Tim Breslin	.25	.50
4	Rene Chapdelaine	.25	.50
5	Sylvain Couturier	.25	.50
6	Phil Crowe	.25	.50
7	Darryl Gilmour, Goalie	.25	.50
8	David Goverde, Goalie	.25	.50
9	Ed Kastelic	.25	.50
10	Rick Kozuback, Asso. Coach	.25	.50
11	Ted Kramer	.25	.50
12	Robert Lang	.25	.50
13	Guy Leveque	.75	1.50
14	Jim Maher	.25	.50
15	Mascot Rocky Roadrunner	.25	.50
16	Brad McCaughey	.25	.50
17	Shawn McCosh	.25	.50
18	John Mokosak	.25	.50
19	Keith Redmond	.25	.50
20	Mike Ruark	.25	.50
21	Brandy Semchuk	.25	.50
22	Dave Stewart	.25	.50
23	Brad Tiley	.25	.50
24	Dave Tretowicz	.25	.50
25	Mike Vukonich	.25	.50
26	Tim Watters	.50	1.00
27	Sean Whyte	.25	.50
28	Darryl Williams	.25	.50

Safeway 1992-93 Pheonix Roadrunners
Card No. 13, Guy Leveque

NHL DRAFT PICKS

ARENA HOLOGRAMS

— 1991 REGULAR ISSUE —

Arena have offered a randomly inserted Pat Falloon Hologram Collector's Card with this set. Also randomly inserted into the sets are autographed cards of each of the thirty-one draft picks. There are 1,000 autographed cards per player, broken down into 667 English and 333 French. English (Silver) French (Gold)

Arena Holograms, 1991 Regular Issue
Card No. 1, Pat Falloon

Card Size: 2 1/2" X 3 1/2"
Face: Four colour, grey stripe at bottom border; Name
Back: Four colour, Number, Resume, Position
Complete Set No.: 33
Complete Set Price: 2.50 5.00
Common Goalie: .05 .10
Common Player: .05 .10
Production: Cases: 9,900; Sets: 198,000

COLLECTOR'S HOLOGRAM CARD

No.	Player	English NRMT	French NRMT
—	Pat Falloon	2.50	2.50

REGULAR ISSUE

No.	Player \ Drafted To	English NRMT	French NRMT
1	Pat Falloon \ Sharks	1.00	1.00
2	Scott Niedermayer \ Devils	.75	.75
3	Scott Lachance \ Islanders	.60	.50
4	Peter Forsberg \ Flyers	1.50	1.50
5	Alek Stojanov \ Canucks	.50	.50
6	Richard Matvichuk \ North Stars	.40	.40
7	Patrick Poulin \ Whalers	.40	.40
8	Martin Lapointe \ Red Wings	.30	.30
9	Tyler Wright \ Oilers	.20	.20
10	Philippe Boucher \ Sabres	.10	.10
11	Patrick Peake \ Capitals	.10	.10
12	Markus Naslund, Error \ Penguins	.10	.10
13	Brent Bilodeau \ Canadiens	.10	.10
14	Glen Murray \ Bruins	.10	.10
15	Niklas Sundblad \ Flames	.10	.10
16	Trevor Halverson \ Capitals	.10	.10
17	Dean McAmmond \ Blackhawks	.10	.10
18	Rene Corbet \ Nordiques	.10	.10
19	Eric Lavigne \ Capitals	.10	.10
20	Steve Staios \ Blues	.10	.10
21	Jim Campbell \ Canadiens	.10	.10
22	Jassen Cullimore \ Canucks	.10	.10
23	Jamie Pushor \ Red Wings	.10	.10
24	Donevan Hextall \ Devils	.10	.10
25	Andrew Verner, Goalie \ Oilers	.10	.10
26	Jason Dawe \ Sabres	.10	.10
27	Jeff Nelson \ Capitals	.10	.10
28	Darcy Werenka \ Rangers	.10	.10
29	Francois Groleau \ Flames	.10	.10
30	Guy Leveque \ Kings	.10	.10
31	Yanic Perreault \ Leafs	.10	.10
32	S. Lachance, P. Falloon Islanders/Sharks	.50	.50
33	Checklist	.10	.10

— 1991 INSERT SET — AUTOGRAPHED CARDS ENGLISH

This 31-card set constituted the chase cards for the 1991 Arena set. They were inserted into the factory sets. There are a total of 1,000 autographed cards, 667 in English and 333 in French. The English cards are numbered _ of 667. The French are numbered _ of 333.

Card Size: 2 1/2" X 3 1/2"
Face: Four colour, grey stripe at bottom border, autographed in permanent marker
Back: Two colour, Number, Resume, Position
Complete Set No.: 31
Complete Set Price: 500.00 500.00
Common Card: 15.00 15.00

No.	Player	English NRMT	French NRMT
1	Pat Falloon, SJ	70.00	70.00
2	Scott Niedermayer, NJ	50.00	50.00
3	Scott Lachance, NYI	40.00	40.00
4	Peter Forsberg, Phi.	70.00	70.00
5	Alek Stojanov, Van.	20.00	20.00
6	Richard Matvichuk, Min	15.00	15.00
7	Patrick Poulin, Hart.	20.00	20.00
8	Martin Lapointe, Det.	15.00	15.00
9	Tyler Wright, Edm.	15.00	15.00
10	Philippe Boucher, Buf.	15.00	15.00
11	Patrick Peake, Wash.	15.00	15.00
12	Marcus Naslund, Error, Pit.	15.00	15.00
13	Brent Bilodeau, Mon.	15.00	15.00
14	Glen Murray, Bos.	15.00	15.00
15	Niklas Sundblad, Cal.	15.00	15.00
16	Trevor Halverson, Wash.	15.00	15.00
17	Dean McAmmond, Chi.	15.00	15.00
18	Rene Corbet, Que.	15.00	15.00
19	Eric Lavigne, Wash.	15.00	15.00
20	Steve Staios, St.L	15.00	15.00
21	Jim Campbell, Mon.	15.00	15.00
22	Jassen Cullimore, Van.	15.00	15.00
23	Jamie Pushor, Det.	15.00	15.00
24	Donevan Hextall, NJ	15.00	15.00
25	Andrew Verner, Goalie, Edm.	15.00	15.00
26	Jason Dawe, Buf.	15.00	15.00
27	Jeff Nelson, Wash.	15.00	15.00
28	Darcy Werenka, NYR	15.00	15.00
29	Francois Groleau, Cal.	15.00	15.00
30	Guy Leveque, LA	15.00	15.00
31	Yanic Perreault, Tor.	15.00	15.00

CLASSIC GAMES

— 1991 HOCKEY DRAFT PICKS —

1991 PROMOTIONAL CARDS

The two Promotional Cards were issued without the back photograph and resume.

Classic Games, 1991 Promotional Cards
Card No. 1, Eric Lindros

Card Size: 2 1/2" X 3 1/2"
Face: Four colour, green border; Draft pick number
Back: Two colour, "For Promotional Purposes Only"

No.	Player	English NRMT	French NRMT
1	Eric Lindros	15.00	15.00
2	Pat Falloon	5.00	5.00

— 1991 REGULAR ISSUE —

Classic Games produced their first hockey "Draft Pick" set in 1991. The 50 card, limited edition, factory set was issued with a numbered authenticity card which also served as a checklist. The set was issued in both English and French.

Classic Games, 1991 Regular Issue
Card No. 3, Scott Niedermayer

Card Size: 2 1/2" X 3 1/2"
Face: Four colour, green border, Draft pick number, Position
Back: Four colour, black on white card stock, Number, Resume, Postion
Imprint: © 1991 Classic Games, Inc., a subsidiary of The Scoreboard, Inc. - all rights reserved. ® Classic is a registered trademark of The Scoreboard, Inc.
Complete Set No.: 50
Complete Set Price: 7.00 7.00
Common Card: .05 .10
Production: 360,000 Sets

BONUS CARD

The set contained a bonus card featuring Raghib "Rocket" Ismail. It was issued with both the English and French factory sets.

No.	Player	English NRMT	French NRMT
B	Raghib "Rocket" Ismail	.50	1.00

REGULAR ISSUE

No.	Player \ Drafted To	English NRMT	French NRMT
1	Eric Lindros \ Quebec	3.00	3.00
2	Pat Falloon \ San Jose	.75	.75
3	Scott Niedermayer \ New Jesey	.75	.75
4	Scott Lachance \ New York (I)	.25	.25
5	Peter Forsberg \ Philadelphia	1.00	1.00
6	Alex Stojanov \ Vancouver	.20	.20
7	Richard Matvichuk \ Minnesota	.20	.20
8	Patrick Poulin \ Hartford	.40	.40
9	Martin Lapointe \ Detroit	.20	.20
10	Tyler Wright \ Edmonton	.20	.20
11	Philippe Boucher \ Buffalo	.05	.10
12	Pat Peake \ Washington	.05	.10
13	Markus Naslund \ Pittsburgh	.05	.10
14	Brent Bilodeau \ Montreal	.05	.10
15	Glen Murray \ Boston	.05	.10
16	Niklas Sundblad \ Calgary	.05	.10
17	Martin Rucinsky \ Edmonton	.05	.10
18	Trevor Halverson \ Washington	.05	.10
19	Dean McAmmond \ Chicago	.05	.10
20	Ray Whitney \ San Jose	.05	.10

1991 PROMOTIONAL CARDS — STAR PICS

No.	Player	English NRMT	French NRMT
21	Rene Corbet \ Quebec	.05	.10
22	Eric Lavigne \ Washington	.05	.10
23	Zigmund Palffy \ New York (I)	.05	.10
24	Steve Staios \ St. Louis	.05	.10
25	Jim Campbell \ Montreal	.05	.10
26	Jassen Cullimore \ Vancouver	.05	.10
27	Martin Hamrlik \ Hartford	.05	.10
28	Jamie Pushor \ Detroit	.05	.10
29	Donevan Hextall \ New Jersey	.05	.10
30	Andrew Verner \ Edmonton	.05	.10
31	Jason Dawe \ Buffalo	.05	.10
32	Jeff Nelson \ Washington	.05	.10
33	Darcy Werenka \ New York R.	.05	.10
34	Jozef Stumpel \ Boston	.05	.10
35	Francois Groleau \ Calgary	.05	.10
36	Guy Leveque \ Los Angeles	.05	.10
37	Jamie Matthews \ Chicago	.05	.10
38	Dody Wood \ San Jose	.05	.10
39	Yanic Perreault \ Toronto	.05	.10
40	Jamie McLennan \ New York (I)	.05	.10
41	Yanick Dupre \ Philadelphia	.05	.10
42	Sandy McCarthy \ Calgary	.05	.10
43	Chris Osgood \ Detroit	.05	.10
44	Fredrik Lindquist \ New Jersey	.05	.10
45	Jason Young \ Buffalo	.05	.10
46	Steve Konowalchuk \ Washington	.05	.10
47	Michael Nylander \ Hartford	.05	.10
48	Shane Peacock \ Pittsburgh	.05	.10
49	Yves Sarault \ Montreal	.05	.10
50	Marcel Cousineau \ Boston	.05	.10
—	Checklist/Certificate of Authenticity	.05	.10

1991 FOUR SPORT DRAFT PICKS

— 1991 PROMOTIONAL CARD —

Classic Games, 1991 Promotional Card
Pat Falloon

Card Size: 2 1/2" X 3 1/2"
Face: Four colour, mottled blue border, Position, Classic logo
Back: Two colour, Number, Resume

No.	Player	EX	NRMT
—	Pat Falloon	7.50	15.00

— 1991 PROMOTIONAL SHEET —

Card Size: 2 1/2" X 3 1/2"
Face: Four colour, mottled blue border, Position, Classic logo
Back: Two colour, Number, Resume

No.	Player	EX	NRMT
—	Introducing Classic Draft Pick Collection Cards, Mini-sheet	12.50	25.00

— 1991 REGULAR ISSUE —

Classic Games produced an exclusive limited edition set of the top draft picks from basketball, baseball, hockey and football. The sets are available in both English and French. Over 70,000 autographed cards were randomly inserted into the 230-card sets. This Standard Catalogue lists only the hockey players for this set.

Classic Games, 1991 Issue
Card No. 8, Patrick Poulin

Card Size: 2 1/2" X 3 1/2"
Face: Four colour, mottled blue border, Position, Classic logo
Back: Two colour, Number, Resume
Complete Set No.: 230
Complete Hockey Set No.: 50

	English	French
Complete Set Price:	17.50	35.00
Hockey Only Price:	3.75	7.50
Common Player:	.05	.05

No.	Player \ Drafted To	English NRMT	French NRMT
1	"Future Superstars", Brien. Taylor, baseball; Larry Johnson, basketball; Eric Lindros, hockey; Russell Maryland, football	1.00	1.00
2	Pat Falloon \ San Jose	.50	.50
3	Scott Niedermayer \ New Jersey	.50	.50
4	Scott Lachance \ New York (I)	.20	.20
5	Peter Forsberg \ Philadelphia	.50	1.50
6	Alex Stojanov \ Vancouver	.05	.05
7	Richard Matvichuk \ Minnesota	.10	.10
8	Patrick Poulin \ Hartford	.20	.20
9	Martin Lapointe \ Detroit	.20	.20
10	Tyler Wright \ Edmonton	.10	.10
11	Philippe Boucher \ Buffalo	.05	.05
12	Pat Peake \ Washington	.20	.20
13	Markus Naslund \ Pittsburgh	.05	.05
14	Brent Bilodeau \ Montreal	.05	.05
15	Glen Murray \ Boston	.20	.20
16	Niklas Sundblad \ Calgary	.05	.05
17	Martin Rucinsky \ Edmonton	.05	.05
18	Trevor Halverson \ Washington	.05	.05
19	Dean McAmmond \ Chicago	.05	.05
20	Ray Whitney \ San Jose	.05	.05
21	Rene Corbet \ Quebec	.05	.05
22	Eric Lavigne \ Washington	.05	.05
23	Zigmund Palffy \ New York (I)	.05	.05
24	Steve Staios \ St. Louis	.05	.05
25	Jim Campbell \ Montreal	.05	.05
26	Jassen Cullimore \ Vancouver	.05	.05
27	Martin Hamrlik \ Hartford	.05	.05
28	Jamie Pushor \ Detroit	.05	.05
29	Donevan Hextall \ New Jersey	.05	.05
30	Andrew Verner \ Edmonton	.05	.05
31	Jason Dawe \ Buffalo	.05	.05
32	Jeff Nelson \ Washington	.05	.05
33	Darcy Werenka \ New York (R)	.05	.05
34	Jozef Stumpel \ Boston	.05	.05
35	Francois Groleau \ Calgary	.05	.05
36	Guy Leveque \ Los Angeles	.05	.05
37	Jamie Matthews \ Chicago	.05	.05
38	Dody Wood \ San Jose	.05	.05
39	Yanic Perreault \ Toronto	.05	.05
40	Jamie McLennan \ New York (I)	.05	.05
41	Yanick Dupre \ Philadelphia	.05	.05
42	Sandy McCarthy \ Calgary	.05	.05
43	Chris Osgood \ Detroit	.05	.05
44	Fredrik Lindquist \ New Jersey	.05	.05
45	Jason Young \ Buffalo	.05	.10
46	Steve Konowalchuk \ Washington	.05	.05
47	Michael Nylander \ Hartford	.05	.10

No.	Checklist	English NRMT	French NRMT
48	Shane Peacock \ Pittsburgh	.05	.10
49	Yves Sarault \ Montreal	.05	.10
50	Marcel Cousineau \ Boston	.05	.10

CHECKLIST

No.	Checklist	English NRMT	French NRMT
227	Checklist 1 (1 to 60)	.05	.05

— 1992 HOCKEY DRAFT PICKS —

1992 PROMOTIONAL CARDS

This 3-card set was issued to promote the Classic set. These cards are unnumbered and are marked "For Promotional Purposes Only" on the back.

Classic Games, 1992 Promotional Cards
Card No. 1, Roman Hamrlik

Card Size: 2-1/2" x 3-1/2"
Face: Four colour, and black and white photos, white border; Name, Position
Back: Four colour, borderless; Name, Team, Resume
Imprint: © 1992 Classic Games, Inc.
Complete Set No.: 3
Complete Set Price: 20.00 / 40.00

No.	Player	EX	NRMT
1	Roman Hamrlik	3.75	7.50
2	Flashback: Mario Lemieux	15.00	30.00
3	Ray Whitney	2.50	5.00

— 1992 HOCKEY DRAFT PICKS COLLECTION —

This 120-card set represents the June 1992 hockey draft. Classic has captured the most important draft picks of the year.

Classic Games, 1992 Hockey Draft Picks
Card No. 6, Robert Petrovicky

Card Size: 2 1/2" x 3 1/2"
Face: Four colour, white border; Name, Position
Back: Four colour, gold border, card stock; Name, Resume
Imprint: © 1992 Classic Games, Inc.
Complete Set No.: 120

	Regular	Gold
Complete Set Price:	12.00	125.00
Common Card:	.10	.75
Foil Pack: (10 Cards)		1.50
Foil Box: (36 Packs)		40.00
Gold Factory Set:		200.00

CLASSIC GAMES — 1992-93 INSERT SETS

No.	Player \ Drafted To	Regular NRMT	Gold NRMT
1	Roman Hamrlik \ Tampa Bay	.25	2.00
2	Alexei Yashin \ Ottawa	1.00	8.00
3	Mike Rathje \ San Jose	.20	1.50
4	Darius Kasparaitis \ New York (I)	.20	1.50
5	Cory Stillman \ Calgary	.15	1.00
6	Robert Petrovicky \ Hartford	.20	1.50
7	Andrei Nazarov \ San Jose	.20	1.50
8	Checklist: Cory Stillman	.10	.75
9	Jason Bowen \ Philadelphia	.15	1.00
10	Jason Smith \ New Jersey	.15	1.00
11	David Wilkie \ Montreal	.10	.75
12	Curtis Bowen \ Detroit	.10	.75
13	Grant Marshall \ Toronto	.10	.75
14	Valeri Bure \ Montreal	.75	5.75
15	Jeff Shantz \ Chicago	.10	.75
16	Justin Hocking \ Los Angeles	.10	.75
17	Mike Peca \ Vancouver	.10	.75
18	Marc Hussey \ Pittsburgh	.10	.75
19	Sandy Allan, Goalie \ Los Angeles	.10	.75
20	Kirk Maltby \ Edmonton	.10	.75
21	Cale Hulse \ New Jersey	.10	.75
22	Sylvain Cloutier \ Detroit	.10	.75
23	Martin Gendron \ Washington	.12	.25
24	Kevin Smyth \ Hartford	.10	.75
25	Jason McBain \ Hartford	.10	.75
26	Lee J. Leslie \ St. Louis	.10	.75
27	Ralph Intranuovo \ Edmonton	.10	.75
28	Martin Reichel \ Edmonton	.10	.75
29	Stefan Ustorf \ Washington	.10	.75
30	Jarkko Varvio \ Minnesota	.10	.75
31	Jere Lehtinen \ Minnesota	.10	.75
32	Janne Gronvall \ Toronto	.10	.75
33	Martin Straka \ Pittsburgh	.75	5.75
34	Libor Polasek \ Vancouver	.10	.75
35	Jozef Cierny \ Buffalo	.10	.75
36	Jan Vopat \ Hartford	.10	.75
37	Ondrej Steiner \ Buffalo	.10	.75
38	Jan Caloun \ San Jose	.10	.75
39	Petr Hrbek \ Detroit	.10	.75
40	Richard Smehlik \ Buffalo	.10	.75
41	Russian Invasion Checklist: Sergei Gonchar	.10	.75
42	Sergei Krivokrasov \ Chicago	.10	.75
43	Sergei Gonchar \ Washington	.10	.75
44	Boris Mironov \ Winnipeg	.10	.75
45	Denis Metliuk \ Philadelphia	.10	.75
46	Sergei Klimovich \ Chicago	.10	.75
47	Sergei Brylin \ New Jersey	.10	.75
48	Andrei Nikolishin \ Hartford	.10	.75
49	Alexander Cherbayev \ San Jose	.10	.75
50	Sergei Zholtok \ Boston	.10	.75
51	Vitali Prokhorov \ St. Louis	.10	.75
52	Nikolai Borschevsky \ Toronto	.10	.75
53	Vitali Tomilin \ New Jersey	.10	.75
54	Alexander Alexeyev \ Winnipeg	.10	.75
55	Roman Zolotov \ Philadelphia	.10	.75
56	Konstantin Korotkov \ Hartford	.10	.75
57	Laperriere Family: Jacques and Daniel Laperriere	.10	.75
58	Lacroix Family: Martin and Eric Lacroix	.10	.75
59	Manon Rheaume, Goalie, Tampa Bay (Try out)	7.00	55.00
60	Checklist #1, Hamrlik/Yashin/Rathje on front	.10	.75
61	Checklist #2, Viktor Kozlov on front	.20	1.50
62	Victor Kozlov (Not eligible until 1993)	.50	4.00
63	College checklist, Denny Felsner on front	.10	.75
64	Denny Felsner \ St. Louis	.10	.75
65	Darrin Madeley, (undrafted free agent)	.10	.75
66	Flashback: Mario Lemieux	1.00	8.00
67	Sandy Moger \ Vancouver	.10	.75
68	Dave Karpa \ Quebec	.10	.75
69	Martin Jiranek \ Washington	.10	.75
70	Dwayne Norris \ Quebec	.10	.75
71	Michael Stewart \ New York (R)	.10	.75
72	Joby Messier \ New York (R)	.10	.75
73	Mike Bales \ Boston	.10	.75
74	Scott Thomas \ Buffalo	.10	.75
75	Daniel Laperriere \ St. Louis	.10	.75
76	Mike Lappin \ Chicago	.10	.75
77	Eric Lacroix \ Toronto	.10	.75
78	Martin Lacroix \ New York (I)	.10	.75

No.	Player \ Drafted To	Regular NRMT	Gold NRMT
79	Scott LaGrand, Goalie \ Philadelphia	.10	.75
80	Jean-Yves Roy \ New York (R)	.10	.75
81	Scott Pellerin \ New Jersey	.10	.75
82	Rob Gaudreau \ Pittsburgh	.10	.75
83	Mike Boback \ Washington	.10	.75
84	Dixon Ward \ Vancouver	.10	.75
85	Jeff McLean \ San Jose	.10	.75
86	Dallas Drake \ Detroit	.10	.75
87	Bret Hedican \ St. Louis	.10	.75
88	Doug Zmolek \ Minnesota	.10	.75
89	Trent Klatt \ Washington	.10	.75
90	Larry Olimb \ Minnesota	.10	.75
91	Duane Derksen, Goalie \ Washington	.10	.75
92	Doug MacDonald \ Buffalo	.10	.75
93	Checklist: Dmitri Kvartalnov	.10	.75
94	Jim Cummins \ New York (R)	.10	.75
95	Lonnie Loach \ Chicago	.10	.75
96	Keith Jones \ Washington	.10	.75
97	Jason Woolley \ Washington	.10	.75
98	Rob Zamuner \ New York (R)	.10	.75
99	Brad Werenka \ Edmonton	.10	.75
100	Brent Grieve \ New York (I)	.10	.75
101	Sean Hill \ Montreal	.10	.75
102	Keith Carney \ Buffalo	.10	.75
103	Peter Ciavagglia \ Calgary	.10	.75
104	David Littman, Goalie \ Buffalo	.10	.75
105	Bill Guerin \ New Jersey	.10	.75
106	Mikhail Kravets \ San Jose	.10	.75
107	J. F. Quintin \ Minnesota	.10	.75
108	Mike Needham \ Pittsburgh	.10	.75
109	Jason Ruff \ St. Louis	.10	.75
110	Mike Vukonich \ Los Angeles	.10	.75
111	Shawn McCosh \ Detroit	.10	.75
112	Dave Tretowicz \ Calgary	.10	.75
113	Todd Harkins \ Calgary	.10	.75
114	Jason Muzzatti \ Calgary	.10	.75
115	Paul Kruse \ Calgary	.10	.75
116	Kevin Wortman \ Calgary	.10	.75
117	Sean Burke, Goalie \ New Jersey	.10	.75
118	Keith Gretzky \ Buffalo	.10	.75
119	Ray Whitney \ San Jose	.10	.75
120	Dmitri Kvartalnov \ Boston	.10	.75
—	Pavel and Valeri Bure, Autographed	—	100.00

Note: Pavel and Valeri Bure autographed cards were available one per Gold factory set.

— 1992-93 INSERT SETS —

1992 MARIO LEMIEUX

1992-93 Insert Set
Mario Lemieux, Autographed

Card Size: 2-1/2" x 3-1/2"
Face: Four colour, whiter border, Name
Back: Four colour, Gold border, Name, Number, Resume
Imprint: © 1992 Classic Games, Inc.

No.	Player	EX	NRMT
SP1	Mario Lemieux	22.50	45.00
—	Mario Lemieux, Autographed	150.00	300.00

1992 EXCLUSIVE LIMITED PRINT INSERT CARDS

This 10-card insert set was randomly inserted in the packs. The set features 10 of the highest profile draft picks from the '92 draft. The cards are numbered LP1 - LP10.

Card Size: 2 1/2" x 3 1/2"
Face: Four colour, borderless; Name
Back: Four colour, gold border, card stock; Name, Resume
Imprint: © 1992 Classic Games, Inc.
Complete Set No.: 10
Complete Set Price: 30.00 60.00

No.	Player \ Drafted To	EX	NRMT
LP1	Roman Hamrlik \ Tampa Bay	3.75	7.50
LP2	Alexei Yashin \ Ottawa	3.75	7.50
LP3	Mike Rathje \ San Jose	2.50	5.00
LP4	Darius Kasparaitis \ New York (I)	3.00	6.00
LP5	Cory Stillman \ Calgary	1.50	3.00
LP6	Dmitri Kvartalnov \ Boston	5.00	10.00
LP7	David Wilkie \ Montreal	1.50	3.00
LP8	Curtis Bowen \ Detroit	1.50	3.00
LP9	Valeri Bure \ Montreal	6.50	13.00
LP10	Joby Messier \ New York (R)	1.50	3.00

— 1992-93 FOUR SPORT DRAFT PICKS —

1992 PROMOTIONAL CARDS

1992 Promotional Card
Card No. PR3, Roman Hamrlik

Card Size: 2 1/2" x 3 1/2"
Face: Four colour, and black and white photos, white border; Name, Position
Back: Four colour, borderless; Name, Team, Resume
Imprint: © 1992 Classic Games, Inc.

No.	Player	EX	NRMT
PR3	Roman Hamrlik	2.50	5.00

— 1992-1993 CLASSIC FOUR SPORT —

DRAFT PICK COLLECTION

Of the 225 cards in this set 75 are hockey. These are listed below.

1992-93 Classic Four Sport
Card No. 152, Alexei Yashin

1991 PROMOTIONAL CARDS — STAR PICS

Card Size: 2 1/2" x 3 1/2"
Face: Four colour; Name, Position, Logo
Back: Four colour; Name, Position, Resume
Imprint: © 1192 Classic Games, Inc.
Complete Set No.: 225
Complete Hockey Set No.: 75
Complete Hockey Set Price: 50.00 10.00
Common Card: .05 .10
Foil Pack: (12 Cards) 2.75
Foil Box: (36 Packs) 10.00
Jumbo Pack: (24 Cards) 5.50
Jumbo Box: (20 Packs) 100.00

No.	Player \ Drafted To	EX	NRMT
151	Roman Hamrlik \ Tampa Bay	.13	.25
152	Alexei Yashin \ Ottawa	.35	.75
153	Mike Rathje \ San Jose	.07	.15
154	Darius Kasparaitis \ New York (I)	.07	.15
155	Cory Stillman \ Calgary	.05	.10
156	Robert Petrovicky \ Hartford	.10	.20
157	Andrei Nazarov \ San Jose	.05	.10
158	Jason Bowen \ Philadelphia	.05	.10
159	Jason Smith \ New Jersey	.05	.10
160	David Wilkie \ Montreal	.05	.10
161	Curtis Bowen \ Detroit	.05	.10
162	Grant Marshall \ Toronto	.05	.10
163	Valeri Bure \ Montreal	.25	.50
164	Jeff Shantz \ Chicago	.05	.10
165	Justin Hocking \ Los Angeles	.05	.10
166	Mike Peca \ Vancouver	.05	.10
167	Marc Hussey \ Pittsburgh	.05	.10
168	Sandy Allen, Goalie \ Los Angeles	.05	.10
169	Kirk Maltby \ Edmonton	.05	.10
170	Cale Hulse \ New Jersey	.05	.10
171	Sylvain Cloutier \ Detroit	.05	.10
172	Martin Gendron \ Washington	.05	.10
173	Kevin Smyth \ Hartford	.05	.10
174	Jason McBain \ Hartford	.05	.10
175	Lee J. Leslie \ St. Louis	.05	.10
176	Ralph Intranuovo \ Edmonton	.05	.10
177	Martin Reichel \ Edmonton	.05	.10
178	Stefan Ustorf \ Washington	.05	.10
179	Jarkko Varvio \ Minnesota	.05	.10
180	Martin Straka \ Pittsburgh	.25	.50
181	Libor Polasek \ Vancouver	.05	.10
182	Jozef Cierny \ Buffalo	.05	.10
183	Sergei Krivokrasov \ Chicago	.10	.20
184	Sergei Gonchar \ Washington	.05	.10
185	Boris Mironov \ Winnipeg	.10	.20
186	Denis Metliuk \ Philadelphia	.05	.10
187	Sergei Klimovich \ Chicago	.05	.10
188	Sergei Brylin \ New Jersey	.05	.10
189	Andrei Nikolishin \ Hartford	.05	.10
190	Alexander Cherbayev \ San Jose	.07	.15
191	Vitali Tomilin \ New Jersey	.05	.10
192	Sandy Moger \ Vancouver	.05	.10
193	Darrin Madeley, Goalie \ Free Agent	.05	.10
194	Denny Felsner \ St. Louis	.07	.15
195	Dwayne Norris \ Quebec	.05	.10
196	Joby Messier \ New York (R)	.05	.10
197	Michael Stewart \ New York (R)	.05	.10
198	Scott Thomas \ Buffalo	.05	.10
199	Daniel LaPerriere \ St. Louis	.05	.10
200	Martin Lacroix \ New York (I)	.05	.10
201	Scott Lagrand, Goalie \ Philadelphia	.05	.10
202	Scott Pellerin \ New Jersey	.05	.10
203	Jean-Yves Roy \ New York (R)	.05	.10
204	Rob Gaudreau \ Pittsburgh	.13	.25
205	Jeff McLean \ San Jose	.05	.10
206	Dallas Drake \ Detroit	.07	.15
207	Doug Zmolek \ Minnesota	.05	.10
208	Duane Derksen, Goalie \ Washington	.05	.10
209	Jim Cummins \ New York (R)	.05	.10
210	Lonnie Loach \ Chicago	.05	.10
211	Rob Zamuner \ New York (R)	.07	.15
212	Brad Werenka \ Edmonton	.05	.10
213	Brent Grieve \ New York (I)	.05	.10
214	Sean Hill \ Montreal	.07	.15
215	Peter Ciavaglia \ Calgary	.05	.10
216	Jason Ruff \ St. Louis	.05	.10
217	Shawn McCosh \ Detroit	.05	.10
218	Dave Tretowicz \ Calgary	.05	.10
219	Mike Vukonich \ Los Angeles	.05	.10
220	Kevin Wortman \ Calgary	.05	.10
221	Jason Muzzatti, Goalie \ Calgary	.05	.10
222	Dmitri Kvartalnov \ Boston	.07	.15
223	Ray Whitney \ San Jose	.07	.15
224	Manon Rheaume, Goalie Tryout \ Tampa Bay	2.50	5.00
225	Viktor Kozlov \ Now with San Jose June '93 draft	.25	.50

— DRAFT PICK COLLECTION INSERT SETS —

AUTOGRAPHED CARDS

These autographed cards were randomly inserted into the foil and jumbo boxes.

Card Size: 2 1/2" x 3 1/2"
Face: Four colour; Name, Position, Autograph in blue sharpie
Back: Black on white card stock;
Imprint: © 1192 Classic Games, Inc.
Complete Set No.: 225
Complete Hockey Set No.: 75
Complete Set Price: 1,400.00 2,800.00
Complete Hockey Set: 65.00 130.00

No.	Player	No. Signed	EX	NRMT
151	Roman Hamrlik	1550	10.00	20.00
153	Mike Rathje	2075	7.50	15.00
155	Cory Stillman	2125	5.00	10.00
158	Jason Bowwn	2075	5.00	10.00
159	Jason Smith	2075	5.00	10.00
165	Justin Hocking	2075	5.00	10.00
170	Cale Hulse	1850	5.00	10.00
181	Libor Polasek	1950	5.00	10.00
185	Boris Mironov	2075	6.00	12.00
192	Sandy Moger	1075	5.00	10.00
195	Dwayne Norris	1075	5.00	10.00
196	Joby Messier	1075	5.00	10.00
207	Doug Smolek	1075	5.00	10.00

1992 - 93 BONUS CARDS

This 20-card bonus set was inserted in the jumbo boxes one per pack. The cards are numbered BC1 - BC20 and have a silver embossed name plate down the left side of the card. This catalogue only lists the hockey cards.

Card Size: 2 1/2" x 3 1/2"
Face: Four colour, borderless; Name on silver foil band
Back: Four colour, borderless, card stock; Name, Resume
Imprint: © 1192 Classic Games, Inc.
Complete Set No.: 6 (Hockey)
Complete Set Price: 11.00 22.00

No.	Player	EX	NRMT
BC7	Roman Hamrlik	.85	1.75
BC8	Valeri Bure	1.50	3.00
BC9	Dalls Drake	1.50	3.00
BC10	Dmitri Kvartalnov	1.50	3.00
BC11	Manon Rheaume	5.00	10.00
BC12	Viktor Kozlov	1.75	3.50

1992 EXCLUSIVE LIMITED PRINT CARDS

1992 Exclusive Limited Print Cards
Card No. LP25, Alexei Yashin

This 25-card set is a selected group of top draft picks from the four sports. These cards differ from the regular issue in their numbering (LP1-LP25) and they have a gold embossed name bar across the left side that states "ONE OF 46,080". This catalogue only lists the hockey player cards.

Card Size: 2-1/2" x 3-1/2"
Face: Four colour borderless; Gold embossed nameplate down the left hand side
Back: Four colour borderless; Dark grey nameplate down left side; Resume on card stock
Imprint: © 1992 Classic Games, Inc.
Complete Set Price: (Hockey) 15.00 30.00

No.	Player	EX	NRMT
LP22	Roman Hamrlik	2.00	4.00
LP23	Mike Rathje	1.00	2.00
LP24	Valeri Bure	5.00	10.00
LP25	Alexei Yashin	5.00	10.00

— 1993 HOCKEY PRO PROSPECTS —

PROMOTIONAL CARDS

1993 Pro Prospects Promotional Card
Card No. PR1, Steve King

Card Size: 2 1/2" x 3 1/2"
Face: Four colour, and black and white photos, white border; Name, Position
Back: Four colour, borderless; Name, Team, Resume
Imprint: © 1992 Classic Games, Inc.

No.	Player	EX	NRMT
PR1	Steve King, NYR	2.50	5.00
PR2	The First Lade of Hockey: Manon Rheaume, Goalie	5.00	10.00

— 1993 HOCKEY PRO PROSPECTS —

This 150-card set was highlighted by the 7-card Manon Rheaume subset. Classic had an exclusive with this female goalie.

1993 Hockey Pro Prospects
Card No. 100, Manon Rheaume

CLASSIC GAMES — 1992 - 1993 INSERT SETS

Card Size: 2 1/2" x 3 1/2"
Face: Four colour, white border; Name, Team
Back: Four colour, grey border, card stock; Name, Position, Resume
Imprint: © 1993 Classic Games, Inc.
Complete Set No.: 150
Complete Set Price: 9.00 / 18.00
Common Card: .05 / .10
Foil Pack: (10 Cards) 1.25
Foil Box: (36 Packs) 40.00
Jumbo Pack: (24 Cards) 2.50
Jumbo Box: (20 Packs) 50.00

No.	Player	EX	NRMT
1	Draveurs Promote Female Goaltender	1.50	3.00
2	Quebec League Welcomes Female Netminder	1.50	3.00
3	Woman Plays Preseason Game	1.50	3.00
4	Atlanta Knights Sign Female Netminder	1.50	3.00
5	Rheaume Makes Pro Hockey History	1.50	3.00
6	Standing Ovation for Hockey Pioneer	1.50	3.00
7	Rheaume Has Golden Touch in Finland	1.50	3.00
8	Oleg Petrov	.12	.25
9	Shjon Podein	.05	.10
10	**Classic All Star:** Alexei Kovalev	.35	.75
11	Roman Oksiuta	.05	.10
12	Dave Tomlinson	.07	.15
13	Jason Miller	.05	.10
14	Andrew McKim	.05	.10
15	Dallas Drake	.10	.20
16	Rob Gaudreau	.12	.25
17	Darrin Madeley	.05	.10
18	Scott Pellerin	.05	.10
19	Scott Thomas	.05	.10
20	**Classic All Star:** Chris Tancil	.05	.10
21	Patric Kjellberg	.05	.10
22	Jim Dowd	.05	.10
23	Daniel Gauthier	.05	.10
24	Mark Beaufait	.05	.10
25	**Classic All Star:** Milan Tichy	.05	.10
26	Chris Osgood	.05	.10
27	Charles Poulin	.05	.10
28	Patrick Lebeau	.05	.10
29	Chris Govedaris	.05	.10
30	**Classic All Star:** Andrei Trefilov, Goalie	.20	.40
31	Kevin Stevens	.12	.25
32	Dmitri Kvartalnov	.07	.15
33	Patrick Roy, Goalie	.35	.75
34	Mark Recchi	.12	.25
35	Adam Oates	.12	.25
36	Patrik Augusta	.05	.10
37	Gerry Fleming	.05	.10
38	Sergei Krivokrasov	.10	.20
39	Mike O'Neill, Goalie	.05	.10
40	**Classic All Star:** Darrin Madeley	.05	.10
41	Lindsay Vallis	.05	.10
42	Todd Nelson	.05	.10
43	Keith Jones	.05	.10
44	"The Legend": Howie Rosenblatt	.05	.10
45	**Classic All Star:** Jason Ruff	.05	.10
46	Robert Lang	.12	.25
47	Andre Faust	.05	.10
48	Steve Bancroft	.05	.10
49	Iain Fraser	.10	.20
50	**Classic All Star:** Roman Hamrlik	.10	.20
51	Pierre Sevigny	.05	.10
52	Jeff Levy, Goalie	.05	.10
53	Len Barrie	.05	.10
54	David Goverde, Goalie	.05	.10
55	**Classic All Star:** Vladimir Malakhov	.20	.40
56	Scott White	.05	.10
57	Dmitri Motkov	.05	.10
58	Jason Herter	.05	.10
59	Drake Berehowsky	.10	.20
60	**Classic All Star:** Steve King	.07	.15
61	Doug Barrault	.05	.10
62	Martin Hamrlik	.05	.10
63	Kevin Miehm	.05	.10
64	Shaun Van Allen	.05	.10
65	**Classic All Star:** Corey Hirsch, Goalie	.12	.25
66	Dwayne Norris	.05	.10
67	Petr Hrbek	.05	.10
68	Philippe Boucher	.05	.10
69	Denis Chervyakov	.05	.10

No.	Player	EX	NRMT
70	**Classic All Star:** Sergei Zubov	.35	.75
71	Geoff Sarjeant, Goalie	.05	.10
72	Les Kuntar, Goalie	.05	.10
73	Byron Dafoe, Goalie	.05	.10
74	**Checklist:** Rangers Connection Kovalev, Zubov, King, and Hirsch	.10	.20
75	**Classic All Star:** Alexandr Andrievski	.05	.10
76	**Checklist:** The Messier Brothers: Joby Messier; Mitch Messier	.05	.10
77	Brian Sullivan	.05	.10
78	Steve Larouche	.05	.10
79	Denis Chasse	.05	.10
80	**Classic All Star:** Felix Potvin, Goalie	.85	1.75
81	Josef Beranek	.12	.25
82	Ken Klee	.05	.10
83	Jozef Stumpel	.10	.20
84	Andrew Verner, Goalie	.05	.10
85	**Classic All Star:** Keith Osborne	.05	.10
86	Igor Malykhin	.05	.10
87	Gilbert Dionne	.07	.15
88	Viktor Gordijuk	.05	.10
89	Glen Murray	.10	.20
90	**Classic All Star:** Scott Pellerin	.05	.10
91	Tommy Soderstrom, Goalie	.12	.25
92	Terry Chitaroni	.05	.10
93	Viktor Kozlov	.25	.50
94	Mikhail Shtalenkov, Goalie	.25	.50
95	Leonid Toropchenko	.05	.10
96	Alex Gaichenyuk	.05	.10
97	Anatoli Fedotov	.05	.10
98	Igor Chibirev	.05	.10
99	Keith Gretzky	.12	.25
100	Manon Rheaume, Goalie	2.50	5.00
101	Sean Whyte	.05	.10
102	Steve Konowalchuk	.05	.10
103	Richard Borgo	.05	.10
104	Paul Di Pietro	.10	.20
105	**Classic All Star:** Patrik Carnback	.05	.10
106	Mike Fountain, Goalie	.05	.10
107	Jamie Heward	.05	.10
108	David St. Pierre	.05	.10
109	Sean O'Donnell	.05	.10
110	**Classic All Star:** Greg Andrusak	.05	.10
111	Damian Rhodes, Goalie	.05	.10
112	Ted Crowley	.05	.10
113	Chris Taylor	.05	.10
114	Terran Sandwith	.05	.10
115	**Classic All Star:** Jesse Belanger	.20	.40
116	Justin Duberman	.05	.10
117	Arturs Irbe, Goalie	.50	1.00
118	Chris LiPuma	.05	.10
119	Mike Torchia, Goalie	.05	.10
120	**Classic All Star:** Niclas Andersson	.05	.10
121	Rick Knickle, Goalie	.07	.15
122	Scott Gruhl	.05	.10
123	Dave Michayluk	.05	.10
124	Guy Leveque	.07	.15
125	**Classic All Star:** Scott Thomas	.05	.10
126	Travis Green	.07	.15
127	Joby Messier	.07	.15
128	Victor Ignatjev	.05	.10
129	Brad Tiley	.05	.10
130	**Classic All Star:** Grigori Panteleyev	.10	.20
131	Vyacheslav Butsayev	.05	.10
132	Danny Lorenz, Goalie	.05	.10
133	Marty McInnis	.05	.10
134	Ed Ronan	.10	.20
135	**Classic All Star:** Vyacheslav Kozlov	.25	.50
136	Kevin St. Jacques	.05	.10
137	Pavel Kostichkin	.05	.10
138	Mike Hurlbut	.05	.10
139	Tomas Forslund	.05	.10
140	**Classic All Star:** Rob Gaudreau	.12	.25
141	Shawn Heaphy	.05	.10
142	Radek Hamr	.10	.20
143	Jaroslav Otevrel	.10	.20
144	Keith Redmond	.05	.10
145	**Classic All Star:** Tom Pederson	.10	.20
146	Jaroslav Modry	.10	.20
147	Darren McCarty	.12	.25
148	Terry Yake	.12	.25
149	Ivan Droppa	.05	.10
150	The "VCR" Line: Shawn Van Allen; Dan Currie; Steven Rice	.05	.10

— 1992 - 1993 INSERT SETS —

AUTOGRAPH CARD

The Dmitri Kvartalnov cards are number _ of 4,000, and the Manon Rheaume cards are numbered _ of 6,500.

1992-93 Autographed Card
Dmitri Kvartalnov

Card Size: 2 1/2" x 3 1/2"
Face: Four colour, white border, Name, Autograph in blue sharpie, Logo's
Back: Green and black, Congratulations
Imprint: None

No.	Player	EX	NRMT
—	Dmitri Kvartalnov	20.00	40.00
—	Manon Rheaume	75.00	125.00

1992 EXCLUSIVE LIMITED PRINT CARDS

This 5-card set was randomly inserted into foil packs. It features the higher ranked prospects and Manon Rheaume. The cards have metallic blue title bars and are numbered LP1 to LP5. This is a limited edition and the cards are numbered _ of 26,000.

1992 Exclusive Limited Print Cards
Card No. LP4, Viktor Kozlov

Card Size: 2 1/2" x 3 1/2"
Face: Four colour, borderless; Name; Team, Position
Back: Four colour, grey border, card stock; Picture; Name; Position; Resume
Imprint: © 1993 Classic Games, Inc.
Complete Set No.: 5
Complete Set Price: 19.00 / 38.00

No.	Player	EX	NRMT
LP1	Manon Rheaume, Goalie, Tampa Bay	10.00	20.00
LP2	Alexei Kovalev, New York Rangers	4.00	8.00
LP3	Rob Gaudreau, San Jose	2.50	5.00
LP4	Viktor Kozlov, San Jose	5.00	10.00
LP5	Dallas Drake, Detroit	2.50	5.00

— 1992 - 93 BONUS CARDS —

This 20-card set was inserted in the jumbo boxes one per pack. The cards are numbered BC1 - BC20 and have a silver embossed name plate down the left side of the card.

Classic Games, 1992-93 Bonus Cards
Card No. BC1, Alexei Kovalev

Card Size: 2 1/2" x 3 1/2"
Face: Four colour, borderless; Name
Back: Four colour, borderless, card stock; Name, Resume
Imprint: © 1992 Classic Games Inc.
Complete Set No.: 20 (6 Hockey)
Complete Set Price: 17.50 35.00
Common Card: .35 .75

No.	Player	EX	NRMT
BC1	Alexei Kovalev	2.00	4.00
BC2	Andrei Trefilou, Goalie	.75	1.50
BC3	Roman Hamrlik	1.00	2.00
BC4	Vladimir Malakov	.75	1.50
BC5	Corey Hirsch, Goalie	1.00	2.00
BC6	Sergei Zubov	1.75	3.50
BC7	Felix Potvin, Goalie	5.00	10.00
BC8	Tommy Soderstrom, Goalie	1.00	2.00
BC9	Victor Kozlov	1.00	2.00
BC10	Manon Rheaume, Goalie	.75	1.50
BC11	Jesse Belanger	1.50	3.00
BC12	Rick Knickle	.35	.75
BC13	Joby Messier	.35	.75
BC14	Vyatcheslav Butsayev	.35	.75
BC15	Tomas Forslund	.35	.75
BC16	Jozef Stumpel	1.00	2.00
BC17	Dmitri Kvartlanov	.85	1.75
BC18	Adam Oates	1.25	2.50
BC19	Dallas Drake	.75	1.50
BC20	Mark Recchi	1.25	2.50

— 1993 HOCKEY DRAFT —

Classic Games, 1993 Hockey Draft
Card No. 1, Alexandre Daigle

Card Size: 2 1/2" X 3 1/2"
Face: Four colour, light blue marble border; Name, Logo
Back: Four colour; Name, Number, Resume, Logo on card stock
Imprint: © 1993 Classic Games, Inc.
Complete Set No.: 150
Complete Set Price: 9.00 18.00
Common Player: .05 .10

TOP TEN

No.	Player \ Drafted To	EX	NRMT
1	Alexandre Daigle \ Ott.	.25	.50
2	Chris Pronger \ Har.	.20	.40
3	Chris Gratton \ TB	.20	.40
4	Paul Kariya \ MDA	.25	.50
5	Rob Niedermayer \ Fl.	.20	.40
6	Viktor Kozlov \ SJ	.15	.30
7	Jason Arnott \ Edm.	.25	.50
8	Niklas Sundstrom \ NYR	.07	.15
9	Todd Harvey \ Dal.	.07	.15
10	Jocelyn Thibault, Goalie Que.	.12	.25

REGULAR ISSUE

No.	Player \ Drafted To	EX	NRMT
11	Checklist 1 (1 - 75)	.05	.10
12	1993 CHL Player Of The Year: Pat Peake \ Wash.	.07	.15
13	Jason Allison \ Wash.	.07	.15
14	Todd Bertuzzi \ NYI	.07	.15
15	Maxim Bets \ St.L	.07	.15
16	Curtis Bowen \ Det.	.07	.15
17	Kevin Brown \ LA	.07	.15
18	Valeri Bure \ Mon.	.10	.20
19	Jason Dawe \ Buf.	.07	.15
20	Adam Deadmarsh \ Que.	.07	.15
21	Aaron Gavey \ TB	.07	.15
22	Nathan Lafayette \ St.L	.12	.25
23	Eric Lecompte \ Chi.	.07	.15
24	Emanuel Legace, Goalie \ Hart.	.07	.15
25	Mike Peca \ Van.	.07	.15
26	Denis Pederson \ NJ	.05	.10
27	Jeff Shantz \ Chi.	.05	.10
28	Nick Stadjuhar \ Edm.	.07	.15
29	Cory Stillman \ Cal.	.07	.15
30	Michal Sykora \ SJ	.07	.15
31	Brent Tully \ Van.	.05	.10
32	Mike Wilson \ Van.	.05	.10
33	Junior Production Line: Kevin Brown, LA ; Pat Peake, Wash.; Bob Wren, LA	.05	.10
34	Checklist 2 (76 - 150) Alexandre Daigle/Alexei Yashin	.12	.25
35	Antti Aalto \ MDA	.05	.10
36	Radim Bicanek \ Ott.	.05	.10
37	Vladimir Chebaturkin \ NYI	.05	.10
38	Alexander Cherbayev \ SJ	.07	.15
39	Markus Ketterer, Goalie \ Buf.	.05	.10
40	Saku Koivu \ Mon.	.12	.25
41	Vladimir Krechin \ Phi.	.05	.10
42	Alexei Kudashov \ Tor.	.05	.10
43	Janne Laukkanen \ Que.	.05	.10
44	Janne Niinimaa \ Phi.	.05	.10
45	Juha Riihijarvi \ Edm.	.05	.10
46	Nikolai Tsulygin \ MDA	.05	.10
47	Vesa Viitakoski \ Cal.	.05	.10
48	David Vyborny \ Edm.	.05	.10
49	Nikolai Zavarukhin \ NJ	.05	.10

THE DAIGLE FILE

No.	Player	EX	NRMT
50	1991 QMJHL Draft	.25	.50
51	QMJHL Rookie, 1991-1992	.25	.50
52	1992 CHL Rookie-Of-The-Year	.25	.50
53	Emerging Superstar, 1992-93	.25	.50
54	No. 1 Overall Pick in 1993 Draft	.25	.50

1993 COLLEGE CHAMPIONS

No.	Player \ Drafted To	EX	NRMT
55	Jim Montgomery \ St.L	.07	.15
56	Mike Dunham, Goalie \ NJ	.05	.10
57	Matt Martin \ Tor.	.07	.15
58	Garth Snow, Goalie \ Que.	.07	.15
59	Shawn Walch, Coach \ Maine	.05	.10

REGULAR ISSUE

No.	Player \ Drafted To	EX	NRMT
60	Mike Bavis \ Buf. Mark Bavis \ NYR	.05	.10
61	Scott Chartier \ MDA	.05	.10
62	Craig Darby \ Mon.	.05	.10
63	Ted Drury \ Cal.	.07	.15
64	Steve Dubinsky \ Chi.	.05	.10
65	Joe Frederick \ Det.	.05	.10
66	Cammi Granato \ Free Agent	.50	1.00
67	Brett Hauer \ Van.	.05	.10
68	Jon Hillebrandt, Goalie \ NYI	.05	.10
69	Ryan Hughes \ Que.	.05	.10
70	Dean Hullet \ LA	.05	.10
71	Kevin O'Sullivan \ NYI	.05	.10
72	Dan Plante \ NYI	.05	.10
73	Derek Plante \ Buf.	.20	.40
74	Travis Richards \ Min.	.05	.10
75	Barry Richter \ Hart.	.05	.10
76	David Roberts \ St.L	.05	.10
77	Chris Rogles \ Chi.	.05	.10
78	Jon Rohloff \ Bos.	.05	.10
79	Brian Rolston \ NJ	.05	.10
80	David Sacco \ Tor.	.07	.15
81	Brian Savage \ Mon.	.07	.15
82	Mike Smith \ Buf.	.05	.10
83	Chris Tamer \ Pit.	.05	.10
84	Chris Therien \ Phi.	.05	.10
85	Aaron Ward \ Win.	.05	.10

1993 WORLD CHAMPIONS

No.	Player \ Drafted To	EX	NRMT
86	Russian Celebration	.05	.10
87	Vyacheslav Butsayev \ Phi.	.05	.10
88	Yan Kaminsky \ Win.	.05	.10
89	Alexander Karpovtsev \ Que.	.07	.15
90	Valeri Karpov \ MDA	.05	.10
91	Sergei Petrenko \ Buf.	.05	.10
92	Andrei Sapozhnikov \ Bos.	.05	.10
93	Sergei Sorokin \ Win.	.05	.10
94	German Titov \ Cal.	.10	.20
95	Andrei Trefilov \ Cal.	.07	.15
96	Alexei Yashin \ Ott.	.20	.40
97	Dimitri Yushkevich \ Phi.	.07	.15

CLASS OF '94

No.	Player \ Drafted To	EX	NRMT
98	Radek Bonk	.25	.50
99	Jason Bonsignore	.20	.40
100	Brad Brown	.05	.10
101	Chris Drury	.05	.10
102	Jeff Freisen	.15	.30
103	Sean Haggerty	.05	.10
104	Jeff Kealty	.05	.10
105	Alexandr Kharlamov	.10	.20
106	Stanislav Neckar	.05	.10
107	Tom O'Connor	.12	.25
108	Jeff O'Neill	.05	.10
109	Deron Quint	.05	.10
110	Vadim Sharifianov	.05	.10
111	Oleg Tverdovsky	.12	.25

HOCKEY ART

No.	Player \ Drafted To	EX	NRMT
112	Manon Rheaume	.25	.50
113	Paul Kariya	.25	.50
114	Alexandre Daigle	.25	.50
115	Jeff O'Neill	.20	.40

FLASHBACKS

No.	Player \ Drafted To	EX	NRMT
116	Mike Bossy \ NYI	.10	.20
117	Pavel Bure \ Van.	.25	.50
118	Chris Chelios \ Mon.	.05	.10
119	Douglas Gilmour \ St.L	.12	.25
120	Roman Hamrlik \ TB	.05	.10
121	Jari Kurri \ Edm.	.05	.10
122	Alexander Mogilny \ Buf.	.12	.25
123	Felix Potvin, Goalie \ Tor.	.25	.50
124	Teemu Selanne \ Win.	.20	.40
125	Tommy Soderstrom, Goalie \ Phi.	.05	.10

REGULAR ISSUE

No.	Player \ Drafted To	EX	NRMT
126	Mike Bales, Goalie \ Bos.	.05	.10
127	Jozef Cierny \ Buf.	.05	.10
128	Ivan Droppa \ Chi.	.05	.10
129	Anders Eriksson \ Det.	.05	.10
130	Anatoli Fedotov \ DA	.05	.10

1993 INSERT SETS (continued)

No.	Player \ Drafted To	EX	NRMT
131	Martin Gendron \ Wash.	.05	.10
132	Daniel Guerard \ Ott.	.05	.10
133	Corey Hirsch, Goalie \ NYR	.07	.15
134	Milos Holan \ Phi.	.05	.10
135	Kenny Jonsson \ Tor.	.05	.10
136	Steven King \ NYR	.05	.10
137	Alexei Kovalev \ NYR	.15	.30
138	Sergei Krivokrassov \ Chi.	.05	.10
139	Mats Lindgren \ Win.	.05	.10
140	Grant Marshall \ Tor.	.05	.10
141	Jesper Mattsson \ Cal.	.05	.10
142	Sandy McCarthy \ Cal.	.05	.10
143	Dean Melanson \ Buf.	.05	.10
144	Robert Petrovicky \ Hart.	.05	.10
145	Mike Rathje \ SJ	.07	.15
146	Manon Rheaume, Goalie \ Atlanta Knights	.35	.75
147	Claude Savoie \ Ott.	.05	.10
148	Mikhail Shtalenkov \ MDA	.05	.10
149	A Season To Remember: Manon Rheaume, Goalie	.35	.75
150	Up Close And Personal: Manon Rheaume	.50	1.00

— 1993 INSERT SETS —
CLASSIC AUTOGRAPHED CARDS

This 12-card autographed set was randomly inserted into foil packs. Some current NHL players along with young minor league talent are included in this set.

1993 Classic Autographed Cards
Card No. 12, Geoff Sanderson

Card Size: 2 1/2" x 3 1/2"
Face: Four colour, borderless; Name, Number, Position, Hand signed autograph, Logo
Back: Grey print stating "Congratulations you havereceived a Limited Edition Classic Games Autographed Card", Logo on white card stock
Imprint: © 1993 Classic Games, Inc.
Complete Set No. 12
Complete Set Price: 225.00 550.00

No.	Player	No. Issued	EX	NRMT
1	Mike Bossy	975	20.00	40.00
2	Pavel Bure	900	50.00	100.00
3	Chris Chelios	1800	20.00	40.00
4	Douglas Gilmour	1850	37.50	75.00
5	Alexander Mogilny	950	25.00	50.00
6	Jim Montgomery	1800	10.00	20.00
7	Rob Niedermayer	2500	25.00	50.00
8	Jeff O'Neill	2225	20.00	40.00
9	Pat Peake	790	17.50	35.00
10	Mark Recchi	1725	25.00	50.00
11	Manon Rheaume, Goalie	1500	50.00	100.00
12	Geoff Sanderson	875	25.00	50.00

CLASS OF 1994

This 7-card acetate set was randomly inserted into foil packs. The cards are all numbered CL_.

1993 Insert Set, Class of 1994
Card No. CL2, Jason Bonsignore

Card Size: 2 1/2" x 3 1/2"
Face: Four colour, borderless; Name, Logo
Back: Blue print on acetate, Name, Number, Resume
Imprint: © 1993 Classic Games, Inc.
Complete Set No. 7
Complete Set Price: 17.50 35.00
Common Card: 1.25 2.50

No.	Player	EX	NRMT
CL1	Jeff O'Neill	3.00	6.00
CL2	Jason Bonsignore	3.00	6.00
CL3	Jeff Friesen	3.00	6.00
CL4	Radek Bonk	7.00	14.00
CL5	Deron Quint	1.25	2.50
CL6	Vadim Sharifanov	1.25	2.50
CL7	Tom O'Connor	1.25	2.50

CLASSIC CRASH

This set is randomly inserted into foil packs. All of these cards are individually numbered _ of 15,000. The cards in the set are numbered N1 to N10.

Card Size: 2 1/2" x 3 1/2"
Face: Four colour, blue border; Name, Logo
Back: Four colour, blue border; Name, Number, Crash number, Resume
Imprint: © 1993 Classic Games, Inc.
Complete Set No. 10
Complete Set Price: 37.50 75.00
Common Card: 3.50 7.00

No.	Player	EX	NRMT
N1	Alexandre Daigle	4.00	8.00
N2	Paul Karuya	7.00	14.00
N3	Jeff O'Neill	4.00	8.00
N4	Jason Bonsignore	4.00	8.00
N5	Teemu Selanne	7.50	15.00
N6	Pavel Bure	7.50	15.00
N7	Alexander Mogilny	5.00	10.00
N8	Manon Rheaume, Goalie	15.00	30.00
N9	Felix Potvin, Goalie	7.50	15.00
N10	Radek Bonk	10.00	20.00

TEAM CANADA

This 7-card insert set was randomly inserted into foil packs. The cards are numbered TC-1 to TC7 and when the complete set is laid down beside each other in order the word CANADA will stand out.

1993 Insert Set, Team Canada
Card No. TC2, Paul Kariya

Card Size: 2 1/2" x 3 1/2"
Face: Four colour, borderless; Name, Letter, Logo
Back: Blue print on acetate; Name, Number, Resume
Imprint: © 1993 Classic Games, Inc.
Complete Set No. 7
Complete Set Price: 10.00 20.00
Common Card: 1.00 2.00

No.	Player	EX	NRMT
TC1	Greg Johnson	1.00	2.00
TC2	Paul Kariya	4.00	8.00
TC3	Brian Savage	1.50	3.00
TC4	Bill Ranford, Goalie	1.00	2.00
TC5	Mark Recchi	2.00	4.00
TC6	Geoff Sanderson	2.00	4.00
TC7	Adam Graves	2.00	4.00

CLASSIC TOP TEN

This 10-card insert acetate ser was randomly inserted into all foil packs. This set is numbered DP1 to DP10.

1993 Insert Set, Classic Top Ten
Card No. DP7, Jason Arnott

Card Size: 2 1/2" x 3 1/2"
Face: Four colour, borderless; Name, Number
Back: Four colour, borderless; Name, Number, Logo, Resume on acetate stock
Imprint: © 1993 Classic Games, Inc.
Complete Set No. 10
Complete Set Price: 17.50 35.00
Common Card: 1.50 3.00

No.	Player	EX	NRMT
DP1	Alexandre Daigle	2.50	5.00
DP2	Chris Pronger	2.00	4.00
DP3	Chris Gratton	2.00	4.00
DP4	Paul Kariya	5.00	10.00
DP5	Rob Niedermayer	2.00	4.00
DP6	Viktor Kozlov	1.50	3.00
DP7	Jason Arnott	5.00	10.00
DP8	Niklas Sundstrom	1.50	3.00
DP9	Todd Harvey	1.50	3.00
DP10	Jocelyn Thibault, Goalie	2.50	5.00

— 1994 CLASSIC PRO HOCKEY PROSPECTS —

Card Size: 2 1/2" X 3 1/2"
Face: Four colour, white border; Name, Team, Position, Logo
Back: Four colour, white border; Name, Number, Resume
Imprint: © 1994 Classic Games, Inc.
Complete Set No.: 250
Complete Set Price: 10.00 20.00
Common Player: .05 .10

THE BONK FILE

No.	Player	EX	NRMT
1	17 Year Old Makes Pro Debut	.35	.75
2	First Las Vegas Thunder Hat Trick	.35	.75
3	Could Be Drafted No. One.??	.35	.75

REGULAR ISSUE

No.	Player	EX	NRMT
4	Vlastimil Kroupa	.10	.20
5	Mattias Norstrom,	.05	.10
6	Jaroslav Nedved	.05	.10
7	Steve Dubinsky	.05	.10
8	Christian Proulx	.05	.10
9	Michal Grosek	.05	.10
10	Pat Neaton	.05	.10

ALL ROOKIE

No.	Player	EX	NRMT
11	Jason Arnott	.50	1.00
12	Martin Brodeur, Goalie	.25	.50
13	Alexandre Daigle	.25	.50
14	Ted Drury	.05	.10
15	Iain Fraser	.05	.10
16	Chris Gratton	.12	.25
17	Greg Johnson	.05	.10
18	Paul Kariya	.20	.40
19	Alexander Karpovtsev	.10	.20
20	Chris Lipuma	.05	.10
21	Kirk Maltby	.05	.10
22	Sandy McCarthy	.05	.10
23	Darren McCarty	.05	.10
24	Jaroslav Modry	.07	.15
25	Jim Montgomery	.07	.15
26	Markus Naslund	.05	.10
27	Rob Niedermayer	.20	.40
28	Chris Osgood, Goalie	.25	.50
29	Pat Peake	.05	.10
30	Derek Plante	.25	.50
31	Chris Pronger	.20	.40
32	Mike Rathje	.05	.10
33	Mikael Renberg	.15	.30
34	Damian Rhodes, Goalie	.15	.30
35	Garth Snow, Goalie	.10	.20
36	Can Stewart	.05	.10
37	Jim Storm	.05	.10
38	Michal Sykora	.05	.10
39	Jocelyn Thibault, Goalie	.15	.30
40	Alexei Yashin	.30	.60

REGULAR ISSUE

No.	Player	EX	NRMT
41	Checklist 1, (1 - 84)	.05	.10
42	Vesa Viitakoski	.05	.10
43	Jake Grimes	.05	.10

BLUE CHIP PROSPECT

No.	Player	EX	NRMT
44	Jim Dowd	.10	.20
45	Craig Ferguson	.10	.20

REGULAR ISSUE

No.	Player	EX	NRMT
46	Mike Boback	.05	.10
47	Francois Groleau	.05	.10
48	Juha Riihijarvi	.05	.10
49	Mikhail Shtalenkov, Goalie	.10	.20
50	Zigmund Palffy	.07	.15

HONORS GRAD

No.	Player	EX	NRMT
51	Felix Potvin, Goalie, Tor.	.25	.50

No.	Player	EX	NRMT
52	Alexei Kovalev, NYR	.25	.50
53	Larry Robinson, Mon.	.07	.15
54	John LeClair, Mon.	.07	.15
55	Dominic Roussel, Goalie	.07	.15
56	Geoff Sanderson, Hart.	.07	.15

REGULAR ISSUE

No.	Player	EX	NRMT
57	Greg Pankewicz	.05	.10
58	Brent Bilodeau	.05	.10
59	Brandon Convery	.07	.15
60	Blue Chip Prospect: Fred Knipscheer	.05	.10
61	Igor Chibirev	.05	.10
62	Anatoli Fedotov	.05	.10
63	Bob Kellogg	.05	.10
64	Mike Maurice	.05	.10
65	Blue Chip Prospect: Chad Penney	.05	.10
66	Mike Bavis	.05	.10
67	Eric Veilleux	.05	.10
68	Parris Duffus, Goalie	.05	.10
69	Daniel Lacroix	.07	.15
70	Blue Chip Prospect: Milos Holan	.05	.10
71	Mike Muller	.05	.10
72	Micah Aivazoff	.10	.20
73	Krzysztop Oliwa	.05	.10
74	Ryan Hughes	.05	.10
75	Blue Chip Prospect: Christian Soucy, Goalie	.05	.10
76	Keith Redmond	.05	.10
77	Mark De Santis	.05	.10
78	Craig Martin	.05	.10
79	Mike Kennedy	.05	.10
80	Blue Chip Prospect: Pauli Jaks, Goalie	.07	.15

MARATHON MAN

No.	Player	EX	NRMT
81	Colin Chin	.05	.10
82	Jody Gage	.05	.10
83	Don Biggs	.05	.10
84	Tim Tookey	.05	.10
85	Clint Malarchuk, Goalie	.07	.15

REGULAR ISSUE

No.	Player	EX	NRMT
86	Jozef Cierny	.05	.10
87	Radek Hamr	.12	.25
88	Jason Dawe	.07	.15
89	Chris Longo	.07	.15
90	Brian Rolston	.07	.15
91	Mike McKee	.05	.10
92	Vitali Prokhorov	.10	.20
93	Chris Snell	.10	.20
94	Martin Brochu, Goalie	.05	.10
95	Dan Plante	.05	.10
96	Darcy Werenka	.05	.10
97	Steffon Walby	.05	.10
98	David Emma	.05	.10
99	San Stiver	.05	.10
100	Radek Bonk	.12	.25
101	Mark Visheau	.05	.10
102	Dean Melanson	.05	.10
103	Vladimir Tsyplakov	.05	.10
104	Mikhail Volkov	.05	.10
105	Blue Chip Prospect: Aaron Miller	.05	.10
106	Alexei Kudashov	.10	.20
107	Shawn Rivers	.05	.10
108	Ladislav Karabin	.05	.10
109	Matt Mallgrave	.05	.10
110	Craig Darby	.05	.10
111	Marcel Cousineau, Goalie	.05	.10
112	Jamie McLennan, Goalie	.05	.10
113	Yanic Perreault	.10	.20
114	Zac Boyer	.05	.10
115	Sergei Zubov	.15	.30
116	Dan Kesa	.05	.10
117	Jim Hiller	.10	.20
118	Dmitri Starostenko	.05	.10
119	Chris Tamer	.05	.10
120	Blue Chip Prospect: Aaron Ward	.05	.10
121	Claude Savoie	.05	.10
122	Jamie Black	.05	.10
123	Jean-Francois Jomphe	.05	.10

— 1991 PROMOTIONAL CARDS — STAR PICS

No.	Player	EX	NRMT
124	Paxton Schulte	.05	.10
125	Blue Chip Prospect: Jarkko Varvio	.10	.20
126	Jaroslav Otevrel	.05	.10
127	Dane Jackson	.05	.10
128	Brent Grieve	.07	.15
129	Checklist 2, (85-168) Rheaume Family	.15	.30
130	Blue Chip Prospect: Rene Corbet	.05	.10
131	Joe Frederick	.05	.10
132	Martin Tanguay	.05	.10
133	Fredrik Jax	.05	.10
134	Jamie Linden	.05	.10
135	Blue Chip Prospect: Jason Smith	.05	.10
136	Rick Kowalsky	.05	.10
137	Dino Grossi	.05	.10
138	Aris Brimanis	.05	.10
130	Jeff McLean	.05	.10
140	Tyler Wright	.07	.15
141	Roman Gorev	.05	.10
142	Dean Hulett	.05	.10
143	Niklas Sundblad	.05	.10
144	Blue Chip Prospect: Jeff Bes	.05	.10
145	Pascal Rheaume	.05	.10
146	Donald Brashear	.05	.10
147	Hugo Belanger	.05	.10
148	Blair Scott	.05	.10
149	Steve Staios	.07	.15
150	Matt Martin	.10	.20
151	Richard Matvichuk	.05	.10
152	Paul Brousseau	.05	.10
153	Evgeny Namestnikov	.05	.10
154	Mike Peca	.05	.10
155	Jeff Nelson	.05	.10
156	Greg Andrusak	.05	.10
157	Norm Batherson	.05	.10
158	Martin Bakula	.05	.10
159	Ed Patterson	.05	.10
160	Blue Chip Prospect: Steve Larouche	.05	.10
161	Libor Polasek	.05	.10
162	Jon Hillebrandt, Goalie	.05	.10
163	Guy Leveque	.07	.15
164	Eric Lacroix	.10	.20
165	Blue Chip Prospect: Scott Walker	.05	.10
166	Robert Burakovsky	.05	.10
167	Markus Ketterer, Goalie	.05	.10
168	Mike Speer	.05	.10
169	Martin Jiranek	.05	.10
170	Andy Schneider	.05	.10
171	Terry Hollinger	.05	.10
172	Mark Lawrence	.05	.10
173	Martin Lapointe	.05	.10
174	Vaclav Prospal	.05	.10
175	Mike Fountain, Goalie	.10	.20
176	Alexander Kerch	.05	.10
177	Oleg Petrov	.10	.20
178	Derek Armstrong	.05	.10
179	Matthew Barnaby	.10	.20
180	Andrei Nazarov	.05	.10
181	Andrei Trefilov, Goalie	.12	.25
182	Jean-Yves Roy	.07	.15
183	Boris Rousson, Goalie	.05	.10
184	Blue Chip Prospect: Daniel Laperriere	.05	.10
185	Blue Chip Prospect: Yan Kaminsky	.07	.15
186	Ralph Intranuovo	.05	.10
187	Sandy Moger	.05	.10
188	Grant Marshall	.05	.10
189	Denny Felsner	.07	.15
190	Blue Chip Prospect: Cory Stillman	.07	.15
191	Eric Lavigne	.07	.15
192	Jarrod Skalde	.05	.10
193	Steve Junker	.05	.10
194	Alexander Cherbayev	.07	.15
195	Nathan Lafayette	.12	.25
196	Ed Ward	.05	.10
197	Harija Vitolinsh	.05	.10
198	Jarmo Kekalainen	.05	.10
199	Neil Eisenhut	.05	.10
200	Radek Bonk	.12	.25
201	Jason Bonsignore	.05	.10

CLASS OF 94

No.	Player	EX	NRMT
202	Jeff Friesen	.20	.40

No.	Players	EX	NRMT
203	Ed Jovanovski	.20	.40
204	Brett Lindros	.25	.50
205	Jeff O'Neill	.15	.30
206	Deron Quint	.07	.15
207	Vadim Sharifjanov	.07	.15
208	Oleg Tverdovsky	.20	.40
209	Checklist #3, (169-250) Jeff Friesen, Jeff O'Neil	.15	.30

REGULAR ISSUE

No.	Player	EX	NRMT
210	Blue Chip Prospect: David Cooper	.05	.10
211	Doug MacDonald	.05	.10
212	Leonid Toropchenko	.05	.10
213	Chris Rogles, Goalie	.05	.10
214	Vyacheslav Kozlov	.15	.30
215	Denis Metlyuk	.05	.10
216	Scott McKay	.05	.10
217	Brian Loney	.05	.10
218	Kevin Hodson, Goalie	.05	.10
219	Bobby House	.05	.10
220	Sergei Krivokrasov	.07	.15
221	Brett Harkins	.05	.10
222	Cale Hulse	.05	.10
223	Marc Tardif	.05	.10
224	Jon Rohloff	.05	.10
225	Blue Chip Prospect: Kevin Smyth	.05	.10
226	Jason Young	.05	.10
227	Sergei Zholtok	.10	.20
228	Todd Simon	.10	.20

BEST OF THE ECHL

No.	Player	EX	NRMT
229	Jerome Bechard	.05	.10
230	Matt Robbins	.05	.10
231	Joe Cook	.05	.10
232	John Brill	.05	.10
233	Dan Goldie	.05	.10
234	Dan Gravelle	.05	.10
235	Shawn Wheeler	.05	.10
236	Brad Harrison	.05	.10
237	Joe Dragon	.05	.10
238	Jason Jennings	.05	.10
239	Manon Rheaume, Goalie	.50	1.00
240	Jamie Steer	.05	.10
241	Scott Rogers	.05	.10
242	Lyle Wildgoose	.05	.10
243	Darren Colbourne	.05	.10
244	Mike Smith	.05	.10
245	Chris Bright	.05	.10
246	Chris Belanger	.05	.10
247	Darren Schwartz	.05	.10

THE WOMEN OF PRO HOCKEY

No.	Player	EX	NRMT
248	Cammi Granato	.50	1.00
249	Erin Whitten, Goalie	.50	1.00
250	Manon Rheaume, Goalie	.75	1.50

PRO PROSPECTS INTERNATIONAL HEROES

Pro Prospects International Heroes
Card No. LP4, Chris Ferraro

This 25 Acetate insert set was randomly inserted into foil packs.
Card Size: 2 1/2" X 3 1/2"
Face: Four colour on acetate; Name, Team
Back: Acetate stock; Name, Number, Resume
Imprint: © 1994 Classic Games, Inc.
Complete Set No.: 25

	EX	NRMT
Complete Set Price:	35.00	70.00
Common Player:	1.50	3.00

No.	Players	EX	NRMT
LP1	Jim Campbell	1.50	3.00
LP2	Ted Drury	1.50	3.00
LP3	Mike Dunham	1.50	3.00
LP4	Chris Ferraro	1.50	3.00
LP5	Peter Ferraro	1.50	3.00
LP6	Darby Hendrickson	1.50	3.00
LP7	Craig Johnson	1.50	3.00
LP8	Todd Marchant	1.50	3.00
LP9	Matt Martin	1.50	3.00
LP10	Brian Rolston	1.50	3.00
LP11	Adrian Aucoin	1.50	3.00
LP12	Martin Gendron	1.50	3.00
LP13	David Harlock	1.50	3.00
LP14	Corey Hirsch, Goalie	2.50	5.00
LP15	Paul Kariya	1.50	3.00
LP16	Emanuel Legace, Goalie	2.50	5.00
LP17	Brett Lindros	6.00	12.00
LP18	Brian Savage	1.50	3.00
LP19	Chris Terrien	1.50	3.00
LP20	Todd Warriner	2.50	5.00
LP21	Radek Bonk	3.50	7.00
LP22	Pavel Bure	4.00	8.00
LP23	Teemu Selanne	3.00	6.00
LP24	Mark Recchi	2.50	5.00
LP25	Alexei Yashin	3.00	6.00

AUTOGRAPHED CARDS

These cards were randomly inserted into foil packs. The cards are hand autographed on the face of the card and the card backs says "congratulate you for receiving the card". This card set is not numbered so they are listed alphabetically.

Card Size: 2 1/2" x 3 1/2"
Face: Four colour, borderless; Name, Number, Autograph, Position
Back: Black print on white card stock. "Congratulations, you have received a limited edition Classic Games Autographed card".
Imprint: © 1993 Classic Games, Inc.
Complete Set No. 9

	EX	NRMT
Complete Set Price:	212.50	425.00
Common Card:	15.00	30.00

No.	Player	No. Issued	EX	NRMT
1	Radek Bonk	2400	37.50	75.00
2	Jason Bonsignore	2450	15.00	30.00
3	Chris Pronger	1400	25.00	50.00
4	Alexei Kovalev	1900	25.00	50.00
5	Manon Rheaume	1900	45.00	90.00
6	Jeff Friesen	2450	15.00	30.00
7	Erin Whitten	1800	35.00	70.00
8	Alexei Yashin	1400	37.50	75.00
9	Joseph Juneau	1370	30.00	60.00

STAR PICS PRO PROSPECTS HOCKEY CARD ART

— 1991 PROMOTIONAL CARDS —

These Promotional Cards were issued in a mini-sheet format. The Scott Lachance photo is repeated within the set, the only difference being the border around the face picture and the placement of the imprints on the back of the card. The back of the Fedorov card is the same as Card No. 30 except for the placement of the imprints, and the face of the card has been changed to a "Flashback" horizontal picture.

Card Size: 2 1/2" x 3 1/2"
Face: Four colour, white face mask on black border
Back: Four colour, white border, Number, Resume, Date drafted
Imprint: © 1991 Star Pics, Inc.

No.	Player	EX	NRMT
—	Sergei Fedorov/Scott Lachance	2.50	5.00

— 1991 REGULAR ISSUE —

This is the first "Draft Picks" hockey set issued by Star Pics. The 72-card set contains two subsets, "Flashback" and "Hall of Fame" both consisting of six cards. Both subsets are borderless cards with "Hall of Fame" printed in sepia and "Flashbacks" printed in red on the respective cards. One in 50 sets were issued with a hand-signed player autographed card. There are no autographed cards for No. 15, Terry Chitaroni and No. 48 Alexei Kovalev. Five complete autographed sets were randomly inserted with the regular sets.

Star Pics, 1991 Issue
Card No. 2, Pat Falloon

Card Size: 2 1/2" x 3 1/2"
Face: Four colour, white face mask on black border
Back: Four colour, white border, Number, Resume, Date drafted
Imprint: © 1991 Star Pics, Inc.
Complete Set No.: 72

	EX	NRMT
Complete Set Price:	3.50	7.00
Common Player:	.05	.10
Case:		200.00

Production:
Individually Numbered Sets: 225,000
Autographed Cards: 4,500
Autographed Sets: 5
Factory Sealed Set: 72 Cards
Factory Sealed Case: 20 Sets

No.	Player \ Drafted To	EX	NRMT
1	Draft Overview	.05	.10
2	Pat Falloon / San Jose	.35	.75
3	Jamie Pushor \ Detroit	.05	.10
4	Hall of Fame: Jean Beliveau, Inducted 1972	.20	.40
5	Martin Lapointe \ Detroit	.12	.25
6	Jamie Matthews \ Chicago	.05	.10
7	Hall of Fame: Rod Gilbert, Inducted 1982	.05	.10
8	Niklas Sunblad \ Calgary	.05	.10
9	Steve Konowalchuk \ Washington	.05	.10
10	Hall of Fame: Alex Delvecchio, Inducted 1977	.05	.10
11	Donevan Hextall \ New Jersey	.05	.10
12	Dody Wood \ San Jose	.05	.10
13	Scott Niedermayer \ New Jersey	.35	.75
14	Trevor Halverson \ Washington	.05	.10
15	Terry Chitaroni \ Toronto	.05	.10
16	Tyler Wright \ Edmonton	.10	.20
17	Andrey Lomakin \ Philadelphia	.05	.10
18	Martin Hamrlik \ Hartford	.05	.10
19	Dmitry Philimonov \ Winnipeg	.05	.10
20	Flashback: Ed Belfour, Goalie	.12	.25
21	Andrew Verner \ Edmonton	.07	.15
22	Yanic Perreault \ Toronto	.07	.15
23	Michael Nylander \ Hartford	.15	.30
24	Scott Lachance \ New York I.	.35	.75
25	Pavel Bure \ Vancouver	1.50	3.00
26	Mike Torchia \ Minnesota	.05	.10
27	Hall of Fame: Frank Mahovlich, Inducted 1981	.07	.15
28	Philippe Boucher \ Buffalo	.07	.15
29	Jiri Slegr \ Vancouver	.05	.10
30	Flashback: Sergei Fedorov	.50	1.00
31	Rene Corbet \ Quebec	.07	.15
32	Jamie McLennan \ New York I.	.12	.25
33	Shane Peacock \ Pittsburgh	.05	.10
34	Mario Nobili \ Edmonton	.05	.10
35	Peter Forsberg \ Philadelphia	.50	1.00
36	All Rookie Team: P. Falloon, T. Wright, P. Poulin P. Boucher, A. Verner, S. Lachance	.05	.10

— 1991 PROMOTIONAL CARDS — STAR PICS 715

No.	Player	EX	NRMT
37	Arturs Irbe \ Minnesota	.85	1.75
38	Alexei Zhitnik \ Los Angeles	.20	.40
39	Pat Peake \ Washington	.25	.50
40	**Flashback:** Adam Oates	.12	.25
41	Markus Naslund \ Pittsburgh	.10	.20
42	Eric Lavigne \ Washington	.05	.10
43	Jeff Nelson \ Washington	.05	.10
44	Yanick Dupre \ Philadelphia	.05	.10
45	Justin Morrison \ Washington	.05	.10
46	Alek Stojanov \ Vancouver	.05	.10
47	Marcel Cousineau \ Boston	.05	.10
48	Alexei Kovalev \ New York R .	.50	1.00
49	Andrey Trefilov \ Calgary	.05	.10
50	**Flashback:** Mats Sundin	.18	.35
51	Steve Staios \ St. Louis	.07	.15
52	**Hall of Fame:** Glenn Hall, Goalie Inducted 1975	.12	.25
53	Brent Bilodeau \ Montreal	.05	.10
54	Darcy Werenka \ New York R.	.05	.10
55	Chris Osgood, Goalie \ Detroit.18	.35	
56	Nathan LaFayette \ St. Louis	.12	.25
57	Richard Matvichuk \ Minnesota	.07	.15
58	Dmitry Mironov \ Toronto	.12	.25
59	Jason Dawe \ Buffalo	.10	.20
60	**Flashback:** Mike Ricci	.12	.25
61	**Hall of Fame:** Gerry Cheevers, Inducted 1985	.12	.25
62	Jim Campbell \ Montreal	.07	.15
63	Francois Groleau \ Calgary	.05	.10
64	Glen Murray \ Boston	.20	.40
65	Jason Young \ Buffalo	.05	.10
66	Dean McAmmond \ Chicago	.07	.15
67	Guy Leveque \ Los Angeles	.05	.10
68	Pat Poulin \ Hartford	.15	.30
69	Bobby House \ Chicago	.05	.10
70	**Flashbacks:** Jaromir Jagr	.35	.75
71	Jassen Cullimore Vancouver	.05	.10
72	Checklist	.05	.10

ULTIMATE TRADING CARD COMPANY

— 1991 PROMOTIONAL CARDS —

Released to introduce the first set of trading cards issued by the Ultimate Trading Card Company.

Card Size: 2 1/2" X 3 1/2"
Face: Four colour
Back: Two colour, Number, Resume
Imprint: © 1991 - All Rights Reserved

No.	Player	EX	NRMT
—	Pat Falloon	10.00	20.00
—	Alex Stojanov	10.00	20.00
—	Mike Torchia	10.00	20.00

— 1991 REGULAR ISSUE —

Sweepstakes Cards are enclosed in every pack allowing the collector to enter a draw for autographed sets and "game worn" equipment. Five hundred autographed sets were available.

Ultimate Trading Card Company,
1991 Issue, Card No. 3, Scott Niedermayer

Card Size: 2 1/2" X 3 1/2"
Face: Four colour, white border, Position
Back: Four colour, Number, Resume
Imprint: © 1991 - ALL RIGHTS RESERVED (SMOKEY'S) logo
Complete Set No.: 90
Autographed Set Price: 500.00
Complete Set Price: 4.00 8.00
Common Card: .10 .10
Foil Pack: (6 Cards) .30
Foil Boxes: (36 Packs) 5.00
Foil Cases: (10 Boxes) 100.00
Set Cases: (20 Sets) 100.00
Production: Foil Cases: 5,000
Set Cases: 6,000

No.	Player \ Drafted To	English NRMT	French NRMT
1	Ultimate / Preview	.10	.10
2	Pat Falloon \ San Jose	.40	.40
3	Scott Niedermayer \ New Jersey	.40	.40
4	Scott La Chance \ New York I.	.15	.15
5	Peter Forsberg \ Philadelphia	.50	.50
6	Alek Stojanov \ Vancouver	.10	.10
7	Richard Matvichuk \ Minnesota	.10	.10
8	Patrick Poulin \ Hartford	.15	.15
9	Martin LaPointe \ Detroit	.15	.15
10	Tyler Wright \ Edmonton	.10	.10
11	Philippe Boucher \ Buffalo	.10	.10
12	Pat Peake \ Washington	.25	.25
13	Markus Nasland \ Philadelphia	.15	.15
14	Brent Bilodeau \ Montreal	.10	.10
15	Glen Murray \ Boston	.25	.25
16	Niklas Sundblad \ Calgary	.10	.10
17	Trevor Halverson \ Washington	.10	.10
18	Dean McCammond \ Chicago	.10	.10
19	Jim Campbell \ Montreal	.10	.10
20	Rene Corbet \ Quebec	.10	.10
21	Eric Lavigne \ Washington	.10	.10
22	Steve Staios \ St. Louis	.10	.10
23	Jassen Cullimore \ Vancouver	.10	.10
24	Jamie Pushor \ Detroit	.10	.10
25	Donevan Hextall \ New Jersey	.10	.10
26	Andrew Verner, Goalie \ Edmonton	.10	.10
27	Jason Dawe \ Buffalo	.10	.10
28	Jeff Nelson \ Washington	.10	.10
29	Darcy Werenka \ New York R.	.10	.10
30	Francois Groleau \ Calgary	.10	.10
31	Guy Leveque \ Los Angeles	.10	.10
32	Jamie Matthews \ Chicago	.10	.10
33	Dody Wood \ San Jose	.10	.10
34	Yanic Perreault \ Toronto	.10	.10
35	Jamie McLellan, Goalie \ New York I.	.10	.10
36	Yanick Dupre \ Philadelphia	.10	.10
37	**Checklist 1:** First Round Group Shot	.10	.10
38	Chris Osgood, Goalie \ Detroit.25		
39	Frederik Lindquist \ New Jersey	.10	.10
40	Jason Young \ Buffalo	.10	.10
41	Steve Konowalchuk \ Washington	.10	.10
42	Mikael Nylander \ Hartford	.20	.20
43	Shane Peacock \ Pittsburgh	.10	.10
44	Yves Sarault \ Montreal	.10	.10
45	Marcel Cousineau, \ Boston, Goalie	.10	.10

No.	Player	English NRMT	French NRMT
46	Nathan Lafayette \ St. Louis	.25	.25
47	Bobby House \ Chicago	.10	.10
48	Terry Toporowski \ San Jose	.10	.10
49	Terry Chitaroni \ Toronto	.10	.10
50	Mike Torchia, Goalie \ Minnesota	.10	.10
51	Mario Nobili \ Edmonton	.10	.10
52	Justin Morrison \ Washington	.10	.10
53	Grayden Reid \ St. Louis	.10	.10
54	**The Underdog:** Yanick Perreault, Tor.	.10	.10
55	**Checklist 2:** Second Round Group Shot	.25	.25
56	Niedermayer, Falloon, La Chance	.10	.10
57	**The Goalies:** A. Verner, Edm.; C. Osgood, Det.; J. McLellan, NYI; M. Cousineau, Bos.; M. Torchia, Min.	.10	.10

FIRST ROUND DRAFT PICK

No.	Player \ Drafted To	English NRMT	French NRMT
58	Pat Falloon \ San Jose	.25	.25
59	Scott Niedermayer \ New Jersey	.20	.20
60	Scott Lachance \ New York I.	.10	.10
61	Peter Forsberg \ Philadelphia	.25	.25
62	Alek Stojanov \ Vancouver	.10	.10
63	Richard Matvichuk \ Minnesota	.10	.10
64	Patrick Poulin \ Hartford	.15	.15
65	Martin LaPointe \ Detroit	.10	.10
66	Tyler Wright \ Edmonton	.10	.10
67	Philippe Boucher \ Buffalo	.10	.10
68	Pat Peake \ Washington	.15	.15
69	Markus Naslund \ Philadelphia	.10	.10
70	Brent Bilodeau \Montreal	.10	.10
71	Glen Murray \ Boston	.10	.10
72	Niklas Sundblad \ Calgary	.10	.10
73	Trevor Halverson \ Washington	.10	.10
74	Dean McCammond \ Chicago	.10	.10

REGULAR ISSUE

No.	Player	English NRMT	French NRMT
75	**Award Winners:** P. Boucher, 1990-91 Canadian Junior Rookie of the Year; J. Nelson, 88-89, 89-90 Canadian Scholastic Player of the Year S, Niedermayer, 1990-91 Canadian Scholastic Player of the Year	.10	.10
76	**The Swedes:** M. Naslund, Phi. P. Forsberg, Phi.	.10	.10
77	**Checklist 3:** 3rd & 4th Round Group Shot	.10	.10

BLACK & WHITE PORTRAITS

No.	Player	English NRMT	French NRMT
78	Pat Falloon, SJ	.25	.25
79	Scott Niedermayer, NJD	.20	.20
80	Falloon & Niedermayer	.20	.20
81	Scott Lachance, NYI	.10	.10
82	Philippe Boucher, Buf.	.10	.10
83	Markus Naslund, Phi.	.10	.10
84	Glen Murray, Bos.	.10	.10
85	Niklas Sundblad, Cal.	.10	.10
86	Jason Dawe, Buf.	.10	.10
87	Yanick Perreault, Tor.	.10	.10

REGULAR ISSUE

No.	Player	English NRMT	French NRMT
88	**Offensive Threats:** Y. Dupre, Phi.; M. Nylander, NYI	.10	.10
89	**Overview: QMJHL -** Top Scorer: R. Corbet Offensive Rookie: Y. Perreault Defensive Rookie: P. Boucher OHL - Top Goaltender: M. Torchia WHL - Rookie of the Year: D. Hextall Top Goaltender: J. McLellan Penalty Leader: K. Toporowski	.10	.10
90	Face The Future/Ultimate	.10	.10

MEMORIAL CUP

7TH INNING SKETCH

— 1990 REGULAR ISSUE —

Issued in 1990 as a limited edition, this set was packaged in a display box and numbered __ of 3000. Also available as an uncut sheet.

1990 Issue
Card No. 1, Len Barrie

Card Size: 2 1/2" X 3 1/2"
Face: Four colour, blue border, League logo
Back: Blue on yellow card stock, Number, Resume, Position
Imprint: 7TH INNING SKETCH, WINDSOR, ONT.
Complete Set No.: 100
Complete Set Price: 150.00   300.00
Common Card: .75   1.50

KAMLOOPS BLAZERS

No.	Player	EX	NRMT
1	Len Barrie	1.50	3.00
2	Zac Boyer	.75	1.50
3	David Chyzowski	.75	1.50
4	Shea Esselmont	.75	1.50
5	Todd Esselmont	.75	1.50
6	Phil Huber	.75	1.50
7	Lance Johnson	.75	1.50
8	Paul Kruse	.75	1.50
9	Cal McGowan	.75	1.50
10	Michael Needham	1.75	3.50
11	Brian Shantz	.75	1.50
12	Daryl Sydor	3.50	7.00
13	Jeff Watchorn	.75	1.50
14	Jarrett Bousquet	.75	1.50
15	Todd Harris	.75	1.50
16	Dean Malkoc	.75	1.50
17	Joey Mittelsteadt	.75	1.50
18	Scott Niedermayer	5.00	10.00
19	Clayton Young	.75	1.50
20	Trevor Sim	.75	1.50
21	Murray Duval	.75	1.50
22	Steve Yule	.75	1.50
23	Craig Bonner	.75	1.50
24	Dale Masson, Goalie	.75	1.50
25	Corey Hirsch, Goalie	2.50	5.00

KITCHENER RANGERS

No.	Player	EX	NRMT
26	Joe McDonnell, Coach	.75	1.50
27	Rick Chambers, Trainer	.75	1.50
28	John Finnie, Goalie	.75	1.50
29	Randy Pearce	.75	1.50
30	Mark Montanari	.75	1.50
31	Mike Torchia, Goalie	1.25	2.50
32	Jason York	.75	1.50
33	Jason Firth	.75	1.50
34	Jamie Israel	.75	1.50
35	Richard Borgo	.75	1.50
36	John Uniac	.75	1.50
37	Steve Smith	.75	1.50
38	Steven Rice	2.50	5.00

No.	Player	EX	NRMT
39	Gilbert Dionne	2.50	5.00
40	Cory Keenan	.75	1.00
41	Rick Allain	.75	1.00
42	John Copley	.75	1.00
43	Gib Tucker	.75	1.00
44	Chris LiPuma	.75	1.00
45	Brad Barton	.75	1.00
46	Rival Fullum	.75	1.00
47	Joey St. Aubin	.75	1.50
48	Jack Williams	.75	1.50
49	Shayne Stevenson	1.25	2.50

LAVAL TITAN

No.	Player	EX	NRMT
50	Pierre Creamer, Coach	.75	1.50
51	Carl Mantha	.75	1.50
52	Julian Cameron, Goalie	.75	1.50
53	Sandy McCarthy	.75	1.50
54	Gino Odjick	2.00	4.00
55	Eric Raymond, Goalie	2.00	4.00
56	Carl Boudreau	.75	1.50
57	Greg MacEachern	.75	1.50
58	Allen Kerr	.75	1.50
59	Patrice Brisebois	2.00	4.00
60	Eric Bissonnette	.75	1.50
61	Martin Lapointe	5.00	10.00
62	Michel Gingras	.75	1.50
63	Sylvain Naud	.75	1.50
64	Patrick Caron	.75	1.50
65	Regis Tremblay	.75	1.50
66	Francois Pelletier	.75	1.50
67	Jason Brousseau	.75	1.50
68	Eric Dubois	.75	1.50
69	Claude Boivin	.75	1.50
70	Denis Chalifoux	.75	1.50
71	Jim Bermingham	.75	1.50
72	Daniel Arsenault	.750	1.50
73	Normand Demers	.750	1.50
74	Serge Anglehart	.750	1.50

OSHAWA GENERALS

No.	Player	EX	NRMT
75	Rick Cornacchia, Coach	.75	1.50
76	Kevin Butt, Goalie	1.25	2.50
77	Fred Brathwaite, Goalie	1.75	3.50
78	Paul O'Hagan	.75	1.50
79	Craig Donaldson	.75	1.50
80	Jean-Paul Davis	.75	1.50
81	Brian Grieve	.75	1.50
82	Bill Armstrong	.75	1.50
83	Wade Simpson	.75	1.50
84	Dave Craievich, Error	.75	1.50
85	Dale Craigwell	.75	1.50
86	Joe Busillo	.75	1.50
87	Cory Banika	.75	1.50
88	Eric Lindros	75.00	150.00
89	Iain Fraser	2.50	5.00
90	Mike Craig	5.00	10.00
91	Jarrod Skalde	3.75	7.50
92	Brent Grieve	.75	1.50
93	Scott Luik	.75	1.50
94	Matt Hoffman	.75	1.50
95	Trevor McIvor	.75	1.50
96	Scott Hollis	.75	1.50
97	Mark Deazeley	.75	1.50
98	Clair Cornish	.75	1.50
99	O.H.L. Champions, Oshawa Generals	65.00	125.00

CHECKLIST

No.	Checklist	EX	NRMT
100	Checklist	.75	1.50

— 1991 REGULAR ISSUE —

Issued in 1991 as a limited edition, this set was packaged in a display box and numbered __ of 20,000. An Eric Lindros card was projected for this set originally but was cancelled at the last minute due to the inability of reaching an agreement. It is estimated that 1300 sets, containing the Lindros card were available at the Memorial Cup Game.

1991 Issue
Card No. 1, Mike Lenarduzzi

Card Size: 2 1/2" X 3 1/2"
Face: Four colour, grey border
Back: Four colour, black on white card stock, Number, Resume, Position
Imprint: © 1990 7th Inning Sketch Printed in Canada
Complete Set No.: 100
Complete Set Price: (W/O Lindros Card) 7.50   15.00
Complete Set Price: (W Lindros Card) 100.00   200.00
Common Card: .10   .20

SAULT STE MARIE GREYHOUNDS

No.	Player	EX	NRMT
1	Mike Lenarduzzi, Goalie	.50	1.00
2	Kevin Hodson, Goalie	.25	.50
3	OHL Action	.10	.20
4	Bob Boughner	.10	.20
5	Adam Foote	.35	.75
6	Brad Tilley	.10	.20
7	Brian Goudie	.10	.20
8	Wade Whitten	.10	.20
9	Jason Denomme	.10	.20
10	David Matsos	.10	.20
11	Rick Kowalsky	.10	.20
12	Jarret Reid	.10	.20
13	Perry Pappas	.10	.20
14	Tom MacDonald	.10	.20
15	Mike DeCoff	.10	.20
16	Joe Busillo	.10	.20
17	Denny Lambert	.10	.20
18	Mark Matier	.10	.20
19	Shaun Imber	.10	.20
20	Ralph Intranuovo	.10	.20
21	Chris Snell, (W/D)	1.50	3.00
22	Tony Iob	.25	.50
23	Colin Miller	.25	.50
24	Ted Nolan, Coach	.25	.50

LES SAGUENEENS DE CHICOUTIMI

No.	Player	EX	NRMT
25	Sylvain Rodigue, Goalie	.10	.20
26	Félix Potvin, Goalie	4.00	8.00
27	Martin Lavallée	.10	.20
28	Eric Brûlé	.75	1.50
29	Steve Larouche	.10	.20
30	Michel St-Jacques	.10	.20
31	Patrick Clément	.10	.20
32	Patrick Bisaillon	.10	.20

CHECKLIST

No.	Checklist	EX	NRMT
33A	Checklist (62 to 131), Original, (W/D)	1.50	3.00
33B	Checklist (62 to 131), Replacement	.10	.20

LES SAGUENEENS DE CHICOUTIMI

No.	Player	EX	NRMT
34	Gilles Bouchard	.10	.20
35	Eric Rochette	.10	.20
36	Rob Dykeman, Goalie (W/D)	1.50	3.00

CHECKLIST

No.	Checklist	EX	NRMT
37A	Checklist (1 to 61), Original, (W/D)	1.50	3.00
37B	Checklist (1 to 61), Replacement	.10	.20

LES SAGUENEENS DE CHICOUTIMI

No.	Player	EX	NRMT
38	Patrice Martineau	.10	.20
39	Danny Beauregard	.10	.20
40	François Bélanger	.10	.20
41	Sébastien Parent	.10	.20
42	Martin Gagné	.10	.20
43	Stéphane Charbonneau	.10	.20
44	Martin Beaupré	.10	.20
45	Daniel Paradis	.10	.20
46	Joe Canale, Coach	.10	.20

REGULAR ISSUE

No.	Player	EX	NRMT
47	OHL Action	.10	.20
48	Jubilation	.10	.20

LES VOLTIGEURS DE DRUMMONDVILLE

No.	Player	EX	NRMT
49	Steve Lupien, Goalie	.10	.20
50	Pierre Gagnon, Goalie	.15	.30
51	Alexandre Legault	.10	.20
52	Martin Charrois	.10	.20
53	Eric Dandenault	.10	.20
54	Denis Chassé	.10	.20
55	Guy Lehoux	.10	.20
56	Ian Laperrière	.10	.20
57	Hugo Proulx	.10	.20
58	Dave Whittom	.10	.20
59	Yanick Dupré	.10	.20
60	Eric Plante	.10	.20
61	Stéphane Desjardins	.10	.20
62	Patrice Brisebois	.35	.75
63	René Corbet	.10	.20
64	Marc Savard	.10	.20
65	Claude Jutras Jr.	.10	.20
66	David Pekarek	.10	.20
67	Roger Larche, Error	.10	.20
68	Dave Paquet	.10	.20
69	Eric Meloche	.10	.20

REGULAR ISSUE

No.	Player	EX	NRMT
70	CHL Action	.10	.20
71	The Celebration	.50	1.00
72	MVP, Felix Potvin, Goalie	4.00	8.00

SPOKANE CHIEFS

No.	Player	EX	NRMT
73	Scott Bailey, Goalie	.10	.20
74	Trevor Kidd, Goalie	.75	1.50
75	Chris Lafreniere	.10	.20
76	Frank Evans	.10	.20
77	Jon Klemm	.10	.20
78	Brent Thurston	.10	.20
79	Jamie McLennan	.10	.20
80	Steve Junker	.10	.20
81	Mark Szoke	.10	.20
82	Ray Whitney	.50	1.00
83	Geoff Grandberg	.10	.20
84	Cam Danyluk	.10	.20
85	Kerry Toporowski	.10	.20
86	Trevor Tovell	.10	.20
87	Pat Falloon	1.50	3.00
88	Bram Vanderkracht	.10	.20

No.	Player	EX	NRMT
89	Mike Jickling	.10	.20
90	Murray Garbutt	.10	.20
91	Calvin Thudium	.10	.20
92	Mark Woolf	.10	.20
93	Shane Maitland	.10	.20
94	Bart Cote	.10	.20
95	Bryan Maxwell, Coach	.10	.20

OSHAWA GENERALS

No.	Player	EX	NRMT
96	Eric Lindros (W/D)	37.50	75.00

PROJECTED DRAFT PICKS

No.	Player	EX	NRMT
97	Scott Niedermayer	1.00	2.00
98	Patrick Poulin	.75	1.50
99	Brent Bilodeau	.35	.75
100	Pat Falloon	1.25	2.50
101	Darcy Werenka	.35	.75
102	Martin Lapointe	.50	1.00
103	Philippe Boucher	.35	.75
104	Jeff Nelson	.35	.75
105	Rene Corbet	.35	.75
106	Pat Peake (W/D)	5.00	10.00
107	Steve Staios (W/D)	2.50	5.00

No.	Player	EX	NRMT
108	Richard Matvichuk	.35	.75
109	Dean McAmmond	.35	.75
110	Alex Stojanov (W/D)	2.00	4.00
111	Glen Murray (W/D)	3.75	7.50
112	Tyler Wright	.35	.75
113	Jason Dawe (W/D)	2.50	5.00
114	Nathan LaFayette (W/D)	3.75	7.50
115	Yanic Perreault	.75	1.50
116	Guy Leveque (W/D)	2.00	4.00
117	Darren Van Impe	.25	.50
118	Shayne Antoski (W/D)	2.00	4.00
119	Eric Lindros (W/D)	37.50	75.00
120	Dennis Perdie (W/D)	2.00	4.00
121	Terry Chitaroni (W/D)	2.00	4.00
122	Jamie Pushor	.25	.50
123	Chris Osgood	.75	1.50
124	Jamie Mathews (W/D)	.20	.40
125	Yves Sarault	.15	.30
126	Yanick Dupre	.20	.40
127	Brad Zimmer	.15	.30
128	Copps Coliseum	.10	.20
129	Jason Widmer	.15	.30
130	Marc Savard	.15	.30

Note: (W/D) denotes cards which were withdrawn from the issue.

7th Inning Sketch 1990 Issue
Card No. 99, O.H.L. Champions, Oshawa Generals

ONTARIO AND QUEBEC HOCKEY LEAGUES

ANONYMOUS

— 1952 - 53 ISSUE —

Card Size: 2" X 3"
Face: Blue tint photo, white border
Back: Black on card stock; Name, Team, Position, Resume, Number
Imprint: None
Complete Set No.: 182
Complete Set Price: 300.00 600.00 1,200.00
Common Player: 5.00 10.00 20.00

WINDSOR

No.	Player	VG	EX	NRMT
1	Dennis Riggin	5.00	10.00	20.00
2	Joe Zorica	5.00	10.00	20.00
3	Larry Hillman	5.00	10.00	20.00
4	Edward Reid	8.00	20.00	40.00
5	Al Arbour	17.50	35.00	75.00
6	Marlin McAlendin	15.00	30.00	60.00
7	Ross Graham	5.00	10.00	20.00
8	Cumming Burton	5.00	10.00	20.00
9	Ed Palamar	5.00	10.00	20.00
10	Elmer Skov	5.00	10.00	20.00
11	Eddie Louttit	5.00	10.00	20.00
12	Gerry Price	5.00	10.00	20.00
13	Lou Dietrich	5.00	10.00	20.00
14	Gaston Marcotte	5.00	10.00	20.00
15	Bob Brown	5.00	10.00	20.00
16	Archie Burton	5.00	10.00	20.00

ST. CATHERINES

No.	Player	VG	EX	NRMT
17	Marven Edwards, Goalie	5.00	10.00	20.00
18	Norman Defelice	5.00	10.00	20.00
19	Pete Kamula	5.00	10.00	20.00
20	Charles Marshall	5.00	10.00	20.00
21	Alex Leslie	5.00	10.00	20.00
22	Minpy Roberts	5.00	10.00	20.00
23	Danny Poliziani	5.00	10.00	20.00
24	Allen Kellog	5.00	10.00	20.00
25	Brian Cullen	11.25	22.50	45.00
26	Ken Schinkel	8.00	20.00	40.00
27	W. Hass	5.00	10.00	20.00
28	Don Nash	5.00	10.00	20.00
29	Robert Maxwell	5.00	10.00	20.00
30	Eddie Mateka	5.00	10.00	20.00
31	Joe Kastelic	8.00	20.00	40.00
32	Hank Ciesla	7.00	15.00	35.00
33	Hugh Barlow	5.00	10.00	20.00
34	Claude Roy, Goalie	5.00	10.00	20.00

THREE RIVERS

No.	Player	VG	EX	NRMT
35	Jean-Guy Gamache	5.00	10.00	20.00
36	Leon Michelin	5.00	10.00	20.00
37	Gerard Bergeron	5.00	10.00	20.00
38	Herve Lalonde	5.00	10.00	20.00
39	J.M. Cossette	5.00	10.00	20.00
40	Jean-Guy Gendron	10.00	20.00	40.00
41	Camille Bedard	5.00	10.00	20.00
42	Alfred Soucy	5.00	10.00	20.00
43	Jean Leclerc	5.00	10.00	20.00
44	Raymond St. Cyr	5.00	10.00	20.00
45	Lester Lahaye	5.00	10.00	20.00
46	Yvan Houle	5.00	10.00	20.00
47	Louis Desrosiers	5.00	10.00	20.00

GUELPH

No.	Player	VG	EX	NRMT
48	Douglas Lessor	5.00	10.00	20.00
49	Irvin Scott	5.00	10.00	20.00
50	Danny Blair, Guelph	5.00	10.00	20.00
51	Jim Connelly, Guelph	5.00	10.00	20.00
52	William Chalmers	5.00	10.00	20.00
53	Frank Bettiol	5.00	10.00	20.00
54	James Holmes	5.00	10.00	20.00
55	Birley Dimme	5.00	10.00	20.00
56	Donald Beattie	5.00	10.00	20.00
57	Terrance Chattington	5.00	10.00	20.00

Anonymous
1952 - 53 Issue
Card No. 26,
Ken Schinkel

Anonymous
1952 - 53 Issue
Card No. 73,
Camille Henri

No.	Player	VG	EX	NRMT
58	Bruce Wallace	5.00	10.00	20.00
59	William McCreary	10.00	20.00	45.00
60	Fred Brady	5.00	10.00	20.00
61	Ronald Murphy	5.00	10.00	20.00
62	Lavi Purola	5.00	10.00	20.00
63	George Whyte	5.00	10.00	20.00

CITADELS

No.	Player	VG	EX	NRMT
64	Marcel Paille, Goalie	10.00	25.00	50.00
65	Maurice Collins	5.00	10.00	20.00
66	Gerard Houle	5.00	10.00	20.00
67	Gilles Laperriere	5.00	10.00	20.00
68	Robert Chevalier	5.00	10.00	20.00
69	Bertrand Lepage	5.00	10.00	20.00
70	Michel Labadie	5.00	10.00	20.00
71	Gabriel Alain	5.00	10.00	20.00
72	Jean-Jacques Pichette	5.00	10.00	20.00
73	Camille Henri	10.00	25.00	50.00
74	Jean-Guy Gignac	5.00	10.00	20.00
75	Leo Amadio	5.00	10.00	20.00
76	Gilles Thibault	5.00	10.00	20.00
77	Gaston Pelletier	5.00	10.00	20.00
78	Adolph Kukulowicz	5.00	10.00	20.00
79	Roland Leclerc	5.00	10.00	20.00
80	Phil Watson	12.00	30.00	60.00
81	Raymond Cyr	5.00	10.00	20.00
82	Jacques Marcotte	5.00	10.00	20.00

OSHAWA

No.	Player	VG	EX	NRMT
83	Floyd Hillman	5.00	10.00	20.00
84	Bob Attersley	5.00	10.00	20.00
85	Harry Sinden	20.00	40.00	85.00
86	Stan Parker, Error	5.00	10.00	20.00
87	Bob Mader	5.00	10.00	20.00
88	Roger Maisonneuve	5.00	10.00	20.00
89	Phil Chapman	5.00	10.00	20.00
90	Don McIntosh	5.00	10.00	20.00
91	Jack Armstrong	5.00	10.00	20.00
92	Carlo Montemurro	5.00	10.00	20.00
93	Ken Courtney, Goalie	5.00	10.00	20.00
94	Bill Stewart	5.00	10.00	20.00
95	Gerald Casey	5.00	10.00	20.00
96	Fred Etcher	5.00	10.00	20.00

BARRIE

No.	Player	VG	EX	NRMT
97	Orrin Carver	5.00	10.00	20.00
98	Ralph Willis	5.00	10.00	20.00
99	Kenneth Robertson	5.00	10.00	20.00
100	Donald Cherry	30.00	60.00	125.00
101	Fred Pletsch	5.00	10.00	20.00
102	Larry Thibault	5.00	10.00	20.00
103	James Robertson	5.00	10.00	20.00
104	Orval Tessier	10.00	25.00	50.00
105	Jack Higgins	5.00	10.00	20.00
106	Robert White	12.00	30.00	60.00
107	Doug Mohns	10.00	25.00	50.00
108	William Sexton	5.00	10.00	20.00
109	John Martan	5.00	10.00	20.00
110	Tony Poeta	12.00	30.00	60.00
111	Don McKenney	10.00	25.00	50.00
112	Bill Harrington	5.00	10.00	20.00
113	Allen Peal	5.00	10.00	20.00

KITCHENER

No.	Player	VG	EX	NRMT
114	John Ford	5.00	10.00	20.00
115	Ken Collins	5.00	10.00	20.00
116	Marc Boileau	5.00	10.00	20.00
117	Doug Vaughan	5.00	10.00	20.00
118	Gilles Boisvert	5.00	10.00	20.00
119	Buddy Horne	5.00	10.00	20.00
120	Graham Joyce	5.00	10.00	20.00
121	Gary Collins	5.00	10.00	20.00
122	Roy Greenan	5.00	10.00	20.00
123	Beryl Klynck	5.00	10.00	20.00

Anonymous
1952 - 53 Issue
Card No. 86, Error,
Team name misspelled
Owhawa on back

— 1989 - 90 REGULAR ISSUE — 7TH INNING SKETCH • 719

No.	Player	VG	EX	NRMT
124	Grieg Hicks	5.00	10.00	20.00
125	Jack Novak	5.00	10.00	20.00
126	Ken Tennant	5.00	10.00	20.00
127	Glen Cressman	5.00	10.00	20.00
128	Curly Davies, Coach / Manager	15.00	35.00	75.00

CANADIAN JR.

No.	Player	VG	EX	NRMT
129	Charlie Hodge, Goalie	22.50	45.00	90.00
130	Bob McCord	5.00	10.00	20.00
131	Gordie Hollingworth	5.00	10.00	20.00
132	Ronald Pilon	5.00	10.00	20.00
133	Brian MacKay	5.00	10.00	20.00
134	Yvon Chasle	5.00	10.00	20.00
135	Denis Boucher	5.00	10.00	20.00
136	Claude Boileau	5.00	10.00	20.00
137	Claude Vinet	5.00	10.00	20.00
138	Claude Provost	15.00	35.00	75.00
139	Henri Richard	65.00	125.00	250.00
140	Les Lilley	5.00	10.00	20.00
141	Phil Goyette	10.00	25.00	50.00
142	Guy Rousseau	5.00	10.00	20.00

ST. MICHAEL'S

No.	Player	VG	EX	NRMT
143	Paul Knox	5.00	10.00	20.00
144	Bill Lee	5.00	10.00	20.00
145	Ted Topazzini	5.00	10.00	20.00
146	Marc Reaume	6.25	12.50	25.00
147	Bill Dineen	15.00	30.00	60.00
148	Ed Plata	5.00	10.00	20.00
149	Noel Price	10.00	25.00	50.00
150	Mike Ratchford	5.00	10.00	20.00
151	Jim Logan	5.00	10.00	20.00
152	Art Clune	5.00	10.00	20.00

Anonymous
1952-53 Issue
Card No. 147,
Bill Dineen

No.	Player	VG	EX	NRMT
153	Jerry MacNamara	10.00	25.00	50.00
154	Jack Caffery	10.00	25.00	50.00
155	Less Duff	5.00	10.00	20.00
156	Murray Costello	10.00	25.00	50.00
157	Ed. Chadwick, Goalie	12.00	30.00	60.00

ROYAL DE MONTREAL

No.	Player	VG	EX	NRMT
158	Mike Desilets	5.00	10.00	20.00
159	Ross Watson	5.00	10.00	20.00
160	Roger Landry	5.00	10.00	20.00
161	Terry O'Connor	5.00	10.00	20.00
162	Ovila Gagnon	5.00	10.00	20.00
163	Dave Broadbelt	5.00	10.00	20.00
164	Sandy Monrisson	5.00	10.00	20.00
165	John MacGillvray	5.00	10.00	20.00
166	Claude Beaupre	5.00	10.00	20.00
167	Eddie Eustache	5.00	10.00	20.00
168	Stan Rodek	5.00	10.00	20.00

GALT

No.	Player	VG	EX	NRMT
169	Maurice Mantha	5.00	10.00	20.00
170	Hector Lalonde	10.00	25.00	50.00
171	Bob Wilson	5.00	10.00	20.00
172	Frank Bonello	5.00	10.00	20.00
173	Peter Kowalchuck	5.00	10.00	20.00
174	Les Binkley	12.00	30.00	60.00
175	John Muckler	10.00	25.00	50.00
176	Ken Wharram	15.00	35.00	75.00
177	John Sleaver	5.00	10.00	20.00
178	Ralph Markarian	5.00	10.00	20.00
179	Ken McMeekin	5.00	10.00	20.00
180	Ron Boomer	5.00	10.00	20.00
181	Kenneth Crawford	5.00	10.00	20.00
182	Jim McBurney	5.00	10.00	20.00

Anonymous
1952-53 Issue
Card No. 154,
Jack Caffery

ONTARIO HOCKEY LEAGUE

7TH INNING SKETCH

— 1989 - 90 REGULAR ISSUE —

Card Size: 2 1/2" X 3 1/2"
Face: Four colour, yellow border
Back: Blue on white card stock, Resume, Position
Imprint: 7TH INNING SKETCH
Complete Set No.: 200

Complete Set Price:	35.00	75.00
Common Card:	.10	.20
Foil Pack: (10 Cards)		2.00
Foil Box: (36 Packs)		70.00
Foil Case: (20 Boxes)		1,300.00
Factory Set:		80.00

OSHAWA GENERALS

No.	Player	EX	NRMT
1	Eric Lindros	5.00	10.00
2	Jarrod Skalde	.35	.75
3	Joe Busillo	.10	.20
4	Dale Craigwell	.35	.75
5	Clair Cornish	.13	.25
6	Jean-Paul Davis	.13	.25
7	Craig Donaldson	.10	.20
8	Wade Simpson	.10	.20
9	Mike Craig	1.00	2.00
10	Mark Deazeley	.10	.20
11	Scott Hollis	.13	.25
12	Brian Grieve	.10	.20

7th Inning Sketch
1989-90 Issue
Card No. 1,
Eric Lindros

No.	Player	EX	NRMT
13	Dave Craievich, Error	.10	.20
14	Paul O'Hagan	.10	.20
15	Matt Hoffman	.25	.50
16	Trevor McIvor	.10	.20
17	Cory Banika	.10	.20
18	Kevin Butt, Goalie	.10	.20
19	Iain Fraser	.50	1.00
20	Bill Armstrong	.10	.20
21	Scott Luik	.25	.50
22	Brent Grieve	.35	.75
23	Fred Brathwaite, Goalie	.60	1.25

LONDON KNIGHTS

No.	Player	EX	NRMT
24	Paul Holden	.10	.20
25	Trevor Dam	.13	.25
26	Chris Taylor	.35	.75
27	Mark Guy	.10	.20
28	Louie DeBrusk	.60	1.25
29	John Battice	.10	.20
30	Chris Crombie	.10	.20
31	Sean Basilio, Goalie	.10	.20
32	Aaron Nagy	.10	.20
33	Greg Ryan	.10	.20
34	Steve Martell	.25	.50
35	Scott MacKay	.25	.50
36	Dennis Purdie	.25	.50
37	Steve Boyd	.10	.20

7TH INNING SKETCH — 1989-90 REGULAR ISSUE

No.	Player	EX	NRMT
38	John Tanner, Goalie	.10	.20
39	David Anderson	.10	.20
40	Rick Corriveau	.75	1.50
41	Todd Hlushko	.25	.50
42	Doug Synishin	.10	.20
43	Dan LeBlanc	.10	.20
44	Dave Noseworthy	.10	.20
45	Karl Taylor	.10	.20
46	Jeff Hogden	.10	.20
47	Mike Kelly / Gary Agnew, Asst. Coaches	.10	.20
48	Wayne Maxner, Coach	.10	.20

OTTAWA 67'S

No.	Player	EX	NRMT
49	Brett Seguin	.25	.50
50	Greg Walters	.10	.20
51	Chris Snell	.25	.50
52	Troy Binnie	.10	.20
53	Joni Lehto	.10	.20
54	Steve Kluczkowski	.10	.20
55	Ryan Kuwabara	.50	1.00
56	Chris Simon	.10	.20
57	Jerrett DeFazio	.25	.50
58	Robert Sangster	.10	.20
59	Greg Clancy	.25	.50
60	Peter Ambroziak	.25	.50
61	Jeff Ricciardi	.25	.50
62	John East	.10	.20
63	Joey McTamney	.10	.20
64	Dan Poirier	.10	.20
65	Gairin Smith	.10	.20
66	Wade Gibson	.10	.20

CHECKLIST

No.	Checklist	EX	NRMT
67	Checklist (1 - 88)	.10	.20

OTTAWA 67'S

No.	Player	EX	NRMT
68	Andrew Brodie	.10	.20
69	Craig Wilson	.10	.20
70	Peter McGlynn, Goalie	.10	.20
71	George Dourian, Goalie	.10	.20

BELLEVILLE BULLS

No.	Player	EX	NRMT
72	Bob Berg	.13	.25
73	Richard Fatrola	.13	.25
74	Craig Fraser	.13	.25
75	Brent Gretzky	1.50	3.00
76	Jake Grimes	.13	.25
77	Darren McCarty	.50	1.00
78	Ted Miskolczi	.25	.50
79	Rob Pearson	1.50	3.00
80	Gordon Pell	.10	.20
81	John Porco	.50	1.00
82	Ken Rowbotham	.10	.20
83	Scott Thornton	.35	.75
84	Shawn Way	.10	.20
85	Steve Bancroft	.10	.20
86	Greg Bignell	.10	.20
87	Scott Boston	.13	.25
88	Scott Feasby	.10	.20
89	Derek Morin	.10	.20
90	Sean O'Reilly	.13	.25
91	Jason Skellet	.10	.20
92	Greg Dreveny	.10	.20
93	Jeff Fife	.10	.20
94	Rob Stopar, Goalie	.10	.20
95	Joe Desrosiers, Trainer	.10	.20
96	Danny Flynn, Head Coach	.10	.20
97	Dr. R.L. Vaughan, Owner	.10	.20

PETERBOROUGH PETES

No.	Player	EX	NRMT
98	Troy Stephens	.25	.50
99	Dan Brown	.10	.20
100	Mike Ricci	2.50	5.00
101	Brent Pope	.10	.20
102	Mike Dagenais	.10	.20
103	Scott Campbell	.10	.20

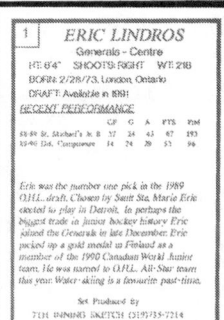

7th Inning Sketch
1989-90 Issue
Card No. 1,
Eric Lindros

7th Inning Sketch
1989-90 Issue
Card No. 82,
Ken Rowbotham

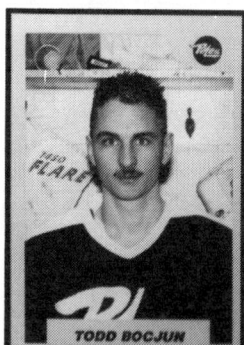

7th Inning Sketch
1989-90 Issue
Card No. 122, Error,
Name misspelled "Bocjun" on face

7th Inning Sketch
1989-90 Issue
Card No. 129,
Geoff Rawson

No.	Player	EX	NRMT
104	Jamie Pegg	.13	.25
105	Joe Hawley	.13	.25
106	Jason Dawe	.50	1.00
107	Paul Mitton	.10	.20
108	Mike Tomlinson	.13	.25
109	David Lorentz	.10	.20
110	Dale McTavish	.13	.25
111	Willie McGarvey	.10	.20
112	Don O'Neill	.10	.20
113	Mark Myles	.10	.20
114	Chris Longo	.20	.40
115	Tom Hopkins	.10	.20
116	Jassen Cullimore	.25	.50
117	Geoff Ingram	.10	.20
118	Twohey/Bovair, Asst. Coaches	.10	.20
119	Doug Searle	.10	.20
120	Bryan Gendron	.10	.20
121	Andrew Verner, Goalie	.35	.75
122	Todd Bojcun, Goalie, Error	.35	.75
123	Dick Todd, Head Coach	.10	.20
124	George Burnett, Head Coach	.10	.20

NIAGARA FALLS THUNDER

No.	Player	EX	NRMT
125	Brad May	1.25	2.50
126	David Benn	.10	.20
127	Brian Mueggler	.10	.20
128	Todd Coopman	.10	.20
129	Geoff Rawson	.10	.20
130	Keith Primeau	1.25	2.50
131	Mark Lawrence	.10	.20
132	Randy Hall, Asst. Coach/GM	.10	.20
133	Greg Suchan	.10	.20
134	Ken Ruddick	.10	.20
135	Jason Winch	.35	.75
136	Paul Wolanski	.25	.50
137	Dennis Scott, Trainer	.10	.20
138	Steve Udvari, Goalie	.10	.20
139	Roch Belley, Goalie	.10	.20
140	Donald Pancoe	.10	.20
141	Paul Bruneau, Asst. Trainer	.10	.20
142	Paul Laus	.10	.20
143	Mike St. John	.10	.20
144	John Johnson	.25	.50
145	Greg Allen	.10	.20
146	Don McConnell	.10	.20
147	Andy Bezeau	.10	.20
148	Jeff Walker	.10	.20

NORTH BAY CENTENNIALS

No.	Player	EX	NRMT
149	John Spoltore	.35	.75
150	Derek Switzer	.35	.75
151	Tyler Ertel	.15	.30
152	Shawn Antoski	.50	1.00
153	Jason Corrigan	.10	.20
154	Derian Hatcher	1.00	2.00
155	John Vary	.10	.20
156	Jamie Caruso	.13	.25
157	Trevor Halverson	.35	.75
158	Robert Deschamps	.10	.20
159	Jeff Gardiner	.10	.20
160	Gary Miller	.10	.20
161	Shayne Antoski	.20	.40
162	John Van Kessel	.10	.20
163	Colin Austin	.10	.20
164	Tom Purcell	.10	.20
165	Joel Morin	.10	.20
166	Tim Favot	.10	.20

CHECKLIST

No.	Checklist	EX	NRMT
167	Checklist (89 - 176)	.10	.20

NORTH BAY CENTENNIALS

No.	Player	EX	NRMT
168	Jason Beaton	.10	.20
169	Chris Ottmann	.10	.20
170	Mike Matuszek, Goalie	.10	.20
171	Rob Fournier, Goalie	.10	.20
172	Ron Bertrand, Goalie	.10	.20

No.	Player	EX	NRMT
173	Bert Templeton, Head Coach/GM	.10	.20
174	Centennials Mascot, Casey Jones	.10	.20
175	Robert Frayn	.10	.20
176	Claude Noel, Asst. Coach	.10	.20

AWARD CARDS

No.	Player	EX	NRMT
177	Sean Basilio, London Knights, P. W. Dinty Moore Trophy	.05	.15
178	Chris Longo, Peterborough Petes, Emms Family Award	.35	.75
179	Cory Keenan, Kitchener Rangers, Memorial Cup All-Star	.05	.15
180	Owen Nolan, Cornwall Royals, Jim Mahon Memorial Trophy	1.50	3.00
181	Steven Rice, Kitchener Rangers, Memorail Cup All-Star	.75	1.50
182	Shayne Stevenson, Kitchener Rangers, Memorial Cup Star	.10	.25
183	Mike Ricci, Peterborough Petes, William Hanley Trophy	1.50	3.00
184	Jason Firth, Kitchener Rangers, Memorial Cup Award	.10	.20
185	John Slaney, Cornwall Royals, Max Kaminsky Trophy	.05	.15
186	Iain Fraser, Oshawa Generals, Leo Lalonde Memorial Trophy	.50	1.00
187	Steven Rice, Kitchener Rangers, O.H.L. Play-Offs	.50	1.00
188	Eric Lindros, Oshawa Generals, O.H.L. Play-Off Leader	3.50	7.00
189	Primeau Scorer	.10	.25
190	Mike Ricci, Peterborough Petes, Red Tilson Trophy	1.00	2.00
191	Mike Torchia, Kitchener Rangers, Goalie, Memorial Cup All-Star	.05	.15
192	Mike Torchia, Kitchener Rangers, Goalie, O.H.L. Star	.05	.15
193	Jarrod Skalde, Oshawa Generals, Champions	.25	.50
194	Paul O'Hagan, Oshawa Generals, Memorial Cup All-Star	.05	.15
195	Eric Lindros, Oshawa Generals, Where in 91?	3.50	7.00
196	Eric Lindros, Oshawa Generals, Memorial Cup All-Star	3.50	7.00
197	Jeff Fife, Belleville Bulls, Goalie O.H.L. Star	.05	.15
198	Iain Fraser, Oshawa Generals, Memorial Cup - MVP	.05	.15
199	Bill Armstrong, Oshawa Generals, Overtime Winner	.05	.15

CHECKLIST
TOMORROW'S STARS TODAY

No.	Checklist	EX	NRMT
200	Checklist (177 - 200)	.10	.20

— 1990 - 91 PROMOTIONAL CARD —

Card Size: 2 1/2" X 3 1/2"
Face: Four colour, white border
Back: Four colour, Number, Resume, Position
Imprint: © 1991 7th Inning Sketch Printed in Canada

No.	Player	EX	NRMT
—	Eric Lindros	5.00	10.00

— 1990 - 91 REGULAR ISSUE —

Card Size: 2 1/2" X 3 1/2"
Face: Four colour, white border
Back: Four colour, Number, Resume, Position
Imprint: © 1991 7th Inning Sketch Printed in Canada
Complete Set No.: 400
Complete Set Price: 15.00 30.00
Common Goalie: .05 .10
Common Player: .05 .10
Foil Pack: (10 Cards) 1.00
Foil Box: (36 Packs) 25.00
Foil Case: (20 Boxes) 400.00
PRODUCTION:
Foil Cases: 5,000
Set Cases: 750 (9,000 individually numbered sets)

7th Inning Sketch
1989-90 Issue
Card No. 178,
Emms Family Award
Chris Longo

7th Inning Sketch
1989-90 Issue
Card No. 180,
Jim Mahon Memorial Trophy,
Owen Nolan

7th Inning Sketch
1990-91 Issue
Card No. 1,
Eric Lindros

1990 - 91 PROMOTIONAL CARD — 7TH INNING SKETCH

DAVID BRANCH CHRISTMAS CARDS

No.	Player	EX	NRMT
—	White card stock	2.50	5.00
—	Silver foil card stock	5.00	10.00

OSHAWA GENERALS

No.	Player	EX	NRMT
1	Eric Lindros, Error	7.50	15.00

ERROR AND VARIATION LISTING

No.	Player	Description
1	Lindros	Photo on back is rotated

BELLEVILLE BULLS

No.	Player	EX	NRMT
2	Greg Dreveny, Goalie, Error	.05	.10
3	Team Checklist, Error	.25	.50
4	Richard Fatrola, Error	.25	.50
5	Craig Fraser	.25	.50
6	Robert Frayn	.05	.10
7	Brent Gretzky	.60	1.25
8	Jake Grimes	.25	.50
9	Darren Hurley	.05	.10
10	Rick Marshall	.05	.10

ERROR AND VARIATION LISTING

No.	Player	Description
2	Dreveny	Photo on back is inverted
3	Checklist	Fatrola's name misspelled Fratrola
4	Fatrola	Incorrectly states "Draft eligible in 1990"

KINGSTON FRONTENACS

No.	Checklist	EX	NRMT
11	Team Checklist, Error	.25	.50

ERROR AND VARIATION LISTING

No.	Checklist	Description
11	Checklist	Name listed as "Bernie John" should be John Bernie

BELLEVILLE BULLS

No.	Players	EX	NRMT
12	Darren McCarty	.25	.50
13	Derek Morin	.05	.10
14	Sean O'Reilly	.15	.30
15A	Rob Pearson, Error	1.00	2.00
15B	Rob Pearson, Corrected	1.50	3.00
16	John Porco	.35	.75
17	Ken Rowbotham	.05	.10
18	Ken Ruddick	.05	.10
19	Jim Sonmez	.13	.25
20	Brad Teichmann, Goalie	.05	.10
21	Chris Varga	.25	.50

ERROR AND VARIATION LISTING

No.	Player	Description
15	Pearson	Listed as a Belleville Bull, plays for Oshawa

CORNWALL ROYALS

No.	Checklist	EX	NRMT
22	Team Checklist	.25	.50

BELLEVILLE BULLS

No.	Player	EX	NRMT
23	Larry Mavety, Coach	.05	.10

See Card Nos. 340 and 346 for more Belleville players

CORNWALL ROYALS

No.	Player	EX	NRMT
24A	Rival Fullum, Variation	.15	.30
24B	Rival Fullum,	.15	.30
25A	Nathan LaFayette, Variation	.75	1.50
25B	Nathan LaFayette,	.75	1.50
26	Darren Bell	.10	.20
27	Craig Brockelhurst	.05	.10
28	Shawn Caplice	.05	.10
29	Mike Cavanagh	.20	.40
30	Jason Cirone	.10	.20
31	Chris Clancy	.05	.10

722 • 7TH INNING SKETCH — 1990 - 91 REGULAR ISSUE

No.	Player	EX	NRMT
32	Mark DeSantis	.05	.10
33	Rob Dykeman, Goalie	.05	.10
34	Shayne Gaffar	.13	.25
35	Ilpo Kauhanen, Goalie	.05	.10
36	Rob Kinghan	.05	.10
37	Dave Lemay	.05	.10
38	Guy Leveque	.50	1.00
39	Matt McGuffin	.05	.10
40	Marcus Middleton	.05	.10
41	Thomas Nemeth	.13	.25
42	Rod Pasma	.05	.10
43	Richard Raymond, Error	.05	.10
44	Jeff Reid	.13	.25
45	Jerry Ribble	.05	.10
46	Jean-Alain Schneider	.10	.20
47	John Slaney	.35	.75
48	Jeremy Stevenson	.10	.20
49	Ryan VandenBussche	.05	.10
50	Marc Crawford, Coach, Error	.55	.75

ERROR AND VARIATION LISTING

No.	Player	Description
24	Fullum	Different typestyle used for team name and card no. on back. Two cards were issued for Fullum: No. 24 - Cornwall Royals, No. 182 - Windsor Spitfires. He was traded from from Cornwall to Windsor
25	LaFayette	Different typestyle used for team name and card no. on back
43	Raymond	Rob Ramage misspelled "Rammage" on back
50	Crawford	Photo on back is inverted

KINGSTON FRONTENACS

No.	Player	EX	NRMT
51	Tony Bella	.05	.10
52	Drake Berehowsky, Error	.75	1.50
53	Jason Chipman, Goalie	.05	.10
54	Tony Cimellaro	.25	.50
55	Keli Corpse	.10	.20
56A	Mike Dawson, Error	.05	.10
56B	Mike Dawson, Corrected	.05	.10
57	Sean Gauthier, Goalie	.05	.10
58	Fred Goltz, Error	.05	.10
59	Gord Harris	.10	.20
60	Tony Iob	.10	.20
61	John Bernie	.05	.10
62	Dale Junkin	.05	.10
63	Nathan Lafayette	.75	1.50
64	Blake Martin	.05	.10
65	Mark McCague	.05	.10
66	Bob McKillop	.20	.40
67	Justin Morrison	.25	.50
68	Bill Robinson	.05	.10
69	Joel Sandie	.05	.10
70	Kevin King	.05	.10
71	Dave Stewart	.13	.25
72	Joel Washkurak	.05	.10
73	Brock Woods	.05	.10
74	Randy Hall, Coach	.05	.10
75A	John Vary, Error	.15	.30
75B	John Vary, Corrected	.15	.30

ERROR AND VARIATION LISTING

No.	Player	Description
52	Berehowsky	Team on back listed as Kingston should be North Bay
56	Dawson	League misspelled on back
58	Goltz	Photos on face and back are not Goltz
75	Vary	Printing error on back

OTTAWA 67'S

No.	Player	EX	NRMT
76	Peter Ambroziak	.13	.25
77	Troy Binnie	.10	.20
78	Curt Bowen	.05	.10
79	Andrew Brodie	.05	.10
80	Team Checklist	.13	.25
81	Greg Clancy	.05	.10
82	Jerrett DeFazio	.25	.50
83	Kris Draper	.75	1.50
84	Wade Gibson	.05	.10
85	Ryan Kuwabara	.13	.25

7th Inning Sketch
1990-91 Issue
Card No. 15A, Error,
Rob Pearson

7th Inning Sketch
1990-91 Issue
Card No. 43, Error,
Richard Raymond

7th Inning Sketch
1990-91 Issue
Card No. 52, Error,
Drake Berehowsky

7th Inning Sketch
1990-91 Issue
Card No. 101, Error,
Kevin Butt

No.	Player	EX	NRMT
86	Joni Lehto	.05	.10
87	Donald MacPherson	.05	.10
88	Grant Marshall	.35	.75
89	Pete McGlynn, Goalie	.05	.10
90	Maurice O'Brien	.05	.10
91	Jeff Ricciardi	.25	.50
92	Brett Seguin	.75	1.50
93A	Lenny DeVuono, Error	.10	.20
93B	Lenny DeVuono, Corrected	.10	.20
94	Gerry Skrypec	.05	.10
95	Chris Snell	.35	.75
96	Jason Snow	.05	.10
97	Sean Spencer, Goalie	.05	.10
98	Brad Spry	.05	.10
99	Matt Stone	.05	.10
100	Brian Kilrea, Coach	.05	.10

ERROR AND VARIATION LISTING

No.	Player	Description
93	DeVuono	Card number misprinted 230

DETROIT COMPUWARE AMBASSADORS

No.	Player	EX	NRMT
101	Kevin Butt, Goalie, Error	.05	.10
102	Glen Craig	.05	.10
103	Paul Doherty	.05	.10
104	Mark Donahue	.05	.10
105	Jeff Gardiner	.20	.40
106	Trent Gleason	.10	.20
107	Troy Gleason	.05	.10
108	Mark Lawrence	.10	.20
109	Trevor McIvor, Error	.05	.10
110	Paul Mitton	.05	.10
111	David Myles	.05	.10
112	Jeff Nolan, Error	.05	.10
113	Rob Papineau	.10	.20
114A	Pat Peake, Error	1.00	2.00
114B	Pat Peake, Corrected	1.00	2.00
115	Chris Phelps	.05	.10
116	John Pinches	.05	.10
117A	Jamie Shea, Goalie, Error	.15	.30
117B	Jamie Shea, Goalie, Corrected	.15	.30
118A	Jamie Sheehan, Error	.05	.10
118B	Jamie Sheehan, Corrected	.05	.10
119	John Stios, Error	.05	.10
120	Tom Sullivan	.10	.20
121	John Wynne	.15	.30

ERROR AND VARIATION LISTING

No.	Player	Description
101	Butt	Photo on back is not Butt
109	McIvor	Photos on face and back are not McIvor
112	Nolan	Name "Jeffrey" should be Jeff
114	Peake	Name "Patrick" should be Pat
117	Shea	Name "James" should be Jamie
118	Sheehan	Name "James" should be Jamie
119	Stos	Name misspelled on face "Jon" Photo on back is inverted

NORTH BAY CENTENNIALS

No.	Player	EX	NRMT
122	Robert Thorpe, Error	.05	.10

ERROR AND VARIATION LISTING

No.	Player	Description
122	Thorpe	Different typestyle on back

DETROIT COMPUWARE AMBASSADORS

No.	Player	EX	NRMT
123	David Benn	.05	.10
124	Andy Weidenbach, Coach, Error	.05	.10
125	Team Checklist	.25	.50

ERROR AND VARIATION LISTING

No.	Player	Description
124	Weidenbach	Name misspelled on back "Weidenback"

LONDON KNIGHTS

No.	Player	EX	NRMT
126	David Anderson	.10	.20
127	Sean Basilio, Goalie, Error	.10	.20

1990 - 91 REGULAR ISSUE — 7TH INNING SKETCH • 723

No.	Player	EX	NRMT
128	Brent Brownlee, Goalie	.05	.10
129	Rick Corriveau	.50	1.00
130	Derrick Crane	.05	.10
131	Chris Crombie	.15	.30
132	Louie DeBrusk	.50	1.00
133	Mark Guy	.10	.20
134	Brett Marietti	.05	.10
135	Steve Martell	.10	.20
136	Scott McKay	.10	.20
137	Aaron Nagy	.05	.10
138	Brett Nicol	.05	.10
139	Barry Potomski	.10	.20
140	Dennis Purdie	.10	.20
141	Kelly Reed	.05	.10
142	Gregory Ryan	.05	.10
143	Brad Smyth	.05	.10

ERROR AND VARIATION LISTING

No.	Player	Description
127	Basilio	Photo on back is inverted

LONDON KNIGHTS

No.	Player	EX	NRMT
144	Nick Stajduhar	.05	.10
145	John Tanner, Goalie, Error	.35	.75
146	Chris Taylor	.13	.25
147	Mark Visheau	.05	.10
148	Gary Agnew, Coach, Error	.05	.10
149	Team Checklist	.10	.20

ERROR AND VARIATION LISTING

No.	Player	Description
145	Tanner	Two cards were issued for Tanner: No. 145 - London Knights No. 377 - Sudbury Wolves He was traded from London to Sudbury
148	Agnew	Photo on back is inverted

SAULT STE. MARIE GREYHOUNDS

No.	Player	EX	NRMT
150	Team Checklist	.25	.50
151	David Babcock	.05	.10
152	Drew Bannister	.05	.10
153	Bob Boughner	.05	.10
154	Joe Busillo, Error	.10	.20
155	Mike DeCoff	.10	.20
156	Jason Denomme	.10	.20
157	Adam Foote	.25	.50
158	Kevin Hodson, Goalie	.05	.10
159	Shaun Imber, Error	.05	.10
160	Ralph Intranuovo	.35	.75
161	Kevin King	.05	.10
162	Rick Kowalsky	.05	.10
163	Chris Kraemer, Error	.05	.10
164	Denny Lambert	.25	.50
165	Mike Lenarduzzi, Goalie	.20	.40
166	Tom MacDonald	.10	.20
167	Mark Matier	.05	.10
168	David Matsos	.05	.10
169	Colin Miller	..10	.20
170	Perry Pappas	.05	.10
171	Jarret Reid	.10	.20
172	Kevin Reid	.05	.10
173	Brad Tiley, Error	.10	.20

ERROR AND VARIATION LISTING

No.	Player	Description
154	Busillo	Incorrectly listed as draft eligible in 1990
159	Imber	Incorrectly listed as draft eligible in 1990
163	Kraemer	Incorrectly listed as draft eligible in 1990
173	Tiley	Defence misspelled "Deffence" on back

WINDSOR SPITFIRES

No.	Checklist	EX	NRMT
174	Team Checklist	.25	.50

SAULT STE. MARIE GREYHOUNDS

No.	Player	EX	NRMT
175	Wade Whitten	.05	.10
176	Ted Nolan	.05	.10

7th Inning Sketch
1990-91 Issue
Card No. 145, Error,
John Tanner

7th Inning Sketch
1990-91 Issue
Card No. 163, Error,
Chris Kraemer

7th Inning Sketch
1990-91 Issue
Card No. 173, Error,
Brad Tiley

7th Inning Sketch
1990-91 Issue
Card No. 178, Error,
Jason Cirone

WINDSOR SPITFIRES

No.	Player	EX	NRMT
177	Sean Burns	.05	.10
178	Jason Cirone, Error	.10	.20
179	John Copley	.05	.10
180	Tyler Ertel	.13	.25
181	Brian Forestell	.05	.10
182	Rival Fullum, Error	.05	.10
183	Steve Gibson	.10	.20
184	Leonard MacDonald	.10	.20
185	Mike Speer, Error	.13	.25
186	Kevin MacKay	.15	.35
187	Ryan Merritt	.13	.25
188	Doug Minor	.05	.10
189	Rick Morton	.05	.10
190	Sean O'Hagan, Goalie	.05	.10
191	Mike Polano	.05	.10
192	Cory Stillman	.25	.50
193	Jason Stos	.10	.20
194	Trevor Walsh	.10	.20
195	Todd Warriner	1.00	2.00
196	Jeff Wilson, Goalie	.15	.30
197	Jason York	.13	.25
198	Jason Zohil, Error	.05	.10
199	Steve Smith, Error	.05	.10
200	Brad Smith, Coach	.05	.10

ERROR AND VARIATION LISTING

No.	Player	Description
178	Cirone	Different typestyle used for team name and card number on back
182	Fullum	Two cards were issued for Fullum: No. 24 - Cornwall Royals No. 182 - Windsor Spitfires; He was traded from Cornwall to Windsor
185	Speer	Different typestyle used for team name and card number on back Two cards were issued for Speer: No. 185 - Windsor Spitfires No. 294 - Owen Sound Platers
198	Zohil	Two cards were issued for Zohil: No. 198 - Windsor Spitfires No. 243 - Kitchener Rangers, Zohil was traded from Windsor to Kitchener
199	Smith	Different typestyle used for team name and card number on back

DUKES OF HAMILTON

No.	Player	EX	NRMT
201	Jeff Bes	.13	.25
202	Ken Blum	.10	.20
203	Sean Brown	.08	.15
204	Darcy Cahill	.10	.20
205	Dale Chokan	.05	.10
206	Chris Code	.10	.20
207	George Dourian, Goalie	.05	.10
208	Todd Gleason	.05	.10
209	Team Checklist, Error,	.13	.25
210	Michael Hartwick	.05	.10
211	Scott Jenkins	.05	.10
212	Rob Leask	.05	.10
213	Gordon Pell	.05	.10
214	Michael Reier	.15	.35
215	Kayle Short	.05	.10
216	Jason Skellett	.05	.10
217	Gairin Smith	.20	.40
218	Jeff Smith	.05	.10
219	Jason Soules	.25	.50
220	Alexandar Stojanov	.25	.50
221	Dan Tanevski, Goalie	.05	.10
222	Gary Taylor	.05	.10
223	Brent Watson	.05	.10
224	Steve Woods	.05	.10
225	Jay Johnston, Coach, Error	.05	.10

ERROR AND VARIATION LISTING

No.	Player	Description
209	Checklist	Team incorrectly called "Hamilton Dukes"
225	Johnston	Number on card shown as "299"

KITCHENER RANGERS

No.	Player	EX	NRMT
226	Mike Allen	.05	.10
227	Brad Barton	.10	.20
228	Richard Borgo	.10	.20

724 • 7TH INNING SKETCH — 1990-91 REGULAR ISSUE

No.	Player	EX	NRMT
229	Justin Cullen	.05	.10

OTTAWA 67'S

No.	Player	EX	NRMT
230	Len DeVuono, Error	.05	.10

ERROR AND VARIATION LISTING

No.	Player	Description
230	Len DeVuono	Traded from Kitchener to Ottawa

KITCHENER RANGERS

No.	Player	EX	NRMT
231	Norman Dezainde	.10	.15
232	Jason Firth	.10	.20
233	Derek Gauthier	.10	.20
234	Jamie Israel	.05	.10
235	Chris LiPuma	.15	.30
236	Tony McCabe	.20	.40
237A	Paul McCallion, Error	.05	.10
237B	Paul McCallion, Corrected	.05	.10
238	Shayne McCosh	.05	.10
239	Rod Saarinen	.05	.10
240	Steve Smith	.05	.10
241	Joey St. Aubin, Error	.10	.20
242	Rob Stopar, Goalie	.05	.10
243	Jason Zohil, Error	.10	.20
244	Mike Torchia, Goalie	.35	.75
245	Gib Tucker	.10	.20
246	John Uniac	.13	.25
247	Jack Williams	.13	.25
248	Joe McDonnell, Coach	.05	.10
249	Steve Rice, Error	.50	1.00
250	Mike Polano, Error	.10	.20

ERROR AND VARIATION LISTING

No.	Player	Description
237	McCallion	Text reads "Jan. 11,1984", no space after comma
241	St. Aubin	Incorrectly listed as draft eligible in 1990
243	Zohil	Missing card number on back
249	McDonnell	Different typestyle used for back
250	Polano	Different typestyle used for team name and card number on back

NIAGARA FALLS THUNDER

No.	Player	EX	NRMT
251	Greg Allen	.10	.20
252	Roch Belley, Goalie	.05	.10
253	Andy Bezeau	.05	.10
254	Derek Booth, Error	.10	.20
255	Kevin Brown	.10	.20
256	Mark Cardiff	.05	.10
257	Jason Coles	.05	.10
258	Todd Coopman	.07	.15
259	Richard Girhiny	.05	.10
260	Brian Holk	.05	.10
261	John Johnson	.35	.75
262	Dan Krisko	.07	.15
263	Manny Legace, Goalie, Error	.35	.75
264	Brad May	.50	1.00
265	Don McConnell	.05	.10
266	Team Checklist, Error	.25	.50
267	Aaron Morrison	.05	.10
268	Cory Pageau	.10	.20
269	Geoff Rawson	.10	.20
270	Todd Simon	.35	.75
271	Steve Staios	.15	.30
272	Jeff Walker	.05	.10
273	Todd Wetzel	.05	.10
274	Jason Winch	.10	.20
275	Paul Wolanski	.10	.20

ERROR AND VARIATION LISTING

No.	Player	Description
254	Booth	Incorrectly listed as draft eligible in 1990
263	Legace	Photo on back is inverted
266	Checklist	Todd Simon incorrectly listed as Jeff Simon

OWEN SOUND PLATERS

No.	Player	EX	NRMT
276	Team Checklist	.25	.50
277	Andrew Brunette	.15	.30

7th Inning Sketch
1990-91 Issue
Card No. 230, Error,
Len DeVuono

7th Inning Sketch
1990-91 Issue
Card No. 237A, Error,
Paul McCallion

7th Inning Sketch
1990-91 Issue
Card No. 263, Error,
Manny Legace

7th Inning Sketch
1990-91 Issue
Card No. 305A, Error,
Jamie Caruso

No.	Player	EX	NRMT
278	Wyatt Buckland	.10	.20
279	Jason Buetow	.05	.10
280	Jason Castellan	.05	.10
281	Trent Cull	.05	.10
282	Robert Deschamps	.05	.10
283	Chris Driscoll	.05	.10
284	Bryan Drury	.05	.10
285	Todd Hunter, Goalie	.05	.10
286	Troy Hutchinson	.05	.10
287	Kirk Maltby	.13	.25
288	Geordie Maynard	.10	.20
289	Kevin McDougall, Goalie	.05	.10
290	Ted Miskolczi	.13	.25
291	Steven Parson	.10	.20
292	Jeff Perry	.13	.25
293	Grayden Reid	.25	.50
294	Mike Speer, Error	.05	.10
295	Mark Strohack	.05	.10
296	Mark Vilneff	.05	.10
297	Keith Whitmore	.13	.25
298	Jim Brown	.10	.20
299	Len McNamara, Coach	.05	.10

ERROR AND VARIATION LISTING

No.	Player	Description
294	Speer	Two cards were issued for Speer: No. 244 - Owen Sound No. 185 - Windsor Spitfires He was traded from Owen Sound to Windsor

OHL COMMISSIONER

No.	Player	EX	NRMT
300	David Branch, Error	.15	.25

ERROR AND VARIATION LISTING

No.	Player	Description
300	Branch	On back Dukes of Hamilton listed as Hamilton Dukes

NORTH BAY CENTENNIALS

No.	Player	EX	NRMT
301	Shayne Antoski	.13	.25
302	Jason Beaton	.05	.10
303	Ron Bertrand, Goalie	.20	.40
304	Michael Burman	.05	.10
305A	Jamie Caruso, Error	.15	.30
305B	Jamie Caruso, Corrected	.20	.40
306	Allan Cox, Error	.05	.10
307	Tim Favot	.05	.10
308	Trevor Halverson	.30	.60
309	Derian Hatcher	.25	.50

ERROR AND VARIATION LISTING

No.	Player	Description
305	Caruso	Name misspelled "James"
306	Cox	Incorrectly listed as draft eligible in 1990

NORTH BAY CENTENNIALS

No.	Player	EX	NRMT
310	Bill Lang	.10	.20
311	Jason MacDonald	.10	.20
312	Gary Miller	.10	.20
313	Chris Ottmann	.05	.10
314	Chad Penney	.10	.20
315	Rick Pollard, Goalie, Error	.05	.10
316	Bradley Shepard	.05	.10
317	John Spoltore	.10	.20
318	Derek Switzer	.10	.20
319	Karl Taylor	.05	.10
320	John Vary	.05	.10
321A	Kevin White, Error	.15	.30
321B	Kevin White, Corrected	.10	.15
322	Billy Wright	.10	.20
323	Bert Templeton, Coach, Error	.05	.10
324	Team Checklist	.25	.50

ERROR AND VARIATION LISTING

No.	Player	Description
315	Pollard	Incorrectly listed as draft eligible in 1990
321	White	Name "K.J. White" name is Kevin J. White
323	Templeton	Photo on back is inverted

1990-91 REGULAR ISSUE — 7TH INNING SKETCH • 725

OSHAWA GENERALS

No.	Player	EX	NRMT
325	Oshawa Checklist	.25	.50
326	Jan Benda	.05	.10
327	Fred Brathwaite, Goalie	.13	.25
328	Markus Brunner	.10	.20
329	Trevor Burgess, Error	.05	.10
330	Clair Cornish	.20	.40
331	Mike Cote	.10	.20
332	David Craievich	.15	.30
333	Dale Craigwell	.35	.75
334	Jean-Paul Davis	.25	.50
335	Mark Deazeley	.10	.20
336	Mike Fountain, Goalie	.35	.75
337	Brain Grieve	.05	.10
338	Matt Hoffman, Error	.13	.25
339	Scott Hollis	.10	.20

ERROR AND VARIATION LISTING

No.	Player	Description
329	Burgess	Photo on face is Brian Grieve
338	Hoffman	Stats incorrectly states "shoots left"

BELLEVILLE BULLS

No.	Player	EX	NRMT
340	Scott Boston	.10	.20

OSHAWA GENERALS

No.	Player	EX	NRMT
341	Scott Luik	.15	.35
342A	Craig Lutes, Error	.05	.10
342B	Craig Lutes, Corrected	.05	.10
343	William MacPherson, Error	.05	.10
344	Paul O'Hagan	.10	.20
345	Wade Simpson	.05	.10

ERROR AND VARIATION LISTING

No.	Player	Description
342	Lutes	Name misspelled "Graig" on back
343	MacPherson	Name wrongly shown as "William" should be B.J. Photo on face and back show Jason Weaver

BELLEVILLE BULLS

No.	Player	EX	NRMT
346A	Jarrod Skalde, Error	.25	.50
346B	Jarrod Skalde, Corrected	.25	.50

ERROR AND VARIATION LISTING

No.	Player	Description
346A	Skalde	Listed as playing for the Oshawa Generals "Lefft" misspelled on back
346B	Skalde	"Lefft" misspelled on back, Osh. Gen. corrected

OSHAWA GENERALS

No.	Player	EX	NRMT
347	Troy Sweet	.05	.10
348	Jason Weaver, Error	.10	.20
349	Rick Cornacchia, Coach	.05	.10
350	The Trophy, Error	.18	.35

ERROR AND VARIATION LISTING

No.	Player	Description
348	Weaver	Photo on face is Craig Lutes
350	Trophy	Incorrectly states "Won in 1990-91" Photo on back is inverted

PETERBOROUGH PETES

No.	Player	EX	NRMT
351	Greg Bailey	.05	.10
352	Ryan Black	.05	.10
353	Todd Bojcun, Goalie, Error	.13	.25
354	Toby Burkitt, Error	.05	.20
355	Scott Campbell	.05	.10
356	Jassen Cullimore	.25	.50
357	Jason Dawe	.35	.75
358	Dan Ferguson	.05	.10
359	Bryan Gendron	.10	.20
360	Michael Harding	.15	.30
361	Joe Hawley	.25	.50
362	Team Checklist, Error	.25	.50
363	Geordie Kinnear	.05	.10
364	Chris Longo, Error	.25	.50
365	Dale McTavish	.15	.30
366	Mark Myles	.10	.20
367	Don O'Neill	.05	.10
368	Jamie Pegg	.15	.30
369	Brent Pope	.05	.10

ERROR AND VARIATION LISTING

No.	Player	Description
353	Bojcun	Photo on face - reversed negative
354	Burkitt	Incorrectly states "Draft Eligible in 1990"
362	Checklist	Jassen Cullimore's name misspelled "Jason"
364	Longo	Missing stats

KITCHENER RANGERS

No.	Player	EX	NRMT
370	Team Checklist, Error	.25	.50

ERROR AND VARIATION LISTING

No.	Player	Description
370	Checklist	Richard Borgo misspelled "Bargo"

PETERBOROUGH PETES

No.	Player	EX	NRMT
371	Douglas Searle	.05	.10
372	Troy Stephens, Error	.10	.20
373	Mike Tomlinson	.25	.50
374	Brent Tully	.05	.10
375	Andrew Verner, Goalie	.15	.30
376	Dick Todd, Coach, Error	.05	.10

ERROR AND VARIATION LISTING

No.	Player	Description
372	Stephens	Photo on back is inverted
376	Todd	Photo on back is inverted

SUDBURY WOLVES

No.	Player	EX	NRMT
377A	John Tanner, Goalie, Error	.10	.20
377B	John Tanner, Goalie, Corrected	.10	.20
378	Adam Bennett	.10	.20
379	Kyle Blacklock	.05	.10

No.	Player	EX	NRMT
380	Terry Chitaroni	.20	.40
381	Brandon Convery	.35	.75
382	J.D. Eaton	.05	.10
383	Derek Etches	.05	.10
384	Rod Hinks	.05	.10
385	Bill Kovacs	.10	.20
386	Alain Laforge, Error	.10	.20
387	Jamie Matthews	.10	.20
388	Glen Murray	.50	1.00
389	Dean Cull, Error	.10	.15
390	Sean O'Donnell	.10	.20
391	Team Checklist	.25	.50
392	Michael Peca, Error	.05	.10
393	Shawn Rivers, Error	.05	.10
394	Dan Ryder, Goalie	.05	.10
395	Alastair Still	.05	.10
396	Michael Yeo	.05	.10
397	Barry Young	.10	.20
398	Jason Young	.10	.20
399	Ken MacKenzie, Coach	.05	.10
400	Bob Berg, Error	.10	.20

ERROR AND VARIATION LISTING

No.	Player	Description
377	Tanner	Different typestyle used on back for team name and card number. Two cards were issued for Tanner: No. 145 - London Knights No. 377 - Sudbury Wolves He was traded from London to Sudbury
386	Laforge	Incorrectly states "Draft Eligible in 1990"
389	Cull	Different typestyle on back
392	Peca	Name misspelled on back "Micheal"
393	Rivers	Incorrectly states "Draft Eligible in 1990"
400	Berg	Different typestyle on back

7th Inning Sketch
1990-91 Issue
Card No. 329, Error,
Trevor Burgess

7th Inning Sketch
1990-91 Issue
Card No. 346A, Error,
Jarrod Skalde

7th Inning Sketch
1990-91 Issue
Card No. 372, Error,
Troy Stephens

7th Inning Sketch
1990-91 Issue
Card No. 400, Error,
Bob Berg

1991 - 92 REGULAR ISSUE

For the first time, this years foil packs contained an insert card. These cards numbered O(ntario) 1 to O 16 were randomly inserted in foil packs at the rate of one or two per foil box. "The Dream" collector's card was randomly inserted in foil packs of the OHL, QMJHL, and WHL

Note: Cards # 147 and 360 do not exist.
Card Size: 2 1/2" X 3 1/2"
Face: Four colour, white border
Back: Four colour, Number, Resume, Position, Bilingual
Imprint: © 1991 7TH Inning Sketch Printed in Canada
Complete Set No.: 383
Complete Set Price: 10.00 20.00
Common Card: .05 .10
Foil Pack: (10 Cards) .75
Foil Box: (36 Packs) 15.00
Foil Case: (20 Boxes) 200.00
Production:
Foil Cases: 3,000
Set Cases: N/A

THE DREAM

No.	Player	EX	NRMT
—	The Dream	2.50	5.00

CORNWALL ROYALS

No.	Player	EX	NRMT
1	John Slaney	.25	.50
2	Jason Meloche	.05	.10
3	Mark DeSantis	.05	.10
4	Richard Raymond	.05	.10
5	Dave Lemay	.05	.10
6	Matt McGuffin	.05	.10
7	Sam Oliveira	.05	.10
8	Jeremy Stevenson	.05	.10
9	Todd Walker	.05	.10
10	Jean-Alain Schneider	.05	.10
11	Guy Leveque	.13	.25
12	Shayne Gaffar	.05	.10
13	Mike Prokopec	.05	.10
14	Nathan Lafayette	.35	.75
15	Larry Courville	.05	.10
16	Chris Clancy	.05	.10
17	Thomas Nemeth	.05	.10
18	Jeff Reid	.05	.10
19	Ilpo Kauhanen, Goalie	.05	.10
20	Rob Dykeman, Goalie	.05	.10
21	Rival Fullum	.05	.10
22	Ryan VandenBussche	.05	.10
23	Gordon Pell	.05	.10
24	Paul Andrea, Error	.05	.10
25	John Lovell, Coach, Error	.05	.10
26	Alan Letang	.05	.10

ERROR AND VARIATION LISTING

No.	Player	Description
24	Andrea	"Generals" should be "Royals"
25	Lovell	"Generals" should be "Royals"

DETROIT COMPUWARE AMBASSADORS

No.	Player	EX	NRMT
27	Chris Phelps	.05	.10
28	John Wynne	.05	.10
29	Rob Kinghan	.05	.10
30	Glen Craig	.05	.10
31	Eric Cairns	.05	.10
32	John Pinches	.05	.10
33	Todd Harvey	.20	.40
34	Craig Fraser	.05	.10
35	Patrick Peake	.35	.75
36	Chris Skoryna	.05	.10
37	Bob Wren	.05	.10
38	Chris Varga	.10	.20
39	David Benn	.05	.10
40	Mark Lawrence	.20	.40
41	Jeff Kostuch	.05	.10
42	J. D. Eaton	.05	.10
43	Derek Etches	.05	.10
44	Jeff Gardiner	.10	.20
45	James Shea, Goalie	.05	.10
46	Brad Teichmann, Goalie	.05	.10
47	Jim Rutherford, GM-Coach	.05	.10
48	Derek Wilkinson	.05	.10

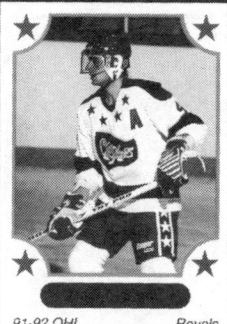

7th Inning Sketch
1991-92 Issue
Card No. 3,
Mark DeSantis

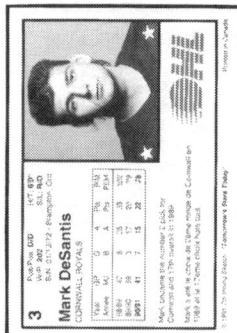

7th Inning Sketch
1991-92 Issue
Card No. 3,
Mark DeSantis

7th Inning Sketch
1991-92 Issue
Card No. 51,
Sandy Allan

7th Inning Sketch
1991-92 Issue
Card No. 80,
Trevor Gallant

91-92 OHL ACTION

No.	Player	EX	NRMT
49	OHL Action	.05	.10
50	OHL Action	.05	.10

NORTH BAY CENTENNIALS

No.	Player	EX	NRMT
51	Sandy Allan, Goalie	.05	.10
52	Ron Bertrand, Goalie	.10	.20
53	Brad Brown	.05	.10
54	Dennis Bonvie	.05	.10
55	Bradley Shepard	.05	.10
56	Allan Cox	.05	.10
57	Jack Williams	.05	.10
58	Chad Penney	.05	.10
59	Jason Firth	.10	.20
60	Bill Lang	.05	.10
61	Ryan Merritt	.05	.10
62	Michael Burman	.05	.10
63	Billy Wright	.15	.30
64	Dave Szabo	.05	.10
65	James Sheehan	.05	.10
66	John Spoltore	.50	1.00
67	Paul Rushforth	.05	.10
68	Jeff Shevalier	.05	.10
69	Robert Thorpe	.05	.10
70	Drake Berehowsky, Error	.25	.50
71	Patrick Barton	.05	.10
72	Bert Templeton, Coach	.05	.10

ERROR AND VARIATION LISTING

No.	Player	Description
70	Barton	"North Bay's" should be "Kingston's"

OTTAWA 67'S

No.	Player	EX	NRMT
73	Wade Gibson	.05	.10

KITCHENER RANGERS

No.	Player	EX	NRMT
74	C. Jay Denomme, Goalie	.05	.10
75	Mike Torchia, Goalie	.10	.20
76	Mike Polano	.05	.10
77	Tony McCabe	.10	.20
78	Chris Kraemer	.05	.10
79	Tim Spitzig	.05	.10
80	Trevor Gallant	.05	.10
81	Yvan Corbin	.05	.10
82	Norman Dezainde	.05	.10
83	Marc Robillard	.05	.10
84	Derek Gauthier	.05	.10
85	Gib Tucker	.05	.10
86	Paul McCallion	.05	.10
87	Eric Manlow	.05	.10
88	James Caruso	.05	.10
89	Gary Miller	.05	.10
90	Jason Stevenson	.05	.10
91	Shayne McCosh	.05	.10
92	Jason Gladney	.05	.10
93	Brad Barton	.05	.10
94	Chris LiPuma	.10	.20
95	Justin Cullen	.05	.10
96	Bill Smith, Scout	.05	.10
97	Joe McDonnell, Coach	.05	.10
98	C. Schucask, Error	.05	.10

ERROR AND VARIATION LISTING

No.	Player	Description
98	Schucask	Improperly numbered "000"

BELLEVILLE BULLS

No.	Player	EX	NRMT
99	Brent Gretzky	.35	.75
100	Gairin Smith	.05	.10
101	Blair Scott	.05	.10
102	Daniel Godbout	.05	.10
103	Dan Preston	.05	.10
104	Ian Keiller	.05	.10
105	Rick Marshall	.05	.10
106	Aaron Morrison	.05	.10
107	Dominic Belanger	.05	.10

1991-92 REGULAR ISSUE — 7TH INNING SKETCH

No.	Player	EX	NRMT
108	Kevin Brown	.05	.10
109	Tony Cimellaro	.05	.10
110	Larry Mavety, Coach	.05	.10
111	Jake Grimes	.10	.20
112	Greg Dreveny, Goalie	.05	.10
113	Darren McCarty	.15	.30
114	Doug Doull	.05	.10
115	Scott Boston	.10	.20
116	Dale Chokan	.05	.10
117	Darren Hurley	.05	.10
118	B. Mielko, Error	.05	.10
119	R. Gallace, Error	.05	.10
120	Shayne Antoski	.05	.10
121	Greg Bailey	.05	.10
122	Keith Redmond	.05	.10

ERROR AND VARIATION LISTING

No.	Player	Description
118	Mielko	Improperly numbered "61"
119	Gallace	Improperly numbered "65"

PETERBOROUGH PETES

No.	Player	EX	NRMT
123	Dick Todd, Coach	.05	.10
124	Scott Turner	.05	.10
125	Colin Wilson	.05	.10
126	Mike Tomlinson	.15	.30
127	Dale McTavish	.05	.10
128	Chris Longo	.20	.40
129	Chad Lang, Goalie	.05	.10
130	Brent Tully	.13	.25
131	Shawn Heins	.05	.10
132	Geordie Kinnear	.05	.10
133	Jeff Walker	.05	.10
134	Chris Pronger	.50	1.00
135	Chad Grills	.05	.10
136	Michael Harding	.05	.10
137	Matt St. Germain	.05	.10
138	Don O'Neill	.05	.10
139	Dave Roche	.05	.10
140	Doug Searle	.05	.10
141	Bryan Gendron	.05	.10
142	Kelly Vipond	.05	.10
143	Andrew Verner, Goalie	.10	.20
144	Ryan Black	.05	.10
145	Jason Dawe	.18	.35
146	Jassen Cullimore	.13	.25
147	Not issued		

OSHAWA GENERALS

No.	Player	EX	NRMT
148	Jason Arnott	1.50	3.00
149	Jan Benda	.05	.10
150	Todd Bradley	.05	.10
151	Markus Brunner	.05	.10
152	Jason Campeau	.05	.10
153	Mark Deazeley	.05	.10
154	Matt Hoffman	.05	.10
155	Scott Hollis	.10	.20
156	Neil Iserhoff	.05	.10
157	Darryl LaFrance	.05	.10
158	B. J. MacPherson	.05	.10
159	Troy Sweet	.05	.10
160	Jason Weaver	.05	.10
161	Stephane Yelle	.05	.10
162	Trevor Burgess	.05	.10
163	Joe Cook	.05	.10
164	Jean-Paul Davis	.10	.20
165	Brian Grieve	.05	.10
166	Rob Leask	.05	.10
167	Wade Simpson	.05	.10
168	Kevin Spero	.05	.10
169	Fred Brathwaite, Goalie	.13	.25
170	Mike Fountain, Goalie	.13	.25
171	Rick Cornacchia, Coach	.05	.10

CHECKLIST

No.	Checklist	EX	NRMT
172	Checklist 1 (1 to 98)	.05	.10

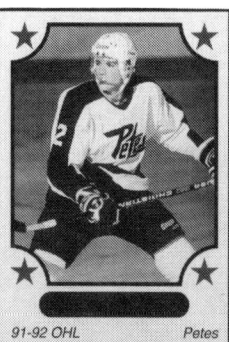

7th Inning Sketch
1991-92 Issue
Card No. 130,
Brent Tully

7th Inning Sketch
1991-92 Issue
Card No. 149,
Jan Benda

7th Inning Sketch
1991-92 Issue
Card No. 181,
Matthew Mullin

7th Inning Sketch
1991-92 Issue
Card No. 196,
OHL Action

WINDSOR SPITFIRES

No.	Player	EX	NRMT
173	Todd Warriner	.50	1.00
174	Reuben Castella	.05	.10
175	Cory Stillman	.25	.50
176	Steve Gibson	.05	.10
177	Trent Cull	.05	.10
178	John Copley	.05	.10
179	Craig Binns	.05	.10
180	Ryan O'Neill	.05	.10
181	Matthew Mullin, Goalie	.05	.10
182	Todd Hunter	.05	.10
183	Jason Stos	.05	.10
184	Robert Frayn, Error	.05	.10
185	Leonard MacDonald	.05	.10
186	Tom Sullivan	.05	.10
187	Steve Smith	.05	.10
188	Bill Bowler	.05	.10
189	James Allison	.05	.10
190	Kevin MacKay	.10	.20
191	David Myles	.05	.10
192	Wayne Maxner, GM-Coach	.05	.10
193	Dave Prpich, Asst. Coach	.05	.10
194	Brady Blain	.05	.10
195	Eric Stamp	.05	.10

ERROR AND VARIATION LISTING

No.	Player	Description
184	Frayn	"Windsor" should be "Spitfires"
193	Prpich	"Windsor" should be "Spitfires"

91-92 OHL ACTION

No.	Player	EX	NRMT
196	OHL Action	.05	.10

NIAGARA FALLS THUNDER

No.	Player	EX	NRMT
197	David Babcock	.05	.10
198	Brad Love	.05	.10
199	Dale Junkin	..05	.10
200	Rick Corriveau	.25	.50
201	Scott Campbell	.05	.10
202	Jason Clarke	.05	.10
203	George Burnett, Coach-GM	.05	.10
204	Ryan Tocher	.05	.10
205	Dennis Maxwell	.05	.10
206	Greg Scott, Goalie	.05	.10
207	Mark Cardiff	.05	.10
208	Neil Fewster	.05	.10
209	Jason Coles	.05	.10
210	Randy Hall, Asst. Coach	.05	.10
211	Todd Simon	.25	.50
212	Ethan Moreau	.05	.10
213	Todd Wetzel	.05	.10
214	Tom Moores	.05	.10
215	Geoff Rawson	.05	.10
216	Dan Krisko	.05	.10
217	Manny Legace, Goalie	.25	.50
218	Kevin Brown	.10	.20
219	Steve Staios	.15	.30

CHECKLIST

No.	Checklist	EX	NRMT
220	Checklist 2 (99 to 196), Error	.05	.10
221	Checklist 3 (197 to 290), Error	.05	.10

ERROR AND VARIATION LISTING

No.	Player	Description
220	Checklist 2	MacDonald misspelled "McDonald"
221	Checklist 3	"Butnett", "Zohil" and "Buckland" are misspelled

KINGSTON FRONTENACS

No.	Player	EX	NRMT
222	Tony Bella	.05	.10
223	Shawn Caplice	.05	.10
224	Keli Corpse	.05	.10
225	Chris Gratton	.05	.10
226	Gord Harris	.05	.10
227	Cory Johnson	.05	.10
228	Kevin King	.05	.10
229	Justin Morrison	.10	.20

7TH INNING SKETCH — 1991-92 REGULAR ISSUE

No.	Player	EX	NRMT
230	Alastair Still	.05	.10
231	Chris Scharf	.05	.10
232	Brian Stagg	.05	.10
233	Mike Dawson	.05	.10
234	Rod Pasma	.05	.10
235	Craig Rivet	.05	.10
236	Dave Stewart	.05	.10
237	John Vary	.15	.30
238	Jason Wadel	.05	.10
239	Joel Yates	.05	.10
240	Marc Lamothe, Goalie	.05	.10
241	Pete McGlynn, Goalie	.05	.10

OHL ACTION

No.	Player	EX	NRMT
242	OHL Action	.05	.10

CHECKLIST

No.	Checklist	EX	NRMT
243	Checklist 4 (291 to 383), Error	.05	.10

ERROR AND VARIATION LISTING

No.	Player	Description
243	Checklist 4	"Baber", "Bes" and "Burkitt" are misspelled

SUDBURY WOLVES

No.	Player	EX	NRMT
244	Joel Sandie	.05	.10
245	Glen Murray	.25	.50
246	Derek Armstrong	.05	.10
247	Michael Peca	.15	.30
248	Barry Young	.05	.10
249	Bernie John	.05	.10
250	Terry Chitaroni	.15	.30
251	Jason Young	.05	.10
252	Rod Hinks	.05	.10
253	Michael Yeo	.05	.10
254	Kyle Blacklock	.05	.10
255	Dan Ryder, Goalie	.05	.10
256	Doug Mason, Asst. Coach	.05	.10
257	Jamie Rivers	.05	.10
258	Brandon Convery	.15	.30
259	Barrie Moore	.05	.10
260	Shawn Rivers	.10	.20
261	Jamie Matthews	.10	.20
262	Tim Favot	.05	.10
263	Bob MacIsaac	.05	.10
264	Sean Gagnon	.05	.10
265	Ken MacKenzie, Coach-GM	.05	.10
266	George Dourian, Error	.05	.10
267	Brian MacKenzie, Asst. Coach	.05	.10
268	Jason Zohil	.05	.10

OWEN SOUND PLATERS

No.	Player	EX	NRMT
269	Rick Tarasuk, Coach	.05	.10
270	James Storr, Goalie	.20	.40
271	Sean Basilio, Goalie	.05	.10
272	Rick Morton	.05	.10
273	Jason Hughes	.05	.10
274	Scott Walker	.05	.10
275	Willie Skilliter	.05	.10
276	Shawn Krueger	.05	.10
277	Jason MacDonald	.05	.10
278	Kirk Maltby	.13	.25
279	Brock Woods	.05	.10
280	Troy Hutchinson	.05	.10
281	Geordie Maynard	.05	.10
282	Luigi Calce	.05	.10
283	Steven Parson	.05	.10
284	Andrew Brunette	.05	.10
285	Robert MacKenzie	.07	.15
286	Jason Buetow	.05	.10
287	Wyatt Buckland	.10	.20
288	Jim Brown	.05	.10
289	Gord Dickie	.05	.10
290	Jeff Smith	.05	.10

7th Inning Sketch
1991-92 Issue
Card No. 245,
Glen Murray

7th Inning Sketch
1991-92 Issue
Card No. 255,
Dan Ryder

7th Inning Sketch
1991-92 Issue
Card No. 266, Error,
Face: Dourian, Back: Dourion

7th Inning Sketch
1991-92 Issue
Card No. 340, Error,
Face: McMurtry, Back: McMurty

OTTAWA 67'S

No.	Player	EX	NRMT
291	Peter Ambroziak	.05	.10
292	Mark O'Donnell	.05	.10

OWEN SOUND PLATERS

No.	Player	EX	NRMT
294	Grayden Reid, Error	.10	.20

ERROR AND VARIATION LISTING

No.	Player	Description
294	Reid	"Platers" should be "67's"
309	Kilrea	Not bilingual

OTTAWA 67'S

No.	Player	EX	NRMT
295	Sean Spencer, Goalie	.05	.10
296	Gerry Skrypec	.05	.10
297	Billy Hall	.05	.10
298	Sean Gawley	.05	.10
299	Grant Marshall	.25	.50
300	Michael Johnson	.05	.10
301	Brett Seguin	.13	.25
302	Chris Coveny	.05	.10
303	Ryan Kuwabara	.10	.20
304	Jeff Ricciardi	.10	.20
305	Curt Bowen	.05	.10
306	Zbynek Kukacka	.05	.10
307	Chris Gignac	.05	.10
308	Steve Washburn	.05	.10
309	Brian Kilrea, Coach, Error	.05	.10
310	Mike Lenarduzzi, Goalie	.13	.25
311	Matt Stone	.05	.10
312	Ken Belanger	.05	.10

SAULT STE. MARIE GREYHOUNDS

No.	Player	EX	NRMT
313	Chris Simon	.10	.20
314	Kiley Hill	.05	.10
315	Chris Grenville	.05	.10
316	Aaron Gavey	.05	.10
317	Briane Thompson	.05	.10
318	Ted Nolan, Coach	.05	.10
319	Perry Pappas	.05	.10
320	Kevin Hodson, Goalie	.05	.10
321	Colin Miller	.10	.20
322	Tom MacDonald	.05	.10
323	Shaun Imber	.05	.10
324	Jarret Reid	.10	.20
325	Tony Iob	.10	.20
326	Mark Matier	.05	.10
327	Drew Bannister	.05	.10
328	Jason Denomme	.05	.10
329	David Matsos	.05	.10
330	Rick Kowalsky	.05	.10
331	Tim Bacik, Goalie	.05	.10
332	Ralph Intranuovo	.10	.20
333	Jonas Rudberg	.05	.10
334	Jeff Toms	.05	.10
335	Jason Julian	.05	.10
336	Brian Goudie	.05	.10
337	Gary Roach	.05	.10
338	Brad Baber	.05	.10
339	Todd Gleason	.05	.10

GUELPH STORM

No.	Player	EX	NRMT
340	Chris McMurty	.05	.10
341	Matt Turek	.05	.10
342	Shane Johnson	.05	.10
343	Grant Pritchett	.05	.10
344	Mike Cote	.05	.10
345	Duane Harmer	.05	.10
346	Jeff Bes	.05	.10
347	Wade Whitten	.05	.10
348	Bill Kovacs	.05	.10
349	Kayle Short	.05	.10
350	Sylvain Cloutier	.05	.10
351	Brent Watson	.05	.10
352	Brent Pope	.05	.10
353	Craig Lutes	.05	.10
354	Michael Hartwick	.05	.10

No.	Player	EX	NRMT
355	Kevin Reid	.05	.10
356	Toby Burkitt	.05	.10
357	Todd Bertuzzi	.05	.10
358	Angelo Amore, Goalie	.05	.10
359	Jeff Pawluk	.05	.10

LONDON KNIGHTS

No.	Player	EX	NRMT
360	Not issued		
361	Gordon Ross	.05	.10
362	Dennis Purdie	.05	.10
363	Dave Gilmore	.05	.10
364	Brent Brownlee, Goalie	.05	.10
365	Aaron Nagy	.05	.10
366	Barry Potomski	.10	.20
367	Steve Smillie	.05	.10
368	Kelly Reed	.05	.10
369	Gary Agnew, Coach	.05	.10
370	Chris Taylor	.15	.30
371	Brett Marietti	.05	.10
372	Cory Evans	.05	.10
373	Brian Stacey	.05	.10
374	Chris Crombie	.15	.30
375	Derrick Crane	.05	.10
376	Scott McKay	.05	.10
377	Gregory Ryan	.10	.20
378	Mark Visheau	.05	.10
379	Gerry Arcella	.05	.10
380	Nick Stajduhar	.05	.10
381	Jason Allison	.05	.10
382	Sean O'Reilly	.05	.10
383	Paul Wolanski	.05	.10

— 1991 - 92 INSERT SET —
THE TEAMS

Inserted into foil packs of the 1991-92 cards. These cards were short printed with one or two cards per foil box.

Card Size: 2 1/2" X 3 1/2"
Face: Four colour, white border
Back: Four colour, Number, Resume, Position
Imprint: © 1991 7th Inning Sketch Printed in Canada
Complete Set No.: 16
Complete Set Price: 3.75 7.50

No.	Player	EX	NRMT
O1	Cornwall Royals	.25	.50
O2	Detroit Ambassadors	.25	.50
O3	Guelph Storm	.25	.50
O4	Kingston Frontenacs	.25	.50
O5	London Knights	.25	.50
O6	Niagara Falls Thunder	.25	.50
O7	North Bay Centennials	.25	.50
O8	Oshawa Generals	.25	.50
O9	Ottawa 67's	.25	.50
O10	Kitchener Rangers	.25	.50
O11	Owen Sound Platers	.25	.50
O12	Peterborough Petes	.25	.50
O13	Sault Ste. Marie Greyhounds	.25	.50
O14	Sudbury Wolves	.25	.50
O15	Windsor Spitfires	.25	.50
O16	Belleville Bulls	.25	.50

7th Inning Sketch
1991-92 Issue
Card No. O1,
Cornwall Royals

7th Inning Sketch
1991 CHL Award Winners
Card No. 1,
Eric Lindros

7th Inning Sketch
1991 CHL Award Winners
Card No. 1,
Eric Lindros

7th Inning Sketch
1991 CHL Award Winners
Card No. 26,
Felix Potvin

1991 CHL AWARD WINNERS'

This 30-card set was issued after the 1991 season to highlight the years top stars. They were only issued in a factory set box.

Card Size:
Face: Four colour, black border; Name, Team, OHL Logo
Back: Four colour, white border; Name, Position, Sponsor's logo
Imprint: © 1992 Seventh Inning Sketch "Tomorrows Stars Today Printed in Canada
Complete Set No.: 30
Complete Set Price: 5.00 10.00
Common Card: .12 .25

O.H.L.

No.	Player	EX	NRMT
1	Top Draft Prospect of the Year: Eric Lindros, Osh.	1.50	3.00
2	Sportsmanlike Player of the Year: Dale Craigwell, Osh.	.13	.25
3	Scholastic Player of the Year: Nathan LaFayette, Corn.	.20	.40
4	Defenceman of the Year: Chris Snell, Ott.67's	.13	.25
5	Rookie Of the Year: Cory Stillman, Windsor Spitfires	.20	.40
6	Goaltender of the Year: Mike Torchia, Kit.	.20	.40
7	Coach of the Year: George Burnett, Nia.	.12	.25
8	Plus-Minus Award of the Year: Eric Lindros, Osh.	1.50	3.00
9	Executive of the Year: Sherwood Bassin, SSM	.12	.25
10	Player of the Year: Eric Lindros, Osh.	1.50	3.00

W.H.L.

No.	Player	EX	NRMT
11	Top Draft Prospect of the Year: Scott Niedermayer, Kam.	.35	.75
12	Sportsmanlike Player of the Year: Pat Falloon, Spo.	.35	.75
13	Scholastic Player of the Year: Scott Niedermayer, Kam.	.35	.75
14	Defenceman of the Year: Darryl Sydor, Kam.	.25	.50
15	Rookie of the Year: Donevan Hextall, PAR	.13	.25
16	Goaltender of the Year: Jamie McLennan, Leth.	.12	.25
17	Coach of the Year: Tom Renney, Kam.	.12	.25
18	Plus-Minus Award of the Year: Frank Evans, Spo.	.12	.25
19	Executive of the Year: Bob Brown, Kam.	.12	.25
20	Player of the Year: Ray Whitney, Spo.	.20	.40

L.H.J.M.Q.

No.	Player	EX	NRMT
21	Top Draft Prospect of the Year: Phillippe Boucher, Gran.	.12	.25
22	Sportsmanlike Player of the Year: Yanic Perreault, Trois.	.13	.25
23	Scholastic Player of the Year: Benoit Larose, Titan	.12	.25
24	Defenceman of the Year: Patrice Brisebois, Drum.	.13	.25
25	Rookie of the Year: Phillippe Boucher, Gran.	.12	.25
26	Goaltender of the Year: Felix Potvin Chic.	1.00	2.00
27	Coach of the Year: Joe Canale, Chic.	.12	.25
28	Plus-Minus Award of the Year: Christian Lariviere, St.H	.12	.25
29	Executive of the Year: Roland Janeliem Drum.	.12	.25
30	Player of the Year: Yanic Perreault, Trois.	.13	.25

QUEBEC HOCKEY LEAGUE

LAVAL DAIRY
— 1951 - 52 ISSUE —

Issued in the province of Quebec and Ottawa region. Scarce

Card Size: 1 3/4" X 2 1/2"
Face: Black and white photo, white border; Name, Position, Number, French
Back: Blank
Imprint: None
Complete Set No.: 109

	VG	EX	NRMT
Complete Set Price:	155.00	315.00	625.00
Common Player:	3.50	7.50	15.00

As DE QUEBEC

No.	Player	VG	EX	NRMT
1	Jean Beliveau	85.00	175.00	350.00
2	Jean Marois, Goalie	3.50	7.50	15.00
3	Joe Crozier	3.50	7.50	15.00
4	Jack Gelineau, Goalie	3.50	7.50	15.00
5	Murdo McKay	3.50	7.50	15.00
6	Arthur Leyte	3.50	7.50	15.00
7	W. Leblanc	3.50	7.50	15.00
8	Robert Hayes	3.50	7.50	15.00
9	Yogi Kraiger	3.50	7.50	15.00
10	Frank King	3.50	7.50	15.00
11	Ludger Tremblay	3.50	7.50	15.00
12	Jackie Leclair	3.50	7.50	15.00
13	Martial Pruneau	3.50	7.50	15.00
14	Armand Gaudreault	3.50	7.50	15.00
15	Marcel Bonin	12.50	25.00	50.00
16	Herbie Carnegie	3.50	7.50	15.00
17	Claude Robert	3.50	7.50	15.00
18	Phil Renaud	3.50	7.50	15.00

CHICOUTIMI

No.	Player	VG	EX	NRMT
19	Roland Hebert	3.50	7.50	15.00
20	Donat Deschesne	3.50	7.50	15.00
21	Jacques Gagnon	3.50	7.50	15.00
22	Normand Dussault	3.50	7.50	15.00
23	Stan Smrke	3.50	7.50	15.00
24	Louis Smrke	3.50	7.50	15.00
25	Floyd Crawford	3.50	7.50	15.00
26	Germain Leger	3.50	7.50	15.00
27	Delphis Franche	3.50	7.50	15.00
28	Dick Wray	3.50	7.50	15.00
29	Guildor Levesque	3.50	7.50	15.00
30	Georges Roy	3.50	7.50	15.00
31	J.P. Lamirande	3.50	7.50	15.00
32	Gerard Glaude	3.50	7.50	15.00
33	Marcel Pelletier	3.50	7.50	15.00
34	Pete Tkachuck	3.50	7.50	15.00
35	Sherman White	3.50	7.50	15.00
36	Jimmy Moore	3.50	7.50	15.00

As DE QUEBEC

No.	Player	VG	EX	NRMT
37	Punch Imlach	20.00	45.00	85.00

SHERBROOKE

No.	Player	VG	EX	NRMT
38	Alex Sandalax	3.50	7.50	15.00
39	William Kyle	3.50	7.50	15.00
40	Kenneth Biggs	3.50	7.50	15.00
41	Peter Wright	3.50	7.50	15.00
42	Rene Pepin	3.50	7.50	15.00
43	Jean-Claude (Tod) Campeau	3.50	7.50	15.00
44	John Smith	3.50	7.50	15.00
45	Thomas McDougall	3.50	7.50	15.00
46	Jos Lepine	3.50	7.50	15.00
47	Guy Labrie	3.50	7.50	15.00
48	Roger Bessette	3.50	7.50	15.00
49	Yvan Dugre	3.50	7.50	15.00
50	James Planche	3.50	7.50	15.00
51	Nils Tremblay	3.50	7.50	15.00

Laval Dairy, 1951-52 Issue, Card No. 13, Martial Pruneau'

Laval Dairy, 1951-52 Issue, Card No. 27, Delphis Franche

Laval Dairy, 1951-52 Issue, Card No. 60, Error, Name misspelled Erinie on face

Laval Dairy 1951-52 Issue Card No. 108, Eddie Emberg

SHAWINIGAN-FALLS

No.	Player	VG	EX	NRMT
52	Bill MacDonagh	3.50	7.50	15.00
53	Georges Ouellet	3.50	7.50	15.00
54	Billy Arcand	3.50	7.50	15.00
55	Johnny Mahaffy	3.50	7.50	15.00
56	Bucky Buchanan	3.50	7.50	15.00
57	Al Miller, Goalie	3.50	7.50	15.00
58	Don Penniston	3.50	7.50	15.00
59	Spike Laliberte	3.50	7.50	15.00
60	Ernie Oakley, Error	3.50	7.50	15.00
61	Jack Bownass	3.50	7.50	15.00
62	Ted Hodgson	3.50	7.50	15.00
63	Lyall Wiseman	3.50	7.50	15.00
64	Erwin Grosse	3.50	7.50	15.00
65	Mel Read	3.50	7.50	15.00
66	Lloyd Henchberger	3.50	7.50	15.00
67	Jack Taylor	3.50	7.50	15.00

VALLEYFIELD

No.	Player	VG	EX	NRMT
68	Marcel Bessette	3.50	7.50	15.00
69	Jack Schmidt	3.50	7.50	15.00
70	Paul Saindon	3.50	7.50	15.00
71	J.P. Bisaillon	3.50	7.50	15.00
72	Eddie Redmond	3.50	7.50	15.00
73	Larry Kwong	3.50	7.50	15.00
74	Andre Corriveau	3.50	7.50	15.00
75	Kitoute Joanette	3.50	7.50	15.00
76	Toe Blake	35.00	70.00	140.00
77	Georges Bougie	3.50	7.50	15.00
78	Jack Irvine	3.50	7.50	15.00
79	Paul Larivee	3.50	7.50	15.00
80	Paul Leclerc	3.50	7.50	15.00
81	Bertrand Bourassa	3.50	7.50	15.00
82	Jacques Deslauriers	3.50	7.50	15.00
83	Bingo Ernst	3.50	7.50	15.00
84	Gaston Gervais	3.50	7.50	15.00

ROYAL DE MONTREAL

No.	Player	VG	EX	NRMT
85	Gerry Plamondon	3.50	7.50	15.00
86	Glen Harmon	3.50	7.50	15.00
87	Bob Friday	3.50	7.50	15.00
88	Rolland Rousseau	3.50	7.50	15.00
89	Billy Goold	3.50	7.50	15.00
90	Lloyd Finkbeiner	3.50	7.50	15.00
91	Clifford Malone	3.50	7.50	15.00
92	Jacques Plante, Goalie	40.00	85.00	175.00
93	Gerard Desaulniers	3.50	7.50	15.00
94	Arthur Rose	3.50	7.50	15.00
95	Jacques Locas	3.50	7.50	15.00
96	Walter Clune	3.50	7.50	15.00
97	Louis Denis	3.50	7.50	15.00
98	Fernand Perreault	3.50	7.50	15.00
99	Douglas McNeil	3.50	7.50	15.00
100	Les Douglas	3.50	7.50	15.00

OTTAWA

No.	Player	VG	EX	NRMT
101	Howard Riopelle	3.50	7.50	15.00
102	Vic Grigg	3.50	7.50	15.00
103	Bobby Roberts	3.50	7.50	15.00
104	Legs Fraser	3.50	7.50	15.00
105	Butch Stahan	3.50	7.50	15.00
106	Fritz Frazer	3.50	7.50	15.00
107	Bill Robinson	3.50	7.50	15.00
108	Eddie Emberg	3.50	7.50	15.00
109	Leo Gravelle	3.50	7.50	15.00

— 1951 - 52 UPDATE —

Believed to be issued during the 1952-53 season as a subset to include new players and trades that took place in the teams for that season.

Card Size: 1 3/4" X 2 1/2"
Face: Black and white photo, white border; Name, Resume, Number, French
Back: Blank
Imprint: None
Complete Set No.: 62
Complete Set Price: 240.00 600.00 1,200.00
Common Player: 4.00 10.00 20.00

As DE QUEBEC

No.	Player	VG	EX	NRMT
7	Al Miller	4.00	10.00	20.00
8	Walter Pawlyshyn	4.00	10.00	20.00
10	Al Baccari	4.00	10.00	20.00
12	Denis Smith	4.00	10.00	20.00
13	Pierre Brillant	4.00	10.00	20.00
14	Frank Mario	4.00	10.00	20.00
15	Danny Nixon	4.00	10.00	20.00
25	Leon Bouchard	4.00	10.00	20.00

CHICOUTIMI

No.	Player	VG	EX	NRMT
26	Pete Taillefer	4.00	10.00	20.00
29	Bucky Buchanen	4.00	10.00	20.00
36	Marius Groleau	4.00	10.00	20.00
38	Fernand Perreault	4.00	10.00	20.00

SHERBROOKE

No.	Player	VG	EX	NRMT
39	Robert Drainville	4.00	10.00	20.00
40	Ronnie Matthews	4.00	10.00	20.00
44	Roger Roberge	4.00	10.00	20.00
46	Pete Wywrot	4.00	10.00	20.00
50	Gilles Dube	4.00	10.00	20.00
52	Bob Pepin	4.00	10.00	20.00
53	Dewar Thompson	4.00	10.00	20.00
55	Irene St. Hilaire	4.00	10.00	20.00
56	Martial Pruneau	4.00	10.00	20.00
57	Jacques Locas	4.00	10.00	20.00

SHAWINIGAN-FALLS

No.	Player	VG	EX	NRMT
59	Nelson Podolsky	4.00	10.00	20.00
60	Bert Giesebrecht	4.00	10.00	20.00
61	Steve Brklacich	4.00	10.00	20.00
65	Jack Hamilton	4.00	10.00	20.00
66	Dave Gatherum	4.00	10.00	20.00
67	Jean-Marie Plante	4.00	10.00	20.00

VALLYFIELD

No.	Player	VG	EX	NRMT
68	Gordie Haworth	4.00	10.00	20.00
70	Bruce Cline	4.00	10.00	20.00
72	Phil Vitale	4.00	10.00	20.00
81	Carl Smelle	4.00	10.00	20.00
84	Tom Smelle	4.00	10.00	20.00

ROYALS DE MONTREAL

No.	Player	VG	EX	NRMT
85	Gerry Plamondon	4.00	10.00	20.00
86	Glen Harmon	6.00	15.00	30.00

SHAWINIGAN-FALLS

No.	Player	VG	EX	NRMT
89	Frank Bathgate	4.00	10.00	20.00
90	Bernie Lemonde	4.00	10.00	20.00

ROYALS DE MONTREAL

No.	Player	VG	EX	NRMT
92	Jacques Plante, Goalie	75.00	150.00	300.00
93	Gerard Desaulniers	4.00	10.00	20.00

SHAWINIGAN-FALLS

No.	Player	VG	EX	NRMT
94	Jean-Claude. Lebrun	4.00	10.00	20.00
95	Bob Leger	4.00	10.00	20.00

Laval Dairy
1951-52 Update
Card No. 10,
Al Baccari

Laval Dairy
1951-52 Update
Card No. 25,
Leon Bouchard

Laval Dairy
1951-52 Update
Card No. 94,
Jean-Claude Lebrun

Laval Dairy
1951-52 Update
Card No. 112,
Jack Giesebrecht

ROYALS DE MONTREA

No.	Player	VG	EX	NRMT
96	Walter Clune	4.00	10.00	20.00
97	Louis Denis	4.00	10.00	20.00

OTTAWA

No.	Player	VG	EX	NRMT
98	Jackie Leclair	6.00	15.00	30.00
99	John Arundel	4.00	10.00	20.00
100	Leslie Douglas	4.00	10.00	20.00
103	Bobby Robertson	4.00	10.00	20.00
104	Ray Fredericks, Goalie	4.00	10.00	20.00
106	Emil Dagenais	4.00	10.00	20.00
108	Al Kuntz	4.00	10.00	20.00
110	Red Johnson	4.00	10.00	20.00
111	John O'Flaherty	4.00	10.00	20.00
112	Jack Giesebrecht	4.00	10.00	20.00
113	Bill Richardson	4.00	10.00	20.00
114	Bep Guidolin	6.00	15.00	30.00

REGULAR ISSUE

No.	Player	VG	EX	NRMT
115	Roger Bedard, Shaw.	4.00	10.00	20.00
116	Renald Lacroix, Val.	4.00	10.00	20.00
117	Gordie Hudson, Que.	4.00	10.00	20.00
118	Dick Wray, Shaw.	4.00	10.00	20.00
119	Ronnie Hurst, Ott.	4.00	10.00	20.00
120	Eddie Joss, Shaw.	4.00	10.00	20.00
121	Lyall Wiseman, Que.	4.00	10.00	20.00

— 1951 - 52 LAC ST. JEAN —

Card Size: 1 3/4" X 2 1/2"
Face: Green tint and white; Name, Number
Back: Blank
Imprint: None
Complete Set No.: 59
Complete Set Price: 200.00 500.00 1,000.00
Common Player: 5.00 10.00 20.00

AS DE JONQUIERE

No.	Player	VG	EX	NRMT
1	Eddy Daoust	5.00	10.00	20.00
2	Guy Gareau	5.00	10.00	20.00
3	Gilles Desrosiers	5.00	10.00	20.00
4	Robert Desbiens	5.00	10.00	20.00
5	James Hayes	5.00	10.00	20.00
6	Paul Gagnon	5.00	10.00	20.00
7	Gerry Perreault	5.00	10.00	20.00
8	Marcel Dufour	5.00	10.00	20.00
9	Armand Bourdon	5.00	10.00	20.00
10	Jean-Marc Pichette	5.00	10.00	20.00
11	Gerry Gagnon	5.00	10.00	20.00
12	Jules Racette	5.00	10.00	20.00
13	Real Marcotte	5.00	10.00	20.00
14	Gerry Theberge	5.00	10.00	20.00
15	Rene Harvey	5.00	10.00	20.00

DOLBEAU (CASTORS)

No.	Player	VG	EX	NRMT
16	Joseph Lacoursiere	5.00	10.00	20.00
17	Fernand Benaquez	5.00	10.00	20.00
18	Andre Boisvert	5.00	10.00	20.00
19	Claude Chretien	5.00	10.00	20.00
20	Nobert Clark	5.00	10.00	20.00
21	Sylvio Lambert	5.00	10.00	20.00
22	Lucien Roy	5.00	10.00	20.00
23	Gerard Audet	5.00	10.00	20.00
24	Jacques Lalancette	5.00	10.00	20.00
25	Maurice St. Jean	5.00	10.00	20.00
26	Camille Lupien	5.00	10.00	20.00
27	Rodrigue Pelchat	5.00	10.00	20.00
28	Conrad L'Heureux	5.00	10.00	20.00
29	Paul Tremblay	5.00	10.00	20.00
30	Robert Vincent	5.00	10.00	20.00

ALMA (ST. JOSEPH)

No.	Player	VG	EX	NRMT
31	Charles Lamirande	5.00	10.00	20.00
32	Leon Gaudreault	5.00	10.00	20.00

ST. LAWRENCE SALES AGENCY — 1952-53 ISSUE

No.	Player	VG	EX	NRMT
33	Maurice Thiffault	5.00	10.00	20.00
34	Marc-Aurele Tremblay	5.00	10.00	20.00
35	Rene Pronovost	5.00	10.00	20.00
36	Victor Corbin	5.00	10.00	20.00
37	Tiny Tamminen	5.00	10.00	20.00
38	Guildor Levesque	5.00	10.00	20.00
39	Gaston Lamirande	5.00	10.00	20.00
40	Guy Gervais	5.00	10.00	20.00
41	Rayner Makila	5.00	10.00	20.00
42	Jules Tremblay	5.00	10.00	20.00
43	Roland Girard	5.00	10.00	20.00
44	Germain Bergeron	5.00	10.00	20.00

PORT ALFRED (ELANS)

No.	Player	VG	EX	NRMT
45	Paul Duchesne	5.00	10.00	20.00
46	Roger Beaudoin	5.00	10.00	20.00
47	Georges Archibal	5.00	10.00	20.00
48	Claude Basque	5.00	10.00	20.00
49	Roger Sarda	5.00	10.00	20.00
50	Edgar Gendron	5.00	10.00	20.00
51	Gaston Labossiere	5.00	10.00	20.00
52	Roland Clantara	5.00	10.00	20.00
53	Florian Gravel	5.00	10.00	20.00
54	Jean-Guy Thompson	5.00	10.00	20.00
55	Yvan Fortin	5.00	10.00	20.00
56	Yves Laporte	5.00	10.00	20.00
57	Claude Germain	5.00	10.00	20.00
58	Gerry Brunet	5.00	10.00	20.00
59	Maurice Courteau	5.00	10.00	20.00

ST. LAWRENCE SALES AGENCY

— 1952 - 53 ISSUE —

Card Size: 1 3/4" X 2 3/4"
Face: Black and white photo, borderless
Back: Black on card stock; Name, Number, Resume, French
Imprint: None
Complete Set No.: 107
Complete Set Price: 400.00 1,000.00 2,000.00
Common Player: 5.00 10.00 20.00

ROYAL DE MONTREAL

No.	Player	VG	EX	NRMT
1	Jacques Plante, Goalie	55.00	110.00	225.00
2	Glenn Harmon	5.00	10.00	20.00
3	Jimmy Moore	5.00	10.00	20.00
4	Gerry Desaulniers	5.00	10.00	20.00
5	Les Douglas	5.00	10.00	20.00
6	Fred Burchell	5.00	10.00	20.00
7	Eddie Litzenberger	10.00	20.00	40.00
8	Rollie Rousseau	5.00	10.00	20.00
9	Roger Leger	5.00	10.00	20.00
10	Phil Samis	5.00	10.00	20.00
11	Paul Masnick	7.00	15.00	35.00
12	Walter Clune	5.00	10.00	20.00
13	Lulu Denis	5.00	10.00	20.00
14	Gerry Plamondon	5.00	10.00	20.00
15	Cliff Malone	5.00	10.00	20.00
16	Pete Morin	5.00	10.00	20.00

VALLEYFIELD

No.	Player	VG	EX	NRMT
17A	Jackie Schmidt	5.00	10.00	20.00
17B	Aldo Guidolin	5.00	10.00	20.00
18	Paul Leclerc	5.00	10.00	20.00
19	Larry Kwong	5.00	10.00	20.00
20	Rosario Joanette	5.00	10.00	20.00
21	Tom Smelle	5.00	10.00	20.00
22	Gordie Haworth	5.00	10.00	20.00
23	Bruce Cline	5.00	10.00	20.00
24	Andre Corriveau	5.00	10.00	20.00
25	Jacques Deslaurier	5.00	10.00	20.00
26	Bingo Ernst	5.00	10.00	20.00
27	Jacques Chartrand	5.00	10.00	20.00
28	Phil Vitale	5.00	10.00	20.00
29	Renald Lacroix	5.00	10.00	20.00
30	J.P. Bisaillon	5.00	10.00	20.00

St. Lawrence Sales
1952-53 Issue
Card No. 1,
Jacques Plante

St. Lawrence Sales
1952-53 Issue
Card No. 54,
Punch Imlach

No.	Player	VG	EX	NRMT
31	Jack Irvine	5.00	10.00	20.00
32	Georges Bougie	5.00	10.00	20.00
33	Paul Larivee	5.00	10.00	20.00
34	Carl Smelle	5.00	10.00	20.00

As DE QUEBEC

No.	Player	VG	EX	NRMT
35	Walter Pawlyschyn	5.00	10.00	20.00
36	Jean Marois	5.00	10.00	20.00
37	Jack Gelineau	5.00	10.00	20.00
38	Danny Nixon	5.00	10.00	20.00
39	Jean Beliveau	70.00	140.00	275.00
40	Phil Renaud	5.00	10.00	20.00
41	Leon Bouchard	5.00	10.00	20.00
42	Dennis Smith	5.00	10.00	20.00
43	Jos Crozier	5.00	10.00	20.00
44	Al Bacari	5.00	10.00	20.00
45	Murdo MacKay	5.00	10.00	20.00
46	Gordie Hudson	5.00	10.00	20.00
47	Claude Robert	5.00	10.00	20.00
48	Yogi Kraiger	5.00	10.00	20.00
49	Ludger Tremblay	5.00	10.00	20.00
50	Pierre Brillant	5.00	10.00	20.00
51	Frank Mario	5.00	10.00	20.00
52	Cooper Leyth	5.00	10.00	20.00
53	Herbie Carnegie	5.00	10.00	20.00
54	Punch Imlach	15.00	35.00	75.00

OTTAWA

No.	Player	VG	EX	NRMT
55	Howard Riopelle	5.00	10.00	20.00
56	Ken Laufman	5.00	10.00	20.00
57	Jackie Leclair	7.00	15.00	35.00
58	Bill Robinson	5.00	10.00	20.00
59	George Ford	5.00	10.00	20.00
60	Bill Johnson	5.00	10.00	20.00
61	Leo Gravelle	5.00	10.00	20.00
62	Jack Giesbrecht	5.00	10.00	20.00
63	John Arundel	5.00	10.00	20.00
64	Vic Gregg	5.00	10.00	20.00
65	B. Guidolin	7.00	15.00	35.00
66	Al Kuntz	5.00	10.00	20.00
67	Emile Dagenais	5.00	10.00	20.00
68	Bill Richardson	5.00	10.00	20.00
69	Bob Robertson	5.00	10.00	20.00
70	Ray Fredericks	5.00	10.00	20.00
71	James O'Flaherty	5.00	10.00	20.00
72	Butch Stahan	5.00	10.00	20.00

SHERBROOKE

No.	Player	VG	EX	NRMT
73	Roger Roberge	5.00	10.00	20.00
74	Guy Labrie	5.00	10.00	20.00
75	Gilles Dube	5.00	10.00	20.00
76	Pete Wywrot	5.00	10.00	20.00
77	Tod Campeau	5.00	10.00	20.00
78	Roger Bessette	5.00	10.00	20.00
79	M. Pruneau	5.00	10.00	20.00
80	Nil Tremblay	5.00	10.00	20.00
81	Jacques Locas	5.00	10.00	20.00
82	Rene Pepin	5.00	10.00	20.00
83	Bob Pepin	5.00	10.00	20.00
84	Tom McDougal	5.00	10.00	20.00
85	Pete Wright	5.00	10.00	20.00
86	Ronnie Mathews	5.00	10.00	20.00
87	Irene St-Hilaire	5.00	10.00	20.00
88	D. Thompson	5.00	10.00	20.00
89	Bob Dainville	5.00	10.00	20.00

CHICOUTIMI

No.	Player	VG	EX	NRMT
90	Marcel Pelletier	5.00	10.00	20.00
91	Delphis Franche	5.00	10.00	20.00
92	Geo. Roy	5.00	10.00	20.00
93	Andy McCallum	5.00	10.00	20.00
94	Lou Smrke	5.00	10.00	20.00
95	J.P. Lamirande	5.00	10.00	20.00
96	Normand Dussault	5.00	10.00	20.00
97	Stan Smrke	5.00	10.00	20.00
98	Jack Bownass	5.00	10.00	20.00

SHAWINIGAN-FALLS

No.	Player	VG	EX	NRMT
99	Billy Arcand	5.00	10.00	20.00 ☐
100	Lyall Wiseman	5.00	10.00	20.00 ☐
101	Jack Hamilton	5.00	10.00	20.00 ☐
102	Bob Leger	5.00	10.00	20.00 ☐
103	Larry Regan	5.00	10.00	20.00 ☐
104	Erwin Grosse	5.00	10.00	20.00 ☐
105	Roger Bedard	5.00	10.00	20.00 ☐
106	Ted Hodgson	5.00	10.00	20.00 ☐
107	Dave Gatherum	5.00	10.00	20.00 ☐

7TH INNING SKETCH

— 1990 - 91 REGULAR ISSUE —

Card Size: 2 1/2" X 3 1/2"
Face: Four colour, white border, Position
Back: Four colour, Number, Resume, Position
Imprint: © 1990 7th Inning Sketch Printed in Canada
Complete Set No.: 268

Complete Set Price:		12.50	25.00 ☐
Common Card:		.05	.10
Foil Pack: (10 Cards)			.75
Foil Box : (36 Packs)			25.00
Foil Case: (20 Boxes)			400.00

Production:
Foil Cases: 1,500
Set Cases: 400 (4,800 Individually numbered sets)

QMJHL CHRISTMAS CARDS

No.	Player	EX	NRMT
—	White card stock	2.50	5.00 ☐
—	Silver foil card stock	5.00	10.00 ☐

ST-HYACINTHE LASER

No.	Player	EX	NRMT
1	Patrick Poulin	.75	1.50 ☐

DRUMMONDVILLE VOLTIGEURS

No.	Player	EX	NRMT
2	Steve Lupien, Goalie	.05	.10 ☐
3	Pierre Gagnon, Goalie	.10	.20 ☐
4	Eric Plante	.10	.20 ☐
5	Stéphane Desjardins	.05	.10 ☐
6	Peter Valenta	.05	.10 ☐
7	Alexandre Legault	.10	.20 ☐
8	Patrice Brisebois	.50	1.00 ☐
9	Martin Charrois	.05	.10 ☐
10	Eric Dandenault	.10	.20 ☐
11	Claude Jutras	.05	.10 ☐
12	David Pekarek	.07	.15 ☐
13	Denis Chassé	.05	.10 ☐
14	Ian Laperrière	.05	.10 ☐
15	Roger Larche	.05	.10 ☐
16	Dave Paquet	.05	.10 ☐
17	Pascal Lebrasseur	.05	.10 ☐
18	Eric Meloche	.05	.10 ☐
19	The Face Off, Action	.05	.10 ☐

CHICOUTIMI SAGUENEENS

No.	Player	EX	NRMT
20	Sylvain Rodrigue, Goalie	.05	.10 ☐
21	Dany Girard	.05	.10 ☐
22	Eric Rochette	.10	.20 ☐
23	Steve Gosselin	.05	.10 ☐
24	Martin Lavallée	.15	.30 ☐

LAVAL TITAN

No.	Player	EX	NRMT
25	Martin Lapointe	1.00	2.00 ☐

CHICOUTIMI SAGUENEENS

No.	Player	EX	NRMT
26	Eric Brûlé, Error	.05	.10 ☐
27	Martin Lacombe	.13	.25 ☐
28	Patrice Martineau	.13	.25 ☐
29	Dave Tremblay	.05	.10 ☐
30	Steve Larouche	.13	.25 ☐
31	Danny Beauregard	.10	.20 ☐

7th Innining Sketch
1990-91 Issue
Card No. 1,
Patrick Poulin

7th Inning Sketch
1990-91 Issue
Card No. 20
Sylvain Rodrigue

7th Inning Sketch
1990-91 Issue
Card No. 26, Error,
Face: Eric Brulé, Back: Eric Brele

7th Inning Sketch
1990-91 Issue
Card No. 40,
Stéphane Charbonneau

No.	Player	EX	NRMT
32	François Bélanger	.25	.50 ☐
33	Michel St-Jacques	.10	.20 ☐
34	Patrick Bisaillon	.08	.15 ☐
35	Felix Potvin, Goalie	3.50	7.00 ☐
36	Sébastien Parent	.13	.25 ☐
37	Eric Duchesne	.05	.10 ☐
38	Gilles Bouchard	.13	.25 ☐
39	Martin Gagné	.13	.25 ☐
40	Stéphane Charbonneau	.13	.25 ☐
41	Martin Beaupré	.10	.20 ☐
42	Daniel Paradis	.08	.15 ☐
43	Joe Canale, Coach	.05	.10 ☐
44	George Vezina Arena	.13	.25 ☐

LAVAL TITAN

No.	Player	EX	NRMT
45	François Leblanc, Goalie	.10	.20 ☐
46	Martin Chaput	.10	.20 ☐
47	Marc Beaucage	.05	.10 ☐
48	Carl Mantha	.10	.20 ☐
49	Jim Bermingham	.13	.25 ☐

GRANBY BISONS

No.	Player	EX	NRMT
50	Philippe Boucher	.50	1.00 ☐

LAVAL TITAN

No.	Player	EX	NRMT
51	Denis Chalifoux	.07	.15 ☐
52	Sylvain Naud	.10	.20 ☐
53	Jean Roberge	.10	.20 ☐
54	Sandy McCarthy	.20	.40 ☐
55	Eric Dubois	.10	.20 ☐
56	Jean Blouin	.10	.20 ☐
57	Jason Brousseau	.10	.20 ☐
58	Pierre Sandke	.05	.10 ☐
59	Benoit Larose	.10	.20 ☐
60	Yannick Fréchette	.10	.20 ☐

GRANBY BISONS

No.	Player	EX	NRMT
61	Pierre Calder	.05	.10 ☐
62	Patrick Grisé	.05	.10 ☐
63	Martin Balleux	.05	.10 ☐
64	Boris Rousson, Goalie	.13	.25 ☐
65	Martin Trudel	.05	.10 ☐
66	Carl Leblanc	.10	.20 ☐
67	Martin Brochu, Goalie	.05	.10 ☐
68	Benoit Therrien	.05	.10 ☐

LAVAL TITAN

No.	Player	EX	NRMT
69	Q.M.J.H.L. Action	.25	.50 ☐
70	Pascal Vincent	.05	.10 ☐

GRANBY BISONS

No.	Player	EX	NRMT
71	Christian Tardif	.10	.20 ☐
72	Christian Campeau	.05	.10 ☐

LAVAL TITAN

No.	Player	EX	NRMT
73	Eric Raymond, Goalie	.15	.30 ☐
74	John Kovacs	.05	.10 ☐

TROIS RIVIERES DRAVEURS

No.	Player	EX	NRMT
75	Steve Arès	.05	.10 ☐

GRANBY BISONS

No.	Player	EX	NRMT
76	Pascal Dufalt	.05	.10 ☐

LAVAL TITAN

No.	Player	EX	NRMT
77	Greg MacEachern	.05	.10 ☐
78	Rémi Belliveau	.05	.10 ☐

7TH INNING SKETCH — 1990 - 91 REGULAR ISSUE

GRANBY BISONS

No.	Player	EX	NRMT
79	Jocelyn Langlois	.05	.10
80	Carl Ménard, Error	.05	.10
81	Sébastien Fortier	.05	.10
82	Jean-Franço Grégoire	.05	.10
83	Normand Demers	.05	.10
84	Nicolas Lefebvre	.05	.10

TROIS RIVIERES DRAVEURS

No.	Player	EX	NRMT
85	Dominic Maltais	.05	.10
86	Mario Thérrien	.05	.10
87	Daniel Thibault	.05	.10
88	Jean-François Labbé, Goalie	.40	.80
89	Alain Côté	.10	.20
90	Eric Prillo	.05	.10
91	Patrick Nadeau	.05	.10
92	Claude Poirier	.10	.20
93	Stéphane Julien	.10	.20
94	Patrice René	.05	.10
95	Francis Courturier, Error	.05	.10
96	Guy Lefebvre	.10	.20
97	Carl Boudreau	.13	.25
98	Jacques Parent	.05	.10

SHAWINIGAN CATARACTES

No.	Player	EX	NRMT
99	Stéphane Bourget	.05	.10

TROIS RIVIERES DRAVEURS

No.	Player	EX	NRMT
100	Yanic Perreault	.75	1.50

SHAWINIGAN CATARACTES

No.	Player	EX	NRMT
101	Yvan Bergeron	.05	.10

BEAUPORT HARFANGS

No.	Player	EX	NRMT
102	Jean-François Rivard, Goalie	.05	.10
103	Daniel Laflamme	.05	.10

SHAWINIGAN CATARACTES

No.	Player	EX	NRMT
104	François Bourdeau	.05	.10
105	Yvan Charrois	.05	.10

BEAUPORT HARFANGS

No.	Player	EX	NRMT
106	Patrick Genest	.05	.10
107	Hervé Lapointe	.05	.10

SHAWINIGAN CATARACTES

No.	Player	EX	NRMT
108	Jean-François Jomphe	.05	.10
109	Marc Tardif	.10	.20

BEAUPORT HARFANGS

No.	Player	EX	NRMT
110	Eric Cardinal	.05	.10
111	Denis Cloutier	.15	.30

SHAWINIGAN CATARACTES

No.	Player	EX	NRMT
112	Q.M.J.H.L. Action	.10	.20
113	Alain Sanscartier, Coach	.05	.10

BEAUPORT HARFANGS

No.	Player	EX	NRMT
114	Marquis Mathieu	.05	.10
115	Stephane Tartari, Error	.05	.10

SHAWINIGAN CATARACTES

No.	Player	EX	NRMT
116	Q.M.J.H.L. Action	.10	.20
117	Q.M.J.H.L. Action	.10	.20

7th Inning Sketch
1990-91 Issue
Card No. 80, Error,
Name misspelled Carol on face

7th Inning Sketch, 1990-91 Issue
Card No. 95, Error
Front: Francis Courturier
Back: Francis Couturier

7th Inning Sketch
1990-91 Issue
Card No. 115, Error,
Name misspelled Stephan on back

7th Inning Sketch
1990-91 Issue
Card No. 119,
David Boudreau

BEAUPORT HARFANGS

No.	Player	EX	NRMT
118	Martin Roy	.05	.10
119	David Boudreau	.10	.20
120	Mario Dumoulin	.05	.10
121	Jean-François Picard	.05	.10
122	Q.M.J.H.L. Action	.10	.20
123	Q.M.J.H.L. Action	.10	.20
124	Maxime Gagné	.05	.10

ST-JEAN LYNX

No.	Player	EX	NRMT
125	Stéphane Ouellet	.15	.30

BEAUPORT HARFANGS

No.	Player	EX	NRMT
126	Steven Paiement	.15	.30

HULL OLYMPIQUES

No.	Player	EX	NRMT
127	François Paquette	.05	.10

BEAUPORT HARFANGS

No.	Player	EX	NRMT
128	Eric Cool	.05	.10
129	Simon Toupin	.05	.10

HULL OLYMPIQUES

No.	Player	EX	NRMT
130	Shane Doiron	.05	.10
131	Todd Sparks	.13	.25

BEAUPORT HARFANGS

No.	Player	EX	NRMT
132	Bruno Lajeunesse	.05	.10
133	Marcel Cousineau, Goalie	.22	.45

HULL OLYMPIQUES

No.	Player	EX	NRMT
134	Claude-Charles Sauriol, Error	.10	.20
135	Eric Bellerose	.22	.45

BEAUPORT HARFANGS

No.	Player	EX	NRMT
136	Q.M.J.H.L. Action	.10	.20
137	Q.M.J.H.L. Action	.10	.20

HULL OLYMPIQUES

No.	Player	EX	NRMT
138	Martin Lepage	.13	.25
139	Michal Longauer	.05	.10
140	Frédéric Boivin	.05	.10
141	Steven Dion	.05	.10
142	Q.M.J.H.L. Action	.10	.20
143	Q.M.J.H.L. Action	.10	.20
144	Dan Paolucci	.05	.10
145	Bruno Villeneuve	.13	.25

CHECKLIST

No.	Team	EX	NRMT
146	Les Draveurs de Trois-Rivieres, Error	.15	.30
147	Les Bisons de Granby, Error	.15	.30

HULL OLYMPIQUES

No.	Player	EX	NRMT
148	Stefan Simoes	.05	.10
149	Joel Blain	.05	.10
150	Eric Lavigne	.25	.50

CHECKLIST

No.	Team	EX	NRMT
151	Le Titan de Laval	.10	.20
152	Le Laser de St-Hyacinthe	.15	.30

HULL OLYMPIQUES

No.	Player	EX	NRMT
153	Robert Melanson	.05	.10
154	Brian Rogger	.05	.10

— 1990-91 REGULAR ISSUE — 7TH INNING SKETCH • 735

CHECKLIST

No.	Team	EX	NRMT
155	Les Lynx de St-Jean	.15	.30
156	Les Olympiques de Hull, Error	.15	.30

HULL OLYMPIQUES

No.	Player	EX	NRMT
157	Francis Ouellette, Goalie	.20	.40
158	Q.M.J.H.L. Action	.10	.20

CHECKLIST

No.	Team	EX	NRMT
159	Les Sagueneens, Error	.15	.30
160	Les Voltigeurs de Drummondville, Error	.15	.30
161	Le College Francais	.15	.30
162	Les Tigres de Victoriaville	.15	.30

DRUMMONDVILLE VOLTIGEURS

No.	Player	EX	NRMT
163	Q.M.J.H.L. Action	.10	.20
164	Q.M.J.H.L. Action	.10	.20

CHECKLIST

No.	Team	EX	NRMT
165	Les Harfangs de Beauport, Error	.15	.30
166	Les Cataractes de Shawinigan	.15	.30

BEAUPORT HARFANGS

No.	Player	EX	NRMT
167	Q.M.J.H.L. Action	.10	.20
168	Q.M.J.H.L. Action	.10	.20

TOIS RIVIERES DRAVEURS

No.	Player	EX	NRMT
169	Pierre Fillion	.05	.10
170	Yanick Degrace, Goalie	.13	.25

ST-JEAN LYNX

No.	Player	EX	NRMT
171	Paul Daigneault	.05	.10
172	Stacy Dallaire	.05	.10

TOIS RIVIERES DRAVEURS

No.	Player	EX	NRMT
173	Steve Searles	.10	.20
174	Todd Gillingham	.25	.50

ST-JEAN LYNX

No.	Player	EX	NRMT
175	Yves Sarault	.25	.50
176	Jason Downey	.10	.20

TOIS RIVIERES DRAVEURS

No.	Player	EX	NRMT
177	Paul Brousseau	.25	.50

ST-JEAN LYNX

No.	Player	EX	NRMT
178	Raymond Delarosbil	.05	.10
179	Yvan Corbin	.05	.10

TOIS RIVIERES DRAVEURS

No.	Player	EX	NRMT
180	Gaston Drapeau, Coach	.05	.10
181	The Celebration	.10	.20

ST-JEAN LYNX

No.	Player	EX	NRMT
182	Reginald Brezeault	.05	.10
183	Eric Lafrance	.05	.10
184	Martin Lavallée, Goalie	.13	.25
185	Sebastien Lavalliere, Error	.05	.10
186	Martin Lefebvre	.05	.10

SHAWINIGAN CATARACTES

No.	Player	EX	NRMT
187	Richard Hamelin	.05	.10
188	Eric Beauvais	.05	.10

7th Inning Sketch, 1990-91 Issue Card No. 159, Error, Shows No. 27 as Richard Boivin should be Martin Lacombe

7th Inning Sketch 1990-91 Issue Card No. 165, Error, Shows Dicard, listed as Picard

7th Inning Sketch 1990-91 Issue Card No. 199, David Morissette

7th Inning Sketch 1990-91 Issue Card No. 195, Patrick Hébert

No.	Player	EX	NRMT
189	Hughes Mongeon	.25	.50
190	Alain Côté	.05	.10
191	Eric Desrochers, Goalie	.05	.10
192	Eric Joyal	.05	.10
193	Steve Dontigny	.05	.10
194	Frederick Lefebvre	.05	.10
195	Patrick Hébert	.05	.10
196	Johnny Lorenzo, Goalie	.05	.10

VICTORIAVILLE TIGRES

No.	Player	EX	NRMT
197	Sylvain Cormier	.05	.10
198	Q.M.J.H.L. Action	.10	.20

SHAWINIGAN CATARACTES

No.	Player	EX	NRMT
199	Dave Morissette	.05	.10

DRUMMONDVILLE VOLITGEURS

No.	Player	EX	NRMT
200	Yanick Dupré	.20	.40

SHAWINIGAN CATARACTES

No.	Player	EX	NRMT
201	Eric Marcoux	.05	.10

VICTORIAVILLE TIGRES

No.	Player	EX	NRMT
202	Bruno Ducharme, Goalie	.05	.10
203	Martin Caron	.05	.10

SHAWINIGAN CATARACTES

No.	Player	EX	NRMT
204	Yves Meunier	.05	.10
205	Eric Bissonnette	.10	.20

ST-JEAN LYNX

No.	Player	EX	NRMT
206	Jason Underhill	.05	.10
207	Dave Belliveau, Error	.05	.10

ST-HYACINTHE LASER

No.	Player	EX	NRMT
208	Steve Lapointe	.05	.10
209	Dean Melanson	.10	.20

ST-JEAN LYNX

No.	Player	EX	NRMT
210	Travor Duhaime	.05	.10
211	Jacques Leblanc	.05	.10

ST-HYACINTHE LASER

No.	Player	EX	NRMT
212	Normand Paquet	.13	.25
213	Hugues Laliberté, Error	.10	.20

ST-JEAN LYNX

No.	Player	EX	NRMT
214	Craig Prior, Goalie	.05	.10
215	Patrick Labrecque, Goalie	.07	.15

ST-HYACINTHE LASER

No.	Player	EX	NRMT
216	Patrick Cloutier	.05	.10
217	Michael Bazinet	.05	.10

ST-JEAN LYNX

No.	Player	EX	NRMT
218	Christian Proulx, Error	.13	.25
219	Q.M.J.H.L. Action	.10	.20

ST-HYACINTHE LASER

No.	Player	EX	NRMT
220	Charles Poulin	.25	.50
221	Christian Larivière	.10	.20
222	Martin Brodeur, Goalie	1.50	3.00
223	Yannik Lemay	.05	.10

7TH INNING SKETCH — 1991-92 REGULAR ISSUE

No.	Player	EX	NRMT
224	Denis Leblanc	.15	.30

SHAWINIGAN CATARACTES

No.	Player	EX	NRMT
225	François Groleau	.20	.40

ST-HYACINTHE LASER

No.	Player	EX	NRMT
226	Pierre Sévigny	.35	.75
227	Pierre Allard	.10	.20
228	Craig Martin	.10	.20

COLLEGE FRANCAIS

No.	Player	EX	NRMT
229	Karl Dykhuis	.35	.75
230	Etienne Lavoie	.05	.10

ST-HYACINTHE LASER

No.	Player	EX	NRMT
231	Stan Melanson	.05	.10

COLLEGE FRANCAIS

No.	Player	EX	NRMT
232	Dominic Rhéaume	.15	.30
233	Mario Nobili	.15	.30

ST-HYACINTHE LASER

No.	Player	EX	NRMT
234	Martin Gendron	.50	1.00
235	Stephane Menard, Goalie	.05	.10

COLLEGE FRANCAIS

No.	Player	EX	NRMT
236	David St-Pierre	.13	.25
237	Yan Arsenault	.05	.10

ST-HYACINTHE LASER

No.	Player	EX	NRMT
238	Norman Flynn, Coach	.05	.10
239	Q.M.J.H.L. Action	.10	.20

COLLEGE FRANCAIS

No.	Player	EX	NRMT
240	Dave Chouinard	.13	.25
241	Robert Guillet	.25	.50
242	Martin Lajeunesse	.05	.10
243	Nichol Cloutier	.05	.10
244	Joel Bouchard	.05	.10
245	Donald Brashear	.05	.10

VICTORIAVILLE TIGRES

No.	Player	EX	NRMT
246	Sébastien Tremblay	.05	.10
247	Dominique Grandmaison, Error	.05	.10
248	Nicolas Lefebvre	.05	.10
249	Joseph Napolitano	.10	.20

DRUMMONDVILLE VOLTIGEURS

No.	Player	EX	NRMT
250	Marc Savard	.20	.40

VICTORIAVILLE TIGRES

No.	Player	EX	NRMT
251	Alain Gauthier, Goalie	.10	.15
252	Patrick Côté	.05	.10
253	Richard Aimonetto	.05	.10
254	Martin Laitre	.05	.10

COLLEGE FRANCAIS

No.	Player	EX	NRMT
255	Carl Lamothe	.05	.10
256	Q.M.J.H.L. Action	.10	.20

VICTORIAVILLE TIGRES

No.	Player	EX	NRMT
257	André Durocher	.05	.10
258	Jocelyn Martel	.05	.10

7th Inning Sketch 1990-91 Issue Card No. 247, Error, Face: Dominique; Back: Dominiqu

7th Inning Sketch 1991-92 Issue Card No. 1, Martin Brodeur

7th Inning Sketch 1991-92 Issue Card No. 1, Martin Brodeur

7th Inning Sketch 1991-92 Issue Card No. 10, Patrick Poulin

COLLEGE FRANCAIS

No.	Player	EX	NRMT
259	Jeanot Ferland	.05	.10
260	Martin Tanguay	.05	.10

VICTORIAVILLE TIGRES

No.	Player	EX	NRMT
261	Claude Savoie	.05	.10
262	Denis Beauchamp	.05	.10

COLLEGE FRANCAIS

No.	Player	EX	NRMT
263	Jean-François Gagnon, Goalie	.10	.20
264	André Bouliane, Goalie	.10	.20

VICTORIAVILLE TIGRES

No.	Player	EX	NRMT
265	Paul-Emile Exantus	.05	.10
266	Dany Nolet	.05	.10

SHAWINIGAN CATARACTES

No.	Player	EX	NRMT
267	Jean Imbeau	.05	.10

TROIS RIVIERES DRAVEURS

No.	Player	EX	NRMT
268	Claude Barthe	.05	.10

— 1991-92 REGULAR ISSUE —

Note: Cards # 66 and 256 do not exist.
Card Size: 2 1/2" X 3 1/2"
Face: Four colour, white border
Back: Four colour, black on white card stock, Number, Resume, Position, Bilingual
Imprint: © 1991 7th Inning Sketch Printed in Canada
Complete Set No.: 298

Complete Set Price:		11.50	23.00
Common Card:		.05	.10
Foil Pack: (10 Cards)			1.00
Foil Box : (36 Packs)			20.00
Foil Case: (20 Boxes)			350.00

Production:
Foil Cases: 1,500
Set Cases: 400 (4,800 Individually numbered sets)

LE LASER DE ST-HYACINTHE

No.	Player	EX	NRMT
1	Martin Brodeur, Goalie	1.50	3.00
2	Normand Paquet	.05	.10
3	David Desnoyers	.05	.10
4	Carlo Colombi	.05	.10
5	Stéphane Ménard, Goalie	.05	.10
6	Sébastien Berube	.05	.10
7	Marc Desgagne	.05	.10
8	Mil Sukovic	.15	.30
9	Patrick Belisle	.05	.10
10	Patrick Poulin	.50	1.00
11	Martin Trudel	.13	.25
12	Charles Poulin	.13	.25
13	Etienne Thibault	.05	.10
14	Pierre Allard	.05	.10
15	François Gagnon	.05	.10
16	Stéphane Huard	.05	.10
17	Yannik Lemay	.05	.10
18	Dany Fortin	.05	.10
19	Carl Menard	.05	.10
20	Serge Labelle	.05	.10
21	Dean Melanson	.05	.10
22	Yves Meunier	.05	.10
23	Pierre Petroni, Coach	.05	.10
24	Mario Pouliot, Asst. Coach, Error	.05	.10
25	Alain Côté, Error	.05	.10
26	Hugues Laliberté	.15	.30
27	Martin Gendron	.25	.50
28	Stan Melanson	.05	.10

1991-92 REGULAR ISSUE — 7TH INNING SKETCH

ERROR AND VARIATION LISTING

No.	Player	Description
24	Pouliot	Face team "Les Bison" should be "Le Laser"
25	Côté	Face team "Les Bison" should be "Le Laser"
		Back team "Kingston Frontenacs" should be "Le Laser de St-Hyacinthe"

LES BISONS DE GRANBY

No.	Player	EX	NRMT
29	Carl Leblanc	.10	.20
30	Patrick Grisé	.10	.20
31	Yves Charron	.05	.10
32	Hughes Mongeon	.05	.10
33	Christian Tardif	.05	.10
34	Patrick Tessier	.05	.10
35	Christian Campeau	.15	.30
36	Mario Therrien	.05	.10
37	Martin Balleux	.10	.20
38	Joel Brassard	.05	.10
39	Sébastien Fortier	.05	.10
40	Jocelyn Langlois	.05	.10
41	Guiseppe Argentos	.05	.10
42	Sylvain Brisson	.05	.10
43	Philippe Boucher	.13	.25
44	Martin Brochu, Goalie	.05	.10
45	Marc Rodgers	.10	.20
46	Pascal Gagnon	.05	.10
47	Benoit Therrien	.05	.10
48	Robin Bouchard	.05	.10
49	Micehl Savoie	.05	.10
50	Jean-Sébastien Boiteau	.05	.10
51	Patrick Lamoureux	.05	.10
52	Stephane Giard, Goalie	.05	.10

LES CATARACTES DE SHAWINIGAN

No.	Player	EX	NRMT
53	Maxime Jean	.05	.10
54	Alain Côté	.05	.10
55	François Groleau	.15	.30
56	Richard Hamelin	.10	.20
57	Eric Beauvis	.05	.10
58	Steve Laplante	.05	.10
59	Yves Meunier	.07	.15
60	Steve Dontigny	.15	.30
61	Simon Roy	.05	.10
62	Jean-François Laroche	.05	.10
63	Patrick Traverse	.05	.10
64	Eric Joyal	.05	.10
65	Jean-François Gregoire	.05	.10
66	Not issued		
67	Jean Imbeau	.10	.20
68	François Bourdeau	.05	.10
69	Alain Savage, Jr.	.05	.10
70	Johnny Lorenzo, Goalie	.10	.20
71	Patrick Lalime, Goalie	.05	.10
72	Patrick Melfi	.05	.10
73	Marc Tardif	.10	.20
74	Marc Savard	.05	.10
75	Alain Sanscartier, Coach	.05	.10
76	Pascal Lebrasseur	.05	.10

CHECKLIST

No.	Checklist	EX	NRMT
77	Checklist 1 (1 to 101)	.05	.10

LES SAGUENEENS DE CHICOUTIMI

No.	Player	EX	NRMT
78	Dany Girard	.05	.10
79	Eddy Gervais	.05	.10
80	Dave Tremblay	.05	.10
81	Dany Larochelle	.05	.10
82	Michel St-Jacques	.10	.20
83	Rodney Petawabano	.05	.10
84	Eric Duchesne	.05	.10
85	Patrick Clement	.05	.10
86	Steve Gosselin	.05	.10
87	Patrick Lacombe	.05	.10
88	Patrice Martineau	.07	.15
89	Danny Beauregard	.10	.20
90	Martin Lamarche	.05	.10
91	Sébastien Parent	.10	.20
92	Christian Caron	.05	.10
93	Sylvain Careau, Goalie	.05	.10

7th Inning Sketch
1991-92 Issue
Card No. 82,
Michel St-Jacques

7th Inning Sketch
1991-92 Issue
Card No. 116,
Carl Boudreau

7th Inning Sketch
1991-92 Issue
Card No. 118,
Eric Bellerose

7th Inning Sketch
1991-92 Issue
Card No. 129,
Robert Guillet

No.	Player	EX	NRMT
94	Martin Beaupré	.05	.10
95	Daniel Paradis	.10	.20
96	Sylvain Rodrigue, Goalie	.05	.10
97	Joe Canale, Coach	.05	.10
98	Patrick Lampron	.05	.10
99	Carl Blondin	.05	.10
100	Carl Wiseman	.05	.10
101	Hugo Hamelin	.05	.10

LES DRAVEURS DE TROIS-RIVIERES

No.	Player	EX	NRMT
102	Claude Poirier	.05	.10
103	Charles Paquette	.05	.10
104	Carl Fleury	.05	.10
105	Paolo Racicot	.05	.10
106	Sébastien Moreau	.05	.10
107	Pascal Trépanier	.05	.10
108	Dominic Maltais	.20	.40
109	Steve Arés	.05	.10
110	Daniel Thibault	.15	.30
111	Eric Messier	.05	.10
112	Stéphane Julien	.05	.10
113	Dave Paquet	.13	.25
114	Nicolas Turmel	.05	.10
115	Pascal Rheaume	.05	.10
116	Carl Boudreau	.18	.35
117	Dave Boudreault	.05	.10
118	Eric Bellerose	.18	.35
119	Steve Searles	.05	.10
120	Patrick Nadeau	.10	.20
121	Stephan Viens	.05	.10
122	Jean-François Labbé, Goalie	.20	.40
123	Jocelyn Thibault, Goalie	.05	.10
124	Gaston Drapeau, Coach	.05	.10

CHECKLIST

No.	Checklist	EX	NRMT
125	Checklist 2 (102 - 198)	.05	.10

LE COLLEGE FRANCAIS DE VERDUN

No.	Player	EX	NRMT
126	Martin Lajeaunes	.10	.20
127	Etienne Lavoie	.05	.10
128	Dominic Rhéaume	.10	.20
129	Robert Guillet	.10	.20
130	François Rivard	.05	.10
131	Phillippe de Rouville, Goalie	.25	.50
132	Andrej Dobrota	.05	.10
133	Pierre Gendron	.05	.10
134	Dave Chouinard	.18	.35
135	Martin Tanguay	.20	.40
136	Jacques Blouin	.05	.10
137	Martin Larochelle	.05	.10
138	Jean-Martin Morin	.05	.10
139	Donald Brashear	.05	.10
140	Stéphane Paradis	.05	.10
141	Jan Simcik	.05	.10
142	Yan Arsenault	.15	.30
143	Joel Bouchard	.05	.10
144	Jean-Sébastien Lefebvre	.05	.10
145	David St. Pierre	.13	.25
146	Mario Nobili	.10	.20
147	Stacy Dallaire	.05	.10
148	Carl Lamothe	.05	.10
149	Andre Bouliane, Goalie	.05	.10
150	Simon Arial	.05	.10

LES LYNX DE ST-JEAN

No.	Player	EX	NRMT
151	Stéphane Madore	.05	.10
152	Hughes Bouchard	.05	.10
153	Steve Decaen	.05	.10
154	Jason Downey	.05	.10
155	Raymond Delarosbil	.05	.10
156	Lino Salvo	.05	.10
157	Réginald Brézeault	.05	.10
158	Nathan Morin	.05	.10
159	Samuel Groleau	.13	.25
160	Patrick Carignan	.13	.25
161	Stéphane St-Amour	.05	.10
162	Marquis Mathieu	.05	.10

738 • 7TH INNING SKETCH — 1991 - 92 REGULAR ISSUE

No.	Player	EX	NRMT
163	Yves Sarault	.20	.40
164	Dave Belliveau	.05	.10
165	Trevor Duhaime	.05	.10
166	Eric O'Connor	.05	.10
167	Christian Proulx	.05	.10
168	Martin Lavallée, Goalie	.05	.10
169	Jean François Gagnon, Goalie	.05	.10
170	Eric Lafrance	.05	.10
171	Enrico Scardocchio	.05	.10
172	David Bergeron	.05	.10

LES HARFANGS DE BEAUPORT

No.	Player	EX	NRMT
173	Guillaume Morin, Goalie	.05	.10
174	Charlie Boucher	.05	.10
175	Marti Rozon	.05	.10
176	Brandon Piccarreto	.05	.10
177	Simon Toupin	.13	.25
178	Jamie Bird	.05	.10
179	Hervé Lapointe	.05	.10
180	Ian Mclantyre	.05	.10
181	Jean-François Rivard, Goalie	.05	.10
182	Alain Chainey, Coach	.05	.10
183	Daniel Laflamme	.05	.10
184	Patrice Paquin	.05	.10
185	Patrick Deraspe	.05	.10
186	Martin Roy	.05	.10
187	Jeannot Ferland	.05	.10
188	Patrick Genest	.07	.15
189	Matthew Barnaby	.05	.10
190	Jean-Guy Trudel	.05	.10
191	Eric Moreau	.05	.10
192	Eric Cool	.13	.25
193	Alexandre Legault	.05	.10
194	Gregg Pineo	.05	.10

LHJMG ACTION

No.	Player	EX	NRMT
195	LHJMQ Action - Quebec	.10	.20

LES HARFANGS DE BEAUPORT

No.	Player	EX	NRMT
196	Radoslav Balaz	.05	.10
197	Stefan Simoes	.05	.10

LHJMG ACTION

No.	Player	EX	NRMT
198	LHJMQ Action - Quebec	.10	.20

LES OLYMPIQUES DE HULL

No.	Player	EX	NRMT
199	François Paquette	.05	.10
200	Paul Macdonald	.05	.10
201	Shane Doiron	.05	.10
202	Michal Longauer	.05	.10
203	Joe Crowley	.05	.10
204	Joey Deliva	.07	.15
205	Pierre-François Lalonde	.07	.15
206	Paul Brousseau	.20	.40
207	Martin Lepage	.05	.10
208	Yanick DeGrace, Goalie	.05	.10
209	Jim Campbell	.05	.10
210	Sebastien Bordeleau	.05	.10
211	Marc Legault, Goalie	.05	.10
212	Joel Blain	.07	.15
213	Claude Jutras	.05	.10
214	Eric Lavigne	.13	.25
215	Todd Sparks	.13	.25
216	Sylvain Lapointe	.05	.10
217	Eric Lecompte	.50	1.00
218	Thierry Mayer	.05	.10
219A	Harold Hersh, Error	.18	.35
219B	Harold Hersh, Corrected	.07	.15
220	Frédéric Boivin	.05	.10
221	Steven Dion	.05	.10
222	Alain Vigneault, Coach	.05	.10

CHECKLIST

No.	Checklist	EX	NRMT
223	Checklist 3 (199 - 298)	.05	.10

7th Inning Sketch
1991-92 Issue
Card No. 192,
Eric Cool

7th Inning Sketch
1991-92 Issue
Card No. 238,
Sylvain Blouin

7th Inning Sketch
1991-92 Issue
Card No. 250,
Bruno Ducharme

7th Inning Sketch
1991-92 Issue
Card No. 269,
Sébastien Tremblay

LE TITAN DE LAVAL

No.	Player	EX	NRMT
224	Petr Valenta	.05	.10

LHJMQ ACTION

No.	Player	EX	NRMT
225	LHJMQ Action - Quebec	.10	.20

LE TITAN DE LAVAL

No.	Player	EX	NRMT
226	Jim Bermingham	.13	.25
227	Yanick Dube	.05	.10
228	Sandy McCarthy	.13	.25
229	Dany Michaud	.05	.10
230	Jason Brousseau	.05	.10
231	Marc Beaucage	.05	.10
232	Eric Cardinal	.05	.10
233	Martin Chaput	.05	.10
234	Jean Roberge	.05	.10
235	Philip Gathercole	.05	.10
236	Michael Gaule	.05	.10
237	Yannick Frechette	.05	.10
238	Sylvain Blolun	.05	.10
239	Davod Pekorek	.05	.10
240	John Kovacs	.05	.10
241	Eric Raymond, Goalie	.05	.10
242	Emmanuel Fernandez	.10	.20
243	Yan St. Pierre	.05	.10
244	Brant Blackned	.05	.10
245	Eric Veilleux	.13	.25
246	Pascal Vincent	.05	.10
247	Benoit Larose	.05	.10
248	Olivier Guillaume	.05	.10

LES TIGRES DE VICTORIAVILLE

No.	Player	EX	NRMT
249	Alain Gauthier, Goalie	.05	.10
250	Bruno Ducharme, Goalie	.05	.10
251	Patrick Charbonneau, Goalie	.05	.10
252	Daniel Germain	.05	.10
253	Pascal Chiasson	.05	.10
254	Marc Thibeault	.05	.10
255	Martin Woods	.05	.10
256	Not issued		
257	Dominic Grand'maison	.05	.10
258	Carl Poirier	.05	.10
259	Stéphane Larocque	.05	.10
260	Mario Dumoulin	.05	.10
261	Yvan Laterreur	.05	.10
262	Claude Savoie	.30	.60
263	Denis Beauchamp	.05	.10
264	Patrick Bisaillon	.07	.15
265	Pascal Bernier	.05	.10
266	Nicolas Lefebvre	.05	.10

LHJMQ ACTION

No.	Player	EX	NRMT
267	LHJMQ Action	.10	.20

LES TIGRES DE VICTORIAVILLE

No.	Player	EX	NRMT
268	Joseph Napolitano	.05	.10
269	Sébastien Tremblay	.10	.20
270	Alexandre Daigle	5.00	10.00
271	Pierre Pillion	.05	.10
272	Yves Lambert, Asst. Coach	.05	.10
273	Pierre Aubry, Coach	.05	.10

LES VOLTIGEURS DE DRUMMONDVILLE

No.	Player	EX	NRMT
274	Yves Loubier, Goalie	.05	.10
275	Peter Sandke	.05	.10
276	Louis Bernard	.05	.10
277	Alain Nasreddine	.05	.10
278	Sylvain Ducharme	.05	.10
279	Jeremy Caissie	.05	.10
280	Eric Meloche	.05	.10
281	Ian Laperriére	.25	.50
282	Hugo Proulx	.25	.50
283	Dave Whittom	.10	.20
284	Yannick Dupre	.15	.30

No.	Player	EX	NRMT
285	Eric Plante	.07	.15
286	Stéphane Desjardins	.05	.10
287	René Corbet	.20	.40
288	David Lessard	.05	.10
289	Eric Marcoux	.05	.10
290	Alexandre Duchesne	.05	.10
291	Maxime Petitclerc	.05	.10
292	Pierre Gagnon, Goalie	.05	.10
293	Roger Larche	.07	.15
294	Jeam Hamel, Coach	.05	.10
295	Alexandre Gaumond	.05	.10
296	Paul-Emile Exentus	.05	.10

LHJMQ ACTION

No.	Player	EX	NRMT
297	LHJMQ Action	.05	.10
298	LHJMQ Action	.05	.10

LES OLYMPIQUES DE HULL

No.	Player	EX	NRMT
XX	Carl Fleur	.50	1.00

Note: The card numbered XX was found inside a wax pack and is not listed on any checklist.

— 1991 - 92 INSERT SET —
THE TEAMS

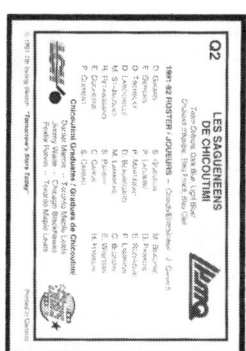

7th Inning Sketch
1991-92 Insert Set
Card No. Q2,
Les Sagueneens de Chicoutimi

Card Size: 2 1/2" X 3 1/2"
Face: Four colour, white border
Back: Four colour, black on white card stock, Number, Resume, Position, Bilingual
Imprint: © 1991 7th Inning Sketch Printed in Canada
Complete Set No.: 11
Complete Set Price: 2.50 5.00

No.	Player	EX	NRMT
Q1	Les Harfangs de Beauport	.25	.50
Q2	Les Sagueneens de Chicoutimi	.25	.50
Q3	Les Voltigeurs de Drummondville	.25	.50
Q4	Les Olympiques de Hull	.25	.50
Q5	Le Titan de Laval	.25	.50
Q6	Le College Francais de Verdun	.25	.50
Q7	Le Laser de St-Hyacinthe	.25	.50
Q8	Les Lynx de St-Jean	.25	.50
Q9	Les Cataractes de Shawinigan	.25	.50
Q10	Les Draveurs de Trois-Rivieres	.25	.50
Q11	Les Tigres de Victoriaville	.25	.50

7th Inning Sketch
1991-92 Insert Set
Card No. Q2,
Les Sagueneens de Chicoutimi

THE CHARLTON STANDARD CATALOGUE OF CANADIAN
BASEBALL & FOOTBALL CARDS
- Fourth Edition -
BASEBALL CARDS FROM 1912 — FOOTBALL CARDS FROM 1949
For Canadian Baseball and Football Card Collectors this Catalogue has it all!

IMPERIAL TOBACCO * MAPLE CRISPETTE * PARKHURST * O-PEE-CHEE * CANADA STARCH * STUART POST *
TOPPS * WORLD WIDE GUM * NALLEYS * DONRUSS - LEAF * EDDIE SARGENT * PROVIGO *
WILLARD * NABISCO * TORONTO BLUE * JAYS * STANDARD OIL * BLUE RIBBON TEA * PANINI
GENERAL MILLS * SCORE * EXHIBITS * HOSTESS * PURITAN MEATS * GULF CANADA * JOGO * VACHON *
ROYAL STUDIOS * NEILSON'S * BEN'S AULT FOODS * COCA-COLA * BAZOOKA * KFC
And All Other Major Manufacturers...

Complete price listings for all Major League Baseball and Canadian Football League cards!
Comprehensive baseball and football minor league card listings!
Regular issues, stickers, inserts, subsets, transfers and much, much more!
All major manufacturers!
Current Pricing for all cards in up to three grades of condition - VG, EX, and NRMT!
All rookie, last, pitcher, quarterback, error and variation cards identified and priced!
Plus Charlton's Fabulous Alphabetical Index!

OVER 300 PAGES * 60,000 PRICES, NEW, LARGER 8 1/2 x 11" FORMAT
RESERVE YOUR COPY TODAY DIRECTLY FROM THE PUBLISHER...

The Charlton Press
2010 YONGE STREET, TORONTO, ONTARIO M4S 1Z9
FOR TOLL FREE ORDERING PHONE 1-800-442-6042 FAX 1-800-442-1542 from anywhere in Canada or the U.S.

740 • CRESCENT ICE CREAM — 1923-24 SELKIRKS HOCKEY CLUB

WESTERN CANADIAN HOCKEY LEAGUE AND WESTERN HOCKEY LEAGUES

CRESCENT ICE CREAM

— 1923 - 24 SELKIRKS HOCKEY CLUB —

Card Size: 1 9/16" X 2 3/8"
Face: Black and white photo
Back: Black on card stock; Number, Premium offer
Imprint: None
Complete Set No.: 14
Complete Set Price: 150.00.00 375.00 750.00
Common Player: 12.00 30.00 60.00

No.	Player	G	VG	EX
1	Cliff O'Meara	12.00	30.00	60.00
2	Leo Benard	12.00	30.00	60.00
3	Pete Speirs	12.00	30.00	60.00
4	Howard Brandow	12.00	30.00	60.00
5	George Clark	12.00	30.00	60.00
6	Unknown	12.00	30.00	60.00
7	Cecil Browne	12.00	30.00	60.00
8	Jack Connelly	12.00	30.00	60.00
9	Charlie Gardner	12.00	30.00	60.00
10	Ward Turvey	12.00	30.00	60.00
11	Connie Johanneson	12.00	30.00	60.00
12	Frank Woodall	12.00	30.00	60.00
13	Harold McMunn	12.00	30.00	60.00
14	Connie Neil	12.00	30.00	60.00

— 1924 - 25 SELKIRKS HOCKEY CLUB —

Sepia variety.
Card Size: 1 9/16" X 2 3/8"
Face: Black and white photo, white border; Team, Name, Position
Back: Black on card stock; Number, Premium offer
Imprint: None
Complete Set No.: 14
Complete Set Price: 150.00 375.00 750.00
Common Player: 12.00 30.00 60.00

No.	Player	G	VG	EX
1	Howard Brandow	12.00	30.00	60.00
2	Jack Hughes	12.00	30.00	60.00
3	Tony Baril	12.00	30.00	60.00
4	Bill Bowman	12.00	30.00	60.00
5	W. Roberts	12.00	30.00	60.00
6	Cecil Browne	12.00	30.00	60.00
7	Errol Gillis	12.00	30.00	60.00
8	Selkirks	12.00	30.00	60.00
9	Fred Comfort	12.00	30.00	60.00
10	Cliff O'Meara	12.00	30.00	60.00
11	Leo Benard	12.00	30.00	60.00
12	Pete Speirs	12.00	30.00	60.00
13	Peter Meurer	12.00	30.00	60.00
14	Billy Borland	12.00	30.00	60.00

— 1924 - 25 FALCON TIGERS HOCKEY CLUB —

Card Size: 1 9/16" X 2 3/8"
Face: Black and white photo, white border; Team, Name, Position
Back: Black on card stock; Number, Premium offer
Imprint: None
Complete Set No.: 14
Complete Set Price: 150.00 375.00 750.00
Common Player: 12.00 30.00 60.00

No.	Player	G	VG	EX
1	Bill Cockburn	12.00	30.00	60.00
2	Wally Byron	12.00	30.00	60.00
3	Wally Fridfinnson	12.00	30.00	60.00
4	Murray Murdoch	12.00	30.00	60.00
5	Oliver Redpath	12.00	30.00	60.00
6	Unknown	12.00	30.00	60.00
7	Ward McVey	12.00	30.00	60.00
8	Tote Mithcell	12.00	30.00	60.00
9	Lorne Carrol	12.00	30.00	60.00
10	Tony Wise	12.00	30.00	60.00
11	Johnny Myres	12.00	30.00	60.00
12	Gordon McKenzie	12.00	30.00	60.00
13	Harry Neal	12.00	30.00	60.00
14	Blake Watson	12.00	30.00	60.00

[PHOTOGRAPH NOT AVAILABLE AT PRESS TIME]

HOLLAND CREAMERIES

— 1924 - 25 WESTERN —

Card Size: 1 1/2" X 2 7/8'
Face: Black and white photo, white border; Name, Position, Number
Back: Black on card stock; Premium offer
Imprint: None
Complete Set No.: 10
Complete Set Price: 110.00 275.00 550.00
Common Player: 12.00 30.00 60.00

No.	Player	G	VG	EX
1	W. Fridfinnson	12.00	30.00	60.00
2	H. McMunn	12.00	30.00	60.00
3	A. Somers	12.00	30.00	60.00
4	F. Woodall	12.00	30.00	60.00
5	F. Fredrickson	12.00	30.00	60.00
6	R.J. Benson	12.00	30.00	60.00
7	H. Neil	12.00	30.00	60.00
8	J.W. Byron	12.00	30.00	60.00
9	C. Neil	12.00	30.00	60.00
10	J. Austman	12.00	30.00	60.00

PAULINS CANDY

— 1923 - 24 ISSUE —

Western Canadian Hockey League. Prize offered for complete set.

Card Size: 1 3/8" X 2 3/4"
Face: Black and white photo, white border; Name
Back: Black on card stock; Number, Premium offer
Imprint: None
ACC No.:V128
Complete Set No.: 70
Complete Set Price: 1,100.00 2,200.00 4,500.00
Common Player: 12.00 30.00 60.00

No.	Player	G	VG	EX
1	Bill Borland	15.00	35.00	75.00
2	Pete Speirs	12.00	30.00	60.00
3	Jack Hughes	12.00	30.00	60.00
4	Errol Gillis	12.00	30.00	60.00
5	Cecil Browne	12.00	30.00	60.00
6	W. Roberts	12.00	30.00	60.00
7	Howard Brandow	12.00	30.00	60.00
8	Fred Comfort	12.00	30.00	60.00
9	Cliff O'Meara	12.00	30.00	60.00
10	Leo Benard	12.00	30.00	60.00
11	Lloyd Harvey	12.00	30.00	60.00
12	Bobby Connors	12.00	30.00	60.00
13	Daddy Dalman	12.00	30.00	60.00
14	Dub Mackie	12.00	30.00	60.00
15	Lorne Chabot, Goalie	40.00	85.00	175.00
16	Phat Wilson	12.00	30.00	60.00
17	Wilf L'Heureux	12.00	30.00	60.00
18	Danny Cox	12.00	30.00	60.00
19	Bill Brydge	12.00	30.00	60.00
20	Alex Gray	12.00	30.00	60.00
21	Albert Pudas	12.00	30.00	60.00
22	Dick Irwin	12.00	30.00	60.00
23	Puss Traub	12.00	30.00	60.00
24	Red McCusker, GOalie	12.00	30.00	60.00
25	Jack Asseltine	12.00	30.00	60.00
26	Duke Dutkowski	12.00	30.00	60.00
27	Charlie McVeigh	12.00	30.00	60.00
28	George Hay	12.00	30.00	60.00
29	Amby Moran	12.00	30.00	60.00
30	Barney Stanley	12.00	30.00	60.00
31	Art Gagne	12.00	30.00	60.00
32	Louis Berlinquette	12.00	30.00	60.00
33	P.C. Stevens	12.00	30.00	60.00
34	W.D. Elmer	12.00	30.00	60.00
35	Bill Cook	50.00	100.00	200.00
36	Leo Reise	12.00	30.00	60.00
37	Curly Headley	12.00	30.00	60.00
38	Newsy Lalonde	50.00	100.00	200.00
39	George Hainsworth, Goalie	60.00	125.00	250.00
40	Laurie Scott	12.00	30.00	60.00

No.	Player	G	VG	EX
41	Joe Simpson	20.00	50.00	100.00
42	Bob Trapp	12.00	30.00	60.00
43	Joe McCormick	12.00	30.00	60.00
44	Ty Arbour	12.00	30.00	60.00
45	Duke Keats	12.00	30.00	60.00
46	Hal Winkler	12.00	30.00	60.00
47	Johnny Sheppard	12.00	30.00	60.00
48	Crutchy Morrison	12.00	30.00	60.00
49	Spunk Sparrow	12.00	30.00	60.00
50	Percy McGregor	12.00	30.00	60.00
51	Harry Tuckwell	12.00	30.00	60.00
52	Chubby Scott	12.00	30.00	60.00
53	Scotty Fraser	12.00	30.00	60.00
54	Bob Davis	12.00	30.00	60.00
55	Clucker White	12.00	30.00	60.00
56	Bob Armstrong	12.00	30.00	60.00
57	Doc Langtry	12.00	30.00	60.00
58	Darb Sommers	12.00	30.00	60.00
59	Frank Hacquoil	12.00	30.00	60.00
60	Stan Evans	12.00	30.00	60.00
61	Eddie Oatman	12.00	30.00	60.00
62	Red Dutton	20.00	50.00	100.00
63	Herb Gardiner	30.00	60.00	120.00
64	Bernie Morris	12.00	30.00	60.00
65	Bobbie Benson	12.00	30.00	60.00
66	Ernie Anderson	12.00	30.00	60.00
67	Cully Wilson	12.00	30.00	60.00
68	Charlie Reid, Goalie	12.00	30.00	60.00
69	Harry Oliver	30.00	60.00	125.00
70	Rusty Crawford	35.00	85.00	175.00

— 1928 - 29 ISSUE —

Issued in Western Canada during 1928 and 1929, this extremely scarce set has two unknown cards (numbers 9 and 20). Card numbers 51, 53, 72, 75, 82, 84, 85, 86 and 90 are players from the Calgary Jimmies who have not been identified.

Card Size: 1 3/8" X 2 5/8"
Face: Black and white photo, white border; Name
Back: Black on card stock; Number, Premium offer
Imprint: None
Complete Set No.: 90

		G	VG	EX
Complete Set Price:		900.00	2250.00	4500.00
Common Team: (1 to 40)		12.00	30.00	60.00
Common Player: (41 to 90)		10.00	25.00	50.00

No.	Player	G	VG	EX
1	University of Manitoba	12.00	30.00	60.00
	Girls Hockey Team	12.00	30.00	60.00
2	Elgin Hockey Team	12.00	30.00	60.00
3	Brandon Schools Boy Champions	12.00	30.00	60.00
4	Port Arthur Hockey Team	12.00	30.00	60.00
5	Enderby Hockey Team	12.00	30.00	60.00
6	Humbolt H.S. Hockey Team	12.00	30.00	60.00
7	Regina Collecgiate Hockey Team	12.00	30.00	60.00
8	Weyburn Beavers	12.00	30.00	60.00
9	Moose Jaw College Jr. Team	12.00	30.00	60.00
10	M.A.C. Junior Hockey	12.00	30.00	60.00
11	Vermilion Agricultural School	12.00	30.00	60.00
12	Rovers, Cranbrook	12.00	30.00	60.00
13	Empire School, Moose Jaw	12.00	30.00	60.00
14	Arts Senior Hockey	12.00	30.00	60.00
15	Juvenile Varsity Hockey	12.00	30.00	60.00
16	St. Peter's College Hockey	12.00	30.00	60.00
17	Arts Girls Hockey Team	12.00	30.00	60.00
18	Swan River Hockey Team	12.00	30.00	60.00
19	UMSU Junior Hockey Team	12.00	30.00	60.00
20	Champion College Hockey Team	12.00	30.00	60.00
21	Drinkwater Hockey Team	12.00	30.00	60.00

PHOTOGRAPH NOT AVAILABLE AT PRESS TIME

No.	Player	VG	EX	NRMT
22	Elks Hockey Team, Biggar, Sask.	12.00	30.00	60.00
23	South Calgary High School	12.00	30.00	60.00
24	Meota Hockey	12.00	30.00	60.00
25	Chartered Accountants	12.00	30.00	60.00
26	Nutana Collegiate Hockey Team	12.00	30.00	60.00
27	MacLeod Hockey Team	12.00	30.00	60.00
28	Arts Junior Hockey	12.00	30.00	60.00
29	Fort William Juniors	12.00	30.00	60.00
30	Swan Lake Hockey Team	12.00	30.00	60.00
31	Dauphin Hockey Team	12.00	30.00	60.00
32	Mount Royal Hockey Team	12.00	30.00	60.00
33	Port Arthur W. End Junior Hockey	12.00	30.00	60.00
34	Hanna Hockey Club	12.00	30.00	60.00
35	Vermilion Junior Hockey	12.00	30.00	60.00
36	Smithers Hockey Team	12.00	30.00	60.00
37	Lloydminster High School	12.00	30.00	60.00
38	Winnipeg Rangers	12.00	30.00	60.00
39	Delisle Intermediate Hockey	12.00	30.00	60.00
40	Moose Jaw College Senior Hockey	12.00	30.00	60.00
41	Art Bonneyman	10.00	25.00	50.00
42	Jimmy Graham	10.00	25.00	50.00
43	Pat O'Hunter	10.00	25.00	50.00
44	Leo Moret	10.00	25.00	50.00
45	Blondie McLennen	10.00	25.00	50.00
46	Red Beatty	10.00	25.00	50.00
47	Frank Peters	10.00	25.00	50.00
48	Lloyd McIntyre	10.00	25.00	50.00
49	Art Somers	10.00	25.00	50.00
50	Ikey Morrison	10.00	25.00	50.00
51	Calgary Jimmies	10.00	25.00	50.00
52	Don Cummings	10.00	25.00	50.00
53	Calgary Jimmies	10.00	25.00	50.00
54	P. Gerlitz	10.00	25.00	50.00
55	A. Kay	10.00	25.00	50.00
56	Paul Runge	10.00	25.00	50.00
57	J. Gerlitz	10.00	25.00	50.00
58	H. Gerlitz	10.00	25.00	50.00
59	C. Biles	10.00	25.00	50.00
60	Jimmy Evans	10.00	25.00	50.00
61	Ira Stuart	10.00	25.00	50.00
62	Berg Irving	10.00	25.00	50.00
63	Cece Browne	10.00	25.00	50.00
64	Nic. Wasnie	10.00	25.00	50.00
65	Gordon Teal	10.00	25.00	50.00
66	Jack Hughes	10.00	25.00	50.00
67	D. Yeatman	10.00	25.00	50.00
68	Connie Johanneson	10.00	25.00	50.00
69	S. Walters	10.00	25.00	50.00
70	Harold McMunn	10.00	25.00	50.00
71	Smokey Harris	10.00	25.00	50.00
72	Calgary Jimmies	10.00	25.00	50.00
73	Burney Morris	10.00	25.00	50.00
74	J. Fowler	10.00	25.00	50.00
75	Calgary Jimmies	10.00	25.00	50.00
76	Pete Spiers	10.00	25.00	50.00
77	Bill Borland	10.00	25.00	50.00
78	Cliff O'Meara	10.00	25.00	50.00
79	F. Porteous	10.00	25.00	50.00
80	W. Brooks	10.00	25.00	50.00
81	Everett McGowan	10.00	25.00	50.00
82	Calgary Jimmies	10.00	25.00	50.00
83	George Dame	10.00	25.00	50.00
84	Calgary Jimmies	10.00	25.00	50.00
85	Calgary Jimmies	10.00	25.00	50.00
86	Calgary Jimmies	10.00	25.00	50.00
87	Heck Fowler	10.00	25.00	50.00
88	Jimmy Hoyle	10.00	25.00	50.00
89	Charlie Gardiner	10.00	25.00	50.00
90	Calgary Jimmies	10.00	25.00	50.00

7TH INNING SKETCH

— 1990 - 91 REGULAR ISSUE —

1990-91 Issue
Card No. 1, Brent Bilodeau

Card Size: 2 1/2" X 3 1/2"
Face: Four colour, white border
Back: Four colour, black on white card stock, Number, Resume, Position
Imprint: © 1991 7th Inning Sketch Printed in Canada
Complete Set No.: 347

	EX	NRMT
Complete Set Price:	15.00	30.00
Common Goalie:	.05	.10
Common Player:	.05	.10
Foil Pack: (10 Cards)		1.50
Foil Box: (36 Packs)		35.00
Foil Case: (20 Boxes)		500.00

Production:
Foil Cases: 2,500
Set Cases: 500 (6,000 individually numbered sets)

WHL CHRISTMAS CARDS

No.	Player	EX	NRMT
—	White card stock	2.50	5.00
—	Silver foil card stock	5.00	10.00

SEATTLE THUNDERBIRDS

No.	Player	EX	NRMT
1	Brent Bilodeau	.50	1.00
2	Craig Chapman	.05	.10
3	Jeff Jubenville	.05	.10
4	Al Kinisky	.10	.20
5	Kevin Malgunas	.05	.10
6	Andy MacIntyre	.05	.10
7	Darren McAusland	.05	.10
8	Mike Seaton	.10	.15
9	Turner Stevenson	.35	.75
10	Lindsay Vallis	.10	.20
11	Dave Wilkie	.05	.10
12	Jesse Wilson	.05	.10
13	Dody Wood	.12	.25
14	Bradley Zavisha	.10	.15
15	Vince Boe	.05	.10
16	Scott Davis	.05	.10
17	Troy Hyatt	.05	.10
18	Trevor Pennock	.05	.10
19	Corey Schwab, Goalie	.07	.15
20	Scott Bellefontaine, Goalie	.05	.10
21	Travis Kelln	.05	.10
22	Peter Anholt, Coach/GM	.05	.10

See Card No. 187, for another Seattle Thunderbirds Player.

MEDICINE HAT TIGERS

No.	Player	EX	NRMT
23	Sonny Mignacca, Goalie, Error	.05	.10
24	Chris Osgood, Goalie	.05	.10
25	Murray Garbutt	.05	.10
26	Kalvin Knibbs	.05	.10
27	Jason Krywulak	.05	.10
28	Jason Miller	.12	.25
29	Rob Niedermayer	1.25	2.50
30	Clayton Norris	.05	.10
31	Jason Prosofsky	.05	.10
32	Dana Rieder	.05	.10
33	Kevin Riehl	.18	.35
34	Tyler Romanchuk	.15	.30
35	Dave Shute	.15	.30
36	Lorne Toews	.05	.10
37	Scott Townsend	.05	.10
38	David Cooper	.25	.50
39	Jon Duval	.05	.10
40	Dan Kordic	.25	.50
41	Mike Rathje	.50	1.00
42	Tim Bothwell, Coach	.05	.10
43	Brent Thompson	.05	.10
44	Jeff Knight	.20	.30

SWIFT CURRENT BRONCOS

No.	Player	EX	NRMT
45	Van Burgess	.05	.10
46	Kimbi Daniels	.25	.50
47	Curtis Friesen	.05	.10
48	Todd Holt	.10	.20
49	Blake Knox	.10	.20
50	Trent McCleary	.10	.20
51	Mark McFarlane	.05	.10
52	Eddie Patterson	.05	.10
53	Lloyd Pellitier	.10	.20
54	Geoff Sanderson	2.50	5.00
55	Andrew Schneider	.12	.25
56	Tyler Wright	.50	1.00
57	Joel Dyck	.05	.10
58	Len MacAusland	.05	.10
59	Evan Marble	.05	.10
60	David Podlubny	.05	.10
61	Kurt Seher	.25	.50
62	Jason Smith	.05	.10
63	Justin Burke, Goalie	.05	.10
64	Kelly Thiessen, Goalie	.05	.10
65	Todd Esselmont	.05	.10
66	Graham James, Coach/GM	.05	.10
67	Chris Herperger	.05	.10
68	Mark McCoy	.05	.10
69	Dean Malkoc	.05	.10
70	Dennis Sproxton, Goalie	.05	.10
71	Centennial Civic Centre	.07	.15
72	Kimbi Daniels (Special Achievement)	.18	.35

SASKATOON BLADES

No.	Player	EX	NRMT
73	Shane Calder	.12	.25
74	Mark Franks	.12	.25
75	Greg Leahy	.05	.10
76	Dean Rambo	.05	.10
77	Scott Scissons	.25	.50
78	David Struch	.05	.10
79	Derek Tibbatts	.15	.30
80	Shawn Yakimishyn	.05	.10
81	Trent Coghill	.05	.10
82	Robert Lelacheur	.10	.20
83	Richard Matvichuk	.50	1.00
84	Mark Raiter	.05	.10
85	Trevor Sherban	.05	.10
86	Mark Wotton	.05	.10
87	Cam Moon, Goalie	.05	.10
88	Trevor Robins, Goalie	.05	.10
89	Jeff Buchanan	.10	.20
90	Ryan Strain	.05	.10
91	Tim Cox	.05	.10
92	Terry Ruskowski, Coach	.07	.15
93	Saskatchewan Place	.07	.15
94	Darin Bader	.05	.10
95	Gaetan Blouin	.07	.15

TRI-CITY AMERICANS

No.	Player	EX	NRMT
96	Rick Kozuback, Coach/GM	.05	.10
97	Jason Bowen	.15	.30
98	Fran Deferenza	.05	.10
99	Terry Degner	.15	.30
100	Devin Derksen	.05	.10
101	Martin Svetlik	.05	.10
102	Jeremy Warring, Goalie	.05	.10
103	Corey Jones, Goalie	.05	.10
104	Dean Tiltgen, Error	.12	.25
105	Ryan Fujita	.12	.25
106	Jeff Fancy	.05	.10
107	Terry Virtue	.05	.10
108	Dennis Pinfold	.05	.10
109	Kyle Reeves	.35	.75
110	Steve McNutt, Error	.10	.20
111	Todd Klassen	.05	.10
112	Darren Hastman	.05	.10
113	Bill Lindsay	.35	.75
114	Brian Sakic, Error	.50	1.00
115	Dan Sherstenka	.05	.10
116	Don Blishen, Goalie	.05	.10
117	Jason Marshall	.50	1.00
118	Dean Zayonce	.10	.20
119	Brad Loring	.05	.10

Note: Card No. 120 not issued.

LETHBRIDGE HURRICANES

No.	Player	EX	NRMT
121	Darcy Austin, Goalie, Error	.07	.15
122	Darcy Werenka	.25	.50
123	Shane Peacock	.05	.10
124	Bob Hartnell, Error	.05	.10
125	Brad Zimmer	.05	.10
126	Allan Egeland	.05	.10
127	Brad Rubachuk	.05	.10
128	Jamie Pushor	.12	.25
129	Jamie McLennan, Goalie, Error	.05	.10
130	Lance Burns	.05	.10
131	Ryan Smith	.10	.15
132	Jason McBain	.05	.10
133	Duane Maruschak, Error	.20	.40
134	Kevin St. Jacques	.12	.25
135	Jason Sorochan	.10	.20
136	Jason Widmer	.05	.10
137	Bob Loucks, Coach	.05	.10
138	Jason Ruff	.18	.35
139	Pat Pylypuik	.05	.10
140	Scott Adair	.05	.10
141	Radek Sip	.20	.40

MOOSE JAW WARRIORS

No.	Player	EX	NRMT
142	Russ West	.05	.10
143	Scott Thomas	.18	.35
144	Kent Staniforth	.05	.10
145	Travis Thiessen	.05	.10
146	Marc Hussey	.05	.10
147	Kevin Masters	.05	.10
148	Todd Johnson	.05	.10
149	Bob Loucks	.05	.10
150	Rob Reimer	.12	.25
151	Jeff Petruic	.05	.10
152	Chris Schmidt	.20	.40
153	Scott Barnstable	.05	.10
154	Ian Layton	.05	.10
155	Kevin Smyth	.15	.30
156	Kim Deck	.05	.10
157	Jason White	.05	.10
158	Peter Cox	.05	.10
159	Jeff Calvert, Goalie, Error	.05	.10
160	Paul Dyck, Error	.07	.15
161	Derek Kletzel	.05	.10
162	Jason Fitzsimmons, Goalie, Error	.05	.10
163	Darcy Jerome	.05	.10

REGINA PATS

No.	Player	EX	NRMT
164	Hal Christiansen	.05	.10
165	Terry Hollinger	.10	.15
166	Mike Risdale, Goalie	.15	.30
167	Jamie Heward	.15	.30
168	Louis Dumont	.05	.10
169	Cory Dosdall	.05	.10
170	Terry Bendera	.05	.10
171	Jamie Hayden	.05	.10
172	Kelly Chotowetz	.05	.10
173	Brad Scott	.12	.25
174	Jeff Shantz	.05	.10
175	Kelly Markwart	.05	.10
176	Gary Pearce	.05	.10
177	Kerry Biette	.05	.10
178	Jamie Splett	.05	.10
179	Frank Kovacs	.05	.10
180	Greg Pankewicz	.05	.10

—1991 - 92 REGULAR ISSUE — 7TH INNING SKETCH • 743

No.	Player	EX	NRMT
181	Colin Ruck	.05	.10
182	Brad Tippett, Coach	.05	.10
183	Dusty Imoo, Goalie	.12	.25
184	Derek Eberle	.05	.10
185	Heath Weenk	.05	.10
186	Mike Sillinger	.50	1.00

SEATTLE THUNDERBIRDS

No.	Player	EX	NRMT
187	Erin Thornton	.05	.10

SPOKANE CHIEFS

No.	Player	EX	NRMT
188	Mike Chrun	.05	.10
189	Pat Falloon	1.50	3.00
190	Bobby House, Error	.12	.25
191	Mike Jickling	.12	.25
192	Trevor Tovell, Error	.05	.10
193	Steve Junker	.20	.40
194	Shane Maitland	.05	.10
195	Chris Lafreniere	.05	.10
196	Frank Evans	.05	.10
197	Jon Klemm	.05	.10
198	Shawn Dietrich, Goalie, Error	.05	.10
199	Dennis Saharachuk, Error	.05	.10
200	Mark Woolf	.20	.40
201	Ray Whitney	.50	1.00
202	Scott Bailey, Goalie	.05	.10
203	Mike Ruark	.05	.10
204	Brent Thurston	.15	.30
205	Dan Faassen	.05	.10
206	Kerry Toporowski	.15	.30
207	Des Christopher, Goalie	.05	.10
208	Geoff Grandberg	.05	.10
209	Bryan Maxwell, Coach	.05	.10
210	Cam Danyluk	.15	.30
211	Bram Vanderkracht	.15	.30
212	Calvin Thudium	.05	.10
213	Mark Szoke, Error	.25	.50

BRANDON WHEAT KINGS

No.	Player	EX	NRMT
214	Kelly McCrimmon, Coach/GM	.05	.10
215	Kevin Robertson, Error	.05	.10
216	Brian Purdy, Error	.15	.30
217	Hardy Sauter	.05	.10
218	Dwayne Gylywoychuk	.05	.10
219	Bart Cote	.05	.10
220	Merv Priest	.05	.10
221	Jeff Hoad	.05	.10
222	Glen Gulutzan	.05	.10
223	Johan Skillgard	.05	.10
224	Byron Penstock, Goalie	.05	.10
225	Mike Vandenberghe, Error	.15	.30
226	Trevor Kidd, Goalie	.50	1.00
227	Dan Kopec	.05	.10
228	Greg Hutchings	.05	.10
229	Chris Constant	.05	.10
230	Glen Webster	.05	.10
231	Rob Puchniak	.05	.10
232	Calvin Flint	.05	.10
233	Stuart Scantlebury	.05	.10
234	Jason White	.05	.10
235	Gary Audette	.07	.15
236	Kevin Schmalz	.05	.10

VICTORIA COUGARS

No.	Player	EX	NRMT
237	Dwayne Newman	.05	.10
238	Chris Catellier	.05	.10
239	Todd Harris	.05	.10
240	Mike Shemko	.05	.10
241	John Badduke	.05	.10
242	Mark Cipriano	.05	.10
243	Brad Bagu	.05	.10
244	Ross Harris	.05	.10
245	Dino Caputo	.05	.10
246	Cam Bristow	.05	.10
247	Jarret Zukiwsky, Error	.05	.10
248	Jason Knox	.05	.10
249	Gerry St. Cyr	.15	.30
250	Larry Woo	.05	.10

No.	Player	EX	NRMT
251	Jason Peters	.05	.10
252	Shane Stangby	.10	.20
253	Dave McMillen	.05	.10
254	Colin Gregor, Error	.05	.10
255	Steve Passmore, Goalie	.05	.10
256	Shayne Green, Error	.20	.40
257	Kevin Koopman, Goalie	.05	.10
258	Lanny Watkins, Error	.10	.15
259	Scott Fukami, Error	.15	.30
260	Rick Hopper, Coach	.05	.10

PRINCE ALBERT RAIDERS

No.	Player	EX	NRMT
261	Laurie Billeck	.05	.10
262	Rob Daum, Coach/GM, Error	.75	1.50
263	Mark Stowe	.05	.10
264	Curtis Regnier, Error	.15	.30
265	David Neilson	.05	10
266	Brain Pellerin	.05	.10
267	Dean McAmmond	.50	1.00
268	Darren Van Impe	.07	.15
269	Troy Neumeier	.05	.10
270	Mike Langen, Goalie	.05	.10
271	Dan Kesa	.20	.40
272	Travis Laycock, Goalie	.05	.10
273	Scott Allison	.15	.30
274	Jeff Gorman	.05	.10
275	Lee J. Leslie	.20	.40
276	Jason Kwiatkowski	.05	.10
277	Donevan Hextall, Error	.35	.75
278	Shane Zulyniak	.05	.10
279	Darren Perkins	.05	.10
280	Chad Seibel	.05	.10
281	Jeff Nelson	.35	.75
282	Troy Hjertas	.05	.10
283	Jamie Linden	.50	1.00

KAMLOOPS BLAZERS

No.	Player	EX	NRMT
284	Zac Boyer	.25	.50
285	Jarret Bousquet	.05	.10
286	Steven Yule	.10	.20
287	Tom Renney, Coach	.05	.10
288	Lance Johnson	.10	.20
289	Scott Niedermayer	.20	.40
290	Ryan Harrison	.05	.10
291	Ed Patterson	.05	.10
292	Jeff Watchorn	.20	.40
293	Cal McGowan	.20	.40
294	Dale Masson, Goalie	.07	.15
295	Joey Mittelsteadt, Error	.07	.15
296	Scott Loucks	.15	.30
297	Shea Esselmont	.05	.10
298	Craig Bonner	.05	.10
299	Mike Mathers	.10	.20
300	Fred Hettle	.05	.10
301	Craig Lyons	.05	.10
302	Murray Duval	.05	.10
303	Jamie Barnes	.05	.10
304	Bryan Gourlie	.05	.10
305	Chad Berezniuk	.05	.10
306	Corey Hirsch, Goalie	.85	1.75
307	Darryl Sydor	.75	1.50
308	Jarrett Deuling	.05	.10
309	Cory Stock	.05	.10

PORTLAND WINTER HAWKS

No.	Player	EX	NRMT
310	Chris Rowland	.12	.25
311	Mike Ruark	.05	.10
312	Steve Konowalchuk	.30	.65
313	Jeff Sebastian	.05	.10
314	Brandon Smith	.05	.10
315	Greg Gatto	.10	.15
316	Brad Harrison	.15	.30
317	Brantt Myhres	.15	.30
318	Jamie Black	.05	.10
319	Colin Foley	.05	.10
320	Cam Danyluk	.05	.10
321	Dean Dorchak	.05	.10
322	Ryan Slemko	.05	.10
323	Kim Deck	.05	.10
324	Kelly Harris	.05	.10

No.	Player	EX	NRMT
325	Murray Bokenfohr	.05	.10
326	Dean Intwert, Goalie	.05	.10
327	Dennis Saharchuk, Error	.05	.10
328	Shane Seiker, Error	.05	.10
329	Terry Virtue	.05	.10
330	Josh Erdman	.05	.10
331	Layne Roland	.07	.15
332	Michel Michon	.05	.10
333	Scott Mydan, Error	.07	.15

CHECKLIST

No.	Team	EX	NRMT
334	Brandon Wheat Kings	.07	.15
335	Moose Jaw Warriors	.07	.15
336	Swift Current Broncos	.07	.15
337	Regina Pats, Error	.07	.15
338	Saskatoon Blades	.07	.15
339	Medicine Hat Tigers	.07	.15

THE GOALMOUTH

No.	Goalmouth	EX	NRMT
340	The Goalmouth	.07	.15

CHECKLIST

No.	Team	EX	NRMT
341	Portland Winter Hawks	.07	.15
342	Kamloops Blazers, Error	.07	.15
343	Victoria Cougars	.07	.15
344	Tri City Americans	.07	.15
345	Spokane Chiefs	.07	.15
346	Seattle Thunderbirds	.07	.15
347	Lethbridge Hurricanes	.07	.15
348	Prince Albert Raiders	.07	.15

—1991 - 92 REGULAR ISSUE —

As with the OHL and QJMHL foil boxes, the WHL packs contains the team insert cards. Note: Cards numbered 233 and 234 do not exist.

1991-92 Issue
Card No. 1, Valeri Bure

Card Size: 2 1/2" X 3 1/2"
Face: Four colour, white border
Back: Four colour, black on white card stock, Number, Resume, Position, Bilingual
Imprint: © 1991 7th Inning Sketch Printed in Canada
Complete Set No.: 360
Complete Set Price: 11.00 22.00
Common Goalie: .07 .15
Common Player: .05 .10
Foil Pack: (10 Cards) .75
Foil Box: (36 Packs) 20.00
Foil Case: (20 Boxes) 325.00
Production:
 Foil Cases: 2,000
 Set Cases: N/A

SPOKANE CHIEFS

No.	Player	EX	NRMT
1	Valeri Bure	1.50	3.00
2	Hardy Sauter	.05	.10
3	Bryan Maxwell, Coach	.07	.15
4	S. Bailey	.05	.10
5	Mike Gray	.05	.10

No.	Player	EX	NRMT
6	Mark Szoke	.05	.10
7	Mike Jickling	.05	.10
8	Frank Evans	.07	.15
9	Steve Junker	.20	.40
10	Greg Gatto	.05	.10
11	Jared Bednar	.05	.10
12	Justin Hocking	.05	.10
13	Paxton Schulte	.05	.10
14	Brad Toporowski	.05	.10
15	Shane Maitland	.05	.10
16	Aaron Boh	.05	.10
17	Ryan Duthie	.05	.10
18	Craig Reichert	.05	.10
19	Danny Faassen	.05	.10
20	Randy Toye	.05	.10
21	Geoff Grandberg	.05	.10
22	Jeremy Warring, Goalie	.07	.15
23	Tyler Romanchuck	.05	.10
24	Jamie Linden	.10	.20
25	90/91 Champs	.07	.15

PORTLAND WINTER HAWKS

No.	Player	EX	NRMT
26	Corey Jones, Goalie	.05	.10
27	Brandon Smith	.05	.10
28	Mike Williamson	.05	.10
29	Adam Murray	.05	.10
30	Steve Konowalchuk	.25	.50
31	Shawn Stone	.05	.10
32	Adam Deadmarsh	.25	.50
33	Rick Mearns	.05	.10
34	Chris Rowland	.07	.15
35	Brandon Coates	.05	.10
36	Dave Cammock	.05	.10
37	Colin Foley	.07	.15
38	Dennis Saharchuk	.05	.10
39	Jiri Beranek	.05	.10
40	Chad Seibel	.05	.10
41	Kelly Harris	.05	.10
42	Layne Roland	.05	.10
43	Cale Hulse	.05	.10
44	Ken Hodge, Coach	.10	.20

MOOSE JAW WARRIORS

No.	Player	EX	NRMT
45	Peter Cox	.05	.10

PORTLAND WINTER HAWKS

No.	Player	EX	NRMT
46	Joaquin Cage, Goalie	.15	.30
47	Brent Peterson, Co-Coach	.05	.10

LETHBRIDGE HURRICANES

No.	Player	EX	NRMT
48	Jason McBain	.05	.10

PORTLAND WINTER HAWKS

No.	Player	EX	NRMT
49	John Badduke	.05	.10

VICTORIA COUGARS

No.	Player	EX	NRMT
50	Rick Hopper, GM	.05	.10
51	Dave Hamilton, Goalie	.07	.15
52	Dwayne Newman	.05	.10
53	Chris Catellier	.05	.10
54	Fran Defrenza	.05	.10
55	Randy Chadney	.05	.10

TRI-CITY AMERICANS

No.	Player	EX	NRMT
56	David Hebky	.05	.10

VICTORIA COUGARS

No.	Player	EX	NRMT
57	Craig Fletcher	.05	.10
58	Kane Chaloner	.05	.10
59	Ross Harris	.10	.20
60	Mike Barrie	.05	.10
61	Steve Lingren	.05	.10
62	Shea Esselmont	.05	.10
63	Matt Smith	.05	.10

No.	Player	EX	NRMT
64	Gerry St. Cyr	.20	.40
65	Andrew Laming	.05	.10

TRI-CITY AMERICANS

No.	Player	EX	NRMT
66	Jeff Fancy	.05	.10

VICTORIA COUGARS

No.	Player	EX	NRMT
67	Ryan Pellaers	.10	.20
68	Scott Fukami	.10	.20
69	Darcy Mattersdorfer	.05	.10
70	Chris Hawes	.05	.10

WHL ACTION

No.	Player	EX	NRMT
72	The Goalies 1	.05	.10

CHECKLIST

No.	Checklist	EX	NRMT
73	Checklist 1 (1 to 97)	.10	.20

KAMLOOPS BLAZERS

No.	Player	EX	NRMT
74	Riverside Coliseum	.05	.10
75	Tom Renney, Coach	.05	.10
76	Corey Hirsch, Goalie	.50	1.00
77	Scott Ferguson	.05	.10
78	Steve Yule	.05	.10

MOOSE JAW WARRIORS

No.	Player	EX	NRMT
79	Todd Johnson,	.05	.10

KAMLOOPS BLAZERS

No.	Player	EX	NRMT
80	Jarrett Bousquet	.05	.10
81	Mike Mathers	.05	.10
82	Rod Stevens	.05	.10
83	Lance Johnson	.05	.10
84	Zac Boyer	.15	.30
85	Craig Lyons	.10	.20
86	Dale Masson, Goalie	.07	.15
87	Scott Loucks	.10	.20
88	Darcy Tucker	.05	.10
89	Shayne Green	.12	.25
90	Micheal Sup	.05	.10
91	Craig Bonner	.05	.10
92	Jeff Watchorn	.05	.10
93	Jarrett Dueling	.07	.15
94	Ed Patterson	.07	.15
95	David Wilkie	.05	.10

WHL ACTION

No.	Player	EX	NRMT
96	The Goalies III	.07	.15
97	A Goal	.07	.15

SEATTLE THUNDERBIRDS

No.	Player	EX	NRMT
98	Andy MacIntyre	.05	.10

TACOMA ROCKETS

No.	Player	EX	NRMT
99	Rhett Trombley	.05	.10

SASKATOON BLADES

No.	Player	EX	NRMT
100	Lorne Molleken, Coach	.05	.10
101	Trevor Robins, Goalie	.07	.15
102	Jeff Buchanan	.10	.20
103	Mark Raiter	.05	.10
104	Bryce Goebel	.05	.10
105	Paul Buczkowski	.05	.10
106	James Startup	.05	.10
107	Chad Rusnak	.05	.10
108	Sean McFatridge	.05	.10
109	Shane Calder	.10	.20
110	Ryan Fujita	.20	.40
111	Derek Tibbatts	.10	.20
112	Glen Gulutzan	.05	.10

No.	Player	EX	NRMT
113	Richard Matvichuk	.25	.50
114	Chad Michalchuk	.05	.10
115	M. Wotton	.05	.10
116	Mark Franks	.07	.15
117	Norm Maracle, Goalie	.12	.25
118	Jason Becker	.05	.10
119	Shawn Yakimishyn	.07	.15

WHL PRESIDENT

No.	Player	EX	NRMT
120	Ed Chynoweth	.05	.10

CHECKLIST

No.	Checklist	EX	NRMT
121	Checklist 2 (98 to 195)	.07	.15

SEATTLE THUNDERBIRDS

No.	Player	EX	NRMT
122	Craig Chapman	.07	.15
123	Jeff Jubenville	.05	.10
124	George Zajankala	.05	.10
125	Turner Stevenson	.18	.35
126	Rob Tallas, Goalie	.07	.15
127	Ryan Brown	.05	.10
128	Andrew Kemper	.05	.10
129	Brendan Witt	.15	.30

No.	Player	EX	NRMT
130	Troy Hyatt	.05	.10
131	Mike Kennedy	.05	.10
132	Jesse Wilson	.10	.20

SWIFT CURRENT BRONCOS

No.	Player	EX	NRMT
133	Kurt Seher	.10	.20

SEATTLE THUNDERBIRDS

No.	Player	EX	NRMT
134	Dody Wood	.12	.25
135	Darren McAusland	.12	.25
136	Jeff Sebastian	.07	.15
137	Eric Bouchard	.05	.10

SWIFT CURRENT BRONCOS

No.	Player	EX	NRMT
138	Joel Dyck	.05	.10
139	Blake Knox	.18	.35

SEATTLE THUNDERBIRDS

No.	Player	EX	NRMT
140	Peter Anholt, Coach	.05	.10
141	Chris Wells	.05	.10
142	Andrew Reimer, Goalie	.07	.15

WHL ACTION

No.	Player	EX	NRMT
143	Along The Boards	.05	.10
144	Which Way Is Up	.05	.10

CHECKLIST

No.	Checklist	EX	NRMT
145	Checklist 3 (196 to 287), Error	.10	.20

ERROR AND VARIATION LISTING

No.	Checklist	Description
145	Checklist	"Dutiaume", "Kelhem", "Theissen" and "Zukiwsky" are misspelled

TACOMA ROCKETS

No.	Player	EX	NRMT
146	Tacoma Dome	.07	.15
147	Opening Ceremonies	.05	.10
148	Marcel Comeau, Coach	.05	.10
149	Donn Clark, Asst. Coach	.05	.10
150	John Varga	.15	.30
151	Joey Young	.05	.10
152	Laurie Billeck	.05	.10
153	Jeff Calvert, Goalie	.07	.15
154	Tuomas Gronman	.05	.10
155	Jason Knox	.05	.10
156	Kevin Malgunas	.05	.10
157	Dave McMillen	.05	.10

No.	Player	EX	NRMT
158	Darryl Onofrychuk, Goalie	.07	.15
159	Mike Piersol	.25	.50
160	Lasse Pirjeta	.05	.10
161	Drew Schoneck	.05	.10
162	Corey Stock	.05	.10
163	Ryan Strain	.05	.10
164	Michal Sykora	.05	.10
165	Scott Thomas	.05	.10
166	Toby Weishaar	.05	.10
167	Jeff Whittle	.05	.10
168	The Rockettes	.05	.10
169	Allan Egeland	.05	.10
170	Van Burgess	.05	.10
171	Trever Fraser	.05	.10
172	Jamie Black	.05	.10

WHL ACTION

No.	Player	EX	NRMT
173	WHL Action	.05	.10

SWIFT CURRENT BRONCOS

No.	Player	EX	NRMT
174	Andy Schneider	.20	.40
175	John McMulkin	.05	.10
176	Rick Girard	.05	.10
177	Shane Hnidy	.05	.10
178	Jason Krywulak	.10	.20
179	Jeremy Riehl	.10	.20

SEATTLE THUNDERBIRDS

No.	Player	EX	NRMT
180	Brent Bilodeau	.18	.35

SWIFT CURRENT BRONCOS

No.	Player	EX	NRMT
181	Mark McCoy	.05	.10
182	Matt Young	.05	.10
183	Dan Sherstenka	.05	.10
184	Jarrod Daniel, Goalie	.07	.15
185	Lennie MacAusland	.05	.10
186	Keith McCambridge	.05	.10
187	Jason Horvath, Error	.05	.10
188	Kevin Koopman, Goalie	.07	.15
189	Chris Herperger	.05	.10
190	Trent McCleary	.05	.10
191	Tyler Wright	.30	.60
192	Todd Holt	.12	.25
193	Ashley Buckberger	.05	.10

SPOKANE CHIEFS

No.	Player	EX	NRMT
194	Bram Vanderkracht	.05	.10

SWIFT CURRENT BRONCOS

No.	Player	EX	NRMT
195	Ken Zilka	.05	.10

MEDICINE HAT TIGERS

No.	Player	EX	NRMT
196	Chris Osgood, Goalie	.35	.75

BRANDON WHEAT KINGS

No.	Player	EX	NRMT
197	Rob Puchniak	.05	.10
198	Todd Dutiaume	.05	.10
199	Mike Maneluk	.05	.10
200	Shawn Dietrich, Goalie	.07	.15
201	Chris Johnston	.05	.10
202	Brian Purdy	.18	.35
203	Mike Chrun	.05	.10
204	Dan Kopec	.05	.10
205	Ryan Smith	.05	.10
206	Marty Murray	.05	.10
207	Merv Priest	.05	.10
208	Bobby House	.12	.25
209	Chris Constant	.10	.20
210	Dwayne Gylywoychuk	.05	.10
211	Stu Scantlebury	.05	.10
212	Mark Kolesar	.05	.10
213	Craig Geekie	.05	.10
214	Terran Sandwith	.10	.20
215	Jeff Hoad	.05	.10
216	Kelly McCrimmon, Coach	.05	.10
217	Carlos Bye	.05	.10

REGINA PATS

No.	Player	EX	NRMT
218	Trevor Hanas	.05	.10
219	Jeff Shantz	.35	.75
220	Heath Weenk	.05	.10
221	Nathan Dempsey	.05	.10
222	Louis Dumont	.12	.35
223	Garry Pearce	.05	.10
224	Terry Bendera	.05	.10
225	Hal Christiansen	.05	.10
226	Jason Smith	.05	.10
227	K. Biette	.05	.10
228	Barry Becker, Goalie	.07	.15
229	Derek Eberle	.05	.10
230	Ken Richardson	.05	.10
231	Niklas Barklund	.05	.10
232	Frank Kovacs	.12	.25
233	Not issued		
234	Not issued		
235	Lloyd Pelletier	.05	.10
236	Dale Vossen, Asst. Coach	.05	.10
237	A. J. Kelham, Error	.05	.10
238	Mike Risdale, Goalie	.07	.15

VICTORIA COUGARS

No.	Player	EX	NRMT
239	Brad Bagu	.05	.10

REGINA PATS

No.	Player	EX	NRMT
240	Niko Ovaska	.05	.10
241	Brad Tippett, Coach	.05	.10

WHL ACTION

No.	Player	EX	NRMT
242	The Goalies II	.05	.10

PRINCE ALBERT RAIDERS

No.	Player	EX	NRMT
243	Lee J. Leslie	.12	.25
244	Darren Perkins	.05	.10
245	Jason Kwiatkowski	.05	.10
246	J. Renard	.05	.10
247	Dan Kesa	.15	.30
248	Jason Klassen	.05	.10
249	Nick Polychronopoulus	.05	.10
250	David Neilson	.10	.20
251	Merv Haney	.05	.10
252	Troy Hjertaas	.05	.10
253	Curt Regnier	.05	.10
254	Dean McAmmond	.20	.40
255	Travis Laycock, Goalie	.10	.20
256	Jeff Lank	.05	.10
257	Barkley Swenson	.05	.10
258	Darren Van Impe	.10	.20
259	Ryan Pisiak	.05	.10
260	Jeff Gorman	.05	.10
261	Stan Matwijiw, Goalie	.07	.15
262	Mike Fedorko, Coach	.05	.10
263	Mark Odnokon, Asst. Coach	.05	.10
264	Shane Zulyniak	.05	.10
265	Jeff Nelson	.20	.40
266	Donevan Hextall	.15	.30

MOOSE JAW WARRIORS

No.	Player	EX	NRMT
267	Kevin Masters	.05	.10
268	C. Schmidt	.12	.25
269	Jeff Budai	.05	.10
270	Bill Hooson	.05	.10

KAMLOOPS BLAZERS

No.	Player	EX	NRMT
271	Fred Hettle	.05	.10

MOOSE JAW WARRIORS

No.	Player	EX	NRMT
272	Kent Staniforth	.05	.10
273	T. Stevenson	.05	.10
274	David Jesiolowski	.05	.10
275	Mike Babcock, Coach	.05	.10
276	Scott Allison	.12	.25
277	Travis Thiessen	.05	.10
278	Marc Hussey	.05	.10
279	Kevin Smyth	.05	.10
280	Jason Fitzsimmons, Goalie	.15	.30
281	Jeff Petruic	.05	.10
282	Russ West	.05	.10
283	Derek Kletzel	.12	.25

KAMLOOPS BLAZERS

No.	Player	EX	NRMT
284	Jarrett Zukiwsky, Error	.05	.10
285	J. Carey	.05	.10

WHL ACTION

No.	Player	EX	NRMT
286	Close Checking	.05	.10

CHECKLIST

No.	Checklist	EX	NRMT
287	Checklist 3 (288 to W15), Error	.07	.10

ERROR AND VARIATION LISTING

No.	Player	Description
287	Checklist	"Kjenstadt", "Mht Tiger" and "Stephenson" misspelled

TRI-CITY AMERICANS

No.	Player	EX	NRMT
288	Jason Bowen	.35	.75
289	Dean Tiltgen	.12	.25
290	Terry Degner	.12	.25
291	J. Murphy	.05	.10
292	Brian Sakic	.25	.50
293	Jamie Barnes	.05	.10
294	Darren Hastman	.05	.10
295	Todd Klassen	.10	.20
296	Mirsad Mujcin, Error	.05	.10
297	Trevor Sherban	.05	.10
298	Chadden Cabana	.05	.10
299	Adam Rettschlag	.05	.10
300	Mark Toljanich	.05	.10
301	Kory Mullin	.05	.10
302	Byron Penstock, Goalie	.05	.10
303	Vladimir Vujtek	.35	.75
304	Bill Lindsay	.35	.75
305	Jeff Cej	.05	.10
306	Mike Busniak, Coach	.05	.10

VICTORIA COUGARS

No.	Player	EX	NRMT
307	Todd Harris	.05	.10

TRI-CITY AMERICANS

No.	Player	EX	NRMT
308	Cory Dosdall	.12	.25
309	Jason Smith	.05	.10
310	Mark Dawkins, Goalie	.05	.10
311	Dan O'Rourke	.05	.10

MEDICINE HAT TIGERS

No.	Player	EX	NRMT
312	Darby Walker	.05	.10
313	Olaf Kjenstadt	.05	.10
314	Sonny Mignacca, Goalie	.07	.15
315	Jon Duval	.05	.10
316	Lorne Toews	.05	.10
317	Dana Rieder	.10	.20
318	Clayton Norris	.12	.25
319	David Cooper	.30	.65
320	Lanny Watkins	.05	.10
321	Evan Marble	.05	.10
322	Scott Lindsay	.05	.10
323	Ryan Petz	.05	.10
324	Jeramie Heistad	.05	.10
325	Scott Townsend	.05	.10
326	Stacy Roest	.05	.10
327	Rob Niedermayer	1.00	2.00
328	Tim Bothwell, Coach	.05	.10
329	Kevin Riehl	.25	.50

746 • 7TH INNING SKETCH — 1991 - 92 INSERT SET —

No.	Player	EX	NRMT
330	Mike Rathje	.35	.75
331	Bryan McCabe	.05	.10
332	MHT Tiger	.05	.10

BRANDON WHEAT KINGS

No.	Player	EX	NRMT
333	Dean Intwert, Goalie	.05	.10
334	Mike Vandenberghe	.05	.10

SPOKANE CHIEFS

No.	Player	EX	NRMT
335	Cam Danyluk	.10	.20

LETHBRIDGE HURRICANES

No.	Player	EX	NRMT
336	Darcy Austin, Goalie	.05	.10
337	Jason Knight	.05	.10
338	Lee Sorochan	.10	.20
339	Al Kinisky	.05	.10
340	Rob Hartnell	.05	.10
341	Radek Sip	.12	.25
342	Jamie Pushor	.12	.25
343	Shane Peacock	.10	.20
344	Cadrin Smart	.05	.10
345	Maurice Meagher	.05	.10
346	Lance Burns	.05	.10
347	Dominic Pittis	.05	.10
348	Todd MacIsaac	.05	.10
349	Brad Zimmer	.05	.10
350	Jason Sorochan	.05	.10
351	Darcy Werenka	.18	.35
352	Kevin St. Jacques	.20	.40
353	David Trofimenkoff	.05	.10
354	Terry Hollinger	.05	.10
355	Travis Munday	.05	.10
356	Slade Stephenson	.05	.10
357	Jason Widmer	.05	.10

PORTLAND WINTER HAWKS

No.	Player	EX	NRMT
358	Brad Zavisha	.05	.10

LETHBRIDGE HURRICANES

No.	Player	EX	NRMT
359	Bob Loucks, Coach	.12	.25
360	Brantt Myrhes, Error	.05	.10

MOOSE JAW WARRIORS

No.	Player	EX	NRMT
	Garfield Henderson	.12	.25

Note: This card is not numbered nor is it listed on any checklist.

— 1991 - 92 INSERT SET —

THE TEAMS

For the first time, this year's foil packs contained an insert card. These cards numbered W(estern) 1 to W 15 were randomly inserted in foil packs at the rate of one or two per foil box.

1991-92 Insert Set
Card No. W8, Swift Current Broncos

Card Size: 2 1/2" X 3 1/2"
Face: Four colour, white border
Back: Four colour, black on white card stock, Number, Resume, Position, Bilingual
Imprint: © 1991 7th Inning Sketch Printed in Canada
Complete Set No.: 11
Complete Set Price: 3.50 7.50

No.	Player	EX	NRMT
W1	Spokane Chiefs	.25	.50
W2	Portland Winterhawks	.25	.50
W3	Victoria Cougars	.25	.50
W4	Kamloops Blazers	.25	.50
W5	Saskatoon Blades	.25	.50
W6	Seattle Thunderbirds	.25	.50
W7	Tacoma Rockets	.25	.50
W8	Swift Current Broncos	.25	.50
W9	Brandon Wheat Kings	.25	.50
W10	Regina Pats	.25	.50
W11	Prince Albert Raiders	.25	.50
W12	Moose Jaw Warriors	.25	.50
W13	Tri-City Americans	.25	.50
W14	Medicine Hat Tigers	.25	.50
W15	Lethbridge Hurricanes	.25	.50

SLASHING

HOOKING

ROUGHING

SASKATCHEWAN JUNIOR HOCKEY LEAGUE

AIR CANADA

— 1991 - 92 REGULAR ISSUE —

Air Canada, 1991-92 Issue
Card No. 1, Jeff Kungle

Card Size: 2 1/2" X 3 1/2"
Face: Four colour, white border; Team, Team and sponsor logos, Jersey number, Name
Back: Black on white card stock; Jersey number, Team logo, Number, Name, Position, Resume
Imprint: Air Canada
Complete Set No.: 250
Complete Set Price: 31.00 / 62.50
Common Player: .05 / .10

ALL STARS

No.	Player	EX	NRMT
1	Jeff Kungle, Mft.	.10	.20
2	Jay Dunn, Nip.	.13	.25
3	Kevin Dickie, Coach, Mft.	.08	.15
4	Martin Smith, NB	.15	.30
5	Jeff Cole, Hum.	.10	.20
6	Trent Hamm, Nip.	.10	.20
7	Kent Rogers, Stn.	.20	.40
8	Dean Gerard, Mft.	.10	.20
9	Jim McLarty, Nip.	.08	.15
10	Malcolm Kostuchenko, NB	.15	.35
11	Mark Scollan, Mvl.	.10	.20
12	Brad Federenko, Mft.	.15	.30
13	Rob Beck, FF	.08	.15
14	Bryce Bohun, NB	.13	.25
15	Kory Karlander, Stn.	.20	.40
16	Scott Christison, ND	.10	.20
17	Tyler Kuhn, FF	.08	.15
18	Corri Moffatt, Mvl.	.10	.20
19	Layne Douglas, Min.	.10	.20
20	Shane Holunga, Wey.	.10	.20
21	Mike Matteucci, Est.	.15	.30
22	Bart Vanstaalduinen, ND	.10	.20
23	Brad McEwen, Gm / Coach, Mvl.	.10	.20
24	Kim Maier, Est.	.13	.25
25	Jamie Ling, ND	.10	.20
26	Dean Seymour, Yor.	.10	.20
27	Derek Crimin, Min.	.10	.20
28	Evan Anderson, Est.	.08	.15
29	Craig Matatall, ND	.08	.15
30	Keith Murphy, Mvl.	.08	.15
31	Jason Feiffer, Wey.	.08	.15
32	Michel Cook, Yor.	.10	.20
33	Rod Krushel, Mvl.	.08	.15
34	Tyler Rice, ND	.10	.20
35	Gerald Tallaire, Est.	.08	.15
36	Richard Nagy, FF	.15	.30
37	Taras Lendzyk, Hum.	.15	.30
38	Jeff Knight, Mft.	.08	.15
39	Darren Opp, Nip.	.15	.30
40	Dwayne Rhinehart, FF	.08	.15
41	Minot Americans All-Stars	.08	.15
42	Scott Bellefontaine, Goalie, Yor.	.08	.15
43	Darren Maloney, Mvl.	.08	.15
44	1992 SJHL North Division All Star Team	.08	.15
45	Yorkton Terriers All-Stars	.08	.15
46	Melville Millionaires All-Stars	.08	.15
47	The 1992 Best All Star Team	.25	.50
48	Estevan Bruins All-Stars	.10	.20
49	Notre Dame Hounds All-Stars	.15	.30
50	Bob Robson, Coach, Est.	.08	.15

REGULAR ISSUE

No.	Player	EX	NRMT
A1	Dean Normand, Hum.	.08	.15
A2	Dan Meyers, Est.	.08	.15
A3	Tyson Balog, Wey.	.08	.15
A4	Tyler McMillan, Wey.	.08	.15
A5	Jason Selkirk, Stn.	.08	.15
A6	Bryce Bohun, NB	.13	.25
A7	Blaire Hornung, Stn.	.08	.15
A8	Craig McKechnie, Mvl.	.08	.15
A9	Rejean Stringer, Nip.	.13	.25
A10	Corri Moffat, Mvl.	.08	.15
A11	Dion Johnson, Min.	.08	.15
A12	Rod Krushel, Mvl.	.08	.15
A13	Mike Langen, Goalie, Wey.	.08	.15
A14	Jeff Hassman, Mvl.	.15	.35
A15	Dean Moore, ND	.08	.15
A16	Trevor Wathen, Min.	.08	.15
A17	Curtis Knight, Hum.	.08	.15
A18	Chris Morgan, Min.	.08	.15
A19	Trevor Thurston, FF	.08	.15
A20	Wayne Filipenko, Min.	.08	.15
A21	Jason Feiffer, Wey.	.08	.15
A22	Layne Douglas, Min.	.08	.15
A23	Dave Gardner, Nip.	.08	.15
A24	Ryan Sandholm, ND	.08	.15
A25	Corey McKee, Mft.	.08	.15
A26	Trevor Schmiess, Hum.	.08	.15
A27	Todd Hollinger, Goalie, Stn.	.08	.15
A28	Jay Dunn, Nip.	.08	.15
A29	Jamie Ling, ND	.13	.25
A30	Todd Small, Stn.	.08	.15
A31	Barret Kropf, Mft.	.08	.15
A32	Dean Gerard, Mft.	.08	.15
A33	Christian Dutil, Goalie, Yor.	.08	.15
A34	Tyler Scheidt, Mft.; Aaron Campbell, Mft.	.15	.30
A35	Dean Sideroff, Hum.	.08	.15
A36	Dan Dufresne, ND	.13	.25
A37	Cam Yager, Goalie, NB	.08	.15
A38	Richard Nagy, Goalie, FF	.13	.25
A39	Aaron Cain, FF	.08	.15
A40	Rob Beck, FF	.08	.15
A41	Blair Wagar, Yor.	.08	.15
A42	Kim Mairer, Est.	.13	.25
A43	Brent Hoiness, NB	.08	.15
A44	Troy Edwards, Est.	.08	.15
A45	Evan Anderson, Est.	.13	.25
A46	Carlin Nordstrom, NB	.08	.15
A47	Dean Seymour, Yor.	.08	.15
A48	Scott Wotton, Yor.	.08	.15
A49	Curtis Joseph, ND	.13	.25
B1	Richard Boscher, Goalie, Stn.	.08	.15
B2	James Schaeffler, Stn.	.05	.10
B3	Wes Rommel, Nip.	.08	.15
B4	Corey Thompson, Nip.	.05	.10
B5	Rob Phillips, Nip.	.05	.10
B6	Jim McLean, Nip.	.08	.15
B7	Trevor Warrener, Stn.	.05	.10
B8	Peter Boake, Wey.	.05	.10
B9	Kevin Riffel, Goalie, Est.	.08	.15
B10	Tom Perry, Hum.	.08	.15
B11	Mark Baird, Hum.	.08	.15
B12	Stacy Prevost, Yor.	.10	.20
B13	Taras Lendzyk, Goalie, Hum.	.10	.20
B14	Shawn Reis, Goalie, Mft.	.05	.10
B15	Shawn Thompson, Mvl.	.15	.30
B16	Curtis Kleisinger, ND	.08	.15
B17	Kent Rogers, Stn.	.20	.40
B18	Scott Christion, Goalie, ND	.10	.20
B19	Gerald Tallaire, Est.	.08	.15
B20	Kelly Hollingshead, Est.	.20	.40
B21	Mike Savard, Goalie, NB	.08	.15
B22	Darren Maloney, Mvl.	.05	.10
B23	Jason Hynd, NB	.05	.10
B24	Scott Stewart, FF	.05	.10
B25	Scott Beattie, Mvl.	.10	.20
B26	Dave McAmmond, FF	.08	.15
B27	Myles Gibb, NB	.05	.10
B28	Ryan Bach, Goalie, ND	.30	.60
B29	Martin Smith, NB	.15	.30
B30	Leigh Brookbank, Yor.	.10	.20
B31	Todd Markus, Mft.	.05	.10
B32	The Boys From PA	.08	.15
B33	Randy Muise, Wey.	.10	.20
B34	George Gervais, Est.	.05	.10
B35	Keith Harris, Wey.	.08	.15
B36	Jamie Stelmak, Goalie, Mvl.	.08	.15
B37	Bart Vanstaalduinen, ND	.10	.20
B38	Scott Murray, Min.	.08	.15
B39	Danny Galarneau, Yor.	.08	.15
B40	Keith Murphy, Mvl.	.10	.20
B41	Jeff Kungle, Mft.	.13	.25
B42	Michel Cook, Yor.	.10	.20
B43	Daryl Krauss, Wey.	.08	.15
B44	Derek Wynne, Min.	.05	.10
B45	Derek Crimin, Min.	.08	.15
B46	Jason Brown, FF	.08	.15
B47	Bruce Matatall, Min.	.05	.10
B48	Chris Hatch, FF	.08	.15
B49	Kurtise Souchotte, Mvl.	.05	.10
B50	Michael Brennan, Hum.	.08	.15
B51	Orrin Hergott, Hum.	.15	.30
C1	Craig Matatall, ND	.05	.10
C2	Brad Prefontaine, Mvl.	.05	.10
C3	Mike Evans, ND	.05	.10
C4	Jody Reiter, NB	.08	.15
C5	Jeremy Mylymok, Mvl.	.13	.25
C6	Dave Doucet, Mvl.	.05	.10
C7	Randy Kerr, Mvl.	.08	.15
C8	Gordon McCann, Mvl.	.08	.15
C9	Quinn Fair, ND	.13	.25
C10	Kyle Niemegeers, Est.	.08	.15
C11	Ryan Smith, NB	.08	.15
C12	Mike Hillock, Min.	.15	.35
C13	Vern Anderson, NB	.08	.15
C14	Trent Hamm, Nip.	.10	.20
C15	Curtis Folkett, Est.	.10	.20
C16	Warren Pickford, Nip.	.05	.10
C17	Craig Volstad, Goalie, Nip.	.08	.15
C18	Sean Tallaire, Est.	.13	.25
C19	Jason Yaganiski, Min.	.05	.10
C20	Jim McLarty, Nip.	.08	.15
C21	Jamie Byfuglien, Min.	.05	.10
C22	Terry Metro, Min.	.08	.15
C23	Todd Kozak, NB	.08	.15
C24	Jeff Huckle, Stn.	.05	.10
C25	Darren McLean, Est.	.05	.10
C26	Bret Mohninger, Stn.	.05	.10
C27	Tim Slukynsky, Yor.	.08	.15
C28	Roman Mrhalek, Yor.	.08	.15
C29	Joel Martinson, Hum.	.08	.15
C30	Ron Patterson, FF	.05	.10
C31	Mark Gorgi, Mft.	.08	.15
C32	Tom Thomson, Stn.	.08	.15
C33	Greg Wahl, Stn.	.08	.15
C34	Craig Perrett, Mft.	.10	.20
C35	Mike Harder, Wey.	.08	.15
C36	Jeff Cole, Hum.	.08	.15
C37	Justin Christoffer, Hum.	.08	.15
C38	Nolan Weir, FF	.08	.15
C39	Jeff Knight, Mft.	.08	.15
C40	Lyle Vaughan, Yor.	.08	.15
C41	Scott Bellefontaine, Goalie, Yor.	.08	.15
C42	Trevor Mathias, Wey.	.13	.25
C43	Chris Schinkel, Goalie, Hum.	.05	.10
C44	Scott Rogers, Mft.	.08	.15

MPS PHOTOGRAPHICS — 1993 REGULAR ISSUE

This 168-card set represents the players of the 1992-93 Saskatchewan Junior Hockey League.

Card Size: 2 1/2" x 3 1/2"
Face: Four colour; Name, Team
Back: Black and white, card stock; Name, Resume
Imprint: MPS Photographics
Complete Set No.: 168

		EX	NRMT
Complete Set Price:		15.00	30.00
Common Goalie:		.10	.20
Common Player:		.10	.20

No.	Player	EX	NRMT
C45	Shane Holunga, Wey.	.13	.25
C46	Dwayne Rhinehart, FF	.08	.15
C47	Eddy Marchant, FF	.08	.15
C48	Travis Smith, Wey.	.10	.20
C49	Not Issued		
C50	Mike Hidlebaugh, Nip.	.10	.20
D1	Darcy Herlick, Wey.	.08	.15
D2	Joel Appleton, Hum.	.08	.15
D3	Bobby Standish, Mft.	.08	.15
D4	Kory Karlander, Stn.	.15	.30
D5	Brett Kinaschuk, Hum.	.08	.15
D6	Kevin Messer, Nip.	.08	.15
D7	Jason Martin, Wey.	.13	.25
D8	Devin Zimmer, Min.	.08	.15
D9	David Foster, Hum.	.08	.15
D10	Bob Schwark, Mft.	.10	.20
D11	Ted Grayling, Mvl.	.08	.15
D12	Travis Vantighem, Mvl.	.08	.15
D13	Darren Houghton, Mvl.	.08	.15
D14	Wade Welte, Mvl.	.05	.10
D15	1991 NB All Stars	.10	.20
D16	Kevin Powell, Min.	.10	.20
D17	Returning Hounds	.08	.15
D18	Dennis Budeau, Min.	.08	.15
D19	Darren Opp, Nip.	.10	.20
D20	Jeff Greenwood, Nip.	.05	.10
D21	Mark Daniels, Stn.	.08	.15
D22	Todd Murphy, Nip.	.08	.15
D23	Scott Weaver, Min.	.08	.15
D24	Robby Bear, Yor.	.08	.15
D25	Nigel Werenka, Yor.	.05	.10
D26	Sean Timmins, ND	.08	.15
D27	Ken Melenfant, Stn.	.08	.15
D28	Greg Taylor, Mft.	.10	.20
D29	Sheldon Bylsma, Yor.	.05	.10
D30	Clint Hooge, Goalie, FF	.05	.10
D31	Bob McIntosh, ND	.05	.10
D32	Dave Lovsin, ND	.08	.15
D33	Jeremy Mathies, NB	.05	.10
D34	Blaine Fomradas, Wey.	.08	.15
D35	Cory Borys, Wey.	.05	.10
D36	Brad Purdie, Wey.	.13	.25
D37	J Sotropa, Stn.	.08	.15
D38	Duane Vardale, NB	.08	.15
D39	Jim Nellis, NB	.05	.10
D40	Brent Sheppard, Hum.	.08	.15
D41	Cam Bristow, Mft.	.08	.15
D42	Steven Brent, Est.	.10	.20
D43	Mike Matteucci, Est.	.10	.20
D44	Bryan Cossette, Est.	.05	.10
D45	Tyler Kuhn, FF	.08	.15
D46	Dave Debusschere, Est.	.08	.15
D47	Darryl Dickson, FF	.05	.10
D48	Derek Meikle, FF	.05	.10
D49	Ex SJHLer: Parris Duffus, Goalie, Mft.	.10	.20
D50	Future Propect: Lance Wakefield, Weyburn Elks	.25	.50
D51	Ex SJHLer: Rod Brind'Amour, ND	.10	.20

ESTEVAN BRUINS

No.	Player	EX	NRMT
1	Troy Edwards	.10	.20
2	Simon Olivier	.10	.20
3	Gerald Tallaire	.10	.20
4	Blair Allison, Goalie	.10	.20
5	Mads True	.10	.20
6	Steve Brent	.10	.20
7	Jay Dobrescu	.10	.20
8	Dave Debusschere	.10	.20
9	Bryan Cossette	.10	.20
10	Brooke Battersby	.10	.20
11	Kyle Niemegeers	.10	.20
12	Darren McLean	.10	.20
13	Carson Cardinal	.10	.20
14	Bill McKay	.10	.20

FLIN FLON BOMBERS

No.	Player	EX	NRMT
15	Chris Hatch	.10	.20
16	Nolan Weir	.10	.20
17	Karl Johnson	.10	.20
18	Jason Brown	.10	.20
19	Tyler Kuhn	.10	.20
20	Daniel Dennis, Goalie	.10	.20
21	Wally Spence	.10	.20
22	Rob Beck	.10	.20
23	Aaron Cain	.10	.20
24	Darryl Dickson	.10	.20
25	Travis Cheyne	.10	.20
26	Mark Leoppky	.10	.20
27	Jason Ahenakew	.10	.20
28	Kyle Paul	.10	.20

HUMBOLDT BRONCOS

No.	Player	EX	NRMT
29	Dean Normand	.10	.20
30	Brett Kinaschuk	.10	.20
31	Darren Schmidt	.10	.20
32	Chris Schinkel, Goalie	.10	.20
33	David Foster	.10	.20
34	Jason Zimmerman	.10	.20
35	Tom Perry	.10	.20
36	Kent Kinsachuk	.10	.20
37	Colin Froese	.10	.20
38	Shawn Zimmerman	.10	.20
39	Lary Empey	.10	.20
40	Curtis Knight	.10	.20
41	Blake Shipley	.10	.20
42	Cory Heon	.10	.20

MELFORT MUSTANGS

No.	Player	EX	NRMT
43	Steve Pashulka	.10	.20

MELVILLE MILLIONAIRES

No.	Player	EX	NRMT
44	Rob Kinch	.10	.20

MELFORT MUSTANGS

No.	Player	EX	NRMT
45	Dean Gerard	.10	.20
46	Matt Desmarais	.10	.20
47	Chad Rusnak	.10	.20
48	Brad Bagu	.10	.20
49	Cam Bristow	.10	.20
50	Derek Simonson	.10	.20
51	Ken Ruddock	.10	.20
52	Tyler Deis	.10	.20
53	Steve Tansowny, Goalie	.10	.20
54	Bill Stait	.10	.20
55	Garfield Henderson	.10	.20
56	Lonny Deobald	.10	.20

MINOT AMERICANS

No.	Player	EX	NRMT
57	Lyle Ehrmantraut	.10	.20

FLIN FLON BOMBERS

No.	Player	EX	NRMT
58	Layne Humenny	.10	.20

MINOT AMERICANS

No.	Player	EX	NRMT
59	Darren Balcombe	.10	.20
60	Jeff McCutheon	.10	.20
61	Trevor Wathen	.10	.20
62	Derek Wynne	.10	.20
63	Matt Russo	.10	.20
64	Bruce Matatall	.10	.20
65	Derek Crimin	.10	.20
66	Chad Crumley	.10	.20
67	Mike Hillock	.10	.20
68	Art Houghton, Goalie	.10	.20
69	Lee Materi	.10	.20
70	Nick Dyhr	.10	.20

MELVILLE MILLIONAIRS

No.	Player	EX	NRMT
71	Darren Maloney	.10	.20
72	Kurtise Souchotte	.10	.20
73	Noel Kamel	.10	.20
74	Trent Harper	.10	.20
75	Ted Grayling	.10	.20
76	Keith Harris	.10	.20
77	Corri Moffat	.10	.20
78	Travis Vantighem	.10	.20
79	Darren Houghton	.10	.20
80	Wade Welte	.10	.20
81	Dave Doucet	.10	.20
82	Jason Prokopetz	.10	.20
83	Gordon McCann	.10	.20
84	Clint Hooge, Goalie	.10	.20

NORTH BATTLEFORD NORTH STARS

No.	Player	EX	NRMT
85	Glen McGillvary	.10	.20
86	Regan Simpson	.10	.20
87	Mike Masse	.10	.20
88	Jeremy Procyshyn	.10	.20
89	Jim Nellis	.10	.20
90	Todd Kozak	.10	.20
91	Brent Holness	.10	.20

WILKIE YOUNGBLOODS

No.	Player	EX	NRMT
92	Josh Welter	.10	.20
	Jason Welter	.10	.20

WEYBURN RED WINGS

No.	Player	EX	NRMT
93	Eldon Barker, Trainer	.10	.20

NORTH BATTLEFORD NORTH STARS

No.	Player	EX	NRMT
94	Duane Vandale	.10	.20

MELVILLE MILLIONAIRS

No.	Player	EX	NRMT
95	Brad McEwen, Coach	.10	.20

NORTH BATTLEFORD NORTH STARS

No.	Player	EX	NRMT
96	Trent Tibbatts	.10	.20
97	Jody Reiter	.10	.20
98	Greg Moore	.10	.20

NOTRE DAME HOUNDS

No.	Player	EX	NRMT
99	Jon Rowe	.10	.20
100	Mike Evans	.10	.20
101	Jason Krug	.10	.20
102	Jon Bracco, Goalie	.10	.20

MPS Photographics
1993 Issue, Card No. 76, Keith Harris

1993 - 94 REGULAR ISSUE — SLAPSHOT IMAGES LTD • 749

No.	Player	EX	NRMT
103	Ryan Sandholm	.10	.20
104	Darryl Sangster	.10	.20
105	Brett Colborne	.10	.20
106	Dean Moore	.10	.20
107	Chris Dechaine	.10	.20
108	Steve McKenna	.10	.20
109	Tony Bergin	.10	.20
110	Tim Murray	.10	.20
111	Casey Kesselring	.10	.20
112	Todd Barth	.10	.20

NIPAWIN HAWKS

No.	Player	EX	NRMT
113	Ryan McConnell	.10	.20
114	Ian Adamson	.10	.20
115	Warren Pickford	.10	.20
116	Todd Murphy	.10	.20
117	Rob Phillips	.10	.20
118	Trevor Demmans	.10	.20
119	Jeff Greenwood	.10	.20
120	Kevin Messer	.10	.20
121	Dion Johnson	.10	.20
122	Rejean Stringer	.10	.20
123	Scott Mead	.10	.20
124	Jeff Lawson	.10	.20
125	Scot Newberry	.10	.20

MELFORT MUSTANGS

No.	Player	EX	NRMT
126	Bill Reid	.10	.20

SASKATOON TITANS

No.	Player	EX	NRTM
127	Chris Winkler	.10	.20
128	Kyle Girgan	.10	.20
129	Trevor Warrener	.10	.20
130	Richard Boscher, Goalie	.10	.20
131	Tom Thomson	.10	.20
132	Mike Wevers	.10	.20
133	Barton Holt	.10	.20
134	Kent Rogers	.10	.20
135	Richard Gibbs	.10	.20
136	Jared Witt	.10	.20
137	Jamie Stelmak	.10	.20
138	Greg Wahl	.10	.20
139	J. Sotropa	.10	.20
140	Mark Pivetz	.10	.20

WEYBURN RED WINGS

No.	Player	EX	NRMT
141	Travis Kirby, Goalie	.10	.20
142	Jason Scanzano	.10	.20
143	Tyson Balog	.10	.20
144	Daryl Krauss	.10	.20
145	Mike Harder	.10	.20
146	Tyler McMillan	.10	.20
147	Darcy Herlick	.10	.20
148	Dave Zwyer	.10	.20
149	Craig McKechnie	.10	.20
150	Cam Cook	.10	.20
151	Derek Bruselinck	.10	.20
152	Travis Smith	.10	.20
153	Daryl Jones	.10	.20
154	Mike Savard. Goalie	.10	.20

YORKTON TERRIERS

No.	Player	EX	NRMT
155	Jeremy Matthies	.10	.20
156	Michel Cook	.10	.20
157	Leigh Brookbank	.10	.20
158	Christian Dutil, Goalie	.10	.20
159	Scott Heshka	.10	.20
160	Danny Galarneau	.10	.20
161	Jamie Dunn	.10	.20
162	Nigel Werenka	.10	.20
163	Steve Sabo	.10	.20
164	Tony Toth	.10	.20
165	Sebastien Moreau	.10	.20
166	Tim Slukynsky	.10	.20
167	Sheldon Bylsma	.10	.20
168	Stacy Prevost	.10	.20

SLAPSHOT IMAGES LTD

— 1993 - 94 REGULAR ISSUE —

DETROIT JR. RED WINGS

Released in February 1994. There are 3,000 sets and 100 numbered uncut sheets.

Detroit Jr. Red Wings
Card No. 1, Todd Harvey

Size: 2 1/2" X 3 1/2"
Face: Four Colour, Red and white border; Name
Back: Four colour, Name, Resume, Sponsor logos
Imprint: Printed in Canada by SLAPSHOT IMAGES LTD. 1994©
Complete Set No.: 25
Complete Set Price: 5.00   10.00

No.	Player	Checklist
1	Todd Harvey	
2	Jason Saal, Goalie	
3	Aaron Ellis, Goalie	
4	Chris Mailloux, Goalie	
5	Robin Lacour	
6	Mike Rucinski	
7	Eric Cairns	
8	Matt Ball	
9	Dale Junkin	
10	Bill McCauley	
11	Jeremy Meehan	
12	Mike Harding	
13	Brad Cook	
14	Jeff Mitchell	
15	Jamie Allison	
16	Dan Pawlaczyk	
17	Kevin Brown	
18	Duane Harmer	
19	Gerry Skrypec	
20	Shayne McCosh	
21	Sean Haggerty	
22	Nic Beaudoin	
23	Paul Maurice, Coach	
24	Pete DeBoer, Asst. Coach	
25	Bob Wren	

LES VOLTIGEURS de DRUMMONDVILLE

Les Voltigeurs de Drummondville
Card No. 10, Ian Laperriere

Released in November 1993. There are 3,000 sets and 275 numbered uncut sheets.

Size: 2 1/2" X 3 1/2"
Face: Four Colour, Purple and Teal border; Name
Back: Four colour, Name, Resume, Sponsor logos
Imprint: Imprime ay Canada par SLAPSHOT IMAGES LTD. 1993©
Complete Set No.: 28
Complete Set Price: 5.00   10.00

No.	Player	Checklist
1	Checklist	
2	Stephane Routhier, Goalie	
3	Yannick Gagnon, Goalie	
4	Sebastien Bety	
5	Martin Latulippe	
6	Nicolas Savage	
7	Sylvain Ducharme	
8	Yan St-Pierre	
9	Emmanuel Labranche	
10	Ian Laperriere	
11	Louis Bernard	
12	Stephane St Amour	
13	Vincent Tremblay	
14	Denis Gauthier Jr.	
15	Eric Plante	
16	Christian Marcoux	
17	Patrice Charbonneau	
18	Raymond Delarosbil	
19	Patrick Livernoche	
20	Luc Decelles	
21	Francois Sasseville	
22	Steve Tardif	
23	Mathieu Sunderland	
24	Alexandre Duchesne	
25	Jean Hamel, Entraineur-chef	
26	Mario Carrier, Entr-Adjoint	
27	Me Andre Lepage, Entraineur	
28	Slapshot Calender	

GUELPH STORM

Released in December, 1993. There are 3,000 sets and 300 uncut numbered sheets.

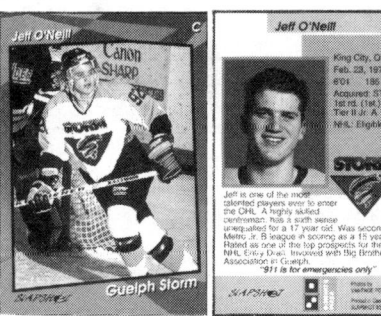

Guelph Storm
Card No. 2, Jeff l'Neill

Size: 2 1/2" X 3 1/2"
Face: Four Colour, Blue and Grey border; Name
Back: Four colour, Name, Resume, Sponsor logos
Imprint: Printed in Canada by SLAPSHOT IMAGES LTD. 1993©
Complete Set No.: 30
Complete Set Price: 5.00   10.00

No.	Player	Checklist
1	Title Card	
2	Jeff O'Neill	
3	Mark McArthur, Goalie	
4	Kayle Short	
5	Ryan Risidore	
6	Mike Rusk	
7	Regan Stocco	
8	Duane Harmer	
9	Sylvain Cloutier	
10	Eric Landry	
11	Jamie Wright	
12	Todd Norman	
13	Mike Pittman	
14	Ken Belanger	
15	Viktor Reuta	
16	Mike Prokopec	
17	Jeff Williams	

750 • SLAPSHOT IMAGES LTD — 1993 - 94 REGULAR ISSUE —

No.	Player	Checklist
18	Chris Skoryna	☐
19	Stephane Lefebvre	☐
20	Jeff Cowan	☐
21	Murray Hogg	☐
22	Andy Adams, Goalie	☐
23	Todd Bertuzzi	☐
24	Grant Pritchett	☐
25	Rumun Ndur	☐
26	**Top Prospect:** Jeff O'Neill	☐
27	Paul Brydges, Asst. Coach	☐
28	John Lovell, Head Coach	☐
29	Team Picture	☐
30	Gurinder Saini, Domibo's Pizza	☐

KINGSTON FRONTENACS

Relased in December 1993. There are 3,000 sets and 200 uncut numbered sheets.

 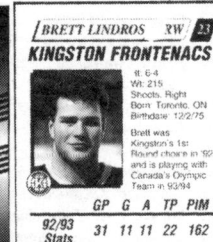

Kingston Frontenacs
Card No. 23, Brett Lindros

Size: 2 1/2" X 3 1/2"
Face: Four Colour, Black and yellow border; Name, Number
Back: Four colour, Name, Number, Team Name, Resume
Imprint: Printed in Canada by SLAPSHOT IMAGES LTD. 1993©
Complete Set No.: 24
Complete Set Price: 15.00 ☐

No.	Player	Checklist
1	Greg Lovell, Goalie	☐
2	Marc Lamothe, Goalie	☐
3	T. J. Moss, Goalie	☐
4	Marc Moro	☐
5	Trevor Doyle	☐
6	Jeff Dacosta	☐
7	Gord Walsh	☐
8	Brian Scott	☐
9	Jason Disher	☐
10	Alexander Zhurik	☐
11	Ken Boone	☐
12	Cail Maclean	☐
13	Bill Marandiuk	☐
14	Martin Sychra	☐
15	Duncan Fader	☐
16	David Ling	☐
17	Chad Kilger	☐
18	Greg Kraemer	☐
19	Trent Cull	☐
20	Steve Parson	☐
21	Craig Rivet	☐
22	Kelo Corpse	☐
23	Brett Lindros	☐
24	David Allison, Head Coach Michael Allison, Asst. Coach	☐

KITCHENER RANGERS PROMO

There are 900 unautographed promo's and 100 autographed promo's that were randomly inserted in Domino's 5-pack pizzas.

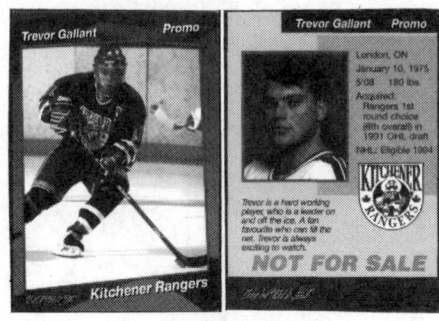

Kitchener Rangers
Card No. 1A, Trevor Gallant

Size: 2 1/2" X 3 1/2"
Face: Four Colour, Blue and red border; Name, Team Name
Back: Four colour, Name, Resume, Sponsor and Team logos
Imprint: Printed in Canada by SLAPSHOT IMAGES LTD. 1993©
Complete Set No.: 1
Complete Set Price: 28.00 ☐

No.	Player	Checklist
1A	Trevor Gallant	3.00 ☐
1B	Trevor Gallant, Autographed	25.00 ☐

KITCHENER RANGERS

Released in January 1994. There are 3,000 sets and 250 uncut numbered sheets.

Kitchener Rangers
Card No. 15, Todd Warriner

Size: 2 1/2" X 3 1/2"
Face: Four Colour, Blue and red border; Name, Team Name
Back: Four colour, Name, Resume, Sponsor and Team logos
Imprint: Printed in Canada by SLAPSHOT IMAGES LTD. 1993©
Complete Set No.: 30
Complete Set Price: 10.00 ☐

No.	Player	Checklist
1	Checklist	☐
2	David Belitski, Goalie	☐
3	Darryl Whyte, Goalie	☐
4	Greg McLean	☐
5	Jason Hughes	☐
6	Gord Dickie	☐
7	Travis Riggin	☐
8	Norm Dezainde	☐
9	Tim Spitzig	☐
10	Trevor Gallant	☐
11	Chris Pittman	☐
12	Ryan Pawluk	☐
13	Jason Morgan	☐
14	James Boyd	☐
15	Todd Warriner	☐
16	Mark Donahue	☐
17	Peter Brearley	☐
18	Andrew Taylor	☐
19	Jason Gladney	☐
20	Wes Swinson	☐

No.	Player	Checklist
21	Matt O'Dette	☐
22	Darren Schmidt	☐
23	Jason Johnson	☐
24	Eric Manlow	☐
25	Jeff Lillie, Goalie	☐
26	Sergei Olympiev	☐
27	Joe McDonnell, Coach	☐
28	Rick Chambers, Trainer	☐
29	**Top Prospects:** Andrew Taylor, Travis Riggin, David Belitski	☐
30	Domino's Pizza	☐

NIAGARA FALLS THUNDER

Released in December 1993. There are 3,000 sets and 250 uncut and numbered sheets.

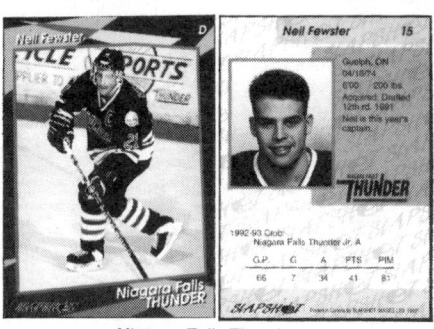

Niagara Falls Thunders
Card No. 15, Neil Fewster

Size: 2 1/2" X 3 1/2"
Face: Four Colour, Purple and green border; Name
Back: Four colour, Name, Resume, Team name
Imprint: Printed in Canada by SLAPSHOT IMAGES LTD. 1993©
Complete Set No.: 28
Complete Set Price: 10.00 ☐

No.	Player	Checklist
1	Checklist	☐
2	Jimmy Hibbert, Goalie	☐
3	Darryl Foster, Goalie	☐
4	Gerry Skrypec	☐
5	Greg de Vries	☐
6	Tim Thompson	☐
7	Joel Yates	☐
8	Yianni Loannou	☐
9	Steve Nimigon	☐
10	Jeff Johnstone	☐
11	Brandon Convery	☐
12	Dale Junkin	☐
13	Ethan Moreau	☐
14	Derek Grant	☐
15	Neil Fewster	☐
16	Jason Reesor	☐
17	Tom Moores	☐
18	Matthew Mayo	☐
19	Bogdon Savenko	☐
20	Corey Bricknell	☐
21	Derek Sylvester	☐
22	Anatoli Filatov	☐
23	Jason Bonsignore	☐
24	Mike Perna	☐
25	**Thunder Alumni:** Emanuel Legrace, Goalie	☐
26	Randy Hall, Coach/GM	☐
27	Chris Johnstone, Coach/Ass't GM	☐
28	**Towering Prospects:** Jason Bonsignore, Ethan Moreau, Brandon Convery	☐

Note: Junior Team Sets are collected as complete sets. Very seldom are they broken up and sold as individual cards. For this reason the cards also are not priced individually. The complete set price is shown in EX and NRMT prices.

NORTH BAY CENTENNIALS

Released in Fenruary 1994. There are 3,000 sets and 250 uncut and numbered sheets.

 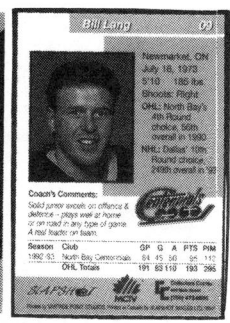

Noth Bay Centennials
Card No. 9, Bill Lang

Size: 2 1/2" X 3 1/2"
Face: Four Colour, Black and yellow border; Name
Back: Four colour, Name, Resume, Sponsor and Team logos
Imprint: Printed in Canada by SLAPSHOT IMAGES LTD. 1993©
Complete Set No.: 25
Complete Set Price: 10.00

No.	Player	Checklist
1	Brad Brown	☐
2	Sandy Allan, Goalie	☐
3	Rob Lave	☐
4	Steve McLaren	☐
5	Andy Delmore	☐
6	Corey Neilson	☐
7	Jason Campeau	☐
8	Jim Ensom	☐
9	Bill Lang	☐
10	Ryan Gillis	☐
11	Michael Burman	☐
12	Stefan Rivard	☐
13	B. J. MacPhearson	☐
14	Lee Jinman	☐
15	Scott Cherrey	☐
16	Damien Bloye	☐
17	Denis Gaudet	☐
18	Bob Thornton	☐
19	John Guirestante	☐
20	Jeff Shevalier	☐
21	Scott Roche, Goalie	☐
22	Vitali Yachmenev	☐
23	Bert Templeton, Coach	☐
24	Rob Kirsch, Asst. Coach	☐
25	**Top Prospects:** Brad Brown, Vitall Yachmeniv	☐

OSHAWA GENERALS

Released in February 1994. There are 3,000 sets and 250 uncut and numbered sheets.

 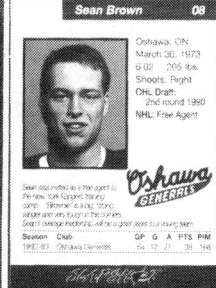

Oshawa Generals
Card No. 8, Sean Brown

Size: 2 1/2" X 3 1/2"
Face: Four Colour, Red and Blue border; Name
Back: Four colour, Name, Resume, Team logos
Imprint: Printed in Canada by SLAPSHOT IMAGES LTD. 1993@
Complete Set No.: 26
Complete Set Price: 10.00

No.	Player	Checklist
1	Checklist	☐
2	Joel Gagnon, Goalie	☐
3	Ken Shepard, Goalie	☐
4	Jan Snopek	☐
5	David Froh	☐
6	Brandon Gray	☐
7	Damon Hardy	☐
8	Sean Brown	☐
9	Jeff Andrews	☐
10	Stephane Yelle	☐
11	Stephane Soulliere	☐
12	Andrew Power	☐
13	Todd Bradley	☐
14	Darryl Lafrance	☐
15	Darryl Moxam	☐
16	Robert Dubois	☐
17	Kevin Vaughan	☐
18	Rob McQuat	☐
19	B. J. Johnston	☐
20	Paul Doherty	☐
21	Eric Boulton	☐
22	Marc Savard	☐
23	Chris Hall	☐
24	Jason McQuat	☐
25	Ryan Lindsay	☐
26	Rick Cornacchia, Wayne Daniels, Brian Drumm, Coaches	☐

PETERBOROUGH PETES

Released in November 1993. There are 3,000 set and 125 uncut and numbered sheets.

 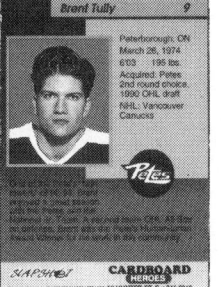

Peterborough Petes
Card No. 9, Brent Tully

Size: 2 1/2" X 3 1/2"
Face: Four Colour, Grey border; Name, Position
Back: Four colour, Name, Resume, Sponsor and Team logos
Imprint: Printed in Canada by SLAPSHOT IMAGES LTD. 1993@
Complete Set No.: 30
Complete Set Price: 15.00

No.	Player	Checklist
1	1992-93 OHL Champions	☐
2	Jonathan Murphy	☐
3	Dave Roche	☐
4	Rob Giffin	☐
5	Mike Harding	☐
6	Tim Hill	☐
7	Darryl Moxam	☐
8	Pat Paone	☐
9	Brent Tully	☐
10	Zac Bierk, Goalie	☐
11	Chad Grills	☐
12	Matt St. Germain	☐
13	Henrik Eppers	☐
14	Rick Emmett	☐
15	Chad Lang, Goalie	☐
16	Cameron Mann	☐
17	Steve Hogg	☐
18	Mike Williams	☐
19	Ryan Nauss	☐
20	Jamie Langenbrunner	☐
21	Ryan Douglas, Goalie	☐
22	Matt Johnson	☐
23	Kelvin Solari	☐
24	Dan Delmonte	☐
25	Quade Loghtbody	☐
26	Adrain Murray	☐
27	**Record Breaker:** Jason Dawe	☐
28	**Record Breaker:** Mike Harding	☐
29	NHL Top Draft Pick: Chris Pronger	☐
30	Cardball Heroes: Greg and Kevin Ball	☐

SAULT STE. MARIE GREYHOUNDS

Released in March 1994. There are 3,400 sets and 100 uncut and numbered sheets.

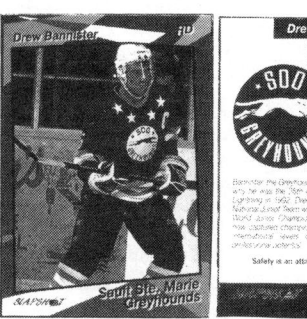 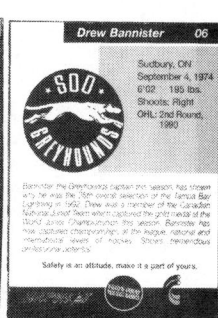

Sault Ste. Marie Greyhounds
Card No. 6, Drew Bannister

Size: 2 1/2" X 3 1/2"
Face: Four Colour, Red and Grey border; Name
Back: Four colour, Name, Resume, Sponsor and Team logos
Imprint: Printed in Canada by SLAPSHOT IMAGES LTD. 1993@
Complete Set No.: 30
Complete Set Price: 10.00

No.	Player	Checklist
1	Andrea Carpano, Goalie	☐
2	Ryan Douglas, Goalie	☐
3	Dan Cloutier, Goalie	☐
4	Oliver Pastinsky	☐
5	Scott King	☐
6	Drew Bannister	☐
7	Sean Gagnon	☐
8	Andre Payette	☐
9	Peter Mackeller	☐
10	Richard Uniacke	☐
11	Steve Zoryk	☐
12	Brad Baber	☐
13	Gary Roach	☐
14	Jeff Gies	☐
15	Tom MacDonald	☐
16	Rhett Trombley	☐
17	Jon VanVolsen	☐
18	Andrew Clark	☐
19	Briane Thompson	☐
20	Aaron Gavey	☐
21	Wade Gibson	☐
22	Chad Grills	☐
23	Jeff Toms	☐
24	Steve Sullivan	☐
25	Jeremy Stevenson	☐
26	Corey Moylan	☐
27	Steve Spina	☐
28	Dave Mayville, Dir. OPS/GM	☐
29	Ted Nolan, Head Coach	☐
30	Dan Flynn, Asst. Coach/GM, Mike Zuke, Asst. Coach	☐

Note: Junior Team Sets are collected as complete sets. Very seldom are they broken up and sold as individual cards. For this reason the cards also are not priced individually. The complete set price is shown in EX and NRMT prices.

752 • SLAPSHOT IMAGES LTD — 1993 - 94 REGULAR ISSUE —

SUDBURY WOLVES

Released in November 1993. There are 3,000 sets. There were no uncut sheets available.

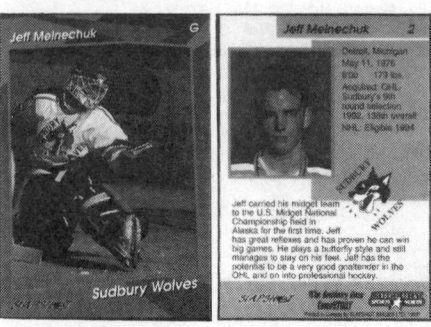

Sudbury Wolves
Card No. 2, Jeff Melnechuk

Size: 2 1/2" X 3 1/2"
Face: Four Colour, Blue and Grey border; Name
Back: Four colour, Name, Resume, Sponsor and Team logos
Imprint: Printed in Canada by SLAPSHOT IMAGES LTD. 1993@
Complete Set No.: 24
Complete Set Price: 10.00 ☐

No.	Player	Checklist
1	Shawn Silver, Goalie	☐
2	Jeff Melnechuk, Goalie	☐
3	Jay McKee	☐
4	Chris McMurtry	☐
5	Rory Fitzpatrick	☐
6	Mike Wilson	☐
7	Shawn Frappier	☐
8	Jamie Rivers	☐
9	Zdenek Nedved	☐
10	Ryan Shanahan	☐
11	Sean Venedam	☐
12	Andrew Dale	☐
13	Mark Giannetti	☐
14	Rick Bodkin	☐
15	Barrie Moore	☐
16	Jamie Matthews	☐
17	Gary Coupal	☐
18	Ilya Lysenko	☐
19	Simon Sherry	☐
20	Steve Potvin	☐
21	Joel Poirier	☐
22	Mike Yeo	☐
23	Bob MacIssac	☐
24	**Legend:** Paul DiPietro	☐

CHARGING

WINDSOR SPITFIRES

Released in January 1994. There are 3,000 sets and 250 uncut and numbered sheets.

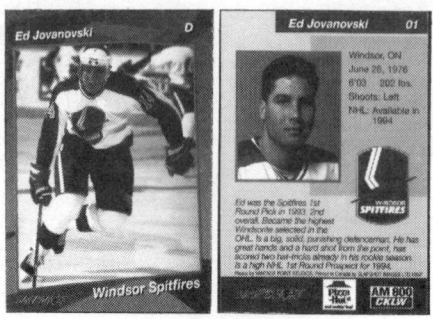

Windsor Spitfires
Card No. 1, Ed Jovanovski

Size: 2 1/2" X 3 1/2"
Face: Four Colour, Blue and Red border; Name
Back: Four colour, Name, Resume, Sponsor logos
Imprint: Printed in Canada by SLAPSHOT IMAGES LTD. 1993@
Complete Set No.: 26
Complete Set Price: 10.00 ☐

No.	Player	Checklist
1	Ed Jovanovski	☐
2	Shawn Silver, Goalie	☐
3	Travis Scott, Goalie	☐
4	Mike Martin	☐
5	Daryl Lavoie	☐
6	Craig Lutes	☐
7	David Pluck	☐
8	Bill Bowler	☐
9	David Green	☐
10	Adam Young	☐
11	Mike Loach	☐
12	Brady Blain	☐
13	Shayne McCosh	☐
14	Rob Shearer	☐
15	Joel Poirier	☐
16	Cory Evans	☐
17	Vladimir Kretchine	☐
18	Dave Roche	☐
19	Ryan Stewart	☐
20	Dave Geris	☐
21	Dan West	☐
22	Luke Clowes	☐
23	John Cooper	☐
24	Akil Adams	☐
25	Pizza Hut	☐
26	Steve Bell, AM800	☐

CROSS-CHECKING

Available in April !

THE CHARLTON STANDARD CATALOGUE OF CANADIAN BASEBALL & FOOTBALL CARDS

- Fourth Edition -

BASEBALL CARDS FROM 1912
FOOTBALL CARDS FROM 1949

For Canadian Baseball and Football Card Collectors this Catalogue has it all!

IMPERIAL TOBACCO * MAPLE CRISPETTE
BAZOOKA *PARKHURST * O-PEE-CHEE
CANADA STARCH * STUART * POST
TOPPS * WORLD WIDE GUM * NALLEYS
DONRUSS - LEAF * EDDIE SARGENT
WILLARD * TORONTO BLUE JAYS
STANDARD OIL * NABISCO * VACHON
BLUE RIBBON TEA * PANINI * PROVIGO
GENERAL MILLS * SCORE * EXHIBITS
HOSTESS * PURITAN MEATS * JOGO
GULF CANADA * ROYAL STUDIOS
BEN'S AULT FOODS * COCA-COLA * KFC
And All Other Major Manufacturers...

Complete price listings for all Major League Baseball and Canadian Football League cards!
Comprehensive baseball and football minor league card listings!
Regular issues, stickers, inserts, subsets, transfers and much, much more!
All major manufacturers!
Current Pricing for all cards in up to three grades of condition - VG, EX, and NRMT!
All rookie, last, pitcher, quarterback, error and variation cards identified and priced!
Plus Charlton's Fabulous Alphabetical Index!

OVER 300 PAGES * 60,000 PRICES
NEW, LARGER 8 1/2 x 11" FORMAT
RESERVE YOUR COPY TODAY
DIRECTLY FROM THE PUBLISHER...

The Charlton Press

**2010 YONGE STREET,
TORONTO, ONTARIO M4S 1Z9**
FOR TOLL FREE ORDERING PHONE
1-800-442-6042 FAX 1-800-442-1542
from anywhere in Canada or the U.S.

**CHAPTER ELEVEN
MINOR LEAGUE TEAM SETS**

ALPHABETICAL LISTING OF MANUFACTURERS
MINOR LEAGUE TEAM SETS

Team	Page
Arizona Icecats	786
Baltimore Skipjacks	755
Belleville Bulls	755
Brandon Wheat Kings	755
Brantford Alexanders	757
Brockville Braves	757
Chicoutimi Sagueneurs	757
Cornwall Royals	757
Flint Sprints	758
Fredericton Canadiens	759
Fredericton Express	758
Halifax Citadels	760
Hamilton Canucks	761
Hamilton Fincups	760
Hamilton Steel City	760
Hull Olympiques	761
Indianapolis Checkers	761
Kamloops Blazers	761
Kelowna Wings	762
Kingston Canadiens	762
Kitchener Rangers	764
Lethbridge Hurricanes	766
London Knights	767
L'Olympiques de Hull	761
Maine Black Bears	768
Medicine Hat Tigers	768
Milwaukee Admirals	768
Minnesota Bulldogs	786
Moncton Alpines	768
Moncton Golden Flames	769
Moncton Hawks	769
Montreal Juniors	770
Nashville Knights	770
Niagara Falls Thunder	771
North Bay Centennials	771
Nova Scotia Oilers	771
Nova Scotia Voyageurs	772
Oshawa Generals	772
Ottawa 67's	774
Peterborough Petes	775
Portland Winterhawks	776
Prince Albert Raiders	776
Quebec Ramparts	776
Rayside Balfour Junior A Canadians	777
Regina Pats	777
Richmond Renegades	778
Les Riveraires de Richelieu	778
Saginaw Gears	779
Saginaw Hawks	779
Salt Lake Golden Eagles	779
Saskatoon Blades	779
Sault Ste. Marie Greyhounds	780
Shawinnigan Falls Cataracts	781
Sherbrooke Canadiens	781
Spokane Chiefs	781
Springfield Indians	781
Sudbury Wolves	782
Toledo Storm (East Coast Hockey League)	785
Toronto Marlboroughs	784
Victoria Cougars	784
Wheeling Thunderbirds	785
Windsor Spitfires	785

BALTIMORE SKIPJACKS

— 1991 - 92 REGULAR ISSUE —

Baltimore Skipjacks, 1992 Issue,
Card No. 12, Steve Seftel

Card Size: 2 1/2" x 3 1/2"
Face: Four colour, white border; Name, Position, Team logo, Jersey number
Back: Black on white card stock; Name, Position, Resume, Sponsors logos, Card _ of 15
Imprint: None
Complete Set No.: 15
Complete Set Price: 4.00   8.00 ☐

No.	Player	Checklist
1	Tim Taylor	☐
2	Brent Hughes	☐
3	Trevor Halverson	☐
4	Bobby Reynolds	☐
5	Ken Lovsin	☐
6	Olaf Kolzig, Goalie	☐
7	Reginald Savage	☐
8	Jim Mathieson	☐
9	Todd Hlushko	☐
10	Mark Ferner	☐
11	John Purves	☐
12	Steve Seftel	☐
13	Craig Duncanson	☐
14	Simon Wheeldon	☐
15	Bob Babcock	☐

BELLEVILLE BULLS

— 1983 - 84 REGULAR ISSUE —

This set was sponsored jointly by Police, Laws and Youth, Board of Commissioners of Police, McDonald's, Canadian Tire, Coca-Cola, GM Bert Jones Bellville, Kiwanis International and "The Intelligencer" CJBQ.

Belleville Bulls, 1983-84 Issue
Card No. 20, Al Iafrate

Card Size: 2 5/8" X 4 1/8"
Face: Four colour, white border; Name, Position, Team logo
Back: Black on white card stock; Number, Hockey tips, Sponsor logos
Imprint: None
Complete Set No.: 30
Complete Set Price: 18.00   36.00 ☐

No.	Player	Checklist
1	Title Card: Belleville Bulls	☐
2	Quinte Sports Centre	☐
3	Dan Quinn	☐
4	Dave MacLean	☐
5	Scott Gardiner	☐
6	Mike Knuude, Trainer	☐
7	Brian Martin	☐
8	Dr. R. Vaughn, Co-Owner	☐
9	John McDonald, Goalie	☐
10	Brian Small	☐
11	Mike Savage	☐
12	Dunc MacIntyre	☐
13	Charlie Moore	☐
14	Jim Andanoff	☐
15	Mario Martini	☐
16	Rick Adolfi	☐
17	Mike Velucci	☐
18	Scott McMichel	☐
19	Ali Butorac	☐
20	Al Iafrate	☐
21	Rob Crocock	☐
22	Craig Coxe	☐
23	Grant Robertson	☐
24	Craig Billington, Goalie	☐
25	Darren Gani	☐
26	Tim Bean	☐
27	Wayne Gretzky, Co-Owner	☐
28	Russ Soule, Assistant Trainer	☐
29	Larry Mavety, Coach and General Manager	☐
30	Team Photo	☐

— 1984 - 85 REGULAR ISSUE —

Card Size: 2 5/8" X 4 1/8"
Face: Four colour, borderless; Name, Position, Date, Logo
Back: Black on white postcrd stock
Imprint: THE BELLEVILLE BULLS 1984-85
Complete Set No.: 31
Complete Set Price: 12.00   24.00 ☐

No.	Player	Checklist
1	Team Photo	☐
2	Dr. R. Vaughan	☐
3	Larry Mavety	☐
4	Dunc MacIntyre	☐
5	Crest	☐
6	Mike Knuude	☐
7	John Purves	☐
8	Charlie Moore	☐
9	Stan Drulia	☐
10	Craig Billington, Goalie	☐
11	Dave MacLean	☐
12	Darren Moxam	☐
13	Shane Doyle	☐
14	Larry Vanherzele	☐
15	Tim Bean	☐
16	Kent Brimmer	☐
17	Angelo Catenaro	☐
18	Steve Linesman	☐
19	Grant Robertson	☐
20	John Reid	☐
21	Dean Whyte	☐
22	Darren Gani	☐
23	Roger Robertson	☐
24	Gary Callachar	☐
25	John Tamer	☐
26	Todd Hawkins	☐
27	Jim Andanoff	☐
28	Chris Rutledge	☐
29	Matt Taylor	☐
30	Maike Hartman	☐
31	Presentation	☐

BRANDON WHEAT KINGS

— 1982 - 83 REGULAR ISSUE—

Card Size: 2 3/8" X 4"
Face: Four colour, white border; Name
Back: Number
Imprint: None
Complete Set No.: 24
Complete Set Price: 11.00   22.00 ☐

No.	Player	Checklist
1	Wheat Kings Logo	☐
2	Kevin Pylypow	☐
3	Dean Kennedy	☐
4	Sonny Sodke	☐
5	Darren Schmidt	☐
6	Cam Plante	☐
7	Sid Cranston	☐
8	Bruce Thompson	☐
9	Dave McDowall	☐
10	Bill Vince	☐
11	Kelly Glowa	☐
12	Tom McMurchy	☐
13	Ed Palichuk	☐
14	Roy Caswell	☐
15	Allan Tarasuk	☐
16	Brent Jessiman	☐
17	Randy Slawson	☐
18	Gord Smith	☐
19	Mike Sturgeon	☐
20	Larry Bumstead	☐
21	Kirk Blomquist	☐
22	Ron Loustel	☐
23	Ron Hextall, Goalie	☐
24	Brandon Police Logo	☐

— 1983 - 84 REGULAR ISSUE —

This set was Sponsored by the Brandon Council, Lions International, Optimist Club of Brandon and the City of Brandon Police.

Brandon Wheat Kings, 1983-84 Issue
Card No. 12, Jay Palmer

Card Size: 2 1/4" X 4"
Face: Four colour, white border; Name, Position, Jersey number,
Back: Black on white card stock; Number, Hockey and safety tips, Sponsor logos
Imprint: Leech Print.
Complete Set No.: 24
Complete Set Price: 11.00   22.00 ☐

No.	Player	Checklist
1	Bryan Wells	☐
2	Jim Agnew	☐
3	Gord Paddock	☐
4	John Dzikowski	☐
5	Kelly Kozack	☐
6	Byron Lomow	☐
7	Pat Loyer	☐
8	Rob Ordman	☐

756 • BRANDON WHEAT KINGS — 1984 - 85 REGULAR ISSUE

No.	Player	Checklist
9	Brad Wells	☐
10	Dave Thomlinson	☐
11	Cam Plante	☐
12	Jay Palmer, Goalie	☐
13	Boyd Lomow	☐
14	Brent Jessiman	☐
15	Paul More	☐
16	Stacy Pratt	☐
17	Team Photo	☐
18	Jack Sangster, Coach	☐
19	Derek Laxdal	☐
20	Ray Ferraro	☐
21	Allan Tarasuk	☐
22	Randy Cameron	☐
23	Dave Curry	☐
24	Ron Hextall, Goalie	☐

— 1984 - 85 REGULAR ISSUE —

Brandon Wheat Kings, 1984-85 Issue
Card No. 20, Pokey Riddick, Goalie

Card Size: 2 1/4" x 3 15/16"
Face: Four colour, white border; Name, Position, Jersey Number
Back: Black on white card stock; Number, Hockey and Safety Tips, Sponsor logos
Imprint: Leech print
Complete Set No.: 24
Complete Set Price: 7.50 15.00 ☐

No.	Player	Checklist
1	Garnet Kazuik	☐
2	Brent Mireau	☐
3	Byron Lomow	☐
4	Dean Shaw, Goalie	☐
5	Dean Sexsmith	☐
6	Brad Mueller	☐
7	John Dzikowski	☐
8	Artie Feher, Goalie	☐
9	Pat Loyer	☐
10	Murray Rice	☐
11	Derek Laxdal	☐
12	Perry Fafard	☐
13	Lee Trim	☐
14	Dan Hart	☐
15	Trent Ciprick	☐
16	Jeff Waver	☐
17	Team Photo	☐
18	Jack Sangster, Coach	☐
19	Darwin McPherson	☐
20	Pokey Riddick, Goalie	☐
21	Boyd Lomow	☐
22	Dave Thomlinson	☐
23	Paul More	☐
24	Brent Severyn	☐

— 1985 - 86 REGULAR ISSUE —

Brandon Wheat Kings, 1985-86 Issue
Card No. 14, Terry Yake

Card Size: 2 1/4" x 3 15/16"
Face: Four colour, white border; Name, Position, Jersey Number
Back: Black on white card stock; Number, Hockey and Safety Tips, Sponsor logos
Imprint: Leech print
Complete Set No.: 24
Complete Set Price: 5.00 10.00 ☐

No.	Player	Checklist
1	Kelly Hitchins	☐
2	Brent Mireau	☐
3	Byron Lomow	☐
4	Bob Heeney	☐
5	Dean Sexsmith	☐
6	Dave Curry	☐
7	John Dzikowski	☐
8	Artie Feher, Goalie	☐
9	Kevin Mayo	☐
10	Murray Rice	☐
11	Derek Laxdal	☐
12	Al Cherniwchan	☐
13	Lee Trim	☐
14	Terry Yake	☐
15	Trent Ciprick	☐
16	Jeff Waver	☐
17	Team Photo	☐
18	Jack Sangster, Coach	☐
19	Mike Morin	☐
20	Jason Phillips	☐
21	Rod Williams	☐
22	Dave Thomlinson	☐
23	Shane Eirickson	☐
24	Randy Hoffart	☐

— 1988 - 89 REGULAR ISSUE —

Brandon Wheat Kings, 1988-89 Issue
Card No. 1, Kevin Cheveldayoff

Card Size: 2 1/4" x 3 15/16"
Face: Four colour, white border; Name, Position, Jersey Number
Back: Black on white card stock; Number, Hockey Tips, Sponsor logos
Imprint: Leech Print
Complete Set No.: 24
Complete Set Price: 4.00 8.00 ☐

No.	Player	Checklist
1	Kevin Cheveldayoff	☐
2	Bob Woods	☐
3	Dwayne Newman	☐
4	Mike Vandenbeaghe	☐
5	Brad Woods	☐
6	Gary Audette	☐
7	Mark Bassen	☐
8	Troy Frederick	☐
9	Troy Kennedy	☐
10	Barry Dreger	☐
11	Bill Whistle	☐
12	Jeff Odgers	☐
13	Sheldon Kowalchuk	☐
14	Chris Robertson	☐
15	Don Laurin	☐
16	Curtis Folkett	☐
17	Team Photo	☐
18	Kelly McCrimmon, Asst. Coach	☐
19	Doug Sauter	☐
20	Kelly Hitchins	☐
21	Trevor Kidd	☐
22	Pryce Wood	☐
23	Cam Brown	☐
24	Greg Hutchings	☐

— 1989 - 90 REGULAR ISSUE —

Brandon Wheat Kings, 1989-90 Issue
Card No. 1, Trevor Kidd

Card Size: 2 1/4" x 3 15/16"
Face: Four colour, tan border; Name, Position, Jersey Number
Back: Black on white card stock; Number, Hockey Tips, Sponsor logos
Imprint: Leech Print
Complete Set No.: 24
Complete Set Price: 4.00 8.00 ☐

No.	Player	Checklist
1	Trevor Kidd, Goalie	☐
2	Troy Frederick	☐
3	Kelly Thiessen	☐
4	Pryce Wood	☐
5	Mike Vandenberghe	☐
6	Chris Constant	☐
7	Hardy Sauter	☐
8	Cam Brown	☐
9	Bart Cote	☐
10	Jeff Hoad	☐
11	Kevin Robertson	☐
12	Dwayne Newman	☐
13	Calvin Flint	☐
14	Glen Webster	☐
15	Greg Hutchings	☐
16	Rob Puchniak	☐
17	Gary Audette	☐

No.	Player	Checklist
18	Kevin Schmalz	☐
19	Dwayne Gylywoychuk	☐
20	Jeff Odgers	☐
21	Brian Purdy	☐
22	Merv Priest	☐
23	Doug Sauter, Coach	☐
24	Team picture	☐

BRANTFORD ALEXANDERS

— 1983 - 84 REGULAR ISSUE —

Card Size: 2 5/8" X 4 1/8"
Face: Four colour
Back: Number
Imprint: None
Complete Set No.: 30
Complete Set Price: 7.50 15.00 ☐

No.	Player	Checklist
1	Ken Gratton	☐
2	Shayne Corson	☐
3	Bob Roberts	☐
4	Bruce Bell	☐
5	Warren Bechard	☐
6	Jason Lafreniere	☐
7	Rob Moffat	☐
8	Jack Calbeck	☐
9	Marc West	☐
10	Larry Van Herzele	☐
11	Doug Stewart	☐
12	Brian MacDonald	☐
13	Dave Draper	☐
14	Jeff Jackson	☐
15	Steve Linseman	☐
16	Steve Short	☐
17	Allan Bester, Goalie	☐
18	John Weir	☐
19	Chris Pusey	☐
20	Mike Millar	☐
21	Chris Glover	☐
22	Bob Pierson	☐
23	Phil Priddle	☐
24	Grant Anderson	☐
25	Ken Gagnier	☐
26	Andy Alway	☐
27	Todd Francis	☐
28	John Meulenbroeks	☐
29	Mike Chettleburgh	☐
30	Bill Dynes	☐

BROCKVILLE BRAVES

— 1987 - 88 REGULAR ISSUE —

Brockville Braves, 1987-88 Issue
Card No. 7, Mark Michaud

Card Size: 2 5/8" x 3 5/8"
Face: Four colour, white border; Name, Position
Back: Black on white card stock; Number, Hockey and Safety tips, Sponsor logos
Imprint: Henderson & Blanchard Ltd.
Complete Set No.: 25
Complete Set Price: 6.00 12.00 ☐

No.	Player	Checklist
1	Brockville Police Crest	☐
2	Steve Harper, Trainer	☐
3	Peter Kelly, Trainer	☐
4	Mac MacLean, Coach / G.M.	☐
5	Mike McCourt	☐
6	Paul MacLean	☐
7	Mark Michaud, Goalie	☐
8	Alain Marchessault	☐
9	Tom Roman	☐
10	Darren Burns	☐
11	Scott Halpenny, Goalie	☐
12	Ray Gallagher	☐
13	Bob Lindsay	☐
14	Brett Harkins	☐
15	Dave Hyrsky	☐
16	Richard Marchessault	☐
17	Scott Boston	☐
18	Steve Hogg, Goalie	☐
19	Chris Webster	☐
20	Stuart Birnie	☐
21	Brett Dunk	☐
22	Charles Cusson	☐
23	Pat Gooley	☐
24	Andy Rodman	☐
25	Peter Radlein	☐

— 1988 - 89 REGULAR ISSUE —

Brockville Braves, 1988-89 Issue
Card No. 23, Chris Weber

Card Size: 2 5/8" x 3 5/8"
Face: Four colour, white border; Name, Position
Back: Black on white card stock; Hockey and safety tips, Sponsor logo
Imprint: Henderson & Blanchard Ltd.
Complete Set No.: 25
Complete Set Price: 9.00 18.00 ☐

No.	Player	Checklist
1	Ray Gallagher	☐
2	Peter Kelly, Trainer	☐
3	Steve Harper	☐
4	Winston Jones, Asst. Coach	☐
5	Mac MacLean, Coach / G.M.	☐
6	Kevin Doherty	☐
7	Stuart Birnie	☐
8	Charles Cusson	☐
9	Paul MacLean	☐
10	Bob Lindsay	☐
11	Darren Burns	☐
12	Rick Pracey, Goalie	☐
13	Mike Malloy	☐
14	Dave Hyrsky	☐
15	Rob Percival	☐
16	Jarrett Eligh	☐
17	Pat Gooley	☐
18	Michael Bracco, Goalie	☐
19	Ken Crook	☐
20	Brad Osborne	☐
21	Todd Reynolds	☐
22	Mike McCourt	☐
23	Chris Webster	☐
24	Kevin Lune	☐
25	Brockville Police Crest	☐

— 1990 - 91 REGULAR ISSUE —

We have no information on this set. We would appreciate hearing from anyone who could supply further information.

Card Size: 2 5/8" X 4 1/8"
Face: Four colour
Back: Unknown
Imprint: None
Complete Set No.: 24
Complete Set Price: 12.50 25.00 ☐

CHICOUTIMI SAGUENEENS

— 1984 - 85 REGULAR ISSUE —

Card Size: 8 1/2" X 11"
Face: Black and white, red border; Name, Resume, Sponsor's logo
Back: Blank
Imprint: None
Complete Set No.: 24
Complete Set Price: 15.00 30.00 ☐

No.	Player	Checklist
1	Bureau Direction	☐
2	Mario Bazinet	☐
3	Pierre Sevigny	☐
4	Gilles Laberge	☐
5	Marc Morin	☐
6	Mario Barbe	☐
7	Daniel Berthiaume, Goalie	☐
8	Francis Breault	☐
9	Greg Choules	☐
10	Luc Dufour	☐
11	Christian Duperron	☐
12	Luc Duval	☐
13	Patrick Emond	☐
14	Marc Fortier	☐
15	Stevem Gauthier	☐
16	Yves Heroux	☐
17	Daniel Jomphe	☐
18	Claude Lajoie	☐
19	Serge Lauzon	☐
20	Roch Marinier	☐
21	Pierre Millier	☐
22	Scott Rettew	☐
23	J. Marc Richard	☐
24	Stephane J. J. Richer	☐

CORNWALL ROYALS

— 1991 - 92 R.A.I.D. —

This set was issued to promote the Royals Against Illegal Drugs campaign. Approximately 5000 to 6000 of each card were produced and distributed at random by Police Officers at all the schools in Cornwall and area. Each student received 3 separate cards and approxiamately 300-400 sets were assembled and sold for $8.00 each in an effort to create a base for next year. Other sets included in the above figure were set aside for the Special Olympics program.

Cornwall Royals, 1991-92 Issue,
Card No. 9, Sam Oliveira

FLINT SPRINTS — 1987 - 88 REGULAR ISSUE —

Card Size: 2 5/8" X 3 3/4"
Face: Four colour, white strip at bottom; Name, Team logo
Back: Black on white card stock; Number, Drug tips, Sponsor logos
Imprint: None
Complete Set No.: 29
Complete Set Price: 6.00 12.00

No.	Player	Checklist
1	Jason Meloche	
2	Mark Desantis	
3	Richard Raymond	
4	Gord Pell	
5	Dave Lemay	
6	John Lovell, Head Coach	
7	Ryan Vandenbussche	
8	David Babcock	
9	Sam Oliveira	
10	Jeremy Stevenson	
11	Todd Walker	
12	Jean-Alain Schneider	
13	Ilpo Kauhanen	
14	Guy Leveque	
15	Shayne Gaffar	
16	Rival Fullum	
17	Mike Prokopec	
18	Nathan Lafayette	
19	Larry Courville	
20	Chris Clancy	
21	Tom Nemeth	
22	Jeff Reid	
23	Paul Andrea	
24	John Slaney	
25	Alan Letang	
26	Rob Dykeman, Goalie	
27	Paul Fixter; Brian O'Leary, Coaching Staff	
28	Claude Shaver, Chief of Police	
29	Checklist	

FLINT SPRINTS

— 1987 - 88 REGULAR ISSUE —

Card Size: 2 1/2" X 3 1/2"
Face: Four colour
Back: Black on white postcard stock; Name, Resume
Imprint: None
Complete Set No.: 20
Complete Set Price: 12.50 25.00

No.	Player	Checklist
1	Mario Chiraroni	
3	John Cullen	
3	Bob Fleming	
4	Keith Gretzky	
5	Todd Hawkins	
6	Mike Hoffman	
7	Curtis Hunt	
8	Dwaine Hutton	
9	Trent Kaese	
10	Tom Karalis	
11	Ray Leblanc	
12	Darren Lowe	
13	Brett MacDonald	
14	Chris McSorley	
15	Mike Mersch	
16	Victor Posa	
17	Kevin Schamehor	
18	Ronald Stern	
19	Don Waddell	
20	Dan Woodley	

Note: Junior Team Sets are collected as complete sets. Very seldom are they broken up and sold as individual cards. For this reason the cards also are not priced individually. The complete set price is shown in EX and NRMT prices.

— 1988 - 89 REGULAR ISSUE —

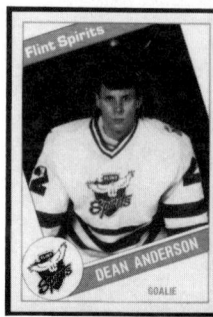

Flint Sprints, 1988-89 Issue
Card No. 1, Dean Anderson

Card Size: 2 1/2" X 3 1/2"
Face: Four colour, white border; Name, Position, Team
Back: Black on white card stock; Name, Position, Resume
Imprint: None
Complete Set No.: 22
Complete Set Price: 10.00 20.00

No.	Player	Checklist
1	Dean Anderson	
2	Rob Bryden	
3	John Devereaux	
4	Stephane Giguere	
5	Steve Harrison	
6	Yves Heroux	
7	Mike Hoffman	
8	Peter Horachek	
9	Guy Jacob	
10	Bob Kennedy	
11	Gary Kruzich	
12	Lonnie Loach	
13	Brett MacDonald	
14	Mike MacWilliam	
15	Moe Mansi	
16	Mike Mersch	
17	Michel Mongeau	
18	Ken Spangler	
19	Mark Vichorek	
20	Troy Vollhoffer	
21	Don Waddell, G/M	
22	Three Amigos: Steve Harrison, Mike Mersch, Mike Hoffman	

FREDERICTON EXPRESS

— 1981 - 82 REGULAR ISSUE —

We have no information on the previous three sets. We would appreciate hearing from anyone who could supply further information.

Card Size: 2 1/2" X 3 1/2"
Face: Four colour
Back: Unknown
Imprint: None
Complete Set No.: 26
Complete Set Price: 17.50 35.00

No.	Player	Checklist

— 1982 - 83 REGULAR ISSUE —

Fredericton Express, 1982-83 Issue
Card No. 6, Clint Malarchuk

Card Size: 2 1/2" X 3 3/4"
Face: Four colour
Back: Number
Imprint: None
Complete Set No.: 26
Complete Set Price: 12.50 25.00

No.	Player	Checklist
1	Express Team Photo	
2	B.J. MacDonald	
3	Sylvain Cote	
4	Michel Bolduc	
5	Gary Lupul	
6	Clint Malarchuk, Goalie	
7	Tony Currie	
8	Tim Tookey	
9	Anders Eldebrink	
10	Basil McRae	
11	Kelly Elcombe	
12	Jacques Demers, Coach	
13	Frank Caprice	
14	Terry Johnson	
15	Grant Martin	
16	Andre Chartrain	
17	Marc Crawford	
18	Gaston Therrien	
19	Andy Schliebener	
20	Christian Tanguay	
21	Art Rutland	
22	Jean Marc Gaulin	
23	Neil Belland	
24	Andre Cote	
25	Jim MacRae	
26	Scott Beckingham and Marty Flynn	

— 1983 - 84 REGULAR ISSUE —

Fredericton Express, 1983-84 Issue
Card No. 3, Michel Dufour

Card Size: 2 1/2" X 3 3/4"
Face: Four colour, white border; Name, Position, Sponsor logos
Back: Black on white card stock; Tips, Number
Imprint: None
Complete Set No.: 27
Complete Set Price: 12.50 25.00

No.	Player	Checklist
1	Title card: Team Photo	☐
2	Frank Caprice, Goalie	☐
3	Michel Dufour, Goalie	☐
4	Brian Ford, Goalie	☐
5	Jean-Marc Lanthier	☐
6	Jim Dobson	☐
7	Mike Hough	☐
8	Rick Lapointe	☐
9	Michel Bolduc	☐
10	Christian Tanguay	☐
11	Tony Currie	☐
12	Moe Lemay	☐
13	Bruce Holloway	☐
14	Neil Belland	☐
15	Richard Turmel	☐
16	Claude Julien	☐
17	André Chartrain	☐
18	Grant Martin	☐
19	Rejean Vignola	☐
20	André Coté	☐
21	Jean-Marc Gaulin	☐
22	Andy Schliebener	☐
23	Stu Kulak	☐
24	Mike Eagles	☐
25	Earl Jessiman, Coach / General Manager	☐
26	Marty Flynn; Scott Beckingham, Trainers	☐
27	Checklist	☐

— 1984 - 85 REGULAR ISSUE —

Card Size: 2 1/2" X 3 3/4"
Face: Four colour, white border; Name, Position
Back: Black on white card stock; Number, Hockey and Safety Tips, Sponsor logos
Imprint: None
Complete Set No.: 28
Complete Set Price: 9.00 18.00 ☐

No.	Player	Checklist
1	Dave Morrison	☐
2	Dave Shaw	☐
3	Bruce Holloway	☐
4	Roger Haegglund	☐
5	Neil Belland	☐
6	Gord Donnelly	☐
7	David Bruce	☐
8	Claude Julien	☐
9	Dan Wood	☐
10	Clint Malarchuk, Goalie	☐
11	Jere Gillis	☐
12	Mike Hough	☐
13	Michel Bolduc	☐
14	Peter Loob	☐
15	Steve Driscoll	☐
16	Newell Brown	☐
17	Jim Dobson	☐
18	Wendell Young, Goalie	☐
19	Mark Kumpel	☐
20	Mike Eagles	☐
21	Tom Thornsbury	☐
22	Grant Martin	☐
23	Marc Crawford	☐
24	Andy Schliebener	☐
25	Earl Jessiman, Coach/G.M.	☐
26	Yvon Vautour	☐
27	Craig Coxe	☐
28	Blake Wesley	☐

Note: Junior Team Sets are collected as complete sets. Very seldom are they broken up and sold as individual cards. For this reason the cards also are not priced individually. The complete set price is shown in EX and NRMT prices.

— 1985 - 86 REGULAR ISSUE —

Fredericton Express, 1985-86 Issue
Card No. 2, David Bruce

Card Size: 2 1/2" X 3 3/4"
Face: Four colour, white border; Name, Position
Back: Black on white card stock; Number, Hockey and Safety tips, Sponsor Logos
Imprint: None
Complete Set No.: 28
Complete Set Price: 9.00 18.00 ☐

No.	Player	Checklist
1	Scott Tottle	☐
2	David Bruce	☐
3	1985-1986 Fredericton Express	☐
4	Marc Crawford	☐
5	Mike Stevens	☐
6	Gary Lupul	☐
7	Alain Lemieux	☐
8	Mike Hough	☐
9	Tony Currie	☐
10	Dunc MacIntyre	☐
11	Jere Gillis	☐
12	Wendell Young, Goalie	☐
13	Jean-Marc Lanthier	☐
14	Ken Quinney	☐
15	Claude Julien	☐
16	Michel Petit	☐
17	Luc Guenette, Goalie	☐
18	Andy Schliebener	☐
19	Mark Kirton	☐
20	Gord Donnelly	☐
21	Tom Karalis	☐
22	Daniel Poudrier	☐
23	Neil Belland	☐
24	Dale Dunbar	☐
25	Marty Flynn; Scott Beckingham, Trainers	☐
26	Jean-Marc Gaulin	☐
27	Al MacAdam	☐
28	Andre Savard, Coach/G.M.	☐

— 1986 - 87 REGULAR ISSUE —

These cards are unnumbered and are listed below in alphabetical order.

Fredericton Express, 1986-87 Issue
Card No. 2, Jim Agnew

Card Size: 2 1/2" X 3 3/4"
Face: Four colour, white border; Name, Position, Resume, Sponsor logos
Back: Black on white card stock; Tips, Bilingual
Imprint: None
Complete Set No.: 26
Complete Set Price: 7.50 15.00 ☐

No.	Player	Checklist
1	Title Card: Team Photo	☐
2	Jim Agnew	☐
3	Brian Bertuzzi	☐
4	David Bruce	☐
5	Frank Caprice, Goalie	☐
6	Marc Crawford	☐
7	Steven Finn	☐
8	Jean-Marc Gaulin	☐
9	Scott Gordon, Goalie	☐
10	Taylor Hall	☐
11	Mike Hough	☐
12	Yves Heroux	☐
13	Tom Karalis	☐
14	Mark Kirton	☐
15	Jean-Marc Lanthier	☐
16	Jean LeBlanc	☐
17	Brett MacDonald	☐
18	Duncan MacIntyre	☐
19	Greg Malone	☐
20	Terry Perkins	☐
21	Daniel Poudrier	☐
22	Jeff Rohlicek	☐
23	André Savard, Coach	☐
24	Mike Stevens	☐
25	Trevor Stienburg	☐
26	Marty Flynn; Scott Beckingham, Trainers	☐

FREDERICTON CANADIENS

— 1992 - 93 REGULAR ISSUE —

Card Size:
Face: Four colour, borderless
Back: Black on white card stock; Resume, Sponsor logos
Imprint: Unknown
Complete Set No.: 28
Complete Set Price: 8.50 17.00 ☐

No.	Player	Checklist
1	Title Card	☐
2	Jesse Belanger'	☐
3	Paulin Bordeleau, Coach	☐
4	Donald Brashear	☐
5	Patrik Carnback	☐
6	Frédéric Chabot	☐
7	Eric Charron	☐
8	Alain Cote	☐
9	Paul DiPietro	☐
10	Craig Ferguson	☐
11	Gerry Fleming	☐
12	Luc Gauthier	☐
13	Robert Guillet	☐
14	Patric Kjellberg	☐
15	Les Kontar	☐
16	Patrick Langois, Equip. Mgr.	☐
17	Ryan Kuwabara	☐
18	Steve Larouche	☐
19	Jacques Parent, Physical Therapist	☐
20	Charles Paulin	☐
21	Oleg Petrov	☐
22	Yves Sarault	☐
23	Pierre Sevigny	☐
24	Darcy Simon	☐
25	Turner Stevenson	☐
26	Mascot: Tricolo	☐
27	Lindsay Vallis	☐
28	Steve Veilleux	☐

HALIFAX CITADELS

— 1989 - 90 REGULAR ISSUE —

Card Size: 2 1/2" X 4 1/4"
Face: Four colour, white border; Name
Back: Black on white card stock; Name, Resume
Imprint: None
Complete Set No.: 26
Complete Set Price: 10.00   20.00

No.	Player	Checklist
1	Joel Baillargeon	
2	Jamie Baker	
3	Mario Brunette	
4	Gerald Bzdel	
5	David Espe	
6	Bryan Fogarty	
7	Robie Ftorek, Coach	
8	Scott Gordon, Goalie	
9	Dean Hopkins	
10	Miroslav Ihnacak	
11	Claude Julien	
12	Kevin Kaminski	
13	Claude Lapointe	
14	McQuaid, Smith	
15	Max Middendorf	
16	Stephan Morin	
17	Dave Pichette	
18	Ken Quinney	
19	J. Marc Richard	
20	J. Marc Routhier	
21	Jaroslav Sevcik	
22	Bent Severyn	
23	Greg Smyth	
24	Trevor Steinburg	
25	Ladislav Tresl	
26	Marc Vermette	

— 1990 - 91 ISSUE —

Halifax Citadels, 1990-91 Issue
Card No. 17, Kip Miller

Card Size: 2 3/4" X 4 1/4"
Face: Four colour, white border; Player's name and jersey number
Back: Black on white card stock; Name, Statistics, Safety tips, Sponsor logo
Imprint: Farmers Co-Operative Dairy Limited
Complete Set No.: 27
Complete Set Price: 9.00   18.00

No.	Player	Checklist
1	Jamie Baker	
2	Mike Bishop, Goalie	
3	Gerald Bzdel	
4	Daniel Dore	
5	Mario Doyon	
6	Dave Espe	
7	Stephane Fiset, Goalie	
8	Scott Gordon, Goalie	
9	Stephane Guerard	
10	Dean Hopkins	
11	Miroslav Ihnacak	

No.	Player	Checklist
12	Jeff Jackson	
13	Clement Jodoin, Coach/G.M.	
14	Claude LaPointe	
15	Dave Latta	
16	Chris McQuaid, Equip. Mgr.	
17	Kip Miller	
18	Stephane Morin	
19	Ken Quinney	
20	Jean-Marc Richard	
21	Serge Roberge	
22	Jaroslav Sercik	
23	Brent Severyn	
24	Greg Smyth	
25	Jim Sprott	
26	Trevor Steinberg	
27	Mark Vermette	

HAMILTON CANUCKS

— 1992 - 93 REGULAR ISSUE —

Card Size: 2 1/2" X 3 1/2"
Face: Four colour; Name, Jersey number, Team, Sponsor's Name
Back: Black on white card stock; Name, Jersey number, Resume, Sponsor logos
Imprint: None
Complete Set No.: 27
Complete Set Price: 9.00   18.00

No.	Player	Checklist
1	Shawn Antoski	
2	Robin Bawa	
3	Jassen Cullimore	
4	Alain Deeks	
5	Neil Eisenhut	
6	Mike Fountain, Goalie	
7	Troy Gamble, Goalie	
8	Jasen Herter	
9	Pat Hickey, President	
10	Innaugural Season Team Photo	
11	Dane Jackson	
12	Dan Kesa	
13	Bob Mason, Goalie	
14	Mario Marios	
15	Mike Maurice	
16	Jay Mazur	
17	Jack McIlhargey, Coach	
18	Sandy Moger	
19	Stephane Morin	
20	Eric Murano	
21	Troy Neumeier	
22	Matt Newsom, General Manager	
23	Opening Night Puck Drop -with Mayor Bob Morrow	
24	Libor Polasek	
25	Doug Torrel	
26	Rick Vaive, Player / Coach	
27	Phil Von Stefenelli	

HAMILTON FINCUPS

— 1975 - 76 REGULAR ISSUE —

Card Size: 2 1/2" X 3 1/2"
Face: Black and white
Back: Unknown
Imprint: None
Complete Set No.: 18
Complete Set Price: 12.50   25.00

No.	Player	Checklist
1	Jack Anderson	
2	Greg Clause	
3	Mike Clarke	
4	Joe Contini	
5	Mike Fedorko	
6	Paul Foley	
7	Greg Hickey	
8	Tony Horvath	
9	Mike Keating	
10	Archie King	
11	Ted Long	
12	Dale McCourt	
13	Dave Norris	
14	Greg (Red) Quest	
15	Glen Richardson	
16	Ron Roscoe	
17	Ric Seiling	
18	Danny Shearer	

HAMILTON STEEL CITY

— DATE UNKNOWN —

These cards are unnumbered and are listed below in alphabetical order.

Hamilton Steel City
Card No. 1, Mike Nuchko

Card Size: 2 1/2" X 3 1/2"
Face: Blue photo, blue border; Team, Name, Jersey number, Position
Back: Blank
Imprint: None
Complete Set No.: 22
Complete Set Price: 7.50   15.00

No.	Player	Checklist
1	Mike Buchko	
2	Pino Caterini, Goalie	
3	Rich Chittley	
4	S. Hutchings	
5	Jim Italiano	
6	Scott Kyle	
7	Fred LeBlanc, President	
8	Stan Malecki	
9	Mike McHugh	
10	Jeff Ninham	
11	Brad Roberts	
12	Chris Roberts	
13	Ange Savelli, Coach	
14	Bruce Shipley	
15	G. Stevenson	
16	John Taylor, Vice President	
17	Keith Taylor	
18	Mark Tonaj	
19	F. Warwick	
20	**Top Scorer:** Pat Windsor	
21	Bill Zenette	
22	Management	

Note: Junior Team Sets are collected as complete sets. Very seldom are they broken up and sold as individual cards. For this reason the cards also are not priced individually. The complete set price is shown in EX and NRMT prices.

L'OUTAOUAIS OLYMPIQUES DE HULL

1987 - 88 REGULAR ISSUE

This 23-card set was numbered in red on the back.

L'Outaouais Olympqies de Hull, 1987-88 Issue
Card No. 7, Jason Glickman

Card Size: 2 3/4" x 4"
Face: Four colour, white border; Team logo
Back: Black on card stock; Name, Number, Sponsor logo
Imprint: Ville de Gatineau Direction de la Securite publique
Complete Set No.: 24
Complete Set Price: 25.00   50.00 ☐

No.	Player	Checklist
1	Joe Aloi	☐
2	Joel Bain	☐
3	Christian Breton	☐
4	Benoit Brunet	☐
5	Guy Dupuis	☐
6	Martin Gelinas	☐
7	Jason Glickman, Goalie	☐
8	Wayne Gretzky, President	☐
9	Denis Heon, Assisant Entraineur	☐
10	Herbie Hohenberger	☐
11	Kenneth MacDermid	☐
12	Craig Martin	☐
13	Mark McLane	☐
14	Stephane Matteau	☐
15	Kelly Nester	☐
16	Jacques Parent, Therapeute athletique	☐
17	Marc Saumier	☐
18	Claude-Charles Sauriol	☐
19	Joe Suk	☐
20	Alain Vigneault, Entraineur	☐
21	George Wilcox	☐
22	L'Equipe des Olympiques de Hull	☐
23	Les Promenades de L'Outaouais Collection des Olympiquesde Hull	☐

HULL OLYMPIQUES

— 1980 REGULAR ISSUE —

We have no information on this set. We would appreciate hearing from anyone who could supply further information.

Card Size: 2 3/4" X 4"
Face: Four colour
Back: Unknown
Imprint: None
Complete Set No.: 24
Complete Set Price: 35.00   65.00 ☐

No.	Player	Checklist

INDIANAPOLIS CHECKERS

— 1981 - 82 REGULAR ISSUE —

This set was issued by Pizza Hut.

Card Size: 2 3/8" X 3 1/2"
Face: Four colour; Name, Position, Team logo
Back: Black on white card; Name, Resume
Imprint: None
Complete Set No.: 20
Complete Set Price: 12.50   25.00 ☐

No.	Player	Checklist
1	Mike Hordy	☐
2	Randy Johnson	☐
3	John Marks	☐
4	Tim Lockridge	☐
5	Darcy Regier	☐
6	Garth MacGuigan	☐
7	Charlie Skjodt	☐
8	Mats Hallin	☐
9	Frank Beaton	☐
10	Kevin Devine	☐
11	Steve Stoyanovich	☐
12	Lorne Stamler	☐
13	Red Laurence	☐
14	Monty Trottier	☐
15	Neil Hawryliw	☐
16	Kelly Davis	☐
17	Glen Duncan	☐
18	Kelly Hrudey, Goalie	☐
19	Rob Holland	☐
20	Bruce Andres	☐

— 1982 - 83 REGULAR ISSUE —

Card Size: 2 3/8" X 3 1/2"
Face: Four colour
Back: Unknown
Imprint: None
Complete Set No.: 21
Complete Set Price: 12.50   25.00 ☐

No.	Player	Checklist
1	Kelly Davis	☐
2	Kevin Devine	☐
3	Gordon Dineen	☐
4	Glen Duncan	☐
5	Greg Gilbert	☐
6	Mike Greeder	☐
7	Mats Hallin	☐
8	Dave Hanson	☐
9	Rob Holland	☐
10	Scott Howson	☐
11	Kelly Hrudey, Goalie	☐
12	Randy Johnson	☐
13	Red Laurence	☐
14	Tim Lockridge	☐
15	Garth MacGuigan	☐
16	Darcy Regier	☐
17	Dan Revell	☐
18	Dave Simpson	☐
19	Lorne Stamler	☐
20	Steve Stoyanovich	☐
21	Monty Trottier	☐

KAMLOOPS BLAZERS

— 1985 - 86 ISSUE —

Card Size: 2 9/4" X 4"
Face: Name, Number, Position, Team logo
Back: Black on white card stock; Hockey and safety tips; Sponsor logos
Imprint: None
Complete Set No. 19
Complete Set Price: 9.00   18.00 ☐

No.	Player	Checklist
1	Robin Bawa	☐
2	Craig Berube	☐
3	Pat Bingham	☐
4	Randy Hansch, Goalie	☐
5	Greg Hawgood	☐
6	Ken Hitchcock, Head Coach	☐
7	Mark Kachowski	☐
8	Troy Kennedy	☐
9	Dave Marcinyshyn	☐
10	Mike Nottingham	☐
11	Doug Pickell	☐
12	Rudy Poeschek	☐
13	Mike Ragot	☐
14	Don Schmidt	☐
15	Ron Shudra	☐
16	Peter Soberlak	☐
17	Lonnie Spink	☐
18	Chris Tarnowski	☐
19	Greg "Spike" Wallace, Trainer	☐

— 1986 - 87 REGULAR ISSUE —

Card Size: 2 1/2" X 3 1/2"
Face: Four colour; Name, Jersey number, Position
Back: Blank
Imprint: None
Complete Set No.: 24
Complete Set Price: 25.00   50.00 ☐

No.	Player	Checklist
1	Warren Babe	☐
2	Robin Bawa	☐
3	Rob Brown	☐
4	Dean Cook	☐
5	Scott Daniels	☐
6	Mario Desjardins	☐
7	Bill Harrington	☐
8	Greg Hawgood	☐
9	Serge Lajoie	☐
10	Dave Marcinyshyn	☐
11	Len Mark	☐
12	Rob McKinley	☐
13	Casey McMillan	☐
14	Darcy Norton	☐
15	Kelly Para	☐
16	Doug Pickell	☐
17	Rudy Poeschek	☐
18	Mark Recchi	☐
19	Don Schmidt	☐
20	Ron Shudra	☐
21	Chris Tarnowski	☐
22	Team Photo	☐
23	Steve Wienke	☐
24	Rich Wiest	☐

— 1987 - 88 REGULAR ISSUE —

Card Size: 2 1/2" X 3 1/2"
Face: Name, Number, Position, Team logo
Back: Black on white card stock; Hockey and safety tips, Sponsor Logos
Imprint: None
Complete Set No.: 24
Complete Set Price: 17.50   35.00 ☐

No.	Player	Checklist
1	Title Card: Team Photo	☐
2	Warren Babe	☐
3	Paul Checknita	☐
4	Dave Chyzowski	☐
5	Dean Cook, Goalie	☐
6	Greg Davies	☐
7	Kim Deck	☐
8	Todd Decker	☐
9	Bill Harrington	☐
10	Greg Hawgood	☐
11	Phil Huber	☐
12	Steve Kloepzig	☐
13	Willie Macdonald, Goalie	☐
14	Pat MacLeod	☐

KELOWNA WINGS

— 1983 - 84 PHOTO ISSUE —
ESSO

Card Size: 8" x 10 3/4"
Face: Blue and white; Name, Team, Date, Facsimile autograph, Logo
Back: Blank
Imprint: None
Complete Set No.: 23
Complete Set Price: 10.00 20.00 ☐

No.	Player	Checklist
1	Craig Butz	☐
2	Bruno Campese	☐
3	Grant Delcourt	☐
4	R. J. Dundas	☐
5	Rocky Dundas	☐
6	Jeff Fenton	☐
7	Mark Fioretti	☐
8	Brent Gilchrist	☐
9	Mikael Johnsson	☐
10	Cam Lazoruk	☐
11	Dave MacDonald	☐
12	Dave McLay	☐
13	Darwein Moeller	☐
14	Ed Palichuk	☐
15	Jeff Sharples	☐
16	Bob Shaw	☐
17	Shawn Vincent	☐
18	Tod Voshell	☐
19	Darcy Wakaluk	☐
20	Chad Walker	☐
21	Stuart Wenaas	☐
22	Terry Zaporkan	☐
23	Greg Zuk	☐

— 1984 - 85 REGULAR ISSUE —

Card Size: 2 1/2" X 3 1/2"
Face: Black and white, white border; Name, Number, Jersey Number, Position
Back: Black on white cardstock; Name, Position, Resume, Safety tips.
Imprint: Unknown
Complete Set No.: 56
Complete Set Price: 20.00 40.00 ☐

No.	Player	Checklist
1	Checklist	☐
2	Darcy Wakaluk, Goalie	☐
3	Stacey Nickel, Goalie	☐
4	Jeff Sharples	☐
5	Greg Zuk	☐
6	Dayrn Sivertson	☐
7	Randy Cameron	☐
8	Mark Fioretti	☐
9	Ron Viglasi	☐
10	Ian Herbers	☐
11	Mike Wegleitner	☐
12	Terry Zaporzon	☐
13	Dwaine Hutton	☐
14	Rod Williams	☐
15	Jeff Rohlicek	☐
16	Brent Gilchrist	☐
17	Rocky Dundas	☐
18	Grant Delcourt	☐
19	Cam Lazoruk	☐
20	Tony Horacek	☐
21	Mark Wingerter	☐
22	Mick Vukota	☐

JUNIOR HOCKEY GRADS

No.	Player	Checklist
23	Danny Gare	☐
24	Rich Sutter	☐
25	Alfie Turcotte	☐
26	Bryan Trottier	☐
27	Bill Derlago	☐
28	Stan Smyl	☐
29	Brent Sutter	☐
30	Mel Bridgman	☐
31	Paul Cyr	☐
32	Gary Lupul	☐
33	Ray Neufeld	☐
34	Brian Propp	☐
35	Bob Nystrom	☐
36	Ryan Walter	☐
37	Russ Courtnall	☐
38	Larry Playfair	☐
39	Ron Delorme	☐
40	Ron Sutter	☐
41	Bobby Clarke	☐
42	Bob Bourne	☐
43	Cam Neely	☐
44	Murray Craven	☐
45	Clark Gillies	☐
46	Ron Flockhart	☐
47	Harold Snepsts	☐
48	Duane Sutter	☐
49	Garth Butcher	☐
50	Bill Hajt	☐
51	Jim Benning	☐
52	Ray Allison	☐
53	Ken Wregget, Goalie	☐
54	Phil Russell	☐
55	Brad McCrimmon	☐
56	Dan Hodgson	☐

— 1988 - 89 REGULAR ISSUE —

Card Size: 2 1/2" X 3 1/2"
Face: Name, Number, Position, Team logo
Back: Black on white card stock; Hockey and safety tips, Sponsor Logos
Imprint: None
Complete Set No.: 24
Complete Set Price: 12.50 25.00 ☐

No.	Player	Checklist
1	Cory Anderson	☐
2	Ed Bertuzzi	☐
3	Pat Bingham	☐
4	Zac Boyer	☐
5	Trevor Buchanan	☐
6	Dave Chysowski	☐
7	Dean Cook	☐
8	Cory Crichton	☐
9	Kim Deck	☐
10	Ryan Harrison	☐
11	Brad Heschuk	☐
12	Corey Hirsch, Goalie	☐
13	Phil Huber	☐
14	Len Jorgenson	☐
15	Paul Kruse	☐
16	Dave Linford	☐
17	Pat MacLeod	☐
18	Darwin McClelland	☐
19	Cal McGowan	☐
20	Mike Needham	☐
21	Don Schmidt	☐
22	Brian Shantz	☐
23	Darryl Sydor	☐
24	Steve Yule	☐
15	Casey McMillan	☐
16	Glenn Mulvenna	☐
17	Mike Needham	☐
18	Darcy Norton	☐
19	Devon Oleniuk	☐
20	Doug Pickell	☐
21	Garth Premak	☐
22	Mark Recchi	☐
23	Don Schmidt	☐
24	Alec Shelfo, Goalie	☐

— 1989 - 90 REGULAR ISSUE —

Card Size: 2 1/2" X 3 1/2"
Face: Name, Number, Position, Team logo
Back: Black on white card stock; Hockey and safety tips, Sponsor Logos
Imprint: None
Complete Set No.: 24
Complete Set Price: 10.00 20.00 ☐

No.	Player	Checklist
1	Len Barrie	☐
2	Craig Bonner	☐
3	Murray Duval	☐
4	Todd Essolmont	☐
5	Todd Harris	☐
6	Corey Hirsch, Goalie	☐
7	Phil Huber	☐
8	Paul Kruse	☐
9	Dale Mason	☐
10	Joey Mittelsteadt	☐
11	Brian Shantz	☐
12	Trevor Sim	☐
13	Lance Johnson	☐
14	Steve Yule	☐
15	Jeff Waatchorn	☐
16	Mike Needham	☐
17	Jarrett Bousquet	☐
18	Clayton Young	☐
19	Cal McGowan	☐
20	Scott Niedermeyer	☐
21	Shea Esselmont	☐
22	Darryl Sydor	☐
23	Dean Malkoc	☐
24	Zac Boyer	☐

KINGSTON CANADIENS

— 1979 - 80 ISSUE —

Card Size: 3" X 6"
Face: Four colour
Back: Unknown
Imprint: None
Complete Set No.: 23
Complete Set Price: 100.00 200.00 ☐

No.	Player	Checklist

— 1980 - 81 ISSUE —

Card Size: 2 5/8" X 4 1/8"
Face: Four colour
Back: Unknown
Imprint: None
Complete Set No.: 25
Complete Set Price: 22.50 45.00 ☐

No.	Player	Checklist

Note: We have no information on the previous two sets and would appreciate hearing from anyone who could supply further information.

— 1981 - 82 ISSUE —

Card Size: 2 5/8" X 4 1/8"
Face: Four colour
Back: Number
Imprint: None
Complete Set No.: 25
Complete Set Price: 15.00 30.00 ☐

No.	Player	Checklist
1	Canadians Logo	☐
2	Scott MacLellan	☐
3	Dave Courtemanche	☐
4	Mark Reade	☐
5	Shawn Babcock	☐
6	Phil Bourque	☐
7	Ian MacInnis	☐
8	Neil Trineer	☐
9	Syl Grandmaitre	☐
10	Carmine Vani	☐
11	Chuck Brimmer	☐
12	Mike Linseman	☐
13	Steve Seguin	☐

No.	Player	Checklist
14	Dan Wood	☐
15	Kirk Muller	☐
16	Jim Aldred	☐
17	Rick Wilson	☐
18	Mike Siltala	☐
19	Howie Scruton	☐
20	Mike Stothers	☐
21	Dennis Smith	☐
22	Steve Richey	☐
23	Mike Moffat	☐
24	Jim Morrison	☐
25	Randy Plumb	☐

— 1982 - 83 REGULAR ISSUE —

Kingston Canadiens, 1982-83 Issue
Card No. 2, Dennis Smith

Card Size: 2 5/8" X 4 1/8"
Face: Four colour, white border; Name, Position, Team logo
Back: Black on white card stock; Number, Tips, sponsor logos
Imprint: WALLACE R. BERRY, PHOTOGRAPHER
COLOUR, FOURWAY GRAPHICS
Complete Set No.: 27
Complete Set Price: 10.00 20.00 ☐

No.	Player	Checklist
1	Jim Morrison, General Manager	☐
2	Dennis Smith	☐
3	Curtis Collin	☐
4	Joel Brown	☐
5	Ron Handy	☐
6	Carmine Vani	☐
7	Al Andrews, Goalie	☐
8	Mike Siltala	☐
9	Syl Grandmaitre	☐
10	Steve Seguin	☐
11	Brian Dobbin	☐
12	Mark Reade	☐
13	John Kemp, Goalie	☐
14	Dan Mahon	☐
15	Keith Knight	☐
16	Ron Sanko	☐
17	John Landry	☐
18	Chris Brant	☐
19	Dave Simurda	☐
20	Mike Lafoy	☐
21	Scott MacLellan	☐
22	Brad Walcot	☐
23	Steve Richey, Goalie	☐
24	Rod Graham, Coach	☐
25	Ben Levesque	☐
26	Checklist	☐
27	International Hockey Hall of Fame & Museum	☐

— 1983 - 84 REGULAR ISSUE —

Kingston Canadiens, 1983-84 Issue
Card No. 2, Dennis Smith

Card Size: 2 5/8" X 3 5/8"
Face: Four colour, white border; Name, Position, Team logo
Back: Black on white card stock; Number, Tips, Sponsor logos
Imprint: WALLACE R. BERRY, PHOTOGRAPHER
COLOUR, FOURWAY GRAPHICS
Complete Set No.: 30
Complete Set Price: 10.00 20.00 ☐

No.	Player	Checklist
1	Kingston Police Crest	☐
2	Dennis Smith	☐
3	Ben Levesque	☐
4	Const. Arie Moraal	☐
5	Tom Allen	☐
6	Mike Plesh	☐
7	Roger Belanger	☐
8	Jeff Chychrun	☐
9	Mike King	☐
10	Scott Metcalfe	☐
11	David Lundmark	☐
12	Tim Salmon	☐
13	Ted Linesman	☐
14	Chris Clifford, Goalie	☐
15	Todd Elik	☐
16	Kevin Conway	☐
17	Barry Burkholder	☐
18	Joel Brown	☐
19	Steve King	☐
20	Craig Kales	☐
21	John Humphries, Trainer	☐
22	David James	☐
23	Dave Simurda	☐
24	Allen Bishop	☐
25	Jeff Hogg, Goalie	☐
26	Rick Cornacchia, Coach	☐
27	Ken Slater, Director	☐
28	Const. Bill Doxtator	☐
29	Checklist	☐
30	International Hockey Hall of Fame & Museum	☐

— 1984 - 85 REGULAR ISSUE —

Kingston Canadiens, 1984-85 Issue
Card No. 6, Scott Metcalfe

Card Size: 2 5/8" X 3 5/8"
Face: Four colour, white border; Name, Position, Team logo
Back: Black on white card stock; Number, Tips, Sponsor logos
Imprint: WALLACE R. BERRY, PHOTOGRAPHER
COLOUR, FOURWAY GRAPHICS
Complete Set No.: 30
Complete Set Price: 9.00 18.00 ☐

No.	Player	Checklist
1	Crest: Kingston Police Force	☐
2	Rick Cornacchia, Coach	☐
3	Cst. Arie Moraal	☐
4	Ken Slater, Director	☐
5	Crest: Kingston Canadians / Checklist	☐
6	Scott Metcalfe	☐
7	Chris Clifford, Goalie	☐
8	Todd Elik	☐
9	Len Spratt, Goalie	☐
10	Mike Plesh	☐
11	Marc Lyons	☐
12	Barry Burkholder	☐
13	Rick Fera	☐
14	David Hoover	☐
15	Andy Rivers	☐
16	Marc Laforge	☐
17	Peter Viscovich	☐
18	Jeff Chycrun	☐
19	Wayne Erskine	☐
20	Todd Clarke	☐
21	Darren Wright	☐
22	Tony Rocca	☐
23	Brian Verbeek	☐
24	Herb Raglan	☐
25	Daril Holmes	☐
26	Len Coyle, Assistant Trainer	☐
27	Ted Linesman	☐
28	Intenational Hockey Hall of Fame	☐
29	Troy MacNevin	☐
30	Peter Campbeil, Head Trainer	☐

— 1985 - 86 REGULAR ISSUE —

Many of the photographs for the 1985-86 issue are the same as those of the 1984-85 issue.

Kingston Canadiens, 1985-86 Issue
Card No. 7, Chris Clifford

Card Size: 2 5/8" X 3 5/8"
Face: Four colour, white border; Name, Position, Team logo
Back: Black on white card stock; Number, Tips, Sponsor logos
Imprint: WALLACE R. BERRY, PHOTOGRAPHER
COLOUR, FOURWAY GRAPHICS
Complete Set No.: 30
Complete Set Price: 8.00 16.00 ☐

No.	Player	Checklist
1	Crest: Kingston Police Force	☐
2	Dale Sandles, Assistant Coach	☐
3	Cst. Arie Moraal	☐
4	Fred O'Donnell, General Manager and Coach	☐
5	Crest: Kingston Canadiens / Checklist	☐
6	Scott Metcalfe	☐
7	Chris Clifford, Goalie	☐
8	Steve Seftel	☐
9	Andy Pearson, Goalie	☐
10	Jeff Cournelius	☐
11	Marc Lyons	☐

KITCHENER RANGERS — 1986 - 87 REGULAR ISSUE —

No.	Player	Checklist
12	Barry Burkholder	☐
13	Bryan Fogarty	☐
14	Jeff Sirkka	☐
15	Scott Pearson	☐
16	Marc Laforge	☐
17	Peter Viscovich	☐
18	Jeff Chycren	☐
19	Wayne Erskine	☐
20	Todd Clarke	☐
21	Darren Wright	☐
22	Mike Maurice	☐
23	Brian Verbeek	☐
24	Mike Fiset	☐
25	Daril Holmes	☐
26	Len Coyle, Asst. Trainer	☐
27	Ted Linesman	☐
28	International Hockey Hall of Fame	☐
29	Troy MacNevin	☐
30	Peter Campbell, Head Trainer	☐

— 1986 - 87 REGULAR ISSUE —

Card Size: 2 5/8" X 3 5/8"
Face: Four colour, white border; Name, Position, Team, Sponsor Logos
Back: Black on white card stock; Number, Hockey and Safety Tips, Sponsor Logos
Imprint: Printed by the Printing Factory
Complete Set No.: 30
Complete Set Price: 9.00   18.00 ☐

No.	Player	Checklist
1	Team Crest/Checklist	☐
2	Fred O'Donnell, Coach/G.M.	☐
3	Cst. Arie Moraal	☐
4	Dale Sandles, Coach	☐
5	Police Crest	☐
6	Brian Tessier, Goalie	☐
7	Franco Giammarco, Goalie	☐
8	Peter Liptrott	☐
9	Chris Clifford, Goalie	☐
10	Scott Metcalfe	☐
11	Scott Pearson	☐
12	Bryan Fogarty	☐
13	Daril Holmes	☐
14	Andy Rivers	☐
15	Troy MacNevin	☐
16	Marc Laforge	☐
17	Wayne Erskine	☐
18	Peter Viscovich	☐
19	Mike Maurice	☐
20	Steve Seftel	☐
21	Chad Badaway	☐
22	Marc Lyons	☐
23	Jeff Sirkka	☐
24	Mike Fiset	☐
25	John Battice	☐
26	Len Coyle, Asst. Trainer	☐
27	Sloan Torti	☐
28	Alain Laforge	☐
29	Ted Linesman	☐
30	Peter Campbell, Head Trainer	☐

1987 - 1988 P.L.A.Y.

Kingston Canadiens, 1987-88 Issue
Card No. 8, Peter Liptrott

Card Size: 2 5/8" x 3 5/8"
Face: Four colour, white border; Name, Team and Sponsor's logo
Back: Black on card stock; Police Tips, Sponsor's logo
Imprint: Printed by The Printing Factory
Complete Set No.: 30
Complete Set Price: 7.50   15.00 ☐

No.	Player	Checklist
1	Checklist	☐
2	Gord Wood, GM	☐
3	Kingston Canadiens / Police Crests	☐
4	Jacques Tremblay, Coach	☐
5	Rhonda Sheridan, Public Relations	☐
6	Jeff Wilson, Goalie	☐
7	Franco Giammarco, Goalie	☐
8	Peter Liptrott	☐
9	David Weiss, Goalie	☐
10	Joel Morin	☐
11	Mark Turner	☐
12	Jeff Sirka	☐
13	James Henckle	☐
14	Mike Bodnarchuk	☐
15	Mike Cavanaugh	☐
16	Darcy Cahill	☐
17	Kevin Falesy	☐
18	Dean Pella	☐
19	Brad Gratton	☐
20	Steve Seftel	☐
21	Bryan Fogarty	☐
22	Scott Pearson	☐
23	Tyler Pella	☐
24	Mike Fiset	☐
25	John Battice	☐
26	Len Coyle, Asst. Trainer	☐
27	Geoff Schneider	☐
28	Chris Lukey	☐
29	Trevor Smith	☐
30	Peter Campbell, Head Trainer	☐

KITCHENER RANGERS

— 1982 - 83 REGULAR ISSUE —

Kitcheners Rangers, 1982-83 Issue
Card No. 6, Kerry Kerch

Card Size: 2 3/4" X 3 1/5"
Face: Four colour, white border
Back: Black on white card stock; Number, Name, Jersey number, Resume, Tips, Sponsor logos
Imprint: DESIGNED & PRINTED BY COBER PRINTING LTD.
Complete Set No.: 30
Complete Set Price: 17.50   35.00 ☐

No.	Player	Checklist
1	Crest: Waterloo Regional Police	☐
2	Harold Basse, Chief of Police	☐
3	Title Card: Sponsor Logos	☐
4	Joe Crozler, General Manager / Coach	☐
5	Crest: Kitchener Rangers / Checklist	☐
6	Kerry Kerch, Goalie	☐
7	Tom St. James	☐
8	Wendell Young, Goalie	☐
9	Dave Shaw	☐
10	Darryl Boudreau, Goalie	☐
11	David Bruce	☐
12	Wayne Presley	☐
13	Garnet McKechney	☐

No.	Player	Checklist
14	Kevin Petendra	☐
15	Brian Wilks	☐
16	Jim Quinn	☐
17	Allan MacInnis	☐
18	Dave Nicholls	☐
19	Mike Eagles	☐
20	Mike Hough	☐
21	Greg Puhalski	☐
22	Darren Wright	☐
23	Todd Steffen	☐
24	John Tucker	☐
25	Kent Paynter	☐
26	Andy O'Brien	☐
27	Les Bradley, Trainer	☐
28	Scott Biggs	☐
29	Chris Martin, Assistant Trainer	☐
30	Dave Webster	☐

— 1983 - 84 REGULAR ISSUE —

Kitchener Rangers, 1983-84 Issue
Card No. 1, Joe Mantione

Card Size: 2 1/2" X 3 1/2"
Face: Four colour, white border; Facsimile autograph
Back: Black on white card stock; Number, Name, Jersey number, Resume, Tips, Sponsor logos
Imprint: COBER PRINTING LTD.
Complete Set No.: 30
Complete Set Price: 12.50   25.00 ☐

No.	Player	Checklist
1	Joe Mantione, Goalie	☐
2	Jim Quinn	☐
3	Crest: Kitchener Rangers / Checklist	☐
4	Rob MacInnis	☐
5	Louie Berardicurti	☐
6	Neil Sandilands	☐
7	Darren Wright	☐
8	Tom Barret, GeneralManager / Coach	☐
9	Brian Wilks	☐
10	Garnet McKechney	☐
11	David Bruce	☐
12	Kent Paynte	☐
13	Title Card: Sponsor Logos	☐
14	Scott Kerr	☐
15	Greg Puhaski	☐
16	Wayne Presley	☐
17	Carmine Vani	☐
18	Shawn Burr	☐
19	Dave Latta	☐
20	John Tucker	☐
21	Mike Stevens	☐
22	Harold Basse, Chief of Police	☐
23	Crest: Waterloo Regional Police	☐
24	Peter Bakovic	☐
25	Brian Ross	☐
26	Brad Balshin	☐
27	Dave Shaw	☐
28	Chris Martin, Assistant Trainer	☐
29	Len Bradley, Trainer	☐
30	Ray LeBlanc, Goalie	☐

— 1984 - 85 REGULAR ISSUE —

Kitchener Rangers, 1984-85 Issue
Card No. 3, Garnet McKechney

Card Size: 2 3/4" X 3 1/2"
Face: Four colour, white border; Facsimile autograph
Back: Black on white card stock; Number, Name, Jersey number, Resume, Tips, Sponsor logos
Imprint: None
Complete Set No.: 30
Complete Set Price: 10.00 20.00 ☐

No.	Player	Checklist
1	Crest: Waterloo Regional Police	☐
2	Harold Basse, Chief of Police	☐
3	Garnet McKechney	☐
4	Tom Barret, General Manager / Coach	☐
5	Crest: Kitchener Rangers / Checklist	☐
6	Mike Bishop, Goalie	☐
7	Craig Wolanin	☐
8	Steve Marcolini	☐
9	Peter Langlois	☐
10	Dave Weiss, Goalie	☐
11	Ken Alexander	☐
12	Ian Pound	☐
13	Doug Stromback	☐
14	Joel Brown	☐
15	Brian Wilks	☐
16	Robin Rubic	☐
17	Kent Paynter	☐
18	Jon Helinski	☐
19	Greg Puhalski	☐
20	Wayne Presley	☐
21	Dave McLlwain	☐
22	Shawn Burr	☐
23	Dave Latta	☐
24	John Keller	☐
25	Mike Stevens	☐
26	Title Card: Sponsor Logos	☐
27	Richard Adolfi	☐
28	Grant Sanders	☐
29	Les Bradley, Trainer	☐
30	Title Card: Sponsor Logos	☐

— 1985 - 86 REGULAR ISSUE —

Kitchener Rangers, 1985-86 Issue
Card No. 6, Dave Weiss

Card Size: 2 3/4" X 3 1/2"
Face: Four colour, white border; Number
Back: Black on white card stock; Number, Name, Jersey number, Resume, Tips, Sponsor logos
Imprint: None
Complete Set No.: 30
Complete Set Price: 10.00 20.00 ☐

No.	Player	Checklist
1	Crest: Waterloo Regional Police	☐
2	Harold Basse, Chief of Police	☐
3	Title Card: Sponsor Logos	☐
4	Tom Barrett, General Manager / Coach	☐
5	Crest: Kitchener Rangers / Checklist	☐
6	Dave Weiss, Goalie	☐
7	Steve Marcolini	☐
8	Kevin Grant	☐
9	Ken Alexander	☐
10	Mike Volpe, Goalie	☐
11	Ian Pound	☐
12	Brett MacDonald	☐
13	Scott Taylor	☐
14	Greg Hankkio	☐
15	Mike Morrison	☐
16	Mike Wolak	☐
17	Craig Booker	☐
18	Jeff Noble	☐
19	Shawn Tyers	☐
20	Peter Lisy	☐
21	Shawn Burr	☐
22	David Latta	☐
23	Ron Sanko	☐
24	Doug Jones	☐
25	Paul Penelton	☐
26	Blair MacPherson	☐
27	Richard Hawkins	☐
28	Brad Sparkes	☐
29	Ron Goodall	☐
30	Kevin Duguay, Trainer	☐

— 1986 - 87 REGULAR ISSUE —

Kitchener Rangers, 1986-87 Issue
Card No. 7, Darren Rumble

Card Size: 2 3/4" X 3 1/2"
Face: Four colour, white border; Number, Name
Back: Black on white card stock; Number, Name, Jersey number, Resume, Tips, Sponsor logos
Imprint: None
Complete Set No.: 30
Complete Set Price: 7.00 14.00 ☐

No.	Player	Checklist
1	Crest: Waterloo Regional Police	☐
2	Harold Basse, Chief of Police	☐
3	Title Card: Sponsor Logos	☐
4	Tom Barrett, General Manager / Coach	☐
5	Crest: Kitchener Rangers / Checklist	☐
6	Dave Weiss, Goalie	☐
7	Darren Rumble	☐
8	Kevin Grant	☐
9	Len Fawcett	☐
10	Darren Beals, Goalie	☐
11	Ed Kister	☐
12	Scott Taylor	☐
13	Darren Moxam	☐
14	Paul Epoch	☐
15	Richard Borgo	☐

No.	Player	Checklist
16	Allan Lake	☐
17	Jeff Noble	☐
18	Mark Montanari	☐
19	Jim Hulton	☐
20	Kelly Gain	☐
21	Craig Booker	☐
22	David Latta	☐
23	Doug Jones	☐
24	Gary Callahan	☐
25	Bruno Lapensee	☐
26	Scott Montgomery, Trainer	☐
27	Ron Goodall	☐
28	Discount Coupon / Sponsor Logos	☐
29	Steve Ewing	☐
30	Joe McDonnell, Assistant Coach	☐

— 1987 - 88 P.L.A.Y. —

Kitchener Rangers, 1987-88 Issue
Card No. 6, Gus Morschauser

Card Size: 2 3/4" X 3 1/2"
Face: Four colour, white border; Number, Name
Back: Black on white card stock; Number, Name, Jersey number, Resume, Tips, Sponsor logo
Imprint: Printed By Cober Printing Ltd.
Complete Set No.: 30
Complete Set Price: 7.00 14.00 ☐

No.	Player	Checklist
1	Crest: Waterloo Regional Police	☐
2	Harold Basse, Chief of Police	☐
3	Children's Bonus Card	☐
4	Joe McDonnell, General Manager / Coach	☐
5	Crest: Kitchener Rangers / Checklist	☐
6	Gus Morschauser, Goalie	☐
7	Rick Allain	☐
8	Kevin Grant	☐
9	Rob Thiel	☐
10	Darren Beals, Goalie	☐
11	Cory Keenan	☐
12	Rival Fullum	☐
13	Tony Crisp	☐
14	Tyler Ertel	☐
15	Richard Borgo	☐
16	Steven Rice	☐
17	Rob Sangster	☐
18	Jeff Noble	☐
19	Mark Montanari	☐
20	Jim Hulton	☐
21	Craig Booker	☐
22	Doug Jones	☐
23	Randy Pearce	☐
24	Darren Rumble	☐
25	Joe Ranger	☐
26	Optimist's Sponsor's Card	☐
27	Ron Goodall	☐
28	Alan Lake	☐
29	Scott Montgomery, Trainer	☐
30	Optimist's Sponsor's Card	☐

— 1988 - 89 REGULAR ISSUE —

Kitchener Rangers, 1988-89 Issue
Card No. 6, Mike Torchia

Card Size: 2 3/4" X 3 1/2"
Face: Four colour, white border; Number, Name
Back: Black on white card stock; Number, Name, Jersey number, Resume, Tips, Sponsor logo
Imprint: Printed By Cober Printing Ltd.
Complete Set No.: 30
Complete Set Price: 6.00 12.00 ☐

No.	Player	Checklist
1	Crest: Waterloo Regional Police	☐
2	Harold Basse, Chief of Police	☐
3	Children's Bonus Card	☐
4	Joe McDonnell, General Manager / Coach	☐
5	Crest: Kitchener Rangers / Checklist	☐
6	Mike Torchia, Goalie	☐
7	Rick Allain	☐
8	John Uniac	☐
9	Rob Thiel	☐
10	Gus Morschauser, Goalie	☐
11	Cory Keenan	☐
12	Rival Fullum	☐
13	Jason Firth	☐
14	Joey St. Aubin	☐
15	Richard Borgo	☐
16	Steven Rice	☐
17	Rob Sangster	☐
18	Gilbert Dionne	☐
19	Mark Montanari	☐
20	Shayne Stevenson	☐
21	Pierre Gagnon	☐
22	Kirk Tomlinson	☐
23	Randy Pearce	☐
24	Brad Barton	☐
25	Chris Li Puma	☐
26	Optimist's Sponsor's Card	☐
27	Steve Herniman	☐
28	Darren Rumble	☐
29	Rick Chambers, Trainer	☐
30	Optimist's Sponsor's Card	☐

— 1989 - 90 REGULAR ISSUE —

Kitchener Rangers, 1989-90 Issue,
Card No. 17, Steven Rice

Card Size: 2 3/4" X 3 1/2"
Face: Four colour, white border; Name, Number
Back: Black on white card stock; Player's name and Jersey number, Number Hockey and Safety Tips, Sponsor Logos
Imprint: Printed by Cober Printing Ltd.
Complete Set No.: 30
Complete Set Price: 7.50 15.00 ☐

No.	Player	Checklist
1	Crest: Waterloo Regional Police	☐
2	Harold Basse, Chief of Police	☐
3	Children's Bonus Card	☐
4	Joe McDonnell, G.M. / Coach	☐
5	1989-90 Checklist	☐
6	Mike Torchia, Goalie	☐
7	Rick Allain	☐
8	John Uniac	☐
9	Jack Williams	☐
10	Dave Schill, Goalie	☐
11	John Copely	☐
12	Cory Keenan	☐
13	Rival Fullum	☐
14	Jason Firth	☐
15	Joey St. Aubin	☐
16	Richard Borgo	☐
17	Steven Rice	☐
18	Rob Sangster	☐
19	Gilbert Dionne	☐
20	Jamie Israel	☐
21	Shayne Stevenson	☐
22	Gib Tucker	☐
23	Randy Pearce	☐
24	Brad Barton	☐
25	Chris Li Puma	☐
26	Optimist's Sponsor's Card	☐
27	Kevin Falesy	☐
28	Steve Smith	☐
29	Rick Chambers, Trainer	☐
30	Optimist's Sponsor's Card	☐

— 1990 - 91 REGULAR ISSUE —

Kitchener Rangers, 1990-91 Issue
Card No. 11, Tony McCabe

Card Size: 2 3/4" X 3 1/2"
Face: Four colour, red border; Name, Date
Back: Black on white card stock; Number Hockey and Safety Tips, Sponsors' logos
Imprint: Printed by Colour Printing Ltd.
Complete Set No.: 30
Complete Set Price: 7.50 15.00 ☐

No.	Player	Checklist
1	Crest: Waterloo Regional Police	☐
2	Harold Basse, Chief of Police	☐
3	Joe McDonnell, G.M. / Coach	☐
4	Rick Chambers, Trainer	☐
5	1990-91 Checklist	☐
6	Mike Torchia, Goalie	☐
7	Len DeVuono	☐
8	John Uniac	☐
9	Steve Smith	☐
10	Rob Stopar, Goalie	☐
11	Tony McCabe	☐
12	Jason Firth	☐
13	Joey St. Aubin	☐
14	Richard Borgo	☐

No.	Player	Checklist
15	Norm Dezainde	☐
16	Jeff Szeryk	☐
17	Derek Gauthier	☐
18	Jamie Israel	☐
19	Shayne McCosh	☐
20	Gib Tucker	☐
21	Paul McCallion	☐
22	Mike Allen	☐
23	Brad Barton	☐
24	Chris Li Puma	☐
25	Justin Cullen	☐
26	Optimist's Sponsor's Card	☐
27	Rob Saarinen	☐
28	Jack Williams	☐
29	Steven Rice	☐
30	Optimist's Sponsor's Card	☐

LETHBRIDGE HURRICANES

— 1988 - 89 REGULAR ISSUE —

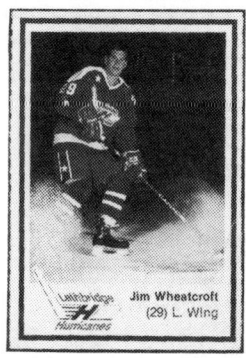

Lethbridge Hurricanes, 1988-89 Issue
Card No. 24, Jim Wheatcroft

Card Size: 2 1/2" X 3 1/2"
Face: Four colour, white border; Name, Position, Jersey number, Team logo
Back: Black on white card stock; Hockey and safety tips, Sponsor logos
Imprint: None
Complete Set No.: 12 Panels of 3 Cards
Complete Set Price: 10.00 20.00 ☐

No.	Player	Checklist
1	Team Card: Team Photo	☐
2	Mark Bassen	☐
3	Pete Berthelsen	☐
4	Bryan Bosch	☐
5	Paul Checknita	☐
6	Kelly Ens	☐
7	Jeff Ferguson, Goalie	☐
8	Scott Fukami	☐
9	Colin Gregor	☐
10	Mark Greig	☐
11	Rob Hale	☐
12	Ted Hutchings	☐
13	Dusty Imoo, Goalie	☐
14	Ivan Jessey	☐
15	Mark Kuntz	☐
16	Corey Lyons	☐
17	Shane Mazutinec	☐
18	Casey McMillan	☐
19	Pat Pylypuik	☐
20	Brad Rubachuk	☐
21	Jason Ruff	☐
22	Chad Seibel	☐
23	Wez Walz	☐
24	Jim Wheatcroft	☐

— 1989 - 90 REGULAR ISSUE —

Lethbridge Hurricanes, 1989-90 Issue
Card No. 17, Pat Pylypuik

Card Size: 2 1/2" X 3 1/2"
Face: Four colour, white border; Name, Position, Jersey number, Team logo
Back: Black on white card stock; Hockey and safety tips, Sponsor logos
Imprint: None
Complete Set No.: 12 Panels of 3 Cards
Complete Set Price: 10.00   20.00 ☐

No.	Player	Checklist
1	Doug Barrault	☐
2	Pete Berthelsen	☐
3	Bryan Bosch	☐
4	Kelly Ens	☐
5	Mark Greig	☐
6	Ron Gunville	☐
7	Rob Hale	☐
8	Neil Hawryluk	☐
9	David Holzer	☐
10	Dusty Imoo, Goalie	☐
11	Darcy Kaminsky, Asst. Coach	☐
12	Bob Loucks, Head Coach	☐
13	Corey Lyons	☐
14	Duane Maruschak	☐
15	Jamie McLennan, Goalie	☐
16	Shane Peacock	☐
17	Pat Pylypuik	☐
18	Gary Reilly	☐
19	Brad Rubachuk	☐
20	Jason Ruff	☐
21	Kevin St. Jacques	☐
22	Wez Walz	☐
23	Darcy Werenka	☐
24	Brad Zimmer	☐

— 1990 - 91 ISSUE —

Card Size: 2 1/2" X 3 1/2"
Face: Four colour
Back: Uknown
Imprint: None
Complete Set No.: 12 Panels of 3 Cards
Complete Set Price: 12.50   25.00 ☐

No.	Player	Checklist
		☐

— 1991 - 92 ISSUE —

Card Size: 2 1/2" X 3 1/2"
Face: Four colour
Back: Uknown
Imprint: None
Complete Set No.: 12 Panels of 3 Cards
Complete Set Price: 12.50   25.00 ☐

No.	Player	Checklist
		☐

Note: We have no information on the two previous sets. We would appreciate hearing from anyone who could supply further information.

— 1992 - 93 REGULAR ISSUE —

Card Size: 2 1/2" X 3 1/2"
Face: Four colour, white border; Name, Position, Jersey number, Team logo
Back: Black on white card stock; Resume, Safety tips, Sponsor logos
Imprint: None
Complete Set No.: 12 Panels of 3 Cards
Complete Set Price: 10.00   20.00 ☐

No.	Player	Checklist
1	Rob Daun, Head Coach	☐
2	Derek Diener	☐
3	Kirk DeWalle	☐
4	Scott Giuco	☐
5	David Jesiolowski	☐
6	Todd MacIsaac	☐
7	Stan Matwijiw	☐
8	Larry McMorran	☐
9	Brad Mehalko	☐
10	Shane Peacock	☐
11	Randy Perry	☐
12	Byron Ritchie	☐
13	Domenic Rittis	☐
14	Bryce Salvador	☐
15	Lee Sorochan	☐
16	Ryan Smith	☐
17	Mark Szoke	☐
18	Scott Townsend	☐
19	David Trofimenkofl	☐
20	Mascot: Twister	☐
21	Ivan Vologjaninov	☐
22	Jason Widmer	☐
23	Derek Wood	☐
24	Aaron Zarowny	☐

LONDON KNIGHTS

— 1985 - 86 REGULAR ISSUE —

London Knights, 1985-86 Issue
Card No. 6, Brendan Shanahan

Card Size: 2 3/4" X 3 1/2"
Face: Four colour, white border; Facsimile autograph
Back: Black on white card stock; Number, Name, Tips, Sponsor logo
Imprint: Kellogg Salada Canada Inc.
Complete Set No.: 30
Complete Set Price: 12.50   25.00 ☐
Album: 2.50   5.00 ☐

No.	Player	Checklist
1	LaVerne Shipley, Chief of Police	☐
2	Joe Ranger	☐
3	Sponsor Card / Checklist	☐
4	Don Boyd, General Manager / Coach	☐
5	Harry E. Sparling, Superintendent	☐
6	Murray Nystrom	☐
7	Bob Halkidis	☐
8	Morgan Watts	☐
9	Brendan Shanahan	☐
10	Brian Dobbin	☐
11	Ed Kister	☐
12	Darin Smith	☐
13	Greg Puhalski	☐
14	Dave Haas	☐
15	Pete McLeod	☐
16	Frank Tremblay	☐
17	Matthew Smyth	☐
18	Glen Leslie	☐
19	Mike Zombo	☐
20	Jamie Groke	☐
21	Brad Schlegel	☐
22	Kelly Cain	☐
23	Tom Allen	☐
24	Rod Gerow	☐
25	Pat Vachon	☐
26	Paul Cook	☐
27	Jeff Reese, Goalie	☐
28	Fred Kean, Director of Public Relations	☐
29	Scott Cumming, Goalie	☐
30	John Williams, Assistant Coach	☐

— 1986 - 87 REGULAR —

London Knights, 1986-87 Issue
Card No. 8, Brad Schlegel

Card Size: 2 3/4" X 3 1/2"
Face: Four colour, white border
Back: Black on white card stock; Number, Name, Jersey number, Tips, Sponsor logo
Imprint: Kellogg Salada Canada Inc.
Complete Set No.: 30
Complete Set Price: 11.00   22.00 ☐
Album: 2.50   5.00 ☐

No.	Player	Checklist
1	LaVerne Shipley, Chief of Police	☐
2	Tom Gosnell, Mayor	☐
3	Sponsor Card / Checklist	☐
4	Wayne Maxner, General Manager / Coach	☐
5	Harry E. Sparling, Superintendent	☐
6	Brendan Shanahan	☐
7	Pat Vachon	☐
8	Brad Schlegel	☐
9	Barry Earhart	☐
10	Jean Marc MacKenzie	☐
11	Jason Simon	☐
12	Jim Sprott	☐
13	Bill Long, Vice President	☐
14	Murray Nystrom	☐
15	Shayne Stevenson	☐
16	Don Martin	☐
17	Ian Pound	☐
18	Peter Lisy	☐
19	Steve Marcolini	☐
20	Craig Majaury	☐
21	Trevor Dam	☐
22	Dave Akey	☐
23	Dennis McEwen	☐
24	Shane Whelan	☐
25	Greg Hankkio	☐
26	Pat Kelly, Asst. Trainer	☐
27	Stephen Titus, Goalie	☐
28	Fred Kean, Director, Error	☐
29	Chris Somers, Goalie	☐
30	Dr. Gord Clark, Team Doctor	☐

MAINE BLACK BEARS

— 1992 - 93 REGULAR ISSUE —
SERIES 2

This set is incomplete. We would appreciate hearing from anyone who could supply further information.

Maine Black Bears, 1992-93 Issue
Card No. 26, Peter Ferraro

Card Size: 2 1/2" X 3 1/2"
Face: Four colour, blue border; Name, Position, Team logo
Back: Black on white card stock; Name, Position, Resume, Card number
Imprint: Copyright © 1993 University of Maine System
Complete Set No.: 36
Complete Set Price: 12.50   25.00 ☐

No.	Player	Checklist
17	Title Card	☐
18	Mike Dunham, Goalie	☐
19	Chris Imes	☐
20	Paul Kariya	☐
21	Mike Latendresse	☐
22	Dan Murphy	☐
23	Dave MacIsaac	☐
24	Dave Lacouture	☐
25	Chris Ferraro	☐
26	Peter Ferraro	☐
27	Jim Montgomery	☐
28	Brad Purdie	☐
29	Lee Saunders	☐
30	Justin Tomberlin	☐
31	Chuck Texeira	☐
32	Martin Mercier	☐
33	Garth Snow, Goalie	☐
34	Cal Ingraham	☐
35	Greg Hirsch, Goalie	☐
36	Jamie Thompson	☐

MEDICINE HAT TIGERS

— 1982 - 83 REGULAR ISSUE —

Card Size: 3" X 4"
Face: Black and white; Name, Jersey Numberm Autograph box, Logo
Back: Blank
Imprint: None
Complete Set No.: 21
Complete Set Price: 9.00   18.00 ☐

No.	Player	Checklist
1	Al Conroy	☐
2	Murray Craven	☐
3	Mark Frank	☐
4	Kevan Guy	☐
5	Jim Hougen	☐
6	Ken Jogenson	☐
7	Matt Kabayama	☐
8	Brent Kisilivich	☐
9	Mike Lay	☐
10	Mark Lamb	☐
11	Dean McArthur	☐
12	Kodie Nelson	☐

No.	Player	Checklist
13	Gord Shmyrko	☐
14	Brnet Meckling	☐
15	Shawn Nagurny	☐
16	Al Pederson	☐
17	Todd Pederson	☐
18	Jay Reid	☐
19	Brent Steblyk	☐
20	Rocky Trottier	☐
21	Dan Turner	☐

— 1983 - 84 REGULAR ISSUE —

Card Size: 2 3/4" X 5"
Face: Four colour; Name
Back: Name
Imprint: None
Complete Set No.: 23
Complete Set Price: 12.50   25.00 ☐

No.	Player	Checklist
1	Murry Craven	☐
2	Shane Churla	☐
3	Don Herczeg	☐
4	Gary Johnson	☐
5	Brent Kisilivich	☐
6	Blair MacGregor	☐
7	Terry Knight	☐
8	Mark Lamb	☐
9	Al Pederson	☐
10	Trevor Semeniuk	☐
11	Dan Turner	☐
12	Brent Steblyk	☐
13	Rocky Trottier	☐
14	Kevan Guy	☐
15	Bobby Bassen	☐
16	Brent Meckling	☐
17	Matt Kabayama	☐
18	Gord Hynes	☐
19	Daryl Henry	☐
20	Jim Kambeitz	☐
21	Mike Lay	☐
22	Gord Shmyrko	☐
23	Al Conroy	☐

— 1985 - 86 REGULAR ISSUE —

Card Size: 2 1/4" X 4"
Face: Four colour; Name
Back: Blank
Imprint: None
Complete Set No.: 24
Complete Set Price: 15.00   30.00 ☐

No.	Player	Checklist
1	Mike Claringbull	☐
2	Doug Houda	☐
3	Mark Kuntz	☐
4	Guy Phillips	☐
5	Rob DiMaio	☐
6	Al Conroy	☐
7	Craige Berube	☐
8	Doug Sauter	☐
9	Deean Chynoweth	☐
10	Scott McCrady	☐
11	Neil Brady	☐
12	Dale Kushner	☐
13	Jeff Weenas	☐
14	Wayne Hynes	☐
15	Troy Gamble	☐
16	Bryan Maxwell	☐
17	Gord Hynes	☐
18	Wayne McBean	☐
19	Mark Pederson	☐
20	Darren Cota	☐
21	Randy Siska	☐
22	Dave Mackey	☐
23	Mark Fitzpatrick, Goalie	☐
24	Doug Ball	☐

MILWAUKEE ADMIRALS

— 1981 - 82 REGULAR ISSUE —

Milwaukee Admirals, 1981-82 Issue
Card No. 1, Pat Rabbitt

Card Size: 2 1/2" X 3 1/2"
Face: Black and white photo, yellow border; Team name, Jersey number, Name, Position
Back: Black on white card stock; Team logo, Name, Jersey number, Resume, Number
Imprint: © TCMA Ltd. Peekskill, N.Y. 10566
Complete Set No.: 15
Complete Set Price: 10.00   20.00 ☐

No.	Player	Checklist
1	Pat Rabbitt	☐
2	Real Paiement	☐
3	Fred Berry	☐
4	Blaine Peerless	☐
5	John Flesch	☐
6	Yves Preston	☐
7	Bruce McKay	☐
8	Dale Yakiwchuk	☐
9	Lorne Bokshowan	☐
10	Danny Lecours	☐
11	Sheldon Currie	☐
12	Doug Robb	☐
13	Rob Polman Tuin, Goalie	☐
14	Bob Collyard	☐
15	Tim Ringler, Trainer	☐

MONCTON ALPINES

— 1982 - 83 REGULAR ISSUE —

We have no information on this set. We would appreciate hearing from anyone who could supply further information.

— 1983 - 84 REGULAR ISSUE —

Moncton Alpines, 1983-84 Issue
Card No. 2, Chris Smith

Card Size: 2 1/2" x 3 3/4"
Face: Four colour, white border; Name, Position, Sponsor logos
Back: Black on white card stock; Jersey number, Name, Resume, Tips, Bilingual
Imprint: None
Complete Set No.: 28
Complete Set Price: 10.00   20.00 ☐

No.	Player	Checklist
1	Doug Messier, Coach	☐
2	Chris Smith, Goalie	☐
3	Marco Baron, Goalie	☐
4	Mike Zanier, Goalie	☐
5	Dwayne Boettger	☐
6	Lowell Loveday	☐
7	Joe McDonnell	☐
8	Peter Dineen	☐
9	John Blum	☐
10	Steve Smith	☐
11	Reg Kerr	☐
12	Tom Rowe	☐
13	Ross Lambert	☐
14	Pat Conacher	☐
15	Paul Miller	☐
16	Bart Yachimec	☐
17	Tom Gorence	☐
18	Jeff Crawford	☐
19	Serge Boisvert	☐
20	Todd Strueby	☐
21	Todd Bidner	☐
22	Dean Dachyshyn	☐
23	Ray Cote	☐
24	Shawn Babcock	☐
25	Shawn Dineen	☐
26	Marc Habscheid	☐
27	Charlie Lavallee; Kevin Ferris, Trainers	☐
—	Checklist	☐

MONCTON GOLDEN FLAMES

— 1984 - 85 REGULAR ISSUE —

Moncton Golden Flames
Card No. 20, Mike Vernon

Card Size: 2 1/2" X 3 3/4"
Face: Four colour, white border; Name, Position
Back: Black on white card stock; Name, Resume, Jersey Number, Hockey and Safety Tips, Sponsor Logos, Bilingual
Imprint: None
Complete Set No.: 26
Complete Set Price: 17.50   35.00 ☐

No.	Player	Checklist
1	Brian Patafie, Trainer	☐
2	Mike Bianni, Trainer	☐
3	Pierre Page, Coach	☐
4	Neil Sheehy	☐
5	George White	☐
6	Mark Lamb	☐
7	Dan Kane	☐
8	Dan Bolduc	☐
9	Lou Kiriakou	☐
10	Joel Otto	☐
11	Dale Degray	☐
12	Mike Clayton	☐
13	Mickey Volcan	☐
14	Ted Pearson	☐
15	Mario Simioni	☐
16	Keith Hanson	☐
17	Yves Courteau	☐
18	Dan Cormier	☐
19	Todd Hooey	☐
20	Mike Vernon, Goalie	☐

No.	Player	Checklist
21	Dave Meszaros, Goalie	☐
22	Bruce Eakin	☐
23	Ed Kastelic	☐
24	Tony Stiles	☐
25	Pierre Rioux	☐
26	Gino Cavallini	☐

— 1985 - 86 REGULAR ISSUE —

Moncton Golden Flames
Card No. 26, Benoit Doucet

Card Size: 2 7/8" X 3 11/16"
Face: Four colour, white border; Name, Position
Back: Black on white card stock; Name, Number, Resume Hockey and safety tips, Sponsor logos, Bilingual
Imprint: None
Complete Set No.: 28
Complete Set Price: 20.00   40.00 ☐

No.	Player	Checklist
1	Terry Crisp, Coach / G.M.	☐
2	Dan Bolduc, Asst. Coach	☐
3	Crisp / Bolduc, Coaches	☐
4	Al Pedersen	☐
5	Dave Meszaros, Goalie	☐
6	George White	☐
7	Mark Lamb	☐
8	Doug Kostynski	☐
9	Brian Bradley	☐
10	Rob Kivell	☐
11	Geoff Courtnall	☐
12	Tony Stiles	☐
13	Jim Buettgen	☐
14	Cleon Daskalakis, Goalie	☐
15	Rick Kosti, Goalie	☐
16	Kevan Guy	☐
17	John Blum	☐
18	Brian Patafie, Mike Baiani, Jamie Druit, Trainers	☐
19	Greg Johnston	☐
20	Dale DeGray	☐
21	John Meulenbroeks	☐
22	Dave Reid	☐
23	Jay Miller	☐
24	Yves Courteau	☐
25	Robin Bartel	☐
26	Benoit Doucet	☐
27	Pete Bakovic	☐
28	Team Photo	☐

Note: Junior Team Sets are collected as complete sets. Very seldom are they broken up and sold as individual cards. For this reason the cards also are not priced individually. The complete set price is shown in EX and NRMT prices.

— 1986 - 87 REGULAR ISSUE —

Moncton Golden Flames, 1986-87 Issue
Card No. 3, Doug Dadswell

Card Size: 2 1/2' X 3 3/4"
Face: Four colour, white border; Sponsor logos, Name, position
Back: Black on white card stock; Jersey number, Name, Resume, Tips, Numbered _ of 28
Imprint: None
Complete Set No.: 28
Complete Set Price: 35.00   70.00 ☐

No.	Player	Checklist
1	Terry Crisp, Coach / G.M.	☐
2	Danny Bolduc, Assistant Coach	☐
3	Doug Dadswell, Goalie	☐
4	Doug Kostynski	☐
5	Bill Ranford, Goalie	☐
6	Brian Patafie	☐
7	Dave Pasin	☐
8	Darwin McCutcheon	☐
9	Team Photo	☐
10	Kevan Guy	☐
11	Kraig Nienhuis	☐
12	Gary Roberts	☐
13	Ken Sabourin	☐
14	Marc D'Amour, Goalie	☐
15	Don Mercier	☐
16	Wade Campbell	☐
17	Mark Paterson	☐
18	Cleon Daskalakis, Goalie	☐
19	Lyndon Byers	☐
20	Brett Hull	☐
21	Bob Sweeney	☐
22	Gord Hynes	☐
23	Peter Bakovic	☐
24	Dave Reid	☐
25	Mike Rucinski	☐
26	Ray Podloski	☐
27	Bob Bodak	☐
28	John Carter	☐

MONCTON HAWKS

— 1987 - 88 REGULAR ISSUE —

Moncton Hawks, 1987-88 Issue
Card No. 6, Bob Essensa

770 • MONTREAL JUNIORS — 1992-93 REGULAR ISSUE —

These cards are unnumbered and are listed in alphabetical order. Sponsors were CKCW, Coke and Shoppers Drug Mart.

Card Size: 2 1/2" X 3 5/8"
Face: Four colour, white border; Sponsors, Name, Position
Back: Black on white card stock; Jersey number, Name, Resume, Tips, Bilingual
Imprint: None
Complete Set No.: 25
Complete Set Price: 12.50   25.00

No.	Player	Checklist
1	Joel Baillargeon	☐
2	Rick Bowness, Coach	☐
3	Bobby Dollas	☐
4	Peter Douris	☐
5	Iain Duncan	☐
6	Bob Essensa, Goalie	☐
7	Todd Flichel	☐
8	Rob Fowler	☐
9	Randy Gilhen	☐
10	Team Photo	☐
11	Matt Hervey	☐
12	Brent Hughes	☐
13	Jamie Husgen	☐
14	Mike Jeffrey	☐
15	Guy Larose	☐
16	Chris Levasseur	☐
17	Len Nielson	☐
18	Roger Ohman	☐
19	Steve Penney, Goalie	☐
20	Ron Pesetti	☐
21	Dave Quigley, Goalie	☐
22	Scott Schneider	☐
23	Ryan Stewart	☐
24	Gord Whitaker	☐
25	Wayne Flemming, Equipment Manager; Rick Carrano, Athletic Therapist	☐

— 1990 - 91 REGULAR ISSUE —

We have no information on this set. We would appreciate hearing from anyone who could supply further information.

Card Size: 2 1/2" X 3 5/8"
Face: Four colour
Back: Unknown
Imprint: None
Complete Set No.: 24
Complete Set Price: 10.00   20.00

No.	Player	Checklist

— 1991 - 92 REGULAR ISSUE —

These cards are unnumbered and are listed in alphabetical order.

Moncton Hawks, 1991-92 Issue
Card No. 2, Jason Cirone

Card Size: 2 1/2" X 3 5/8"
Face: Four colour, white border; Name, Sponsor's logo
Back: Black on white card stock; Name, Jersey number, Resume, Tips, Bilingual
Imprint: None
Complete Set No.: 26
Complete Set Price: 12.50   25.00

No.	Player	Checklist
1	Luciano Borsato	☐
2	Jason Cirone	☐
3	Rob Cowie	☐
4	Lee Davidson	☐
5	Kris Draper	☐
6	Dallas Eakins	☐
7	Dave Farrish, Coach / G.M.	☐
8	Sean Gauthier, Goalie	☐
9	Ken Gernander	☐
10	Tod Hartje	☐
11	Bob Joyce	☐
12	Claude Julien	☐
13	Chris Kiene	☐
14	Mark Kumpel, Asst. Coach	☐
15	Derek Langille	☐
16	Tyler Larter	☐
17	John LeBlanc	☐
18	Scott Levins	☐
19	Rob Murray	☐
20	Kent Paynter	☐
21	Rudy Poescheck	☐
22	Dave Prior, Goaltending Coach	☐
23	Warren Rychel	☐
24	Rick Tabaracci, Goalie	☐
25	Darren Veitch	☐
26	The Hawk, Mascot	☐

MONTREAL JUNIORS

— 1979 - 80 POSTCARD ISSUE —
BLACK AND WHITE

These cards are unnumbered and are listed in alphabetical order.

Card Size: 3 3/4" X 5 7/8"
Face: Black and white; Name
Back: Blank
Imprint: Paul Sauvé Studios
Complete Set No.: 30
Complete Set Price: 12.50   25.00

No.	Player	Checklist
1	Jeff Barratt	☐
2	Andre Begin	☐
3	Denis Champagne	☐
4	Denis Cyr	☐
5	Ghyslain Cyr	☐
6	Roland Diotte	☐
7	Pierre Dubois	☐
8	Sylvain Gagne	☐
9	Guy Jacob	☐
10	Michael Krushelnysky	☐
11	Ron Lapointe	☐
12	Richard Lavallee	☐
13	Daniel Laxton	☐
14	Francois Laxton	☐
15	Francois Lecompte	☐
16	Eikke Leime	☐
17	Pierre Martin	☐
18	Menick	☐
19	William Mulcahy	☐
20	Caetano Orlando	☐
21	Patrice Pare	☐
22	Mario Patry	☐
23	Fabian Pavlin	☐
24	Roger Poitras	☐
25	Constant Priondolo	☐
26	Denis Savard	☐
27	Eric Taylor	☐
28	Denis Tremblay	☐
29	J. Jacques Vezina	☐
30	Taras Zytysky	☐

— 1979 - 80 POSTCARD ISSUE —
FOUR COLOUR

This set was produced in colour at the end of the 1979-80 season and replaced the black and white issue produced earlier in the year. The cards are unnumbered and are listed below alphabetical order.

Card Size: 3 3/8" X 4 7/8"
Face: Four colour; Name
Back: Blank
Imprint: Paul Sauvé Studios
Complete Set No.: 25
Complete Set Price: 12.50   25.00

No.	Player	Checklist
1	Jeff Barratt	☐
2	Andre Begin	☐
3	Alain Bouchard	☐
4	Denis Champagne	☐
5	Denis Cyr	☐
6	Roland Diotte	☐
7	J. Pierre Dubois	☐
8	Sylvain Gagne	☐
9	Guy Jacob	☐
10	Mike Klassen	☐
11	Michael Krushelnysky	☐
12	Richard Lavallee	☐
13	Francois Lecompte	☐
14	Eikke Leime	☐
15	Pierre Martin	☐
16	Eric Morin	☐
17	William Mulcahy	☐
18	Gaetano Orlando	☐
19	Patrice Pare	☐
20	Constant Priondolo	☐
21	Denis Savard	☐
22	Jacques St.Jean	☐
23	Team Photo	☐
24	J. Jacques Vezina	☐
25	Taras Zytynsky	☐

NASHVILLE KNIGHTS

— 1989 - 90 REGULAR ISSUE —

This set was produced by Lee's Country Ckicken. The cards are unnumbered and are listed here in alphabetical order.

Nashville Knights, 1989-90 Issue,
Card No. 1, Pat Bingham

Card Size: 2 1/2" x 3 1/2"
Face: Four colour, white border; Name
Back: Black on white card stock; Name, Resume
Imprint: None
Complete Set No.: 23
Complete Set Price: 12.50   25.00

No.	Player	Checklist
1	Pat Bingham	☐
2	Andre Brassard	☐
3	Mike Bukta	☐
4	Chris Cambio	☐
5	Craig Jenkins, Announcer; Dave Cavaliere, Trainer	☐
6	Glen Engevik	☐
7	Ron Fuller, Owner; Bob Polk, Owner	☐
8	Matt Gallagher, Director; Scott Greer, Assistant General Manager	☐
9	Archie Henderson, Coach	☐

No.	Player	Checklist
10	Billy Huard	☐
11	Todd Jenkins	☐
12	Brock Kelly, Error	☐
13	Eddie Krayer	☐
14	Garth Lamb	☐
15	Rob Levasseur	☐
16	Dan O'Brien	☐
17	John Reid, Goalie	☐
18	John Reid, Goalie	☐
19	Jeff Salzbrunn	☐
20	Mike Schwalb	☐
21	Ron Servatius	☐
22	Jason Simon	☐
23	Chick-E-Lee	☐

NIAGARA FALLS THUNDER

— 1988 - 89 REGULAR ISSUE —

Card Size: 2 5/8" x 4 1/8"
Face: Four colour; Name, Team logo
Back: Black on white cardstock; Resume
Imprint: 25
Complete Set No.: 25
Complete Set Price: 15.00   30.00 ☐

No.	Player	Checklist
1	Title Card: Team Crest	☐
2	Bill Laforge	☐
3	Benny Rogano	☐
4	Heavy Evason	☐
5	Greg Allan	☐
6	Stan Drulia	☐
7	Bryan Fogarty	☐
8	Ron Fournier	☐
9	Alain Laforge	☐
10	Paul Laus	☐
11	Mark Lawrence	☐
12	Jamie Leach	☐
13	Steve Locke	☐
14	Brad May	☐
15	Shawn McCosh	☐
16	Colin Miller	☐
17	Keith Osborne	☐
18	Don Pancoe	☐
19	Scott Pearson	☐
20	Keith Primeau	☐
21	Mike Rosati	☐
22	Jason Soules	☐
23	Adrian Vanderslot	☐
24	Dennis Vial	☐
25	Paul Wolanski	☐

— 1989 - 90 REGULAR ISSUE —

These cards were only available at Arby's or Pizza Pizza. They are unnumbered and are listed in alphabetical order.

Niagara Falls Thunder, 1988-89 Issue
Card No. 2, Greg Allen

Card Size: 2 5/8" X 4 3/16"
Face: Four colour, white border; Team logo, Name
Back: Black on white card stock; Team logo, Name, Resume, Sponsor logos
Imprint: None
Complete Set No.: 25
Complete Set Price: 6.00   12.00 ☐

No.	Player	Checklist
1	Title Card: Team Logo	☐
2	Greg Allen	☐
3	Roch Belley, Goalie	☐
4	David Benn	☐
5	Andy Bezeau	☐
6	Paul Bruneau, Assistant Trainer; Dennis Scott, Athletic Therapist	☐
7	George Burnett, Coach	☐
8	Randy Hall, Assistant Coach	☐
9	Todd Coopman	☐
10	John Johnson	☐
11	Paul Laus	☐
12	Mark Lawrence	☐
13	Brad May	☐
14	Don McConnell	☐
15	Brian Mueggler	☐
16	Don Pancoe	☐
17	Keith Primeau	☐
18	Geoff Rawson	☐
19	Ken Ruddick	☐
20	Greg Suchan	☐
21	Steve Udvari, Goalie	☐
22	Jeff Walker	☐
23	Jason Winch	☐
24	Paul Wolanski	☐
25	Checklist	☐

NORTH BAY CENTENNIALS

— 1982 - 83 REGULAR ISSUE —

These unnumbered cards were produced by Aunt May's / CFCH 600. They are listed below in alphabetical order.

North Bay Centennials, 1982-83 Issue
Card No. 9, Mark Hatcher

Card Size: 2 1/2" X 3 7/8"
Face: Four colour, white border; Name, Position
Back: Black on white card stock; Name, Jersey number, Resume, Sponsor logos
Imprint: None
Complete Set No.: 24
Complete Set Price: 13.00   26.00 ☐

No.	Player	Checklist
1	Allen Bishop	☐
2	John Capel	☐
3	Rob Degagne	☐
4	Phil Drouillard	☐
5	Jeff Eatough	☐
6	Tony Gilliard	☐
7	Paul Gillis	☐
8	Pete Handley	☐
9	Mark Hatcher	☐
10	Tim Helmer	☐
11	Craig Kales	☐

No.	Player	Checklist
12	Bob Laforest	☐
13	Mark Laforest, Goalie	☐
14	Bill Maguire	☐
15	Andrew McBain	☐
16	Ron Meighan	☐
17	Rick Morocco	☐
18	Alain Raymond	☐
19	Joe Reekie	☐
20	Joel Smith, Goalie	☐
21	Bert Templeton, Coach	☐
22	Kevin Vescio	☐
23	Peter Woodgate	☐
24	Don Young	☐

— 1983 - 84 REGULAR ISSUE —

These cards unnumbered were produced by Aunt May's / CFCH 600. They are listed below in alphabetical order.

Card Size: 2 1/2" X 3 7/8"
Face: Four colour, white border; Name
Back: Black on white card stock; Name, Jersey number Resume, Sponsor logos
Imprint: None
Complete Set No.: 25
Complete Set Price: 13.00   28.00 ☐

No.	Player	Checklist
1	Sponsor Card	☐
2	Peter Abric	☐
3	Richard Benoit	☐
4	Scott Birnie	☐
5	John Capel	☐
6	Curtis Collin	☐
7	Rob Degagne	☐
8	Kevin Hatcher	☐
9	Marc Hatcher	☐
10	Tim Helmer	☐
11	Jim Hunter	☐
12	Kevin Kerr	☐
13	Nicholas Kypreos	☐
14	Mike Larouche	☐
15	Greg Larsen	☐
16	Mark Lavarre	☐
17	Brett MacDonald	☐
18	Wayne MacPhee	☐
19	Peter McGrath	☐
20	Rob Nichols	☐
21	Ron Sanko	☐
22	Kevin Vescio	☐
23	Mike Webber	☐
24	Peter Woodgate	☐
25	Bert Templeton	☐

NOVA SCOTIA OILERS

— 1984 - 85 REGULAR ISSUE —

Nova Scotia Oilers, 1984-85 Issue
Card No. 1, Mark Holden

ARIZONA ICECATS — 1985-86 ISSUE

Card Size: 2 1/2" X 3 3/4"
Face: Four colour, white border; Sponsor logos, Name, Position
Back: Black on white card stock; Jersey number, Name, Resume, Numbered _ of 26
Imprint: None
Complete Set No.: 26
Complete Set Price: 11.00 22.00

No.	Player	Checklist
1	Mark Holden, Goalie	
2	Dave Allison	
3	Dwayne Boettger	
4	Lowell Loveday	
5	Rejean Cloutier	
6	Ray Cote	
7	Pat Conacher	
8	Ken Berry	
9	Steve Graves	
10	Todd Strueby	
11	Steve Smith	
12	Archie Henderson	
13	Dean Dachyshyn	
14	Marc Habscheid	
15	Larry Melnyk	
16	Raimo Summanen	
17	Jim Playfair	
18	Mike Zanier, Goalie	
19	Ian Wood, Goalie	
20	Dean Hopkins	
21	Norm Aubin	
22	Tony Currie	
23	Ross Lambert	
24	Terry Martin	
25	**The Coaches:** Ed Chadwick; Larry Kish; Bob Boucher	
26	**The Trainers:** Lou Christian; Kevin Farris	

— 1985-86 REGULAR ISSUE —

Nova Scotia Oilers, 1985-86 Issue
Card No. 1, Dean Hopkins

Card Size: 2 1/2" X 3 3/4"
Face: Four colour, white border; Sponsor logos, Name, Position
Back: Black on white card stock; Jersey number, Name, Position, Resume, Numbered _ of 28
Imprint: None
Complete Set No.: 28
Complete Set Price: 10.00 20.00

No.	Player	Checklist
1	Dean Hopkins	
2	Jeff Larmer	
3	Mike Moller	
4	Dean Dachyshyn	
5	Bruce Boudreau	
6	Ken Solheim	
7	Jeff Beukeboom	
8	Mark Lavarre	
9	John Ollson	
10	Lou Crawford	
11	Warren Skorodenski, Goalie	
12	Dwayne Boettger	
13	Daryl Reaugh, Goalie	
14	John Miner	
15	Jim Ralph, Goalie	

No.	Player	Checklist
16	Wayne Presley	
17	Steve Graves	
18	Tom McMurchy	
19	Darin Sceviour	
20	Kent Paynter	
21	Larry Kish, Coach / General Manager	
22	Jim Playfair	
23	Kevin Farris; Ralph Mosher, Trainers	
24	Mickey Volcan	
25	Ron Low, Assistant Coach	
26	Don Biggs	
27	Bruce Eakin	
28	Team Photo	

NOVA SCOTIA VOYAGEURS

— 1983-84 REGULAR ISSUE —

Nova Scotia Voyageurs, 1983-84 Issue
Card No. 1, Mark Holden

Card Size: 2 1/2" X 3 3/4"
Face: Four colour, white border; Jersey number, Name, Sponsor logos
Back: Black on white card stock; Jersey number, Name, Position, Resume, Tips, Number
Imprint: None
Complete Set No.: 24
Complete Set Price: 11.00 22.00

No.	Player	Checklist
1	Mark Holden	
2	Bill Kitchen	
3	Dave Allison	
4	Stephane Lefebvre	
5	Stan Hennigar	
6	Steve Marengere	
7	John Goodwin	
8	John Newberry	
9	Bill Rilay	
10	Norman Baron	
11	Brian Skrudland	
12	Mike Lalor	
13	Blair Barnes	
14	Remi Gagne	
15	Steve Penney, Goalie	
16	Michel Therrien	
17	Dave Stoyanovich	
18	Brian Patafie; Lou Christian, Trainers	
19	Mike McPhee	
20	Wayne Thompson	
21	Ted Fauss	
22	Jeff Teal	
23	Larry Landon	
24	Greg Moffett	

Note: Junior Team Sets are collected as complete sets. Very seldom are they broken up and sold as individual cards. For this reason the cards also are not priced individually. The complete set price is shown in EX and NRMT prices.

OSHAWA GENERALS

— 1980-81 REGULAR ISSUE —

Oshawa General, 1980-81 Issue
Card No. 1, O.H.A. Oshawa Generals Logo

Card Size: 2 5/8" X 4 1/8"
Face: Four colour, white border; Position, Team logo, Name
Back: Black on white card stock; Safety tip, Sponsor logos
Imprint: DESIGNED AND PRODUCED BY STUDIO 601 WHITBY, ONTARIO, CANADA
Complete Set No.: 25
Complete Set Price: 87.50 175.00
Common Player: 1.75 3.50

No.	Player	EX	NRMT
1	O.H.A. Oshawa Generals Logo	2.50	5.00
2	Ray Flaherty	1.75	3.50
3	Craig Kitchener	1.75	3.50
4	Dan Revell	1.75	3.50
5	Bob Kucheran	1.75	3.50
6	Pat Poulin	2.50	5.00
7	David Andreychuk	12.50	25.00
8	Barry Tabobondung	1.75	3.50
9	Steve Konroyd	2.50	5.00
10	Paul Edwards	1.75	3.50
11	Dale Degray	2.50	5.00
12	Joe Cirella	6.00	12.00
13	Norm Schmidt	1.75	3.50
14	Markus Lehto	1.75	3.50
15	Mitch Lamoureaux	1.75	3.50
16	Tony Tanti	6.00	12.00
17	Bill Laforge, Coach	1.75	3.50
18	Greg Gravel	1.75	3.50
19	Mike Lekun	1.75	3.50
20	Chris Smith, Goalie	1.75	3.50
21	Peter Sidorkiewicz, Goalie	4.00	8.00
22	Greg Stefan, Goalie	5.00	10.00

EX-GENERALS

No.	Player	EX	NRMT
23	Tom McCarthy	1.75	3.50
24	Rick Lanz	1.75	3.50
25	Bobby Orr	6.50	13.00

— 1981-82 REGULAR ISSUE —

Card Size: 2 5/8" X 4 1/8"
Face: Four colour, white border, Position, Team logo
Back: Black on white card stock, Safety tip
Imprint: DESIGNED AND PRODUCED BY STUDIO 601 WHITBY, ONTARIO, CANADA
Complete Set No.: 25
Complete Set Price: 60.00 120.00
Common Player: 1.75 3.50

No.	Player	EX	NRMT
1	O.H.A. Oshawa Generals Logo	2.50	5.00
2	Chris Smith, Goalie	1.75	3.50
3	Peter Sidorkiewicz, Goalie	3.25	6.50
4	Ali Butorac	1.75	3.50
5	Dan Revell	1.75	3.50
6	Mitch Lamoureux	1.75	3.50
7	Norm Schmidt	1.75	3.50
8	Paul Edwards	1.75	3.50

No.	Player	EX	NRMT
9	Dan Nicholson	1.75	3.50
10	John Hutchings	1.75	3.50
11	Dave Gans	1.75	3.50
12	David Andreychuk	9.00	18.00
13	Mike Stern	1.75	3.50
14	Dale Degray	2.50	5.00
15	Mike Lekun	1.75	3.50
16	Greg Gravel	1.75	3.50
17	Dave MacLean	1.75	3.50
18	Toni Tanti	3.75	7.50
19	John MacLean	6.00	12.00
20	Jim Uens	1.75	3.50
21	Guy Jacob	1.75	3.50
22	Jeff Steffan	1.75	3.50
23	Paul Theriault, Coach	1.75	3.50
24	Sherwood Bassin, Manager	1.75	3.50
25	Durham Regional Police Logo	1.75	3.50

— 1982 - 83 REGULAR ISSUE —

Oshawa Generals, 1982-83 Issue
Card No. 5, Joe Cirella

Card Size: 2 5/8" X 4 1/8"
Face: Four colour, white border, Position, Team Logo
Back: Black on white card stock, Safety Tip
Imprint: ARJAY PRINTERS LTD.
Complete Set No.: 25
Complete Set Price: 60.00 120.00
Common Player: 1.50 3.00

No.	Player	EX	NRMT
1	O.H.L. Oshawa Generals Logo	2.50	5.00
2	Jeff Hogg, Goalie	1.50	3.00
3	Peter Sidorkiewicz, Goalie	3.00	6.00
4	Dale Degray	2.50	5.00
5	Joe Cirella	3.50	7.00
6	Todd Smith	1.50	3.00
7	Scott Brydges	1.50	3.00
8	Jeff Steffen	1.50	3.00
9	Don Biggs	1.50	3.00
10	Todd Hooey	1.50	3.00
11	Tony Tanti	3.75	7.50
12	Danny Gratton	1.50	3.00
13	Steve King	1.50	3.00
14	Dean Defazio	1.50	3.00
15	John MacLean	5.00	10.00
16	Tim Burgess	1.50	3.00
17	Mike Stern	1.50	3.00
18	Dan Nicholson	1.50	3.00
19	David Gans	1.50	3.00
20	John Hutchings	1.50	3.00
21	Norm Schmidt	1.50	3.00
22	Todd Charlesworth	1.50	3.00
23	Paul Theriault, Coach	1.50	3.00
24	Sherwood Bassin, General Manager	1.50	3.00
25	Durham Regional Police Logo	1.50	3.00

— 1983 - 84 REGULAR ISSUE —

Oshawa Generals, 1983-84 Issue
Card No. 1, Peter Sidorkiewicz

Card Size: 2 5/8" X 4 1/8"
Face: Four colour, white border, Position, Team logo
Back: Black on white card stock, Safety Tip
Complete Set No.: 30
Complete Set Price: 50.00 100.00
Common Player: 1.50 3.00

No.	Player	EX	NRMT
1	Peter Sidorkiewicz, Goalie	2.00	5.00
2	Kirk McLean, Goalie	7.50	15.00
3	Todd Charlesworth	1.50	3.00
4	Ian Ferguson	1.50	3.00
5	John Hutchings	1.50	3.00
6	O.H.L. Oshawa Generals Logo	1.50	3.00
7	Mark Haarmann	1.50	3.00
8	Joel Curtis	1.50	3.00
9	Dan Gratton	1.50	3.00
10	Steve Hedington	1.50	3.00
11	Scott Brydges	1.50	3.00
12	CKAR 1350 Motor City Music	1.50	3.00
13	Brad Walcot	1.50	3.00
14	Paul Theriault, Coach	1.50	3.00
15	Jon Jenkins, Chief of Police	1.50	3.00
16	Sherry Bassin, General Manager	1.50	3.00
17	Craig Morrison	1.50	3.00
18	Bolahood's Sports Haven Logo	1.50	3.00
19	Bruce Melanson	1.50	3.00
20	Mike Stern	1.50	3.00
21	Gary McColgan	1.50	3.00
22	Lee Giffin	1.50	3.00
23	Brent Maki	1.50	3.00
24	Ronald McDonald	1.50	3.00
25	Jeff Steffen	1.50	3.00
26	John Stevens	1.50	3.00
27	David Gans	1.50	3.00
28	Don Biggs	1.50	3.00
29	Chip Crandall	1.50	3.00
30	Durham Regional Police Logo	1.50	3.00

— 1989 - 90 REGULAR ISSUE —

Oshawa Generals, 1989-90 Issue
Card No. 31, Eric Lindros

Card Nos. 1 to 30 were issued in the Fall of 1989 as the Durham Police Set. Card Nos. 31 to 35 were issued in January 1990 as an update set. Ten thousand sets were issued with the update set being double printed.

Card Size: 2 5/8" X 4 1/8"
Face: Four colour, white border, Position, Team logo
Back: Black on white card stock, Safety Tip
Imprint: Magill Business Forms
Complete Set No.: 35
Complete Set Price: 62.50 125.00
Common Player: .10 .20

No.	Player	EX	NRMT
1	Cory Banika	.10	.20
2	David Craievich	.10	.20
3	Scott Hollis	.10	.20
4	Mike Decoff	.10	.20
5	Joe Busillo	.20	.40
6	Matt Hoffman	.10	.20
7	Craig Donaldson	.25	.50
8	Jason Denomme	.10	.20
9	Brian Grieve	.10	.20
10	Wade Simpson	.10	.20
11	Dale Craigwell	.50	1.00
12	Mike Lenarduzzi	.10	.20
13	Rick Cornacchia, Head Coach	.25	.50
14	David Edwards, Chief of Police	.25	.50
15	Kevin Butt, Goalie	.10	.20
16	Oshawa Generals Team	.10	.20
17	Clair Cornish	.10	.20
18	Jarrod Skalde	.50	1.00
19	Mark Deazeley	.10	.20
20	Jean-Paul Davis	.10	.20
21	Todd Coopman	.10	.20
22	Trevor McIvor	.10	.20
23	Mike Craig	2.00	4.00
24	Paul O'Hagan	.10	.20
25	Iain Fraser	1.50	3.00
26	Brent Grieve	.50	1.00
27	Lions International Logo	.10	.20
28	National Sports Centre Logo	.10	.20
29	Durham Regional Police Logo	.10	.20
30	Oshawa Generals 1989-90 Logo	.10	.20
31	Eric Lindros	35.00	75.00
32	Bill Armstrong	.10	.20
33	Chris Vanclief	.10	.20
34	Scott Luik	.35	.75
35	Fred Brathwaithe, Goalie	.50	1.00

Note: Card No. 31 Eric Lindros has been counterfeited

— 1990 - 91 REGULAR ISSUE —

This is the last set issued by the Durham Regional Police.

Oshawa Generals, 1990-91 Issue
Card No. 2, Mike Cote

Card Size: 2 5/8" X 3 3/4"
Face: Four colour, white border, Team logo
Back: Black on white card stock, Safety Tip
Imprint: Magill Business Forms
Complete Set No.: 30
Complete Set Price: 27.50 55.00
Common Player: .10 .20

No.	Player	EX	NRMT
1	Lions International Logo	.10	.20
2	Mike Cote	.10	.20

774 • ARIZONA ICECATS — 1985 - 86 ISSUE

No.	Player	EX	NRMT
3	Fred Brathwaite, Goalie	.35	.75
4	Scott Luik	.25	.50
5	National Sports Centre Logo	.10	.20
6	Mike Fountain, Goalie	.10	.20
7	Rick Cornacchia, Head Coach	.10	.20
8	David Edwards, Chief of Police	.10	.20
9	Troy Sweet	.10	.20
10	Jan Benda	.10	.20
11	David Dorosh	.10	.20
12	Craig Lutes	.10	.20
13	Eric Lindros	25.00	50.00
14	David Craievich	.10	.20
15	Wade Simpson	.10	.20
16	Dale Craigwell	.35	.75
17	Oshawa Generals 1990-91 Logo	.10	.20
18	Matt Hoffman	.50	1.00
19	Rob Pearson	1.25	2.50
20	Paul O'Hagan	.10	.20
21	Brian Grieve	.10	.20
22	Mark Deazeley	.10	.20
23	Clair Cornish	.25	.50
24	B. J. MacPherson	.10	.20
25	Jason Weaver	.15	.30
26	Markus Brunner	.10	.20
27	Trevor Burgess	.10	.20
28	Jean-Paul Davis	.25	.50
29	Durham Regional Police Logo	.10	.20
30	Scott Hollis	.25	.50

— 1991 - 92 REGULAR ISSUE —

Domino's Pizza in conjunction with Coca-Cola issued the Oshawa Generals 1991-92 thirty-two card "Environmental" set. The set was released over a six week period with any food and coke purchased at Domino's Pizza. An uncut sheet limited to 5,000 was produced as well for the 8th Annual United Way Face-Off Breakfast.

Oshawa Generals, 1991-92 Issue
Card No. 1, Mike Fountain

Card Size: 2 1/2" X 3 1/2"
Face: Four colour, white border, Jersey number, Team logo
Back: Blue and red on white card stock, Number, Resume, Environmental Tips
Imprint: Printed by Precision Litho, Ajax
Photos by Prosport Photography
Complete Set No.: 32
Complete Set Price: 10.00 20.00
Common Player: .05 .10

No.	Player	EX	NRMT
1	Mike Fountain, Goalie	.10	.20
2	The Quality Choice: Brian Grieve 91-92	.10	.20
3	Trevor Burgess	.05	.10
4	Wade Simpson	.05	.10
5	Ken Shepard, Goalie	.05	.10
6	Stephane Yelle	.05	.10
7	Matt Hoffman	.05	.10
8	Neil Iserhoff	.05	.10
9	Rob Leask	.05	.10
10	Kevin Spero	.05	.10
11	Scott Hollis	.25	.50
12	Sean Brown	.05	.10
13	Todd Bradley	.05	.10
14	Darry LaFrance	.05	.10
15	Markus Brunner	.05	.10
16	B. J. MacPherson	.05	.10

No.	Player	EX	NRMT
17	Jason Campeau	.10	.20
18	Jason Weaver	.15	.30
19	Jan Benda	.05	.10
20	Jason Arnott	2.00	4.00
21	Eric Lindros	6.00	12.00
22	Wayne Daniels, Director of Operations	.05	.10
23	Joe Cook	.05	.10
24	Can't Beat the Real Thing 91-92	.05	.10
25	Experience The Domino's Effect 92-92	.05	.10
26	Mark Deazeley	.10	.20
27	Jean-Paul Davis	.10	.20
28	Brian Grieve	.05	.10
29	Oshawa Generals 1991/92	.10	.20
30	Ian Young, Larry Marson, Rick Cornacchia, Coaching Staff 91-92	.10	.20
31	Checklist 91-92	.10	.20
32	Prosport's Action 91-92	.05	.10
	Uncut Sheet	12.50	25.00

OTTAWA 67'S

— 1981 - 82 PHOTO ISSUE —

Ottawa 67's, 1981-82 Photo Issue
Photo No. 19, Jim Ralph

Card Size: 5 1/2" X 8 1/2"
Face: Black and white, white border; Name, Jersey number, Facsimile autograph
Back: Blank
Imprint: None
Complete Set No.: 25
Complete Set Price: 22.50 45.00

No.	Player	Checklist
1	James Allson	
2	John Boland	
3	Randy Boyd	
4	Adam Creighton	
5	Bill Dowd	
6	Dwayne Davison	
7	Alan Hepple	
8	Mike James	
9	Brian Kilrea	
10	Moe Lemay	
11	Danny Longe	
12	Paul Louttit	
13	Don Maclaren	
14	John Ollson	
15	Brian Patafie	
16	Mark Paterson	
17	Phil Patterson	
18	Larry Power	
19	Jim Ralph, Goalie	
20	Darcy Roy	
21	Brad Shaw	
22	Brian Small	
23	Doug Stewart	
24	Jeff Vaive	
25	Fraser Wood	

— 1982 - 83 REGULAR ISSUE —

Card Size: 2 5/8" X 4 1/8"
Face: Four colour, white border; Name, Jersey number
Back: Blank
Imprint: None
Complete Set No.: 27
Complete Set Price: 14.00 28.00

No.	Player	Checklist
1	Brian Kilrea	
2	Gordon Hamilton	
3	Jim Jackson	
4	Gordon C. Hamilton Jr.	
5	Larry McAndrew	
6	Bruce Cassidy	
7	Greg Coram	
8	Adam Creighton	
9	Bill Dowd	
10	Scott Hammond	
11	Alan Hepple (2)	
12	Alan Hepple	
13	Mike James	
14	Paul Louttit	
15	Brian McKinnon	
16	Don Maclaren	
17	John Ollson	
18	Darren Pang	
19	Mark Paterson	
20	Phil Patterson	
21	Larry Power	
22	Gary Roberts	
23	Brian Rome	
24	Darcy Roy	
25	Brad Shaw	
26	Doug Stewart	
27	Jeff Vaive	

— 1983 - 84 REGULAR ISSUE —

These cards are unnumbered and are listed below in alphabetical order. Sponsor's are M.O.M. Printing, Coca-Cola and Channel Twelve.

Ottawa 67's, 1983-84 Issue
Card No. 18, Darren Pang

Card Size: 2 5/8" X 4 1/8"
Face: Four colour, whtie border; Name, Jersey number
Back: Black on white card stock; Name, Jersey number, Resume, Sponsor logos
Imprint: *Photo by Toomey Photography
Complete Set No.: 27
Complete Set Price: 10.00 20.00

No.	Player	Checklist
1	Bruce Cassidy	
2	Greg Coram, Goalie	
3	Adam Creighton	
4	Bill Dowd	
5	Gord Hamilton	
6	Gord C. Hamilton Jr.	
7	Scott Hammond	
8	Alan Hepple	
9	Alan Hepple	
10	Jim Jackson	
11	Mike James	

— 1984 - 85 REGULAR ISSUE — PETERBOROUGH PETES • 775

No.	Player	EX	NRMT
12	Brian Kilrea		
13	Paul Louttit		
14	Larry MacAndrew		
15	Brian McKinnon		
16	Don McLaren		
17	John Oilson		
18	Darren Pang, Goalie		
19	Mark Paterson		
20	Phil Patterson		
21	Larry Power		
22	Gary Roberts		
23	Brian Rome		
24	Darcy T. Roy		
25	Brad Shaw		
26	Doug Stewart		
27	Jeff Vaive		

— 1984 - 85 REGULAR ISSUE —

These cards are unnumbered and are listed below in alphabetical order. Sponsors are M.O.M. Printing, Coca-Cola and Channel Twelve.

Oshawa Generals, 1984-85 Issue
Card No. 6, Adam Creighton

Card Size: 2 11/16" x 4 1/8"
Face: Four colour, white border; Name, Jersey number
Back: Black on white card stock; Name, Jersey number, Resume, Sponsor logos
Imprint: *Photo by Toomey Photography
Complete Set No.: 45
Complete Set Price: 11.00   22.00

No.	Player	Checklist
1	Richard Adolfi	
2	Bill Bennett	
3	Bruce Cassidy	
4	Todd Clarke	
5	Greg Coran, Goalie	
6	Adam Creighton	
7	Bob Giffin	
8	Gord Hamilton, Assistant Coach	
9	Gord C. Hamilton Jr., Assistant Trainer	
10	Scott Hammond	
11	John Hanna	
12	Tim Helmer	
13	Steve Hrynewich	
14	Jim Jackson, Assistant Trainer	
15	Mike James	
16	Brian Kilrea, Coach / General Manager	
17	Larry MacAndrew, Trainer	
18	Brian McKinnon	
19	Don McLaren	
20	Roy Myllari	
21	Darren Pang, Goalie	
22	Mark Paterson	
23	Phil Patterson	
24	Gary Roberts	
25	Darcy Roy	
26	Brad Shaw	
27	Steve Simoni	
28	Jeff Vaive	

— 1985 - 86 REGULAR ISSUE —

These cards are unnumbered and are listed below in alphabetical order. Sponsors are M.O.M. Printing, Coca-Cola and Channel Twelve.

Card Size: 2 11/16" x 4 1/8"
Face: Four colour, white border; Name, Jersey number
Back: Black on white card stock; Name, Jersey number, Resume, Sponsor logos
Imprint: *Photo by Toomey Photography
Complete Set No.: 45
Complete Set Price: 11.00   22.00

No.	Player	Checklist
1	Tom Allen	
2	Bill Bennett	
3	Bruce Cassidy	
4	Greg Coram, Goalie	
5	Bob Ellett, Coach	
6	Tony Geesink	
7	Bob Giffen	
8	John Hanna	
9	Tim Helmer	
10	Andy Helmuth	
11	Steve Hrynewich	
12	Rob Hudson	
13	Jim Jackson, Asst. Trainer	
14	Steve Kayser	
15	Bill Kuchna	
16	Mike LaRouche	
17	Tom Lawson, Asst. Manager	
18	Richard Lessard	
19	Gary Roberts	
20	Jerry Scott	
21	John Shephard -Director of Public Relations	
22	Steve Simoni	
23	Greg Sliz	
24	Gord Thomas, Trainer	
25	Chris Vickers	
26	Bert Weir	
27	Dennis Wigle	

— 1992 - 93 REGULAR ISSUE —

This 24-card set features the 25th Anniversary team packaged in a wax paper pouch with seal of Ottawa 67's 25th crest.

Ottawa 67's, 1992-93 Issue
Card No. 7, Chris Coveny

Card Size: 2 1/2" x 3 1/2"
Face: Four colour, purple border; Name, Position, Number, Logo
Back: Two colour, black border, card stock; Name, Resume; Sponsor's logo
Imprint: None
Complete Set No.: 24
Complete Set Price: 5.00   10.00

No.	Player	Checklist
1	Ken Belanger	
2	Curt Bowen	
3	Rich Bronilla	
4	Mathew Burnett	
5	Shawn Caplice	
6	Mike Carr	
7	Chris Coveny	
8	Howard Darwin, Founder	
9	Shean Donovan	

No.	Player	Checklist
10	Mark Edmundson	
11	Billy Hall	
12	Mike Johnson	
13	Brian Kilrea, Coach/GM	
14	Grayson Lafoley	
15	Grant Marshall	
16	Cory Murphy	
17	Mike Peca	
18	Greg Ryan	
19	Jeff Salajko, Goalie	
20	Gerry Skrypec	
21	Sean Spencer, Goalie	
22	Steve Washburn	
23	Mark Yakabuski	
24	25th Anniversary Card	

PETERBOROUGH PETES

— 1991 - 92 REGULAR ISSUE —

Peterborough Petes, 1991-92 Issue
Card No. 7, Chris Longo

Card Size: 2 1/2" X 3 3/4"
Face: Black and white
Back: Unknown
Imprint: None
Complete Set No.: 30
Complete Set Price: 17.50   35.00

No.	Player	Checklist
—	Pet. Commission of Police	
—	Kiwanis International	
—	Quaker	
1	Jason Dawe	
2	Chris Pronger	
3	Scott Turner	
4	Chad Grills	
5	Brent Tulley	
6	Mike Harding	
7	Chris Longo	
8	Slapshot, Mascot	
9	Doug Searle	
10	Mike Thomlinson	
11	Bryan Gendron	
12	Andrew Verner, Goalie	
13	Ryan Black	
14	Don O'Neill	
15	Jeff Twohey, Asst. Coach	
16	Dale McTavish	
17	Jeff Walker	
18	Matt St-Germain	
19	Dave Roche	
20	Colin Wilson	
21	Jason Cullimore	
22	Chad Lang	
23	Dick Todd, Coach	
24	Geordie Kinnear	
25	Shawn Heins	
26	John Johnson	
27	Kelly Vipond	

776 • PORTLAND WINTERHAWKS — 1992 REGULAR ISSUE —

— 1992 REGULAR ISSUE —

Card Size: 2 1/2" x 3 3/4"
Face: Four colour, white border, Name, Team Logo
Back: Three colour on white card stock
Imprint: Designed and Produced by C.P. Graphics, Peterborough, Ontario.
Complete Set No.: 27
Complete Set Price: 7.50 15.00

No.	Player	Checklist
--	Title Card	
7	Chris Longo	
10	Mike Thomlinson	
11	Bryan Gendron	
12	Andrew Verner, Goalie	
15	Jeff Twohey, AM/Coach	
21	Jason Cullimore	
22	Chad Lang, Goalie	
25	Shawn Heins	
27	Kelly Vipond	

PORTLAND WINTERHAWKS

— 1986 - 87 REGULAR ISSUE —

These cards are numbered and are listed here aphabetically.

Card Size: 2 1/2" X 3 1/2"
Face: Four colour, white border; Name, Position, Jersey Number
Back: Black on white card stock; Number, Resume
Imprint: None
Complete Set No.: 24
Complete Set Price: 11.00 22.00

No.	Player	Checklist
1	Dave Archibald	
2	Bruce Basken	
3	Thomas Bjuhr	
4	Shawn Clouston	
5	Jeff Finley	
6	Bob Foglietta	
7	Brian Gerrits	
8	Darryl Gilmour, Goalie	
9	Dennis Holland	
10	Steve Kloepzig	
11	Jim Latos	
12	Dave McLay	
13	Scott Melnyk	
14	Troy Mick	
15	Roy Mitchell	
16	Jamie Nicolls	
17	Trevor Pohl	
18	Troy Pohl	
19	Glen Seymour, Goalie	
20	Jeff Sharples	
21	Jay Stark	
22	Jim Swan, Goalie	
23	Glen Wesley	
24	Dan Woodley	

— 1988 - 89 REGULAR ISSUE —

These cards are numbered and are listed here aphabetically.

Card Size: 2 1/2" X 3 1/2"
Face: Four colour, white border; Name, Position, Jersey number
Back: Black on white card stock; Number, Resume,
Imprint: None
Complete Set No.: 21
Complete Set Price: 7.50 15.00

No.	Player	Checklist
1	Wayne Anchikoski	
2	Eric Badzgon, Goalie	
3	Chad Biafore	
4	James Black	
5	Terry Black	
6	Shaun Clouston	
7	Byron Dafoe, Goalie	
8	Brent Fleetwood	

No.	Player	Checklist
9	Rob Flintoft	
10	Bryan Gourlie	
11	Mark Greyeyes	
12	Dennis Holland	
13	Kevin Jorgenson	
14	Greg Leahy	
15	Troy Mick	
16	Roy Mitchell	
17	Joey Mitelsteadt	
18	Mike Moore	
19	Scott Mydan	
20	Calvin Thudium	
21	Wild Cherry Pepsi Coupon	

— 1989 - 90 REGULAR ISSUE —

These cards are numbered and are listed here aphabetically.

Card Size: 2 1/2" X 3 1/2"
Face: Four colour, white border; Name, Jersey number, Position
Back: Black on white card stock; Number, Resume
Imprint: None
Complete Set No.: 21
Complete Set Price: 7.50 15.00

No.	Player	Checklist
1	Jamie Black	
2	Vince Coccioio	
3	Byron Dafoe, Goalie	
4	Cam Danyluk	
5	Kim Deck	
6	Dean Dorchak	
7	Brent Fleetwood	
8	Rick Fry	
9	Bryan Gourlie	
10	Brad Harrison	
11	Judson Innes	
12	Dean Intwert, Goalie	
13	Kevin Jorgenson	
14	Todd Kinniburgh	
15	Greg Leahy	
16	Jamie Linden	
17	Scott Mydan	
18	Mike Ruark	
19	Jeff Sebastian	
20	Brandon Smith	
21	Steve Young	

— 1993 - 94 REGULAR ISSUE —

These cards are numbered and are listed here aphabetically.

Card Size: 2 1/2" X 3 1/2"
Face: Four colour, white border; Name, Jersey number, Position
Back: Black on white card stock; Name, Number, Team logo
Imprint: None
Complete Set No.: 30
Complete Set Price: 7.50 15.00

No.	Player	Checklist
1	Mike Arbulic	
2	Lonny Bohonos	
3	Shannon Briske	
4	Dave Cammock	
5	Shawn Collins	
6	Matt Davidson	
7	Adam Deadmarsh	
8	Jake Deadmarsh	
9	Brett Fizzell	
10	Colin Foley	
11	Brad Isbister	
12	Scott Langkow, Goalie	
13	Mike Little	
14	Dmitri Markovsky	
15	Jason McBain	
16	Scott Nichol	
17	Brent Peterson, Coach	
18	Nolan Pratt	
19	Scott Rideout, Goalie	
20	Layne Roland	

No.	Player	Checklist
21	Dave Scatchard	
22	Brandon Smith	
23	Brad Swanson	
24	Brad Symes	
25	Jason Wiemer	
26	Mike Williamson	
27	Great Moments	
28	Great Moments	
29	Great Moments	
30	Great Moments	

PRINCE ALBERT RAIDERS

— 1984 - 85 STICKER ISSUE —

These stickers were issued by Ronald McDonald House. They are unnumbered and listed below in alphabetical order.

Prince Albert Raiders, 1984-85 Issue
Sticker No. 1, Ken Baumgartner

Sticker Size: 15/16" X 1 3/4"
Face: Black and white photo, borderless; Jersey number
Back: Blank
Imprint: None
Complete Set No.: 22
Complete Set Price: 12.50 25.00

No.	Player	Checklist
1	Ken Baumgartner	
2	Brad Bennett	
3	Dean Braham	
4	Rod Dallman	
5	Neil Davey	
6	Pat Elynuik	
7	Collin Feser	
8	Dave Goertz	
9	Steve Gotaas	
10	Tony Grenier	
11	Roydon Gunn	
12	Doug Hobson	
13	Dan Hodgson	
14	Curtis Hunt	
15	Kim Issel	
16	Ward Komonosky	
17	David Manson	
18	Dale McFee	
19	Ken Morrison	
20	Dave Pasin	
21	Don Schmidt	
22	Emanuel Viveiros	

QUEBEC RAMPARTS

— 1980 - 81 REGULAR ISSUE —

Card Size: 2" X 3"
Face: Four colour, white strip at bottom; Team logo, Jersey number, Name, French
Back: Blank
Imprint: None
Complete Set No.: 22
Complete Set Price: 10.00 20.00

No.	Player	Checklist
1	Marc Bertrand	
2	Jacques Chouinard	
3	Roger Côtè	

No.	Player	Checklist
4	Gaston Drapeau, Instructeur	
5	Claude Drouin	
6	Gaëtan Duchesne	
7	Scott Fraser	
8	Jean Paul Larivière	
9	Andrè Larocque	
10	Roberto Lavoie	
11	Stèphane Lessard	
12	Marc Lemay	
13	Paul Lèvesque	
14	Richard Linteau	
15	Patrice Massè	
16	Jean-Marc Lanthier	
17	David Pretty	
18	Guy Riel	
19	Daniel Rioux	
20	Roberto Romano	
21	Michel Therrien	
22	Gilles Tremblay	

RAYSIDE BALFOUR JUNIOR A CANADIANS

— 1990 - 91 REGULAR ISSUE —

Rayside Balfour Junior A Canadiens
1990-91 Issue
Card No. 23, Sean Van Amburg

Card Size: 2 3/8" X 3 5/16"
Face: Four colour, borderless; Name, Jersey number
Back: Black on white card stock; Sponsor logos
Imprint: None
Complete Set No.: 23
Complete Set Price: 7.50   15.00 ☐

No.	Player	Checklist
1	Title Card	
2	Dan Baston	
3	Jon Boeve, Goalie	
4	Jordan Boyle	
5	Serge Coulombe	
6	Mike Dore	
7	Denis Gosselin	
8	Mike Gratton	
9	Jason Hall, Goalie	
10	Grant Healey	
11	Marc Lafreniere	
12	Alain Leclair	
13	Mike Longo	
14	Troy Mallette	
15	Matthew Mooney	
16	Virgil Nose	
17	Trevor Oystrick, Goalie	
18	Steve Proceviat	
19	Chris Puskas	
20	Yvon Quenneville	
21	Michael Sullivan	
22	Trevor Tremblay	
23	Sean Van Amburg	

— 1991 - 92 REGULAR ISSUE —

Card Size: 2 3/8" X 3 5/16"
Face: Four colour, borderless; Name, Number, Team name
Back: Black on white card stock; Sponsor logos
Imprint: None
Complete Set No.: 23
Complete Set Price: 7.50   15.00 ☐

No.	Player	Checklist
1	Title Card	
2	Dan Baston	
3	Don Cucksey	
4	Dean Cull	
5	Mike Dore	
6	Denis Gosselin	
7	Jason Hall, Goalie	
8	Grant Healey	
9	Marc Lafreniere	
10	Mike Longo	
11	Scott MacLellan	
12	Matt Mooney	
13	Rob Moxness, Goalie	
14	Virgil Nose	
15	Trent Oystrick	
16	Jon Stewart	
17	Jon Stos	
18	Dave Sutton	
19	Scott Sutton	
20	Trevor Tremblay	
21	Jaak Valiots	
22	Sean Van Amburg	
23	Jason Young 1982 - 83 Stickboy	

REGINA PATS

— 1981 - 82 REGULAR ISSUE —

Card Size: 2 3/4" X 4 1/8"
Face: Four colour; Name
Back: Blank
Imprint: None
Complete Set No.: 25
Complete Set Price: 12.50   25.00 ☐

No.	Player	Checklist
1	Regina Pats Logo	
2	Garth Butcher	
3	Lyndon Byers	
4	Jock Callander	
5	Marc Centrone	
6	Dave Goertz	
7	Evans Dobni	
8	Dale Derkatch	
9	Jeff Crawford	
10	Jim Clarke	
11	Jayson Meyer	
12	Gary Leeman	
13	Bruce Holloway	
14	Ken Heppner	
15	Taylor Hall	
16	Wally Schreiber	
17	Kevin Pylypow	
18	Ray Plamondon	
19	Brent Pascal	
20	Dave Michayluk	
21	Barry Trotz	
22	Al Tuer	
23	Tony Vogel	
24	Martin Wood	
25	Regina Police Logo	

Note: Junior Team Sets are collected as complete sets. Very seldom are they broken up and sold as individual cards. For this reason the cards also are not priced individually. The complete set price is shown in EX and NRMT prices.

— 1982 - 83 REGULAR ISSUE —

Card Size: 2 3/4" X 4 1/8"
Face: Four colour; Name
Back: Blank
Imprint: None
Complete Set No.: 25
Complete Set Price: 12.50   25.00 ☐

No.	Player	Checklist
1	Regina Pats and Police Logo	
2	Todd Lumbard, Goalie	
3	Jamie Reeve, Goalie	
4	Dave Goertz	
5	John Milner	
6	Doug Trapp	
7	R.J. Dundas	
8	Stu Grimson	
9	Al Tuer	
10	Rick Herbert	
11	Tony Vogel	
12	John Bekkers	
13	Dale Derkatch	
14	Gary Leeman	
15	Nevin Markwart	
16	Kurt Wickenheiser	
17	Jeff Frank	
18	Marc Centrone	
19	Taylor Hall	
20	Lyndon Byers	
21	Jayson Meyers	
22	Jeff Crawford	
23	Don Boyd	
24	Barry Trapp	
25	Pats Big Blue Mascot	

— 1983 - 84 REGULAR ISSUE —

Regina Pats, 1983-84 Issue
Card No. 2, Todd Lumbard

Card Size: 2 5/8" X 4 1/8"
Face: Four colour, white border; Jersey number, Name, Position
Back: Black on white card stock; Number, Tips, Sponsor logos
Imprint: photos by Royal Studios
Complete Set No.: 25
Complete Set Price: 10.00   20.00 ☐

No.	Player	Checklist
1	Title Card: Regina Pats	
2	Todd Lumbard, Goalie	
3	Jamie Reeve, Goalie	
4	Dave Goertz	
5	John Miner	
6	Doug Trapp	
7	R.J. Dundas	
8	Stu Grimson	
9	Al Tuer	
10	Rick Herbert	
11	Tony Vogel	
12	John Bekkers	
13	Dale Derkatch	
14	Gary Leeman	
15	Nevin Markwart	
16	Kurt Wickenheiser	

RICHMOND RENEGADES — 1985-86 REGULAR ISSUE

No.	Player	Checklist
17	Jeff Frank	☐
18	Marc Centrone	☐
19	Taylor Hall	☐
20	Lyndon Byers	☐
21	Jayson Meyer	☐
22	Jeff Crawford	☐
23	Don Boyd, Head Coach	☐
24	Barry Trapp, Assistant Coach	☐
25	K-9 Big Blue, Mascot	☐

— 1985-86 REGULAR ISSUE —

We have no information on this set. We would appreciate hearing from anyone who could supply further information.

Card Size: 2 1/2" X 3 1/2"
Face: Four colour
Back: Unknown
Imprint: None
Complete Set No.: 31
Complete Set Price: 12.50   25.00 ☐

— 1986-87 REGULAR ISSUE —

These cards were issued by Royal Studios. They are unnumbered and are listed below in alphabetical order.

Card Size: 2 1/2" X 3 1/2"
Face: Four colour, white and red border; Name, Jersey number, Team
Back: Black on white card stock; Name, Resume
Imprint: ROYAL STUDIOS PRINTED BY: FORBES-ANDERSON PRESS LTD.
Complete Set No.: 30
Complete Set Price: 7.50   15.00 ☐

No.	Player	Checklist
1	Troy Bakogeorge	☐
2	Grant Chorney	☐
3	Gary Dickie	☐
4	Milan Dragicevic	☐
5	Mike Dyck	☐
6	Craig Endean	☐
7	Mike Gibson	☐
8	Erin Ginnell	☐
9	Brad Hornung (2)	☐
10	Mark Janse	☐
11	Trent Kachur	☐
12	Craig Kalawsky	☐
13	Dan Logan	☐
14	Mascot: K-9	☐
15	Jim Mathieson	☐
16	Darrin McKechnie	☐
17	Darin McInnes	☐
18	Rob McKinley, Goalie	☐
19	Brad Miller	☐
20	Stacy Nickel	☐
21	Cregg Nicol	☐
22	Len Nielsen	☐
23	Darren Parsons	☐
24	Doug Sauter	☐
25	Ray Savard	☐
26	Dennis Sobchuk	☐
27	Chris Tarnowski	☐
28	Mike Van Slooten	☐
29	Brian Wilkie	☐
30	Rod Williams	☐

Note: Junior Team Sets are collected as complete sets. Very seldom are they broken up and sold as individual cards. For this reason the cards also are not priced individually. The complete set price is shown in EX and NRMT prices.

— 1987-88 REGULAR ISSUE —

These cards were issued by Royal Studios. They are unnumbered and are listed below in alphabetical order.

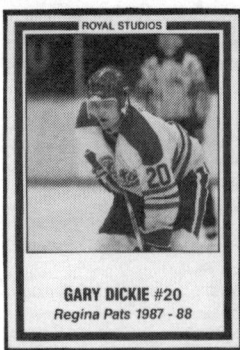

Regina Pats, 1987-88 Issue
Card No. 2, Gary Dickie

Card Size: 2 1/2" X 3 1/2"
Face: Four colour, white and red border; Name, Jersey number, Team
Back: Black on white card stock; Name, Resume
Imprint: ROYAL STUDIOS PRINTED BY: FORBES-ANDERSON PRESS LTD.
Complete Set No.: 28
Complete Set Price: 5.50   11.00 ☐

No.	Player	Checklist
1	Kevin Clemens	☐
2	Gary Dickie	☐
3	Milan Dragicevic	☐
4	Mike Dyck	☐
5	Craig Endean	☐
6	Kevin Gallant, Director	☐
7	Jamie Heward	☐
8	Rod Houk, Goalie	☐
9	Mark Janssens	☐
10	Trent Kachur	☐
11	Craig Kalawsky	☐
12	Frank Kovacs	☐
13	Darren Kwiatkowski	☐
14	Brian Leibel	☐
15	Tim Logan	☐
16	Jim Mathieson	☐
17	Darrin McKechnie	☐
18	Rob McKinley, Goalie	☐
19	Brad Miller	☐
20	Cregg Nicol	☐
21	Doug Sauter, Coach	☐
22	Dan Sexton	☐
23	Mike Sillinger	☐
24	Dennis Sobchuk, Assistant General Manager / Coach	☐
25	Stanley Szumlak, Certified Athletic Therapist	☐
26	Mike Van Slooten	☐
27	K-9, Mascot	☐
28	1974 Memorial Cup Champions	☐

— 1988-89 ROYAL STUDIOS —

These cards were issued by Royal Studios. They are unnumbered and are listed below in alphabetical order.

Card Size: 2 1/2" X 3 1/2"
Face: Four colour, white and red border; Name, Jersey number, Team
Back: Black on white card stock; Name, Resume
Imprint: ROYAL STUDIOS PRINTED BY: FORBES-ANDERSON PRESS LTD.
Complete Set No.: 24
Complete Set Price: 5.00   10.00 ☐

No.	Player	Checklist
1	Shane Bogden	☐
2	Cam Braver	☐
3	Scott Daniels	☐
4	Gary Dickie	☐
5	Mike Dyck	☐
6	Kevin Haller	☐
7	Jamie Heward	☐
8	Terry Hollinger	☐
9	Rod Houk	☐
10	Frank Kovacs	☐
11	Brian Leibel	☐
12	Bernie Lynch	☐
13	Kelly Markwart	☐
14	Jim Mathieson	☐
15	Brad McGinnis	☐
16	Brad Miller	☐
17	Dwayne Monteith	☐
18	Curtis Nykyforuk	☐
19	Darren Parsons	☐
20	Cory Paterson	☐
21	Jeff Sebastian	☐
22	Mike Sillinger	☐
23	Chad Silver	☐
24	Jamie Splett	☐

— 1989-90 ISSUE —

We have no information on this set. We would appreciate hearing from anyone who could supply further information.

Card Size: 4" X 6"
Face: Four colour
Back: Unknown
Imprint: None
Complete Set No.: 22
Complete Set Price: 12.50   25.00 ☐

RICHMOND RENEGADES

— 1990-91 ISSUE —

We have no information on this set. We would appreciate hearing from anyone who could supply further information.

Card Size: 2 1/2" X 3 1/2"
Face: Four colour
Back: Unknown
Imprint: None
Complete Set No.: 18
Complete Set Price: 15.00   30.00 ☐

LES RIVERAINES DE RICHELIEU

— 1988-89 REGULAR ISSUE —

Card Size: 2 7/8" x 4"
Face: Four colour; Name
Back: Black on white card stock; Name, Jersey number
Imprint: None
Complete Set No.: 30
Complete Set Price: 7.50   15.00 ☐

No.	Player	Checklist
1	Team Photo	☐
2	Bertrand Cournoyer	☐
3	Stephane Valois	☐
4	Andre Millette	☐
5	Michel Deguise	☐
6	Yves Cournoyer	☐
7	Guy Caplette	☐
8	Roger Laporte	☐
9	Jacques Provencal	☐
10	Denis Benoit	☐
11	Alain Rancourt	☐
12	Marc Beaurivage	☐
13	Jonathan Black	☐
14	Richard Boisvert	☐
15	Hughes Bouchard	☐
16	Francois Bourdeau	☐

No.	Player	Checklist
17	Parick Grise	
18	Robert Guillet	
19	Jimmy Lachance	
20	Frederic Lefebvre	
21	Frederic Maltais	
22	Joseph Napolitano	
23	Remy Patoine	
24	Jean Plamondon	
25	Steve Plasse	
26	Jean-Fra. Poirier	
27	Francois St-Germain	
28	Frederic Savard	
29	Martin Tanguay	
30	Richard Valois	

SAGINAW GEARS

— 1978 - 79 REGULAR ISSUE —

Saginaw Gears, 1978-79 Issue
Card No. 5, Bob Froese

Card Size: 2 1/2" x 3 1/2"
Face: Black and white, white border; Name, Position
Back: Blank
Imprint: None
Complete Set No.: 20
Complete Set Price: 15.00   30.00

No.	Player	Checklist
1	Wrena. Blair, Owner	
2	Marcel Comeau	
3	Dennis Desrosiers	
4	Jon Fontas	
5	Bob Froese, Goalie	
6	"Gunner" Garrett, Trainer	
7	Bob Gladney	
8	Warren Holmes	
9	Stu Irving	
10	Larry Hopkins	
11	Scott Jessee	
12	Lynn Jorgenson	
13	Doug Keans, Goalie	
14	Claude Larochelle	
15	Paul McIntosh	
16	Don Perry	
17	Greg Steel	
18	Mark Suzor	
19	Mark Toffolo	
20	Dave Westner	

Note: Junior Team Sets are collected as complete sets. Very seldom are they broken up and sold as individual cards. For this reason the cards also are not priced individually. The complete set price is shown in EX and NRMT prices.

SAGINAW HAWKS

— 1988 - 89 REGULAR ISSUE —

Saginaw Hawk, 1988-89 Issue
Card No. 1, Ray Gallagher

Card Size: 2 5/8" X 3 5/8"
Face: Four colour, white border; Team logo, Name, Position
Back: Black on white card stock; Number, Tips, Sponsor logos
Imprint: None
Complete Set No.: 25
Complete Set Price: 5.50   11.00

No.	Player	Checklist
1	Ray Gallagher	
2	Peter Kelly, Trainer	
3	Steve Harper, Trainer	
4	Winston Jones, Assistant Coach	
5	Mac MacLean, Coach/General Manager	
6	Kevin Doherty	
7	Stuart Birnie	
8	Charles Cusson	
9	Paul MacLean	
10	Bob Lindsay	
11	Darren Burns	
12	Rick Pracey, Goalie	
13	Mike Malloy	
14	Dave Hyrsky	
15	Rob Percival	
16	Jarrett Eligh	
17	Pat Gooley	
18	Michael Bracco, Goalie	
19	Ken Crook	
20	Brad Osborne	
21	Todd Reynolds, Goalie	
22	Mike McCourt	
23	Chris Webster	
24	Kevin Lune	
25	Crest: Brockville Police	

SALT LAKE GOLDEN EAGLES

— 1988 - 89 REGULAR ISSUE —

Card Size: 2 1/2" X 3 1/2"
Face: Four colour; Name, Positon, Sponsor Logos
Back: Black on white card stock; Number, Resume
Imprint: None
Complete Set No.: 23
Complete Set Price: 25.00   50.00

No.	Player	Checklist
1	Rick Barkovich	
2	Michael Dark	
3	Terry Perkins	
4	Peter Lappin	
5	Wayne Cowley	
6	Rich Chernomaz	
7	Steve Smith	
8	Theoren Fleury	
9	Dave Reierson	
10	Not Issued	
11	Martin Simard	
12	Stu Grimson	
13	Darwin McCutcheon	
14	Doug Clarke	
15	Doug Pickell	
16	Randy Bucyk	
17	Jim Johannson	
18	Rick Lessard	
19	Ken Sabourin	
20	Chris Biotti	
21	Jeff Wenaas	
22	Mark Holmes	
23	Bob Bodak	
24	Marc Bureau	

SASKATOON BLADES

— 1981 - 82 REGULAR ISSUE —

Card Size: 2 1/2" X 3 7/8"
Face: Four colour; Name
Back: Black on white card stock; Resume
Imprint: None
Complete Set No.: 25
Complete Set Price: 13.00   26.00

No.	Player	Checklist
1	Blades Team Photo	
2	Daryl Stanley	
3	Leroy Gorski	
4	Don Clark	
5	Brad Duggan	
6	Dave Chartier	
7	Dave Brown	
8	Adams Thompson	
9	Bruce Eakin	
10	Brian Skudland	
11	Roger Kortko	
12	Ron Dreger	
13	Daryl Lubiniecki	
14	Marc Habscheid	
15	Saskatoon Police Logo	
16	Todd Strueby	
17	Craig Hurley	
18	Bill Hlynsky	
19	Lane Lambert	
20	Mike Bloski	
21	Bruce Gordon	
22	Perry Ganchar	
23	Ron Loustel	
24	Blades Logo	
25	Checklist	

— 1983 - 84 REGULAR ISSUE —

Card Size: 2 1/2" X 3 3/4"
Face: Four colour
Back: Number
Imprint: None
Complete Set No.: 25
Complete Set Price: 17.50   35.00

No.	Player	Checklist
1	Team Photo	
2	Trent Yawney	
3	Grant Jennings	
4	Duncan MacPherson	
5	Greg Holtby	
6	Dan Leier	
7	Dwaine Hutton	
8	Wendel Clark	
9	Kerry Laviolette	
10	Dave Chartier	
11	Dale Henry	
12	Randy Smith	
13	Kevin Kowalchuk	
14	Todd McLellan	
15	Saskatoon Police	
16	Larry Korchinski	
17	Curtis Chamberlin	
18	Greg Lebsack	

SAULT STE. MARIE GREYHOUNDS — 1984 - 85 REGULAR ISSUE —

No.	Player	Checklist
19	Ron Dreger	☐
20	Doug Kyle	☐
21	Rick Smith	☐
22	Joey Kocur	☐
23	Alan Larochelle	☐
24	Mark Thietke	☐
25	Checklist	☐

— 1984 - 85 REGULAR ISSUE —

These stickers were issued by Ronald McDonald House. They are unnumbered and are listed below in alphabetical order.

Saskatoon Blades, 1984-85 Issue
Card No. 3, Wendel Clark

Sticker Size: 2" X 1 3/4"
Face: Black and white photo, borderless; Jersey number
Back: Blank
Imprint: None
Complete Set No.: 20
Complete Set Price: 15.00   30.00 ☐

No.	Player	Checklist
1	Jack Bowkus	☐
2	Curtis Chamberlin	☐
3	Wendel Clark	☐
4	Ron Dreger	☐
5	Randy Hoffart	☐
6	Mark Holick	☐
7	Greg Holtby	☐
8	Grant Jennings	☐
9	Kevin Kowalchuk	☐
10	Bryan Larkin	☐
11	James Latos	☐
12	Duncan MacPherson	☐
13	Rod Matechuk	☐
14	Todd McLellan	☐
15	Darren Moren	☐
16	Mike Morin	☐
17	Devon Oleniuk	☐
18	Grant Tkachuk	☐
19	Troy Vollhoffer	☐
20	Trent Yawney	☐

— 1986 - 87 PHOTO ISSUE —

These photos were issued by Shell Oil and were inserted home game programs.

Card Size: 8 1/2" x 11"
Face: Blue and white
Back: Blue and white; Name, Team, Sponsor's logo
Imprint: None
Complete Set No.: 25
Complete Set Price: 15.00   30.00 ☐

No.	Player	Checklist
1	Blair Atcheynum	☐
2	Colin Bayer	☐
3	Jack Bowkus	☐
4	Mike Butka	☐
5	Kelly Chase	☐
6	Tim Cheveldae, Goalie	☐
7	Blaine Chrest	☐
8	Jason Christie	☐
9	Kerry Clark	☐
10	Brian Glynn	☐
11	Mark Holick	☐
12	Kevin Kaminski	☐

No.	Player	Checklist
13	Tracy Katelnikoff	☐
14	Kory Kocur	☐
15	Brian Larkin	☐
16	Curtis Leschyshyn	☐
17	Dan Logan	☐
18	Todd McLellan	☐
19	Devon Oleniuk	☐
20	Marty Prazma	☐
21	Mary Reimer	☐
22	Walter Shutter	☐
23	Grant Tkachuk	☐
24	Tony Twist	☐
25	Shaun Van Allen	☐

SAULT STE. MARIE GREY-HOUNDS

— 1980 - 81 REGULAR ISSUE —

Card Size: 2 1/2" X 4"
Face: Four colour; Name
Back: Black on white card stock
Imprint: None
Complete Set No.: 25
Complete Set Price: 13.00   26.00 ☐

No.	Player	Checklist
1	Ken Porteous	☐
2	Brian Petterle	☐
3	Gord Dineen	☐
4	Tony Cella	☐
5	Doug Shedden	☐
6	Terry Tait	☐
7	Greyhounds Logo	☐
8	Steve Smith	☐
9	Hugh Larkin	☐
10	Steve Gatzos	☐
11	Tim Zwijack	☐
12	Vic Morin	☐
13	John Vanbiesbrouck, Goalie	☐
14	Ron Francis	☐
15	Tony Butorac	☐
16	John Goodwin	☐
17	Ron Handy	☐
18	Jim Pavese	☐
19	Sault Ste. Marie Police Logo	☐
20	Rick Morocco	☐
21	Ken Latta	☐
22	Dirk Rueter	☐
23	OMJHL Logo	☐
24	Terry Crisp	☐
25	Marc D'Amour	☐

— 1981 - 82 REGULAR ISSUE —

These cards are unnumbered and are listed below in alphabetical order.

Card Size: 2 1/2" X 4"
Face: Four colour; Jersey number
Back: Black on white card stock
Imprint: None
Complete Set No.: 28
Complete Set Price: 13.00   28.00 ☐

No.	Player	Checklist
1	Jim Alfred	☐
2	Dave Andreoli	☐
3	Richard Beaulne	☐
4	Bruce Bell	☐
5	Chuck Brimmer	☐
6	Tony Cella	☐
7	Kevin Conway	☐
8	Terry Crisp, Coach	☐
9	Marc D'Amour	☐
10	Gord Dineen	☐
11	Chris Felix	☐
12	Ron Francis	☐
13	Steve Graves	☐

No.	Player	Checklist
14	Wayne Groulx	☐
15	Huey Larkin	☐
16	Ken Latta	☐
17	Mike Lococo	☐
18	Jim Pavese	☐
19	Dirk Rueter	☐
20	Steve Smith	☐
21	Terry Tait	☐
22	Rick Tocchet	☐
23	John Vanbiesbrouck, Goalie	☐
24	Harry Wolfe	☐
25	J.D. Yari	☐
26	Bluebird Bakery Limited Logo	☐
27	Canadian Tire Logo	☐
28	Coca-Cola Logo	☐

— 1982 - 83 REGULAR ISSUE —

These cards are unnumbered and are listed below in alphabetical order.

Card Size: 2 1/2" X 4"
Face: Four colour, Jersey number
Back: Black on white card stock
Imprint: None
Complete Set No.: 25
Complete Set Price: 12.50   25.00 ☐

No.	Player	Checklist
1	Jim Aldred	☐
2	John Armelin	☐
3	Jeff Beaukeboom	☐
4	Richard Beaulne	☐
5	Tony Cella	☐
6	Kevin Conway	☐
7	Terry Crisp, Coach	☐
8	Chris Felix	☐
9	Steve Graves	☐
10	Gus Greco	☐
11	Wayne Groulx	☐
12	Sam Haidy	☐
13	Tim Hoover	☐
14	Pat Lahey	☐
15	Huey Larkin	☐
16	Mike Lococo	☐
17	Mike Neill	☐
18	Ken Sabourin	☐
19	Steve Smith	☐
20	Terry Tait	☐
21	Rick Tocchet	☐
22	John Vanbiesbrouck, Goalie	☐
23	Harry Wolfe	☐
24	Bluebird Bakery Ltd.	☐
25	Station Mall	☐

— 1983 - 84 REGULAR ISSUE —

These cards are unnumbered and are listed below in alphabetical order.

Card Size: 2 1/4" X 4"
Face: Four colour
Back: Black on white card stock
Imprint: None
Complete Set No.: 25
Complete Set Price: 11.50   23.00 ☐

No.	Player	Checklist
1	Jeff Beukeboom	☐
2	Graeme Bonar	☐
3	Cris Brant	☐
4	John English	☐
5	Chris Felix	☐
6	Rick Fera	☐
7	Marc Fournier	☐
8	Steve Graves	☐
9	Gus Greco	☐
10	Wayne Groulx	☐
11	Sam Haidy	☐
12	Tim Hoover	☐
13	Jerry Iuliano	☐

No.	Player	Checklist
14	Pat Lahey	☐
15	Mike Lococo	☐
16	Jean Marc MacKenzie	☐
17	Mike Oliverio	☐
18	Brit Peer	☐
19	Joey Rampton	☐
20	Ken Sabourin	☐
21	Jim Samec	☐
22	Rick Tocchet	☐
23	Harry Wolfe	☐
24	Coca-Cola	☐
25	IGA	☐

— 1984 - 85 REGULAR ISSUE —

These cards are unnumbered and are listed below in alphabetical order.

Card Size: 2 1/4" X 4"
Face: Four colour
Back: Black on white card stock
Imprint: None
Complete Set No.: 25
Complete Set Price: 11.50   23.00 ☐

No.	Player	Checklist
1	Marty Abrams	☐
2	Jeff Beukeboom	☐
3	Chris Brant	☐
4	Terry Crisp, Coach	☐
5	Chris Felix	☐
6	Scott Green	☐
7	Wayne Groulx	☐
8	Steve Hollett	☐
9	Tim Hoover	☐
10	Derek King	☐
11	Tyler Larter	☐
12	Jean Marc MacKenzie	☐
13	Scott Mosey	☐
14	Mike Oliverio	☐
15	Grit Peer	☐
16	Wayne Presley	☐
17	Bob Probert	☐
18	Brian Rome	☐
19	Ken Sabourin	☐
20	Rob Veccia	☐
21	Harry Wolfe, Voice of the Greyhounds	☐
22	IGA	☐
23	Coke is it	☐

— 1987 - 88 REGULAR ISSUE —

Card Size: 2 5/8" x 3 3/4"
Face: Four colour, white border; Name
Back: Black on white card stock; Number, Hockey and safety tips, Sponsor logos
Imprint: None
Complete Set No.: 35
Complete Set Price: 35.00   65.00 ☐

No.	Player	Checklist
1	Police Chief Barry King -Checklist	☐
2	Dan Currie	☐
3	Mike Glover	☐
4	Tyler Larter	☐
5	Bob Jones	☐
6	Cst. Lyndon Slewidge	☐
7	Brad Jones	☐
8	Ron Francis	☐
9	Dale Turnbull	☐
10	Don McConnell	☐
11	Chris Felix	☐
12	Steve Udvari	☐
13	Shawn Simpson	☐
14	Rob Zettler	☐
15	Phil Esposito	☐
16	John VanBiesbrouck, Goalie	☐
17	Mike Oliverio	☐
18	Colin Ford	☐

No.	Player	Checklist
19	Steve Herniman	☐
20	Troy Mallette	☐
21	Craig Hartsburg	☐
22	Don Boyd	☐
23	Peter Fiorentino	☐
24	Jeff Columbus	☐
25	Brad Stepan	☐
26	Rick Tocchet	☐
27	Shane Sargant	☐
28	Wayne Muir	☐
29	Wayne Gretzky	☐
30	Gary Luther	☐
31	Harry Wolfe, Voice of the Hounds	☐
32	Rod Thacker	☐
33	Terry Tait, Ted Nolan, Mark Pavoni, Asst Coaches	☐
34	Brian Hoard	☐
35	Glen Johnston	☐

SHAWINNIGAN FALLS CATRACTS

— 1980 REGULAR ISSUE —

We have no information on this set. We would appreciate hearing from anyone who could supply further information.

Card Size: 3" x 4 3/8"
Face: Four colour
Back: Unknown
Imprint: None
Complete Set No.: 22
Complete Set Price: 20.00   40.00 ☐

No.	Player	Checklist

SHERBROOKE CANADIENS

— 1986 - 87 REGULAR ISSUE —

Card Size: 2 1/2" x 3 1/2"
Face: Four colour; Name
Back: Four colour; Name, Resume
Imprint: None
Complete Set No.: 30
Complete Set Price: 25.00   50.00 ☐

No.	Player	Checklist
1	Entraineurs 1986-87	☐
2	Soigneurs 1986-87	☐
3	Coupe Stanley 1986	☐
4	Joel Baillargeon	☐
5	Daniel Berthiaume, Goalie	☐
6	Serge Boisvert	☐
7	Graeme Bonar	☐
8	Randy Bucyk	☐
9	Bill Campbell	☐
10	Jose Charbonneau	☐
11	Rejean Cloutier	☐
12	Bobby Dollas	☐
13	Peter Douris	☐
14	Steben Fletcher	☐
15	Perry Ganchar	☐
16	Luc Gauthier	☐
17	Randy Gilhen	☐
18	Scott Harlow	☐
19	Rick Hayward	☐
20	Kevin Houle	☐
21	Rick Knickle	☐
22	Vincent Riendeau, Goalie	☐
23	Guy Rouleau	☐
24	Scott Sandelin	☐
25	Karel Svoboda	☐
26	Peter Taglianeti	☐
27	Gilles Thibaudeau	☐
28	Ernie Vargas	☐
29	Andre Villeneuve	☐
30	Brian Williams	☐

SPOKANE CHIEFS

— 1989 - 90 REGULAR ISSUE —

This set is unnumbered and is listed alphabetically.

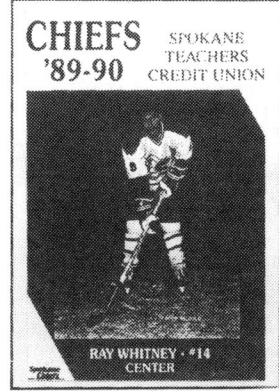

Spokane Chiefs, 1989-90 Issue
Card No. 17, Ray Whitney

Card Size: 2 1/2" x 3 1/2"
Face: Four colour, white border; Name, Position, Jersey number
Back: Black on white card stock; Name, Position, Jersey number Resume, Hockey and Safety Tips
Imprint: None
Complete Set No.: 17
Complete Set Price: 10.00   20.00 ☐

No.	Player	Checklist
1	Mike Chrun	☐
2	Shawn Dietrich	☐
3	Milan Dragicevic	☐
4	Frank Evans	☐
5	Pat Falloon	☐
6	Jeff Ferguson	☐
7	Travis Green	☐
8	Bobby House	☐
9	Mick Jickling	☐
10	Jon Klemm	☐
11	Steve Junker	☐
12	Chris Rowland	☐
13	Dennis Saharchuk	☐
14	Kerry Toporowski	☐
15	Trevor Tovell	☐
16	Bram Vanderkracht	☐
17	Ray Whitney	☐

SPRINGFIELD INDIANS

— 1983 - 84 REGULAR ISSUE —

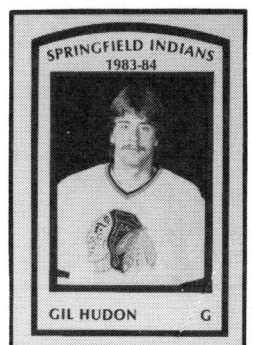

Springfield Indians, 1983-84 Issue
Card No. 1, Gil Hudon

Card Size: 2 1/2" X 3 1/2"
Face: Black and white photo, blue, red and white border; Team, Name, Position
Back: Black on white card stock; Number, Team logo
Imprint: None
Complete Set No.: 25
Complete Set Price: 10.00   20.00 ☐

ARIZONA ICECATS — 1985-86 ISSUE

No.	Player	Checklist
1	Gil Hudon, Goalie	☐
2	Jim Ralph, Goalie	☐
3	Todd Bergen	☐
4	Len Hachborn	☐
5	John Olison	☐
6	Steve Tsujiura	☐
7	Gordie Williams	☐
8	Dave Brown	☐
9	Dan Frawley	☐
10	Tom McMurchy	☐
11	Dave Michayluk	☐
12	Bob Mormina	☐
13	Perry Pelensky	☐
14	Andy Brickley	☐
15	Ross Fitzpatrick	☐
16	Florent Robidoux	☐
17	Jeff Smith	☐
18	Rod Willard	☐
19	Darrell Anholt	☐
20	Steve Blyth	☐
21	Don Dietrich	☐
22	Steve Smith	☐
23	Daryl Stanley	☐
24	Taras Zytynsky	☐
25	Doug Sauter, Coach	☐

— 1984 - 85 REGULAR ISSUE —

Springfield Indians, 1984-85 Issue
Card No. 13, Rob Flockhart

Card Size: 2 1/2" x 3 7/16"
Face: Black and white, blue red and white border;
Name, Position
Back: Black on white card stock; Name, Number, Position
Imprint: None
Complete Set No.: 25
Complete Set Price: 10.00   20.00 ☐

No.	Player	Checklist
1	Mike Sands, Goalie	☐
2	Lorne Molleken, Goalie	☐
3	Todd Lombard, Goalie	☐
4	Randy Velischek	☐
5	David Jensen	☐
6	Ken Leiter	☐
7	Vern Smith	☐
8	Alan Kerr	☐
9	Scott Howson	☐
10	Tim Coulis	☐
11	Terry Tait	☐
12	Tim Trimper	☐
13	Rob Flockhart	☐
14	Ron Handy	☐
15	Jiri Poner	☐
16	Chris Pryor	☐
17	Dale Henry	☐
18	Mark Hamway	☐
19	Monty Trottier	☐
20	Miroslav Maly	☐
21	Dirk Graham	☐
22	Roger Kortko	☐
23	Bob Bodak	☐
24	Lorne Henning, Coach	☐
25	Checklist	☐

SUDBURY WOLVES
— 1984 - 85 POSTCARD ISSUE —

Sudbury Wolves, 1984-85 Issue,
Card No. 7, Jeff Brown

Card Size: 3 9/16" x 5 1/4"
Face: Four colour, white border; Name, Number, Jersey number
Back: Black on white card stock; Name, Position, Resume
Imprint: None
Complete Set No.: 16
Complete Set Price: 7.50   15.00 ☐

No.	Player	Checklist
1	Andy Spruce, Coach	☐
2	Sean Evoy, Goalie	☐
3	Mario Martini	☐
4	Brent Daugherty	☐
5	Mario Chitaroni	☐
6	Dan Chiasson	☐
7	Jeff Brown	☐
8	Todd Sepkowski	☐
9	Brad Belland	☐
10	Glenn Greenough	☐
11	John Landry	☐
12	Max Middendorf	☐
13	David Moylan	☐
14	Jamie Nadjiwan	☐
15	Warren Rychel	☐
16	Ed Smith	☐

— 1985 - 86 REGULAR ISSUE —

Sudbury Wolves, 1985-86 Issue
Card No. 6, Sean Evoy

Card Size: 2 3/4" x 4"
Face: Four colour, white border; Facsimile autograph
Back: Black on card stock; Name, Tips from Police
Imprint: Printed in Sudbury by Journal Printing
Complete Set No.: 26
Complete Set Price: 7.50   15.00 ☐

No.	Player	Checklist
1	Sudbury Regional Police Logo	☐
2	Sponsor's Card	☐
3	Checklist	☐
4	R. Zanibbi, Chief of Police	☐
5	Wayne Maxner, Coach/GM	☐
6	Sean Evoy, Goalie	☐
7	Todd Lalonde	☐
8	Costa Papista	☐
9	Robin Rubic	☐
10	David Moylan	☐
11	Brent Daugherty	☐
12	Glenn Greenough	☐
13	Mario Chitaroni	☐
14	Ken McRae	☐
15	Mike Hudson	☐
16	Andy Paquette	☐
17	Ed Lemaire	☐
18	Mark Turner	☐
19	Craig Duncanson	☐
20	Jeff Brown	☐
21	Team Photograph	☐
22	Max Middendorf	☐
23	Keith Van Rooyen	☐
24	Brad Walcot	☐
25	Rob Wilson	☐
26	Bill White, Goalie	☐

— 1986 - 87 REGULAR ISSUE —

Card Size: 3" x 4 1/8"
Face: Four colour; Name, Number, Position
Back: Black on card stock; Name, Number, Tips from Police
Imprint: Printed in Sudbury by Journal Printing
Complete Set No.: 26
Complete Set Price: 7.50   15.00 ☐

No.	Player	Checklist
1	Mascot	☐
2	Ted Mielczarek	☐
3	Dan Gatenby	☐
4	Todd Lalonde	☐
5	Justin Corbeil	☐
6	Jordan Fois	☐
7	Rodney Lapointe	☐
8	Dave Akey	☐
9	Jim Smith	☐
10	Fred Pennell	☐
11	Joey Simon	☐
12	Luciano Fagioli	☐
13	Robb Graham	☐
14	John Uniac	☐
15	Dave Carrie	☐
16	Pierre Gagnon	☐
17	Peter Hughes	☐
18	Scott McCullough	☐
19	Dean Guitard	☐
20	Pat Holley	☐
21	Chad Bradawey	☐
22	Paul Dipietro	☐
23	Derek Thompson	☐
24	Scott Luce	☐
25	Rob Wilson	☐
26	R. Zaninni, Chief of Police	☐

— 1987 - 88 REGULAR ISSUE —

We have no information on this set. We would appreciate hearing from anyone who could supply further information.

Card Size: 3" X 4 1/8""
Face: Four colour
Back: Unknown
Imprint: None
Complete Set No.: 26
Complete Set Price: 13.00   28.00 ☐

No.	Player	Checklist

— 1988 - 89 REGULAR ISSUE —

— 1988 - 89 REGULAR ISSUE —

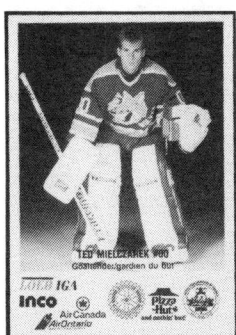

Sudbury Wolves, 1988-89 Issue
Card No. 3, Ted Mielczarek

Card Size: 3" x 4 1/8"
Face: Four colour, white border; Name, Sponsor's logo
Back: Black on card stock; Name, Resume
Imprint: Printed in Sudbury by Journal Printing
Complete Set No.: 26
Complete Set Price: 7.00   15.00

No.	Player	Checklist
1	Checklist	
2	David Goverde, Goalie	
3	Ted Mielczarek, Goalie	
4	Adam Bennett	
5	Kevin Grant	
6	Jordan Fois	
7	Sean O'Donnell	
8	Kevin Meisner	
9	Jim Smith	
10	Fred Pennell	
11	Tyler Pella	
12	Dean Pella	
13	Darren Bell	
14	Derek Thompson	
15	Terry Chitaroni	
16	Sean Stansfield	
17	Alastair Still	
18	Jim Sonmez	
19	Shannon Bolton	
20	Andy Paquette	
21	Mark Turner	
22	Paul DiPietro	
23	Robert Knesaurek	
24	Todd Lalonde	
25	Scott Herniman	
26	R. Zanibbi, Chief of Police	

— 1989 - 90 REGULAR ISSUE —

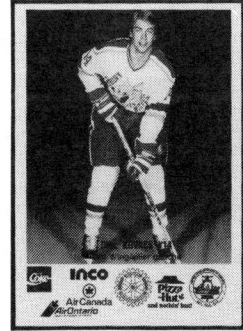

Sudbury Wolves, 1989-90 Issue
Card No. 3, Bill Kovacs

Card Size: 3" x 4 1/4"
Face: Four colour, white border; Name, Sponsor's logo
Back: Black on card stock; Name
Imprint: Printed in Sudbury by Journal Printing
Complete Set No.: 25
Complete Set Price: 7.50   15.00

No.	Player	Checklist
1	Checklist	
2	Alistair Still	
3	Bill Kovacs	
4	Darren Bell	
5	Scott Mahoney	
6	Glen Murray	
7	Alain LaForge	
8	Jamie Matthews	
9	Adam Bennett	
10	Jon Boeve, Goalie	
11	Derek Etches	
12	Marcus Middleton	
13	Jim Sonmez	
14	Leonard MacDonald	
15	Paul DePietro	
16	Neil Ethier	
17	Sean O'Donnell	
18	Andy MacVicar	
19	David Goverde, Goalie	
20	Jason Young	
21	Wade Bartley	
22	Barry Young	
23	R. Zanibbi, Chief of Police	
24	Terry Chitaroni	
25	Rob Knesaurek	

— 1990 - 91 REGULAR ISSUE —

Card Size: 3 X 4 1/4"
Face: Four colour
Back: Black on card stock; Name, Tips from Police, Sponsors logos
Imprint: None
Complete Set No.: 25
Complete Set Price: 7.50   15.00

No.	Player	Checklist
1	Darryl Paquette	
2	Adam Bennett	
3	Barry Young	
4	Jon Boeve	
5	Kyle Blacklock	
6	Sean O'Donnell	
7	Dan Ryder	
8	Wade Bartley	
9	Jamie Matthews	
10	Rod Hinks	
11	Derek Etches	
12	Brandon Convery	
13	Glen Murray	
14	Bill Kovacs	
15	Terry Chitaroni	
16	Jason Young	
17	Alastair Still	
18	Shawn Rivers	
19	Alain Laforge	
20	J. D. Eaton	
21	Mike Peca	
22	Howler, Mascot	
23	Mike Yeo	
24	Not Issued	
25	R. Zanibbi, Chief of Police	

Note: Junior Team Sets are collected as complete sets. Very seldom are they broken up and sold as individual cards. For this reason the cards also are not priced individually. The complete set price is shown in EX and NRMT prices.

— 1991 - 92 REGULAR ISSUE —

Sudbury Wolves, 1991-92 Issue
Card No. 24, Jason Young

Card Size: 3" x 4 1/8"
Face: Four colour, white border; Name, Sponsor's logo
Back: Black on card stock; Name
Imprint: Printed in Sudbury
Complete Set No.: 25
Complete Set Price: 7.50   15.00

No.	Player	Checklist
1	R. Zanibbi, Chief of Police	
2	Lil/Howler, Rookie Card	
3	Team Photo Checklist	
4	Kyle Blacklock	
5	Sean Gagnon	
6	Bernie John	
7	Bob MacIsaac	
8	Jamie Rivers	
9	Shawn Rivers	
10	Joel Sandie	
11	Barry Young	
12	George Dourian, Goalie	
13	Dan Ryder, Goalie	
14	Derek Armstrong	
15	Terry Chitaroni	
16	Brandon Convery	
17	Tim Favot	
18	Rod Hinks	
19	Jamie Matthews	
20	Barrie Moore	
21	Glen Murray	
22	Michael Peca	
23	Michael Yeo	
24	Jason Young	
25	Jason Zohil	

— 1992 - 93 REGULAR ISSUE —

Card Size: 3" x 4 1/4"
Face: Four colour, white border; Name, Sponsor's logos
Back: Black on card stock; Name
Imprint: Printed in Sudbury by Journal Printing
Complete Set No.: 27
Complete Set Price: 7.50   15.00

No.	Player	Checklist
1	Howler and Little Rookie	
2	R. Zanibbi (Chief)	
3	Bob Macisaac	
4	Joel Sandie	
5	Rory Fitzpatrick	
6	Mike Wilson	
7	Sjawn Frappier	
8	Bernie John	
9	Jamie Rivers	
10	Jamie Matthews	
11	Zdener Nedueb	
12	Ryan Shanahan	
13	Corey Crane	
14	Matt Kiereck	
15	Rick Bodkin	
16	Derek Armstrong	
17	Barrie Moore	
18	Rod Hinks	
19	Kayle Short	

784 • ARIZONA ICECATS — 1985 - 86 ISSUE

No.	Player	Checklist
20	Michael Yeo	☐
21	Gary Coupal	☐
22	Dennis Maxwell	☐
23	Steve Potvin	☐
24	Joel Poirier	☐
25	Greg Dreveng, Goalie	☐
26	Mark Gowan	☐
27	Steve Stavis	☐

TORONTO MARLBOROUGHS

— DATE UNKNOWN —

We have no inofrmation on this set. We would appreciate hearing from anyone who could supply further information.

Card Size:
Face: Unknown
Back: Unknown
Imprint: Unknown
Complete Set No.: Unknown
Complete Set Price: Unknown ☐

No.	Player	Checklist

VICTORIA COUGARS

— 1981 - 82 REGULAR ISSUE —

These cards are unnumbered and are listed below in alphabetical order.

Victoria Cougars, 1981-82 Issue
Card No. 8, Wade Jenson

Card Size: 3" X 5"
Face: Four colour; Name
Back: Black on white card stock
Imprint: None
Complete Set No.: 16
Complete Set Price: 13.00   26.00 ☐

No.	Player	Checklist
1	Bob Bales	☐
2	Greg Barber	☐
3	Ray Benik	☐
4	Rich Chernomaz	☐
5	Daryl Colwell	☐
6	Geoff Courtnall	☐
7	Paul Cyr	☐
8	Wade Jenson	☐
9	Stu Kulak	☐
10	Peter Martin	☐
11	John Mokosak	☐
12	Mark Morrison	☐
13	Bryant Seaton	☐
14	Jack Shupe	☐
15	Eric Thurston	☐
16	Randy Wickware	☐

— 1982 - 83 REGULAR ISSUE —

These cards are unnumbered and are listed below in alphabetical order.

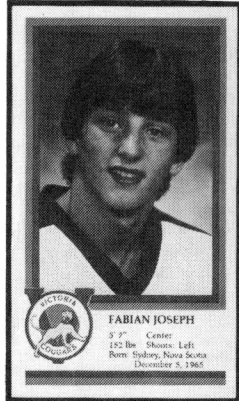

Victoria Cougars, 1982-83 Issue
Card No. 8 Fabian Joseph

Card Size: 3" X 5"
Face: Four colour, white border; Team logo, Name, Resume
Back: Black on white card stock; Name, Sponsor logos
Imprint: None
Complete Set No.: 13
Complete Set Price: 12.50   25.00 ☐

No.	Player	Checklist
1	Steve Bayliss	☐
2	Ray Benik	☐
3	Rich Chernomaz	☐
4	Geoff Courtnall	☐
5	Russ Courtnall	☐
6	Paul Cyr	☐
7	Shawn Green	☐
8	Fabian Joseph	☐
9	Stu Kulak	☐
10	Brenn Leach	☐
11	Jack MacKeigan	☐
12	Dave MacKey	☐
13	Mark McLeary	☐
14	Dan Moberg	☐
15	John Mokosak	☐
16	Mark Morrison	☐
17	Eric Thurston	☐
18	Ron Viglasi	☐

GRADUATION SERIES

No.	Player	Checklist
19	Curt Fraser	☐
20	Grant Fuhr, Goalie	☐
21	Gary Lupul	☐
22	Brad Palmer	☐
23	Barry Pederson	☐

— 1983 - 84 POLICE —

Cards are unnumbered and are listed below in alphabetical order.

Victoria Cougars, 1983-84 Issue
Card No. 1, Misko Antisin

Card Size: 3" X 5"
Face: Four colour, white border; Team logo, Name, Resume
Back: Black on white card stock; Name, Sponsor logos
Imprint: Photograph by: Scope Photography Ltd.
Complete Set No.:
Complete Set Price: 10.50   21.00 ☐

No.	Player	Checklist
1	Misko Antisin	☐
2	Steve Bayliss	☐
3	Paul Bifano	☐
4	Russ Courtnall	☐
5	Greg Davies	☐
6	Dean Drozdiak	☐
7	Jim Gunn	☐
8	Richard Hajdu	☐
9	Randy Hansch, Goalie	☐
10	Matt Hervey	☐
11	Fabian Joseph	☐
12	Rob Kivell	☐
13	Brenn Leach	☐
14	Jack MacKeigan	☐
15	Dave Mackey	☐
16	Tom Martin	☐
17	Darren Moren, Goalie	☐
18	Adam Morrison	☐
19	Dan Sexton	☐
20	Randy Siska	☐
21	Eric Thurston	☐
22	Simon Wheeldon	☐

GRADUATION SERIES

No.	Player	Checklist
23	Murray Bannerman, Goalie	☐
24	Gord Roberts	☐

— 1984 - 85 REGULAR ISSUE —

Cards are unnumbered ane are listed below in alphabetical order.

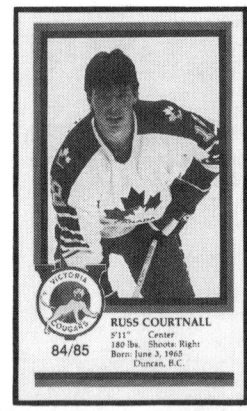

Victoria Cougars, 1984-85 Issue
Card No. 5, Russell Courtnall

Card Size: 3" X 5"
Face: Four colour, white border; Team logo, Name, Resume
Back: Black on white card stock; Name, Sponsor logos
Imprint: None
Complete Set No.: 24
Complete Set Price: 8.00   16.00 ☐

No.	Player	Checklist
1	Misko Antisin	☐
2	Greg Batters	☐
3	Chris Calverly	☐
4	Darin Choquette	☐
5	Russell Courtnall	☐
6	Rick Davidson	☐
7	Bill Gregoire	☐
8	Richard Hajdu	☐
9	Randy Hansch, Goalie	☐
10	Rob Kivell	☐
11	Brad Melin	☐
12	Jim Mentis	☐
13	Adam Morrison	☐

No.	Player	Checklist
14	Mark Morrison	☐
15	Kodie Nelson	☐
16	Ken Priestlay	☐
17	Bruce Pritchard	☐
18	Trevor Semeniuk	☐
19	Dan Sexton	☐
20	Randy Siska	☐
21	Chris Tarnowski	☐

GRADUATION SERIES

No.	Player	Checklist
22	Mel Bridgman	☐
23	Geoff Courtnall	☐
24	Torrie Robertson	☐

— 1989 - 90 REGULAR ISSUE —

These cards are unnumbered and are listed below in alphabetical order. Sponsors were Safeway, Romeo's and Flynn Printing.

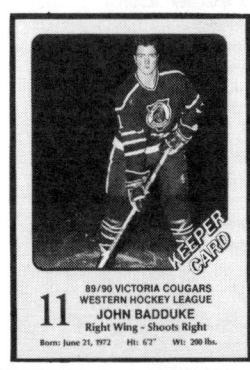

Victoria Cougars, 1989-90 Issue
Card No. 1, John Badduke

Card Size: 2 3/4" X 3 15/16"
Face: Four colour, yellow border; Jersey number, Name, Position, Resume
Back: Red and black on white card stock; Tips, Sponsor logos
Imprint: None
Complete Set No.:
Complete Set Price: 5.00   10.00 ☐

No.	Player	Checklist
1	John Badduke	☐
2	Terry Bendera	☐
3	Trevor Buchanan	☐
4	Jaret Burgoyne, Goalie	☐
5	Dino Caputo	☐
6	Chris Catellier	☐
7	Mark Cipriano	☐
8	Milan Dragicevic	☐
9	Dean Dyer	☐
10	Shayne Green	☐
11	Ryan Harrison	☐
12	Corey Jones, Goalie	☐
13	Terry Klapstein	☐
14	Jason Knox	☐
15	Curtis Nykyforuk	☐
16	Jason Peters	☐
17	Blair Scott	☐
18	Mike Seaton	☐
19	Rob Sumner	☐
20	Larry Woo	☐
21	Jarret Zukiwsky	☐

Note: Junior Team Sets are collected as complete sets. Very seldom are they broken up and sold as individual cards. For this reason the cards also are not priced individually. The complete set price is shown in EX and NRMT prices.

WHEELING THUNDERBIRDS

— 1992 - 93 REGULAR ISSUE —

Wheeling Thunderbirds, 1992-93 Issue
Card No. 10, Mike Millham

Card Size: 2 1/2" x 3 1/2"
Face: Four colour, grey border; Name, Position, Team
Back: Black on card stock; Name, Resume
Imprint: Those Guys Productions
Complete Set No.: 24
Complete Set Price: 2.50   5.00 ☐

No.	Player	Checklist
1	Wheeling Thunderbirds Checklist	☐
2	Claude Barthe	☐
3	Joel Blain	☐
4	Derek DeCosty	☐
5	Marc Deschamps	☐
6	Tom Dion	☐
7	Devin Edgerton	☐
8	Pete Heine	☐
9	Kim Maier	☐
10	Mike Millham, Goalie	☐
11	Cory Paterson	☐
12	Trevor Pochipinski	☐
13	Tim Roberts	☐
14	Mark Rodgers	☐
15	Darren Schwartz	☐
16	Trevor Senn	☐
17	Tim Tisdale	☐
18	John Uniac	☐
19	Denny MaGruder, GM	☐
20	"Those Guys": Chuck Greenwood; Jim Smith	☐
21	Larry Kish, VP/GM	☐
22	Doug Sauter, Coach	☐
23	"T-Bird", Mascot	☐
24	Doug Bacon	☐

WINDSOR SPITFIRES

— 1989 - 90 REGULAR ISSUE —

Windsor Spitfires, 1989-90 Issue
Card No. 1, Sean Burns

Card Size: 2 1/2" X 3 1/2"
Face: Four colour, white border; Name
Back: Black on white card stock; Name, Resume
Imprint: None
Complete Set No.: 22
Complete Set Price: 5.00   10.00 ☐

No.	Player	Checklist
1	Sean Burns	☐
2	Glen Craig	☐
3	Brian Forestell	☐
4	Chris Fraser	☐
5	Trent Gleason	☐
6	Jon Hartley	☐
7	Ron Jones	☐
8	Bob Leeming	☐
9	Kevin MacKay	☐
10	Kevin McDougall	☐
11	Ryan Merritt	☐
12	David Myles	☐
13	Sean O'Hagan	☐
14	Mike Polano	☐
15	Brad Smith, Coach	☐
16	Jason Snow	☐
17	Jason Stos	☐
18	Jon Stos	☐
19	Jamie Vargo	☐
20	Trevor Walsh	☐
21	K.J. White	☐
22	Jason Zohil	☐

EAST COAST HOCKEY LEAGUE

— 1992 - 1993 REGULAR ISSUE —

TOLEDO STORM

Toledo Storm, 1992-93 Issue
Card No. 19, Derek Booth

Card Size: 2 3/8" x 3 1/2"
Face: Four colour, white border; Name, Team and Sponsor's logo
Back: Black on grey and white card stock; Name, Resume, Team logo
Imprint: © None
Complete Set No.: 55
Complete Set Price: 5.00   10.00 ☐

SERIES 1

No.	Player	Checklist
1	Checklist	☐
2	Chris McSorley, Coach	☐
3	Scott Luhrmann, Equipment Specialist	☐
4	Barry Soskin, President/GM	☐
5	Tim Mouser, Dir. of Sales	☐
6	Jeff Gibbons, Dir. of Broadcasting	☐
7	Mike Williams, Goalie	☐
8	Scott King, Goalie	☐
9	Alex Hicks	☐
10	Rick Judson	☐
11	Brent Sapergia	☐
12	Iain Duncan	☐
13	Mark Deazeley	☐
14	Jeff Jablonski	☐
15	Bruce MacDonald	☐
16	Rick Corriveau	☐

786 • ARIZONA ICECATS — 1985-86 ISSUE

No.	Player	Checklist
17	Pat Pylypuik	☐
18	Alex Roberts	☐
19	Derek Booth	☐
20	Andy Suhy	☐
21	Jason Stos	☐
22	Greg Puhalski	☐
23	Wade Bartley	☐
24	Distillery Crew	☐
25	The Dawnbusters, Broadcasters	☐
26	Becky Shock, Broadcaster	☐
27	Don Davis, Broadcaster	☐
28	Beth Daniels	☐
29	Dennis O'Brien, Broadcaster	☐
30	Will Worster, Broadcaster	☐

SERIES 2

No.	Player	Checklist
1	Checklist	☐
2	Chris McSorley, Coach	☐
3	Scott Luhrmann, Equipment Specialist	☐
4	Barry Soskin, President/GM	☐
5	Tim Mouser, Director of Sales	☐
6	Jeff Gibbons, Director of Broadcasting	☐
7	Claude Scott, The Happy Trumpeter	☐
8	Scott King, Goalie	☐
9	Andy Suhy	☐
10	Pat Pylypuik	☐
11	Alex Roberts	☐
12	Mark Deazeley	☐
13	John Johnson	☐
14	Jeff Rohlicek	☐
15	Dan Wiebe	☐
16	Jeff Jablonski	☐
17	Greg Puhalski	☐
18	Bruce MacDonald	☐
19	Iain Duncan	☐
20	Rick Judson	☐
21	Alex Hicks	☐
22	Barry Potomski	☐
23	Derek Booth	☐
24	Rick Corriveau	☐
25	Mark Richards, Goalie	☐

SLOW WHISTLE

UNIVERSITY OF MINNESOTA - DULUTH
MINNESOTA BULLDOGS

— 1985 - 86 REGULAR ISSUE —

Minnesota Bulldogs, 1985-86 Issue
Card No. 28, Brett Hull

Card Size: 2 1/2" X 3 1/2"
Face: Four colour, white border; Name, Jersey number, Position
Back: Black on white card stock; Team logo, Name, Resume
Imprint: TIM & LARRY'S SPORTS CARDS • DULUTH, MN
Complete Set No.: 36
Complete Set Price: 22.50   45.00 ☐

No.	Player	Checklist
1	Skeeter Moore	☐
2	Terry Shold, Error	☐
3	Mike DeAngelis	☐
4	Rob Pallin, Error	☐
5	Norm Maciver	☐
6	Wayne Smith	☐
7	Dave Cowan, Error	☐
8	Darin Illikainen	☐
9	Rick Hayko, Goalie	☐
10	Guy Gosselin	☐
11	Paul Roff, Error	☐
12	Jim Toninato	☐
13	Tom Hanson	☐
14	Mike Cortes, Goalie	☐
15	Matt Christensen	☐
16	Bruce Fishback	☐
17	Mark Odnokon	☐
18	Brian Johnson	☐
19	Bob Alexander	☐
20	Tom Lorentz	☐
21	Roman Sindelar	☐
22	Jim Sprenger	☐
23	Dan Tousignant, Error	☐
24	Sean Toomey	☐
25	Brian Durand	☐
26	John Hyduke, Goalie, Error	☐
27	Brian Nelson, Error	☐
28	Brett Hull, Error	☐
29	Joe DeLisle	☐
30	Pat Janostin, Error	☐
31	Ben Duffy	☐
32	Sean Krakiwsky, Error	☐
33	Mike Sertich, Head Coach	☐
34	Coaches; Trainers; Assistants	☐
35	1985 - 86 U.M.D. Hockey Cheerleaders	☐
36	Jay Jackson, The Maroon Loon, Mascot	☐

ERROR LISTING

Universeity of Minnesota
Minnesota Bulldogs, 1985-86 Issue

Card No. 2, Jersey No. 26, number on jersey is 22
Card No. 3, Jersey No. 3, number on jersey is 6
Card No. 7, Jersey No. 17, number on jersey is 13
Card No. 7, Jersey number missing
Card No. 23, Jersey No. 13, number on jersey is 4
Card No. 26, Jersey No. 31, number on jersey is 35
Card No. 27, Jersey No. 11, number on jersey is 10
Card No. 28, Jersey No. 29, number on jersey is 23
Card No. 30, Jersey No. 23, number on jersey is 9
Card No. 32, Jersey No. 13, number on jersey is 26

UNIVERSITY OF ARIZONA
ARIZONA ICECATS

— 1985 - 86 REGULAR ISSUE —

Card Size: 2 1/8" X 3"
Face: Four colour, white border; Name, Jersey number, Position
Back: Negative image of face side
Imprint: None
Complete Set No.: 20
Complete Set Price: 5.00   10.00 ☐

UNCUT SHEET

No.	Player	Checklist
1	Title card: Arizona Icecats	☐
2	Dan Anderson	☐
3	Don Carlson, Goalie	☐
4	Dan Divjak	☐
5	Shane Fausel, Goalie	☐
6	Flavio Gentile	☐
7	Leo Golembiewski, Coach	☐
8	Jeremy Goltz	☐
9	Glenn Hall, Honorary Captain	☐
10	Steve Hutchings	☐
11	Icecat Leaders	☐
12	Aaron Joffe	☐
13	Greg Mitchell	☐
14	Cory Oleson	☐
15	Ricky Pope	☐
16	Drew Sibr	☐
17	Dean Sives	☐
18	Tommy Smith	☐
19	Nate Soules	☐
20	Kelly Walker	☐

BOARDING

**CHAPTER TWELVE
ERROR CARDS**

788 • ERROR CARDS

IMPERIAL TOBACCO

1910-11 POSTCARD ISSUE

No.	Player	Descriptoin
26	S. Ronan	Name misspelled Skein on face, should be Skene

SEET CAPORAL

1934-35 PHOTO ISSUE

No.	Player	Descriptoin
12	G. Carson	Name misspelled Jerry on face should be Gerry
18	W. Larochelle	Name shown as Victor not Wildor

WILLIAM PATERSON LTD

1924-25 REGULAR ISSUE

No.	Player	Description
7	Cy Denneny	Name misspelled Dennenay on face
20	Jesse Spring	Name misspelled Jess on face

ANONYMOUS

1925-26 "BORDERLESS" ISSUE

No.	Player	Description
41	S. Cleghorn	Pictured with Montreal, listed with Boston

1926-27 "BORDER" ISSUE

No.	Player	Description
6	Albert Leduc	
7	W. Larochelle	Name shown as Victor not Wildor
47	L. Berlinquette	Pictured with Montreal, listed with Toronto
100	S. Rothschild	Name misspelled Rotchild

DOMINION CHOCOLATE

1925 DOMINION ATHLETIC STARS

No.	Player	Description
69	H. Smith	Name misspelled Hooly on face and back, should be "Hooley"
117	O. Cleghorn	Name misspelled Ogie on face and back

O-PEE-CHEE

1934-35 REGULAR ISSUE - SERIES B

No.	Player	Description
51	L. Aurie	Name shown as Laurie on face and back

1935-36 REGULAR ISSUE - SERIES C

No.	Player	Description
92	R. Jenkins	Name misspelled Rogers on back should be "Roger"

1936-37 REGULAR ISSUE - SERIES D

No.	Player	Description
113	A. Wiebe	Name misspelled Weibe on face

1937-38 REGULAR ISSUE - SERIES E

No.	Player	Description
151	B. MacKenzie	Name misspelled McKenzie on back

No.	Player	Description
165	E. Robinson	Name misspelled Earle in facsimile signature
176	R. Lorraine	Name misspelled Lorrain on back
179	G. Shannon	Name misspelled Jerry on face and back

1939-40 REGULAR ISSUE

No.	Player	Description
11	W. Stanowski	Name misspelled Stanowsky on face

1968-69 REGULAR ISSUE

No.	Player	Description
3	D. Awrey	Photo on front Skip Krake
43	S. Krake	Photo on front Don Awrey
55	P. MacDonald	Name on back: Jacques Parker; should be: Calvin Parker Macdonald
177	Barclay Plager	Card shows Bob Plager
183	A. Stanley	Name misspelled Alan on back, should be "Allan"
193	K. McCreary	Keith McCreary, "Without Number"

1968-69 PUCK STICKERS

No.	Player	Description
13	Glenn Hall	Name misspelled Glen on face

1969-70 REGULAR ISSUE

No.	Player	Description
162	Nick Libett	Name misspelled Libbett on face and back
205A	Phil Esposito	Card numbered 214 on back

1970-71 REGULAR ISSUE

No.	Player	Description
284A	Bobby Orr	No Overprint

1971-72 REGULAR ISSUE

No.	Player	Description
26	Garry Unger	Name misspelled Gary on back
29	M. Tardif	Name misspelled Tardiff on face
145	G. Lapointe	Shows Lapointe wearing jersey #10 which was Lafleur's number
146	C. Larose	Name misspelled La Rose on face and back
148	G. Lafleur	Name misspelled La Fleur on face and back
225	P. McDuffe	Stats show position played as defenceman should be goalie
256	J. Plante	"63" shutouts, should be "77".

1972-73 REGULAR ISSUE

No.	Player	Description
19	Checklist	Same as Card No. 190
23	R. Smith	Total games should be 262, not 265
48A	Jean Ratelle	Position shown as defence on face should be centre
85A	Brad Park	Position shown as centre should be defence.
100	R. Vachon	Name misspelled Ragatien on back Should be "Rogatien"
162	D. Balon	Name misspelled Ballon on back
182	NHL Action	Card shows Gilbert Perreault, should be Rick Martin
184	D. DeJordy	Back shows team as Atlanta Flames, face shows correct team as Detroit Red Wings
231	C. Larose	Name misspelled LaRose on face
240	G. Sheppard	Name misspelled Greg Shepherd on face and back, should be Gregg Sheppard
256	K. Schinkel	Name misspelled Shinkel on face
278	G. O'Flaherty	Name misspelled Jerry on face, should be "Gerry"
284	R. Smith	
334A	Checklist 3	Numbers 335 to 341 incorrectly listed
337	W. Carleton	Name misspelled Carlton on face

1973-74 REGULAR ISSUE

No.	Player	Description
8	G. Sheppard	Name misspelled Greg on face and back, should be Gregg

No.	Player	Description
129	Checklist	Card is the same as No. 263
235	Gregg Boddy	Name misspelled Greg on face;

1974-75 REGULAR ISSUE

No.	Player	Description
24	J. Lemaire,	Jacques Lemaire in Buffalo Sabres uniform should be Montreal Canadiens uniform
28	Boston Bruins	Card face shows John Bucyk (22.3), back of card lists Ken Hodge (19.9)
54	Checklist 1	
107	B. Plager	Shows Barclay Plager should be Bob
178	C. Lefley	Shows Pierre Bouchard
233	New York (I)	B. Harris and R. Stewart, Goals D. Potvin, Assists, Points; R. Stewart; Scoring Pct. Name misspelled Steward under Scoring Pct.
275	G. Goldup	Name misspelled Glen on face, should be Glenn
292	W. Paiement	Name misspelled Paiemont on face
298	F. Thomson	Name misspelled Thompson on face
311	Checklist 3	Name misspelled Gilies Marotte
321	H. Richard	Points total incorrect
330	Montreal Canadiens Checklist	Name misspelled Glen Holdup
349	Gregg Boddy	Name misspelled Greg on face
353	Glenn Resch	Name misspelled Glen on face
360	D. Tallon	Name misspelled Talon on face
365	T. Bergman	Name misspelled Tommie on face, should be Thommie

1975-76 REGULAR ISSUE

No.	Player	Description
70	Y. Cournoyer	Name misspelled Yvon on face should be Yvan
99	Checklist 1	#11 Name misspelled Edestand, #70 Name misspelled Yvon
107	D. Risebrough	Card shows Bob Gainey
126	G. Lafleur	Shows position played as defense should be centre
223	M. Tremblay	Shows Craig McTavish
244	T. Irvine	Shows Ted Harris;should be Ted Irvine
267B	Checklist 4	#362 Name misspelled Laroque; #396 Name misspelled Snepts
337	T. Crisp	Shows Don Saleski
359A	P. Jarry	Missing "Traded" banner
382	S. Gilbertson	Shows Denis Dupere

1976-77 REGULAR ISSUE

No.	Player	Description
267	B. McKenzie	Name misspelled KcKenzie on face
326	J.P. LeBlanc	Name misspelled LaBlanc on face and back
348	L. McDonald	Name misspelled MacDonald on face and back

1977-78 REGULAR ISSUE

No.	Player	Description
133	J.P. LeBlanc	Name misspelled Leblanc on face
249	Checklist 2	#133 Name misspelled Leblanc
312	R. Bourbonnais	Shows Bernie Federko
369	J. Lynch	Shows Bill Collins

1978-79 REGULAR ISSUE

No.	Player	Description
216	B. Maxwell	Shows Brad Maxwell; should be Bryan Maxwell

1979-80 REGULAR ISSUE

No.	Player	Description
59	R. Smith	Kingston misspelled Kinston on back
137	R. Pierce	Shows Ron Delorme
141	T. Ruskowski	Name misspelled Ruskouski on face and back
147	P. Marsh	
158	G. Croteau	
237	Checklist 2	#245, Bruins name misspelled Buins
306	J. Bob Kelly	"Now With Oilers" shows Bob Kelly

ERROR CARDS • 789

1980 - 81 REGULAR ISSUE

No.	Player	Description
275	D. Risebrough	Shows Serge Savard

1981 - 82 REGULAR ISSUE

No.	Player	Description
330	P. Brasar	Shows Brent Ashton
338	R. Lanz	Shows Thomas Gradin
366	D. Hoyda	Shows Doug Lecuyer
374	M. Mattson	Name misspelled Mattsson on face

1982 - 83 REGULAR ISSUE

No.	Player	Description
346	Ivan Hlinka	Shows Jiri Bubla

1983 - 84 REGULAR ISSUE

No.	Player	Description
105	S. Larmer	Shows Steve Ludzik
106	S. Ludzik	Shows Steve Larmer
126	C. Micalef	Name misspelled Carrado on face should be Corrado

1984 - 85 REGULAR ISSUE

No.	Player	Description
260	L. DeBlois	Name misspelled Deblois on face and back
297	A. Bester	Name misspelled Alan on face and back should be Allan

1986 - 87 REGULAR ISSUE

No.	Player	Description
226	Ullie Hiemer	Name misspelled Uli on face and back
247	J. Otto	Shows Moe Lemay
249	M. Lemay	Shows Joel Otto

1987 - 88 REGULAR ISSUE

No.	Player	Description
9	R. Carlyle	Name misspelled Calryle on face and back
24	M. Thelven	Name misspelled Thelvin on face and back
67	G. Gallant	Name misspelled Gerald on face and back should be Gerard
183	B. Nicholls	Name misspelled Nichols on face and back
184	Dirk Graham	Name misspelled Dick on face and back
220	M. Marois	Name misspelled Marios on face and back

1988 - 89 REGULAR ISSUE

No.	Player	Description
99A	Checklist 1	
120	W. Gretzky	"C" for position missing from top left corner
229	K. Lowe	Shows Gretzky's stats on back
233	M. Marois	Name misspelled Marios on face and back
241	M. Osborne	Name misspelled Osbourne on face and back

1989 - 90 REGULAR ISSUE

No.	Player	Description
274	M. Osborne	Name misspelled Osbourne on face and back
292	H. Jarvenpaa	Name misspelled Jaryenpaa on face
326	B. Leetch	Shows David Shaw

1990 - 91 REGULAR ISSUE

No.	Player	Description
5	Jari Kurri	Name misspelled Jarri on face and back
54	Carey Wilson	Name misspelled Cary on face and back
120	W. Gretzky	Total assists should be 1,302
131	J. Patrick	Border colour incorrect for New York Rangers cards

1990 - 91 REGULAR ISSUE

No.	Player	Description
235	S. Leach,	Name misspelled Stephan on face and back, should be Stephen
401	J. Kordic	Position should read left wing not defence
445	S. Mylnikov	Name misspelled Sergi on face and back, should be Sergei
501	Arturs Irbe	Name misspelled Artur on face and back

1990 - 91 PREMIER ISSUE

No.	Player	Description
19	M. Craig	Position centre, should be right wing
24	P. Olav Djoos	Shoots left, should be right
96	M. Ricci	Birthdate, November 27, 1971, should be October 27, 1971

1991 - 92 REGULAR ISSUE

No.	Player	Description
8	S. Fedorov	Name misspelled Federov on face
45	F. Olausson	Name misspelled Clausson on face
80	P. LaFontaine	First 'A' in surname is reversed
322	T. Fleury	Name misspelled Fluery on back
357	N. Lacombe	Name misspelled Norman on face and back, should be Normand
431	C. Lapointe	Name misspelled LaPointe on face and back
439	A. Kasatonov	Name misspelled Alexi on back, should be Alexei
471	A. Godynyuk	Name misspelled Godynuk on face and back

1991 - 92 REGULAR ISSUE INSERT SET - SAN JOSE/RUSSIA

No.	Player	Description
8S	J. Myllys	'Shoots right 'should be 'Catches left'
15R	V. Gordijuk	Name misspelled Victor on face and back, should be Viktor
16R	Y. Khmylev	Name misspelled Khmiliov on face and back
37R	I. Korolev	Name misspelled Korolyov on face and back
40R	A. Lomakin	Name misspelled Adrei on face, should be Andrei
44R	S. Sorokin	Name misspelled Serguei on face and back, should be Sergei
62R	I. Ulanov	Name misspelled Vlanov on face and back

1991 - 92 PREMIER ISSUE

No.	Player	Description
118A	V. Konstantinov	Back shows Nicklas Lidstrom; Also reads:"11th Overall...", should be "12th Overall..."
189	M. Krushelnyski	Name misspelled Krushelnynski on back

WORLD WIDE GUM

1933 - 34 ICE KINGS

No.	Player	Description
3	A. Joliat	Name misspelled Aurele on face and back should be Aurel
8	B. Siebert	Name misspelled Seibert on face

V129 ANONYMOUS

1933 - 34 ISSUE

No.	Player	Description
28	B. Siebert	Name misspelled Seibert on face
35	R. Beattie	Name misspelled Beatty on face

ST. LAWRENCE STARCH COMPANY

BEE HIVE VARIATIONS
GROUP ONE PHOTOS - 1934 TO 1944

No.	Player	Description
70	R. Mitchell	Name misspelled Mitchel on face
83	L. Trudel	Name misspelled Trudell on face
100	G. Giesebrecht	Name misspelled Geisebrecht on face
146	T. DeMers	Name misspelled Demers on face
163	L. Lamoureux	Name misspelled Lamoureaux on face
192	Gerry Carson	Name misspelled Jerry on face
204	Gerry Shannon	Name misspelled Jerry on face
252	P. Slobodzian	Name misspelled Slobodian on face
318	Jimmy Fowler	Name misspelled Jimmie on face
348	W. Stanowski	Name misspelled Stanowsky on face

GROUP TWO PHOTOS - 1944 TO 1963

No.	Player	Description
124	Gerry Melnyk	Name misspelled Jerry on face
158	Gerry Couture	Name misspelled Jerry on face
169B	F. Gauthier	
196	Gerry Melnyk	Name misspelled Jerry on face
231	F. Curry	Name misspelled Currie on face
357B	Jean Ratelle	Name misspelled John on face
394B	B. Cullen	Photo of Brian Cullen
412	Gerry James	Name misspelled Jerry on face
454A	Allan Stanley	Name misspelled Alan on face

GROUP THREE PHOTOS - 1964 TO 1967

No.	Player	Description
25	R. Schock	Name misspelled Shock on face
35	G. Hall	Name misspelled Glen on face, should be Glenn

SWEET CAPORAL

1934 - 1935 PHOTO ISSUE

No.	Player	Description
12	G. Carson	Name misspelled Jerry on face, should be Gerry
18	W. Larochelle	
112	A. Joliat	Name misspelled Aurele on face, should be Aurel

QUAKER OATS

1945 - 54 PHOTOS

No.	Player	Description
29A	R. Leger	Name misspelled Liger on face
29B	R. Leger	Name misspelled Liger on face
29C	R. Leger	Name misspelled Liger on face

1955 - 56 PHOTOS

No.	Player	Description
62	B. Siebert	Name misspelled Seibert on face and back

CHLP / CKAC / CKVL RADIO

No.	Player	Description
42	T. DeMers	Name misspelled Demers on face

PARKHURST

1951 - 52 REGULAR ISSUE

No.	Player	Description
33	E. Kryznowski	Name misspelled Kryanowski
46	L. (Lee) Fogolin	

ERROR CARDS

1952-53 REGULAR ISSUE

No.	Player	Description
3	B. Geoffrion	Name misspelled Gioffrion on back
29	E. Kryznowski	Name misspelled Krysanowski on face and back

1953-54 REGULAR ISSUE

No.	Player	Description
37	A. Arbour	Photo shows Bill Dineen
38	B. Dineen	Photo shows Al Arbour
88	J. Peirson	Name misspelled Pierson on back

1954-55 REGULAR ISSUE

No.	Player	Description
32	J. Thomson	Name misspelled Thompson on back
65	J. Bower	Name misspelled Bowers on back

1955-56 REGULAR ISSUE

No.	Player	Description
62	B. Siebert	Name misspelled Seibert on face and back

1957-58 REGULAR ISSUE

No.	Player	Description
19	A. MacNeil	Name misspelled McNeil on face and back
23	Allan Stanley	Name misspelled on face - Allen and on back - Alan
46	J. Bower	Name misspelled Bowers on face

1960-61 REGULAR ISSUE

No.	Description
28	Gerry Melnyk — Name misspelled Jerry on face and back

1961-62 REGULAR ISSUE

No.	Player	Description
44	W. Connelly	Name misspelled Connolly on face and back and he played 61-62 season for Boston

1991-92 ENGLISH ISSUE SERIES ONE

No.	Player	Description
3	V. Ruzicka	Name misspelled Vladimar on face should be Vladimir
20	T. Forslund	Name misspelled Thomas on back should be Tomas
37	N. Lidstrom	Name misspelled Niklas on face should be Nicklas
107	G. Healy	Name misspelled Healey on face

1991-92 ENGLISH ISSUE SERIES TWO

No.	Player	Description
266	V. Kozlov	Name misspelled Vyacheslav on face and back should be Viacheslav

1991-92 FRENCH ISSUE SERIES ONE

No.	Player	Description
3	V. Ruzicka	Name misselled Ruzika
20	T. Forslund	Name misspelled Thomas on back
37	N. Lidstrom	Name misspelled Niklas on face
107	G. Healy	Name misspelled Healey on back

1991-92 FRENCH ISSUE SERIES TWO

No.	Player	Description
266	V. Kozlov	Name misspelled Vyacheslav should be Viacheslav

TOPPS

1957-58 REGULAR ISSUE

No.	Player	Description
35	T. Sawchuk	Name misspelled Sawchuck on face

1958-59 REGULAR ISSUE

No.	Player	Description
8	Gordie Howe	Name misspelled Gordy on face
45	J. Toppazzini	Name misspelled Toppazini on face
47	P. Goegan	Name misspelled Geogan on face

1959-60 REGULAR ISSUE

No.	Player	Description
8	A. Delvecchio	Delvecchio listed as "wing" on back should be "centre"
9	D. McKenney	Name misspelled McKenny on face
25	Barry Cullen	French resume refers to his brother Brian
40	Charlie Burns	Name misspelled Charley on face
47	B. Hull	Hull listed as "centre" should be "left wing"

1960-61 REGULAR ISSUE

No.	Player	Description
34	F. Frederickson	Name misspelled Fredrickson on face
40	D. McKenney	Name misspelled McKenny on face

1961-62 REGULAR ISSUE

No.	Player	Description
4	D. Smith	Position shown as forward should be defense

1962-63 REGULAR ISSUE

No.	Player	Description
9	D. Smith	
38	A. McDonald	Name misspelled MacDonald on face and back
64	P. Hannigan	Name misspelled Hanninigan on back

1963-64 REGULAR ISSUE

No.	Player	Description
37	A. McDonald	

1965-66 REGULAR ISSUE

No.	Player	Description
28	Garry Peters	Name misspelled Gary on face
40	Poul Popiel	Name misspelled Paul on face and back
76	Y. Cournoyer	Name misspelled Yvon on face and back, should be Yvan

1967-68 REGULAR ISSUE

No.	Player	Description
37	D. Awrey	Card shows Skip Krake
93	S. Krake	Card shows Don Awrey

1968-69 REGULAR ISSUE

No.	Player	Description
3	D. Awrey	Card shows Skip Krake
43	S. Krake	Card shows Don Awrey

1970-71 REGULAR ISSUE

No.	Player	Description
56	C. Larose	Name misspelled LaRose on face and back
122	Poul Popiel	Name misspelled Paul on face and back

1973-74 REGULAR ISSUE

No.	Player	Description
8	G. Sheppard	Name misspelled Greg on face and back, should be Gregg

1974-75 REGULAR ISSUE

No.	Player	Description
24	J. Lemaire	Lemaire in Buffalo Sabres Uniform should be Montreal Canadiens
107	B. Plager	Card shows Barclay Plager
178	C. Lefley	Card shows Pierre Bouchard

1975-76 REGULAR ISSUE

No.	Player	Description
70	Y. Cournoyer	Name misspelled Yvon on face should be Yvan
83	Buffalo Sabres	Name misspelled Gary on back
84	Chicago Black Hawks	
88	Kansas City Scouts	Name misspelled Dennis on back
95	Philadelphia Flyers	Philadelphia misspelled on back
97	Vancouver Canucks	Mike Robitaille's card shown as 242 should be 24 and Dennis Ververgaert, Card No. 42 not shown on checklist
101	G. Gagnon	Name misspelled Germain on face and back, should be Germaine
107	D. Risebrough	Card shows Bob Gainey
126	G. Lafleur	Listed as defence
244	T. Irvine	Card shows Ted Harris

1977-78 REGULAR ISSUE

No.	Player	Description
138A	B. MacAdam	

1978-79 REGULAR ISSUE

No.	Player	Description
216	B. Maxwell	Card shows Brad Maxwell

1979-80 REGULAR ISSUE

No.	Player	Description
137	R. Pierce	Card shows Ron Delorme

1987-88 REGULAR ISSUE

No.	Player	Description
24	M. Thelven	Name misspelled Thelvin on face
67	G. Gallant	Name misspelled Gerald on face, should be Gerard
183	B. Nicholls	Name misspelled Nichols on face and back
184	D. Graham	

1990-91 REGULAR ISSUE

No.	Player	Description
5	Jari Kurri	Name misspelled Jarri on face
54	Carey Wilson	Name misspelled Cary on face and back
120	W. Gretzky	Assist total on back should be 1,302
131	James Patrick	Border colour should be blue to match teammates
204	Daren Puppa	Name misspelled Darren on face and back
235	Stephen Leach	Name misspelled Stephan on face
299	D. McLlwain	

1991-92 REGULAR ISSUE

No.	Player	Description
8	S. Fedorov	Name misspelled Federov on face
45	F. Olausson	Name misspelled Clausson on face
78	D. Khristich	Name misspelled Dmitri on face and back should be Dimitri
322	T. Fleury	Name misspelled Fluery on back
357	N. Lacombe	Name misspelled Norman on face and back should be Normand
431	C. Lapointe	Name misspelled LaPointe on face and back
439	A. Kasatonov	Name misspelled Alexi on back, should be Alexei

ERROR CARDS • 791

No.	Player	Description
471	A. Godynyuk	Name misspelled Godynuk on face and back

1991 - 92 INSERT SET '90-'91 TEAM SCORING LEADERS

No.	Player	Description
14	T. Fleury	Name misspelled Fleury on back

1991 - 92 STADIUM CLUB

No.	Player	Description
102	P. Verbeek	Sarnia misspelled Sarina
359	D. Khristich	Name misspelled Dmitri on face and back should be Dimitri
363	N. Lacombe	Name misspelled Norman on face and back should be Normand

1992 - 93 REGULAR ISSUE

No.	Player	Description
115	E. Davydov	

1992 - 93 INSERT SET GOLD ISSUE

No.	Player	Description
115	E. Davydov	
120	F. Olausson	

1992 - 93 STADIUM CLUB SERIES ONE

No.	Player	Description
192	P. Ahola	No hockey team shown on back

SERIES TWO

No.	Player	Description
264	J. Reekie	
298	J. Chychrun	

THE TORONTO STAR

1963 - 64 HOCKEY STARS IN ACTION

No.	Player	Description
11	A. Delvecchio	Name misspelled Alec on face and back should be Alex
22	M. Pronovost	Name misspelled Provost on face and back

SHIRRIFF

1960 - 61 HOCKEY COINS

No.	Player	Description
51	Gerry Melnyk	Name misspelled Jerry on face

1961 - 62 SHIRRIFF / SALADA HOCKEY COINS

No.	Player	Description
38	Gerry Melnyk	Name misspelled Jerry on face

COLGATE

1970 - 71 STAMPS

No.	Player	Description
17	M. Tardif	Name misspelled

1971 - 72 HEADS

No.	Player	Description
15b	N. Ullman	Name misspelled Ullmann

ESSO

1970 - 71 POWER PLAYERS

No.	Player	Description
63	K. Magnuson	Name misspelled Magnusson on face

EDDIE SARGENT PROMOTIONS LTD

1972 - 73 STICKERS

No.	Player	Description
130	Denis DeJordy	Name misspelled Dennis on face

LIPTON SOUP

1974 - 75 ISSUE

No.	Player	Description
36	J. Pappin	Name misspelled Papin on face

PEPSICO

1980 - 81 CAPS

No.	Player	Description
6	K. LaVallee	Name misspelled Lavalee on face

HOCKEY HALL OF FAME

1983 REGULAR ISSUE

No.	Player	Description
49	F. Frederickson	Name misspelled Fredrickson on back
236	S. Schriner	Name misspelled Sweeney on back should be Sweeny

1987 REGULAR ISSUE

No.	Player	Description
49	F. Frederickson	Name misspelled Fredrickson on back
236	S. Schriner	Name misspelled Sweeney on back, should be Sweeny

VACHON FOODS

1983 - 84 ISSUE

No.	Player	Description
96A	W. Poddubny	Shows Peter Inhacek

KRAFT

1986 - 87 DRAWINGS DREAM TEAM COLLECTABLE CARDS

No.	Player	Description
69	S. Smyl	Name misspelled Syml on face

BOWMAN

1990 - 91 ISSUE

No.	Player	Description
12	A. Secord	Card shows Duane Sutter
46	P. Svoboda	Card shows Chris Chelios
136	D. McLlwain	Position on card should be "Shoots Left"
181	C. Donatelli	Birthdate should be 11/22/65

1990 - 91 INSERT SET HAT TRICKS

No.	Player	Description
HT8	M. Gartner	Pictured with Minnesota listed with Toronto

1991 - 92 REGULAR ISSUE

No.	Player	Description
50	S. Fedorov	Name misspelled Federov on back
184	M. McSorley	Name misspelled McSorely on face
248	N. Lacombe	Name misspelled Norman on face and back should be Normand
307	D. Khristich	Name misspelled Dmitri on face and back should be Dimitri
350	G. Wesley	Name misspelled Glenn on face and back should be Glen

1992 - 93 REGULAR ISSUE

No.	Player	Description
257	J. Chychrun	Name misspelled Chychurn on face

PRO SET

1990 - 1991 SERIES TWO

No.	Name	Description
406	A. Brickley	Back reads C/LW; Should read LW
428	J. Cloutier	Position and jersey number in wrong colour
470A	T. Ewen	Shows Eric Desjardins on back
475	R. Walter	Position should read "LW" on face and back
480	A. Stewart	Name misspelled Alan on face and back should be Allan
533A		Inverted trademark
556	P. Zezel	Missing trade stats
593	S. Matteau	Position on face should read "RW"
596	K. Sabourin	Position on face should read "D"
597	T. Sweeney	Position on face and back should read "LW"
598	E. Belfour	Hometown misspelled "Carmen"
600	M. McNeill	Position on back should read "C"
613	M. Craig	Listed as #20 but jersey shows #50
623	D. Marcinyshyn	Card number is smaller than others
632	J. Jagr	Noticeable red blotch on back
634	S. Gordon	Team name misspelled Nordique on back

1991 - 92 ENGLISH ISSUE

No.	Player	Description
15	P. Turgeon	Birthday shown as Aug. 28, should be Aug. 29
17	B. Hogue	Back shows Hogue played for Winnipeg 88/89, 90/91; He always played for Buffalo
19	D. Bodger	Shows first season stats with Sabres as second highest should be third highest
130B	G. Carbonneau	Face: Guy Carbonneau, Back: shows the back of Card No. 4
328	Neil Wilkinson	Shows birthplace as Selkirk, Minnesota; should be Selkirk, Manitoba
527	T. Forslund	Name misspelled Thomas on face and back should be Tomas
531	N. Lidstrom	Name misspelled Niklas on face
547	S. Niedermayer	Name misspelled Neidermayer on face
603	K. McLean	Leader logo shows PPG should be GAA

1991 - 92 FRENCH ISSUES

No.	Player	Description
15	P. Turgeon	Birthday shown as Aug. 28 should be Aug. 29
17	B. Hogue	Back shows Hogue played for Winnipeg in 88/89, 90/91. Hogue played for Buffalo
19	D. Bodger	Shows first season stats Sabres, had second highest, should be third highest
47	R. McGill	Reads Drafted By San Jose should read Sélectionné San Jose
120	S. Lebeau	Name misspelled Stéphane on face and back should be Stéphan
527	T. Forslund	Name misspelled Thomas on face and back should be Tomas

ERROR CARDS

SCORE

1990 - 91 CANADIAN ISSUE

No.	Player	Description
52	M. Vernon	Vernon won WHL MVP only once
102A	M. Fitzpatrick	"Catches Right"; Corrected: "Catches left"
202	J. Johnson	Back should read "New Hope, Min."
231A	D. McLlwain	"Shoots Right"; Corrected: "Shoots Left"
259A	D. Evason	Reversed Photo
282	S Beauregard	Back should read Fort Wayne
407A	J. Waite	Back: "Catches Right" should read "Catches Left"

1990 - 91 AMERICAN ISSUE

No.	Player	Description
52	M. Vernon	Vernon won WHL MVP only once
102A	M. Fitzpatrick	" Catches Right" should read " Catches Left"
202	J. Johnson	Back should read "New Hope, Minn."
259A	D. Evason	Photo reversed
282	S Beauregard	Played for Fort Wayne not Fort Worth

1991 - 92 CANADIAN ISSUE

No.	Player	Description
346	D. Hasek	Name misspelled Dominic on face and back should be Dominik
394	N. Lacombe	Name misspelled Norman on face and back should be Normand

1991 - 92 BILINGUAL ISSUE

No.	Player	Description
346	D. Hasek	Name misspelled Dominic on face and back should be Dominik
394	N. Lacombe	Name misspelled Norman on face and back should be Normand

1991 - 92 AMERICAN ISSUE

No.	Player	Description
316	D. Hasek	Name misspelled Dominic on face and back

1991 ROOKIE AND TRADED

No.	Player	Description
71T	N. Lidstrom	Name misspelled Niklas on face and back, should be Nicklas

1993 - 94 CANADIAN ISSUE

No.	Player	Description
209	D. Mirinov	Name misspelled Dimitri on face nd back, should be Dmitri

UPPER DECK

1990 - 91 LOW NUMBERS - ENGLISH

No.	Player	Description
228	D. Chyzowski	Face: Uniform #9; should be #89

1990 - 91 LOW NUMBERS - FRENCH

No.	Player	Description
228	D. Chyzowski	Face: Uniform #9; should be #89

1991 - 92 LOW NUMBERS - ENGLISH

No.	Player	Description
3	D. Filimonov	Name misspelled Dmitri on face and back should be Dimitri
26	N. Lidstrom	Name misspelled Niklas on face and back should be Nicklas

1991 - 92 HIGH NUMBERS - ENGLISH

No.	Player	Description
587	N. Lidstrom	Name misspelled Niklas on face and back should be Nicklas

1991 - 92 LOW NUMBERS - FRENCH

No.	Player	Description
3	D. Filimonov	Name misspelled Dmitri on face and back should be Dimitri
26	N. Lidstrom	Name misspelled Niklas on face and back should be Nicklas

1991 - 92 HIGH NUMBERS - FRENCH

No.	Player	Description
587	N. Lidstrom	Name misspelled Niklas on face and back should be Nicklas

1992 - 93 LOW NUMBERS

No.	Player	Description
83	D. Mironov	Name misspelled Dimitri Mirinov on face and back

N.H.L. TEAM SETS

EDMONTON OILERS

TEAM ISSUES

1979 - 80 POSTCARD ISSUE

No.	Player	Description
18A	E. Mio	Birthdate reads Jan. 31, 1979, should be Jan. 31, 1954

RED ROOSTER

1984 - 85 REGULAR ISSUE

No.	Player	Description
19	W. Lindstrom	Name misspelled Willie on face should be Willi

ACTION MAGAZINE

1988 - 89 TENTH ANNIVERSARY

No.	Player	Description
138	B. Baltimore	Name misspelled Bryon on face and back should be Byron

HARTFORD WHALERS

THE GROUND ROUND JUNIOR WHALERS

1988 - 89 POSTCARD ISSUE

No.	Player	Description
12	B. Peterson	Jersey number missing from back
18	C. Wilson	Jersey number missing

MINNESOTA NORTH STARS

TEAM ISSUES

1984 - 85 ISSUE

No.	Player	Description
2	W. Plett	Name misspelled Willie on face

VACHON

1988 SUPER COLLECTION

No.	Player	Description
11A	J. Laperriere	Missing number
17A	M. McPhee	Missing number
60A	M. Lalor	Missing number

MONTREAL CANADIENS

O-PEE-CHEE

1993 HOCKEYFEST PROMOTIONAL SHEET

No.	Player	Description
21	A. Joliat	Name misspelled Joliate on card

SMOKEY

1990 - 91 REGULAR ISSUE

No.	Player	Description
3	P. Bondra	Name misspelled Bondran on face

WINNIPEG JETS

TEAM ISSUES

1986 - 87 POSTCARD ISSUE

No.	Player	Description
19	F. Olausson	

POLICE

1984 - 85 REGULAR ISSUE

No.	Player	Description
17	P. Pooley	Name misspelled Paul on face should be Poul

WORLD HOCKEY ASSOCIATION

O-PEE-CHEE

1973 - 74 POSTERS

No.	Player	Description
19	B. Campbell	Name misspelled Brian on face should be Bryan

1974 - 75 REGULAR ISSUE

No.	Player	Description
53	Checklist	Misspelled #36 J.P . Leblanc

1975 - 76 REGULAR ISSUE

No.	Player	Description
3	S. Aubry	Name misspelled Aubrey on face
9	B. Baltimore	Name misspelled Bryon on face and back should be Byron
15	V-P. Ketola	Hyphen missing from name on face and back should be Veli-Pekka Ketola
85	N. Lapointe	Name misspelled LaPoint on back
87	GARY Jarrett	Name misspelled Garry on face and back
89	G. Labossierre	Name misspelled Labossiere on face and back
109	L-E. Sjoberg	Name misspelled Sjoverg on face
131	Checklist	Misspelled #9 Bryon; #15 without hyphen, misspelled #87 Garry

ERROR CARDS • 793

1977 - 78 REGULAR ISSUE

No.	Player	Description
58	Checklist	Misspelled #13 Leduc should be LeDuc

WORLD HOCKEY

PANINI

1979 STICKERS

No.	Player	Description
140	V. Tretiak	Name misspelled Vladislav Tretjak on face

RED ACE INTERNATIONAL

1992 RUSSIAN NHL STARS

No.	Player	Description
4	N. Bortchevski	Name misspelled Bortchevsky on face and back
6	V. Butsayev	Name misspelled Viacheslav on face and back should be Vyacheslav
7	A. Cherbayev	Name misspelled Cherbajev on face and back

1992 RUSSIAN STARS

No.	Player	Description
1	D. Kasparaitis	Name misspelled Kasparajtis on face and back
13	Arturs Irbe	Name misspelled Artur on face and back
21	S. Ozolinch	Name misspelled Ozolinsh on face and back
32	L. Berdichevsky	Name misspelled Berdichevski on face and back

AMERICAN AND INTERNATIONAL HOCKEY LEAGUES

PROCARDS

1988 - 89 AMERICAN HOCKEY LEAGUE

No.	Player	Description
52	L. Carson	Name misspelled Lindsy on face
238	J. Ralph	Stats missing from back of card

1988 - 89 INTERNATIONAL HOCKEY LEAGUE

No.	Player	Description
117	J. Torkki	

1990 - 1991 AHL IHL

No.	Player	Description
21	R. Bennett	Face: "Ric", Back: "Eric";; should be Ric

1991 - 1992 AHL IHL

No.	Player	Description
24	Rochester Americans,	Incorrect: Card No. 24 Di Vita Correct: Card No. 17 Di Vita
92	Fredericton Canadiens,	Incorrect: Card No. 92 Dary Correct: Card No. 71 Darcy
238	Cape Breton Oilers,	Incorrect: Card No. 238, Haywood Correct: Card No. 226, Hawgood
262	Fort Wayne Komets,	Incorrect: Card No. 262 Shanunessy Correct: Cards No. 247 Shaunessey
405	R. Backstrom	Card shows No. 404 should be No. 405
406	R. Kozuback	Shows No. 405 should be No. 406
407	Phoenix Roadrunners	Shows No. 406, should be No. 407
428	Utica Devils	Incorrect: Card No. 428 Hankinson Correct: Card No. 413 Hankison
619	C. Fraser	Numbered 618 should be 619

ARENA HOLOGRAMS

1991 ENGLISH ISSUE

No.	Player	Description
12	M.. Naslund	Name misspelled Marcus on face, should be Markus

1991 INSERT SET AUTOGRAPHED CARDS ENGLISH

No.	Player	Description
12	M.. Naslund	Name misspelled Marcus on face should be Markus

1991 FRENCH ISSUE

No.	Player	Description
12	M.. Naslund	Name misspelled Marcus on face Should be Markus

1991 INSERT SET AUTOGRAPHED CARDS - FRENCH

No.	Player	Description
12	M.. Naslund	Name misspelled Marcus on face should be Markus

MEMORIAL CUP 7TH INNING SKETCH

1990 REGULAR ISSUE

No.	Player	Description
84	D. Cralevich	

1991 REGULAR ISSUE

No.	Player	Description
67	R. Larche	Name misspelled Larohe on face

ONTARIO AND QUEBEC HOCKEY LEAGUES

ANONYMOUS

1952 - 53 ISSUE

No.	Player	Description
86	S. Parker	Team name misspelled Owhawa on back

LAVAL DIARY

1951 - 52 ISSUE

No.	Player	Description
60	E. Oakley	

MINOR LEAGUE TEAM SETS

LONDON KNIGHTS

1985 - 86 P.L.A.Y.

No.	Player	Description
28	F. Kean	"Director of Public and Marketing; Director of Public and Marketing Relations"

UNIVERSITY OF MINNESOTA - DULUTH

MINNESOTA BULLDOGS

1985 - 86 ISSUE

No.	Player	Description
2	T. Shold	Jersey No. 26, number on jersey is 22
4	R. Pallin	
7	D. Cowan	Jersey No. 17, number on jersey is 13. Jersey number missing
11	P. Roff	
23	D. Tousignant	Jersey No. 13, number on jersey is 4
26	J. Hyduke	Jersey No. 31, number on jersey is 35
27	B. Nelson	Jersey No. 11, number on jersey is 10
28	B. Hull	Jersey No. 29, number on jersey is 23
30	P. Janostin	Jersey No. 23, number on jersey is 9
32	S. Krakiwsky	Jersey No. 13, number on jersey is 26

KNEEING

GLOSSARY OF TERMS

ACC: Acronym for American Card Catalog coding system.
AS: All Star player.
G: All-Time Great player.
Checklist Card: A card listing the players name and associated card numbers making up a set or subset. Unmarked checklist cards have a high value.
Album: A paper or plastic booklet issued by the company to hold a specific set of cards.
Facsimile Autograph: A player's autograph produced mechanically on a card or photograph, as opposed to an actual signature.
C Card: A cigarette card produced and issued in Canada.
Coin: A disk made of plastic or metal containing the picture of a player.
Common: A regular card of no premium value.
Collector Issue: A complete set of cards sold directly by the supplier without any associated product or sponsor.
Combination Card: A card depicting two or more players but not a team.
Coupon: See Tab.
Crease: A card wrinkle resulting from improper handling.
Dealer: A person who buys, trades, and sells collectibles and supplies to make a profit.
Die-cut: A card partially cut with perforations allowing part of the card to be folded or removed.
Disc: A circular-shaped card.
Display Card: A sheet of three to nine cards used by maunfacturers as advertising on product packages. The backs of these cards contain advertisements.
Error Card: A card with erroneous information not corrected by the producer.

Full Sheet: A sheet containing a number of cards which have not been cut into individual cards.
Hall of Famer: A player inducted into the Hockey Hall of Fame.
HL: Player highlight card.
HOF: Acronym for Hall of Fame.
Horz: Horizontal pose on card.
IA: In Action card depicting one or several players during game action.
Insert: An item of a different sort inserted into a package of a standard card series. The item may be a stamp, sticker, poster, etc.
Issue: A set of cards in reference to its manufacturer.
Last Card (LC): Last Card issued of a player by a manufacturer in the regular issue
Layering: The peeling of layers of a card, especially at the corners.
Panel: A card composed of two or more individual cards without perforations, usually forming the back part of a product package.
Plastic Sheet: A clear plastic page punched with standard three-ring spacing, comprising several pockets into which cards may be inserted for display and preservation.
Premium: A card purchased in conjunction with another card or product or received in redemption for a coupon.
Rare: A subjective term used to denote cards of very limited availability.
RB: A Record Breaker card.
Regional: A card distributed in a limited geographical area. Usually the issuer is a not a major producer of cards.

Regular Issue (Set): The Standard Set issued by a manufacturer which is avalable in wax or foil packs on a more or less national bases
Rookie Card (RC): The first card ever produced of a player by a major issuer in a regular issue.
Scarce: A subjective term used to denote a card of limited availability.
Series: The complete set of cards issued by a producer for a particular year. May also refer to a specific sequentially numbered group of cards of a set produced at the same time.
Set: A collection of every single card of the same type produced by an issuer for any given year.
Skip-numbered: A set containing card numbering that is not sequential—certain card numbers were not printed.
SP: A special card containing information other than that relating to an individual player or a team.
Tab: A portion of a card usually set off by perforations so that it may be removed without damaging the main body of the card.
Team Card: A card depicting an entire team.
Trimmed: A card with the edges trimmed to improve the condition. Trimming decreases the value.
V Card: A candy or gum card produced and issued in Canada.
Variation: A corrected or different version of the same card number or player pose in a set. Sometimes one of the variations is scarce.
Vert: The standard vertical pose on a card.

ABBREVIATIONS

NHL TEAMS

Atl.: Atlanta Flames
Bos.: Boston Bruins
Buf.: Buffalo Sabres
Ca.: California Golden Seals
Cal.: Calgary Flames
Chi.: Chicago Black Hawks
Cle.: Cleveland Barons
Col.: Colorado Rockies
Det.: Detroit Red Wings
Edm.: Edmonton Oilers
Har.: Hartford Whalers
Hou.: Houston Aeros
KC: Kansas City Scouts
LA: Los Angeles Kings
Min.: Minnesota North Stars
Mon.: Montreal Canadiens
NJ: New Jersey Devils
NYI: New York Islanders
NYR: New Yor Rangers
Oak.: Oakland Seals
Phi.: Philadelphia Flyers
Pit.: Pittsburgh Penguins
Ott.: Ottawa Senators
Que.: Quebec Nordiques
SJ: San Jose Sharks
St. L.: St. Louis Blues
TB: Tampa Bay Lightning
Tor.: Toronto Maple Leafs
Van.: Vancouver Canucks
Wash.: Washington Capitals
Win.: Winnipeg Jet

WHA TEAMS

AlO: Alberta Oilers
BiB: Birmingham Bulls
CaC: Calgary Cowboys
ChC: Chicago Cougars
CiS: Cincinnati Stingers
ClC: Cleveland Crusaders
EdO: Edmonton Oilers
HoA: Houston Aeros
InR: Indianapolis Racers
LAS: Los Angeles Sharks
MiS: Michigan Stags
MFS: Minnesota Fighting Saints
NEW: New England Whalers
NJR: New Jersey Knights
NeR: New York Raiders
OtC: Ottawa Civics
OtN: Ottawa Nationals
PhB: Philadelphia Blazers
PhR: Phoenix Roadrunners
QuN: Quebec Nordiques
SDM: San Diego Mariners
ToT: Toronto Toros
VaB: Vancouver Blazers
WiN: Winnipeg Jets

JUNIOR AND MINOR LEAGUES

AHL: American Hockey League
IHL: International Hockey League
OHL: Ontario Hockey League
QMJHL: Quebec Major Junior Hockey League
SJHL: Saskatchewan Junior Hockey League
USC: United States College League
WHL: Western Hockey League

ALPHABETICAL INDEX OF ISSUERS

Issuer	Page
7-Eleven	317
7th Inning Sketch	
Memorial Cup	717
Ontario Hockey League	720
Quebec Minor Junior Hockey League	731
Western Hockey League	741
Abalene Sales and Promotions Ltd.	419
Action Packed	339
Adventure Gum	269
Air Canada (SJHL)	748
Alberta Lotteries (Team Canada)	673
Amalgamated Press	153
American International Hockey Leagues	693
Anonymous	
National Hockey League	26
Ontario and Quebec Hockey Leagues	719
Arena Holograms	707
Atlanta Flames	579
Bauer Skates	282
Bazooka	293
Bee Hive Variations	144
Belleville Bulls	755
Berk Ross	157
Boston Bruins	580
Bowman	340
Brandon Wheat Kings	755
Brantford Alexanders	757
Brockville Braves	757
Buffalo Sabres	582
Bufford Litho	3
Calgary Flames	588
Calumel Hockey Club of Laurium	10
Canada Cycle and Motor Company (CCM)	29
Canada Junior Team	685
Canada Starch	152
Canadian Chewing Gum Sales Ltd	29
Celebrity Watch Inc.	339
Champ's Cigarette Cards	20
Chex	275
Chicago Black Hawks	590
Chicoutimi Sagueneurs	757
CHLP / CKAC / CKVL Radio	156
Clarke, A. R. and Co. Limited	10
Classic Games	707
Cleveland Crusaders (WHA)	662
Coca-Cola	276
Colgate	289
Colorado Rockies	592
Cornwall Royals	757
Crescent Ice Cream (WCHL)	741
Dad's Cookies	290
Detroit Red Wings	593
Dimanche / Derniere Heure	298
Diamond Match Company, The	30
Dominion Chocolate	27
Donruss	440
Durivage	420
Eaton's	278
Eddie Sargent Promotions Ltd	283
Edmonton Oilers	596
El Producto	275
Esso	290
Fleer Ultra	421
Fredericton Canadiens	759
Fredericton Express	758
Frito-Lay	339
Funmate Canada Ltd	314
Future Trends (Team Canada)	671
Gillette	419
Gottmann and Kretchmer	5
Goudey Gum	33
Great Atlantic and Pacific Tea Co. (The)	4
Halifax Citadels	760
Hamilton Canucks	761
Hamilton Fincups	760
Hamilton Gum	33
Hamilton King Cigarettes	13
Hamilton Steel City	760
Hartford Whalers	601
Highliner	436
Hockey Hall of Fame	309
Hockey Hall of Fame and Museum	437
Hockey Wit	444
Holland Creameries (WCHL)	741
Houston Aeros (WHA)	662
Hull Olympiques	761
Humpty Dumpty	437
Imperial Tobacco	17
Indianapolis Checkers	761
Ivan Fiodorov Press	677
Kamloops Blazers	761
Kellogg's	294
Kelowna Wings	762
Kenner	444
Kingston Canadiens	762
Kitchener Rangers	764
Kraft	318
La Patrie	187
La Presse	28
Laval Dairy (QHL)	731
Leaf	
National Hockey League	447
World Hockey - Finland	686
Les Riveraires de Richelieu	778
Lethbridge Hurricanes	766
Letraset	301
Lipton Soup	302
Loblaws	302
London Knights	767
Los Angeles Kings	603
Los Angeles Sharks (WHA)	662
L'Outaouais Olympiques de Hull	761
MPS Photographics	749
Mac's Milk	302
Maine Black Bears	768
Maple Crispette	26
Mayer, F. Boot and Shoe Co.	4
McDonald's Restaurants	308
Medicine Hat Tigers	768
Milwaukee Admirals	768
Minnesota Bulldogs	786
Minnesota North Stars	605
Moncton Alpines	768
Moncton Golden Flames	769
Moncton Hawks	769
Montreal Canadiens	608
Montreal Juniors	770
Murad Cigarettes College Series	13
Nabisco	268
Nashville Knights	770
New England Whalers (WHA)	662
New Jersey Devils	616
New York Islanders	618
New York Rangers	620
Niagra Falls Thunder	771
North Bay Centennials	771
Northern Hardware Company	9
Nova Scotia Oilers	771
Nova Scotia Voyageurs	771
O'Keefe Beverages	28
O-Pee-Chee	
National Hockey League	33
Team Canada	671
World Hockey Association	679
Oshawa Generals	772
Ottawa Nationals (WHA)	663
Ottawa Senators	621
Ottawa 67's	774
Panini	
National Hockey League	324
World Hockey	657
Parkhurst	157
Paulin's Candy (WCHL)	741
PepsiCo	306
Peterborough Petes	775
Phoenix Road Runners (WHA)	663
Philadelphia Flyers	622
Pittsburgh Penguins	624
Popsicle	305
Portland Winterhawks	776
Post Cereal	278
Prince Albert Raiders	776
Pro Set	346
ProCards (AHL/IHL)	693
Quaker Oats	
National Hockey League	153
World Hockey Association	361
Quebec Nordiques	
National Hockey League	627
World Hockey Association	663
Quebec Ramparts	776
Rayside Balfour Junior A Canadians	777
Red Ace International	677
Regina Pats	777
Richmond Renegades	778
Royal Desserts	187
Russian Team Sets	677
Safeway Phoenix Roadrunners	705
Saginaw Gears	779
Saginaw Hawks	779
Salt Lake Golden Eagles	779
San Jose Sharks	632
Saskatchewan Junior Hockey League	748
Saskatoon Blades	779
Sault Ste. Marie Greyhounds	780
Score	364
Scotia Bank (Team Canada)	671
Season's	438
Sega - E M Sports	445
Shawinnigan Falls Cataracts	781
Sherbrooke Canadiens	781
Shirriff	269
Slapshot Images Ltd.	750
Spokane Chiefs	781
Sportscaster Cards	305
Springfield Indians	781
St. Lawrence Sales Agency (QHL)	733
St. Lawrence Starch Company	143
St. Louis Blues	630
Star Pics	715
Sudbury Wolves	782
Sweet Caporal	20
TCMA Ltd.	307
Tampa Bay Lightning	634
The Toronto Star	265
Topps	188
Toronto Maple Leafs	635
Toronto Marlboroughs	784
Toronto Sun	296
Towers / Bonimart	301
Tri-Globe International (World Hockey)	678
Ultimate Trading Card Company	
Minor Leagues	716
National Hockey League	438
Upper Deck	
National Hockey League	398
Canada Junior Team	685
U.S.A. Olympic Team (World Hockey)	681
V129 Anonymous	141
Vachon Foods	316
Vancouver Blazers (WHA)	664
Vancouver Canucks	641
Vancouver Millionairs	646
Victoria Cougars	784
Warwick Bro's. and Rutter Ltd.	9
Washington Capitals	647
Wheeling Thunderbirds	785
Willards Chocolate	28
William Paterson Ltd	25
Windsor Spitfires	785
Winnipeg Jets	
National Hockey League	650
World Hockey Association	664
Wonder Bread	269
World Wide Gum	140
York Peanut Butter	273
Zellers	439

THE CHARLTON CONTRIBUTOR'S PAGE

Dear Collector:

In our continuing efforts to improve our pricing publications, we're asking that you fax or mail information you may have concerning the listings in this catalogue to our editorial offices in Toronto.

Please make note of any price changes you've seen over the past several months together with other relevant comments you may have on any of the products listed herein. The Charlton Press is interested in hearing from collectors and dealers. We would like to hear about any sets that have been overlooked or any other items or information that may not have been included.

Everyone who contributes will receive acknowledgement in the next edition.

Please send us your response before July 1st, 1995 to allow us adequate time to include your contribution in the Seventh Edition of *The Charlton Standard Catalogue of Hockey Cards*.

Thank you for helping to make Charlton Press publications the best they can be.

Please send your contributions together
with your name, address and phone number to:

**Editorial Office
The Charlton Press
2010 Yonge Street
Toronto, Ontario M4S 1Z9
Fax (416) 488-4656**